The Europa World Year Book 1991

VOLUME I

PART ONE   INTERNATIONAL ORGANIZATIONS
PART TWO   AFGHANISTAN–JORDAN

EUROPA PUBLICATIONS LIMITED

First published 1926

© **Europa Publications Limited 1991**
18 Bedford Square, London, WC1B 3JN, England

All rights reserved. No part of this
publication may be photocopied, recorded,
or otherwise reproduced, stored in a retrieval
system or transmitted in any form or by any
electronic or mechanical means without the
prior permission of the copyright owner.

Australia and New Zealand
James Bennett (Collaroy) Pty Ltd, 4 Collaroy Street,
Collaroy, NSW 2097, Australia

India
UBS Publishers' Distributors Ltd,
5 Ansari Road, POB 7015, New Delhi 110 002

Japan
Maruzen Co Ltd, POB 5050, Tokyo International 100-31

ISBN 0-946653-69-0
ISSN 0956-2273
Library of Congress Catalog Card Number 59-2942

Printed and bound in England by
Staples Printers Rochester Limited, Love Lane, Rochester, Kent.

FOREWORD

THE EUROPA WORLD YEAR BOOK (formerly THE EUROPA YEAR BOOK: A WORLD SURVEY) was first published in 1926. Since 1960 it has appeared in annual two-volume editions, and has become established as an authoritative reference work, providing a wealth of detailed information on the political, economic and commercial institutions of the world.

Volume I contains international organizations and the first part of the alphabetical survey of countries of the world, from Afghanistan to Jordan. A chapter on the united Germany appears, for the first time, in this edition. Volume II contains countries from Kenya to Zimbabwe.

Readers are referred to our six regional books, THE MIDDLE EAST AND NORTH AFRICA, AFRICA SOUTH OF THE SAHARA, THE FAR EAST AND AUSTRALASIA, SOUTH AMERICA, CENTRAL AMERICA AND THE CARIBBEAN, WESTERN EUROPE and THE USA AND CANADA, for additional information on the geography, history and economy of these areas.

The information is revised annually by a variety of methods, including direct mailing to all the institutions listed. Many other sources are used, such as national statistical offices, government departments and diplomatic missions. The editors thank the innumerable individuals and organizations throughout the world whose generous co-operation in providing current information for this edition is invaluable in presenting the most accurate and up-to-date material available, and acknowledge particular indebtedness for material from the following publications: the United Nations' *Demographic Yearbook*, *Statistical Yearbook* and *Industrial Statistics Yearbook*; the Food and Agriculture Organization of the United Nations' *Production Yearbook*, *Yearbook of Fishery Statistics* and *Yearbook of Forest Products*; the International Monetary Fund's *International Financial Statistics*; and *The Military Balance 1990–91*, published by the International Institute for Strategic Studies, 23 Tavistock Street, London, WC2E 7NQ.

March 1991.

FOREWORD

THE EUROPA WORLD YEAR BOOK (formerly THE EUROPA YEAR BOOK: A WORLD SURVEY) was first published in 1926. Since 1960 it has appeared in annual two-volume editions and has become established as an authoritative reference work, providing a wealth of detailed information on the political, economic and commercial institutions of the world.

Volume I contains international organizations and the first part of the alphabetical survey of countries of the world, from Afghanistan to Jordan (a chapter on the United Germany appears for the first time). In this edition Volume II contains countries from Kenya to Zimbabwe.

Readers are referred to our sister-annual books, THE MIDDLE EAST AND NORTH AFRICA, AFRICA SOUTH OF THE SAHARA, THE FAR EAST AND AUSTRALASIA, SOUTH AMERICA, CENTRAL AMERICA AND THE CARIBBEAN, WESTERN EUROPE and THE USA AND CANADA, for additional information on the geography, history and economy of those areas.

The information is revised annually by a variety of methods, including direct mailing to all the institutions listed. Many other sources are tapped, such as national statistical offices, governmental departments and diplomatic missions. The editors thank the innumerable individuals and organizations throughout the world whose generous co-operation in providing current information for this edition is invaluable in presenting the most accurate and up-to-date material available, and acknowledge transferred information (or material) from the following publications: the United Nations' Demographic Yearbook, Statistical Yearbook and Industrial Statistics Yearbook; the Food and Agriculture Organization of the United Nations, FAO's (1989) Yearbook (Yearbook of Fishery Statistics and Yearbook of Forest Products; the International Monetary Fund's International Financial Statistics and The Military Balance 1990/91, published by the International Institute for Strategic Studies, 23 Tavistock Street, London WC2E 7NQ.

March 1991

CONTENTS

Abbreviations	Page xi
International Comparisons	xiv
Late Information	xix

PART ONE
International Organizations*

The United Nations	3
Members	3
Permanent Missions	4
Observers	6
Information Centres	7
Budget	8
Charter of the United Nations	9
Secretariat	17
General Assembly	18
Security Council	19
Economic and Social Council—ECOSOC	19
International Court of Justice	20
United Nations Training and Research Institutes	21
United Nations Regional Commissions	24
Economic Commission for Europe—ECE	24
Economic and Social Commission for Asia and the Pacific—ESCAP	25
Economic Commission for Latin America and the Caribbean—ECLAC	27
Economic Commission for Africa—ECA	28
Economic and Social Commission for Western Asia—ESCWA	31
Other United Nations Bodies	33
International Sea-Bed Authority	33
Office of the United Nations Disaster Relief Co-Ordinator—UNDRO	34
United Nations Centre for Human Settlements—UNCHS (Habitat)	35
United Nations Children's Fund—UNICEF	36
United Nations Conference on Trade and Development—UNCTAD	37
United Nations Development Programme—UNDP	39
United Nations Environment Programme—UNEP	41
United Nations High Commissioner for Refugees—UNHCR	43
United Nations Observer Missions and Peace-keeping Forces	46
United Nations Population Fund—UNFPA	47
United Nations Relief and Works Agency for Palestine Refugees in the Near East—UNRWA	48

World Food Council—WFC	Page 50
World Food Programme—WFP	51
Membership of the United Nations and its Specialized Agencies	52
Specialized Agencies within the UN System	55
Food and Agriculture Organization—FAO	55
General Agreement on Tariffs and Trade—GATT	58
International Atomic Energy Agency—IAEA	60
International Bank for Reconstruction and Development—IBRD (World Bank)	62
International Development Association—IDA	66
International Finance Corporation—IFC	67
Multilateral Investment Guarantee Agency—MIGA	68
International Civil Aviation Organization—ICAO	68
International Fund for Agricultural Development—IFAD	70
International Labour Organisation—ILO	72
International Maritime Organization—IMO	73
International Monetary Fund—IMF	74
International Telecommunication Union—ITU	78
United Nations Educational, Scientific and Cultural Organization—UNESCO	79
United Nations Industrial Development Organization—UNIDO	82
Universal Postal Union—UPU	83
World Health Organization—WHO	84
World Intellectual Property Organization—WIPO	86
World Meteorological Organization—WMO	88
African Development Bank—ADB	91
Andean Group	93
Arab Bank for Economic Development in Africa—BADEA	95
Arab Fund for Economic and Social Development—AFESD	97
Arab Monetary Fund	98
Asian Development Bank—ADB	100
Association of South East Asian Nations—ASEAN	103
Bank for International Settlements—BIS	106
Caribbean Community and Common Market—CARICOM	108
Central American Common Market—CACM	110
The Colombo Plan for Co-operative Economic and Social Development in Asia and the Pacific	112
The Commonwealth	113
Communauté Economique de l'Afrique de l'Ouest—CEAO	120
Conseil de l'Entente	122
Co-operation Council for the Arab States of the Gulf	123
Council for Mutual Economic Assistance—CMEA	125
Council of Arab Economic Unity	127
Council of Europe	129

* A complete Index of International Organizations is to be found on p. 1551.

CONTENTS

Economic Community of West African States—ECOWAS	Page 133
The European Community	135
European Free Trade Association—EFTA	154
The Franc Zone	156
Inter-American Development Bank—IDB	158
International Bank for Economic Co-operation—IBEC	160
International Chamber of Commerce—ICC	161
International Confederation of Free Trade Unions—ICFTU	163
International Investment Bank	165
International Olympic Committee	166
International Organization for Migration—IOM	167
International Red Cross and Red Crescent Movement	168
International Committee of the Red Cross—ICRC	168
League of Red Cross and Red Crescent Societies—LRCS	169
Islamic Development Bank	170
Latin American Integration Association—LAIA	172
League of Arab States	174
Nordic Council	179
Nordic Council of Ministers	180
North Atlantic Treaty Organisation—NATO	183
Organisation for Economic Co-operation and Development—OECD	186
International Energy Agency	188
OECD Nuclear Energy Agency—NEA	188
Organization of African Unity—OAU	190
Organization of American States—OAS	194
Organization of Arab Petroleum Exporting Countries—OAPEC	197
Organization of the Islamic Conference—OIC	198
Organization of the Petroleum Exporting Countries—OPEC	200
OPEC Fund for International Development	203
South Pacific Commission—SPC	205
South Pacific Forum	207
South Pacific Forum Secretariat	207
Southern African Development Co-ordination Conference—SADCC	209
Warsaw Treaty of Friendship, Co-operation and Mutual Assistance—The Warsaw Pact	211
Western European Union—WEU	212
World Confederation of Labour—WCL	213
World Council of Churches—WCC	214
World Federation of Trade Unions—WFTU	215
Other International Organizations	217

PART TWO
Afghanistan–Jordan

Afghanistan	281
Albania	296
Algeria	309
Andorra	328
Angola	332
Antarctica	345
Antigua and Barbuda	Page 347
Argentina	354
Australia	375
Australian External Territories:	401
Christmas Island	401
Cocos (Keeling) Islands	402
Norfolk Island	403
Other Territories	405
Austria	406
The Bahamas	425
Bahrain	432
Bangladesh	441
Barbados	459
Belgium	466
Belize	489
Benin	496
Bhutan	508
Bolivia	516
Botswana	531
Brazil	542
Brunei	567
Bulgaria	573
Burkina Faso	592
Burma—see Myanmar, Vol. II	
Burundi	603
Cambodia	612
Cameroon	623
Canada	638
Cape Verde	668
The Central African Republic	674
Chad	685
Chile	697
China, People's Republic	715
China (Taiwan)	743
Colombia	758
The Comoros	778
The Congo	784
Costa Rica	795
Côte d'Ivoire	808
Cuba	822
Cyprus	839
Czechoslovakia	855
Denmark	875
Danish External Territories:	897
Faeroe Islands	897
Greenland	900
Djibouti	904
Dominica	910
The Dominican Republic	916
Ecuador	929
Egypt	945
El Salvador	968
Equatorial Guinea	982
Ethiopia	988
Fiji	1003
Finland	1012
Finnish External Territory:	1031
Åland Islands	1031

CONTENTS

France	Page 1033
French Overseas Possessions:	1078
Overseas Departments:	1078
French Guiana	1078
Guadeloupe	1081
Martinique	1085
Réunion	1089
Overseas Collectivités Territoriales:	1094
Mayotte	1094
Saint Pierre and Miquelon	1096
Overseas Territories:	1099
French Polynesia	1099
French Southern and Antarctic Territories	1104
New Caledonia	1105
Wallis and Futuna Islands	1110
Gabon	1114
The Gambia	1127
Germany	1134
Ghana	1188
Greece	1201
Grenada	1220
Guatemala	1227
Guinea	1242
Guinea-Bissau	Page 1251
Guyana	1257
Haiti	1267
Honduras	1279
Hungary	1291
Iceland	1312
India	1321
Indonesia	1361
Iran	1381
Iraq	1398
Ireland	1417
Israel	1436
Italy	1459
The Ivory Coast—see Côte d'Ivoire	
Jamaica	1491
Japan	1504
Jordan	1536
Index of International Organizations	1551

An Index of Territories is to be found at the end of Volume II.

ABBREVIATIONS

AB	Aktiebolag (Joint Stock Company)
Abog.	Abogado (Lawyer)
Acad.	Academician; Academy
ACT	Australian Capital Territory
ADB	African Development Bank; Asian Development Bank
Adm.	Admiral
admin.	administration
AG	Aktiengesellschaft (Joint Stock Company)
a.i.	ad interim
AID	(US) Agency for International Development
AIDS	Acquired Immunodeficiency Syndrome
Al.	Aleja (Alley, Avenue)
Ala	Alabama
ALADI	Asociación Latino-Americana de Integración
Alt.	Alternate
Alta	Alberta
AM	Amplitude Modulation
amalg.	amalgamated
AP	Andhra Pradesh
Apdo	Apartado (Post Box)
approx.	approximately
Apt	Apartment
Ariz	Arizona
Ark	Arkansas
A/S	Aktieselskab (Joint Stock Company)
ASEAN	Association of South East Asian Nations
asscn	association
assoc.	associate
asst	assistant
Aug.	August
auth.	authorised
Ave	Avenue
Avda	Avenida (Avenue)
Avv.	Avvocato (Lawyer)
BC	British Columbia
Bd	Board
Bd, Bld, Blv., Blvd	Boulevard
b/d	barrels per day
Bhd	Berhad (Public Limited Company)
Bldg	Building
BP	Boîte postale (Post Box)
br.(s)	branch(es)
Brig.	Brigadier
Bt	Baronet
bte	boîte (box)
BTN	Brussels Tariff Nomenclature
bul.	bulvar (boulevard)
C	Centigrade
c.	circa; cuadra(s) (block(s))
CACM	Central American Common Market
Cad.	Caddesi (Street)
Calif	California
cap.	capital
Capt.	Captain
CARICOM	Caribbean Community
CCL	Caribbean Congress of Labour
Cdre	Commodore
Cen.	Central
CEO	Chief Executive Officer
CFA	Communauté Financière Africaine; Co-opération Financière en Afrique centrale
CFP	Communauté française du Pacifique; Comptoirs français du Pacifique
Chair.	Chairman/woman
CI	Channel Islands
Cia	Companhia
Cía	Compañía
Cie	Compagnie
c.i.f.	cost, insurance and freight
C-in-C	Commander-in-Chief
circ.	circulation
cm	centimetre(s)
CMEA	Council for Mutual Economic Assistance
Cnr	Corner
Co	Company; County
Col	Colonel
Col.	Colonia
Colo	Colorado
Comm.	Commission; Commendatore
Commdr	Commander
Commdt	Commandant
Commr	Commissioner
Confed.	Confederation
Conn	Connecticut
Cont.	Contador (Accountant)
Corpn	Corporation
CP	Case Postale; Caixa Postal; Casella Postale (Post Box); Communist Party
CPSU	Communist Party of the Soviet Union
Cres.	Crescent
CSTAL	Confederación Sindical de los Trabajadores de América Latina
CTCA	Confederación de Trabajadores Centro-americanos
Cttee	Committee
cu	cubic
cwt	hundredweight
DC	District of Columbia; Distrito Central
DDR	Deutsche Democratische Republik (German Democratic Republic)
DE	Departamento Estatal
Dec.	December
Del	Delaware
Del.	Delegación
Dem.	Democratic; Democrat
Dep.	Deputy
dep.	deposits
Dept	Department
devt	development
DF	Distrito Federal
Diag.	Diagonal
Dir	Director
Div.	Division(al)
DM	Deutsche Mark
DN	Distrito Nacional
Doc.	Docent
Dott.	Dottore
Dr	Doctor
Dr.	Drive
Dra	Doctora
dr.(e)	drachma(e)
Drs	Doctorandus
dwt	dead weight tons
E	East; Eastern
EC	European Community
ECA	(United Nations) Economic Commission for Africa
ECE	(United Nations) Economic Commission for Europe
ECLAC	(United Nations) Economic Commission for Latin America and the Caribbean
Econ.	Economist; Economics
ECOSOC	(United Nations) Economic and Social Council
ECOWAS	Economic Community of West African States
ECU	European Currency Unit
ECWA	(United Nations) Economic Commission for Western Asia
Edif.	Edificio (Building)
edn	edition
EEC	European Economic Community
EFTA	European Free Trade Association
e.g.	exempli gratia (for example)
eKv	electron kilovolt
eMv	electron megavolt
Eng.	Engineer; Engineering
Esc.	Escuela; Escudos; Escritorio
ESCAP	(United Nations) Economic and Social Commission for Asia and the Pacific

ABBREVIATIONS

esq.	esquina (corner)	kv.	kvartal (apartment block)
est.	established; estimate; estimated	kW	kilowatt(s)
etc.	et cetera	kWh	kilowatt hours
eV	eingetragener Verein	Ky	Kentucky
excl.	excluding		
exec.	executive	La	Louisiana
Ext.	Extension	lb	pound(s)
		Lic.	Licenciado
F	Fahrenheit	Licda	Licenciada
f.	founded	LNG	liquefied natural gas
FAO	Food and Agriculture Organization	LPG	liquefied petroleum gas
Feb.	February	Lt, Lieut	Lieutenant
Fed.	Federation; Federal	Ltd	Limited
Fla	Florida		
FM	frequency modulation	m	metre(s)
fmrly	formerly	m.	million
f.o.b.	free on board	Maj.	Major
Fr	Father	Man	Manitoba
Fr.	Franc	Man.	Manager; managing
FRG	Federal Republic of Germany	Mass	Massachusetts
Fri.	Friday	mbH	mit beschränkter Haftung (with limited liability)
ft	foot (feet)	Mc/s	megacycles per second
		Md	Maryland
g	gram(s)	Me	Maine
Ga	Georgia	mem.	member
GATT	General Agreement on Tariffs and Trade	MEP	Member of the European Parliament
GDP	gross domestic product	MEV	mega electron volts
GDR	German Democratic Republic	mfrs	manufacturers
Gen.	General	Mgr	Monseigneur; Monsignor
GeV	giga electron volts	MHz	megahertz
GmbH	Gesellschaft mit beschränkter Haftung (Limited Liability Company)	Mich	Michigan
		Mil.	Military
GNP	gross national product	Minn	Minnesota
Gov.	Governor	Miss	Mississippi
Govt	Government	Mlle	Mademoiselle
grt	gross registered tons	mm	millimetre(s)
GWh	gigawatt hours	Mme	Madame
		Mo	Missouri
ha	hectares	Mon.	Monday
HE	His (or Her) Eminence; His (or Her) Excellency	Mont	Montana
hf	hlutafelag (Company Limited)	MP	Member of Parliament; Madhya Pradesh
hl	hectolitre(s)	MSS	Manuscripts
HM	His (or Her) Majesty	MW	megawatt(s); medium wave
Hon.	Honorary (or Honourable)	MWh	megawatt hour(s)
hp	horsepower		
HQ	Headquarters	N	North; Northern
HRH	His (or Her) Royal Highness	n.a.	not available
		nab.	naberezhnaya (embankment, quai)
IBRD	International Bank for Reconstruction and Development (World Bank)	nám.	náměstí (square)
		Nat.	National
ICC	International Chamber of Commerce	NATO	North Atlantic Treaty Organization
ICFTU	International Confederation of Free Trade Unions	NB	New Brunswick
		NC	North Carolina
IDA	International Development Association	NCO	Non-Commissioned Officer
IDB	Inter-American Development Bank	ND	North Dakota
i.e.	id est (that is to say)	Neb	Nebraska
Ill	Illinois	Nev	Nevada
ILO	International Labour Organisation/Office	Nfld	Newfoundland
IMF	International Monetary Fund	NH	New Hampshire
in (ins)	inch (inches)	NJ	New Jersey
Inc, Incorp.,		NM	New Mexico
Incd	Incorporated	NMP	net material product
incl.	including	no	número (number)
Ind	Indiana	no.	number
Ind.	Independent	Nov.	November
INF	Intermediate-Range Nuclear Forces	nr	near
Ing.	Engineer	nrt	net registered tons
Insp.	Inspector	NS	Nova Scotia
Int.	International	NSW	New South Wales
Inzå.	Engineer	NV	Naamloze Vennootschap (Limited Company)
IRF	International Road Federation	NY	New York
irreg.	irregular	NZ	New Zealand
Is	Islands		
ISIC	International Standard Industrial Classification	OAPEC	Organization of Arab Petroleum Exporting Countries
Jan.	January	OAS	Organization of American States
Jnr	Junior	OAU	Organization of African Unity
Jr	Jonkheer (Netherlands); Junior	Oct.	October
Jt	Joint	OECD	Organisation for Economic Co-operation and Development
Kans	Kansas	OECS	Organization of East Caribbean States
kg	kilogram(s)	Of.	Oficina (Office)
KG	Kommandit Gesellschaft (Limited Partnership)	OIC	Organization of the Islamic Conference
kHz	kilohertz	Okla	Oklahoma
KK	Kaien Kaisha (Limited Company)	Ont	Ontario
km	kilometre(s)	OPEC	Organization of Petroleum Exporting Countries

ABBREVIATIONS

opp.	opposite	Sok.	Sokak (Street)
Ore	Oregon	SP	São Paulo
Org.	Organization	SpA	Società per Azioni (Joint Stock Company)
ORIT	Organización Regional Interamericana de Trabajadores	Sq.	Square
		sq	square (in measurements)
		Sr	Senior; Señor
p.	page	Sra	Señora
p.a.	per annum	Srl	Società a Responsabilità Limitata (Limited Company)
Pa	Pennsylvania		
Parl.	Parliament(ary)	SSR	Soviet Socialist Republic
per.	pereulok (lane, alley)	St	Saint; Street
Perm. Rep.	Permanent Representative	Sta	Santa
PK	Post Box (Turkish)	Ste	Sainte
pl.	platz; place; ploshchad (square)	subs.	subscriptions; subscribed
PLC	Public Limited Company	Sun.	Sunday
PLO	Palestine Liberation Organization	Supt	Superintendent
PMB	Private Mail Bag		
POB	Post Office Box	Tas	Tasmania
Pr.	prospekt (avenue)	TD	Teachta Dála (Member of Parliament)
Pres.	President	tech., techn.	technical
Prin.	Principal	tel.	telephone
Prof.	Professor	Tenn	Tennessee
Propr	Proprietor	Tex	Texas
Prov.	Province; Provincial; Provinciale (Dutch)	Thur.	Thursday
PT	Perseroan Tarbates (Limited Company)	Treas.	Treasurer
Pte	Private	Tue.	Tuesday
Pty	Proprietary	TV	television
p.u.	paid up		
publ.	publication; published	u.	utca (street)
Publr	Publisher	u/a	unit of account
Pvt.	Private	UAE	United Arab Emirates
		UDEAC	Union Douanière et Economique de l'Afrique Centrale
Qld	Queensland		
Qué	Québec	UEE	Unidade Económica Estatal
q.v.	quod vide (to which refer)	UK	United Kingdom
		ul.	ulitsa (street)
Rag.	Ragioniere (Accountant)	UN	United Nations
Rd	Road	UNCTAD	United Nations Conference on Trade and Development
R(s)	rupee(s)		
reg., regd	register; registered	UNDP	United Nations Development Programme
reorg.	reorganized	UNESCO	United Nations Educational, Scientific and Cultural Organization
Rep.	Republic; Republican; Representative		
Repub.	Republic	UNHCR	United Nations High Commissioner for Refugees
res	reserve(s)	Univ.	University
retd	retired	UNRWA	United Nations Relief and Works Agency for Palestine Refugees in the Near East
Rev.	Reverend		
RI	Rhode Island	UP	Uttar Pradesh
RJ	Rio de Janeiro	USA	United States of America
Rm	Room	USAID	United States Agency for International Development
ro-ro	roll-on roll-off		
Rp.(s)	rupiah(s)	USSR	Union of Soviet Socialist Republics
RSFSR	Russian Soviet Federative Socialist Republic		
Rt	Right	Va	Virginia
		VAT	Value Added Tax
S	South; Southern; San	VEB	Volkseigener Betrieb (Public Company)
SA	Société Anonyme, Sociedad Anónima (Limited Company); South Australia	Ven.	Venerable
		VHF	Very High Frequency
SADCC	Southern African Development Co-ordination Conference	Vic	Victoria
		viz.	videlicet (namely)
SARL	Sociedade Anônima de Responsabilidade Limitada (Joint Stock Company of Limited Liability)	Vn	Veien (Street)
		vol.(s)	volume(s)
		Vt	Vermont
Sask	Saskatchewan		
Sat.	Saturday		
SC	South Carolina	W	West; Western
SD	South Dakota	WA	Western Australia
Sdn Bhd	Sendirian Berhad (Private Limited Company)	Wash	Washington (State)
SDR(s)	Special Drawing Right(s)	WCL	World Confederation of Labour
Sec.	Secretary	Wed.	Wednesday
Secr.	Secretariat	WFTU	World Federation of Trade Unions
Sen.	Senior; Senator	WHO	World Health Organization
Sept.	September	Wis	Wisconsin
SER	Sua Eccellenza Reverendissima (His Eminence)	W Va	West Virginia
SFRY	Socialist Federal Republic of Yugoslavia	Wy	Wyoming
SITC	Standard International Trade Classification		
SJ	Society of Jesus	yr	year
Soc.	Society		

INTERNATIONAL COMPARISONS

The following table provides a general comparison of area, population, life expectancy and gross national product for every independent state (excluding the Vatican City) and every other territory with more than 25,000 inhabitants (excluding the Gaza Strip). An attempt has been made to provide comparable information under each heading, and the figures in the table refer to the latest period for which uniform data are available in each category.

Area figures refer to total area, including inland water. Unless otherwise indicated, population figures are mid-year estimates. Most of the data refer to *de facto* population (persons actually present in the area), though some are estimates of *de jure* population (persons normally resident). Figures for life expectancy are estimates, prepared in the Population Division of the United Nations, of the average number of years of life remaining to a new-born child if subject to the mortality conditions (recorded or assumed) of the period 1985-90. It should be stressed that the figures refer to the average life expectancy *at birth* for both sexes. In many developing countries mortality rates are high during the first few years of life, but persons who survive infancy have a life expectancy much greater than the average at birth. It is also noteworthy that in all developed countries the life expectancy of females is greater than that of males.

Figures for gross national product (GNP) may be taken as indicators of the comparative sizes of the various national economies, while data on GNP per head facilitate international comparisons of average levels of economic activity. Owing to variations in price levels and the unequal distribution of income, a figure for GNP per head is only an approximate measure of a country's wealth or poverty, and should not be regarded as a reliable indicator of the relative standard of living in each country. Sources are quoted at the end of the tables, but it must be stressed that the data on total GNP and on GNP per head are, to a considerable extent, estimates, and may be used only as a general guide. In particular, a wide margin of error may be expected in estimates for centrally planned economies, and in figures for GNP per head of less than $350, where the subsistence sector is unusually important and the degree of precision tends to decrease as the ratio of subsistence production to total GNP increases. Figures refer to GNP at market prices, converted to US dollars, with GNP per head usually rounded to the nearest $10. The conversion factor from national currencies to US dollars is the average of exchange rates for three consecutive years, e.g. for 1989 the base period is 1987-89. Data on GNP per head are based on World Bank figures for population, which may differ from figures shown elsewhere in the table.

Country	Area (sq km)	Mid-1989 population ('000)	Mid-1989 population density (per sq km)	Average population increase, 1985-89 (% per year)	Life expectancy at birth, 1985-90 (years)	1989 Gross national product ($ million)	1989 GNP per head ($)
Afghanistan[1,2,3,4]	652,090	18,614	29	2.6	41.5	3,518	242
Albania[5]	28,748	3,202	111	2.0	71.6	1,930	740
Algeria[3,6]	2,381,741	22,971	9.6	3.2	62.5	53,116	2,170
American Samoa[7]	195	38	196	1.7	n.a.	190	5,410
Andorra	467	50	107	2.7	n.a.	n.a.	n.a.
Angola	1,246,700	9,747*	7.8	2.7	44.5	6,010	620
Antigua and Barbuda[8]	442	78	178	0.7	n.a.	302	3,880
Argentina	2,766,889	31,929	12	1.3	70.6	68,780	2,160
Aruba[9,10,11,12]	193	61	316	0.0	n.a.	n.a.	n.a.
Australia[13]	7,682,300	16,807	2.2	1.6	76.1	242,131	14,440
Austria	83,857	7,618	91	0.2	74.1	131,899	17,360
Bahamas	13,878	249	18	1.8	n.a.	2,820	11,370
Bahrain[8]	678	489	721	4.1	70.7	3,009	6,360
Bangladesh	143,998	106,507	740	1.9	50.7	19,913	180
Barbados	430	256	595	0.3	73.9	1,622	6,370
Belgium[10,11]	30,519	9,883	324	0.1	74.7	162,026	16,390
Belize[10,11]	22,965	180	7.8	2.7	n.a.	294	1,600
Benin	112,622	4,591	41	3.2	46.5	1,753	380
Bermuda[8,10,11,12]	53	60	1,132	2.3	n.a.	1,389	24,370
Bhutan[8,14]	47,000	1,165	25	n.a.	47.9	266	190
Bolivia	1,098,581	7,193	6.5	2.8	53.1	4,301	600
Botswana[8]	581,730	1,256	2.2	3.9	58.5	1,105	940
Brazil[15]	8,511,965	147,404	17	2.1	64.9	375,146	2,550
Brunei[12,16,17]	5,765	249	43	2.9	n.a.	3,317	14,120
Bulgaria[10,11,18]	110,994	8,981	81	0.1	72.0	20,860	2,320
Burkina Faso	274,200	8,770	32	2.7	47.2	2,716	310
Burundi	27,834	5,302	190	3.0	49.0	1,149	220
Cambodia[19]	181,035	8,055*	44	2.5	48.4	585	78
Cameroon	475,442	11,540	24	3.2	51.0	11,661	1,010
Canada	9,970,610	26,248	2.6	1.1	76.7	500,337	19,020
Cape Verde[20,21]	4,033	347	86	2.4	61.0	281	760
Cayman Islands[10,11]	259	25	97	6.0	n.a.	n.a.	n.a.
Central African Republic[2,3]	622,984	2,740	4.4	2.9	45.5	1,144	390
Chad	1,284,000	5,538*	4.3	2.5	45.5	1,038	190
Channel Islands[7,10,11]	195	137	703	1.0	n.a.	1,350	10,390
Chile	756,945	12,961	17	1.7	71.5	22,910	1,770
China, People's Republic[22,23,24]	9,571,300	1,133,683	118	1.5	69.4	393,006	360
China (Taiwan)[25,26]	36,000	20,000	556	1.1	68.2	150,393	7,518
Colombia	1,138,914	32,317	28	2.0	64.8	38,607	1,190

See notes on page xvii

(continued opposite)

INTERNATIONAL COMPARISONS

(continued)

Country	Area (sq km)	Mid-1989 population ('000)	Mid-1989 population density (per sq km)	Average population increase, 1985–89 (% per year)	Life expectancy at birth, 1985–90 (years)	1989 Gross national product ($ million)	1989 GNP per head ($)
Comoros[27, 28, 29]	2,235	484	217	4.2	52.0	209	460
Congo[30, 31]	342,000	1,843	5.4	3.1	48.5	2,045	930
Costa Rica[32, 33]	51,100	2,489	49	2.3	74.7	4,898	1,790
Côte d'Ivoire[34, 35]	322,463	9,300	29	4.1	52.5	9,305	790
Cuba[4]	110,861	10,514	95	1.0	74.0	15,487	1,548
Cyprus	9,251	694	75	1.1	75.7	4,892	7,050
Czechoslovakia[36]	127,899	15,639	122	0.2	71.1	89,260	5,820
Denmark	43,093	5,132	119	0.1	75.4	105,263	20,510
Djibouti[2, 3, 19]	23,200	456	20	4.2	47.0	423	1,169
Dominica[8, 10, 37, 38]	751	81	108	0.9	70.4	136	1,670
Dominican Republic	48,734	7,012	144	2.2	65.9	5,513	790
East Timor[39, 40]	14,874	715	48	3.1	42.5	100	150
Ecuador[41]	283,561	10,490	37	2.8	65.4	10,774	1,040
Egypt	1,001,449	53,080	53	2.3	60.6	32,501	630
El Salvador	21,041	5,207	247	2.0	62.1	5,356	1,040
Equatorial Guinea[42]	28,051	341	12	2.2	46.5	149	430
Ethiopia	1,221,900	49,513	41	3.4	41.0	5,953	120
Faeroe Islands[10, 11, 17, 43]	1,399	47	34	1.2	73.9	686	14,600
Fiji[44, 45]	18,274	727	40	0.5	70.4	1,218	1,640
Finland	338,145	4,962	15	0.3	74.8	109,705	22,060
France	543,965	56,160	103	0.4	75.6	1,000,866	17,830
French Guiana[19, 21, 46]	90,000	90	1.0	3.8	n.a.	231	2,718
French Polynesia[7, 16, 47, 48, 49]	4,000	189	47	2.6	56.7	1,370	7,840
Gabon[32]	267,667	1,206	4.5	n.a.	51.5	3,060	2,770
Gambia[50, 51]	11,295	688	61	3.4	43.0	196	230
German Democratic Republic[36, 52]	108,333	16,630	154	−0.0	73.2	120,940	7,180
Germany, Federal Republic[52, 53]	248,628	61,990	249	0.4	74.8	1,272,959	20,750
Ghana[54, 55]	238,533	13,391	56	2.6	54.0	5,503	380
Gibraltar[7, 56]	5.5	31	5,580	0.5	n.a.	130	4,370
Greece	131,957	10,020	76	0.2	75.6	53,626	5,340
Greenland[10, 11, 12, 57]	2,175,600	55	0.03	1.0	n.a.	465	8,780
Grenada[38, 58, 59]	344	97	282	1.4	70.4	179	1,900
Guadeloupe[7, 16, 21, 46]	1,705	338	198	0.4	73.3	1,100	3,300
Guam[7, 21, 54, 60]	541	126	233	2.4	69.6	670	5,470
Guatemala	108,889	8,935	82	2.9	62.0	8,205	920
Guinea[10, 11]	245,857	5,071	21	2.8	42.2	2,372	430
Guinea-Bissau[61, 62]	36,125	943	26	2.4	45.0	173	180
Guyana[32, 63]	214,969	790	3.7	0.8	69.7	248	310
Haiti	27,750	5,609	202	1.5	54.7	2,256	400
Honduras	112,088	4,951	44	3.2	64.0	4,495	900
Hong Kong[16, 64]	1,074	5,761	5,364	1.4	76.2	59,202	10,320
Hungary[18]	93,033	10,576	114	−0.2	70.1	27,078	2,560
Iceland[10, 11]	103,000	250	2.4	1.2	77.5	5,351	21,240
India[65]	3,287,590	811,817	247	2.0	57.9	287,383	350
Indonesia[39]	1,904,569	178,421	94	2.1	56.0	87,936	490
Iran[19]	1,648,000	54,203	33	3.2	65.2	183,843	3,716
Iraq[19, 66, 67]	438,317	16,278	37	3.1	63.9	43,794	2,659
Ireland[68]	70,283	3,515	50	−0.2	74.1	30,054	8,500
Isle of Man[7, 10, 11]	572	66	115	1.6	n.a.	380	5,910
Israel[69]	20,770	4,509	217	1.6	75.4	44,131	9,750
Italy	301,277	57,517	191	0.2	75.6	871,955	15,150
Jamaica	10,990	2,375	216	0.7	74.0	3,011	1,260
Japan	377,815	123,116	326	0.5	78.1	2,920,310	23,730
Jordan[70]	97,740	4,102*	42	4.0	66.0	5,291	1,730
Kenya[2, 3]	580,367	21,163	36	4.0	58.4	8,785	380
Kiribati[10, 60, 71]	861	68	79	2.0	69.6	48	700
Korea, Democratic People's Republic[4, 72]	120,538	22,418*	186	2.4	69.3	17,670	846
Korea, Republic[72]	99,222	42,380	427	1.0	69.3	186,467	4,400
Kuwait	17,818	2,048	115	4.6	72.8	33,082	16,380
Laos[73]	236,800	3,585	15	n.a.	48.5	693	170
Lebanon[19]	10,400	2,897*	279	2.1	67.0	949	350
Lesotho	30,355	1,700	56	2.7	55.9	816	470
Liberia[17]	111,369	2,508	23	3.5	54.5	1,051	450
Libya[8, 31, 74]	1,759,540	3,637	2.1	4.5	60.7	22,976	5,410
Liechtenstein[12, 48]	160	28	177	1.2	n.a.	n.a.	n.a.
Luxembourg[75, 76]	2,586	378	146	0.7	74.3	9,408	24,860
Macau[77]	17	448	25,700	3.4	n.a.	810	2,710
Madagascar[32, 78]	587,041	9,985	17	2.8	53.5	2,543	230
Malawi[67, 79]	118,484	7,983	67	3.7	47.0	1,475	180
Malaysia[10, 11]	329,749	16,942	51	2.6	69.5	37,005	2,130
Maldives[12]	298	206	691	2.9	n.a.	87	420

See notes on page xvii *(continued overleaf)*

INTERNATIONAL COMPARISONS

(continued)

Country	Area (sq km)	Mid-1989 population ('000)	Mid-1989 population density (per sq km)	Average population increase, 1985–89 (% per year)	Life expectancy at birth, 1985–90 (years)	1989 Gross national product ($ million)	1989 GNP per head ($)
Mali[45]	1,240,192	7,960	6.4	1.7	44.0	2,109	260
Malta	316	350	1,108	1.0	72.7	2,041	5,820
Martinique[7, 11, 16, 61]	1,102	337	306	0.5	74.2	1,400	4,280
Mauritania[80, 81]	1,025,520	1,339	1.3	n.a.	46.0	953	490
Mauritius	2,040	1,068	524	1.2	69.0	2,068	1,950
Mexico	1,958,201	84,490	43	2.0	68.9	170,053	1,990
Monaco[82, 83]	2.0	27	13,878	1.1	n.a.	n.a.	n.a.
Mongolia[4, 84, 85]	1,566,500	2,043	1.3	2.5	63.5	1,408	716
Morocco[80]	446,550	24,521*	55	2.6	60.7	22,069	900
Mozambique[86]	801,590	15,326	19	2.6	46.5	1,193	80
Myanmar[51, 57, 87]	676,578	38,541	57	2.0	60.0	7,450	200
Namibia[57, 88]	824,292	1,817*	2.2	3.2	56.2	1,150	1,020
Nauru[60, 89, 90]	21	8	378	1.6	69.6	n.a.	n.a.
Nepal	140,797	18,442	131	2.5	50.9	3,206	170
Netherlands	40,844	14,835	363	0.6	76.8	237,415	16,010
Netherlands Antilles[7, 9, 12, 91]	800	189	236	n.a.	n.a.	1,610	6,110
New Caledonia[7, 16, 42, 49, 92]	19,103	164	8.6	2.1	65.9	860	5,760
New Zealand[93, 94]	267,844	3,389	13	0.6	74.7	39,437	11,800
Nicaragua[2, 3, 17]	130,000	3,384	26	3.6	63.3	2,911	830
Niger[95, 96]	1,267,000	7,250	5.7	3.4	44.5	2,195	290
Nigeria[10]	923,768	104,957	114	n.a.	50.5	28,314	250
Norway	323,877	4,227	13	0.4	76.8	92,097	21,850
Oman	212,457	1,422*	6.7	3.4	55.4	7,756	5,220
Pacific Islands (Trust Territory)[34, 60, 97, 98, 99]	1,779	142	80	2.4	69.6	160	1,100
Pakistan[1, 100]	796,095	108,678	137	3.1	56.5	40,134	370
Panama	77,082	2,370	31	2.1	72.1	4,211	1,780
Papua New Guinea	462,840	3,593	7.8	2.1	54.0	3,444	900
Paraguay	406,752	4,157	10	3.0	66.9	4,299	1,030
Peru[15]	1,285,216	21,792	17	2.6	61.4	23,009	1,090
Philippines	300,000	60,097	200	2.4	63.5	42,754	700
Poland[18]	312,683	37,854	121	0.4	71.4	66,974	1,760
Portugal	92,389	10,467	113	0.8	73.3	44,058	4,260
Puerto Rico[10, 11]	8,897	3,293	370	0.1	74.9	20,118	6,010
Qatar[8, 45]	11,000	422	38	4.1	69.3	4,077	9,920
Réunion[16, 21, 46, 57]	2,510	570	227	1.5	71.2	2,120	3,940
Romania[18, 101]	237,500	23,152	97	0.5	70.1	57,030	2,540
Rwanda[63, 102]	26,338	6,274	238	3.6	48.5	2,157	310
Saint Christopher and Nevis[2, 8, 12]	262	44	167	n.a.	n.a.	119	2,860
Saint Lucia[38]	622	148	238	1.9	70.4	267	1,810
Saint Vincent and the Grenadines[8, 38, 91, 103]	388	113	291	1.1	70.4	135	1,200
San Marino[12, 104]	61	23	379	0.6	n.a.	n.a.	n.a.
São Tomé and Príncipe[56]	964	116	120	2.4	n.a.	43	360
Saudi Arabia[105]	2,149,690	14,435	6.7	5.0	63.4	89,986	6,230
Senegal[106, 107]	196,722	6,882	35	2.6	45.8	4,716	650
Seychelles[12]	308	67	218	0.6	n.a.	285	4,170
Sierra Leone	71,740	4,046*	56	2.5	41.0	813	200
Singapore	626	2,685	4,287	1.2	72.8	28,058	10,450
Solomon Islands[10, 49, 108]	27,556	299	11	3.5	41.1	181	570
Somalia	637,657	7,339*	12	3.5	45.0	1,035	170
South Africa[88]	1,221,037	34,492*	28	2.2	60.4	86,029	2,460
Spain[109]	504,782	38,811	77	0.2	76.5	358,352	9,150
Spanish North Africa[40, 109, 110, 111]	32	129	4,041	−0.2	n.a.	90	720
Sri Lanka	65,610	16,806	256	1.5	70.3	7,268	430
Sudan[8, 112]	2,505,813	20,564	8.2	n.a.	49.8	10,094	420
Suriname[113, 114]	163,265	389	2.4	2.2	69.5	1,314	3,020
Swaziland[108, 115]	17,364	681	39	3.3	55.5	683	900
Sweden	440,945	8,493	19	0.4	77.1	184,230	21,710
Switzerland	41,293	6,647	161	0.7	77.0	197,984	30,270
Syria	185,180	11,719	63	3.4	65.0	12,444	1,020
Tanzania[116]	945,087	24,802	26	3.4	53.0	3,079	120
Thailand	513,115	55,448	108	1.8	65.0	64,437	1,170
Togo[117, 118]	56,785	3,296	58	3.3	53.0	1,364	390
Tonga[49, 108, 119]	748	95	127	0.5	55.2	89	910
Trinidad and Tobago[10, 11]	5,130	1,212	236	1.0	70.2	4,000	3,160
Tunisia[2, 3]	163,610	7,465	46	2.6	65.3	10,089	1,260
Turkey	779,452	56,741	73	3.1	64.1	74,731	1,360
Tuvalu[101, 120, 121]	25	8	329	2.0	n.a.	5	680
Uganda[122, 123]	235,880	12,636	54	2.7	51.0	4,254	250
USSR[36, 85, 124]	22,402,200	286,717	13	0.9	69.5	1,212,030	4,550
United Arab Emirates[34, 98]	83,600	1,206	14	5.9	70.7	28,449	18,430

See notes on opposite page

(continued opposite)

INTERNATIONAL COMPARISONS

(continued)

Country	Area (sq km)	Mid-1989 population ('000)	Mid-1989 population density (per sq km)	Average population increase, 1985-89 (% per year)	Life expectancy at birth, 1985-90 (years)	1989 Gross national product ($ million)	1989 GNP per head ($)
United Kingdom	244,103	57,205	234	0.3	75.2	834,166	14,570
USA	9,372,614	248,760	27	1.0	75.4	5,237,707	21,100
US Virgin Islands[16, 21, 54, 57]	342	106	310	1.2	n.a.	1,074	9,760
Uruguay	177,414	3,077	17	0.6	71.0	8,069	2,620
Vanuatu[49, 85, 125]	12,190	143	12	2.4	44.6	131	860
Venezuela[15]	912,050	19,246	21	2.7	69.7	47,164	2,450
Viet-Nam[4, 85, 126]	329,566	64,412	195	2.1	61.3	7,630	124
Western Sahara[80, 127, 128]	266,000	165	0.6	8.9	n.a.	n.a.	n.a.
Western Samoa[12, 114, 129]	2,831	159	56	0.5	n.a.	14	720
Yemen Arab Republic[130, 131]	195,000	9,274	48	n.a.	50.9	7,203	640
Yemen, People's Democratic Republic[130, 132, 133]	332,968	2,345	7.0	2.6	50.8		
Yugoslavia	255,804	23,690	93	0.6	71.9	59,080	2,490
Zaire[45]	2,345,409	34,491	15	3.1	52.5	8,841	260
Zambia	752,614	7,804	10	3.8	53.4	3,060	390
Zimbabwe[45]	390,580	9,122	23	2.8	58.3	6,076	640

* United Nations estimate.

[1] Figures for population and increase rate assume stable growth and take no account of inward or outward migration.

[2] Figures for population and density refer to mid-1986.

[3] The population increase rate refers to 1980-86.

[4] Figures for GNP refer to estimates of net material product, measured at current prices, for 1986 or (in the case of Afghanistan) the year ending 20 March 1987 (Source: UN, *National Accounts Statistics*).

[5] Figures for GNP refer to 1978 and are estimated on a 1977-79 base period.

[6] Figures for population and density refer to the census of April 1987.

[7] Figures for GNP refer to 1985 and are estimated on a 1983-85 base period.

[8] Figures for GNP refer to 1988 and are estimated on a 1986-88 base period.

[9] Aruba, listed separately, was part of the Netherlands Antilles prior to 1 January 1986. Data relating to GNP for the Netherlands Antilles include Aruba.

[10] Figures for population and density refer to mid-1988.

[11] The population increase rate refers to 1985-88.

[12] Although no estimates are available of 1985-90 life expectancy for both sexes, the UN *Demographic Yearbook* includes separate figures of life expectancy for males and females at another date.

[13] Figure for life expectancy includes Australian dependencies: Christmas Island, the Cocos (Keeling) Islands and Norfolk Island.

[14] Figures for population and density refer to mid-1980.

[15] Population figures exclude Indian jungle inhabitants.

[16] Figures for GNP refer to estimates of gross domestic product.

[17] Figures for GNP refer to 1987 and are estimated on a 1985-87 base period.

[18] Figures for the GNP of Bulgaria, Hungary, Poland and Romania are not comparable with those of other centrally planned economies.

[19] Figures for GNP refer to estimates of gross domestic product, measured at current prices, for 1986 or (in the case of Iran) the year ending 20 March 1987 (Source: UN, *National Accounts Statistics*).

[20] Figures for population and density refer to 31 December 1987.

[21] The population increase rate refers to 1980-87.

[22] Figures for population and density refer to the census of 1 July 1990.

[23] The population increase rate refers to 1982-90.

[24] The figure for life expectancy refers to the whole of China, including Taiwan.

[25] The estimate of life expectancy refers to 1965-70.

[26] Figures for GNP are in terms of current prices, rather than being adjusted to a three-year base period.

[27] Except for GNP, figures include the island of Mayotte (estimated population 73,000 at 1 January 1988), which has remained under French administration since the Comoros became independent in July 1975.

[28] Figures for population and density refer to 31 December 1986.

[29] The population increase rate refers to 1973-86.

[30] Figures for population and density refer to the census of 22 December 1984.

[31] The population increase rate refers to 1974-84.

[32] Figures for population and density refer to mid-1985.

[33] The population increase rate refers to 1973-84.

[34] Figures for population and density refer to mid-1983.

[35] The population increase rate refers to 1979-83.

[36] Figures for GNP are provisional data for 1980 and are estimated on a 1978-80 base period.

[37] The population increase rate refers to 1981-88.

[38] The figure for life expectancy is the average for the Windward Islands (Dominica, Grenada, Saint Lucia and Saint Vincent and the Grenadines).

[39] East (formerly Portuguese) Timor, listed separately, was incorporated into Indonesia on 17 July 1976. Figures for Indonesia, except the data on GNP, exclude East Timor.

[40] Figures for GNP refer to 1974 and are estimated on a 1973-75 base period.

[41] Population figures exclude nomadic Indian tribes.

[42] The population increase rate refers to 1983-89.

[43] The figure for life expectancy is the 1965-70 average for the Faeroe Islands and Iceland.

[44] Figures for population and density refer to 31 December 1989.

[45] The population increase rate refers to 1986-89.

[46] Figures for population and density refer to 1 January 1988.

[47] Figures for population and density refer to the census of 6 September 1988.

[48] The population increase rate refers to 1983-88.

[49] The estimate of life expectancy refers to 1965.

[50] Figures for population and density refer to the census of 15 April 1983.

[51] The population increase rate refers to 1973-83.

[52] The German Democratic Republic and the Federal Republic of Germany merged on 3 October 1990.

[53] Figures include data for West Berlin.

[54] Figures for population and density refer to mid-1987.

[55] The population increase rate refers to 1984-87.

[56] The population increase rate refers to 1981-89.

[57] Figures for GNP refer to 1986 and are estimated on a 1984-86 base period.

[58] Figures for population and density refer to 30 April 1987.

[59] The population increase rate refers to 1981-87.

[60] The figure for life expectancy is the average for Micronesia.

[61] Figures for population and density refer to 1 January 1989.

INTERNATIONAL COMPARISONS

[62] The population increase rate refers to 1979-88.

[63] The population increase rate refers to 1980-85.

[64] Population figures exclude Vietnamese refugees.

[65] Figures include the Indian-held part of the disputed territory of Jammu and Kashmir.

[66] Figures for population and density refer to the census of 17 October 1987.

[67] The population increase rate refers to 1977-87.

[68] Figures for population and density refer to 15 April 1989.

[69] Including East Jerusalem, annexed from Jordan in 1967. Population figures also include Israeli residents in other territories under military occupation.

[70] Figures for GNP relate to the East Bank region only (estimated population 2,796,000 at 31 December 1986).

[71] The population increase rate refers to 1978-85.

[72] The area excludes the demilitarized zone (1,262 sq km) separating the Democratic People's Republic of Korea and the Republic of Korea.

[73] Figures for population and density refer to the census of 1 March 1985.

[74] Figures for population and density refer to the census of 31 July 1984.

[75] Figures for population and density refer to 1 January 1990.

[76] The population increase rate refers to 1985-90.

[77] Figures for GNP refer to 1982 and are estimated on a 1980-82 base period.

[78] The population increase rate refers to 1981-85.

[79] Figures for population and density refer to the census of 1-21 September 1987.

[80] Western (formerly Spanish) Sahara, listed separately, was partitioned in 1976 between Mauritania and Morocco. Mauritania withdrew in August 1979, when Morocco annexed the former Mauritanian area. Figures for the area, population and life expectancy of these countries exclude their respective portions of the territory.

[81] Figures for population and density refer to the census of 1 January 1977.

[82] Figures for population and density refer to the census of 4 March 1982.

[83] The population increase rate refers to 1975-82.

[84] Figures for population and density refer to the census of 5 January 1989.

[85] The population increase rate refers to 1979-89.

[86] Figures for population and density refer to 1 August 1989.

[87] Figures for population and density refer to 1 October 1987.

[88] The area and population of Walvis Bay, an integral part of South Africa, are included with Namibia.

[89] Figures for population and density refer to the census of 13 May 1983.

[90] The population increase rate refers to 1977-83.

[91] Figures for population and density refer to 31 December 1988.

[92] Figures for population and density refer to the census of 4 April 1989.

[93] Figures for population and density refer to 28 February 1990.

[94] The population increase rate refers to 1986-90.

[95] Figures for population and density refer to the census of 10-24 May 1988.

[96] The population increase rate refers to 1977-88.

[97] Comprising the Marshall Islands, the Federated States of Micronesia, the Northern Mariana Islands and Palau.

[98] The population increase rate refers to 1980-83.

[99] Figures for GNP refer to 1984 and are estimated on a 1982-84 base period.

[100] Figures exclude the disputed territory of Jammu and Kashmir (total area 222,802 sq km, of which 83,807 sq km is held by Pakistan).

[101] Figures for GNP refer to 1981 and are estimated on a 1979-81 base period.

[102] Figures for population and density refer to 31 December 1985.

[103] The population increase rate refers to 1980-88.

[104] Figures for population and density refer to 30 September 1989.

[105] The population increase rate refers to 1974-89.

[106] Figures for population and density refer to the census of 20 May-5 June 1988.

[107] The population increase rate refers to 1976-88.

[108] The population increase rate refers to 1976-86.

[109] Data for Spanish North Africa (Ceuta and Melilla) are also included with the figures for Spain.

[110] Figures for population and density refer to the census of 1 March 1981.

[111] The population increase rate refers to 1970-81.

[112] Figures for population and density refer to the census of 1 February 1983.

[113] Figures for population and density refer to 31 December 1984.

[114] The population increase rate refers to 1980-84.

[115] Figures for population and density refer to the census of 25 August 1986.

[116] Figures for GNP refer to mainland Tanzania only, excluding Zanzibar (population 643,000 at mid-1989).

[117] Figures for population and density refer to 31 January 1988.

[118] The population increase rate refers to 1982-88.

[119] Figures for population and density refer to the census of 28 November 1986.

[120] Figures for population and density refer to the census of June 1985.

[121] The population increase rate refers to 1979-85.

[122] Figures for population and density refer to the census of 18 January 1980.

[123] The population increase rate refers to 1969-80.

[124] Figures for population and density refer to the census of 12 January 1989.

[125] Figures for population and density refer to the census of 15 May 1989.

[126] Figures for population and density refer to the census of 1 April 1989.

[127] Figures for population and density refer to mid-1979.

[128] The population increase rate refers to 1975-79.

[129] Figures for population and density refer to mid-1984.

[130] The Yemen Arab Republic and the People's Democratic Republic of Yemen merged to form the Republic of Yemen on 22 May 1990.

[131] Figures for population and density refer to the census of 1-18 February 1986, including nationals living abroad.

[132] Figures for population and density refer to the census of 29 March 1988.

[133] The population increase rate refers to 1973-88.

Principal Sources: Population estimates taken from the United Nations *Population and Vital Statistics Report* (quarterly); figures for area taken mainly from the United Nations *Demographic Yearbook 1988*; data on life expectancy taken mainly from *World Population Prospects: 1988* (UN Population Studies, No. 106); estimates of gross national product and GNP per head taken from *The World Bank Atlas* (International Bank for Reconstruction and Development, 1990).

LATE INFORMATION

UNITED NATIONS SECRETARIAT (p. 17)
Under-Secretary-General for Technical Co-operation for Development: JI CHAOZU (People's Republic of China) (appointed January 1991).
Under-Secretary-General for Special Political Questions, Regional Co-operation, Decolonization and Trusteeship: JAMES O. C. JONAH (Sierra Leone) (from 1 January 1991).

INTERNATIONAL COURT OF JUSTICE (p. 20)
President: Sir ROBERT JENNINGS (United Kingdom).
Vice-President: SHIGERU ODA (Japan) (from February 1991).

UNITED NATIONS HIGH COMMISSIONER FOR REFUGEES—UNHCR (p. 43)
High Commissioner: SADAKO OGATA (Japan) (from 1 January 1991).

UNITED NATIONS RELIEF AND WORKS AGENCY FOR PALESTINE REFUGEES IN THE NEAR EAST—UNRWA (p. 48)
Commissioner-General: ILTER TÜRKMEN (Turkey) (appointed January 1991).

GENERAL AGREEMENT ON TARIFFS AND TRADE—GATT (p. 59)
The 'Uruguay Round' of trade negotiations, due to be concluded in December 1990, was adjourned in that month after participants failed to reach an agreement on the reduction of the European Community's subsidies for agriculture. Negotiations were resumed in February 1991.

INTERNATIONAL MONETARY FUND—IMF (p. 75)
The following Executive Directors took office in November 1990 (the names of the outgoing Executive Directors, representing the same groups of countries, are given in parentheses): ANGEL TORRES (Spain) (replacing LEONOR FILARDO); L. B. MONYAKE* (Lesotho) (EL TAYEB EL KOGALI); ALEJANDRO VÉGH (Uruguay) (ERNESTO FELDMAN); ABBAS MIRAKHOR (Iran) (MOHAMMED REZA GHAZIMI); CORENTINO V. SANTOS (Cape Verde) (MAWAKANI SAMBA). In December BERND GOOS became the Executive Director for Germany.
* Also representing Angola.

BANK FOR INTERNATIONAL SETTLEMENTS—BIS (p. 106)
President: BENGT DENNIS (Sweden) (appointed November 1990).

COUNCIL OF EUROPE (p. 129)
In February 1991 Czechoslovakia became a member of the Council of Europe.

WARSAW TREATY (p. 211)
In February 1991 an agreement was concluded by the signatories of the Warsaw Treaty (Warsaw Pact)—Bulgaria, Czechoslovakia, Hungary, Poland, Romania and the USSR—dismantling the military structures of the organization with effect from 1 April.

AFGHANISTAN (p. 290)
Government Changes
(January 1991)
Dr ABDOL WAHED SORABI, Deputy Prime Minister and Minister of Planning, was given the additional post of Vice-President.

(February 1991)
Deputy Prime Minister and Minister of Economic Affairs: ABDOL SAMAD SALIM.
Deputy Prime Minister and Minister of Social and Cultural Affairs: Pohanwal MOHAMMAD ANWAR ARGHANDIWAL.
Minister of Planning: GHOLAM MOHAYODDIN SHAHBAZ.
Minister of Central Statistics: Pohandoy DR MOHAMMAD NAZIR SHAHEDI.
Minister of Civil Aviation and Tourism: Pohand Dr WADIR SAFI.

ALBANIA (p. 304)
Government and PLA Changes
In mid-December 1990 the following were removed from the Political Bureau of the Central Committee of the Party of Labour of Albania (PLA): MUHO ASLLANI, FOTO ÇAMI, HAJREDIN ÇELIKU, LENKA ÇUKO, SIMON STEFANI, PIRRO KONDI and QIRJAKO MIHALI. NEXHMIJE HOXHA resigned from the chair of the General Council of the Democratic Front and was replaced by ADIL ÇARÇANI. In late December SPIRO DEDE became a Secretary of the PLA Central Committee. Several changes in the composition of the Council of Ministers were made. Further government changes followed in January 1991. On 20 February, however, against a background of increasing unrest, Ramiz Alia declared presidential rule. An eight-member Presidential Council was established, and a provisional Council of Ministers was appointed.

Presidential Council
FATOS NANO
KLEANTHI KOÇI
KIÇO BLUSHI
HAXHI LLESHI
LEFTER XHUVELI
REXHEP MEJDANI
MINELLA DALANI
XHENET MUCO

Provisional Council of Ministers
Chairman: FATOS NANO.
Deputy Chairman: SHKELQIM CANI.
Secretary-General: ALEKS LUARASI.
Minister of Foreign Affairs: MUHAMET KAPLLANI
Minister of People's Defence: KIÇO MUSTAQI.
Minister of Internal Affairs: GRAMOZ RUCAJ.
Minister of Justice: DASHAMIR KORE.
Chairman of the State Planning Commission: LEONTJEV CUCI.
Minister of Industry, Mines and Energy: DRINI MEZINI.
Minister of Finance: QEMAL DISHA.
Minister of Food and Light Industry: YLLI BUFI
Minister of Agriculture: AHMET OSJA.
Minister of Foreign Trade and Economic Co-operation with Foreign Countries: SHANE KORBECI.
Minister of Domestic Trade: ALTIN YLLI.
Minister of Construction: LEONARD NANO.
Minister of Transport: SALVADOR FRANJA.
Minister of Education: KASTRIOT ISLAMI.
Minister of Health: SABIT BROKA.
Chairman of the State Control Commission: ZYDI PEPA.

The general election scheduled for 10 February 1991 was postponed until 31 March.

ANDORRA (p. 330)
Government Change
(February 1991)
General Council of the Valleys
First Syndic: ALBERT GELABERT.

ANGOLA (p. 340)
Government Changes
(January 1991)
Minister of Agriculture: ISAAC FRANCISCO MARIA DOS ANJOS.
Minister of Education: ANTÓNIO VALENTIN DA SILVA NETO.
Minister of Energy and Petroleum: JOÃO LOURENÇO LANDOITE.
Minister of Industry: JUSTINO JOSÉ FERNANDES.
Minister of Trade: AMBROSO ANTÓNIO DE OLIVEIRA SILVESTRE.

In February 1991 the following Ministries were abolished: Ministry of Construction, Ministry of Energy and Petroleum, Ministry of Labour and Social Security, Ministry of State Security, Ministry of Trade; the following Ministries were created: Ministry of Commerce, Ministry of Petroleum, Ministry of Public Works and Urbanization, Ministry for Territorial Administration.

ARGENTINA (p. 364)
Government Changes
(January 1991)
Minister of the Economy: DOMINGO CAVALLO.
Minister of Foreign Affairs: GUIDO DI TELLA.
Minister of National Defence: ANTONIO ERMÁN GONZÁLEZ.

LATE INFORMATION

AUSTRIA (p. 414)
Government Changes
(December 1990)

Minister of Employment and Social Affairs: Josef Hesoun (SPÖ).
Minister of Health, Consumer Protection and Sport: Ing. Harald Ettl (SPÖ).
Minister of Justice: Dr Nikolaus Michalek (Independent).
Minister of National Defence: Dr Werner Fasslabend (ÖVP).
Minister of Education and Arts: Dr Rudolf Scholten (SPÖ).
Minister of Women's Affairs in the Federal Chancellery: Johanna Dohnal (SPÖ).
Secretaries of State to the Federal Chancellery: Dr Peter Jankowitsch (SPÖ), Dr Peter Kostelka (SPÖ).
Secretary of State in the Ministry of Economic Affairs: Dr Maria Fekter (ÖVP).

BANGLADESH (p. 441)

Following the resignation of President Ershad in December 1990, an interim Council of Advisers took office, pending a general election for the Jatiya Sangsad, held on 27 February 1991. Preliminary results indicated that the Bangladesh Nationalist Party (BNP), led by Begum Khalida Zia, had won 140 of the 300 elective seats, the Awami League 95, the Jatiya Dal 35, the Jamaat-e-Islami Bangladesh 18, and others 6. Four counts had yet to be completed in constituencies where partial re-polling had been ordered. The two remaining seats were vacant, and by-elections were pending. A few days after the election, the BNP was ensured a small working majority in the Jatiya Sangsad, following discussions with the Jamaat-e-Islami Bangladesh, and was, thus, enabled to appoint deputies to 28 of the 30 parliamentary seats reserved for women. Begum Khalida Zia was expected to form a new Council of Ministers.

BARBADOS (p. 462)
Government Changes
(January 1991)

Minister of Justice and Public Safety: Keith Simmons.
Minister of Labour, Consumer Affairs and the Environment: Warwick Franklin.
Minister of Tourism and Sports: Wes Hall.
Minister of Agriculture, Food and Fisheries: Harcourt Lewis.
Minister of Trade, Industry and Commerce: Carl Clarke.
Minister of Community Development and Culture: David Thompson.
Minister of State in the Ministry of Finance and Economic Affairs: Harold Blackman.

House of Assembly
General Election, 22 January 1991

Party	Seats
Democratic Labour Party (DLP)	18
Barbados Labour Party (BLP)	10
Total	28

BENIN (p. 504)

As many as 24 political organizations were reported to have participated in elections to Benin's new legislative body on 17 February 1991. Official election results were due to be published on 2 March. Fifteen candidates were expected to contest the presidential election, scheduled to take place on 10 March, with a second round of voting (if necessary) on 24 March.

BRAZIL (p. 553)
Gubernatorial elections (first round), 3 October 1990

Pernambuco: Joaquim Francisco (PFL).

Election results from the state of Alagoas were annulled, following allegations of electoral malpractice. A fresh election was scheduled for early 1991.

Gubernatorial elections (second round), 25 November 1990

Acre: Edmundo Pinto (PDS).
Amapá: Annibal Barcellos (PFL).
Espírito Santo: Albuíno Azeredo (PDT).
Maranhão: Edison Lobão (PFL).
Minas Gerais: Hélio Garcia (PRS).
Pará: Jáder Barbalho (PMDB).
Paraíba: Ronaldo Cunha Lima (PMDB).
Paraná: Roberto Requião (PMDB).
Piauí: Antônio Freitas Neto (PFL).
Rio Grande do Norte: José Agripino Maia (PFL).
Rio Grande do Sul: Alceu Collares (PDT).
Rondônia: Osvaldo Pianna (PTR).
Roraima: Otomar Pinto (PTB).
São Paulo: Luís Antônio Fleury (PMDB).
Tocantins: Moises Avelino (PMDB).

BURUNDI (p. 609)
Government Changes
(February 1991)

Minister of Land Use, Tourism and the Environment: Louis Nduwimana.
Minister of the Interior and Development of Local Collectives: Libère Bararunyeretse.
Minister of Justice: Sébastien Ntahuga.
Minister of Higher Education and Scientific Research: Gilbert Midende.
Minister of Commerce and Industry: Astère Girukwigomba.
Minister of Handicrafts, Professional Training and Youth: Adolphe Nahayo.
Minister of Energy and Mines: Bonaventure Bangurambona.
Minister of Labour and Social Security: Julie Ngiriye.
Minister of the Civil Service: Charles Karikurubu.
Minister of Women's Advancement and Social Protection: Victoire Ndikumana.
Minister of Communications, Culture and Sport: Frederick Ngenzebuhoro.
Secretary of State in charge of Public Security: Laurent Kagimbi.

CAMBODIA (p. 621)

In January 1991 the Prime Minister, Hun Sen, replaced Chea Sim as the Chairman of the National Assembly.

In February the State of Cambodia announced that three members of the Supreme National Council, Sin Song, Kong Sam-ol and Chem Snguon, had resigned. They were replaced by Dit Munty. Im Chhunlim and Sin Sen.

CAPE VERDE (p. 668)
Assembléia Nacional Popular
Legislative Election, 14 January 1991

Party	Seats
Movimento parce Democracia (MPD)	56
Partido Africano da Independência de Cabo Verde (PAICV)	23
Total	79

Following the election, the Prime Minister, Gen. Pedro Verona Rodriques Pires, resigned. On 28 January Carlos Veiga, the Chairman of the MPD, was appointed Prime Minister in a transitional administration. At a presidential election, held on 17 February, the MPD candidate, António Mascarenhas Monteiro, obtained 72% of the votes cast, while the incumbent President, Aristides Maria Pereira, obtained only 26.2% of the votes. António Mascarenhas Monteiro was subsequently to form a new government, based on the results of the legislative election.

CHILE (p. 706)
Government Change
(February 1991)

Minister for Women's Affairs: María Soledad Alvear.

PEOPLE'S REPUBLIC OF CHINA (p. 731)
Government Changes

In March 1991 the Minister of Construction, Lin Hanxiong, and the Minister of Communications, Qian Yongchang, were dismissed. They were replaced by Hou Jie and Huang Zhendong respectively.

EL SALVADOR (p. 976)
Government Change
(February 1991)

Minister of Justice: Dr René Hernández Valiente.

PART ONE
International Organizations

PART ONE

International Organizations

THE UNITED NATIONS

Address: United Nations Plaza, New York, NY 10017, USA.
Telephone: (212) 963-1234.

The United Nations was founded in 1945 to maintain international peace and security and to develop international co-operation in economic, social, cultural and humanitarian problems.

The United Nations was a name devised by President Franklin D. Roosevelt of the United States. It was first used in the Declaration by United Nations of 1 January 1942, when representatives of 26 nations pledged their governments to continue fighting together against the Axis powers.

The United Nations Charter (see p. 9) was drawn up by the representatives of 50 countries at the United Nations Conference on International Organization, which met at San Francisco from 25 April to 26 June 1945. The representatives deliberated on the basis of proposals worked out by representatives of China, the USSR, the United Kingdom and the United States at Dumbarton Oaks in August–October 1944. The Charter was signed on 26 June 1945. Poland, not represented at the Conference, signed it later but nevertheless became one of the original 51 members.

The United Nations officially came into existence on 24 October 1945, when the Charter had been ratified by China, France, the USSR, the United Kingdom and the United States, and by a majority of other signatories. United Nations Day is now celebrated annually on 24 October.

Membership

MEMBERS OF THE UNITED NATIONS

(with assessments for percentage contributions to the UN budget for 1989, 1990 and 1991, and year of admission)

Country	Assessment	Year
Afghanistan	0.01	1946
Albania	0.01	1955
Algeria	0.15	1962
Angola	0.01	1976
Antigua and Barbuda	0.01	1981
Argentina	0.66	1945
Australia	1.57	1945
Austria	0.74	1955
Bahamas	0.02	1973
Bahrain	0.02	1971
Bangladesh	0.01	1974
Barbados	0.01	1966
Belgium	1.17	1945
Belize	0.01	1981
Benin	0.01	1960
Bhutan	0.01	1971
Bolivia	0.01	1945
Botswana	0.01	1966
Brazil	1.45	1945
Brunei	0.04	1984
Bulgaria	0.15	1955
Burkina Faso	0.01	1960
Burundi	0.01	1962
Byelorussian SSR[1]	0.33	1945
Cambodia (Kampuchea)[2]	0.01	1955
Cameroon	0.01	1960
Canada	3.09	1945
Cape Verde	0.01	1975
Central African Republic	0.01	1960
Chad	0.01	1960
Chile	0.08	1945
China, People's Republic[3]	0.79	1945
Colombia	0.14	1945
Comoros	0.01	1975
Congo	0.01	1960
Costa Rica	0.02	1945
Côte d'Ivoire	0.02	1960
Cuba	0.09	1945
Cyprus	0.02	1960
Czechoslovakia	0.66	1945
Denmark	0.69	1945
Djibouti	0.01	1977
Dominica	0.01	1978
Dominican Republic	0.03	1945
Ecuador	0.03	1945
Egypt	0.07	1945
El Salvador	0.01	1945
Equatorial Guinea	0.01	1968
Ethiopia	0.01	1945
Fiji	0.01	1970
Finland	0.51	1955
France	6.25	1945
Gabon	0.03	1960
The Gambia	0.01	1965
Germany	n.a.	1973
Ghana	0.01	1957
Greece	0.40	1945
Grenada	0.01	1974
Guatemala	0.02	1945
Guinea	0.01	1958
Guinea-Bissau	0.01	1974
Guyana	0.01	1966
Haiti	0.01	1945
Honduras	0.01	1945
Hungary	0.21	1955
Iceland	0.03	1946
India	0.37	1945
Indonesia	0.15	1950
Iran	0.69	1945
Iraq	0.12	1945
Ireland	0.18	1955
Israel	0.21	1949
Italy	3.99	1955
Jamaica	0.01	1962
Japan	11.38	1956
Jordan	0.01	1955
Kenya	0.01	1963
Kuwait	0.29	1963
Laos	0.01	1955
Lebanon	0.01	1945
Lesotho	0.01	1966
Liberia	0.01	1945
Libya	0.28	1955
Liechtenstein	n.a.	1990
Luxembourg	0.06	1945
Madagascar	0.01	1960
Malawi	0.01	1964
Malaysia	0.11	1957
Maldives	0.01	1965
Mali	0.01	1960
Malta	0.01	1964
Mauritania	0.01	1961
Mauritius	0.01	1968
Mexico	0.94	1945
Mongolia	0.01	1961
Morocco	0.04	1956
Mozambique	0.01	1975
Myanmar	0.01	1948
Namibia	0.01	1990
Nepal	0.01	1955
Netherlands	1.65	1945
New Zealand	0.24	1945
Nicaragua	0.01	1945
Niger	0.01	1960
Nigeria	0.20	1960
Norway	0.55	1945
Oman	0.02	1971
Pakistan	0.06	1947
Panama	0.02	1945
Papua New Guinea	0.01	1975
Paraguay	0.03	1945
Peru	0.06	1945
Philippines	0.09	1945
Poland	0.56	1945
Portugal	0.18	1955
Qatar	0.05	1971
Romania	0.19	1955
Rwanda	0.01	1962
Saint Christopher and Nevis	0.01	1983
Saint Lucia	0.01	1979
Saint Vincent and the Grenadines	0.01	1980
São Tomé and Príncipe	0.01	1975

INTERNATIONAL ORGANIZATIONS

United Nations

Saudi Arabia	1.02	1945
Senegal	0.01	1960
Seychelles	0.01	1976
Sierra Leone	0.01	1961
Singapore	0.11	1965
Solomon Islands	0.01	1978
Somalia	0.01	1960
South Africa	0.45	1945
Spain	1.95	1955
Sri Lanka	0.01	1955
Sudan	0.01	1956
Suriname	0.01	1975
Swaziland	0.01	1968
Sweden	1.21	1946
Syria	0.04	1945
Tanzania[4]	0.01	1961
Thailand	0.10	1946
Togo	0.01	1960
Trinidad and Tobago	0.05	1962
Tunisia	0.03	1956
Turkey	0.32	1945
Uganda	0.01	1962
Ukrainian SSR[1]	1.25	1945
USSR	9.99	1945
United Arab Emirates	0.19	1971
United Kingdom	4.86	1945
USA	25.00	1945
Uruguay	0.04	1945
Vanuatu	0.01	1981
Venezuela	0.57	1945
Viet-Nam	0.01	1977
Western Samoa	0.01	1976
Yemen[5]	n.a.	1947/67
Yugoslavia	0.46	1945
Zaire	0.01	1960
Zambia	0.01	1964
Zimbabwe	0.02	1980

Total Membership: 159 (October 1990)

[1] The Byelorussian SSR and the Ukrainian SSR are integral parts of the USSR and not independent countries, but they have separate UN membership.
[2] Representing the Supreme National Council, established in 1990 in accordance with a plan formulated by the five permanent members of the UN Security Council.
[3] From 1945 until 1971 the Chinese seat was occupied by the Republic of China (confined to Taiwan since 1949).
[4] Tanganyika was a member of the United Nations from December 1961 and Zanzibar was a member from December 1963. From April 1964, the United Republic of Tanganyika and Zanzibar continued as a single member, changing its name to United Republic of Tanzania in November 1964.
[5] The Yemen Arab Republic (admitted to the UN in 1947) and the People's Democratic Republic of Yemen (admitted in 1967) were amalgamated in 1990.

SOVEREIGN COUNTRIES NOT IN THE UNITED NATIONS
(October 1990)

Andorra	Nauru
China (Taiwan)	San Marino
Kiribati	Switzerland
Democratic People's Republic of Korea	Tonga
	Tuvalu
Republic of Korea	Vatican City (Holy See)
Monaco	

Diplomatic Representation

MEMBER STATES' PERMANENT MISSIONS TO THE UNITED NATIONS
(with Permanent Representatives—October 1990)

Afghanistan: 866 United Nations Plaza, Suite 520, New York, NY 10017; tel. (212) 754-1191; NOOR AHMAD NOOR.

Albania: 320 East 79th St, New York, NY 10021; tel. (212) 249-2059; BASHKIM PITARKA.

Algeria: 15 East 47th St, New York, NY 10017; tel. (212) 750-1960; fax (212) 759-9538.

Angola: 125 East 73rd St, New York, NY 10021; tel. (212) 861-5656; fax (212) 861-9295; MANUEL PEDRO PACAVIRA.

Antigua and Barbuda: 610 Fifth Ave, Suite 311, New York, NY 10020; tel. (212) 541-4117; fax (212) 757-1607; LIONEL HURST.

Argentina: 1 United Nations Plaza, 25th Floor, New York, NY 10017; tel. (212) 688-6300; fax (212) 980-8395; Dr JORGE VÁZQUEZ.

Australia: 1 Dag Hammarskjöld Plaza, 885 Second Ave, 16th Floor, New York, NY 10017; tel. (212) 421-6910; fax (212) 371-5843; Dr PETER WILENSKI.

Austria: 809 United Nations Plaza, 7th Floor, New York, NY 10017; tel. (212) 949-1840; fax (212) 953-1302; PETER HOHENFELLNER.

Bahamas: 767 Third Ave, 9th Floor, New York, NY 10017; tel. (212) 421-6925; fax (212) 759-2135; JAMES B. MOULTRIE.

Bahrain: 2 United Nations Plaza, 25th Floor, New York, NY 10017; tel. (212) 223-6200; fax (212) 319-0687; MUHAMMAD ABDUL GHAFFAR.

Bangladesh: 821 United Nations Plaza, 8th Floor, New York, NY 10017; tel. (212) 867-3434; fax (212) 972-4038; A. H. G. MOHIUDDIN.

Barbados: 800 Second Ave, 18th Floor, New York, NY 10017; tel. (212) 867-8431; BESLEY MAYCOCK.

Belgium: 809 United Nations Plaza, 2nd Floor, New York, NY 10017; tel. (212) 599-5250; fax (212) 599-6843; PAUL NOTERDAEME.

Belize: 820 Second Ave, Suite 922, New York, NY 10017; tel. (212) 599-0233; fax (212) 599-3391; CARL L. B. ROGERS.

Benin: 4 East 73rd St, New York, NY 10021; tel. (212) 249-6014; RENÉ MONGBE.

Bhutan: 2 United Nations Plaza, 27th Floor, New York, NY 10017; tel. (212) 826-1919; fax (212) 826-2998; UGYEN TSHERING.

Bolivia: 211 East 43rd St, 8th Floor (Room 802), New York, NY 10017; tel. (212) 682-8132; fax (212) 687-4642; HUGO NAVAJAS-MOGRO.

Botswana: 103 East 37th St, New York, NY 10016; tel. (212) 889-2277; fax (212) 725-5061; LEGWAILA JOSEPH LEGWAILA.

Brazil: 747 Third Ave, 9th Floor, New York, NY 10017; tel. (212) 832-6868; fax (212) 371-5716; PAULO SARDENBERG.

Brunei: 866 United Nations Plaza, Room 248, New York, NY 10017; tel. (212) 838-1600; fax (212) 980-6478; Dato Paduka Haji JAYA BIN ABDUL LATIF.

Bulgaria: 11 East 84th St, New York, NY 10028; tel. (212) 737-4790; fax (212) 472-9865; DIMITAR T. KOSTOV.

Burkina Faso: 115 East 73rd St, New York, NY 10021; tel. (212) 288-7515; GAËTAN RIMWANGUIYA OUEDRAOGO.

Burundi: 201 East 42nd St, 28th Floor, New York, NY 10017; tel. (212) 687-1180; fax (212) 687-1197; BENOÎT SEBURYAMO.

Byelorussian Soviet Socialist Republic: 136 East 67th St, New York, NY 10021; tel. (212) 535-3420; GUENNADI N. BURAVKIN.

Cambodia (Kampuchea): 747 Third Ave, 8th Floor, New York, NY 10017; tel. (212) 888-6646; fax (212) 980-1041.

Cameroon: 22 East 73rd St, New York, NY 10021; tel. (212) 794-2295; fax (212) 249-0533; PASCAL BILOA TANG.

Canada: 866 United Nations Plaza, Suite 250, New York, NY 10017; tel. (212) 751-5600; fax (212) 486-1295; YVES FORTIER.

Cape Verde: 27 East 69th St, New York, NY 10021; tel. (212) 472-0333; fax (212) 794-1398; HUMBERTO BETTENCOURT SANTOS.

Central African Republic: 386 Park Ave South, Room 1614, New York, NY 10016; tel. (212) 689-6195; JEAN-PIERRE SOHAHONG-KOMBET.

Chad: 211 East 43rd St, Suite 1703, New York, NY 10017; tel. (212) 986-0980; MAHAMAT ALI ADOUM.

Chile: 809 United Nations Plaza, 4th Floor, New York, NY 10017; tel. (212) 687-7547; fax (212) 972-9875; JUAN O. SOMAVIA.

China, People's Republic: 155 West 66th St, New York, NY 10023; tel. (212) 787-3838; fax (212) 870-0333; LI DAOYU.

Colombia: 140 East 57th St, 5th Floor, New York, NY 10022; tel. (212) 355-7776; fax (212) 371-2813; Dr ENRIQUE PEÑALOSA.

Comoros: 336 East 45th St, New York, NY 10017; tel. (212) 972-8010; fax (212) 983-4712; AMINI ALI MOUMIN.

Congo: 14 East 65th St, New York, NY 10021; tel. (212) 744-7840; Dr MARTIN ADOUKI.

Costa Rica: 211 East 43rd St, Room 903, New York, NY 10017; tel. (212) 986-6373; fax (212) 986-6842; CRISTIÁN TATTENBACH.

Côte d'Ivoire: 866 United Nations Plaza, Room 566, New York, NY 10017; tel. (212) 371-7036; fax (212) 935-5347; AMARA ESSY.

Cuba: 315 Lexington Ave and 38th St, New York, NY 10016; tel. (212) 689-7215; fax (212) 779-1697; RICARDO ALARCÓN DE QUESADA.

Cyprus: 13 East 40th St, New York, NY 10016; tel. (212) 481-6023; fax (212) 685-7316; ANDREAS MAVROMMATIS.

Czechoslovakia: 1109–1111 Madison Ave, New York, NY 10028; tel. (212) 535-8814; fax (212) 772-0586; EDUARD KUKAN.

Denmark: 2 United Nations Plaza, 26th Floor, New York, NY 10017; tel. (212) 308-7009; fax (212) 308-3384; KJELD MORTENSEN.

INTERNATIONAL ORGANIZATIONS
United Nations

Djibouti: 866 United Nations Plaza, Suite 4011, New York, NY 10017; tel. (212) 753-3163; fax (212) 223-1276; ROBLE OLHAYE.

Dominica: 820 Second Ave, New York, NY 10017; tel. (212) 949-0853; fax (212) 808-4975; FRANKLIN ANDREW BARON.

Dominican Republic: 144 East 44th St, 4th Floor, New York, NY 10017; tel. (212) 867-0833.

Ecuador: 866 United Nations Plaza, Room 516, New York, NY 10017; tel. (212) 935-1680; fax (212) 935-1835; Dr JOSÉ AYALA LASSO.

Egypt: 36 East 67th St, New York, NY 10021; tel. (212) 879-6300; fax (212) 794-3874; AMRE M. MOUSSA.

El Salvador: 46 Park Ave, New York, NY 10016; tel. (212) 679-1616; Dr RICARDO G. CASTANEDA-CORNEJO.

Equatorial Guinea: 57 Magnolia Ave, Mount Vernon, NY 10553; DAMASO-OBIANG NDONG.

Ethiopia: 866 United Nations Plaza, Room 560, New York, NY 10017; tel. (212) 421-1830; fax (212) 754-0360; TESFAYE TADESSE.

Fiji: 1 United Nations Plaza, 26th Floor, New York, NY 10017; tel. (212) 355-7316; fax (212) 319-1896; WINSTON THOMPSON.

Finland: 866 United Nations Plaza, 2nd Floor, New York, NY 10017; tel. (212) 355-2100; fax (212) 759-6156; Dr KLAUS TÖRNUDD.

France: 1 Dag Hammarskjöld Plaza, 245 East 47th St, New York, NY 10017; tel. (212) 308-5700; PIERRE-LOUIS BLANC.

Gabon: 18 East 41st St, 6th Floor, New York, NY 10017; tel. (212) 686-9720; fax (212) 689-5769; DENIS DANGUE REWAKA.

The Gambia: 820 Second Ave, 9th Floor, New York, NY 10017; tel. (212) 949-6640; fax (212) 808-4975; OUSMAN AHMADU SALLAH.

Germany: 600 Third Ave, 41st Floor, New York, NY 10016; tel. (212) 949-9200; fax (212) 490-0857; Dr OTTO BRÄUTIGAM.

Ghana: 19 East 47th St, New York, NY 10017; tel. (212) 832-1300; Dr KOFI AWOONOR.

Greece: 733 Third Ave, 23rd Floor, New York, NY 10017; tel. (212) 490-6060; ANTONIOS EXARCHOS.

Grenada: 820 Second Ave, Suite 900D, New York, NY 10017; tel. (212) 599-0301; EUGENE PURSOO.

Guatemala: 57 Park Ave, New York, NY 10016; tel. (212) 679-4760; fax (212) 685-8741; FRANCISCO VILLAGRAN DE LEÓN.

Guinea: 140 East 39th St, New York, NY 10016; tel. (212) 687-8115; fax (212) 687-8248; ZAÏNOUL ABIDINE SANOUSSI.

Guinea-Bissau: 211 East 43rd St, Room 604, New York, NY 10017; tel. (212) 661-3977; BOUBACAR TOURE.

Guyana: 866 United Nations Plaza, Suite 555, New York, NY 10017; tel. (212) 527-3232; fax (212) 935-7548; SAMUEL R. INSANALLY.

Haiti: 801 Second Ave, Room 300, New York, NY 10017; tel. (212) 370-4840; fax (212) 661-8698; YVES L. AUGUSTE.

Honduras: 866 United Nations Plaza, Suite 417, New York, NY 10017; tel. (212) 752-3370; fax (212) 223-0498; ROBERTO FLORES BERMÚDEZ.

Hungary: 10 East 75th St, New York, NY 10021; tel. (212) 535-8660; fax (212) 734-6036; ANDRÉ ERDÖS.

Iceland: 370 Lexington Ave, 5th Floor, New York, NY 10017; tel. (212) 686-4100; fax (212) 532-4138; BENEDIKT GRÖNDAL.

India: 866 United Nations Plaza, Suite 505, New York, NY 10017; tel. (212) 751-0900; fax (212) 751-1393; CHINMAYA RAJANINATH GHAREKHAN.

Indonesia: 325 East 38th St, New York, NY 10016; tel. (212) 972-8333; NANA S. SUTRESNA.

Iran: 622 Third Ave, 34th Floor, New York, NY 10017; tel. (212) 687-2020; fax (212) 867-7086; KAMAL KHARRAZI.

Iraq: 14 East 79th St, New York, NY 10021; tel. (212) 737-4434; fax (212) 772-1794; Dr ABDUL AMIR A. AL-ANBARI.

Ireland: 1 Dag Hammarskjöld Plaza, 885 Second Ave, 19th Floor, New York, NY 10017; tel. (212) 421-6934; fax (212) 223-0926; FRANCIS MAHON HAYES.

Israel: 800 Second Ave, New York, NY 10017; tel. (212) 351-5200; fax (212) 697-6272; YORAM ARIDOR.

Italy: 2 United Nations Plaza, 24th Floor, New York, NY 10017; tel. (212) 486-9191; fax (212) 486-1036; VIERI TRAXLER.

Jamaica: 866 Second Ave, 15th Floor, 2 Dag Hammarskjöld Plaza, New York, NY 10017; tel. (212) 688-7040; fax (212) 308-3730; HERBERT SAMUEL WALKER.

Japan: 866 United Nations Plaza, 2nd Floor, New York, NY 10017; tel. (212) 223-4300; fax (212) 751-1966; YOSHIO HATANO.

Jordan: 866 United Nations Plaza, Room 550–552, New York, NY 10017; tel. (212) 752-0135; fax (212) 826-0830; ABDULLAH SALAH.

Kenya: 866 United Nations Plaza, Room 486, New York, NY 10017; tel. (212) 421-4740; MICHAEL GEORGE OKEYO.

Kuwait: 321 East 44th St, New York, NY 10017; tel. (212) 973-4300; fax (212) 370-1733; MOHAMMAD A. ABULHASAN.

Laos: 820 Second Ave, Suite 400, New York, NY 10017; tel. (212) 986-0227; SALY KHAMSY.

Lebanon: 866 United Nations Plaza, Room 531–533, New York, NY 10017; tel. (212) 355-5460; fax (212) 838-2819; K. MAKKAWI.

Lesotho: 204 East 39th St, New York, NY 10016; tel. (212) 661-1690; MONYANE P. PHOOFOLO.

Liberia: 820 Second Ave, 4th Floor, New York, NY 10017; tel. (212) 687-1033; WILLIAM BULL.

Libya: 309-315 East 48th St, New York, NY 10017; tel. (212) 752-5775; Dr ALI A. TREIKI.

Liechtenstein: 405 Lexington Ave, 43rd Floor, New York, NY 10017; tel. (212) 599-0220; fax (212) 599-0064; CLAUDIA FRITSCHE.

Luxembourg: 801 Second Ave, New York, NY 10017; tel. (212) 370-9850; fax (212) 697-5529; JEAN FEYDER.

Madagascar: 801 Second Ave, Suite 404, New York, NY 10017; tel. (212) 986-9491; fax (212) 986-6271; BLAISE RABETAFIKA.

Malawi: 600 Third Ave, 30th Floor, New York, NY 10016; tel. (212) 949-0180; ROBERT B. MBAYA.

Malaysia: 140 East 45th St, 43rd Floor, New York, NY 10017; tel. (212) 986-6310; fax (212) 490-8576; ISMAIL RAZALI.

Maldives: 820 Second Ave, Suite 800C, New York, NY 10017; tel. (212) 599-6195; fax (212) 972-3970; HUSSEIN MANIKFAN.

Mali: 111 East 69th St, New York, NY 10021; tel. (212) 737-4150; NOUMOU DIAKITE.

Malta: 249 East 35th St, New York, NY 10016; tel. (212) 725-2345; fax (212) 779-7097; Dr ALEXANDER BORG OLIVIER.

Mauritania: 9 East 77th St, New York, NY 10021; tel. (212) 737-7780; fax (212) 472-3314; MOHAMEDOU OULD MOHAMED MAHMOUD.

Mauritius: 211 East 43rd St, 15th Floor, New York, NY 10017; tel. (212) 949-0190; fax (212) 697-3829; Dr SATTEEANUND PEERTHUM.

Mexico: 2 United Nations Plaza, 28th Floor, New York, NY 10017; tel. (212) 752-0220; fax (212) 688-8862; Dr JORGE MONTAÑO.

Mongolia: 6 East 77th St, New York, NY 10021; tel. (212) 861-9460; fax (212) 861-9464; MANGALYN DUGERSUREN.

Morocco: 767 Third Ave, 30th Floor, New York, NY 10017; tel. (212) 421-1580; fax (212) 980-1512; AZIZ HASBI.

Mozambique: 70 East 79th St, New York, NY 10021; tel. (212) 517-4550; fax (212) 517-4553; PEDRO COMISSARIO AFONSO.

Myanmar: 10 East 77th St, New York, NY 10021; tel. (212) 535-1310; fax (212) 737-2421; KYAW MIN.

Namibia: 135 East 36th St, New York, NY 10016; tel. (212) 685-2003; fax (212) 685-1561.

Nepal: 820 Second Ave, Suite 202, New York, NY 10017; tel. (212) 370-4188; fax (212) 953-2038; JAI PRATAP RANA.

Netherlands: 711 Third Ave, 9th Floor, New York, NY 10017; tel. (212) 697-5547; fax (212) 370-1954; ROBERT J. VAN SCHAIK.

New Zealand: 1 United Nations Plaza, 25th Floor, New York, NY 10017; tel. (212) 826-1960; fax (212) 758-0827; TERENCE O'BRIEN.

Nicaragua: 820 Second Ave, 8th Floor, New York, NY 10017; tel. (212) 490-7997; Dr ROBERTO MAYORGA-CORTES.

Niger: 417 East 50th St, New York, NY 10022; tel. (212) 421-3260; Col MOUMOUNI DJERMAKOYE.

Nigeria: 733 Third Ave, 15th Floor, New York, NY 10017; tel. (212) 953-9130; fax (212) 697-1970; Prof. IBRAHIM A. GAMBARI.

Norway: 825 Third Ave, 18th Floor, New York, NY 10017; tel. (212) 421-0280; fax (212) 688-0554; MARTIN JOHANNES HUSLID.

Oman: 866 United Nations Plaza, Suite 540, New York, NY 10017; tel. (212) 355-3505; fax (212) 644-0070; SALIM BIN MUHAMMAD AL-KHUSSAIBY.

Pakistan: 8 East 65th St, New York, NY 10021; tel. (212) 879-8600; fax (212) 744-7348; JAMSHEED K. A. MARKER.

Panama: 866 United Nations Plaza, Suite 509, New York, NY 10017; tel. (212) 421-5420; fax (212) 421-2694; Dr CÉSAR PEREIRA BURGOS.

Papua New Guinea: 866 United Nations Plaza, Suite 322, New York, NY 10017; tel. (212) 832-0043; fax (212) 832-0918; RENAGI RENAGI LOHIA.

Paraguay: 211 East 43rd St, Room 1202, New York, NY 10017; tel. (212) 687-3490; fax (212) 818-1282; ALFREDO CAÑETE.

Peru: 820 Second Ave, Suite 1600, New York, NY 10017; tel. (212) 687-3336; fax (212) 972-6975; Dr RICARDO V. LUNA.

Philippines: 556 Fifth Ave, 5th Floor, New York, NY 10036; tel. (212) 764-1300; fax (212) 840-8602; SEDREY A. ORDOÑEZ.

Poland: 9 East 66th St, New York, NY 10021; tel. (212) 744-2506; ; fax (212) 517-6771; Dr STANISŁAW PAWLAK.

INTERNATIONAL ORGANIZATIONS

United Nations

Portugal: 777 Third Ave, 27th Floor, New York, NY 10017; tel. (212) 759-9444; fax (212) 355-1124; Fernando José Reino.

Qatar: 747 Third Ave, 22nd Floor, New York, NY 10017; tel. (212) 486-9335; fax (212) 758-4952; Dr Hassan Ali Hussain al-Ni'mah.

Romania: 573–577 Third Ave, New York, NY 10016; tel. (212) 682-3273; fax (212) 682-9746; Aurel Dragoş Munteanu.

Rwanda: 124 East 39th St, New York, NY 10016; tel. (212) 696-0644; fax (212) 689-3304; Oswald Rukashaza.

Saint Christopher and Nevis: 414 East 75th St, 5th Floor, New York, NY 10021; tel. (212) 535-1234; fax (212) 879-4789; Dr William Herbert.

Saint Lucia: 820 Second Ave, Suite 900, New York, NY 10017; tel. (212) 697-9360; fax (212) 808-4975; Dr Charles S. Flemming.

Saint Vincent and the Grenadines: 801 Second Ave, 21st Floor, New York, NY 10017; tel. (212) 687-4490; Kingsley Layne.

São Tomé and Príncipe: 801 Second Ave, Suite 1504, New York, NY 10017; tel. (212) 697-4211; fax (212) 687-8389; Joaquim Rafael Branco.

Saudi Arabia: 405 Lexington Ave, 56th Floor, New York, NY 10017; tel. (212) 697-4830; fax (212) 983-4895; Samir Shihabi.

Senegal: 238 East 68th St, New York, NY 10021; tel. (212) 517-9030; fax (212) 737-7461; Absa Claude Diallo.

Seychelles: 820 Second Ave, Room 900F, New York, NY 10017; tel. (212) 687-9766; fax (212) 808-4975.

Sierra Leone: 57 East 64th St, New York, NY 10021; tel. (212) 570-0030; Dr Tom Obaleh Kargbo.

Singapore: 2 United Nations Plaza, 25th Floor, New York, NY 10017; tel. (212) 826-0840; fax (212) 826-2964; Dr Chan Heng Chee.

Solomon Islands: 820 Second Ave, Suite 800A, New York, NY 10017; tel. (212) 599-6193; fax (212) 972-3970; Francis Bugotu.

Somalia: 425 East 61st St, Suite 703, New York, NY 10021; tel. (212) 688-9410; Abdillahi Said Osman.

South Africa: 326 East 48th St, New York, NY 10017; tel. (212) 371-8154; fax (212) 371-7577; Jeremy B. Shearar.

Spain: 809 United Nations Plaza, 6th Floor, New York, NY 10017; tel. (212) 661-1050; Francisco Villar y Ortiz de Urdía.

Sri Lanka: 630 Third Ave, 20th Floor, New York, NY 10017; tel. (212) 986-7040; fax (212) 986-1838; Daya Perera.

Sudan: 210 East 49th St, New York, NY 10017; tel. (212) 421-2680; Lt-Gen. Joseph Lagu.

Suriname: 866 United Nations Plaza, Suite 320, New York, NY 10017; tel. (212) 826-0660; Kriesnadath Nandoe.

Swaziland: 866 United Nations Plaza, Suite 420, New York, NY 10017; tel. (212) 371-8910; Dr Timothy L. L. Dlamini.

Sweden: 885 Second Ave, 46th Floor, New York, NY 10017; tel. (212) 751-5900; fax (212) 832-0389; Jan K. Eliasson.

Syria: 820 Second Ave, 10th Floor, New York, NY 10017; tel. (212) 661-1313; fax (212) 983-4439; Dia-Allah el-Fattal.

Tanzania: 205 East 42nd St, 13th Floor, New York, NY 10017; tel. (212) 972-9160; fax (212) 682-5232; Anthony B. Nyakyi.

Thailand: 628 Second Ave, New York, NY 10016; tel. (212) 689-1004; fax (212) 683-6017; Nitya Pibulsonggram.

Togo: 112 East 40th St, New York, NY 10016; tel. (212) 490-3455; Soumi-Biova Pennaneach.

Trinidad and Tobago: 675 Third Ave, 22nd Floor, New York, NY 10017; tel. (212) 697-7620; fax (212) 682-3580; Dr Marjorie R. Thorpe.

Tunisia: 405 Lexington Ave, 65th Floor, New York, NY 10174; tel. (212) 557-3344; fax (212) 697-4099; Ahmed Ghezal.

Turkey: 821 United Nations Plaza, 11th Floor, New York, NY 10017; tel. (212) 949-0150; fax (212) 949-0086; Mustafa Akşin.

Uganda: 336 East 45th St, New York, NY 10017; tel. (212) 949-0110; fax (212) 687-4517; Prof. Perezi Karukubiro-Kamunanwire.

Ukrainian Soviet Socialist Republic: 136 East 67th St, New York, NY 10021; tel. (212) 535-3418; Guennadi I. Oudovenko.

USSR: 136 East 67th St, New York, NY 10021; tel. (212) 861-4900; fax (212) 628-0252; Yuli M. Vorontsov.

United Arab Emirates: 747 Third Ave, 36th Floor, New York, NY 10017; tel. (212) 371-0480; fax (212) 319-5433; Muhammad Hussain al-Shaali.

United Kingdom: 845 Third Ave, 10th Floor, New York, NY 10022; tel. (212) 752-2710; fax (212) 745-0316; Sir David Hannay.

United Republic of Tanzania: (see Tanzania).

USA: 799 United Nations Plaza, New York, NY 10017; tel. (212) 415-4000; fax (212) 415-4443; Thomas R. Pickering.

Uruguay: 747 Third Ave, 37th Floor, New York, NY 10017; tel. (212) 752-8240; fax (212) 593-0935; Ramiro Piriz-Ballon.

Vanuatu: 416 Convent Ave, New York, NY 10031; tel. (212) 926-3311; fax (212) 926-4131; Robert F. van Lierop.

Venezuela: 335 East 46th St, New York, NY 10017; tel. (212) 557-2055; fax (212) 557-3528.

Viet-Nam: 20 Waterside Plaza (Lobby), New York, NY 10010; tel. (212) 679-3779; fax (212) 686-8534; Trinh Xuan Lang.

Western Samoa: 820 Second Ave, Suite 800D, New York, NY 10017; tel. (212) 599-6196; fax (212) 972-3970; Dr Fili Wendt.

Yemen: 866 United Nations Plaza, Room 435, New York, NY 10017; tel. (212) 355-1730; Abdalla Saleh al-Ashtal.

Yugoslavia: 854 Fifth Ave, New York, NY 10021; tel. (212) 879-8700; fax (212) 879-8705; Darko Silović.

Zaire: 767 Third Ave, 25th Floor, New York, NY 10017; tel. (212) 754-1966; fax (212) 754-1970; Bagbeni Adeito Nzengeya.

Zambia: 237 East 52nd St, New York, NY 10022; tel. (212) 758-1110; fax (212) 758-1319; Lt-Gen. Peter Dingiswaye Zuze.

Zimbabwe: 19 East 47th St, New York, NY 10017; tel. (212) 980-9511; fax (212) 755-4188; Simbarashe Mumbengegwi.

OBSERVERS

Non-member states, inter-governmental and other organizations which have received an invitation to participate in the sessions and the work of the General Assembly as Observers, maintaining permanent offices at the UN.

Non-member states

Holy See: 20 East 72nd St, New York, NY 10021; tel. (212) 734-2900; fax (212) 988-3633; The Most Rev. Mgr Renato Raffaele Martino.

Korea, Democratic People's Republic: 225 East 86th St, New York, NY 10028; tel. (212) 722-3536; fax (212) 534-3612; Pak Gil Yon.

Korea, Republic: 866 United Nations Plaza, Suite 300, New York, NY 10017; tel. (212) 371-1280; Hong-Choo Hyun.

Monaco: 845 Third Ave, 19th Floor, New York, NY 10022; tel. (212) 759-5227; fax (212) 754-9320; John Dubé.

San Marino: 745 Fifth Ave, Suite 1208, New York, NY 10151; tel. (212) 751-1234; fax (212) 751-1436; Ghazi Aita.

Switzerland: 757 Third Ave, 21st Floor, New York, NY 10017; tel. (212) 421-1480; fax (212) 751-2104; Dieter Chenaux-Repond.

Inter-governmental organizations*

Asian-African Legal Consultative Committee: 404 East 66th St, Apt 12C, New York, NY 10021; tel. (212) 734-7608; K. Bhagwat-Singh.

Commonwealth Secretariat: 820 Second Ave, Suite 800A, New York, NY 10017; tel. (212) 599-6190; fax (212) 972-3970.

European Community: 3 Dag Hammarskjöld Plaza, 12th Floor, 305 East 47th St, New York, NY 10017; tel. (212) 371-3804; fax (212) 758-2718; the Observer is the Permanent Representative to the UN of the country currently exercising the Presidency of the Council of Ministers of the Community.

International Committee of the Red Cross: 780 Third Ave, Suite 2802, New York, NY 10017; tel. (212) 371-0771; fax (212) 838-5397.

League of Arab States: 747 Third Ave, 35th Floor, New York, NY 10017; tel. (212) 838-8700; fax (212) 355-3909.

Organization of African Unity: 346 East 50th St, New York, NY 10022; tel. (212) 319-5490; fax (212) 319-3571; Ibrahima Sy.

Organization of the Islamic Conference: 130 East 40th St, 5th Floor, New York, NY 10016; tel. (212) 883-0140; fax (212) 883-0143.

* The following inter-governmental organizations have a standing invitation to participate as Observers, but do not maintain permanent offices at the United Nations:
  African, Caribbean and Pacific Group of States.
  African Development Bank.
  Agency for Cultural and Technical Co-operation.
  Agency for the Prohibition of Nuclear Weapons in Latin America and the Caribbean.
  Council of Europe.
  Organization of American States.
  Sistema Económica Latinoamericana.

The Council for Mutual Economic Assistance (CMEA–COMECON) is represented by the Permanent Mission of the country currently holding the Presidency of the CMEA.

Other organization

Palestine Liberation Organization: 115 East 65th St, New York, NY 10021; tel. (212) 288-8500; fax (212) 517-2377.

INTERNATIONAL ORGANIZATIONS

United Nations Information Centres

Afghanistan: POB 5; Shah Mahmoud Ghazi Watt, Kabul.
Algeria: POB 823; 19 ave Chahid el-Ouali, Mustapha Sayed, Algiers.
Argentina: Junín 1940, 1° piso, 1113 Buenos Aires (also covers Uruguay).
Australia: GPO Box 4045; Suite 1, 2nd Floor, 125 York St, Sydney, NSW 2001 (also covers Fiji, Kiribati, Nauru, New Zealand, Tonga, Tuvalu, Vanuatu and Western Samoa).
Austria: POB 500; Vienna International Centre, Wagramerstrasse 5, 1220 Vienna (also covers Germany and Hungary).
Bahrain: POB 26004: House 131, Rd 2803, Segaya 328, Manama (also covers Qatar and the United Arab Emirates).
Bangladesh: POB 3658; House 25, Rd 11, Dhanmandi, Dhaka 1209.
Belgium: 40 ave de Broqueville, 1200 Brussels (also covers Luxembourg and the Netherlands).
Bolivia: POB 9072; Edif. Naciones Unidas, Plaza Isabel la Católica, Planta Baja, La Paz.
Brazil: Palacio Itamaraty, Avda Marechal Floriano 196, 20080 Rio de Janeiro.
Burkina Faso: POB 135; 218 rue de la Gare, Secteur no 3, Ouagadougou (also covers Chad, Mali and Niger).
Burundi: POB 2160; ave de la Poste 7, place de l'Indépendance, Bujumbura.
Cameroon: POB 836; Immeuble Kamden, rue Joseph Clère, Yaoundé (also covers the Central African Republic and Gabon).
Chile: Edif. Naciones Unidas, Avda Dag Hammarskjöld, Casilla 179-D, Santiago.
Colombia: Apdo Aéreo 058964; Calle 72, No. 12-65, 2° piso, Bogotá 2 (also covers Ecuador and Venezuela).
Congo: POB 13210; ave Foch, Case Ortf 15, Brazzaville.
Czechoslovakia: Panská 5, 110 00 Prague 1.
Denmark: 37 H. C. Andersens Blvd, 1553 Copenhagen V (also covers Finland, Iceland, Norway and Sweden).
Egypt: POB 262; 1 Osiris St, Tagher Bldg, Garden City, Cairo (also covers Saudi Arabia and Yemen).
El Salvador: POB 2157; Edif. Escalón, 2° piso, Paseo General Escalón y 87 Avda Norte, Colonia Escalón, San Salvador.
Ethiopia: POB 3001; Africa Hall, Addis Ababa.
France: 1 rue Miollis, 75732 Paris Cedex 15.
Ghana: Roman Ridge Ambassadorial Estate, Extension Area, Plot N78, Accra (also covers Sierra Leone).
Greece: 36 Amalia Ave, 105 58 Athens (also covers Cyprus and Israel).
India: 55 Lodi Estate, New Delhi 110003 (also covers Bhutan).
Indonesia: Gedung Dewan Pers, 5th Floor, 32-34 Jalan Kebon Sirih, Jakarta.
Iran: POB 15875-4557; ave Boharest Maydan, Argantine 74, Teheran.
Iraq: POB 27; Amiriya, Airport St, Baghdad.
Italy: Palazzetto Venezia, Piazza San Marco 50, Rome (also covers the Holy See and Malta).
Japan: Shin Aoyama Bldg Nishikan, 22nd Floor, 1-1 Minami Aoyama 1-chome, Minato-ku, Tokyo 107 (also covers the Trust Territory of the Pacific Islands).
Kenya: POB 34135; United Nations Office, Gigiri, Nairobi (also covers Seychelles and Uganda).
Lebanon: POB 4656; Apt No. 1, Fakhoury Bldg, Montée Bain Militaire, Ardati St, Beirut (also covers Jordan, Kuwait and Syria).
Lesotho: POB 301; Corner Kingsway and Hilton Rds, opposite Sanlam Centre, Maseru 100.
Liberia: POB 274; LBDI Bldg, Tubman Blvd, Monrovia.
Libya: POB 286; Sharia Muzzafar al-Aftas, Hay al-Andalous, Tripoli.
Madagascar: POB 1348; 22 rue Rainitovo, Antasahavola, Antananarivo.
Mexico: Presidente Mazaryk 29, 7° piso, México 11570, DF (also covers Cuba and the Dominican Republic).
Morocco: POB 601; Angle Charia Moulay Ibnouzaid et Zankat Roundanat No. 6, Rabat.
Myanmar: 6 Natmauk Rd, POB 230, Yangon.
Nepal: POB 107; Pulchowk, Patan, Kathmandu.
Nicaragua: POB 3260; Bolonia, de Plaza España, 2 cuadros abajo, Managua.
Nigeria: POB 1068; 17 Kingsway Rd, Ikoyi, Lagos.
Pakistan: POB 1107; House No. 26, 88th St, Ramna 6/3, Islamabad.
Panama: POB 6-9083, El Dorado; Urbanización Obarrio, Calle 54 y Avda Tercera Sur, Casa No. 17, Panama City.
Paraguay: Casilla de Correo 1107, Asunción.
Peru: POB 14-0199; Mariscal Blas Cerdeña 450, San Isidro, Lima.
Philippines: POB 7285 (ADC); NEDA Bldg, Ground Floor, 106 Amorsolo St, Legaspi Village, Makati, Metro Manila (also covers Papua New Guinea and Solomon Islands).
Portugal: Rua Latina Coelho No. 1, Edif. Aviz, Bloco A1, 10°, 1000 Lisbon.
Romania: POB 1-701; 16 Aurel Vlaicu St, Bucharest.
Senegal: POB 154; 72 blvd de la République, Dakar (also covers Cape Verde, Côte d'Ivoire, The Gambia, Guinea, Guinea-Bissau and Mauritania).
Spain: POB 3400, 28080; Avda General Perón 32-1°, 28020 Madrid.
Sri Lanka: POB 1505; 202-204 Bauddhaloka Mawatha, Colombo 7.
Sudan: POB 1992; UN Compound, University Ave, Khartoum (also covers Somalia).
Switzerland: Palais des Nations, 1211 Geneva 10 (also covers Bulgaria and Poland).
Tanzania: POB 9224; Matasalamat Bldg, 1st Floor, Samora Machel Ave, Dar es Salaam.
Thailand: United Nations Bldg, Rajadamnern Ave, Bangkok 10200 (also covers Cambodia, Hong Kong, Laos, Malaysia, Singapore and Viet-Nam).
Togo: POB 911; 107 blvd de 13 janvier, Lomé (also covers Benin).
Trinidad and Tobago: POB 130; 16 Victoria Ave, Port of Spain (also covers Antigua and Barbuda, the Bahamas, Barbados, Belize, Dominica, Grenada, Guyana, Jamaica, the Netherlands Antilles, Saint Christopher and Nevis, Saint Lucia, Saint Vincent and the Grenadines and Suriname).
Tunisia: POB 863, 61 blvd Bab Benat, Tunis.
Turkey: PK 407; 197 Atatürk Bulvarı, Ankara.
USSR: 4/16 Ulitsa Lunacharskogo, Moscow 121002 (also covers the Byelorussian SSR and the Ukrainian SSR).
United Kingdom: 20 Buckingham Gate, London, SW1E 6LB (also covers Ireland).
USA: 1889 F St, NW, Washington, DC 20006.
Yugoslavia: POB 157; Svetozara Markovica 58, Belgrade 11001 (also covers Albania).
Zaire: POB 7248: Bâtiment Deuxième République, blvd du 30 juin, Kinshasa.
Zambia: POB 32905, Lusaka (also covers Botswana, Malawi and Swaziland).
Zimbabwe: POB 4408; Dolphin House, 123 Moffat St/Union Ave, Harare.

United Nations Publications

Yearbook of the United Nations.
The UN Chronicle (quarterly).
United Nations Documents Index (quarterly).
Current Bibliographical Information (monthly).
Monthly Bulletin of Statistics.
Population and Vital Statistics Report (monthly).
Objective: Justice (2 a year).
Bulletin on Narcotics (quarterly).
CTC Reporter (Centre on Transnational Corporations; 3 a year).
Documents (of the General Assembly; the Security Council; the Economic and Social Council; the Trusteeship Council.

Other UN publications are listed in the chapters dealing with the agencies concerned.

Finance

The United Nations Budget is mainly financed by contributions from member states (in the proportions shown on pp. 3-4). In 1986 and 1987 there was a serious financial crisis, as a result of arrears in payments by some members. The USA (which pays some 25% of the budget) withheld part of its contributions, demanding financial reforms and the introduction of 'weighted' voting (in proportion to members' contributions) on budgetary matters. An 18-member panel of experts was established in December 1985 to review UN administration and finance. Its report was presented to the UN Secretary-General in August 1986, and the recommendations were approved by the General Assembly later in the year. The reforms were to include: a limit on the number of UN conferences to be held each year; a reduction in numbers of staff (by 15% at lower levels and by 25% at the most senior levels), together with a restructuring of the principal administrative departments; a reduction in the volume of documents produced by the UN; and more efficient collaboration between UN agencies. The most important innovation was made in response to demands by the principal contributors to the UN budget (including both the USA and the USSR) for greater control over spending: from 1990 the budget was to be drafted by the 21-member Committee for Programme and Co-ordination (expanded to 34 members in 1987), and to be adopted by consensus, giving the major contributors a power of veto for the first time (although the budget would still be subject to approval by the General Assembly). In September 1988 the US Government, expressing its satisfaction with the reforms, authorized the immediate payment of $144m. and the eventual payment of $520m. in current and overdue contributions.

The extension of UN peace-keeping activities (e.g. to Iran and Iraq, Namibia and Angola) resulted in a significant increase in expenditure in 1989 and 1990.

In September 1990 the total amount owed by member countries was reported to be $660m. (of which almost $522m. was owed by the USA: of this amount, $288m. was carried over from previous years, and $233m. was for the current year).

TWO-YEAR BUDGET OF THE UNITED NATIONS (US dollars)

	1988–89*	1990–91†
Overall policy-making, direction and co-ordination	48,426,300	59,705,000
Political and Security Council affairs; peace-keeping activities	110,474,500	107,470,700
Political affairs, trusteeship and decolonization	27,964,800	35,988,200
Policy-making organs (economic and social activities)	1,847,700	2,163,100
Office of the Director-General for Development and International Economic Co-operation	4,378,300	4,670,800
Regional Commissions' New York Office	780,800	855,300
Department of International Economic and Social Affairs	40,422,100	46,814,800
Activities on global social development issues	10,216,700	9,985,700
Department of Technical Co-operation for Development	21,881,500	23,853,200
Transnational corporations	10,423,100	10,919,200
Economic Commission for Europe	31,627,900	33,089,300
Economic and Social Commission for Asia and the Pacific	34,895,100	39,791,400
Economic Commission for Latin America and the Caribbean	40,696,800	49,010,700
Economic Commission for Africa	48,081,000	57,725,700
Economic and Social Commission for Western Asia	34,255,800	38,595,400
United Nations Conference on Trade and Development	73,060,900	73,107,600
International Trade Centre	12,453,200	15,400,800
Centre for Science and Technology for Development	3,894,800	4,298,800
United Nations Environment Programme	10,214,900	11,195,600
United Nations Centre for Human Settlements (Habitat)	7,523,900	9,937,800
International drug control	7,896,000	8,333,600
Office of the United Nations High Commissioner for Refugees	37,042,900	34,180,100
Office of the United Nations Disaster Relief Co-ordinator	7,283,600	6,481,200
Human rights	16,112,500	16,105,700
Regular programme of technical co-operation	32,759,000	36,163,200
International Court of Justice	13,056,900	13,333,000
Legal activities	16,062,400	18,766,500
Public information	77,224,700	87,225,400
Administration and management	381,045,300	397,759,500
Conference and library services	332,028,900	352,777,600
United Nations bond issue	3,523,400	—
Staff assessment	255,818,300	298,390,400
Construction, alteration, improvement and major maintenance of premises	18,939,700	70,538,700
Grand total	**1,772,313,700**	**1,974,634,000**

* Budget approved December 1988 and revised December 1989.
† Budget approved December 1989.

Charter of the United Nations

We the peoples of the United Nations determined

to save succeeding generations from the scourge of war, which twice in our lifetime has brought untold sorrow to mankind, and

to reaffirm faith in fundamental human rights, in the dignity and worth of the human person, in the equal rights of men and women and of nations large and small, and

to establish conditions under which justice and respect for the obligations arising from treaties and other sources of international law can be maintained, and

to promote social progress and better standards of life in larger freedom,

And for these ends

to practise tolerance and live together in peace with one another as good neighbours, and

to unite our strength to maintain international peace and security, and

to ensure, by the acceptance of principles and the institution of methods, that armed force shall not be used, save in the common interest, and

to employ international machinery for the promotion of the economic and social advancement of all peoples,

Have resolved to combine our efforts to accomplish these aims.

Accordingly, our respective Governments, through representatives assembled in the city of San Francisco, who have exhibited their full powers found to be in good and due form, have agreed to the present Charter of the United Nations and do hereby establish an international organization to be known as the United Nations.

I. PURPOSES AND PRINCIPLES

Article 1

The Purposes of the United Nations are:

1. To maintain international peace and security, and to that end: to take effective collective measures for the prevention and removal of threats to the peace, and for the suppression of acts of aggression or other breaches of the peace, and to bring about by peaceful means, and in conformity with the principles of justice and international law, adjustment or settlement of international disputes or situations which might lead to a breach of the peace:

2. To develop friendly relations among nations based on respect for the principle of equal rights and self-determination of peoples, and to take other appropriate measures to strengthen universal peace;

3. To achieve international co-operation in solving international problems of an economic, social, cultural, or humanitarian character, and in promoting and encouraging respect for human rights and for fundamental freedoms for all without distinction as to race, sex, language, or religion; and

4. To be a centre for harmonizing the accusations of nations in the attainment of these common ends.

Article 2

The Organization and its Members, in pursuit of the Purposes stated in Article 1, shall act in accordance with the following Principles.

1. The Organization is based on the principle of the sovereign equality of all its Members.

2. All Members, in order to ensure to all of them the rights and benefits resulting from membership, shall fulfil in good faith the obligations assumed by them in accordance with the present Charter.

3. All Members shall settle their international disputes by peaceful means in such a manner that international peace and security, and justice, are not endangered.

4. All Members shall refrain in their international relations from the threat or use of force against the territorial integrity or political independence of any state, or in any manner inconsistent with the Purposes of the United Nations.

5. All Members shall give the United Nations every assistance in any action it takes in accordance with the present Charter, and shall refrain from giving assistance to any state against which the United Nations is taking preventive or enforcement action.

6. The Organization shall ensure that states which are not Members of the United Nations act in accordance with these Principles so far as may be necessary for the maintenance of international peace and security.

7. Nothing contained in the present Charter shall authorize the United Nations to intervene in matters which are essentially within the domestic jurisdiction of any state or shall require the Members to submit such matters to settlement under the present Charter; but this principle shall not prejudice the application of enforcement measures under Chapter VII.

II. MEMBERSHIP

Article 3

The original Members of the United Nations shall be the states which, having participated in the United Nations Conference on International Organization at San Francisco, or having previously signed the Declaration by United Nations of January 1, 1942, sign the present Charter and ratify it in accordance with Article 110.

Article 4

1. Membership in the United Nations is open to all other peace-loving states which accept the obligations contained in the present Charter and, in the judgement of the Organization, are able and willing to carry out these obligations.

2. The admission of any such state to membership in the United Nations will be effected by a decision of the General Assembly upon the recommendation of the Security Council.

Article 5

A member of the United Nations against which preventive or enforcement action has been taken by the Security Council may be suspended from the exercise of the rights and privileges of membership by the General Assembly upon the recommendation of the Security Council. The exercise of these rights and privileges may be restored by the Security Council.

Article 6

A Member of the United Nations which has persistently violated the Principles contained in the present Charter may be expelled from the Organization by the General Assembly upon the recommendation of the Security Council.

III. ORGANS

Article 7

1. There are established as the principal organs of the United Nations: a General Assembly, a Security Council, an Economic and Social Council, a Trusteeship Council, an International Court of Justice, and a Secretariat.

2. Such subsidiary organs as may be found necessary may be established in accordance with the present Charter.

Article 8

The United Nations shall place no restrictions on the eligibility of men and women to participate in any capacity and under conditions of equality in its principal and subsidiary organs.

IV. THE GENERAL ASSEMBLY

Composition

Article 9

1. The General Assembly shall consist of all the Members of the United Nations.

2. Each Member shall have not more than five representatives in the General Assembly.

Functions and Powers

Article 10

The General Assembly may discuss any questions or any matters within the scope of the present Charter or relating to the powers and functions of any organs provided for in the present Charter, and, except as provided in Article 12, may make recommendations to the Members of the United Nations or to the Security Council or to both on any such questions or matters.

Article 11

1. The General Assembly may consider the general principles of co-operation in the maintenance of international peace and security, including the principles governing disarmament and the regulation of armaments, and may make recommendations with regard to such principles to the Members or to the Security Council or to both.

2. The General Assembly may discuss any questions relating to the maintenance of international peace and security brought before it by any Member of the United Nations, or by the Security Council, or by a state which is not a Member of the United Nations in accordance with Article 35, paragraph 2, and, except as provided in Article 12, may make recommendations with regard to any such question to the state or states concerned or to the Security Council or both. Any such question on which action is necessary shall be referred to the Security Council by the General Assembly either before or after discussion.

3. The General Assembly may call the attention of the Security Council to situations which are likely to endanger international peace and security.

4. The powers of the General Assembly set forth in this Article shall not limit the general scope of Article 10.

Article 12

1. While the Security Council is exercising in respect of any dispute or situation the functions assigned to it in the present Charter, the General Assembly shall not make any recommendations with regard to that dispute or situation unless the Security Council so requests.

2. The Secretary-General, with the consent of the Security Council, shall notify the General Assembly at each session of any matters relative to the maintenance of international peace and security which are being dealt with by the Security Council and shall similarly notify the General Assembly, or the Members of the United Nations if the General Assembly is not in session, immediately the Security Council ceases to deal with such matters.

Article 13

1. The General Assembly shall initiate studies and make recommendations for the purpose of:

(a) promoting international co-operation in the political field and encouraging the progressive development of international law and its codification;

(b) promoting international co-operation in the economic, social, cultural, educational, and health fields, and assisting in the realization of human rights and fundamental freedoms for all without distinction as to race, sex, language, or religion.

2. The further responsibilities, functions and powers of the General Assembly with respect to matters mentioned in paragraph 1(b) above are set forth in Chapters IX and X.

Article 14

Subject to the provision of Article 12, the General Assembly may recommend measures for the peaceful adjustment of any situation, regardless of origin, which it deems likely to impair the general welfare or friendly relations among nations, including situations resulting from a violation of the provisions of the present Charter setting forth the Purposes and Principles of the United Nations.

Article 15

1. The General Assembly shall receive and consider annual and special reports from the Security Council; these reports shall include an account of the measures that the Security Council has decided upon or taken to maintain international peace and security.

2. The General Assembly shall receive and consider reports from the other organs of the United Nations.

Article 16

The General Assembly shall perform such functions with respect to the international trusteeship system as are assigned to it under Chapters XII and XIII, including the approval of the trusteeship agreements for areas not designated as strategic.

Article 17

1. The General Assembly shall consider and approve the budget of the Organization.

2. The expenses of the Organization shall be borne by the Members as apportioned by the General Assembly.

3. The General Assembly shall consider and approve any financial and budgetary arrangements with specialized agencies referred to in Article 57 and shall examine the administrative budgets of such specialized agencies with a view to making recommendations to the agencies concerned.

Voting

Article 18

1. Each Member of the General Assembly shall have one vote.

2. Decisions of the General Assembly on important questions shall be made by a two-thirds majority of the members present and voting. These questions shall include: recommendations with respect to the maintenance of international peace and security, the election of the non-permanent Members of the Security Council, the election of the Members of the Economic and Social Council, the election of Members of the Trusteeship Council in accordance with paragraph 1(c) of Article 86, the admission of new Members to the United Nations, the suspension of the rights and privileges of membership, the expulsion of Members, questions relating to the operation of the trusteeship system, and budgetary questions.

3. Decisions on other questions, including the determination of additional categories of questions to be decided by a two-thirds majority, shall be made by a majority of the members present and voting.

Article 19

A Member of the United Nations which is in arrears in the payment of its financial contributions to the Organization shall have no vote in the General Assembly if the amount of its arrears equals or exceeds the amount of the contributions due from it for the preceding two full years. The General Assembly may, nevertheless, permit such a Member to vote if it is satisfied that the failure to pay is due to conditions beyond the control of the Member.

Procedure

Article 20

The General Assembly shall meet in regular annual sessions and in such special sessions as occasion may require. Special sessions shall be convoked by the Secretary-General at the request of the Security Council or of a majority of the members of the United Nations.

Article 21

The General Assembly shall adopt its own rules of procedure. It shall elect its President for each session.

Article 22

The General Assembly may establish such subsidiary organs as it deems necessary for the performance of its functions.

V. THE SECURITY COUNCIL
Composition

Article 23

1. The Security Council shall consist of 11 Members of the United Nations. The Republic of China, France, the Union of Soviet Socialist Republics, the United Kingdom of Great Britain and Northern Ireland, and the United States of America shall be permanent members of the Security Council. The General Assembly shall elect six other Members of the United Nations to be non-permanent members of the Security Council, due regard being specially paid, in the first instance to the contribution of Members of the United Nations to the maintenance of international peace and security and to the other purposes of the Organization, and also to equitable geographical distribution.

2. The non-permanent members of the Security Council shall be elected for a term of two years. In the first election of the non-permanent members, however, three shall be chosen for a term of one year. A retiring member shall not be eligible for immediate re-election.

3. Each member of the Security Council shall have one representative.

Functions and Powers

Article 24

1. In order to ensure prompt and effective action by the United Nations, its Members confer on the Security Council primary responsibility for the maintenance of international peace and security, and agree that in carrying out its duties under this responsibility the Security Council acts on their behalf.

2. In discharging these duties the Security Council shall act in accordance with the Purposes and Principles of the United Nations. The specific powers granted to the Security Council for the discharge of these duties are laid down in Chapters VI, VII, VIII and XII.

3. The Security Council shall submit annual and, when necessary, special reports to the General Assembly for its consideration.

Article 25

The Members of the United Nations agree to accept and carry out the decisions of the Security Council in accordance with the present Charter.

Article 26

In order to promote the establishment and maintenance of international peace and security with the least diversion for armaments of the world's human and economic resources, the Security Council shall be responsible for formulating, with the assistance of the Military Staff Committee referred to in Article 47, plans to be submitted to the Members of the United Nations for the establishment of a system for the regulation of armaments.

Voting

Article 27

1. Each member of the Security Council shall have one vote.

2. Decisions of the Security Council on procedural matters shall be made by an affirmative vote of seven members.

3. Decisions of the Security Council on all other matters shall be made by an affirmative vote of seven members including the concurring votes of the permanent members; provided that, in decisions under Chapter VI, and under paragraph 3 of Article 52, a party to a dispute shall abstain from voting.

Procedure

Article 28

1. The Security Council shall be so organized as to be able to function continuously. Each member of the Security Council shall for this purpose be represented at all times at the seat of the Organization.

2. The Security Council shall hold periodic meetings at which each of its members may, if it so desires, be represented by a member of the government or by some other specially designated representative.

3. The Security Council may hold meetings at such places other than the seat of the Organization as in its judgment will best facilitate its work.

Article 29

The Security Council may establish such subsidiary organs as it deems necessary for the performance of its functions.

Article 30

The Security Council shall adopt its own rules of procedure, including the method of selecting its President.

Article 31

Any Member of the United Nations which is not a member of the Security Council may participate, without vote, in the discussion of any question brought before the Security Council whenever the latter considers that the interests of that Member are specially affected.

Article 32

Any Member of the United Nations which is not a member of the Security Council or any state which is not a Member of the United Nations, if it is a party to a dispute under consideration by the Security Council, shall be invited to participate, without vote, in the discussion relating to the dispute. The Security Council shall lay down such conditions as it deems just for the participation of a state which is not a Member of the United Nations.

VI. PACIFIC SETTLEMENT OF DISPUTES

Article 33

1. The parties to any dispute, the continuance of which is likely to endanger the maintenance of international peace and security, shall, first of all, seek a solution by negotiation, enquiry, mediation, conciliation, arbitration, judicial settlement, resort to regional agencies or arrangements, or other peaceful means of their own choice.

2. The Security Council shall, when it deems necessary, call upon the parties to settle their disputes by such means.

Article 34

The Security Council may investigate any dispute, or any situation which might lead to international friction or give rise to a dispute, in order to determine whether the continuance of the dispute or situation is likely to endanger the maintenance of international peace and security.

Article 35

1. Any Member of the United Nations may bring any dispute, or any situation of the nature referred to in Article 34, to the attention of the Security Council or of the General Assembly.

2. A state which is not a Member of the United Nations may bring to the attention of the Security Council or of the General Assembly any dispute to which it is a party if it accepts in advance, for the purposes of the dispute, the obligations of pacific settlement provided in the present Charter.

3. The proceedings of the General Assembly in respect of matters brought to its attention under this Article will be subject to the provisions of Articles 11 and 12.

Article 36

1. The Security Council may, at any stage of a dispute of the nature referred to in Article 33 or of a situation of like nature, recommend appropriate procedures or methods of adjustment.

2. The Security Council should take into consideration any procedures for the settlement of the dispute which have already been adopted by the parties.

3. In making recommendations under this Article the Security Council should also take into consideration that legal disputes should as a general rule be referred by the parties to the International Court of Justice in accordance with the provisions of the statute of the Court.

Article 37

1. Should the parties to a dispute of the nature referred to in Article 33, fail to settle it by the means indicated in that Article, they shall refer it to the Security Council.

2. If the Security Council deems that the continuance of the dispute is in fact likely to endanger the maintenance of international peace and security, it shall decide whether to take action under Article 36 or to recommend such terms of settlement as it may consider appropriate.

Article 38

Without prejudice to the provisions of Articles 33 to 37, the Security Council may, if all the parties to any dispute so request, make recommendations to the parties with a view to a pacific settlement of the dispute.

VII. ACTION WITH RESPECT TO THREATS TO THE PEACE, BREACHES OF THE PEACE, AND ACTS OF AGGRESSION

Article 39

The Security Council shall determine the existence of any threat to the peace, breach of the peace, or act of aggression and shall make recommendations, or decide what measures shall be taken in accordance with Articles 41 and 42, to maintain or restore international peace and security.

Article 40

In order to prevent an aggravation of the situation, the Security Council may, before making the recommendations or deciding upon the measures provided for in Article 39, call upon the parties concerned to comply with such provisional measures as it deems necessary or desirable. Such provisional measures shall be without prejudice to the rights, claims, or position of the parties concerned. The Security Council shall duly take account of failure to comply with such provisional measures.

Article 41

The Security Council may decide what measures not involving the use of armed force are to be employed to give effect to its decisions, and it may call upon the Members of the United Nations to apply such measures. These may include complete or partial interruption of economic relations and of rail, sea, air, postal, telegraphic, radio, and other means of communication, and the severance of diplomatic relations.

Article 42

Should the Security Council consider that measures provided for in Article 41 would be inadequate or have proved to be inadequate, it may take such action by air, sea, or land forces as may be necessary to maintain or restore international peace and security. Such action may include demonstrations, blockade, and other operations by air, sea, or land forces of Members of the United Nations.

Article 43

1. All Members of the United Nations, in order to contribute to the maintenance of international peace and security, undertake to make available to the Security Council, on its call and in accordance with a special agreement or agreements, armed forces, assistance, and facilities, including rights of passage, necessary for the purpose of maintaining international peace and security.

2. Such agreement or agreements shall govern the numbers and types of forces, their degree of readiness and general location, and the nature of the facilities and assistance to be provided.

3. The agreement or agreements shall be negotiated as soon as possible on the initiative of the Security Council. They shall be concluded between the Security Council and Members or between the Security Council and groups of Members and shall be subject to ratification by the signatory states in accordance with their respective constitutional processes.

Article 44

When the Security Council has decided to use force it shall, before calling upon a Member not represented on it to provide armed forces in fulfilment of the obligations assumed under Article 43, invite that Member, if the Member so desires, to participate in the decisions of the Security Council concerning the employment of contingents of that Member's armed forces.

Article 45

In order to enable the United Nations to take urgent military measures, Members shall hold immediately available national airforce contingents for combined international enforcement action. The strength and degree of readiness of these contingents and plans for their combined action shall be determined, within the limits laid down in the special agreement and agreements referred to in Article 43, by the Security Council with the assistance of the Military Staff Committee.

Article 46

Plans for the application of armed force shall be made by the Security Council with the assistance of the Military Staff Committee.

Article 47

1. There shall be established a Military Staff Committee to advise and assist the Security Council on all questions relating to the Security Council's military requirements for the maintenance of international peace and security, the employment and command of forces placed at its disposal, the regulation of armaments, and possible disarmament.

2. The Military Staff Committee shall consist of the Chiefs of Staff of the permanent members of the Security Council or their representatives. Any Member of the United Nations not permanently represented on the Committee shall be invited by the Committee to be associated with it when the efficient discharge of the Committee's responsibilities requires the participation of that Member in its work.

3. The Military Staff Committee shall be responsible under the Security Council for the strategic direction of any armed forces placed at the disposal of the Security Council. Questions relating to the command of such forces shall be worked out subsequently.

4. The Military Staff Committee, with the authorization of the Security Council and after consultation with appropriate regional agencies, may establish regional sub-committees.

Article 48

1. The action required to carry out the decisions of the Security Council for the maintenance of international peace and security shall be taken by all the Members of the United Nations or by some of them, as the Security Council may determine.

2. Such decisions shall be carried out by the Members of the United Nations directly and through their action in the appropriate international agencies of which they are members.

Article 49

The Members of the United Nations shall join in affording mutual assistance in carrying out the measures decided upon by the Security Council.

Article 50

If preventive or enforcement measures against any state are taken by the Security Council, any other state, whether a Member of the United Nations or not, which finds itself confronted with special economic problems arising from the carrying out of those measures shall have the right to consult the Security Council with regard to a solution of those problems.

Article 51

Nothing in the present Charter shall impair the inherent right of individual or collective self-defence if an armed attack occurs against a Member of the United Nations, until the Security Council has taken measures necessary to maintain international peace and security. Measures taken by Members in the exercise of this right of self-defence shall be immediately reported to the Security Council and shall not in any way affect the authority and responsibility of the Security Council under the present Charter to take at any time such action as it deems necessary in order to maintain or restore international peace and security.

VIII. REGIONAL ARRANGEMENTS

Article 52

1. Nothing in the present Charter precludes the existence of regional arrangements or agencies for dealing with such matters relating to the maintenance of international peace and security as are appropriate for regional action, provided that such arrangements or agencies and their activities are consistent with the Purposes and Principles of the United Nations.

2. The Members of the United Nations entering into such arrangements or constituting such agencies shall make every effort to achieve pacific settlement of local disputes through such regional agencies before referring them to the Security Council.

3. The Security Council shall encourage the development of pacific settlement of local disputes through such regional arrangements or by such regional agencies either on the initiative of the states concerned or by reference from the Security Council.

4. This Article in no way impairs the application of Articles 34 and 35.

Article 53

1. The Security Council shall, where appropriate, utilize such regional arrangements or agencies for enforcement action under its authority. But no enforcement action shall be taken under regional arrangements or by regional agencies without the authorization of the Security Council, with the exception of measures against any enemy state, as defined in paragraph 2 of this Article, provided for pursuant to Article 107 or in regional arrangements directed against renewal of aggressive policy on the part of any such state, until such time as the Organization may, on request of the Governments concerned, be charged with the responsibility for preventing further aggression by such a state.

2. The term enemy state as used in paragraph 1 of this Article applies to any state which during the Second World War has been an enemy of any signatory of the present Charter.

Article 54

The Security Council shall at all times be kept fully informed of activities undertaken or in contemplation under regional arrangements or by regional agencies for the maintenance of international peace and security.

IX. INTERNATIONAL ECONOMIC AND SOCIAL CO-OPERATION

Article 55

With a view to the creation of conditions of stability and wellbeing which are necessary for peaceful and friendly relations among nations based on respect for the principle of equal rights and self-determination of peoples, the United Nations shall promote:

(a) higher standards of living, full employment, and conditions of economic and social progress and development;

(b) solutions of international economic, social, health, and related problems; and international cultural and educational co-operation; and

(c) universal respect for, and observance of, human rights and fundamental freedoms for all without distinction as to race, sex, language, or religion.

Article 56

All Members pledge themselves to take joint and separate action in co-operation with the Organization for the achievement of the purposes set forth in Article 55.

Article 57

1. The various specialized agencies, established by intergovernmental agreement and having wide international responsibilities, as defined in their basic instruments, in economic, social, cultural, educational, health, and related fields, shall be brought into relationship with the United Nations in accordance with the provisions of Article 63.

2. Such agencies thus brought into relationship with the United Nations are hereinafter referred to as specialized agencies.

Article 58

The Organization shall make recommendations for the co-ordination of the policies and activities of the specialized agencies.

Article 59

The Organization shall, where appropriate, initiate negotiations among the states concerned for the creation of any new specialized agencies required for the accomplishment of the purposes set forth in Article 55.

Article 60

Responsibility for the discharge of the functions of the Organization set forth in this Chapter shall be vested in the General Assembly and, under the authority of the General Assembly, in the Economic and Social Council, which shall have for this purpose the powers set forth in Chapter X.

X. THE ECONOMIC AND SOCIAL COUNCIL

Composition

Article 61

1. The Economic and Social Council shall consist of 18 Members of the United Nations elected by the General Assembly.

2. Subject to the provisions of paragraph 3, six members of the Economic and Social Council shall be elected each year for a term of three years. A retiring member shall be eligible for immediate re-election.

3. At the first election, 18 members of the Economic and Social Council shall be chosen. The term of office of six members so chosen shall expire at the end of one year, and of six other members at the end of two years, in accordance with arrangements made by the General Assembly.

4. Each member of the Economic and Social Council shall have one representative.

Functions and Powers

Article 62

1. The Economic and Social Council may make or initiate studies and reports with respect to international economic, social, cultural, educational, health, and related matters and may make recommendations with respect to any such matters to the General Assembly, to the Members of the United Nations, and to the specialized agencies concerned.

2. It may make recommendations for the purpose of promoting respect for, and observance of, human rights and fundamental freedoms for all.

3. It may prepare draft conventions for submission to the General Assembly, with respect to matters falling within its competence.

4. It may call, in accordance with the rules prescribed by the United Nations, international conferences on matters falling within its competence.

Article 63

1. The Economic and Social Council may enter into agreements with any of the agencies referred to in Article 57, defining the terms on which the agency concerned shall be brought into relationship with the United Nations. Such agreements shall be subject to approval by the General Assembly.

2. It may co-ordinate the activities of the specialized agencies through consultation with and recommendations to such agencies and through recommendations to the General Assembly and to the Members of the United Nations.

Article 64

1. The Economic and Social Council may take appropriate steps to obtain regular reports from the specialized agencies. It may make arrangements with the Members of the United Nations and with specialized agencies to obtain reports on the steps taken to give effect to its own recommendations and to recommendations on matters falling within its competence made by the General Assembly.

2. It may communicate its observations on these reports to the General Assembly.

Article 65

The Economic and Social Council may furnish information to the Security Council and shall assist the Security Council upon its request.

Article 66

1. The Economic and Social Council shall perform such functions as fall within its competence in connection with the carrying out of the recommendations of the General Assembly.

2. It may, with the approval of the General Assembly, perform services at the request of Members of the United Nations and at the request of specialized agencies.

3. It shall perform such other functions as are specified elsewhere in the present Charter or as may be assigned to it by the General Assembly.

Voting

Article 67

1. Each member of the Economic and Social Council shall have one vote.

2. Decisions of the Economic and Social Council shall be made by a majority of the members present and voting.

Procedure

Article 68

The Economic and Social Council shall set up commissions in economic and social fields and for the promotion of human rights, and such other commissions as may be required for the performance of its functions.

Article 69

The Economic and Social Council shall invite any Member of the United Nations to participate, without vote, in its deliberations on any matter of particular concern to that Member.

Article 70

The Economic and Social Council may make arrangements for representatives of the specialized agencies to participate, without vote, in its deliberations and in those of the commissions established by it, and for its representatives to participate in the deliberations of the specialized agencies.

Article 71

The Economic and Social Council may make suitable arrangements for consultation with non-governmental organizations which are concerned with matters within its competence. Such arrangements may be made with international organizations and, where appropriate, with national organizations after consultation with the Member of the United Nations concerned.

Article 72

1. The Economic and Social Council shall adopt its own rules of procedure, including the method of selecting its President.

2. The Economic and Social Council shall meet as required in accordance with its rules, which shall include provision for the convening of meetings on the request of a majority of its members.

XI. NON-SELF-GOVERNING TERRITORIES

Article 73

Members of the United Nations which have or assume responsibilities for the administration of territories whose peoples have not yet attained a full measure of self-government recognize the principle that the interests of the inhabitants of these territories are paramount, and accept as a sacred trust the obligation to promote to the utmost, within the system of international peace and security established by the present Charter, the well-being of the inhabitants of these territories, and, to this end:

(a) to ensure, with due respect for the culture of the peoples concerned, their political, economic, social, and educational advancement, their just treatment, and their protection against abuses;

(b) to develop self-government, to take due account of the political aspirations of the peoples, and to assist them in the progressive development of their free political institutions, according to the particular circumstances of each territory and its peoples and their varying stages of advancement;

(c) to further international peace and security;

(d) to promote constructive measures of development, to encourage research, and to co-operate with one another and, when and where appropriate, with specialized international bodies with a view to the practical achievement of the social, economic, and scientific purposes set forth in this Article; and

(e) to transmit regularly to the Secretary-General for information purposes, subject to such limitations as security and constitutional considerations may require, statistical and other information, of a technical nature relating to economic, social, and educational conditions in the territories for which they are respectively responsible other than those territories to which Chapters XII and XIII apply.

Article 74

Members of the United Nations also agree that their policy in respect of the territories to which this Chapter applies, no less than in respect of their metropolitan areas, must be based on the general principles of good-neighbourliness, due account being taken of the interests and well-being of the rest of the world, in social, economic, and commercial matters.

XII. INTERNATIONAL TRUSTEESHIP SYSTEM

Article 75

The United Nations shall establish under its authority an international trusteeship system for the administration and supervision of such territories as may be placed thereunder by subsequent individual agreements. These territories are hereinafter referred to as trust territories.

Article 76

The basic objectives of the trusteeship system, in accordance with the Purposes of the United Nations laid down in Article 1 of the present Charter, shall be:

(a) to further international peace and security;

(b) to promote the political, economic, social, and educational advancement of the inhabitants of the trust territories, and their progressive development towards self-government or independence as may be appropriate to the particular circumstances of each territory and its peoples and the freely expressed wishes of the peoples concerned, and as may be provided by the terms of each trusteeship agreement;

(c) to encourage respect for human rights and for fundamental freedoms for all without distinction as to race, sex, language, or religion, and to encourage recognition of the interdependence of the peoples of the world; and

(d) to ensure equal treatment in social, economic, and commercial matters for all Members of the United Nations and their nationals, and also equal treatment for the latter in the administration of justice, without prejudice to the attainment of the foregoing objectives and subject to the provisions of Article 80.

Article 77

1. The trusteeship system shall apply to such territories in the following categories as may be placed thereunder by means of trusteeship agreements.

(a) territories now held under mandate;

(b) territories which may be detached from enemy states as a result of the Second World War; and

(c) territories voluntarily placed under the system by states responsible for their administration.

2. It will be a matter for subsequent agreement as to which territories in the foregoing categories will be brought under the trusteeship system and upon what terms.

Article 78

The trusteeship system shall not apply to territories which have become Members of the United Nations, relationship among which shall be based on respect for the principle of sovereign equality.

Article 79

The terms of trusteeship for each territory to be placed under the trusteeship system, including any alteration or amendment, shall be agreed upon by the states directly concerned, including the mandatory power in the case of territories held under mandate by a Member of the United Nations, and shall be approved as provided for in Articles 83 and 85.

Article 80

1. Except as may be agreed upon in individual trusteeship agreements, made under Articles 77, 79, and 81, placing each territory under the trusteeship system, and until such agreements have been concluded, nothing in this Chapter shall be construed in or of itself to alter in any manner the rights whatsoever of any states or any peoples or the terms of existing international instruments to which Members of the United Nations may respectively be parties.

2. Paragraph 1 of this Article shall not be interpreted as giving grounds for delay or postponement of the negotiation and conclusion of agreements for placing mandated and other territories under the trusteeship system as provided for in Article 77.

Article 81

The trusteeship agreement shall in each case include the terms under which the trust territory will be administered and designate the authority which will exercise the administration of the trust territory. Such authority, hereinafter called the administering authority, may be one or more states or the Organization itself.

Article 82

There may be designated, in any trusteeship agreement, a strategic area or areas which may include part or all of the trust territory to which the agreement applies, without prejudice to any special agreement or agreements made under Article 43.

Article 83

1. All functions of the United Nations relating to strategic areas, including the approval of the terms of the trusteeship agreements and of their alteration or amendment, shall be exercised by the Security Council.

2. The basic objectives set forth in Article 76 shall be applicable to the people of each strategic area.

3. The Security Council shall, subject to the provisions of the trusteeship agreements and without prejudice to security considerations, avail itself of the assistance of the Trusteeship Council to perform those functions of the United Nations under the trusteeship system relating to political, economic, social, and educational matters in the strategic areas.

Article 84

It shall be the duty of the administering authority to ensure that the trust territory shall play its part in the maintenance of international peace and security. To this end the administering authority may make use of volunteer forces, facilities, and assistance from the trust territory in carrying out the obligations towards the Security Council undertaken in this regard by the administering authority, as well as for local defence and the maintenance of law and order within the trust territory.

Article 85

1. The functions of the United Nations with regard to trusteeship agreements for all areas not designated as strategic, including the approval of the terms of the trusteeship agreements and of their alteration or amendment, shall be exercised by the General Assembly.

2. The Trusteeship Council, operating under the authority of the General Assembly, shall assist the General Assembly in carrying out these functions.

XIII. THE TRUSTEESHIP COUNCIL

Composition

Article 86

1. The Trusteeship Council shall consist of the following Members of the United Nations:

(a) those Members administering trust territories:

(b) such of those Members mentioned by name in Article 23 as are not administering trust territories; and

(c) as many other Members elected for three-year terms by the General Assembly as may be necessary to ensure that the total number of members of the Trusteeship Council is equally divided between those Members of the United Nations which administer trust territories and those which do not.

2. Each member of the Trusteeship Council shall designate one specially qualified person to represent it therein.

Functions and Powers

Article 87

The General Assembly and, under its authority, the Trusteeship Council, in carrying out their functions, may:

(a) consider reports submitted by the administering authority;

(b) accept petitions and examine them in consultation with the administering authority;

(c) provide for periodic visits to the respective trust territories at times agreed upon with the administering authority; and

(d) take these and other actions in conformity with the terms of the trusteeship agreements.

Article 88

The Trusteeship Council shall formulate a questionnaire on the political, economic, social, and educational advancement of the inhabitants of each trust territory, and the administering authority for each trust territory within the competence of the General Assembly shall make an annual report to the General Assembly upon the basis of such questionnaire.

Voting

Article 89

1. Each member of the Trusteeship Council shall have one vote.

2. Decisions of the Trusteeship Council shall be made by a majority of the members present and voting.

Procedure

Article 90

1. The Trusteeship Council shall adopt its own rules of procedure, including the method of selecting its President.

2. The Trusteeship Council shall meet as required in accordance with its rules, which shall include provision for the convening of meetings on the request of a majority of its members.

Article 91

The Trusteeship Council shall, when appropriate, avail itself of the assistance of the Economic and Social Council and of the specialized agencies in regard to matters with which they are respectively concerned.

XIV. THE INTERNATIONAL COURT OF JUSTICE

Article 92

The International Court of Justice shall be the principal judicial organ of the United Nations. It shall function in accordance with the annexed Statute, which is based upon the Statute of the

Permanent Court of International Justice and forms an integral part of the present Charter.

Article 93

1. All Members of the United Nations are *ipso facto* parties to the Statute of the International Court of Justice.

2. A state which is not a Member of the United Nations may become a party to the Statute of the International Court of Justice on condition to be determined in each case by the General Assembly upon the recommendation of the Security Council.

Article 94

1. Each Member of the United Nations undertakes to comply with the decision of the International Court of Justice in any case to which it is a party.

2. If any party to a case fails to perform the obligations incumbent upon it under a judgment rendered by the Court, the other party may have recourse to the Security Council, which may, if it deems necessary, make recommendations or decide upon measures to be taken to give effect to the judgment.

Article 95

Nothing in the present Charter shall prevent Members of the United Nations from entrusting the solution of their differences to other tribunals by virtue of agreements already in existence or which may be concluded in the future.

Article 96

1. The General Assembly or the Security Council may request the International Court of Justice to give an advisory opinion on any legal question.

2. Other organs of the United Nations and specialized agencies, which may at any time be so authorized by the General Assembly, may also request advisory opinions of the Court on legal questions arising within the scope of their activities.

XV. THE SECRETARIAT

Article 97

The Secretariat shall comprise a Secretary-General and such staff as the Organization may require. The Secretary-General shall be appointed by the General Assembly upon the recommendation of the Security Council. He shall be the chief administrative officer of the Organization.

Article 98

The Secretary-General shall act in that capacity in all meetings of the General Assembly, of the Security Council, of the Economic and Social Council, and of the Trusteeship Council, and shall perform such other functions as are entrusted to him by these organs. The Secretary-General shall make an annual report to the General Assembly on the work of the Organization.

Article 99

The Secretary-General may bring to the attention of the Security Council any matter which in his opinion may threaten the maintenance of international peace and security.

Article 100

1. In the performance of their duties the Secretary-General and the staff shall not seek or receive instructions from any government or from any other authority external to the Organization. They shall refrain from any action which might reflect on their position as international officials responsible only to the Organization.

2. Each Member of the United Nations undertakes to respect the exclusively international character of the responsibilities of the Secretary-General and the staff and not to seek to influence them in the discharge of their responsibilities.

Article 101

1. The staff shall be appointed by the Secretary-General under regulations established by the General Assembly.

2. Appropriate staffs shall be permanently assigned to the Economic and Social Council, the Trusteeship Council, and, as required, to other organs of the United Nations. These staffs shall form a part of the Secretariat.

3. The paramount consideration in the employment of the staff and in the determination of the conditions of service shall be the necessity of securing the highest standards of efficiency, competence, and integrity. Due regard shall be paid to the importance of recruiting the staff on as wide a geographical basis as possible.

XVI. MISCELLANEOUS PROVISIONS

Article 102

1. Every treaty and every international agreement entered into by any Member of the United Nations after the present Charter comes into force shall as soon as possible be registered with the Secretariat and published by it.

2. No party to any such treaty or international agreement which has not been registered in accordance with the provisions of paragraph 1 of this Article may invoke that treaty or agreement before any organ of the United Nations.

Article 103

In the event of a conflict between the obligations of the Members of the United Nations under the present Charter and their obligations under any other international agreement, their obligations under the present Charter shall prevail.

Article 104

The Organization shall enjoy in the territory of each of its Members such legal capacity as may be necessary for the exercise of its functions and the fulfilment of its purposes.

Article 105

1. The Organization shall enjoy in the territory of each of its Members such privileges and immunities as are necessary for the fulfilment of its purposes.

2. Representatives of the Members of the United Nations and officials of the Organization shall similarly enjoy such privileges and immunities as are necessary for the independent exercise of their functions in connection with the Organization.

3. The General Assembly may make recommendations with a view to determining the details of the application of paragraphs 1 and 2 of this Article or may propose conventions to the Members of the United Nations for this purpose.

XVII. TRANSITIONAL SECURITY ARRANGEMENTS

Article 106

Pending the coming into force of such special agreements referred to in Article 43 as in the opinion of the Security Council enable it to begin the exercise of its responsibilities under Article 42, the parties to the Four-Nation Declaration signed at Moscow, October 30, 1943, and France, shall, in accordance with the provisions of paragraph 5 of that Declaration, consult with one another and as occasion requires with other Members of the United Nations with a view to such joint action on behalf of the Organization as may be necessary for the purpose of maintaining international peace and security.

Article 107

Nothing in the present Charter shall invalidate or preclude action, in relation to any state which during the Second World War has been an enemy of any signatory to the present Charter, taken or authorized as a result of that war by the Governments having responsibility for such action.

XVIII. AMENDMENTS

Article 108

Amendments to the present Charter shall come into force for all Members of the United Nations when they have been adopted by a vote of two-thirds of the members of the General Assembly and ratified in accordance with their respective constitutional processes by two-thirds of the Members of the United Nations, including all the permanent members of the Security Council.

Article 109

1. A General Conference of the Members of the United Nations for the purpose of reviewing the present Charter may be held at a date and place to be fixed by a two-thirds vote of the members of the General Assembly and by a vote of any seven members of the Security Council. Each Member of the United Nations shall have one vote in the conference.

2. Any alteration of the present Charter recommended by a two-thirds vote of the conference shall take effect when ratified in accordance with their respective constitutional processes by two-thirds of the Members of the United Nations including all the permanent members of the Security Council.

3. If such a conference has not been held before the tenth annual session of the General Assembly following the coming into force of the present Charter, the proposal to call such a conference shall be placed on the agenda of that session of the General Assembly, and the conference shall be held if so decided by a majority vote of the members of the General Assembly and by a vote of any seven members of the Security Council.

XIX. RATIFICATION AND SIGNATURE

Article 110

1. The present Charter shall be ratified by the signatory states in accordance with their respective constitutional processes.

2. The ratifications shall be deposited with the Government of the United States of America, which shall notify all the signatory states of each deposit as well as the Secretary-General of the Organization when he has been appointed.

3. The present Charter shall come into force upon the deposit of ratifications by the Republic of China, France, the Union of Soviet Socialist Republics, the United Kingdom of Great Britain and Northern Ireland, and the United States of America, and by a majority of the other signatory states. A protocol of the ratifications deposited shall thereupon be drawn up by the Government of the United States of America which shall communicate copies thereof to all the signatory states.

4. The states signatory to the present Charter which ratify it after it has come into force will become original Members of the United Nations on the date of the deposit of their respective ratifications.

Article 111

The present Charter, of which the Chinese, French, Russian, English, and Spanish texts are equally authentic, shall remain deposited in the archives of the Government of the United States of America. Duly certified copies thereof shall be transmitted by that Government to the Governments of the other signatory states.

IN FAITH WHEREOF the representatives of the Governments of the United Nations have signed the present Charter.

DONE at the city of San Francisco the twenty-sixth day of June, one thousand nine hundred and forty-five.

Amendments

The following amendments to Articles 23 and 27 of the Charter came into force in August 1965.

Article 23

1. The Security Council shall consist of 15 Members of the United Nations. The Republic of China, France, the Union of Soviet Socialist Republics, the United Kingdom of Great Britain and Northern Ireland, and the United States of America shall be permanent members of the Security Council. The General Assembly shall elect 10 other Members of the United Nations to be non-permanent members of the Security Council, due regard being specially paid, in the first instance to the contribution of Members of the United Nations to the maintenance of international peace and security and to the other purposes of the Organization, and also to equitable geographical distribution.

2. The non-permanent members of the Security Council shall be elected for a term of two years. In the first election of the non-permanent members after the increase of the membership of the Security Council from 11 to 15, two of the four additional members shall be chosen for a term of one year. A retiring member shall not be eligible for immediate re-election.

3. Each member of the Security Council shall have one representative.

Article 27

1. Each member of the Security Council shall have one vote.

2. Decisions of the Security Council on procedural matters shall be made by an affirmative vote of nine members.

3. Decisions of the Security Council on all other matters shall be made by an affirmative vote of nine members including the concurring votes of the permanent members; provided that, in decisions under Chapter VI and under paragraph 3 of Article 52, a party to a dispute shall abstain from voting.

The following amendments to Article 61 of the Charter came into force in September 1973.

Article 61

1. The Economic and Social Council shall consist of 54 Members of the United Nations elected by the General Assembly.

2. Subject to the provisions of paragraph 3, 18 members of the Economic and Social Council shall be elected each year for a term of three years. A retiring member shall be eligible for immediate re-election.

3. At the first election after the increase in the membership of the Economic and Social Council from 27 to 54 members, in addition to the members elected in place of the nine members whose term of office expires at the end of that year, 27 additional members shall be elected. Of these 27 additional members, the term of office of nine members so elected shall expire at the end of one year, and of nine other members at the end of two years, in accordance with arrangements made by the General Assembly.

4. Each member of the Economic and Social Council shall have one representative.

The following amendment to Paragraph 1 of Article 109 of the Charter came into force in June 1968.

Article 109

1. A General Conference of the Members of the United Nations for the purpose of reviewing the present Charter may be held at a date and place to be fixed by a two-thirds vote of the members of the General Assembly and by a vote of any nine members of the Security Council. Each Member of the United Nations shall have one vote in the conference.

Secretariat

SECRETARY-GENERAL

The Secretary-General is the UN's chief administrative officer, elected for a five-year term by the General Assembly on the recommendation of the Security Council. He acts in that capacity at all meetings of the General Assembly, the Security Council, the Economic and Social Council, and the Trusteeship Council, and performs such other functions as are entrusted to him by those organs. He is required to submit an annual report to the General Assembly and may bring to the attention of the Security Council any matter which in his opinion may threaten international peace. (See Charter, p. 15.)

Secretary-General: JAVIER PÉREZ DE CUÉLLAR (Peru) (1982–91).

HEADQUARTERS STAFF
(October 1990)

Office of the Director-General for Development and International Economic Co-operation
Director-General: ANTOINE BLANCA (France).
Assistant Secretary-General: ENRIQUE TER HORST (Venezuela).

Executive Office of the Secretary-General
Chef de Cabinet: VIRENDRA DAYAL (India).
Assistant Secretary-General: ALVARO DE SOTO (Peru).
Assistant Secretary-General, Chief of Protocol: ALI Y. TEYMOUR (Egypt).

Office for Special Political Affairs
Under-Secretary-General: MARRACK I. GOULDING (United Kingdom).

Office for Research and the Collection of Information
Assistant Secretary-General: JAMES O. C. JONAH (Sierra Leone)

Office for Political and General Assembly Affairs and Secretariat Services
Under-Secretary-General: RONALD I. SPIERS (USA).

Office of Legal Affairs
Under-Secretary-General, The Legal Counsel: CARL-AUGUST FLEISCHHAUER (Germany).

Office of the Secretary-General in Afghanistan and Pakistan
Assistant Secretary-General, Personal Representative of the Secretary-General: BENON SAVAN (Cyprus).

Department of Political and Security Council Affairs
Under-Secretary-General: VASILIY S. SAFRONCHUK (USSR).

Department for Disarmament Affairs
Under-Secretary-General: YASUSHI AKASHI (Japan).

Department for Special Political Questions, Regional Co-operation, Decolonization and Trusteeship
Under-Secretary-General: ABDULRAHIM A. FARAH (Somalia).

Department of International Economic and Social Affairs
Under-Secretary-General: RAFEEUDDIN AHMED (Pakistan).

Department of Technical Co-operation for Development
Under-Secretary-General: XIE QIMEI (People's Republic of China).

Department of Administration and Management
Under-Secretary-General: MARTTI AHTISAARI (Finland).

Office of Programme Planning, Budget and Finance
Assistant Secretary-General, Controller: KOFI ANNAN (Ghana).

Office of Human Resources Management
Assistant Secretary-General: ABDOU CISS (Senegal).

Office of General Services
Assistant Secretary-General: J. RICHARD FORAN (Canada).

Department of Conference Services
Under-Secretary-General: EUGENIUSZ WYZNER (Poland).

Department of Public Information
Under-Secretary-General: THÉRÈSE PAQUET-SÉVIGNY (Canada).

Office of the Special Representative of the Secretary-General for Humanitarian Affairs in South-East Asia
Under-Secretary-General: RAFEEUDDIN AHMED (Pakistan).

Office for Ocean Affairs and the Law of the Sea
Under-Secretary-General, Special Representative of the Secretary-General for the Law of the Sea: SATYA N. NANDAN (Fiji).

United Nations Centre against Apartheid
Assistant Secretary-General: SOTIRIOS MOUSOURIS (Greece).

The chief administrative staff of the UN Regional Commissions and of all the subsidiary organs of the UN are also members of the Secretariat staff and are listed in the appropriate chapters. The Secretariat staff also includes a number of special missions and special appointments, including some of senior rank. In 1986 and 1987 there were reductions in the number of staff, as a result of budgetary restrictions.

On 30 June 1990 the total number of staff of the Secretariat holding appointments continuing for a year or more was 12,600, including those serving away from the headquarters. They comprised 3,782 professional, expert and higher-level staff and 8,818 in the General Service, Field Service and other categories.

On 31 December 1989 the total number of staff in the whole United Nations system (including the specialized agencies) was 51,422. This comprised 19,033 professional, expert and higher-level staff and 32,389 in the General Service and other categories.

GENEVA OFFICE

Address: Palais des Nations, 1211 Geneva 10, Switzerland.
Telephone: (022) 310211.
Director-General: Under-Sec.-Gen. JAN MARTENSON (Sweden)

VIENNA OFFICE

Address: Vienna International Centre, POB 500, 1400 Vienna, Austria.
Director-General: Under-Sec.-Gen. MARGARET JOAN ANSTEE (United Kingdom).

UN CONFERENCES, 1990–91

Amendment Conference on the Treaty Banning Nuclear Weapon Tests in the Atmosphere, in Outer Space and under Water: New York, June 1990, January 1991.

Eighth United Nations Congress on the Prevention of Crime and the Treatment of Offenders: Havana, August–September 1990.

Fourth Review Conference of the Parties to the Treaty on the Non-Proliferation of Nuclear Weapons: Geneva, August–September 1990.

Second United Nations Conference on the Least-Developed Countries: Paris, September 1990.

Second United Nations Conference to Review All Aspects of the Set of Multilaterally Agreed Equitable Principles and Rules for the Control of Restrictive Business Practices: Geneva, November–December 1990.

Third Review Conference of the Parties to the Convention on the Prohibition of the Development, Production and Stockpiling of Bacteriological (Biological) and Toxin Weapons and on their Destruction: Geneva, 1991.

United Nations Conference on Trade and Development (Eighth Session) 1991.

International Conference of Plenipotentiaries on the Draft Convention on the Liability of Operators of Transport Terminals in International Trade: Vienna, April 1991.

General Assembly

The General Assembly was established as a principal organ of the United Nations under the UN Charter (see p. 9). It first met on 10 January 1946. It is the main deliberative organ of the United Nations, and the only one composed of representatives of all the UN member states. Each delegation consists of not more than five representatives and five alternates, with as many advisers as may be required. The Assembly meets regularly for three months each year, and special sessions may also be held. It has specific responsibility for electing the Secretary-General and members of other UN councils and organs, and for approving the UN budget and the assessments for financial contributions by member states. It is also empowered to make recommendations (but not binding decisions) on questions of international security and co-operation.

After the election of its President and other officers, the Assembly opens its general debate, a three-week period during which the head of each delegation makes a formal statement of his or her government's views on major world issues. The Assembly then begins examination of the principal items on its agenda: it acts directly on a few agenda items, but most business is handled by the seven Main Committees (listed below), which study and debate each item and present draft resolutions to the Assembly. After a review of the report of each Main Committee, the Assembly formally approves or rejects the Committee's recommendations. On designated 'important questions', such as recommendations on international peace and security, the admission of new members to the United Nations, or budgetary questions, a two-thirds majority is needed for adoption of a resolution. Other questions may be decided by a simple majority. In the Assembly, each member has one vote. Voting in the Assembly is sometimes replaced by an effort to find consensus among member states, in order to strengthen support for the Assembly's decisions: the President consults delegations in private to find out whether they are willing to agree to adoption of a resolution without a vote; if they are, the President can declare that a resolution has been so adopted.

Special sessions of the Assembly may also be held to discuss issues which require particular attention. By September 1990 there had been 18 such sessions, on issues which included the problems of Palestine, Namibia, the African economic situation, illicit drugs, apartheid, and disarmament. Nine 'emergency special sessions' had also been held to discuss situations on which the UN Security Council had been unable to reach a decision: the Middle East (1958 and 1967), Hungary (1956), Suez (1956), the Congo (1960), Afghanistan (1980), Palestine (1980), Namibia (1981) and the occupied Arab territories (1982).

President of 45th Session (from September 1990): GUIDO DE MARCO (Malta).

MAIN COMMITTEES

There are seven Main Committees, on which all members have a right to be represented. The first six were appointed in 1946. An *ad hoc* Political Committee was first established in November 1948 and re-established annually until November 1956, when it was made permanent and renamed Special Political Committee.

First Committee: Disarmament and Related International Security Questions.
Special Political Committee.
Second Committee: Economic and Financial.
Third Committee: Social, Humanitarian and Cultural.
Fourth Committee: Decolonization.
Fifth Committee: Administrative and Budgetary.
Sixth Committee: Legal.

OTHER SESSIONAL COMMITTEES

General Committee: f. 1946; composed of 29 members, including the Assembly President, the 21 Vice-Presidents and the Chairmen of the seven Main Committees.
Credentials Committee: f. 1946; composed of nine members elected at each Assembly session.

POLITICAL AND SECURITY MATTERS

Special Committee on Peace-keeping Operations: f. 1965; 33 appointed members.
Disarmament Commission: f. 1978 (replacing body f. 1952); composed of all UN members.
UN Scientific Committee on the Effects of Atomic Radiation: f. 1955; 20 members.
UN Scientific Advisory Committee: f. 1954 under different title; seven members.
Committee on the Peaceful Uses of Outer Space: f. 1959; 53 members; has a Legal Sub-Committee and a Scientific and Technical Sub-Committee.
Special Committee against Apartheid: f. 1962; 19 members.
Committee of Trustees of the UN Trust Fund for South Africa: f. 1965; five members.
Ad Hoc Committee on the Indian Ocean: f. 1972; 48 members.
Ad Hoc Committee on the Implementation of the Collective Security Provisions of the Charter of the United Nations: f. 1983.
Committee on the Exercise of the Inalienable Rights of the Palestinian People: f. 1975; 23 members.
Special Committee on the Implementation of the Declaration on Decolonization: f. 1961; 24 members.
Advisory Committee on the UN Educational and Training Programme for Southern Africa: f. 1968; 13 members.

DEVELOPMENT

Intergovernmental Committee on Science and Technology for Development: f. 1980; open to all states.
Committee on the Development and Utilization of New and Renewable Sources of Energy: f. 1983; open to all states.
United Nations Environment Programme (UNEP) Governing Council: f. 1972; 58 members.
World Food Council: f. 1974; 36 members.

LEGAL QUESTIONS

International Law Commission: f. 1947; 34 members elected for a five-year term; originally established in 1946 as the Committee on the Progressive Development of International Law and its Codification.
Advisory Committee on the UN Programme of Assistance in Teaching, Study, Dissemination and Wider Appreciation of International Law: f. 1965; 13 members.
UN Commission on International Trade Law: f. 1966; 36 members.
Special Committee on the Charter of the United Nations and on the Strengthening of the Role of the Organization: f. 1975; 47 members.
Special Committee on Enhancing the Effectiveness of the Principle of Non-Use of Force in International Relations: f. 1977; 35 members.

There is also a UN Administrative Tribunal and a Committee on Applications for Review of Administrative Tribunal Judgments.

ADMINISTRATIVE AND FINANCIAL QUESTIONS

Advisory Committee on Administrative and Budgetary Questions: f. 1946; 16 members appointed for three-year terms.
Committee on Contributions: f. 1946; 18 members appointed for three-year terms.
International Civil Service Commission: f. 1948; 15 members appointed for four-year terms.
Committee on Information: f. 1978, formerly the Committee to review UN Policies and Activities; 69 members.

There is also a Board of Auditors, Investments Committee, UN Joint Staff Pension Board, Joint Inspection Unit, UN Staff Pension Committee, Committee on Conferences, and Committee for Programme and Co-ordination.

TRUSTEESHIP COUNCIL

The Trusteeship Council (comprising the People's Republic of China—a non-active member until May 1989—France, the USSR, the United Kingdom and the USA) has supervised United Nations Trust Territories through the administering authorities to promote the political, economic, social and educational advancement of the inhabitants towards self-government or independence. (See Charter, p. 14.) By 1990 the only territory remaining under United Nations trusteeship was the Trust Territory of the Pacific Islands, now comprising only the Republic of Palau (part of the archipelago of the Caroline Islands), administered by the USA.

Security Council

The Security Council was established as a principal organ under the United Nations Charter; its first meeting was held on 17 January 1946. Its task is to promote international peace and security in all parts of the world. (See Charter, p. 10 and p. 16.)

MEMBERS

Permanent members:

People's Republic of China, France, USSR, United Kingdom, USA.

The remaining 10 members are normally elected by the General Assembly for two-year periods (five countries from Africa and Asia, two from Latin America, one from Eastern Europe, and two from Western Europe and others). Non-permanent members from 1 January 1991: Austria, Belgium, Côte d'Ivoire, Cuba, Ecuador, India, Romania, Yemen, Zaire, Zimbabwe.

ORGANIZATION

The Security Council has the right to investigate any dispute or situation which might lead to friction between two or more countries, and such disputes or situations may be brought to the Council's attention either by one of its members, by any member state, by the General Assembly, by the Secretary-General or even, under certain conditions, by a state which is not a member of the United Nations.

The Council has the right to recommend ways and means of peaceful settlement and, in certain circumstances, the actual terms of settlement. In the event of a threat to or breach of international peace or an act of aggression, the Council has powers to take 'enforcement' measures in order to restore international peace and security. These include severance of communications and of economic and diplomatic relations and, if required, action by air, land and sea forces.

All members of the United Nations are pledged by the Charter to make available to the Security Council, on its call and in accordance with special agreements, the armed forces, assistance and facilities necessary to maintain international peace and security. These agreements, however, have not yet been concluded.

The Council is organized to be able to function continuously. The Presidency of the Council is held monthly in turn by the member states in English alphabetical order. Each member of the Council has one vote. On procedural matters decisions are made by the affirmative vote of any nine members. For decisions on other matters the required nine affirmative votes must include the votes of the five permanent members. This is the rule of 'great power unanimity' popularly known as the 'veto' privilege. In practice, an abstention by one of the permanent members is not regarded as a veto. Any member, whether permanent or non-permanent, must abstain from voting in any decision concerning the pacific settlement of a dispute to which it is a party.

The Council held 69 meetings in 1989. Of these, 26 were devoted to the situation in the Middle East and related questions, including the situation in the occupied Arab territories, the deportation of Palestinians, the deteriorating situation in Lebanon, the United Nations Interim Force in Lebanon (UNIFIL) and the United Nations Disengagement Observer Force (UNDOF). Eleven meetings considered the implementation of the United Nations plan for Namibia and charges of South African non-compliance with certain aspects of the relevant agreements. Regarding events in Central America, the Council devoted 10 meetings to consideration of regional peace efforts and charges of interference, including complaints brought by Panama, Nicaragua and El Salvador. Seven meetings were devoted to the continuing hostilities in Afghanistan, six to the shooting down by US forces of two Libyan aircraft on 4 January 1989, two to the activities of the United Nations Iran-Iraq Military Observer Group (UNIIMOG) and two to the work of the United Nations Peace-keeping Force in Cyprus (UNFICYP); one considered proposals concerning the detectability of plastic explosives; one discussed the prevention of hostage-taking and political abduction; and two concerned an election to fill a vacancy on the International Court of Justice. One of the Council's meetings was held in private to adopt its report to the General Assembly. In 1990 the Security Council's activities included discussions on a peaceful settlement in Cambodia, and an agreement to impose economic sanctions on Iraq, following the Iraqi invasion of Kuwait.

SUBSIDIARY BODIES

Military Staff Committee: Consists of the Chiefs of Staff (or their representatives) of the five permanent members of the Security Council: assists the Council on all military questions.

(See also UN Observer Missions and Peace-keeping Forces.)

STANDING COMMITTEES

There are three standing committees, each composed of representatives of all Council members: Committee of Experts (to examine provisional rules of procedure and other matters); Committee on Council Meetings Away from Headquarters; Committee on the Admission of New Members.

Economic and Social Council—ECOSOC

ECOSOC promotes world co-operation on economic, social, cultural and humanitarian problems. (See Charter, p. 13 and p. 16.)

MEMBERS

Fifty-four members are elected by the General Assembly for three-year terms: 18 are elected each year. Membership is allotted by regions as follows: Africa 14 members, Western Europe and others 13, Asia 11, Latin America 10, Eastern Europe 6.

ORGANIZATION

The Council, normally meeting twice a year in New York and Geneva, is mainly a central policy-making and co-ordinating organ. It has a co-ordinating function between the UN and the specialized agencies, and also makes consultative arrangements with approved voluntary or non-governmental organizations which work within the sphere of its activities. The Council has functional and regional commissions to carry out much of its detailed work.

SESSIONAL COMMITTEES

Each sessional committee comprises the 54 members of the Council: there is a First (Economic) Committee, a Second (Social) Committee and a Third (Programme and Co-ordination) Committee.

FUNCTIONAL COMMISSIONS

Statistical Commission: Standardizes terminology and procedure in statistics and promotes the development of national statistics; 24 members.

Population Commission: Advises the Council on population matters and their relation to socio-economic conditions; 27 members.

Commission for Social Development: Plans social development programmes; 32 members.

Commission on Human Rights: Seeks greater respect for the basic rights of man, the prevention of discrimination and the protection of minorities; reviews specific instances of human rights violation, provides policy guidance; works on declarations, conventions and other instruments of international law; 43 members. There is a Sub-Commission on Prevention of Discrimination and Protection of Minorities.

Commission on the Status of Women: Aims at equality of political, economic and social rights for women; 32 members.

Commission on Narcotic Drugs: Mainly concerned in combating illicit traffic; 40 members. There is a Sub-Commission on Illicit Drug Traffic and Related Matters in the Near and Middle East.

COMMITTEES AND SUBSIDIARY BODIES

Committee on Non-Governmental Organizations: f. 1946.

Committee on Negotiations with Intergovernmental Agencies: f. 1946.

INTERNATIONAL ORGANIZATIONS

Committee for Development Planning: f. 1965.
Committee on Natural Resources: f. 1970.
Committee on Crime Prevention and Control: f. 1972.
Commission on Transnational Corporations: f. 1974.
Commission on Human Settlements: f. 1977.

REGIONAL COMMISSIONS
(see pp. 24–32)

Economic Commission for Europe—ECE.
Economic and Social Commission for Asia and the Pacific—ESCAP.
Economic Commission for Latin America and the Caribbean—ECLAC.
Economic Commission for Africa—ECA.
Economic and Social Commission for Western Asia—ESCWA.

RELATED BODIES

UNICEF Executive Board: 41 members, elected by ECOSOC (see p. 36).

UNHCR Executive Committee: 41 members, elected by ECOSOC (see p. 43).

UNDP Governing Council: 48 members, elected by ECOSOC (see p. 39).

Committee on Food Aid Policies and Programmes: one-half of the 30 members are elected by ECOSOC, one-half by FAO; governing body of the World Food Programme (see p. 51).

International Narcotics Control Board: f. 1964; 13 members.

Board of Trustees of the International Research and Training Institute for Women (INSTRAW): 11 members.

International Court of Justice

Address: Peace Palace, 2517 KJ The Hague, Netherlands.
Telephone: (070) 392-44-41.
Telex: 32323.
Fax: (070) 364-99-28.

Set up in 1945, the Court is the principal judicial organ of the UN. All members of the UN, and also Switzerland and San Marino, are parties to the Statute of the Court. (See Charter, p. 14.)

THE JUDGES
(October 1990; in order of precedence)

	Term Ends*
President: José María Ruda (Argentina)	1991
Vice-President: Kéba Mbaye (Senegal)	1991
Judges:	
Manfred Lachs (Poland)	1994
Taslim Olawale Elias (Nigeria)	1994
Shigeru Oda (Japan)	1994
Roberto Ago (Italy)	1997
Mohamed Shahabuddeen (Guyana)	1997
Stephen M. Schwebel (USA)	1997
Sir Robert Jennings (United Kingdom)†	1991
Mohammed Bedjaoui (Algeria)	1997
Ni Zhengyu (People's Republic of China)	1994
Jens Evensen (Norway)	1994
Nikolai K. Tarassov (USSR)	1997
Gilbert Guillaume (France)†	1991
Raghunandan Swarup Pathak (India)	1991

* Each term ends on 5 February of the year indicated.
† Re-elected for term beginning February 1991. Andrés Aguilar Mawdsley (Venezuela), Christopher Weeramantry (Sri Lanka), and Raymond Ranjeva (Madagascar) were also elected to the Court with effect from February 1991.

The Court is composed of 15 judges, each of a different nationality, elected with an absolute majority by both the General Assembly and the Security Council. Representation of the main forms of civilization and the different legal systems of the world are borne in mind in their election. Candidates are nominated by national panels of jurists.

The judges are elected for nine years and may be re-elected; elections for five seats are held every three years. The Court elects its President and Vice-President for each three-year period. Members may not have any political, administrative, or other professional occupation, and may not sit in any case with which they have been otherwise connected than as a judge of the Court. For the purposes of a case, each side—consisting of one or more States—may, unless the Bench already includes a judge with a corresponding nationality, choose a person from outside the Court to sit as a judge on terms of equality with the Members. Judicial decisions are taken by a majority of the judges present, subject to a quorum of nine Members. The President has a casting vote.

FUNCTIONS

The International Court of Justice operates in accordance with a Statute which is an integral part of the UN Charter. Only States may be parties in cases before the Court; those not parties to the Statute may have access in certain circumstances and under conditions laid down by the Security Council.

The Jurisdiction of the Court comprises:

1. All cases which the parties refer to it jointly by special agreement (indicated in the list below by a stroke between the names of the parties).

2. All matters concerning which a treaty or convention in force provides for reference to the Court. About 700 bilateral or multilateral agreements make such provision. Among the more noteworthy: Treaty of Peace with Japan (1951), European Convention for Peaceful Settlement of Disputes (1957), Single Convention on Narcotic Drugs (1961), Protocol relating to the Status of Refugees (1967), Hague Convention on the Suppression of the Unlawful Seizure of Aircraft (1970).

3. Legal disputes between States which have recognized the jurisdiction of the Court as compulsory for specified classes of dispute. Declarations by the following 52 States accepting the compulsory jurisdiction of the Court are in force: Australia, Austria, Barbados, Belgium, Botswana, Cambodia (Kampuchea), Canada, Colombia, Costa Rica, Cyprus, Denmark, the Dominican Republic, Egypt, El Salvador, Finland, The Gambia, Guinea-Bissau, Haiti, Honduras, India, Japan, Kenya, Liberia, Liechtenstein, Luxembourg, Malawi, Malta, Mauritius, Mexico, Nauru, the Netherlands, New Zealand, Nicaragua, Nigeria, Norway, Pakistan, Panama, the Philippines, Poland, Portugal, Senegal, Somalia, Sudan, Suriname, Swaziland, Sweden, Switzerland, Togo, Uganda, the United Kingdom, Uruguay and Zaire.

Disputes as to whether the Court has jurisdiction are settled by the Court.

Judgments are without appeal, but are binding only for the particular case and between the parties. States appearing before the Court undertake to comply with its Judgment. If a party to a case fails to do so, the other party may apply to the Security Council, which may make recommendations or decide upon measures to give effect to the Judgment.

Advisory opinions on legal questions may be requested by the General Assembly, the Security Council or, if so authorized by the Assembly, other United Nations organs or specialized agencies.

Rules of Court governing procedure are made by the Court under a power conferred by the Statute.

CONSIDERED CASES

Judgments

By September 1990, 62 cases had been referred to the Court by States. Some were removed from the list as a result of settlement or discontinuance, or on the grounds of a lack of basis for jurisdiction. Cases which have been the subject of a Judgment by the Court include: Corfu Channel (United Kingdom v. Albania); Fisheries (United Kingdom v. Norway); Asylum (Colombia/Peru), Haya de la Torre (Colombia v. Peru); Rights of Nationals of the United States of America in Morocco (France v. United States); Ambatielos (Greece v. United Kingdom); Anglo-Iranian Oil Co. (United Kingdom v. Iran); Minquiers and Ecrehos (France/United Kingdom); Nottebohm (Liechtenstein v. Guatemala); Monetary Gold Removed from Rome in 1943 (Italy v. France, United Kingdom and United States); Certain Norwegian Loans (France v. Norway); Right of Passage over Indian Territory (Portugal v. India); Application of the Convention of 1902 Governing the Guardianship of Infants (Netherlands v. Sweden); Interhandel (Switzerland v. United States); Sovereignty over Certain Frontier Land (Belgium/Netherlands); Arbitral Award made by the King of Spain on 23 December 1906 (Honduras v. Nicaragua); Temple of Preah Vihear (Cambodia v. Thailand); South West Africa (Ethiopia and Liberia v. South Africa); Northern Cameroons (Cameroon v. United Kingdom); Barcelona Traction, Light and Power Co, Ltd (New Application: 1962) (Belgium v. Spain); North Sea Continental Shelf (Federal Republic of Germany/Denmark and Netherlands); Appeal relating to the Jurisdiction of the ICAO Council (India v. Pakistan); Fisheries Jurisdiction (United Kingdom v. Iceland; Federal Republic of Germany v. Iceland); Nuclear Tests (Australia v. France; New Zealand v. France); Aegean Sea Continental Shelf (Greece v. Turkey); United States Diplomatic and Consular Staff in Teheran (USA v. Iran); Continental Shelf (Tunisia/Libya); Delimitation of the Maritime Boundary in the Gulf of Maine Area (Canada/USA); Continental Shelf (Libya/Malta); Application for revision and interpretation of the Judgment of 24 February 1982 in the case concerning the Continental Shelf (Tunisia v. Libya); Military and Paramilitary Activities in and against Nicaragua (Nicaragua v. USA); Frontier Dispute (Burkina Faso/Mali); Delimitation of Maritime Boundary (Denmark v. Norway); Border and Transborder Armed Actions (Nicaragua v. Honduras); Elettronica Sicula SpA (USA v. Italy).

The cases under consideration in 1990 were: Land, Island and Maritime Frontier Dispute (El Salvador/Honduras) (in one aspect of which Nicaragua has been permitted to intervene); Certain Phosphate Lands in Nauru (Nauru v. Australia); a case brought by Iran against the USA, concerning the shooting-down of an Iranian airliner in 1988; a case brought by Denmark against Norway concerning the maritime boundary between Greenland and Jan Mayen island; a case brought by Guinea-Bissau against Senegal concerning an arbitral award on maritime boundaries; and a territorial dispute between Libya and Chad.

Advisory Opinions

Advisory Opinions on the following matters have been given by the Court at the request of the United Nations General Assembly or an organ thereof: Condition of Admission of a State to Membership in the United Nations; Competence of the General Assembly for the Admission of a State to the United Nations; Reparation for Injuries Suffered in the Service of the United Nations; Interpretation of the Peace Treaties with Bulgaria, Hungary and Romania; International Status of South West Africa; Voting Procedure on Questions relating to Reports and Petitions concerning the Territory of South West Africa; Admissibility of Hearings of Petitioners by the Committee on South West Africa; Reservations to the Convention on the Prevention and Punishment of the Crime of Genocide; Effect of Awards of Compensation Made by the United Nations Administrative Tribunal (UNAT); Certain Expenses of the United Nations; Western Sahara; Application for Review of UNAT Judgment No. 158; Application for Review of UNAT Judgment No. 273; Application for Review of UNAT Judgment No. 333; Applicability of the Obligation to Arbitrate under Section 21 of the United Nations Headquarters Agreement of 26 June 1947 (relating to the closure of the Observer Mission to the United Nations maintained by the Palestine Liberation Organization).

An Advisory Opinion has been given at the request of the Security Council: Legal Consequences for States of the continued presence of South Africa in Namibia (South West Africa) notwithstanding Security Council resolution 276 (1970). In 1989 (at the request of the UN Economic and Social Council) the Court gave an Advisory Opinion on the Applicability of Article 6, Section 22, of the Convention on the Privileges and Immunities of the United Nations.

The Court has also, at the request of UNESCO, given an Advisory Opinion on Judgments of the Administrative Tribunal of the ILO upon Complaints made against UNESCO and, at the request of IMCO, on the Constitution of the Maritime Safety Committee of the Inter-Governmental Maritime Consultative Organization.

In December 1980 the Court gave the World Health Organization an advisory opinion concerning the Interpretation of the Agreement of 25 March 1951 between WHO and Egypt.

FINANCE

The budget for the two years 1990-91 amounted to US $13.3m., financed entirely by the United Nations.

PUBLICATIONS

Reports (Judgments, Opinions and Orders): series.

Pleadings (Written Pleadings and Statements, Oral Proceedings, Correspondence): series.

Yearbook (published in 3rd quarter each year).

Bibliography (annually).

Catalogue (irregular).

Acts and Documents, No. 5 (contains Statute and Rules of the Court, the Resolution concerning its internal judicial practice and other documents).

United Nations Training and Research Institutes

UNITED NATIONS INSTITUTE FOR DISARMAMENT RESEARCH—UNIDIR

Address: Palais des Nations, 1211 Geneva 10, Switzerland.
Telephone: (022) 7346011.
Telex: 412962.
Fax: 7339879.

UNIDIR is an autonomous institution within the United Nations. It was established by the General Assembly in 1980 and its statute became effective on 1 January 1985. Its purpose is to undertake independent research on disarmament and related problems, particularly international security issues, in order to provide the international community with more diversified and complete data and to assist negotiations on disarmament.

Research projects are conducted within the Institute, or commissioned to individual experts or research organizations. For some major studies, multinational groups of experts are established. There is a fellowship programme to enable scholars from developing countries to conduct research at the Institute.

In 1991 the Institute's work programme included the following research projects: national security concepts; examination of verification methods, procedures and techniques of treaties and agreements currently in force and those envisaged in proposals under negotiation; technical, legal and strategic aspects of verification in the field of conventional disarmament; analysis of existing and proposed international disarmament verification organizations; high technology, surveillance and verification of arms control and disarmament; international security implications of the peaceful uses of outer space; international co-operation in chemical disarmament; examination of south-east European issues in the context of European security in the 1990s; regional approaches to disarmament, security and stability; nuclear non-proliferation; confidence-building measures for maritime security; unilateral measures for disarmament and security and their juridical, political and strategic consequences. There is a computerized information and documentation data base service on selected topics. The following meetings were planned for 1990: Conference of Disarmament Research Institutes in Africa; Conference on the United Nations in Disarmament and Security; and a Conference of Disarmament Research Institutes in Latin America and the Caribbean was planned for 1991.

The Institute's budget for 1991 amounted to US $1.6m. It is financed mainly by voluntary contributions from governments and public or private organizations. A contribution to the costs of the Director and staff may be provided from the UN regular budget.

Director: Jayantha Dhanapala (Sri Lanka).
Publications: *UNIDIR Newsletter* (quarterly); research reports.

UNITED NATIONS INSTITUTE FOR TRAINING AND RESEARCH—UNITAR

Address: 801 United Nations Plaza, New York, NY 10017, USA.

UNITAR was established in 1965 as an autonomous body within the United Nations to improve, by means of training and research, the effectiveness of the United Nations, in particular the maintenance of peace and security and the promotion of economic and social development.

Training is given at various levels, with particular attention given to the needs of officials from developing countries. The Institute organizes seminars and short courses for delegates to the UN, including new delegates to the General Assembly and new members of permanent missions, and briefing seminars on issues currently before the UN, such as international economic development and international negotiations. Courses are also held for officials other than diplomats, e.g. training in the modernization of public administration, the management of public enterprises and finance. UNITAR has also organized special programmes at the request of member states, including courses on basic diplomacy and multinational co-operation.

UNITAR's research is divided between those studies which focus on the short- and medium-term needs of the UN, and those dealing with longer-term trends. Since 1966 the Institute has published many studies on peace and security, international organization and development, and the first of a series of studies on the effectiveness of various parts of the UN system and aspects of regional co-operation (including case studies of the Economic and Social Council, the International Law Commission and the Law of the Sea Conference, which have been debated by the General Assembly).

The 'Project on the Future' includes studies and conferences on two broad themes: (a) policy choices related to the creation of a new international economic order, and (b) the meaning of physical limits and supply constraints in energy and natural resources. A major project on Technology, Domestic Distribution and North-South Relations is to prepare a new model of economic growth relevant to the social and economic circumstances of the developing countries. Conferences have been organized dealing with aspects of energy, including two on small-scale resources and two on heavy crude and tar sands.

UNITAR's grant from the UN regular budget was reduced from US $1,500,000 for the two years 1984–85 to $600,000 for 1986–87, and thereafter it received no support from the UN budget.

Executive Director: MICHEL DOO KINGUÉ (Cameroon).

UNITED NATIONS INTERNATIONAL RESEARCH AND TRAINING INSTITUTE FOR THE ADVANCEMENT OF WOMEN—INSTRAW

Address: POB 21747, Santo Domingo, Dominican Republic.
Telephone: 685-2111.
Telex: 326-4280.

The Institute was established in 1979 as an autonomous institution within the United Nations, to encourage the advancement of women and their integration in the development process at all levels.

INSTRAW provides training in the compiling of statistics related to women and their role in development, and conducts research on measuring women's contribution to household income and national economies. Other studies include 'Women and the World Economy' and sectoral issues, e.g. women, water and sanitation; women and food security. There is a network of 'focal points' in 21 countries. INSTRAW has an annual budget of about US $2.5m.

Director: DUNJA PASTIZZI-FERENCIC.
Publications: *INSTRAW News* (3 a year); studies.

UNITED NATIONS RESEARCH INSTITUTE FOR SOCIAL DEVELOPMENT—UNRISD

Address: Palais des Nations, 1211 Geneva 10, Switzerland.
Telephone: (022) 7988400.
Telex: 289696.

UNRISD was established in 1964 as an autonomous body within the United Nations, to conduct research into problems and policies of social and economic development during different phases of economic growth.

The Institute focuses its research on the implications of dominant social and economic processes, at national and local levels. Research therefore concentrates on the social structures and forces associated with these processes, and on practical policy alternatives. Studies are undertaken in a wide variety of national settings to facilitate comparative analysis. During the 1980s major research themes included Food Systems and Society (the impact of the 'green revolution' and the extent and causes of food insecurity), and Popular Participation (studying less-privileged social groups and their organized efforts to increase their control over resources and institutions). UNRISD's medium-term programme for 1988–89 involved research in the following areas:

Adjustment, Livelihood and Power: the Social Impact of the Economic Crisis. This project was to assess the impact of the prolonged economic crisis that affected a large number of developing countries in the 1980s, investigating the origins of the crisis, survival strategies of vulnerable groups, and the impact of the crisis on social movements and balance of political power.

Food Policy in the World Recession. This project was to study the socio-economic and political implications of reforms in food pricing and marketing of the type implemented in many developing countries during the 1980s.

Refugees, Returnees and Local Society in Developing Countries: a study of the impact of refugees on the living conditions of host populations, and the reintegration of refugees returning to their country of origin, looking particularly at how government and international policies and programmes affect this process.

Democracy, Participation and Development: includes studies of: social participation in economic reform; participation in various socialist contexts; social and political movements which have espoused violence; and ethnic conflict.

Sustainable Development and Participation: studies people's participation in resource management, and women's involvement in the management of natural resources and the local environment.

The Institute is supported by voluntary grants from governments, and also receives financing from other UN organizations, and from various other national and international agencies. Estimated income and expenditure for 1989 was US $2m.

There are five full-time professional researchers (together with five supporting staff) and a number of consultants and collaborators, particularly in the developing countries.

Director: DHARAM GHAI (Kenya).
Publications: *Research Notes* (annually), studies.

UNITED NATIONS UNIVERSITY—UNU

Address: Toho Seimei Building, 15-1, Shibuya 2-chome, Shibuya-ku, Tokyo 150, Japan.
Telephone: (03) 499-2811.
Telex: 25442.
Fax: (03) 499-2828.

The University is sponsored jointly by the United Nations and UNESCO. It is an autonomous institution within the United Nations, guaranteed academic freedom by a charter approved by the General Assembly in 1973. It is governed by a 24-member University Council of scholars and scientists, who are appointed by the Secretary-General of the UN and the Director-General of UNESCO. The University is not traditional in the sense of having students or awarding degrees, but works through networks of collaborating institutions and individuals. These include Associated Institutions (universities and research institutes linked with the UNU under general agreements of co-operation). The UNU undertakes multi-disciplinary research on problems of human survival, development and welfare that are the concern of the United Nations and its agencies, and works to strengthen research and training capabilities in developing countries. It provides post-graduate fellowships for scientists and scholars from developing countries, and conducts various training activities in association with its programme. In 1990 work was being undertaken in the following areas of study: peace, governance and culture; analysis of the world economy; threats to global life-support systems; the application and impact of advances in science and technology; urbanization and demographic change; food and nutrition; human health and welfare. In 1984 the UNU established the World Institute of Development Economics Research (UNU/WIDER) in Helsinki, Finland. By 1990 a second research and training centre, the UNU Institute for New Technologies (UNU/INTECH) had been established in Maastricht, the Netherlands, and three other centres were in various stages of development: an Institute for Natural Resources in Africa (to be based in Yamoussoukro, Côte d'Ivoire, and Lusaka, Zambia); an International Institute for Software Technology (Macau); and an institute of advanced studies (Tokyo, Japan). A programme on biotechnology in Latin America and the Caribbean (based in Venezuela) had also been established.

Rector: Prof. HEITOR GURGULINO DE SOUZA (Brazil).
Chairman of Council: Prof. MIHÁLY SIMAI.

INTERNATIONAL ORGANIZATIONS — *United Nations*

UNIVERSITY FOR PEACE

Address: Apdo postal 199, 1.250 Escazú, Costa Rica.
Telephone: 49-10-72.
Telex: 2331.

The University for Peace was established by the United Nations in 1980 to conduct research on disarmament, mediation, the resolution of conflicts and the relationship between peace and economic development.

Rector: ADOLFO PÉREZ ESQUIVEL.

Publication: *Carta Informativa*.

UNITED NATIONS REGIONAL COMMISSIONS

Economic Commission for Europe—ECE

Address: Palais des Nations, 1211 Geneva 10, Switzerland.
Telephone: (022) 7346011.
Telex: 412962.

The UN Economic Commission for Europe was established in 1947. Representatives of all European countries (including Cyprus and Turkey) and of the USA and Canada study the economic, environmental and technological problems of the region and recommend courses of action.

MEMBERS

Albania	Luxembourg
Austria	Malta
Belgium	Netherlands
Bulgaria	Norway
Byelorussian SSR	Poland
Canada	Portugal
Cyprus	Romania
Czechoslovakia	Spain
Denmark	Sweden
Finland	Switzerland
France	Turkey
Germany	Ukrainian SSR
Greece	USSR
Hungary	United Kingdom
Iceland	USA
Ireland	Yugoslavia
Italy	

Organization
(October 1990)

COMMISSION

ECE, with ECAFE (now ESCAP), was the earliest of the five regional economic commissions set up by the UN Economic and Social Council. The Commission holds an annual plenary session and meetings of subsidiary bodies are convened throughout the year.

President: OLLI ADOLF MENNANDER.

SECRETARIAT

The Secretariat services the meetings of the Commission and its subsidiary bodies and publishes periodic surveys and reviews, including a number of specialized statistical bulletins on coal, timber, steel, chemicals, engineering, housing and building, electric power, gas, general energy and transport (see list of publications below). It maintains close and regular liaison with the United Nations Secretariat in New York, with the secretariats of the other UN regional commissions, and with the UN Specialized Agencies. The Executive Secretary also carries out secretarial functions for the executive body of the 1979 Convention on Long-range Transboundary Air Pollution and its protocols. The ECE Secretariat also services the ECOSOC Committee of Experts on the Transport of Dangerous Goods.

Executive Secretary: GERALD HINTEREGGER (Austria).

Activities

The principal topics in the ECE work programme are: environmental protection; scientific and technical co-operation; energy; transport policies; trade and industrial co-operation between eastern and western Europe; and economic projections. Work is carried out by the subsidiary bodies listed below, assisted by sub-committees, working parties and meetings of experts.

Committee on Agricultural Problems: Reviews agricultural developments in the region and conditions in major commodity markets; elaborates commercial quality standards for perishable produce in international trade, and deals with a wide range of economic and technical problems relating to the production and marketing of crop and animal products. Mechanization of agriculture, questions of agrarian structure, farm rationalization and management, and regional developments, are studied and discussed in joint FAO/ECE working parties.

Timber Committee: Regularly reviews markets for softwoods, hardwoods, wood-based panels and industrial wood raw material; analyses medium- and long-term prospects for timber; keeps under review developments in forest industries, including environmental and energy-related aspects. Subsidiary bodies run jointly with the FAO deal with forest technology, management and training and with forest economics and statistics.

Coal Committee: Concentrates on problems of demand, production (underground and open-cast), upgrading, conversion, trade (including world trade) and use; studies related research and development activities; analyses market developments; exchanges information on policies; undertakes demand projections.

Committee on Electric Power: Analyses the electric power situation and its prospects, studies the planning and operation of large power systems, as well as particular aspects of hydroelectric, thermal and nuclear generation, international interconnections, the efficient use of electricity, and the relation between electricity and the environment.

Committee on Gas: Deals with gas resources, the economic and technical aspects of the production, transport and utilization of gas, natural and manufactured as well as liquefied petroleum gases; monitors trade in gas, and forecasts demand.

Committee on Housing, Building and Planning: Reviews trends and policies in the field of human settlements. Undertakes studies and organizes seminars on these issues. Promotes international co-operation in the field of urban and regional research. Also promotes international harmonization of building regulations and standards. Human settlements problems of southern Europe receive special consideration.

Senior Advisers to ECE Governments on Environmental and Water Problems: Promotes co-operation among member governments in developing and implementing policies for environmental protection, rational use of natural resources, and sustainable economic development; seeks solutions to environmental problems, particularly those of a transboundary nature; harmonizes at regional level legal, administrative and technical procedures; develops international agreements on the environment; and assesses national policies and legislation.

Inland Transport Committee: Covers road, rail and inland water transport, customs, contracts, transport of dangerous and perishable goods, equipment, statistics, road traffic safety and construction of vehicles. A number of international agreements, adopted through ECE, are continuously updated and supplemented.

Steel Committee: Annually reviews trends in the European and world markets, changes in price policy, growth of capacity supply factors and future prospects. Also studies long-term economic prospects and technological issues in the iron and steel industry, and compiles quarterly statistics on production of and trade in steel products.

Committee on the Development of Trade: A forum for studying means of expanding and diversifying trade among European countries, as well as with countries in other regions, and for drawing up recommendations on how to achieve these ends. Analyses trends, problems and prospects in intra-European trade; explores means of removing or reducing obstacles to the development of trade; promotes new or improved methods of trading by means of marketing, industrial co-operation, standardization, contractual guides, and the facilitation of international trade procedures.

Conference of European Statisticians: Promotes improvement of national statistics and their international comparability in economic, social, demographic and environmental fields; facilitates exchange of information between European countries. A joint study group is held with the FAO on food and agriculture statistics.

Senior Economic Advisers to ECE Governments: Brings together high-level governmental experts for an exchange of views on current, medium- and long-term economic development; organizes groups of experts, joint research projects and seminars on selected issues of common interest; in 1988 the group completed an Overall Economic Perspective of the ECE region to the year 2000.

Chemical Industry Committee: Regularly reviews the market of chemical products and their raw materials in Europe, USA and elsewhere. Compiles annual statistics on production of and trade in chemical products. Carries out studies on special problems

INTERNATIONAL ORGANIZATIONS — United Nations (Regional Commissions)

arising in connection with the development of the chemical industry.

Senior Advisers to ECE Governments on Science and Technology: Keeps under review developments in the sphere of science and technology. Major activities are: review and analysis of national scientific and technological policies; evaluation of research and development; innovation policies; technological forecasting; transfer of technology, including licensing procedures; study of selected issues, such as biotechnology and economic development; prediction of earthquakes; and assessment of medium- and long-term perspectives in science and technology. The Working Party on Engineering Industries and Automation regularly reviews medium- and long-term developments in engineering industries, compiles and analyses annual statistics on production and trade in engineering products, and undertakes studies (e.g. on new manufacturing and information technologies, environmental and resource-saving issues, and bio-medical engineering).

Senior Advisers to ECE Governments on Energy: Exchanges information on general energy problems, including energy resources and national policies; work programme comprises programmes, policies and prospects; demand and supply; trade and co-operation; conservation; statistics.

BUDGET

ECE's budget for the two years 1990–91 was US $33.1m.

PUBLICATIONS

ECE Annual Report.
Economic Bulletin for Europe.
Economic Survey of Europe.
Prices of Agricultural Products and Selected Inputs in Europe and North America—Annual ECE/FAO Price Review.
Review of the Agricultural Situation in Europe.
Timber Bulletin for Europe.
Annual Review of the Chemical Industry.
Annual Review of Engineering Industries and Automation.
Annual Bulletin of Coal Statistics for Europe.
Annual Bulletin of Electrical Energy Statistics for Europe.
Annual Bulletin of General Energy Statistics for Europe.
Annual Bulletin of Gas Statistics for Europe.
Annual Bulletin of Housing and Building Statistics for Europe.
Annual Bulletin of Steel Statistics for Europe.
Statistics of World Trade in Steel.
Annual Bulletin of Trade in Chemical Products.
Annual Bulletin of Transport Statistics for Europe.
Annual Bulletin of Statistics on World Trade in Engineering Products.
The Steel Market.
Statistical Indicators of Short-term Economic Changes in ECE Countries.
Statistics of Road Traffic Accidents in Europe.

Series of studies on air pollution, the environment, trade facilitation, industrial co-operation, energy, joint ventures, and economic reforms in Eastern Europe.

Reports, proceedings of meetings, technical documents, etc.

Economic and Social Commission for Asia and the Pacific—ESCAP

Address: United Nations Bldg, Rajadamnern Ave, Bangkok 10200, Thailand.
Telephone: (02) 282-9161.
Telex: 82392.

The Commission was founded in 1947 to encourage the economic and social development of Asia and the Far East; it was originally known as the Economic Commission for Asia and the Far East (ECAFE). The title ESCAP, which replaced ECAFE, was adopted after a reorganization in 1974.

MEMBERS

Afghanistan	Japan	Philippines
Australia	Korea, Republic	Singapore
Bangladesh	Laos	Solomon Islands
Bhutan	Malaysia	Sri Lanka
Brunei	Maldives	Thailand
Cambodia	Mongolia	Tonga
China, People's Republic	Myanmar	Tuvalu
	Nauru	USSR
Fiji	Nepal	United Kingdom
France	Netherlands	USA
India	New Zealand	Vanuatu
Indonesia	Pakistan	Viet-Nam
Iran	Papua New Guinea	Western Samoa

ASSOCIATE MEMBERS

American Samoa	Kiribati	Niue
Cook Islands	Marshall Islands	Northern Mariana Islands
Guam	Federated States of Micronesia	
Hong Kong		Palau

Organization
(October 1990)

COMMISSION

The Commission meets annually at ministerial level to examine the region's problems, to review progress, to establish priorities and to launch new projects.

Committees of officials dealing with the specific areas of work listed below meet annually or every two years; *ad hoc* conferences may also be held on subjects not otherwise covered.

SECRETARIAT

Executive Secretary: S. A. M. S. KIBRIA (Bangladesh).
Deputy Executive Secretary: SHIGENOBU NAGAI (Japan).
Chief, Programme Co-ordination and Monitoring Office: SEIKO TAKAHASHI.

The secretariat includes the Programme Co-ordination and Monitoring Office, the Information Service and three specialized units: the ESCAP/CTC Joint Unit on Transnational Corporations (working with the UN Centre for Transnational Corporations), the Operation Evaluation Unit, and the Regional Energy Development Programme. ESCAP's work is covered by 11 Divisions: Administration; Agriculture and Rural Development; Development Planning; Industry, Human Settlements and Environment; International Trade and Tourism; Natural Resources; Population; Social Development; Statistics; Transport and Communications; and Technical Co-operation.

PACIFIC OFFICE

Pacific Operations Centre: Port Vila, Vanuatu; f. 1984 by merging the ESCAP Pacific Liaison Office (Nauru) and the UN Development Advisory Team (Fiji).

Activities

ESCAP acts as a UN regional centre, providing the only intergovernmental forum for the whole of Asia and the Pacific, and executing a wide range of development programmes through technical assistance, advisory services to governments, research, training and information.

AGRICULTURE AND RURAL DEVELOPMENT

ESCAP undertakes programmes aimed at helping farming communities to improve their livelihood and to increase the production of food. It collects and disseminates information through a quarterly bulletin, and also issues periodicals on agro-chemicals and fertilizers. It provides training in farm broadcasting and in the safe use of pesticides. In co-operation with other UN agencies (especially FAO and ILO) it assists low-income farmers and the landless, by introducing innovative credit schemes, and organizing groups of landless workers and co-operatives. A Fertilizer Advisory, Development and Information Network for Asia and the

Pacific is run in co-operation with UNIDO and FAO. ESCAP also monitors the effects of weather on certain crops, enabling prediction of food shortages.

Regional Co-ordination Centre for Research and Development of Coarse Grains, Pulses, Roots and Tuber Crops: Jalan Merdeka 99, Bogor 16111, Indonesia; tel. (0251) 26290; telex 48369; f. 1981 to provide technical services for research on the production of and trade in these crops in the humid tropics of Asia and the Pacific. Publ. *Palawija News* (quarterly). Dir SHIRO OKABE.

DEVELOPMENT PLANNING

This division undertakes research and provides information on and technical assistance for regional planning. It publishes studies on specific development issues, together with an annual Economic and Social Survey of the region. Its research programme includes issues relating to external debt, trade in primary commodities, foreign investment and public finance. Two special sub-programmes cover the least-developed countries of the region and the Pacific islands.

INDUSTRY, HUMAN SETTLEMENTS AND ENVIRONMENT

In co-operation with the UN Industrial Development Organization (UNIDO), ESCAP provides support for industrial development, through industrial reviews of developing countries, studies on policy reorientation, investment promotion, advisory services, information and training. It carries out feasibility studies for the establishment of industries away from metropolitan areas, and promotes 'catalyst' industries in the least-developed countries of the region. It encourages foreign investment and provides tax advice.

Asian and Pacific Centre for Transfer of Technology: 49 Palace Rd, POB 115, Bangalore 560052, India; tel. 76931; telex 845-2719; f. 1977 to assist countries of the ESCAP region in technology development and transfer. Dir (vacant). Publs *Asia Pacific Tech Monitor* (every 2 months), monographs, proceedings.

Regional Network for Agricultural Machinery: c/o UNDP, POB 7285, 1300 Domestic Rd, Pasay City, Metro Manila, Philippines; tel. 3470; telex 72222250; f. 1977 to promote the local manufacture of agricultural machinery, to increase agricultural output and productivity, and to improve the working conditions and income of farmers; assists members to implement mechanization policies, and to develop and demonstrate tools and machines, through national institutes in each member country. Mems: Bangladesh, People's Republic of China, India, Indonesia, Iran, Republic of Korea, Nepal, Pakistan, Philippines, Sri Lanka, Thailand. Project Man. Dr ZIA UR RAHMAN. Publs *RNAM Newsletter* (3 a year), technical bulletins.

INTERNATIONAL TRADE AND TOURISM

The International Trade and Tourism Division organizes intergovernmental meetings for trade negotiations and the formulation of measures for expanding trade. It provides training and advisory services in export promotion and market development. It conducts programmes for the promotion of trade in manufactured goods, regional joint ventures, and the development of human resources. ESCAP has helped to establish a number of regional groups linking producers of coconuts, jute, rubber and other commodities. Technical assistance is given to land-locked and remote island countries of the region for the improvement of transport facilities.

MARINE RESOURCES

The ESCAP Programme on Marine Affairs (established in 1986) helps member countries to benefit under the UN Convention on the Law of the Sea (1982) which established 'exclusive economic zones' for coastal states: ESCAP advises on the planning of policies and legislation, and offers training in the assessment and exploitation of marine resources.

NATURAL RESOURCES

ESCAP assists the countries of the region to benefit from their mineral resources, by encouraging exploration and assessment of land and marine areas, conducting studies of mineral commodities, promoting interdisciplinary research, sponsoring technical co-operation, and stressing the environmental impact of the exploitation of these resources.

ESCAP's Regional Energy Development Programme encourages co-operation in the planning and management of energy programmes, the efficient use of energy and development of new sources of energy, with special emphasis on augmenting rural energy supplies. There is also a special Pacific Energy Development Programme. ESCAP assists countries in the efficient use of fossil energy supplies, and sponsors the investigation of new and renewable energy sources in the region. It provides a regional network of information and advisory services on solar, wind and biomass energy.

ESCAP's Regional Remote Sensing Programme promotes advanced techniques in compiling and analysing remote-sensing data, gathered by aircraft and satellites, for use in agriculture, forestry, and exploration for mineral and water resources. Special training was provided during the period 1985-87 for about 50 trainees annually. A special programme provides training and other assistance for the planning of human settlements, taking into account geological and hydrological features.

The development of water resources through national water plans (covering irrigation, drinking-water supply and sanitation, hydroelectric power, and control of flood and storm damage) also forms part of the work of this division.

ESCAP/WMO Typhoon Committee: c/o UNDP, POB 7285 ADC, Pasay City, Metro Manila, Philippines; tel. 922-8055; telex 42021; f. 1968; an intergovernmental body sponsored by ESCAP and WMO for mitigation of typhoon damage. It aims at establishing efficient typhoon and flood warning systems through improved meteorological and telecommunication facilities. Other activities include promotion of disaster preparedness, training of personnel and co-ordination of research. The committee's programme is supported from national resources and also by UNDP and other international and bilateral assistance. Mems: Cambodia, People's Republic of China, Hong Kong, Japan, Republic of Korea, Laos, Malaysia, the Philippines, Thailand, Viet-Nam. Co-ordinator of Secretariat: Dr ROMAN L. KINTANAR.

WMO/ESCAP Panel on Tropical Cyclones: Technical Support Unit, c/o Dept of Meteorology, Colombo, Sri Lanka; tel. 93943; f. 1973 to mitigate damage caused by tropical cyclones in the Bay of Bengal and the Arabian Sea; mems: Bangladesh, India, Maldives, Myanmar, Pakistan, Sri Lanka, Thailand.

POPULATION

The region's high density of population means that population control has an important place in development planning. ESCAP makes comparative demographic studies of individual member countries, and reviews national family-planning programmes. ESCAP co-ordinates a population information network for the region, and member governments receive advice on demography and family planning. Much of ESCAP's work in this field is funded by the UN Population Fund (UNFPA).

SOCIAL DEVELOPMENT

ESCAP's social development programme aims to encourage participation in development by disadvantaged groups, namely the disabled, women, the young and the old. ESCAP attempts to increase the self-reliance of women by providing a regional women's information network for the sharing of expertise, and provides advice for policy-makers in the area of women's participation in development. In 1986 ESCAP began a programme of assistance for member governments on improving national programmes for disability prevention and the rehabilitation of disabled persons.

STATISTICS

Recognizing the importance of statistical data in drawing up and evaluating development programmes, ESCAP undertakes periodical reviews of national statistical systems, provides training and advisory services, and organizes technical meetings. A major objective is to develop national statistical services in the region. Particular emphasis is placed on household surveys as a means of compiling demographic information. ESCAP also collects and publishes a wide range of statistical information on the Asia-Pacific region.

Statistical Institute for Asia and the Pacific: Akasaka POB 13, Tokyo 107-91, Japan; tel. (03) 357-8351; telex 32217; f. 1970; trains government statisticians; prepares teaching materials, provides facilities for special studies and research of a statistical nature, assists in the development of statistical education and training at all levels in national and sub-regional centres. Dir S. A. MEEGAMA.

TRANSPORT AND COMMUNICATIONS

At the 40th session of ESCAP, delegates agreed to designate the period 1985-94 as the Transport Decade for Asia and the Pacific, owing to the vital part played by transport improvements in the process of development.

Intergovernmental meetings of road experts are regularly held by ESCAP to discuss road transport. The Asian Highway Network Project comprises a network of 65,000 km of roads in 15 countries; ESCAP publishes maps of the network and reports on its development. ESCAP also publishes manuals on labour-intensive rural road construction and maintenance, and conducts training courses for officials in charge of roadworks.

ESCAP aims to help developing maritime members to adopt up-to-date technology in shipping, ports and inland waterways.

INTERNATIONAL ORGANIZATIONS United Nations (Regional Commissions)

Programme activities include regular reviews of developments in this field; compilation of statistics; guidelines for maritime legislation; the expansion of container transport; maintaining an information system on ports management; promotion of the interests of maritime transport users; and rehabilitation of inland waterways.

ESCAP gives technical assistance to member countries for modernizing railways. An Asia-Pacific Railway Co-operation Group was established by transport ministers in 1983. Studies have been made by ESCAP on container transport by rail in selected countries, and on the feasibility of the electrification of railways in Thailand.

ESCAP also assists member countries in matters relating to integrated transport planning, urban transport, the environmental impact of transport planning, and the facilitation of international traffic.

FINANCE

For the two-year period 1988-89 ESCAP's regular budget, an appropriation from the UN budget, was US $34.9m., and for 1990-91 it was $39.8m. The regular budget is supplemented annually by funds from various sources for technical assistance, expected to amount to $50.7m. in 1990-91.

PUBLICATIONS

Economic and Social Survey of Asia and the Pacific (annually).
Small Industry Bulletin for Asia and the Pacific.
Industry and Technology Development News for Asia and the Pacific.
Transport and Communications Bulletin for Asia and the Pacific.
Review of Developments in Shipping, Ports and Inland Waterways.
Agricultural Information Development Bulletin (quarterly).
Agro-chemicals News in Brief (quarterly).
Fertilizer Trade Information (monthly).
Economic Bulletin (2 a year).
Development Papers (occasional).
Atlas of Stratigraphy.
Atlas of Mineral Resources of the ESCAP Region.
ESCAP Energy News.
Electric Power in Asia and the Pacific (2 a year).
Water Resources Journal.
Confluence (water resources newsletter).
Asia-Pacific Population Journal.
Statistical Yearbook for Asia and the Pacific.
Quarterly Bulletin of Statistics for Asia and the Pacific.
Sample Surveys in the ESCAP Region (annually).
Bibliographies; trade profiles; commodity prices; statistics.

Economic Commission for Latin America and the Caribbean—ECLAC

Address: Edif. Naciones Unidas, Avda Dag Hammarskjöld, Casilla 179D, Santiago, Chile.
Telephone: (2) 485051.
Telex: 340295.

The UN Economic Commission for Latin America was founded in 1948 to co-ordinate policies for the promotion of economic development in the Latin American region. In 1984 the title 'Economic Commission for Latin America and the Caribbean' was adopted.

MEMBERS

Antigua and Barbuda
Argentina
Bahamas
Barbados
Belize
Bolivia
Brazil
Canada
Chile
Colombia
Costa Rica
Cuba
Dominica
Dominican Republic
Ecuador
El Salvador
France
Grenada
Guatemala
Guyana
Haiti
Honduras
Jamaica
Mexico
Netherlands
Nicaragua
Panama
Paraguay
Peru
Portugal
Saint Christopher and Nevis
Saint Lucia
Saint Vincent and the Grenadines
Spain
Suriname
Trinidad and Tobago
United Kingdom
USA
Uruguay
Venezuela

ASSOCIATE MEMBERS

Aruba
British Virgin Islands
Montserrat
Netherlands Antilles
United States Virgin Islands

Organization

(October 1990)

COMMISSION

The Commission normally meets every two years in one of the Latin American capitals. It has established permanent bodies with various sub-committees:

Committee of the Whole.
Central American Economic Co-operation Committee: sub-committees on trade; statistical co-ordination; transport; housing, building and planning; electric power; industrial initiatives; and agricultural development.
Committee of High-Level Government Experts.
Caribbean Development and Co-operation Committee.

SECRETARIAT

The Executive Secretariat comprises the Executive Secretary; Deputy Executive Secretary; the Programme Planning and Co-ordination Office; the Secretary of the Commission, with a conference service unit; and the UN Information Service.

There is a library, a computer centre, and a service for producing documents and publications. In addition, work in specific fields is carried out by divisions of the Secretariat as indicated below under 'Activities'.

There is a sub-regional office in Mexico, a sub-regional headquarters for the Caribbean, and offices in Bogotá, Brasília, Buenos Aires, Montevideo and Washington.

Executive Secretary: GERT ROSENTHAL (Guatemala).

Activities

ECLAC collaborates with regional governments in the investigation and analysis of regional and national economic problems, and provides guidance in the formulation of development plans. Many of its activities are undertaken in co-operation with other UN agencies. Under the programme headings listed below, ECLAC conducts: research; analysis; publication of information; provision of technical assistance; participation in seminars and conferences; training courses; and co-operation with national, regional and international organizations.

  Development Issues and Policies
  Energy
  Environment (Joint ECLAC/UNEP Development and Environment Unit)
  Food and Agriculture (Joint ECLAC/FAO Agriculture Division)
  Human Settlements (Joint ECLAC/UNCHS Human Settlements Unit)
  Industrial Development
  International Trade and Development Financing
  Natural Resources
  Population (see CELADE below)
  Science and Technology
  Social Development and Humanitarian Affairs
  Statistics

INTERNATIONAL ORGANIZATIONS

Transnational Corporations
Transport

In January 1987 ECLAC organized a special conference to discuss national and international strategies for the region's economic recovery and development. A regional conference on poverty was held in August 1988. In May 1990 the Commission discussed the economic prospects for the region in the 1990s, and presented a proposal for the consideration of member states' governments, concerning the transformation of the productive structures of the region in a context of progressively greater social equity. Such a process was intended to overcome the setbacks suffered by the region during the 1980s, by allowing economic growth, improvement of income distribution, increased democracy, protection of the environment, and improvement of the quality of life of the entire population

Latin American and Caribbean Institute for Economic and Social Planning—ILPES: Edif. Naciones Unidas, Avda Dag Hammarskjöld, Casilla 1567, Santiago, Chile; tel. (2) 485051; telex 340295; fax (2) 480252; f. 1962; undertakes research and provides training and advisory services; encourages co-operation among the planning services of the region. Dir ALFREDO COSTA-FILHO.

Latin American Demographic Centre—CELADE: Edif. Naciones Unidas, Avda Dag Hammarskjöld, Casilla 91, Santiago, Chile; tel. (2) 485051; telex 340295; fax (2) 480252; f. 1957, became an integral part of the Commission in 1975; provides technical assistance to governments, universities and research centres in demographic analysis, population policies, integration of population factors in development planning, and data processing; conducts annual postgraduate course and various national and regional seminars; provides demographic estimates and projections, documentation, data processing and training. Dir REYNALDO BAJRAJ.

BUDGET

ECLAC's share of the UN budget for the two years 1990–91 was US $49m. In addition, voluntary extrabudgetary contributions are received.

PUBLICATIONS

Revista de la CEPAL (Spanish and English, 3 a year).
Economic Survey of Latin America (Spanish and English, annually).
Boletín de planificación (2–3 a year).
Temas de planificación (3 a year).
PLANINDEX (2 a year).
Boletín demográfico (2 a year).
DOCPAL Resúmenes (population studies, 2 a year).
Notas de Población (3 a year).
Boletín del Banco de Datos del CELADE (annually).
Statistical Yearbook for Latin America (Spanish and English, annually).
CEPALINDEX (2 a year).
Studies, reports, bibliographical bulletins.

Economic Commission for Africa—ECA

Address: Africa Hall, POB 3001, Addis Ababa, Ethiopia.
Telephone: 447200.
Telex: 976 21029.

The UN Economic Commission for Africa was founded in 1958 by a resolution of ECOSOC to initiate and take part in measures for facilitating Africa's economic development.

MEMBERS*

Algeria
Angola
Benin
Botswana
Burkina Faso
Burundi
Cameroon
Cape Verde
Central African Republic
Chad
Comoros
Congo
Côte d'Ivoire
Djibouti
Egypt
Equatorial Guinea
Ethiopia
Gabon
The Gambia
Ghana
Guinea
Guinea-Bissau
Kenya
Lesotho
Liberia
Libya
Madagascar
Malawi
Mali
Mauritania
Mauritius
Morocco
Mozambique
Namibia
Niger
Nigeria
Rwanda
São Tomé and Príncipe
Senegal
Seychelles
Sierra Leone
Somalia
Sudan
Swaziland
Tanzania
Togo
Tunisia
Uganda
Zaire
Zambia
Zimbabwe

* South Africa's membership was suspended in 1965.

Organization

(October 1990)

COMMISSION

The Commission may only act with the agreement of the government of the country concerned. It is also empowered to make recommendations on any matter within its competence directly to the government of the member or associate member concerned, to governments admitted in a consultative capacity, and to the UN Specialized Agencies. The Commission is required to submit for prior consideration by ECOSOC any of its proposals for actions that would be likely to have important effects on the international economy.

CONFERENCE OF MINISTERS

The Conference is attended by ministers responsible for economic or financial affairs, planning and development of governments of member states, and is the main deliberative body of the Commission. It meets annually. A Technical Preparatory Committee of the Whole, representing all member states, was established in 1979 to deal with matters submitted for the consideration of the Conference.

The Commission's responsibility to promote concerted action for the economic and social development of Africa is vested primarily in the Conference, which considers matters of general policy and the priorities to be assigned to the Commission's programmes, considers inter-African and international economic policy and makes recommendations to member states in connection with such matters. It reviews the course of programmes being implemented in the preceding year and examines and approves the programmes proposed for the next.

OTHER POLICY-MAKING BODIES

Conference of African Ministers of Finance.
Conference of African Ministers of Industry.
Conference of African Ministers of Social Affairs.
Conference of African Ministers of Trade.
Conference of African Ministers of Transport, Communications and Planning.
Conference of Ministers Responsible for Human Resources Planning, Development and Utilization.
Conference of Ministers of Finance.
Councils of Ministers of the MULPOCs (see below).

SECRETARIAT

The Secretariat provides the services necessary for the meeting of the Conference of Ministers and the meetings of the Commission's subsidiary bodies, carries out the resolutions and implements the programmes adopted there.

The headquarters of the Secretariat is in Addis Ababa, Ethiopia. It comprises a Cabinet Office and 11 Divisions.

Cabinet Office of the Executive Secretary:
  Policy and Programme Co-ordination Office
  Economic Co-operation Office

Office of the Secretary of the Commission
Technical Assistance Co-ordination and Operations Office
Information Service
Pan-African Documentation and Information Service (PADIS)
African Training and Research Centre for Women
Security and Safety Unit

Divisions:
Socio-Economic Research and Planning
Trade and Development Finance
Joint ECA/FAO Food and Agriculture
Industry and Human Settlements
Natural Resources
Transport, Communications and Tourism
Public Administration, Human Resources and Social Development
Statistics
Population
Administration and Conference Services

Executive Secretary: ADEBAYO ADEDEJI (Nigeria).

Subsidiary Bodies

Joint Conference of African Planners, Statisticians and Demographers.
Intergovernmental Committee of Experts for Science and Technology Development.
Intergovernmental Regional Committee on Human Settlements and Environment.
Follow-up Committee on Industrialization in Africa.
Intergovernmental Committee of Experts of African Least-Developed Countries.
Conference of Ministers of African Least-Developed Countries.

Regional Operational Centres

Multinational Programming and Operational Centres (MULPOC) act as 'field agents' for the implementation of regional development programmes. The Centres are located in Yaoundé, Cameroon (serving central Africa), Gisenyi, Rwanda (Great Lakes Community), Lusaka, Zambia (east and southern Africa), Niamey, Niger (west Africa) and Tangier, Morocco (north Africa). Each centre holds regular ministerial meetings.

Activities

The Commission's 1984–89 work programme was largely derived from the 'Development Strategy for Africa for the United Nations' Third Development Decade', which was drawn up by the ECA Conference of Ministers and approved by the OAU summit conference in 1979. The plan for the implementation of this strategy, known as the Lagos Plan of Action, was adopted by the OAU in 1980: it envisaged the economic integration of the continent (an 'African Common Market') by the end of the century. The Commission's work is also based on the UN Programme of Action for African Economic Recovery and Development (1986–90) and on the 'Strategies for the Advancement of Women' adopted in 1985 by the conference held in Nairobi to mark the end of the UN Decade for Women.

POLICY AND PROGRAMME CO-ORDINATION

The Policy and Programme Co-ordination Office assists the Executive Secretary in directing the Commission's work programme. It submits proposals on African development to the policy-making bodies of the UN and OAU, and co-ordinates the ECA side of the ECA/OAU Intersecretariat Committee and other inter-agency committees. It services the annual conference of ministers, and attempts to ensure that policy decisions are reflected in the planning of ECA activities. It prepares reports for the evaluation of programme performance.

SOCIO-ECONOMIC RESEARCH AND PLANNING

Monitoring economic and social trends in the African region and studying the development problems concerning it are among the fundamental tasks of the Commission. The annual *Survey of Economic and Social Conditions in Africa* analyses past trends and prospects. Studies of specific issues are also carried out at the request of member states of the Commission.

The Commission gives assistance to governments in general economic analysis, in fiscal, financial and monetary issues and in planning. Studies on planning are carried out in the Secretariat in order to provide African planning departments with better tools. A project under way in 1988 aimed to develop short-term forecasting techniques suitable to the needs and means of African countries. Special assistance is given to least-developed, land-locked and island countries which have a much lower income level than other countries and which are faced with heavier constraints than others. Studies are also undertaken to assist longer-term planning.

The Conference of African Planners, Statisticians and Demographers, which is held every two years, provides an important opportunity for African governments to exchange views and experiences, to obtain information on new techniques and to discuss the most appropriate approaches to development problems.

In 1989 ECA published a report entitled *African Alternative Framework to Structural Adjustment Programmes for Socio-Economic Recovery and Transformation*, which argued that programmes of strict economic reform, as imposed by the International Monetary Fund and the World Bank, had not resulted in sustained economic growth in Africa over the past decade.

INFORMATION

The Pan-African Documentation and Information Service (PADIS) was established in 1980. The main objectives of PADIS are: to provide access to numerical and other information on African social, economic, scientific and technological development issues; to assist African countries in their efforts to develop national information handling capabilities; to establish teledata-transmission linkages within and beyond Africa; and to design sound technical specifications, norms and standards to minimize technical barriers in the exchange of information.

STATISTICS

The Statistics Division of ECA, which comprises two sections (Statistical Development and Economic Statistics) promotes the development and co-ordination of national statistical services in the region and the improvement and comparability of statistical data. It prepares documents to assist in the improvement of statistical methodology and undertakes the collection, evaluation and dissemination of statistical information. During the 1980s ECA's efforts in the field of statistics were concentrated in five main areas:

(i) The African Household Survey Capability Programme (AHSCP), which aims at helping African countries in the collection and analysis of integrated demographic, social and economic data on households and household members, on a continuing basis;

(ii) The Statistical Training Programme for Africa (STPA), which aims to make the region self-sufficient in statistical personnel at all levels;

(iii) The Regional Advisory Service in Demographic Statistics (RASDS), which provides technical advisory services for population censuses, demographic surveys and civil registration;

(iv) The National Accounts Capability Programme (NACP), which aims at improving economic statistics generally by building up a capability in each country for the collection, processing and analysis of economic data;

(v) The Statistical Data Base, part of PADIS (see above), which provides on-line statistical information to users.

POPULATION

ECA assists its member states in (i) population data collection and data processing, which is done by the Statistics Division of the Commission (q.v.); (ii) analysis of demographic data obtained from censuses or surveys: this assistance is given by the Population Division; (iii) training demographers at the Regional Institute for Population Studies (RIPS) in Accra (Ghana) and at the Institut de formation et de recherche démographiques (IFORD) in Yaoundé (Cameroon); (iv) formulation of population policies and integrating population variables in development planning, through advisory missions and through the organization of national seminars on population and development; and (v) dissemination of information through its *Newsletter*, *Demographic Handbook for Africa*, the *African Population Studies* series and other publications, and the Population Information Network for Africa (POPIN-Africa), which comprises regional and national information centres. The Commission conducts studies on population dynamics and their relationship to development.

The second African Population Conference was held in Arusha, Tanzania, in January 1984; it adopted 93 recommendations for the future management of the regional population. The Fifth Joint Conference of African Planners, Statisticians and Demographers was held in 1988.

TRANSPORT AND COMMUNICATIONS

For the United Nations Transport and Communications Decade in Africa (UNTACDA), a comprehensive programme was adopted by ECA for the period 1978–88, to encourage the formation of efficient and reliable transport and communications links among all African countries.

The programme included the construction of the following trans-African roads: Lagos-Mombasa (6,300 km); Dakar-N'Djamena (4,600 km); Nouakchott-Lagos (4,600 km); Cairo-Gaborone (9,027 km); and Algiers-Lagos, the Trans-Saharan Highway (5,929 km). The programme also envisaged uniform road traffic regulations, signs, signals and a highway code.

The UNTACDA programme aimed to enable inter-connection of some African railway networks, extension of some into the land-locked countries, modernization of track and rolling stock and the introduction of uniform operating and training procedures. Efforts were also made to establish the manufacturing of spare parts and components in Africa.

The programme aimed to strengthen international and coastal shipping in Africa through the pooling of resources on a subregional basis, the rationalization of sailing schedules, port modernization, and the establishment of joint training and repair facilities in the continent. ECA assisted in the formation of the Port Management Associations of West and Central Africa and of Eastern and Southern Africa.

In the air transport subsector, the programme aimed to introduce a four-zone air-route grid system covering the entire region, development of a regional air navigational plan, joint acquisition of aircraft and equipment, establishment of joint maintenance and repair facilities, establishment of regional and sub-regional training institutions and the harmonization of tariffs and charges within the region.

ECA and the International Telecommunication Union (ITU) collaborate with the OAU in assisting member states towards completion of the Pan-African Telecommunication network (PANAFTEL). Projects on low-cost broadcasting systems have also been undertaken, in collaboration with UNESCO. In 1986 funds were secured for a feasibility study for a Regional Satellite Communications System.

SOCIAL DEVELOPMENT, ENVIRONMENT AND HUMAN SETTLEMENTS

The Social Development, Environment and Human Settlements Division undertakes studies, produces technical publications and organizes meetings. It provides advisory services to member states on formulating policies relating to overall social development, integrated rural development, youth and social welfare, and housing. It co-ordinates environmental activities in Africa with UNEP and other agencies.

In January 1980 the African Centre for Applied Research and Training in Social Development (ACARTSOD) was inaugurated in Tripoli, Libya, to provide training of high-level personnel required for research and development programmes, and to organize seminars and conduct research.

AGRICULTURE

The attainment of self-sufficiency in food is a paramount objective. The Regional Food Plan for Africa, prepared by ECA in collaboration with FAO, was adopted by the African ministers of agriculture in 1978. ECA has undertaken the implementation of the Regional Food Plan along with the various intergovernmental organizations working in Africa. During 1986-89 its work fell into three main categories: (i) agricultural planning, including the conservation of forest and land resources; (ii) promotion of integrated rural development, particularly institution-building, agricultural research and improvement of livestock and fisheries; (iii) marketing of produce, with emphasis on prevention of food losses and providing incentives for increasing food production. In 1986, as part of the UN Programme of Action for African Economic Recovery, ECA drew up strategies for improving Africa's preparedness to meet emergencies without losing sight of the need for long-term development; it emphasized food security, agricultural research, development of livestock, inter-state co-operation, and rational exploitation of forests.

INDUSTRY

The UN Industrial Development Decade for Africa covered the years 1980-90. It initiated plans for the setting-up of African multinational corporations in these areas. The preparatory phase of the Decade (1982-84) was for reviewing and adjusting the industrial plans of a number of African countries in order to lay the foundation for self-sustained industrial development in the ensuing years. The economic crisis aggravated by drought and famine during 1983-85 meant that African countries were forced to use their foreign exchange earnings for food imports rather than for industrial investment. The Decade's aim that Africa should produce at least 1.4% of world industrial production by the year 1990 could not therefore be achieved. In 1986 the UN General Assembly initiated a Programme of Action for African Economic Recovery and Development (UNPAAERD) for 1986-90, which was to include restructuring of the industrial sector in African countries, rationalization of existing industries, promotion of small-scale industries, and improving the allocation of resources. Particular emphasis was to be given to industries that supply fertilizers, implements and other requisites for agriculture.

The African Industrial Development Fund was established in 1979 to provide resources for pre-investment activities for developing industrial projects, especially multinational ones. The African Regional Centre for Engineering Design and Manufacturing (Ibadan, Nigeria) was established in 1980.

In 1987 a project on the development of the building materials industry was begun, with the aim of increasing the production of affordable building materials and allowing the exchange of information on suitable locally-made bricks and tiles.

SCIENCE AND TECHNOLOGY

ECA activities in this field concentrate on the application of science and technology to economic development, on the provision of training facilities and on promoting regional co-operation. The African Regional Centre for Technology (Dakar, Senegal) became operational in 1980, aiming to assist African countries in the development of indigenous technologies, the improvement of negotiating capabilities for imported technologies and related areas. The Secretariat undertakes advisory missions to member states, and promotes regional co-operation through the Intergovernmental Committee of Experts for Science and Technology Development. Technical support is given to regional institutions.

NATURAL RESOURCES

The Eastern and Southern African Mineral Resources Development Centre at Dodoma, Tanzania, provides information on the development of mineral resources, practical courses in geology and mining, advisory services, pre-feasibility studies and specialized laboratory services. A similar Central African multinational centre was established in 1983 at Brazzaville, Congo. The third Regional Conference on the Development and Utilization of Mineral Resources, held in 1988, adopted a programme of action including surveys on precious and semi-precious stones, surveys on trade in copper and aluminium-based products among African countries, evaluating prospects for financing mineral development projects in Africa, development of raw materials for fertilizers, and the formation of national and regional policies for exploitation and use of minerals.

Three Regional Centres, for Services in Surveying, Mapping and Remote Sensing (Nairobi, Kenya), for Remote Sensing (Ouagadougo, Burkina Faso) and for Training in Aerospace Surveys (Ile-Ife, Nigeria), provide specialized services for an inventory of natural resources. Standardized specifications for basic topographical mapping in Africa were drawn up in 1985. In 1989 ground stations (in Burkina Faso and Kenya) were being planned to receive signals from US and European remote-sensing satellites and process the data received on mineral, land and water resources. Two ECA-sponsored organizations were amalgamated in 1987 to form the African Organization for Cartography and Remote Sensing. The seventh UN Regional Cartographic Conference was held in 1989. An African Centre of Meteorological Applications for Development was being constructed in Niamey (Niger) in 1990.

Member states are assisted in the assessment and use of water resources, and the development of lakes and river-basins common to more than one country. A programme of activities for marine development was begun in 1983, with particular reference to the effects of the United Nations Convention on the Law of the Sea (adopted in 1982), and the subsequent establishment of 'exclusive economic zones' for coastal states.

ENERGY

Assistance is given (in the form of training and advisory services) in the development of energy resources, in planning and efficient utilization. A study of African coal resources was completed in 1988. Investigations are being made on development and use of non-conventional sources of energy including solar, geothermal and biogas energy. Maps of the primary energy resources of Africa were updated and published in 1984, and work on an atlas of energy resources continued. A study on the prospects of nuclear energy in Africa was completed in 1987, and a technical advisory committee was established in 1989 to co-ordinate the development of nuclear technology in the region. The African Regional Centre for Solar Energy, in Bujumbura, Burundi, was inaugurated in 1989.

INTERNATIONAL TRADE AND FINANCE

ECA assists African countries in expanding trade among themselves and with other regions of the world and in promoting financial and monetary co-operation. ECA attempts to ensure that African countries should participate effectively in current international negotiations. To this end, assistance has been provided to member states in negotiations under UNCTAD and GATT; in the annual conferences of the IMF and IBRD; in negotiations with the European Community; and in meetings related to economic co-operation among developing countries. Studies have been prepared on problems and prospects likely to arise for the African region from the implementation of the Common Fund Agreement; the Generalized System of Trade Preferences; the impacts of exchange rate fluctuations on the economies of African countries; and on long-term implications of different debt arrangements for African economies. ECA assists individual member states by undertaking studies on domestic trade, expansion of inter-African trade, transnational corporations, integration of women in trade and development, and strengthening the capacities of state-trading organizations. ECA promotes co-operation between developing countries, and the expansion of African trade with overseas countries.

The expansion of trade within Africa is constrained by the low level of industrial production, and by the strong emphasis on commodity trade. ECA encourages the diversification of production and the expansion of domestic trade structures, within regional economic groupings. ECA was instrumental in the establishment of the Preferential Trade Area for Eastern and Southern Africa (1983) and of the Economic Community of Central African States (1985). In West Africa, assistance has been provided to harmonize the trade liberalization programmes of the Economic Community of West African States (ECOWAS), the Communauté économique de l'Afrique de l'ouest (CEAO) and the Mano River Union. ECA encouraged the founding in 1974 of the Association of African Trade Promotion Organizations, based in Morocco, and the establishment in 1984 of the Federation of African Chambers of Commerce.

In June 1987 ECA organized an international conference on African economic recovery, held in Abuja, Nigeria, which discussed the region's heavy external debts and the need for more favourable trading conditions for African commodities.

PUBLIC ADMINISTRATION, HUMAN RESOURCES AND SOCIAL DEVELOPMENT

The Division aims to assist governments and public corporations in, for example, public administration and financial management; planning of human resources; and youth work and social development. It conducts studies and analyses, provides advisory services and training programmes in public administration, administers fellowships, and produces technical publications.

The Division services the Conference of Ministers Responsible for Human Resources Planning, Development and Utilization, the Conference of Ministers of Social Affairs, and the Conference of heads of institutions of higher education. It supports regional and sub-regional institutions such as the African Institute for Higher Technical Training and Research in Nairobi, Kenya, and the Eastern and Southern African Management Institute in Arusha, Tanzania. Support is also given to various African professional bodies.

BUDGET

ECA's share of the (revised) UN budget for the two years 1988–89 was US $48.1m., increasing to $57.7m. for 1990–91.

PUBLICATIONS

ECA Annual Report.
Report of the Executive Secretary (every 2 years).
Foreign Trade Statistics for Africa series.
  Direction of Trade (quarterly).
  Summary Table (annually).
African Statistical Yearbook.
Statistical Information Bulletin for Africa (annually).
Statistical Newsletter (2 a year).
Directory of African Statisticians (every 2 years).
African Compendium on Environmental Statistics (irregular).
African Socio-Economic Indicators (annually).
Focus on African Industry (2 a year).
Survey on Economic and Social Conditions in Africa (annually).
African Directory of Demographers (irregular).
African Population Newsletter (2 a year).
African Population Studies Series (irregular).
POPINDEX—Africa (annually).
Demographic Handbook for Africa (irregular).
African Trade Bulletin (2 a year).
Bulletin of ECA-sponsored Institutions (irregular).
Rural Progress (2 a year).
Flash on Trade Opportunities (quarterly).
Africa Index (3 a year).
Devindex Africa (quarterly).
PADIS Newsletter (quarterly).

Economic and Social Commission for Western Asia—ESCWA

Address: Amiriyah, POB 27, Baghdad, Iraq.
Telephone: 5569400.
Telex: 213303.

The UN Economic Commission for Western Asia was established in 1974 by a resolution of the UN Economic and Social Council (ECOSOC), to provide facilities of a wider scope for those countries previously served by the UN Economic and Social Office in Beirut (UNESOB). The name 'Economic and Social Commission for Western Asia' (ESCWA) was adopted in 1985.

MEMBERS

Bahrain
Egypt
Iraq
Jordan
Kuwait
Lebanon
Oman
Palestine Liberation Organization (PLO)
Qatar
Saudi Arabia
Syria
United Arab Emirates
Yemen

Organization

(October 1990)

COMMISSION

The sessions of the Commission (held every two years) are attended by representatives of member states, of UN bodies and specialized agencies, of regional and intergovernmental organizations, and of other states attending as observers.

SECRETARIAT

In 1982 the Commission established its permanent headquarters in Baghdad, Iraq.

Divisions:
  Development Planning
  Joint ESCWA/FAO Agriculture
  Joint ESCWA/UNIDO Industry
  Natural Resources, Science and Technology
  Human Settlements and Environment
  Transport, Communications and Tourism
  Social Development and Population
  Statistics
  General Economic Analysis
  Administration

Executive Secretary: TAYSEER ABDEL JABER (Jordan).

Activities

ESCWA undertakes or sponsors studies of economic and technological problems of the region, collects and disseminates information, and provides advisory services.

ESCWA's development plans for the 1980s comprised the following points: making the best use of natural resources; strengthening the regional economy so as to reduce dependence on external sources, such as food imports, and to cut trade imbalances; planned use of petroleum energy; development of human resources; regu-

INTERNATIONAL ORGANIZATIONS

United Nations (Regional Commissions)

lation of the movement of workers between countries; integration of women in development.

Owing to limits on recruitment imposed, from 1987 onwards, by the budgetary crisis affecting the United Nations, the Commission's work programme was curtailed.

Much of ESCWA's work is carried out in co-operation with other UN bodies. It conducts industrial studies for individual countries in conjunction with UNIDO. It co-operates with FAO in regional planning, food security and management of agricultural resources; in 1983-84, for example, a joint mission was undertaken with FAO and UNDP to Egypt, Iraq, Kuwait and Saudi Arabia, to assess training needs in agricultural planning and project analysis. UNDP supports ESCWA's work on household surveys in western Asia and the Arab Planning Institute in Kuwait. Work is also undertaken with UNFPA in population programmes, with ILO in statistical surveys on labour, with UNCTAD in development planning and maritime transport training, and with UNEP in integrating environmental considerations (particularly control of desertification) into development programmes.

The programme of work and priorities comprises studies of various technical and socio-economic problems, particularly those demanding inter-country and sub-regional co-operation. The main areas are:

food and agriculture;

development planning (particularly in the least-developed countries in the region);

human settlement (particularly housing finance and city management);

industrial development (appraisal of potential, co-ordination of policies);

international trade (identification of intra-regional trade and integration opportunities);

labour, management and employment (making the best use of available manpower, development of required skills);

natural resources (energy planning, minerals and water development);

science and technology (problems of dependence on imported technology; training of manpower);

social development (welfare, participation in development, training and planning);

statistics (improvement of procedures, adopting uniform standards);

transport, communications and tourism (multinational shipping enterprises, railway networks, road construction and maintenance, and tourism development);

transnational corporations.

BUDGET

ESCWA's share of the UN budget for the two years 1990-91 was US $38.6m.

PUBLICATIONS

Agriculture and Development (annually).

Population Bulletin (2 a year).

Studies on Development Problems in Selected Countries of the Middle East (annually).

Statistical Abstract (annually).

Survey of Economic and Social Developments in the ESCWA Region (annually).

External Trade Bulletin.

National Accounts Studies.

Reports and studies.

OTHER UNITED NATIONS BODIES

International Sea-Bed Authority

The Authority is to be established one year after the United Nations Convention on the Law of the Sea, adopted in 1982, has been ratified by 60 countries. The seat of the Authority is to be in Kingston, Jamaica.

Organization
(October 1990)

ASSEMBLY
The Assembly is to be the supreme organ of the Authority, consisting of representatives of all parties to the Convention, and will establish policies, approve the budget and elect council members.

COUNCIL
The Council will be elected by the Assembly, and is to consist of 36 members, of whom 18 are to be elected from four 'major interest groups'—the four states who are the largest investors in sea-bed minerals, the four major importers of sea-bed minerals, the four major land-based exporters of the same minerals, and six developing countries representing special interests—while 18 are to be elected on a general basis, but ensuring that all regions of the world are represented. The Council is to decide on the most important questions by consensus rather than by voting.

OTHER ORGANS
The Council is to be assisted by an Economic Planning Commission, which will review supply, demand and pricing of sea-bed minerals and monitor the effects of sea-bed production on land-based mining concerns; and by a Legal and Technical Commission which will supervise sea-bed activities. Each Commission is to have 15 members, elected by the Council with regard for equitable geographical distribution and the representation of special interests. The Sea-Bed Disputes Chamber of the International Tribunal for the Law of the Sea will adjudicate on disputes with respect to activities.

PREPARATORY COMMISSION
Address: Office for Ocean Affairs and the Law of the Sea, United Nations Plaza, New York, NY 10017, USA.
Special Representative of the Secretary-General for the Law of the Sea: SATYA N. NANDAN (Fiji).

The Preparatory Commission, which first met in 1983 and holds annual sessions, was formed to set up the different organs of the Authority pending the entering into force of the Convention. It is also to act as an executive body when registering the applications of pioneer investors.

The Law of the Sea Convention

The third UN Conference on the Law of the Sea (UNCLOS) began its work in 1973, with the aim of regulating maritime activities by defining zones and boundaries, ensuring fair exploitation of resources, and providing machinery for settlement of disputes. Negotiations, involving over 160 countries, continued until 1982, having been delayed in 1981 when the newly elected US Government decided to review its policy. The UN Convention on the Law of the Sea was finally adopted by UNCLOS in April 1982; 130 states voted in its favour, while the USA, Israel, Turkey and Venezuela voted against, and there were 17 abstentions including the Federal Republic of Germany, the USSR and the United Kingdom. The Convention was opened for signing in December for a two-year period: by 1987 159 states had signed, but the USA, the United Kingdom, and the Federal Republic of Germany refused to sign, and by July 1990, 43 states had ratified the Convention, which requires 60 ratifications before it can come into force. The main provisions of the Convention are as follows:

- Coastal states are allowed sovereignty over their territorial waters of up to 12 miles in breadth; foreign vessels are to be allowed 'innocent passage' through these waters.
- Ships and aircraft of all states are allowed 'transit passage' through straits used for international navigation.
- Archipelagic states (composed of islands) have sovereignty over a sea area enclosed by straight lines drawn between the outermost points of the islands.
- Coastal states have sovereign rights in a 200-mile exclusive economic zone with respect to natural resources and jurisdiction over certain activities (such as protection and preservation of the environment), and rights over the adjacent continental shelf up to 350 miles from the shore under specified circumstances.
- All states have freedom of navigation, overflight, scientific research and fishing on the high seas, but must co-operate in measures to conserve living resources.
- A 'parallel system' is to be established for exploiting the international sea-bed, where all activities are to be supervised by the International Sea-Bed Authority. The Authority will conduct its own mining operations and also contract with private and state ventures to give them mining rights.
- States are bound to control pollution and co-operate in forming preventive rules, and incur penalties for failing to combat pollution.
- Marine scientific research in the zones under national jurisdiction is subject to the prior consent of the coastal state, but consent may be denied only under specific circumstances.
- States must submit disputes on the application and interpretation of the Convention to a compulsory procedure entailing decisions binding on all parties. An International Tribunal for the Law of the Sea is to be established.

The objections of the USA and other industrialized nations which have refused to support the Convention concern the provisions for exploitation of the international ocean bed, and particularly the minerals to be found there (chiefly manganese, cobalt, copper and nickel), envisaged as the 'common heritage of mankind'. It is argued that those countries which possess adequate technology for deep-sea mining would be insufficiently represented in the new Authority; the operations of private mining consortia, according to the objectors, would be unacceptably limited by the stipulations that their technology should be shared with a supranational mining enterprise, and that production should be limited in order to protect land-based producers.

Office of the United Nations Disaster Relief Co-ordinator—UNDRO

Address: Palais des Nations, 1211 Geneva 10, Switzerland.
Telephone: (022) 7346011.
Telex: 28148.
Fax: (022) 7335623.

UNDRO was established in 1972 to mobilize and co-ordinate international emergency relief to disaster-stricken areas, and to co-operate in promoting disaster preparedness and prevention.

Organization
(October 1990)

DISASTER RELIEF CO-ORDINATOR

In March 1972 a Disaster Relief Co-ordinator was appointed, at Under-Secretary-General level, to report directly to the UN Secretary-General. UNDRO is a separate entity within the UN Secretariat and consists of a Relief Co-ordination Branch and a Disaster Mitigation Branch.
Co-ordinator: M'HAMED ESSAAFI (Tunisia).

FIELD ORGANIZATION

UNDRO is represented in developing countries by the Resident Representatives of UNDP (q.v.). UNDRO also has a Liaison Office at UN headquarters in New York.
New York Office: Room 2935A, United Nations, New York, NY 10017; tel. (212) 963-5704; telex 023-175715; fax (212) 644-0702.

Activities

The Co-ordinator's mandate derives from a number of General Assembly resolutions on assistance in case of natural disaster and other disaster situations. The Office has four main functions: relief co-ordination; disaster preparedness; disaster prevention; and the provision of public information, data processing services and communications. UNDRO has also entered into agreements (Memoranda of Understanding) with other UN agencies, defining areas and means of co-operation, in order to strengthen the collective response of the United Nations system to disasters.

RELIEF CO-ORDINATION

The Office aims to ensure that, in case of natural or other disaster, all emergency relief activities are mobilized and co-ordinated so as to supply the needs of the disaster-stricken country in a timely and effective manner. UNDRO provides 24-hour monitoring of natural disasters and emergency situations as they occur. Once a disaster situation requiring international assistance is recognized, and a request from the government of the affected country is received, the UNDP Resident Representative, often assisted by an UNDRO relief co-ordination officer, reviews the damage and the immediate relief needs with the competent local authorities, and communicates the findings to UNDRO headquarters. The extent and the compound nature of disasters often calls for an assessment by specialists in various spheres, and multi-agency missions are organized in which representatives of specialized agencies and other organizations take part. Close co-operation is maintained with the other organizations of the UN system and with other intergovernmental and non-governmental organizations. UNDRO places emphasis on obtaining and disseminating all relevant information in good time, so as to avoid waste or misuse of resources, and to determine the timing of the response. During the period January 1987 to mid-1989 UNDRO was involved in 136 disaster situations, of which eight were of a long-standing nature, requiring UNDRO assistance over a lengthy period. The more complex situations often require concerted relief programmes whereby bilateral donors, the United Nations system and other agencies provide assistance to the stricken population. During 1989 major disasters requiring UNDRO involvement included fires in Burma; earthquakes in the People's Republic of China and the USSR; floods in China, Djibouti, Guyana, Malawi, Sri Lanka, Tanzania and the People's Democratic Republic of Yemen; an outbreak of meningitis in Ethiopia; an influx of returnees (as a result of unrest) in Mauritania and Senegal; a cyclone in Mauritius; civil strife in Mozambique; and a typhoon in Viet-Nam. UNDRO was given responsibility for co-ordinating UN relief efforts for foreign workers fleeing from Iraq and Kuwait (following the Iraqi invasion of Kuwait in August 1990).

DISASTER PREPAREDNESS AND PREVENTION

UNDRO promotes the integration of human and material resources and of different skills and disciplines into an effective national system of readiness, in order to minimize the loss of lives and the damage when a disaster strikes.

Disaster preparedness advisory missions are usually undertaken by consultants recruited by UNDRO, who advise governments on the best methods of improving their organization to deal with all kinds of disasters, and not just those which arise from natural causes. The recommendations of these missions sometimes call for specific projects to be carried out, and if these cannot be funded by the government then UNDRO may be asked to seek the necessary financing from donors. Preparedness organizations naturally need trained personnel, and UNDRO arranges or takes part in many seminars for disaster managers and others concerned in relief work, in the preparation and issue of warnings, and in the application of new technologies to disaster work generally. UNDRO is also engaged in attempts to remove obstacles to the rapid delivery of international relief, and this requires willingness by donors as well as by potential recipients to streamline procedures and to waive normal legal requirements for the movement of relief goods and personnel.

In the area of disaster prevention UNDRO is engaged in the development and application of techniques of vulnerability analysis, and in promoting the use of legislation, land-use planning and other inexpensive methods of reducing or eliminating disaster risks. UNDRO is also engaged, jointly with other UN agencies, in attempts to reduce both the hazards created by industrial activities and the effects of industrial accidents.

In the late 1980s projects for disaster prevention and preparedness, both national and regional, incuded: the Seismic Risk Reduction Project in the Balkans area of eastern Europe, the Co-operative Project for Seismic Risk Reduction in the Mediterranean Region, the Pan-Caribbean Disaster Preparedness and Prevention Project, and seminars on earthquake prediction and mitigation. A disaster mitigation programme for the Pacific area was being prepared during this period, together with a regional prevention and preparedness programme for Latin America. In 1986-88 national projects were co-ordinated in Colombia, Egypt, Haiti, Indonesia, Madagascar, Nepal and Niger.

In 1986 UNDRO established a warehouse in Pisa, Italy, which stocks relief supplies (including medicines, blankets, tents, plastic water-tanks, generators and tools) ready for shipment anywhere in the world at short notice.

In 1988, following a decision by the UN General Assembly to designate the 1990s as the International Decade for Natural Disaster Reduction, UNDRO was host to the first meetings of an inter-agency working group and a group of experts preparing for the Decade, and was to provide a secretariat for the Decade.

PUBLIC INFORMATION, DATA PROCESSING AND COMMUNICATIONS

As well as issuing the publications listed below, UNDRO maintains a reference library and a data processing and communications unit. There is a large and comprehensive data base of disaster-related information, also available to other organizations. A computer-based information network for internal disaster management, UNIENET, is also accessible to any individual or organization actively engaged in disaster management. UNIENET provides an electronic mail service, a bulletin board and access to data bases, and is connected to all other UN information networks.

FINANCE

The amount allocated to UNDRO in the regular budget of the UN for the two years 1984-85 was US $4.8m., and UNDRO's share for 1986-87 amounted to $5.6m. In 1986-87 voluntary contributions to cover operational and administrative costs amounted to $2.2m., and a further $21m. was channelled through UNDRO for relief and technical assistance. The programme budget for 1988-89 amounted to $6.8m.

As a co-ordinating office, UNDRO is not itself regarded as a principal source of relief assistance, although the Co-ordinator has the authority to make a contribution from the regular budget not

INTERNATIONAL ORGANIZATIONS

United Nations (Other Bodies)

exceeding $50,000 for any one disaster (and not exceeding in total $360,000 in one year) to meet immediate needs, e.g. for medicines, food or the transport of life-saving equipment. The Co-ordinator is also empowered to receive contributions in kind or in cash to be used for providing relief supplies. However, the greater part of the international assistance provided goes direct to the country concerned, and it is normally expected that the amount and nature of these contributions will be based upon the information given in UNDRO 'situation reports' which are sent by telex to donor sources and other interested organizations throughout the world. During 1988 emergency relief recorded by UNDRO amounted to just under $1,000m.

PUBLICATIONS

Annual Report to the UN General Assembly.

UNDRO News (6 a year).

Disaster News in Brief (annually).

Disaster Prevention and Mitigation: a Compendium of Current Knowledge (12 vols).

Guidelines for Disaster Prevention (3 vols).

Shelter after Disaster: Guidelines for Assistance.

Volcanic Emergency Management.

Disasters and the Disabled.

Technical papers, case reports, Disaster Assessment Mission reports.

United Nations Centre for Human Settlements—UNCHS (Habitat)

Address: POB 30030, Nairobi, Kenya.
Telephone: 333930/520600.
Telex: 22996.
Fax: 520724.

UNCHS (Habitat) was established in October 1978 to service the intergovernmental Commission on Human Settlements, and to serve as a focus for human settlements activities in the UN system.

Organization
(October 1990)

UN COMMISSION ON HUMAN SETTLEMENTS

The Commission (see ECOSOC, p. 19) is the governing body of UNCHS (Habitat). It meets every two years and has 58 members, serving for four years. Sixteen members are from Africa, 13 from Asia, six from Eastern European countries, 10 from Latin America and 13 from Western Europe and other countries.

CENTRE FOR HUMAN SETTLEMENTS

The Centre's work covers technical co-operation, research and development (incorporating settlement planning and policies, shelter and community services, construction and infrastructure, and training) and information, audio-visual and documentation. Other units include the Office of the Executive Director and the Division of Administration. The Habitat and Human Settlements Foundation (HHSF) serves as the financial arm of the Centre.

The Executive Director oversees the work of the Centre, which is to service the Commission on Human Settlements and to implement its resolutions; to ensure the integration and co-ordination of technical co-operation, research and the exchange and dissemination of information; and to execute human settlements projects funded by the United Nations Development Programme (UNDP), funds-in-trust or other contributions.

Executive Director: Dr ARCOT RAMACHANDRAN (India).

Activities

UNCHS (Habitat) assists governments in activities related to human settlements. It supports and conducts research, provides technical co-operation and disseminates information, under the eight sub-programmes listed below. At the end of 1988 activities included 238 technical co-operation projects in 93 countries, with project budgets exceeding US $22m. for 1988; of these, 87 were in Africa, 53 in Latin America and the Caribbean, 55 in Asia and the Pacific, 25 in western Asia and 12 in Europe.

UNCHS (Habitat) also conducts research and training and organizes meetings of experts. Advisory services are provided to governments on building materials and methods, financing procedures, and the application of advanced technology to human settlements planning. UNCHS (Habitat) runs an informal network of human settlements planners who use microcomputers.

In 1988 the Commission on Human Settlements approved a Global Strategy for Shelter to the Year 2000. This was unanimously adopted by the UN General Assembly in December 1988.

Settlement Policies and Strategies

This sub-programme aims to identify high-priority settlements policy issues and to prepare guidelines for formulating and implementing national policies.

Settlements Planning

UNCHS (Habitat) promotes the use of effective methods of settlements planning in both urban and rural areas. In 1986-87 the main emphasis was on forecasting settlements trends and prospects, and on the planning and development of rural settlements. During 1986 training courses in community participation were in operation in Bolivia, Sri Lanka and Zambia.

Shelter and Community Services

This sub-programme assists in improving conditions and services for low-income settlements in urban and rural areas, by upgrading squatter settlements, rehabilitating inner-city slums and supporting co-operative housing: community participation is seen as an essential part of this work.

Development of the Indigenous Construction Sector

Work under this sub-programme concentrates on increasing the capacity of the construction sector to meet demand. Reports being prepared during 1986 covered earth construction; planning of the construction industry using indigenous methods; reformulation of building acts, regulations and codes in African countries; and the use of selected indigenous building materials with potential for wide application in developing countries. Manuals were being prepared on construction using lime, stone and earth.

Low-cost Infrastructure for Human Settlements

UNCHS (Habitat) encourages the development of appropriate infrastructure. In 1985-86 reports were published on traffic in low-income urban settlements and on low-cost vehicles, and the Centre was in the process of preparing guidelines for legislation on water supply and sanitation; a design manual on shallow sewerage; and guidelines for the operation of low-cost water supply and sanitation systems. It published reports on the use of solar energy, and on natural forces in the design of buildings, and studies on energy-efficient housing.

Land

This sub-programme promotes effective government measures for developing land for human settlements, essentially through evaluating regulations on land use, analysing methods of land acquisition and allocation, and collecting data on land use.

Mobilization of Finance

This sub-programme aims to mobilize financial resources for the development of human settlements. Particular emphasis is placed on monitoring the performance of human settlements finance institutions, the role of non-conventional finance mechanisms and support to community-based institutions.

INTERNATIONAL ORGANIZATIONS

Human Settlements Institutions and Management
UNCHS (Habitat) helps to establish or strengthen institutions and management capabilities through case studies, guidelines and training.

FINANCE
The amount allocated to the Centre in the UN budget for the two years 1988–89 was US $7.5m., and extra-budgetary resources were expected to amount to $40m., while contributions to the HHSF were expected to total $10m.

PUBLICATIONS
UNCHS Habitat News (3 a year).

Shelter Bulletin (3 a year).

Technical reports and studies, occasional papers, bibliographies, directories.

United Nations Children's Fund—UNICEF

Address: 3 United Nations Plaza, New York, NY 10017, USA.
Telephone: (212) 326-7000.
Telex: 760-7848.

UNICEF was established in 1946 by the General Assembly as the UN International Children's Emergency Fund, to meet the emergency needs of children in post-war Europe and China. In 1950 its mandate was changed to respond to the needs of children in developing countries. In 1953 the General Assembly decided that UNICEF should continue its work, as a permanent arm of the UN system, with an emphasis on programmes giving long-term benefits to children everywhere, particularly those in developing countries who are in the greatest need.

Organization
(October 1990)

EXECUTIVE BOARD
The governing body of UNICEF meets once a year to establish policy, review programmes and commit funds. Membership comprises 41 governments from all regions, elected in rotation for a three-year term by ECOSOC.

SECRETARIAT
The Executive Director of UNICEF is appointed by the UN Secretary-General in consultation with the Executive Board. The administration of UNICEF and the appointment and direction of staff are the responsibility of the Executive Director, under policy directives laid down by the Executive Board, and under a broad authority delegated to the Executive Director by the Secretary-General. UNICEF has a network of country and regional offices serving 121 countries in the developing world; these offices are supported by partner national committees and other voluntary agencies.

Executive Director: JAMES P. GRANT (USA).

MAJOR UNICEF OFFICES
Europe: Palais des Nations, 1211 Geneva 10, Switzerland.
Eastern and Southern Africa: POB 44145, Nairobi, Kenya.
Middle East and North Africa: POB 811721, Amman, Jordan.
Central and West Africa: BP 443, Abidjan 04, Côte d'Ivoire.
The Americas and the Caribbean: Apdo Aéreo 7555, Bogotá, Colombia.
East Asia and Pakistan: POB 2-154, Bangkok 10200, Thailand.
South Central Asia: UNICEF House, 73 Lodi Estate, New Delhi 110003, India.
Australia and New Zealand: GPO Box Q143, Sydney, NSW 2000, Australia.
Japan: c/o UN Information Centre, 22nd Floor, Shin Aoyama Bldg, Nishikan, 1-1, Minami-Aoyama 1-chome, Minato-ku, Tokyo 107, Japan.

NATIONAL COMMITTEES
There are 33 National Committees, mostly in industrialized countries, whose volunteer members raise money through various activities, including the sale of greetings cards; the Committees also undertake advocacy efforts within their own societies and act as focal points of local support for governmental fund-raising.

Activities

UNICEF's efforts for the 1980s concentrated on the drastic reduction of infant mortality rates through an attack on the principal causes of preventable death and disease, using community-based health and other first-level services and drawing on a wide variety of national and community organizations for support in mobilizing the necessary human and financial resources. UNICEF works with the governments of developing countries by assisting in the development, administration and evaluation of services benefiting children; delivery of technical supplies, equipment and other aid for extending those services; and providing funds to strengthen training of national personnel. UNICEF facilitates the exchange of programming experience among developing countries, and encourages governments to undertake a regular review of the situation of their children and to incorporate a national policy for children in their comprehensive development plans. UNICEF provides assistance on the basis of mutually agreed priorities for children in collaboration with the governments concerned. Priority is given by UNICEF to aiding children in the lower-income groups in the least-developed countries.

Community participation is the key element of the 'basic services' approach adopted by UNICEF in 1975. This approach emphasizes meeting the basic needs of children through community involvement in the planning and running of services. By mobilizing community energies, drawing on local skills through simple training, and the use of relevant and available technology, a great deal can be done to improve maternal and child care, introduce safe water supplies and sanitation, expand primary and non-formal education, including nutrition education for mothers and children, improve the household production of nutritious foods and improve the situation of women, particularly through training and support for income-generating activities.

Economic stringency in the 1980s intensified the search for innovative, low-cost solutions to development problems. Alternative approaches to tackling such major problems of child health and nutrition as immunizable diseases, diarrhoeal dehydration and others have made possible a virtual revolution in child survival and development, with a substantial reduction of death and disease. Since 1982 UNICEF has advocated a concerted international effort to make this potential a reality, focusing on: (a) immunizable, child-killing diseases such as measles, diphtheria, tuberculosis, whooping cough, tetanus and poliomyelitis; (b) diarrhoeal disease; (c) early detection of malnutrition through growth monitoring; (d) promotion of breast-feeding and proper weaning; (e) female education; and (f) birth spacing. The new approaches depend crucially upon community participation and therefore build upon the community-based services strategy which UNICEF has been advocating and supporting since 1975. An allied dimension is social mobilization, by which community organizations and other groups and sectors of society involve themselves in broad, mutually-reinforcing efforts, often on a nation-wide basis, such as national immunization campaigns.

In several crucial health areas, new medical technologies have substantially improved the chances of success. In particular, the widespread use (since 1980) of a simple mixture of salt plus sugar or cereal starch in water (oral rehydration therapy) has revolutionized family and community-level treatment of diarrhoeal dehydration, one of the leading causes of death for infants and young children.

UNICEF estimated that about 1.5m. child deaths were being averted each year during the mid-1980s by oral rehydration therapy and immunization. Sustained efforts of this kind against the major killers of children, it was felt, could reduce child death and disability by 50% in much of the developing world by the early 1990s.

INTERNATIONAL ORGANIZATIONS

United Nations (Other Bodies)

In the course of the 1980s, UNICEF assisted in drafting a Convention on the Rights of the Child, which was adopted by the UN General Assembly in November 1989 and entered into force in September 1990, following ratification by 30 states and signature by 105 states. The Convention's 54 provisions included the right of a child to live with its parents and to receive health care and education; the right to protection from abuse, neglect and harmful labour practices; and safeguards for children who are adopted. Also in September 1990, heads of state and government from more than 70 countries attended a 'World Summit for Children', organized by UNICEF, and committed their nations to reducing the number of deaths of children under five years of age, and of women who die in childbirth; they also undertook to reduce malnutrition, and to guarantee access to clean water, sanitation and basic education.

In emergency relief and rehabilitation, UNICEF works closely with other UN agencies (as well as with numerous non-governmental organizations); in 1988 it provided about US $32m. worth of assistance to 43 countries affected by disasters. Aid was in the form of shelter materials, medicaments, water supply equipment, food supplements, and the support or strengthening of essential services. UNICEF supports the initiative of the UN Secretary-General, aimed at mobilizing extra resources for the victims of drought, famine and conflict in the African continent. In Lebanon, where a significant role has been undertaken since 1974, UNICEF is continuing to co-operate in a major UN programme of rehabilitation.

FINANCE

UNICEF's work is accomplished with voluntary contributions from both governments and non-governmental sources. Total income in 1988 came to US $709m. Income from governments accounted for about 75% of this.

UNICEF's income is divided between contributions for general resources and contributions for specific purposes or emergencies. General resources are the funds available to fulfil commitments for co-operation in country programmes approved by the Executive Board, and to meet administrative and programme support expenditures. They include contributions from governments, the net income from greetings cards sales, funds contributed by the public (mainly through National Committees) and other income. These funds amounted to $437m. in 1988. Contributions for specific purposes are those sought by UNICEF from governments and intergovernmental organizations as supplementary funds to support projects for which general resources are insufficient, or for relief and rehabilitation programmes in emergency situations. Supplementary funding in 1988 amounted to $233m.

UNICEF PROGRAMME EXPENDITURE BY SECTOR
(1988)

	Cost (US $ million)
Child health	158
Water supply	69
Nutrition	23
Community and family-based services for children	29
Formal and non-formal education	37
Planning and project support	52
Emergency relief	32
Total	**400**

PUBLICATIONS

State of the World's Children (annually, in English, French, Spanish and Arabic).

UNICEF Annual Report (summarizes UNICEF policies and programmes; in English, French and Spanish).

Facts about UNICEF (annually, in English, French and Spanish).

Les Carnets de l'Enfance/Assignment Children (concerned with planning development for women, children and youth; in English and French).

United Nations Conference on Trade and Development—UNCTAD

Address: Palais des Nations, 1211 Geneva 10, Switzerland.
Telephone: (022) 7346011.
Telex: 289696.
Fax: (022) 7339879.

UNCTAD was established by the UN General Assembly as one of its permanent organs in December 1964. Its role is to promote international trade, particularly that of developing countries, with a view to accelerating economic development. It is the principal instrument of the General Assembly for deliberation and negotiation in respect of international trade and related issues of international economic co-operation.

Organization
(October 1990)

CONFERENCE

The Conference of government ministers concerned with trade and development is held every four years in different capitals of member states. Seventh session: Geneva, Switzerland, July 1987. UNCTAD has 166 members, including all the UN member states, and a number of organizations have observer status.

SECRETARIAT

As well as servicing the Conference, the UNCTAD secretariat undertakes research and policy analysis; implementation or follow-up of decisions of intergovernmental bodies; technical co-operation in support of UNCTAD's policy objectives, particularly as an executing agency of the United Nations Development Programme; and information exchanges and consultations of various types. It provided support for the United Nations Programme of Action for African Economic Recovery and Development, 1986–1990 (UNPAAERD).

Secretary-General: KENNETH DADZIE (Ghana).

Deputy Secretaries-General: YVES BERTHELOT (France), DIOGO DE GASPAR (Brazil).

TRADE AND DEVELOPMENT BOARD

Between Conferences, the continuing work of the organization is carried out by UNCTAD's executive body, the Trade and Development Board (which normally meets twice a year to review topics related to trade and economic interdependence), together with its various committees and subsidiary bodies.

INTERGOVERNMENTAL COMMITTEES

Several intergovernmental committees, reporting to the Trade and Development Board, and often drawing on the work of expert bodies, review trends and make policy recommendations in specific areas: commodities; manufactures; development finance; insurance; shipping and ports; transfer of technology; and economic co-operation among developing countries. A special committee monitors the Generalized System of Preferences. Another group of experts reviews the impact of restrictive business practices on the trade of developing countries.

Activities

The main recurring themes addressed by governments through UNCTAD, and in the supporting activities of its secretariat, are:

the expansion and diversification of the exports of goods and services of developing countries, which are their main source of external finance for development; and the need for developed countries to adopt policies and measures to support this aim, in particular by opening their markets and adjusting their productive structures;

the stabilization and strengthening of international commodity markets, on which most developing countries remain dependent for export earnings; the enhancement of such earnings through increased participation in processing, marketing and distribution of commodities; and the reduction of that dependence through diversification of their economies;

the enhancement of the export capacity of developing countries through mobilizing domestic and external resources, including development assistance and foreign investment, strengthening technological capabilities, developing merchant shipping, and promoting appropriate national trade and transport policies;

the alleviation of the impact of debt on the economies of developing countries and the reduction of their debt burden;

special measures in support of the 'least developed countries', a classification now comprising 41 of the world's poorest and most vulnerable countries, and of other particularly disadvantaged countries; and support for the expansion of trade and economic co-operation among developing countries, as a mutually beneficial complement to their traditional economic links with developed economies and as a contribution to the growth of the world economy.

In all these areas, UNCTAD seeks to promote intergovernmental consensus, as a basis for action through the UNCTAD machinery, the General Assembly or the organizations of the United Nations system, as well as for national policy formulation. Such action can take various forms. These include concluding legally-binding or non-binding instruments and codes of behaviour; elaborating policy frameworks for concrete measures and decisions by countries; and generating intellectual and political impulses for the adoption of international as well as national policies.

During the 1980s, UNCTAD brought about the negotiation (by producer and consumer countries) of fixed-term agreements on specific commodities, such as natural rubber (1987), cocoa (1986), olive oil (1986) and tin (1981). These agreements had as their principal objective the stabilization of conditions in the international trade of the commodities concerned and, for this purpose, established pricing and supply arrangements. Development agreements which came into force in 1984 and 1985 concerned jute (1982) and tropical timber (1983). (See also the section on Other International Organizations—Commodities.) The agreement of 1980 establishing the Common Fund for Commodities entered into effect in 1989, providing capital of US $470m. to assist the functioning of international commodity agreements, together with voluntary contributions of about $255m., intended for longer-term purposes such as research, market promotion and conservation of resources.

UNCTAD is responsible for the Generalized System of Preferences (GSP), initiated in 1971, whereby a certain proportion of manufactured goods that are exported by developing countries receive preferential tariff treatment by developed countries. By 1990 the GSP covered some US $50,000m. of annual exports from developing countries.

In 1978 UNCTAD adopted a resolution providing for the retroactive adjustment of terms for the official development assistance debt of low-income countries (which, by 1990, had yielded debt relief amounting to $6,500m. for more than 50 such countries). In 1980 UNCTAD drafted a set of guidelines for international action in the area of debt-rescheduling. In the same year UNCTAD adopted a set of rules for the control of restrictive business practices that adversely affect international trade. The Trade and Development Board has also been mandated to follow closely developments and issues that are of particular concern to developing countries in the 'Uruguay Round' of multilateral trade negotiations (see GATT). The Secretariat provides technical assistance to developing countries on request, in connection with the Uruguay Round.

UNCTAD also seeks to help developing countries to increase their participation in world shipping, to improve the efficiency of their activities in shipping and ports and to acquire new technology in shipping, multimodal transport and ports. These objectives are pursued through the development of appropriate international policies in related fields, through increased regional and subregional co-operation among developing countries, and through the provision of technical assistance to developing countries involving the supply of both expertise and training. UNCTAD's work has resulted in the negotiation of several Conventions, such as the UN Convention on a Code of Conduct for Liner Conferences, which was adopted in 1974 and came into force in 1983. This Convention provides for the national shipping lines of developing countries to participate on an equal basis with the shipping lines of developed countries, as well as for a more equal relationship between the providers and users of liner shipping services. Other UNCTAD initiatives have resulted in the adoption of the UN Convention on the Carriage of Goods by Sea (Hamburg Rules) in 1978, and the UN Convention on International Multimodal Transport in 1980. These two Conventions have adopted a modern liability limitation system which takes into account the post-war technological and structural developments in maritime and multimodal transport and which, when in force, will increase the efficiency and harmonization of international transport practices between shippers and carriers. In addition, the UN Convention on Conditions for Registration of Ships, which seeks to set up a uniform international regime relating to the registration of ships and to the jurisdiction and control over ships by the flag state, including the definition of the principle of a genuine link, was adopted in 1986. By September 1990, the Hamburg Rules had received 17 ratifications (entry into force requires 20 contracting parties); the Multimodal Convention, five ratifications (entry into force requires 30 contracting parties); and the Registration of Ships Convention, six ratifications (entry into force requires 40 contracting parties accounting for 25% of the world tonnage).

In 1981 UNCTAD serviced the UN Conference on the Least Developed Countries (LDCs), which adopted the 'Substantial New Programme of Action' for the 1980s for the 36 poorest countries; a mid-term review of this programme was carried out by UNCTAD in October 1985. Another Conference, held in 1990, reported that none of the targets agreed at the previous conference (concerning average growth in agricultural and industrial production, and the proportion of donors' gross national product to be used for development aid) had been met. The 1990 conference adopted a new 'Programme of Action', embodying commitments by the LDCs and their development partners.

At the 1987 session of UNCTAD, developing countries failed to persuade the developed countries to increase debt relief or to reduce interest rates, but the Conference agreed on the need for flexibility in the rescheduling of debts, so that the medium-term economic plans of debtor governments were not imperilled by the short-term austerity measures imposed by creditors. The Conference also agreed on the importance of reducing restrictive trade practices through the current round of negotiations under the General Agreement on Tariffs and Trade (q.v.). In 1988 UNCTAD proposed (in its annual *Trade and Development Report*) that at least 30% of debts owed to commercial banks by the 15 most heavily indebted countries (principally Argentina, Brazil and Mexico) should be cancelled.

The International Trade Centre in Geneva is operated jointly by GATT and UNCTAD.

FINANCE

The expenses of UNCTAD are borne by the regular budget of the UN. The amount approved by the UN General Assembly for the two-year period 1988–89 was US $77m. Technical co-operation activities, financed separately, were expected to cost $22m. in 1990.

PUBLICATIONS

UNCTAD Bulletin (6 a year, in English and French).
Trade and Development Report (annually).
The Least Developed Countries Report (annually).
Handbook of International Trade and Development Statistics (annually).
UNCTAD Commodity Yearbook.
Monthly Commodity Price Bulletin.
Review of Maritime Transport (annually).
UNCTAD Review (occasional).
UNCTAD Statistical Pocket Book (occasional).
Guide to UNCTAD Publications (annually).

United Nations Development Programme—UNDP

Address: One United Nations Plaza, New York, NY 10017, USA.
Telephone: (212) 906-5000.

The Programme was established in 1965 by the UN General Assembly to help the developing countries increase the wealth-producing capabilities of their natural and human resources.

Organization
(October 1990)

UNDP is responsible to the UN General Assembly, to which it reports through ECOSOC.

GOVERNING COUNCIL

The Council, which meets annually, is the policy-making body of UNDP, and comprises representatives of 48 countries; 27 seats are filled by developing countries and 21 by economically more advanced countries; one-third of the membership changes each year.

SECRETARIAT

Administrator: William H. Draper (USA).
Associate Administrator: Luis María Gómez (Argentina).

REGIONAL BUREAUX

Headed by assistant administrators, the regional bureaux share the responsibility for implementing the programme with the Administrator's office. Within certain limitations, large-scale projects may be approved and funding allocated by the Administrator, and smaller-scale projects by the Resident Representatives, based in 112 countries.

The four regional bureaux, all at the Secretariat in New York, cover: Africa; Asia and the Pacific; the Arab states and Europe; and Latin America and the Caribbean; there is also a Division for Global and Interregional Projects.

FIELD OFFICES

In almost every country receiving UNDP assistance there is a Country Office, headed by the UNDP Resident Representative, who co-ordinates all UN technical assistance, advises the Government on formulating the country programme, sees that field activities are carried out, and acts as the leader of the UN team of experts working in the country. Resident Representatives are normally designated as co-ordinators for all UN operational development activities; the field offices function as the primary presence of the UN in most developing countries.

Activities

As the world's largest source of grant technical assistance in developing countries, UNDP works with more than 150 governments and 36 international agencies for faster economic growth and better standards of living throughout the world. Agriculture (including forestry and fisheries) is the largest component of UNDP activities, accounting for about 22% of project expenditure in 1989 (see table). Most of the work is carried out in the field by the various United Nations agencies, or by the government of the country concerned.

Assistance is mostly non-monetary, comprising the provision of experts' services, consultancies, equipment, and fellowships for advanced study abroad. In 1989 about 46% of spending on projects was for the services of experts, 24% was for equipment, 12% was for training, and the remainder was for other costs, such as maintenance of equipment. Most UNDP projects incorporate training for local workers. Developing countries themselves provide 50% or more of the total project costs in terms of personnel, facilities, equipment and supplies.

Project work covers five main areas: locating, assessing and activating latent natural resources and other development assets; stimulating capital investment to help realize these possibilities; support for professional and vocational training; expansion of scientific research and applied technology; and strengthening of national and regional development planning. In 1989 there were 6,904 ongoing projects, and in that year 1,441 new projects were approved.

During 1989 UNDP made available the services of 17,569 national and international experts, and awarded 11,113 fellowships for nationals of developing countries to study abroad.

Countries receiving UNDP assistance are allocated an indicative planning figure (IPF) for a five-year period. The IPF represents the approximate total funding that a country can expect to receive, based on a formula taking per caput gross national product (GNP), population size and other criteria into account. In partnership with UNDP's Country Offices, governments calculate their technical assistance requirements on the basis of this formula. Activities covering more than one region are developed by UNDP's Division for Global and Interregional Projects, in consultation with the relevant national and regional institutions.

In UNDP's fourth programming cycle (1987–91), 80% of the resources available was to be devoted to the poorest developing countries, with per caput GNP of US $750 or less; within this group, countries with per caput GNP of less than $375 were to receive particular attention. For 1987–91 UNDP drew up 152 country programmes of medium-term technical assistance. In 1990 the Governing Council stipulated that for the 1992–96 programming cycle 87% of funds should be reserved for countries with per caput GNP of $750 or less, and 55% to the 41 countries designated as least-developed. The following were to be observed as priorities during the cycle: elimination of poverty; environmental protection; involvement of women in development; improvement of management skills; and technology transfers to developing countries.

During 1986 UNDP created a Division for Women and Development, to ensure that women should play a greater part in UNDP-supported activities, and a Division for Non-Governmental Organizations, to encourage a more effective partnership with such organizations in development work. In the same year a system for providing short-term advisory services was initiated. A Management Development Programme began operating in 1989, with the purpose of strengthening the management capacity of governments on a long-term basis. The Programme was allocated $60m. for the period 1989–91.

UNDP supports the Caribbean Project Development Facility (established in 1981) and the Africa Project Development Facility (established in 1986), which are administered by the International Finance Corporation (q.v.), and which aim to encourage private investment in these regions.

UNDP also takes part in emergency relief operations with UNDRO and other agencies.

FINANCE

The Development Programme is financed by the voluntary contributions of members of the United Nations and the Programme's participating agencies. Total expenditure in 1989 was estimated at $1,200m., of which $890m. was for field programmes (see table below) and the remainder was for planning, management and co-ordination by UNDP's headquarters staff and field offices, and support costs for 31 executing agencies.

UNDP PROJECT EXPENDITURE BY SECTOR (1989)

	Estimated cost (US $ m. equivalent)
Agriculture, forestry and fisheries	192.3
General development, policies and planning	170.7
Industry	103.8
Transport and communications	95.7
Natural resources	90.2
Science and technology	49.0
Employment	41.4
Health	39.0
Education	37.0
Population, human settlements, humanitarian aid	30.7
Total (incl. other)	890.0

INTERNATIONAL ORGANIZATIONS

UNDP PROJECT EXENDITURE BY REGION (1989)

	Estimated expenditure (US $ million)
Africa	315.1
Asia and the Pacific	307.9
Latin America and the Caribbean	135.1
Arab states and Europe	90.1
Interregional and global	41.8
Total	**890.0**

PUBLICATIONS

Annual Report.
Update (every 2 weeks).
World Development (every 2 months).
Co-operation South (quarterly).
Source (quarterly).

Associated Funds

UNITED NATIONS CAPITAL DEVELOPMENT FUND—UNCDF

The Fund was established in 1966 and became fully operational in 1974. It assists developing countries by supplementing existing sources of capital assistance, through grants and loans on concessionary terms. Rapid assistance is available to governments for small-scale projects directly and immediately benefiting the low-income groups who have not benefited from earlier development efforts. Assistance may be given to any of the member states of the UN system, and is not necessarily limited to specific projects. The Fund is mainly used for the benefit of the least-developed countries. Voluntary contributions pledged for 1989 amounted to US $36.7m.

Examples of projects financed by UNCDF include: creation of 'revolving funds' for village co-operatives to obtain supplies of seeds and fertilizers; credit for low-cost housing or small businesses; provision of facilities for irrigation, drinking-water and food storage; construction of roads, schools and health centres; and reafforestation of land.

UNITED NATIONS DEVELOPMENT FUND FOR WOMEN—UNIFEM

This Fund (formerly the Voluntary Fund for the UN Decade for Women) became an associated fund of UNDP in 1985. Its purpose is to involve women in development and to support innovative activities benefiting women in all regions, e.g. credit funds, small-scale group enterprises to raise incomes, and training in work-saving and fuel-conserving technologies. Pledges for 1990 totalled $6.7m.

Director: SHARON CAPELING-ALAKIJA (Canada).

UNITED NATIONS FUND FOR SCIENCE AND TECHNOLOGY FOR DEVELOPMENT—UNFSTD

UNFSTD was established in 1982 to help developing countries acquire the capacity to formulate science and technology policies linked to their development goals. Advisory services and the exchange of information are its principal activities. In 1989 UNFSTD received $1.2m. in contributions. Income is also obtained from cost-sharing and sub-trust funds.

Director: RUSTAM LALKAKA (India).

UNITED NATIONS REVOLVING FUND FOR NATURAL RESOURCES EXPLORATION—RFNRE

The RFNRE was established in 1974 to provide risk capital to finance exploration for natural resources (particularly minerals) in developing countries and, when discoveries are made, to help to attract investment. The revolving character of the Fund, which distinguishes it from most other UN technical co-operation programmes, lies in the undertaking of contributing governments to make replenishment contributions to the Fund when the projects it finances lead to commercial production. Contributions pledged to the Fund amounted to $2.5m. for 1989.

Director: SHIGEAKI TOMITA (Japan).

UNITED NATIONS SUDANO-SAHELIAN OFFICE—UNSO

UNSO's responsibility is to help the countries of the Sahel region of western Africa to combat drought and desertification. Activities include planting improved crop strains; setting up food storage facilities; establishing agricultural implement workshops; developing transport and communications; agrometeorological and hydrological services; forest conservation and expansion; water resources management; sand dune fixation; and the development of alternative systems for energy production and overall policy planning. Voluntary contributions pledged for 1989 amounted to $6.7m., and other income (from trust funds and cost-sharing) was $21.8m.

UN Sahelian Regional Office: BP 366, ave Dimdolobsom, Ouagadougou, Burkina Faso; tel. 367-81; telex 5262.

UNITED NATIONS VOLUNTEERS—UNV

The United Nations Volunteers is an important source of middle-level skills for the UN development system supplied at modest cost, particularly in the least-developed countries. Volunteers expand the scope of UNDP project activities by supplementing the work of international and host-country experts and by extending the influence of projects to local community levels. One of the most important parts of UNV's work is the support of technical co-operation within and among the developing countries by encouraging volunteers from the countries themselves and by forming regional exchange teams made up of such volunteers. UNV is also engaged in a variety of activities to increase youth participation in development and to promote the involvement of domestic development services.

In 1989 2,355 volunteers from both developed and developing nations were serving in 108 countries. Voluntary contributions to the programme amounted to $1.2m. in that year.

OTHER FUNDS

Other special funds include the International Initiative against Avoidable Disablement; the Partners in Development Fund to support local non-governmental organizations; the Special Fund for Landlocked Developing Countries; and the Energy Account, which works with the World Bank to carry out energy sector assessments in developing countries.

United Nations Environment Programme—UNEP

Address: POB 30552, Nairobi, Kenya.
Telephone: 333930.
Telex: 22068.
Fax: (2542) 520711.

The United Nations Environment Programme was established in 1972 by the UN General Assembly following recommendations of the 1972 UN Conference on the Human Environment, in Stockholm, Sweden, to encourage international co-operation in matters relating to the human environment.

Organization
(October 1990)

GOVERNING COUNCIL
The main function of the Governing Council, which meets every two years, is to provide general policy guidelines for the direction and co-ordination of environmental programmes within the UN system. It comprises representatives of 58 states, elected by the UN General Assembly on a rotating basis.

SECRETARIAT
The Secretariat serves as a focal point for environmental action within the UN system.
Executive Director: MOSTAFA K. TOLBA (Egypt).

REGIONAL OFFICES
Europe: Pavillon du Petit Saconnex, 16 ave Jean Trembley, 1209 Geneva, Switzerland; tel. (022) 7999400; telex 28877.
Asia and the Pacific: UN Bldg, 10th Floor, Rajadamnern Ave, Bangkok 10200, Thailand; tel. 2829161; telex 82392.
Latin America and the Caribbean: Presidente Mazaryk 29, Ap. Postal 6-718, México 5, DF, Mexico; tel. 2501555; telex 01771055.
West Asia: 1083 Road No 425, Jufair 342, Manama, Bahrain; tel. 729040; telex 8337.
Africa: UNEP Headquarters (see above).
North America: UNDC Two Bldg, Room 0803, 2 United Nations Plaza, New York, NY 10017, USA; tel. (212) 754-8139; telex 420544.

OTHER OFFICES
Convention on International Trade in Endangered Species of Wild Fauna and Flora (CITES): 6 rue du Maupas, CP 78, 1000 Lausanne 9, Switzerland; tel. (021) 200081; telex 24584; fax (021) 200084; Sec.-Gen. EUGÈNE LAPOINTE.
International Register for Potentially Toxic Chemicals Programme Activity Centre (IRPTC/PAC): Palais des Nations, 1211 Geneva 10, Switzerland; tel. (022) 7988400; telex 28877.
UNEP Industry and Environmental Office (IEO): Tour Mirabeau, 39-43, Quai André Citroen, 57539 Paris Cedex 15, France; tel. (1) 40-58-88-50; telex 204997; fax (1) 40-58-88-88.

Activities

UNEP aims to maintain a constant watch on the changing state of the environment; to analyse the trends; to assess the problems using a wide range of data and techniques; and to promote projects leading to environmentally sound development. It plays a catalytic and co-ordinating role within and beyond the UN system. Many UNEP projects are implemented in co-operation with other UN agencies, particularly FAO, UNESCO and WHO. About 40 intergovernmental organizations outside the UN system have official observer status on UNEP's Governing Council, and, through the Environment Liaison Centre in Nairobi, UNEP is linked to more than 6,000 non-governmental bodies concerned with the environment.

ENVIRONMENT AND DEVELOPMENT
UNEP encourages the integration of environmental considerations in development planning; in 1986, for example, it convened a conference of experts in Canberra (Australia) and 'workshops' in New Delhi (India) and Beijing (People's Republic of China), on the economics of dry-land degradation and rehabilitation; assisted the Government of Cyprus in analysis of local needs and environmentally sound planning; co-operated with the World Bank in developing guidelines on how to introduce considerations of environmental resources into national income accounting; and worked with the Government of Jamaica on planning improved management of river-basins. Training courses for those involved in planning are also provided. In 1985 UNEP (with the OAU and ECA) convened the first African Ministerial Conference on the Environment, and in 1986 a similar conference was held for government ministers from the Arab states.

UNEP makes comparative assessments of the environmental impact of different energy sources, and encourages the development of new and renewable sources of energy. Work on the more efficient use of fuel-wood was being undertaken in Bolivia, Brazil and Kenya during 1986, and a meeting of experts was held to discuss energy conservation in western Asia.

UNEP draws up and reviews international environmental law. It administers the Convention on International Trade in Endangered Species of Wild Fauna and Flora (CITES—see above), to which 102 states were parties in 1989. In October 1989 a CITES conference adopted a ban on international trade in ivory, in order to conserve the world's dwindling population of elephants. UNEP also organizes working groups of experts to develop legal guidelines and principles on, for example, the protection of the earth's ozone layer, management of hazardous wastes, and marine pollution. UNEP also provides technical assistance for drawing up national legislation.

UNEP works with industry and governments to prepare technical guidelines, information and training programmes on environmentally sound industrial development. Particular emphasis is given to promoting cleaner production methods, to sound methods of managing industrial wastes, and to emergency preparedness for industrial accidents.

ENVIRONMENTAL AWARENESS
UNEP encourages the inclusion of environmental issues in education. The joint UNEP/UNESCO International Programme in Environmental Education, launched in 1975, includes the training of teachers, publications and technical assistance to governments for the incorporation of environmental education at all levels of general education.

UNEP attempts to enhance the capabilities of countries to deal with environmental concerns by providing trained decision-makers, planners and managers, particularly in developing countries. It encourages the incorporation of environmental concerns into the training activities of ILO, other UN agencies, non-governmental organizations and national governments. UNEP supports regional networks of training institutions, and provides help for universities in developing courses in environmental management.

UNEP provides information through its publications (see below), and press releases. A News and Data team provides information for the news media and operates a data base.

ENVIRONMENTAL ASSESSMENT
UNEP's environmental assessment programme, known as Earthwatch, aims to study the interaction between man and the environment, provide early warning of potential environmental hazards, and determine the state of natural resources. The Global Environment Monitoring System (GEMS), which began in 1975, collects data on the following topics: renewable resources; atmosphere; environmental pollution; long-range transport of pollutants; integrated monitoring of pollutants and ecosystems; and oceans (handled through its programme for oceans and coastal areas). In September 1988 UNEP and WHO held a meeting of experts to discuss reports on the findings of long-term GEMS studies on air pollution, water pollution and food contamination by chemicals. To convert the data collected into information usable by decision-makers, a global resource information data-base (GRID) was set up in 1985. The INFOTERRA programme forms a network of 129 national 'focal points' for the exchange of environmental information, including the annual compilation of a Directory of Sources.

UNEP conducts research on the 'outer limits' of tolerance of the biosphere and its subsystems to the demands made on it by human activities, and undertakes climate impact studies, e.g. assessing the effect of carbon dioxide emission on climate—the 'greenhouse effect', which is predicted to result in potentially catastrophic climatic changes. UNEP organized an international conference on global warming, attended by representatives of 72 countries, in November 1989. The conference failed to adopt proposals to 'freeze' carbon dioxide emissions by the year 2000, and postponed any decision on levels of reduction to be made.

INTERNATIONAL ORGANIZATIONS

United Nations (Other Bodies)

In 1985 a study was completed by UNEP on the effects of chlorofluorocarbon (CFC) production on the layer of ozone in the earth's atmosphere, warning that serious consequences to human health were likely to result if governments did not limit such production. Following the adoption in 1985 of the Vienna Convention for the Protection of the Ozone Layer, UNEP began a programme of legal and technical activities, with the aim of securing agreement on a protocol to the Convention that would impose legal limits on the production of CFCs. Agreement was reached by 24 nations in September 1987, in Montreal, Canada. The 'Montreal protocol' was intended to reduce production of CFCs by 50% by the year 2000. By mid-1990 50 nations had ratified the protocol. In June 1990, however, UNEP organized further negotiations in an attempt to strengthen the protocol, and it was agreed that the production of CFCs should be phased out completely by 2000. A fund was established to assist developing countries in making the necessary technological adaptations.

In 1989 the Basel Convention on the Control of Transboundary Movements of Hazardous Wastes and their Disposal was adopted. It governs the transport and disposal of hazardous wastes, with the aim of preventing the 'dumping' of wastes from industrialized countries in countries that have no processing facilities.

OCEANS

UNEP co-operates with other agencies in assessing marine pollution, chiefly through its regional seas programme: by the end of 1986 action plans had been adopted in nine regions (the Mediterranean; the seas around Kuwait; the Caribbean; the West and Central African region; the East African region; the East Asian region; the Red Sea and the Gulf of Aden; the South Pacific; and the South-East Pacific), and regional conventions had been signed by member states in six of these regions. With FAO, a joint Plan of Action for the Conservation, Management and Utilization of Marine Mammals was drawn up in 1984.

WATER AND LAND ECOSYSTEMS

UNEP supports research and training in the management of inland water resources and the protection of fresh-water ecosystems. The EMINA programme promotes an environmentally sound approach to the development of water resources. UNEP monitors and attempts to combat topsoil erosion, the destruction of tropical forests and the misuse of agricultural pesticides. It works with FAO and other agencies in the development of 'Tropical Forestry Action Plans'. It collaborates with the International Union for the Conservation of Nature and Natural Resources (IUCN, q.v.) in the protection of endangered species and habitats, and provides a secretariat for the Ecosystem Conservation Group (consisting of UNEP, FAO, UNESCO and IUCN), which sends expert missions to help prepare national conservation strategies. UNEP supports a number of projects which collect and conserve plant and animal genetic resources, including a 'gene bank' for crops and trees, and also supports six regional Microbiological Resources Centres which undertake training and research in this field.

DESERTIFICATION CONTROL

UNEP co-ordinates the UN Plan of Action to Combat Desertification (begun in 1978), which is particularly active in the Sudano-Sahelian region. Individual countries are assisted in formulating plans of action, including the planting of shrubs and trees, and prevention of the encroachment of sand-dunes. In 1986 and 1987 UNEP assisted in the formation of regional networks of non-governmental organizations engaged in anti-desertification activities, in Africa, Latin America and Asia and the Pacific.

HEALTH AND HUMAN SETTLEMENTS

UNEP promotes increased awareness of environmental health problems, particularly those caused by chemical contamination and the side-effects of pesticides. It maintains the International Register of Potentially Toxic Chemicals, and provides guidance on chemical hazards and waste management. UNEP collaborates with other UN agencies, especially UNCHS, in combating deteriorating environmental standards in towns; in 1986 it completed work on guidelines for the control of environmental pollution in human settlements of developing countries, and took part in preparations for the International Year of Shelter for the Homeless (1987).

FINANCE

UNEP derives its finances from the regular budget of the United Nations (from which US $10.65m. was allotted to it for the two years 1988–89), and from voluntary contributions to the Environment Fund, which amounted to about $34.9m. in 1988.

ENVIRONMENT FUND: COMMITMENTS FOR PROGRAMME ACTIVITIES, 1990

Purpose	Commitments (US dollars)
Monitoring and assessment	2,865,486
Information exchange	2,261,849
Oceans	2,524,773
Water	1,088,981
Terrestrial ecosystems management	1,449,903
Desertification control	3,067,818
Environmental health	420,780
Peace, arms race and the environment	218,047
Technology and the environment	1,407,735
Support measures	4,375,168
Technical and regional co-operation	1,314,572
Fund programme reserve	939,664
Total	**21,934,776**

GEOGRAPHICAL DISTRIBUTION OF FUND EXPENDITURE, 1990

Region	Amount (US dollars)
Africa	2,494,222
Asia	1,979,509
Latin America	1,225,464
North America	35,578
Europe	51,799
Inter-regional	1,224,496
Global	14,923,708
Total	**21,934,776**

PUBLICATIONS

Annual Report of the Executive Director.

State of the Environment Report (annually).

Our Planet (quarterly).

Desertification Control Bulletin (2 a year).

Industry and Environment Bulletin (quarterly).

INFOterra Bulletin (quarterly).

INFOterra International Directory of Sources.

IRPTC Bulletin (3 a year: on toxic chemicals).

Environmental Events Record (monthly).

Ozone Layer Bulletin (annually).

The Siren (quarterly, on regional seas programme).

Catalogue of Publications (every 2 years).

Catalogue of Audio-Visual Material (every 2 years).

UNESCO-UNEP Newsletter (quarterly).

Studies, reports, legal texts, technical guidelines, etc.

INTERNATIONAL ORGANIZATIONS — United Nations (Other Bodies)

United Nations High Commissioner for Refugees—UNHCR

Address: Case postale 2500, 1211 Geneva 2 dépôt, Switzerland.
Telephone: (22) 7398111.
Telex: 415740.
Fax: (022) 7319546.

The Office of the High Commissioner was established in 1951 to provide international protection for refugees and to seek permanent solutions to their problems.

Organization
(November 1990)

HIGH COMMISSIONER
The High Commissioner is elected by the United Nations General Assembly on the nomination of the Secretary-General, and is responsible to the General Assembly and to the UN Economic and Social Council (ECOSOC).

High Commissioner: (vacant).
Deputy High Commissioner: DOUGLAS STAFFORD (USA).

EXECUTIVE COMMITTEE
The Executive Committee of the High Commissioner's Programme, established by ECOSOC, gives the High Commissioner policy directives in respect of material assistance programmes and advice at his request in the field of international protection. It meets once a year, usually at Geneva. It includes representatives of 43 states, both members and non-members of the UN.

ADMINISTRATION
Headquarters includes the High Commissioner's Office, the Division of Refugee Law and Doctrine, and five Regional Bureaux (Africa; Asia and Oceania; Europe and North America; Latin America and the Caribbean; South West Asia, the Middle East and North Africa). In 1990 the High Commissioner had more than 100 field offices.

Activities

The competence of the High Commissioner extends to any person who, owing to well-founded fear of being persecuted for reasons of race, religion, nationality or political opinion, is outside the country of his or her nationality and is unable or, owing to such fear or for reasons other than personal convenience, remains unwilling to accept the protection of that country; or who, not having a nationality and being outside the country of his or her former habitual residence, is unable or, owing to such fear or for reasons other than personal convenience, is unwilling to return to it. Refugees meeting these criteria are entitled to the protection of the Office of the High Commissioner irrespective of their geographical location. Refugees who are assisted by other United Nations agencies, or who have the same rights or obligations as nationals of their country of residence, are outside the mandate of UNHCR.

INTERNATIONAL PROTECTION
As laid down in the Statute of the Office, one of the two primary functions of UNHCR is to extend international protection to refugees. In the exercise of this function, UNHCR seeks to ensure that refugees and asylum-seekers are protected against *refoulement* (forcible return), that they receive asylum, and that they are treated according to internationally recognized standards of treatment. UNHCR pursues these objectives by a variety of means which include promoting the conclusion and ratification by states of international conventions for the protection of refugees.

The most comprehensive instrument concerning refugees which has been elaborated at the international level is the 1951 United Nations Convention relating to the Status of Refugees. This Convention, the scope of which was extended by a Protocol adopted in 1967, defines the rights and duties of refugees and contains provisions dealing with a variety of matters which affect the day-to-day lives of refugees. The application of the 1951 United Nations Refugee Convention and the 1967 Protocol is supervised by UNHCR. Important provisions for the treatment of refugees are also contained in a number of instruments adopted at the regional level. These include the OAU Convention of 1969 Governing the Specific Aspects of Refugee Problems, the European Agreement on the Abolition of Visas for Refugees, and the 1969 American Convention on Human Rights.

UNHCR has actively encouraged states to accede to the 1951 United Nations Refugee Convention and the 1967 Protocol: 107 states had accepted either or both of these basic refugee instruments by June 1990. An increasing number of states have also adopted domestic legislation and/or administrative measures to implement the international instruments, particularly in the field of procedures for the determination of refugee status. Such measures provide an important guarantee that refugees will be accorded the standards of treatment which have been internationally established for their benefit.

A continuing concern of UNHCR has been to ensure that states scrupulously observe the fundamental principle of *non-refoulement* according to which no-one may be forcibly returned to a territory where he or she has reason to fear persecution. While this principle is now widely reflected in the practice of states, violations still occur. UNHCR has also continued to promote the adoption of liberal practices of asylum by states, so that refugees and asylum seekers are granted admission, at least on a temporary basis. Major problems have arisen in regard to violation of the physical safety of refugees as a result of piracy, abduction and armed attack. UNHCR has urged the international community to find solutions to these problems as a matter of priority. In 1981 the High Commissioner launched an anti-piracy campaign in the Gulf of Thailand. The campaign was continued in subsequent years, and the number of attacks on boats carrying refugees decreased, but it was nevertheless estimated that in 1989 nearly 100 such attacks took place, with 18 people reported killed and 734 missing. UNHCR has also attempted to deal with the problem of military attacks on refugee camps in southern Africa and elsewhere, by formulating and encouraging the acceptance of a set of principles to ensure the safety of refugees.

MATERIAL ASSISTANCE TO REFUGEES
Emergency relief is provided to refugees when food supplies, medical aid or other forms of assistance are required on a large scale at short notice. Other members of the UN system, as well as inter-governmental and non-governmental organizations, co-operate closely with UNHCR in this field.

Even in the more stable refugee situations, UNHCR is often called upon to provide material assistance beyond the initial emergency phase, while permanent solutions are being sought. This assistance can take various forms, including the provision of food, shelter, medical care and essential supplies. Also covered in many instances are basic services, including education and counselling. Whenever possible, measures of this kind are accompanied by efforts to encourage maximum levels of self-reliance among the refugee population.

As far as possible, assistance is geared towards the identification and implementation of durable solutions to refugee problems—this being the second statutory responsibility of UNHCR. Such solutions generally take one of three forms: voluntary repatriation, local integration or resettlement in another country. Where voluntary repatriation is feasible, the Office assists refugees to overcome obstacles preventing their return to their country of origin. This may be done through negotiations with governments involved, or by providing funds either for the physical movement of refugees or for the rehabilitation of returnees once back in their own country.

When voluntary repatriation is not feasible, efforts are made to assist refugees to integrate locally and to become self-supporting in their countries of asylum. In Europe, this has generally been done either by granting loans to refugees, or by assisting them, through vocational training or in other ways, to learn a skill and to set themselves up in gainful occupations. One major form of assistance to help refugees re-establish themselves outside camps is the provision of housing.

In contrast to the situation in Europe, the majority of refugees in Africa, and some of those in Asia, are assisted through local settlement in agriculture. In Africa, the consolidation of refugee settlements frequently requires close co-operation between UNHCR and other members of the UN system which provide development assistance to the areas affected. The problem of needy individual refugees in search of employment or educational opportunities in urban areas of Africa, and who are mainly without agricultural skills, also claims special attention. Assistance is provided through special refugee counselling services, in some cases in co-operation with the OAU Bureau for African Refugees.

In cases where resettlement through emigration is the only viable solution to a refugee problem, UNHCR negotiates with governments in an endeavour to obtain suitable resettlement opportunities, to encourage liberalization of admission criteria and to draw up special immigration schemes.

ASIA AND THE MIDDLE EAST

Since 1975 UNHCR assistance activities in the Far East and Australasia have been dominated by the problems of refugees and displaced persons in and from the Indo-Chinese peninsula: Laotians, Cambodians and Vietnamese, needing both immediate assistance in the countries of temporary asylum to which they had fled, and help in finding a place of permanent resettlement. Between 1975 and 1988 1.5m. Indo-Chinese refugees were resettled, chiefly in the USA (714,782), the People's Republic of China (284,000), Canada (121,182), Australia (117,997) and France (108,241). A special programme, launched in 1980, continued to assist about 400,000 Cambodians who had returned to their homeland from Thailand, Viet-Nam and Laos.

In May 1979 UNHCR and Viet-Nam signed a 'memorandum of understanding' on the orderly departure of persons wishing to leave: under the Orderly Departure Programme which resulted, 165,000 persons had left Viet-Nam by mid-1989. Nevertheless, from 1986 the number of Vietnamese 'boat people' arriving in asylum camps began to increase. In 1988 the increasing difficulty of finding resettlement places for refugees led to stricter policies of deterrence being adopted by countries of first asylum, particularly Thailand and Hong Kong, on the grounds that many of those arriving were fleeing for economic reasons rather than for political ones, and were therefore not 'genuine' refugees. In June Hong Kong adopted a policy of 'screening' Vietnamese arrivals to determine whether or not they were 'genuine' political refugees or economic migrants. In March 1990 a similar 'screening' policy was adopted by the ASEAN member states.

In June 1989 there were 85,000 Vietnamese refugees in camps in South-East Asia: of these some 43,000 were in Hong Kong, where there were reported to be about 500 new arrivals every day. In addition, there were still some 75,000 Laotian refugees in camps in northern Thailand. In that month an international conference was convened by UNHCR in Geneva to discuss the Indo-Chinese refugee problem. The participants (representing 58 states, including Viet-Nam) adopted a plan providing for the 'screening' of all Vietnamese arrivals in the region to determine their refugee status, the resettlement of 'genuine' refugees and the repatriation (described as voluntary 'in the first instance') of those deemed to be economic migrants. A committee representing 15 nations was to supervise the plan. In December 51 Vietnamese (classified as economic migrants rather than refugees) were forcibly repatriated from Hong Kong. UNHCR opposed this action on the grounds that it impeded efforts to encourage voluntary repatriation. UNHCR urged the USA and other governments to address the problem at its source, by giving economic aid to Viet-Nam. At another international conference, held in January 1990, participants failed to agree on a time-limit after which mandatory repatriation should begin: the USA insisted that a 12-month 'moratorium' should be imposed before further mandatory repatriation was undertaken. By August more than 4,000 Vietnamese had accepted voluntary repatriation and had returned from Hong Kong to Viet-Nam, where their reintegration was monitored by UNHCR. During the first half of 1990 the number of Vietnamese refugees arriving in Hong Kong decreased to 2,993 (compared with 23,335 in the first half of 1989), but there was an increase in the number of arrivals in Indonesia. In July ASEAN member states threatened to abandon the principle of granting first asylum to refugees (Malaysia had already refused to allow several thousand to land during the previous 12 months). In September an agreement was reached by UNHCR and the Governments of the United Kingdom and Viet-Nam on the repatriation of Vietnamese who, although not 'volunteers' are 'not opposed' to returning.

In Papua New Guinea there were 1,225 refugees from the Indonesian province of Irian Jaya at the beginning of 1984, and this number increased to 10,500 by mid-1986.

As a result of events in Afghanistan, almost 1m. refugees crossed into the North-West Frontier and Baluchistan provinces of Pakistan between January 1979 and mid-1980. By the end of 1987 there were an estimated 3.2m. Afghan refugees living in officially established villages. UNHCR provided immediate relief assistance, health care, education, vocational training and the promotion of income-generating and self-help programmes, in collaboration with the World Food Programme, the International Labour Organisation and the World Bank. The UNHCR budget allocated US $74m. to Pakistan for 1988. UNHCR also provided assistance for Afghan refugees in Iran, who were estimated to number 2.35m. at the end of 1987. In April 1988 the Afghan and Pakistani Governments signed an agreement on the withdrawal of Soviet troops from Afghanistan and on the subsequent voluntary repatriation of Afghan refugees. UNHCR agreed to provide assistance in the repatriation programme (in co-operation with the office of the UN Co-ordinator for Humanitarian and Economic Assistance to Afghanistan), both in ensuring the rights of the returning population and in providing material assistance such as transport, immunization, and supplies of food and other essentials. Meanwhile, UNHCR's services to Afghan refugees in Pakistan and Iran were to continue. In early 1990 it was reported that few refugees were willing to return to Afghanistan, in view of the continuing political instability and economic hardship there.

During 1987 UNHCR began to provide emergency assistance to Kurdish refugees arriving in Iran from Iraq: they numbered 95,000 by mid-1990. At the end of 1988 the Turkish Government also requested assistance from UNHCR for some 40,000 Iraqi Kurdish refugees in Turkey.

From 1974 onwards UNHCR acted as co-ordinator of the UN Humanitarian Programme of Assistance for Cyprus, assisting displaced persons on the island. An estimated $9.5m. was allocated to Cyprus for 1988.

In 1988 assistance was provided for about 70,000 displaced persons and refugees who had come to the Yemen Arab Republic from the People's Democratic Republic of Yemen.

REFUGEES OF CONCERN TO UNHCR*
(1 January 1989 unless otherwise stated)

Host Country	Number of registered refugees
Africa	
Angola	91,950
Burundi	267,500
Cameroon	51,200
Ethiopia	679,500
Kenya	12,500
Malawi	628,150
Rwanda	22,200
Somalia	834,000
Sudan	745,000
Swaziland	28,800
Tanzania	265,150
Uganda	102,000
Zaire	340,700
Zambia	143,600
Zimbabwe	174,500
Asia and Oceania	
Australia	90,900
China, People's Republic	284,300
Hong Kong	56,700†
Malaysia	104,400
Thailand	107,800
Viet-Nam	25,000
Europe	
Austria	17,400
Belgium	23,000
Denmark	27,300
France	184,500
Germany, Federal Republic	150,000
Italy	11,000
Netherlands	26,000
Norway	11,000
Sweden	139,800
Switzerland	29,600
United Kingdom	101,300
North America, Latin America and the Caribbean	
Argentina	13,600
Belize	30,100
Canada	380,200
Costa Rica	278,600
Guatemala	223,100
Honduras	237,100
Mexico	356,400
USA	1,000,000
South-West Asia, Middle East and North Africa	
Algeria	170,000
Iran	2,850,000
Pakistan	3,257,600

* The table shows only those countries where more than 10,000 refugees were present. The figures do not include Palestine refugees, who come under the care of UNRWA (q.v.), nor non-registered refugees (e.g. Ethiopians living in Somalia outside official refugee camps), nor returnees and persons displaced within their own country (e.g. in Cambodia). Most figures are based on government estimates.

† Figure as at October 1989.

INTERNATIONAL ORGANIZATIONS United Nations (Other Bodies)

UNHCR co-ordinates humanitarian assistance for Sahrawis in the Tindouf area of Algeria; there were 167,000 registered refugees in Algeria in early 1989.

AFRICA

The total number of refugees and displaced persons in Africa (including North Africa) increased from about 1m. in 1975 to over 5m. in 1980: the main groups had fled from Ethiopia to Djibouti, Somalia and Sudan, from Chad to Cameroon and Nigeria, from Burundi to Tanzania and from Uganda to Zaire.

In April 1981 the first International Conference on Assistance to Refugees in Africa (ICARA) was held, with the object of focusing public attention on the plight of refugees in Africa, mobilizing additional resources for refugee programmes there, and strengthening the economic capacity of countries affected by large influxes of refugees. A total of US $566.9m. was pledged by donor governments as a result of the conference: the original target had been $1,150m. A second conference (ICARA II) was held in July 1984, with the particular aim of helping host countries, themselves poor, to cope with large numbers of refugees.

In 1984 UNHCR established emergency programmes for refugees in Ethiopia, Somalia and Sudan, and for limited periods in the Central African Republic and Djibouti. By the end of 1985 the situation had improved, but UNHCR continued to provide relief assistance for Sudanese refugees in Ethiopia, for Ethiopian refugees in Somalia, and for refugees from Ethiopia, Uganda and Chad in Sudan. As a result of favourable rains, emergency programmes in Ethiopia, Somalia and Sudan were phased out in early 1987. There were, however, new influxes of Sudanese refugees into Ethiopia during 1986 and early 1987.

UNHCR provided assistance for large numbers of refugees who were able to return home in 1986-89, to Chad (mostly from the Central African Republic and Sudan), to Ethiopia (mostly from Djibouti, Somalia and Sudan) and to Uganda (mostly from Sudan). In 1987, owing to the security crisis in Mozambique, there was massive movement of Mozambican refugees into neighbouring countries: by early 1988 there were an estimated 800,000 Mozambican refugees, mostly in Malawi. During 1988 there was a new influx of refugees from Sudan into Ethiopia (numbering more than 300,000), and in June and July 100,000 refugees from Somalia also entered Ethiopia. In July UNHCR issued an appeal for $42m to assist newly-arrived refugees in Ethiopia and Malawi. In September an appeal was also issued for $4.7m. to assist 55,000 refugees from Burundi who had fled to Rwanda after tribal massacres. By the end of the year most had returned home, with assistance from UNHCR.

In January 1989 the Governments of Malawi and Mozambique and UNHCR agreed to establish a joint commission for the voluntary repatriation of Mozambican refugees currently in Malawi. By the end of the year 11,000 refugees had returned to safe areas of Mozambique. In 1989 UNHCR undertook responsibility for the repatriation (beginning in June) of some 41,000 Namibian refugees, mostly from Angola to Namibia, in preparation for the Namibian independence process. In the same year UNHCR provided assistance for Senegalese refugees in Mauritania and for Mauritanian refugees in Senegal, following ethnic conflicts in both countries. In 1990 UNHCR gave assistance to victims of civil war in Liberia who had fled to Côte d'Ivoire, Guinea and Sierra Leone.

CENTRAL AND SOUTH AMERICA

UNHCR's budget for Central America amounted to $34.2m. in 1988, when it continued to provide emergency relief to newly-arrived groups of refugees, and to implement self-sufficiency programmes, including, in some Central American countries, 'active refugee centres' which aim to combine a degree of agricultural self-sufficiency with increasing access for refugees to the local economy and labour market. In May 1989, when an International Conference on Central American Refugees (CIREFCA) was held in Guatemala, there were some 150,000 refugees receiving UNHCR assistance in the region, as well as an estimated 1.8m. other refugees and displaced persons, mostly from El Salvador, Guatemala and Nicaragua: the principal host countries were Costa Rica, Honduras and Mexico. CIREFCA adopted a plan of action for the voluntary repatriation of refugees in the region, and established national co-ordinating committees to assist in this process.

UNHCR also provides assistance for numbers of refugees in South America (particularly Chileans and Uruguayans). At the beginning of 1989 there were about 13,600 refugees in Argentina and some 9,400 in other countries of the region.

EUROPE AND NORTH AMERICA

UNHCR's material assistance activities in Europe are limited in scale as assistance is, in most cases, provided by governments and private organizations. At the beginning of 1989 there were 745,225 refugees in Europe. During 1988 about 350,000 people requested asylum in European countries and North America, compared with 240,000 in 1987.

Canada and the USA are major countries of resettlement for refugees: Canada admitted 13,000 government-sponsored refugees in 1989, while the USA imposed a limit of 125,000 on the number of admissions in the year beginning October 1989. UNHCR provides counselling and legal services for asylum-seekers in these countries.

Finance

UNHCR administrative expenditure is financed under the United Nations Regular Budget. General Programmes of material assistance are financed from voluntary contributions made by governments and also from non-governmental sources. In addition, UNHCR undertakes a number of Special Programmes, as requested by the UN General Assembly, the Secretary-General of the UN or a member state, to assist returnees and, in some cases, displaced persons. In 1990 the High Commissioner reported that financial constraints were severely curtailing the organization's ability to provide protection and assistance for refugees: projected needs for that year were $680m., while funds received were likely to be $550m.

UNHCR Expenditure (US $'000)

Source	1987	1988 estimates	1989 projections
UN Regular Budget	17,946.9	19,558.0	19,327.0
Voluntary funds:			
General Programmes	335,549.9	407,780.5	400,103.0
Special Programmes	124,836.2	90,088.8	44,171.1
Total	478,333.0	517,427.3	463,601.1

UNHCR Expenditure by Region (US $'000)

	1987	1988 estimates
Africa	186,686.5	205,403.3
Asia and Oceania	72,534.0	89,305.9
Europe and North America	21,182.3	24,145.0
Latin America and the Caribbean	40,125.9	37,556.1
South West Asia, North Africa and the Middle East*	114,662.7	99,482.2
Headquarters programmes, global and regional projects	43,141.6	61,534.8
Total	478,333.0	517,427.3

* Including Pakistan.

PUBLICATIONS

Refugees (monthly, in English and French).
UNHCR Handbook for Emergencies.
Refugee Abstracts.
Press releases, reports.

United Nations Observer Missions and Peace-keeping Forces

Address: Office for Special Political Affairs, United Nations, New York, NY 10017, USA.

United Nations peace-keeping operations have been conceived as instruments of conflict control. Each operation has been established with a specific mandate. The UN has used these operations in various conflicts, with the consent of the parties involved, to maintain peaceful conditions, without prejudice to the positions or claims of parties, in order to facilitate the search for political settlements through peaceful means such as mediation and the good offices of the Secretary-General. United Nations peace-keeping operations fall into two categories: peace-keeping forces and observer missions.

Peace-keeping forces are composed of contingents of lightly-armed troops, made available by member states. These forces assist in preventing the recurrence of fighting, restoring and maintaining peace, and promoting a return to normal conditions. To this end, peace-keeping forces are authorized as necessary to undertake negotiations, persuasion, observation and fact-finding. They run patrols and interpose physically between the opposing parties. Peace-keeping forces are permitted to use their weapons only in self-defence.

Military observer missions are composed of officers (usually unarmed), who are made available, on the Secretary-General's request, by member states. A mission's function is to observe and report to the Secretary-General (who in turn informs the UN Security Council) on the maintenance of a cease-fire, to investigate violations and to do what it can to improve the situation.

Peace-keeping forces and observer missions must at all times maintain complete impartiality and avoid any action that might affect the claims or positions of the parties.

UNITED NATIONS TRUCE SUPERVISION ORGANIZATION—UNTSO

Headquarters: Government House, Jerusalem.
Chief of Staff: Maj.-Gen. HANS CHRISTENSEN (Finland).

UNTSO was established initially to supervise the truce called by the UN Security Council in Palestine in May 1948 and has assisted in the application of the 1949 Armistice Agreements. Its activities have evolved over the years, in response to developments in the Middle East and in accordance with the relevant resolutions of the Security Council.

UNTSO observers assist the UN peace-keeping forces in the Middle East (see below), UNIFIL and UNDOF. In addition, a small group of observers remains in the Sinai region of Egypt to maintain a UN presence. There are also small detachments of observers in Beirut, Lebanon and Amman, Jordan. Another group of observers was temporarily redeployed to UNGOMAP (see below) from 1988 to March 1990. UNTSO observers have been available at short notice to form the nucleus of other peace-keeping operations.

The authorized strength of UNTSO in July 1990 was 298 military observers from 19 countries.

UNTSO expenditures are covered by the regular budget of the United Nations. For the two years 1990–91, a sum of US $48.5m. was appropriated by the General Assembly.

UNITED NATIONS DISENGAGEMENT OBSERVER FORCE—UNDOF

Headquarters: Damascus, Syria.
Commander: Maj.-Gen. ADOLF RADAUER (Austria).

UNDOF was established for an initial period of six months by a UN Security Council resolution in May 1974, following the signature in Geneva of a disengagement agreement between Syrian and Israeli forces. The mandate has since been extended by successive resolutions. The initial task of the Force was to take over territory evacuated in stages by the Israeli troops, in accordance with the disengagement agreement, to hand over territory to Syrian troops, and to establish an area of separation on the Golan Heights.

UNDOF continues to man the area of separation, from which Syrian and Israeli forces are excluded; it carries out inspections of the areas of limited armaments and forces, and it uses its best efforts to maintain the ceasefire. The Force operates exclusively on Syrian territory.

In July 1990 the Force comprised 1,330 troops from Austria, Canada, Finland and Poland, and seven military observers detailed from UNTSO. Another 95 UNTSO military observers assist UNDOF in the performance of its tasks.

In December 1989 the UN General Assembly authorized expenditure for UNDOF at a rate of US $3.36m. per month.

UNITED NATIONS INTERIM FORCE IN LEBANON—UNIFIL

Headquarters: Naqoura, Lebanon.
Commander: Lt-Gen. LARS-ERIC WAHLGREN (Sweden).

UNIFIL was established by a UN Security Council resolution in March 1978 (after an invasion of Lebanon by Israeli forces), for a six-month period, subsequently extended by successive resolutions. The mandate of the force is to confirm the withdrawal of Israeli forces, to restore international peace and security, and to assist the Government of Lebanon in ensuring the return of its effective authority in southern Lebanon. UNIFIL has also extended humanitarian assistance to the population of the area, particularly after the second Israeli invasion of Lebanon in 1982.

In July 1990 the Force comprised 5,850 troops from nine countries. A group of 65 UNTSO military observers assists UNIFIL in the performance of its tasks. They form the Observer Group, Lebanon.

In December 1989, the UN General Assembly authorized expenditures for UNIFIL at a rate of US $12m. per month. Owing to the failure of some states (notably the USA) to pay their assessed contributions, UNIFIL had an accumulated financial shortfall of more than $307m. by mid-1990.

UNITED NATIONS PEACE-KEEPING FORCE IN CYPRUS—UNFICYP

Headquarters: Nicosia, Cyprus.
Special Representative of the UN Secretary-General: OSCAR CAMILION (Argentina).
Commander: Maj.-Gen. CLIVE MILNER (Canada).

UNFICYP was established in March 1964 by a UN Security Council resolution (for a three-month period, subsequently extended) to prevent a recurrence of fighting between the Greek and Turkish Cypriot communities, and to contribute to the maintenance of law and order and a return to normal conditions. The Force controls a 180-km buffer zone, established (following the Turkish intervention in 1974) between the cease-fire lines of the Turkish forces and the Cyprus National Guard.

In July 1990 the Force comprised 2,108 military personnel, and 36 civilian police, from eight countries.

The estimated cost to the United Nations of maintaining the Force during the six months from 15 June 1990 was US $13.8m., to be covered entirely by voluntary contributions; an additional (larger) part of the costs was absorbed by the countries contributing troops. In May 1990 the UN Secretary-General appealed for an increase in voluntary contributions to meet an accumulated deficit of $179m.

UNITED NATIONS GOOD OFFICES MISSION IN AFGHANISTAN AND PAKISTAN—UNGOMAP

UNGOMAP was established in April 1988 to monitor the withdrawal of Soviet troops from Afghanistan, as well as non-interference and non-intervention between Afghanistan and Pakistan, as stipulated in the peace agreements signed in Geneva in that month. In 1989 the mission comprised 40 military observers from 10 countries. The operation was concluded on 15 March 1990.

UNITED NATIONS IRAN-IRAQ MILITARY OBSERVER GROUP—UNIIMOG

Headquarters: Baghdad, Iraq, and Teheran, Iran.
Commander: Maj.-Gen. SLAVKO JOVIĆ (Yugoslavia).

UNIIMOG was established in August 1988 by the UN Security Council, for an initial period of six months (subsequently extended), following the announcement of a cease-fire in the war between Iran and Iraq. In July 1990 UNIIMOG comprised 400 military observers from 25 countries, plus about 500 military and civilian support staff. The Group's principal tasks were to monitor the two sides' compliance with the cease-fire, to supervise the withdrawal of troops to internationally-recognized boundaries, and to obtain the agreement of the parties to other arrangements which, pending a comprehensive settlement, might help to reduce tension and build confidence between them.

UNITED NATIONS MILITARY OBSERVER GROUP IN INDIA AND PAKISTAN— UNMOGIP

Headquarters: Rawalpindi, Pakistan (November–April), Srinagar (May–October).

Chief Military Observer: Brig.-Gen. JEREMIAH ENRIGHT (Ireland).

The Group was established in 1948 by UN Security Council resolutions aiming to restore peace in the region of Jammu and Kashmir, whose status had become a matter of dispute between the Governments of India and Pakistan. Following a cease-fire which came into effect in January 1949, the military observers of UNMOGIP were deployed to assist in its observance. In July 1990 there were 35 observers, deployed on both sides of the 'line of control' that had been agreed upon by India and Pakistan in 1972.

UNITED NATIONS ANGOLA VERIFICATION MISSION—UNAVEM

Headquarters: Luanda, Angola.

Chief Military Observer: Brig.-Gen. PÉRICLES FERREIRA GOMES (Brazil).

UNAVEM was established by the UN Security Council in December 1988, at the request of the Governments of Angola and Cuba. Its task was to verify the redeployment of Cuban troops northwards, and their phased and total withdrawal from Angola, in accordance with the timetable agreed by the two governments. The mission's mandate was for a period of 31 months, ending one month after the anticipated completion of the withdrawal of the Cuban troops. The military observers began their mission in January 1989. In July 1990 there were 60 observers from 10 countries

UNITED NATIONS TRANSITION ASSISTANCE GROUP—UNTAG

UNTAG was established in 1978 by UN Security Council Resolution 435, implementation of which began in April 1989, when the group comprised 4,500 troops from 20 countries (with 2,350 in reserve) and 500 civilian police from 15 countries. The Group's principal task was the supervision of elections to a Constituent Assembly and to ensure a peaceful transition to independence for Namibia. The operation was concluded on 21 March 1990.

UNITED NATIONS OBSERVER GROUP IN CENTRAL AMERICA—ONUCA

Headquarters: Tegucigalpa, Honduras.

Chief Military Observer: Maj.-Gen. AGUSTÍN QUESADA GÓMEZ (Spain).

ONUCA was established in November 1989 by the Security Council, initially for a six-month period, extended in May and November 1990 for further six month periods. Its original mandate was to verify the undertakings by five Central American governments—those of Costa Rica, El Salvador, Guatemala, Honduras and Nicaragua—to cease aid to irregular forces and not to use the territory of one state for attacks on other states.

In July 1990 the Group comprised 301 military observers and 124 military support personnel from 11 countries.

Between March and June 1990 ONUCA strength was temporarily augmented by the addition of a Venezuelan battalion of 700 troops, in order to assist in the voluntary demobilization of the Nicaraguan resistance.

In December 1989 the UN General Assembly authorized expenditure for ONUCA at the rate of US $4.5m. per month.

United Nations Population Fund—UNFPA

Address: 220 East 42nd St, New York, NY 10017, USA.
Telephone: (212) 963-1234.
Telex: 422031.
Fax: (212) 370-0201.

Created in 1967 as the Trust Fund for Population Activities, the UN Fund for Population Activities (UNFPA) was established as a Fund of the UN General Assembly in 1972 and was made a subsidiary organ of the UN General Assembly in 1979, with the UNDP Governing Council designated as its governing body. In 1987 UNFPA's name was changed to the United Nations Population Fund (retaining the same acronym).

Organization

(October 1990)

EXECUTIVE DIRECTOR

The Executive Director, who has the rank of Under-Secretary-General of the UN, is responsible for the overall direction of the Fund, working closely with governments, United Nations bodies and agencies, regional groups, and non-governmental organizations to ensure the most effective programming and use of resources in population activities.

Executive Director: Dr NAFIS SADIK (Pakistan).
Deputy Executive Director: TATSURO KUNUGI (Japan).

EXECUTING AGENCIES

In most projects assistance is extended through member organizations of the UN system; ultimate responsibility for execution of projects lies with recipient governments, using the services of the UN organizations as required. The Fund may also call on the services of non-governmental organizations in this role and sometimes it acts as its own executing agency.

FIELD ORGANIZATION

UNFPA Deputy Representatives and Senior Advisers on Population, attached to the offices of the UNDP Resident Representatives, assist governments in formulating requests for aid and co-ordinate the work of the executing agencies in any given country or area.

Activities

At the end of 1989 UNFPA was providing assistance for 3,538 projects, of which 1,156 were in Africa, 907 in Asia and the Pacific, 583 in Latin America and the Caribbean, 444 in the Arab states and Europe, 291 inter-regional, and 157 global. UNFPA approved 372 new country projects during 1989, at a total cost of US $42.5m. Many UNFPA-supported projects are executed by other UN agencies, notably WHO, UNESCO and ILO, or by the government of the country concerned. A total of 119 assessment missions were undertaken between 1977 and 1989 to assist governments in drawing up or reviewing population programmes.

Priority programme areas are as follows:

1. Family planning. In 1989 46.3% of total programme expenditure allocations were for family planning, concentrating on extending acceptance of family planning and expanding the delivery of services to rural and marginal urban areas. The emphasis is on combining family planning services with maternal and child health care. UNFPA also supports research into contraceptives and training in contraceptive technology.

2. Information, education and communication. This accounted for 16.8% of total programme allocations in 1989. UNFPA assists broadcasting, poster campaigns and itinerant drama groups which

INTERNATIONAL ORGANIZATIONS

convey family planning information, and supports education programmes for school pupils and adults.

3. Basic data collection. This accounted for 10.9% of programme expenditure in 1989. UNFPA provides assistance and training for national statistical offices in undertaking censuses and demographic surveys.

4. Utilization of population data and research for policy formulation and development planning. This accounted for 19.7% of programme expenditure in 1989. UNFPA provides assistance for analysis of demographic and socio-economic data, for research on population trends and for the formulation of government policies. It supports a programme of fellowships in demographic analysis, data processing and cartography.

5. Women, population and development. In 1989 UNFPA assistance in this area amounted to 3.1% of programme expenditure. The Fund aims to enhance the status of women and ensure that their needs and concerns are taken into account when development and population programmes are being planned. It supports training and monitoring services for this purpose.

UNFPA also has special programmes on youth, on ageing, and on AIDS, involving national and regional seminars and training programmes. It produces publications (see below) and audio-visual aids, promotes conferences, and encourages wider coverage of population issues in the media.

In November 1989 UNFPA organized the International Forum on Population in the Twenty-First Century, which involved representatives of 79 countries and numerous UN and other agencies. The Forum adopted a declaration recommending specific objectives to be achieved by the year 2000, including: an increase in the number of couples using family planning, from the current level of 326m. to 535m. (i.e. 56% of women of reproductive age would be using contraceptives); a reduction in early marriage and teenage pregnancy; a reduction of infant mortality rates to 50 per 1,000 live births, and of maternal mortality rates by at least 50% (particularly in regions where maternal mortality currently exceeded 100 per 100,000 live births); and an increase in life expectancy at birth, to at least 62 years, in countries with a high mortality rate.

FINANCE

Total expenditure (provisional) in 1989 was US $217.0m. (compared with $167.2m. in 1988), of which $157.4m. was spent on projects. The USA, formerly the largest donor, pledged no funds to UNFPA in 1986–89 (in protest at the Fund's support for the 'one child per family' policy of the People's Republic of China), but the shortfall was largely compensated for by other donors.

Project expenditure:
allocations by region, 1989 (percentages)

Africa south of the Sahara	25.8
Arab states and Europe	12.1
Asia and the Pacific	36.2
Latin America and the Caribbean	13.3
Inter-regional and global	12.6
Total	**100.0**

PUBLICATIONS

Annual Report.
State of World Population Report (annually).
Population (newsletter, monthly in Arabic, English, French and Spanish).
Populi (quarterly).
Inventory of Population Projects Around the World (annually).
Global Population Assistance Report (1982–88).
Reports and reference works; also videotapes.

United Nations Relief and Works Agency for Palestine Refugees in the Near East—UNRWA

Addresses: POB 700, 1400 Vienna, Austria;
POB 484, Amman, Jordan.

Telephone (Vienna): (0222) 26310.

Telex (Vienna): 135310.

UNRWA began operations in 1950 to provide relief, health, education and welfare services for Palestine refugees in the Near East.

Organization

(October 1990)

UNRWA employs an international staff of 131 and 18,300 local staff, mainly Palestine refugees. The Commissioner-General is assisted by an Advisory Commission consisting of representatives of the governments of:

Belgium
Egypt
France
Japan
Jordan
Lebanon
Syria
Turkey
United Kingdom
USA

Commissioner-General: GIORGIO GIACOMELLI (Italy).

REGIONAL OFFICES

Gaza Strip: UNRWA Field Office, POB 61, Gaza.

Jordan: UNRWA Field Office, POB 484, Amman.

West Bank: UNRWA Field Office, POB 19149, Jerusalem.

Lebanon: UNRWA Field Office, POB 947, Beirut.

Syria: UNRWA Field Office, POB 4313, Damascus.

Egypt: UNRWA Liaison Office, 2 Dar-esh-Shifa St, Garden City, POB 277, Cairo.

United States: UNRWA Liaison Office, Room DC 2-0550, United Nations, New York, NY 10017.

Activities

SERVICES FOR PALESTINE REFUGEES

Since 1950, UNRWA has provided relief, health and education services for the needy among the Palestine refugees in Lebanon, Syria, Jordan, the West Bank and the Gaza Strip. For UNRWA's purposes, a Palestine refugee is one whose normal residence was in Palestine for a minimum of two years before the 1948 conflict and who, as a result of the Arab–Israeli hostilities, lost his home and means of livelihood. To be eligible for assistance, a refugee must reside in one of the 'host' countries in which UNRWA operates and be in need. A refugee's children and grandchildren who fulfil certain criteria are also eligible for UNRWA assistance. At March 1990, the registered refugee population numbered 2,397,600 (about half the estimated total number of Palestinians), living in five areas administered by four governments. There were 764,370 registered refugees (plus about 52,000 unregistered) living in 61 camps, while the remaining refugees have settled in the towns and villages already existing.

UNRWA's activities fall into the categories of education and training; health services; and relief and welfare services.

Education (under the technical supervision of UNESCO) takes up about two-thirds of UNRWA's annual budget. In the 1989/90 school year there were 357,713 pupils in 628 UNRWA schools (76 schools in Lebanon, 110 in Syria, 197 in Jordan, 98 on the West Bank and 147 in the Gaza Strip) and 12,601 staff. At three-quarters of the schools, morning and afternoon shifts are held in order to accommodate more pupils. UNRWA also runs eight vocational and teacher-training centres with 5,026 places. UNRWA awarded 450 scholarships for study at Arab universities in 1989/90.

Health services accounted for about 20% of UNRWA expenditure in 1989. There are 3,325 medical staff posts, 98 health units, 86 specialist clinics and laboratories, and 93 mother and child health clinics; over 6m. visits by patients are made each year to UNRWA medical units. UNRWA also runs a supplementary feeding programme, mainly for children, to combat malnutrition: there are 94 feeding centres. Technical supervision for the health programme is provided by WHO.

Relief services (which accounted for 10% of UNRWA expenditure in 1989) comprise the distribution of food rations, the provision of emergency shelter and the organization of welfare programmes for about 150,000 of the poorest refugees.

AID TO DISPLACED PERSONS

After the renewal of Arab–Israeli hostilities in the Middle East in June 1967, hundreds of thousands of people fled from the fighting and Israeli-occupied areas to east Jordan, Syria and Egypt. UNRWA provided emergency relief for displaced refugees and was additionally empowered by a UN General Assembly resolution to provide 'humanitarian assistance, as far as practicable, on an emergency basis and as a temporary measure' for those persons other than Palestine refugees who were newly displaced and in urgent need. In practice, UNRWA has lacked the funds to aid the other displaced persons and the main burden of supporting them has fallen on the Arab governments concerned. The Agency, as requested by the Government of Jordan in 1967 and on that Government's behalf, distributes rations to displaced persons in Jordan who are not registered refugees of 1948.

With the agreement of the Israeli Government, UNRWA has continued to provide assistance for registered refugees living in the Israeli-occupied territories of the West Bank and the Gaza Strip.

RECENT EMERGENCIES

Beginning with the 1975–1976 civil war, Palestine refugees and UNRWA's services have been adversely affected by the continuing disturbances in Lebanon. UNRWA launched an emergency relief programme following the Israeli invasion of the south in March 1978, which caused the temporary evacuation of most of the 60,000 refugees living there and the flight of 17,000 refugees in other parts of the country.

In 1979 UNRWA again launched an emergency appeal for aid to southern Lebanon because of continuing Israeli and other attacks. In 1981 civil strife and Israeli attacks disrupted UNRWA activities. The education programme was hardest hit, with up to 50 school days lost in some schools during the 1980/81 school year.

The Israeli invasion of June 1982 meant that over 150,000 persons were displaced, necessitating an emergency relief programme costing US $52m. Many UNRWA schools, clinics and offices were destroyed or damaged. The emergency programme was extended to spring 1984 and an appeal for $13m. was made to provide funds for reconstruction of UNRWA facilities, refugee shelters and refugee camp infrastructure.

During the first half of 1985 UNRWA organized two emergency relief operations in Lebanon, providing food and medical care for 40,000 displaced refugees during factional fighting in the Sidon area in March and April, and emergency assistance to 35,000 displaced refugees when refugee camps in Beirut were besieged in May and June. Two similar emergency operations were also mounted in the first half of 1986. UNRWA also provides cash grants to refugees whose homes have been damaged or destroyed in the fighting. In late 1986 and early 1987 UNRWA faced another emergency in Lebanon. Three camps in Beirut and Tyre were besieged for some months, and 48,000 refugees were displaced. In February 1987 the Agency launched an emergency appeal for $20.6m. to finance emergency relief and repair of thousands of refugee homes, and a number of Agency schools, clinics and other installations.

Meanwhile, UNRWA faced increasing problems in the Israeli-occupied territories of the West Bank and the Gaza Strip, where unrest broke out in December 1987. By March 1990 780 Palestinians, including many registered refugees, had been killed, and thousands injured. Schools in the West Bank were closed for the first four months of 1988, and for more than six months of 1989, and UNRWA services in both territories were frequently interrupted as curfews were imposed on camps. UNRWA began an appeal which raised US $65m. in financial and material assistance for the refugees in the two territories by June 1989.

FINANCE

For the most part, UNRWA's income is made up of voluntary contributions, almost entirely from governments, the remainder being provided by voluntary agencies, business corporations and private sources. Much of UNRWA's budget is used to pay its educational and medical staff. However, the cost of 131 international staff is funded by the UN, WHO and UNESCO, and a further nine international staff are paid from UNRWA's budget.

Contributions dropped from US $190.6m. in 1980 to about $174m. in 1985, despite UNRWA's rising expenses. Planned expenditure for 1985 had to be cut by $43m., through deferral of pay and cost-of-living increases to 12,000 field staff, a cut in overhead costs and supplies and cuts in construction, maintenance and the purchase of new equipment. Austerity measures continued during 1986, but the Agency was able to find the funds for most programmes, although construction plans were not fully funded. UNRWA's financial situation subsequently improved, but it was expected that an annual increase of 5% in the budget would be necessary to maintain operations at current levels. The estimated budget for 1990 was $230m., plus $6.4m. for the Lebanon emergency budget and $14.3m. for the first six months of emergency measures in the occupied territories.

STATISTICS

Refugees Registered with UNRWA (30 June 1989)

	Refugees in camps	Refugees not in camps	Total registered refugees
Jordan	190,847	708,964	899,811
West Bank	104,977	293,414	398,391
Gaza Strip	253,970	215,415	469,385
Lebanon	145,538	148,734	294,272
Syria	69,015	203,763	272,778
Total	764,347*	1,570,290	2,334,637

* The figure excludes a further 52,000 persons, not registered refugees, living in camps: about 37,000 of these are persons displaced as a result of the June 1967 hostilities.

Displaced Persons

Apart from the Palestine refugees of 1948 who are registered with UNRWA and who are UNRWA's main concern (see table above), considerable numbers of people have, since 1967, been displaced within the UNRWA areas of operations, and others have had to leave these areas. According to government estimates, there were 210,000 displaced persons in Jordan and 125,000 in Syria in June 1988.

UNRWA Schools (1988/89)

	Number of schools	Number of teachers	Number of pupils
Jordan	197	3,736	134,435
West Bank	98*	1,340	39,275
Gaza Strip	147	2,619	91,222
Lebanon	76	1,183	32,826
Syria	110	1,557	53,378
Total	628	10,435	351,136†

* In accordance with Israeli military orders, 90 of the 98 schools on the West Bank were closed for almost all of the 1988/89 school year.
† The figure excludes 110,339 refugee pupils attending government and private schools, and includes all non-eligible children attending UNRWA schools (numbering 55,790).

PUBLICATIONS

Annual Report of the Commissioner-General of UNRWA.

UNRWA—a Survey of United Nations Assistance to Palestine Refugees (every 2 years).

Palestine Refugees Today—the UNRWA Newsletter (quarterly).

UNRWA Report (quarterly).

UNRWA News (fortnightly).

Catalogues of publications and audio-visual materials.

INTERNATIONAL ORGANIZATIONS
United Nations (Other Bodies)

World Food Council—WFC

Address: Via delle Terme di Caracalla, 00100 Rome, Italy.
Telephone: (06) 57971.
Telex: 610181.
Fax: (06) 5745091.

The World Food Council was created in December 1974 by the UN General Assembly, upon the specific recommendation of the World Food Conference held in November 1974. It aims to stimulate governments and the international community to adopt the necessary policies and programmes required to alleviate world hunger and improve the global food system.

Organization

(October 1990)

COUNCIL

The Council meets annually and consists of ministers of agriculture representing 36 member states, elected by the UN General Assembly: one-third retire each year. Membership is drawn from regional groups in the following proportions: nine from Africa, eight from Asia, seven from Latin America, four from Eastern Europe, and eight from Western Europe and North America. A President and four regional Vice-Presidents are elected every two years.

SECRETARIAT

With the help of various multilateral and bilateral organizations and research institutions, the Secretariat reviews the current world food situation and recommends to the Council appropriate policy changes designed to improve food production and nutritional well-being, particularly in the developing countries.

Executive Director: GERALD I. TRANT (Canada).

Activities

The Council is required to review, on a regular basis, the major problems and policy issues affecting the world food situation, and also the proposals that are advanced by governments and institutions to address them. It works closely with other UN agencies, such as FAO, IFAD (which it helped to establish) and the World Food Programme, but, unlike these, it is exclusively an instrument of policy and guidance, and does not administer operational assistance programmes.

The Council concentrates on promoting the international political consensus necessary (1) to increase food production in the developing countries, most notably in sub-Saharan Africa; (2) to improve national and international food security measures through policies that link food production, agricultural trade and nutritional concerns; (3) to assure the greater effectiveness of food aid; and (4) to reduce barriers to trade in agricultural commodities between developed and developing countries.

In 1979 a system of 'food strategies' was launched, whereby individual developing countries, in collaboration with a particular developed country or institution, were to prepare overall food plans so as to enable a more co-ordinated approach and the best use of aid: strategies would include consideration of such issues as the stimulation of production by price incentives; improvement of marketing and distribution infrastructure; the effect of exchange rates on production; research on higher-yielding crops; improved supply of fertilizers and pesticides; land-holding reforms; and the supply of credit to small farmers. By 1987 more than 50 developing countries had adopted such a scheme, with assistance from developed countries, the World Bank, FAO, ILO, IFAD, UNDP, the African Development Bank and the Inter-American Development Bank.

In July 1980 a new Food Aid Convention entered into force, increasing the guaranteed minimum level of food aid from grain-exporting countries to developing countries in need from 4.2 to 7.6m. tons a year, which was, however, still short of the 10m. minimum recommended by the WFC. The 1985 Council called for a clearer distinction between food aid and the disposal of highly subsidized surpluses, which has disruptive effects on markets and production incentives; it criticized the 'dumping' of surplus cereals by industrialized countries.

At the 13th session of the Council, held in Beijing, the People's Republic of China, in June 1987, the ministers noted that, although total food production had increased since the 1974 World Food Conference, the number of undernourished people in the world had risen. They stated that hunger is often not caused by scarcity of food, but rather by lack of access to food: reduced economic activity, falling national incomes and net capital outflows, and programmes aiming to bring about stabilization and adjustment, had led in many countries to significant reductions in purchasing power, growing unemployment, and rising food prices. In their discussion of 'South-South' co-operation the ministers recognized the will of the developing countries to work together, particularly in food and agriculture, and recommended four priority areas for attention in such co-operation: food production; institution-building, including training and enhancement of management capability; development of agro-industries; and trade.

The Council considered the impact of international trade and related national policies on food and development, and concluded that growing protectionism, the decline in commodity prices, the deterioration in the terms of trade, and limited access to markets had had a negative impact on international agricultural trade, and impeded the efforts of developing countries to overcome hunger and malnutrition. The Council urged the OECD member countries to avoid excessive market support for agricultural products, and requested that food surpluses should be used to assist the developing countries.

At its 14th session, held in Nicosia, Cyprus, in May 1988, the Council noted that food consumption per person had decreased further in all developing regions in 1987, while the living conditions of the poorest people had continued to deteriorate. It requested a joint effort by all countries and international agencies to improve the nutritional levels of low-income groups during periods of economic adjustment. The Council decided to launch the 'Cyprus Initiative against Hunger in the World' in an attempt to balance access to food, by asking countries with a food surplus to contribute part of their over-production to nations that are short of food; developed nations without a surplus would be asked to contribute cash, while food-deficit nations would be asked to deploy domestic resources in order to bring maximum benefit to the poor and hungry. The Council also discussed sustainable food security, with reference to a report by the UN Environment Programme on the ecological stress caused by increasing food cultivation on marginal lands.

At its 15th session, held in Cairo, Egypt, in May 1989, the Council adopted a programme of co-operative action for the 1990s, aiming to achieve: the elimination of starvation and death caused by famine; a substantial reduction of malnutrition and mortality among young children; a tangible reduction in chronic hunger; and the elimination of major nutritional-deficiency diseases. The Council agreed to make a major effort to raise the level of political support for the elimination of hunger and malnutrition.

At its 16th session, held in Bangkok, Thailand, in May 1990, the Council noted that, during the 1980s, the number of hungry people had increased to some 550m., and the number of malnourished children had increased. Persistent economic problems (including debt, increases in interest rates, declining commodity prices, trade protectionism, increasing populations and environmental degradation) had particularly affected the hungry poor. Output of cereals had fallen short of consumption for three consecutive years, leaving stocks only just above the level deemed necessary for global food security. The meeting requested the Secretariat to undertake reviews of the role of the private sector in national agricultural development strategies, and of national and international research on the extension of the 'Green Revolution' (using new technology to increase food production). It pointed out the need for the incorporation of food-security objectives into national economic adjustment programmes, to protect low-income groups and ensure long-term reductions of hunger and malnutrition. The Council urged an improvement in co-ordination between relevant international agencies (including a consultative mechanism to be established by WFC, FAO, WFP and IFAD).

World Food Programme—WFP

Address: Via Cristoforo Colombo 426, 00145 Rome, Italy.
Telephone: (06) 57971.
Telex: 626675.
Fax: (06) 57975652.

WFP, the food aid arm of the United Nations, became operational in 1963. It aims to stimulate economic and social development through food aid and to provide emergency relief.

Organization
(October 1990)

COMMITTEE ON FOOD AID POLICIES AND PROGRAMMES (CFA)

The Committee has 30 members: 15 elected by the UN Economic and Social Council (ECOSOC, q.v.) and 15 by FAO.

SECRETARIAT

Executive Director: JAMES INGRAM (Australia).

Activities

Member governments make voluntary contributions of commodities, cash, and services (particularly shipping) to WFP, which uses the food to support economic and social development projects in the developing countries. The food is supplied, for example, as an incentive in development self-help schemes, as part wages in labour-intensive projects of many kinds, particularly in the rural economy, but also in the industrial field, and in support of institutional feeding schemes where the emphasis is mainly on enabling the beneficiaries to have an adequate and balanced diet. One of the criteria for WFP aid to projects is that the recipient country can continue them after the aid has ceased. Priority is given to low-income, food-deficit countries and to vulnerable groups such as pregnant women and children. Some WFP projects are intended to alleviate the effects of structural adjustment programmes (particularly programmes which involve reductions in public expenditure and in subsidies for basic foods).

WFP also provides emergency food aid for victims of natural and man-made disasters, chiefly from the International Emergency Food Reserve, which it manages. In 1987 donors contributed 531,300 metric tons of food (worth US $161.6m.) to the Reserve.

By the end of December 1988, 1,484 projects in 115 countries had been approved since the beginning of the Programme's operations, at a total cost to WFP of $9,310m. In addition, 1,001 emergency operations had been undertaken in 105 countries at a total cost to the Programme of $2,435m.

In 1988 310 projects, valued at $3,600m., were operational in 86 countries. By the end of the year, pledges in food aid and cash (including pledges to the International Emergency Food Reserve) for the two years 1987–88 amounted to $1,619m. A total of $779m. was committed to new and expanded development projects in 1988; of this, 86% was for low-income, food-deficit countries. More than 50% of development assistance went to agricultural and rural development projects, while the remainder was invested in human resource development, including food for vulnerable groups and primary schools.

Examples of projects being supported by WFP food aid in 1989 and 1990 included: a poultry-rearing scheme for women in Bangladesh; anti-desertification work in Burkina Faso; women's co-operative groups in Guatemala; irrigation and water supply projects and restoration of forest cover in India; soil and water conservation in Haiti; a project to prevent wastage of rain-water in Tunisia; and school farming projects in Uganda.

In 1988 WFP also committed $254m. to provide emergency food aid to an estimated 15m. people. About two-thirds of this was for refugees, and the remainder was for victims of drought, hurricanes, typhoons and floods.

PUBLICATION

World Food Programme Journal (every 3 months).

INTERNATIONAL ORGANIZATIONS United Nations (Membership)

Membership of the United Nations and its Specialized Agencies

	UN	IAEA	IBRD	IDA	IFC	IMF	FAO	IFAD	GATT	IMO[2]	ICAO[3]	ILO	ITU[4]	UNESCO	UNIDO	UPU[5]	WHO[6]	WMO[7]	WIPO
Afghanistan	x	x	x	x	x	x	x	x			x	x	x	x	x	x	x	x	
Albania[1]	x	x					x						x	x		x	x	x	x
Algeria[1]	x	x	x	x	x	x	x	x		x	x	x	x	x	x	x	x	x	x
Angola[1]	x		x	x	x	x	x	x		x	x	x	x	x	x	x	x	x	x
Antigua and Barbuda	x		x	x	x	x	x		x	x	x		x	x		x	x	x	
Argentina	x	x	x	x	x	x	x	x	x	x	x	x	x	x	x	x	x	x	x
Australia	x	x	x	x	x	x	x	x	x	x	x	x	x	x	x	x	x	x	x
Austria	x	x	x	x	x	x	x	x	x	x	x	x	x	x	x	x	x	x	x
Bahamas[1]	x		x		x	x	x			x	x		x	x		x	x	x	
Bahrain[1]	x		x			x	x			x	x	x	x	x	x	x	x	x	
Bangladesh	x	x	x	x	x	x	x	x	x	x	x	x	x	x	x	x	x	x	x
Barbados	x		x		x	x	x		x	x	x	x	x	x	x	x	x	x	
Belgium	x	x	x	x	x	x	x	x	x	x	x	x	x	x	x	x	x	x	x
Belize	x		x	x	x	x	x		x		x	x	x	x	x	x	x	x	
Benin	x		x	x	x	x	x	x	x	x	x	x	x	x	x	x	x	x	x
Bhutan	x		x	x		x	x	x					x		x	x	x		
Bolivia	x	x	x	x	x	x	x	x		x	x	x	x	x	x	x	x	x	x
Botswana	x		x	x	x	x	x	x			x	x	x	x	x	x	x	x	
Brazil	x	x	x	x	x	x	x	x	x	x	x	x	x	x	x	x	x	x	x
Brunei[1]	x									x	x		x	x		x	x	x	
Bulgaria	x	x					x		x	x	x	x	x	x	x	x	x	x	x
Burkina Faso	x		x	x	x	x	x	x	x		x	x	x	x	x	x	x	x	x
Burundi	x		x	x	x	x	x	x			x	x	x	x	x	x	x	x	x
Byelorussian SSR	x	x									x	x	x	x	x	x	x	x	x
Cambodia[1]	x		x	x	x	x	x				x	x	x	x		x	x	x	
Cameroon	x		x	x	x	x	x	x	x	x	x	x	x	x	x	x	x	x	x
Canada	x	x	x	x	x	x	x	x	x	x	x	x	x	x	x	x	x	x	x
Cape Verde[1]	x		x	x		x	x	x		x	x	x	x	x	x	x	x	x	
Central African Republic	x		x	x	x	x	x	x	x		x	x	x	x	x	x	x	x	x
Chad	x		x	x	x	x	x	x	x		x	x	x	x	x	x	x	x	
Chile	x	x	x	x	x	x	x	x	x	x	x	x	x	x	x	x	x	x	x
China, People's Republic	x	x	x	x	x	x	x	x		x	x	x	x	x	x	x	x	x	x
Colombia	x	x	x	x	x	x	x	x	x	x	x	x	x	x	x	x	x	x	x
Comoros	x		x	x		x	x				x		x	x	x	x	x	x	
Congo	x		x	x	x	x	x	x		x	x	x	x	x	x	x	x	x	x
Costa Rica	x	x	x	x	x	x	x	x	x	x	x	x	x	x	x	x	x	x	x
Côte d'Ivoire	x	x	x	x	x	x	x	x	x	x	x	x	x	x	x	x	x	x	x
Cuba	x	x					x		x	x	x	x	x	x	x	x	x	x	x
Cyprus	x	x	x	x	x	x	x	x	x	x	x	x	x	x	x	x	x	x	x
Czechoslovakia	x	x					x		x	x	x	x	x	x	x	x	x	x	x
Denmark	x	x	x	x	x	x	x	x	x	x	x	x	x	x	x	x	x	x	x
Djibouti	x		x	x		x	x			x	x	x	x	x		x	x	x	
Dominica[1]	x		x	x		x	x						x	x	x	x	x		
Dominican Republic	x		x	x	x	x	x	x	x	x	x	x	x	x	x	x	x	x	x
Ecuador	x	x	x	x	x	x	x	x	x	x	x	x	x	x	x	x	x	x	x
Egypt	x	x	x	x	x	x	x	x	x	x	x	x	x	x	x	x	x	x	x
El Salvador	x	x	x	x	x	x	x	x	x	x	x	x	x	x	x	x	x	x	x
Equatorial Guinea[1]	x		x	x		x	x				x	x	x	x	x	x	x		
Ethiopia	x	x	x	x	x	x	x	x		x	x	x	x	x	x	x	x	x	
Fiji[1]	x		x	x	x	x	x			x	x	x	x	x		x	x	x	x
Finland	x	x	x	x	x	x	x	x	x	x	x	x	x	x	x	x	x	x	x
France	x	x	x	x	x	x	x	x	x	x	x	x	x	x	x	x	x	x	x
Gabon	x	x	x	x	x	x	x	x	x	x	x	x	x	x	x	x	x	x	x
The Gambia	x		x	x	x	x	x	x	x		x	x	x	x	x	x	x	x	
Germany	x	x	x	x	x	x	x	x	x	x	x	x	x	x	x	x	x	x	x
Ghana	x	x	x	x	x	x	x	x	x	x	x	x	x	x	x	x	x	x	x
Greece	x	x	x	x	x	x	x	x	x	x	x	x	x	x	x	x	x	x	x
Grenada[1]	x		x	x		x	x				x		x	x	x	x	x		
Guatemala	x	x	x	x	x	x	x	x		x	x	x	x	x	x	x	x	x	x
Guinea	x		x	x	x	x	x	x	x	x	x	x	x	x	x	x	x	x	x
Guinea-Bissau[1]	x		x	x		x	x	x		x	x	x	x	x	x	x	x	x	x
Guyana	x		x	x	x	x	x	x	x		x	x	x	x	x	x	x	x	
Haiti	x	x	x	x	x	x	x	x	x	x	x	x	x	x	x	x	x	x	x
Honduras	x		x	x	x	x	x	x	x	x	x	x	x	x	x	x	x	x	x
Hungary	x	x	x	x	x	x	x		x	x	x	x	x	x	x	x	x	x	x
Iceland	x	x	x			x	x		x	x	x	x	x	x		x	x	x	x
India	x	x	x	x	x	x	x	x	x	x	x	x	x	x	x	x	x	x	x
Indonesia	x	x	x	x	x	x	x	x		x	x	x	x	x	x	x	x	x	x
Iran	x	x	x	x	x	x	x			x	x	x	x	x	x	x	x	x	

continued

INTERNATIONAL ORGANIZATIONS

United Nations (Membership)

	UN	IAEA	IBRD	IDA	IFC	IMF	FAO	IFAD	GATT	IMO[2]	ICAO[3]	ILO	ITU[4]	UNESCO	UNIDO	UPU[5]	WHO[6]	WMO[7]	WIPO
Iraq	x	x	x	x	x	x	x	x		x	x	x	x	x	x	x	x	x	x
Ireland	x	x	x	x	x	x	x	x	x	x	x	x	x	x	x	x	x	x	x
Israel	x	x	x	x	x	x	x	x	x	x	x	x	x	x	x	x	x	x	x
Italy	x	x	x	x	x	x	x	x	x	x	x	x	x	x	x	x	x	x	x
Jamaica	x	x	x	x	x	x	x	x	x	x	x	x	x	x	x	x	x	x	x
Japan	x	x	x	x	x	x	x	x	x	x	x	x	x	x	x	x	x	x	x
Jordan	x	x	x	x	x	x	x	x		x	x	x	x	x	x	x	x	x	x
Kenya	x	x	x	x	x	x	x	x	x	x	x	x	x	x	x	x	x	x	x
Kiribati[1]			x	x	x						x		x				x	x	
Korea, Democratic People's Republic		x					x	x		x	x		x	x	x	x	x	x	x
Korea, Republic		x	x	x	x	x	x	x		x	x		x	x	x	x	x	x	x
Kuwait	x	x	x	x	x	x	x	x	x	x	x		x	x	x	x	x	x	x
Laos	x		x	x		x	x	x			x	x	x	x	x	x	x	x	x
Lebanon	x	x	x	x	x	x	x	x		x	x	x	x	x	x	x	x	x	
Lesotho	x		x	x	x	x	x	x	x		x	x	x	x	x	x	x	x	x
Liberia	x	x	x	x	x	x	x	x		x	x	x	x	x	x	x	x	x	x
Libya	x	x	x	x	x	x	x	x		x	x	x	x	x	x	x	x	x	x
Liechtenstein		x									x					x			x
Luxembourg	x	x	x	x	x	x	x	x	x	x	x	x	x	x	x	x	x	x	x
Madagascar	x	x	x	x	x	x	x	x		x	x	x	x	x	x	x	x	x	x
Malawi	x		x	x	x	x	x	x	x	x	x	x	x	x	x	x	x	x	x
Malaysia	x	x	x	x	x	x	x		x	x	x	x	x	x	x	x	x	x	x
Maldives	x		x	x		x	x			x	x		x	x	x	x	x	x	
Mali[1]	x	x	x	x	x	x	x	x		x	x	x	x	x	x	x	x	x	x
Malta	x		x		x	x	x	x		x	x	x	x	x	x	x	x	x	x
Mauritania	x		x	x	x	x	x	x		x	x	x	x	x	x	x	x	x	x
Mauritius	x	x	x	x	x	x	x	x	x	x	x	x	x	x	x	x	x	x	x
Mexico	x	x	x	x	x	x	x	x		x	x	x	x	x	x	x	x	x	x
Monaco		x								x	x		x	x		x	x	x	x
Mongolia	x	x					x				x	x	x	x	x	x	x	x	x
Morocco	x	x	x	x	x	x	x	x	x	x	x	x	x	x	x	x	x	x	x
Mozambique[1]	x		x	x	x	x	x	x		x	x	x	x	x	x	x	x	x	x
Myanmar	x	x	x	x		x	x	x		x	x	x	x	x	x	x	x	x	
Namibia	x		x		x								x	x	x	x		x	
Nauru										x	x		x			x			
Nepal	x		x	x	x	x	x	x		x	x	x	x	x	x	x	x	x	
Netherlands	x	x	x	x	x	x	x	x	x	x	x	x	x	x	x	x	x	x	x
New Zealand	x	x	x	x	x	x	x	x	x	x	x	x	x	x	x	x	x	x	x
Nicaragua	x	x	x	x	x	x	x	x	x	x	x	x	x	x	x	x	x	x	x
Niger	x	x	x	x	x	x	x	x		x	x	x	x	x	x	x	x	x	x
Nigeria	x	x	x	x	x	x	x	x	x	x	x	x	x	x	x	x	x	x	x
Norway	x	x	x	x	x	x	x	x	x	x	x	x	x	x	x	x	x	x	x
Oman	x		x	x	x	x	x			x	x		x	x	x	x	x	x	
Pakistan	x	x	x	x	x	x	x	x	x	x	x	x	x	x	x	x	x	x	x
Panama	x	x	x	x	x	x	x	x		x	x	x	x	x	x	x	x	x	x
Papua New Guinea[1]	x		x	x	x	x	x	x		x	x	x	x	x	x	x	x	x	
Paraguay	x	x	x	x	x	x	x	x		x	x	x	x	x	x	x	x	x	x
Peru	x	x	x	x	x	x	x	x	x	x	x	x	x	x	x	x	x	x	x
Philippines	x	x	x	x	x	x	x	x	x	x	x	x	x	x	x	x	x	x	x
Poland	x	x	x	x		x			x	x	x	x	x	x	x	x	x	x	x
Portugal	x	x	x		x	x	x	x	x	x	x	x	x	x	x	x	x	x	x
Qatar[1]	x	x	x			x	x	x		x	x	x	x	x	x	x	x	x	x
Romania	x	x	x			x	x	x	x	x	x	x	x	x	x	x	x	x	x
Rwanda	x		x	x	x	x	x	x	x		x	x	x	x	x	x	x	x	x
Saint Christopher and Nevis[1]	x		x	x		x	x							x	x	x	x	x	
Saint Lucia[1]	x		x	x	x		x	x		x	x	x		x	x	x	x	x	
Saint Vincent and the Grenadines[1]	x					x	x	x		x	x		x	x	x	x	x		
San Marino											x		x	x		x	x	x	
São Tomé and Príncipe[1]	x		x	x			x	x			x	x	x	x	x	x	x		
Saudi Arabia	x	x	x	x	x	x	x	x		x	x	x	x	x	x	x	x	x	x
Senegal	x	x	x	x	x	x	x	x	x	x	x	x	x	x	x	x	x	x	x
Seychelles[1]	x		x	x	x	x	x			x	x		x	x	x	x	x	x	
Sierra Leone	x	x	x	x	x	x	x	x	x	x	x	x	x	x	x	x	x	x	
Singapore	x	x	x	x	x	x			x	x	x	x	x		x	x	x	x	x
Solomon Islands[1]	x		x	x		x	x	x			x	x	x		x	x	x	x	
Somalia	x		x	x		x	x	x		x	x	x	x		x	x	x	x	x
South Africa	x	x	x	x	x	x	x		x		x		x			x	x	x	x
Spain	x	x	x	x	x	x	x	x	x	x	x	x	x	x	x	x	x	x	x
Sri Lanka	x	x	x	x	x	x	x	x	x	x	x	x	x	x	x	x	x	x	x
Sudan	x	x	x	x	x	x	x	x		x	x	x	x	x	x	x	x	x	x
Suriname	x		x			x	x	x		x	x	x	x	x	x	x	x	x	x
Swaziland[1]	x		x	x	x	x	x	x			x	x	x		x	x	x		x
Sweden	x	x	x	x	x	x	x	x	x	x	x	x	x	x	x	x	x	x	x
Switzerland		x					x	x	x	x	x	x	x	x	x	x	x	x	x
Syria	x	x	x	x	x	x	x	x			x	x	x	x	x	x	x	x	

continued

INTERNATIONAL ORGANIZATIONS   United Nations (Membership)

	UN	IAEA	IBRD	IDA	IFC	IMF	FAO	IFAD	GATT	IMO[2]	ICAO[3]	ILO	ITU[4]	UNESCO	UNIDO	UPU[5]	WHO[6]	WMO[7]	WIPO
Tanzania	x	x	x	x	x	x	x	x	x	x	x	x	x	x	x	x	x	x	x
Thailand	x	x	x	x	x	x	x	x	x	x	x	x	x	x	x	x	x	x	x
Togo	x		x	x	x	x	x	x	x	x	x	x	x	x	x	x	x	x	x
Tonga[1]							x	x	x	x	x		x	x	x	x	x		
Trinidad and Tobago	x		x	x	x	x	x	x	x	x	x	x	x	x	x	x	x		x
Tunisia	x	x	x	x	x	x	x	x	x	x	x	x	x	x	x	x	x	x	x
Turkey	x	x	x	x	x	x	x	x	x	x	x	x	x	x	x	x	x	x	x
Tuvalu[1]																x			
Uganda	x	x	x	x		x	x	x	x		x	x	x	x	x	x	x	x	x
Ukrainian SSR	x	x										x	x	x	x	x	x	x	x
USSR	x	x								x	x	x	x	x	x	x	x	x	x
United Arab Emirates[1]	x	x	x	x	x	x	x	x		x	x	x	x	x	x	x	x	x	x
United Kingdom	x	x	x	x	x	x	x	x	x	x	x	x	x	x	x	x	x	x	x
USA	x	x	x	x	x	x	x	x	x	x	x	x	x		x	x	x	x	x
Uruguay	x	x	x	x	x	x	x	x	x	x	x	x	x	x	x	x	x	x	x
Vanuatu	x					x	x	x		x	x		x		x	x	x		
Vatican City		x									x		x			x			x
Venezuela	x	x	x		x	x	x	x		x	x	x	x	x	x	x	x	x	x
Viet-Nam	x	x	x	x	x	x	x	x		x	x	x	x	x	x	x	x	x	x
Western Samoa	x		x	x	x	x	x						x	x			x		x
Yemen	x		x	x	x	x	x	x			x	x	x	x	x	x	x		x
Yugoslavia	x	x	x	x	x	x	x	x	x	x	x	x	x	x	x	x	x	x	x
Zaire	x	x	x	x	x	x	x	x	x	x	x	x	x	x	x	x	x	x	x
Zambia[1]	x	x	x	x	x	x	x	x			x	x	x	x	x	x	x	x	x
Zimbabwe	x	x	x	x	x	x	x	x			x	x	x	x	x	x	x	x	x

[1] Countries to whose territories GATT has been applied and which now, as independent states, maintain a *de facto* application of the GATT pending final decisions as to their future commercial policy.
[2] Hong Kong and Macau are associate members of IMO.
[3] The Cook Islands, the Federated States of Micronesia and the Marshall Islands are members of ICAO.
[4] Members also include British Overseas Territories, French Overseas Territories, Macau and United States Territories.
[5] Members also include British Overseas Territories, French Overseas Territories, Macau, the Netherlands Antilles and United States Territories.
[6] The Cook Islands is a member of WHO.
[7] Members also include British Caribbean Territories, French Polynesia, Hong Kong, the Netherlands Antilles and New Caledonia, all of which maintain their own meteorological service. South Africa's membership was suspended in 1975.

SPECIALIZED AGENCIES WITHIN THE UN SYSTEM

Food and Agriculture Organization—FAO

Address: Via delle Terme di Caracalla, 00100 Rome, Italy.
Telephone: (06) 57971.
Telex: 610181.
Fax: (06) 57973152.

FAO, the first specialized agency of the UN to be founded after World War II, was established in Quebec, Canada, in October 1945. The Organization fights malnutrition and hunger and serves as a co-ordinating agency for development programmes in the whole range of food and agriculture, including forestry and fisheries. It helps developing countries to promote educational and training facilities and institution-building.

MEMBERS

157 members: see Table on pp. 52-54.

Organization

(October 1990)

CONFERENCE

The governing body is the FAO Conference of member nations. It meets every two years, formulates policy, determines the Organization's programme and budget on a biennial basis, and elects new members. It also elects the Director-General of the Secretariat and the Independent Chairman of the Council. Every other year, FAO also holds conferences in each of its five regions (the Near East, Asia and the Pacific, Africa, Latin America and the Caribbean, and Europe).

COUNCIL

The FAO Council is composed of representatives of 49 member nations, elected by the Conference for staggered three-year terms. It is the interim governing body of FAO between sessions of the Conference. The most important standing Committees of the Council are: the Finance and Programme Committees, the Committee on Commodity Problems, the Committee on Fisheries, the Committee on Agriculture and the Committee on Forestry.

SECRETARIAT

The total number of staff at FAO headquarters in late 1989 was 3,175, while staff in field, regional and country offices numbered 3,052; there were also 70 associate experts at headquarters and 311 in field, regional and country offices. Work is supervised by the following Departments: Administration and Finance; General Affairs and Information; Economic and Social Policy; Agriculture; Forestry; Fisheries; and Development.

Director-General (1976-92): EDOUARD SAOUMA (Lebanon).

REGIONAL OFFICES

Africa: UN Agency Bldg, North Maxwell Rd, POB 1628, Accra, Ghana; tel. 666851; telex 2139; Regional Rep. R. T. N'DAW.

Asia and the Pacific: Maliwan Mansion, Phra Atit Rd, Bangkok 10200, Thailand; tel. 2817844; telex 82815; Regional Rep. H. TSUCHIYA (acting).

Europe: Via delle Terme di Caracalla, 00100 Rome, Italy; tel. 57971; telex 610181; Regional Rep. ALESSANDRO BOZZINI.

Latin America and the Caribbean: Avenida Santa Maria 6700, Casilla 10095, Santiago, Chile; tel. 462061; telex 228 8056; Regional Rep. RAFAEL MORENO ROJAS.

Near East: Via delle Terme di Caracalla, 00100 Rome, Italy; tel. 57971; telex 610181; Regional Rep. ATIF Y. BUKHARI.

LIAISON OFFICES

North America: Suite 300, 1001 22nd St, NW, Washington, DC 20437, USA; telex 64255; Dir H. W. HJORT.

United Nations: Suite DC1-1125, 1 United Nations Plaza, New York, NY 10017, USA; tel. (212) 754-6036; telex 236350; Rep. JEAN S. CAMARA.

Activities

FAO published its fifth World Food Survey in 1985. It showed that during the 1970s, for the first time on record, the proportion of the world's population recorded as undernourished fell (from 19% to 15%). But with increasing populations, the estimated total number of undernourished people increased by about 10m.; by the most conservative criteria, there were at least 335m. undernourished people in the world in 1980. World population increased by 178m. in the two years 1988-89, and 90% of the increase occurred in the developing countries. FAO estimated that there were 500m. undernourished people in the world by the end of 1989.

FAO aims to raise levels of nutrition and standards of living, by improving the production and distribution of food and other commodities derived from farms, fisheries and forests. Its work falls into four basic categories: analysis and dissemination of information; advising governments on policy and planning; promoting consultations and co-operation among member countries; and providing technical advice and assistance.

FAO's total field programme expenditure for 1989 was an estimated US $358m., slightly more than the $341m. spent in 1988. An estimated 50% of the expenditure was in Africa, 24% in Asia and the Pacific, 13% in the Near East, 8% in Latin America and the Caribbean, 1% in Europe, and 4% was spent on inter-regional or global projects.

AGRICULTURE

In the two years 1988-89 about 25% of FAO's Field Programme expenditure was devoted to increasing agricultural production, through demonstrating techniques that will enable small farmers to increase production, by a number of methods, including improved seeds and fertilizer use, soil conservation and reforestation, better water resource management techniques, upgrading storage facilities, and improvements in processing and marketing.

Cereal and food legume production continue to be a primary focus of FAO's activities, with emphasis on demonstrations at the farm level. During 1989, for example, FAO assisted in promoting the production of under-exploited traditional food crops, such as cassava, yams, breadfruit, sweet potato and plantains, throughout the developing world, especially by means of training sessions for agricultural extension staff and small farmers. FAO has developed a 'wheatless bread' that can be made using cassava, sorghum or millet flour and may considerably reduce future dependence on wheat imports in developing countries. The Organization also supports large-scale regional programmes to promote these crops. During 1988 FAO tested improved lines of the pigeon pea, yam and cassava in 14 Latin American and Caribbean countries, to foster their production and reduce food import costs. Through the International Rice Commission FAO promotes the development of the world's most important single food crop. Particular attention is given to methods of integrating rice cultivation with other produce—allowing farmers with little land to produce more rice and, for example, fish, small animals, or mushrooms.

Plant protection, weed control, and animal health programmes form an important part of FAO's work as farming methods become more intensive, and pests more resistant to control methods. At the FAO Conference in November 1985 the member nations approved an International Code of Conduct on the Distribution and Use of Pesticides. In 1989 the Conference adopted an additional clause concerning 'Prior Informed Consent', whereby governments are to inform FAO when a pesticide has been banned or its use restricted. The clause aims to supply importing countries with vital information about the hazards of toxic chemicals, while keeping the pesticides industry informed of control actions and encouraging governments to take proper measures to curb trade in highly toxic agrochemicals. FAO's Joint Division with the International Atomic Energy Agency (IAEA), tests controlled-release formulas of pesticides and herbicides that gradually free their substances and can limit the amount of agrochemicals needed to protect crops. The Joint FAO-IAEA Division is engaged in exploring biotechnologies and in developing non-toxic fertilizers (especially those that are locally available) and improved strains of food crops (especially from indigenous varieties). In animal production and health, the Joint Division has developed progesterone-measuring and disease-diagnostic kits, and in 1988 delivered more than 1m. kits to developing countries.

In 1986 FAO established the Emergency Centre for Locust Operations (ECLO) to co-ordinate international action against five species of locusts and grasshoppers which threatened agriculture in much of Africa. At the beginning of 1988 the infestations of desert locusts in north and west Africa were the worst for 30 years. Major control campaigns were mounted in northern Africa in early 1988 and in sub-Saharan Africa in mid- and late 1988. Over 14.5m. ha were treated during the year. By the end of 1988 the principal infestations were confined to Morocco, Saudi Arabia and the western Sahel region.

During the late 1980s, to protect indigenous livestock species from extinction, FAO helped to establish regional animal gene banks and was to continue to mobilize support for germplasm collection throughout the 1990s. Hundreds of plant species, too, are in danger of disappearing and FAO is intensifying its activities to save them. The 1989 Conference approved an interpretation of the International Undertaking on Plant Genetic Resources which recognizes the rights of farmers and plant breeders to be compensated. The Undertaking aims to ensure that plant genetic resources of economic and/or social interest, particularly for agriculture, will be explored, preserved, evaluated and made available for plant breeding and scientific purposes. FAO, through its International Fund for Plant Genetic Resources, supports plant genetic conservation, management and utilization programmes, especially in the developing countries.

FISHERIES

In 1984 FAO held the first World Conference on Fisheries Management and Development, which approved five 'action programmes' on planning and management, small-scale fisheries, aquaculture, trade in fish and fish products, and promoting the role of fisheries in alleviating under-nutrition.

FAO has developed micro-computer software to help developing countries assess the state of their fish stocks. In 1989 the Fisheries Department was studying a series of software that will help developing countries to assess fisheries management options in biological and socio-economic terms. Software packages are tested at FAO workshops and training courses. Among FAO's many fisheries activities is the Programme for Integrated Development of Artisanal Fisheries in West Africa (IDAF), which includes improving boats and gear, better processing and marketing, and improving infrastructure and health care. The programme stresses local participation at all stages and aims to enhance the self-sufficiency of small fisheries communities, in the long term. By the end of 1989, 20 countries had participated in the programme.

FORESTRY

In 1985 FAO introduced a Tropical Forestry Action Plan in response to international alarm over the spread of deforestation and desertification and their consequences on the environment, and the resulting depletion of natural resources. The Plan aims to improve the lives of rural people; to increase food production; to safeguard proper methods of shifting cultivation; to ensure the sustainable use of forests; to increase supplies of fuelwood and its efficient use; and to expand income and employment opportunities in the forest products industry and trade. The 1989 Conference stressed the need to promote the Action Plan on a global scale, and recommended that additional resources be mobilized for its implementation. The Organization warned that by the year 2000 more than half the population of the developing world (some 2,800m. people) would either be short of fuelwood or lack it altogether, and would be caught in a destructive cycle of deforestation, fuelwood scarcity, poverty and malnutrition. A Plan of Action for the tropical forests of Latin America and the Caribbean was drawn up in 1988 after an FAO study. The Organization concluded that without sound resource management, much of the future demand in the region for industrial forest products would have to be met by imports. The plan analysed production potential and suggested ways to introduce better management practices. Other forestry activities include schemes to introduce more efficient domestic stoves and ovens, and to encourage tree-planting, in efforts to reduce deforestation.

PROCESSING AND MARKETING

An estimated 20% of all food harvested is lost before it can be consumed, and in some developing countries the proportion is much higher. FAO helps reduce immediate post-harvest losses, with the introduction of improved processing methods and storage systems. It also advises on the distribution and marketing of agricultural produce and on the selection and preparation of foods for optimum nutrition. Many of these activities form part of wider rural development projects. Many developing countries rely on agricultural products as their main source of foreign earnings, but the terms under which they are traded are usually more favourable to the industrialized countries, as was emphasized during the Uruguay Round of GATT negotiations (q.v.). FAO continues to favour the elimination of export subsidies and related discriminatory practices, such as protectionist measures that hamper international trade in agricultural commodities.

FOOD SECURITY

FAO's food security policy aims to encourage the production of adequate food supplies, to maximize stability in the flow of supplies, and to ensure access on the part of those who need them. The Global Information and Early Warning System monitors the world food situation and identifies countries threatened by shortages to guide potential donors. An environmental monitoring system, ARTEMIS (Africa Real-Time Environmental Monitoring using Imaging Satellites), installed in 1988, processes data from orbiting and stationary satellites to provide continuous monitoring of rainfall and vegetation conditions across Africa, the Near East and Southwest Asia. Twenty-one projects to set up subregional or national early warning systems were being implemented in 1989. As world cereal stocks decreased for the third consecutive year in 1989, they were at the minimum level (17% of world consumption) that FAO considers necessary for world food security.

FAO INVESTMENT CENTRE

The Investment Centre was established in 1964 to help countries prepare viable investment projects that will attract external financing. By the end of 1989 it had assisted some 750 investment projects, generating US $34,000m. of agricultural investment in 108 countries. Each year the Centre undertakes about 200 missions under its own responsibility, and participates in about 100 missions led by co-operating financial institutions.

EMERGENCY RELIEF

The Office for Special Relief Operations (OSRO) was set up in 1973 in response to the disastrous drought in the Sahel in that year. In 1975 the office was expanded to handle such emergencies globally. As well as providing emergency aid, OSRO aims to rehabilitate agricultural production following disasters. Jointly with the United Nations, FAO is responsible for the World Food Programme (q.v.) which provides emergency food supplies, and food aid in support of development projects.

INFORMATION AND RESEARCH

FAO issues regular statistical reports, commodity studies, and technical manuals in local languages (see list of publications below).

General and specialized computerized data bases co-ordinated by FAO contain information on every area of food and agriculture; the Current Agricultural Research Information System (CARIS), for example, enables over 70 countries to exchange information on current research; other systems provide information on agricultural sciences and technology (AGRIS), commodities (ICS), fisheries (ASFIS, GLOBEFISH and FISHDAB) and forest resources (FORIS).

FAO's Research and Technology Development Division helps to co-ordinate and support members' agricultural research. Missions to review and plan research are sent to member countries, on request.

FAO Councils and Commissions

(Based at the Rome headquarters unless otherwise indicated.)

African Commission on Agricultural Statistics: c/o FAO Regional Office for Africa, POB 1628, Accra, Ghana: f. 1961 to advise member countries on the development and standardization of food and agricultural statistics.

African Forestry Commission: f. 1959 to advise on the formulation of forest policy and to review and co-ordinate its implementation on a regional level; to exchange information and advise on technical problems.

Asia and Pacific Commission on Agricultural Statistics: c/o FAO Regional Office, Maliwan Mansion, Phra Atit Rd, Bangkok 2, Thailand; f. 1962 to review the state of food and agricultural statistics in the region and to advise member countries on the development and standardization of agricultural statistics.

Asia and Pacific Plant Protection Commission: c/o FAO Regional Office, Maliwan Mansion, Phra Atit Rd, Bangkok 2, Thailand; f. 1956 (new title 1983) to strengthen international co-operation in plant protection to prevent the introduction and spread of destructive plant diseases and pests.

Asia-Pacific Forestry Commission: f. 1949 to advise on the formulation of forest policy, and review and co-ordinate its

INTERNATIONAL ORGANIZATIONS

United Nations (Specialized Agencies)

implementation throughout the region; to exchange information and advise on technical problems.

Caribbean Plant Protection Commission: f. 1967 to preserve the existing plant resources of the area.

Commission for Controlling the Desert Locust in the Eastern Region of its distribution area in South West Asia: f. 1964 to carry out all possible measures to control plagues of the desert locust in Afghanistan, India, Iran and Pakistan.

Commission for Controlling the Desert Locust in the Near East: f. 1965 to carry out all possible measures to control plagues of the desert locust within the Middle East and to reduce crop damage.

Commission for Controlling the Desert Locust in North-West Africa: f. 1971 to promote research on control of the desert locust in NW Africa.

Commission for Inland Fisheries of Latin America: f. 1976 to promote, co-ordinate and assist national and regional fishery and limnological surveys and programmes of research and development leading to the rational utilization of inland fishery resources.

Commission on African Animal Trypanosomiasis: f. 1979 to develop and implement programmes to combat this disease.

Commission on Fertilizers: f. 1973 to provide guidance on the effective distribution and use of fertilizers.

Commission on Plant Genetic Resources: f. 1983 to provide advice on programmes dealing with crop improvement through plant genetic resources.

European Commission for the Control of Foot-and-Mouth Disease: f. 1953 to promote national and international action for the control of the disease in Europe and its final eradication.

European Commission on Agriculture: f. 1949 to encourage and facilitate action and co-operation in technological agricultural problems among member states and between international organizations concerned with agricultural technology in Europe.

European Forestry Commission: f. 1947 to advise on the formulation of forest policy and to review and co-ordinate its implementation on a regional level; to exchange information and to make recommendations.

European Inland Fisheries Advisory Commission: f. 1957 to promote improvements in inland fisheries and to advise member governments and FAO on inland fishery matters.

FAO Regional Commission on Farm Management for Asia and the Far East: c/o FAO Regional Office, Maliwan Mansion, Phra Atit Rd, Bangkok 2, Thailand; f. 1959 to stimulate and co-ordinate farm management research and extension activities and to serve as a clearing-house for the exchange of information and experience among the member countries in the region.

FAO/WHO Codex Alimentarius Commission: f. 1962 to make proposals for the co-ordination of all international food standards work and to publish a code of international food standards.

General Fisheries Council for the Mediterranean—GFCM: f. 1952 to develop aquatic resources, to encourage and co-ordinate research in the fishing and allied industries, to assemble and publish information, and to recommend the standardization of equipment, techniques and nomenclature.

Indian Ocean Fishery Commission: c/o FAO Regional Office, Maliwan Mansion, Phra Atit Rd, Bangkok 2, Thailand; f. 1967 to promote national programmes, research and development activities, and to examine management problems.

Indo-Pacific Fishery Commission: c/o FAO Regional Office, Maliwan Mansion, Phra Atit Rd, Bangkok 2, Thailand; f. 1948 to develop fisheries, encourage and co-ordinate research, disseminate information, recommend projects to governments, propose standards in technique and nomenclature.

International Poplar Commission: f. 1947 to study scientific, technical, social and economic aspects of poplar and willow cultivation; to promote the exchange of ideas and material between research workers, producers and users; to arrange joint research programmes, congresses, study tours; to make recommendations to the FAO Conference and to National Poplar Commissions.

International Rice Commission: f. 1948 to promote national and international action on production, conservation, distribution and consumption of rice, except matters relating to international trade.

Joint FAO/WHO/OAU Regional Food and Nutrition Commission for Africa: c/o FAO Regional Office for Africa, POB 1628, Accra, Ghana; f. 1962 to provide liaison in matters pertaining to food and nutrition, and to review food and nutrition problems in Africa.

Latin American Forestry Commission: f. 1948 to advise on formulation of forest policy and review and co-ordinate its implementation throughout the region; to exchange information and advise on technical problems.

Near East Forestry Commission: f. 1953 to advise on formulation of forest policy and review and co-ordinate its implementation throughout the region; to exchange information and advise on technical problems.

Near East Regional Commission on Agriculture: f. 1983 to conduct periodic reviews of agricultural problems in the region; to promote policies and regional and national programmes for improving production of crops and livestock; to expand agricultural services and research; to promote the transfer of technology and regional technical co-operation; and to provide guidance on training and manpower development.

Near East Regional Economic and Social Policy Commission: f. 1983 to review developments relating to food, agriculture and food security; to recommend policies on agrarian reform and rural development; to review and exchange information on food and nutrition policies and on agricultural planning; and to compile statistics.

North American Forestry Commission: f. 1959 to advise on the formulation and co-ordination of national forest policies in Canada, Mexico and the USA; to exchange information and to advise on technical problems.

Regional Animal Production and Health Commission for Asia, the Far East and the South-West Pacific: c/o FAO Regional Office, Maliwan Mansion, Phra Atit Rd, Bangkok 2, Thailand; f. 1973 to promote livestock development in general, and national and international research and action with respect to animal health and husbandry problems in the region.

Regional Commission on Food Security for Asia and the Pacific: c/o FAO Regional Office, Maliwan Mansion, Phra Atit Rd, Bangkok 2, Thailand; f. 1982 to review regional food security; to assist member states in preparing programmes for strengthening food security and for dealing with acute food shortages; and to encourage technical co-operation.

Regional Commission on Land and Water Use in the Near East: f. 1967 to review the current situation with regard to land and water use in the region; to identify the main problems concerning the development of land and water resources which require research and study and to consider other related matters.

Regional Fisheries Advisory Commission for the Southwest Atlantic: f. 1961 to advise FAO on fisheries in the South-west Atlantic area, to advise member countries (Argentina, Brazil and Uruguay) on the administration and rational exploitation of marine and inland resources; to assist in the collection and dissemination of data, in training, and to promote liaison and co-operation.

Western Central Atlantic Fishery Commission: f. 1973 to assist international co-operation for the conservation, development and utilization of the living resources, especially shrimps, of the Western Central Atlantic.

FINANCE

FAO's Regular Programme, which is financed by contributions from member governments, covers the cost of the FAO's Secretariat, its Technical Co-operation Programme and part of the cost of several special action programmes. The budget for the two years 1990–91 amounted to US $568.8m. Much of FAO's technical assistance programme is funded from extra-budgetary sources. The single largest contributor is the United Nations Development Programme (UNDP), which in 1989 accounted for US $164.3m., or 46% of field project expenditures. Equally important are the trust funds that come mainly from donor countries and international financing institutions. They totalled $163.8m., or 45.7% of technical assistance funds. FAO's contribution under its Technical Co-operation programme (TCP, FAO's regular budgetary funds for the Field Programme) was some $29.9m.

During the late 1980s FAO was reported to be undergoing a financial crisis, owing to arrears in payments by member countries: by the end of 1989 outstanding payments amounted to $175m., of which $142m. was owed by the USA, FAO's single largest contributor. (The delay in payment was partly attributed to the dissatisfaction expressed by some member states at a lack of consultation in FAO's budgetary procedures.) As a result, reductions in staffing levels, delays in filling vacant posts, and cancellations of meetings and publications, became necessary.

FAO PUBLICATIONS

Quarterly Bulletin of Statistics.
Food Outlook (monthly).
Production Yearbook.
Yearbook of Fishery Statistics.
Yearbook of Forest Products.
Trade Yearbook.
Fertilizer Yearbook.

INTERNATIONAL ORGANIZATIONS / United Nations (Specialized Agencies)

Animal Health Yearbook.
Commodity Review and Outlook (annually).
The State of Food and Agriculture (annually).
Plant Protection Bulletin (quarterly).

Ceres (every 2 months).
Unasylva (quarterly).
Environment and Energy Bulletin.
Commodity reviews; studies; manuals.

General Agreement on Tariffs and Trade—GATT

Address: Centre William Rappard, 154 rue de Lausanne, 1211 Geneva 21, Switzerland.
Telephone: (022) 7395111.
Telex: 412324.
Fax: (022) 7314206.

GATT was established in 1948 as a multilateral treaty aiming to liberalize world trade and place it on a secure basis.

CONTRACTING PARTIES TO GATT

At mid-September 1990 there were 99 contracting parties (including Hong Kong, which became a member in its own right in 1986); a further 28 in practice apply the rules of GATT to their commercial policy: see Table on pp. 52–54.

Organization
(October 1990)

SESSIONS

The sessions of contracting parties are usually held annually, in Geneva. The session is the highest body of GATT. Decisions are generally arrived at by consensus, not by vote. On the rare occasions that voting takes place, each contracting party (member country) has one vote. Most decisions by vote are taken by simple majority; but a two-thirds majority, with the majority comprising more than half the member countries, is needed for 'waivers': authorizations, in particular cases, to depart from specific obligations under the General Agreement. Outside the sessions, votes may be taken by postal ballot.

COUNCIL OF REPRESENTATIVES

Meets as necessary (generally about 10 times a year) to deal with urgent and routine matters arising between sessions of contracting parties and to supervise the work of committees and working groups.

SECRETARIAT

The secretariat, numbering about 400 people, consists of experts in trade policy and economics and an administrative staff (including translators and interpreters). It prepares and runs the sessions of contracting parties and services the work of the Council and of the committees, working groups and panels of independent experts. It is also responsible for organizing multilateral trade negotiations held within the framework of GATT.
Director-General: ARTHUR DUNKEL (Switzerland).
Deputy Directors-General: MADAN MATHUR (India), CHARLES CARLISLE (USA).

COMMITTEES AND WORKING PARTIES

Standing committees or councils exist to direct GATT work on trade and development issues; to carry on trade negotiations among developing countries; to examine the situation of countries using trade restrictions to protect their balance of payments; to supervise implementation of the various Tokyo Round agreements; to supervise the Arrangement Regarding International Trade in Textiles (Multi-fibre Arrangement); and to deal with budget, financial and administrative questions.

A Consultative Group of Eighteen, consisting of high-level representatives with responsibility for trade policy in their countries, was established in 1975. It meets at least once a year.

Working parties (ad hoc committees) are set up to deal with current questions, such as requests for accession to GATT; verification that agreements concluded by member countries are in conformity with GATT; or studies of issues on which the member countries will later wish to take a joint decision. Panels of independent experts are often set up to investigate disputes and report their conclusions to the Council. Ten panel reports were adopted in 1989.

INTERNATIONAL TRADE CENTRE

Address: 54–56 rue de Montbrillant, 1202 Geneva, Switzerland.
Telephone: (022) 7346021.
Telex: 289052.

Established by GATT in 1964, the Centre has been jointly operated since 1968 by GATT and the UN (the latter through UNCTAD). It assists developing countries to formulate and implement trade promotion programmes, provides information and advice on export markets and marketing techniques, helps to develop export promotion and marketing institutions and services, and trains national personnel. In 1984 it became an executing agency of the UN Development Programme (UNDP, q.v.), directly responsible for carrying out UNDP-financed projects related to trade promotion.
Executive Director: GÖRAN M. ENGBLOM (Sweden).

The Agreement

GATT is based on a few fundamental principles. First, as directed in the famous 'most-favoured-nation' clause, trade must be conducted on the basis of non-discrimination: all contracting parties are bound to grant to each other treatment as favourable as they give to any country in the application and administration of import and export duties and charges. Exceptions—principally for customs unions and free trade areas and for measures in favour of and among developing countries (see Tokyo Round 'framework' agreements below)—are granted only subject to strict rules.

Second, protection should be given to domestic industry essentially through the customs tariff. The aim of this rule is to make the extent of protection clear and to make competition possible.

Third, a stable and predictable basis for trade is provided by the binding of the tariff levels negotiated among the contracting parties. These bound items are listed for each country in tariff schedules which form an integral part of the General Agreement. A return to higher tariffs is discouraged by the requirement that any increases are compensated for; consequently this provision is seldom invoked.

Consultation, to avoid damage to the trading interests of contracting parties, is another fundamental principle of GATT. Members are able to call on GATT for a fair settlement of cases in which they think their rights under the General Agreement are being withheld or compromised by other members.

There are 'waiver' procedures whereby a country may, when its economic or trade circumstances so warrant, seek a derogation from a particular GATT obligation or obligations. There are also escape provisions for emergency action against imports in certain defined circumstances.

The trade problems of developing countries receive special attention in GATT. In 1965 a new chapter on Trade and Development was added to the General Agreement; a key provision is that developing countries should not be expected to offer reciprocity in negotiations with developed countries. GATT members have also relaxed the most-favoured-nation rule to accommodate the Generalized System of Preferences by developed for developing countries and to allow an exchange of preferential tariff reductions among developing countries. (See UNCTAD.)

Finally, GATT offers a framework within which negotiations are held for the reduction of tariffs and other barriers to trade and a structure for putting the results of such negotiations into a legal instrument.

Activities

Much of GATT's regular work consists of consultations and negotiations on specific trade problems affecting individual commodities or member countries.

INTERNATIONAL ORGANIZATIONS

United Nations (Specialized Agencies)

From time to time, major multilateral trade negotiations also take place under GATT auspices. There have been seven rounds of such negotiations: in 1947 (in Geneva), in 1949 (Annecy, France), 1951 (Torquay, England), 1956 (Geneva), 1960–61 (Geneva, the 'Dillon Round'), 1964–67 (Geneva, the 'Kennedy Round'), and 1973–79 (Geneva, the 'Tokyo Round', so called because the negotiations were launched at a ministerial meeting in the Japanese capital in 1973). A further round (the 'Uruguay Round') began at Punta del Este, Uruguay, in September 1986 (see below).

Ninety-nine countries participated in the Tokyo Round. In November 1979 the negotiations were concluded with agreements covering: an improved legal framework for the conduct of world trade (which includes recognition of tariff and non-tariff treatment in favour of and among developing countries as a permanent legal feature of the world trading system); non-tariff measures (subsidies and countervailing duties; technical barriers to trade; government procurement; customs valuation; import licensing procedures; and a revision of the 1967 GATT anti-dumping code); bovine meat; dairy products; tropical products; and an agreement on free trade in civil aircraft. The agreements contain provisions for special and more favourable treatment for developing countries.

Participating countries also agreed to reduce tariffs on thousands of industrial and agricultural products, for the most part by annual cuts over a period of seven years beginning on 1 January 1980. By the beginning of 1987 all contracting parties had implemented the final tariff cuts negotiated in the Tokyo Round: cuts worth some US $300,000m. had reduced the average level of industrial tariffs in the developed countries by 34% (from 7.0% to 4.7%).

The agreements providing an improved framework for the conduct of world trade took effect in November 1979. The other agreements took effect on 1 January 1980, except for those covering government procurement and customs valuation, which took effect on 1 January 1981, and the concessions on tropical products which began as early as 1977. Committees were established to supervise implementation of the agreements.

A work programme was established in November 1979, giving priority to full implementation of the Tokyo Round agreements, future trade liberalization and further efforts to assist the trade of developing countries; the Committee on Trade and Development is largely responsible for these efforts, and its role was strengthened in the work programme. Two sub-committees were established in 1981: one to examine any new protective measures taken by developed countries against imports from developing countries, and the other to consider the trade problems of the least-developed countries.

A considerable proportion of world trade in textiles and clothing is carried out by the 40 signatories participating in the Arrangement Regarding International Trade in Textiles (Multi-fibre Arrangement), which entered into force in January 1974 under GATT auspices for a period of four years. (The European Community counts as one signatory.) The aim of the Multi-fibre Arrangement was to allow the major importers (the USA, Japan and the European Community) to reorganize their textile industries in the face of low-cost production by developing countries. Under the Arrangement all fibres, fabrics and garments are divided into categories, and within each category bilateral agreements are negotiated between suppliers and importers for every product that is likely to cause disruption in the importer's domestic textile industry. In December 1977 the signatory Governments of the Arrangement decided to extend it for four years, and at the end of 1981 the Arrangement was extended for a further period of four years and seven months, from 1 January 1982 to 31 July 1986. Although many developing countries demanded that the Arrangement should be abolished and that trade in textiles should be covered by normal GATT procedures, a new Arrangement was agreed with effect from 1 August 1986, for five years. A negotiating group on textiles and clothing was established in 1987 under the Uruguay Round of negotiations (see below).

The 1982 session of contracting parties was held in Geneva in November and included a ministerial-level meeting (the first for nine years), attended by some 70 ministers from the GATT member countries, who adopted a joint declaration, affirming their commitment against protectionism and calling for a renewed consensus in support of the GATT. The declaration also set out a programme of work covering many aspects of trade policy, with emphasis on the following aims: to identify the means of bringing agriculture more fully into the multilateral trading system; to revise the GATT rules on emergency 'safeguard' action against imports; to identify and examine quantitative restrictions and other non-tariff barriers and to consider their possible elimination or liberalization; to review the implementation of GATT rules relating to developing countries; to examine the scope for trade liberalization in textiles and clothing; to look at problems affecting trade in certain natural resource products; and to review the operation of the Tokyo Round agreements and arrangements. Reports on much of this work were presented to the session of contracting parties in November 1984, and it was subsequently continued.

During 1985 and 1986 preparations were made for a new round of multilateral trade negotiations. Many developing countries opposed the USA's proposal that the agenda should include liberalizing trade in services (such as tourism, banking and insurance), an area not previously covered by GATT, but eventually a compromise was reached whereby negotiations on services were to be conducted by a separate committee, supervised by GATT but outside its legal framework. Proposals by the USA and others to discuss distortion of agricultural trade by export subsidies and farm support policies were adopted, despite opposition from the European Community. The Uruguay Round began in September 1986 and was expected to be completed in four years. Participants agreed that during the course of the negotiations they would observe a 'standstill' in measures that restrict or distort trade, and a 'rollback' or phasing-out of existing trade practices that were inconsistent with GATT rules. Negotiations were conducted by 14 groups dealing with trade in goods: tariffs; non-tariff measures; tropical products; products based on natural resources (particularly fish, forestry products, non-ferrous metals and minerals); textiles and clothing, agriculture; GATT articles (a review of existing GATT provisions); safeguards; improvement or expansion of Tokyo Round agreements; subsidies and countervailing measures; dispute settlement; trade-related aspects of intellectual property protection, including trade in counterfeit goods; trade-related investment measures; and functioning of the GATT system. The separate group, discussing trade in services, was to establish principles and rules for this trade, including the elaboration of possible disciplines for individual service sectors.

By mid-1989 the following results had been achieved: an agreement on liberalization of trade in tropical products (an important sector for developing countries, covering some $20,000m. annually in trade); the streamlining of GATT procedures for the settlement of disputes; and the establishment of a review mechanism for trade policy, under which individual members would be subject to regular examination. Guidelines were agreed on long-term reform of agricultural policy, and on a short-term 'freeze' on government support for agriculture and market access in 1989–90. Ministers of trade reviewing the Round in December 1988 and April 1989, agreed that tariff cuts should be at least as substantial as those negotiated in the Tokyo Round (i.e. in excess of 30%). In September 1990 107 countries were taking part in the negotiations. During 1990 the progress of negotiations was impeded by serious disagreements, particularly in the following areas: the alleged abuse of 'anti-dumping' measures (measures intended to prevent the export of products at lower prices than those at which they are sold within the exporting country) to protect the importing countries' domestic industries, in contravention of GATT rules; the liberalization of agricultural trade, with the USA and the 'Cairns Group' of agricultural exporters demanding the elimination by the EEC of subsidies granted to agricultural exporters and of restrictions on agricultural imports; and the progressive dissolution of the Multi-fibre Arrangement. The final ministerial meeting of the Uruguay Round began in December 1990, but continuing disagreement over agricultural subsidies made it appear unlikely that the negotiations would be successfully concluded (see Late Information).

FINANCE

Payments are based on each member's share of the total trade between members. The budget for 1989 amounted to 64.8m. Swiss francs, and that for 1990 to 74.5m. Swiss francs.

PUBLICATIONS
(available in English, French and Spanish editions).

International Trade (annual report on the main developments in international trade).

Trade Policy Reviews (by country).

GATT Activities (annual).

GATT Focus (newsletter, 10 a year).

Basic Instruments and Selected Documents series. Annual supplements record the formal decisions of the Members, important committee papers, etc. Volume IV gives the current text of the General Agreement.

GATT Studies in International Trade (occasional series of staff papers).

GATT: What it is, What it does.

The Tokyo Round of Multilateral Trade Negotiations. A two-volume report by the Director-General. Copies of the multilateral agreements concluded in the Tokyo Round are also available.

INTERNATIONAL ORGANIZATIONS *United Nations (Specialized Agencies)*

International Atomic Energy Agency—IAEA

Address: POB 100, Wagramerstrasse 5, 1400 Vienna, Austria.
Telephone: (0222) 2360.
Telex: 1-12645.
Fax: (0222) 234564.

The International Atomic Energy Agency (IAEA) is an intergovernmental organization, established in 1957 in accordance with a decision of the General Assembly of the United Nations. Although it is autonomous, the IAEA is administratively a member of the United Nations, and reports on its activities once a year to the UN General Assembly. Its main objectives are to enlarge the contribution of atomic energy to peace, health and prosperity throughout the world and to ensure, so far as it is able, that assistance provided by it or at its request or under its supervision or control is not used in such a way as to further any military purpose.

MEMBERS

112 members: see Table on pp. 52–54.

Organization

(October 1990)

GENERAL CONFERENCE

The Conference, comprising representatives of all member states, convenes each year for general debate on the Agency's policy, budget and programme. It elects members to the Board of Governors, and approves the appointment of the Director-General; it admits new member states.

BOARD OF GOVERNORS

The Board of Governors consists of 35 member states: 22 elected by the General Conference for two-year periods and 13 designated by the Board from among member states which are advanced in nuclear technology. It is the principal policy-making body of the Agency and is responsible to the General Conference. Under its own authority, the Board approves all safeguards agreements, important projects and safety standards.

SECRETARIAT

The Secretariat, comprising about 2,100 staff, is headed by the Director-General, who is assisted by five Deputy Directors-General. The Secretariat is divided into five departments: Technical Co-operation; Nuclear Energy and Safety; Research and Isotopes; Safeguards; Administration. A Standing Advisory Group on Safeguards Implementation advises the Director-General on technical aspects of safeguards.

Director-General: HANS BLIX (Sweden).

Activities

The IAEA's functions can be divided into two main categories: technical co-operation (assisting research on and practical application of atomic energy for peaceful uses); and safeguards (ensuring that special fissionable and other materials, services, equipment and information made available by the Agency or at its request or under its supervision are not used for any military purpose).

TECHNICAL CO-OPERATION AND TRAINING

During 1989 1,135 technical co-operation projects and applications were being undertaken in 80 countries, with IAEA assistance in the form of experts, training and equipment. The IAEA organized 106 regional and inter-regional training courses, and assigned 2,144 experts to provide specialized help on specific nuclear applications.

FOOD AND AGRICULTURE

In co-operation with FAO (q.v.), the Agency conducts programmes of applied research on the use of radiation and isotopes in six main fields: efficiency in the use of water and fertilizers; improvement of food crops by induced mutations; eradication or control of destructive insects by the introduction of sterilized insects; improvement of livestock nutrition and health; studies on improving efficacy and reducing residues of pesticides, and increasing utilization of agricultural wastes; and food preservation by irradiation.

LIFE SCIENCES

In co-operation with the World Health Organization (WHO, q.v.), IAEA promotes the use of nuclear techniques in medicine, biology and health-related environmental research, provides training, and conducts research on techniques for improving the accuracy of radiation dosimetry.

The IAEA/WHO Network of Secondary Standard Dosimetry Laboratories (SSDLs) comprises about 50 member laboratories. The Agency's Dosimetry Laboratory performs dose inter-comparisons for both SSDLs and radiotherapy centres. The IAEA undertakes maintenance plans for nuclear laboratories; national programmes of quality control for nuclear medicine instruments; quality control of radioimmunoassay techniques; radiation sterilization of medical supplies; and improvement of cancer therapy.

PHYSICAL SCIENCES AND LABORATORIES

The Agency's programme in physical sciences includes industrial applications of isotopes and radiation technology; application of nuclear techniques to mineral exploration and exploitation; radiopharmaceuticals; and hydrology, involving the use of isotope techniques for assessment of water resources. Nuclear data services are provided, and training is given for nuclear scientists from developing countries. The IAEA Laboratory at Seibersdorf, Austria, supports the Agency's research, radio-isotope and safeguards programmes, while the Safeguards Analytical Laboratory analyses nuclear fuel-cycle samples collected by IAEA safeguards inspectors. The International Laboratory of Marine Radioactivity, in Monaco, studies radionuclides and other ocean pollutants. From 1979 onwards the European Community, Japan, the USA and the USSR worked as partners on the International Tokamak Reactor (INTOR) for controlled fusion. In 1987 the four agreed to begin a conceptual design study for an international thermonuclear experimental reactor (ITER) as a continuation of work on INTOR.

NUCLEAR POWER

At the end of 1989 there were 426 nuclear power plants in operation throughout the world, with a total generating capacity of 318,271 MW, providing about 17% of total electrical energy generated during the year. There were also 96 reactors under construction, with a generating capacity of 78,907 MW. The Agency helps developing member states to introduce nuclear-powered electricity-generating plants through assistance with planning, feasibility studies, surveys of manpower and infrastructure, and safety measures. It publishes books on numerous aspects of nuclear power, and provides training courses on safety in nuclear power plants and other topics. An energy data bank collects and disseminates information on nuclear technology, and a power-reactor information system monitors the technical performance of nuclear power plants.

RADIOACTIVE WASTE MANAGEMENT

The Agency provides practical help to member states in the management of radioactive waste. The Waste Management Advisory Programme (WAMAP) was established in 1987, and undertook 12 missions in 1988. A code of practice to prevent the illegal dumping of radioactive waste was drawn up in 1989, and another on the international trans-boundary movement of waste was drawn up in 1990.

NUCLEAR SAFETY

The IAEA's nuclear safety programme encourages international co-operation in the exchange of information, promoting implementation of its safety standards and providing advisory safety services. It includes the IAEA Incident Reporting System; an emergency preparedness programme; operational safety review teams; and a safety research co-ordination programme.

The revised edition of the Basic Safety Standards for Radiation Protection (IAEA Safety Series No. 9) was published in 1982. The Nuclear Safety Standards programme, initiated in 1974 with five codes of practice and more than 60 safety guides, was revised in 1987.

In 1982, to provide member states with advice on achieving and maintaining a high level of safety in the operation of nuclear power plants, the Agency established operational safety review teams, which will visit a power plant on request. By mid-1989 34 such missions had visited 19 countries. Co-ordinated research programmes establish risk criteria for the nuclear fuel cycle and identify cost-effective means to reduce risks in energy systems. The International Nuclear Safety Advisory Group (INSAG) comprises experts from nuclear safety licensing authorities, nuclear industry and research, and aims to provide a forum for exchange of information and to identify important current safety issues.

During 1988 there were 70 technical co-operation projects under way in the field of radiation protection. Missions visited 12 countries to assist with radiation protection.

Following the serious accident at the Chernobyl nuclear power plant in the Ukraine, in April 1986, the IAEA convened a series of meetings to consider the implications of the disaster and ways of improving the response to such emergencies. Two conventions were drawn up and entered into force in October: the first commits parties to provide early notification and information about nuclear accidents with possible trans-boundary effects (it had 37 parties in April 1989); and the second commits parties to endeavour to provide assistance in the event of a nuclear accident (it had 32 parties in April 1989). During 1990 the IAEA organized an assessment of the consequences of the Chernobyl accident, undertaken by an international team of experts.

DISSEMINATION OF INFORMATION

The International Nuclear Information System (INIS) provides a computerized indexing and abstracting service. Information on the peaceful uses of atomic energy is collected by member states and international organizations and sent to the IAEA for processing and dissemination (see list of publications below). IAEA also co-operates with the FAO in an information system for agriculture (AGRIS). The IAEA Nuclear Data Section provides cost-free data centre services and co-operates with other national and regional nuclear and atomic data centres in the systematic worldwide collection, compilation, dissemination and exchange of nuclear reaction data, nuclear structure and decay data, and atomic and molecular data for fusion.

SAFEGUARDS

The Treaty on the Non-Proliferation of Nuclear Weapons (NPT), which entered into force in 1970, requires each non-nuclear-weapon state (one which had not manufactured and exploded a nuclear weapon or other nuclear explosive device prior to 1 January 1967) Party to the Treaty to conclude a safeguards agreement with the IAEA. Under such an agreement the State undertakes to accept IAEA safeguards on all nuclear material in all its peaceful nuclear activities for the purpose of verifying that such material is not diverted to nuclear weapons or other nuclear explosive devices. By the end of 1989 140 states had ratified and acceded to the Treaty, but more than 50 non-nuclear-weapon states had not complied, within the prescribed time-limit, with their obligations under the Treaty regarding the conclusion of the relevant safeguards agreement with the Agency.

Two nuclear-weapon states, the United Kingdom and the USA, both Party to the NPT, concluded safeguards agreements with the Agency (in 1978 and 1980 respectively) that permit the application of IAEA safeguards to all their nuclear activities, excluding those with 'direct national significance'. A third nuclear-weapon state, France, concluded a similar agreement in 1981 under which it accepts IAEA safeguards on nuclear material in facilities to be designated by France. In February 1985 an agreement was signed by the IAEA and the USSR on the application of IAEA safeguards to certain peaceful nuclear installations in the USSR. A safeguards agreement with the People's Republic of China was signed in September 1988.

The Treaty for the prohibition of Nuclear Weapons in Latin America (Tlatelolco Treaty) entered into force in 1968, aiming to create a zone free of nuclear weapons in Latin America. The IAEA administers full applications of safeguards in relation to the Treaty. In addition, the IAEA applies safeguards in 10 states under agreements other than those in connection with the NPT and the Tlatelolco Treaty.

In 1988 2,128 inspections were carried out under safeguards agreements at 920 nuclear installations in 57 non-nuclear-weapon states and four nuclear-weapon states. Some 320 automatic photographic and television surveillance systems operated in the field, and 15,500 seals applied to nuclear material were detached and subsequently verified. About 1,170 samples of uranium and plutonium were analysed.

INTERNATIONAL CENTRE FOR THEORETICAL PHYSICS

The Centre, in Trieste, Italy, brings together scientists from the developed and the developing countries. With support from the Italian government, the Centre has been operated jointly by the IAEA and UNESCO since 1970. Each year it offers seminars followed by a research workshop, as well as short topical seminars, training courses, symposia and panels. Independent research is also carried out. The programme concentrates on solid-state physics, high-energy and elementary particle physics, physics of nuclear structure and reactions, applicable mathematics and, to a lesser extent, on physics of the earth and the environment, physics of energy, biophysics, microprocessors and physics of technology.

NUCLEAR FUEL CYCLE

The Agency promotes the exchange of information between Member States on technical, safety, environmental, and economic aspects of nuclear fuel cycle technology, including uranium prospecting and the treatment and disposal of radioactive waste; it provides assistance to Member States in the planning, implementation and operation of nuclear fuel cycle facilities and assists in the development of advanced nuclear fuel cycle technology. Every two years, in collaboration with the OECD, the Agency prepares estimates of world uranium resources, demand and production.

BUDGET

The Agency is financed by regular and voluntary contributions from member states. The regular budget for 1990 envisaged expenditure of US $162.8m., and the target for voluntary contributions to finance the IAEA technical assistance programme in 1990 was $45.5m. Expenditure of $178.9m. was approved under the regular budget for 1991, and the target for technical assistance contributions was $49m.

PUBLICATIONS

Annual Report.
Nuclear Safety Review (annually).
IAEA Newsbriefs (monthly).
IAEA Bulletin (quarterly).
Nuclear Fusion (monthly).
Meetings on Atomic Energy (quarterly).
Technical Directories.
Panel Proceedings Series.
Safety Series.
Legal Series.
Technical Reports Series.
INIS Atomindex (bibliography, 2 a month).
INIS Reference Series.
Publications Catalogue (annually).

International Bank for Reconstruction and Development—IBRD (World Bank)

Address: 1818 H St, NW, Washington, DC 20433, USA.
Telephone: (202) 477-1234.
Telex: 248423.
Fax: (202) 477-6391.

The IBRD was established on 27 December 1945. Initially it was concerned with post-war reconstruction in Europe; since then its aim has been to assist the economic development of member nations by making loans where private capital is not available on reasonable terms to finance productive investments. Loans are made either direct to governments, or to private enterprises with the guarantee of their governments. The IBRD has three affiliates, the International Development Association (IDA, q.v.), the International Finance Corporation (IFC, q.v.) and the Multilateral Investment Guarantee Agency (MIGA, q.v.). The 'World Bank', as it is commonly known, comprises the IBRD and IDA.

MEMBERS

There are 153 members: see Table on pp. 52–54. Only members of the International Monetary Fund (IMF, q.v.) may be considered for membership in the World Bank. Subscriptions to the capital stock of the Bank are based on each member's quota in the IMF, which is designed to reflect the country's relative economic strength. Voting rights are related to shareholdings.

Organization
(October 1990)

Officers and staff of the IBRD serve concurrently as officers and staff in the International Development Association (IDA). The World Bank has offices in New York, Paris, Geneva and Tokyo; regional missions in Nairobi (for eastern Africa), Abidjan (for western Africa) and Bangkok; and resident missions in 45 countries.

BOARD OF GOVERNORS

The Board of Governors consists of one Governor appointed by each member nation. Typically, a Governor is the country's finance minister, central bank governor, or a minister or an official of comparable rank. The Board normally meets once a year.

EXECUTIVE DIRECTORS

With the exception of certain powers specifically reserved to them by the Articles of Agreement, the Governors of the Bank have delegated their powers for the conduct of the general operations of the World Bank to a Board of Executive Directors that performs its duties on a full-time basis at the Bank's headquarters. There are 22 Executive Directors; each Director selects an Alternate. Five Directors are appointed by the five members having the largest number of shares of capital stock, and the rest are elected by the Governors representing the other members. The President of the Bank is Chairman of the Board.

The Executive Directors fulfil dual responsibilities. First, they represent the interests of their country or groups of countries. Second, they exercise their authority as delegated by the Governors in overseeing the policies of the Bank and evaluating completed projects. Since the Bank operates on the basis of consensus (formal votes are rare), this dual role involves frequent communication and consultations with governments so as to reflect accurately their views in Board discussions.

The Directors consider and decide on Bank policy and on all loan and credit proposals. They are also responsible for presentation to the Board of Governors at its Annual Meetings of an audit of accounts, an administrative budget, the *Annual Report* on the operations and policies of the World Bank, and any other matter that, in their judgement, requires submission to the Board of Governors. Matters may be submitted to the Governors at the Annual Meetings or at any time between Annual Meetings.

OFFICERS

President and Chairman of Executive Directors: BARBER B. CONABLE.
Senior Vice-President, Policy, Research and External Affairs: WILFRIED P. THALWITZ.
Senior Vice-President, Operations: MOEEN A. QURESHI.
Senior Vice-President, Finance: ERNEST STERN.

OFFICES

New York Office and World Bank Mission to the United Nations: 747 Third Ave (26th Floor), New York, NY 10017, USA; Special Rep. to UN G. DAVID LOOS.
European Office: 66 ave d'Iéna, 75116 Paris, France; tel (1) 40-69-30-00; telex 842-620628; fax (1) 47-20-19-66; Dir OLIVIER LAFOURCADE.
Regional Mission in Eastern Africa: POB 30577; Reinsurance Plaza, Taifa Rd, Nairobi, Kenya; Dir PETER EIGEN.
Regional Mission in Western Africa: BP 1850; Corner Booker Washington and Jacques AKA Sts, Abidjan 01, Côte d'Ivoire; Chief ELKYN CHAPARRO.
Regional Mission in Thailand: Udom Vidhya Bldg, 956 Rama IV Rd, Sala Daeng, Bangkok 10500, Thailand; Chief PHILIPPE E. ANNEZ.

Activities
FINANCIAL OPERATIONS

IBRD capital is derived from members' subscriptions to capital shares, the calculation of which is based on their quotas in the International Monetary Fund (q.v.). In April 1988 the Board of Governors approved an increase of about 80% in the IBRD's authorized capital, to US $171,000m. On 30 June 1990 the total subscribed capital of the IBRD was US $125,262m. of which the paid-in portion is 9%; the remainder is subject to call if required. Most of the IBRD's lendable funds come from its borrowing, on commercial terms, in world capital markets, and also from its retained earnings and the flow of repayments on its loans. IBRD loans carry a variable interest rate, rather than a rate fixed at the time of borrowing.

IBRD loans usually have a 'grace period' of five years and are repayable over 15 years or fewer. Loans are made to governments, or must be guaranteed by the government concerned, and are normally made for projects likely to offer a commercially viable rate of return. In 1980 the World Bank introduced structural adjustment lending, which (instead of financing specific projects) supports programmes and changes necessary to modify the structure of an economy so that it can restore or maintain its growth and viability in its balance of payments over the medium term.

The IBRD and IDA together made new lending and investment commitments totalling $20,702m. during the year ending 30 June 1990, compared with $21,367m. in the previous year. During the year, the IBRD alone approved 121 loans to 36 countries and two regions, totalling $15,179.7m., compared with $16,433m. in the previous year, the largest borrowers being Brazil, India, Indonesia and Mexico (see table). Disbursements by the IBRD in the year ending 30 June 1990 amounted to $13,859m., compared with $11,310m. in the previous year. (For details of IDA operations, see separate chapter on IDA.)

IBRD operations were supported by borrowings in international capital markets, which totalled $11,720m. in the year ending 30 June 1990 ($9,286m. in the previous year). During the year the IBRD made a profit of $1,046m.

In 1987 the World Bank undertook to strengthen its work in alleviating poverty, and to attempt to mitigate the social effects of economic adjustment programmes. It subsequently increased its focus on operations which promote productive employment and give the poor greater access to health care, education and physical infrastructure; in particular, emphasis was placed on operations designed to improve conditions for women. Improvements in food security were also to be given greater support. A 'Special Programme of Assistance' for sub-Saharan Africa (1988–90, extended to 1993) increased concessional lending to heavily-indebted and impoverished African countries. During the late 1980s priority was also given to assisting 17 heavily-indebted middle-income countries (of which 11 were in Latin America). From 1987 the World Bank accorded greater importance to the protection of the environment and to monitoring the impact of projects (particularly in agriculture and energy) on the environment. In 1989/90 systematic 'screening' of all new projects was introduced, in order to assess their environmental impact. In the same year, the Bank began a 'core poverty programme' for the direct alleviation of poverty among specific groups. Economic adjustment operations received 19% of IBRD

INTERNATIONAL ORGANIZATIONS

United Nations (Specialized Agencies)

EXECUTIVE DIRECTORS AND THEIR VOTING POWER (June 1990)

Executive Director	Casting Votes of	IBRD Total votes	IBRD % of total	IDA Total votes	IDA % of total
Appointed:					
E. Patrick Coady	United States	162,773	15.37	1,189,128	17.41
Masaki Shiratori	Japan	94,020	8.88	664,752	9.73
Gerhard Boehmer	Federal Republic of Germany	72,649	6.86	478,598	7.01
Frank Cassell	United Kingdom	69,647	6.58	392,447	5.74
Jean-Pierre Landau	France	55,477	5.24	267,428	3.91
Elected:					
Jacques de Groote (Belgium)	Austria, Belgium, Hungary, Luxembourg, Turkey	53,945	5.09	236,777	3.47
Paul Arlman (Netherlands)	Cyprus, Israel, Netherlands, Romania*, Yugoslavia	46,871	4.42	218,038	3.19
Frank Potter (Canada)	Antigua and Barbuda*, The Bahamas*, Barbados*, Belize, Canada, Dominica, Grenada, Guyana, Ireland, Jamaica*, Saint Christopher and Nevis, Saint Lucia, Saint Vincent and the Grenadines	46,808	4.42	293,978	4.30
Jorge Pinto (Mexico)	Costa Rica, El Salvador, Guatemala, Honduras, Mexico, Nicaragua, Panama, Spain, Venezuela*	43,300	4.09	186,970	2.74
Jonas H. Haralz (Iceland)	Denmark, Finland, Iceland, Norway, Sweden	42,326	4.00	324,257	4.75
Chang-Yuel Lim (Republic of Korea)	Australia, Kiribati, Korea (Republic), New Zealand, Papua New Guinea, Solomon Islands, Vanuatu, Western Samoa	39,580	3.74	165,277	2.42
Cesare Caranza (Italy)	Greece, Italy, Malta*, Poland, Portugal*	39,570	3.74	391,478	5.73
J. S. Baijal (India)	Bangladesh, Bhutan, India, Sri Lanka	38,497	3.63	293,094	4.29
Zhang Junyi (China)	People's Republic of China	35,221	3.33	138,951	2.03
Fawzi Hamad al-Sultan (Kuwait)	Bahrain*, Egypt, Iraq, Jordan, Kuwait, Lebanon, Maldives, Oman, Pakistan, Qatar*, Syria, United Arab Emirates, Yemen Arab Republic†	32,337	3.05	255,712	3.74
Mourad Benachenhou (Algeria)	Afghanistan, Algeria, Ghana, Iran, Libya, Morocco, Tunisia, Yemen (People's Democratic Republic)†	30,469	2.88	120,777	1.77
Vibul Aunsnunta (Thailand)	Fiji, Indonesia, Laos, Malaysia, Myanmar, Nepal, Singapore*, Thailand, Tonga, Viet-Nam	29,523	2.79	200,362	2.93
Eduardo Wiesner (Colombia)	Brazil, Colombia, Dominican Republic, Ecuador, Haiti, Philippines, Suriname*, Trinidad and Tobago	28,641	2.70	213,146	3.12
J. S. A. Funna (Sierra Leone)	Botswana, Burundi, Ethiopia, The Gambia, Guinea, Kenya, Lesotho, Liberia, Malawi, Mozambique, Nigeria, Seychelles*, Sierra Leone, Sudan, Swaziland, Tanzania, Uganda, Zambia, Zimbabwe	25,623	2.42	230,481	3.37
Ibrahim A. al-Assaf (Saudi Arabia)	Saudi Arabia	25,390	2.40	226,623	3.32
Raymundo Morales (Peru)	Argentina, Bolivia, Chile, Paraguay, Peru, Uruguay*	24,745	2.34	138,856	2.03
André Milongo (Congo)	Benin, Burkina Faso, Cameroon, Cape Verde, Central African Republic, Chad, Comoros, Congo, Côte d'Ivoire, Djibouti, Equatorial Guinea, Gabon, Guinea-Bissau, Madagascar, Mali, Mauritania, Mauritius, Niger, Rwanda, São Tomé and Príncipe, Senegal, Somalia, Togo, Zaire	21,843	2.06	204,717	3.00

* Members of IBRD only (not IDA).
† From 13 July 1990 the newly-formed Republic of Yemen, comprising the former Yemen Arab Republic and People's Democratic Republic of Yemen, was substituted for these countries in the World Bank's records as being a single member. The Republic of Yemen was allocated 1,491 votes in the IBRD, and 20,029 votes in IDA. Fawzi Hamad al-Sultan was to be the Executive Director casting the votes of Yemen.

Note: Angola (2,926 votes in IBRD and 45,662 votes in IDA), Cambodia (464 votes in IBRD and 7,826 in IDA) and South Africa (13,712 votes in IBRD and 20,119 in IDA) did not participate in the 1988 regular election of Executive Directors. Angola joined the World Bank in September 1989. Bulgaria, Czechoslovakia and Namibia joined the World Bank in September 1990.

and IDA commitments in the year to 30 June 1990; agricultural projects received 18%, energy 16% and transport 13%.

TECHNICAL ASSISTANCE

The provision of technical assistance to member countries has become a major component of World Bank activities. The economic, sector and project analysis undertaken by the Bank in the normal course of its operations is the vehicle for considerable technical assistance. In addition, project loans and credits may include funds earmarked specifically for feasibility studies, resource surveys, management or planning advice, and training. During the calendar year 1989, technical assistance components of loans amounted to $1,185.8m. In addition, 12 free-standing technical assistance loans were approved, amounting to about $126m.

The Bank serves as an executing agency for projects financed by the UN Development Programme. At mid-1990 the number in progress was 162, with a total allocation of $260.9m. The Bank also administers projects financed by various trust funds.

Technical assistance (usually reimbursable) is also extended to countries that do not need Bank financial support, e.g. for training and transfer of technology.

ECONOMIC RESEARCH AND STUDIES

The World Bank's research, carried out by its own research staff, is intended to provide a source of policy advice to members, and to encourage the development of indigenous research. The principal areas of research in 1989/90 included: external debt issues; food security and alleviation of poverty; debt and the effects of economic adjustment policies; public-sector management; development of the private sector; conservation of the environment; and reform of socialist economies. The last three topics were to be given priority from 1990.

Consultative Group for International Agricultural Research—CGIAR: founded in 1971 under the sponsorship of the World Bank, FAO and UNDP. The Bank is chairman of the group (which includes governments, private foundations and multilateral development agencies) and provides its secretariat. The group was formed to raise financial support for international agricultural research work for improving crops and animal production in the developing countries. The group supports 13 research centres; donations for the calendar year 1989 amounted to $225m. (of which the Bank provided $33m.). Exec. Sec. Alexander von der Osten-Sacken.

INTERNATIONAL ORGANIZATIONS — United Nations (Specialized Agencies)

CO-OPERATION WITH OTHER ORGANIZATIONS

The World Bank co-operates closely with other UN bodies through consultations, meetings, and joint activities; co-operation with UNDP and WHO, in their programmes to improve health, nutrition and sanitation, is especially important. It collaborates with the IMF in implementing economic adjustment programmes in developing countries. The Bank holds regular consultations with the European Community and OECD on development issues, and the Bank-NGO Committee provides an annual forum for discussion with non-governmental organizations (NGOs). The Bank chairs meetings of donor governments and organizations for the co-ordination of aid to particular countries.

The Bank conducts co-financing and aid co-ordination projects with official aid agencies, export credit institutions, and commercial banks. During the year ending 30 June 1990 a total of 127 IBRD and IDA projects involved co-financers' contributions amounting to $12,978.5m. In 1983 the Bank announced the introduction of a set of new co-financing instruments designed to increase the participation of commercial banks in project loans. In 1989/90 commercial co-financing under these instruments amounted to $657m.

EVALUATION

The World Bank's Operations Evaluation Department studies and publishes the results of projects after a loan has been fully disbursed, so as to identify problems and possible improvements in future activities. Internal auditing is also carried out, to monitor the effectiveness of the Bank's management.

IBRD INSTITUTIONS

Economic Development Institute—EDI: founded in 1955. Training is provided for government officials at the middle and upper levels of responsibility who are concerned with development programmes and projects. Courses are in national economic management and project analysis. The EDI has become one of the most important of the Bank's activities in technical assistance. In its overseas courses, the aim is to build up local capability to conduct projects courses in future. The Institute also produces training materials, and administers a fellowships scheme and the World Bank graduate scholarship programme (funded by the Government of Japan), which awarded 43 scholarships for post-graduate development studies in the 1989/90 academic year. In the year ending 30 June 1990 99 EDI courses and seminars were held, mostly abroad. Dir AMNON GOLAN.

International Centre for Settlement of Investment Disputes—ICSID: founded in 1966 under the Convention of the Settlement of Investment Disputes between States and Nationals of Other States. The Convention was designed to encourage the growth of private foreign investment for economic development, by creating the possibility, always subject to the consent of both parties, for a Contracting State and a foreign investor who is a national of another Contracting State to settle any legal dispute that might arise out of such an investment by conciliation and/or arbitration before an impartial, international forum. The governing body of the Centre is its Administrative Council, composed of one representative of each Contracting State, all of whom have equal voting power. The President of the World Bank is (ex officio) the non-voting Chairman of the Administrative Council.

By the end of June 1990, 92 states had signed and ratified the Convention. At mid-1990 there were six disputes before the Centre. Sec.-Gen. IBRAHIM F. I. SHIHATA.

PUBLICATIONS

World Bank Catalog of Publications.
World Bank News (weekly).
World Bank Annual Report.
World Development Report (annually).
World Bank Economic Review (3 a year).
World Bank Research Observer.
Research News (quarterly).
World Bank Atlas (annually).
Abstracts of Current Studies: The World Bank Research Program (annually).
Annual Review of Project Performance Results.
Staff Working Papers.
ICSID Annual Report.
ICSID Review—Foreign Investment Law Journal (2 a year).

World Bank Statistics

LENDING OPERATIONS, BY PURPOSE
(year ending 30 June 1990; US $ million)

	IBRD	IDA	Total
Agriculture and rural development	1,994.5	1,661.6	3,656.1
Development finance companies	945.0	326.7	1,271.7
Education	530.1	956.5	1,486.6
Energy	2,998.5	219.8	3,218.3
Industry	650.5	145.1	795.6
Non-project	2,600.0	444.0	3,044.0
Population, health and nutrition	524.6	408.8	933.4
Public-sector management	480.0	45.6	525.6
Small-scale enterprises	50.0	157.5	207.5
Technical assistance	96.0	45.0	141.0
Telecommunications	592.2	24.5	616.7
Transportation	2,250.2	535.1	2,785.3
Urban development	702.7	299.4	1,002.1
Water supply and sewerage	697.4	252.4	931.8
Total	**15,179.7**	**5,522.0**	**20,701.7**

IBRD INCOME AND EXPENDITURE
(US $'000, year ending 30 June)

Revenue	1989	1990
Income from loans:		
Interest	6,393,924	6,627,871
Commitment charges	271,695	139,223
Income from investments	1,586,002	1,491,928
Other income	22,260	58,117
Total income	**8,273,881**	**8,317,139**

Expenditure	1989	1990
Interest on borrowings	6,139,685	6,077,627
Amortization of issuance costs	155,996	152,003
Administrative expenses	462,352	494,119
Provision for loan losses	357,607	357,416
Other financial expenses	4,117	10,599
Total	**7,119,757**	**7,091,764**
Operating income	**1,154,124**	**1,225,375**
Contributions to special programmes	60,237	74,015
Cumulative effect of change in accounting principle	—	105,500
Net income	**1,093,887**	**1,045,860**

INTERNATIONAL ORGANIZATIONS — United Nations (Specialized Agencies)

IBRD LOANS AND IDA CREDITS APPROVED, BY REGION (1 July 1989–30 June 1990)

	IBRD Loans[1]		IDA Credits[1]		Total[1]	
	Number[2]	US $ m.	Number[2]	US $ m.	Number[2]	US $ m.
Africa:						
Benin	—	—	1	2.5	1	2.5
Burkina Faso	—	—	1	22.2	1	22.2
Burundi	—	—	2	71.2	2	71.2
Cameroon	3	51.5	—	—	3	51.5
Central African Republic	—	—	3	126.0	3	126.0
Chad	—	—	1	13.4	1	13.4
Côte d'Ivoire	6	497.9	—	—	6	497.9
Djibouti	—	—	1	5.8	1	5.8
Ethiopia	—	—	2	75.2	2	75.2
Gabon	1	5.0	—	—	1	5.0
The Gambia	—	—	2	21.6	2	21.6
Ghana	—	—	4	185.7	4	185.7
Guinea	—	—	5	175.0	5	175.0
Guinea-Bissau	—	—	1	23.6	1	23.6
Kenya	—	—	5	201.6	5	201.6
Lesotho	—	—	1	12.1	1	12.1
Madagascar	—	—	5	148.4	5	148.4
Malawi	—	—	3	140.4	3	140.4
Mali	—	—	1	53.0	1	53.0
Mauritania	—	—	3	75.0	3	75.0
Mauritius	1	30.0	—	—	1	30.0
Mozambique	—	—	4	143.1	4	143.1
Niger	—	—	1	19.9	1	19.9
Nigeria	6	533.1	1	120.0	7	653.1
Rwanda	—	—	2	44.4	2	44.4
São Tomé and Príncipe	—	—	1	9.8	1	9.8
Senegal	—	—	5	185.0	5	185.0
Somalia	—	—	2	54.6	2	54.6
Sudan	—	—	1	82.2	1	82.2
Tanzania	—	—	5	513.6	5	513.6
Togo	—	—	—	0.2	—	0.2
Uganda	—	—	3	214.5	3	214.5
Western Africa region	1	15.0	—	40.0	1	55.0
Zaire	—	—	1	5.9	1	5.9
Zimbabwe	1	14.5	—	—	1	14.5
Total	19	1,147.0	67	2,785.9	86	3,932.9
Asia:						
Bangladesh	—	—	5	540.1	5	540.1
China, People's Republic	—	—	5	590.0	52	590.0
Fiji	1	16.2	—	—	1	16.2
India	10	1,100.0	1	832.4	11	1,940.4
Indonesia	9	1,632.8	—	—	9	1,632.8
Korea, Republic	3	110.6	—	—	3	110.6
Laos	—	—	2	44.7	2	44.7
Malaysia	2	154.2	—	—	2	154.2
Maldives	—	—	1	7.5	1	7.5
Nepal	—	—	1	47.2	1	47.2
Papua New Guinea	2	67.2	—	—	2	67.2
Philippines	7	941.8	—	—	7	941.8
Sri Lanka	—	—	2	143.4	2	143.4
Thailand	2	144.0	—	—	2	144.0
Tonga	—	—	1	3.0	1	3.0
Western Samoa	—	—	1	14.0	1	14.0
Total	36	4,174.8	19	2,222.3	55	6,397.1
Europe, Middle East, and North Africa:						
Algeria	4	457.5	—	—	4	457.5
Cyprus	1	25.0	—	—	1	25.0
Egypt	2	61.5	—	—	2	61.5
Hungary	3	366.0	—	—	3	366.0
Jordan	2	175.0	—	—	2	175.0
Morocco	5	482.5	—	—	5	482.5
Pakistan	4	617.5	2	208.3	6	825.8
Poland	5	781.0	—	—	5	781.0
Tunisia	2	147.0	—	—	2	147.0
Turkey	3	326.2	—	—	3	326.2
Yemen Arab Republic	—	—	2	30.0	2	30.0
Yemen, People's Democratic Republic	—	—	3	37.5	3	37.5
Yugoslavia	2	692.0	—	—	2	692.0
Total	33	4,131.2	7	275.8	40	4,407.0
Latin America and the Caribbean:						
Bolivia	—	—	4	100.2	4	100.2
Brazil	8	1,569.0	—	—	8	1,569.0
Caribbean region	1	20.0	—	12.0	1	32.0
Chile	2	354.0	—	—	2	354.0
Colombia	3	157.2	—	—	3	157.2
Costa Rica	1	60.0	—	—	1	60.0
Ecuador	1	50.0	—	—	1	50.0
Guyana	—	—	2	81.0	2	81.0
Haiti	—	—	2	39.6	2	39.6
Jamaica	2	55.0	—	—	2	55.0
Mexico	7	2,607.5	—	—	7	2,607.5
Saint Lucia	1	2.5	—	5.2	1	7.7
Trinidad and Tobago	2	44.0	—	—	2	44.0
Uruguay	2	127.5	—	—	2	127.5
Venezuela	3	680.0	—	—	3	680.0
Total	33	5,726.7	8	238.0	41	5,964.7
Grand total	121	15,179.7	101	5,522.0	222	20,701.7

[1] Supplements are included in amounts, but are not counted as separate lending operations.
[2] Joint IBRD/IDA operations are counted only once, as IBRD operations.

INTERNATIONAL ORGANIZATIONS   United Nations (Specialized Agencies)

IBRD OPERATIONS AND RESOURCES, 1981-90 (years ending 30 June)

	1980/81	1981/82	1982/83	1983/84	1984/85	1985/86	1986/87	1987/88	1988/89	1989/90
Amounts in US $ m.										
Loans approved*	8,809	10,330	11,138	11,947	11,356	13,179	14,188	14,762	16,433	15,180
Disbursements†	5,063	6,326	6,817	8,580	8,645	8,263	11,383	11,636	11,310	13,859
Total income	2,999	3,372	4,232	4,655	5,529	6,815	7,689	8,549	8,274	8,317
Net income	610	598	752	600	1,137	1,243	1,113	1,004	1,094	1,046
General reserve	2,567	2,772	3,052	3,337	3,586	4,896	6,284	7,242	7,576	9,196
New borrowings	5,069	8,521	10,292	9,831	11,086	10,609	9,321	10,832	9,286	11,720
Subscribed capital	36,614	43,165	52,089	56,011	58,846	77,526	85,231	91,436	115,668	125,262
Operations, Countries										
Operations approved	140	150	136	129	131	131	127	118	119	121
Recipient countries	50	43	43	43	44	41	39	37	38	36

* Excludes loans to IFC.
† Excludes disbursements on loans to IFC.
Source: *World Bank Annual Report 1990*.

International Development Association—IDA

Address: 1818 H Street, NW, Washington, DC 20433, USA.
Telephone: (202) 477-1234.
Telex: 248423.
Fax: (202) 477-6391.

The International Development Association began operations in November 1960. Affiliated to the IBRD (see above), IDA advances capital to the poorer developing member countries on more flexible terms than those offered by the IBRD.

MEMBERS

136 members: see Table on pp. 52-54.

Organization

Officers and staff of the IBRD serve concurrently as officers and staff of IDA.
President and Chairman of Executive Directors: BARBER B. CONABLE (ex officio).

Activities

IDA assistance is aimed at the poorer developing countries, numbering more than 40 (i.e. those with a per caput GNP of less than US $650 in 1988 dollars). Under IDA lending conditions, credits can be extended to countries whose balance of payments could not sustain the burden of repayment required for IBRD loans. Terms are more favourable than those provided by the IBRD; credits are for a period of 35 or 40 years, with a 'grace period' of 10 years, and no interest charges.

IDA's total resources, consisting of members' subscriptions and supplementary resources (additional subscriptions and contributions) amounted to US $54,628m. on 30 June 1990. Resources are replenished periodically by contributions from the more affluent member countries. Owing to a decision by the government of the USA to cut its annual contributions by 20% to $750m., a total of $9,000m. was made available for the seventh replenishment (covering the period 1984-87), compared with the IDA target figure of $16,000m., and the previous three-year replenishment amounting to $12,000m. Supplementary funding of $1,200m. was provided by developed countries (excluding the USA). Negotiations on an eighth replenishment of $12,400m. were concluded in 1986, and a ninth, of $15,500m., was approved in 1989 for 1991-93.

A Special Facility for Sub-Saharan Africa, administered by IDA, was established in 1985 with funds of $1,250m., to finance structural adjustment, sectoral reform programmes and rehabilitation. The funds were fully disbursed by June 1990.

During the year ending 30 June 1990, 101 IDA operations were approved for 43 countries, at a cost of $5,522m. Some 30% of IDA assistance approved was for agriculture and rural development, 17% for education and 10% for transport. About 50% of assistance was for Africa and 40% was for Asia (excluding Pakistan) (see table on p. 65). During 1991-93 priority was to be given to the reduction of poverty, support for 'sound macroeconomic and sectoral policies' and the protection of the environment.

IDA OPERATIONS AND RESOURCES, 1981-90 (years ending 30 June)

	1980/81	1981/82	1982/83	1983/84	1984/85	1985/86	1986/87	1987/88	1988/89	1989/90
Amounts in US $ m.										
Commitments	3,482	2,686	3,341	3,575	3,028	3,140	3,486	4,459	4,934	5,522
Disbursements	1,878	2,067	2,596	2,524	2,491	3,155	3,088	3,397	3,597	3,845
Operations, Countries										
Operations approved*	106	97	107	106	105	97	108	99	106	101
Recipient countries	40	42	44	43	45	37	39	36	42	43

*Joint IBRD/IDA operations are counted only once, as IBRD operations.
Source: *World Bank Annual Report 1990*.

INTERNATIONAL ORGANIZATIONS *United Nations (Specialized Agencies)*

International Finance Corporation—IFC

Address: 1818 H Street, NW, Washington, DC 20433, USA.
Telephone: (202) 477-1234.
Telex: 248423.
Fax: (202) 477-6391.

IFC was founded in 1956 as an affiliate of the World Bank to encourage the growth of productive private enterprise in its member countries, particularly in the less-developed areas.

MEMBERS
138 members: see Table on pp. 52–54.

Organization
(October 1990)

IFC is a separate legal entity in the World Bank Group. Executive Directors of the World Bank also serve as Directors of IFC. The President of the World Bank is ex-officio Chairman of the IFC Board of Directors, which has appointed him President of IFC. Subject to his overall supervision, the day-to-day operations of IFC are conducted by its staff under the direction of the Executive Vice-President. In June 1990 IFC had 595 regular members of staff.

PRINCIPAL OFFICERS
President: BARBER B. CONABLE.
Executive Vice-President: Sir WILLIAM RYRIE.

REGIONAL OFFICES
There are Regional Missions in Côte d'Ivoire (for western Africa), Egypt (for the Middle East), India, Indonesia, Kenya (for eastern Africa), Morocco (for North Africa), Pakistan, the Philippines, Thailand and Zimbabwe (for southern Africa). There are also offices in Austria, France, Japan and the United Kingdom, and Resident Missions in Brazil, Nigeria and Turkey. The Africa Project Development Facility and the Caribbean Project Development Facility are both based at IFC's Washington headquarters.

Activities

IFC functions as follows:

1. In association with private investors, invests without government guarantee in productive private enterprises of economic priority in member countries where sufficient private capital is not available on reasonable terms.
2. Stimulates the international flow of private capital to developing countries.
3. Encourages the development of local capital markets.
4. Invests in and gives technical help to development finance companies, and assists other institutions which also support economic development and follow policies generally consistent with those of IFC.
5. Commits limited amounts of funds for promotional purposes, to help bring development enterprises into being.
6. Revolves its portfolio by sales of its investments to other investors.

IFC's authorized capital is US $1,300m., following the authorization of $650m. in new shares in 1985. At 30 June 1990 paid-in capital was $1,072m. The World Bank was originally the principal source of borrowed funds, but IFC also borrows from private capital markets, which provided 81% of total borrowings in 1989/90. IFC's net income almost doubled to $196.5m. in 1988/89, decreasing to $157m. in 1989/90.

In the year ending 30 June 1990 investments approved by IFC amounted to $2,201m. for 122 projects (compared with $1,710m. for 92 projects in the previous year). Of the total approved, $1,200m. was for loans and $257m. was for equity or equity-like investments. Participation by other investors brought the total amount invested in these projects to $9,377m.: in other words, for every $1 that IFC agreed to invest, other investors were to invest about $5.2. Disbursements for IFC's account amounted to $1,001m. (compared with $870m. in the previous year).

Projects approved during the year were located in 38 countries; one was regional and three world-wide in scope. The largest proportion of investment finance was allocated to Latin America and the Caribbean (33%); Asia received 32%, Africa (including Morocco and Tunisia) 16% and Europe and the Middle East 11%. About 22% of IFC's investment was in countries with a per caput annual income of less than $830. The Corporation invested in a wide variety of business and financial institutions in the following sectors: capital markets and financial services; food and agribusiness; mining; energy; tourism; and various types of manufacturing, including cement, chemicals, electronics, wood and paper, shipbuilding, and textiles. IFC also undertakes technical assistance for attracting foreign investment, the creation of new enterprises and the restructuring of existing ones, often in co-operation with the UN Development Programme (UNDP).

IFC's five-year programme for 1985–89 included four major objectives: to provide technical and financial assistance to firms which, although otherwise sound, are faced with severe market and financial difficulties and must re-structure their businesses; to give increased attention to high-priority development projects in low-income countries, especially in agriculture and agro-industry; to increase investment in petroleum and gas exploration and development; and to expand its activities in Africa south of the Sahara. Real net investment was expected to expand by about 7% per year during the period. During 1986/87 the Board made certain adjustments to the programme: restructuring activities were to be intensified; more attention was to be given to special services of an innovative nature in sub-Saharan Africa; and the energy exploration and development initiative was to be revised in response to changing market needs and opportunities. During the period IFC also adopted new approaches to loan funding that bring to borrowers advantages arising from developments in international financial markets. IFC's clients were in future to have access to some of the new financial instruments and techniques actively in use in the industrialized countries, but seldom offered to the private sector of the developing countries.

It was decided by the Board of Directors that, from 1989/90 onwards, IFC would adopt a 'rolling' three-year planning process, with annual updating of objectives for the next three years. Emphasis was to be placed on closer co-operation with the World Bank, particularly in the following areas: development of the financial sector in member countries; privatization of public enterprises; encouraging private investment; and conducting research and policy studies. IFC was expected to play an important part in the development of the private sector in eastern Europe from 1990 onwards.

IFC acts as the executing agency of the Caribbean Project Development Facility (CPDF), established by UNDP in 1981 to raise funds for new investment in the Caribbean: operations were extended to six Central American countries in 1989. In 1989 CPDF provided advisory services for nine proposed new projects. In 1986 IFC, in co-operation with UNDP and the African Development Bank, launched the Africa Project Development Facility (APDF). IFC manages the Facility, which consists of two teams of experts based in Nairobi, Kenya (covering eastern Africa), Abidjan, Côte d'Ivoire (covering western and central Africa), and Harare, Zimbabwe (covering southern Africa). APDF aims to support the private sector of African countries by helping African entrepreneurs to develop sound investment projects (small and medium-sized businesses) and to find financing for them. During 1989 APDF provided advisory services for 24 projects, and helped to secure financing for them. In 1990 a similar facility was established for the South Pacific region.

The Emerging Markets Growth Fund (EMGF) was initiated in 1987 to invest in publicly listed shares in certain developing countries, and a similar fund, the Emerging Markets Investment Fund (directed mainly towards Japanese investors) was established in 1988. The technique known as Guaranteed Recovery of Investment Principal (GRIP) was introduced during 1986/87, as a means of sharing the risks with foreign equity investors in certain cases.

In April 1989 IFC (with UNDP, the African Development Bank and other agencies and governments) began operating a new facility, the African Management Services Company, which helps to find qualified senior executives from around the world to work with African companies, assist in the training of local managers, and provide supporting services. In July 1988 IFC established the Africa Enterprise Fund, with capital of $60m., to provide financial and non-financial assistance directly to small and medium-sized enterprises. The Fund was expected to invest in about 100 projects over an initial three-year period.

The Foreign Investment Advisory Service is operated jointly by IFC and MIGA (q.v.), and provides advice to governments on attracting foreign investment.

PUBLICATION

Annual Report.

INTERNATIONAL ORGANIZATIONS   United Nations (Specialized Agencies)

IFC OPERATIONS AND RESOURCES, 1981–90 (fiscal years ending 30 June)

	1981	1982	1983	1984	1985	1986	1987	1988	1989†	1990†
Approved investments										
Number of new projects	56	65	58	62	75	85	92	95	92	122
Amount (gross US $ million)	811	612	845	696	937	1,156	920	1,270	1,710	2,201
Total project costs* (US $ million)	3,340	2,936	2,894	2,473	2,768	3,588	4,343	5,010	9,698	9,377
Disbursements (IFC's own account)	292	246	228	238	266	325	328	762	870	1,001
Resources and income (US $ million)										
Borrowings	509	531	536	582	825	1,223	1,581	2,047	2,255	3,580
Paid-in capital	392	497	544	544	546	602	722	850	948	1,072
Accumulated earnings	159	181	204	230	258	284	338	438	635	792
Net income	19.5	21.6	23.0	26.3	28.3	25.4	53.8	100.6	196.5	157.0

* Including investment mobilized from other sources.
† Includes Africa Enterprise Fund projects.

Multilateral Investment Guarantee Agency—MIGA

Address: 1818 H Street, NW, Washington, DC 20433, USA.
Telephone: (202) 477-1234.
Telex: 248423.
Fax: (202) 477-6391.

MIGA was founded in 1988 as an affiliate of the World Bank, to encourage the flow of investments for productive purposes among its member countries, especially developing countries, through the mitigation of non-commercial barriers to investment (especially political risk).

MEMBERS

By mid-1990 MIGA had 58 member countries. Membership is open to all countries that are members of the World Bank, and Switzerland.

Organization
(October 1990)

MIGA is legally and financially separate from the World Bank. It is supervised by a Board of Directors.
President: BARBER B. CONABLE.
Executive Vice-President: YOSHIO TERASAWA.

Activities

The convention establishing MIGA took effect in April 1988. Authorized capital was US $1,082m. By October 1990 the convention had been signed by 95 countries.

MIGA's purpose is to guarantee eligible investments against losses resulting from non-commercial risks, under four main categories:

transfer risk resulting from host government restrictions on currency conversion and transfer;

risk of loss resulting from legislative or administrative actions of the host government;

repudiation by the host government of contracts with investors in cases in which the investor has no access to a competent forum;

the risk of armed conflict and civil unrest.

MIGA also provides policy and advisory services to promote foreign investment in developing countries. Jointly with IFC, MIGA operates the Foreign Investment Advisory Service (FIAS), which advises governments on their legislation and policies relating to foreign investment.

During its first full year of operations (1989/90), MIGA issued guarantees for four projects, in Chile (two), Hungary and Indonesia, involving one Canadian and three US investors. Policy and advisory services were provided to 22 countries, and investment promotion conferences were held in Ghana and Hungary.

International Civil Aviation Organization—ICAO

Address: 1000 Sherbrooke St West, Montreal, PQ H3A 2R2, Canada.
Telephone: (514) 285-8219.
Telex: 05-24513.
Fax: (514) 288-4772.

The Convention on International Civil Aviation was signed in Chicago in 1944. As a result ICAO was founded in 1947 to develop the techniques of international air navigation and to help in the planning and improvement of international air transport.

MEMBERS
161 members: see Table on pp. 52–54.

Organization
(October 1990)

ASSEMBLY
Composed of representatives of all member states, the Assembly is the organization's legislative body and meets at least once in three years. It reviews the work of the organization, sets out the work programme for the next three years, approves the budget and determines members' contributions.

COUNCIL
Composed of representatives of 33 member states, elected by the Assembly. It is the executive body, and establishes and supervises subsidiary technical committees and makes recommendations to member governments; meets in virtually continuous session; elects the President, appoints the Secretary-General, and administers the finances of the organization. The functions of the Council are:

to adopt international standards and recommended practices and incorporate them as annexes to the Convention on International Civil Aviation;

to arbitrate between member states on matters concerning aviation and implementation of the Convention;

to investigate any situation which presents avoidable obstacles to development of international air navigation;

to take whatever steps are necessary to maintain safety and regularity of operation of international air transport;

to provide technical assistance to the developing countries under the UN Development Programme and other assistance programmes.

President of the Council: Dr ASSAD KOTAITE (Lebanon).
Secretary-General: Dr SHIVINDER SINGH SIDHU (India).

AIR NAVIGATION COMMISSION

The Commission comprises 15 members.
President: V. J. SINGH.

STANDING COMMITTEES

These include the Air Transport Committee, the Committee on Joint Support of Air Navigation Services, the Finance Committee, the Legal Committee, the Committee on Unlawful Interference, the Personnel Committee, and the Edward Warner Award Committee.

REGIONAL OFFICES

Western and Central Africa: BP 2356, Dakar, Senegal.
Eastern and Southern Africa: POB 46294, Nairobi, Kenya.
Asia and Pacific: 252/1 Vipavadee Rangsit Rd, Ladyao, Bangkhen, Bangkok 10900, Thailand.
Europe: 3 bis, Villa Emile-Bergerat, 92522 Neuilly-sur-Seine Cedex, France.
Middle East: 9 Shagaret el-Dorr, Zamalek, Cairo, Egypt.
North America, Central America and the Caribbean: Apartado Postal 5-377, CP 11590, México 5, DF, Mexico.
South America: Apartado 4127, Lima 100, Peru.

Activities

ICAO aims to ensure the safe and orderly growth of civil aviation; to encourage skills in aircraft design and operation; to improve airways, airports and air navigation; to prevent the waste of resources in unreasonable competition; to safeguard the rights of each contracting party to operate international air transport; and to prevent discriminatory practices.

ICAO SPECIFICATIONS

These are contained in annexes to the Chicago Convention, and in three sets of Procedures for Air Navigation Services (PANS Documents). The specifications are periodically revised in keeping with developments in technology and changing requirements. The 18 annexes to the Convention include personnel licensing, rules relating to the conduct of flights, meteorological services, aeronautical charts, air-ground communications, safety specifications, identification, air traffic control, rescue services, environmental protection, security and the transporting of dangerous goods. Technical Manuals and Circulars are issued to facilitate implementation.

ICAO REGIONAL PLANS

These set out the technical requirements for air navigation facilities in the nine ICAO regions; Regional Offices offer assistance (see addresses above). Because of growth in air traffic and changes in the pattern of air routes, the Plans are periodically amended.

EUROPEAN AIR NAVIGATION PLANNING GROUP

Reviews current problems and the need for changes in the air navigation facilities in the European Region.

ICAO PROJECTS

Studies of current problems aiming to apply new technology, including: airworthiness of aircraft, all-weather navigation, aircraft separation, obstacle clearances, noise abatement, operation of aircraft and carriage by air of dangerous goods, automated data interchange systems, aviation security and use of space technology in air navigation.

ENVIRONMENT

International standards and guidelines for noise certification of aircraft and international provisions for the regulation of aircraft engine emissions have been adopted and published in Annex 16 to the Chicago Convention.

AIR TRANSPORT

Continuing functions include preparation of regional air transport development studies; studies of regulatory policy regarding international air transport; studies on international air transport fares and rates; review of the economic situation of airports and route facilities; development of guidance material on civil aviation forecasting and planning; collection and publication of statistics; facilitation of passenger and freight clearance formalities; and multilateral financing of certain air navigation facilities.

TECHNICAL ASSISTANCE BUREAU

The Bureau assists developing countries in the execution of various projects, financed by UNDP and other sources (see under Finance, below).

LEGAL COMMITTEE

The general work programme of the Committee in 1990 included the following subjects: the UN Convention on the Law of the Sea and its implications for the application of the Chicago Convention, its annexes and other international air law instruments; the liability of air traffic control agencies; study of the status of the instruments of the 'Warsaw System'; the institutional and legal aspects of future air navigation systems; and the legal aspects of global air-to-ground communications.

FINANCE

ICAO is financed mainly by contributions from member states; the annual budget required US $33.8m. in contributions for 1990, and $35.5m. for 1991. The administrative and operational costs of ICAO's technical assistance programme are financed mainly from funds provided by UNDP (q.v.); net expenditure was estimated at $8.3m. for 1990 and $8.4m. for 1991.

PUBLICATIONS

Catalogue of ICAO Publications.
ICAO Journal (monthly, in English, French and Spanish; quarterly digest in Russian).
Digest of Statistics.
Minutes and Documents of the Legal Committee.
Lexicon of terms.
The 18 Annexes to the Convention.
Procedures for Air Navigation Services.
ICAO Training Manual.
Regional Air Navigation Plans.
Aircraft Accident Digest.

INTERNATIONAL ORGANIZATIONS   United Nations (Specialized Agencies)

International Fund for Agricultural Development—IFAD

Address: Via del Serafico 107, 00142 Rome, Italy.
Telephone: (06) 54591.
Telex: 620330.
Fax: (06) 5043463.

Following a decision by the 1974 UN World Food Conference, IFAD was established in 1976 to fund rural development programmes specifically aimed at the poorest of the world's people. It began operations in December 1977.

MEMBERS

144 members: see Table on pp. 52–54.

Category I	Category II	Category III
Australia	Algeria	111 developing countries
Austria	Gabon	
Belgium	Indonesia	
Canada	Iran	
Denmark	Iraq	
Finland	Kuwait	
France	Libya	
Germany	Nigeria	
Greece	Qatar	
Ireland	Saudi Arabia	
Italy	United Arab Emirates	
Japan	Venezuela	
Luxembourg		
Netherlands		
New Zealand		
Norway		
Spain		
Sweden		
Switzerland		
United Kingdom		
USA		

Organization

(October 1990)

GOVERNING COUNCIL

Each member state is represented in the Governing Council by a Governor and an Alternate. There are three categories of members: industrialized countries (OECD members) forming Category I; petroleum-exporting developing countries (OPEC members) forming Category II; recipient developing countries (Category III). Categories I and II *shall* contribute to the resources of the Fund while Category III *may* do so. All the powers of the Fund are vested in the Governing Council. It may, however, delegate certain powers to the Executive Board. Sessions are held annually with special sessions as required. The Governing Council elects the President of the Fund by a two-thirds majority for a four-year term. He is eligible for re-election. The President is also the Chairman of the Executive Board.

EXECUTIVE BOARD

Consists of 18 members and 17 alternates, elected by the Governing Council, one-third by each category of membership. Members serve for three years. The Executive Board is responsible for the conduct and general operation of IFAD and approves loans and grants for projects; it meets three or four times a year.

The total number of votes in the Governing Council and the Executive Board is 1,800, distributed equally between the three categories of membership. Thus two-thirds of the votes lie with the developing countries (Categories II and III) which will therefore have a major influence on the investment decisions of the Fund. At the same time two-thirds of the votes are held by donor countries (Categories I and II).

President and Chairman of Executive Board: IDRISS JAZAIRY.

DEPARTMENTS

IFAD has three main administrative departments: the Economic and Planning Department (with Divisions for Planning and Economic Analysis, Policy Review, and Monitoring and Evaluation); the Project Management Department (with four regional Divisions, a Loan Implementation Unit and a Technical Advisory Unit); and the General Affairs Department. In November 1988 IFAD had 189 regular staff, of whom about 40% were in executive or technical positions.

Activities

The Fund's objective is to mobilize additional resources to be made available on concessional terms for agricultural development in developing member states. IFAD provides financing primarily for projects designed to improve food production systems and to strengthen related policies and institutions. In allocating resources IFAD is guided by: the need to increase food production in the poorest food-deficit countries; the potential for increasing food production in other developing countries; and the importance of improving the nutritional level of the poorest people in developing countries and the conditions of their lives. All projects focus on those who often do not benefit from other development programmes: small farmers, artisanal fishermen, nomadic pastoralists, women, and the rural landless.

IFAD is empowered to make both grants and loans. Under its Agreement, grants are limited to 12.5% of the resources committed in any one financial year. There are three kinds of loan: highly concessional loans, which carry no interest but have an annual service charge of 1% and a maturity period of 50 years, including a grace period of 10 years; intermediate term loans, which have an annual interest rate of 4% and a maturity period of 20 years, including a grace period of five years; and ordinary term loans which have an interest rate of 8% and a maturity period of 15–18 years, including a grace period of three years. To avoid duplication of work, the administration of loans, for the purposes of disbursements and supervision of project implementation, is entrusted to competent international financial institutions, with the Fund retaining an active interest. In order to increase the impact of its lending resources on food production, the Fund seeks as much as possible to attract other external donors and beneficiary governments as co-financiers of its projects.

In 1986 IFAD launched a Special Programme for Sub-Saharan Africa, aiming to spend $300m. over the next three years on improving food production (with an emphasis on traditional food crops and biological pest control) and water conservation in Africa, in addition to operations in the region carried out under its regular programme.

Between 1978 and the end of 1989 the Fund approved loans for 266 projects in 93 countries, and 326 technical assistance grants, at a cost of about US$2,900m. from its own resources. IFAD's investment represented some 26% of total project costs, while 34% was provided by other external donors and 40% by recipient governments. During this period about two-thirds of loans were in the highly concessional category.

In 1988 IFAD approved total loans (including those under the Special Programme for Sub-Saharan Africa) amounting to SDR 176.45m., or about US $230m. (The average value of the SDR—Special Drawing Right—in 1988 was US $1.34392.) Of this total, 49.6% was for sub-Saharan Africa, 23% for Asia (including the Pacific), 16% for the Near East and North Africa, and 11% for Latin America. Technical assistance grants amounting to SDR 9.82m. (for research, training and project preparation) were also made, bringing the total financial assistance approved to SDR 186.27m. This represented an increase over the total of SDR 175.4m. approved in 1987, but was still considerably less than the annual average of SDR 280m. approved in 1979–83 (reflecting a reduction in IFAD's resources: see Finance, below). Loan disbursements during 1988 amounted to SDR 156.2m. In 1989 IFAD approved 23 new loans (of which seven were for the Special Programme for Sub-Saharan Africa) and 35 technical assistance grants, amounting to US $273m.

IFAD's development projects usually include a number of components, such as infrastructure (e.g. improvement of water supplies, small-scale irrigation and road construction); input supply (e.g. improved seeds, fertilizers and pesticides); institutional support (e.g. research, training and extension services); and producer incentives (e.g. pricing and marketing improvements). IFAD also attempts to enable the landless to acquire income-generating assets: by increasing the provision of credit for the rural poor, it seeks to free them from dependence on the unorganized and exploitative capital market and to generate productive activities. An example is IFAD's support for the Grameen Bank in Bangladesh, which at the beginning of 1987 was handling 215,000 small loans (70% of which were to women) and had a credit recovery rate of 99%.

During the late 1980s, increased emphasis was given to environmental conservation, in an effort to alleviate poverty that results from the deterioration of natural resources. In addition to promoting small-scale irrigation (which has proved more economically and

INTERNATIONAL ORGANIZATIONS

ecologically viable than large-scale systems), projects include low-cost anti-erosion measures, land improvement, soil conservation, agro-forestry systems, improved management of arid rangeland, and safe biological control of pests.

In addition to its regular efforts to identify projects and programmes, IFAD organizes special programming missions to certain selected countries to undertake a comprehensive review of the constraints affecting the rural poor, and to help countries to design strategies for the removal of these constraints. Based on the recommendations of these missions, a number of projects have been identified or prepared. In general, these projects tend to focus on institutional improvements at the national and local level to direct inputs and services to small farmers and the landless rural poor. Monitoring and evaluation missions are also sent to check the progress of projects.

PROJECTS APPROVED BY IFAD IN 1988

Region and Country	Loan Amount (SDR million)
Africa	46.95
Burundi	6.90
Cameroon	8.30
Madagascar	10.30
Nigeria	11.50
Rwanda	8.60
São Tomé and Príncipe	1.35
Asia and the Pacific	41.20
Bangladesh	5.60
Bhutan	2.00
China (People's Republic)	13.40
Pakistan	12.50
Solomon Islands	1.15
Sri Lanka	4.85
Tonga	1.70
Latin America and the Caribbean	19.50
Argentina	8.20
Costa Rica	3.50
Venezuela	7.80
Near East and North Africa	28.30
Algeria	10.90
Tunisia	9.30
People's Democratic Republic of Yemen	28.30
Total (regular programmes)	135.95
Special Programme for Sub-Saharan Africa	40.50
Guinea	11.40
Lesotho	6.00
Mali	7.80
Senegal	8.50
Sudan	6.80
Total loans	176.45
Technical assistance grants	9.82
Total operations in 1988	186.27

United Nations (Specialized Agencies)

FINANCE

The total initial resources pledged by members, valued as at 31 December 1981, amounted to US $1,015m. In 1982 agreement was reached on the first replenishment of the Fund's resources. Member countries offered to provide contributions totalling about US $1,100m. for the period 1981–83 (later extended to 1984). This comprised $620m. (56%) from the developed (Category I) countries, $450m. (41%) from petroleum-exporting developing (Category II) countries and $30m. (3%) from other developing (Category III) countries. Together with the carrying-over of available resources, this would have enabled the Fund to undertake an operational programme of about $1,350m. during 1981–84. However, actual payments (particularly those of the USA) were slower than expected. As a result, the size of IFAD's lending operations decreased from 1982 until 1986.

Negotiations on a second replenishment for 1985–87 began in July 1983, and continued until January 1986, when members finally agreed on a replenishment of $460m. This was to be supplemented by an extra $300m. for a Special Programme for Sub-Saharan Africa: by April 1988 the amount required for this Programme had been fully pledged by donor countries.

Consultations on a third replenishment were conducted in 1989, with a target figure of $750m. Agreement was reached in June on a replenishment amounting to $522.9m.

PUBLICATION

Annual Report.

International Labour Organisation—ILO

Address: 4 route des Morillons, 1211 Geneva 22, Switzerland.
Telephone: (022) 7996111.
Telex: 415647.
Fax: (22) 7988685.

ILO was founded in 1919 to work for social justice as a basis for lasting peace. It carries out this mandate by promoting decent living standards, satisfactory conditions of work and pay and adequate employment opportunities. Methods of action include the creation of international labour standards; the provision of technical co-operation services; and research and publications on social and labour matters. In 1946, ILO became a specialized agency associated with the UN. It was awarded the Nobel Peace Prize in 1969.

MEMBERS

148 members: see Table on pp. 52–54.

Organization

(October 1990)

INTERNATIONAL LABOUR CONFERENCE

The supreme deliberative body of ILO, the Conference normally meets annually in Geneva, with a session devoted to maritime questions when necessary; it is attended by about 2,000 delegates, advisers and observers. National delegations are composed of two government delegates, one employers' delegate and one workers' delegate. Non-governmental delegates can speak and vote independently of the views of their government. Conference elects the Governing Body and adopts the Budget and International Labour Conventions and Recommendations.

The President and Vice-Presidents hold office for the term of the Conference only.

GOVERNING BODY

ILO's executive council; normally meets three or four times a year in Geneva to decide policy and programmes. Composed of 28 Government members, 14 employers' members and 14 workers' members. Ten seats are reserved for 'states of chief industrial importance': Brazil, the People's Republic of China, France, Germany, India, Italy, Japan, the USSR, the United Kingdom and the USA. The remaining 18 are elected from other countries every three years. Employers' and workers' members are elected as individuals, not as national candidates.

Chairman (1990/91): GERD MUHR (Germany).
Employers' Vice-Chairman: JEAN-JACQUES OECHSLIN (France).
Government Vice-Chairman: ALFREDO PADILLA PRADO (Venezuela).

INTERNATIONAL LABOUR OFFICE

The International Labour Office is ILO's secretariat, operational headquarters and publishing house. It is staffed in Geneva and in the field by about 1,900 people of some 110 nationalities. Operations are decentralized to regional, area and branch offices in nearly 40 countries.

Director-General: MICHEL HANSENNE (Belgium).

REGIONAL OFFICES

Regional Office for Africa: 01 BP 3960, Abidjan 01, Côte d'Ivoire.
Regional Office for the Americas: Apdo Postal 3638, Lima 1, Peru.
Regional Office for Arab States: ILO, 4 route des Morillons, 1211 Geneva 22, Switzerland.
Regional Office for Asia and the Pacific: POB 1759, Bangkok 2, Thailand.

Activities

INTERNATIONAL LABOUR CONFERENCE

74th session (maritime): Sept.-Oct. 1987. Adopted a Convention and Recommendation on seafarers' welfare at sea and in port, a Convention on social security protection for seafarers, a Convention on health protection and medical care, and a revised Convention and Recommendation on repatriation.

75th session: June 1988. Adopted a Convention and Recommendation on employment promotion and protection against unemployment, and a Convention and Recommendation on safety and health in construction. The session began the two-year process of updating standards relating to indigenous and tribal populations.

76th session: June 1989. Adopted a convention on indigenous and tribal peoples in independent countries. The session also held first discussions on the revision of standards relating to night work, and on safety in the use of chemicals at work.

77th session: June 1990. Adopted conventions and recommendations on night work and on the use of chemicals at work. Also held a first discussion on new standards relating to working conditions in hotels and restaurants, and a general discussion on self-employment.

INTERNATIONAL LABOUR STANDARDS

One of the ILO's primary functions is the adoption by the International Labour Conference of Conventions and Recommendations setting minimum labour standards. Through ratification by member states, Conventions create binding obligations to put their provisions into effect. Recommendations provide guidance as to policy and practice. A total of 171 Conventions and 178 Recommendations have been adopted, ranging over a wide field of social and labour matters, including basic human rights such as freedom of association, abolition of forced labour and elimination of discrimination in employment. Together they form the International Labour Code. By July 1990 more than 5,500 ratifications of the Conventions had been registered by member states.

TECHNICAL CO-OPERATION

Technical co-operation continues to be a major ILO activity. About US $143m. from all sources, including the United Nations Development Programme, was spent in 1989 for the promotion of employment, the development of human resources and social institutions, and the improvement of living and working conditions. Of the total figure, 44.7% was provided by UNDP, 36.5% by bilateral aid agencies in trust fund arrangements, and 7.6% by the UN Population Fund, the ILO regular budget contributing 11.2%.

WORLD EMPLOYMENT PROGRAMME

The employment objective has been incorporated by the United Nations as a key policy factor in the Second United Nations Development Decade. The ILO has the role of catalyst in bringing employment considerations to the fore in the activities of all agencies within the UN system, and for this purpose launched the World Employment Programme.

The aim of the programme is to assist decision makers in identifying and putting into effect specific employment-promoting development policies. This is accomplished through comprehensive employment strategy missions and exploratory country employment missions; through regional employment teams for Africa, Asia and Latin America and the Caribbean; and through country employment teams.

The programme also includes research activities which cover eight major project areas: technology and employment, income distribution and employment, population and employment, education and training and employment, rural employment, promotion, urbanization and employment, trade expansion and employment, and emergency employment schemes.

MEETINGS

Among meetings held during 1990, in addition to the regular International Labour Conference and Governing Body sessions, were the fifth Tripartite Technical Meeting for Mines other than Coal Mines, a Meeting of Experts on Statistics of Strikes and Lock-outs, a Joint Meeting on Conditions of Employment and Work of Fire-fighting Personnel, a Meeting of Experts on Safety and Health in Surface Mining Operations, and the Eighth Session of the Joint ILO/IMO Committee on Training. Due to be held later in the year were a Meeting of Experts on the Social Protection of Homeworkers, a Meeting of Experts on the Prevention of Major Hazards, a Meeting of Experts on Civil Aviation, the Eleventh Session of the Advisory Committee on Rural Redevelopment, a Tripartite Symposium on Equality of Opportunity and Treatment for Men and Women Workers in Industrialized Countries, a Tripartite Meeting on Conditions of Employment and Work of Journalists, and the Third Tripartite Technical Meeting for the Printing and Allied Trades.

INTERNATIONAL ORGANIZATIONS United Nations (Specialized Agencies)

INTERNATIONAL INSTITUTE FOR LABOUR STUDIES

Established in 1960 and based at the ILO's Geneva headquarters, the Institute is an advanced educational and research institution dealing with social and labour policy, and brings together international experts representing employers, management, workers and government interests. Activities include international and regional study courses, and are financed by grants and an Endowment Fund to which governments and other bodies contribute.

INTERNATIONAL CENTRE FOR ADVANCED TECHNICAL AND VOCATIONAL TRAINING

Address: Via Ventimiglia 201, 10127 Turin, Italy.

The Centre became operational in 1965. It provides programmes for directors in charge of technical and vocational institutions, training officers, senior and middle-level managers in private and public enterprises, trade union leaders, and technicians, primarily from the developing regions of the world. The ILO Director-General is Chairman of the Board of the Centre.

FINANCE

The net expenditure budget for the two years 1990–91 was US $330m. (compared with $357m. for 1988–89).

PUBLICATIONS

(in English, French and Spanish unless otherwise indicated)

International Labour Review (6 a year).
Official Bulletin (3 a year).
Legislative Series (selected labour and social security laws and regulations; 2 a year).
Bulletin of Labour Statistics (quarterly).
Social and Labour Bulletin (quarterly).
Year Book of Labour Statistics.
International studies, surveys, works of practical guidance or reference on questions of social policy, manpower, industrial relations, working conditions, social security, training, management development, etc.
Training and Development Abstracts (a service providing digests of articles, laws, reports on vocational guidance and training and management development).
Reports for the annual sessions of the International Labour Conference, etc. (in English, French, German, Russian, Spanish).
ILO-Information (bulletin issued in 17 languages).

International Maritime Organization—IMO

Address: 4 Albert Embankment, London, SE1 7SR, England.
Telephone: (071) 735-7611.
Telex: 23588.

The Inter-Governmental Maritime Consultative Organization (IMCO) began operations in 1959, as a specialized agency of the UN to facilitate co-operation among governments on technical matters affecting international shipping. Its main functions are the achievement of safe and efficient navigation, and the control of pollution caused by ships and craft operating in the marine environment. IMCO became IMO in 1982.

MEMBERS

133 members and two associate members: see Table on pp. 52–54.

Organization

(October 1990)

ASSEMBLY

The Assembly consists of delegates from all member countries, who each have one vote. Associate members and observers from other governments and the international agencies are also present. Regular sessions are held every two years. The Assembly is responsible for the election of members to the Council. It considers reports from all subsidiary bodies and decides the action to be taken on them; it votes the agency's budget and determines the work programme and financial policy.

The Assembly also recommends to members measures to promote maritime safety and to prevent and control maritime pollution from ships.

COUNCIL

The Council is the governing body of the Organization between the biennial sessions of the Assembly. Its members, representatives of 32 states, are elected by the Assembly for a term of two years. The Council appoints the Secretary-General; transmits reports by the subsidiary bodies, including the Maritime Safety Committee, to the Assembly and reports on the work of the Organization generally; submits budget estimates and financial statements with comments and recommendations to the Assembly. The Council normally meets twice a year.

Chairman: M. S. TIGHILT (Algeria).

Facilitation Committee: Constituted by the Council in May 1972 as a subsidiary body, this Committee deals with measures to facilitate maritime travel and transport and matters arising from the 1965 Facilitation Convention. Membership open to all IMO member states.

MARITIME SAFETY COMMITTEE

The Maritime Safety Committee is open to all IMO members. The Committee meets at least once a year and submits proposals to the Assembly on technical matters affecting shipping, including prevention of marine pollution.

Sub-Committees:
Bulk Chemicals.
Containers and Cargoes.
Carriage of Dangerous Goods.
Fire Protection.
Life-Saving, Search and Rescue.
Radiocommunications.
Safety of Navigation.
Standards of Training and Watchkeeping.
Ship Design and Equipment.
Stability and Load Lines and Fishing Vessel Safety.

LEGAL COMMITTEE

Established by the Council in June 1967 to deal initially with problems connected with the loss of the tanker *Torrey Canyon*, and subsequently with any legal problems laid before IMO. Membership open to all IMO Member States.

MARINE ENVIRONMENT PROTECTION COMMITTEE

Established by the eighth Assembly (1973) to co-ordinate IMO's work on the prevention and control of marine pollution from ships, and to assist IMO in its consultations with other UN bodies, and with international organizations and expert bodies in the field of marine pollution. Membership is open to all IMO members.

TECHNICAL CO-OPERATION COMMITTEE

Constituted by the Council in May 1972, this Committee evaluates the implementation of UN Development Programme projects for which IMO is executing agency and generally reviews IMO's technical assistance programmes. Its membership is open to all IMO member states.

SECRETARIAT

The Secretariat consists of the Secretary-General and a staff appointed by the Secretary-General and recruited on as wide a geographical basis as possible.

Secretary-General: W. A. O'NEIL (CANADA).

Divisions of the Secretariat:
Maritime Safety
Navigation (Sub-Division)
Technology (Sub-Division)
Marine Environment
Legal Affairs and External Relations
Administrative
Conference
Technical Co-operation

Activities

In addition to the work of its committees and sub-committees, the organization works in connection with the following Conventions, of which it is the depository:

International Convention for the Prevention of Pollution of the Sea by Oil, 1954. IMO has taken over administration from the United Kingdom.

Convention on Facilitation of International Maritime Traffic, 1965. Came into force in March 1967.

International Convention on Load Lines, 1966. Came into force in July 1968.

INTERNATIONAL ORGANIZATIONS

United Nations (Specialized Agencies)

International Convention on Tonnage Measurement of Ships, 1969. Convention embodies a universal system for measuring ships' tonnage. Came into force in 1982.

International Convention relating to Intervention on the High Seas in Cases of Oil Pollution Casualties, 1969. Came into force in May 1975.

International Convention on Civil Liability for Oil Pollution Damage, 1969. Came into force in June 1975.

Intenational Convention on the Establishment of an International Fund for Compensation for Oil Pollution Damage, 1971. Came into force in October 1978.

Convention on the International Regulations for Preventing Collisions at Sea, 1972. Came into force in July 1977.

International Convention for Safe Containers, 1972. Came into force in September 1977.

International Convention on the Prevention of Pollution from Ships, 1973 (as modified by the Protocol of 1978). Came into force in October 1983.

International Convention for Safety of Life at Sea, 1974. Came into force in May 1980. A Protocol drawn up in 1978 came into force in May 1981.

Athens Convention relating to the Carriage of Passengers and their Luggage by Sea, 1974. Came into force in April 1987.

Convention on the International Maritime Satellite Organization, 1976. Came into force in July 1979.

Convention on Limitation of Liability for Maritime Claims, 1976. Came into force in December 1986.

International Convention for the Safety of Fishing Vessels, Torremolinos, 1977. Will come into force 12 months after 15 countries whose combined fishing fleets constitute 50% of world fishing fleets of 24 metres in length and over have become parties.

International Convention on Standards of Training, Certification and Watchkeeping for Seafarers, 1978. Came into force in April 1984.

International Convention on Maritime Search and Rescue, 1979. Came into force in June 1985.

International Convention for the Suppression of Unlawful Acts against the Safety of International Shipping, 1988. To come into force 90 days after acceptance by 15 states.

International Convention on Salvage, 1989. To come into force one year after acceptance by 15 states.

BUDGET

Contributions are received from the member states. The budget appropriation for 1990-91 was £25.4m.

PUBLICATIONS

IMO News (quarterly, English and French).

Numerous specialized publications, including international conventions of which IMO is depositary.

International Monetary Fund—IMF

Address: 700 19th St, NW, Washington, DC 20431, USA.
Telephone: (202) 623-7430.
Telex: 440040.
Fax: (202) 623-4661.

The IMF was established at the same time as the World Bank in December 1945, to promote international monetary co-operation, to facilitate the expansion and balanced growth of international trade and to promote stability in foreign exchange.

MEMBERS

154 members: see Table on pp. 52-54.

Organization

(October 1990)

Managing Director: MICHEL CAMDESSUS (France).
Deputy Managing Director: RICHARD D. ERB (USA).

BOARD OF GOVERNORS

The highest authority of the Fund is exercised by the Board of Governors, on which each member country is represented by a Governor and an Alternate Governor. Normally the Board of Governors meets once a year, but the Governors may take votes by mail or other means between annual meetings. The Board of Governors has delegated many of its powers to the Executive Directors. However, the conditions governing the admission of new members, adjustment of quotas, election of Executive Directors, as well as certain other important powers remain the sole responsibility of the Board of Governors. The voting power of each member in the Board of Governors is related to its quota in the Fund (see p. 77).

The Interim Committee of the Board of Governors, established in 1974, usually meets twice a year. It comprises 22 members, representing the same countries or groups of countries as those on the Board of Executive Directors (see below). It reviews the international monetary system and advises the Board of Governors.

The Development Committee (the Joint Ministerial Committee of the Boards of Governors of the World Bank and the IMF on the Transfer of Real Resources to Developing Countries) was also set up in 1974, with a structure similar to that of the Interim Committee, to review development policy issues and financing requirements.

BOARD OF EXECUTIVE DIRECTORS

The 22-member Board of Executive Directors, responsible for the day-to-day operations of the Fund, is in continuous session in Washington, under the chairmanship of the Fund's Managing Director. The USA, the United Kingdom, Germany, France, Japan and Saudi Arabia each appoint one Executive Director, while 15 of the remaining Executive Directors are elected by groups of member countries with similar interests; there is also a Director from the People's Republic of China. As in the Board of Governors, the voting power of each member is related to its quota in the Fund, but in practice the Executive Directors normally operate by consensus.

The Managing Director of the Fund serves as head of its staff, which is organized into departments by function and area. On 30 April 1989 the Fund staff comprised 1,691 people from 100 countries.

Activities

The purposes of the IMF, as set out in the Articles of Agreement, are:

(i) To promote international monetary co-operation through a permanent institution which provides the machinery for consultation and collaboration on monetary problems.

(ii) To facilitate the expansion and balanced growth of international trade, and to contribute thereby to the promotion and maintenance of high levels of employment and real income and to the development of members' productive resources.

(iii) To promote exchange stability, to maintain orderly exchange arrangements among members, and to avoid competitive exchange depreciation.

(iv) To assist in the establishment of a multilateral system of payments in respect of current transactions between members and in the elimination of foreign exchange restrictions which hamper the growth of trade.

(v) To give confidence to members by making the general resources of the Fund temporarily available to them, under adequate safeguards, thus providing them with the opportunity to correct maladjustments in their balance of payments, without resorting to measures destructive of national or international prosperity.

(vi) In accordance with the above, to shorten the duration of and lessen the degree of disequilibrium in the international balances of payments of members.

In joining the Fund, each country agrees to co-operate with the above objectives, and the Fund monitors members' compliance by

INTERNATIONAL ORGANIZATIONS

United Nations (Specialized Agencies)

BOARD OF EXECUTIVE DIRECTORS (August 1990)

Director	Casting Votes of	Total Votes	%
Appointed:			
Thomas C. Dawson	USA	179,433	19.11
David Peretz	United Kingdom	62,190	6.62
Günter Grosche	Federal Republic of Germany	54,287	5.78
Jean-Pierre Landau	France	45,078	4.80
Koji Yamazaki	Japan	42,483	4.52
Muhammad al-Jasser	Saudi Arabia	32,274	3.44
Elected:			
Renato Filosa (Italy)	Greece, Italy, Malta, Poland, Portugal	45,357	4.83
Leonor Filardo (Venezuela)*	Costa Rica, El Salvador, Guatemala, Honduras, Mexico, Nicaragua, Spain, Venezuela	44,401	4.73
G. A. Posthumus (Netherlands)	Cyprus, Israel, Netherlands, Romania, Yugoslavia	40,425	4.30
Jacques de Groote (Belgium)	Austria, Belgium, Hungary, Luxembourg, Turkey	40,178	4.28
Mohamed Finaish (Libya)	Bahrain, Egypt, Iraq, Jordan, Kuwait, Lebanon, Libya, Maldives, Oman, Pakistan, Qatar, Somalia, Syria, United Arab Emirates, Yemen	39,276	4.18
C. Scott Clark (Canada)	Antigua and Barbuda, Bahamas, Barbados, Belize, Canada, Dominica, Grenada, Ireland, Jamaica, Saint Christopher and Nevis, Saint Lucia, Saint Vincent and the Grenadines	38,709	4.12
E. A. Evans (Australia)	Australia, Kiribati, Republic of Korea, New Zealand, Papua New Guinea, Philippines, Seychelles, Solomon Islands, Vanuatu, Western Samoa	33,254	3.54
Markus Fogelholm (Finland)	Denmark, Finland, Iceland, Norway, Sweden	32,338	3.44
G. K. Arora (India)	Bangladesh, Bhutan, India, Sri Lanka	28,208	3.00
Alexandre Kafka (Brazil)	Brazil, Colombia, Dominican Republic, Ecuador, Guyana, Haiti, Panama, Suriname, Trinidad and Tobago	27,582	2.94
Julius Emmanuel Ismael (Indonesia)	Fiji, Indonesia, Laos, Malaysia, Myanmar, Nepal, Singapore, Thailand, Tonga, Viet-Nam	27,094	2.89
El Tayeb El Kogali (Sudan)*	Botswana, Burundi, Ethiopia, The Gambia, Kenya, Lesotho, Liberia, Malawi, Mozambique, Nigeria, Sierra Leone, Sudan, Swaziland, Tanzania, Uganda, Zambia, Zimbabwe	26,738	2.85
Dai Qianding	People's Republic of China	24,159	2.57
Ernesto Feldman (Argentina)*	Argentina, Bolivia, Chile, Paraguay, Peru, Uruguay	23,373	2.49
Mohammed Reza Ghazimi (Iran)*	Afghanistan, Algeria, Ghana, Iran, Morocco, Tunisia	21,691	2.31
Mawakani Samba (Zaire)*	Benin, Burkina Faso, Cameroon, Cape Verde, Central African Republic, Chad, Comoros, Congo, Côte d'Ivoire, Djibouti, Equatorial Guinea, Gabon, Guinea, Guinea-Bissau, Madagascar, Mali, Mauritania, Mauritius, Niger, Rwanda, São Tomé and Príncipe, Senegal, Togo, Zaire	18,940	2.02

Note: Votes in the General Department and the SDR Department totalled 937,075 in August 1990, including the votes of Angola (which became a member in September 1989), Cambodia and South Africa, which did not participate in the 1988 Regular Election of Executive Directors. The number of votes in the Executive Board was 927,468. Bulgaria, Czechoslovakia and Namibia joined the IMF in September 1990. Applications for membership by Mongolia and Switzerland were also under consideration.

* Replaced by newly-elected Directors on 1 November 1990 (see Late Information).

holding an annual consultation with each country, in order to survey the country's exchange rate policies and determine its need for assistance.

SPECIAL DRAWING RIGHTS

The special drawing right (SDR) was introduced in 1970 as a substitute for gold in international payments: it is intended eventually to become the principal reserve asset in the international monetary system. SDRs are allocated to members in proportion to their quotas. Originally SDR 9,300m. were allocated, and by 1990 six further allocations of approximately SDR 4,000m. each had been made, bringing the total of SDRs in existence to SDR 21,400m. or about 4% of international non-gold reserves.

From 1974 to 1980 the SDR was valued on the basis of the market exchange rate for a basket of 16 currencies, belonging to the members with the largest exports of goods and services; since 1981 it has been based on the currencies of the five largest exporters (France, the Federal Republic of Germany, Japan, the United Kingdom and the USA). The value of the SDR at 31 July 1990 was US $1.36564.

The Second Amendment to the Articles of Agreement (1978) altered and expanded the possible uses of the SDR in transactions with other participants. 'Other holders' of the SDRs have the same degree of freedom as Fund members to buy and sell SDRs and to receive or use them in loans, pledges, swaps, donations or settlement of financial obligations. In October 1990 there were 16 'other holders': the African Development Bank and the African Development Fund, the Andean Reserve Fund, the Arab Monetary Fund, the Asian Development Bank, the Bank for International Settlements, the Bank of Central African States, the Central Bank of West African States, the East African Development Bank, the Eastern Caribbean Central Bank, the International Bank for Reconstruction and Development and the International Development Association, the International Fund for Agricultural Development, the Islamic Development Bank, the Nordic Investment Bank and the Swiss National Bank.

QUOTAS

Each member is assigned a quota related to its national income, monetary reserves, trade balance and other economic indicators. A member's subscription is equal to its quota and is payable partly in SDRs and partly in its own currency. The quota approximately determines a member's voting power, the amount of foreign exchange it may purchase from the Fund, and its allocation of SDRs.

Quotas are reviewed at intervals of not more than five years, to take into account the state of the world economy and members' different rates of development. General increases were made in 1959, 1966, 1970, 1978 and 1980, while special increases were made for the People's Republic of China in April 1980, for a group of 11 members in December 1980, and for Saudi Arabia in April 1981. The eighth general review of quotas resulted in March 1983 in an agreement to raise quotas by 47.5% to SDR 90,035m., subject to approval by national legislatures. The early review (two years ahead of schedule) was considered necessary in view of the debt crisis afflicting some member states. By April 1984 all of the 142 members that had consented to increases in quotas had completed payments of their subscriptions, raising the total of IMF quotas to SDR 89,236.3m. At 31 July 1990 total quotas in the Fund amounted to SDR 90,100m. (see table below). Proposals for a ninth general review of quotas were adopted in June 1990. Total quotas were increased by 50% to SDR 135,200m. The increase was to come into effect by December 1991 (subject to approval by member states holding at least 85% of current quotas).

RESOURCES

Members' subscriptions form the basic resource of the IMF. They are supplemented by borrowing. Under the General Arrangements to Borrow (GAB), established in 1962, the 'Group of Ten' industrialized nations (Belgium, Canada, France, Germany, Italy, Japan, the Netherlands, Sweden, the United Kingdom and the USA) and Switzerland (before 1990 not a member of the IMF, but a full participant in the GAB from April 1984) undertake to lend the Fund up to SDR 17,000m. in their own currencies, so as to help meet the balance-of-payments requirements of any member of the group, or to meet requests to the Fund from countries with balance-of-payments problems that could threaten the stability of the international monetary system. In July 1983 the Fund entered into an agreement with Saudi Arabia, in association with the GAB, making available SDR 1,500m., and other borrowing arrangements were completed in 1984 with the BIS, the Saudi Arabian Monetary Agency, Belgium and Japan, making available a further SDR 6,000m. In December 1986 another borrowing arrangement with Japan made available SDR 3,000m.

As part of the effort to reduce the monetary role of gold, a third of the Fund's gold holdings was sold between 1976 and 1980: one-half of this amount was sold at public auction for the benefit of developing member states. Of the resulting US $4,640m., part was allotted to the 104 eligible members according to their quotas, and part was put into a Trust Fund making low-interest loans. By the time the Trust Fund was wound up in April 1981 it had disbursed $3,560m. Repayments of Trust Fund loans are used to make further concessionary loans, for example under the structural adjustment facility described below.

DRAWING ARRANGEMENTS

Exchange transactions within the Fund take the form of members' purchases (i.e. drawings) from the Fund of the currencies of other members for the equivalent amounts of their own currencies. Fund resources are available to eligible members on an essentially short-term and revolving basis to provide members with temporary assistance to contribute to the solution of their payments problems. Before making a purchase, a member must show that its balance of payments or reserve position make the purchase necessary. Apart from this requirement, reserve tranche purchases (i.e. purchases that do not bring the Fund's holdings of the member's currency to a level above its quota) are permitted unconditionally.

With further purchases, however, the Fund's policy of 'conditionality' means that a member requesting assistance must agree to adjust its economic policies, as stipulated by the IMF. All requests other than for use of the reserve tranche are examined by the Executive Board to determine whether the proposed use would be consistent with the Fund's policies, and a member must discuss its proposed adjustment programme (including fiscal, monetary, exchange and trade policies) with IMF staff. Purchases outside the reserve tranche are made in four credit tranches, each equivalent to 25% of the member's quota; a member must reverse the transaction by repurchasing its own currency (with SDRs or currencies specified by the Fund) within a specified time. A credit tranche purchase is usually made under a 'stand-by arrangement' with the Fund, or under the extended Fund facility. A stand-by arrangement is normally of one or two years' duration, and the amount is made available in instalments, subject to the member's observance of 'performance criteria'; repurchases must be made within three-and-a-quarter to five years. An extended arrangement is normally of three years' duration, and the member must submit detailed economic programmes and progress reports for each year; repurchases must be made within four-and-a-half to 10 years. A member whose payments imbalance is large in relation to its quota may make use of temporary facilities established by the Fund using borrowed resources, namely the 'enlarged access policy' established in 1981, which helps to finance stand-by and extended arrangements for such a member, up to a limit of between 90% and 110% of the member's quota annually. Repurchases are made within three-and-a-half to seven years.

In addition, there are special-purpose arrangements, all of which are subject to the member's co-operation with the Fund to find an appropriate solution to its difficulties. The buffer stock financing facility (established in 1969) enables members to pay their contributions to the buffer stocks which are intended to stabilize primary commodity markets. Members may draw up to 45% of their quota for this purpose. Repurchases are made within three-and-a-quarter to five years. In August 1988 the Fund established the compensatory and contingency financing facility (CCFF), which replaced and expanded the former compensatory financing facility, established in 1963. The CCFF provides compensation to members whose export earnings are reduced owing to circumstances beyond their control, or who are affected by excess costs of cereal imports. Contingency financing is provided to help members maintain their efforts at economic adjustment even when affected by a sharp increase in interest rates or other externally-derived difficulties. Repurchases are made within three-and-a-quarter to five years.

In March 1986 the Fund established a structural adjustment facility (SAF) to provide balance of payments assistance on concessional terms to low-income developing countries. The facility was to be funded with about SDR 2,700m., expected to become available during 1985–91 from repayments of Trust Fund loans. SAF loans carry an interest rate of 0.5%, repayable within 10 years, including a five-and-a-half-year grace period. The member concerned may draw up to 70% of its quota over three years, and must develop a three-year adjustment programme (with assistance given jointly by staff of the Fund and of the World Bank) to restore sustainable economic growth. At mid-1989 62 countries were eligible for assistance under the SAF (but two, the People's Republic of China and India, had indicated that they would not avail themselves of the facility, thus enlarging the amount available for other countries). By August 1989 SAF arrangements had been approved for 31 countries, with total commitments of SDR 1,600m.

In December 1987 the Fund established an enhanced structural adjustment facility (ESAF), which was to provide new resources of SDR 6,000m. (in addition to SDR 2,200m. as yet undisbursed under the SAF), to assist the adjustment efforts of, in particular, heavily-indebted countries. Maximum access was to be set at 250% of the member's quota, and conditions for repayment were to be similar to those imposed under the SAF.

In May 1989 the Fund approved guidelines for further assistance to indebted countries, allowing about 25% of resources under a country's extended or stand-by arrangement to be used to support operations involving reduction of debt principal; the Fund was also to approve additional funding (up to 40% of a member's quota) for interest support in connection with reduction of debt or debt-servicing.

In the year ending 30 April 1990, the IMF made commitments of SDR 11,336.9m. to member countries (compared with SDR 4,559.7m. in the previous 12 months). Of this amount, SDR 3,249m. was committed under 16 stand-by arrangements, SDR 7,627m. under three extended arrangements, and SDR 460.5m. under seven SAF and ESAF arrangements.

Overdue financial obligations to the Fund increased to SDR 3,300m. in 1989/90. In June 1990 the Board of Governors adopted a Third Amendment to the IMF's Articles of Agreement, providing for the suspension of voting rights and certain related rights when a member persistently fails to fulfil its obligations.

TECHNICAL ASSISTANCE

This is provided by special missions or resident representatives who advise members on every aspect of economic management. The Central Banking Department and the Fiscal Affairs Department are particularly involved in technical assistance. The IMF Institute, founded in 1964, trains officials from member countries in financial analysis and policy, balance of payments methodology and public finance: it also gives assistance to national and regional training centres.

PUBLICATIONS

Annual Report.

Annual Report on Exchange Arrangements and Exchange Restrictions.

International Financial Statistics (monthly and annually).

Balance of Payments Statistics (monthly and annually).

Government Finance Statistics Yearbook.

Direction of Trade Statistics (monthly and annually).

IMF Survey (2 a month).

Finance and Development (quarterly, published jointly with the World Bank).

Staff Papers (quarterly economic journal).

International Capital Markets (annually).

World Economic Outlook (annually).

Occasional papers, publications brochure.

INTERNATIONAL ORGANIZATIONS

United Nations (Specialized Agencies)

Statistics

QUOTAS (million SDRs)

	August 1990	Proposed quotas under Ninth General Review
Afghanistan	86.7	120.4
Algeria	623.1	914.4
Angola	145.0	207.3
Antigua and Barbuda	5.0	8.5
Argentina	1,113.0	1,537.1
Australia	1,619.2	2,333.2
Austria	775.6	1,188.3
Bahamas	66.4	94.9
Bahrain	48.9	82.8
Bangladesh	287.5	392.5
Barbados	34.1	48.9
Belgium	2,080.4	3,102.3
Belize	9.5	13.5
Benin	31.3	45.3
Bhutan	2.5	4.5
Bolivia	90.7	126.2
Botswana	22.1	36.6
Brazil	1,461.3	2,170.8
Burkina Faso	31.6	44.2
Burundi	42.7	57.2
Cambodia	25.0	25.0
Cameroon	92.7	135.1
Canada	2,941.0	4,320.3
Cape Verde	4.5	7.0
Central African Republic	30.4	41.2
Chad	30.6	41.3
Chile	440.5	621.7
China, People's Republic	2,390.9	3,385.2
Colombia	394.2	561.3
Comoros	4.5	6.5
Congo	37.3	57.9
Costa Rica	84.1	119.0
Côte d'Ivoire	165.5	238.2
Cyprus	69.7	100.0
Denmark	711.0	1,069.9
Djibouti	8.0	11.5
Dominica	4.0	6.0
Dominican Republic	112.1	158.8
Ecuador	150.7	219.2
Egypt	463.4	678.4
El Salvador	89.0	125.6
Equatorial Guinea	18.4	24.3
Ethiopia	70.6	98.3
Fiji	36.5	51.1
Finland	574.9	861.8
France	4,482.8	7,414.6
Gabon	73.1	110.3
The Gambia	17.1	22.9
Germany	5,403.7	8,241.5
Ghana	204.5	274.0
Greece	399.9	587.6
Grenada	6.0	8.5
Guatemala	108.0	153.8
Guinea	57.9	78.7
Guinea-Bissau	7.5	10.5
Guyana	49.2	67.2
Haiti	44.1	60.7
Honduras	67.8	95.0
Hungary	530.7	754.8
Iceland	59.6	85.3
India	2,207.7	3,055.5
Indonesia	1,009.7	1,497.6
Iran	660.0	1,078.5
Iraq	504.0	864.8
Ireland	343.4	525.0
Israel	446.6	666.2
Italy	2,909.1	4,590.7
Jamaica	145.5	200.9
Japan	4,223.3	8,241.5
Jordan	73.9	121.7
Kenya	142.0	199.4

—continued	August 1990	Proposed quotas under Ninth General Review
Kiribati	2.5	4.0
Korea, Republic	462.8	799.6
Kuwait	635.3	995.2
Laos	29.3	39.1
Lebanon	78.7	146.0
Lesotho	15.1	23.9
Liberia	71.3	96.2
Libya	515.7	817.6
Luxembourg	77.0	135.5
Madagascar	66.4	90.4
Malawi	37.2	50.9
Malaysia	550.6	832.7
Maldives	2.0	5.5
Mali	50.8	68.9
Malta	45.1	67.5
Mauritania	33.9	47.5
Mauritius	53.6	73.3
Mexico	1,165.5	1,753.3
Morocco	306.6	427.7
Mozambique	61.0	84.0
Myanmar	137.0	184.9
Nepal	37.3	52.0
Netherlands	2,264.8	3,444.2
New Zealand	461.6	650.1
Nicaragua	68.2	96.1
Niger	33.7	48.3
Nigeria	849.5	1,281.6
Norway	699.0	1,104.6
Oman	63.1	119.4
Pakistan	546.3	758.2
Panama	102.2	149.6
Papua New Guinea	65.9	95.3
Paraguay	48.4	72.1
Peru	330.9	466.1
Philippines	440.4	633.4
Poland	680.0	988.5
Portugal	376.6	557.6
Qatar	114.9	190.5
Romania	523.4	754.1
Rwanda	43.8	59.5
Saint Christopher and Nevis	4.5	6.5
Saint Lucia	7.5	11.0
Saint Vincent and the Grenadines	4.0	6.0
São Tomé and Príncipe	4.0	5.5
Saudi Arabia	3,202.4	5,130.6
Senegal	85.1	118.9
Seychelles	3.0	6.0
Sierra Leone	57.9	77.2
Singapore	92.4	357.6
Solomon Islands	5.0	7.5
Somalia	44.2	60.9
South Africa	915.7	1,365.4
Spain	1,286.0	1,935.4
Sri Lanka	223.1	303.6
Sudan	169.7	233.1
Suriname	49.3	67.6
Swaziland	24.7	36.5
Sweden	1,064.3	1,614.0
Syria	139.1	209.9
Tanzania	107.0	146.9
Thailand	386.6	573.9
Togo	38.4	54.3
Tonga	3.25	5.0
Trinidad and Tobago	170.1	246.8
Tunisia	138.2	206.0
Turkey	429.1	642.0
Uganda	99.6	133.9
United Arab Emirates	202.6	392.1
United Kingdom	6,194.0	7,414.6
USA	17,918.3	26,526.8
Uruguay	163.8	225.3
Vanuatu	9.0	12.5
Venezuela	1,371.5	1,951.3
Viet-Nam	176.8	241.6
Western Samoa	6.0	8.5
Yemen	120.5	176.5
Yugoslavia	613.0	918.3
Zaire	291.0	394.8
Zambia	270.3	363.5
Zimbabwe	191.0	261.3

FINANCIAL ACTIVITIES (SDR million, year ending 30 April)

Type of Transaction	1985	1986	1987	1988	1989	1990
Total disbursements	6,060	3,941	3,307	4,562	2,682	5,266
Purchases by facility (General Resources Account)*	6,060	3,941	3,168	4,117	2,128	4,440
Credit tranches	2,768	2,841	2,325	2,313	1,702	1,183
Buffer stock financing facility	—	—	—	—	—	—
Compensatory and contingency financing facility	1,248	601	593	1,544	238	808
Extended Fund facility	2,044	498	250	260	188	2,449
Loans under SAF/ESAF arrangements	—	—	139	445	554	826
Special Disbursement Account resources	—	—	139	445	380	584
ESAF Trust resources	—	—	—	—	174	242
By region: developing countries	6,060	3,941	3,307	4,562	2,682	5,267
Africa	1,018	842	647	955	701	1,289
Asia	747	844	1,282	804	469	525
Europe	838	323	68	—	338	268
Middle East	57	—	—	116	—	66
Western Hemisphere	3,401	1,933	1,311	2,688	1,174	3,119
Repurchases and repayments	3,041	4,687	6,741	8,463	6,705	6,398
Repurchases†	2,829	4,274	6,162	7,935	6,258	6,042
Trust Fund loan repayments	212	413	579	528	447	356
Total outstanding credit provided by Fund (end of year)	37,622	36,877	33,443	29,543	25,520	24,389
Of which:						
General Resources Account	34,973	34,640	31,646	27,829	23,700	22,098
Special Disbursement Account	—	—	139	584	965	1,549
Administered Accounts						
Trust Fund	2,650	2,237	1,658	1,129	682	327
ESAF Trust	—	—	—	—	174	416

* Excluding reserve tranche purchases.
† Including sales of currencies, which have the effect of repurchases.
Source: *International Monetary Fund Annual Report 1990.*

International Telecommunication Union—ITU

Address: Place des Nations, 1211 Geneva 20, Switzerland.
Telephone: (022) 7305111.
Telex: 421000.
Fax: (022) 7337256.

Founded in 1865, ITU became a Specialized Agency of the UN in 1947. It acts to encourage world co-operation in the use of telecommunication, to promote technical development and to harmonize national policies in the field.

MEMBERS
164 members: see Table on pp. 52-54.

Organization
(October 1990)

PLENIPOTENTIARY CONFERENCE

The supreme organ of ITU; meets about every five years. Each member has one vote at the Conference, whose main tasks are to establish policies, revise the Convention (see below) and approve limits on budgetary spending. The 1989 Conference (May/June) was held in Nice, France. It adopted a new constitution for ITU.

WORLD ADMINISTRATIVE CONFERENCES

The World Administrative Telegraph and Telephone Conference revises telegraph and telephone regulations. The World Administrative Radio Conference revises radio regulations and reviews the activities of the International Frequency Registration Board. World Administrative Conferences meet at irregular intervals according to technical needs, and there may also be regional Administrative Conferences held to consider specific issues of a regional nature.

ADMINISTRATIVE COUNCIL

The Administrative Council meets annually in Geneva and is composed of 43 members elected by the Plenipotentiary Conference.

The Council ensures the efficient co-ordination of the work of the Union in all matters of policy, administration and finance, in the interval between Plenipotentiary Conferences, and approves the annual budget.

GENERAL SECRETARIAT

The Secretary-General is elected by the Plenipotentiary Conference, and is responsible to it for the General Secretariat's work, and for the Union's administrative and financial services. The General Secretariat's staff totals 750; the working languages are Arabic, Chinese, English, French, Russian and Spanish.

Secretary-General: Dr Pekka Tarjanne (Finland).

Convention

The International Telecommunication Convention is the definitive convention of the Union, member countries being those who signed it in 1932 or acceded to it later. Since 1932 it has been superseded by new versions at successive plenipotentiary conferences. The Convention current in 1990 was adopted in 1982 and entered into force in 1984; it was to be superseded by the Convention and constitution adopted in 1989, once they came into force.

The Convention deals with the purposes and structure of the Union, the general provisions relating to telecommunications, special provisions for radio, relations with the UN and other organizations, and the application of the Convention and the Regulations.

TELECOMMUNICATIONS REGULATIONS

The Telecommunications Regulations were adopted in 1988 and entered into force in 1990. They establish the general principles relating to the provision and operation of international telecommunication services offered to the public. They also establish rules applicable to administrations and recognized private operating agencies. Their provisions are applied to both wire and wireless telegraph and telephone communications in so far as the Radio Regulations and the Additional Radio Regulations do not provide otherwise.

INTERNATIONAL ORGANIZATIONS

United Nations (Specialized Agencies)

RADIO REGULATIONS

The Radio Regulations include general rules for the assignment and use of frequencies and the associated orbital positions for space stations. They include a Table of Frequency Allocations (governing the use of radio frequency bands between 9kHz and 400 GHz) for the various radio services (radio broadcasting, television, radio astronomy, navigation aids, point-to-point service, maritime mobile, amateur).

The 1979 World Administrative Radio Conference undertook a complete revision of the radio spectrum allocation. Partial revisions were also made by subsequent world and regional administrative radio conferences, particularly with reference to space radio-communications, using satellites.

Activities

INTERNATIONAL FREQUENCY REGISTRATION BOARD—IFRB

IFRB records assignments of radio frequencies and provides technical advice to enable members of the Union to operate as many radio channels as possible in overcrowded parts of the radio spectrum. It also investigates cases of harmful interference and makes recommendations for their solution.

INTERNATIONAL TELEGRAPH AND TELEPHONE CONSULTATIVE COMMITTEE—CCITT

The work of the Committee is done by 15 study groups, covering telecommunications networks and network components, telecommunications services and tariffs, and subjects of specific interest to developing countries. Handbooks are published.

Director: T. IRMER (Germany).

INTERNATIONAL RADIO CONSULTATIVE COMMITTEE— CCIR

The work of CCIR is done by 12 study groups covering sound and television broadcasting, satellite broadcasting, broadcast programme transmissions, computer applications, spectrum utilization and monitoring, space research and radioastronomy, radio-wave propagation, fixed satellite service, etc.

Director: RICHARD C. KIRBY (USA).

PLAN COMMITTEES

The Plan Committees are joint CCIR/CCITT committees responsible for preparing plans establishing circuit and routing requirements for international telecommunications and for giving estimates of the growth of international traffic. They comprise a World Plan Committee and four regional committees, for Africa, for Latin America, for Asia and Oceania and for Europe and the Mediterranean Basin.

TECHNICAL CO-OPERATION

ITU's programme of technical co-operation in developing countries is mainly financed by UNDP (q.v.), at an annual cost of about US $30m. In 1990 a Telecommunications Development Bureau was established to implement projects: it undertakes research and field studies, provides advice and training, and attempts to ensure the strict application of international technical and operational standards.

INFORMATION

ITU issues numerous technical and statistical publications (see below) and maintains a library and archives.

FINANCE

The total 1990 budget amounted to 136m. Swiss francs (compared with 132m. Swiss francs in 1989).

PUBLICATIONS

List of Publications (2 a year).

Telecommunication Journal (monthly).

Conventions, statistics, technical documents and manuals, conference documents.

United Nations Educational, Scientific and Cultural Organization—UNESCO

Address: 7 place de Fontenoy, 75700 Paris.
Telephone: (1) 45-68-10-00.
Telex: 204461.
Fax: (1) 45-67-16-90.

UNESCO was established in 1946 'for the purpose of advancing, through the educational, scientific and cultural relations of the peoples of the world, the objectives of international peace and the common welfare of mankind'.

MEMBERS

156 members: see Table on pp. 52-54.

Organization

(October 1990)

GENERAL CONFERENCE

The supreme governing body of the Organization, the Conference meets in ordinary session once in two years and is composed of representatives of the member states.

EXECUTIVE BOARD

The Board, comprising 50 members, prepares the programme to be submitted to the Conference and supervises its execution; it meets twice or sometimes three times a year.

SECRETARIAT

Director-General: FEDERICO MAYOR ZARAGOZA (Spain).
Director of the Executive Office: LUIS MARQUES (Spain).

CO-OPERATING BODIES

In accordance with UNESCO's Constitution, national Commissions have been set up in most member states. These help to integrate work within the member states and the work of UNESCO.

UNESCO REGIONAL OFFICES

Africa

Regional Office for Education in Africa: BP 3311, Dakar, Senegal; tel. 23-50-82; telex 51410; fax 23-83-93; Dir THOMAS KELLER.

Regional Office for Science and Technology for Africa: POB 30592, Nairobi, Kenya; tel. 333930; telex 22275; f. 1965 to execute UNESCO's regional science programme, and to assist in the planning and execution of national programmes. Dir Prof. P. LISSOUBA.

Latin America and the Caribbean

Regional Centre for Higher Education in Latin America and the Caribbean (CRESALC): Altos de Sebucan, Avda Los Chorros/Cruce, Calle Acueducto, Edificio Asovincar, Apdo 62090, Caracas 1060, Venezuela.

Regional Office for Culture in Latin America and the Caribbean: Calzada 551, esq. a D, Vedado, Apdo 4158, Havana, Cuba; tel. 32-7741; telex 51-2154; Dir H. CRESPO TORAL.

Regional Office for Education in Latin America and the Caribbean: POB 3187, Santiago, Chile; tel. 223-5582; telex 340258; fax 491875.

Regional Office for Science and Technology for Latin America and the Caribbean: 1320 Bulevar Artigas, Casilla 859, 11000 Montevideo, Uruguay; tel. 41.18.07; telex 22340; Dir E. M. DEL CAMPO.

Asia and the Pacific

Office for the Pacific States: POB 5766, Matautu, Apia, Western Samoa; tel. 24276; telex 209; Chief of Mission F. L. HIGGINSON.

Principal Regional Office for Asia and the Pacific (including the Asian Centre for Educational Innovation for Development): 920 Sukhumvit Rd, POB 920 Prakanong Post Office, Bangkok 10110, Thailand; tel. 391-0577; telex 20591; fax 391-0866; Dir HEDEYAT AHMED.

Regional Office for Book Development in Asia and the Pacific: POB 2043A, Islamabad, Pakistan; tel. 822071; telex 5886; fax 823783.

Regional Office for Science and Technology for South and Central Asia: UNESCO House, 15 Jor Bagh, New Delhi 110003, India; tel. 618092; telex 31-65896; fax 615176; Dir Dr M. P. DERKATCH.

Regional Office for Science and Technology for South-East Asia: UN Building (2nd Floor), Jl. Thamrin 14, Tromol Pos 273/JKT, Jakarta, Indonesia; tel. 321308; telex 44178.

Arab States and Europe

European Centre for Higher Education (CEPES): Palatul Kretulescu, Stirbei Voda 39, Bucharest, Romania; tel. 159956; telex 11658.

Regional Office for Education in the Arab States: 7 place de Fontenoy, 75700 Paris, France.

Regional Office for Science and Technology in the Arab States: POB 950492, Amman, Jordan; tel. 606559; telex 24357; Dir Dr OSMAN ABAYAZID.

Activities

UNESCO's activities, which take three main forms as outlined below, are funded through a regular budget provided by member states and also through other sources, particularly UNDP. UNESCO co-operates with many other UN agencies and international non-governmental organizations.

International Intellectual Co-operation: UNESCO assists the interchange of experience, knowledge and ideas through a world network of specialists. Apart from the work of its professional staff, UNESCO co-operates regularly with the national associations and international federations of scientists, artists, writers and educators, some of which it helped to establish. UNESCO convenes conferences and meetings, and co-ordinates international scientific efforts; it helps to standardize procedures of documentation and provides clearing house services; it offers fellowships; and it publishes a wide range of specialized works, including source books and works of reference. UNESCO promotes various international agreements, including the International Copyright Convention and the World Cultural and National Heritage Convention, which member states are invited to accept.

Operational Assistance: UNESCO has established missions which advise governments, particularly in the developing member countries, in the planning of projects; and it appoints experts to assist in carrying them out. The projects are concerned with the teaching of functional literacy to workers in development undertakings; teacher training; establishing of libraries and documentation centres; provision of training for journalists, radio, television and film workers; improvement of scientific and technical education; training of planners in cultural development; and the international exchange of persons and information.

Promotion of Peace: UNESCO organizes various research efforts on racial problems, and is particularly concerned with prevention of discrimination in education, and improving access for women to education. It also promotes studies and research on conflicts and peace, violence and obstacles to disarmament, and the role of international law and organizations in building peace. It is stressed that human rights, peace and disarmament cannot be dealt with separately, as the observance of human rights is a prerequisite to peace and vice versa.

In 1984 the government of the USA (which had been due to provide about 25% of UNESCO's budget for the two years 1984–85) withdrew from the organization, alleging inefficiency, financial mismanagement and political bias against Western countries. The United Kingdom and Singapore also withdrew from UNESCO at the end of 1985. In April 1990 the Governments of both the United Kingdom and the USA announced that reforms undertaken by UNESCO's administration had not been sufficient for them to consider rejoining the organization in the near future.

EDUCATION

UNESCO's most important activities, as stipulated in its programme for 1990–95, are in the sphere of education, particularly the spread of literacy, adult education, and the encouragement of universal primary education. It places special emphasis on the attainment of education by women and the handicapped, and on literacy as an integral part of rural development. During the two years 1986–87 this sector was allocated US $71m. from the organization's regular budget of $307m.

Each year expert missions are sent to member states on request to advise on all matters concerning education. In 1987 UNESCO provided about 5,000 fellowships and travel grants. In these forms of assistance priority is given to the rural regions of developing member countries.

Examples of activities include: co-operation with UNRWA (q.v.) to provide schooling for Palestinian refugee children; educational assistance for African refugees; studies on the establishment of regional industries to provide educational equipment; and about 90 teacher-training schemes. The International Institute for Educational Planning and the International Bureau of Education (q.v.) carry out training, research and the exchange of information on aspects of education.

UNESCO was given responsibility for organizing International Literacy Year (1990), which was proclaimed by the UN as a means of initiating a plan of action for the spread of literacy (based on regional literacy programmes that had been established by UNESCO over the past decade in Africa, Latin America and the Caribbean, the Arab states and Asia and the Pacific). The principal aims of the International Literacy Year were to increase action by governments to eliminate illiteracy among women and disadvantaged groups; and to increase public awareness of the extent and implications of illiteracy.

In March 1990 UNESCO, with other UN agencies, sponsored the World Conference on Education for All.

NATURAL SCIENCES AND TECHNOLOGY

UNESCO's science and technology programme was allocated US $49m. from the organization's regular budget of $307m. for 1986–87. While the main emphasis in UNESCO's work in science and technology is on harnessing these to development, and above all on meeting the needs of developing countries, the Organization is also active in promoting and fostering collaborative international projects among the highly industrialized countries. UNESCO's activities can be divided into three levels: international, regional and sub-regional, and national.

At the international level, UNESCO has over the years established various forms of intergovernmental co-operation concerned with the environmental sciences and research on natural resources. Examples of these are the Man and Biosphere Programme (MAB) which by 1988 had undertaken 1,000 programmes in 100 countries, involving local people in solving practical problems of environmental resource management in arid lands, humid tropical zones, mountain ecosystems, urban systems, etc.; the International Geological Correlation Programme (IGCP), run jointly with the International Union of Geological Sciences (q.v.); the International Hydrological Programme (IHP), dealing with the scientific aspects of water resources assessment and management; and the Intergovernmental Oceanographic Commission (q.v.) which promotes scientific investigation into the nature and resources of the oceans through the concerted action of its member states. Another programme, the Intergovernmental Informatics Programme, encourages co-operation between developed and developing countries in computer sciences. In the basic sciences, UNESCO helps promote international and regional co-operation in close collaboration with the world scientific communities, with which it maintains close co-operative links particularly through its support to ICSU and member unions. Major disciplinary programmes are promoted in the fields of physics (including support to the International Centre for Theoretical Physics), the chemical sciences, life sciences, including applied microbiology, mathematics, informatics and new sources of energy.

At the regional and sub-regional level, UNESCO develops co-operative scientific and technological research programmes through organization and support of scientific meetings and contacts with research institutions, and the establishment or strengthening of co-operative networks; the African Network of Scientific and Technological Institutions, for example, was launched in 1980 at UNESCO's Nairobi Regional Office, to encourage collaboration among these institutions, and in 1982 a regional network of engineering institutions was established in the Middle East. Periodically, regional ministerial conferences are organized on science and technology policy and on the application of science and technology to development. A second conference of ministers responsible for the application of science and technology to development in Africa was held in July 1987. More specialized regional and sub-regional meetings are also organized.

At the national level, UNESCO assists member states, upon request, in policy-making and planning in the field of science and technology generally, and by organizing training and research programmes in basic sciences, engineering sciences and environmental sciences, particularly work relevant to development, such as projects concerning the use of small scale energy sources for rural and dispersed populations. In 1989 a two-year programme was set up to assist the teaching of the natural sciences in universities in the developing countries, through grants for the production of low-cost laboratory equipment and teaching materials, and training courses for university teachers and laboratory technicians.

SOCIAL SCIENCES

The social and human sciences programme aims to encourage the development of the social sciences throughout the world by strengthening national and regional institutions, the conceptual development of the social sciences, training, the exchange and diffusion of information, and co-operation with international non-governmental organizations. The programme was allocated US $14m. from UNESCO's 1986-87 budget of $307m.

The activities concerning human rights and peace include two major programmes: the elimination of prejudice, intolerance, racism and apartheid; and a programme for peace, international understanding, human rights and the rights of peoples.

CULTURE

UNESCO's cultural heritage programme was allocated US $19m. from the organization's budget of $307m. for 1986-87. The programme is in three parts: activities designed to foster the world-wide application of three international conventions that aim to protect and conserve cultural property; international safeguarding campaigns to help member states to conserve and restore monuments and sites (in 1988 there were 22 such campaigns in progress); and the training of museum managers and conservationists and promotion of public awareness of the cultural heritage.

UNESCO's World Heritage Programme, launched in 1978, aims to protect historic sites and natural landmarks of outstanding universal significance, in accordance with the 1972 UNESCO Convention Concerning the Protection of the World Cultural and Natural Heritage, by providing financial aid for restoration, technical assistance, training and management planning. By the beginning of 1989 the 'World Heritage List' comprised 315 sites in 67 countries: for example, the Great Barrier Reef in Australia, the Galapagos Islands (Ecuador), Chartres Cathedral (France), the Taj Mahal (India), Auschwitz concentration camp (Poland), the historic sanctuary of Machu Picchu (Peru), and the Serengeti National Park (Tanzania). UNESCO has participated in the restoration of the Buddhist temple at Borobudur, Indonesia (1973-83), the re-siting of the temples of Abu Simbel, Egypt, preliminary work on preserving the ancient city of Moenjodaro, Pakistan, and many other conservation projects.

The seventh volume of an eight-volume history of Africa was published in 1985, and in 1988 work was also in progress on histories of Latin America, the Caribbean and the civilizations of Central Asia, and on a six-volume publication on Islamic culture. A 10-year programme for the collection and safeguarding of the non-physical heritage (oral traditions, music, dance, medicine, etc.) was begun in 1988. UNESCO encourages the translation and publication of literary works, publishes albums of art, and produces records, audiovisual programmes and travelling art exhibitions. It supports the development of book publishing and distribution and the training of editors and managers in publishing. UNESCO is active in preparing and encouraging the enforcement of international legislation on copyright.

COMMUNICATION

UNESCO's programme aims at fostering a free flow of information among individuals, communities and countries, The international movement of persons and circulation of materials are promoted through measures for the reduction of obstacles of a legislative, administrative or economic nature. The communication programme received US $13m. in the 1986-87 budget.

Assistance is provided to member states in the formulation of national communication policies, and a series of regional intergovernmental conferences on this subject has been organized since 1976. UNESCO also promotes research in the field of communication.

At the General Conference in October 1980 a 'New World Information and Communication Order' (NWICO) (including plans for an international code of journalistic ethics and for the 'licensing' of journalists) was approved, in spite of objections from the United Kingdom and USA; those in favour of NWICO argued that established agencies and commercial interests had too much control over news and information, while their opponents maintained that the new proposals infringed press freedom. Following the approval of NWICO, the Intergovernmental Programme for the Development of Communication (IPDC) was established, under which UNESCO executes a number of programmes both in individual countries and at the regional and sub-regional levels, to provide advisory services and help advance professional training in communication skills. Projects included the Pan-African News Agency,

a regional training centre for the Arab states, a Latin American information service and, in Asia, a network of information exchange and a 'bank' of films and television programmes. Two international projects were also planned: a study on the role of satellites in the exchange of information, and a project on rural communications.

FINANCE

UNESCO's Regular Programme budget for the two years 1984-85 was US $374.4m.; for 1986-87 it was $307m., and for 1988-89 it was $350.4m. Extra-budgetary funds were expected to amount to $213m. in 1988-89. The budget for 1990-91 envisaged expenditure of $380m.

PUBLICATIONS

(mostly in English, French and Spanish editions; Arabic, Chinese and Russian versions are also available in many cases)

UNESCO Courier (monthly, in 35 languages).

UNESCO Sources (monthly).

Copyright Bulletin (quarterly).

Museum (quarterly).

Impact of Science on Society (quarterly).

International Social Science Journal (quarterly).

Nature and Resources (quarterly review of the Man and Biosphere programme, the International Hydrological Programme and the International Geological Correlation Programme).

Prospects (quarterly review on education).

Books, statistics, scientific maps and atlases.

INTERNATIONAL INSTITUTE FOR EDUCATIONAL PLANNING—IIEP

Address: 7-9 rue Eugène Delacroix, 75116 Paris, France.

Telephone: (1) 45-04-28-22.

Telex: 640032.

Fax: (1) 40-72-83-66.

The Institute was established by UNESCO in 1963 to serve as a world centre for advanced training and research in educational planning. Its purpose is to help all member states of UNESCO in their social and economic development efforts, by enlarging the fund of knowledge about educational planning and the supply of competent experts in this field.

Legally and administratively a part of UNESCO, the Institute is autonomous, and its policies and programme are controlled by its own Governing Board, under special statutes voted by the General Conference of UNESCO.

Chairman of Governing Board: Prof. MALCOLM S. ADISESHIAH.

Director: JACQUES HALLAK.

INTERNATIONAL BUREAU OF EDUCATION—IBE

Address: POB 199, 1211 Geneva 20, Switzerland.

Telephone: (022) 7981455.

Telex: 415771.

Fax: (022) 7981486.

Founded in 1925, the IBE became an intergovernmental organization in 1929 and was incorporated into UNESCO in 1969 as an international centre of comparative education. The Bureau provides information on developments and innovations in education; it has a library of 100,000 volumes, with 300,000 research reports on microfiche. It publishes a quarterly bulletin and newsletter, and various reference works. The Council of the IBE is composed of representatives of 24 Member States designated by the General Conference of UNESCO. The International Conference on Education is held every two years.

Director: GEORGES TOHMÉ.

INTERGOVERNMENTAL COMMITTEE FOR PHYSICAL EDUCATION AND SPORT—ICPES

Address: 7 place de Fontenoy, 75700 Paris.

Established by UNESCO in 1978 to serve as a permanent intergovernmental body in the field of physical education and sport.

The Committee is composed of 30 representatives of member states of UNESCO, elected by the General Conference.

United Nations Industrial Development Organization—UNIDO

Address: POB 300, 1400 Vienna, Austria.
Telephone: (01) 21-13-10.
Telex: 135612.
Fax: (01) 23-21-56.

UNIDO began operations in 1967, as an autonomous organization within the UN Secretariat, and became a specialized agency of the UN on 1 January 1986. Its objective is to promote industrial development in developing countries, so as to help in the establishment of a new international economic order.

MEMBERS
151 members: see Table on pp. 52-54.

Organization
(October 1990)

GENERAL CONFERENCE
The General Conference meets every two years and consists of representatives of all member states. It is the chief policy-making body of the Organization.

INDUSTRIAL DEVELOPMENT BOARD
The Board consists of 53 members elected by the General Conference for a three-year period: 33 members are from developing countries, 15 from developed market-economy countries, and five from countries with centrally-planned economies.

PROGRAMME AND BUDGET COMMITTEE
The Committee consists of 27 members, elected by the General Conference for a two-year term.

SECRETARIAT
At the beginning of 1990 there were 1,358 staff members in the UNIDO Secretariat. The Secretariat comprises the office of the Director-General and five departments, each headed by a Deputy Director-General: Programme and Project Development; Industrial Operations; Industrial Promotion, Consultations and Technology; External Relations, Public Information, Language and Documentation Services; and Administration.

Director-General: DOMINGO L. SIAZON, Jr.

FIELD REPRESENTATION
UNIDO's Country Directors work in developing countries, in collaboration with the Resident Representatives of UNDP. In 1989 there were 37 Country Directors and 69 Junior Professional Officers. A total of 2,131 experts were engaged in field work.

Activities

Activities cover macro-economic and micro-economic aspects of industrial development. At macro-economic level, questions are considered concerning the formulation of industrial development policies, planning, programming, surveys, infrastructure and structure, and institutional services to industry. At micro-economic level, assistance is provided in problems of pre-feasibility and feasibility of industry or plant, investment and financing, production and productivity, product development and design, technology and techniques, management, marketing, quality and research.

Technical assistance is provided on request to developing countries through governments, industries or other bodies. Such assistance usually consists of expert services, but can also include supply of equipment or fellowships for training. During 1989 UNIDO's technical assistance activities included support for regional development of hides, skins, leather and leather products in Africa, for glass production in Viet-Nam and for modernization of the manufacturing sector in Brazil. International workshops were held on enterprise-to-enterprise co-operation in the food-processing sector; on welding and electro-smelting technology; on liquid natural rubber; on railway transport development; and on industrialization of least-developed countries. Studies were published on industrial development in Angola, Bangladesh, Cameroon, Djibouti, Mauritania, Namibia, Sudan, the Yemen Arab Republic and the People's Democratic Republic of Yemen.

The Secretariat provides contacts between industrialized and developing countries and identifies possibilities for the solution of specific problems in developing countries. The Industrial and Technological Information Bank provides information on technologies developed or adapted for developing countries.

There are Investment Promotion Offices in Cologne, Milan, Paris, Seoul, Tokyo, Vienna, Warsaw, Washington and Zürich to publicize investment opportunities and provide information to investors. UNIDO also co-sponsors (with the governments concerned) investment promotion meetings in a particular country or region, identifying projects and bringing together potential investors. During 1989 'Investment Forums' were held in Freetown, Sierra Leone, and Hanover, Federal Republic of Germany (for the People's Republic of China).

The System of Consultations, introduced in 1977, is designed to help developing countries increase their share of total world production as much as possible. During 1989 Consultations were held on the food-processing industry, electronics, capital goods and small and medium-sized enterprises. These meetings are attended by representatives of government, labour, industry, consumer interests and financial institutions, who examine prospects and targets for the growth of production of the commodity concerned in both developed and developing countries.

UNIDO assisted in establishing the International Centre for Genetic Engineering and Biotechnology, based in Trieste (Italy) and New Delhi (India), and linked with national centres. The Centre began an interim programme of work in 1988.

During 1989 UNIDO awarded 1,896 fellowships (1,422 in 1988). A total of 85 group training programmes were carried out, and training was provided for 1,451 nationals of developing countries through fellowships, group training programmes and workshops in factories, study tours and as counterparts attached to field projects.

In 1989 UNIDO carried out 1,896 projects at a cost of $133.8m., of which 40.6% was for expert personnel, 28.0% for equipment and 15.1% for training and fellowships.

UNIDO project expenditure (1989)

Purpose	Amount (US $ million)
Chemical industries	30.2
Engineering industries	17.2
Agro-industries	14.6
Metallurgical industries	9.1
Institutional infrastructure	15.0
Industrial human resource development	6.4
Feasibility studies	7.0
Industrial planning	8.1
Industrial management and rehabilitation	7.5

FINANCE
The regular budget for the two years 1990-91 amounted to US $156.7m. An operational budget of $34.2m. was approved for 1990-91. The Industrial Development Fund is used by UNIDO to finance development projects which fall outside the usual systems of multilateral funding. In 1988 and 1989 the Industrial Development Board appealed for an increase in contributions to the Fund to a level of $50m. annually. In 1990 serious arrears in contributions (amounting to $88.2m.) were reported.

PUBLICATIONS
Annual Report.
UNIDO Newsletter (monthly).

UNIDO Update (quarterly).
Industry and Development (annually).
Industry Africa (2 a year).
Handbook of Industrial Statistics (annually).
Guide to Information Sources (about 6 a year).
Transfer of Technology Series (6 to 8 a year).

Guide to Training Opportunities for Industrial Development (annually).
Manual for the Preparation of Industrial Feasibility Studies (10 languages).

Numerous working papers and reports (listed in *UNIDO Newsletter* as they appear).

Universal Postal Union—UPU

Address: Case postale, 3000 Berne 15, Switzerland.
Telephone: (031) 432211.
Telex: 912761.
Fax: (031) 432210.

The General Postal Union was founded by the Treaty of Berne (1874), beginning operations in July 1875. Three years later its name was changed to the Universal Postal Union. In 1948 UPU became a Specialized Agency of the UN.

MEMBERS
167 members: see Table on pp. 52–54.

Organization
(October 1990)

CONGRESS
The supreme body of the Union is Congress, which meets every five years. Its duties are legislative and consist mainly of revision of the Acts (see below). The 20th Congress was held in Washington, DC, USA, in 1989.

EXECUTIVE COUNCIL
Between Congresses, an Executive Council, created by the Paris Congress, 1947, meets annually at Berne. It is composed of 40 member countries of the Union elected by Congress on the basis of an equitable geographical distribution. It ensures continuity of the Union's work in the interval between Congresses, supervises the activities of the International Bureau, undertakes studies, draws up proposals, and makes recommendations to the Congress. It is responsible for encouraging, supervising and co-ordinating international co-operation in the form of postal technical assistance and vocational training.

CONSULTATIVE COUNCIL FOR POSTAL STUDIES
At the Ottawa Congress, 1957, a Consultative Committee for Postal Studies was established, which, at the Tokyo Congress, 1969, became the Consultative Council for Postal Studies (CCPS). Its 35 member countries meet annually, generally at Berne. It is responsible for organizing studies of major problems affecting postal administrations in all UPU member countries, in the technical operations and economic fields and in the sphere of technical co-operation. The CCPS also provides information and opinions on these matters, and examines teaching and training problems arising in the new and developing countries.

INTERNATIONAL BUREAU
The day-to-day administrative work of UPU is executed through the International Bureau, stationed at Berne. It serves as an instrument of liaison, information and consultation for the postal administration of the member countries, provides secretarial services for UPU bodies, promotes technical assistance and organizes conferences.

Director-General of the International Bureau: A. C. BOTTO DE BARROS (Brazil).

Activities
The essential principles of the Union are the following:

1. Formation of one single postal territory.
2. Unification of postal charges and weight steps.
3. Non-sharing of postage paid for ordinary letters between the sender country and the country of destination.
4. Guarantee of freedom of transit.
5. Settlement of disputes by arbitration.
6. Establishment of a central office under the name of the International Bureau paid for by all members.
7. Periodical meeting of Congress.
8. Promotion of the development of international postal services and postal technical assistance to Union members.

The common rules applicable to the international postal service and to the letter-post provisions are contained in the Universal Postal Convention and its Detailed Regulations. Owing to their importance in the postal field and their historical value, these two Acts, together with the Constitution and the General Regulations, constitute the compulsory Acts of the Union. It is therefore not possible to be a member country of the Union without being a party to these Acts and applying their provisions.

The activities of the international postal service, other than letter mail, are governed by Special Agreements. These are binding only for the countries which have acceded to them. There are eight such Agreements:

1. Agreement concerning Insured Letters and Boxes.
2. Agreement concerning Postal Parcels.
3. Agreement concerning Postal Money Orders and Postal Travellers' Cheques.
4. Agreement concerning Giro Transfers.
5. Agreement concerning Cash on Delivery Items.
6. Agreement concerning the Collection of Bills.
7. Agreement concerning the International Savings Bank Service.
8. Agreement concerning Subscriptions to Newspapers and Periodicals.

FINANCE
The Executive Council fixed 22.2m. Swiss francs as the maximum figure for annual gross expenditure in the year 1989, and 26.2m. Swiss francs for 1990. Members are listed in eight classes, establishing the proportion that they should pay.

PUBLICATIONS
Union Postale (quarterly, in French, German, English, Arabic, Chinese, Spanish and Russian).

Other UPU publications are listed in *Liste des publications du Bureau international*; all are in French, some also in English, Arabic and Spanish.

World Health Organization—WHO

Address: Avenue Appia, 1211 Geneva 27, Switzerland.
Telephone: (022) 7912111.
Telex: 415416.
Fax: (022) 7910746.

WHO was established in 1948 as the central agency directing international health work. Of its many activities, the most important single aspect is technical co-operation with national health administrations, particularly in the developing countries.

MEMBERS

165 members: see Table on pp. 52–54.

Organization
(October 1990)

WORLD HEALTH ASSEMBLY

The Assembly usually meets in Geneva, once a year; it is responsible for policy making, and the biennial programme and budget; appoints the Director-General, admits new members and reviews budget contributions.

EXECUTIVE BOARD

The Board is composed of 31 health experts designated by, but not representing, their governments; they serve for three years, and the World Health Assembly elects 10 or 11 member states each year to the Board. It meets at least twice a year to review the Director-General's programme, which it forwards to the Assembly with any recommendations that seem necessary. It advises on questions referred to it by the Assembly and is responsible for putting into effect the decisions and policies of the Assembly. It is also empowered to take emergency measures in case of epidemics or disasters.

SECRETARIAT

Director-General: Dr Hiroshi Nakajima (Japan).
Deputy Director-General: Dr Mohamed Abdelmoumène (Algeria).
Assistant Directors-General: Dr Hu Ching-Li (People's Republic of China), Dr Jean-Paul Jardel (France), Dr Nikolai P. Napalkov (USSR), Dr Ralph H. Henderson (USA), Denis G. Aitken (UK).

Administrative Divisions and Programmes:
Office of Research Promotion and Development.
Special Programme of Research, Development and Research Training in Human Reproduction.
Programme for External Coordination.
Division of Noncommunicable Diseases.
Health and Biomedical Information Programme.
Parasitic Diseases Programme.
Pharmaceuticals.
Division of Health Manpower Development.
Special Programme for Research and Training in Tropical Diseases.
Expanded Programme on Immunization.
Division of Budget and Finance.
Health for all Strategy Coordination.
Division of Environmental Health.
Action Programme on Essential Drugs.
Division of Information Systems Support.
Global Programme on AIDS.
Diarrhoeal and Acute Respiratory Diseases Control.
Division of Personnel and General Services.
Malaria Action Programme.
Division of Family Health.
Staff Development and Training.
Internal Audit.
Division of Mental Health.
Division of Vector Biology and Control.
Division of Strengthening of Health Services.
Division of Communicable Diseases.
Division of Epidemiological Surveillance and Health Situation and Trend Assessment.
National Health Systems and Policies.
Division of Diagnostic, Therapeutic and Rehabilitative Technology.
Division of Emergency Relief Operations.
Programme on Substance Abuse.

REGIONAL OFFICES

Each of WHO's six geographical regions has its own organization consisting of a regional committee representing the member states and associate members in the region concerned, and a regional office staffed by experts in various fields of health.

Africa: POB 6, Brazzaville, Congo; tel. 813860; telex 5217; Prof. Gottlieb Lobe Monekosso.

Americas: Pan-American Sanitary Bureau, 525 23rd St, NW, Washington, DC 20037, USA; tel. (202) 861-3200; telex 248338; Dir Dr Carlyle Guerra de Macedo.

Eastern Mediterranean: POB 1517, Alexandria 21511, Egypt; tel. (02) 4830090; telex 54028; Dir Dr Hussein Abdul-Razzaq Gezairy.

Europe: 8 Scherfigsvej, 2100 Copenhagen Ø, Denmark; tel. (01) 29-01-11; telex 15348; Dir Dr Jo Erik Asvall.

South-East Asia: Indraprastha Estate, Mahatma Gandhi Rd, New Delhi 110002, India; tel. (11) 3317804; telex 3165095; Dir Dr U Ko Ko.

Western Pacific: POB 2932, Manila 2801, Philippines; tel. (02) 5218421; telex 27652; Dir Dr Sang Tae Han.

Activities

WHO's objective is stated in the constitution as 'the attainment by all peoples of the highest possible level of health'.

It acts as the central authority directing international health work, and establishes relations with professional groups and government health authorities on that basis.

It supports, on request from member states, programmes to control or eradicate disease, train health workers best suited to local needs and strengthen national health systems. Aid is provided in emergencies and natural disasters.

A global programme of collaborative research and exchange of scientific information is carried out in co-operation with about 900 national institutions. Particular stress is laid on the widespread communicable diseases of the tropics, and the countries directly concerned are assisted in developing their research capabilities.

It keeps communicable diseases under constant surveillance, promotes the exchange of prompt and accurate information, and administers the International Health Regulations. It sets standards for the quality control of drugs, vaccines and other substances affecting health.

It collects and disseminates health data and carries out statistical analyses and comparative studies in such diseases as cancer, heart disease and mental illness.

It receives reports on drugs observed to have shown adverse reactions in any country, and transmits the information to other member states. All available information on effects on human health of the pollutants in the environment is critically reviewed and published.

Co-operation among scientists and professional groups is encouraged, and the organization may propose international conventions and agreements. It assists in developing an informed public opinion on matters of health.

HEALTH FOR ALL

In May 1981 the 34th World Health Assembly adopted a Global Strategy in support of 'Health for all by the year 2000', or the attainment by all citizens of the world of a level of health that will permit them to lead a socially and economically productive life. Almost all members indicated a high level of commitment to this goal, and guiding principles for national, regional and global plans of action were prepared, in response to the UN General Assembly resolution concerning health as an integral part of development. Primary health care is seen as the key to 'Health for all', with the following as minimum requirements:

Safe water in the home or within 15 minutes' walking distance, and adequate sanitary facilities in the home or immediate vicinity;

Immunization against diphtheria, pertussis (whooping cough), tetanus, poliomyelitis, measles and tuberculosis;

Local health care, including availability of at least 20 essential drugs, within one hour's travel;

Trained personnel to attend childbirth, and to care for pregnant mothers and children up to at least one year old.

The Eighth General Programme of Work, for the period 1990-95, comprises activities supporting the 'Health for All' strategy outlined above.

DISEASE PREVENTION AND CONTROL

One of WHO's major achievements was the eradication of smallpox, which, following a massive international campaign of vaccination and surveillance, begun in 1958 and intensified in 1967, was declared to have been achieved in 1977. In 1988 the World Health Assembly declared its commitment to the similar eradication of poliomyelitis by the year 2000; and in 1990 the Assembly resolved to eliminate iodine deficiency (causing mental handicap) by 2000.

WHO's Expanded Programme on Immunization (EPI), launched in 1974, aims to provide immunization for all children by 1990 against six diseases which constitute a major cause of death and disability in the developing countries: diphtheria, pertussis (whooping cough), tetanus, poliomyelitis, measles and tuberculosis. In July 1990 WHO reported that 70% of the world's children under one year of age had been immunized against these diseases (compared with 20% in the early 1980s), and that 10m. child deaths were being prevented annually by vaccination (although each year 3m. children were still dying of diseases preventable by vaccines). The programme costs WHO some US $8m. annually. An essential requirement is the 'cold chain' providing special containers and refrigerators for the transport of vaccines in tropical climates; WHO has developed appropriate equipment and training manuals for this purpose, and organizes special training courses for health workers.

Since 1960 WHO's Division of Vector Biology and Control has maintained a programme for the control of vector-borne diseases such as malaria, African trypanosomiasis (sleeping-sickness), American trypanosomiasis (Chagas disease), onchocerciasis (river-blindness), filariases, dengue and dengue haemorrhagic fever—all of which are transmitted by insects—and schistosomiasis (bilharzia), transmitted by a water-snail. WHO evaluates the insecticides developed to control these vectors (including the environmental effects of the chemicals used), and also conducts research on biological control, using the natural enemies of the vectors, such as larva-eating fish. It also encourages the environmental management of potential breeding-grounds for vectors. The programme aimed to establish, by 1989, national vector control strategies in at least 50% of the countries affected. A special programme for research and training in tropical diseases, sponsored jointly by WHO, UNDP and the World Bank, was established in 1975, and comprises a worldwide network of about 4,000 scientists, working on the development of vaccines, new drugs, diagnostic kits, non-chemical insecticides and other methods of control. The programme aims to strengthen research institutions in developing countries, and to encourage participation by scientists from the countries most affected.

WHO helped in preparations for the UN International Drinking Water Supply and Sanitation Decade (1981-90) by participating in regional and national meetings to plan strategies for the Decade and by drawing up new guidelines for drinking water quality. In 1987 a review of progress showed that despite some major achievements (provision of access to clean water for some 300m. people since the beginning of the Decade), by 1990, owing to the expected growth in population, there were likely to be more people without access to clean water and sanitation than at the beginning of the decade, particularly in rural areas. WHO's Diarrhoeal Diseases Control Programme encourages national programmes based on improved hygienic practices and the use of simple oral rehydration therapy to prevent infant deaths. A programme for the elimination of dracunculiasis (guinea-worm disease) among poor rural communities, through education and the provision of clean drinking-water, was being undertaken in 1990.

WHO's Global Programme on AIDS (Acquired Immunodeficiency Syndrome) began in 1987. At the beginning of September 1990, WHO had received reports of 283,010 cases of AIDS from 157 countries, and estimated the true number of cases to be 1.2m. (including an estimated 400,000 cases in children under five years of age, of which 90% were in Africa south of the Sahara); the number of adults infected with the human immunodeficiency virus (HIV), which causes AIDS, was estimated at between 8m. and 10m. (including some 3m. women of child-bearing age). The aims of WHO's Global Programme are to prevent HIV transmission, to care for HIV-infected people, and to unify national and international efforts against AIDS. In March 1988 WHO formed an 'alliance' with UNDP, aiming to expand the struggle against AIDS by using UNDP's already existing network of resident representatives and development programmes. WHO supports national AIDS control plans, which (in the absence of a vaccine) stress education and information as vital in stopping the spread of the HIV. Programmes also include funds for training medical personnel; improving facilities for screening and protecting blood supplies; epidemiological surveillance; and establishing or expanding laboratory facilities for diagnosing AIDS and treatment facilities for AIDS patients. WHO's Global Programme on AIDS required an estimated US $90.7m. in funding for 1990 (of which 70% was to support national programmes). The Global Commission on AIDS, comprising biomedical and social scientists and other experts, held its inaugural meeting in 1989.

WHO's Tobacco or Health Programme aims to reduce the use of tobacco, which is estimated to be responsible for more than 2.5m. deaths annually (through lung cancer, heart disease, chronic bronchitis and other effects). The Programme aims to educate tobacco-users and to prevent young people from adopting the habit.

'Inter-Health', a programme to combat non-communicable diseases (such as those arising from an unhealthy diet) was initiated in 1990, with the particular aim of preventing an increase in the incidence of such diseases in developing countries.

MATERNAL HEALTH

WHO's Safe Motherhood Initiative supports a programme of action for women's health and the reduction of maternal mortality (estimated to claim 500,000 victims annually).

NUTRITION

WHO collaborates with FAO, the World Food Programme and other UN agencies to ensure that health needs are included in their nutrition programmes. A joint WHO/UNICEF Nutrition Support Programme assists long-term national nutrition plans for children. Jointly with FAO, WHO establishes food standards (through the FAO/WHO Codex Alimentarius Commission) and evaluates food additives for safety. WHO's Food Safety Programme aims to reduce the occurrence of food-borne diseases, caused by microbiologically contaminated food. The programme emphasizes the enforcement of regulations on food safety, and the education of consumers.

In co-operation with FAO, WHO was to organize an international conference on nutrition in 1992.

In May 1981 the International Code of Marketing of Breastmilk Substitutes was adopted by the World Health Assembly, aiming to provide safe and adequate nutrition for infants by promoting breast-feeding and by ensuring the proper use of breastmilk substitutes, when necessary, with controls on production, storage and advertising.

DRUGS

The WHO Action Programme on Essential Drugs and Vaccines aims to prevent the inappropriate and excessive prescription of drugs and to ensure the availability of a selected number of safe and effective drugs and vaccines of acceptable quality and at low cost, in support of primary health care. WHO maintains and regularly revises a Model List of Essential Drugs, numbering 250 substances that will treat over 80% of the health problems of a given population, and should be available in adequate quantities at all times, in the appropriate dosage forms.

WHO is also active in monitoring and controlling drug abuse. Guidelines for member states on the assessment of drug abuse problems were prepared in 1986, together with a manual for primary health care workers in drug dependence and alcohol-related problems. A Programme on Substance Abuse was initiated by WHO in 1990, to survey and combat the global increase in drug abuse, by reducing the demand for drugs and controlling the supply of psychoactive substances.

DISASTER RELIEF

WHO acts as the 'health arm' of disaster relief carried out within the UN system, particularly by UNDP, UNDRO and UNICEF (q.v.). It works in close co-operation with the UN High Commissioner for Refugees, appointing joint health co-ordinators and providing technical advice, for example in listing essential drugs needed for refugee camps.

HEALTH DAYS

World Health Day is held on 7 April every year, and is used to promote awareness of a particular health topic. In 1990 the theme was 'Our Planet—Our Health'. The third 'No Tobacco Day' was held on 31 May, and the second 'World AIDS Day' was held on 1 December.

ASSOCIATED AGENCY

International Agency for Research on Cancer: 150 Cours Albert Thomas, 69372 Lyon Cedex 08, France. Established in 1965 as a self-governing body within the framework of WHO, the Agency organizes international research on cancer. It has its own laboratories and runs a programme of research on the environmental factors causing cancer. Members: Australia, Belgium, Canada,

INTERNATIONAL ORGANIZATIONS

Denmark, Finland, France, Germany, Italy, Japan, Netherlands, Norway, Sweden, Switzerland, USSR, United Kingdom, USA.
Director: Dr LORENZO TOMATIS (Italy).

FINANCE

WHO's regular budget is provided by assessment of member states and associate members. An additional fund for specific projects is provided by voluntary contributions from members and other sources. Funds are received from the UN Development Programme for particular projects and from UNFPA for appropriate programmes.

Total budget appropriations for the two years 1986–87 amounted to US $554m., but delays in the payment of government contributions meant that implementation of the budget had to be reduced by $35m. The budget for 1988–89 amounted to $609m., representing a slight decrease from the previous biennial total in real terms. Another 'zero-growth' budget of $653.7m. was approved for 1990-91. Extra-budgetary funds were expected to amount to $770m. during this period.

WHO Budget appropriations by region, 1986–87

Region	Amount (US dollars)	% of total budget
Africa	101,164,000	18.26
Americas	58,076,000	10.48
South-East Asia	69,873,000	12.62
Europe	36,503,000	6.59
Eastern Mediterranean	62,405,000	11.26
Western Pacific	51,288,000	9.26
Global and inter-regional	167,689,100	30.27
World Health Assembly & Executive Board	7,001,900	1.26
Total	554,000,000	100.00

Budget appropriations by purpose, 1986–87

Purpose	Amount (US dollars)	% of total budget
Direction, co-ordination and management	64,450,700	11.63
Health system infrastructure	180,705,500	32.62
Health science and technology—health promotion and care	102,513,300	18.51
Health science and technology—disease prevention and control	85,377,400	15.41
Programme support	120,953,100	21.83
Total	554,000,000	100.00

PUBLICATIONS

Full catalogue of publications supplied free on request.
World Health (6 a year in English, French, Portuguese, Russian and Spanish; quarterly in Arabic and Farsi).
Technical Report Series.
Public Health Papers.
WHO AIDS Series.
WHO Drug Information (quarterly).
Bulletin of WHO (6 a year).
Official Records.
Weekly Epidemiological Record.
World Health Statistics Report (quarterly).
World Health Statistics Annual.
International Digest of Health Legislation (quarterly).
Reports on the World Health Situation: (approximately every 6 years) the sixth report (January 1981) covers the period 1973–77.
World Health Forum (quarterly, in Arabic, Chinese, English, French, Russian and Spanish).

World Intellectual Property Organization—WIPO

Address: 34 chemin des Colombettes, 1211 Geneva 20, Switzerland.
Telephone: (022) 7309111.
Telex: 412912.
Fax: (022) 7335428.

WIPO was established by a Convention signed in Stockholm in 1967, which came into force in 1970. It became a specialized agency of the UN in December 1974.

MEMBERS
125 members: see Table on pp. 52–54.

Organization
(October 1990)

INTERNATIONAL BUREAU

The secretariat of WIPO and the Unions which it administers (see below). It is controlled by the member states in the General Assembly and Conference of WIPO, and in the separate Assemblies and Conferences of Representatives held by its constituent Unions. The Paris and Berne Unions elect Executive Committees from among their members and the joint membership of these two Committees constitutes the Co-ordination Committee of WIPO.

The International Bureau prepares the meetings of the various bodies of WIPO and the Unions, mainly through the provision of reports and working documents. It organizes the meetings, and sees that the decisions are communicated to all concerned, and, as far as possible, that they are carried out.

The International Bureau carries out projects and initiates new ones to promote international co-operation in the field of intellectual property. It acts as an information service and publishes reviews. It is also the depositary of most of the treaties administered by WIPO.

Director General: Dr ARPAD BOGSCH (USA).
Deputy Directors General: SHAHID ALIKHAN, LEV KOSTIKOV, ALFONS SCHÄFERS.

Activities

WIPO is responsible for promoting the protection of intellectual property throughout the world. Intellectual property comprises two principal branches: industrial property (patents and other rights in technological inventions, rights in trademarks, industrial designs, appellations of origin, etc.) and copyright and neighbouring rights (in literary, musical and artistic works, in films and records, etc.).

WIPO administers various international treaties, of which the most important are the Paris Convention for the Protection of Industrial Property (1883) and the Berne Convention for the Protection of Literary and Artistic Works (1886). WIPO carries out a programme of activities in the field of intellectual property, in order to promote creative intellectual activity and to facilitate the transfer of technology, especially to and among developing countries.

CO-OPERATION WITH DEVELOPING COUNTRIES

In the field of industrial property, the main objectives of WIPO's co-operation with developing countries are: to encourage and increase, in quantity and quality, the creation of patentable inventions by their own nationals and in their own enterprises, and thereby to increase the degree of their technological self-reliance; to improve the conditions of acquisition of foreign patented technology; to increase the competitiveness of developing countries in international trade through better protection of the trademarks and service marks of relevance in such trade; and to facilitate access by developing countries to the technological information contained in patent documents. In order to achieve these objectives, most developing countries need to create or modernize domestic legislation and governmental institutions; to accede to international treaties; to employ more specialists in government, in industry and in the legal professions; and to acquire more patent documents and better methods of analysing their contents.

These activities are supervised by the WIPO Permanent Committee for Development Co-operation Related to Industrial Property, membership of which is voluntary and carries no financial obligation with it. By September 1990, 106 States were members of the Permanent Committee.

In the field of copyright, the main objectives of WIPO's co-operation with developing countries are: to encourage and increase the creation of literary and artistic works by their own nationals, and thereby to maintain their national culture in their own languages and/or corresponding to their own ethnic and social traditions and aspirations; and to improve the conditions of acquisition of the right to use or enjoy the literary and artistic works in which copyright is owned by foreigners. In order to achieve these objectives, most developing countries are in need of creating or modernizing domestic legislation and institutions, acceding to international treaties and having more specialists, all in the field of copyright.

Most of these development co-operation activities are kept under review by the WIPO Permanent Committee for Development Co-operation Related to Copyright and Neighbouring Rights, membership of which is voluntary and carries no financial obligation with it. By September 1990, this Committee had 88 States as members.

In both industrial property and copyright, WIPO's development co-operation consists mainly of advice, training and the furnishing of documents and equipment. The advice is given by the staff of WIPO, experts chosen by WIPO or international meetings called by WIPO. The training is individual (on-the-job) or collective (courses, seminars and workshops).

LEGAL AND TECHNICAL

Revision of treaties; revision of classifications of goods and services; preparation for entry into force of new treaties, and for other possible new international instruments.

WIPO Permanent Committee on Industrial Property Information: composed of representatives of 70 states and five organizations; encourages co-operation between national and regional industrial property offices in all matters concerning documentation and information on industrial property.

SERVICES

International registration of trademarks: operating since 1893; by September 1990 645,500 registrations and renewals of trademarks had been made, of which 14,500 were made during the first eight months of 1990; publ. *Les Marques internationales* (monthly).

International deposit of industrial designs: operating since 1928; by September 1990 94,500 deposits had been made, of which 2,900 were made during the first eight months of 1990; publ. *International Designs Bulletin* (monthly).

International registration of appellations of origin: operating since 1966; by September 1990 727 appellations had been registered; publ. *Les Appellations d'origine* (irreg.).

International applications for patents: operating since 1978; by September 1990 91,000 record copies of international applications for patents under the Patent Co-operation Treaty (PCT) had been received.

THE UNIONS

International Union for the Protection of Industrial Property (Paris Convention): the treaty was signed in Paris in 1883; there were 100 member states in September 1990. Member states must accord to nationals and residents of other member states the same advantages under their laws relating to the protection of inventions, trademarks and other subjects of industrial property as they accord to their own nationals.

The treaty contains provisions concerning the conditions under which a state may license the use of a patent in its territory; for example, that the owner of the patent does not exploit it to unfair advantage in that country.

Diplomatic conferences were held in 1980, 1981, 1982 and 1984, for the revision of the Paris Convention, with the particular aim of meeting the needs of developing countries. The fourth Consultative Meeting on the revision took place in September 1987.

International Union for the Protection of Literary and Artistic Works (Berne Union): the treaty was signed in Berne in 1886 and last revised in 1971; there were 85 member states in September 1990. Member states must accord the same protection to the copyright of nationals of other member states as to their own. The treaty also prescribes minimum standards of protection, for example, that copyright protection generally continues throughout the author's life and for 50 years after. It includes special provision for the developing countries.

OTHER AGREEMENTS

Signatories of the agreements form unions similar to those described above.

International Protection of Industrial Property:

Madrid Agreement of 14 April 1891, for the Repression of False or Deceptive Indications of Source on Goods.

Madrid Agreement of 14 April 1891, Concerning the International Registration of Marks.

The Hague Agreement of 6 November 1925, Concerning the International Deposit of Industrial Designs.

Nice Agreement of 15 June 1957, Concerning the International Classification of Goods and Services for the Purposes of the Registration of Marks.

Lisbon Agreement of 31 October 1958, for the Protection of Appellations of Origin and their International Registration.

Locarno Agreement of 8 October 1968, Establishing an International Classification for Industrial Designs.

Patent Co-operation Treaty of 19 June 1970 (PCT).

Strasbourg Agreement of 24 March 1971, Concerning the International Patent Classification (IPC).

Vienna Agreement of 12 June 1973, Establishing an International Classification of the Figurative Elements of Marks.

Budapest Treaty of 28 April 1977, on the International Recognition of the Deposit of Micro-organisms for the Purposes of Patent Procedure.

Nairobi Treaty of 26 September 1981, on the Protection of the Olympic Symbol.

Special International Protection of the Rights of Performers, Producers of Phonograms and Broadcasting Organizations ('Neighbouring Rights'):

Rome Convention, 26 October 1961, for the Protection of Performers, Producers of Phonograms and Broadcasting Organizations.

Geneva Convention, 29 October 1971, for the Protection of Producers of Phonograms against Unauthorized Duplication of their Phonograms.

Brussels Convention, 21 May 1974, Relating to the Distribution of Programme-carrying Signals Transmitted by Satellite.

In 1989 three separate diplomatic conferences were convened by WIPO, and adopted the following (which had not yet entered into force by October 1990):

Treaty on the International Registration of Audiovisual Works.

Treaty on Intellectual Property in Respect of Integrated Circuits.

Protocol Relating to the Madrid Agreement Concerning the International Registration of Works.

FINANCE

The budget for the two years 1990–91 amounted to 153.4m. Swiss francs.

PUBLICATIONS

Copyright (monthly in English and French; quarterly in Spanish).

Industrial Property (monthly in English and French; quarterly in Spanish).

International Designs Bulletin (monthly in English and French).

Les marques internationales (monthly in French).

Newsletter (irregular in Arabic, English, French, Portuguese, Russian and Spanish).

PCT Gazette (fortnightly in English and French).

Les appellations d'origine (irregular in French).

Intellectual Property in Asia and the Pacific (quarterly in English).

World Meteorological Organization—WMO

Address: Case postale 2300, 41 ave Giuseppe Motta, 1211 Geneva 2, Switzerland.
Telephone: (022) 7308111.
Telex: 23260.
Fax: (022) 7342326.

The WMO started activities and was recognized as a Specialized Agency of the UN in 1951, aiming to improve the exchange of weather information and its applications.

MEMBERS

158 members, of which one is suspended; see Table on pp. 52–54.

Organization
(October 1990)

WORLD METEOROLOGICAL CONGRESS

The supreme organ of the Organization, the Congress is convened every four years and represents all members; it adopts regulations, approves policy, programme and budget. Tenth session: May 1987.

EXECUTIVE COUNCIL

The Council has 36 members and meets at least yearly to prepare studies and recommendations for the Congress; it supervises the implementation of Congress resolutions and regulations, informs members on technical matters and offers advice.

SECRETARIAT

The secretariat acts as an administrative, documentary and information centre; undertakes special technical studies; produces publications; organizes meetings of WMO constituent bodies; acts as a link between the meteorological and hydrometeorological services of the world, and provides information for the general public. At the beginning of 1989 there were 274 staff members in Geneva and in two regional offices, together with 48 experts and 32 local staff employed in technical assistance projects in 23 countries.

Secretary-General: Prof. G. O. P. OBASI (Nigeria).
Deputy Secretary-General: DAVID AXFORD (UK).

REGIONAL ASSOCIATIONS

Members are grouped in six Regional Associations (Africa, Asia, Europe, North and Central America, South America and South-West Pacific), whose task is to co-ordinate meteorological activity within their regions and to examine questions referred to them by the Executive Council. Sessions are held at least once every four years.

TECHNICAL COMMISSIONS

The Technical Commissions are composed of experts nominated by the members of the Organization. Sessions are held at least once every four years. The Commissions cover the following areas: Basic Systems; Climatology; Instruments and Methods of Observation; Atmospheric Sciences; Aeronautical Meteorology; Agricultural Meteorology; Hydrology; Marine Meteorology.

Activities

WORLD WEATHER WATCH PROGRAMME

Combining facilities and services provided by the members, the Programme's primary purpose is to make available meteorological and related geophysical and environmental information enabling them to maintain efficient meteorological services. Facilities in regions outside any national territory (outer space, ocean areas and Antarctica) are maintained by members on a voluntary basis.

Global Observing System: Simultaneous observations are made at more than 9,500 land stations. Meteorological information is also received from 3,000 aircraft, 7,400 ships, 300 fixed and drifting buoys, 200 background pollution monitoring stations and 10 polar orbiting and geostationary meteorological satellites. About 150 members operate some 300 ground stations equipped to receive picture transmissions from the satellites.

Global Data Processing System: consists of World Meteorological Centres (WMCs) at Melbourne (Australia), Moscow (USSR) and Washington, DC (USA), 29 Regional/Special Meteorological Centres (RSMCs) and 148 National Meteorological Centres. The WMCs and RSMCs provide analyses, forecasts and warnings for exchange on the Global Telecommunications System. Some centres concentrate on the monitoring and forecasting of special weather phenomena, such as tropical cyclones, monsoons, droughts, etc., which have a major impact on human safety and national economies. These analyses and forecasts are designed to assist the members in making local and specialized forecasts.

Global Telecommunication System: consists of (a) the Main Telecommunication Network (MTN), (b) the regional telecommunication networks, and (c) the national telecommunication networks. The system operates through 160 national meteorological centres, 30 Regional Telecommunications Hubs and three WMCs.

Executive Council Working Group on Antarctic Meteorology: co-ordinates WMO activities related to the Antarctic, in particular the surface and upper-air observing programme, plans the regular exchange of observational data and products needed for operational and research purposes, studies problems related to instruments and methods of observation peculiar to the Antarctic and develops appropriate regional coding practices. It maintains active contacts with scientific bodies dealing with Antarctic research and co-operates with relevant WMO constituent bodies and with other international organizations on aspects of Antarctic meteorology.

Executive Council Panel of Experts on Satellites: co-ordinates WMO's satellite-related activities, examines and records plans for new satellites and satellite operations in member countries and promotes the use of satellite data in WMO programmes. It makes appropriate recommendations to WMO bodies and considers ways in which the processing and distribution of information from satellites may best meet the needs of the members.

Tropical Cyclone Programme: established in response to UN General Assembly Resolution 2733 (XXV), aims at the development of national and regionally co-ordinated systems to ensure that the loss of life and damage caused by tropical cyclones are reduced to a minimum. The programme supports the transfer of technology, and includes five regional tropical cyclone bodies, to improve warning systems and for collaboration with other international organizations in activities related to disaster preparedness.

WORLD CLIMATE PROGRAMME

Adopted by the Eighth World Meteorological Congress (1979), the World Climate Programme (WCP) comprises the following components: World Climate Data Programme (WCDP), World Climate Applications Programme (WCAP), World Climate Impact Studies Programme (WCIP), World Climate Research Programme (WCRP). The objectives of the WCP are: to use existing climate information to improve economic and social planning; to improve the understanding of climate processes through research, so as to determine the predictability of climate and the extent of man's influence on it; and to detect and warn governments of impending climate variations or changes, either natural or man-made, which may significantly affect critical human activities.

Co-ordination of the overall Programme is the responsibility of the WMO, along with direct management of the WCDP and WCAP. The UN Environment Programme (q.v.) has accepted responsibility for the WCIP, while the WCRP is a joint effort between WMO and the International Council of Scientific Unions (ICSU, q.v.). Other organizations involved in the Programme include UNESCO, FAO, WHO, IFAD and the Consultative Group for International Agricultural Research.

World Climate Data Programme: aims to make available reliable climate data, through four main projects: the Climate Data Information Service; transfer of technology in the use of computer-based climate data; the Climate Monitoring System; and the Data Rescue Project.

World Climate Applications Programme: promotes applications of climate knowledge in the areas of food production, water, energy (especially solar and wind energy), urban planning and building, human health, transport, tourism and recreation.

World Climate Research Programme: organized jointly with the International Council of Scientific Unions, to determine to what extent climate can be predicted, and the extent of man's influence on climate. Its three specific objectives are: establishing the physical basis for weather predictions over time ranges of one to two months; understanding the variability of the global climate over periods of several years; and studying the long-term variations and the response of climate to natural or man-made influence over periods of several decades. Studies include: the 'greenhouse effect' of changes in the atmosphere caused by emissions of carbon dioxide and other gases, the effect of cloudiness on the radiation balance; the effect of ground water storage and vegetation on evaporation;

and the effects of oceanic circulation changes on the global atmosphere.

World Climate Impact Studies Programme: aims to make reliable estimates of the socio-economic impact of climate changes, and to assist in forming national policies accordingly. It concentrates on: study of the impact of climate variations on national food systems; assessment of the impact of man's activities on the climate, especially through increasing the amount of carbon dioxide and other radiatively active gases in the atmosphere; and developing the methodology of climate impact assessments.

RESEARCH AND DEVELOPMENT PROGRAMME

This major programme aims to help members to implement research projects; to disseminate relevant scientific information; to draw the attention of members to outstanding research problems of major importance, such as atmospheric composition and climate changes; and to encourage and help members to incorporate the results of research into operational forecasting or other appropriate techniques, particularly when such changes of procedure require international co-ordination and agreement.

Global Atmosphere Watch (GAW): This is the main worldwide system which integrates most monitoring and research activities involving the measurement of atmospheric composition, and is intended to serve as an early warning system to detect further changes in atmospheric concentrations of 'greenhouse' gases, changes in the ozone layer and in long-range transport of pollutants, including acidity and toxicity of rain, as well as the atmospheric burden of aerosols. The instruments of these globally standardized observations and related research are the WMO Global Ozone Observing System, operating about 140 stations in more than 60 countries, and the WMO Background Air Pollution Monitoring Network (BAPMoN) having nearly 200 stations in more than 90 countries. Through GAW, WMO collaborates with the UN Economic Commission for Europe (ECE) and is responsible for the meteorological part of the Monitoring and Evaluation of the Long-range Transmission of Air Pollutants in Europe. In this respect, WMO has arranged for the establishment of two Meteorological Synthesizing Centres (Oslo and Moscow) which provide daily analysis of the transport of pollution over Europe. The GAW also gives attention to atmospheric chemistry studies, prepares assessments and encourages integrated environmental monitoring.

Weather Prediction Research Programmes: The programmes assist members in exchanging the results of research on weather prediction, organize international conferences, and publish technical reports and progress reports on numerical weather prediction, in order to improve members' weather services. The Programme on Short- and Medium-Range Weather Prediction Research aims at strengthening members' research in short- and medium-range weather forecasting, including local forecasting techniques. The main objective of the Programme on Long-Range Forecasting Research is to improve the level of members' capabilities in monthly and seasonal weather forecasting.

Tropical Meteorology Research Programme: aims at the promotion and co-ordination of members' research efforts into such important problems as monsoons, tropical cyclones, droughts in the arid zones of the tropics, rain-producing tropical weather systems, and the interaction between tropical and mid-latitude weather systems. This should lead to a better understanding of tropical systems and forecasting, and thus be of economic benefit to tropical countries.

Cloud Physics and Weather Modification Programme: encourages scientific research on weather modification, based on cloud physics, particularly precipitation enhancement ('rain-making') and hail suppression. It provides information on world-wide weather modification projects, and guidance in the design and evaluation of experiments. It also studies the chemistry of clouds and their role in the transport of pollution.

APPLICATIONS OF METEOROLOGY PROGRAMME

Services to ocean activities: Supervised by the Commission for Marine Meteorology, international arrangements are made for the provision of marine meteorological and other related geophysical information, including sea ice and wave information, to shipping, fishing operations and other marine activities; the preparation of marine climatological information is also arranged internationally for multiple applications. Close collaboration is maintained with the Intergovernmental Oceanographic Commission to undertake joint programmes in ocean services and oceanic research.

Aeronautical meteorology programme: concerned with the provision of operational meteorological information required in the interests of the safety, regularity and efficiency of air navigation. Supervised by the Commission for Aeronautical Meteorology, the programme is aimed at the global introduction of common standards in providing services on the basis of internationally agreed requirements provided by ICAO.

Applications to agriculture: the study of weather and climate as they affect agriculture, the selection of crops and their protection from disease and deterioration in storage, soil conservation, phenology and physiology of crops and farm animals; the Commission for Agricultural Meteorology supervises the applications projects and also advises the Secretary-General in his efforts to co-ordinate activities in support of food production. There are also special activities in agrometeorology to monitor and combat drought and desertification, to apply climate information in agricultural planning and to help improve the efficiency of the use of water and energy in agriculture; close co-operation is maintained with the UN Environment Programme.

HYDROLOGY AND WATER RESOURCES PROGRAMME

This major programme concentrates on promoting world-wide co-operation in the evaluation of water resources and the development of hydrological networks and services, including data collection and processing, hydrological forecasting and warnings and the supply of meteorological and hydrological data for design purposes. The three components of the programme are:

Operational Hydrology Programme: Planned and executed under the auspices of the Commission of Hydrology, this Programme deals with all aspects of hydrological data, including instruments, methods of observation and transmission, systems of forecasting and their application to water resources projects. The regional implementation of this Programme is the responsibility of the WMO Regional Associations.

Hydrological Operational Multipurpose Subprogramme: consists of the organized transfer of hydrological technology used in network design, observations, collection, processing and storage of data and hydrological modelling. Manuals of procedures and general guidance, descriptions of equipment and computer software are produced.

Applications and Services to Water Resources: directed towards achieving the targets of various water-dependent sectors, it also contributes to WMO projects which have important hydrological aspects, such as those in the Tropical Cyclone and World Climate programmes.

Co-operation with Water-Related Programmes of other International Organizations: includes participation in the International Hydrological Programme of UNESCO, joint activities with other UN agencies, and participation in regional projects concerned with large international river basins such as the Rhine and the Danube.

EDUCATION AND TRAINING PROGRAMME

Activities include surveys of personnel training requirements, the development of appropriate training programmes, the establishment and improvement of regional training centres, the organization of training courses, seminars and conferences and the preparation of training materials. The Programme also arranges individual training programmes and the provision of fellowships. There are about 600 trainees in any one year. About 250 fellowships are awarded annually. Advice is given on training facilities, and there is a library of training materials for meteorological and related instruction. The focal point of WMO's education and training activities is the Panel of Experts on Education and Training set up by the Executive Council.

TECHNICAL CO-OPERATION PROGRAMME

United Nations Development Programme: WMO provides assistance in the development of national meteorological and hydrological services, in the application of meteorological and hydrological data to national economic development, and in the training of personnel. Assistance in the form of expert missions, fellowships and equipment was provided to 119 countries in 1989 at a cost of US $15.1m., financed by UNDP.

Voluntary Co-operation Programme: WMO assists members in implementing the World Weather Watch Programme to develop an integrated observing and forecasting system. Member governments contribute equipment, services and fellowships for training. In 1989 272 projects were approved under this programme.

WMO also carries out assistance projects under Trust Fund arrangements, financed by national authorities, either for activities in their own country or in a beneficiary country. Several such projects, at a cost of $4.7m., were in progress in 1989.

Financial support from WMO's regular budget for fellowships, group training, technical conferences and study tours amounted to $0.8m. in 1989.

CO-OPERATION WITH OTHER BODIES

As a Specialized Agency of the UN, WMO is actively involved in the activities of the UN system. In addition, WMO has concluded a number of formal agreements and working arrangements with international organizations both within and outside the UN system,

INTERNATIONAL ORGANIZATIONS

United Nations (Specialized Agencies)

at the inter-governmental and non-governmental level. As a result, WMO participates in major international conferences convened under the auspices of the United Nations or other organizations. The Intergovernmental Panel on Climate Change (IPCC) was jointly established in 1988 by the Secretary-General of WMO and the Executive Director of UNEP, to assess scientific information on changes in climate and to formulate a realistic response.

FINANCE

WMO is financed by contributions from members on a proportional scale of assessment. The budget for the four years 1988-91 was 170m. Swiss francs. Outside this budget, WMO implements a number of projects as executing agency for the UNDP or else under trust-fund arrangements.

PUBLICATIONS

Annual Report.

WMO Bulletin (quarterly in English, French, Russian and Spanish).

Reports, technical notes and training publications.

AFRICAN DEVELOPMENT BANK—ADB

Address: 01 BP 1387, Abidjan 01, Côte d'Ivoire.
Telephone: 20-44-44.
Telex: 23717.
Fax: 22-70-04.

Established in August 1963, the Bank began operations in July 1966.

AFRICAN MEMBERS

Algeria
Angola
Benin
Botswana
Burkina Faso
Burundi
Cameroon
Cape Verde
Central African Republic
Chad
Comoros
Congo
Côte d'Ivoire
Djibouti
Egypt
Equatorial Guinea
Ethiopia
Gabon
The Gambia
Ghana
Guinea
Guinea-Bissau
Kenya
Lesotho
Liberia
Libya
Madagascar
Malawi
Mali
Mauritania
Mauritius
Morocco
Mozambique
Namibia
Niger
Nigeria
Rwanda
São Tomé and Príncipe
Senegal
Seychelles
Sierra Leone
Somalia
Sudan
Swaziland
Tanzania
Togo
Tunisia
Uganda
Zaire
Zambia
Zimbabwe

There are also 25 non-African members.

Organization
(October 1990)

BOARD OF GOVERNORS

The highest policy-making body of the Bank. Each member country nominates one Governor, usually its Minister of Finance and Economic Affairs, and an alternate Governor. The Board meets once a year. It elects the Board of Directors and the President.

BOARD OF DIRECTORS

The Board consists of 18 members (of whom six are non-African and hold 36.57% of the voting power) elected by the Board of Governors for a term of three years; it is responsible for the general operations of the Bank. It holds ordinary meetings twice a month.

OFFICERS

The President is responsible for the organization and the day-to-day operations of the Bank under guidance of the Board of Directors. The President is elected for a five year term and serves as the Chairman of the Board of Directors. He is assisted by five Vice-Presidents, elected for a three-year term by the Board of Directors on his recommendation.

During 1986 the Bank's organization was restructured, in preparation for the expected increase in capital (see below) and the resultant expansion of operations. Activities were divided into three sections (for eastern, western and central Africa) and a separate department for disbursements was created, while greater emphasis was to be placed on the evaluation of projects. There are regional offices in Cameroon, Ethiopia, Guinea, Kenya, Morocco, Nigeria and Zimbabwe.

Executive President and Chairman of Board of Directors: BABACAR N' DIAYE (Senegal).
Secretary-General: A. B. BEYE.

FINANCIAL STRUCTURE

The Bank uses a unit of account (UA) which is equivalent to one United States dollar before the devaluation of 1971.

The capital stock of the Bank was at first exclusively open for subscription by African countries, with each member's subscription consisting of an equal number of paid-up and callable shares. In 1978, however, the Governors agreed to open the capital stock of the Bank to subscription by non-regional states on the basis of nine principles aimed at maintaining the African character of the institution. The decision was finally ratified in May 1982, and the participation of non-regional countries became effective on 30 December. It was agreed that African members should still hold two-thirds of the share capital, that all loan operations should be restricted to African members, and that the Bank's President should always be an African national. In 1986 a special committee established by the Board of Governors approved an increase in the Bank's authorized capital from UA 5,400m. (US $6,500m.) to UA 16,200m. ($19,600m.) (with paid-up capital as a proportion of the whole to be reduced from 25% to 6¼%). This took effect from June 1987. At the end of 1989 subscribed capital was $18,647.7m. (of which the paid-up portion was $2,173.4m.).

Activities

The ADB Group of development financing institutions comprises the African Development Fund (ADF) and the Nigeria Trust Fund (NTF), which provide concessionary loans, and the African Development Bank itself.

At the end of 1989 total loan approvals by the ADB Group since the beginning of its operations amounted to US $15,618.5m. In 1989 the group approved loans of $2,856m., compared with $2,177m. in 1987. Disbursement of loans during 1989 increased to $1,503m. from $1,167m. in 1988. Agricultural projects received the largest proportion of group loans (19.7%), while public utilities received 18.2%, transport 15.3%, education and health 14.6%, industry 10.4%, and multi-sector activities 21.7%. In response to pressure from non-African members of the group, the proportion of non-project lending (for structural and sectoral reforms) declined from 35.7% in 1987 to 25.7% in 1988, and to 20.2% in 1989.

The ADB contributed funds for the establishment in 1986 of the Africa Project Development Facility, which assists the private sector in Africa by providing advisory services and finance for entrepreneurs: it is managed by the International Finance Corporation (q.v.).

The Bank also provides technical assistance in the form of experts' services, pre-investment studies, and staff training; much of this assistance is financed through bilateral aid funds contributed by developed member states. In 1988 it created a 'round table' of African business executives, to hold regular meetings and encourage private enterprise. A conference on private investment and enterprise in Africa was sponsored by the Bank in March 1990.

AFRICAN DEVELOPMENT BANK (ADB)

The Bank makes loans at a variable annual interest rate (7.5% in 1990), plus commission and commitment fees of 1% each. Loan approvals increased from $1,343m. for 24 loans in 1987 to $1,405m. for 27 loans in 1988 and to $1,865m. for 36 loans in 1989. The capital increase approved in 1986 (see above) was intended to support a programme of lending amounting to $6,050m. in 1987-91.

AFRICAN DEVELOPMENT FUND (ADF)

The Fund commenced operations in 1973. It grants interest-free loans to African countries for projects with repayment over 50 years (including a 10-year grace period) and with a service charge of 0.75% per annum. Grants for project feasibility studies are made to the poorest countries.

In 1987 donor countries agreed on a fifth replenishment of the Fund's resources, amounting to $2,700m. for 1988-90. In future 85% of available resources were to be reserved for the poorest countries (those with annual GDP per caput of less than $510, at 1985 prices). Commitments approved by the ADF in 1988 amounted to $763m. for 57 operations, increasing to $982m. for 103 operations in 1989.

INTERNATIONAL ORGANIZATIONS

African Development Bank

NIGERIA TRUST FUND (NTF)

The Agreement establishing the Nigeria Trust Fund was signed in February 1976 by the Bank and the Government of Nigeria. The Fund is administered by the Bank and its loans are granted for up to 25 years, including grace periods of up to five years, and carry 0.75% commitment charges and 4% interest charges. The loans are intended to provide financing for projects in co-operation with other lending institutions.

In 1988 lending amounted to $8.07m. for one loan (compared with $27.6m. for three loans in 1987). Commitments totalled $9.2m. for two loans in 1989.

Summary of Bank Group Activities (US $ million)

	1988	1989	Cumulative total*
ADB loans			
Amount approved	1,405.11	1,864.95	9,455.04
Disbursements	784.14	996.63	4,163.94
ADF loans and grants			
Amount approved	763.99	982.19	5,971.62
Disbursements	373.04	492.88	2,482.39
NTF loans			
Amount approved	8.07	9.20	191.79
Disbursements	9.72	13.84	108.83
Group total			
Amount approved	2,177.17	2,856.34	15,618.45
Disbursements	1,166.90	1,503.35	6,755.16

* Since the initial operations of the three institutions (1967 for ADB, 1974 for ADF and 1976 for NTF).

Bank Group Loan and Grant Approvals by Region, 1988–89
(US $ million)

Country	1988	%	1989	%
Central Africa	331.41	15.22	815.12	28.54
Angola	—		4.68	
Burundi	11.04		11.12	
Cameroon	9.09		175.19	
Central African Republic	1.81		24.21	
Chad	—		51.31	
Congo	8.80		43.33	
Equatorial Guinea	17.20		—	
Gabon	91.91		57.88	
Rwanda	8.07		14.53	
São Tomé & Príncipe	29.16		—	
Zaire	154.31		407.00	
Multinational	—		25.87	
East Africa	224.54	10.31	363.87	12.74
Djibouti	8.86		18.98	
Ethiopia	127.12		166.61	
Kenya	14.66		98.90	
Madagascar	16.93		54.04	
Mauritius	6.73		1.20	
Seychelles	50.24		9.94	
Somalia	—		10.39	
Uganda	—		3.82	
North Africa	632.20	29.04	877.20	30.71
Algeria	53.83		249.61	
Egypt	282.60		131.20	
Mauritania	41.86		16.73	
Morocco	68.63		297.21	
Sudan	104.55		2.30	
Tunisia	80.74		180.15	
Southern Africa	246.73	11.33	148.10	5.18
Botswana	25.32		39.00	
Lesotho	23.10		3.40	
Malawi	14.77		19.06	
Mozambique	115.42		12.10	
Swaziland	—		11.82	
Tanzania	17.08		18.14	
Zambia	33.17		38.43	
Zimbabwe	17.86		2.92	
Multinational	—		3.21	
West Africa	738.31	33.91	650.27	22.77
Benin	16.11		—	
Burkina Faso	19.09		44.64	
Cape Verde	13.76		0.33	
Côte d'Ivoire	322.01		79.08	
Gambia	9.15		21.84	
Ghana	160.42		—	
Guinea	1.61		89.43	
Guinea-Bissau	9.13		53.34	
Liberia	—		2.97	
Mali	49.19		26.35	
Niger	10.04		24.21	
Nigeria	60.49		301.18	
Senegal	—		4.07	
Sierra Leone	—		1.43	
Togo	18.59		—	
Multinational	48.71		1.41	
Multiregional	4.00	0.18	1.77	0.06
Total	**2,177.17**	**100.00**	**2,856.34**	**100.00**

ASSOCIATED INSTITUTIONS

The ADB actively participated in the establishment of four associated institutions:

Africa Reinsurance Corporation—Africa-Re: Reinsurance House, 46 Marina, PMB 12765, Lagos, Nigeria; f. 1977; started operations in 1978; its purpose is to foster the development of the insurance and reinsurance industry in Africa and to promote the growth of national and regional underwriting capacities. Africa-Re has an authorized capital of US $15m., of which the ADB holds 10%; paid-up capital was $9.6m. in December 1988. There are nine Directors, one appointed by the Bank. Mems: 40 countries and the ADB. Gen. Man. E. ZAFU.

Association of African Development Finance Institutions—AADFI: c/o ADB, 01 BP 1387, Abidjan 01, Côte d'Ivoire; tel. 20-44-44; telex 23717; f. 1975; aims to promote co-operation among the development banks of the region in matters relating to development ideas, project design and financing. Mems: 120 institutions. Sec.-Gen. MOHAMED O. CHEIKH-SIDIA.

Shelter-Afrique (Société pour l'habitat et le logement territorial en Afrique): Mamlaka Rd, POB 41479, Nairobi, Kenya; tel. 722305; telex 25355; fax 722024; f. 1982 to finance housing in ADB member countries. Share capital is US $300m., held by 28 African countries, the ADB, Africa-Re and the Commonwealth Development Corporation. Dir EBENEZER OLUSEYI LUFADEJU.

Société internationale financière pour les investissements et le développement en Afrique—SIFIDA: 22 rue François-Perréard, BP 310, 1225 Chêne-Bourg, Switzerland; tel. (022) 486000; telex 418647; fax (022) 482161; f. 1970; holding company which aims to promote the establishment and growth of productive enterprises in Africa. It finances industrial projects, organizes syndicated loans, project identification and development, and export finance. Its shareholders include the ADB, IFC and about 130 financial, industrial and commercial institutions in the USA, Europe and Asia; authorized share capital US $20.8m., subscribed capital $20.8m. Chair. DEREK C. PEY; Man. Dir PHILIPPE SÉCHAUD.

PUBLICATIONS

Annual Report.

ADB News (monthly).

Quarterly Statement.

Basic Information (2 a year).

Statistical Handbook (annually).

Summaries of operations in each member country.

ANDEAN GROUP
(ACUERDO DE CARTAGENA)

Address: Avda Paseo de la República 3895, Lima 27; Casilla 18-1177, Lima 18, Peru.
Telephone: (14) 414212.
Telex: 20104.
Fax: 420911.

The organization, officially known as the Acuerdo de Cartagena (from the Cartagena Agreement which established it in 1969) and also known as the Grupo Andino (Andean Group) or the Pacto Andino (Andean Pact), aims to accelerate the harmonious development of the member states through economic and social integration. The group covers an area of 4,710,000 sq km, with about 80m. inhabitants.

MEMBERS

Bolivia   Colombia   Ecuador   Peru   Venezuela

Chile withdrew from the Group in January 1976.

Organization
(October 1990)

COMMISSION

This is the supreme authority of the Group, consisting of a plenipotentiary representative from each member country. Each country has the presidency in turn. The Commission is assisted by two Consultative Councils, each comprising four representatives from each country, elected respectively by national employers' organizations and by trades unions.

ANDEAN COUNCIL

The Council consists of the ministers of foreign affairs of the member countries, meeting annually or whenever it is considered necessary, to formulate a common external policy and to co-ordinate the process of integration.

JUNTA

Technical body which ensures that the Agreement is implemented and that the Commission's decisions are complied with. It submits proposals to the Commission for facilitating the fulfilment of the Agreement. Members are appointed for a three-year term. They supervise technical officials assigned to the following Departments: External Relations, Agricultural Development, Press Office, Economic Policy, Physical Integration, Programme of Assistance to Bolivia, Industrial Development, Programme Planning, Legal Affairs, Technology.

PARLIAMENT

Parlamento Andino: Carrera 7A, No 13-58, Oficina 401, Bogotá, Colombia; tel. (1) 2844191; telex 42380; fax (1) 2843270; f. 1979; comprises five members from each country, and meets in each capital city in turn; makes recommendations on regional policy. Pres. WILFRIDO LUCERO; Exec. Sec. MILOS ALCALAY.

COURT OF JUSTICE

Tribunal de Justicia del Acuerdo de Cartagena: Calle Roca 450, Casilla 9054 Suc. 7, Quito, Ecuador; tel. (2) 529-990; telex 21263; fax (2) 554-543; f. 1979, began operating in 1984; its function is to resolve disputes and interpret legislation. It comprises five judges, one from each member country, appointed for a renewable period of six years. The Presidency is assumed annually by each judge in turn, by alphabetical order of country. Judges: Dr GALO PICO MANTILLA (Ecuador), Dr EDGAR BARRIENTOS CAZAZOLA (Bolivia), Dr FERNANDO URIBE RESTREPO (Colombia), Dra CARMEN ELENA CRESPO DE HERNÁNDEZ (Venezuela), Dr HUGO POPPE ENTRAMBASAGUAS (Bolivia), Dr JUAN VICENTE UGARTE DEL PINO (Peru).

RESERVE FUND

Fondo Andina de Reservas: Carrera 13, No. 27-47, 10°, Bogotá, Colombia; tel. (1) 2858511; fax (1) 2881117; f. 1978 to support the balance of payments of member countries, provide credit, guarantee loans, and contribute to the harmonization of monetary and financial policies. In 1984 it began operating in the foreign exchange market. It is administered by an Assembly of the ministers of finance and economy of the member countries, and a Board of Directors comprising the presidents of the central banks of member states. In October 1985 it was decided that the Fund's capital should be expanded from US $100m. to $500m. In 1988 the admission of other Latin American countries, to create the Fondo Latinoamericano de Reservas, was approved. Exec. Pres. GUILLERMO CASTAÑEDA MUNGI (Peru).

DEVELOPMENT CORPORATION

Corporación Andina de Fomento: Torre Central, Avda Luis Roche, Altamira, Pisos 5°-10°, Apdo 5086, Caracas, Venezuela; tel. (2) 284-2221; telex 22587; f. 1968, began operations in 1970; aims to encourage the integration of the Andean countries by specialization and an equitable distribution of investments. It conducts research to identify investment opportunities, and prepares the resulting investment projects; gives technical and financial assistance; and attracts internal and external credit. Authorized capital: US $1,000m., subscribed by the member states; shares worth about $200m. were to be offered to non-regional countries in 1986, and in 1987 it was announced that shares would also be offered to banks and other private organizations. The Board of Directors comprises representatives of each country at ministerial level. Exec. Pres. JOSÉ C. CARDENAS (Ecuador).

Activities

In May 1979, at Cartagena, Colombia, the Presidents of the five member countries signed the 'Mandate of Cartagena', which called for greater economic and political co-operation in the 1980s, including the establishment of more sub-regional development programmes (especially in industry).

The operations of the Group have frequently been hindered by political problems: Bolivia threatened to withdraw in September 1980 following criticism of its Government by other members of the group, while Ecuador also suspended its membership temporarily at the beginning of 1981, following border disputes with Peru. In 1983 the Presidents of the five member states reaffirmed their commitment to regional integration, particularly in agriculture, trade, industry, finance, science and technology, physical integration, and aid to Bolivia and Ecuador.

In May 1987 representatives of member countries signed the Quito Protocol, modifying the Cartagena Agreement. The protocol included a relaxation of the strict rules that had formerly been imposed on foreign investors in the region (see below). It came into force in May 1988.

In May 1989 the Presidents of four member countries, together with the Bolivian Minister of Foreign Affairs, undertook to 'revitalize' the process of Andean integration, by withdrawing measures that obstructed the programme of trade liberalization, and by complying with tariff reductions that had already been agreed upon. They agreed that member states should conduct studies on the adoption of a common passport. In May 1990 another meeting of heads of state agreed to co-ordinate negotiations with creditors, improve co-operation in industrial development, and adopt a common policy on exports of energy. They also agreed to hold such meetings twice a year, and to hold direct elections to the Andean Parliament.

TRADE

Trade between members amounted to US $1,400m. in 1980, or about 4.5% of their foreign trade, compared with $111m. (2.5%) between the same countries in 1970. Trade within the group increased by about 37% annually between 1978 and 1980. Tariff reduction on manufactured goods traded between Colombia, Peru and Venezuela was almost complete by 1980, although agreement on a common external tariff had not yet been made. A council for customs affairs met for the first time in January 1982, aiming to harmonize national legislation within the group. Owing to the world recession trade within the group fell by some 40% during 1983. In response the Junta undertook schemes to promote exports and to establish a barter system.

In December 1983 an agreement was signed with the European Community, to eliminate obstacles in trade between the two regions and to develop co-operation programmes. The first joint meeting under the agreement was to be held in December 1987.

In December 1984 the member states launched a new common currency, the Andean peso, aiming to reduce dependence on the US dollar and to increase regional trade. The new currency was to be backed by special contributions to the Fondo Andina de Reservas amounting to $80m., and was to be 'pegged' to the US dollar, taking the form of financial drafts rather than notes and coins.

In May 1986 a new formula for trade among member countries was agreed, in order to restrict the number of products exempted from trade liberalization measures: under the new agreement each country could retain trade restrictions on up to 40 'sensitive' products.

INDUSTRY

Negotiations began in 1970 for the formulation of joint industrial programmes, particularly in the petrochemicals, metal-working and motor vehicle industries, but disagreements over the allocation of different plants, and the choice of foreign manufacturers for co-operation, prevented progress and by 1984 the more ambitious schemes had been abandoned. Instead, emphasis was to be placed on assisting small- and medium-sized industries, particularly in the agro-industrial and electronics sectors, in co-operation with national industrial organizations.

From 1971, in accordance with a Commission directive (Decision 24), foreign investors were required to transfer 51% of their shares to local investors within 15 years, in order to qualify for the preferential trade arrangements. Transfers were to be completed by 1989 for Colombia, Peru and Venezuela, and by 1994 for Bolivia and Ecuador. Foreign-owned companies were not to repatriate dividends of more than 14% (later raised to 20%), except with approval of the Commission, on pain of disqualification from preferential tariffs. In addition, foreign investors were forbidden to participate in transport undertakings, public utilities, banking and insurance, and were not to engage in activities already adequately covered by existing national enterprises. In early 1985 individual Pact members began to liberalize these laws, recognizing that the Group's policy, by deterring foreign investors, had contributed to its collective foreign debt of some US $70,000m., and in February 1986 ministers discussed a relaxation of the 'Decision 24' rules for foreign investors.

The Quito Protocol, modifying the Cartagena Agreement, was signed by members in May 1987 and entered into force one year later. It finally annulled Decision 24, and replaced it with Decision 220, allowing greater freedom for individual countries to establish their own rules on foreign investment. Each government was to decide which sectors were to be closed to foreign participation, and the period within which foreign investors must transfer a majority shareholding to local investors was extended to 30 years (37 years in Bolivia and Ecuador).

A further directive (Decision 169), in force since 1982, covers the formation of 'Empresas Multinacionales Andinas' (multinational enterprises) with capital from two or more member countries and non-member countries. At the end of 1985 there were 11 such enterprises (six in industry and the rest in agro-industry, trade, transport and construction).

In November 1988 member states established a bank, the Banco Intermunicipal Andino, which was to finance public works.

AGRICULTURE

The Andean Agricultural Development Programme was formulated in 1976. Twenty-two resolutions aimed at integrating the Andean agricultural sector were approved there. In 1984 the Andean Food Security System was created to develop the agrarian sector, replace imports progressively with local produce, and improve rural living conditions.

TRANSPORT AND COMMUNICATIONS

In 1982 member governments adopted a plan of action for improving road and maritime transport. In 1983 the Commission drew up a plan to assist Bolivia by giving attention to its problems as a landlocked country, particularly through improving roads connecting it with the rest of the region and with the Pacific. Studies on the improvement of regional posts and telecommunications were undertaken in 1984, and a scheme for attracting tourists to the region was drawn up.

Asociación de Empresas Estatales de Telecomunicaciones: Avda Coruña 2669 y González Suárez, Casilla 6042, Quito, Ecuador; tel. (2) 547-572; undertakes improvements of the postal and telecommunications systems in the region. Sec.-Gen. JAIME AGUILERA BLANCO.

SOCIAL DEVELOPMENT

Three Secretariats co-ordinate activities in social development and welfare:

Health: Paseo de la República 3832, 3° Piso, Casilla 5170, San Isidro, Lima, Peru; tel. 414212; telex 21444. Exec. Sec. Dr NAZARIO ROMÁN ARMENDÁRIZ

Labour Affairs: Luis Felipe Borja y Ponce s/n, Edif. Géminis, 9°, Casilla 601 A, Quito, Ecuador; tel. (2) 545-374. Exec. Sec. WASHINGTON BARRIGA LÓPEZ.

Education, Science and Culture: Carrera 19, No 80-64, Apdo Aéreo 53465, Bogotá, Colombia; tel. (1) 2560221; telex 45569; fax 2579378. Exec. Sec. HERNANDO OCHOA NÚÑEZ.

ARAB BANK FOR ECONOMIC DEVELOPMENT IN AFRICA

(BANQUE ARABE POUR LE DÉVELOPPEMENT ÉCONOMIQUE EN AFRIQUE—BADEA)

Address: Sayed Abdar-Rahman el-Mahdi Ave, POB 2640, Khartoum, Sudan.
Telephone: 73646, 74709.
Telex: 22248, 22739.

The Bank was created by the Arab League at the Sixth Arab Summit Conference in Algiers, November 1973. Operations began in early 1975. The purpose of the Bank is to contribute to Africa's economic development by providing all or part of the financing required for development projects and by supplying technical assistance to African countries.

MEMBERS

Subscribing countries: all members of the Arab League except Djibouti, Somalia and Yemen. Egypt's membership was suspended in April 1979, but restored in April 1988.

Recipient countries: all member countries of the Organization of African Unity except the member countries of the Arab League. A total of 41 countries are eligible for BADEA aid.

Organization
(October 1990)

BOARD OF GOVERNORS

The Board of Governors, the highest authority of the Bank, is composed of finance ministers of Arab League member states; it meets annually, examines the Bank's activities in the past year and provides the resources required for the tasks assigned to it in the coming year. Only the Board of Governors has the power to increase the Bank's capital.

BOARD OF DIRECTORS

The Board meets four times a year to make recommendations concerning policy to the Board of Governors and supervises the implementation of their decisions; it performs all the executive functions of the Bank. The Board comprises a chairman, appointed by the Board of Directors for a two-year term, and 10 other members. Countries with 200 or more shares each have a permanent seat on the Board (Algeria, Iraq, Kuwait, Libya, Qatar, Saudi Arabia and the United Arab Emirates); appointments to the remaining four seats are made by the Governors for a four-year term.

Chairman: AHMAD ABDALLAH AL-AKEIL (Saudi Arabia).
Director-General: AHMAD AL-HARTI AL-OUARDI (Morocco).

SUBSCRIPTIONS TO CAPITAL STOCK
(US $ million at 31 December 1988)

Algeria	42.6	Oman	15.6
Bahrain	2.1	Palestine	2.1
Egypt	2.1	Qatar	85.2
Iraq	149.1	Saudi Arabia	255.6
Jordan	2.1	Sudan	2.1
Kuwait	156.2	Syria	1.4
Lebanon	7.1	Tunisia	8.9
Libya	170.4	United Arab Emirates	127.8
Mauritania	2.1		
Morocco	15.6	**Total**	**1,048.3**

Paid-up capital: US $1,045.5m.

Activities

BADEA aid consists mainly of loans on concessional terms for development projects, not exceeding US $15m. or 50% of the total cost of each project (80% for loans of under $10m.). Technical assistance (e.g. pre-investment studies, training and assistance for institutions) is also provided, and Arab investment in Africa is encouraged.

The Special Arab Assistance Fund for Africa (SAAFA), established in 1972 to provide loans for Africa, was integrated with BADEA in 1977 after disbursing aid to the total of US $214.2m. to 32 African countries.

By December 1989 BADEA had approved loans and grants amounting to US $946.39m. (or $1,160.6m. when SAAFA operations are included) involving 142 projects, nine lines of credit and 49 grants for technical assistance for a total of 38 African countries. Most projects are co-financed with other organizations or countries, chiefly Arab or predominantly Arab aid organizations (including the OPEC Fund and the Islamic Development Bank), western industrialized countries, the World Bank and the African Development Bank. Total disbursements to the end of 1988 (including SAAFA loans) amounted to $656m., or about 60% of total commitments.

The sectoral distribution of aid is determined by development priorities adopted by the African countries themselves. The average distribution has been weighted in favour of projects for infrastructural development, which received 50% of total aid (excluding SAAFA aid) up to the end of 1989. The commitments to agriculture, industrial and energy development projects in 1975–89 were 27%, 12% and 9% respectively.

In 1988 $66.7m. was allocated for nine projects and three technical assistance operations. Projects for which loans were approved in that year were: improvements in water supply in Benin ($4m.), Guinea ($9.5m.) and Senegal ($8.1m.); road-building in Burkina Faso ($10m.), Madagascar ($10m.), Rwanda ($9.5m.) and Zimbabwe ($10m.); sugar production in Burundi ($1m.); and power rehabilitation in the Central African Republic ($4m.).

In 1989 loans and grants totalled $72m. Projects supported in that year included road-building in Botswana ($6.3m.). The Gambia ($3m.) and Senegal ($7m.); a line of credit to the Angolan national bank ($4m.); forestry in Zimbabwe ($9.4m.); and urban electrification in Mozambique ($10m.).

During the first half of 1990 loans and grants totalling $49m. were approved by the Bank bringing the cumulative total to $995.6m. (or $1,209.9m. including SAAFA activities).

INTERNATIONAL ORGANIZATIONS *Arab Bank for Economic Development in Africa*

LOANS AND GRANTS APPROVED BY BADEA*
(US $ million cumulative to 31 December 1987)

Country	Amount	Country	Amount
Angola	32.4	Liberia	10.6
Benin	38.7	Madagascar	36.8
Botswana	33.0	Mali	39.7
Burkina Faso	33.3	Mauritius	12.7
Burundi	35.9	Mozambique	55.0
Cameroon	31.9	Niger	35.9
Cape Verde	28.2	Rwanda	35.8
Central African Republic	13.2	São Tomé and Príncipe	20.7
Chad	10.7	Senegal	41.0
Comoros	27.7	Seychelles	6.1
Congo	33.8	Sierra Leone	25.1
Côte d'Ivoire	3.3	Swaziland	4.2
Equatorial Guinea	8.0	Tanzania	34.2
Ethiopia	14.7	Togo	8.6
The Gambia	9.1	Uganda	45.2
Ghana	46.8	Zaire	22.4
Guinea	35.5	Zambia	47.7
Guinea-Bissau	22.2	Zimbabwe	37.3
Kenya	30.4	Unspecified	9.7
Lesotho	25.6	**Total**	**1,043.1**

* Including grants made by the Special Arab Assistance Fund for Africa before 1977, totalling $214.2m.

TOTAL BADEA COMMITMENTS BY SECTOR
(US $ million)

Sector	1988	1975–88
Infrastructure	40.0	449.2
Roads	39.8	256.9
Railways	—	23.2
Maritime and river transport	—	45.6
Air transport	0.2	35.5
Telecommunications	—	19.4
Water supply	—	19.9
Dams, bridges and public services	—	48.9
Agriculture	22.6	225.1
Rural development	21.6	98.2
Food production	—	39.7
Livestock	—	19.6
Fishing	—	38.8
Agro-industry	1.0	21.2
Forestry development	—	8.0
Industry	—	109.3
Building materials industry	—	50.4
Chemical industry	—	20.0
Small and medium-sized industry	—	34.2
Textile industry	—	4.7
Energy infrastructure and electric power	4.0	74.2
Special programme (emergency aid)	—	14.6
Technical assistance	0.1	2.0
Human resources	—	0.1
Support for institutions	0.1	1.9
Total	**66.7**	**874.4**

PUBLICATIONS

Annual Report.
Co-operation for Development (quarterly).
Studies on Afro-Arab Co-operation.

ARAB FUND FOR ECONOMIC AND SOCIAL DEVELOPMENT—AFESD

Address: POB 21923, Safat, 13080 Kuwait.*
Telephone: 2451580.
Telex: 22153.
Fax: 2416758.

* Relocated to Bahrain, 1990.

Established in 1968 by the Economic Council of the Arab League, the Fund began its operations in 1973. It participates in the financing of economic and social development projects in the Arab states.

MEMBERSHIP

Twenty countries and the Palestine Liberation Organization (see table of subscriptions below).

Organization
(October 1990)

BOARD OF GOVERNORS

The Board of Governors consists of a Governor and an Alternate Governor appointed by each member of the Fund. The Board of Governors is considered as the General Assembly of the Fund, and has all powers.

BOARD OF DIRECTORS

The Board of Directors is composed of six Directors elected by the Board of Governors from among Arab citizens of recognized experience and competence. They are elected for a renewable term of two years.

The Board of Directors is charged with all the activities of the Fund and exercises the powers delegated to it by the Board of Governors.

Director-General and Chairman of the Board of Directors: ABD AL-LATIF YOUSUF AL-HAMAD.

FINANCIAL STRUCTURE

The authorized capital at commencement of operations in April 1973 was 100m. Kuwaiti dinars (KD). In 1982 the capital was increased to KD 800m., divided into 80,000 shares having a value of KD 10,000 each. At the end of 1988 subscribed capital was KD 694.8m., and paid-up capital was KD 644.3m. (see table below).

SUBSCRIPTIONS (KD million, December 1988)*

Country	Amount	Country	Amount
Algeria	64.78	Palestine Liberation Organization	1.10
Bahrain	2.16	Qatar	6.75
Djibouti	0.20	Saudi Arabia	159.07
Egypt†	21.75	Somalia	0.21
Iraq	31.76	Sudan	11.06
Jordan	17.30	Syria	24.0
Kuwait	169.70	Tunisia	6.16
Lebanon	2.0	United Arab Emirates	28.00
Libya	59.85	Yemen Arab Republic‡	4.25
Mauritania	0.82	Yemen, People's Democratic Republic‡	0.20
Morocco	16.0		
Oman	17.28	**Total**	**644.22**

* 100 Kuwaiti dinars = US $355.30 (December 1988).

† In April 1979 all aid to and economic relations with Egypt were suspended, but finance for projects already in progress continued. In April 1988 Egypt was reintegrated into the Fund.

‡ Amalgamated to form the Republic of Yemen in May 1990.

Activities

The Fund participates in the financing of economic and social development projects in the Arab states and countries by:

1. Financing economic projects of an investment character by means of loans granted on easy terms to governments, and to public or private organizations and institutions, giving preference to economic projects of interest specifically to Arab peoples, and to joint Arab projects.

2. Encouraging, directly or indirectly, the investment of public and private capital in such a manner as to ensure the development and growth of the Arab economy.

3. Providing technical expertise and assistance in the various fields of economic development.

The Fund co-operates with other Arab organizations such as the Arab Monetary Fund, the League of Arab States and OAPEC in preparing regional studies and conferences, and acts as the secretariat of the Co-ordination Group of Arab National and Regional Development Institutions.

By the end of 1988 the Fund had made 222 loans for 173 projects in 17 countries, since the beginning of its operations. The total value of these loans was KD 1,000.98m. Disbursements amounted to KD 499.55m. by the end of 1988.

During 1988 the Fund approved 14 loans totalling KD 100.75m. for 12 projects (see table below). Agricultural projects and electric power projects each received some 26% of total commitments. Disbursements of loans during the year amounted to KD 45.5m.

Technical assistance grants reached KD 22.3m. by the end of 1988. During 1988 33 new grants were approved, totalling KD 4.9m., of which the largest proportion (79%) was for training and institutional support, particularly for Palestinians in the Israeli-occupied territories.

LOANS BY SECTOR, 1988

Sector	Amount (KD million)	%
Transport and telecommunications	16.30	16.2
Energy	26.10	25.9
Water and sewerage	19.85	19.7
Industry and mining	12.50	12.4
Agriculture, livestock and fisheries	26.00	25.8
Total (incl. others)	**100.75**	**100.0**

LOANS BY COUNTRY, 1988

Country	Project	Amount (KD million)
Algeria	Water supply, electricity and irrigation	17.00
Iraq	Industrial credit	8.00
Mauritania	Electricity	7.50
	Road improvements	3.10
Morocco	Irrigation	17.00
Sudan	Textiles	4.50
Syria	Road-building	8.00
Tunisia	Irrigation	5.50
	Road improvements	2.70
Yemen Arab Republic	Agricultural development	3.50
	Road improvements	2.50
	Electricity	8.60
Yemen, People's Democratic Republic	Electricity	10.00
	Water supply	2.85
Total		**100.75**

ARAB MONETARY FUND

Address: POB 2818, Abu Dhabi, United Arab Emirates.
Telephone: 215000.
Telex: 22989.
Fax: 326454.

The Agreement establishing the Arab Monetary Fund was approved by the Economic Council of Arab States in Rabat, Morocco, in April 1976 and entered into force on 2 February 1977.

MEMBERS

Algeria	Oman
Bahrain	Palestine Liberation Organization
Egypt*	Qatar
Iraq	Saudi Arabia
Jordan	Somalia
Kuwait	Sudan
Lebanon	Syria
Libya	Tunisia
Mauritania	United Arab Emirates
Morocco	Yemen

* Egypt's membership was suspended in April 1979, but resumed in April 1988.

Organization
(October 1990)

BOARD OF GOVERNORS

The Board of Governors is the highest authority of the Arab Monetary Fund. It formulates policies on Arab economic integration and liberalization of trade among member states. With certain exceptions, it may delegate to the Board of Executive Directors any of its powers. The Board of Governors is composed of a governor and a deputy governor appointed by each member state for a term of five years. It meets at least once a year; meetings may also be convened at the request of half the members, or of members holding half of the total voting power.

BOARD OF EXECUTIVE DIRECTORS

The Board of Executive Directors exercises all powers vested in it by the Board of Governors and may delegate to the Director-General such powers as it deems fit. It is composed of the Director-General and eight non-resident directors elected by the Board of Governors. Each director holds office for three years and may be re-elected.

DIRECTOR-GENERAL

The Director-General of the Fund is appointed by the Board of Governors for a renewable five-year term, and serves as Chairman of the Board of Executive Directors.

The Director-General supervises a Committee on Loans and a Committee on Investments to make recommendations on loan and investment policies to the Board of Executive Directors, and is required to submit an Annual Report to the Board of Governors.

Director-General and Chairman of the Board of Executive Directors: OSAMA J. FAQUIH.

FINANCE

The Arab Accounting Dinar (AAD) is a unit of account equivalent to 3 IMF Special Drawing Rights (The average value of the SDR in 1989 was US $1.281251.)

Each member paid, in convertible currencies, 5% of the value of its shares at the time of its ratification of the Agreement and another 20% when the Agreement entered into force. In addition, each member paid 2% of the value of its shares in its national currency regardless of whether it is convertible. The second 25% of the capital was to be subscribed by the end of September 1979, bringing the total paid-up capital in convertible currencies to AAD 131.5m. (SDR 394.5m.). An increase in requests for loans led to a resolution by the Board of Governors in April 1981, giving members the option of paying the balance of their subscribed capital. This payment became obligatory in July 1981, when total approved loans exceeded 50% of the already paid-up capital in convertible currencies. In April 1983 the authorized capital of the Fund was increased from AAD 288m. to AAD 600m. The new capital stock comprised 12,000 shares, each having the value of AAD 50,000. At the end of 1989 total subscribed capital was AAD 326m., and paid-up capital was AAD 311.84m.

CAPITAL SUBSCRIPTIONS
(million Arab Accounting Dinars, 31 December 1989)

Member	Authorized capital	Paid-up capital	Votes
Algeria	60.00	42.40	923
Bahrain	9.00	5.00	175
Egypt	60.00	20.00	715
Iraq	60.00	42.40	923
Jordan	11.00	5.40	183
Kuwait	60.00	32.00	715
Lebanon	13.00	5.00	175
Libya	30.00	13.44	344
Mauritania	9.00	5.00	175
Morocco	35.00	15.00	375
Oman	9.00	5.00	175
Palestine Liberation Organization	4.00	—	118
Qatar	24.00	10.00	275
Saudi Arabia	90.00	48.40	1,043
Somalia	9.00	4.00	155
Sudan	25.00	10.00	275
Syria	20.00	7.20	219
Tunisia	15.00	7.00	215
United Arab Emirates	36.00	19.20	459
Yemen Arab Republic	12.00	10.40	283
Yemen, People's Democratic Republic	9.00	5.00	125
Total	**600.00**	**311.84**	**8,095**

Activities

The creation of the Arab Monetary Fund was seen as a step towards the goal of Arab economic integration. It assists member states in balance of payments difficulties, and also has a broad range of aims.

The Articles of Agreement define the Fund's aims as follows:

(a) to correct disequilibria in the balance of payments of member states;

(b) to promote the stability of exchange rates among Arab currencies, to render them mutually convertible, and to eliminate restrictions on current payments between member states;

(c) to establish policies and modes of monetary co-operation to speed up Arab economic integration and economic development in the member states;

(d) to tender advice on the investment of member states' financial resources in foreign markets, whenever called upon to do so;

(e) to promote the development of Arab financial markets;

(f) to promote the use of the Arab dinar as a unit of account and to pave the way for the creation of a unified Arab currency;

(g) to co-ordinate the positions of member states in dealing with international monetary and economic problems; and

(h) to provide a mechanism for the settlement of current payments between member states in order to promote trade among them.

The Arab Monetary Fund functions both as a fund and a bank. It is empowered:

(a) to provide short- and medium-term loans to finance balance of payments deficits of member states;

(b) to issue guarantees to member states to strengthen their borrowing capabilities;

INTERNATIONAL ORGANIZATIONS
Arab Monetary Fund

LOANS APPROVED, 1989

Borrower	Type of loan	Amount (AAD million)
Algeria	Ordinary	41.64
Egypt	Automatic	5.25
Iraq	Automatic	3.30
Jordan	Ordinary	5.32
Morocco	Extended	17.15
Syria	Extension of ordinary	1.08
Total*		**73.74**

* Excludes a compensatory loan to Egypt (AAD 6.625m.) and an extended loan to Mauritania (AAD 6.86m.), approved at the end of 1989, with disbursements starting in early 1990.

LOANS APPROVED, 1978–89

Type of loan	Number of loans	Amount (AAD '000)
Automatic	50	237,585
Extended	8	95,980
Ordinary	9	93,630
Compensatory	8	60,740
Inter-Arab Trade Facility	11	64,730
Total	**86**	**552,665**

(c) to act as intermediary in the issuance of loans in Arab and international markets for the account of member states and under their guarantees;

(d) to co-ordinate the monetary policies of member states;

(e) to manage any funds placed under its charge by member states;

(f) to hold periodic consultations with member states on their economic conditions; and

(g) to provide technical assistance to banking and monetary institutions in member states.

Loans are intended to finance an overall balance of payments deficit and a member may draw up to 75% of its paid-up subscription, in convertible currencies, for this purpose unconditionally (automatic loans). A member may, however, obtain loans in excess of this limit, subject to agreement with the Fund on a programme aimed at reducing its balance of payments deficit (ordinary and extended loans, equivalent to 175% and 225% of its quota respectively). From 1981 a country receiving no extended loans was entitled to a loan under the Inter-Arab Trade Facility (discontinued in 1989) of up to 100% of its quota. In addition, a member has the right to borrow up to 100% of its paid-up capital in order to cope with an unexpected deficit in its balance of payments resulting from a decrease in its exports of goods and services or a large increase in its imports of agricultural products following a poor harvest (compensatory loans). Over the period 1978–89, 88 loans were extended to 12 member countries.

Automatic and compensatory loans are repayable within three years, while ordinary and extended loans are repayable within five and seven years respectively. Loans are granted at concessionary and uniform rates of interest which increase with the length of the period of the loan.

At the end of 1989 total approved loans amounted to AAD 566.15m., of which AAD 510.97m. had been disbursed and AAD 268.93m. repaid.

The Fund's lending declined from AAD 85m. in 1983 to AAD 18.5m. in 1984 (when investigations were being conducted into alleged financial malpractice by senior officials of the Fund between 1977 and 1982). Lending increased to AAD 51m. in 1985, comprising nine loans to five member states. In 1986 the Fund extended 11 loans amounting to AAD 33.5m., and in 1987 it approved three loans totalling AAD 29.1m.

In 1988 the Fund's executive directors agreed to modify their policy on lending, placing an emphasis on specific projects that would directly increase economic growth in the country concerned. They also agreed to replace direct trade financing with an export credit guarantee scheme. During 1988 the Fund made 14 loans amounting to AAD 121m. During 1989 the Fund approved six loans amounting to AAD 73.74m. (see table).

In March 1989 Arab financial institutions agreed to establish an Arab Trade Financing Program (ATFP), to increase inter-Arab trade in goods and services (excluding petroleum) (see below).

The Fund also undertakes studies and surveys on inter-Arab trade; provides technical assistance, in the form of training courses or placements for trainees, seminars, and expert advisory services; and co-operates with other regional organizations by participating in meetings. An Economic Policy Institute was established by the Fund in 1988 to conduct research and training for economists and policy-makers, to organize meetings and to publish information.

TRADE PROMOTION

Arab Trade Financing Program (ATFP): POB 26799, Abu Dhabi, United Arab Emirates; tel. 316999; telex 24166; fax 316793; f. 1989 to develop and liberalize trade between Arab countries, and to enhance the competitive ability of Arab exporters; operates by extending lines of credit to national agencies (designated by Arab governments) for exports and imports. The Arab Monetary Fund was to provide 50% of the ATFP's capital of US $500m., and participation was also invited from private and official Arab financial institutions and joint Arab/foreign institutions. Chief Executive OSAMA J. FAQUIH.

PUBLICATIONS

Annual Report.
The Arab Countries: Economic Indicators.
Cross Exchange Rates of Arab Currencies.
Foreign Trade of the Arab Countries.
Joint Arab Economic Report (annually).
Money and Credit in the Arab Countries.
National Accounts of the Arab Countries.
Balance of Payments and Public Debt of the Arab Countries.
Reports on commodity structure (by value and quantity) of member countries' imports from and exports to other Arab countries.

ASIAN DEVELOPMENT BANK—ADB

Address: 2330 Roxas Blvd, 1300 Metro Manila, Philippines; POB 789, 1099 Manila, Philippines.
Telephone: 8344444; (632) 7113851 (international calls).
Telex: 23103.
Fax: (632) 741-7961.

The Bank commenced operations in December 1966; its aims are to raise funds from private and public sources for development purposes in the region, to assist member states in co-ordinating economic policies, and to give technical assistance in development projects.

MEMBERS
There are 34 member countries and territories within the ESCAP region and 15 others (see list of subscriptions below).

Organization
(October 1990)

BOARD OF GOVERNORS
All powers of the Bank are vested in the Board which may delegate its powers to the Board of Directors except in such matters as admission of new members, changes in the Bank's authorized capital stock, election of Directors and President, amendment of the Charter. One Governor and one Alternate Governor are appointed by each member country. The Board meets at least once a year.

BOARD OF DIRECTORS
The Board of Directors is responsible for general direction of operations and exercises all powers delegated by the Board of Governors, which elects it. Of the 12 Directors, eight represent constituency groups of member countries within the ESCAP region (with about 65% of the voting power) and four represent the rest of the member countries. Each Director serves for two years and may be re-elected. The President of the Bank, though not a Director, is Chairman of the Board.

Chairman of Board of Directors and President: KIMIMASA TARUMIZU (Japan).
Vice-Presidents: IN YONG CHUNG (Republic of Korea); WILLIAM R. THOMSON (USA); GÜNTHER SCHULZ (Germany).

ADMINISTRATION
There were 1,665 Bank staff from 40 countries on 31 December 1989.
Departments: Programs (East and West), Agriculture, Infrastructure, Energy and Industry, Private Sector, Budget, Personnel and Management Systems, Controller's, Treasurer's, Economics and Development Resource Center.
Offices: President, Secretary, General Counsel, Development Policy, Central Projects Services, Administrative Services, Special Projects, Environment, Information, Computer Services, Internal Audit, Post-Evaluation. There are Resident Offices in Bangladesh, Indonesia, Nepal and Pakistan. The Regional Office for the South Pacific is in Vanuatu.
Secretary: ARUN B. ADARKAR (India).
General Counsel: CHUN PYO JHONG (Republic of Korea).

FINANCIAL STRUCTURE
The Bank's ordinary capital resources (which are used for loans to the more advanced developing countries in the region) are held and used entirely separately from its Special Funds resources (see below). A third general capital increase, of 105%, was authorized in April 1983.

At 31 December 1989 the position of subscriptions to the capital stock was as follows: Authorized US $22,111m.; Subscribed $21,138m.; Paid-in $2,552m.

The Bank also borrows funds from the world capital markets. Total borrowings during 1989 amounted to $645m. (compared with $435m. in 1988).

In July 1986 the Bank abolished the system of fixed lending rates, under which ordinary operations loans had carried interest rates fixed at the time of loan commitment for the entire life of the loan. Under the new system the lending rate is adjusted every six months, to take into account changing conditions in international financial markets. The lending rate was fixed at 6.36% per annum for the six months to 31 December 1990.

SUBSCRIPTIONS AND VOTING POWER*
(31 December 1989)

Country	Total subscriptions to capital stock (US $'000)	Voting power (% of total)
Regional:		
Afghanistan	15,704	0.485
Australia	1,345,306	5.517
Bangladesh	237,390	1.324
Bhutan	1,445	0.431
Cambodia	11,499	0.469
China, People's Republic	1,498,142	6.096
Cook Islands	618	0.428
Fiji	15,809	0.485
Hong Kong	126,619	0.905
India	1,471,925	5.996
Indonesia	1,266,193	5.218
Japan	3,165,483	12.406
Kiribati	933	0.429
Korea, Republic	1,171,219	4.858
Laos	3,233	0.438
Malaysia	633,097	2.822
Maldives	933	0.429
Myanmar	126,619	0.905
Nepal	34,181	0.555
New Zealand	357,057	1.777
Pakistan	506,477	2.342
Papua New Guinea	21,815	0.508
Philippines	553,945	2.522
Singapore	79,112	0.725
Solomon Islands	1,551	0.431
Sri Lanka	134,833	0.936
Taiwan	253,239	1.384
Thailand	316,542	1.624
Tonga	933	0.429
Vanuatu	1,551	0.431
Viet-Nam	79,349	0.726
Western Samoa	762	0.428
Sub-total	13,433,514	64.459
Non-regional:		
Austria	79,112	0.725
Belgium	79,112	0.725
Canada	1,216,163	5.028
Denmark	79,112	0.725
Finland	79,112	0.725
France	541,145	2.474
Germany, Fed. Repub.	1,005,780	4.232
Italy	420,203	2.016
Netherlands	238,481	1.328
Norway	79,112	0.725
Spain	79,112	0.725
Sweden	31,645	0.545
Switzerland	135,687	0.939
United Kingdom	474,820	2.223
USA	3,165,483	12.406
Sub-total	7,704,079	35.541
Total	21,137,593	100.000

* In April 1990, Marshall Islands and the Federated States of Micronesia were admitted to membership. Mongolia and Turkey also applied to join in 1990.

INTERNATIONAL ORGANIZATIONS
Asian Development Bank

SPECIAL FUNDS

The Asian Development Fund (ADF) was established in 1974 in order to provide a systematic mechanism for mobilizing and administering resources for the Bank to lend on concessionary terms to the least-developed member countries. Administration of the earlier Special Funds—the Multi-Purpose Special Fund (MPSF) and the Agricultural Special Fund (ASF)—had been complicated by the fact that contributions of individual donors had been made voluntarily at the initiative of the countries concerned and were frequently tied to procurement in those countries.

Successive replenishments of the Fund's resources amounted to $809m. for the period 1976–78, $2,150m. for 1979–82, and $3,214m. for 1983–86. A further replenishment (ADF V) was approved in 1986, and came into effect in May 1987, providing $3,600m. for the four years 1987–90.

The Bank provides technical assistance grants from its Technical Assistance Special Fund. By the end of 1989, direct voluntary contributions to this fund amounted to $173m. The Japan Special Fund was established in 1988 to provide finance for technical assistance and equity investment. Two scholarship programmes were also established in 1988.

Activities

Loans by the Bank are usually aimed at specific projects, resulting in the creation of real physical assets. In responding to requests from member governments for loans, the Bank's staff assesses the financial and economic viability of projects and the way in which they fit into the economic framework and priorities of development of the country concerned. In 1987 the Bank adopted a policy of lending in support of programmes of sectoral adjustment, not limited to specific projects; such lending was not to exceed 15% of total Bank lending. In 1985 the Bank decided to expand its assistance to the private sector, hitherto comprising loans to development finance institutions, under government guarantee, for lending to small and medium-sized enterprises; a programme was now formulated for direct financial assistance, in the form of equity and loans without government guarantee, to private enterprises. In addition, the Bank was to increase its support for financial institutions and capital markets and, where appropriate, give assistance for the privatization of public sector enterprises.

In 1989 the Bank approved 69 loans for 60 projects in 15 developing member countries, amounting to US $3,623.6m., (compared with $3,145.6m. in 1988). Loans from ordinary capital resources totalled $2,260.3m., while loans from the ADF amounted to $1,363.3m. The Bank also approved 14 equity investments totalling $56.4m. Two underwriting commitments, for a total of $11.2m., were also approved. Co-financing by other institutions amounted to $1,273m. Disbursements of loans during 1989 amounted to $2,235m., compared with $1,649m. in the previous year.

During 1989 the agriculture and agro-industry sector received the largest proportion (23%) of total loan approvals: these included

BANK ACTIVITIES BY SECTOR

Sector	Loan Approvals (US $ million)			
	1989		1968–89	
	Amount	%	Amount	%
Agriculture and agro-industry.	846.26	23.36	8,225.61	28.76
Energy	604.93	16.69	6,390.78	22.35
Industry and non-fuel minerals	760.70	20.99	4,683.99	16.38
Transport and communications	586.10	16.18	4,556.95	15.94
Social infrastructure	756.60	20.88	4,466.61	15.62
Multi-sector	69.00	1.90	272.71	0.95
Total	**3,623.59**	**100.00**	**28,596.65**	**100.00**

LENDING ACTIVITIES BY COUNTRY (US $ million)

Country	Loans approved in 1989			Cumulative 1968–89			
	Ordinary Capital	ADF	Total	Ordinary Capital	ADF	Total	%
Afghanistan	—	—	—	—	95.10	95.10	0.33
Bangladesh	—	338.30	338.30	11.40	2,787.09	2,798.49	9.79
Bhutan	—	—	—	—	31.63	31.63	0.11
Cambodia	—	—	—	—	1.67	1.67	0.01
China, People's Republic	39.70	—	39.70	455.90	—	455.90	1.59
Cook Islands	—	—	—	—	5.25	5.25	0.02
Fiji	9.60	—	9.60	103.10	—	103.10	0.36
Hong Kong	—	—	—	101.50	—	101.50	0.35
India	503.90	—	503.90	1,644.50	—	1,644.50	5.75
Indonesia	667.30	105.00	772.30	5,219.15	482.38	5,701.53	19.94
Kiribati	—	—	—	—	3.90	3.90	0.01
Korea, Republic	—	—	—	2,319.63	3.70	2,323.33	8.12
Laos	—	59.00	59.00	—	176.64	176.64	0.62
Malaysia	138.20	—	138.20	1,529.34	3.30	1,532.64	5.36
Maldives	—	—	—	—	15.88	15.88	0.06
Myanmar	—	—	—	6.60	524.26	530.86	1.86
Nepal	—	122.10	122.10	2.00	860.26	862.26	3.02
Pakistan	337.80	386.20	724.00	2,352.32	2,785.65	5,137.97	17.97
Papua New Guinea	32.43	61.00	93.43	174.68	201.34	376.02	1.31
Philippines	421.40	137.00	558.40	2,967.44	444.26	3,411.70	11.93
Singapore	—	—	—	178.08	3.00	181.08	0.63
Solomon Islands	—	—	—	—	38.11	38.11	0.13
Sri Lanka	—	127.26	127.26	14.13	869.19	910.32	3.18
Taiwan	—	—	—	100.39	—	100.39	0.35
Thailand	110.00	—	110.00	1,831.00	72.10	1,903.10	6.65
Tonga	—	5.00	5.00	—	19.55	19.55	0.07
Vanuatu	—	—	—	—	10.85	10.85	0.04
Viet-Nam	—	—	—	3.93	40.67	44.60	0.16
Western Samoa	—	22.40	22.40	—	78.78	78.78	0.28
Total	**2,260.33**	**1,363.26**	**3,623.59**	**19,015.09**	**9,581.56**	**28,596.65**	**100.00**

Source: *ADB Annual Report 1989*.

INTERNATIONAL ORGANIZATIONS
Asian Development Bank

loans in support of adjustment in the agricultural sector in Laos, Papua New Guinea, the Philippines, Sri Lanka and Western Samoa; forestry projects in Bangladesh, Indonesia and the Philippines; and projects supporting agricultural diversification (e.g. horticulture in Bangladesh, brackish-water aquaculture in Indonesia, and secondary crops in Nepal). Industry and non-fuel minerals received 21% of loans, mainly through lending to national development finance institutions which provide credit for small and medium-sized enterprises. Social infrastructure (water supply and sanitation, urban development, housing, education and health) received 21% of loans, energy projects 17% and transport and communications (chiefly road improvements) 16%.

Loans and grants for technical assistance (e.g. project preparation, consultant services and training) amounted to $239.2m. for 241 projects in 1989. The Bank's Post-Evaluation Office prepares reports on completed projects, in order to assess achievements and problems.

The Bank co-operates with other international organizations active in the region, particularly the World Bank group and UNDP, and participates in meetings of aid donors for developing member countries.

BUDGET
Internal administrative expenses amounted to US $106.3m. in 1989, and were expected to come to $120m. in 1990.

PUBLICATIONS
Annual Report.
Asian Development Outlook (annually).
ADB Quarterly Review.
Energy Indicators of Major Developing Member Countries (annually).
Key Indicators of Developing Member Countries of ADB (annually).
Asian Development Review (2 a year).
ADB Business Opportunities (monthly).
Project Profiles for Commercial Co-financing (quarterly).
Handbooks, guidelines, sample bidding documents.

ASSOCIATION OF SOUTH EAST ASIAN NATIONS—ASEAN

Address: Jalan Sisingamangaraja, POB 2072, Jakarta, Indonesia.
Telephone: 712272.
Telex: 47214.

ASEAN was established in August 1967 at Bangkok, Thailand, to accelerate economic progress and to increase the stability of the South-East Asian region.

MEMBERS

Brunei	Malaysia	Singapore
Indonesia	Philippines	Thailand

Organization
(October 1990)

SUMMIT MEETING

The highest authority of ASEAN, bringing together the Heads of Government of member countries. The first meeting was held in Bali, Indonesia, in February 1976; the second in Kuala Lumpur, Malaysia, in August 1977. A third summit meeting was held in Manila, the Philippines, in December 1987.

MINISTERIAL CONFERENCES

The ministers of foreign affairs of member states meet annually in each member country in turn. Ministers of economic affairs also meet about once a year, to direct ASEAN economic co-operation, and other ministers meet when necessary. Ministerial meetings are serviced by the committees described below.

STANDING COMMITTEE

The Standing Committee normally meets every two months. It consists of the minister of foreign affairs of the host country and ambassadors of the other five.

SECRETARIATS

A permanent secretariat was established in Jakarta, Indonesia, in 1976 to form a central co-ordinating body. The post of Secretary-General rotates among the member countries in alphabetical order every three years. In each member country day-to-day work is co-ordinated by an ASEAN national secretariat.

Secretary-General: RUSLI NOOR (Indonesia).

COMMITTEES

Economic co-operation is directed by ministers of economic affairs through five Committees, on Food, Agriculture and Forestry; Finance and Banking; Industry, Minerals and Energy; Transport and Communications; and Trade and Tourism.

Other ministerial meetings are serviced by the following three Committees: Culture and Information; Science and Technology; and Social Development.

These committees are serviced by a network of subsidiary technical bodies comprising sub-committees, expert groups, ad-hoc working groups, working parties, etc.

To support the conduct of relations with other countries and international organizations, ASEAN committees (composed of heads of diplomatic missions) have been established in 10 foreign capitals: those of Australia, Belgium, Canada, France, Germany, Japan, New Zealand, Switzerland, the United Kingdom and the USA.

Activities

ASEAN was established in 1967 with the signing of the ASEAN Declaration, otherwise known as the Bangkok Declaration, by the ministers of foreign affairs of Indonesia, Malaysia, the Philippines, Singapore and Thailand. Brunei joined the organization in January 1984, shortly after attaining independence. The ASEAN Declaration sets out the objectives of the organization as follows:

(i) To accelerate economic growth, social progress and cultural development in the region through joint endeavours in the spirit of equality and partnership in order to strengthen the foundation for a prosperous and peaceful community of South East Asian nations;

(ii) To promote regional peace and stability through abiding respect for justice and the rule of law in the relationship among countries of the region and adherence to the principles of the United Nations Charter;

(iii) To promote active collaboration and mutual assistance on matters of common interest in the economic, social, cultural, technical, scientific and administrative fields;

(iv) To provide assistance to each other in the form of training and research facilities in the educational, professional, technical and administrative spheres;

(v) To collaborate more effectively for the greater utilization of their agriculture and industries, the expansion of their trade, including the study of the problems of international commodity trade, the improvement of their transportation and communication facilities and the raising of the living standards of their people;

(vi) To promote South-East Asian studies; and

(vii) To maintain close and beneficial co-operation with existing international and regional organizations with similar aims and purposes, and explore all avenues for even closer co-operation among themselves.

ASEAN's first summit meeting was held at Denpasar, Bali, Indonesia, in February 1976. Two major documents were signed:

Treaty of Amity and Co-operation, laying down principles of mutual respect for the independence and sovereignty of all nations; non-interference in the internal affairs of one another; settlement of disputes by peaceful means; and effective co-operation among the five countries. (Amended in 1987 by a Protocol which would allow other states within and outside the region to accede to the Treaty.)

Declaration of Concord, giving guidelines for action in economic, social and cultural relations, including: the maintenance of political stability; the establishment of a 'Zone of Peace, Freedom and Stability'; the promotion of social justice and improvement of living standards; mutual assistance in the event of natural disasters; and co-operation in economic development.

EXTERNAL RELATIONS

The European Community: In March 1980 a co-operation agreement was signed between ASEAN and the EEC, following a joint ministerial conference. The agreement, which entered into force on 1 October, provided for the strengthening of existing trade links and increased co-operation in the scientific and agricultural spheres. A joint co-operation committee met in Manila in November (and annually thereafter); it drew up a programme of scientific and technological co-operation, approved measures to promote contacts between industrialists from the two regions, and agreed on the financing of ASEAN regional projects by the Community. An ASEAN-EEC Business Council was launched in December 1983 to provide a forum for businessmen from the two regions and to identify joint projects. The first meeting of ministers of economic affairs from ASEAN and EEC member countries took place in October 1985, and agreed to encourage European investment in the ASEAN region (then estimated at 13% of total foreign investment, compared with 28% for Japanese investment and 17% for the USA). In 1986 a joint group of experts on trade was set up, to examine problems of access to ASEAN markets and similar matters, and in 1987 joint investment committees were established in all the ASEAN capital cities. In 1988 it was agreed that a joint management centre should be established in Brunei. At a meeting held in February 1990 ASEAN and EEC ministers discussed the likely effects of the completion of the European single market in 1992, and of the expansion of EEC aid to East European countries.

Japan: The ASEAN-Japan Forum was established in 1977 to discuss matters of mutual concern in trade, investment, technology transfer and development assistance. In 1981 the Japanese Government approved yen-based credits worth $870m. for Indonesia, Malaysia, the Philippines and Thailand. Further support was offered in 1983 in the form of increased financial aid for Indonesia, Malaysia and Thailand and a scheme for renovating industrial installations originally built with Japanese assistance. Discussions were also held concerning Japanese restrictions on imports of

ASEAN agricultural produce: Thailand and the Philippines in particular expressed concern over their trade deficit with Japan. Tariff cuts on certain ASEAN exports were made by Japan in 1985, but ASEAN members continued to criticize Japan's attitude and called for Japan to import more manufactured products rather than raw materials. In 1987 Japan established an 'ASEAN-Japan Development Fund' of about $2,000m. for assistance to ASEAN members over the next three years, particularly in private-sector industrial development.

Other countries: ASEAN holds regular 'Dialogues' on trade and other matters with a number of countries, and receives assistance for various development projects. Under the ASEAN-Australia Economic Co-operation Programme, Australia gives financial support for ASEAN activities, including (in 1987) training in water quality management, prevention of drug abuse, and development education. A joint Business Council was set up in 1980. New Zealand has given technical and financial assistance in forestry development, dairy technology, veterinary management and legal aid training. The USA gives assistance for the development of small and medium-sized businesses and other projects, and supports a Center for Technology Exchange. ASEAN-Canada co-operation projects include fisheries technology, a joint programme to reduce post-harvest crop losses, and a forest seed centre.

In July 1989 ASEAN took part in discussions initiated by Australia on economic co-operation by Asian and Pacific nations, but expressed opposition to proposals for the establishment of a formal regional trade grouping. However, in November ASEAN participated in the formation (with Australia, Canada, Japan, the Republic of Korea, New Zealand and the USA) of Asia-Pacific Economic Co-operation (APEC), envisaged as a forum for regular discussions on questions of trade.

Indo-China: The question of relations with the new communist governments in Indo-China was prominent at the Bali summit in February 1976. The documents signed at the summit made clear that ASEAN countries wished to form a zone of peace, freedom and neutrality, a concept adopted by ASEAN in 1971, and would respect the independence and sovereignty of all nations. ASEAN was to be an economic and diplomatic forum, with no question of a military alliance. Diplomatic relations with the communist governments were established in 1976. In 1978 the hostilities between Viet-Nam, Kampuchea (Cambodia) and the People's Republic of China caused both Viet-Nam and China to seek closer ties with ASEAN and to negotiate with ASEAN as a group, not in bilateral terms. Fears of Viet-Nam's military ambitions, stirred by the invasion of Kampuchea in December 1978, and the severe strain placed on the ASEAN countries by the exodus of refugees from Viet-Nam, however, caused ASEAN to reassess its relations with Viet-Nam, which it accused of trying to destabilize South-East Asia, and to seek new ways of establishing peace. At the 12th meeting of ministers of foreign affairs in June 1979 grave concern was expressed over the thousands of displaced persons from Indo-China, and the delegates deplored the fact that Viet-Nam had not taken effective measures to stop the exodus. The ASEAN Foreign Ministers also reiterated their support for the right of the Kampuchean people to self-determination. In July 1981 the United Nations held a conference on Kampuchea, sponsored by ASEAN: the ASEAN countries proposed a coalition of the three main factions in Kampuchea, the withdrawal of Vietnamese troops, and elections supervised by the UN (see chapter on Viet-Nam). ASEAN made it clear that it would not, as a group, supply arms to any faction.

In September 1983 ASEAN issued an 'Appeal for Kampuchean Independence', in which it called for phased withdrawals of Vietnamese troops, supervised by a peace-keeping force, and for safe areas to be established for Kampuchean refugee camps; these actions were seen as the first steps in a comprehensive political settlement. This appeal was rejected by Viet-Nam in October.

In February 1985 a meeting of ASEAN ministers of foreign affairs, repeating their previous demands for Vietnamese withdrawal from Kampuchea, also requested military aid from foreign countries to the anti-Vietnamese coalition in Kampuchea. In July ASEAN proposed 'proximity' talks to be held (through an intermediary) between Viet-Nam and the Kampuchean coalition, but Viet-Nam refused to take part. In July 1988 an 'informal' meeting was held at Bogor, Indonesia, between representatives of Viet-Nam, Laos, ASEAN and the Kampuchean factions, to discuss a possible political settlement in Kampuchea, and further discussions were held in October and in February 1989. In July ASEAN ministers reiterated that a UN peace-keeping force should be established in Cambodia (as it was now known) after the withdrawal of Vietnamese troops, which took place in September 1989. ASEAN participated in the international conference on Cambodia which was held in Paris, France in July/August, and in further negotiations held in Jakarta, Indonesia in February 1990, neither of which achieved a political settlement. In July 1990 ASEAN ministers criticized the US Government's decision to withdraw its support for the representation of the Cambodian resistance coalition at the UN, and to begin direct negotiations with Viet-Nam; and they urged the formation of a Supreme National Council (SNC), on which the Vietnamese-backed government of Cambodia and the three opposition groups would be represented, and which would fill Cambodia's seat at the UN. In August the UN Security Council proposed the formation of an SNC in Cambodia, and the holding of elections there, under UN supervision. The plan was accepted by all the Cambodian factions at a conference held in Jakarta in September, and further negotiations were expected to take place in Paris in November.

In July 1988 ASEAN officials took part in discussions with the Vietnamese Government on the voluntary repatriation of Vietnamese who had fled to ASEAN countries. In March 1989 ASEAN announced that Vietnamese asylum-seekers would no longer automatically be treated as eligible for resettlement, but would be 'screened' to establish whether they were economic migrants or 'genuine' refugees. In July 1990 ASEAN criticized the US Government's refusal to approve the forcible repatriation of Vietnamese asylum-seekers who had been classified as economic migrants rather than as refugees. ASEAN members also threatened to refuse to allow further arrivals to land on their shores.

INDUSTRY

In 1976 ASEAN ministers agreed to set up five equity-sharing medium-sized industries; a 60% share of each was to be owned by the host country, and the remaining 40% by the other four members. The projects originally comprised the manufacture of diesel engines in Singapore, urea for fertilizers in Indonesia and Malaysia, superphosphates in the Philippines, and soda ash in Thailand. In 1978 the text of the Basic Agreement on ASEAN Industrial Projects was agreed. By 1982, however, only the urea projects in Indonesia and Malaysia were ready to be implemented. The Indonesian project had its ASEAN company incorporated in March 1979 and was inaugurated in January 1984, with an annual production capacity of 570,000 metric tons. The Malaysian project, with an annual production capacity of 495,000 tons of urea and 330,000 tons of ammonia, began operations in 1985. The Singapore diesel engine project was abandoned and an alternative scheme, the establishment of a hepatitis vaccine plant, was approved in 1984, but was also abandoned in 1987. The Thai soda ash project was also abandoned in 1985 owing to falling demand, and the Philippine superphosphates scheme proved not to be feasible and was abandoned in favour of a copper fabrication project.

The ASEAN Industrial Complementation programme, begun in 1981, encourages member countries to produce complementary products in specific industrial sectors for preferential exchange among themselves, for example components to be used in the automobile industry. The establishment of ASEAN Industrial Joint Ventures was approved in 1983. This scheme, initiated by ASEAN chambers of commerce and industry, aims to set up projects with at least 51% participation (reduced to 40% in 1987) by private sector companies from two or more ASEAN member states; the resultant products would receive preferential treatment (tariff reductions of 75%, increased to 90% in 1987) from the participating countries, and, after four years, preferential treatment from other member states. By August 1988 15 joint projects had been approved, including the manufacture of vehicle components and security paper (for banknotes), production of potash, feldspar and quartz, and meat processing, and by September 1990 seven ventures were reported to be in operation.

In 1988 the ASEAN Fund was established, with capital of $150m. (of which $15m. was contributed by the Asian Development Bank), to provide finance for portfolio investments in ASEAN countries, in particular for small and medium-sized companies.

TRADE

A Basic Agreement on the Establishment of ASEAN Preferential Trade Arrangements was concluded in 1977. This was not intended to lead directly to the formation of a free trade zone. The Philippines, Thailand and Singapore had favoured trade liberalization, and early in 1977 they concluded bilateral agreements for 10% tariff cuts on a wide range of items traded between themselves. Indonesia, on the other hand, had opposed trade liberalization, taking the view that its own economy would be at a disadvantage under free trade. The ASEAN agreement therefore provided for negotiations to lead to the introduction of preferences product by product. In July 1980 it was decided that all imports with trade values of less than US $50,000 (as recorded in the trade statistics for 1978) should have the existing tariff reduced by 20%, bringing the number of items under the preferential trading arrangements to over 6,000. A system of uniform tariff reductions of 20%–25% was adopted in 1982 to replace the 'product-by-product' approach. An import value ceiling of US $1m. for these cuts, imposed in January, was raised to $2.5m. in May and to $10m. in November. Tariff cuts of 50% were approved in November for certain non-food products. In February 1985 the uniform tariff reduction was raised to 25% (instead of 20%–25% as previously). Although by mid-1987 almost 19,000 items were included on the list of products granted preferential import tariff rates, most of these items were insignificant in regional trade. Because individual countries are permitted to exclude any 'sensitive' products from preferential import tariffs, the system only covered about 5% of trade between the members. In December 1987 the meeting of ASEAN heads of government resolved to reduce such exclusions to a maximum of 10% of the number of items traded and to a maximum of 50% of the value of trade, over the next five years (seven years for Indonesia and the Philippines).

FINANCE AND BANKING

In 1987 heads of government agreed to accelerate regional co-operation in this field, in order to support intra-ASEAN trade and investment; they adopted measures to increase the role of ASEAN currencies in regional trade, to assist negotiations on the avoidance of double taxation, and to improve the efficiency of tax and customs administrators. An ASEAN Reinsurance Corporation was to be established in 1988, with initial authorized capital of US $10m.

AGRICULTURE

The ASEAN Agricultural Development Planning Centre was set up in 1981 to conduct research and training and to draw up regional production plans.

An emergency grain reserve agreement was signed in 1979. During the year an emergency reserve of 50,000 tons of rice was established, available to any member country at three days' notice. Other areas of co-operation include: a Plant Quarantine Training Institute; an Agricultural Development Planning Centre; a Forest Tree Seed Centre; and a post-harvest programme for conserving grain. An ASEAN centre for training and research in poultry diseases was opened in 1988.

In October 1983 a ministerial agreement on fisheries co-operation was concluded, providing for the joint management of fish resources, the sharing of technology, and co-operation in marketing. An agreement on the co-ordination and development of aquaculture was signed in 1987.

The first ASEAN Forestry Congress was held in October 1983 to discuss the state of the regional timber industry and the problems of forest depletion. In January 1985 it was announced that an ASEAN Institute for Forest Management was to be set up in Malaysia, with assistance from Canada.

ENERGY

In 1983 a ministerial meeting on energy co-operation resulted in the formation of a Committee on Energy Co-operation, the commissioning of a study on coal power development, a scheme for petroleum sharing, and nine co-operative projects. In 1986 member states signed an agreement on regional sharing of petroleum supplies in the event of an emergency.

TRANSPORT AND COMMUNICATIONS

Joint transport projects being undertaken in 1988 included the Pan Borneo Highway (linking Brunei with Indonesia and Malaysia), and improvement of roads and ferry links. An agreement on the mutual recognition of driving licences came into effect in 1988. Four centres for training in civil aviation were in operation in 1988, and two more were to be opened in 1989. In 1987 heads of government agreed to promote shipping links among member states and to investigate the feasibility of joint facilities for shipping companies.

JOINT RESEARCH AND TECHNOLOGY

The ASEAN Committee on Science and Technology has co-ordinated the Protein Project, investigating low-cost alternative sources of protein; research in food technology and the management of food waste materials; completion of a Climatic Atlas and Regional Compendium of Climatic Statistics; a nature conservation scheme; and non-conventional energy research. The ASEAN-US Center for Technology Exchange (based in New York, with a regional office in Kuala Lumpur, Malaysia) was opened in 1984. The first ASEAN Science and Technology Week was held in 1986, and the second was held in 1989. In 1987 heads of government adopted a programme of action for regional co-operation in biotechnology, materials science, micro-electronics and new sources of energy; the programme was also to include the establishment of regional research networks. In 1987 the principle of 'sustainable development' was adopted by heads of government, and an environment programme for 1988–92 was also adopted.

EDUCATION

Under the ASEAN Development Education Programme five projects (financed by Australia) have been set up: Special Education; Education Management Information System; Teacher Education Reform; Work-oriented Education; Test Development. A National Agency of Development Education has been set up in each country.

SOCIAL DEVELOPMENT

Activities include a Population Programme to co-ordinate demographic research; co-operation against drug abuse; mutual assistance in natural disasters; collaboration in health and nutrition programmes; technical co-operation in the production of pharmaceuticals; a youth programme; and a women's programme. A ministerial-level conference on drug abuse and illicit trafficking was held in June 1987.

TOURISM

An ASEAN Tourism Forum is held annually to assist in co-ordinating the region's tourism industry. In 1986 ASEAN ministers of foreign affairs approved the establishment of a Tourism Promotion Centre, to be situated in Kuala Lumpur, Malaysia. In 1987 it was decided that 1992 should be designated 'Visit ASEAN year'.

CULTURE

Joint cultural activities being undertaken in the late 1980s included: preparation of an ASEAN literary anthology; archaeological excavations; studies of children's rhymes and chants, and of traditional games and sports; and exchanges of librarians. In 1987 an ASEAN Performing Arts Festival and an ASEAN Song Festival were held in Brunei and Singapore respectively, and a Theatre Festival was held in the Philippines in 1988. ASEAN finances seminars for journalists and news agencies, and operates a News Exchange.

PUBLICATIONS

Annual Report of the ASEAN Standing Committee.

ASEAN Newsletter (every 2 months).

ASEAN Journal on Science and Technology for Development (2 a year).

Information Series and *Documents Series*.

BANK FOR INTERNATIONAL SETTLEMENTS—BIS

Address: Centralbahnplatz 2, 4002 Basel, Switzerland.
Telephone: (061) 2808080.
Telex: 962487.
Fax: (061) 2809100.

The Bank for International Settlements was founded pursuant to the Hague Agreements of 1930 to promote co-operation among national central banks and to provide additional facilities for international financial operations.

Organization

(October 1990)

GENERAL MEETING

The General Meeting is held annually. The right of representation and of voting is exercised, in proportion to the number of shares subscribed in each country, by the central banks (or the financial institutions acting in their stead) of the following countries: Australia, Austria, Belgium, Bulgaria, Canada, Czechoslovakia, Denmark, Finland, France, Germany, Greece, Hungary, Iceland, Ireland, Italy, Japan, the Netherlands, Norway, Poland, Portugal, Romania, South Africa, Spain, Sweden, Switzerland, Turkey, the United Kingdom, the USA and Yugoslavia (i.e. 24 European countries and five others).

BOARD OF DIRECTORS

The Board of Directors is responsible for the conduct of the Bank's operations at the highest level, and comprises the Governors in office of the central banks of Belgium, France, Germany, Italy and the United Kingdom, each of whom appoints another member of the same nationality. The USA does not occupy the two seats to which it is entitled. The statutes also provide for the election to the Board of not more than nine Governors of other member central banks: those of the Netherlands, Sweden and Switzerland are also members of the Board.

Chairman of the Board and President of the Bank: Dr W. F. DUISENBERG (Netherlands).

Vice-Chairman: BERNARD CLAPPIER (France).

CHIEF EXECUTIVE OFFICER

General Manager: Prof. Dr ALEXANDRE LAMFALUSSY (Belgium).

The Bank has a staff of about 390 employees.

Activities

The BIS is a financial institution whose special role is to promote the co-operation of central banks, and to fulfil the function of a 'central banks' bank'. Although it has the legal form of a company limited by shares, it is an international organization governed by international law, and enjoys special privileges and immunities in keeping with its role (a Headquarters Agreement was concluded with Switzerland in 1987). The participating central banks were originally given the option of subscribing to the shares themselves or arranging for their subscription in their own countries: thus the BIS also has some private shareholders, but they have no right of participation in the General Meeting and 85% of the total share capital is in the hands of central banks.

FINANCE

The authorized capital of the Bank is 1,500m. gold francs, divided into 600,000 shares of 2,500 gold francs each.

Statement of Account*
(In gold francs; units of 0.29032258 ... gram of fine gold—Art. 4 of the Statutes; 30 June 1990)

Assets		%
Gold	4,959,048,967	10.6
Cash on hand and on sight a/c with banks	12,785,382	0.0
Treasury bills	928,900,416	2.0
Time deposits and advances	33,589,352,583	72.1
Securities at term	7,095,191,828	15.3
Miscellaneous	6,632,591	0.0
Total	**46,591,911,767**	**100.0**

Liabilities		%
Authorized cap.: 1,500,000,000		
Issued cap.: 1,182,812,500 viz. 473,125 shares of which 25% paid up	295,703,125	0.6
Reserves	1,180,483,397	2.5
Deposits (gold)	4,471,696,254	9.6
Deposits (currencies)	39,390,890,287	84.6
Staff pension scheme	140,988,413	0.3
Miscellaneous	1,079,819,767	2.3
Dividend payable on 1 July 1989	32,330,524	0.1
Total	**46,591,911,767**	**100.0**

* Assets and liabilities in US dollars are converted at US $208 per fine ounce of gold (equivalent to 1 gold franc = US $1.94149 ...) and all other items in currencies on the basis of market rates against the US dollar.

BANKING OPERATIONS

The BIS assists central banks in managing and investing their monetary reserves: in 1990 about 80 central banks from all over the world had deposits with the BIS, which managed more than 10% of world foreign exchange reserves.

The BIS uses the funds deposited with it partly for lending to central banks. Its credit transactions may take the form of swaps against gold; covered credits secured by means of a pledge of gold or marketable short-term securities; credits against gold or currency deposits of the same amount and for the same duration held with the BIS; unsecured credits in the form of advances or deposits; or standby credits, which in individual instances are backed by guarantees given by member central banks. In addition, the Bank undertakes operations in foreign exchange and in gold, both with central banks and with the markets.

In late 1982, faced with the increasingly critical debt situation of some Latin American countries and the resultant threat to the viability of the international financial system, the BIS granted comparatively large-scale loans to central banks that did not number among its shareholders: the central banks of Argentina, Brazil and Mexico were granted bridging loans pending the disbursement of balance-of-payments credits extended by the IMF. These facilities amounted to almost US $3,000m., all of which had been repaid by the end of 1983. The Bank subsequently made similar loans, but with decreasing frequency. During 1986 financial assistance was arranged for the Mexican central bank (a facility of $1,100m., of which the BIS contributed $400m.) and the Nigerian central bank (a facility of $250m., of which the BIS contributed $176m.). In 1987 two bridging facilities were arranged for the Central Bank of Argentina (totalling $1,000m., of which the BIS contributed $525m.). In 1988 bridging facilities were granted to the central banks of Yugoslavia ($250m., of which the BIS contributed $200m.), Brazil ($500m., of which the BIS contributed $250m.), and Argentina ($500m., of which the BIS contributed $190.5m.). In 1989 a bridging facility was arranged for the Central Bank of Mexico ($2,000m., of which the BIS contributed $700m.), and in 1990 bridging facilities were arranged for the central banks of Venezuela ($400m., of which the BIS contributed $296m.), Guyana ($178m., of which the BIS contributed $133.5m.), and Hungary ($280m., of which the BIS contributed $260m.).

Between 1981 and 1984 the BIS provided a facility of SDR 675m. to the IMF to enable the latter to anticipate the availability of cash resulting from the eighth review of IMF quotas. In April 1984 the BIS concluded an agreement with the IMF to provide a credit of SDR 2,505m. in order to cover the 'commitment gap' in connection with the policy of enlarged access to the IMF.

The BIS also engages in traditional types of investment: funds not required for lending to central banks are placed in the market as deposits with commercial banks and purchases of short-term negotiable paper, including Treasury bills. Such operations constitute a major part of the Bank's business.

Because the central banks' monetary reserves must be available at short notice, they can only be placed with the BIS at short term, for fixed periods and with clearly defined repayment terms. The BIS has to match its assets to the maturity structure and nature of its commitments, and must therefore conduct its business with special regard to maintaining a high degree of liquidity.

The Bank's operations must be in conformity with the monetary policy of the central banks of the countries concerned. It is not permitted to make advances to governments or to open current accounts in their name. Real estate transactions are also excluded.

INTERNATIONAL MONETARY CO-OPERATION

Governors of central banks meet for regular discussions at the BIS to co-ordinate international monetary policy and ensure orderly conditions on the international financial markets. There is close co-operation with the IMF and, since its membership includes central banks of eastern European countries, the BIS also provides a forum for contacts between East and West.

The BIS provides the secretariat for the Committee of Governors of the EEC Central Banks and for the Board of Governors of the European Monetary Co-operation Fund.

A Euro-currency Standing Committee was set up at the BIS in 1971 to provide the central bank Governors of the 'Group of Ten' industrialized countries (see p. 76) and Switzerland with information concerning the monetary policy aspects of the Eurocurrency markets. Since 1982 it has provided a regular critical survey of the entire international credit system.

In 1974 the Governors of central banks of the Group of Ten and Switzerland set up the Committee on Banking Regulations and Supervisory Practices (whose secretariat is provided by the BIS) to co-ordinate banking supervision at the international level. The Committee pools information on banking supervisory regulations and surveillance systems, including the supervision of banks' foreign currency business, identifies possible danger areas and proposes measures to safeguard the banks' solvency and liquidity.

The Bank also organizes and provides the secretariat for periodic meetings of experts, such as the Group of Computer Experts, the Group of Experts on Payment Systems and the Group of Experts on Monetary and Economic Data Bank Questions, which aims to develop a data bank service for the central banks of the Group of Ten countries and the BIS.

RESEARCH

The Bank's Monetary and Economic Department conducts research, particularly into monetary questions; collects and publishes data on international banking developments; and organizes a data bank for central banks. The BIS Annual Report provides an independent analysis of monetary and economic developments. Statistics on international banking and on external indebtedness are also published regularly.

AGENCY AND TRUSTEE FUNCTIONS

The BIS acts as an agent for the European Monetary Co-operation Fund, conducting operations in connection with the working of the European Monetary System (EMS) and with borrowing and lending by the European Community. In 1986 the Bank assumed the functions of agent in a private international clearing and settlement system for bank deposits denominated in European Currency Units (ECUs). The Bank also acts as trustee for certain international governmental loans.

PUBLICATIONS

Annual Report.

Quarterly press release on international banking developments; half-yearly reports (jointly with the OECD) on external indebtedness.

CARIBBEAN COMMUNITY AND COMMON MARKET— CARICOM

Address: Bank of Guyana Building, POB 10827, Georgetown, Guyana.
Telephone: (02) 69280.
Telex: 2263.
Fax: (02) 56194.

CARICOM was formed by the Treaty of Chaguaramas in 1973 as a movement towards unity in the Caribbean; it replaced the Caribbean Free Trade Association (CARIFTA), founded in 1965.

MEMBERS

Antigua and Barbuda	Jamaica
Bahamas	Montserrat
Barbados	Saint Christopher and Nevis
Belize	Saint Lucia
Dominica	Saint Vincent and the Grenadines
Grenada	Trinidad and Tobago
Guyana	

OBSERVERS

Anguilla	Netherlands Antilles
Dominican Republic	Puerto Rico
Haiti	Suriname
Mexico	Venezuela

In 1990 applications for full membership by the British Virgin Islands, the Dominican Republic and the Turks and Caicos Islands were being considered.

Organization
(October 1990)

HEADS OF GOVERNMENT CONFERENCE

The Conference is the final authority of the Community and determines policy. It is responsible for the conclusion of treaties on behalf of the Community and for entering into relationships between the Community and international organizations and states. The Conference is also responsible for making the financial arrangements to meet the expenses of the Community, but has delegated this function to the Common Market Council. Decisions of the Conference are generally taken unanimously. Heads of Government met in November 1982 (the first meeting for seven years) and thereafter annually.

COMMON MARKET COUNCIL

The principal organ of the Common Market, the Council consists of a minister of government designated by each member state. It is responsible for the development and smooth running of the Common Market, and for the settlement of any problems arising out of its functioning. However, the Conference may issue directives to the Council. The Council generally takes decisions unanimously.

INSTITUTIONS

There are several institutions of the Caribbean Community responsible for formulating policies and supervising co-operation in services such as education, health, labour matters and foreign policy. Each member state is represented on each institution by a minister of government. These institutions are the Conference of Ministers Responsible for Health and the Standing Committees of Ministers Responsible (respectively) for Education; Labour; Foreign Affairs; Finance; Agriculture; Industry; Transport; Energy, Mines and Natural Resources; Science and Technology; Tourism; Environment.

The observers listed above enjoy observer status in various Community institutions. Further co-operation with these countries is pursued through Joint Technical Groups.

SECRETARIAT

The Secretariat is organized into five divisions: Trade and Agriculture; Economics and Industry; Functional Co-operation; General Services and Administration; Office of the Legal Counsel. The functions of the Secretariat are: to service meetings of the Community and of its Institutions or Committees; to take appropriate follow-up action on decisions made at such meetings; to carry out studies on questions of economic and functional co-operation relating to the region as a whole; to provide services to member states at their request in respect of matters relating to the achievement of the objectives of the Community.

Secretary-General: RODERICK RAINFORD (Jamaica).
Deputy Secretary-General: FRANK O. ABDULAH (Trinidad and Tobago).

Activities

REGIONAL INTEGRATION

In 1989 CARICOM heads of government established the 15-member West Indian Commission to study regional political and economic integration. From July 1990 the Commission (led by Sir Shridath Ramphal, the former Secretary-General of the Commonwealth) was to travel to all the CARICOM member countries for consultation.

CO-ORDINATION OF FOREIGN POLICY

The Community's Standing Committee of ministers responsible for foreign affairs meets at least twice a year. Activities for the co-ordination of foreign policy include: strengthening of member states' position in international organizations; joint diplomatic action on issues of particular interest to the Caribbean; and the evaluation of the Community's relations with third countries and organizations, together with joint co-operation arrangements.

CARICOM's trading relations with the USA and Canada are regulated, respectively, under the Caribbean Basin Initiative of 1983 and the 'Caribcan' agreement of 1986, under which duty-free access was permitted for Caribbean products, with, however, important exceptions.

ECONOMIC CO-OPERATION

The Caribbean Community's main field of activity is economic integration, by means of a Caribbean Common Market which replaced the former Caribbean Free Trade Association (CARIFTA). The Secretariat and the Caribbean Development Bank carry out research on the best means of facing economic difficulties, and meetings of the Chief Executives of commercial banks and of central bank officials are also held with the aim of strengthening regional co-operation.

During the 1980s the economic difficulties of member states hindered the development of intra-regional trade, which accounted for 10.2% of imports in 1985, falling to 7.5% in 1986, when their value was less than half the 1981 level. The value of Community trade fell from US $555m. in 1982 to about $290m. in 1986. Among the reasons for this decline were currency fluctuations within the region, import-licensing measures taken by individual members (notably Trinidad and Tobago), and the collapse in 1983 of the Community's trade payments facility, the Multilateral Clearing Facility (MCF), after it had exceeded its credit limit. Another problem was the difficulty of applying the CARICOM Rules of Origin, which attempt to verify that imported goods genuinely come from within the community; the garment industry is particularly affected by illegal imports. At the annual Conference held in June/July 1987, the heads of government agreed to dismantle all obstacles to trade within CARICOM by October 1988. This was implemented as planned, but a three-year period was permitted during which 17 products from the OECS states would be allowed protection. The value of trade within the Community increased by 8% in 1987, by 14.6% in 1988, and by 20% (to US $436m.) in 1989.

In July 1984 heads of government agreed to establish a common external tariff on certain products, such as steel, cement and fertilizers. They also issued the 'Nassau Understanding' calling for structural adjustment in the economies of the region, including measures to expand production and reduce imports. The revised target date for the implementation of the common external tariff was January 1989. In July 1986 the Conference agreed to establish a trade credit facility to replace the defunct MCF, in the form of a Caribbean Export Bank, based in Barbados, which was to begin operations in early 1988, with initial equity of US $17m.; it was envisaged that the Bank would provide pre-shipment financing for a maximum of two years, and post-shipment financing for up to five years, covering most of the region's exports, except for well-established ones such as sugar, bananas and bauxite. However, the beginning of operations was delayed owing to difficulty in attracting finance from external donors, and in July 1988 it was announced that the establishment of the bank had been postponed for the time being. Instead, it was proposed by the CARICOM Conference that an export credit facility should be established within the Caribbean Development Bank. In November 1989 the CARICOM Export Development Council was established, and undertook a three-year export development project to stimulate trade within CARICOM and to promote exports outside the region.

In 1989 the Conference of Heads of Government agreed to implement, by July 1993 (the 20th anniversary of the signing of the Treaty of Chaguaramas, which brought CARICOM into being), a series of measures to encourage the creation of a single Caribbean market. These included the establishment of a CARICOM Industrial Programming Scheme; the bringing into operation (by January 1990) of the CARICOM Enterprise Regime; abolition of passport requirements for CARICOM nationals travelling within the region (by December 1990); re-establishment (by December 1990) of the MCF; full implementation of the common external tariff by January 1991; free movement of skilled workers by January 1991; removal of all remaining regional barriers to trade by July 1991; establishment of a regional system of air and sea transport by July 1992; and the introduction of a scheme for regional capital movement by 1993.

In August 1989 a meeting of heads of government of CARICOM states and Venezuela agreed to form (with representatives of other Latin American countries, if they wished) a working group on ways to develop regional economic co-operation, including greater self-sufficiency in food, joint exploration for mineral resources, joint trading policies, and co-operation in communications and transport systems. The working group was established in January 1990: Brazil and Colombia also became members.

INDUSTRY AND ENERGY

CARICOM aims to promote the development of joint ventures in exporting industries (particularly the woodwork, furniture, ceramics and foundry industries) through an agreement on an industrial programming scheme, expected to enter into effect in 1990. Work on an investors' guide for each member state was completed in 1984. CARICOM's Export Development Council gives training and consultancy services to regional manufacturers. Regional manufacturers' exhibitions (CARIMEX) are held every three years. A regional exporters' directory was due to be completed in 1988. The Caribbean Trade Information System (CARTIS) comprises computer data-bases covering country and product profiles, trade statistics, trade opportunities, institutions and bibliographical information; it links the national trade centres of CARICOM members.

The Secretariat has established a national standards bureau in each member country to harmonize technical standards, and supervises the metrication of weights and measures.

The CARICOM Alternative Energy Systems Project provides training, assesses energy needs and conducts energy audits.

TRANSPORT

The West Indies Shipping Corporation (WISCO) forms the official carrier in the region, and in 1983 a special CARICOM committee was formed to encourage co-operation between WISCO and the national shipping lines. A Caribbean Confederation of Shippers' Councils represents the interests of regional exporters and importers. In early 1990 CARICOM studied proposals for the restructuring and co-ordination of regional air services.

AGRICULTURE

In 1985 the New Marketing Arrangements for Primary Agricultural Products and Livestock were instituted, with the aim of increasing the flow of agricultural commodities within the region. The Regional Agricultural Sector Programme for 1987-91 gives targets for crop and livestock production, fisheries and forestry, and also covers marketing, research, training and agricultural finance. A computer-based Caribbean Agricultural Marketing Information System was being prepared in 1987. The Caribbean Agricultural Research and Development Institute (CARDI), founded in 1975, devises and transfers appropriate technology for small-scale farmers, and provides training and advisory services. The Caribbean Food Corporation, established in 1976, implements joint-venture projects with investors from the private and public sectors; at the end of August 1987 there were 26 projects under way.

HEALTH AND EDUCATION

In 1986 CARICOM and the Pan-American Health Organization launched 'Caribbean Co-operation in Health' with projects to be undertaken in six main areas: environmental protection, including the control of disease-bearing pests; development of human resources; chronic non-communicable diseases and accidents; strengthening health systems; food and nutrition; maternal and child health care, and population activities.

CARICOM educational programmes have included the improvement of reading in schools through assistance for teacher-training; and ensuring the availability of low-cost educational material throughout the region. A survey of the facilities for technical and vocational training was being undertaken in 1987.

ASSOCIATE INSTITUTIONS

Caribbean Development Bank: POB 408, Wildey, St Michael, Barbados; tel. 431-1600; telex 2287; fax 426-7269; f. 1969 to stimulate regional economic growth through support for agriculture, industry, transport and other infrastructure, tourism, housing and education; cap. US $693.6m. (June 1990). In 1989 loan approvals totalled $73.6m. (for 20 projects) and disbursements $58.8m. In 1990 it was agreed to establish a Special Development Fund of $124m. Mems: CARICOM states, and Anguilla, British Virgin Islands, Canada, Cayman Islands, Colombia, France, Germany, Italy, Mexico, Turks and Caicos Islands, United Kingdom, Venezuela. Pres. NEVILLE NICHOLLS.

Organisation of Eastern Caribbean States—OECS: POB 179, The Morne, Castries, Saint Lucia; tel. 22537; telex 6248; fax 31628; Economic Affairs Secretariat: POB 822, St John's, Antigua; f. 1981 by the seven states which formerly belonged to the West Indies Associated States (f. 1966). Principal institutions are: the Authority of Heads of Government (the supreme policy-making body), the Foreign Affairs Committee, the Defence and Security Committee, and the Economic Affairs Committee. An export development agency (based in Dominica) was established in 1990. Mems: Antigua and Barbuda, Dominica, Grenada, Montserrat, Saint Christopher and Nevis, Saint Lucia, Saint Vincent and the Grenadines; assoc. mem.: British Virgin Islands. Dir-Gen. Dr VAUGHAN A. LEWIS.

Eastern Caribbean Central Bank: POB 89, Basseterre, St Christopher and Nevis; tel. 2537; telex 6828; f. 1983 by OECS governments; maintains regional currency (Eastern Caribbean dollar) and advises on the economic development of member states. Gov. DWIGHT VENNER.

Other Associate Institutions of CARICOM, in accordance with its constitution, are: the Caribbean Examinations Council, the Caribbean Meteorological Institute, the Council of Legal Education, the West Indies Shipping Corporation, the University of Guyana and the University of the West Indies. In 1989 the Conference of Heads of Government agreed to establish an assembly of CARICOM members of parliament, and a Caribbean Court of Appeal.

CENTRAL AMERICAN COMMON MARKET—CACM

(MERCADO COMÚN CENTROAMERICANO)

Address: 4A Avda 10-25, Zona 14, Apdo Postal 1237, 01901 Guatemala City, Guatemala.

Telephone: (2) 682151.

Telex: 5676.

Fax: (2) 681071.

CACM was established by the Organization of Central American States (ODECA, q.v.) under the General Treaty of Central American Economic Integration (Tratado General de Integración Económica Centroamericana) signed in Managua on 15 December 1960. It was ratified by all countries by September 1963.

MEMBERS

Costa Rica	El Salvador	Nicaragua
Guatemala	Honduras	

Organization

(October 1990)

MINISTERIAL MEETINGS

The organization's policy is formulated by regular meetings of Ministers and Vice-Ministers of Central American Integration; meetings of other ministers, and of presidents of central banks, also play an important part.

PERMANENT SECRETARIAT

Secretaría Permanente del Tratado General de Integración Económica Centroamericana—SIECA: supervises the correct implementation of the legal instruments of economic integration, carries out relevant studies at the request of the Common Market authorities, and arranges the meetings of the main bodies. There are departments of: industry; agriculture; taxes and tariffs; physical integration; commercial policy; statistics; economic and social programmes; finance and administration; and science and technology.

Secretary-General: Marco Antonio Villamar Contreras.

Activities

The General Treaty envisaged the eventual liberalization of intra-regional trade and the establishment of a free-trade area and a customs union. Economic integration in the region, however, has been hampered by ideological differences between governments, difficulties in internal supply, protectionist measures by overseas markets, external and intra-regional debts, adverse rates of exchange and high interest rates.

By 1969, 95% of customs items had been awarded free-trade status; the remaining 5% consisted of goods covered by international agreements and other special arrangements. In 1970, however, following a dispute with El Salvador, Honduras reintroduced duties on imports from other CACM countries; trade between El Salvador and Honduras was not resumed until 1982, and Honduras' trade with the other members continued to be governed by bilateral agreements. Regular meetings of senior customs officials aim to increase co-operation, to develop a uniform terminology, and to recommend revisions of customs legislation. CACM member-countries also aim to pursue a common policy in respect of international trade agreements on commodities, raw materials and staples. SIECA participates in meetings with other regional organizations (such as SELA and ECLAC, q.v.) and represents the region at meetings of international organizations, such as UNCTAD.

Little headway has been made in industrial integration, mainly because of the continuing heavy external dependence of the region's economies. Under the Convention for Fiscal Incentives for Industrial Development, which came into operation in 1969, a wide range of tax benefits are applied to various categories of industries in the region, to encourage productivity. SIECA carries out studies on the industrial sector, compiles statistics, and provides information to member governments. It also analyses energy consumption in the region and gives assistance to governments in drawing up energy plans, aiming to reduce dependence on imported petroleum.

A co-ordinating commission supervises the marketing of four basic crops (maize, rice, beans and sorghum), recording and forecasting production figures and recommending minimum guarantee prices. Information on other crops is also compiled. A permanent commission for agricultural research and extension services monitors and co-ordinates regional projects in this field.

SIECA gives technical assistance to governments in improving their transport systems. In 1983 regional Ministers of Transport agreed to establish in each country, in collaboration with existing bodies, a mechanism for encouraging regional co-operation in transport and related matters.

An agreement to establish a Central American Monetary Union was signed in 1964, with the eventual aim of establishing a common currency (the Central American peso, at par with the US dollar) and aligning foreign exchange and monetary policies. The Central American Monetary Council, comprising the presidents of the member states' central banks, meets regularly to consider monetary policy and financial affairs. A Fund for Monetary Stabilization, founded in 1969 by the central banks of member states, provides short-term financial assistance to members facing temporary balance-of-payments difficulties.

In 1971 the Secretariat began work on a new integration model for the region and a draft treaty for a Central American Economic and Social Community was finalized in March 1976. It provided for the establishment of new top-level administrative organizations and a number of regional institutions, for a free-trade area, a customs union, and common industrial policies similar to those contained in the 1960 General Treaty. It also called for the harmonization of fiscal and financial policies, the establishment of a monetary union and the enactment of common programmes for social and economic development. Member states' legislatures, however, failed to ratify the new treaty, and CACM's achievements remained limited.

Trade within the region increased in value from US $33m. in 1960 to $1,129m. in 1980, but subsequently diminished every year until 1986, when it amounted to $421m. The decline was due to a number of factors: low prices for the region's main export commodities, and heavy external debts, both resulting in a severe shortage of foreign exchange; and intra-regional trade 'freezes' provoked by trade debts amounting to $700m. at mid-1986 (Guatemala and Costa Rica being the chief creditors, and Nicaragua and El Salvador the main debtors). In January 1986 a new CACM tariff and customs agreement came into effect, imposing standard import duties for the whole region (aimed at discouraging the import of non-essential goods from outside the region), and a uniform tariff nomenclature. Honduras, however, continued to insist on bilateral tariff agreements with other member countries. In July CACM members agreed on a new payments mechanism for mutual trade, based on the Derecho de Importación Centroamericano (DICA—Central American Import Right), a voucher issued by central banks and used as currency to avoid using scarce US dollars. In 1987 intra-regional trade increased to $500m., and in 1989 it increased to $750m.

An agreement with the European Community was signed in November 1985, providing for economic co-operation and EEC aid for the region. In February 1989 the EEC agreed to provide ECU 800m. (about US $930m.) for Central America, including ECU 150m. in support of CACM's efforts to increase regional trade, ECU 200m. for the Central American Bank for Economic Integration (see below), and ECU 450m. in credits for the member states of CACM. In November it agreed to provide a further ECU 120m. in support of CACM's regional integration plans over the next three years.

PUBLICATIONS

Carta Informativa (monthly).

Anuario Estadístico Centroamericano de Comercio Exterior.

Cuadernos de la SIECA (2 a year).

Series Estadísticas Seleccionadas de Centroamérica y Panamá (annually).

Estadísticas Macroeconómicas de Centroamérica (annually).

INTERNATIONAL ORGANIZATIONS   *Central American Common Market*

Institutions

FINANCE

Banco Centroamericano de Integración Económica—BCIE (Central American Bank for Economic Integration): Apdo Postal 772, Tegucigalpa, Honduras; tel. 372230; telex 1103; fax 370793; f. 1961 to promote the economic integration and balanced economic development of member countries; finances public and private development projects, particularly those related to industrialization and infrastructure. By June 1990 cumulative lending amounted to US $2,021m., mainly for roads, hydroelectricity projects, housing and telecommunications. Authorized capital: $600m. Exec. Pres. ROLANDO RAMÍREZ PANIAGUA. Publs *Annual Report*, *Revista de la Integración*.

Consejo Monetario Centroamericano: Apdo 5438, 1000 San José, Costa Rica; tel. 336044; telex 2234; fax 215643; f. 1964 by the presidents of CACM central banks, to co-ordinate monetary policies. Exec. Sec. OLIVIER CASTRO. Publs *Boletín Estadístico* (annually), *Informe Económico* (annually), *Serie de Estudios Técnicos*.

TRADE AND INDUSTRY

Federación de Cámaras de Comercio del Istmo Centroamericano (Federation of Central American Chambers of Commerce): Avda Balboa y Calle 41, Apdo 74, Panamá 1, Panama; tel. 27-0033; telex 2434; f. 1961; for planning and co-ordinating industrial and commercial exchanges and exhibitions. Pres. RAÚL ADAMES.

Federación de Cámaras y Asociaciones Industriales Centroamericanas—FECAICA (Federation of Industrial Chambers and Associations in Central America): 12 Calle No 1-25, Zona 10, Edificio Géminis 10, Torre Norte, 11° nivel, Of. 1103, Guatemala City, Guatemala; established in 1959 by the Chambers of Commerce and Industry of the CACM countries to promote commerce and industry, principally by interchange of information.

Instituto Centroamericano de Administración de Empresas (Central American Institute for Business Administration): Apdo 2485, Managua, Nicaragua; tel. (2) 58403; telex 2360; fax (2) 58617; Apdo 960, 4050 Alajuela, Costa Rica; tel. 412255; telex 7040; fax 439101; f. 1964; provides postgraduate programme in business administration; executive training programmes; management research and consulting; libraries of 60,000 vols. Dean Dr MELVYN COPEN.

Instituto Centroamericano de Investigación y Tecnología Industrial (Central American Research Institute for Industry): Apdo Postal 1552, Avda La Reforma 4-47, Zona 10, Guatemala City; tel. (2) 310631; telex 5312; fax (2) 317470; f. 1956 by the five Central American Republics, with assistance from the United Nations, to provide technical advisory services to regional governments and private enterprise. Dir W. LUDWIG INGRAM (Nicaragua).

PUBLIC ADMINISTRATION

Instituto Centroamericano de Administración Pública (Central American Institute of Public Administration): POB 10.025-1000, San José, Costa Rica; tel. 223133; telex 2180; fax 232843; f. 1954 by the five Central American Republics and the United Nations, with later participation by Panama. The Institute aims to train the region's public servants, provide technical assistance and carry out research leading to reforms in public administration. Dir Lic. CARMEN MARÍA ROMERO.

EDUCATION AND HEALTH

Confederación Universitaria Centroamericana (Central American University Confederation): Apdo 37, Universidad de Costa Rica, San José, Costa Rica; tel. 252744; telex 3011; fax 340071; f. 1948 to guarantee academic, administrative and economic autonomy for universities and to encourage regional integration of higher education; Council of 14 mems. Mems.: seven universities, in Costa Rica (two), El Salvador, Guatemala, Honduras, Nicaragua and Panama. Sec.-Gen. Dr RODRIGO FERNÁNDEZ (Costa Rica). Publs *Estudios Sociales Centroamericanas* (quarterly), *Cuadernos de Investigación* (monthly), *Carta Informativa de la Secretaría General* (monthly).

Instituto de Nutrición de Centro América y Panamá—INCAP (Institute of Nutrition of Central America and Panama): Apdo 1188, Carretera Roosevelt, Zona 11, 01901 Guatemala City, Guatemala; tel. (2) 723762; telex 5696; fax (2) 715658; f. 1949 to promote the development of nutritional sciences and their application and to strengthen the technical capacity of member countries to solve problems of food and nutrition; provides training and technical assistance for nutrition education and planning; conducts research. Divisions: agricultural and food sciences; nutrition and health; food and nutrition planning. Maintains library (including about 600 periodicals). Administered by the Pan American Health Organization (PAHO) and the World Health Organization. Mems: CACM mems and Panama. Dir Dr HERNÁN L. DELGADO. Publs *Boletín PROPAG* (quarterly), *Boletín ASI* (quarterly), annual report, compilations.

TRANSPORT AND COMMUNICATIONS

Comisión Centroamericana de Ferrocarriles—COCAFER (Central American Railways Commission): c/o SIECA, 4A Avda 10-25, Zona 14, Apdo Postal 1237, 01901 Guatemala City, Guatemala; tel. (2) 682151; telex 5676; fax (2) 681071.

Comisión Centroamericana de Transporte Marítomo—COCATRAM (Central American Maritime Transport Commission): c/o SIECA, 4A Avda 10-25, Zona 14, Apdo Postal 1237, 01901 Guatemala City, Guatemala; tel. (2) 682151; telex 5675; fax (2) 681071.

Comisión Técnica de las Telecomunicaciones de Centroamerica—COMTELCA (Technical Commission for Telecommunications in Central America): Apdo 1793, Tegucigalpa, Honduras; tel. 329527; telex 1235; f. 1966 to co-ordinate and improve the regional telecommunications network. Dir RAFAEL LEMUS.

Corporación Centroamericana de Servicios de Navegación Aérea—COCESNA (Central American Air Navigation Service Corporation): Apdo 660, Tegucigalpa, Honduras; tel. 331141; fax 331219; f. 1960; offers air traffic control services, aeronautical telecommunications services and radio assistance services for air navigation. Gen. Man. FERNANDO A. CASTILLO R.

THE COLOMBO PLAN FOR CO-OPERATIVE ECONOMIC AND SOCIAL DEVELOPMENT IN ASIA AND THE PACIFIC

Address: 12 Melbourne Ave, POB 596, Colombo 4, Sri Lanka.
Telephone: 581813.
Telex: 21537.
Fax: 580721.

Founded by seven Commonwealth countries in 1950 (as the Colombo Plan for Co-operative Economic Development in South and South-East Asia), the Colombo Plan was subsequently joined by more countries in Asia and the Pacific as well as the USA and Japan. The purpose of the Plan is to make a collective international effort to encourage the economic and social development of member countries in the Asia and Pacific region.

MEMBERS

Afghanistan
Australia
Bangladesh
Bhutan
Cambodia
Canada
Fiji
India
Indonesia
Iran
Japan
Korea, Republic
Laos
Malaysia
Maldives
Myanmar
Nepal
New Zealand
Pakistan
Papua New Guinea
Philippines
Singapore
Sri Lanka
Thailand
United Kingdom
USA

Organization
(August 1990)

CONSULTATIVE COMMITTEE

The Committee is the principal policy-making and deliberative body of the Colombo Plan, consisting of ministers representing member governments. It meets every two years in a member country. It reviews the progress of member countries, discusses how available resources can best be used for development, and exchanges views on specific development issues.

COLOMBO PLAN COUNCIL

The Council consists of the heads of member countries' diplomatic missions in Colombo, who meet several times a year to identify development issues of current interest for consideration by the Consultative Committee, and gives guidance for the functioning of the Colombo Plan Bureau and the Drug Advisory Programme.

COLOMBO PLAN BUREAU

The only permanent institution of the Plan, with its headquarters in Colombo, the Bureau services meetings of the Council, carries out research, arranges seminars and workshops and maintains a record of aid flows among member countries.

Director: GILBERT SHEINBAUM (USA).

Activities

The basic principles and policies governing assistance under the Plan are agreed upon by ministers at the meetings of the Consultative Committee. Specific aid programmes are then negotiated bilaterally on a government-to-government basis, within the framework of the policies adopted. There is no centralized programming, nor a common fund to finance national development projects.

ASSISTANCE PROVIDED IN 1988

Donor country	US $ million
Australia	461.3
Canada	420.0
Japan	4,404.1
New Zealand	9.5
United Kingdom	399.0
USA	1,035.4
Total	6,729.3

CAPITAL AID

Capital aid under the Plan takes the form of grants and concessional loans for national projects, mainly from six developed countries to the developing member countries of the Plan. It covers many aspects of social and economic development, including projects in agriculture, industry, communications, energy and education.

TECHNICAL CO-OPERATION

Under the Technical Co-operation programme experts and volunteers are provided, training fellowships are awarded and equipment for training and research is supplied, to assist recipient countries in agriculture, fisheries, industry, planning, education, health, and many other aspects of economic and social development. Examples of projects being undertaken in 1988 included the following (the donor country is indicated in parentheses): provision of consultancy services, training, equipment and research collaboration to promote the health of Indian coal miners (United Kingdom); provision of technical assistance for a tropical rain forest research project in Indonesia (Japan); agricultural research, improvement of fertilizer distribution and climatic/environmental monitoring projects to increase agricultural productivity in Bangladesh (USA); and capital and technical assistance for the development of exotic pine forests and timber exports in Fiji (New Zealand).

During 1988, 35,002 students and trainees received training, and 9,841 experts and volunteers were engaged under technical assistance programmes. The total value of technical co-operation disbursements in 1988 amounted to US $1,020.7m.

The largest number of fellowship awards (9,699) during 1986 was provided by Japan. Among recipients, Indonesia was the chief beneficiary, receiving 3,486 awards; the other main recipients were India, Thailand, Malaysia, the Philippines and the Republic of Korea. Of the total of 10,306 experts financed in 1986, Japan provided 6,091 and the USA 2,589. Indonesia received the largest number of experts (2,094).

A major objective of the Colombo Plan is to foster economic and technical co-operation among developing member countries themselves. During 1988 developing member countries (principally India and the Republic of Korea) financed 69 experts, 600 students and 1,756 trainees. Their technical co-operation expenditure during the year amounted to $9.8m.

DRUG ADVISORY PROGRAMME

The programme was launched in 1973 to help develop co-operative schemes to eliminate the causes and ameliorate the effects of drug abuse in member states. Seminars are held in member countries to inform governments and the public and to help organize remedial measures. Assistance is given in training narcotics officials in all aspects of drug abuse prevention by means of exchanges, fellowships, study, training and observation. Member countries are helped in establishing narcotics control offices or boards, revising legislation on narcotics, improving law enforcement, treatment, rehabilitation and prevention education, and in improving public understanding of these matters by the use of mass media, workshops and seminars.

TRAINING COLLEGE

Colombo Plan Staff College for Technician Education: POB 7500, Domestic Airport Post Office, Domestic Rd, Pasay City 1300, Philippines; tel. 673-1925; telex 43175; fax 673-0891; f. 1974 as a specialized institution of the Colombo Plan, funded by contributions from member governments; trains staff for the education of technicians, conducts conferences and research, and provides advisory services. Dir Dr THAMRONGSAK MOENJAK (Thailand). Publs *Annual Report*, *Newsletter* (quarterly), technical books.

PUBLICATIONS

The Colombo Plan Newsletter (quarterly).
Proceedings and Conclusions of the Consultative Committee (every 2 years).
Annual Report of the Colombo Plan Council.
The Colombo Plan Brochure.
Development Perspectives: Country Issues Papers by Member Governments to the Consultative Committee (every 2 years).

THE COMMONWEALTH

Address: Marlborough House, Pall Mall, London, SW1Y 5HX, England.
Telephone: (071) 839-3411.
Telex: 27678.

The Commonwealth is a voluntary association of 50 independent states, comprising about one-quarter of the world's population. It includes the United Kingdom and most of its former dependencies, and former dependencies of Australia and New Zealand (themselves Commonwealth countries).

The evolution of the Commonwealth began with the introduction of self-government in Canada in the 1840s; Australia, New Zealand and South Africa became independent before the first world war. At the Imperial Conference of 1926 the United Kingdom and the four Dominions, as they were then called, were described as 'autonomous communities within the British Empire, equal in status', and this change was enacted into law by the Statute of Westminster, in 1931.

The modern Commonwealth began with the entry of India and Pakistan in 1947, and of Sri Lanka (then Ceylon) in 1948. In 1950 India became a republic, and the Commonwealth Heads of Government then decided that allegiance to the same monarch need not be a condition of membership. This was a precedent for a number of other members (see Heads of State and Heads of Government, below).

MEMBERS*

Antigua and Barbuda	Namibia
Australia	Nauru†
Bahamas	New Zealand
Bangladesh	Nigeria
Barbados	Pakistan
Belize	Papua New Guinea
Botswana	Saint Christopher and Nevis
Brunei	Saint Lucia
Canada	Saint Vincent and the Grenadines
Cyprus	Seychelles
Dominica	Sierra Leone
The Gambia	Singapore
Ghana	Solomon Islands
Grenada	Sri Lanka
Guyana	Swaziland
India	Tanzania
Jamaica	Tonga
Kenya	Trinidad and Tobago
Kiribati	Tuvalu†
Lesotho	Uganda
Malawi	United Kingdom
Malaysia	Vanuatu
Maldives	Western Samoa
Malta	Zambia
Mauritius	Zimbabwe

* Ireland, South Africa and Pakistan withdrew from the Commonwealth in 1949, 1961 and 1972 respectively. In October 1987 Fiji's membership was declared to have lapsed (following the proclamation of a republic there). Pakistan rejoined the Commonwealth in October 1989.

† Nauru and Tuvalu are special members of the Commonwealth; they have the right to participate in functional activities but are not represented at Meetings of Heads of Government.

Dependencies and Associated States

Australia:
  Australian Antarctic Territory
  Christmas Island
  Cocos (Keeling) Islands
  Coral Sea Islands Territory
  Heard and McDonald Islands
  Norfolk Island
New Zealand:
  Cook Islands
  Niue
  Ross Dependency
  Tokelau
United Kingdom:
  Anguilla
  Bermuda
  British Antarctic Territory
  British Indian Ocean Territory
  British Virgin Islands
  Cayman Islands
  Channel Islands
  Falkland Islands
  Gibraltar
  Hong Kong
  Isle of Man
  Montserrat
  Pitcairn Islands
  St Helena
    Ascension
    Tristan da Cunha
  South Georgia and South Sandwich Islands
  Turks and Caicos Islands

HEADS OF STATE AND HEADS OF GOVERNMENT

In November 1990, 22 member countries were monarchies and 28 were republics. All Commonwealth countries accept Queen Elizabeth II as the symbol of the free association of the independent member nations and as such the Head of the Commonwealth. Of the 28 republics, the offices of Head of State and Head of Government were combined in 20: Bangladesh, Botswana, Cyprus, The Gambia, Ghana, Guyana, Kenya, Kiribati, Malawi, Maldives, Namibia, Nauru, Nigeria, Seychelles, Sierra Leone, Sri Lanka, Tanzania, Uganda, Zambia and Zimbabwe. The two offices were separated in the remaining eight: Dominica, India, Malta, Pakistan, Singapore, Trinidad and Tobago, Vanuatu and Western Samoa.

Of the monarchies, the Queen is Head of State of the United Kingdom and of 16 others, in each of which she is represented by a Governor-General: Antigua and Barbuda, Australia, the Bahamas, Barbados, Belize, Canada, Grenada, Jamaica, Mauritius, New Zealand, Papua New Guinea, Saint Christopher and Nevis, Saint Lucia, Saint Vincent and the Grenadines, Solomon Islands and Tuvalu. Brunei, Lesotho, Malaysia, Swaziland and Tonga are also monarchies, where the traditional monarch is Head of State.

The Governors-General are appointed by the Queen on the advice of the Prime Ministers of the country concerned. They are wholly independent of the Government of the United Kingdom.

HIGH COMMISSIONERS

Governments of member countries are represented in other Commonwealth countries by High Commissioners, who have a status equivalent to that of Ambassadors.

Organization
(October 1990)

The Commonwealth is not a federation: there is no central government nor are there any rigid contractual obligations such as bind members of the United Nations.

The Commonwealth has no written constitution but its members subscribe to the ideals of the Declaration of Commonwealth Principles (see below) unanimously approved by a meeting of Heads of Government in Singapore in 1971. Members also approved the 1977 statement on apartheid in sport (the Gleneagles Agreement); the 1979 Lusaka Declaration on Racism and Racial Prejudice; the 1981 Melbourne Declaration on relations between developed and developing countries; the 1983 New Delhi Statement on Economic Action; the 1983 Goa Declaration on International Security; the 1985 Nassau Declaration on World Order; the 1987 Vancouver Declaration on World Trade; the Okanagan Statement and Programme of Action on Southern Africa (1987); and the Langkawi Declaration on the Environment (1989).

MEETINGS OF HEADS OF GOVERNMENT

Meetings are private and informal and operate not by voting but by consensus. The emphasis is on consultation and exchange of views for co-operation. A communiqué is issued at the end of every meeting. Meetings are held every two years in different capitals in the Commonwealth. The 1989 meeting was held in Kuala Lumpur, Malaysia, and the 1991 meeting was to be held in Harare, Zimbabwe.

OTHER CONSULTATIONS

Meetings at ministerial and official level are also held regularly. Since 1959 Finance Ministers have met in a Commonwealth country in the week prior to the annual meetings of the IMF and the World Bank. Education Ministers usually meet about every three years. Ministers of Health and of Employment and Labour hold annual meetings, and the Commonwealth Youth Affairs Council, at ministerial level, meets every two years.

Senior officials—Cabinet Secretaries, Permanent Secretaries to Heads of Government and others—meet regularly in the year between meetings of Heads of Government to provide continuity and to exchange views on various developments.

COMMONWEALTH SECRETARIAT

The Secretariat, established by Commonwealth Heads of Government in 1965, operates as an international organization at the

INTERNATIONAL ORGANIZATIONS
The Commonwealth

service of all Commonwealth countries. It organizes consultations between governments and runs programmes of co-operation. Meetings of heads of government, ministers and senior officials decide these programmes and provide overall direction.

The Secretariat is headed by a Secretary-General (elected by Heads of Government), with two Deputy Secretaries-General and two Assistant Secretaries-General. One Deputy is responsible for political affairs (divisions of international affairs, legal affairs, information, and administration and conference services), the other for economic affairs (divisions of economic affairs, export market development, and food production and rural development). One Assistant Secretary-General is responsible for the Human Resource Development Group (education, training, management, medical, women's and youth programmes) and the science division, the other for the Commonwealth Fund for Technical Co-operation (CFTC).

Secretary-General: Chief E. CHUKWUEMEKA (EMEKA) ANYAOKU (Nigeria).
Deputy Secretary-General (Political): ANTHONY SIAGURU.
Deputy Secretary-General (Economic): PETER UNWIN (UK).
Assistant Secretaries-General: WILLIAM MONTGOMERY (Canada), MANMOHAN MALHOUTRA (India).
Director, Administration Division: Tunku ABDUL AZIZ (Malaysia).
Director, Information Division: PATSY ROBERTSON (Jamaica).

BUDGET

The Secretariat's budget for 1988/89 was £6,792,610, and the budget for 1989/90 was £7,357,690. Member governments meet the cost of the Secretariat through subscriptions on a scale related to income and population, similar to the scale for contributions to the United Nations.

Activities

INTERNATIONAL AFFAIRS

The most publicized achievement of the 1979 Lusaka meeting of Heads of Government was the nine-point plan to direct Zimbabwe-Rhodesia towards internationally recognized independence, formulated by a group of leaders—from Australia, Jamaica, Nigeria, Tanzania, the United Kingdom and Zambia, together with the Commonwealth Secretary-General—and endorsed at a special session of all heads of delegation. The leaders issued the Lusaka Declaration on Racism and Racial Prejudice as a formal expression of their abhorrence of all forms of racist policy.

At their 1981 meeting in Melbourne, the Heads of Government issued the Melbourne Declaration in which they asserted that the current 'gross inequality of wealth and opportunity' was a 'fundamental source of tension and instability in the world', and declared their common resolve 'to advance the dialogue between developing and developed countries; to infuse an increased sense of urgency and direction into the resolution of these common problems of mankind'. The meeting confirmed the Commonwealth's commitment to independence for Namibia, and condemned South Africa's attempts to destabilize neighbouring states.

In November 1983 the Heads of Government, meeting in New Delhi, issued the Goa Declaration on International Security, demanding 'a concerted effort ... to restore constructive dialogue to the conduct of East-West relations', and the cessation of the nuclear arms race, and asking for funds released by disarmament to be used in world development. The leaders expressed concern at the vulnerability of small states to external attack and interference in their affairs. The Secretary-General subsequently established a Commonwealth Consultative Group to undertake a study of the special needs of such states.

In October 1985 Heads of Government, meeting at Nassau, Bahamas, issued the Nassau Declaration on World Order, reaffirming Commonwealth commitment to the United Nations, to international co-operation for development and to the eventual elimination of nuclear weapons. The same meeting issued the Commonwealth Accord on Southern Africa, calling on the South African authorities to dismantle apartheid and open dialogue with a view to establishing a representative government. The meeting also established a Commonwealth 'Eminent Persons Group'. It visited South Africa in February and March 1986 and attempted unsuccessfully to establish a dialogue between the South African Government and opposition leaders. In August the Heads of Government of seven Commonwealth countries (Australia, the Bahamas, Canada, India, the United Kingdom, Zambia and Zimbabwe) met to consider the Group's report, and (with the exception of the United Kingdom) agreed to adopt a series of measures to exert economic pressure on the South African Government, and to encourage other countries to adopt such measures. These included bans on the following: air links with South Africa; government assistance to investment in, and trade with, South Africa; government contracts with majority-owned South African companies; promotion of tourist visits to South Africa; new bank loans to South Africa; imports of uranium, coal, iron and steel from South Africa.

In October 1987 Heads of Government, meeting at Vancouver, Canada, issued the Okanagan Statement and Programme of Action on Southern Africa, to strengthen the Commonwealth effort to end apartheid and bring about political freedom in South Africa. They also established the Commonwealth Committee of Foreign Ministers on Southern Africa, comprising the ministers of foreign affairs of Australia, Canada, Guyana, India, Nigeria, Tanzania, Zambia and Zimbabwe (and, subsequently, of Malaysia). The Committee was to provide impetus and guidance in furtherance of the objectives of the Statement. The Vancouver meeting also issued the Vancouver Declaration on World Trade, condemning protectionism and reaffirming the leaders' commitment to work for a durable and just world trading system. They pledged to work to strengthen the General Agreement on Tariffs and Trade (GATT), and gave their support to the Uruguay Round of multilateral trade negotiations (begun in 1986).

In October 1989 Heads of Government, meeting in Kuala Lumpur, Malaysia, issued the Langkawi Declaration on the Environment, a 16-point joint programme of action to combat environmental degradation and ensure sustainable development. They reaffirmed their commitment to the eradication of apartheid in South Africa and to the use of economic sanctions as a means to this end.

International Affairs Division: assists consultation among member governments on international and Commonwealth matters of common interest. In association with host governments, it organizes the meetings of Heads of Government and senior officials. Since 1978 the Division has organized and serviced Commonwealth regional Heads of Government meetings for the Asia-Pacific region (CHOGRM): these meetings discuss regional political trends and establish programmes of co-operation in trade, energy, industry, agriculture and maritime issues. The Division services committees and special groups set up by Heads of Government dealing with political matters. The Secretariat has observer status at the United Nations, and manages an office in New York to enable small states, which would otherwise be unable to afford facilities there, to maintain a presence at the United Nations. The Division monitors political developments in the Commonwealth and international progress in such matters as disarmament, the concerns of small states, dismantling of apartheid and the Law of the Sea. It also undertakes research on matters of common interest to member governments, and reports back to them. The Division is involved in diplomatic training and consular co-operation. A Unit for the Promotion of Human Rights in the Commonwealth was established within the Division in 1985.

Director: MAX GAYLARD (Australia).

LAW

Legal Division: services the meetings of law ministers and attorneys-general. It runs a Commonwealth commercial crime service, administers a training programme for legislative draftsmen, and assists co-operation and exchange of information on law reform, taxation policy, extradition, the reciprocal enforcement of judgments, the Commonwealth Scheme for Mutual Assistance in Criminal Matters, the scheme for the Transfer of Convicted Offenders within the Commonwealth, and other legal matters. It liaises with the Commonwealth Magistrates' Association, the Commonwealth Legal Education Association, the Commonwealth Lawyers' Association, the Commonwealth Association of Legislative Counsel, and with other international organizations. It also provides in-house legal advice for the Secretariat, and helps to prepare the triennial Commonwealth Law Conference for the practising profession. An annual 'colloquium' of chief justices is also held. The quarterly *Commonwealth Law Bulletin* reports on legal developments in and beyond the Commonwealth.

Director: JEREMY D. POPE (New Zealand).

ECONOMIC CO-OPERATION

Economic Affairs Division: organizes and services the regular meetings of Commonwealth ministers of finance, and of labour and employment, and assists in servicing the biennial meetings of Heads of Government. It engages in research and analysis on economic issues of interest to member governments; organizes seminars and conferences of government officials and experts; and publishes regular bulletins on commodities, international development policies, capital markets, regional co-operation and on basic statistics of small countries. The Division initiated a major programme of technical assistance to enable developing Commonwealth countries to participate in the Uruguay Round of

INTERNATIONAL ORGANIZATIONS
The Commonwealth

multilateral trade negotiations (begun in 1986). The Division also services expert groups commissioned by governments. Such groups have reported on, among other things, protectionism; obstacles to the North-South negotiating process; reform of the international financial and trading system; the debt crisis; management of technological change; the special needs of small states; and youth unemployment. The Division undertook preparatory work for the establishment of a Commonwealth Equity Fund, initiated in September 1990, to allow developing member countries to improve their access to private institutional investment.

Director: Dr BISHNODAT PERSAUD (Barbados).

Export Market Development Division: assists governments to improve foreign exchange earnings through identification and exploration of export markets, using trade promotion events such as export business intensification programmes, buyer-seller meetings, integrated marketing programmes and contact promotion programmes. It gives advice on production development and adaptation, packaging, standardization, quality control and pricing; provides assistance for small states, regional organizations and countries with recently-established industries; and organizes conferences and seminars. The Division is financed by the CFTC.

Director: ARVIND G. BARVE (Kenya).

Food Production and Rural Development Division: offers expert technical advice and training in food production and rural development. It derives its mandate from meetings of ministers of agriculture. Priority is given to institutional development; food and agriculture policy; project planning and management; conservation and land-use planning; and livestock. The division is financed by the CFTC.

Director: JOSHUA K. MUTHAMA (Kenya).

HUMAN RESOURCES

Human Resource Development Group (HRDG): set up in 1983, brings together six previously separate programmes (see below) whose primary purpose is the development of human resources in Commonwealth countries. The group encourages inter-programme collaboration and multi-disciplinary activity, with emphasis on operational projects in the field. The group aims to assist member countries in a number of important areas of human resource development and the improvement of professional skills.

Assistant Secretary-General, HRDG: MANMOHAN MALHOUTRA (India).

The **Education Programme** arranges specialist seminars and co-operative projects and commissions studies in areas identified by education ministers, whose three-yearly meetings it also services. Its present areas of emphasis include Commonwealth student mobility and co-operation in higher education, distance teaching and new technologies in education, education and work, education in small states and education in science and technology.

The **Fellowships and Training Programme** (financed by the CFTC) provides awards, finds training places and arranges training attachments and study visits. Applicants must be nominated by their governments. In 1988/89 the Programme supported about 3,600 trainees. The majority of trainees are at middle management and technician level and most training is provided in developing countries. The Programme has established distance education units for Namibians and South Africans (in Lusaka, Zambia and Dar es Salaam, Tanzania, respectively), and a Nassau Fellowship Scheme, for South Africans who are victims of apartheid, was begun in 1986. Awards for practical training attachments are provided under the Commonwealth Industrial Training and Experience Programme.

The **Management Development Programme** (financed by the CFTC) assists governments (particularly those of small states) in improving public management systems and practice, through seminars, training programmes, consultations, project studies and publications; it provides opportunities for policy-makers to share their experience, and acts as a clearing-house for information.

The **Health Programme**, guided by the meetings of Commonwealth health ministers, assists governments to strengthen their health services. It supports the work of regional health organizations, undertakes studies and provides advisory services at the request of governments.

The **Women and Development Programme** seeks to enhance women's participation in and benefits from development through training, policy analysis, research, and consultancies on issues such as employment and income, women and the environment, and violence against women.

The **Commonwealth Youth Programme**, funded through separate contributions from governments, seeks to promote the involvement of young people in the economic and social development of their countries. It provides policy advice for governments and operates regional training programmes for youth workers and policy-makers through its centres in Africa, Asia, the Caribbean and the Pacific. It conducts a Youth Study Fellowship scheme, a Youth Project Fund, a Youth Exchange Programme (in the Caribbean), and a Youth Service Awards Scheme, holds conferences and seminars, carries out research and disseminates information.

SCIENCE

Science Division: provides the secretariat of the Commonwealth Science Council of 34 governments; organizes regional and global programmes to enhance the scientific and technological capabilities of member countries, through co-operative research, training and the exchange of information. Work is carried out in the areas of energy, water and mineral resources, biological resources, environmental planning, agriculture, industrial support, and science management and organization.

Science Adviser: Dr G. THYAGARAJAN (India).

TECHNICAL CO-OPERATION

Commonwealth Fund for Technical Co-operation: financed by voluntary subscriptions from all member governments, provides technical assistance to developing Commonwealth countries. It provides consultancy and advisory services, assigns experts to work in member countries, and finances specialized training. The CFTC also funds the Fellowships and Training Programme (see under Human Resources). CFTC expenditure during the year ending 30 June 1990 was expected to be £25.5m. The number of experts on long-term assignments was 180 in February 1990, with about 50 more experts on assignments of less than six months' duration.

The **General Technical Assistance Division** of the CFTC supplies experts and consultants and commissions specialist studies. Each year it provides governments with more than 200 experts in (for example) economics, telecommunications, computers, transport and agriculture.

The CFTC's **Technical Assistance Group** is an in-house consultancy providing governments with assistance (including financial, legal and policy advice) in negotiations on natural resources and other investment projects, maritime boundary delimitation and fisheries, macroeconomic policies and debt management.

The **Industrial Development Unit** of the CFTC assists governments in the development and implementation of industrial projects; assistance includes investment planning and project design, entrepreneurial development, transfer of technology, and upgrading enterprises.

CFTC Managing Director: WILLIAM MONTGOMERY (Canada).

SELECTED PUBLICATIONS

The Commonwealth Today (revised every 2 years).
The Commonwealth Factbook.
Report of the Commonwealth Secretary-General (every 2 years).
Commonwealth Currents (every 2 months).
Commonwealth Organisations (directory).
Notes on the Commonwealth (series of reference leaflets).
In Common (quarterly newsletter of the Youth Programme).
Link In (quarterly newsletter of the Women and Development Programme).
International Development Policies (quarterly).
Meat and Dairy Products (2 a year).
Fruit and Tropical Products (2 a year).
Hides and Skins (2 a year).
Tobacco Quarterly.
Wool Quarterly.
Wool Statistics (annually).
Science and Technology News.
Numerous reports, studies and papers (catalogue available).

Commonwealth Organizations
(In England, unless otherwise stated)

AGRICULTURE AND FORESTRY

CAB International (CABI): Wallingford, Oxon, OX10 8DE, England; tel. (0491) 32111; telex 847964; fax (0491) 33508; f. 1929; formerly Commonwealth Agricultural Bureaux; consists of four Institutes, 11 Bureaux and a development services unit, under the control of an Executive Council comprising representatives from

INTERNATIONAL ORGANIZATIONS

member countries which contribute to its funds. Its functions are to provide:

(i) a world information service for agricultural scientists and other professional workers in the same and allied fields;

(ii) a biological control service; and

(iii) a pest and disease identification service.

Each Institute and Bureau is concerned with its own particular branch of agricultural science and acts as an effective clearing house for the collection, collation and dissemination of information of value to research workers. The information, compiled from worldwide literature, is published in 26 main journals, 21 specialist journals and several serial publications. Annotated bibliographies provide information on specific topics, and review articles, books, maps and monographs are also issued. The CAB ABSTRACTS database is accessible online through the following retrieval services: DIALOG (USA), BRS (USA), CAN/OLE (Canada), ESA-IRS (Italy), DIMDI (Federal Republic of Germany), DATASTAR and JICST (Japan); many organizations provide SDI services from CABI tapes.

In addition, Institutes of Entomology, Mycology and Parasitology provide identification and taxonomic services and the Institute of Biological Control undertakes field work in biological control throughout the world. There are regional offices in Malaysia and Trinidad and Tobago. Dir-Gen. D. MENTZ.

The following Bureaux are based at the CABI address shown above.

CABI Bureau of Agricultural Economics: f. 1966; provides an information service on agricultural economics and business, rural sociology, rural development in low-income countries, rural extension, education and training, tourism, leisure and recreation. Man. Editor MARGOT BELLAMY. Publs *World Agricultural Economics and Rural Sociology Abstracts* (monthly), *Rural Development Abstracts* (quarterly), *Leisure, Recreation and Tourism Abstracts* (quarterly).

CABI Bureau of Animal Breeding and Genetics: f. 1929 for the collection and abstracting of the world's literature on the breeding and the genetics of animals, and for the dissemination of this information throughout the world. Man. Editor J. D. TURTON. Publs *Animal Breeding Abstracts* (monthly), *Poultry Abstracts* (monthly), *AgBiotech News and Information* (every 2 months).

CABI Bureau of Animal Health: f. 1929 to provide information on veterinary science. Man. Editor G. PHILLIPS. Publs *Index Veterinarius* (monthly), *Veterinary Bulletin* (monthly), *Review of Medical and Veterinary Entomology* (monthly), *Small Animal Abstracts* (annually), *Animal Disease Occurrence* (annually), *Helminthological Abstracts, Review of Medical and Veterinary Mycology* (quarterly), *Protozoological Abstracts*.

CABI Bureau of Crop Protection: f. 1987 for the collection and abstracting of world scientific literature on crop protection, including the biology and control of weeds, insects and other pests, plant nematodes, pathogenic fungi, bacteria and viruses. Man. Editor P. R. SCOTT. Publs *Review of Plant Pathology, Review of Agricultural Entomology, Weed Abstracts, Nematological Abstracts*, bibliographies.

CABI Bureau of Dairy Science and Technology: f. 1938 for the collection, collation, and distribution of scientific and technological information on dairy husbandry, milk and milk products, and the economics, physiology, microbiology, chemistry and physics of dairying for the benefit of research workers, teachers, advisory officers, etc. Man. Editor P. D. WILSON. Publs *Dairy Science Abstracts* (monthly).

CABI Bureau of Horticulture and Plantation Crops: f. 1929. Man. Editor Dr K. K. S. BHAT. Publs *Horticultural Abstracts, Ornamental Horticulture, Cotton and Tropical Fibres Abstracts, Sorghum and Millets Abstracts, Tropical Oil Seeds Abstracts* (all monthly).

CABI Bureau of Nutrition: f. 1929 to collect and abstract the world's literature in the field of human and animal nutrition, and to disseminate this information world-wide. Man. Editor E. DODSWORTH. Publs *Nutrition Abstracts and Reviews: Series A—Human and Experimental* (monthly), *Series B—Livestock Feeds and Feeding* (monthly).

CABI Bureau of Pastures and Field Crops: f. 1929; publishes abstracts compiled from the world's scientific literature on grasses and grasslands, herbage plants, rangelands and annual field crops, and produces annotated bibliographies on selected subjects within its scope. Man. Editor P. WIGHTMAN. Publs *Herbage Abstracts, Field Crop Abstracts, Crop Physiology Abstracts, Potato Abstracts, Rice Abstracts, Seed Abstracts, Soyabean Abstracts* (all monthly), *Faba Bean Abstracts* (quarterly), *Lentil Abstracts* (annually), and occasional publications.

CABI Bureau of Plant Breeding and Genetics: f. 1929 to abstract and review current world literature on the breeding and genetics of plants of economic importance and to maintain an information service on all these subjects. Man. Editor RAY WATKINS. Publs *Plant Breeding Abstracts* (monthly), *Maize Abstracts* (every 2 months), *Wheat, Barley and Triticale Abstracts* (every 2 months), *AgBiotech* (every 2 months).

CABI Bureau of Soils: f. 1929 for the collection and dissemination of information from the world scientific literature on all aspects of soils, the use of fertilizers, and the relationship between plants and soils, particularly plant nutrition. Man. Editor J. NOWLAND. Publs *Soils and Fertilizers* (monthly), *Irrigation and Drainage Abstracts* (quarterly), series of technical communications (occasional).

CABI Forestry Bureau: f. 1938 for the collection and abstracting of the world's literature on forestry, forest products and their utilization, and for the dissemination of this information throughout the world. Man. Editor K. BECKER. Publs *Forestry Abstracts* (monthly), *Forest Products Abstracts* (every 2 months), *Agroforestry Abstracts*.

International Institute of Biological Control: Silwood Park, Buckhurst Rd, Ascot, Berks, SL5 7TA; tel. (0990) 872999; telex 93121-02255; fax (0990) 872901; f. 1927 as the Farnham House Laboratory of the Imperial Institute of Entomology; transferred to Canada 1940 and to Trinidad 1962; since 1983 its main research and administrative centre has been in the United Kingdom; its purpose is the biological control of injurious insects and noxious weeds, and the collection and distribution throughout the world of beneficial organisms with which to attack the pests. Dir Dr D. J. GREATHEAD. Publs *Natural Enemy Databank, Biocontrol News and Information* (quarterly).

International Institute of Entomology: 56 Queen's Gate, London, SW7 5JR; tel. (071) 584-0067; telex 93121-02251; fax (071) 581-1676; f. 1913 for the collection, co-ordination and dissemination of all information concerning injurious and useful insects and other arthropods; undertakes identifications; organizes international training courses and workshops on applied taxonomy of insects and mites. Dir Dr K. M. HARRIS. Publs *Bulletin of Entomological Research* (quarterly), *Distribution Maps of Pests* (18 a year), bibliographies and monographs.

International Institute of Parasitology: 395A Hatfield Rd, St Albans, Herts, AL4 0XU; tel. (0727) 833151; telex 93121-02254; fax (0727) 868721; f. 1929; undertakes identifications and conducts taxonomic and applied research on animal and human helminths and on plant parasitic nematodes; provides advisory and consultancy services and training. Dir R. MULLER.

International Mycological Institute: Ferry Lane, Kew, Surrey, TW9 3AF; tel. (081) 940-4086; telex 265871; fax (081) 332-1171; f. 1920 for the collection and dissemination of information on the fungal, bacterial, virus and physiological disorders of plants; on fungal diseases of man and animals; and on the taxonomy of fungi; undertakes identifications of micro-fungi and plant pathogenic bacteria from all over the world; incorporates major collection of fungus cultures and a biodeterioration and industrial services centre; consultancy services, especially in industrial mycology and surveys of plant diseases; holds training courses. Dir Prof. D. L. HAWKSWORTH. Publs *Biodeterioration Abstracts* (quarterly), *Distribution Maps of Plant Diseases* (42 a year), *Index of Fungi* (2 a year), *Mycological Papers* (irregular), *Phytopathological Papers* (irregular), *Descriptions of Pathogenic Fungi and Bacteria* (4 sets a year), *Bibliography of Systematic Mycology* (2 a year), *Systema Ascomycetum* (2 a year), books on mycology and plant pathology.

Commonwealth Forestry Association: c/o Oxford Forestry Institute, South Parks Rd, Oxford, OX1 3RB; tel. (0865) 275072; fax (0865) 275074; f. 1921; produces, collects and circulates information relating to forestry and the commercial utilization of forest products and provides a means of communications in the Commonwealth and other interested countries. Mems: 1,600. Chair. R. L. NEWMAN. Publs *Commonwealth Forestry Review* (quarterly), *Commonwealth Forestry Handbook*.

Standing Committee on Commonwealth Forestry: Forestry Commission, 231 Corstorphine Rd, Edinburgh, EH12 7AT, Scotland; tel. (031) 334-0303; telex 727879; fax (031) 334-3047; f. 1923 to provide continuity between Conferences, and to provide a forum for discussion on any forestry matters of common interest to member governments which may be brought to the Committee's notice by any member country or organization; mems about 50. Sec. P. BAYLIS. Publs *Newsletter*.

COMMONWEALTH STUDIES

Institute of Commonwealth Studies: 28 Russell Sq., London, WC1B 5DS; tel. (071) 580-5876; fax (071) 255-2160; f. 1949 to promote advanced study of the Commonwealth; provides a library and meeting place for postgraduate students and academic staff engaged in research in this field. Incorporates the Sir Robert

Menzies Centre for Australian Studies. Dir SHULA MARKS; Publs *Annual Report, Commonwealth Papers* (series), *Collected Seminar Papers, Newsletter*.

COMMUNICATIONS

Commonwealth Air Transport Council: 2 Marsham St, Room S5/05A, London, SW1P 3EB; tel. (071) 276-5436; telex 22221; fax (071) 276-5390; f. 1945 to keep under review the development of Commonwealth civil air transport. Meetings every three years. Mems: governments of Commonwealth Countries and British Dependent Territories. Sec. Miss P. BRAUNTON. Publs *Commonwealth Air Transport Review* (3 a year), *Commonwealth Air Transport Electronics News* (2 a year), *Selected R & D Abstracts* (2 a year), *Civil Aviation Training Facilities in Commonwealth Countries* (every 3 years).

Commonwealth Telecommunications Organization: 26–27 Oxendon St, London, SW1Y 4EL; tel. (071) 930-5511; fax (071) 930-4248; f. 1967 to enhance the development of international telecommunications in Commonwealth countries through financial and technical collaborative arrangements. Gen. Sec. GRAHAM H. CUNNOLD.

EDUCATION

Association of Commonwealth Universities: John Foster House, 36 Gordon Sq., London, WC1H 0PF; tel. (071) 387-8572; fax (071) 387-2655; f. 1913; holds quinquennial Congresses and other meetings in intervening years; publishes factual information about Commonwealth universities and access to them; acts as a general information centre and provides an advisory appointments service; supplies secretariats for the Commonwealth Scholarship Commission in the United Kingdom and the Marshall Aid Commemoration Commission; administers various fellowships and scholarships. Mems: 351 universities in 30 countries or regions. Sec. Gen. Dr A. CHRISTODOULOU. Publs include *Commonwealth Universities Yearbook, ACU Bulletin of Current Documentation, British Universities' Guide to Graduate Study, University Entrance: the Official Guide, Awards for Commonwealth University Academic Staff, Awards for Postgraduate Study at Commonwealth Universities, Financial Aid for First Degree Study at Commonwealth Universities, Grants for Study Visits by University Administrators and Librarians, Higher Education in the United Kingdom, Graduate Study Abroad* (series), *Taking a First Degree Abroad* (series), *Who's Who of Commonwealth University Vice-Chancellors, Presidents and Rectors*.

Commonwealth Association of Science, Technology and Mathematics Educators—CASTME: c/o Education Programme, HRDG, Commonwealth Secretariat, Marlborough House, Pall Mall, London, SW1Y 5HX; tel. (071) 839-3411; telex 27678; f. 1974; special emphasis is given to the social significance of education in these subjects. Organizes an Awards Scheme to promote effective teaching and learning in these subjects, and biennial regional seminars. Pres. Dr MAURICE GOLDSMITH; Hon. Sec. E. APEA. Publ. *CASTME Journal* (quarterly).

Commonwealth Council for Educational Administration: c/o Faculty of Education, Nursing and Professional Studies, University of New England, Armidale, NSW 2351, Australia; tel. (067) 732543; telex 66050; fax (067) 733363; f. 1970; aims to foster quality in professional development and links among educational administrators; holds national and regional conferences, as well as visits and seminars. Mems: 30 affiliated groups representing 6,000 persons. Pres. Dr BILL MUDFORD; Exec. Dir JOHN WEEKS. Publs *Newsletter* (2 a year), *Studies in Educational Administration* (2 a year), *Directory of Courses*.

League for the Exchange of Commonwealth Teachers: 7 Lion Yard, Tremadoc Rd, London, SW4 7NQ; tel. (071) 498-1101; telex 919186; fax (071) 720-5403; f. 1901; promotes educational exchanges for a period of one year between teachers in Australia, the Bahamas, Barbados, Bermuda, Canada, Guyana, India, Jamaica, Kenya, New Zealand, Pakistan and Trinidad and Tobago. Dir PATRICIA SWAIN. Publ. *Annual Report*.

HEALTH

Commonwealth Medical Association: c/o BMA House, Tavistock Sq., London, WC1H 9JP; tel. (071) 383-6266; telex 265929; fax (071) 383-6233; f. 1962 for the exchange of information; provision of technical co-operation and advice; formulation and maintenance of a code of ethics; provision of continuing medical education; development and promotion of health education programmes; and liaison with WHO and the UN on health issues; meetings of its Council are held every three years. Mems: medical associations in Commonwealth countries. Sec. Dr J. D. J. HAVARD. Publ. *CMA Quarterly Bulletin*.

Commonwealth Pharmaceutical Association: 1 Lambeth High St, London, SE1 7JN; tel. (071) 735-9141; telex 93121-131542; fax (071) 735-7629; f. 1969 to promote the interests of pharmaceutical sciences and the profession of pharmacy in the Commonwealth; to maintain high professional standards, encourage links between members and the creation of national associations; and to facilitate the dissemination of information. Holds conferences (every four years) and regional meetings. Mems: 36 pharmaceutical associations. Sec. RAYMOND DICKINSON. Publ. *Quarterly Newsletter*.

Commonwealth Society for the Deaf: Dilke House, Malet St, London, WC1E 7JA; tel. (071) 631-5311; promotes the health, education and general welfare of the deaf in developing Commonwealth countries; encourages and assists the development of educational facilities, the training of teachers of the deaf, and the provision of support for parents of deaf children; organizes visits by volunteer specialists to work for 2–3 weeks with local communities; provides audiological equipment and encourages the establishment of maintenance services for such equipment; conducts research into the causes and prevention of deafness. Admin. Sec. Miss E. LUBIENSKA. Publs *Annual Report, Research Report*.

Sight Savers (Royal Commonwealth Society for the Blind): POB 191, Haywards Heath, Sussex, RH16 1FN; tel. (0444) 412424; telex 87167; fax (0444) 415866; f. 1950 to prevent blindness and to promote the education, employment and welfare of blind people in the developing world; operates through governments and non-governmental organizations to contribute to the development of national and regional programmes; gives high priority to training local staff; Chair. Sir FRANK MILLS; Dir A. W. JOHNS. Publs *Annual Report, Horizons* (newsletter).

INFORMATION AND THE MEDIA

Commonwealth Broadcasting Association: Broadcasting House, London, W1A 1AA; tel. (071) 580-4468, ext. 6023; telex 265781; f. 1945; General Conferences are held every two years. Mems: 59 national public service broadcasting organizations in 52 Commonwealth countries. Pres. CHEUNG MAN YEE; Sec.-Gen. ALVA CLARKE. Publs *COMBROAD* (quarterly), *CBA Handbook* (updated every 2 years).

Commonwealth Institute: Kensington High St, London, W8 6NQ; tel. (071) 603-4535; telex 8955822; fax (071) 602-7374; f. 1887 as the Imperial Institute; a centre for public information and educational services, the Institute houses a permanent exhibition designed to express countries of the modern Commonwealth in visual terms, art galleries showing contemporary works of art, information and educational resources centres, and an Arts Centre with a continuous programme of dance, drama, music and films. Dir-Gen. JAMES PORTER.

Commonwealth Institute, Scotland: 8 Rutland Sq., Edinburgh, EH1 2AS, Scotland; tel. (031) 229-6668; fax (031) 229-6041; Dir C. G. CARROL.

Commonwealth Journalists' Association: Castle House, 25 Castlereagh St, London, W1H 5YR; tel. (071) 262-1054; telex 296033; fax (071) 724-6925; f. 1978 to improve standards of journalism, promote co-operation between journalists in Commonwealth countries, and foster interest in Commonwealth affairs. Pres. RAY EKPU; Exec. Dir LAWRIE BREEN.

Commonwealth Press Union (Association of Commonwealth Newspapers, News Agencies and Periodicals): Studio House, 184 Fleet St, London, EC4A 2DU; tel. (071) 242-1056; telex 936565; fax (071) 831-4923; f. 1950 (succeeding the Empire Press Union, f. 1909) to promote the welfare of the Commonwealth press by defending its freedom and providing training for journalists; organizes biennial conferences. Mems: about 500 newspapers, news agencies, periodicals in 30 countries. Pres. Sir PETER GIBBINGS; Chair. of Council LYLE TURNBULL; Dir JAYANATH C. RAJEPAKSE. Publs *CPU News, Annual Report*.

LAW

Commonwealth Lawyers' Association: c/o The Law Society, 50 Chancery Lane, London, WC2A 1SX; tel. (071) 242-1222; telex 261203; fax (071) 831-0057; f. 1983 (fmrly the Commonwealth Legal Bureau); seeks to maintain and promote the rule of law throughout the Commonwealth, by ensuring that the people of the Commonwealth are served by an independent and efficient legal profession; upholds professional standards and promotes the availability of legal services; assists in organizing the triennial Commonwealth law conferences. Pres. Dr R. M. A. CHONGWE; Exec. Sec. HAMISH C. ADAMSON. Publ. *Commonwealth Lawyer* (2 a year).

Commonwealth Legal Advisory Service: c/o British Institute of International and Comparative Law, Charles Clore House, 17 Russell Sq., London, WC1B 5DR; tel. (071) 636-5802; fax (071) 323-2016; financed by the British Institute and by contributions from the Commonwealth Governments; besides operating the advisory service, the British Institute prepares surveys and organizes lectures, study courses and conferences. Dir ROGER ROSE. Publ. *ICLQ, Bulletin of Legal Developments*.

INTERNATIONAL ORGANIZATIONS

The Commonwealth

Commonwealth Legal Education Association: Legal Division, Commonwealth Secretariat, Marlborough House, Pall Mall, London, SW1Y 5HX; tel. (071) 839-3411; f. 1971; to promote contacts and exchanges; to provide information. Hon. Sec. JEREMY POPE. Publs *Commonwealth Legal Education Newsletter, List of Schools of Law in the Commonwealth* (every 2 years), *Compendium of Post-Graduate Law Courses in the Commonwealth*.

Commonwealth Magistrates' Association: 28 Fitzroy Sq., London, W1P 6DD; tel. (071) 387-4889; fax (071) 383-0757; f. 1970 to advance the administration of the law by promoting the independence of the judiciary, to further education in law and crime prevention and to disseminate information; conferences and study tours; corporate membership for associations of the judiciary or courts of limited jurisdiction; associate membership for individuals. Pres. ANDREAS LOIZOU; Sec. Dr J. S. BUCHANAN. Publ. *Commonwealth Judicial Journal* (2 a year).

PARLIAMENTARY AFFAIRS

Commonwealth Parliamentary Association: 7 Old Palace Yard, London, SW1P 3JY; tel. (071) 799-1460; telex 911569; fax (071) 222-6073; f. 1911 to promote understanding and co-operation between Commonwealth parliamentarians; organization: Executive Committee of 25 Members of Parliament responsible to annual General Assembly; 115 branches throughout the Commonwealth; holds annual Commonwealth Parliamentary Conferences and seminars, and also regional conferences and seminars; Sec.-Gen. DAVID TONKIN. Publ. *The Parliamentarian* (quarterly).

PROFESSIONAL AND INDUSTRIAL RELATIONS

Commonwealth Association of Architects: 66 Portland Place, London, W1N 4AD; tel. (071) 636-8276; telex 22914; fax (071) 255-1541; f. 1964; an association of 35 societies of architects in various Commonwealth countries. Objects: to facilitate the reciprocal recognition of professional qualifications; to provide a clearing house for information on architectural practice, and to encourage collaboration. Plenary Conferences every two years; regional Conferences are held. Sec. GEORGE WILSON. Publs *Handbook, Architectural Education in the Commonwealth, Issues in Architectural Practice, List of Recognised Schools of Architecture*.

Commonwealth Foundation: Marlborough House, Pall Mall, London, SW1Y 5HY; tel. (071) 930-3783; fax (071) 839-8157; f. 1966 to administer a fund to promote closer professional co-operation within the Commonwealth (reconstituted as an international organization 1983). The Foundation is an autonomous body assisting professionals from Commonwealth countries to visit other Commonwealth countries to attend conferences and undertake advisory and study visits and training attachments. Also supports Commonwealth professional associations and professional centres; runs short-term fellowship schemes. Funds are provided by 43 Commonwealth governments: in 1990/91 £1.5m. was available for grant-making. Chair. ROBERT STANFIELD (Canada); Dir 'INOKE FALETAU (Tonga).

Commonwealth Trade Union Council: c/o TUC, Congress House, 23–28 Great Russell St, London, WC1B 3LS; tel. (071) 636-4030; telex 266006; fax (071) 436-0301; f. 1979 to promote the interests of workers in the Commonwealth and encourage the development of trades unions in developing countries of the Commonwealth; provides assistance for training. Dir PATRICK QUINN (UK).

SCIENCE AND TECHNOLOGY

Commonwealth Advisory Aeronautical Research Council: Room 9145, St Christopher House, Southwark St, London, SE1 0TD; tel. (071) 921-1355; f. 1946; encourages and co-ordinates aeronautical research throughout the Commonwealth. Sec. D. B. HALLIDAY.

Commonwealth Engineers' Council: c/o Institution of Civil Engineers, 1–7 Great George St, London, SW1P 3AA; tel. (071) 222-7722; telex 935637; fax (071) 222-7500; f. 1946; the Conference meets every 2 years to provide an opportunity for officers of engineering institutions of Commonwealth countries to exchange views on collaboration; there is a standing committee on engineering education and training; organizes seminars on related topics. Sec. J. C. MCKENZIE.

Commonwealth Geological Surveys Consultative Group: c/o Commonwealth Science Council, CSC Earth Services Programme, Marlborough House, Pall Mall, London, SW1Y 5HX; tel. (071) 839-3411; telex 27678; fax (071) 930-0827; f. 1948 (as the Commonwealth Committee on Mineral Resources and Geology) to promote collaboration in geological, geochemical, geophysical and remote sensing techniques and the exchange of information. Sec. Dr SIYAN MALOMO; Publ. *Earth Sciences Newsletter*.

SPORT

Commonwealth Games Federation: 197 Knightsbridge, London, SW7 1RZ; tel. (071) 225-5555; telex 919156; fax (071) 225-5197; the Games were first held in 1930 and are now held every four years; participation is limited to amateur teams representing the member countries of the Commonwealth; held in Auckland, New Zealand, in 1990 and to be held in Victoria, Canada, in 1994. Mems: 65 affiliated bodies. Chair. A. O. DE SALES; Hon. Sec. DAVID DIXON.

YOUTH

Commonwealth Youth Exchange Council: 7 Lion Yard, Tremadoc Rd, London, SW4 7NQ; tel. (071) 498-6151; fax (071) 720-5403; f. 1970; promotes contact between groups of young people of the United Kingdom and other Commonwealth countries by means of educational exchange visits, provides information for organizers and allocates grants; 188 member organizations. Dir V. S. G. CRAGGS. Publs *Contact* (handbook), *Exchange* (newsletter).

Duke of Edinburgh's Award Scheme: 5 Prince of Wales Terrace, London, W8 5PG; tel. (071) 938-4545; telex 923753; f. 1956; offers a programme of leisure activities for young people, comprising service, expeditions, sport and skills, operating in over 40 countries (not confined to the Commonwealth). Dir Maj.-Gen. MICHAEL F. HOBBS; International Sec.-Gen. DAVID NEWING. Publs *Award World* (3 a year), handbooks and guides.

MISCELLANEOUS

British Commonwealth Ex-services League: 48 Pall Mall, London, SW1Y 5JG; tel. (071) 930-8131, ext. 263; links the ex-service organizations in the Commonwealth, assists ex-servicemen of the Crown and their dependants who are resident abroad; holds triennial conferences. Sec.-Gen. Brig. M. J. DOYLE. Publ. *Triennial Report*.

Commonwealth Countries League: 14 Thistleworth Close, Isleworth, Middx, TW7 4QQ; tel. (081) 568-9868; f. 1925 to secure equal opportunities and status between men and women in the Commonwealth, and the social and political education of women, to act as a link between Commonwealth women's organizations, and to promote and finance secondary education of disadvantaged girls of high ability in their own countries, through the CCL Educational Fund; holds meetings with speakers and an annual Conference, organizes the annual Commonwealth Fair for fund-raising; individual mems and affiliated socs in the Commonwealth. Sec.-Gen. SHEILA O'REILLY. Publ. *CCL Newsletter* (3 a year).

Commonwealth War Graves Commission: 2 Marlow Rd, Maidenhead, Berks, SL6 7DX; tel. (0628) 34221; telex 847526; fax (0628) 771208; f. 1917 (as Imperial War Graves Commission); provides for the marking and permanent care of the graves of members of the Commonwealth Forces who died during the wars of 1914–18 and 1939–45; maintains over 1m. graves in some 140 countries and commemorates by name on memorials more than 750,000 who have no known grave or who were cremated. Mems: Australia, Canada, India, New Zealand, South Africa, United Kingdom. Pres. HRH The Duke of KENT; Dir-Gen. J. SAYNOR.

Joint Commonwealth Societies' Council: c/o Commonwealth Trust, Commonwealth House, 18 Northumberland Ave, London, WC2N 5BJ; tel. (071) 930-6733; fax (071) 930-9705; co-ordinates the activities of recognized societies promoting mutual understanding in the Commonwealth; mems: 13 unofficial Commonwealth organizations and four official bodies. Chair. Sir DONALD TEBBIT; Sec. JENNY GROVES.

Royal Commonwealth Society: 18 Northumberland Ave, London, WC2N 5BJ; tel. (071) 930-6733; fax (071) 930-9705; to promote knowledge and understanding among the people of the Commonwealth; branches in principal Commonwealth countries; has full residential club facilities, lectures and library. Sec.-Gen. Sir DAVID THORNE. Publ. *Newsletter* (3 a year), *Library Notes*, conference reports.

Royal Over-Seas League: Over-Seas House, Park Place, St James's St, London, SW1A 1LR; tel. (071) 408-0214; telex 268995; fax (01) 499-6738; f. 1910 to promote friendship and understanding in the Commonwealth; membership is open to all British subjects and Commonwealth citizens. Chair. Sir LAWRENCE BYFORD; Dir-Gen. Capt. J. B. RUMBLE. Publ. *Overseas* (quarterly).

Victoria League for Commonwealth Friendship: 18 Northumberland Ave, London, WC2N 5BJ; tel. (071) 930-1671; f. 1901 to further personal friendship among Commonwealth peoples; about 41,000 mems. Pres. HRH Princess MARGARET, Countess of Snowdon; Chair. Sir ZELMAN COWEN; Sec. Mrs SYLVIA BARNETT.

Declaration of Commonwealth Principles

Agreed by the Commonwealth Heads of Government Meeting at Singapore, 22 January 1971.

The Commonwealth of Nations is a voluntary association of independent sovereign states, each responsible for its own policies, consulting and co-operating in the common interests of their peoples and in the promotion of international understanding and world peace.

Members of the Commonwealth come from territories in the six continents and five oceans, include peoples of different races, languages and religions, and display every stage of economic development from poor developing nations to wealthy industrialized nations. They encompass a rich variety of cultures, traditions and institutions.

Membership of the Commonwealth is compatible with the freedom of member-governments to be non-aligned or to belong to any other grouping, association or alliance. Within this diversity all members of the Commonwealth hold certain principles in common. It is by pursuing these principles that the Commonwealth can continue to influence international society for the benefit of mankind.

We believe that international peace and order are essential to the security and prosperity of mankind; we therefore support the United Nations and seek to strengthen its influence for peace in the world, and its efforts to remove the causes of tension between nations.

We believe in the liberty of the individual, in equal rights for all citizens regardless of race, colour, creed or political belief, and in their inalienable right to participate by means of free and democratic political processes in framing the society in which they live. We therefore strive to promote in each of our countries those representative institutions and guarantees for personal freedom under the law that are our common heritage.

We recognize racial prejudice as a dangerous sickness threatening the healthy development of the human race and racial discrimination as an unmitigated evil of society. Each of us will vigorously combat this evil within our own nation.

No country will afford to regimes which practise racial discrimination assistance which in its own judgment directly contributes to the pursuit or consolidation of this evil policy. We oppose all forms of colonial domination and racial oppression and are committed to the principles of human dignity and equality.

We will therefore use all our efforts to foster human equality and dignity everywhere, and to further the principles of self-determination and non-racialism.

We believe that the wide disparities in wealth now existing between different sections of mankind are too great to be tolerated. They also create world tensions. Our aim is their progressive removal. We therefore seek to use our efforts to overcome poverty, ignorance and disease, in raising standards of life and achieving a more equitable international society.

To this end our aim is to achieve the freest possible flow of international trade on terms fair and equitable to all, taking into account the special requirements of the developing countries, and to encourage the flow of adequate resources, including governmental and private resources, to the developing countries, bearing in mind the importance of doing this in a true spirit of partnership and of establishing for this purpose in the developing countries conditions which are conducive to sustained investment and growth.

We believe that international co-operation is essential to remove the causes of war, promote tolerance, combat injustice, and secure development among the peoples of the world. We are convinced that the Commonwealth is one of the most fruitful associations for these purposes.

In pursuing these principles the members of the Commonwealth believe that they can provide a constructive example of the multi-national approach which is vital to peace and progress in the modern world. The association is based on consultation, discussion and co-operation.

In rejecting coercion as an instrument of policy they recognize that the security of each member state from external aggression is a matter of concern to all members. It provides many channels for continuing exchanges of knowledge and views on professional, cultural, economic, legal and political issues among member states.

These relationships we intend to foster and extend, for we believe that our multi-national association can expand human understanding and understanding among nations, assist in the elimination of discrimination based on differences of race, colour or creed, maintain and strengthen personal liberty, contribute to the enrichment of life for all, and provide a powerful influence for peace among nations.

The Gleneagles Agreement on Sporting Contacts with South Africa

In 1977 Commonwealth Heads of Government, meeting at Gleneagles in Scotland, reached the following agreement on discouraging sporting links with South Africa:

They were conscious that sport is an important means of developing and fostering understanding between the people, and especially between the young people, of all countries. . . .

Mindful of these and other considerations, they accepted it as the urgent duty of each of their Governments vigorously to combat the evil of apartheid by withholding any form of support for, and by taking every practical step to discourage contact or competition by their nationals with sporting organizations, teams or sportsmen from South Africa or from any other country where sports are organized on the basis of race, colour or ethnic origin.

They fully acknowledged that it was for each Government to determine in accordance with its law the methods by which it might best discharge these commitments. But they recognized that the effective fulfilment of their commitments was essential to the harmonious development of Commonwealth sport hereafter. . . .

Heads of Government specially welcomed the belief, unanimously expressed at their Meeting, that in the light of their consultations and accord there were unlikely to be future sporting contacts of any significance between Commonwealth countries or their nationals and South Africa while that country continues to pursue the detestable policy of apartheid. . . .

The Lusaka Declaration on Racism and Racial Prejudice

The Declaration, adopted by Heads of Government in 1979, includes the following statements:

United in our desire to rid the world of the evils of racism and racial prejudice, we proclaim our faith in the inherent dignity and worth of the human person and declare that:

(i) the peoples of the Commonwealth have the right to live freely in dignity and equality, without any distinction or exclusion based on race, colour, sex, descent, or national or ethnic origin;

(ii) while everyone is free to retain diversity in his or her culture and lifestyle this diversity does not justify the perpetuation of racial prejudice or racially discriminatory practices;

(iii) everyone has the right to equality before the law and equal justice under the law; and

(iv) everyone has the right to effective remedies and protection against any form of discrimination based on the grounds of race, colour, sex, descent, or national or ethnic origin.

We reject as inhuman and intolerable all policies designed to perpetuate apartheid, racial segregation or other policies based on theories that racial groups are or may be inherently superior or inferior.

We reaffirm that it is the duty of all the peoples of the Commonwealth to work together for the total eradication of the infamous policy of apartheid which is internationally recognized as a crime against the conscience and dignity of mankind and the very existence of which is an affront to humanity.

We agree that everyone has the right to protection against acts of incitement to racial hatred and discrimination, whether committed by individuals, groups or other organizations. . . .

Inspired by the principles of freedom and equality which characterise our association, we accept the solemn duty of working together to eliminate racism and racial prejudice. This duty involves the acceptance of the principle that positive measures may be required to advance the elimination of racism, including assistance to those struggling to rid themselves and their environment of the practice.

Being aware that legislation alone cannot eliminate racism and racial prejudice, we endorse the need to initiate public information and education policies designed to promote understanding, tolerance, respect and friendship among peoples and racial groups. . . .

We note that racism and racial prejudice, wherever they occur, are significant factors contributing to tension between nations and thus inhibit peaceful progress and development. We believe that the goal of the eradication of racism stands as a critical priority for governments of the Commonwealth committed as they are to the promotion of the ideals of peaceful and happy lives for their people.

COMMUNAUTÉ ÉCONOMIQUE DE L'AFRIQUE DE L'OUEST—CEAO

(WEST AFRICAN ECONOMIC COMMUNITY)

Address: rue Agostino Neto, BP 643, Ouagadougou, Burkina Faso.
Telephone: 33-22-32.
Telex: 5212.
Established in January 1974 to replace the West African Customs Union (UDEAO).

MEMBERS

Benin   Mali   Niger
Burkina Faso   Mauritania   Senegal
Côte d'Ivoire
Observers: Guinea, Togo.

Organization
(October 1990)

CONFERENCE OF HEADS OF STATE
The Conference of Heads of State is the supreme organ of the Community. It is held every two years in one of the member states, and its President is the Head of State of the host country. Decisions of the Conference must be unanimous. It appoints the officers of the Community.
President (1990–91): Brig. ALI SAÏBOU (Niger).

COUNCIL OF MINISTERS
The Council of Ministers meets at least twice a year, usually at the seat of the Community. Each member state is represented by its Minister of Finance or a member of government, according to the subject under discussion. Decisions are taken unanimously.

GENERAL SECRETARIAT
The Secretariat is responsible for carrying out decisions of the Conference of Heads of State and the Council of Ministers. It comprises four main departments: trade; rural development; industrial development; administration and finance. The Secretary-General is appointed for a four-year term.
Secretary-General: MAMADOU HAIDARA (Mali).

Activities

The Community has three main areas of activity: trade, regional economic co-operation and economic integration through Community projects.

TRADE
Of the three categories of produce traded within the Community, non-manufactured, crude products may be imported and exported within the Community without import taxes, paying only internal taxes; traditional handicrafts are exempted from import taxes, and subject to the payment of internal taxes only, according to an agreement in June 1979; and industrial products of member states, when exported to other member states, may benefit from the special preferential system based on the substitution for customs duties and taxes of a sole tax called Regional Co-operation Tax. The main purpose of the tax is to encourage exchanges within the Community; it is always lower than the ones payable in the member states. The tax came into force on 1 January 1976: by mid-1985 it had been applied to 428 products or groups of products from 253 enterprises, of which 127 were from Côte d'Ivoire and 75 from Senegal. Trade in these products increased sevenfold from 4,500m. francs CFA in 1976 to 32,000m. in 1984. By 1989, however, trade between CEAO member states still amounted to only 6% of their total trade.

In 1984 a three-year programme was begun, aiming to harmonize customs procedure and the codification of merchandise, and to establish a common tariff for imports from outside the community. Other projects included the improvement of statistical data; commercial training (through, for example, regional seminars on marketing and exporting); and the establishment of a Centre Régional d'Information et de Documentation Commerciale. In 1984 the Conference of Heads of State adopted a convention harmonizing rates of taxation for nationals of member states, and in 1985 the first part of a common investment code was completed.

RURAL AND INDUSTRIAL DEVELOPMENT
Proposals for regional rural development projects approved in 1984 (and yet to come into effect in 1990) comprised the establishment of a seed-production centre in Baguinéda, Mali, of an agricultural training centre in Ouagadougou, Burkina Faso, and of rural savings banks. Studies were also being made during the late 1980s for a programme of industrial co-operation (particularly in the production of fertilizers, glass and metals); the harmonization of national investment laws; co-operation in traditional medicine; development of regional tourism; setting up a community shipping line; a regional transport plan; and a programme of agricultural and veterinary research. A five-year plan (1988–92) for transport and communications was adopted by regional ministers of transport in 1987, and a study was commissioned on the access of land-locked states to the sea.

ECONOMIC INTEGRATION
In 1978, 1982 and 1983 the conferences of Heads of State approved the formation of common programmes and institutions, at a cost of over 60,000m. francs CFA, to be financed by a number of donors (notably the African Development Bank and African Development Fund, BADEA, the Islamic Development Bank, the World Bank, the OPEC Fund, France, the Federal Republic of Germany and Kuwait). The projects comprised: a rural water programme throughout the region, to provide 2,634 village wells at a cost of some 23,000m. francs CFA; a regional solar energy centre in Bamako, Mali, to be completed in late 1986 (8,146m. francs CFA); a corporation for the manufacture of railway rolling-stock, to be based in Burkina Faso and Senegal; a centre for higher studies in management, opened in Dakar, Senegal in 1985 (2,217m. francs CFA); a college of geology and mining, to be constructed in Niamey, Niger, by 1987 (11,046m. francs CFA); a college for textile studies in Ségou, Mali, construction of which began in 1986 (5,002m. francs CFA); a community fisheries company, based in Mauritania (17,136m. francs CFA); and two centres for research and training in fisheries, in Mauritania and Côte d'Ivoire.

In 1983 a total of 800m. francs CFA was allotted to member states affected by drought, and in 1984 a second rural waterworks programme was approved, to provide a further 500 village wells and boreholes in each of the member states. In 1989 Kuwait agreed to provide 2,500m. francs CFA for this programme.

COMMUNITY DEVELOPMENT FUND—FCD
The Fund is financed by member states according to their respective shares in the trade of industrial products within the Community. The sum is decided annually, at the Conference of Heads of State, in relation to the revenue from the Regional Co-operation Tax. It compensates for certain types of trade loss and finances economic development projects. The Fund's budget for 1985 amounted to 10,571m. francs CFA. Members' difficulties in paying their subscriptions, however, have severely hampered the Fund's activities: by June 1985 overdue contributions amounted to 15,333m. francs CFA.

SOLIDARITY AND INTERVENTION FUND
Fonds de Solidarité et d'Intervention pour le Développement—FOSIDEC (Solidarity and Intervention Fund): BP 2529, Ouagadougou, Burkina Faso; tel. 33-47-94; telex 5342; f. 1977 to contribute to regional equilibrium by granting and guaranteeing loans, financing studies and granting subsidies. The Fund's initial capital was 5,000m. francs CFA. By June 1985 the Fund's interventions amounted to 26,267.6m. francs CFA, of which 49.5% was for industrial projects, 32.3% for water development and 14.4% for agriculture and agro-industry. In November 1984 the Fund's director was dismissed, and in April 1986 he was convicted (together with a former secretary-general of the CEAO) of the embezzlement of 6,400m. francs CFA. In 1989 the Conference of Heads of State agreed to impose a 'community solidarity levy' on imports from outside the Community, in order to finance integration projects and service debts. In 1990 the African Development Bank, the World Bank and the French Government agreed to provide 70m. francs CFA for studies on the revival of the Fund. Dir-Gen. AMADOU BABA SY.

INTERNATIONAL ORGANIZATIONS

CO-OPERATION AGREEMENTS

An agreement of non-aggression and mutual co-operation was signed by the member countries in June 1977, and an agreement on free circulation and the right to establish residence was signed in October 1978.

Communauté Économique de l'Afrique de l'Ouest

PUBLICATIONS

Rapport annuel (annually).

Intégration africaine (2 a year).

CONSEIL DE L'ENTENTE
(ENTENTE COUNCIL)

Address: Fonds d'Entraide et de Garantie des Emprunts, 01 BP 3734, Abidjan 01, Côte d'Ivoire.
Telephone: 33-28-35.
Telex: 23558.
Fax: 33-11-49.

The Conseil de l'Entente, founded in 1959, is a political and economic association of four states which were formerly part of French West Africa, and Togo, which joined in 1966. It gives priority to economic co-ordination in member states.

MEMBERS

Benin   Burkina Faso   Côte d'Ivoire   Niger   Togo

Organization
(October 1990)

THE COUNCIL

The Council consists of the Heads of State and the ministers concerned with the items on the agenda of particular meetings.

The Council meets annually, the place rotating each year between the member states, and is chaired by the President of the host country. Secretariat services are provided by the Secretariat of the Mutual Aid and Guarantee Fund. Extraordinary meetings may be held at the request of two or more members.

FONDS D'ENTRAIDE ET DE GARANTIE DES EMPRUNTS

The Mutual Aid and Loan Guarantee Fund is responsible for carrying out the economic projects decided on by the Council. Its Management Committee, comprising three representatives of each member state, meets twice a year, and a small group of professional advisers assists development institutions in member countries in the preparation of projects and the presentation of requests for aid. Financial resources comprise annual contributions from member states, subsidies and grants (mainly from the French Government), and investment returns and commissions from guarantee operations. At the end of 1989 the Fund's capital amounted to 15,797m. francs CFA.

Administrative Secretary: PAUL KAYA.

Activities

The Entente Council, through the Mutual Aid and Loan Guarantee Fund, aims to promote economic development in the region; to assist in preparing specific projects and to mobilize funds from other sources; to act as a guarantee fund to encourage investments in the region; and to encourage trade and investment between the member states. It is empowered to finance the reduction of interest rates and the extension of maturity periods of foreign loans to member countries.

Between 1978 and 1980 the Fund initiated eight agricultural projects for improving and rehabilitating crop production, at a cost of 9,000m. francs CFA, and seven projects for the development of livestock, at a cost of 3,000m. francs CFA. In 1987 the Fund began a five-year programme of agricultural projects, one in each of the five member countries, with emphasis on training and organizing farmers and modernizing methods of production. The programme was expected to cost 5,000m. francs CFA.

Between 1983 and 1985 a programme of hydraulics was undertaken in four of the five member countries (excluding Togo), providing 1,475 wells and 1,641 pumps at a cost of 6,330m. francs CFA. The second phase of the programme, begun in 1986, envisaged the provision of a further 2,000 wells in these countries: by the end of 1989, 1,386 wells had been completed.

The Fund's programme of assistance to industry, begun in 1972 with financial aid from the USA, had led to the creation or expansion of 860 small and medium-sized enterprises by the end of 1989. In 1989 assistance amounting to 29m. francs CFA was given for credit schemes and for technical assistance. Studies on industrial standardization were undertaken in 1985, and identified the following priorities: training for industrial inspectors, the creation of a standards bureau (particularly for food products and building materials), a system for standardizing electrical equipment, and safety regulations for public buildings. The first project to be undertaken in this field, providing training in quality control, was completed in 1988 and new projects, providing training for industrial inspectors and standardization of electrical equipment, began in that year.

The Fund also supports two centres (in Niamey, Niger, and Ouagadougou, Burkina Faso) for the training of motor mechanics and drivers of heavy goods vehicles; research into new sources of energy (particularly the exploitation of biogas and the use of vegetable waste, such as coffee-bean husks, as fuel); conducting energy 'audits' for transport companies, factories and public buildings and recommending economies; provision of electricity for villages, using solar power; the building of hotels and encouragement of tourism; and support for national schools of administration and technical training.

Loans guaranteed by the Fund included assistance for extension of the port of Lomé, Togo, in 1981 (1,276m. francs CFA), for building a telecommunications station in Benin in 1982 (1,000m. francs CFA), for the development of coffee and cotton cultivation in Togo in 1983 (6,750m. francs CFA), for a hydroelectric scheme to benefit Benin and Togo in 1984 (4,300m. francs CFA), and for construction of presidential offices in Burkina Faso in 1989 (3,000m. francs CFA).

In 1989 the Fund recorded expenditure of 1,558m. francs CFA (compared with 1,371m. francs CFA in 1988 and 1,217m. francs CFA in 1987). Assistance from France amounted to 485m. francs CFA for 1988 and to 206m. francs CFA for 1989.

PUBLICATIONS

Entente Africaine (quarterly).

Rapport d'activité (annually).

ASSOCIATED ORGANIZATION

Communauté économique du bétail et de la viande du Conseil de l'Entente (Livestock and Meat Economic Community of the Entente Council): BP 638, Ouagadougou, Burkina Faso; f. 1970 to promote the production, processing and marketing of livestock and meat; negotiates between members and with third countries on technical and financial co-operation and co-ordinated legislation; attempts to co-ordinate measures to combat drought and cattle disease. Budget (1987): 105.4m. francs CFA. Mems: states belonging to the Conseil de l'Entente. Sec. Dr ALOUA MOUSSA.

CO-OPERATION COUNCIL FOR THE ARAB STATES OF THE GULF

Address: POB 7153, Riyadh 11462, Saudi Arabia.
Telephone: 482-7777.
Telex: 403635.
More generally known as the Gulf Co-operation Council (GCC), the organization was established on 25 May 1981 by six Arab states.

MEMBERS

Bahrain	Oman	Saudi Arabia
Kuwait	Qatar	United Arab Emirates

Organization
(October 1990)

SUPREME COUNCIL

The Supreme Council comprises the heads of member states, meeting annually in ordinary session, and in emergency session if demanded by two or more members. The Presidency of the Council is undertaken by each state in turn, in alphabetical order. The Supreme Council draws up the overall policy of the organization; it discusses recommendations and laws presented to it by the Ministerial Council and the Secretariat General in preparation for endorsement. A body for resolving disputes is also to be attached to and formed by the Supreme Council.

MINISTERIAL COUNCIL

The Ministerial Council consists of the foreign ministers of member states, meeting every three months, and in emergency session if demanded by two or more members. It prepares for the meetings of the Supreme Council, and draws up policies, recommendations, studies and projects aimed at developing co-operation and co-ordination among member states in various spheres.

SECRETARIAT GENERAL

The Secretariat assists member states in implementing recommendations by the Supreme and Ministerial Councils, and prepares reports and studies, budgets and accounts. The Secretary-General is appointed by the Supreme Council, upon the recommendation of the Ministerial Council, for a renewable three-year term. All member states contribute in equal proportions towards the budget of the Secretariat, which amounted to US $27m. for 1985/86.
Secretary-General: ABDULLAH YACOUB BISHARA (Kuwait).
Assistant Secretary-General for Political Affairs: SAIF BIN HASHIL AL-MASKERY (Oman).
Assistant Secretary-General for Economic Affairs: Dr ABDULLAH AL-KUWAIZ (Saudi Arabia).

Activities

The Council was set up following a series of meetings of foreign ministers of the states concerned, culminating in an agreement on the basic details of its constitution on 10 March 1981. The Constitution was signed by the six heads of state on 25 May. It describes the organization as providing 'the means for realizing co-ordination, integration and co-operation' in all economic, social and cultural affairs. A series of ministerial meetings subsequently began to put the proposals into effect.

ECONOMIC CO-OPERATION

In June 1981 Gulf finance ministers drew up an economic co-operation agreement covering investment, petroleum, the abolition of customs duties, harmonization of banking regulations and financial and monetary co-ordination. In November 1982 Heads of State approved the formation of a Gulf Investment Corporation with capital of US $2,100m., to be based in Kuwait (see below). Customs duties on domestic products of the Gulf states were abolished in March 1983, and new regulations allowing free movement of workers and vehicles between member states were also introduced. In 1985 unified patent legislation was discussed, to deal with the increasing problem of counterfeit goods in the region. A common minimum customs levy (of between 4% and 20%) on foreign imports was imposed in 1986. In February 1987 the governors of the member states' central banks agreed in principle to co-ordinate their rates of exchange, and this was approved by the Supreme Council in November of that year, but disagreement remained over whether to link the Gulf currencies to the US dollar, the SDR or a 'basket' of other currencies. In May 1989 GCC ministers of industry suggested the imposition of higher tariffs on imports that were regarded as a threat to GCC manufacturing industries. Ministers of finance, meeting in the following month, agreed to divide imports into four categories for tariff purposes, but were reported to have failed to reach agreement on exact levels of tariffs. In October 1990, following the Iraqi invasion of Kuwait, GCC governments agreed to provide support for regional banks affected by the crisis.

TRADE

In 1982 a ministerial committee was formed to co-ordinate trade development in the region. A feasibility study was commissioned on the establishment of strategic food reserves for the member states, and the joint purchase of rice was undertaken. In November 1986 the Supreme Council approved a measure whereby citizens of GCC member states were enabled to undertake certain retail trade activities in any other member state, with effect from 1 March 1987. The ministerial committee in charge of trade also forms the board of directors of the GCC Standards and Metrology Organization, which approves minimum standards for goods produced in or imported to the region: by mid-1988 99 Gulf standards had been approved. A joint trade exhibition is held annually.

INDUSTRY

In 1985, following a series of meetings of the GCC ministers of industry, the Supreme Council endorsed a common industrial strategy for the GCC states. It approved regulations stipulating that priority should be given to imports of GCC industrial products, and permitting GCC investors to obtain loans from GCC industrial development banks. In November 1986 resolutions were adopted on the protection of industrial products, and on the co-ordination of industrial projects, in order to avoid duplication. During 1988 unified legislation was being prepared on the investment of foreign capital in the GCC states. A number of studies of investment opportunities, and feasibility studies for joint industrial projects, were undertaken in the late 1980s.

AGRICULTURE

In January 1983 ministers of agriculture met to draw up a unified agricultural policy, which was endorsed by the Supreme Council in November 1985. Between 1983 and 1987 ministers also approved proposals for harmonizing legislation relating to water conservation, veterinary vaccines, insecticides, fertilizers, fisheries and seeds. Studies on the establishment of two joint veterinary laboratories (for diagnosis of virus diseases and for production of vaccines), and on agricultural and veterinary quarantine, have also been undertaken. In 1987 two private Saudi Arabian companies were designated as official GCC producers of seed and poultry.

TRANSPORT AND COMMUNICATIONS

During 1985 feasibility studies were being undertaken on new rail and road links between member states, and on the establishment of a joint coastal transport company. In December it was announced that implementation of a scheme to build a 1,700-km railway to link all the member states and Iraq (and thereby the European railway network) had been postponed, owing to its high cost (estimated at US $4,000m.). In January 1986 ministers agreed to establish a joint telecommunications network.

ENERGY

In 1982 a ministerial committee was established to co-ordinate hydrocarbons policies and prices. Sub-committees were also formed to exchange information on marketing and prices; to discuss the development of the hydrocarbons refining industry; to examine domestic energy consumption and subsidies; to co-ordinate training by national oil companies; and to co-ordinate exploration for minerals. Specific studies were undertaken on the expansion of hydrocarbons refining in Oman, and on the building of a pipeline from the Gulf oilfields to the coast of Oman, which would mean that petroleum no longer had to be carried by sea through the Strait of Hormuz. In 1982 ministers also adopted a petroleum security plan to safeguard individual members against a halt in their production, to form a stockpile of petroleum products, and to organize a boycott of any non-member country when appropriate. A unified policy on the acquisition of technology was also approved. Feasibility studies on the integration of member states' electricity networks to form a regional power grid were commissioned in March 1983, and were still being conducted in 1990. In December 1987 the Supreme Council adopted a plan whereby a member state whose petroleum production was disrupted could 'borrow' petroleum from other members, in order to fulfil its export obligations.

REGIONAL SECURITY

Although no mention of defence or security was made in the original constitution, the summit meeting which ratified the constitution also issued a statement rejecting any foreign military presence in the region. The Supreme Council meeting in November 1981 agreed to include defence co-operation in the activities of the organization: as a result, defence ministers met in January 1982 to discuss a common security policy, including a joint air defence system and standardization of weapons. Ground forces of the member states held a joint military exercise in October 1983, followed by naval and air exercises in 1984. In November 1984 member states agreed to form a joint defence force for rapid deployment against external aggression, comprising units from the armed forces of each country under a central command.

In 1981 the Council jointly endorsed the Saudi Arabian 'Fahd Plan' (see under Arab League) for peace in the Middle East. Between 1982 and 1986 the Council made repeated offers to mediate in the war between Iraq (supported by the member states individually) and Iran. In July 1987 GCC ministers of foreign affairs approved the UN Security Council resolution (No. 598) which recommended that Iran and Iraq should settle their conflict through negotiation, and they offered their support to the UN Secretary-General in his efforts to mediate. In October (following an Iranian missile attack on Kuwait) GCC ministers of foreign affairs issued a statement declaring that aggression against one member state was regarded as aggression against them all. In December the Supreme Council studied a report by ministers of defence on protecting vessels and coastal installations against Iranian attacks, and approved a joint pact on regional co-operation in matters of security. The meeting issued a statement regretting Iran's 'procrastination' in implementing the UN Security Council resolution No. 598. Following the cease-fire between Iran and Iraq in August 1988, the Supreme Council, meeting in November, failed to agree on a common policy on improving relations with Iran. In December 1989 the Supreme Council agreed to undertake new diplomatic efforts to secure a lasting peace between Iran and Iraq. In August 1990, following the Iraqi invasion of Kuwait, the Ministerial Council issued a statement describing the invasion as a violation of sovereignty, and demanding the withdrawal of Iraqi troops from Kuwait.

EXTERNAL RELATIONS

In 1984 and 1985 representatives of the GCC and the European Community discussed access to European markets by GCC petrochemical products (with reference to tariffs that were imposed on GCC petrochemicals by the EEC in June 1984). In June 1988 an agreement was signed by GCC and EEC ministers on economic co-operation: the EEC agreed to assist the GCC states in developing their agriculture and industry. Negotiations took place subsequently on trade liberalization and in particular on the reduction of tariffs imposed by the EEC on petrochemical imports: a full free-trade agreement was, however, opposed by some EEC member governments, who were apprehensive that this would adversely affect the European petrochemicals industry. In October 1989 the Commission of the EEC proposed to EEC member governments that Community tariffs on imports of petrochemicals from the GCC should be phased out over a period of 12–16 years. In March 1990 GCC and EEC ministers of foreign affairs undertook to hold negotiations on a free-trade agreement: discussions began in October.

INVESTMENT CORPORATION

Gulf Investment Corporation: POB 3402, Safat 13035, Kuwait; tel. 2431911; telex 44002; fax 2448894; f. 1983 by the six member states of the GCC, each contributing US $350m. of the total capital of $2,100m.; paid-up capital $540m., total assets $1,938m. (Dec. 1989); investment chiefly in the Gulf region, financing industrial projects (including pharmaceuticals, chemicals, steel wire, aircraft engineering, aluminium, dairy produce and chicken-breeding). By the end of 1988 120 proposed projects had been reviewed, and 11 (with equity participation by the Corporation amounting to $45m.) had been approved. Chair. MUHAMMAD ABALKHALI (Saudi Arabia); Chief Exec. Dr KHALED AL-FAYEZ.

COUNCIL FOR MUTUAL ECONOMIC ASSISTANCE—CMEA

Address: 121205 Moscow, Prospekt Kalinina 56, USSR.
Telephone: (095) 290-91-11.
Telex: 411141.

The CMEA (sometimes known as COMECON) was founded in 1949 to assist the economic development of its member states through the sharing of resources and the co-ordination of efforts.

MEMBERS

Bulgaria	Hungary	Romania
Cuba	Mongolia	USSR
Czechoslovakia	Poland	Viet-Nam

Albania ceased to participate in the activities of the Council at the end of 1961. The Mongolian People's Republic was admitted in 1962, the Republic of Cuba in 1972 and the Socialist Republic of Viet-Nam in 1978. The German Democratic Republic, a member since 1950, was reunified with the Federal Republic of Germany in October 1990.

OBSERVERS

In accordance with Article XI of the Charter, the Council may invite participation of non-member countries in the work of its organs, or in spheres agreed by arrangement with the relevant countries. Afghanistan, Angola, Ethiopia, Laos, Mozambique, Nicaragua and Yemen participate as observers in the work of certain CMEA organs. In 1964 an agreement was concluded whereby Yugoslavia can participate in certain defined spheres of the Council's activity.

Organization*
(October 1990)

MEETING OF HEADS OF STATE

A summit meeting of heads of state of member countries (the first since 1969) was held in June 1984, and another took place in November 1986.

COUNCIL

The Council meets once a year in the capital of each member state in turn, all members being represented, usually by heads of government. It examines the reports of the Executive Committee, discusses economic, scientific and technical co-operation and determines the main directions of activities.

EXECUTIVE COMMITTEE

The Executive Committee, the chief executive organ of the CMEA, is composed of the representatives of the member states at the level of deputy heads of government. It meets at least once every three months to examine proposals from member states, the Permanent Commissions and the Secretariat. It guides all co-ordinating work, in agreement with the decisions of the Session of the Council. The Chair is taken in turn by representatives of each country.

COMMITTEES

The CMEA has committees for co-operation in the following areas: planning; science and technology; machine-building; electronics; agro-industry; external economic relations; fuel and raw materials.

PERMANENT COMMISSIONS

There are Permanent Commissions on co-operation in the areas of: statistics; electricity and nuclear power engineering; the chemical industry; metallurgy; light industry; transport; standardization; communications and postal services; environmental protection; monetary and financial matters; and legal matters.

CONFERENCES

Certain conferences are established in the CMEA structure as permanent representative bodies. These include conferences of heads of water management bodies; ministers of internal trade; heads of agencies for inventions; legal experts; heads of pricing agencies; heads of state labour organizations; representatives of freight organizations and shipowners' organizations.

SECRETARIAT

Secretary of Council: VYACHESLAV VLADIMIROVICH SYCHEV (USSR).

* Extensive changes in the structure and activities of the CMEA were under discussion in 1990 (see below).

Activities

The CMEA's original aim was to unite and co-ordinate the efforts of the member countries in order to improve the development of socialist economic integration; to achieve more rapid economic and technical progress in these countries, and particularly a higher level of industrialization in countries where this was lacking; to achieve a steady growth of labour productivity; to work gradually towards a balanced level of development in the different regions, and a steady increase in standards of living in the member states.

Trade between member states was planned by yearly agreements until 1951 and thereafter by long-term bilateral and multilateral trade agreements linked to the development plans of the member countries. In 1985 trade between member countries comprised about 60% of their foreign trade, which was wholly state-controlled and conducted under a 'barter' system.

In 1971 the Council adopted the 'Comprehensive Programme for Further Extension and Improvement of Co-operation and the Development of Socialist Economic Integration among CMEA Countries'. Reviewing the first 10 years of this programme in 1981, the Council noted that CMEA industrial production had increased by 84% during the period, and trade among members by over 300%. In 1979 the Council adopted long-term specific programmes for energy, fuel, raw materials, agriculture, food production, machine building and transport for the period up to 1990.

Until 1990 the national five-year economic plans of member states were co-ordinated by the CMEA secretariat, in consultation with national planning offices. The original emphasis on mutual trade shifted to co-operation in production, involving specialization, joint ventures and the standardization of equipment and components, supervised by the various Permanent Commissions listed above. A number of joint organizations (listed on the following page) were established to co-ordinate members' planning in various branches of industry and transport.

Joint power engineering projects and supply networks were established in the 1980s, with particular emphasis on the development of nuclear and solar power and the reduction of petroleum consumption.

In industry, the programme for the 1980s gave special attention to the electronics industry and the standardization of electronic components. A major plan for the introduction of robots in industry was agreed in 1982. Member countries also agreed to co-operate in attempts to protect the environment from pollution caused by industry (especially the chemicals industry). In December 1985 the Council adopted a 'Comprehensive Programme for the Scientific and Technical Progress of the CMEA Countries to the Year 2000', covering electronics, industrial automation (robotics), development of new industrial materials and computer technology, biotechnology, and nuclear energy. A new organization, Interrobot, was established to co-ordinate industrial automation.

Agricultural co-operation emphasized the improved availability and nutritional quality of food supplies, through higher-yielding crop varieties, more extensive use of fertilizers, and collaboration in producing up-to-date equipment for processing foodstuffs.

Problems affecting economic co-operation during the 1980s included the members' dependence on the USSR for subsidized imports of energy; the cumbersome procedures of state trading organizations; and the lack of a convertible currency for trade between members. Use of the non-convertible 'transferable rouble' as the CMEA's unit of account for trade between members meant that any country achieving a trade surplus could not spend it on imports from other CMEA or western countries, and there was thus little incentive for improving or expanding production.

In 1988 a reorganization of the CMEA's administrative structure took place, involving the amalgamation of a number of existing bodies and the creation of new ones (notably a Committee for External Economic Relations, and a Permanent Commission for Environmental Protection). In July the Council discussed economic reforms and the need to stimulate trade between members and to improve production-sharing: it adopted the 'Collective Concept of the Socialist Division of Labour', which was intended to encourage industrial modernization and make more effective use of the mutual division of labour. The creation of a convertible currency was supported by all the members except the German Democratic Republic and Romania. The meeting approved special programmes of assistance for Cuba, Mongolia and Viet-Nam.

Following the domestic political changes which took place in eastern European countries in 1989 and 1990, and the coming into office of non-communist governments there, a Council meeting held in January 1990 established a commission to recommend radical changes in the structure and activities of the CMEA. It was agreed that each member should have sovereignty in economic decision-making, and that trade should be conducted bilaterally, in convertible currencies and at international market prices. These changes were to be introduced in phases, and trade preferences were to be retained for the least-developed members (Cuba, Mongolia and Viet-Nam). It was apparently envisaged that the CMEA's activities would eventually be confined to statistical research and analysis.

EXTERNAL RELATIONS

In accordance with an agreement concluded in 1964, Yugoslavia participates in the work of some CMEA bodies: areas of co-operation include foreign trade, monetary and financial matters, scientific and technological co-operation, metallurgy and engineering. Between 1973 and 1988 Finland signed 120 multilateral and bilateral agreements and protocols with the CMEA, including agreements on co-operation in engineering, timber production, petroleum and gas, environmental protection and transport. Other co-operation agreements were signed with Iraq (1975), Mexico (1975), Nicaragua (1983), Mozambique (1985), Angola (1986), Ethiopia (1986), the People's Democratic Republic of Yemen (1986) and Afghanistan (1987). Special commissions meet regularly to discuss and organize co-operation with each of these countries. At the beginning of 1984 there were over 300 industrial co-operation projects in developing countries, particularly India. The CMEA has observer status at the United Nations.

In June 1985 CMEA leaders agreed to propose the establishment of official links with the European Community, and formal relations were established in June 1988. Bilateral agreements on trade and economic co-operation were subsequently concluded between the EEC and Hungary (September 1988), Poland (September 1989), the USSR (December 1989), Czechoslovakia, Bulgaria and the German Democratic Republic (all in May 1990); an agreement with Romania, due to be signed in 1990, was suspended in June, following the violent suppression of anti-government demonstrations in Romania. In July 1989 the EEC undertook to co-ordinate a programme of extensive aid from the OECD countries for Hungary and Poland, later extended to include the other east European countries. Following the reunification of Germany in October 1990, its trade with the former German Democratic Republic's CMEA partners was to be permitted to continue until 1992 without being subject to the normal EEC tariffs.

International Economic Bodies established by CMEA member countries

INDUSTRIAL ORGANIZATIONS

Assofoto: Moscow 2, Smolenskii per. 1/4, USSR; f. 1973; photo-chemical industry; joint planning; co-operation in all stages of the reproduction process.

Central Dispatching Organization of the Interconnected Power Systems: Jungmannova 29, 111 32 Prague 1, Czechoslovakia; tel. (2) 225323; telex 121042; fax (2) 368339; f. 1962; responsible for co-ordinating the exchange of electric power. Dir ROLF MITSCHKE.

Computers: Moscow, ul. Chaikovskogo 11, USSR; f. 1969; computer engineering, establishment of standardized computer technology; joint planning of international industrial complex.

Interatomenergo: Moscow, ul. Kitaiskii proezd 7, USSR; f. 1973; nuclear power plant construction; co-ordination of research, development and production; specialization and co-operation of production; mutual support in planning and training.

Interatominstrument: 00-791 Warsaw, ul. Chocimska 28, Poland; nuclear-technical apparatus construction; co-operation in research, production and sales, industrial co-ordination.

Interchim: Thälmannplatz 5, PSF 726, Halle 4020, Germany; tel. 38401; telex 4322; f. 1970; branches of chemical industry. Specialization and co-operation in production; co-ordination of production plans. Dir J. SCHNEIDER.

Interchimvolokno: Bucharest, Piaţa Rosetti, Sector 1, Romania; f. 1974; organizes and co-ordinates research and production in the chemical fibres industry, promotes the development of trade and co-ordinates the supply of raw materials and equipment.

Interelektro: Moscow, ul. 1 Smolenskaya 7, USSR; f. 1973; selected branches of electrotechnology; joint planning and prognostics; specialization and co-operation of production; scientific and technical co-operation; co-ordination of mutual goods supplies.

Intermetall: 1146 Budapest, Cházár András ul. 9, Hungary; tel. 121-7500; telex 22-5043; f. 1964; ferrous metallurgy; specialization and co-operation in production; assortment exchange.

Interoceanmetall: Szczecin, Poland; f. 1987 to undertake sea-bed mining.

Interrobot: f. 1985; for co-ordination of industrial automation.

Intertextilmash: Moscow, ul. Shchepkina 49, USSR; f. 1973; selected branches of textile machinery construction; co-ordination of research, development and production; specialization and co-operation in production, research, development, construction, sales and service.

Organization for Co-operation in the Roller-Bearings Industry: Warsaw, ul. Senatorska 13/15, Poland; tel. 261546; telex 813489; f. 1964; co-ordinates production of anti-friction roller-bearings for use in engineering; carries out research into standardization and improvements in design and equipment.

JOINT RESEARCH INSTITUTES AND ASSOCIATIONS

Institute for Standardization: 121205 Moscow, Prospekt Kalinina 56, USSR; tel. (095) 290-87-89; telex 411141; f. 1962; prepares technical and industrial standards and conducts quality assessment. Dir M. A. DOVBENKO.

Interetalonpribor: Moscow, Ezdakov per, USSR; f. 1972; measurement technology, joint research, development and production of measuring apparatus.

Interkosmos: 117901 Moscow, Leninskii prospekt 14, USSR; f. 1970; space research.

International Centre for Scientific and Technological Information: Moscow, ul. Kuusinena 21B, USSR; f. 1969; develops methods and technical aspects of information work, provides an information service for participating countries.

International Institute for Economic Problems of the Socialist World System: 103051 Moscow, ul. Stretenka 27–29, USSR; tel. (095) 223-22-18; f. 1970.

Joint Institute for Nuclear Research: 101000 Moscow, POB 79, USSR; tel. (095) 200-22-83; telex 412621; f. 1956 to promote the development of nuclear research among member countries; Committee of Government Plenipotentiaries meets annually to determine future policy and finance; Institute includes research laboratories for: Nuclear Problems, High Energies, Theoretical Physics, Neutron Physics, Nuclear Reactions, Computing and Automation, New Methods of Acceleration. Mems: CMEA countries and the Democratic People's Republic of Korea. Dir D. KISS (Hungary).

TRANSPORT ORGANIZATIONS

International Shipowners Association: 81-376 Gdynia, Sieroszewskiego 7, Poland; tel. 210974; telex 54250; f. 1970; members co-operate in technical, operational, documentary and legal matters concerning maritime traffic. Mems: four national associations and five shipping companies from nine countries. Pres. J. STRANSKY; Sec.-Gen. A. I. FROLOV.

Interport: 70-464 Szczecin, ul. Armii Czerwonej 37, Poland; f. 1973; co-ordination and rationalization of seaport capacities.

OPW: ul. Italska 37, Prague, Czechoslovakia; f. 1963; railway freight transport.

Ship-chartering Co-ordination Bureau: 121205 Moscow, Prospekt Kalinina 56, USSR; tel. 290-97-46; telex 411159; f. 1952; co-operation in rationalizing maritime freight. Dir G. P. KOSTYLEV.

CURRENCY AND CREDIT ORGANIZATIONS

See chapters on the International Bank for Economic Co-operation and the International Investment Bank.

PUBLICATIONS

Statistical Yearbook.

Survey of CMEA Activities (annually).

Economic Co-operation of the CMEA Member Countries (monthly in Russian; quarterly in English and Spanish).

Press Bulletin.

International Agricultural Journal.

Books (between 10 and 15 a year) and press releases.

COUNCIL OF ARAB ECONOMIC UNITY

Address: POB 925100, Amman, Jordan.
Telephone: 664326-9.
Telex: 21900.
The first meeting of the Council was held in 1964.

MEMBERS

Egypt
Iraq
Jordan
Kuwait
Libya
Mauritania
Palestine Liberation Organization
Somalia
Sudan
Syria
United Arab Emirates
Yemen

Organization
(October 1990)

COUNCIL

The Council consists of representatives of member states, usually ministers of economy, finance and trade. It meets twice a year; meetings are chaired by the representative of each country for one year.

GENERAL SECRETARIAT

Entrusted with the implementation of the Council's decisions and with proposing work plans, including efforts to encourage participation by member states in the Arab Economic Unity Agreement. The Secretariat also compiles statistics, conducts research and publishes studies on Arab economic problems and on the effects of major world economic trends.
Secretary-General: HASAN IBRAHIM.
Assistant Secretary-General: MAHMOUD KHALIL EL-GAZZAR.

COMMITTEES

There are seven standing committees: preparatory, follow-up and Arab Common Market development; Permanent Delegates; budget; economic planning; fiscal and monetary matters; customs and trade planning and co-ordination; statistics. There are also seven 'ad hoc' committees, including meetings of experts on tariffs, trade promotion and trade legislation.

Activities

A five-year work plan for the General Secretariat in 1986-90 was approved in December 1985. Like the previous five-year plan, it included the co-ordination of measures leading to a customs union subject to a unified administration; market and commodity studies; unification of statistical terminology and methods of data collection; studies for the formation of new joint Arab companies and federations; formulation of specific programmes for agricultural and industrial co-ordination and for improving road and railway networks.

ARAB COMMON MARKET

Members: Egypt, Iraq, Jordan, Libya, Mauritania, Syria and Yemen.

Based on a resolution passed by the Council in August 1964; its implementation is supervised by the Council and does not constitute a separate organization. Customs duties and other taxes on trade between the member countries were eliminated in annual stages, the process being completed in 1971. The second stage was to be the adoption of a full customs union, and ultimately all restrictions on trade between the member countries, including quotas, and restrictions on residence, employment and transport, were to be abolished. In practice, however, the trading of national products has not been freed from all monetary, quantitative and administrative restrictions.

Between 1978 and 1989, the following measures were undertaken by the Council for the development of the Arab Common Market:

Introduction of flexible membership conditions for the least developed Arab states (Mauritania, Somalia, Sudan, People's Democratic Republic of Yemen, Yemen Arab Republic).

Approval in principle of a fund to compensate the least developed countries for financial losses incurred as a result of joining the Arab Common Market.

Approval of legal, technical and administrative preparations for unification of tariffs levied on products imported from non-member countries.

Formation of a committee of ministerial deputies to deal with problems in the application of market rulings and to promote the organization's activities.

Adoption of unified customs legislation and of an integrated programme aimed at enhancing trade between member states and expanding members' productive capacity.

MULTILATERAL AGREEMENTS

The Council has initiated the following multilateral agreements aimed at achieving economic unity:

Agreement on Basic Levels of Social Insurance.
Agreement on Reciprocity in Social Insurance Systems.
Agreement on Labour Mobility.
Agreement on Organization of Transit Trade.
Agreement on Avoidance of Double Taxation and Elimination of Tax Evasion.
Agreement on Co-operation in Collection of Taxes.
Agreement on Capital Investment and Mobility.
Agreement on Settlement of Investment Disputes between Host Arab Countries and Citizens of Other Countries.

JOINT VENTURES

A number of multilateral organizations in industry and agriculture have been formed on the principle that faster development and economies of scale may be achieved by combining the efforts of member states. In industries that are new to the member countries, Arab Joint Companies are formed, while existing industries are co-ordinated by the setting up of Arab Specialized Unions. The unions are for closer co-operation on problems of production and marketing, and to help companies deal as a group in international markets. The companies are intended to be self-supporting on a purely commercial basis; they may issue shares to citizens of the participating countries. The joint ventures are:

Arab Joint Companies (cap. = capital; figures in Kuwaiti dinars unless otherwise stated):

Arab Company for Drug Industries and Medical Appliances: POB 925161, Amman, Jordan; cap. 60m.

Arab Company for Industrial Investment: POB 2154, Baghdad, Iraq; cap. 150m.

Arab Company for Livestock Development: POB 5305, Damascus, Syria; tel. 666037; telex 11376; cap. 60m.

Arab Mining Company: POB 20198, Amman, Jordan; telex 21169; cap. 120m.

Specialized Arab Unions and Federations:

Arab Co-operative Federation: POB 57640, Baghdad, Iraq; telex 2685.

Arab Federation for Cement and Building Materials: POB 9015, Damascus, Syria.

Arab Federation of Chemical Fertilizers Producers: POB 23696, Kuwait.

Arab Federation of Engineering Industries: POB 509, Baghdad, Iraq; tel. 776-1101; telex 2724.

Arab Federation of Leather Industries: POB 2188, Damascus, Syria.

Arab Federation of Paper Industries: POB 5456, Baghdad, Iraq.

Arab Federation of Shipping Industries: POB 1161, Baghdad, Iraq.

Arab Federation of Textile Industries: POB 620, Damascus, Syria.

Arab Seaports Federation: Basrah, Iraq.

Arab Sugar Federation: POB 195, Khartoum, Sudan.

INTERNATIONAL ORGANIZATIONS   Council of Arab Economic Unity

Arab Union of Fish Producers: POB 15064, Baghdad, Iraq; tel. 551-1261.
Arab Union of Food Industries: POB 13025, Baghdad, Iraq.
Arab Union of Land Transport: POB 926324, Amman, Jordan.
Arab Union of Pharmaceutical Manufacturers and Medical Appliance Manufacturers: POB 1124, Amman, Jordan; tel. 665320; telex 21528.
Arab Union of Railways: POB 6599, Aleppo, Syria; tel. 220302; telex 331009.

PUBLICATIONS
Economic Report of the General Secretary (2 a year).
Progress Report (2 a year).
Arab Economic Unity Bulletin (2 a year).
Statistical Yearbook for Arab Countries.
Annual Bulletin for Arab Countries' Foreign Trade Statistics.
Yearbook for Intra-Arab Trade Statistics.
Yearbook of National Accounts for Arab Countries.
Demographic Yearbook for Arab Countries.
Annual Bulletin for Official Exchange Rates of Arab Currencies.
Annual Bibliography.
Guide to Studies prepared by Secretariat.

128

THE COUNCIL OF EUROPE

Address: BP 431, R6-67006 Strasbourg Cedex, France.
Telephone: (88) 41-20-00.
Telex: 870943.
Fax: (88) 41-27-81.

The Council was founded in May 1949 to achieve a greater unity between its members, to facilitate their economic and social progress and to uphold the principles of parliamentary democracy. Membership has risen from the original 10 to 24.

MEMBERS*

Austria	Liechtenstein
Belgium	Luxembourg
Cyprus	Malta
Denmark	Netherlands
Finland	Norway
France	Portugal
Germany	San Marino
Greece	Spain
Hungary	Sweden
Iceland	Switzerland
Ireland	Turkey
Italy	United Kingdom

* Czechoslovakia, Poland and Yugoslavia applied for full membership in 1990, and Bulgaria and Romania declared their intention of applying.

Organization
(October 1990)

COMMITTEE OF MINISTERS

The Committee consists of the Ministers of Foreign Affairs of all member states; it decides with binding effect all matters of internal organization, makes recommendations to governments and may also draw up conventions and agreements; it also discusses matters of political concern, such as European co-operation and North-South relations, United Nations activities, the protection of human rights and prevention of terrorism. It usually meets in April/May and November each year.

CONFERENCES OF SPECIALIZED MINISTERS

There are 19 Conferences of specialized ministers, meeting regularly for intergovernmental co-operation in various fields.

MINISTERS' DEPUTIES

Senior diplomats are accredited to the Council as permanent representatives of their governments, and deal with most of the routine work at monthly meetings. Any decision reached by the Deputies has the same force as one adopted by the Ministers.

PARLIAMENTARY ASSEMBLY

President: ANDERS BJÖRCK (Sweden).
Chairman of the Socialist Group: KARL AHRENS (Germany).
Chairman of the Group of the European People's Party: ADOLFO SARTI (Italy).
Chairman of the European Democratic (Conservative) Group: Sir GEOFFREY FINSBERG (UK).
Chairman of the Liberal Democratic and Reformers' Group: BJØRN ELMQUIST (Denmark).
Chairman of the United European Left Group: INGER HARMS (Denmark).

Members are elected or appointed by their national parliaments from among the members thereof; political parties in each delegation follow the proportion of their strength in the national parliament. Members do not represent their governments; they are spokesmen for public opinion. The Assembly has 183 members: 18 each for France, Germany, Italy and the United Kingdom; 12 each for Spain and Turkey; seven each for Belgium, Greece, the Netherlands and Portugal; six each for Austria, Hungary, Sweden and Switzerland; five each for Denmark, Finland and Norway; four for Ireland; three each for Cyprus, Iceland, Luxembourg and Malta; and two each for Liechtenstein and San Marino. Israel has permanent observer status, while the legislative assemblies of Bulgaria, Czechoslovakia, Poland, the USSR and Yugoslavia enjoy 'guest status'. A delegation from Albania attended the Assembly as an observer in 1990.

The Assembly meets in ordinary session once a year for not more than a month. The session is usually divided into three parts held in January–February, April–May and September–October. The Assembly may submit recommendations to the Committee of Ministers, pass resolutions, discuss reports and any matters of common European interest. It is also a consultative body to the Committee of Ministers, and elects the Secretary-General, the Deputy Secretary-General, the Clerk of the Assembly and the members of the European Court of Human Rights.

Standing Committee: Represents the Assembly when it is not in session, and may adopt Recommendations to the Committee of Ministers and Resolutions on behalf of the Assembly. Consists of the President, Vice-Presidents, Chairmen of the Ordinary Committees and a number of ordinary members. Meets at least three times a year (once in 'mini' session).

Ordinary Committees: political, economic and development, social, health and family affairs, legal, culture and education, science and technology, environment, regional planning and local authorities, migration, refugees and demography, rules of procedure, agriculture, relations with European non-member countries, parliamentary and public relations, budget and intergovernmental work programme.

SECRETARIAT

Secretary-General: CATHERINE LALUMIÈRE (France).
Deputy Secretary-General: GAETANO ADINOLFI (Italy).
Clerk of the Parliamentary Assembly: HEINRICH KLEBES (Germany).

Activities

In an effort to harmonize national laws, to put the citizens of member countries on an equal footing and to pool certain resources and facilities, the Council has concluded a number of Conventions and Agreements covering particular aspects of European co-operation. By September 1989 a total of 133 treaties had been concluded, of which 24 had not yet come into force. In May 1989 the Council of Ministers adopted a Declaration on the future role of the organization, undertaking to increase co-operation with the European Community and with Eastern European countries.

HUMAN RIGHTS

The promotion and development of human rights is one of the major tasks of the Council of Europe. All member states are parties to the European Convention for the Protection of Human Rights and Fundamental Freedoms of 1950. The Steering Committee for Human Rights is responsible for inter-governmental co-operation in human rights and fundamental freedoms; it works to strengthen the effectiveness of systems for protecting human rights, to identify potential threats and challenges to human rights, and to encourage education and provide information on the subject. It was responsible for the preparation of the European Ministerial Conference on Human Rights (1985), and the elaboration of the European Convention for the Prevention of Torture, which entered into force in February 1989. The Convention provides for the establishment of an independent committee of experts, empowered to visit all places where persons are deprived of their liberty by a public authority.

European Commission of Human Rights

The Commission has 23 members. It is competent to examine complaints made either by a contracting party, or in certain cases, by an individual, non-governmental organization or group of individuals, that the European Convention for the Protection of Human Rights and Fundamental Freedoms has been violated by one or more of the contracting parties. If the Commission decides to admit the application, it then ascertains the full facts of the case and places itself at the disposal of the parties in order to try and reach a friendly settlement. If no settlement is reached, the

INTERNATIONAL ORGANIZATIONS

Council of Europe

Commission sends a report to the Committee of Ministers in which it states an opinion as to whether there has been a violation of the Convention. It is then for the Committee of Ministers or, if the case is referred to it, the Court to decide whether or not a violation has taken place. By the end of 1988 14,400 human rights applications had been lodged.

President: Prof. CARL AAGE NØRGAARD (Denmark).
First Vice-President: Prof. Dr JOCHEN A. FROWEIN (Germany).
Second Vice-President: Prof. STEPHAN TRECHSEL (Switzerland).
Secretary: HANS-CHRISTIAN KRÜGER (Germany).

European Court of Human Rights

The Court comprises 23 judges. It may deal with a case only after the Commission has acknowledged the failure of efforts for a friendly settlement. The following may bring a case before the Court, provided that the High Contracting Party or Parties concerned have accepted its compulsory jurisdiction or, failing that, with the consent of the High Contracting Party or Parties concerned: the Commission, a High Contracting Party whose national is alleged to be a victim, a High Contracting Party which referred the case to the Commission, and a High Contracting Party against which the complaint has been lodged. In the event of dispute as to whether the Court has jurisdiction, the matter is settled by the Court. The judgment of the Court is final. The Court may, in certain circumstances, give advisory opinions at the request of the Committee of Ministers.

President: ROLV RYSSDAL (Norway).
Vice-President: JOHN J. CREMONA (Malta).
Registrar: MARC-ANDRÉ EISSEN (France).

MASS MEDIA

In 1982 the Committee of Ministers adopted a Declaration on the freedom of expression and information, which forms the basis for the Council of Europe's mass media activities. Activities in the media field are carried out by a steering committee of governmental experts and cover all aspects of mass communication—legal, political, cultural, economic, social and technical—notably as far as current developments relating to broadcasting are concerned.

From 1984 onwards, the Committee of Ministers adopted a number of recommendations concerning principles on television advertising (in particular when it is transmitted by satellite), use of satellite capacity for television and sound radio, promotion of audio-visual production, copyright aspects of television by satellite and cable, private copying of videograms and phonograms, audio-visual piracy and the distribution of videograms having a violent or pornographic content.

In early 1987 the Committee of Ministers instructed its Steering Committee on the Mass Media (CDMM) to draw up a European Convention on transfrontier television. The Convention was adopted in March 1989, and by September it had been signed by 10 member states. It establishes a framework for the transfrontier circulation of television programme services. It guarantees freedom of reception and establishes the principle of non-restriction of the retransmission of services conforming to minimum standards embodied in it.

The CDMM is responsible for preparing European ministerial conferences on mass media policy, of which the third was to be held in 1991. During 1989 the CDMM was engaged in considering: sponsorship and new forms of commercial promotion; exclusivity rights for major events; finance and taxation in the audio-visual sector; measures to promote European audio-visual works; collection of data on media legislation; new developments in sound radio broadcasting; copyright issues relating to reprography, satellite broadcasting and cable distribution; and unauthorized use of television signals.

SOCIAL WELFARE

The European Social Charter, in force since 1965, is now applied in Austria, Cyprus, Denmark, France, Germany, Greece, Iceland, Ireland, Italy, Malta, the Netherlands, Norway, Spain, Sweden and the United Kingdom; it lays down the rights and principles which are the basis of the Council's social policy, and guarantees a number of social and economic rights to the citizen, including the right to work, the right to form workers' organizations, the right to social security and social assistance, the right of the family to protection and the right of migrant workers to protection and assistance. In May 1988 the Charter was completed by an Additional Protocol which extends these rights.

The European Code of Social Security and its Protocol entered into force in 1968; by 1990 the Code and Protocol had been ratified by Belgium, Germany, Luxembourg, the Netherlands, Norway, Portugal and Sweden, while the Code alone had been ratified by Denmark, France, Greece, Ireland, Italy, Switzerland, Turkey and the United Kingdom. These instruments set minimum standards for medical care and the following benefits: sickness, old-age, unemployment, employment injury, family, maternity, invalidity and survivor's benefit. A revision of these instruments, aiming to provide higher standards and greater flexibility, was completed for signature in 1990.

The European Convention on Social Security, in force since 1977, now applies in Austria, Belgium, Luxembourg, the Netherlands, Portugal, Spain and Turkey; most of the provisions apply automatically, while others are subject to the conclusion of additional multilateral or bilateral agreements. The Convention is concerned with establishing equality of treatment for nationals of member states and with ensuring the granting and maintenance of social security rights by such means as the adding together of insurance periods completed in more than one state; two interim agreements are also in force, which will progressively be superseded by the Convention.

A number of resolutions passed by the Committee of Ministers give guidance for intergovernmental action on particular aspects of social policy, welfare or labour law. Eight states are co-operating in drawing up common standards on the protection of safety and health at work.

The Council of Europe operates annual social research programmes, in which groups of specialists make comparative studies in social welfare and labour, covering up to 20 states.

HEALTH

Through a series of expert committees, the Council aims at ensuring constant co-operation in Europe in a variety of health-related fields: e.g., promotion of education for health, evaluation of programmes for the prevention of diseases, assessment and implementation of new methods of treatment and techniques, adaptation of training curricula for health personnel. It strives to formulate cost-effective policies in order to contain the rising costs of health care.

A programme of Medical Fellowships enables members of the health professions to study new techniques and participate in co-ordinated research programmes. Availability of blood and blood products (also of very rare groups) has been ensured through European Agreements and a network of co-operating transfusion centres. Advances in this field and in histocompatibility are continuously assessed by expert committees.

Twelve states co-operate in establishing common standards regarding the use of pesticides, food additives, flavouring substances, and plastic materials that come into contact with food. They also deal with pharmaceutical and cosmetic products, residues of veterinary drugs in food of animal origin, and wood protection products.

Thirteen states co-operate in establishing a coherent policy on the rehabilitation of disabled people, aiming to allow such people the greatest possible degree of independence, equality and participation. Assistance is given in the assessment of national legislation in this field.

In the co-operation group to combat drug abuse and illicit drug trafficking (Pompidou Group), 19 states work together at ministerial level to counteract drug abuse. The Group follows a multi-disciplinary approach embracing in particular legislation, law enforcement, prevention, treatment, rehabilitation and data collection.

The European Agreement on the restriction of the use of certain detergents in washing and cleaning products entered into force in 1971 (amended by a protocol, 1984). There are 10 parties to the Agreement.

The Convention on the Elaboration of a European Pharmacopoeia (establishing standards for medicinal substances) entered into force in May 1974: in 1989 19 states were parties to the Convention and WHO and the EEC participate in the meetings. Publication of a second edition began in 1980: it covered about 700 substances by 1988.

POPULATION

The European Population Committee, an intergovernmental committee of scientists and government officials engaged in demography, monitors and analyses population trends in member states and informs governments and the public of developments that may require political action. It compiles an annual review of demographic developments and publishes the results of studies of particular aspects of population, for example the implications of declining fertility, the changing age structure of European populations, parental responsibilities, and the demographic consequences for Europe of the increase in world population. Seminars and conferences are held; a Population Conference is planned for 1992.

MIGRANT WORKERS AND REFUGEES

The European Convention on the Legal Status of Migrant Workers, in force since 1983, was applicable by 1989 to France the Netherlands, Norway, Portugal, Spain, Sweden and Turkey. The Convention is based on the principle of equality of treatment for migrant workers and the nationals of the host country as to housing, working conditions, and social security. The convention also upholds the principle of the right to family reunion.

During 1986–91 the European Committee on Migration was engaged on a multi-disciplinary project on community relations. Experiments in inter-cultural education are sponsored. Vocational training grants are awarded to student-instructors and instructor-trainees.

SOCIAL DEVELOPMENT FUND

The Council of Europe Social Development Fund was created in 1956 (as the Resettlement Fund) to make loans for the resettlement of refugees or those made homeless by natural disasters, and to assist in job creation, vocational training and health education schemes. In 1989 20 countries were members of the Fund and the loans granted since the Fund's inception amounted to about US $7,500m.

LEGAL MATTERS

The European Committee on Legal Co-operation supervises the work programme for international, administrative, civil and commercial law. Specialized committees of legal experts work under its direction. There are also committees concerned with the movement of persons, refugees and bio-ethics. Numerous conventions have been adopted, on matters which include: foreign liabilities; information on foreign law; consular functions; bearer securities; state immunity; motorists' liability; adoption; nationality; animal protection; mutual aid in administrative matters; custody of children; data protection; insider trading; bankruptcy; and the legal status of non-governmental organizations. In February 1990 ministers agreed to introduce a legally-binding code of ethics on medical research, and in June the Secretary-General proposed the adoption of a convention for the protection of the human person with regard to the biomedical sciences. Conferences of ministers of justice of member states, although not formally under the Council of Europe, make proposals for the Council's work programme.

CRIME

The European Committee on Crime Problems has prepared conventions on such matters as extradition, mutual assistance, recognition and enforcement of foreign judgments, the transfer of proceedings, the suppression of terrorism, the transfer of prisoners and the compensation to be paid to victims of violent crime. A number of resolutions on various questions relating to penal law, penology and criminology have been adopted by the Committee of Ministers.

The Criminological Scientific Council is composed of specialists in law, psychology, sociology and related sciences. It advises the European Committee on Crime Problems and criminological research conferences.

Penological matters are examined by the directors of prison administrations whose resolutions and conclusions serve as guidelines to the member states for the penal policy to be adopted. A Committee on Co-operation in Prison Affairs prepared new European Prison Rules in 1987 and was preparing Rules for alternatives to imprisonment in 1989.

EDUCATION AND CULTURE

The Council for Cultural Co-operation implements the educational and cultural programme which gives priority to primary education, human rights education in schools, education and cultural development of migrants, modern language teaching, reform and development of tertiary education, adult education and social development, cultural development policies at regional and local level, evaluation of national cultural policies, and action to promote reading, poetry and translation. It administers the Cultural Fund, which was established to promote and finance educational and cultural activities in accordance with the statute of the Council of Europe. Mems: member states and other signatories of the Cultural Convention, namely Yugoslavia and the Holy See. The Parliamentary Assembly is also represented. Other activities include the European Schools Day Competition, and the management of the European Documentation and Information System in Education (EUDISED).

The Council also organizes Council of Europe Higher Education scholarships, teacher-training courses and bursaries, and European Art Exhibitions.

Secretariat services are provided by the Council of Europe for the standing conference of European ministers of education. Sessions are held every two years. The conference of European ministers responsible for cultural affairs is held every three years.

YOUTH

The European Youth Centre (EYC) is equipped with audio-visual workshops, reading and conference rooms; provides about 40 residential courses a year for youth leaders, on European affairs, problems of modern society, the role of youth, and techniques of leading and organizing youth movements. About 1,500 people can be accommodated annually. A notable feature of the EYC, which it shares with the European Youth Foundation, is its decision-making structure, by which decisions on its programme and general policy matters are, taken by a Governing Board composed of an equal number of youth organizations and government representatives. Each year the EYC organizes symposia on topics of interest to youth organizations.

The European Youth Foundation (EYF) aims to provide financial assistance to European activities of non-governmental youth organizations and began operations in 1973. Since that time more than 150 organizations have received financial aid for carrying out international activities. The total number of young people taking part in meetings supported by the Foundation amounted to about 80,000 by 1989, coming from more than 30 countries. More than 87m. French francs have been distributed.

The European Steering Committee for Intergovernmental Co-operation in the Youth Field conducts research in youth-related matters and prepares for ministerial conferences.

SPORT

The Committee for the Development of Sport, founded in November 1977, has the same membership as the Council for Cultural Co-operation (see above) and administers the Sports Fund. Its activities concentrate on the implementation of the European Sport for All Charter (1975); the role of sport in society (e.g. medical, political, ethical and educational aspects); the practice of sport (activities, special projects, etc.); the diffusion of sports information and co-ordination of sports research. The Committee is also responsible for preparing the conference of European ministers responsible for sport. In 1984 the conference adopted an Anti-Doping Charter for Sport, and in 1985 it adopted the European Convention on Spectator Violence and Misbehaviour at Sports Events. A Charter on Sport for Disabled Persons was adopted in 1986, and an Anti-Doping Convention in 1989.

ENVIRONMENT AND REGIONAL PLANNING

The Steering Committee for the Conservation and Management of the Environment and Natural Habitats, founded in 1962, prepares policy recommendations and promotes co-operation in all environmental questions. It introduced a European Water Charter in 1968, a Soil Charter in 1974 and a Charter on Invertebrates in 1986. The Committee awards the European Diploma for protection of areas of European significance, supervises a network of biogenetic reserves, and maintains 'red lists' of threatened animals and plants.

Sixteen member states, two non-members and the European Community have ratified a Convention on the Conservation of European Wildlife and Natural Habitats, which entered into force in June 1982 and gives total protection to 119 species of plants, 55 mammals, 294 birds, 34 reptiles, 17 amphibians, 115 freshwater fishes, 81 invertebrates and their habitats. A European Campaign for the Countryside was undertaken in 1987–88, attempting to reconcile development with conservation. The Council's NATUROPA Centre provides information and documentation on the environment. Information campaigns on Farming and Wildlife, Mediterranean Coastlines, and Freshwater Fish were under way in 1989.

Regional disparities constitute a major obstacle to the process of European integration. Conferences of ministers of regional planning are held, and in the late 1980s they adopted 'principles of a new land-use policy' aiming at the rational use of land.

LOCAL AND REGIONAL GOVERNMENT

The standing conference of local and regional authorities in Europe was created in 1957 as a representative assembly of regions and municipalities of the member states of the Council of Europe; since April 1976 annual sessions have been chiefly concerned with local government matters, regional planning, regional problems, protection of the environment, town and country planning and social and cultural affairs. Ad hoc conferences and public hearings are also held.

The Steering Committee on Local and Regional Authorities was established in 1988 as a forum for senior officials from ministries of local government, for the exchange of experience between national governments, and for a common approach to the development of the national structures and legislature. The committee studies participation in local affairs and problems of local and regional finance. In 1985 a European Charter of Local Self-Government was opened for signature.

INTERNATIONAL ORGANIZATIONS
Council of Europe

MONUMENTS AND SITES

The Cultural Heritage Committee maintains contact between authorities in charge of historic buildings and encourages public interest. A third conference of ministers responsible for conservation of the architectural heritage was to be held in 1990/91.

A Convention for the Conservation of the Architectural Heritage of Europe, signed by 18 member states, entered into force in 1987.

EXTERNAL RELATIONS

Agreements providing for co-operation and exchange of documents and observers have been concluded with the United Nations and its Agencies, and with most of the European inter-governmental organizations and the Organization of American States. Particularly close relations exist with the European Community, OECD, EFTA and Western European Union.

Israel is represented in the Parliamentary Assembly by an observer, and certain European and other non-member countries have been invited to participate in or send observers to certain meetings of technical committees and specialized conferences.

Relations with non-member states, other organizations and non-governmental organizations are co-ordinated within the Secretariat by the Directorate of Political Affairs.

In 1988 the Council of Europe organized a Campaign on North-South Interdependence and Solidarity, to raise public awareness of global interdependence: this resulted in the 'Madrid Appeal', a series of propositions for action on North-South issues, and an 'Africa-Europe Encounter' held in Benin in September 1989.

FINANCE

The ordinary budget for 1990 was 477m. French francs, of which France, Germany, Italy and the United Kingdom each contributed 16.85%; other states make smaller contributions.

PUBLICATIONS

Forum (quarterly, in English, French, German and Italian).

Catalogue of Publications (annually).

ECONOMIC COMMUNITY OF WEST AFRICAN STATES—ECOWAS

Address: 6 King George V Rd, PMB 12745, Lagos, Nigeria.
Telephone: 636841.
Telex: 22633.

The Treaty of Lagos, establishing ECOWAS, was signed in May 1975 by 15 states, with the object of promoting trade, co-operation and self-reliance in West Africa. Outstanding protocols bringing certain key features of the Treaty into effect were ratified in November 1976. Cape Verde joined in 1977.

MEMBERS

Benin	Guinea	Niger
Burkina Faso	Guinea-Bissau	Nigeria
Cape Verde	Liberia	Senegal
Côte d'Ivoire	Mali	Sierra Leone
The Gambia	Mauritania	Togo
Ghana		

Organization
(October 1990)

CONFERENCE OF HEADS OF STATE AND GOVERNMENT

The Conference, the highest authority of ECOWAS, meets once a year. The Chairman is drawn from the member states in turn.

COUNCIL OF MINISTERS

The Council consists of two representatives from each country; a chairman is drawn from each country in turn. It meets twice a year, and is responsible for the running of the Community.

TRIBUNAL

The treaty provides for a Community Tribunal, whose composition and competence are determined by the Authority of Heads of State and Government; it interprets the provisions of the treaty and settles disputes between member states that are referred to it.

EXECUTIVE SECRETARIAT

The Headquarters of the Executive Secretariat is in Lagos. There was a staff of about 240 in 1986. The Executive Secretary is elected for a four-year term, which may be renewed once only. The Secretariat's operational budget for 1988 was US $7m.
Executive Secretary: Dr ABASS BUNDU (Sierra Leone).

SPECIALIZED COMMISSIONS

There are five commissions:
   (i) Trade, Customs, Immigration, Monetary and Payments;
   (ii) Industry, Agriculture and Natural Resources;
   (iii) Transport, Communications and Energy;
   (iv) Social and Cultural Affairs;
   (v) Administration and finance.

FUND FOR CO-OPERATION, COMPENSATION AND DEVELOPMENT

Address: ave du 24 janvier, Lomé, Togo.
Telex: 5339.

The Fund is administered by a Board of Directors. The chief executive of the Fund is the Managing Director, who holds office for a renewable term of four years. There is a staff of 50. The authorized capital of the Fund was raised from US $90m. to $360m. in 1986. The Fund's first loan was approved in November 1982, amounting to $12.5m. for the initial phase of a telecommunications improvement scheme involving seven member states (see below). By the end of 1985 loans (totalling $6m.) had also been approved for the construction of bridges in Benin and a major highway in Liberia; grants amounting to $665,221 had been approved for Liberia, Mali and Togo, for feasibility studies on the proposed Trans-West African Highway. Grants were also made to finance studies by the Secretariat on energy and monetary affairs. The Fund's investment budget for 1986 amounted to $25.7m. In 1988 agreements were reached with the African Development Bank and the Islamic Development Bank on the co-financing of projects and joint training of staff, and it was agreed that the Fund should be opened to non-regional participants.
Managing Director: MAHANTA FALL (Senegal).

Activities

ECOWAS aims to promote co-operation and development in economic, social and cultural activity, particularly in the fields for which specialized commissions (see above) are appointed, to raise the standard of living of the people of the member countries, increase and maintain economic stability, improve relations among member countries and contribute to the progress and development of Africa.

The treaty provides for compensation for states whose import duties are reduced through trade liberalization and contains a clause permitting safeguard measures in favour of any country affected by economic disturbances through the application of the treaty.

The treaty also contains a commitment to abolish all obstacles to the free movement of people, services and capital, and to promote: harmonization of agricultural policies; common projects in marketing, research and the agriculturally based industries; joint development of economic and industrial policies and elimination of disparities in levels of development; and common monetary policies.

Lack of success in many of ECOWAS' aims has been attributed to the existence of numerous other intergovernmental organizations in the region (such as the francophone CEAO and the Mano River Union, q.v.), and to member governments' lack of commitment, shown by their reluctance to implement policies at the national level, their failure to provide the agreed financial resources (arrears in contributions were reported to total US $58m. at mid-1990), and the absence of national links with the Secretariat.

CUSTOMS UNION

Elimination of tariffs and other obstructions to trade among member states, and the establishment of a common external tariff, were planned over a transitional period of 15 years. At the 1978 Conference of Heads of State and Government it was decided that from 28 May 1979 no member state might increase its customs tariff on goods from another member. This was regarded as the first step towards the abolition of customs duties within the Community. During the first two years import duties on intra-community trade were to be maintained, and then eliminated in phases over the next eight years. Quotas and other restrictions of equivalent effect were to be abolished in the first 10 years. In the remaining five years all differences between external customs tariffs were to be abolished.

The 1980 Conference of Heads of State and Government decided to establish a free trade area for unprocessed agricultural products and handicrafts from May 1981. Tariffs on industrial products made by specified community enterprises were also to be abolished from that date, but implementation was delayed by difficulties in defining the enterprises. From 1 January 1990 tariffs were lifted from 25 listed items manufactured in ECOWAS member states. Over the ensuing decade, tariffs on other industrial products were to be eliminated as follows: the 'most-developed' countries of ECOWAS (Côte d'Ivoire, Ghana, Nigeria and Senegal) were to abolish tariffs on 'priority' products within four years and on 'non-priority' products within six years; the second group (Benin, Guinea, Liberia, Sierra Leone and Togo) were to abolish tariffs on 'priority' products within six years, and on 'non-priority' products within eight years; and the 'least-developed' members (Burkina Faso, Cape Verde, The Gambia, Guinea-Bissau, Mali, Mauritania and Niger) were to abolish tariffs on 'priority' products within eight years and on 'non-priority' products within 10 years.

The 1983 Conference of Heads of State and Government decided to initiate studies on the formation of a single ECOWAS monetary zone. In the same year a programme was approved for the establishment of a computer unit (ASYCUDA) in Lomé, to process customs and trade statistics and to calculate the loss of revenue resulting from the liberalization of intra-community trade. The system was being installed in early 1990.

TRAVEL, TRANSPORT AND COMMUNICATIONS

At the 1979 Conference of Heads of State a Protocol was signed relating to free circulation of the region's citizens and to rights of residence and establishment. The first provision (the right of entry without a visa) came into force in July 1980, following ratification by eight members. The second provision, allowing unlimited rights of residence, was signed in 1986 (although Nigeria indicated that unskilled workers and certain categories of professionals would not be allowed to stay for an indefinite period); by mid-1990, however, the protocol on rights of residence had yet to come into effect.

The Conference also adopted a programme for the improvement and extension of the internal and interstate telecommunications network, 'Intelcom', estimated to cost US $60m. The first and second phases of the programme, comprising the construction of microwave telephone, telex and television links between Ghana and Burkina Faso, Benin and Burkina Faso, Nigeria and Niger, and Mali and Côte d'Ivoire, were completed in October 1988.

A programme for the development of regional transport was adopted by the 1980 Conference. It includes the harmonization of road signs and laws and the construction of new road and rail links between member states. A regional motor insurance ('Brown Card') scheme was launched in July 1984, and a revised regional road map was being drawn up in collaboration with the UN Economic Commission for Africa. In April 1988 a meeting of donor organizations, led by the World Bank, agreed to provide finance amounting to US $276m. for constructing and improving roads in the region.

A feasibility study on the establishment of an ECOWAS shipping line was completed in 1984, and a programme on air traffic safety was begun with the co-operation of the International Civil Aviation Organization. In 1986 a data bank was established to monitor traffic in West African ports, with the aim of improving efficiency.

ECONOMIC DEVELOPMENT

Pre-feasibility studies on the establishment of a private regional investment bank were undertaken by the ECOWAS Secretariat in 1984. The creation of the bank (known as Ecobank Transnational Inc, based in Lomé, Togo) was approved by heads of state and government in November. It opened in March 1988. ECOWAS has a 10% share in the bank. By mid-1990 Ecobank affiliates had been opened in Benin, Côte d'Ivoire, Ghana, Nigeria and Togo. The ECOWAS Reinsurance Corporation (Eco-Re) was expected to begin operations in 1989.

The West African Industrial Forum, sponsored by ECOWAS, is held every two years to promote regional industrial investment. The ninth Forum was to be held in Dakar, Senegal, in December 1990, with assistance from the European Community and UNIDO.

In 1987 ECOWAS launched an Economic Recovery Programme (ERP) for 1988-91. The ERP originally envisaged expenditure of US $920m. (later increased to $1,670m.) for 136 regional projects, of which 64 were concerned with rural development, 21 with transport improvements and 23 with industry. By December 54 projects were described as ready for execution, while 66 were at the stage of feasibility studies, and 16 still awaited funding.

In November 1988 a conference of regional ministers of finance and governors of central banks was convened to discuss member countries' indebtedness.

In June 1990 the Conference of Heads of State and Government agreed to adopt measures that would create a single monetary zone in the region by 1994. The Conference also discussed the likely effects of the completion of the European Community's 'single market', scheduled for 1992.

DEFENCE

At the third Conference of Heads of State and Government a protocol of non-aggression was signed. Thirteen members signed a protocol on mutual defence assistance at the 1981 Conference. A mutual defence force and defence council were planned. In 1990 a Standing Mediation Committee was formed to mediate in disputes between member states. In July ECOWAS ministers attempted to mediate in civil conflict in Liberia, and in August they sent an ECOWAS Monitoring Group (ECOMOG—comprising about 4,000 troops from The Gambia, Ghana, Guinea, Nigeria and Sierra Leone) to Liberia, to try to bring about a cease-fire between the rival factions there, to restore public order, and to establish an interim government, until elections could be held. In September ECOMOG failed to prevent the capture and killing of the Liberian President, Samuel Doe, by rebel forces, and fighting between rival groups continued. In October it was announced that the size of ECOMOG was to be increased to 9,000 troops.

ENERGY

The 1981 Conference agreed on a work programme for energy development, involving a regional analysis of energy use and plans for increasing efficiency and finding alternative sources. The creation of an Energy Resources Development Fund was approved in 1982. In October 1983 it was announced that (in co-operation with UNESCO) a regional information centre and data base was to be set up in Dakar, Senegal, to disseminate information on renewable energy. In 1987 plans were announced for the construction of an ECOWAS refinery, to supply refined petroleum products for the region.

AGRICULTURE

An Agricultural Development Strategy was adopted in 1982, aiming at sub-regional self-sufficiency by the year 2000. The strategy included plans for selecting seeds and cattle species, and called for solidarity among member states during international commodity negotiations. Seven seed selection and multiplication centres and eight livestock-breeding centres were designated in 1984. In 1988 it was announced that ECOWAS was to establish a cattle-ranch in southern Mali, over an area of 18,000 ha, to breed cattle for distribution in the ECOWAS region. A tsetse-fly control programme was also undertaken.

The years 1983-93 were designated as an ECOWAS tree-planting decade by the 1982 Conference.

SOCIAL PROGRAMME

Four organizations have been established within ECOWAS by the Executive Secretariat: the Organization of Trade Unions of West Africa, which held its first meeting in 1984; the West African Youth Association; the West African Universities' Association; and the West Africa Women's Association (whose statutes were approved by a meeting of ministers of social affairs in May 1987). Regional sports competitions are held annually. The West African Health Organization (q.v.) was formed in 1989 by ECOWAS member states.

TOURISM

In March 1987 regional ministers of tourism met for the first time and agreed to integrate policies on the development of tourism and to exchange information.

ENVIRONMENT

The 1988 Conference adopted a resolution condemning the dumping of nuclear and industrial waste in Africa by countries outside the region. All members agreed to promulgate domestic legislation prohibiting such dumping, and in 1989 it was announced that a treaty was to be drafted on the subject.

THE EUROPEAN COMMUNITY

No final decision has been made on a headquarters for the Community. Meetings of the principal organs take place in Brussels, Luxembourg and Strasbourg.

The European Coal and Steel Community (ECSC) was created by a treaty signed in Paris on 18 April 1951 (effective from 25 July 1952) to pool the coal and steel production of the six original members (see below). It was seen as a first step towards a united Europe. The European Economic Community (EEC) and European Atomic Energy Community (Euratom) were established by separate treaties signed in Rome on 25 March 1957 (effective from 1 January 1958), the former to create a Common Market and to approximate economic policies, the latter to promote growth in nuclear industries. The common institutions of the three Communities were established by a treaty signed in Brussels on 8 April 1965 (effective from 1 July 1967). The three institutions are normally regarded, in practice, as a single entity, the European Community, and since 1967 they have been supervised by a single Commission (see p. 140).

MEMBERS

Belgium*	Greece	Netherlands*
Denmark	Ireland	Portugal
France*	Italy*	Spain
Germany*	Luxembourg*	United Kingdom

* Original members. Denmark, Ireland and the United Kingdom joined on 1 January 1973, and Greece on 1 January 1981. In a referendum held in February 1982, the inhabitants of Greenland voted to end their membership of the Community, entered into when under full Danish rule. Greenland's withdrawal took effect from 1 February 1985. Portugal and Spain became members on 1 January 1986. Following the reunification of Germany in October 1990, the former German Democratic Republic immediately became part of the Community, although a transitional period was to be allowed before certain Community legislation took effect there.

PERMANENT REPRESENTATIVES OF MEMBER STATES

Belgium: 62 Belliardstraat, 1040 Brussels; tel. (02) 233-21-11; P. DE SCHOUTHEETE.

Denmark: 73 rue d'Arlon, 1040 Brussels; tel. (02) 233-08-11; JAKOB RYTTER.

France: 67 rue Ducale, 1000 Brussels; tel. (02) 511-49-55; telex 21265; JEAN VIDAL.

Germany: 19–21 rue J. de Lalaing, 1040 Brussels; tel. (02) 238-18-11; telex 21745; JÜRGEN TRUMPF.

Greece: 71 ave de Cortenberg, 1040 Brussels; tel. (02) 739-56-11; CONSTANTINOS LYBEROPOULOS.

Ireland: 5 ave Galilée, bte 22, 1030 Brussels; tel. (02) 218-06-05; telex 26730; JOHN CAMPBELL.

Italy: 74 rue de la Loi, 1040 Brussels; tel. (02) 230-81-70; telex 01121462; PIETRO CALAMIA.

Luxembourg: 211 rue du Noyer, 1040 Brussels; tel. (02) 735-20-60; telex 21707; JOSEPH WEYLAND.

Netherlands: 46 ave des Arts, 1040 Brussels; tel. (02) 513-77-75; telex 26125; fax (02) 513-08-29; P. C. NIEMAN.

Portugal: 11-13 rue Marie-Thérèse, 1040 Brussels; tel. (02) 211-12-11; JOSÉ CÉSAR PAVLOVRO DAS NEVES.

Spain: 52 blvd du Régent, 1000 Brussels; tel. (02) 509-86-11; CARLOS WESTENDORP Y CABEZA.

United Kingdom: 6 rond-point Robert Schumann, 1040 Brussels; tel. (02) 230-62-05; telex 24312; J. O. KERR.

PERMANENT MISSIONS TO THE EUROPEAN COMMUNITIES, WITH AMBASSADORS
(September 1990)

Afghanistan: 32 ave Raphaël, 75016 Paris, France; tel. (1) 45-27-66-09; Chargé d'affaires: ABDULLAH KESHTMAND.

Algeria: 209 ave Molière, 1060 Brussels; tel. (02) 343-50-78; NOUREDDINE KERROUM.

Angola: 182 rue Franz Merjay, 1180 Brussels; tel. (02) 344-49-80; telex 63170; EMÍLIO JOSÉ DE CARVALHO GUERRA.

Antigua and Barbuda: 15 Thayer St, London, W1, England; tel. (071) 486-7073; telex 8814503; JAMES A. E. THOMAS.

Argentina: 225 ave Louise (7e étage), 1050 Brussels; tel. (02) 648-93-71; telex 23079; DIEGO RAMIRO GUELAR.

Australia: 6/8 rue Guimard, 1040 Brussels; tel. (02) 231-05-00; telex 21834; PETER C. J. CURTIS.

Austria: 35–36 ave des Klauwaerts, 1050 Brussels; tel. (02) 649-00-83; telex 21407; WOLFGANG WOLTE.

Bahamas: 10 Chesterfield St, London, W1X 8AH, England; tel. (071) 408-4488; telex 892617; PATRICIA RODGERS.

Bangladesh: 29–31 rue Jacques Jordaens, 1050 Brussels; tel. (02) 640-55-00; telex 63189; A. K. M. KAMALUDDIN CHOWDHURY.

Barbados: 14 ave Lloyd George, 1050 Brussels; tel. (02) 648-12-28; telex 63926; RASHID ORLANDO MARVILLE.

Belize: 200 Sutherland Ave, London, W9 1RX, England; tel. (071) 266-3485; telex 8814503; Sir EDNEY CAIN.

Benin: 5 ave de l'Observatoire, 1180 Brussels; tel. (02) 374-91-91; telex 24568; MAMADOU TAÏROU DJAOUGA.

Bhutan: 17–19 chemin Champs-d'Amier, 1209 Geneva, Switzerland; tel. (022) 7987971; Dasho NADO RINCHHEN.

Bolivia: 176 ave Louise, 1050 Brussels; tel. (02) 647-27-18; telex 63494; EDUARDO RUÍZ GARCÍA.

Botswana: 169 ave de Tervuren, 1150 Brussels; tel. (02) 735-20-70; telex 22849; ERNEST SIPHO MPOFU.

Brazil: 350 ave Louise (6e étage), 1050 Brussels; tel. (02) 640-20-40; fax (02) 648-80-40; GERALDO EGIDIO DA COSTA HOLANDA CAVALCANTI.

Brunei: 49 Cromwell Rd, London, SW7 2ED, England; tel. (071) 581-0521; telex 888369; fax (071) 225-0804; Pengiran SETIA RAJA Pengiran Haji JAYA.

Bulgaria: 58 ave Hamoir, 1180 Brussels; tel. (02) 374-59-63; ATANAS G. GUINEV.

Burkina Faso: 16 place Guy d'Arezzo, 1060 Brussels; tel. (02) 345-99-11; AMADÉ OUEDRAOGO.

Burundi: 46 square Marie-Louise, 1040 Brussels; tel. (02) 230-45-35; telex 23572; JULIAN NAHAYO.

Cameroon: 131 ave Brugmann, 1060 Brussels; tel. (02) 345-18-70; telex 24117; ISABELLE BASSONG.

Canada: 2 ave de Tervuren, 1040 Brussels; tel. (02) 735-91-25; DANIEL MOLGAT.

Cape Verde: 44 Koninginnegracht, 2514 AK The Hague, Netherlands; tel. (070) 46-96-23; telex 34321; LUÍS DE MATOS MONTEIRO DA FONSECA.

Central African Republic: 416 blvd Lambermont, 1030 Brussels; tel. (02) 242-28-80; telex 0222 493; JOSÉ-MARIE PEHOUA.

Chad: 52 blvd Lambermont, 1030 Brussels; tel. (02) 215-19-75; ABDOULAYE LAMANA.

Chile: 326 ave Louise, Boîte 22 (5e étage), 1050 Brussels; tel. (02) 649-94-83; telex 61442; DIEGO VALENZUELA RODRÍGUEZ.

China, People's Republic: 445 ave de Tervuren, 1150 Brussels; tel. (02) 771-58-57; XIA DAOSHENG.

Colombia: 44 rue Van Eyck (2e étage), 1050 Brussels; tel. (02) 649-56-79; telex 25254; MANUEL JOSÉ CARDENAS.

Comoros: 15 rue de la Néva, 75008 Paris, France; tel. (1) 47-63-81-78; telex 642390; ALI MLAHAILI.

Congo: 16 ave F. D. Roosevelt, 1050 Brussels: tel. (02) 648-38-56; telex 23677; AMBROISE GAMBOUELE.

Costa Rica: 489 ave Louise, bte 23, 1050 Brussels; tel. (02) 640-55-41.

Côte d'Ivoire: 234 ave F. D. Roosevelt, 1050 Brussels; tel. (02) 672-23-57; telex 21993; CHARLES VALY TUHO.

Cuba: 77 rue Robert Jones, 1180 Brussels; tel. (02) 343-00-20; TERESITA AVERHOFF PURÓN.

Cyprus: 83–85 rue de la Loi, 1040 Brussels; tel. (02) 230-12-95; NICOS AGATHOCLEOUS.

Czechoslovakia: 152 ave Adolphe Buyl, 1050 Brussels; tel. (02) 647-68-09; KAREL LUKAS.

Djibouti: 24 ave F. D. Roosevelt, 1050 Brussels; tel. (02) 646-41-51; telex 27242; HASSAN IDRISS AHMED.

Dominica: 12 rue des Bollandistes, 1040 Brussels; tel. (02) 733-43-28; CHARLES SAVARIN.

INTERNATIONAL ORGANIZATIONS — European Community

Dominican Republic: 160A ave Louise, 1050 Brussels; tel. (02) 646-08-40.

Ecuador: 70 chaussée de Charleroi, 1060 Brussels; tel. (02) 537-91-30; XAVIER PÉREZ MARTÍNEZ.

Egypt: 44 ave Léo Errera, 1180 Brussels; tel. (02) 345-52-53; telex 23716; HOUSSEIN MOHAMED EL KAMEL.

El Salvador: 3 blvd Saint-Michel, 1040 Brussels; tel. (02) 733-04-85; ANA CRISTINA SOL.

Equatorial Guinea: 6 rue Alfred de Vigny, 75008 Paris, France; tel. (1) 47-66-44-33.

Ethiopia: 32 blvd Saint-Michel, 1040 Brussels; tel. (02) 733-49-29; telex 62285; fax (02) 732-18-51; WOLDE AMANUEL HAILU.

Fiji: 66 ave de Cortenberg (7e étage, boîte 7), 1040 Brussels; tel. (02) 736-90-50; telex 26934; KALIOPATE TAVOLA.

Finland: 489 ave Louise, 1050 Brussels; tel. (02) 648-84-84; telex 23099; LEIF BLOMQVIST.

Gabon: 112 ave Winston Churchill, 1180 Brussels; tel. (02) 343-00-55; MICHEL LESLIE TEALE.

The Gambia: 126 ave F. D. Roosevelt, 1050 Brussels; tel. (02) 640-10-49; telex 24344; ABDULLAH M. K. BOJANG.

Ghana: 44 rue Gachard, 1050 Brussels; tel. (02) 649-01-63; fax (02) 649-24-83; JOSEPH AHWA LARYEA.

Grenada: 24 ave des Arts, 1040 Brussels; tel. (02) 230-62-65; telex 64015.

Guatemala: 53 blvd Général Wahis, 1030 Brussels; tel. (02) 736-03-40; telex 25130; CARLOS HUMBERTO JIMÉNEZ-LICONA.

Guinea: 75 ave Roger Vandendriessche, 1150 Brussels; tel. (02) 771-01-26.

Guinea-Bissau: 70 ave F. D. Roosevelt, 1050 Brussels; tel. (02) 647-08-90; telex 63631; BUBACAR TURÉ.

Guyana: 21–22 ave des Arts, 1040 Brussels; tel. (02) 230-60-65; telex 26180; JAMES HENRY E. MATHESON.

Haiti: 160A ave Louise, 1050 Brussels; tel. (02) 649-73-81.

Holy See: 5–9 ave des Franciscains, 1150 Brussels; tel. (02) 762-20-05; Apostolic Nuncio: Mgr GIOVANNI MORETTI.

Honduras: 3 ave des Gaulois (5e étage), 1040 Brussels; tel. (02) 734-00-00; MANUEL LÓPEZ LUNA.

Hungary: 41 rue Edmond Picard, 1180 Brussels; tel. (02) 343-67-90; GÁBOR GÖBÖLYÖS.

Iceland: 5 rue Archimède, 1040 Brussels; tel. (02) 231-03-95; telex 29459; fax (02) 230-81-46; EINAR BENEDIKTSSON.

India: 217 chaussée de Vleurgat, 1050 Brussels; tel. (02) 640-91-40; M. G. V. RAMAKRISHNA.

Indonesia: 294 ave de Tervuren, 1150 Brussels; tel. (02) 771-20-12; telex 21200; fax (02) 771-22-91; ATMONO SURYO.

Iran: 415 ave de Tervuren, 1150 Brussels; tel. (02) 762-37-45; MOHAMED REZA BAKHTIARI.

Iraq: 131 ave de la Floride, 1180 Brussels; tel. (02) 374-59-91; telex 26414; fax (02) 374-76-15; Dr ZAID HWAISHAN HAIDAR.

Israel: 40 ave de l'Observatoire, 1180 Brussels; tel. (02) 374-90-80; AVRAHAM PRIMOR.

Jamaica: 83–85 rue de la Loi, 1040 Brussels; tel. (02) 230-11-70; LESLIE ARMON WILSON.

Japan: 58 ave des Arts (7e étage), 1040 Brussels; tel. (02) 513-92-00; TAKEHIKO NISHIYANA.

Jordan: 104 ave F. D. Roosevelt, 1050 Brussels; tel. (02) 640-77-55; telex 62513.

Kenya: 1–5 ave de la Joyeuse Entrée, 1040 Brussels; tel. (02) 230-30-65; telex 62568; FRANCIS KIRIMI MUTHAURA.

Korea, Republic: 249 ave de Tervuren, 1150 Brussels; tel. (02) 772-32-00; fax 7723051; TONG MAN KWUN.

Kuwait: 43 ave F. D. Roosevelt, 1050 Brussels; tel. (02) 647-79-50; AHMAD A. EL-EBRAHIM IBRAHIM.

Laos: 74 ave Raymond Poincaré, 75116 Paris, France; tel. (1) 45-53-70-47; telex 610711; PHOUNE KHAMMOUNHEUANG.

Lebanon: 2 rue Guillaume Stocq, 1050 Brussels; tel. (02) 649-94-60; telex 22547; SAID AL-ASSAAD.

Lesotho: 66 ave de Cortenberg, 1040 Brussels; tel. (02) 736-39-76; telex 25852; MABOTSE LEROTHOLI.

Liberia: 55 ave F. D. Roosevelt, 1050 Brussels; tel. (02) 640-84-46; telex 61384.

Libya: 28 ave Victoria, 1050 Brussels; tel. (02) 649-21-12; telex 23398; MOHAMED S. ALFAITURI.

Madagascar: 276 ave de Tervuren, 1150 Brussels; tel. (02) 770-17-26; telex 61197; CHRISTIAN RÉMI RICHARD.

Malawi: 15 rue de la Loi, 1040 Brussels; tel. (02) 231-09-80; telex 24128; LAWRENCE P. ANTHONY.

Malaysia: 414A ave de Tervuren, 1150 Brussels; tel. (02) 762-67-67; telex 26396; Dato DALI MAHMUD HASHIM.

Maldives: 212 East 47th St, New York, NY 10017, USA; tel. (212) 688-07-76; telex 960945.

Mali: 487 ave Molière, 1060 Brussels; tel. (02) 345-74-32; telex 22508; LAMINE KEITA.

Malta: 44 rue Jules Lejeune, 1060 Brussels; tel. (02) 343-01-95; telex 26616; JOSEPH LICARI.

Mauritania: 127 ave Gustave Demey, 1160 Brussels; tel. (02) 672-47-47; telex 26034; ELY OULD ALLAF.

Mauritius: 68 rue des Bollandistes, 1040 Brussels; tel. (02) 733-99-88; RAYMOND CHASLE.

Mexico: 164 chaussée de la Hulpe, 1170 Brussels; tel. (02) 676-07-11; telex 22355; fax (02) 676-07-77; ALFREDO DEL MAZO GONZÁLEZ.

Mongolia: 5 ave Robert Schumann, 92100 Boulogne-Billancourt, France; tel. (1) 46-05-28-12; LUVSANDORJIIN MUNDAGBAATAR.

Morocco: 29 blvd Saint-Michel, 1040 Brussels; tel. (02) 736-11-00; telex 21233; ABDALLAH LAHLOU.

Mozambique: 97 blvd St Michel, 1040 Brussels; tel. (02) 736-25-64; telex 65478; fax (02) 735-62-07; FRANCES VITÓRIA VELHO RODRIGUES.

Myanmar: 5300 Bonn, Schumannstrasse 112, Germany; tel. (0228) 210091; telex 8869560; U WING AUNG.

Nepal: 53 Bonn-Bad Godesberg, Im Hag 15, Germany; tel. (0228) 343097.

New Zealand: 47–48 blvd du Régent, 1000 Brussels; tel. (02) 512-10-40; telex 22025; fax (02) 513-48-56; GERARD FRANCIS THOMPSON.

Nicaragua: 55 ave de Wolvendael, 1180 Brussels; tel. (02) 375-64-34; telex 63553; fax (02) 375-71-88; ALVARO PORTA BERMÚDEZ.

Niger: 78 ave F. D. Roosevelt, 1050 Brussels; tel. (02) 648-61-40; telex 22857; AMADOU ZADA.

Nigeria: 288 ave de Tervuren, 1150 Brussels; tel. (02) 762-52-00; telex 22435; MAURICE B. EKPANG.

Norway: 17 rue Archimède, 1040 Brussels; tel. (02) 234-11-11; telex 21071; fax (02) 234-11-50; EIVINN BERG.

Oman: 50 ave d'Iéna, 75116 Paris, France; tel. (1) 47-23-01-63; telex 613765; MUNIR BIN ABDULNABI BIN YOUSUF MAKKI.

Pakistan: 57 ave Delleurs, 1170 Brussels; tel. (02) 673-80-07; telex 61816; MUNIR AKRAM.

Panama: 8 blvd Brand Whitlock, 1040 Brussels; tel. (02) 733-90-89; telex 25169; fax (02) 733-77-79; ROBERTO ALEMÁN HEALY.

Papua New Guinea: 17–19 ave Montoyer, 1040 Brussels; tel. (02) 512-31-26; telex 62249; BROWN BAI.

Paraguay: 42 ave de Saturne, 1180 Brussels; tel. (02) 374-87-48; telex 26535; DIDO FLORENTIN-BAGADO.

Peru: 179 ave de Tervuren, 1150 Brussels; tel. (02) 733-33-19; fax (02) 733-48-19; JULIO EGO-AGUIRRE-ALVAREZ.

Philippines: 299 ave Molière, 1060 Brussels; tel. (02) 343-68-32; fax (02) 347-08-56; ROBERTO R. ROMULO.

Poland: 18 ave de l'Horizon, 1150 Brussels; tel. (02) 771-32-62; telex 20555; fax (02) 771-49-10; JAN KULAKOWSKI.

Qatar: 71 ave F. D. Roosevelt, 1050 Brussels; tel. (02) 640-29-00; telex 63754.

Romania: 37A rue Washington, 1050 Brussels; tel. (02) 647-96-14; CONSTANTIN PARVUTOIU.

Rwanda: 1 ave des Fleurs, 1150 Brussels; tel. (02) 763-07-21; telex 26653; FRANÇOIS NGARUKIYINTWALI.

Saint Lucia: 10 Kensington Court, London, W8, England; tel. (071) 937-9522; ALAN RICHARD GUNN.

Saint Vincent and the Grenadines: 10 Kensington Court, London W8, England; tel. (071) 937-9522; ALAN RICHARD GUNN.

San Marino: 44 ave Brugmann, 1060 Brussels; tel. (02) 344-60-67; GIAN NICOLA FILIPPI BALESTRA.

São Tomé and Príncipe: 42 ave Brugmann, 1060 Brussels; tel. (02) 347-53-75; telex 65313.

Saudi Arabia: 45 ave F. D. Roosevelt, 1050 Brussels; tel. (02) 649-57-25; telex 61600; Prince MUHAMMAD IBN NAWAF IBN ABD AL-AZIZ AS-SA'UD.

Senegal: 196 ave F. D. Roosevelt, 1050 Brussels; tel. (02) 673-00-97; FALILOU KANE.

Seychelles: 53 bis rue François Ier, 75008 Paris, France; tel. (1) 47-23-98-11; telex 649634.

Sierra Leone: 410 ave de Tervuren, 1150 Brussels; tel. (02) 771-00-52; telex 63624; MARIAN JUDITH TANNER KAMARA.

Singapore: 198 ave F. D. Roosevelt, 1050 Brussels; tel. (02) 660-30-98; JAYALEKSHIMI MOHIDEEN.

Solomon Islands: c/o Ministry of Foreign Affairs, Honiara, Solomon Islands; WILSON IFUNAOA.

Somalia: 66 ave F. D. Roosevelt, 1050 Brussels; tel. (02) 640-16-69; telex 24807; Ali Hassan Ali.
South Africa: 26 rue de la Loi, 1040 Brussels; tel. (02) 231-17-25; telex 63060; Bhadra Galu Ranchod.
Sri Lanka: 21-22 ave des Arts, 1040 Brussels; tel. (02) 230-48-90; Tyrrel Dissanayaka.
Sudan: 124 ave F. D. Roosevelt, 1050 Brussels: tel. (02) 647-51-59; Saeed Saad Mahgoub Saad.
Suriname: 379 ave Louise, 1050 Brussels: tel. (02) 640-11-72; Donald McLeod.
Swaziland: 71 rue Joseph II (5e étage), 1040 Brussels; tel. (02) 230-00-44; telex 26254; fax (02) 230-50-89; John Dhlamini.
Sweden: 6 rond-point Robert Schumann, 1040 Brussels; tel. (02) 237-01-11; telex 26126; fax (02) 230-77-57; Stig Brattström.
Switzerland: 53 rue d'Arlon, 1040 Brussels; tel. (02) 230-14-90; telex 21660; Bénédict de Tscharner.
Syria: 3 ave F. D. Roosevelt, 1050 Brussels; tel. (02) 648-01-35; Siba Nasser.
Tanzania: 363 ave Louise, 1050 Brussels; tel. (02) 640-65-00; telex 63616.
Thailand: 2 square du Val de la Cambre, 1050 Brussels; tel. (02) 640-68-10; telex 63510; fax (02) 648-30-66; Danai Tulalamba.
Togo: 264 ave de Tervuren, 1150 Brussels; tel. (02) 770-17-91; telex 25093; fax (02) 771-50-75; Assiongbon Agbenou.
Tonga: New Zealand House (12th floor), Haymarket, London, SW1Y 4TE, England; tel. (071) 839-3287; telex 8954094.
Trinidad and Tobago: 14 ave de la Faisanderie, 1150 Brussels; tel. (02) 762-94-00; telex 23539; fax (02) 772-27-83; Terrence Baden-Semper.
Tunisia: 278 ave de Tervuren, 1150 Brussels; tel. (02) 771-73-95; telex 22078; Rachid Sfar.
Turkey: 4 rue Montoyer, 1040 Brussels; tel. (02) 513-28-34; Ozdem Sanberk.
Uganda: 317 ave de Tervuren, 1150 Brussels; tel. (02) 762-58-25; telex 62814; Charles Kakuru Katungi.
USSR: 56 ave Louis Lepoutre, 1060 Brussels; tel. (02) 343-03-39; Vladimir G. Shemiatenkov.
United Arab Emirates: 73 ave F. D. Roosevelt, 1050 Brussels; tel. (02) 640-60-00; fax (02) 646-24-73; Salem Rached al-Agroobi.
USA: 40 blvd du Régent, 1000 Brussels; tel. (02) 513-44-50; Alfred Thomas Niles.
Uruguay: 437 ave Louise, 1050 Brussels; tel. (02) 649-46-26; telex 24663; José María Araneo.
Venezuela: 5 square Vergote, 1200 Brussels; tel. (02) 736-10-23; telex 61742; fax (02) 732-24-87; César Gil.
Western Samoa: 95 ave F. D. Roosevelt, 1050 Brussels; tel. (02) 660-84-54; telex 25657; Afamasaga Faamatala Toleafoa.
Yemen: Surinamestraat 9, 2585 GC The Hague, Netherlands; tel. (070) 65-39-36; telex 33290; Mohammed Abdul Rehman al-Robaee.
Yugoslavia: 11 ave Emile de Mot, 1050 Brussels; tel. (02) 649-83-49; telex 26156; Mihajlo Crnobrnja.
Zaire: 30 rue Marie de Bourgogne, 1040 Brussels; tel. (02) 513-66-10; telex 21983; Kimbulu Moyanso wa Lokwa.
Zambia: 469 ave Molière, 1060 Brussels; tel. (02) 343-56-49; telex 63102; Kapembe Nsingo.
Zimbabwe: 21-22 ave des Arts, 1040 Brussels; tel. (02) 230-85-35; telex 24133; Andrew Hama Mtetwa.

Source: Directorate-General for External Relations.

Summary of the Treaty establishing the European Economic Community (Treaty of Rome)

(effective from 1 January 1958)

PART I. PRINCIPLES

The aim of the Community is, by establishing a Common Market and progressively approximating the economic policies of the member states, to promote throughout the Community a harmonious development of economic activities, a continuous and balanced expansion, an increased stability, an accelerated raising of the standard of living and closer relations between its member states. With these aims in view, the activities of the Community will include:

(a) the elimination between member states of customs duties and of quantitative restrictions in regard to the importation and exportation of goods, as well as of all other measures with equivalent effect;

(b) the establishment of a common customs tariff and a common commercial policy towards third countries;

(c) the abolition between member states of the obstacles to the free movement of persons, services and capital;

(d) the inauguration of a common agricultural policy;

(e) the inauguration of a common transport policy;

(f) the establishment of a system ensuring that competition shall not be distorted in the Common Market;

(g) the application of procedures that will make it possible to co-ordinate the economic policies of member states and to remedy disequilibria in their balance of payments;

(h) the approximation of their respective municipal law to the extent necessary for the functioning of the Common Market;

(i) the creation of a European Social Fund in order to improve the possibilities of employment for workers and to contribute to the raising of their standard of living;

(j) the establishment of a European Investment Bank intended to facilitate the economic expansion of the Community through the creation of new resources; and

(k) the association of overseas countries and territories with the Community with a view to increasing trade and to pursuing jointly their effort toward economic and social development.

Member states, acting in close collaboration with the institutions of the Community, shall co-ordinate their respective economic policies to the extent that is necessary to attain the objectives of the Treaty; the institutions of the Community shall take care not to prejudice the internal and external financial stability of the member states. Within the field of application of the Treaty and without prejudice to certain special provisions which it contains, any discrimination on the grounds of nationality shall be hereby prohibited.

The Common Market shall be progressively established in the course of a transitional period of 12 years. This transitional period shall be divided into three stages of four years each.

PART II. BASES OF THE COMMUNITY

Free Movement of Goods

Member states shall refrain from introducing between themselves any new import or export customs duties, or charges with equivalent effect, and from increasing such duties or charges as they apply in their commercial relations with each other. Member states shall progressively abolish between themselves all import and export customs duties, charges with an equivalent effect, and also customs duties of a fiscal nature. Independently of these provisions, any member state may, in the course of the transitional period, suspend in whole or in part the collection of import duties applied by it to products imported from other member states, or may carry out the foreseen reductions more rapidly than laid down in the Treaty if its general economic situation and the situation of the sector so concerned permit.

A common customs tariff shall be established, which, subject to certain conditions (especially with regard to the Italian tariff), shall be at the level of the arithmetical average of the duties applied in the four customs territories (i.e. France, Germany, Italy and Benelux) covered by the Community. This customs tariff shall be applied in its entirety not later than at the date of the expiry of the transitional period. Member states may follow an independent accelerating process similar to that allowed for reduction of inter-Community customs duties.

Member states shall refrain from introducing between themselves any new quantitative restrictions or measures with equivalent effect, and existing restrictions and measures shall be abolished not later than at the end of the first stage of the transitional period. These provisions shall not be an obstacle to prohibitions or restrictions in respect of importation, exportation or transit which are justified on grounds of public morality, health or safety, the protection of human or animal life or health, the preservation of plant life, the protection of national treasures of artistic, historic or archaeological value or the protection of industrial and commercial property. Such prohibitions or restrictions shall not, however, constitute either a means of arbitrary discrimination or a disguised restriction on trade between member states. Member states shall progressively adjust any state monopolies of a commercial character in such a manner as will ensure the exclusion, at the end of the transitional period, of all discrimination between the nationals of member states in regard to conditions of supply and marketing of goods. These provisions shall apply to any body by means of which a member state shall *de jure* or *de facto* either directly or indirectly, control or appreciably influence importation or exportation between member states, and also to monopolies assigned by the state. In the case of a commercial monopoly which is accompanied by regulations designed to facilitate the marketing or the valorisation of agricultural products, it should be ensured that in the application of these provisions equivalent guarantees are provided in respect of the employment and standard of living of the producers concerned.

The obligations incumbent on member states shall be binding only to such extent as they are compatible with existing international agreements.

Agriculture

The Common Market shall extend to agriculture and trade in agricultural products. The common agricultural policy shall have as its objectives:

(a) the increase of agricultural productivity by developing technical progress and by ensuring the rational development of agricultural production and the optimum utilization of the factors of production, particularly labour;

(b) the ensurance thereby of a fair standard of living for the agricultural population;

(c) the stabilization of markets;

(d) regular supplies;

(e) reasonable prices in supplies to consumers.

Due account must be taken of the particular character of agricultural activities, arising from the social structure of agriculture and from structural and natural disparities between the various agricultural regions; of the need to make the appropriate adjustments gradually; and of the fact that in member states agriculture constitutes a sector which is closely linked with the economy as a whole. With a view to developing a common agricultural policy during the transitional period and the establishment of it not later than at the end of the period, a common organization of agricultural markets shall be effected.

Free Movement of Persons, Services and Capital

Workers: The free movement of workers shall be ensured within the Community not later than at the date of the expiry of the transitional period, involving the abolition of any discrimination based on nationality between workers of the member states as regards employment, remuneration and other working conditions. This shall include the right to accept offers of employment actually made, to move about freely for this purpose within the territory of the member states, to stay in any member state in order to carry on an employment in conformity with the legislative and administrative provisions governing the employment of the workers of that state, and to live, on conditions which shall be the subject of implementing regulations laid down by the Commission, in the territory of a member state after having been employed there. (These provisions do not apply to employment in the public administration.)

In the field of social security, the Council shall adopt the measures necessary to effect the free movement of workers, in particular, by introducing a system which permits an assurance to be given to migrant workers and their beneficiaries that, for the purposes of qualifying for and retaining the rights to benefits and of the calculation of these benefits, all periods taken into consideration by the respective municipal law of the countries concerned shall be added together, and that these benefits will be paid to persons resident in the territories of the member states.

Right of Establishment: Restrictions on the freedom of establishment of nationals of a member state in the territory of another member state shall be progressively abolished during the transitional period, nor may any new restrictions of a similar character be introduced. Such progressive abolition shall also extend to restrictions on the setting up of agencies, branches or subsidiaries. Freedom of establishment shall include the right to engage in and carry on non-wage-earning activities and also to set up and manage enterprises and companies under the conditions laid down by the law of the country of establishment for its own nationals, subject to the provisions of this Treaty relating to capital.

Services: Restrictions on the free supply of services within the Community shall be progressively abolished in the course of the transitional period in respect of nationals of member states who are established in a state of the Community other than that of the person to whom the services are supplied; no new restrictions of a similar character may be introduced. The Council, acting by a unanimous vote on a proposal of the Commission, may extend the benefit of these provisions to cover services supplied by nationals of any third country who are established within the Community.

Particular services involved are activities of an industrial or artisan character and those of the liberal professions.

Capital: Member states shall during the transitional period progressively abolish between themselves restrictions on the movement of capital belonging to persons resident in the member states, and also any discriminatory treatment based on the nationality or place of residence of the parties or on the place in which such capital is invested. Current payments connected with movements of capital between member states shall be freed from all restrictions not later than at the end of the first stage of the transitional period.

Member states shall endeavour to avoid introducing within the Community any new exchange restrictions which affect the movement of capital and current payments connected with such movements, and making existing rules more restrictive.

Transport

With a view to establishing a common transport policy, the Council of Ministers shall, acting on a proposal of the Commission and after consulting the Economic and Social Committee and the European Parliament, lay down common rules applicable to international transport effected from or to the territory of a member state or crossing the territory of one or more member states, conditions for the admission of non-resident carriers to national transport services within a member state and any other appropriate provisions. Until these have been enacted and unless the Council of Ministers gives its unanimous consent, no member state shall apply the various provisions governing this subject at the date of the entry into force of this Treaty in such a way as to make them less favourable, in their direct or indirect effect, for carriers of other member states by comparison with its own national carriers.

Any discrimination which consists in the application by a carrier, in respect of the same goods conveyed in the same circumstances, of transport rates and conditions which differ on the ground of the country of origin or destination of the goods carried, shall be abolished in the traffic of the Community not later than at the end of the second stage of the transitional period.

A Committee with consultative status, composed of experts appointed by the governments of the member states, shall be established and attached to the Commission, without prejudice to the competence of the transport section of the Economic and Social Committee.

PART III. POLICY OF THE COMMUNITY

Common Rules

Enterprises: The following practices by enterprises are prohibited: the direct or indirect fixing of purchase or selling prices or of any other trading conditions; the limitation of control of production, markets, technical development of investment; market-sharing or the sharing of sources of supply; the application to parties to transactions of unequal terms in respect of equivalent supplies, thereby placing them at a competitive disadvantage; the subjection of the conclusion of a contract to the acceptance by a party of additional supplies which, either by their nature or according to commercial usage, have no connection with the subject of such contract. The provisions may be declared inapplicable if the agreements neither impose on the enterprises concerned any restrictions not indispensable to the attainment of improved production, distribution or technical progress, nor enable enterprises to eliminate competition in respect of a substantial proportion of the goods concerned.

Dumping: If, in the course of the transitional period, the Commission, at the request of a member state or of any other interested party, finds that dumping practices exist within the Common Market, it shall issue recommendations to the originator of such practices with a view to bringing them to an end. Where such practices continue, the Commission shall authorise the member state injured to take protective measures of which the Commission shall determine the conditions and particulars.

Re-importation within the Community shall be free of all customs duties, quantitative restrictions or measures with equivalent effect.

Aid granted by States: Any aid granted by a member state or granted by means of state resources which is contrary to the purposes of the treaty is forbidden. The following shall be deemed to be compatible with the Common Market:

(a) aids of a social character granted without discrimination to individual consumers;

(b) aids intended to remedy damage caused by natural calamities or other extraordinary events;

(c) aids granted to the economy of certain regions of the Federal German Republic affected by the division of Germany, to the extent that they are necessary to compensate for the economic disadvantages caused by the division.

The following may be deemed to be compatible with the Common Market:

(a) aids intended to promote the economic development of regions where the standard of living is abnormally low or where there exists serious under-employment;

(b) aids intended to promote the execution of important projects of common European interest or to remedy a serious economic disturbance of the economy of a member state;

(c) aids intended to facilitate the development of certain activities or of certain economic regions, provided that such aids do not change trading conditions to such a degree as would be contrary to the common interest;

(d) such other categories of aids as may be specified by a decision of the Council of Ministers acting on a proposal of the Commission.

The Commission is charged to examine constantly all systems of aids existing in the member states, and may require any member state to abolish or modify any aid which it finds to be in conflict with the principles of the Common Market.

Fiscal Provisions: A member state shall not impose, directly or indirectly, on the products of other member states, any internal charges of any kind in excess of those applied directly or indirectly to like domestic products. Furthermore, a member state shall not impose on the product of other member states any internal charges of such a nature as to afford indirect protection to other productions. Member states shall, not later than at the beginning of the second stage of the transitional period, abolish or amend any provisions existing at the date of the entry into force of the Treaty which are contrary to these rules. Products exported to any member state may not benefit from any drawback on internal charges in excess of those charges imposed directly or indirectly on them. Subject to these conditions, any member states which levy a turnover tax calculated by a cumulative multi-stage system may, in the case of internal charges imposed by them on imported products or of drawbacks granted by them on exported products, establish average rates for specific products or groups of products.

Approximation of Laws: The Council, acting by means of a unanimous vote on a proposal of the Commission, shall issue directives for the approximation of such legislative and administrative provisions of the member states as have a direct incidence on the establishment or functioning of the Common Market. The European Parliament and the Economic and Social Committee shall be consulted concerning any directives whose implementation in one or more of the member states would involve amendment of legislative provisions.

Economic Policy

Balance of Payments: Member states are charged to co-ordinate their economic policies in order that each may ensure the equilibrium of their overall balances of payments and maintain confidence in their currency, together with a high level of employment and stability of prices. In order to promote this co-ordination a Monetary Committee is established.

Each member state engages itself to treat its policy with regard to exchange rates as a matter of common interest. Where a member state is in difficulties or seriously threatened with dificulties as regards its balance of payments as a result either of overall disequilibrium of the balance of payments or of the kinds of currency at its disposal, and where such difficulties are likely, in particular, to prejudice the functioning of the Common Market or the progressive establishment of the common commercial policy, the Commission shall examine the situation and indicate the measures which it recommends to the state concerned to adopt; if this action proves insufficient to overcome the difficulties, the Commission shall, after consulting the Monetary Committee, recommend to the Council of Ministers the granting of mutual assistance. This mutual assistance may take the form of:

(a) concerted action in regard to any other international organization to which the member states may have recourse;

(b) any measures necessary to avoid diversions of commercial traffic where the state in difficulty maintains or re-establishes quantitative restrictions with regard to third countries;

(c) the granting of limited credits by other member states, subject to their agreement.

Furthermore, during the transitional period, mutual assistance may also take the form of special reductions in customs duties or enlargements of quotas. If the mutual assistance recommended by the Commission is not granted by the Council, or if the mutual assistance granted and the measures taken prove insufficient, the Commission shall authorise the state in difficulties to take measures of safeguard, of which the Commission shall determine the conditions and particulars. In the case of a sudden balance-of-payments crisis, any member state may take immediate provisional measures of safeguard, which must be submitted to the consideration of the Commission as soon as possible. On the basis of an opinion of the Commission and after consulting the Monetary Committee, the Council may decide that the state concerned shall amend, suspend or abolish such measures.

Commercial Policy: Member states shall co-ordinate their commercial relations with third countries in such a way as to bring about, not later than at the expiry of the transitional period, the conditions necessary to the implementation of a common policy in the matter of external trade. After the expiry of the transitional period, the common commercial policy shall be based on uniform principles, particularly in regard to tariff amendments, the conclusion of tariff or trade agreements, the alignment of measures of liberalisation, export policy and protective commercial measures, including measures to be taken in cases of dumping or subsidies. The Commission will be authorised to conduct negotiations with third countries. As from the end of the transitional period, member states shall, in respect of all matters of particular interest in regard to the Common Market, within the framework of any international organizations of an economic character, only proceed by way of common action. The Commission shall for this purpose submit to the Council of Ministers proposals concerning the scope and implementation of such common action. During the transitional period, member states shall consult with each other with a view to concerting their action and, as far as possible, adopting a uniform attitude.

Social Policy

Social Provisions: Without prejudice to the other provisions of the Treaty and in conformity with its general objectives, it shall be the aim of the Commission to promote close collaboration between member states in the social field, particularly in matters relating to employment, labour legislation and working conditions, occupational and continuation training, social security, protection against occupational accidents and diseases, industrial hygiene, the law as to trade unions and collective bargaining between employers and workers.

Each member state shall in the course of the first stage of the transitional period ensure and subsequently maintain the application of the principle of equal pay for men and women.

The European Social Fund: See p. 153.

The European Investment Bank: See p. 143.

PART IV. OVERSEAS COUNTRIES AND TERRITORIES

The member states agree to bring into association with the Community the non-European countries and territories which have special relations with Belgium, France, Italy and the Netherlands in order to promote the economic and social development of these countries and territories and to establish close economic relations between them and the Community as a whole.

Member states shall, in their commercial exchanges with the countries and territories, apply the same rules which they apply among themselves pursuant to the Treaty. Each country or territory shall apply to its commercial exchanges with member states and with other countries and territories the same rules which it applied in respect of the European state with which it has special relations. Member states shall contribute to the investments required by the progressive development of these countries and territories.

Customs duties on trade between member states and the countries and territories are to be progressively abolished according to the same timetable as for trade between the member states themselves. The countries and territories may, however, levy customs duties which correspond to the needs of their development and to the requirements of their industrialisation or which, being of a fiscal nature, have the object of contributing to their budgets.

(The Convention implementing these provisions is concluded for a period of five years only from the date of entry into force of the Treaty.)

PART V. INSTITUTIONS OF THE COMMUNITY

Provisions Governing Institutions

For the achievement of their aims and under the conditions provided for in the Treaty, the Council and the Commission shall adopt regulations and directives, make decisions and formulate recommendations or opinions. Regulations shall have a general application and shall be binding in every respect and directly applicable in each member state. Directives shall bind any member state to which they are addressed, as to the result to be achieved, while leaving to domestic agencies a competence as to form and means. Decisions shall be binding in every respect for the addressees named therein. Recommendations and opinions shall have no binding force.

Financial Provisions

Estimates shall be drawn up for each financial year for all revenues and expenditures of the Community and shall be shown in the budget.

The revenues of the budget shall comprise the financial contributions of member states assessed by reference to a fixed scale.

The Commission shall implement the budget on its own responsibility and within the limits of the appropriations made. The Council of Ministers shall:

(a) lay down the financial regulations specifying, in particular, the procedure to be adopted for establishing and implementing the budget, and for rendering and auditing accounts;

(b) determine the methods and procedure whereby the contributions by member states shall be made available to the Commission; and

(c) establish rules concerning the responsibility of pay-commissioners and accountants and arrange for the relevant supervision.

PART VI. GENERAL AND FINAL PROVISIONS

Member states shall, in so far as is necessary, engage in negotiations with each other with a view to ensuring for the benefit of their nationals:

(a) the protection of persons as well as the enjoyment and protection of rights under the conditions granted by each state to its own nationals;

(b) the elimination of double taxation within the Community;

(c) the mutual recognition of companies, the maintenance of their legal personality in cases where the registered office is transferred from one country to another, and the possibility for companies subject to the municipal law of different member states to form mergers; and

(d) the simplification of the formalities governing the reciprocal recognition and execution of judicial decisions and arbitral awards.

Within a period of three years after the date of the entry into force of the Treaty, member states shall treat nationals of other member states in the same manner, as regards financial participation by such nationals in the capital of companies, as they treat their own nationals, without prejudice to the application of the other provisions of the Treaty.

The Treaty shall in no way prejudice the system existing in member states in respect of property.

The provisions of the Treaty shall not detract from the following rules:

(a) no member state shall be obliged to supply information the disclosure of which it considers contrary to the essential interests of its security.

(b) any member state may take the measures which it considers necessary for the protection of the essential interests of its security, and which are connected with the production of or the trade in arms, ammunition and war material; such measures shall not, however, prejudice conditions of competition in the Common Market in respect of products not intended for specifically military purposes.

The list of products to which (b) applies shall be determined by the Council in the course of the first year after the date of entry into force of the Treaty. The list may be subsequently amended by the unanimous vote of the Council on a proposal of the Commission.

Member states shall consult one another for the purpose of enacting in common the necessary provisions to prevent the functioning of the Common Market from being affected by measures which a member state may be called upon to take in case of serious internal disturbances affecting public order, in case of war or in order to carry out undertakings into which it has entered for the purpose of maintaining peace and international security.

In the course of the transitional period, where there are serious difficulties which are likely to persist in any sector of economic activity or difficulties which may seriously impair the economic situation in any region, any member state may ask for authorization to take measures of safeguard in order to restore the situation and adapt the sector concerned to the Common Market economy.

The provisions of the Treaty shall not affect those of the Treaty establishing the European Coal and Steel Community, nor those of the Treaty establishing the European Atomic Energy Community; nor shall they be an obstacle to the existence or completion of regional unions between Belgium and Luxembourg, and between Belgium, Luxembourg and the Netherlands, in so far as the objectives of these regional unions are not achieved by the application of this Treaty.

The government of any member state of the Commission may submit to the Council proposals for the revision of the Treaty.

Any European state may apply to become a member of the Community.

The Community may conclude with a third country, a union of states or an international organization agreements granting an association embodying reciprocal rights and obligations, joint actions and special procedures.

The Treaty is concluded for an unlimited period.

OTHER TREATIES

The following additional treaties have been signed by the members of the European Communities:

Treaty Instituting a Single Council and a Single Commission of the European Communities: signed in Brussels on 8 April 1965 by the six original members.

Treaty Modifying Certain Budgetary Arrangements of the European Communities and of the Treaty Instituting a Single Council and a Single Commission of the European Communities: signed in Luxembourg on 22 April 1970 by the six original members.

Treaty Concerning the Accession of the Kingdom of Denmark, Ireland, the Kingdom of Norway and the United Kingdom of Great Britain to the European Economic Community and the European Atomic Energy Community: signed in Brussels on 22 January 1972 (amended on 1 January 1973, owing to the non-accession of Norway).

Treaty of Accession of the Hellenic Republic to the European Economic Community and to the European Atomic Energy Community: signed in Athens on 28 May 1979.

Treaty of Accession of the Portuguese Republic and the Kingdom of Spain to the European Economic Community and to the European Atomic Energy Community: signed in Lisbon and Madrid on 12 June 1985.

(Accession of new members to the European Coal and Steel Community is enacted separately, by a Decision of the Council of the European Communities.)

THE SINGLE EUROPEAN ACT

On 1 July 1987 amendments to the Treaty of Rome, in the form of the 'Single European Act', came into effect, following ratification by all the member states. The Act contained provisions which aimed to complete by 1992 the creation of a single Community market—'an area without internal frontiers in which the free movement of goods, persons, services and capital is ensured'. Other provisions increased Community co-operation in research and technology, social policy (particularly the improvement of working conditions), economic and social cohesion (reduction of disparities between regions), environmental protection, creation of economic and monetary union, and foreign policy. It allowed the Council of Ministers to take decisions by a qualified majority vote on matters which previously, under the Treaty of Rome, had required unanimity: this applied principally to matters relating to the establishment of the internal market (see below under the heading Council of Ministers). The Act increased the powers of the European Parliament to delay and amend legislation, although the Council retained final decision-making powers. The Act also provided for the establishment of a secretariat for European political co-operation on matters of foreign policy.

ECONOMIC AND POLITICAL UNION

Parallel inter-governmental conferences on political union and on economic and monetary union were to be held in December 1990, and were expected to make further amendments to the Treaty of Rome.

Community Institutions

Originally each of the Communities had its own Commission (High Authority in the case of the ECSC) and Council, but a treaty transferring the powers of these bodies to a single Commission and a single Council came into effect in 1967.

COMMISSION OF THE EUROPEAN COMMUNITIES

Address: 200 rue de la Loi, 1049 Brussels, Belgium.
Telephone: (02) 235-11-11.
Telex: 21877.
Fax: (02) 235-01-22.

MEMBERS OF THE COMMISSION
(with their responsibilities: October 1990)

President: JACQUES DELORS (France): Secretariat-General; Legal Service; Spokesman's Service; Joint Interpreting and Conference Service; Security Office; Monetary Affairs.

Vice-Presidents:

FRANS ANDRIESSEN (Netherlands): External Relations; Trade Policy; Co-operation with other European countries.

INTERNATIONAL ORGANIZATIONS

European Community

HENNING CHRISTOPHERSEN (Denmark): Economic and Financial Affairs; Structural Funds; Statistical Office.

MANUEL MARÍN (Spain): Co-operation and Development; Fisheries.

FILIPPO MARIA PANDOLFI (Italy): Research and Science; Telecommunications; Information Technology and Innovation; Joint Research Centre.

MARTIN BANGEMANN (Germany): Internal Market; Industrial Affairs; Relations with the European Parliament.

Sir LEON BRITTAN (UK): Competition Policy; Financial Institutions.

Other members:

CARLO RIPA DI MEANA (Italy): Environment; Nuclear Safety; Civil Protection.

ANTÓNIO CARDOSO E CUNHA (Portugal): Energy; Tourism; Small and Medium-sized Businesses; Personnel and Administration.

ABEL MATUTES (Spain): Mediterranean Policy; Relations with Latin America; North-South Relations.

PETER SCHMIDHÜBER (Germany): Budget; Financial Control.

CHRISTIANE SCRIVENER (France): Taxation and Customs Union.

BRUCE MILLAN (UK): Regional Policy.

JEAN DONDELINGER (Luxembourg): Cultural Affairs; Audiovisual Affairs; Information; Citizens' Europe; Publications.

RAY MCSHARRY (Ireland): Agriculture and Rural Development.

KAREL VAN MIERT (Belgium): Transport; Credit and Investment; Consumer Affairs.

VASSO PAPANDREOU (Greece): Employment; Industrial Relations; Social Affairs; Education and Training; Economic and Social Committee.

The functions of the Commission are fourfold: to ensure the application of the provisions of the Treaties and of the provisions enacted by the institutions of the Communities in pursuance thereof; to formulate recommendations or opinions in matters which are the subject of the Treaties, where the latter expressly so provides or where the Commission considers it necessary; to dispose, under the conditions laid down in the Treaties, of a power of decision of its own and to participate in the preparation of acts of the Council of Ministers and of the European Parliament; and to exercise the competence conferred on it by the Council of Ministers for the implementation of the rules laid down by the latter.

The Commission may not include more than two members having the nationality of the same state; the number of members of the Commission may be amended by a unanimous vote of the Council of Ministers. In the performance of their duties, the members of the Commission are forbidden to seek or accept instructions from any Government or other body, or to engage in any other paid or unpaid professional activity.

The members of the Commission are appointed by the Governments of the member states acting in common agreement for a renewable term of four years; the President and Vice-Presidents are appointed for renewable terms of two years. Any member of the Commission, if he no longer fulfils the conditions required for the performance of his duties, or if he commits a serious offence, may be declared removed from office by the Court of Justice. The Court may furthermore, on the petition of the Council of Ministers or of the Commission itself, provisionally suspend any member of the Commission from his duties.

ADMINISTRATION

Offices are at the address of the European Commission: 200 rue de la Loi, 1049 Brussels, Belgium; tel. (02) 235-11-11; fax (02) 235-01-22; telex 21877 (unless otherwise stated).

Secretariat-General of the Commission: Sec.-Gen. DAVID WILLIAMSON.

Legal Service: Dir-Gen. JEAN-LOUIS DEWOST.

Spokesman's Service: Spokesman BRUNO DETHOMAS (acting).

Joint Interpreting and Conference Service: Dir-Gen. RENÉE VAN HOOF.

Statistical Office: Bâtiment Jean Monnet, rue Alcide de Gasperi, 2920 Luxembourg; tel. 430-11; telex 3423; Dir-Gen. YVES FRANCHET.

Directorates-General:

I **(External Relations):** Dir-Gen. HORST KRENZLER.

II **(Economic and Financial Affairs):** Dir-Gen. GIOVANNI RAVASIO.

III **(Internal Market and Industrial Affairs):** Dir-Gen. RICCARDO PERISSICH.

IV **(Competition):** Dir-Gen. CLAUS-DIETER EHLERMANN.

V **(Employment, Industrial Relations and Social Affairs):** Dir-Gen. JEAN DEGIMBE.

Task Force for Human Resources, Education, Training and Youth: Dir HYWEL CERI JONES.

VI **(Agriculture):** Dir-Gen. GUY LEGRAS.

VII **(Transport):** Dir-Gen. EDUARDO PEÑA ABIZANDA.

VIII **(Development):** Dir-Gen. DIETER FRISCH.

IX **(Personnel and Administration):** Dir-Gen. RICHARD HAY.

Translation Service: Dir-Gen. EDUARD BRACKENIERS.

X **(Information, Communication and Culture):** Dir-Gen. COLETTE FLESCH.

XI **(Environment, Consumer Protection and Nuclear Safety):** Dir-Gen. LAURENS JAN BRINKHORST.

XII **(Science, Research and Development):** Dir-Gen. PAOLO FASELLA.

Joint Research Centre: Dir-Gen. JEAN-PIERRE CONTZEN.

XIII **(Telecommunications, Information Industries and Innovation):** Dir-Gen. MICHEL CARPENTIER.

XIV **(Fisheries):** Dir-Gen. (vacant).

XV **(Financial Institutions and Company Law):** Dir-Gen. GEOFFREY FITCHEW.

XVI **(Regional Policy):** Dir-Gen. ENEKO LANDABURU.

XVII **(Energy):** Dir-Gen. CONSTANTINOS MANIATOPOULOS.

XVIII **(Credit and Investments):** Centre A. Wagner, rue Alcide de Gasperi, 2920 Luxembourg-Kirchberg; tel. 430-11; telex 3423; fax 436322; Dir-Gen. ENRICO CIOFFI.

XIX **(Budgets):** Dir-Gen. JEAN-PAUL MINGASSON.

XX **(Financial Control):** Dir-Gen. LUCIEN DE MOOR (acting).

XXI **(Customs Union and Indirect Taxation):** Dir-Gen. PETER WILMOTT.

XXII **(Co-ordination of Structural Instruments):** Dir-Gen. THOMAS O'DWYER.

XXIII **(Enterprise Policy, Commerce, Tourism and Social Economy):** Dir-Gen. HEINRICH VON MOLTKE.

Euratom Supply Agency: Dir-Gen. MICHAEL GOPPEL.

Security Office: Dir PIETER DE HAAN.

THE EUROPEAN COUNCIL

The Heads of State or of Government of the member countries meet twice a year, in the capital of the member state which currently exercises the presidency of the Council of Ministers, or in Brussels.

Until 1975 summit meetings were held at rather less frequent intervals and were often required to take decisions which came to be regarded as the major guidelines for the development of the Community.

In answer to the evident need for more frequent consultation at the highest level it was decided at the summit meeting in Paris in December 1974 to hold the meetings on a regular basis. The Council discusses matters relating to the Community and matters handled by the 'Political Co-operation' system (under which the Foreign Ministers of the member states meet at least four times a year to co-ordinate foreign policy).

COUNCIL OF MINISTERS OF THE EUROPEAN COMMUNITIES

General Secretariat: 170 rue de la Loi, 1048 Brussels, Belgium.

Telephone: (02) 234-61-11.

Telex: 21711.

Secretary-General: NIELS ERSBØLL (Denmark).

The Council of Ministers has the double responsibility of ensuring the co-ordination of the general economic policies of the member states and of taking the decisions necessary for carrying out the Treaties.

The Council is composed of representatives of the member states, each Government delegating to it one of its members, according to the subject to be discussed. The Councils of foreign affairs, economics and finance and agriculture normally meet once a month. About 60 Council sessions are held each year. The office of President is exercised for a term of six months by each member of the Council in rotation according to the alphabetical order of the member states. Meetings of the Council are called by the President acting on his or her own initiative or at the request of a member or of the Commission.

The Treaty of Rome prescribed three types of voting: simple majority, qualified majority and unanimity. Where conclusions require a qualified majority, the votes of its members are weighted

INTERNATIONAL ORGANIZATIONS   *European Community*

as follows: France, Germany, Italy and the United Kingdom 10; Spain 8; Belgium, Greece, the Netherlands and Portugal 5; Denmark and Ireland 3; Luxembourg 2 (Total 76). Majorities are required for the adoption of any conclusions as follows: 54 votes in cases where the Treaty requires a previous proposal of the Commission, or 54 votes including a favourable vote by more than half the members in all other cases. It was declared at a meeting of the Council of Ministers in 1966 that when decisions affecting very important national interests were at stake, discussions should be continued for a reasonable length of time, so that mutually acceptable solutions could be found, giving each member what amounted to a right of veto. Amendments to the Treaty of Rome, effective from July 1987 (following ratification by national legislatures), restricted the right of 'veto', and were expected to speed up the development of a genuine common market: they allowed proposals relating to the dismantling of barriers to the free movement of goods, persons, services and capital to be approved by a majority vote in the Council, rather than by a unanimous vote. Unanimity would still be required, however, for certain areas, including harmonization of indirect taxes, legislation on health and safety, veterinary controls, and environmental protection; individual states would also retain control over immigration rules, prevention of terrorism and drug-trafficking.

The amendments also introduced a 'co-operation procedure' whereby a proposal adopted by a qualified majority in the Council must be submitted to the European Parliament for approval: if the Parliament rejects the Council's common position, unanimity shall be required for the Council to act on a second reading, and if the Parliament suggests amendments, the Commission must re-examine the proposal and forward it to the Council again.

PERMANENT REPRESENTATIVES

Preparation and co-ordination of the Council's work is entrusted to a Committee of Permanent Representatives (COREPER), meeting in Brussels, consisting of the ambassadors of the member countries to the Communities, and aided by committees of national civil servants.

EUROPEAN PARLIAMENT

Address: Centre Européen, Plateau de Kirchberg, 2929 Luxembourg.

Telephone: 43001.

Telex: 2894.

Fax: 437009.

PRESIDENT AND MEMBERS
(October 1990)

President: ENRIQUE BARÓN CRESPO (Spain).

Members: 518 members, apportioned as follows: France, Germany, Italy and the United Kingdom 81 members each; Spain 60; the Netherlands 25; Belgium, Greece and Portugal 24 each; Denmark 16; Ireland 15; Luxembourg 6. Members are elected by direct universal suffrage by the citizens of the member states. Members sit in the Chamber in political, not national, groups.

Political Groupings

	Distribution of seats (October 1990)
Socialist Group	180
European People's Party (Christian Democratic Group)	121
Liberal and Democratic Reformist Group	49
European Democratic Group	34
The Green Group in the European Parliament	29
Group of the European Unitarian Left	28
Group of the European Democratic Alliance	22
Technical Group of the European Right	17
Left Unity	14
Rainbow Group in the European Parliament	14
Non-attached	10
Total	**518**

The tasks of the European Parliament are: advising on legislation, scrutinizing the Community budget and exercising a measure of democratic control over the executive organs of the European Communities, the Commission and the Council. It has the power to dismiss the Commission by a vote of censure. An increase in parliamentary powers was brought about by the amendments to the Treaty of Rome, known as the Single European Act, which were adopted in 1986 and which entered into force on 1 July 1987: in certain circumstances where the Council of Ministers normally adopts legislation through majority voting, a co-operation procedure involving a second parliamentary reading comes into force, enabling Parliament to amend legislation. (During the first 16 months of the operation of this system, about one-half of the amendments proposed by Parliament were accepted by the Council.) Community agreements with third countries now require parliamentary approval. The reforms fell far short of demands by members of Parliament for full powers of joint decision-making.

Parliament has an annual session, divided into about 12 one-week meetings, normally held in Strasbourg. The session opens with the March meeting. Committees normally meet in Brussels.

The budgetary powers of Parliament (which, with the Council, forms the Budgetary Authority of the Communities) were increased to their present status by a treaty of 22 July 1975. Under this treaty, it can amend non-agricultural spending and reject the draft budget, acting by a majority of its members and two-thirds of the votes cast.

The Parliament is run by a Bureau comprising the President, and 14 vice-presidents elected from its members by secret ballot to serve for two-and-a-half years. Parliament has 18 specialized committees, which deliberate on proposals for legislation put forward by the Commission before Parliament's final opinion is delivered by a resolution in plenary session.

There are Standing Committees on Political Affairs; Agriculture, Fisheries and Rural Development; Budgets; Budgetary Control; Economic and Monetary Affairs and Industrial Policy; Energy, Research and Technology; External Economic Relations; Legal Affairs and Citizens' Rights; Social Affairs, Employment and the Working Environment; Regional Policy and Planning; Transport and Tourism; Environment, Public Health and Consumer Protection; Youth, Culture, Education, the Media and Sport; Development and Co-operation; Rules of Procedure, the Verification of Credentials and Immunities; Institutional Affairs; Petitions; Women's Rights.

The first direct elections to the European Parliament took place in June 1979. The directly elected Parliament met for the first time in July 1979. The second elections were held from 14–17 June 1984 (with separate elections held in Portugal and Spain in 1987, following the accession of these two countries to the Community), and the third elections were held on 15–18 June 1989.

COURT OF JUSTICE OF THE EUROPEAN COMMUNITIES

Address: Palais de la Cour de Justice, 2925 Luxembourg.

Telephone: 4303-1.

Telex: 2510.

Fax: 433766.

The task of the Court of Justice is to ensure the observance of law in the interpretation and application of the Treaties setting up the three Communities, and in implementing regulations issued by the Council or the Commission. The 13 Judges and the six Advocates General are appointed for renewable six-year terms by the Governments of the member states. The President of the Court is elected by the Judges from among their number for a renewable term of three years. The majority of cases, including all those of major importance, are dealt with by a full bench of 13 judges. The remainder are dealt with by one of the six chambers, each of which consists of a President of Chamber and two or four judges. The Court has jurisdiction to award damages. It may review the legality of acts (other than recommendations or opinions) of the Council or the Commission and is competent to give judgment on actions by a member state, the Council or the Commission on grounds of lack of competence, of infringement of an essential procedural requirement, of infringement of a Treaty or of any legal rule relating to its application, or of misuse of power. Any natural or legal person may, under the same conditions, appeal against a decision addressed to him or against a decision which, although in the form of a regulation or decision addressed to another person, is of direct and individual concern to him.

The Court is also empowered to hear certain other cases concerning the contractual and non-contractual liability of the Communities and disputes between member states in connection with the objects of the Treaties. It also gives preliminary rulings at the request of national courts on the interpretation of the Treaties, of Community legislation, and of the Brussels Convention on Jurisdiction and the Enforcement of Judgments in Civil and Commercial Matters. During 1989 385 new cases were brought before the Court, of which 139 were cases referred to it for preliminary rulings by the national courts of the member states. In the same period 188 judgments and interim orders were delivered.

INTERNATIONAL ORGANIZATIONS

European Community

Composition of the Court (in order of precedence, October 1990)

Judge O. DUE, President.
Judge G. F. MANCINI, President of the Sixth Chamber.
Judge T. F. O'HIGGINS, President of the Second Chamber.
Judge J. C. MOITINHO DE ALMEIDA, President of the Third and Fifth Chambers.
Judge G. C. RODRÍGUEZ IGLESIAS, President of the First Chamber.
Judge M. DIEZ DE VELASCO, President of the Fourth Chamber.
First Advocate General F. G. JACOBS.
Judge Sir GORDON SLYNN.
Judge C. N. KAKOURIS.
Advocate General C. O. LENZ.
Advocate General M. DARMON.
Judge R. JOLIET.
Judge F. A. SCHOCKWEILER.
Advocate General J. MISCHO.
Judge F. GREVISSE.
Judge M. ZULEEG.
Advocate General W. VAN GERVEN.
Advocate General G. TESAURO.
Judge P. J. G. KAPTEYN.
J.-G. GIRAUD, Registrar.

By a decision of 24 October 1988 the Council of the European Communities, exercising powers conferred upon it by the Single European Act, established a Court of First Instance with jurisdiction to hear and determine certain categories of cases brought by natural or legal persons and which had hitherto been dealt with by the Court of Justice. Those categories are:
Cases arising under the competition rules of the EEC Treaty
Cases brought under the ECSC Treaty
Cases brought by European Community officials.

Composition of the Court of First Instance (in order of precedence, October 1990)

Judge J. L. DA CRUZ VILAÇA, President.
Judge A. SAGGIO, President of the Second Chamber.
Judge C. YERARIS, President of the Third Chamber.
Judge R. SCHINTGEN, President of the Fourth Chamber.
Judge C. P. BRIET, President of the Fifth Chamber.
Judge D. P. M. BARRINGTON.
Judge D. A. O. EDWARD.
Judge H. KIRSCHNER.
Judge B. VESTERDORF.
Judge R. GARCÍA-VALDECASAS Y FERNÁNDEZ.
Judge J. BIANCARELLI.
Judge K. LENAERTS.
H. JUNG, Registrar.

COURT OF AUDITORS OF THE EUROPEAN COMMUNITIES

Address: 12 rue Alcide de Gasperi, 1615 Luxembourg.
Telephone: 4398-1.
Telex: 3512.
Fax: 439342.

The Court of Auditors was created by a Treaty which came into force on 1 July 1977. It is the body responsible for the external audit of the resources managed by the three Communities. It consists of 12 Members who are appointed for six-year terms by unanimous decision of the Council of Ministers, after consultation with the European Parliament. The Members elect the President from among their number for a term of three years.

The Court is organized and acts as a corporate body. It adopts its decisions by a majority of its Members. Each Member, however, has a direct responsibility to audit certain Community sectors.

The Court examines the accounts of all expenditure and revenue of the European Communities and of any body created by them in so far as the relevant constituent instrument does not preclude such examination. It examines whether all revenue has been received and all expenditure incurred in a lawful and regular manner and whether the financial management has been sound. The audit is based on records, and if necessary is performed on the spot in the institutions of the Communities and in the member states. In the member states the audit is carried out in liaison with the national audit bodies. The Court draws up an annual report after the close of each financial year. It may also, at any time, submit observations on specific questions and deliver opinions at the request of one of the institutions of the Communities. It assists the Assembly and the Council in exercising their powers of control over the implementation of the budget, and gives its prior opinion on the financial regulations, on the methods and procedure whereby the budgetary revenue is made available to the Commission, and on the laying-down of rules concerning the responsibility of authorizing officers and accounting officers and concerning appropriate arrangements for inspection.

President: ALDO ANGIOI* (Italy).
Audit Group I: JOHN CAREY (UK), CONSTANTINOS ANDROUTSOPOULOS (Greece), DANIEL STRASSER* (France).
Audit Group II: ANDRÉ MIDDELHOEK (Netherlands), JOSEP SUBIRATS (Spain), CARLOS MORENO* (Portugal), BERNHARD FRIEDMANN (Germany).
Audit Group III: RICHIE RYAN* (Ireland), FERNAND HEBETTE (Belgium), OLÉ WARBERG (Denmark), MAURICE THOSS (Luxembourg).
* Ad Hoc Group members.
Secretary-General: PATRICK EVERARD.

EUROPEAN INVESTMENT BANK

Address: 100 blvd Konrad Adenauer, 2950 Luxembourg.
Telephone: 4379-1.
Telex: 3530.
Fax: 437704.

Board of Governors: One Minister (usually the Finance Minister) from each member state.

Board of Directors: Three directors and two alternates each come from France, Germany, Italy and the United Kingdom; two directors come from Spain and one from Portugal, and both countries have a joint alternate; one director each comes from Belgium, Luxembourg and the Netherlands, who jointly have one alternate; Denmark, Greece and Ireland each have one director and jointly one alternate. The Commission of the European Communities has one director and one alternate.

Management Committee:

President: ERNST-GÜNTHER BRÖDER (Germany).

Vice-Presidents: ROGER LAVELLE (UK), LUCIO IZZO (Italy), ALAIN PRATE (France), M. ARNEDO ORBAÑANOS (Spain), HANS DUBORG (Denmark), LUDOVICUS MEULEMANS (Belgium).

The European Investment Bank (EIB) was created in 1958 by the six founder member states of the European Economic Community. In 1990 the capital subscribed by the 12 member states stood at 28,800m. ECUs, of which 9.01% was paid-in or to be paid-in. Capital structure was as follows: France, Germany, Italy and the United Kingdom 19.1% each; Spain 7.0%; Belgium and the Netherlands 5.3% each; Denmark 2.7%; Greece 1.4%; Portugal 0.9%; Ireland 0.7%; Luxembourg 0.1%. From 1 January 1991, the EIB's capital was to be doubled to 57,600m. ECUs. The bulk of the EIB's resources, however, comes from borrowings, principally public or private bond issues on capital markets inside and outside the Community. In 1989 the Bank borrowed 9,034.5m. ECUs, compared with 7,666m. in 1988.

The EIB's principal task is laid down in Article 130 of the Treaty: working on a non-profit basis, the Bank makes or guarantees loans for investment projects which contribute to the balanced and steady development of the common market. Throughout the Bank's history, priority has been given to financing investment projects which further regional development within the Community. The EIB also finances projects of common interest to several member countries, or the Community as a whole, particularly projects which meet the Community's energy objectives and large infrastructure projects, and gives support to industrial modernization and conversion. During the 1980s, the Bank increased its lending for investments in environmental protection and the development and introduction of advanced technology. The EIB also provides finance for developing countries in Africa, the Caribbean and the Pacific, under the terms of the Lomé Convention (q.v.).

In 1978 the New Community Instrument for Borrowing and Lending (NCI) was set up to raise funds for financing structural investment projects to reflect the Community's priorities, particularly for energy, industrial conversion and infrastructure, and (more recently) for small and medium-sized enterprises. Funds are deposited with the European Investment Bank.

In 1989 total financing operations by the EIB, both inside and outside the Community, amounted to 12,246.1m. ECUs, of which 12,041.8m. ECUs were from the EIB's own resources and 204.3m. ECUs were from resources supplied by the Community. Loans granted for projects within the Community totalled 11,634.2m. ECUs (of which 78.3m. ECUs was from NCI resources). About

INTERNATIONAL ORGANIZATIONS

two-thirds of this amount was for regional development projects. Transport and telecommunications infrastructure, particularly the improvement of road and air links, accounted for 3,766m. ECUs; loans for the energy sector amounted to 1,716m. ECUs, and loans for environmental protection to 1,728m. ECUs. Operations outside the Community totalled 612m. ECUs, of which 486m. ECUs was from the EIB's own resources. Mediterranean countries (Algeria, Egypt, Israel, Jordan, Morocco, Tunisia and Yugoslavia) received 343m. ECUs, and (under the Lomé Convention) the Community's African, Caribbean and Pacific partners received 155m. ECUs from the EIB's own resources and 114m. ECUs in risk capital. In late 1989 the Board of Governors authorized the EIB to grant loans from its own resources to finance investment of 1,000m. ECUs in Hungary and Poland.

FINANCING PROVIDED (million ECUs)

Recipient	1988 Amount	1988 %	1984–88 Amount	1984–88 %
Community				
Belgium	11.6	0.1	205.1	0.6
Denmark	494.1	5.2	1,718.6	4.7
France	1,350.5	14.3	5,428.1	14.8
Federal Republic of Germany	603.0	6.4	1,547.0	4.2
Greece	186.5	2.0	1,372.8	3.7
Ireland	154.8	1.6	944.0	2.6
Italy	3,371.9	35.6	15,521.6	42.3
Luxembourg	—	—	36.2	0.1
Netherlands	259.7	2.7	455.0	1.2
Portugal	560.4	5.9	1,140.6[1]	3.1
Spain	1,018.5	10.8	2,135.2[1]	5.8
United Kingdom	1,178.7	12.4	5,746.5	15.7
Non-member countries[2]	285.0	3.0	468.7	1.2
Sub-total	9,474.8	100.0	36,709.5[3]	100.0
Outside the Community				
from the Bank's own resources	520.1		2,295.7	
from budgetary resources	180.1		638.8	
Sub-total	700.2		2,934.5	
Total	10,175.0		39,644.0	

[1] Excluding pre-accession aid (Portugal 725m. ECUs; Spain 550m. ECUs).
[2] Loans granted for energy projects in Austria, Norway and Tunisia but of direct importance to the Community.
[3] Including loans granted from the resources of the New Community Instrument for borrowing and lending, i.e. a total of 3,262m. ECUs in 1984–88.

CONSULTATIVE BODIES

ECONOMIC AND SOCIAL COMMITTEE

Address: 2 rue Ravenstein, 1000 Brussels.
Telephone: (02) 519-90-11.
Telex: 25 983.
Fax: (02) 513-48-93.

The Committee is advisory and is consulted by the Council of Ministers or by the Commission of the European Communities, particularly with regard to agriculture, free movement of workers, harmonization of laws and transport, as well as legislation adopted under the Euratom Treaty. In addition, the Committee has the power to deliver opinions on its own initiative.

The Committee has 189 members representing economic and social fields, 24 each from France, Germany, Italy and the United Kingdom, 21 from Spain, 12 each from Belgium, Greece, the Netherlands and Portugal, nine from Denmark and Ireland, and six from Luxembourg. One-third represent each side of industry and one-third the general economic interest. The Committee is appointed for a renewable term of four years by the unanimous vote of the Council of Ministers of the European Communities. Members are appointed in their personal capacity and are not bound by any mandatory instructions.

President: FRANÇOIS STAEDELIN.
Secretary-General: JACQUES MOREAU.

European Community

ECSC CONSULTATIVE COMMITTEE

The Committee is advisory and is attached to the Commission. Its members are appointed by the Council of Ministers for two years and are not bound by any mandate from the organizations that designated them in the first place.

There are 84 members representing, in equal proportions, producers, workers and consumers and dealers in the coal and steel industries.

AGRICULTURAL ADVISORY COMMITTEES

There is one Committee for the organization of the market of each sector; two for dealing with social questions in agriculture; and one for structures.

In addition to the consultative bodies listed above there are several hundred special interest groups representing every type of interest within the Community. All these hold unofficial talks with the Commission.

Activities of the Community

AGRICULTURE

Co-operation in the Community is at its most highly-organized in the area of agriculture. The objectives of the Common Agricultural Policy (CAP) are described in the Treaty of Rome (see p. 137). The markets for agricultural products have been progressively organized following three basic principles: (i) unity of the market (products must be able to circulate freely within the Community and markets must be organized according to common rules); (ii) Community preference (products must be protected from low-cost imports and from fluctuations on the world market); (iii) common financial responsibility: the European Agricultural Guidance and Guarantee Fund: finances, through its Guarantee Section, all public expenditure intervention, storage costs, marketing subsidies and export rebates, at a cost, in 1990, of 27,522m. ECUs, or some 59% of total Community expenditure.

From 1969 the operation of the CAP was hindered by the unstable monetary situation. A system of 'monetary compensatory amounts' (MCAs) was therefore introduced: MCAs are added or deducted in agricultural exchanges between member states to take account of fluctuations between the reference rate of exchange (the 'green' currencies) and the real rate. Thus a subsidy is paid to the supplier in a country whose currency has appreciated against a reference rate of exchange, and a tax is paid by the supplier where the currency has depreciated or not appreciated as much. In practice, however, the MCA system has led to wide variations in prices within the Community, and has proved disadvantageous to any country which is a net food exporter with a weak currency. In 1984 it was decided that the system should eventually be phased out, thereby restoring a single market. In 1989 the relative stability of currencies made it possible to abolish MCAs for all countries that were full members of the European Monetary System. The system was to be completely dismantled by the end of 1992.

Agricultural prices are, in theory, fixed each year at a common level for the community as a whole, taking into account the rate of inflation and the need to discourage surplus production of certain commodities. Export subsidies are paid to enable farmers to sell produce at the lower world market prices without loss. These subsidies account for some 50% of agricultural spending.

An intervention price has been established for certain cereals, sugar, some fruits and vegetables, dairy produce and meat: when market prices fall below this level the Community intervenes, and buys a certain quantity which is then stored until prices recover. During the 1980s expanding production led to food surpluses, costly to maintain, particularly in dairy produce, beef, cereals and wine, or to the destruction of large quantities of fruit and vegetables.

Agriculture is by far the largest item on the Community budget, accounting for over two-thirds of annual expenditure, mainly for supporting prices. In 1984 ministers of agriculture adopted proposals for adapting the CAP so as to limit the burden on the Community budget and make the agricultural sector more responsive to the level of supply and demand. They agreed to eliminate the system of MCAs, in phases (see above). Lower milk production quotas were to be imposed in most countries. The guaranteed prices for most agricultural products were 'frozen' between 1984 and 1987, with adjustments in the 'green' currencies being made to alleviate the effect on producers. As a result of the imposition of quotas, milk production decreased slightly, but consumption also fell, and by 1986 surplus dairy produce had reached record levels, despite the Community's efforts to dispose of surplus butter by selling it cheaply within and outside Europe, and to use skimmed milk powder as animal feed. In 1986 and 1987 further reductions in milk production quotas were imposed, and by mid-1988 surpluses of dairy produce had been considerably reduced.

In February 1988 the Council agreed upon budgetary reforms which included a legally-enforceable 'ceiling' on agricultural expenditure. The annual rate of increase in spending on agricultural guarantees was not to exceed 74% of the year's increase in the Community's gross national product. Existing 'stabilizers' on agricultural production were extended: a guarantee threshold of 160m. metric tons per year was imposed for cereals for the period 1988-92, with any excess production being penalized by a cut of 3% in the guaranteed intervention price for the ensuing year. Guarantee thresholds were also imposed on oilseeds and protein feed crops, while subsequent meetings of ministers of agriculture imposed similar 'stabilizers' on production of wine, sugar, fruit and vegetables, tobacco, olive oil, cotton and sheep-meat. The system of milk production quotas was extended until 1992. The Council meeting in February also agreed to adopt a 'set-aside' scheme whereby farmers would be compensated for withdrawing land from cultivation. Ministers of agriculture agreed once again to a virtual 'freeze' of guaranteed prices for 1988/89 and for 1989/90. In 1990 increasing surpluses of beef and dairy products were again reported, while a fall of 10% in the price of lamb was expected to lead to an increase in payments of subsidies, and a decline in international wheat prices increased the cost to the Community of exporting surplus wheat; it was therefore feared that budgetary spending on agriculture for 1991 would have to be increased more than originally envisaged, while the absorption of the former German Democratic Republic into the Community was also expected to lead to considerable extra expenditure on the agricultural sector there. In 1990 the CAP came under attack in the 'Uruguay Round' of negotiations on the General Agreement on Tariffs and Trade (GATT, q.v.). The US Government demanded a reduction of 75% in the EEC's agricultural subsidies, and of 90% in export subsidies, on the grounds that they disrupted world markets. In November Community ministers of agriculture agreed to accept proposals by the Commission for a reduction of 30% in agricultural subsidies, despite the serious effect that this would have on farmers' incomes.

In 1989 the Court of Auditors reported evidence of serious fraud in the operation of the CAP, arising particularly from inadequate customs controls and false claims for subsidies and intervention payments. In July the Council agreed to increase budgetary allocations for the prevention of fraud.

FISHERIES

The Common Fisheries Policy (CFP) came into effect in January 1983 after seven years of negotiations, particularly over the problem of access to fishing-grounds. In 1973 a 10-year agreement had been reached, whereby member states could have exclusive access to waters up to six nautical miles (11.1 km) or in some cases 12 miles from their shores; 'historic rights' were reserved in certain cases for foreign fishermen who had traditionally fished within a country's waters. In 1977 the Community set up a 200-mile (370-km) fishing zone around its coastline (excluding the Mediterranean) within which all members would have access to fishing. The 1983 agreement confirmed the 200-mile zone and allowed exclusive national zones of six miles with access between six and 12 miles from the shore for other countries according to specified 'historic rights'. Rules furthering conservation (e.g. standards for fishing tackle) are imposed under the policy, with checks by a Community fisheries inspectorate. Total allowable catches are fixed annually by species, divided into national quotas.

The organization of fish marketing involves common rules on quality and packing, and a system of guide prices established annually by the Council of Ministers. Fish are withdrawn from the market if prices fall too far below the guide price, and compensation may then be paid to the fishermen. As with agricultural produce, export subsidies are paid to enable the export of fish onto the lower-priced world market, and import levies are imposed to prevent competition from low-priced imports.

The Community supports re-structuring of the fishing industry by offering grants for equipment and building. A three-year plan, beginning in 1983 and involving expenditure of 250m. ECUs, supported capacity reduction (scrapping or laying-up of fishing-vessels), the exploration and development of new grounds and the modernization of existing facilities.

Agreements have been signed with other countries (Norway, Sweden, Canada and the USA) allowing reciprocal fishing rights and other advantages, and with some African countries which receive assistance in building up their fishing industries in return for allowing EEC boats to fish in their waters. Following the withdrawal of Greenland from the Community in February 1985, Community vessels retained fishing rights in Greenland waters, in exchange for financial compensation under a 10-year agreement.

SCIENCE AND TECHNOLOGY

In September 1981 the Commission brought together under a single Directorate-General all the departments responsible for scientific research, and proposed the formation of a common research and development policy, aiming to make the most of national potential, with emphasis on industrial and agricultural applications.

In the amendments to the Treaty of Rome, effective from July 1987, a section on research and technology was included for the first time, defining the extent of Community co-operation and introducing new decision-making structures. In 1987 the Council adopted a programme of research and technological development for 1987-91, with a budget of 5,396m. ECUs. The programme was divided into eight areas: quality of life (health; radiation protection; environment); towards a common market and an information and communications society (information technology, telecommunications, services); modernization of industrial sectors (manufacturing industry, advanced materials, raw materials and recycling, technical standards); exploitation of biological resources (biotechnology, agro-industry, agricultural resources); energy (nuclear safety; controlled thermonuclear fusion; non-nuclear energy and rational use of energy); science and technology for development; exploitation of the sea-bed and use of marine resources (marine science; fisheries); and improvement of European co-operation (human resources; joint use of major installations; forecasting, assessment and statistics, dissemination of research results).

In 1989 the Council adopted a revised programme on research and technological development for the period 1990-94, requiring total Community finance of 5,700m. ECUs, divided as follows: information and communications technologies 2,221m., industrial and materials technologies 888m., environment 518m., life sciences and technologies 741m., energy 814m., human capital and mobility 518m.

The Community's Joint Research Centre (JRC), following a reorganization in 1989, comprises nine institutes based at Ispra (Italy), Geel (Belgium), Karlsruhe (Germany) and Petten (Netherlands). The institutes' work covers: nuclear measurements; transuranium elements; advanced materials; remote sensing applications; the environment; systems engineering; safety technology; information technologies and electronics; and prospective technological studies.

Another major area of research is information technology: in November 1982 the Council approved a series of pilot projects preparing for the 10-year European Strategic Research Programme in Information Technology (ESPRIT), which concentrates on five key areas: advanced micro-electronics; software technology; advanced information processing; office automation; and computer integrated manufacturing. The programme, launched in 1984, is financed half by the EEC and half by research institutes, universities and industrial companies. By 1990 there were about 5,500 scientists working on more than 200 projects under the second phase of the ESPRIT programme.

In 1987 the Council agreed on the main phase of a joint programme for 1987-91 of research and development in advanced communications technology in Europe (RACE), aiming to establish an integrated broad-band telecommunications network.

The Community also supports biotechnological research, aiming to promote the use of modern biology in agriculture and industry. The 1985-89 biotechnology programme involved 93 transnational joint research projects. This was followed by a new programme of biotechnology research, known as 'Bridge' for 1990-94: the budget was 100m. ECUs. The 'Eclair' programme of agro-industrial research, based on biotechnology, was to take place in 1989-93, with a budget of 80m. ECUs, and the 'Flair' programme of research on food science and technology was to cover the same period.

A second research project on forecasting and assessment in science and technology (FAST) took place in 1983-87, with a budget of 8.5m. ECUs: its work covered the effects of new technology on work and employment; the development of renewable natural resources; technological change in the service industries; and new industrial systems, particularly in the communications and food industries. A third FAST programme was envisaged for 1988-92.

In 1985 the Council adopted a programme of basic research in industrial technologies (Brite), with Community funding of 125m. ECUs for 1985-88, aiming to develop new methods for the benefit of existing industries, such as aeronautics, chemicals, textiles and metalworking. A 'Euram' research programme on raw materials and advanced materials was also undertaken for 1986-89. A joint 'Brite-Euram' programme was undertaken for 1989-92, with a proposed budget of 440m. ECUs.

An experimental project was approved by the Council in June 1983 to encourage joint scientific research, for example in pharmaco-biology, solid state physics, optics, combustion, photometry/photoacoustics, interface phenomena and climatology. The means of stimulating joint research include grants, twinning laboratories in different countries, developing specific multinational projects and encouraging the mobility of research workers. The project proved successful and led to a four-year programme (1985–88) for stimulating joint research, with an appropriation of 60m. ECUs. The Community also co-operates with non-member countries in specific research projects, for example (in 1988) with Switzerland (on wood and advanced materials), with Sweden (on wood and waste recycling), with Austria (on advanced materials) and with Finland (on wood). In 1985 the Commission and 18 European countries (including the members of the Community as individuals) adopted the draft charter for the EUREKA programme of research in advanced technology.

The Direct Information Access Network (Euronet DIANE), inaugurated in 1980, comprises more than 750 data bases and banks, managed by national posts and telecommunications administrations and easily accessible to individuals or organizations seeking information on thousands of scientific, medical, technological or economic topics.

ENERGY

The treaty setting up the European Atomic Energy Community (Euratom) came into force on 1 January 1958, to encourage the growth of the nuclear energy industry in the Community through conducting research, providing access to information, supplying nuclear fuels, building reactors, and establishing common laws and procedures for the nuclear industry. A common market for nuclear materials was introduced in 1959, and there is a common insurance scheme against nuclear risks. The Commission is empowered to make loans on behalf of Euratom to finance investment in nuclear power stations and the enrichment of fissile materials. Loans made during 1987 amounted to 313.7m. ECUs for five firms, bringing the total since 1977 (when such operations began) to 2,753.1m. ECUs. There were no new loans in 1988 or 1989. An agreement with the International Atomic Energy Authority entered into force in 1977, to facilitate co-operation in research on nuclear safeguards and controls. The Community's Joint Research Centre (see under Science and Technology) conducts research on nuclear safety and the management of radioactive waste.

The Joint European Torus (JET) is an experimental thermonuclear machine designed to pioneer new processes of nuclear fusion, using the 'Tokamak' system of magnetic confinement to heat gases to very high temperatures and bring about the fusion of tritium and deuterium nuclei. Sweden and Switzerland are also members of the JET project. Since 1974 work has been proceeding at Culham in the United Kingdom, and the project was formally inaugurated in April 1984. In 1982 a five-year programme of research in the field of controlled thermonuclear fusion was established, and subsequently extended: the Community was to contribute 735m. ECUs for thermonuclear fusion research from January 1988 to March 1992. The programme also includes preparation of the Next European Torus (NET), the intermediate stage in the development of a demonstration reactor: work on possible alternative methods of nuclear fusion is also being undertaken. In 1988 work began with representatives of Japan, the USSR and the USA on the joint design of an International Thermonuclear Experimental Reactor (ITER).

The Commission has consistently urged the formation of an effective overall energy policy. Energy objectives for the decade to 1995 were adopted by the Council in 1986: they aimed to restrict the Community's reliance on petroleum to 40% of energy consumption, and to keep net petroleum imports at less than 30% of energy consumption; to improve energy efficiency by at least 20%; to reduce the proportion of electricity generated using petroleum to less than 15%; and to increase the use of new and renewable energy sources.

In 1990 Community legislation on the completion of the 'internal energy market' was adopted: it aimed to encourage the sale of electricity and gas across national borders in the Community, by opening national networks to foreign supplies, obliging suppliers to publish their prices, and co-ordinating investment in energy.

INDUSTRY

Industrial co-operation was the earliest activity of the Community, or more accurately of the European Coal and Steel Community (ECSC). The treaty establishing the ECSC came into force in July 1952, and by the end of 1954 nearly all barriers to trade in coal, coke, steel, pig-iron and scrap iron had been removed. The Community fixes prices and supervises production levels, and assists investment and redevelopment programmes by granting loans, from funds raised on the capital market (see below).

In other sectors the Community has less influence, although the European Commission has to approve state aid to industry by Community members, and forbids measures which might result in unfair competition. Community aid is given to certain sectors. Steel, textiles and shipbuilding have been given particular attention as areas with special difficulties.

'Anti-crisis' measures for the steel industry, first adopted in 1977 in the face of a fall in world demand and a 50% price slump between 1974 and 1977, were renewed in December 1979, mainly consisting of minimum price rules, guide prices and arrangements with 17 major steel-exporting countries. In October 1980 the Council agreed to proclaim a state of 'manifest crisis' in the steel industry, enabling compulsory production quotas to be imposed so as to maintain price levels. In 1981 a new aid code for the steel industry was introduced, ensuring that assistance is granted only to firms implementing a restructuring programme which will reduce their capacity and restore their competitiveness and financial viability. By late 1985 the industry had lost 30m. metric tons of annual production capacity. In July ministers of industry agreed to phase out state aids to steel and production quotas by the end of 1988. Stricter controls on state aid to the coal industry were also envisaged over the same period. The quota system for steel production was abolished on 30 June 1988.

Through redeployment loans and non-reimbursable aid for retraining, the Community attempted to compensate for the loss of about 350,000 jobs in the steel industry between 1974 and 1984. During 1989 the Community granted 193m. ECUs in 'readaptation aid' for workers in the coal and steel industries affected by restructuring measures.

The European textile and clothing industry has been affected by overseas competition: 15% of the Community's textile firms closed between 1973 and 1980, with an average loss of 115,000 jobs per year during that period. The Community participates in the Multifibre Arrangement (see GATT), to limit imports from low-cost suppliers overseas. The European Regional Development Fund gives particular support to regions where textiles formerly provided a large proportion of industrial employment, while the European Social Fund also assists in retraining workers.

In the Community's shipyards, production fell by 50% in 1976–80, while the workforce was reduced by 40%. In 1981 the Council adopted a fifth directive on aid to shipbuilding, providing a framework for aid in reorganizing the industry and increasing efficiency, while discouraging any increase in capacity; this directive was extended until the end of 1986, after which the Council adopted a sixth directive, involving rigorous curbs on state aids to shipbuilding. A programme of assistance to shipbuilding workers for the period 1987–90 (worth 350m. ECUs) was announced in 1987.

The Commission has made a number of proposals on a joint strategy for developing the information technology industry in Europe, particularly in view of the superiority of Japan and the USA in the market for advanced electronic circuits. The ESPRIT research programme (see under Science and Technology) aims to build the technological foundations for a fully competitive European industry. In 1988 the Commission issued a directive requiring member states to liberalize their rules on the supply of telecommunications terminal equipment, thus ending the monopolies enjoyed by national telecommunications authorities. In 1989 ministers agreed to liberalize the market in telecommunications services (apart from voice telephone services and telex).

Harmonization of national company law to form a common legal structure had led by the end of 1989 to the adoption of 12 directives concerning disclosure of information, company capital, internal mergers, the accounts of companies and of financial institutions, division of companies, the qualification of auditors, and single-member private limited companies; other directives on cross-frontier mergers of public limited liability companies, on take-over bids, on participation in management by workers, and on company taxation were being considered in 1989. The Community Patent Convention, providing for the issue of a Community patent valid for all members, was signed in 1975, subject to ratification by all member states. A Community Trade Mark Office was to be in operation by 1990. As part of the process of completing the internal market, numerous directives have been adopted on the technical harmonization and standardization of products (e.g. on safety devices in motor vehicles, labelling of foodstuffs and of dangerous substances, and classification of medicines).

In October 1988 the Council approved a directive on the liberalization of government procurement: contracts for public works worth more than 5m. ECUs were to be offered for tender throughout the Community. In 1990 the legislation was extended to include public water, energy, transport and telecommunications utilities (but not the purchase of fuel).

In September 1990 new regulations entered into force concerning mergers of large companies that might create unfair competition. Approval by the Community's 'Mergers Task Force' was henceforth to be required for all mergers involving companies with a total world-wide turnover of more than 5,000m. ECUs, and a turnover within the EEC of more than 250m. ECUs (except when more than two-thirds of each party's sales are conducted in a single member state).

The Business Co-operation Centre, created by the Commission in 1973, supplies information to businesses and introduces busi-

INTERNATIONAL ORGANIZATIONS   European Community

nesses from different countries wishing to co-operate or form links. It gives particular attention to small and medium-sized concerns, and to companies in applicant countries wishing to acquaint themselves with the Community market. In 1986 the Council adopted an action programme for small and medium-sized enterprises, including simplified tax procedures and easier access to capital, and in 1988 the Commission initiated a programme of training for the managers of such enterprises, in preparation for the completion of the single market in 1992. A network of 39 'Euro-Info-Centres' (aimed particularly at small businesses) began work in 1987, and a further 148 such Centres were in operation by 1990.

TRANSPORT

The establishment of a common transport policy is stipulated in the EEC Treaty (see p. 138), with the aim of gradually standardizing national regulations which hinder the free movement of traffic within the Community, such as the varying safety and licensing rules, diverse restrictions on the size of lorries, and frontier-crossing formalities.

Revised proposals for a common policy for inland transport, issued by the Commission in February 1983, included: co-operation in removing physical and legislative obstacles to a unified railway network; creation of Community authorizations for specific types of road transport; adjustment of national taxation systems for commercial vehicles; a permanent pricing system for international road haulage; harmonization of national scrapping schemes to reduce surplus capacity on inland waterways; negotiations with non-member countries such as Yugoslavia and Austria on transit and combined services; and the establishment of a Community system for paying infrastructure costs.

In 1986 transport ministers agreed on a system of Community-wide permits for commercial vehicles, to allow easier crossing of frontiers. In December 1989 a regulation was adopted, aiming to introduce (over a transitional period from 1990 to 1993) freedom to provide road haulage services in the domestic market of a member state. At the same time a single system of rate-fixing for road haulage was introduced (with effect from 1 January 1990).

In 1984 and 1985 the Commission made proposals on the development of a Community air transport policy (to apply only to flights within the Community, and aiming to produce a more flexible system, with greater scope for competition and more moderate fares). In April 1986 the European Court of Justice confirmed that the Community's rules on competition applied to air transport, and the Commission subsequently threatened to begin legal proceedings against European airlines operating a price-fixing 'cartel'. In 1987 ministers of transport reached an agreement on the liberalization of air transport, which included the deregulation of air fares and of route-sharing. In 1990 they agreed to make further reductions in guaranteed quotas for a country's airlines on routes to another country, and approved the introduction, from 1992, of a 'double disapproval' system whereby cheaper fares offered for flights between two countries would automatically be valid unless vetoed by both governments. In 1989 measures were adopted for the improvement of air traffic congestion, including the centralization of air traffic control facilities.

In 1986 progress was made towards the establishment of a common maritime transport policy, with the adoption of regulations on unfair pricing practices, safeguard of access to cargoes, application of competition rules, and the phasing-out by 1990 of unilateral cargo reservation and discriminatory cargo-sharing arrangements. In 1989 the Commission proposed the establishment of a Community shipping register ('Euros') and freedom for shipping companies to provide maritime transport anywhere within the Community.

In 1989 the Commission approved proposals on railway policy with the aim of achieving greater integration, including technical harmonization (e.g. standardization of track gauges and signalling) and guaranteed rights of transit for joint ventures between railways of different member states. In that year the Commission studied plans for an integrated high-speed rail network, and held consultations with Austria, Switzerland and Yugoslavia on co-operation in rail transport and infrastructure.

In 1988 the Commission proposed a five-year transport infrastructure programme (already approved in principle by the Council) whereby support would be given from Community funds for projects deemed to be of European importance, such as improvement of road and rail links with Portugal and Spain and with Scandinavia, and the Channel tunnel between France and the United Kingdom.

EDUCATION, CULTURE AND BROADCASTING

The postgraduate European University Institute was founded in Florence in 1972, with departments of history and civilization, economics, law, and political and social sciences; it had about 180 students in 1988. In June 1980 the Council approved the following recommendations by the Commission: intensification of modern language teaching; promotion of the study of the European Community in schools; development of a common policy on the admission of higher-education students from other member states; equality of education and vocational training for girls.

In September 1980 an educational information network known as EURYDICE began operations, with a central unit in Brussels and national units providing data on the widely varying systems of education within member states. In 1987 the Council adopted a European Action Scheme for the Mobility of University Students (ERASMUS), which supports university co-operation schemes (1,507 in 1989/90, at a cost of 16m. ECUs) and makes grants enabling university students to spend a study period in another Community country (at a cost of 26m. ECUs for 1989/90).

In 1985 the Council approved a programme of education and training for technology (COMETT), comprising a network of university/industry training partnerships and exchange schemes, to be undertaken in 1987–89, with a budget of 45m. ECUs: a second phase of the programme was to take place in 1990–94.

Although it has no common cultural policy as such, the Community has given practical help for cultural activities. Grants are given to young musicians and cultural workers, and to conservation and restoration centres. A programme of sponsoring translations of works from member states began in 1982 with 20 titles. In 1985 the Community sponsored a 'European Music Year' jointly with the Council of Europe. Under the Community's programme for conserving the European architectural heritage, 30 projects were approved in 1988.

In 1989 ministers of education adopted the LINGUA programme to encourage the learning by young people of Community languages other than their own. The programme was initially to run for five years from 1990, with a proposed budget of 250m. ECUs.

In 1989 ministers of foreign affairs adopted a directive establishing minimum standards for television programmes which could be broadcast freely across European frontiers: limits were placed on the amount of time devoted to advertisements, and governments were to be allowed to forbid the transmission of programmes considered morally harmful.

SOCIAL POLICY

The Single European Act, which entered into force in 1987, added to the original EEC Treaty articles which emphasized the need for 'economic and social cohesion' in the Community and the reduction of disparities between the various regions, principally through the existing 'structural funds'—the European Regional Development Fund, the European Social fund, and the Guidance Section of the European Agricultural Guidance and Guarantee Fund (for details of these funds see p. 153). In February 1988 the Council declared that Community operations through the structural funds, the European Investment Bank and other financial instruments should have five priority objectives:

  (i) Promoting the development and structural adjustment of the less-developed regions (where gross domestic product per caput is less than 75% of the Community average);
 (ii) Converting the regions, frontier regions or parts of regions seriously affected by industrial decline;
(iii) Combating long-term unemployment among people above the age of 25;
 (iv) Providing employment for young people (aged under 25);
  (v) With a view to the reform of the common agricultural policy: speeding up the adjustment of agricultural structures and promoting the development of rural areas.

A number of Community directives have been adopted on equal rights for women in pay, access to employment and social security, and the Commission has undertaken legal proceedings against several member states before the European Court of Justice for infringements. In 1982 the Council adopted the Community Action Programme on the Promotion of Equal Opportunities for Women (1982–85), involving concrete action by national governments (including positive discrimination where necessary) in combating unemployment among women; bringing about equal treatment for men and women in occupational social schemes (e.g. sick pay and pensions) and in self-employed occupations, including agriculture; and legislation on parental leave. A second programme (1986–90) was aproved in 1986 to encourage more effective action by member states. In 1987 the Commission adopted a programme to improve the working and living conditions of workers and reduce accidents and occupational diseases.

In 1989 the Commission proposed a Charter of Fundamental Social Rights of Workers, covering freedom of movement, fair remuneration, improvement of working conditions, the right to social security, freedom of association and collective wage agreements, the development of participation by workers in management, and sexual equality. The Charter was approved by the heads of government of all Community member states except the United Kingdom in December.

CONSUMER PROTECTION

The Community's second five-year Consumer Protection Programme was approved by the Council in 1981, based on the same principles as those of the first programme (protection of health and safety, with procedures for withdrawal of goods from the market; standardization of rules for food additives and packaging; rules for machines and equipment; authorization procedures for new products). The second programme also included measures for monitoring the quality and durability of products, improving after-sale service, legal remedies for unsatisfactory goods and services, and the encouragement of consumer associations. The Consumers' Consultative Council represents European consumers' organizations, and gives opinions on consumer matters. In 1983 the European Council approved a proposal for a Community system for the rapid exchange of information whenever a particular consumer product is found to present an immediate risk to consumers. In 1986-90 it adopted directives on permitted levels of pesticide residues in food; on rules for consumer credit; on the approximation of the laws of member states concerning products which, appearing to be other than they are, endanger the health or safety of consumers; on the safety of toys; on the indication of prices; on standardizing calculation of consumer credit; and on the contractual liability of tour operators.

ENVIRONMENT POLICY

The second environment Action Programme (1977-81) laid down the following principles for action: reduction of pollution and nuisance, protection of natural resources, organization of relevant research and participation in international efforts to improve the environment. A third Action Programme (1982-86) laid greater emphasis on prevention, and included the introduction of environmental impact assessment in all forms of planning, improved monitoring techniques and co-operation with developing countries. A fourth Action Programme (1987-92) was adopted in 1986, aiming to make environmental protection an integral part of economic and social policies.

By 1988 more than 60 directives had been adopted, obliging member states to make regulations on air and water pollution (e.g. 'acid rain' and lead emissions from vehicles), the transport of toxic waste, waste treatment, noise abatement and the protection of natural resources. In 1985 the Community (and a number of individual member states) signed an international agreement, the Vienna Convention for the Protection of the Ozone Layer, and in 1987 the Community signed a protocol to the treaty, controlling the production of chlorofluorocarbons.

In 1981 the Council adopted a five-year programme (1981-85) for environmental research done on a shared-cost basis by various scientific institutions; the programme included measurements of pollutants, development of 'clean technologies', and climatology. The programme for 1986-90 comprised research on environmental protection, climatology and natural hazards, and technological hazards.

In 1989 ministers of the environment undertook to ban production of the most harmful chlorofluorocarbons altogether by the year 2000. Limits were also imposed on the emission of harmful exhaust fumes by cars. In 1990 ministers of the environment agreed to establish a network of installations for disposing of hazardous waste, allowing the Community to be self-sufficient in waste disposal. In the same year they discussed the imposition of limits on emissions of carbon dioxide, responsible for 'global warming': in October they agreed to stabilize emissions at 1990 levels by the year 2000 (2005 for the United Kingdom). Also in 1990 they agreed to establish a European environment agency, to be responsible for information-gathering, with the possibility that its powers would later be extended to monitoring the implementation of environmental legislation. East European countries were also invited to join the agency.

FINANCIAL SERVICES AND CAPITAL MOVEMENTS

A directive on Community banking, adopted in 1977, laid down common prudential criteria for the establishment and operation of banks in member states. A second banking directive, adopted by ministers of finance in December 1989, aimed to create a single community licence for banking, whereby the authorization initially given to a bank by its country of origin is automatically valid for the whole Community: in other words, a bank established in one member country can open branches in any other.

Proposals on the liberalization of non-life insurance, giving insurance companies from one member state free access to customers in other member states without having to establish a base there, were also approved by the Council in 1987.

Freedom of capital movements and the creation of a uniform financial area were regarded as vital for the completion of the internal market by 1992. In 1987, as part of the liberalization of the flow of capital, a Council directive came into force, whereby member states were obliged to remove restrictions on three categories of transactions: long-term credits related to commercial transactions; acquisition of securities; and the admission of securities to capital markets. Portugal and Spain were allowed extra time to comply (until the end of 1992 and 1990 respectively), while temporary protective measures were applied for Greece, Ireland and Italy. In June 1988 the Council of Ministers approved a directive whereby all restrictions on capital movements (financial loans and credits, current and deposit account operations, transactions in securities and other instruments normally dealt in on the money market) were to be removed by 1 July 1990 (except in Belgium, Greece, Ireland, Luxembourg, Portugal and Spain, which were to be permitted to exercise certain restrictions until the end of 1992). Member states were to be allowed to reintroduce restrictions on short-term capital movements for a maximum of six months, should their monetary or exchange-rate policies be disrupted.

ECONOMIC AND MONETARY UNION

A report on the economic situation is presented annually by the Commission, analysing recent developments and short- and medium-term prospects. Economic policy guidelines for the following year are adopted annually by the Council.

The following objectives for the end of 1973 were agreed by the Council in 1971, as the first of three stages towards European economic and monetary union:

  the narrowing of exchange rate margins to 2.25%;

  creation of a medium-term pool of reserves;

  co-ordination of short- and medium-term economic and budgetary policies;

  a joint position on international monetary issues;

  harmonization of taxes;

  creation of the European Monetary Co-operation Fund;

  creation of the European Regional Development Fund.

The narrowing of exchange margins (the 'snake') came into effect in 1972; but Denmark, France, Ireland, Italy and the United Kingdom later floated their currencies, with only Denmark permanently returning to the arrangement. Sweden and Norway also linked their currencies to the 'snake'; but Sweden withdrew from the arrangement in August 1977, and Norway withdrew in December 1978.

The European Monetary System (EMS) came into force in March 1979, with the aim of creating closer monetary co-operation, leading to a zone of monetary stability in Europe, principally through an exchange rate mechanism (ERM), which is supervised by the ministries of finance and the central banks of member states. Not all Community members participate in the ERM: Spain joined only in June 1989, and the United Kingdom in October 1990, while Greece and Portugal remained outside. To prevent wide fluctuations in the value of members' currencies against each other, the ERM fixes for each currency a central rate in European Currency Units (ECUs, see below), which are based on a 'basket' of national currencies; a reference rate in relation to other currencies is fixed for each currency, with established fluctuation margins (6% for the pound sterling and the Spanish peseta, 2.25% for others). Central Banks of the participating states intervene by buying or selling currencies when the agreed margin is likely to be exceeded. Each member places 20% of its gold reserves and dollar reserves respectively into the European Monetary Co-operation Fund, and receives a supply of ECUs to regulate Central Bank interventions. Short- and medium-term credit facilities are given to support the balance of payments of member countries. The EMS was initially put under strain by the wide fluctuations in the exchange rates of non-Community currencies and by the differences in economic development among members, which led to nine realignments of currencies in 1979-83. Subsequently, however, greater stability was achieved, with only two realignments of currencies between 1984 and 1988. In June 1985 measures were adopted by the governors of the Community's central banks, aiming to strengthen the EMS by expanding the use of the ECU, e.g. by allowing international monetary institutions and the central banks of non-member countries to become 'other holders' of ECUs.

In September 1988 a committee (chaired by Jacques Delors, the President of the European Commission, and comprising the governors of member countries' central banks, representatives of the European Commission and outside experts) was established to discuss European monetary union. The resulting 'Delors plan', presented to heads of government in June 1989, envisaged the first stage of the process of monetary union beginning on 1 July 1990, when governments would be required to begin drafting a treaty on monetary union. The plan also recommended the inclusion of as many members as possible in the ERM, and a greater advisory role for central bank governors in the formation of monetary policy. The second stage would begin following the

INTERNATIONAL ORGANIZATIONS

European Community

conclusion of the treaty on monetary union, and would include the creation of a European central bank and a European System of Central Banks (which would eventually assume responsibility for a common monetary policy); medium-term guidelines would be established for the economic policies of member states, together with non-binding limits for budgetary deficits. In the third stage, exchange rates would be irrevocably fixed, budgetary limits would become compulsory, and the ECU would be established as a single Community currency. In June 1989 heads of government agreed to embark on the first stage in July 1990, and in October 1990 they agreed (with the exception of the United Kingdom) to begin the second stage in January 1994. An intergovernmental conference was to be held in December 1990 to make the necessary changes to the Treaty of Rome.

The European Currency Unit

With the creation of the European Monetary System (EMS) a new monetary unit, the European Currency Unit (ECU) was adopted. Its value and composition were identical to those of the European Unit of Account (EUA) already used in the administrative fields of the Community. The ECU is a composite monetary unit, in which the relative value of each currency is determined by the gross national product and the volume of trade of each country.

The ECU, which has been assigned the function of the unit of account used by the European Monetary Co-operation Fund, is also used as the denominator for the exchange rate mechanism; as the denominator for operations in both the intervention and the credit mechanisms; and as a means of settlement between monetary authorities of the European Community.

From April 1979 onwards the ECU was also used as the unit of account for the purposes of the common agricultural policy. From 1981 it replaced the EUA in the general budget of the Community; the activities of the European Development Fund under the Lomé Convention; the balance sheets and loan operations of the European Investment Bank; and the activities of the European Coal and Steel Community. It is now the only unit of account used in the Community.

In June 1989 it was announced that, with effect from 20 September, the Portuguese and Spanish currencies were to be included in the composition of the ECU. From that date the amounts of the national currencies included in the composition of the ECU were to be 'weighted' as follows (in percentages). Belgian franc 7.6; Danish krone 2.45; French franc 19.0; Deutsche Mark 30.1; Greek drachma 0.8; Irish pound 1.1; Italian lira 10.15; Luxembourg franc 0.3; Netherlands guilder 9.4; Portuguese escudo 0.8; Spanish peseta 5.3; United Kingdom pound sterling 13.0.

The ECU's value in national currencies is calculated and published daily. Its value on 30 September 1990 was US $1.31545.

External Relations

Although there is no single Community institution dealing with foreign affairs, the Community acts as a single entity in many aspects of international affairs. It had diplomatic relations in its own right with 142 countries in September 1990 (see p. 135), and with international organizations, and participates as a body in international conferences on trade and development and the 'North-South dialogue'. It has observer status at the United Nations.

Under the Single European Act, which came into force on 1 July 1987 (amending the Treaty of Rome), it was formally stipulated for the first time that member states should inform and consult each other on foreign policy matters (as was already, in practice, often the case) and a secretariat was to be established to assist the Presidency in preparing and implementing the activities of European political co-operation and in administrative matters. In 1990 ministers of foreign affairs discussed proposals for co-ordination of foreign policy and for closer co-operation with Western European Union (q.v.).

Agreements have been signed with numerous countries and groups of countries, allowing for co-operation in trade and other matters. The Community is also a party to 37 international conventions (in 17 of these to the exclusion of the individual member states).

EUROPE

Association agreements, intended to lead to customs union or possible accession, were signed between the Community and Greece (1961), Turkey (1963), Malta (1970) and Cyprus (1972). The agreements established free access to the Community market for most industrial products and tariff reductions for most agricultural products. Annexed are financial protocols under which the Community provides concessional finance to these countries. Aid to Turkey (which had originally been allocated 600m. ECUs for the period 1981–86) was suspended owing to the violation of human rights there following the coup in 1980. With a view to the progressive normalization of relations with Turkey, a meeting with Turkish government ministers (the first for six years) was held in October 1986. In April 1987 Turkey applied for membership of the Community. In 1989 the European Commission stated that formal negotiations on Turkish membership could not take place until 1993, and that it would first be necessary for Turkey to restructure its economy, improve its observance of human rights, and harmonize its relations with Greece. The Commission undertook, however, to increase the Community's financial assistance for Turkey. Additional aid was to be provided for Turkey to alleviate the effects on its economy of the Iraqi invasion of Kuwait in August 1990. In 1987 an agreement was concluded with Cyprus, setting out the details for the progressive establishment of a customs union over a 15-year period. In July 1990 Cyprus made a formal application to join the Community. In the same month Malta also applied for membership.

A co-operation agreement was signed with Yugoslavia in 1980 (but not ratified until April 1983), allowing tariff-free imports (with 'ceilings' for a number of sensitive items) and Community loans of 200m. ECUs over five years. In 1987 a new financial protocol, providing loans of 550m. ECUs over six years, was concluded. At the same time the trade agreement was renewed, with improvements in the conditions of access to the Community market for certain Yugoslav industrial and agricultural products.

Trade negotiations with state trading (including Eastern European) countries were proposed by the Community in 1974, but progress over the ensuing decade was confined to sectoral agreements on textiles, steel and certain agricultural products with Bulgaria, Czechoslovakia, Hungary, Poland and Romania. A proposal for talks leading to closer co-operation with the Community was made by the CMEA in June 1985; in 1986 discussions were opened with several of the European CMEA countries and with the CMEA itself on the normalization of relations and the possibility of more far-reaching agreements. In 1988 agreement was reached on the establishment of diplomatic relations between the Community and most of the East European countries, including the USSR, and on official relations between the Community and the CMEA. During the next two years the extensive political changes and reforms in East European countries led to a further strengthening of links with the Community. Agreements on trade and economic co-operation were concluded with Hungary (September 1988), Poland (September 1989), the USSR (December 1989), Czechoslovakia (December 1988—on trade only—and May 1990), Bulgaria (May 1990), the German Democratic Republic (GDR—May 1990) and Romania (October 1990). In July 1989 the EEC was entrusted with the co-ordination of OECD member states' aid to Hungary and Poland ('Operation Phare'—Poland/Hungary Aid for Restructuring of Economies): this programme was extended in February 1990 to include Bulgaria, Czechoslovakia, the GDR, Romania and Yugoslavia. Community heads of government agreed in December 1989 to establish a European Bank for Reconstruction and Development (with participation by OECD and CMEA member states) to promote investment in Eastern Europe. In March 1990 Community ministers of finance approved assistance of some 2,000m. ECUs for Eastern Europe over the next three years. Aid projects laid particular emphasis on agricultural improvements and the prevention of pollution. Food aid was also provided in 1990. In October heads of government discussed providing long-term aid to the USSR, but concluded that the Soviet Government's plans for economic reform must first be finalized: they agreed, however, to send emergency aid if necessary.

Following the introduction on 1 July 1990 of monetary, economic and social union between the Federal Republic of Germany and the GDR, and the formal integration of the two countries on 3 October, Community legislation was to take effect within the former GDR over a transitional period, lasting until the end of 1992 (with the exception of certain measures, particularly those concerned with environmental protection, which were to take effect after a longer period). The Commission estimated that financial assistance from the Community's structural funds for the former GDR would need to total 3,000m. ECUs over the period 1991-93, while additional agricultural expenditure arising from German reunification was estimated at more than 1,000m. ECUs per year for 1991 and 1992.

The members of EFTA (Austria, Finland, Iceland, Norway, Sweden and Switzerland) each have bilateral Free Trade Agreements with the EEC and the ECSC. The agreements mainly concern the industrial sector. Free trade was introduced by the immediate abolition of quantitative restrictions and the elimination of tariffs in stages. For certain 'sensitive' industrial products, which could have had a disruptive effect on the Community market, the transition period was longer. Customs duties for the majority of products were abolished in July 1977. On 1 January 1984 the last tariff barriers were eliminated, thus establishing full free trade for industrial products. In July 1989 Austria made a formal application to join the Community. Formal negotiations on the creation of a 'European Economic Area', which would mean the formation of a single market for goods, services, capital and labour among EEC and EFTA members, began in June 1990.

THE MIDDLE EAST

Co-operation agreements came into force with Israel in 1975, with the Maghreb countries (Algeria, Morocco and Tunisia) in 1976 and with the Mashreq countries (Egypt, Jordan, Lebanon and Syria) in 1977, covering free access to the Community market for industrial products, customs preferences for certain agricultural products, and financial aid in the form of grants and loans from the European Investment Bank. In order to ensure that the enlargement of the Community would not have an adverse effect on the traditional agricultural exports of these countries to the Community (mainly citrus fruit, wines and olive oil), protocols to the agreements were concluded with most of these countries in 1987, containing provisions designed to ensure that traditional trade patterns are maintained. A non-preferential co-operation agreement was negotiated with the Yemen Arab Republic in 1984. In July 1987 Morocco applied to join the Community, but its application was rejected on the grounds that it is not a European country. A fisheries agreement with Morocco was concluded in 1988.

Three protocols were negotiated in 1987 on assistance to Israel for the period 1987–91, and on modification of the co-operation agreement with Israel to take into account the accession of Portugal and Spain to the Community; however, approval of these protocols was delayed by the European Parliament until October 1988, as a protest against Israel's response to unrest in the occupied territories of the West Bank and the Gaza Strip. In January 1989 the Community and Israel eliminated the last tariff barriers to full free trade for industrial products.

In June 1990 the European Commission proposed the provision (subject to approval by member governments) of 3,000m. ECUs in loans and grants for the Maghreb and Mashreq countries and Israel, over the five-year period from November 1991. This amount was to include 600m. ECUs for loans to support structural adjustment programmes, undertaken in conjunction with the IMF and the World Bank, in particular to compensate for the adverse social effects of adjustment programmes (for example the effects on poor people of a reduction in subsidies for essential goods). Particular emphasis was also to be placed on increasing production of food, promoting investment, the development of small and medium-sized businesses, and protection of the environment. An additional 60m. ECUs was to be provided for Palestinians in the Israeli-occupied territories.

In 1984 discussions began with the Gulf Co-operation Council (GCC) on the possibility of concluding a comprehensive co-operation agreement covering trade, energy and industrial matters. During 1984–87 talks took place in particular on access to European markets for GCC refined petroleum products, after tariffs were imposed by the EEC in 1984 on certain petrochemicals from the region. In June 1988 an agreement was signed with the countries of the GCC, providing for co-operation in industry, energy, technology and other fields, and discussions subsequently began on a second agreement, designed to expand and liberalize trade between the parties. A meeting on industrial co-operation was held in February 1990. In March it was agreed that negotiations on a full free-trade pact should begin, but it was expected that any agreement would involve transition periods of some 12 years for the reduction of European tariffs on 'sensitive products' (i.e. petrochemicals).

Contacts with the Arab world in general take place within the framework of the 'Euro-Arab Dialogue', established in 1973 to provide a forum for discussion of economic issues through working groups on specific topics. In December 1989 a meeting of ministers of foreign affairs of Arab and EEC countries agreed to reactivate the Dialogue, entrusting political discussions to an annual ministerial meeting, and economic, technical, social and cultural matters to the General Committee of the Dialogue.

Following the Iraqi invasion of Kuwait in August 1990, the Community agreed to enforce a trade embargo against Iraq, and to provide emergency aid for refugees leaving Iran and Kuwait. Aid amounting to 1,500m. ECUs was approved in October for three countries whose economies had been seriously affected by the crisis, Egypt, Jordan and Turkey.

LATIN AMERICA

A non-preferential trade agreement was signed with Uruguay in 1974 and economic and commercial co-operation agreements with Mexico in 1975 and Brazil in 1980. A five-year co-operation agreement with the members of the Central American Common Market and with Panama entered into force in 1987, as did a similar agreement with the member countries of the Andean Group. Priority was given to technology transfer, rural development, training, promotion of trade and investment, and co-operation in the energy sector. In March 1989 the Community agreed to provide 800m. ECUs in aid for Central America over the next two years.

ASIA AND AUSTRALASIA

Non-preferential co-operation agreements were signed with the EEC by India (1973 and 1981), Bangladesh (1976), Sri Lanka (1975) and Pakistan (1976 and 1986). A trade agreement was signed with the People's Republic of China in 1978, and renewed and expanded in May 1985. A co-operation agreement was signed with the countries of the Association of South East Asian Nations (ASEAN) in 1980.

Under the 1989 programme of aid to non-associated developing countries, the EEC allocated about 191m. ECUs for Asia, principally for agricultural projects. In 1990 the European Commission proposed to increase its aid to less-developed Asian countries, with emphasis on assistance for environmental protection, urban improvements and support for economic adjustment policies.

Textiles exports by Asian countries have caused concern in the EEC, owing to the depressed state of its own textiles industry. During 1982 bilateral negotiations were held under the Multi-Fibre Arrangement (see GATT) with Asian producers, notably Hong Kong, the Republic of Korea and Macau, which, together with Taiwan (not a party to the Multi-Fibre Arrangement), accounted for some 40% of EEC textile imports. Agreements were eventually reached involving cuts in clothing quotas of between 8% and 10% for the four dominant countries, 'anti-surge' clauses to prevent flooding of European markets, and measures to be imposed in the event of fraud. In 1986 new bilateral negotiations were held and agreements were reached with the principal Asian textile exporters, for the period 1987-91: in most cases a slight increase in quotas was permitted by the EEC.

Numerous discussions have been held since 1981 on the Community's increasing trade deficit with Japan. The Community has requested in particular a greater opening of the Japanese market to European goods and moderation in Japanese exports of certain sensitive products. Between 1981 and 1985 the Japanese Government announced seven series of external economic measures in order to improve access to the Japanese market. Moderation of exports of certain products to the Community was exercised between 1983 and 1985, but during the late 1980s European heads of government repeated their concern at the continuing trade deficit with Japan, amounting to some 19,100m. ECUs in 1989, and at the failure of the Japanese market to accept more European exports. In 1990 the EEC and Japan established a joint committee to attempt to correct the imbalance of trade, working within the current round of GATT negotiations.

Regular consultations are held with Australia at ministerial level. During the 1980s Australia repeatedly criticized the Community's agricultural export subsidies and their effect on Australia's own agriculture, while the EEC criticized industrial protectionism in Australia. In 1984 Australia received assurances that the Community would not extend its export subsidies to markets in the Far East, and in 1987 discussions were held on improving access to the European market for Australian produce. An agreement was reached in 1989 on maintaining until 1992 the United Kingdom's imports of butter from New Zealand, despite the surplus of dairy produce within the Community.

CANADA AND THE USA

A framework agreement for commercial and economic co-operation between the Community and Canada was signed in Ottawa in July 1976, the Community's first non-preferential co-operation agreement concerned not only with trade promotion but also with wide-ranging economic co-operation.

A number of specific agreements have been concluded between the Community and the USA: a co-operation agreement on the peaceful use of atomic energy entered into force in 1959, and agreements on environmental matters and on fisheries came into force in 1974 and 1984 respectively. Additional agreements provide for co-operation in other fields of scientific research and development, while bilateral contacts between officials and government ministers occur in many areas not covered by a formal agreement. In 1988 trade between the Community and the USA amounted to US $164,000m., while direct investment flows amounted to $279,000m.

The USA has frequently criticized the Common Agricultural Policy, which it sees as creating unfair competition for American exports by its system of export refunds and preferential agreements. In 1990, during GATT negotiations, the USA, supported by Canada, Australia and other agricultural exporters, demanded that the EEC should reduce its subsidies to agriculture by 75%, and its support for exports of agricultural produce by 90%.

A similar criticism has been levelled at Community subsidies to the steel industry, and a dispute arose over certain categories of steel products of which Community exports to the USA trebled between 1981 and 1984. In October 1985 and September 1986 agreements were reached on Community exports of steel to the USA until September 1989 (subsequently extended until March 1992).

New trade legislation, enacted in the USA in 1988, gave rise to concern in the Community, which considered that several of the provisions were incompatible with GATT rules. The impact on the USA of the Community's 1992 programme was also the subject of frequent discussions in 1989 and 1990.

GENERALIZED PREFERENCES

In July 1971 the Community introduced a system of generalized tariff preferences (GSP) in favour of developing countries: in 1986 the list of beneficiaries covered 128 independent states and 22 dependent territories. In line with objectives agreed by UNCTAD (q.v.), the scheme provides for duty-free entry of all otherwise dutiable manufactured and semi-manufactured industrial products, including textiles—but subject in certain circumstances to preferential limits. Preferences, usually in the form of a tariff reduction, are also offered on some agricultural products. In 1980 the Council agreed to the extension of the scheme for a second decade (1981-90): at the same time it adopted an operational framework for industrial products, which gives individual preferential limits based on the degree of competitiveness of the developing country concerned. Since 1977 the Community has progressively liberalized GSP access for the least-developed countries by according them duty-free entry on all products and by exempting them from virtually all preferential limits. In 1989 the GSP was extended to Hungary and Poland.

OVERSEAS AID

The main channels for Community aid to developing countries are the Lomé Convention (see below) and the Mediterranean Financial Protocols, but technical and financial aid, and assistance for refugees, training, trade promotion and co-operation in industry, energy, science and technology (about 400m. ECUs in 1988) is also given to about 30 countries in Asia and Latin America. During 1989 food aid, including about 1.2m. metric tons of cereals and 92,700 tons of milk powder, was provided for developing countries. Emergency aid of 38.6m. ECUs was provided for victims of disasters in Africa and elsewhere. Assistance of about 79m. ECUs was also granted through non-governmental organizations, in the form of co-financing for projects.

THE LOMÉ CONVENTION

The First Lomé Convention (Lomé I), which was concluded at Lomé, Togo, in February 1975 and came into force on 1 April 1976, replaced the Yaoundé Conventions and the Arusha Agreement (under which some of the former overseas possessions of France and the United Kingdom retained privileged access to the European market, together with financial assistance). Lomé I was designed to provide a new framework of co-operation, taking into account the varying needs of developing African, Caribbean and Pacific (ACP) countries. The Second Lomé Convention came into force on 1 January 1981. The Third Lomé Convention came into force on 1 March 1985 (trade provisions) and 1 May 1986 (aid). The Fourth Lomé Convention was signed in December 1989: its trade provisions entered into force on 1 March 1990, and the remainder was expected to enter into force in 1991. In October 1990 69 ACP states were parties to the Convention.

ACP-EEC INSTITUTIONS

Council of Ministers: one minister from each signatory state; one co-chairman from each of the two groups; meets annually.

Committee of Ambassadors: one ambassador from each signatory state; chairmanship alternates between the two groups; meets at least every six months.

Joint Assembly: EEC and ACP are equally represented; attended by delegates of the ACP countries and members of the European Parliament; one co-chairman from each of the two groups; meets twice a year.

Centre for the Development of Industry: 28 rue de l'Industrie, 1040 Brussels, Belgium; tel. (02) 513-41-00; telex 61427; fax (02) 511-75-93; f. 1977 to encourage investment in the ACP states by providing contracts and advice, holding promotion meetings, and helping to finance feasibility studies; Dir PAUL FRIX.

Technical Centre for Agricultural and Rural Co-operation: Postbus 380, 6700 AJ Wageningen, Netherlands; tel. (08380) 20484; telex 20577; fax (08380) 31052; f. 1983 to provide ACP states with better access to information, research, training and innovations in agricultural development and extension; Dir ASSOUMOU MBA.

ACP INSTITUTIONS

ACP Council of Ministers.

ACP Committee of Ambassadors.

ACP Secretariat: ACP House, 451 ave Georges Henri, Brussels, Belgium; tel. (02) 733-96-00; Sec.-Gen. GHEBRAY BERHANE.

THE ACP STATES

Angola	Madagascar
Antigua and Barbuda	Malawi
Bahamas	Mali
Barbados	Mauritania
Belize	Mauritius
Benin	Mozambique
Botswana	Namibia
Burkina Faso	Niger
Burundi	Nigeria
Cameroon	Papua New Guinea
Cape Verde	Rwanda
Central African Republic	Saint Christopher and Nevis
Chad	Saint Lucia
Comoros	Saint Vincent and the Grenadines
Congo	São Tomé and Príncipe
Côte d'Ivoire	Senegal
Djibouti	Seychelles
Dominica	Sierra Leone
Dominican Republic	Solomon Islands
Equatorial Guinea	Somalia
Ethiopia	Sudan
Fiji	Suriname
Gabon	Swaziland
The Gambia	Tanzania
Ghana	Togo
Grenada	Tonga
Guinea	Trinidad and Tobago
Guinea-Bissau	Tuvalu
Guyana	Uganda
Haiti	Vanuatu
Jamaica	Western Samoa
Kenya	Zaire
Kiribati	Zambia
Lesotho	Zimbabwe
Liberia	

FUNCTIONS

Under the First Lomé Convention (Lomé I) the Community committed 3,052.4m. ECUs for aid and investment in developing countries. Provision was made for over 99% of ACP (mainly agricultural) exports to enter the EEC market duty free, while certain products which compete directly with Community agriculture were given preferential treatment but not free access: for certain commodities, such as sugar, imports of fixed quantities at internal Community prices were guaranteed. The Stabex (Stabilization of Export Earnings) scheme was designed to help developing countries to withstand fluctuations in the price of their agricultural products, by paying compensation for reduced export earnings. The Convention also provided for Community funds to help finance projects in ACP countries through grants and loans from the European Investment Bank (q.v.) and from the European Development Fund (EDF), which is not included in the Community budget (except for its administrative expenditure) but is financed separately by the member states.

The Second Lomé Convention (1 January 1981–28 February 1985) envisaged Community expenditure of 5,530m. ECUs: it extended some of the provisions of Lomé I, and introduced new fields of co-operation. One of the most important innovations was a scheme (Sysmin), similar to Stabex, to safeguard exports of mineral products. Other chapters concerned new rules on investment protection, migrant labour, fishing, sea transport, co-operation in energy policy and agricultural development, and procedures to speed the administration of aid.

Negotiations for a Third Lomé Convention began in October 1983. The ACP states expressed dissatisfaction with the current arrangements, particularly the inadequacy of Stabex funds (which had been unable to cover more than 50% of the amounts requested during 1979-83) and the presence of non-tariff barriers which restricted their access to European markets. Lomé III, which came into force on 1 March 1985 (trade provisions) and 1 May 1986 (aid), and was due to expire on 28 February 1990, made commitments of 8,500m. ECUs, including loans of 1,100m. ECUs from the European Investment Bank. Innovations included an emphasis on agriculture and fisheries, and measures to combat desertification; assistance for rehabilitating existing industries or sectoral improvements, rather than new individual capital projects; improvements in the efficiency of the Stabex system (now covering a list of 48 agricultural products) and of Sysmin; simplification of the rules of origin of products exported to the EEC; an undertaking to promote private investment; co-operation in transport and communications, particularly shipping; cultural and social co-operation; restructuring of emergency aid, and more efficient procedures for technical and financial assistance.

The Fourth Lomé Convention entered partially into force (trade provisions) on 1 March 1990: its duration was to be 10 years. The budget for financial and technical co-operation for the first five years amounted to 12,000m. ECUs, of which 10,800m. ECUs was from the EDF (including 1,500m. ECUs for Stabex and 480m. ECUs for Sysmin) and 1,200m. ECUs from the EIB. Innovations included the provision of assistance for structural adjustment programmes (amounting to 1,150m. ECUs); increased support for the private sector, environmental protection, and control of growth in population; and measures to avoid increasing the recipient countries' indebtedness (e.g. by providing Stabex and Sysmin assistance in the form of grants, rather than loans).

COMMITMENTS MADE UNDER THE LOMÉ CONVENTION
(million ECUs)

	1989	1976–89
Development of production	563.26	7,382.30
Industrialization	262.11	3,590.61
Tourism	9.07	70.72
Rural production	292.08	3,720.97
Economic infrastructure, transport and communications	275.17	3,074.22
Social development	179.47	1,506.85
Education and training	58.16	690.30
Health	50.54	304.43
Hydraulics, environment	70.77	512.12
Trade promotion	14.24	147.66
Emergency aid	33.53	432.19
Stabex	274.08	2,121.49
Relaunch and rehabilitation plan	0.12	100.43
Refugee aid	31.98	25.09
Imports programme	127.89	377.77
Other	12.94	253.54
Total	**1,512.68**	**15,421.54**

Source: Directorate-General for Development.

Finance

THE COMMUNITY BUDGET

The general budget of the European Communities covers all EEC and Euratom expenditure and the administrative expenditure of the ECSC. The Commission is responsible for implementing the budget. (The ECSC, like the EIB, has its own resources and conducts its own financial operations.) Under the Council decision of 24 June 1988 all revenue (except that expressly designated for supplementary research and technological development programmes) is used without distinction to finance all expenditure, and all budget expenditure must be covered in full by the revenue entered in the budget. Any amendment of this decision requires the unanimous approval of the Council and must be ratified by the member states. The Treaty of Rome requires member states to release funds to cover the appropriations entered in the budget.

Each Community institution draws up estimates of its expenditure, and sends them to the Commission before 1 July of the year preceding the financial year (1 January–31 December) in question. The Commission consolidates these estimates in a preliminary draft budget, which it sends to the Council by 1 September. Expenditure is divided into two categories: that necessarily resulting from the Treaties (compulsory expenditure) and other (non-compulsory) expenditure. The draft budget must be approved by a qualified majority in the Council, and presented to Parliament by 5 October. Parliament may propose modifications to compulsory expenditure, and may (within the limits of the 'maximum rate of increase', dependent on growth of member states' gross national product—GNP—and budgets) amend non-compulsory expenditure. The budget must normally be declared finally adopted 75 days after the draft is presented to Parliament. If the budget has not been adopted by the beginning of the financial year, monthly expenditure may amount to one-twelfth of the appropriations adopted for the previous year's budget. The Commission may (even late in the year during which the budget is being executed) revise estimates of revenue and expenditure, by presenting supplementary and/or amending budgets.

Expenditure under the general budget is financed by 'own resources', comprising agricultural levies (on imports of agricultural produce from non-member states), customs duties, application of value-added tax (VAT) on goods and services, and (since 1988) a levy based on the GNP of member states. Member states are

BUDGET EXPENDITURE (ECUs)

	Appropriations for payments*		Appropriations for commitments*	
	1990†	1991 (preliminary draft)	1990†	1991 (preliminary draft)
Administration				
Expenditure relating to persons working with the institution	1,056,427,000	1,154,647,000	1,056,427,000	1,154,647,000
Buildings, equipment and miscellaneous operating expenditure	288,127,500	313,679,000	288,127,500	313,679,000
Expenditure resulting from special functions carried out by the institution	185,211,360	202,577,000	185,211,360	202,577,000
Total	1,529,765,860	1,670,903,000	1,529,765,860	1,670,903,000
Operations				
EAGGF Guarantee section	27,522,000,000	31,356,000,000	27,522,000,000	31,356,000,000
Structural operations and fisheries	10,911,175,000	13,809,700,000	12,532,475,000	15,056,400,000
Training, youth, culture, information and other social operations	272,725,000	340,020,000	279,635,000	353,622,000
Energy, Euratom nuclear safeguards and environment	178,080,000	183,329,000	115,380,000	225,955,000
Consumer protection, internal market, industry and innovation technology	251,583,000	284,865,000	290,583,000	329,380,000
Research and technological development	1,412,075,000	1,551,040,000	1,727,000,000	2,024,300,000
Co-operation with developing countries and third countries	1,503,590,000	1,694,620,000	1,902,270,000	2,376,080,000
Repayments and refunds to Member States	2,335,091,812	1,147,438,073	2,335,091,812	1,147,438,073
Reserves and provisions	—	—	−38,400,000	—
Operations—Total	44,386,319,812	50,367,012,073	46,666,034,812	52,869,175,073
Commission—Total	45,916,085,672	52,037,915,073	48,195,800,672	54,540,078,073
Other institutions	847,661,982	932,000,000	847,661,982	932,000,000
Grand total	46,763,747,654	52,969,915,073	49,043,462,654	55,472,078,073

* Appropriations for payments cover the expenditure needed to honour commitments entered into during the current budget year or in previous years and falling due in the current budget year. Appropriations for commitments cover the total cost, during the current budget year, of the legal obligations entered into for operations to be carried out over a number of years. In any given budget year the totals for these two types of appropriation normally differ, since commitments appropriations are required ahead of the matching payment appropriations.

† 1990 figures are updated as at September 1990, and include two supplementary budgets.

INTERNATIONAL ORGANIZATIONS

European Community

MEMBER STATES' CONTRIBUTIONS

Country	Contribution for 1990 (forecast) (million ECUs)	% of total
Belgium	1,726.1	4.1
Denmark	855.8	2.0
France	8,368.8	19.8
Federal Republic of Germany	10,949.2	26.0
Greece	551.3	1.3
Ireland	363.6	0.9
Italy	6,338.7	15.0
Luxembourg	68.4	0.2
Netherlands	2,652.1	6.3
Portugal	499.2	1.2
Spain	3,364.5	8.0
United Kingdom	6,421.4	15.2

REVENUE (million ECUs)

Source of revenue	1990	1991 (estimate)
Agricultural levies	1,037.2	1,096.2
Sugar and isoglucose levies	1,246.1	1,091.4
Customs duties	11,349.9	11,872.8
VAT own resources	28,431.9	29,782.2
GNP-based own resources	94.6	8,020.2
Budget balance from previous year	3,481.0	780.1
Other revenue	304.0	327.0
Balance of EAGGF monetary reserve from previous year	819.0	–
Total	**46,763.7**	**52,969.9**

obliged to collect 'own resources' on the Community's behalf. From May 1985 arrangements were introduced for the correction of budgetary imbalances, as a result of which the United Kingdom received compensation in the form of reductions in VAT payments. In 1988 it was decided by the Community's heads of government that (from 1992) the maximum amount of 'own resources' that might be called up in any one year was to be equivalent to 1.2% of member states' total GNP.

The general budget contains the expenditures of the five main Community institutions—the Commission, the Council, Parliament, the Court of Justice and the Court of Auditors—of which Commission expenditure (covering administrative costs and expenditure on operations) forms the largest proportion. The Common Agricultural Policy accounts for about two-thirds of total expenditure, principally in agricultural guarantees. In 1988 it was decided (as part of a system of budgetary discipline agreed by the Council) that the rate of increase in spending on agricultural guarantees between 1988 and a given year was not to exceed 74% of the growth rate of Community GNP during the same period.

In 1990 the Council considered proposals by the Commission that, to assist the completion of the internal market by 1992, national rates of VAT and excise duties should be aligned, and VAT should be levied in the country of origin before export, thus reducing the risk of fraud if border checks were eliminated.

STRUCTURAL FUNDS

The Community's 'structural funds' comprise the Guidance Section of the European Agricultural Guidance and Guarantee Fund, the European Regional Development Fund and the European Social Fund. In accordance with the Single European Act (1987) reforms of the Community's structural funds were adopted by the Council with effect from 1 January 1989, with the aim of more accurate identification of priority targets, and greater selectivity to enable action to be concentrated in the least-favoured regions (see Social Policy, p. 147). Commitments for the structural funds were to double, in real terms, by 1993 from their 1987 level of 7,200m. ECUs.

European Agricultural Guidance and Guarantee Fund (EAGGF)—Guidance Section

Created in 1962, the European Agricultural Guidance and Guarantee Fund is administered by the Commission. The Guidance section covers expenditure on Community aid for projects to improve farming conditions in the member states. It includes aid for conversion projects in specific branches of agriculture, for farm modernization and reforestation programmes, the payment of annuities to farmers who give up farming, and subsidies to farms in mountainous and other less-favoured areas. This aid is usually granted in the form of financial contributions to programmes also supported by the member governments themselves. Commitments of some 1,500m. ECUs were made for 1989.

European Regional Development Fund—ERDF

Payments began in 1975. The Fund is intended to compensate for the unequal rate of development in different regions of the Community, by encouraging investment and improving infrastructure in 'problem regions'. Initially, funds were spent entirely according to a system of national quotas, but in 1979 an additional non-quota section was adopted, allowing the financing of specific Community measures to aid, for example, frontier areas or different areas affected by the same problem. In 1984 agreement was reached on a revision of the Fund, whereby a larger proportion (up to 15%) could be allocated to supra-national programmes, initiated by the Commission but subject to a veto by the governments concerned. In addition, more flexible national quotas were drawn up, with upper and lower limits. In 1989 the Fund made commitments of 4,666.2m. ECUs and payments of 3,920.0m. ECUs.

European Social Fund

The Fund was established in 1960, with the aim of improving employment opportunities by assisting training and workers' mobility. From 1972 there was a new emphasis on job creation schemes as well as on training. Under new rules approved in 1983 the Fund was to increase its aid for the employment of young people (aged under 25), reserving 75% of its resources for this purpose, while a guaranteed minimum of 40% was to be spent in the Community's poorest regions. Areas of high unemployment and industrial decline were also to be given priority, while about 5% of aid was to be used for pilot projects experimenting with new training methods, job creation schemes, or job-sharing projects.

Appropriations for commitments by the Fund in 1989 amounted to 3,524m. ECUs, of which about 18% was for the United Kingdom, 17% each for Italy and Spain, and 12% for France. Appropriations for payments amounted to 2,950m. ECUs in that year. From 1986 stricter rules were applied for selection of suitable schemes, but in 1989 eligible applications still exceeded available resources by about 78%.

PUBLICATIONS*

General Report on the Activities of the European Communities (annually).

Bulletin of the European Communities (11 a year).

The Courier (every 2 months, on ACP-EEC affairs).

European Economy (quarterly, with supplements).

Publications of the European Communities (quarterly).

Information sheets, background reports and statistical documents.

* Most publications are available in all the official languages of the Community. They are obtainable from the Office for Official Publications of the European Communities, 2 rue Mercier, 2985 Luxembourg; tel. 499281; telex 1324; fax 495719.

EUROPEAN FREE TRADE ASSOCIATION—EFTA

Address: 9-11 rue de Varembé, 1211 Geneva 20, Switzerland.
Telephone: (022) 7491111.
Telex: 22660.
Fax: (022) 7339291.

Established in 1960, EFTA aims to bring about free trade in industrial goods and an expansion of trade in agricultural goods between its member countries, and to contribute to the liberalization and expansion of world trade.

MEMBERS

Austria	Iceland	Sweden
Finland	Norway	Switzerland

Three founder members subsequently left EFTA and joined the European Community: Denmark (1973), the United Kingdom (1973) and Portugal (1986). Finland, formerly an associate member of EFTA, became a full member on 1 January 1986. In July 1989 Austria applied to join the EEC.

Organization
(October 1990)

COUNCIL

Council delegations are led by Ministers (normally twice a year) or by the Heads of National Delegations (usually weekly). The Chair is held for six months by each country in turn.

Heads of Permanent Delegations:
Austria: F. CESKA
Finland: A. HYNNINEN
Iceland: K. JOHANNSSON
Norway: E. SELMER
Sweden: L. ANELL
Switzerland: W. ROSSIER

EFTA STANDING COMMITTEES

Committee of Trade Experts.
Committee of Origin and Customs Experts.
Committee on Technical Barriers to Trade.
Group of Legal Experts.
Economic Committee.
Consultative Committee.
Committee of Members of Parliament of the EFTA Countries.
Budget Committee.
Economic Development Committee.
Committee on Agriculture and Fisheries.

SECRETARIAT

Secretary-General: GEORG REISCH (Austria).
Deputy Secretary-General: BERNDT OLOF JOHANSSON (Finland).

Activities

EFTA unites in one free trade area the markets of its member countries, as a means of working towards a sustained growth in economic activity and a continuous improvement in living standards in EFTA countries, and of contributing to the growth of world trade.

The creation of a single market including all the countries in Western Europe was the ultimate objective of EFTA when it was created in 1960. Its first target, the creation of free trade in industrial goods between its members, was achieved by the end of 1966.

Following the departure of Denmark and the United Kingdom from EFTA at the end of 1972, to become members of the EEC, agreements between the remaining EFTA countries and the EEC came into force which established free trade in most industrial goods between them from 1 July 1977. The last restrictions on free industrial trade were abolished from 1 January 1984. In April of that year ministers from all EFTA and EEC member countries agreed on general guidelines for developing the EFTA-EEC relationship. Their Declaration (known as the Luxembourg Declaration) recommended intensified efforts to promote the free movement of goods between their countries, and closer co-operation in a number of other fields, including research and development. In 1989 the European Community accounted for 59% of EFTA's imports and for 56% of EFTA's exports. In March 1989 the EFTA heads of government issued a declaration reaffirming their commitment to establish a homogeneous and dynamic European Economic Area (EEA), consisting of all the member states of EFTA and the EEC, and welcoming the proposal of the President of the EEC Commission to seek a more structured partnership with common decision-making and administrative institutions. An intensive fact-finding programme was duly initiated; it was completed by the end of 1989 and formal negotiations for an EEA treaty opened in June 1990. The treaty was scheduled to come into force by 1 January 1993, to coincide with the completion of the EC's internal market.

Although Portugal left EFTA in 1985, EFTA decided to maintain the Industrial Development Fund for Portugal, which was set up in 1976, for the 25-year period originally foreseen. A similar fund for Yugoslavia, amounting to US $100m., was established at the end of 1989. This complements the work of the Joint EFTA-Yugoslavia Committee, set up in 1978 to promote the expansion of trade and industrial co-operation with Yugoslavia. In June 1990 declarations of co-operation were signed between the EFTA countries and Hungary, Poland and Czechoslovakia. These declarations covered many areas of co-operation and were expected to play an important role in the evolution of relations between these three countries and the EFTA countries.

EFTA's policy for the 1990s envisaged its main task to be contributing to the development of the European Economic Area. However, it still carries out its traditional tasks of ensuring the efficient functioning of free trade between its members and of acting as a forum for consultations or co-ordination between its members, not only on trade matters but also on wider economic questions—including those which are dealt with by large international organizations.

EFTA TRADE, 1989
Imports, c.i.f. (US $ million)

	EFTA	EEC	USA	Japan	Eastern Europe	Rest of world	World
Importing country:							
Austria	2,768.2	26,399.8	1,406.6	1,924.1	2,351.5	4,050.3	38,900.5
Finland	4,620.5	10,895.1	1,553.0	1,795.4	3,347.1	2,408.9	24,620.0
Iceland	266.9	715.3	154.0	68.4	91.3	104.7	1,400.6
Norway	4,909.1	10,178.1	1,756.2	877.1	561.4	5,359.0	23,640.9
Sweden	8,331.7	26,848.3	4,008.3	2,981.3	1,703.6	5,072.8	48,946.0
Switzerland	4,222.3	41,250.4	3,724.9	2,646.3	722.1	5,670.5	58,236.5
Total EFTA	25,118.9	116,287.1	12,603.1	10,292.6	8,777.0	22,665.8	195,744.5

INTERNATIONAL ORGANIZATIONS — European Free Trade Association

Exports, f.o.b. (US $ million)

	EFTA	EEC	USA	Japan	Eastern Europe	Rest of world	World
Exporting country:							
Austria	3,461.7	20,719.3	1,130.4	471.7	2,923.4	3,763.5	32,470.0
Finland	4,648.6	9,964.5	1,481.1	470.9	3,702.9	3,017.4	23,285.4
Iceland	154.2	791.0	200.1	99.3	69.5	87.1	1,401.2
Norway	4,378.7	17,605.8	1,830.7	453.9	315.8	2,451.8	27,036.7
Sweden	9,821.8	27,466.8	4,813.9	979.4	1,139.4	7,372.4	51,593.7
Switzerland	3,425.6	29,178.7	4,573.1	2,154.2	1,658.0	10,562.7	51,552.3
Total EFTA	25,890.7	105,726.2	14,029.4	4,629.3	9,808.9	27,254.9	187,339.4

EFTA trade with the European Community, 1989

	Imports		Exports		Trade balance (US $ million)
	Value in US $ million	% of total imports	Value in US $ million	% of total exports	
Austria	26,399.8	67.9	20,719.3	63.8	−5,680.5
Finland	10,895.1	44.3	9,964.5	42.8	−930.6
Iceland	715.3	51.1	791.0	56.5	75.7
Norway	10,178.1	43.1	17,605.8	65.1	7,427.7
Sweden	26,848.3	54.9	27,466.8	53.2	618.5
Switzerland	41,250.4	70.8	29,178.7	56.6	−12,071.7
Total EFTA	116,287.1	59.4	105,726.2	56.4	−10,560.9

Source: UN COMTRADE data base.

FINANCE

Net budget for 1990/91: 26.9m. Swiss francs. The basis for contributions, determined by reference to the GNP at factor cost of the EFTA countries, was as follows: Austria 17.59%, Finland 13.79%, Iceland 1.72%, Norway 12.59%, Sweden 24.83%, Switzerland 29.48%.

PUBLICATIONS

EFTA Bulletin (4 a year).

EFTA Annual Report.

Annual Report of EFTA Industrial Development Fund for Portugal.

THE FRANC ZONE

Address: Direction Générale des Services Etrangers (Service des Relations avec la Zone Franc), Banque de France, 39 rue Croix-des-Petits-Champs, BP 140-01, Paris Cedex 01, France.
Telephone: (1) 42-92-42-92.
Telex: 220932.
Fax: (1) 42-96-04-23.

MEMBERS

Benin	Equatorial Guinea
Burkina Faso	French Republic*
Cameroon	Gabon
Central African Republic	Mali
Chad	Niger
Comoros	Senegal
Congo	Togo
Côte d'Ivoire	

* Metropolitan France, Mayotte, St Pierre and Miquelon and the Overseas Departments and Territories.

The Franc Zone embraces all those countries and groups of countries whose currencies are linked with the French franc at a fixed rate of exchange and who agree to hold their reserves mainly in the form of French francs and to effect their exchange on the Paris market. Each of these countries or groups of countries has its own central issuing Bank and its currency is freely convertible into French francs. This monetary union is based on agreements concluded between France and each country or group of countries.

Apart from Guinea and Mauritania, all of the countries that formerly comprised French West and Equatorial Africa are members of the Franc Zone. The former West and Equatorial African territories are still grouped within the currency areas that existed before independence, each group having its own currency issued by a central bank.

Mali withdrew from the Franc Zone in 1962, setting up its own currency, the Mali franc, and its own issuing Bank. Mali rejoined the Franc Zone in 1968, and the Mali franc returned to full convertibility with the French franc: agreement was reached on the establishment of a central issuing bank, jointly administered by France and Mali, until Mali rejoined UMOA (see below) in 1984.

A number of states left the Franc Zone during the period 1958–73: Guinea, Tunisia, Morocco, Algeria, Mauritania and Madagascar.

The Comoros, formerly a French Overseas Territory, did not join the Franc Zone on achieving independence in 1975. However, francs CFA were used as the currency of the new state and the Institut d'émission des Comoros continued to function as a Franc Zone organization. In 1976 the Comoros formally assumed membership. In July 1981 the Banque centrale des Comores replaced the Institut d'émission des Comores, establishing its own currency, the Comoros franc.

Equatorial Guinea, a former Spanish colony, joined the Franc Zone in January 1985.

EXCHANGE REGULATIONS

Currencies of the Franc Zone are freely convertible into the French franc at a fixed rate, through 'Operations Accounts' established by agreements concluded between the French Treasury and the individual issuing Banks. It is backed fully by the French Treasury, which also provides the issuing Banks with overdraft facilities.

The monetary reserves of the CFA countries are normally held in French francs in the French Treasury. However, the Banque centrale des états de l'Afrique de l'ouest and the Banque des états de l'Afrique centrale are authorized to hold up to 35% of their foreign exchange holdings in currencies other than the franc. Exchange is effected on the Paris market. Part of the reserves earned by richer members can be used to offset the deficits incurred by poorer countries.

Regulations drawn up in 1967 provided for the free convertibility of currency with that of countries outside the Franc Zone. Restrictions were removed on the import and export of CFA banknotes, although some capital transfers are subject to approval by the governments concerned.

When the French government instituted exchange control to protect the French franc in May 1968, other Franc Zone countries were obliged to take similar action in order to maintain free convertibility within the Franc Zone. The franc CFA was devalued following devaluation of the French franc in August 1969. Since March 1973 the French authorities have ceased to maintain the franc–US dollar rate within previously agreed margins, and, as a result, the value of the franc CFA has fluctuated on foreign exchange markets in line with the French franc.

CURRENCIES OF THE FRANC ZONE

French franc (= 100 centimes): used in Metropolitan France, in the Overseas Departments of Guadeloupe, French Guiana, Martinique, Réunion, and in the Overseas Collectivités Territoriales of Mayotte and St Pierre and Miquelon.

1 franc CFA=2 French centimes. CFA stands for Communauté financière africaine in the West African area and for Coopération financière en Afrique centrale in the Central African area. Used in the monetary areas of West and Central Africa respectively.

1 Comoros franc=2 French centimes. Used in the Comoros, where it replaced the franc CFA in 1981.

1 franc CFP=5.5 French centimes. CFP stands for Comptoirs français du Pacifique. Used in New Caledonia, French Polynesia and the Wallis and Futuna Islands.

WEST AFRICA

Union monétaire ouest-africaine—UMOA (West African Monetary Union): established by Treaty of November 1973, entered into force 1974; comprises Benin, Burkina Faso, Côte d'Ivoire, Niger, Senegal (all parts of former French West Africa) and Togo; Mali, which left the Union in 1962 after creating its own currency, rejoined in June 1984.

Banque centrale des états de l'Afrique de l'ouest—BCEAO: ave Abdoulaye Fadiga, BP 3108, Dakar, Senegal; tel. 23-16-15; telex 21815; fax 23-93-35; f. 1955 under the title 'Institut d'émission de l'AOF et du Togo' and re-created under present title by a treaty between the West African states and a convention with France in 1962, both of which were modified in 1973; central bank of issue for the members of UMOA; cap. and res 217,441m. francs CFA (Sept. 1989). Gov. (vacant); Dep. Govs. OUSMANE OUEDRAOGO (Burkina Faso), OUMAROU SIDIKOU (Niger); Sec.-Gen. JACQUES DIOUF (Senegal). Publs *Annual Report, Notes d'Information et Statistiques* (monthly).

Banque ouest-africaine de développement—BOAD: BP 1172, Lomé, Togo; tel. 21-42-44; telex 5289; f. 1973 by heads of member states of UMOA, to promote the balanced development of member states and the economic integration of West Africa; cap. (authorized) 140,000m. francs CFA, (subscribed) 117,500m. francs CFA (Oct. 1990). Mems: Benin, Burkina Faso, Côte d'Ivoire, Mali, Niger, Senegal, Togo. Pres. ABOU BAKAR BABA-MOUSSA; Vice-Pres. ALPHA TOURE. Publ. *Rapport Annuel*.

CENTRAL AFRICA

Union douanière et économique de l'Afrique centrale—UDEAC (Customs and Economic Union of Central Africa): BP 969, Bangui, Central African Republic; tel. 61-09-22; telex 5254; f. 1966 by the Brazzaville Treaty of 1964 (revised in 1974); forms customs union, with free trade between members and a common external tariff for imports from other countries. UDEAC has a common code for investment policy and a Solidarity Fund to counteract regional disparities of wealth and economic development. UDEAC co-sponsored the Central African Industrial Forum, held in December 1985 and December 1987, aiming to promote industrial investment by the European Community and other industrialized nations. In December 1988 a meeting of heads of state of the Franc Zone countries urged the immediate implementation of the following schemes: a common market in meat; joint production of pharmaceuticals; a UDEAC training school for telecommunications engineers; joint agricultural research centres; tax harmonization; and the construction of new roads that would link the Central African Republic and Gabon to the Trans-African Highway (Lagos–Mombasa). Budget (1990) 1,331m. francs CFA. Mems: Cameroon, Central African Republic, Chad, Congo, Equatorial Guinea, Gabon. Sec.-Gen. AMBROISE FOALEM (Cameroon). Publs *Annuaire du Commerce Extérieur de l'UDEAC, Bulletin des Statistiques Générales* (quarterly).

At the summit meeting in December 1981, UDEAC leaders agreed in principle to form an economic community of Central African states (Communauté économique des états d'Afrique centrale—CEEAC), to include UDEAC members and Burundi,

Rwanda, São Tomé and Príncipe and Zaire. CEEAC (q.v.) began operations in 1985.

Banque des états de l'Afrique centrale: BP 1917, Yaoundé, Cameroon; tel. 22-25-05; telex 8343; fax 23-33-29; f. 1973 as the central bank of issue of Cameroon, the Central African Republic, Chad, Congo, Equatorial Guinea and Gabon; cap. 36,000m. francs CFA, res 162,037m. francs CFA (June 1989). Gov. JEAN-FÉLIX MAMALEPOT; Vice-Gov. JEAN-EDOUARD SATHOUD (Congo). Publs *Rapport annuel, Etudes et statistiques* (monthly).

Banque de développement des états de l'Afrique centrale: BP 1177, Brazzaville, Congo; tel. 81-02-12; telex 5306; f. 1976; cap. 41,880m. francs CFA (June 1988); non-African shareholders comprise govts of France, Germany and Kuwait; Dir-Gen. CÉLESTIN LEROY GAOMBALET.

CENTRAL ISSUING BANKS

Banque des états de l'Afrique centrale: see above.

Banque centrale des états de l'Afrique de l'ouest: see above.

Banque centrale des Comores: BP 405, Moroni, Comoros; tel. 73-10-02; telex 213; f. 1981; Gov. MOHAMED HALIFA.

Institut d'émission des départements d'outre-mer: Cité du Retiro, 35/37 rue Boissy d'Anglas, 75379 Paris Cedex 08, France; tel. 40-06-41-41; issuing authority for the French Overseas Departments and the French Overseas Collectivité Territoriale of St Pierre and Miquelon; Pres. DENIS FERMAN; Dir-Gen. PHILIPPE JURGENSEN.

Institut d'émission d'outre-mer: Cité du Retiro, 35/37 rue Boissy d'Anglas, 75379 Paris Cedex 08, France; tel. 40-06-41-41; issuing authority for the French Overseas Territories and the French Overseas Collectivité Territoriale of Mayotte; Pres. DENIS FERMAN; Dir-Gen. PHILIPPE JURGENSEN.

Banque de France: 1 rue de la Vrillière, Paris, France; f. 1800; issuing authority for Metropolitan France; Gov. J. DE LAROSIÈRE; Dep. Govs DENIS FERMAN, PHILIPPE LAGAYETTE.

FRENCH ECONOMIC AID

France's ties with the African Franc Zone countries involve not only monetary arrangements, but also include comprehensive French assistance in the forms of budget support, foreign aid, technical assistance and subsidies on commodity exports.

Official French financial aid and technical assistance to developing countries is administered by the following agencies:

Fonds d'aide et de coopération—FAC: 20 rue Monsieur, 75007 Paris, France; in 1959 FAC took over from FIDES (Fonds d'investissement pour le développement économique et social) the administration of subsidies and loans from the French government to the former French African states. FAC is administered by the Ministry of Co-operation, which allocates budgetary funds to it.

Caisse centrale de coopération économique—CCCE: Cité du Retiro, 35/37 rue Boissy d'Anglas, 75379 Paris Cedex 08, France; tel. (1) 40-06-31-31; telex 212632; f. 1941, and given present name in 1958. French development bank which lends money to member states and former member states of the Franc Zone and several other states, and executes the financial operations of the FAC. Loans for Franc Zone countries approved in 1989 totalled 3,480m. French francs; Dir-Gen. PHILIPPE JURGENSEN.

INTER-AMERICAN DEVELOPMENT BANK—IDB

Address: 1300 New York Ave, NW, Washington, DC 20577, USA.
Telephone: (202) 623-1397.
Fax: (202) 789-2835.

The Bank was founded in 1959 to promote the individual and collective development of regional developing member countries through the financing of economic and social development projects and the provision of technical assistance. Membership was increased in 1976 and 1977 to include countries outside the region.

MEMBERS

Argentina	Finland	Panama
Austria	France	Paraguay
Bahamas	Germany	Peru
Barbados	Guatemala	Portugal
Belgium	Guyana	Spain
Bolivia	Haiti	Suriname
Brazil	Honduras	Sweden
Canada	Israel	Switzerland
Chile	Italy	Trinidad and Tobago
Colombia	Jamaica	United Kingdom
Costa Rica	Japan	USA
Denmark	Mexico	Uruguay
Dominican Republic	Netherlands	Venezuela
Ecuador	Nicaragua	Yugoslavia
El Salvador	Norway	

Organization
(October 1990)

BOARD OF GOVERNORS

All the powers of the Bank are vested in a Board of Governors, consisting of one Governor and one alternate appointed by each member country. The Board meets annually, with special meetings when necessary.

BOARD OF EXECUTIVE DIRECTORS

There are 12 executive directors and 12 alternates. Each Director is elected by a group of two or more countries, except the Directors representing Canada and the USA. The USA holds 34.6% of votes on the Board, proportional to its contribution to the Bank's capital.

ADMINISTRATION

The Bank has eight departments: operations; finance; economic and social development; project analysis; legal affairs; plans and programmes; administrative; and secretariat. There are External Relations, Controller's and Auditor General's Offices, an External Review and Evaluation Office, and field offices in 25 countries. At the end of 1989 there were 1,524 Bank staff.

President: ENRIQUE V. IGLESIAS (Uruguay).
Executive Vice-President: JAMES W. CONROW (USA).

Activities

Loans are made to governments, and to public and private entities for specific economic and social development projects and (from 1990) for sectoral reforms. These loans are repayable in the currencies lent and their terms range from 15 to 40 years. Total lending authorized by the Bank by the end of 1989 amounted to US $41,599m. During 1988 the Bank approved loans totalling $1,682m., compared with loans amounting to $2,361m. in 1987 and $3,037m. in 1986. The decline in lending was attributed to the stagnation of the Latin American economy as a whole, making it difficult for governments to pay their share of project costs; and to uncertainty over the replenishment of the Bank's capital (see below). In 1989, however, lending (36 loans) increased to $2,618m., while disbursements totalled $2,549m.

The subscribed ordinary capital stock, including inter-regional capital, which was merged into it in 1987, totalled $34,455m. at the end of 1989, of which $2,642m. is paid-in and $31,813m. is callable. The callable capital constitutes, in effect, a guarantee of the securities which the Bank issues in the capital markets in order to increase its resources available for lending. Replenishments are made every four years: the sixth replenishment, agreed in 1983, raised the authorized capital to $35,000m. During 1987 and 1988 agreement on a seventh replenishment of the Bank's capital was delayed by the US Government's demands for a restructuring of lending policies. Previously, a simple majority of directors' votes was sufficient to ensure the approval of a loan; developing member countries had nearly 54% of the voting power. The USA now proposed that a 65% majority should be necessary, thus giving the USA and Canada combined a virtual power of veto. The US Government also criticized the Bank's policy of lending mostly for specific projects, rather than in support of economic adjustment programmes. In March 1989 it was agreed that authorized capital should be increased by $26,500m. This was expected to lead to a lending programme amounting to $22,500m. in 1990-93. The proposal for loan approvals by a 65% majority was not accepted, but it was agreed that opposition by one shareholder could delay approval of a loan for two months, opposition by two for another five months, while opposition by three shareholders, holding at least 40% of the votes, could delay approval by a further five months, after which approval was to be decided by a simple majority of shareholders.

In 1989 the Bank borrowed $1,983.6m. on the international capital markets. Net earnings during the year amounted to $220.6m., and at the end of the year the Bank's total reserves were $3,296m.

The Fund for Special Operations enables the Bank to make concessional loans for economic and social projects where circumstances call for special treatment, such as lower interest rates and longer repayment terms than those applied to loans from the ordinary resources. During 1989 the Fund made 12 loans totalling $342m. In 1989 the Board of Governors approved $200m. in new contributions to the Fund.

Several donor countries have placed sums under the Bank's administration for assistance to Latin America, outside the framework of the Ordinary Resources and the Bank's Special Operations. These include the United States Social Progress Trust Fund (set up in 1961), which had made loans amounting to $538m. by the end of 1987; the Venezuelan Trust Fund (set up in 1975), which had made loans totalling $725m. by the end of 1987; and other funds administered on behalf of Argentina, Canada, Japan, Norway, Sweden, Switzerland and the United Kingdom. Total cumulative lending from all these funds amounted to $1,448m. at the end of 1989. In October 1988 the Spanish Government agreed to establish a $500m. 'Quincentennial Fund' at the IDB, together with a $150m. compensation account to subsidize interest rates and thereby allow the approval of concessional loans.

In 1989 the energy sector received the largest share of IDB lending (27.6%), followed by agriculture and fisheries (22.1%) (see table). Following the capital increase approved in 1989, the Bank was to undertake sectoral lending for the first time, devoting up to 25% of its financing to loans which would allow countries to make

Distribution of loans (US $ million)

Sector	1989	%	1961–89	%
Productive Sectors				
Agriculture and fisheries	621	23.7	9,181	22.1
Industry and mining	18	0.7	5,557	13.4
Tourism	—	—	523	1.3
Physical Infrastructure				
Energy	892	34.1	11,486	27.6
Transportation and communications	378	14.4	5,421	13.0
Social Infrastructure				
Environmental and public health	101	3.9	4,175	10.0
Education, science and technology	155	6.0	1,815	4.4
Urban development	381	14.5	1,932	4.6
Other				
Export financing	66	2.5	929	2.2
Preinvestment	6	0.2	386	0.9
Other	—	—	194	0.5
Total	2,618	100.0	41,599	100.0

INTERNATIONAL ORGANIZATIONS

Inter-American Development Bank

Lending in 1989 and cumulative lending, 1961–89 (US $ million; after cancellations and exchange adjustments)

Country	Total Amount 1989	Total Amount 1961–89	Ordinary Capital 1989	Ordinary Capital 1961–89	Fund for Special Operations 1989	Fund for Special Operations 1961–89	Funds in Administration 1989	Funds in Administration 1961–89
Argentina	11.4	4,201.2	11.4	3,633.1	—	519	—	49.1
Bahamas	—	120.5	—	118.5	—	—	—	2.0
Barbados	9.4	154.5	9.5	92.6	—	43.2	0.2	18.7
Bolivia	169.9	1,530.0	56.9	690.0	103.8	775.8	9.1	64.2
Brazil	525.1	6,757.3	474.5	5,378.5	50.7	1,246.1	—	132.7
Chile	640.0	3,583.4	640.0	3,336.2	—	203.3	—	43.9
Colombia	40.0	3,883.9	35.7	3,153.7	4.3	665.8	—	64.4
Costa Rica	200.8	1,347.7	188.8	895.0	—	355.5	12.0	97.2
Dominican Republic	171.3	1,063.6	106.8	398.5	62.0	590.2	2.5	74.9
Ecuador	58.5	2,284.1	2.3	1,359.5	56.2	834.2	—	90.4
El Salvador	4.3	940.4	—	274.5	—	549.5	4.3	116.4
Guatemala	0.1	1,124.3	—	531.9	—	532.4	0.2	60.0
Guyana	46.4	304.6	—	103.0	46.4	193.6	—	8.0
Haiti	—	289.3	—	—	—	282.4	—	6.9
Honduras	0.1	970.6	—	300.9	—	616.5	0.2	53.2
Jamaica	115.3	707.4	104.3	433.6	—	178.6	11.0	95.2
Mexico	143.1	5,139.6	143.1	4,538.5	—	566.1	—	35.0
Nicaragua	—	461.4	—	92.6	—	317.5	—	51.3
Panama	—	847.0	—	529.4	—	283.0	—	34.6
Paraguay	18.8	618.2	—	163.6	18.8	442.3	—	12.3
Peru	—	1,602.8	—	987.3	—	412.1	—	203.4
Suriname	—	21.7	—	18.7	—	3.0	—	0.0
Trinidad and Tobago	67.8	184.2	66.1	151.6	—	27.3	1.6	5.3
Uruguay	26.2	737.6	26.2	579.1	—	104.7	—	41.8
Venezuela	120.0	1,411.8	120.0	1,237.5	—	101.4	—	72.9
Regional	250.0	1,311.6	250.0	1,103.3	—	194.2	—	14.1
Total	2,618.5	41,598.7	2,235.6	30,113.1	342.2	10,037.7	41.1	1,447.9

policy changes and improve their institutions. An environmental protection division was also formed in 1989.

A special programme provides financing for small projects run by, for example, co-operatives or local producers' associations, which would normally fail to obtain credit from conventional sources: the beneficiaries are low-income farmers, small-scale entrepreneurs and craftsmen. During 1989 19 projects were financed at a cost of $8.1m.

The Bank provides grants and technical co-operation for the countries of the region. Such assistance amounted to $61m. for 210 projects in 1989.

In March 1986 the charter of the Inter-American Investment Corporation (IIC), an affiliate of the Bank, entered into force, with the aim of promoting private-sector investment in the region (particularly in small- and medium-sized industries).

AFFILIATED INSTITUTIONS

Instituto para la Integración de América Latina (Institute for Latin American Integration): Esmeralda 130, 16°, Casilla de Correo 39, Sucursal 1, Buenos Aires, Argentina; f.1964 as a permanent department of the Inter-American Development Bank. Its functions are: to study the regional integration process; to carry out research into problems which the integration movement poses for individual countries; to organize training courses and seminars; to conduct, at the request of member countries, preliminary studies on joint development schemes and on economic integration alternatives available to individual countries; to provide advisory services to the Bank and to other public and private institutions; to offer courses on the economic, political, social, institutional, legal, scientific and technological aspects of regional integration. Dir EDUARDO ZALDUENDO.

Inter-American Investment Corporation—IIC: f. 1986 as an affiliate of the Inter-American Development Bank, to promote private-sector investment in the region. The IIC's initial capital stock was to be US $200m., of which 55% was contributed by developing member nations, 25.5% by the USA, and the remainder by non-regional members. Emphasis is placed on investment in small and medium-sized enterprises. Gen. Man. GUNTHER H. MULLER.

PUBLICATIONS

Integración Latinoamericana (monthly).

Annual Report (annually, in English and Spanish).

The Process of Integration in Latin America (annually, in English and Spanish).

INTERNATIONAL BANK FOR ECONOMIC CO-OPERATION—IBEC

Address: 11 Ul. M. Poryvaevoi, 107078 Moscow, USSR.
Telephone: 204-72-20.
Telex: 411391.

The Bank was founded in October 1963 with eight member countries, and commenced operations in January 1964 to assist in the economic co-operation and development of member countries (see also CMEA, p. 125, and International Investment Bank, p. 165).

MEMBERS

Bulgaria	Hungary	Romania
Cuba*	Mongolia	USSR
Czechoslovakia	Poland	Viet-Nam*

* Cuba joined the Bank in 1974, and Viet-Nam in 1977. The German Democratic Republic was a member until its reunification with the Federal Republic of Germany in October 1990.

Organization

(October 1990)

THE COUNCIL

The Council is composed of representatives of all member countries. Each country has one vote irrespective of its share in the capital of the Bank. The Council considers and decides questions of policy, determining the general policy of the Bank and the orientation of the development of its activities. It meets about twice a year.

THE BOARD

The Board is the executive body subordinate to the Council; there is one permanent representative from each of the member states.

Chairman: V. S. Khokhlov (USSR).

Activities

The Bank acts as the central institution of the CMEA member countries for credit and settlements. Its main purpose is to effect multilateral settlements in the collective currency of its members, the transferable rouble (TR), and to grant credits in TRs to the authorized banks of the member countries and to international economic organizations. Favourable credit conditions are granted to Cuba, Mongolia and Viet-Nam. Settlements in the collective currency include trade-related and non-commercial payments. The Bank also carries out credit and other transactions in convertible currencies with members and non-member countries.

The total volume of the Bank's operations amounted to 667,800m. TR in 1989; operations in transferable roubles totalled 325,700m. TR. At 31 December 1989 the balance total of the IBEC amounted to 6,780m. TR, compared with 5,801m. TR one year previously.

During 1989 the volume of settlements among member countries channelled through the IBEC was 220,400m. TR, compared with the previous year's total of 225,200m. TR. The volume of trade-related settlements, accounting for 93% of the total, met the targets of the authorized banks. Credits extended by the IBEC to the banks of member countries amounted to 19,100m. TR, compared with 12,900m. TR in 1988.

Following extensive political changes in Eastern Europe in 1989 and 1990, discussions took place in 1990 on the restructuring of the CMEA (q.v.), including the introduction of trade in convertible currencies, and corresponding changes were expected to take place in the activities of the IBEC.

CAPITAL (31 December 1989; million transferable roubles)

	Authorized	Paid-up
Bulgaria	17.0	12.9
Cuba	4.4	3.3
Czechoslovakia	45.0	34.0
German Democratic Republic	55.0	41.6
Hungary	21.0	15.9
Mongolia	3.0	1.7
Poland	27.0	20.4
Romania	16.0	12.1
USSR	116.0	87.7
Viet-Nam	0.9	0.7
Total	**305.3**	**230.3**

BALANCE SHEET (31 December; transferable roubles)

Assets	1988	1989
Monetary funds	1,323,870,764	1,312,346,689
Current accounts and cash on hand	17,249,385	19,438,030
Time deposits	1,306,621,379	1,292,908,659
Credits granted	4,407,509,779	5,391,303,111
Property of the Bank	878,104	941,231
Other assets	69,124,170	75,563,945
Total	**5,801,382,817**	**6,780,154,976**

Liabilities	1988	1989
Capital funds of the Bank	468,748,199	480,220,785
Capital paid up	230,316,560	230,316,560
Reserve capital	238,431,639	249,904,225
Deposits	4,735,533,171	5,552,990,902
Current accounts	629,434,153	1,963,555,254
Time deposits	4,106,099,018	3,589,435,648
Credits received	441,248,344	565,132,366
Other liabilities	120,950,689	143,100,978
Net profit	34,902,414	38,709,945
Total	**5,801,382,817**	**6,780,154,976**

INTERNATIONAL CHAMBER OF COMMERCE—ICC

Address: 38 Cours Albert 1er, 75008 Paris, France.
Telephone: (1) 45-62-34-56.
Telex: 650770.
Fax: (1) 42-25-86-63.

The ICC was founded in 1919 to promote free trade and private enterprise, provide practical services and represent business interests at governmental and inter-governmental levels.

MEMBERS

At the end of 1989 membership consisted of about 5,360 individual corporations and 1,700 organizations (mainly trade and industrial organizations and chambers of commerce). In the following 59 countries National Committees or Councils have been formed to co-ordinate certain functions at the national level, while the ICC is also represented in 50 other countries and territories.

Argentina	India	Saudi Arabia
Australia	Indonesia	Senegal
Austria	Iran	Singapore
Belgium	Ireland	South Africa
Brazil	Israel	Spain
Burkina Faso	Italy	Sri Lanka
Cameroon	Japan	Sweden
Canada	Jordan	Switzerland
Colombia	Republic of Korea	Syria
Côte d'Ivoire	Kuwait	Taiwan
Cyprus	Lebanon	Togo
Denmark	Luxembourg	Tunisia
Ecuador	Madagascar	Turkey
Egypt	Mexico	United Kingdom
Finland	Morocco	USA
France	Netherlands	Uruguay
Gabon	Nigeria	Venezuela
Germany	Norway	Yugoslavia
Greece	Pakistan	Zaire
Iceland	Portugal	

Organization

(October 1990)

COUNCIL

The Council is the governing body of the organization. It is composed of members nominated by the National Committees and meets twice a year.

President: PETER WALLENBERG (Sweden).
Vice-President: JOSEPH E. CONNOR (USA).

EXECUTIVE BOARD

The Executive Board consists of 12–15 members appointed by the Council on the recommendation of the President and six ex-officio members. Members serve for a three-year term, one-third of the members retiring at the end of each year. It ensures close direction of ICC activities and meets four times a year.

INTERNATIONAL SECRETARIAT

The ICC secretariat is based at International Headquarters in Paris, with additional offices maintained in Geneva and New York principally for liaison with the United Nations and its agencies.
Secretary-General: FRANCIS LAGREULA (acting).

NATIONAL COMMITTEES AND GROUPS

Each affiliate is composed of leading business organizations and individual companies. It has its own secretariat, monitors issues of concern to its national constituents, and draws public and government attention to ICC policies.

CONGRESS

The ICC's supreme assembly, to which all member companies and organizations are invited to send senior representatives. Congresses are held every three years, in a different place on each occasion, with up to 2,000 participants. The 29th Congress was held in New Delhi, India, in February 1987, and the 30th Congress was held in Hamburg, Federal Republic of Germany, in June 1990.

CONFERENCE

Conferences with about 250 participants take place in non-Congress years. The eighth Conference was held in Istanbul, Turkey, in September 1988, and the ninth was to take place in Dublin, Ireland, in October 1991.

Activities

The various Commissions of the ICC (listed below) are composed of practising businessmen and experts from all sectors of economic life, nominated by National Committees. ICC recommendations must be adopted by a Commission following consultation with National Committees, and then approved by the Council or Executive Board, before they can be regarded as official ICC policies. Meetings of Commissions are generally held twice a year. Working Parties are frequently constituted by Commissions to undertake specific projects and report back to their parent body. Officers of Commissions, and specialized Working Parties, often meet in the intervals between Commission sessions. The Commissions produce a wide array of specific codes and guidelines of direct use to the world business community; draw up statements and initiatives for presentation to governments and international bodies; and comment constructively and in detail on proposed actions by inter-governmental organizations that are likely to affect business.

ICC works closely with the United Nations and its various organizations. The ICC-UN, GATT Economic Consultative Committee, for example, brings together ICC members and the heads of UN economic organizations and the OECD for annual discussions on the world economy. The Commission on International Trade Policy campaigns against protectionism in world trade and in support of the General Agreement on Tariffs and Trade (GATT, q.v.), and ensures that ICC views are represented in the multilateral trade negotiations which take place under GATT auspices. The ICC also works closely with the European Community, commenting on EEC directives and making recommendations on, for example, tax harmonization and laws relating to competition.

ICC plays a part in combating international crime connected with commerce. The ICC International Maritime Bureau combats maritime fraud, for example insurance fraud and the theft of cargoes. The ICC Counterfeiting Intelligence Bureau was established in 1985 to investigate counterfeiting in trade-marked goods, copyrights and industrial designs. Commercial disputes are submitted to the ICC Court of Arbitration: during 1989 309 new cases were registered and 140 partial or final awards were made, together with 20 awards made with the consent of the parties.

Policy and Technical Commissions:

Commission on International Trade Policy
Commission on International Monetary Relations
Commission on Multinational Enterprises and International Investments
Commission on Industrial Property
Commission on Taxation
Commission on Law and Practices Relating to Competition
Commission on Insurance
Commission on Marketing
Commission on Energy
Commission on Environment
Commission on Computing, Telecommunications and Information Policy
Commission on Sea Transport
Commission on Air Transport
Commission on Trade Regulations and Procedures
Commission on International Commercial Practice
Commission on Banking Technique and Practice
Commission on International Arbitration
East-West Committee

Bodies for the Settlement of Disputes:

Court of Arbitration
International Centre for Technical Expertise
International Maritime Arbitration Organization

INTERNATIONAL ORGANIZATIONS

International Chamber of Commerce

Other Bodies:
ICC-UN, GATT Economic Consultative Committee
International Bureau of Chambers of Commerce
ICC International Maritime Bureau
ICC Counterfeiting Intelligence Bureau
ICC Centre for Maritime Co-operation
ICC Institute of International Business Law and Practice
ICC International Environmental Bureau
ICC Corporate Security Services

FINANCE

The International Chamber of Commerce is a private organization financed partly by contributions from National Committees and other members, according to the economic importance of the country which each represents, and partly by revenue from fees for various services and from sales of publications. The operating budget for 1987 was about 55m. French francs.

PUBLICATIONS

Annual Report.
Contact.
Handbook.
IGO Report.
ICC International Court of Arbitration Bulletin.
Numerous publications on general and technical business and trade-related subjects.

INTERNATIONAL CONFEDERATION OF FREE TRADE UNIONS—ICFTU

Address: 37-41 rue Montagne aux Herbes Potagères, 1000 Brussels, Belgium.
Telephone: (02) 217-80-85.
Telex: 26785.
Fax: (02) 218-84-15.

ICFTU was founded in 1949 by trade union federations which had withdrawn from the World Federation of Trade Unions (see p. 215). It aims to promote the interests of working people and to secure recognition of workers' organizations as free bargaining agents; to reduce the gap between rich and poor; and to defend fundamental human and trade union rights. See also the World Confederation of Labour (p. 213).

MEMBERS

144 organizations in 101 countries with 99m. members (May 1990).

Organization

(October 1990)

WORLD CONGRESS

The Congress, the highest authority of ICFTU, normally meets every four years. The 14th Congress was held in Melbourne, Australia, in March 1988.

Delegations from national federations vary in size according to membership. The Congress examines past activities, maps out future plans, elects the Executive Board and the General Secretary, considers the functioning of the regional machinery, examines financial reports and social, economic and political situations. It works through plenary sessions and through technical committees which report to the plenary sessions.

EXECUTIVE BOARD

The Board meets twice a year, for about three days, usually at Brussels, or at the Congress venue; it consists of 37 members elected by Congress and nominated by areas of the world. The General Secretary is an ex-officio member. After each Congress the Board elects a President and at least seven Vice-Presidents.

The Board considers administrative questions; hears reports from field representatives, missions, regional organizations and affiliates, and makes resultant decisions; and discusses finances, applications for affiliation, and problems affecting world labour. It elects a sub-committee of nine to deal with urgent matters between Board meetings.
President: P. P. NARAYANAN (Malaysia).

PERMANENT COMMITTEES

Finance and General Purposes Committee. Administers the General Fund made up of affiliation fees and the International Solidarity Fund constituting additional voluntary contributions.
Economic and Social Committee.
Education Policy Committee.
Peace, Security and Disarmament Committee.
Women's Committee.
ICFTU/ITS Working Group on Young Workers' Questions.
ICFTU/ITS Working Party on Multinational Companies.
Working Group on International Trade and Monetary Questions.

SECRETARIAT

The headquarters staff numbers 97, comprising some 25 different nationalities.

The four departments are: Administration; Development Co-operation; Economic and Social Policy; Finance. There are also the African Desk; Electronic Data Processing Unit; Information Division; Personnel; and Women's Bureau.
General Secretary: JOHN VANDERVEKEN.

BRANCH OFFICES

ICFTU Geneva Office: 46 avenue Blanc, 1202 Geneva, Switzerland.

ICFTU United Nations Office: Room 404, 104 East 40th St, New York, NY 10016, USA.

There are also Permanent Representatives accredited to FAO (Rome) to the UN, UNIDO and IAEA (Vienna) and to UNEP and Habitat (Nairobi).

REGIONAL ORGANIZATIONS

ICFTU African Regional Organization—AFRO: c/o Sierra Leone Labour Congress, POB 1333, Freetown, Sierra Leone; Sec. KANDEH YILLA (Sierra Leone).
Inter-American Regional Organization of Workers—ORIT: POB 7039, 06000 México, DF, Mexico; tel. 566-7024; telex 1771699; Pres. A. MADARIAGA; Gen. Sec. LUIS ANDERSON.
ICFTU Asian and Pacific Regional Organization—APRO: Trade Union House, Shenton Way, Singapore 0106; tel. 2226294; telex 24480; Pres. GOPESHWAR; Gen. Sec. T. IZUMI.

There are Liaison Offices in Indonesia and Thailand and Field Representatives in Argentina, Australia, Kenya and Zimbabwe. In addition, a number of Project Planners for development co-operation travel in different countries.

FINANCE

Affiliated federations pay a standard fee of 5,658 Belgian francs (1990), or its equivalent in other currencies, per 1,000 members per annum, which covers the establishment and routine activities of the ICFTU headquarters in Brussels, and partly subsidizes the regional organizations.

An International Solidarity Fund was set up in 1956 to assist unions in developing countries, and workers and trade unionists victimized by repressive political measures. It provides legal assistance and supports educational activities. In cases of major natural disasters affecting workers token relief aid is granted.

PUBLICATIONS

Free Labour World (official journal, fortnightly).
World Economic Review (annually).
Survey of Violations of Trade Union Rights (annually).
Occupational Health and Safety Bulletin.

All these periodicals are issued in English, French, German and Spanish. In addition the Congress report is issued in English. Numerous other publications on labour, economic and trade union training have been published in various languages.

Associated International Trade Secretariats

International Federation of Building and Woodworkers: POB 733, 1215 Geneva 15 Aéroport, Switzerland; tel. (022) 7880888; telex 415327; fax (022) 7880716; f. 1934. Mems: national unions with a membership of 3m. workers. Organization: Congress, Executive Committee. Pres. KONRAD CARL (Germany); Sec.-Gen. U. ASP (Sweden). Publs *Bulletin* (quarterly).

International Federation of Chemical, Energy and General Workers' Unions—ICEF: 109 ave Emile de Béco, 1050 Brussels, Belgium; tel. (02) 647-02-35; telex 20847; fax (02) 648-43-16; f. 1907. Mems: 189 national unions covering 6.3m. people in 59 countries. Holds Congress (every four years). Pres. HERMANN RAPPE; Gen. Sec. MICHAEL BOGGS. Publs *Bulletin* (quarterly), *ICEF Info* (monthly).

International Federation of Commercial, Clerical, Professional and Technical Employees—FIET: 15 ave de Balexert, 1219 Châtelaine-Geneva, Switzerland; tel. (022) 7962733; telex 418736; fax (022) 7965321; f. 1904. Mems: 325 national unions of non-manual workers comprising 10m. people in 100 countries. Holds World Congresses (every four years); has seven trade sections (for bank workers, insurance workers, workers in social insurance and health care, commercial workers, salaried employees in industry, hairdressers and workers in property services), regional organizations for Europe, Western Hemisphere, Asia and Africa. Pres. BENGT LLOYD (Sweden); Sec.-Gen. PHILIP J. JENNINGS (UK) (acting). Publs *FIET INFO* (monthly in English, French, German and Spanish).

International Federation of Free Teachers' Unions: Herengracht 54–56, 1015 BN Amsterdam, Netherlands; tel. (020) 24 90 72; telex 17118; fax (020) 27-42-05; f. 1951. Mems: 77 national organizations of teachers' trade unions covering 7m. members in 54 countries. Holds Congress (every four years). Pres. A. SHANKER (USA); Gen. Sec. FRED VAN LEEUWEN (Netherlands). Publs *International Action* (monthly), *Workers in Education* (5 a year) (both in English, French and Spanish).

International Federation of Journalists: IPC, blvd Charlemagne 1, Bte 5, 1041 Brussels, Belgium; tel. (02) 238-09-51; telex 61275; fax (02) 230-36-33; f. 1952 to link national unions of professional journalists dedicated to the freedom of the press, to defend the rights of journalists, and to raise professional standards; it conducts surveys, assists in trade union training programmes, organizes seminars and provides information; it arranges fact-finding missions in countries where press freedom is under pressure, and issues protests against the persecution and detention of journalists and the censorship of the mass media. Mems: 50 unions in 43 countries, comprising 175,000 individuals. Pres. MIA DOORNAERT (Belgium); Gen. Sec. AIDAN WHITE (United Kingdom).

International Federation of Plantation, Agricultural and Allied Workers: 17 rue Necker, 1201 Geneva, Switzerland; tel. (022) 7313105; telex 4122494; fax (022) 7380114; f. 1959. Mems: unions covering approx. 6m. workers. Holds Congress (every six years). Pres P. P. NARAYANAN (Malaysia); Gen. Sec. BÖRJE SVENSSON (Sweden). Publ. *News* (quarterly).

International Graphical Federation: 17 rue des Fripiers, Galerie du Centre (Block 2), 1000 Brussels, Belgium; tel. (02) 512-39-29; telex 222044; fax (02) 512-38-14; f. 1949. Mems: 45 national organizations in 37 countries, covering 835,386 individuals. Holds Congress (every three years). Pres. ERWIN FERLEMANN (Germany); Gen. Sec. ROBERT W. TOMLINS. Publs *Journal of the IGF* (2 a year), reports.

International Metalworkers' Federation: Route des Acacias 54 bis, 1227 Geneva, Switzerland; tel. (022) 436150; telex 423298; fax (022) 431510; f. 1893. Mems: national organizations covering 13m. workers in 70 countries. Holds Congress (every four years); has seven regional offices; six industrial departments; World Company Councils for unions in multinational corporations. Pres. F. STEINKUHLER (Germany); Gen. Sec. MARCELLO MALENTACCHI. Publ. *IMF News* (every 2 weeks, seven languages).

International Secretariat for Arts, Mass Media and Entertainment Trade Unions: 15 ave de Balexert, 1219 Châtelaine-Geneva, Switzerland; tel. (022) 7962733; telex 418736; fax (022) 7965321; f. 1965; Pres. WALTER BACHER; Sec.-Gen. IRENE ROBADEY.

International Textile, Garment and Leather Workers' Federation: rue Joseph Stevens 8, 1000 Brussels, Belgium; tel. (02) 512-26-06; fax (02) 511-09-04; f. 1970. Mems: 160 unions covering 5.9m. workers in 76 countries. Pres. B. KELLER (Germany); Gen. Sec. NEIL KEARNEY (Ireland).

International Transport Workers' Federation: 133–135 Great Suffolk St, London, SE1 1PD, England; tel. (071) 403-2733; telex 8811397; fax (071) 357-7871; f. 1896. Mems: national trade unions covering 4.5m. workers in 90 countries. Holds Congress (every four years); has eight Industrial Sections. Pres. JIM HUNTER (Canada); Gen. Sec. HAROLD LEWIS (UK). Publ. *ITF News* (monthly).

International Union of Food and Allied Workers' Associations: 8 rampe du Pont-Rouge, 1213 Petit-Lancy, Switzerland; tel. (022) 793-22-33; telex 429292; fax (022) 7932238; f. 1920. Mems: national organizations covering about 2.1m workers in 80 countries. Holds Congress (every four years). Pres. LAGE ANDREASSON (Sweden); Gen. Sec. DAN GALLIN (Switzerland). Publs monthly bulletins.

Miners' International Federation: 109 ave Emile de Béco, 1050 Brussels, Belgium; tel. (02) 646-21-20; telex 20847; fax (02) 648-43-16; f. 1890. Mems: 43 national unions covering 2.1m. miners in 41 countries. Holds Congress (every four years). Pres. A. STENDALEN (Sweden); Gen. Sec. P. MICHALZIK (Germany).

Postal, Telegraph and Telephone International: 38 ave du Lignon, 1219 Geneva, Switzerland; tel. (022) 7968311; fax (022) 7963975; f. 1920. Mems: national trade unions covering 4.2m. workers in 102 countries. Holds Congress (every four years). Pres. AKIRA YAMAGISHI (Japan); Gen. Sec. PHILIP BOWYER. Publs *PTTI News* (six languages, monthly), *PTTI Studies* (four languages, quarterly).

Public Services International: 45 ave Voltaire, 01210 Ferney-Voltaire, France; tel. 50-40-64-64; telex 390559; fax 50-40-73-20; f. 1907; Mems: 250 unions and professional associations covering 8.9m. workers in 80 countries. Holds Congress (every four years). Pres. MONIKA WULF-MATHIES (Germany); Gen. Sec. HANS ENGELBERTS (Netherlands). Publs *INFO* (10 a year), *Focus*.

Universal Alliance of Diamond Workers: Lange Kievitstraat 57 (Bus 1), 2018 Antwerp, Belgium; tel. (03) 232-91-51; f. 1905. Mems: 10,100 in six countries. Pres. J. MEIJNIKMAN (Netherlands); Gen. Sec. C. DENISSE (Belgium).

INTERNATIONAL INVESTMENT BANK

Address: 17 Presnensky Val, Moscow 123557, USSR.
Telephone: 253-80-24.
Telex: 411358.
Fax: 253-97-83.

Established by an intergovernmental Agreement of the members of the Council for Mutual Economic Assistance (see p. 125) in 1970, the Bank commenced operations on 1 January 1971.

MEMBERS*

Bulgaria	Hungary	Romania
Cuba	Mongolia	USSR
Czechoslovakia	Poland	Viet-Nam

* The German Democratic Republic was a member until its reunification with the Federal Republic of Germany in October 1990.

Organization
(October 1990)

COUNCIL

The Council of the Bank is the highest authority and consists of representatives of all the member countries. Each member country, irrespective of the amount of its quota, has one vote in the Council. Major decisions require a unanimous vote. The Council meets as often as necessary but not less than twice a year.

BOARD

The Board is the executive body of the Bank and consists of a Chairman and three Deputies appointed by the Council. Its task is to supervise the Bank's activities in accordance with the Agreement, the Statutes of the Bank and the decisions of the Council.
Chairman: ALBERT N. BELICHENKO (USSR).

Activities

Under Article II of the Agreement on the Establishment of the International Investment Bank the fundamental task of the Bank is to grant long-term and medium-term credits for projects connected with the international socialist division of labour, specialization and co-operation in production, expenditure for expansion of raw materials and fuel resources in the members' collective interest, for the construction of enterprises of mutual concern to member countries in other branches of the economy, for the construction of projects for the development of the national economies of member countries and for other purposes established by the Council. Credits are granted for a period of up to 15 years, and may be granted to:

(i) banks, economic organizations and enterprises of member countries;
(ii) international economic organizations and enterprises of member countries;
(iii) banks and economic organizations of other countries.

The Bank may:

(i) form reserve capital and create its own special funds;
(ii) attract funds in collective currency (transferable roubles), in national currencies of interested countries and in convertible currency;
(iii) issue interest-bearing bond loans placed on international capital markets;
(iv) place surplus funds with other banks, buy and sell currency, gold and securities, grant guarantees and conduct other banking operations;
(v) co-operate with the Council for Mutual Economic Assistance, the International Bank for Economic Co-operation (q.v.) and other economic organizations of the member countries of the Bank;
(vi) make contact and establish business relations with international and other financial and credit institutions as well as with banks;
(vii) conclude international agreements and the like, as well as making business transactions within its competence.

In 1974, a Special Fund was formed for financing programmes of economic and technical assistance to developing countries.

As at 1 January 1990, the Bank's authorized capital was 1,071.3m. transferable roubles, of which the paid-up portion was 589.2m. transferable roubles. Total assets amounted to 3,159.1m. transferable roubles. By the end of 1989 the Bank had authorized credits for 139 projects, totalling 5,799m. transferable roubles. The largest proportion of credits granted between 1971 and the end of 1989 was for the energy and fuel sector (57%), while 23% was for machine-building and metal-working (including electrical engineering and electronics), 11% was for metallurgy and 5% for the chemical industry. During 1989 credits amounting to 234m. transferable roubles were approved for 13 projects (compared with 600m. transferable roubles for 23 projects in 1988). During 1989 projects assisted included modernization of a petroleum-refining plant in Hungary; production of food-industry and textiles equipment in the German Democratic Republic; a joint Soviet/Yugoslav venture producing plastic items; production of polymer film in the USSR; production of construction machinery in Poland; a joint Soviet/Polish venture producing aircraft engines; production and processing of citrus fruit in Cuba; a coal extraction plant in Viet-Nam, to be constructed by a Hungarian enterprise; and plants producing garments, shoes, packing materials and cement in Viet-Nam. In 1989 the Bank participated for the first time in financing leasing operations: a credit was granted to a Bulgarian leasing company to improve production capacity at a joint Bulgarian/Swiss/Soviet stationery venture.

Following extensive political changes in Eastern Europe in 1989 and 1990, discussions took place in 1990 on the restructuring of the CMEA (q.v.), including the introduction of trade in convertible currencies. Corresponding changes were expected to take place in the activities of the Bank, including an expansion of credit assistance and increased links with Western financial institutions.

AUTHORIZED CAPITAL
(million transferable roubles as at 1 January 1990)

Country	Amount
Bulgaria	85.1
Cuba	15.7
Czechoslovakia	129.9
German Democratic Republic	176.1
Hungary	83.7
Mongolia	4.5
Poland	121.4
Romania	52.6
USSR	399.3
Viet-Nam	3.0
Total	**1,071.3**

INTERNATIONAL INVESTMENT BANK ACTIVITIES

Year	Assets	Loans granted (cumulative)	Net Profit	Number of projects (cumulative)
	(million transferable roubles)			
1971	189	182	—	16
1975	943	2,885	17	40
1980	2,165	3,305	19	73
1985	2,355	3,866	23	94
1986	2,566	4,762	24	103
1987	2,720	4,959	26	111
1988	2,980	5,565	30	126
1989	3,159	5,799	35	139

INTERNATIONAL OLYMPIC COMMITTEE

Address: Château de Vidy, 1007 Lausanne, Switzerland.
Telephone: 253271.
Telex: 454024.
Fax: 241552.

The International Olympic Committee was founded in 1894 to ensure the regular celebration of the Olympic Games.

Organization
(October 1990)

INTERNATIONAL OLYMPIC COMMITTEE

The International Olympic Committee (IOC) is a non-governmental international organization comprising 94 members, who are representatives of the IOC in their countries and not their countries' delegates to the IOC. The members meet in session at least once a year.

The IOC is the final authority on all questions concerning the Olympic Games and the Olympic movement. There are 166 recognized National Olympic Committees, which are the sole authorities responsible for the representation of their respective countries at the Olympic Games. The IOC may give recognition to International Federations which undertake to adhere to the Olympic Charter, and which govern sports that comply with the IOC's criteria.

EXECUTIVE BOARD

The session of the IOC delegates to the Executive Board the authority to manage the IOC's affairs. The President of the Board is elected for an eight-year term, and is eligible for re-election for successive terms of four years. The Vice-Presidents are elected for four-year terms, and may be re-elected after a minimum interval of four years. Members of the Board are elected to hold office for four years.

President: JUAN ANTONIO SAMARANCH (Spain).
First Vice-President: RICHARD W. POUND (Canada).
Second Vice-President: Judge KÉBA MBAYE (Senegal).
Third Vice-President: HE ZHENLIANG (People's Republic of China).
Fourth Vice-President: KEVAN GOSPER (Australia).
Members of the Board:
CHIHARU IGAYA (Japan).
GUNNAR ERICSSON (Sweden).
UN YONG KIM (Republic of Korea).
ROBERT HELMICK (USA).
MARC HODLER (Switzerland).
FLOR ISAVA-FONSECA (Venezuela).

ADMINISTRATION

The administration of the IOC is under the authority of the Director-General and the Secretary-General, who are appointed by the Executive Board.
Director-General: FRANÇOIS CARRARD.
Secretary-General: FRANÇOISE ZWEIFEL.

Activities

According to Rule 1 of the Olympic Charter, the aims of the Olympic movement are:

to promote the development of those physical and moral qualities which are the basis of sport,

to educate young people through sport in a spirit of better understanding between each other and of friendship, thereby helping to build a better and more peaceful world,

to spread the Olympic principles throughout the world, thereby creating international goodwill,

to bring together the athletes of the world in the great four-yearly sport festival, the Olympic Games.

THE GAMES OF THE OLYMPIAD

The Olympic Summer Games take place during the first year of the Olympiad (period of four years) which they are to celebrate. They are the exclusive property of the IOC, which entrusts their organization to a host city seven years in advance.

1896	Athens	1956	Melbourne
1900	Paris	1960	Rome
1904	St Louis	1964	Tokyo
1908	London	1968	Mexico City
1912	Stockholm	1972	Munich
1920	Antwerp	1976	Montreal
1924	Paris	1980	Moscow
1928	Amsterdam	1984	Los Angeles
1932	Los Angeles	1988	Seoul
1936	Berlin	1992	Barcelona
1948	London	1996	Atlanta
1952	Helsinki		

The programme of the Games must include at least 15 of the total number of Olympic sports (sports governed by recognized International Federations and admitted to the Olympic programme by decision of the IOC at least six years before the Games). The Olympic summer sports are: archery, athletics, badminton (from 1992), baseball (from 1992), basketball, boxing, canoeing, cycling, equestrian sports, fencing, football, gymnastics, handball, field hockey, judo, modern pentathlon, rowing, shooting, swimming, table tennis, tennis, volleyball, water polo, weight-lifting, wrestling, yachting.

OLYMPIC WINTER GAMES

The Olympic Winter Games comprise competitions in sports practised on snow and ice. From 1994 onwards, they are to be held in the second calendar year following that in which the Games of the Olympiad take place.

1924	Chamonix	1968	Grenoble
1928	St Moritz	1972	Sapporo
1932	Lake Placid	1976	Innsbruck
1936	Garmisch-Partenkirchen	1980	Lake Placid
1948	St Moritz	1984	Sarajevo
1952	Oslo	1988	Calgary
1956	Cortina d'Ampezzo	1992	Albertville
1960	Squaw Valley	1994	Lillehammer
1964	Innsbruck		

The Winter Games may include skiing, skating, ice hockey, bobsleigh, luge and biathlon.

INTERNATIONAL ORGANIZATION FOR MIGRATION—IOM

Address: 17 route des Morillons, POB 71, 1211 Geneva 19, Switzerland.
Telephone: (022) 7179111.
Telex: 415722.
Fax: (022) 7986150.

The Intergovernmental Committee for Migration (ICM) was founded in 1951 as a non-political and humanitarian organization with a predominantly operational mandate, including the handling of orderly and planned migration to meet specific needs of emigration and immigration countries; and the processing and movement of refugees, displaced persons and other individuals in need of international migration services to countries offering them resettlement opportunities. In 1989 ICM's name was changed to the International Organization for Migration (IOM).

MEMBERS

Argentina	Ecuador	Nicaragua
Australia	El Salvador	Norway
Austria	Germany	Panama
Belgium	Greece	Paraguay
Bolivia	Guatemala	Peru
Canada	Honduras	Philippines
Chile	Israel	Portugal
Colombia	Italy	Switzerland
Costa Rica	Kenya	Thailand
Cyprus	Korea, Republic	USA
Denmark	Luxembourg	Uruguay
Dominican Republic	Netherlands	Venezuela

Observers: Belize, Brazil, Cape Verde, Egypt, Finland, France, Ghana, Guinea-Bissau, Holy See, Japan, Mexico, New Zealand, San Marino, Somalia, Spain, Sweden, Turkey, Uganda, United Kingdom, Yugoslavia, Zimbabwe.

Organization
(October 1990)

IOM is governed by a Council which is composed of representatives of all member governments, and has the responsibility for making final decisions on policy, programmes and financing. An Executive Committee of 10 member governments elected by the Council prepares the work of the Council and makes recommendations on the basis of reports from the Sub-Committee on Budget and Finance and the Sub-Committee on the Co-ordination of Transport. IOM had a network of 46 offices in 1990.

Director General: JAMES N. PURCELL (USA).
Deputy Director General: HÉCTOR CHARRY SAMPER (Colombia).

Activities

Upon request from member governments, IOM arranges the organized transfer of migrants, refugees, displaced persons and other individuals in need of international migration services. This includes (for refugees) processing, medical services to respond to entry requirements in resettlement countries, and language and cultural orientation courses; and (for migrants) counselling, recruitment, selection, processing in country of origin, reception, placement and integration assistance in the receiving country, and language courses. IOM co-ordinates its refugee activities with the UN High Commissioner for Refugees (q.v.) and with governmental and non-governmental organizations.

IOM's programmes of 'Migration for Development' aim at contributing towards alleviating economic and social problems through recruitment and selection of high-level workers and professionals to fill positions in priority sectors of the economy in developing countries for which qualified persons are not available locally (particularly in Latin America and Africa). Under such programmes, IOM identifies, selects, recruits, places and transfers the qualified personnel. The programmes comprise Selective Migration and Integrated Experts—to provide highly qualified professionals and technicians; Return of Talent—to facilitate the return of qualified nationals to their home countries or region after they have acquired skills and experience in industrialized countries; and Horizontal Co-operation in the field of qualified human resources, through the exchange of governmental experts and the intraregional transfer of professionals and technicians. During 1983–89 868 qualified African nationals returned to Africa from industrialized countries under these programmes, and in 1989 2,572 professionals, technicians and highly-skilled workers were transferred to Latin America. A pilot project to assign experts to Malaysia and the Philippines was being implemented in 1989.

IOM provides advisory services and carries out studies to assist member governments in the formation and implementation of their migration policy, legislation and administration.

International Seminars are organized by IOM on international migration issues. These IOM Seminars serve as a forum for exchange of information and ideas among member and observer governments, governmental and non-governmental organizations, with a view to devising practical recommendations on current migration problems.

A number of UN agencies, 13 international governmental and 24 non-governmental organizations co-operate in the programmes which IOM carries out within the framework of the policies of its member governments.

During 1989 IOM handled 212,354 people (including 202,257 refugees), bringing to more than 4m. the total number of persons resettled in 126 new home countries since the organization began operations in 1952. In 1989 the largest group of refugees resettled by IOM comprised Indochinese refugees from countries of asylum in south-east Asia (63,815). IOM arranges the movement of persons emigrating directly from Viet-Nam under the 'Orderly Departure Programme' (43,983 in 1989). During the year, IOM assisted in the resettlement or repatriation of 14,343 Latin American refugees and displaced people; about 48,000 Soviet citizens and 21,000 other Eastern Europeans; and 5,704 African and Middle Eastern refugees. IOM assisted 3,400 Portuguese who obtained immigration opportunities abroad. Some 10,000 people were also assisted in resettlement or repatriation through programmes for asylum-seekers in Belgium and the Federal Republic of Germany.

Following the Iraqi invasion of Kuwait in August 1990, IOM organized the repatriation by air of thousands of (mainly Asian) migrant workers who had fled from Iraq and Kuwait into Jordan.

FINANCE

The IOM budget for 1989 amounted to US $137.9m. for operations and $18.5m. for administration: the principal item of expenditure ($53.7m.) was for assistance to refugees in Asia. The projected budget for 1990 was $153.0m. (operational).

PUBLICATIONS

Monthly Dispatch.
International Migration (quarterly).
IOM Latin American Migration Journal (3 a year).

INTERNATIONAL RED CROSS AND RED CRESCENT MOVEMENT

The International Red Cross and Red Crescent Movement is a world-wide independent humanitarian organization, comprising two bodies working at an international level: one in time of armed conflict, the International Committee of the Red Cross (ICRC), founded in 1863; and the other in peace time, the League of Red Cross and Red Crescent Societies (LRCS), founded in 1919, and 148 National Red Cross and Red Crescent Societies working mainly at national level.

Organization

INTERNATIONAL CONFERENCE

The supreme deliberative body of the Movement, the Conference comprises delegations from the ICRC, the League and the National Societies, and of representatives of States Parties to the Geneva Conventions (see below). The Conference's function is to determine the general policy of the Movement and to ensure unity in the work of the various bodies. It usually meets every four years, and is hosted by the National Society of the country in which it is held.

STANDING COMMISSION

The Commission meets at least twice a year in ordinary session. It promotes harmony in the work of the Movement, and examines matters which concern the Movement as a whole. It is formed of two representatives of the ICRC, two of the League, and five members of National Societies elected by the Conference.

COUNCIL OF DELEGATES

The Council comprises delegations from the National Societies, from the International Committee and from the League. The Council is the body where the representatives of all the components of the Movement meet to discuss matters which concern the Movement as a whole.

Principles of the Movement

Humanity. The International Red Cross and Red Crescent Movement, born of a desire to bring assistance without discrimination to the wounded on the battlefield, endeavours, in its international and national capacity, to prevent and alleviate human suffering wherever it may be found. Its purpose is to protect life and health and to ensure respect for the human being.

Impartiality. It makes no discrimination as to nationality, race, religious beliefs, class or political opinions. It endeavours to relieve the suffering of individuals, being guided solely by their needs, and to give priority to the most urgent cases of distress.

Neutrality. In order to continue to enjoy the confidence of all, the Movement may not take sides in hostilities or engage in controversies of a political, racial, religious or ideological nature.

Independence. The Movement is independent. The National Societies, while auxiliaries in the humanitarian services of their governments and subject to national laws, must retain their autonomy so that they may always be able to act in accordance with the principles of the Movement.

Voluntary Service. It is a voluntary relief movement not prompted by desire for gain.

Unity. There must be only one Red Cross or Red Crescent Society in any one country. It must be open to all. It must carry on its humanitarian work throughout the territory.

Universality. The Movement is a world-wide organization in which all National Societies have equal status and share equal responsibilities and duties in helping each other.

International Committee of the Red Cross—ICRC

Address: 19 avenue de la Paix, 1202 Geneva, Switzerland.
Telephone: (022) 7346001.
Telex: 414226.
Fax: (022) 7332057.

Organization
(October 1990)

INTERNATIONAL COMMITTEE

The ICRC is an independent institution of a private character. It is exclusively composed of Swiss nationals. Members are co-opted, and their total number may not exceed 25. The international character of the ICRC is based on its mission and not on its composition.

President: CORNELIO SOMMARUGA.
Vice-Presidents: MAURICE AUBERT, CLAUDIO CARATSCH.

EXECUTIVE COUNCIL

The Executive Council meets weekly.
President: CORNELIO SOMMARUGA.
Members: ATHOS GALLINO, RUDOLF JÄCKLI, PIERRE KELLER, ANDRÉ GHELFI, ANNE PETITPIERRE, CLAUDIO CARATSCH.

DIRECTORATE

The Directorate is responsible for administration, in accordance with decisions taken by the International Committee, the Executive Council and the President. It was restructured in 1988 and comprises six departments: operations; operational support; principles and law and relations with the movement; finance and administration; human resources; communications. The ICRC employed about 4,000 people at mid-1990, of whom more than 80% were working in the field among its 47 delegations.

Activities

The International Committee of the Red Cross was founded in 1863, in Geneva, by Henry Dunant and four of his friends. The original purpose of the Committee was to assist wounded soldiers on the battlefield. The present activities of the ICRC consist in giving legal protection and material assistance to military and civilian victims of wars (international wars, internal strife and disturbances). In 1990 the ICRC was granted the status of an observer at the United Nations.

The ICRC promoted the foundation in each country of the world of National Committees of the Red Cross or Red Crescent, which later became the National Societies of the Red Cross or Red Crescent.

As well as providing medical aid and emergency food supplies in many countries, the ICRC plays an important part in inspecting prison conditions and in tracing missing persons, and in disseminating humanitarian principles in an attempt to protect non-combatants from violence. Examples of its activities during the late 1980s included the following:

Africa: visits to detainees in several countries; food or medical aid in Angola, Somalia, Ethiopia, Mozambique, Sudan, Uganda and other countries; programmes for the rehabilitation of the disabled in several countries.

Latin America: relief activities, medical aid, visits to detainees.

Asia: medical assistance in Afghanistan, Cambodia and Thailand, visits to detainees in Afghanistan, Indonesia, the Philippines and Sri Lanka; dealing with enquiries about missing relatives among refugees from Viet-Nam and Cambodia; medical assistance programme for Afghan refugees in Pakistan.

Middle East: emergency action in Lebanon, providing medical supplies and evacuating the wounded and refugees; repatriation of prisoners following the cease-fire in the war between Iran and Iraq in 1988; visits to detainees in Israel and the Israeli-occupied territories.

INTERNATIONAL ORGANIZATIONS

THE GENEVA CONVENTIONS

In 1864, one year after its foundation, the ICRC submitted to the states called to a Diplomatic Conference in Geneva a draft international treaty for 'the Amelioration of the Condition of the Wounded in Armies in the Field'. This treaty was adopted and signed by twelve states, which thereby bound themselves to respect as neutral wounded soldiers and those assisting them. This was the first Geneva Convention.

With the development of technology and weapons, the introduction of new means of waging war, and the manifestation of certain phenomena (the great number of prisoners of war during World War I; the enormous number of displaced persons and refugees during World War II; the internationalization of internal conflicts in recent years) the necessity was felt of having other international treaties to protect new categories of war victims. The ICRC, for more than 127 years now, has been the leader of a movement to improve and complement international humanitarian law.

There are now four Geneva Conventions, adopted on 12 August 1949: I—to protect wounded and sick in armed forces on land, as well as medical personnel; II—to protect the same categories of people at sea, as well as the shipwrecked; III—concerning the treatment of prisoners of war; IV—for the protection of civilians in time of war; and there are two Additional Protocols of 8 June 1977, for the protection of victims in international armed conflicts (Protocol I) and in non-international armed conflicts (Protocol II).

In August 1990 165 states were parties to the Geneva Conventions; 97 were parties to Protocol I and 87 to Protocol II.

FINANCE

The ICRC's work is financed by a voluntary annual grant from governments parties to the Geneva Conventions, voluntary contributions from National Red Cross and Red Crescent Societies and by gifts and legacies from private people. The ICRC's various budgets for 1989 amounted to some 500m. Swiss francs.

PERIODICALS AND PUBLICATIONS

International Review of the Red Cross (every 2 months, French, English and Spanish editions; short edition *Extracts* in German).

ICRC Bulletin (monthly, French, English, Spanish and German editions).

Annual Report (editions in Arabic, English, French, German and Spanish).

The Geneva Conventions: texts and commentaries.

The Protocols Additional.

Various publications on humanitarian law and subjects of Red Cross interest.

League of Red Cross and Red Crescent Societies—LRCS

Address: 17 Chemin des Crêts, Petit-Saconnex, Case Postale 372, 1211 Geneva 19, Switzerland.

Telephone: (022) 7345580.

Telex: 22555.

Fax: (022) 7330395.

The League was founded in 1919. It is the world federation of all Red Cross and Red Crescent Societies. The general aim of the League is to inspire, encourage, facilitate and promote at all times all forms of humanitarian activities by the National Societies, with a view to the prevention and alleviation of human suffering, and thereby contribute to the maintenance and promotion of peace in the world.

MEMBERS

National Red Cross and Red Crescent Societies in 148 countries in October 1990, with an aggregate youth and adult membership of over 250m.

Organization
(October 1990)

GENERAL ASSEMBLY

The General Assembly is the highest authority of the League and meets every two years in commission sessions (for development, disaster relief, health and community services, and youth) and plenary sessions. It is composed of representatives from all National Societies that are members of the League.

President: Dr MARIO VILLARROEL LANDER (Venezuela).

EXECUTIVE COUNCIL

The Council, which meets every six months, is composed of the President of the League, nine Vice-Presidents and 16 National Societies elected by the Assembly. Its functions include the implementation of decisions of the General Assembly; it also has powers to act between meetings of the Assembly.

ASSEMBLY AND FINANCE COMMISSIONS

Development Commission.
Disaster Relief Commission.
Health and Community Services Commission.
Youth Commission.
Finance Commission.
Permanent Scale of Contributions Commission.

The Advisory Commissions meet, in principle, once every two years, at the same time as the General Assembly. Members are elected by the Assembly under a system that ensures each Society a seat on one Commission. The Finance Commission, which has seven members, meets twice a year, and the Permanent Scale of Contributions Commission, also with seven members, meets annually.

SECRETARIAT

Secretary General: PÄR STENBÄCK (Finland).

Treasurer-General: AL-MEHDI BENNOUNA (Morocco).

Activities

RELIEF

The Secretariat assumes the statutory responsibilities of the League in the field of relief to victims of natural disasters, refugees and civilian populations who may be displaced or exposed to abnormal hardship. This activity has three main aspects:

(i) Relief Operations: for the co-ordination of relief operations on the international level and execution by the National Society of the stricken country or by the League itself;

(ii) Supply, Logistics and Warehouses: for the co-ordination and purchase, transport and warehousing of relief supplies;

(iii) Disaster Preparedness: for co-ordination of assistance to National Societies situated in disaster-prone areas in the study and execution of practical measures calculated to prevent disasters and diminish their effects.

SERVICES TO NATIONAL SOCIETIES

The Secretariat promotes and co-ordinates assistance to National Societies in developing their basic structure and their services to the community. The Secretariat is equipped to advise Societies in the fields of health, social welfare, information, nursing, first aid and training; and the operation of blood programmes. It also promotes the establishment and development of educational and service programmes for children and youth.

The League maintains close relations with many inter-governmental organizations, the United Nations and its Specialized Agencies, and with non-governmental organizations, and represents member Societies in the international field.

FINANCE

The permanent Secretariat of the League is financed by the contributions of Member Societies on a pro-rata basis. Each relief action is financed by separate, voluntary contributions, and development programme projects are also financed on a voluntary basis.

PUBLICATIONS

(in English, French and Spanish; the *Annual Review* and *Weekly News* also appear in Arabic)

Annual Review.

Red Cross, Red Crescent (quarterly).

Weekly News.

Transfusion International (quarterly).

ISLAMIC DEVELOPMENT BANK

Address: POB 5925, Jeddah 21432, Saudi Arabia.
Telephone: 6361400.
Telex: 601137.
Fax: 6366871.

An international financial institution established following a conference of finance ministers of member countries of the Organization of the Islamic Conference (q.v.), held in Jeddah in December 1973. Its aim is to encourage the economic development and social progress of member countries and of Muslim communities in non-member countries, in accordance with the principles of the Islamic Shari'a (sacred law). The Bank formally opened in October 1975.

MEMBERS

There are 44 members (see table of subscriptions below).

Organization
(October 1990)

BOARD OF GOVERNORS

Each member country is represented by a governor, usually its Finance Minister, or an alternate. The Board of Governors is the Supreme Authority of the Bank, and meets annually.

BOARD OF EXECUTIVE DIRECTORS

The Board consists of 11 members, five of whom are appointed by the four largest subscribers to the capital stock of the Bank; the remaining six are elected by Governors representing the other subscribers. Members of the Board of Executive Directors are elected for three-year terms. The Board is responsible for the direction of the general operations of the Bank.

President of the Bank and Chairman of the Board of Executive Directors: Dr AHMAD MUHAMMAD ALI (Saudi Arabia).

FINANCIAL STRUCTURE

The authorized capital of the Bank is 2,000m. Islamic Dinars divided into 200,000 shares having a value of 10,000 Islamic Dinars each. The Islamic Dinar (ID) is the Bank's unit of account and is equivalent to the value of one Special Drawing Right of the IMF (SDR 1 = US $1.24362 at the end of May 1989).

In April 1989 subscribed capital amounted to ID 1,960.87m., and paid-up capital was ID 1,642.45m.

SUBSCRIPTIONS (million Islamic Dinars, as at April 1989)

Country	Amount	Country	Amount
Afghanistan	2.5	Mauritania	2.5
Algeria	63.1	Morocco	12.6
Bahrain	7.0	Niger	6.3
Bangladesh	25.0	Oman	7.0
Benin	2.5	Pakistan	63.1
Brunei	6.3	Palestine Liberation Organization	5.0
Burkina Faso	6.3		
Cameroon	6.3		
Chad	2.5	Qatar	50.0
Comoros	2.5	Saudi Arabia	506.37
Djibouti	2.5	Senegal	6.3
Egypt	25.0	Sierra Leone	2.5
Gabon	7.5	Somalia	2.5
The Gambia	2.5	Sudan	25.2
Guinea	6.3	Syria	2.5
Guinea-Bissau	6.3	Tunisia	5.0
Indonesia	63.1	Turkey	160.0
Iran	2.5	Uganda	6.3
Iraq	25.2	United Arab Emirates	194.7
Jordan	10.1		
Kuwait	252.2	Yemen Arab Republic*	6.3
Lebanon	2.5		
Libya	315.3	Yemen, People's Democratic Republic*	6.3
Malaysia	40.4		
Maldives	2.5		
Mali	2.5	**Total**	**1,900.87**

* Formed Republic of Yemen, May 1990.

Activities

The Bank adheres to the Islamic principle forbidding usury, and does not grant loans or credits for interest. Instead, its methods of financing are: provision of interest-free loans (with a service fee) mainly for infrastructural projects which are expected to have a marked impact on long-term socio-economic development; provision of technical assistance (e.g. for feasibility studies); equity participation in industrial and agricultural projects; leasing operations, involving the leasing of equipment such as ships, and instalment sale financing; and profit-sharing operations. Funds not immediately needed for projects are used for foreign trade financing, particularly for importing commodities to be used in development (i.e. raw materials and intermediate industrial goods, rather than consumer goods); priority is given to the import of goods from other member countries (see table). A longer-term trade financing scheme was introduced in 1987/88. In addition, the Special Assistance Account provides emergency aid and other assistance, with particular emphasis on education in Islamic communities in non-member countries.

By August 1987 the Bank had approved a total of ID 1,565.3m. for project financing and technical assistance, and a total of ID 4,354.8m. for foreign trade financing. During the Islamic year 1407, from 5 September 1986 to 24 August 1987, the Bank approved a total of ID 587.3m. for 101 operations (excluding those covered by the Special Assistance Account), compared with ID 740.7m. for 93 projects in the previous year. The decrease reflected restrictions on borrowing imposed on some member countries by their economic difficulties. Of financing approved in the year to 24 August 1987 (excluding the Special Assistance Account), 23% was for ordinary operations and 77% for foreign trade financing.

The Bank approved 11 interest-free loans in the year ending 24 August 1987, amounting to ID 36.08m. (compared with seven loans of ID 28.27m. in the previous year). These loans supported the following projects: reconstruction of Cotonou port, Benin; petroleum storage in the Comoros; road-building in The Gambia and the Yemen Arab Republic; primary education in rural areas of Guinea; building schools in Maldives and Niger; a dam in Morocco; railway improvements in Pakistan; rice-growing in Senegal; and

Operations approved, 5 September 1986–24 August 1987

Type of operation	Number of operations	Total amount (milllion Islamic Dinars)
Ordinary operations	48	134.22
Project financing	24	128.16
Loan	11	36.08
Equity	1	0.75
Leasing	1*	10.00
Profit-sharing	—	—
Instalment sales	11	81.34
Technical assistance	24	6.06
Foreign trade financing	53	453.03
Operations financed from the Special Assistance Account	12	9.12
Total	**113**	**596.44**

* A combined equity and leasing operation.

Project financing and technical assistance by sector, 5 September 1986–24 August 1987

Sector	Amount (million Islamic Dinars)	%
Agriculture	25.77	19.2
Industry and mining	19.51	14.6
Transport and communications	36.06	26.9
Utilities	30.91	23.0
Social services	11.22	8.4
Other	10.75	8.0
Total	**134.22**	**100.0**

INTERNATIONAL ORGANIZATIONS   *Islamic Development Bank*

the Middle East Technical University, Turkey. During the same year the Bank approved only one equity project and one combined line of equity and leasing. Instalment sale financing was approved for 11 projects and amounted to ID 81.34m.

The Bank approved 24 technical assistance operations during the year, amounting to ID 6.06m., of which about 38% was in the form of grants.

Nineteen member countries are among the world's least-developed countries (as designated by the United Nations). During the year 67.5% of loan financing was directed to these countries.

Foreign trade financing approved during the year amounted to ID 453.03m. for 53 operations in 12 member countries: of this amount 49% was for imports of crude petroleum, 28% for intermediate industrial goods, and 6% for vegetable oil.

Under the Bank's Special Assistance Account, 12 operations were approved during the year, amounting to ID 9.12m., mostly for Islamic education centres. Implementation of a special programme of emergency aid to Sahelian member countries suffering from drought (approved two years previously, at a cost of ID 49m.) continued during the year. The Bank's scholarships programme sponsored 223 students from 16 countries during the year to 24 August 1987. The Bank also undertakes the distribution of meat sacrificed by Muslim pilgrims: during the year meat from 478,994 head of sheep was distributed to the needy in 19 member countries.

Disbursements during the year ending 24 August 1987 totalled ID 523.92m. (compared with ID 557.16m. in the previous year). Of this total ID 89m. was for project financing and technical assistance, and ID 427.83m. was for foreign trade financing, while ID 7.1m. was provided from the Special Assistance Account.

During the Islamic year 1408 (ending 12 August 1988) the Bank approved ID 596.35m. for 108 operations (excluding ID 12.37m. for 15 operations financed from the Special Assistance Account). Project financing received ID 155.63m., technical assistance ID 5.07m. and foreign trade financing ID 435.64m. Of total project financing and technical assistance during the year, some 35% was for public utilities, 18% for industry and mining, 16% for social services, 15% for transport and 10% for agriculture.

RESEARCH AND TRAINING INSTITUTE

Islamic Research and Training Institute: POB 9201, Jeddah 21413, Saudi Arabia; tel. 6361400; telex 601407; f. 1982 for research enabling economic, financial and banking activities to conform to Islamic law, and to provide training for staff involved in development activities in the Bank's member countries.

PUBLICATION

Annual Report.

LATIN AMERICAN INTEGRATION ASSOCIATION—LAIA

(ASOCIACIÓN LATINOAMERICANA DE INTEGRACIÓN—ALADI)

Address: Cebollatí 1461, Casilla 577, Montevideo, Uruguay.
Telephone: (2) 401121.
Telex: 26944.
Fax: (2) 490649.

The Latin American Integration Association was established in August 1980 to replace the Latin American Free Trade Association, set up in February 1960.

MEMBERS

Argentina
Bolivia
Brazil
Chile
Colombia
Ecuador
Mexico
Paraguay
Peru
Uruguay
Venezuela

Observers: Costa Rica, Cuba, Dominican Republic, El Salvador, Guatemala, Honduras, Italy, Nicaragua, Panama, Portugal and Spain; also the UN Economic Commission for Latin America and the Caribbean (ECLAC), the UN Development Programme (UNDP), the European Community, the Inter-American Development Bank and the Organization of American States.

Organization

(October 1990)

COUNCIL OF MINISTERS

The Council of Ministers of Foreign Affairs is responsible for the adoption of the Association's policies. It meets when convened by the Committee of Representatives.

EVALUATION AND CONVERGENCE CONFERENCE

The Conference, comprising plenipotentiaries of the member governments, assesses the Association's progress and encourages negotiations betwen members. It meets when convened by the Committee of Representatives.

COMMITTEE OF REPRESENTATIVES

The Committee, the permanent political body of the Association, comprises a permanent and a deputy representative from each member country, and 16 permanent observers (see above). Its task is to ensure the correct implementation of the Treaty and its supplementary regulations. There are eight auxiliary bodies:

Council for Financial and Monetary Affairs: comprises the Presidents of member states' central banks, who examine all aspects of financial, monetary and exchange co-operation.

Advisory Commission on Financial and Monetary Affairs.

Meeting of Directors of National Customs Administrations.

Council on Transport for Trade Facilitation.

Advisory Council for Export Financing.

Tourism Council.

Advisory Entrepreneurial Council.

Advisory Nomenclature Commission.

SECRETARIAT

The Secretariat is the technical body of the Association; it submits proposals for action, carries out research and evaluates activities. The Secretary-General is appointed for a three-year term.

Secretary-General: JORGE LUIS ORDÓÑEZ (Colombia).

Deputy Secretaries-General: ANTONIO J. C. ANTÚNES (Brazil), JORGE CAÑETE ARCE (Paraguay).

Activities

The Latin American Free Trade Association (LAFTA) was an intergovernmental organization, created by the Treaty of Montevideo in February 1960 with the object of increasing trade between the Contracting Parties and of promoting regional integration, thus contributing to the economic and social development of the member countries. The Treaty provided for the gradual establishment of a free trade area, which would form the basis for a Latin American Common Market. Reduction of tariff and other trade barriers was to be carried out gradually up to 1980.

This scheme, however, made little progress. By 1980 only 14% of annual trade among members could be attributed to LAFTA agreements, and it was the richest states which were receiving most benefit. In June 1980 it was decided that LAFTA should be replaced by a less ambitious and more flexible organization, the Latin American Integration Association (LAIA), established by the 1980 Montevideo Treaty, which came into force in March 1981, and was fully ratified in March 1982. Instead of across-the-board tariff cuts, the Treaty envisaged an area of economic preferences, comprising a regional tariff preference for goods originating in member states (in effect from 1 July 1984) and regional and partial scope agreements (on economic complementation, trade promotion, trade in agricultural goods, scientific and technical co-operation, the environment, tourism, and other matters), taking into account the different stages of development of the members, and with no definite timetable for the establishment of a full common market.

The members of LAIA are divided into three categories: most developed (Argentina, Brazil and Mexico); intermediate (Chile, Colombia, Peru, Uruguay and Venezuela); and least developed (Bolivia, Ecuador and Paraguay), enjoying a special preferential system. By the end of 1983 the transition from LAFTA to LAIA had been completed with the renegotiation of over 23,000 tariff cuts granted among the partners from 1962 onwards. During 1981 the value of exports within LAIA accounted for 13% of member countries' total exports; the proportion fell to 8.1% in 1985, and stood at 11.6% in 1986 and 10.7% in 1987, 1988 and 1989.

Certain LAFTA institutions were retained and adapted by LAIA, e.g. the Reciprocal Payments and Credits Agreement (1965, modified in 1982) and the Multilateral Credit Agreement to Alleviate Temporary Shortages of Liquidity, known as the Santo Domingo Agreement (1969, extended in 1981 to include mechanisms for counteracting global balance-of-payments difficulties and for assisting in times of natural disaster).

A feature of LAIA is its 'outward' projection, allowing for multilateral links or agreements with Latin American non-member countries or integration organizations, and with other developing countries or economic groups outside the continent.

By mid-1990 the following agreements had entered into force: 34 renegotiation agreements (concerning the former LAFTA tariff cuts); 23 trade agreements (mostly on the basis of former LAFTA industrial complementation pacts); 13 economic complementation agreements; one agricultural agreement; three agreements on tourism; one agreement on cultural co-operation; two agreements with Latin American non-member countries; three regional market-opening agreements in favour of the least developed members; an agreement on regional tariff preferences (whereby a member state would allow imports from another to enter with tariffs lower than those imposed on imports from non-member states); and a regional agreement for the recovery and expansion of intra-LAIA trade. A new system of tariff nomenclature, based on the 'harmonized system', was adopted from 1 January 1990 as a basis for common trade negotiations and statistics. General regimes on safeguards and rules of origin entered into force in 1987.

The Secretariat convenes meetings of entrepreneurs in various private industrial sectors, to encourage regional trade and co-operation. In all, 26 such meetings were planned for 1989.

A regional round of negotiations was launched by LAIA members in April 1986, aiming to develop a renewed preferential trade and payments system in the region, open to the participation of Latin American non-member countries. The agenda comprised four main fields of negotiation: trade expansion and regulation; co-operation and economic complementarity; payments and export financing; and preferential measures for the less-developed members. In early 1987 multilateral programmes were approved for the elimination of non-tariff barriers, the recovery and expansion of intra-LAIA trade and for alleviating trade imbalances between partners; new rules on origin and safeguards were also approved.

In May 1990 the Council of Ministers approved guidelines for a stronger role for the organization in the context of a renewed approach to Latin American integration: the aim was to strengthen relationships between members, to modernize their productive structure, to diversify fields of co-operation (particularly in science, technology, finance, transport and communications), to harmonize macro-economic policies, and to foster a more active participation by different social groups in the process of integration. These aims

INTERNATIONAL ORGANIZATIONS

Latin American Integration Association

were to be implemented in a three-year programme of action (1990–92), which also included measures to expand intra-LAIA trade, additional support for the less-developed members, strengthening of LAIA institutions, and co-operation in tourism, culture, the environment, border integration and information activities. In June 1990 member countries agreed to increase the average level of regional tariff preferences from 10% to 20% (varying according to the level of development of the exporting and importing countries).

PUBLICATIONS

Síntesis ALADI (monthly, in Spanish).

Ambito Empresarial (monthly for entrepreneurs).

Reports, studies, texts of agreements, and trade statistics.

LEAGUE OF ARAB STATES

Address: 37 avenue Khereddine Pacha, Tunis, Tunisia.
Telephone: 890 100.
Telex: 14411.
Fax: 781801.

(The League began to move back to its former headquarters in Cairo, Egypt, at the end of October 1990.)

The League of Arab States (more generally known as the Arab League) is a voluntary association of sovereign Arab states designed to strengthen the close ties linking them and to co-ordinate their policies and activities and direct them towards the common good of all the Arab countries. It was founded in March 1945 (see Pact of the League, p. 177).

MEMBERS

Algeria	Oman
Bahrain	Palestine†
Djibouti	Qatar
Egypt*	Saudi Arabia
Iraq	Somalia
Jordan	Sudan
Kuwait	Syria
Lebanon	Tunisia
Libya	United Arab Emirates
Mauritania	Yemen
Morocco	

* In March 1979 Egypt's membership of the Arab League was suspended, and it was decided to make Tunis the temporary headquarters of the League, its Secretariat and its permanent committees. Egypt was readmitted to the League in May 1989.

† Palestine is considered an independent state, as explained in the Charter Annex on Palestine, and therefore a full member of the League.

Organization
(October 1990)

COUNCIL

The supreme organ of the Arab League, the Council consists of representatives of the member states, each of which has one vote, and a representative for Palestine. Unanimous decisions of the Council shall be binding upon all member states of the League; majority decisions shall be binding only on those states which have accepted them.

The Council may, if necessary, hold an extraordinary session at the request of two member states. Invitations to all sessions are extended by the Secretary-General. The ordinary sessions are presided over by representatives of the member states in turn.

Sixteen committees are attached to the Council:

Political Committee: studies political questions and reports to the Council meetings concerned with them. All member states are members of the Committee. It represents the Council in dealing with critical political matters when the Council is meeting. Usually composed of the foreign ministers.

Cultural Committee: in charge of following up the activities of the Cultural Department and the cultural affairs within the scope of the secretariat; co-ordinates the activities of the general secretariat and the various cultural bodies in member states.

Economic Committee: complemented by the Economic Council since 1953.

Communications Committee: supervises land, sea and air communications, together with weather forecasts and postal matters.

Social Committee: supports co-operation in such matters as family and child welfare.

Legal Committee: an extension of the Nationality and Passports Committee abolished in 1947; studies and legally formulates draft agreements, bills, regulations and official documents.

Arab Oil Experts Committee: for study of oil affairs; also investigates methods to prevent the smuggling of Arab oil into Israel; and for co-ordination of oil policies in general.

Information Committee: studies information projects, suggests plans and carries out the policies decided by the Council of Information Ministers.

Health Committee: for co-operation in health affairs.

Human Rights Committee: studies subjects concerning human rights, particularly violations by Israel; collaborates with the Information and Cultural Committees.

Permanent Committee for Administrative and Financial Affairs.

Permanent Committee for Meteorology.

Committee of Arab Experts on Co-operation.

Arab Women's Committee.

Organization of Youth Welfare.

Conference of Liaison Officers: co-ordinates trade activities among commercial attachés of various Arab embassies abroad.

The Arab League maintains a permanent office at the United Nations in New York, and has observer status at the UN General Assembly.

GENERAL SECRETARIAT

The administrative and financial offices of the League. The Secretariat carries out the decisions of the Council, and provides financial and administrative services for the personnel of the League. Administrative departments comprise: Arab Affairs, Economic Affairs, International Affairs, Palestine Affairs, Legal Affairs, Social and Cultural Affairs, Information, and Administrative and Financial Affairs.

The Secretary-General is appointed by the League Council by a two-thirds majority of the member states, for a five-year term. He appoints the assistant Secretaries-General and principal officials, with the approval of the Council. He has the rank of ambassador, and the assistant Secretaries-General have the rank of ministers plenipotentiary.

Secretary-General (acting) and Assistant Secretary-General for Arab Affairs: ASSAD AL-ASSAD (Lebanon).

Assistant Secretaries-General:
International Affairs: ADNAN OMRAN (Syria).
Palestine Affairs: Dr MUHAMMAD AL-FARRA (Jordan).
Special Adviser: LAKHDAR AL-IBRAHIMI (Algeria).
Social and Cultural Affairs: MAHDI MUSTAFA AL-HADI (Sudan).

DEFENCE AND ECONOMIC CO-OPERATION

Groups established under the Treaty of Joint Defence and Economic Co-operation, concluded in 1950 to complement the Charter of the League.

Arab Unified Military Command: f. 1964 to co-ordinate military policies for the liberation of Palestine.

Economic Council: to compare and co-ordinate the economic policies of the member states; the Council is composed of ministers of economic affairs or their deputies. Decisions are taken by majority vote. The first meeting was held in 1953.

Joint Defence Council: supervises implementation of those aspects of the treaty concerned with common defence. Composed of foreign and defence ministers; decisions by a two-thirds majority vote of members are binding on all.

Permanent Military Commission: established 1950; composed of representatives of army general staffs; main purpose: to draw up plans of joint defence for submission to the Joint Defence Council.

ARAB DETERRENT FORCE

Set up in June 1976 by the Arab League Council to supervise successive attempts to cease hostilities in Lebanon, and afterwards to maintain the peace. The mandate of the Force has been successively renewed. The Arab League Summit Conference in October 1976 agreed that costs were to be paid in the following percentage contributions: Saudi Arabia and Kuwait 20% each, United Arab Emirates 15%, Qatar 10% and other Arab states 35%.

OTHER INSTITUTIONS OF THE LEAGUE

Other bodies established by resolutions adopted by the Council of the League:

Academy of Arab Music: POB 6150, Baghdad, Iraq; tel. 552 15 37; Sec.-Gen. MUNIR DAGHIR.

INTERNATIONAL ORGANIZATIONS
League of Arab States

Administrative Tribunal of the Arab League: f. 1964; began operations 1966.

Arab Fund for Technical Assistance to African and Arab Countries—AFTAAAC: 37 ave Khereddine Pacha, Tunis, Tunisia; tel. 890 100; telex 13242; f. 1975 to provide technical assistance for development projects by providing African and Arab experts, grants for scholarships and training, and finance for technical studies. Exec. Sec. MAHDI MUSTAFA AL-HADI.

Special Bureau for Boycotting Israel: POB 437, Damascus, Syria.

SPECIALIZED ORGANIZATIONS

All member states of the Arab League are also members of the Specialized Agencies, which constitute an integral part of the Arab League. (See also chapters on the Arab Bank for Economic Development in Africa, the Arab Fund for Economic and Social Development, the Arab Monetary Fund, the Council of Arab Economic Unity and the Organization of Arab Petroleum Exporting Countries.)

Arab Administrative Development Organization: POB 17159, Amman, Jordan; tel. 811394; telex 21594; fax 816972; f. 1969 (as Arab Organization of Administrative Sciences), to improve Arab administrative systems, develop Arab administrative organizations and enhance the capabilities of Arab civil servants, through training, consultancy research and documentation. Dir-Gen. Dr NASSIR AL-SAIGH. Publs *Arab Journal of Administration* (quarterly), research series.

Arab Centre for the Study of Arid Zones and Dry Lands (ACSAD): POB 2440, Damascus, Syria; tel. 755713; telex 412697; f. 1971 to conduct regional research and development programmes related to water and soil resources, plant and animal production, agro-meteorology, and socio-economic studies of arid zones. The Centre holds conferences and training courses and encourages the exchange of information by Arab scientists. Dir-Gen. MUHAMMAD EL-KHASH.

Arab Civil Aviation Council: POB 4410, 17 Al-Nasr St, Rabat, Morocco; tel. 74178; telex 32817; created 1965, began operations 1967; aims to develop the principles, techniques and economics of air transport in the Arab world; to co-operate with the International Civil Aviation Organization and to attempt to standardize laws and technical terms; also deals with Arab air rates. Pres N AL-KHANI. Publs *Air Transport Activities in Arab Countries, Lexicon of Civil Aviation Terminology* (Arabic); *Unified Air Law for Arab States* (Arabic and English).

Arab Industrial Development Organization: POB 3156, Al-Sa'adoun, Baghdad, Iraq; tel. 7184655; telex 2823; f. 1980; conducts sectoral studies on the situation and prospects of Arab industry, assists national industrial surveys, and provides consultation and training services. Dir-Gen. HATEM ABD AR-RASHEED. Publs *Bulletin, Journal of Arab Industrial Development* (in Arabic), reports and studies.

Arab Labour Organization: Sa'adoun Ave, POB 3237, Baghdad, Iraq; tel. 96191; telex 212746; established in 1965 for co-operation between member states in labour problems; unification of labour legislation and general conditions of work wherever possible; research; technical assistance; social insurance; training, etc.; the organization has a tripartite structure: governments, employers and workers. Dir-Gen. HASHEMI AL-BANANI. Publs *Bulletin* (monthly), *Arab Labour Review* (quarterly).

Arab League Educational, Cultural and Scientific Organization—ALECSO: BP 1120, ave Mohamed V, Tunis, Tunisia; tel. 784-466; telex 13825; f. 1970 to promote and co-ordinate educational, cultural and scientific activities in the Arab region. Dir-Gen. Dr MOHEDDINE SABER. Publs *Arab Journal of Language Studies, Arab Journal of Information, Arab Journal of Educational Research, Arab Journal of Culture, Arab Journal of Science, Arab Educational Statistical Bulletin, Yearbook of Science, Yearbook of Arab Culture*.

Arab Maritime Transport Academy: POB 1552, Sharjah, United Arab Emirates; tel. 358866; telex 68167; fax 372869; f. 1975. Dir-Gen. Capt. ABDUL WAHAB M. AL-DIWANI.

Arab Organization for Agricultural Development: POB 474, Khartoum, Sudan; tel. 43330; telex 22554; f. 1970 to contribute to co-operation in agricultural activities, and in the development of natural and human resources for agriculture; compiles data, conducts studies, training and food security programmes; has regional offices in eight countries; includes Arab Forestry and Pastures Institute, Syria. Dir-Gen. Dr HASSAN FAHMI JUMAH.

Arab Organization for Standardization and Metrology: POB 926161, Amman, Jordan; tel. 663834; telex 22463; began activity in 1968 to co-ordinate standards and metrology in the Arab states, and standardize methods of analysis and testing of products; sponsors seminars and training courses in standardization, metrology, and quality control; has 33 technical committees in 18 Arab countries; runs an Arab Centre for Information and Documentation; assists in the establishment of national bodies and collaborates with international standards activities. Sec.-Gen. Dr MAHDI H. HNOOSH. Publs *Annual Report* (Arabic and English), *Standardization* (10 a year, Arabic, English and French).

Arab Postal Union: POB 7999, Dubai, United Arab Emirates; tel. 690508; telex 46284; f. 1952; aims to establish more strict postal relations between the Arab countries than those laid down by the Universal Postal Union, to pursue the development and modernization of postal services in member countries. Sec.-Gen. HUSSEIN AL-HAMDANI. Publ. *Review* (quarterly).

Arab Satellite Communication Organization—ASCO: POB 1038, Riyadh, Saudi Arabia; tel. 478 9995; telex 201300; plans ARABSAT project, under which the first satellite was launched in February 1985, for the improvement of telephone, telex, data transmission and radio and television in Arab countries. Dir-Gen. ABD AL-KADER BAIRI.

Arab States Broadcasting Union—ASBU: POB 65, 17 rue el-Mensoura, el-Mensah 4, Tunis 1014, Tunisia; tel. 238044; telex 13398; fax 766551; f. 1969 to promote Arab fraternity, co-ordinate and study broadcasting subjects, to exchange expertise and technical co-operation in broadcasting; conducts training and audience research. Mems: 21 Arab radio and TV stations and seven foreign associates. Sec.-Gen. RAOUF BASTI. Publ. *ASBU Review* (2 a year).

Arab Telecommunications Union: POB 2397, Baghdad, Iraq; tel. 776-1713; telex 212007; f. 1953 to co-ordinate and develop telecommunications between the 21 member countries; to exchange technical aid and encourage research. Sec.-Gen. ABDUL JABBAR HASSAN KHALAF IBRAHIM AL-ANI. Publs *Economic and Technical Studies; Arab Telecommunications Union Journal* (quarterly).

Council of Arab Ministers of the Interior: POB 490, Hashad, Tunis, Tunisia; tel. 237320; telex 14887; f. 1983 to reinforce internal security and combat crime; Sec.-Gen. Dr AKRAM NASHA'T.

Arab Bureau for Narcotics: POB 17225, Amman, Jordan; tel. 813012; telex 21020; f. 1961 to supervise anti-drug campaigns and co-ordinate efforts to prevent the illegal production and smuggling of drugs.

Arab Bureau for Prevention of Crime: POB 5687, Baghdad, Iraq.

Arab Bureau of Criminal Police: Immeuble Union Sportive, ave Mayssaloume, Damascus, Syria.

Inter-Arab Investment Guarantee Corporation: POB 23568, Safat 13096, Kuwait; tel. 2404740; telex 22562–46312; fax 2405406; operating from its office in Riyadh, Saudi Arabia; f. 1975; insures Arab investors for non-commercial risks, and export credits for commercial and non-commercial risks; authorized capital 25m. Kuwaiti dinars (Dec. 1988). Mems: 22 Arab governments. Dir-Gen. MAMOUN I. HASSAN. Publ. *News Bulletin* (monthly), *Arab Investment Climate Report* (annually).

External Relations

ARAB LEAGUE OFFICES AND INFORMATION CENTRES ABROAD

Set up by the Arab League to co-ordinate work at all levels among Arab embassies abroad.

Argentina: Avda 3 de Febrero 1358, 1426 Buenos Aires.
Austria: Grimmelshausengasse 12, 1030 Vienna.
Belgium: 106 ave Franklin D. Roosevelt, 1050 Brussels.
Brazil: Shis-Qi 15, Conj. 7, Casa 23, 71600 Brasília, DF.
Canada: 170 Laurier Ave West, Suite 709, Ottawa K1P 5VP.
Ethiopia: POB 5768, Addis Ababa.
France: 114 blvd Malesherbes, 75017 Paris.
Germany: Friedrich Wilhelm Str. 2A, 5300 Bonn 1.
Greece: 10 Antheon St, Palaio Psychico, Athens.
India: 61 Golf Links, New Delhi 110003.
Italy: Piazzale delle Belle Arti 6, 00196 Rome.
Japan: 1-1-12 Moto Asabu, Minato-ku, Tokyo 106.
Kenya: POB 30770, Nairobi.
Mexico: Monte Altai 524, Lomas de Chapultepec, 11000 México, DF.
Netherlands: Lange Voorhout 12, 2514 ED The Hague.
Senegal: 41 rue el-Hadji Amadou, Assane Ndoye, Dakar.
Switzerland: 9 rue du Valais, 1202 Geneva.
United Kingdom: 52 Green St, London W1Y 3RH.
USA: 747 Third Ave, New York, NY 10017; 1100 17th St, NW, Suite 901, Washington, DC 20036; and in Chicago, Dallas and San Francisco.

Record of Events

1945 Pact of the Arab League signed, March.
1946 Cultural Treaty signed.
1950 Joint Defence and Economic Co-operation Treaty.
1952 Agreements on extradition, writs and letters of request, nationality of Arabs outside their country of origin.
1953 Formation of Economic Council.
Convention on the privileges and immunities of the League.
1954 Nationality Agreement.
1956 Agreement on the adoption of a Common Tariff Nomenclature.
Sudan joined Arab League.
1961 Kuwait joined League.
Syrian Arab Republic rejoined League as independent member.
1962 Arab Economic Unity Agreement.
1964 First Summit Conference of Arab kings and presidents, Cairo, January.
First meeting of Economic Unity Council, June. Arab Common Market approved by Arab Economic Unity Council, August.
Second Summit Conference welcomed establishment of Palestine Liberation Organization (PLO), September.
1965 Arab Common Market established, January.
1969 Fifth Summit Conference, Rabat. Call for mobilization of all Arab nations against Israel.
1971 Bahrain, Qatar and Oman admitted to Arab League, September.
1973 Mauritania admitted to Arab League, December.
1974 Somalia admitted to Arab League, February.
1977 Djibouti admitted to membership, September.
Tripoli Declaration, December. Decision of Algeria, Iraq, Libya and Yemen PDR to boycott League meetings in Egypt in response to President Sadat's visit to Israel.
1978 69th meeting of Arab League Council in Cairo, March, boycotted by 'rejectionist' states.
1979 Council meeting in Baghdad, March: various resolutions were adopted of which the main points were: to withdraw Arab ambassadors from Egypt; to recommend severance of political and diplomatic relations with Egypt; to suspend Egypt's membership of the League on the date of the signing of the peace treaty with Israel; to make the city of Tunis the temporary HQ of the League, its Secretariat, ministerial councils and permanent technical committees; to condemn United States' policy regarding its role in concluding the Camp David agreements and the peace treaty; to halt all bank loans, deposits, guarantees or facilities, as well as all financial or technical contributions and aid to Egypt; to prohibit trade exchanges with the Egyptian state and with private establishments dealing with Israel.
1980 Meeting of Arab foreign and economic ministers (as the Arab Economic and Social Council), Amman, July. An Iraqi plan for investment of at least $10,000m. over 10 years, to aid development in poorer Arab states (particularly Djibouti, Mauritania, Somalia, Sudan and the two Yemens), was discussed. The November Summit Conference in Amman was boycotted by the Palestine Liberation Organization, Algeria, Lebanon, Libya, Syria and the People's Democratic Republic of Yemen, maintaining that the conference should have been postponed because of the serious differences in the Arab world over the Iran–Iraq war and the approach to negotiations on Israel. The Summit Conference agreed to set up a $5,000m. fund for the benefit of poorer Arab states, with Iraq, Kuwait, Qatar, Saudi Arabia and the United Arab Emirates as donors: assistance was to take the form of 20-year development loans, and the fund was to be administered by the Arab Fund for Social and Economic Development (q.v.). The conference also approved a wider 'Strategy for Joint Arab Economic Action', covering pan-Arab development planning up to the year 2000.
1981 In March the Council of Ministers set up a conciliation mission to try to improve relations between Morocco and Mauritania.
Twelfth Summit Conference, Fez, Morocco, November. The meeting was suspended after a few hours, following disagreement over a Saudi Arabian proposal known as the Fahd Plan, which includes not only the Arab demands on behalf of the Palestinians, as approved by the UN General Assembly, but also an implied *de facto* recognition of Israel.
1982 In February the conference of Arab ministers set up a ministerial commission to consider retaliatory measures against states supporting Israel.
Second Arab Energy Conference held in Qatar, March.
Twelfth Summit Conference reconvened, Fez, September: peace plan, similar to the Fahd Plan mentioned above, adopted. The plan demanded Israel's withdrawal from territories occupied in 1967, and removal of Israeli settlements in these areas; freedom of worship for all religions in the sacred places; the right of the Palestinian people to self-determination, under the leadership of the Palestine Liberation Organization; temporary UN supervision for the West Bank and the Gaza Strip; the creation of an independent Palestinian state, with Jerusalem as its capital; and a guarantee of peace for all the states of the region by the UN Security Council. An Arab League delegation, led by King Hussein of Jordan, subsequently visited Washington, Paris, Moscow and Beijing seeking support for the peace plan.
1983 The summit meeting due to be held in November was postponed owing to members' differences of opinion concerning Syria's opposition to Yasser Arafat's chairmanship of the PLO, and Syrian support of Iran in the war against Iraq.
1984 In March an emergency meeting established an Arab League committee to encourage international efforts to bring about a negotiated settlement of the Iran–Iraq war. In May ministers of foreign affairs adopted a resolution calling on Iran to stop attacking non-belligerent ships and installations in the Gulf region: similar attacks by Iraq were not mentioned.
1985 The Third Arab Energy Conference, sponsored by the Arab League and OAPEC, was held in Algeria in May. In August an emergency Summit Conference was boycotted by Algeria, Lebanon, Libya, Syria and the People's Democratic Republic of Yemen, while of the other 16 members only nine were represented by their heads of state. The conference reaffirmed its support for the peace plan adopted in 1982 (see above), but was non-committal on proposals made by Jordan and the Palestine Liberation Organization, envisaging eventual talks with Israel on Palestinian rights. Two commissions were set up to mediate in disagreements between Arab states (between Jordan and Syria, Iraq and Syria, Iraq and Libya, and Libya and the PLO).
1986 Proposals to hold an emergency summit meeting in May, in response to the US bombing of Libyan cities in April, were unsuccessful. In July King Hassan of Morocco announced that he was resigning as chairman of the next League Summit Conference (for which no date had yet been fixed), after criticism by several Arab leaders of his meeting with the Israeli Prime Minister earlier that month. In August it was announced that more than one-half of the League's members were in arrears with their contributions to the annual budget of some US $30m., and that a financial crisis was imminent. A ministerial meeting held in October condemned any attempt at direct negotiation with Israel, and reiterated that an international conference convened by the United Nations would be the only acceptable means of bringing about a peaceful settlement in the Middle East. In December a special ministerial committee was created to attempt to stop the fighting for control of the Palestinian refugee camps in Lebanon between Palestinian guerrillas and the Shi'ite Amal militia.
1987 In April the Council demanded that Iran should accept a settlement of the conflict with Iraq by peaceful means, in compliance with the UN Charter. In August the Council agreed on a resolution criticizing Iran for persisting in its hostilities against Iraq and for making threats against the Gulf states. An extraordinary Summit Conference was held in November, mainly to discuss the war between Iran and Iraq. Contrary to expectations, the participants (including President Assad of Syria) unanimously agreed on a statement expressing support for Iraq in its defence of its legitimate rights, and condemning Iran for its aggression against Iraq and for its procrastination in accepting the UN Security Council resolution No. 598 of July 1987, which had recommended a cease-fire in the Iran-Iraq war and negotiations on a settlement of the conflict. The meeting also stated that the resumption of diplomatic relations with Egypt was a matter to be decided by individual states.
1988 In June a Summit Conference was held in Algiers to discuss the seven-month uprising by Palestinians in Israeli-occupied territories. The meeting agreed to provide finance for the PLO to continue the uprising. It reiterated the Arab League's demand for an international conference, attended

by the PLO, to seek to bring about a peaceful settlement in the Middle East (thereby implicitly rejecting recent proposals by the US Government for a conference that would exclude the PLO). At the conference, the leaders of Algeria, Libya, Mauritania, Morocco and Tunisia met informally to discuss the formation of a Maghreb regional grouping.

1989 In January (responding to the deteriorating political situation in Lebanon) an Arab League mediation group, comprising six ministers of foreign affairs, began discussions with the two rival Lebanese governments on the possibility of a political settlement in Lebanon. In April the League issued a provisional peace plan, which would involve a cease-fire in Lebanon, supervised by a force of Arab military observers. At a Summit Conference, held in May, Egypt was readmitted to the League. The Summit Conference expressed support for the chairman of the PLO, Yasser Arafat, in his recent peace proposals made before the UN General Assembly, and reiterated the League's support for proposals that an international conference should be convened to discuss the rights of Palestinians: in so doing, it accepted UN Security Council Resolutions 242 and 338 on a peaceful settlement in the Middle East and thus gave tacit recognition to the state of Israel. The meeting also supported Arafat in rejecting Israeli proposals for elections in the Israeli-occupied territories of the West Bank and the Gaza Strip. A new mediation committee, comprising the heads of state of Algeria, Morocco and Saudi Arabia, was established, with a six-month mandate to negotiate a cease-fire in Lebanon, and to reconvene the Lebanese legislature with the aim of holding a presidential election and restoring constitutional government in Lebanon. In September the principal factions in Lebanon agreed to observe a cease-fire, and the surviving members of the Lebanese legislature (originally elected in 1972) met at Taif, in Saudi Arabia, in October, and approved the League's proposed 'charter of national reconciliation' (see chapter on Lebanon).

1990 In March member states' ministers of foreign affairs agreed, in principle, to return the League's headquarters from Tunis to Cairo. In May a Summit Conference, held in Baghdad, Iraq (which was boycotted by Syria and Lebanon), condemned the recent increase in the emigration of Jews from the USSR to Israel, and strongly criticized the US Government's support for Israel. The meeting also criticized recent efforts by Western governments to prevent the development of advanced weapons technology in Iraq. The mandate of the Lebanon mediation committee was extended for a further six months. In August an emergency Summit Conference was held to discuss the invasion and annexation of Kuwait by Iraq. Twelve members (Bahrain, Djibouti, Egypt, Kuwait, Lebanon, Morocco, Oman, Qatar, Saudi Arabia, Somalia, Syria and the United Arab Emirates) approved a resolution condemning Iraq's action, and demanding the withdrawal of Iraqi forces from Kuwait and the reinstatement of the Government. The 12 states expressed support for the Saudi Arabian Government's invitation to the USA to send forces to defend Saudi Arabia; they also agreed to impose economic sanctions on Iraq, and to provide troops for an Arab defensive force in Saudi Arabia. The remaining member states, however, condemned the presence of foreign troops in Saudi Arabia, and their ministers of foreign affairs refused to attend a meeting held at the end of August to discuss possible solutions to the crisis. The dissenting countries also rejected the decision, taken earlier in the year, to return the League's headquarters to Cairo. In September the Secretary-General of the League, Chedli Klibi, resigned, reportedly after incurring criticism by moderate Arab leaders, and the League's representative at the UN, Clovis Maksoud, also resigned, deploring both the Iraqi invasion and the Western military presence in Saudi Arabia. The official transfer of the League's headquarters to Cairo took place on 31 October.

PUBLICATIONS

Sh'oun Arabiyya (*Journal of Arab Affairs*, quarterly).
Information Bulletin (Arabic and English, daily).
Bulletins of treaties and agreements concluded among the member states.
New York Office: *Arab World* (monthly), and *News and Views*.
Geneva Office: *Le Monde Arabe* (monthly), and *Nouvelles du Monde Arabe* (weekly).
Buenos Aires Office: *Arabia Review* (monthly).
Paris Office: *Actualités Arabes* (fortnightly).
Brasília Office: *Oriente Arabe* (monthly).
Rome Office: *Rassegna del Mondo Arabo* (monthly).
London Office: *The Arab* (monthly).
New Delhi Office: *Al Arab* (monthly).
Bonn Office: *Arabische Korrespondenz* (fortnightly).
Ottawa Office: *Spotlight on the Arab World* (fortnightly), *The Arab Case* (monthly).

The Pact of the League of Arab States

(22 March 1945)

Article 1. The League of Arab States is composed of the independent Arab States which have signed this Pact.

Any independent Arab state has the right to become a member of the League. If it desires to do so, it shall submit a request which will be deposited with the Permanent Secretariat-General and submitted to the Council at the first meeting held after submission of the request.

Article 2. The League has as its purpose the strengthening of the relations between the member states; the co-ordination of their policies in order to achieve co-operation between them and to safeguard their independence and sovereignty; and a general concern with the affairs and interests of the Arab countries. It has also as its purpose the close co-operation of the member states, with due regard to the organization and circumstances of each state, on the following matters:

(*a*) Economic and financial affairs, including commercial relations, customs, currency, and questions of agriculture and industry.

(*b*) Communications: this includes railways, roads, aviation, navigation, telegraphs and posts.

(*c*) Cultural affairs.

(*d*) Nationality, passports, visas, execution of judgments, and extradition of criminals.

(*e*) Social affairs.

(*f*) Health problems.

Article 3. The League shall possess a Council composed of the representatives of the member states of the League; each state shall have a single vote, irrespective of the number of its representatives.

It shall be the task of the Council to achieve the realization of the objectives of the League and to supervise the execution of agreements which the member states have concluded on the questions enumerated in the preceding article, or on any other questions.

It likewise shall be the Council's task to decide upon the means by which the League is to co-operate with the international bodies to be created in the future in order to guarantee security and peace and regulate economic and social relations.

Article 4. For each of the questions listed in Article 2 there shall be set up a special committee in which the member states of the League shall be represented. These committees shall be charged with the task of laying down the principles and extent of co-operation. Such principles shall be formulated as draft agreements, to be presented to the Council for examination preparatory to their submission to the aforesaid states.

Representatives of the other Arab countries may take part in the work of the aforesaid committees. The Council shall determine the conditions under which these representatives may be permitted to participate and the rules governing such representation.

Article 5. Any resort to force in order to resolve disputes arising between two or more member states of the League is prohibited. If there should rise among them a difference which does not concern a state's independence, sovereignty, or territorial integrity, and if the parties to the dispute have recourse to the Council for the settlement of this difference, the decision of the Council shall then be enforceable and obligatory.

In such a case, the states between whom the difference has arisen shall not participate in the deliberations and decisions of the Council.

The Council shall mediate in all differences which threaten to lead to war between two member states, or a member state and a third state, with a view to bringing about their reconciliation.

Decisions of arbitration and mediation shall be taken by majority vote.

Article 6. In case of aggression or threat of aggression by one state against a member state, the state which has been attacked or threatened with aggression may demand the immediate convocation of the Council.

The Council shall by unanimous decision determine the measures necessary to repulse the aggression. If the aggressor is a member state, its vote shall not be counted in determining unanimity.

If, as a result of the attack, the government of the state attacked finds itself unable to communicate with the Council, that state's representative in the Council shall have the right to request the convocation of the Council for the purpose indicated in the foregoing paragraph. In the event that this representative is unable to communicate with the Council, any member state of the League shall have the right to request the convocation of the Council.

Article 7. Unanimous decisions of the Council shall be binding upon all member states of the League; majority decisions shall be binding only upon those states which have accepted them.

In either case the decisions of the Council shall be enforced in each member state according to its respective basic laws.

Article 8. Each member state shall respect the systems of government established in the other member states and regard them as exclusive concerns of those states. Each shall pledge to abstain from any action calculated to change established systems of government.

Article 9. States of the League which desire to establish closer co-operation and stronger bonds than are provided by this Pact may conclude agreements to that end.

Treaties and agreements already concluded or to be concluded in the future between a member state and another state shall not be binding or restrictive upon other members.

Article 10. The permanent seat of the League of Arab States is established in Cairo. The Council may, however, assemble at any other place it may designate.

Article 11. The Council of the League shall convene in ordinary session twice a year, in March and in September. It shall convene in extraordinary session upon the request of two member states of the League whenever the need arises.

Article 12. The League shall have a permanent Secretariat-General which shall consist of a Secretary-General, Assistant Secretaries, and an appropriate number of officials.

The Council of the League shall appoint the Secretary-General by a majority of two-thirds of the states of the League. The Secretary-General, with the approval of the Council, shall appoint the Assistant Secretaries and the principal officials of the League.

The Council of the League shall establish an administrative regulation for the functions of the Secretariat-General and matters relating to the Staff.

The Secretary-General shall have the rank of Ambassador and the Assistant Secretaries that of Ministers Plenipotentiary.

Article 13. The Secretary-General shall prepare the draft of the budget of the League and shall submit it to the Council for approval before the beginning of each fiscal year.

The Council shall fix the share of the expenses to be borne by each state of the League. This share may be reconsidered if necessary.

Article 14. The members of the Council of the League as well as the members of the committees and the officials who are to be designated in the administrative regulation shall enjoy diplomatic privileges and immunity when engaged in the exercise of their functions.

The building occupied by the organs of the League shall be inviolable.

Article 15. The first meeting of the Council shall be convened at the invitation of the head of the Egyptian Government. Thereafter it shall be convened at the invitation of the Secretary-General.

The representatives of the member states of the League shall alternately assume the presidency of the Council at each of its ordinary sessions.

Article 16. Except in cases specifically indicated in this Pact, a majority vote of the Council shall be sufficient to make enforceable decisions on the following matters:

(a) Matters relating to personnel.

(b) Adoption of the budget of the League.

(c) Establishment of the administrative regulations for the Council, the Committees, and the Secretariat-General.

(d) Decisions to adjourn the sessions.

Article 17. Each member state of the League shall deposit with the Secretariat-General one copy of every treaty or agreement concluded or to be concluded in the future between itself and another member state of the League or a third state.

Article 18. (deals with withdrawal).

Article 19. (deals with amendment).

Article 20. (deals with ratification).

ANNEX REGARDING PALESTINE

Since the termination of the last great war the rule of the Ottoman Empire over the Arab countries, among them Palestine, which has become detached from that Empire, has come to an end. She has come to be autonomous, not subordinate to any other state.

The Treaty of Lausanne proclaimed that her future was to be settled by the parties concerned.

However, even though she was as yet unable to control her own affairs, the Covenant of the League (of Nations) in 1919 made provision for a regime based upon recognition of her independence.

Her international existence and independence in the legal sense cannot, therefore, be questioned, any more than could the independence of the Arab countries.

Although the outward manifestations of this independence have remained obscured for reasons beyond her control, this should not be allowed to interfere with her participation in the work of the Council of the League.

The states signatory to the Pact of the Arab League are therefore of the opinion that, considering the special circumstances of Palestine and until that country can effectively exercise its independence, the Council of the League should take charge of the selection of an Arab representative from Palestine to take part in its work.

ANNEX REGARDING CO-OPERATION WITH COUNTRIES WHICH ARE NOT MEMBERS OF THE COUNCIL OF THE LEAGUE

Whereas the member states of the League will have to deal in the Council as well as in the committees with matters which will benefit and affect the Arab world at large;

And whereas the Council has to take into account the aspirations of the Arab countries which are not members of the Council and has to work toward their realization;

Now therefore, it particularly behoves the states signatory to the Pact of the Arab League to enjoin the Council of the League, when considering the admission of those countries to participation in the committees referred to in the Pact, that it should do its utmost to co-operate with them, and furthermore, that it should spare no effort to learn their needs and understand their aspirations and hopes; and that it should work thenceforth for their best interests and the safeguarding of the future with all the political means at its disposal.

NORDIC COUNCIL

Address: Tyrgatan 7, Box 19506, 10432 Stockholm, Sweden.
Telephone: (08) 14-34-20.
Telex: 12 867.
Fax: (08) 11-75-36.

The Nordic Council was founded in 1952 for co-operation between the Nordic parliaments and governments. The four original members were Denmark, Iceland, Norway and Sweden; Finland joined in 1955, and the Faeroe Islands and Åland Islands were granted representation in 1970 within the Danish and Finnish delegations respectively. Greenland had separate representation within the Danish delegation from 1984. Co-operation was first regulated by a Statute, and subsequently by the Helsinki Treaty of 1962. The Nordic region has a population of about 23 million.

MEMBERS

Denmark (with the autonomous territories of the Faeroe Islands and Greenland)
Finland (with the autonomous territory of the Åland Islands)
Iceland
Norway
Sweden

Organization
(October 1990)

COUNCIL

The Nordic Council is not a supranational parliament, but a place where representatives of all the Nordic parliaments take decisions guiding Nordic co-operation. The Nordic Council of Ministers (see next page) represents the governments of the Nordic countries when decisions are to be implemented.

The Council convenes annually in a plenary session of about one week's duration. Following an introductory general debate, the Session considers proposals put forward by Council members, by the Council of Ministers or national governments. The Session also follows up the outcome of past decisions and the work of the various Nordic institutions.

The Council comprises 87 members, elected annually by and from the parliaments of the respective countries (Denmark 16 members; Faeroes 2; Greenland 2; Finland 18; Åland 2; Iceland 7; Norway 20; Sweden 20). The various parties are proportionately represented in accordance with their representation in the national parliaments.

The Council initiates and follows up co-operative efforts among the Nordic countries. It does this by issuing recommendations and statements of position to the Council of Ministers and the respective governments. The recommendations of the Council, which express political judgements and opinions with solid foundations in the Nordic parliaments, generally result in the taking of measures on the part of Councils of Ministers of the national governments in question.

The 38th session of the Council, held in February/March 1990, dealt with 36 members' proposals and 12 proposals by the Council of Ministers. The proposals submitted by members of the Council covered a wide range of subjects, including a Nordic nuclear-weapon-free zone, support for co-operation on ecological farming, several proposals on Council working methods and decision-making, uniform Nordic firearms legislation, expansion of the Nordplus exchange scheme, the financial position of artists, a Nordic cultural festival in 1992, telecommunications for the disabled, exporting of wastes, children's rights, a programme to combat youth unemployment, research into the problems caused by amalgam fillings, action to tackle air pollution, and direct air links between towns in northern central areas of Norway, Sweden and Finland. The 36 members' proposals were assigned to the Nordic Council's standing committees as follows: fifteen to the Social and Environmental Committee, nine to the Legal Committee, six to the Cultural Committee, four to the Economic Committee and two to the Communications Committee.

Four of the 12 Council of Ministers proposals related to the cultural sector, involving amendments to the agreement establishing the Nordic Council Fund, an action programme to promote mutual understanding of the languages of the Nordic region, new guidelines for the Nordic Science Policy Council, and a Nordic labour market for people with at least three years' higher education entitling them to practise a vocation or profession. The Social and Environmental Committee also considered four proposals from the Council of Ministers, on better working environments in the Nordic countries, a Nordic plan of action against marine pollution, an action programme on cleaner technologies, wastes and recycling, and an action plan to combat air pollution. The Economic Committee stated its views on four Council of Ministers proposals, dealing with a regional policy co-operation programme for 1990–94, supplementary measures under the Nordic agriculture and forestry action programme, a Nordic environmental finance corporation, and an increase in the Nordic Investment Bank's project investment loan facility.

STANDING COMMITTEES

Council members are assigned to six Standing Committees.

The **Economic Committee** is responsible for fiscal and monetary issues, industry and energy, trade, regional policy, development assistance, agriculture and forestry, and construction and housing.

The **Legal Committee** deals with legislation and other legal matters, including refugee issues, equality between women and men, consumer affairs, food issues, and the Council's internal rules.

The **Communications Committee's** responsibilities include transport, road safety, computer and other technology, tourism, telecommunications and postal services.

The **Cultural Committee** is responsible for culture, research, education, the media, sport, and young people.

The **Social and Environmental Committee** is concerned with health care, social services, employment, the working environment, and protection of the natural environment.

The **Budget and Control Committee** co-ordinates scrutiny of the Council of Ministers' budget proposals by the specialized standing committees and monitors activities paid for out of Council of Ministers funds.

PRESIDIUM

The day-to-day work of the Nordic Council is directed by a Presidium, made up of 11 MPs, 10 full members and one observer. The Presidium is the Council's highest decision-making body between sessions.

SECRETARIATS

Each delegation to the Nordic Council has a secretariat at its national parliament. The secretaries of the six standing committees are attached to the secretariat of the Presidium in Stockholm.

PUBLICATIONS

Yearbook of Nordic Statistics (in English and Swedish).
Nordiska Samarbetsorgan (list of all Nordic institutions, with their names in English).
Nordisk Kontakt (magazine, in the languages of the region).
The Nordic Council (handbook).
Books and pamphlets on Nordic co-operation; summaries of Council sessions.

NORDIC COUNCIL OF MINISTERS

Address: Store Strandstraede 18, 1255 Copenhagen K, Denmark.
Telephone: 33-11-47-11.
Telex: 15544.
Fax: 33-11-47-11.

The Governments of Denmark, Finland, Iceland, Norway and Sweden co-operate through the Nordic Council of Ministers. This co-operation is regulated by the Treaty of Co-operation between Denmark, Finland, Iceland, Norway and Sweden of 1962 (amended in 1971, 1974, 1983 and 1985) and the Treaty between Denmark, Finland, Iceland, Norway and Sweden concerning cultural co-operation of 1971 (amended in 1983 and 1985). The Prime Ministers and the Ministers of Defence and Foreign Affairs do not meet within the Nordic Council of Ministers. These ministers, however, meet on an informal basis.

MEMBERS
Denmark Finland Iceland Norway Sweden

Organization
(October 1990)

COUNCIL OF MINISTERS
The Nordic Council of Ministers holds formal and informal meetings and is attended by ministers with responsibility for the subject under discussion. Each member state also appoints a minister in its own cabinet as Minister for Nordic Co-operation.

Decisions of the Council of Ministers must be unanimous, except for procedural questions, which may be decided by a simple majority of those voting. Abstention constitutes no obstacle to a decision. Decisions are binding on the individual countries, provided that no parliamentary approval is necessary under the constitution of any of the countries. If such approval is necessary, the Council of Ministers must be so informed before its decision.

Meetings are concerned with: agreements and treaties, guidelines for national legislation, recommendations from the Nordic Council, financing joint studies, setting up Nordic institutions.

The Council of Ministers reports each year to the Nordic Council on progress in all co-operation between member states as well as on future plans.

SECRETARIAT
The Office of the Secretary-General deals with co-ordination and legal matters (including co-ordination of work related to the European integration process and to the development of Eastern Europe).
There are departments for:
1. Budget and administration;
2. Cultural and educational co-operation;
3. Research, advanced education, computer technology, protection of the environment, energy;
4. Labour market questions, occupational environment, social policy and health care, equality;
5. Finance and monetary policy, industry, housing and construction, trade and development aid;
6. Regional policy, transport, communications, tourism, farming, forestry, fishing and consumer questions;
7. Information.

Secretary-General: FRIDTJOV CLEMET.

COMMITTEES
Committee of Ministers' Deputies: for final preparation of material for the meetings of Ministers of Nordic Co-operation.
Senior Executives' Committees: prepare the meetings of the Council of Ministers and conduct research at its request. There are a number of sub-committees. The Committees cover the subjects listed under the Secretariat (above).

Activities

ECONOMIC CO-OPERATION
Economic co-operation is undertaken in the following areas: freer markets for goods and services; measures on training and employment; elimination of trade barriers; liberalization of capital movements; research and development; export promotion; taxes and other levies; and regional policy. During 1989 a new economic plan of action was adopted for the four year period 1989–92, with particular regard to the planned completion by 1992 of the European Community's internal market. Promotion of the competitiveness of Nordic industry (particularly with regard to advanced technology) was to be given high priority during the early 1990s. The national administrations for overseas development have carried out several projects as a group, and consult with one another frequently.

Nordic Investment Bank: founded under an agreement of December 1975 to provide finance and guarantees for the implementation of investment projects and exports; authorized and subscribed capital 1,600m. IMF Special Drawing Rights. The main sectors of the Bank's activities are energy, metal and wood-processing industries (including petroleum extraction) and manufacturing. In 1982 a separate scheme for financing investments in developing countries was established.

Nordic Industrial Fund: f. 1973 to provide grants, subsidies and loans for industrial research and development projects of interest to more than one member country.

Nordic Economic Research Council: f. 1980 to promote research and analysis on Nordic economic issues, including regional interdependence and closer co-operation.

NORDTEST: f. 1973 as an inter-Nordic agency for technical testing and standardization of methods and of laboratory accreditation.

Nordic Project Fund: f. 1982 to strengthen the international competitiveness of Nordic exporting companies, and to promote industrial co-operation in international projects (e.g. in environmental protection).

COMMUNICATIONS AND TRANSPORT
A Nordic agreement for transport and communications entered into force in 1973. The main areas of co-operation have been concerned with international transport, the environment, infrastructure, road research, transport for the disabled and road safety. Earlier agreements cover co-operation in post and telecommunications. Passports are not required for travel by Nordic citizens within the region. An agreement on the liberalization of road haulage between the Nordic countries came into force on 1 January 1989.

EMPLOYMENT
In 1954 an agreement entered into force on a free labour market between Denmark, Finland, Norway and Sweden. Iceland became a party to the agreement in 1982, when it was revised to include worker training and job-oriented rehabilitation. There is a joint centre for labour market training at Övertorneå in Sweden. A Nordic agreement on compensation for unemployment was concluded in 1985, and a convention on the working environment was signed in 1989.

SEXUAL EQUALITY
A Nordic co-operation programme on equality between women and men began in 1974. Projects completed by 1990 focused on working conditions, education, social welfare and family policy, housing and social planning, and women's participation in politics. In 1989–93 emphasis was to be placed on the role of women in economic development, and on opportunities for women and men in combining family life with work outside the home.

ENVIRONMENT
The Nordic Convention on the protection of the environment was signed in 1974, entering into force in October 1976. The member states undertake to harmonize regulations for protecting the environment, and to assess certain measures affecting neighbouring countries.

The coastal states have also signed a Convention on the Marine Environment of the Baltic, which entered into force in May 1980; special agreements have been concluded between Denmark and Sweden on pollution in the Öresund, and between Finland and Sweden on pollution in the Gulf of Bothnia.

A new programme of long-term goals for Nordic environmental co-operation was drawn up by the Council of Ministers in 1988, together with a plan of action against marine pollution. The year 1990 was designated as Nordic Environment and Biology Year.

ENERGY

A four-year agreement on energy co-operation entered into force in 1989; co-operation was to include studies on energy-saving, energy and the environment, the energy market, and the introduction of new and renewable sources of energy. A supplementary agreement entered into force in 1990, covering co-operation in ensuring a safe supply of energy and in long-term investment.

CONSUMER AFFAIRS

The main areas of co-operation are in safety legislation, consumer education and information and consumers' economic and legal interests.

FOOD AND NUTRITION

Co-operation in this sector began in 1982, and includes projects in food legislation, diet and nutrition, toxicology, risk evaluation and food controls.

AGRICULTURE AND FISHERIES

In 1989 a five-year programme of co-operation in the Nordic fisheries sector was adopted, with the aim of undertaking joint projects on the marine environment, aquaculture and marketing. An action programme for 1985–95 on Nordic co-operation in agriculture and forestry included joint research on gene banks and plant-breeding, removal of technical barriers to trade, and environmental protection in rural areas.

LAW

The five countries have similar legal systems and tend towards uniformity in legislation and interpretation of law. Much of the preparatory committee work within the national administrations on new legislation involves consultation with the neighbour countries.

Citizens of one Nordic country working in another are in many respects given the status of nationals. In all the Nordic countries they already have the right to vote in local elections in the country of residence. The changing of citizenship from one Nordic country to another has been simplified, and legislation on marriage and on children's rights amended to achieve the greatest possible parity.

There are special extradition facilities between the countries and further stages towards co-operation between the police and the courts have been adopted.

There is a permanent Council for Criminology, a Nordic Institute for Maritime Law in Oslo and a permanent committee for Penalty Law.

REGIONAL POLICY

Under a joint programme, covering the period 1990–94, the Council of Ministers agreed to develop new forms of co-operation between various regions within the Nordic countries; to give greater priority to developing skills and exchanging knowledge and information; to devise joint regional support schemes; and to strengthen joint Nordic action on international issues.

SOCIAL WELFARE AND HEALTH

Under the Convention on Social Security, 1955 (renewed in 1981), Nordic citizens have the same rights, benefits and obligations in each Nordic country, with regard to sickness, parenthood, occupational injury, unemployment, disablement and old-age pension. Uniform provisions exist concerning basic pension and supplementary pension benefits when moving from one Nordic country to another.

In 1981 an agreement was concluded for doctors, dentists, nurses, pharmacists and members of several other professions on the standards of competence required for obtaining work in other Nordic countries.

Institutions:
Nordic School of Public Health, Gothenburg, Sweden;
Scandinavian Institute of Dental Materials, Oslo;
Nordic Council on Medicines, Uppsala, Sweden;
Nordic Council on Alcohol and Drug Research, Helsinki;
Nordic Committee on Disability, Stockholm.
Nordic Staff Training Centre for Deaf-Blind Services, Dronninglund, Denmark.

Other Permanent Bodies:
Scandiatransplant, under Nordic Committee on Kidney Transplantation, Århus, Denmark;
Nordic Medico-Statistical Committee, Copenhagen;
Nordic Committee of Social Security Statistics, Copenhagen.
Nordic Clinical Chemistry Institute, Helsinki.

EDUCATIONAL AND SCIENTIFIC CO-OPERATION

Education: Nordic co-operation in the educational field includes the objective content and means of education, the structure of the educational system and pedagogical development work.

Joint projects include:
Nordic Co-operation in Adult Education
Nordic Educational Courses
Nordic Folk Academy
Nordic School of Journalism
Nordic Language Secretariat
Nordic Language and Information Centre
Nordic Federation for Medical Education
Nordic School of Nutritional and Textile Sciences
Nordic School Co-operation

Research: Nordic co-operation in research comprises information on research activities and research findings, joint research projects, joint research institutions, the methods and means in research policy, the organizational structure of research and a co-ordination of the national research programmes.

Much of the research co-operation activities at the more permanent joint research institutions consists of establishing science contacts in the Nordic areas by means of grants, visiting lecturers, courses and symposia.

The research institutions and research bodies listed below receive continuous financial support via the Nordic cultural budget. In many cases, these joint Nordic institutions ensure a high international standard that would otherwise have been difficult to maintain at a purely national level.

Nordic Accelerator Committee
Nordic Council for Arctic Medical Research
Nordic Institute of Asian Studies
Nordic Documentation Centre for Mass Communication Research
Nordic Committee on East European Studies
Nordic Council for Ecology
Nordic Institute of Folklore
Nordic Geoexcursions to Iceland
Nordic Co-operation Committee for International Politics
Nordic Council for Marine Biology
Nordic Institute of Maritime Law
Nordic Council for Physical Oceanography
Nordic Institute for Studies in Urban and Regional Planning
Nordic Academy for Training of Researchers
Nordic Association for Research on Latin America
Nordic Council for Scientific Information and Research Libraries
Nordic Summer University
Nordic Institute for Theoretical Physics
Nordic Volcanological Institute
Nordic Council for Co-operation in Silvicultural Research
Nordic Gene Bank
Nordic Science Policy Council

Cultural activities: Cultural co-operation is concerned with artistic and other cultural exchange between the Nordic countries; activities relating to libraries, museums, radio, television, and film; promotion of activities within organizations with general cultural aims, including youth and sports organizations; the improvement of conditions for the creative and performing arts; and encouragement for artists and cultural workers. Exhibitions and performances of Nordic culture are organized abroad.

Joint projects include:
Nordic Co-operation among Adult Education Organizations
Nordic Amateur Theatre Council
Nordic Art Association
Nordic Arts Centre
Nordic Co-operation in Athletics
Nordic Council Literature Prize
Nordic Council Music Prize
Nordic Film and Television Production Fund
Nordic House in Reykjavík
Nordic House in the Faeroe Islands
Nordic Arts Committee
Nordic Music Co-operation
Nordic Sami Institute
Nordic Theatre and Dance Committee
Nordic Writers' Courses
Nordic Youth Co-operation Committee
Nordic Literature and Libraries Committee
Nordic Cultural Manifestations

NORDIC CULTURAL FUND

The Nordic Cultural Fund was founded in 1966 to promote cultural co-operation by making grants for Nordic cultural projects within the region. A Board of 10 members (meeting four times a year) administers and distributes the resources of the Fund and super-

INTERNATIONAL ORGANIZATIONS

Nordic Council of Ministers

vises its activities. Five of the members are appointed by the Nordic Council and five by the Nordic Council of Ministers (of culture and education), for a period of two years. The Fund is located within and administered by the Secretariat of the Nordic Council of Ministers. It considers applications for assistance for research, education and general cultural activities; grants may also be made for disseminating information concerning Nordic culture within and outside the region. In 1987 the Fund was allotted 11m. Danish kroner.

FINANCE

Joint expenses are divided according to an agreed scale in proportion to the relative national product of the member countries. The 1990 budget of the Nordic Council of Ministers amounted to 678m. Danish kroner, of which Sweden was to contribute 37.1%, Denmark 21.8%, Finland 20.7%, Norway 19.4% and Iceland 1.0%. Various forms of co-operation are also financed directly from the national budgets.

NORTH ATLANTIC TREATY ORGANISATION—NATO

Address: 1110 Brussels, Belgium.
Telephone: (02) 728-41-11.
Telex: 23867.
Fax: (02) 728-45-79.

NATO was founded in 1949 by the North Atlantic Treaty as an international collective defence organization linking a group of European states (then numbering 10) with the USA and Canada. Member countries agree to treat an armed attack on any one of them as an attack against all.

MEMBERS*

Belgium	Iceland	Spain
Canada	Italy	Turkey
Denmark	Luxembourg	United Kingdom
France	Netherlands	USA
Germany	Norway	
Greece	Portugal	

* Greece and Turkey acceded to the Treaty in 1952, and the Federal Republic of Germany in 1955. France withdrew from the integrated military structure of NATO in 1966, although remaining a member of the Atlantic Alliance. Following the Turkish invasion of Cyprus in 1974, Greece also announced a partial withdrawal from the integrated military structure of NATO; it re-joined in October 1980. Spain joined NATO in May 1982.

Organization
(October 1990)

NORTH ATLANTIC COUNCIL

The highest authority of the alliance, composed of representatives of the 16 member states. It meets at the level of Permanent Representatives, ministers of foreign affairs, or heads of state and government. Ministerial meetings are held at least twice a year. At the level of Permanent Representatives the Council meets at least once a week.

The Secretary General of NATO is chairman of the Council. Annually, the minister of foreign affairs of a member state is nominated honorary President, following the English alphabetical order of countries.

Decisions are taken by common consent and not by majority vote. The Council is a forum for wide consultation between member governments on major issues, including political, military, economic and other subjects. It also gives political guidance to the military authorities.

PERMANENT REPRESENTATIVES

Belgium: PROSPER THUYSBAERT
Canada: GORDON SCOTT SMITH
Denmark: OLE BIERRING
France: GABRIEL ROBIN
Germany: Dr HANS-FRIEDRICH VON PLOETZ
Greece: IOANNIS BOURLOYANNIS-TSANGARIDIS
Iceland: SVERRIR HAUKUR GUNNLAUGSSON
Italy: FRANCESCO PAOLO FULCI
Luxembourg: FRANÇOIS BREMER (acting)
Netherlands: ADRIAAN JACOBOVITS DE SZEGED
Norway: BJØRN INGE KRISTVIK
Portugal: JOSÉ GREGÓRIO FARIA
Spain: MÁXIMO CAJAL
Turkey: ÜNAL ÜNSAL
United Kingdom: Sir MICHAEL ALEXANDER
USA: WILLIAM H. TAFT IV

DEFENCE PLANNING COMMITTEE

Most defence matters are dealt with in the Defence Planning Committee, composed of representatives of all member countries except France. Within the field of its responsibilities the Defence Planning Committee has the same functions and authority as the Council. Like the Council it meets regularly at ambassadorial level and assembles twice a year in ministerial sessions, when member countries are represented by their ministers of defence.

NUCLEAR PLANNING GROUP

The Nuclear Planning Group follows a similar pattern of meetings at ambassadorial level and at the level of ministers of defence and has the same functions and authority for decisions on nuclear matters as the Council and Defence Planning Committee have in their own spheres. All member countries except France participate. Iceland participates as an observer.

OTHER COMMITTEES

There are also committees for political affairs, economics, armaments, defence review, science, infrastructure, logistics, communications, civil emergency planning, information and cultural relations, and civil and military budgets. The Committee on the Challenges of Modern Society examines methods of improving allied co-operation in creating a better environment. In addition other committees deal with specialized subjects such as NATO pipelines, European air space co-ordination, etc.

INTERNATIONAL SECRETARIAT

The Secretary General is Chairman of the North Atlantic Council, the Defence Planning Committee, the Nuclear Planning Group, and the Committee on the Challenges of Modern Society. He is the head of the International Secretariat, with staff drawn from the member countries. He proposes items for NATO consultation and is generally responsible for promoting consultation and co-operation in accordance with the provisions of the North Atlantic Treaty. He is empowered to offer his help informally in cases of disputes between member countries, to facilitate procedures for settlement.

Secretary General: MANFRED WÖRNER (Germany).
Deputy Secretary General: AMEDEO DE FRANCHIS (Italy).

There is an Assistant Secretary General for each of the divisions listed below.

PRINCIPAL DIVISIONS

Division of Political Affairs: maintains political liaison with national delegations and international organizations. Prepares reports on political subjects for the Secretary General and the Council, and provides the administrative structure for the management of the Alliance's political responsibilities, including arms control. Asst Sec. Gen. Dr HENNING WEGENER (Germany).

Division of Defence Planning and Policy: studies all matters concerning the defence of the Alliance, and co-ordinates the defence review and other force planning procedures of the Alliance. Asst Sec. Gen. MICHAEL LEGGE (UK).

Division of Defence Support: promotes the most efficient use of the Allies' resources in the production of military equipment and its standardization. Asst Sec. Gen. PHILIP MERRILL (USA).

Division of Infrastructure, Logistics and Civil Emergency Planning: supervises the technical and financial aspects of the infrastructure programme. Provides guidance, co-ordination and support to the activities of NATO committees or bodies active in the field of consumer logistics and civil emergency planning. Asst Sec. Gen. LAWRENCE E. DAVIES (Canada).

Division of Scientific and Environmental Affairs: advises the Secretary-General on scientific matters of interest to NATO. Responsible for promoting and administering scientific exchange programmes between member countries, research fellowships, advanced study institutes and special programmes of support for the scientific and technological development of less-advanced member countries. Asst Sec. Gen. JACQUES DUCUING (France).

Military Organization

MILITARY COMMITTEE

Composed of the allied Chiefs-of-Staff, or their representatives, of all member countries except France: the highest military body in NATO under the authority of the Council. Meets at least twice a year at Chiefs-of-Staff level and remains in permanent session with Permanent Military Representatives. It is responsible for making recommendations to the Council and Defence Planning Committee on military matters and for supplying guidance on military questions to Supreme Allied Commanders and subordinate military authorities.

France maintains a Military Mission to the Military Committee for regular consultation.

President: Adm. D. WELLERSHOF (Germany).
Chairman: Gen. VIGLEIK EIDE (Norway).
Deputy Chairman: Lt-Gen. C. P. OTSTOTT (USA).

INTERNATIONAL MILITARY STAFF
Director: Lt-Gen. CORRADO MELILLO (Italy).

COMMANDS
European Command: Casteau, Belgium—Supreme Headquarters Allied Powers Europe—SHAPE. Supreme Allied Commander Europe—SACEUR: Gen. JOHN R. GALVIN (USA).

Atlantic Ocean Command: Norfolk, Virginia, USA. Supreme Allied Commander Atlantic—SACLANT: Admiral LEON A. EDNEY (USA).

Channel Command: Northwood, England. Allied Commander-in-Chief Channel—CINCHAN: Admiral Sir BENJAMIN BATHURST (UK).

Activities

The common security policy of the members of the North Atlantic Alliance is to safeguard peace through the maintenance of political solidarity and adequate defence at the lowest level of military forces needed to deter all possible forms of aggression. Each year, member countries take part in a Defence Review, designed to assess their contribution to the common defence in relation to their respective capabilities and constraints. Allied defence policy is reviewed periodically by ministers of defence and, following a decision of the NATO heads of state and government, a review of NATO's overall strategy was undertaken in 1990 (see below).

During the 1980s the Alliance was also actively involved in co-ordinating policies with regard to arms control and disarmament issues designed to bring about negotiated reductions in conventional forces, intermediate and short-range nuclear forces and strategic nuclear forces.

Political consultations within the Alliance take place on a permanent basis, under the auspices of the North Atlantic Council, on all matters affecting the common security interests of the member countries, including developments in Central and Eastern Europe, as well as events outside the North Atlantic Treaty area.

Co-operation in scientific and technological fields as well as co-operation on environmental challenges takes place in the NATO Science Committee and in its Committee on the Challenges of Modern Society. Both these bodies operate an expanding international programme of science fellowships, advance study institutes and research grants. A Science for Stability Programme was established in 1980 to help Greece, Portugal and Turkey develop their scientific and technological capabilities, and new programmes were being developed in 1990 with a view to enhancing participation of scientists from other non-NATO countries.

At a summit meeting held in London in July 1990, NATO heads of state and government published a far-reaching declaration on steps being undertaken within the Alliance to adapt its policies and objectives in the light of the fundamental changes which had taken place in Central and Eastern Europe. The 'London Declaration' stated that the leaders intended to 'enhance the political component' of the Alliance; and that NATO would remain a 'defensive alliance' with no 'aggressive intentions... We will never be the first to use force'. It proposed to member states of the Warsaw Pact 'a joint declaration in which we solemnly state that we are no longer adversaries', invited President Gorbachev of the USSR and other leaders of Warsaw Pact countries to address the North Atlantic Council and to establish regular diplomatic liaison with NATO, and suggested intensification of military contacts. The declaration committed NATO to restructuring and reducing its forces, following the expected conclusion, later in 1990, of a treaty on the reduction of conventional forces in Europe, and proposed new negotiations on the reduction of short-range nuclear forces, to begin immediately afterwards. It recommended that the Conference on Security and Co-operation in Europe (CSCE) should be given much greater importance in determining the political and military future of Europe.

NATO AGENCIES
1. Civilian production and logistics organizations responsible to the Council:

Central European Operating Agency—CEOA: Versailles, France; f. 1957 to supervise the integrated military pipeline network in Central Europe.

Nato Airborne Early Warning and Control Programme Management Organisation—NAPMO: Brunssum, Netherlands; f. 1978 to manage the procurement aspects of the NATO Airborne Early Warning and Control System.

NATO Communications and Information Systems Organisation—NACISO: Brussels, Belgium; f. 1985 by expansion of NATO Integrated Communications System Organisation; supervises planning and implementation of an integrated voice, telegraph and data communications system, to improve the Alliance's capability for crisis management and for the command and control of NATO forces.

NATO European Fighter Aircraft Development, Production and Logistics Management Organisation—NEFMO: Munich, Federal Republic of Germany; f. 1987; mems: Germany, Italy, Spain, UK.

NATO HAWK Management Office: Rueil-Malmaison, France; f. 1959 to supervise the multinational production of the HAWK surface-to-air missile system in Europe.

NATO Maintenance and Supply Agency—NAMSA: Luxembourg; f. 1958; supplies spare parts and logistic support for a number of jointly-used weapon systems, missiles and electronic systems; all member nations except Iceland participate.

NATO MRCA Development and Production Management Organisation—NAMMO: Munich, Germany; f. 1969 to supervise development and production of the Multi-Role Combat Aircraft project; mems: Germany, Italy, UK.

2. Responsible to the Military Committee:

Advisory Group for Aerospace Research and Development—AGARD: Neuilly-sur-Seine, France; f. 1952; brings together aerospace scientists from member countries for exchange of information and research co-operation; provides scientific and technical advice for the Military Committee, for other NATO bodies and for member nations.

Allied Communications Security Agency—ACSA: Brussels, Belgium; f. 1953.

Allied Data Systems Interoperability Agency—ADSIA: Brussels, Belgium; f. 1979 to improve interoperability within the NATO Command, Control and Information Systems.

Allied Long Lines Agency—ALLA: Brussels, Belgium; f. 1951 to formulate policies to meet the long lines communications requirements of NATO.

Allied Naval Communications Agency—ANCA: London, England; f. 1951 to establish reliable communications for maritime operations.

Allied Radio Frequency Agency—ARFA: Brussels, Belgium; f. 1951 to establish policies concerned with military use of the radio frequency spectrum.

Allied Tactical Communications Agency—ATCA: Brussels, Belgium; f. 1972 to establish policies concerned with tactical communications for land and air operations.

NATO MILITARY FORCES AND EXPENDITURE
(1990 estimates)

	Number of armed forces personnel ('000)	Defence expenditure as % of GDP
Europe		
Belgium	110	2.6
Denmark	31	2.1
France	554	3.7
Germany, Federal Republic	496	2.8
Greece	201	5.6
Italy	450	2.4
Luxembourg	1	0.2
Netherlands	107	2.8
Norway	40	3.3
Portugal	105	3.2
Spain	308	2.1
Turkey	780	3.5
United Kingdom	322	4.2
North America		
Canada	89	2.0
United States	2,242	5.9

Iceland has no armed forces
Source: Statistical Analysis Service, NATO

Military Agency for Standardization—MAS: Brussels, Belgium; f. 1951 to improve military standardization of equipment for NATO forces.

NATO Defense College—NADEFCOL: Rome, Italy; f. 1951 to train officials for posts in NATO organizations or in national ministries.

3. Responsible to Supreme Allied Commander Atlantic (SACLANT):

SACLANT Undersea Research Centre—SACLANTCEN: La Spezia, Italy; f. 1962 for research in submarine detection and oceanographic problems.

4. Responsible to Supreme Allied Commander Europe (SACEUR):

SHAPE Technical Centre—STC: The Hague, Netherlands; f. 1960 to provide scientific and technical advice, originally on the formation of an integrated air defence system, subsequently on a broader programme covering force capability and structure; command and control; communications.

FINANCE

As NATO is an international, not a supra-national, organization, its member countries themselves decide the amount to be devoted to their defence effort and the form which the latter will assume. Thus, the aim of NATO's defence planning is to develop realistic military plans for the defence of the alliance at reasonable cost. Under the annual defence planning process, political, military and economic factors are considered in relation to strategy, force requirements and available resources. The procedure for the co-ordination of military plans and defence expenditures rests on the detailed and comparative analysis of the capabilities of member countries. All installations for the use of international forces are financed under a common-funded infrastructure programme.

PUBLICATIONS

NATO publications (in English and French, with some editions in other languages) include:

NATO Review (6 a year in English, French, Danish, Dutch, German, Italian and Spanish; quarterly editions in Greek, Norwegian, Portuguese and Turkish; annual edition in Icelandic).

NATO Facts and Figures.

NATO Basic Documents.

NATO Final Communiqués.

NATO Handbook.

Economic and scientific publications.

ORGANISATION FOR ECONOMIC CO-OPERATION AND DEVELOPMENT—OECD

Address: 2 rue André-Pascal, 75775 Paris Cedex 16, France.
Telephone: (1) 45-24-82-00.
Telex: 620160.
Fax: (1) 45-24-85-00.

OECD was founded in 1961, replacing the Organisation for European Economic Co-operation (OEEC) which had been set up in 1948 in connection with the Marshall Plan. It constitutes a forum where representatives of the governments of the industrialized democracies discuss and attempt to co-ordinate their economic and social policies.

MEMBERS

Australia	Greece	Norway
Austria	Iceland	Portugal
Belgium	Ireland	Spain
Canada	Italy	Sweden
Denmark	Japan	Switzerland
Finland	Luxembourg	Turkey
France	Netherlands	United Kingdom
Germany	New Zealand	USA

Yugoslavia participates in the work of OECD with a special status. The Commission of the European Communities also takes part in the Organisation's work.

Organization

(October 1990)

COUNCIL

The governing body of OECD is the Council on which each member country is represented. The Council meets from time to time (usually once a year) at the level of government ministers, and regularly at official level, when it comprises the heads of Permanent Delegations to OECD (diplomatic missions headed by ambassadors). It is responsible for all questions of general policy and may establish subsidiary bodies as required to achieve the aims of the Organisation. Decisions and recommendations of the Council are adopted by mutual agreement of all its members. The Chairman of the Council at ministerial level is a member of government from the country elected to the chairmanship for that year. The Chairman of the Council at official level is the Secretary-General.

Heads of Permanent Delegations (with ambassadorial rank):
Australia: ED VISBORD
Austria: GEORG LENNKH
Belgium: JUAN CASSIER
Canada: MICHAEL BERRY
Denmark: JENS CHRISTENSEN
Finland: WILHELM BREITENSTEIN
France: BERNARD BOCHET
Germany: KLAUS MEYER
Greece: DIMITRIS KOULOURIANOS
Iceland: ALBERT GUDMUNDSSON
Ireland: TADHG O'SULLIVAN
Italy: LUIGI FONTANA GIUSTI
Japan: HIROAKI FUJII
Luxembourg: PIERRE WURTH
Netherlands: A. G. O. SMITSENDONK
New Zealand: JUDITH TROTTER
Norway: BJØRN BARTH
Portugal: FERNANDO DOS SANTOS MARTINS
Spain: ELOY IBÁÑEZ
Sweden: BO KJELLEN
Switzerland: ERIC ROETHLISBERGER
Turkey: MUSTAFA ASULA
United Kingdom: J. W. D. GRAY
USA: PHILIP LARSON

Participants with Special Status:
Yugoslavia. ZARKO PAPIĆ
Commission of the European Communities: RAYMOND PHAN VAN PHI

EXECUTIVE COMMITTEE

Each year the Council designates 14 of its members to form the Executive Committee which prepares the work of the Council. It is also called upon to carry out specific tasks where necessary. Apart from its regular meetings, the Committee meets occasionally in special sessions attended by senior government officials.

SECRETARIAT

The Council, the committees and other bodies in OECD are assisted by an independent international secretariat headed by the Secretary-General.
Secretary-General: JEAN-CLAUDE PAYE (France).
Deputy Secretaries-General: R. A. CORNELL (USA), PIERRE VINDE (Sweden), MAKOTO TANIGUCHI (Japan).

AUTONOMOUS AND SEMI-AUTONOMOUS BODIES

International Energy Agency (see p. 188).
Nuclear Energy Agency (see p. 188).
Development Centre: f. 1962; includes all member countries except New Zealand. Pres. LOUIS EMMERIJ (see also under Development Co-operation, next page).
Centre for Educational Research and Innovation: includes all member countries and Yugoslavia. Dir THOMAS J. ALEXANDER (see also under Manpower, Social Affairs and Education, next page).

Activities

The greater part of the work of OECD, which covers all aspects of economic and social policy, is prepared and carried out in about 200 specialized bodies (Committees, Working Parties, etc.); all members are normally represented on these bodies, except on those of a restricted nature. Participants are usually civil servants coming either from the capitals of member states or from the Permanent Delegations to OECD. The main bodies are:

Economic Policy Committee
Economic and Development Review Committee
Environment Committee
Group on Urban Affairs
Development Assistance Committee
Technical Co-operation Committee
Trade Committee
Payments Committee
Committee on Capital Movements and Invisible Transactions
Committee on International Investment and Multinational
  Enterprises
Committee on Financial Markets
Committee on Fiscal Affairs
Committee on Competition Law and Policy
Committee on Consumer Policy
Tourism Committee
Maritime Transport Committee
Committee for Agriculture
Fisheries Committee
Committee for Scientific and Technological Policy
Committee for Information, Computer and Communications
  Policy
Education Committee
Industry Committee
Steel Committee
Committee for Energy Policy
Manpower and Social Affairs Committee
Steering Committee of the Programme of Co-operation in the
  Field of Road Research
Steering Committee of the Programme on Educational Building
High Level Group on Commodities
Group on North-South Economic Issues

ECONOMIC POLICY

The main organ for the consideration and direction of economic policy among the member countries is the Economic Policy Committee, which comprises governments' chief economic advisors and central bankers, and meets two or three times a year to review

INTERNATIONAL ORGANIZATIONS
OECD

the economic and financial situation and policies of member countries. It has several working parties and groups, the most important of which are Working Party No. 1 on Macro-Economic and Structural Policy Analysis, Working Party No. 3 on Policies for the Promotion of Better International Payments Equilibrium and the Working Group on Short-Term Economic Prospects.

The Economic and Development Review Committee is responsible for the annual examination of the economic situation of each member country. Usually, a report is issued each year on each country, after an examination carried out by a panel of representatives of a number of other member countries; this process of mutual examination, has been extended also to other branches of the Organisation's work (agriculture, manpower and social affairs, scientific policy and development aid efforts).

ENERGY

Work in the field of energy includes co-ordination of members' energy policies, assessment of short-, medium- and long-term energy prospects; a long-term programme of energy conservation, development of alternative energy sources and energy research and development; a system of information on the international oil and energy markets; and improvement of relations between oil-producing and oil-consuming countries. This work is carried out in OECD's International Energy Agency (IEA: see below), an autonomous body in which 21 member countries of OECD and the Commission of the European Communities participate, as well as within the context of OECD as a whole under the Committee for Energy Policy. Co-operation in the development of nuclear power is undertaken by the Nuclear Energy Agency (see below).

DEVELOPMENT CO-OPERATION

The Development Assistance Committee (DAC) consists of representatives of the main OECD capital-exporting countries; it discusses methods for making national resources available for assisting countries and areas in the process of economic development anywhere in the world, and for expanding and improving the flow of development assistance and other long-term funds.

The Group on North-South Economic Issues deals with the wide range of subjects involved in economic relationships between OECD countries and developing countries. It is particularly concerned with the treatment of these issues in the various fora of international economic discussion, such as UNCTAD.

A Technical Co-operation Committee has the task of drawing up and supervising the programmes of technical assistance arranged for the benefit of member countries, or areas of member countries, in the process of development.

The OECD Development Centre (a semi-autonomous body) was set up in 1962 for the collection and dissemination of information in the field of economic development, research into development problems and the training of specialists both from the industrialized and developing countries.

INTERNATIONAL TRADE

The activities of the Trade Committee are aimed at maintaining the degree of trade liberalization achieved, avoiding the emergence of new trade barriers, and improving further the liberalization of trade on a multilateral and non-discriminatory basis. These activities include examination of issues concerning trade relations among member countries as well as relations with non-member countries, in particular developing countries. The existing procedures allow, inter alia, any member country to obtain prompt consideration and discussions by the Trade Committee of trade measures taken by another member country which adversely affect its own interests.

The task of the High-Level Group on Commodities is to find a more active and broader approach to commodity problems, notably with a view to contributing to a greater stability in the markets.

FINANCIAL AND FISCAL AFFAIRS

The progressive abolition of obstacles to the international flow of services and capital is the responsibility of various OECD Committees. The Committee on Capital Movements and Invisible Transactions watches over the implementation of the Codes of Liberalization of Invisible Transactions and of Capital Movements. The Committee on International Investment and Multinational Enterprises prepared a Code of Behaviour (called 'Guidelines') for multinational enterprises, recommended to them by all member governments; the Committee is to follow up the implementation of these guidelines in order to improve the effectiveness of co-operation among member countries in international investment and multinational enterprises. Other specialized committees have been set up to deal with financial markets, fiscal matters, competition law and policy, tourism, maritime transport, consumer policy, etc.

FOOD, AGRICULTURE AND FISHERIES

The Committee for Agriculture reviews major developments in agricultural policies, deals with the adaptation of agriculture to changing economic conditions, elaborates forecasts of production and market prospects, holds consultations on import and export practices and assesses implications of world developments in food and agriculture for member countries' policies. A separate Fisheries Committee carries out similar tasks in its own sector.

ENVIRONMENT

The Environment Committee is responsible for the economic and policy aspects of OECD's work in this field. The Committee is assisted by various Sector Groups. Its work has led to agreements adopted by member countries setting out guiding principles on the international trade aspects of environment policies (e.g. the 'Polluter pays' principle), and on trans-frontier movements of hazardous waste. A special Chemicals Programme promotes co-operation and mutual assistance in controlling the 80,000 chemicals on the commercial market. The Committee also deals with policies for air and water management, noise abatement, trans-frontier pollution, etc.

Urban problems in OECD countries are dealt with by a Group on Urban Affairs, covering economic, social and administrative issues in cities, as well as ecological aspects of the built-up environment.

SCIENCE, TECHNOLOGY AND INDUSTRY

The Committee for Scientific and Technological Policy is responsible for encouraging co-operation among member countries in scientific and technological policies with a view to contributing to the achievement of their economic and social aims.

The Committee for Information, Computer and Communications Policy is to examine policy issues arising from the development and application of technologies in the field of information, computer and communications systems and services, including the impact of such issues on the economy and on society in general.

The Steel Committee enables governments, consistent with general economic policies, to act promptly to cope with crisis situations, to keep steel trade as unrestricted and undistorted as possible and to facilitate the necessary structural adjustment of the industry.

The Industry Committee has overall responsibility for all aspects of the Organisation's work in the field of industry which require co-operation and confrontation among member governments.

MANPOWER, SOCIAL AFFAIRS AND EDUCATION

The Manpower and Social Affairs Committee is concerned with the development of manpower and selective employment policies to ensure the utilization of manpower at the highest possible level and to improve the quality and flexibility of working life as well as the integration of social policies. Its work includes such aspects as the role of women in the economy, industrial relations, intra-European migration movements and the development of social indicators.

The Committee for Education relates educational planning to educational policy and evaluates the implications of policy for the allocation and use of resources. The Committee reviews educational trends, develops statistics and indicators and analyses policies for greater equality of educational opportunity, new options for youth and learning opportunities for adults. Together, the Manpower and Education Committees seek to provide for greater integration of manpower and educational policy.

The OECD's Centre for Educational Research and Innovation (CERI) promotes the development of research activities in education together with experiments of an advanced nature designed to test innovations in educational systems and to stimulate research and development. Yugoslavia is also a member.

RELATIONS WITH OTHER INTERNATIONAL ORGANIZATIONS

Under a Protocol signed at the same time as the OECD Convention, the Commission of the European Communities generally takes part in the work of OECD. EFTA may also send representatives to OECD meetings. Formal relations exist with a number of other international organizations, including the ILO, FAO, IMF, IBRD, UNCTAD, IAEA and the Council of Europe. A few non-governmental organizations have been granted consultative status, notably the Business and Industry Advisory Committee to OECD (BIAC) and the Trade Union Advisory Committee to OECD (TUAC).

PUBLICATIONS

News from OECD (monthly).

The OECD Observer (every 2 months).

Activities of OECD (Secretary-General's Annual Report).

INTERNATIONAL ORGANIZATIONS OECD

Main Economic Indicators (monthly).
The OECD Economic Outlook (2 a year).
Economic Surveys by OECD (annually for each country).
OECD Employment Outlook (annually).
Foreign Trade Statistics (monthly).
Financial Statistics (24 a year).
National Accounts (annually).
Development Assistance Efforts and Policies (annually).
Tourism Policy and International Tourism.
Oil and Gas Statistics (quarterly).
Energy Balances (annually).

Numerous specialized reports, books and statistics on economic and social subjects (about 130 titles a year, both in English and French) are also published.

International Energy Agency

Address: 2 rue André Pascal, 75775 Paris Cedex 16, France.

The Agency was set up by the Council of OECD in 1974 to develop co-operation on energy questions among participating countries.

MEMBERS

Australia
Austria
Belgium
Canada
Denmark
Germany
Greece
Ireland
Italy
Japan
Luxembourg
Netherlands
New Zealand
Norway
Portugal
Spain
Sweden
Switzerland
Turkey
United Kingdom
USA

The Commission of the European Communities is also represented.

Activities

The Agreement on an International Energy Programme was signed in November 1974 and formally entered into force in January 1976. The Programme commits the participating countries of the International Energy Agency to share oil in emergencies, to strengthen their long-term co-operation in order to reduce dependence on oil imports, to increase the availability of information on the oil market and to develop relations with the oil-producing and other oil-consuming countries.

The emergency oil-sharing plan has been established and the IEA ensures that the necessary technical information and facilities are in place so that it can be readily used in the event of a reduction in oil supplies.

The IEA Long-Term Co-operation Programme is designed to strengthen the security of energy supplies and promote stability in world energy markets. It provides for co-operative efforts to conserve energy, to accelerate the development of alternative energy sources by means of both specific and general measures, to step up research and development of new energy technologies and to remove legislative and administrative obstacles to increased energy supplies. Regular reviews of member countries' efforts in the fields of energy conservation and accelerated development of alternative energy sources assess the effectiveness of national programmes in relation to the objectives of the Agency.

The Agency has developed an extensive system of information and consultation on the oil market with a view to obtaining a better idea of probable future developments in the oil market. Another function of the Agency is to develop a long-term co-operative relationship among oil-producing and consuming countries.

GOVERNING BOARD

Composed of ministers or senior officials of the member governments. Decisions may be taken by a weighted majority on a number of specified subjects, particularly concerning emergency measures and the emergency reserve commitment; a simple weighted majority is required for procedural decisions and decisions implementing specific obligations in the agreement. Unanimity is required only if new obligations, not already specified in the agreement, are to be undertaken.

The Governing Board is assisted by four Standing Groups and a high-level Committee, dealing respectively with emergency questions; long-term co-operation; oil market; relations with producer and other consumer countries; and energy research and development.

There is also a Coal and an Oil Industry Advisory Board, composed of industrial executives.

SECRETARIAT

Executive Director: HELGA STEEG (Germany).

Deputy Executive Director: JOHN FERRITER (USA).

OECD Nuclear Energy Agency—NEA

Address: 38 boulevard Suchet, 75016 Paris, France.
Telephone: (1) 45-24-82-00.
Telex: 630668.
Fax: (1) 45-24-96-24.

The NEA was established in 1958 to further the peaceful uses of nuclear energy. Originally a European agency, it has since admitted four of the five OECD members outside Europe.

MEMBERS

All members of OECD except New Zealand.

Organization

(October 1990)

STEERING COMMITTEE FOR NUCLEAR ENERGY

Chairman: RICHARD KENNEDY (USA).

SECRETARIAT

Director-General: Dr KUNIHIKO UEMATSU.
Deputy Director-General: PIERRE STROHL.
Deputy Director (Science and Computer Processing): JOHNNY ROSEN.
Deputy Director (Safety and Regulation): KLAUS STADIE.

MAIN COMMITTEES

Committee for Technical and Economic Studies on Nuclear Energy Development and the Fuel Cycle;
Committee on the Safety of Nuclear Installations;
Committee on Nuclear Regulatory Activities;
Committee on Radiation Protection and Public Health;
Radioactive Waste Management Committee;
NEA Nuclear Data Committee (NEANDC);
NEA Committee on Reactor Physics (NEACRP);
Group of Governmental Experts on Third Party Liability in the Field of Nuclear Energy.

Activities

The main purpose of the Agency is to promote international co-operation within the OECD area for the development and application of nuclear power for peaceful purposes through international research and development projects and exchange of scientific and technical experience and information. The Agency also maintains a continual survey with the co-operation of other organizations, notably the International Atomic Energy Agency (IAEA, q.v.), of world uranium resources, production and demand, and of economic and technical aspects of the nuclear fuel cycle.

A major part of the Agency's work is devoted to the safety and regulation of nuclear power, including co-operative studies and projects related to the prevention of nuclear accidents and the long-term safety of radioactive waste disposal systems.

JOINT PROJECTS

Halden Project: Halden, Norway; experimental boiling heavy water reactor, which became an OECD project in 1958. From 1964, under successive agreements with participating countries, the reactor has been used for long-term testing of water reactor fuels and for research into automatic computer-based control of nuclear power stations. Nuclear energy research institutions and authorities in 10 countries support the project.

Co-operative Programme on Three Mile Island: a multinational programme (established in 1986) which examines samples taken from the Three Mile Island nuclear reactor in Pennsylvania, USA (following the accident which took place there in 1979) and develops computer codes for analysis of severe accidents. The objective of this programme is to contribute to a better understanding of the accident, in particular of the sequence of events and the behaviour of fission products. Eleven countries participate in the programme.

International Stripa Project: set up in early 1980, this project is conducting experiments in an abandoned iron mine in Sweden, on the use of hard crystalline rock for isolating nuclear waste. Nine countries participate in the project.

Incident Reporting System: introduced in 1980 to exchange experience in operating nuclear power plants in OECD member countries and to improve nuclear safety by facilitating feedback of this experience to nuclear regulatory authorities, utilities and manufacturers.

Chemical Thermodynamic Data Base: the objective of this project, set up in 1983, is to compile fundamental chemical thermodynamic data which permit the quantification of mass transfers in chemical reactions occurring in ground water and in water-rock reactions. Such data can be used in geochemical modelling of waste disposal systems performance assessments to predict the concentration of radioelements under various conditions.

Alligator Rivers Analogue Project: an international research project, established in 1988 to gain further insight into the long-term physical and chemical processes likely to influence the transport of radionuclides through rock masses. Research involves the study of geochemical and hydrogeological processes acting upon the Koongarra uranium ore deposit in Australia, which may resemble those processes acting upon high-level radioactive waste disposal facility.

Decommissioning of Nuclear Installations: this co-operative programme, set up in 1985, provides for an exchange of scientific and technical information to develop the operational experience and data base needed for the future decommissioning of large nuclear power plants. Nine countries are participating in this programme.

COMMON SERVICE

NEA Data Bank: Saclay, France; set up in 1978 in succession to the Computer Programme Library and the Neutron Data Compilation Centre, the Data Bank allows the 17 participating countries to share large computer programmes used in reactor calculations, and nuclear data applications. It also operates as one of a worldwide network of four nuclear data centres.

FINANCE

The Agency's budget for 1989 amounted to 60m. French francs.

PUBLICATIONS

Annual Report.
NEA Newsletter (2 a year).
Nuclear Law Bulletin (2 a year).
Nuclear Energy Data (annually).
Reports and proceedings.

ORGANIZATION OF AFRICAN UNITY—OAU

Address: POB 3243, Addis Ababa, Ethiopia.
Telephone: 517700.
Telex: 21046.

The Organization was founded in 1963 to promote unity and solidarity among African states.

FORMATION

There were various attempts at establishing an inter-African organization before the OAU Charter was drawn up. In November 1958 Ghana and Guinea (later joined by Mali) drafted a Charter which was to form the basis of a Union of African States. In January 1961 a conference was held at Casablanca, attended by the Heads of State of Ghana, Guinea, Mali, Morocco, and representatives of Libya and of the provisional government of the Algerian Republic (GPRA). Tunisia, Nigeria, Liberia and Togo declined the invitation to attend. An African Charter was adopted and it was decided to set up an African Military Command and an African Common Market.

Between October 1960 and March 1961 three conferences were held by French-speaking African countries, at Abidjan, Brazzaville and Yaoundé. None of the 12 countries which attended these meetings had been present at the Casablanca Conference. These conferences led eventually to the signing in September 1961, at Tananarive, of a charter establishing the Union africaine et malgache, later the Organisation commune africaine et mauricienne (OCAM).

In May 1961 a conference was held at Monrovia, Liberia, attended by the Heads of State or representatives of 19 countries: Cameroon, Central African Republic, Chad, Congo Republic (ex-French), Côte d'Ivoire, Dahomey, Ethiopia, Gabon, Liberia, Madagascar, Mauritania, Niger, Nigeria, Senegal, Sierra Leone, Somalia, Togo, Tunisia and Upper Volta. They met again (with the exception of Tunisia and with the addition of the ex-Belgian Congo Republic) in January 1962 at Lagos, Nigeria, and set up a permanent secretariat and a standing committee of finance ministers, and accepted a draft charter for an Organization of Inter-African and Malagasy States.

It was the Conference of Addis Ababa, held in 1963, which finally brought together African states despite the regional, political and linguistic differences which divided them. The Foreign Ministers of 32 African states attended the Preparatory Meeting held in May: Algeria, Burundi, Cameroon, Central African Republic, Chad, Congo (Brazzaville) (now the Congo), Congo (Léopoldville) (now Zaire), Côte d'Ivoire, Dahomey (now Benin), Ethiopia, Gabon, Ghana, Guinea, Liberia, Libya, Madagascar, Mali, Mauritania, Morocco, Niger, Nigeria, Rwanda, Senegal, Sierra Leone, Somalia, Sudan, Tanganyika (now Tanzania), Togo, Tunisia, Uganda, the United Arab Republic (Egypt) and Upper Volta (now Burkina Faso).

The topics discussed by the meeting were: (i) creation of the Organization of African States; (ii) co-operation among African states in the following fields: economic and social; education, culture and science; collective defence; (iii) decolonization; (iv) apartheid and racial discrimination; (v) effects of economic grouping on the economic development of Africa; (vi) disarmament; (vii) creation of a Permanent Conciliation Commission; and (viii) Africa and the United Nations.

The Heads of State Conference which opened on 23 May drew up the Charter of the Organization of African Unity, which was then signed by the heads of 30 states on 25 May 1963. The Charter was essentially functional and reflected a compromise between the concept of a loose association of states favoured by the Monrovia Group and the federal idea supported by the Casablanca Group, and in particular by Ghana.

SUMMARY OF OAU CHARTER

Article I. Establishment of the Organization of African Unity. The Organization to include continental African states, Madagascar, and other islands surrounding Africa.

Article II. Aims of the OAU:

1. To promote unity and solidarity among African states.
2. To intensify and co-ordinate efforts to improve living standards in Africa.
3. To defend sovereignty, territorial integrity and independence of African states.
4. To eradicate all forms of colonialism from Africa.
5. To promote international co-operation in keeping with the Charter of the United Nations.

Article III. Member states adhere to the principles of sovereignty, non-interference in internal affairs of member states, respect for territorial integrity, peaceful settlement of disputes, condemnation of political subversion, dedication to the emancipation of dependent African territories, and international non-alignment.

Article IV. Each independent sovereign African state shall be entitled to become a member of the Organization.

Article V. All member states shall have equal rights and duties.

Article VI. All member states shall observe scrupulously the principles laid down in Article III.

Article VII. Establishment of the Assembly of Heads of State and Government, the Council of Ministers, the General Secretariat, and the Commission of Mediation, Conciliation and Arbitration.

Articles VIII-XI. The Assembly of Heads of State and Government co-ordinates policies and reviews the structure of the Organization.

Articles XII-XV. The Council of Ministers shall prepare conferences of the Assembly, and co-ordinate inter-African co-operation. All resolutions shall be by simple majority.

Articles XVI-XVIII. The General Secretariat. The Administrative Secretary-General and his staff shall not seek or receive instructions from any government or other authority external to the Organization. They are international officials responsible only to the Organization.

Article XIX. Commission of Mediation, Conciliation and Arbitration. A separate protocol concerning the composition and nature of this Commission shall be regarded as an integral part of the Charter.

Articles XX-XXII. Specialized Commissions shall be established, composed of Ministers or other officials designated by Member Governments. Their regulations shall be laid down by the Council of Ministers.

Article XXIII. The Budget shall be prepared by the Secretary-General and approved by the Council of Ministers. Contributions shall be in accordance with the scale of assessment of the United Nations. No Member shall pay more than 20% of the total yearly amount.

Article XXIV. Texts of the Charter in African languages, English and French shall be equally authentic. Instruments of ratification shall be deposited with the Government of Ethiopia.

Article XXV. The Charter shall come into force on receipt by the Government of Ethiopia of the instruments of ratification of two-thirds of the signatory states.

Article XXVI. The Charter shall be registered with the Secretariat of the United Nations.

Article XXVII. Questions of interpretation shall be settled by a two-thirds majority vote in the Assembly of Heads of State and Government.

Article XXVIII. Admission of new independent African states to the Organization shall be decided by a simple majority of the Member States.

Articles XXIX-XXXIII. The working languages of the Organization shall be African languages, English and French. The Secretary-General may accept gifts and bequests to the Organization, subject to the approval of the Council of Ministers. The Council of Ministers shall establish privileges and immunities to be accorded to the personnel of the Secretariat in the territories of Member States. A State wishing to withdraw from the Organization must give a year's written notice to the Secretariat. The Charter may only be amended after consideration by all Member States and by a two-thirds majority vote of the Assembly of Heads of State and Government. Such amendments will come into force one year after submission.

INTERNATIONAL ORGANIZATIONS   *Organization of African Unity*

MEMBERS*

Algeria	Libya
Angola	Madagascar
Benin	Malawi
Botswana	Mali
Burkina Faso	Mauritania
Burundi	Mauritius
Cameroon	Mozambique
Cape Verde	Namibia
Central African Republic	Niger
Chad	Nigeria
The Comoros	Rwanda
Congo	São Tomé and Príncipe
Côte d'Ivoire	Senegal
Djibouti	Seychelles
Egypt	Sierra Leone
Equatorial Guinea	Somalia
Ethiopia	Sudan
Gabon	Swaziland
The Gambia	Tanzania
Ghana	Togo
Guinea	Tunisia
Guinea-Bissau	Uganda
Kenya	Zaire
Lesotho	Zambia
Liberia	Zimbabwe

* The Sahrawi Arab Democratic Republic (Western Sahara) was admitted to the OAU in February 1982, following recognition by 26 of the 50 members, but its membership was disputed by Morocco and other states which claimed that a two-thirds majority was needed to admit a state whose existence was in question. Morocco withdrew from the OAU with effect from November 1985.

Organization

(October 1990)

ASSEMBLY OF HEADS OF STATE

The Assembly of Heads of State and Government meets annually to co-ordinate policies of African states. Resolutions are passed by a two-thirds majority, procedural matters by a simple majority. A chairman is elected at each meeting from among the members, to hold office for one year.

Chairman (1990/91): Lt-Gen YOWERI KAGUTA MUSEVENI (Uganda).

COUNCIL OF MINISTERS

Consists of ministers of foreign affairs and others and meets twice a year, with provision for extraordinary sessions. Each session elects its own Chairman. Prepares meetings of, and is responsible to, the Assembly of Heads of State.

GENERAL SECRETARIAT

The permanent headquarters of the organization. It carries out functions assigned to it in the Charter of the OAU and by other agreements and treaties made between member states. Departments: Political; Finance; Education, Science, Culture and Social Affairs; Economic Development and Co-operation; Administration and Conferences. The Secretary-General is elected for a four-year term by the Assembly of Heads of State.

Secretary-General: SALIM AHMED SALIM (Tanzania).

ARBITRATION COMMISSION

Commission of Mediation, Conciliation and Arbitration: Addis Ababa; f. 1964; consists of 21 members elected by the Assembly of Heads of State for a five-year term; no state may have more than one member; has a Bureau consisting of a President and two Vice-Presidents, who shall not be eligible for re-election. Its task is to hear and settle disputes between member states by peaceful means.

SPECIALIZED COMMISSIONS

There are specialized commissions for economic, social, transport and communications affairs; education, science, culture and health; defence; human rights; and labour.

LIBERATION COMMITTEE

Co-ordinating Committee for the Liberation Movements of Africa: Dar es Salaam, Tanzania; f. 1963; to provide financial and military aid to nationalist movements in dependent countries; regional offices in Maputo, Mozambique, Lusaka, Zambia, and Luanda, Angola.

Executive Secretary: Brig. HASHIM MBITA (Tanzania).

BUDGET

Member states contribute in accordance with their United Nations assessment. No member state is assessed for an amount exceeding 20% of the yearly regular budget of the Organization. The budget for 1987/88 was estimated at $23.2m. The budget for 1988/89 was estimated at $25.03m., and that for 1989/90 at $28m. Arrears in payments of contributions by members were reported to amount to $80m. at the beginning of 1990.

Principal Events, 1980–90

1980

May	An economic summit meeting resolved to take steps towards establishment of an African Common Market by year 2000; adopted 'Lagos Plan of Action' to this end.
July	The 17th Assembly of Heads of State postponed a decision on admitting the Sahrawi Arab Democratic Republic (SADR), proclaimed by the Frente Popular para la Liberación de Sakiet el Hamra y Río de Oro, known as the Frente Polisario (Polisario Front) in Western Sahara (the former Spanish Sahara, claimed by Morocco), after Morocco threatened to leave the OAU if admission were granted.
Sept.	The OAU committee on Western Sahara announced a six-point ceasefire plan, to include a referendum organized by the OAU with assistance from the UN.

1981

Jan.	A conference on Chad and Libya condemned the proposed merger of the two countries, demanded the withdrawal of all foreign forces from Chad and decided to send an African force to maintain peace there and supervise elections. A meeting of Ministers of Justice approved an African Charter on Human and People's Rights which (subject to ratification by a majority of OAU members) would establish a Commission to investigate violations of human rights.
Feb.	Ministers of foreign affairs supported proposals for an intensified guerrilla war in Namibia and mandatory economic sanctions against South Africa to persuade the South African Government to negotiate on Namibian independence.
June	At the 18th Assembly of Heads of State, Morocco agreed to hold a referendum in Western Sahara. A ministerial committee was created to investigate the Nigeria-Cameroon border dispute.
Nov.	The first members of the OAU peace-keeping force (from Nigeria, Senegal and Zaire) arrived in Chad to replace the Libyan troops previously supporting the Government against opposition forces.

1982

Feb.	The OAU committee on Chad established a timetable for ceasefire, negotiations, a provisional constitution and elections in Chad, and announced that the OAU peace-keeping force's mandate would cease at the end of June. The committee on Western Sahara empowered Pres. Moi of Kenya to conduct negotiations for a ceasefire between Morocco and the Polisario Front. At a meeting of Ministers of Foreign Affairs, the admission of a representative of the SADR led to a walk-out by 19 countries.
March–April	Ordinary OAU business was disrupted because boycotts by opponents and supporters of Polisario meant that three ministerial meetings were without a quorum of members. Discussions by a special group representing nine countries failed to solve the deadlock.
Aug.	The 19th Assembly of Heads of State, due to be held in Tripoli, Libya, failed to achieve a quorum when 19 states boycotted the meeting owing to the dispute over the admission of the SADR. A five-member committee was set up to try to convene another summit before the end of the year.
Nov.	A second attempt to hold the 19th Assembly of Heads of State in Tripoli was abandoned after a dispute over the representation of Chad: the Libyan leader, Col Gaddafi, and others opposed the presence of Pres. Hissène Habré in favour of the former Pres. Goukouni Oueddei, leading to a boycott by representatives of 14 moderate states.

1983

June	The 19th Assembly of Heads of State met in Addis Ababa: SADR representatives agreed not to attend, in order to avoid a boycott of the meeting by their opponents. The

Assembly again called for a referendum in Western Sahara and for direct negotiations between Morocco and the SADR.

1984

Jan. The OAU-sponsored talks between the rival factions in Chad, held in Addis Ababa, broke down without result, chiefly owing to the refusal of Pres. Habré to attend.

March The council of ministers of foreign affairs discussed cumulative budgetary arrears amounting to over US $34m.: less than one-third of contributions due for the 1983/84 period had been paid. The SADR delegation again agreed not to attend the meeting, but declared that they would be present at the next Assembly of Heads of State.

Nov. The 20th Assembly was held in Addis Ababa. Nigeria became the 30th OAU member to recognize the Sahrawi Arab Democratic Republic. A delegation from the SADR was admitted to the Assembly, and Morocco immediately announced its resignation from the OAU (to take effect after one year); only Zaire supported Morocco by withdrawing from the meeting. The Assembly concentrated on economic matters, discussing Africa's balance-of-payments problems, debts and the drought affecting many countries. An emergency fund was set up to combat the effects of drought, with initial contributions of US $10m. each from Algeria and Libya.

1985

July The 21st Assembly of Heads of State was held in Addis Ababa, and again discussed mainly economic issues. It resulted in the Addis Ababa Declaration, in which member countries reiterated their commitment to the Lagos Plan of Action (see under 1980) and adopted a priority programme for the next five years, emphasizing the rehabilitation of African agriculture: they agreed to increase agriculture's share of public investment to between 20% and 25% by the year 1989. The meeting also expressed concern at Africa's heavy external debt (expected to total over US $170,000m. by the end of 1985) and called for a special conference of creditors and borrowers to seek a solution to the problem, and for an increase in concessional financial resources. The Assembly also agreed on the appointment of a new Secretary-General. A special emergency fund was created by the Assembly to combat drought and famine in Africa.

1986

May At a special session of the UN General Assembly on the economic problems of Africa, the OAU (represented by its Chairman) presented a programme, prepared jointly with the UN Economic Commission for Africa, calling for debt relief and an increase in assistance for agricultural investment.

July The 22nd Assembly of Heads of State called for comprehensive economic sanctions against South Africa, and strongly criticized the governments of the United Kingdom and the USA for opposing sanctions. Among other resolutions the Assembly condemned outside interference in Angola; called upon France to return the island of Mayotte to the Comoros; and resolved to continue efforts (led by the OAU Chairman) to bring about reconciliation in Chad. A council of 'wise men', comprising former African heads of state, was established to mediate, when necessary, in disputes between member countries. The Assembly reiterated its call for an international conference on Africa's foreign debt.

1987

Feb. The OAU Chairman, President Sassou-Nguessou of the Congo, undertook a tour of Europe to discuss the possibility of a negotiated settlement in Chad; the political situation in South Africa; and African debt.

July The Assembly of Heads of State reiterated its demands that Western countries should impose economic sanctions on South Africa. It renewed the mandate of the special OAU committee which had been attempting to resolve the dispute between Chad and Libya. It also discussed the spread of the disease AIDS in Africa; and approved the establishment of an African commission on human rights, now that the African Charter on Human and People's Rights (approved in 1981) had been ratified by a majority of member states.

Nov. A summit meeting on the subject of Africa's external debt (now estimated to total US $200,000m.) was held in Addis Ababa (but was attended by only 10 heads of state and government). The meeting issued a statement requesting the conversion of past bilateral loans into grants, a 10-year suspension of debt-service payments, reduction of interest rates and the lengthening of debt-maturity periods. It asked that creditors should observe the principle that debt-servicing should not exceed a 'reasonable and bearable' percentage of the debtor country's export earnings. A 'contact group' was established to enlist support for an international conference on African debt.

1988

May The Assembly of Heads of State recognized that no conference on debt was likely to be held in 1988, owing to the reluctance of creditors to participate. It condemned the links with South Africa still maintained by some African countries, and protested at the recently-reported unauthorized disposal of toxic waste in Africa by industrial companies from outside the continent.

Aug. The OAU organized an international conference in Oslo, Norway, on refugees and displaced persons in southern Africa.

1989

Jan. A meeting on apartheid, organized by the OAU, resulted in the formation of the African Anti-Apartheid Committee (see below).

Feb. The OAU Council of Ministers discussed the independence process in Namibia, and criticized the UN Security Council's decision to limit the size of the UN military observer force (UNTAG) which was to supervise the process.

May The OAU Chairman, President Traoré of Mali, undertook a mission of mediation between the governments of Mauritania and Senegal, following ethnic conflict between the citizens of the two countries.

July The Assembly of Heads of State discussed the Namibian independence process, and urged that the UN should ensure that the forthcoming elections there would be fairly conducted. They again requested that an international conference on Africa's debts should be held.

Sept.–Dec. The newly-elected OAU Chairman, Hosni Mubarak, and the newly-appointed OAU Secretary-General, Salim Ahmed Salim, attempted to mediate in the dispute between Mauritania and Senegal. In November a mediation committee, comprising representatives of six countries, visited Mauritania and Senegal.

1990

March A monitoring group was formed by the OAU to report on events in South Africa. The OAU urged the international community to continue imposing economic sanctions on South Africa.

July The Assembly of Heads of State reviewed the implications for Africa of recent socio-economic and political changes in Eastern Europe, and of the European Community's progress towards monetary and political union.

Specialized Agencies

African Anti-Apartheid Committee: Brazzaville, Congo; f. 1989; aims to link anti-apartheid movements within and outside Africa, and to co-ordinate anti-apartheid strategy. Chair. DANIEL ABIBI (Congo).

African Bureau for Educational Sciences: BP 14, Kisangani, Zaire.

African Civil Aviation Commission—AFCAC: 15 blvd de la République, BP 2356, Dakar, Senegal; tel. 22-30-30; telex 3182; f. 1969 to encourage co-operation in all civil aviation activities; promotes co-ordination and better utilization and development of African air transport systems and the standardization of aircraft, flight equipment and training programmes for pilots and mechanics; organizes working groups and seminars, and compiles statistics. Pres. VASSIRIKI SAVANE (Côte d'Ivoire); Sec. EDOUARD LOMBOLOU.

International Scientific Council for Trypanosomiasis Research and Control: Joint Secretariat, OAU/STRC, PM Bag 2359, Lagos, Nigeria; tel. 633289; telex 22199; f. 1949 to review the work on tsetse and trypanosomiasis problems carried out by organizations and workers concerned in laboratories and in the field; to stimulate further research and discussion and to promote co-ordination between research workers and organizations in the different countries in Africa, and to provide a regular opportunity for the discussion of particular problems and for the exposition of new experiments and discoveries. Exec. Sec. Prof. A. OLUFEMI WILLIAMS; Publ. Proceedings of ISCTR Conferences.

Organization of African Trade Union Unity—OATUU: POB M386, Accra, Ghana; tel. 774531; f. 1973 as a single continental trade union organization, independent of international trade union organizations; has affiliates from all African trade unions. Congress, composed of four delegates from all affiliated trade union centres, meets at least every four years as supreme policy-making body; General Council, composed of one representative from all affiliated trade unions, meets annually to implement Congress decisions and to approve annual budget. Mems: trade union movements in 50 independent African countries, including trade unions within the liberation movements. Sec.-Gen. HASSAN SUNMONU (Nigeria). Publ. *Voice of African Workers*.

Pan-African News Agency—PANA: BP 4056, Dakar, Senegal; tel. 22-61-20; telex 3261 3307; regional headquarters in Khartoum, Sudan; Lusaka, Zambia; Kinshasa, Zaire; Lagos, Nigeria; Tripoli, Libya; began operations in May 1983; receives information from national news agencies and circulates news in English and French. Dir AUGUSTE MPASSI-MUBA (Congo).

Pan-African Postal Union—PAPU: POB 6026, Arusha, Tanzania; tel. 3910; telex 42096; f. 1980; Admin. Council representing 16 countries elected on regional basis (merger with PATU—see below—announced March 1990). Sec.-Gen. COMLANVI AMOUSSOU (Togo).

Pan-African Telecommunications Union—PATU: BP 8634, Kinshasa, Zaire; tel. 22175; telex 21049; f. 1977 for co-ordination of telecommunications development (merger with PAPU—see above—announced March 1990). Sec.-Gen. RAJABU MABULA YUSUF.

Scientific, Technical and Research Commission—OAU/STRC: Nigerian Ports Authority Bldg, PMB 2359, Marina, Lagos, Nigeria; tel. 633289; telex 22199; f. 1965 to succeed the Commission for Technical Co-operation in Africa (f. 1954). Supervises the Inter-African Bureau for Animal Resources (Nairobi, Kenya), the Inter-African Bureau for Soils (Bangui, Central African Republic) and the Inter-African Phytosanitary Commission (Yaoundé, Cameroon) and several joint research projects (see also International Scientific Council on Trypanosomiasis Research and Control, above); a centre for Fertilizer Development was to be established in 1988. The Commission provides training in agricultural management, and conducts pest control programmes. Exec. Sec. Prof. A. OLUFEMI WILLIAMS.

Supreme Council for Sports in Africa: BP 1363, Yaoundé, Cameroon; tel. 22-27-11; telex 8295. Sec.-Gen. AMADOU LAMINE BA.

Union of African Railways: BP 687, Kinshasa, Zaire; tel. 23861; telex 21258; f. 1972 to standardize, expand, co-ordinate and improve members' railway services; the ultimate aim is to link all systems; main organs: General Assembly, Executive Board, General Secretariat, five technical cttees. Mems in 30 African countries. Pres. TOM MMARI; Sec.-Gen. ROBERT GEBE NKANA (Malawi).

ORGANIZATION OF AMERICAN STATES—OAS

Address: 1889 F St, NW, Washington, DC 20006, USA.
Telephone: (202) 458-3000.
Telex: 440118.

The OAS was founded at Bogotá, Colombia, in 1948 (succeeding the International Union of American Republics, founded in 1890) to foster peace, security, mutual understanding and co-operation among the nations of the Western Hemisphere.

MEMBERS

Antigua and Barbuda	Haiti
Argentina	Honduras
Bahamas	Jamaica
Barbados	Mexico
Bolivia	Nicaragua
Brazil	Panama
Canada	Paraguay
Chile	Peru
Colombia	Saint Christopher and Nevis
Costa Rica	Saint Lucia
Cuba*	Saint Vincent and the Grenadines
Dominica	Suriname
Dominican Republic	Trinidad and Tobago
Ecuador	USA
El Salvador	Uruguay
Grenada	Venezuela
Guatemala	

Permanent Observers: Algeria, Austria, Belgium, Belize, Cyprus, Egypt, Equatorial Guinea, Finland, France, Germany, Greece, Guyana, the Holy See, Israel, Italy, Japan, the Republic of Korea, Morocco, the Netherlands, Pakistan, Portugal, Romania, Saudi Arabia, Spain, Switzerland, and the European Community.

* The Cuban Government was suspended from OAS activities in 1962.

Organization
(October 1990)

GENERAL ASSEMBLY
The Assembly meets annually and can also hold special sessions when convoked by the Permanent Council. Supreme organ of the OAS, it decides general action and policy.

MEETINGS OF CONSULTATION OF MINISTERS OF FOREIGN AFFAIRS
Meetings are held to consider problems of an urgent nature and of common interest to member states; they may be held at the request of any member state.

PERMANENT COUNCIL
The Council meets regularly throughout the year at OAS headquarters. It is composed of one representative of each member state with the rank of ambassador; each government may accredit alternate representatives and advisers and when necessary appoint an interim representative. The office of Chairman is held in turn by each of the representatives, following alphabetical order according to the names of the countries in Spanish. The Vice-Chairman is determined in the same way, following reverse alphabetical order. Their terms of office are three months.

The Council acts as an organ of consultation and oversees the maintenance of friendly relations between members. It supervises the work of the OAS and promotes co-operation with a variety of other international bodies including the United Nations. The official languages are English, French, Portuguese and Spanish.

INTER-AMERICAN ECONOMIC AND SOCIAL COUNCIL
The Council holds annual meetings of expert representatives and of ministers of finance and economy. Its aim is to promote co-operation among the countries of the region, in order to accelerate economic and social development. The permanent executive committee of the Council provides technical assistance.
Executive Secretary: Augusto Galli (Venezuela).

INTER-AMERICAN COUNCIL FOR EDUCATION, SCIENCE AND CULTURE
The Council is composed of one representative from each member state, appointed by the respective governments; it meets annually at the level of ministers of education. Its principal purpose is to promote friendly relations and mutual understanding between the peoples of the Americas through educational, scientific and cultural co-operation and exchange between member states.

The council has a permanent executive committee and three committees in charge of carrying out regional development programmes in the fields of education, science and technology, and culture.
Executive Secretary: Enrique Martín del Campo (Mexico).

INTER-AMERICAN JURIDICAL COMMITTEE
Address: Rua Senador Vergueiro 81, Rio de Janeiro, RJ, Brazil; tel. (21) 225-1361. Composed of 11 jurists, nationals of different member states, elected for a period of four years with the possibility of re-election once. The Committee's purpose is to serve as an advisory body to the Organization on juridical matters; to promote the progressive development and codification of international law and to study juridical problems related to the integration of the developing countries in the hemisphere, and in so far as may appear desirable, the possibility of attaining uniformity in legislation.

INTER-AMERICAN COMMISSION ON HUMAN RIGHTS
The Commission was established in 1960 and comprises seven members. It promotes the observance and protection of human rights in the member states of the OAS; it examines and reports on the human rights situation in member countries, and provides consultative services.

INTER-AMERICAN COURT OF HUMAN RIGHTS
Based in San José, Costa Rica, the Court was established in 1978, as an autonomous judicial institution whose purpose is to apply and interpret the American Convention on Human Rights (which entered into force in 1978 and had been ratified by 19 OAS member states by the end of June 1990). The Court comprises seven jurists from OAS member states.

GENERAL SECRETARIAT
The central and permanent organ of the Organization, carries out the duties entrusted to it by the General Assembly, Meetings of Consultation of Ministers of Foreign Affairs and the Councils.
Secretary-General: João Clemente Baena Soares (Brazil).
Assistant Secretary-General: Christopher Thomas (Trinidad and Tobago).

Record of Events

1826	First Congress of American States, convened by Simón Bolívar at Panama City. The Treaty of Perpetual Union, League and Confederation was signed by Colombia, the United Provinces of Central America, Peru, and Mexico.
1889–90	First International Conference of American States (Washington) founded the International Union of American Republics and established a central office, the Commercial Bureau, the purpose of which was the 'prompt collection and distribution of commercial information'.
1910	Fourth Conference (Buenos Aires) changed the organization's name to Union of American Republics. The name of its principal organ was changed from Commercial Bureau to Pan American Union.
1923	Fifth Conference (Santiago, Chile) changed the title to Union of Republics of the American Continent, with the Pan American Union as its permanent organ.
1928	Sixth Conference (Havana): the Governing Board and Pan American Union were prohibited from exercising political functions

1945	Inter-American Conference on Problems of War and Peace: Mexico City. The Act of Chapultepec established a system of Continental Security for the American States.
1947	The Inter-American Treaty of Reciprocal Assistance set up a joint security pact for the defence of the Western Hemisphere against attack from outside and for internal security.
1948	Ninth Conference (Bogotá). Member Governments signed the Charter of the Organization of American States.
1954	The OAS adopted the Declaration of Solidarity for the Preservation of the Political Integrity of the American States against the Intervention of International Communism.
1959	An Act was passed by 21 American States to establish the Inter-American Development Bank (q.v.).
1962	Cuba was suspended from the OAS, which supported the USA in its demand for the removal of missile bases in Cuba.
1964	The OAS mediated in dispute between USA and Panama, and voted for sanctions against Cuba by 15 votes to 4 (Bolivia, Chile, Mexico and Uruguay).
1965	An Inter-American Peace Force was created in reaction to events in the Dominican Republic.
1967	A treaty for the establishment of a Latin American nuclear-free zone was signed in Mexico City. In April a regional summit conference agreed to create a Latin American Common Market based on existing integration systems LAFTA and CACM.
1969	El Salvador and Honduras called on the OAS to investigate alleged violation of human rights of Salvadoreans in Honduras. A committee was sent to investigate after fighting broke out. Observers from OAS member nations supervised cease-fire and exchange of prisoners.
1970	Entry into force of the Protocol of Buenos Aires, establishing the General Assembly as the highest body of the OAS, replacing the Inter-American Conferences, and the three Councils as its main organs. The General Assembly held two special sessions to establish the new system and to discuss other current problems, in particular kidnapping and extortion.
1971	First regular session of the General Assembly of the OAS at San José, Costa Rica, in April.
1976	Sixth General Assembly; chief resolutions concerned human rights, the US Trade Act of 1974 and transnational enterprises. It also resolved to hold a Special Assembly to review matters concerning inter-American co-operation for development. The Assembly proclaimed a Decade of Women 1976–85: Equality, Development and Peace. Honduras and El Salvador signed the Act of Managua to end a series of border incidents between them.
1977	The Seventh General Assembly was held in Grenada, a new member state. The delegations adopted four resolutions on human rights and a resolution condemning terrorist activities. 1978 was declared Inter-American Rural Youth Year.
1978	The Eighth General Assembly was held in Washington, DC; resolutions included one calling for member states to co-operate with the Inter-American Commission on Human Rights in on-site inspections, and another recommending the establishment of an Inter-American Court of Human Rights in San José, Costa Rica. In view of the USA's announced intention to reduce its quota, the Permanent Council received a mandate to develop a new formula to finance the OAS programme budget. Funds were authorized for purchase of new OAS headquarters under construction in Washington, DC.
1979	The Inter-American Court of Human Rights was formally established in San José, Costa Rica, its members installed, and the statutes governing its operation were adopted.
1980	The Permanent Council met in July and passed a resolution condemning the military coup in Bolivia and deploring the interruption of the return to democracy there. In November the Tenth General Assembly named Argentina, Chile, El Salvador, Haiti, Paraguay and Uruguay as countries of special concern with regard to human rights violations (but avoided condemning them outright after Argentina threatened to withdraw from the organization if this was done).
1981	In February ministers of foreign affairs urged Ecuador and Peru to stop military operations in their border area: both countries agreed to a cease-fire monitored by a committee composed of representatives of Argentina, Brazil, Chile and the USA.
1982	In May ministers of foreign affairs urged Argentina and the United Kingdom to cease hostilities over the Falkland (Malvinas) Islands and to resume negotiations for a peaceful settlement of the conflict, taking into account Argentina's 'rights of sovereignty' and the interests of the islanders.
1984	In November the General Assembly discussed the political crisis in Central America and the increasing foreign debts incurred by Latin American countries; it agreed to attempt to 'revitalize' the OAS during the next year, so that the Organization could play a more effective part in solving regional problems.
1985	In December amendments to the OAS Charter were adopted by the General Assembly (subject to ratification by two-thirds of the member states, which was expected to take several years). The amendments increased the executive powers of the OAS Secretary-General, who would henceforth be allowed to take the initiative in bringing before the Permanent Council matters that 'might threaten the peace and security of the hemisphere or the development of the member states', something which previously only a member country had been permitted to do. The OAS also gained greater powers of mediation through an amendment allowing the Permanent Council to try to resolve a dispute between members, whether or not all the parties concerned had (as previously stipulated) agreed to take the matter before the OAS.
1986	In November the General Assembly passed a resolution expressing 'strong concern' over the United Kingdom's decision, in the previous month, to establish an exclusive 'conservation and management zone' extending for 150 nautical miles around the Falkland Islands. The Assembly also expressed its support for the negotiations conducted by the Contadora Group (q.v.) with the aim of bringing about peace in Central America.
1987	Following the signing in August of the 'Esquipulas II' agreement (in which the heads of government of Costa Rica, El Salvador, Guatemala, Honduras and Nicaragua agreed to implement a cease-fire between government forces and rebel groups, an amnesty for rebels, and democratic political processes) the Secretary-General of the OAS was invited to serve as a member of the international commission which was established to oversee compliance with the agreement.
1988	The OAS Secretary-General was invited to witness negotiations held in March between the Nicaraguan Government and rebel forces, and, following the signing of a cease-fire agreement with effect from 1 April, he continued to serve as a member of the verification commission established by the agreement. In November the Protocol of Cartagena, containing amendments to the OAS Charter, entered into force.
1989	In May ministers of foreign affairs met to consider the situation in Panama (where the Government had declared the recent elections invalid following an apparent victory by its opponents) and instructed a four-member group, comprising the OAS Secretary-General and three ministers, to attempt to bring about democratic reforms in Panama. The mission made five visits to Panama, but failed to bring about a transfer of power. The OAS Secretary-General was invited to observe the electoral process in Nicaragua (where elections were due to be held in February 1990), and in July 1989 he established a team of observers for this purpose. The OAS Secretary-General, together with the UN Secretary-General, was requested to verify the dismantling of the Nicaraguan resistance forces, as agreed upon by Central American heads of state in August. In December the OAS adopted a resolution deploring the USA's invasion of Panama two days previously, and urging that hostilities should cease immediately.
1990	Following the elections held in Nicaragua in February, OAS observers were invited to remain in the country during the transitional period leading to the inauguration of the new President in April. At the 20th General

Assembly, held in June, Latin American heads of state issued a declaration reaffirming their commitment to (among other things) protection of the environment, repudiation of terrorism, finding a solution to the regional drugs crisis, consolidation of democracy and respect for human rights.

FINANCE

The total funds managed by the OAS in 1989 amounted to US $90m. in quotas and contributions of the member states, together with counterpart contributions from them, and additional contributions from Permanent Observers and other organizations. Serious arrears in members' payments were reported in 1988, and a 'financial crisis' was reported at mid-1989, with a deficit of $30m. expected by the end of the year.

PUBLICATIONS
(in English and Spanish)

Catalog of Publications (annually).
Américas (6 a year).
Annual Report.
Ciencia Interamericana (quarterly).
La Educación (quarterly).
Statistical Bulletin (quarterly).
Numerous cultural, legal and scientific reports and studies.

SPECIALIZED ORGANIZATIONS OF THE OAS

Inter-American Children's Institute: Avda 8 de Octubre 2904, Montevideo, Uruguay; tel. (2) 47-2150; f. 1927 to achieve better health, education, social legislation, social services and statistics. Dir-Gen. EUGENIA M. ZAMORA (Costa Rica). Publ. *Boletín*.

Inter-American Commission of Women: General Secretariat of the OAS, 1889 F St, NW, Washington, DC 20006, USA; tel. (202) 458-6084; fax (202) 458-3967; f. 1928 for the extension of civil, political, economic, social and cultural rights for women. Pres. MILAGRO AZCÚNAGA DE MELÉNDEZ (El Salvador).

Inter-American Indian Institute: Avda Insurgentes Sur 1690, Col. Florida, México 01030, DF, Mexico; tel. (5) 6600007; fax (5) 5348090; f. 1940 to direct research for the better understanding of Indian groups and the solution of their educational, economic and social problems; provides technical assistance for programmes of Indian community development and trains personnel. Dir Dr JOSÉ MATOS MAR (Peru). Publs *América Indígena* (quarterly), *Anuario Indigenista*, *Indian News of the Americas*, *Noticias Indigenistas de América* (every 4 months).

Inter-American Institute for Co-operation on Agriculture: Apdo 55–2200 Coronado, San José, Costa Rica; tel. 290222; telex 21441; f. 1942 (as the Inter-American Institute of Agricultural Sciences: new name 1980); supports the efforts of member states to improve agricultural development and rural well-being; encourages co-operation between regional organizations, and provides a forum for the exchange of experience. Dir Dr MARTÍN E. PIÑEIRO (Argentina).

Pan American Health Organization: 525 23rd St, NW, Washington, DC 20037, USA; tel. (202) 861-3200; telex 248338; fax (202) 223-5971; f. 1902; co-ordinates regional efforts to improve health; maintains close relations with national health organizations and serves as the Regional Office for the Americas of the World Health Organization. Dir Dr CARLYLE GUERRA DE MACEDO (Brazil).

Pan-American Institute of Geography and History: Ex-Arzobispado 29, 11860 México, DF, Mexico; tel. (5) 2775888; fax (5) 2716172; f. 1928; co-ordinates and promotes the study of cartography, geophysics, geography, history, anthropology, archaeology, and other related scientific studies. Pres. CLARENCE W. MINKEL (USA); Sec.-Gen. CHESTER ZELAYA-GOODMAN (Costa Rica). Publs *Boletín Aéreo*, *Revista Cartográfica*, *Revista Geográfica*, *Revista de Historia de América*, *Revista de Arqueología Americana*, *Revista Geofísica*, *Folklore Americano*.

ASSOCIATED ORGANIZATIONS

Inter-American Defense Board: 2600 16th St, NW, Washington, DC 20441, USA; tel. (202) 939-6600; works in liaison with member governments to plan the common defence of the western hemisphere; operates the Inter-American Defense College. Chair. Maj.-Gen. BERNARD LOEFFKE (USA).

Inter-American Nuclear Energy Commission: General Secretariat of the OAS, 17th St and Constitution Ave, NW, Washington, DC 20006, USA; tel. (202) 458-3368; telex 64128; fax (202) 458-3167; f. 1959 to assist member countries in developing and co-ordinating nuclear energy research; organizes periodic conferences and gives fellowships and financial assistance to research institutions. Exec. Sec. MIGUEL LAUFER (Venezuela).

ORGANIZATION OF ARAB PETROLEUM EXPORTING COUNTRIES—OAPEC

Address: POB 20501, Safat, 13066 Kuwait.
Telephone: 2448200.
Telex: 22166.
Fax: 2426885.

OAPEC was established in 1968 to safeguard the interests of members and to determine ways and means for their co-operation in various forms of economic activity in the petroleum industry. In 1988 member states produced 22.4% of total world petroleum production.

MEMBERS*

Algeria	Kuwait	Syria
Bahrain	Libya	United Arab Emirates
Egypt	Qatar	
Iraq	Saudi Arabia	

* Egypt's membership was suspended in April 1979, and restored in May 1989. Tunisia ceased to be a member from 1 January 1987.

Organization
(October 1990)

MINISTERIAL COUNCIL

The Council consists normally of the ministers of petroleum of the member states, and forms the supreme authority of the Organization, responsible for drawing up its general policy, directing its activities and laying down its governing rules. It meets twice yearly as a minimum requirement and may hold extraordinary sessions. Chairmanship is on an annual rotation basis.

EXECUTIVE BUREAU

Assists the Council to direct the management of the Organization, approves staff regulations, reviews the budget, and refers it to the Council, considers matters relating to the Organization's agreements and activities and draws up the agenda for the Council. The Bureau comprises one senior official from each member state. Chairmanship is by rotation. The Bureau normally convenes twice a year before meetings of the Ministerial Council.

SECRETARIAT

Secretary-General: ABD AL-AZIZ AL-TURKI (Saudi Arabia).

Besides the Office of the Secretary-General, there are four departments: Finance and Administrative Affairs, Information and Library, Technical Affairs and Economics Departments. The last two form the Arab Centre for Energy Studies (which was established in 1983).

JUDICIAL TRIBUNAL

The Tribunal comprises nine judges from Arab countries. Its task is to settle differences in interpretation and application of the OAPEC Agreement, arising between members and also between OAPEC and its affiliates; disputes among member countries on oil activities falling within OAPEC's jurisdiction and not under the sovereignty of member countries; and disputes that the Ministerial Council decides to submit to the Tribunal.

President: FARIS ALWAGAYAN.

Activities

OAPEC co-ordinates different aspects of the Arab petroleum industry through the joint undertakings described below. It co-operates with the League of Arab States and other Arab organizations, and attempts to link petroleum research institutes in the Arab states. It organizes or participates in conferences and seminars, many of which are held in co-operation with non-Arab organizations; examples include the Fifth Arab Conference on Mineral Resources and the fourth Arab Energy Conference (1988), and seminars on the Arab refining industry in the 1990s, on the hydrocarbon-producing potential of deep geological formations in the Arab countries and techniques for exploring them, and on the utilization of natural gas in the Arab world (all in 1989). One of the principal features of OAPEC's 1987–91 programme of activities was the promotion of inter-Arab trade in petroleum products and petrochemicals.

OAPEC provides training in technical matters and in documentation and information. The General Secretariat also conducts technical and feasibility studies and carries out market reviews. It provides information through a library, data base and the publications listed below.

OAPEC's budget for 1989 was about US $4.2m., compared with $4.5m. for 1988.

The invasion of Kuwait by Iraq in August 1990, and the subsequent international embargo on petroleum exports from Iraq and Kuwait, severely disrupted OAPEC's activities.

JOINTLY SPONSORED UNDERTAKINGS

Arab Maritime Petroleum Transport Company—AMPTC: POB 22525, Safat, 13086 Kuwait; tel. 2411815; telex 23175; f. 1973 to undertake transport of crude oil, gas, refined products and petrochemicals, and thus to increase Arab participation in the tanker transport industry; capital (authorized and subscribed) $500m. Chair. RASHID AWEIDAH ATH-THANI; Man.-Dir SULEIMAN AL-BASSAM.

Arab Petroleum Investments Corporation—APICORP: POB 448, Dhahran Airport 31932, Saudi Arabia; tel. 864-74-00; telex 870068; fax 8945076; f. 1975 to finance investments in petroleum and petrochemicals projects and related industries in the Arab world and in developing countries, with priority being given to Arab joint ventures. Projects financed include gas liquefaction plants, petrochemicals, tankers, oil refineries, pipelines, exploration, detergents, fertilizers and process control instrumentation. Authorized capital: US $1,200m.; subscribed capital: $400m. Shareholders: Kuwait, Saudi Arabia and United Arab Emirates (17% each), Libya (15%), Iraq and Qatar (10% each), Algeria (5%), Bahrain, Egypt and Syria (3% each). Chair. JAMAL HASSAN JAWA; Gen.-Man. Dr NUREDDIN FARRAG.

Arab Petroleum Services Company—APSC: POB 12925, Tripoli, Libya; tel. 45861; telex 20405; f. 1977 to provide petroleum services through the establishment of companies specializing in various activities, and to train specialized personnel. Authorized capital: 100m. Libyan dinars; subscribed capital: 15m. Libyan dinars. Chair. AYYAD AD-DALY; Gen.-Man. ISMAIL AL-KORAITLI.

Arab Drilling and Workover Company: POB 680, Tripoli, Libya; f. 1980 as a subsidiary of APSC; subscribed capital: 12m. Libyan dinars; Gen. Man. MUHAMMAD AHMAD ATTIGA.

Arab Geophysical Exploration Services Company: POB 12925, Tripoli, Libya; tel. 38700; telex 20405; f. 1985.

Arab Well Logging Company: POB 6225, Baghdad, Iraq; tel. 5411125; telex 213688; f. 1983; provides well-logging services and data interpretation.

Arab Petroleum Training Institute: POB 6037, Al-Tajeyat, Baghdad, Iraq; f. 1979; tel. 5234100; telex 212728; Dir BARAK SAID YEHYA.

Arab Shipbuilding and Repair Yard Company—ASRY: POB 50110, Manama, Bahrain; tel. 671111; telex 8455; fax 670236; f. 1974 to undertake repairs and servicing of vessels; operates a dry dock in Bahrain. Capital (authorized and subscribed) $340m. Chair. Sheikh DAIJ BIN KHALIFA AL-KHALIFA; Gen. Man. ANTÓNIO MACHADO LOPES.

PUBLICATIONS

Secretary-General's Annual Report (Arabic and English editions).
Oil and Arab Cooperation (quarterly, Arabic).
OAPEC Monthly Bulletin (Arabic and English editions).
Energy Bibliography (annually, Arabic and English).
Energy Resources Monitor (quarterly, Arabic).
OAPEC Library Index of Periodical Articles (2 a year, Arabic and English).
Papers, studies, conference proceedings.

ORGANIZATION OF THE ISLAMIC CONFERENCE—OIC

Address: Kilo 6, Mecca Rd, POB 178, Jeddah, Saudi Arabia.
Telephone: 6873880.
Telex: 401366.

The Organization was established in May 1971, following a summit meeting of Muslim heads of state at Rabat, Morocco, in September 1969, and the Islamic Foreign Ministers' Conference in Jeddah in March 1970, and in Karachi, Pakistan, in December 1970.

MEMBERS

Afghanistan*	Libya
Algeria	Malaysia
Bahrain	Maldives
Bangladesh	Mali
Benin	Mauritania
Brunei	Morocco
Burkina Faso	Niger
Cameroon	Oman
Chad	Pakistan
The Comoros	Palestine Liberation Organization
Djibouti	
Egypt†	Qatar
Gabon	Saudi Arabia
The Gambia	Senegal
Guinea	Sierra Leone
Guinea-Bissau	Somalia
Indonesia	Sudan
Iran	Syria
Iraq	Tunisia
Jordan	Turkey
Kuwait	Uganda
Lebanon	United Arab Emirates
	Yemen

* Afghanistan's membership was suspended in January 1980, but in March 1989 delegates of the self-declared Mujaheddin Government of Afghanistan were admitted to membership.

† Egypt's membership was suspended in May 1979 and restored in March 1984.

Note: Observer status has been granted to the 'Turkish Federated State of Cyprus' (which declared independence as the 'Turkish Republic of Northern Cyprus' in November 1983). Mozambique and Nigeria also have observer status.

Organization
(October 1990)

SUMMIT CONFERENCES

The supreme body of the Organization is the Conference of Heads of State, which met in 1969 at Rabat, Morocco, in 1974 at Lahore, Pakistan, and in January 1981 at Mecca, Saudi Arabia, when it was decided that summit conferences would be held every three years in future. Fifth Conference: Kuwait, January 1987.

CONFERENCES OF MINISTERS OF FOREIGN AFFAIRS

Conferences take place annually, to consider the means for implementing the general policy of the Organization.

SECRETARIAT

The executive organ of the Organization, headed by a Secretary-General and four Assistant Secretaries-General.

Secretary-General: HAMID ALGABID (Niger).

SPECIALIZED COMMITTEES

Al-Quds Committee: f. 1975 to implement the resolutions of the Islamic Conference on the status of Jerusalem (Al-Quds); since 1979 it has met at the level of foreign ministers, under the chairmanship of King Hassan II of Morocco.

Islamic Commission for Economic, Cultural and Social Affairs: f. 1976.

Permanent Finance Committee.

Standing Committee for Scientific and Technical Co-operation: f. 1981.

Standing Committee for Economic and Trade Co-operation: f. 1981.

Standing Committee for Information and Cultural Affairs: f. 1981.

Activities

The Organization's aims, as set out in the Charter adopted in 1972 are:

(i) To promote Islamic solidarity among member states;

(ii) To consolidate co-operation among member states in the economic, social, cultural, scientific and other vital fields, and to arrange consultations among member states belonging to international organizations;

(iii) To endeavour to eliminate racial segregation and discrimination and to eradicate colonialism in all its forms;

(iv) To take necessary measures to support international peace and security founded on justice;

(v) To co-ordinate all efforts for the safeguard of the Holy Places and support of the struggle of the people of Palestine, and help them to regain their rights and liberate their land;

(vi) To strengthen the struggle of all Muslim people with a view to safeguarding their dignity, independence and national rights; and

(vii) To create a suitable atmosphere for the promotion of co-operation and understanding among member states and other countries.

The first summit conference of Islamic leaders (representing 24 states) took place in 1969 following the burning of the Al Aqsa Mosque in Jerusalem. At this conference it was decided that Islamic governments should 'consult together with a view to promoting close co-operation and mutual assistance in the economic, scientific, cultural and spiritual fields, inspired by the immortal teachings of Islam'. Thereafter the foreign ministers of the countries concerned met annually, and adopted the Charter of the Organization of the Islamic Conference in 1972.

At the second Islamic summit conference (Lahore, Pakistan, 1974), the Islamic Solidarity Fund was established, together with a committee of representatives which later evolved into the Islamic Commission for Economic, Social and Cultural Affairs. Subsequently, numerous other subsidiary bodies have been set up (see below).

ECONOMIC CO-OPERATION

A general agreement for economic, technical and commercial co-operation came into force in 1981, providing for the establishment of joint investment projects and trade co-ordination. This was followed by an agreement on promotion, protection and guarantee of investments among member states. A plan of action to strengthen economic co-operation was adopted at the third Islamic summit conference in 1981, aiming to promote collective self-reliance and the development of joint ventures in all sectors. In April 1983 the Islamic Reinsurance Corporation was launched by the OIC with authorized capital of US $200m.

A meeting of ministers of industry was held in February 1982, and agreed to promote industrial co-operation, including joint ventures in agricultural machinery, engineering and other basic industries.

In December 1988 it was announced that a committee of experts, established by the OIC, was to draw up a 10-year programme of assistance to developing countries (mainly in Africa) in science and technology.

CULTURAL CO-OPERATION

The Organization supports education in Muslim communities throughout the world, and, through the Islamic Solidarity Fund, has helped to establish Islamic universities in Niger, Uganda and Malaysia. It organizes seminars on various aspects of Islam, and encourages dialogue with the other monotheistic religions. Support is given to publications on Islam both in Muslim and Western countries.

In March 1989 the Conference of Ministers of Foreign Affairs denounced as an apostate the author of the controversial novel *The Satanic Verses* (Salman Rushdie), demanded the withdrawal of the book from circulation, and urged member states to boycott publishing houses which refused to comply.

HUMANITARIAN ASSISTANCE

Assistance is given to Muslim communities affected by wars and natural disasters, in co-operation with UN organizations, particularly UNHCR. The countries of the Sahel region (Burkina Faso, Capo Verde, Chad, The Gambia, Guinea, Guinea-Bissau, Mali, Mauritania, Niger and Senegal) receive particular attention as victims of drought.

POLITICAL CO-OPERATION

The Organization is also active at a political level. From the beginning it called for vacation of Arab territories by Israel, recognition of the rights of Palestinians and of the Palestine Liberation Organization as their sole legitimate representative, and the restoration of Jerusalem to Arab rule. The 1981 summit conference called for a *jihad* (holy war—though not necessarily in a military sense) 'for the liberation of Jerusalem and the occupied territories'; this was to include an Islamic economic boycott of Israel.

In January 1980 an extraordinary conference of ministers of foreign affairs demanded the immediate and unconditional withdrawal of Soviet troops from Afghanistan and suspended Afghanistan's membership of the organization. The conference also reaffirmed the importance of the Iranian Islamic Republic's sovereignty, territorial integrity and political independence, and adopted a resolution opposing any foreign pressures exerted on Islamic countries in general and Iran in particular. The conference further asked members not to participate in the 1980 Olympics unless the Soviet troops had withdrawn from Afghanistan; and adopted a resolution condemning armed aggression against Somalia and denouncing the presence of military forces of the USSR and some of its allies in the Horn of Africa.

In May 1980 a special committee was set up to conduct consultations on Afghanistan. Mediation in the Gulf war between Iran and Iraq was also attempted: an Islamic Peace Committee, headed by the Secretary-General of the Organization, was established in September 1980 and suggested a cease-fire supervised by an observer force of troops drawn from Islamic countries, but the terms were rejected by the protagonists.

The third Islamic summit conference (Mecca, Saudi Arabia, January 1981) repeated the demand for Soviet withdrawal from Afghanistan and affirmed Afghanistan's political independence. It also decided to continue attempts at mediation between Iran and Iraq.

In 1982 Islamic ministers of foreign affairs decided to set up Islamic offices for boycotting Israel and for military co-operation with the Palestine Liberation Organization. The OIC endorsed the peace plan proposed by the League of Arab States.

The 1984 summit conference agreed to reinstate Egypt as a member of the Organization, although the resolution was opposed by seven states.

The fourth summit conference, held in Kuwait in January 1987, again discussed the continuing Iran-Iraq war, and agreed that the Islamic Peace Committee should attempt to prevent the sale of military equipment to the parties in the conflict. The conference also discussed the conflicts in Chad and Lebanon, and requested the holding of a United Nations conference to define international terrorism, as opposed to legitimate fighting for freedom. The conference also approved proposals for joint development of modern technology, and for improving scientific and technical skills in the less-developed Islamic countries.

In March 1989 ministers of foreign affairs agreed to readmit Afghanistan, as represented by the 'interim government' formed by the Mujaheddin (rebels), following the withdrawal of Soviet troops from Afghanistan.

In August 1990 a majority of ministers of foreign affairs condemned Iraq's recent invasion of Kuwait, and demanded the withdrawal of Iraqi forces.

SUBSIDIARY ORGANS

Al-Quds Fund: f. 1976.

International Commission for the Islamic Heritage: f. 1980.

International Islamic Law Commission: f. 1982.

Islamic Centre for the Development of Trade: Complexe Commerciale des Habous, ave des FAR, BP 13545, Casablanca, Morocco; tel. 31 49 74; telex 22026; opened 1983 to encourage regular commercial contacts, harmonize policies and promote investments among OIC members.

Islamic Centre for Technical and Vocational Training and Research: KB Bazar, Joydebpur, Gazipur Dist., Dhaka, Bangladesh; tel. 390154; telex 642739; f. 1979 to provide skilled technicians and instructors in mechanical, electrical, electronic and chemical technology, and to conduct research; expected to begin operations in 1986, with 650 students, later to increase to 1,150. Dir Dr RAFIQ ED-DIN AHMAD.

Islamic Commission for the International Crescent: f. 1980.

Islamic Foundation for Science, Technology and Development—IFSTAD: POB 9833, Jeddah 21423, Saudi Arabia; tel. 6322273; telex 604081; f. 1981 to promote co-operation in science and technology within the Islamic world. Dir-Gen. (vacant).

Islamic Jurisprudence Academy: f. 1982.

Islamic Solidarity Fund: c/o OIC Secretariat, POB 178, Jeddah, Saudi Arabia; f. 1974 to meet the needs of Islamic communities by providing emergency aid and the wherewithal to build mosques, Islamic centres, hospitals, schools and universities. Exec. Dir HASSAN M. DAOUD.

Research Centre for Islamic History, Art and Culture: POB 24, Beşiktaş 80692, Istanbul, Turkey; tel. 1605988; telex 26484; fax 1584385; f. 1979; library of 25,000 vols; Dir-Gen. E. IHSANOĞLU. Publ. *Newsletter* (3 a year).

Statistical, Economic and Social Research and Training Centre for the Islamic Countries: Attar Sok. 4, GOP, Ankara, Turkey; tel. 1286105; telex 43163; f. 1978; Dir Dr ŞADI CINDORUK.

OTHER INSTITUTIONS WITHIN THE OIC SYSTEM

International Islamic News Agency: Prince Fahd St, POB 5054, Jeddah, Saudi Arabia; f. 1972. Dir-Gen. AHMAD FARRAG.

Islamic Capitals Organization: c/o Mayor of Mecca, Mecca, Saudi Arabia; f. 1978.

Islamic Chamber of Commerce, Industry and Commodity Exchange: Clifton Road, POB 3831, Karachi, Pakistan; tel. 530535; telex 25533; f. 1979. Pres. Sheikh ISMAIL ABU DAWOOD; Sec.-Gen. ALIOUNE DAT. Publ. *Quarterly Information Bulletin*.

Islamic Development Bank (q.v.).

Islamic Educational, Scientific and Cultural Organization: BP 755, Agdal, Rabat, Morocco; tel. 724-33; telex 326-45; fax 774-59; f. 1982. Dir-Gen. ABD AL-HADI BOUTALEB. Publs *ISESCO Bulletin* (quarterly), *Islam Today* (annually), *ISESCO Triennial*.

Islamic States Broadcasting Organization: c/o Pakistan Broadcasting Corpn, Broadcasting House, Constitution Ave, Islamabad, Pakistan; tel. 820114; telex 5816; f. 1975. Dir-Gen. AGHA NASIR.

At the summit conference in January 1981 it was decided that an Islamic Court of Justice should be established to adjudicate in disputes between Muslim countries. Experts met in January 1983 to draw up a constitution for the court. In 1987 it was decided that an Islamic Institute of Agriculture was to be established in Dakar, Senegal, by 1990.

ORGANIZATION OF THE PETROLEUM EXPORTING COUNTRIES—OPEC

Address: Obere Donaustrasse 93, 1020 Vienna, Austria.

Telephone: (01) 21-11-20.

Telex: 134474.

Fax: (01) 26-43-20.

OPEC was established in 1960 to link countries whose main source of export earnings is petroleum; it aims to unify and co-ordinate members' petroleum policies and to safeguard their interests generally. The OPEC Fund for International Development is described on p. 203.

OPEC's share of world petroleum production was 33.8% in 1988 (compared with 45% in 1980 and a peak of 55.5% in 1973). At the end of 1988 OPEC members were estimated to possess 77% of the world's known reserves of crude petroleum, and 11.6% of world refining capacity. In 1986 OPEC members possessed about 33% of known reserves of natural gas.

MEMBERS

Algeria
Ecuador
Gabon
Indonesia
Iran
Iraq
Kuwait
Libya
Nigeria
Qatar
Saudi Arabia
United Arab Emirates
Venezuela

Organization

(October 1990)

CONFERENCE

The Conference is the supreme authority of the Organization, responsible for the formulation of its general policy. It consists of representatives of member countries, who examine reports and recommendations submitted by the Board of Governors. It approves the appointment of Governors from each country and elects the Chairman of the Board of Governors. It works on the unanimity principle, and meets at least twice a year.

BOARD OF GOVERNORS

The Board directs the management of the Organization; it implements resolutions of the Conference and draws up an annual budget. It consists of one governor for each member country, and meets at least twice a year.

ECONOMIC COMMISSION

A specialized body operating within the framework of the Secretariat, with a view to assisting the Organization in promoting stability in international oil prices at equitable levels; consists of a board, national representatives and a commission staff; meets at least twice a year.

SECRETARIAT

Office of the Secretary-General: Provides the Secretary-General with executive assistance in carrying out contacts with governments, organizations and delegations, in matters of protocol and in the preparation for and co-ordination of meetings.

Secretary-General: Dr SUBROTO (Indonesia).

Deputy Secretary-General: (vacant).

Energy Studies Department: Conducts a continuous programme for research in energy and related matters; monitors, forecasts and analyses developments in the energy and petrochemical industries; and evaluates hydrocarbons and products and their non-energy uses.

Economics and Finance Department: Analyses economic and financial issues of significant interest; in particular those related to international financial and monetary matters, and to the international petroleum industry.

Data Services Department: Computer Section maintains and expands information services to support the research activities of the Secretariat and those of member countries. Statistics Section collects, collates and analyses statistical information from both primary and secondary sources.

Personnel and Administration Department: Responsible for all organization methods, provision of administrative services for all meetings, personnel matters, budgets accounting and internal control.

Public Information Department: Responsible for a central public relations programme; production and distribution of publications, films, slides and tapes; and communication of OPEC objectives and decisions to the world at large.

Legal Office: Undertakes special and other in-house legal studies and reports to ascertain where the best interests of the Organization and member countries lie.

OPEC NEWS AGENCY

Founded 1980 to provide information on OPEC to about 80 countries and counteract inaccurate reporting by some other sources: covers member countries' petroleum and energy issues; activities of the OPEC Secretariat; co-operation with other developing countries; news on oil companies; technical and policy information on the upstream and downstream sectors of the industry; energy supply and demand; and economic and social development in member countries.

Record of Events

1960 The first OPEC Conference was held in Baghdad in September, attended by representatives from Iran, Iraq, Kuwait, Saudi Arabia and Venezuela.

1961 Second Conference, Caracas, January. Qatar was admitted to membership; a Board of Governors was formed and statutes agreed.

1962 Fourth Conference, Geneva, April and June. Protests were addressed to oil companies against price cuts introduced in August 1960. Indonesia and Libya were admitted to membership.

1965 In July the Conference reached agreement on a two-year joint production programme, implemented from 1965 to 1967, to limit annual growth in output to secure adequate prices.

1967 Abu Dhabi was admitted to membership.

1968 Fifteenth Conference (extraordinary), Beirut, January. OPEC accepted an offer of elimination of discounts submitted by oil companies following negotiations in November 1967.

1969 Algeria was admitted to membership.

1970 Twenty-first Conference, Caracas, December. Tax on income of oil companies was raised to 55%.

1971 A five-year agreement was concluded in February between the six producing countries in the Gulf and 23 international oil companies (Teheran Agreement).
Twenty-fourth Conference, Vienna, July. Nigeria was admitted to membership.

1972 In January oil companies agreed to adjust oil revenues of the largest producers after changes in currency exchange rates (Geneva Agreement).

1973 Agreement with companies was reached under which posted prices of crude oil were raised by 11.9% and a mechanism was installed to make monthly adjustments to prices in future (Second Geneva Agreement).
Negotiations with oil companies on revision of the Teheran Agreement broke down in October and the Gulf states unilaterally declared 70% increases in posted prices, from $3.01 to $5.11 per barrel.
Thirty-sixth Conference, Teheran, December. The posted price was to increase by nearly 130%, from $5.11 to $11.65 per barrel, from 1 January 1974. Ecuador was admitted to full membership and Gabon became an associate member.

1974 As a result of Saudi opposition to the December price increase, prices were held at current level for first quarter (and subsequently for the remainder of 1974). Abu Dhabi's membership was transferred to the United Arab Emirates.

A meeting in June increased royalties charged to oil companies from 12.5% to 14.5% in all member states except Saudi Arabia.

A meeting in September increased governmental take by about 3.5% through further increases in royalties on equity crude to 16.67% and in taxes to 65.65%, except in Saudi Arabia.

1975 OPEC's first summit conference was held in Algiers in March. Gabon was admitted to full membership.

A ministerial meeting in September agreed to raise prices by 10% for the period until June 1976.

1976 The OPEC Special Fund for International Development was created in May.

In December, a general 15% rise in basic prices was proposed and supported by 11 member states. This was to take place in two stages: a 10% rise as of 1 January 1977, and a further 5% rise as of 1 July 1977. However, Saudi Arabia and the United Arab Emirates decided to raise their prices by 5% only.

1977 Following an earlier waiver by nine members of the 5% second stage of the price rise agreed at Doha, Saudi Arabia and the United Arab Emirates announced in July that they would both raise their prices by 5%. As a result, a single level of prices throughout the organization was restored.

Because of continued disagreements between the 'moderates', led by Saudi Arabia and Iran, and the 'radicals', led by Algeria, Libya and Iraq, the year's second Conference at Caracas, December, was unable to settle on an increase in prices.

1978 In May a ministerial committee from six member states was established to draw up long-term pricing and production strategy. Production ceilings of members were lowered.

Fifty-first Conference, Geneva, June. Price levels were to remain stable until the end of 1978. A committee of experts, chaired by Kuwait, met in July to consider ways of compensating for the effects of the depreciation of the US dollar.

In December 1978 it was decided to raise prices by instalments of 5%, 3.8%, 2.3% and 2.7%. These would bring a rise of 14.5% over nine months, but an average increase of 10% for 1979.

1979 At an extraordinary meeting in Geneva at the end of March it was decided to raise prices by 9%. Many members maintained surcharges they had imposed in February after Iranian exports were halted.

In June the Conference agreed minimum and maximum prices which seemed likely to add between 15% and 20% to import bills of consumer countries.

The December Conference recommended replenishment of the OPEC Fund and agreed in principle to convert the Fund into a development agency with its own legal personality. An OPEC News Agency was to be set up, based at the Secretariat.

1980 In June the Conference decided to set the price for a marker crude at US $32.00 per barrel, and that the value differentials which could be added above this ceiling (on account of quality and geographical location) should not exceed $5.00 per barrel.

It was decided to begin studies on the feasibility of an OPEC Institute of Higher Education, for technological research and training.

The planned OPEC summit meeting in Baghdad in November was postponed indefinitely because of the Iran–Iraq war, but the scheduled price-fixing meeting of petroleum ministers went ahead in Bali in December, with both Iranians and Iraqis present. A ceiling price of US $41.00 per barrel was fixed for premium crudes.

1981 In May attempts to achieve price reunification were made, but Saudi Arabia refused to increase its $32.00 per barrel price unless the higher prices charged by other countries were lowered. Most of the other OPEC countries agreed to cut production by 10% so as to reduce the surplus. An emergency meeting in Geneva in August again failed to unify prices, although Saudi Arabia agreed to reduce production by 1m. barrels per day, with the level of output to be reviewed monthly.

In October OPEC countries agreed to increase the Saudi marker price by 6% to $34 per barrel, with a ceiling price of $38 per barrel. This price structure was intended to remain in force until the end of 1982. Saudi Arabia also announced that it would keep its production below 8.5m.b/d.

1982 The continuing world oil glut (resulting from a fall in demand to a predicted 46m. b/d in 1982, compared with 52m. in 1979) forced prices below the official mark of $34 per barrel in some producer countries. In March an emergency meeting of petroleum ministers was held in Vienna and agreed (for the first time in OPEC's history) to defend the Organization's price structure by imposing an overall production ceiling of 18m. b/d, effectively 17.5m. b/d with Saudi Arabia's separate announcement of a cut to 7m. b/d in its own production. Measures were taken to support Nigerian prices following a slump in production.

In December the Conference agreed to limit OPEC production to 18.5m. b/d in 1983 (representing about one-third of total world production) but postponed the allocation of national quotas pending consultations among the respective governments.

1983 In January an emergency meeting of petroleum ministers, fearing a collapse in world oil prices, decided to reduce the production ceiling to 17.5m. b/d (itself several million b/d above actual current output) but failed to agree on individual production quotas or on adjustments to the differentials in prices charged for the high-quality crude petroleum produced by Algeria, Libya and Nigeria compared with that produced by the Gulf States.

In February Nigeria cut its prices to $30 per barrel, following a collapse in its production. To avoid a 'price war' OPEC set the official price of marker crude at $29 per barrel, and agreed to maintain existing differentials among the various OPEC crudes at the level agreed on in March 1982, with the temporary exception that the differentials for Nigerian crudes should be $1 more than the price of the marker crude. It also agreed to maintain the production ceiling of 17.5m. b/d and allocated quotas for each member country except Saudi Arabia, which was to act as a 'swing producer' to supply the balancing quantities to meet market requirements. It called on member countries to avoid giving discounts in any form, and to refrain from 'dumping' petroleum products into the world oil market at prices which would endanger the crude oil pricing structure. The official marker price and production ceiling were maintained throughout the year, although actual production by members was believed to be in excess of 18m. b/d at the end of the year. Despite demands for revised quotas by some countries, and Iran's attempt to restore the marker price to $34 per barrel, the meeting agreed to maintain the existing production and pricing agreement as the policy most likely to restore stability to the world petroleum market.

1984 The production ceiling of 17.5m. b/d and the official price of $29 per barrel were maintained until October, when the production ceiling was lowered to 16m. b/d. In December price differentials for light (more expensive) and heavy (cheaper) crudes were slightly altered in an attempt to counteract price-cutting by non-OPEC producers, particularly Norway and the United Kingdom. An auditing commission was set up to monitor members' adherence to production limits.

1985 In January members (except Algeria, Iran and Libya) effectively abandoned the marker price system: the price of Arabian light crude (the former marker price) was lowered to $28 per barrel, and price differentials between the cheapest and most expensive grades were cut from $4 to $2.40; this system was also adopted by Iran in February.

During the year production in excess of quotas by OPEC members, unofficial discounts and barter deals by members, and price cuts by non-members (such as Mexico, which had hitherto kept its prices in line with those of OPEC) contributed to a weakening of the market. Saudi Arabia indicated that it was not prepared to continue cutting its own output, to make up for others' increases, in an attempt to support world prices. In July, 10 members agreed to small price cuts of $0.50 and $0.20 per barrel respectively for heavy and medium crudes. Ecuador, Gabon and Iraq demanded larger production quotas, and when, in October, discussion of the redistribution of quotas was postponed, Ecuador announced that it was 'temporarily' leaving OPEC, the first member country to do so. In December ministers of petroleum of OPEC member states resolved to 'secure and defend for OPEC a fair share in the world market consistent with the income necessary for member countries' development'. A special committee was established to determine what OPEC's share of the world market should be, and how it should be defended in the face of falling prices and the steady production levels maintained by some non-members.

1986 During the first half of the year prices dropped to below $10 per barrel. In April ministers from 10 member states agreed to set OPEC production at 16.7m. b/d for the third quarter of 1986 and at 17.3m. b/d for the fourth quarter. Algeria, Iran and Libya dissented, arguing that production should be reduced to 14.5m. b/d and 16.8m. b/d respectively for those periods, in order to restore prices. Discussions were also held with non-member countries (Angola, Egypt, Malaysia, Mexico and Oman), which agreed to co-operate in limiting production. However, requests by OPEC that the United Kingdom should reduce its petroleum production levels continued to be rejected by the British Government. In August all members, with the exception of Iraq (which demanded to be allowed the same quota as Iran and, when this was denied it, refused to be a party to the agreement), agreed upon a return to production quotas, with the aim of cutting production to 14.8m. b/d (about 16.8m. b/d including Iraq's production) for the ensuing two months. This measure resulted in an increase in prices to about $15 per barrel, and in October the agreement was extended until the end of the year, with a slight increase in collective output to 15m. b/d (excluding Iraq's production). In December members (with the exception of Iraq) agreed to return to a fixed pricing system at a level of $18 per barrel as the OPEC reference price, with effect from 1 February 1987 (following a one-month phase-out period on existing contracts). It was also agreed that, in order to support the reference price, cuts in production should be made: OPEC's total production for the first and second quarters of 1987 was not to exceed 15.8m. b/d.

1987 At their meeting in June ministers noted that the agreement reached in the previous December had succeeded in stabilizing prices, despite the fact that production was believed to have exceeded the agreed limit during the first half of the year. The Conference decided that production during the third and fourth quarters of the year should be limited to 16.6m. b/d (including Iraq's production). It established a committee of three heads of delegations to visit member countries, to motivate them to comply with the agreement, while another group of five heads of delegations undertook to seek the co-operation of non-member producers. During the third and fourth quarters, however, total production was reported to be at least 1m. b/d above the agreed level. In December ministers decided to extend the existing agreement for the first half of 1988, although Iraq, once more, refused to participate.

1988 By March petroleum prices had fallen below $15 per barrel. In April non-OPEC producers offered to reduce the volume of their petroleum exports by 5% if OPEC members would do the same. Saudi Arabia, however, refused to accept further reductions in production, saying that existing quotas should first be more strictly enforced. In June the previous production limit (15.06m. b/d, excluding Iraq's production) was again renewed for six months, in the hope that increasing demand would be sufficient to raise prices. By October, however, petroleum prices were below $12 per barrel. OPEC members (excluding Iraq) were estimated to be producing about 21m. b/d. In November a new agreement was reached, limiting total production (including that of Iraq) to 18.5m. b/d, with effect from 1 January 1989. Iran and Iraq finally agreed to accept identical quotas. It was hoped that the agreement would raise prices to $18 per barrel.

1989 In June (when prices had returned to about $18 per barrel) ministers agreed to increase the production limit to 19.5m. b/d for the second half of 1989. However, Kuwait and the United Arab Emirates indicated that they would not feel bound to observe this limit. In September the production limit was again increased, to 20.5m. b/d, and in November the limit for the first half of 1990 was increased to 22m. b/d.

1990 Actual output of petroleum by OPEC members was estimated in March at about 24m. b/d, with Kuwait, Saudi Arabia and the United Arab Emirates, in particular, exceeding their quotas. A decline in prices of some 25% between January and May resulted in a declaration by over-producing members in May that they would reduce their production to the agreed limit. By late June, however, it was reported that total production had decreased by only 400,000 b/d, and prices remained at about $14 per barrel. In July Iraq threatened to take military action against Kuwait unless it reduced its petroleum production. In the same month OPEC members agreed to raise prices to $21 per barrel, and to limit output to 22.5m. b/d. In August, however, Iraq invaded Kuwait, and petroleum exports by the two countries (estimated to have a combined production capacity of 5m. b/d) were halted by an international embargo. Petroleum prices immediately increased to exceed $25 per barrel. Later in the month an informal consultative meeting of OPEC ministers placed the July agreement in abeyance, and permitted a temporary increase in production of petroleum, of between 3m. and 3.5m. b/d (mostly by Saudi Arabia, the United Arab Emirates and Venezuela). In September and October prices fluctuated in response to political developments in the Gulf region, reaching a point in excess of $40 per barrel in early October, but falling to about $25 per barrel by the end of the month. In October OPEC officials urged the industrialized countries to release their stocks of petroleum, in order to prevent further price increases.

FINANCE

The budget for 1989 amounted to 235.3m. Austrian schillings, and that for 1990 was 235.6m. schillings.

PUBLICATIONS

OPEC Bulletin (10 a year).
OPEC Review (quarterly).
Annual Report.
Annual Statistical Bulletin.
Facts and Figures.
OPEC Information.
OPEC at a Glance.
OPEC Official Resolutions and Press Releases.

OPEC FUND FOR INTERNATIONAL DEVELOPMENT

Address: POB 995, 1011 Vienna, Austria.
Telephone: (01) 51-56-40.
Telex: 131734.
Fax: (01) 513-92-38.
The Fund was established by OPEC member countries in 1976.

MEMBERS
Member countries of OPEC (q.v.).

Organization
(October 1990)

ADMINISTRATION
The Fund is administered by a Ministerial Council and a Governing Board. Each member country is represented on the Council by its minister of finance. The Board consists of one representative and one alternate for each member country.
Chairman, Ministerial Council: JASIM MUHAMMAD AL-KHARAFI (Kuwait).
Chairman, Governing Board: OSAMAH FAQUIH (Saudi Arabia).
Director-General of the Fund: YESUFU SEYYID ABDULAI (Nigeria).

FINANCIAL STRUCTURE
The resources of the Fund, whose unit of account is the US dollar, consist of contributions by OPEC member countries, and income received from operations or otherwise accruing to the Fund.

The initial endowment of the Fund amounted to US $800m. Its resources have been replenished three times, and have been further increased by the profits accruing to seven OPEC member countries through the sales of gold held by the International Monetary Fund. The pledged contributions to the OPEC Fund amounted to US $3,435m. at the end of 1989, and paid-in contributions totalled $2,701m.

Activities

The OPEC Fund for International Development is a multilateral agency for financial co-operation and assistance. Its objective is to reinforce financial co-operation between OPEC member countries and other developing countries through the provision of financial support to the latter on appropriate terms, to assist them in their economic and social development. The Fund was conceived as a collective financial facility which would consolidate the assistance extended by its member countries; its resources are additional to those already made available through other bilateral and multilateral aid agencies of OPEC members. It is empowered to:

(a) Provide concessional loans for balance-of-payments support;

(b) Provide concessional loans for the implementation of development projects and programmes;

(c) Make contributions and/or provide loans to eligible international agencies; and

(d) Finance technical assistance and research through grants.

The eligible beneficiaries of the Fund's assistance are the governments of developing countries other than OPEC member countries, and international development agencies whose beneficiaries are developing countries. The Fund gives priority to the countries with the lowest income.

The Fund may undertake technical, economic and financial appraisal of a project submitted to it, or entrust such an appraisal to an appropriate international development agency, the executing national agency of a member country, or any other qualified agency. Most projects financed by the Fund have been co-financed by other development finance agencies. In each such case, one of the co-financing agencies may be appointed to administer the Fund's loan in association with its own. This practice has enabled the Fund to extend its lending activities to 90 countries over a short period of time and in a simple way, with the aim of avoiding duplication and complications. As its experience grew, the Fund increasingly resorted to parallel, rather than joint financing, taking up separate project components to be financed according to its rules and policies. In addition, it started to finance some projects completely on its own. These trends necessitated the issuance in 1982 of guidelines for the procurement of goods and services under the Fund's loans, allowing for a margin of preference for goods and services of local origin or originating in other developing countries: the general principle of competitive bidding is, however, followed by the Fund. The loans are not tied to procurement from Fund member countries or from any other countries. The margin of preference for goods and services obtainable in developing countries is allowed on the request of the borrower and within defined limits.

The Fund's ninth lending programme, covering the period 1990–91, was approved in 1989. Besides extending loans for project and programme financing and balance of payments support, the Fund also undertakes other operations, including grants in support of technical assistance and other activities (mainly research), and financial contributions to other international institutions.

By the end of December 1989 the number of loans extended by the Fund was 500, totalling US $2,407.4m., of which 66% was for project financing, 30% was for balance-of-payments support and 4% was for programme financing. About 73% of the amount committed had been disbursed.

Direct loans are supplemented by grants to support technical assistance, food aid and research. By the end of December 1989, 267 grants, amounting to $214m., had been extended, including $83.6m. to the Common Fund for Commodities, and a special contribution of $20m. to the International Fund for Agricultural Development (IFAD). In addition, the Fund had contributed $971.9m. to other international institutions by the end of 1989, comprising OPEC members' contributions to the resources of IFAD, and irrevocable transfers in the name of its members to the IMF Trust Fund.

During the year ending 31 December 1989, the Fund's total commitments amounted to $121.5m. (compared with $93.3m. in 1988 and $140.7m. in 1987). Of the 1989 total, 71% was for project financing. The largest proportion of project loans (21%) was for the transport sector, financing road improvements in Chad, The Gambia, Mozambique, Rwanda and the Yemen Arab Republic. Energy projects (in Jordan, Mauritania and the People's Democratic Republic of Yemen) received 20% of loans; health projects (in Bangladesh and India) 19%; water supply and sewerage (in Benin, Burkina Faso, Haiti, Mali, Mauritania, Niger, Saint Lucia and Senegal) 16%; and education (in Madagascar and Myanmar) 14%. Programme loans totalling $32.8m. were made to Cape Verde, Guinea-Bissau, Mali, Nepal, Sudan and Tanzania to finance imports of essential goods. Grants made for technical assistance and research amounted to $2.2m.

During the first eight months of 1990 agreements on 20 loans, amounting to $79.7m., were signed with 20 developing countries, and grants amounting to $920,500 were allocated.

OPEC FUND COMMITMENTS AND DISBURSEMENTS
(1989, US $ million).

	Commitments	Disbursements
Lending operations:	119.345	65.725
Project financing	86.525	61.617
Balance of payments support	—	3.883
Programme financing	32.820	0.225
Grant Programme	2.158	8.510
Technical assistance	1.875	2.534
Research and other intellectual activities	0.283	0.323
Total	121.503	74.235

INTERNATIONAL ORGANIZATIONS

Project loans approved in 1989 (US $ '000)

Region and country	Loans approved
Africa	31,500
Benin	1,300
Burkina Faso	2,200
Chad	4,500
The Gambia	2,000
Madagascar	5,000
Mali	2,500
Mauritania	3,500
Mozambique	3,500
Niger	1,500
Rwanda	4,000
Senegal	1,500
Asia and the Middle East	47,800
Bangladesh	10,000
India	6,500
Jordan	10,000
Myanmar	7,300
Yemen Arab Republic	9,000
People's Democratic Republic of Yemen	5,000
Caribbean	7,225
Haiti	5,325
Saint Lucia	1,900
Total	86,525

OPEC Fund for International Development

PUBLICATIONS

Annual Report (in Arabic, English, French and Spanish).

OPEC Fund Newsletter (3 a year).

OPEC Aid and OPEC Aid Institutions—A Profile (annually).

Occasional books and papers.

SOUTH PACIFIC COMMISSION—SPC

Address: BP D5, Nouméa Cedex, New Caledonia.
Telephone: 26-20-00.
Telex: 3139.
Fax: 26-38-18.

The Commission was established by an agreement signed in Canberra, Australia, by the governments of Australia, France, the Netherlands, New Zealand, the United Kingdom and the USA, in February 1947, effective from July 1948. (The Netherlands withdrew from the Commission in 1962, when it ceased to administer the former colony of Dutch New Guinea, now Irian Jaya, part of Indonesia.) The Commission provides technical advice, training and assistance in economic, social and cultural development to the countries of the region. It serves a population of about 5m. people, scattered over some 30m. sq km., over 98% of which is sea.

MEMBERS

American Samoa	Northern Mariana Islands
Australia	Palau
Cook Islands	Papua New Guinea
Federated States of Micronesia	Pitcairn Islands
Fiji	Solomon Islands
France	Tokelau
French Polynesia	Tonga
Guam	Tuvalu
Kiribati	United Kingdom
Marshall Islands	USA
Nauru	Vanuatu
New Caledonia	Wallis and Futuna Islands
New Zealand	Western Samoa
Niue	

Organization
(October 1990)

SOUTH PACIFIC CONFERENCE

The Conference is held annually and since 1974 has combined the former South Pacific Conference, attended by delegates from the countries and territories within the Commission's area of action, and the former Commission Session, attended by representatives of the participating governments. Each government and territorial administration has the right to send a representative and alternates to the Conference and each representative (or alternate) has the right to cast one vote on behalf of the government or territorial administration which he or she represents.

The Conference is the supreme decision-making body of the Commission; it examines and adopts the Commission's work programme and budget for the coming year, and discusses any other matters within the competence of the Commission.

COMMITTEE OF REPRESENTATIVES OF GOVERNMENTS AND ADMINISTRATIONS

This Committee comprises representatives of all 27 member states and territories, having equal voting rights. It meets twice a year: it recommends the administrative budget, evaluates the effectiveness of the past year's work programme, examines the draft budget and work programme presented by the Secretary-General, and nominates the principal officers of the Commission.

SECRETARIAT

The Secretariat has a Management Committee which has a supervisory and advisory role over all Commission activities. Committee members are the Principal Officers of the Commission. The Secretary-General is the chief executive officer of the Commission. The Commission has about 170 staff members

Secretary-General: ATANRAOI BAITEKE (Kiribati).
Director of Programmes: JON JONASSEN (Cook Islands).
Deputy Director of Programmes: HÉLÈNE COURTE (New Caledonia).

Activities

The Commission provides, on request of its member countries, technical assistance, advisory services, information and clearing-house services. The organization also conducts regional conferences and technical meetings, as well as training courses, workshops and seminars at the regional or country level. Although not a funding organization, SPC provides small grants-in-aid and awards to meet specific requests and needs of members. Its activities are closely co-ordinated with those of the Pacific countries, and its annual work programme is approved each year by the South Pacific Conference, a process which is intended to ensure that the Commission remains responsive to the expressed needs of the island countries.

FOOD AND MATERIALS

The Commission's tropical agriculture programme aims to develop and diversify subsistence and commercial agriculture, in order to reduce dependence on imports, increase exports and improve nutrition. The programme provides appropriate support to local agricultural programmes, particularly in the promotion of food production and nutrition, food crop diversification, livestock development, coconut development and training. These activities take the form of technical and financial assistance, training and consultancies. The Plant Protection Service provides assistance to member governments in the development of national plant protection services. Advice, information and direct assistance are provided by the four specialist programme officers of the Service, based in Suva. Areas of expertise include: plant quarantine, safe transfer of plant germplasm, biological control, information, pest and disease control, pesticides, and legislation.

MARINE RESOURCES

Assistance to member countries in fisheries development is the Commission's largest single activity. The Fisheries programme is comprised of seven principal projects, covering coastal and oceanic fisheries. The Deep Sea Fisheries Development Project is a village-level, rural development project, with several roving master fishermen. It promotes the development and expansion of artisanal fisheries that are at present under-utilized, in order to generate income-earning opportunities. The project develops and evaluates new and simple fishing technology, gear and techniques, and provides practical training to local fishermen and government fisheries extension officers. The Gear Development Sub-Project was established to adapt new or unfamiliar fishing gears and methods to Pacific island countries, in order to improve productivity in established fisheries and to promote the capture of locally under-exploited species in a manner appropriate to local conditions. The Regional Fisheries Training Project co-ordinates all ongoing SPC fisheries training activities. Training courses are held in specialized areas such as fisheries refrigeration, fish-handling and processing, fish catching methods, extension and communication skills, echo sounding, micro-computer training and fisheries systems. The Pacific Island Fisheries Officers Training Course is held annually in New Zealand. The Fish Handling and Processing Project provides expert advice to help countries utilize the catch to its maximum potential by upgrading fish-handling practices at all levels in national fishing industries. It develops and promotes the use of simple processing techniques, and assists with identification and development of marketing opportunities. The Fisheries Information Project collects and disseminates fisheries information and supports special interest groups which serve as information and communication networks for fisheries researchers with common interests. The Inshore Fisheries Research Project assists in the management of national inshore and coastal fishery resources, in the face of increasing levels of inshore exploitation in many Pacific island fisheries. The project's activities include enhancing the national capabilities of Pacific island countries to carry out resource surveys and assessments and supporting the establishment and maintenance of national small-scale fishery statistics collection and analysis programmes, by providing advice, technical assistance and training. The Tuna and Billfish Assessment Programme provides statistical services to national fisheries departments and SPC programmes, and conducts scientific research on stocks of tunas and billfish in the SPC region and on the environmental factors which affect them, in order to help countries develop, manage and rationally exploit the renewable oceanic resources of the region.

ENVIRONMENT MANAGEMENT

The South Pacific Regional Environment Programme (SPREP) was initiated as a joint programme of SPC, the South Pacific Forum Secretariat, the United Nations Environment Programme (UNEP), and the Economic and Social Commission for Asia and the Pacific (ESCAP); it aims to ensure that resource development is in harmony with the unique environmental quality of the region and with sound principles of sustained resource management. SPC was the implementing agency for SPREP until 1990, when it was decided that SPREP should become an independent organization, with financial autonomy, retaining associate status with SPC. Activities currently focus on the following areas: natural resource management; protected area management and species conservation; coastal and marine activities; monitoring, research and control of pollution in coastal and open waters; land-based and water pollution prevention; environmental education and training; environmental information; environmental planning and administration; climatic change and sea level rise.

RURAL DEVELOPMENT AND TECHNOLOGY

The overall objective of the Rural Development Programme is to assist in improving the quality of life in the rural areas and outer islands of the region by complementing the rural development activities of island countries. SPC promotes active participation of the rural population and encourages the use of traditional practices and knowledge in the formulation of rural development projects. The rural development training project aims to promote project planning, implementation and management techniques, as well as community development skills. The Technology Programme aims to provide technical assistance, advice and monitoring of pilot regional programmes, with emphasis on new and rural technologies, as well as technology transfer. Activities include the development of solar energy, bee-keeping, coconut-processing, and training in aircraft maintenance.

COMMUNITY HEALTH

The aim of the Community Health Programme is to improve the health of Pacific islanders through disease prevention and primary health care on a community level, using a multi-sectoral approach. The community health services work as a fully integrated team to assist governments in strengthening their health and development programmes by conducting projects and activities in the following areas: rural health, sanitation and water supply; health education; nutrition and food composition; epidemiology and disease surveillance and control; and dental health.

SOCIO-ECONOMIC STATISTICAL SERVICES

The statistics section assists governments and administrations in the region to develop the range of socio-economic statistics produced, and to improve their quality and reliability. It encourages co-operation between government statistical agencies in the region, and promotes the widespread use of international standards and classifications. It provides a statistical information service, by the issue of regional publications, and the supply of regional data and analytical reports, and organizes training courses. The economics section assists governments of the region through the provision of advisory services in economic development planning, agricultural development policies, marketing and price stabilization and economic development policies in general. Training courses are also organized, with emphasis on the techniques of development planning, project analysis, farm management and negotiations with overseas interests. The section also undertakes research on economic development issues. The Population Programme assists governments to plan, carry out, process and analyse population censuses and demographic surveys. It provides the services of experienced specialists, disseminates information and research data on population and development, and provides training.

COMMUNITY EDUCATION SERVICES

The Pacific Women's Resource Bureau aims to assist national women's offices in upgrading their skills to deal with women's problems at local, national and regional levels, to establish an information network among Pacific women, and develop national and regional programmes on issues and problems facing women. It assists governments, on request, in bringing about the active participation of women in national development efforts. The SPC Community Education Training Centre (CETC) at Narere, Fiji, conducts a community development training course for about 30 women community workers annually, with the objective of training women in methods of community education so that they can help others to achieve better living conditions for island families and communities. The SPC Regional Media Centre, based in Suva, Fiji, conducts practical workshops and training courses in graphic design, publication and printing, photography, radio broadcasting, video/television production, and other selected areas of audio-visual communication media for islanders who use communication skills in their professional activities. The Youth and Adult Education Programme provides non-formal education and support for youth, community workers and young adults in community development subjects.

CULTURAL CONSERVATION AND EXCHANGE

SPC was instrumental in setting up the Festival of Pacific Arts and acts as the Secretariat of the Council of Pacific Arts. A Revolving Fund supports activities designed to promote the culture and traditions of Pacific island member countries, with emphasis on the Festival of Pacific Arts.

FINANCE

Contributions to the regular budget of the Commission are made by member governments and administrations, according to a formula based on per caput income. In addition to projects funded from the regular budget, the Commission carries out activities funded by special voluntary contributions from governments, international organizations and other sources. Assessed and extra-budgetary contributions for 1990 were expected to total 1,780m. francs CFP (about US $16.5m.), of which extra-budgetary contributions represented about 70%.

PUBLICATIONS

Annual Report.
Report of the South Pacific Conference.
Pacific Impact (quarterly).
Regional Tuna Bulletin (quarterly).
Environment Newsletter (quarterly).
Youthlink (quarterly).
Women's Newsletter (quarterly).
Plant Protection News.
Technical publications, statistical bulletins, advisory leaflets and reports.

SOUTH PACIFIC FORUM

MEMBERS

Australia	New Zealand
Cook Islands	Niue
Fiji	Papua New Guinea
Kiribati	Solomon Islands
Marshall Islands	Tonga
Federated States of	Tuvalu
Micronesia	Vanuatu
Nauru	Western Samoa

The South Pacific Forum is the gathering of Heads of Government of the independent and self-governing states of the South Pacific. Its first meeting was held on 5 August 1971, in Wellington, New Zealand. It provides an opportunity for informal discussions to be held on a wide range of common issues and problems and meets annually or when issues require urgent attention. The Forum has no written constitution or international agreement governing its activities nor any formal rules relating to its purpose, membership or conduct of meeting. Decisions are always reached by consensus, it never having been found necessary or desirable to vote formally on issues.

The 16th Forum was held in August 1985 in Rarotonga, Cook Islands. It adopted a treaty declaring a nuclear-free zone in the South Pacific and prohibiting the possession, testing and use of nuclear weapons in the region (which would come into force following ratification by eight member states). France, the United Kingdom, the USA, the People's Republic of China and the USSR were invited to sign protocols committing them to support the treaty. The Forum also reaffirmed its support for self-determination in the French Overseas Territory of New Caledonia, and set up a group to observe developments there. The SPARTECA agreement (see below) was discussed, and its scope was widened.

The 17th Forum, held in August 1986 in Suva, Fiji, agreed unanimously to bring the question of New Caledonia before the UN Special Committee on Decolonization, on the grounds that the French Government which had taken office earlier that year appeared to be committed to retaining New Caledonia as a French territory. The Forum also approved an amendment in the protocols to the nuclear-free zone treaty, being offered to the non-regional powers for signature: this would allow the signatories to withdraw if unforeseen circumstances made it necessary for their national interest. The meeting expressed concern over the lack of progress in negotiations with the USA over fishing rights in the region.

The treaty on the South Pacific nuclear-free zone came into effect in December 1986, following ratification by eight states. In the same month the USSR signed the protocols in support of the treaty, and the People's Republic of China did so in February 1987; the other three major nuclear powers, however, intimated that they did not intend to adhere to the treaty.

The 18th Forum, held in May 1987 in Apia, Western Samoa, took place earlier in the year than usual, in anticipation of the referendum on independence due to be held in New Caledonia. The meeting denounced the referendum as 'divisive and futile' on the grounds that the voting procedure to be followed favoured the European settlers in New Caledonia, and recommended that a UN-sponsored referendum should be held instead. The Forum also expressed grave concern over the military coup which had taken place in Fiji earlier that month, and offered to send a mission to Fiji to assist in establishing an acceptable government there. The Forum welcomed the signing of a Multilateral Fisheries Treaty with the USA in April 1987, and strongly condemned the illegal fishing activities of United States and other foreign vessels in the region. It was decided that a Committee on Regional Institutional Arrangements should be established to examine ways to increase international recognition of the Forum, and to examine the concept of a single regional organization.

The 19th Forum, held in September 1988 in Tonga, discussed the threat posed to low-lying island countries in the region (such as Kiribati, Tonga and Tuvalu) by the predicted rise in sea-level caused by heating of the earth's atmosphere as a result of pollution (the 'greenhouse effect'). The Forum agreed to establish a network of stations to monitor climatic change in the Pacific region. The meeting also discussed the establishment of a regional telecommunications network (to be based on a satellite station in Sydney, Australia), and agreed to seek multilateral (rather than bilateral) negotiations with Japan on fishing rights in the Pacific.

The 20th Forum, held in July 1989 in Tarawa, Kiribati, discussed the problem of drift-net fishing, as practised by the Japanese and Taiwanese fleets, which was reported to have increased tuna catches in the region to considerably more than the agreed maximum sustainable level, while also indiscriminately destroying many other marine species. In November members adopted a regional convention banning the practice.

The 21st Forum, held in August 1990 in Vanuatu, welcomed announcements made by Japan and Taiwan in the previous month that they would suspend drift-net fishing in the region. The members criticized the US Government's use of the US external territory of Johnston Atoll for the destruction of chemical weapons. The meeting urged industrialized countries to reduce the emission of gases that contribute to the 'greenhouse effect'. A ministerial committee was established to monitor political developments in New Caledonia.

South Pacific Forum Secretariat

Address: GPO Box 856, Suva, Fiji.

Telephone: 312600.

Telex: 2229.

The South Pacific Bureau for Economic Co-operation (SPEC) was established by an agreement signed on 17 April 1973, at the third meeting of the South Pacific Forum in Apia, Western Samoa. SPEC was renamed the South Pacific Forum Secretariat in 1988.

Organization

(October 1990)

COMMITTEE

The Committee is the Secretariat's executive board. It comprises representatives and senior officials from all member countries. It meets twice a year, immediately before the meetings of the South Pacific Forum and at the end of the year, to discuss in detail the Secretariat's work programme and annual budget.

SECRETARIAT

The Secretariat carries out the day-to-day activities of the Forum. It is headed by a Secretary-General, with an executive staff of 25 drawn from the member countries.

Secretary-General: HENRY FATI NAISALI.

Activities

The Secretariat's aim is to facilitate continuing co-operation and consultation between members on trade, economic development, transport, tourism and other related matters.

The Secretariat's trade activities cover trade promotion, the identification and development of export-oriented industries, and the negotiation of export opportunities. Following a study of trade relations and industrial development in the South Pacific, SPEC co-ordinated and assisted island countries in negotiating the South Pacific Regional Trade and Economic Co-operation Agreement (SPARTECA) which came into force in 1981, aiming to redress the trade deficit of the South Pacific countries with Australia and New Zealand. It is a non-reciprocal trade agreement under which Australia and New Zealand offer duty-free and unrestricted access or concessional access for specified products originating from the developing island member countries of the Forum. In August 1985

Australia agreed to further liberalization of trade by abolishing (from the beginning of 1987) duties and quotas on all Pacific products except steel, cars, sugar, footwear and garments. The Secretariat also investigates the prospects for closer economic co-operation between members, and has conducted market surveys in Japan and the USA, and surveys on regional industry, the harmonization of industrial incentives, national investment policies, possibilities of bulk purchasing and regional crop insurance. It provides support for national trade promotion and trade information services.

Regional transport forms an important part of the Secretariat's activities. A Regional Shipping Council was set up by the Forum in 1974, and a Regional Civil Aviation Council and Advisory Committee in 1976. In 1984 these bodies undertook a regional transport survey, to compile a comprehensive data base on transport in the region. The South Pacific Forum established the Pacific Forum Line and the Association of South Pacific Airlines (see below), and the Secretariat is involved in formulating regional maritime standards and in supervising wage rates and working conditions for seamen. In 1986 the South Pacific Maritime Development Programme was established. Its initial work programme comprised assistance for regional maritime training, and for the development of regional maritime administrations and legislation; and approaches to international aid donors for capital-intensive projects, including the possible replacement of domestic fleets in the region. The South Pacific Civil Aviation Development Programme provides technical assistance for civil aviation planning, and in 1989 undertook a major project for the upgrading of five international airports in the region.

The Secretariat acts as the co-ordinating agency for telecommunications work undertaken in the region by UNDP and other agencies. In 1983 the 14th South Pacific Forum approved the establishment of the South Pacific Telecommunications Development Programme, to be conducted over the next decade and to include the provision of affordable satellite services for remote areas.

The Secretariat acts as overall regional energy co-ordinator. An Energy Unit was formed in 1982: its work includes research on alternative energy sources, financed by the European Community. The Secretariat was to manage a solar electrification project for remote areas, established in 1990 with finance from the European Community. A Regional Petroleum Unit provides advice on the purchase, transport and storage of petroleum.

The Secretariat services the Pacific Group Council of ACP states receiving assistance from the European Community under the Lomé Convention (q.v.). It also manages a regional disaster relief fund and a Fellowship Scheme to provide in-service training in island member countries for about 25 candidates per year, financed by Australia, New Zealand and the Commonwealth Fund for Technical Co-operation. With funds from UNDP, the Secretariat recruits specialists to carry out short-term advisory services in the islands of the region. A Pacific Regional Advisory Service was established in 1981, to maintain a register of locally-available skills and to co-ordinate the transfer of these skills from one member to another, through the exchange of advisers and consultants. The Secretariat participates in the South Pacific Regional Environment Programme (SPREP) with the South Pacific Commission (q.v.).

BUDGET

The Governments of Australia and New Zealand each contribute one-third of the annual budget and the remaining third is equally shared by the other member Governments. Regular budgetary expenditure approved for 1989 amounted to $F 2,104,000, while extra-budgetary funding was expected to total $F 3,599,000.

Associated and Affiliated Organizations

Association of South Pacific Airlines—ASPA: POB 9817, Nadi Airport, Nadi, Fiji; tel. 73526; telex 5139; fax 790196; f. 1979 at a meeting of airlines in the South Pacific, convened to promote co-operation among the member airlines for the development of regular, safe and economical commercial aviation within, to and from the South Pacific. Mems: 19 regional airlines, three associates. Chair. PAUL AISA; Sec.-Gen. GEORGE E. FAKTAUFON.

Pacific Forum Line: POB 796, Auckland, New Zealand; tel. (09) 396700; telex 60460; fax (09) 392683; f. 1977 as a joint venture by 10 South Pacific countries, to provide shipping services to meet the special requirements of the region; operates five container vessels; conducts shipping agency services in Fiji, New Zealand and Western Samoa, and stevedoring in Western Samoa. Chair. D. TUFUI; CEO W. J. MACLENNAN.

South Pacific Forum Fisheries Agency—FFA: POB 629, Honiara, Solomon Islands; tel. (677) 21-124; telex 66336; fax (677) 23995; f. 1978 by the South Pacific Forum to promote co-operation in fisheries among coastal states in the region; collects and disseminates information and advice on the living marine resources of the region, including the management, exploitation and development of these resources; provides assistance in the areas of law (treaty negotiations, drafting legislation, and co-ordinating surveillance and enforcement), fisheries development, research, economics, computers, and information management. The Agency signed a five-year agreement with the USA in April 1987, allowing fishing rights to the US fishing fleet in exchange for payments amounting to US $60m. Dir P. A. MULLER. Publs *FFA News Digest* (monthly), *FFA Export Market Report* (quarterly).

South Pacific Trade Commission: 225 Clarence St, Sydney, NSW 2000, Australia; tel. 290-2833; telex 70342; fax 262-2320; f. 1979 to identify and develop markets in Australia for investments in and exports from the Pacific islands; funded by the Australian govt. Trade Commr WILLIAM T. MCCABE.

PUBLICATIONS

Annual Report.

Forum Secretariat Directory of Aid Agencies.

SPARTECA (guide for Pacific island exporters).

Forum Secretariat Series for Trade and Investment in the South Pacific.

Reports of Forum and Bureau meetings.

SOUTHERN AFRICAN DEVELOPMENT CO-ORDINATION CONFERENCE—SADCC

Address: Private Bag 0095, Gaborone, Botswana.
Telephone: 51863.
Telex: 2555.

The first Conference was held at Arusha, Tanzania, in July 1979, to harmonize development plans and to reduce the region's economic dependence on South Africa.

MEMBERS

Angola	Mozambique	Zambia
Botswana	Namibia	Zimbabwe
Lesotho	Swaziland	
Malawi	Tanzania	

Organization
(October 1990)

SUMMIT MEETING
The meeting is held annually and is attended by heads of state and government or their representatives.

COUNCIL OF MINISTERS
Representatives of SADCC member countries at ministerial level meet at least twice a year; in addition, special meetings are held to co-ordinate regional policy in a particular field by, for example, ministers of energy and ministers of transport.

CONFERENCES ON CO-OPERATION
A conference with SADCC's 'international co-operating partners' (donor governments and international agencies) is held annually to review progress in the various sectors of the SADCC programme and to present new projects requiring assistance.

SECRETARIAT
Executive Secretary: Dr SIMBARASHE MAKONI (Zimbabwe).

SECTORAL CO-ORDINATION OFFICES
Southern Africa Transport and Communications Commission (SATCC): CP 2677, Maputo, Mozambique; tel. 20246; telex 6597.
Energy Sector Technical and Administrative Unit: CP 172, Luanda, Angola; tel. 23382; telex 3170.
Agricultural Research and Animal Disease Control: Ministry of Agriculture, Private Bag 003, Gaborone, Botswana; tel. 350581; telex 2543.
Tourism: Lesotho Tourist Board, POB 1378, Maseru 100, Lesotho; tel. 323760; telex 4820; fax 310108.
Soil and Water Conservation and Utilisation: Ministry of Agriculture, Co-operatives and Marketing, POB 24, Maseru 100, Lesotho; tel. 322741; telex 4330.
Fisheries, Wildlife and Forestry: Ministry of Forestry and Natural Resources, Private Bag 350, Lilongwe 3, Malawi; tel. 731322; telex 4465.
Manpower Development: Dept of Economic Planning and Statistics, POB 602, Mbabane, Swaziland; tel. 43765; telex 2109.
Trade and Industrial Co-ordination Division: Ministry of Industries and Trade, POB 9503, Dar es Salaam, Tanzania; tel. 27251; telex 41686.
Mining: Ministry of Mines, POB 31969, Lusaka, Zambia; tel. 227653; telex 45970.
Food Security Technical and Administrative Unit: Ministry of Lands, Agriculture and Rural Resettlement, Private Bag 7701, Causeway, Harare, Zimbabwe; tel. 706081; telex 22455.

Activities

In July 1979 the first Southern African Development Co-ordination Conference was attended by delegations from Angola, Botswana, Mozambique, Tanzania and Zambia, with representatives from donor governments and international agencies; the group was later joined by Lesotho, Malawi, Swaziland and Zimbabwe, and Namibia became a member in 1990. In April 1980 a regional economic summit conference was held in Lusaka, Zambia, and the Lusaka Declaration, a statement of strategy entitled 'Southern Africa: Towards Economic Liberation', was approved, together with a programme of action allotting specific studies and tasks to member governments (see list of co-ordinating offices, above). The members aimed to reduce their dependence on South Africa for rail and air links and port facilities, imports of raw materials and manufactured goods, and the supply of electric power. In 1985, however, an SADCC report noted that since 1980 the region had become still more dependent on South Africa for its trade outlets, and the 1986 summit meeting, although it recommended the adoption of economic sanctions against South Africa, failed to establish a timetable for doing so.

In August 1989 it was reported that US $2,537m. of the $6,313m. required for SADCC projects had been secured. At the donors' conference held in January 1990, the World Bank announced that it was to provide $4,000m. for SADCC member states over the next five years.

TRANSPORT AND COMMUNICATIONS
Transport is seen as the most important area to be developed, on the grounds that, as the Lusaka Declaration noted, 'The dominance of the Republic of South Africa has been reinforced by its transport system. Without the establishment of an adequate regional transport and communications system, other areas of co-operation become impractical'. Priority was to be given to the improvement of road and railway services into Mozambique, so that the land-locked countries of the region could transport their goods through Mozambican ports instead of South African ones.

Rehabilitation of the railway between Malawi and Beira on the coast of Mozambique was under way in 1982, while work on the line from Malawi to the port of Nacala in Mozambique began in 1983. Other proposed railway projects include improvement of lines and equipment in Angola and Botswana, between Mozambique and Swaziland, and between Tanzania and Zambia. In early 1988 plans were announced for a 10-year rehabilitation plan (to cost $575m.) for the Benguela railway, leading to the port of Lobito in Angola, and for the second phase of the rehabilitation of the Limpopo railway, running from Zimbabwe to Maputo, Mozambique. In February 1989 donors agreed to provide $90m. for the first phase of the Benguela railway scheme.

Port facilities are to be improved at Luanda in Angola, Beira, Maputo and Nacala in Mozambique, and Dar es Salaam, Tanzania. There are plans for the rehabilitation and upgrading of roads throughout the region, and, in particular, work on the main roads connecting Mozambique with Swaziland (from 1986) and with Zimbabwe, and on the road between Tanzania and Zambia. Civil aviation projects include a new airport at Maseru, Lesotho, completed in 1985, and improvements of major airports in Mozambique, Swaziland, Zambia and Zimbabwe, together with studies on the joint use of maintenance facilities, on regional airworthiness certification and aviation legislation, and on navigational aids. A 10-year plan for the development of civil aviation in the region was discussed by ministers in June 1989. Work on a satellite earth station in Swaziland had been completed by 1984, while two more, in Angola and Zimbabwe, were being constructed, and microwave communications links are planned throughout the region.

In August 1989 it was reported that financing secured for the transport and communications programme now amounted to $2,054m. for 201 projects: the total required was $5,097m.

ENERGY
The energy programme consists of 80 projects, with total funding requirements of US $427m., as at August 1989, when $129m. had been secured. The main areas of work comprised: a study on regional self-sufficiency in the supply of petroleum products; exploitation of the region's coal resources; development of hydroelectric power, and the linking of national electricity grids (Botswana-Zimbabwe, Botswana-Zambia, Mozambique-Swaziland and Zimbabwe-Mozambique); and new and renewable sources of energy, including pilot projects in solar energy and wind-power and the developing of integrated energy systems for villages.

TRADE, INDUSTRY AND MINING
In the industry and trade sector 14 projects were being planned in August 1989, at a total cost of $14m., of which $3m. had been secured.

INTERNATIONAL ORGANIZATIONS

Southern African Development Co-ordination Conference

In 1986 it was announced that, as well as attempting to improve the region's physical infrastructure, SADCC would also place more emphasis on increasing the production of goods and on stimulating intra-regional trade, which accounted for only about 5% of the members' total external trade. A trade promotion programme was approved in 1986: it included the possible formation of a regional export credit facility. The annual co-operation conference held in February 1987 was attended by about 120 representatives of private-sector businesses, and it was hoped that this would stimulate private investment in the region.

At the end of August 1989, 39 planned mining projects required financing of $70m., of which $36m. had been secured. Studies on the manufacturing of mining machinery and spare parts, repairing and reconditioning facilities, and the development of a regional iron and steel industry had been completed by 1986, and studies on the availability of skilled manpower, small-scale mining and a geological inventory were being undertaken.

In March 1989, following a meeting of national business organizations, it was announced that an SADCC regional investment council was to be established, with the aim of identifying and promoting opportunities for investment in the member states.

MANPOWER

SADCC aims to meet the region's requirements in skilled manpower by providing training in the following categories: high-level managerial personnel; high- and medium-level technicians; artisans; and instructors. In August 1989 the funding required for 29 manpower projects was US $26m., of which $9m. had been secured.

FOOD AND AGRICULTURE

In August 1989 funding required for 119 projects in this sector was US $670m., of which $304m. had been secured. Priority is given to regional food security and to self-sufficiency in basic foods. During 1986 work was under way on a regional early warning system for anticipating food shortages, and an inventory of agricultural resources. In 1989 a regional food programme (including price incentives for farmers and the construction of strategic storage facilities) was established. Improvement of inland and marine fisheries, livestock production and the control of animal diseases also form an important part of the work in this sector. The Southern African Centre for Co-operation in Agricultural Research (SACCAR), in Gaborone, Botswana, began operations in 1985. It co-ordinates national research systems and operates a small research grants programme. Its three initial programmes covered sorghum and millet improvement, grain legume improvement, and land and water management. Other projects undertaken by SADCC include wildlife protection and forestry.

SADCC PROJECT FINANCING BY SECTOR (August 1989)

Sector	Number of projects	Total cost (US $ million)	Funding secured (US $ million)*
Energy	80	427	129
Food, agricultural and natural resources	119	670	304
Industry and trade	14	14	3
Manpower development	29	26	9
Mining	39	70	36
Tourism	8	10	2
Transport and communications	201	5,097	2,054
Total	490	6,313	2,537

* Includes both local and foreign resources.

PUBLICATIONS

Annual Progress Report.
SADCC Energy Bulletin.
SACCAR Newsletter.
Soil and Water Conservation and Land Utilization Newsletter.

THE WARSAW TREATY OF FRIENDSHIP, CO-OPERATION AND MUTUAL ASSISTANCE— THE WARSAW PACT

Headquarters of the Joint Command: Moscow, USSR.

The Warsaw Treaty of Friendship, Co-operation and Mutual Assistance (the Warsaw Pact) was signed in Warsaw in May 1955. It was automatically extended for a further 10 years in June 1975, and renewed, before its expiry, for a further period of 20 years (with an option to extend it for a further 10 years) in April 1985: the terms of the treaty were unchanged. The treaty was supplemented by an interlocking system of treaties between the member countries. Albania, one of the original signatories, ceased to participate in 1961 and formally withdrew from the Treaty in 1968. The other signatories were Bulgaria, Czechoslovakia, the German Democratic Republic (GDR), Hungary, Poland, Romania and the USSR.

Organization*

(October 1990)

POLITICAL CONSULTATIVE COMMITTEE (PCC)

Following the renewal of the Warsaw Treaty in April 1985 the PCC met annually. Until 1989 delegations of member states were normally led by the General Secretary of the national Communist Party, supported by the Head of Government, ministers of foreign affairs and defence and others. Meetings are normally attended by the Commander-in-Chief, Warsaw Pact Joint Armed Forces. Summit meetings of leaders of Pact countries (not formally described as PCC meetings) also take place from time to time.

MINISTERIAL COMMITTEES

A Committee of Ministers of Defence was established by the PCC in 1969, as part of a reorganization of the Treaty's military structure; it meets annually. A Committee of Ministers of Foreign Affairs was established in 1976.

MILITARY COUNCIL

Established by the PCC in 1969, the Council comprises national Chiefs of Staff or deputy ministers of defence, with status of Deputy Commanders-in-Chief of the Warsaw Pact Joint Armed Forces. It normally meets twice a year, in each member country in turn, under the chairmanship of the Commander-in-Chief of the Joint Armed Forces.

JOINT SECRETARIAT

The Secretariat was formally established in Moscow in 1956, and reinstituted in 1976, after a period of inactivity.

JOINT COMMAND OF THE ARMED FORCES

The Joint Command was established in 1955, under the general supervision of the PCC.

Commander-in-Chief: Army Gen. PETR G. LUSHEV (USSR).

Chief of Staff and First Deputy Commander-in-Chief: Army Gen. VLADIMIR N. LOBOV (USSR).

Deputy Commanders-in-Chief: The members of the Military Council.

The Combined General Staff comprises representatives of the member states, with headquarters in Moscow. It services meetings of the Committee of Ministers of Defence and of the Military Council, and plans and evaluates manoeuvres and exercises of Warsaw Pact Joint Armed Forces.

* Following the extensive political changes which took place in Eastern Europe in 1989 and 1990, the PCC agreed, in June 1990, to undertake a major review of the character and functions of the Warsaw Pact, so as to transform it into 'a pact of sovereign and equal states, based on democratic principles'. The meeting recommended collaboration with NATO and with neutral and non-aligned European countries, to form a new European security structure. In the same month Hungary declared that it would not take part in Warsaw Pact military exercises in 1990, and that it planned to leave the Pact by the end of 1991. In September the German Democratic Republic formally left the Pact, prior to its reunification with the Federal Republic of Germany (and consequent absorption into NATO). In November member countries signed an agreement on the maximum level of conventional (non-nuclear) armaments to be permitted for each member, in anticipation of an agreement that was concluded with NATO on reductions in conventional forces, at a meeting of the Conference on Security and Co-operation in Europe (CSCE), later in November. A Warsaw Pact summit conference of heads of government, scheduled to be held in early November, was postponed until after the CSCE meeting. The conference was expected to discuss the dissolution of the Pact's military structure.

WESTERN EUROPEAN UNION—WEU

Address: 9 Grosvenor Place, London, SW1X 7HL, England.
Telephone: (071) 235-5351.

Based on the Brussels Treaty of 1948, Western European Union was set up in 1955. Member States seek to harmonize their views on security and defence questions.

MEMBERS

Belgium	Netherlands
France	Portugal
Germany	Spain
Italy	United Kingdom
Luxembourg	

Organization
(October 1990)

COUNCIL

The Council of Western European Union consists of the ministers of foreign affairs and of defence of the member countries, or the Ambassadors resident in London and an Under-Secretary of the British Foreign and Commonwealth Office. As supreme authority of WEU, it is responsible for formulating policy and issuing directives to the Secretary-General and the Agencies for Security Questions (see below). The Council meets twice a year at ministerial level, and at permanent (ambassadorial) level as often as required (usually twice a month). Each country holds the Presidency of the Council for one year, beginning on 1 July.

SECRETARIAT-GENERAL

Secretary-General: WILLEM VAN EEKELEN (Netherlands).
Deputy Secretary-General: H. HOLTHOFF (Germany).

AGENCIES FOR SECURITY QUESTIONS

Address: 43 ave du Président Wilson, 75775 Paris Cedex 16, France.

Agency for the Study of Arms Control and Disarmament Questions.
Agency for the Study of Security and Defence Questions.
Agency for the Development of Co-operation in the Field of Armaments.

ASSEMBLY

Address: 43 ave du Président Wilson, 75775 Paris Cedex 16, France.

The Assembly of Western European Union consists of the delegates of the member countries to the Parliamentary Assembly of the Council of Europe. It meets twice a year in Paris. The Assembly considers defence policy in Western Europe, besides other matters concerning member states in common, and may make recommendations or transmit opinions to the Council, to national parliaments, governments and international organizations. An annual report is presented to the Assembly by the Council.

President: CHARLES GOERENS (Luxembourg).
Clerk: GEORGES MOULIAS (France).

PERMANENT COMMITTEES OF THE ASSEMBLY

There are permanent committees on: Defence Questions and Armaments; General Affairs; Scientific Questions; Budgetary Affairs and Administration; Rules of Procedure and Privileges; and Parliamentary and Public Relations.

Activities

The Brussels Treaty was signed in 1948 by Belgium, France, Luxembourg, the Netherlands and the United Kingdom. It foresaw the potential for international co-operation in Western Europe and provided for collective defence and collaboration in economic, social and cultural activities. Within this framework, NATO and the Council of Europe (see chapters) were formed in 1949.

On the collapse in 1954 of plans for a European Defence Community, a nine-power conference was convened in London to try to reach a new agreement. This conference's decisions were embodied in a series of formal agreements drawn up by a ministerial conference held in Paris in October 1954. The agreements entailed: arrangements for the Brussels Treaty to be strengthened and modified to include the Federal Republic of Germany and Italy, the ending of the occupation regime in the Federal Republic of Germany, and the invitation to the latter to join NATO. These agreements were ratified on 6 May 1955, on which date the seven-power Western European Union came into being.

The new organization was given the task of settling the future of the Saar region. Under a Franco-German agreement of October 1954, the Saar was to have a European statute within the framework of WEU, subject to approval by referendum. In October 1955 the Saar population voted against the statute and expressed the wish for incorporation in the Federal Republic of Germany. Political and economic incorporation were achieved in January 1957 and July 1959 respectively.

The modified Brussels Treaty provided for a system of co-operation in social and cultural affairs: these activities were transferred in June 1960 to the Council of Europe.

A meeting of ministers of defence and of foreign affairs, held in Rome in October 1984, agreed to 'reactivate' WEU by restructuring its organization and by holding more frequent ministerial meetings, in order to harmonize members' views on defence questions, arms control and disarmament, developments in East-West relations, Europe's contribution to the Atlantic alliance, and European armaments co-operation.

In October 1987 the Council adopted a 'Platform on European Security Interests', declaring its intention to develop a 'more cohesive European defence identity', while affirming that 'the substantial presence of US conventional and nuclear forces plays an irreplaceable part in the defence of Europe'. The document also resolved to improve consultations and extend co-ordination in defence and security matters, and to use existing resources more effectively by expanding bilateral and regional military co-operation.

In November 1988 Portugal and Spain were admitted to membership of WEU (subject to approval by the legislatures of member states, a process which was concluded in March 1990).

In April 1990 WEU ministers of foreign affairs and defence discussed the implications of recent political changes in Eastern Europe, and agreed to organize contacts with the newly-elected governments there. Following the Iraqi invasion of Kuwait in August, the military response of Western European countries was co-ordinated by WEU.

A WEU Institute for Security Studies was established in Paris in July 1990.

PUBLICATIONS

Assembly of Western European Union: Texts adopted and Brief Account of the Session (2 a year).

Annual Report of the Council.

Assembly documents and reports.

WORLD CONFEDERATION OF LABOUR—WCL

Address: 33 rue de Trèves, 1040 Brussels, Belgium.
Telephone: (02) 230-62-95.
Telex: 26966.
Fax: (02) 230-87-22.

Founded in 1920 as the International Federation of Christian Trade Unions (IFCTU); reconstituted under present title in 1968. (See also the International Confederation of Free Trade Unions and the World Federation of Trade Unions.)

MEMBERS

Affiliated national federations and trade union internationals; about 15,000,000 members in 78 countries.

Organization
(October 1990)

CONGRESS

The supreme and legislative authority. The most recent meeting was held in October 1985 in Baden, Austria. Congress consists of delegates from national confederations and trade internationals. Delegates have votes according to the size of their organization. Congress receives official reports, elects the Executive Board, considers the future programme and any proposals.

CONFEDERAL BOARD

The Board meets annually, and consists of 36 members (including 15 representatives of national confederations and 11 representatives of trade internationals) elected by Congress from among its members for four-year terms. It issues executive directions and instructions to the Secretariat.

SECRETARIAT-GENERAL

Secretary-General: CARLOS LUIS CUSTER (Argentina).

REGIONAL OFFICES

Latin America: Latin-American Confederation of Workers, Apdo 6681, Caracas 1010, Venezuela. Sec.-Gen. EMILIO MASPERO.
Asia: Brotherhood of Asian Trade Unionists (BATU), 1839 Dr Antonio Vasquez St, Malate, Manila, Philippines. Pres. J. TAN.
North America: c/o National Alliance of Postal and Federal Employees, 1628 11th St, NW, Washington, DC 20001, USA.

INTERNATIONAL INSTITUTES OF TRADE UNION STUDIES

Africa: Fondation panafricaine pour le développement économique, social et culturel (Fopadesc), Lomé, Togo.
Asia: BATU Social Institute, Manila, Philippines.
Latin America:
Instituto Andino de Estudios Sociales, Lima, Peru.
Instituto Centro-Americano de Estudios Sociales (ICAES), San José, Costa Rica.
Instituto de Formación del Caribe, Willemstad, Curaçao, Netherlands Antilles.
Instituto del Cono Sur (INCASUR), Buenos Aires, Argentina.
Universidad de Trabajadores de América Latina (UTAL).

FINANCE

Income is derived from affiliation dues, contributions, donations and capital interest.

PUBLICATIONS

Labor Press and Information Bulletin (8 a year; in English, French, German, Dutch and Spanish).
Flash (in English, French, German, Dutch and Spanish).
Reports of Congresses; Study Documents.

International Trade Federations

International Federation of Textile and Clothing Workers: 27 Koning Albertlaan, 9000 Ghent, Belgium; fax (091) 20-45-59; f. 1901. Mems: unions covering 400,000 workers in 19 countries. Organization: Congress (every three years), Bureau, Secretariat. Pres. A. DUQUET (Belgium); Sec. D. UYTTENHOVE (Belgium).

International Federation of Trade Unions of Employees in Public Service—INFEDOP: 33 rue de Trèves, 1040 Brussels, Belgium; tel. (02) 230-60-90; f. 1922. Mems: national federations of workers in public service, covering 4m. workers. Organization: World Congress (at least every five years), World Confederal Board (meets every year), six Trade Groups, Secretariat. Pres. A. HENGCHEN (Belgium); Sec.-Gen. JOS DE CEULAER (Belgium). Publ. *Labor Professional Action* (6 a year).

INFEDOP has four regional organizations:
EUROFEDOP: 33 rue de Trèves, 1040 Brussels, Belgium.
CLASEP: Apartado 6681, Caracas 101, Venezuela.
CLTC: Apartado 4456, Caracas 101, Venezuela.
ASIAFEDOP: POB 163, Manila, Philippines.

International Federation of Trade Unions of Transport Workers—FIOST: 26 ave d'Auderghem, 1040 Brussels, Belgium; tel. (02) 231-00-90; fax (02) 231-11-44; f. 1921. Mems: national federations in 28 countries covering 600,000 workers. Organization: Congress (every four years), Committee (meets twice a year), Executive Board. Pres. JOHN JANSSENS (Belgium); Sec.-Gen. ALFRED GOSSELIN (Belgium). Publ. *Labor* (6 a year).

World Confederation of Teachers: 33 rue de Trèves, 1040 Brussels, Belgium; tel. (02) 230-60-90; telex 26966; fax (02) 230-87-22; f. 1963. Mems: national federations of unions concerned with teaching. Organization: Congress (every four years), Council (at least once a year), Steering Committee. Pres. L. VAN BENEDEN; Sec.-Gen. R. DENIS (Belgium).

World Federation of Agriculture and Food Workers: 31 rue de Trèves, 1040 Brussels, Belgium; tel. (02) 230-60-90; f. 1982 (merger of former World Federation of Agricultural Workers and World Federation of Workers in the Food, Drink, Tobacco and Hotel Industries). Mems: national federations covering 2,800,000 workers in 38 countries. Organization: Congress (every five years), World Board, Daily Management Board. Pres. JORGE LASSO; Sec. E. VERVLIET (Belgium). Publ. *Labor* (8 a year).

World Federation of Building and Woodworkers Unions: 31 rue de Trèves, 1040 Brussels, Belgium; f. 1936. Mems: national federations covering 2,438,000 workers in several countries. Organization: Congress, Bureau, Permanent Secretariat. Pres. A. DESLOOVERE; Sec. G. DE LANGE (Netherlands). Publ. *Bulletin*.

World Federation of Clerical Workers: 1 Beggaardenstraat, 2000 Antwerp, Belgium; f. 1921. Mems: national federations of unions and professional associations covering 400,000 workers in 11 countries. Organization: Congress (every two years), Council, Executive Bureau, Secretariat. Pres. L. STRAGIER (Belgium). Publ. *Revue* (every 2 years).

World Federation of Industry Workers: 33 rue de Trèves, 1040 Brussels, Belgium; f. 1985. Mems: regional and national federations covering about 500,000 workers in 30 countries. Organization: Congress (every five years), World Board (every year), Executive Committee, six World Trade Councils. Pres. L. DUSOLEIL; Sec.-Gen. M. SOMMEREYNS. Publ. *Labor*.

WORLD COUNCIL OF CHURCHES—WCC

Address: 150 route de Ferney, POB 2100, 1211 Geneva 2, Switzerland.
Telephone: (022) 7916111.
Telex: 415730.
Fax: (022) 7910361.

The Council was founded in 1948 to promote co-operation between Christian Churches and to prepare for a clearer manifestation of the unity of the Church.

MEMBERS

There are 316 member Churches in over 100 countries, of which 30 are associate members. Chief denominations: Anglican, Baptist, Congregational, Lutheran, Methodist, Moravian, Old Catholic, Orthodox, Presbyterian, Reformed and Society of Friends. The Roman Catholic Church is not a member but sends official observers to meetings.

Organization
(October 1990)

ASSEMBLY

The governing body of the World Council, consisting of delegates of the member Churches, it meets every six or seven years to frame policy and consider some main theme. The sixth Assembly was held at Vancouver, Canada, in 1983.

Presidium: Dame R. NITA BARROW (Barbados), Dr MARGA BUEHRIG (Switzerland), Metropolitan PAULOS MAR GREGORIOS (India), Bishop JOHANNES HEMPEL (Germany), Patriarch IGNATIOS IV (Syria), Most Rev. W. P. KHOTSO MAKHULU (Botswana), Very Rev. Dr LOIS WILSON (Canada).

CENTRAL COMMITTEE

Appointed by the Assembly to carry out its policies and decisions, the Committee consists of 150 members chosen from Assembly delegates. It meets annually.

Moderator: Rev. Dr HEINZ JOACHIM HELD (Germany).
Vice-Moderators: Metropolitan CHRYSTOSTOMOS of Myra (Turkey), Dr SYLVIA TALBOT (USA).

EXECUTIVE COMMITTEE

Consists of the Presidents, the Officers and 16 members chosen by the Central Committee from its membership to prepare its agenda, expedite its decisions and supervise the work of the Council between meetings of the Central Committee. Meets every six months.

GENERAL SECRETARIAT

The General Secretariat implements the policies laid down by the WCC, and co-ordinates the work programme units described below. It includes a Communication Department, a Finance Department and a Library, and supervises the work of the Ecumenical Institute at Bossey, Switzerland, which provides training in ecumenical leadership.

General Secretary: Rev. Dr EMILIO CASTRO (Uruguay).

Activities

The work of the WCC is carried out by three programme units:

FAITH AND WITNESS

This unit studies the theological questions which divide the churches (producing, for example, recent statements on baptism, the Eucharist and the ministry) and the problems facing the Church in the modern world; it assists the Christian community in sharing information and resources for mission and evangelism; and conducts dialogues with people of non-Christian faiths.

JUSTICE AND SERVICE

The mandate of the unit on Justice and Service is 'to assist the churches in combating poverty, injustice and oppression and to facilitate ecumenical co-operation in service to human need and in promoting freedom, justice, peace, human dignity and world community.' The five sub-units reflect these tasks: Commission on Inter-Church Aid, Refugee and World Service (CICARWS), Commission of the Churches in International Affairs (CCIA), Programme to Combat Racism (PCR), Commission on the Churches' Participation in Development (CCPD) and Christian Medical Commission (CMC). Unit-wide programme priorities are covered by the Programme on Justice, Peace and the Integrity of Creation. The Human Rights Resources Office for Latin America assists many programmes and initiatives in Latin Amercia and the Caribbean, in close consultation with the local churches, in the area of human rights.

EDUCATION AND RENEWAL

This unit aims to increase participation by women, young people and lay people generally in the activities of the Church and of society; to serve theological education institutions and stimulate new developments in Christian education; and to help make the ecumenical movement a reality at parish level.

FINANCE

The WCC's budget for 1990 amounted to 42.5m. Swiss francs. The main contributors are the churches and their agencies, with funds for certain projects contributed by other organizations. Of total income, about 44% was allotted to the Justice and Service Unit, 14% to the Faith and Witness Unit, and 18% to the Education and Renewal Unit; the General Secretariat, Communication Department, Governing Bodies, administrative services and Library together account for 19%; and the Ecumenical Institute, Bossey, 5%.

PUBLICATIONS

Catalogue of periodicals, books and audio-visuals.
One World (monthly).
Ecumenical Review (quarterly).
International Review of Mission (quarterly).
Ecumenical Press Service (weekly).

WORLD FEDERATION OF TRADE UNIONS—WFTU

Address: Vinohradská 10, 12147 Prague 2, Czechoslovakia*.
Telephone: (2) 353565.
Telex: 121525.
Fax: (2) 354393.

* In November 1990 the Czechoslovak Government requested that WFTU should leave its Prague offices in 1991.

The Federation was founded in 1945, on a world-wide basis. A number of members withdrew from the Federation in 1949 to set up the International Confederation of Free Trade Unions (see p. 163). (See also the World Confederation of Labour, p. 213.)

MEMBERS
In 1989 there were 94 affiliated national federations in 82 countries, with 214m. members. Membership was reported to have declined to 190m. in 1990.

Organization
(October 1990)

WORLD TRADE UNION CONGRESS
The Congress meets every four years. It reviews WFTU's work, endorses reports from the executives, and elects the General Council and Bureau. The size of the delegations is based on the total membership of national federations. The Congress is also open to participation by non-affiliated organizations. The 12th Congress was held in November 1990, in Moscow.

GENERAL COUNCIL
The General Council meets once a year and comprises members and deputies, representing 82 countries and 11 Trade Unions Internationals, and elected by Congress from nominees of national federations. Every affiliated organization has one member and one deputy member.

The Council receives reports from the Bureau, approves the budget, plans the Congress agenda, and elects the General Secretary and Secretariat officers.

BUREAU
President: (vacant).
Vice-Presidents: ERNEST BOATSWAIN (Australia), INDRAJIT GUPTA (India), ELIAS EL-HABR (Lebanon), KAREL HOFFMANN (Czechoslovakia), HENRI KRASUCKI (France), B. LUVSATSEREN (Mongolia), IZZEDINE NASSER (Syria), VALENTIN PACHO (Peru), STEPAN A. SHALAYEV (USSR), TADESSE TAMERAT (Ethiopia), ROBERTO VEIGA (Cuba), ROMAIN VILON GUEZO (Benin), MIROSLAV ZAVADIL (Czechoslovakia), ANDREAS ZIARTIDES (Cyprus).

The Bureau, which has 40 members, meets twice a year and conducts most of the executive work of WFTU.

SECRETARIAT
The Secretariat consists of the General Secretary and eight secretaries. It is appointed by the General Council and is responsible for economic and social affairs, national trade union liaison, press and information, the Trade Unions Internationals, women's affairs, solidarity activities, education, administration and finance. In 1990 the Czechoslovak Government asked the Secretariat to leave its premises in Prague by June 1991, on the grounds that no Czechoslovak trade union organization now belonged to WFTU.
General Secretary: IBRAHIM ZAKARIA.

BUDGET
Income is derived from affiliation dues, which are based on the number of members in each trade union federation.

PUBLICATIONS
World Trade Union Movement (monthly; published in 10 languages).
Flashes from the Trade Unions (weekly; published in five languages).

Trade Unions Internationals
The following autonomous Trade Unions Internationals are associated with WFTU:

Trade Unions International of Agricultural, Forestry and Plantation Workers: Bolshaya Serpoukloukskaya 44, 113093 Moscow, USSR; f. 1949. Mems: 106 unions grouping over 70m. workers in 66 countries. Pres. A. KYRIACOU (Cyprus); Sec.-Gen. ANDRÉ HEMMERLÉ (France). Publ. *Bulletin* (every 2 months in Arabic, French, Spanish, English and Russian).

Trade Unions International of Chemical, Oil and Allied Workers (ICPS): 1415 Budapest, Hungary; tel. 1428-558; f. 1950. Mems: about 14m., grouped in 106 unions in 60 countries; Industrial Commissions for Oil, Chemicals, Rubber, Paper-board and Glass/Pottery. Pres. FERENC DAJKA (Hungary); Gen. Sec. ALAIN COVET (France). Publs *Information Bulletin*, *Information Sheet* (French, English, Spanish, Russian, German, Arabic, Japanese).

Trade Unions International of Food, Tobacco, Hotel and Allied Industries Workers: Stamboliiski St 3, Sofia 1000, Bulgaria; tel. 88-57-59; f. 1949. Mems: 115 unions grouping 22m. individuals in 54 countries. Pres. FREDDY HUCK (France); Gen. Sec. R. MARTÍNEZ MASDEU (Cuba). Publ. *News Bulletin*.

Trade Unions International of Metal Workers: POB 158, Pouchkinskaya 5/6, Moscow 109003, USSR; tel. and fax (095) 200-02-23; telex 411370; f. 1949. Mems: 62 unions grouping 22.5m. workers from 43 countries. Gen. Sec. GILBERT LE BESCOND (France). Publs *Informations*, *Bulletin*.

Trade Unions International of Public and Allied Employees: 1086 Berlin, Französische Str. 47, Germany; tel. 2292662; telex 114326; f. 1949. Mems: 39m. in 152 unions in 54 countries. Branch Commissions: State, Municipal, Postal and Telecommunications, Health, Banks and Insurance. Pres. ALAIN POUCHOL (France); Gen. Sec. JOCHEN MEINEL (Germany). Publs *Public Services* (in English, French and Spanish), *Information Bulletin* (in seven languages).

Trade Unions International of Textile, Clothing, Leather and Fur Workers: Opletalova 57, 110 00 Prague 1, Czechoslovakia; f. 1949. Mems: 12m. workers in 71 organizations in 58 countries. Pres. GILBERTO MORALES (Colombia); Sec.-Gen. JAN HÜBNER (Czechoslovakia). Publ. *Information Courier*.

Trade Unions International of Transport Workers: Váci u. 73, 1139 Budapest, Hungary; tel. 209-601; telex 225861; f. 1949. Mems: 173 unions grouping 20m. workers from 72 countries. Pres. G. LANOUE (France); Gen. Sec. J. TOTH. Publs *Bulletin* (monthly, in English, French and Spanish).

Trade Unions International of Workers in Commerce: Opletalova 57, 110 00 Prague I, Czechoslovakia; f. 1959. Mems: 70 national federations in 61 countries, grouping 23m. members. Pres. JANOS VAS (Hungary); Sec.-Gen. ALVARO VILLAMARÍN (Colombia).

Trade Unions International of Workers in Energy: 36/40 ul. Kopernika, 00-924 Warsaw, Poland; tel. 264316; telex 816913; fax 381653; f. 1949. Mems: 37 unions with 7.5m. mems. in 34 countries. Pres. FRANÇOIS DUTEIL (France); Gen. Sec. MIECZYSŁAW JUREK (Poland). Publ. *Information Bulletin*.

Trade Unions International of Workers of the Building, Wood and Building Materials Industries: Box 281, Helsinki 10, Finland; tel. 693-10-50; f. 1949. Mems: 78 unions in 60 countries, grouping 17m. workers. Pres. LOTHAR LINDNER (Germany); Sec.-Gen. MAURI PERÄ (Finland). Publ. *Bulletin*.

World Federation of Teachers' Unions: 1026 Berlin, Wallstrasse 61/65, Germany; tel. 2793461; telex 114809; f. 1946. Mems: 132 national unions of teachers and educational and scientific workers in 85 countries, representing over 25m. individuals. Pres. LESTURUGE ARIYAWANSA (Sri Lanka); Gen. Sec. GERARD MONTANT (France). Publs *Teachers of the World* (quarterly, in English, French, German and Spanish), *International Teachers' News* (8 a year, in seven languages), reports and papers.

OTHER INTERNATIONAL ORGANIZATIONS

Agriculture, Food, Forestry and Fisheries	*page* 219	Religion	*page* 250
Aid, Development and Economic Co-operation	222	Science	252
Arts and Culture	225	Social Sciences and Humanistic Studies	259
Commodities	227	Social Welfare	261
Economics and Finance	230	Sport and Recreations	265
Education	231	Technology	266
Government and Politics	235	Tourism	270
Industrial and Professional Relations	238	Trade and Industry	271
Law	240	Transport	275
Medicine and Health	242	Youth and Students	277
Posts and Telecommunications	248		
Press, Radio and Television	248	**Index at end of volume**	

OTHER INTERNATIONAL ORGANIZATIONS

Agriculture, Food, Forestry and Fisheries

(For organizations concerned with agricultural commodities, see Commodities, p. 227)

African Timber Organization: BP 1077, Libreville, Gabon; tel. (241) 732928; telex 5620; f. 1976 to enable members to study and co-ordinate ways of influencing prices of wood and wood products by ensuring a continuous flow of information on forestry matters; to harmonize commercial policies and carry out industrial and technical research. Mems: Angola, Cameroon, Central African Republic, Congo, Côte d'Ivoire, Equatorial Guinea, Gabon, Ghana, Liberia, Tanzania, São Tomé and Príncipe, Zaire. Sec.-Gen. MOHAMMED LAWAL GARBA.

Asian Vegetable Research and Development Center: POB 42, Shanhua, Tainan 74199, Taiwan; tel. (06) 5837801; telex 73560; fax (06) 583009; f. 1971 to improve diet and standard of living of rural populations in the humid tropics by increased production of vegetable crops through the breeding of better varieties and the development of improved cultural methods; research programme includes plant breeding, plant pathology, plant physiology, soil science, entomology, crop management, cropping systems, agricultural economics, and chemistry; the Centre has an experimental farm, laboratories, gene-bank, greenhouses, library and weather station and provides training for research and production specialists in tropical vegetables. It undertakes scientific publishing. Mems: Australia, France, Germany, Japan, Republic of Korea, Philippines, Taiwan, Thailand, USA. Dir-Gen. Dr EMIL O. JAVIER. Publs *Annual Report*, *Newsletter*, *Technical Bulletin*, *CENTERPOINT*, directories of researchers.

Association for the Advancement of Agricultural Science in Africa—AAASA: POB 30087, Addis Ababa, Ethiopia; f. 1968 to promote the development and application of agricultural sciences and the exchange of ideas; to encourage Africans to enter training; holds several seminars each year in different African countries. Mems: individual agronomists, research institutes, organizations in the agricultural sciences in Africa. Sec.-Gen. Prof. M. EL-FOULY (acting). Publs *Journal* (2 a year), *Newsletter* (quarterly).

Caribbean Food and Nutrition Institute: Jamaica Centre, UWI Campus, POB 140, Kingston 7, Jamaica; tel. (809) 927-1540; telex 3705; Trinidad Centre, UWI Campus, St. Augustine, Trinidad; tel. 66 31544; f. 1967 to serve the governments and people of the region and to act as a catalyst among persons and organizations concerned with food and nutrition through research and field investigations, training in nutrition, dissemination of information, advisory services and production of educational material. Mems: all English-speaking Caribbean territories, including the mainland countries of Belize and Guyana. Dir Dr ADELINE WYNANTE PATTERSON. Publs *Cajanus* (quarterly), *Nyam News* (monthly), educational material.

Collaborative International Pesticides Analytical Council Ltd.—CIPAC: c/o Plantenziektenkundige Dienst, Postbus 9102, 6700 HC Wageningen, Netherlands; tel. 8370-96420; telex 45163; fax 8370-21701; f. 1957 to organize international collaborative work on methods of analysis for pesticides used in crop protection. Mems: individuals in 15 countries and corresponding mems. in 19 countries. Chair. Dr H. P. BOSSHARDT (Switzerland); Sec. Dr A. MARTIJN (Netherlands).

Common Organization for the Control of Desert Locust and Bird Pests—OCLALAV: BP 1066, Dakar, Senegal; f. 1965 to destroy insect pests, in particular the desert locust, and grain-eating birds, in particular the quelea-quelea, and to sponsor related research projects. Mems: Benin, Burkina Faso, Cameroon, Chad, Côte d'Ivoire, The Gambia, Mali, Mauritania, Niger, Senegal. Dir-Gen. ABDULLAHI OULD SOUEÏD AHMED.

Dairy Society International—DSI: 7185 Ruritan Drive, Chambersburg, Pa 17201, USA; tel. (717) 375-4392; f. 1946 to foster the extension of dairy and dairy industrial enterprise internationally through an interchange and dissemination of scientific, technological, economic, dietary and other relevant information; organizer and sponsor of the first World Congress for Milk Utilization. Mems: in 50 countries. Pres. JAMES E. CLICK (USA); Man. Dir G. W. WEIGOLD (USA). Publs *DSI Report to Members*, *DSI Bulletin*, *Market Frontier News*, *Dairy Situation Review*.

Desert Locust Control Organization for Eastern Africa: POB 4255, Addis Ababa, Ethiopia; tel. 611465; telex 21510; f. 1962 to promote most effective control of desert locust in the region and to carry out research into the locust's environment and behaviour, and pesticides residue analysis; assists member states in the monitoring and extermination of other migratory pests such as the quelea-quelea (grain-eating birds), the army worm and the tsetse fly; bases at Asmara and Dire Dawa (Ethiopia), Mogadishu and Hargeisa (Somalia), Nairobi (Kenya), Khartoum (Sudan), Arusha (Tanzania) and Djibouti. Mems: Djibouti, Ethiopia, Kenya, Somalia, Sudan, Tanzania, Uganda. Dir-Gen. Prof. HOSEA Y. KAYUMBO. Publs *Desert Locust Situation Reports* (monthly), *Annual Report*.

European and Mediterranean Plant Protection Organization: 1 rue Le Nôtre, 75016 Paris, France; tel. (1) 45-20-77-94; telex 614148; fax (1) 42-24-89-43; f. 1951, present name adopted in 1955; aims to promote international co-operation between government plant protection services and in preventing the introduction and spread of pests and diseases of plants and plant products. Mems: governments of 33 countries and territories. Chair. J. THIAULT; Dir-Gen. I. M. SMITH. Publs *EPPO Bulletin*, *Data Sheets on Quarantine Organisms*, *Guidelines for the Biological Evaluation of Pesticides*, *Crop Growth Stage Keys*, *Summary of the Phytosanitary Regulations of EPPO Member Countries*, *Reporting Service*.

European Association for Animal Production (Fédération européenne de zootechnie): Via A. Torlonia 15A, 00161 Rome, Italy; tel. (06) 8840785; f. 1949 to help improve the conditions of animal production and meet consumer demand; holds annual meetings. Mems: associations in 31 member countries. Pres. Prof. A. NARDONE (Italy); Sec.-Gen. Prof. Dr J. BOYAZOGLU. Publ. *Livestock Production Science* (12 a year).

European Association for Research on Plant Breeding—EUCARPIA: c/o POB 128, 6700 AC Wageningen, Netherlands; tel. (08370) 19112; f. 1956 to promote scientific and technical co-operation in the plant breeding field. Mems: 1,150 individuals, 80 corporate mems; 12 sections and several working groups. Pres. Dr Y. DATTEE (France); Sec. M. MESKEN. Publ. *Bulletin*.

European Confederation of Agriculture: CP 87, 5200 Brugg, Aargau, Switzerland; tel. (056) 413177; telex 825110; f. 1889 as International Confederation, re-formed in 1948 as European Confederation; represents the interests of European agriculture in the international field; social security for independent farmers and foresters in the member countries. Mems: 436 ordinary and 43 advisory mems. from 20 countries. Pres. HEINRICH ORSINI-ROSENBERG (Austria); Gen. Sec. WILLY STRAUB. Publs *CEA Dialog*, *Rapport sur le marché international du lait et des produits laitiers* (quarterly).

European Grassland Federation: c/o Dr W. H. Prins, Badhuisweg 13G, 2597 JN 's-Gravenhage, Netherlands; tel. (070) 3525071; fax (070) 3521451; f. 1963 to facilitate and maintain liaison between European grassland organizations and to promote the interchange of scientific and practical knowledge and experience; a general meeting is held every two years (1992 in Finland) and symposia at other times. Mems: 21 organizations and three individuals from 24 countries. Pres. Dr S. PULLI; Federation Sec. Dr W. H. PRINS.

European Livestock and Meat Trading Union: 81A rue de la Loi, 1040 Brussels, Belgium; tel. (02) 230-46-03; telex 64685; fax (02) 230-94-00; f. 1952 to study problems of the European livestock and meat trade and inform members of all legislation affecting it, and to act as an international arbitration commission; conducts research on agricultural markets, quality of livestock, and veterinary regulations. Mems: national organizations in Austria, Belgium, Denmark, France, Germany, Greece, Ireland, Italy, Luxembourg, Netherlands, Portugal, Spain, Sweden, Switzerland; and the European Association of Livestock Markets. Pres. A. ANORO; Sec.-Gen. J.-L. MERIAUX.

Inter-American Association of Agricultural Librarians and Documentalists (Asociación Interamericana de Bibliotecarios y Documentalistas Agrícolas—AIBDA): c/o IICA-CIDIA, Apdo 55-2200 Coronado, Costa Rica; tel. 29-0222; telex 2144; fax 29-4741; f. 1953 to promote professional improvement of its members through technical publications and meetings, and to promote improvement of library services in agricultural sciences. Mems: about 400 in 31 countries. Pres. NITZIA BARRANTES DE CEBALLOS; Exec. Sec. GHISLAINE POITEVIEN. Publs *Boletín Informativo* (quarterly), *Boletín Especial* (irregular), *Revista AIBDA* (2 a year), *Páginas* *de Contenido: Ciencias de la Información* (quarterly), *AIBDA Actualidades* (irregular), *Guía para Bibliotecas Agrícolas*.

Inter-American Tropical Tuna Commission—IATTC: c/o Scripps Institution of Oceanography, La Jolla, Calif 92093, USA; tel. (619) 546-7100; telex 697115; fax (619) 546-7133; f. 1950; investigates the biology of the tunas of the eastern Pacific Ocean to determine the effects of fishing and natural factors on stocks; recommends appropriate conservation measures to maintain stocks at levels which will afford maximum sustainable catches; attempts to maintain porpoise stocks and avoid the needless killing of porpoise by tuna-fishers. Mems: Costa Rica, France, Japan, Nicaragua, Panama, USA. Dir JAMES JOSEPH. Publs *Bulletin* (irregular), *Annual Report*.

International Association for Cereal Science and Technology: Wiener Strasse 22A, POB 77, 2320 Schwechat, Austria; tel. (0222) 77-72-02; telex 133316; fax (0222) 77-72-04; f. 1955 (as the International Association for Cereal Chemistry; name changed 1984) to standardize the methods of testing and analysing cereals and cereal products. Mems: 33 member states. Sec.-Gen. Dr Dipl. Ing. H. GLATTES (Austria).

International Association for Vegetation Science: 3400 Göttingen, Wilhelm-Weber-Str. 2, Germany; tel. (0551) 395700; f. 1938. Mems: 970 from 51 countries. Chair. Prof. Dr S. PIGNATTI; Sec. Prof. Dr H. DIERSCHKE. Publs *Phytocoenologia, Vegetatio, Journal of Vegetation Science*.

International Association of Agricultural Economists: 1211 West 22nd St, Oak Brook, Ill 60521, USA; f. 1929 to foster development of the sciences of agricultural economics and further the application of the results of economic investigation in agricultural processes and the improvement of economic and social conditions relating to agricultural and rural life. Mems: 1,552 from 76 countries. Pres. JOHN W. LONGWORTH (Australia); Sec. and Treas. R. J. HILDRETH (USA).

International Association of Agricultural Information Specialists: c/o Drs J. van der Burg, PUDOC, PO Box 4, 6700 AA Wageningen, Netherlands; telex 45015; fax (08370) 84761; f. 1955 to promote agricultural library science and documentation, and the professional interests of agricultural librarians and documentalists; affiliated to the International Federation of Library Associations and to the Fédération Internationale de Documentation. Mems: 600 in 80 countries. Pres. J. HOWARD (USA); Sec.-Treas. Drs J. VAN DER BURG (Netherlands). Publs *Quarterly Bulletin, Current Agricultural Serials* (2 vols.), *Primer for Agricultural Libraries, IAALD News, World Directory of Agricultural Information Resource Centres*.

International Association of Horticultural Producers: Postbus 93099, 2509 AB The Hague, Netherlands; tel. (070) 814631; telex 31 406; fax (070) 477176; f. 1948; represents the common interests of commercial horticultural producers in the international field by frequent meetings, regular publications, press-notices, resolutions and addresses to governments and international authorities; authorizes international horticultural exhibitions. Mems: national associations in 25 countries. Pres. R. MATHIS; Gen. Sec. Drs J. B. M. ROTTEVEEL. Publ. *Yearbook of International Horticultural Statistics*.

International Bee Research Association: 18 North Rd, Cardiff, CF1 3DY, Wales; tel. (0222) 372409; telex 262433; f. 1949 to further and co-ordinate research on bees, etc. (including pollination) in all countries. Mems: 1,200 in 130 countries. Dir DAVID A. FRANCIS. Publs *Bee World* (quarterly), *Apicultural Abstracts* (quarterly), *Journal of Apicultural Research* (quarterly).

International Centre for Tropical Agriculture (Centro Internacional de Agricultura Tropical): Apdo Aéreo 6713, Cali, Colombia; tel. (57-23) 675050; telex 05769; fax (57-23) 647243; f. 1969 to accelerate agricultural and economic development and to increase agricultural productivity in the tropics; research and training focuses on production problems of the tropics concentrating on field beans, cassava, rice and tropical pastures. Dir-Gen. Dr GUSTAVO A. NORES. Publs *Annual Report, CIAT International* (2 a year), catalogue of publications.

International Commission for Agricultural and Food Industries: 35 rue du Général Foy, 75008 Paris, France; tel. (1) 42-93-19-24; fax (1) 43-87-71-92; f. 1934 to study scientific, technical and economic questions related to the food and agricultural industries in various countries, to co-ordinate investigations in these areas and to assemble and distribute relevant documentation for these industries (the information centre is managed by CDIUPA, Le Noyer Lambert, 91305 Massy, France); to organize yearly international congresses for agricultural and food industries. Pres. FERNANDO MÉNDEZ DE ANDES; Gen. Sec. GUY DARDENNE (France). Publs *Comptes Rendus des Congrès Internationaux des Industries Agricoles*.

International Commission for the Conservation of Atlantic Tunas: Calle Príncipe de Vergara 17, 28001 Madrid, Spain; tel. 431 03 29; telex 46330; f. 1969 to promote the conservation and rational exploitation of tuna resources in the Atlantic Ocean and adjacent seas. Exec. Sec. O. RODRÍGUEZ MARTÍN.

International Commission for the Southeast Atlantic Fisheries: Paseo de la Habana 65, 28036 Madrid, Spain; tel. 458 8766; telex 45533; f. 1971 under the Convention for the Conservation of the Living Resources of the Southeast Atlantic; monitors fish stocks and determines quotas. Mems: 17 countries. Chair. Capt. K. N. GAYDAROV (Bulgaria); Exec. Sec. R. LAGARDE.

International Commission of Sugar Technology: 1 Aandorenstraat, 3300 Tienen, Belgium; tel. 80-12-11; telex 22251; fax 82-04-38; f. 1948 to organize meetings with a view to discussing past investigations and promoting scientific and technical research work. Pres. of Scientific Cttee. G. MANTOVANI (Italy); Gen. Sec. R. PIECK (Belgium).

International Committee for Recording the Productivity of Milk Animals: Via A. Torlonia 15A, 00161 Rome, Italy; tel. (06) 8840785; f. 1951 to extend and improve the work of milk recording, standardize methods; 27th session, France, July 1990. Mems: in 28 countries. Pres. Dr K. MEYN (Germany); Sec.-Gen. Prof. Dr J. BOYAZOGLU.

International Crops Research Institute for the Semi-Arid Tropics—ICRISAT: Patancheru, Andhra Pradesh 502 324, India; tel. (0842) 224016; telex 422203; fax (0842) 241239; f. 1972 as world centre for genetic improvement of sorghum, pearl millet, pigeonpea, chickpea and groundnut, and for research on the management of resources in the world's semi-arid tropics; research covers all physical and socio-economic aspects of improving farming systems on unirrigated land. Dir LESLIE D. SWINDALE (New Zealand). Publs *Annual Report, Research Highlights, SAT News* (quarterly), *Sorghum and Millet Information Center Newsletter* (3 a year), *International Chickpea Newsletter* (2 a year), *International Pigeonpea Newsletter* (2 a year), *International Arachis Newsletter* (2 a year), *Research/Information Bulletin* (occasional).

International Dairy Federation: 41 Square Vergote, 1040 Brussels, Belgium; tel. (02) 733-98-88; telex 63818; fax (02) 733-04-13; f. 1903 to link all dairy associations in order to encourage the solution of scientific, technical and economic problems affecting the dairy industry. Mems: national committees in 35 countries. Sec.-Gen. E. HOPKIN (UK). Publs *Bulletin of IDF, IDF News, Mastitis Newsletter, Packaging News, Dairy Education and Training Newsletter*.

International Federation of Agricultural Producers—IFAP: 21 rue Chaptal, 75009 Paris, France; tel. (1) 45-26-05-53; telex 281210; fax (1) 48-74-72-12; f. 1946 to represent, in the international field, the interests of agricultural producers; to exchange information and ideas and help develop understanding of world problems and their effects upon agricultural producers; to encourage efficiency of production, processing, and marketing of agricultural commodities; holds conference every two years. National farmers' organizations and agricultural co-operatives of 51 countries are represented in the Federation. Pres. H. O. A. KJELDSEN (Denmark); Sec.-Gen. D. KING. Publs *IFAP Newsletter* (monthly), *World Agriculture/IFAP News* (quarterly), *Farming for Development* (quarterly), *IFAP Tropical Commodity Newsletter* (monthly), *Proceedings of General Conferences*.

International Federation of Beekeepers' Associations—APIMONDIA: Corso Vittorio Emanuele 101, 00186 Rome, Italy; tel. (6) 65121; telex 612533; fax 6548578; f. 1949; collects and brings up to date documentation concerning international beekeeping; studies the particular problems of beekeeping through its permanent committees; organizes international congresses, seminars, symposia and meetings; stimulates research into new techniques for more economical results; co-operates with other international organizations interested in beekeeping, in particular with FAO. Mems: 80 associations from 68 countries. Pres. RAYMOND BORNECK; Sec.-Gen. Dr SILVESTRO CANNAMELA. Publ. *Apiacta* (quarterly, in English, French, German, Russian and Spanish), *Dictionary of Beekeeping Terms*, studies.

International Hop Growers' Convention: c/o Institut za hmeljarstvo in pivovarstvo, 63310 Žalec, Yugoslavia; tel. (063) 711221; telex 33 514; f. 1950 to act as a centre for the collection of data on hop production, and to conduct scientific, technical and economic commissions. Mems: national associations in Australia, Belgium, Czechoslovakia, France, Germany, Hungary, Poland, Spain, United Kingdom, USA, Yugoslavia. Pres. J. F. BLANCHARD (UK); Gen. Sec. ALOJZ ČETINA (Yugoslavia). Publ. *Hopfen-Rundschau* (fortnightly).

International Institute for Sugar Beet Research: 47 rue Montoyer, 1040 Brussels, Belgium; tel. (02) 509-15-33; telex 21287; fax (02) 512-65-06; f. 1931 to promote research and exchange of information, by organizing meetings and study groups. Mems: 517 in 39 countries. Pres. of the Admin. Council D. MARCHIORI; Sec.-Gen. L. WEICKMANS.

OTHER INTERNATIONAL ORGANIZATIONS
Agriculture, Food, Forestry and Fisheries

International Institute of Tropical Agriculture—IITA: Oyo Rd, PMB 5320, Ibadan, Nigeria; tel. 400300; telex 31417; f. 1967; principal financing arranged by the Consultative Group on International Agricultural Research (CGIAR), co-ordinated by the IBRD. The four main research programmes comprise farming systems, grain legume improvement, cereal improvement and root and tuber improvement; training programme for researchers in tropical agriculture; library of 35,000 vols. Dir LAURENCE D. STIFEL. Publs *Annual Report*, technical bulletins, research reports.

International Laboratory for Research on Animal Diseases—ILRAD: POB 30709, Nairobi, Kenya; tel. 592311; telex 22040; fax 593499; f. 1973; conducts laboratory and field research on improved immunological and other controls of animal trypanosomiasis and theileriosis; training programme for researchers in animal disease control as well as technical and other staff; regular seminars, conferences; specialized library. Dir-Gen. Dr A. R. GRAY. Publs *Annual Scientific Report, ILRAD Reports* (quarterly), *Annual Report, Highlights*.

International Livestock Centre for Africa—ILCA: POB 5689, Addis Ababa, Ethiopia; tel. 613215; telex 21207; fax 611892; f. 1974; an international research centre supported by and financed largely through the Consultative Group on International Agricultural Research of the IBRD; a multidisciplinary research, information and training institute concerned with livestock and agricultural production, animal traction, feed resources, tolerance of disease, and livestock policy; collaborates with national and international research programmes; research sites in Ethiopia, Kenya, Mali, Niger and Nigeria. Dir-Gen. JOHN WALSH. Publs *Annual Report, ILCA Bulletin, ILCA Newsletter*, research reports, bibliographies, manuals.

International Maize and Wheat Improvement Centre—CIMMYT: Apdo. Postal 6-641, 06600 México, DF, Mexico; tel. (905) 7613311; telex 177 2023; conducts world-wide research programme for increasing production of maize, wheat and triticale, with emphasis on food production in developing countries. Dir-Gen. Dr DONALD WINKELMANN.

International North Pacific Fisheries Commission: 6640 N.W. Marine Drive, Vancouver, British Columbia, V6T 1X2, Canada; tel. (604) 228-1128; fax (604) 228-1135; f. 1953. Mems: Canada, Japan, USA. Publs *Annual Report, Bulletin and Statistical Yearbook*.

International Organization for Biological Control of Noxious Animals and Plants: Institut für Phytomedizin, Swiss Federal Institute of Technology (ETH), 8092 Zürich, Switzerland; tel. (01) 2563921; telex 53178; fax (01) 2520192; f. 1955 to promote and co-ordinate research on the more effective biological control of harmful insects and plants; re-organized in 1971 as a central council with world-wide affiliations and largely autonomous regional sections in different parts of the world: the West Palaearctic (Europe, North Africa, the Middle East), the Western Hemisphere, South-East Asia, Pacific Region and Tropical Africa. Pres. Dr J. COULSON (USA); Sec.-Gen. Dr J.-P. AESCHLIMANN (Switzerland). Publs *Entomophaga* (quarterly), *Newsletter*.

International Organization of Citrus Virologists: c/o Dr L. W. Timmer, University of Florida, IFAS, 700 Experiment Station Rd, Lake Alfred, Fla 33850, USA; tel. (813) 956-1151; fax (813) 956-4631; f. 1957 to promote research on citrus virus diseases at international level by standardizing diagnostic techniques and exchanging information relating to these diseases and their control. Mems: 250. Chair. Dr LUIS NAVARRO; Sec.-Treas. Dr L. W. TIMMER.

International Red Locust Control Organization for Central and Southern Africa: POB 240252, Ndola, Zambia; tel. 612433; telex 30072; f. 1971 to control locusts in eastern, central and southern Africa, and assists in the control of African army-worm and queleaquelea. Mems: nine countries. Dir E. K. BYARUHANGA. Publs *Annual Report, Monthly Report* and scientific reports.

International Regional Organization of Plant Protection and Animal Health (Organismo Internacional Regional de Sanidad Agropecuaria—OIRSA): Apdo (01) 61, Edif. Carbonell 2, Carretera a Santa Tecla, San Salvador, El Salvador; tel. 232391; telex (0373) 20746; fax 242331; f. 1953 for the prevention of the introduction of animal and plant pests and diseases unknown in the region; research, control and eradication programmes of the principal pests present in agriculture; technical assistance and advice to the ministries of agriculture and livestock of member countries; education and qualification of personnel. Mems: Costa Rica, El Salvador, Guatemala, Honduras, Mexico, Nicaragua, Panama. Exec. Dir Ing. RAFAEL ERNESTO MATA PEREIRA.

International Rice Research Institute—IRRI: POB 933, Manila, Philippines; tel. 818-1926; telex 45365; fax 817-8470; f. 1960; conducts a comprehensive basic research programme on the rice plant and its management with the objective of increasing the quantity and quality of rice; maintains a library to collect and provide access to the world's technical rice literature; publishes and disseminates research results; conducts regional rice research projects in co-operation with scientists in rice-producing countries; offers a resident training programme in rice research methods and techniques for staff members of organizations concerned with rice; organizes international conferences and symposia. Dir-Gen. KLAUS LAMPE. Publs *Annual Report, IRRI Reporter, The International Bibliography of Rice Research, International Rice Research Newsletter, IRRI Research Paper Series, Research Highlights*.

International Seed Testing Association: Reckenholz, POB 412, 8046 Zürich, Switzerland; tel. (01) 3713133; fax (01) 3777201; f. 1906 (reconstituted 1924) to promote uniformity and accurate methods of seed testing and evaluation in order to facilitate efficiency in production, processing, distribution and utilization of seeds; organizes triennial conventions, meetings, workshops, symposia and training courses. Mems: 60 countries. Pres. E. MADSEN (Denmark); Hon. Sec. Treas. Prof. A. LOVATO (Italy). Publs *Seed Science and Technology* (3 a year), *ISTA News Bulletin* (quarterly).

International Sericultural Commission: 25 quai Jean-Jacques Rousseau, 69350 La Mulatière, France; tel. 78-50-41-98; fax 78-86-09-57; f. 1948 to encourage the development of silk production. Library of 8,000 vols. Mems: governments of Brazil, Egypt, France, India, Japan, Lebanon, Madagascar, Mauritius, Philippines, Romania, Thailand, Tunisia. Sec.-Gen. Dr H. BOUVIER (France). Publ. *Sericologia* (quarterly).

International Service for National Agricultural Research—ISNAR: POB 93375, 2509 AJ The Hague, Netherlands; tel. (070) 349-61-00; telex 33746; fax (070) 381-96-77; f. 1980 by the Consultative Group on International Agricultural Research (q.v.) to strengthen national agricultural research systems in developing countries; to link these systems to sources of technical assistance and co-operation. Chair. HENRI CARSALADE; Dir-Gen. Dr CHRISTIAN BONTE FRIEDHEIM.

International Society for Horticultural Science: Englaan 1, 6703 ET Wageningen, Netherlands; tel. (08370) 21747; telex 45760; fax (08370) 21586; f. 1959 to co-operate in the research field. Mems: 54 member-countries, 265 organizations, 3,050 individuals. Pres. Prof. Dr R. SAKIYAMA (Japan); Sec.-Gen. and Treas. Ir. H. H. VAN DER BORG (Netherlands). Publs *Chronica Horticulturae* (4 a year), *Acta Horticulturae, Scientia Horticulturae* (monthly), *Horticultural Research International*.

International Society for Soilless Culture—ISOSC: POB 52, 6700 AB Wageningen, Netherlands; tel. (08370) 13809; fax (08370) 23457; f. 1955 as International Working Group on Soilless Culture, to promote world-wide distribution and co-ordination of research, advisory services, and practical application of soilless culture; international congress held every four years. Mems: 433 from 67 countries. Pres. Prof. Dr FRANZ PENNINGSFELD; Sec.-Gen. Ing. Agr. ABRAM A. STEINER. Publs *Bibliography on Hydroponics* (annually).

International Society of Soil Science: c/o Institute of Soil Science, University of Agriculture, Gregor-Mendel-Strasse 33, 1180 Vienna, Austria; tel. (0222) 34-25-00; fax (0222) 36-91-659; f. 1924. Mems: 8,000 individuals and associations in 135 countries. Pres. Dr A. AGUILAR S. (Mexico); Sec.-Gen. Prof. Dr W. E. H. BLUM (Austria). Publ. *Bulletin* (2 a year).

International Union of Forestry Research Organizations—IUFRO: 1131 Vienna, Schönbrunn-Tirolergarten, Austria; tel. (01) 82-01-51; telex 753-12646; fax (01) 82-93-55; f. 1890/92. Mems: 600 organizations in 100 countries, more than 15,000 individual mems. Pres. Dr SALLEH MOHD NOR (Malaysia); Sec. HEINRICH SCHMUTZENHOFER (Austria). Publs *Annual Report, IUFRO News* (quarterly).

International Veterinary Association for Animal Production: c/o Sociedad Veterinaria de Zootecnia, Isabel la Católica 12, 4° izq., 28013 Madrid, Spain; tel. 2471838; holds world congresses on livestock genetics, animal feeding and zootechnology. Mems: about 1,400 veterinary specialists. Pres of Exec. Cttee Prof. A. DE VUYST (Belgium); Sec.-Gen. Prof. Dr CARLOS LUIS DE CUENCA (Spain). Publs *Zootechnia* (4 a year).

Northwest Atlantic Fisheries Organization: POB 638, Dartmouth, Nova Scotia, B2Y 3Y9, Canada; tel. (902) 469-9105; telex 019-31475; fax (902) 469-5729; f. 1979 (formerly International Commission for the Northwest Atlantic Fisheries); aims at optimum use, management and conservation of resources, promotes research and compiles statistics. Pres. K. HOYDAL; Exec. Sec. J. C. E. CARDOSO. Publs *Annual Report, Statistical Bulletin, Journal of Northwest Atlantic Fishery Science, Scientific Council Reports, Scientific Council Studies, Sampling Yearbook, Proceedings, List of Fishing Vessels*.

World Association for Animal Production: Via A. Torlonia 15A, 00161 Rome, Italy; tel. (06) 8840785; f. 1965; holds world conference on animal production every five years; encourages, sponsors and participates in regional meetings, seminars and symposia. Pres.

Prof. Dr R. BLAIR (Canada); Sec.-Gen. Prof. Dr J. BOYAZOGLU. Publ. *News Items* (2 a year).

World Association of Veterinary Food-Hygienists: Institut für Veterinärmedizin des Bundesgesundheitsamtes, Postfach 330013, 1000 Berlin 33, Germany; tel. (030) 83082705; telex 184016; fax (030) 83082741; f. 1955 to promote hygienic food control and discuss research. Mems: 36 member countries. Pres. Dr RONALD E. ENGEL; Sec. Treas. Dr P. TEUFEL.

World Association of Veterinary Microbiologists, Immunologists and Specialists in Infectious Diseases: Ecole Nationale Vétérinaire d'Alfort, 7 ave du Général de Gaulle, 94704 Maisons-Alfort Cedex, France; f. 1967 to facilitate international contacts in the fields of microbiology, immunology and animal infectious diseases. Pres. Prof. CH. PILET (France). Publs *Comparative Immunology, Microbiology and Infectious Diseases*.

World Ploughing Organization—WPO: Whiteclose, Longtown, Carlisle, Cumbria, CA6 5TY, England; tel. (0228) 791153; f. 1952 to promote World Ploughing Contest in a different country each year, to improve techniques and promote better understanding of soil cultivation practices through research and practical demonstrations. Affiliates in 27 countries. Gen. Sec. ALFRED HALL. Publs *WPO Handbook* (annual), *WPO Bulletin of News and Information* (irregular).

World's Poultry Science Association: 3102 Hermannsburg, Peter-Schütze-Weg 11, Germany; tel. (05052) 775; f. 1912 to exchange knowledge in the industry, to encourage research and teaching, to publish information relating to production and marketing problems; to promote World Poultry Congresses and co-operate with governments. Mems: individuals in 95 countries, branches in 40 countries. Pres. Prof. YUKIO YAMADA (Japan); Sec. Prof. ROSE-MARIE WEGNER (Germany). Publ. *The World Poultry Science Journal* (3 a year).

World Veterinary Association: Isabel la Católica 12, 28013 Madrid, Spain; tel. 247 18 38; f. 1959 as a continuation of the International Veterinary Congresses; first Congress 1863. Mems: organizations in 72 countries and 18 organizations of veterinary specialists as associate members. Pres. Dr J. F. FIGUEROA (Peru); Sec.-Treas. Prof. Dr CARLOS L. DE CUENCA. Publs *WVA Informative Bulletin*, *World Directory of Veterinary Education Establishments*.

Aid, Development and Economic Co-operation

African Training and Research Centre in Administration for Development (Centre africain de formation et de recherches administratives pour le développement—CAFRAD): ave Mohamed V, BP 310, Tangier, Morocco; tel. 36430; telex 33664; f. 1964 by agreement between Morocco and UNESCO; undertakes research into administrative problems in Africa, documentation of results, provision of a consultation service for governments and organizations; holds frequent seminars. Mems: 27 African countries. Pres. ABDERRAHIM BENABDEJLIL; Dir-Gen. MAMADOU THIAM. Publs *Cahiers Africains d'Administration Publique* (4 a year), *African Administrative Studies* (2 a year), *ANAI Index*, *Répertoire des Consultants*, *CAFRAD News* (3 a year, in English, French and Arabic).

Afro-Asian Housing Organization—AAHO: POB 523, 30 26th July St, Cairo, Egypt; tel. 750139; f. 1965 to promote co-operation between African and Asian countries in housing, reconstruction, physical planning and related matters. Sec.-Gen. AHMED A. H. ZANFALY (Egypt).

Afro-Asian Rural Reconstruction Organization—AARRO: A-2/31 Safdarjung Enclave, New Delhi 110029, India; tel. 672045; telex 72326; f. 1962 to act as a catalyst for co-operative restructuring of rural life in Africa and Asia; to explore collectively opportunities for co-ordination of efforts for promoting welfare and eradicating hunger, thirst, disease, illiteracy and poverty amongst the rural people; and to assist the formation of organizations of farmers and other rural people. Activities include collaborative research on development issues, training; assistance in forming organizations of farmers and other rural people; the exchange of information; international conferences and seminars; and awarding 100 individual training fellowships at nine institutes in Egypt, India, Japan, the Republic of Korea and Taiwan. Mems: 10 African, 12 Asian countries, and one African associate. Sec.-Gen. B. C. GANGOPADHYAY. Publs *Annual Report*, *Rural Reconstruction* (2 a year), *AARRO Newsletter* (2 a year).

Agence de coopération culturelle et technique: 13 quai André Citroën, 75015 Paris, France: tel. (1) 45-75-62-41; telex 2011916; f. 1970, Niamey, Niger, to exchange knowledge of the cultures of French-speaking countries, to provide technical assistance, to assist relations between member countries. Technical and financial assistance has been given to projects in every member country, mainly to aid rural people. Mems: 30 countries, mainly African; associates: Cameroon, Egypt, Guinea-Bissau, Laos, Mauritania, Morocco; participants: Saint Lucia and the Canadian provinces of Quebec and New Brunswick. Sec.-Gen. JEAN-LOUIS ROY (Canada). Publ. *Agecoop Liaison* (monthly).

Arab Authority for Agricultural Investment and Development—AAAID: POB 2102, Khartoum, Sudan; tel. 41423; telex 23017; f. 1976 to accelerate agricultural development in the Arab world and to ensure food security; acts principally by equity participation in agricultural projects in Iraq, Sudan and Tunisia; authorized capital US $542m., paid-in capital $345m. (Dec. 1987). Mems: Algeria, Egypt, Iraq, Kuwait, Mauritania, Morocco, Qatar, Saudi Arabia, Somalia, Sudan, Syria, Tunisia, United Arab Emirates. Pres. Dr HUSAIN YOUSUF AL-ANI.

Arab Co-operation Council: Amman, Jordan; f. 1989 to promote economic co-operation between member states, including free movement of workers, joint projects in transport, communications and agriculture, and eventual integration of trade and monetary policies. Mems: Egypt, Iraq, Jordan, Yemen. Sec.-Gen. HELMI NAMAR (Egypt).

Arab Gulf Programme for the United Nations Development Organizations—AGFUND: POB 18371, Riyadh 11415, Saudi Arabia; tel. 4416240; telex 404071; fax 4412963; f. 1981 to provide grants for projects in mother and child care carried out by United Nations organizations and co-ordinate assistance by the nations of the Gulf; between 1981 and July 1989 AGFUND committed a total of US $176.6m. for the benefit of 115 countries. Contributions to AGFUND stood at US $207.8m. in July 1989. Pres. HRH Prince TALAL IBN ABDUL AZIZ AL-SAUD.

Asia-Pacific Economic Co-operation—APEC: f. 1989 as a forum for regular discussion on regional trade questions and economic co-operation. Mems: ASEAN countries (Brunei, Indonesia, Malaysia, Philippines, Singapore, Thailand), Australia, Canada, Japan, Republic of Korea, New Zealand, USA.

Association of Development Financing Institutions in Asia and the Pacific: c/o Private Development Corporation of the Philippines, PDCP Building, Ayala Ave, Makati, Manila, Philippines; tel. 816-16-72; telex 45022; f. 1976 to promote the interest and economic development of the respective countries of its member-institutions, and the Asia-Pacific region as a whole, through development financing. Mems: 52 ordinary, five special, 16 associate and five co-operating mems. Chair. Management Cttee S. S. NADKARNI (India); Sec.-Gen. ORLANDO P. PEÑA (Philippines).

BAM International (Frères des Hommes): 45 bis rue de la Glacière, 75013 Paris, France; tel. (1) 47-07-00-00; f. 1965 to support local partners helping the under-privileged to have more control of their own development, to increase public awareness and mobilization with regard to participatory development and international solidarity. Affiliated organizations in Belgium, Italy, Luxembourg, Spain and the United Kingdom. Mems: approx. 1,000. Pres. JEAN ALLAIN. Publ. *Newsletter* (4 a year).

Benelux Economic Union: 39 rue de la Régence, 1000 Brussels, Belgium; tel. (02) 519-38-11; fax (02) 513-42-06; f. 1960 to bring about the economic union of Belgium, Luxembourg and the Netherlands; structure comprises: the Committee of Ministers; the Council, consisting of one chairman from each country and the presidents of the eight Committees, on foreign economic relations, monetary and financial matters, industry and commerce, agriculture, food and fisheries, customs and taxation, transport, social affairs and movement of persons; the Court of Justice; the Consultative Inter-Parliamentary Council; the Economic and Social Advisory Council; and the Secretariat-General. Sec.-Gen. Drs B. M. J. HENNEKAM (Netherlands), MARIE-ROSE BERNA (Luxembourg), L. LENAERTS (Belgium). Publs *Benelux Newsletter* (monthly), *Benelux Review* (quarterly), *Benelux Textes de Base*, *Bulletin Benelux*.

Caritas Internationalis (International Confederation of Catholic Organizations for charitable and social action): Palazzo San Calisto, 00120 Città del Vaticano; tel. 6987197; telex 504/2014; fax 6987237; f. 1950 to study problems arising from poverty, their causes and possible solutions; national member organizations undertake assistance and development activities. The Confederation co-ordinates emergency relief and development projects, and represents members at international level. Mems: 120 national organizations. Pres. Cardinal ALEXANDRE DO NASCIMENTO (Angola); Sec.-Gen. Dr GERHARD MEIER (Switzerland). Publs *Intercaritas* (quarterly).

Club of Dakar: 76 rue Lecourbe, 75015 Paris, France; tel. (1) 42-67-16-00; f. 1974; an informal international forum for dialogue and development research, particularly concerned with Africa. Mems: 200 administrators, industrial executives, scientists and bankers from many industrialized and developing countries. Pres. AMADOU SEYDOU; Dir E. GUILLON.

Club of the Sahel (Club du Sahel): c/o OECD, 2 rue André Pascal, 75775 Paris, France; tel. (1) 45-24-89-59; telex 620160; fax (1) 45-

24-90-31; f. 1976; an informal forum of donor countries and member states of the permanent Inter-State Committee on Drought Control in the Sahel—CILSS (q.v.), for promoting the co-ordination of long-term policies and programmes in key development sectors affecting food production and drought control in the nine member countries of the CILSS; formed by the CILSS in association with the OECD. The Club collects information, conducts studies and helps to mobilize resources for the development of the Sahel region in agriculture livestock, cereals pricing policy, ecology, forestry and village water supplies.

Communauté Economique des Etats de l'Afrique Centrale—CEEAC (Economic Community of Central African States): BP 2112, Libreville, Gabon; f. 1983; operational 1 January 1985; aims to promote co-operation between member states by abolishing trade restrictions, establishing a common external customs tariff, linking commercial banks, and setting up a development fund, over a period of 12 years. Budget (1990): US $3.9m. Membership comprises the states belonging to UDEAC (q.v.) and five others: Burundi, Cameroon, Central African Republic, Chad, Congo, Equatorial Guinea, Gabon, Rwanda, São Tomé and Príncipe, Zaire; Angola has observer status.

Conference of Regions in North-West Europe: POB 107, 8000 Bruges 1, Belgium; f. 1955 to co-ordinate regional studies with a view to planned development in the area around the North Sea and in the Scheldt, Meuse and Rhine valleys; also compiles cartographical documents. Mems: individual scholars and representatives of planning offices in Belgium, France, Germany, Luxembourg, Netherlands and the United Kingdom. Pres. Sir JACK STEWART-CLARKE (UK); Sec.-Gen. Prof. I. B. F. KORMOSS (Belgium).

Council of American Development Foundations—SOLIDARIOS: Calle 6 No. 10 Paraiso, POB 620, Santo Domingo, Dominican Republic; tel. (809) 544-2121; fax (809) 544-0550; f. 1972; exchanges information and experience, arranges technical assistance, raises funds to organize training programmes and scholarships; administers development fund to finance programmes carried out by members through a guarantee programme; provides consultancy services. Member foundations provide technical and financial assistance to low-income groups for rural, housing and handicraft projects. Mems: 28 institutional mems in 14 Latin American and Caribbean countries. Pres. J. MANUEL PITTALUGA; Sec.-Gen. ENRIQUE A. FERNÁNDEZ P. Publs *Solidarios* (quarterly), *Annual Report*.

Economic Community of the Great Lakes Countries (Communauté économique des pays des Grands Lacs—CEPGL): POB 58, Gisenyi, Rwanda; telex 602; f. 1976; main organs: annual Conference of Heads of State, Council of Ministers of Foreign Affairs, Permanent Executive Secretariat, Consultative Commission, three Specialized Technical Commissions. There are four specialized agencies: a development bank, the Banque de Développement des Etats des Grands Lacs (BDEGL) at Goma, Zaire; an energy centre at Bujumbura, Burundi; the Institute of Agronomic and Zootechnical Research, Gitega, Burundi; and a regional electricity company (SINELAC) at Bukavu, Zaire. A five-year plan (1987-91) was adopted in 1986, requiring financing of about US $3.87m. for agricultural, industrial and energy projects. Mems: Burundi, Rwanda, Zaire. Exec. Sec. ANTOINE NDUWAYO (Burundi). Publs *Grands Lacs* (quarterly review), and an annual journal.

Economic Co-operation Organization—ECO: 5 Hejab Ave, Blvd Keshavarz, POB 14155-6176, Teheran, Iran; tel. 658045; telex 213774; f. 1964 (as Regional Co-operation for Development, renamed 1985), a tripartite arrangement aiming at closer co-operation; members aim to co-operate in certain industrial projects and standards, trade, tourism, transport (including the building of road and rail links), communications and cultural affairs. A joint postal organization (the South and West Asia Postal Union) was established in 1988, and a joint Chamber of Commerce and Industry in 1990; the establishment of a preferential tariff arrangement, a joint investment and development bank, a joint reinsurance company and a joint shipping company were under consideration in 1990. Mems: Iran, Pakistan, Turkey. Sec.-Gen. ALI REZA SALARI (Iran).

European Bank for Reconstruction and Development—EBRD: Broadgate, London, EC2, England; f. May 1990 (expected to begin operations early 1991, following ratification of articles by the legislatures of two-thirds of the shareholding countries). Object: to contribute to the progress and economic reconstruction of the countries of central and eastern Europe which undertake to respect and put into practice the principles of multi-party democracy and a market economy. Capital 10,000m. ECUs (of which EEC members, together with the European Commission and the European Investment Bank, hold 51%, central and east European countries 13.5%, the USA 10%, Japan 8.5%). The Bank was to reserve 60% of its lending for the development of the private economy, and 40% for infrastructure; for the first three years of operations, the USSR was not to borrow more than the equivalent of its paid-in capital. Mems: EEC member countries, the European Commission and the European Investment Bank; EFTA member countries; central and east European countries—Bulgaria, Czechoslovakia, Hungary, Poland, Romania, the USSR and Yugoslavia; and other countries—Australia, Canada, Cyprus, Egypt, Israel, Japan, Republic of Korea, Liechtenstein, Malta, Mexico, Morocco, New Zealand, Turkey, USA. Pres. JACQUES ATTALI (France); Sec.-Gen. BART LE BLANC (Netherlands).

Food Aid Committee: c/o International Wheat Council, Haymarket House, 28 Haymarket, London, SW1Y 4SS, England; tel. (071) 930-4128; telex 916128; fax (071) 839-6907; f. 1967; responsible for administration of the Food Aid Convention (1986), a constituent element of the International Wheat Agreement. The 22 donor members are pledged to supply 7.5m. metric tons of grain annually to developing countries, mostly as gifts: in practice aid has exceeded 10m. tons annually. Publ. *Report on shipments* (annually).

Gambia River Basin Development Organization—OMVG: BP 2353, 13 rue Le Blanc, Dakar, Senegal; tel. 22-31-59; f. 1978 by Senegal and The Gambia; Guinea joined in 1981 and Guinea-Bissau in 1983. Plans include the construction of dams on the 1,100-km river at Balingho, The Gambia, and Kekreti, Senegal, to provide irrigation and hydroelectricity, at a cost of about US $400m.; feasibility studies were undertaken in 1984, but by 1990 no progress towards beginning construction of the dams had been reported; maintains documentation centre. High Commissioner MALICK JOHN; Sec.-Gen. NASSIROU DIALLO.

Indian Ocean Commission—IOC: Q4, Ave Sir Guy Forget, BP 7, Quatre Bornes, Mauritius; tel. 425-9564; telex 5273; fax 425-1209; f. 1982 to promote regional co-operation, particularly in economic development; principal projects under way in the late 1980s (at a cost of 4,000m. francs CFA) comprised tuna-fishing development and the development of new and renewable energy systems, with assistance principally from the European Community; tariff reduction is also envisaged. Permanent technical committees cover: tuna-fishing; regional industrial co-operation; regional commerce; air transport; tourism; environment; maritime transport; education, training and culture; labour; sports. The IOC organizes an annual regional trade fair (1991: Mauritius). Mems: Comoros, France (representing the French Overseas Department of Réunion), Madagascar, Mauritius, Seychelles. Sec.-Gen. H. RASOLONDRAIBE. Publ. *Guide Import/Export*.

Inter-American Planning Society (Sociedad Interamericana de Planificación—SIAP): Apdo postal 27-716, 06760 México, DF, Mexico; f. 1956 to promote development of comprehensive planning as a continuous and co-ordinated process at all levels. Mems: 55 institutions and 2,460 individuals in 25 countries. Pres. Arq. HERMES MARROQUÍN (Guatemala); Exec. Sec. LUIS E. CAMACHO (Colombia). Publs *Correo Informativo* (quarterly), *Inter-American Journal of Planning* (quarterly).

Intergovernmental Authority on Drought and Development—IGADD: BP 2653, Djibouti; tel. (253) 354200; telex 5978; f. 1986 by six drought-affected states to co-ordinate measures to combat the effects of drought and desertification; donor countries meeting in March 1987 agreed to provide technical and financial support for 63 projects in the region. Mems: Djibouti, Ethiopia, Kenya, Somalia, Sudan, Uganda. Exec. Sec. MAKONNEN KEBRET (Ethiopia).

International Co-operation for Development and Solidarity—CIDSE: 1-2 ave des Arts, 1040 Brussels, Belgium; tel. (02) 219-00-80; telex 64208; f. 1967 to study the means of rendering more effective the co-operation amongst member organizations in the field of socio-economic development aid; to promote the creation of new organizations in both developed and developing countries, the co-ordination of its members, development aid projects and programmes by means of a computerized central registration of all development projects introduced to the affiliated organizations. Mems: Catholic agencies in 13 countries. Pres. BERNARD HOLZER; Sec.-Gen. PATRICE ROBINEAU.

Lake Chad Basin Commission: BP 727, N'Djamena, Chad; tel. 514137; telex 5251; f. 1964 to encourage co-operation in developing the Lake Chad region and to attract financial and technical assistance for research; the 1986-91 programme emphasizes anti-desertification measures; co-ordinated protection of crops, animals and forestry, and of Lake Chad; and improvements in road and railway links between member countries; proposed operating budget (1988) 455.5m. francs CFA; capital budget 500m. francs CFA. Mems: Cameroon, Chad, Niger, Nigeria. Exec. Sec. ABUBAKAR B. JAURO.

Latin American Association of Development Financing Institutions (Asociación Latinoamericana de Instituciones Financieros de Desarrollo—ALIDE): POB 3988, Lima 100, Peru; tel. 422400; telex 21037; fax 428105; f. 1968 to promote co-operation among regional development financing bodies. Mems: about 170 financing institutions and development organizations in 30 countries. Pres. JESÚS

VILLAMIZAR; Sec.-Gen. CARLOS GARATEA YORI. Publs *Memoria anual, Directorio Latinoamericano de Instituciones Financieras de Desarrollo, Boletín Informativo, ALIDE Noticias.*

Latin American Economic System (Sistema Económico Latinoamericano—SELA): Apdo 17035, El Conde, Caracas 1010, Venezuela; tel. 9514233; telex 23508; f. 1975 by the Panama Convention; aims to accelerate the economic and social development of its members through intra-regional co-operation, and to provide a permanent system of consultation and co-ordination in economic and social matters. The Latin American Council meets annually at ministerial level; there are also Action Committees and a Permanent Secretariat. The following organizations have also been created within SELA:
Trade Information and Foreign Trade Support Programme;
Latin American Tourism Training Institute;
Latin American Housing and Human Settlements Development Organization;
Latin American Multinational Fertilizer Marketing Enterprise;
Latin American Features Agency;
Latin American Fisheries Development Organization;
Latin American Shipping Organization;
Latin American Commission for Science and Technology.
Pres. CARLOS ALZAMORA;
Perm. Sec. CARLOS PÉREZ DE CASTILLO.

Liptako-Gourma Integrated Development Authority: POB 619, ave M. Thevenond, Ouagadougou, Burkina Faso; telex 5247; f. 1972; scope of activities includes water infrastructure, telecommunications and construction of roads and railways; in 1986 undertook study on development of water resources in the basin of the Niger river (for hydroelectricity and irrigation). Budget (1988) 161.4m. francs CFA. Mems: Burkina Faso, Mali, Niger. Sec.-Gen. SILIMANE GANOU (Niger).

Mano River Union: Private Male Bag 133, Freetown, Sierra Leone; tel. 22811; f. 1973 to establish a customs and economic union between member states to improve living standards. A common external tariff was instituted in April 1977. Intra-union free trade was officially introduced in May 1981, as the first stage in progress towards a customs union. An industrial development unit was set up in 1980 to identify projects and encourage investment. Construction of a Freetown-Monrovia road and other road projects was partially completed by 1990. Feasibility studies for a hydroelectric scheme were completed in 1983. Joint institutes have been set up to provide training in posts and telecommunications, forestry, and maritime activities. Decisions are taken at meetings of a joint ministerial cttee formed by the ministers of member states. Mems: Guinea, Liberia, Sierra Leone. Sec.-Gen. Dr ABDOULAYE DIALLO (Guinea).

Niger Basin Authority (Autorité du bassin du Niger): BP 729, Niamey, Niger; f. 1964 (as River Niger Commission; name changed 1980) to harmonize national programmes concerned with the River Niger Basin and to execute an integrated development plan; activities comprise: statistics; navigation regulation; hydrological forecasting; environmental control; infrastructure and agro-pastoral development; and arranging assistance for these projects. Mems: Benin, Burkina Faso, Cameroon, Chad, Côte d'Ivoire, Guinea, Mali, Niger, Nigeria. Exec. Sec. ALIYU MAGAGI (Nigeria). Publ. *Bulletin.*

Organization for the Development of the Senegal River (Organisation pour la Mise en Valeur du Fleuve Sénégal—OMVS): 46 rue Carnot, BP 3152, Dakar, Senegal; tel. 22-36-79; telex 670; f. 1972 to use the Senegal river for hydroelectricity, irrigation and navigation. The Djama dam in Senegal (completed in 1986) provides a barrage to prevent salt water from moving upstream, and the Manantali dam in Mali (completed in 1988) is intended to provide a reservoir for irrigation of about 400,000 ha of land and (eventually) for production of hydroelectricity and provision of year-round navigation for ocean-going vessels. In 1988 the formation of a joint company to manage future projects was announced (capital was to be held 50% by member countries and 50% by the private business sector). Mems: Mali, Mauritania, Senegal; the admission of Guinea was approved in principle by heads of state of the member countries in 1987, but by 1990 it had still not taken effect. High Commr AHMED MOHAMED AG HAMANI (Mali); Sec.-Gen. FOUNÉKÉ KEITA (Mali).

Organization for the Management and Development of the Kagera River Basin (Organisation pour l'aménagement et le développement du bassin de la rivière Kagera): BP 297, Kigali, Rwanda; tel. 84665; telex 0909 22567; f. 1978; joint development and management of resources, including the construction of an 80-MW hydroelectric dam at Rusumo Falls, on the Rwanda-Tanzania border, and a 2,000-km railway network between the four member countries, and a telecommunications network between member states (financed by US $16m. from the African Development Bank). A tsetse-fly control project began in 1990. Budget (1988) $2.3m.

Mems: Burundi, Rwanda, Tanzania, Uganda. Exec. Sec. GRÉGOIRE BANYIYEZAKO.

Pacific Basin Economic Council: Industry House, Barton, ACT 2000, Australia; tel. (06) 2732311; telex 62733; fax (06) 2733106; f. 1967; a businessmen's organization composed of the representatives of business circles of Australia, Chile, Canada, Hong Kong, Japan, Republic of Korea, Mexico, New Zealand, Peru, Taiwan, USA and the countries of the Pacific Basin, which co-operates with government and international institutions in the overall economic development of the Pacific Area and the advancement of the livelihood of the population; promotes economic collaboration among the member countries and co-operates with the developing countries in their effort to achieve self-sustaining economic growth; holds annual International General Meeting. Chair. R. J. FYNMORE (Australia); Dir-Gen. M. J. OVERLAND.

Pacific Economic Co-operation Conference: no permanent secretariat; f. 1980; annual meetings of business representatives, academic staff and government officials, to discuss regional economic matters; standing committee of 17 mems, including mems from the ASEAN states, Australia, Canada, the People's Republic of China, Japan, the Republic of Korea, New Zealand, the Pacific islands, Taiwan and the USA; 1989 Conference held in Wellington, New Zealand (November).

Pan-African Institute for Development—PAID: BP 4056, Douala, Cameroon; tel. 42-10-61; telex 6048; f. 1964 to train rural development officers from Africa at intermediate and senior levels; emphasis in education is given to: women in development; promotion of small and medium-sized enterprises; involvement of local populations in development; staff training for national centres; preparation of projects for regional co-operation; consultation, applied research, local project support and specialized training. There are four regional institutes: Central Africa (Douala), Sahel (Ouagadougou, Burkina Faso) (French-speaking), West Africa (Buéa, Cameroon), Eastern and Southern Africa (Kabwe, Zambia) (English-speaking). Sec.-Gen. Prof. A. C. MONDJANAGNI. Publs *Newsletter* (3 a year), *PAID Report* (2 a year).

Pan American Development Foundation—PADF: 1889 F St, NW, Washington, DC 20006, USA; tel. (202) 458-3969; telex 64128; fax (202) 458-6316; f. 1962 to support development activities in Latin America and the Caribbean through providing low-interest credit for small-scale entrepreneurs, vocational training, improved health care, agricultural development and reforestation, and to strengthen the ability of the private sector in the region to participate in development activities; provides emergency disaster relief and reconstruction assistance. Chair. JOÃO CLEMENTE BAENA SOARES; Pres. J. JOHN JOVA; Exec. Dir MARVIN WEISSMAN. Publ. *PADF Newsletter* (2 a year).

Permanent Inter-State Committee on Drought Control in the Sahel—CILSS: POB 7049, Ouagadougou, Burkina Faso; f. 1973; works in co-operation with UN Sudano-Sahelian Office (UNSO, q.v.); aims to combat the effects of chronic drought in the Sahel region (where the deficit in grain production was estimated at 1.7m. metric tons for 1988), by improving irrigation and food production, halting deforestation and creating food reserves. Budget (1990): 489m. francs CFA. Mems: Burkina Faso, Cape Verde, Chad, The Gambia, Guinea-Bissau, Mali, Mauritania, Niger, Senegal. Exec. Sec. ALI DIARD DJALBORD (Chad).

Population Council: 1 Dag Hammarskjöld Plaza, New York, NY 10017, USA; tel. (212) 644-1300; telex 234722; fax (212) 755-6052; f. 1952; social and health science programmes and research relevant to developing countries, and conducts biomedical research to develop and improve contraceptive technology; provides advice and technical assistance; disseminates information and publications. Five regional offices, in Indonesia, Mexico, Egypt, Kenya and Senegal. Chair. MCGEORGE BUNDY; Pres. GEORGE ZEIDENSTEIN. Publs *Studies in Family Planning* (every 2 months), *Population and Development Review* (quarterly).

Preferential Trade Area for Eastern and Southern African States—PTA: POB 30051, Lusaka, Zambia; tel. 229725; telex 40127; f. 1981 with the aim of improving commercial and economic co-operation in the region, and transforming the structure of production of national economies in the region; promotes regional trade and the creation of institutional mechanisms, including monetary arrangements, for facilitating trade; supports inter-country co-operation in the rationalization of existing national excess capacity and high-cost industries, and the development of basic and strategic industries; promotes co-operation in agricultural development and improvement of transport links, and the development of technical and professional skills. The Reserve Bank of Zimbabwe operates a clearing house (f. 1984) for transactions for goods and services within the PTA, enabling member states to conduct multilateral trade in their own currencies. From July 1984 tariff reductions (of between 10% and 70%) were introduced for selected commodities, and in 1987 it was announced that further reductions

OTHER INTERNATIONAL ORGANIZATIONS

(of 10% every two years) were to be made for these commodities. PTA travellers' cheques, denominated in the PTA unit of account (UAPTA, equal to one IMF Special Drawing Right), were introduced in 1988. A PTA Trade and Development Bank, based in Bujumbura, Burundi, became operational in 1986, with an authorized share capital of UAPTA 400m. The PTA Federation of Chambers of Commerce and Industry, the Association of PTA Commercial Banks, and the PTA Centre for Commercial Arbitration, were also formed. A Regional Investment Projects Forum was organized in 1990. Mems: Angola, Burundi, the Comoros, Djibouti, Ethiopia, Kenya, Lesotho, Malawi, Mauritius, Mozambique, Namibia, Rwanda, Somalia, Sudan, Swaziland, Tanzania, Zaire, Zambia, Zimbabwe. Sec.-Gen. BINGU WA MUTHARIKA (Malawi).

Society for International Development: Palazzo Civiltà del Lavoro, EUR, 00144 Rome, Italy; tel. (06) 5917897; telex 616484; fax (06) 5919836; f. 1957 to provide a forum for an exchange of ideas, facts and experience among persons concerned with the problems of economic and social development in both developed and developing countries. Mems: 10,000 (90 brs in 132 countries). Pres. ENRIQUE IGLESIAS; Sec.-Gen. MAURICE WILLIAMS; Exec. Dir ROBERT CASSANI. Publs *Development* (quarterly), *Compass* (quarterly).

South Asian Association for Regional Co-operation—SAARC: GPO Box 4222, Kathmandu, Nepal; tel. 221785; telex 2561; fax 227033; f. 1985 by the leaders of seven South Asian nations, to accelerate economic growth, social progress and cultural development, and to strengthen collective self-reliance. There are 12 agreed areas of co-operation: agriculture and forestry; education; health and population; meteorology; rural development; telecommunications; transport; science and technology; postal services; sports, arts and culture; women in development; prevention of drugs-trafficking and drug abuse. Other schemes include the SAARC Audio Visual Exchange Programme, SAARC Documentation Centre, SAARC fellowships and scholarships, a youth volunteers' programme and organized tourism. A regional convention on the suppression of terrorism, and an agreement on establishing a food security reserve, were signed in 1987. Studies were conducted in 1988–90 on natural disasters, protection of the environment, intra-regional trade expansion, and joint ventures in agriculture, industry and energy. The SAARC charter stipulates that decisions should be made unanimously, and that 'bilateral and contentious issues' should not be discussed; meetings of heads of governments are held annually, and ministers of foreign affairs meet at least twice a year. Mems: Bangladesh, Bhutan, India, Maldives, Nepal, Pakistan, Sri Lanka. Sec.-Gen. K. K. BHARGAVA (India).

South Commission: CP 228, 1211 Geneva 19, Switzerland; f. 1987 by the summit meeting of the Non-aligned Movement, to conduct studies on development issues and to promote self-reliant development and improved South-North relations. Chair. Dr JULIUS NYERERE.

Union of the Arab Maghreb: Quartier administratif, Rabat, Morocco (secretariat to change annually, according to the chairmanship of the Union); f. 1989; aims to encourage joint ventures and to create a single market; structure comprises a council of heads of state (meeting twice a year), a council of ministers of foreign affairs, a consultative council of 10 delegates from each national legislature, and a court with 2 judges from each country; chairmanship rotates every six months between heads of state. By mid-1990 joint projects that had been approved or were under consideration included: creation of a free market in energy products; free movement of citizens within the region; joint transport undertakings, including a joint airline (eventually integrating existing airlines) and road and railway improvements; formation of a Maghreb union of textile and leather industries; and the creation (by 1995) of a customs union. Mems: Algeria, Libya, Mauritania, Morocco, Tunisia.

Vienna Institute for Development and Co-operation (Wiener Institut für Entwicklungsfragen und Zusammenarbeit): 1010 Vienna, Austria; tel. (01) 713-35-94; f. 1987 (fmrly Vienna Institute for Development, f. 1964); disseminates information on the problems and achievements of developing countries; encourages increased aid-giving and international co-operation; conducts research. Pres. FRANZ VRANITZKY; Dir ERICH ANDRLIK.

World University Service—WUS: 5 chemin des Iris, 1216 Geneva, Switzerland; tel. (022) 7988711; telex 415537; fax (022) 7980829; f. 1920; links students, faculty and administrators in post-secondary institutions concerned with economic and social development, and seeks to protect their academic freedom and autonomy; seeks to extend technical, personal and financial resources of post-secondary institutions to under-developed areas and communities; provides scholarships at university level for refugees from South Africa and Latin America and supports informal education projects for women in these areas; the principle is to assist people to improve and develop their own communities. WUS is independent and is

Aid, Development etc., Arts and Culture

governed by an assembly of national committees. Pres. HUGO MIRANDA (Chile); Gen. Sec. NIGEL HARTLEY (UK). Publs *WUS Activities, WUS and Human Rights* (quarterly).

Arts and Culture

Europa Nostra: Lange Voorhout 35, 2514 EC The Hague, Netherlands; tel. (070) 3560333; fax (070) 3617865; f. 1963; an international federation of non-governmental associations for the protection of Europe's natural and cultural heritage; has consultative status with the Council of Europe. Mems: c. 200 associations; associated corporate membership open to all European local authorities. Pres. HRH The Prince Consort of Denmark; Chair. HENRI J. DE KOSTER (Netherlands); Hon. Sec.-Gen. Dr MAURICE LINDSAY (UK).

European Association of Conservatoires, Music Academies and Music High Schools: Kramgasse 36, 3011 Berne, Switzerland; tel. (031) 226221; fax (031) 212053; f. 1953 to establish and foster contacts and exchanges between members. Mems: 100. Sec.-Gen. URS FRAUCHIGER.

European Cultural Centre (Centre Européen de la Culture): Villa Moynier, 122 rue de Lausanne, 1211 Geneva 21, Switzerland; tel. (022) 7322803; telex 412585; fax (022) 7384012; f. 1950 to contribute to the union of Europe by encouraging cultural pursuits, providing a meeting place, and conducting research in the various fields of European Studies; holds conferences on European subjects, European documentation and archives. Groups the Secretariats of the European Association of Music Festivals and the Association of Institutes of European Studies. Pres. JACQUES FREYMOND (Switzerland); Sec.-Gen. GÉRARD DE PUYMÈGE (France). Publ. *Cadmos* (quarterly), *Newsletter* (2 a year).

European Society of Culture: Dorsoduro 909 (Zattere ai Gesuati/Campo Sant'Agnese), 30123 Venice, Italy; tel. (041) 5230210; fax (041) 5231033; f. 1950 to unite artists, poets, scientists, philosophers and others through mutual interests and friendship in order to safeguard and improve the conditions required for creative activity; library of 10,000 volumes. Mems: 2,000. Pres. Prof. VINCENZO CAPPELLETTI (Italy); Gen. Sec. Dott. MICHELLE CAMPAGNOLO-BOUVIER.

Inter-American Music Council (Consejo Interamericano de Musica—CIDEM): 1889 F St, NW, 230-C, Washington, DC 20006, USA; tel. (202) 458-3158; telex 64128; fax (202) 458-3967; f. 1956 to promote the exchange of works, performances and information in all fields of music, to study problems relative to music education, to encourage activity in the field of musicology, to promote folklore research and music creation, to establish distribution centres for music material of the composers of the Americas, etc. Mems: national music societies of 32 American countries. Sec.-Gen. EFRAIN PAESKY.

Interfilm (International Interchurch Film Centre): POB 515, 1200 AM Hilversum, Netherlands; tel. (035) 17645; f. 1955 to promote film criticism and film education; ecumenical, associated with the World Council of Churches; makes awards and recommendations at international film festivals, holds study conferences. Mems: organizations in 40 countries. Pres. Dr AMAL DIBO (Lebanon); Gen. Sec. Dr JAN HES (Netherlands). Publ. *Interfilm Information* (quarterly).

International Association of Art (Painting-Sculpture-Graphic Art) (Association internationale des arts plastiques—Peinture, Sculpture, Arts Graphiques): Maison de l'UNESCO, 1 rue Miollis, 75015 Paris, France; tel. (1) 45-68-26-55; fax (1) 45-67-59-76; f. 1954. Mems: 81 national committees. Pres. EDUARDO ARENILLAS; Sec.-Gen. LILA SKARVELI.

International Association of Art Critics: 9 rue Berryer, 75008 Paris, France; tel. (1) 42-56-17-53; fax (1) 42-56-08-42; f. 1949 to increase co-operation in plastic arts, promote international cultural exchanges and protect the interests of members. Mems: 3,000, in 55 countries. Pres. JACQUES LEENHARDT (France); Sec.-Gen. LÉONE DE LA GRANDVILLE.

International Association of Bibliophiles: Bibliothèque nationale, 58 rue Richelieu, 75084 Paris Cedex 02, France; fax (1) 42-96-84-47; f. 1963 to create contacts between bibliophiles and to encourage book-collecting in different countries; to organize or encourage congresses, meetings, exhibitions, the award of scholarships, the publication of a bulletin, yearbooks, and works of reference or bibliography. Mems: 500. Pres. ANTHONY R. A. HOBSON (UK); Sec.-Gen. ANTOINE CORON (France). Publ. *Le Bulletin du Bibliophile*.

International Association of Literary Critics: 38 rue du Faubourg St-Jacques, 75014 Paris, France; tel. (1) 43-54-18-66; telex 206963; f. 1969; organizes congresses. Pres. ROBERT ANDRÉ. Publ. *Revue* (2 a year).

International Association of Museums of Arms and Military History—IAMAM: Bayerisches Armeemuseum, 8070 Ingolstadt, Neues Schloss, Paradeplatz 4, Germany; tel. (0841) 35067; f. 1957;

OTHER INTERNATIONAL ORGANIZATIONS

Arts and Culture

links museums and other scientific institutions with public collections of arms and armour and military equipment, uniforms, etc.; triennial conferences and occasional specialist symposia. Mems: 252 institutions in 50 countries. Pres. BENGT HOLMQUIST (Sweden); Sec.-Gen. Dr ERNST AICHNER (Germany). Publs *Repertory of Museums of Arms and Military History, Triennial Report, Glossarium Armorum*, reports on symposia.

International Board on Books for Young People—IBBY: Nonnenweg 12, Postfach, 4003 Basel, Switzerland; tel. (061) 232917; fax (061) 232757; f. 1953 to support and link bodies in all countries connected with children's book work; to encourage the distribution of good children's books; to promote scientific investigation into problems of juvenile books; to organize educational aid for developing countries; presents the Hans Christian Andersen Award every two years to a living author and a living illustrator whose work is an outstanding contribution to juvenile literature, and the IBBY-Ashai Reading Promotion Award annually to an organization which has made a significant contribution to children's literature; sponsors International Children's Book Day (2 April). Mems: national sections and individuals in 60 countries. Pres. Dr RONALD JOBE (Canada); Sec. LEENA MAISSEN. Publs *Bookbird* (quarterly, in English), *Congress Papers, IBBY Honour List* (every 2 years); special bibliographies.

International Centre for the Study of the Preservation and Restoration of Cultural Property—ICCROM: Via di San Michele 13, 00153 Rome, Italy; tel. 580 9021; telex 613114; f. 1959; assembles documents on preservation and restoration of cultural property; stimulates research and proffers advice in this domain; organizes missions of experts; undertakes training of specialists and organizes regular courses on (i) Architectural Conservation; (ii) Conservation of Mural Paintings; (iii) Scientific Principles of Conservation; (iv) Preventive Conservation in Museums; (v) Conservation of Paper. Mems: 79 countries. Dir Prof. ANDRZEJ TOMASZEWSKI. Publ. *Newsletter* (annually, English and French).

International Centre of Films for Children and Young People—ICFCYP: 9 rue Bargue, 75015 Paris, France; tel. (1) 40-56-00-67; f. 1957; a clearing house of information about: entertainment films (cinema and television) for children and young people, influence of films on the young, and regulations in force for the protection and education of young people; promotes production and distribution of suitable films and their appreciation; to this end it encourages the setting up of National Centres. Mems: 33 full mems (National Centres), 23 associated organizations. Pres. PREDRAG GOLUBOVIĆ (Yugoslavia); Dir MONIQUE GRÉGOIRE. Publ. *Young Cinema International*.

International Committee for the Diffusion of Arts and Literature through the Cinema (Comité international pour la diffusion des arts et des lettres par le cinéma—CIDALC): 24 blvd Poissonnière, 75009 Paris, France; tel. (1) 42-46-65-36; f. 1930 to promote the creation and release of educational, cultural and documentary films and other films of educational value in order to contribute to closer understanding between peoples; awards medals and prizes for films of exceptional merit. Mems: national committees in 25 countries. Pres. JEAN-PIERRE FOUCAULT (France); Sec.-Gen. MARIO VERDONE (Italy). Publ. *Annuaire CIDALC*.

International Comparative Literature Association: c/o L. Metzger, Dept of English, Emory University, Atlanta, Ga 30322, USA; f. 1954 to work for the development of the comparative study of literature in modern languages. Member societies and individuals in 58 countries. Sec. LORE METZGER. Publ. *ICLA Bulletin*.

International Confederation of Societies of Authors and Composers—World Congress of Authors and Composers: 11 rue Keppler, 75116 Paris, France; tel. (1) 45-53-59-37; f. 1926 to protect the rights of authors and composers; documentation centre. Mems: 99 member societies from 49 countries. Pres. EDGAR FAURE (France); Sec.-Gen. JEAN-ALEXIS ZIEGLER.

International Council of Graphic Design Associations: POB 398, London, W11 4UG, England; tel. (071) 603-8494; fax (071) 371-6040; f. 1963; aims to raise standards of graphic design, to exchange information, and to organize exhibitions and congresses. Mems: 54 associations in 35 countries. Pres. HELMUT LANGER (Germany); Sec.-Gen. MARY MULLIN. Publs *Newsletter* (quarterly), *Graphic Design World Views*.

International Council of Museums—ICOM: Maison de l'UNESCO, 1 rue Miollis, 75732 Paris Cedex 15, France; tel. (1) 47-34-05-00; telex 270602; fax (1) 43-06-78-62; f. 1946 to further international co-operation among museums and to advance museum interests; maintains with UNESCO the most extensive museum documentation centre in the world. Mems: 9,000 individuals and institutions from 119 countries. Pres. A. O. KONARE (Mali); Sec.-Gen. P. CARDON (USA). Publ. *ICOM News Nouvelles de l'ICOM* (quarterly).

International Council on Monuments and Sites—ICOMOS: 75 rue du Temple, 75003 Paris, France; tel. (1) 42-77-35-76; telex 240918; fax (1) 42-77-57-42; f. 1965 to promote the study and preservation of monuments and sites; to arouse and cultivate the interest of public authorities, and people of every country in their monuments and sites and in their cultural heritage; to liaise between public authorities, departments, institutions and individuals interested in the preservation and study of monuments and sites; to disseminate the results of research into the problems, technical, social and administrative, connected with the conservation of the architectural heritage, and of centres of historic interest; holds triennial General Assembly and Symposium. Mems: 3,500; 13 International Committees, 66 National Committees. Pres. ROBERTO DI STEFANO (Italy); Sec.-Gen. HELMUT STELZER (Germany). Publ. *ICOMOS Information* (quarterly).

International Federation for Theatre Research: 14 Woronzow Rd, London, NW8 6QE, England; f. 1955 by 21 countries at the International Conference on Theatre History, London. Chair. Prof. W. GREISENEGGER; Joint Secs-Gen. Prof. J.-C. GODIN, Prof. MICHAEL J. ANDERSON, Publs *Theatre Research International* (in association with Oxford University Press) (3 a year), *Bulletin* (3 a year).

International Federation of Film Archives: c/o B. van der Elst, 70 Coudenberg, 1000 Brussels, Belgium; tel. (02) 511-13-90; telex 26146; fax (02) 514-58-10; f. 1938 to encourage the creation of archives in all countries for the collection and conservation of the film heritage of each land; to facilitate co-operation and exchanges between these film archives; to promote public interest in the art of the cinema; to aid research in this field and to compile new documentation; conducts research; publishes manuals, etc.; holds annual congresses. Mems in 57 countries. Pres. ROBERT DAUDELIN (Canada); Sec.-Gen. EVA ORBANZ (Germany).

International Federation of Film Producers' Associations: 33 ave des Champs-Elysées, 75008 Paris, France; tel. (1) 42-25-62-14; fax (1) 42-56-16-52; f. 1933 to represent film production internationally, to defend its general interests and promote its development, to study all cultural, legal, economic, technical and social problems of interest to the activity of film production. Mems: national associations in 21 countries. Pres. FRANCO CRISTALDI (Italy); Sec.-Gen. ANDRÉ CHAUBEAU (France).

International Institute for Children's Literature and Reading Research (Internationales Institut für Jugendliteratur und Leseforschung): 1040 Vienna, Mayerhofgasse 6, Austria; tel. (01) 65-03-59; f. 1965 as an international documentation, research and advisory centre of juvenile literature and reading; maintains specialized library; arranges conferences and exhibitions; compiles recommendation lists. Mems: individual and group members in 28 countries. Pres. Dr HERMANN LEIN; Dir Dr LUCIA BINDER. Publs *Bookbird* (quarterly in co-operation with the International Board on Books for Young People), *1000 & 1 Buch* (6 a year in co-operation with the Austrian Ministry of Education, *Schriften zur Jugendlektüre, PA-Kontakte* (published irregularly).

International Institute for Conservation of Historic and Artistic Works: 6 Buckingham St., London, WC2N 6BA, England; tel. (071) 839-5975; fax (071) 976-1564; f. 1950. Mems: 3,350 individual, 450 institutional members. Pres. Prof. E. T. HALL; Sec.-Gen. Prof. H. W. M. HODGES. Publs *Studies in Conservation* (quarterly), *Art and Archaeology Technical Abstracts—IIC* (2 a year).

International Liaison Centre for Cinema and Television Schools (Centre international de liaison des écoles de cinéma et de télévision): 8 rue Thérésienne, 1000 Brussels, Belgium; tel. (02) 511-98-39; fax (02) 511-02-79; f. 1955 to co-ordinate teaching standards and to develop plans for creation of cultural, artistic, teaching and technical relations between mems. Pres. COLIN YOUNG (UK); Sec.-Gen. RAYMOND RAVAR (Belgium).

International Music Council—IMC: Maison de l'UNESCO, 1 rue Miollis, 75732 Paris Cedex 15, France; tel. (1) 45-68-25-50; fax (1) 43-06-87-98; f. 1949 to foster the exchange of musicians, music (written and recorded), and information between countries and cultures; to support contemporary composers and young professional musicians. Mems: 23 international non-governmental organizations, national committees in 65 countries. Pres. LUPWISHI MBUYAMBA (Zaire); Sec.-Gen. CAMILLE SWINNEN (Belgium); Exec. Sec. GUY HUOT.

Members of IMC include:

European Association of Music Festivals: 122 rue de Lausanne, 1211 Geneva 21, Switzerland; tel. (022) 7322803; telex 412585; fax (022) 7384012; f. 1951; aims to maintain high artistic standards and the representative character of music festivals; holds annual General Assembly. Mems: 53 regularly-held music festivals in 23 European countries, Israel and Japan. Pres. FRANS DE RUITER. Publs *Season* (annually), *Festivals* (annually).

International Association of Music Libraries, Archives and Documentation Centres—IAML: Svenskt Musikhistoriskt

Arkiv, Box 16326, 10326 Stockholm, Sweden; tel. (8) 11-91-92; f. 1951. Mems: 1,830 institutions and individuals in 41 countries. Pres. CATHERINE MASSIP (France); Sec.-Gen. V. HEINTZ (Sweden). Publ. *Fontes artis musicae* (every 4 months).

International Council for Traditional Music: Dept of Music, Columbia University, New York, NY 10027; tel. (212) 678-0332; telex 220094; f. 1947 (as International Folk Music Council) to further the study, practice, documentation, preservation and dissemination of traditional music of all countries; conferences held every two years. Mems: 1,200. Pres. Dr ERICH STOCKMANN (Germany); Sec.-Gen. Prof. DIETER CHRISTENSEN (USA). Publs *Yearbook for Traditional Music, Bulletin* (2 a year), *Directory of Traditional Music* (every 2 years).

International Federation of 'Jeunesses Musicales': Palais des Beaux-Arts, 10 rue Royale, 1000 Brussels, Belgium; tel. (02) 513-97-74; telex 61825; f. 1945 to promote the development of musical appreciation among young people, to encourage the creation of new societies and to ensure co-operation between national societies. Mems: organizations in 40 countries. Sec.-Gen. ALEXANDER SCHISCHLIK.

International Federation of Musicians: Hofackerstrasse 7, 8032 Zürich, Switzerland; tel. (01) 556611; fax (01) 556502; f. 1948 to promote and protect the interests of musicians in affiliated unions; promotes international exchange of musicians. Mems: 37 unions totalling 293,687 individuals in 31 countries. Pres. JOHN MORTON (UK); Gen. Sec. YVONNE BURCKHARDT (Switzerland).

International Institute for Comparative Music Studies and Documentation (Internationales Institut für Vergleichende Musikstudien und Dokumentation): 1000 Berlin 33, Winklerstrasse 20, Germany; tel. (030) 8262853; telex 182875; fax (030) 8259991; f. 1963 to promote traditional folk music and non-European traditional music, by maintaining archives and encouraging the exchange of performers and scholars. Mems from 13 countries. Dir MAX PETER BAUMANN. Publs *The World of Music* (3 a year), *Intercultural Music Studies* (book series), *Traditional Music of the World* (record series).

International Jazz Federation: Borupvej 66, 4683 Ronnede, Denmark; f. 1969 to promote the knowledge and appreciation of jazz throughout the world; arranges jazz education conferences and competitions for young jazz groups; encourages co-operation among national societies. Mems: 16 national organizations. Pres. ARNVID MEYER (Denmark). Publ. *Jazz Forum* (6 a year).

International Music Centre (Internationales Musikzentrum—IMZ): 1030 Vienna, Lothringerstr. 20, Austria; tel. (01) 713-07-77; telex 753-11745; fax (01) 713-07-7717; f. 1961 for the study and dissemination of music through the technical media (film, television, radio, gramophone); co-operates with other international organizations such as EBU and OIRT; organizes congresses, seminars and screenings on music in the audio-visual media; courses and competitions to strengthen the relationship between performing artists and the audio-visual media. Mems: 110 ordinary mems and 30 associate mems in 33 countries, including 50 broadcasting organizations. Pres. DENNIS MARKS (UK); Sec.-Gen. WILFRIED SCHEIB (Austria); Exec. Dir ERIC MARINITSCH. Publ. *Music in the Media* (10 a year in English, French and German).

International Society for Contemporary Music: c/o Swedish National Radio, RH7C, 105 10 Stockholm, Sweden; tel. (8) 784-18-01; telex 10000; fax (8) 661-80-25; f. 1922 to promote the development of contemporary music and to organize annual World Music Days. Member organizations in 34 countries. Pres. ZYGMUNT KRAUZE (Poland); Sec.-Gen. TRYGVE NORDWALL.

World Federation of International Music Competitions: 104 rue de Carouge, 1205 Geneva, Switzerland; tel. (022) 213620; f. 1957 to co-ordinate the arrangements for affiliated competitions, to exchange experience, etc.; a General Assembly is held every April. Mems: 88. Pres. ROBERT DUNAND; Sec.-Gen. JACQUES HALDENWANG.

International PEÑ (A World Association of Writers): 38 King St, London, WC2E 8JT, England; tel. (071) 379-7939; f. 1921 to promote co-operation between writers. There are 101 centres throughout the world, with total membership about 12,000. International Pres. GYÖRGY KONRÁD; International Sec. ALEXANDRE BLOKH. Publ. *PEN International* (in English and French, with the assistance of UNESCO).

International Theatre Institute—ITI: Maison de l'UNESCO, 1 rue Miollis, 75015 Paris, France; tel. (1) 45-68-26-50; fax (1) 43-06-87-98; f. 1948 to facilitate cultural exchanges and international understanding in the domain of the theatre; conferences, publications, etc. Mems: 77 member nations, each with an ITI national centre. Pres. MARTHA COIGNEY (USA); Sec.-Gen. ANDRÉ-LOUIS PERINETTI.

International Typographic Association: 4142 Münchenstein, Gutenbergstrasse 1, Switzerland; tel. (061) 468820; f. 1957 to co-ordinate the ideas of those whose profession or interests have to do with the art of typography and to obtain effective international legislation to protect type designs. Mems: 400. Pres. MARTIN FEHLE.

Royal Asiatic Society of Great Britain and Ireland: 60 Queen's Gardens, London, W2; f. 1823 for the study of history and cultures of the East. Mems: c. 1,000, branch societies in Asia. Dir R. H. PINDER WILSON; Sec. L. COLLINS. Publ. *Journal* (3 a year).

Society of African Culture: 64 rue Carnot, Dakar, Senegal; tel. 24-10-31; f. 1956 to create unity and friendship among scholars in Africa for the encouragement of their own cultures. Mems: from 45 countries. Pres. AIMÉ CÉSAIRE; Sec.-Gen. CHRISTIANE YANDÉ DIOP. Publ. *Présence Africaine* (quarterly).

United Towns Organization: 22 rue d'Alsace, 92300 Levallois-Perret, France; tel. (1) 47-39-36-86; telex 610472; fax (1) 47-39-36-85; f. 1957 by Le Monde Bilingue (f. 1951); since 1960 has specialized in twinning towns in developed areas with those in less developed areas; aims to set up permanent links between towns throughout the world, leading to social, cultural, economic and other exchanges favouring world peace, understanding and development; encourages the spread of bilingualism. Mems: 3,500 towns throughout the world. World Pres. PIERRE MAUROY; Sec.-Gen. HUBERT LESIRE-OGREL. Publs *Cités Unies* (quarterly, French, English and Spanish), *United Towns Newsletter* (quarterly, English), *Cités Unies Informations* (monthly), *Notiziario* (quarterly), *Mitteilungsblatt* (quarterly), quarterly newsletter in Arabic, *Index of International Relations of Towns of World*.

World Crafts Council: POB 2045, 1012 Copenhagen K, Denmark; tel. (01) 46-10-60; telex 16600; f. 1964; aims to strengthen the status of crafts as a vital part of cultural life, to link craftsmen around the world, and to foster wider recognition of their work. Mems: national organizations in more than 80 countries. Pres. ANDERS CLASON (Sweden); Sec.-Gen. JOHN VEDEL-RIEPER (Denmark). Publs *Annual Report, Craft International Newsletter* (quarterly), *Craft Reports from All Around the World* (annually).

World Union of French Speakers (Union mondiale des voix françaises): BP 56-05, 75222 Paris Cedex 05, France; f. 1960; cultural exchange in the French language by records, tape recordings, etc. Mems: 1,000. Pres. B. LABONDE; Sec.-Gen. P. ROBERT. Publ. *Via Vox Contact*.

Commodities

African Groundnut Council: Trade Fair Complex, Badagry Expressway Km 15, POB 3025, Lagos, Nigeria; tel. 880982; telex 21366; f. 1964 to advise producing countries on marketing policies. Mems: The Gambia, Mali, Niger, Nigeria, Senegal, Sudan. Chair. CHEICK HAMIDOU KANE (Senegal); Exec. Sec. Elhadj MOUR MAMADOU SAMB (Senegal).

African Petroleum Producers' Association: Brazzaville, Congo; f. 1986 by African petroleum-producing countries to reinforce co-operation among regional producers and to stabilize prices. Mems: Algeria, Angola, Benin, Cameroon, Congo, Côte d'Ivoire, Egypt, Gabon, Libya, Nigeria, Zaire. Exec. Sec. MOHAMMED SOUIDI (Algeria).

Asian and Pacific Coconut Community: POB 1343, 3rd Floor, Wisma Bakrie Bldg, Jalan H. R. Rasuna Said Kav. Bl., Kuningan, Jak-Selatan 10002, Indonesia; tel. 510073; telex 62863; fax 510073; f. 1969 to promote, co-ordinate, and harmonize all activities of the coconut industry towards better production, processing, marketing and research. Mems: Fiji, India, Indonesia, Malaysia, Federated States of Micronesia, Papua New Guinea, Philippines, Solomon Islands, Sri Lanka, Thailand, Vanuatu, Viet-Nam, Western Samoa; assoc. mem.: Palau. Exec. Dir P. G. PUNCHIHEWA. Publs *COCOMUNITY* (every 2 weeks, with quarterly supplement), *CORD* (2 a year), *Statistical Yearbook, Directory of Coconut Products Exporters.*

Association of Iron Ore Exporting Countries—APEF: Le Château, 14 chemin Auguste Vilbert, 1218 Grand Saconnex, Geneva, Switzerland; tel. (022) 982955; telex 289443; f. 1975 to collect and disseminate information on iron ore. Mems: nine countries. Sec.-Gen. L. ROIGART.

Association of Natural Rubber Producing Countries—ANRPC: Natural Rubber Bldg, 148 Jalan Ampang, 50450 Kuala Lumpur, Malaysia; tel. 2611900; fax 2613014; f. 1970 to co-ordinate the production and marketing of natural rubber, to promote technical co-operation amongst members and to bring about fair and stable prices for natural rubber. A joint regional marketing system has been agreed in principle. Seminars, meetings and training courses on technical and statistical subjects are held. Mems: India, Indonesia, Malaysia, Papua New Guinea, Singapore, Sri Lanka, Thailand. Sec.-Gen. Dr ABDUL MADJID. Publs *Quarterly Statistical Bulletin, ANRPC News.*

OTHER INTERNATIONAL ORGANIZATIONS
Commodities

Association of Tin Producing Countries (ATPC): Menara Dayabumi, 4th Floor, Jalan Sultan Hishamuddin, 50050 Kuala Lumpur, Malaysia; tel. (03) 2747620; telex 32721; fax (03) 2740669; f. 1983; promotes co-operation in marketing of tin, supports research, compiles and analyses data. Mems: Australia, Bolivia, Indonesia, Malaysia, Nigeria, Thailand, Zaire. Observer: Brazil. Sec.-Gen. REDZWAN SUMUN (Malaysia).

Cadmium Association: 42 Weymouth St, London, W1N 3LQ, England; tel. (071) 499-8425; telex 261286; fax (071) 493-1555; f. 1976; covers all aspects of the production and use of cadmium and its compounds; includes almost all producers and users of cadmium outside the USA. Chair. N. D. HOYLE (UK); Dir M. E. COOK (UK).

Cocoa Producers' Alliance: POB 1718, Western House, 8–10 Broad St, Lagos, Nigeria; tel. 635506; f. 1962 to exchange technical and scientific information; to discuss problems of mutual concern to producers; to ensure adequate supplies at remunerative prices; to promote consumption. Mems: Brazil, Cameroon, Côte d'Ivoire, Dominican Republic, Ecuador, Gabon, Ghana, Malaysia, Mexico, Nigeria, São Tomé and Príncipe, Togo, Trinidad and Tobago. Sec.-Gen. DJEUMO SILAS KAMGA.

European Aluminium Association: 4000 Dusseldorf 1, Königsallee 30, POB 1207, Germany; tel. (0211) 80871; telex 8587407; fax (0211) 324098; f. 1981 to encourage studies, research and technical co-operation, to make representations to international bodies and to assist national associations in dealing with national authorities. Mems: individual producers of primary aluminium, 15 national groups for wrought producers, the Organization of European Aluminium Smelters, representing producers of secondary aluminium and the European Aluminium Foil Association, representing foil rollers and converters. Chair. J. SCHIRNER; Sec.-Gen. H. SEEBAUER.

European Association for the Trade in Jute and Related Products: Adriaan Goekooplaan 5, 2517 JX The Hague, Netherlands; tel. (070) 354-68-11; fax (070) 351-27-77; f. 1970 to maintain contacts between national associations and carry out scientific research; to exchange information and to represent the interests of the trade. Mems: enterprises in Belgium, Denmark, France, Germany, Netherlands, Spain, Switzerland, United Kingdom. Sec.-Gen. L. ANTONINI (Netherlands).

European Committee of Sugar Manufacturers: 45 ave Montaigne, 75008 Paris, France; tel. (1) 47-23-68-25; telex 280401; f. 1954 to collect statistics and information, conduct research and promote co-operation between national organizations. Mems: national associations in Austria, Belgium, Denmark, Finland, France, Germany, Greece, Ireland, Italy, Netherlands, Spain, Sweden, Switzerland, United Kingdom. Pres. O. ADRIAENSEN; Dir-Gen. M. DE LA FOREST DIVONNE.

Group of Latin American and Caribbean Sugar Exporting Countries—GEPLACEA: Ejército Nacional 373, 1°, 11520 México DF, Mexico; tel. 250-75-66; telex 01771042; fax 250-7591; f. 1974 to serve as a forum of consultation on the production and sale of sugar; to contribute to the adoption of agreed positions at international meetings on sugar; to provide training and the transfer of technology; to exchange scientific and technical knowledge on agriculture and the sugar industry; to co-ordinate the various branches of sugar processing; to co-ordinate policies of action in order to achieve fair and remunerative prices. Mems: 22 Latin American and Caribbean countries and the Philippines (accounting for about 45% of world sugar exports and 66% of world cane sugar production). Exec. Sec. JOSÉ ANTONIO CERRO.

Inter-African Coffee Organization—IACO: BP V210, Abidjan, Côte d'Ivoire; tel. 21-61-31; telex 22406; f. 1960. Mems: 25 coffee-producing countries in Africa. Pres. FILOMENO CEITA (Angola); Sec.-Gen. AREGA WORKU (Ethiopia). Publs *African Coffee* (quarterly), *Directory of African Exporters* (every 2 years).

Intergovernmental Council of Copper Exporting Countries (Conseil intergouvernemental des pays exportateurs de cuivre—CIPEC): 39 rue de la Bienfaisance, 75008 Paris, France; tel. (1) 42-25-00-24; telex 649077; fax (1) 42-89-89-11; f. 1967 to co-ordinate research and information policies among the members. Mems: Chile, Peru, Zaire, Zambia. Observer: Yugoslavia. Sec.-Gen. JORGE FERNÁNDEZ MALDONADO SOLARI. Publ. *CIPEC Quarterly Review*.

International Bauxite Association: 36 Trafalgar Rd, POB 551, Kingston 5, Jamaica; tel. 92-64535; telex 2428; fax 92-67157; f. 1974 to promote the development of the bauxite industry, to co-ordinate policies of the producing countries and to ensure a fair price for exports of bauxite and its products. Mems: Australia, Ghana, Guinea, Guyana, India, Indonesia, Jamaica, Sierra Leone, Suriname, Yugoslavia. Sec.-Gen. IBRAHIMA BAH (Guinea). Publ. *Quarterly Review*.

International Cocoa Organization—ICCO: 22 Berners St, London, W1P 3DB, England; tel. (071) 637 3211; telex 28173; fax (071) 631-0114; f. 1973 under the first International Cocoa Agreement, 1972 (renewed in 1975 and 1980; the fourth agreement entered into force in January 1987, and was extended, without its economic clauses, for two years from October 1990). ICCO supervises the implementation of the agreement, and provides member governments with conference facilities and up-to-date information on the world cocoa economy and the operation of the agreement (price-stabilizing activities were suspended in March 1990). Mems: 18 exporting countries which account for 81% of world cocoa exports, and 22 importing countries which account for over 61% of world cocoa imports. (The EEC participates as an intergovernmental organization; the USA is not a member.) Chair. D. K. ANINAKWAH (Ghana); Exec. Dir E. KOUAMÉ (Côte d'Ivoire); Buffer Stock Manager J. PLAMBECK (Germany). Publs *Quarterly Bulletin of Cocoa Statistics*, *Annual Report*, studies on the world cocoa economy.

International Coffee Organization: 22 Berners St, London, W1P 4DD, England; tel. (071) 580-8591; telex 267659; f. 1963 under the International Coffee Agreement, 1962, which was renegotiated in 1968, 1976 and 1983 (extended to 1992); aims to achieve a reasonable balance between supply and demand on a basis which will assure adequate supplies at fair prices to consumers and expanding markets at remunerative prices to producers; system of export quotas, to stabilize prices, was abandoned in July 1989. Mems: 50 exporting countries accounting for over 99% of world coffee exports, and 22 importing countries accounting for approximately 90% of world imports. Chair. of Council KAORU ISHIKAWA (Japan); Exec. Dir ALEXANDRE F. BELTRÃO.

International Confederation of European Sugar Beet Growers: 29 rue du Général Foy, 75008 Paris, France; tel. (1) 42-94-41-00; telex 640241; f. 1925 to act as a centre for the co-ordination and dissemination of information about beet sugar production and the industry; to represent the interests of sugar beet growers at an international level. Member associations in Austria, Belgium, Denmark, Finland, France, Germany, Greece, Ireland, Italy, Netherlands, Spain, Sweden, Switzerland, United Kingdom. Pres. F. GHAYE (Belgium); Sec.-Gen. H. CHAVANES (France).

International Cotton Advisory Committee: 1901 Pennsylvania Ave, NW, Suite 201, Washington, DC 20006, USA; tel. (202) 463-6660; telex 701517; f. 1939 to keep in touch with developments affecting the world cotton situation; to collect and disseminate statistics; to suggest to the governments represented any measures for the furtherance of international collaboration in maintaining and developing a sound world cotton economy. Mems: 44 countries. Exec. Dir Dr L. H. SHAW. Publs *Cotton—Review of the World Situation*, *Cotton—World Statistics*, *The ICAC Recorder*.

International Institute for Cotton: Suite 627, 1511 K St NW, Washington, DC 20005, USA; tel. (202) 347-4220; f. 1966 to increase world consumption of raw cotton and cotton products through utilization research, market research, sales promotion, education and public relations; to form a link between cotton exporting countries and the main importers. Mems: nine countries. Pres. Dr SHAILENDRA K. AGNIHOTRI (India); Exec. Dir PETER PEREIRA (UK); Sec. HARPAL LUTHER (India).

International Jute Organization: 95A Rd No 4, Banani, POB 6073, Gulshan, Dhaka, Bangladesh; tel. 883256; fax 883641; f. 1984 in accordance with an agreement made by 48 producing and consuming countries in 1982, under the auspices of UNCTAD (new agreement negotiated in 1989); aims to improve the jute economy by research and development projects, market promotion and cost reduction. Mems: five exporting and 27 importing countries. Exec. Dir SHAMSUL HAQUE CHISHTY (Bangladesh). Publ. *Jute* (quarterly).

International Lead and Zinc Study Group: Metro House, 58 St James's St, London, SW1A 1LD, England; tel. (071) 499-9373; telex 299819; fax (071) 493-3725; f. 1959, for intergovernmental consultation on world trade in lead and zinc; conducts studies and provides information on trends in supply and demand. Standing committee usually meets early in the year in London, and the study group and all committees in October in Geneva. Mems: 32 countries. Chair. J. T. REBEL (Netherlands); Sec.-Gen. R. W. BOEHNKE. Publs *Lead and Zinc Statistics* (monthly).

International Molybdenum Association: 280 Earls Court Rd, London, SW5 9AS, England; tel. (071) 373-7413; telex 889077; fax (071) 373-8047; f. 1989; collates statistics, promotes the use of molybdenum, monitors health and environmental issues. Pres. S. JOHNSON; Sec. MICHAEL BUBY.

International Natural Rubber Organization—INRO: POB 10374, 50712 Kuala Lumpur, Malaysia; tel. 2486466; telex 31570; f. 1980 to stabilize natural rubber prices by operating a buffer stock, and to seek to ensure an adequate supply, under the International Natural Rubber Agreement (1979), which entered into force in April 1982, and was extended for two years in 1985; a second agreement came into effect in 1989. Mems: 22 importing countries (including the European Community) and three exporting countries (Indonesia, Malaysia and Thailand). Exec. Dir PONG SONO (Thailand).

OTHER INTERNATIONAL ORGANIZATIONS — Commodities

International Olive Oil Council: Juan Bravo 10, 2°-3°, 28006 Madrid, Spain; tel. 5774735; telex 48197; fax 4316127; f. 1959 to administer the International Agreement on Olive Oil and Table Olives, the objectives of which are as follows: to promote international co-operation in connection with problems of the world economy for olive products; to prevent the occurrence of any unfair competition in the world olive products trade; to encourage the production and consumption of, and international trade in, olive products, and to reduce the disadvantages due to fluctuations of supplies on the market. Mems: of the 1986 Agreement (Fourth Agreement): five mainly producing countries, one mainly importing country, and the European Economic Community. Dir FAUSTO LUCHETTI. Publs *Information Sheet of the IOOC* (fortnightly, French and Spanish), *OLIVAE* (5 a year, in English, French, Italian and Spanish), *National Policies for Olive Products* (annually).

International Pepper Community: 3rd Floor, Wisma Bakrie, Jalan H. R. Rasuna Said, Kav. B1, Kuningan, Jakarta 12920, Indonesia; tel. 5200401; telex 62218; f. 1972 for promoting pepper and co-ordinating activities relating to the pepper economy; mems: Brazil, India, Indonesia, Malaysia. Exec. Dir MOHAMED ISMAIL.

International Rubber Study Group: 8th Floor, York House, Empire Way, Wembley, HA9 0PA, England; tel. (081) 903-7727; telex 8951293; fax (081) 903-2848; f. 1944 to provide a forum for the discussion of problems affecting synthetic and natural rubber and to provide statistical and other general information on rubber. Mems: 27 governments. Sec.-Gen. Dr B. C. SEKHAR. Publs *Rubber Statistical Bulletin* (monthly), *International Rubber Digest* (monthly), *Proceedings of Group Meetings and Assemblies*, *Records of International Rubber Forums* (annually), *World Rubber Statistics Handbook*.

International Silk Association: 20 rue Joseph Serlin, 69001 Lyon, France; tel. (33) 78-39-18-41; telex 330949; fax (33) 78-27-17-84; f. 1949 to promote closer collaboration between all branches of the silk industry and trade, develop the consumption of silk and foster scientific research; collects and disseminates information and statistics relating to the trade and industry; organizes triennial Congresses. Mems: employers' and technical organizations in 36 countries. Pres. BERNARD MOREL JOURNEL (France); Gen. Sec. R. CURRIE. Publs *ISA Newsletter* (monthly), standards, trade rules, etc.

International Spice Group: c/o Commonwealth Secretariat, Marlborough House, Pall Mall, London, SW1Y 5HX, England; tel. (071) 839-3411; telex 27678; f. 1983 to provide forum for producers and consumers of spices, and to attempt to increase the consumption of spices. Mems: 26 producer countries.

International Sugar Organization: 28 Haymarket, London, SW1Y 4SP, England; tel. (071) 930-3666; telex 24143; fax (071) 930-0401; administers the International Sugar Agreement (1987); the agreement does not include measures for stabilizing markets. Mems: 36 exporting countries and nine importing countries. Exec. Dir ALFREDO A. RICART; Sec. (vacant). Publs *Sugar Year Book*, *Monthly Statistical Bulletin*, *Annual Report*, *World Sugar Economy, Structure and Policies*.

International Tea Committee Ltd: Sir John Lyon House, 5 High Timber St, London, EC4V 3NH, England; tel. (071) 248-4672; telex 887911; fax (071) 248-3011; f. 1933 to administer the International Tea Agreement; now serves as a statistical and information centre; in 1979 membership was extended to include consuming countries. Producer Mems: national tea boards or associations of Bangladesh, India, Indonesia, Kenya, Malawi, Sri Lanka, Zimbabwe; Consumer Mems: United Kingdom Tea Association, Tea Association of the USA Inc., Comité Européen du Thé and the Tea Council of Canada; Assoc. Mems: Netherlands and UK ministries of agriculture. Chair. J. F. HILDITCH; Sec. PETER ABEL. Publs *Bulletin of Statistics* (annually), *Statistical Summary* (monthly).

International Tea Promotion Association: POB 20064, Tea Board of Kenya, Nairobi, Kenya; tel. 20241; telex 987-22190; fax 331650; f. 1979. Mems: eight countries (Bangladesh, Indonesia, Kenya, Malawi, Mauritius, Mozambique, Tanzania, Uganda), accounting for about 35% of world exports of black tea. Chair. GEORGE M. KIMANI; Liaison Officer NGOIMA WA MWAURA. Publ. *International Tea Journal* (annually).

International Tropical Timber Organization: 8F Sangyo Boeki Centre Bldg, 2 Yamashita-cho, Naka-ku, Yokohama 231, Japan; tel. 671-7045; telex 3822480; fax 671-7007; f. 1985 under the International Tropical Timber Agreement (1983); provides forum for consultation and co-operation between producers and consumers of tropical timber, in order to strike a balance between utilization and conservation; promotes research and development, reforestation and forest management, further processing of tropical timber in producing countries, and establishment of market intelligence and economic information; no provision is made for price stabilization. Mems: 47 producing and consuming countries. Exec. Dir Dr B. C. Y. FREEZAILAH (Malaysia).

International Tungsten Industry Association: 280 Earls Court Rd, London, SW5 9AS, England; tel. (071) 373-7413; telex 889077; fax (071) 373-8047; f. 1988 (fmrly Primary Tungsten Asscn, f. 1975); promotes use of tungsten, collates statistics, prepares market reports, monitors health and environmental issues. Mems: 66. Pres. W. LENTON; Sec. MICHAEL MABY. Publ. *Bulletin*.

International Vine and Wine Office: 11 rue Roquépine, 75008 Paris, France; tel. (1) 42-65-04-16; telex 281196; fax (1) 42-66-90-63; f. 1924 to study all the scientific, technical, economic and human problems concerning the vine and its products; to spread knowledge by means of its publications; to assist contacts between researchers and establish international research programmes. Mems: 33 countries. Dir ROBERT TINLOT. Publs *Bulletin de l'OIV* (every 2 months), *Lexique de la Vigne et du Vin*, *Recueil des méthodes internationales d'analyse des vins*, *Code international des Pratiques oenologiques*, *Codex oenologique international*, numerous scientific publications.

International Wheat Council: Haymarket House, 28 Haymarket, London, SW1Y 4SS, England; tel. (071) 930-4128; telex 916128; fax (071) 839-6907; f. 1949; responsible for the administration of the Wheat Trade Convention of the International Wheat Agreement, 1986; aims to further international co-operation in all aspects of trade in wheat and other grains, to promote international trade in grains, and to secure the freest possible flow of this trade in the interests of members, particularly developing member countries; and to contribute to the stability of the international grain market; acts as forum for consultations between members, and provides comprehensive information on the international grain market and factors affecting it. Mems: 47 countries and the EEC. Exec. Dir. J. H. PAROTTE. Publs *World Wheat Statistics* (annually), *Record of Shipments of Wheat and Flour*, *Report for the Crop Year* (annually), *Grain Market Report* (monthly), *Secretariat Papers* (occasional).

International Wool Secretariat: Wool House, 6 Carlton Gardens, London, SW1Y 5AE; tel. (071) 930-7300; telex 263926; fax (071) 930-8884; f. 1937 to expand the use and usefulness of wool through promotion and research. Financed by Australia, New Zealand, South Africa and Uruguay, it has an international policy of promoting wool irrespective of the country of origin. A non-trading organization, IWS has branches in over 30 countries and Technical Offices in Italy, Japan, Netherlands, United Kingdom and the USA. Man. Dir J. MCPHEE.

International Wool Study Group: Ashdown House, 123 Victoria St, London, SW1E 6RB, England; tel. (071) 215-6215; telex 8813148; f. 1946 to collect and collate statistics relating to world supply of and demand for wool; to review developments and to consider possible solutions to problems and difficulties unlikely to be resolved in the ordinary course of world trade in wool. Mems: 14 countries. Sec.-Gen. L. J. LAMONT.

Lead Development Association: 42 Weymouth St, London, W1N 3LQ, England; tel. (071) 499-8422; telex 261286; fax (071) 493-1555; f. 1954; provides authoritative information on the use of lead and its compounds; maintains a library and abstracting service in collaboration with the Zinc Development Association (see below). Financed by lead producers and users in the United Kingdom, Europe and elsewhere. Dir Dr D. N. WILSON (UK); Chief Exec. F. D. WARD (UK).

Mutual Assistance of the Latin American Government Oil Companies (Asistencia Recíproca Petrolera Estatal Latinoamericana—ARPEL): Javier de Viana 2345, 11200 Montevideo, Uruguay; tel. 406993; telex 22560; fax 237023; f. 1965 to study and recommend the implementation of mutually beneficial agreements among members in order to promote technical and economic development; to further Latin-American integration; to promote the interchange of technical assistance and information; to plan congresses, lectures, and meetings concerning the oil industry. Mems: state enterprises in Argentina, Bolivia, Brazil, Canada, Chile, Colombia, Costa Rica, Ecuador, Jamaica, Mexico, Paraguay, Peru, Suriname, Trinidad and Tobago, Uruguay, Venezuela. Sec.-Gen. ALVARO ALVES TEIXEIRA. Publ. *Boletín Técnico ARPEL*.

Sugar Association of the Caribbean (Inc.): POB 719C, Bridgetown, Barbados; tel. (809) 425-0010; fax (809) 425-3505; f. 1942. Mems: six national associations. Chair. H. B. DAVIS; Sec. D. H. A. JOHNSON. Publs *SAC Handbook*, *SAC Annual Report*, *Proceedings of Meetings of WI Sugar Technologists*.

Union of Banana-Exporting Countries—UPEB: Apdo 4273, Panamá 5, Panama; tel. 636266; telex 2568; fax 648355; f. 1974 as an intergovernmental agency to further the banana industry; mems: Colombia, Costa Rica, Dominican Republic, Guatemala, Nicaragua, Panama, Venezuela. Exec. Dir HAROLDO RODAS. Publs *Informe Mensual UPEB*, *Boletín Mensual de Estadísticas*, *BIBLIOBAN* (annually), bibliographies.

West Africa Rice Development Association—WARDA: 01 BP 2551 Bouaké 01, Côte d'Ivoire; tel. 63-45-14; telex 69138; fax 63-

47-14; f. 1970; undertakes research on rice for West Africa; has three regional research stations in Côte d'Ivoire, Senegal and Sierra Leone; provides training and consulting services; budget (1989) US $6.8m.; funded by the CGIAR and member countries. Mems: Benin, Burkina Faso, Chad, Côte d'Ivoire, The Gambia, Ghana, Guinea, Guinea-Bissau, Liberia, Mali, Mauritania, Niger, Nigeria, Senegal, Sierra Leone, Togo. Dir.-Gen. Dr EUGENE ROBERT TERRY (Sierra Leone). Publ. *Annual Report*.

West Indian Sea Island Cotton Association (Inc.): c/o Barbados Agricultural Development Corporation, Fairy Valley, Christ Church, Barbados. Pres. E. LEROY WARD; Sec. MICHAEL I. EDGHILL.

World Federation of Diamond Bourses: 62 Pelikaanstraat, 2018 Antwerp, Belgium; tel. (03) 232-76-55; fax (03) 226-40-73; f. 1947 to protect the interests of affiliated organizations and their individual members and to settle or arbitrate in disputes. Mems: 20 in 12 countries. Pres. E. GOLDSTEIN (UK); Sec.-Gen. PH. BLONDIN (Belgium).

World Gold Council: 1 rue de la Rôtisserie, 1204 Geneva, Switzerland; tel. (022) 219666; telex 428471; fax (022) 288160; f. 1987 as worldwide international association of gold producers, to promote the sale of gold. Chair. HUGH M. MORGAN; CEO ELLIOT M. HOOD.

Zinc Development Association: 42 Weymouth St, London, W1N 3LQ, England; tel. (071) 499-6636; telex 261286; fax (071) 493-1555; provides authoritative advice on the uses of zinc, its alloys and its compounds; maintains a library in collaboration with the Lead Development Association (q.v.). Affiliates are: Zinc Alloy Die Casters Association and Zinc Pigment Development Association. Financed by zinc producers and users in the United Kingdom, Europe and elsewhere. Chair. L. HENNIKER-HEATON (UK).

Economics and Finance

African Centre for Monetary Studies: 15 blvd Franklin Roosevelt, BP 1791, Dakar, Senegal; tel. 23-38-21; telex 61256; began operations 1978; aims to promote better understanding of banking and monetary matters; to study monetary problems of African countries and the effect on them of international monetary developments; seeks to enable African countries to co-ordinate strategies in international monetary affairs. Established as an organ of the Association of African Central Banks (AACB) as a result of a decision by the OAU Heads of State and Government. Mems: all mems of AACB (q.v.).

African Insurance Organization: BP 5860, Douala, Cameroon; tel. 424162; telex 5504; f. 1972 to promote the expansion of the insurance and reinsurance industry in Africa, and to increase regional co-operation; holds annual conference, and arranges meetings for reinsurers, brokers, consultants, supervisory authorities and actuaries in Africa; has established African insurance 'pools' for aviation and fire risks, and has created associations of African insurance educators, supervisory authorities and insurance brokers and consultants. Sec.-Gen. Y. ASEFFA.

Arab Bankers Association: 1/2 Hanover St, London, W1R 9WB; tel. (071) 629-5423; telex 297338; fax (071) 629-8631; f. 1980 to co-ordinate interests of Arab bankers, improve relations with other countries, prepare studies for development projects in the Arab world, administer a code for arbitration between financial institutions, and provide training for Arab bankers. Mems: 400. Chair. MUSTAPHA SERAGELDIN; Gen. Man. GHAYTH ARMANAZI. Publ. *Arab Banker* (every 2 months).

Asian Clearing Union—ACU: c/o Central Bank of the Islamic Republic of Iran, POB 11365/8531, Teheran, Iran; tel. 232076; telex 213120; fax 237677; f. 1974 to provide clearing arrangements to economize on the use of foreign exchange and promote the use of domestic currencies in trade transactions among developing countries; part of ESCAP's Asian trade expansion programme; the Central Bank of Iran is the Union's agent. Mems: Bangladesh, India, Iran, Myanmar, Nepal, Pakistan, Sri Lanka. Gen.-Man. MOHAMMAD FIROUZDOR. Publs *Annual Report, Newsletter* (monthly).

Asian Confederation of Credit Unions: POB 24-171, Bangkok 10240, Thailand; tel. 374-5321; telex 82234; fax 374-5321; links and promotes credit unions in Asia, provides research facilities and training programmes. Mems: Bangladesh, Hong Kong, Indonesia, Japan, Republic of Korea, Papua New Guinea, Philippines, Sri Lanka, Taiwan, Thailand; assoc. mems in India and Malaysia. Gen. Man. SOMCHIT SUPABANPOT. Publs *Asia-Con News* (every 2 months), *Annual Report and Directory*.

Asian Reinsurance Corporation: Sinthon Bldg, 6th Floor, 132 Wireless Rd, Lumpini, Bangkok 10500, Thailand; tel. 250-1476; telex 87231; fax 154-4845; f. 1979 by ESCAP with UNCTAD, to operate as a professional reinsurer, giving priority in retrocessions to national insurance and reinsurance markets of member countries, and as a development organization providing technical assistance to national markets; cap. (auth.) US $15m., (p.u.) US $4.5m. Mems: Afghanistan, Bangladesh, Bhutan, People's Republic of China, India, Republic of Korea, Philippines, Sri Lanka, Thailand. Gen. Man. M. S. WIJENAIKE.

Association of African Central Banks: 15 blvd Franklin Roosevelt, BP 1791, Dakar, Senegal; tel. 23-38-21; telex 61256; f. 1968 to promote contacts in the monetary and financial sphere in order to increase co-operation and trade among member states; to strengthen monetary and financial stability on the African continent. Mems: 34 African central banks representing 45 states. Chair. ABDUL R. TURAY (Sierra Leone).

Association of African Tax Administrators: c/o ECA, POB 3001, Addis Ababa, Ethiopia; f. 1980 to promote co-operation in the field of taxation policy, legislation and administration among African countries. Mems: 20 states. Chair. ABDERREZAG NAILI-DOUAOUDA (Algeria).

Association of European Institutes of Economic Research (Association d'instituts européens de conjoncture économique): 3 place Montesquieu, BP 4, 1348 Louvain-la-Neuve, Belgium; tel. (10) 47-41-52; fax (10) 47-29-97; f. 1955; provides a means of contact between member institutes; organizes two meetings yearly, in the spring and autumn, at which discussions are held, on the economic situation and on a special theoretical subject. Mems: 40 institutes in 20 European countries. Admin. Sec. PAUL OLBRECHTS.

Association of International Bond Dealers: Postfach, 8033 Zürich, Switzerland; tel. (01) 3634222; telex 815812; f. 1969 for discussion of questions relating to the international securities markets, to issue rules governing their functions, and to maintain a close liaison between the primary and secondary markets. Mems: 881 banks and major financial institutions in 38 countries. Chair. JAN EKMAN (Sweden), JOHN L. LANGTON (Switzerland). Publs *International Bond Manual*, daily Eurobond listing, electronic price information, weekly Eurobond guide, yield book, reports, etc.

Centre for Latin American Monetary Studies (Centro de Estudios Monetarios Latinoamericanos): Durango 54, Col. Roma, Del. Cuauhtémoc, 06700 México, DF, Mexico; tel. 533-03-00; telex 1771229; fax 514-65-54; f. 1952; organizes technical training programmes on monetary policy, development finance, etc., applied research programmes on monetary and central banking policies and procedures, regional meetings of banking officials. Mems: 30 associated members (Central Banks of Latin America and the Caribbean), 29 co-operating members (development agencies, regional financial agencies and non-Latin American Central Banks). Dir JÉSUS SILVA-HERZOG. Publs *Bulletin* (every 2 months), *Monetaria* (quarterly), *Money Affairs* (2 a year).

Comité Européen des Assurances (European Insurance Committee): 3 bis rue de la Chaussée d'Antin, 75009 Paris, France; tel. (1) 48-24-66-00; telex 281829; fax (1) 47-70-03-75; f. 1953. Mems: national insurance associations of 19 western European countries, and one observer. Pres. Dr G. BÜCHNER (Germany); Sec.-Gen. F. LOHEAC (France).

Econometric Society: Dept of Economics, Northwestern University, Evanston, Ill 60208, USA; tel. (312) 491-3615; f. 1930 to promote studies that aim at a unification of the theoretical-quantitative and the empirical-quantitative approach to economic problems. Mems: 6,000. Exec. Dir and Sec. JULIE P. GORDON. Publ. *Econometrica* (6 a year).

Eurofinas: 267 ave de Tervuren, 1150 Brussels, Belgium; tel. (02) 771-21-08; telex 63804; fax (02) 770-75-36; f. 1959 to study the development of instalment credit financing in Europe, to collate and publish instalment credit statistics, to promote research into instalment credit practice; mems: finance houses and professional associations in Austria, Belgium, Finland, France, Germany, Ireland, Italy, Netherlands, Norway, Spain, Sweden, Switzerland, United Kingdom. Chair. J. R. DE BUGALLAL (Spain); Sec.-Gen. MARC BAERT. Publs *Eurofinas Newsletter* (monthly), *Study Reports*.

European Federation of Financial Analysts Societies: c/o SAFE, 45 rue des Petits Champs, 75001 Paris, France; tel. (1) 42-61-90-93; fax (1) 47-03-98-34; f. 1962 to co-ordinate the activities of all European associations of financial analysts. Mems: 9,000 in 16 societies. Chair. J.-G. DE WAEL; Sec.-Gen. PETER VAN DE PAVERD.

European Financial Management and Marketing Association: 16 rue d'Aguesseau, 75008 Paris, France; tel. (1) 47-42-52-72; telex 280288; fax (1) 47-42-56-76; f. 1971 to link financial institutions by organizing seminars, conferences and training sessions and an annual World Convention, and by providing documentation services. Mems: 130 European financial institutions. Pres. DANIEL CARDON DE LICHTBUER; Sec.-Gen. MICHEL BARNICH (acting). Publ. *Newsletter*.

European Venture Capital Association: 6 Minervastraat, Box 6, 1930 Zaventem, Belgium; tel. (02) 720-60-10; fax (02) 725-30-36;

f. 1983 to link venture capital companies within the European Community and to encourage joint investment projects, particularly in support of small and medium-sized businesses; holds annual symposium, seminars. Mems: 135 (corporate and individual), and 65 associate mems, in 22 countries. Sec.-Gen. YVES FASSIN.

Inter-American Institute of Capital Markets: Apdo 1766, Caracas 1010-A, Venezuela; f. 1977 under the joint sponsorship of the OAS and the Venezuelan Government, to assist member countries in the development of their capital markets; organizes international conferences. Mems: 28 countries. Pres. BERNARDO PAUL. Publ. *Boletín Bibliográfico.*

International Accounting Standards Committee—IASC: 41 Kingsway, London, WC2B 6YU, England; tel. (071) 240-8781; telex 295177; fax (071) 379-0048; f. 1973 to formulate and publish in the public interest standards to be observed in the presentation of financial statements and to promote worldwide acceptance and observance, and to work for the improvement and harmonization of regulations, accounting standards and procedures relating to the presentation of financial statements. Mems: over 90 accounting bodies representing 900,000 accountants in 70 countries. Chair. ARTHUR WYATT; Sec.-Gen. DAVID H. CAIRNS. Publs *Statements of International Accounting Standards, Exposure Drafts, IASC News* (4 a year), *Discussion Papers.*

International Association for Research in Income and Wealth: 48 Morton St, New York, NY 10014, USA; tel. (212) 924-4386; f. 1947 to further research in the general field of national income and wealth and related topics by the organization of periodic conferences and by other means. Mems: approx. 350. Chair. JÁNOS ARVAY (Hungary); Exec. Sec. JANE FORMAN (USA). Publ. *Review of Income and Wealth* (quarterly).

International Association of Islamic Banks: POB 4992, Jeddah, Saudi Arabia; branches in Cairo, Egypt (POB 2838), and Karachi, Pakistan (POB 541); f. 1977 to link Islamic banks, which do not deal at interest but work on the principle of participation: activities include training and research. Chair. Prince MOHAMED AL-FAISAL AL-SAUD; Sec.-Gen. Dr AHMED AL-NAGGAR.

International Bureau of Fiscal Documentation: 'Muiderpoort', Sarphatistraat 124, POB 20237, 1000 HE Amsterdam, Netherlands; tel. (020) 267726; telex 13217; fax (020) 228658; f. 1938 to supply information on fiscal law and its application; library on international taxation. Pres. A. NOOTEBOOM; Man. Dir H. M. A. L. HAMAEKERS. Publs *Bulletin for International Fiscal Documentation, European Taxation, Supplementary Service to European Taxation* (all monthly), *Tax News Service* (fortnightly); studies, data bases.

International Centre for Local Credit: Koninginnegracht 2, 2514 AA The Hague, Netherlands; f. 1958 to promote local authority credit by gathering, exchanging and distributing information and advice on member institutions and on local authority credit and related subjects; studies important subjects in the field of local authority credit. Mems: 23 financial institutions in 15 countries. Pres. F. NARMON (Belgium); Sec.-Gen. W. GRIFFIOEN (Netherlands). Publs *Bulletin, Newsletter,* special reports.

International Economic Association: 23 rue Campagne Première, 75014 Paris, France; tel. (1) 43-27-91-44; telex 264918; fax (1) 43-39-00-99; f. 1949 to promote international collaboration for the advancement of economic knowledge and develop personal contacts between economists, and to encourage provision of means for the dissemination of economic knowledge. Member associations in 59 countries. Pres. Prof. ANTHONY B. ATKINSON (UK); Sec.-Gen. Prof. JEAN-PAUL FITOUSSI (France).

International Federation of Accountants: 540 Madison Ave, 21st Floor, New York, NY 10022, USA; tel. (212) 486-2446; telex 640428; f. 1977 to develop a co-ordinated worldwide accounting profession with harmonized standards. Mems: 105 accountancy bodies in 78 countries. Pres. ROBERT L. MAY (USA); Exec. Dir ROBERT SEMPIER (USA).

International Federation of Stock Exchanges: 22 blvd de Courcelles, 75017 Paris, France; tel. (1) 47-63-17-60; telex 642720; f. 1961 to promote among its members a co-operation that is not detrimental to the traditional relations which some of them may maintain with stock exchanges of third countries; represents its members at meetings of international organizations. Mems: 15 European and 18 other stock exchanges. Pres. Dr GERNOT ERNST; Sec.-Gen. JEANNE ABBEY.

International Fiscal Association: World Trade Center, POB 30215, 3001 DE Rotterdam, Netherlands; tel. (010) 4052990; telex 23229; fax (010) 4055031; f. 1938 to study international and comparative public finance and fiscal law, especially taxation; holds annual congresses. Mems in 85 countries and national branches in 39 countries. Pres. K. BEUSCH (Germany); Sec.-Gen. J. FRANS SPIERDIJK (Netherlands). Publs *Cahiers de Droit Fiscal International, Yearbook of the International Fiscal Association, IFA Congress Seminar Series.*

International Institute of Public Finance: University of the Saar, 6600 Saarbrücken 11, Germany; f. 1937; a private scientific organization aiming to establish contacts between people of every nationality, whose main or supplementary activity consists in the study of public finance; holds one meeting a year devoted to a certain scientific subject. Acting Pres. VITO TANZI (USA).

International Savings Banks Institute: 1–3 rue Albert Gos, 1206 Geneva, Switzerland; tel. (022) 477466; telex 428702; f. 1925 to act as an intelligence and liaison centre for savings banks. Mems: 124 savings banks and savings banks associations in 82 countries. Pres. Dr ALAIN LERAY; Gen. Man. J. M. PESANT (France). Publs (in English, French and German) *Savings Banks International* (quarterly), *International Information* (monthly), *International Savings Banks Directory, Savings Banks Foreign Business Directory.*

International Union of Housing Finance Institutions: 3 Savile Row, London, W1X 1AF, England; tel. (071) 437-0655; telex 24538; f. 1914 to foster world-wide interest in savings and home-ownership and co-operation among members; to encourage comparative study of methods and practice in housing finance; to encourage appropriate legislation on housing finance. Sec.-Gen. MARK BOLEAT. Publs *Housing Finance International* (quarterly), *Directory, International Housing Finance Factbook* (every 2 years), *IUBSSA Newsletter* (3 a year).

Latin American Banking Federation (Federación Latino-americana de Bancos—FELABAN): Apdo Aéreo 091959, Bogotá, DE8, Colombia; tel. 2560875; telex 45548; fax 6111153; f. 1965 to co-ordinate efforts towards a wide and accelerated economic development in Latin American countries. Mems: 19 Latin American national banking associations. Pres. of Board Dr JOSÉ JUÁN DE OLLOQUI; Sec.-Gen. Dra MARICIELO GLEN DE TOBÓN (Colombia).

West African Clearing House: PMB 218, Freetown, Sierra Leone; tel. 24485; telex 3368; f. 1975; administers transactions between its nine member central banks in order to promote local trade and currency transactions. Mems: Banque Centrale des Etats de l'Afrique de l'Ouest (serving Benin, Burkina Faso, Côte d'Ivoire, Mali, Niger, Senegal, Togo) and the central banks of The Gambia, Ghana, Guinea, Guinea-Bissau, Liberia, Mauritania, Nigeria and Sierra Leone. Exec. Sec. CHRIS E. NEMEDIA (Nigeria).

World Council of Credit Unions—WOCCU: POB 2982, 5810 Mineral Point Rd, Madison, WI 53701, USA; tel. (608) 231-7130; telex 467918; fax (608) 238-8020; f. 1970 to link credit unions and similar co-operative financial institutions and assist them in expanding and improving their services; provides technical and financial assistance to credit union associations in developing countries. Mems: 43,000 credit unions in 76 countries. Pres. G. A. CHARBONNEAU. Publs *WOCCU Statistical Report and Directory* (annually), *World Reporter* (quarterly), *Credit Union Technical Reporter* (quarterly).

Education

African Association for Literacy and Adult Education: POB 50768, Finance House, 6th Floor, Loita St, Nairobi, Kenya; tel. 331512; telex 22096; fax 340849; f. 1984, combining the former African Adult Education Association and the AFROLIT Society (both f. 1968); aims to promote adult education and literacy in Africa, to study the problems involved, and to allow the exchange of information; holds Conference every three years. Mems: 21 national education associations and 267 institutions. Chair. Dr ANTHONY SETSABI (Lesotho); Sec.-Gen. PAUL WANGOOLA (Uganda). Publs *AALAE Newsletter* (quarterly, French and English), *Journal* (2 a year).

Association for Childhood Education International: 11141 Georgia Ave, Suite 200, Wheaton, Md 20902, USA; tel. (301) 942-2443; f. 1892 to work for the education of children (from infancy through early adolescence) by promoting desirable conditions in schools, raising the standard of teaching, co-operating with all groups concerned with children, informing the public of the needs of children. Mems: 12,000. Pres. VERL SHORT; Exec. Dir A. GILSON BROWN. Publs *Childhood Education* (5 a year), *ACEI Exchange Newsletter* (6 a year), *Journal of Research in Childhood Education* (2 a year), leaflets on current educational subjects (3 a year).

Association of African Universities: POB 5744, Accra North, Ghana; tel. 665461; telex 2284; f. 1967 to promote exchanges, contact and co-operation among African university institutions and to collect and disseminate information on research and higher education in Africa. Mems: 92 university institutions. Sec.-Gen. Prof. DONALD E. U. EKONG (Nigeria). Publs *AAU Newsletter* (3 a year), *Directory of African Universities* (every 2 years).

Association of Arab Universities: POB 401, Jubeyha, Amman, Jordan; tel. 845131; telex 23855; fax 832994; f. 1964. Mems: 74 universities. Sec.-Gen. Dr MOHAMMAD F. DOGHAIM. Publs. *Bulletin* (annually and quarterly, in Arabic).

OTHER INTERNATIONAL ORGANIZATIONS

Association of Caribbean Universities and Research Institutes: POB 11532, Caparra Heights Station, San Juan, Puerto Rico 00922; tel. (809) 720-4381; f. 1968 to foster contact and collaboration between member universities and institutes; conferences, meetings, seminars, etc.; circulation of information through newsletters, bulletins; facilitates co-operation and the pooling of resources in research; encourages exchange of staff and students. Mems: 50. Sec.-Gen. Dr THOMAS MATHEWS. Publ. *Caribbean Educational Bulletin* (quarterly).

Association of Institutes for European Studies (Association des Instituts d'Etudes Européennes—AIEE): 122 rue de Lausanne, 1202 Geneva, Switzerland; tel. (022) 322803; f. 1951, to co-ordinate activities of member institutes in teaching and research, exchange information, provide a centre for documentation. Mems: 32 institutes in nine countries. Pres. Prof. E. CEREXHE (Belgium); Sec.-Gen. Prof. DUSAN SIDJANSKI. Publ. *Bulletin intérieur* (2 a month).

Association of Partially or Wholly French-Language Universities (Association des universités partiellement ou entièrement de langue française—AUPELF): Université de Montréal, BP 6128, Montreal, Canada H3C 3J7; tel. (514) 343-6630; telex 055-60955; fax (514) 343-2107; f. 1961; aims: documentation, co-ordination, co-operation, exchange. Mems: 172, and 371 assoc. mems. Pres. BAKARY TIO-TOURÉ; Sec.-Gen. MAURICE-ETIENNE BEUTLER. Publs *Perspectives universitaires* (2 a year), *Idées* (irregular), *Universités* (quarterly).

Association of South-East Asian Institutions of Higher Learning—ASAIHL: Secretariat, Ratasastra Bldg 2, Chulalongkorn University, Henri Dunant Rd, Bangkok 10330, Thailand; tel. (02) 251-6966; telex 72432; fax (02) 225-5007; f. 1956 to promote the economic, cultural and social welfare of the people of South-East Asia by means of educational co-operation and research programmes. Mems: 115 university institutions in 11 countries. Pres. Dr IAM CHAYA-NGAM (Thailand); Sec.-Gen. Dr NINNAT OLANVORAVUTH. Publs *Newsletter*, *Handbook* (every 3 years).

Catholic International Education Office: 60 rue des Eburons, 1040 Brussels, Belgium; tel. (02) 230-72-52; f. 1952 for the study of the problems of Catholic education throughout the world; co-ordination of the activities of members; and representation of Catholic education at international bodies. Mems: 84 countries, 16 assoc. mems, 13 collaborating mems, 5 corresponding mems. Pres. Mgr A. FERNANDES (acting); Sec.-Gen. PAULUS ADAMS, FSC. Publs *OIEC Bulletin* (every 2 months in English, French and Spanish), *L'éducation sociale des jeunes à l'école* (French and Spanish).

Catholic International Federation for Physical and Sports Education: 22 rue Oberkampf, 75011 Paris, France; tel. (1) 43-38-50-57; f. 1911 to group Catholic associations for physical education and sport of different countries and to develop the principles and precepts of Christian morality by fostering meetings, study and international co-operation. Mems: 14 affiliated national federations representing about 2.8m. members. Pres. Dr J. FINDER (Austria); Sec.-Gen. ROBERT PRINGARBE (France).

Comparative Education Society in Europe: 51 rue de la Concorde, 1050 Brussels, Belgium; tel. (02) 512-17-34; telex 21504; fax (02) 512-32-65; f. 1961 to promote teaching and research in comparative and international education; the Society organizes conferences and promotes literature. Mems in 39 countries. Pres. Prof. H. VAN DAELE (Belgium). Publ. *Newsletter* (quarterly).

European Bureau of Adult Education: Nieuweweg 4, POB 367, 3800 AJ Amersfoort, Netherlands; tel. (33) 631114; fax (33) 616627; f. 1953 as a clearing-house and centre of co-operation for all groups concerned with adult education in Europe. Mems: 150 in 18 countries. Pres. K. L. OGLESBY (UK); Dir W. BAX. Publs *Conference Reports*, *Directory of Adult Education Organisations in Europe*, *Newsletter*, *Survey of Adult Education Legislation*, *Glossary of Terms*.

European Cultural Foundation: Jan van Goyenkade 5, 1075 HN Amsterdam, Netherlands; tel. (20) 760222; telex 18710; fax (20) 752231; f. 1954 as a non-governmental organization, supported by private sources, to promote activities of mutual interest to European countries, concerning basic values, culture, education, environment, East-West cultural relations, media, social issues, or the problems of European society in general (excluding strictly scientific or medical subjects); national committees in 20 countries; has established a transnational network of 11 institutes and centres: European Institute of Education and Social Policy, Paris (with Erasmus Bureau, Brussels); Institute for European Environmental Policy, Bonn, London, Arnhem and Paris; European Co-operation Fund, Brussels; European Centre for Work and Society, Maastricht and Brussels; EURYDICE Central Unit (the Education Information Network of the European Community), Brussels; European Institute for the Media, Manchester; European Foundation Center, Brussels; Central and East European Publishing Project, Oxford; Institute for Human Sciences, Vienna; Concordo East/West, Brussels. A grants programme, for projects involving at least three European countries, is also conducted. Pres. HRH Princess MARGRIET of the Netherlands; Sec.-Gen. R. GEORIS. Publs *Annual Report*, *Newsletter* (2 a year).

European Federation for Catholic Adult Education: Kapuzinerstrasse 84, 4020 Linz, Austria; tel. (0732) 27-44-41; f. 1963 to strengthen international contact between members, to assist international research and practical projects in adult education; to help communications between its members and other international bodies; holds conference every two years. Pres. Dr WALTER SUK (Austria).

European Foundation for Management Development: 40 rue Washington, 1050 Brussels, Belgium; tel. (02) 648-03-85; telex 65080; f. 1971 through merger of European Association of Management Training Centres and International University Contact for Management Education; aims to help improve the quality of management development within the economic, social and cultural context of Europe and in harmony with its overall needs. Mems: more than 550 institutions and individuals. Pres. PEDRO NUENO; Dir-Gen. GAY HASKINS. Publs *European Management Development* (quarterly), *Documentation on Books, Cases and other teaching Material in Management* (every 2 months).

European Union of Arabic and Islamic Scholars: c/o Institut für Orientalistik, Liebiggasse 6, 1010 Vienna, Austria; tel. (01) 03-25-93; f. 1970 to organize congresses of Arabic and Islamic Studies; congresses are held every two years. Mems: about 250. Sec. Dr ARNE A. AMBROS.

Graduate Institute of International Studies (Institut universitaire de hautes études internationales): POB 36, 132 rue de Lausanne, Geneva, Switzerland; tel. (022) 7311730; telex 412151; fax (022) 7384306; f. 1927 to establish a centre for advanced studies in international relations of the present day, juridical, historical, political, economic and social. Library of 120,000 vols. Dir Prof. LUCIUS CAFLISCH; Sec.-Gen. J.-C. FRACHEBOURG.

Inter-American Centre for Research and Documentation on Vocational Training (Centro Interamericano de Investigación y Documentación sobre Formación Profesional—CINTERFOR): Avda Uruguay 1238, Casilla de correo 1761, Montevideo, Uruguay; tel. 920557; telex 22573; fax 921305; f. 1964 by the International Labour Organisation (q.v.) for mutual help among the Latin American and Caribbean countries in planning vocational training; services are provided in documentation, research, exchange of experience; holds seminars and courses. Dir JOÃO CARLOS ALEXIM. Publs *Bulletin* (4 a year), *Documentation* (2 a year), *Bibliographical Series*, *Studies*, *Monographs and Abstracts*.

Inter-American Confederation for Catholic Education (Confederación Interamericana de Educación Católica): Calle 78 No 12–16 (ofna 101), Apdo Aéreo 90036, Bogotá 8 DE, Colombia; tel. 255-3676; f. 1945 to defend and extend the principles and rules of Catholic education, freedom of education, and human rights; organizes congress every three years. Pres. CÉSAR BLONDET SABROSO; Sec.-Gen. MARIO IANTORNO. Publs *Educación Hoy: Perspectivas Latinoamericanas* (every 3 months), *Colección CENTRAL*, *Colección RADIAR*, *Colección Textos*.

International Association for Educational and Vocational Guidance—IAEVG: Dept of Economic Development, Gloucester House, Chichester St, Belfast, BT1 4RA, Northern Ireland; tel. (0232) 321200; f. 1951 to contribute to the development of vocational guidance and promote contact between persons associated with it. Mems: 40,000 from 60 countries. Pres. Prof. WILLIAM C. BINGHAM (USA); Sec.-Gen. KATHLEEN M. V. HALL (UK). Publs *Bulletin* (2 a year), *Newsletter* (3 a year).

International Association for Educational and Vocational Information: 20 rue de l'Estrapade, 75005 Paris, France; f. 1956 to facilitate co-operation between national organizations concerned with supplying information to university and college students and secondary pupils and their parents. Mems: national organizations in 50 countries. Pres. C. VIMONT (France); Sec.-Gen. J. L. C. BOUVIER (Belgium); Dir L. TODOROV. Publ. *Informations universitaires et professionnelles internationales* (quarterly).

International Association for the Development of Documentation, Libraries and Archives in Africa: BP 375, Dakar, Senegal; f. 1957 to organize and develop documentation and archives in all African countries. Sec.-Gen. ZACHEUS SUNDAY ALI (Nigeria).

International Association of Papyrologists: Fondation Egyptologique Reine Elisabeth, Parc du Cinquantenaire 10, 1040 Brussels, Belgium; tel. (02) 741-73-64; f. 1947; Mems: about 500. Pres. Prof. HANS-ALBERT RUPRECHT (Germany); Sec. Prof. JEAN BINGEN (Belgium).

International Association of Physical Education in Higher Education: Institut Supérieur d'Education Physique, Université de Liège au Sart Tilman, 4000 Liège, Belgium; tel. (041) 56-38-90; telex 41397; fax (041) 66-57-00; f. 1962; organizes congresses, exchanges, and research in physical education. Mems: institutions in 51 countries. Sec.-Gen. Dr MAURICE PIERON.

International Association of Universities—IAU/International Universities Bureau—IUB: 1 rue Miollis, 75732 Paris Cedex 15, France; tel. (1) 45-68-25-45; telex 250615; fax (1) 47-34-76-05; f. 1950 to allow co-operation at the international level among universities and other institutions of higher education; provides clearing-house services and operates the joint IAU/UNESCO Information Centre on Higher Education; conducts meetings and research on issues concerning higher education. Ninth General Conference, University of Helsinki, Finland, 1990. Mems: about 1,000 universities and institutions of higher education in 120 countries; assoc. mems: nine international university organizations. Pres. WALTER KAMBA; Sec.-Gen. FRANZ EBERHARD. Publs *Higher Education Policy* (quarterly), *International Handbook of Universities* (every 2 years), *World List of Universities* (every 2 years).

International Association of University Professors and Lecturers—IAUPL: 18 rue du Docteur Roux, 75015 Paris, France; tel. (1) 47-83-31-65; f. 1945 for the development of academic fraternity amongst university teachers and research workers; the protection of independence and freedom of teaching and research; the furtherance of the interests of all university teachers; and the consideration of academic problems. Mems: federations in 17 countries. Hon. Sec.-Gen. Dr L. P. LAPRÉVOTE. Publ. *Communication*.

International Baccalaureate Organization—IBO: Route des Morillons 15, Grand-Saconnex 1218, Geneva, Switzerland; tel. (022) 7910274; telex 265871; fax (022) 7910277; f. 1967 to plan curricula and an international university entrance examination, the International Baccalaureate, recognized by major universities in Europe, North and South America, Africa, Middle East and Australia; provides international board of examiners. Mems: 400 participating schools. Chair. of Council Dr PIET GATHIER (Netherlands); Dir-Gen. ROGER M. PEEL.

International Council for Adult Education: 720 Bathurst St, Suite 500, Toronto, Ont, Canada M5S 2R4; tel. (416) 588-1211; telex 06-986766; fax (416) 588-5725; f. 1973 to promote the education of adults in relation to the need for healthy growth and development of individuals and communities; undertakes research and training; organizes seminars, the exchange of information, and co-operative publishing; General Assembly meets every four years. Mems: six regional organizations and national associations in 76 countries. Pres. FRANCISCO VIO GROSSI; Sec.-Gen. BUDD HALL. Publ. *Convergence, ICAE News*.

International Council for Distance Education: Gjerdrums Vei 12, 0486 Oslo 4, Norway; tel. (02) 950630; fax (02) 950719; f. 1938 (name changed 1982); furthers distance (correspondence) education by promoting research, encouraging regional links, providing information and organizing conferences. Mems: 120 institutions, 600 individuals in 50 countries. Pres. Dr DAVID SEWART (UK); Sec.-Gen. REIDAR ROLL (Norway).

International Federation for Parent Education: 1 ave Léon Journault, 92311 Sèvres Cedex, France; tel. (1) 45-07-21-64; f. 1964 to gather in congresses and colloquia experts from different scientific fields and those responsible for family education in their own countries and to encourage the establishment of family education where it does not exist. Mems: 120. Pres. JEAN AUBA (France). Publs *Quarterly Bulletin*.

International Federation of Catholic Universities: 78A rue de Sèvres, 75341 Paris Cedex 07, France; tel. (1) 42-73-36-25; fax (1) 45-67-06-22; f. 1948; to ensure a strong bond of mutual assistance among all Catholic universities in the search for truth; to help to solve problems of growth and development, and to co-operate with other international organizations. Mems: 172 in 36 countries. Pres. MICHEL FALISE (France); Sec.-Gen. LUCIEN MICHAUD (Canada). Publ. *Quarterly Newsletter*.

International Federation of 'Ecole Moderne' Movements: 24 ave des Armes, BP 109, 06322 Cannes-la-Bocca Cedex, France; tel. 93-47-96-11; f. 1957 to bring into contact associations devoted to the improvement of school organization and to work for the adoption of techniques advocated by C. Freinet; conducts courses for teachers, promotes interschool exchange of correspondence and magazines. Mems: associations of teachers in 40 countries. Pres. HENRY LANDROIT. Publs *L'Educateur* (2 a month), *Art Enfantin* (bi-monthly), *Bibliothèque de Travail Sonore, Bibliothèque de l'Ecole Moderne, Bibliothèque de Travail* (bi-monthly), *Bibliothèque de Travail Junior* (monthly), *Bibliothèque de Travail Second degré, La Multilettre*.

International Federation of Library Associations and Institutions—IFLA: c/o Royal Library, POB 95312, 2509 CH The Hague, Netherlands; tel. (070) 3140884; telex 34402; fax (070) 3834827; f. 1927 to promote international co-operation in librarianship and bibliography. Mems: 178 associations, representing 129 countries, 1,065 institutions and individual members. Pres. Dr HANS-PETER GEH; Sec.-Gen. Dr PAUL NAUTA. Publs *IFLA Annual, IFLA Directory, IFLA Journal, International Cataloguing and Bibliographic Control* (quarterly), *IFLA Professional Reports*.

International Federation of Organisations for School Correspondence and Exchange: 29 rue d'Ulm, 75230 Paris Cedex 05, France; tel. (1) 46-57-11-17; f. 1929 to contribute to the knowledge of foreign languages and civilizations and to bring together young people of all nations by furthering international scholastic exchanges including correspondence, individual and group visits to foreign countries, individual accommodation with families, placements in international holiday camps, etc. Mems: comprises 78 national bureaux of scholastic correspondence and exchange in 36 countries. Pres. A. H. MALE (UK); Gen. Sec. A. ELMARY (France).

International Federation of Physical Education: 4 Cleevecroft Ave, Bishops Cleeve, Cheltenham, GL52 4JZ, England; f. 1923; studies physical education on scientific, pedagogic and aesthetic bases in order to stimulate health, harmonious development or preservation, healthy recreation, and the best adaptation of the individual to the general needs of social life; organizes international congresses and courses. Mems: from 112 countries. Pres. JOHN C. ANDREWS. Publ. *FIEP Bulletin* (quarterly in Arabic, French, English, Portuguese and Spanish).

International Federation of Secondary Teachers—FIPESO: 7 rue de Villersexel, 75007 Paris, France; tel. (1) 40-63-29-35; fax (1) 40-63-29-36; f. 1912 to contribute to the progress of secondary education. Mems: 47 associations with 850,000 members in 30 countries. Gen. Sec. LOUIS WEBER. Publs *FIPESO Newsletter* (8 a year), *International Bulletin* (2 a year).

International Federation of Teachers' Associations: 3 rue de La Rochefoucauld, 75009 Paris, France; tel. (1) 48-74-58-44; f. 1926 to raise the level of popular education and improve teaching methods; to protect interests of teachers; to promote international understanding. Mems: 59 national associations. Pres. FERD MILBERT (Luxembourg); Sec.-Gen. JEAN-BERNARD GICQUEL (France). Publs *Feuilles d'Informations* (9 or 10 a year), *FIAI-IFTA-Informations* (2 a year).

International Federation of Teachers of Modern Languages: Seestrasse 247, 8038 Zürich, Switzerland; tel. (01) 4825040; telex 815250; fax (01) 4816124; f. 1931; holds meetings on every aspect of foreign-language teaching; has consultative status with UNESCO. Mems: 33 national and regional language associations and six international unilingual associations (teachers of English, French, German, Italian and Spanish). Pres. EDWARD M. BATLEY; Sec.-Gen. GYÖRGY SZÉPE. Publ. *FIPLV World News* (quarterly in English, French and Spanish).

International Federation of University Women: 37 Quai Wilson, 1201 Geneva, Switzerland; tel. (022) 7312380; fax (022) 7380440; f. 1919 to promote understanding and friendship among university women of the world; to encourage international co-operation; to further the development of education; to represent university women in international organizations; to encourage the full application of members' skills to the problems which arise at all levels of public life. Affiliates: 52 national associations with over 230,000 mems. Pres. Dr MARY H. PURCELL (USA); Exec. Sec. D. DAVIES (UK). Publs *IFUW News* (monthly), *Communiqué* (annually), triennial report.

International Federation of Workers' Educational Associations: Histadrut, 93 Arlosoroff St, Tel Aviv 61002, Israel; tel. 03-262335; telex 342488; f. 1947 to promote co-operation between national non-governmental bodies concerned with workers' education, through clearing-house services, exchange of information, publications, international seminars, conferences, summer schools, etc. Pres. Prof. KURT PROKOP (Austria); Sec.-Gen. DAVID FARAN-FRANKFURTER (Israel).

International Institute for Adult Literacy Methods: POB 13145-654, Teheran, Iran; f. 1968 by UNESCO and the government of Iran; a clearing-house for information on activities concerning literacy in various countries; carries out comparative studies of the methods, media and techniques used in literacy programmes; maintains documentation service and library on literacy; arranges seminars. Dir Dr HASSAN SADOGH VANINI.

International Institute of Philosophy—IIP (Institut international de philosophie—IIP): 8 rue Jean-Calvin, 75005 Paris, France; tel. (1) 43-36-39-11; f. 1937 to clarify fundamental issues of contemporary philosophy in annual meetings and to promote mutual understanding among thinkers of different backgrounds and traditions; a maximum of 115 members are elected, chosen from all countries and representing different tendencies. Mems: 106 in 36 countries. Pres. RUTH BARCAN MARCUS (USA); Sec.-Gen. P. AUBENQUE (France). Publs *Bibliography of Philosophy* (quarterly), *Proceedings* of annual meetings, *Chroniques, Philosophy and World Community* (series), *Philosophical Problems Today*.

International Institute of Public Administration: 2 ave de l'Observatoire, 75272 Paris Cedex 06; tel. (1) 43-26-49-00; telex 270229; fax (1) 46-33-26-38; f. 1967; trains high-ranking civil servants from

OTHER INTERNATIONAL ORGANIZATIONS

abroad; administrative, economic, financial and diplomatic programmes; Africa, Latin America, Asia, Europe and Near East departments; research department, library of 80,000 vols; Documentation Centre. Dir M. FRANC. Publs *Revue française d'administration publique* (quarterly), *L'année administrative* (annually).

International Montessori Association: Koninginneweg 161, 1075 CN Amsterdam, Netherlands; tel. (20) 798932; f. 1929 to propagate the ideals and educational methods of Dr Maria Montessori on child development, without racial, religious or political prejudice; organizes training courses for teachers in 14 countries. Pres. G. J. PORTIELJE; Sec. FAHMIDA MALIK. Publ. *Communications* (quarterly).

International Reading Association: 800 Barksdale Rd, POB 8139, Newark, Del 19714-8139, USA; tel. (302) 731-1600; telex 5106002813; fax (302) 731-1057; f. 1956 to improve the quality of reading instruction at all levels, to promote the habit of lifelong reading, and to develop every reader's proficiency. Mems: 94,000 in 100 countries. Pres. Dr CARL BRAUN. Publs *The Reading Teacher* (9 a year), *Journal of Reading* (9 a year), *Reading Research Quarterly*, *Lectura y Vida* (quarterly in Spanish), *Reading Today* (6 a year).

International Schools Association—ISA: CIC CASE 20, 1211 Geneva 20, Switzerland; tel. (022) 7336717; f. 1951 to co-ordinate work in international schools and promote their development; member schools maintain the highest standards and accept pupils of all nationalities, irrespective of race and creed. ISA carries out curriculum research; convenes annual conferences on problems of curriculum and educational reform; organizes occasional teachers' training workshops and specialist seminars. Mems: 80 schools throughout the world. Pres. BERNARD IVALDI. Publs *Education Bulletin* (2 a year), *ISA Magazine* (annually), *Conference Report* (annually), curriculum studies (occasional).

International Society for Business Education: Hunderupvej 122A, 5230 Odense M, Denmark; f. 1901 to encourage international exchange of information and organize international courses and congresses on business education; 2,200 mems, national organizations and individuals in 16 countries. Pres. CHRISTIAN THIERSTEIN (Switzerland); Dir ERIK LANGE (Denmark). Publ. *International Review for Business Education*.

International Society for Education through Art: c/o NSEAD, 7A High St, Corsham, Wilts, SN13 0ES, England; tel. (0249) 714825; fax (0249) 716138; f. 1951 to unite art teachers throughout the world, to exchange information and to co-ordinate research into art education; organizes international congresses and exhibitions of children's art. Pres. Prof. ELLIOT EISNER (USA); Sec. JOHN STEERS. Publ. *INSEA News*.

International Society for Music Education: Music Education Centre, University of Reading, Bulmershe Court, Reading, RG6 1HY, England; tel. (0734) 318846; fax (0734) 352080; f. 1953 to organize international conferences, seminars and publications on matters pertaining to music education; acts as advisory body to UNESCO in matters of music education. Mems: national committees and individuals in 58 countries. Pres. JOHN RITCHIE (New Zealand); Sec.-Gen. RONALD SMITH (UK). Publs *ISME Conference Proceedings*, *Journal*.

International Society for the Study of Medieval Philosophy: Collège Thomas More, 1 Chemin d'Aristote, 1348 Louvain-la-Neuve, Belgium; tel. (010) 47-48-07; telex 59037; fax (010) 47-48-19; f. 1958 to promote the study of medieval thought and the collaboration between individuals and institutions concerned in this field; organizes international congresses. Mems: 478. Pres. Prof. TULLIO GREGORY (Italy); Sec. Dr JACQUELINE HAMESSE (Belgium). Publ. *Bulletin de Philosophie Médiévale* (annually).

International Youth Library (Internationale Jugendbibliothek): 8000 Munich 60, Schloss Blutenburg, Germany; tel. (089) 8112028; fax (089) 8117553; f. 1948, since 1953 an associated project of UNESCO, to promote the international exchange of children's literature and to provide study opportunities for specialists in children's books. Maintains a library of 500,000 volumes in about 120 languages. Dir Dr ANDREAS BODE. Publs *The White Ravens*, *IJB Bulletin*, *IJB Report*, catalogues.

League of European Research Libraries—LIBER: Biblioteca Nacional, 83 Campo Grande, 1751 Lisbon, Portugal; tel. (01) 767639; fax (01) 7933607; f. 1971 to establish close collaboration between the general research libraries of Europe, and national and university libraries in particular; and to help in finding practical ways of improving the quality of the services these libraries provide. Mems: 180. Pres. MICHAEL SMETHURST; Sec. MARIA LUÍSA CABRAL. Publs *LIBER Quarterly*, *LIBER News Sheet* (2 or 3 a year).

Organization for Museums, Monuments and Sites in Africa: Centre for Museum Studies, PMB 2031, Jos, Nigeria; f. 1975 to foster the collection, study and conservation of the natural and cultural heritage of Africa; co-operation between member countries through seminars, workshops, conferences, etc., exchange of personnel, training facilities. Mems from 30 countries. Pres. Dr J. M. ESSOMBA (Cameroon); Sec.-Gen. KWASI MYLES.

Organization of Ibero-American States for Education, Science and Culture (Organización de Estados Iberoamericanos para la Educación, la Ciencia y la Cultura): Ciudad Universitaria, 28040 Madrid, Spain; tel. 449 69 54; telex 48422; fax 449 36 78; f. 1949 (as the Ibero-American Bureau of Education); provides information on education, science and culture; encourages exchanges and organizes training courses; the General Assembly (at ministerial level) meets every four years. Mems: governments of 20 countries. Sec.-Gen. SIMÓN ROMERO LOZANO. Publs *Educación—Noticias de Educación, Ciencia y Cultura Iberoamericana* (every 2 months), *Sumarios de Revistas de Educación* (2 a year), studies.

Organization of the Catholic Universities of Latin America (Organización de Universidades Católicas de América Latina—ODUCAL): c/o Rev. Dr A. E. Fosbery, Univ. del Norte Santo Tomas de Aquino, 9 de Julio 165, CP 4000, San Miguel de Tucuman, Argentina; f. 1953 to assist the social, economic and cultural development of Latin America through the promotion of Catholic higher education in the continent. Mems: 24 Catholic universities in Argentina, Brazil, Chile, Colombia, Dominican Republic, Ecuador, Mexico, Nicaragua, Paraguay, Peru, Puerto Rico, Venezuela. Pres. Rev. Dr ANNIBAL ERNESZT FOSBERY (Argentina); Publs *Anuario; Sapientia; Universitas*.

Regional Centre for Adult Education and Functional Literacy in Latin America (Centro Regional de Educación de Adultos y Alfabetización Funcional para América Latina): Quinta Eréndira s/n, Pátzcuaro, Michoacán, Mexico; tel. 20005; f. 1951 by UNESCO and OAS to encourage literacy and rural development through adult education and co-operative research; library of 60,000 vols. Dir Dr LUIS G. BENAVIDES ILIZALITURRI. Publ. *Retablos de Papel*, *Cuadernos del CREFAL*.

Southeast Asian Ministers of Education Organization—SEAMEO: Darakarn Bldg, 920 Sukhumvit Rd, Bangkok 10110, Thailand; tel. 3910144; telex 22683; fax 3812587; f. 1965 to promote co-operation among the Southeast Asian nations through projects in education, science and culture; SEAMEO has eight regional centres: BIOTROP for tropical biology, in Bogor, Indonesia; INNOTECH for educational innovation and technology, and a Non-Formal Education Programme (SNEP), at Quezon City, Philippines; RECSAM for education in science and mathematics, in Penang, Malaysia; RELC for languages, in Singapore; SEARCA for graduate study and research in agriculture, in Los Baños, Philippines; SPAFA for archaeology and fine arts with sub-centres in Indonesia, Philippines and Thailand and a co-ordinating unit in Bangkok, Thailand; TROPMED for tropical medicine and public health with national centres in Indonesia, Malaysia, Philippines and Thailand and a central office in Bangkok, Thailand; and VOC-TECH for vocational and technical education. Mems: Brunei, Cambodia, Indonesia, Laos, Malaysia, Philippines, Singapore, Thailand. Assoc. mems: Australia, Canada, France, Germany, New Zealand. Dir Prof. Dr JAKUB ISMAN. Publs *Annual Report*, *SEAMEO Quarterly*, *Calendar of Activities*, *Catalogue of Publications*.

Standing Conference of Rectors, Presidents and Vice-Chancellors of the European Universities (Conférence permanente des recteurs, présidents et vice-chanceliers des universités européennes—CRE): 10 rue du Conseil Général, 1211 Geneva 4, Switzerland; tel. (022) 292644; telex 428380; fax (022) 292821; f. 1959; holds two conferences a year, a General Assembly every five years, and special seminars; sponsors inter-university co-operation projects ('Columbus', with Latin American universities, and 'Copernicus', linking European universities on the theme of sustainable growth and environment). Mems: 440 university heads in 27 countries. Pres. Prof. HINRICH SEIDEL; Sec.-Gen. Dr ANDRIS BARBLAN. Publ. *CRE-action* (4 a year).

Union of Latin American Universities (Unión de Universidades de América Latina—UDUAL): Edificio UDUAL, Apdo postal 70-232, Ciudad Universitaria, Del. Coyoacán, 04510 México, DF, Mexico; tel. 548-9786; telex 1764112; fax 548-97-86; f. 1949 to further the improvement of university association, to organize the interchange of professors, students, research fellows and graduates and generally encourage good relations between the Latin American universities; arranges conferences, conducts statistical research; centre for university documentation. Mems: 151 universities. Pres. Dr JORGE CARPIZO (Mexico); Sec.-Gen. Dr JOSÉ LUIS SOBERANES. Publs *Universidades* (annually), *Gaceta UDUAL* (quarterly), *Censo* (every 2 years).

Universal Esperanto Association: Nieuwe Binnenweg 176, 3015 BJ Rotterdam, Netherlands; tel. (010) 4361044; telex 23721; fax (010) 4361751; f. 1908 to assist the spread of the international language, Esperanto, and to facilitate the practical use of the language. Mems: 49 affiliated national associations and 43,148 individuals in 101 countries. Pres. Prof JOHN C. WELLS (UK); Gen. Sec. OSMO BULLAR (Finland). Publs *Esperanto* (monthly), *Kontakto* (every 2 months), *Jarlibro* (yearbook), *Esperanto Documento*.

World Association for Educational Research: Rijksuniversiteit Gent, Pedagogisch Laboratorium, 1 Henri Dunantlaan, 9000 Ghent, Belgium; tel. (91) 25-41-00; f. 1953, present title adopted 1977; aims to encourage research in educational sciences by organizing congress, issuing publications, the exchange of information, etc. Member societies and individual members in 50 countries. Pres. Prof. Dr Miroslav Cipro (Czechoslovakia); Gen. Sec. Prof. Dr M.-L. van Herreweghe (Belgium). Publ. *Communicationes* (2 a year).

World Confederation of Organizations of the Teaching Profession: 5 ave du Moulin, 1110 Morges, Vaud, Switzerland; tel. (021) 8017467; telex 458 219; fax (021) 8017469; f. 1952 to foster a conception of education directed toward the promotion of international understanding and goodwill; to improve teaching methods, educational organization and the training of teachers to equip them better to serve the interests of youth; to defend the rights and the material and moral interests of the teaching profession; to promote closer relationships between teachers in different countries. Mems: 191 national teachers' associations in 120 countries. Pres. Mary Hatwood Futrell; Sec.-Gen. Robert Harris. Publs *WCOTP Biennial Report* (in English, French, Spanish), *Echo* (quarterly, in English, French, Spanish, Japanese, Chinese and German).

World Education Fellowship: 33 Kinnaird Ave, London, W4 3SH, England; tel. (081) 994-7258; f. 1921 to promote education for international understanding, and the exchange and practice of ideas together with research into progressive educational theories and methods. Sections and groups in 20 countries. Chair. Prof. John Stephenson; Sec. Rosemary Crommelin. Publ. *The New Era in Education* (3 a year).

World Union of Catholic Teachers (Union Mondiale des Enseignants Catholiques—UMEC): Piazza San Calisto 16, 00120 Città del Vaticano; tel. 698-7286; f. 1951; encourages the grouping of Catholic teachers for the greater effectiveness of the Catholic school, distributes documentation on Catholic doctrine with regard to education, and facilitates personal contacts through congresses, seminars, etc., nationally and internationally. Mems: 63 organizations in 56 countries. Pres. Harry Mellon; Sec.-Gen. Giuseppe Cicolini. Publ. *Nouvelles de l'UMEC*.

Government and Politics

African Association for Public Administration and Management: POB 60087, Addis Ababa, Ethiopia; tel. 150389; telex 21029; f. 1971 to provide senior officials with opportunities for exchanging ideas and experience, to promote the study of professional techniques and encourage research in particular African administrative problems. Mems: over 500 corporate and individual. Pres William N. Wamalwa; Sec.-Gen. Gelase Mutahaba. Publs *Newsletter* (quarterly), *Annual Seminar Report*, studies.

Afro-Asian Peoples' Solidarity Organization—AAPSO: 89 Abdel Aziz Al-Saoud St, 11451-61 Manial, Cairo, Egypt; tel. 3622946; telex 92627; fax 3637361; f. 1957; acts among and for the peoples of Africa and Asia in their struggle for genuine independence, sovereignty, socio-economic development, peace and disarmament; sixth Congress held in 1984 (the first since 1972). Mems: 82 national committees and 10 affiliated European organizations. Pres. Dr Mourad Ghaleb; Sec.-Gen. Nouri Abdar-Razzak (Iraq). Publ. *Afro-Asian Solidarity* (quarterly).

Agency for the Prohibition of Nuclear Weapons in Latin America and the Caribbean (Organismo para la Proscripción de las Armas Nucleares en la América Latina y el Caribe—OPANAL): Temístocles 78, Col. Polanco, CP 11560, México, DF, Mexico; tel. 250-62-22; f. 1969 to ensure compliance with the Treaty for the Prohibition of Nuclear Weapons in Latin America (Treaty of Tlatelolco), 1967; to ensure the absence of all nuclear weapons in the application zone of the Treaty; to contribute to the movement against proliferation of nuclear weapons; to promote general and complete disarmament; to prohibit all testing, use, manufacture, acquisition, storage, installation and any form of possession, by any means, of nuclear weapons. Holds General Conference every two years. Mems: 24 states which have fully ratified the Treaty: Antigua and Barbuda, Bahamas, Barbados, Bolivia, Colombia, Costa Rica, Dominica, Dominican Republic, Ecuador, El Salvador, Grenada, Guatemala, Haiti, Honduras, Jamaica, Mexico, Nicaragua, Panama, Paraguay, Peru, Suriname, Trinidad and Tobago, Uruguay and Venezuela. The Treaty has two additional Protocols; the first signed and ratified by the UK, the Netherlands and the USA, and signed by France; the second signed and ratified by China, the USA, France, the UK and the USSR. Sec.-Gen. Dr Antonio Stempel París (Venezuela).

ANZUS: c/o Dept of Foreign Affairs and Trade, Bag 8, Queen Victoria Terrace, Canberra, ACT 2600, Australia; tel. (062) 619111; telex 62007; the ANZUS Security Treaty was signed in San Francisco, USA, in September 1951 by Australia, New Zealand and the USA, and ratified in April 1952 to co-ordinate partners' efforts for collective defence for the preservation of peace and security in the Pacific area, through the exchange of technical information and strategic intelligence, and a programme of exercises, exchanges and visits. Following the election of a Labour Government in New Zealand in July 1984, New Zealand refused to allow visits by US naval vessels carrying nuclear weapons, and this led to the cancellation of joint ANZUS military exercises planned for March and October 1985. In August 1986 the USA formally announced the suspension of its security commitment to New Zealand under ANZUS. Instead of the annual ANZUS Council meetings, bilateral talks were subsequently held every year between Australia and the USA. Free access to Australian ports for US naval vessels continued. ANZUS continued to govern security relations between Australia and the USA, and between Australia and New Zealand; security relations between New Zealand and the USA were the only aspect of the treaty to be suspended. The Australian and US Governments expressed the hope that at some time in the future a change in policy by New Zealand would allow a return to full trilateral co-operation.

Association of Secretaries General of Parliaments: c/o Committee Office, House of Commons, London, SW1, England; tel. (071) 219-5777; f. 1938; studies the law, practice and working methods of different Parliaments and proposes measures for improving those methods and for securing co-operation between the services of different Parliaments; operates as a consultative body to the Inter-Parliamentary Union (q.v.), and assists the Union on subjects within the scope of the Association. Mems: about 170, representing about 80 countries. Pres. Christodoulos Hadjioannou (Cyprus); Joint Sec. A. R. Kennon (UK). Publ. *Constitutional and Parliamentary Information* (2 a year).

Atlantic Treaty Association: 185 rue de la Pompe, 75116 Paris, France; tel. (1) 45-53-28-80; fax (1) 47-55-49-63; f. 1954 to inform public opinion on the North Atlantic Alliance and to promote the solidarity of the peoples of the North Atlantic; holds annual assemblies, seminars, study conferences for teachers and young politicians. Mems: national associations in the 16 member countries of NATO (q.v.). Chair. Bernardino Gomes (Portugal); Sec.-Gen. Jean Beliard (France).

Celtic League: 58 Flordd Eryri, Parc Hendre, Caernarvon, Wales; f. 1961 to foster co-operation between the six Celtic nations (Ireland, Scotland, Man, Wales, Cornwall and Brittany), especially those who are actively working for political autonomy by non-violent means; campaigns politically on issues affecting the Celtic countries; monitors military activity in the Celtic countries; co-operates with national cultural organizations to promote the languages and culture of the Celts. Mems: approx. 1,400 individuals in the Celtic communities and elsewhere. Chair. P. Beresford Ellis; Gen. Sec. D. Fear. Publ. *Carn* (quarterly).

Christian Democrat International: 16 rue de la Victoire, Boîte 1, 1060 Brussels, Belgium; tel. (02) 537-13-22; telex 61118; fax (02) 537-93-48; f.1961; to serve as a platform for the co-operation of political parties of Christian Social inspiration. Mems: parties in 56 countries (of which 25 in Europe). Sec.-Gen. André Louis. Publ. *CD-Info* (quarterly, in nine languages).

Confederation of the Socialist Parties of the European Community: 79 rue Belliard, 1047 Brussels, Belgium; tel. (02) 284-29-78; telex 62184; fax (02) 230-17-66; f. 1974; affiliated to the Socialist International (q.v.). Mems: 16 full member parties, five associate, four with observer status. Chair. Guy Spitaels (Belgium); Sec.-Gen. Axel Hamisch (Germany).

Conference on Security and Co-operation in Europe—CSCE: secretariat to be established in Prague, Czechoslovakia; reviews the Helsinki Agreement of 1975 on East-West relations (covering military security, economic co-operation and the observance of human rights), which was signed by all European countries (except Albania), Canada and the USA. Conferences were held in 1977–78 (Belgrade), 1980–83 (Madrid) and 1986–89 (Vienna). In July 1990 heads of government of the NATO member countries proposed to increase the role of the CSCE 'to provide a forum for wider political dialogue in a more united Europe'. They proposed a permanent CSCE secretariat, regular meetings of government leaders, a parliamentary body (based on the existing assembly of the Council of Europe), a mechanism for monitoring elections, and a military forum for the prevention of conflict. A CSCE summit meeting of heads of government met in November 1990 to sign an agreement on the reduction of conventional forces in Europe, and a 'Charter for a New Europe', undertaking to respect democracy and human rights, and to settle disputes by peaceful means.

Eastern Regional Organization for Public Administration—EROPA: POB 474, Manila, Philippines; tel. 995411; f. 1960 to promote regional co-operation in improving knowledge, systems and practices of governmental administration to help accelerate economic and social development; organizes regional conferences, seminars, special studies, surveys and training programmes. There are three regional centres: Training Centre (New Delhi), Local Government Centre (Tokyo), Development Management Centre (Seoul). Mems: 13 countries, 79 organizations, 256 individuals. Chair. BIMAL RAJ BASNYAT (Nepal); Sec.-Gen. RAUL P. DE GUZMAN (Philippines). Publs *EROPA Bulletin* (quarterly), *Asian Review of Public Administration*.

European Movement: 98 rue du Trône, 1050 Brussels, Belgium; tel. (02) 512-44-44; fax (02) 512-66-73; f. 1947 by a liaison committee of representatives from European organizations, to study the political, economic and technical problems of a European Union and suggest how they can be solved; to inform and lead public opinion in the promotion of integration. Conferences have led to the creation of the Council of Europe, College of Europe, etc. Mems: European movements and national councils in Austria, Belgium, Denmark, France, Germany, Greece, Ireland, Italy, Luxembourg, Malta, Netherlands, Norway, Spain, Sweden, Switzerland, United Kingdom; and several international social and economic organizations. Pres. VALÉRY GISCARD D'ESTAING (France); Sec.-Gen. J. H. C. MOLENAAR (Netherlands).

European Union of Women—EUW: Kärtnerstr. 51, 1010 Vienna, Austria; f. 1955 to increase the influence of women in the political and civic life of their country and of Europe. Mems: 16 member countries. Pres. M. FLEMMING; Publ. *Bulletin* (biennial).

European Young Christian Democrats—EYCD: 16 rue de la Victoire, 1060 Brussels, Belgium; tel. (02) 537-41-47; telex 63885; fax (02) 537-93-48; f. 1947; holds monthly seminars and meetings for young political leaders; conducts training in international political matters. Mems: 26 organizations in 22 European countries, Pres. ANDREA DE GUTTRY (Italy); Sec.-Gen. MARC BERTRAND (Belgium). Publ. *Newsletter* (monthly), *CD-Future* (quarterly).

Group of Rio: f. 1987 at a meeting in Acapulco, Mexico, of eight Latin American government leaders, who agreed to establish a 'permanent mechanism for joint political action'. The group discussed, in particular, the region's foreign debt, and demanded a reduction in interest rates and a limit on debt-service payments. Mems: Argentina, Bolivia, Brazil, Chile, Colombia, Ecuador, Mexico, Panama (suspended 1988), Paraguay, Peru, Uruguay, Venezuela.

Hansard Society for Parliamentary Government: 16 Gower St, London, WC1E 6DP, England; tel. (071) 323-1131; fax (071) 636-1536; f. 1944 to promote political education and research and the informed discussion of all aspects of modern parliamentary government. Dir DAVID HARRIS. Publ. *Parliamentary Affairs—A Journal of Comparative Politics* (quarterly).

Inter-African Socialists and Democrats: 6 rue al-Waquidi 1004, al-Menzah IV, Tunis, Tunisia; tel. 231-138; telex 15415; f. 1981 (as Inter-African Socialist Organization; name changed 1988). Chair. ABDOU DIOUF (Senegal); Sec.-Gen. SADOK FAYALA (Tunisia).

International Alliance of Women: 1st Floor, Jebb Wing, Regent's College, Inner Circle, Regent's Park, London, NW1 9NS, England; tel. (01) 487-7437; f. 1904 to obtain equality for women in all fields and to encourage women to take up their responsibilities; to join in international activities. Mems: 75 national affiliates in 65 countries. Pres. Mrs OLIVE BLOOMER. Publ. *International Women's News* (quarterly).

International Association of Educators for World Peace: POB 3282, Mastin Lake Station, Huntsville, Alabama 35810, USA; tel. (205) 534-5501; telex 91024-05482; fax (205) 851-9157; f. 1969 to develop the kind of education which will contribute to the promotion of peaceful relations at personal, community and international levels, to communicate and clarify controversial views in order to achieve maximum understanding and to help put into practice the Universal Declaration of Human Rights. Mems: 17,500 in 52 countries. Pres. Dr SURYA NATH PRASAD (India); Exec. Vice-Pres. Dr CHARLES MERCIECA (USA); Sec.-Gen. Prof. FRANCIS DESSART (Begium). Publs *Peace Progress* (annually), *IAEWP Newsletter* (quarterly), *Peace Education* (2 a year).

International Commission for the History of Representative and Parliamentary Institutions: c/o M. S. Corciulo, Via A. Baldassarri 25, 00139 Rome, Italy; tel. (06) 8125156; f. 1936. Mems: 300 individuals in 31 countries. Pres. S. MASTELLONE (Italy); Sec. M. S. CORCIULO (Italy). Publs *Parliaments, Estates and Representation*; many monographs.

International Democrat Union: 48 Westminster Palace Gardens, Artillery Row, London, SW1P 1RR, England; tel. (071) 222-0847; telex 8955242; fax (071) 222-1459; f. 1983; group of centre-right political parties; holds conference every six months; Mems: 28 political parties within and outside Europe. Exec. Sec. GRAHAM WYNN.

International Federation of Resistance Movements: 1021 Vienna II, Alliiortonstrasse 2-4/5, Austria; tel. (01) 247135; f. 1951; supports the medical and social welfare of former victims of fascism, works for peace, disarmament and human rights, against fascism and neo-fascism. Mems: 75 national organizations in 27 European countries and in Israel. Pres. ARIALDO BANFI (Italy); Sec.-Gen. ALIX LHOTE (France). Publs *Résistance Unie—Service d'Information* (5 a year, in French and German), *Cahier d'informations médicales, sociales et juridiques* (in French and German).

International Institute for Peace: 1040 Vienna, Mollwaldplatz 4, Austria; f. 1957; studies the possibilities, principles and forms of peaceful co-existence and co-operation between the two social world systems. Mems: individuals and corporate bodies invited by the executive board. Pres. Dr GEORG FUCHS (Austria); Vice-Pres. Prof. Dr RAIMO VÄYRYNEN (Finland), Prof. Dr OLEG BYKOV (USSR). Publ. *Peace and the Sciences* (in English and German).

International Institute for Strategic Studies: 23 Tavistock St, London, WC2E 7NQ, England; tel. (071) 379-7676; telex 94081492; fax (071) 836-3108; f. 1958; concerned with the study of the role of force in international relations, including problems of international strategy, disarmament and arms control, peace-keeping and intervention, defence economics, etc.; is independent of any government. Mems: 3,000. Dir FRANÇOIS HEISBOURG. Publs *Survival* (every 2 months), *The Military Balance* (annually), *Strategic Survey* (annually), *Adelphi Papers* (10 a year).

International League for Human Rights: 432 Park Avenue South, 11th Floor, New York, NY 10016, USA; tel. (212) 684-1221; f. 1942 to implement political, civil, social, economic and cultural rights contained in the Universal Declaration of Human Rights adopted by the United Nations and to support and protect defenders of human rights world-wide. Mems: individuals, national affiliates and correspondents throughout the world. Exec. Dir FELICE D. GAER. Publs *Review*, *Human Rights Bulletin*, human rights reports.

International Peace Bureau: 41 rue de Zürich, 1201 Geneva, Switzerland; tel. and fax (022) 7316429; f. 1892; promotes international co-operation for general and complete disarmament and the non-violent solution of international conflicts; co-ordinates and represents peace movements at the UN. Mems: international organizations, national peace councils or other federations co-ordinating peace movements in their respective countries, national and local organizations, totalling 98 organizations in 37 countries, with a total affiliated membership of about 30m. Pres. BRUCE KENT; Sec.-Gen. COLIN ARCHER. Publs *Geneva Monitor* (every 2 months), *IPB Geneva News*.

International Political Science Association: c/o Institute of Political Science, University of Oslo, PB 1097, Blindern, 0317 Oslo 3, Norway; tel. (2) 45-51-68; telex 72425; fax (2) 45-44-11; f. 1949; aims to promote the development of political science. Mems: 39 national associations, 105 institutions, 1,200 individual mems. Pres. GUILLERMO O'DONNELL (Argentina); Sec.-Gen. FRANCESCO KJELLBERG (Norway). Publs *Newsletter* (3 a year), *International Political Science Abstracts* (bi-monthly), *International Political Science Review* (quarterly), *Advances in Political Science* (annually).

International Union of Local Authorities: POB 90646, 2509 LP, The Hague, Netherlands; tel. (070) 3244032; telex 30510; fax (070) 3246916; f. 1913 to promote local government, improve local administration and encourage popular participation in public affairs. Functions include organization of conferences, seminars, and biennial international congress; servicing of specialized committees (municipal insurance, wholesale markets, European affairs, technical); research projects; comparative courses for local government officials, primarily from developing countries; development of inter-municipal relations to provide a link between local authorities of all countries; maintenance of a permanent office for the collection and distribution of information on municipal affairs. Members in 70 countries; six regional sections. Pres. LARS ERIC ERICSSON (Sweden); Sec.-Gen. JACEK ZAPASNIK. Publs *Local Government* (monthly).

International Union of Young Christian Democrats—IUYCD: 16 rue de la Victoire, 1060 Brussels, Belgium; f. 1962. Mems: 42 national organizations. Sec.-Gen. MARCOS VILLASMIL (Venezuela). Publs *Information* (monthly), *Documents* (quarterly).

Inter-Parliamentary Union: place du Petit-Saconnex, CP 438, 1211 Geneva 19, Switzerland; tel. (022) 7344150; telex 289784; fax (022) 7333141; f. 1889; brings together representatives of the legislatures of sovereign states. As the focal point for world-wide parliamentary dialogue, the IPU works for peace and co-operation among peoples and for the firm establishment of representative institutions; holds two conferences annually, bringing together national groups of MPs to study political, economic, social, cultural and environmental problems; there are five Committees comprising representatives of all national groups. The Union operates an International Centre for Parliamentary Documentation, and co-ordinates a technical co-operation programme to help strengthen the infrastructures of legislatures in developing countries. Budget (1000) 6.2m. Swiss francs. Mems: 113 Inter-Parliamentary Groups. Assoc. Mems: the European Parliament, the Andean Parliament. Pres. of Inter-Parliamentary Council DAOUDA SOW (Senegal); Sec.-

Gen. PIERRE CORNILLON (France). Publs. *Inter-Parliamentary Bulletin* (quarterly), *World Directory of Parliaments* (annually), *Chronicle of Parliamentary Elections and Developments* (annually), *Parliaments of the World: A Reference Compendium*.

Inuit Circumpolar Conference: POB 300, Kuujjuaq, PQ J0M 1C0, Canada; f. 1977 to protect the indigenous culture, environment and rights of the Inuit people (Eskimoes), and to encourage co-operation among the Inuit; conferences held every three years. Mems: Inuit communities in Canada, Greenland and Alaska. Pres. HANS-PAVIA ROSING.

Jewish Agency for Israel: POB 91920, Jerusalem, Israel; f. 1929 as an instrument through which world Jewry could build up a national home. It is now the executive arm of the World Zionist Organization. Mems: Zionist federations in 45 countries. Exec. Chair. LEON DULZIN; Sec.-Gen. HARRY M. ROSEN. Publs *Israel Digest* (weekly), *Economic Horizons* (monthly in USA), *Folk und Zion* (monthly in Yiddish).

Latin American Parliament (Parlamento Latinoamericano): Avda Abancay 210, Casilla de Correo 6041, Lima Peru; f. 1965; permanent democratic institution, representative of all existing political trends within the national legislative bodies of Latin America; aims to promote the movement towards economic, political and cultural integration of the Latin American republics, and to uphold human rights, peace and security. Sec.-Gen. ANDRÉS TOWNSEND EZCURRA (Peru). Publs *Acuerdos, Resoluciones de las Asambleas Ordinarias* (annually), *Revista del Parlamento Latinoamericano* (annually); statements and agreements.

Liberal International: 1 Whitehall Place, London, SW1A 2HE, England; tel. (071) 839-5905; telex 8956551; fax (071) 925-2685; f. 1947 to bring together people of liberal ideas and principles all over the world and to secure international co-operation amongst the political parties which accept the Manifesto (1947), the Liberal Declaration of Oxford (1967) and the Appeal of Rome (1981), and are affiliated to the International. Pres. ADOLFO SUÁREZ GONZÁLEZ (Spain); Exec. Vice-Pres. URS SCHÖTTLI (Switzerland).

Non-aligned Movement: Co-ordination Bureau, c/o Federal Secretariat for Foreign Affairs, 11000 Belgrade, ul. Kneza Miloša 24, Yugoslavia; f. 1961 by a meeting of 25 Heads of State, aiming to link countries which refuse to adhere to the main East-West military and political blocs; co-ordination bureau established in 1973; works for the establishment of a new international economic order, and especially for better terms for countries producing raw materials; maintains special funds for agricultural development, improvement of food production and the financing of buffer stocks; 'South Commission' (q.v.) promotes co-operation between developing countries. Ninth summit conference: Belgrade, Yugoslavia, 1989. Mems: 102.

North Atlantic Assembly: 3 place du Petit Sablon, 1000 Brussels, Belgium; tel. (02) 513-28-65; telex 24809; fax (02) 514-18-47; f. 1955 as the NATO Parliamentarians' Conference; name changed 1966; the inter-parliamentary assembly of the North Atlantic Alliance; holds two plenary sessions a year and meetings of committees (Political, Defence and Security, Economic, Scientific and Technical, Civilian Affairs, Special Committee on Alliance Strategy and Arms Control) where North Americans and Europeans examine the problems confronting the Alliance. Pres. P. DUFFY (UK); Sec.-Gen. PETER CORTERIER (Germany).

Open Door International (for the Economic Emancipation of the Woman Worker); 16 rue Américaine, 1050 Brussels, Belgium; tel. (02) 537-67-61; f. 1929 to obtain equal rights and opportunities for women in the whole field of work. Mems in 10 countries. Pres. ESTHER HODGE (UK); Hon. Sec. ADÈLE HAUWEL (Belgium).

Organization of Central American States (Organización de Estados Centroamericanos—ODECA): Pino Alto, Paseo Escalón, San Salvador, El Salvador; tel. (503) 235136; f. 1951 to strengthen unity in Central America, settle disputes, provide mutual assistance and promote economic, social and cultural development through joint action. Mems: Costa Rica, El Salvador, Guatemala, Honduras, Nicaragua. Gen. Sec. RICARDO JUÁREZ MÁRQUEZ (Guatemala).

Organization of Solidarity of the Peoples of Africa, Asia and Latin America (Organización de Solidaridad de los Pueblos de Africa, Asia y América Latina—OSPAAAL): Apdo 4224, Havana 10400, Cuba; tel. 30-5520; telex 512259; f. 1966 at the first Conference of Solidarity of the Peoples of Africa, Asia and Latin America, to unite, co-ordinate and encourage national liberation movements in the three continents, to oppose foreign intervention in the affairs of sovereign states, colonial and neo-colonial practices, and to fight against racialism and all forms of racial discrimination; favours the establishment of a new international economic order. Mems: revolutionary organizations in 82 countries. Sec.-Gen. Dr RENÉ ANILLO CAPOTE. Publ. *Tricontinental* (every 2 months, in English, French and Spanish).

Organization of the Cooperatives of America (Organización de las Cooperativas de América): Calle 97A No 11-31, Apdo Aéreo 13568, Apdo Postal 241263, Bogotá, DE, Colombia; tel. 2552867; telex 45103; fax 2189130; f. 1963 for improving socio-economic, cultural and moral conditions through the use of the co-operatives system; works in every country of the continent; regional offices sponsor plans of activities based on the most pressing needs and special conditions of individual countries. Mems: 7,000. Pres. Dr ARMANDO TOVAR PARADA; Exec. Sec. Dr CARLOS JULIO PINEDA. Publs *OCA News* (monthly), *Cooperative America* (every 4 months, in Spanish).

Parliamentary Association for Euro-Arab Co-operation: 33-35 ave d'Auderghem, 1040 Brussels, Belgium; tel. (02) 231-13-00; fax (02) 231-06-46; f. 1974 as an association of more than 650 parliamentarians of all parties from the national parliaments of the Council of Europe countries and from the European Parliament, to promote friendship and co-operation between Europe and the Arab world; Executive Committee holds joint meetings with Arab Inter-Parliamentary Union; represented in Council of Europe, Western European Union and European Parliament; works for the progress of the Euro-Arab Dialogue and a settlement in the Middle East which takes into account the national rights of the Palestinian people. Joint Chair. MICHELE ACHILLI (Italy), RUI AMARAL (Portugal); Sec.-Gen. HANS-PETER KOTTHAUS (Germany).

Socialist International: Maritime House, Old Town, Clapham, London, SW4 0JW, England; tel. (071) 627-4449; telex 261735; fax (071) 720-4448; f. 1864; the world's oldest and largest association of political parties, grouping democratic socialist, labour and social democratic parties from every continent; provides a forum for political action, policy discussion and the exchange of ideas; works with many international organizations and trades unions (particularly members of ICFTU, q.v.); holds Congress every three years; the Council meets twice a year, and regular conferences and meetings of party leaders are also held; committees and councils on a variety of subjects and in different regions meet frequently. Mems: 56 full member parties and 23 consultative parties in 72 countries. There are three fraternal organizations (see below) and nine associated organizations, including: the Asia-Pacific Socialist Organization; the Confederation of Socialist Parties of the European Community (q.v.); the Socialist Group of the European Parliament; and the International Federation of the Socialist and Democratic Press (q.v.). Pres. WILLY BRANDT (Germany); Gen. Sec. LUIS AYALA (Chile); Publ. *Socialist Affairs* (quarterly).

International Falcon Movement—Socialist Educational International: Waelhemstraat 71, 1030 Brussels, Belgium; tel. (02) 215-79-27; telex 25074; fax (02) 245-00-83; f. 1924 to promote international understanding, develop a sense of social responsibility and to prepare children and adolescents for democratic life; co-operates with several institutions concerned with children, youth and education. Mems: about 1m.; 62 co-operating organizations in all countries. Pres. JERRY SVENSSON (Sweden); Sec.-Gen. JACQUI COTTYN (Belgium). Publs *IFM-SEI Bulletin* (quarterly), *IFM-SEI Documents, Euro-Newsletter, Asian Regional Bulletin, Latin American Regional Bulletin*.

International Union of Socialist Youth: 1070 Vienna, Neustiftgasse 3, Austria; tel. (01) 931267; telex 75312469; fax (01) 523124385; f. 1907 as Socialist Youth International, present name from 1946 to educate young people in the principles of free and democratic socialism and further the co-operation of democratic socialist youth organizations; conducts international meetings, symposia, etc. Mems: 95 youth and student organizations in 65 countries. Pres. SVEN-ERIC SÖDER; Gen. Sec. RICARD TORRELL. Publ. *IUSY Newsletter*.

Socialist International Women: Maritime House, Old Town, Clapham, London, SW4 0JW, England; tel. (071) 627-4449; telex 261735; fax (071) 720-4448; f. 1955 to strengthen relations between its members, to exchange experience and views, to promote the understanding among women of the aims of democratic socialism, to promote programmes to oppose any discrimination in society and to work for human rights in general and for development and peace. Mems: 73 organizations. Pres. ANITA GRADIN; Gen. Sec. MARÍA RODRÍGUEZ-JONAS. Publ. *Women and Politics* (quarterly).

Stockholm International Peace Research Institute—SIPRI: Pipers väg 28, 171 73 Solna, Sweden; tel. (8) 55-97-00; f. 1966; studies relate to disarmament and arms control, e.g. the implications of new weapon technology, production and transfer of arms, military expenditure, etc. About 55 staff mems, half of whom are research workers. Dir Dr WALTHER STÜTZLE (Germany); Chair. Dr INGA THORSSON (Sweden). Publs *SIPRI Yearbook, Monographs*, and research reports.

Trilateral Commission: 345 East 46th St, New York, NY 10017, USA; tel. (212) 661-1180; telex 650-252-5637; fax (212) 949-7268; (also offices in Paris and Tokyo); f. 1973 by private citizens of Western Europe, Japan and North America, to encourage closer co-operation among these regions on matters of common concern; by analysis of major issues the Commission seeks to improve public understanding of such problems, to develop and support proposals for handling them jointly, and to nurture the habit of working together in the 'trilateral' area. The Commission issues 'task force' reports on such subjects as monetary affairs, political co-operation, trade issues, the energy crisis and reform of international institutions. Mems: about 300 individuals eminent in academic life, industry, finance, labour, etc.; those currently engaged as senior government officials are excluded. Chairmen DAVID ROCKEFELLER, GEORGES BERTHOIN, ISAMU YAMASHITA; Dirs CHARLES B. HECK, PAUL REVAY, TADASHI YAMAMOTO. Publs *Task Force Reports, Triangle Papers*.

War Resisters' International: 55 Dawes St, London, SE17 1EL, England; tel. (071) 703-7189; fax (071) 708-2545; f. 1921; encourages refusal to participate in or support wars or military service, collaborates with peace and non-violent social change movements. Mems: approx. 200,000. Chair. NARAYAN DESAI; Secs HOWARD CLARK, CHRIS BOOTH. Publs *Peace News* (monthly).

Women's International Democratic Federation: 1080 Berlin, Unter den Linden 13, Germany; tel. 2000958; telex 115080; f. 1945 to unite women regardless of nationality, race, religion and political opinion, so that they may work together to win and defend their rights as citizens, mothers and workers, to protect children and to ensure peace and progress, democracy and national independence. Structure: Congress, Council, Bureau, Secretariat and Finance Control Commission. Mems: 138 organizations in 124 countries as well as individual mems. Pres. FREDA BROWN (Australia). Publs *Women of the Whole World* (6 a year), *Documents and Information, News in Brief, Women in Action* (4 languages).

World Association for World Federation: Leliegracht 21, 1016 GR Amsterdam, Netherlands; tel. (020) 227502; f. 1947 to achieve a just world order through a strengthened United Nations; to acquire for the UN the authority to make and enforce laws for peaceful settlement of disputes, to govern the high seas and outer space, and to raise revenue under limited taxing powers; to establish better international co-operation in areas of environment, development and disarmament. Mems: 25,000 in 20 countries. Pres. Dr J. F. LEDDY. Publs *World Federalist News* (quarterly).

World Council of Indigenous Peoples: 555 King Edward Ave, Ottawa, Ontario K1N 6N5, Canada; tel. (613) 230-9030; telex 0533338; fax (613) 230-9340; f. 1975 to promote the rights of indigenous peoples and to support their cultural, social and economic development. The Council comprises representatives of indigenous organizations from five regions: North, South and Central America, Pacific-Asia and Scandinavia; a general assembly is held every three years. Pres. DONALD ROJAS MAROTO. Publ. *WCIP Newsletter* (4-6 a year), *Tri-Annual Report*.

World Disarmament Campaign: 45–47 Blythe St, London, E2 6LX, England; tel. (071) 729-2523; f. 1980 to encourage governments to take positive and decisive action to end the arms race, acting on the four main commitments called for in the Final Document of the UN's First Special Session on Disarmament; aims to mobilize people of every country in a demand for multilateral disarmament, to encourage consideration of alternatives to the nuclear deterrent for ensuring world security, and to campaign for a strengthened role for the UN in these matters. Chair. Dr FRANK BARNABY, Dr TONY HART.

World Federation of United Nations Associations—WFUNA: c/o Palais des Nations, 1211 Geneva 10, Switzerland; tel. (022) 7330730; telex 412962; fax (022) 7334838; f. 1946 to encourage popular interest and participation in United Nations programmes, discussion of the role and future of the UN, and education for international understanding. Plenary Assembly meets every two years; WFUNA founded International Youth and Student Movement for the United Nations (q.v.). Mems: national associations in 73 countries. Sec.-Gen. Dr MAREK HAGMAJER (Poland). Publ. *WFUNA Bulletin* (quarterly).

World Peace Council: Lönnrotinkatu 25A/VI, SF 00180 Helsinki 18, Finland; tel. 649004; telex 121680; f. 1950 at the Second World Peace Congress, Warsaw. Principles: the prevention of nuclear war; the peaceful co-existence of the various socio-economic systems in the world; settlement of differences between nations by negotiation and agreement; complete disarmament; elimination of colonialism and racial discrimination; respect for the right of peoples to sovereignty and independence. Mems: Representatives of c. 2,500 political parties and national organizations from 139 countries, and of 30 international organizations; Presidential Committee of 228 mems elected by the Council. Sec.-Gen. ROMESH CHANDRA. Publs *New Perspectives* (every 2 months), *Peace Courier* (monthly).

Industrial and Professional Relations

See also the chapters on ICFTU, WCL and WFTU.

Arab Federation of Petroleum, Mining and Chemicals Workers: POB 1905, Tripoli, Libya; f. 1961; runs the Arab Petroleum Institute for Labour Studies, Cairo. Mems: 18 affiliated unions in 12 countries. Sec.-Gen. ANWAR ASHMAWI MOHAMED (Egypt). Publs *Arab Petroleum* (monthly), specialized publications and statistics.

Association for Systems Management: 24587 Bagley Rd, Cleveland, Ohio 44138, USA; tel. (216) 243-6900; f. 1947; an international professional organization for the advancement and self-renewal of management information systems analysis throughout business and industry. Mems: 10,000 in 35 countries. Pres. JAMES T. HERLIKY; Exec. Dir RICHARD L. IRWIN. Publ. *Journal of Systems Management*.

Caribbean Congress of Labour: Room 405, Norman Centre, Broad St, Bridgetown, Barbados; tel. 429-5517; f. 1960 to fight for the recognition of trade union organizations; to build and strengthen the ties between the Free Trade Unions of the Caribbean and the rest of the world; to support the work of ICFTU (q.v.); to encourage the formation of national groupings and centres. Mems: 28 in 17 countries. Pres. LEROY TROTMAN (Barbados); Sec.-Treas. KERTIST AUGUSTUS (Dominica).

European Association for Personnel Management: 4000 Düsseldorf, Niederkasseler Lohweg 16, Germany; f. 1962 to disseminate knowledge and information concerning the personnel function of management, to establish and maintain professional standards, to define the specific nature of personnel management within industry, commerce and the public services, and to assist in the development of national associations. Mems: 14 national associations. Sec.-Gen. H. WIRTH.

European Civil Service Federation: 48 rue Franklin, 1040 Brussels, Belgium; tel. (02) 733-22-59; telex 21877; f. 1962 to foster the idea of a European civil service of staff of international organizations operating in Western Europe or pursuing regional objectives; upholds the interests of civil service members. Sec.-Gen. L. RIJNOUDT. Publ. *Eurechos*.

European Federation of Conference Towns: 40 rue Washington, 1050 Brussels, Belgium; tel. (02) 452-98-30; telex 20429; lays down standards for conference towns; provides advice and assistance to its members and other organizations holding conferences in Europe; undertakes publicity and propaganda for promotional purposes; helps conference towns to set up national centres. Perm. Sec. RITA DE LANDTSHEER.

European Industrial Research Management Association—EIRMA: 38 cours Albert 1, 75008 Paris, France; tel. (1) 42-25-60-44; telex 643 908; f. 1966 under auspices of the OECD (q.v.); a permanent body in which European science-based firms meet to discuss and study industrial research policy and management and take joint action in trying to solve problems in this field. Mems: 170 in 18 countries. Pres. R. JUNNILA; Gen. Sec. Dr R. SCHULZ. Publs *Annual Report, Conference Reports, Working Group Reports*.

European Trade Union Confederation: 37 rue Montagne aux Herbes Potagères, 1000 Brussels, Belgium; tel. (02) 218-31-00; telex 62241; f. 1973; comprises 36 national trade union confederations in 21 western European countries, representing over 43m. workers; holds congress every three years. Gen. Sec. MATHIAS HINTERSCHEID.

Federation of International Civil Servants' Associations: Palais des Nations, 1211 Geneva 10, Switzerland; tel. (022) 7988400; telex 412962; fax (022) 7330096; f. 1952 to co-ordinate policies and activities of member associations and unions, to represent staff interests before inter-agency and legislative organs of the UN and to promote the development of an international civil service. Mems: 28 associations and unions consisting of staff of UN organizations, 19 consultative associations and five inter-organizational federations with observer status. Pres. ETTORE DENTI. Publs *Annual Report, FICSA News, Newsletter*.

Graphical International Federation: Valeriusplein 30, 1075 BJ Amsterdam, Netherlands; tel. (020) 71-32-79; telex 18695; f. 1925. Mems: national federations in 15 countries, covering 100,000 workers. Pres. L. VAN HAUDT (Belgium); Sec.-Gen. R. E. VAN KESTEREN (Netherlands).

International Association of Conference Interpreters: 10 ave de Sécheron, 1202 Geneva, Switzerland; tel. (022) 7313323; fax (022) 7324151; f. 1953 to represent professional conference interpreters, ensure the highest possible standards and protect the legitimate interests of members. Establishes criteria designed to improve the standards of training and recognizes schools meeting the required standards. Has consultative status with the UN and several of its

OTHER INTERNATIONAL ORGANIZATIONS — Industrial and Professional Relations

agencies. Mems: 1,800 in 53 countries. Pres. GISELA SIEBOURG (Germany); Vice-Pres. MONIQUE DUCROUX (Switzerland). Publs *Code of Professional Conduct, Yearbook* (listing interpreters), etc.

International Association of Conference Translators: 15 route des Morillons, 1218 Le Grand-Saconnex, Geneva, Switzerland; tel. (022) 7910666; f. 1962; aims to examine problems of revisers, translators, précis writers and editors working for international conferences and organizations, to protect the interests of those in the profession and help maintain high standards; establishes links with international organizations and conference organizers. Mems: 495 in 33 countries. Pres. SHEILA HALL (UK); Exec. Sec. GENEVIÈVE SERIOT (Switzerland); Publ. *Directory, Bulletin*.

International Association of Crafts and Small and Medium-Sized Enterprises—IACME: Schwarztorstrasse 26, 3007 Berne, Switzerland; tel. (031) 257785; telex 912947; f. 1947 to defend undertakings and the freedom of enterprise within private economy, to develop training, to encourage the creation of national organizations of independent enterprises and promote international collaboration, to represent the common interests of members and to institute exchange of ideas and information. Mems: organizations in 26 countries which also belong to one of the international organic federations composing the IACME: International Federation of Master Craftsmen (IFC), International Federation of Small and Medium-Sized Industrial Enterprises (IFSMI) and International Federation of Small and Medium-Sized Commercial Enterprises (IFSMC). Chair. PAUL SCHNITKER; Gen. Sec. BALZ HORBER.

International Association of Medical Laboratory Technologists: c/o SLF/SSF, Ostermalmsgatan 19, 114 26 Stockholm, Sweden; tel. (8) 10-30-31; f. 1954 to afford opportunities for meetings and communication between medical laboratory technologists, to raise training standards and to standardize training in different countries in order to facilitate free exchange of labour; holds international congress every second year. Mems: 150,000 in 33 countries. Pres. ULLA-BRIT LINDHOLM; Exec. Dir MARGARETTA HAAG. Publ. *MedTecInternational* (2 a year).

International Association of Mutual Insurance Companies: 114 rue La Boétie, 75008 Paris, France; tel. (1) 42-25-84-86; fax (1) 42-56-04-49; f. 1964 for the establishment of good relations between its members and the protection of the general interests of private insurance based on the principle of mutuality. Mems: over 250 in 25 countries. Pres. W. DIENER (Switzerland); Sec.-Gen. A. TEMPELAERE (France). Publs *Mutuality* (2 a year), *AISAM dictionary, Newsletter* (3 a year).

International Confederation of Executive and Professional Staffs (Confédération internationale des cadres): 30 rue de Gramont, 75002 Paris, France; telex 215116; f. 1950 to improve the material and moral status of executive staffs. Mems: national organizations in Belgium, Denmark, France, Federal Republic of Germany, Italy, Luxembourg, Monaco, Netherlands, Portugal, Spain, UK, and international professional federations for chemistry and allied industries (FICCIA), mines (FICM), transport (FICT), metallurgical industries (FIEM), agriculture (FIDCA) and insurance (AECA). Pres. Dr FAUSTO D'ELIA (Italy); Sec.-Gen. JEAN DE SANTIS (France). Publ. *Cadres*.

International European Construction Federation: 9 rue La Pérouse, 75116 Paris, France; tel. (1) 47-20-80-74; telex 613456; f. 1905. Mems: 25 national employers' organizations in 18 countries. Pres. PAUL WILLEMEN (Belgium); Sec.-Gen. ERIC LEPAGE (France). Publ. *L'Entreprise Européenne*.

International Federation of Actors: 31A Thayer St, London, W1M 5LH, England; tel. (01) 487-4699; fax (01) 487-5809; f. 1952. Mems: actors' unions totalling 200,000 individuals in 43 countries. Pres. PETER HEINZ KERSTEN (Austria); Sec.-Gen. ROLF REMBE.

International Federation of Air Line Pilots' Associations: Interpilot House, 116 High St, Egham, Surrey, TW20 9HQ, England; tel. (0784) 437361; telex 8951918; fax (0784) 432045; f. 1948 to aid in the establishment of fair conditions of employment; to contribute towards safety within the industry; to provide an international basis for rapid and accurate evaluation of technical and industrial aspects of the profession. Mems: 73 associations, 60,000 pilots. Pres. Capt. L. H. D. BAKKER; Exec. Administrator T. V. MIDDLETON.

International Federation of Business and Professional Women: Studio 16, Cloisters Business Centre, 8 Battersea Park Rd, London, SW8 4BG, England; tel. (071) 738-8323; fax (071) 622-8528; f. 1930 to promote interests of business and professional women and secure combined action by them. Mems: national federations, associate clubs and individual associates, totalling more than 200,000 mems in 75 countries. Pres. YVETTE SWAN; Gen. Sec. MARIANNE HASLEGRAVE. Publ. *Widening Horizons* (quarterly).

International Industrial Relations Association: c/o International Labour Office, 1211 Geneva 22, Switzerland; tel. (022) 7996841; telex 415647; fax (022) 7988685; f. 1966 to encourage development of national associations of specialists, facilitate the spread of information, organize conferences, and to promote internationally planned research, through study groups and regional meetings; a World Congress is held every three years. Mems: 26 associations, 45 institutions and 900 individuals. Pres. Prof. Dr JOHN NILAND; Sec. Dr A. GLADSTONE. Publs *IIRA Bulletin* (3 a year).

International Organisation of Employers—IOE: 28 chemin de Joinville, 1216 Cointrin/Geneva, Switzerland; tel. (022) 7981616; telex 415463; fax (022) 7988862; f. 1920, reorganized 1948; aims to represent the interests of private employers, to defend free enterprise, to maintain contacts in labour matters. General Council meets annually; there is an Executive Committee and a General Secretariat. Mems: 99 federations in 101 countries. Chair. JEAN-JACQUES OECHSLIN (France); Sec.-Gen. COSTAS KAPARTIS (Cyprus). Publ. *The Free Employer*.

International Organization of Experts—ORDINEX: 163 rue Saint-Honoré, 75001 Paris, France; tel. (1) 42-60-54-41; fax (1) 42-61-65-52; f. 1961 to establish co-operation between experts on an international level. Mems: 2,400. Pres. EUGÈNE GELBERT (Switzerland). Publ. *General Yearbook*.

International Public Relations Association—IPRA: Case Postale 126, 1211 Geneva 20, Switzerland; tel. (022) 7910550; fax (022) 7880336; f. 1955 to provide for an exchange of ideas, technical knowledge and professional experience among those engaged in international public relations, and to foster the highest standards of professional competence. Mems: 900 in 63 countries. Pres. CHARLES VAN DER STRATEN WAILLET (Belgium); Sec.-Gen. ROGER HAYES. Publs *Newsletter* (6 a year), *International Public Relations Review* (4 a year).

International Society of City and Regional Planners—ISoCaRP: Mauritskade 23, 2514 HD The Hague, Netherlands; tel. (070) 3462654; fax (070) 3617909; f. 1965 to promote better planning practice through the exchange of knowledge. Mems: 430 in 49 countries. Pres. JAVIER DE MESONES (Spanish); Sec.-Gen. H. W. STRUBEN (Netherlands). Publ. *News Bulletin* (2 a year).

International Union of Architects: 51 rue Raynouard, 75016 Paris, France; tel. (1) 45-24-36-88; telex 614 855; fax (1) 45-24-02-78; f. 1948; holds triennial congress. Mems: 90 countries. Pres. OLUFEMI MAJEKODUNMI (Nigeria); Sec.-Gen. NILS CARLSON. Publ. *Lettre d'informations* (monthly).

Latin American Federation of Agricultural and Food Industry Workers (Federación Latinoamericana de Trabajadores Campesinos y de la Alimentación): Apdo 1422, Caracas 1010A, Venezuela; tel. (032) 721549; telex 29873; fax (032) 720463; f. 1961 to represent the interests of agricultural workers and workers in the food and hotel industries in Latin America. Mems: national unions in 28 countries and territories. Sec.-Gen. JOSÉ LASSO. Publ. *Boletín Luchemos* (quarterly).

Nordic Federation of Factory Workers' Unions (Nordiska Fabriksarbetarefederationen): Box 1114, 111 81 Stockholm, Sweden; f. 1901 to promote collaboration between affiliates in Denmark, Finland, Iceland, Norway and Sweden; supports sister unions economically and in other ways in labour market conflicts. Mems: 400,000 in 12 unions. Pres. UNO EKBERG (Sweden); Sec. RAGNAR CARLSSON (Sweden).

Pan-African Employers' Federation: c/o Federation of Kenya Employers, POB 48311, Nairobi, Kenya; tel. 721929; telex 22642; f. 1986 to link African employers' organizations and to represent them at the UN, the International Labour Organisation and the OAU. Pres. HENRI GEORGET (Niger); Sec.-Gen. TOM DIJU OWUOR (Kenya).

World Federation of Scientific Workers: 6 Endsleigh St, London, WC1H 0DX, England; tel. (01) 387-5096; f. 1946 to improve the position of science and scientists, to assist in promoting international scientific co-operation and to promote the use of science for beneficial ends; studies and publicizes problems of general, nuclear, biological and chemical disarmament; surveys the position and activities of scientists. Member organizations in 35 countries, totalling over 300,000 mems. Sec.-Gen. S. DAVISON (UK). Publ. *Scientific World* (quarterly in English, Esperanto, German and Russian).

World Movement of Christian Workers—WMCW: 90 rue des Palais, 1210 Brussels, Belgium; tel. (02) 216-56-96; f. 1961 to unite national movements which advance the spiritual and collective well-being of workers; general assembly every four years. Mems: 49 affiliated movements in 42 countries. Sec.-Gen. JACQUES PULH. Publ. *Infor-WMCW*.

World Union of Professions (Union mondiale des professions libérales): 28 rue Hamelin, 75116 Paris, France; tel. (1) 47-23-00-02; fax (1) 47-20-29-35; f. 1987 to represent and link members of the liberal professions. Mems: 23 national inter-professional organizations, two regional groups and nine international federations. Pres. ALAIN TINAYRE.

OTHER INTERNATIONAL ORGANIZATIONS

Law

Asian-African Legal Consultative Committee: 27 Ring Rd, Lajpat Nagar-IV, New Delhi 110024, India; tel. 6415280; f. 1956 to consider legal problems referred to it by member countries and to be a forum for Afro-Asian co-operation in international law and economic relations; provides background material for conferences, prepares standard/model contract forms suited to the needs of the region; promotes arbitration as a means of settling international commercial disputes; trains officers of member states; has permanent UN observer status. Mems: 40 states. Pres. MATHEW GUY MULI (Kenya); Sec.-Gen. FRANK X. NJENGA (Kenya).

Council of the Bars and Law Societies of the European Community—CCBE: 40 rue Washington, 1050 Brussels, Belgium; tel. (02) 640-42-74; telex 65080; fax (02) 647-79-41; f. 1960 to ensure liaison between the bars and law societies of the member countries as between these and the European Community authorities (Parliament, Economic and Social Committee, Court and Commission). Mems: 12 delegations, and observers from Austria, Cyprus, Finland, Norway, Sweden and Switzerland. Pres. PIET WACKIE EYSTEN (Netherlands); Sec.-Gen. JEAN-RÉGNIER THYS (Belgium).

Hague Conference on Private International Law: Scheveningseweg 6, 2517 KT The Hague, Netherlands; tel (70) 3633303; telex 33383; fax (70) 3604867; f. 1893 to work for the unification of the rules of private international law, Permanent Bureau f. 1955. Mems: 23 European and 13 other countries. Sec.-Gen. Dr G. A. L. DROZ.

Institute of International Law (Institut de droit international): 22 ave William Favre, 1207 Geneva, Switzerland; tel. (022) 7360772; f. 1873 to promote the development of international law by endeavouring to formulate general principles in accordance with civilized ethical standards, and by giving assistance to genuine attempts at the gradual and progressive codification of international law. Mems: limited to 132 members and associates from all over the world. Sec.-Gen. NICOLAS VALTICOS (Greece). Publ. *Annuaire de l'Institut de Droit international*.

Inter-American Bar Association: 1889 F St, NW, Suite LL-2, Washington, DC 20006–4499, USA; tel. (202) 789-2747; telex 64128; fax (202) 842-2608; f. 1940 to promote the rule of law and to establish and maintain relations between associations and organizations of lawyers in the Americas. Mems: 90 associations and 3,500 individuals in 27 countries. Sec.-Gen. GROVER PREVATTE HOPKINS (USA). Publs *Newsletter* (quarterly), *Conference Proceedings*.

Intergovernmental Copyright Committee: Division of Books and Copyright, UNESCO, 7 place de Fontenoy, 75700 Paris, France; tel. (1) 45-68-10-00; telex 204461; fax (1) 42-73-04-01; established to study the application and operation of the Universal Copyright Convention and to make preparations for periodic revisions of this Convention; and to study any other problems concerning the international protection of copyright, in co-operation with various international organizations. Mems: 18 states. Chair. ROBERT DITTRICH.

International Association for the Protection of Industrial Property: Bleicherweg 58, Postfach, 8027 Zürich 27, Switzerland; tel. (01) 2041212; telex 815656; fax (01) 2027502; f. 1897 to encourage legislation regarding the international protection of industrial property and the development and extension of international conventions, and to make comparative studies of existing legislation with a view to its improvement and unification; holds triennial congress. Mems: 6,400 (national and regional groups and individual mems) in 96 countries. Exec. Pres. MASAHIKO TAKEDA (Japan); Sec.-Gen. Dr MARTIN J. LUTZ (Switzerland).

International Association of Democratic Lawyers: 263 ave Albert, 1180 Brussels, Belgium; tel. (02) 345-14-71; fax (02) 343-35-96; f. 1946 to facilitate contacts and exchange between lawyers, to encourage study of legal science and international law and support the democratic principles favourable to maintenance of peace and co-operation between nations; conducts research on banning atomic weapons, on labour law, private international law, agrarian law, etc.; consultative status with UN. Mems: in 96 countries. Pres. STEFANO RODOTA (Italy); Sec.-Gen. AMAR BENTOUMI (Algeria). Publs *International Review of Contemporary Law*, in French, English and Spanish (every 6 months).

International Association of Juvenile and Family Court Magistrates: Tribunal pour Enfants, Palais de Justice, 75055 Paris, France; f. 1928 to consider questions concerning child welfare legislation and to encourage research in the field of juvenile courts and delinquency. Activities: international congress, study groups and regional meetings. Pres. A. BARBOSA (Portugal); Gen.-Sec. LUCIEN BEAULIEU (Canada).

International Association of Law Libraries: c/o The Law School Library, University of Chicago, 1121 East 60th St, Chicago, Ill 60637, USA; tel. (312) 702-9599; fax (312) 702-0730; f. 1959 to encourage and facilitate the work of librarians and others concerned with the bibliographic processing and administration of legal materials. Mems: 600 from more than 50 countries (personal and institutional). Pres. ADOLF SPRUDZS (USA); Sec. TIMOTHY KEARLEY (USA). Publ. *International Journal of Legal Information* (3 a year), *The IALL Messenger* (irregular).

International Association of Legal Sciences (Association internationale des sciences juridiques): c/o CISS, 1 rue Miollis, 75015 Paris, France; tel. (1) 45-68-25-59; f. 1950 to promote the mutual knowledge and understanding of nations and the increase of learning by encouraging throughout the world the study of foreign legal systems and the use of the comparative method in legal science. Governed by a president and an executive bureau of 10 members known as the International Committee of Comparative Law. National committees in 47 countries. Sponsored by UNESCO. Pres. Prof. D. MITROVIĆ (Yugoslavia); Sec.-Gen. Dr S. FRIEDMAN (France).

International Association of Penal Law: c/o Prof. R. Ottenhof, Faculté de Droit, Université de Pau, 19 ave Montebello, 64000 Pau, France; f. 1924 to establish collaboration between those from different countries who are working in penal law, studying criminology, and promoting the theoretical and practical development of an international penal law. Mems: 1,500. Pres. Prof. M. C. BASSIOUNI. Publ. *Revue Internationale de Droit Pénal* (biannual).

International Bar Association: 2 Harewood Place, Hanover Sq., London, W1R 9HB, England; tel. (071) 629-1206; telex 8812664; fax (071) 409-0456; f. 1947; a non-political federation of national bar associations and law societies; aims to discuss problems of professional organization and status; to advance the science of jurisprudence; to promote uniformity and definition in appropriate fields of law; to promote administration of justice under law among peoples of the world; to promote in their legal aspects the principles and aims of the United Nations. Mems: 124 member organizations in 71 countries, 13,500 individual members in 129 countries. Pres. W. REECE SMITH (USA); Exec. Dir Mrs MADELEINE MAY (UK); Sec.-Gen. ANTHONY F. SMITH (Australia). Publs *International Business Lawyer* (11 a year), *International Bar News* (4 a year), *International Legal Practitioner* (quarterly), *Journal of Energy and Natural Resources Law* (quarterly).

International Commission of Jurists: POB 120, 109 route de Chêne, 1224 Chêne-Bougeries, Geneva, Switzerland; tel. (022) 493545; telex 418531; fax (022) 493145; f. 1952 to strengthen the Rule of Law in its practical manifestations and to defend it by mobilizing world legal opinion. There are 59 sections in 49 countries. Pres. ANDRÉS AGUILAR MAWDSLEY (Venezuela); Sec.-Gen. ADAMA DIENG (acting). Publs *The Rule of Law and Human Rights*, *The Review*, *ICJ Newsletter*, *Bulletin of the Centre for the Independence of Judges and Lawyers (CIJL)*, special reports.

International Commission on Civil Status: Faculté de Droit et des Sciences politiques, place d'Athènes, 67084 Strasbourg Cedex, France; f. 1950 for the establishment and presentation of legislative documentation relating to the rights of individuals, and research on means of simplifying the judicial and technical administration concerning civil status. Mems: governments of Austria, Belgium, France, Germany, Greece, Italy, Luxembourg, Netherlands, Portugal, Spain, Switzerland, Turkey. Pres. W. BREUKELAAR (Netherlands); Sec.-Gen. J. M. BISCHOFF (France).

International Copyright Society: 1000 Berlin 15, Kurfürstendamm 35, Germany; tel. (030) 8833077; telex 184578; fax (030) 8817105; f. 1954 to enquire scientifically into the natural rights of the author and to put the knowledge obtained to practical application all over the world, in particular in the field of legislation. Mems: 393 individuals and corresponding organizations in 52 countries. Pres. Prof. Dr ERICH SCHULZE; Gen. Sec. VERA MOVSESSIAN. Publs *Schriftenreihe* (61 vols), *Yearbook*.

International Council of Environmental Law: 5300 Bonn 1, Adenauerallee 214, Germany; tel. (0228) 2692-240; f. 1969 to exchange information and expertise on legal, administrative and policy aspects of environmental questions. Exec. Governor Dr WOLFGANG BURHENNE. Publs *Directory*, *References*, *Environmental Policy and Law*.

International Criminal Police Organization—INTERPOL: POB 205, 26 rue Armengaud, 92210 Saint Cloud, France; tel. (1) 46-02-55-50; telex 270658; f. 1923, reconstituted 1946; aims to promote and ensure the widest possible mutual assistance between police forces within the limits of laws existing in different countries, to establish and develop all institutions likely to contribute to the prevention and suppression of ordinary law crimes; co-ordinates activities of police authorities of member states in international affairs, centralizes records and information regarding international criminals; operates a radio network of 70 stations. The General Assembly is held annually. Mems: official bodies of 154 countries. Pres. YVES BARROT (France); Sec.-Gen. R. E. KENDALL. Publs

OTHER INTERNATIONAL ORGANIZATIONS
Law

International Criminal Police Review (6 a year), *Counterfeits and Forgeries, International Crime Statistics.*

International Customs Tariffs Bureau: 38 rue de l'Association, 1000 Brussels, Belgium; tel. (02) 516-87-74; the executive instrument of the International Union for the Publication of Customs Tariffs; f. 1890, to translate and publish all customs tariffs in five languages—English, French, German, Italian, Spanish. Mems: 76. Pres. F. ROELANTS (Belgium); Dir RICHARD J. PERKINS. Publs *International Customs Journal, Annual Report.*

International Development Law Institute: Via Paolo Frisi 23, 00197 Rome, Italy; tel. 872008; telex 622381; f. 1983 to strengthen the lawyer's role in solving development problems, by offering training and technical assistance to legal advisers and contract negotiators from developing countries; the 1988 training programme includes seminars on international business transactions and courses for development lawyers; provides specially-designed training 'workshops' for particular countries on request. Dir L. MICHAEL HAGER.

International Federation for European Law—FIDE: Claudio Coelle 20, 28001 Madrid, Spain; fax 5773774; f. 1961 to advance studies on European law among members of the European Community by co-ordinating activities of member societies and by organizing conferences every two years. Mems: 12 national associations. Pres. EDUARDO GARCÍA DE ENTERÍA; Sec.-Gen. SANTIAGO MARTÍNEZ LAGE.

International Federation of Senior Police Officers: 4400 Münster, Feldkamp 4, Postfach 480 164, Germany; tel. (02501) 7171; f. 1950 to unite policemen of different nationalities, adopting the general principle that prevention should prevail over repression, and that the citizen should be convinced of the protective role of the police; seeks to develop methods, and studies problems of traffic police. Set up International Centre of Crime and Accident Prevention, 1976. Mems: 16 national groups and individuals of 48 different nationalities. Pres. HERMAN BERGER (Norway); Vice-Pres. Dr HUBERT HOLLER (Austria), Col WARICHET (Belgium); Sec.-Gen. G. KRATZ (Germany). Publ. *International Police Information* (every 3 months, French, German and English).

International Institute for the Unification of Private Law—UNIDROIT: Via Panisperna 28, 00184 Rome, Italy; tel. (06) 6841372; telex 623196; fax (06) 6841394; f. 1926 to undertake studies of comparative law, to prepare for the establishment of uniform legislation, to prepare drafts of international agreements on private law and to organize conferences and publish works on such subjects; holds international congresses on private law and meetings of organizations concerned with the unification of law; library of 215,000 vols. Mems: governments of 53 countries. Pres. RICCARDO MONACO (Italy); Sec.-Gen. MALCOLM EVANS (UK). Publs *Uniform Law Review* (2 a year), *Digest of Legal Activities of International Organizations, News Bulletin* (quarterly), etc.

International Institute of Space Law—IISL: 3-5 rue Mario Nikis, 75015 Paris, France; tel. (1) 45-67-42-60; telex 205917; fax (1) 42-73-21-20; f. 1959 at the XI Congress of the International Astronautical Federation; organizes annual Space Law colloquium; studies juridical and sociological aspects of astronautics and makes awards. Mems: individuals from many countries, elected for life. Pres. I. DIEDERICKS-VERSCHOOR (Netherlands). Publs *Proceedings of Annual Colloquium on Space Law, Survey of Teaching of Space Law in the World.*

International Juridical Institute: Permanent Office for the Supply of International Legal Information, 't Hoenstraat 5, 2596 HX The Hague, Netherlands; tel. (070) 3460974; fax (070) 3453226; f. 1918 to supply information on any matter of international interest, not being of a secret nature, respecting international, municipal and foreign law and the application thereof. Pres. C. D. VAN BOESCHOTEN; Sec. P. A. M. MEIJKNECHT; Dir A. L. G. A. STILLE.

International Law Association: Charles Clore House, 17 Russell Square, London, WC1B 5DR, England; tel. (071) 323-2978; fax (071) 323-3580; f. 1873 for the study and advancement of international law, public and private; the promotion of international understanding and goodwill. Mems: 4,000 in 40 regional branches. Pres. Sir LAURENCE STREET (Australia); Chair. Exec. Council Sir GORDON SLYNN (UK); Sec.-Gen. BRUCE MAULEVERER.

International Maritime Committee (Comité Maritime International): Mechelsesteenweg 203, 2018 Antwerp 1, Belgium; tel. (03) 218-48-87; telex 31653; fax (03) 218-67-21; f. 1897 to contribute to the unification of maritime law by means of conferences, publications, etc. and to encourage the creation of national associations; work includes drafting of conventions on collisions at sea, salvage and assistance at sea, limitation of shipowners' liability, maritime mortgages, etc. Mems: national associations in 49 countries. Pres. FRANCESCO BERLINGIERI (Italy); Secs-Gen. JAN RAMBERG (Exec.), HENRI VOET (Admin. and Treas.). Publs *CMI Newsletter, Year Book.*

International Nuclear Law Association: 29 sq. de Meeûs, 1040 Brussels, Belgium; f. 1972 to promote international studies of legal problems related to the peaceful use of nuclear energy, particularly the protection of man and the environment; holds conference every two years. Mems: 450 in 30 countries. Pres. F. VANDENABEELE (Belgium); Sec.-Gen. FERNAND LACROIX (Belgium).

International Penal and Penitentiary Foundation: c/o Dr K. Hobe, Bundesministerium der Justiz, Postfach 200 365, 5300 Bonn 2, Germany; tel. (0228) 584226; telex 228506; fax (0228) 584525; f. 1951 to encourage studies in the field of prevention of crime and treatment of delinquents. Mems in 21 countries (membership limited to three people from each country) and corresponding mems. Pres. JORGE DE FIGUEIREDO DIAS (Portugal); Sec.-Gen. KONRAD HOBE (Germany).

International Police Association—IPA: Postbus 100, 3970 AC Driebergen, Netherlands; tel. (03438) 35676; fax (03438) 17308; f. 1950 to exchange professional information, create ties of friendship between all sections of police service, organize group travel, studies, etc. Mems: 260,000 in 52 countries. Sec. T. A. LEENDERS. Publs *Police World* (quarterly), *International Bibliography of the Police, Annual Scholarship Report, Youth Gatherings, Police and Public, Police Participation in the Council of Europe.*

International Society for Labour Law and Social Security: ILO, Case 500, 1211 Geneva 22, Switzerland; f. 1958 to encourage collaboration between specialists; holds World Congress every three years as well as irregular regional congresses (Europe, Asia and Americas). Mems: 1,000 in 60 countries. Pres. Prof. L. NAGY (Hungary); Sec.-Gen. J.-M. SERVAIS (Belgium).

International Union of Latin Notaries (Unión Internacional del Notariado Latino): Via Senato 37, 20121 Milan, Italy; f. 1948 to study and standardize notarial legislation and promote the progress, stability and advancement of the Latin notarial system. Mems: organizations and individuals in 42 countries. Sec. FEDERICO GUASTI. Publ. *Revista Internacional del Notariado* (quarterly).

International Union of Lawyers: 103 ave Charles de Gaulle, 92200 Neuilly, France; tel. (1) 47-38-13-11; telex 620101; f. 1927 to promote the independence and freedom of lawyers, and defend their ethical and material interests on an international level; to contribute to the development of international order based on law. Mems: 55 associations in 41 countries. Publs *Bulletin* (quarterly). Sec. NATHALIE FLORNOY.

Law Association for Asia and the Pacific—Lawasia: 10th Floor, 170 Phillip St, Sydney, NSW 2000, Australia; tel. (02) 221-2970; telex 73063; f. 1966 to promote the administration of justice, the protection of human rights and the maintenance of the rule of law within the region, to advance the standard of legal education, to promote uniformity within the region in appropriate fields of law and to advance the interests of the legal profession. Mems: 52 asscns in 21 countries; 2,000 individual mems. Pres. G. T. S. SIDHU (Malaysia); Sec.-Gen. Dr D. H. GEDDES. Publs *Lawasia* (annual journal), *Lawasia Human Rights Bulletin, Lawasia Newsletter, Lawasia Human Rights Newsletter.*

Permanent Court of Arbitration: Carnegieplein 2, 2517 KJ The Hague, Netherlands; tel. (070) 3469680; fax (070) 3561338; f. by the Convention for the Pacific Settlement of International Disputes (1899, 1907) to enable immediate recourse to be made to arbitration for international disputes which cannot be settled by diplomacy, to facilitate the solution of disputes by international inquiry and conciliation commissions. Mems: governments of 76 countries. Sec.-Gen. HANS JONKMAN (Netherlands).

Society of Comparative Legislation: 28 rue Saint-Guillaume, 75007 Paris, France; tel. (1) 45-44-44-67; fax (1) 45-49-41-65; f. 1869 to study and compare laws of different countries, and to investigate practical means of improving the various branches of legislation. Mems: 1,700 in 48 countries. Pres. JACQUES BOUTET (France); Sec.-Gen. XAVIER BLANC-JOUVAN (France). Publs *Revue Internationale de Droit Comparé* (quarterly), *Journées de la Société de Législation comparée* (annually).

Union of Arab Jurists: POB 6026, Al-Mansour, Baghdad, Iraq; tel. 5375820; telex 21-2661; f. 1975 to facilitate contacts between Arab lawyers, to safeguard the Arab legislative and judicial heritage; to encourage the study of Islamic jurisprudence; and to defend human rights. Mems: 16 bar associations in 16 countries and individual mems. Sec.-Gen. SHIBIB LAZIM AL-MALIKI. Publ. *Al-Hukuki al-Arabi* (Arab Jurist).

Union of International Associations: 40 rue Washington, 1050 Brussels, Belgium; tel. (02) 640-41-09; telex 65080; fax (02) 649-32-69; f. 1907, present title adopted 1910. Aims: to serve as a documentation centre on international organizations, to undertake and promote research into the phenomenon of 'organization' and into the legal, administrative and technical problems common to international organizations, to publicize their work and to encourage mutual contacts. Mems: 200 in 54 countries. Pres. F. A. CASADIO (Italy); Sec.-Gen. JACQUES RAEYMAECKERS (Belgium).

Publs *Transnational Associations* (6 a year), *International Congress Calendar* (quarterly), *Yearbook of International Organizations*, *International Organization Participation* (annually), *Global Action Network* (annually), *Encyclopedia of World Problems and Human Potential*, *Documents for the Study of International Non-Governmental Relations*, *International Congress Science* series, *International Association Statutes* series, *Who's Who in International Organizations*.

World Jurist Association—WJA: Suite 202, 1000 Connecticut Ave, NW, Washington, DC 20036, USA; tel. (202) 466-5428; telex 440456; fax (202) 452-8540; f. 1963; promotes the continued development of international law and legal maintenance of world order; holds biennial world conferences, World Law Day, demonstration trials; organizes research programmes. Mems: lawyers, jurists and legal scholars in 155 countries. Pres. CHARLES S. RHYNE; Exec. Vice-Pres. MARGARETHA M. HENNEBERRY (USA). Publs *The World Jurist* (English, every 2 months), Research Reports, *Law and Judicial Systems of Nations*, 3rd revised edn (directory), *World Legal Directory* (biennial), *Law and Computer Technology* (quarterly), *World Law Review* Vols I-V (World Conference Proceedings), *The Chief Justices and Judges of the Supreme Courts of Nations* (directory), etc.

World Association of Judges—WAJ: f. 1966 to advance the administration of judicial justice through co-operation and communication among ranking jurists of all countries. Sec.-Gen. Dr KARL-GEORG ZIERLEIN.

World Association of Law Professors—WALP: f. 1975 to improve scholarship and education in dealing with matters related to international law; Chair. V. P. NANDA (USA); Sec.-Gen. DIETER C. UMBACH (FRG).

World Association of Lawyers—WAL: f. 1975 to develop international law and improve lawyers' effectiveness in dealing with it; Pres. RAUL I. GOCO (Philippines).

Medicine and Health

Council for International Organisations of Medical Sciences—CIOMS: c/o WHO, ave Appia, 1211 Geneva 27, Switzerland; tel. (022) 7913406; telex 415416; fax (022) 7910746; f. 1949; general assembly every three years. Mems: 90 organizations. Pres. Prof F. VILARDELL; Exec. Sec. Dr Z. BANKOWSKI. Publs *Calendar of International and Regional Congresses* (annual), *Proceedings of CIOMS*, *Round Table Conferences*, *International Nomenclature of Diseases*.

MEMBERS OF CIOMS

Members of CIOMS include the following:

International Academy of Legal and Social Medicine: c/o 49A ave Nicolai, BP 8, 4802 Verviers, Belgium; tel. (087) 22-98-21; f. 1938; holds an international Congress and General Assembly every three years, and interim meetings. Mems in 50 countries. Exec. Sec. and Treas. ELIZABETH FRANCSON. Publs *Acta Medicinae Legalis et Socialis* (annually), *Newsletter* (3 a year).

International Association for the Study of the Liver: c/o R. Groszmann, VA Medical Center, Hepatic Hemodynamic Lab. 111C, West Haven, CT 06516, USA. Pres. Dr LUIZ CARLOS DA COSTA GAYOTTO; Sec. ROBERTO GROSZMANN.

International Association of Allergology and Clinical Immunology: 611 East Wells St, Milwaukee, WI 53202, USA; tel. (414) 276-6445; fax (414) 276-3349; f. 1945 to further work in the educational, research and practical medical aspects of allergic and immunological diseases; 1991 Congress: Kyoto, Japan. Mems: 40 national societies. Pres. Prof. J. CHARPIN (France); Sec.-Gen. Dr O. L. FRICK (USA); Exec. Sec. R. IBER (USA). Publ. *Allergy and Clinical Immunology News* (6 a year).

International College of Surgeons: 1516 N. Lake Shore Drive, Chicago, Ill 60610, USA; tel. (312) 642-3555; telex 324629; fax (312) 787-1624; f. 1935, as a world-wide institution for the advancement of the art and science of surgery, to create a common bond among the surgeons of all nations and promote the highest standards of surgery without regard to nationality, creed, or colour; sends teams of surgeons to developing countries to teach local surgeons; organizes research and scholarship programme and International Surgical Congresses; maintains the International Museum of Surgical Science in Chicago. Mems: about 15,000 in 100 countries. Pres. Prof. TEHEMTON E. UDWADIA; Corporate Sec. Dr ROBERT H. HUX. Publ. *International Surgery* (quarterly).

International Dental Federation: 64 Wimpole St, London, W1M 8AL, England; tel. (071) 935-7852; telex 25247; fax (071) 486-0183; f. 1900. Mems: 88 national dental associations in 100 countries and 21 affiliates. Pres. Dr R. GONZALES GIRALDA (Spain); Exec. Dir Dr P. Å. ZILLÉN (Sweden). Publs *International Dental Journal* (every 2 months) and *FDI News* (every 2 months).

International Diabetes Federation: 40 rue Washington, 1050 Brussels, Belgium; tel. (02) 647-44-14; telex 65080; fax (02) 649-32-69; f. 1949 to help in the collection and dissemination of information regarding diabetes and to improve the welfare of people suffering from that disease. Mems: associations in 100 countries. Pres. Prof J. J. HOET (Belgium); Sec. HILARY WILLIAMS. Publ. *IDF News Bulletin* (quarterly), *IDF Bulletin* (3 a year).

International Federation of Clinical Neurophysiology: c/o Dr B. R. Tharp, Dept of Neurology, H3160, Stanford Medical Center, Stanford, Ca 94305, USA; tel. (415) 725-6903; fax (415) 725-7459; f. 1949 to attain the highest level of knowledge in the field of electro-encephalography and clinical neurophysiology in all the countries of the world. Mems: 48 organizations. Pres. Dr J. KIMURA (Japan); Sec. Dr B. R. THARP (USA). Publ. *The EEG Journal* (monthly), *Evoked Potentials* (every 2 months).

International Federation of Oto-Rhino-Laryngological Societies: 91-12 Fruithoflaan, 2600 Antwerp, Belgium; tel. (03) 440-20-21; fax (03) 440-20-22; f. 1965 to initiate and support programmes to protect hearing and prevent hearing impairment; Congresses every four years. Pres. T. SACRISTÁN ALONSO (Spain); Exec. Dir Prof. J. MARQUET (Belgium). Publ. *IFOS Newsletter* (6 a year).

International Federation of Physical Medicine and Rehabilitation: Mount Sinai Hospital, Dept of Rehabilitation Medicine, 600 University Ave, Toronto, Canada M5G 1X5; f. 1952 to link national societies, organize conferences (every four years) and disseminate information to developing countries. Next conference: Dresden, Germany, 1992. Pres. Dr C. M. GODFREY; Sec. Dr J. JIMÉNEZ.

International Federation of Surgical Colleges: c/o Prof. W. A. L. MacGowan, Royal College of Surgeons in Ireland, 123 St Stephen's Green, Dublin 2, Ireland; tel. 780200; telex 30795; fax 782100; f. 1958 to encourage high standards of surgery and surgical training; co-operates closely with the World Health Organization in compiling standard lists of surgical requirements in developing countries and evaluating surgical manpower. Mems: colleges or associations in 35 countries, and 210 individual associates. Pres. Dr ROBERT B. SALTER (Canada); Sec. Prof. W. A. L. MACGOWAN (Ireland).

International League Against Rheumatism: 58 rue Ernest Bloch, 1207 Geneva, Switzerland; tel. (022) 7351688; telex 423118; fax (022) 7351874; f. 1927 to promote international co-operation for the study and control of rheumatic diseases; to encourage the foundation of national leagues against rheumatism; to organize regular international congresses and to act as a connecting link between national leagues and international organizations. Mems: 13,000. Pres. Dr KEN MUIRDEN (Australia); Sec.-Gen. Prof. JOHN EDMONDS (Australia). Publs *Annals of the Rheumatic Diseases* (in England), *Revue du Rhumatisme* (in France), *Reumatismo* (in Italy), *Arthritis and Rheumatism* (USA), etc.

International Leprosy Association: Sasakawa Hall 6F, 3-12-12 Kita, Minato-ku, Tokyo 108, Japan; f. 1931 to promote international co-operation in work on leprosy, from which about 15m. people in the world are suffering. Thirteenth Congress, The Hague, 1988. Sec. Dr YO YUASA (Japan). Publ. *International Journal of Leprosy and Other Mycobacterial Diseases* (quarterly).

International Pediatric Association: Château de Longchamp, Carrefour de Longchamp, Bois de Boulogne, 75016 Paris, France; tel. (1) 45-27-15-90; telex 648379; fax (1) 45-25-73-67; f. 1912; holds triennial congresses and regional meetings. Mems: 110 national paediatric societies, associations or academies in 102 countries. Pres. Prof. PERLA SANTOS-OCAMPO (Philippines); Exec. Dir Prof. IHSAN DOGRAMACI (Turkey). Publ. *International Child Health* (quarterly).

International Rehabilitation Medicine Association: 1333 Moursund Ave, A-221, Houston, Texas 77030, USA; tel. (713) 799-5086; fax (713) 799-5058; f. 1968. Mems: 2,005 in 72 countries. Pres. Prof. M. GRABOIS (USA). Publ. *News and Views* (quarterly).

International Rhinologic Society: c/o Prof. Clement, ENT-Dept, AZ-VUB, Laarbeeklaan 101, 1090 Brussels, Belgium; f. 1965; holds congress every four years. Pres. Prof. R. TAKAHASHI (Japan); Sec. Prof. P. A. R. CLEMENT (Belgium). Publ. *Journal of Rhinology*.

International Society and Federation of Cardiology: CP 117, 1211 Geneva 12, Switzerland; tel. (022) 476755; fax (022) 471028; f. 1978 through merger of the International Society of Cardiology and the International Cardiology Federation; aims to promote the study, prevention and relief of cardiovascular diseases through scientific and public education programmes and the exchange of materials between its affiliated societies and foundations and with other agencies having related interests. Organizes World Congresses every four years. Mems: national cardiac societies and heart foundations in 64 countries. Pres. Dr W. RUTISHAUSER (Switzerland); Sec. Dr E. SALAZAR (Mexico); Exec. Sec. M. B. DE FIGUEIREDO. Publ. *Heartbeat* (quarterly).

OTHER INTERNATIONAL ORGANIZATIONS

International Society of Audiology: 330–332 Gray's Inn Rd, London, WC1X 8EE, England; tel. (071) 837-8855, ext. 4322; f. 1962. Mems: 300 individuals. Pres. Prof. W. NIEMEYER (Germany); Gen. Sec. R. HINCHCLIFFE. Publ. *Audiology* (every 2 months).

International Society of Dermatology (Tropical, Geographic and Ecologic): 200 First St, SW, Rochester, Mn 55901, USA. Pres. Dr FRANCISCO KERDEL-VEGAS; Sec.-Gen. Dr SIGFRID A. MULLER.

International Society of Internal Medicine: Dept. of Medicine, Regionalspital, 4900 Langenthal, Switzerland; tel. (063) 293131; f. 1948 to encourage research and education in internal medicine. Mems: 37 national societies, 3,000 individuals in 54 countries. Congresses: Brussels 1988, Stockholm 1990. Pres. Prof. F. CHALÉM (Colombia); Sec. Dr ROLF A. STREULI (Switzerland).

International Union against Cancer: 3 rue du Conseil Général, 1205 Geneva, Switzerland; tel. (022) 201811; telex 429724; fax (022) 201810; f. 1933 to promote on an international level the campaign against cancer in its research, therapeutic and preventive aspects; organizes International Cancer Congress every four years; administers the American Cancer Society Eleanor Roosevelt International Cancer Fellowships, the International Cancer Research Technology Transfer Project and the Yamagiwa-Yoshida Memorial International Cancer Study Grants; conducts worldwide programmes of campaign organization, public education and patient support, detection and diagnosis, epidemiology and prevention, smoking and cancer, tumour biology, etc. Mems: voluntary national organizations, private or public cancer research and treatment organizations and institutes and governmental agencies in 82 countries. Pres. Dr S. ECKHARDT (Hungary); Sec.-Gen. Dr G. P. MURPHY (USA); Exec. Dir A. J. TURNBULL. Publs *UICC International Directory of Cancer Institutes and Organizations* (every 2 years), *International Journal of Cancer* (18 a year), *UICC News* (quarterly), *International Calendar of Meetings on Cancer* (2 a year).

Latin American Association of National Academies of Medicine: Apdo Aéreo 88951, Bogotá 8, Colombia; tel. 2-493122; f. 1967. Mems: nine national Academies. Pres. Dr PLUTARCO NARANJO (Peru); Sec. Dr ALBERTO CÁRDENAS-ESCOVAR (Colombia).

Medical Women's International Association: 5000 Cologne 41, Herbert-Levin-Strasse 5, Germany; tel. (221) 4004558; telex 08882161; f. 1919 to facilitate contacts between medical women and to encourage their co-operation in matters connected with international health problems. Mems: national associations in 44 countries, and individuals. Pres. Dr IL OK CHOO (Republic of Korea); Sec.-Gen. CAROLYN MOTZEL (Germany).

World Federation for Medical Education: c/o University of Edinburgh, Teviot Place, Edinburgh, EH8 9AG, Scotland; tel. (031) 226-3125; telex 727442; fax (031) 667-7938; f. 1972; promotes and integrates medical education world-wide; links regional and international associations. Pres. Prof. H. J. WALTON.

World Federation of Associations of Paediatric Surgeons: c/o Prof. J. Boix-Ochoa, Clinica Infantil 'Vall d'Hebrón', Departamento de Cirugía Pediátrica, Valle de Hebrón, s/n, Barcelona 08035, Spain; f. 1974. Mems: 50 associations. Pres. J. R. PYNEYRO; Sec. Prof. J. BOIX-OCHOA.

World Federation of Neurology: London Neurological Centre, 110 Harley St, London W1N 1DG, England; tel. (071) 935-3546; f. 1955 as International Neurological Congress, present title adopted 1957. Aims to assemble members of various congresses associated with neurology, and organize co-operation of neurological researchers. Organizes Congress every four years. Mems: 22,000 in 68 countries. Pres. Lord WALTON OF DETCHANT (UK); Sec.-Treas. F. CLIFFORD ROSE (UK). Publs *Journal of the Neurological Sciences, Acta Neuropathologica, World Neurology* (quarterly).

World Medical Association: 28 ave des Alpes, 01210 Ferney-Voltaire, France; tel. (50) 40-75-75; telex 385755; fax (50) 40-59-37; f. 1947 to achieve the highest international standards in all aspects of medical practice, to promote closer ties among doctors and national medical associations by personal contact and all other means, to study problems confronting the medical profession and to present its views to appropriate bodies. Structure: annual General Assembly and Council (meets twice a year). Mems: 45 national medical associations. Pres. Dr RAM ISHAY (Israel); Sec.-Gen. Dr ANDRÉ WYNEN (Belgium). Publ. *The World Medical Journal* (6 a year).

World Organization of Gastroenterology: Department of Medicine, Royal Infirmary, Edinburgh EH3 9YW, Scotland; tel. (031) 229-2477; telex 727442; fax (031) 229-2948; f. 1958 to promote clinical and academic gastroenterological practice throughout the world, and to ensure high ethical standards. Mems in 73 countries. Sec.-Gen. Prof. IAN A. D. BOUCHIER (UK).

World Psychiatric Association: Dept of Psychiatry, Kommunehospitalet, 1399 Copenhagen K, Denmark; tel. (33) 938500, ext. 3390; fax (33) 324240; f. 1961 for the exchange of information concerning the problems of mental illness and the strengthening of relations between psychiatrists in all countries; organizes World Psychiatric Congresses and regional and inter-regional scientific meetings. Mems: 81 societies totalling 75,000 psychiatrists. Sec.-Gen. Prof. FINI SCHULSINGER (Denmark).

ASSOCIATE MEMBERS OF CIOMS

Associate members of CIOMS include the following:

Asia Pacific Academy of Ophthalmology: Dept of Ophthalmology, Juntendo University School of Medicine, 3-1-3 Hongo Bunkyo-ku, Tokyo 113, Japan; tel. 03-813-3111 (ext. 3354); f. 1956; holds congress every two years (12th congress: Seoul, Republic of Korea, 1989). Pres. Prof. CALVIN RING; Sec.-Gen. Dr AKIRA NAKAJIMA (Japan).

International Association of Medicine and Biology of the Environment: c/o 115 rue de la Pompe, 75116 Paris, France; tel. (1) 45-53-45-04; telex 614584; f. 1972 with assistance from the UN Environment Programme; aims to contribute to the solution of problems caused by human influence on the environment; structure includes 13 technical commissions. Mems: individuals and organizations in 71 countries. Hon. Pres. Prof. R. DUBOS; Pres. Dr R. ABBOU.

International Committee of Military Medicine and Pharmacy: 79 rue Saint-Laurent, 4000 Liège, Belgium; tel. (41) 22-21-83; fax (41) 22-21-50; f. 1921. Mems: official delegates from 91 countries. Pres. Gen. Dr A. LAIN GONZÁLEZ (Spain); Sec.-Gen. Lt.-Col Dr M. COOLS (Belgium). Publ. *Revue Internationale des Services de Santé des Forces Armées* (quarterly).

International Congress on Tropical Medicine and Malaria: c/o Prof. M. Miller, Faculty of Medicine, University of Calgary, Calgary T2N 1N4, Canada; to work towards the solution of problems concerning malaria and tropical diseases. Sec. Prof. MAX MILLER.

International Council for Laboratory Animal Science: POB 6, 70211 Kuopio 10, Finland; tel. 163080; telex 42218; fax 163410; f. 1976. Pres. S. ERICHSEN (Norway); Sec.-Gen. O. HÄNNINEN (Finland).

International Federation of Clinical Chemistry: c/o Dr P. Garcia-Webb, Dept of Clinical Biochemistry, Queen Elizabeth II Medical Centre, Nedlands, Western Australia 6009, Australia; tel. (9) 3892632; telex 93446; fax (9) 3893882; f. 1952. Mems: 53 national societies (about 26,000 individuals). Pres. Prof. G. SIEST (France); Sec. Dr. P. GARCIA-WEBB (Australia). Publs *Journal* (6 a year), *Annual Report*.

International Medical Society of Paraplegia: National Spinal Injuries Centre, Stoke Mandeville Hospital, Aylesbury, Bucks, HP21 8AL, England; tel. (0296) 84111. Pres. Prof. R. E. CARTER (USA); Sec. I. NUSEIBEH. Publ. *Paraplegia*.

International Society of Blood Transfusion: BP 100, 91943 Les Ulis Cedex, France; tel. (1) 69-07-20-40; telex 603218; fax (1) 69-07-41-85; f. 1937. Mems: about 1,935 in 100 countries. Pres. G. ARCHER (Australia); Sec.-Gen. M. GARRETTA. Publ. *Transfusion Today* (quarterly).

Rehabilitation International: 25 East 21st St, New York, NY 10010, USA; tel. (212) 420-1500; telex 446412; fax (212) 505-0871; f. 1922 to advance the welfare of the disabled through the exchange of information and research on equipment and methods of assistance; organizes international conferences and co-operates with UN agencies and other international organizations. Mems: national organizations in 80 countries. Pres. FENMORE R. SETON; Sec.-Gen. SUSAN R. HAMMERMAN. Publs *International Rehabilitation Review* (3 a year), *International Journal of Rehabilitation Research* (quarterly), *Rehabilitación* (2 a year).

Transplantation Society: c/o Dr R. Ferguson, Dept of Surgery, Room 259, Means Hall, 1654 Upham Drive, Ohio State University, Columbus, Ohio 43210, USA; tel. (614) 293-8545; fax (614) 293-4670. Pres. Dr J. RICHARD BATCHELOR; Secs Prof. R. F. M. WOOD, Dr RONALD FERGUSON (USA).

World Federation of Associations of Clinical Toxicology Centres and Poison Control Centres: c/o Prof. L. Roche, 150 cours Albert-Thomas, 69372 Lyon Cedex 2, France; tel. 78-74-16-74. Pres. Prof. A. FURTADO RAHDE; Sec. Prof. L. ROCHE.

OTHER ORGANIZATIONS

Aerospace Medical Association: 320 So. Henry St, Alexandria, Va 22314, USA; tel. (703) 739-2240; f. 1929 as Aero Medical Association; to advance the science and art of aviation and space medicine; to establish and maintain co-operation between medical and allied sciences concerned with aerospace medicine; to promote, protect, and maintain safety in aviation and astronautics. Mems: individual, constituent and corporate in 75 countries. Pres. SARAH A. NUNNELEY (USA); Exec. Vice-Pres. RUFUS R. HESSBERG (USA). Publ. *Aviation Space and Environmental Medicine* (monthly).

OTHER INTERNATIONAL ORGANIZATIONS
Medicine and Health

Asian-Pacific Dental Federation: 841 Mountbatten Rd, Singapore 1543; tel. 3453125; telex 34189; fax 3442116; f. 1955 to establish closer relationship among dental associations in Asian and Pacific countries and to encourage research, with particular emphasis on dental health in the region; holds congress every two years. Mems: 17 national associations. Sec.-Gen. Dr OLIVER HENNEDIGE. Publ. *APDF/APRO Newsletter* (3 a year).

Association for Paediatric Education in Europe: Juliana Children's Hospital, POB 60604, 2506 LP The Hague, Netherlands; f. 1970 to encourage improvements and promote research in paediatric education. Mems: 70 in 20 European countries. Pres. O. NEYZI (Turkey); Sec. Dr M. LOURDES LEVY (Portugal).

Association of National European and Mediterranean Societies of Gastro-enterology—ASNEMGE: Gastroenterology Unit, 18th Floor, Guy's Tower, Guy's Hospital, London, SE1 9RT, England; tel. (071) 855-4564; fax (071) 407-6689; f. 1947 to facilitate the exchange of ideas between gastro-enterologists and disseminate knowledge; organizes International Congress of Gastroenterology every four years. Mems in 30 countries, national societies and sections of national medical societies. Pres. Prof. ALDO TORSOLI; Sec. Prof. R. H. DOWLING (UK).

Balkan Medical Union: 1 rue Gabriel Peri, 70148 Bucharest, Romania; tel. 16-78-46; f. 1932; studies medical problems, particularly ailments specific to the Balkan region, to promote a regional programme of public health; enables exchange of information between doctors in the region; organizes research programmes and congresses. Mems: doctors and specialists from Albania, Bulgaria, Cyprus, Greece, Romania, Turkey and Yugoslavia. Pres. Dr M. POPESCU BUZEU (Romania); Sec.-Gen. Dr P. FIRU (Romania). Publs *Archives de l'union médicale Balkanique* (6 a year), *Bulletin de l'union médicale Balkanique* (6 a year), *Annuaire, Bulletin de l'Entente Médicale Méditerranéenne* (annually).

European Association for Cancer Research: c/o Dr M. R. Price, Cancer Research Campaign Laboratories, University of Nottingham, University Park, Nottingham, NG7 2RD, UK; tel. (0602) 484848 (ext. 3401); f. 1968 to facilitate contact between cancer research workers and to organize scientific meetings in Europe. Mems: over 1,300 in 40 countries in and outside Europe. Pres. Prof. Dr P. BANNASCH (Germany); Sec. Dr M. R. PRICE (UK).

European Association for Health Information and Libraries: 60 rue de la Concorde, 1050 Brussels, Belgium; tel. (02) 511-80-63; fax (02) 512-32-65; f. 1987; serves professionals in health information and biomedical libraries of the member states of the Council of Europe; holds regular conferences of medical librarians. Pres. M. CLELAND (Switzerland); Sec. B. BLUM (Switzerland). Publ. *Newsletter to European Health Librarians* (quarterly).

European Association for the Study of Diabetes: Auf'm Hennekamp 32, 4000 Dusseldorf 1, Germany; tel. (0211) 316738; f. 1965 to support research in the field of diabetes, to promote the rapid diffusion of acquired knowledge and its application; holds annual scientific meetings within Europe. Mems: 3,000 in 62 countries, not confined to Europe. Pres. Prof. P. LEFEBVRE (Belgium); Exec. Dir Dr VIKTOR JOERGENS. Publ. *Diabetologia* (12 a year).

European Association of Internal Medicine: Clinique Médicale B, 1 place de l'Hôpital, 67091 Strasbourg, France; tel. 88-16-12-50; f. 1969 to promote internal medicine from the ethical, scientific and professional points of view; to bring together European internists; to organize meetings, etc. Mems: 400 in 20 European countries. Pres. Prof. E. COCHE (Belgium); Sec. Prof J. F. BLICKLE (France). Publ. *European Journal of Internal Medicine*.

European Association of Radiology: c/o Prof. A. Baert, Universitarie Ziekenhuizen, Gasthuisberg, Herestraat 49, 3000 Leuven, Belgium; f. 1962 to develop and co-ordinate the efforts of radiologists in Europe by promoting radiology in both biology and medicine, studying its problems, developing professional training and establishing contact between radiologists and professional, scientific and industrial organizations. Mems: national associations in 25 countries. Sec.-Gen. Prof. ALBERT BAERT.

European Association of Social Medicine: Via Sacchi 24, 10128 Turin, Italy; f. 1953 to provide co-operation between national associations of preventive medicine and public health. Mems: associations in 10 countries. Pres. Prof. Dr JEAN-BAPTISTE BOUVIER (France); Sec.-Gen. Prof. Dr ENRICO BELLI (Italy).

European Brain and Behaviour Society: c/o G. Mohn, Univ.-Augenklinik, 7400 Tübingen, Schleichstr. 12, Germany; tel. (07071) 293734; holds two conferences a year. Pres. Prof. M. JEANNEROD; Sec. Dr G. MOHN.

European Committee for the Protection of the Population against the Hazards of Chronic Toxicity—EUROTOX: Faculté des Sciences Pharmaceutiques et Biologiques, Laboratoire de Toxicologie et d'Hygiène Industrielle, 4 ave de l'Observatoire, Paris 6e, France; tel. (1) 43-26-71-22; f. 1957; studies risks of long-term build-up of toxicity. Gen. Sec. Prof. R. TRUHAUT (France).

European Healthcare Management Association: Vergemount Hall, Clonskeagh, Dublin 6, Ireland; tel. 839299; f. 1966 to promote collaboration between European countries in the organization and development of training programmes in hospital and health services administration; to encourage studies and research. Mems: 100 (corporate) in 21 countries, and 23 associate mems. Pres. Prof. Dr K.-D. HENKE; Dir PHILIP C. BERMAN; Publ. *Newsletter* (quarterly), *Directory* (every 2 years).

European League against Rheumatism: Witikonerstr. 68, 8032 Zürich, Switzerland; tel. (01) 3839690; fax (01) 3839810; f. 1947 to co-ordinate research and treatment of rheumatic complaints, conducted by national societies; holds annual symposia, and congress every four years. Mems in 32 countries. Exec. Sec. F. WYSS. Publ. *Bulletin*.

European Organization for Caries Research—ORCA: c/o Prof. C. Robinson, Dept of Oral Biology, School of Dentistry, University of Leeds, Leeds, LS2 9LU, England; tel. (0532) 336159; f. 1953 to promote and undertake research on dental health, encourage international contacts, and make the public aware of the importance of care of the teeth. Mems: research workers in 23 countries. Pres. Prof. J. ARENDS (Netherlands); Sec.-Gen. Prof. C. ROBINSON (UK).

European Orthodontic Society: Flat 31, 49 Hallam St, London, W1N 5LL, England; tel. (01) 935-2795; f. 1907 to advance the science of orthodontics and its relations with the collateral arts and sciences. Mems: 1,630 in 51 countries. Sec. Prof. J. MOSS. Publ. *European Journal of Orthodontics* (quarterly).

European Union of Medical Specialists: 20 ave de la Couronne, Brussels 1050, Belgium; tel. (02) 649-51-64; fax (02) 649-26-90; f. 1958 to safeguard the interests of medical specialists. Mems: two representatives each from Belgium, Denmark, France, Federal Republic of Germany, Greece, Ireland, Italy, Luxembourg, Netherlands, Portugal, Spain, United Kingdom. Pres. Dr A. KUTTNER (Germany); Sec.-Gen. Dr R. PEIFFER (Belgium).

Eurotransplant Foundation: c/o University Hospital, Leiden 2333 AA, Netherlands; tel. (071) 268008; telex 39266; fax (071) 149480; f. 1967; co-ordinates the exchange of organs for transplants in Germany, Austria, Belgium, the Netherlands; keeps register of almost 10,000 patients with all necessary information for matching with suitable donors in the shortest possible time; organizes transport of the organ and the transplantation; collaboration with similar organizations in Western and Eastern Europe. Chair. Prof. Dr J. J. VAN ROOD; Dir Drs B. COHEN, Dr G. G. PERSIJN.

Federation of French-Language Obstetricians and Gynaecologists (Fédération des gynécologues et obstetriciens de langue française): Clinique Baudelocque, 123 blvd de Port-Royal, 75674 Paris Cedex 14, France; tel. (1) 42-34-11-43; f. 1920 for the scientific study of phenomena having reference to obstetrics, gynaecology and reproduction in general. Mems: 1,500 in 50 countries. Pres. Prof. P. AUDET LAPOINTE (Canada); Gen. Sec. Prof. J. R. ZORN (France). Publ. *Journal de Gynécologie Obstétrique et Biologie de la Reproduction* (8 a year).

Federation of the European Dental Industry: 5000 Cologne 1, Pipinstrasse 16, Germany; tel. (0221) 215993; telex 8882226; fax (0221) 245013; f. 1957 to promote the interests of the dental industry. Mems: national associations in Austria, Denmark, France, Germany, Italy, Netherlands, Sweden, Switzerland, United Kingdom. Pres. and Chair. A. D'HOLLOSY (Netherlands); Sec. HARALD RUSSEGGER (Germany).

Federation of World Health Foundations: c/o WHO, Ave Appia, 1211 Geneva 27, Switzerland; f. 1967 to co-ordinate the work of the members and to maintain relations between them and the World Health Organization. The General Council of representatives of the member foundations is assisted by a steering committee. The Federation examines projects to be considered by the foundations, seeks to establish new foundations, provides advice and training. Mems: 10 national health foundations which have entered into formal agreement with WHO, in Canada, Hong Kong, Indonesia, Ireland, Philippines, Sri Lanka, Switzerland, USA. Pres., CEO MILTON P. SIEGEL.

General Association of Municipal Health and Technical Experts: 9 rue de Phalsbourg, 75017 Paris, France; tel. (1) 42-27-38-91; f. 1905 to study all questions related to urban and rural health—the control of preventable diseases, disinfection, distribution and purification of drinking water, construction of drains, sewage, collection and disposal of household refuse, etc. Mems in 35 countries. Pres. J. M. HIRTZ; Sec.-Gen. M. BRÈS (France). Publ. *TSM-Techniques, Sciences, Méthodes* (monthly).

Inter-American Association of Sanitary and Environmental Engineering: Rua Nicolau Gagliardi 354, 05429 São Paulo, SP, Brazil; tel. (011) 212-4080; telex 81453; fax (011) 814-2441; f. 1946 to assist the development of water supply and sanitation. Mems: 23 countries. Publ. *Revista Ingeniería Sanitaria* (quarterly).

International Academy of Aviation and Space Medicine: Infante Stanto 66-3A, Lisbon 3, Portugal; f. 1955; to facilitate international co-operation in research and teaching in the fields of aviation and space medicine. Mems: in 40 countries. Sec.-Gen. Dr ANTONIO CASTELO-BRANCO.

International Academy of Cytology: Universitäts Frauenklinik, 7800 Freiburg i. Br., Hugstetterstr. 55, Germany; tel. (0761) 270-3076; fax (0761) 3122; f. 1957 to foster and facilitate international exchange of knowledge and information on specialized problems of clinical cytology and to stimulate research in clinical cytology; to standardize terminology. Mems: 1,975. Pres. MICHAEL DRAKE; Sec. MANUEL HILGARTH. Publ. *Acta Cytologica*.

International Agency for the Prevention of Blindness: c/o National Eye Institute, National Institutes of Health, Bldg 31, Room 6A03, Bethesda, Md 20892, USA; tel. (301) 496-2234; telex 248232; fax (301) 496-2297; f. 1975 to collaborate with the World Health Organization and other UN organizations in promoting and co-ordinating global action for the prevention of blindness, with emphasis on the major blinding diseases of the developing world. Operates through national committees in 64 countries and regional organizations in eight areas. Pres. CARL KUPFER. Publ. *IAPB Newsletter* (2 a year).

International Anatomical Congress: Prof. L. J. A. DiDio, Dept of Anatomy, Medical College of Ohio, CS 10008 Toledo, OH 43699, USA; f. 1903; runs congresses for anatomists from all over the world to discuss research, teaching methods and terminology in the fields of gross and microscopical anatomy, histology, cytology, etc. Pres. Prof. L. J. A. DiDio (USA); Sec.-Gen. Prof. J. A. E. PINA (Portugal).

International Association for Child and Adolescent Psychiatry and Allied Professions: Dept of Child and Adolescent Psychiatry, Malmö General Hospital, 21401 Malmö, Sweden; tel. (40) 331674; fax (40) 331701; f. 1948 to promote scientific research in the field of child psychiatry by collaboration with allied professions. Mems: national associations and individuals in 39 countries. Sec.-Gen. KARI SCHLEIMER. Publ. *International Yearbook of Child Psychiatry*.

International Association for Dental Research: 1111 14th St, NW, Suite 1000, Washington, DC 20005, USA; tel. (202) 898-1050; fax (202) 789-1033; f. 1920 to encourage research in dentistry and related fields, and to publish the results; holds annual meetings, triennial conferences and divisional meetings. Pres. WILLIAM H. BOWEN; Exec. Dir Dr JOHN J. CLARKSON.

International Association of Agricultural Medicine and Rural Health: Saku Central Hospital, 197 Usuda-machi, Minamisaku-Gun, Nagano 384-03, Japan; tel. (0267) 82-3131; fax (0267) 82-9638; f. 1961 to study the problems of medicine in agriculture in all countries and to prevent the diseases caused by the conditions of work in agriculture. Mems: 405. Pres. Prof. J. TÉNYI (Hungary); Sec.-Gen. Prof. TOSHIKAZU WAKATSUKI (Japan).

International Association of Applied Psychology: Graduate School of Management, Monash University, Clayton, Vic. 3168, Australia; f. 1920, present title adopted in 1955; aims to establish contacts between those carrying out scientific work on applied psychology, to promote research and the adoption of measures contributing to this work. Mems: 3,000 in 90 countries. Pres. Prof. H. C. TRIANDIS (USA); Sec.-Gen. Prof. M. C. KNOWLES (Australia). Publ. *Applied Psychology: An International Review* (quarterly).

International Association of Asthmology—INTERASMA: c/o Prof. F. Michel, ave du Major Flandre, 34059 Montpellier, France; f. 1954 to advance medical knowledge of bronchial asthma and allied disorders. Mems: 1,100 in 54 countries. Pres. Prof. BELLANTI (USA); Sec. Prof. GODARD (France). Publ. *Allergologia et Immunopathologia* (every 2 months).

International Association of Gerontology: Avda Prolongación División del Norte No. 4273, Col. Prado Coapa, Coyoacan 14350, México DF, Mexico; tel. 6843204; fax 6795842; f. 1950 to promote research and training in all fields of gerontology and to protect interests of gerontologic societies and institutions. Mems: 56 national societies in 52 countries. Pres. Dr S. BRAVO-WILLIAMS (Mexico); Sec.-Gen. Dr J. GONZÁLEZ-ARAGÓN (Mexico). Publ. *Newsletter* (annually).

International Association of Group Psychotherapy: Viale San Gimignano 10, 20146 Milan, Italy; tel. (02) 4154072; f. 1954; holds congresses every three years. Mems: 500 individuals in 30 countries; 20 organizations in 10 countries. Pres. GRETE A. LEUTZ (Germany); Sec.-Treas. GIOVANNI BORIA (Italy). Publ. *Newsletter*.

International Association of Hydatid Disease: Florida 460, Piso 3, 1005 Buenos Aires, Argentina; tel. 322-3431; telex 23414; f. 1941. Mems: 500 in 40 countries. Pres. Dr MIGUEL PÉREZ GALLARDO (Spain); Sec.-Gen. Prof. Dr RAUL MARTÍN MENDY (Argentina). Publ. *Archivos Internacionales de la Hidatidosis* (every 4 years), *Boletín de Hidatidosis* (quarterly).

International Association of Logopedics and Phoniatrics: 6 ave de la Gare, 1003 Lausanne, Switzerland; f. 1924 to promote standards of training and research in human communication disorders in all countries, to establish information centres and communicate with kindred organizations. Mems: 400 individuals and 50 societies from 31 countries. Pres. Dr ANDRÉ MULLER; Gen. Sec. M. DE MONTFORT. Publ. *Folia Phoniatrica* (6 a year).

International Association of Oral and Maxillofacial Surgeons: c/o Medical College of Virginia, Box 410, MCV Station, Richmond, VA 23298-0410, USA; tel. (804) 371-8515; fax (804) 786-0753; f. 1963 to advance the science and art of oral surgery. Mems: 2,000. Pres. Dr R. V. WALKER (USA); Sec.-Gen. Dr D. M. LASKIN (USA). Publs *International Journal of Oral and Maxillofacial Surgery* (every 2 months), *Newsletter* (every 6 months).

International Brain Research Organization—IBRO: 51 blvd de Montmorency, 75016 Paris, France; f. 1958 to further all aspects of brain research. Mems: 31 corporate, 13 academic and 21,000 individual. Pres. Prof. D. P. PURPURA (USA); Sec.-Gen. Dr D. OTTOSON. Publs *IBRO News*, *Neuroscience* (bi-monthly), *IBRO Membership Directory*.

International Bronchoesophagological Society: Mayo Clinic, Scottsdale, Ariz 65258, USA; f. 1951 to promote by all means the progress of bronchoesophagology and to provide a forum for discussion among broncho-esophagologists of various specialities; holds congress every three years. Mems: 500 in 49 countries. Exec. Sec. Dr DAVID SANDERSON.

International Bureau for Epilepsy: POB 21, 2100 AA Heemstede, Netherlands; tel. (023) 33-90-60; fax (023) 29-43-24; f. 1961 to collect and disseminate information about social and medical care for people with epilepsy, to organize international and regional meetings; to advise and answer questions on social aspects of epilepsy. Mems: 37 national epilepsy organizations. Sec.-Gen. HANNEKE M. DE BOER. Publ. *International Epilepsy News* (quarterly).

International Cell Research Organization: c/o UNESCO, 7 place de Fontenoy, 75700 Paris, France; f. 1962 to create, encourage and promote co-operation between scientists of different disciplines throughout the world for the advancement of fundamental knowledge of the cell, normal and abnormal; organizes every year eight to ten international laboratory courses on modern topics of cell and molecular biology and biotechnology for young research scientists in important research centres all over the world. Mems: 400. Chair. Prof. L. ERNSTER (Sweden); Exec. Sec. Prof. G. N. COHEN (France).

International Chiropractors' Association: 1110 North Glebe Rd, Arlington, Va 22201, USA; tel. (703) 528-5000; f. 1926 to promote advancement of the art and science of chiropractic. Mems: 7,000 individuals in addition to affiliated associations. Pres. FRED BARGE; Sec.-Treas. ANDREW WYMORE. Publs *International Review of Chiropractic* (every 2 months), *ICA Today* (every 2 months).

International Commission on Occupational Health: 10 ave Jules-Crosnier, 1206 Geneva, Switzerland; tel. (022) 476184; f. 1906 (present name 1985) to study and prevent pathological conditions arising from industrial work; arranges congresses on occupational medicine and the protection of workers' health; provides information for public authorities and learned societies. Mems: 1,200 from 75 countries. Pres. Dr ROBERT MURRAY (UK); Sec.-Treas. Prof. LUIGI PARMEGGIANI (Italy). Publ. *Newsletter* (quarterly).

International Commission on Radiological Protection—ICRP: POB 35, Didcot, OX11 0RJ, England; tel. (0235) 833929; telex 838897; fax (0235) 832832; f. 1928 to provide technical guidance and promote international co-operation in the field of radiation protection; committees on Radiation Effects, Secondary Limits, Protection in Medicine, and the application of recommendations. Mems: about 70. Chair. Dr D. BENINSON (Argentina); Scientific Sec. Dr H. SMITH (UK). Publ. *Annals of the ICRP*.

International Committee of Catholic Nurses: 43 Square Vergote, 1040 Brussels, Belgium; tel. (02) 732-10-50; fax (02) 734-84-60; f. 1933 to group professional catholic nursing associations; to represent Christian thought in the general professional field at international level; to co-operate in the general development of the profession and to promote social welfare. Mems: 49 full, 20 corresponding mems. Pres. LILIANA FIORI; Gen. Sec. ANN VERLINDE. Publs *Nouvelles/News/Nachrichten* (every 4 months).

International Council for Physical Fitness Research—ICPFR: Dept of Pediatrics, McMaster University, Hamilton, Ont L8N 3Z5, Canada; f. 1964 to construct international standardized physical fitness tests, to obtain information on world standards of physical fitness, to promote comparative studies and to encourage health and physical fitness in all countries through the exchange of scientific knowledge. Mems: in 25 countries. Pres. Prof. O. BAR-OR.

International Council of Nurses—ICN: 3 place Jean-Marteau, 1201 Geneva, Switzerland; tel. (022) 7312960; fax (022) 7381036; f. 1899 to provide a medium through which national associations of nurses may share their common interests, working together to develop the contribution of nursing to the promotion of the health

OTHER INTERNATIONAL ORGANIZATIONS
Medicine and Health

of people and the care of the sick. Quadrennial congresses are held in different countries. Mems: 102 national nurses' associations. Pres. Dr Mo Im Kim (Republic of Korea); Exec. Dir Constance Holleran. Publ. *The International Nursing Review* (6 a year, in English).

International Cystic Fibrosis (Mucoviscidosis) Association: 3 Lecky St, London, SW7 3QP, England; tel. (071) 373-8300; fax (071) 353-5422; f. 1964 to disseminate current information on cystic fibrosis in those areas of the world where the disease occurs and to stimulate the work of scientific and medical researchers attempting to discover its cure. Conducts annual medical symposia. Mems: 34 national organizations. Pres. Martin Weibel (Switzerland); Sec. Robert Johnson (UK).

International Epidemiological Association—IEA: c/o Dr A. Aromaa, Research Institute for Social Security, Social Insurance Institution, PO Box 78, 00381 Helsinki, Finland; tel. (90) 4343560; telex 122375; f. 1954. Mems: 1,700. Pres. and Chair. Dr Walter W. Holland; Sec. Dr Arpo Aromaa. Publ. *International Journal of Epidemiology* (quarterly).

International Federation for Hygiene, Preventive Medicine and Social Medicine: Via Salaria 237, 00199 Rome, Italy; tel. 8457928; f. 1951. Eleventh Conference: Madrid, Spain, September 1986. Mems: national associations and individual members in 74 countries. Pres. Prof. Dr G. A. Canaperia (Italy); Sec.-Gen. Dr Ernst Musil (Austria). Publ. *Bulletin*.

International Federation for Medical and Biological Engineering: c/o O. Z. Roy, National Research Council of Canada, Room 307, Bldg M-50, Ottawa, Ont. K1A 0R8, Canada; tel. (613) 993-1686; telex 053-4134; f. 1959. Mems: national associations in 33 countries. Sec.-Gen. Orest Z. Roy (Canada).

International Federation for Medical Psychotherapy: c/o Dr M. Geyer, 7010 Leipzig, Karl-Tauchnitz-Str. 25, Germany; f. 1946 to further research and teaching of psychotherapy, to organize international congresses. Mems: 3,200 psychotherapists from 24 countries, 36 societies. Pres. Dr Edgar Heim (Switzerland); Sec.-Gen. Prof. Dr M. Geyer (Germany). Publ. *Psychotherapy and Psychosomatics*.

International Federation of Fertility Societies: Michaelisstrasse 16, 2300 Kiel 1, Germany; tel. (0431) 5972040; fax (0431) 5972149; Pres. Prof. Dr Kurt Semm.

International Federation of Gynecology and Obstetrics: 27 Sussex Place, Regent's Park, London, NW1 4RG, England; tel. (071) 723-2951; fax (071) 724-7725; f. 1954; assists and contributes to research in gynaecology and obstetrics; aims to facilitate the exchange of information and perfect methods of teaching; organizes international congresses. Membership: national societies in 86 countries. Pres. of Bureau Prof. J. A. Pinotti (Brazil); Sec.-Gen. Prof. D. V. I. Fairweather (UK). Publ. *Journal*.

International Federation of Multiple Sclerosis Societies: 3/9 Heddon St, London, W1R 7LE, England; tel. (071) 734-9120; fax (071) 287-2587; f. 1965 to co-ordinate and further the work of 31 national multiple sclerosis organizations throughout the world, to stimulate and encourage scientific research in this and related neurological diseases, to aid member societies in helping individuals who are in any way disabled as a result of these diseases, to collect and disseminate information and to provide counsel and active help in furthering the development of voluntary national multiple sclerosis organizations. Pres. William P. Benton; Sec.-Gen. Tom Petzal. Publs *Federation Update* (quarterly), *Annual Report*.

International Federation of Ophthalmological Societies: c/o Prof. A. Deutman, Institute of Ophthalmology, University of Nijmegen, 15 Philips van Leydenlaan, 6525 EX Nijmegen, Netherlands; tel. (080) 513138; fax (080) 540522; f. 1953; holds international congress every four years. Pres. Prof. A. Nakajima (Japan); Sec. Prof. A. Deutman.

International Federation of Thermalism and Climatism: 16 rue de l'Estrapade, 75005 Paris, France; tel. (1) 43-25-11-85; telex 203187; f. 1947. Mems in 26 countries. Pres. Dr G. Ebrard; Gen. Sec. M. Vitu.

International Guild of Opticians: 40 Portland Place, London, W1N 4BA, England; tel. (071) 637-2507; fax (071) 436-8852; f. 1951 to promote the science of, and to maintain and advance standards and effect co-operation in optical dispensing. Central Sec. A. P. D. Westhead (UK).

International Hospital Federation: 2 St Andrew's Place, London, NW1 4LB, England; tel. (071) 935-9487; f. 1947 for information exchange and education in hospital and health service matters; represents institutional health care in discussions with WHO; conducts conferences and courses on management and policy issues. Mems in five categories: national hospital and health service organizations, professional associations, regional organizations and individual hospitals; individual mems, professional and industrial mems; honorary mems. Dir.-Gen. Dr E. N. Pickering. Publ. *Yearbook, Journal, Newsletter*.

International League against Epilepsy: c/o Dr R. J. Porter, National Institutes of Health, Bethesda, Md 20892, USA; f. 1910 to link national professional associations and to encourage research, including classification and anti-epileptic drugs; collaborates with the International Bureau for Epilepsy (q.v.) and with WHO. Mems: 33 associations. Pres. H. Meinardi (Netherlands); Sec.-Gen. R. J. Porter.

International Medical Association for the Study of Living Conditions and Health: Institute of Nutrition, blvd D. Nestorov 15, 1431 Sofia, Bulgaria; tel. 58 121 707; f. 1951 to co-ordinate research in a wide range of subjects relating to living, working and environmental conditions which favour man's healthy physical and moral development; holds international congresses. Mems: doctors in 35 countries. Pres. Prof. T. Tashev (Bulgaria). Publ. *Acta Medica et Sociologica*, congress and conference reports.

International Narcotics Control Board—INCB: 1400 Vienna, POB 500, Austria; tel. 26310; telex 135612; f. 1961 to supervise the implementation of the Drug Control Treaties by governments. Mems: 13 individuals. Pres. Sahibzada Raoof Ali Kiian; Sec. Abdelaziz Bahi (Tunisia). Publ. *Annual Report* (with two statistical supplements).

International Optometric and Optical League: 10 Knaresborough Place, London, SW5 0TG, England; tel. (071) 370-4765; fax (071) 373-1143; f. 1927 to co-ordinate efforts to provide a good standard of ophthalmic optical (optometric) care throughout the world; enables exchange of ideas between different countries; a large part of its work is concerned with optometric education, and advice upon standards of qualification. The League also interests itself in legislation in relation to optometry throughout the world. Mems: 64 optometric organizations in 50 countries. Pres. G. B. Holmes; Sec. D. A. Leason. Publs *Interoptics* (quarterly).

International Organization for Medical Physics: c/o Prof. C. G. Orton, Gershenson Radiation Oncology Center, Harper Hospital, 3990 John R. St, Detroit, Mich 48201, USA; tel. (313) 745-2489; f. 1963 to organize international co-operation in medical physics, to promote communication between the various branches of medical physics and allied subjects, to contribute to the advancement of medical physics in all its aspects and to advise on the formation of national organizations. Mems: national organizations in medical physics in 40 countries. Pres. Prof. John R. Cunningham (Canada); Sec.-Gen. Prof. Colin G. Orton (USA). Publ. *Medical Physics World*.

International Pharmaceutical Federation: Alexanderstraat 11, 2514 JL The Hague, Netherlands; tel. (070) 63-19-25; telex 32781; fax (070) 63-39-14; f. 1912 to promote the development of pharmacy both as a profession and as an applied science; holds Assembly of Pharmacists every two years, International Congress every year. Mems: 69 national pharmaceutical organizations in 53 countries, 75 associate collective mems, 3,650 individuals. Dir L. Félix-Faure. Publ. *International Pharmacy Journal* (every 2 months).

International Psycho-Analytical Association: Broomhills, Woodside Lane, London, N12 8UD, England; tel. (071) 446-8324; fax (071) 445-4729; f. 1908 to hold meetings to define and promulgate the theory and teaching of psychoanalysis, to act as a forum for scientific discussions, to control and regulate training and to contribute to the interdisciplinary area which is common to the behavioural sciences. Mems: 6,700. Pres. Prof. Joseph Sandler; Sec. Dr Jacqueline Amati-Mehler. Publs *Bulletin, Newsletter*.

International Society for Cardiovascular Surgery: 13 Elm St, POB 1565, Manchester, MA 01944-0865, USA; tel. (508) 526-8330; fax (508) 526-4018; telex 940103; f. 1950 to stimulate research in the diagnosis and therapy of cardiovascular diseases and to exchange ideas on an international basis. Sec.-Gen. James A. Deweese (USA). Publ. *Journal of Cardiovascular Surgery*.

International Society for Mental Imagery Techniques: 12 rue St Julien-le-Pauvre, 75005 Paris, France; tel. (1) 46-33-52-47; f. 1968; a group of research workers, technicians and psychotherapists using oneirism techniques under waking conditions, with the belief that a healing action cannot be dissociated from the restoration of creativity. Mems: in 17 countries. Pres. Dr André Virel (France); Sec. Odile Drecq (France).

International Society for Research on Civilization Diseases and Environment: POB 1715, 1017 Luxembourg; f. 1973 to study environmental conditions, non-transmissive diseases and occupational medicine; holds annual congress and one or two workshops a year. Mems: associations and individuals in 61 countries. Pres. Dr S. Klein (Belgium); Sec.-Gen. Jean-Paul Risch.

International Society of Art and Psychopathology: Centre Hospitalier St Anne, 100 rue de la Santé, 75014 Paris, France; tel. (1) 45-89-55-21; f. 1959 to bring together the various specialists interested in the problems of expression and artistic activities in connection with psychiatric, sociological and psychological research, as well as in the use of methods applied to other fields than that of mental illness. Mems: 625. Pres. Prof. VOLMAT (France); Sec.-Gen. Dr C. WIART (France).

International Society of Developmental Biologists: c/o Prof. J. Gurdon, University of Cambridge, Dept of Zoology, Downing St, Cambridge, CB2 3EJ, England; f. 1911 as International Institute of Embryology. Objects: to promote the study of developmental biology and to promote international co-operation among the investigators in this field. Mems: 850 in 33 countries. Pres. Prof. J. GURDON; Sec.-Treas. Dr J. KNOWLAND. Publ. *Cell Differentiation and Development.*

International Society of Geographical Pathology—ISGP: c/o Prof. W. Dutz, Pathologisches Institut, Krankenhaus Lainz, 1130 Vienna, Austria; f. 1931 to study the relations between diseases and the geographical environments in which they occur. Mems: national and regional committees in 42 countries. Sec.-Gen. Prof. WERNER DUTZ.

International Society of Lymphology: 1501 North Campbell Ave, Room 4406, Tucson, Ariz 85724, USA; tel. (602) 626-6118; fax (602) 626-0822; f. 1966 to further progress in lymphology through personal contact and exchange of ideas among members. Mems: 400 in 43 countries. Pres. W. OLSZEWSKI (Poland); Sec.-Gen. M. H. WITTE (USA). Publ. *Lymphology* (quarterly).

International Society of Neuropathology: c/o Dr S. Ludwin, Dept of Pathology, Queen's University, Kingston, Ontario K7L 3N6, Canada. Pres. Prof. J. H. ADAMS; Sec.-Gen. Dr S. LUDWIN.

International Society of Orthopaedic Surgery and Traumatology: 40 rue Washington, 1050 Brussels, Belgium; tel. (02) 648-68-23; telex 65080; fax (02) 649-32-69; f. 1929; congresses are convened every three years. Mems: 77 countries, 3,000 individuals. Pres. LEONARDO ZAMUDIO (Mexico); Sec.-Gen. JACQUES WAGNER (Belgium). Publ. *International Orthopaedics* (quarterly).

International Society of Radiology: Dept of Medical Radiology, University Hospital, 8091 Zürich, Switzerland; tel. (01) 2552900; fax (01) 255-44-43; f. 1953 to promote diagnostic radiology and radiation oncology through its International Commissions on Radiation Units and Measurements, on Radiation Protection, on Radiological Education and on Rules and Regulations; organizes quadrennial International Congress of Radiology; collaborates with the World Health Organization. Mems: 64 national radiological societies. Sec. W. A. FUCHS.

International Society of Surgery: POB 411, 4153 Reinach BL 1, Switzerland; tel. (061) 7117036; fax (061) 7117303; f. 1902; organizes congresses: 34th World Congress of Surgery, Stockholm, Sweden, August 1991. Mems: 3,500. Sec.-Gen. Prof. MARTIN ALLGOWER. Publ. *World Journal of Surgery* (every 2 months).

International Union against Tuberculosis and Lung Disease: 68 blvd St Michel, 75006 Paris, France; tel. (1) 46-33-08-30; telex 270945; fax (1) 43-29-90-87; f. 1920 to co-ordinate the efforts of antituberculosis and respiratory disease associations, to mobilize public interest, to assist control programmes and research around the world, to collaborate with governments and the WHO, to promote conferences. Mems: associations in 118 countries, numerous individual mems. Pres. Dr J. SWOMLEY; Chair. Exec. Cttee Prof. J. CHRÉTIEN; Exec. Dir Dr ANNIK ROUILLON. Publ. *Bulletin* (in English, French and Spanish); incl. conference proceedings.

International Union for Health Education: 15/21 rue de l'Ecole de Médecine, 75270 Paris Cedex 06, France; tel. (1) 43-26-90-82; fax (1) 48-56-22-22; f. 1951; provides an international network for the exchange of practical information on developments in health education; promotes research into effective methods and techniques in health education and encourages professional training in health education for health workers, teachers, social workers and others; holds regional and world conferences. Mems: in 75 countries. Pres. DENNIS TOLSMA (USA). Publ. *HYGIE-International Journal of Health Education* (quarterly).

International Union of Therapeutics: c/o Prof. A. Pradalier, Hôpital Rothschild, 33 blvd de Picpus, 75571 Paris Cedex 12, France; tel. (1) 40-19-33-63; f. 1934; international congresses every other year. Mems: 500 from 22 countries. Pres. Dr J. DRY; Gen. Sec. Prof. A. PRADALIER.

Middle East Neurosurgical Society: c/o Dr Fuad S. Haddad, Neurosurgical Department, American University Medical Centre, POB 113-6044, Beirut, Lebanon; tel. 347348; telex 20801; f. 1958 to promote clinical advances and scientific research among its members and to spread knowledge of neurosurgery and related fields among all members of the medical profession in the Middle East. Mems: 684 in nine countries. Pres. Dr STAMATIS COMNINOS; Hon. Sec. Dr FUAD S. HADDAD.

Organization for Co-ordination and Co-operation in the Struggle against Endemic Diseases (Organisation de coordination et de coopération pour la lutte contre les grandes endémies—OCCGE): 01 BP 153, Bobo-Dioulasso 01, Burkina Faso; tel. 98-27-62; telex 8260; fax 98-13-72; f. 1960; conducts research, provides training and maintains a documentation centre and computer information system. Mems: governments of Benin, Burkina Faso, Côte d'Ivoire, Mali, Mauritania, Niger, Senegal, Togo; assoc. mem: France. Sec.-Gen. Dr EMMANUEL AKINOCHO. Publs *Rapport annuel, OCCGE Info.*

Research centres:

Centre de Recherches alimentaires et nutritionelles: Lomé, Togo.

Centre de Recherches sur les Méningites et les Schistosomiases: BP 10 887, Niamey, Niger; tel. 72-39-69.

Centre Muraz: 01 BP 153, Bobo-Dioulasso 01, Burkina Faso; tel. 98-18-72; telex 8260; f. 1939; multi-discipline research centre with special interest in epidemiology of tropical diseases and training of health workers. Dir Prof. JEAN-PAUL CHIRON.

Centre Régional de Recherches Entomologiques: Cotonou, Benin.

Institut de Recherche sur la Tuberculose et les Infections respiratoires aiguës: Nouakchott, Mauritania.

Institut d'Ophtalmologie Tropicale en Afrique: BP 248, Bamako, Mali; tel. 22-27-22; fax 22-51-86; Dir Dr SERGES RESNIKOFF.

Institut Marchoux: BP 251, Bamako, Mali; tel. 22-25-31; telex 1200; fax 22-48-45; research on leprosy, epidemiology, training. Dir Dr PIERRE BOBIN.

Institut Pierre Richet: BP 1500, Bouaké, Côte d'Ivoire; tel. 63-37-46; research on trypanosomiasis and onchocerciasis; Dir JEAN-PIERRE EDUZAN.

Office de Recherches sur l'Alimentation et la Nutrition africaine: BP 2098, Dakar, Senegal; tel. 22-58-92; Dir Dr MAKHTAR N'DIAYE.

In 1990 it was announced that the West African Health Community was to be amalgamated with the Organization for Co-ordination and Co-operation in the Struggle against Endemic Diseases to form the West African Health Organization, covering all the member states of ECOWAS (subject to ratification by member states).

Organization for Co-ordination in the Struggle against Endemic Diseases in Central Africa (Organisation de coordination pour la lutte contre les endémies en Afrique Centrale—OCEAC): BP 288, Yaoundé, Cameroon; tel. 23 22 32; telex 8411; f. 1965 to standardize methods of controlling endemic diseases, to co-ordinate national action, and to negotiate programmes of assistance and training on a regional scale. Mems: Cameroon, Central African Republic, Chad, Congo, Equatorial Guinea, Gabon. Pres. SISSINIO MBANA NSORO MBANA; Sec.-Gen. Dr DANIEL KOUKA BEMBA. Publs *EPI–Notes* (quarterly), *Bulletin de Liaison et de Documentation* (quarterly).

Pan-American Association of Ophthalmology: 1301 South Bowen Rd, Suite 365, Arlington, Texas 76013, USA; tel. (817) 265-2831; fax (817) 275-3961; f. 1939 to promote friendship and dissemination of scientific information among the profession throughout the Western Hemisphere; holds annual meetings. Mems: national ophthalmological societies and other bodies in 39 countries. Pres. Dr ENRIQUE MALBRAN (Argentina); Exec. Dir Dr FRANCISCO CONTRERAS (Peru). Publs *Ojo-Eye-Olho* (2 a year), *El Noticiero* (quarterly).

Pan-Pacific Surgical Association: 733 Bishop St, Honolulu, Hawaii 96813, USA; f. 1929 to bring together surgeons to exchange scientific knowledge relating to surgery and medicine, and to promote the improvement and standardization of hospitals and their services and facilities; congresses are held every two years. Mems: 2,716 regular, associate and senior mems from 44 countries. Chair. RAYMOND TANIGUCHI.

Society of French-speaking Neuro-Surgeons (Société de neurochirurgie de langue française): Hôpital Neurologique, 59 blvd Pinel, BP Lyon-Montchat, 69394 Lyon Cedex 3, France; tel. 72-35-72-11; f. 1949; holds annual convention and congress. Mems: 600 in numerous countries. Pres. F. COHADON (France); Sec. G. FISCHER (France). Publ. *Neuro-Chirurgie* (6 a year).

Transnational Association of Acupuncture and Taoist Medicine: 48 ave Kléber, 75116 Paris, France; tel. (1) 47-27-05-95; f. 1963 to develop and promote knowledge of acupuncture in the world. Mems: national societies and individuals in 70 countries. Pres. Dr J. C. DE TYMOWSKI; Sec.-Gen. J. DE KERGUENEC. Publ. *Ecomédecine* (monthly).

World Association of Societies of (Anatomic and Clinical) Pathology—WASP: c/o Prof. T. Kawai, Jichi Medical School, Minami-Kawachi-machi, Tochigi 32904, Japan; tel. (0285) 442111; fax (0285) 448249; f. 1947 to link national societies and to co-ordinate their scientific and technical means of action; and to promote the development of anatomic and clinical pathology, especially by convening conferences, congresses and meetings, and by the interchange of publications and personnel. Membership: 47 national associations. Pres. TYRA T. HUTCHENS (USA); Sec. Prof. T. KAWAI. Publ. *Newsletter* (quarterly).

OTHER INTERNATIONAL ORGANIZATIONS

Medicine and Health, Posts and Telecommunications, etc.

World Confederation for Physical Therapy: 16-19 Eastcastle St, London, W1N 7PA, England; tel. (071) 637-2104; fax (071) 637-4694; f. 1951 to encourage improved standards of physical therapy in training and practice; to promote exchange of information between nations; to assist the development of informed public opinion regarding physical therapy. Mems: 48 organizations. Pres. B. DAVEY; Sec.-Gen. M. H. O'HARE. Publs *Newsletter* (2 a year), *Programmes of Physical Therapy Education, Registration Requirements and Working Conditions.*

World Federation for Mental Health: 1021 Prince St, Alexandria, Va 22314, USA; tel. (703) 684-7722; fax (703) 684-5968; f. 1948 to promote among all nations the highest possible standard of mental health; to work with agencies of the United Nations in promoting mental health; to help other voluntary associations in the improvement of mental health services. Mems: 118 national or international associations in 53 countries. Pres. Dr STANISLAS FLACHE (Switzerland); Dir-Gen. Dr EUGENE B. BRODY; Deputy Sec.-Gen. RICHARD HUNTER. Publs *Newsletter* (5 a year).

World Federation of Neurosurgical Societies: c/o Dr H. A. D. Walder, Bergweg 12, 6523 MD Nijmegen, Netherlands; tel. (80) 231146; f. 1957 to assist the development of neurosurgery and to help the formation of associations; to assist the exchange of information and to encourage research. Mems: 57 societies representing 56 countries. Pres. Prof. W. KEMP CLARK; Sec. Dr H. ALPHONS D. WALDER.

World Federation of Occupational Therapists: University of Western Ontario, Occupational Therapy Dept, Health Sciences Bldg, London, Ontario N6A 5C1, Canada; tel. (519) 661-2179; fax (519) 661-3894; f. 1952 to further the rehabilitation of the physically and mentally disabled by promoting the development of occupational therapy in all countries; to facilitate the exchange of information and publications; to promote research in occupational therapy; international congresses are held every four years. Mems: national professional associations in 37 countries, with total membership of approximately 36,000. Pres. MARIA SCHWARZ (Switzerland); Hon. Sec.-Treas. BARBARA POSTHUMA (Canada). Publs *Bulletin* (2 a year).

World Federation of Public Health Associations: c/o Catherine Savino, American Public Health Asscn, 1015 15th St, NW, Washington, DC 20005, USA; tel. (202) 789-5600; fax (202) 789-5661; f. 1967. Triennial Congress: Atlanta, Ga, USA, 1991. Mems: 45 national public health associations. Exec. Sec. CATHERINE SAVINO (USA). Publs *Salubritas* (newsletter in English, French and Spanish), *WFPHA News* (in English), and occasional technical papers.

World Federation of Societies of Anaesthesiologists—WFSA: Pantai Medical Centre, 59100 Kuala Lumpur, Malaysia; tel. (03) 7575077; telex 32234; fax (03) 2558148; f. 1955 to make available the highest standards of anaesthesia to all peoples of the world. Mems: 84 national societies. Pres. Dr JOHN S. M. ZORAB (UK); Sec. Dr SAYWAN LIM (Malaysia). Publ. *Newsletter* (2 a year), *Annual Report, Lectures in Anaesthesiology* (2 a year), *Career Guide.*

Posts and Telecommunications

African Posts and Telecommunications Union: ave Patrice Lumumba, BP 44, Brazzaville, Congo; tel. 832778; telex 5212; f. 1961 to improve postal and telecommunication services between member administrations. Mems: 12 countries. Sec.-Gen. MAHMOUDOU SAMOURA.

Asia-Pacific Telecommunity: No. 12/49, Soi 5, Chaengwattana Rd, Thungsonghong, Bangkok 10210, Thailand; tel. 573-0044; f. 1979 to cover all matters relating to telecommunications in the region. Mems: Afghanistan, Australia, Bangladesh, Brunei, People's Republic of China, India, Indonesia, Iran, Japan, Republic of Korea, Laos, Malaysia, Maldives, Myanmar, Nauru, Nepal, Pakistan, Philippines, Singapore, Sri Lanka, Thailand, Viet-Nam; assoc. mems: Cook Islands, Hong Kong; two affiliated mems each in the Republic of Korea, Hong Kong, Japan and Thailand, and five in the Philippines. Exec. Dir CHAO THONGMA.

Asian-Pacific Postal Union: Post Office Bldg, 1000 Manila, Philippines; tel. 47-07-60; f. 1962 to extend, facilitate and improve the postal relations between the member countries and to promote cooperation in the field of postal services. Mems: 23 countries. Chair. SOMBUT UTHAISANG (Thailand); Dir TAGUMPAY R. JARDINIANO. Publs *Annual Report, Exchange Program of Postal Officials, Newsletter.*

European Conference of Postal and Telecommunications Administrations: Dept of Trade and Industry, Telecommunications and Posts Division, Kingsgate House, 66-74 Victoria St, London, SW1E 6SW, England; tel. (071) 215-8149; telex 936069; f. 1959 to strengthen relations between member administrations and to harmonize and improve their technical services; set up Eurodata Foundation, for research and publishing. Mems: 26 countries. Publ. *Bulletin.*

European Telecommunications Satellite Organization—EUTELSAT: Tour Maine Montparnasse, 33 ave du Maine, 75755 Paris Cedex, France; tel. (1) 45-38-47-47; telex 203823; fax (1) 45-38-37-00; f. 1977 to develop and operate the European satellite telecommunications system; operates EUTELSAT I fleet of four telecommunications satellites for domestic and international communications in Europe; the EUTELSAT II system of medium-power satellites was to be introduced from 1990. Mems: 26 national telecommunications administrations.

INMARSAT—International Maritime Satellite Organization: 40 Melton St, London, NW1 2EQ, England; tel. (071) 387-9089; telex 297201; fax (071) 387-2115; f. 1979 to provide (from February 1982) global communications for shipping via satellites on a commercial basis; satellites in geo-stationary orbit over the Atlantic, Indian and Pacific Oceans provide telephone, telex, facsimile, telegram, low to high speed data services and distress and safety communications for ships of all nations and structures such as oil rigs; in 1985 the operating agreement was amended to include aeronautical communications, and in 1988 amendments were approved which allow provision of global land-mobile communications. Organs: Assembly of all Parties to the Convention (every 2 years); council of representatives of 22 national telecommunications administrations; executive Directorate. Mems: 59 countries. Chair. of Council J. SANDER (Netherlands); Dir-Gen. OLOF LUNDBERG (Sweden). Publ. *Ocean Voice* (quarterly), *Aeronautical Satellite News* (quarterly), *Transat* (quarterly).

International Telecommunications Satellite Organization—INTELSAT: 3400 International Drive, NW, Washington, DC 20008-3098, USA; tel. (202) 944-6800; telex 892707; f. 1964 to establish a global commercial satellite communications system. Assembly of Parties attended by representatives of member governments, meets every two years to consider policy and long-term aims and matters of interest to members as sovereign states. Meeting of Signatories to the Operating Agreement held annually. Thirteen INTELSAT satellites in synchronous orbit provide a global communications service; INTELSAT provides most of the world's overseas traffic. Mems: 117 governments. Dir-Gen. DEAN BURCH.

Pacific Telecommunications Council: 1110 University Ave, Suite 308, Honolulu, Hawaii 96826; tel. (808) 941-3789; telex 7430550; fax (808) 944-4874; f. 1980 to promote the development, understanding and beneficial use of telecommunications throughout the Pacific region; provides forum for users and providers of communications services; sponsors annual conference and seminars. Mems: 275 (corporate, government, academic and individual). Pres. ROBERT ENGELBARDT; Exec. Dir RICHARD J. BARBER. Publ. *Pacific Telecommunications* (quarterly).

Postal Union of the Americas and Spain (Unión Postal de las Américas y España): Calle Cebollatí 1468/70, Casilla de Correos 20.042, Montevideo, Uruguay; tel. 400070; telex 22073; f. 1911 to extend, facilitate and study the postal relationships of member countries. Mems: 24 countries. Sec.-Gen. Ing. PEDRO MIGUEL CABERO (Argentina).

Press, Radio and Television

Asia-Pacific Broadcasting Union—ABU: POB 1164, Jalan Pantai Bahru, 59700 Kuala Lumpur, Malaysia; tel. 2743592; telex 32227; fax 2305292; f. 1964 to assist in the development of radio and television in the Asia/Pacific area, particularly in its use for educational purposes. Mems: 39 full, nine additional and 26 associates. Pres. BEVERLEY WAKEM (New Zealand); Sec.-Gen. HUGH LEONARD. Publs *ABU News* (every 2 months), *ABU Technical Review* (every 2 months).

Association for the Promotion of the International Circulation of the Press—DISTRIPRESS: 8002 Zürich, Beethovenstrasse 20, Switzerland; tel. (01) 2024121; telex 815591; fax (01) 2021025; f. 1955 to assist in the promotion of the freedom of the press throughout the world, supporting and aiding UNESCO in promoting the free flow of ideas. Organizes meetings of publishers and distributors of newspapers, periodicals and paperback books, to promote the exchange of information and experience among members. Mems: 441. Pres. ALAN FRASER (UK); Man. Dr ARNOLD E. KAULICH (Switzerland). Publs *Distripress News, Distripress Letter, Who's Who.*

Association of European Journalists: Kastanienweg 26, 5300 Bonn 2, Germany; tel. (0228) 324381; f. 1963 to participate actively in the development of a European consciousness; to promote deeper knowledge of European problems and secure appreciation by the general public of the work of European institutions; and to facilitate members' access to sources of European information,

Mems: 1,500 individuals and national associations in 12 countries. Sec.-Gen. GUENTHER WAGENLEHNER.

Broadcasting Organizations of Non-aligned Countries—BONAC: c/o Cyprus Broadcasting Corporation, POB 4828, Nicosia, Cyprus; tel. (02) 422231; telex 2333; fax (02) 314050; f. 1977 to ensure an equitable, objective and comprehensive flow of information through broadcasting; assists in training of broadcasters, maintains programme bank, and organizes radio and TV festival and competition; General Conference held every three years; Secretariat moves to the broadcasting organization of host country. Mems: in 102 countries. Chair. DEMETRIOS KYPRIANOU.

European Alliance of Press Agencies: c/o ANSA, Via della Dataria 94, 00187 Rome; tel. 67741; telex 610242; fax 6787630; f. 1957 to assist co-operation among members and to study and protect their common interests; annual assembly. Mems in 26 countries. Sec.-Gen. ARRIGO ACCORNERO.

European Broadcasting Union—EBU: Ancienne-Route 17A, CP 67, 1218 Grand-Saconnex, Geneva, Switzerland; tel. (022) 7987766; telex 415700; fax (022) 7985997; f. 1950 in succession to the International Broadcasting Union; a professional association of broadcasting organizations, supporting the interests of members and assisting the development of broadcasting in all its forms; activities include the Eurovision news and programme exchanges (linking 37 television services in 29 countries). Mems: 98 active (European) and associate in 69 countries. Pres. J. B. MÜNCH (Germany); Sec.-Gen. Dr R. DE KALBERMATTEN (Switzerland). Publs *EBU Review* (monthly in English and French).

Inca-Fiej Research Association: Washingtonplatz 1, 6100 Darmstadt, Germany; tel. (06151) 70050; telex 0419273; fax (06151) 784542; f. 1961 to develop methods, machines and techniques for the newspaper industry; to evaluate standard specifications for raw materials for use in newspaper production; to investigate economy and quality improvements for newspaper printing and publishing. Mems: 766 newspapers, 66 suppliers. Pres. JOSÉ MARIA BERGARECHE BUSQUET; Man. Dir Dr F. W. BURKHARDT. Publ. *Newspaper Techniques* (monthly in English, French and German).

Inter-American Press Association (Sociedad Interamericana de Prensa): 2911 NW 39th St, Miami, Fla 33142, USA; tel. (305) 634-2465; telex 522873; f. 1942 to guard the freedom of the press in the Americas; to promote and maintain the dignity, rights and responsibilities of the profession of journalism; to foster a wider knowledge and greater interchange among the peoples of the Americas. Mems: 1,400. Exec. Dir W. P. WILLIAMSON, Jr. Publ. *IAPA News* (monthly in English and Spanish).

International Alliance of Distribution by Cable: 1 blvd Anspach, boîte 28, 1000 Brussels, Belgium; tel. (02) 211-94-49; telex 11473; fax (02) 211-99-07; f. 1955 to encourage the development of distribution by cable and defend its interests; to ensure exchange of documentation and carry out research on relevant technical and legal questions. Mems: 20 organizations in 14 countries. Pres. M. DE SUTTER; Sec.-Gen. PETER KOKKEN.

International Association of Broadcasting (Asociación Internacional de Radiodifusión—AIR): 25 de Mayo 520, Montevideo, Uruguay; tel. 95-8141; telex 23225; fax 96-1703; f. 1946 to preserve free and private radio broadcasting; to promote co-operation between the corporations and public authorities; to defend freedom of expression. Mems: national associations of broadcasters. Pres. LUIZ EDUARDO BORGERTH; Dir-Gen. Dr HÉCTOR OSCAR AMENGUAL. Publ. *La Gaceta de AIR* (every 2 months).

International Association of Sound Archives: c/o Sven Allerstrand, ALB, Box 7371, 103 91 Stockholm, Sweden; tel. (8) 14-39-60; fax (8) 20-69-68; f. 1969; involved in the preservation and exchange of sound recordings, and in developing recording techniques; holds annual conference. Mems: institutions in 42 countries, and 10 international and regional organizations. Pres. GERALD GIBSON (USA); Sec.-Gen. SVEN ALLERSTRAND (Sweden). Publ. *Phonographic Bulletin* (2 a year).

International Catholic Union of the Press (Union catholique internationale de la presse—UCIP): 37–39 rue de Vermont, Case Postale 197, 1211 Geneva 20, Switzerland; tel (022) 7340017; telex 412040, f. 1927 to link all Catholics who influence public opinion through the press, to inspire a high standard of professional conscience and to represent the interest of the Catholic press at international organizations. Mems: International Federation of Catholic Press Agencies, International Federation of Catholic Journalists, International Federation of Catholic Dailies and Periodicals, International Catholic Association of Teachers in Information and Communication, International Federation of Church Press Associations, UCIP Africa, UCIP Asia, UCIP Latin America. Sec.-Gen. Rev. BRUNO HOLTZ (Switzerland). Publ. *UCIP-Informations*.

International Council for Film, Television and Audiovisual Communication: 1 rue Miollis, 75732 Paris Cedex 15, France; tel. (1) 45-68-25-56; f. 1958 to arrange meetings and co-operation generally. Mems: 36 international film and television organizations. Pres. GÉRARD BOLLA; Exec. Sec. EMMANUEL FLIPO. Publ. *Letter of Information* (monthly).

International Council of French-speaking Radio and Television Organizations: (Conseil international des radios-télévisions d'expression française): 23 rue Gourgas, 1205 Geneva, Switzerland; tel. (022) 281211; telex 428274; fax (022) 205177; f. 1978 to establish links between French-speaking radio and television organizations. Mems: 42 organizations. Pres. ROBERT STEPHANE (Belgium); Sec.-Gen. ANDRÉ MIGNOLET (Belgium) (acting).

International Federation of Newspaper Publishers—FIEJ: 6 rue du Faubourg Poissonnière, 75010 Paris, France; tel. (1) 45-23-38-88; telex 290513; f. 1948 to defend the freedom of the press, to safeguard the ethical and economic interests of newspapers and to study all questions of interest to newspapers at international level. Mems: national organizations in 30 countries, individual publishers in five others, and 13 news agencies. Pres. GIOVANNI GIOVANNINI (Italy); Sec.-Gen. JAN J. NOUWEN.

International Federation of Press Cutting Agencies: Streulistrasse 19, POB 8030 Zürich, Switzerland; tel. (01) 3834983; telex 816543; fax (01) 3834357; f. 1953 to improve the standing of the profession, prevent infringements, illegal practices and unfair competition; and to develop business and friendly relations among press cuttings agencies throughout the world. Mems: 62 agencies. Pres. LAURENCE D'ARAINON (France); Gen. Sec. Dr DIETER HENNE (Switzerland).

International Federation of the Cinematographic Press—FIPRESCI: 8000 Munich 40, Schleissheimer Str. 83, Germany; tel. (089) 182303; telex 214674; fax (089) 184766; f. 1930 to develop the cinematographic press and promote cinema as an art; organizes international meetings and juries in film festivals. Mems: national organizations or corresponding members in 68 countries. Pres. MARCEL MARTIN (France); Sec.-Gen. KLAUS EDER (Germany).

International Federation of the Periodical Press: Press Foundation House, 5 St Matthew St, London, SW1P 2JT, England; tel. (071) 873-8158; fax (071) 873-8167; f. 1925 to protect and promote the material and moral interests of the periodical press, facilitate contacts between members and develop the free exchange of ideas and information. Mems: 104 national associations and publishing companies in 31 countries Pres. S. LAAKSO (Finland), Dir M. J. FINLEY (UK).

International Federation of the Socialist and Democratic Press: CP 737, 20101 Milan, Italy; tel. (02) 8050105; f. 1953 to promote co-operation between editors and publishers of socialist newspapers; affiliated to the Socialist International (q.v.). Mems: about 100. Sec. UMBERTO GIOVINE.

International Institute of Communications: Tavistock House South, Tavistock Sq., London, WC1H 9LF, England; tel. (071) 388-0671; telex 24578; fax (071) 380-0623; f. 1969 (as the International Broadcast Institute) to link all working in the field of communications, including policy makers, broadcasters, industrialists and engineers; holds local, regional and international meetings, undertakes and sponsors research and gathers information. Mems: over 80 corporate and institutional. Pres. BRIAN QUINN (UK); Exec. Dir VICTORIA RUBENSÖHN.

International Maritime Radio Association: Southbank House, Black Prince Rd, London, SE1 7SJ, England; tel. (071) 587-1245; telex 295555; fax (071) 587-1436; f. 1928 to study and develop means of improving marine wireless communications and radio aids to marine navigation. Mems: 52 organizations and companies operating wireless stations on vessels of the merchant marine and fishing boats of practically all the maritime nations of the world. Pres. W. NIPPIERD (Norway); Sec.-Gen. and Chair. of Technical Cttee M. P. FOX (UK).

International Organization of Journalists: Pařížská 9, 110 01 Prague 1, Czechoslovakia; tel. 2328015; telex 122631; f. 1946 to defend the freedom of the press and of journalists and to promote their material welfare. Activities include the maintenance of international training centres and international recreation centres for journalists. Mems: national organizations and individuals in 120 countries. Chair. KAARLE NORDENSTRENG (Finland); Sec.-Gen. GERALD GATINO. Publs *The Democratic Journalist* (monthly in English, French, Russian and Spanish), *Interpressgrafik* (quarterly), *Interpressmagazin* (every 2 months), *IOJ Newsletter* (2 a month, in Arabic, English, French, German, Russian and Spanish).

International Press Institute—IPI: Dilke House, Malet St, London, WC1E 7JA, England; tel. (071) 636-0703; telex 25950; fax (071) 580-8349; f. 1951 as a non-governmental association of editors, publishers and news broadcasters who support the principles of a free and responsible press; activities: defence of press freedom, regional meetings of members, training programmes, research and library; annual general assembly. Mems: about 2,000 from 64 countries. Pres. PER-ERIK LÖNNFORS (Finland); Dir PETER GALLINER (UK). Publ. *IPI Report* (monthly).

International Press Telecommunications Council: c/o O. Robinson, Studio House, 184 Fleet St, London, EC4, England; tel. (071) 405-2608; f. 1965 to safeguard and promote the interests of the Press on all matters relating to telecommunications; keeps its members informed of current and future telecommunications developments. The Council meets once a year and maintains five committees. Mems: 26 press associations, newspapers and news agencies. Chair. JOSEPH P. RAWLEY; Dir OLIVER G. ROBINSON. Publ. *IPTC News* (3 a year).

International Radio and Television Organization (OIRT): ul. Skokanská 1, 169 56 Prague 6, Czechoslovakia; tel. 342004; telex 122144; fax 3115897; f. 1946 as the International Broadcasting Organization in succession to Union internationale de radiodiffusion; present name adopted 1959; links broadcasting and television services in member countries and exchanges information on technical developments and programmes; includes Technical Commission (with five study groups), Radio Programme Commission (with six specialized groups), Television Programme Commission (Intervision Council); Technical Centre; Intervision network to link members' television services; holds annual general assembly. Mems: broadcasting organizations from Afghanistan, Algeria, Bulgaria, Byelorussian SSR, Cambodia, Cuba, Czechoslovakia, Estonian SSR, Finland, Germany, Hungary, Democratic People's Republic of Korea, Laos, Latvian SSR, Lithuanian SSR, Moldavian SSR, Mongolia, Nicaragua, Poland, Romania, Ukrainian SSR, USSR, Viet-Nam, Yemen. Sec.-Gen. Dr GENNADIJ CODR.

Latin-American Catholic Press Union: Apdo Postal 21-178, Quito, Ecuador; tel. 548046; fax 501658; f. 1959 to co-ordinate, promote and improve the Catholic press in Latin America. Mems: national groups and local associations in Latin America. Pres. ISMAR DE OLIVEIRA SOARES (Brazil); Sec. ELENA S. OSHIRO (Argentina).

Organization of Asia-Pacific News Agencies—OANA: Antara News Agency, POB 257, Wisma Antara, 19th Floor, 17 Merdeka Selatan, Jakarta 10002, Indonesia; tel. 344379; telex 44305; fax 363052; f. 1961 to promote co-operation in professional matters and mutual exchange of news, features, etc. among the news agencies of Asia and the Pacific via the Asia-Pacific News Network (ANN). Mems: Anadolu Ajansi (Turkey), Antara (Indonesia), APP (Pakistan), Bakhtar Information Agency (Afghanistan), BERNAMA (Malaysia), BSS (Bangladesh), ENA (Bangladesh), Hindustan Samachar (India), IRNA (Iran), KCNA (Korea, Democratic People's Republic), KPL (Laos), Kyodo (Japan), Lankapuvath (Sri Lanka), Montsame (Mongolia), PNA (Philippines), PPI (Pakistan), PTI (India), RSS (Nepal), Samachar Bharati (India), TASS (USSR), TNA (Thailand), UNI (India), Viet-Nam News Agency, Xinhua (People's Republic of China), Yonhap (Republic of Korea). Pres. HANDJOJO NITIMIHARDJO (Indonesia); Sec.-Gen. PARNI HADI (Indonesia).

Press Foundation of Asia: POB 1843, 1500 Roxas Blvd, Manila, Philippines; tel. 598633; telex 27674; f. 1967; an independent, non-profit making organization governed by its newspaper members; acts as a professional forum for about 200 newspapers in Asia; aims to reduce cost of newspapers to potential readers, to improve editorial and management techniques through research and training programmes and to encourage the growth of the Asian press; operates *Depthnews* feature service. Mems: 200 newspapers. Chair. KIM SANG MAN (Republic of Korea); Dir-Gen. ROMEO ABUNDO. Publ. *Pressasia* (quarterly), *Asian Women and Children* (quarterly), *Environment Folio* (quarterly).

Union of National Radio and Television Organizations of Africa—URTNA: 101 rue Carnot, BP 3237, Dakar, Senegal; tel. 21-59-70; telex 650; f. 1962; co-ordinates radio and television services, including monitoring and frequency allocation, the exchange of information and coverage of national and international events among African countries; maintains programme exchange centre (Nairobi, Kenya), technical centre (Bamako, Mali) and a centre for rural radio studies (Ouagadougou, Burkina Faso); in 1988 URTNA decided to establish a centre for the exchange of television news in Algiers, Algeria. Mems: 44 organizations and eight associate members. Sec.-Gen. KASSAYE DEMENA (Ethiopia). Publs *URTNA Review* (English and French, 2 a year), *Family Health and Communication Bulletin* (monthly), reports.

World Association for Christian Communication—WACC: 357 Kennington Lane, London, SE11 5QY, England; tel. (071) 582-9139; telex 8812669; fax (071) 735-0340; f. 1975; works among churches, church-related organizations and individuals to promote more effective use of all forms of media (including radio, television, newspapers, books, film, cassettes, dance, drama etc.) for proclaiming the Christian gospel, particularly with reference to ethical and social issues. Mems in 61 countries. Pres. PHILIP J. NAYLOR; Gen. Sec. CARLOS A. VALLE. Publs *Action* newsletter (10 a year), *Media Development* (quarterly).

Religion

Agudath Israel World Organisation: Hacherut Sq, POB 326, Jerusalem 91002, Israel; tel. 384357; f. 1912 to help solve the problems facing Jewish people all over the world in the spirit of the Jewish tradition; holds World Rabbinical Council (every five years), and an annual Central Council comprising 100 mems nominated by affiliated organizations. Mems: over 500,000 in 25 countries. Sec.-Gen. A. HIRSCH (Jerusalem). Publs *Hamodia* (daily newspaper), *Jewish Tribune* (London, weekly), *Jewish Observer* (New York, monthly), *Dos Yiddishe Vort* (New York, monthly), *Coalition* (New York), *Perspectives* (Toronto, monthly), *La Voz Judia* (Buenos Aires, monthly), *Jüdische Stimme* (Zürich, monthly).

All Africa Conference of Churches—AACC: Waiyaki Way, POB 14205, Nairobi, Kenya; tel. 61166; telex 22175; f. 1958; an organ of co-operation and continuing fellowship among Protestant, Orthodox and independent churches and Christian Councils in Africa. Mems: 117 churches and 20 associated councils in 39 African countries. Pres. Archbishop DESMOND TUTU (South Africa); Gen. Sec. Rev. JOSÉ CHIPENDA (Angola). Publ. *The African Challenge* (quarterly).

Alliance Israélite Universelle; 45 rue La Bruyère, 75425 Paris Cedex 09, France; tel. (1) 42-80-35-00; f. 1860 to work for the emancipation and moral progress of the Jews; maintains 39 schools in the Mediterranean area; library of 100,000 vols. Mems: 12,000 in 20 countries. Pres. ADY STEG; Dir JACQUES LEVY (France). Publs *Cahiers de l'Alliance Israélite Universelle* (2 a year) in French, *The Alliance Review* in English, *Les Nouveaux Cahiers* (quarterly) in French.

Bahá'í International Community: Bahá'í World Centre, POB 155, 31 001 Haifa, Israel; tel. (04) 510344; telex 46626; fax 358522; f. 1844 in Persia to promote the unity of mankind and world peace through the teachings of the Bahá'í religion, including the equality of men and women and the elimination of all forms of prejudice; maintains schools for children and adults worldwide, and maintains educational and cultural radio stations in the USA and Latin America; has 25 publishing trusts throughout the world. Governing body: Universal House of Justice (nine mems elected by 151 National Spiritual Assemblies). Mems: in 108,000 centres (168 countries). Sec.-Gen. RONALD BATES (UK). Publs *Bahá'í World*, *La Pensée Bahá'íe* (quarterly), *World Order* (quarterly), *Opinioni Bahá'í* (quarterly), *One Country* (English, French, Chinese).

Baptist World Alliance: 6733 Curran St, McLean, Va 22101-6005, USA; tel. (703) 790-8980; fax (703) 893-5160; f. 1905 as an association of national Baptist conventions and unions; 16th World Congress, Seoul, Republic of Korea, 1990. Mems in 150 countries. Pres. KNUD WÜMPELMANN (Denmark); Gen. Sec. Dr DENTON LOTZ. Publ. *The Baptist World* (quarterly).

Caribbean Conference of Churches: POB 616, Bridgetown, Barbados; tel. (809) 427-2681; telex 2335; fax (809) 429-2075; f. 1973; holds Assembly every five years; conducts study and research programmes and supports education and community development projects. Mems: 34 churches. Sec.-Gen. Rev. ALLAN F. KIRTON.

Christian Conference of Asia: 6–10 Nakagawa Nishi 2-chome, Ikuno-ku, Osaka 544, Japan; tel. (06) 712-2719; telex 65433; fax (06) 718-0988; f. 1959 to promote co-operation and joint study in matters of common concern among the Churches of the region and to encourage interaction with other regional Conferences and the World Council of Churches. Mems: 110 churches and national councils of churches. Gen. Sec. Bishop J. V. SAMUEL. Publ. *CCA News* (monthly).

Christian Peace Conference: 111 21 Prague 1, Jungmannova 9, Czechoslovakia; tel. 2360289; telex 123363; fax 2350251; f. 1958 as an international movement of theologians, clergy and laymen, aiming to bring Christendom to recognize its share of guilt in both world wars and to dedicate itself to the service of friendship, reconciliation and peaceful co-operation of nations, to concentrate on united action for peace, and to co-ordinate peace groups in individual churches and facilitate their effective participation in the peaceful development of society. It works through regional committees and member churches in many countries. Moderator Rev. Dr RICHARD ANDRIAMANJATO; Co-ordinator Canon KENYON E. WRIGHT. Publs *CPC News Bulletin* (2 a month in English and German), occasional *Study Volume* and *Summary of Information* (in French and Spanish).

Conference of European Churches—CEC: POB 2100, 150 route de Ferney, 1211 Geneva 2, Switzerland; tel. (022) 7916111; telex 415730; fax (022) 7910361; f. 1957 as a regional ecumenical organization for Europe and a meeting-place for European churches from East and West, and for members and non-members of the World Council of Churches; conferences every few years (latest: Stirling, 1986). Mems: 118 Protestant, Anglican and Orthodox churches in 27 European countries. Pres. Metropolitan ALEXIJ of Moscow and All Russia; Gen. Sec. JEAN FISCHER. Publ. *CEC News*.

OTHER INTERNATIONAL ORGANIZATIONS   Religion

Conference of International Catholic Organizations: 37–39 rue de Vermont, Geneva, Switzerland; f. 1927 to encourage collaboration and agreement between the different Catholic international organizations in their common interests, and to contribute to international understanding; organizes international assemblies and meetings to study specific problems. Permanent commissions deal with human rights, the new international economic order, social problems, the family health, education, etc. Mems: 30 Catholic international organizations. Administrator RUDI RUEGG (Switzerland).

Consultative Council of Jewish Organizations—CCJO: 420 Lexington Ave, New York, NY 10170, USA; tel. (212) 808-5437; f. 1946 to co-operate and consult with the UN and other international bodies directly concerned with human rights and to defend the cultural, political and religious rights of Jews throughout the world. Sec.-Gen. WARREN GREEN (USA).

European Baptist Federation: 2000 Hamburg 61, Albertinenhaus, Süntelstr. 11A, Germany; tel. 5509723; fax 5509725; f. 1949 to promote fellowship and co-operation among Baptists in Europe; to further the aims and objects of the Baptist World Alliance; to stimulate and co-ordinate evangelism in Europe; to provide for consultation and planning of missionary work in Europe and elsewhere in the world. Mems: Baptist Unions in 23 European countries. Pres. Rev. PETER BARBER (UK); Sec.-Treas. Rev. KARL-HEINZ WALTER (Germany).

Evangelical Alliance: 186 Kennington Park Rd, London, SE11 4BT, England; tel. (071) 582-0228; fax (071) 582-6221; f. 1846 to promote Christian unity and co-operation, religious freedom and evangelization; affiliated to the European Evangelical Alliance and the World Evangelical Fellowship. Pres. Rt Rev. TIMOTHY DUDLEY-SMITH; Gen. Dir CLIVE CALVER. Publs *Idea* (every 2 months).

Friends (Quakers) World Committee for Consultation: Drayton House, 30 Gordon St, London, WC1H 0AX, England; tel. (01) 388-0497; f. 1937 to encourage and strengthen the spiritual life within the Religious Society of Friends; to help Friends to a better understanding of their vocation in the world; to promote consultation among Friends of all countries; representation at the United Nations as a non-governmental organization. Mems: appointed representatives and individuals from 56 countries. Gen. Sec. VAL FERGUSON. Publs *Friends World News* (2 a year), *Calendar of Yearly Meetings* (annually), *Finding Friends around the World* (handbook), *Quaker Information Network* (6 a year).

International Association for Religious Freedom—IARF: 6000 Frankfurt 70, Dreieichstr. 59, Germany; tel. (069) 628772; fax (069) 621680; f. 1900 as a world community of religions, subscribing to the principle of openness; conducts intercultural encounters, inter-religious dialogues, a social service network and development programme. Regional conferences and triennial congress. Mems: 55 groups in 21 countries. Pres. PUNYABRATA ROYCHOUDHURY (India); Gen. Sec. Rev. Dr ROBERT TRAER (Gerrmany). Publ. *IARF World* (2 a year).

International Association of Buddhist Studies: c/o Prof. L. Gomez, Dept of Religious Studies, Bldg 70, Stanford University, Stanford, Ca 94305, USA; f. 1976; holds international conference every two years; supports studies of Buddhist literature. Gen. Sec. LUIS GOMEZ. Publ. *Journal* (2 a year).

International Council of Christians and Jews: 6148 Heppenheim, Werlestrasse 2, Postfach 129, Germany; tel. 62525041; fax 6252-68331; f. 1955 to promote mutual respect and co-operation; holds annual international colloquium, seminars, meetings for young people. Mems: national councils in 23 countries. Pres. Dr MARTIN STÖHR; Chair. Exec. Cttee Sir SIGMUND STERNBERG; Sec.-Gen. Dr JACOBUS SCHONEVELD.

International Council of Jewish Women: 19 rue de Téhéran, 75008 Paris, France; tel. (1) 46-24-78-34; telex 612874; f. 1912 to promote friendly relations and understanding among Jewish women throughout the world; exchanges information on community welfare activities, promotes volunteer leadership, sponsors field work in social welfare and fosters Jewish education. Mems: affiliates totalling over 1 million members in 37 countries. Pres. STELLA ROZAN (France); Sec. JANINE GDALIA (France). Publ. *Newsletter* (2 a year, English and Spanish).

International Fellowship of Reconciliation: Spoorstraat 38–40, 1815 BK Alkmaar, Netherlands; tel. (072) 12-30-14; fax (072) 15-11-02; f. 1919; a transnational inter-religious movement committed to non-violence as a principle of life and to forming a world community of peace and liberation. Branches in 30 countries. Pres. DIANA FRANCIS (UK); Gen. Sec. DAVID C. ATWOOD. Publ. *Reconciliation International* (quarterly).

International Humanist and Ethical Union: Oudkerkof 11, 3512 GH Utrecht, Netherlands; tel. (30) 31-21-55; fax (30) 36-71-04; f. 1952 to bring into association all those interested in promoting ethical and scientific humanism. Mems: national organizations and individuals in 51 countries. Pres Prof. Dr P. KURTZ (USA), K. VIGELAND (Norway), Dr R. A. P. TIELMAN (Netherlands). Publ. *International Humanist* (quarterly).

International Organization for the Study of the Old Testament: Faculteit der Godgeleerdheid, POB 9515, 2300 RA Leiden, Netherlands; f. 1950. Holds triennial congresses (next congress: Paris, July 1992). Pres. A. CAQUOT (France); Sec. Prof. A. VAN DER KOOIJ (Netherlands). Publ. *Vetus Testamentum* (quarterly).

Islamic Council of Europe: 16 Grosvenor Crescent, London, SW1X 7EP, England; tel. (071) 235-9832; telex 894240; f. 1973 as a co-ordinating body for Islamic centres and organizations in Europe; an autonomous Council collaborating with the Islamic Secretariat and other Islamic organizations; aims to develop a better understanding of Islam and Muslim culture in the West. Sec.-Gen. SALEM AZZAM.

Latin American Council of Churches (Consejo Latinoamericano de Iglesias—CLAI): Casilla 85-22, Av. Patria 640 y Amazonas, Of. 1001, Quito, Ecuador; tel. 561-539; telex 21150; fax 504-377; f. 1982. Mems: 97 churches in 19 countries, and nine associated organizations. Pres. Bishop FEDERICO J. PAGURA; Gen. Sec. Rev. FELIPE ADOLF.

Latin American Episcopal Council: Apartado Aéreos 5278 y 51086, Bogotá, Colombia; tel. 6121620; telex 41388; fax 6121929; f. 1955 to study the problems of the Roman Catholic Church in Latin America; to co-ordinate Church activities. Mems: the Episcopal Conferences of Central and South America and the Caribbean. Pres. Rt Rev. DARÍO CASTRILLÓN (Colombia).

Lutheran World Federation: 150 route de Ferney, 1211 Geneva 2, Switzerland; tel. (022) 7916111; telex 415730; fax (022) 7988616; f. 1947; confederation of 106 Lutheran Churches of 87 countries. Current activities: inter-church aid; relief work in various areas of the globe; service to refugees including resettlement; aid to missions; theological research, conferences and exchanges; scholarship aid in various fields of church life; inter-confessional dialogue with Roman Catholic, Reformed, Anglican and Orthodox churches; religious communications projects and international news and information services; eighth Assembly, Brazil, 1990. Pres. Rev. Dr GOTTFRIED BRAKEMEIER; Gen. Sec. Rev. Dr GUNNAR JOHAN STAALSETT (Norway). Publs *Lutheran World Information* (English and German, weekly and monthly editions), *LWF Report* and *LWF Documentation* (English and German, 6 a year).

Middle East Council of Churches: Makhoul St, Deep Bldg, POB 5376, Beirut, Lebanon; tel. 344894; telex 22662; f. 1974. Mems: 24 churches. Pres Patriarch IGNATIUS ZAKKA I IWAS, Patriarch IGNATIUS IV, Rt Rev. SAMIR KAFITY, Archbishop YOUSUF EL-KHOURY; Gen. Sec. GABRIEL HABIB.

Moral Re-Armament: Mountain House, Caux, 1824 Vaud, Switzerland; tel. (021) 9634821; fax (021) 9635260; other international centres at Panchgani, India, Petropolis, Brazil, London and Tirley Garth, UK, and Gweru, Zimbabwe; f. 1921; aims: a new social order for better human relations and the elimination of political, industrial and racial antagonism. Legally incorporated bodies in 20 countries. Pres. MARCEL GRANDY. Publs *Changer* (French, monthly), *For a Change* (English, monthly), *Caux Information* (German, monthly).

Muslim World League (Rabitat al-Alam al-Islami): POB 537-538, Mecca al-Mukarramah, Mecca, Saudia Arabia; tel. (02) 5422733; f. 1962 to advance Islamic unity and solidarity; provides financial assistance for Islamic education, medical care and relief work; has 30 offices throughout the world. Sec.-Gen. Dr ABDULLAH OMAR NASSEEF. Publs *Majalla al-Rabita* (monthly, Arabic), *Akhbar al-Alam al Islami* (weekly, Arabic), *Journal* (monthly, English).

Opus Dei (Prelature of the Holy Cross and Opus Dei): Viale Bruno Buozzi 73, 00197 Rome, Italy; tel. 870562; f. 1928 by Mgr Escrivá de Balaguer to spread, at every level of society, a profound awakening of consciences to the universal calling to sanctity and apostolate in the course of members' own professional work. Mems: 74,710 laymen and 1,385 priests. Prelate Mgr ALVARO DEL PORTILLO. Publ. *Romana, Bulletin of the Prelature* (every six months).

Pacific Conference of Churches: POB 208, 4 Thurston St, Suva, Fiji; tel. 302332; f. 1961. Mems: 28 churches, councils and associations; holds assembly every five years. Chair. Rt Rev. LESLIE BOSETO; Gen. Sec. Rev. SIONE K. F. MOTU'AHALA. Publ. *PCC News* (quarterly).

Pax Romana International Catholic Movement for Intellectual and Cultural Affairs—ICMICA; and International Movement of Catholic Students—IMCS: 37–39 rue de Vermont, POB 85, 1211 Geneva 20, Switzerland; f. 1921 (IMCS), 1947 (ICMICA), to encourage in members an awareness of their responsibilities as men and Christians in the student and intellectual milieux; to promote contacts between students and graduates throughout the world and co-ordinate the contribution of Catholic intellectual circles to

OTHER INTERNATIONAL ORGANIZATIONS   Religion, Science

international life. Mems: 80 student and 60 intellectual organizations in 80 countries. ICMICA—Pres. WILLIAM NEVILLE (Australia); Gen. Sec. VICTOR KARUNAN (India); IMCS—Pres. CARLES TORNER; Sec.-Gen. ETIENNE BISIMWA. Publ. *Convergence* (every 2 months).

Salvation Army: International HQ, 101 Queen Victoria St, London, EC4P 4EP, England; tel. (071) 236-5222; telex 8954847; fax (071) 236-4981; f. 1865 to spread the Christian gospel and relieve poverty; emphasis is placed on the need for personal discipleship, and to make its evangelism effective it adopts a quasi-military form of organization. Social, medical and educational work is also performed in the 94 countries where the Army operates. Gen. EVA BURROWS; Chief of Staff Commissioner RON COX; Chancellor Commissioner PETER HAWKINS. Publs: 132 periodicals in 31 languages.

Soroptimist International: 87 Glisson Rd, Cambridge, CB1 2HG, England; tel. (0223) 311833; f. 1921 to maintain high ethical standards in business, the professions, and other aspects of life; to strive for human rights for all people and, in particular, to advance the status of women; to develop friendship and unity among Soroptimists of all countries; to contribute to international understanding and universal friendship. Mems: 87,000 in 2,605 clubs in 85 countries and territories. International Pres. MARILYNN K. HOFSTETTER (USA); Exec. Officer DOREEN ASTLEY (UK). Publ. *International Soroptimist* (quarterly).

Theosophical Society: Adyar, Madras 600 020, India; tel. (044) 412815; f. 1875; aims at universal brotherhood, without distinction of race, creed, sex, caste or colour; study of comparative religion, philosophy and science; investigation of unexplained laws of nature and powers latent in man. Mems: 35,000 in 70 countries. Pres. RADHA S. BURNIER; Sec. Dr HUGH GRAY (UK). Publs *The Theosophist* (monthly), *Adyar News Letter* (quarterly), *Brahmavidya* (annually).

United Bible Societies: 7th Floor, Reading Bridge House, Reading, RG1 8PJ, England; tel. (0734) 500200; telex 848541; fax (0734) 500857; f. 1946. Mems: 78 Bible Societies and 32 Bible Society Offices at work throughout the world. Pres. Rt Rev. Dr EDUARD LOHSE (Germany); Gen. Sec. (vacant). Publs *United Bible Societies Bulletin*, *The Bible Translator* (quarterly), *Prayer Booklet* (annually), *World Report* (monthly).

United Lodge of Theosophists: Theosophy Hall, 40 New Marine Lines, Bombay 400020, India; tel. 299024; f. 1929 to form the nucleus of a Universal Brotherhood of Humanity, without distinction of race, creed, sex, caste or colour; Mems: 22 lodges in nine countries. Publs *Theosophy*, *The Theosophical Movement* (monthly), *The Aryan Path* (bi-monthly), *Bulletin* (quarterly).

Watch Tower Bible and Tract Society: 25 Columbia Heights, Brooklyn, New York, NY 11201, USA; tel. (718) 625-3600; f. 1881; 94 branches; serves as legal agency for Jehovah's Witnesses, whose membership is 3.7m. Pres. FREDERICK W. FRANZ; Sec. and Treas. LYMAN SWINGLE. Publs *The Watchtower* (2 a month, in 108 languages), *Awake!* (2 a month, in 61 languages).

World Alliance of Reformed Churches (Presbyterian and Congregational): 150 route de Ferney, 1211 Geneva 2, Switzerland; tel. (022) 7916111; telex 415730; fax (022) 7916505; f. 1970 by merger of WARC (Presbyterian) (f. 1875) with International Congregational Council (f. 1891) to promote fellowship among Reformed, Presbyterian and Congregational churches. Mems: 178 churches in 84 countries. Gen. Sec. Prof. MILAN OPOCENSKY (Czechoslovakia). Publs *Reformed World* (quarterly).

World Conference on Religion and Peace: 14 chemin Auguste-Vilbert, 1218 Grand Saconnex, Geneva, Switzerland; tel. (022) 7985162; fax (022) 7910034; f. 1970 to co-ordinate education and action of various world religions for world peace and justice. Mems: religious organizations and individuals in 50 countries. Pres. Dr M. ARAM; Sec.-Gen. Dr JOHN B. TAYLOR. Publ. *Religion for Peace* (quarterly newsletter).

World Congress of Faiths: 28 Powis Gdns, London, W11 1JG, England; tel. (071) 727-2607; f. 1936 to promote a spirit of fellowship among mankind through religion, to bring together people of all nationalities, backgrounds and creeds, to encourage the study and understanding of world faiths, and to promote welfare and peace. Mems: about 500. Pres. Rev. Dr EDWARD CARPENTER; Chair. Prof. KEITH WARD. Publs *World Faith Insight*, *Interfaith News* (3 a year).

World Federation of Christian Life Communities: Borgo S. Spirito 8, Casella Postale 6139, 00195 Rome, Italy; tel. (06) 6868079; f. 1953 as World Federation of the Sodalities of our Lady (first group founded 1563) as a lay movement (based on the teachings of Ignatius Loyola) to integrate Christian faith and daily living. Mems: groups in 55 countries representing about 100,000 individuals. Pres. BRENDAN MCLOUGHLIN (Ireland); Exec. Sec. JOSÉ REYES (Chile). Publ. *Progressio* (every 2 months in English, French, Spanish).

World Fellowship of Buddhists: 33 Sukhumvit Rd, (between Soi 1 and Soi 3), Bangkok 10110, Thailand; f. 1950 to promote practice, teaching and philosophy of Buddhism; holds annual General Congress; has 94 regional centres in 37 countries. Pres. SANYA DHARMASAKTI; Hon. Gen. Sec. PRASERT RUANGSKUL. Publ. *WFB Review* (quarterly).

World Jewish Congress: 501 Madison Ave, New York, NY 10022, USA; tel. (212) 755-5770; fax (212) 755-5883; f. 1936; a voluntary association of representative Jewish communities and organizations throughout the world, aiming to foster the unity of the Jewish people and to ensure the continuity and development of their heritage. Mems: Jewish communities in 63 countries. Pres. EDGAR M. BRONFMAN; Sec.-Gen. ISRAEL SINGER. Publs *Patterns of Prejudice* (quarterly, London), *Gesher* (Hebrew quarterly, Israel), *Christian Jewish Relations* (quarterly, London), *Boletín Informativo OJI* (fortnightly, Buenos Aires).

World Methodist Council: International Headquarters, POB 518, Lake Junaluska, NC 28745, USA; tel. (704) 456-9432; fax (704) 456-9453; f. 1881 to deepen the fellowship of the Methodist peoples, to encourage evangelism, to foster Methodist participation in the ecumenical movement, and to promote the unity of Methodist witness and service. Mems: 64 Church bodies in 90 countries, comprising 25m. individuals. Chair. Bishop LAWI IMATHIU (Kenya); Gen. Sec. JOE HALE (USA). Publ. *World Parish* (6 a year).

World Sephardi Federation: 13 rue Marignac, 1206 Geneva, Switzerland; tel. (022) 473313; telex 427569; f. 1951 to strengthen the unity of Jewry and Judaism among Sephardi and Oriental Jews, to defend and foster religious and cultural activities of all Sephardi and Oriental Jewish communities and preserve their spiritual heritage, to provide moral and material assistance where necessary and to co-operate with other similar organizations. Mems: 50 communities and organizations in 33 countries. Pres. Sec.-Gen. SHIMON DERY.

World Student Christian Federation: 5 route des Morillons, Grand-Saconnex, 1218 Geneva, Switzerland; tel. (022) 7988953; telex 415730; fax (022) 7910361; f. 1895 to proclaim Jesus Christ as Lord and Saviour in the academic community, and to present students with the claims of the Christian faith over their whole life. Gen. Assembly every four years. Mems: 67 national Student Christian Movements, and 34 national correspondents. Chair. Bishop POULOSE MAR POULOSE (India); Sec.-Gen. CHRISTINE LEDGER (Australia), MANUEL QUINTERO (Cuba).

World Union for Progressive Judaism: 838 Fifth Ave, New York, NY 10021, USA; tel. (212) 249-0100; f. 1926; promotes and co-ordinates efforts of Reform, Liberal and Progressive congregations throughout the world; supports new congregations; assigns and employs rabbis; sponsors seminaries and schools; organizes international conferences; maintains a youth section. Mems: organizations and individuals in 23 countries. Exec. Dir Rabbi RICHARD G. HIRSCH (Israel). Publs *AMMI* (quarterly), *Telem* (monthly in Hebrew), *International Conference Reports*, *European Judaism* (bi-annual).

World Union of Catholic Women's Organisations: 20 rue Notre-Dame-des-Champs, 75006 Paris, France; tel. (1) 45-44-27-65; fax (1) 42-84-04-80; f. 1910 to promote and co-ordinate the contribution of Catholic women in international life, in social, civic, cultural and religious matters. Mems: 30,000,000. Pres.-Gen. M. T. VAN HETEREN-HOGENHUIS (Netherlands); Sec.-Gen. GERALDINE MACCARTHY. Publ. *Newsletter* (quarterly in four languages).

Science

International Council of Scientific Unions—ICSU: 51 blvd de Montmorency, 75016 Paris, France; tel. (1) 45-25-03-29; telex 630 553; fax (1) 42-88-94-31; f. 1919 as International Research Council; present name adopted 1931; new statutes adopted 1990; to co-ordinate international co-operation in theoretical and applied sciences and to promote national scientific research through the intermediary of affiliated national organizations; General Assembly of representatives of national and scientific members meets every three years to formulate policy. The following committees have been established: Scientific Cttee on the Application of Science to Agriculture, Fisheries and Aquaculture, Scientific Cttee on Antarctic Research, Scientific Cttee on Oceanic Research, Cttee on Space Research, ICSU-UATI Co-ordinating Cttee on Water Research, Scientific Cttee on Solar-Terrestrial Physics, Cttee on Science and Technology in Developing Countries, Cttee on Data for Science and Technology, Cttee on the Teaching of Science, Scientific Cttee on Problems of the Environment, Cttee on Genetic Experimentation, Cttee on Biotechnology and Scientific Cttee on International Geosphere-Biosphere Programme. The following services and Inter-Union Committees and Commissions have been established: Federation of Astronomical and Geophysical Services, Inter-Union Commission on Frequency Allocations for Radio

OTHER INTERNATIONAL ORGANIZATIONS
Science

Astronomy and Space Science, Inter-Union Commission on Radio Meteorology, Inter-Union Commission on Spectroscopy, Inter-Union Commission on Lithosphere. National mems: academies or research councils in 75 countries; Scientific mems and assocs: 20 international unions (see below) and 26 scientific associates. Pres. Prof. M. G. K. MENON (India); Sec.-Gen. Prof. J. W. M. LA RIVIÈRE (Netherlands). Publs *ICSU Yearbook*, *Science International* (quarterly).

UNIONS FEDERATED TO THE ICSU

International Astronomical Union: 98 bis blvd d'Arago, 75014 Paris, France; f. 1919 to facilitate co-operation between the astronomers of various countries and to further the study of astronomy in all its branches; last General Assembly was held in 1988 in Baltimore, USA. Mems: organizations in 57 countries, and 7,000 individual mems. Pres. Prof. Y. KOZAI (Japan); Gen. Sec. Dr D. MCNALLY (UK). Publs *IAU Information Bulletin* (2 a year).

International Geographical Union—IGU: Dept of Geography, University of Alberta, Edmonton, Alberta, T6G 2H4, Canada; tel. (403) 492-3287; telex 037-2979; fax (403) 492-7219; f. 1922 to encourage the study of problems relating to geography, to promote and co-ordinate research requiring international co-operation, and to organize international congresses and commissions. Mems: 60, and six associates. Pres. Prof. ROLAND J. FUCHS (USA); Sec.-Gen. Prof. L. A. KOSIŃSKI (Canada). Publs *IGU Bulletin* (1–2 a year), Circular Letter, congress proceedings.

International Mathematical Union: c/o IMPA, Estrada Dona Castorina 110, Jardem Botânico, Rio de Janeiro, RJ 22460, Brazil; tel. (55) 21-294-9032; telex 2121145; fax 21-512-4115; f. 1952 to support and assist the International Congress of Mathematicians and other international scientific meetings or conferences; to encourage and support other international mathematical activities considered likely to contribute to the development of mathematical science—pure, applied or educational. Mems: 52 countries. Pres. J. L. LIONS; Sec.-Gen. Prof. JACOB PALIS, Jr.

International Union for Pure and Applied Biophysics: Institute of Biophysics, Medical University, 7643 Pécs, Hungary; tel. (72) 14017; telex 12311; fax (72) 26244; f. 1961 to organize international co-operation in biophysics and promote communication between biophysics and allied subjects, to encourage national co operation between biophysical societies, and to contribute to the advancement of biophysical knowledge. Mems: 41 adhering bodies. Pres. Prof. L. D. PEACHEY (USA); Sec.-Gen. Prof. J. TIGYI (Hungary). Publ. *Quarterly Reviews of Biophysics*.

International Union of Biochemistry: Dept of Biochemistry, Duke University Medical Center, POB 3711, Durham, NC 27710, USA; tel. (919) 684-5326; telex 802829; f. 1955 to sponsor the International Congresses of Biochemistry, to co-ordinate research and discussion, to organize co-operation between the societies of biochemistry, to promote high standards of biochemistry throughout the world and to contribute to the advancement of biochemistry in all its international aspects. Mems: 51 bodies. Pres. Dr E. C. SLATER (UK); Sec.-Gen. Dr R. L. HILL (USA).

International Union of Biological Sciences: 51 blvd de Montmorency, 75016 Paris, France; tel. (1) 45-25-00-09; telex 630553; fax (1) 42-88-94-31; f. 1919. Mems: 42 national bodies, 72 scientific bodies. Exec. Sec. Dr T. YOUNES. Publ. *Biology International* (2 a year, plus special issues), *IUBS Monographs*, *IUBS Methodology*, *Manual Series*.

International Union of Crystallography: c/o Dr J. N. King, 5 Abbey Sq., Chester, CH1 2HU, England; tel. 342878; f. 1947 to facilitate international standardization of methods, of units, of nomenclature and of symbols used in crystallography; and to form a focus for the relations of crystallography to other sciences. Mems in 34 countries. Pres. Prof. A. AUTHIER (France); Gen. Sec. Prof. A. HORDVIK (Norway); Exec. Sec. Dr J. N. KING. Publs *Acta Crystallographica*, *Journal of Applied Crystallography*, *Structure Reports* (2 volumes a year), *International Tables for Crystallography*, *World Directory of Crystallographers*, *IUCr Crystallographic Symposia*, *IUCr Monographs on Crystallography*, *IUCr Texts on Crystallography*.

International Union of Geodesy and Geophysics—IUGG: Observatoire Royal de Belgique, 3 ave Circulaire, 1180 Brussels, Belgium; tel. (02) 373-02-11; telex 21565; fax (02) 374-98-22; f. 1919; federation of seven associations representing Geodesy, Seismology and Physics of the Earth's Interior, Physical Sciences of the Ocean, Volcanology and Chemistry of the Earth's Interior, Scientific Hydrology, Meteorology and Atmospheric Physics, Geomagnetism and Aeronomy, which meet at the General Assemblies of the Union. In addition, there are Joint Committees of the various associations either among themselves or with other unions. The Union organizes scientific meetings and also sponsors various permanent services, to collect, analyse and publish geophysical data. Mems: in 78 countries. Pres. Prof. V. KEILIS-BOROK (USSR); Gen. Sec. Prof. P. MELCHIOR (Belgium). Publs *IUGG Chronicle* (6 a year), *Geodetic Bulletin* (quarterly), *International Bibliography of Geodesy* (irregular), *International Seismological Summary* (yearly), *Bulletin Volcanologique* (2 a year), *Bulletin mensuel du Bureau Central Sismologique* (monthly), *Bulletin de l'Association Internationale d'Hydrologie Scientifique* (quarterly), *International Bibliography of Hydrology*, *Catalogue des Volcans Actifs* (both irregular).

International Union of Geological Sciences—IUGS: c/o R. Sinding-Larsen, Leiv Erikssons vei 39, POB 3006, 7002 Trondheim, Norway; tel. (7) 90-43-15; telex 55417; f. 1961 to encourage the study of geoscientific problems, facilitate international and interdisciplinary co-operation in geology and related sciences, and support the quadrennial International Geological Congress. IUGS organizes international meetings and co-sponsors joint programmes, including the International Geological Correlation Programme (with UNESCO). Mems from 95 countries. Pres. Prof. U. G. CORDANI (Brazil); Sec.-Gen. R. BRETT (USA).

International Union of Immunological Societies: Dept of Chemical Immunology, Weizmann Institute of Science, Rehovot, Israel; tel. (8) 469712; telex 381300; f. 1969; holds triennial international congress. Mems: national societies in 41 countries. Pres. JACOB B. NATVIG; Sec.-Gen. Dr RUTH ARNON (Israel).

International Union of Microbiological Societies—IUMS: Dept of Biochemistry and Genetics, Catherine Cookson Bldg, Framlington Place, Newcastle-upon-Tyne, NE2 4HH, England; tel. (091) 222-7695; telex 53654; fax (091) 261-1182; f. 1930. Mems: 94 national microbiological societies. Pres. Prof. S. SASAKI (Japan); Sec.-Gen. Prof. S. W. GLOVER. Publs *International Journal of Systematic Bacteriology* (quarterly), *Intervirology* (monthly), *International Journal of Food Microbiology* (every 2 months), *Advances in Microbial Ecology* (annually), *Journal of Biological Standardization* (quarterly), *World Journal of Microbiology and Biotechnology* (every 2 months).

International Union of Nutritional Sciences: c/o Dept of Human Nutrition, Agricultural University, POB 8129, 6700 EV Wageningen, Netherlands; tel. (08370) 82589; telex 45015; fax (08370) 83342; f. 1946 to promote international co-operation in the scientific study of nutrition and its applications, to encourage research and exchange of scientific information by holding international congresses and issuing publications. Mems: 66 organizations. Pres. J. E. DUTRA DE OLIVEIRA (Brazil); Sec.-Gen. Prof. J. G. A. J. HAUTVAST (Netherlands). Publs *IUNS Directory*, *Newsletter*.

International Union of Pharmacology: Laboratoire de Pharmacologie, UCL 7350, 73 ave E. Mounier, 1200 Brussels, Belgium; tel. (02) 764-73-50; fax (02) 764-73-50; f. 1963 to promote international co-ordination of research, discussion and publication in the field of pharmacology, including clinical pharmacology, drug metabolism and toxicology; co-operates with WHO in all matters concerning drugs and drug research; holds international congresses. Mems: 48 national and three regional societies. Pres. S. EBASHI (Japan); Sec.-Gen. T. GODFRAIND (Belgium). Publ. *TIPS (Trends in Pharmacological Sciences)*.

International Union of Physiological Sciences: c/o Prof. R. Naquet, Laboratoire de Physiologie Nerveuse, CNRS, ave de la Terrasse, 91190 Gif-sur-Yvette, France; tel. (1) 69-07-61-45; telex 691137; f. 1955. Mems: 48 national and six assoc. mems. Pres. Sir ANDREW HUXLEY (UK); Sec.-Gen. Prof. R. NAQUET.

International Union of Psychological Science: c/o Prof. K. Pawlik, Psychologisches Institut I, Von-Melle-Park II, 2000 Hamburg 13, Germany; tel. (040) 4123-4723; f. 1951 to contribute to the development of intellectual exchange and scientific relations between psychologists of different countries. Mems: national societies in 48 countries. Pres. Prof. MARK R. ROSENZWEIG (USA); Sec.-Gen. Prof. KURT PAWLIK (Germany). Publs *International Journal of Psychology* (quarterly), *International Directory of Psychologists* (irregular).

International Union of Pure and Applied Chemistry—IUPAC: Bank Court Chambers, 2–3 Pound Way, Cowley Centre, Oxford, OX4 3YF, England; tel. (0865) 747744; telex 83220; fax (0865) 747510; f. 1919 to organize permanent co-operation between chemical associations in the member countries, to study topics of international importance requiring regulation, standardization or codification, to co-operate with other international organizations in the field of chemistry and to contribute to the advancement of all aspects of chemistry. Biennial General Assembly. Mems: in 45 countries. Pres. Prof. Y. P. JEANNIN (France); Sec.-Gen. Prof. T. S. WEST (UK). Publs *Chemistry International* (bi-monthly), *Pure and Applied Chemistry* (monthly).

OTHER INTERNATIONAL ORGANIZATIONS

International Union of Pure and Applied Physics: Gothenburg University, Vasaparken, 411 24 Göteborg, Sweden; tel. (031) 63-18-83; telex 2369; fax (031) 63-46-60; f. 1922 to promote and encourage international co-operation in physics. Mems: in 45 countries. Pres. Prof. L. Kerwin (Canada); Sec.-Gen. Jan S. Nilsson (Sweden).

International Union of Radio Science: c/o Observatoire Royal de Belgique, 3 ave Circulaire, 1180 Brussels, Belgium; tel. (02) 374-13-08; f. 1919 to encourage and organize scientific research in radio science, particularly where international co-operation is required; and to promote the development of uniform methods of measurement and standardized measuring instruments on an international basis, to stimulate and co-ordinate studies of the scientific aspects of telecommunications using electro-magnetic waves, guided and unguided. There are 40 national committees. Pres. A. L. Cullen (UK); Sec.-Gen. Prof. J. Van Bladel (Belgium). Publs *URSI Information Bulletin*, *Review of Radio Science*.

International Union of the History and Philosophy of Science: Division of the History of Science: Office for History of Science, Uppsala University, Uppsala, Sweden; tel. (18) 18-15-79; Division of the History of Logic, Methodology and Philosophy of Science: Dept of Philosophy, University of Turku, 20500 Turku 50, Finland; f. 1954 to promote research into the history and philosophy of science. There are 34 national committees. DHS Council (Montreal): Pres. Prof. W. Shea (Canada); Sec. T. Frängmyr (Sweden). DLMPS Council: Pres. Prof. Jonathan Cohen (UK); Sec. R. Hilpinen (Finland).

International Union of Theoretical and Applied Mechanics: Pfaffenwaldring 9, University of Stuttgart, 7000 Stuttgart 80, Germany; telex 7255445; fax (0711) 685-6400; f. 1947 to form a link beween persons and organizations engaged in scientific work (theoretical or experimental) in mechanics or in related sciences; to organize international congresses of theoretical and applied mechanics, through a standing Congress Committee, and to organize other international meetings for subjects falling within this field; and to engage in other activities meant to promote the development of mechanics as a science. Mems: from 37 countries. Pres. Prof. P. Germain (France); Sec. Prof. W. Schiehlen (Germany). Publ. *Annual Report*.

OTHER ORGANIZATIONS

Association for the Taxonomic Study of the Flora of Tropical Africa: National Herbarium and Botanic Gardens of Malawi, POB 528, Zomba, Malawi; tel. 523145; telex 45252; fax 522108; f. 1950 to facilitate co-operation and liaison between botanists engaged in the study of the flora of tropical Africa south of the Sahara including Madagascar; maintains a library. Mems: about 800 botanists in 63 countries. Sec.-Gen. Dr J. H. Seyani. Publs *AETFAT Bulletin* (annual), *Proceedings*.

Association of African Geological Surveys: c/o CIFEG, POB 6517, ave de Concyr, 45065 Orléans Cedex 2, France; tel. 38-64-36-57; telex 780258; fax 38-64-35-18; f. 1929 to synthesize the geological knowledge of Africa and neighbouring countries and encourage research in geological and allied sciences; operates PANGIS (Pan-African Network for a Geological Information System), aiming to install bibliographical data-bases; affiliated to the International Union of Geological Sciences (q.v.). Mems: about 60 (Official Geological Surveys, public and private organizations). Pres. G. O. Kesse (Ghana); Sec.-Gen. M. Bensaïd (Morocco). Publs *African Geology*, maps and studies.

Association of European Atomic Forums—FORATOM: 22 Buckingham Gate, London, SW1Y 4SL, England; tel. (071) 828-0116; fax (071) 828-0110; f. 1960; holds periodical conferences. Mems: atomic 'forums' in Austria, Belgium, Finland, France, Germany, Italy, Luxembourg, Netherlands, Norway, Spain, Sweden, Switzerland, United Kingdom. Pres. Olavi Vapaavuori; Sec. Gen. Jim Corner.

Association of Geoscientists for International Development—AGID: c/o Dr J. L. Rau, Asian Institute of Technology, POB 2754, Bangkok 10501, Thailand; tel. 529-0100-13, ext. 2528; telex 84276; fax 529-0374; f. 1974 to encourage communication between those interested in the application of the geosciences to international development; to give priority to the developing countries in these matters; to organize meetings and publish information; affiliated to the International Union of Geological Sciences (q.v.). Mems: in 116 countries (individuals, and 44 institutions). Sec.-Treas. Dr Jon L. Rau (Thailand). Publ. *AGID News* (quarterly).

Biometric Society: Dept of Applied Statistics, University of Reading, Whiteknights, POB 217, Reading, RG6 2AN, England; tel. (0734) 875123; telex 847813; fax (0734) 753169; f. 1947 for the advancement of quantitative biological science through the development of quantitative theories and the application, development and dissemination of effective mathematical and statistical techniques; the Society has 16 regional organizations and 8 national groups, is affiliated with the International Statistical Institute and the World Health Organization, and constitutes the Section of Biometry of the International Union of Biological Sciences (q.v.). Mems: over 6,000 in more than 60 countries. Pres. Prof. R. Tomassone (France); Sec. Prof. R. Mead (UK). Publ. *Biometrics* (quarterly).

Council for the International Congresses of Entomology: c/o CSIRO Division of Entomology, POB 1700, Canberra, ACT 2601, Australia; tel. (062) 465227; telex 62309; fax (062) 497302; f. 1910 to act as a link between quadrennial congresses and to arrange the venue for each congress; the committee is also the entomology section of the International Union of Biological Sciences (q.v.). Chair. Dr R. Galun (Israel); Sec. Dr M. J. Whitten (Australia).

European Association of Exploration Geophysicists: Utrechtseweg 62, POB 298, 3700 AG Zeist, Netherlands; tel. (3404) 56997; fax (3404) 62640; f. 1951 to facilitate contacts between exploration geophysicists, disseminate information to members, arrange annual meetings, technical exhibitions, and courses. Mems 3,750, and 1,030 subscribers in 82 countries throughout the world. Treas./Sec. P. Kennett (UK). Publs *Geophysical Prospecting* (8 a year), *First Break* (monthly), *Tidal Gravity Corrections* (annually).

European Atomic Energy Society: UKAEA, 11 Charles II St, London, SW1Y 4QP; tel. (071) 930-5454; telex 22565; fax (071) 930-5454, ext. 274; f. 1954 to encourage co-operation in atomic energy research. Mems: national atomic energy commissions in Austria, Belgium, Denmark, Finland, France, Germany, Greece, Italy, Netherlands, Norway, Portugal, Spain, Sweden, Switzerland, United Kingdom. Pres. Prof. C. M. Malbrain; Exec. Vice-Pres. R. N. Simeone.

European Molecular Biology Organization—EMBO: 6900 Heidelberg 1, Postfach 1022.40, Germany; tel. (6221) 383031; telex 461613; fax (6221) 387306; f. 1964 to promote collaboration in the field of molecular biology; to establish fellowships for training and research; to establish a European Laboratory of Molecular Biology where a majority of the disciplines comprising the subject will be represented. Mems: 750. Chair. Prof. M. Birnstiel (Austria); Sec.-Gen. Prof. P. Chambon (France); Exec. Sec. Dr J. Tooze (Germany). Publ. *EMBO Journal* (13 a year).

European Organization for Nuclear Research—CERN: European Laboratory for Particle Physics, 1211 Geneva 23, Switzerland; tel. (022) 7676111; telex 419000; fax (022) 7677555; f. 1954 to provide for collaboration among European states in nuclear research of a pure scientific and fundamental character; the work of CERN is for peaceful purposes only and concerns subnuclear, high-energy and elementary particle physics; it is not concerned with the development of nuclear reactors or fusion devices. Council comprises two representatives of each member state. Major experimental facilities: Synchro-Cyclotron (of 600 MeV), Proton Synchrotron (of 25–28 GeV), and Super Proton Synchrotron (of 450 GeV). A Large Electron-Positron Collider (LEP) of 27 km circumference (of 50 GeV per beam) was commissioned in July 1989. Budget (1989) 809m. Swiss francs. Mems: Austria, Belgium, Denmark, Finland (subject to ratification), France, Germany, Greece, Italy, Netherlands, Norway, Portugal, Spain, Sweden, Switzerland, United Kingdom; Observers: Poland, Turkey, Yugoslavia. Dir-Gen. Prof. Carlo Rubbia (Italy). Publs *CERN Courier* (monthly), *Annual Report*, *Scientific Reports*.

European Space Agency—ESA: 8-10 rue Mario Nikis, 75738 Paris Cedex 15, France; tel. (1) 42-73-76-54; telex 202746; fax (1) 42-73-75-60; f. 1975 to promote co-operation among European states in space research and technology and their application for peaceful purposes. Council composed of representatives of member states is the governing body. The Agency runs ESTEC (European Space Research and Technology Centre), ESOC (European Space Operations Centre) and ESRIN (Space Documentation Centre). The Agency's 'Ariane' programme (begun in 1979) develops rockets to launch satellites for telecommunications, meteorology and other scientific and industrial purposes. In 1987 member governments approved a programme to include a new type of Ariane launcher, a manned space-shuttle (Hermes), and collaboration with the USA on a manned space-station. Mems: Austria, Belgium, Denmark, France, Germany, Ireland, Italy, Netherlands, Norway, Spain, Sweden, Switzerland, United Kingdom; associated states: Canada, Finland. Chair. Dr H. Grage (Denmark); Man. Dir Jean-Marie Luton. Publs *Annual Report*, *ESA Bulletin*, *ESA Journal*.

European-Mediterranean Seismological Centre: 5 rue René Descartes, 67084 Strasbourg Cedex, France; tel. 88-41-63-69; telex 890 826; f. 1976 for rapid determination of seismic hypocentres in the region; maintains data base. Mems: institutions in 14 countries. Sec.-Gen. J. Bonnin. Publ. monthly list of preliminary hypocentral determinations.

Federation of Arab Scientific Research Councils: POB 13027, Baghdad, Iraq; tel. 5381090; telex 212466; f. 1976 to encourage co-operation in scientific research, to promote the establishment of new institutions and plan joint regional research projects. Mems: national science bodies in 15 countries. Sec.-Gen. Dr TAHA AL-NUEIMI. Publs *Journal, Newsletter*.

Federation of Asian Scientific Academies and Societies—FASAS: c/o Indian National Science Academy, Bahadur Shah Zafar Marg, New Delhi 110002, India; tel. (11) 331-3153; telex 3161835; fax (11) 331-3153; f. 1984 to stimulate regional co-operation and promote national and regional self-reliance in science and technology, by organizing meetings, training and research programmes and encouraging the exchange of scientists and of scientific information. Mems: national scientific academies and societies from Afghanistan, Bangladesh, People's Republic of China, India, Republic of Korea, Malaysia, Nepal, Pakistan, Philippines, Singapore, Sri Lanka, Thailand. Pres. Prof. YAN DONGSHENG (China); Sec. Prof. S. K. JOSHI (India).

Federation of European Biochemical Societies: c/o Prof. V. Turk, Dept of Biochemistry, Jozef Stefan Institute, Jamova 39, 61000 Ljubljana, Yugoslavia; tel. (61) 219143; telex 31296; fax (61) 273594; f. 1964 to promote the science of biochemistry through meetings of European biochemists, provision of fellowships and advanced courses and issuing publications. Mems: 40,000 in 27 societies. Chair. Dr P. FRIEDRICH; Sec.-Gen. Prof. V. TURK. Publs *European Journal of Biochemistry, FEBS Letters, FEBS Bulletin*.

Foundation for International Scientific Co-ordination (Fondation 'Pour la science', Centre international de synthèse): 12 rue Colbert, 75002 Paris, France; tel. (1) 42-97-50-68; f. 1924. Dir JEAN-CLAUDE PERROT. Publs *Revue de Synthèse, Revue d'Histoire des Sciences, Semaines de Synthèse, L'Evolution de l'Humanité, Bibliothèque de Synthèse*.

Intergovernmental Oceanographic Commission: UNESCO, 7 place de Fontenoy, 75700 Paris, France; tel. (1) 45-68-39-83; telex 204461; fax (1) 40-56-93-16; f. 1960 to promote scientific investigation with a view to learning more about the nature and resources of the oceans through the concerted action of its members. Mems: 117 governments. Chair. Prof. ULF LIE (Norway); Sec. Dr GUNNAR KULLENBERG. Publs *IOC Technical Series* (irregular), *IOC Manuals* and *Guides* (irregular), *IOC Workshop Reports* (irregular) and *IOC Training Course Reports* (irregular).

International Academy of Astronautics—IAA: 6 rue Galilee, POB 1268-16, 75766 Paris Cedex 15, France; tel. (1) 47 23 82-15; telex 051767; fax (1) 47-23-82-16; f. 1960; fosters the development of astronautics for peaceful purposes, holds scientific meetings and makes scientific studies, reports, awards and book awards; maintains 19 scientific cttees and develops a multilingual terminology data base (20 languages). Mems: 681 and 382 corresponding mems in 4 trustee sections: basic sciences, engineering sciences, life sciences and social sciences from 57 countries. Sec.-Gen. Dr JEAN-MICHEL CONTANT. Publ. *Acta Astronautica* (monthly).

International Association for Earthquake Engineering: Kenchiku Kaikan, 3rd Floor, 5-26-20, Shiba, Minato-ku, Tokyo 108, Japan; f. 1963 to promote international co-operation among scientists and engineers in the field of earthquake engineering through exchange of knowledge, ideas and results of research and practical experience. Mems: 38 countries. Pres. GIUSEPPE GRANDORI (Italy).

International Association for Ecology—INTECOL: Savannah River Ecology Laboratory, Drawer E, Aiken, Sc 29802, USA; tel. (803) 725-2472; fax (803) 725-3309; f. 1967 to provide opportunities for communication between ecologists; to co-operate with organizations and individuals having related aims and interests; to encourage studies in the different fields of ecology; affiliated to the International Union of Biological Sciences (q.v.). Mems: 35 national and international ecological societies, and 1,000 individuals. Pres. W. HABER (Germany); Sec.-Gen. R. SHARITZ (USA).

International Association for Mathematical Geology: c/o Prof. J. C. Davis, Kansas Geological Survey, 1930 Constant Ave, Lawrence, Kan 66046, USA; tel. (913) 864-4991; f. 1968 for the preparation and elaboration of mathematical models of geological processes; the introduction of mathematical methods in geological sciences and technology; assistance in the development of mathematical investigation in geological sciences; the organization of international collaboration in mathematical geology through various forums and publications; educational programmes for mathematical geology; affiliated to the International Union of Geological Sciences (q.v.). Mems: c. 800. Pres. Prof. J. C. DAVIS (USA); Sec.-Gen. Dr R. B. MCCAMMON (USA). Publs *Journal of the International Association for Mathematical Geology* (8 a year), *Computers and Geosciences* (4 a year), *Newsletter* (quarterly).

International Association for Mathematics and Computers in Simulation: c/o Institut Montefiore, Bâtiment B28, Sart Tilman, 4000 Liège, Belgium; tel. (41) 56-37-10; f. 1955 to further the study of mathematical tools and computer software and hardware, analogue, digital or hybrid computers for simulation of soft or hard systems. Mems: 1,100 and 27 assoc. mems. Pres. R. VICHNEVETSKY (USA); Sec. J. ROBERT (Belgium). Publs *Mathematics and Computers in Simulation* (6 a year), *Applied Numerical Mathematics* (6 a year).

International Association for the Physical Sciences of the Ocean—IAPSO: POB 1161, Del Mar, Ca 92014-1161, USA; f. 1919 to promote the study of scientific problems relating to the oceans and interactions occurring at its boundaries, chiefly in so far as such study may be carried out by the aid of mathematics, physics and chemistry; to initiate, facilitate and co-ordinate research; to provide for discussion, comparison and publication; affiliated to the International Union of Geodesy and Geophysics (q.v.). Mems: 71 member states. Pres. Prof. JAMES J. O'BRIEN (USA); Sec.-Gen. Dr ROBERT E. STEVENSON (USA). Publs *Publications Scientifiques* (irregular).

International Association for Plant Physiology—IAPP: c/o Dr D. Graham, Food Research Laboratories, CSIRO, POB 52, North Ryde, NSW, Australia 2113; tel. (02) 887-8333; telex 23407; fax (02) 887-3107; f. 1955 to promote the development of plant physiology at the international level through congresses, symposia and workshops, by maintaining communication with national societies and by encouraging interaction between plant physiologists in developing and developed countries; affiliated to the International Union of Biological Sciences (q.v.). Pres. Prof. Dr J. B. BRUINSMA; Sec.-Treas. Dr D. GRAHAM.

International Association for Plant Taxonomy: Botanisches Museum, Königin Luisestr. 6–8, 1000 Berlin 33, Germany; tel. (030) 8300-6132; f. 1950 to promote the development of plant taxonomy and encourage contacts between people and institutes interested in this work; affiliated to the International Union of Biological Sciences (q.v.). Mems: institutes and individuals in 85 countries. Pres. F. A. STAFLEN (Netherlands); Sec.-Gen. W. GREUTER (Germany). Publs *Taxon* (quarterly), *Regnum vegetabile* (irregular).

International Association of Biological Standardization: Biostandards, CP 456, 1211 Geneva 4, Switzerland; telex 421859; fax (22) 475610; f. 1955 to connect producers and controllers of immunological products (sera, vaccines, etc.) for the study and the development of methods of standardization; supports international organizations in their efforts to solve problems of standardization. Mems: 650. Pres. C. HUYGELEN (Belgium); Sec.-Gen. D. GAUDRY (France). Publs *Newsletter* (quarterly), *Biologicals* (quarterly).

International Association of Botanic Gardens: c/o Dr B. Morley, Botanic Gardens of Adelaide, North Terrace, Adelaide, SA 5000, Australia; tel. (08) 228-2320; fax (08) 223-1809; f. 1954 to promote co-operation between scientific collections of living plants, including the exchange of information and specimens; to promote the study of the taxonomy of cultivated plants; and to encourage the conservation of rare plants and their habitats; affiliated to the International Union of Biological Sciences (q.v.). Pres. Prof. PETER ASHTON (USA); Sec. Dr BRIAN D. MORLEY (Australia).

International Association of Geodesy: 136 bis rue de Grenelle, 75700 Paris, France; tel. (1) 43-98-82-69; telex 204989; fax (1) 45-55-07-85; f. 1922 to promote the study of all scientific problems of geodesy and encourage geodetic research; to promote and co-ordinate international co-operation in this field; to publish results; affiliated to the International Union of Geodesy and Geophysics (q.v.). Mems: national committees in 73 countries. Pres. I. I. MUELLER (USA); Sec.-Gen. M. LOUIS (France); Asst. Sec.-Gen. C. BOUCHER (France). Publs *Bulletin géodésique, Travaux de l'AIG, Bibliographie géodésique internationale*.

International Association of Geomagnetism and Aeronomy—IAGA: Physics Dept, Aberdeen University, Aberdeen, AB9 2UE, Scotland; tel. (0224) 574585; telex 73458; f. 1919 for the study of questions relating to geomagnetism and aeronomy and the encouragement of research; holds General and Scientific Assemblies every four years; affiliated to the International Union of Geodesy and Geophysics (IUGG, q.v.). Mems: the countries which adhere to the IUGG. Pres. R. E. GENDRIN (France); Sec.-Gen. M. GADSDEN (UK). Publs *IAGA Bulletin* (including annual *Geomagnetic Data*), *IAGA News* (annually).

International Association of Hydrological Sciences: Committee for Hydrological Research TNO, POB 297, 2501 BD The Hague, Netherlands; tel. (070) 49-65-37; telex 31660; fax (070) 85-57-00; f. 1922 to promote co-operation in the study of hydrology and water resources. Pres. VIT KLEMES (Canada); Sec.-Gen. H. J. COLENBRANDER. Publs *Journal* (every 2 months), *Newsletter* (3 a year).

International Association of Meteorology and Atmospheric Physics—IAMAP: Institute for Meteorology and Geophysics, University of Innsbruck, 6020 Innsbruck, Austria; f. 1919; permanent commissions on atmospheric ozone, radiation, atmospheric chemistry and global pollution, dynamic meteorology, polar meteorology, clouds and precipitation, climate, atmospheric electricity, planetary atmospheres and their evolution, and meteorology of the upper atmosphere; general assemblies held once every four years; special assemblies held once between general assemblies; affiliated to the

OTHER INTERNATIONAL ORGANIZATIONS

International Union of Geodesy and Geophysics (q.v.). Pres. Dr G. B. TUCKER (Australia); Sec.-Gen. Prof. M. KUHN (Austria).

International Association of Photobiology: c/o Rex M. Tyrrell, Institut Suisse de Recherches Expérimentales sur le Cancer, 1066 Epalinges, Lausanne, Switzerland; tel. (021) 333061; telex 26156; fax (021) 326933; f. 1928; stimulation of scientific research concerning the physics, chemistry and climatology of non-ionizing radiations (ultra-violet, visible and infra-red) in relation to their biological efffects and their applications in biology and medicine; 18 national committees represented; affiliated to the International Union of Biological Sciences (q.v.). International Congresses held every four years. Pres. Prof. T. YOSHIZAWA; Sec.-Gen. Dr R. M. TYRRELL (Switzerland).

International Association of Sedimentologists: c/o Prof. F. Surlyk, Geologisk Centralinstitut, Øster Voldgade 10, 1350 Copenhagen K, Denmark; f. 1952; affiliated to the International Union of Geological Sciences (q.v.). Mems: 2,100. Pres. Prof. G. G. ZUFFA (Italy); Gen. Sec. Prof. FINN SURLYK (Denmark). Publ. *Sedimentology* (every 2 months).

International Association of Theoretical and Applied Limnology (Societas Internationalis Limnologiae): Dept of Biology, University of Alabama, Tuscaloosa, Ala 35487-0344, USA; tel. (205) 348-1793; fax (205) 348-1786; f. 1922; study of physical, chemical and biological phenomena of lakes and rivers; affiliated to the International Union of Biological Sciences (q.v.). Mems: about 3,200. Pres. P. M. JÓNASSON (Denmark); Gen. Sec. and Treas. ROBERT G. WETZEL (USA).

International Association of Volcanology and Chemistry of the Earth's Interior—IAVCEI: c/o Institut Mineralogie, Ruhr Universität Bochum, 4630 Bochum, Germany; tel. (0234) 7003520; telex 0825-860; f. 1919 to examine scientifically all aspects of volcanology; affiliated to the International Union of Geodesy and Geophysics (q.v.). Pres. S. ARAMAKI; Sec.-Gen. H.-U. SCHMINKE (Germany). Publs *Bulletin of Volcanology, Catalogue of the Active Volcanoes of the World, Newsletter.*

International Association of Wood Anatomists: c/o Institute of Systematic Botany, University of Utrecht, Netherlands; tel. 030-532643; f. 1931 for the purpose of study, documentation and exchange of information on the structure of wood. Mems: 500 in 61 countries. Exec. Sec. B. J. H. TER WELLE. Publ. *IAWA Bulletin.*

International Association on Water Pollution Research and Control: 1 Queen Anne's Gate, London, SW1H 9BT, England; tel. (071) 222-3848; telex 918518; fax (071) 233-1197; f. 1965 to encourage international communication, co-operative effort, and a maximum exchange of information on water quality management; to sponsor conferences every two years; to publish research reports. Mems: 47 national, 420 corporate and 2,720 individuals. Pres. Prof. P. GRAU; Exec. Dir A. MILBURN. Publs *Water Research* (monthly), *Water Science and Technology* (12 a year), *Water Quality International* (quarterly), *Yearbook; Scientific and Technical Reports.*

International Astronautical Federation—IAF: 3-5 rue Mario-Nikis, 75015 Paris, France; tel. (1) 45-67-42-60; telex 205917; fax (1) 42-73-21-20; f. 1950 to foster the development of astronautics for peaceful purposes at national and international levels. The IAF has created the International Academy of Astronautics (IAA) and the International Institute of Space Law (IISL). Mems: 106 national astronautical societies in 37 countries. Pres. ALVARO AZCARRAGA (Spain); Exec. Sec. M. CLAUDIN.

International Botanical Congress: c/o Prof. K. Iwatsuki, Botanical Gardens, University of Tokyo, Hakusan 3-7-1, Bunkyo-ku, Tokyo 112, Japan; tel. (03) 814-2625; fax (03) 814-0139; f. 1864 to inform botanists of recent progress in the plant sciences; the Nomenclature Section of the Congress attempts to provide a uniform terminology and methodology for the naming of plants; other Divisions deal with developmental, metabolic, structural, systematic and evolutionary, ecological botany; genetics and plant breeding; next Congress: Tokyo, 1993; affiliated to the International Union of Biological Sciences (q.v.). Sec. Prof. K. IWATSUKI.

International Bureau of Weights and Measures: Pavillon de Breteuil, 92312 Sèvres Cedex, France; tel. (1) 45-07-70-70; telex 631351; fax (1) 45-34-20-21; f. 1875 for the international unification of physical measures; establishment of fundamental standards and of scales of the principal physical dimensions; preservation of the international prototypes; determination of national standards; precision measurements in physics. Mems: 47 states. Pres. D. KIND (Germany); Sec. J. KOVALEVSKY (France); Dir T. J. QUINN (UK).

International Cartographic Association: 24 Strickland Rd, Mt Pleasant, Western Australia 6153, Australia; tel. (09) 364-5380; telex 95791; f. 1959 for the advancement, instigation and co-ordination of cartographic research involving co-operation between different nations. Particularly concerned with furtherance of training in cartography, study of source material, compilation, graphic design, drawing, scribing and reproduction techniques of maps; organizes international conferences, symposia, meetings, exhibitions. Mems: 64 nations. Sec.-Treas. DON PEARCE (Australia). Publs *ICA Newsletter* (2 a year).

International Centre of Insect Physiology and Ecology: POB 30772, Nairobi, Kenya; tel. 802501; telex 22053; fax 803360; f. 1979 to increase food production by undertaking research on pests of major crops, vectors of livestock diseases, and insect carriers of human diseases critical to tropical rural health; and to increase the capacity of developing countries in pest management research and its application, by training scientists and technologists; field stations in Ethiopia, Kenya, the Philippines, Rwanda, Somalia and Zambia. Dir Prof. THOMAS R. ODHIAMBO (Kenya). Publs *Insect Science and its Application* (every 2 months), *Annual Report, DUDU* (quarterly).

International Commission for Optics: Institut d'Optique/CNRS, POB 147, 91403 Orsay Cedex, France; tel. (1) 69-41-68-44; telex 602166; fax (1) 69-41-31-92; f. 1948 to contribute to the progress of theoretical and instrumental optics, to assist in research and to promote international agreement on specifications; Gen. Assembly every three years. Mems: national committees in 35 countries. Pres. Prof. J. C. DAINTY (UK); Sec.-Gen. Dr P. CHAVEL (France). Publs *ICO Newsletter.*

International Commission for Plant-Bee Relationships: c/o Dr S. N. Holm, Royal Veterinary and Agricultural University, Department of Crop Science, Research Station, Højbakkegaard, 2630 Taastrup, Denmark; tel. 42-99-26-13; fax 43-71-04-14; f. 1950 to promote research and its application in the field of bee biology, and collect and spread information; to organize meetings, etc., and collaborate with scientific organizations; affiliated to the International Union of Biological Sciences (q.v.). Mems: 175 in 34 countries. Pres. Dr INGRID WILLIAMS; Sec. J. N. TASEI.

International Commission for the Scientific Exploration of the Mediterranean Sea (Commission internationale pour l'exploration scientifique de la mer Méditerranée—CIESM): 16 blvd de Suisse, 98030 Monaco Cedex; tel. (93) 30-38-79; f. 1919 for scientific exploration of the Mediterranean Sea; includes 12 scientific committees. Mems: 1,650 scientists, 17 member countries. Pres. SAS The Prince RAINIER III of MONACO; Sec.-Gen. Cdt. J. Y. COUSTEAU (France).

International Commission on Physics Education: c/o Prof. J. Barojas, POB 55534, 09340 México DF, Mexico; tel. 686-35-19; f. 1960 to encourage and develop international collaboration in the improvement and extension of the methods and scope of physics education at all levels; collaborates with UNESCO and organizes international conferences. Mems: appointed triennially by the International Union of Pure and Applied Physics. Sec. Prof. J. BAROJAS.

International Commission on Radiation Units and Measurements—ICRU: 7910 Woodmont Ave, Suite 800, Bethesda, Md 20814, USA; tel. (301) 657-2652; fax (301) 907-8768; f. 1925 to develop internationally acceptable recommendations regarding: (1) quantities and units of radiation and radioactivity, (2) procedures suitable for the measurement and application of these quantities in clinical radiology and radiobiology, (3) physical data needed in the application of these procedures. Makes recommendations on quantities and units for radiation protection (see below, International Radiation Protection Association). Mems: from about 18 countries. Chair. A. ALLISY; Sec. R. S. CASWELL; Exec. Sec. W. R. NEY. Publs *Reports.*

International Commission on Zoological Nomenclature: c/o The Natural History Museum, Cromwell Rd, London, SW7 5BD, England; tel. (071) 938-9387; f. 1895; has judicial powers to determine all matters relating to the interpretation of the International Code of Zoological Nomenclature and also plenary powers to suspend the operation of the Code where the strict application of the Code would lead to confusion and instability of nomenclature; the Commission is responsible also for maintaining and developing the Official Lists and Official Indexes of Names in Zoology; affiliated to the International Union of Biological Sciences (q.v.). Pres. Prof. Dr O. KRAUS (Germany); Exec. Sec. Dr P. K. TUBBS (UK). Publs *International Code of Zoological Nomenclature, Bulletin of Zoological Nomenclature, Official Lists and Indexes of Names and Works in Zoology.*

International Council for Bird Preservation: 32 Cambridge Rd, Girton, CB3 0PJ, England; tel. (0223) 277318; telex 818794; fax (0223) 277200; f. 1922; determines status of bird species throughout the world and compiles data on all endangered species; identifies conservation problems and priorities; initiates and co-ordinates conservation projects and international conventions. Representatives in 47 countries; national sections in 63 countries. Pres. Dr R. W. PETERSON (USA); Dir Dr CHRISTOPH IMBODEN (UK). Publs *Bulletin, ICBP/IUCN Bird Red Data Book, World Birdwatch.*

International Council for Scientific and Technical Information: 51 blvd de Montmorency, 75016 Paris, France; tel. (1) 45 25 65 92;

OTHER INTERNATIONAL ORGANIZATIONS

telex 630553; f. 1984; aims to increase accessibility to scientific and technical information; fosters communication and interaction among all participants in the information transfer chain. Mems: 45 organizations. Pres. H. E. KENNEDY (USA); Exec. Sec. M. ORFUS (France).

International Council for the Exploration of the Sea—ICES: Palaegade 2-4, 1261 Copenhagen K, Denmark; tel. 33-15-42-25; telex 22498; fax 33-93-42-15; f. 1902 to encourage concerted biological and hydrographical investigations for the promotion of a planned exploitation of the resources of the Atlantic Ocean and its adjacent seas, and primarily the North Atlantic; library of 15,000 vols. Membership: governments of 18 countries. Gen. Sec. Dr E. D. ANDERSON. Publs *Journal du Conseil, Bulletin Statistique, ICES Oceanographic Data Lists and Inventories, Co-operative Research Reports, Fiches d'Identification du Plancton, Fiches d'Identification des Maladies et Parasites des Poissons, Crustacés et Mollusques*.

International Council of Psychologists: POB 62, Hopkinton, RI 02833-0062, USA; tel. (608) 238-5373; f. 1959 to advance psychology and the application of its findings throughout the world; holds annual conventions. Mems: 1,800 qualified psychologists. Sec.-Gen. Dr PATRICIA J. FONTES. Publs. *International Psychologist* (quarterly).

International Council of the Aeronautical Sciences: c/o Royal Aeronautical Society, 4 Hamilton Place, London, W1V 0BQ, England; tel. (01) 493-7945; telex 262826; fax (01) 499-6230; f.1957 to encourage free interchange of information on all phases of mechanical flight; holds biennial Congresses. Mems: national associations in 28 countries. Pres. B. LASCHKA (Germany); Exec. Sec. A. D. YOUNG (UK).

International Earth Rotation Service: Central Bureau, Paris Observatory, 61 ave de l'Observatoire, 75014 Paris, France; f. 1988 (fmrly International Polar Motion Service and Bureau International de l'Heure); maintained by the International Astronomical Union and the International Union of Geodesy and Geophysics; defines and maintains terrestrial and celestial reference systems; determines earth orientation parameters (terrestrial and celestial co-ordinates of the pole and universal time) connecting these systems; organizes collection, analysis and dissemination of data. Dir of Directing Board Prof. K. YOKOYAMA.

International Federation for Cell Biology: c/o Dr A. M. Zimmerman, Dept of Zoology, University of Toronto, 25 Harbord St, Toronto M5S 1A1, Canada; f. 1972 to foster international co-operation, and organize conferences. Pres. Prof. F. CLEMENTI; Sec.-Gen. Dr A. M. ZIMMERMAN. Publs *Cell Biology International* (monthly), reports.

International Federation of Operational Research Societies: c/o IMSOR, Bldg 321, Technical University of Denmark, 2800 Lyngby, Denmark; tel. 42-88-22-22; telex 37529; fax 42-88-13-97; f. 1959 for development of operational research as a unified science and its advancement in all nations of the world. Mems: about 30,000 individuals, 39 national societies, five kindred societies. Pres. Prof. WILLIAM PIERSKALLA (USA); Sec. HELLE R. WELLING. Publs *International Abstracts in Operational Research, IFORS Bulletin*.

International Federation of Scientific Editors' Associations: BioSciences Information Service, 2100 Arch St, Philadelphia, Pa 19103, USA; tel. (215) 587-4815; telex 831739; f. 1978; links associations of editors in different branches of science; recommends standards and practices for manuscript preparation; co-operates with secondary sources in facilitating information retrieval. Pres. J. WATSON (Canada); Sec.-Gen. E. M. ZIPF (USA).

International Federation of Societies for Electron Microscopy: Dept of Cell Biology, Institute of Anatomy, University of Aarhus, Aarhus, Denmark; f. 1955. Mems: representative organizations of 40 countries. Pres. Prof. G. THOMAS (USA); Gen.-Sec. Prof. A. MAUNSBACH (Denmark).

International Food Information Service: UK Office (IFIS Publishing), Lane End House, Shinfield, Reading, RG2 9BB, England; tel. (0734) 883895; telex 847204; f. 1968 by the Gesellschaft für Information und Dokumentation (Frankfurt), the Institute of Food Technologists (Chicago), the Commonwealth Agricultural Bureaux (now CAB International) and the Centrum voor Landbouwpublikaties en Landbouwdocumentaties (Wageningen) for the collection and dissemination of scientific and technological information on foods and their processing. Gen. Man. Dr JOHN R. METCALFE; Man. Dir (IFIS GmbH) GUNTHER KALBSKOPF. Publ. *Food Science and Technology Abstracts* (monthly).

International Foundation of the High-Altitude Research Stations Jungfraujoch and Gornergrat: Sidlerstrasse 5, 3012 Berne, Switzerland; tel. (031) 654052; telex 912643; fax (031) 654405; f. 1931; international research centre which enables scientists from many scientific fields to carry out experiments at high altitudes. Seven countries contribute to support the station: Austria,

Science

Belgium, France, Germany, Italy, Switzerland, United Kingdom. Pres. Prof. H. DEBRUNNER.

International Glaciological Society: Lensfield Rd, Cambridge, CB2 1ER, England; tel. (0223) 355974; f. 1936 to stimulate interest in and encourage research into the scientific and technical problems of snow and ice in all countries. Mems: 850 in 33 countries. Pres. Dr G. K. C. CLARKE (Canada); Sec.-Gen. H. RICHARDSON. Publs *Journal of Glaciology* (3 a year), *Ice* (News Bulletin—3 a year), *Annals of Glaciology*.

International Group of Scientific, Technical and Medical Publishers: Keizersgracht 462, 1016 GE Amsterdam, Netherlands; tel. (020) 22-52-14; fax (020) 38-15-66; f. 1969 to deal with problems of international copyright protection and assist publishers and authors in disseminating scientific information by both conventional and advanced methods; holds seminars and study groups. Sec. PAUL NIJHOFF ASSER. Publs *STM Newsletter, STM Copyright Bulletin, STM Innovations Bulletin*.

International Hydrographic Organization: ave Président J. F. Kennedy, BP 445, Monte Carlo, 98011 Monaco Cedex; tel. 506587; telex 479164; fax 25-20-03; f. 1921 to link the hydrographic offices of its member governments and co-ordinate their work with a view to rendering navigation easier and safer on all the seas of the world; to obtain as far as possible uniformity in charts and hydrographic documents; to encourage the adoption of the best methods of conducting hydrographic surveys and improvements in the theory and practice of the science of hydrography, and to encourage surveying in those parts of the world where accurate charts are lacking; to extend and facilitate the application of oceanographic knowledge for the benefit of navigators and specialists in marine sciences; to render advice and assistance to developing countries upon request, facilitating their application for financial aid from the UNDP for creation or extension of their hydrographic capabilities; to fulfil the role of world data centre for bathymetry; provides computerized Tidal Constituent Data Bank. Next conference: 1992. Mems: 57 states. Directing Committee: Pres. Rear Adm. Sir DAVID W. HASLAM (UK); Dirs Rear Adm. A. CIVETTA (Italy), A. J. KERR (Canada). Publs *International Hydrographic Review* (2 a year), *International Hydrographic Bulletin* (monthly), *IHO Yearbook*.

International Institute of Refrigeration: 177 blvd Malesherbes, 75017 Paris, France; tel. (1) 42-27-32-35; telex 643269; fax (1) 47-63-17-98; f. 1908 to further the development of the science and practice of refrigeration on a world-wide scale; to investigate, discuss and recommend any aspects leading to improvements in the field of refrigeration; maintains FRIGINTER data-base. Mems: 57 national organizations and 800 associates. Dir A. GAC (France). Publs *Bulletin* (every 2 months), *International Journal of Refrigeration* (every 2 months).

International Mineralogical Association: Institute of Mineralogy, University of Marburg, 3550 Marburg, Germany; tel. 28-5617; telex 482372; f. 1958 to further international co-operation in the science of mineralogy; affiliated to the International Union of Geological Sciences (q.v.). Mems: national societies in 31 countries. Sec. Prof. S. S. HAFNER.

International Organisation of Legal Metrology: 11 rue Turgot, 75009 Paris, France; tel. (1) 48-78-12-82; telex 215463; fax (1) 42-82-17-27; f. 1955 to serve as documentation and information centre on the verification, checking, construction and use of measuring instruments, to determine characteristics and standards to which measuring instruments must conform for their use to be recommended internationally, and to determine the general principles of legal metrology. Mems: governments of 50 countries. Dir B. ATHANÉ (France). Publ. *Bulletin* (quarterly).

International Palaeontological Association: c/o Dr M. Kato, Dept of Geology and Mineralogy, Hokkaido University, Sapporo 060, Japan; tel. (11) 716-2111; f. 1933; affiliated to the International Union of Geological Sciences and the International Union of Biological Sciences (q.v.). Pres. A. HALLAM (UK); Sec.-Gen. M. KATO (Japan). Publs *Lethaia* (quarterly), *Directory*.

International Peat Society: Unioninkatu 40B, 00170 Helsinki, Finland; tel. 358-0-1924340; f. 1968 to encourage co-operation in the study and use of mires, peatlands, peat and related material, through international meetings, research groups and the exchange of information. Mems: 14 National Cttees, 225 research institutes and other organizations, and 500 individuals from 41 countries. Pres. Dr Y. PESSI (Finland); Sec.-Gen. V. KONDRATIEV (USSR). Publs *IPS Bulletin* (annually), *International Peat Journal* (annually).

International Phonetic Association—IPA: Dept of Linguistics and Phonetics, University of Leeds, LS2 9JT, England; f. 1886 to promote the scientific study of phonetics and its applications. Mems: 800. Sec. P. J. ROACH (UK). Publ. *Journal* (2 a year).

International Phycological Society: c/o Dept of Biology, Dalhousie University, Halifax, NS, Canada B3H 4J1; tel. (902) 424-2168; telex 921863; f. 1961 to promote the study of algae, the distribution of information, and international co-operation in this field. Mems: about 1,000. Sec. A. R. O. CHAPMAN (Canada). Publ. *Phycologia* (quarterly).

International Primatological Society: c/o Dr G. Epple, 3500 Market St, Philadelphia, Pa 19104, USA; f. 1964 to promote primatological science in all fields. Mems: about 900. Pres. Dr JOHN P. HEARN (UK); Sec.-Gen. Dr GISELA EPPLE (FRG).

International Radiation Protection Association—IRPA: POB 662, 5600 AR Eindhoven, Netherlands; tel. (040) 47-33-55; fax (040) 43-50-20; f. 1966 to unite in an international scientific society, individuals and societies throughout the world concerned with protection against ionizing radiations and allied effects, and to be representative of doctors, health physicists, radiological protection officers and others engaged in radiological protection, radiation safety, nuclear safety, legal, medical and veterinary aspects and in radiation research and other allied activities. Mems: 13,000, in 31 societies. Pres. J. R. A. LAKEY (UK); Sec.-Gen. C. J. HUYSKENS (Netherlands). Publ. *IRPA Bulletin*.

International Society for General Semantics: POB 2469, San Francisco, Calif 94126, USA; f. 1943 to advance knowledge of and inquiry into non-Aristotelian systems and general semantics. Mems: 3,000 individuals in 28 countries. Pres. MARY MORAIN (USA); Exec. Dir RUSSELL JOYNER (USA).

International Society for Human and Animal Mycology—ISHAM: c/o C. de Vroey, Laboratory for Mycology, Institute of Tropical Medicine, 155 Nationalestraat, 2000 Antwerp 1, Belgium; tel. (03) 247-63-35; telex 31648; fax (03) 216-14-31; f. 1954 to pursue the study of fungi pathogenic for man and animals; holds congresses (1991 Congress: Montreal, Canada). Mems: 820 from 71 countries. Pres. D. W. R. MACKENZIE; Gen. Sec. C. DE VROEY. Publ. *Journal of Medical and Veterinary Mycology* (6 a year).

International Society for Rock Mechanics: c/o Laboratório Nacional de Engenharia Civil, 101 Av. do Brasil, 1799 Lisboa Codex, Portugal; tel. (1) 8482131; telex 16760; fax (1) 897660; f. 1962 to encourage and co-ordinate international co-operation in the science of rock mechanics; to assist individuals and local organizations to form national bodies primarily interested in rock mechanics; to maintain liaison with other organizations that represent sciences of interest to the Society, including geology, geophysics, soil mechanics, mining engineering, petroleum engineering and civil engineering. The Society organizes international meetings and encourages the publication of the results of research in rock mechanics. Mems: c. 6,000. Pres. Dr JOHN FRANKLIN; Sec.-Gen. JOSÉ DELGADO RODRIGUES. Publ. *News* (quarterly).

International Society for Stereology: c/o Dr T. Mattfeldt, Institute of Pathology, 6900 Heidelberg, Im Neuenheimer Feld 220/221, Germany; tel. (06221) 562624; f. 1961; an interdisciplinary society gathering scientists from metallurgy, geology, mineralogy and biology to exchange ideas on three-dimensional interpretation of two-dimensional samples (sections, projections) of their material by means of stereological principles; seventh Congress: Caen, France 1987. Mems: 470. Pres. JEAN-LOUIS CHERMANT; Sec. Dr TORSTEN MATTFELDT.

International Society for Tropical Ecology: c/o Botany Dept, Banaras Hindu University, Varanasi, 221005 India; f. 1956 to promote and develop the science of ecology in the tropics in the service of man; to publish a journal to aid ecologists in the tropics in communication of their findings; and to hold symposia from time to time to summarize the state of knowledge in particular or general fields of tropical ecology. Mems: 500. Sec. Dr K. C. MISRA (India); Editor Prof. J. S. SINGH. Publ. *Tropical Ecology* (2 a year).

International Society of Biometeorology: 440 Witikonerstrasse, 8053 Zürich, Switzerland; f. 1956 to unite all biometeorologists working in the fields of agricultural, botanical, cosmic, entomological, forest, human, medical, veterinarian, zoological and other branches of biometeorology. Mems: 450 individuals, nationals of 46 countries. Pres. Dr W. H. WEIHE (Switzerland); Sec. Dr B. P. PRIMAULT (Switzerland). Publ. *Biometeorology* (Proceedings of the Congress of ISB), *International Journal of Biometeorology* (quarterly), *Progress in Biometeorology*.

International Society of Criminology: 4 rue de Mondovi, 75001 Paris, France; tel. (1) 42-61-80-22; f. 1934 to promote the development of the sciences in their application to the criminal phenomenon. Mems: in 63 countries. Sec.-Gen. GEORGES PICCA. Publ. *Annales internationales de Criminologie* (2 a year).

International Translations Centre: Schuttersveld 2, 2611 WE Delft, Netherlands; tel. (015) 142242; telex 38104; fax (015) 158535; f. 1961 as the European Translations Centre, by the OECD; an international clearing house for scientific and technical translations prepared from all languages into Western languages; over 200 organizations regularly send notifications of translations to the Centre, or deposit a copy; through the World Translations Index over 315,000 translations are made available. Chair. Dr D. WOOD (UK); Dir M. RISSEEUW (Netherlands). Publs *World Translations Index* (10 a year, annual cumulative edition), *WTI Database* (ESA/IRS and Dialog), *Journals in Translation* (irregular).

International Union for Conservation of Nature and Natural Resources—IUCN: 1196 Gland, Switzerland; tel. (022) 649114; telex 419605; fax (022) 644238; f. 1948 to promote the conservation of natural resources by the scientific monitoring of their conditions, by determining scientific priorities for conservation, mobilizing the scientific and professional resources to investigate the most serious conservation problems and recommend solutions to them, developing programmes to protect and sustain the most important and threatened species and eco-systems and assisting governments to devise and carry out conservation projects; maintains a conservation library and documentation centre and units for monitoring traffic in wildlife. Mems: governments of 63 countries, 111 government agencies, 414 national and 39 international non-governmental organizations and 37 affiliates. Pres. SHRIDATH RAMPHAL (Guyana); Dir-Gen. Dr MARTIN W. HOLDGATE (UK). Publs *IUCN Bulletin* (every 3 months) incl. annual report, *Red Data Book* (on mammals, plants, invertebrates, amphibians and reptiles), *World Conservation Strategy*, *United Nations List of National Parks and Protected Areas*, Environmental Policy and Law Papers.

International Union for Quaternary Research—INQUA: Ingenieurgeologie, ETH-Hönggerberg, 8093 Zürich, Switzerland; tel. (01) 3772521; telex 823474; f. 1928 to co-ordinate research on the quaternary geological era throughout the world. Pres. N. W. RUTTER (Canada); Sec. C. SCHLÜCHTER (Switzerland).

International Union of Food Science and Technology: c/o National Food Centre, Dunsinea, Castleknock, Dublin 15, Ireland; tel. (01) 383222; telex 31947; fax (01) 383684; f. 1970; sponsors international symposia and congresses. Mems: 46 national groups. Pres. E. VON SYDOW (Sweden); Sec.-Gen. D. E. HOOD (Ireland). Publ. *IUFOST Newsletter* (2 a year).

International Waterfowl and Wetlands Research Bureau: Slimbridge, Glos, GL2 7BX, England; tel. (0453) 890624; telex 437145; fax (0453) 890827; f. 1954 to stimulate and co-ordinate research on and conservation of waterfowl and their wetland habitats, particularly through the Ramsar Convention; co-ordinates research by institutes and individuals (professional and amateur) throughout the world; alerts governments and organizations when wetlands are threatened. Mems: 40 countries. Dir Dr MIKE MOSER. Publs *IWRB News* (every 6 months), *Annual Report*, conference proceedings.

Nordic Society for Cell Biology (Nordisk Forening for Celleforskning): c/o Dr Vibeke Dantzer, Dept of Anatomy, Royal Veterinary and Agricultural College, Bülowsvej 13, 1870 Frederiksberg C, Denmark; tel. (01) 351788; f. 1960 to promote contact between cell biologists through symposia and a congress every two years. Mems: 150 in Denmark, Finland, Iceland, Norway, Sweden. Chair. OLLE HEBY (Sweden); Sec. Dr V. DANTZER (Denmark).

Pacific Science Association: POB 17801, Honolulu, Hawaii 96817; tel. (808) 847-3511; fax (808) 841-8968; f. 1920 to promote co-operation in the study of scientific problems relating to the Pacific region, more particularly those affecting the prosperity and wellbeing of Pacific peoples; sponsors Pacific Science Congresses and Inter-Congresses. Mems: institutional representatives from 35 areas, scientific societies, individual scientists. Seventh Inter-Congress, Okinawa, 1993; 17th Congress, Hawaii, 1991. Pres. Dr W. D. DUCKWORTH; Exec. Sec. Dr L. G. ELDREDGE. Publ. *Information Bulletin* (4 a year).

Pugwash Conferences on Science and World Affairs: 63A Great Russell St, London, WC1B 3BG; tel. (071) 405-6661; fax (071) 831-5657; f. 1957 to organize international conferences of scientists to discuss problems arising from development of science, particularly the dangers to mankind from weapons of mass destruction. Mems: national Pugwash groups in 38 countries. Pres. Prof. JOSEPH ROTBLAT; Sec.-Gen. Prof. FRANCESCO CALOGERO. Publ. *Pugwash Newsletter* (quarterly), *Annals of Pugwash*.

Unitas Malacologica (Malacological Union): Dr E. Gittenberger, Rijksmuseum van Natuurlijke Historie, POB 9517, 2300 RA Leiden, Netherlands; tel. (071) 14-38-44; fax (071) 133344; f. 1962 to further the study of molluscs; affiliated to the International Union of Biological Sciences (q.v.); holds triennial congress. Mems: 400 in over 30 countries. Pres. Dr F. GIUSTI (Italy); Sec. Dr E. GITTENBERGER. Publ. *UM Newsletter* (annually).

World Organisation of Systems and Cybernetics—WOSC: c/o Prof. R. Vallée, 2 rue de Vouillé, 75015 Paris, France; tel. (1) 45-33-62-46; f. 1969 to act as clearing-house for all societies concerned with cybernetics and systems, to aim for the recognition of cybernetics as fundamental sciences, to organize and sponsor international exhibitions of automation and computer equipment, congresses and symposia, and to promote and co-ordinate research in systems and cybernetics. Mems: national and international societies in 30 countries. Dir-Gen. Prof. R. VALLÉE (France). Publs

International Journal of Cybernetics and Systems (Kybernetes), International Journal of Information, Education and Research in Robotics and Artificial Intelligence (Robotica).

World Wide Fund for Nature—WWF: World Conservation Centre, ave du Mont-Blanc, 1196 Gland, Switzerland; tel. (022) 649111; telex 419618; fax (022) 644238; f. 1961 (as World Wildlife Fund) to conserve the world's flora, fauna and natural resources and environment; to attract moral and financial support for safeguarding the living world and to convert such support into action based on scientific priorities. Mems: 23 national organizations, and four associates. Pres. HRH The Prince PHILIP, Duke of EDINBURGH; Dir-Gen. CHARLES DE HAES. Publs *Conservation Yearbook* (every 2 years), *The New Road* (quarterly), *WWF News* (every 2 months), *WWF Reports* (every 2 months), *WWF Year Review* (annually).

Social Sciences and Humanistic Studies

International Council for Philosophy and Humanistic Studies—ICPHS: Maison de l'UNESCO, 1 rue Miollis, 75732 Paris Cedex 15, France; tel. (1) 45-68-26-85; fax (1) 40-65-94-80; f. 1949 under the auspices of UNESCO to encourage respect for cultural autonomy by the comparative study of civilization and to contribute towards international understanding through a better knowledge of man; to develop international co-operation in philosophy, humanistic and kindred studies and to encourage the setting up of international organizations; to promote the dissemination of information in these fields; to sponsor works of learning, etc. Mems: organizations (see below) representing 145 countries. Pres. STEPHEN A. WURM (Austria); Sec.Gen. JEAN D'ORMESSON (France). Publs *Bulletin of Information* (biennially), *Diogenes* (quarterly).

UNIONS FEDERATED TO THE ICPHS

International Academic Union: Palais des Academies, 1 rue Ducale, 1000 Brussels, Belgium; tel. (02) 512-60-79; fax (02) 502-04-24; f. 1919 to promote international co-operation through collective research in philology, archaeology, art history, history and social sciences. Mems: academic institutions in 35 countries. Pres. G. MAY (USA); Sec. PHILIPPE ROBERTS-JONES.

International Association for the History of Religions: c/o Philipps-Universität, FG Religionswissenschaft, Liebigstrasse 37, 3550 Marburg, Germany; tel. (06421) 283662; f. 1950 to promote international collaboration of scholars, to organize congresses and to stimulate research. Mems: 24 countries. Pres. UGO BIANCHI; Sec.-Gen. MICHAEL PYE.

International Committee for the History of Art: 7 rue du Faisan, 67450 Mundolsheim, France; f. 1900 by the 12th International Congress on the History of Art, for collaboration in the scientific study of the history of art. International congress every five years, and two colloquia between congresses. Mems: National Committees in 31 countries. Pres. Prof. IRVING LAVIN (USA); Sec. Prof. A. A. SCHMID (Switzerland). Publs *Répertoire d'Art et d'Archéologie* (quarterly), *Corpus international des vitraux*, *Bulletin du CIHA.*

International Committee of Historical Sciences: 28 rue Guynemer, 75006 Paris, France; f. 1926 to work for the advancement of historical sciences by means of international co-ordination; 10 internal commissions; an international congress is held every five years. Mems: 47 national committees and 24 affiliated international organizations. Pres. E. DE LA TORRE VILLAR (Mexico); Sec.-Gen. HÉLÈNE AHRWEILER. Publs *Bulletin d'Information du CISH*, *Bibliographie internationale des sciences historiques.*

International Congress of African Studies: Institute of African and Asian Studies, University of Khartoum, POB 321, Khartoum, Sudan; f. 1962. Pres. YUSUF FADL HASSAN (Sudan); Sec.-Gen. SAYYID H. HURREIZ (Sudan).

International Federation for Modern Languages and Literatures: c/o D. A. Wells, Dept of German, Birkbeck College, Malet St, London, WC1E 7HX; tel. (071) 631-6103; fax (071) 631-6270; f. 1928 to establish permanent contact between historians of literature, to develop or perfect facilities for their work and to promote the study of modern languages and literature. Congress every three years. Mems: 20 associations, with individual mems in 98 countries. Sec.-Gen. D. A. WELLS (UK).

International Federation of Philosophical Societies: c/o E. Agazzi, Séminaire de Philosophie, Université, 1700 Fribourg, Switzerland; tel. (037) 219448; fax (037) 219703; f. 1948 under the auspices of UNESCO, to encourage international co-operation in the field of philosophy; holds World Congress of Philosophy every five years. Mems: 112 societies from 47 countries; 27 international societies. Pres. EVANDRO AGAZZI (Switzerland); Sec.-Gen. IOANNA KUÇURADI (Turkey). Publs *International Bibliography of Philosophy*, *Chroniques de Philosophie*, *Contemporary Philosophy*, *Philosophical Problems Today.*

International Federation of Societies of Classical Studies: c/o Prof. F. Paschoud, 6 chemin aux Folies, 1293 Bellevue, Switzerland; tel. (022) 7742656; f. 1948 under the auspices of UNESCO. Mems: 69 societies in 39 countries. Pres. Prof. J. IRIGOIN (France); Sec. Prof. F. PASCHOUD (Switzerland). Publs *L'Année Philologique*, other bibliographies, dictionaries, reference works, *Thesaurus linguae Latinae.*

International Musicological Society: CP 1561, 4001 Basel, Switzerland. Pres. CHRISTOPH MAHLING (Germany); Sec.-Gen. RUDOLF HAUSLER (Switzerland).

International Union for Oriental and Asian Studies: 77 quai du Port-au-Fouarre, 94100 Saint Maur, France; f. 1951 by the 22nd International Congress of Orientalists under the auspices of UNESCO, to promote contacts between orientalists throughout the world, and to organize congresses, research and publications. Mems: in 64 countries. Pres. R. N. DANDEKAR (India); Sec.-Gen. LOUIS BAZIN (France). Publs Four oriental bibliographies, *Philologiae Turcicae Fundamenta*, *Materialien zum Sumerischen Lexikon*, *Sanskrit Dictionary*, *Corpus Inscriptionum Iranicarum*, *Linguistic Atlas of Iran*, *Matériels des parlers iraniens*, *Turcica.*

International Union of Anthropological and Ethnological Sciences: c/o Prof. E. Sunderland, University College of North Wales, Bangor, Gwynedd, LL57 2DG, Wales; tel. (0248) 351151, ext. 2000; telex 61100; fax (0248) 370451; f. 1948 under the auspices of UNESCO; has 15 international research commissions. Mems: institutions and individuals in 100 countries. Pres. Prof. Dr LOURDES ARIZPE (Mexico); Sec.-Gen. Prof. E. SUNDERLAND (UK). Publs *IUAES Newsletter* (3 a year), *Anthropological Index* (4 a year).

International Union of Prehistoric and Protohistoric Sciences: c/o Prof. J. Nenquin, Séminaire d'archéologie de l'Université de Gand, Blandijnberg 2, 9000 Ghent, Belgium; tel. (91) 25-75-71; f. 1931 to promote congresses and scientific work in the fields of pre- and proto-history. Mems: 120 countries. Pres. Prof. B. CHROPOVSKY (Czechoslovakia); Sec.-Gen. Prof. JACQUES NENQUIN (Belgium).

Permanent International Committee of Linguists: Dr Kuyperlaan 11, 2215 NE Voorhout, Netherlands; tel. (02522) 11852; f. 1928 to further linguistic research, to co-ordinate activities undertaken for the advancement of linguistics, and to make the results of linguistic research known internationally; holds Congress every five years. Mems: 48 countries and two international linguistic organizations. Pres. R. H. ROBINS (UK); Sec.-Gen. E. M. UHLENBECK (Netherlands). Publs *Linguistic Bibliography* (annually).

OTHER ORGANIZATIONS

Arab Towns Organization: PO Box 4954, Safat 13050, Kuwait; tel. 2435540; telex 46390; f. 1967 to help Arab towns in solving problems, preserving the natural environment and cultural heritage; runs a fund to provide loans on concessional terms for needy members, and an Institute for Urban Development (AUDI) based in Riyadh, Saudi Arabia; provides training courses for officials of Arab municipalities and holds seminars on urban development and other relevant subjects; offers awards for preservation of Arabic architecture. Mems: 350 towns. Dir-Gen. TALEB T. AT-TAHER; Sec.-Gen. ABD AL-AZIZ Y. AL-ADASANI. Publ. *Al-Madinah Al-Arabiyah* (every 2 months).

Association for the Study of the World Refugee Problem—AWR: Piazzale di Porta Pia 121, 00198 Rome, Italy; tel. 22424; f. 1961 to promote and co-ordinate scholarly research on refugee problems. Mems: 475 in 19 countries. Pres. FRANCO FOSCHI (Italy); Sec.-Gen. ALDO CLEMENTE (Italy). Publ. *AWR Bulletin* (quarterly) in English, French, Italian and German; treatises on refugee problems (17 vols).

Council for the Development of Economic and Social Research in Africa—CODESRIA: BP 3304, Dakar, Senegal; tel. 23-02-11; telex 61339; fax 24-12-89; f. 1973; promotes research, provides conferences, working groups and information services. Mems: research institutes and university faculties in all African countries. Exec. Sec. THANDIKA MKANDAWIRE. Publs *Africa Development* (quarterly), *CODESRIA Bulletin* (quarterly).

Eastern Regional Organisation for Planning and Housing: 4A Ring Rd, Indraprastha Estate, New Delhi 110002, India; tel. 274809; f. 1958 to promote and co-ordinate the study and practice of housing and regional town and country planning. Offices in Japan, India and Indonesia. Mems: 71 organizations and 160 individuals in 13 countries. Sec.-Gen. C. S. CHANDRASEKHARA (India). Publs *EAROPH News and Notes* (monthly), *Town and Country Planning* (bibliography).

English-Speaking Union of the Commonwealth: Dartmouth House, 37 Charles St, Berkeley Square, London, W1X 8AB, England; tel. (071) 493-3328; fax (071) 495-6108; f. 1918 to promote

OTHER INTERNATIONAL ORGANIZATIONS

international understanding between Britain, the Commonwealth, the United States and Europe, in conjunction with the ESU of the USA. Mems: 70,000 (incl. USA). Chair. Lord PYM; Dir-Gen. DAVID HICKS. Publ. *Concord*.

European Association for Population Studies: POB 11676, 2502 AR The Hague, Netherlands; tel. (070) 469482; telex 31138; fax (070) 647187; f. 1983 to conduct research and provide information on European population problems; organizes conferences, seminars and workshops. Mems: demographers from 29 countries. Sec.-Treas. Prof. GUILLAUME WUNSCH. Publ. *European Journal of Population/Revue Européenne de Démographie* (quarterly).

European Co-ordination Centre for Research and Documentation in Social Sciences: 1010 Vienna, Grünangergasse 2, Austria; tel. (0222) 512-43-33-0; f. 1963 for promotion of contacts between East and West European countries in all areas of social sciences. Activities include co-ordination of international comparative research projects; training of social scientists in problems of international research; organization of conferences; exchange of information and documentation; administered by a Board of Directors (23 social scientists from East and West) and a permanent secretariat in Vienna. Pres. ØRJAR ØYEN (Norway); Dir L. KIUZADJAN (USSR). Publs *Vienna Centre Newsletter, ECSSID Bulletin*, and books.

European Society for Rural Sociology: c/o Prof. H. Newby, University of Essex, Colchester CO4 35Q, England; f. 1957 to further research in, and co-ordination of, rural sociology and provide a centre for documentation of information. Mems: 360 individuals, institutions and associations in 21 European countries and 16 countries outside Europe. Chair. Prof. H. NEWBY (UK); Sec. H. J. BECKER (Germany). Publ. *Sociologia Ruralis* (quarterly).

Experiment in International Living: POB 595, Main St, Putney, Vermont 05346, USA; tel. (802) 387-4210; telex 6503490251; fax (802) 387-5783; an international federation of non-profit educational and cultural exchange institutions; f. 1932 to create mutual understanding and respect among people of different nations, as a means of furthering peace. Mems: over 100,000; national offices in 27 countries. Exec. Sec. ROBIN BITTERS.

Institute for International Sociological Research: POB 100705, Cologne 40, Wiener Weg 6, Germany; tel. (0221) 486019; f. 1964; diplomatic and international affairs, social and political sciences, moral and behavioural sciences, arts and literature. Mems: 132 Life Fellows, 44 Assoc. Fellows; 14 research centres; affiliated institutes: Academy of Diplomacy and International Affairs, International Academy of Social and Moral Sciences, Arts and Letters. Pres., Chair. Exec. Cttee and Dir-Gen. Consul Dr EDWARD S. ELLENBERG. Publs *Diplomatic Observer* (monthly), *Newsletter, Bulletin* (quarterly), *Annual Report*, etc.

International African Institute: Connaught House (H. 708), Aldwych, London, WC2A 2AE, England; tel. (071) 831-3068; f. 1926 to promote the study of African peoples, their languages, cultures and social life in their traditional and modern settings; international seminar programme brings together scholars from Africa and elsewhere; links scholars so as to facilitate research projects, especially in the social sciences. Mems: 1,500 in 97 countries. Chair. Prof. WILLIAM A. SHACK; Dir Prof. PETER LLOYD. Publs *Africa, Ethnographic Survey, International African Library* (monograph series), *International African Seminar Series*.

International Association for Mass Communication Research: c/o Prof. Dr Cees Hamelink, Institute of Social Studies, POB 90733, 2509 LS The Hague, Netherlands; tel. (070) 3510100; telex 31491; fax (070) 3549851; f. 1957 to stimulate interest in mass communication research and the dissemination of information about research and research needs, to improve communication practice, policy and research and training for journalism, to provide a forum for researchers and others involved in mass communication to meet and exchange information. Mems: over 1,000 in 65 countries. Pres. Prof. Dr CEES HAMELINK (Netherlands); Sec.-Gen. T. SZECSKO (Hungary).

International Association of Applied Linguistics: c/o Dr M. Spoelders, Seminarie en Laboratorium voor Pedagogiek, 1 Henri Dunantlaan, 9000 Ghent, Belgium; tel. (091) 25-41-00; telex 12754; f. 1964; organizes seminars on applied linguistics, and a World Congress every three years (1990 Congress: Thessaloniki, Greece). Mems: associations in 37 countries. Pres. Prof. Dr ALBERT VALDMAN (USA); Sec.-Gen. Prof. Dr MARC SPOELDERS (Belgium). Publs. *AILA Review* (annually), *AILA News* (quarterly).

International Association of Documentalists and Information Officers—IAD: 74 rue des Saints-Pères, Paris 7e, France; f. 1962 to serve the professional interests of documentalists and to work on the problems of documentation at an international level. Mems: approx. 700. Gen. Sec. Dr JACQUES SAMAIN. Publ. *Monthly News*.

International Association of Metropolitan City Libraries—INTAMEL: Pestalozzigesellschaft, Zähringerstr. 17, 8001 Zürich,

Social Sciences and Humanistic Studies

Switzerland; tel. (01) 2617811; f. 1967. Pres. M. P. K. BARNES (UK); Sec. C. RELLY (Switzerland).

International Committee for Social Sciences Information and Documentation: c/o Prof. J. Meyriat, 27 rue Saint-Guillaume, 75007 Paris, France; tel. (1) 45-49-50-50; telex 201002; fax (1) 42-22-31-26; f. 1950 to collect and disseminate information on documentation services in social sciences, help improve documentation, advise societies on problems of documentation and to draw up rules likely to improve the presentation of all documents. Members from international associations specializing in social sciences or in documentation, and from other specialized fields. Sec.-Gen. JEAN MEYRIAT (France). Publs *International Bibliography of the Social Sciences* (annually), occasional reports, etc.

International Council on Archives: 60 rue des Francs-Bourgeois, 75003 Paris, France; tel. (1) 40-27-63-49; f. 1948. Mems: 1,100 in 140 countries. Pres. JEAN FAVIER (France); Exec. Sec. CHARLES KECSKEMETI (France). Publs *Archivum* (annually), *Janus* (2 a year), *ICA Bulletin* (2 a year).

International Ergonomics Association: c/o H. W. Hendrick, College of Systems Science, University of Denver, Denver, Colo 80208, USA; tel. (303) 871-3619; fax (303) 871-2067; f. 1957 to bring together organizations and persons interested in the scientific study of human work and its environment; to establish international contacts among those specializing in this field, co-operate with employers' associations and trade unions in order to encourage the practical application of ergonomic sciences in industries, and promote scientific research in this field. Mems: 17 federated societies. Pres. ILKKA KUORINKA (Finland); Sec.-Gen. HAL W. HENDRICK (USA). Publ. *Ergonomics* (monthly).

International Federation for Housing and Planning: Wassenaarseweg 43, 2596 CG The Hague, Netherlands; tel. (070) 3244557; telex 31578; fax (070) 3282085; f. 1913 to study and promote the improvement of housing, the theory and practice of town planning inclusive of the creation of new agglomerations and the planning of territories at regional, national and international levels. Mems: 400 organizations and 500 individuals in 65 countries. Pres. Prof. R. RADOVIĆ (Yugoslavia); Sec.-Gen. J. H. LÉONS (Netherlands). Publs *Prospect* (quarterly).

International Federation of Institutes for Socio-religious Research: 1/21 place Montesquieu, Bte 21, 1348 Louvain-la-neuve, Belgium; f. 1958; federates centres engaged in undertaking scientific research in order to analyse and discover the social and religious phenomena at work in contemporary society. Mems: institutes in 26 countries. Pres. V. COSMAO (France); Vice-Pres. Canon Fr. HOUTART (Belgium); Sec.-Gen. F. DASSETTO (Italy). Publ. *Social Compass (International Review of Sociology of Religion)* (4 a year, in English and French).

International Federation of Social Science Organizations: 40 Czechoslovak Academy of Sciences, Institute of State and Law, Narodni Trida 18, 116 Prague 1, Czechoslovakia; f. 1979 to assist research and teaching in the social sciences, and to facilitate co-operation and enlist mutual assistance in the planning and evaluation of programmes of major importance to members. Mems: 31 organizations. Pres. Prof. A. O. PHILLIPS; Sec.-Gen. Prof. J. BLAHOZ. Publs *Newsletter, International Directory of Social Science Organizations*.

International Federation of Vexillological Associations: Box 580, Winchester, Mass 01890, USA; tel. (617) 729-9410; fax (617) 721-4817; f. 1967 to promote through its member organizations the scientific study of the history and symbolism of flags, and especially to hold International Congresses every two years and sanction international standards for scientific flag study. Mems: 21 associations in 15 countries. Pres. Rev. HUGH BOUDIN (Belgium); Sec.-Gen. Dr WHITNEY SMITH (USA). Publs *Recueil* (every 2 years), *The Flag Bulletin* (every 2 months), *Info FIAV* (every 4 months).

International Institute for Ligurian Studies: Museo Bicknell, via Romana 39 bis, 18012 Bordighera, Italy; tel. (0184) 263601; f. 1947 to conduct research on ancient monuments and regional traditions in the north-west arc of the Mediterranean (France and Italy). Library of 55,000 vols. Mems: in France, Italy, Spain, Switzerland. Dir Dott FRANCISCA PALLARÉS (Italy).

International Institute of Administrative Sciences: 1 rue Defacqz, Bte 11, 1050 Brussels, Belgium; tel. (02) 538-91-65; telex 65933; fax (02) 537-97-02; f. 1930 for comparative examination of administrative experience in the various countries; research and programmes for improving administrative law and practices and for technical assistance; library of 11,400 vols; consultative status with UN and UNESCO; international congresses. Mems: 47 mem. states, 46 national sections, 39 corporate and individual members. Pres. A. ZUCK (USA); Dir.-Gen. CARLOS ALMADA (Mexico). Publs *International Review of Administrative Sciences* (quarterly), *Interadmin* (3 a year), *Infoadmin* (2 a year).

International Institute of Sociology: c/o Facoltà di Scienze Politiche, Università di Roma 'La Sapienza', Piazzale A. Moro 5, 00185

OTHER INTERNATIONAL ORGANIZATIONS

Rome, Italy; tel. (06) 3451017; fax (06) 3451017; f. 1893 to enable sociologists to meet and study sociological questions. Mems: 300, representing 45 countries. Pres. PAOLO AMMASSARI (Italy); Gen. Sec. ALAN HEDLEY. Publ. *The Annals of the IIS*.

International Numismatic Commission: Oslo University Coin Collection, Frederiksgate 2, 0164 Oslo 1, Norway; tel. (02) 41-63-00; fax (02) 41-10-12; f. 1936; enables co-operation between scholars studying coins and medals. Mems: numismatic organizations in 35 countries. Pres. K. SKAARE (Norway); Sec. R. WEILLER (Luxembourg).

International Peace Academy: 777 United Nations Plaza, New York, NY 10017, USA; tel. (212) 949-8480; telex 6503307142; f. 1967 to educate government officials in the procedures needed for conflict resolution, peace-keeping, mediation and negotiation, through international training seminars and publications; off-the-record meetings are also conducted to gain complete understanding of a specific conflict. Chair. Maj.-Gen. INDAR JIT RIKHYE (retd) (India); Exec. Dir THOMAS WEISS. Publ. *Annual Report*.

International Peace Research Association: Antioch College, Yellow Springs, OH 45387, USA; tel. (513) 767-7331; fax (513) 767-1891; f. 1964 to encourage interdisciplinary research on the conditions of peace and the causes of war. Mems: 125 corporate, 13 national and regional associations, 816 individuals, in 70 countries. Sec.-Gen. PAUL SMOKER (UK). Publ. *IPRA Newsletter* (4 a year).

International Social Science Council—ISSC: Maison de l'UNESCO, 1 rue Miollis, Paris 75015, France; tel. (1) 45-68-25-58; f. 1952; since 1973 a federation of the organizations listed below. Aims: the advancement of the social sciences throughout the world and their application to the major problems of the world; the spread of co-operation at an international level between specialists in the social sciences. ISSC has a Standing Committee for Conceptual and Terminological Analysis (COCTA, established in co-operation with IPSA and ISA); a Standing Committee on Human Dimensions of Global Environmental Change; also created the European Co-ordination Centre for Research and Documentation in the Social Sciences, in Vienna. Pres. C. MENDES (Brazil); Sec.-Gen. L. I. RAMALLO (Spain).

Associations Federated to the ISSC

(details of these organizations will be found under their appropriate category elsewhere in the International Organizations section)

International Association of Legal Sciences (p. 240).
International Economic Association (p. 231).
International Federation of Social Science Organizations (p. 260).
International Geographical Union (p. 253).
International Institute of Administrative Sciences (p. 260).
International Law Association (p. 241).
International Peace Research Association (p. 261).
International Political Science Association (p. 236).
International Sociological Association (p. 261).
International Studies Association (p. 261).
International Union for the Scientific Study of Population (p. 261).
International Union of Anthropological and Ethnological Sciences (p. 259).
International Union of Psychological Science (p. 253).
World Association for Public Opinion Research (p. 261).
World Federation for Mental Health (p. 248).

International Society of Social Defence: c/o Centro nazionale di prevenzione e difesa sociale, Piazza Castello 3, 20121 Milan, Italy; tel. (02) 870-695; telex 315896; fax (02) 875-942; f. 1945 to combat crime, to protect society and to prevent citizens from being tempted to commit criminal actions. Mems in 34 countries. Pres. SIMONE ROZES (France); Sec.-Gen. A. BERIA DI ARGENTINE (Italy). Publ. *Cahiers de défense sociale* (annually).

International Sociological Association: Calle Pinar 25, 28006 Madrid, Spain; tel. 2617483; fax 2617185; f. 1949 to promote sociological knowledge, facilitate contacts between sociologists, encourage the dissemination and exchange of information and facilities and stimulate research; has 42 research committees on various aspects of sociology; holds World Congresses every four years (12th Congress: Madrid, Spain, 1990). Pres. T. K. OOMMEN (India); Exec. Sec. IZABELA BARLINSKA. Publs *Current Sociology* (3 a year), *International Sociology* (4 a year), *Sage Studies in International Sociology* (based on World Congress).

International Statistical Institute: POB 950, Prinses Beatrixlaan 428, 2270 AZ Voorburg, Netherlands; tel. (70) 3694341; telex 32260; f. 1885; devoted to the development and improvement of statistical methods and their application throughout the world; administers among others a statistical education centre in Calcutta in co-operation with UNESCO and the Indian Statistical Institute;

Social Sciences and Humanistic Studies, Social Welfare

executes international research programmes. Mems: 1,540 ordinary mems; 8 hon. mems; 109 ex-officio mems; 49 corporate mems; 10 international organizations; 32 national statistical societies. Pres. G. KULLDORF; Dir Permanent Office DENISE LIEVESLEY. Publs *Bulletin of the International Statistical Institute* (proceedings of biennial sessions), *International Statistical Review* (3 a year), *Statistical Education Newsletter* (3 a year), *Short Book Reviews* (3 a year), *Statistical Theory and Method Abstracts* (quarterly), *International Statistical Information* (newsletter, 3 a year), *Directories* (annually).

International Studies Association: c/o Dr W. Welsh, James F. Byrnes Bldg, University of South Carolina, Columbia, SC 29208, USA; tel. (803) 777-2933; fax (803) 777-6839; f. 1959; links those whose professional concerns extend beyond their own national boundaries (government officials, representatives of business and industry, and scholars). Mems: 2,422 in 56 countries. Pres. CHARLES F. HERMANN; Exec. Dir Dr WILLIAM A. WELSH. Publs *International Studies Quarterly, ISA Newsletter*.

International Union for the Scientific Study of Population: 34 rue des Augustins, 4000 Liège, Belgium; tel. (041) 22-40-80; telex 42648; fax (041) 22-38-47; f. 1928 to advance the progress of quantitative and qualitative demography as a science. Mems: 1,900 in 124 countries. Pres. M. LIVI BACCI (Italy); Sec.-Gen. A. HILL (UK). Publs *IUSSP Newsletter* and books on population.

Mensa International: 15 The Ivories, 6–8 Northampton St, London, N1 2HY; tel. (071) 226-6891; f. 1946 to identify and foster intelligence for the benefit of humanity. Members are individuals who score in a recognized intelligence test higher than 98% of people in general: there are 85,000 mems world-wide. Pres. Chair. DAVID SCHULMAN (Ireland); Exec. Dir E. J. VINCENT (UK). Publ. *Mensa Journal International* (monthly).

Third World Forum: BP 3501, Dakar, Senegal; f. 1973 to link social scientists and others from the developing countries, to discuss alternative development policies and encourage research. Regional offices in Egypt, Mexico, Senegal and Sri Lanka. Mems: individuals in more than 50 countries. Dir SAMIR AMIN.

World Association for Public Opinion Research: c/o The School of Journalism, University of North Carolina, CB 3365, Howell Hall, Chapel Hill, NC 27599-3365, USA; tel. (919) 962-4078; fax (919) 962-0620; f. 1947 to establish and promote contacts between persons in the field of survey research on opinions, attitudes and behaviour of people in the various countries of the world; to further the use of objective, scientific survey research in national and international affairs. Mems: 430 from 57 countries. Gen. Sec. VAL LAUDER. Publs *WAPOR Newsletter* (quarterly), *International Journal of Public Opinion* (quarterly).

World Society for Ekistics: c/o Athens Centre of Ekistics, 24 Strat. Syndesmou St, 106 73 Athens, Greece; tel. 3623-216; telex 215227; f. 1965; aims to promote knowledge and ideas concerning human settlements through research, publications and conferences; to recognize the benefits and necessity of an inter-disciplinary approach to the needs of human settlements. Pres. GERALD B. DIX; Sec.-Gen. P. PSOMOPOULOS.

World Union of Catholic Philosophical Societies: c/o Prof. G. F. McLean, School of Philosophy, Catholic University of America, Washington, DC 20064, USA; tel. (202) 319-5636; fax (202) 319-6089; f. 1948. Mems: societies and individuals in 44 countries. Pres. Prof. JEAN LADRIÈRE (Belgium); Sec.-Gen. Prof. GEORGE F. McLEAN (USA). Publ. *Circulaires* (1 or 2 issues a year).

Social Welfare

Aid to Displaced Persons and its European Villages: 35 rue du Marché, 5200 Huy, Belgium; tel. (085) 21-34-81; f. 1957 to carry on and develop work begun by the Belgian association Aid to Displaced Persons; aims to provide material and moral aid for refugees; European Villages established at Aachen, Bregenz, Augsburg, Berchem-Ste-Agathe, Spiesen, Euskirchen, Wuppertal as centres for refugees. Pres. J. EECKHOUT (Belgium).

Amnesty International: 1 Easton St, London, WC1X 8DJ, England; tel. (071) 433-5500; telex 28502; fax (071) 956-1157; f. 1961; an independent worldwide movement working impartially for the release of all prisoners of conscience, fair and prompt trials for all political prisoners, and the abolition of torture and the death penalty; financed by donations. Mems: 700,000, with 4,000 volunteer groups; nationally organized sections in 44 countries. Chair. PETER DUFFY (UK); Sec.-Gen. IAN MARTIN (UK). Publs *Newsletter* (monthly), *Annual Report*.

Anti-Slavery International: 180 Brixton Rd, London, SW9 6AT, England; tel. (071) 582-4040; f. 1839 to eradicate slavery and forced labour in all their forms, to promote the well-being of indigenous peoples, and to protect human rights in accordance with the Universal Declaration of Human Rights, 1948. Mems: 900 members

OTHER INTERNATIONAL ORGANIZATIONS

Social Welfare

in 30 countries. Chair. MICHAEL HARRIS; Dir LESLEY ROBERTS. Publs *Annual Report, Anti-Slavery Reporter* (annually) and special reports on research.

Associated Country Women of the World: Vincent House, Vincent Square, London, SW1P 2NB; tel. (071) 834-8635; f. 1930 to aid the economic and social development of countrywomen and home-makers of all nations; to promote study of an interest in home-making, housing, health, education, and aspects of food and agriculture. Mems: approx. 9m. Gen. Sec. JENNIFER PEARCE. Publ. *The Countrywoman* (quarterly).

Association Internationale de la Mutualité (International Association for Mutual Benefit Funds): 8-10 rue de Hesse, 1204 Geneva, Switzerland; tel. (022) 214528; fax (022) 214541; f. 1950 to propagate and develop mutual benefits funds in all countries. Mems: national and regional institutions in 17 countries. Pres. ROBERT VAN DEN HEUVEL (Belgium); Sec.-Gen. RENÉ-NOËL BESSI (France).

Association of Social Work Education in Africa: POB 1176, Addis Ababa, Ethiopia; tel. 126827; f. 1971 to promote teaching and research in social development, to improve standards of institutions in this field, to exchange information and experience. Mems: schools of social work, community development training centres, other institutions and centres; 53 training institutions and 140 social work educators in 32 African countries, 22 non-African assoc. mems. in Europe and North America. Exec. Sec. AREGA YIMAN. Publs *Journal for Social Work Education in Africa*.

Aviation sans frontières—ASF: Brussels National Airport, Bldg 2, LC 142, 1930 Zaventem, Belgium; tel. (02) 722-35-35; telex 22569; f. 1980 to make available the resources of the aviation industry to humanitarian organizations, for carrying supplies and equipment at minimum cost, both on long-distance flights and locally. Mems: about 200 pilots and other airline staff. Pres. JEAN-LUC STORDER; Man. YVON LEPEZ.

Catholic International Union for Social Service: 111 rue de la Poste, 1030 Brussels, Belgium; tel. (02) 217-29-87; f. 1925 to develop social service on the basis of Christian doctrine; to unite Catholic social schools and social workers' associations in all countries to promote their foundation; to represent at the international level the Catholic viewpoint as it affects social service. Mems: 172 schools of social service, 26 associations of social workers, 52 individual members. Exec. Sec. ALEXANDRE CARLSON. Publs *Service Social dans le monde* (quarterly), *News Bulletin, Bulletin de Liaison, Boletín de Noticias* (quarterly).

Co-ordinating Committee for International Voluntary Service—CCIVS: Maison de l'UNESCO, 1 rue Miollis, 75015 Paris, France; tel. (1) 45-68-27-31; f. 1948; acts as an information centre and co-ordinating body for voluntary service organizations all over the world. Affiliated mems: 110 organizations. Dir A. KROUGLOO. Publs *News from CCIVS* (4 a year), handbook, directories.

EIRENE—International Christian Service for Peace: 5450 Neuwied 1, Engerser Str. 74B, Germany; f. 1957; works in North Africa, Asia and Latin America (professional training, apprenticeship programmes, agricultural work and co-operatives), Europe and the USA (volunteer programmes in co-operation with peace groups). Gen. Sec. JOSEF FREISE.

European Federation for the Welfare of the Elderly—EURAG: 8010 Graz, Schmiedg. 26 (Amtshaus), Austria; tel. (0316) 872-3008; fax (0316) 8723019; f. 1962 for the exchange of experience among member associations; practical co-operation among member organizations to achieve their objectives in the field of ageing; representation of the interests of members before international organizations; promotion of understanding and co-operation in matters of social welfare; to draw attention to the problems of old age. Mems: organizations in 25 countries. Pres. NELLA M. BERTO (Italy); Sec.-Gen. EDUARD PUMPERNIG (Austria). Publs. (in English, French, German and Italian) *EURAG Newsletter* (quarterly), *EURAG Information* (monthly).

Federation of Asian Women's Associations—FAWA: Centro Escolar University, 9 Mendiola St, San Miguel, Manila, Philippines; tel. 741-04-46; f. 1959 to provide closer relations, and bring about joint efforts among Asians, particularly among the women, through mutual appreciation of cultural, moral and socio-economic values. Mems: 415,000. Pres. Dr H. SJAMSINOOR ADNOES; Sec. Mrs NICOLASA J. TRIA TIRONA (Philippines). Publ. *FAWA News Bulletin* (every 3 months).

Inter-American Conference on Social Security (Comité Permanente Interamericano de Seguridad Social): Apdo postal 99089, CP 10100 México DF, Mexico; tel. 595-01-07; telex 1775793; fax 683-85-24; f. 1942 to facilitate and develop co-operation between social security administrations and institutions in the American states; 15th General Assembly, 1989. Mems: governments and social security institutions in 28 countries. Pres. Lic. RICARDO GARCÍA SÁINZ (Mexico); Sec.-Gen. AGUSTÍN DARDADORI KUDLI (Mexico). Publs *Seguridad Social, Boletín Informativo*.

International Abolitionist Federation: 47 rue de Rivoli, 75001 Paris, France; tel. (1) 45-08-97-52; f. 1875 for the abolition of the organization and exploitation of the prostitution of others and the regulation of prostitution by public authorities; holds international congress every three years. Affiliated organizations in 21 countries. Corresponding mems in 60 countries. Pres. ANIMA BASAK (Austria); Gen. Sec. MARIE-RENÉE JAMET (France). Publs *Revue abolitionniste* (2 a year).

International Association against Noise: Hirschenplatz 7, 6004 Lucerne, Switzerland; tel. (041) 513013; f. 1959 to promote noise-control at an international level; to promote co-operation and the exchange of experience and prepare supranational measures; issues information, carries out research, organizes conferences, and assists national anti-noise associations. Mems: 17, and three associate mems. Pres. JUDITH LANG; Sec. Dr WILLY AECHERLI (Switzerland).

International Association of Children's International Summer Villages—CISV International: Mea House, Ellison Place, Newcastle upon Tyne, England; tel. (091) 232-4998; telex 53373; fax (091) 261-4710; f. 1950 to conduct International Camps for children and young people between the ages of 11 and 18. Mems: 40,268. International Pres. RUTH LUND; Sec.-Gen. JOSEPH G. BANKS. Publ. *CISV News* (2 a year), *Voices* (annually), *Local Work Magazine* (3 a year), *Interspectives* (annually).

International Association for Education to a Life without Drugs (Internationaler Verband für Erziehung zu suchtmittelfreiem Leben—IVES): Lyshoj 6, 6300 Graasten, Denmark; f. 1954 (as the International Association for Temperance Education) to promote international co-operation in education on the dangers of alcohol and drugs; collection and distribution of information on drugs; maintains regular contact with national and international organizations active in these fields; holds conferences. Mems: 17,000 in seven countries. Pres. WILLY STUBER; Sec. JÜRGEN KLAHN.

International Association for Suicide Prevention: 1811 Trousdale Drive, Burlingame, Calif 94010, USA; tel. (415) 877-5604; f. 1960 to establish an organization where individuals and agencies of various disciplines and professions from different countries can find a common platform for interchange of acquired experience, literature and information about suicide; disseminates information; arranges special training; encourages and carries out research; organizes the Biannual International Congress for Suicide Prevention. Mems: 730 individuals and societies, in 42 countries of all continents. Vice-Pres. CHARLOTTE P. ROSS (USA). Publ. *Crisis* (2 a year).

International Association of Schools of Social Work: 1010 Vienna, Josefs Platz 6, Austria; tel. (222) 513-4297; fax (222) 513-8468; f. 1928 to provide international leadership and encourage high standards in social work education. Mems: 1,600 schools of social work in 70 countries, and 25 national associations of schools. Pres. Dr RALPH GARBER (Canada); Sec.-Gen. VERA MEHTA (India). Publs *International Social Work* (quarterly), *Directory of Members, IASSW News*.

International Association of Workers for Troubled Children and Youth: 66 chaussée d'Antin, 75009 Paris, France; f. 1951 to promote the profession of specialized social workers for maladjusted children; to provide a centre of information about child welfare and encourage co-operation between the members; 1990 Congress: USA. Mems: national and regional public or private associations from 19 countries and individual members in many other countries. Pres. DANIEL DUPIED (France); Sec.-Gen. BRUNO NEFF (France).

International Catholic Migration Commission: CP 96, 37-39 rue de Vermont, 1211 Geneva 20, Switzerland; tel. (022) 7334150; telex 28100; fax (022) 7347929; f. 1951; offers migration aid programmes to those who are not in a position to secure by themselves their resettlement elsewhere; grants interest-free travel loans; assists refugees on a worldwide basis, helping with all social and technical problems. Sub-committees dealing with Europe and Latin America. Mems: in 76 countries. Pres. EDWARD DE BRANDT; Sec.-Gen. Dr ANDRÉ N. VAN CHAU (USA). Publs *Annual Report, Migrations, Migration News, ICMC Newsletter*.

International Children's Centre (Centre international de l'enfance): Château de Longchamp, carrefour de Longchamp, Bois de Boulogne, 75016 Paris, France; tel. (1) 45-20-79-92; telex 648379; fax (1) 45-25-73-67; f. 1949 to improve the health and well-being of children and families, especially in developing countries; financed by the French Government and other sources; three departments: Education and Training (organizing courses, seminars and working groups all over the world), Communicable Diseases and Immunization (developing immunization techniques); Information (documentation centre, publications and bibliographical data base), and External Relations Office. Pres. of Admin. Council Prof. PIERRE ROYER; Dir-Gen. JEAN BROUSTE. Publs *Children in the Tropics*, bibliographical bulletins, studies.

OTHER INTERNATIONAL ORGANIZATIONS — Social Welfare

International Christian Federation for the Prevention of Alcoholism and Drug Addiction: c/o DKSN, Alvsjö Gardsvag 7, 125 30 Alvsjö, Sweden; f. 1960, reconstituted 1980 to promote worldwide education and remedial work through the churches, to co-ordinate Christian concern about alcohol and drug abuse, in co-operation with the World Council of Churches and WHO. Chair. Rev. FRANK S. GIBSON (UK); Gen. Sec. JONATHAN N. GNANADASON (India).

International Civil Defence Organisation: 10–12 chemin Surville, 1213 Petit-Lancy-Geneva, Switzerland; tel. (022) 7934433; telex 423786; fax (022) 7934428; f. 1931, present statutes in force 1972; aims to intensify and co-ordinate on a world-wide scale the development and improvement of organization, means and techniques for preventing and reducing the consequences of natural disasters in peacetime or of the use of weapons in time of conflict. Sec.-Gen. SADOK ZNAÏDI (Tunisia). Publs *International Civil Defence Journal* (quarterly, in English, French, Spanish and Arabic).

International Commission for the Prevention of Alcoholism and Drug Dependency: 12501 Old Columbia Pike, Silver Spring, MD 20904-6600 USA; tel. (301) 680-6719; telex 440186; fax (301) 680-6090; f. 1953 to encourage scientific research on intoxication by alcohol, its physiological, mental and moral effects on the individual, and its effect on the community; eighth World Congress, Kuala Lumpur, Malaysia, 1991. Mems: individuals in 90 countries. Exec. Dir THOMAS R. NESLUND. Publ. *ICPA Quarterly*.

International Commission for the Protection of the Rhine against Pollution: 5400 Koblenz, Hohenzollernstrasse 18, POB 309, Germany; tel. (0261) 12495; telex 862499; fax (0261) 36572; f. 1950 to prepare and commission research to establish the nature of the pollution of the Rhine; to propose measures of protection to the signatory governments. Mems: 23 delegates from France, Germany, Luxembourg, Netherlands, Switzerland and the EEC. Pres. Dr M. CASPARI; Sec. J. M. GOPPEL. Publ. *Annual Report*.

International Council of Voluntary Agencies: 13 rue Gautier, 1201 Geneva, Switzerland; tel. (022) 7326600; telex 22891; fax (022) 7389904; f. 1962 to provide a forum for voluntary humanitarian and development agencies. Mems: 80 non-governmental organizations. Chair. FRANK JUDD; Exec. Dir ANTHONY J. KOZLOWSKI. Publs *Annual Report*, *NGO Management* (quarterly in English and French).

International Council of Women: c/o 13 rue Caumartin, 75009 Paris, France; tel. (1) 47-42-19-40; f. 1888 to bring together in international affiliation National Councils of Women from all continents for consultation and joint action in order to promote equal rights for men and women and the integration of women in development and in decision-making; 14 standing committees. Mems: 75 national councils. Pres. LILY BOEYKENS; Sec.-Gen. JACQUELINE BARBET-MASSIN.

International Council on Alcohol and Addictions: CP 189, 1001 Lausanne, Switzerland; tel. (021) 209865; telex 450666; fax (021) 209817; f. 1907; organizes training courses, congresses, symposia and seminars in different countries. Mems: affiliated organizations in 62 countries, as well as individual members. Pres. STEIN BERG (Norway); Exec. Dir ARCHER TONGUE (UK). Publs *ICAA News* (quarterly), *Alcoholism* (2 a year), *Drug and Alcohol Dependence* (bi-monthly).

International Council on Disability: c/o Rehabilitation International, 25 East 21st St, New York, NY 10010, USA; tel. (212) 420-1500; telex 446412; f. 1953 to assist the UN and its specialized agencies to develop a well co-ordinated international programme for rehabilitation of the handicapped. Mems: 66 organizations. Chair. NORMAN ACTON.

International Council on Jewish Social and Welfare Services: 75 rue de Lyon, 1211 Geneva 13, Switzerland; tel. (022) 449000; telex 23163; f. 1961; functions include the exchange of views and information among member agencies concerning the problems of Jewish social and welfare services including medical care, old age, welfare, child care, rehabilitation, technical assistance, vocational training, agricultural and other resettlement, economic assistance, refugees, migration, integration and related problems; representation of views to governments and international organizations. Mems: six national and international organizations. Exec. Sec. CHERYL MARINER.

International Council on Social Welfare: 1060 Vienna, Koestlergasse 1/29, Austria; tel. (022) 587-81-64; f. 1928 to provide an international forum for the discussion of social work and related issues; to promote interest in social welfare; holds international conference every two years; provides documentation and information services. Mems: 68 national committees, 25 international organizations. Pres. KHUNYING A. MEESOOK (Thailand); Sec.-Gen. INGRID GELINEK (Austria). Publs *International Social Work* (quarterly), *ICSW Newsletter* (quarterly).

International Dachau Committee: 65 rue de Haerne, 1040 Brussels, Belgium; f. 1958 to perpetuate the memory of the political prisoners of Dachau; to manifest the friendship and solidarity of former prisoners whatever their beliefs or nationality; to maintain the ideals of their resistance, liberty, tolerance and respect for persons and nations; and to maintain the former concentration camp at Dachau as a museum and international memorial. Sec.-Gen. GEORGES-VALÉRY WALRAEVE. Publ. *Bulletin Officiel du Comité International de Dachau* (2 a year).

International Federation of Blue Cross Societies: CP 658, 2501 Bienne, Switzerland; tel. (032) 227565; telex 934333; f. 1877 to aid the victims of intemperance and drug addicts, and to take part in the general movement against alcoholism. Pres. Dr HANS SCHAFFNER (Switzerland); Gen. Sec. ERIC ZIEHLI.

International Federation of Disabled Workers and Civilian Handicapped: c/o Reichsbund, 5300 Bonn 2, Beethovenallee 56–58, Federal Republic of Germany; tel. (0228) 363071; telex 885557; fax (0228) 361550; f. 1953 to bring together representatives of the disabled and handicapped into an international non-political organization under the guidance of the disabled themselves; to promote greater opportunities for the disabled; to create rehabilitation centres; to act as a co-ordinating body for all similar national organizations. Mems: national groups from Austria, Czechoslovakia, Denmark, Finland, France, Germany, Hungary, Iceland, Italy, Netherlands, Norway, Poland, Spain, Sweden, Switzerland, Yugoslavia. Pres. ALBERT CAMINADA (Liechtenstein); Gen. Sec. MARIJA ŠTIGLIC (Germany). Publs *Bulletin*, *Nouvelles*.

International Federation of Educative Communities: Rämistrasse 27, 8001 Zürich, Switzerland; tel. (01) 470247; f. 1948 under the auspices of UNESCO to co-ordinate the work of national associations, and to promote children's communities. Mems: national associations from 18 European countries, Israel, Canada and the USA. Pres. Prof. Dr HEINRICH TUGGENER (Switzerland); Gen. Sec. Dr FRANZ ZÜSLI-NISCOSI (Switzerland). Publs *Etudes Pédagogiques*, *Documents*, *Recherches et Témoignages*.

International Federation of Human Rights: 27 rue Jean-Dolent, 75014 Paris, France; tel. (1) 43-31-94-95; f. 1922 to uphold the principles of justice, liberty and equality; conducts missions of enquiry, makes protests and representations to governments concerning violations of human rights. Mems: national leagues in 36 countries and territories. Pres. DANIEL JACOBY. Publ. *Lettre* (weekly).

International Federation of Social Workers—IFSW: 33 rue de l'Athénée, 1206 Geneva, Switzerland; tel. (022) 471236; f. 1928 as International Permanent Secretariat of Social Workers; present name adopted 1950; aims to promote social work as a profession through international co-operation concerning standards, training, ethics and working conditions; represents the profession at international meetings; assists in welfare programmes sponsored by international organizations. Mems: national associations in 50 countries. Pres. Prof. GAYLE G. JAMES (Canada); Sec.-Gen. ANDREW M. APOSTOL (Switzerland).

International Fellowship of Former Scouts and Guides—IFOFSAG: 9 rue du Champ de Mars, bte 14, 1050 Brussels, Belgium; tel. (02) 511-46-95; f. 1953 to help former scouts and guides to keep alive the spirit of the Scout and Guide Promise and Laws in their own lives; to bring that spirit into the communities in which they live and work; to establish liaison and co-operation between national organizations for former scouts and guides; to encourage the founding of an organization in any country where no such organization exists; to promote friendship amongst former scouts and guides throughout the world. Mems: 62,000 in 33 member states. Chair. of Council MARGARETE SCHOPPER; Sec.-Gen. NAÏC PIRARD. Publ. *The Fellowship Bulletin* (quarterly).

International League of Societies for Persons with Mental Handicap: 248 ave Louise, bte 17, 1050 Brussels, Belgium; tel. (02) 647-61-80; fax (02) 647-29-69; f. 1960 to promote the interests of the mentally handicapped without regard to nationality, race or creed, furthers co-operation between national bodies, organizes congresses. Mems: 54 national associations and 70 affiliates in 78 countries, and five associates (regional). Pres. ELOISA G. E. DE LORENZO (Uruguay); Sec.-Gen. V. WAHLSTRÖM (Sweden).

International Lifeboat Federation: c/o Royal National Lifeboat Institution, West Quay Rd, Poole, Dorset, BH15 1HZ, England; tel. (0202) 671133; telex 41328; f. 1924; conferences held at four-yearly intervals; next Conference: Norway, 1991. Sec. RAY KIPLING. Publ. *Lifeboat International*.

International Planned Parenthood Federation—IPPF: Regent's College, Inner Circle, Regent's Park, London, NW1 4NS, England; tel. (071) 486-0741; telex 919573; fax (071) 487-7950; f. 1952; aims to initiate and support family planning services throughout the world, and to increase understanding of population problems; offers technical assistance and training; collaborates with other international organizations and provides information. Mems: independent family planning associations in 134 countries. Pres. Dr FRED T. SAI; Sec.-Gen. Dr HALFDAN MAHLER. Publs *People* (quart-

OTHER INTERNATIONAL ORGANIZATIONS

Social Welfare

erly, in English and French), *Medical Bulletin* (every 2 months, in English, French and Spanish), publications list.

International Prisoners Aid Association: c/o Dr Ali, Department of Sociology, University of Louisville, Louisville, Ky 40292, USA; tel. (502) 588-6836; f. 1950; to improve prisoners' aid services for rehabilitation of the individual and protection of society. Mems: national federations in 29 countries. Pres. Dr WOLFGANG DOLE-ISCH (Austria); Exec. Dir Dr BADR-EL-DIN ALI. Publ. *Newsletter* (3 a year).

International Social Security Association: Case Postale No. 1, 1211 Geneva 22, Switzerland; telex 22271; f. 1927 to promote the development of social security through the improvement of techniques and administration. Mems: 312 institutions in 125 countries. Pres. JÉRÔME DEJARDIN (Belgium); Sec.-Gen. VLADIMIR RYS (UK). Publs *International Social Security Review* (quarterly, English, French, German, Spanish), *Estudios de la Seguridad Social* (irregular), *World Bibliography of Social Security* (2 a year, English, French, Spanish, German), *African News Sheet* (English and French), *Asian News Sheet*, *Caribbean News Sheet*, *Social Security Documentation* (African, Asian, European and American series), *Current Research in Social Security* (2 a year, English, French, German and Spanish), *ISSA News* (2 a year).

International Social Service: 32 quai du Seujet, 1201 Geneva, Switzerland; tel. (022) 7317454; telex 412758; fax (022) 7380949; f. 1921 to aid families and individuals whose problems require services beyond the boundaries of the country in which they live and where the solution of these problems depends upon co-ordinated action on the part of social workers in two or more countries; to study from an international standpoint the conditions and consequences of emigration in their effect on individual, family, and social life. Operates on a non-sectarian and non-political basis. Mems: branches in 15 countries, two affiliated offices, and correspondents in some 100 other countries. Pres. FRANCIS BLANCHARD (France); Sec.-Gen. DAMIEN NGABONZIZA.

International Union of Family Organisations: 28 place Saint-Georges, 75009 Paris, France; tel. (1) 48-78-07-59; f. 1947 to bring together all organizations throughout the world which are working for family welfare; conducts permanent commissions on standards of living, housing, marriage guidance, work groups on family movements, rural families, etc.; there are five regional organizations: the Pan-African Family Organisation (Dakar, Senegal), the Arab Family Organisation (Tunis, Tunisia), the Asian Union of Family Organisations (New Delhi, India), the European regional organization (Vienna, Austria) and the Latin American Secretariat (Bogotá, Colombia). Mems: national associations, groups and governmental departments in 55 countries. Pres. MARIA TERESA DA COSTA MACEDO (Portugal); Sec.-Gen. ANDRÉ RAUGET (France).

International Union of Societies for the Aid of Mental Health: Croix Marine, 39 rue Charles Monselet, 33000 Bordeaux, France; tel. 56-81-60-05; f. 1964 to group national societies and committees whose aim is to help mentally handicapped or maladjusted people. Gen. Pres Mme DELAUNAY, Dr DEMANGEAT; Secs Dr CADORET, Dr BROUSTRA.

International Union of Tenants: Box 7514, 10392 Stockholm, Sweden; tel. (08) 24-63-50; fax (08) 20-53-24; f. 1955 to collaborate in safeguarding the interests of tenants; participates in activities of UNCHS (Habitat); holds triennial congress. Mems: national tenant organizations in 15 European countries and Tanzania. Chair. LARS ANDERSTIG; Sec. NIC NILSSON. Publ. *IUT International Information* (quarterly).

International Workers' Aid (Entraide Ouvrière Internationale): 5300 Bonn, Oppelner Strasse 130, Germany; tel. (0228) 66850; telex 8869654; f. 1950 to support welfare services for youth (especially the unemployed), the elderly and disadvantaged groups, to assist refugees and displaced persons, to take action as a relief organization in cases of catastrophes or political disturbances and to work for social justice and human solidarity. Members in Austria, Belgium, Denmark, France, Germany, Israel, Italy, Luxembourg, Norway, Portugal, Spain, Switzerland, United Kingdom. Pres. HERMANN BUSCHFORT (Germany); Sec.-Gen. RICHARD HAAR.

Inter-University European Institute on Social Welfare—IEISW: 179 rue du Débarcadère, 6001 Marcinelle, Belgium; tel. (71) 36-62-73; f. 1970 to promote, carry out and publicize scientific research on social welfare and community work. Chair. Board of Dirs JACQUES HOCHEPIED (Belgium); Gen. Sec. P. ROZEN (Belgium). Publ. *COMM*.

Lions Clubs International: 300 West 22nd St, Oak Brook, Ill 60570-0001, USA; tel. (708) 571-5466; telex 297236; fax (708) 571-8890; f. 1917 to foster understanding among people of the world; to promote principles of good government and citizenship; and an interest in civic, cultural, social and moral welfare; to encourage service-minded people to serve their community without financial reward. Mems: 1.36m. with over 39,000 clubs in 166 countries and geographic areas. Exec. Admin. MARK C. LUKAS. Publ. *The Lion* (10 a year, in 18 languages).

Médecins sans frontières—MSF: 8 rue Saint Sabin, 75011 Paris, France; tel. (1) 40-21-29-29; telex 214360; fax (1) 48-06-68-68; f. 1971; composed of physicians and other members of the medical profession; aims to provide medical assistance to victims of war and natural disasters, and medium-term programmes of nutrition, immunization, sanitation, public health, and rehabilitation of hospitals and dispensaries. Mems: 3,000 in France, groups in other European countries. Pres. Dr RONY BRAUMAN; Dir-Gen. Dr FRANCIS CHARHON.

Pan-Pacific and South East Asia Women's Association—PPSEAWA: 2234 New Petchburi Rd, Bangkok 10310, Thailand; f. 1928 to strengthen the bonds of peace by fostering better understanding and friendship among women of all Pacific and South-East Asian areas, and to promote co-operation among women of these regions for the study and improvement of social conditions; holds international conference every three years. Pres. THANPUYING SUMALEE CHARTIKAVANIJ. Publ. *PPSEAWA Bulletin*.

Rotary International: 1560 Sherman Ave, Evanston, Ill 60201, USA; tel. (312) 866-3000; telex 724465; f. 1905 to foster the ideal of service as a basis of worthy enterprise, to promote high ethical standards in business and professions and to further international understanding, goodwill and peace. Mems: over 1,060,000 in 23,800 Rotary Clubs in 162 countries and regions. Pres. HUGH ARCHER; Gen. Sec. PHILIP H. LINDSEY (USA). Publs *The Rotarian* (monthly, English), *Revista Rotaria* (bi-monthly, Spanish).

Service Civil International—SCI: Draakstraat 37, 2018 Antwerp, Belgium; tel. (03) 235-94-73; fax (03) 235-29-73; f. 1920 to promote peace and understanding through voluntary service projects (workcamps, local groups, long-term community development projects and education). Mems: 10,000 in 22 countries; projects in 20 countries. Pres. LESLEY HIGGINS. Publ. *Action* (quarterly).

Society of Saint Vincent de Paul: 5 rue du Pré-aux-Clercs, Paris 7e, France; tel. (1) 42-61-50-25; telex 264918; fax (1) 42-61-72-56; f. 1833 to conduct charitable activities such as child care, youth work, work with immigrants, adult literacy programmes, residential care for the sick, handicapped and elderly, social counselling and work with prisoners and the unemployed—all conducted through personal contact. Mems: over 850,000 in 114 countries. Pres. AMIN A. DE TARRAZI; Sec.-Gen. COLETTE GLANDIÈRES. Publ. *Vincenpaul* (monthly, in French, English and Spanish).

World Blind Union: 58 ave Bosquet, 75007 Paris, France; tel. (1) 45-55-67-54; telex 206471; fax (1) 45-56-07-40; f. 1984 (amalgamating the World Council for the Welfare of the Blind and the International Federation of the Blind) to work for the prevention of blindness and the welfare of blind and visually-impaired people; encourages development of braille, talking book programmes and other media for the blind; rehabilitation, training and employment; prevention and cure of blindness in co-operation with the International Agency for the Prevention of Blindness; co-ordinates aid to the blind in developing countries; conducts studies on technical, social and educational matters, maintains the Louis Braille birthplace as an international museum. Mems in 140 countries. Pres. DUNCAN A. WATSON (UK); Sec.-Gen. PEDRO ZURITA (Spain). Publs *World Blind* (3 a year, in English, English Braille and on cassette, in Spanish and Spanish Braille and in French).

World Federation of the Deaf—WFD: 120 via Gregorio VII, 00165, Rome, Italy; tel. (06) 6377041; f. 1951 for the social rehabilitation of the deaf and the fight against deafness; aims to promote and exchange information; to facilitate the union and federation of national associations; organize international meetings and protect the rights of the deaf. Mems: 72 member countries. Pres. Dr Y. ANDERSSON; Sec.-Gen. Dr C. MAGAROTTO (Italy). Publ. *The Voice of Silence* (quarterly).

World ORT Union: ORT House, Sumpter Close, Finchley Rd, POB 346, London, NW3 5HR, England; tel. (071) 431-1333; telex 8953281; fax (071) 435-4784; f. 1880 for the development of industrial, agricultural and artisan work among the Jews, training and generally improving the economic situation; conducts vocational training programmes for adolescents and adults, including instructors' and teachers' education and apprenticeship training in more than 40 countries, including technical assistance programmes in co-operation with interested governments. Mems: committees in 30 countries. Dir-Gen. JOSEPH HARMATZ. Publs *Annual Report*, *Yearbook*, *Technical and Pedagogical Bulletin*, *ORT data*, *ORT Magazine*.

World Society for the Protection of Animals: 106 Jermyn St, London, SW1Y 6EE, England; tel. (071) 839-3026; f. 1981, incorporating the World Federation for the Protection of Animals (f. 1950) and the International Society for the Protection of Animals (f. 1950); promotes animal welfare and conservation by humane education; disseminates literature to encourage humane management and slaughter of food animals, control of domestic and wild animal communities. Dir-Gen. GORDON WALWYN.

World Veterans Federation: 16 rue Hamelin, 75116 Paris, France; tel. (1) 47-04-33-00; telex 643253; fax (1) 47-04-20-84; f. 1950 to maintain international peace and security by the application of the San Francisco Charter and helping to implement the Universal Declaration of Human Rights and related international conventions, to defend the spiritual and material interests of war veterans and war victims. It promotes practical international co-operation in disarmament, human rights problems, economic development, rehabilitation of the handicapped, accessibility of the man-made environment, legislation concerning war veterans and war victims, and development of international humanitarian law; in 1986 established International Socio-Medical Information Centre (Oslo, Norway) for psycho-medical problems resulting from stress. Regional committees for Africa, Asia and the Pacific, and Europe. Mems: national organizations in 54 countries, representing more than 20,000,000 war veterans and war victims. Pres. W. Ch. J. M. VAN LANSCHOT (Netherlands); Sec.-Gen. SERGE WOURGAFT (France). Publs special studies (disarmament, human rights, rehabilitation).

Zonta International: 557 W. Randolph St, Chicago, Ill 60606, USA; tel. (312) 930-5848; telex 190200; fax (312) 930-0951; f. 1919; executive service organization; international and community service projects to promote the status of women. Mems: 35,000 in 53 countries. Pres. LANEEN FORDE (Australia); Exec. Dir BONNIE KOENIG. Publ. *The Zontian* (quarterly).

Sport and Recreations

Arab Sports Confederation: POB 6040, Riyadh, Saudi Arabia; tel. 482-4727; telex 403099; fax 482-1951; f. 1976 to encourage regional co-operation in sport. Mems: 21 national Olympic Committees, 30 Arab sports federations. Pres. Prince FAISAL BIN FAHD ABD AL-AZIZ; Sec.-Gen. OTHMAN M. AL-SAAD.

Fédération Aéronautique Internationale (International Aeronautical Federation): 10/12 rue du Capitaine Ménard, 75015 Paris, France; tel. (1) 45-79-24-77; telex 201327; fax (1) 45-79-73-15; f. 1905 to encourage all aeronautical sports; organizes world championships and makes rules through Air Sports Commissions; endorses world aeronautical and astronautical records. Mems: in 77 countries. Pres. CLIFTON VON KANN; Dir Dr CENEK KEPAK. Publs *Annual Bulletin, FAI News* (2 a year).

General Association of International Sports Federations—GAISF: 7 blvd de Suisse, Monte Carlo, Monaco; tel. 93-50-74-13; telex 479459; fax 93-25-28-73; f. 1967 to act as a forum for the exchange of ideas and discussion of common problems in sport; to collect and circulate information; to provide secretarial and translation services for members, organize meetings and provide technical documentation and consultancy services; and to co-ordinate the main international competitions. Mems: 75 international sports organizations; Pres. Dr UN YONG KIM; Sec.-Gen. LUC NIGGLI (Monaco). Publs *Calendar of International Sports Competitions* (2 a year), *GAISF News* (monthly, in English and French), *GAISF Calendar, Sport and Education* and *Sport and Media*.

International Amateur Athletic Federation: 3 Hans Crescent, Knightsbridge, London, SW1X 0LN, England; tel. (071) 581-8771; telex 296859; fax (071) 584-5907; f. 1912 to ensure co-operation and fairness among members, and to combat discrimination in athletics; to affiliate national governing bodies, to compile athletic competition rules and to organize championships at all levels; to settle disputes between members, and to conduct a programme of development for members who need coaching, judging courses, etc., and to frame regulations for the establishment of World, Olympic and other athletic records. Mems: 184 countries. Pres. P. NEBIOLO (Italy); Gen. Sec. J. B. HOLT (UK). Publs *IAAF Handbook* (English and French editions, every 2 years), *IAAF Magazine/Newsletter* (6 a year each in English and French), *New Studies in Athletics* (quarterly).

International Amateur Boxing Association: 0-1136 Berlin, Postamt Volkradstrasse, Postlagernd, Germany; tel. (2) 2081647; telex 115149; fax (2) 2084292; f. 1946 as the world body controlling amateur boxing for the Olympic Games, continental, regional and inter-nation championships and tournaments in every part of the world. Mems: 155 nations. Pres. Prof. A. CHOWDHRY (Pakistan); Sec.-Gen. KARL-HEINZ WEHR (Germany). Publ. *World Amateur Boxing Magazine* (quarterly).

International Amateur Radio Union: POB AAA, Newington, CT 06111, USA; tel. (203) 666-1541; telex 6502155052; fax (203) 665-7531; f. 1925 to link national amateur radio societies and represent the interests of two-way amateur radio communication. Mems: 127 national amateur radio societies. Pres. RICHARD L. BALDWIN; Sec. LARRY E. PRICE.

International Amateur Swimming Federation (Fédération internationale de natation amateur—FINA): 425 Walnut St, Suite 1610, Cincinnati, Oh 45202, USA; tel. (513) 381-2963; telex 810-461-2623; fax (513) 381-2964; f. 1908 to promote amateur swimming and swimming sports internationally; to administer rules for swimming sports, for competitions and for establishing records; to organize world championships and FINA events; development programme to increase the popularity and quality of aquatic sports. Mems: 124 countries. Pres. MUSTAPHA LARFAOUI (Algeria); Sec. ROSS WALES (USA). Publs *Handbook* (every 4 years), *FINA News* (monthly).

International Amateur Wrestling Federation: 3 ave Ruchonnet, 1003 Lausanne, Switzerland; tel. (021) 3128426; telex 455958; fax (021) 236073; f. 1912 to encourage the development of amateur wrestling and promote the sport in countries where it is not yet practised; to further friendly relations between all members; to oppose any form of political, racial or religious discrimination. Mems: 112 federations. Pres. MILAN ERCEGAN; Sec.-Gen. MICHEL DUSSON. Publs *News Bulletin, Theory and Practice of Wrestling*.

International Council for Health, Physical Education, and Recreation: 1900 Association Drive, Reston, Va 22091, USA; f. 1958 by the World Confederation of Organizations of the Teaching Profession; f. as separate organization in 1959 to encourage the development of programmes in health, physical education, and recreation throughout the world.

International Cricket Council: Lord's Cricket Ground, London, NW8 8QN, England; tel. (071) 289-1611; telex 297329; fax (071) 289-9100; f. 1909; concerns itself with the game at the international level. Annual conference; seven full and 18 associate mems. Sec. Lt-Col J. R. STEPHENSON.

International Cycling Union: 6 rue Amat, 1202 Geneva, Switzerland; tel. (022) 7322914; telex 412878; fax (022) 7318042; f. 1900 to develop, regulate and control all forms of cycling as a sport. Mems: 146 federations. Exec. Pres. VALERY SYSSOEV; Gen. Sec. MICHAL JEKIEL. Publs *Le Monde Cycliste Magazine* (4 a year), *International Calendar* (annually).

International Federation of Association Football (Fédération internationale de football association—FIFA): Hitzigweg 11, POB 85, 8030 Zürich, Switzerland; tel. (01) 555400; telex 817240; fax (01) 556239; f. 1904 to promote the game of association football and foster friendly relations among players and national associations; to control football and uphold the laws of the game as laid down by the International Football Association Board; to prevent discrimination of any kind between players; and to provide arbitration in any disputes between national associations; organizes World Cup competition every four years. Mems: 166 national associations, six regional confederations. Pres. Dr JOÃO HAVELANGE (Brazil); Gen. Sec. J. S. BLATTER (Switzerland). Publs. *FIFA News* (monthly), *FIFA Magazine* (quarterly) (both in English, French, Spanish and German).

International Federation of Park and Recreation Administration—IFPRA: The Grotto, Lower Basildon, Reading, Berkshire, RG8 9NE, England; tel. (0491) 873558; fax (0491) 874059; f. 1957 to provide a world centre where members of government departments, local authorities, and all organizations concerned with recreational services can discuss relevant matters. Mems: 300 in 34 countries. Pres. GRAHAM BRADBOURNE (New Zealand); Gen. Sec. ALAN SMITH (UK).

International Gymnastic Federation: rue des Oeuches 10, CP 333, 2740 Moutier 1, Switzerland; tel. (032) 936666; telex 934961; fax (032) 936671; f. 1881 to promote the exchange of official documents and publications on gymnastics. Mems: 93 affiliated federations. Pres. YURI TITOV (USSR); Gen. Sec. NORBERT BUECHE (Switzerland). Publ. *Bulletin* (4 a year).

International Hockey Federation: Boîte 5, 1 ave des Arts, 1040 Brussels, Belgium; tel. (02) 219-45-37; telex 63393; f. 1924 to fix the rules of outdoor and indoor hockey for all affiliated national associations; to control the game of hockey and indoor hockey; to control the organization of international tournaments, such as the Olympic Games and the World Cup. Mems: 101 national associations. Pres. ETIENNE GLICHITCH (France); Sec.-Gen. JUAN ANGEL CALZADO DE CASTRO. Publ. *World Hockey* (quarterly).

International Judo Federation: 106 Berlin, PSF 380, Germany; tel. 2291633; telex 112137; fax 2299392; f. 1949 to promote cordial and friendly relations between members; to protect the interests of judo throughout the world; to organize World Championships and the judo events of the Olympic Games; to develop and spread the techniques and spirit of judo throughout the world. Pres. LAWRIE HARGRAVE; Sec.-Gen. HEINZ KEMPA.

International Philatelic Federation: Zollikerstrasse 128, 8008 Zürich, Switzerland; tel. (01) 553839; fax (01) 3831446; f. 1926 to promote philately internationally. Pres. D. N. JATIQ; Sec.-Gen. M. L. HEIRI.

International Rowing Federation (Fédération internationale des Sociétés d'Aviron—FISA): 3653 Oberhofen am Thunersee, Switzerland; tel. (33) 435053; fax (33) 435073; f. 1892 to establish contacts

OTHER INTERNATIONAL ORGANIZATIONS   *Sport and Recreations, Technology*

between oarsmen in all countries and to draw up racing rules. Mems: national organizations in 65 countries. Pres. DENIS OSWALD.

International Shooting Union: 8000 Munich 2, Bavariaring 21, Germany; tel. (089) 531012; telex 5216792; fax (089) 5309481; f. 1907 to promote and guide the development of the amateur shooting sports; to organize World Championships; to control the organization of continental and regional championships; to supervise the shooting events of the Olympic and Continental Games under the auspices of the International Olympic Committee. Mems: in 113 countries. Pres. OLEGARIO VÁZQUEZ-RAÑA (Mexico); Sec.-Gen. HORST G. SCHREIBER (Germany). Publ. *UIT Journal, International Shooting Sport* (6 a year).

International Skating Union: Promenade 73, 7270 Davos-Platz, Switzerland; tel. (081) 437577; telex 853123; fax (081) 436671; f. 1892; holds regular conferences. Mems: 47 skating organizations in 37 countries. Pres. OLAF POULSEN; Sec.-Gen. BEAT HÄSLER.

International Ski Federation: 3653 Oberhofen am Thunersee, Switzerland; tel. (33) 446161; telex 921109; fax (33) 435353; f. 1924 to further the sport of skiing; to prevent discrimination in skiing matters on racial, religious or political grounds; to organize World Ski Championships and regional championships and, as supreme international skiing authority, to establish the international competition calendar and rules for all ski competitions approved by the FIS, and to arbitrate in any disputes. Mems: 62 national ski associations. Pres. MARC HODLER (Switzerland); Sec.-Gen. GIAN-FRANCO KASPER (Switzerland). Publ. *FIS Bulletin* (4 times a year).

International Table Tennis Federation: 53 London Rd, St Leonards-on-Sea, East Sussex, TN37 6AY, England; tel. (0424) 721414; telex 95277; fax (0424) 431871. Pres. ICHIRO OGIMURA; Sec.-Gen. TONY BROOKS.

International Tennis Federation: Palliser Rd, Barons Court, London, W14 9EN, England; tel. (071) 381-8060; telex 919253; fax (071) 381-3989; f. 1913 to govern the game of tennis throughout the world and promote its teaching; to preserve its independence of outside authority; to produce the Rules of Tennis, to promote the Davis Cup Competition for men, the Federation Cup for women, nine cups for veterans and the World Youth Cup for players of 16 years old and under; to organize tournaments. Mems: 94 full and 65 associate. Pres. PHILIPPE CHATRIER (France). Publs *World of Tennis* (annually), *President's Newsletter* (monthly), *ITF News* (monthly).

International Weightlifting Federation: PF 614, 1374 Budapest, Hungary; tel. 1318153; telex 227553; fax 1532108; f. 1905 to control international weightlifting; to set up technical rules and to train referees; to supervise World Championships, Olympic Games, regional games and international contests of all kinds; to supervise the activities of national and continental federations; to register world records. Mems: in 133 countries. Pres. GOTTFRIED SCHÖDL (Austria); Gen. Sec. TAMÁS AJAN (Hungary). Publs *IWF Constitution and Rules* (every 4 years), *World Weightlifting* (quarterly).

International Yacht Racing Union: 60 Knightsbridge, London, SW1X 7JX, England; tel. (071) 235-6221; telex 915487; fax (071) 245-9861; f. 1907; controlling authority of sailing in all its forms throughout the world; establishes and amends international yacht racing rules, organizes the Olympic Yachting Regatta and other championships. Mems: 93 national yachting authorities. Pres. PETER TALLBERG; Exec. Dir MIKE EVANS.

World Bridge Federation: 56 route de Vandoeuvres, 1253 Geneva, Switzerland; tel. (022) 7501541; telex 422887; fax (022) 7501620; f. 1958 to promote the game of contract bridge throughout the world, federate national bridge associations in all countries, conduct bridge associations in all countries, conduct world championships competitions, establish standard bridge laws. Mems: 89 countries. Pres. DENIS HOWARD (Australia); Sec. ERNESTO D'ORSI (Brazil). Publ. *World Bridge News* (quarterly).

World Chess Federation: Abendweg 1, 6006 Lucerne, Switzerland; tel. (041) 513378; telex 862845; fax (041) 515846; f. 1924; controls chess competitions of world importance and awards international chess titles. Pres. FLORENCIO CAMPOMANES (Philippines); Gen. Sec. CASTO ABUNDO (Philippines).

World Underwater Federation: 47 rue du Commerce, 75015 Paris, France; tel. (1) 45-75-42-75; telex 205734; f. 1959 to develop underwater activities; to form bodies to instruct in the techniques of underwater diving; to perfect existing equipment and encourage inventions and to experiment with newly marketed products, suggesting possible improvements; to organize international competitions. Mems: 74 countries. Gen. Sec. MARCEL BIBAS (France). Publs *International Year Book of CMAS, Bulletin News* (every 3 months).

Technology

Union of International Technical Associations (Union des associations techniques internationales—UATI): UNESCO House, Room S1.27, 1 rue Miollis, 75015 Paris, France; tel. (1) 45-66-94-10; telex 204461; fax (1) 43-06-29-27; f. 1951 under the auspices of UNESCO to co-ordinate activities of member organizations and represent their interests; helps to arrange international congresses and the publication of technical material. Mems: 30 organizations. Chair. ROGER GINOCCHIO (France); Sec.-Gen. PIERRE PECOUX. Publ. *Bulletin* (quarterly).

MEMBER ORGANIZATIONS

Members of UATI include the following:

International Association for Hydraulic Research: c/o Delft Hydraulics Laboratory, Rotterdamseweg 185, POB 177, 2600 MH Delft, Netherlands; tel. (015) 569353; fax (015) 619674; f. 1935; holds biennial congresses. Mems: 2,300 individual, 270 corporate. Sec. J. E. PRINS (Netherlands). Publs *Directory of Hydraulic Research Institutes and Laboratories, Journal of Hydraulic Research*

International Association of Lighthouse Authorities: 13 rue Yvon Villarceau, 75116 Paris, France; tel. (1) 45-00-38-60; telex 610 480; fax (1) 45-00-29-02; f. 1957; holds technical conference every five years; working groups study special problems and formulate technical recommendations, guidelines and manuals. Mems in 80 countries. Sec.-Gen. NORMAN F. MATTHEWS. Publs *Bulletin* (quarterly), technical dictionary (in English, French, German and Spanish).

International Bridge, Tunnel and Turnpike Association: 2120 L St, NW, Suite 305, Washington, DC 20037, USA; tel. (202) 659-4620; telex 275445; fax (202) 659-0500; f. 1932. Pres. HENRI CYNA; Exec. Dir. NEIL D. SCHUSTER. Publ. *Tollways* (monthly).

International Commission of Agricultural Engineering: Station de Recherche de Génie Rural, 115 Van Gansberghelaan, 9220 Merelbeke, Belgium; tel. (091) 52-18-21; fax (091) 52-15-83; f. 1930. Mems: associations from 27 countries, individual mems from six countries. Pres. Prof. MCNULTY (Ireland); Sec.-Gen. J. DAELEMANS (Belgium). Publs *Yearbook*, technical reports.

International Commission on Glass: Stazione Sperimentale del Vetro, Via Briati 10, Venezia-Tucci, Italy; tel. (041) 739422; f. 1950 to co-ordinate research in glass and allied products, exchange information and organize conferences. Mems: 24 organizations. Pres. J.-P. CAUSSE; Sec.-Gen. F. NICOLETTI.

International Commission on Irrigation and Drainage: 48 Nyaya Marg, Chanakyapuri, New Delhi 110021, India; tel. (11) 301 68 37; telex 031-65920; f. 1950; holds triennial congresses. Mems: 69 national committees. Pres. J. R. HENNESSY (UK); Sec.-Gen. Dr R. S. VARSHNEY (India). Publs *Bulletin* (2 a year), *Bibliography* (annually), *World Irrigation, Multilingual Technical Dictionary, World Flood Control*, technical books.

International Committee of Foundry Technical Associations: Obstgartenstr. 19, Case Postale 7190, 8023 Zürich, Switzerland; tel. (01) 3613060; telex 817538; fax (01) 3628351. Pres. M. GRAND-PIERRE; Sec. M. J. GERSTER.

International Federation for the Theory of Machines and Mechanisms: Dolejskova 5, 18200 Prague 8, Czechoslovakia; telex 122018; f. 1969. Pres. G. BIANCHI; Sec.-Gen. L. PUST.

International Federation of Automatic Control—IFAC: 2361 Laxenburg, Schlossplatz 12, Austria; tel. (02236) 71447; telex 79248; fax (02236) 72859; f. 1957 to serve those concerned with the theory and application of automatic control and systems engineering. Mems: 42 national associations. Pres. Prof. B. TAMM (USSR); Sec. G. HENCSEY. Publs *Automatica* (bi-monthly), *Newsletter*.

International Federation of Industrial Energy Consumers: Rhône-Poulenc SA, 25 quai Paul-Doumer, 92408 Courbevoie Cedex, France; tel. (1) 47-68-16-98. Pres. A. DE CARVALHO; Sec.-Gen. A. MONGON.

International Gas Union: c/o Swissgas, Grütlistrasse 44, POB 658, 8027 Zürich, Switzerland; tel. (01) 2028075; telex 817816; fax (01) 2017803; f. 1931 to study all aspects and problems of the gas industry with a view to promoting international co-operation and the general improvement of the industry. Mems: national organizations in 46 countries. Pres. H. RICHTER (Germany); Sec.-Gen. J.-P. LAUPER (Switzerland).

International Institute of Welding: 11/12 Pall Mall, London, SW1Y 5LU, England; tel. (071) 925-0082; telex 81183; f. 1948. Mems: 50 societies in 37 countries. Pres. R. V. SALKIN (Belgium); Sec.-Gen. P. D. BOYD (UK). Publ. *Welding in the World* (7 a year).

International Measurement Confederation: POB 457, 1371 Budapest 5, Hungary; tel. 1531-562; fax 156-1215. Sec.-Gen. T. KEMENY.

International Union for Electro-heat: Tour Atlantique, 92080 Paris-la-Défense Cedex 6; tel. (1) 47-78-99-34; telex 615739; f. 1953, present title adopted 1957. Aims to study all questions relative to electro-heat, except commercial questions; links national groups

OTHER INTERNATIONAL ORGANIZATIONS — Technology

and organizes international congresses on electro-heat. Mems: national committees and titular members in 24 countries. Pres. L. C. Gaya Goya (Spain); Gen. Sec. A. Dailliet (Belgium).

International Union of Air Pollution Prevention Associations: 136 North St, Brighton, BN1 1RG, England; tel. (0273) 26313; fax (0273) 735802. Pres. S. Hart; Dir-Gen. J. Langston.

International Union of Producers and Distributors of Electrical Energy: 27 rue Jacques Ibert, 75858 Paris Cedex 17, France; tel. (1) 40-42-37-08; telex 616305; fax (1) 40-42-60-52; f. 1925 for study of all questions relating to the production, transmission and distribution of electrical energy. Mems: 46 countries. Pres. Christophe Babaiantz; Sec.-Gen. Bruno d'Onghia.

International Union of Testing and Research Laboratories for Materials and Structures: Ecole Normale Supérieure, Pavillon du CROUS, 61 ave du Président Wilson, 94235 Cachan Cedex, France; tel. (1) 47-40-23-97; telex 250948; fax (1) 47-40-01-13; f. 1947 for the exchange of information and the promotion of co-operation on experimental research concerning structures and materials, for the study of research methods with a view to improvement and standardization. Mems: laboratories and individuals in 73 countries. Pres. Dr I. Dunstan (UK); Sec.-Gen. M. Fickelson (France). Publ. *Materials and Structures—Testing and Research* (bi-monthly).

Permanent International Association of Navigation Congresses—PIANC: 155 rue de la Loi, 1040 Brussels, Belgium; tel. (02) 733-96-70; f. 1885, present form adopted 1902; fosters progress in the construction, maintenance and operation of inland and maritime waterways, of inland and maritime ports and of coastal areas; publishes information in this field, undertakes studies, organizes international and national meetings. Congresses are held every four years. Mems: 40 governments, 2,786 others. Pres. Ir. R. de Paepe; Sec.-Gen. H. Vandervelden. Publs *Bulletin* (quarterly), *Illustrated Technical Dictionary* (in 6 languages), technical reports, Congress papers, etc.

Permanent International Association of Road Congresses: 27 rue Guénégaud, 75006 Paris, France; tel. (1) 46-33-71-90; fax (1) 46-33-84-60; f. 1909 to promote the construction, improvement, maintenance, use and economic development of roads; organizes technical committees and study sessions. Mems: governments, public bodies, organizations and private individuals in 70 countries. Pres. M. E. Balaguer (Spain); Sec.-Gen. M. B. Fauveau (France). Publs *Bulletin, Technical Dictionary*, technical reports.

World Energy Council: 34 St James's St, London, SW1A 1HD, England; tel. (071) 930-3966; telex 264707; fax (071) 925-0452; f. 1924 to link all branches of energy and resources technology and maintain liaison between world experts; holds congresses every three years. Mems: 95 committees. Pres. Dr J. S. Foster (Canada); Sec.-Gen. I. D. Lindsay (UK). Publs energy supply and demand projections, resources surveys, technical assessments, reports.

OTHER ORGANIZATIONS

African Organization of Cartography and Remote Sensing: BP 102, Hussein Dey, Algiers, Algeria; tel. 77-79-34; telex 65474; f. 1988 by amalgamation of African Association of Cartography and African Council for Remote Sensing; aims to encourage the development of cartography and of remote sensing by satellites; organizes conferences and other meetings, promotes establishment of training institutions; four regional training centres (in Burkina Faso, Kenya, Nigeria and Tunisia). Mems: principal cartographic services of African countries. Sec.-Gen. Mohamed Boualga.

African Regional Centre for Technology: Ave Cheikh Anta Diop, BP 2435, Dakar, Senegal; tel. 25-77-12; telex 61282; fax 25-77-13; f. 1980 to encourage the development of indigenous technology and to improve the terms of access to imported technology; assists the establishment of national centres. Dir (vacant). Publs *African Technodevelopment, Alert Africa*.

Bureau International de la Récupération (International Recycling Bureau): 13 place du Samedi, 1000 Brussels, Belgium; tel. (02) 217-82-51; telex 61965; fax (02) 217-22-74; f. 1948 as the world federation of the reclamation and recycling industries, to promote international trade in scrap iron and steel, non-ferrous metals, paper, textiles, plastics and rubber. Mems: associations and individuals in 50 countries. Sec.-Gen. Francis Veys.

European Builders of Thermal and Electric Locomotives: 12 rue Bixio, 75007 Paris, France; tel. (1) 47-05-36-62; telex 270105; fax (1) 47-05-29-17; f. 1953 as an information centre on economic and technical matters relating to the production, distribution and consumption of locomotives throughout the world. Mems: 40 firms, in 12 countries. Chair. B. G. Sephton; Gen. Sec. R. de Planta.

European Computer Manufacturers Association—ECMA: 114 rue de Rhône, 1204 Geneva, Switzerland; tel. (022) 7353634; telex 413237; fax (022) 7865231; f. 1961 to study and develop, in co-operation with the appropriate national and international organizations, as a scientific endeavour and in the general interest, methods and procedures in order to facilitate and standardize the use of data processing systems; and to promulgate various standards applicable to the functional design and use of data processing equipment. Mems: 31 ordinary and 15 associate. Sec.-Gen. D. Hekimi. Publ. *ECMA Standards*, technical reports.

European Convention for Constructional Steelwork: 32/36 ave des Ombrages, bte 20, 1200 Brussels, Belgium; tel. (02) 762-04-29; fax (02) 762-09-35; f. 1955 for the consideration of problems involved in metallic construction. Member organizations in Australia, Austria, Belgium, Canada, Denmark, Finland, France, Germany, Italy, Japan, Luxembourg, Netherlands, Norway, Sweden, Switzerland, Turkey, United Kingdom, USA, Yugoslavia. Gen. Sec. J. van Neste.

European Federation of Chemical Engineering: c/o Institution of Chemical Engineers, Davis Bldg, 165-171 Railway Terrace, Rugby, Warwickshire, CV21 3HQ, England; tel. (0788) 578214; telex 311780; fax (0788) 560833; f. 1953 to encourage co-operation in Europe between non-profit-making scientific and technical societies for the advancement of chemical engineering and its application in the process industries. Mems: 56 societies in 22 European countries; 12 corresponding societies in other countries.

European Federation of Corrosion: 1 Carlton House Terrace, London, SW1Y 5DB, England; tel. (071) 839-4071; telex 8814813; fax (071) 839-1702; f. 1955 to encourage co-operation in research on corrosion and methods of combating it. Member societies in 20 countries. Hon. Secs R. Mas (France), Dieter Behrens (Germany), R. B. Wood (UK).

European Federation of National Engineering Associations—FEANI: 4 rue de la Mission Marchand, 75016 Paris, France; tel. (1) 42-24-91-43; fax (1) 42-24-53-80; f. 1951 to bring together engineers in Europe and to strive for their unity; to affirm the position, role and responsibility of engineers in society; and to facilitate the mutual recognition of professional qualifications of engineers in Europe. Mems: 1 for each of the 21 mem. countries. Pres. L. G. de Steur (Netherlands); Sec.-Gen. M. Guerin (France). Publ. *FEANI Letter*.

European Organization for Civil Aviation Equipment—EUROCAE: 11 rue Hamelin, 75783 Paris Cedex 16, France; tel. (1) 45-05-71-88; telex 611045; fax (01) 45-53-03-93; f. 1963; studies and advises on problems related to the application of electronics and electronic equipment to aeronautics and assists international bodies in the establishment of international standards. Mems: 65 manufacturers, airlines and research bodies. Pres. B. Dubois; Sec.-Gen. Bernard Perret.

Eurospace: 16 bis ave Bosquet, 75007 Paris, France; tel. (1) 45-55-83-53; telex 270716; fax (1) 45-51-99-23; f. 1961; an association of European aerospace industrial companies, banks, press organizations and national associations for promoting space activity in the fields of telecommunication, television, aeronautical, maritime, meteorological, educational and press usage satellites, as well as launchers (conventional and recoverable). The Association carries out studies on the legal, economic, technical and financial aspects. It acts as an industrial adviser to the European Space Agency. Mems (direct or associate) in Belgium, Denmark, Finland, France, Germany, Italy, Netherlands, Norway, Spain, Sweden, Switzerland, United Kingdom. Pres. Jean Delorme; Sec.-Gen. Yves Demerliac; Tech. Sec. Rex Turner.

Federation of Scientific and Technical Organizations of the Socialist Countries—FENTO: c/o MTESZ, 1055 Budapest, Kossuth Lajos tér 6-8, Hungary; tel. 533-333; telex 225792; f. 1962. Pres. Jenő Fock; Gen. Sec. János Tóth.

Inter-African Committee for Hydraulic Studies—CIEH: 01 BP 369, Ouagadougou, Burkina Faso; tel. 30-71-12; telex 5277; f. 1960 to ensure co-operation in hydrology, hydrogeology, climatology, urban sanitation and other water sciences, through exchange of information and co-ordination of research and other projects; administrative budget (1988/89): 110m. francs CFA; investment budget 400m. francs CFA. Mems: 13 African countries. Sec.-Gen. Abdou Hassane. Publs *Bulletin de Liaison technique* (quarterly), research studies.

International Association for Bridge and Structural Engineering: ETH—Hönggerberg, 8093 Zürich, Switzerland; tel. (01) 3772647; fax (01) 3712131; f. 1929 to promote the interchange of knowledge and research work results concerning bridge and structural engineering and to foster co-operation among those connected with this work. Mems: 3,200 government departments, local authorities, universities, institutes, firms and individuals in 80 countries. Pres. Prof. H. von Gunten (Switzerland); Exec. Dir A. Golay. Publs *Structural Engineering International* (quarterly), *Congress Report, IABSE Report, Structural Engineering Documents*.

International Association for Cybernetics: c/o C. Aigret, Palais des Expositions, place André Rijckmans, 5000 Namur, Belgium; tel. (081) 73-52-09; telex 59101; fax (081) 23-09-45; f. 1957 to ensure

OTHER INTERNATIONAL ORGANIZATIONS
Technology

liaison between research workers engaged in various sectors of cybernetics, to promote the development of the science and of its applications and to disseminate information about it. Mems: firms and individuals in 42 countries. Sec.-Gen. CARINE AIGRET. Publs *Cybernetica* (quarterly).

International Association of Rolling Stock Builders: 12 rue Bixio, 75007 Paris, France; tel. (1) 47-05-36-62; telex 270105; fax (1) 47-05-29-17; f. 1934; an information centre on economic and technical questions relating to the production, distribution and consumption of railway rolling stock throughout the world. Mems: 52 firms in 13 countries. Chair. C. BERNSTEIN; Gen. Del. R. DE PLANTA.

International Association of Technological University Libraries: c/o Helsinki University of Technology Library, Otaniementie 9, 02150 Espoo, Finland; tel. (90) 4514112; telex 121591; fax (90) 4514132; f. 1955 to promote co-operation between member libraries and stimulate research on library problems. Mems: about 190 university libraries in 39 countries. Pres. Prof. ELIN TÖRNUDD (Finland); Sec. Dr N. FJÄLLBRANT (Sweden). Publ. *IATUL Quarterly*.

International Cargo Handling Co-ordination Association—ICHCA: 71 Bondway, London, SW8 1SH, England; tel. (071) 793-1022; telex 261106; fax (071) 820-1703; f. 1952 to foster economy and efficiency in the movement of goods from origin to destination. Mems: 2,000 in 90 countries. Pres. STIG LARSSON (Sweden); Dir JOHN T. WARBURTON. Publs *Cargo Systems International* (monthly), *ICHCA Quarterly Bulletin*, *Biennial Report*, *Who's Who in Cargo Handling* (annually), *International Cargo Handling, Buyers' Guide to Manufacturers* (annually).

International Colour Association: c/o Dr J. Walraven, Institute for Perception TNO, POB 23, 3769 ZG Soesterberg, Netherlands; tel. (034) 63-62-11; f. 1967 to encourage research in colour in all its aspects, disseminate the knowledge gained from this research and promote its application to the solution of problems in the fields of science, art and industry; holds international congresses and symposia. Mems: organizations in 21 countries. Pres. Dr H. TERSTIEGE (Germany); Sec. Dr J. WALRAVEN (Netherlands).

International Commission on Illumination—CIE: Kegelgasse 27, 1030 Vienna, Austria; tel. (01) 75-31-87; telex 111151; fax (01) 713-08-38; f. 1900 as International Commission on Photometry, present name 1913; aims to provide an international forum for all matters relating to the science and art of light and lighting; to exchange information; to develop and publish international standards, and to provide guidance in their application. Mems: 38 national committees and five individuals. Exec. Sec. J. SCHANDA. Publs standards, technical reports.

International Commission on Large Dams: 151 blvd Haussmann, 75008 Paris, France; tel. (1) 40-42-67-33; telex 641320; fax (1) 40-42-60-71; f. 1928; holds triennial congresses. Mems in 79 countries. Pres. J. A. VELTROP (USA); Sec.-Gen. J. COTILLON. Publs *Technical Bulletin*, *World Register of Dams*, *World Register of Mine and Industrial Wastes*, *Technical Dictionary on Dams*, studies.

International Committee on Aeronautical Fatigue—ICAF: c/o Prof. J. Schijve, Faculty of Aerospace Engineering, TUD, Kluyverweg 1, 2629 HS Delft, Netherlands; tel. (015) 78-13-41; telex 38151; fax (015) 78-18-22; f. 1951 for collaboration on fatigue of aeronautical structures among aeronautical bodies and laboratories by means of exchange of documents and by organizing periodical conferences. Mems: national centres in 13 countries. Sec. Prof. J. SCHIJVE (Netherlands).

International Conference on Large High-Voltage Electric Systems—CIGRE: 112 blvd Haussmann, 75008 Paris, France; tel. (1) 45-22-65-12; telex 650445; fax (1) 45-22-21-16; f. 1921 to facilitate and promote the exchange of technical knowledge and information between all countries in the general field of electrical generation and transmission at high voltages; holds general sessions (every two years), symposia. Mems: 3,500 in 79 countries. Pres. J. LEPECKI; Sec.-Gen. G. LEROY (France). Publ. *Electra* (every 2 months).

International Council for Building Research, Studies and Documentation—CIB: POB 20704, 3001 JA Rotterdam, Netherlands; premises at Kruisplein 25, 3014 DB Rotterdam; tel. (010) 411-02-40; fax (010) 433-43-72; f. 1953 to encourage and facilitate co-operation in building research, studies and documentation in all aspects. Mems: governmental and industrial organizations and qualified individuals in 70 countries. Pres. G. SEADEN (Canada); Gen. Sec. GY. SEBESTYEN. Publ. *Information Bulletin* (bi-monthly).

International Electrotechnical Commission—IEC: 3 rue de Varembé, POB 131, 1211 Geneva 20, Switzerland; tel. (022) 340150; telex 28872; f. 1906 as the authority for world standards for electrical and electronic engineering; its standards are used as the basis for regional and national standards, and are used in preparing specifications for international trade. Mems: national committees representing all branches of electrical and electronic activities in 40 countries. Gen.-Sec. A. M. RAEBURN. Publs *International Standards and Reports, IEC Bulletin, Annual Report, Report on Activities, Catalogue of Publications*.

International Special Committee on Radio Interference: British Electrotechnical Committee, British Standards Institution, 2 Park St, London, W1A 2BS, England; tel. (071) 629-9000; telex 266933; f. 1934; special committee of the IEC to promote international agreement on the protection of radio reception from interference by equipment other than authorized transmitters; recommends limits of such interference and specifies equipment and methods of measurement; determines requirements for immunity of sound and TV broadcasting receivers from interference and the impact of safety regulations on interference suppression. Mems: national committees of IEC and seven other international organizations. Sec. M. H. LOCKTON.

International Federation for Information and Documentation: POB 90402, 2509 LK The Hague, Netherlands; tel. (070) 314-06-71; telex 34402; fax (070) 314-06-67; f. 1895 to promote, through international co-operation, research in and development of information science, information management and documentation, which includes the organization, storage, retrieval, repackaging, dissemination, and evaluation of information, however recorded, in the fields of science, technology, industry, social sciences, arts and humanities; regional commissions for Latin America, Asia and Oceania, Western, Eastern and Southern Africa, and for North Africa and the Near East. Mems: 69 national, four international, some 300 affiliates. Pres. RITVA T. LAUNO; Exec. Dir BEN G. GOEDEGEBUURE. Publs *International Forum on Information and Documentation* (quarterly), *FID News Bulletin* (monthly), *FID/ET Newsletter on Education and Training Programmes for Information Personnel* (quarterly), *FID Directory* (every 2 years).

International Federation for Information Processing: c/o Bull SA, 121 ave de Malakoff, 75016 Paris, France; tel. (1) 40-65-03-83; f. 1960 to promote information science and technology; to stimulate research, development and application of information processing in science and human activities; to further the dissemination and exchange of information on information processing; to encourage education in information processing; to advance international co-operation in the field of information processing. Mems: 46 national organizations representing 64 countries. Pres. B. SENDOV (Bulgaria); Exec. Sec. J. FOUROT (France).

International Federation of Airworthiness—IFA: 58 Whiteheath Ave, Ruislip, Middx, HA4 7PW, England; tel. (0895) 672504; telex 8951771; fax (0895) 676656; f. 1964 to provide a forum for the exchange of international experience in maintenance, design and operations; holds annual conference; awards international aviation scholarship annually. Mems: 117, comprising 47 airlines, 17 airworthiness authorities, 23 aerospace manufacturing companies, 17 service and repair organizations, three consultancies, six professional societies, two aviation insurance companies, one aircraft leasing company, and the Flight Safety Foundation (USA). Pres. JOSEPH SUTTER; Exec. Dir J. M. RAINBOW (UK). Publ. *IFA News* (quarterly).

International Federation of Automotive Engineering Societies: Steinacherstrasse 59, 8308 Ober-Illnau, Zürich, Switzerland; f. 1947 to promote the technical development of mechanical transport engineering and research; congresses every two years. Mems: national organizations in 19 countries. Sec.-Gen. W. LEMMENMEYER. Publ. *Bulletin*.

International Federation of Consulting Engineers: 13c ave du Temple, POB 86, 1000 Lausanne 12, Switzerland; tel. (021) 335003; telex 454698; fax (021) 335432; f. 1913 to encourage international co-operation and the setting up of standards for consulting engineers. Mems: national associations in 50 countries, comprising some 26,000 individual members. Pres. S. C. GENTRY.

International Federation of Hospital Engineering: 69 Evans Lane, Kidlington, Oxford, OX5 2JA, England; tel. (0865) 2769; f. 1970 to promote internationally the standards of hospital engineering and to provide for the interchange of knowledge and ideas. Mems: 50. Pres. BASIL HERMON.

International Information Management Congress: 345 Woodcliff Drive, Fairport, NY 14450, USA; tel. (716) 383-8330; telex 6714921; fax (716) 383-8442; f. 1962 (as the International Micrographic Congress) to promote co-operation in document-based information management; to provide an international clearing-house for information, exchange publications and encourage the establishment of international standards; to promote international product exhibitions, seminars and conventions. Mems: 30 associations, 116 regular and 700 affiliate mems from 64 countries. Exec. Dir GEORGE D. HOFFMANN (USA). Publ. *IMC Journal* (every 2 months).

International Institute of Seismology and Earthquake Engineering: Building Research Institute, Ministry of Construction, 1

Tatehara, Tsukuba-shi, Ibaraki Pref., Japan; tel. (0298) 64-2151; telex 3652560; f. 1962 to work on seismology and earthquake engineering for the purpose of reducing earthquake damage in the world; trains seismologists and earthquake engineers from the seismic countries and undertakes surveys, research, guidance and analysis of information on earthquakes and related matters. Mems: 51 countries. Dir S. OKAMOTO.

International Institution for Production Engineering Research: 10 rue Mansart, 75009 Paris, France; tel. (1) 45-26-21-80; telex 281029; fax (1) 40-16-40-75; f. 1951 to promote by scientific research the study of the mechanical processing of all solid materials including checks on efficiency and quality of work. Mems: 179 active and honorary, 99 corresponding, 134 associates, in 40 countries. Pres. W. KÖNIG; Sec.-Gen. R. GESLOT. Publ. *Annals*.

International Iron and Steel Institute—IISI: 120 rue Col Bourg, 1140 Brussels, Belgium; tel. (02) 735-90-75; telex 22639; fax (02) 735-80-12; f. 1967 to promote the welfare and interest of the world's steel industries; to undertake research in all aspects of steel industries; to serve as a forum for exchange of knowledge and discussion of problems relating to steel industries; to collect, disseminate and maintain statistics and information; to serve as a liaison body between international and national steel organizations. Mems: in 43 countries. Chair. HIROSHI SAITO; Sec.-Gen. LENHARD J. HOLSCHUH.

International Organization for Standardization: POB 56, 1 rue de Varembé, 1211 Geneva 20, Switzerland; tel. (022) 7490111; telex 412205; fax (022) 7333430; f. 1947 to reach international agreement on industrial and commercial standards. Mems: national standards institutions of 90 countries. Pres. R. PHILLIPS; Sec.-Gen. LAWRENCE D. EICHER. Publs *ISO International Standards, ISO Memento* (annually), *ISO Catalogue* (annually), *ISO Bulletin* (monthly).

International Research Group on Wood Preservation: Box 5607, 114 86 Stockholm, Sweden; tel. (08) 10-14-53; telex 14445; fax (08) 10-80-81; f. 1965 as Wood Preservation Group by OECD; independent since 1969; consists of five working groups and 16 sub-groups; holds plenary annual meeting. Mems: 315 in 51 countries. Pres. Prof. HUBERT WILLEITNER (Germany); Sec.-Gen. JÖRAN JERMER (Sweden). Publs technical documents and books, *Annual Report*.

International Rubber Research and Development Board—IRRDB: Chapel Building, Brickendonbury, Hertford, SG13 8NP, England; tel. (0992) 584966; telex 817449; fax (0992) 554837; f. 1937. Mems: 15 research institutes. Sec. P. W. ALLEN.

International Society for Photogrammetry and Remote Sensing: c/o Institute of Industrial Science, University of Tokyo, 7-22 Roppongi, Minato-ku, Tokyo, Japan; tel. (03) 4026231, ext. 2560; telex 720242; f. 1910; holds congress every four years, and technical symposia. Mems: 81 countries. Pres. K. TORLEGÅRD (Sweden); Sec.-Gen. S. MURAI (Japan). Publs *International Archives of Photogrammetry and Remote Sensing, Photogrammetria*.

International Society for Soil Mechanics and Foundation Engineering: Engineering Dept, Trumpington St, Cambridge, CB2 1PZ, England; tel. (0223) 355020; telex 81239; fax (0223) 332662; f. 1936 to promote international co-operation among scientists and engineers in the field of geotechnics and its engineering applications; maintains 27 technical committees; holds quadrennial international conference, regional conferences and specialist conferences. Mems: 18,000 individuals, 61 national societies. Pres. Prof. N. R. MORGENSTERN; Gen. Sec. Dr R. PARRY. Publs *Newsletter* (quarterly), *Lexicon of Soil Mechanics Terms* (in eight languages).

International Solar Energy Society: 124, Caulfield East, Victoria 3145, Australia; tel. (03) 571-7557; telex 154087; fax (03) 563-5173; f. 1954 to foster science and technology relating to the applications of solar energy, to encourage research and development, to promote education and to gather, compile and disseminate information in this field; holds international conferences. Mems: 4,000 in 95 countries. Pres. D. LORRIMAN (Canada); Sec.-Treas. W. R. READ (Australia). Publs *Journal* (monthly), *Newsletter* (quarterly), *Sunworld* (quarterly).

International Solid Wastes and Public Cleansing Association: Vester Farimagsgade 29, 1780 Copenhagen V, Denmark; tel. 33-15-65-65; fax 33-93-71-71. Pres. J. A. DEN DULK (Netherlands); Sec.-Gen. JEANNE MØLLER (Denmark).

International Tin Research Institute: Kingston Lane, Uxbridge, Middx, UB8 3PJ, England; tel. (0895) 72406; f. 1932 to develop world consumption of tin; engages in scientific research, technical development and aims to spread knowledge of tin throughout the world by publishing research articles, issuing handbooks, giving lectures and demonstrations, and taking part in exhibitions and trade fairs. Dir B. T. K. BARRY. Publs *Annual Report, Tin and its Uses* (quarterly, in English, French, German, Japanese and Spanish).

International Union for Vacuum Science, Technique and Applications: c/o Dr J. S. Colligon, Dept of Electronic and Electrical Engineering, University of Salford, Salford, M5 4WT, England; tel. (061) 745-5247; telex 668680; fax (061) 745-5999; f. 1958; collaborates with the International Standards Organization in defining and adopting technical standards; holds triennial International Vacuum Congress and International Conference on Solid Surfaces; regulates the Welch Foundation for postgraduate research in vacuum science and technology; scientific divisions for surface science, applied surface science, thin film physics, vacuum science, electronic materials and processes, fusion technology and vacuum metallurgy. Mems: organizations in 26 countries. Pres. Dr J. L. DE SEGOVIA (Spain); Sec.-Gen. Dr JOHN S. COLLIGON (UK). Publs *News Bulletin* (every 2 months).

International Union of Heat Distributors: Bahnhofplatz 3, 8023 Zürich, Switzerland; tel. (01) 2113635; f. 1954 to study the various problems concerning the development and distribution of heat for all purposes by means of pipes laid underground. The Union assembles the results of research and tests and puts statistical information at the disposal of the members; holds conference every two years. Mems: 150 companies in 16 countries. Pres. NIELS NEDERGAARD (Denmark); Sec. Dr E. KEPPLER (Switzerland). Publ. *Bulletin* (quarterly).

International Union of Metal: Seestrasse 105, 8002 Zürich, Switzerland; tel. (01) 2017376; telex 817671; fax (01) 2023497; f. 1954 for liaison between national bodies to exchange documentation and study common problems. Mems: national federations from Austria, Belgium, Germany, Luxembourg, Netherlands, Sweden, Switzerland. Pres. FRANÇOIS BICHEL (Luxembourg); Sec. HANS-JÖRG FEDERER (Switzerland).

International Water Resources Association: 205 North Mathews Ave, Urbana, Ill 61801 USA; tel. (217) 333-0536; telex 5101011969; fax (217) 333-8046; f. 1972 to promote collaboration in and support for international water resources programmes; holds conferences; conducts training in water resources management. Pres. ASIT K. BISWAS (UK); Sec.-Gen. GLENN E. STOUT (USA). Publ. *Water International* (quarterly).

International Water Supply Association: 1 Queen Anne's Gate, London, SW1H 9BT, England; tel. (071) 222-8111; telex 918518; fax (071) 222-7243; f. 1947 to co-ordinate technical, legal and administrative aspects of public water supply; congresses held every two years. Mems: national organizations, water authorities and individuals in 107 countries. Pres. W. H. RICHARDSON; Sec.-Gen. L. R. BAYS (UK). Publs *Aqua* (6 a year), *Water Supply* (quarterly).

Latin-American Energy Organization (Organización Latino-americana de Energía—OLADE): Av. Occidental, OLADE Bldg, Sector San Carlos, POB 6413 CCI, Quito, Ecuador; tel. 538-122; f. 1973 to act as an instrument of co-operation in using and conserving the energy resources of the region. Mems: 26 Latin-American and Caribbean countries. Exec. Sec. GABRIEL SÁNCHEZ SIERRA. Publ. *Revista Energética*.

Latin-American Iron and Steel Institute: Dario Urzua 1994, Casilla 16065, Santiago 9, Chile; tel. 2237581; telex 340348; fax 2253111; f. 1959 to help achieve the harmonious development of iron and steel production, manufacture and marketing in Latin America; conducts economic surveys on the steel sector; organizes technical conventions and meetings; disseminates industrial processes suited to regional conditions; prepares and maintains statistics on production, end uses, prices, etc., of raw materials and steel products within this area. Mems: 91, and 92 associates. Chair. GUILLERMO BECKER; Sec.-Gen. ANÍBAL GÓMEZ. Publs *Siderurgia Latinoamericana* (monthly), *Statistical Year Book, Directory of Latin American Iron and Steel Companies* (every 2 years).

Regional Centre for Services in Surveying, Mapping and Remote Sensing: POB 18118, Nairobi, Kenya; tel. 803320; telex 25258; f. 1975 to provide services in the professional techniques of map-making, and the application of satellite and remote sensing data in resource analysis and development planning; undertakes research and provides advisory services to African governments. Mems: 12 signatory and 10 non-signatory governments. Dir-Gen. SAMUEL L. OKEC (acting).

Regional Centre for Training in Aerospace Surveys: PMB 5545, Ile-Ife, Nigeria; tel. (036) 230050; telex 34262; f. 1972 for training, research and advisory services; administered by the ECA. Mems: eight governments. Dir Prof. O. O. AYENI.

World Association of Industrial and Technological Research Organizations—WAITRO: c/o Danish Technological Institute, Teknologiparken, 8000 Aarhus C, Denmark; tel. 86-14-24-00; telex 68722; fax 86-14-77-22; f. 1970 by the UN Industrial Development Organization to encourage co-operation in industrial and technological research, through financial assistance for training and joint activities, arranging international seminars, and allowing the exchange of information. Mems: 83 research institutes in 52 countries. Pres. Dr J. K. NIGAM (India); Sec.-Gen. R. W. SHORT. Publs *Communique* (quarterly).

OTHER INTERNATIONAL ORGANIZATIONS   Technology, Tourism

World Association of Nuclear Operators—WANO: 35 ave de Friedland, 75008 Paris, France; f. 1989 by operators of nuclear power plants; aims to assist in the exchange of information on the design and operation of nuclear reactors, and to prevent accidents; four 'early warning centres' (in France, Japan, the USA and the USSR). Mems in 31 countries.

World Bureau of Metal Statistics: 27A High St, Ware, Herts, SG12 9BA, England; tel. (0920) 461274; telex 817746; fax (0920) 464258; f. 1949; statistics of production, consumption, stocks, prices and international trade in copper, lead, zinc, tin, nickel, aluminium and several other minor metals. Gen. Man. J. L. T. DAVIES. Publs *World Metal Statistics* (monthly).

World Federation of Engineering Organizations—WFEO: c/o C. Herselin, 19 rue Blanche, 75009 Paris, France; tel. (1) 45-26-34-82; telex 650594; f. 1968 to advance engineering as a profession in the interests of the world community; to foster co-operation between engineering organizations throughout the world; to undertake special projects through co-operation between members and in co-operation with other international bodies. Mems: 80 national, five international. Pres. S. BEN JEMAA (Tunisia); Sec.-Gen. C. HERSELIN (France).

World Petroleum Congresses: 61 New Cavendish St, London, W1M 8AR, England; tel. (071) 636-1004; telex 264380; fax (071) 255-1472; f. 1933 to provide an international congress as a forum for petroleum science, technology, economics and management; to publish the proceedings, and to undertake related information and liaison activities; executive board represents 16 member countries. Pres. Dr KLAUS L. MAI (USA); Sec.-Gen. D. C. PAYNE (UK).

Tourism

Alliance Internationale de Tourisme: 2 quai Gustave Ador, 1207 Geneva, Switzerland; tel. (022) 7352727; telex 413103; fax (022) 7352326; f. 1898, present title adopted 1919; represents motoring organizations and touring clubs around the world; aims to study all questions relating to international touring and to suggest reforms, to encourage the development of tourism and all matters concerning the motorist, traffic management, the environment, road safety, consumer protection and to defend the interests of touring associations. Mems: 125 associations totalling 80m. members in 86 countries. Pres. L. H. VIDELA PACHECO (Chile); Sec.-Gen. J. WARD (UK).

Arab Tourism Organization: POB 2354, Amman, Jordan; tel. 30840; telex 21471; f. 1954. Mems: national tourist organizations of 21 Arab countries, and four associate members in the private sector. Sec.-Gen. Dr ABDUL RAHMAN ABU RABAH (Jordan). Publs *Arab Tourism Magazine* (every 2 months), *Bulletin* (monthly), studies.

Caribbean Tourism Organization: Bridgetown, Barbados; tel. 427-5242; fax 429-3065; offices in New York (tel. (212) 682-0435) and London (tel. (071) 839-8480); f. 1951 to encourage tourism in the Caribbean region (present name 1989). Mems: 28 Caribbean governments and 400 allied mems. Sec.-Gen. JEAN HOLDER.

East Asia Travel Association: c/o Japan National Tourist Organization, 2-10-1 Yurakucho, Chiyoda-ku, Tokyo, Japan; tel. (03) 216-2910; telex 24132; fax (03) 214-7680; f. 1966 to promote tourism in the East Asian region, encourage and facilitate the flow of tourists to that region from other parts of the world, and to develop regional tourist industries by close collaboration among members. Mems: seven national tourist organizations, seven airlines and one travel association. Pres. TAIICHIRO ANDO; Sec.-Gen. KOICHI SOGABE.

European Motor Hotel Federation—EMF: Jutfaseweg 206, 3522 HS Utrecht, Netherlands; tel. (030) 892282; f. 1956 to represent the interests of European motel-owners. Mems: 133. Sec. H. J. KLOOSTERHUIS (Netherlands).

European Travel Commission: 2 rue Linois, 75015 Paris, France; tel. (1) 45-75-62-16; telex 270974; fax (1) 45-77-11-49; f. 1948 to promote tourism in and to Europe, to foster co-operation and the exchange of information, to organize research. Mems: national tourist organizations of 24 European countries. Exec. Dir ROBERT HOLLIER (France); Sec. E. P. KEARNEY.

International Academy of Tourism: 9 rue Princesse Marie de Lorraine, 98000 Monte-Carlo, Monaco; tel. 93-30-97-68; f. 1951 to develop the cultural and humanistic aspects of international tourism and to establish an accepted vocabulary for tourism. Mems: 117. Pres. TIMOTHY O'DRISCOLL; Chancellor LOUIS NAGEL. Publs *Revue, Dictionnaire Touristique International*.

International Association of Scientific Experts in Tourism: Varnbüelstrasse 19, 9000 St Gallen, Switzerland; tel. (071) 302530; fax (071) 302536; f. 1949 to encourage scientific activity by its members; to support tourist institutions of a scientific nature; to organize conventions. Mems: 345 from 40 countries. Pres. Prof. Dr CLAUDE KASPAR (Switzerland); Gen. Sec. Dr HANSPETER SCHMIDHAUSER (Switzerland). Publ. *The Tourist Review* (quarterly).

International Congress and Convention Association: Concertgebouwplein 27, POB 75343, 1070 AH Amsterdam, Netherlands; tel. (020) 664-74-21; telex 11629; fax (020) 664-92-65; f. 1963 to establish worldwide co-operation between all involved in organizing congresses, conventions and exhibitions (including travel agents, airlines, hotels, congress centres and professional congress organizers). Mems: 400 in 70 countries. Sec.-Gen. DICK OUWEHAND. Publ. *TW/ICCA News* (every 2 months).

International Federation of Popular Travel Organizations: Tour Maine Montparnasse, 33 ave du Maine, 75755 Paris Cedex 15, France; tel. (1) 45-38-28-28; telex 260938; f. 1950. Mems: 23 organizations. Pres. ANDRÉ GUIGNAND (France); Sec.-Gen. FLORENCE FOUQUIER (France).

International Federation of Tourist Centres: Brennerstrasse 30, 4820 Bad Ischl, Austria; f. 1949. Mems: Austria, Belgium, France, Germany, Finland, Italy, Liechtenstein, Netherlands, Norway, Sweden, Switzerland, United Kingdom. Pres. Dr ALDO DEBENE (Austria); Sec.-Gen. KONRAD BERTHOLD (Liechtenstein).

International Ho-Re-Ca: Blumenfeldstrasse 20, Postfach, 8046 Zürich, Switzerland; tel. (01) 3775111; fax (01) 3718909; f. 1949 to bring together national associations of hotel, restaurant and café proprietors to further the interests of the trade, international tourism, etc. Mems: 29 national organizations. Pres. JOCHEN KOEPP (Germany); Gen. Sec. Dr XAVER FREI (Switzerland).

International Hotel Association: 80 rue de la Roquette, 75544 Paris Cedex 11, France; tel. (1) 47-00-84-57; telex 216410; fax (1) 47-00-64-55; f. 1946 to link internationally national hotel associations and hotels active in international tourism; to consider all questions of interest to the international hotel industry; to assist in the employment of qualified hotel staff and the exchange of students; to distribute information. Mems: 106 national hotel associations, 101 national and international hotel chains, and 3,305 hotels; also affiliate members. Pres. SAM FEDERMANN (Israel); Gen. Sec. RAYMOND K. FENELON (UK). Publs *Hotels* (monthly), *International Hotel Guide* (annually), *Directory of Travel Agencies* (every 2 years), *Opportunities Newsletter* (6 a year), *Dialogue* (every 2 months).

Latin-American Confederation of Tourist Organizations: Viamonte 640, 8°, 1053 Buenos Aires, Argentina; tel. 392-4003; telex 23385; fax (541) 112272; f. 1957 to link Latin American national associations of travel agents and their members with other tourist bodies around the world. Mems: in 19 countries and affiliate mems in 70 countries. Pres. ARMANDO ESPINEL; Sec.-Gen. SANTIAGO TARANTO. Publ. *Revista COTAL* (monthly).

Pacific Asia Travel Association—PATA: 1 Montgomery St, Suite 1750, San Francisco, Calif 94104, USA; tel. (415) 986-4646; f. 1951 for the promotion of travel to and between the countries and islands of the Pacific; regional offices in Singapore and Sydney; holds annual conference, seminars. Mems: governments, carriers, travel agents, tour operators and hotels in 68 countries and territories. Exec. Vice-Pres. R. KANE RUFE. Publs *Pacific Travel News* (monthly).

Tourism Council of the South Pacific: POB 13119, Suva, Fiji; tel. 315277; fax 301995; aims to co-ordinate the development of tourism and increase its contribution to regional socio-economic development; funded principally by the EEC. Mems: American Samoa, Cook Islands, Fiji, Kiribati, Niue, Papua New Guinea, Solomon Islands, Tahiti, Tonga, Tuvalu, Vanuatu, Western Samoa.

Universal Federation of Travel Agents' Associations—UFTAA: 17 rue Grimaldi, 98000 Monaco; tel. 93-50-00-28; fax 93-15-96-77; f. 1966 to unite travel agents associations, to represent the interests of travel agents at the international level, to help in international legal differences; issues literature on travel, etc. Mems: national associations of travel agencies in 83 countries. Sec.-Gen. GARETH J. DAVIES.

World Association of Travel Agencies: 37 Quai Wilson, 1201 Geneva, Switzerland; tel. (022) 7314760; telex 22447; fax (022) 7328161; f. 1949 to foster the development of tourism, to help the rational organization of tourism in all countries, to collect and disseminate information and to participate in all commercial and financial operations which will foster the development of tourism. Individual travel agencies may use the services of the world-wide network of 250 members. Pres. URS BAUER (Switzerland); Sec.-Gen. HERVÉ CHOISY (Switzerland).

World Tourism Organization: Calle Capitán Haya 42, 28020 Madrid, Spain; tel. 5710628; telex 42188; fax 5713733; f. 1975 to promote travel and tourism; undertakes technical co-operation, and the protection of tourists and tourist facilities; provides training and information (including statistics). There are six regional commissions and a General Assembly is held every two years. Mems: governments of 105 countries, also four associate members, one observer, and 158 affiliated tourism organizations. Sec.-Gen. WILLIBALD PAHR.

Trade and Industry

African Regional Organization for Standardization: POB 57363, Nairobi, Kenya; tel. 24561; telex 22097; fax 729228; f. 1977 to promote standardization, quality control, certification and metrology in the African region, formulate regional standards, and co-ordinate participation in international standardization activities. Mems: 24 states. Sec.-Gen. ZAWDU FELLEKE.

Arab Iron and Steel Union—AISU: BP 4, Cheraga, Algiers, Algeria; tel. 78 15 78; telex 63158; f. 1972 to develop commercial and technical aspects of Arab steel production by helping member associations to commercialize their production in Arab markets, guaranteeing them high quality materials and intermediary products, informing them of recent developments in the industry and organizing training sessions. Mems: 43 companies in 12 Arab countries. Gen. Sec. MUHAMMAD LAID LACHGAR. Publs *Arab Steel Review* (monthly), *Information Bulletin* (2 a month), *Directory* (annually).

Asian Productivity Organization: 4-14 Akasaka, 8-chome, Minato-ku, Tokyo 107, Japan; tel. (03) 4087221; telex 26477; fax (03) 4087220; f. 1961 to strengthen the productivity movement in the Asian region and disseminate technical knowledge. Mems: 17 countries. Sec.-Gen. NAGAO YOSHIDA. Publs *APO News* (monthly), *Annual Report*.

Association of African Trade Promotion Organizations—AATPO: BP 23, Tangier, Morocco; tel. 41687; telex 33695; f. 1975 under the auspices of the OAU and the ECA to foster regular contact between African states in trade matters and to assist in the harmonization of their commercial policies in order to promote intra-African trade; conducts research and training; organizes meetings and trade information missions. Mems: 26 states. Sec.-Gen. Dr FAROUK SHAKWEER. Publs *FLASH: African Trade* (monthly), *Directory of Trade Information Sources in Africa*, *Directory of State Trading Organizations*, *Directory of Importers and Exporters of Food Products in Africa*.

Association of European Chambers of Commerce (EUROCHAMBERS): 5 rue Archimède, 1040 Brussels, Belgium; tel. (02) 231-07-15; telex 25315; fax (02) 230-00-38; f. 1958 to promote the exchange of experience and information among its members and to bring their joint opinions to the attention of the institutions of the European Community; conducts studies and seminars. Mems: associations in the EEC member states; eight associate and three corresponding mems; Pres. R. DELOROZOY (France); Sec.-Gen. H. J. VON BÜLOW (Germany).

Cairns Group: c/o Department of Foreign Affairs and Trade, Bag 8, Queen Victoria Terrace, Canberra, ACT 2600, Australia; f. 1986 by major agricultural exporting countries, aiming to bring about reforms in international agricultural trade, including reductions in export subsidies, in barriers to access and in internal support measures; represents members' interests in GATT negotiations. Mems: Argentina, Australia, Brazil, Canada, Chile, Colombia, Fiji, Hungary, Indonesia, Malaysia, New Zealand, Philippines, Thailand, Uruguay. Chair. Dr NEAL BLEWETT (Australia).

Committee for European Construction Equipment—CECE: 22-26 Dingwall Rd, Croydon, Surrey, CR0 9XF, England; tel. (081) 688-2727; telex 9419625; fax (081) 681-2134; f. 1959 to further contact between manufacturers, to improve market conditions and productivity and to conduct research into techniques. Mems: representatives from Belgium, Finland, France, Germany, Italy, Netherlands, Spain, Sweden, United Kingdom. Pres. A. LEONI (Italy); Sec.-Gen. D. BARRELL (UK).

Committee of European Foundry Associations: 2 rue de Bassano, 75783 Paris Cedex 16, France; tel. (1) 47-23-55-50; telex 620617; fax (1) 47-20-44-15; f. 1953 to safeguard the common interests of European foundry industries; to collect and exchange information. Mems: associations in 13 countries. Pres. M. ZIMMERMANN (Austria); Sec.-Gen. J. P. BURDEAU.

Confederation of Asia-Pacific Chambers of Commerce and Industry: 10th Floor, 122 Tunhua North Rd, Taipei 10590, Taiwan; tel. 7163016; telex 11144; fax 7183683; f. 1966; holds biennial conferences to examine regional co-operation; undertakes liaison with governments in the promotion of laws conducive to regional co-operation; serves as a centre for compiling and disseminating trade and business information; encourages contacts between businesses; conducts training and research. Mems: national chambers of commerce and industry of Australia, Hong Kong, India, Indonesia, Japan, Republic of Korea, Malaysia, New Zealand, Papua New Guinea, Philippines, Singapore, Sri Lanka, Taiwan, Thailand; also affiliate, associate and special mems. Dir-Gen. JOHNSON C. YEN. Publs *CACCI Profile* (monthly), *CACCI Journal of Commerce and Industry*.

Confederation of European Soft Drinks Associations—CESDA: 51 ave Général de Gaulle, 1050 Brussels, Belgium; tel. (02) 649-12-86; f. 1961 to promote co-operation among the national associations of soft drinks manufacturers on all industrial and commercial matters, to stimulate the sales and consumption of soft drinks, to deal with matters of interest to all member-associations and to represent the common interests of member-associations and authorities; holds a congress every two years. Pres. R. DELVILLE; Gen. Sec. P. E. FOSSEPREZ.

Confederation of International Contractors' Associations: 128 rue la Boétie, 75008 Paris, France; tel. (1) 49-53-50-50; telex 290918; fax (1) 45-63-52-84; f. 1974 to promote co-operation and the exchange of information among building contractors' federations. Mems: four international associations (Europe, Asia and the Western Pacific, North America and Latin America). Pres. FRANS DE VILDER; Sec.-Gen. ERIC LEPAGE.

Co-ordinating Committee for Multilateral Export Controls—COCOM: 58 bis rue la Boétie, 75008 Paris, France; f. 1949; aims to prevent the transfer of military technology to communist countries, by controlling the sale of strategically important goods by Western exporters; reduction and simplification of list of embargoed products undertaken in 1990. Mems: governments belonging to NATO (with the exception of Iceland), Australia and Japan.

Customs Co-operation Council: 26-38 rue de l'Industrie, 1040 Brussels, Belgium; tel. (02) 513-99-00; telex 61597; fax (02) 514-33-72; f. 1950 to study all questions relating to co-operation in customs matters, and examine technical aspects, bearing in mind economic factors, of customs systems with a view to attaining uniformity; preparation of conventions and recommendations; ensuring uniform interpretation and application of customs conventions (e.g. on valuation and tariff nomenclature), and conciliatory action in case of dispute; circulation of information and advice regarding Customs regulations and procedures and co-operation with other international organizations. Mems: governments of 107 countries or territories. Chair. H. M. RÍOS RODRÍGUEZ (Spain); Sec.-Gen. T. P. HAYES (Australia). Publs *Bulletin* (annually), *CCC News*.

European Association of Advertising Agencies: 28 ave du Barbeau, 1160 Brussels, Belgium; tel. (02) 672-43-36; fax (02) 672-00-14; f. 1960 to maintain and to raise the standards of service to advertisers of all European advertising agencies, and to strive towards uniformity in fields where this would be of benefit; to serve the interests of all agency members in Europe. Mems: 16 national advertising agency associations and 24 multinational agency groups. Pres. ANDRÉ BERNARD; Sec.-Gen. RONALD BEATSON. Publ. *Bulletin*.

European Association of Manufacturers of Radiators—EURORAD: Obstgartenstr. 19, 8023 Zürich, Switzerland; telex 817538; fax (01) 3628351; f. 1966 to represent the national associations of manufacturers of radiators made of steel and cast iron, intended to be attached to central heating plants and which convey heat by natural convection and radiation without the need for casing. Mems: in 12 countries. Pres. G. VANDENSCHRIECK (Belgium); Gen. Sec. K. EGLI (Switzerland).

European Association of National Productivity Centres: 60 rue de la Concorde, 1050 Brussels, Belgium; tel. (02) 511-71-00; f. 1966 to enable members to pool knowledge about their policies and activities, specifically as regards the relative importance of various productivity factors, and the ensuing economic and social consequences. Mems: 18 European, North American and Australasian centres. Pres. PIERRE LOUIS RÉMY; Sec.-Gen. A. C. HUBERT. Publs *EPI* (quarterly), *EUROproductivity* (monthly), *Annual Report*.

European Brewery Convention: POB 510, 2380 BB Zoeterwoude, Netherlands; tel. (071) 45-60-47; telex 39390; fax (071) 41-00-13; f. 1947, present name adopted 1948; aims to promote scientific co-ordination in malting and brewing. Mems: national associations in Austria, Belgium, Denmark, Finland, France, Germany, Italy, Luxembourg, Netherlands, Norway, Portugal, Spain, Sweden, Switzerland, United Kingdom. Pres. T. M. ENARI (Finland); Sec.-Gen. Mrs M. VAN WIJNGAARDEN (Netherlands).

European Chemical Industry Federation: 250 ave Louise, bte 71, 1050 Brussels, Belgium; tel. (02) 640-20-95; telex 62444; fax (02) 640-19-81; f. 1972; represents and defends the interests of the chemical industry relating to legal and trade policy, internal market, environmental and technical matters; liaises with intergovernmental organizations. Mems: 15 national federations and 39 major Europe-based companies. Dir.-Gen. Drs H. H. LEVER.

European Committee for Standardization (Comité européen de normalisation—CEN): 2 rue Bréderode, Bte 5, 1000 Brussels, Belgium; tel. (02) 519-68-11; telex 26257; fax (02) 519-68-19; f. 1961 to promote European standardization and provide the CEN conformity certification marking system and the CEN system of mutual recognition of test and inspection results, so as to eliminate obstacles caused by technical requirements in order to facilitate

OTHER INTERNATIONAL ORGANIZATIONS
Trade and Industry

the exchange of goods and services. Mems: 16 national standards bodies. Sec.-Gen. EVANGELOS VARDAKAS.

European Committee of Associations of Manufacturers of Agricultural Machinery: 19 rue Jacques Bingen, 75017 Paris, France; tel. (1) 47-66-02-20; telex 640362; fax (1) 40-54-95-60; f. 1959 to study economic and technical problems, to protect members' interests and to disseminate information. Mems: Austria, Belgium, Denmark, Finland, France, Germany, Italy, Netherlands, Norway, Spain, Sweden, Switzerland, United Kingdom. Pres. G. VEZZALINI (Italy); Sec.-Gen. H. VINCENT (France).

European Committee of Textile Machinery Manufacturers: Kirchenweg 4, Postfach, 8032 Zürich, Switzerland; tel. (01) 3844844; telex 816519; fax (01) 3844848; f. 1952; organizes international textile machinery exhibitions. Mems: organizations in Belgium, France, Germany, Italy, Netherlands, Spain, Switzerland, United Kingdom. Pres. G. GILBOS (Belgium); Sec. Dr J. MERMOD (Switzerland).

European Confederation of Iron and Steel Industries—EUROFER: 5 square de Meeûs, Bte 9, 1040 Brussels, Belgium; tel. (02) 512-98-30; telex 62112; f. 1976 as a confederation of national federations or companies in the steel industries of member states of the European Coal and Steel Community, to foster co-operation between the member federations and to represent their common interests to the EEC and other international organizations. Mems: Belgium, Denmark, France, Germany, Ireland, Italy, Luxembourg, Netherlands, Portugal, Spain, United Kingdom. Dir-Gen. D. VAN HÜLSEN.

European Confederation of Paint, Printing Ink and Artists' Colours Manufacturers' Associations: 49 square Marie Louise, 1040 Brussels, Belgium; tel. (02) 238-97-96; telex 23167; fax (02) 230-14-09; f. 1951 to study questions relating to paint and printing ink industries, to take or recommend measures for their development and interests, to exchange information. Mems: national associations in 16 European countries. Pres. Q. KNIGHT; Gen. Sec. H.-A. LENTZE (Belgium).

European Confederation of Woodworking Industries: 109-111 rue Royale, 1000 Brussels, Belgium; tel. (02) 217-63-65; telex 64143; fax (02) 217-59-04; f. 1952 to act as a liaison between national organizations, to undertake research and to defend the interests of the industry. Mems: national federations in 13 European countries and European sectoral organizations in woodworking. Pres. H. GOTSCHY (Germany); Sec.-Gen. Dr G. VAN STEERTEGEM.

European Federation of Associations of Insulation Enterprises: 10 rue du Débarcadère, 75852 Paris Cedex 17, France; tel. (1) 40-55-13-70; telex 644044; fax (1) 40-55-13-69; f. 1970; groups the organizations in Europe representing insulation firms including thermal insulation, sound-proofing and fire-proofing insulation; aims to facilitate contacts between member associations, to study any problems of interest to the profession, to safeguard the interests of the profession and represent it in international forums. Mems: professional organizations in 15 European countries. Chair. T. WREDE.

European Federation of Associations of Particle Board Manufacturers: 63 Giessen, Wilhelmstrasse 25, Germany; tel. (0641) 78091; telex 482877; fax (0641) 72145; f. 1958 to develop and encourage international co-operation in the particle board industry. Pres. J. M. PENA MÖLLER (Spain); Sec.-Gen. A. KRIER (Germany). Publs *Annual Report*, technical documents.

European Federation of Handling Industries: POB 179, Kirchenweg 4, 8032 Zürich, Switzerland; tel. (01) 3844844; telex 816519; fax (01) 3844848; f. 1953 to facilitate contact between members of the profession, conduct research, standardize methods of calculation and construction and promote standardized safety regulations. Mems: organizations in 13 European countries. Pres. Dr G. WENDT; Sec. Dr K. MEIER (Switzerland).

European Federation of Management Consultants' Associations: 3 rue Léon Bonnat, 75016 Paris, France; tel. (1) 45-24-43-53; telex 612938; fax (1) 42-88-26-84; f. 1960 to bring management consultants together and promote a high standard of professional competence in all European countries concerned, by encouraging discussions of, and research into, problems of common professional interest. Mems: 17 associations. Gen. Sec. E. LABOUREAU.

European Federation of Plywood Industry: 30 ave Marceau, 75008 Paris, France; f. 1957 to organize joint research between members of the industry at international level. Mems: associations in nine European countries. Pres. T. FULCONIS (France); Sec.-Gen. PIERRE LAPEYRE.

European Federation of Productivity Services: c/o Aros M Gruppen, Box 520, 72109 Västerås, Sweden; tel. (21) 101052; fax (21) 148967; f. 1961 to promote throughout Europe the application of productivity services; to promote and support the development of the practice and techniques of industrial and commercial productivity and efficiency; and to provide a contact network for the exchange of information and ideas. Mems: 14, and three corresponding organizations. Pres. W. HELMS; Exec. Sec. K. HELMRICH.

European Federation of Tile and Brick Manufacturers: Obstgartenstrasse 28, 8035 Zürich, Switzerland; tel. (01) 3619650; fax (01) 3610205; f. 1952 to co-ordinate research between members of the industry, improve technical knowledge, encourage professional training. Mems: associations in Austria, Belgium, Denmark, Finland, France, Germany, Greece, Ireland, Italy, Netherlands, Norway, Spain, Sweden, Switzerland, United Kingdom. Chair. C. KOREVAAR; Dir Dr W. P. WELLER.

European Furniture Manufacturers Federation: 15 rue de l'Association, 1000 Brussels; tel. (02) 218-18-89; fax (02) 219-27-01; f. 1950 to determine and support general interests of the European furniture industry and to facilitate contacts between members of the industry. Mems: organizations in Belgium, Denmark, Finland, France, Germany, Italy, Netherlands, Norway, Portugal, Spain, Sweden, Switzerland, United Kingdom, Yugoslavia. Pres. R. RODRÍGUEZ; Sec.-Gen. B. DE TURCK.

European General Galvanizers Association: c/o Zinc Development Association, 42 Weymouth St, London, W1N 3LQ, England; tel. (071) 499-6636; telex 261286; fax (071) 493-1555; f. 1955 to promote co-operation between members of the industry, especially in improving processes and finding new uses for galvanized products; maintains a film and photographic section and library. Mems: associations in Austria, Belgium, Denmark, Finland, France, Germany, Italy, Netherlands, Norway, Portugal, Spain, Sweden, Switzerland, United Kingdom. Pres. A. MOHRENSCHILDT (Italy).

European Glass Container Manufacturers' Committee: Northumberland Rd, Sheffield, S10 2UA, England; tel. (0742) 686201; fax (0742) 681073; f. 1951 to facilitate contacts between members of the industry, inform them of legislation regarding it. Mems: representatives from 15 European countries. Sec. D. K. BARLOW (UK).

European Organization for Quality—EOQ: POB 5032, 3001 Berne, Switzerland; tel. (031) 216166; telex 913278; fax (031) 263257; f. 1956 to encourage the use and application of quality control with the intent to improve quality, reduce costs and increase productivity; organizes annual conferences for the exchange of information, documentation, etc. Member organizations in 25 European countries. Pres. HORST FUHR; Sec.-Gen. MAX CONRAD (Switzerland). Publs *Quality* (quarterly), *Glossary*, *Sampling Books*, *Specifications Guide*, *Quality Survey in Automotive Industry*, *Reliability Book*.

European Packaging Federation: c/o Nederlands Verpakkingscentrum NVC, Postbus 164, 2800 AD Gouda, Netherlands; tel. (01820) 12411; fax (01820) 12769; f. 1953 to encourage the exchange of information between national packaging institutes and to promote technical and economic progress. Mems: organizations in Austria, Belgium, Denmark, Finland, France, Germany, Hungary, Italy, Netherlands, Poland, Spain, Switzerland, United Kingdom. Pres. Prof. DIETER BERNDT (Germany); Sec.-Gen. PAUL F. M. JANSSEN (Netherlands).

European Patent Office—EPO: 8000 Munich 2, Erhardtstrasse 27, Germany; tel. (089) 2399-0; telex 523656; fax (089) 2399 4465; f. 1977 to grant European patents according to the Munich convention of 1973; conducts searches and examination of patent applications. Mems: Austria, Belgium, Denmark, France, Germany, Greece, Italy, Liechtenstein, Luxembourg, Netherlands, Spain, Sweden, Switzerland, United Kingdom. Pres. P. BRAENDLI (Switzerland); Chair. Admin. Council JEAN-CLAUDE COMBALDIEU (France). Publs *Annual Report*, *Official Journal* (monthly), *European Patent Bulletin*, *European Patent Applications*, *Granted Patents*.

European Society for Opinion and Marketing Research—ESOMAR: J. J. Viottastraat 29, 1071 JP Amsterdam, Netherlands; tel. (020) 664-21-41; telex 18535; fax (020) 664-29-22; f. 1948 to further professional interests and encourage high technical standards. Mems: about 2,400 in 50 countries. Pres. JEAN-LOUIS LABORIE (France); Dir FERNANDA MONTI (Netherlands). Publs *Marketing and Research Today* (quarterly), *Newsbrief* (6 a year), *Marketing Research in Europe* (annually), *ESOMAR Directory* (annually).

European Union of Coachbuilders: 46 Woluwedal, bte 14, 1200 Brussels, Belgium; tel. (02) 771-17-42; f. 1948 to promote research on questions affecting the industry, exchange information, and establish a common policy for the industry. Mems: national federations in Belgium, France, Germany, Italy, Luxembourg, Netherlands, Switzerland, United Kingdom. Pres. G. BAETEN (Belgium); Sec.-Gen. HILDE VANDER STICHELE (Belgium).

European Union of the Natural Gas Industry—EUROGAS: 4 ave Palmerston, 1040 Brussels, Belgium; tel. (02) 237-11-11; fax (02) 230-44-80. Mem. organizations in Austria, Belgium, Denmark, Germany, France, Ireland, Italy, Netherlands, Spain, Sweden, Switzerland, United Kingdom. Pres. F. GUTMANN (France); Gen. Sec. P. CLAUS (Belgium).

OTHER INTERNATIONAL ORGANIZATIONS   *Trade and Industry*

Federation of European Marketing Research Associations—FEMRA: Studio 38, Wimbledon Business Centre, Riverside Road, London, SW17 0BA; tel. (081) 879-0709; fax (081) 947-2637; f. 1965 to facilitate contacts between researchers; holds annual conferences and seminars; main specialist divisions: European chemical marketing research; European technological forecasting; paper and related industries; industrial materials; automotive; textiles; methodology; information technology. Mems: 700. Pres. DAVID A. CLARK (France).

General Union of Chambers of Commerce, Industry and Agriculture for Arab Countries: POB 11-2837, Beirut, Lebanon; tel. 814269; telex 20347; fax 806840; f. 1951 to foster Arab economic collaboration, to increase and improve production and to facilitate the exchange of technical information in Arab countries. Mems: Chambers of Commerce, Industry and Agriculture in 21 Arab countries. Gen. Sec. BURHAN DAJANI. Publ. *Arab Economic Report* (Arabic and English).

Gulf Organization for Industrial Consulting: POB 5114, Doha, Qatar; tel. 831234; telex 4619; f. 1976 by seven Gulf Arab states to pool industrial expertise and encourage joint development of projects; undertakes feasibility studies, market diagnosis, assistance in policy-making, legal consultancies, project promotion and technical training. Sec.-Gen. Dr ABDULRAHMAN A. AL-JAAFARY. Publs *Arab Gulf Industry* (quarterly), *Bulletin* (monthly), *Gulf Industrial Focus* (every 2 months), *Annual Report*.

Inter-American Commercial Arbitration Commission: 1889 F St, NW, Room LL-3, Washington, DC 20006, USA; tel. (202) 458-3000; telex 64128; fax (202) 828-0157; f. 1934 to establish an inter-American system of arbitration for the settlement of commercial disputes by means of tribunals. Mems: national committees, commercial firms and individuals in 22 countries. Dir CHARLES R. NORBERG.

International Advertising Association Inc: 342 Madison Ave, Suite 2000, New York, NY 10017, USA; tel. (212) 557-1133; telex 237969; fax (212) 983-0455; f. 1938 to raise the general level of advertising and marketing efficiency throughout the world; to promote the concept of freer trade and facilitate the interchange of ideas, experience and information. Mems: 2,700. Pres. ROGER NEILL (UK); Exec. Dir RICHARD M. CORNER (USA). Publs *IAA Membership Directory and Annual Report*, *International Advertiser Magazine*.

International Association of Buying Groups: 5000 Cologne 1, Lindenstr. 20, Germany; tel. (0221) 219456; f. 1951 for research, documentation and compilation of statistics; holds congress every three years. Mems: 80 buying groups in 12 countries. Sec.-Gen. Dr GÜNTER OLESCH.

International Association of Chain Stores: 61 quai d'Orsay, 75007 Paris, France; tel. (1) 47-05-48-43; telex 206387; fax (1) 45-51-59-83; f. 1953; links general merchandise and food retail companies and their suppliers; organizes annual congress and symposia to exchange ideas on trends, techniques and practices, and to improve professional standards and consumer service. Mems: 500 companies in 32 countries. Chair. DON MARSH; CEO ETIENNE LAURENT. Publ. *CIES Communication* (2 a year).

International Association of Congress Centres (Association internationale des palais de Congrès—AIPC): c/o Muzejski prostor, Jezuitski trg 4, POB 19, 41000 Zagreb, Yugoslavia; tel. (041) 433-722; telex 22398; f. 1958 to unite conference centres fulfilling certain criteria, to study the administration and technical problems of international conferences, to promote a common commercial policy and co-ordinate all elements of conferences. Mems: 73 from 29 countries. Pres. MATTHIAS FUCHS; Sec.-Gen. RADOVAN VOLMUT (Yugoslavia). Publ. list of principal conferences of the world (3 a year).

International Association of Department Stores: 72 blvd Haussmann, 75008 Paris, France; tel. (1) 43-87-25-80; fax (1) 43-87-66-84; f. 1928 to conduct research, exchange information and statistics on management, organization and technical problems; centre of documentation. Mems: large-scale retail enterprises in Andorra, Belgium, Denmark, Finland, France, Germany, Italy, Netherlands, Norway, Spain, Sweden, Switzerland, United Kingdom; associate mem. in Japan. Pres. JOERGEN BASSE (Denmark); Gen. Sec. E. KALDEREN (Sweden). Publ. *Retail News Letter* (monthly).

International Association of Electrical Contractors: 5 rue Hamelin, 75116 Paris, France; tel. (1) 47-27-97-49; telex 620 993; fax (1) 47-55-00-47. Pres. HANS BARTOSCH; Gen. Sec. ROLAND AUBER.

International Association of Insurance and Reinsurance Intermediaries (Bureau International des Producteurs d'Assurances et de Réassurances—BIPAR): 40 ave Albert-Elisabeth, 1200 Brussels, Belgium; tel. (02) 735-60-48; fax (02) 732-14-18; f. 1937. Mems: 41 associations from 22 countries, representing approx. 250,000 brokers and agents. Pres. HENRI VAN DUYNEN; Dir HARALD KRAUSS. Publ. *EC Bulletin* (5 a year).

International Association of Scholarly Publishers: c/o Tønnes Bekker-Nielsen, Århus Universitetsforlag, Århus Universitet, 8000 Århus C, Denmark; tel. 86-19-70-33; f. 1972 for the exchange of information and experience on scholarly and academic publishing by universities and others; assists in the transfer of publishing skills to developing countries. Mems: 139 in 40 countries. Pres. TØNNES BEKKER-NIELSEN (Denmark); Sec.-Gen. PETER J. GIVLER (USA). Publs *IASP Newsletter* (every 2 months), *International Directory of Scholarly Publishers*.

International Association of Textile Dyers and Printers: Reedham House, 31 King St West, Manchester, M3 2PF, England; tel. (061) 832-9279; telex 666737; fax (061) 833-1740; f. 1967 to defend and promote the interests of members in international affairs and to provide a forum for discussion of matters of mutual interest. Mems: national trade associations representing dyers and printers in nine countries. Pres. JAN JONGBLOET (Belgium); Sec.-Gen. BARRY G. HAZEL (UK).

International Booksellers Federation—IBF: 6000 Frankfurt, Grosser Hirschgraben 17-21, Germany; tel. (069) 1306318; fax (069) 1306309; f. 1956 to promote the booktrade and the exchange of information and to protect the interests of booksellers when dealing with other international organizations; special committees deal with questions of postage, resale price maintenance, book market research, advertising, customs and tariffs, the problems of young booksellers, etc. Mems: 200 in 20 countries. Pres. HANS-JÜRGEN WITT; Sec.-Gen. JOCHEN GRÖNKE. Publs *IBF-bulletin* (2 a year), *Booksellers International*.

International Bureau for the Standardization of Man-Made Fibres (BISFA): 25 rue de Maubeuge, 75009 Paris, France; tel. (1) 42-81-97-62; telex 282591; fax (1) 42-81-97-63; f. 1928 to examine and establish rules for the standardization, classification and naming of various categories of man-made fibres. Mems: 56. Sec.-Gen. P. BARDON.

International Confederation for Printing and Allied Industries—INTERGRAF: 18 square Marie-Louise, bte 25, 1040 Brussels, Belgium; tel. (02) 230-86-46; telex 64393; f. 1983 (formerly EUROGRAF, f. 1975) to defend the common interests of the printing and allied interests in member countries. Mems: federations in 15 countries. Pres. RICO BÜCHLER; Sec.-Gen. GEOFFREY WILSON.

International Confederation of Art Dealers: 1 bis rue Clément Marot, 75008 Paris, France; f. 1936 to co-ordinate the work of associations of dealers in works of art and paintings and to contribute to artistic and economic expansion. Mems: associations in 14 countries. Pres. EMILE BOURGEY (France).

International Confederation of the Butchers' and Delicatessen Trade: Steinwiesstrasse 59, 8028 Zürich, Switzerland; tel. (01) 2527766; f. 1946 to safeguard common interests. Sec.-Gen. Dr H. GERBER.

International Co-operative Alliance—ICA: 15 route des Morillons, 1218 Grand-Saconnex, Geneva, Switzerland; tel. (022) 984121; telex 27935; f. 1895 for the pursuit of co-operative aims: regional offices in India, Tanzania and Côte d'Ivoire; Congress meets every four years; 13 auxiliary committees exist for the sharing of technical expertise by co-operative organizations in the following fields: agriculture, banking, fisheries, consumer affairs, wholesale distribution, housing, insurance, women's participation and industrial and artisanal co-operatives; annual budget about £500,000 obtained from subscriptions. Mems: 500m. individuals in 705,640 co-operative societies. Pres. LARS MARCUS (Sweden); Dir R. BEASLEY (USA). Publs *Review of International Co-operation* (quarterly).

International Council of Shopping Centres: 665 Fifth Ave, New York, NY 10022, USA; tel. (212) 421-8181; telex 128185; f. 1957 as a trade association for the shopping centre industry, to promote professional standards of performance in the development, construction, financing, leasing and management of shopping centres throughout the world; organizes training courses; gives awards for new centres. Exec. Vice-Pres. JOHN T. RIORDAN.

International Council of Societies of Industrial Design—ICSID: Kluuvikatu 1D, 00100 Helsinki, Finland; tel. (90) 626661; telex 124723; fax (90) 175890; f. 1957 to encourage the development of high standards in the practice of industrial design; to improve and expand the contribution of industrial design throughout the world. Mems: in 38 countries. Pres. ANTTI NURMESNIEMI (Finland); Sec.-Gen. KAARINA POHTO. Publs *ICSID News* (5 or 6 a year), *World Directory of Design Schools*.

International Council of Tanners: 192 High St, Lewes, East Sussex, BN7 2NP, England; tel. (0273) 472149; telex 878149; f. 1926 to study all questions relating to the leather industry and maintain contact with national associations. Mems: national tanners' organizations in 36 countries. Pres. JOHN KOPPANY (Argentina); Sec. GUY G. REAKS (UK).

International Exhibitions Bureau: 56 ave Victor Hugo, Paris 16e, France; tel. (1) 45-00-38-63; f. 1928, revised by Protocol 1972, for the authorization and registration of international exhibitions falling under the 1928 Convention. Mems: 43 states. Pres. Jacques Sol-Rolland; Sec.-Gen. Marie-Hélène Defrene.

International Federation for Household Maintenance Products: 49 sq. Marie-Louise, 1040 Brussels, Belgium; tel. (02) 238-97-11; telex 23167; f. 1967 to promote in all fields the manufacture and use of a wide range of cleaning products, polishes, bleaches, disinfectants and insecticides, to develop the exchange of statistical information and to study technical, scientific, economic and social problems of interest to its members. Mems: in 10 countries. Pres. R. Young; Sec. P. Costa (Belgium).

International Federation of Associations of Specialists in Occupational Safety and Industrial Hygiene: BP 567, 59308 Valenciennes Cedex, France; tel. 27-46-19-24; f. 1952 (as European Federation of Associations of Engineers and Heads of Industrial Safety Services); promotes the prevention of accidents at work and of occupational illnesses; provides information exchange, training and education programmes, and international conferences. Pres. Gilbert Bresson.

International Federation of Associations of Textile Chemists and Colourists—IFATCC: Hollenweg 8A, 4153 Reinach, Switzerland; f. 1930 for liaison on professional matters between members; and the furtherance of scientific and technical collaboration in the development of the textile finishing industry and the colouring of materials. Mems: in 13 countries. Pres. Dr W. Krucker (Switzerland); Sec. Dr Pierre Albrecht (Switzerland).

International Federation of Grocers' Associations—IFGA: Falkenplatz 1, 3001 Berne, Switzerland; tel. (031) 237646; fax (031) 237646; f. 1927; initiates special studies and works to further the interests of members having special regard to new conditions resulting from European integration and developments in consuming and distribution. Mems: 500,000. Sec.-Gen. Peter Schuetz (Switzerland).

International Federation of Pharmaceutical Manufacturers Associations—IFPMA: 67 rue St Jean, 1201 Geneva, Switzerland; tel. (022) 7326317; telex 27042; fax (022) 7386418; f. 1968 for the exchange of information and international co-operation in all questions of interest to the pharmaceutical industry, particularly in the field of health legislation, science and research; development of ethical principles and practices and co-operation with national and international organizations, governmental and non-governmental. Mems: the pharmaceutical manufacturers associations of the EEC, EFTA, Latin America, Australia, Canada, Hong Kong, India, Israel, Japan, Kenya, Republic of Korea, Malaysia, New Zealand, Pakistan, Philippines, Singapore, South Africa, Spain, Sri Lanka, Thailand, Turkey and USA. Pres. P. Joly; Exec. Vice-Pres. Dr Richard B. Arnold.

International Federation of the Phonographic Industry: 54 Regent St, London, W1R 5PJ, England; tel. (071) 434-3521; telex 919044; fax (071) 439-9166; f. 1933; association of the worldwide sound and music video recording industry, making representations to governments and international bodies and generally defending the interests of its members. Mems: 890 in 62 countries. Pres. Nesuhi Ertegun; Dir-Gen. I. D. Thomas.

International Fertilizer Industry Association: 28 rue Marbeuf, 75008 Paris, France; tel. (1) 42-25-27-07; telex 640481; fax (1) 42-25-24-08. Pres. W. Klassen; Sec.-Gen. L. M. Maene.

International Fragrance Association—IFRA: 8 rue Charles-Humbert, 1205 Geneva, Switzerland; tel. (022) 7213548; telex 428354; fax (022) 7811860; f. 1973 to collect and study scientific data on fragrance materials and to make recommendations on their safe use. Mems: national Associations in 14 countries. Pres. Horst F. W. Gerberding; Sec.-Gen. F. Grundschober.

International Fur Trade Federation: 20–21 Queenhithe, London, EC4V 3AA, England; tel. (071) 489-8159; telex 917513; f. 1949 to promote and organize joint action by fur trade organizations for promoting, developing and protecting trade in furskins and/or processing thereof. Mems: 32 organizations in 29 countries. Pres. J. E. Poser (USA); Sec. J. Bailey.

International Group of National Associations of Manufacturers of Agrochemical Products: 79A ave Albert Lancaster, 1180 Brussels, Belgium; tel. (02) 375-68-60; telex 62120; f. 1967 to encourage the rational use of chemicals in agriculture, the harmonization of national and international legislation, and the respect of industrial property rights; encourages research on chemical residues and toxicology. Mems: associations in 50 countries. Dir-Gen. Hans G. van Loeper.

International Organization for Motor Trades and Repairs: Kosterijland 15, 3981 AJ Bunnik, Netherlands; tel. (03405) 95301; telex 70381; fax (03405) 67835; f. 1947 to collect and disseminate information about all aspects of the trade; to hold meetings and congresses. Mems: 37 associations in 24 countries. Pres. J. P. Allais (France); Gen. Sec. J. A. Hoerzema (Netherlands). Publ. Newsletter.

International Organization of Consumers' Unions—IOCU: Emmastraat 9, 2595 EG The Hague, Netherlands; tel. (070) 347-63-31; telex 33561; fax (070) 383-49-76; f. 1960; links consumer groups worldwide through information networks and international seminars; supports new consumer groups and international consumers' interests at the international level. Mems: 170 national associations in 63 countries. Dir-Gen. Michel van Hulten. Publs IOCU Newsletter (10 a year), Consumer Currents (10 a year).

International Organization of Motor Manufacturers: 4 rue de Berri, 75008 Paris; tel. (1) 43-59-00-13; telex 290012; fax (1) 45-63-84-41; f. 1919 to co-ordinate and further the interests of the automobile industry, to promote the study of economic and other matters affecting automobile construction; to control automobile manufacturers' participation in international exhibitions in Europe. Full mems: manufacturers' associations of 15 European countries, Japan, China and the USA. Assoc. mems: three importers' associations. Corresponding mems: four automobile associations. Pres. R. Ravenel (France); Gen. Sec. J. M. Muller. Publ. *Yearbook of the World's Motor Industry*.

International Organization of the Flavour Industry—IOFI: 8 rue Charles-Humbert, 1205 Geneva, Switzerland; tel. (022) 7213548; telex 428354; fax (022) 7811860; f. 1969 to support and promote the flavour industry; active in the fields of safety evaluation and regulation of flavouring substances. Mems: national associations in 21 countries. Pres. P. van Berge; Sec.-Gen. F. Grundschober. Publs *Documentation Bulletin* (monthly), *Information Letters*, *Code of Practice*.

International Publishers' Association: 3 ave de Miremont, 1206 Geneva, Switzerland; tel. (022) 463018; telex 421883; fax (022) 475717; f. 1896 to defend the freedom of publishers, promote their interests and foster international co-operation; helps the international trade in books and music, works on international copyright, and translation rights. Mems: 54 professional book publishers' organizations in 46 countries and music publishers' associations in 20 countries. Pres. Andrew Neilly; Sec.-Gen. J. Alexis Koutchoumow.

International Rayon and Synthetic Fibres Committee: 29 rue de Courcelles, Paris 8e, France; tel. (1) 45-63-87-10; telex 650931; f. 1950 to improve the quality and use of man-made fibres and of products made from fibres. Mems: national associations and individual producers in 19 countries. Pres. M. de Rosen (France); Dir-Gen. Prof. J. L. Juvet.

International Shopfitting Organisation: Schmelzbergstr. 56, 8044 Zürich, Switzerland; tel. (01) 261-35-40; fax (01) 261-10-36; f. 1959 to promote friendship and interchange of ideas between individuals and firms concerned with the common interests of shopfitting. Mems: companies in 16 countries. Pres. K. Benschop; Sec. Petra Isenberg.

International Textile Manufacturers Federation—ITMF: Am Schanzengraben 29, Postfach, 8039 Zürich, Switzerland; tel. (01) 2017080; telex 817578; fax (01) 2017134; f. 1904, present title adopted 1978. Aims to protect and promote the interests of its members, to disseminate information, and encourage co-operation. Mems: national textile trade associations in 44 countries. Pres. Tom Bell (Canada); Dir Dr Herwig Strolz (Austria). Publs *Newsletter*, *State of Trade Report* (quarterly), statistics.

International Union of Marine Insurance: Aeschengraben 21, 4002 Basel, Switzerland; f. 1873 to collect and distribute information on marine insurance on a world-wide basis. Mems: 50 associations. Pres. A. W. Kamp; Gen. Sec. E. Burckhardt.

International Whaling Commission: The Red House, Station Rd, Histon, Cambridge, CB4 4NP, England; tel. (0223) 233971; fax (0223) 232876; f. 1946 under the International Convention for the Regulation of Whaling, for the conservation of the world whale stocks; aims to review the regulations covering the operations of whaling; to encourage research relating to whales and whaling, to collect and analyse statistical information and to study and disseminate information concerning methods of increasing whale stocks; a ban on commercial whaling was passed by the Commission in July 1982, to take effect three years subsequently (although, in some cases, a phased reduction of commercial operations was not completed until 1988). An assessment of the effects on whale stocks of this ban was being made in 1990, so that possible modifications could be considered in 1991. Mems: governments of 36 countries. Chair. S. Irberger (Sweden); Sec. Dr R. Gambell. Publ. *Annual Report*.

International Wool Textile Organisation: 165 Queen Victoria St, London, EC4 4DD, England; tel. (081) 788-8876; f. 1929 to link wool textile organizations in member-countries and represent their interests; holds annual International Wool Conference. Mems: in 28 countries. Pres. Jean-Marie Segard (France); Sec.-Gen. W. H. Lakin (UK).

International Wrought Copper Council: 6 Bathurst St, Sussex Sq., London, W2 2SD, England; tel. (071) 724-7465; telex 23556;

OTHER INTERNATIONAL ORGANIZATIONS

fax (071) 724-0308; f. 1953 to bind together and represent the copper fabricating industries in the member countries, and to represent the views of copper consumers to raw material producers; organizes specialist activities on technical work and the development of copper. Mems: 18 national groups representing non-ferrous metals industries in all West European countries, Australia and Japan. Chair. N. Brodersen; Sec. S. N. Payton.

Liaison Group of the European Mechanical, Electrical, Electronic and Metalworking Industries: 99 rue de Stassart, 1050 Brussels, Belgium; tel. (02) 511-34-84; telex 21078; fax (02) 512-99-70; f. 1954 to provide a permanent liaison between the mechanical, electrical and electronic engineering, and metalworking industries of member countries. Mems: 23 trade associations in 15 West European countries. Pres. Sir William Barlow (UK); Sec.-Gen. Trevor Gay.

Union of Industrial and Employers' Confederations of Europe—UNICE: 40 rue Joseph II, 1040 Brussels, Belgium; tel. (02) 237-65-11; telex 26013; fax (02) 231-14-45; aims to ensure that European Community policy-making takes account of the views of industry; committees and working groups work out joint positions in the various fields of interest to industry and submit them to the Community institutions concerned. The Council of Presidents (of member federations) lays down general policy; the Executive Committee (of Directors-General of member federations) is the managing body; and the Committee of Permanent Delegates, consisting of federation representatives in Brussels, ensures permanent liaison with members. Mems: 17 industrial and employers' federations from the EC member states, and 15 federations from non-Community countries. Pres. Carlos Ferrer; Sec.-Gen. Zygmunt Tyszkiewicz. Publ. *UNICE Information* (every 2 months).

Union of International Fairs: 35 bis, rue Jouffroy, 75017 Paris, France; tel. (1) 42-67-99-12; telex 644097; fax (1) 42-27-19-29; f. 1925 to increase co-operation between international fairs, safeguard their interests and extend their operations; holds annual congress and educational seminars. The Union has defined the conditions to be fulfilled to qualify as an international fair, and is concerned with the standards of the fairs. It studies improvements which could be made in the conditions of the fairs and organizes training seminars. Mems: 141 organizers, 65 general fairs and 344 specialized exhibitions. Pres. C. Y. De Vriese (Netherlands); Sec.-Gen. Gerda Marquardt (France).

World Council of Management—CIOS: c/o RKW, 6236 Eschborn, Düsseldorfstr. 40, POB 5867, Germany; tel. (06196) 495366; telex 4072755; fax (06196) 495304; f. 1926 to promote the understanding of the principles and the practice of the methods of modern management; to organize conferences, congresses and seminars on management; to exchange information on management techniques; to promote training programmes. Mems: national organizations in 45 countries. Pres. John Diebolu (USA); Sec. Herbert Müller (Germany). Publ. *Newsletter*.

World Federation of Advertisers: 54 rue des Colonies, Bte 13, 1000 Brussels; tel. (02) 219-06-98; telex 63801; fax (02) 219-54-94; f. 1953; promotes and studies advertising and its related problems. Mems: associations in 33 countries and 30 international companies. Pres. Jacques Glain; Dir-Gen. Paul P. de Win.

World Packaging Organisation: 42 ave de Versailles, 75016 Paris, France; tel. (1) 42-88-29-74; telex 648838; fax (1) 45-25-02-73; f. 1967 to provide a forum for the exchange of knowledge of packaging technology and, in general, to create conditions for the conservation, preservation and distribution of world food production; holds annual congress and competition. Mems: Asian, North American, Latin American and European packaging federations. Pres. G. K. Townshend (UK); Gen. Sec. Pierre J. Louis (France).

World Trade Centers Association: One World Trade Center, Suite 7701, New York, NY 10048, USA; tel. (212) 313-4600; telex 285472; fax (212) 488-0064; f. 1968 to promote trade through the establishment of world trade centres, including education facilities, information services and exhibition facilities; operates an electronic trading and communication system (World Trade Center Network). Mems: trade centres, chambers of commerce and other organizations in 53 countries. Pres. Guy F. Tozzoli; Chair. Tadayoshi Yamada. Publs *WTCA News* (monthly), *World Traders* (quarterly).

Transport

African Airlines Association: POB 20116, Nairobi, Kenya; tel. 502645; f. 1968 to give African air companies expert advice in technical, financial, juridical and market matters; to improve communications in Africa; to represent the mem. airlines; and to develop manpower resources. Mems: 35 national carriers. Pres. Abdullahi Bello (Nigeria).

Arab Air Carriers' Organization—AACO: POB 130468, Chouran, Beirut, Lebanon; tel. 861294; telex 22370; f. 1965 to co-ordinate and promote co-operation in the activities of Arab airline companies. Mems: 16 Arab air carriers. Pres. Muftah Eddlew (Libya); Sec.-Gen. Adli Dajani.

Arab Union of Railways: POB 6599, Aleppo, Syria; tel. 220302; telex 331009; f. 1979 to stimulate co-operation between railways in Arab countries, and to co-ordinate the interconnection of Arab railways with each other and with international railways; holds Symposium every two years. Mems: 16, comprising railways of Algeria, Iraq, Jordan, Lebanon, Morocco, Sudan, Syria, Tunisia; construction companies in Morocco, Tunisia and Syria; the Arab Union of Land Transport; and the Palestine Liberation Organization. Gen. Sec. Mourhaf Sabouni. Publs *Al Sikak Al Arabie* (Arab Railways, quarterly), *Statistics of Arab Railways* (annually), *Glossary of Railway Terms* (Arabic, English, French and German).

Association of European Airlines: 350 ave Louise, Bte 4, 1050 Brussels, Belgium; tel. (02) 640-31-75; telex 22918; fax (02) 648-40-17; f. 1954 to carry out research on political, commercial, economic and technical aspects of air transport; maintains statistical data bank. Mems: 21 airlines. Pres. Dr C. M. Kozlu; Sec.-Gen. Karl-Heinz Neumeister.

Baltic and International Maritime Council—BIMCO: Bagsværdvej 161, 2880 Bagsværd, Denmark; tel. 44-44-45-00; telex 19086; fax 44-44-44-50; f. 1905 to unite shipowners and other persons and organizations connected with the shipping industry. Mems: in 106 countries, representing nearly 50% of world merchant tonnage. Pres. Sir Ian Denholm (from April 1991); Sec.-Gen. Torben C. Skaanild.

Central Commission for the Navigation of the Rhine: Palais du Rhin, 67082 Strasbourg Cedex, France; tel. (88) 32-35-84; f. 1815 to ensure free movement of traffic and standard river facilities to ships of all nations; draws up navigational rules, standardizes customs regulations, arbitrates in disputes involving river traffic, approves plans for river maintenance work; there is an administrative centre for social security for boatmen, and a tripartite commission for labour conditions. Mems: Belgium, France, Germany, Netherlands, Switzerland, United Kingdom. Pres. C. Bauwens; Sec.-Gen. R. Doerflinger (France).

Central Office for International Carriage by Rail: Thunplatz, Gryphenhübeliweg 30, 3006 Berne, Switzerland; tel. (031) 431762; telex 912063; fax (031) 431164; f. 1893; maintains and publishes lists of lines on which international carriage is undertaken; circulates communications from the contracting States and railways to other States and railways; publishes information on behalf of international transport services; undertakes conciliation, gives an advisory opinion or assists in arbitration on disputes arising between railways; examines requests for the amendment of the Conventions concerning International Carriage by Rail, and convenes conferences. Mems: 35 states. Dir-Gen. C. Mossu (acting). Publ. *Bulletin des Transports Internationaux ferroviaires* (quarterly, in French and German).

Danube Commission: Benczúr utca 25, 1068 Budapest, Hungary; tel. 228-083; f. 1948 to supervise facilities for shipping on the Danube; holds annual sessions; approves projects for river maintenance, supervises a uniform system of traffic regulations on the whole navigable portion of the Danube and on river inspection. Mems: Austria, Bulgaria, Czechoslovakia, Hungary, Romania, Ukraine, USSR, Yugoslavia. Pres. S. Pop (Romania); Sec. R. Sova (Yugoslavia). Publs *Basic Regulations for Navigation on the Danube, Hydrological Yearbook, Statistical Yearbook*, proceedings of sessions.

European Civil Aviation Conference—ECAC: 3 bis Villa Emile-Bergerat, 92522 Neuilly-sur-Seine Cedex, France; tel. (1) 46-37-95-45; telex 610075; fax (1) 46-24-18-18; f. 1955 to review the development of European civil aviation with the object of promoting its co-ordination, better utilization and orderly development, and to consider any special problem that might arise in this field. Mems: 25 European states. Vice-Pres. C.-E. Calas; Sec. Edward Hudson.

European Conference of Ministers of Transport—ECMT: 19 rue Franqueville, 75775 Paris Cedex 16, France; tel. (1) 45 24 82 00; telex 611040; fax (1) 45-24-97-42; f. 1953 to achieve the maximum use and most rational development of European inland transport. Council of Ministers of Transport meets twice yearly; Committee of Deputy Ministers meets six times a year and is assisted by Subsidiary Bodies concerned with: General Transport Policy, Railways, Roads, Inland Waterways, Investment, Road and Traffic Signs and Signals, Urban Safety, Economic Research, and other matters. Mems: 19 European countries; Associate Mems: Australia, Canada, Japan, USA. Chair. S. Andersson (Sweden); Sec.-Gen. Dr J.-C. Terlouw.

European Organisation for the Safety of Air Navigation—EUROCONTROL: 72 rue de la Loi, 1040 Brussels, Belgium; tel. (02) 233-02-11; telex 21173; fax (02) 233-03-53; f. 1963 to strengthen co-operation among member states in matters of air navigation; representatives of contracting parties form the Permanent Com-

OTHER INTERNATIONAL ORGANIZATIONS — Transport

mission (governing body). The EUROCONTROL External Services comprise the Eurocontrol Experimental Centre, the EUROCONTROL Institute of Air Navigation Services, the Central Route Charges Office and the Upper Area Control Centre at Maastricht, Netherlands. Budget (1989) 147.5m. ECUs. Mems: Belgium, Cyprus, France, Germany, Greece, Ireland, Luxembourg, Malta, Netherlands, Portugal, Spain, Switzerland, Turkey, United Kingdom. Pres. Perm. Commission SÉAMUS BRENNAN (Ireland); Pres. Cttee of Management LOUIS PAILHAS (France); Dir-Gen. KEITH MACK (UK).

European Passenger Train Time-Table Conference: Direction générale des chemins de fer fédéraux suisses, Hochschulstrasse 6, 3030 Berne, Switzerland; tel. (031) 601111; telex 991121; f. 1923 to arrange international passenger connections by rail and water and to help obtain easing of customs and passport control at frontier stations. Mems: rail and steamship companies and administrations. Administered by the Directorate of the Swiss Federal Railways.

European Railway Wagon Pool—EUROP: SNCB, Département Transport, 85 rue de France, 1070 Brussels, Belgium; tel. (02) 525-41-30; telex 24607; fax (02) 525-21-38; f. 1953 for the common use of wagons put into the pool by member railways. Mems: nine national railway administrations. Managing railway: Belgian Railways. Pres. J. DEKEMPENEER.

Institute of Air Transport: 103 rue la Boétie, 75008 Paris, France; tel. (1) 43-59-38-68; telex 642584; fax (1) 43-59-47-37; f. 1945 to serve as an international centre of research on economic, technical and policy aspects of air transport, and on the economy and sociology of transport and tourism; acts as economic and technical consultant in carrying out research requested by members on specific subjects; maintains a data bank, a library and a consultation and advice service; organizes training courses on air transport economics. Mems: organizations involved in air transport, production and equipment, universities, banks, insurance companies, private individuals and government agencies in 79 different countries. Pres. HENRI SAUVAN; Dir-Gen. JACQUES PAVAUX; Sec.-Gen. JEAN-MARIE HERVÉ. Publs in French and English, *ITA Magazine* (every 2 months), *ITA Press* (2 a month), *ITA Studies and Reports* (quarterly).

International Air Transport Association—IATA: 33 route de l'Aéroport, CP 672, 1215 Geneva 15; tel. (022) 7992525; f. 1945 to promote safe, regular and economic air transport, to foster air commerce and to provide a means of international air transport collaboration. Fields of activity: finance (through IATA Clearing House for international accounts), technical problems, air traffic fares and documentation, international law on conditions of contract and carriage, documentation and information research and international co-operation. Exec. Cttee of 25 members, assisted by Financial, Technical and Traffic Cttees; Tariff Co-ordinating Conferences on fares and rates meet regularly; there are Traffic Service Offices in Montreal and Singapore; Regional Technical Offices for Africa in Nairobi and Dakar, Europe in Geneva, Middle East, North Atlantic/North America in London, South America/Caribbean in Rio de Janeiro and South East Asia/Pacific in Bangkok. Mems: 200 companies. Dir-Gen. GÜNTER ESER; Corporate Sec. H. LAROSE.

International Association for the Rhine Vessels Register—IVR: Vasteland 12E, 3011 BL Rotterdam (POB 23210, 3001 KE Rotterdam), Netherlands; tel. (010) 4116070; fax (010) 4129091; f. 1947 for the classification of Rhine ships, the organization and publication of a Rhine ships register and for the unification of general average rules, etc. Mems: shipowners and associations, insurers and associations, shipbuilding engineers, average adjusters and others interested in Rhine traffic. Gen. Sec. Ing. H. A. F. VAN DER WERF.

International Association of Ports and Harbors: Kotohira-Kaikan Bldg, 2-8 Toranomon 1-chome, Minato-ku, Tokyo 105, Japan; tel. (03) 591-4261; telex 02222516; fax (03) 580-0364; f. 1955 to increase the efficiency of ports and harbours through the dissemination of information relative to the fields of port organization, management, administration, operation, development and promotion; to encourage the growth of water-borne commerce; holds conference every two years. Mems: 340 in 80 states. Pres. J. H. MCJUNKIN (USA); Sec.-Gen. HIROSHI KUSAKA (Japan). Publs *Ports and Harbors* (10 a year), *Membership Directory* (annually).

International Automobile Federation: 8 place de la Concorde, 75008 Paris, France; tel. (1) 42-65-99-51; telex 290442; fax (1) 49-24-98-00; f. 1904 to develop international automobile sport and motor touring. Mems: 112 national automobile clubs or associations in 95 countries. Pres. JEAN-MARIE BALESTRE; Sec.-Gen. J. J. FREVILLE.

International Chamber of Shipping: 30/32 St Mary Axe, London, EC3A 8ET, England; tel. (071) 283-2922; telex 884008; fax (071) 626-8135; f. 1921 to co-ordinate the views of the international shipping industry on matters of common interest, in the policy-making, technical and legal fields of shipping operations. Mems: national associations representative of free-enterprise shipowners and operators in 34 countries, covering 50% of world merchant shipping. Sec.-Gen. J. C. S. HORROCKS.

International Civil Airports Association—ICAA: Bâtiment 226, Orly Sud 103, 94396 Orly Aérogare Cedex, France; tel. (1) 49-75-44-70; telex 261120; fax (1) 49-75-44-85; f. 1962 to develop relations and co-operation among civil airports throughout the world and promote the interests of air transport in general. Mems: 250 from 90 countries and territories. Pres. LIM HOCK SAN (Singapore); Dir-Gen. JACQUES BLOCK (France). Publs *ICAA INFO* (every 2 months), *ICAA News*.

International Container Bureau: 14 rue Jean Rey, 75015 Paris, France; tel. (1) 47-34-68-13; telex 270835; f. 1933 to group representatives of all means of transport and activities concerning containers, to promote combined door-to-door transport by the successive use of several means of transport; to examine and bring into effect administrative, technical and customs advances and to centralize data on behalf of its members. Mems: 800. Sec.-Gen. P. FOURNIER. Publs *Containers* (quarterly), *Container Bulletin*.

International Federation of Freight Forwarders' Associations: Baumackerstr. 24, P.O. Box, 8050 Zürich, Switzerland; tel. (01) 3116511; telex 823579; fax (01) 3119044; f. 1926 to protect and represent its members at international level. Mems: 68 organizations and 1,700 associate members in 120 countries. Pres. C. STJERNLÖF; Sec.-Gen. T. ALBARELLI. Publ. *FIATA News* (quarterly).

International Rail Transport Committee—CIT: Direction générale des chemins de fer fédéraux suisses, Division juridique, 43 Mittelstrasse, 3030 Berne, Switzerland; tel. (031) 602565; telex 991212; fax (031) 604007; f. 1902 for the development of international law relating to railway transport on the basis of the Convention concerning International Carriage by Rail (COTIF) and its Appendices (CIV, CIM), and for the adoption of standard rules on other questions relating to international transport law. Mems: 300 transport undertakings in 34 countries. Pres. M. EISENRING (Switzerland); Sec. M. BERTHERIN (Switzerland).

International Railway Congress Association: 36 rue Ravenstein, B7, 1000 Brussels, Belgium; tel. (02) 513-92-80; telex 25035; fax (02) 512-93-84; f. 1885 to facilitate the progress and development of railways by holding periodical congresses and by issuing publications. Mems: governments, railway administrations and national or international organizations. Pres. E. SCHOUPPE; Sec.-Gen. A. MARTENS. Publs *Rail International* (monthly in French, German, Russian and English).

International Road Federation—IRF: 525 School St, SW, Washington, DC 20024, USA; tel. (202) 554-2106; telex 44036; fax (202) 479-0828; f. 1948 to encourage the development and improvement of highways and highway transportation; organizes World Highway Conferences. Mems: 68 national road associations and 500 individual firms and industrial associations. *Geneva:* Chair. F. CARPI DE RESMINI; Dir-Gen. M. W. WESTERHUIS; *Washington:* Chair. HENRY MICHEL; Dir-Gen. RICHARD B. ROBERTSON. Publs *World Road Statistics* (annually, Geneva), *Routes du Monde* (8 a year), *World Highways* (6 a year), *IRF Directory of World Road Administrators* (Geneva/Washington).

International Road Safety: 75 rue de Mamer, 8081 Luxembourg-Bertrange; tel. 31-83-41; telex 2338; fax 31-14-60; f. 1959 for exchange of ideas and material on road safety; organizes international action; assists non-member countries. Mems: 58 national organizations. Pres. L. NILLES.

International Road Transport Union—IRU: Centre International, 3 rue de Varembé, BP 44, 1202 Geneva, Switzerland; tel. (022) 7341330; telex 27107; fax (022) 7330660; f. 1948 to study all problems of road transport, to promote unification and simplification of regulations relating to road transport, and to develop the use of road transport for passengers and goods. Mems: 120 national federations for road transport and interested groups, in 52 countries. Sec.-Gen. A.-J. WESTERINK.

International Shipping Federation Ltd: 30/32 St Mary Axe, London, EC3A 8ET, England; tel. (071) 283-2922; telex 884008; fax (071) 283-9138; f. 1909 to consider all personnel questions affecting the interests of shipowners; responsible for Shipowners' Group at conferences of the International Labour Organisation. Mems: national shipowners' organizations in 30 countries. Pres. A. G. HATCHETT (UK); Dir J. C. S. HORROCKS; Sec. D. A. DEARSLEY.

International Union for Inland Navigation: 7 quai du Général Koenig, 67085 Strasbourg Cedex, France; tel. 88-36-28-44; f. 1952 to promote the interests of inland waterways carriers. Mems: national waterways organizations of Belgium, France, Germany, Italy, Luxembourg, Netherlands, Switzerland, United Kingdom. Pres. C. MEISTERMANN (France); Sec. M. RUSCHER. Publs annual and occasional reports.

International Union of Public Transport: 19 ave de l'Uruguay, 1050 Brussels, Belgium; tel. (02) 673-61-00; telex 63916; fax (02)

660-10-72; f. 1885 to study all problems connected with the urban and regional public passenger transport industry. Mems: 447 public transport systems in 64 countries, 269 contractors and services and 991 personal members. Pres. J. M. OSSEWAARDE (Netherlands); Sec.-Gen. PIERRE LACONTE. Publs *Review* (quarterly), *Biblio-Index* (monthly), Compendium of Statistics, congress reports, bibliographies.

International Union of Railways: 16 rue Jean-Rey, 75015 Paris, France; tel. (1) 42-73-01-20; telex 270835; fax (1) 42-73-01-40; f. 1922 for the harmonization of railway operations; compiles information concerning economic, management and technical aspects of railways. Mems: 84 railways. Pres. P. LANGAGER; Sec.-Gen. M. WALRAVE. Publs *Rail International*, jointly with the International Railway Congress Association (IRCA) (monthly, in English, French and German), *International Railway Statistics* (annually, in English, French and German), *Annual Report*.

Northern Shipowners' Defence Club (Nordisk Skibsrederforening): Kristinelundv. 22, POB 3033 El., 0207 Oslo 2, Norway; tel. (2) 55-47-20; telex 76825; fax (2) 43-00-35; f. 1889 to assist members in disputes over contracts, taking the necessary legal steps on behalf of members and bearing the cost of such claims. Members are mainly Finnish, Swedish and Norwegian and some non-Scandinavian shipowners, representing about 1,700 ships and drilling rigs with gross tonnage of about 46 million. Man. Dir NICHOLAS HAMBRO; Chair. FRIDTJOF LORENTZEN. Publ. *A Law Report of Scandinavian Maritime Cases* (annually).

Organisation for the Collaboration of Railways: Hoża 63–67, 00681 Warsaw, Poland; tel. 21 61 54; f. 1956 for the development of international traffic and technical and scientific co-operation in the sphere of railway and road traffic. Conference of Ministers of member countries meets annually. Mems: ministries of transport of the People's Republic of China, Cuba, Democratic People's Republic of Korea, Mongolia, Viet-Nam, Albania, Bulgaria, Czechoslovakia, Hungary, Poland, Romania, USSR. Chair. Dr RYSZARD STAWROWSKI (Poland). Publ. *O.S.SH.D. Journal* (every 2 months; in Chinese, German and Russian).

Orient Airlines Association: POB 161 MCPO, Metro Manila 1299, Philippines; premises at 5/F Standard Bldg, 151 Paseo de Roxas, Makati, Metro Manila 1200; tel. 8190151; fax 8103518; f. 1966; member carriers exchange information and plan the development of the industry within the region by means of commercial, technical and management information committees. Mems: Air New Zealand, Air Niugini, All Nippon Airways, Cathay Pacific Airways Ltd, China Airlines, Garuda Indonesia, Japan Airlines, Korean Air, Malaysia Airlines, Philippine Airlines, Qantas Airways Ltd, Singapore Airlines, Royal Brunei Airlines and Thai Airways International. Sec.-Gen. IBRAHIM MOHD TAIB. Publ. *Annual Report*.

Pan American Railway Congress Association (Asociación del Congreso Panamericano de Ferrocarriles): Av. 9 de Julio 1925, 13°, 1332 Buenos Aires, Argentina; tel. 38 4625; telex 22507; fax 814-1823; f. 1907; present title adopted 1941; aims to promote the development and progress of railways in the American continent; holds Congresses every three years. Mems: government representatives, railway enterprises and individuals in 21 countries. Pres. JUAN CARLOS DE MARCHI (Argentina); Gen. Sec. CAYETANO MARLETTA RAINIERI (Argentina). Publ. *Technical Bulletin* (every 2 months).

Union of European Railway Industries: 12 rue Bixio, 75007 Paris, France; tel. (1) 47-05-36-62; telex 270105; fax (1) 47-05-29-17; f. 1975 as a union of associations which represent companies concerned in the manufacture of railway equipment in Europe, in order to represent their collective interests towards all European and international organizations concerned. Chair. M. O. J. BRONCHART; Sec.-Gen. R. DE PLANTA.

Union of European Railway Road Services: Direction générale de la Société Nationale des Chemins de Fer Français (SNCF), 88 rue Saint-Lazare, 75436 Paris, France; f. 1950/1951; runs the EUROPABUS international railway road services, an international network of scheduled coach services covering 100,000 km. Mems: railway administrations in Austria, Belgium, Denmark, France, Germany, Greece, Hungary, Italy, Luxembourg, Netherlands, Norway, Portugal, Spain, Sweden, Switzerland, United Kingdom. Pres. LOUIS LACOSTE (France); Sec.-Gen. (vacant).

World Airlines Clubs Association: c/o IATA, Suite 3050, 2000 Peel St, Montreal, Quebec, Canada H3A 2R4; f. 1966; holds a General Assembly annually, regional meetings, international events and sports tournaments. Mems: 98 clubs in 42 countries. Pres. JULIO SEIZ; Man. JOSEPH LEDWOS. Publs *WACA World*, *WACA Contact*, *WACA World News*, annual report.

Youth and Students

Asian Students' Association: 511 Nathan Rd, 1/F, Kowloon, Hong Kong; tel. 880515; telex 52988; f. 1969 to help in the solution of local and regional problems; to assist in promotion of an Asian identity; to promote programmes of common benefit to member organizations; since 1972 the organization has opposed all forms of colonialism or foreign intervention in Asia; activities: Conference, Seminars, Workshops. There are Student Commissions for Economics, Education, Students' Rights, Women's Affairs, and a Nuclear-Free and Independent Pacific. Mems: 14 national or regional student unions, 12 associate co-operating mems. Co-Secs. EMMANUEL CALONZO, BOONTHAN T. VERAWONGSE. Publ. *Asian Student News*.

Council of European National Youth Committees—CENYC: 8 ave des Courses, 1050 Brussels, Belgium; tel. (02) 648-91-01; fax (02) 648-96-40; f. 1963 to further the consciousness of European youth and to represent the European National Co-ordinating Committees of youth work vis-à-vis European institutions. Activities include research on youth problems in Europe; projects, seminars, study groups, study tours; the Council provides a forum for the exchange of information, experiences and ideas between members, and represents European youth organizations in relations with other regions; furthers contact between young people in eastern and western Europe. Mems: national committees in 17 countries. Sec.-Gen. RACHEL KYTE (UK). Publ. *CENYC Contact* (quarterly).

Council on International Educational Exchange: 205 East 42nd St, New York, NY 10017, USA; tel. (212) 661-1414; telex 423227; fax (212) 972-3231; f. 1947; issues International Student Identity Card entitling holders to discounts and basic insurance, arranges passage on intra-European student flights and trans-Atlantic transport; arranges overseas work programmes for students; co-ordinates summer programmes in the USA for foreign students and teachers; sponsors conferences on educational exchange; publications list overseas study, work and voluntary service programmes for high school and college students and sources of information on student travel abroad. Mems: 208 colleges, universities and international educational organizations. Exec. Dir JACK EGLE. Publs include *Work, Study, Travel Abroad: The Whole World Handbook*, *Campus Update* (monthly), *Volunteer!*

International Association for the Exchange of Students for Technical Experience—IAESTE: POB 3101, 10210 Athens, Greece; tel. (01) 3613930; fax (01) 3626792; f. 1948. Mems: 52 national committees. Gen. Sec. Prof. BERNARDO J. HEROLD. Publ. *Annual Report*.

International Association of Dental Students: 64 Wimpole St, London, W1M 8AL, England; f. 1951 to represent dental students and their opinions internationally, to promote dental student exchanges and international congresses. Mems: 20,000 students in 19 countries (and 15,000 corresponding mems). Pres. S. SMITH (UK); Sec.-Gen. JILL ADAM (UK). Publ. *IADS Newsletter* (3 a year).

International Association of Students in Economics and Management (AIESEC International): 40 rue Washington, Box 10, 1050 Brussels, Belgium; tel. (02) 646-24-20; telex 65080; fax (02) 646-37-64; f. 1948 to contribute to the development of member countries through international education programmes, e.g. trainee exchanges, seminars, conferences and cultural programmes. Mems: 50,000 from 681 universities in 70 countries. Pres. LENNART BJURSTRÖM. Publs *Annual Report*, *AIESEC Link*, *Corporate Bulletin*.

International Federation of Medical Students Associations: 1090 Vienna, Liechtensteinstr. 13, Austria; tel. (022) 31-55-66; telex 116706; f. 1951 to study and promote the professional interests of medical students throughout the world; to improve medical education, and arrange international exchanges and projects in primary health care. Mems: national associations in 65 countries, corresponding mems in 34 countries. Sec.-Gen. KLEOPATRA ORMOS. Publ. *Intermedica*.

International Pharmaceutical Students' Federation: Alexanderstraat 11, 2514 JL The Hague, Netherlands; tel. (070) 63-19-25; f. 1949 to study and promote the interests of pharmaceutical students and to encourage international co-operation. Mems: 27 national organizations and 17 local associations. Pres. RUI DOS SANTOS IVO; Sec.-Gen. JO W. JAMES. Publ. *IPSF News Bulletin* (3 a year).

International Union of Students: POB 58, 17 November St, 110 01 Prague 01, Czechoslovakia; tel. 2312812; telex 122858; fax 2316100; f. 1946 to defend the rights and interests of students and strive for peace, disarmament, the eradication of illiteracy and of all forms of discrimination; operates research centre and student travel bureau; activities include conferences, meetings, solidarity campaigns, relief projects, award of 30–40 scholarships annually, travel and exchange, sports events, cultural projects. Mems: 109 organizations from 105 countries. Pres. JOSEF SKALA; Gen. Sec. GIORGOS MICHAELIDES (Cyprus). Publs *World Student News* (monthly), *IUS Newsletter*, *Student Life* (monthly), *DE—Democratization of Education* (quarterly).

International Young Christian Workers: 11 rue Plantin, 1070 Brussels, Belgium; tel. (02) 521-69-83; f. 1945, on the inspiration of

OTHER INTERNATIONAL ORGANIZATIONS — Youth and Students

the Priest-Cardinal Joseph Cardijn; aims to educate young workers to take on present and future responsibilities in their commitment to the working class, and to confront all the situations which prevent them from fulfilling themselves. Pres. FÉLIX OLLARVES SÁNCHEZ (Venezuela); Sec.-Gen. GLYNN CLOETE (South Africa). Publs *International INFO* (3 a year), *IYCW Bulletin* (quarterly).

International Youth and Student Movement for the United Nations—ISMUN: c/o Palais des Nations, 1211 Geneva 10, Switzerland; tel. (022) 330861; f. 1948 by the World Federation of United Nations Associations, independent since 1949; an international non-governmental organization of students and young people dedicated especially to supporting the principles embodied in the United Nations Charter and Universal Declaration of Human Rights; encourages constructive action in building economic, social and cultural equality and in working for national independence, social justice and human rights on a worldwide scale; regional offices in Austria, France, Ghana, Panama and the USA. Mems: associations in 53 countries. Sec.-Gen. JUAN CARLOS GIACOSA. Publs *ISMUN Newsletter* (monthly).

International Youth Hostel Federation: 9 Guessens Rd, Welwyn Garden City, Herts., AL8 6QW, England; tel. (0707) 324170; telex 298784; fax (0707) 323980; f. 1932; facilitates international travel by members of the various youth hostel associations and advises and helps in the formation of youth hostel associations in all countries where no such organizations exist; records over 36m. overnight stays annually in 5,300 youth hostels. Mems: 60 national associations with 3.7m. individual members; 10 associated national organizations. Pres. JOHN PARFITT (UK); Sec.-Gen. RAWDON LAU (Hong Kong). Publs *Annual Report, Guidebook on World Hostels* (annually), *Manual, Monthly News Bulletin, Phrase Book*.

Junior Chamber International (JCI), Inc.: 400 University Drive (POB 140-577), Coral Gables, Fla 33134-0577, USA; tel. (305) 446-7608; telex 441084; fax (305) 442-0041; f. 1944 to encourage and advance international understanding and goodwill. Junior Chamber organizations throughout the world provide young people with opportunities for leadership training, promoting goodwill through international fellowship, solving civic problems by arousing civic consciousness and discussing social, economic and cultural questions. Mems: over 400,000 in 90 countries. Pres. E. JORGE SUNCAR M.; Sec.-Gen. W. DANIEL LAMEY. Publ. *JCI News* (quarterly, in English).

Latin American Confederation of Young Men's Christian Associations (Confederación Latinoamericana de Asociaciones Cristianas de Jóvenes): Culpina 272, 1406 Buenos Aires, Argentina; tel. and fax 613-3747; telex 17125; f. 1914 to encourage the moral, spiritual, intellectual, social and physical development of young men; to strengthen the work of the Associations and to sponsor the establishment of new Associations. Mems: affiliated YMCAs in 17 countries, with over 500,000 individuals. Pres. JORGE E. RODRÍGUEZ (Costa Rica); Gen. Sec. NORBERTO D. RODRÍGUEZ (Argentina). Publs *Articulos Técnicos, Revista Trimestral, Informes Internacionales*.

Pan-African Youth Movement (Mouvement pan-africain de la jeunesse): 19 rue Debbih Chérif, BP 72, Plateau Saulière, Algiers, Algeria; tel. 57-19-78; telex 61244; f. 1962; promotes political independence and the economic, social and cultural development of Africa; serves as the voice of African youth in regional and international forums. Mems: over 40 organizations. Sec.-Gen. HAMADOUN IBRAHIM ISSEBERE. Publ. *MPJ News* (quarterly).

World Alliance of Young Men's Christian Associations: 37 quai Wilson, 1201 Geneva; tel. (022) 7323100; telex 412332; fax (022) 7384015; f. 1855 to unite the National Alliances of Young Men's Christian Associations throughout the world. Mems: national alliances and related associations in 100 countries. Pres. ALEJANDRO VASSILAQUI; Sec.-Gen. LEE SOO-MIN. Publ. *World Communique* (quarterly).

World Assembly of Youth: Ved Bellahøj 4, 2700 Brønshøj, Copenhagen, Denmark; tel. 31-60-77-70; telex 21465; fax 31-60-57-97; f. 1949 as co-ordinating body for youth councils and organizations; organizes conferences, training courses and practical development projects. Pres. OLE L. SIMONSEN; Sec.-Gen. SHIV KHARE. Publs *WAY Information, Youth Press Service, Youth Roundup, Youth & AIDS Update* (all every 2 months), *WAY Forum*.

World Association of Girl Guides and Girl Scouts: Olave Centre, 12C Lyndhurst Rd, London, NW3 5PQ, England; tel. (071) 794-1181; fax (071) 431-3764; f. 1928 to promote unity of purpose and common understanding in the fundamental principles of the Girl Guide and Girl Scout Movement throughout the world and to encourage friendship amongst girls of all nations within frontiers and beyond; World Conference meets every three years. Mems: about 8m. individuals in 118 national organizations. Chair. World Cttee BARBARA HAYES; Dir World Bureau JAN HOLT; Publs *Triennial Report, Trefoil Round the World, Newsletter, Our World News*.

World Council of Service Clubs: 8 Whitney St, Blenheim 7301, New Zealand; tel. (057) 87159; fax (057) 88968; f. 1946 to provide a means of exchange of information and news for furthering international understanding and co-operation, to facilitate the extension of service clubs, and to create in young people a sense of civic responsibility. Mems: 4,000 clubs (about 100,000 individuals) in 76 countries. Gen. Sec. MARK PETERS (New Zealand).

World Federation of Democratic Youth—WFDY: POB 147, 1389 Budapest, Hungary; tel. 1154-095; telex 22-7197; fax 1352-746; f. 1945 to strive for peace and disarmament and joint action by democratic and progressive youth movements in support of national independence, democracy, social progress and youth rights; to support liberation struggles in Asia, Africa and Latin America; and to work for a new and more just international economic order. Mems: 270 organizations in 115 countries. Pres. ALI MAWLA (Lebanon); Gen. Sec. GYÖRGY SZABÓ (Hungary). Publs *WFDY News* (fortnightly, in English, French and Spanish), *World Youth* (monthly, in English, French and Spanish).

World Organization of the Scout Movement: Case Postale 241, 1211 Geneva 4, Switzerland; tel. (022) 204233; telex 428139; f. 1922 to promote unity and understanding of scouting throughout the world; to develop good citizenship among young people by forming their characters for service, co-operation and leadership; to provide aid and advice to members and potential member associations. The World Scout Bureau (Geneva) has regional offices in Costa Rica, Egypt, Kenya, the Philippines and Switzerland. Mems: over 16m. in 160 countries and territories. Sec.-Gen. Dr JACQUES MOREILLON (Switzerland). Publs *World Scouting News* (monthly), *Triennial Report*.

World Union of Jewish Students: POB 7914, 91077 Jerusalem, Israel; tel. (02) 639314; telex 25615; fax (02) 637605; f. 1924; organization for national student bodies concerned with educational and political matters, where possible in co-operation with non-Jewish student organizations, UNESCO, etc.; divided into six regions; organizes Congress every three years. Mems: 35 national unions representing over 700,000 students. Chair. YOSEF I. ABRAMOWITZ; Exec. Dir DANIEL YOSSEF (UK). Publs *Shofar, WUJS Report*.

World Young Women's Christian Association—World YWCA: 37 quai Wilson, 1201 Geneva, Switzerland; tel. (022) 7323100; f. 1894 for the linking together of national YWCAs in 88 countries for their mutual help and development and the initiation of work in countries where the Association does not yet exist; works for international understanding, for improved social and economic conditions and for basic human rights for all people. Pres. JEWEL GRAHAM; Gen. Sec. ELAINE H. STEEL. Publs *Annual Report, Programme of International Co-operation, Programme Material, Common Concern*.

Youth for Development and Co-operation—YDC: Leliegracht 21, 1016 GR Amsterdam, Netherlands; tel. (020) 261993; works for a new international order fulfilling the conditions for responsible use and fair distribution of the world's resources, full realization of human rights, and decentralization of decision-making; seminars, conferences and campaigns on issues related to the development of the Third World, and on important problems dealt with by the UN and specialized agencies (food, population, debt, environment, etc.). Mems: 37 organizations. Chair. J. R. MOLINA. Publs *FLASH* (every 2 months), *Progress Report* (bi-monthly), *LLDCs—Campaign Newsletter* (quarterly).

PART TWO
Afghanistan–Jordan

AFGHANISTAN

Introductory Survey

Location, Climate, Language, Religion, Flag, Capital

The Republic of Afghanistan is a land-locked country in south-western Asia. Its neighbours are the USSR to the north, Iran to the west, the People's Republic of China to the north-east and Pakistan to the east and south. The climate varies sharply between the highlands and lowlands; the temperature in the south-west in summer reaches 48.8°C (120°F), but in the winter, in the Hindu Kush mountains of the north-east, it falls to −26°C (−15°F). Of the many languages spoken in Afghanistan, the principal two are Pashtu and Dari (a dialect of Persian). The majority of Afghans are Muslims of the Sunni sect; there are also minority groups of Hindus, Sikhs and Jews. The national flag has three equal horizontal stripes, of red, black and green, with a superimposed emblem of an open book under a candle, surrounded by stylized heads of grain. The capital is Kabul.

Recent History

The last King of Afghanistan, Muhammad Zahir Shah, reigned from 1933 to 1973. His country was neutral during both World Wars and became a staunch advocate of non-alignment. In 1953 the King's cousin, Lt-Gen. Sardar Mohammad Daud Khan, became Prime Minister and, securing aid from the USSR, initiated a series of economic plans for the modernization of the country. In 1963 Gen. Daud resigned and Dr Mohammad Yusuf became the first Prime Minister not of royal birth. He introduced a new democratic constitution which combined western ideas with Islamic religious and political beliefs, but the King never allowed political parties to operate. Afghanistan made little progress under the succeeding Prime Ministers.

In July 1973, while King Zahir was in Italy, the monarchy was overthrown by a coup, in which the main figure was the former Prime Minister, Gen. Daud. The 1964 Constitution was abolished and Afghanistan was declared a republic. Daud renounced his royal titles and took office as Head of State, Prime Minister and Minister of Foreign Affairs and Defence.

A Loya Jirgah (Supreme National Tribal Assembly), appointed from among notable elders by provincial governors, was convened in January 1977 and adopted a new constitution, providing for presidential government and a one-party state. Daud was elected to continue as President for six years and the Assembly was then dissolved. In March 1977 President Daud formed a new civilian government, nominally ending military rule. However, during 1977 there was growing discontent with Daud, especially within the armed forces, and in April 1978 a coup, known (from the month) as the 'Saur Revolution', ousted the President, who was killed with several members of his family.

Nur Mohammad Taraki, imprisoned leader of the formerly banned People's Democratic Party of Afghanistan (PDPA), was released and installed as President of the Revolutionary Council and Prime Minister. The country was renamed the Democratic Republic of Afghanistan, the year-old Constitution was abolished and no political parties other than the communist PDPA were allowed to function. Afghanistan's already close relations with the USSR were further strengthened. However, opposition to the new regime led to armed insurrection, particularly by fiercely traditionalist Muslim rebel tribesmen (known, collectively, as the Mujaheddin), in almost all provinces, and the flight of thousands of refugees to Pakistan and Iran. In spite of purges of the army and civil service, Taraki's position became increasingly insecure, and in September 1979 he was ousted by Hafizullah Amin, who had been Deputy Prime Minister and Minister of Foreign Affairs since March. Amin's imposition of rigorous communist policies was unsuccessful and unpopular. In December 1979 he was removed and killed in a coup that was supported by the entry into Afghanistan of about 80,000 combat troops from the USSR. This incursion by Soviet armed forces into a traditionally non-aligned neighbouring country aroused world-wide condemnation. Babrak Karmal, a former Deputy Prime Minister under Taraki, was installed as the new Head of State, having been flown into Kabul by a Soviet aircraft from virtual exile in Eastern Europe.

Riots, strikes and inter-factional strife and purges continued into 1980 and 1981. President Karmal centralized his authority by reorganizing government departments within the Prime Minister's Office in July 1980. Sultan Ali Keshtmand, hitherto a Deputy Prime Minister, replaced Karmal as Prime Minister in June 1981. In the hope of strengthening the position of Karmal's Parcham ('Flag') faction of the PDPA over the Khalq ('Masses') faction of the party, the Revolutionary Council and the Politburo were enlarged. In the same month the regime launched the long-awaited National Fatherland Front (NFF), incorporating the PDPA and other organizations, with the aim of promoting national unity. Neither measure appeared to be achieving its aim, so the Council of Ministers was reshuffled again in August and September 1982, further strengthening Karmal's Parcham faction. At its 12th plenum in July 1983, the PDPA Central Committee elected 10 new full members and 16 new alternate members, nearly all of them Parcham supporters. However, the PDPA regime continued to fail to win widespread popular support. As a result, the Government attempted to broaden the base of its support: in April 1985 it summoned a Loya Jirgah, comprising indirectly-elected tribal elders, who ratified a new constitution for Afghanistan; a non-PDPA member was appointed chairman of the NFF in May 1985; elections were held between August 1985 and March/April 1986 for new local government organs (it was claimed that 60% of those elected were non-party members), and several non-party members were appointed to high-ranking government posts between December 1985 and February 1986.

In May 1986, however, Dr Najibullah Ahmadzai (the former head of the state security service, KHAD) succeeded Karmal as General Secretary of the PDPA. Karmal was allowed to retain the lesser post of President of the Revolutionary Council. In the same month Dr Najibullah (like Karmal, a member of the Parcham faction) announced the formation of a collective leadership comprising himself, Karmal and Prime Minister Keshtmand. In November 1986, however, Karmal was relieved of all party and government posts. Muhammad Chamkani, formerly First Vice-President (and a non-PDPA member), became Acting President of the Revolutionary Council, pending the introduction of a new constitution and the establishment of a permanent legislature.

In December 1986 an extraordinary plenum of the PDPA Central Committee approved a policy of national reconciliation, which involved a unilateral cease-fire for six months from 15 January 1987, negotiations with opposition groups, and the proposed formation of a coalition government of national unity. On 3 January 1987 a Supreme Extraordinary Commission for National Reconciliation, led by Abd ar-Rahim Hatif (the Chairman of the National Committee of the NFF), was formed to conduct the negotiations. The NFF was renamed the National Front (NF), and became a separate organization from the PDPA. The new policy of reconciliation won some support from former opponents, but the seven-party opposition alliance (Ittehad-i-Islami Afghan Mujaheddin, Islamic Unity of Afghan Mujaheddin—IUAM) refused to observe the cease-fire or to participate in negotiations, while continuing to demand a complete and unconditional Soviet withdrawal.

In July 1987, as part of the process of national reconciliation, several important developments occurred: a law permitting the formation of other political parties (according to certain provisions) was introduced; a six-month extension of the cease-fire was announced; Dr Najibullah announced that the PDPA would be prepared to share power with representatives of opposition groups in the event of the formation of a coalition government of national unity; and the draft of a new constitution was approved by the Presidium of the Revolutionary Council. The main innovations to be incorporated in this draft constitution were: the formation of a multi-party political system, under the auspices of the NF; the formation of a bicameral legislature, called the Meli Shura (National Assembly), which was composed of a Sena (Senate) and a Wolasi Jirgah (House of Representatives); the granting of a permanent constitutional status to the PDPA; the bestowal of unlimited power on the

President, who was to hold office for seven years; and the change in the name of the country from the Democratic Republic to the Republic of Afghanistan. A Loya Jirgah ratified the new Constitution in November, and a third six-month extension of the cease-fire was announced.

A further round of local elections throughout the country began in August 1987. A considerable number of those elected were reported to be non-PDPA members. On 30 September Dr Najibullah was unanimously elected as President of the Revolutionary Council, and Haji Muhammad Chamkani resumed his former post as First Vice-President. In order to strengthen his position, Dr Najibullah ousted all the remaining supporters of the former President, Babrak Karmal, from the Central Committee and Politburo of the PDPA in October, a few days before opening the second nation-wide PDPA conference in Kabul. In November a Loya Jirgah unanimously elected Dr Najibullah as President of the State.

In April 1988 elections were held to both houses of the new National Assembly, which replaced the Revolutionary Council. Although the elections were boycotted by the Mujaheddin, the Government left vacant 50 of the 234 seats in the House of Representatives, and a small number of seats in the Senate, in the hope that the guerrillas would abandon their armed struggle and present their own representatives to participate in the new administration. The PDPA itself won only 46 seats in the House of Representatives, but was guaranteed support from the NF, which gained 45, and from the various newly-recognized left-wing parties, which won a total of 24 seats. In May Dr Muhammad Hasan Sharq (a non-PDPA member and a Deputy Prime Minister since June 1987) replaced Sultan Ali Keshtmand as Prime Minister, and in June a new Council of Ministers was appointed.

On 18 February 1989, following the completion of the withdrawal of Soviet troops from Afghanistan (see below), Najibullah implemented a government reshuffle, involving the replacement of non-communist ministers with loyal PDPA members. On the same day, the Prime Minister, Dr Sharq (who had been one of the main promoters of the policy of national reconciliation), resigned from his post and was replaced by the former Prime Minister, Sultan Ali Keshtmand. Following the declaration of a state of emergency by Najibullah (citing his allegations of repeated violations of the Geneva accords by Pakistan and the USA) on 19 February, a PDPA-dominated 20-member Supreme Council for the Defence of the Homeland was established. The Council, which was headed by President Najibullah and was composed of ministers, Politburo members and high-ranking military figures, assumed full responsibility for the country's economic, political and military policies (although the Council of Ministers continued to function). In accordance with the state of emergency law, the legislative power vested in the Meli Shura was transferred to the Council of Ministers. In May a Loya Jirgah was convened in Kabul. Najibullah's efforts to persuade the guerrilla commanders to attend failed. At the Loya Jirgah, Najibullah announced the creation of a non-party National Mediatory Commission to confer with the Mujaheddin. This Commission has, as yet, proved relatively powerless. In June Najibullah appointed a former political adversary, Mahmud Barialay, to the senior government position of First Deputy Prime Minister, in a move which was widely viewed as an attempt to consolidate the position of his Soviet-backed regime. In mid-October, claiming a number of positive developments in the policy of national reconciliation, Najibullah reassigned to the Meli Shura the powers that had been transferred to the Council of Ministers under the state of emergency.

In early March 1990 the Minister of Defence, Lt-Gen. Shahnawaz Tanay, with the alleged support of the air force and some divisions of the army, led an unsuccessful coup attempt against Najibullah's Government. Following the defeat of the conspirators, Najibullah carried out thorough purges of PDPA and army leaders and decided to move quickly back towards some form of constitutional civilian government. On 20 May the state of emergency was lifted; the Supreme Council for the Defence of the Homeland was disbanded; and a new Council of Ministers (in which PDPA members kept the most important posts), under the premiership of Fazle Haq Khalikyar, the governor of the western province of Herat, was appointed. At the end of the month a Loya Jirgah was convened in Kabul, which considered and ratified constitutional amendments, greatly reducing Afghanistan's socialist orientation; ending the PDPA's and the NF's monopoly over executive power and paving the way for democratic elections acceptable to everyone in Afghanistan; introducing greater political and press freedom; encouraging the development of the private sector and further foreign investment; lessening the role of the State and affording greater prominence to Islam. The extensive powers of the presidency were, however, retained. In addition, the PDPA ended its congress in Kabul in late June by changing its name to the Homeland Party (Hizb-i Watan), and by dissolving the Politburo and the Central Committee and replacing them with an Executive Board and a Central Council. Najibullah was unanimously elected as Chairman of the Homeland Party. An important factor in Najibullah's decision to continue with, and to extend, the process of national reconciliation was the fact that the USSR's own internal problems made the Soviet administration unwilling to sustain, for much longer, the supplies of arms, goods and credits which helped to uphold the Kabul regime.

Fighting between the Mujaheddin and Afghan army units had begun in the eastern provinces after the 1978 coup and was aggravated by the implementation of social and economic reforms by the new administrations. The Afghan army relied heavily upon Soviet military aid in the form of weapons, equipment and expertise, but morale and resources were severely affected by defections to the rebels' ranks: numbers fell from about 80,000 men in 1978 to about 40,000 in 1985. A vigorous recruitment drive and stricter conscription regulations, implemented by Dr Najibullah in June 1986, failed to increase the size of the Afghan army by any great extent, and the defections continued.

In 1984–89 the guerrilla groups, which had been poorly armed at first, received ever-increasing support (both military and financial) from abroad, notably from the USA (which began to supply them with sophisticated anti-aircraft weapons in 1986), the United Kingdom and the People's Republic of China. Despite the Government's decision to seal the border with Pakistan, announced in September 1985, and the strong presence of Soviet forces there, foreign weapons continued to reach the guerrillas via Pakistan. Many of the guerrillas established bases in the North-West Frontier Province of Pakistan (notably in the provincial capital, Peshawar). Major efforts were made by the Government to enlist the support of border tribes by offering important concessions, financial inducements and guns in return for their support. A frontier tribal jirgah (assembly), held in September 1985, decided to establish anti-Mujaheddin militias on both sides of the Pakistan border. From 1985 the fighting intensified, especially in areas close to the border between Afghanistan and Pakistan. There were many violations of the border, involving shelling, bombing and incursions into neighbouring airspace. The general pattern of the war, however, remained the same: the regime held the main towns and a few strategic bases, and relied on bombing of both military and civilian targets, and occasional attacks in force, together with conciliatory measures such as the provision of funds for local development, while the rebel forces dominated rural areas and could cause serious disruption.

With the civil war came famine in parts of Afghanistan, and there was a mass movement of population from the countryside to Kabul (whose population increased from about 750,000 in 1978 to 1,420,000, according to a Kabul Radio report, in February 1989), and of refugees to Pakistan and Iran. In mid-1988 a UNHCR estimate assessed the number of Afghan refugees in Pakistan at 3.15m., and the number in Iran at 2.35m. Supply convoys were often prevented from reaching the cities, owing to the repeated severing of major road links by the guerrillas. Kabul, in particular, began to suffer from severe shortages of food and fuel, which were only partially alleviated by airlifts of emergency supplies, organized by the UN, the USSR and India. As a result of the increasing danger and hardship, a number of countries, including the USA, the UK, the Federal Republic of Germany and Japan, temporarily closed their embassies in the capital.

From 1980, extensive international negotiations took place to try to achieve the complete withdrawal of Soviet forces. The UN General Assembly demanded the withdrawal of foreign troops from Afghanistan in nine successive resolutions between 1980 and 1987. Between June 1982 and September 1987, seven rounds of indirect talks, the last in several phases, took place between the Afghan and Pakistani Ministers of Foreign Affairs in Geneva, under the auspices of the UN. In October 1986 the USSR made a token withdrawal of six regiments (6,000–8,000 men) from Afghanistan. As a result of

AFGHANISTAN

Introductory Survey

the discussions in Geneva, an agreement was finally signed on 14 April 1988. The Geneva accords consisted of five documents: detailed undertakings by Afghanistan and Pakistan, relating to non-intervention and non-interference in each other's affairs; international guarantees of Afghan neutrality (with the USA and the USSR as the principal guarantors); arrangements for the voluntary and safe return of Afghan refugees from Pakistan and Iran; a document linking the preceding documents with a timetable for a Soviet withdrawal; and the establishment of a UN monitoring force, to be known as the United Nations Good Offices Mission in Afghanistan and Pakistan (UNGOMAP) and to be based in Kabul and Islamabad, which was to monitor both the Soviet troop departures and the return of the refugees. The withdrawal of Soviet troops (numbering 100,000, according to Soviet figures, or 115,000, according to Western sources) commenced on 15 May.

Neither the Mujaheddin nor Iran played any role in the formulation of the Geneva accords, and, in spite of protests by Pakistan, the accords did not incorporate an agreement regarding the composition of an interim coalition government in Afghanistan, or the 'symmetrical' cessation of Soviet aid to Najibullah's regime and US aid to the Mujaheddin. Therefore, despite the withdrawal of the Soviet troops, the supply of weapons to both sides was not stopped, and the fighting continued. Pakistan repeatedly denied accusations, made by the Afghan and Soviet Governments, that it had violated the accords by continuing to harbour Afghan guerrillas and to act as a conduit for arms supplies to the latter from various sympathizers. Despite the sudden death of the Pakistani President, Gen. Zia ul-Haq (who had been one of the Mujaheddin's staunchest allies), in August 1988, Pakistan and the USA continued to support the guerrillas' cause. At the end of November Soviet officials held direct talks with representatives of the Mujaheddin in Peshawar, Pakistan, the first such meeting since the start of the 10-year conflict. High-level discussions, regarding various aspects of the Afghanistan crisis, were held in early December in Saudi Arabia between Prof. Burhanuddin Rabbani, the Chairman of the IUAM, and Yuliy Vorontsov, who had recently been appointed Soviet ambassador to Afghanistan (while retaining his post as First Deputy Minister of Foreign Affairs). These discussions collapsed, however, when the Mujaheddin leaders reiterated their demand that no members of Najibullah's regime should be incorporated in any future Afghan government, while the Soviet officials continued to insist on a government role for the PDPA. In spite of the unabated violence, the USSR, adhering to the condition specified in the Geneva accords, had withdrawn all of its troops from Afghanistan by mid-February 1989.

In mid-1988 the Mujaheddin had intensified their military activities, attacking small provincial centres and launching missiles against major cities, several of which were unsuccessfully besieged (notably Jalalabad and Khost). By November 1990, owing mainly to their lack of organization and limited experience of modern strategic warfare, the Mujaheddin had failed to achieve any significant military successes and their limited control was confined to rural areas (including several small provincial capitals). The guerrillas also failed to make any important advances on the political front. Talks between the IUAM and the Islamic Coalition Council of Afghanistan (ICCA) repeatedly failed to reach any agreement as to the composition of a broadly-based interim government. Consequently, in February 1989 the IUAM convened its own Shura (Assembly) in Rawalpindi, Pakistan, at which an interim government-in-exile was elected. The Mujaheddin government, however, was officially recognized by only four countries. The government-in-exile also failed to gain any substantial support or recognition from the guerrilla commanders, who were beginning to establish their own unofficial alliances inside the country, with the aim of overthrowing Najibullah's regime. In June, however, the Mujaheddin government received a type of informal diplomatic recognition, when the US Government appointed a special envoy to the Mujaheddin, with the rank of personal ambassador. In the following month, the USA decided to increase the flow and the quality of armaments to the Mujaheddin to counter the growing influx of weapons to the Afghan army from the USSR. In mid-1989 the unity of the Mujaheddin forces was seriously weakened by an increase in internecine violence between the various moderate and fundamentalist guerrilla groups. In August Gulbuddin Hekmatyar's faction of the fundamentalist Hizb-i Islami suspended its participation in the Mujaheddin government until elections were held in Afghanistan. The guerrillas suffered a further setback in September, when the Iranian Government terminated military aid to the ICCA-backed Shi'a Mujaheddin in Afghanistan, advising them that it was in their interest to co-operate with Najibullah's Government. In an attempt to reduce factional infighting among Mujaheddin groups, the USA, Saudi Arabia and Pakistan began to reduce financial aid and military supplies to the IUAM in Peshawar, and to undertake the difficult task of delivering weapons and money directly to guerrilla commanders and tribal leaders inside Afghanistan. In early 1990, however, attempts by the Mujaheddin government to form a Shura to elect a new and more broadly-based alternative government to the Kabul regime foundered on factional rivalries. In May local Mujaheddin field commanders formed a separate council in Afghanistan to represent their own interests. Towards the end of the year, reflecting its disillusionment with the guerrilla cause, the US Government was planning to reduce aid to the Mujaheddin by one-third, to US $200m., in 1991.

Government

In November 1987 a new constitution was ratified by a Loya Jirgah (Supreme National Tribal Assembly). A new bicameral legislature, called the Meli Shura (National Assembly), was formed to replace the Revolutionary Council. The National Assembly is composed of a 192-member Sena (Senate) and a 234-member Wolasi Jirgah (House of Representatives). A small number of seats in the Senate and 50 seats in the House of Representatives have been reserved for members of the opposition. The President is elected by the majority vote of a Loya Jirgah for a term of seven years. The President appoints the Prime Minister, who, in turn, appoints the members of the Council of Ministers. The 31 provinces of Afghanistan are each administered by an appointed governor.

Defence

Every able-bodied Afghan male (excepting religious scholars and preachers) between the ages of 15 and 40 years has to serve four years in the army (with a break of three years at the end of the second year), which was estimated to number 58,000 men in June 1990, but conscription is difficult to enforce and desertions are frequent. Equipment and training are provided largely by the USSR. The withdrawal of Soviet troops was completed in February 1989. The Afghan air force, which numbered an estimated 8,000, is equipped with supersonic jet aircraft. Paramilitary forces include a gendarmerie (Sarandoy) of about 20,000, a state security service (KHAD) of around 25,000, a border guard of about 20,000 and numerous regional militias; police security forces come under the Ministry of the Interior (gendarmarie) and the Ministry of State Security (KHAD). A Special Guard was formed to defend the capital city in 1988.

Economic Affairs

According to government figures, Afghanistan's gross national product (GNP) in 1986/87 amounted to US $3,156m., an increase of 5.2% compared with 1985/86, and GNP per head stood at $155-$160. The economy, according to government estimates, expanded by less than 2% annually between 1980 and 1986.

Agriculture (including hunting, forestry and fishing) contributed an estimated 64.5% of net material product (NMP) in 1986/87. More than 65% of the settled labour force are employed in agriculture. The principal commercial products of the sector are fruit and nuts (which accounted for around 46.7% of total export earnings, according to the IMF, in 1989/90), wool and cotton, and processed hides and skins. The Government claimed that the volume of agricultural production increased by 0.7% in 1987/88.

Industry (including mining, manufacturing, construction and power) contributed an estimated 21.1% of NMP in 1986/87. Official sources claimed that the volume of industrial output increased by 3.5% in 1987.

Mining and quarrying employed about 1.5% of the settled labour force in 1979. Natural gas is the major mineral export. Salt, hard coal, copper, lapis lazuli, barytes and talc are also mined. In addition, Afghanistan has small reserves of petroleum and iron ore.

Manufacturing employed about 10.9% of the settled labour force in 1979. Afghanistan's major manufacturing industries include food products, cotton textiles, chemical fertilizers, cement, leather and plastic goods.

AFGHANISTAN

Energy is derived principally from petroleum (which is imported from Iran and the USSR) and coal. The Government plans to increase internal sources of energy by establishing hydro- and thermal electric power stations.

In 1989, according to the IMF, Afghanistan recorded a visible trade deficit of US $220.6m., and there was a deficit of $217.1m. on the current account of the balance of payments. According to government figures, the Eastern bloc countries accounted for 68% (USSR 60%) of the total foreign trade turnover (imports plus exports) in 1986/87. The principal exports are natural gas, fruit (dried and fresh) and nuts, carpets and rugs, Karakul fur skins and cotton. The principal imports are vehicles and spare parts, petroleum products, fertilizers, basic manufactured goods and foodstuffs (notably wheat).

In 1987 the Government estimated that financial contributions from the USSR constituted 40% of the country's civilian budget. In 1988/89 the USSR and other member countries of the Council for Mutual Economic Assistance (CMEA, see p. 125) were to contribute 97% (USSR 81%) of foreign aid to Afghanistan, which totalled an estimated US $223.3m., an increase of 14.5% compared with 1987/88. In 1987 Afghanistan's total external debt was $1,499m. During 1981–85 the annual rate of inflation remained at about 20%.

It is extremely difficult to provide an accurate economic profile of Afghanistan, owing to the continuing civil war, population movement, communication problems and lack of reliable official statistics. Government figures often appear highly optimistic. Both the agricultural and industrial sectors have been severely disrupted by the unrest, and Afghanistan relies heavily on the USSR and other communist countries in addressing all aspects of its faltering economy. Despite the Government's policy of national reconciliation, which was introduced in 1986, and the Soviet troop withdrawal, which was completed in early 1989, the economy, as a whole, showed no real signs of improvement, and the ambitious targets of the Five-Year Economic and Social Development Plan (1986–91), including a 25% growth in the economy over the Plan period, appeared highly unlikely to be attained. In June 1988 the UN launched an appeal to raise US $1,160m. towards the implementation of a large-scale, 18-month, programme for reconstruction and rehabilitation in Afghanistan. In October the USSR pledged to contribute $600m. in humanitarian aid. World-wide response, however, was rather poor.

Social Welfare

Workers and employees are entitled to free hospital treatment. Most private companies have their own doctor and hospitals. Disabled people are looked after in social welfare centres in the provincial capitals. In 1982 Afghanistan had 68 hospital establishments, with a total of 4,837 beds, and there were 1,160 physicians working in the government health service. Serious damage was reported to have been caused to hospital facilities by the disturbances from 1980 onwards. The estimated average life expectancy at birth in 1980–85 had fallen by two years from the 1970 figure to 36 years, the lowest in Asia. Between 1980 and 1985, according to UN estimates, there were 194 deaths of children under 12 months old for every 1,000 live births, the highest infant mortality rate in Asia. In 1980 only 20% of the urban population and 3% of the rural population had access to safe water supplies. In the same year the average daily intake of calories per person had fallen to 1,775, also the lowest in Asia, although this figure had risen to 2,280 by 1982, according to government sources. In 1982/83 estimated expenditure on social services was Afs 2,315m., about 20% of the ordinary budget. In 1988 government officials assessed the combined total of medical centres and hospitals at 196 and physicians at 1,931.

Education

Primary education, which is officially compulsory, begins at seven years of age and lasts for eight years. Secondary education, beginning at 15 years of age, lasts for a further four years. As a proportion of the school-age population, the total enrolment at primary and secondary schools declined from 29% (boys 46%; girls 11%) in 1981 to only 14% (boys 19%; girls 10%) in 1986. Enrolment at primary schools declined from 1,198,286 in 1981 to 449,948 in 1982, rising to 611,106 in 1986. Primary enrolment in 1985 included an estimated 15% of children in the relevant age-group (boys 20%; girls 10%). The number of pupils enrolled at general secondary schools declined from 144,858 in 1981 to 89,448 (equivalent to only 6% of children in the secondary age-group) in 1986.

Afghanistan has one of the highest levels of adult illiteracy in Asia, with an average rate of 76.3% (males 61.1%; females 92.2%) in 1985, according to estimates by UNESCO. In 1987 the Government claimed that there were more than 20,000 literacy courses, attended by a total of about 400,000 students, throughout Afghanistan. According to the Government, about 857,000 pupils were studying at 1,348 schools in September 1988, compared with 700,544 pupils at 1,236 schools in 1986. Since 1979 higher education has been disrupted by the departure of many teaching staff from Afghanistan. In 1987 an estimated 15,000 Afghan students and trainees were receiving education at establishments in the USSR. In 1988 there were eight vocational colleges, 15 technical colleges and five universities (including an Islamic university in Kabul) in Afghanistan.

Public Holidays

The Afghan year 1369 runs from 21 March 1990 to 20 March 1991, and the year 1370 runs from 21 March 1991 to 20 March 1992.

1991: 17 March* (first day of Ramadan), 21 March (Nau-roz: New Year's Day, Iranian calendar), 16 April* (Id al-Fitr, end of Ramadan), 27 April (Revolution Day), 1 May (Workers' Day), 23 June* (Id al-Adha, Feast of the Sacrifice), 22 July* (Ashura, Martyrdom of Iman Husayn), 18 August (Independence Day), 21 September* (Roze-Maulud, Birth of Prophet Muhammad).

1992: 5 March* (first day of Ramadan), 21 March (Nau-roz: New Year's Day, Iranian calendar), 4 April* (Id al-Fitr, end of Ramadan), 27 April (Revolution Day), 1 May (Workers' Day), 11 June* (Id al-Adha, Feast of the Sacrifice), 11 July* (Ashura, Martyrdom of Iman Husayn), 18 August (Independence Day), 10 September* (Roze-Maulud, Birth of Prophet Muhammad).

* These holidays are dependent on the Islamic lunar calendar and may vary by one or two days from the dates given.

Weights and Measures

The metric system has been officially adopted but traditional weights are still used. One 'seer' equals 16 lb (7.3 kg).

AFGHANISTAN

Statistical Survey

Source (unless otherwise stated): Central Statistics Authority, Block 4, Macroraion, Kabul; tel. (93) 24883.

Area and Population

AREA, POPULATION AND DENSITY

Area (sq km)	652,225*
Population (census results)	
23 June 1979†	
Males	6,712,377
Females	6,338,981
Total	13,051,358
Population (official estimates at mid-year)‡	
1984	17,672,000
1985	18,136,000
1986	18,614,000
Density (per sq km) at mid-1986	28.5

* 251,773 sq miles.
† Figures exclude nomadic population, estimated to total 2,500,000. The census data also exclude an adjustment for underenumeration, estimated to have been 5% for the urban population and 10% for the rural population.
‡ These data include estimates for nomadic population (2,734,000 in 1983), but take no account of emigration by refugees. Assuming an average net outflow of 703,000 persons per year in 1980–85, the UN Population Division has estimated Afghanistan's total mid-year population (in '000) as: 14,519 in 1985; 14,529 in 1986; 14,709 in 1987 (Source: UN, *World Population Prospects: 1988*). In 1988, according to UNHCR estimates, the total Afghan refugee population numbered 5.5m., of whom 3.15m. were living in Pakistan and 2.35m. in Iran.

Population (official estimates, excluding nomads, at mid-year): 15,219,000 in 1987; 15,513,000 in 1988; 15,814,000 in 1989.

PROVINCES (estimates, March 1982)*

	Area (sq km)	Population	Density (per sq km)	Capital (with population)
Kabul	4,585	1,517,909	331.1	Kabul (1,036,407)
Kapesa†	1,871	262,039	140.1	Mahmudraki (1,262)
Parwan	9,399	527,987	56.2	Sharikar (25,117)
Wardag†	9,023	300,796	33.3	Maidanshar (2,153)
Loghar†	4,652	226,234	48.6	Baraiki Barak (1,164)
Ghazni	23,378	676,416	28.9	Ghazni (31,985)
Paktia	9,581	506,264	52.8	Gardiz (10,040)
Nangarhar	7,616	781,619	102.6	Jalalabad (57,824)
Laghman	7,210	325,010	45.0	Mehterlam (4,191)
Kunar	10,479	261,604	25.0	Asadabad (2,196)
Badakhshan	47,403	520,620	10.9	Faizabad (9,564)
Takhar	12,376	543,818	43.9	Talukan (20,947)
Baghlan	17,109	516,921	30.2	Baghlan (41,240)
Kunduz	7,827	582,600	74.4	Kunduz (57,112)
Samangan	15,465	273,864	17.7	Aibak (5,191)
Balkh	12,593	609,590	48.4	Mazar-i-Sharif (110,367)
Jawzjan	25,553	615,877	24.1	Shiberghan (19,969)
Fariab	22,279	609,703	27.3	Maymana (40,212)
Badghis	21,858	244,346	11.2	Kalainow (5,614)
Herat	61,315	808,224	13.2	Herat (150,497)
Farah	47,788	245,474	5.1	Farah (19,761)
Neemroze	41,356	108,418	2.6	Zarang (6,809)
Helmand	61,829	541,508	8.8	Lashkargha (22,707)
Qandahar	47,676	597,954	12.5	Qandahar (191,345)
Zabul	17,293	187,612	10.8	Qalat (6,251)
Uruzgan	29,295	464,556	15.5	Terincot (3,534)
Ghor	38,666	353,494	9.1	Cheghcheran (3,126)
Bamian	17,414	280,859	16.1	Bamian (7,732)
Paktika	19,336	256,470	13.3	Sheran (1,469)
Total	652,225	13,747,786	21.1	

* Population figures refer to settled inhabitants only, excluding kuchies (nomads), estimated at 2,600,000 for the whole country.
† Formed in 1981.

Note: Two new provinces, named Sar-e Pol and Nurestan, were formed in April 1988 and July 1988 respectively, bringing the total number of provinces in Afghanistan to 31.

PRINCIPAL TOWNS (estimated population at March 1982)

Kabul (capital)	1,036,407	Kunduz	57,112
Qandahar	191,345	Baghlan	41,240
Herat	150,497	Maymana	40,212
Mazar-i-Sharif	110,367	Pul-i-Khomri	32,695
Jalalabad	57,824	Ghazni	31,985

BIRTHS AND DEATHS

1979 (demographic survey): Live births 627,619 (birth rate 48.1 per 1,000); Deaths 290,974 (death rate 22.3 per 1,000).

ECONOMICALLY ACTIVE POPULATION* (ISIC Major Divisions, persons aged 8 years and over, 1979 census)

	Males	Females	Total
Agriculture, hunting, forestry and fishing	2,358,821	10,660	2,369,481
Mining and quarrying	57,492	1,847	59,339
Manufacturing	170,908	252,465	423,373
Electricity, gas and water	11,078	276	11,354
Construction	50,670	416	51,086
Wholesale and retail trade	135,242	2,618	137,860
Transport, storage and communications	65,376	867	66,243
Other services	716,511	32,834	749,345
Total	3,566,098	301,983	3,868,081

* Figures refer to settled population only and exclude 77,510 persons seeking work for the first time (66,057 males; 11,453 females).

AFGHANISTAN

Agriculture

PRINCIPAL CROPS ('000 metric tons)

	1987	1988	1989
Wheat*	1,925	1,925	1,925
Rice (paddy)	344	490	490*
Barley*	250	250	250
Maize	685	838	750*
Millet	40	40*	45*
Potatoes*	300	300	300
Pulses*	40	40	41
Sesame seed*	25	26	27
Cottonseed†	74	80	40
Cotton (lint)†	37	40	20
Vegetables	632	212	220*
Watermelons*	31	31	32
Melons*	114	115	117
Grapes*	475	450	430
Sugar cane*	60	50	50
Sugar beets*	2	2	2
Plums*	37	37	37
Oranges*	24	24	24
Apricots*	37	37	37
Other fruit*	228	230	231

* FAO estimate(s).   † Unofficial figures.
Source: FAO, *Production Yearbook*.

LIVESTOCK
('000 head, year ending 30 September)

	1987	1988	1989
Horses*	400	400	400
Mules*	30	30	30
Asses	1,300	1,300*	1,300*
Cattle*	1,500	1,550	1,600
Camels	300	265	265*
Sheep*	10,500	11,500	12,500
Goats*	2,000	2,050	2,100

Poultry (estimates, million): 7 in 1987; 7 in 1988; 7 in 1989.
* FAO estimate(s).
Source: FAO, *Production Yearbook*.

LIVESTOCK PRODUCTS (FAO estimates, '000 metric tons)

	1987	1988	1989
Beef and veal	65	65	65
Mutton and lamb	100	105	110
Goats' meat	20	21	22
Poultry meat	13	13	13
Other meat	8	9	10
Cows' milk	300	315	330
Sheep's milk	130	150	170
Goats' milk	36	37	38
Cheese	14.2	15.3	16.4
Butter and ghee	9.0	9.5	10.3
Hen eggs	14.2	14.2	14.2
Honey	3.0	3.0	3.0
Wool:			
greasy	13.0	14.0	15.0
clean	7.4	7.9	8.5
Cattle hides	10.6	10.6	10.6
Sheep skins	15.6	16.4	17.2
Goat skins	3.0	3.1	3.3

Source: FAO, *Production Yearbook*.

Forestry

ROUNDWOOD REMOVALS
(FAO estimates, '000 cu m, excluding bark)

	1986	1987	1988
Sawlogs, veneer logs and logs for sleepers*	856	856	856
Other industrial wood	600	603	614
Fuel wood	4,329	4,352	4,431
Total	5,785	5,811	5,901

* Assumed to be unchanged from 1976.
Source: FAO, *Yearbook of Forest Products*.

SAWNWOOD PRODUCTION (FAO estimates, '000 cu m)

	1974	1975	1976
Total (incl. boxboards)	410	330	400

1977–88: Annual production as in 1976 (FAO estimates).
Source: FAO, *Yearbook of Forest Products*.

Fishing

1964–88: Total catch 1,500 metric tons each year (FAO estimate).

Mining

('000 metric tons, unless otherwise indicated)

	1985	1986	1987
Hard coal	151	160	167
Salt (unrefined)*	51	37	10†
Gypsum (crude)	8	12	3†
Natural gas (petajoules)	111	111	113

* Production during 12 months beginning 21 March of year stated.
† Provisional.
Source: UN, *Industrial Statistics Yearbook*.

Industry

SELECTED PRODUCTS (year ending 20 March, '000 metric tons, unless otherwise indicated)

	1984/85	1985/86	1986/87
Margarine	2.7	3.6	3.5
Vegetable oil	3	4	5
Wheat flour†	154	174	187
Wine ('000 hectolitres)†	262	264	289
Soft drinks ('000 hectolitres)	7,300	7,600	8,500
Woven cotton fabrics (million metres)	45.3	55.0	58.1
Woven woollen fabrics (million square metres)*	0.5	0.4	0.4
Footwear—excl. rubber ('000 pairs)†	344	380	613
Rubber footwear ('000 pairs)†	2,400	2,400	2,200
Nitrogenous fertilizers‡	48.8	55.2	56.1*
Cement	112	128	103
Electric energy (million kWh)†	1,045	1,060	1,171

* Provisional.
† Production in calendar years 1984, 1985 and 1986.
‡ Production in terms of nitrogen in year ending 30 June (Source: FAO).
Source: mainly UN, *Industrial Statistics Yearbook*.

AFGHANISTAN   Statistical Survey

Finance

CURRENCY AND EXCHANGE RATES

Monetary Units
100 puls (puli) = 2 krans = 1 afghani (Af).

Denominations
Coins: 25 and 50 puls: 1, 2, and 5 afghanis.
Notes: 10, 20, 50 and 100 afghanis.

Sterling and Dollar Equivalents (30 September 1990)
£1 sterling = 94.80 afghanis;
US $1 = 50.60 afghanis;
1,000 afghanis = £10.549 = $19.763.

Exchange Rate
The official rate has been maintained at US $1 = 50.60 afghanis since September 1981.

BUDGET (million afghanis, year ending 21 September)

Revenue	1977/78	1978/79	1979/80
Direct taxes	2,428	2,535	2,461
Indirect taxes	6,830	6,913	4,794
Revenue from monopolies and other enterprises	1,316	1,192	1,407
Natural gas revenue	1,510	2,637	3,874
Revenue from other property and services	2,357	1,954	2,456
Other revenue	480	1,224	796
Total revenue	14,921	16,455	15,788

Expenditure	1977/78	1978/79	1979/80
Administration	1,255	1,690	4,218
Defence, security	2,656	3,007	6,294
Social services	2,538	3,186	3,279
Economic services	870	985	1,092
Total ministries	7,319	8,868	14,883
Foreign debt service	2,087	2,493	1,029
Subsidies (exchange, etc.)	2,532	1,024	870
Total ordinary	11,938	12,385	16,782
Development budget	5,200	6,845	5,374

1980/81 (estimates in million afghanis): Revenue: internal sources 23,478, grants-in-aid from USSR 1,735, loans and project assistance 8,546, total revenue 33,759; Expenditure: ministries' allocation 19,213, development budget 14,546, total expenditure 33,759.
In January 1986 the Government announced a Five-Year Economic and Social Development Plan (March 1986–91), involving proposed expenditure of Afs 115,000m. (US $2,300m.).

BANK OF AFGHANISTAN RESERVES*
(US $ million at December)

	1987	1988	1989
IMF special drawing rights	14.91	12.80	10.63
Reserve position in IMF	6.87	6.53	6.41
Foreign exchange	257.90	241.80	226.65
Total	279.68	261.12	243.69

* Figures exclude gold reserves, totalling 965,000 troy ounces since 1980. Assuming a gold price of 12,850 afghanis per ounce, these reserves were officially valued at US $245.06 million in December of each year 1985–89.
Source: IMF, *International Financial Statistics*.

MONEY SUPPLY (million afghanis at 21 December)

	1987	1988	1989
Currency outside banks	112,488	152,330	222,720
Private sector deposits at Bank of Afghanistan	9,564	12,695	12,838
Demand deposits at commercial banks	5,642	9,531	n.a.

Source: IMF, *International Financial Statistics*.

COST OF LIVING
(retail price index, excluding rent; base: 1985 = 100)

	1987	1988	1989
All items	115.9	141.4	242.9

Source: IMF, *International Financial Statistics*.

NATIONAL ACCOUNTS
('000 million afghanis at constant 1978 prices, year ending 20 March)

Net Material Product (NMP)* by Economic Activity

	1984/85	1985/86	1986/87
Agriculture, hunting, forestry and fishing	65.4	65.2	67.1
Mining and quarrying			
Manufacturing	15.3	16.4	17.1
Electricity, gas and water			
Construction	3.9	3.9	4.8
Trade, restaurants and hotels	10.1	10.0	10.4
Transport, storage and communications	3.7	2.7	2.9
Other services	1.8	1.7	1.7
Total	100.2	99.9	104.0

* Defined as the total net value of goods and 'productive' services, including turnover taxes, produced by the economy. This excludes economic activities not contributing directly to material production, such as public administration, defence and personal and professional services.
Source: UN, *National Accounts Statistics*.

BALANCE OF PAYMENTS (US $ million)

	1987	1988	1989
Merchandise exports f.o.b.	538.7	453.8	395.7
Merchandise imports f.o.b.	−904.5	−731.8	−616.3
Trade balance	−365.8	−278.0	−220.6
Exports of services	54.8	92.9	28.3
Imports of services	−167.6	−131.5	−112.3
Balance on goods and services	−478.6	−316.6	−304.6
Unrequited transfers (net)	311.7	342.8	87.5
Current balance	−166.9	26.2	−217.1
Long-term capital (net)	113.6	22.4	−196.0
Short-term capital (net)	−147.5	−26.5	122.7
Net errors and omissions	211.6	−47.9	270.4
Total (net monetary movements)	10.8	−25.8	−20.0
Valuation changes (net)	10.4	7.2	2.6
Changes in reserves	21.2	−18.6	−17.4

Source: IMF, *International Financial Statistics*.

AFGHANISTAN   *Statistical Survey*

External Trade

PRINCIPAL COMMODITIES (US $ '000, year ending 20 March)

Imports c.i.f.	1980/81	1981/82	1983/84*
Wheat	798	18,100	38,251
Sugar	40,833	50,328	25,200
Tea	28,369	n.a.	23,855
Cigarettes	5,114	7,219	12,755
Vegetable oil	17,320	26,332	30,481
Drugs	4,497	4,195	3,768
Soaps	9,991	17,256	8,039
Tyres and tubes	16,766	12,764	28,823
Textile yarn and thread	16,800	24,586	n.a.
Cotton fabrics	873	6,319	n.a.
Rayon fabrics	6,879	9,498	n.a.
Other textile goods	52,546	49,036	n.a.
Vehicles and spare parts	89,852	141,062	n.a.
Petroleum products	124,000	112,093	n.a.
Footwear (new)	2,058	5,275	5,317
Bicycles	2,042	488	1,952
Matches	1,171	1,542	1,793
Sewing machines	140	285	266
Electric and non-electric machines	2,333	765	n.a.
Chemical materials	7,464	6,636	n.a.
Agricultural tractors	1	8,280	n.a.
Fertilizers	8,325	3,300	3,904
Used clothes	2,523	1,875	5,334
Television receivers	5,391	3,241	10,139
Other items	106,662	92,307	n.a.
Total	**551,748**	**622,416**	**846,022**

* Figures for 1982/83 are not available.

Total imports c.i.f. (US $ '000, year ending 20 March): 1,194,200 in 1985/86; 1,403,500 in 1986/87; 995,900 in 1987/88; 900,300 in 1988/89; 821,700 in 1989/90 (Source: IMF, *International Financial Statistics*).

Exports f.o.b.	1980/81	1981/82	1983/84*
Fresh fruit	39,762	50,544	66,374
Dried fruit	169,478	174,933	191,971
Hides and skins	14,491	11,711	15,547
Karakul fur skins	33,299	18,845	9,592
Oil-seeds	6,412	2,031	3,888
Wool and other animal hair	12,308	23,364	25,380
Cotton	39,650	22,566	10,175
Casings	5,369	4,617	3,336
Medicinal herbs and caraway seeds	4,206	11,511	16,524
Natural gas	233,128	272,589	305,276
Carpets and rugs	103,590	72,680	50,361
Other commodities	43,551	28,901	30,155
Total	**705,244**	**694,292**	**728,579**

* Figures for 1982/83 are not available.

1985/86 (US $ '000, year ending 20 March): Fruit and nuts 94,500; Karakul fur skins 5,700; Natural gas 309,400; Wool 22,500; Carpets 58,400; Cotton 19,200; Total (incl. others) 556,800.
1986/87 (US $ '000, year ending 20 March): Fruit and nuts 134,900; Karakul fur skins 10,500; Natural gas 259,600; Wool 14,600; Carpets 39,500; Cotton 9,800; Total (incl. others) 551,900.
1987/88 (US $'000, year ending 20 March): Fruit and nuts 128,600; Karakul fur skins 8,300; Natural gas 204,500; Wool 3,800; Carpets 48,900; Cotton 8,900; Total (incl. others) 511,900.
1988/89 (US $'000, year ending 20 March): Fruit and nuts 142,100; Karakul fur skins 6,100; Natural gas 143,000; Wool 30,900; Carpets 39,100; Cotton 12,300; Total (incl. others) 432,700.
1989/90 (US $'000, year ending 20 March): Fruit and nuts 110,200; Karakul fur skins 3,600; Natural gas n.a.; Wool 5,500; Carpets 38,000; Cotton 900; Total (incl. others) 235,900 (Source: IMF, *International Financial Statistics*).

PRINCIPAL TRADING PARTNERS (US $ '000)

Imports	1980/81	1981/82	1983/84*
Germany, Federal Republic	16,959	16,779	17,076
Hong Kong	18,586	27,386	n.a.
India	20,572	17,024	28,985
Japan	98,207	76,670	111,061
Pakistan	14,895	11,737	14,882
USSR	290,496	365,000	526,319
USA	14,216	7,156	8,721
Total (incl. others)	**551,748**	**622,416**	**846,022**

* Figures for 1982/83 are not available.

Exports	1980/81	1981/82	1983/84*
Czechoslovakia	14,585	12,088	4,836
Germany, Federal Republic	51,513	41,801	26,130
India	54,746	43,212	84,212
Pakistan	52,101	61,249	118,080
Saudi Arabia	21,188	19,214	n.a.
USSR	417,872	412,635	400,756
United Kingdom	51,844	36,340	25,137
Total (incl. others)	**705,244**	**694,292**	**728,579**

* Figures for 1982/83 are not available.

Transport

ROAD TRAFFIC (motor vehicles in use)

	1979/80	1980/81	1981/82
Passenger cars	34,192	34,080	34,908
Commercial vehicles	27,555	28,714	30,800

CIVIL AVIATION ('000)

	1984	1985
Kilometres flown	3,800	3,900
Passengers carried	220	226
Passenger-km	173,000	175,000
Freight ton-km	19,800	19,900
Mail ton-km	200	200

Source: UN, *Statistical Yearbook*.

1987: Passengers carried 217,916; Passenger-km ('000) 174,676; Freight ton-km ('000) 8,093. Source: International Air Transport Association.

Tourism

INTERNATIONAL TOURIST ARRIVALS BY COUNTRY

	1978	1979	1980
Australia	3,070	967	28
France	4,781	1,153	234
Germany, Federal Republic	7,496	1,817	258
India	9,744	4,350	992
Pakistan	23,663	10,126	2,466
United Kingdom	9,102	1,850	128
USA	6,389	1,039	79
Others	27,744	8,902	2,438
Total	**91,989**	**30,204**	**6,623**

Total tourist arrivals (estimates): 9,200 in 1981, 9,500 in 1982.

Receipts from tourism (US $ million): 28 in 1978, 1 in 1979, 1 in 1980.

Communications Media

Telephones in use: 23,680 in 1979/80. Radio receivers in use: an estimated 1.5m. in 1986. Television receivers in use: an estimated 115,000 in 1986.

Education

(1986)

	Institutions	Teachers	Pupils
Pre-primary	195	n.a.	18,002
Elementary	886	16,414	611,106
Secondary*	n.a.	n.a.	89,448

* Figures refer to general education only, excluding vocational training (teachers 1,262 in 1980; pupils 12,410 in 1980, 14,532 in 1981).

Higher education (1982): Universities, etc.: 1,212 teachers, 13,611 students; Other institutions: 512 teachers, 6,041 students.

Source: UNESCO, *Statistical Yearbook*.

Directory

The Constitution

Immediately after the coup of 27 April 1978 (the Saur Revolution), the 1977 Constitution was abolished. Both Nur Muhammad Taraki (Head of State from April 1978 to September 1979) and his successor, Hafizullah Amin (September–December 1979), promised to introduce new constitutions, but these leaders were removed from power before any drafts had been prepared by special commissions which they had appointed. On 21 April 1980 the Revolutionary Council ratified the Basic Principles of the Democratic Republic of Afghanistan. These were superseded by a new constitution ratified in April 1985. Another new constitution was ratified during a meeting of a Loya Jirgah (Supreme National Tribal Assembly), held on 29–30 November 1987. This constitution was amended in May 1990. The following is a summary of the Constitution as it stood in May 1990.

GENERAL PROVISIONS

The fundamental duty of the State is to defend the independence, national sovereignty and territorial integrity of the Republic of Afghanistan. National sovereignty belongs to the people. The people exercise national sovereignty through the Loya Jirgah and the Meli Shura.

Foreign policy is based on the principle of peaceful co-existence and active and positive non-alignment. Friendship and co-operation are to be strengthened with all countries, particularly neighbouring and Islamic ones. Afghanistan abides by the UN Charter and the Universal Declaration of Human Rights and supports the struggle against colonialism, imperialism, Zionism, racism and fascism. Afghanistan favours disarmament and the prevention of the proliferation of nuclear and chemical weapons. War propaganda is prohibited.

Islam is the religion of Afghanistan and no law shall run counter to the principles of Islam.

Political parties are allowed to be formed, providing that their policies and activities are in accordance with the provisions of the Constitution and the laws of the country. A party that is legally formed cannot be dissolved without legal grounds. Judges and prosecutors cannot be members of a political party during their term of office.

Pashtu and Dari are the official languages.

The capital is Kabul.

The State shall follow the policy of understanding and co-operation between all nationalities, clans and tribes within the country to ensure equality and the rapid development of backward regions.

The family constitutes the basic unit of society. The State shall adopt necessary measures to ensure the health of mothers and children.

The State protects all forms of legal property, including private property. The hereditary right to property shall be guaranteed according to Islamic law.

For the growth of the national economy, the State encourages foreign investment in the Republic of Afghanistan and regulates it in accordance with the law.

RIGHTS AND DUTIES OF THE PEOPLE

All subjects of Afghanistan are equal before the law. The following rights are guaranteed: the right to life and security, to complain to the appropriate government organs, to participate in the political sphere, to freedom of speech and thought, to hold peaceful demonstrations and strikes, to work, to free education, to protection of health and social welfare, to scientific, technical and cultural activities, to freedom of movement both within Afghanistan and abroad, to observe the religious rites of Islam and of other religions, to security of residence and privacy of communication and correspondence, and to liberty and human dignity.

In criminal cases, an accused person is considered innocent until guilt is recognized by the court. Nobody may be arrested, detained or punished except in accordance with the law.

Every citizen is bound to observe the Constitution and the laws of the Republic of Afghanistan, to pay taxes and duties to the State in accordance with the provisions of the law, and to undertake military service, when and as required.

LOYA JIRGAH

This is the highest manifestation of the will of the people of Afghanistan. It is composed of: the President and Vice-Presidents, members of the Meli Shura (National Assembly), the General Prosecutor, the Council of Ministers, the Attorney-General, his deputies and members of the Attorney-General's Office, the chairman of the Constitution Council, the heads of the provincial councils, representatives from each province, according to the number of their representatives in the Wolasi Jirgah (House of Representatives), elected by the people by a general secret ballot, and a minimum of 50 people, from among prominent political, scientific, social and religious figures, appointed by the President.

The Loya Jirgah is empowered: to approve and amend the Constitution; to elect the President and to accept the resignation of the President; to consent to the declaration of war and armistice; and to adopt decisions on major questions regarding the destiny of the country. The Loya Jirgah shall be summoned, opened and chaired by the President. Sessions of the Loya Jirgah require a minimum attendance of two-thirds of the members. Decisions shall be adopted by a majority vote. In the event of the dissolution of the Wolasi Jirgah (House of Representatives), its members shall retain their membership of the Loya Jirgah until a new Wolasi Jirgah is elected. Elections to the Loya Jirgah shall be regulated by law and the procedure laid down by the Loya Jirgah itself.

THE PRESIDENT

The President is the Head of State and shall be elected by a majority vote of the Loya Jirgah for a term of seven years. No person can be elected as President for more than two terms. The President is accountable, and shall report, to the Loya Jirgah. The Loya Jirgah shall be convened to elect a new President 30 days before the end of the term of office of the outgoing President. Any Muslim citizen of the Republic of Afghanistan who is more than 40 years of age can be elected as President.

The President shall exercise the following executive powers: the supreme command of the armed forces; the ratification of the resolutions of the Meli Shura; the appointment of the Prime Minister; the approval of the appointment of ministers, judges and army officials; the granting of citizenship and the commuting of punishment; the power to call a referendum, to proclaim a state of emergency, and to declare war (with the consent of the Loya Jirgah). Should a state of emergency continue for more than three months, the consent of the Loya Jirgah is imperative for its extension.

In the event of the President being unable to perform his duties, the presidential functions and powers shall be entrusted to the first Vice-President. In the event of the death or resignation of the President, the first Vice-President shall ask the Loya Jirgah to elect a new President within one month. In the event of resignation, the President shall submit his resignation directly to the Loya Jirgah.

MELI SHURA

The Meli Shura (National Assembly) is the highest legislative organ of the Republic of Afghanistan. It consists of two houses: the Wolasi Jirgah (House of Representatives) and the Sena (Senate). Members of the Wolasi Jirgah (representatives) are elected by general secret ballot for a legislative term of five years. Members of the Sena (senators) are elected and appointed in the following manner: two people from each province are elected for a period of five years; two people from each provincial council are elected by the council for a period of three years; and the remaining one-third of senators are appointed by the President for a period of four years.

The Meli Shura is vested with the authority: to approve, amend and repeal laws and legislative decrees, and to present them to the President for his signature; to interpret laws; to ratify and annul international treaties; to approve socio-economic development plans and to endorse the Government's reports on their execution; to approve the state budget and to evaluate the Government's report on its execution; to establish and make changes to administrative units; to establish and abolish ministries; to appoint and remove Vice-Presidents, on the recommendation of the President; and to endorse the establishment of relations with foreign countries and international organizations. The Wolasi Jirgah also has the power to approve a vote of confidence or no confidence in the Council of Ministers or one of its members.

At its first session, the Wolasi Jirgah elects, from among its members, an executive committee, composed of a chairman, two deputy chairmen and two secretaries, for the whole term of the legislature. The Sena elects, from among its members, an executive committee, composed of a chairman for a term of five years, and two deputy chairmen and two secretaries for a term of one year.

Ordinary sessions of the Meli Shura are held twice a year and do not normally last longer than three months. An extraordinary session can be held at the request of the President, the chairman of either house, or one-fifth of the members of each house. The houses of the Meli Shura can hold separate or joint sessions. Sessions require a minimum attendance of two-thirds of the members of each house and decisions shall be adopted by a majority vote. Sessions are open, unless the houses decide to meet in closed sessions.

The following authorities have the right to propose the introduction, amendment or repeal of a law in either house of the Meli Shura: the President, the standing commissions of the Meli Shura, at least one-tenth of the membership of each house, the Council of Ministers, the Supreme Court, and the office of the Attorney-General.

If the decision of one house is rejected by the other, a joint committee, consisting of an equal number of members from both houses, shall be formed. A decision by the joint committee, which will be agreed by a two-thirds majority, will be considered valid after approval by the President. If the joint committee fails to resolve differences, the matter shall be discussed in a joint session of the Meli Shura, and a decision reached by a majority vote. The decisions that are made by the Meli Shura are enforced after being signed by the President.

After consulting the chairman of the Wolasi Jirgah, the chairman of the Sena, the Prime Minister, the Attorney-General and the chairman of the Constitution Council, the President can declare the dissolution of the Wolasi Jirgah, stating his justification for doing so. Re-elections shall be held within 3 months of the dissolution.

COUNCIL OF MINISTERS

The Council of Ministers is composed of: a Prime Minister, deputy Prime Ministers and Ministers. The Council of Ministers is appointed by the Prime Minister. It is empowered: to formulate and implement domestic and foreign policies; to formulate economic development plans and state budgets; and to ensure public order.

The Council of Ministers is dissolved under the following conditions: the resignation of the Prime Minister, chronic illness of the Prime Minister, the withdrawal of confidence in the Council of Ministers by the Meli Shura, the end of the legislative term, or the dissolution of the Wolasi Jirgah or the Meli Shura.

THE JUDICIARY

(See section on the Judicial System.)

THE CONSTITUTION COUNCIL

The responsibilities of this body are: to evaluate and ensure the conformity of laws, legislative decrees and international treaties with the Constitution; and to give legal advice to the President on constitutional matters. The Constitution Council is composed of a chairman, a vice-chairman and eight members, who are appointed by the President.

LOCAL ADMINISTRATIVE ORGANS

For the purposes of local administration, the Republic of Afghanistan is divided into provinces, districts, cities and wards. These administrative units are led, respectively, by governors, district administrators, mayors and heads of wards. In each province a provincial council and district councils are formed in accordance with the law. Provincial councils and district councils each elect a chairman and a secretary from among their members. The term of office of a provincial council and a district council is three years.

FINAL PROVISIONS

Amendments to the Constitution shall be made by the Loya Jirgah. Any amendment shall be on the proposal of the President, or on the proposal of one-third and the approval of two-thirds of the members of the Meli Shura. Amendment to the Constitution during a state of emergency is not allowed.

The Government

HEAD OF STATE

President: Dr Najibullah Ahmadzai (took office 30 November 1987).

First Vice-President: Sultan Ali Keshtmand.

Vice-Presidents: Abd ar-Rahim Hatif, Lt-Gen. Muhammad Rafi, Abd al-Hamid Mohtat, Mohammed Eshaq Tokhi.

COUNCIL OF MINISTERS
(November 1990)

Prime Minister: Fazle Haq Khalikyar.

Deputy Prime Ministers: Mahmud Barialay, Dr Namatollah Pazhwak, Abdol Qayum Nurzay, Muhammad Sarwar Mangal, Mahbubollah Koshani.

Deputy Prime Minister and Minister of Planning: Dr Abdol Wahed Sorabi.

Minister of Finance: Mohammad Hakim.

Minister of the Interior: Dr Raz Mohammad Paktin.

Minister of Defence: Gen. Muhammad Aslam Watanjar.

Minister of Foreign Affairs: Abd al-Wakil.

Minister of State Security: Gen. Ghulam Faruq Yaqubi.

Minister of Justice: Prof. Gholam Mahaynodin Darez.

Minister of Commerce: Zakim Shah.

Minister of Islamic Affairs and Endowment: Mohammed Sediq Saylani.

Minister of Higher and Vocational Education: Dr Prof. Mohammad Anwar Shamas.

Minister of Public Health: Prof. Mehr Mohammad Ejazi.

Minister of Agriculture and Land Reform: Eng. Muhammad Ghofran.

Minister of Border Affairs: Sarjang Zazi.

Minister of Returnees' Affairs: Fateh Mohammad Tarin.

Minister of Education and Training: Masoma Esmati Wardak.

Minister of Civil Aviation and Tourism: Hamidollah Tarzi.

Minister of Transport: Khalilullah.

Minister of Mines and Industries: Abdol Samad Salah.

Minister of Water and Electricity: Mir Abdol Ghafur Rahim.

Minister of Construction Affairs: Dr Faqir Mohammad Nekzad.

Minister of Communications: Eng. Sayed Nasem Ulowi.

Minister of Revival and Rural Development: Eng. Hayatollah Azizi.

Minister of Light Industries and Foodstuffs: Dr Mohammad Anwar Dost.

Minister of Information and Culture: Abdol Bashir Roygar.

Minister of Social Security: Saleha Faruq Etemadi.

Minister of Central Statistics: Gholam Mayhudin Shabaz.

Ministers without Portfolio: Dr Nur Ahmad Barets, Dr Faqir Mohammad Yaqubi, Dr Shah Wali, Sayd Ekram Paygir.

AFGHANISTAN
Directory

MINISTRIES

Office of the Council of Ministers: Shar Rahi Sedarat, Kabul; tel. (93) 26926.

Office of the Prime Minister: Shar Rahi Sedarat, Kabul; tel. (93) 26926.

Ministry of Agriculture and Land Reform: Jamal Mina, Kabul; tel. (93) 41151.

Ministry of Border Affairs: Shah Mahmud Ghazi Ave, Kabul; tel. (93) 21793.

Ministry of Civil Aviation and Tourism: POB 165, Ansari Wat, Kabul; tel. (93) 21015.

Ministry of Commerce: Darulaman Wat, Kabul; tel. (93) 41041; telex 234.

Ministry of Communications: Puli Bagh-i-Omomi, Kabul; tel. (93) 21341; telex 297.

Ministry of Construction Affairs: Micro-Rayon, Kabul; tel. (93) 63701.

Ministry of Defence: Darulaman Wat, Kabul; tel. (93) 41232; telex 325.

Ministry of Education: Mohd Jan Khan Wat, Kabul; tel. (93) 25151.

Ministry of Energy: Micro-Rayon, Kabul; tel. (93) 25109.

Ministry of Finance: Shar Rahi Pashtunistan, Kabul; tel. (93) 26041.

Ministry of Foreign Affairs: Shah Mahmud Ghazi St, Shar-i-Nau, Kabul; tel. (93) 25441; telex 232.

Ministry of Higher and Vocational Education: Jamal Mina, Kabul; tel. (93) 40041.

Ministry of Information and Culture: Mohd Jan Khan Wat, Kabul.

Ministry of the Interior: Shar-i-Nau, Kabul; tel. (93) 32441.

Ministry of Islamic Affairs: Kabul.

Ministry of Justice: Shar Rahi Pashtunistan, Kabul; tel. (93) 23404.

Ministry of Light Industries and Foodstuffs: Ansari Wat, Kabul; tel. (93) 41551.

Ministry of Mines and Industries: Shar Rahi Pashtunistan, Kabul; tel. (93) 25841; telex 260.

Ministry of Planning: Shar-i-Nau, Kabul; tel. (93) 21273.

Ministry of Public Health: Micro-Rayon, Kabul; tel. (93) 40851.

Ministry of State Security: Kabul.

Ministry of Transport: Ansari Wat, Kabul; tel. (93) 25541.

Ministry of Water Resources Development and Irrigation: Darulaman Wat, Kabul; tel. (93) 40743.

EXECUTIVE BOARD OF THE CENTRAL COUNCIL OF THE HOMELAND PARTY

Full Members: Dr Najibullah, Dr Raz Mohammad Paktin, Sultan Ali Keshtmand, Suleiman La'eq, Abd al-Wakil, Gen. Ghulam Faruq Yaqubi, Farid Ahmad Mazdak, Gen. Muhammad Aslam Watanjar, Gen. Muhammad Rafi, Mahmud Barialay, Najmuddin Kawiani, Nazar Muhammad, Nur Ahmad Nur.

Candidate Members: Sayed Ekram Paygir, Abdul Qodus Ghorbandi.

Legislature

MELI SHURA
(National Assembly)

The Meli Shura, which was established in 1987 and replaced the Revolutionary Council, is composed of two houses: the Wolasi Jirgah (House of Representatives) and the Sena (Senate). Elections were held to both houses in April 1988.

Wolasi Jirgah

Representatives are elected for five years. Of the total 234 seats, 184 were contested in the general election in April 1988. The remaining 50 seats were reserved for members of the opposition.

Chairman: Dr Khalil Ahmad Abawi.

Deputy Chairmen: Dr Saleh Mohammad Zerai, Zohorullah Zohori.

Sena

The Sena comprises 192 members. One-third of its members are elected for five years, one-third are elected for three years, and one-third are appointed for three years. At the general election in 1988, 115 senators were elected, while the majority of the remaining 77 seats were filled by senators appointed by the President. A small number of seats were reserved for members of the opposition.

Chairman: Dr Mahmud Habibi.

Deputy Chairmen: Helaludin Badri, Prof. Shah Ali Akbar Shahritany.

Political Organizations

Homeland Party (Hizb-i Watan): Kabul; f. 1965 as People's Democratic Party of Afghanistan (PDPA), split 1967; refounded 1976, when the Khalq (Masses) Party and its splinter Parcham (Flag) Party reunited and absorbed the Musawat Party; renamed Homeland Party in 1990; 205,000 mems; Chair. Dr Najibullah; Vice-Chair. Suleiman La'eq, Farid Ahmad Mazdak, Abdul Mobin, Najmuddin Kawiani, Nazar Muhammad.

National Front (NF): POB 2514, Kabul; tel. (93) 62006; f. 1981, as National Fatherland Front, as union of PDPA representatives, nat. and tribal groups; aims to promote nat. unity, reconciliation and reconstruction; became a collective organization for all legal political activity in 1987, when it was renamed National Front; merged with the Peace Front of Afghanistan in 1990; Exec. Board of 39 mems; Chair. Cen. Council Farid Ahmad Mazdak (acting); First Dep. Chair. Abdul Qodus Ghorbandi; more than 1m. mems.

In July 1987 a law permitting the formation of other political parties was introduced. In order to be officially recognized, a party must support national reconciliation, have at least 500 members and be based in Kabul.

The following organizations have been approved and registered as political parties by the Government since November 1987:

Hezbollah-e Afghanistan: Kabul; f. 1990; Chair. Alhaj Shaikh Ali Wosoqusalam Wosoqi.

Islamic Party of the People of Afghanistan (IPPA): Kabul; Chair. Qari Abd as-Satar Serat; Vice-Chair. Maulvi Nasrollah Hanifi.

Ittehad-i-Ansarollah (Union of Followers of God): Kabul; f. 1988; Islamic; became collective mem. of NF in Jan. 1989; Pres. Haji Zafar Muhammad Khadem.

Kargaran-e Jawan-e Afghanistan (KJA) (Young Workers' Organization of Afghanistan): Kabul; f. 1989; First Sec. Abdol Ghafar Sharifi.

Pashtun khwa Meli Awami Party: f. 1989.

Peasants' National Unity (PNU) (Bazgari Meli Ittehad): Kabul; f. as Peasants' Justice Party of Afghanistan; renamed the PNU in 1990; Chair. Abd al-Hakim Tawana.

Solidarity Movement of Afghan People: Kabul; f. 1988; Chair. Mohammad Sarwar Lemach.

Toilers' Organization of Afghanistan (TOA): Kabul; left-wing; signed co-operation agreement with the PDPA in 1987; First Sec. Hamidollah Gran.

Toilers' Revolutionary Organization of Afghanistan (TROA): Kabul; f. 1968; left-wing; signed co-operation agreement with the PDPA in 1987; Leaders Mahbubullah Koshani, Muhammad Bashir Baghlani, Muhammad Eshaq Kawa.

Unity of Strugglers for Peace and Progress in Afghanistan (Etafaq-e Mabarezan-e Solha wa taraqi Afghanistan): Kabul; f. 1990.

There are many insurgent groups of Mujaheddin fighting against the Soviet-backed Government in Afghanistan. The different groups co-operate to varying degrees, but relations are often strained by rivalry and feuding. In May 1985 seven major groups (each with its headquarters in Pakistan) formed a grand alliance, called the **Ittehad-i-Islami Afghan Mujaheddin** (Islamic Unity of Afghan Mujaheddin—IUAM; POB 185, Charsadda Rd, Peshawar, Pakistan; the leadership is changed every three months; c. 100,000 mems), comprising three moderate/traditionalist groups:

Harakat-i-Inqilab-i-Islami (Movement for Islamic Revolution): Leader Mawlawi Mohammad Nabi Mohammadi; c. 20,000 supporters.

Jebha-i-Nejat-i-Melli Afghanistan (Afghan National Liberation Front): Leader Prof. Sibghatullah Mojaddedi; Sec.-Gen. Zabihollah Mojaddedi; c. 35,000 supporters.

Mahaz-i-Melli-i-Islami (National Islamic Front): Leader Pir Sayed Ahmad Gailani; c. 20,000 supporters.

and four fundamentalist (Sunni) groups:

Hizb-i Islami (Islamic Party): split into two factions in 1979; Leaders Gulbuddin Hekmatyar (c. 35,000 supporters) and Maulvi Muhammad Yunus Khalis (c. 10,000 supporters).

Jamiat-i Islami (Islamic Society): f. 1970; Leader Prof. Burhanuddin Rabbani; c. 20,000 supporters.

AFGHANISTAN

Ittehad-i-Islami (Islamic Unity): Leader Prof. ABD AR-RASUL SAYEF; Deputy Leader AHMAD SHAH; c. 15,000 supporters.

In June 1987 eight Afghan Islamic (Shi'a) factions (originally based in Teheran, Iran) formed the **Islamic Coalition Council of Afghanistan** (ICCA Leader: ABDUL KARIM KHALEELI), comprising: the **Afghan Nasr Organization** (c. 50,000 supporters), the **Guardians of Islamic Jihad of Afghanistan**, the **United Islamic Front of Afghanistan**, the **Islamic Force of Afghanistan**, the **Dawa Party of Islamic Unity of Afghanistan**, the **Harakat-e Eslami Afghanistan** (the Islamic Movement of Afghanistan; Leader: Ayatollah ASEF MOHSENI; 20,000 supporters), the **Hezbollah** (c. 4,000 supporters), and the **Islamic Struggle for Afghanistan**. The Consultative Council of the ICCA transferred its headquarters to Peshawar, Pakistan, in September 1990.

Diplomatic Representation

EMBASSIES IN AFGHANISTAN*

Austria: POB 24, Zarghouna Wat, Kabul; tel. (93) 32720; telex 218; Ambassador: (vacant).

Bangladesh: POB 510, House 19, Sarak 'H', Wazir Akbar Khan Mena, Kabul; tel. (93) 25783; Chargé d'affaires a.i.: MAHMOOD HASAN.

Bulgaria: Wazir Akbar Khan Mena, Kabul; tel. (93) 22996; Ambassador: IVAN IVANOV MATEEV.

China, People's Republic: Shah Mahmud Wat, Shar-i-Nau, Kabul; tel. (93) 20446; Chargé d'affaires a.i.: ZHANG DELIANG.

Cuba: Shar Rahi Haji Yaqub, opp. Shar-i-Nau Park, Kabul; tel. (93) 30863; Ambassador: REGINO FARINAS CANTERO.

Czechoslovakia: Taimani Wat, Kala-i-Fatullah, Kabul; tel. (93) 32082; Ambassador: BOHUSLAV HANDL.

Denmark: Kabul; Ambassador: (vacant).

France: Shar-i-Nau, Kabul; tel. (93) 23631; Chargé d'affaires: THIERRY BERNADAC.

Germany: Ghazi Ayub Khan Wat, Shar-i-Nau, Kabul; tel. (93) 20782; telex 249; Ambassador: HORST LINDNER.

Hungary: POB 830, Sin 306-308, Wazir Akbar Khan Mena, Kabul; tel. (93) 24281; Ambassador: MIHÁLY GOLUB.

India: Malalai Wat, Shar-i-Nau, Kabul; tel. (93) 30557; Ambassador: VIJAY K. NAMBIAR.

Indonesia: POB 532, Wazir Akbar Khan Mena, District 10, House 93, Kabul; tel. (93) 23334; telex 239; Chargé d'affaires a.i.: HAFIZ ABDOL GHANI.

Iran: Shar-i-Nau, Kabul; tel. (93) 26255; Chargé d'affaires a.i.: AHMAD KHUDADADI.

Iraq: POB 523, Wazir Akbar Khan Mena, Kabul; tel. (93) 24797; Ambassador: BURHAN KHALIL GHAZAL.

Italy: POB 606, Khoja Abdullah Ansari Wat, Kabul; tel. (93) 24624; telex 55; Chargé d'affaires a.i.: Mr CALAMAI.

Japan: POB 80, Wazir Akbar Khan Mena, Kabul; tel. (93) 26844; telex 216; Chargé d'affaires a.i.: KEIKI HIRAGA.

Korea, Democratic People's Republic: Wazir Akbar Khan Mena, House 28, Sarak 'H' House 103, Kabul; tel. (93) 22161; Ambassador: OH IN-YONG.

Libya: 103 Wazir Akbar Khan Mena, Kabul; tel. (93) 25947; Secretary: SALEM A. EL-HUNI.

Mongolia: Wazir Akbar Khan Mena, Sarak 'T' House 8714, Kabul; tel. (93) 22138; Ambassador: (vacant).

Pakistan: Zarghouna Wat, Shar-i-Nau, Kabul; tel. (93) 21374; Chargé d'affaires a.i.: S. FIDA YUNAS.

Poland: Gozargah St, Kabul; tel. (93) 42461; Ambassador: EDWARD PORADKO.

Turkey: Shar-i-Nau, Kabul; tel. (93) 20072; Chargé d'affaires a.i.: SALIH ZEKI KARACA.

USSR: Darulaman Wat, Kabul; tel. (93) 41541; Ambassador: BORIS NIKOLAYEVICH PASTUKHOV.

United Kingdom: Karte Parwan, Kabul; tel. (93) 30511; Chargé d'affaires a.i.: IAN W. MACKLEY.

USA: Wazir Akbar Khan Mena, Kabul; tel. (93) 62230; Chargé d'affaires a.i.: JON D. GLASSMANN.

Viet-Nam: 3 Nijat St, Wazir Akbar Khan Mena, Kabul; tel. (93) 26596; Ambassador: (vacant).

Yugoslavia: POB 53, 923 Main Rd, Wazir Akbar Khan Mena, Kabul; tel. (93) 61671; telex 272; Chargé d'affaires a.i.: VELIBOR DULOVIĆ

* Not all of the above mentioned countries recognize the Soviet-backed administration as the legitimate government of Afghanistan.

Judicial System

The functions and structure of the judiciary are established in Articles 107–121 of the Constitution ratified by the Loya Jirgah in November 1987 and amended in May 1990.

The courts apply the provisions of the Constitution and the laws of the Republic of Afghanistan, and, in cases of ambivalence, will judge in accordance with the rules of Shari'a (Islamic religious law). Trials are held in open session except when circumstances defined by law deem the trial to be held in closed session. Trials are conducted in Pashtu and Dari or in the language of the majority of the inhabitants of the locality. The right to speak in court in one's mother tongue is guaranteed to the two sides of the lawsuit.

The judiciary comprises the Supreme Court and those courts which are formed in accordance with the directives of the law. The State may establish specialized courts within the unified system of the judiciary.

The highest judicial organ is the Supreme Court, which consists of a Chief Justice, deputy Chief Justices and judges, all of whom are appointed by the President in accordance with the law. It supervises the judicial activities of the courts and ensures the uniformity of law enforcement and interpretation by those courts.

Death sentences are carried out after ratification by the President.

Chief Justice of the Supreme Court: ABDOL KARIM SHADAN.

Deputy Chief Justice of the Supreme Court: ABDOL HAKIM SHARAI JOWZJANI.

The public prosecutor's office consists of the Attorney-General's office and those other attorneys' offices which are formed in accordance with the directives of the law. The Attorney-General supervises the activities of all the attorney offices, which are independent of local organs and answerable only to the Attorney-General himself. The Attorney-General and his deputies, who are appointed by the President in accordance with the law, supervise the implementation and observance of all laws.

Attorney-General: SYED SHARAFUDDIN SHARAF.

Deputy Attorney-General: ABDOL HAKIM SHARAI JOWZJANI.

Religion

The official religion of Afghanistan is Islam. Muslims comprise 99% of the population, approximately 80% of them of the Sunni and the remainder of the Shi'ite sect. There are small minority groups of Hindus, Sikhs and Jews.

ISLAM

The High Council of Ulema and Clergy of Afghanistan: Kabul; f. 1980; 7,000 mems; Gen. Dir Alhaj GHOLAM SARWAR MANZUR; Dep. Dirs ABDUL AZIZE QIASARI, MOHAMMED MUSA TAHERI.

The Press

The newspapers and periodicals marked * were reported to be the only ones appearing regularly in 1988.

PRINCIPAL DAILIES

Akhbar-e-Hafta: Kabul; f. 1989; pro-Homeland Party; Editor ZAHER TANIN.

***Anis:** (Friendship): Kabul; f. 1927; evening; independent; Dari and Pashtu; news and literary articles; organ of the NF; Chief Editor MOHAMMAH S. KHARNIKASH; circ. 25,000.

Badakhshan: Faizabad; f. 1945; Dari and Pashtu; Chief Editor HADI ROSTAQI; circ. 3,000.

Bedar: Mazar-i-Sharif; f. 1920; Dari and Pashtu; Chief Editor ROZEQ FANI; circ, 2,500.

Ettehadi-Baghlan: Baghlan; f. 1930; Dari and Pashtu; Chief Editor SHAFIQULLAH MOSHFEQ; circ. 1,200.

***Haqiqat-e Enqelab-e Saur** (Truth of the April Revolution): Kabul; f. 1980; Dari; organ of the Homeland Party; Editor BAREQ SHAFII; circ. 50,000.

***Hewad:** Kabul; f. 1959; Dari and Pashtu; state-owned; Editor-in-Chief ABDULLAH BAKHTIANAE; circ. 12,200.

***Ittifak Islam:** Herat; Dari and Pashtu.

Jawzjan: Jawzjan; f. 1942; Dari and Pashtu; Chief Editor A. RAHEM HAMRO; circ. 1,500.

***Kabul New Times:** POB 983, Ansari Wat, Kabul; tel. (93) 01841; f. 1962 as Kabul Times, renamed 1980; English; state-owned; Editor-in-Chief M. SEDDIQ RAHPOE; circ. 5,000.

AFGHANISTAN
Directory

Nangarhor: Jalalabad; f. 1919; Pashtu; Chief Editor MORAD SANGARMAL; circ. 1,500.

Payam (Message): Kabul; f. 1988; organ of the Homeland Party.

Sanae: Parwan; f. 1953; Dari and Pashtu; Chief Editor G. SAKHI ESHANZADA; circ. 1,700.

*****Seistan:** Farah; f. 1947; Dari and Pashtu; Editor-in-Chief M. ANWAR MAHAL; circ. 1,800.

Tulu-i-Afghan: Qandahar; f. 1924; Pashtu; Chief Editor TAHER SHAFEQ; circ. 1,500.

Wolanga: Paktia; f. 1943; Pashtu; Chief Editor M. ANWAR; circ. 1,500.

PERIODICALS

*****Adalat** (Justice): Kabul; f. 1988; monthly; organ of the Peasants' National Unity.

*****Afghanistan:** Historical Society of Afghanistan, Kabul; tel. (93) 30370; f. 1948; quarterly; English and French; historical and cultural; Editor MALIHA ZAFAR.

*****Afghanistan Today:** Block 106, Ansari Wat, Kabul; tel. (93) 61868; telex 333; f. 1985; every 2 months; state-owned; socio-political, economics and cultural; CEO KARIM HOQOUQ; circ. 10,500.

*****Al-Eslam:** Kabul; f. 1988; monthly; organ of the Islamic Party of the People of Afghanistan; Editor-in-Chief Mawlawi NASROLLAH HANIFI; circ. 5,000.

*****Aryana:** Historical Society of Afghanistan, Kabul; tel. (93) 30370; f. 1943; quarterly; Pashtu and Dari; cultural and historical; Editor ABD AL-HADI HAND.

*****Awaz:** Kabul; f. 1940; monthly; Pashtu and Dari; radio and television programmes; Editor NASIR TOHORI; circ. 20,000.

*****Erfan:** Ministry of Education, Mohd Jan Khan Wat, Kabul; tel. (93) 21612; f. 1923; monthly; Dari and Pashtu; education, psychology, mathematics, religion, literature and technology; Chief Editor MOHAMMAD QASEM HILAMAN; circ. 8,000.

Ershad-e-Islam (Islamic Precepts): Kabul; f. 1987; publ. by the Ministry of Islamic Affairs; Editor MUHAMMAD SALEM KHARES.

*****Gharjestan:** Kabul; f. 1988; every two months; political and cultural; for the people of Hazara.

Gorash: Ministry of Information and Culture, Mohd Jan Khan Wat, Kabul; f. 1979; weekly; Turkmani; Chief Editor S. MISEDIQ AMINI; circ. 1,000.

*****Haqiqat-e-Sarbaz:** Ministry of Defence, Kabul; f. 1980; 3 a week; Dari and Pashtu; Chief Editor MER JAMALUDDIN FAKHR; circ. 18,370.

Helmand: Bost; f. 1954; 2 a week; Pashtu; Editor-in-Chief M. OMER FARHAT BALEGH; circ. 1,700.

Herat: Ministry of Information and Culture, Mohd Jan Khan Wat, Kabul; f. 1923; monthly; Dari and Pashtu; Chief Editor JALIL SHABGER FOLADYON.

*****Kabul:** Afghanistan Academy of Sciences, Research Centre for Languages and Literature, Akbar Khan Mena, Kabul; f. 1931; monthly; Pashtu; literature and language research; Editor N. M. SAHEEM.

*****Kar:** POB 756, Kabul; tel. (93) 24435; telex 372; monthly; publ. by the Central Council of the National Union of Afghanistan Employees; Editor-in-Chief A. R. ASHTY; circ. 10,000.

*****Kunar Periodical Journal:** Asadabad; f. 1987; Pashtu; news and socio-economic issues; circ. 5,000.

Meli Jabha: Kabul; weekly; organ of the National Front.

Mojala-e-Ariana (Light): Kabul; f. 1978; monthly; Dari and Pashtu; Editor-in-Chief RASHID ASHTI; circ. 1,000.

*****Muhasel-e-Emroz** (Today's Student): Kabul; f. 1986; monthly; state-owned; juvenile; circ. 5,000.

Nengarhar: Kabul; f. 1919; weekly; Pashtu; Editor-in-Chief KARIM HASHIMI; circ. 1,500.

Palwasha: Kabul; f. 1988; fortnightly; Publr and Editor-in-Chief SHAH ZAMAN WREZ STANIZAI.

*****Pamir:** Micro-Rayon, Kabul; tel. (93) 20585; f. 1952; fortnightly; Dari and Pashtu; combined organ of the Kabul Cttee and Municipality; Chief Editor ENAYET POZHOHAN GURDANI; circ. 30,000.

Payam-e-Haq: Kabul; f. 1953; monthly; Dari and Pashtu; Editor-in-Chief FARAH SHAH MOHIBI; circ. 1,000.

Samangon: Aibak; f. 1978; weekly; Dari; Editor-in-Chief M. MOHSEN HASSAN; circ. 1,500.

Sawad (Literacy): Kabul; f. 1954; monthly; Dari and Pashtu; Editor-in-Chief MALEM GOL ZADRON; circ. 1,000.

*****Seramiasht:** POB 3066, Afghan Red Crescent Society, Puli Artal, Kabul; tel. (93) 30969; telex 318; f. 1958; 2 a month; Dari, Pashtu and English; Editor H. R. JADIR; circ. 2,000.

Sob: Kabul; tel. (93) 25240; f. 1979; weekly; Baluchi; Editor-in-Chief WALIMUHAMMAD ROKHSHONI; circ. 1,000.

Talim wa Tarbia (Education): Kabul; f. 1954; monthly; publ. by Institute of Education.

Urdu (Military): Kabul; f. 1922; quarterly; Dari and Pashtu; military journal; issued by the Ministry of Defence; Chief Editor KHALIL-ULAH AKBARI; circ. 500.

*****Voice of Peace:** The Extraordinary Supreme Commission for National Reconciliation of Afghanistan, Kabul; f. 1987; fortnightly; Dari and Pashtu; peace and reconciliation.

*****Yulduz** (Star): Ministry of Information and Culture, Mohd Jan Khan Wat, Kabul; f. 1979; weekly; Uzbeki and Turkmani; Chief Editor EKHAN BAYONI; circ. 2,000.

*****Zendagi-e Hezbi** (Party Life): Kabul; f. 1987; 6 a year; Dari and Pashtu; issued by the Homeland Party.

Zeray: Afghanistan Academy of Sciences, Research Centre for Languages and Literature, Akbar Khan Mena, Kabul; f. 1938; weekly; Pashtu; Pashtu folklore, literature and language; Editor MUHAMMAD NASSER; circ. 1,000.

*****Zhwandoon** (Life): Kabul; tel. (93) 26849; f. 1944; weekly; Pashtu and Dari; illustrated; Editor ROHELA ROSEKH KHORAMI; circ. 1,400.

NEWS AGENCIES

Bakhtar News Agency: Ministry of Information and Culture, Mohd Jan Khan Wat, Kabul; tel. (93) 24089; telex 210; f. 1939; Pres. GHOLAM SARWAR YURESH; Dir ABD AL-QUDDUS TANDER.

Foreign Bureaux

Československá tisková kancelář (ČTK) (Czechoslovakia): POB 673, Kabul; tel. (93) 23419; telex 79.

The following foreign agencies are also represented in Kabul: IAN (USSR; Correspondent ALEKSANDR TRUBIN) and Tanjug (Yugoslavia).

PRESS ASSOCIATION

Union of Journalists of Afghanistan: Wazir Akbar Khan Mena, St 13, Kabul; f. 1980; Chair. MOHAMMAD HASAN BAREQ SHAFAI; Sec. MAHMUD HABIBI.

Publishers

Afghan Book: POB 206, Kabul; f. 1969; books on various subjects, translations of foreign works on Afghanistan, books in English on Afghanistan and Dari language textbooks for foreigners; Man. Dir JAMILA AHANG.

Afghanistan Today Publishers: POB 983, c/o The Kabul New Times, Ansari Wat, Kabul; tel. (93) 61847; publicity materials; answers enquiries about Afghanistan.

Balhaqi Book Publishing and Importing Institute: POB 2025, Kabul; tel. (93) 26818; f. 1971 by co-operation of the Government Printing House, Bakhtar News Agency and leading newspapers; publishers and importers of books; Pres. MUHAMMAD ANWAR NUMYALAI.

Book Publishing Institute: Herat; f. 1970 by co-operation of Government Printing House and citizens of Herat; books on literature, history and religion.

Book Publishing Institute: Qandahar; f. 1970; supervised by Government Printing House; mainly books in Pashtu language.

Educational Publications: Ministry of Education, Mohd Jan Khan Wat, Kabul; tel. (93) 21716; textbooks for primary and secondary schools in the Pashtu and Dari languages; also three monthly magazines in Pashtu and in Dari.

Franklin Book Programs Inc: POB 332, Kabul.

Historical Society of Afghanistan: Kabul; tel. (93) 30370; f. 1931; mainly historical and cultural works and two quarterly magazines: *Afghanistan* (English and French), *Aryana* (Dari and Pashtu); Pres. AHMAD ALI MOTAMEDI.

Institute of Geography: Kabul University, Kabul; geographical and related works.

International Center for Pashtu Studies: Kabul; f. 1975 by the Afghan Govt with the assistance of UNESCO; research work on the Pashtu language and literature and on the history and culture of the Pashtu people; Pres. and Assoc. Chief Researcher J. K. HEKMATY; publs *Pashtu* (quarterly).

Kabul University Press: Kabul; tel. (93) 42433; f. 1950; textbooks; two quarterly scientific journals in Dari and in English, etc.

Research Center for Linguistics and Literary Studies: Afghanistan Academy of Sciences, Akbar Khan Mena, Kabul; tel. (93)

AFGHANISTAN

26912; f. 1978; research on Afghan languages (incl. Pashtu, Dari, Baluchi and Uzbek) and Afghan folklore; Pres. Prof. MOHAMMED R. ELHAM; publs *Kabul* (Pashtu), *Zeray* (Pashtu weekly) and *Khurasan* (Dari).

Government Publishing House

Government Printing House: Kabul; tel. (93) 26851; f. 1870 under supervision of the Ministry of Information and Culture; four daily newspapers in Kabul, one in English; weekly, fortnightly and monthly magazines, one of them in English; books on Afghan history and literature, as well as textbooks for the Ministry of Education; 13 daily newspapers in 13 provincial centres and one journal and also magazines in three provincial centres; Dir MUHAMMAD AYAN AYAN.

Radio and Television

In 1986 there were an estimated 1.5m. radio receivers and 115,000 television receivers in use. Television broadcasting in colour began in August 1978 with a transmission range of 50 km. In March 1985 new radio stations were commissioned in Qandahar, Herat, Jalalabad, Ghazni and Asadabad, in addition to existing main stations in the provinces of Kabul and Nangarhar. Further radio stations were to be established in the provinces of Paktia, Farah and Badakhshan.

State Committee for Radio, Television and Cinematography: Ansari Wat, Kabul; tel. (93) 25241; telex 288; Chair. (vacant).

Radio Afghanistan and TV Afghanistan: POB 544, Ansari Wat, Kabul; tel. (93) 25241; under the supervision of the Ministry of Communications; in 1988 TV Afghanistan was broadcast 10 hours daily; home service (Radio) in Dari, Pashtu, Pashai, Nuristani, Uzbeki, Turkmani and Balochi; foreign service in Urdu, Arabic, English, Russian, German, Dari and Pashtu; Pres. (Radio) SAYED YAQUB WASIQ; Pres. (Television) ABDULLAH SHADAN.

Finance

(cap. = capital; auth. = authorized; p.u. = paid up; res = reserves; m. = million; brs = branches; amounts in afghanis unless otherwise stated)

BANKING

In June 1975 all banks were nationalized. There are no foreign banks operating in Afghanistan.

Da Afghanistan Bank (Central Bank of Afghanistan): Ibne Sina Wat, Kabul; tel. (93) 24075; telex 223; f. 1939; main functions: banknote issue, foreign exchange regulation, credit extensions to banks and leading enterprises and companies, govt and private depository, govt fiscal agency; cap. 4,000m., res 5,299m., dep. 15,008m. (1985); Gov. ABDUL WAHAB ASEFI; Pres. ABD AL-BASHIR RANJBAR; 65 brs.

Agricultural Development Bank of Afghanistan: POB 414, Cineme Pamir Bldg, Jade Maiwand, Kabul; tel. (93) 24459; telex 274; f. 1959; makes available credits for farmers, co-operatives and agro-business; aid provided by IBRD and UNDP; cap. 666.8m., res 498.7m., total resources 3,188.3m. (March 1987); Chair. Dr M. KABIAR; Pres. Dr ABDULLAH NAQSHBANDI.

Banke Milli Afghan (Afghan National Bank): Ibne Sina Wat, Kabul; tel. (93) 25451; telex 231; f. 1932; cap. p.u. 1,000m., res 100.7m., total resources 6,954.8m. (1986); Chair. HAMIDULLAH TARZI; Pres. Dr ABDUL HADI AHMADYAR; 68 brs.

Export Promotion Bank of Afghanistan: 24 Mohd Jan Khan Wat, Kabul; tel. (93) 24447; telex 202; f. 1976; provides financing for exports and export-oriented investments; total assets 12,904.1m. (March 1988); Pres. MOHAMMAD YAQUB NEDA; Vice-Pres. BURHANUDDIN SHAHIM.

Industrial Development Bank of Afghanistan: POB 14, Shar-i-Nau, Kabul; tel. (93) 33336; f. 1973; provides financing for industrial development; total financial resources including cap. 2,500m. (1990); Pres. HAYATULLAH AZIZ; Vice-Pres. A. YARMAND.

Mortgage and Construction Bank: Bldg No. 2, First Part Jade Maiwand, Kabul; tel. (93) 23341; f. 1955 to provide short- and long-term building loans; auth. cap. 200m.; cap. p.u. 100m. (1987); Pres. FAIZ MUHAMMAD ALOKOZI.

Pashtany Tejaraty Bank (Afghan Commercial Bank): Mohd Jan Khan Wat, Kabul; tel. (93) 26551; telex 243; f. 1954 to provide short-term credits, forwarding facilities, opening letters of credit, purchase and sale of foreign exchange; cap. p.u. 1,000m., dep. 7,085.7m., total assets 19,826.4m. (1987); Chair. Dr BASIR RANJBAR; Pres. and CEO ZIR GUL WARDAK; 14 brs.

INSURANCE

There is one national insurance company:

Afghan National Insurance Co: POB 329, Afghan Insurance Bldg, Char-ra-hi-Share Nau, Kabul; tel. (93) 31643; telex 231; f. 1964; mem. of Asian Reinsurance Corpn; marine, aviation, fire, motor and accident insurance; cap. 450m.; Pres. M. Y. DEEN; Vice-Pres. ABD AR-RAZAQ.

No foreign insurance companies are permitted to operate in Afghanistan.

Trade and Industry

CHAMBERS OF COMMERCE AND INDUSTRY

Afghan Chamber of Commerce and Industry: Mohd Jan Khan Wat, Kabul; tel. (93) 26796; telex 245; Pres. MUHAMMAD HAKIM; Vice-Pres. AMAN CAMRAN.

Federation of Afghan Chambers of Commerce and Industry: Darulaman Wat, Kabul; f. 1923; includes chambers of commerce and industry in Ghazni, Qandahar, Kabul (Chair. Mr KARIMZADA), Herat (Chair. Mr SIDIQI), Mazar-i-Sharif, Fariab, Jawzjan, Kunduz, Jalalabad and Andkhoy; Pres. MEHAR CHAND VERMA; Deputy Pres. MUHAMMAD HAKIM.

TRADING CORPORATIONS

Afghan Carpet Exporters' Guild: POB 3159, Darulaman Wat, Kabul; tel. (93) 41765; telex 234; f. 1967; a non-profit making organization of carpet manufacturers and exporters; Pres. ZIAUDDIN ZIA; c. 1,000 mems.

Afghan Cart Company: POB 61, Zarghona-Maidan, Kabul; tel. (93) 21952; telex 57; the largest export/import company in Afghanistan.

Afghan Fruit Processing Co: POB 261, Industrial Estate, Puli Charkhi, Kabul; tel. (93) 65186; telex 261; f. 1960; exports raisins, other dried fruits and nuts.

Afghan Raisin and Other Dried Fruits Institute: POB 3034, Sharara Wat, Kabul; tel. (93) 30463; telex 48; exporters of dried fruits and nuts; Pres. NAJMUDDIN MUSLEH.

Afghan Wool Enterprises: Shar-i-Nau, Kabul; tel. (93) 31963.

Afghanistan Karakul Institute: POB 506, Puli Charkhi, Kabul; tel. (93) 61852; telex 234; f. 1967; exporters of furs; Pres. G. M. BAHEER.

Afghanistan Plants Enterprise: POB 122, Puli Charkhi, Kabul; tel. (93) 31962; exports medicines, plants and spices.

Handicraft Promotion and Export Centre: POB 3089, Sharara Wat, Kabul; tel. (93) 32935; telex 34; Pres. MOMENA RANJBAR.

TRADE UNIONS

In December 1988 union membership stood at 293,703.

National Union of Afghanistan Employees (NUAE): POB 756, Kabul; tel. (93) 23040; telex 372; f. 1978, as Central Council of Afghanistan Trade Unions, to establish and develop the trade union movement, including the formation of councils and organizational cttees in the provinces; changed name in 1990; 285,000 mems; Pres. ABD AS-SATAR PURDELI; Vice-Pres Prof. FAQIR MOHAMMAD ZMARY, AHMADULLAH POYA.

Balkh Council of Trade Unions: Mazar-i-Sharif; Pres. MUHAMMAD KABIR KARGAR.

Central Council of the Union of Craftsmen: Kabul; f. 1987; c. 58,000 mems.

Commerce and Transport Employees' Union: Kabul; Gen. Sec. AHMAD ZIA SIDDIQI.

Construction Employees' Union: Kabul; Gen. Sec. AMINULLAH.

Kabul Union of Furriers: Kabul; Leader ABD AL-KHALIQ.

Mines and Industries Employees' Union: Kabul; Gen. Sec. MOHAMMED AMIN.

Nangarhar Council of Trade Unions: Jalalabad; Deputy Chair. MUQREBUDDIN KARGAR.

Public Health Employees' Union: Kabul; Pres. Prof. M. RAHIM KHUSHDEL.

Public Services Employees' Union: Kabul; Gen. Sec. ABDUL MEJJER TEMORY.

Science and Culture Employees' Union: Kabul; Gen. Sec. T. HABIBZAI.

Traders' Union of Afghanistan: Kabul; Chair. REZWANQOL TAMANA.

Union of Peasant Co-operatives of the Republic of Afghanistan (UPCRA): POB 3272, Dehmazang, Kabul; tel. (93) 42683; telex 241; 1,370,000 mems; Chair. FAZULLAH ALBURZ.

AFGHANISTAN

Weaving and Sewing Employees' Union: Kabul; Gen. Sec. A. W. KARGAR.

Writers' Union of Afghanistan: Kabul; Chair. MOHAMMAD AZAM RAHNAWARD ZARYAB; Vice-Chair. ABDOLLAH BAKHTIANI, AKBAR KARKAR.

Transport

RAILWAYS

In 1977 the Government approved plans for the creation of a railway system. The proposed line (of 1,815 km) was to connect Kabul to Qandahar and Herat, linking with the Iranian State Railways at Islam Quala and Tarakun, and with Pakistan Railways at Chaman. By 1990, however, work had not yet begun on the proposed railway.

A combined road and rail bridge was completed across the Amu-Dar'ya (Oxus) river in 1982, linking the Afghan port of Hairatan with the Soviet port of Termez. There were also plans for a 200-km railway line from Hairatan to Pul-i-Khomri, 160 km north of Kabul, but work had not begun by 1990. It has been reported that Afghan personnel are receiving training in the USSR.

ROADS

Ministry of Communications and **Ministry of Construction Affairs:** Kabul; in 1986 there were 22,000 km of roads. All-weather highways now link Kabul with Qandahar and Herat in the south and west, Jalalabad in the east and Mazar-i-Sharif and the Amu-Dar'ya river in the north.

Land Transport Company: Khoshal Mena, Kabul; tel. (93) 20345; f. 1943; commercial transport within Afghanistan.

Afghan International Transport Company: Kabul.

Afghan Container Transport Company Ltd: POB 3234, Shar-i-Nau, Kabul; tel. (93) 23088; telex 17.

Afghan Transit Company: POB 530, Ghousy Market, Mohd Jan Khan Wat, Kabul; tel. (93) 22654; telex 76.

The Milli Bus Enterprise: Ministry of Transport, Ansari Wat, Kabul; tel. (93) 25541; state-owned and -administered; 721 buses; Pres. Eng. AZIZ NAGHABAN.

INLAND WATERWAYS

There are 1,200 km of navigable inland waterways, including the Amu-Dar'ya (Oxus) river. River ports on the Amu-Dar'ya are linked by road to Kabul.

CIVIL AVIATION

There are international airports at Kabul and Qandahar. There are 30 local airports.

Ministry of Civil Aviation and Tourism: POB 165, Ansari Wat, Kabul; tel. (93) 21015; Dir-Gen. of Air Operations ABD AL-WASEH HAIDARI.

National Airline

Ariana Afghan Airlines: POB 76, Afghan Air Authority Bldg, Ansari Wat, Kabul; tel. (93) 21015; telex 228; f. 1955; merged with Bakhtar Afghan Airlines Co Ltd in October 1985; internal services between Kabul and 18 regional locations; external services to the USSR, Czechoslovakia, India and the UAE; CEO GHOLAM MOHAMMAD MINAYAR; fleet of 2 Boeing 727-100, 2 Tu-154M, 2 Antonov-26, 2 Antonov-24, 2 YAK-40.

Tourism

Afghanistan's potential attractions for the foreign visitor include: Bamian, with its high statue of Buddha and thousands of painted caves; Bandi Amir, with its suspended lakes; the Blue Mosque of Mazar; Herat, with its Grand Mosque and minarets; the towns of Qandahar and Girishk; Balkh (ancient Bactria), 'Mother of Cities', in the north; Bagram, Hadda and Surkh Kotal (of interest to archaeologists); and the high mountains of the Hindu Kush. There were an estimated 9,200 visitors (including 4,700 from the USSR) in 1981, and about the same number in 1982.

Afghan Tour: Ansari Wat, Shar-i-Nau, Kabul; tel. (93) 30152; official travel agency supervised by ATO; Pres. M. OMAR KARIMZADA.

Afghan Tourist Organization (ATO): Ansari Wat, Shar-i-Nau, Kabul; tel. (93) 30323; f. 1958; Pres. M. OMAR KARIMZADA.

Atomic Energy

Atomic Energy Commission: Faculty of Science, Kabul University, Kabul; Pres. Dr MUHAMMAD RASUL.

ALBANIA

Introductory Survey

Location, Climate, Language, Religion, Flag, Capital

The People's Socialist Republic of Albania lies in south-eastern Europe. It is bordered by Yugoslavia to the north and east, by Greece to the south and by the Adriatic and Ionian Seas (parts of the Mediterranean Sea) to the west. The climate is Mediterranean throughout most of the country. The sea plays a moderating role, although frequent cyclones in the winter months make the weather unstable. The average temperature is 14°C (57°F) in the north-east and 18°C (64°F) in the south-west. The language is Albanian, the principal dialects being Gheg (north of the Shkumbini river) and Tosk (in the south). The literary language is being formed on the basis of a strong fusion of the two dialects, with the phonetic and morphological structure of Tosk prevailing. The State recognizes no religion and supports atheist propaganda. All religious institutions were closed in 1967. Before 1946 Islam was the predominant faith, and there were small groups of Christians (mainly Roman Catholic in the north and Eastern Orthodox in the south). The national flag (proportions 7 by 5) is red, with a two-headed black eagle, above which is a gold-edged, five-pointed red star, in the centre. The capital is Tirana (Tiranë).

Recent History

On 28 November 1912, after more than 400 years of Turkish rule, Albania declared its independence under a provisional government. The country was occupied by Italy in 1914 but its independence was re-established in 1920. A republic was proclaimed in 1925 and Ahmet Beg Zogu was elected President. He was proclaimed King Zog in 1928 and reigned until the occupation of Albania by Italy in April 1939, after which Albania was united with the Italian crown for four years. Albania was occupied by German forces in 1943, but they withdrew after a year. A provisional government was formed in October 1944.

The Communist-led National Liberation Front (NLF), established with help from Yugoslav Communists in 1941, was the most successful wartime resistance group and took power on 29 November 1944. Elections in December 1945 were based on a single list of candidates, sponsored by the Communists. The new regime was led by Enver Hoxha, head of the Albanian Communist Party since 1943. King Zog was deposed and the People's Republic of Albania was proclaimed on 11 January 1946. The Communist Party was renamed the Party of Labour of Albania (PLA) in 1948.

The NLF regime had close links with Yugoslavia, including a monetary and customs union, until the latter's expulsion from the Cominform in 1948. Albania's leaders, fearing Yugoslav expansionism, quickly turned against their former mentors. Albania became a close ally of the USSR and joined the Moscow-based Council for Mutual Economic Assistance (CMEA) in 1949. Albania's adherence to the Eastern bloc was weakened by the relaxation of Soviet policy towards Yugoslavia after the death of Marshal Stalin, the Soviet leader, in 1953.

Hoxha resigned as Head of Government in 1954 but retained effective national leadership as First Secretary of the PLA. Albania joined the Warsaw Pact in 1955 but relations with the USSR deteriorated when Soviet leaders attempted a *rapprochement* with Yugoslavia. Albania supported Beijing in the Sino-Soviet ideological dispute. The USSR denounced Albania and broke off relations in 1961. Albania turned increasingly to the People's Republic of China for support, ended participation in the CMEA in 1962 and withdrew from the Warsaw Pact in 1968. However, following the improvement of relations between China and the USA after 1972, Albania became disenchanted with its alliance with Beijing. Sino-Albanian relations deteriorated further upon the death of Mao Zedong, the Chinese leader, in 1976. A new constitution was adopted in December 1976, declaring Albania a People's Socialist Republic, and reaffirming its policy of self-reliance.

In 1974 the Minister of Defence, Gen. Beqir Balluku, was dismissed, but it was not until 1978 that the Government chose to reveal that he had been involved in a plot against it on behalf of China, and that he had been executed in 1975. In 1978 Albania announced its full support of Viet-Nam in its dispute with Beijing, and China formally terminated all economic and military co-operation with Albania.

In September 1979 Hysni Kapo, a member of the PLA's Political Bureau and one of Hoxha's closest collaborators, died. A government reshuffle took place in April 1980, and Mehmet Shehu, Chairman of the Council of Ministers (Prime Minister) since 1954, was relieved of his concurrent post of Minister of Defence. In December 1981 Shehu died as a result of a shooting incident. It was officially reported that he had committed suicide, but other sources suggested his involvement in a leadership struggle with Hoxha. (A year later Hoxha claimed that Shehu had been the leader of a plot to assassinate him, and in March 1985, amidst suggestions that Shehu had in fact been executed—which were subsequently denied by the Government—allegations that Shehu had worked as a secret agent, successively for the USA, the USSR and Yugoslavia, were repeated.) Following the death of Shehu, a new government was formed under Adil Çarçani, hitherto First Deputy Chairman. Feçor Shehu, Minister of the Interior and nephew of Mehmet Shehu, was not reappointed.

In September 1982 a group of armed Albanian exiles landed on the coast, but were promptly disposed of by the authorities. The Pretender to the throne of Albania, Leka I, while not directly involved, admitted his acquaintance with the rebels' leader. In November Ramiz Alia replaced Haxhi Lleshi as President of the Presidium of the People's Assembly (Head of State), and the Council of Ministers was reshuffled. A number of former state and PLA officials, including Feçor Shehu and two other former Ministers, were reportedly executed in September 1983. In February 1984 an additional Deputy Chairman of the Council of Ministers was appointed.

Enver Hoxha died in April 1985. No foreign delegations were permitted to attend the funeral, and a Soviet message of condolence was rejected. Ramiz Alia replaced Hoxha as First Secretary of the PLA, and pledged that he would uphold the independent policies of his predecessor. In mid-1985 the Chairman of the State Planning Commission and the Minister of Finance were replaced. To celebrate the 40th anniversary of the proclamation of the Republic, in January 1986 an amnesty for certain categories of prisoners was announced. In March 1986 Nexhmije Hoxha, widow of Enver Hoxha, was elected to the chair of the General Council of the Democratic Front of Albania.

The Ninth PLA Congress was held in November 1986. The new Central Committee re-elected Ramiz Alia as First Secretary, and the number of full members of the Political Bureau was increased from 10 to 13. Following the election of a new People's Assembly in February 1987, Ramiz Alia was also re-elected President of its Presidium. Adil Çarçani was reappointed Chairman of the Council of Ministers, and the number of Deputy Chairmen was increased from three to four. The Ministry of Light and Foodstuff Industry was divided into two separate Ministries, and a State Control Commission was established at ministerial level. In February 1988 Farudin Hoxha was appointed to the newly-created post of Minister to the Presidium of the Council of Ministers.

In February 1989 an extensive reshuffle of the Government and PLA leadership took place. Changes included the replacement of three Deputy Chairmen of the Council of Ministers and the establishment of the new post of General Secretary of the Council of Ministers, in order to ease the workload of the Chairman. Two of the four Secretaries of the PLA Central Committee were transferred to posts within the Council of Ministers.

In November 1989, on the 45th anniversary of Albania's liberation from Nazi occupation, an amnesty for certain prisoners was declared. A number of political detainees, including some imprisoned for having attempted to flee the country and others convicted on charges of agitation and propaganda against the State, were among those to benefit. In previous years, similar amnesties had excluded political prisoners.

ALBANIA

Yugoslav reports, in December 1989, of anti-Government demonstrations in the town of Shkodër (which were alleged to have been brutally suppressed) and of an incident in October, in which four Albanian citizens of Greek origin were said to have been tortured and killed following an attempt to escape across the border, were strongly denied by the Albanian authorities. At the end of December, encouraged by the dramatic events in Eastern Europe, from exile in South Africa Leka I urged Albanians to rise up and emulate the people of Romania in ousting the country's leadership. In January 1990 Yugoslav sources alleged that public hangings had taken place in Shkodër. In the same month, again according to the Yugoslav media, as many as 7,000 demonstrators were reported to have taken part in a further protest in Shkodër, at which numerous arrests were made.

While continuing to deny the reports of internal unrest, in late January 1990 Ramiz Alia announced proposals for modest political and economic reforms. The principle of offering a choice of candidates at elections was to be introduced, although the leading role of the PLA was to be upheld. Limitations on the terms of office of certain party and state officials were to be imposed, and the powers of the PLA's local organizations were to be expanded. Proposed economic reforms included a degree of decentralization of planning.

A report released in December 1984 by the human rights organization, Amnesty International, had been critical of Albania's detention of thousands of political and religious dissidents. The precise number of detainees remained a subject of much speculation. In February 1990, however, in an unprecedented statement, the Minister of Internal Affairs gave the total prison population as 3,850, of whom only 83 had been convicted for the attempted overthrow of the State by means of violence. The Minister also stated that no prisoner had been detained on grounds of religious activity.

During March and April 1990 further displays of public discontent reportedly took place, protesters being critical of the anti-reformist elements of the PLA and in particular of Nexhmije Hoxha. A strike by 2,000 textile workers at a factory in Berat was believed to be unprecedented.

Extensive reforms of the judicial system were approved by the People's Assembly in May 1990, shortly before a visit to Tirana by the UN Secretary-General, Javier Pérez de Cuéllar. The Ministry of Justice was re-established. The number of capital offences was reduced from 34 to 11, anti-State agitation and propaganda ceasing to be such a crime. Although Albania was to remain an atheist state, religious propaganda would henceforth be tolerated. Furthermore, Albanians were to be granted the right to a passport for the purposes of foreign travel, while the penalty for attempting to flee the country illegally was reduced. Various economic reforms, announced at the same time, included a review of the constitutional ban on the acceptance of foreign credits and investment.

In July 1990 there was renewed unrest, when anti-Government demonstrators took to the streets of Tirana and were violently dispersed by the security forces. In desperation, a number of Albanians fled to the Federal German embassy in search of asylum. Within days, more than 3,000 citizens had followed, while others sought refuge in the embassies of Italy, France, Greece, Turkey, Poland, Hungary and Czechoslovakia, the total soon exceeding 5,000. Living conditions inside the missions rapidly deteriorated. Although denounced by the Albanian authorities, the refugees were nevertheless granted permission to leave the country. A multinational relief operation, co-ordinated by the UN, facilitated the safe evacuation of the Albanians, most of whom ultimately travelled to the Federal Republic of Germany. The Federal German, French and Italian embassies in Tirana were subsequently closed, ostensibly for cleaning.

Meanwhile, during the refugee crisis, both the Council of Ministers and the Political Bureau of the PLA had been reshuffled. A number of prominent 'hardliners' were among those replaced. Hekuran Isai replaced Simon Stefani as Deputy Chairman of the Council of Ministers and Minister of Internal Affairs, the latter being appointed Chairman of the State Control Commission in place of Manush Myftiu, who also lost his position as Deputy Chairman of the Council of Ministers (the number of Deputy Chairmen therefore being reduced to two). Simon Stefani remained a member of the Political Bureau, but Manush Myftiu and two others were removed.

As the process of moderate reform gathered momentum during the course of 1990, the Government suffered a set-back in October when Ismail Kadare, the country's foremost author, who had become increasingly critical of the limitations of the reforms, defected while in Paris. He was immediately granted political asylum in France, causing considerable embarrassment to the Albanian authorities.

In November 1990, against a background of mounting pressure for the pace of reform to be accelerated, Ramiz Alia announced proposals for more radical political changes, urging that the leading role of the PLA be redefined. The new electoral procedure was confirmed, requiring the presentation of at least two candidates for every polling centre at the 1991 elections. A special commission was established for the purpose of examining the need for amendments to the Constitution. In early December it was announced that elections to the People's Assembly were to be held on 10 February 1991.

Albania has diplomatic relations with more than 100 countries. Until 1990 Albania remained hostile to the USSR, Soviet attempts to renew links having been repeatedly rebuffed. Throughout 1989 the Albanian leadership had continued to express its criticism of the reforms taking place in the USSR. Having frequently reiterated its determination not to have any relations with either the USSR or the USA, Albania reversed its policy in April 1990, when Ramiz Alia expressed his willingness to establish relations with both countries. In July Albania and the USSR formally agreed to restore diplomatic relations and to reopen their respective embassies. Delegations from the US Congress visited Albania during 1990, and in October, having addressed the UN General Assembly in New York, Alia visited the Albanian community in Boston.

Following the rift with Beijing in the mid-1970s, Albania had begun to show an interest in emerging from its isolation and in improving relations with Western European nations. The gradual relaxation of isolationist policies culminated in 1990 in a declaration of Albania's desire to establish good relations with all countries, irrespective of their social system. Two separate border incidents during 1984, in which a Frenchman employed on the Greek island of Corfu and a Greek citizen were shot dead by Albanian frontier guards, created only temporary set-backs. In 1985 delegations from the Italian and the French Ministries of Foreign Affairs visited Tirana, and it was reported that secret talks were taking place between Albania and the United Kingdom with a view to re-establishing diplomatic relations (severed as a result of the sinking of two British warships in the Corfu channel in 1946; negotiations continued in 1990). In October 1985 the Albanian Minister of Foreign Trade, Shane Korbeci, visited Italy and was received by the Italian Prime Minister, Bettino Craxi. Relations between the two countries were subsequently strained, however, following an incident involving six Albanian citizens who entered the Italian embassy in Tirana in December 1985 in search of political asylum. In May 1990 the Albanian family was finally permitted to leave for Italy. In December 1986 two Italian trawlers were seized by the Albanian authorities while allegedly fishing illegally in Albania's territorial waters in the vicinity of Vlorë. The eight fishermen concerned were brought to trial in January 1987. Six Italians received suspended prison sentences of between four and 10 months, and the one-year sentences of the two captains were also suspended upon appeal to the Supreme Court. In 1988 a delegation from the French National Assembly was received in Tirana, and the French Secretary of State for Foreign Affairs also visited Albania. In March 1989 Reis Malile became the first Albanian Minister of Foreign Affairs to undertake an official visit to France. Diplomatic relations with Spain were established in September 1986, and with Canada and the Federal Republic of Germany in September 1987. In October 1987 the Federal German Minister of Foreign Affairs paid an official visit to Albania, and in September 1988 the Albanian Minister of Foreign Affairs went to Bonn. Reciprocal visits by official delegations in 1989 maintained this improvement in relations, while links with the German Democratic Republic were also strengthened. Albania welcomed the reunification of Germany in October 1990.

Negotiations between Albania and Greece took place in Athens in 1984, and in December the visit to Tirana by the Greek Minister of State for Foreign Affairs resulted in the signing of several co-operation agreements. In January 1985 the Albanian/Greek border crossing at Kakavija was reopened. In August 1987 Greece formally ended the technical state of war with Albania, in existence since 1945. Relations with Greece continued to improve in 1989, following a further visit to that country in February by the Albanian Minister of

Foreign Affairs. However, the question of the status of the Greek minority in Albania, unofficially estimated to number between 200,000 and 400,000, remains a sensitive issue, as does that of the 2m. ethnic Albanians resident in Yugoslavia. Ideological differences also prevent friendly relations with Yugoslavia. Following riots in the Yugoslav province of Kosovo in 1981 by ethnic Albanians demanding better conditions, relations between Albania and Yugoslavia were strained. During 1985, however, talks on trade and transport between the two countries were successful. In October 1986 the Albanian Minister of Foreign Affairs and the Yugoslav Federal Secretary for Foreign Affairs held discussions at the UN in New York. The meeting was reportedly the first between the two countries' Foreign Ministers since 1946. In 1987 tension was renewed, owing to the failure of the Shkodër–Titograd railway line, but in December the Yugoslav Secretary for Foreign Trade visited Tirana for talks on bilateral co-operation. Relations with Yugoslavia deteriorated sharply in early 1989, when many ethnic Albanian demonstrators were killed during renewed unrest in Kosovo. Links with Turkey were strengthened in August 1988 and February 1989, when the Turkish and Albanian Ministers of Foreign Affairs met for discussions, and in June 1990 the Albanian Chairman of the Council of Ministers visited Turkey. In August 1988 the Japanese Deputy Minister of Foreign Affairs had talks in Tirana. In March 1989 an official visit to the People's Republic of China by the Albanian Deputy Minister of Foreign Affairs (reciprocated in August 1990) indicated a significant modification in Albanian policy.

Albania was not represented at the 1984 Stockholm Conference on Security and Co-operation in Europe (CSCE), but was granted observer status at the 1990 CSCE summit meeting, held in Paris. In February 1988 Albania attended a meeting of Balkan Foreign Ministers, held in Yugoslavia. At the conference, the first of all six Balkan nations for more than 50 years, the Albanian Minister of Foreign Affairs displayed a positive approach and emphasized the need for realism in regional co-operation. The participants agreed that ministerial delegations should meet on a regular basis in order to discuss multilateral co-operation. A meeting of Foreign Ministry officials was held in Tirana in January 1989. Meetings of Balkan Ministers of Energy and of Ministers of Foreign Affairs were also convened in Albania, in May and October 1990 respectively. An Albanian delegation attended an international conference on the prohibition of chemical weapons, held in Paris in January 1989. In August 1990 Albania announced that it was to become a signatory of the Treaty on the Non-Proliferation of Nuclear Weapons.

Government

Nominally the supreme organ of government is the People's Assembly, a single-chamber legislature of 250 deputies. In practice the Assembly meets for only a few days each year to ratify actions taken in its name by the Presidium of the Assembly, whose President is Head of State. Executive authority is held by the Council of Ministers, whose Chairman is Head of Government. The Council is elected by the Assembly.

Real power is held by leaders of the (Communist) Party of Labour of Albania, or Workers' Party, the only political party in the country. The Party has a political monopoly; it controls the entire functioning of government, and all the country's leaders are members. The Party Congress, convened every five years, elects the Central Committee (85 full members and 46 candidate members were elected in November 1986), which, in turn, elects the Political Bureau (Politburo) and the Secretariat.

Elections to the People's Assembly, held every four years, are based on a single list of candidates standing for the Communist-led Democratic Front of Albania.

For local government, Albania is divided into 26 districts, each under a People's Council elected every three years.

Defence

Defence in Albania is conducted under the auspices of the People's Army, which was founded in 1943. Military service lasts for two years in the Army, and three years in the Air Force, Navy and paramilitary units. In June 1990, according to Western estimates, the total strength of the armed forces was 48,000 (including 22,400 conscripts), comprising Army 35,000, Air Force 11,000 and Navy 2,000. The internal security forces number 5,000 and the frontier force 7,000. Defence expenditure in 1990 was estimated at 1,030m. lekë.

Economic Affairs

In 1986, according to unofficial estimates, Albania's gross national product (GNP) was US $2,800m., equivalent to $930 per head. During the seventh Five-Year Plan (1981–85) net material product (NMP) grew by 16%, compared with a target of 35–37%. In comparison with the previous year, NMP expanded by 7.2% in 1986. Figures for 1987 and 1988 were unavailable, but in 1989 NMP was reported to have increased by 10%. Between 1980 and 1988 the population increased by an annual average rate of 2.1%.

The agricultural sector contributed 31.5% of NMP and employed 51.7% of the working population in 1988. In that year co-operatives accounted for almost 75% of agricultural output. From 1990 a limited degree of private enterprise was permitted. The principal crops are wheat, maize, potatoes, sugar beet, citrus fruit, grapes, olives and tobacco. In 1981–85 agricultural production increased by 13%. Compared with the previous year, output rose by 9.7% in 1989.

Industry accounted for 46.3% of NMP and employed 22.9% of the labour force in 1988. In 1981–85 industrial output went up by 27%. In comparison with the previous year, production increased by 5.6% in 1989. Albania is one of the world's largest producers of chromite (chromium ore), output being estimated at 239,000 metric tons (chromium content) in 1987. Copper, nickel and coal are also mined. Albania has adequate petroleum resources and its own refining facilities, and in 1990 invited Western European and US companies to assist in the exploration of both onshore and offshore reserves. (The acceptance of foreign capital in order to establish joint ventures was authorized in 1990.) In 1987 the light and foodstuffs industries provided more than 85% of domestic requirements, while accounting for 38% of gross industrial production and for 40% of the country's total exports. Important industrial products include fertilizers, machinery, building materials, cigarettes, textiles, wine, olive oil and raw sugar.

Hydroelectric generation accounted for more than 80% of total electricity production in 1988. Output of electric energy reached an estimated 3,984m. kWh in 1988, having increased by 150% between 1980 and 1988.

In 1988 imports totalled 3,218m. lekë and exports totalled 2,709m. lekë, resulting in a trade deficit of 509m. lekë. Albania's principal trading partners in 1988 were Italy, the Federal Republic of Germany, Czechoslovakia and Yugoslavia. Trade relations with the USSR were restored in 1990. The main imports are minerals, metals, machinery, chemicals and paper and rubber products. The most important exports are chromite, ferro-nickel ore, copper wire, electricity (rainfall conditions permitting—see below), foodstuffs, tobacco products and handicrafts. In 1988 exports increased by 13%.

The 1990 state budget envisaged revenue of 9,650m. lekë and expenditure of 9,600m. lekë., thus giving a surplus of 50m. During 1986–90 capital investment was to total 24,450m. lekë. In 1989 Albania had no external debt. Until 1990 the Constitution prohibited the acceptance of foreign credits. Retail prices were reported to be stable in 1990.

The eighth Five-Year Plan (1986–90) continued to stress the development of energy and mineral resources, particularly the petroleum industry. Compared with 1985, NMP was to rise by 35–37% and the volume of industrial production by 29–31%. In comparison with the 1981–85 period, average annual agricultural output was to increase by 35–37%. The volume of foreign trade was to expand by 34–36%. Real income per head in 1990 was to be 7–9% higher than in 1985. Recurrent drought, however, led to shortfalls in the agricultural and hydroelectric sectors. The winter of 1988/89 was reported to be the driest for at least 40 years. By 1990 the lack of rain had become an extremely serious problem. Albania was unable to maintain its exports of electricity, thus losing a valuable source of revenue, and production targets for bread grain, industrial crops, potatoes and other agricultural commodities were not fulfilled. Albania was therefore obliged to import supplies of electric energy and foodstuffs. Many factories were unable to operate at full capacity. The 'new economic mechanism', introduced in July 1990 and to be fully implemented in January 1991, allowed industrial and other organizations greater independence. The services and handicrafts sectors were reorganized to permit some free enterprise.

Social Welfare

All medical services are free of charge, and medicines are supplied free to children up to one year of age. Between 1985

ALBANIA

and 1990 expenditure on the health service was to be increased by 17.3%. The 1987 state budget allocated 499m. lekë to the health sector. In 1987 the number of hospitals totalled 158, and there were 12,212 beds available. There were 5,341 doctors and dentists, or one for every 577 persons. Kindergartens and nursery schools receive large subsidies. Women are entitled to 180 days' maternity leave, receiving 80% of salary. There is a non-contributory state social insurance system for all workers, with 70–100% of salary being paid during sick leave, and a pension system for the old and disabled. Retirement pensions represent 70% of the average monthly salary. Men retire between the ages of 50 and 60, and women between 45 and 55.

Education

Education in Albania is provided free at primary and secondary level. Students in higher education pay a fee in accordance with the family income. The state budget allocated 946m. lekë to education and culture in 1987. Children in the age group of three to six years may attend nursery school (kopshte). Children between the ages of seven and 15 years attend an 'eight-year school', which is compulsory. In 1988/89 about 73% of pupils leaving the 'eight-year school' went on to secondary education. Secondary schools in Albania may be divided into three main categories, namely '12-year schools' (shkollat 12-vjeçare) giving four-year general courses, secondary technical-professional schools (shkollat e mesme tekniko-profesionale) which combine vocational training with a general education, and lower vocational schools (shkollat e ulte profesionale) which train workers in the fields of agriculture and industry. The school-year in secondary schools lasts six and a half months. All secondary-school graduates are required to spend a year working in factories or on collective farms.

In the 1988/89 school year a total of 760,000 pupils and students enrolled at educational institutes. The Enver Hoxha University at Tirana has eight faculties and had 12,000 full- and part-time students in 1989/90. Students at higher education institutes spend seven months of every year at the institute, two months in production or construction work, one month in physical culture and military training, and two months on vacation.

Public Holidays

1991: 1 January (New Year's Day), 11 January (Proclamation of the Republic), 1 May (May Day), 7 November (Victory of the October Socialist Revolution), 28 November (Proclamation of Independence), 29 November (Liberation Day 1944).

1992: 1 January (New Year's Day), 11 January (Proclamation of the Republic), 1 May (May Day), 7 November (Victory of the October Socialist Revolution), 28 November (Proclamation of Independence), 29 November (Liberation Day 1944).

Weights and Measures

The metric system is in force.

Statistical Survey

Source (unless otherwise stated): Drejtoria e Statistikës, Tirana.

Area and Population

AREA, POPULATION AND DENSITY

Area (sq km)	
Land	27,398
Inland water	1,350
Total	28,748*
Population (census results)	
January 1979	2,591,000
2 April 1989	3,182,417
Population (official estimates at mid-year)	
1987	3,082,700†
1988	3,143,200
1989	3,208,000
Density (per sq km) at mid-1989	111.6

* 11,100 sq miles.
† Comprising 1,588,500 males and 1,494,200 females.

Ethnic Groups (census of 2 April 1989): Albanian 3,117,601; Greek 58,758; Macedonian 4,697; Montenegrin, Serbian, Croatian, etc. 100; others 1,261.

DISTRICTS (1988)

	Area (sq km)	Population (annual average)	Density (per sq km)
Berat	1,027	173,700	169.1
Dibër	1,568	148,200	94.5
Durrës	848	242,500	286.0
Elbasan	1,481	238,600	161.1
Fier	1,175	239,700	204.0
Gramsh	695	43,800	63.0
Gjirokastër	1,137	65,500	57.6
Kolonjë	805	24,600	30.5
Korçë	2,181	213,200	97.8
Krujë	607	105,300	157.2
Kukës	1,330	99,400	74.7
Lezhë	479	61,100	127.5
Librazhd	1,013	70,800	69.9
Lushnjë	712	132,200	185.7
Mat	1,028	75,900	73.5
Mirditë	867	49,700	57.3
Përmet	929	39,400	42.4
Pogradec	725	70,500	97.2
Pukë	1,034	48,200	46.6
Sarandë	1,097	86,800	78.9
Shkodër	2,528	233,000	92.2
Skrapar	775	45,800	59.1
Tepelenë	817	49,100	60.1
Tiranë	1,238	363,100	293.3
Tropojë	1,043	44,200	42.4
Vlorë	1,600	171,000	108.1
Total	**28,748**	**3,138,100**	**109.2**

Source: *Statistical Yearbook of the PSR of Albania*.

ALBANIA

PRINCIPAL TOWNS (population at mid-1987)

Tiranë (Tirana, the capital)	225,700
Durrës (Durazzo)	78,700
Elbasan	78,300
Shkodër (Scutari)	76,300
Vlorë (Vlonë or Valona)	67,700
Korçë (Koritsa)	61,500
Berat	40,500
Fier	40,300
Lushnjë	26,900
Kavajë	24,200
Gjirokastër	23,800
Qyteti Stalin	20,600

Source: *Statistical Yearbook of the PSR of Albania.*

BIRTHS, MARRIAGES AND DEATHS

	Registered live births		Registered marriages		Registered deaths	
	Number	Rate (per 1,000)	Number	Rate (per 1,000)	Number	Rate (per 1,000)
1984	79,177	27.3	26,397	9.1	16,618	5.7
1985	77,535	26.2	25,271	8.5	17,179	5.8
1986	76,435	25.3	25,718	8.5	17,369	5.7
1987	79,696	25.9	27,370	8.9	17,119	5.6
1988	80,241	25.5	28,174	9.0	17,027	5.4

Average Life Expectation (1987/88): 72.0 years (Males 69.4 years, Females 74.9 years).

Source: *Statistical Yearbook of the PSR of Albania.*

ECONOMICALLY ACTIVE POPULATION
(ILO estimates, '000 persons at mid-1980)

	Males	Females	Total
Agriculture, etc.	338	339	677
Industry	237	74	311
Services	144	79	223
Total	**719**	**492**	**1,211**

Source: ILO, *Economically Active Population Estimates and Projections, 1950–2025.*

Mid-1988 (estimates in '000): Agriculture, etc. 739; Total 1,483 (Source: FAO, *Production Yearbook*).

EMPLOYMENT IN THE 'SOCIALIZED' SECTOR
(excluding agricultural co-operatives)

	1986	1987
Industry	272,300	287,000
Construction	78,300	77,800
Agriculture	182,100	190,300
Transport and communications	38,000	39,600
Trade	55,400	56,400
Education and culture	55,800	57,600
Health service	37,200	37,700
Others	40,300	41,800
Total	**759,400**	**788,200**

1988: Total: 811,000.
Source: *Statistical Yearbook of the PSR of Albania.*

Agriculture

PRINCIPAL CROPS ('000 metric tons)

	1986*	1987*	1988
Wheat and spelt	555	565	589
Rice (paddy)	11	11	11
Barley	36	38	40*
Maize	320	320	306
Rye	10	10	11*
Oats	30	30	30*
Sorghum	36	36	38*
Potatoes	131	135	137*
Dry beans	21	21	21*
Sunflower seed	33	30	27*
Seed cotton	15	14	14*
Cotton seed	9	9	9*
Olives	40	40	42*
Vegetables	187	188	188*
Grapes	85	88	88*
Sugar beet	330	360	360*
Apples	18	19	20*
Plums	20	21	23*
Oranges	14	15	16*
Tobacco (leaves)	20†	20†	29*
Cotton (lint)	4	4	4*

* FAO estimate(s). † Unofficial estimate.
Source: FAO, *Production Yearbook.*

LIVESTOCK

	1986	1987	1988
Horses	53,100	56,400	
Mules	18,200	17,900	176,000
Asses	90,800	95,300	
Cattle	618,600	671,900	696,000
Pigs	209,200	214,400	197,000
Sheep	1,346,500	1,432,300	1,525,000
Goats	918,900	979,100	1,076,000
Poultry	n.a.	5,221,000	5,062,000

Source: *Statistical Yearbook of the PSR of Albania.*

LIVESTOCK PRODUCTS (FAO estimates, metric tons)

	1986	1987	1988
Beef and veal	27,000	28,000	28,000
Mutton and lamb	18,000	18,000	19,000
Goats' meat	8,000	8,000	8,000
Pig meat	9,000	9,000	9,000
Poultry meat	14,000	14,000	15,000
Cows' milk	345,000	346,000	347,000
Sheep's milk	45,000	45,000	46,000
Goats' milk	31,000	32,000	32,000
Cheese	13,200	13,900	14,400
Butter	3,838	3,879	3,919
Hen eggs	13,200	13,200	14,000
Wool:			
greasy	3,200	3,300	3,400
scoured (clean)	1,920	2,000	2,100
Cattle hides	3,982	4,030	4,068
Sheep and lamb skins	2,394	2,402	2,413
Goat and kid skins	664	665	665

Source: FAO, *Production Yearbook.*

Forestry

ROUNDWOOD REMOVALS ('000 cubic metres)

Annual total 2,330 (Industrial wood 722, Fuel wood 1,608) in 1976–88 (FAO estimates).

ALBANIA

SAWNWOOD PRODUCTION ('000 cubic metres)
Annual total 200 (coniferous 105, broadleaved 95) in 1977–82 (official estimates) and in 1983–88 (FAO estimates).
Source: FAO, *Yearbook of Forest Products*.

Fishing

('000 metric tons, live weight)

	1985	1986	1987
Inland waters	3.1	3.2	3.2
Mediterranean Sea	9.2	8.8	9.3
Total catch	12.3	12.0	12.5

Source: FAO, *Yearbook of Fishery Statistics*.

Mining

PRODUCTION (estimates, '000 metric tons)

	1985	1986	1987
Brown coal (incl. lignite)	2,150	2,300	2,300
Crude petroleum	3,100	3,000	3,000
Natural gas (terajoules)	15,000	15,000	15,000
Copper*†	15.0	15.0	15.0
Nickel*†	10.0	10.0	10.5
Chromium*‡	237	245	239

* Figures relate to the metal content of ores.
† Estimated by Metallgesellschaft Aktiengesellschaft (Frankfurt).
‡ Estimated by the US Bureau of Mines.
Source: UN, *Industrial Statistics Yearbook*.
1988: Lignite 2,184,000 metric tons (Source: *Statistical Yearbook of the PSR of Albania*).

Industry

MAIN INDUSTRIAL PRODUCTS
('000 metric tons, unless otherwise indicated)

	1980	1985	1988
Electric energy (million kWh)	3,717	3,147	3,984
Blister copper	9.8	11	15
Copper wires and cables	5.7	9.4	11.6
Carbonic ferrochrome	12.2	11.9	38.7
Metallurgical coke	173	250	291
Rolled wrought steel	96	107	96
Phosphatic fertilizers	150	157	165
Ammonium nitrate	109	95	96
Urea	88	78	77
Sulphuric acid	72	73	81
Caustic soda	25	29	31
Soda ash	23	22	22
Machinery and equipment (million lekë)	350	465	496
Spare parts (million lekë)	327	407	493
Cement	826	642	746
Bricks and tiles (million pieces)	294	295	319
Refractory bricks	4.8	28	30
Furniture (million lekë)	86	112	131
Heavy cloth (million metres)	12.5	12.3	11.3
Knitwear (million pieces)	9.8	11.0	12.1
Footwear ('000 pairs)	4,735	4,800	5,396
Television receivers ('000)	21	21.3	16.5
Radio receivers ('000)	8	16	25
Beer ('000 hectolitres)	150	199	237
Cigarettes (million)	4,950	5,348	5,310
Soap and detergent	14.7	18.2	21.5

Source: *Statistical Yearbook of the PSR of Albania*.
1985: Wine 230,000 hectolitres (FAO estimate).
1986: Raw sugar 35,000 metric tons (estimated by International Sugar Organization, London).
1987: Olive oil 4,000 metric tons (FAO estimate).

Finance

CURRENCY AND EXCHANGE RATES
Monetary Units
100 qindarka (qintars) = 1 new lek.

Denominations
Coins: 5, 10, 20 and 50 qintars; 1 lek.
Notes: 1, 3, 5, 10, 25, 50 and 100 lekë.

Sterling and Dollar Equivalents (31 July 1990)
£1 sterling = 11.53 lekë;
US $1 = 6.20 lekë (non-commercial rates);
1,000 lekë = £86.72 = $161.29.

Exchange Rate
The non-commercial rate, applicable to tourism, was fixed at US $1 = 7.000 lekë between June 1979 and September 1988. A revised rate of $1 = 6.000 lekë was introduced in September 1988 and remained in force until September 1989.

STATE BUDGET (million lekë, provisional)

Revenue	1988	1989	1990
National economy	9,140	9,194	9,323
Non-productive sector and other income from the socialist sector	360	356	327
Total revenue	9,500*	9,550	9,650

* Final total: 8,558m. lekë.

Expenditure	1988	1989	1990
National economy	5,120	4,998	4,933
Socio-cultural measures	2,747	2,908	3,042
Defence	1,060	1,075	1,030
Administration	161	163	175
Total expenditure (incl. others)	9,450*	9,500	9,600

* Final total: 8,552m. lekë.
Source: *Zëri i Popullit*.

INVESTMENT
Capital investment during the 1986–90 Five-Year Plan was estimated at 24,450 million lekë, 2,800 million more than during the previous Five-Year Plan.
Source: Albanian Telegraphic Agency.

NATIONAL ACCOUNTS
Net Material Product
(percentages at 1986 prices)

Activities of the Material Spere	1987	1988
Industry	45.8	46.3
Agriculture	33.3	31.5
Construction	6.4	6.5
Transport, trade, etc.	14.5	15.7
Total	100.0	100.0

External Trade

(million lekë)

	1985	1987	1988
Imports c.i.f.	2,520	2,650	3,218
Exports f.o.b.	2,236	2,650	2,709

Source: *Statistical Yearbook of the PSR of Albania*. Figures for 1986 are not available.

ALBANIA

PRINCIPAL COMMODITIES (%)

Imports	1985	1987	1988
Machinery and equipment	25.1	26.2	28.5
Spare parts and bearings	5.3	6.7	4.8
Fuels, minerals and metals	27.0	28.2	25.2
Chemical and rubber products	14.1	14.2	13.1
Construction materials	1.4	0.1	0.1
Raw materials of plant or animal origin	12.8	12.7	14.0
Foodstuffs	8.3	5.4	8.1
Other consumer goods	6.0	6.5	6.2
Total	100.0	100.0	100.0

Exports	1985	1987	1988
Fuels	15.1	11.0	7.9
Electricity	7.8	13.1	7.3
Minerals and metals	31.2	29.3	39.8
Chemical products	0.7	1.2	0.8
Construction materials	1.0	1.3	1.5
Raw materials of plant or animal origin	14.6	16.8	16.1
Processed foodstuffs	10.8	9.1	8.7
Unprocessed foodstuffs	8.1	8.2	8.2
Other consumer goods	10.7	10.0	9.7
Total	100.0	100.0	100.0

Source: *Statistical Yearbook of the PSR of Albania*. Figures for 1986 are not available.

PRINCIPAL TRADING PARTNERS (%)

Exports	1986	1987	1988
Austria	1.5	3.5	5.4
Bulgaria	7.5	7.5	9.4
China, People's Republic	4.9	6.1	5.1
Cuba	1.7	1.0	1.3
Czechoslovakia	12.1	12.4	10.0
Egypt	1.0	1.5	1.2
France	1.9	2.0	1.6
German Democratic Republic	5.7	6.8	8.2
Germany, Federal Republic	3.2	4.0	4.2
Greece	6.8	5.5	1.8
Hungary	5.1	6.2	5.9
Italy	3.5	4.4	6.3
Japan	1.2	1.6	1.8
Poland	7.0	6.0	7.5
Romania	9.5	9.3	9.7
Sweden	5.0	3.3	4.6
Switzerland	3.0	4.3	2.5
Yugoslavia	13.9	11.1	7.1
Total (incl. others)	100.0	100.0	100.0

Source: *Statistical Yearbook of the PSR of Albania*. Percentages for imports are not available.

Transport

RAILWAYS (traffic)

	1987	1988
Passengers carried ('000)	10,601	10,966
Passengers-km (million)	661.6	703.0
Freight carried ('000 metric tons)	7,666	7,659
Freight ton-km (million)	629	626

Source: *Statistical Yearbook of the PSR of Albania*.

ROAD TRAFFIC

	1987	1988
Passengers carried*	59,210	77,287
Passenger-km (million)*	1,174.0	1,380.2
Freight carried ('000 metric tons)	76,840	76,982
Freight ton-km (million)	1,268	1,269

* Figures refer to operations by the Ministry of Transport only.
Source: *Statistical Yearbook of the PSR of Albania*.

INTERNATIONAL SEA-BORNE SHIPPING
(estimated freight traffic, '000 metric tons)

	1983	1984	1985
Goods loaded	1,150	1,150	1,077
Goods unloaded	631	635	626

Source: UN, *Monthly Bulletin of Statistics*.

1987: Total sea-borne freight: 1,025,000 metric tons; ton-kilometres: 2,437m.
1988: Total sea-borne freight: 1,095,000 metric tons; ton-kilometres: 2,563m.
Source: *Statistical Yearbook of the PSR of Albania*.

Communications Media

	1984	1985	1986
Book production:			
Titles*	1,130	939	959
Copies ('000)*	6,506	5,710	6,665
Daily newspapers:			
Number	2	n.a.	2
Average circulation	145,000	n.a.	135,000
Radio receivers in use	n.a.	493,000	500,000
Television receivers in use	n.a.	232,000	250,000

* Figures include pamphlets (158 titles and 494,000 copies in 1984; 95 titles and 300,000 copies in 1985; 52 titles and 380,000 copies in 1986).

1987: Radio receivers in use: 514,000; Television receivers in use: 255,000.
Source: UNESCO, *Statistical Yearbook*.

1987: Daily newspapers: number: 2; average circulation: 150,000.
1988: Book production: titles: 1,018; copies: 7,440,000.
Source: *Statistical Yearbook of the PSR of Albania*.

Education
(1988)

	Institutions	Teachers	Pupils
Pre-primary	3,251	5,299	121,000
Primary (8-year)	1,691	27,862	547,000
Secondary:			
general	43	1,783	59,000
vocational	442	7,221	135,000
Higher	8	1,659	25,000

Source: *Statistical Yearbook of the PSR of Albania*

Directory

The Constitution

A new constitution was adopted on 28 December 1976. A special commission was established in November 1990 to review the Constitution. The following is a summary of the main provisions of the 1976 Constitution:

THE SOCIAL ORDER

The Political Order

Articles 1-15. Albania is a People's Socialist Republic, based on the dictatorship of the proletariat. The Party of Labour of Albania (Workers' Party) is the sole leading political force of the State and society. Marxism-Leninism is the ruling ideology.

The representative bodies are the People's Assembly and the People's Councils, elected by the people through universal suffrage by equal, direct and secret ballot. Officials serve the people and render account to them. They also participate directly in production work, in order to prevent the creation of a privileged stratum.

In the construction of socialism, Albania relies primarily on its own efforts.

The Economic Order

Articles 16-31. The economy is a socialist economy, which relies on the socialist ownership of the means of production. Socialist property is inviolable and state property belongs to all the people. The State works to narrow the differences between the countryside and the cities. The personal property of the citizens is recognized and protected by the State.

Foreign trade is a state monopoly.

The granting of concessions to, and the creation of foreign or joint economic or financial institutions with, capitalist, bourgeois and revisionist monopolies and states, as well as the acceptance of credits from them, is prohibited. (This clause ceased to be effective in 1990.)

Citizens pay no levies or taxes whatsoever. (This was under review in 1990.)

Education, Science and Culture

Articles 32-37. The State carries out broad ideological and cultural activity for the communist education of the working people. Education is organized by the State and is free of charge.

The State organizes the development of science and technology.

The State recognizes no religion and supports and carries out atheist propaganda.

THE FUNDAMENTAL RIGHTS AND DUTIES OF CITIZENS

Articles 38-65. The rights and duties of citizens are founded on the reconciliation of the interests of the individual with those of the socialist society.

All citizens are equal before the law. Women enjoy the same rights as men.

Citizens reaching the age of 18 have the right to take part in voting for, and to be elected to, all organs of state power.

Citizens enjoy the right to work and to recreation. Workers are guaranteed the necessary material means for life in old age and sickness.

Marriage and the family are under the care and protection of the State and society. Marriage is contracted before the competent state organs.

Citizens enjoy freedom of speech.

The creation of all organizations of a fascist, anti-democratic, religious or anti-socialist nature is prohibited.

SUPREME BODIES OF STATE POWER

The People's Assembly

Articles 66-74. The People's Assembly is the supreme body of state power and sole law-making body. It defines the main directions of the domestic and foreign policy of the State. It elects, appoints and dismisses the Presidium of the People's Assembly, the Council of Ministers, the Supreme Court, the Attorney-General and his deputies.

The People's Assembly is composed of 250 deputies, elected for a period of four years, and meets in regular session twice a year.

The Presidium of the People's Assembly

Articles 75-79. The Presidium of the People's Assembly is the supreme body of state power, with permanent activity, and is composed of a President, three Vice-Presidents, a Secretary and 10 members. It convenes the sessions of the People's Assembly and, between sessions, supervises the implementation of the laws and decisions of the People's Assembly, and controls all state organs.

The Presidium directs and controls the activity of the People's Councils.

The Supreme Organs of State Administration

Articles 80-86. The Council of Ministers is the supreme executive and order-issuing body, and is composed of the Chairman, Deputy Chairmen and ministers. It directs activity for the realization of the domestic and foreign policies of the State. It directs and controls the activity of the ministries, other central organs of the state administration and the executive committees of the People's Councils.

The Chairman and Deputy Chairmen of the Council of Ministers constitute the Presidium of the Council of Ministers.

The Country's Defence and the Armed Forces

Articles 87-91. The State protects the victories of the people's revolution and of socialist construction, and defends the freedom, national independence and territorial integrity of the country.

The armed forces are led by the Party of Labour of Albania. The First Secretary of the Central Committee of the Party of Labour of Albania is the Supreme Commander of the armed forces and Chairman of the Defence Council. The stationing of foreign bases and military forces in Albania is not permitted.

LOCAL ORGANS OF STATE POWER AND STATE ADMINISTRATION

Articles 92-100. The People's Councils are organs of state power, which carry out the administration in the respective administrative-territorial units with the broad participation of the working masses. The People's Councils are elected for a term of three years.

A Higher People's Council may dissolve a lower People's Council. Executive committees are an executive and order-issuing organ of the People's Councils.

THE PEOPLE'S COURTS

Articles 101-103. The People's Courts are bodies which administer justice. At the head of the organs of justice stands the Supreme Court, which directs and controls the activity of the courts. The Supreme Court is elected at the first session of the People's Assembly. The other People's Courts are elected by the people.

THE ATTORNEY-GENERAL'S OFFICE

Articles 104-106. It is the duty of the Attorney-General's Office to supervise the implementation of the laws. The Attorney-General and his deputies are appointed at the first session of the People's Assembly. Attorneys are appointed by the Presidium of the Assembly.

THE EMBLEM, THE FLAG, THE CAPITAL

Articles 107-109. The emblem of the People's Socialist Republic of Albania consists of a black double-headed eagle, encircled by two sheaves of wheat with a five-pointed red star at the top and tied at the bottom by a red ribbon bearing the inscription '24th May 1944'.

The state flag has a red background with a black double-headed eagle in the middle and a red five-pointed star outlined in gold at the top.

The capital is Tirana.

FINAL PROVISIONS

Articles 110-112. The Constitution is the fundamental law of the State. Drafts for amendments may be presented by the Presidium of the People's Assembly, the Council of Ministers or two-fifths of the deputies. The approval of the Constitution and amendments to it requires a two-thirds majority of all deputies.

The Government

(November 1990)

HEAD OF STATE

President of the Presidium of the People's Assembly: RAMIZ ALIA (elected 22 November 1982, re-elected 19 February 1987).

ALBANIA

PRESIDIUM OF THE PEOPLE'S ASSEMBLY
President: Ramiz Alia.
Vice-Presidents: Rita Marko, Xhafer Spahiu, Emine Guri.
Secretary: Sihat Tozaj.
Members:
Simon Ballabani
Faik Çinaj
Petrit Gaçe
Rahman Hanku
Sotir Koçollari
Terezina Marubi
Stefan Qirjako
Kristaq Rama
Lumturi Rexha
Eleni Selenica

COUNCIL OF MINISTERS
Chairman (Prime Minister): Adil Çarçani.
Deputy Chairman and Minister of Internal Affairs: Hekuran Isai.
Deputy Chairman and Minister of Agriculture: Pali Miska.
Chairman of the State Control Commission: Simon Stefani.
Minister of Foreign Affairs: Reis Malile.
Minister of People's Defence: Kiço Mustaqi.
Chairman of the State Planning Commission: Bujar Kolaneci.
Minister of Finance: Andrea Nako.
Minister of Industry and Mining and of Energy (acting): Besnik Bekteshi.
Minister of Light Industry: Bashkim Sykaj.
Minister of the Foodstuff Industry: Ylli Bufi.
Minister of Construction: Ismail Ahmeti.
Minister of Transport: Hajredin Çeliku.
Minister of Domestic Trade: Pajtim Ajazi.
Minister of Foreign Trade: Shane Korbeci.
Minister of Public Services: (vacant).
Minister of Education: Skënder Gjinushi.
Minister of Health Service: Ahmet Kamberi.
Minister of Justice: Enver Halile.
Minister to the Presidium of the Council of Ministers: Farudin Hoxha.
Minister, Secretary-General of the Council of Ministers: Niko Gjyzari.

MINISTRIES
All Ministries are in Tirana.
Council of Ministers: Këshilli i Ministrave, Tirana; telex 4201.
Ministry of Agriculture: Ministria e Bujqësisë, Tirana; telex 4209.
Ministry of Construction: Ministria e Ndertimit, Tirana; telex 4208.
Ministry of Domestic Trade: Ministria e Tregetisë të Brendeshme, Tirana; telex 4290.
Ministry of Education: Ministria e Arsimit, Tirana; telex 4203.
Ministry of Energy: Ministria e Energjetikes, Tirana; telex 4296.
Ministry of Finance: Ministria e Financave, Tirana; telex 4297.
Ministry of Foreign Affairs: Ministria e Punëvet të Jashtme, Tirana; telex 2164.
Ministry of Foreign Trade: Ministria e Tregetisë të Jashtme, Tirana; telex 2152.
Ministry of Health Service: Ministria e Shendetesisë, Tirana; telex 4205.
Ministry of Industry and Mining: Ministria e Industrisë dhe Minierave, Tirana; telex 4204.
Ministry of Light Industry: Ministria e Industrise të Lehte, Tirana; telex 4206.
Ministry of Transport: Ministria e Transporteve, Tirana; telex 4207.
State Planning Commission: Komiteti i Planit të Shtetit, Tirana; telex 4295.

POLITICAL BUREAU OF THE CENTRAL COMMITTEE OF THE PARTY OF LABOUR OF ALBANIA
Full Members:
Ramiz Alia
Muho Asllani
Besnik Bekteshi
Foto Çami
Adil Çarçani
Hajredin Çeliku
Vangjel Çërrava
Lenka Çuko
Xhelil Gjoni
Hekuran Isai
Pali Miska
Kiço Mustaqi
Simon Stefani

Candidate Members:
Xhemal Dymylja
Llambi Gegprifti
Niko Gjyzari
Pirro Kondi
Qirjako Mihali

Legislature

KUVENDI POPULLOR
(People's Assembly)
President: Petro Dode.
Vice-Presidents: Mrs Vitori Curri, Ibrahim Hamza.
Secretary: Sali Shijaku.

The Assembly has 250 members, elected (unopposed) for a four-year term. At the general election held on 1 February 1987, it was reported that 100% of the electorate voted: 1,830,652 votes were cast in favour of the 250 candidates and one vote was invalid.

Political Organizations

Partia e Punës e Shqipërisë (Party of Labour of Albania, PLA): Tirana; telex 4291; f. 1941; the Communist Party of Albania, which adopted its present name in 1948; also known as the Workers' Party; the country's only permitted political party; Marxist-Leninist; Central Cttee of 85 full and 46 candidate mems elected in Nov. 1986; 147,000 mems and candidate mems (Nov. 1986); First Sec. of Central Cttee Ramiz Alia; Secs Abdyl Backa, Foto Çami, Xhelil Gjoni.

Fronti Demokratik i Shqipërisë (Democratic Front of Albania): Tirana; tel. (42) 27957; f. 1942 to succeed National Liberation Front; works towards political union and mobilization of the masses in the construction of socialism and in the defence of freedom and independence, for the active participation of the masses in governing the country and in the solution of major social and state problems; in consultation with the social organizations and the masses, the Democratic Front nominates candidates in elections; Gen. Council of 185 mems elected in June 1989; Chair. of Gen. Council Nexhmije Hoxha; Sec. Leka Shkurti.

Bashkimi i Rinisë së Punës të Shqipërisë (Union of Working Youth of Albania): Tirana; tel. (42) 27818; f. 1941; political organization for young people, sponsored by the Party of Labour of Albania, playing an important role in the political, economic, social, educational and cultural life of the country; at the 9th Congress, held in October 1987, 15 mems and 6 candidate mems were elected to the Presidium of the Central Cttee; 175 mems were elected to the Central Cttee; First Sec. of the Central Cttee Lisen Bashkurti.

Bashkimi të Grave të Shqipërisë (Women's Union of Albania): Tirana; tel. (42) 27959; f. 1943 for the ideological, political and social education of women, aiming to achieve their complete emancipation, to help build a socialist society, and to consolidate the international solidarity of women; at the 9th Congress, held in June 1983, a General Council of 167 mems, a Presidium of 27 and a Secretariat of 5 were elected; Pres. of General Council Lumturi Rexha; Sec.-Gen. Leonora Çaro.

Diplomatic Representation

EMBASSIES IN ALBANIA

Bulgaria: Rruga Skënderbeu 12, Tirana; tel. (42) 22672; Ambassador: Stefan Naumov.
China, People's Republic: Rruga Skënderbeu 57, Tirana; tel. (42) 22600; telex 2148; Ambassador: Gu Maoxuan.
Cuba: Rruga Kongresi i Përmetit 13, Tirana; tel. (42) 25176; telex 2155; Ambassador: Julio C. Cancio Ferrer.
Czechoslovakia: Rruga Skënderbeu 10, Tirana; telex 2162; Ambassador: Anton Šimkovič.
Egypt: Rruga Skënderbeu 43, Tirana; tel. (42) 23013; telex 2156; Ambassador: Manzur Ahmad al-Dali.
France: Rruga Skënderbeu 14, Tirana; tel. (42) 22804; telex 2150; Ambassador: Michel Boulmer.
Germany: Rruga Skënderbeu, Tirana; tel. (42) 23481; telex 2254; Ambassador: Friedrich Kroneck.
Greece: Rruga Frederick Shiroka 3, Tirana; tel. (42) 26850; Ambassador: Spyridon A. Dokianos.
Hungary: Rruga Skënderbeu 16, Tirana; tel. (42) 22004; telex 2257; Ambassador: Ferenc Poka.
Italy: Rruga Labinoti 103, Tirana; tel. (42) 22800; telex 2166; Ambassador: Giorgio de Andreis.
Korea, Democratic People's Republic: Rruga Skënderbeu 55, Tirana; tel. (42) 22258; Ambassador: Kim U-Chong.
Poland: Rruga Kongresi i Përmetit 123, Tirana; Ambassador: Władysław Ciaston.

ALBANIA

Romania: Rruga Themistokli Gërmenji 2, Tirana; tel. (42) 22259; Ambassador: GHEORGHE MIKU.

Turkey: Rruga Konferenca e Pezës 31, Tirana; tel. (42) 22449; Ambassador: TEOMAN SÜRENKÖK.

Viet-Nam: Rruga Lek Dukagjini, Tirana; tel. (42) 22556; telex 2253; Ambassador: NGUYEN CHI THANH.

Yugoslavia: Rruga Kongresi i Përmetit 192–196, Tirana; tel. (42) 23042; telex 2167; Ambassador: NOVAK PRIBICEVIĆ.

Judicial System

The judicial system is administered by the Ministry of Justice, re-established in 1990, which supervises the organization and functioning of the Supreme Court, the Territorial Division Courts, and the District Courts. The Supreme Court is elected for a four-year term by the People's Assembly; between sessions of the Assembly, individual members of the Court are elected by the Presidium of the People's Assembly. The Territorial Division Courts are elected for a three-year term by the People's Councils of the districts in which they exercise their jurisdiction. The District Courts are elected for a three-year term by all voting citizens through a direct and secret ballot. The Village, City and City Quarter Courts are bodies of a social or unofficial character, operating at the People's Councils, and are elected by the people for a three-year term. Military Tribunals are held at the Supreme Court and at District Courts. Courts of Justice are independent in the exercise of their functions, and are separated from the administration.

A revised Penal Code came into effect in October 1977, followed by a Code of Penal Procedure (1980), a Labour Code (1980), a Civil Code, together with a Code of Civil Procedure (1982) and a Family Code (1982). Trials are held in public. The accused is assured the right of defence, and the principle of presumption of innocence is sanctioned by the Code of Penal Procedure. First-degree cases are normally tried by District Courts or, exceptionally, by Territorial Division Courts or the Supreme Court. For first-degree cases, the tribunal comprises a professional judge and two assistant judges. Trials in the Village, City and City Quarter Courts are held before an assistant judge from the District Court and two social activists. These Courts try simple cases, and are empowered to punish a guilty person with a fine or social reprimand. Second-degree cases are held in the Territorial Division Courts or in the Supreme Court, before three judges and two assistant judges. The verdicts of the lower courts may be altered, within the law, by the higher courts, and judges may be recalled before the expiration of their term by their electors or the organ that has elected them. Both the President of the Supreme Court and the Attorney-General have the right to issue a demand for the protection of legality against the peremptory verdicts of the courts. The demand for the protection of legality is presented, within the law, before the Penal Tribunal (College), the Civil Tribunal, the Military Tribunal or the Plenary Meeting of the Supreme Court.

The Office of Investigation is a state organ that investigates criminal acts. This department is separated from the organs of internal affairs and from the other administrative organs. The Chairman of the General Department of Investigation and his deputies are appointed by the People's Assembly. The chairmen of the district's offices of investigation are appointed by the Chairman of the General Department of Investigation. Attorneys' offices are state organs that control strictly and uniformly the application of the laws from Ministries and other central and local organs, from courts, organs of investigation, enterprises, institutions and citizens' organizations. The Attorney-General and his deputies are appointed by the People's Assembly, and District Attorneys by the Presidium of the People's Assembly.

Extensive reforms of the judicial system were announced in May 1990. In addition to the re-establishment of the Ministry of Justice (the Minister being empowered to overturn court rulings), defendants were guaranteed the right to a defence lawyer. The number of capital offences was reduced from 34 to 11, women being exempt from the death penalty.

President of the Supreme Court: KLEANTHI KOÇO.

Attorney-General: RRAPI MINO.

Chairman of the General Department of Investigation: QEMAL LAME.

Religion

There is no formal practice of the previously predominant Muslim religion, although certain social traditions persist. All religious institutions were closed by the Government in 1967. Many places of worship were converted into museums, sports halls, etc. Article 37 of the 1976 Constitution states that Albania recognizes no religion and supports and carries out atheist propaganda. In 1990, however, the reopening of mosques and churches was reportedly under consideration. Formerly the population was approximately 70% Muslim, 10% Roman Catholic (in the north) and 20% Eastern Orthodox (in the south). A small number of Albanians are believed to be adherents of the Jewish faith.

CHRISTIANITY
The Roman Catholic Church

Albania formally comprises the archdioceses of Durrës (directly responsible to the Holy See) and Shkodrë (Shkodër), three dioceses, one territorial abbacy and Southern Albania (previously the responsibility of an Apostolic Administrator). There are no longer any resident prelates holding office in the country. In November 1990 it was reported that 5,000 Catholics had attended a mass at a chapel in Shkodër, the first to be held since 1967.

Apostolic Administrator of Durrës and Lezhë: NICOLA TROSHANI, Titular Bishop of Cisamo (Cisamus).

Apostolic Administrator of Shkodrë: ERNESTO ÇOBA, Titular Bishop of Mideo (Midaëum).

The Press

The Albanian press recognizes itself as a powerful medium of educational and organizational propaganda with a profound Marxist-Leninist ideological content. It expresses party doctrine forcefully. There are numerous local newspapers, generally the organs of the regional party committees. In 1985 the 23 newspapers and 77 magazines had a total circulation of 64m. copies. The most important publications are the Party of Labour daily, *Zëri i Popullit*, and *Bashkimi*, the organ of the Democratic Front. In 1987 there were 14 district newspapers, published twice a week. The Albanian Telegraphic Agency (ATA) has a monopoly of news distribution in Albania.

PRINCIPAL DAILIES

Zëri i Popullit (The Voice of the People): Bulevardi Stalin, Tirana; tel. (42) 27808; telex 4251; fax (42) 27813; f. 1942; daily except Mon.; publ. by the Central Committee of the Party of Labour; Editor-in-Chief SPIRO DEDE; circ. 120,000.

Bashkimi (Unity): Bulevardi Stalin, Tirana; tel. (42) 28110; f. 1943; publ. by the Democratic Front; Editor-in-Chief HAMIT BORIÇI; circ. 30,000.

PERIODICALS
Tirana

Bibliografia Kombëtare e Librit Shqiptar (National Bibliography of Albanian Books): Tirana; quarterly; publ. by the National Library of Albania.

Bibliografia Kombëtare e Periodikeve Shqip (National Bibliography of Albanian periodicals): Tirana; monthly; publ. by the National Library of Albania.

Bujqësia Socialiste (Socialist Agriculture): Tirana; monthly; publ. by the Ministry of Agriculture; Editor FAIK LABINOTI.

Buletini i Shkencave Bujqësore (Agricultural Sciences Bulletin): Tirana; quarterly; summaries in French; publ. by the Agricultural Scientific Research Institute; Editor-in-Chief LEFTER VESHI.

Buletini i Shkencave Gjeologjike (Bulletin of Geological Sciences): Tirana; tel. (42) 22511; telex 4204; fax (42) 34031; f. 1965; quarterly; publ. by Geological Research and Designs Institute and Faculty of Geology and Mines of Enver Hoxha University; Editor AFAT SERJANI; circ. 650.

Buletini i Shkencave Mjekësore (Medical Sciences Bulletin): Tirana; quarterly; summaries in French; publ. by the Enver Hoxha University of Tirana; Editor-in-Chief YLVI VEHBIU.

Buletini i Shkencave të Natyrës (Natural Sciences Bulletin): Tirana; f. 1957; quarterly; summaries in French; publ. by the Enver Hoxha University of Tirana; Editor-in-Chief MUHARREM FRASHERI.

Buletini i Shkencave Teknike (Technical Sciences Bulletin): Tirana; quarterly; summaries in French; publ. by the Enver Hoxha University of Tirana.

Drejtësia Popullore (People's Law): Tirana; f. 1948; quarterly; publ. of organs of justice; Chief Editor ELENI SELENICA.

Drita (The Light): Baboci 37z, Tirana; f. 1960; weekly; publ. by Union of Writers and Artists of Albania; Chief Editor ZIJA ÇELA.

Estrada (Variety Shows): Tirana; every 2 months; publ. by the Central House of Popular Creativity.

Fatosi (The Valiant): Tirana; tel. (42) 23024; f. 1959; fortnightly; literary and artistic magazine for children; publ. by Cen. Cttee of

ALBANIA

Union of Working Youth; Editor-in-Chief XHEVAT BEQARAJ; circ. 21,200.

Gazeta Zyrtare e RPS të Shqipërisë (Official Gazette of the PSR of Albania): Presidium of the People's Assembly, Tirana; tel. (42) 29385; telex 4298; f. 1945; occasional government review.

Gjuha Jonë (Our Language): Tirana; 3 a year; organ of the Institute of Language and Literature at the Academy of Sciences; Editor ALI DHRIMO.

Horizonti (Horizon): Tirana; tel. (42) 29204; f. 1979; monthly; scientific and technical magazine for children; publ. by Cen. Cttee of Union of Working Youth; Editor-in-Chief THANAS QERAMA; circ. 18,850.

Hosteni (The Goad): Tirana; f. 1945; fortnightly; political review of humour and satire; publ. by the Union of Journalists; Editor-in-Chief NIKO NIKOLLA.

Iliria (Illyria): Qendra e Kërkimeve Arkeologjike, Tirana; tel. (42) 26501; f. 1971; 2 a year; summaries in French; publ. by Centre of Archaeological Research at the Academy of Sciences; Chief of Editorial Bd Dr M. KORKUTI; circ. 900.

Kënga Jonë (Our Song): Tirana; f. 1960; every 2 months; publ. by the Central House of Popular Creativity.

Kultura Popullore (Popular Culture): Tirana; 2 a year; annually in French; publ. by the Institute of Folk Culture at the Academy of Sciences; Editor-in-Chief ALFRED UÇI.

Les Lettres Albanaises: Rruga Konferenca e Pezës, Tirana; tel. (42) 22691; quarterly; in French; literary and artistic review; publ. by Union of Writers and Artists of Albania; Editor DIANA ÇULI.

Luftëtari (The Fighter): Tirana; f. 1945; 2 a week; publ. by the Ministry of National Defence; Editor-in-Chief DEMOKRAT ANASTASI.

Mbrëmje Tematike (Evening Parties): Tirana; publ. by the Central House of Popular Creativity.

Mësuesi (The Teacher): Tirana; f. 1961; weekly; publ. by the Ministry of Education and Culture; Editor-in-Chief THOMA QENDRO.

Monumentet (Monuments): Tirana; f. 1971; 2 a year; summaries in French; publ. by the Institute of Monuments and Culture; Editor-in-Chief SOTIR KOSTA.

Ndërtuesi (The Builder): Tirana; quarterly; publ. by the Ministry of Construction.

Në shërbim të popullit (In the Service of the People): Tirana; f. 1955; Editor-in-Chief THOMA NAQE.

Në skenën e fëmijëve (On the Children's Stage): Tirana; publ. by the Central House of Popular Creativity.

Nëna dhe Fëmija (Mother and Child): Tirana; 3 a year; publ. by Ministry of Public Health.

Nëntori (November): Baboci 37z, Tirana; f. 1954; monthly; publ. by the Union of Writers and Artists of Albania; Chief Editor KIÇO BLUSHI.

Për Mbrojtjen e Atdheut (For the Defence of the Fatherland): Tirana; f. 1948; publ. of the Ministry of National Defence; Editor-in-Chief BEGE TENA.

Përmbledhje Studimesh (Collection of Studies): Tirana; quarterly; summaries in French; bulletin of the Ministry of Industry and Mining.

Pionieri (The Pioneer): Tirana; f. 1944; fortnightly; publ. by the Cen. Cttee of the Union of Working Youth; Editor-in-Chief SKENDER HASKO; circ. 38,000.

Probleme Ekonomike: Tirana; quarterly; organ of Institute for Economic Studies.

Puna (Labour): Bulevardi Dëshmorët e Kombit, Tirana; f. 1945; 2 a week; also quarterly in French; organ of the Central Council of Albanian Trade Unions; Editor-in-Chief KRISTAQ LAKA.

Radio Përhapja: Tirana; fortnightly; organ of Albanian Radio and Television.

Revista Mjekësore (Medical Review): Tirana; every 2 months; publ. by Ministry of Health.

Revista Pedagogjike: Tirana; quarterly; organ of the Institute of Pedagogical Studies; Editor SOTIR TEMO.

Rruga e Partisë (The Party's Road): Tirana; f. 1954; monthly; publ. by Cen. Cttee of the Party of Labour; Editor STEFI KOTMILO; circ. 9,000.

Shëndeti (Health): Tirana; f. 1949; monthly; publ. by the Ministry of Public Health; Editor-in-Chief ROZA THEOHARI.

Shkenca dhe Jeta (Science and Life): Tirana; every 2 months; organ of the Central Committee of the Union of Working Youth; Editor-in-Chief KUDRET ISAI.

Shqipëria e Re (New Albania): Rruga Asim Vokshi 2, Tirana; f. 1947; published monthly in Albanian; every 2 months in Arabic, English, French, German, Italian, Russian and Spanish; organ of the Committee for Foreign Cultural Relations; illustrated political and social magazine; Editor YMER MINXHOZI; circ. 170,000.

Shqipëria Sot (Albania Today): Tirana; every 2 months; published in English, French, German, Italian and Spanish; political, cultural and social review; Editor-in-Chief DHIMITER VERLI.

Shqiptarja e Re (The New Albanian Woman): Tirana; f. 1943; monthly; publ. by the Women's Union of Albania; political and socio-cultural review; Editor-in-Chief VALENTINA LESKAJ.

Skena dhe Ekrani (Stage and Screen): Tirana; quarterly; publ. by the Committee for Culture and Arts.

Socio-Political Studies: Tirana; tel. (42) 28395; telex 4291; f. 1981 in Albanian, 1984 in English and French; 2 a year in Albanian, annually in English and French; publ. by Institute of Marxist-Leninist Studies; Chief of Editorial Bd Prof. SOTIR MADHI; circ. 3,000 (Albanian), 1,000 (English and French).

Sporti Popullor (People's Sport): Tirana; f. 1945; weekly; publ. by the Ministry of Education and Culture; Editor BESNIK DIZDARI; circ. 60,000.

Studenti (The Student): Tirana; f. 1967; weekly; publ. by the Committee of the University Working Youth Union.

Studia Albanica: Tirana; f. 1964; 2 a year; history and philology; in French; publ. by the Albanian Academy of Sciences; Editor-in-Chief LUAN OMARI.

Studime Filologjike (Philological Studies): Tirana; f. 1964; quarterly; summaries in French; publ. by the Institute of Language and Literature at the Albanian Academy of Sciences; Editor-in-Chief ANDROKLI KOSTALLARI.

Studime Historike (Historical Studies): Tirana; f. 1964; quarterly; summaries in French; publ. by the Institute of History at the Albanian Academy of Sciences; historical sciences; Editor-in-Chief STEFANAQ POLLO.

Teknika (Technology): Tirana; f. 1954; quarterly; publ. by the Ministry of Industry and Mining; Editor NATASHA VARFI.

Teatri (Theatre): Tirana; f. 1960; every 2 months; publ. by the Central House of Popular Creativity.

Tirana: Tirana; f. 1987; publ. by Tirana District Party of Labour Cttee.

Tregtia e Jashtme Popullore (Albanian Foreign Trade): Rruga Konferenca e Pezës 6, Tirana; tel. (42) 22934; telex 2179; f. 1961; every 2 months; in English and French; organ of the Albanian Chamber of Commerce; Editor AGIM KORBI.

Tribuna e Gazetarit (The Journalist's Tribune): Tirana; every 2 months; publ. by the Union of Journalists of Albania; Editor ADRIATIK KANANI.

Vatra e Kulturës (Centre of Culture): Tirana; publ. by the Central House of Popular Creativity.

Ylli (The Star): Tirana; f. 1951; monthly; socio-political and literary review; Editor-in-Chief NEVRUZ TURHANI.

Yllkat (Little Stars): Tirana; monthly; publ. by Institute of Pedagogical Studies.

Zëri i Rinisë (The Voice of the Youth): Tirana; f. 1942; 2 a week; publ. by Cen. Cttee of the Union of Albanian Working Youth; Editor-in-Chief REMZI LANI; circ. 53,000.

10 Korriku (10 July): Tirana; f. 1947; monthly; publ. by the Ministry of People's Defence; Editor-in-Chief SELAMI VEHBIU.

Other Towns

Adriatiku (Adriatic): Durrës; f. 1967; 2 a week; publ. by Durrës District Party of Labour Cttee.

Draper e Çekan (Hammer and Sickle): Fier; f. 1967; 2 a week.

Fitorjë (Victory): Sarandë; f. 1971; 2 a week; Editor-in-Chief BELUL KORKUTI.

Jehona e Skraparit (Echo of Skrapar): Skrapar; 2 a week.

Jeta e Re (New Life): Shkodër; f. 1967; 2 a week.

Kastrioti: Krujë; f. 1971; 2 a week; publ. by Krüje District Party of Labour Cttee.

Kukësi i Ri (New Kukës): Kukës; 2 a week.

Kushtrimi (Clarion Call): Berat; f. 1967; 2 a week.

Laiko Vima (People's Step): Gjirokastër; f. 1945; 2 a week; monthly literary edn; in Greek; publ. by the Democratic Front for the Greek minority; Editor-in-Chief VASIL ÇAMI.

Pararoja (Vanguard): Gjirokastër; f. 1967; 2 a week; publ. by Gjirokastër District Party of Labour Cttee.

Përpara (Forward): Korçë; f. 1967; 2 a week; publ. by Korçë District Party of Labour Cttee; Editor-in-Chief STRATI MARKO; circ. 4,000.

Shkëndija (The Spark): Lushnjë; f. 1971; 2 a week; publ. by Lushnjë District Party of Labour Cttee.

ALBANIA

Directory

Shkumbimi: Elbasan; 2 a week; publ. by Elbasan District Party of Labour Cttee; Editor-in-Chief MEFAIL PUPULEKU.

Ushtimi i Maleve (Rumble of the Mountains): Peshkopi; 2 a week.

Zëri i Vlorës (The Voice of Vlorë): Vlorë; f. 1967; 2 a week; publ. by Vlorë District Party of Labour Cttee; Editor-in-Chief DASHO METODASHAJ.

In addition, 11 new local newspapers, published by the District Party Committees of Lezhë, Përmet, Pukë, Pogradec, Mirditë, Tepelenë, Mat, Gramsh, Kolonjë, Tropojë and Librazhd, were established in 1988.

NEWS AGENCY

Albanian Telegraphic Agency (ATA): Bulevardi Marcel Cachin 23, Tirana; tel. (42) 24412; telex 2142; f. 1945; domestic and foreign news; branches in provincial towns; Dir TAQO ZOTO.

Foreign Bureau

Xinhua (New China) News Agency (People's Republic of China): Rruga Skënderbeu 57, Tirana; tel. (42) 33139; fax (42) 33139; Bureau Chief LI JIYU.

PRESS ASSOCIATION

Bashkimi i Gazetarëve të Shqipërisë (Union of Journalists of Albania): Tirana; tel. (42) 27977; f. 1949; Chair. MARASH HAJATI; Sec.-Gen. YMER MINXHOZI.

Publishers

In 1986 a total of 859 book titles (including 770 first editions) were published.

Drejtoria Qëndrore e Përhapjes dhe e Propagandimit të Librit (Central Administration for the Dissemination and Propagation of the Book): Tirana; tel. (42) 27841; directed by the Ministry of Education and Culture.

Botime të Akademisë së Shkencave të RPSSH: Tirana; publishing house of the Albanian Academy of Sciences.

Botime të Drejtorisë së Arsimit Shëndetësor dhe të Shtëpisë së Propagandës Bujqësore: Tirana; medicine, sciences and agriculture.

Botime të Institutit të Lartë Bujqësor: Tirana; publishing house of the Higher Institute of Agriculture.

Botime të Shtëpisë Botuese 8 Nëntori: Tirana; tel. (42) 28064; f. 1972; books on Albania and other countries, political and social sciences, translations of Albanian works into foreign languages, technical and scientific books, illustrated albums, etc.; Dir XHEMAL DINI.

Botime të Shtëpisë Botuese të Librit Shkollor: Tirana; f. 1967; educational books; Dir FEJZI KOÇI.

Shtepia Botuese e Librit Universitar: Rruga Dora d'Istria, Tirana; tel. (42) 25659; telex 2211; f. 1988; publishes university textbooks on sciences, engineering, geography, history, literature, foreign languages, economics, etc.; Dir MUSTAFA FEZGA.

Shtëpia Botuese Naim Frashëri: Tirana; tel. (42) 27906; f. 1947; fiction, poetry, drama, criticism, children's literature, translations; Dir GAQO BUSHAKA.

Government Publishing House

N.I.SH. Shtypshkronjave Mihal Duri (Mihal Duri State Printing House): Tirana; government publications, politics, law, education; Dir HAJRI HOXHA.

WRITERS' UNION

Lidhja e Shkrimtarëve dhe e Artistëve të Shqipërisë (Union of Writers and Artists of Albania): Baboci 37z, Tirana; tel. (42) 27989; f. 1945, 1,750 mems, Chair. DRITËRO AGOLLI.

Radio and Television

In 1987 there were an estimated 514,000 radio receivers and 255,000 television sets in use.

Radiotelevisioni Shqiptar: Rruga Ismail Qemali, Tirana; tel. (42) 28134; telex 2216; f. 1944; Dir-Gen. SEFEDIN ÇELA; Dir of Domestic Radio THIMI NIKA.

RADIO

Radio Tirana: telex 4158; broadcasts more than 24 hours of internal programmes daily from Tirana; regional stations in Berat, Fier, Gjirokastër, Korçë, Kükes, Pukë, Rogozhina, Sarandë and Shkodër; wire-relay service in Tirana and in factories, mines and clubs all over the country.

External Service: broadcasts for 83 hours daily in Albanian, Arabic, Bulgarian, Chinese, Czech, English, French, German, Greek, Hungarian, Indonesian, Italian, Persian, Polish, Portuguese, Romanian, Russian, Serbo-Croat, Spanish, Swedish and Turkish; Dir AGIM PAPAPROKO.

TELEVISION

There are stations at Tirana, Berat, Elbasan, Gjirokastër, Kükes, Peshkopi and Pogradec. Programmes are broadcast for 4 hours daily (9½ hours on Sundays).

Finance

Banka e Shtëtit Shqiptar (Albanian State Bank): Head Office: Sheshi Skënderbeu 1, Tirana; tel. (42) 22435; telex 2153; f. 1945; bank of issue; sole credit institution; handles all foreign exchange transactions; branches in 34 towns; Gen. Dir QIRJAKO MIHALI.

State Agricultural Bank: Tirana; tel. (42) 27738; f. 1970; gives short- and long-term credits to agricultural co-operatives and enterprises; Dir S. KUCI.

Drejtoria e Përgjithshme e Kursimeve dhe Sigurimeve (Directorate of Savings and Insurance): Tirana; tel. (42) 22542; f. 1949; Dir KOSTAQ POSTOLI.

In 1987 there were 3,950 savings banks in operation, and deposits totalled 1,329m. lekë.

Trade and Industry

CHAMBER OF COMMERCE

Dhoma e Tregtisë e Republikës Popullore Socialiste të Shqipërisë (Chamber of Commerce of the People's Socialist Republic of Albania): Rruga Konferenca e Pezës 6, Tirana; tel. (42) 27997; telex 2179; f. 1958; Chair. LIGOR DHAMO; Vice-Chair. SIMON POREÇI.

Durrës Chamber of Commerce: Durrës; f. 1988; promotes trade with southern Italy.

Gjirokastër Chamber of Commerce: Gjirokastër; f. 1988; promotes trade with Greek border area; Chair. NAXHI MAMANI; Sec. GENCI SHEHU.

Shkodër Chamber of Commerce: Shkodër; promotes trade with Yugoslav border area; Sec. ENVER DIBRA.

There are also chambers of commerce in Korçë, Kukës, Peshkopi, Pogradec and Sarandë.

SUPERVISORY ORGANIZATION

Albkontroll: Bulevardi Enver Hoxha 45, Durrës; tel. (52) 23-54; telex 2181; f. 1962; brs throughout Albania; independent control body for inspection of goods for import and export, means of transport, etc.; Gen. Man. HITO MINGA.

NATIONAL FOREIGN TRADE ORGANIZATIONS

Agroeksport: Rruga 4 Shkurti 6, Tirana; tel. (42) 25227; telex 2137; exports vegetables, fruit, canned fish, wine, tobacco, etc.; imports rice, coffee and other foodstuffs, paper products, etc.; Gen. Man. LUAN SHAHU.

Agrokoop: Rruga 4 Shkurti 6, Tirana; telex 2248; specializes in foodstuffs and consumer goods.

Albkoop: Rruga 4 Shkurti 6, Tirana; tel. (42) 24179; telex 2187; f. 1986; import and export of consumer goods, incl. clothing, textiles, handicrafts, stationery, jewellery; Gen. Man. JETON HAJDARAJ.

Arteksportimport: Rruga 4 Shkurti 6, Tirana; tel. (42) 24540; telex 2140; f. 1989; exports handicrafts and products of the light industry; imports chemicals, textiles and items required by Albanian industries.

Eksimagra: Rruga Gjon Muzaka, Tirana; tel. (42) 23128; telex 2111; f. 1989; exports fresh vegetables and fruit, figs, pheasants, etc.; imports meat, cereals, edible fats, packaging, etc.; Gen. Man. VIKTOR NUSHI.

Ihtimpeks: Rruga Siri Kodra 32, Tirana; tel. (42) 22287; f. 1990; exports fresh fish, molluscs and mussels, and live eels; imports fishing nets and other equipment.

Industrialimpeks: Rruga 4 Shkurti 6, Tirana; tel. (42) 26123; telex 2112; exports copper wires, furniture, kitchenware, paper, timber, wooden articles, cement, etc.; imports fabrics, cement, chemicals, paper, cardboard, school and office items, etc.; Gen. Man. HAZBI GJIKONDI.

ALBANIA

Makinaimpeks: Rruga 4 Shkurti 6, Tirana; tel. (42) 25220; telex 2128; imports vehicles, factory installations, machinery and parts; Gen. Man. THEODHOR DUMA.

Mekalb: Rruga Kongresi i Përmetit, Tirana; Tel. (42) 28655; telex 4166; f. 1990; exports spare parts for tractors, agricultural machinery, etc.; imports machine tools, radio and TV components and metal items.

Metalimport: Rruga 4 Shkurti 6, Tirana; tel. (42) 23848; telex 2116; imports ferrous and non-ferrous metals, electrodes, oil lubricants, minerals, etc.; Dir T. BORODNI.

Mineralimpeks: Rruga 4 Shkurti 6, Tirana; tel. (42) 23370; telex 2123; exports chromium ore, ferro-nickel ore, electricity, etc.; imports coal, coke, oils, etc.; Gen. Man. NIQIFOR ALIKAJ.

Minergoimpeks: Rruga Marcel Cachin, Tirana; tel. (42) 22148; telex 2238; f. 1990; exports products of the mining, metallurgical and oil industries; imports machinery and equipment, lubricating oils and raw materials.

Teknoimport: Rruga 4 Shkurti 6, Tirana; tel. (42) 25222; telex 2127; fax 42-32-67; f. 1990; imports industrial and agricultural equipment.

Transshqip: Rruga 4 Shkurti 6, Tirana; tel. (42) 23076; telex 2131; f. 1960; transport of foreign trade goods by sea, road and rail; agents in Durrës, Vlorë and Sarandë; Gen. Man. GJOLEK ZENELI.

REGIONAL FOREIGN TRADE ORGANIZATIONS

Durrësimpeks: Rruga Skënderbeu 177, Durrës; tel. (52) 21-99; telex 2181; f. 1988; handles border trade with Southern Italy (Puglia); industrial and agricultural goods; Dir TAQO KOSTA.

Gjirokastërimpeks: Rruga Kombëtare 55, Gjirokastër; tel. 707; f. 1988; handles border trade with Greece; industrial and agricultural goods.

Korçaimpeks: Korçë; handles border trade with Greece.

Kukësimpeks: Kukës; handles trade with Yugoslavia (Kosovo and Macedonia); Dir ASIM BARUTI.

Pogradecimpeks: Pogradec; handles border trade with Yugoslavia (Macedonia).

Sarandaimpeks: Sarandë; handles trade with Corfu and other regions of Southern Greece.

Shkodërimpeks: Shkodër; handles trade with Yugoslavia (Montenegro); industrial and agricultural goods.

CO-OPERATIVE ORGANIZATIONS

Centrocoop: Sheshi Skënderbeu, Tirana; co-operative import and export organization.

Bashkimi Qëndror i Kooperativave të Artizanatit (Central Union of Handicraft Workers' Co-operatives): Tirana; Pres. KRISTO THEMELKO.

Bashkimi Qëndror i Kooperativave Tregtare (Central Union of Commercial Co-operatives): Tirana.

Bashkimi Qëndror i Kooperativave të Shit-Blerjes (Central Union of Buying and Selling Co-operatives): Tirana.

TRADE UNIONS

The principal function of Albanian trade unions is to mobilize the working class to carry out the task of socialist construction. In every work and production centre there is a trade union grass-root organization which elects the trade union committee, while in each ward and district there is a ward committee and a district council.

Këshilli Qëndror i Bashkimeve Profesionale të Shqiperisë (Central Council of Albanian Trade Unions): Bulevardi Dëshmorët e Kombit, Tirana; f. 1945; 743,894 mems; a 201-member General Council, a 21-member Presidium and four secretaries were elected at the 10th Congress, held in June 1987; Pres. of Gen. Council SOTIR KOÇOLLARI.

Transport

RAILWAYS

In 1988 there were 509 km of railway track, with lines linking Tirana–Vorë–Durrës, Durrës–Kavajë–Rrogozhinë–Elbasan–Librazhd–Prenjas–Pogradec, Rrogozhinë–Lushnjë–Fier–Ballsh, Vorë–Laç–Lezhë–Shkodër and Selenicë–Vlorë. A standard-gauge line is being built between Fier and Selenicë. A new 35-km line between Fier and Vlorë was opened in 1985. In March 1986 work began on the Milot–Rrëshen–Klos railway, to comprise 66 km of main line and 34 km of secondary lines. The Milot–Rrëshen section opened in October 1987.

In 1979 Albania and Yugoslavia agreed to construct a 50-km line between Shkodër and Titograd. Construction of the 35-km extension from Laç to Shkodër was completed in 1981, and the Shkodër–Hani i Hotit link (35.5 km) was completed in 1984. Work on the Yugoslav section was completed in late 1985. The Shkodër–Titograd line opened to international freight traffic in September 1986. In mid-1988, however, Yugoslavia suspended all traffic on the Titograd–Shkodër line, following heavy financial losses. Albania continued to operate a regular cargo service.

Drejtoria e Hekurudhave: Tirana; railways administration; Gen. Dir VIKTOR CAPRAZI.

ROADS

In 1988 the road network comprised 6,700 km of main roads and 10,000 km of other roads. All regions are linked by the road network, but many roads in mountainous districts are unsuitable for motor transport. Private cars are banned in Albania. Bicycles and mules are widely used. Proposals to construct a 200-km motorway between Durrës and the border with Greece, in co-operation with a group of Greek companies, were under consideration in 1990.

SHIPPING

Albania's merchant fleet had an estimated total displacement of 56,000 grt in 1982. The chief ports are the Enver Hoxha Port of Durrës, Vlorë, Sarandë and Shëngjin. Durrës harbour has been dredged to allow for bigger ships. In 1980 construction of a new port near Vlorë began. When completed, by 1990, the port was to have a cargo-handling capacity of more than 4m. tons per year. A ferry service between the Enver Hoxha Port of Durrës and Trieste (Italy) was inaugurated in November 1983. An agreement to establish a ferry service between Albania and the Greek island of Corfu was confirmed in 1988.

Drejtoria e Agjensisë së Vaporave: Enver Hoxha Port of Durrës; shipping administration.

CIVIL AVIATION

Albania has air links with Athens, Berlin, Bucharest, Budapest, Frankfurt, Paris, Rome, Vienna (summer only) and Zürich. An occasional charter service operates from London. There is a small but modern airport at Rinas, 28 km from Tirana. There is no regular internal air service.

Albtransport: Rruga Kongresi i Përmetit 202, Tirana; tel. (42) 23026; telex 2154; air agency.

Tourism

In 1989 a total of 14,435 tourists (incl. 3,830 from Greece) were permitted to enter Albania. The main tourist centres include Tirana, Durrës, Sarandë and Shkodër. The Roman amphitheatre at Durrës is one of the largest in Europe. The ancient towns of Apollonia and Butrint are important archaeological sites, and there are many other towns of historic interest.

Albturist: Bulevardi Dëshmorët e Kombit 6, Tirana; tel. (42) 23860; telex 2148; brs in main towns and all tourist centres; hotels in 14 towns; Gen. Man. RUHI SHEQI.

ALGERIA

Introductory Survey

Location, Climate, Language, Religion, Flag, Capital

The Democratic and Popular Republic of Algeria lies in north Africa, with the Mediterranean Sea to the north, Mali and Niger to the south, Tunisia and Libya to the east, and Morocco and Mauritania to the west. The climate on the Mediterranean coast is temperate, becoming more extreme in the Atlas mountains immediately to the south. Further south is part of the Sahara, a hot and arid desert. Temperatures in Algiers, on the coast, are generally between 9°C (48°F) and 29°C (84°F), while in the interior they may exceed 50°C (122°F). Arabic is the official language but French is still widely used. There is a considerable Berber-speaking minority. Islam is the state religion, and almost all Algerians are Muslims. The national flag (proportions 3 by 2) has two equal vertical stripes, of green and white, with a red crescent moon and a five-pointed red star superimposed in the centre. The capital is Algiers (el-Djezaïr).

Recent History

Algeria was conquered by French forces in the 1830s and annexed by France in 1842. For most of the colonial period, official policy was to colonize the territory with French settlers, and many French citizens became permanent residents. Unlike most of France's overseas possessions, Algeria was not formally a colony but was 'attached' to metropolitan France. However, political and economic power within Algeria was largely held by the white settler minority, as the indigenous Muslim majority did not have equal rights.

On 1 November 1954 the major Algerian nationalist movement, the Front de Libération Nationale (FLN), began a war for national independence, in the course of which about 1m. Muslims were killed or wounded. Despite resistance from the Europeans in Algeria, the French Government agreed to a cease-fire in March 1962 and independence was declared on 3 July 1962. In August the Algerian provisional government transferred its functions to the Political Bureau of the FLN, and in September a National Constituent Assembly was elected (from a single list of FLN candidates) and the Republic proclaimed. A new government was formed, with Ahmed Ben Bella, founder of the FLN, as Prime Minister. As a result of the nationalist victory, about 1m. French settlers emigrated from Algeria.

A draft constitution, providing for a presidential regime with the FLN as the sole party, was adopted by the Constituent Assembly in August 1963. In September the Constitution was approved by popular referendum and Ben Bella was elected President. Under his leadership, economic reconstruction was begun and the foundation was laid for a single-party socialist state. However, the failure of the FLN to function as an active political force left real power with the bureaucracy and the army. In June 1965 the Minister of Defence, Col Houari Boumedienne, deposed Ben Bella in a bloodless coup and took control of the State as President of a Revolutionary Council of 26 members, chiefly army officers.

Boumedienne faced considerable opposition from left-wing members of the FLN, but by 1971 the Government felt strong enough to adopt a more active social policy. French petroleum interests were nationalized and an agrarian reform programme was initiated. In June 1975 Boumedienne announced a series of measures to consolidate the regime and his personal power, including the drawing up of a National Charter and a new constitution, and the holding of elections for a President and National Assembly. Following public discussion of the National Charter, which formulated the principles and plans for creating a socialist system and maintaining Islam as the state religion, a referendum was held in June 1976, at which the Charter was adopted by 98.5% of the electorate. In November a new constitution was approved by another referendum, and in December Boumedienne was elected President unopposed, winning more than 99% of the votes cast. The new formal structure of power was completed in February 1977 by the election of FLN members to the National Assembly.

In December 1978 President Boumedienne died, and the Council of the Revolution (now consisting of only eight members) took over the government. An FLN Congress in January 1979 adopted a new party structure, electing a Central Committee which was envisaged as the highest policy-making body both of the party and of the nation as a whole: this Committee was to choose a party leader who would automatically become the sole presidential candidate. Their choice of Col Ben Djedid Chadli, commander of Oran military district, was upheld by a national referendum in February, and was seen as representing a compromise between liberal and radical contenders. Unlike Boumedienne, Chadli appointed a Prime Minister, Col Muhammad Abd al-Ghani, anticipating constitutional changes which were approved by the National Assembly in June and which included the obligatory appointment of a Prime Minister. Further changes in the party structure of the FLN were made in June 1980, when the FLN authorized Chadli to form a smaller Political Bureau of seven members (increased to 10 in July 1981) with more limited responsibilities, thereby increasing the power of the President. Membership of the National Assembly was increased to 281 in the legislative elections of March 1982, when the electorate was offered a choice of three candidates per seat. Of the successful candidates, 55 were FLN party officials and 142 were government officials, so executive control of the Assembly was expected to increase.

At the fifth conference of the FLN, held in December 1983, Chadli was re-elected to the post of Secretary-General of the party, and became the sole candidate for the presidential election, which was held on 12 January 1984. His candidature was endorsed by 95.4% of the electorate, and he was therefore returned to office for another five years. Immediately after his re-election, President Chadli named a new Prime Minister, Abd al-Hamid Brahimi, the former Minister of Planning. In 1985 Chadli initiated a public debate on Boumedienne's National Charter of 1976, which resulted in the adoption of a new National Charter at a special congress of the FLN in December. The revised Charter sought a balance between socialism and Islam as the state ideology, and encouraged the development of the private sector. At a referendum in January 1986, 98.37% of the votes cast (with 95.92% of the electorate participating) favoured the adoption of the new Charter. The number of seats in the National Assembly was increased to 295, all candidates being nominated by the FLN, for a general election in February 1987, when a record 87.29% of the electorate participated. Of the votes cast, however, 15.26% were invalid. In June a new Minister of the Interior was appointed, and Chadli introduced further changes in the military hierarchy, in order to strengthen the position of the Chief of Staff of the Army and to create a more professional army. In July the National Assembly passed legislation to permit the formation of local organizations without prior government authorization. The new law, however, continued to forbid associations that were deemed to threaten Algeria's security or the policies of the Charter.

Meanwhile, the Government encountered criticism and violent protests from students, Islamic fundamentalists and the Berbers of the Kabyle region, who felt that their culture and language were being suppressed. In 1985, 18 alleged supporters of Ben Bella were sentenced to terms of imprisonment, following their conviction on charges of threatening state security. In a separate trial, a total of 22 human rights and Berber cultural activists were found guilty of membership of illegal organizations, and received short prison sentences. In November 1986 four people were killed and 186 people were arrested during three days of rioting at Constantine and Sétif, which followed protests by students against government plans to reform the *baccalauréat* examination, and against poor living conditions and tuition facilities at the University of Constantine. The 186 detainees later received prison sentences for unlawful assembly, disturbing the peace and damage to property. Several human rights activists were exiled to southern Algeria, and in January 1987 security forces shot dead the leader, Mustafa Bouiali, and several other members of a clandestine Islamic fundamentalist group, who had been in hiding for 18 months, following the theft of weapons from a police barracks. In March and April the Government issued amnesties to human rights activists and to the 186 people imprisoned after the riots in Constantine, and approved the formation of a new human rights organization. In June 12 alleged supporters of Ben Bella received 'moderate' sentences of between two and 10 years' imprisonment for attacking the State, distributing subversive literature and receiving funds from abroad. At the end of a large trial in July, involving 202 defendants charged with involvement in the activities of Bouiali's Islamic fundamentalist group, four people received death sentences for plotting against the State, murder, armed attacks and robbery. Other defendants received sentences ranging from life to one year's imprisonment, while 15 people were acquitted. During an amnesty to commemorate the 25th anniversary of Algerian independence in August, the four death sentences were commuted to life imprisonment.

In response to a sharp decline in the price of petroleum in 1986 and an increase in Algeria's external debt, the Government introduced austerity measures and began to remove state controls from various economic sectors. In November 1987 the Ministry of Planning and Land Management, which had previously been responsible for the close supervision of every aspect of Algeria's economy, was abolished, in accordance with the latter policy. In the same month a new Ministry of Education and Training was created, in response to increasing demands for employment and educational opportunities for young people. With the aim of accelerating the implementation of new economic measures, in December President Chadli announced a series of administrative reforms, intended to improve the efficiency of Algeria's slow-moving and complex bureaucratic procedures. In February 1988 Chadli appointed 'technocratic' ministers to deal with the economic problems of the health and agricultural sectors.

Meanwhile, Algeria's economic difficulties and the rapid increase in the country's population, along with the Government's austerity policies, had resulted in decaying infrastructure, shortages of food and other essential goods, high prices, unemployment and increasing social polarization. Since July 1988 there had been a wave of strikes, but in September President Chadli reaffirmed his commitment to economic reform and vowed to dismiss any officials attempting to obstruct the implementation of austerity measures. Rumours subsequently emerged of government plans to introduce further austerity measures, including a rise in bread prices. There were demands for a general strike, and in early October riots broke out in the working-class districts of Algiers. As violent unrest spread through the capital and to Oran and Annaba, the Government declared a state of emergency, and armed soldiers were deployed at Algiers harbour and outside important buildings. Official sources announced that 3,743 people had been arrested, and that 176 had died during clashes with government forces, although other estimates of deaths ranged from 200 to 500. After six days, the state of emergency was revoked and Chadli promised to introduce political reforms. It was subsequently announced that a referendum would be held on 3 November, seeking approval for a series of constitutional amendments which included proposals to transfer some of the President's powers to the Prime Minister and to make the Prime Minister accountable to the National Assembly, rather than to the FLN. Meanwhile, food and other essential goods, drawn from emergency stockpiles, were delivered to shops in Algiers, and 923 detainees, mostly minors, were released. In late October Chadli dismissed the uncompromising Muhammad Cherif Messaadia from the deputy leadership of the FLN and replaced him with the more liberal Abd al-Hamid Mehri. Chadli also announced plans to make the FLN more democratic by broadening its membership and by introducing elections for most party posts. It was also proposed that non-party members would be allowed to contest seats in popularly-elected organizations. These plans were to form the subject of a referendum in early 1989.

At the referendum held on 3 November 1988, 92.27% of votes cast (with 83.10% of the electorate participating) favoured the adoption of the constitutional reforms proposed in October. Immediately after the referendum, Chadli appointed Kasdi Merbah, who had been the Minister of Health since February, to be Prime Minister. Merbah appointed a new 22-member Council of Ministers, which included 13 newcomers. The principal ministries were allocated to 'technocrats' or to veteran politicians. The new Government subsequently presented the National Assembly with an emergency programme of reforms, which aimed to remove causes of discontent by addressing problems experienced by Algerian youth and by the unemployed. In November the FLN congress approved further constitutional amendments and nominated Chadli as sole candidate in the forthcoming presidential election. In early December the President instituted changes in the army, replacing commanders in 11 important military posts with younger, more professional officers.

On 22 December 1988 Chadli was re-elected to a third term of office, receiving 81% of the votes cast, and proceeded with his programme of political reform. At a referendum held on 23 February 1989 the further amendments to the Constitution were approved by 73.4% of votes cast (with 79% of the electorate participating). Adoption of the amendments signified the ending of the one-party socialist state and permitted the formation of political associations outside the ruling FLN. Under the provisions of the amended Constitution, the army lost its role of developing socialism in the State. The right of employees to strike was also established. Executive, legislative and judicial functions were separated, and brought under the supervision of a Constitutional Council.

The process of political reform continued in subsequent months. In March 1989 army officers requested to be relieved of their duties as members of the FLN Central Committee, on the grounds that the army should be concerned solely with the defence of the nation. Following the electorate's approval of the constitutional amendments, several political groups were created. On 2 July Algeria officially became a multi-party state, with the adoption of the law on political associations. However, political organizations were permitted only if approved by the Ministry of Interior, and by September only five parties had been granted legal recognition: the Parti Social-Démocrate (PSD); the Rassemblement pour la Culture et la Démocratie (RCD); the Parti d'Avant-Garde Socialiste (PAGS); the Front Islamique du Salut (FIS); and the Parti National pour la Solidarité et le Développement (PNSD). In response to demands from journalists for independent status, a new Information Code, which guaranteed the freedom of the press, was introduced in late July. However, the FLN was granted control of the two major daily newspapers, *Al-Moudjahid* and *Ach-Cha'ab*, a move which attracted severe criticism.

Meanwhile, an economic crisis arose in mid-1989, when numerous strikes and demonstrations over the shortage of housing, rising food prices and a lack of basic consumer goods took place. On 10 September Chadli dismissed the Prime Minister, Kasdi Merbah, apparently owing to the latter's slow implementation of political and economic reforms. Chadli appointed one of his closest colleagues, Mouloud Hamrouche, to be Prime Minister, and a new government was announced six days later. In late September Hamrouche obtained the support of the Government for a programme of radical economic policies and political liberalization. However, the security of the new Government was threatened by the spread of Muslim fundamentalism, which swiftly gained popularity among young people. In October an Islamic demonstration, numbering an estimated 20,000, commemorated the anniversary of the previous year's riots. The Islamic fundamentalist party, the FIS, declined in popularity, however, when it was revealed that it had organized its own security force to apprehend and punish suspected criminals. The existence of such a force was widely condemned, and its revelation was regarded as detrimental not only to the FIS but also to other fundamentalist parties hoping for recognition.

An extraordinary congress of the FLN, held at the end of November 1989, elected a new Central Committee, comprising 272 members. In late December a 15-member Political Bureau was selected to replace the Executive Secretariat of the Central Committee. By early 1990 more than 20 political parties, including the revived socialist party, Front des Forces Socialistes (FFS), and the moderate Islamic party, Mouvement pour la Démocratie en Algérie (MDA), which was founded by Ben Bella in 1984, had been granted legal recognition. Municipal and provincial elections, scheduled for December 1989, were postponed until June 1990 to allow the newly-formed opposition parties more time for preparation. A new electoral law, adopted in March 1990, introduced a system of partial proportional representation to be applied in the forthcoming elections (see Government, p. 312). Demands by opposition parties for a further postponement of the elections were rejected, and in

April the FFS and MDA announced a boycott, claiming that they had been granted insufficient time to prepare.

Meanwhile, the widespread strikes and demonstrations, which continued in early 1990, were attributed by the Government to the growing influence of Islamic fundamentalism. In April members of the FIS demonstrated in favour of the dissolution of the National Assembly and the introduction of Islamic law. Municipal and provincial elections were held on 14 June 1990. The FIS received 55.42% of votes cast (with 66.15% of the electorate participating), and obtained a majority in 853 municipalities and 32 provinces, while the FLN won only 31.64% of the votes and secured control of 487 municipalities and 14 provinces. The FIS subsequently demanded the dissolution of the National Assembly and immediate parliamentary elections. In July the Central Committee of the FLN agreed to relieve five government members of their duties within the Political Bureau in order to reduce the influence of the FLN in the Government. In the same month President Chadli implemented an extensive ministerial reshuffle, which included, for the first time since 1965, the separation of the office of Minister of Defence from that of President. Shortly afterwards, Chadli announced that elections to the National Assembly were to be held in March 1991.

In August 1990 the Government declared a general amnesty, which permitted the release of large numbers of political prisoners. The return from exile, in September, of Ahmad Ben Bella, the former President and the leader of the MDA, was expected to improve the prospects of the MDA in the forthcoming parliamentary elections. In late 1990 unpopular economic reforms continued to provoke dissension within the FLN. The resignation, in October, of the President of the National Assembly, Rabah Bitat, was apparently prompted by disagreement over the Government's economic policy. Fears of division within the FLN were physically realized when the former Prime Minister, Kasdi Merbah, announced his resignation from the Central Committee and the formation of his own breakaway faction. In November his party, the Mouvement Algérien pour la Justice et le Développement, comprised 2,000 members, including three former ministers and three parliamentary deputies. In the same month a further revision of the electoral law was announced.

Since independence, Algeria has been one of the world's most prominent non-aligned states. The Government has supported various liberation movements in Africa and the Middle East, providing military, financial and diplomatic aid for the Polisario Front in Western Sahara (see chapter on Morocco).

In the early 1980s there was a noticeable improvement in relations with the USA, culminating, in April 1985, in a meeting between the US and Algerian Presidents in Washington. As a result of this visit, Chadli succeeded in having Algeria removed from the list of countries that the US Government had declared 'ineligible' to purchase US military equipment. Algeria's relations with the USA were temporarily strained in April 1988, when Algeria successfully negotiated the release of hostages being held on a hijacked Kuwaiti airliner, while agreeing to provide the hijackers with a safe passage from Algiers airport to Iran or Lebanon. The Algerian authorities' decision to allow the hijackers to escape unpunished attracted severe criticism from the USA and the UK. However, any tension with the USA was defused shortly afterwards by the visit to Algeria of the US Deputy Secretary of State, John Whitehead, who used the occasion to request Algeria to assist in the release of US hostages being held in Lebanon. In August 1989 Algeria played an active role in delaying the threatened execution of an American hostage, Joseph Cicippio, who was being held in captivity by a pro-Iranian Shia group in Lebanon. Chadli, intervening at the personal request of the US President, George Bush, sent a senior mediator to Lebanon.

The protracted struggle in Western Sahara embittered Algeria's relations with France, which supported the claims of Morocco and Mauritania. Algeria also criticized French military intervention elsewhere in Africa, while further grievances were the heavy trade surplus in France's favour, and France's determination to reduce the number of Algerians resident in France. By the early 1980s, relations had improved, and in 1982 President Chadli made the first official visit to France by an Algerian head of state since independence. In September 1986 relations were strained by the French Government's announcement of proposals to introduce visa requirements for visitors from non-EEC countries to France. In October Algeria retaliated by introducing similar requirements for French visitors. In the same month, however, the French Government expelled 13 Algerian members of the MDA from France and banned the party's newspaper, Al-Badil, after Algerian security forces co-operated with France following a series of bombings in Paris. In April 1987 the Algerian Government agreed to release the assets of former French settlers, which had been 'frozen' since independence. Further agreements allowed former French property-owners to sell their land in Algeria to the Algerian State, and permitted French workers in Algeria to transfer their income to France. In return, the French Government agreed to provide financial assistance to Algeria for three years. In July the two countries concluded an agreement relating to children from mixed Algerian-French marriages, and the French authorities suppressed another MDA publication. In the following months Algeria assisted in negotiations between France and Iran over the blockading of the French embassy in Teheran and the Iranian embassy in Paris. Algeria also conducted negotiations with Islamic groups in Lebanon, in an attempt to obtain the release of French hostages. Meanwhile, in January 1988 France announced the arrests of two MDA members on charges which included illegal possession of arms. In June Algeria and France signed an agreement guaranteeing French mothers access to children living with their Algerian fathers. The two countries also agreed to establish a bilateral commission to adjudicate on contentious cases of child custody. In July the French Government banned the MDA newspaper, Al-Badil démocratique, which had been established as a replacement for the outlawed Al-Badil. In September, however, relations between France and Algeria cooled, as parents occupied the French embassy in Algiers to protest against the Algerian Government's decision that children from Algerian-French marriages should attend Arabic-speaking schools. Relations continued to deteriorate during the riots in Algiers in October (see above), as Algerian state newspapers accused the French media of exaggerating the extent of the unrest, and the Algerian Government criticized the French Minister of Co-operation for objecting to the stern measures taken against rioters. Meanwhile, the French Prime Minister maintained an embarrassed silence on the unrest, in an attempt to balance French support for human rights with the French interest in preventing the unrest from spreading across the Maghreb and into the North African community in France. However, during a visit to Algiers in March 1989, the French President, François Mitterrand, demonstrated his support for Chadli and the recently-introduced reforms. In June the Association for Algerian-French Friendship was created with the aim of strengthening links between the two countries.

Relations with Spain improved in 1987, after deteriorating in 1986 owing to Algerian suspicion of Spain's pro-Moroccan position in the conflict in Western Sahara and the presence in Algiers of a leader of ETA, the Basque separatist movement. In December 1986 the Spanish Deputy Prime Minister visited President Chadli, and in the following month Spain announced that Algeria would be incorporated into its programme of overseas military co-operation. In August the two countries signed a pact which allowed an Algerian security official to be stationed in Spain to monitor the activities of Algerian dissidents, in exchange for closer supervision of members of ETA exiled in Algeria. In December an MDA activist was arrested by the Spanish authorities and expelled to Algeria. In April and May 1989, 16 ETA members were expelled from Algeria, following the breakdown of peace talks with the Spanish Government and a resumption of ETA violence in Spain.

Algeria's relations with other Maghreb states (Libya, Mauritania, Morocco and Tunisia) improved considerably in the 1980s. Algeria partially opened its frontier with Morocco in February 1983, and signed the Maghreb Fraternity and Co-operation Treaty, which normalized relations with Tunisia, in March. It was hoped that this treaty would eventually form the basis of the long-discussed Great Arab Maghreb. It was, therefore, left open for other countries to sign; Mauritania did so in December 1983. However, the rapprochement with Morocco continued to be hindered by Algeria's continuing support of the Polisario Front. In May 1987 President Chadli met King Hassan of Morocco at a location on the Algeria/Morocco border, under the auspices of King Fahd of Saudi Arabia. After the meeting, the two leaders issued a communiqué announcing that consultations to resolve existing problems between the two countries would continue. Later in the month, the Algerian Government released 150 Moroccan soldiers, in exchange for 102 Algerian prisoners, held in Morocco.

Meanwhile, relations with Libya improved, following President Chadli's meetings with the Libyan Secretary for Foreign Liaison in November 1985, and with Col Muammar al-Qaddafi, the Libyan leader, in January 1986. In an attempt to consolidate its good relations with Algeria, Libya advocated a treaty of union with Algeria in March and June 1986. In June 1987 a proposal for a political union between Libya and Algeria was submitted to Chadli by Col Qaddafi's deputy, Maj. Abd as-Salam Jalloud, during his visit to Algeria. After Jalloud's visit, Algeria suggested that the Maghreb Fraternity and Co-operation Treaty of 1983 already provided a framework for a new Algerian-Libyan relationship. Later in June, Col Qaddafi arrived unexpectedly in Algeria to attempt to persuade Chadli to agree to the union proposals, but he succeeded only in gaining several minor co-operation agreements. In the following month Chadli visited Tunisia to discuss the Libyan proposals with Habib Bourguiba, the Tunisian President. The two leaders subsequently issued a joint communiqué announcing that discussions had been held on the means of developing unity within the Maghreb region. In October Algeria agreed, in principle, to a treaty of political union with Libya, but the official announcement of the treaty was postponed, following diplomatic pressure from the USA (in addition to opposition from within the Algerian Government), and Chadli again proposed that Libya should sign the Maghreb Fraternity and Co-operation Treaty.

Towards the end of 1987 and during 1988 the process of achieving Maghreb unity gained momentum. In November 1987 President Chadli received the Moroccan Minister of Foreign Affairs, and they discussed means of accelerating the establishment of the Great Arab Maghreb and of resolving the conflict in Western Sahara. In January 1988, during a meeting in Tunis, Chadli and the new Tunisian President, Zine al-Abidine ben Ali, issued directives to intensify bilateral co-operation, demanded a just resolution of the Western Sahara conflict, and pledged to work for regional stability and the early creation of the Great Arab Maghreb. Chadli then visited Col Qaddafi in an apparent attempt to persuade him to sign the Maghreb Fraternity and Co-operation Treaty in March, on the fifth anniversary of its inception. At a tripartite meeting in Tunis in February, Chadli, President Ben Ali of Tunisia and Col Qaddafi of Libya all expressed their determination to work towards the creation of the Great Arab Maghreb. Libya's failure to sign the Maghreb Fraternity and Co-operation Treaty was a major factor underlying Algeria's subsequent efforts to improve relations with Morocco. In early May the head of the secretariat (i.e. deputy leader) of the FLN, Muhammad Cherif Messaadia, visited Rabat to invite King Hassan to a 'summit' conference of the Arab League in Algiers, which Chadli had convened for June, with the aim of rallying support for the Palestinian uprising in the Israeli-occupied territories. A few days later, King Hassan dispatched two senior advisers to Algiers for further consultations, and on 16 May the two countries announced the re-establishment of diplomatic relations at ambassadorial level. The Moroccan-Algerian border was subsequently opened in early June, before the Arab League 'summit'.

The creation of the Great Arab Maghreb became a reality in June 1988, when the first meeting of the five Heads of State of the Maghreb countries was held in Algiers, following the conclusion of the Arab League 'summit'. The five leaders issued a joint communiqué announcing the creation of a Maghreb commission whose responsibility was to focus on the establishment of a semi-legislative, semi-consultative council to harmonize legislation in the region, and to prepare joint economic projects. At the end of June, Algeria and Libya agreed to hold referendums on a proposed union of the two countries. Unlike the proposals issued by Col Qaddafi in 1987 (which envisaged a total merger), this revised proposal aimed merely to establish a federation between the two countries. In July 1988 Algeria signed a co-operation agreement with Morocco, and the two countries announced plans to harmonize their railway, postal and telecommunications systems. Later in the month, the Maghreb commission met in Algiers and announced the creation of five working groups to examine areas of regional integration. The working groups, each chaired by a representative of a member country, met during the following three months, in order to prepare for the second meeting of the Maghreb commission in October. In February 1989 the treaty creating the Union of the Arab Maghreb (see p. 225) was signed in Morocco by the leaders of Algeria, Libya, Mauritania, Morocco and Tunisia. In June the five nations formed a joint parliament. In May Boualem Bessaïeh, the Algerian Minister for Foreign Affairs, and his Moroccan counterpart ratified the agreement demarcating the state frontier between Algeria and Morocco, a significant move towards a stable Maghreb. At a 'summit' meeting in July 1990 the five nations agreed to introduce unified tariffs on imports by 1991 and to establish a full customs union by 1995.

Government

Under the 1976 Constitution (with modifications adopted by the National Assembly in June 1979 and with further amendments approved by popular referendum in November 1988 and in February 1989), Algeria is a multi-party state, with parties subject to approval from the Ministry of the Interior. The Head of State is the President of the Republic, who is nominated by a Congress of the FLN and is elected for a five-year term by universal adult suffrage. The President presides over a Council of Ministers and a High Security Council. The President may appoint Vice-Presidents and must appoint a Prime Minister, who initiates legislation and appoints a Council of Ministers. The Prime Minister is responsible to the unicameral National People's Assembly, which comprises 295 members, elected by universal adult suffrage for a five-year term. The President is empowered to legislate by decree, after consultations with the Prime Minister, when the Assembly is not in session. The country is divided into 48 departments (wilayat), sub-divided into communes. Each wilaya and commune has an elected assembly. Under a new electoral law, which was adopted in March 1990 and which introduced a system of partial proportional representation, elections to the National Assembly would henceforth comprise only one round of voting, the winning list of candidates in each constituency receiving all the seats. At local elections any list of candidates obtaining more than 50% of the votes would win all the seats. If no party secured the requisite majority, the winning list would be allocated one-half of the seats, the remainder being distributed proportionately among other parties that had received a minimum of 7% of the votes.

Defence

In June 1990 the estimated strength of the armed forces was 125,500 (including 70,000 conscripts), comprising an army of 107,000, a navy of 6,500 and an air force of 12,000. The 1990 defence budget was estimated at 8,100m. dinars. The USSR provides military equipment and training. Military service is compulsory for 18 months, and there is a gendarmerie of 23,000, controlled by the Ministry of the Interior.

Economic Affairs

In 1988, according to estimates by the World Bank, Algeria's gross national product (GNP), measured at average 1986–88 prices, was US $58,250m., equivalent to $2,450 per head. During 1980–88, it was estimated, GNP increased, in real terms, at an average annual rate of 3.0%. GNP per head in 1988 was the same, in real terms, as in 1980. Over the period 1980–88, the population increased by an annual average of 3.1%. Algeria's gross domestic product (GDP) increased, in real terms, by an annual average of 3.5% in 1980–88.

Agriculture (including forestry and fishing) is an important sector of the Algerian economy, employing about 25% of the country's work-force, and contributing 13% of GDP, in 1988. The principal crops are grapes, wheat, barley and oats. Olives, citrus fruits and tobacco are also grown. During 1980–88 agricultural production increased at an average annual rate of 5.6%.

Industry (including mining, manufacturing, construction and power) contributed 43% of GDP in 1988, and employed 32.6% of the labour force in 1985. During 1980–88 industrial production increased by an annual average of 3.8%.

The major mineral exports are petroleum and natural gas. Reserves of iron ore, phosphates, lead and zinc are also exploited. In addition, Algeria has deposits of antimony, tungsten, manganese, mercury, copper and salt.

Manufacturing represented 12% of GDP in 1988; the most important sectors, measured by gross value of output, are food-processing, machinery and transport equipment, and textiles. During 1980–88 the output of the manufacturing sector increased by an annual average of 6.1%.

ALGERIA

Energy is derived principally from natural gas and petroleum. However, nuclear power is exploited as an additional source of energy; the first nuclear reactor was installed in 1989. Imports of mineral fuels comprised only 2% of the value of total imports in 1987.

In 1988 Algeria recorded a visible trade surplus of US $946m., but there was a deficit of $2,040m. on the current account of the balance of payments. The principal source of imports continued to be France (24.0% in 1986), which was also the principal market for exports (21.6% in 1986). Other major trading partners were Italy, the Federal Republic of Germany, the USA and the Netherlands. The principal exports in 1987 were petroleum and natural gas, with hydrocarbons accounting for 97.4% of total export revenue. Other exports included vegetables, tobacco, hides, dates, and phosphates. The principal imports were machinery and transport equipment, basic manufactures and food.

The 1990 budget envisaged a deficit of 3,500m. dinars. Algeria's total external public debt amounted to US $24,500m. at the end of 1989. The cost of debt-servicing represented 70.5% of export earnings (goods and services) in that year. The annual rate of inflation averaged 9.3% in 1989. An estimated 25% of the work-force were unemployed in late 1990.

Algeria is a member of the Union of the Arab Maghreb (see p. 225), which aims to promote economic integration of member states, and also of OPEC (see p. 200).

Scarcity of food is a severe problem in Algeria; agricultural development is affected by such problems as drought and flood, and in 1988 Algeria suffered from a plague of locusts over the Sahel region. Therefore, investment in agriculture has been made a priority. In 1990 the Government planned to refinance part of the foreign debt and to reduce the debt-service ratio by obtaining loans, to be secured by collateral, through a group of French banks. A four-year development plan (1990–94), supported by loans from the World Bank and IMF, was designed to liberalize the economy, allowing companies to become more independent of the State and encouraging further foreign investment in Algeria. The aim was to reduce the country's reliance on food imports and to provide exports other than hydrocarbons. However, the success of the Algerian economy continued to depend heavily on international prices for crude petroleum and natural gas. In 1990 an increase in revenue from the export of petroleum was expected to convert the current account deficit to a surplus.

Social Welfare

Since 1974, all Algerian citizens have had the right to free medical care. In 1979 Algeria had 367 hospital establishments, with a total of 47,116 beds, and there were 6,881 physicians working in the country. In 1984 the Government announced a new health plan, under which several new health centres and clinics were to be built, an institution for training health care administrators was to be founded, and vaccinations were to be made more readily available. In 1987 the administrative budget allocated 3,961m. dinars to expenditure on health.

Education

In accordance with the National Charter, the various primary and secondary schools were unified in 1976, private education was abolished and a nine-year 'enseignement fondamental' was introduced. Education is officially compulsory for nine years between six and 15 years of age. Primary education begins at the age of six and lasts for six years. Secondary education begins at 12 years of age and lasts for up to seven years (a first cycle of four years and a second of three years). In 1988 the total enrolment at primary and secondary schools was equivalent to 76% of the school-age population (84% of boys; 67% of girls). Enrolment at primary schools in 1988 included an estimated 89% of children in the relevant age-group (97% of boys; 82% of girls). Enrolment at secondary schools in 1988 was equivalent to 54% of children in the relevant age-group (61% of boys; 46% of girls). More than 14% of total planned expenditure in the 1990 budget was allocated to education and training. Priority is being given to teacher-training, to the development of technical and scientific teaching programmes, and to adult literacy and training schemes. In 1987 there were eight universities and a number of 'Centres Universitaires' and technical colleges. In 1986/87 there were about 156,700 undergraduates and post-graduates studying at university. In 1985, according to UNESCO estimates, the average rate of adult illiteracy was 50.4% (males 37%; females 63%).

Public Holidays

1991: 1 January (New Year), 16 April* (Id al-Fitr, end of Ramadan), 1 May (Labour Day), 19 June (Ben Bella's Overthrow), 23 June* (Id al-Adha, Feast of the Sacrifice), 5 July (Independence), 13 July* (Islamic New Year), 22 July* (Ashoura), 21 September* (Mouloud, Birth of Muhammad), 1 November (Anniversary of the Revolution).

1992: 1 January (New Year), 4 April* (Id al-Fitr, end of Ramadan), 1 May (Labour Day), 11 June* (Id al-Adha, Feast of the Sacrifice), 19 June (Ben Bella's Overthrow), 2 July* (Islamic New Year), 5 July (Independence), 11 July* (Ashoura), 10 September* (Mouloud, Birth of Muhammad), 1 November (Anniversary of the Revolution).

* Religious holidays, which are dependent on the Islamic lunar calendar, may differ by one or two days from the dates given.

Weights and Measures

The metric system is in force.

ALGERIA

Statistical Survey

Source (unless otherwise stated): Office National des Statistiques, Ministère de la Planification et de l'Aménagement du Territoire (abolished in November 1987), 8 rue des Moussebiline, BP 55, Algiers; tel. 64-77-90; telex 52620.

Area and Population

AREA, POPULATION AND DENSITY

Area (sq km)	2,381,741*
Population (census results)†	
12 February 1977‡	16,948,000
April 1987‡	22,971,558
Population (UN estimates at mid-year)‡	
1987	23,102,000
1988	23,841,000
1989	24,597,000
Density (per sq km) at mid-1989	10.3

* 919,595 sq miles.
† Provisional.
‡ Excluding Algerian nationals residing abroad, numbering an estimated 828,000 at 1 January 1978.

AREA AND POPULATION BY WILAYA (ADMINISTRATIVE DISTRICT)*

	Area (sq km)	Population (estimates at 1 Jan. 1984)†
Adrar	422,498.0	161,936
el-Asnam (ech-Cheliff)	8,676.7	1,040,563
Laghouat	112,052.0	391,817
Oum el-Bouaghi (Oum el-Bouagul)	8,123.0	464,806
Batna	14,881.5	691,079
Béjaia	3,442.2	659,040
Biskra (Beskra)	109,728.0	662,778
Béchar	306,000.0	184,069
Blida (el-Boulaïda)	3,703.8	1,126,303
Bouira	4,517.1	454,805
Tamanrasset (Tamenghest)	556,000.0	62,680
Tébessa (Tbessa)	16,574.5	439,638
Tlemcen (Tilimsen)	9,283.7	678,025
Tiaret (Tihert)	23,455.6	731,542
Tizi-Ouzou	3,756.3	1,028,864
Algiers (el-Djezaïr)	785.7	2,442,303
Djelfa (el-Djelfa)	22,904.8	403,500
Jijel	3,704.5	604,319
Sétif (Stif)	10,350.4	1,776,673
Saida	106,777.4	450,594
Skikda	4,748.3	597,530
Sidi-Bel-Abbès	11,648.2	604,773
Annaba	3,489.3	650,096
Guelma	8,624.4	633,733
Constantine (Qacentina)	3,561.7	807,245
Médéa (Lemdiyya)	6,704.1	575,305
Mostaganem (Mestghanem)	7,023.6	396,765
M'Sila	19,824.6	540,013
Mascara (Mouaskar)	5,845.6	526,644
Ouargla (Wargla)	559,234.0	261,760
Oran (Ouahran)	1,820.0	889,800
Total	**2,381,741.0**	**20,841,000**

* In December 1983 an administrative reorganization created 17 new wilayat, bringing the total number to 48.
† Excluding Algerian nationals abroad, estimated to total 828,000 at 1 January 1978.

PRINCIPAL TOWNS (estimated population at 1 January 1983)

Algiers (el-Djezaïr, capital)	1,721,607	Tlemcen (Tilimsen)	146,089
Oran (Ouahran)	663,504	Skikda	141,159
Constantine (Qacentina)	448,578	Béjaia	124,122
Annaba	348,322	Batna	122,788
Blida (el-Boulaïda)	191,314	El-Asnam (ech-Cheliff)	118,996
Sétif (Stif)	186,978	Boufarik	112,000*
Sidi-bel-Abbès	146,653	Tizi-Ouzou	100,749
		Médéa (Lemdiyya)	84,292

* 1977 figure.

April 1987 (census results, not including suburbs): Algiers 1,483,000; Constantine 438,000; Oran 590,000.

BIRTHS AND DEATHS (UN estimates, annual averages)

	1975–80	1980–85	1985–90
Birth rate (per 1,000)	45.0	42.5	40.2
Death rate (per 1,000)	13.4	10.7	9.1

Source: UN, *World Population Prospects: 1988*.

EMPLOYMENT
(household survey, '000 persons, excluding armed forces, 1985)

	Males	Females	Total
Agriculture, hunting, forestry and fishing	987	12	999
Mining and quarrying			
Manufacturing	556	39	595
Electricity, gas and water			
Construction	661	9	670
Trade, restaurants and hotels	302	9	311
Transport, storage and communications	192	10	202
Financing, insurance, real estate and business services	860	247	1,107
Community, social and personal services			
Total	**3,558**	**326**	**3,884**

Source: ILO, *Year Book of Labour Statistics*.

Agriculture

PRINCIPAL CROPS ('000 metric tons)

	1987	1988	1989
Wheat	1,175	614	850
Barley	820	390	870†
Oats	68	30	54
Potatoes	905	899	1,030
Pulses	67	36	61
Sugar beets	114*	115*	117*
Onions (dry)	200	200	200*
Tomatoes	457	490*	500*
Carrots	135	150*	160*
Grapes	282†	301†	360*
Olives	200†	170†	173*
Oranges	183	208	177
Tangerines, mandarins, clementines and satsumas	84	93	95*
Dates	224	196	210
Water-melons	360	320*	330*
Tobacco (leaves)	5*	4*	4*

* FAO estimate. † Unofficial figure.

Source: FAO, *Production Yearbook*.

ALGERIA

LIVESTOCK ('000 head, year ending September)

	1987	1988	1989
Sheep	14,300	14,325†	12,500†
Goats	3,500	3,570*	3,600*
Cattle	1,523	1,520*	1,410†
Horses	185	187*	190*
Mules	127	113	130*
Asses	354	327	300
Camels	134	114	135*

Poultry (FAO estimates, million): 23 in 1987; 23 in 1988; 23 in 1989.
* FAO estimate.   † Unofficial figure.
Source: FAO, *Production Yearbook*.

LIVESTOCK PRODUCTS ('000 metric tons)

	1987	1988	1989
Beef and veal	74	81	80*
Mutton and lamb	80*	75	70
Goat's meat	15	15	15
Poultry meat	63*	64*	64*
Other meat	9	10	10
Cows' milk	590†	585†	595†
Sheep's milk	201*	203*	204*
Goats' milk	166*	168*	170*
Hen eggs	143.8†	154.0	165.0
Wool:			
greasy	43.0*	45.0*	46.0*
clean	21.8*	23.7*	24.6*
Cattle hides	7.6*	7.4*	6.7*
Sheep skins	12.5*	12.6*	10.2*
Goat skins	2.9*	3.0*	3.0*

* FAO estimate.   † Unofficial figure.
Source: FAO, *Production Yearbook*.

Forestry

ROUNDWOOD REMOVALS
(FAO estimates, '000 cu m, excluding bark)

	1986	1987	1988
Sawlogs, veneer logs and logs for sleepers*	20	20	20
Other industrial wood	216	223	230
Fuel wood	1,705	1,760	1,815
Total	1,941	2,003	2,065

* Assumed to be unchanged since 1975.
Source: FAO, *Yearbook of Forest Products*.

Fishing*
(FAO estimates, '000 metric tons, live weight)

	1984	1985	1986
European sardine (pilchard)	36.4	36.6	38.9
Other marine fishes	26.2	26.4	28.0
Marine crustaceans	2.9	3.0	3.2
Total catch	65.5	66.0	70.0

1987: Catch as in 1986 (FAO estimates).
* Figures exclude catch from inland waters (258 metric tons in 1987).
Source: FAO, *Yearbook of Fishery Statistics*.

Mining
('000 metric tons, unless otherwise indicated)

	1985	1986	1987
Hard coal*	8	9	8
Crude petroleum	31,264	31,334	33,090
Natural gas (petajoules)	1,161.5	1,187.9	1,312.9
Iron ore:			
gross weight*	3,780	3,360	3,380
metal content	1,823	1,814	1,827
Copper concentrates†	0.2	—	—
Lead concentrates†	3.9	3.8	2.1
Zinc concentrates†	14.3	14.2	9.4
Mercury (metric tons)	804	766	756
Phosphate rock	1,221	1,203	1,209
Salt (unrefined)	168	190	106
Gypsum (crude)	250‡	250*	77

* Provisional or estimated data.
† Figures refer to the metal content of concentrates.
‡ Estimate by the US Bureau of Mines.
Source: UN, *Industrial Statistics Yearbook* and *Monthly Bulletin of Statistics*.

1988: Crude petroleum 30,830,000 metric tons; Natural gas 1,560 petajoules.
1989: Crude petroleum 32,450,000 metric tons.

Industry

SELECTED PRODUCTS
('000 metric tons, unless otherwise indicated)

	1985	1986	1987
Olive oil (crude)	16‡	15	10
Margarine	16.0	15.9	18.0
Raw sugar*	13‡	14‡	15‡
Wine ('000 hectolitres)	1,338	1,347	1,250
Cigarettes (metric tons)	1,850	1,900*	1,769
Woven cotton fabrics (million sq metres)*	103	n.a.	n.a.
Footwear—excl. rubber ('000 pairs)	17,909	18,421	18,100
Nitrogenous fertilizers (a)†	105.8	112.5	117.0
Phosphate fertilizers (b)†	71.1	53.8	55.1
Naphtha	4,060	4,400	4,460
Motor spirit (petrol)	1,800	1,889	1,846
Kerosene	130	110	100
Jet fuel	500	511	525
Distillate fuel oils	6,866	7,673	7,522
Residual fuel oils	6,402	6,782	6,262
Liquefied petroleum gas	2,300*	2,890	3,780
Cement	6,096	6,448	7,541
Pig-iron	1,462	1,246	1,478
Crude steel	1,213	1,120	1,378
Television receivers ('000)	223	259	318
Buses and coaches—assembled (number)	636	730	625
Lorries—assembled (number)	5,772	6,671	5,785
Electric energy (million kWh)	12,274	12,981	13,400

* Provisional or estimated data.
† Production in terms of (a) nitrogen or (b) phosphoric acid. Phosphate fertilizers include ground rock phosphate.
‡ Data from the FAO.
Source: mainly UN, *Industrial Statistics Yearbook*.

1988 ('000 metric tons): Olive oil 8 (unofficial estimate); Raw sugar 15 (FAO estimate); Nitrogenous fertilizers 105.5; Phosphate fertilizers 70.7.

ALGERIA

Statistical Survey

Finance

CURRENCY AND EXCHANGE RATES

Monetary Units
100 centimes = 1 Algerian dinar (AD).

Denominations
Coins: 1, 2, 5, 10, 20 and 50 centimes; 1 and 5 dinars.
Notes: 10, 20, 50, 100 and 200 dinars.

Sterling and Dollar Equivalents (30 September 1990)
£1 sterling = 17.783 dinars;
US $1 = 9.492 dinars;
1,000 Algerian dinars = £56.23 = $105.35.

Average Exchange Rate (dinars per US $)
1987 4.8497
1988 5.9148
1989 7.6086

ADMINISTRATIVE BUDGET (estimates, million AD)

Expenditure	1985	1986	1987*
Presidency	611.8	640.0	585.0
National defence	4,793.1	5,459.0	5,805.0
Foreign affairs	583.5	619.3	583.0
Light industry	137.6	149.5	132.0
Housing and construction	359.4	460.9	439.0
Finance	1,252.4	1,446.1	1,613.0
Home affairs	n.a.	3,543.0	4,003.0
Commerce	130.6	146.8	148.0
Youth and sport	403.6	446.6	396.0
Information	350.8	384.8	373.0
Ex-servicemen	2,984.5	3,289.0	3,192.0
Culture and tourism	218.3	258.2	226.0
Agriculture and fishing	766.0	838.1	772.0
Health	2,720.6	3,518.3	3,961.0
Transport	373.7	414.0	413.0
Justice	477.4	556.4	668.0
Professional training	1,397.9	1,539.8	1,562.0
Religious affairs	363.7	403.1	473.0
Public works	690.8	784.1	697.0
Education	11,026.7	13,626.7	15,886.0
Higher education and scientific research	2,764.4	2,931.6	3,494.0
Heavy industry	94.6	108.3	107.0
Water, environment and forests	798.3	866.0	810.0
Energy and petrochemicals industries	201.5	220.9	216.0
Planning and land development	n.a.	165.9	—
Social protection	476.7	530.1	501.0
Extra expenditure	25,197.5	23,384.4	15,779.0
Total (incl. others)	**62,200.0**	**67,000.0**	**63,000.0**

* As announced in November 1985. A revised administrative budget, announced in April 1986, projected total expenditure of 59,500 million AD.

1988 (million AD): Revenue 103,000; Administrative expenditure 64,500.
1989 (million AD): Revenue 114,700; Administrative expenditure 71,900.
1990 (million AD): Revenue 136,500; Administrative expenditure 84,000.

INVESTMENT BUDGET (million AD)

Expenditure	1988
Hydrocarbons	700
Manufacturing industries	1,300
Mines and energy (incl. rural electrification)	1,000
Agriculture and water projects	7,450
Services	135
Economic and administrative infrastructure	8,369
Education and training	7,100
Social and cultural infrastructures	3,294
Construction	2,142
Infrastructure and training linked to the reform of state enterprises	470
Grants to new enterprises	150
Financial restructuring of state enterprises	3,400
Total (incl. others)	**47,500**

Source: *Al-Moudjahid*.

CENTRAL BANK RESERVES (US $ million at 31 December)

	1987	1988	1989
Gold*	277	263	257
IMF special drawing rights	202	2	4
Reserve position in IMF	153	—	—
Foreign exchange	1,285	898	843
Total	**1,917**	**1,163**	**1,104**

* Valued at 35 SDRs per troy ounce.

Source: IMF, *International Financial Statistics*.

MONEY SUPPLY (million AD at 31 December)

	1987	1988	1989
Currency outside banks	96,892	109,755	119,870
Demand deposits at deposit money banks	103,801	115,527	101,893
Checking deposits at post office	22,247	25,881	26,955
Private sector demand deposits at treasury	929	1,044	1,295
Total money	**223,869**	**252,207**	**250,013**

Source: IMF, *International Financial Statistics*.

COST OF LIVING (Consumer Price Index for Algiers; average of monthly figures; base: 1982 = 100)

	1985	1986	1987
Food	127.5	149.2	160.6
Clothing	118.3	123.9	133.2
Rent, electricity, gas and water	115.7	127.5	139.0
All items (incl. others)	**126.6**	**142.2**	**152.8**

1988: Food 166.7; All items 161.8.
1989: Food 181.8; All items 176.9.

Source: ILO, mainly *Year Book of Labour Statistics*.

ALGERIA

NATIONAL ACCOUNTS (million AD at current prices)
Expenditure on the Gross Domestic Product

	1986	1987	1988
Government final consumption expenditure	53,500	56,300	60,000
Private final consumption expenditure	152,000	152,800	158,800
Increase in stocks	−2,500	500	1,000
Gross fixed capital formation	95,300	92,800	97,300
Total domestic expenditure	298,300	302,400	317,100
Exports of goods and services	39,100	45,500	48,900
Less Imports of goods and services	50,900	40,000	46,000
GDP in purchasers' values	286,500	307,900	320,000

Source: IMF, *International Financial Statistics*.

BALANCE OF PAYMENTS (US $ million)

	1986	1987	1988
Merchandise exports f.o.b.	8,065	9,029	7,620
Merchandise imports f.o.b.	−7,879	−6,616	−6,675
Trade balance	185	2,413	946
Exports of services	721	675	542
Imports of services	−3,900	−3,464	−3,917
Balance on goods and services	−2,994	−376	−2,429
Private unrequited transfers (net)	765	522	385
Government unrequited transfers (net)	−1	−5	5
Current balance	−2,230	141	−2,040
Long-term capital (net)	364	21	767
Short-term capital (net)	226	289	−23
Net errors and omissions	142	−802	335
Total (net monetary movements)	−1,498	−352	−960
Valuation changes (net)	339	332	19
Official financing (net)	—	—	201
Changes in reserves	−1,159	−20	−740

Source: IMF, *International Financial Statistics*.

External Trade

Note: Data exclude military goods. Exports include stores and bunkers for foreign ships and aircraft.

PRINCIPAL COMMODITIES
(distribution by SITC, US $ million)

Imports c.i.f.	1984	1985	1986
Food and live animals	1,742.9	2,142.3	1,806.3
Dairy products and birds' eggs	344.7	439.2	381.1
Milk and cream	193.1	268.1	242.1
Cereals and cereal preparations	734.0	1,031.7	677.7
Wheat and meslin (unmilled)	367.9	542.8	381.4
Crude materials (inedible) except fuels	438.4	419.3	380.5
Cork and wood	214.8	182.8	173.8
Mineral fuels, lubricants, etc.	216.1	190.0	278.4
Petroleum, petroleum products, etc.	103.4	114.7	215.3
Animal and vegetable oils, fats and waxes	198.8	306.4	172.1
Fixed vegetable oils and fats	159.9	251.0	142.8
Soft fixed vegetable oils	102.8	215.0	91.9
Chemicals and related products	686.2	745.0	992.5
Medicinal and pharmaceutical products	209.6	218.9	328.4

Imports c.i.f.—*continued*	1984	1985	1986
Medicaments	192.4	202.6	302.1
Artificial resins, plastic materials, etc.	198.5	167.0	220.5
Basic manufactures	3,247.1	2,310.9	2,071.1
Textile yarn, fabrics, etc.	272.8	261.8	239.4
Non-metallic mineral manufactures	862.5	500.5	353.6
Articles of cement, concrete or artificial stone	588.8	246.4	99.8
Iron and steel	645.2	576.0	562.1
Bars, rods, angles, shapes and sections	320.4	234.2	257.3
Bars and rods	238.0	116.8	151.6
Structures and parts of iron and steel	552.7	196.9	129.8
Machinery and transport equipment	3,238.5	3,249.9	3,068.9
Power generating machinery and equipment	302.6	365.8	365.9
Machinery specialized for particular industries (excl. metalworking)	472.7	546.3	400.4
General industrial machinery and equipment	740.3	740.3	802.3
Electrical machinery, apparatus and appliances	643.2	513.6	551.8
Switchgear, etc., and parts	208.5	135.0	133.7
Road vehicles and parts*	739.6	671.8	595.9
Motor vehicles for goods transport, etc.	324.0	251.6	242.3
Goods vehicles (lorries and trucks)	270.7	196.1	186.2
Parts and accessories for cars, buses, lorries, etc.*	234.6	256.5	270.2
Miscellaneous manufactured articles	462.5	404.1	416.2
Total (incl. others)	10,288.9	9,842.3	9,234.5

* Excluding tyres, engines and electrical parts.

Source: UN, *International Trade Statistics Yearbook*.

1987 (million AD): Foodstuffs 8,524; Semi-finished products 8,850; Raw materials 2,424; Industrial equipment 9,064; Consumer goods 4,374; Total (incl. others) 34,196.

Source: Direction Générale des Douanes, *Actualité Economique*.

(distribution by SITC, US $ million)

Exports f.o.b.	1984	1985	1986
Mineral fuels, lubricants, etc.	11,595.3	9,900.9	7,640.7
Petroleum, petroleum products, etc.	8,458.8	6,376.5	5,004.4
Crude petroleum oils, etc.	4,434.0	2,539.8	3,120.6
Refined petroleum products	4,021.5	3,833.4	1,875.3
Motor spirit (petrol) and other light oils	1,434.7	1,393.3	573.1
Kerosene and other medium oils	264.5	107.8	35.7
Gas oils (distillate fuels)	1,273.8	1,274.3	696.3
Residual fuel oils	1,037.3	1,058.0	569.9
Gas (natural and manufactured)	3,135.1	3,522.9	2,632.5
Liquefied petroleum gases	2,432.2	2,595.6	1,845.8
Petroleum gases, etc. in the gaseous state	702.8	927.2	786.7
Total (incl. others)	11,885.7	10,149.1	7,830.6

Source: UN, *International Trade Statistics Yearbook*.

1987 (million AD): Foodstuffs 145; Energy and lubricants 38,137; Semi-finished products 518; Total (incl. others) 39,156.

Source: Direction Générale des Douanes, *Actualité Economie*.

ALGERIA

Statistical Survey

PRINCIPAL TRADING PARTNERS (US $ million)*

Imports c.i.f.	1984	1985	1986
Argentina	83.6	50.2	101.3
Austria	175.0	223.7	241.9
Belgium/Luxembourg	446.8	415.9	279.1
Brazil	282.4	284.0	224.3
Canada	398.5	402.5	203.5
China, People's Republic	114.5	38.5	29.4
Denmark	139.5	81.0	30.3
Finland	126.0	107.4	65.8
France	2,421.4	2,555.8	2,214.1
Germany, Federal Republic	1,099.5	1,106.8	1,020.9
Greece	103.7	99.6	93.1
Hungary	135.3	92.0	54.9
Italy	903.4	1,076.8	1,193.2
Japan	838.5	570.1	420.5
Netherlands	260.2	284.9	274.9
Spain	452.0	135.1	423.5
Sweden	162.0	153.9	104.8
Switzerland	106.9	121.3	173.1
Tunisia	36.2	68.0	102.6
Turkey	146.0	151.5	205.8
United Kingdom	355.4	297.1	234.5
USA	580.9	642.6	711.9
Yugoslavia	169.6	163.2	141.7
Total (incl. others)	10,263.2	9,813.5	9,234.4

Exports f.o.b.	1984	1985	1986
Austria	110.8	33.4	79.7
Belgium/Luxembourg	91.2	12.3	494.5
Brazil	82.5	150.5	112.2
Bulgaria	35.5	185.6	15.3
Canada	89.0	200.3	2.9
France	3,379.5	3,019.8	1,687.6
Germany, Federal Republic	357.4	347.0	247.6
Greece	164.9	145.3	22.0
Italy	2,154.6	2,335.1	1,560.0
Japan	81.2	104.8	100.8
Netherlands	1,424.7	931.7	1,113.4
Spain	409.1	601.7	448.0
Turkey	131.0	142.2	51.5
United Kingdom	171.4	178.7	88.6
USA	2,575.8	1,010.6	1,360.6
Yugoslavia	185.1	350.2	148.2
Total (incl. others)	11,885.7	10,149.1	7,830.6

* Imports by country of production; exports by country of last consignment.

Source: UN, *International Trade Statistics Yearbook*.

Transport

RAILWAYS (traffic)

	1982	1983	1984
Passengers carried ('000)	24,842	34,043	35,700
Freight carried ('000 metric tons)	11,355	11,437	11,400
Passenger-km (million)	1,774	1,804	1,835
Freight ton-km (million)	2,765	2,671	2,631

1987: Passengers carried ('000) 43,000, Freight carried ('000 metric tons) 12,700.

ROAD TRAFFIC (motor vehicles in use at 31 December)

	1977	1978	1981*
Passenger cars	355,125	411,894	573,573
Lorries and vans	174,801	186,169	248,258
Coaches and buses	5,484	6,401	8,417
Motorcycles	16,637	16,812	17,608

* Figures for 1979 and 1980 are not available.

Source: Ministère de la Planification et de l'Aménagement du Territoire, Algiers; and (1981) International Road Federation.

INTERNATIONAL SEA-BORNE SHIPPING
(estimated freight traffic, '000 metric tons)

	1983	1984	1985
Goods loaded	54,677	53,370	50,543
Goods unloaded	16,676	15,865	15,450

Source: UN, *Monthly Bulletin of Statistics*.

CIVIL AVIATION (traffic on scheduled services)

	1983	1984	1985
Kilometres flown ('000)	31,200	36,400	42,200
Passengers carried ('000)	3,411	3,781	3,966
Passenger-km (million)	2,798	3,312	3,597
Freight ton-km ('000)	28,200	14,900	21,000
Mail ton-km ('000)	1,900	1,900	1,800
Total ton-km ('000)	282,000	306,000	354,000

Source: UN, *Statistical Yearbook*.

Tourism

FOREIGN VISITORS BY COUNTRY OF ORIGIN

	1984	1985	1986
France	167,811	108,278	91,181
Germany, Federal Republic	27,562	19,720	17,347
Italy	30,844	23,318	21,937
Morocco	1,537	821	624
Tunisia	9,233	8,203	10,169
United Kingdom	9,684	7,969	6,868
USA	4,070	3,279	2,607
Total (incl. others)	250,747	171,588	150,733

Hotel Capacity (1986): 200 hotels; 32,862 beds.
Total Visitors (1988): 353,723.

Source: Ministère de la Culture et du Tourisme, Algiers.

ALGERIA
Statistical Survey, Directory

Communications Media

	1982	1983	1984
Radio receivers ('000 in use)	4,200	4,400	n.a.
Television receivers ('000 in use)	n.a.	1,325	n.a.
Book production: titles*	504	n.a.	718
Daily newspapers:			
Number	4	n.a.	5
Average circulation ('000 copies)	445	n.a.	570
Non-daily newspapers:			
Number	15	n.a.	n.a.
Average circulation ('000 copies)	309	n.a.	n.a.
Other periodicals:			
Number	27	n.a.	n.a.
Average circulation ('000 copies)	476	n.a.	n.a.

* Including pamphlets (167 in 1984).

1986: Radio receivers ('000 in use) 5,000; Television receivers ('000 in use) 1,610; Daily newspapers 6 (average circulation 812,000 copies).
1987: Radio receivers ('000 in use) 5,250; Television receivers ('000 in use) 1,607.
Source: UNESCO, *Statistical Yearbook*.
Telephones: ('000 in use): 709 in 1984; 769 in 1985; 822 in 1986 (Source: UN, *Statistical Yearbook*).
1989: 5.5m. radio receivers in use; 1.6m. television receivers in use (incl. more than 300,000 colour receivers).

Education

(state institutions only, 1986)

	Institutions	Teachers	Pupils
Primary	11,427	133,250	3,635,332
Middle and Secondary			
General	1,250*	88,758	1,877,553
Teacher training	40†	2,458‡	23,238
Technical	174*	2,528	98,300
Higher (Universities, etc.)	13*	12,204	154,700

* 1981/82 figures.
† 1978/79 figure.
‡ 1985/86 figure.

1988: Primary education: 12,240 institutions, 139,917 teachers, 3,911,388 pupils; General secondary education: 107,786 teachers, 1,954,869 pupils; Technical education: 5,313 teachers, 156,423 pupils.

Source: mainly UNESCO, *Statistical Yearbook*.

Directory

The Constitution

A new constitution for the Democratic and Popular Republic of Algeria, approved by popular referendum on 19 November 1976, was promulgated on 22 November 1976. The Constitution was amended by the National People's Assembly on 30 June 1979. Further amendments were approved by referendum on 3 November 1988, and on 23 February 1989. The main provisions of the Constitution, as amended, are summarized below:

The preamble recalls that Algeria owes its independence to a war of liberation which led to the creation of a modern sovereign state, guaranteeing social justice, equality and liberty for all. It emphasizes Algeria's Islamic heritage, and stresses that, as an Arab Mediterranean and African country, it forms an integral part of the Great Arab Maghreb.

FUNDAMENTAL PRINCIPLES OF THE ORGANIZATION OF ALGERIAN SOCIETY

The Republic
Algeria is a popular, democratic state. Islam is the state religion and Arabic is the official national language.

The People
National sovereignty resides in the people and is exercised through its elected representatives. The institutions of the State consolidate national unity and protect the fundamental rights of its citizens. The exploitation of one individual by another is forbidden.

The State
The State is exclusively at the service of the people. Those holding positions of responsibility must live solely on their salaries and may not, directly or by the agency of others, engage in any remunerative activity.

Fundamental Freedoms and the Rights of Man and the Citizen
Fundamental rights and freedoms are guaranteed. All discrimination on grounds of sex, race or belief is forbidden. Law cannot operate retrospectively and a person is presumed innocent until proved guilty. Victims of judicial error shall receive compensation from the State.

The State guarantees the inviolability of the home, of private life and of the person. The State also guarantees the secrecy of correspondence, the freedom of conscience and opinion, freedom of intellectual, artistic and scientific creation, and freedom of expression and assembly.

The State guarantees the right to form political associations, to join a trade union, the right to strike, the right to work, to protection, to security, to health, to leisure, to education, etc. It also guarantees the right to leave the national territory, within the limits set by law.

Duties of citizens
Every citizen must respect the Constitution, and must protect public property and safeguard national independence. The law sanctions the duty of parents to educate and protect their children, as well as the duty of children to help and support their parents.

The National Popular Army
The army safeguards national independence and sovereignty.

Principles of foreign policy
Algeria subscribes to the principles and objectives of the UN. It advocates international co-operation, the development of friendly relations between states, on the basis of equality and mutual interest, and non-interference in the internal affairs of states.

POWER AND ITS ORGANIZATION

The Executive
The President of the Republic is Head of State, Head of the Armed Forces and responsible for national defence. He must be of Algerian origin, a Muslim and more than 40 years old. He is elected by universal, secret, direct suffrage. His mandate is for five years, and is indefinitely renewable. The President embodies the unity of the nation. The President presides over joint meetings of the party and the executive. The President presides over meetings of the Council of Ministers. He decides and conducts foreign policy and appoints the Head of Government, who is responsible to the National People's Assembly. The Head of Government must appoint a Council of Ministers. He drafts, co-ordinates and implements his government's programme, which he must present to the Assembly for ratification. Should the Assembly reject the programme, the Head of Government and the Council of Ministers resign, and the President appoints a new Head of Government. Should the newly-appointed Head of Government's

ALGERIA   Directory

programme be rejected by the Assembly, the President dissolves the Assembly, and a general election is held. Should the President be unable to perform his functions, owing to a long and serious illness, the President of the National People's Assembly assumes the office for a maximum period of 45 days (subject to the approval of a two-thirds majority in the National Assembly). If the President is still unable to perform his functions after 45 days, the Presidency is declared vacant by the Constitutional Council. Should the Presidency fall vacant, the President of the National People's Assembly temporarily assumes the office and organizes presidential elections within 45 days. He may not himself be a candidate in the election. The President presides over a High Security Council which advises on all matters affecting national security.

The Legislature

The National People's Assembly prepares and votes the law. Its members are elected by universal, direct, secret suffrage for a five-year term. The deputies enjoy parliamentary immunity. The Assembly sits for two ordinary sessions per year, each of not more than three months' duration. The commissions of the Assembly are in permanent session. The Assembly may be summoned to meet for an extraordinary session on the request of the President, or of the Head of Government, or of two-thirds of the members of the Assembly. Both the Head of Government and the Assembly may initiate legislation. The Assembly may legislate in all areas except national defence.

The Judiciary

Judges obey only the law. They defend society and fundamental freedoms. The right of the accused to a defence is guaranteed. The Supreme Court regulates the activities of courts and tribunals. The Higher Court of the Magistrature is presided over by the President of the Republic; the Minister of Justice is Vice-President of the Court. All magistrates are answerable to the Higher Court for the manner in which they fulfil their functions.

The Constitutional Council

The Constitutional Council is responsible for ensuring that the Constitution is respected, and that referendums, the election of the President of the Republic and legislative elections are conducted in accordance with the law. The Constitutional Council comprises seven members, of whom two are appointed by the President of the Republic, two elected by the National People's Assembly and two elected by the Supreme Court. The Council's members serve for a six-year term of office.

Constitutional revision

The Constitution can be revised on the initiative of the President of the Republic by a two-thirds majority of the National Assembly, and must be approved by national referendum. The basic principles of the Constitution may not be revised.

The Government

HEAD OF STATE

President and Commander-in-Chief of the Armed Forces: BEN DJEDID CHADLI (elected 7 February 1979; re-elected 12 January 1984 and 22 December 1988).

COUNCIL OF MINISTERS
(November 1990)

President: BEN DJEDID CHADLI.
Prime Minister: MOULOUD HAMROUCHE.
Minister of Foreign Affairs: SID-AHMAD GHOZALI.
Minister of Justice: ALI BEN FLIS.
Minister of Defence: Maj.-Gen. KHALED NEZZAR.
Minister of Religious Affairs: SAÏD CHIBANE.
Minister of the Interior: MUHAMMAD SALAH MUHAMMADI.
Minister of Education and Training: ALI BEN MUHAMMAD.
Minister of Youth: ABD AL-KADER BOUDJEMAA.
Minister of the Economy: GHAZI HIDOUCI.
Minister of Social Affairs: MUHAMMAD GHRIB.
Minister of Agriculture: ABD AL-KADER BENDAOUD.
Minister of Transport: HASSEN KALOUCHE.
Minister of Equipment: MUHAMMAD KEHIFED.
Minister of Mines and Industry: SADOK BOUSSENA.
Minister of Posts and Telecommunications: MUHAMMAD SERRADJ.
Minister of Health: HAMID SIDI SAÏD.
Minister Delegate for Local Authorities: BENALI HENNI.

Minister Delegate for Universities: MUSTAPHA CHERIF.
Minister Delegate for Professional Training: ABD EN-NOUR KERAMANE.
Minister Delegate for the Organization of Commerce: SMAIL GOUMEZIANE.
Minister Delegate for Employment: AMAR KARA MUHAMMAD.
Minister with Special Responsibility for Research and Technology: CHERIF HADJ-SLIMANE.
Secretary of State for Maghreb Affairs: ABD AL-AZIZ KHELLEF.
Secretary-General of the Government: AHMAD MEDJHOUDA.

MINISTRIES

Office of the President: Présidence de la République, el-Mouradia, Algiers; tel. (2) 60-03-60; telex 53761.
Office of the Prime Minister: Palais du Gouvernement, Algiers; tel. (2) 60-23-40; telex 52073.
Ministry of Agriculture: 12 blvd Col Amirouche, Algiers; tel. (2) 63-89-50; telex 52984.
Ministry of Culture and Tourism: Algiers.
Ministry of Defence: ave des Tagarins, Algiers; tel. (2) 61-15-15; telex 52627.
Ministry of the Economy: Palais du Gouvernement, Algiers; tel. (2) 63-23-40; telex 52062.
Ministry of Education and Training: 8 ave de Pékin, el-Mouradia, Algiers; tel. (2) 60-54-41; telex 52443.
Ministry of Equipment: le Grand Seminaire, Kouba, Algiers; tel. (2) 58-95-00; telex 62560.
Ministry of Foreign Affairs: 6 rue 16n- Batran, el-Mouradia, Algiers; tel. (2) 60-47-44; telex 52794.
Ministry of Health: 25 blvd Laala Abd ar-Rahmane, el-Madania, Algiers; tel. (2) 66-33-15; telex 51263.
Ministry of Higher Education: 1 rue Bachir Attar, Palais du 1er Mai, Algiers; tel. (2) 66-33-61; telex 52720.
Ministry of Industry: rue Ahmad Bey, Immeuble le Colisée, Algiers; tel. (2) 60-11-14; telex 52707.
Ministry of the Interior: Palais du Government, Algiers; tel. (2) 63-23-40; telex 52073.
Ministry of Justice: 8 rue de Khartoum, el-Biar, Algiers; tel. (2) 78-20-90; telex 52761.
Ministry of Mines and Industry: 80 ave Ahmad Ghermoul, Algiers; tel. (2) 67-33-00; telex 52790.
Ministry of Posts and Telecommunications: 4 blvd Salah Bouakouir, Algiers; tel. (2) 61-12-20; telex 52020.
Ministry of Religious Affairs: 4 ave Timgad, Hydra, Algiers; tel. (2) 60-85-55; telex 66118; fax (2) 60-09-36.
Ministry of Social Affairs: rue Farid Zouieoueche, Kouba, Algiers; tel. (2) 77-91-33; telex 53447.
Ministry of Transport: chemin Abd al-Kader Gadouche, Hydra, Algiers; tel. (2) 60-60-33; telex 52775.
Ministry of Youth: 3 place du 1er Mai, Algiers; tel. (2) 66-33-70; telex 65054.

Legislature

ASSEMBLÉE NATIONALE POPULAIRE

The National People's Assembly comprises 295 deputies, elected by universal suffrage for a five-year term. The most recent general election took place on 26 February 1987. A single-party list of candidates was presented by the FLN, but the electorate was offered a choice of three candidates per seat. Electoral participation was 87.29%.

Under a new electoral law adopted in March 1990, elections to the National Assembly would henceforth comprise only one round of voting, the winning list of candidates in each constituency receiving all the seats. At local elections any list of candidates obtaining more than 50% of the votes would win all the seats. If no party secured the requisite majority, the winning list would be allocated one-half of the seats, the remainder being distributed proportionately among other parties that had each received a minimum of 7% of the votes. A revision of electoral legislation, approved in November 1990, provided for the reorganization of voter registration.

President of the National Assembly: ABD AL-AZIZ BELKHADEM.

Political Organizations

Until 1989 the FLN was the only legal party in Algeria. The February 1989 amendments to the Constitution permitted the

ALGERIA

formation of other political associations, with some restrictions. Numerous political parties subsequently emerged, and by late 1990 there were more than 20. The most important of these are listed below.

Alliance Centriste et Démocrate (ACD): Algiers; informal alliance, f. 1990, to unite social-democratic and central candidates for electoral purposes; includes:

Association du Peuple pour l'Unité et l'Action (APUA): Bachdajarah, Algiers; f. 1990 as a legal party; Leader AL-MEHDI ABBES ALLALOU.

Front National de Renouvellement (FNR): Algiers; Leader ZINEDDINE CHERIFI.

Parti National pour la Solidarité et le Développement (PNSD): Algiers; Leader RABAH BENCHERIF.

Parti Social-Démocrate (PSD): Algiers; f. 1989; centre party; advocates economic liberalization; Leader ABDERRAHMANE ABJERID; Sec.-Gen. ABD AL-KADER BOUZAR.

Parti Social-Libéral (PSL): Leader AHMAD KHELIL.

El-Oumma (The Community): Algiers; f. 1990 as a legal party; advocates the application of Islam in political life; Leader BENYOUSSEF BEN KHEDDA.

Front des Forces Socialistes (FFS): f. 1963; revived 1990; Leader HOCINE AIT AHMAD.

Front Islamique du Salut (FIS): Algiers; f. 1989; aims to emphasize the importance of Islam in political and social life; gained control of 32 provinces and 853 local councils at local elections in June 1990; Leader ABBASI MADANI.

Front de Libération Nationale (FLN): blvd Zirout Yousuf, Algiers; telex 53931; f. 1954; sole legal party until 1989; socialist in outlook, the party is organized into a Secretariat, a Central Committee, Federations, Kasmas and cells; at the 6th FLN Congress, held in November 1988, a new Central Committee of 155 mems was elected, and the Political Bureau was dissolved; until November 1988, the Secretary-General (chosen by the Central Committee) automatically became the candidate for the Presidency, but the revision of the Constitution in February 1989 formally separated the two roles; a new Central Committee of 272 mems. was elected at an extraordinary congress, held on 28–30 November 1989, and a 15-mem. Political Bureau (replacing the Executive Secretariat of the Central Committee) was elected in December 1989; under the aegis of the FLN are various mass political organizations, including the Union Nationale de la Jeunesse Algérienne (UNJA) and the Union Nationale des Femmes Algériennes (UNFA); Sec.-Gen. ABD AL-HAMID MEHIRI.

Mouvement Algérien pour la Justice et le Développement: Algiers; f. 1990; reformist party; Leader KASDI MERBAH.

Mouvement pour la Démocratie en Algérie (MDA): Algiers; f. 1990 as a legal party; Leader AHMAD BEN BELLA.

Parti d'Avant-Garde Socialiste (PAGS): 8 rue des Frères, BP 513, Algiers; tel. (2) 63-38-20; communist; operated clandestinely between 1966 and 1989; Sec.-Gen. HADJERES SAOLEK.

Parti Démocratique Progressif (PDR): Algiers; f. 1990 as a legal party; Leader SACI MABROUK.

Parti Républicain Progressif (PRP): Algiers; f. 1990 as a legal party; Sec.-Gen. KADIR DRISS.

Parti d'Unité Arabe Islamique-Démocratique (PUAID): Menaa; f. 1990 as a legal party; advocates creation of a pan-Arab state under Islamic law; Leader BELHADJ KHALIL HARFI.

Rassemblement Arabique-Islamique (RAI): Algiers; f. 1990; aims to increase the use of Arabic in social and cultural life; Leader ME LAID GRINE.

Rassemblement pour la Culture et la Démocratie (RCD): Tizi-Ouzou; f. 1989; secular party; advocates recognition of Berber as national language; Sec.-Gen. SAÏD SAADI.

Other political parties include the following: Hezbollah (Algerian Party for Maghreb Rebirth), Parti du Peuple Algérien (PPA), Parti National Algérien (PNA), Parti du Renouveau Algérien (PRA, Leader NOURREDDINE BOUKROUH), Parti Socialiste des Travailleurs (PST), Union des Forces Démocratiques (UFD).

Diplomatic Representation

EMBASSIES IN ALGERIA

Albania: 19 bis rue Abdelkrim Lagoune, el-Mouradia, Algiers; Ambassador: DHIMITËR STAMO.

Angola: 34 chemin Abd al-Kader, el-Mouradia, Algiers; tel. (2) 56-15-24; telex 62204; Ambassador: HENRIQUE TELES CARREIRA.

Argentina: 7 rue Hamani, Algiers; tel. (2) 64-74-08; telex 67485; Ambassador: VICENTE ESPECHE-GIL.

Australia: 12 ave Emile Marquis, Djenane-el-Malik, Hydra, Algiers; tel. (2) 60-28-46; telex 66105; fax (2) 592081; Ambassador: M. P. F. SMITH.

Austria: Les Vergers, rue 2, Villa 9, DZ-16330 Bir Khadem, Algiers; tel. (2) 56-26-99; telex 62302; Ambassador: HANS G. KNITEL.

Bangladesh: 149 blvd Salah Bouakouir, Algiers; telex 66363; Ambassador: MAHBUBUL HUQ.

Belgium: 22 chemin Youcef Tayebi, el-Biar, Algiers; tel. (2) 78-57-12; telex 61365; Ambassador: ANDRÉ ADAM.

Benin: rue 3, Villa no. 4, Beaulieu, el-Harrach, Algiers; telex 52447; Ambassador: ANTOINE LALEYE.

Brazil: 48 blvd Muhammad V, Algiers; telex 52470; Ambassador: RONALD L. M. SMALL.

Bulgaria: 13 blvd Col Bougara, Algiers; Ambassador: GRIGOR TODOROV KRUCHMARSKI.

Burundi: 116 bis blvd des Martyrs, Algiers; telex 53501; Ambassador: ANDRÉ NADAYIRAGE.

Cameroon: 26 chemin Cheikh Bachir Ibrahimi, el-Biar, Algiers; telex 52421; Ambassador: SIMON NKO'O ETOUNGOU.

Canada: 27 bis rue Ali Massoudi, POB 225, Hydra, Algiers; tel. (2) 60-66-11; telex 66043; Ambassador: GILLES MATHIEL.

Chad: 6 rue Sylvain Fourastier, Le Golf, Algiers; telex 52642; Ambassador: MBAILAOU NAIMBAYE LOSSIMIAN.

Chile: Algiers.

China, People's Republic: 34 blvd des Martyrs, Algiers; telex 53233; Ambassador: JIN SEN.

Congo: 13 rue Rabah Noël, Algiers; telex 52069; Ambassador: BENJAMIN BOUNKOULOU.

Côte d'Ivoire: Immeuble 'Le Bosquet', Le Paradou, Hydra, Algiers; telex 52881; Ambassador: LAMBERT AMON TAMOH.

Cuba: 22 rue Larbi Alik, Hydra, Algiers; telex 66163; Ambassador: ULISES ESTRADA LESCAILLE.

Czechoslovakia: Villa Malika, 7 chemin Zyriab, BP 999, Algiers; tel. (2) 60-05-25; telex 66281; Ambassador: FRANTIŠEK KAN.

Denmark: 29 blvd Zirout Youcef, BP 500, DZ-16000 Alger-Gare, Algiers; tel. (2) 63-88-71; telex 67328; fax (2) 64-51-52; Ambassador: PREBEN HANSEN.

Egypt: 16300, Algiers; tel. 60-16-73; telex 66058; Ambassador: Dr HUSSAIN AHMAD AMIN.

Finland: BP 256, 16035 Hydra, Algiers; tel. (2) 59-32-92; telex 66296; fax (2) 59-46-37; Ambassador: RISTO RÄNNÄLI.

France: 6 rue Larbi Alik, Hydra, Algiers; telex 52644; Ambassador: JEAN AUDIBERT.

Gabon: 136 bis blvd Salah Bouakouir au 80 rue Allili, BP 85, Algiers; tel. (2) 72-02-64; telex 52242; Ambassador: YVES ONGOLLO.

Germany: 165 chemin Sfindja, BP 664, Algiers; tel. (2) 74-19-56; telex 67343; Ambassador: Dr WILFRIED M. HOFMANN.

Ghana: 62 rue des Frères Bénali Abdellah, Hydra, Algiers; tel. (2) 60-64-44; telex 62234; Ambassador: ISAAC O. TWUM-AMPOFO.

Greece: 31 rue A. les Crêtes, 16035 Hydra, Algiers; tel. (2) 60-08-55; telex 66071; Ambassador: GEORGES HELMIS.

Guinea: 43 blvd Central Said Hamdine, Hydra, Algiers; telex 53451; Ambassador: FODE BERETE.

Guinea-Bissau: Cité DNC, rue Ahmad Kara, Hydra, Algiers; tel. (2) 60-01-51; Ambassador: Dr LEONEL VIEIRA (also representing Cape Verde).

Holy See: 1 rue Nourredine Mekiri, 16090 Bologhine, Algiers; tel. (2) 62-34-30; Pro-Nuncio: Mgr EDMOND FARHAT.

Hungary: 18 ave des Frères Oughlis, BP 68, el-Mouradia, Algiers; tel. (2) 60-77-09; telex 62217; Ambassador: ZOLTÁN ZSIGMOND.

India: 119 ter rue Didouche Mourad, Algiers; tel. (2) 59-46-00; telex 66138; Ambassador: V. K. NAMBIAR.

Indonesia: 6 rue Muhammad Chemlal, BP 62, 16070 el Mouradia, Algiers; tel. (2) 60-20-51; telex 62214; Ambassador: MUHAMMAD SINGGIH HADIPRANOWO.

Iran: 60 rue Didouche Mourad, Algiers; telex 52880; Ambassador: SIAVASH ZARGARAN YAQOUBI.

Iraq: 4 rue Arezki Abri, Hydra, Algiers; telex 53067; Ambassador: IBRAHIM SHUJAA SULTAN.

Italy: 18 rue Muhammad Ouidir Amellal, el-Biar, Algiers; tel. (2) 78-33-99; telex 61357; Ambassador: MICHELANGELO JACOBUCCI.

Japan: 1 chemin Macklay, el-Biar, Algiers; tel. (2) 78-62-00; telex 61389; Ambassador: NISHIYAMA TAKEHIKO.

Jordan: 6 rue du Chenoua, Algiers; telex 52464; Ambassador: YASIN ISTANBULI.

Korea, Democratic People's Republic: 49 rue Hamlia, Bologtrine, Algiers; telex 53929; Ambassador: LI MAN-SOK.

ALGERIA

Korea, Republic: Algiers.
Kuwait: 1 ter rue Didouche Mourad, Algiers; telex 52267; Ambassador: ABDEL-LATIF HAMAD AL-SALIH.
Lebanon: 9 rue Kaïd Ahmad, el-Biar, Algiers; telex 52416; Ambassador: SALHAD NASRI.
Libya: 15 chemin Cheikh Bachir Ibrahimi, Algiers; telex 52700; Ambassador: ABDEL-FATTAH NAAS.
Madagascar: 22 rue Abd al-Kader Aouis Bologhine, Algiers; tel. (2) 62-31-96; telex 61156; Ambassador: SAMUEL LAHADY.
Mali: Villa no. 15, Cité DNC/ANP, chemin du Kaddous, Algiers; telex 52631; Ambassador: BOUBACAR KASSE.
Mauritania: BP 276, el-Mouradia, Algiers; telex 53437; Ambassador: OULD MUHAMMAD MAHMOUD MUHAMMADOU.
Mexico: 8 chemin du Kaddous, BP 880, DZ-16300 Alger-Gare, Algiers; tel. (2) 59-12-13; telex 66090; Ambassador: JORGE PALACIOS.
Mongolia: 4 rue Belkacem Amani, Hydra, Algiers; tel. (2) 60-26-12; Ambassador: BURENJARGALYN ORSOO.
Morocco: Algiers; Ambassador Prof. ABD AL-LATIF BERBICHE.
Netherlands: 23 chemin Cheikh Bachir Ibrahimi, BP 72, El-Biar, Algiers; tel. (2) 78-28-29; telex 61364; fax (2) 78-07-70; Ambassador: Dr PATRICK S. J. RUTGERS.
Niger: 54 rue Vercors Rostamia Bouzareah, Algiers; telex 52625; Ambassador: MOUSTAPHA TAHI.
Nigeria: 27 bis rue Blaise Pascal, BP 629, Algiers; tel. (2) 60-60-50; telex 52523; Ambassador: B. A. OKI.
Oman: 126 rue Didouche Mourad, Algiers; telex 52223; Ambassador: SALEM ISMAIL SUWAID.
Pakistan: 14 ave Soudani Boudjemâa, Algiers; tel. (2) 60-57-81; telex 66277; Ambassador: KARAMATULLAH KHAN GHORI.
Philippines: Algiers; Ambassador: PACIFICO CASTRO.
Poland: 37 ave Mustafa Ali Khodja, el-Biar, Algiers; telex 52562; Ambassador: STANISŁAW PICHLA.
Portugal: 67 chemin Muhammad Gacem, Algiers; tel. (2) 56-61-95; telex 62202; Ambassador: FERNANDO ANDRESEN GUIMARÃES.
Qatar: BP 118, 25 bis allée Centrale, Clairval, Algiers; tel. (2) 79-80-56; telex 52224; Ambassador: KHALIFA SULTAN AL-ASSIRY.
Romania: 24 rue Si Arezki, Hydra, Algiers; telex 52915; Ambassador: TUDOR ZAMFIRA.
Saudi Arabia: 4 rue Arezki Abri, Hydra, Algiers; telex 53039; Ambassador: HASAN FAQQI.
Senegal: 1 rue Arago, Algiers; tel. (2) 60-32-85; telex 52133; Ambassador: IBRAHIMA WONE.
Somalia: 11 impasse Tarting, blvd des Martyrs, Algiers; telex 52140; Ambassador: ABD AL-HAMID ALI YOUCEF.
Spain: 10 rue Azil Ali, Algiers; telex 67330; Ambassador: GUMERSINDO RICO Y RODRÍGUEZ VILLAR.
Sweden: BP 623, DZ-16035, Hydra, Algiers; tel. (2) 59-43-00; telex 66046; fax (2) 59-17-17; Ambassador: TOM G. R. TSCHERNING.
Switzerland: 27 blvd Zirout Youcef, DZ-16000 Alger-Gare, Algiers; tel. (2) 63-39-02; telex 67342; Ambassador: O. UHL.
Syria: Domaine Tamzali, chemin A. Gadouche, Hydra, Algiers; telex 52572; Ambassador: AHMAD MADANIYA.
Tunisia: 11 rue du Bois de Boulogne, Hydra, Algiers; telex 52968; Ambassador: M'HEDI BACCOUCHE.
Turkey: Villa dar el Ouard, chemin de la Rochelle, blvd Col Bougara, Algiers; tel. (2) 60-12-57; telex 66244; Ambassador: OMER ERSUN.
USSR: impasse Boukhandoura, el-Biar, Algiers; telex 52511; Ambassador: VASILIY TARATOUTA.
United Arab Emirates: 26 rue Aouis Mokrane, POB 454, el-Mouradia, Algiers; tel. (2) 56-46-47; telex 62208; Ambassador: MUHAMMAD I. AL-JOWAIED.
United Kingdom: Résidence Cassiopée, Bâtiment B, 7 chemin des Glycines, BP 43, DZ-16000 Alger-Gare, Algiers; tel. (2) 60-56-01; telex 66151; fax (2) 60-44-10; Ambassador: CHRISTOPHER C. R. BATTISCOMBE.
USA: 4 chemin Cheikh Bachir Brahimi, BP 549, Alger-Gare, 16000 Algiers; tel. (2) 60-11-86; telex 66047; Ambassador: CHRISTOPHER ROSS.
Venezuela: 3 impasse Ahmed Kara, BP 813, Algiers; telex 66642; fax (2) 60-75-55; Ambassador: FRANCISCO SALAZAR MARTÍNEZ.
Viet-Nam: 30 rue de Chenoua, Hydra, Algiers; telex 52147; Ambassador: VO TOAN.
Yemen Arab Republic*: 74 rue Bouraba, Algiers; telex 53582; Ambassador: HAMOD MUHAMMAD BAYDER.
Yemen, People's Democratic Republic*: 12 ave Chahid el-Wali Mustafa Sayed, Algiers; Ambassador: ABD AL-WAKIL ISMAIL AS-SAROURI.
Yugoslavia: 7 rue des Frères Benhafid, BP 662, Hydra, Algiers; tel. (2) 60-47-04; telex 66076; Ambassador: BORISLAV MILOŠEVIĆ.
Zaire: 12 rue A, Les Crêtes, Hydra, Algiers; telex 52749; Ambassador: IKOLO BOLELAMA W'OKONDOLA.
Zimbabwe: 24 rue Arab Si Ahmad, Birkhadem, Algiers; Ambassador: SOLOMON RAKOBE NKOMO.

* Merged to form the Republic of Yemen since May 1990.

Judicial System

The highest court of justice is the Supreme Court (Cour suprême) in Algiers. Justice is exercised through 183 courts (tribunaux) and 31 appeal courts (cours d'appel), grouped on a regional basis. Three special Criminal Courts were set up in Oran, Constantine and Algiers in 1966 to deal with economic crimes against the State. From these there is no appeal. In April 1975 a Cour de sûreté de l'état, composed of magistrates and high-ranking army officers, was established to try all cases involving state security. The Cour des comptes was established in 1979. A new penal code was adopted in January 1982, retaining the death penalty.

President of Supreme Court: A. MEDJHOUDA.
Procurator-General: Y. BEKKOUCHE.

Religion

ISLAM

Islam is the official religion, and the whole Algerian population, with a few rare exceptions, is Muslim.

President of the Superior Islamic Council: AHMAD HAMANI; place Cheik Abd al-Hamid ibn Badis, Algiers.

CHRISTIANITY

The European inhabitants, and a few Arabs, are generally Christians, mostly Roman Catholics.

The Roman Catholic Church

Algeria comprises one archdiocese and three dioceses (including one directly responsible to the Holy See). In December 1988 there were an estimated 43,238 adherents in the country.

Bishops' Conference: Conférence Episcopale Régionale du Nord de l'Afrique, 13 rue Khélifa-Boukhalfa, DZ-16000 Alger-Gare, Algiers; tel. (2) 63-42-44; f. 1985; Pres. Most Rev. HENRI TEISSIER, Archbishop of Algiers; Sec-Gen. Fr JEAN LANDOUSIES.

Archbishop of Algiers: Most Rev. HENRI TEISSIER, Archevêché, 13 rue Khélifa-Boukhalfa, DZ-16000 Alger-Gare, Algiers; tel. (2) 63-42-44.

Protestant Church

Protestant Church of Algeria: 31 rue Reda Houhou, 16000 Algiers; tel. (2) 71-62-38; telex 65172; three parishes; 1,000 mems; Pastors (Algiers) Dr HUGH G. JOHNSON, STEVEN H. DICKIE; Pastor (Oran) Dr DAVID W. BUTLER; Pastor (Constantine) KAYIJ-A-MUTOMBU.

The Press

DAILIES

Ach-Cha'ab (The People): 1 place Maurice Audin, Algiers; f. 1962; FLN journal in Arabic; Dir KAMEL AVACHE; circ. 80,000.

Al-Badil: Algiers; relaunched 1990; MDA journal in French and Arabic; circ. 130,000.

Horizons: 20 rue de la Liberté, Algiers; tel. (2) 73-70-30; telex 66310; f. 1985; evening; French; circ. 300,000.

Al-Joumhouria (The Republic): 6 rue ben Senoussi Hamida, Oran; f. 1963; Arabic; Editor MOHAMED KAOUCHE; circ. 70,000.

Al-Massa: Algiers; f. 1985; evening; Arabic; circ. 100,000.

Al-Moudjahid (The Fighter): 20 rue de la Liberté, Algiers; f. 1965; FLN journal in French and Arabic; Dir ZOUBIR ZEMZOUM; circ. 392,000.

An-Nasr (The Victory): Zone Industrielle, BP 388, La Palma, Constantine; tel. (4) 93-92-16; f. 1963; Arabic; Editor ABDALLAH CHERIANI; circ. 340,000.

Le Soir d'Algérie: Algiers; f. 1990; evening; 'independent' information journal in French; Editors ZOUBIR SOUISSI, MAAMAR FARRAH.

ALGERIA

WEEKLIES

Algérie Actualité: 2 rue Jacques Cartier, 16000 Algiers; tel. (2) 63-54-20; telex 66475; f. 1965; French; Dir KAMEL BELKACEM; circ. 250,000.

Al-Hadef (The Goal): Zone Industrielle, BP 388, La Palma, Constantine; tel. (4) 93-92-16; f. 1972; sports; French; Editor-in-Chief MUSTAFA MANCERI; circ. 110,000.

Révolution Africaine: 7 rue du Stade, Hydra, Algiers; FLN journal in French; socialist; Dir ZOUBIR ZEMZOUM; circ. 50,000.

OTHER PERIODICALS

Al-Acala: 4 rue Timgad, Hydra, Algiers; tel. (2) 60-85-55; telex 66118; fax (2) 60-09-36; f. 1970; published by the Ministry of Religious Affairs; fortnightly; Editor MUHAMMAD AL-MAHDI.

Algérie Médicale: 3 blvd Zirout Youcef, Algiers; f. 1964; publ. of Union médicale algérienne; 2 a year; circ. 3,000.

Alouan (Colours): 119 rue Didouche Mourad, Algiers; f. 1973; cultural review; monthly; Arabic.

Arab Steel: BP 4, Cheriga, Algiers; telex 52553; monthly; Arabic, English and French.

Bibliographie de l'Algérie: Bibliothèque Nationale, 1 ave Docteur Fanon, Algiers 16000; tel. (2) 63-06-32; f. 1964; lists books, theses, pamphlets and periodicals published in Algeria; 2 a year; Arabic and French.

Ach-Cha'ab ath-Thakafi (Cultural People): Algiers; f. 1972; cultural monthly; Arabic.

Ach-Chabab (Youth): 2 rue Khélifa Boukhalfa; journal of the UNJA; bi-monthly; French and Arabic.

Culture et Société: 7 blvd Ché Guévara, Algiers; tel. (2) 71-24-36; telex 65761; fax (2) 57-85-08; f. 1984; summary of items issued by state news agency; monthly; Dir BELKACEM AHCENE-DJABALLAH.

Développement et Wilayate: 7 blvd Ché Guévara, Algiers; tel. (2) 71-24-36; telex 65761; fax (2) 57-85-08; f. 1984; summary of items issued by state news agency; monthly; Dir-Gen. MUHAMMAD HAMDI.

Al-Djeza'ir Réalités (Algeria Today): BP 95–96, Bouzareah, Algiers; f. 1972; organ of the Popular Assembly of the Wilaya of Algiers; monthly; French and Arabic.

Al-Djeza'iria (Algerian Woman): Villa Joly, 24 ave Franklin Roosevelt, Algiers; f. 1970; organ of the UNFA; monthly; French and Arabic.

Al-Djeich (The Army): Office de l'Armée Nationale Populaire, 3 chemin de Gascogne, Algiers; f. 1963; monthly; Algerian army review; Arabic and French; circ. 10,000.

Economie: 7 blvd Ché Guévara, Algiers; tel. (2) 71-24-36; telex 65761; fax (2) 57-85-08; f. 1984; monthly; summary of items issued by state news agency; Dir-Gen. MUHAMMAD HAMDI.

Journal Officiel de la République Algérienne Démocratique et Populaire: 7, 9 and 13 ave A. ben Barek; f. 1962; French and Arabic.

Al-Kitab (The Book): 3 blvd Zirout Youcef, Algiers; f. 1972; bulletin of SNED; every 2 months; French and Arabic.

Libyca: 3 blvd Zirout Youcef, Algiers; f. 1953; anthropology and ethnography; irregular; French; Dir MOULOUD MAMMERI.

Nouvelles Economiques: 6 blvd Amilcar Cabral, Algiers; f. 1969; publ. of Institut Algérien du Commerce Extérieur; monthly; French and Arabic.

Politique Internationale: 7 blvd Ché Guévara, Algiers; tel. (2) 71-24-36; telex 65761; fax (2) 57-85-08; f. 1988; summary of items issued by state news agency; Dir-Gen. MUHAMMAD HAMDI.

Révolution et Travail: 1 rue Abdelkader Benbarek, place du 1er mai, Algiers; tel. (2) 66-73-53; telex 65051; journal of UGTA (central trade union) with Arabic and French editions; monthly; Editor-in-Chief LAKHDARI MOHAMED LAKHDAR.

Revue Algérienne du Travail: Algiers; f. 1964; labour publication; quarterly; French.

Revue d'Histoire et de Civilisation du Maghreb: 3 blvd Zirout Youcef, Algiers; f. 1966; history and civilization; irregular; French and Arabic; circ. 4,000; Dir M. KADDACHE.

Ath-Thakafa (Culture): 2 place Cheikh ben Badis, BP 96, Algiers; tel. (2) 62-20-73; f. 1971; every 2 months; cultural review; circ. 10,000; Editor-in-Chief CHEBOUB OTHMANE.

NEWS AGENCIES

Algérie Presse Service (APS): 7 blvd Ché Guévara, Algiers; tel. (2) 71-24-36; telex 66380; f. 1962; Dir-Gen. BELKACEM AHCENE-DJABALLAH.

Foreign Bureaux

Agence France-Presse (AFP): 6 rue Abd al-Karim el-Khettabi, Algiers; tel. (2) 63-62-01; telex 67427; Chief YVES LEERS.

Agencia EFE (Spain): 4 ave Pasteur, Algiers; tel. (2) 61-64-16; telex 66458; fax (2) 61-39-49; Chief MANUEL OSTOS.

Agenzia Nazionale Stampa Associata (ANSA) (Italy): 4 ave Pasteur, Algiers; tel. (2) 63-73-14; telex 66467; fax (2) 63-59-42; Representative RACHID KHIARI.

Allgemeiner Deutscher Nachrichtendienst (ADN) (Germany): 38 rue Larbi Alik, Hydra, Algiers; tel. (2) 60-07-14; telex 66167; Chief DIETER GRAU.

Associated Press (AP) (USA): 4 ave Pasteur, BP 769, Algiers; tel. (2) 63-59-41; telex 67365; fax (2) 63-59-42; Representative RACHID KHIARI.

Bulgarska Telegrafna Agentsia (BTA) (Bulgaria): Zaatcha 5, el-Mouradia, Algiers; Chief GORAN GOTEV.

Informatsionnoye Agentstvo Novosti (IAN) (USSR): BP 24, el-Mouradia, Algiers; Chief Officer YURI S. BAGDASAROV.

Reuters (UK): 6 blvd Mohamed Khemisti, Algiers; tel. (2) 644677; telex 67487.

Telegrafnoye Agentstvo Sovetskovo Soyuza (TASS) (USSR): 21 rue de Boulogne, Algiers; Chief KONSTANTIN DUDAREV.

Xinhua (New China) News Agency (People's Republic of China): 32 rue de Carthage, Hydra, Algiers; tel. (2) 60-76-85; telex 66204; Chief BAI GUORUI.

Wikalat al-Maghreb al-Arabi (Morocco) and the Middle East News Agency (Egypt) are also represented.

Publishers

Entreprise Nationale du Livre (ENAL): 3 blvd Zirout Youcef, BP 49, Algiers; tel. (2) 63-97-12; telex 53845; f. 1966 as Société Nationale d'Edition et de Diffusion, name changed 1983; publishes books of all types, and is sole importer, exporter and distributor of all printed material, stationery, school and office supplies; also holds state monopoly for commercial advertising; Dir-Gen. SEGHIR BENAMAR.

Office des Publications Universitaires: 1 place Centrale de Ben, Aknoun, Algiers; tel. (2) 78-87-18; telex 61396; publishes university textbooks.

Radio and Television

In 1989 there were 5.5m. radio receivers and 1.6m. television receivers in use, of which more than 300,000 were colour receivers.

Radiodiffusion Télévision Algérienne (RTA): Immeuble RTA, 21 blvd des Martyrs, Algiers; tel. (2) 60-23-00; telex 52042; government-controlled; Dir of RTA MUHAMMAD OUZEGHDOU; Dirs of Radio M. ABD AL-KADER, HACHEMI SOUAMI; Dir of TV ABD AL-KADER BRAHIMI.

RADIO

Arabic Network: transmitters at Adrar, Aïn Beïda, Algiers, Béchar, Béni Abbès, Djanet, El Goléa, Ghardaia, Hassi Messaoud, In Aménas, In Salah, Laghouat, Les Trembles, Ouargla, Reggane, Tamanrasset, Timimoun, Tindouf.

French Network: transmitters at Algiers, Constantine, Oran and Tipaza.

Kabyle Network: transmitter at Algiers.

TELEVISION

The principal transmitters are at Algiers, Batna, Sidi-Bel-Abbès, Constantine, Souk-Ahras and Tlemcen. The national network was completed during 1970. Television is taking a major part in the national education programme. Plans for a second national television service, to begin transmitting in December 1991, were announced in early 1990. The new station will broadcast in Arabic, French and English for 20 hours per day.

Finance

(cap. = capital; dep. = deposits; res = reserves; brs = branches; m. = million; amounts in Algerian dinars)

BANKING

Central Bank

Banque Centrale d'Algérie: 8 blvd Zirout Youcef, 16000 Algiers; tel. (2) 64-75-00; telex 52046; fax (2) 61-87-46; f. 1962; cap. 40m.; bank of issue; Gov. ABD AR-RAHMANE HADJ NACER; Gen. Man. BACHIR SAÏL; 50 brs.

ALGERIA

Nationalized Banks

From November 1967 only the following nationalized banks (with the exception of the Banque du Maghreb Arabe pour l'Investissement et le Commerce) were authorized to conduct exchange transactions and to deal with banks abroad, and by May 1972 these three banks had absorbed all foreign and private banks. New legislation regarding the restructuring of the banking and credit sector, approved in August 1986, enabled the five commercial banks (Banque Extérieure d'Algérie, Banque Nationale d'Algérie, Crédit Populaire d'Algérie, Banque de l'Agriculture et du Développement Rural and Banque de Développement Local) to improve their project assessment capabilities. In addition, the Central Bank was given a greater role in managing money supply, the exchange rate and foreign exchange reserves, and was authorized to borrow internationally.

Banque Extérieure d'Algérie (BEA): 11 blvd Col Amirouche, Algiers; tel. (2) 61-12-52; telex 52755; f. 1967; cap. 1,000m., dep. 52,882m., res 12,625m. (1987); chiefly concerned with energy and maritime transport sectors; Chair. ABD AL-KADER DJERIDI; Dir Gen. HOCINE HANNACHI; 60 brs.

Banque du Maghreb Arabe pour l'Investissement et le Commerce: Algiers; owned by the Algerian Govt (50%) and the Libyan Govt (50%); Pres. HAKIKI; Dir Gen. OUERSELLI.

Banque Nationale d'Algérie (BNA): 8 blvd Ernesto Ché Guévara, Algiers; tel. (2) 62-05-44; telex 61224; f. 1966; cap. 1,000m., res 5,343.1m. (1988); specializes in industry, transport and trade sectors; Chair. HOCINE MOUFFOK; Gen. Man. ABD AL-MADJID NASSOU; 143 brs.

Crédit Populaire d'Algérie (CPA): 2 blvd Col Amirouche, 16000 Algiers; tel. (2) 61-13-34; telex 67147; fax (2) 64-40-41; f. 1966; cap. 800m., dep. 18,723m. (1989); bank for building and public works, light industry, transport and tourism; Chair. OMAR BENDERRA; Gen. Man. MAHFOUD ZEROUTA; 90 brs.

Development Banks

Banque de l'Agriculture et du Développement Rural (BADR): 17 blvd Col Amirouche, BP 484, Algiers; tel. (2) 74-61-17; telex 62240; f. 1982; cap. 1,000m., total assets 81,863m. (1988); finance for the agricultural sector; Man. Dir MUSTAFA ACHOUR; 239 brs.

Banque Algérienne de Développement (BAD): 12 blvd Col Amirouche, Algiers; tel. (2) 73-89-50; telex 67220; fax (2) 74-62-56; f. 1963; cap. 1,000m. (1989), dep. 3,596.5m. (Dec. 1984); a public establishment with fiscal sovereignty, to contribute to Algerian economic development through long-term investment programmes; Dirs RAFIK IDRI, MUHAMMAD ARSLANE BACHTARZI; 4 brs.

Banque de Développement Local (BDL): 5 rue Gaci Amar, Staoueli, (W. Tipaza); tel. (2) 81-58-00; telex 53355; f. 1985; regional development bank; cap. 500m. (1987), dep. 6,457m. (1986); Dir-Gen. MUHAMMAD MALEK; 83 brs.

Caisse Nationale d'Epargne et de Prévoyance (CNEP): 42 rue Khélifa Boukhalfa, Algiers; tel. (2) 66-33-53; telex 65196; fax (2) 65-28-64; f. 1964; savings and housing bank; Man. LAKHDAR BENOUATAF.

FOREIGN BANKS

Banque Nationale de Paris (BNP): 53 rue No 5, Le Paradou; tel. (2) 59-11-90; telex 66209; fax (2) 59-38-22; Dir CLAUDE GIORDAN.

Crédit Lyonnais: 2 blvd Khémisti, Algiers; tel. (2) 63-30-75; telex 67460; fax (2) 63-30-76; Dir DENIS VAGANEY.

Société Générale: 53 rue Abri Arezki, Algiers; tel. (2) 59-02-93; Dir JEAN-YVES TUFFERY.

INSURANCE

Insurance is a state monopoly.

Caisse Nationale de Mutualité Agricole: 24 blvd Victor Hugo, Algiers; tel. (2) 63-76-82; telex 67333; Dir-Gen. YAHIA CHERIF BRAHIM.

Compagnie Algérienne d'Assurance: 48 rue Didouche Mourad, Algiers; tel. (2) 64-54-32; telex 66669; f. 1963 as a public corporation; Pres. MAHFOUD BATTATA.

Compagnie Centrale de Réassurance: 21 blvd Zirout Youcef, Algiers; tel. (2) 63-72-88; telex 67092; f. 1973; general; Chair. DJAMEL-EDDINE CHOUAÏB CHOUITER; Gen. Man. AHMAD AL-AZHAR NECHACHBY.

Société Algérienne d'Assurances (SAA): 5 blvd Ernesto Ché Guévara, Algiers; tel. (2) 63-29-44; telex 61216; f. 1963; state-sponsored company; Chair. MAHFOUD BATTATA; Dir-Gen. ABD AL-KRIM DJAFRI.

Trade and Industry

CHAMBERS OF COMMERCE

Chambre Française de Commerce et d'Industrie en Algérie (CFCIA): 1 rue du Languedoc, Algiers; tel. (2) 63-25-25; telex 66505; fax (2) 63-75-33; f. 1965; Pres. MICHEL DE CAFFARELLI; Dir GEORGES FAULX-BRIOLE.

Chambre Nationale de Commerce (CNC): Palais Consulaire, rue Amilcar Cabral, BP 100, Algiers; tel. (2) 57-55-55; telex 61345; f. 1980; Dir-Gen. HAMZA MASMOUDI.

TRADE AND INDUSTRIAL ORGANIZATIONS

Association Nationale des Fabrications et Utilisateurs d'Emballages Metalliques: Gué de Constantine, BP 245, Algiers; telex 64415; Pres. OTHMANI.

Groupement pour l'Industrialisation du Bâtiment (GIBAT): 1 et 3 ave Colonel Driant, BP 51, 55102 Verdun; tel. 29-86-09; telex 930212; Dir ARMAND MANFE.

Institut Algérien de Normalisation et de Propriété Industrielle (INAPI): 5–7 rue Abou Hamou Moussa, 16000 Algiers; tel. (2) 63-51-80; telex 66409; f. 1973; Dir-Gen. HADJ SADOK.

Institut National Algérien du Commerce Extérieur (COMEX): 6 bldg Anatole-France, Algiers; tel. (2) 62-70-44; telex 52763; Dir-Gen. SAAD ZERHOUNI.

Institut National des Industries Légères (INIL): Boumerdes; tel. (2) 64-33-71; telex 53603.

DEVELOPMENT ORGANIZATIONS

Entreprise Nationale de Développement des Industries Alimentaires (ENIAL): 2 rue Ahmed Aït Muhammad, Algiers; tel. (2) 76-51-42; telex 54816; Dir-Gen. MOKRAOUI.

Entreprise Nationale de Développement des Industries d'Articles de Sport, Jouets et Instruments de Musique (DEJIMAS): 5 rue Abane Ramdane, Algiers; tel. (2) 63-22-17; telex 52873; Dir-Gen. FAROUK NADI.

Entreprise Nationale de Développement des Industries Manufacturières (ENEDIM): 22 rue des Fusillés, El Anasser, Algiers; tel. (2) 68-13-43; telex 52871; f. 1983; Dir-Gen. ISLI.

Entreprise Nationale de Développement et de Recherche Industriels des Matériaux de Construction (ENDMC): Gué de Constantine, BP 78, Kouba, Algiers; tel. (2) 76-85-66; telex 52205; f. 1982; Dir-Gen. HASSAM.

Entreprise Nationale d'Engineering et de Développement des Industries Légères (EDIL): 50 rue Khélifa Boukhalfa, BP 1140, Algiers; tel. (2) 66-33-90; telex 52883; f. 1982; Dir-Gen. MISSOUM ABD AL-HAKIM.

Institut National de la Production et du Développement Industriel (INPED): 126 rue Didouche Mourad, Boumerdes; tel. (2) 41-52-50; telex 52488.

NATIONALIZED INDUSTRIES

A large part of Algerian industry is nationalized. Following the implementation of an economic reform programme in the 1980s, however, more than 300 of the 450 nationalized companies had been transferred to the private sector by late 1990.

The following are some of the most important nationalized industries, each controlled by the appropriate Ministry.

Entreprise Nationale d'Ammeublement et de Transformation du Bois (ENATB): route de Chréa, BP 18, Bouinan; tel. (3) 48-35-82; telex 63418; f. 1982; furniture and other wood products; Dir-Gen. ALI SLIMANI.

Entreprise Nationale d'Ascenseurs (ENASC): 86 rue Hassiba Ben Bouali, Algiers; tel. (2) 65-99-40; telex 65222; f. 1989; manufacture of elevators; Dir-Gen. MUHAMMAD FERRAH.

Entreprise Nationale de Bâtiments Industrialisés (BATIMETAL): BP 89, Ain Defla; tel. (3) 45-24-31; telex 53312; f. 1983; study and commercialization of buildings; Dir-Gen. ABD AL-KADER RAHAL.

Entreprise Nationale de Cellulose et de Papier (CELPAP): route de la Salamandre, BP 128, Mostaganem; tel. (6) 26-54-99; telex 14058; pulp and paper; Man. Dir ENWAR TEWFIK BERBAR.

Entreprise Nationale de Charpentes et de Chaudronnerie (ENCC): 13 rue Marcel Cerdan, BP 1547, Oran; tel. (6) 33-29-32; telex 22107; f. 1983; manufacture of boilers; Dir-Gen. DRISS TANDJAOUI.

Entreprise Nationale de Commerce: 6–9 rue Belhaffat-Ghazali, Hussein Dey, Algiers; tel. (2) 77-43-20; telex 52063; monopoly of imports and distribution of materials and equipment; Dir-Gen. MUHAMMAD LAID BELARBIA.

Entreprise Nationale de Construction de Matériels et d'Equipements Ferroviaires: route d'El Hadjar, BP 63, Annaba; tel. (8)

ALGERIA

83-77-41; telex 81998; f. 1983; production, import and export of railway equipment; Dir-Gen. SEBIT OTHMANE BOUSSADIA.

Entreprise Nationale de Développement et de Coordination des Industries Alimentaires (ENIAL): Bab Ezzouar, 5 route nationale, Algiers; tel. (2) 76-21-06; telex 64112; f. 1965; semolina, pasta, flour and couscous; Dir-Gen. BOILATTABI MUHAMMAD.

Entreprise Nationale de Distribution du Matériel Electrique (EDIMEL): 4 et 6 blvd Muhammad V, Algiers; tel. (2) 63-70-82; telex 67161; f. 1983; distribution of electrical equipment; Dir-Gen. ABD AR-RAZAK KEBBAB.

Entreprise Nationale de Manufacture de Chaussures et de Maroquinerie (EMAC): route de Mascara, BP 150, Sig; tel. (6) 33-91-40; telex 22692; f. 1983; manufacture of shoes and leather goods; Dir-Gen. DJELLOUL BENDJEDID.

Entreprise Nationale de Production de Produits Pharmaceutiques: Aïn d'Hab, Médéa; tel. (3) 50-54-64; telex 74018; f. 1983; production of chemicals; Dir-Gen. MOULOUD BELKEBIR.

Entreprise Nationale de Produits Métalliques Utilitaires: Carrefour de Meftah, BP 25, Algiers; tel. (2) 76-64-12; telex 64524; manufacture of metal products; Dir-Gen. MUHAMMAD SAID MOUACI.

Entreprise Nationale de Produits Miniers Non-Ferreux et des Substances Utiles (ENOF): 31 rue Muhammad Hattab, Belfort; tel. (2) 76-62-42; telex 64161; f. 1983; production and distribution of minerals; Dir-Gen. HOCINE ANANE.

Entreprise Nationale des Appareils de Mesure et de Contrôle (AMC): route de Batna, BP 2, El Eulma; tel. (5) 85-92-72; telex 85901; production of measuring equipment; Dir-Gen. MOKHTAR TOUIMER.

Entreprise Nationale des Corps Gras (ENCG): 13 ave Mustapha Sayed El-Ouali, Algiers; tel. (02) 59-34-22; telex 66075; f. 1982 to replace SOGEDIA; oils, margarines and soaps; Dir-Gen. RACHID HAMOUCHE.

Entreprise Nationale des Emballages en Papier et Cartons (ENAPC): route d'Alger, BP 490, Bordj-Bou-Arreridj; tel. (5) 99-58-48; telex 86823; f. 1985; wrapping paper and cardboard containers.

Entreprise Nationale des Gaz Industriels (ENGI): route de Baraki, Gué de Constantine, BP 247, Algiers; tel. (2) 75-12-70; telex 64413; production and distribution of gas; Dir-Gen. ABD AR-RAHMANE MAKHOUKH.

Entreprise Nationale des Industries du Cable (ENICAB): 62 blvd Salah Bouakouir, BP 94, Algiers; tel. (2) 64-94-32; telex 66497; f. 1983; consortium of cable manufacturers; Dir-Gen. MUHAMMAD BELLAG.

Entreprise Nationale des Industries de Confection et de Bonneterie (ECOTEX): route des Aures, BP 107, Bejaia; tel. (5) 92-29-60; telex 83054; consortium of textiles and clothing manufacturers; Dir-Gen. AMAR CHERIF.

Entreprise Nationale des Industries de l'Electro-Ménager (ENIEM): BP 71, 15000 Poste Chikhi; tel. (3) 40-29-71; telex 76954; consortium of manufacturers of household equipment; Dir-Gen. CHAABANE HAMMAD.

Entreprise Nationale des Jus et Conserves Alimentaires (ENAJUC): 1 route nationale, BP 108, Boufarik; tel. (3) 48-22-13; telex 52437; f. 1982; manufacture of food products; Dir-Gen. OUSSALAH.

Entreprise Nationale des Pêches (ENAPECHES): Quai d'Aigues Mortes, Port d'Alger; tel. (2) 71-52-67; telex 61346; f. 1979 to replace (with ECOREP which deals with fishing equipment) former Office Algérien des Pêches; production, marketing, importing and exporting fish; Man. Dir EL-OKBI BENOUAAR.

Entreprise Nationale de Sidérurgie (SIDER): Chaiba, el-Hadjar, BP 342, Annaba; tel. (8) 83-49-99; telex 81661; f. 1964 as Société Nationale de Sidérurgie, restructured 1983; steel, cast iron, zinc and products; Man. Dir MESSAOUD CHETTIH.

Entreprise Nationale de Transformation de Produits Longs (ENTPL): 19 ave Mekki, BP 1005, El Manouar; tel. (6) 34-52-40; telex 22953; f. 1983; production and distribution of girders; Dir-Gen. MUHAMMAD BOUTCHACHA.

Entreprise Nationale de Travaux d'Electrification: Villa Malwall, Ain d'Heb, Médéa; tel. (3) 50-61-27; telex 74061; f. 1982; study of electrical infrastructure; Dir-Gen. ABD AL-BAKI BELABDOUN.

Entreprise Nationale de Tubes et de Transformation de Produits Plats (ENTTPP): route de la Gare, BP 131, Reghaia, Algiers; tel. (2) 80-91-86; telex 68116; f. 1983; manufacture and distribution of tubing; Dir-Gen. RACHID BELHOUS.

Entreprise Nationale du Fer et du Phosphate (FERPHOS): Zhun 2, BP 122, Tebessa; tel. (8) 97-49-58; telex 95004; f. 1983; production, import and export of iron and phosphate products; Dir-Gen. AHMAD BENSLIMANE.

Office Régional des Produits Oléicoles du Centre (ORPO Centre): rue Bey Muhammad, Domaine Garidi, Kouba, Algiers;

Directory

tel. (2) 58-41-70; telex 77098; production and marketing of olives and olive oil; Dir-Gen. MUSTAFA CHABOUR.

Pharmacie Centrale Algérienne: 2 rue Bichat, Algiers; tel. (2) 65-18-27; telex 52993; f. 1969; pharmaceutical products; Man. Dir M. MORSLI.

Secrétariat d'Etat aux Forêts et au Reboisement: Immeuble des Forêts, Bois du Petit Atlas, el-Mouradia, Algiers; tel. (2) 60-43-00; telex 52854; f. 1971; production of timber, care of forests; Man. Dir DANIEL BELBACHIR.

Société Entreprise Nationale de Véhicules Industriels (SNVI): 5 route nationale, BP 153, Rouiba; tel. (2) 80-69-65; telex 68134; f. 1981; vehicles; Dir-Gen. FENARDJI.

Société Nationale de l'Artisanat Traditionnel (SNAT): Algiers; tel. (2) 62-68-02; telex 53093; traditional crafts; Man. Dir SAÏD AMRANI.

Société Nationale de Constructions Mécaniques (SONACOME): Birkhadem, Algiers; tel. (2) 65-93-92; telex 52800; f. 1967; to be reorganized into 11 smaller companies, most of which will specialize in manufacture or distribution of one of SONACOME's products; Dir DAOUD AKROUF.

Société Nationale de Constructions Métalliques (SN METAL): Algiers; tel. (2) 63-29-30; telex 52889; f. 1968; production of metal goods; Chair. HACHEM MALIK; Man. Dir ABD AL-KADER MAIZA.

Société Nationale des Eaux Minérales Algériennes (SN-EMA): 21 rue Bellouchat Mouloud, Hussein Dey, Algiers; tel. (2) 77-17-91; telex 52310; mineral water; Man. Dir TAHAR KHENEL.

Société Nationale de l'Electricité et du Gaz (SONELGAZ): 2 blvd Salah Bouakouir, BP 841, Algiers; tel. (2) 64-82-60; telex 66381; monopoly of production, distribution and transportation of electricity and gas; Man. Dir MUSTAFA HARRATI.

Société Nationale de Fabrication et de Montage du Matériel Electrique (SONELEC): 4 & 6 blvd Muhammad V, Algiers; tel. (2) 63-70-82; telex 52867; electrical equipment.

Société Nationale des Industries Chimiques (SNIC): 4-6 blvd Muhammad V, BP 641, Algiers; tel. (2) 64-07-73; telex 52802; production and distribution of chemical products; Dir-Gen. RACHID BEN IDDIR.

Société Nationale des Industries des Lièges et du Bois (SNLB): 1 rue Kaddour Rahim, BP 61, Hussein Dey, Algiers; tel. (2) 77-99-99; telex 52726; f. 1973; production of cork and wooden goods; Chair. MALEK BELLANI.

Société Nationale des Industries des Peaux et Cuirs (SONIPEC): 100 rue de Tripoli, BP 113, Hussein Dey, Algiers; tel. (2) 77-66-00; telex 52832; f. 1967; hides and skins; Chair. MUHAMMAD CHERIF AZI; Man. Dir HASSAN BEN YOUNES.

Société Nationale des Industries Textiles (SONITEX): 4-6 rue Patrice Lumumba, Algiers; tel. (2) 63-41-35; telex 52929; f. 1966; split in 1982 into separate cotton, wool, industrial textiles, silk, clothing and distribution companies; 22,000 employees; Man. Dir MUHAMMAD AREZKI ISLI.

Société Nationale des Matériaux de Construction (SNMC): Algiers; tel. (2) 64-35-13; telex 52204; f. 1968; production and import monopoly of building materials; Man. Dir ABD AL-KADER MAIZI.

Société Nationale de Recherches et d'Exploitations Minières (SONAREM): 127 blvd Salah Bouakouiz, BP 860, Algiers; tel. (2) 63-15-55; telex 52910; f. 1967; mining and prospecting; Dir-Gen. OUBRAHAM FERHAT.

Société Nationale pour la Recherche, la Production, le Transport, la Transformation et la Commercialisation des Hydrocarbures (SONATRACH): 10 rue du Sahara, Hydra, Algiers; tel. (2) 56-18-56; telex 62103; f. 1963; exploration, exploitation, transport and marketing of petroleum, natural gas and their products; Dir-Gen. SADOK BOUSENA.

In May 1980 SONATRACH was disbanded, and its functions were divided among 12 companies (including SONATRACH itself). The other 11 were:

Entreprise Nationale de Canalisation (ENAC): ave de la Palestine, BP 514, Algiers; tel. (2) 70-35-90; telex 42939; piping; Dir-Gen. HAMID MAZRI.

Entreprise Nationale de Raffinage et de Distribution des Produits Pétroliers (ENRDP): route des Dunes, BP 73, Chéraga, Algiers; tel. (2) 81-09-69; telex 53079; f. 1980; export and internal distribution of products; Dir-Gen. ABD AL-MADJID KAZI-TANI.

Entreprise Nationale d'Engineering Pétrolier (ENEP): 2 blvd Muhammad V, Algiers; tel. (2) 63-08-92; telex 66493; engineering.

Entreprise Nationale de Forage (ENAFOR): BP 211, Hassi Messaoud, Algiers; tel. (2) 73-85-40; telex 44077; drilling; Dir-Gen. ABD AR-RACHID ROUABAH.

Entreprise Nationale de Génie Civil et Bâtiments (ENGCB): route de Corso, BP 23, Boudouaou, Algiers; tel. (2) 41-65-26; telex 53653; civil engineering; Dir-Gen. MUHAMMAD TAHAR ZEMZOUM.

ALGERIA

Entreprise Nationale de Géophysique (ENAGEO): BP 213, Hassi Messaoud, Ouargla; tel. (9) 78-80-03; telex 44053; geophysics; Dir-Gen. ALI OUARTSI.

Entreprise Nationale des Grands Travaux Pétroliers (ENGTP): Zone Industrielle, BP 09, Reghaïa, Boumerdes; tel. (2) 80-06-80; telex 68150; fax (2) 80-59-20; major industrial projects; Dir-Gen. A. BENAMEUR; Asst Dir-Gen. M. BEN AMEUR.

Entreprise Nationale de Pétrochimie et d'Engrais (ENPE): route des Dunes, Chéraga, Algiers; tel. (2) 81-09-69; telex 53876; petrochemicals and fertilizers.

Entreprise Nationale des Plastiques et de Caoutchouc (ENPC): rue des Frères Meslim, BP 452, Aïn Turk, Sétif; tel. (5) 90-33-40; telex 86040; production and marketing of rubber and plastics; Dir-Gen. MAHIEDDINE ECHIKH.

Enterprise Nationale de Raffinage des Produits Pétroliers (ENRP): f. 1987; refining of products.

Entreprise Nationale de Service aux Puits (ENSP): BP 83, Hassi Messaoud, Ouargla; tel. (9) 73-89-85; telex 44018; fax (9) 73-82-01; oil-well servicing; Dir-Gen. O. BENDAHOU.

Entreprise Nationale des Travaux aux Puits (ENTP): BP 71, In-Amenas, Illizi; telex 44052; oil-well construction; Dir-Gen. ABD AL-AZIZ KRISSAT.

Société Nationale des Tabacs et Alumettes (SNTA): 40 rue Hocine-Nourredine, Algiers; tel. (2) 66-18-68; telex 52780; monopoly of manufacture and trade in tobacco, cigarettes and matches; Dir-Gen. MUHAMMAD TAHAB BOUZEGHOUB.

STATE TRADING ORGANIZATIONS

Since 1972 all international trading has been carried out by state organizations, of which the following are the most important:

Entreprise Nationale d'Approvisionnement en Bois et Dérivés (ENAB): 2 blvd Muhammad V, Algiers; tel. (2) 63-85-32; telex 52508; wood and derivatives; Dir-Gen. MIMOUN HADDOU.

Entreprise Nationale d'Approvisionnement en Outillage et Produits de Quincaillerie Générale (ENAOQ): 6 rue Amar Semaous, Hussein-Dey, Algiers; tel. (2) 77-45-03; telex 65566; tools and general hardware; Dir-Gen. ALI HOCINE.

Entreprise Nationale d'Approvisionnements en Produits Alimentaires (ENAPAL): 29 rue Larbi ben M'hidi, BP 659, Algiers; tel. (2) 76-10-11; telex 64278; f. 1983; monopoly of import, export and bulk trade in basic foodstuffs; brs in more than 40 towns; Chair. LAID SABRI; Man. Dir BRAHIM DOUAOURI.

Entreprise Nationale d'Approvisionnement et de Régulation en Fruits et Légumes (ENAFLA): 12 ave des 3 Frères Bouadou, BP 42, Birmandreis, Algiers; tel. (2) 56-90-83; telex 62113; f. 1983; division of the Ministry of Commerce; fruit and vegetable marketing, production and export; Man. Dir ALI BENSEGUENI.

Office Algérien Interprofessionel des Céréales (OAIC): 5 rue Ferhat-Boussaad, Algiers; tel. (2) 66-38-14; telex 52121; f. 1962; monopoly of trade in wheat, rice, maize, barley and products derived from these cereals; Man. Dir M. DOUAOURI.

Office National de la Commercialisation des Produits Viti-Vinicoles (ONCV): 112 Quai-Sud, Algiers; tel. (2) 63-09-40; telex 67074; f. 1968; monopoly of importing and exporting products of the wine industry; Man. Dir DOUAOURI BRAHIM.

TRADE FAIR

Foire Internationale d'Alger: Palais des Expositions, Pins Maritimes, BP 656, Algiers; tel. (2) 76-31-00; telex 64212.

PRINCIPAL TRADE UNIONS

Union Générale des Travailleurs Algériens (UGTA): Maison du Peuple, place du 1er mai, Algiers; tel. 66-89-47; telex 65051; f. 1956; 1,000,000 mems; Sec.-Gen. ABD AL-HAK BENHAMOUDA.

There are 10 national 'professional sectors' affiliated to UGTA. These are:

Secteur Alimentation, Commerce et Tourisme (Food, Commerce and Tourist Industry Workers): Gen. Sec. ABD AL-KADER GHRIBLI.

Secteur Bois, Bâtiments et Travaux Publics (Building Trades Workers): Gen. Sec. LAIFA LATRECHE.

Secteur Education et Formation Professionnelle (Teachers): Gen. Sec. SAÏDI BEN GANA.

Secteur Energie et Pétrochimie (Energy and Petrochemical Workers): Gen. Sec. ALI BELHOUCHET.

Secteur Finances (Financial Workers): Gen. Sec. MUHAMMAD ZAAF.

Secteur Information, Formation et Culture (Information, Training and Culture).

Secteur Industries Légères (Light Industry): Gen. Sec. ABD AL-KADER MALKI.

Secteur Industries Lourdes (Heavy Industry).

Secteur Santé et Sécurité Sociale (Health and Social Security Workers): Gen. Sec. ABD AL-AZIZ DJEFFAL.

Secteur Transports et Télécommunications (Transport and Telecommunications Workers): Gen. Sec. EL-HACHEMI BEN MOUHOUB.

Union Nationale des Paysans Algériens—UNPA: f. 1973; 700,000 mems; Sec.-Gen. AÏSSA NEDJEM.

Al-Haraka al-Islamiyah lil-Ummal al-Jazarivia (Islamic Movement for Algerian Workers): Tlemcen; f. 1990; based on teachings of Islamic faith.

Transport

RAILWAYS

In 1982 plans were announced for the investment of US $11,000m. in constructing new railways by 1990. Studies were undertaken in 1982 for an underground railway in Algiers, which was eventually to cover a 64-km network. When the economy encountered difficulties in 1985–86, the construction of the metro system and other major projects were postponed or cancelled, and emphasis was given to the rehabilitation of the existing network. A new authority, Infrafer (Entreprise Nationale de Réalisation des Infrastructures Ferroviares), was established in 1987 to take responsibility for the construction of new track. In February 1988 the metro project was revived in a modified form. Work on the first 26-km line of the network, to be constructed by local companies with foreign assistance, began in 1990. It was projected that the line would take 10 years to complete.

Société Nationale des Transports Ferroviaires (SNTF): 21–23 blvd Muhammad V, Algiers; tel. (2) 61-15-10; telex 52455; f. 1976 to replace Société Nationale des Chemins de Fer Algériens; 3,898 km of track, of which 296 km are electrified and 1,112 km are narrow gauge; daily passenger services from Algiers to the principal provincial cities and a service to Tunis; Dir-Gen. M. MAHERZI.

ROADS

There are about 82,000 km of roads and tracks, of which 24,000 km are main roads and 19,000 km are secondary roads. The total is made up of 55,000 km in the north, including 24,000 km of good roads, and 27,000 km in the south, including 3,200 km with asphalt surface. The French administration built a good road system, partly for military purposes, which since independence has been allowed to deteriorate in parts, and only a small percentage of roads are surfaced. New roads have been built linking the Sahara oil fields with the coast, and the Trans-Sahara highway is a major project. The first 360-km stretch of the highway, from Hassi Marroket to Aïn Salah, was opened in April 1973, and the next section, ending at Tamanrasset, was opened in June 1978. In 1987 Algeria received a loan of US $120m. from the World Bank to rehabilitate 386 km of primary roads and to establish a road maintenance project.

Société Nationale des Transports Routiers (SNTR): 27 rue des 3 Frères Bouadou, Birmandreis, Algiers; tel. (2) 56-21-21; telex 52962; f. 1967; holds a monopoly of goods transport by road; Chair. HAOUSSINE EL-HADJ; Dir-Gen. BEN AOUDA BEN EL-HADJ DJELLOUL.

Société Nationale des Transports des Voyageurs (SNTV): 19 rue Rabah Midat, Algiers; tel. (2) 66-00-52; telex 52603; f. 1967; holds monopoly of long-distance passenger transport by road; Man. Dir M. DIB.

SHIPPING

Algiers is the main port, with anchorage of between 23 m and 29 m in the Bay of Algiers, and anchorage for the largest vessels in Agha Bay. The port has a total quay length of 8,380 m. There are also important ports at Annaba, Arzew, Béjaia, Djidjelli, Ghazaouet, Mostaganem, Oran and Skikda. The contract for a new port for steel at Djenden was awarded to an Italian firm in 1984. Petroleum and liquefied gas are exported through Arzew, Béjaia and Skikda. Algerian crude petroleum is also exported through the Tunisian port of La Skhirra.

Compagnie Algéro-Libyenne de Transports Maritimes (CALTRAM): 21 rue des Frères, Bouadou, Birmandreis, Algiers; tel. (2) 63-58-07; telex 62112; Chair. M. O. DAS.

Entreprise Nationale de Consignation et d'Activités Annexes aux Transports Maritimes (ENCATM): 2 rue de Beziers, Algiers;

ALGERIA

tel. (2) 64-27-82; telex 66577; fax (2) 63-24-98; f. 1987 as part of restructuring of SNTM-CNAN; responsible for merchant traffic.

Entreprise Nationale de Réparations Navales (ERENAV): Algiers; f. 1987; ship repairs.

Entreprise Nationale de Transport Maritime de Voyageurs—Algérie Ferries (ENTMV): Algiers; f. 1987 as part of restructuring of SNTM-CNAN; responsible for passenger transport; operates coastal car ferry services between Algiers, Annanba and Oran.

NAFTAL Direction Aviation Maritime: Aéroport Houari Boumedienne, Dar-el-Beida, BP 70, Algiers; tel. (2) 75-73-75; telex 64315; Dir Z. Ben Merabet.

Office National des Ports (ONP): quai d'Arcachon, BP 830, Algiers-Port; tel. (2) 62-57-48; telex 52738; f. 1971; responsible for management and growth of port facilities and sea pilotage; Man. Dir M. Harrati.

Société Nationale de Manutention (SONAMA): 6 rue de Béziers, Algiers; tel. (2) 64-65-61; telex 52339; monopoly of port handling; Man. Dir Amos Belalem.

Société Nationale de Transports Maritimes et Compagnie Nationale Algérienne de Navigation (SNTM-CNAN): 2 quai d'Ajaccio, Nouvelle Gare Maritime, BP 280, Algiers; tel. (2) 71-14-78; telex 66580; f. 1963; state-owned company which has the monopoly of conveyance, freight, chartering and transit facilities in all Algerian ports; operates fleet of freight and passenger ships; office in Marseilles and reps. in Paris, most French ports and the principal ports in many other countries. In September 1987 the company was restructured, and two new shipping companies were formed to deal with passenger transport and merchant traffic; Chair. Lazhar Hani; Man. Dir Ammar Bousbah.

Société Nationale de Transports Maritimes des Hydrocarbures et des Produits Chimiques (SNTM-HYPROC): BP 60, Arzew; tel. (6) 37-30-99; telex 12097; fax (6) 37-28-30; Dir-Gen. Mourad Belguedj.

CIVIL AVIATION

Algeria's main airport, Dar-el-Beïda, 20 km from Algiers, is a class A airport of international standing. At Constantine, Annaba, Tlemcen and Oran there are also airports which meet international requirements. There are also 65 aerodromes of which 20 are public, and a further 135 airstrips connected with the petroleum industry.

Air Algérie (Entreprise Nationale d'Exploitation des Services Aériens Internationaux de Transport Public) and **Inter-Air Services (Entreprise Nationale d'Exploitation des Services Aériens de Transport Intérieur et Travail Aériens):** 1 place Maurice Audin, Immeuble el-Djazair, BP 858, Algiers; tel. (2) 63-12-82; telex 52436; Air Algérie f. 1953 by merger of the original Air Algérie (f. 1949) and Compagnie Air Transport; state-owned from 1972; divided into Inter-Air Services (internal flights) and Air Algérie (external flights) 1983; internal services and extensive services to Europe, North, Central and West Africa, the Middle East and Asia; Dir-Gen. Haroussine el-Hadj; fleet of 2 Airbus A310-200, 10 Boeing 727-200, 13 Boeing 737-200C, 3 Boeing 737-200C, 3 Lockheed L-100-30, 8 Fokker F27.

Air Maghreb: consortium of the national airlines of Algeria, Libya, Mauritania, Morocco and Tunisia; to operate co-ordinated schedules within the region from November 1990.

Tourism

Algeria's tourist attractions include the Mediterranean coast, the Atlas mountains and the desert. In 1988 a total of 353,723 tourists visited Algeria. Receipts from tourism totalled about US $60m. in 1983. In 1986 there were 200 hotels, with a total of 32,862 beds, and in 1987 a development programme planned to provide a further 120,000 beds by 1999, through joint ventures with foreign companies. The Government identified 19 potential tourist centres and aimed to attract 900,000 tourists per year by 1999.

Entreprise de Gestion Touristique du Centre (EGT CENTRE): Hotel Essafir, Algiers; tel. (2) 63-50-40; telex 52142; Dir-Gen. Salah Eddine Senni.

Office National Algérien de l'Animation de la Promotion et de l'Information Touristique (ONAT): 25-27 rue Khélifa-Boukhalfa, 16000 Algiers; tel. (2) 74-33-76; telex 66339; fax (2) 74-32-14; f. 1962; Dir-Gen. Kassoussi Abd al-Djalil.

Office National du Tourisme (ONT): 27 rue Khelifa Boukhalfa, Algiers; tel. (2) 61-26-55; telex 66383; f. 1990; state institution; oversees tourism development policy; Dir-Gen. Atmane Sahnoun.

Société de Développement de l'Industrie Touristique en Algérie (SODITAL): 2 rue Asselah Hocine, Algiers; f. 1989; Dir-Gen. Noureddine Salhi.

Atomic Energy

Haut Commissariat à la Recherche (HCR): 2 blvd Frantz Fanon, Algiers; tel. (2) 66-33-25; telex 65303; f. 1986; formerly Commissariat aux Energies Nouvelles; government-funded; research and development in the field of renewable sources of energy, including atomic, solar, wind and geothermal energy.

Subsidiary organizations include:

Centre for the Development of Advanced Techniques: robotics, remote sensing, laser technology, plasma physics, systems design, micro-computers, electronic instruments.

Centre for the Development of Energy Conversion: reactor physics and technology, nuclear and process instrumentation, turbo-machinery, heat-transfer technology.

Centre for the Development of Materials: ore processing, metallurgy, semi-conductors, analytical chemistry, geochemistry.

Centre for the Development of Technics in Health Physics and Nuclear Safety: regulations and standards on ionizing radiation, radioactive release, inspection and security during conversion, transport and storage of radioactive materials.

Centre for Experimentation on Solar Energy Equipment: research and development of alternative energy sources, including solar, wind and geothermal energy.

Centre for Nuclear and Solar Studies: basic and applied research, nuclear physics, gamma irradiation technology, training.

ANDORRA

Introductory Survey

Location, Climate, Language, Religion, Flag, Capital

The Valleys of Andorra form an autonomous co-principality in western Europe. The country lies in the eastern Pyrenees, bounded by France and Spain, and is situated roughly midway between Barcelona and Toulouse. The climate is alpine, with much snow in winter and a warm summer. The official language is Catalan, but French and Spanish are also widely spoken. Most of the inhabitants are Christians, mainly Roman Catholics. The flag (proportions 3 by 2) has three equal vertical stripes, of blue, yellow and red, with the state coat of arms (a quartered shield above the motto *Virtus unita fortior*) in the centre of the yellow stripe. The capital is Andorra la Vella.

Recent History

Owing to the lack of distinction between the competence of the General Council of Andorra and the co-princes who have ruled the country since 1278, the Andorrans have encountered many difficulties during recent years in their attempts to gain international status for their country and control over its essential services.

Until 1970 the franchise was granted only to third-generation Andorran males who were more than 25 years of age. Thereafter, women, persons aged between 21 and 25, and second-generation Andorrans were allowed to vote in elections to the General Council. In 1977 the franchise was extended to include all first-generation Andorrans of foreign parentage who were aged 28 and over. The electorate remained small, however, when compared with the size of the population, and Andorra's foreign residents (who comprise 70% of the total population) increased their demands for political and nationality rights. Immigration is on a quota system, being restricted to French and Spanish nationals intending to work in Andorra.

Political parties are not directly represented in the General Council, but there are loose groupings with liberal and conservative sympathies. The country's only political organization, the Partit Democràtic d'Andorra, is technically illegal, and in the 1981 elections to the General Council the party urged its supporters to cast blank votes.

During discussions on institutional reform, held in 1980, representatives of the co-princes and the General Council agreed that an executive council should be formed, and that a referendum should be held on changes in the electoral system. In January 1981 the co-princes formally requested the General Council to prepare plans for reform, in accordance with these proposals. After elections to the General Council in December 1981, the new Council elected Oscar Ribas Reig as President of Government in January 1982. He appointed an executive of six ministers who expressed their determination to give Andorra a full constitution, to defend local industry and to encourage private investment.

Severe storm damage in November 1982, and the general effects of the world recession, led to a controversial vote by the General Council, in August 1983, in favour of the introduction of income tax, to help to alleviate Andorra's budgetary deficit of 840m. pesetas, and to provide the Government with extra revenue to pursue development projects. Subsequent government proposals for an indirect tax on bank deposits, hotel rooms and property sales encountered strong opposition from financial and tourism concerns, and prompted the resignation of the Government in April 1984. Josep Pintat Solans, a local businessman, was elected unopposed by the General Council as President of Government in May. In August, however, the Ministers of Finance, and Industry, Commerce and Agriculture resigned from their posts over disagreements concerning the failure to implement economic reforms. Major extensions of citizenship rights were proposed in August 1985.

In December 1985 a general election was held for the General Council, which later re-elected Francesc Cerqueda i Pascuet to the post of First Syndic. The electorate was increased by about 27% as a result of the newly-introduced lower minimum voting age of 18 years. The Council also re-elected Josep Pintat Solans as President of Government in January 1986, when he won the support of 27 of its 28 members.

In September 1986 President François Mitterrand of France (the French co-prince of Andorra) and his Spanish counterpart, Dr Joan Martí Alanis (the Bishop of Urgel), met in Andorra to discuss the co-principality's status in relation to the EEC, and the question of free exchange of goods between the members of the Community and Andorra, following Spain's admission to the EEC in January 1986.

In April 1987 the Consejo Sindical Interregional Pirineos-Mediterráneo (CSI), a collective comprising French and Spanish trade unions, in association with the Andorran Asociación de Residentes Andorranos (ARA) began to claim rights, including those of freedom of expression and association and the right to strike, for 20,000 of its members who were employed as immigrant workers in Andorra.

A document proposing further institutional reforms was approved by the General Council in October 1987. The transfer to the Andorran Government of responsibility for such matters as public order was proposed, while the competence of the co-princes in the administration of justice was recognized. The document also envisaged the drafting of a constitution for Andorra. The implementation of the reforms, however, was dependent on the agreement of the co-princes. In 1988 a commission from the Council of Europe (see p. ???) investigated the question of human rights in Andorra.

In December 1987 municipal elections were held, in which 80% of the electorate voted. The number of citizens eligible to vote, however, represented only 13% of Andorra's total population. For the first time, the election campaign involved the convening of meetings and the use of the media, in addition to the traditional 'door-to-door' canvassing. Although Andorra has no political parties as such, four of the seven seats were won by candidates promoting a conservative stance.

In April 1988 Andorra enacted a law recognizing the Universal Declaration of Human Rights, adopted by the UN General Assembly in 1948. In June 1988 the first Andorran workers' trade union was established by the French unions, CFDT and FO, and by the Spanish union, UGT. (There are about 26,000 salaried workers in Andorra, 90% of whom are of French or Spanish origin.) In the following month, however, the General Council unanimously rejected the formation of the union, as it did not recognize the right of association of workers and prohibited the existence of any union. It warned the foreign members of the union that they risked immediate expulsion from Andorra.

It was reported in July 1989 that the Council of Europe Commission for Political Affairs had proposed that a referendum be held in Andorra on the adoption of a written constitution incorporating citizens' rights. The Commission also recommended the introduction of a system of proportional representation for elections, the extension of the right of association, and increased flexibility in the law governing the acquisition of Andorran nationality.

On 10 December 1989 a general election, was held for the General Council, which later elected Josep Maria Beal Benedico, with 15 votes, to the post of First Syndic. There were 7,185 registered voters, of whom more than 80% voted. The Council elected Oscar Robas Reig as President of Government in January 1990, when he won the support of 22 of its 28 members (he had previously held the post in 1982–84). In June the General Council voted unanimously to establish a special commission to draft a constitution. The proposed constitution was to promulgate popular sovereignty and to constitutionalize the co-princes.

In April 1990, following an improvement in Andorra's foreign relations and an increase in the number of Andorran citizens travelling abroad, Spain officially assumed the responsibility of representing Andorran interests abroad, both at diplomatic level and otherwise.

Government

Andorra has no proper constitution, and its peculiar autonomy is a legacy of feudal conditions; the country, although administratively independent, has no clear international status.

ANDORRA

Andorra is a co-principality, under the suzerainty of the President of France and the Spanish Bishop of Urgel. The valleys pay a nominal biannual tax, the *questia*, to France and to the Bishop of Urgel. The French President is represented in Andorra by the Veguer de França, and the Bishop by the Veguer Episcopal. Each co-ruler has set up a permanent delegation for Andorran affairs. The Permanent Delegates are, respectively, the prefect of the French department of Pyrénées-Orientales and one of the vicars general of the Urgel diocese.

The General Council of the Valleys submits motions and proposals to the permanent delegation. The 28 members of the Council (four from each of the seven parishes) are elected by Andorran citizens for a term of four years, one-half of the Council being renewed every two years until December 1981, when an election was held for the whole Council. The Council elects as its head, for a three-year term, the First Syndic (Syndic Procurador General), who until 1982 also acted as chief executive, and the Second Syndic, who cease to be members of the Council on their election. The General Council appointed an Executive Council, headed by a President of Government, for the first time in January 1982. This constituted the separation of powers between an executive and a legislature and represented an important step towards institutional reform. Proposals for further reforms were approved by the General Council in October 1987.

In a 'popular consultation' on electoral reform, held in May 1982, some 30% of voters supported the existing majority vote system, while 42% preferred a new system of proportional representation; approval of such a reform, however, still depended on the consent of the co-princes.

In June 1990 the General Council voted unanimously to establish a special commission to draft a constitution, which was to promulgate popular sovereignty and to constitutionalize the co-princes.

Defence

Andorra has no defence budget.

Economic Affairs

In 1987 Andorra's gross domestic product (GDP) per head was estimated at US $9,834. Traditionally an agricultural country, Andorra's principal crops are potatoes, cereals and tobacco. In 1981 production of potatoes and tobacco was 472 and 264 metric tons respectively. Livestock is also important, and in 1982 there were approximately 9,000 sheep and 1,115 cattle. Industry is limited in Andorra, although iron, lead, alum, stone and timber are produced.

Energy is derived mainly from hydroelectric power. In November 1987 the Andorran Government announced its intention of acquiring two electricity companies, Forces Hidroelèctriques Andorranes SA and Electricidad Andorrana SA, for 3,500m. pesetas. The two companies were to be merged to form Forces Elèctriques d'Andorra (FEDA).

After 1945 Andorra's economy expanded rapidly, as a result of the co-principality's development as a market for numerous European and overseas goods, owing to favourable excise conditions. The trade in low-duty consumer items and tourism are therefore the most important sources of revenue. The number of visitors totalled 12m. in 1988. The absence of income tax and other forms of direct taxation favoured the development of Andorra as a 'tax haven'. The banking sector makes a significant contribution to the economy.

Andorra's external trade is dominated by the import of consumer goods destined for sale to visitors (see below, however). In 1987 imports were valued at 86,490m. pesetas. In 1986 the principal source of imports (42.2%) was France, which was also the principal market for exports (54.3%). Spain is Andorra's other main trading partner, providing 27.0% of imports and purchasing 32.8% of exports in 1986.

The 1988 budget estimated expenditure at 13,515.6m. pesetas and revenue at 9,486.3m. pesetas. The Government derives its revenue from a small levy on imports, indirect taxes on petrol and other items, stamp duty and the sale of postage stamps. There is reportedly no unemployment in Andorra.

In March 1990 Andorra approved a trade agreement with the EEC (necessitated by Spain's accession to the Community in January 1986) constituting the former's first international treaty for about 700 years. The treaty, which was adopted unanimously by the General Council, allowed for the establishment of a customs union with the EEC, whereby industrial goods, under a uniform customs tariff, would flow unrestrictedly between Andorra and members of the Community, but the Community's external tariffs would be applied by Andorra to third countries. The new customs union presented a considerable threat to Andorra's lucrative trade in consumer goods (Andorra had originally sought to secure an agreement granting the country special status within the EEC in an attempt to preserve this trade).

Education

Education is provided by both French- and Spanish-language schools. Instruction in Catalan has only recently become available, at a school under the control of the local Roman Catholic Church. In 1987/88 there were a total of 8,769 pupils attending the 18 schools. The total number of teaching staff in 1982 was 305.

Public Holidays

1991: 1 January (New Year's Day), 29 March (Good Friday), 1 April (Easter Monday), 8 September (National Holiday), 25–26 December (Christmas).

1992: 1 January (New Year's Day), 17 April (Good Friday), 20 April (Easter Monday), 8 September (National Holiday), 25–26 December (Christmas).

Each Parish also holds its own annual festival, which is taken as a public holiday, usually lasting for three days, in July, August or September.

Weights and Measures

The metric system is in force.

Statistical Survey

AREA AND POPULATION

Area: 467 sq km (180 sq miles).

Population: 50,528 (1989), comprising 14,003 Andorrans, 26,734 Spanish, 3,932 French and 5,859 others. *Capital:* Andorra la Vella, population 19,566. Source: Conselleria de Treball i Benestar Social.

Births, Marriages and Deaths (1989): Live births 634 (birth rate 12.6 per 1,000); Marriages (1987) 125 (Marriage rate 2.6 per 1,000); Deaths 209 (death rate 4.2 per 1,000).

FINANCE

Currency and Exchange Rates: French and Spanish currencies are both in use. *French currency:* 100 centimes = 1 franc. *Coins:* 1, 5, 10, 20 and 50 centimes; 1, 2, 5 and 10 francs. *Notes:* 10, 20, 50, 100 and 500 francs. *Sterling and Dollar Equivalents* (30 September 1990): £1 sterling = 9.8225 francs; US $1 = 5.2425 francs; 1,000 French francs = £101.81 = $190.75. *Average Exchange Rate* (francs per US dollar): 6.011 in 1987; 5.957 in 1988; 6.380 in 1989. *Spanish currency:* 100 céntimos = 1 peseta. *Coins:* 50 céntimos; 1, 5, 25, 50 and 100 pesetas. *Notes:* 100, 500, 1,000 and 5,000 pesetas. *Sterling and Dollar Equivalents* (30 September 1990): £1 sterling = 182.95 pesetas; US $1 = 98.00 pesetas; 1,000 Spanish pesetas = £5.466 = $10.204. *Average Exchange Rate* (pesetas per US dollar): 123.48 in 1987; 116.49 in 1988; 118.38 in 1989.

Budget (million pesetas, 1988): *Expenditure:* General 94.3, Head of Government's services 4,327.2, Finance 259.2, Education and culture 1,440.0, Public services 5,378.8, Agriculture, commerce and industry 310.6, Employment and social welfare 600.7, Tourism and sports 723.8, Financial charges 381.0, Total 13,515.6; *Revenue:* Import duties 8,660.5, Other 825.8, Total 9,486.3. Source: Conselleria de Finances.

EXTERNAL TRADE

Imports (1986): from France 31,525,222,000 pesetas; from Spain 20,036,199,000 pesetas; Total (incl. others) 74,312,755,085 pesetas.

ANDORRA

Exports (1986): to France 1,261,917 pesetas; to Spain 762,196 pesetas (estimate); Total (incl. others) 2,325,252 pesetas.

TOURISM

Tourist Arrivals (1977): via France 2,200,000; via Spain 4,500,000; Total 6,700,000. Source: data supplied by French and Spanish Customs.

COMMUNICATIONS MEDIA

Radio Receivers (1987): 9,000 in use.
Television Receivers (1987): 6,000 in use.

EDUCATION

Enrolment (1987/88): 3- to 6-year-olds 1,865; 7- to 15-year-olds 5,579; 16 and over 1,325; Total 8,769.

Directory

The Government

(November 1990)

Episcopal Co-Prince: Dr JOAN MARTÍ ALANIS, Bishop of Urgel.
French Co-Prince: FRANÇOIS MITTERRAND.
Permanent Episcopal Delegate: NEMESI MARQUES.
Permanent French Delegate: MAURICE JOUBERT.
Veguer Episcopal: FRANCESC BADIA-BATALLA.
Veguer de França: LLUÍS DEBLÉ.

EXECUTIVE COUNCIL

President of Government: OSCAR RIBAS REIG.
Minister of Finance, Commerce and Industry: JAUME BARTOMEU CASSANY.
Minister of Public Services: JOAN SANTAMARIA TARRE.
Minister of Tourism and Sport: CANDIT NAUDI MORA.
Minister of Health, Labour and Welfare: ANTONI ARMENGOL ALEIX.
Minister of Agriculture and Natural Patrimony: GUILLEM BENAZET RIBA.

Legislature

CONSELL GENERAL DE LAS VALLS D'ANDORRÀ
(General Council of the Valleys)

First Syndic: JOSEP MARIA BEAL BENEDICO.
Second Syndic: ANTONI GARRALLÀ ROSSELL.

There are 28 members (four from each of the seven parishes), directly elected for a term of four years. The most recent general election was held on 10 December 1989.

Political Organizations

Although political parties are not officially allowed in Andorra, conservative and liberal groupings exist, in addition to the following party:

Partit Democràtic d'Andorra (PDA): Andorra la Vella; f. 1979 to succeed Agrupament Democràtic d'Andorra; technically illegal; advocates representative and parliamentary democracy, while accepting Andorra's status as a co-principality.

Judicial System

In Civil Law judicial power is exercised in civil matters in the first instance by four judges (Battles), two appointed by the French Veguer and two by the Veguer Episcopal. There is a Judge of Appeal appointed alternately by France and Spain, and in the third instance (Tercera Sala) cases are heard in the Supreme Court of Andorra at Perpignan or in the court at Urgel.

Criminal Law is administered by the Tribunal des Corts, consisting of the two Veguers, the Judge of Appeal, the two Battles and two members of the General Council (Parladors).

The Press

Correu Andorrá: Avinguda Meritxell 114, Andorra la Vella; tel. 22500; fax 22938; Dir CRISTINA CORNELLA.

Poble Andorra: Carretera de la Comella, Andorra la Vella; tel. 22506; telex 211; fax 26696; f. 1974; weekly; Dir M. CARME GRAU; circ. 3,000.

Radio and Television

In 1987 there were an estimated 9,000 radio receivers and 6,000 television receivers in use. In February 1987 a private TV company, Antena 7, began to transmit one hour of Andorran-interest programmes daily from the Spanish side of the border.

RADIO

Radio Andorra: BPI, Avinguda Meritxell, Andorra la Vella; f. 1984 as an Andorran-owned commercial public broadcasting service, to replace two stations which closed in 1981, following the expiry of their contracts with French and Spanish companies; Dir GUALBERTO OSSORIO.

TELEVISION

Antena 7: Avinguda les Escoles 16, Escaldes-Engordany; tel. 24433; telex 427; fax 26088.

Finance

(cap. = capital; res = reserves; dep. = deposits; m. = million; brs = branches; amounts in Spanish pesetas)

PRINCIPAL BANKS

Banc Agricol i Comercial d'Andorra SA: Carrer Mossèn Cinto Verdaguer 6, Andorra la Vella; tel. 21333; telex 201; fax 60133; f. 1930; cap. 2,400m., res 5,410m., dep. 93,562m. (Dec. 1989); Pres. MANUEL CERQUEDA-DONADEU; Dir and Gen. Man. JOSEP MONTAÑES ALSO; 7 brs.

Banc Internacional SA: Avinguda Meritxell 32, POB 8, Andorra la Vella; tel. 20037; telex 206; f. 1958; affiliated to Banco de Bilbao, Spain; cap. 5,292m., res 7,840m., dep. 108,868m. (Dec. 1989); Chair. JOAN MORA FONT; Gen. Man. MANUEL DOMINGO NARVARTE; 3 brs.

Banca Cassany SA: Avinguda Meritxell 39-41, Andorra la Vella; tel. 20138; f. 1958; Dir ALAIN FRECHU; Sec. J. PIERRE CANTURRI.

Banca Mora SA: Plaça Coprinceps 2, Les Escaldes; tel. 20607; telex 222; fax 29980; f. 1952; affiliated to Banco de Bilbao; cap. 1,512m., res 3,026m., dep. 95,874m. (Dec. 1989); Chair. FRANCESC MORA FONT; Man. Dir JORDI ARISTOT MORA; 7 brs.

Banca Reig: Sant Julià de Lòria; tel. 41074; telex 240; fax 41833; Chair. J. REIG; 2 brs.

Crèdit Andorrà: Avinguda Princep Benlloch 19, Andorra la Vella; tel. 20326; telex 200; f. 1955; cap. 5,000m., res 6,337m., dep. 157,508m. (Dec. 1988); Chair. A. PINTAT; Man. Dir P. ROQUET; 11 brs.

Transport

RAILWAYS

There are no railways in Andorra, but the nearest stations are Ax-les-Thermes, Hospitalet and La Tour de Carol, in France (with trains from Toulouse and Perpignan), and Puigcerdà, in Spain, on the line from Barcelona. There is a connecting bus service from all four stations to Andorra.

ROADS

Roads are maintained by the General Council of Andorra. A good road connects the Spanish and French frontiers, passing through

ANDORRA

Andorra la Vella. In 1990 two new road tunnels through the Pyrenees were under construction. When completed, they will substantially improve Andorra's communications with both France and Spain.

In 1989 there were 32,480 registered motor vehicles in use, of which 29,046 were cars and 3,434 were lorries and vans.

CIVIL AVIATION

There is an airport at Seo de Urgel in Spain, 20 km from Andorra la Vella, with three flights daily from Barcelona. In late 1989 the bus service connecting to Andorra was not in operation.

Tourism

Andorra has attractive mountain scenery. Winter sports facilities are available at five skiing centres.

Consellería de Turisme i Esports: Govern d'Andorra, Edifici Administratiu, Andorra la Vella; tel. 29345; telex 469; fax 60184.

Sindicat d'Initiativa de las Valls d'Andorra: Carrer Dr Vilanova, Andorra la Vella; tel. 20214.

ANGOLA

Introductory Survey

Location, Climate, Language, Religion, Flag, Capital

The People's Republic of Angola lies on the west coast of Africa. The Cabinda district is separated from the rest of the country by the estuary of the River Congo and Zairean territory, with the Congo lying to its north. Angola is bordered by Zaire to the north, Zambia to the east and Namibia to the south. The climate is tropical, locally tempered by altitude. There are two distinct seasons (wet and dry) but little seasonal variation in temperature. It is very hot and rainy in the coastal lowlands but temperatures fall inland. The official language is Portuguese, but African languages (mainly Ovimbundu, Kimbundu, Bakongo and Chokwe) are also in common use. Much of the population follows traditional African beliefs, although there is a large minority of Christians, mainly Roman Catholics. The flag (proportions 3 by 2) has two equal horizontal stripes, of red and black; superimposed in the centre, in gold, are a five-pointed star, half a cog-wheel and a machete. The capital is Luanda.

Recent History

Formerly a Portuguese colony, Angola became an overseas province in 1951. African nationalist groups began to form in the 1950s and 1960s, including the Movimento Popular de Libertação de Angola (MPLA) in 1956, the Frente Nacional de Libertação de Angola (FNLA) in 1962 and the União Nacional para a Independência Total de Angola (UNITA) in 1966. There was an unsuccessful nationalist rebellion in 1961. Severe repression ensued but, after a new wave of fighting in 1966, nationalist guerrilla groups were able to establish military and political control in large parts of eastern Angola and to press westward. Following the April 1974 coup d'état in Portugal, Angola's right to independence was recognized, and negotiations between the Portuguese Government and the nationalist groups began in September. After the formation of a common front by these groups, it was agreed that Angola would become independent in November 1975.

In January 1975 a transitional government was established, comprising representatives of the MPLA, the FNLA, UNITA and the Portuguese Government. However, violent clashes between the MPLA and the FNLA occurred in March, as a result of the groups' political differences, and continued throughout the country. By the second half of 1975 control of Angola was effectively divided between the three major nationalist groups, each aided by foreign powers. The MPLA (which held the capital) was supported by the USSR and Cuba, the FNLA by Zaire and Western powers (including the USA), while UNITA was backed by South African forces. The FNLA and UNITA formed a united front to fight the MPLA.

The Portuguese Government proclaimed Angola independent from 11 November 1975, transferring sovereignty to 'the Angolan people' rather than to any of the liberation movements. The MPLA proclaimed the People's Republic of Angola and the establishment of a government in Luanda under the presidency of the movement's leader, Dr Agostinho Neto. The FNLA and UNITA proclaimed the People's Democratic Republic of Angola and a coalition government, based in Nova Lisboa (renamed Huambo). The involvement of South African and Cuban troops caused an international furore. By the end of February 1976, however, the MPLA, aided by Cuban technical and military expertise, had effectively gained control of the whole country. South African troops were withdrawn from Angola in March, but Cuban troops remained to assist the MPLA regime in countering guerrilla activity by the remnants of the defeated UNITA forces.

In May 1977 an abortive coup, led by Nito Alves (a former minister), resulted in a purge of state and party officials, severely hampering the task of national reconstruction. In December 1977 the MPLA was restructured as a political party, the Movimento Popular de Libertação de Angola—Partido de Trabalho (MPLA—PT), but further divisions became evident in December 1978, when President Neto abolished the post of Prime Minister and ousted several other ministers.

President Neto died in September 1979, and José Eduardo dos Santos, then Minister of Planning, was unanimously elected party leader and President by the MPLA—PT Central Committee. President dos Santos continued to encourage strong links with the Soviet bloc, and led campaigns to eliminate corruption and inefficiency. Elections to the National People's Assembly, which replaced the Council of the Revolution, were first held in 1980. Fresh elections, due to be held in 1983, were postponed until 1986, owing to political and military problems.

The MPLA—PT Government's recovery programme was continually hindered by security problems. Although the FNLA rebel movement reportedly surrendered to the Government in 1984, UNITA conducted sustained and disruptive guerrilla activities, mainly in southern and central Angola, throughout the 1980s. In addition, forces from South Africa, which was providing UNITA with considerable military aid, made numerous armed incursions over the Angolan border with Namibia, ostensibly in pursuit of guerrilla forces belonging to the South West Africa People's Organisation (SWAPO), which was supported by the Angolan Government. In July 1983 regional military councils were established in the provinces affected by the fighting. Although the Government's military campaign against UNITA appeared to be increasingly successful during 1985, the rebels' position was strengthened in April 1986, when US military aid began to arrive. A visit to the European Parliament by Jonas Savimbi, the President of UNITA, in October 1986 failed to improve the international standing of the group. The US Government, however, continued to provide covert military aid to UNITA during the period 1987–90. Nevertheless, UNITA was excluded from a series of major peace negotiations which commenced in May 1988. In July and August Jonas Savimbi travelled to the USA and to several European and African capitals to seek support for UNITA's demands to be included in the negotiations. Although movement for a negotiated settlement between the MPLA—PT Government and UNITA then gathered momentum, UNITA's position became vulnerable in August, when a cease-fire between Angola and South Africa was declared and when South African troops were reportedly withdrawn from Angola. UNITA, which openly refused to adhere to the cease-fire, continued to be active. Following the conclusion of the New York accords on Angola and Namibia in December, whereby South Africa undertook to discontinue its military support for UNITA (see below), the US Government renewed its commitment to the rebels.

During late 1988 peace initiatives emerged from within Africa with regard to the Angolan civil war. Efforts by President Botha of South Africa to improve the diplomatic standing of his country in the region included an official visit, in October, to Zaire, where the security situation in Angola was discussed. At that time, Zaire was one of several African states involved in efforts, supported by the USA, to pressurize the Angolan Government into negotiating an internal settlement with UNITA.

In early February 1989 the Angolan Government offered a 12-month amnesty to members of the rebel organization; UNITA, restating its aim of entering into a transitional coalition government with the MPLA—PT as a prelude to multi-party elections, responded to the amnesty by launching a major offensive against Angolan government targets. This was abandoned shortly afterwards, following the intercession of President Houphouët-Boigny of Côte d'Ivoire. In early March President dos Santos announced that he was willing to attend a regional 'summit' conference on the Angolan civil war; Savimbi, in turn, announced that he would honour a unilateral moratorium on offensive military operations until mid-July. In mid-May eight African Heads of State attended a conference in Luanda, at which President dos Santos presented a peace plan that envisaged the cessation of US aid to UNITA and offered the rebels reintegration into society; this was rejected by UNITA. Nevertheless, in mid-June both President dos Santos and Dr Savimbi attended a conference at Gbadolite, in Zaire, convened by the Zairean President, Mobutu Sese

Seko, at which 18 African Heads of State were present; dos Santos had previously released 700 UNITA prisoners as a gesture of goodwill. President Mobutu succeeded in mediating a peace agreement between the Angolan Government and UNITA, in accordance with which a cease-fire came into effect on 24 June. The full terms of the accord were not, however, made public at that time, and it subsequently became apparent that these were interpreted differently by each party: government claims that Savimbi had agreed to go into temporary exile and that members of UNITA were to be absorbed into existing Angolan institutions were strongly denied by the rebels. Within one week, each side had accused the other of violating the cease-fire, and in late August Savimbi announced a resumption of hostilities.

In September 1989, after boycotting a conference of eight African Heads of State in Kinshasa, Zaire, at which the June peace accord had been redrafted, Savimbi announced a series of counter-proposals, envisaging the creation of an African peace-keeping force, to supervise a renewed cease-fire, and the commencement of negotiations between UNITA and the Government, with the objective of agreeing a settlement which would lay the foundation of a multi-party democracy in Angola. In early October, following a meeting with President Bush of the USA, Savimbi agreed to resume peace talks with the Angolan Government, with President Mobutu of Zaire acting as mediator: indirect exploratory talks between the two sides were held in mid-October. In late December President dos Santos proposed an eight-point peace plan which envisaged some political reform, but did not include provisions for a multi-party political system; the plan was rejected by UNITA.

During early 1990 fighting intensified between government troops and the UNITA rebels in the Mavinga region of southern Angola, a UNITA stronghold. Initially, the government forces made substantial advances. In April UNITA agreed to respect an immediate cease-fire and requested direct discussions with the Government: exploratory talks between representatives of the two sides were held in Portugal later that month. During May UNITA guerrillas succeeded in regaining control of Mavinga, and in the following month the Government announced that it was to withdraw its troops from the region as a gesture of goodwill. Unproductive direct talks were held between the two sides in mid-June.

In early July 1990 the Central Committee of the MPLA—PT announced that the Government would allow Angola to 'evolve towards a multi-party system', thus conceding one of UNITA's principal demands. This recommendation was ratified in December by the third Congress of the MPLA—PT, together with proposals to replace the party's official Marxist-Leninist ideology with a commitment to 'democratic socialism', and for constitutional changes under which the President and the legislature would be chosen by secret ballot in direct elections. It was also agreed to terminate the party's direct link with the armed forces. The Congress decisions were to be submitted to public debate in early 1991 and subsequently to formal legislative approval.

Meanwhile, in August 1990, representatives of UNITA and the MPLA—PT Government had resumed discussions in Portugal. A fourth round in September, at which it was agreed that the USA, the USSR and Portugal should act as guarantors of a cease-fire, was followed by a fifth round of discussions in November, at which UNITA insisted that the UN should monitor the cease-fire arrangements. This demand was rejected by the Angolan Government on the grounds that such monitoring would infringe national sovereignty. Further negotiations between the two sides were to take place in January 1991.

Throughout the 1980s, Angola, along with the other 'frontline' states, supported proposals for the attainment of independence by Namibia, following a UN-supervised cease-fire and elections. From 1982, however, South Africa and the USA insisted that any withdrawal of South African troops from Namibia must be preceded, or at least accompanied, by the withdrawal of Cuban troops from Angola. The rejection by the Angolan Government of this stipulation prevented progress towards a settlement of the Namibia issue until December 1983, when South Africa proposed a complete withdrawal of its forces from Angola, on condition that the Angolan Government undertook to prevent SWAPO and Cuban forces from entering the areas vacated by the South African troops. Angola eventually accepted this proposal, and a cease-fire was established in the occupied area in early 1984. Although some South African forces remained inside Angolan territory during 1984, the cease-fire was maintained, and in September and October, in talks held with US delegates, President dos Santos proposed a peace plan for Namibia, involving a phased withdrawal of most of the Cuban forces in Angola. Under the plan, the Cuban withdrawal would be conditional on the evacuation of the remaining South African forces from Angola, and would begin only after the procedure leading to Namibian independence was under way. The peace proposals were conveyed to South Africa by the USA in November, but differences between South Africa and Angola concerning the timetable for (and the extent of) the Cuban withdrawal prevented the conclusion of an agreement, although by April 1985 South Africa claimed to have withdrawn virtually all of its remaining troops from Angola.

South Africa, however, continued to deploy military forces in Angolan territory. By mid-1987 it was apparent that South African security forces were becoming increasingly active inside Angola and in Namibia, along the southern border with Angola. As that year progressed, the security situation in Angola deteriorated considerably: in October the South African Government confirmed, for the first time, that it was maintaining a 'limited presence' of troops inside Angola. In November South Africa confirmed that it was providing military support to UNITA, and announced that it had engaged in direct action against Soviet and Cuban forces. Later in that month, the UN Security Council demanded the unconditional withdrawal of South African troops from Angola within two weeks. Having eventually agreed to comply with this demand, South Africa nevertheless continued to be active in Angola in the first half of 1988. When negotiations aiming to achieve a peace settlement in Angola and Namibia commenced in May 1988, the security situation worsened, as the parties involved in the discussions attempted, through military consolidation, to strengthen their bargaining positions. Following progress in the peace negotiations (see below), a cease-fire was announced in August, and South African troops had withdrawn from Angola by the end of that month.

From the mid-1980s, Angolan relations with the USA deteriorated, largely as a result of the reverse in US policy towards UNITA. In July 1985 the US Congress repealed legislation (the so-called Clark Amendment) which had prohibited US military support for UNITA since 1976. Angola subsequently suspended all contacts with the USA, although the Angolan proposals of 1984, concerning the Cuban withdrawal, remained valid. Following a visit by Jonas Savimbi to the USA in January 1986, the Reagan administration announced its decision, endorsed by the US Congress in September 1986, to provide covert military aid to UNITA. (The US Government continued to grant UNITA covert military aid in 1987–90.)

In April 1987 Angola and the USA finally resumed discussions concerning a negotiated settlement over Namibia, and the Angolan Government made considerable efforts to secure diplomatic recognition from the USA. In July it was reported that the discussions concerning Namibia had failed to produce agreement, but negotiations were resumed in September and in January 1988. Angola's readiness to establish good relations with the USA was reflected in the change in the direction of the Government's economic policy, indicated in August 1987 by President dos Santos' announcement that Angola was applying for membership of the International Monetary Fund (IMF). In the following month the President made visits to several European capitals, including Paris and Lisbon, aimed at securing economic and, in some cases, military aid, and at obtaining support for Angola's proposed membership of the IMF. The visit to Lisbon was particularly significant, in that it was the first by an Angolan President to Portugal since Angola gained independence in 1975.

In March 1988 it appeared that, in spite of an intensification of armed hostilities, a state of military deadlock had again been reached, and a series of negotiations subsequently took place. During discussions between Angola, Cuba and the USA in March, Angola indicated a willingness to be flexible regarding the timetable for the evacuation of Cuban forces from southern Angola. The USA and the USSR played a prominent role in negotiations, and in early June they announced a target date of 29 September 1988 for reaching a peace settlement. The USA also acted as unofficial mediator in a series of major discussions which began in May 1988 between Angola, Cuba and South Africa. By mid-July the participants had agreed to a document containing 14 'essential principles' for a peaceful settlement, which provided for independence for Namibia, in accordance with the terms of the UN Security Council's Resolution 435 (see chapter on Namibia, Vol. II), and for the withdrawal of Cuban troops from Angola. Discussions in early August resulted in an agreement on a 'sequence of steps' for a peace settlement, leading to the commencement of the implementation of independence for Namibia on 1 November. In accordance with the provisions of this agreement, a cease-fire began on 8 August and South African troops were evacuated from Angola in late August, when further discussions were held at Brazzaville, in the Congo, between Angola, Cuba and South Africa (and the USA) regarding the proposed formulation of a timetable for the total withdrawal of Cuban troops from Angola. Although the participants in these talks failed to reach an agreement on a timetable for the Cuban withdrawal by the target date of 1 September, the cease-fire remained in force. Further negotiations on an exact schedule for the evacuation of Cuban troops were held in September, October and November, and an agreement in principle was finally reached in mid-November, although the signing of a formal protocol was delayed until mid-December, owing to South African dissatisfaction with procedures for the verification of the Cuban withdrawal. On 22 December 1988, in New York, a bilateral agreement was signed by Angola and Cuba, and a tripartite accord by Angola, Cuba and South Africa: Cuba undertook to complete a phased withdrawal of its estimated 50,000 troops from Angola by July 1991, while 1 April 1989 was designated as the date of commencement for a seven-month transition process, culminating in a general election in November, in preparation for Namibian independence. (Namibia became independent on 21 March 1990.) Angola, Cuba and South Africa were to establish a joint commission, in which the USA and the USSR would be represented as observers. All prisoners of war were to be exchanged, and the signatories of the tripartite accord were to refrain from supporting subversive organizations in each other's territories (the latter clause necessitated the curtailment of South African aid to UNITA). The UN Security Council authorized the creation of a UN Angola Verification Mission (UNAVEM, see p. 47) to monitor the Cuban troop redeployment and withdrawal. By late 1990 some 39,000 Cuban troops had been withdrawn from Angola.

The USA has hitherto made the withdrawal of Cuban forces a precondition for diplomatic recognition of the Angolan Government, which has been withheld since independence. Angola has diplomatic and economic links with most other countries, both Eastern and Western. In January 1982 Angola and the USSR signed a major agreement on economic co-operation. In 1983 diplomatic relations were established with the People's Republic of China, which had supported the MPLA's opponents in the independence struggle. In February 1985 Angola and Zaire signed a defence and security agreement which reportedly included an undertaking that neither country would allow its territory to be used as a base for attacks against the other. The efficacy of this agreement was brought into question in March 1986, when it appeared that a UNITA raid on the diamond-mining town of Andrada in northern Angola, in which 178 foreign workers were taken hostage, had been launched from Zaire. The two countries reaffirmed the terms of the 1985 agreement at talks held in July 1986. Zaire's tacit complicity with Jonas Savimbi was, however, indicated by the spread of UNITA activity in the area that borders Zaire in late 1986 and early 1987, and by the reputed use of Zairean territory by the US Government to transfer military aid to UNITA during the late 1980s. Nevertheless, in April 1987 Angola, Zaire and Zambia signed a declaration of intent to restore services on the Benguela railway, which had been effectively closed since 1975. Although efforts by Zaire to mediate in the armed conflict in Angola during 1988 were resisted by President dos Santos (owing to Zaire's alleged support for UNITA), relations between Angola and Zaire improved in 1989, and from mid-1989 President Mobutu of Zaire played a prominent role in an initiative to achieve a settlement to the Angolan civil war. In September it was announced that Angola and Zaire were to conduct joint patrols of their common border.

Government

According to the 1975 Constitution (amended in October 1976 and September 1980), the Movimento Popular de Libertação de Angola—Partido do Trabalho (Workers' Party) or MPLA—PT, a Marxist-Leninist vanguard party, is responsible for the country's political, economic and social leadership. No other political parties are permitted. The MPLA—PT's supreme organ is the Congress, which normally meets every four years. In December 1985 the Congress elected the MPLA—PT's President and a 90-member Central Committee (75 full and 15 alternate members) to supervise the movement's work. The Committee elected an eight-member Secretariat to recommend policies to the Council of Ministers. In addition, the Central Committee appointed a Political Bureau, comprising a maximum of 13 full members and two alternate members; the Political Bureau is the principal policy-making body of the MPLA—PT, and is effectively senior to the Central Committee Secretariat.

The supreme organ of state is the National People's Assembly, which comprises 318 members (including 29 alternate members) chosen by electoral colleges, composed of representatives elected by all 'loyal' citizens. The Assembly's term of office is five years. The Head of State is the President of the Republic, who is also President of the MPLA—PT, Commander-in-Chief of the armed forces, Chairman of the Political Bureau of the MPLA—PT and Chairman of the Council of Ministers. The President appoints the Council of Ministers to exercise executive authority.

In December 1990 the third Congress of the MPLA—PT approved proposals permitting Angola to 'evolve towards a multi-party system'. Arrangements were agreed for constitutional reform, whereby the President and the National People's Assembly would be elected directly by secret ballot.

Defence

All men between 18 and 35 years of age are liable to compulsory conscription; military service is voluntary for women. In June 1990 the armed forces, FAPLA (Forças Armadas Populares de Libertação de Angola), had an estimated total strength of 100,000: 91,500 (including 10,000 guerrilla forces and 24,000 conscripts) serving in the army, 1,500 in the navy and 7,000 in the air force. The Directorate of People's Defence and Territorial Troops (formerly the People's Defence Organization), a people's militia, has about 50,000 members. The border guard numbers 7,000. In addition, there were about 1,100 Soviet advisers in Angola in 1990. In accordance with agreements signed by Angola, Cuba and South Africa in December 1988 (see Recent History), the estimated 50,000 Cuban troops stationed in Angola at that time were to be withdrawn, in phases, by July 1991. A UN Angola Verification Mission (UNAVEM) was established to monitor the withdrawal. By late 1990 some 39,000 Cuban troops had been withdrawn. The defence budget for 1988 was 24,790m. kwanza.

Economic Affairs

In 1986, according to estimates by the UN, Angola's gross domestic product (GDP), measured at current prices, was US $4,774m., equivalent to $531 per head. During 1980–86 GDP increased, in real terms, by an estimated average annual rate of 3.4%, although real GDP per head increased by an annual average of only 0.4% over the same period. In 1985–88 Angola's population increased by an average annual rate of 2.7%.

Agriculture and fishing contributed 10.4% of GDP in 1985. An estimated 71% of the total labour force were employed in the agricultural sector in 1988. The principal cash crops are coffee, sugar cane, cotton and sisal. The main subsistence crops are cassava, maize, sweet potatoes and bananas.

Industry (including mining, manufacturing, construction and power) contributed 46.9% of GDP in 1985, and employed an estimated 9.5% of the labour force in 1980. Mining and manufacturing contributed 41.7% of GDP in 1985, the petroleum sector accounting for 32.5%. Angola's principal mineral exports are petroleum and diamonds. In addition, there are reserves of iron ore, copper, lead, zinc, gold, manganese, phosphates, salt and uranium. Petroleum refining is the most important industry. Petroleum and petroleum products provided more than 90% of Angola's export earnings in 1985. The principal manufacturing activities include food-processing, brewing and the production of electrical goods, textiles and construction materials. Energy is derived mainly from hydroelectric power. Angola's power potential exceeds its needs.

In 1986 Angola recorded a visible trade surplus of US $220m. There was a deficit of $447m. on the current account of the balance of payments in that year. In 1985 the principal source

ANGOLA

of imports was Portugal and the main market for exports was the USA. Other trading partners included Brazil, the United Kingdom, the Netherlands and France. The principal exports in 1985 were petroleum and petroleum products. The principal imports were foodstuffs, transport equipment, electrical equipment and base metals.

The 1987 state budget envisaged a deficit of $789m. Angola's total external debt was estimated at $6,000m. in late 1990, the USSR being the principal creditor.

Angola is a member of both the Preferential Trade Area for Eastern and Southern African States (see p. 224) and the Southern African Development Co-ordination Conference (see p. 209), which seeks to reduce the economic dependence of southern African states on South Africa.

Angola has extensive mineral reserves and abundant fertile land, but during the 1980s economic activity, with the exception of the petroleum sector, was severely impaired by the poor security situation and an acute shortage of skilled personnel. During 1989 and 1990 widespread drought caused severe famine in many rural areas. In January 1988 the Government initiated the Saneamento Económico e Financeiro (SEF), a programme of economic and financial restructuring, which aimed to improve the efficiency and productivity of state enterprises, and envisaged the transfer of some state enterprises to private ownership. In September 1989 Angola was admitted to the International Monetary Fund (IMF). It was hoped that this would generate Western financial aid for the SEF. In August 1990 the Government approved a series of economic austerity measures, including a devaluation of the national currency (the kwanza) by more than 50%, which was implemented in October.

Social Welfare

Medical care is provided free of charge, but its availability is limited by a shortage of trained personnel and medicines. At independence there were 24 hospitals in Angola (eight of them in Luanda), but these were left without trained staff. In 1981 there were 460 foreign physicians in the country, mainly from Cuba, and a major training programme produces about 1,000 Angolan paramedics per year, and helps to spread basic medical knowledge to village communities. An agreement with the USSR, signed in 1984, provided for the completion and equipment of hospitals in Lubango, Luanda and Malanje. In the same year Spain approved a loan of US $3m. to Angola for the construction of a medical school. The 1985 budget allocated 18,780m. kwanza (20.8% of total expenditure) to social services. A scheme to rehabilitate the national referral hospital, Américo Boavida, towards which the EEC and Italy provided $28m., commenced in 1989. War veterans receive support from the Ministry of Defence.

Education

Education is officially compulsory for eight years, between seven and 15 years of age, and is provided free of charge. Primary education begins at seven years of age and lasts for four years. Secondary education, beginning at the age of 11 and lasting for up to six years, comprises a first cycle of four years and a second of two years. In 1973, under Portuguese rule, primary school pupils numbered only 300,000, but by 1986/87 there were 1,400,252. Enrolment at secondary schools (including students receiving vocational instruction and teacher-training) increased from 57,829 in 1970 to 190,702 in 1980. Secondary pupils totalled 151,759 in 1984. As a proportion of the school-age population, the total enrolment at primary and secondary schools increased from 37% in 1970 to 80% in 1980, but declined to 49% in 1984. Higher education is also being encouraged. The only university, Agostinho Neto University in Luanda, had 5,736 students in 1986/87. Much education is now conducted in vernacular languages rather than Portuguese. At independence the estimated rate of adult illiteracy was more than 85%. A national literacy campaign was launched in 1976, and the average rate of adult illiteracy in 1985 was officially estimated at 59% (males 51%, females 67%).

In 1990 the Government announced that religious and other private bodies would be permitted to establish professional training institutions.

Public Holidays

1991: 1 January (New Year's Day), 4 February (Anniversary of the outbreak of the armed struggle against Portuguese colonialism), 27 March (Victory Day), 14 April (Youth Day)*, 1 May (Workers' Day), 1 August (Armed Forces' Day)*, 17 September (National Hero's Day, birthday of Dr Agostinho Neto), 11 November (Independence Day), 1 December (Pioneers' Day)*, 10 December (Anniversary of the Foundation of the MPLA), 25 December (Family Day).

1992: 1 January (New Year's Day), 4 February (Anniversary of the outbreak of the armed struggle against Portuguese colonialism), 27 March (Victory Day), 14 April (Youth Day)*, 1 May (Workers' Day), 1 August (Armed Forces' Day)*, 17 September (National Hero's Day, birthday of Dr Agostinho Neto), 11 November (Independence Day), 1 December (Pioneers' Day)*, 10 December (Anniversary of the Foundation of the MPLA), 25 December (Family Day).

* Although not officially recognized as public holidays, these days are popularly treated as such.

Weights and Measures

The metric system is in force.

ANGOLA   *Statistical Survey*

Statistical Survey

Sources (unless otherwise stated): Direcção dos Serviços de Estatística, Luanda.

Area and Population

AREA, POPULATION AND DENSITY

Area (sq km)	1,246,700*
Population (census results)	
30 December 1960	4,480,719
15 December 1970	
Males	2,943,974
Females	2,702,192
Total	5,646,166
Population (UN estimates at mid-year)†	
1987	9,226,000
1988	9,481,000
1989	9,747,000
Density (per sq km) at mid-1989	7.8

* 481,354 sq miles.
† Source: UN, *World Population Prospects: 1988*.
1986: Population 8,989,800 (official estimate).

DISTRIBUTION OF POPULATION BY DISTRICT
(1986 estimates)

	Area (sq km)	Population	Density (per sq km)
Cabinda	7,270	138,400	19.0
Zaire	40,130	135,700	3.4
Uíge	58,698	714,700	12.2
Luanda	2,418	1,227,100	507.5
Cuanza Norte	24,110*	343,700	14.3
Cuanza Sul	55,660*	616,900	11.1
Malanje	87,246*	805,800	9.2
Lunda-Norte	102,783	272,300	2.6
Lunda-Sul	56,985	149,600	2.6
Benguela	31,788	584,100	18.4
Huambo	34,274	1,350,400	39.4
Bié	70,314	995,200	14.2
Moxico	223,023	283,100	1.3
Cuando-Cubango	199,049	124,100	0.6
Namibe	58,137	95,700	1.6
Huíla	75,002	787,800	10.5
Bengo	31,371*	150,800	4.8
Cunene	89,342	214,400	2.4
Total	**1,246,700**	**8,989,800**	**7.2**

* Provisional estimates.
Source: Instituto Nacional de Estatística, Angola.

PRINCIPAL TOWNS (population at 1970 census)

Luanda (capital)	480,613*		Benguela	40,996
Huambo (Nova			Lubango (Sá da	
Lisboa)	61,885		Bandeira)	31,674
Lobito	59,258		Malanje	31,559

* 1982 estimate: 1,200,000.

BIRTHS AND DEATHS (UN estimates, annual averages)

	1970-75	1975-80	1980-85
Birth rate (per 1,000)	48.0	47.5	47.3
Death rate (per 1,000)	25.4	23.6	22.2

Source: UN, *World Population Prospects: 1988*.

ECONOMICALLY ACTIVE POPULATION
(ILO estimates, '000 persons at mid-1980)

	Males	Females	Total
Agriculture, etc.	1,281	1,237	2,518
Industry	304	22	326
Services	442	128	569
Total	**2,027**	**1,386**	**3,414**

Source: ILO, *Economically Active Population Estimates and Projections, 1950–2025*.

Mid-1988 (estimates in '000): Agriculture, etc. 2,766; Total (incl. others) 3,918. Source: FAO, *Production Yearbook*.

Agriculture

PRINCIPAL CROPS
(FAO estimates, unless otherwise indicated '000 metric tons)

	1982	1983	1984
Wheat	10	10	10
Rice (paddy)	20	22	22
Maize	250	275	260
Millet and sorghum	50	50	50
Potatoes	40	40	40
Sweet potatoes	180	180	180
Cassava (Manioc)	1,950	1,950	1,950
Dry beans	40	40	40
Groundnuts (in shell)	20	20	20
Sunflower seed	10	10	10
Cottonseed	22	22	22
Cotton (lint)	11	11	11
Palm kernels	12	12	12
Palm oil	40	40	40
Vegetables	227	227	227
Citrus fruit	80	80	80
Pineapples	35	35	35
Bananas	280	280	280
Sugar cane	250	350	240
Coffee (green)	17	22†	27†
Tobacco	3	3	3
Sisal	n.a.	3	3

1985: Harvests assumed to be unchanged since 1984, with the following exceptions ('000 metric tons): Wheat 3*; Maize 250*; Sugar cane 270*; Coffee (green) 12†.
1986: Harvests assumed to be unchanged since 1985, with the following exceptions ('000 metric tons): Wheat 2; Rice 20*; Maize 280; Millet and sorghum 54; Cassava (Manioc) 1,970*; Sugar cane 320*; Coffee (green) 14†; Sisal 1†.
1987: Harvests assumed to be unchanged since 1986, with the following exceptions ('000 metric tons): Maize 300; Millet and sorghum 60; Coffee (green) 16†; Tobacco 4†.
1988: Harvests assumed to be unchanged since 1987, with the following exceptions ('000 metric tons): Maize 270; Cassava (Manioc) 1,980*; Sugar cane 330*; Coffee 15†; Tobacco 5†.

* FAO estimates.   † Unofficial estimates.
Source: FAO, *Production Yearbook*.

LIVESTOCK (FAO estimates, '000 head, year ending September)

	1986	1987	1988
Cattle	3,380	3,390	3,400
Pigs	470	475	480
Sheep	255	260	265
Goats	965	970	975

Poultry (FAO estimates, million): 6 in 1986; 6 in 1987; 6 in 1988.
Source: FAO, *Production Yearbook*.

ANGOLA

LIVESTOCK PRODUCTS (FAO estimates, '000 metric tons)

	1984	1985	1986
Beef and veal	53	54	55
Goats' meat	3	3	3
Pig meat	15	16	16
Poultry meat	7	7	7
Other meat	7	6	6
Cows' milk	148	148	148
Butter	0.8	0.8	0.8
Cheese	2.5	2.5	2.5
Hen eggs	3.9	3.9	3.9
Cattle hides	7.7	7.9	8.1

Honey: 15,000 metric tons per year (FAO estimate).

1987: Figures assumed to be unchanged since 1986, with the following exceptions (FAO estimates, '000 metric tons): Other meat 7; Cattle hides 8.3.

1988: Figures assumed to be unchanged since 1987, with the following exceptions (FAO estimates, '000 metric tons): Beef and veal 56; Pig meat 17; Other meat 6; Cattle hides 8.6.

Source: FAO, *Production Yearbook*.

Forestry

ROUNDWOOD REMOVALS ('000 cubic metres, excluding bark)

	1986	1987*	1988*
Sawlogs, veneer logs and logs for sleepers	108	108	108
Pulpwood*†	140	140	140
Other industrial wood*	755	775	796
Fuel wood*	3,997	4,102	4,214
Total	5,000	5,125	5,258

* FAO estimates.   † Assumed to be unchanged since 1973.
Source: FAO, *Yearbook of Forest Products*.

SAWNWOOD PRODUCTION ('000 cubic metres)

	1986	1987	1988
Total (incl. boxboards)	5	5*	5

* FAO estimate.
Source: FAO, *Yearbook of Forest Products*.

Fishing

('000 metric tons, live weight)

	1985	1986	1987
Freshwater fishes*	8.0	8.0	8.0
Cunene horse mackerel	19.3	19.1	17.6
Sardinellas	28.7	21.6	8.0
Other marine fishes (incl. unspecified)	17.6	9.8	47.6
Total fish	73.6	58.4	81.2
Crustaceans and molluscs	0.9	0.1	0.2
Total catch	74.5	58.5	81.3

* Assumed to be unchanged since 1973.
Source: FAO, *Yearbook of Fishery Statistics*.

Mining

('000 metric tons, unless otherwise indicated)

	1985	1986	1987
Crude petroleum	11,452	13,926	17,506
Natural gas (petajoules)	5	5	6
Salt (unrefined)*	10	10	10
Diamonds ('000 carats)*	714	250	180†
Gypsum (crude)*	20	20	20

* Based on estimates by the US Bureau of Mines.
† Figure represents production of gem diamonds only.
Source: UN, *Industrial Statistics Yearbook*.

Crude petroleum (million metric tons): 22.32 in 1988; 22.64 in 1989 (Source: UN, *Monthly Bulletin of Statistics*).

Industry

SELECTED PRODUCTS
('000 metric tons, unless otherwise indicated)

	1985	1986	1987
Raw sugar*	50	50	n.a.
Cigarettes (million)†	2,400	2,400	2,400
Jet fuels	173	150	145
Motor spirit	104	100	105
Distillate fuel oils	354	315	310
Residual fuel oils	679	650	640
Cement	205	390‡	n.a.
Crude steel§	10	10	10
Electric energy (million kWh)	1,790	1,790	1,800

* Estimates by the International Sugar Organization.
† Estimates by the US Department of Agriculture (output assumed to be unchanged since 1979).
‡ Estimate.
§ Estimates by the US Bureau of Mines.
Source: UN, *Industrial Statistics Yearbook*.

Finance

CURRENCY AND EXCHANGE RATES

Monetary Units
100 lwei (LW) = 1 new kwanza (NKZ).

Denominations
Coins: 50 lwei; 1, 2, 5, 10 and 20 new kwanza.
Notes: 20, 50, 100, 500, 1,000 and 5,000 new kwanza.

Sterling and Dollar Equivalents (30 September 1990)
£1 sterling = 55.49 new kwanza;
US \$1 = 29.62 new kwanza;
1,000 new kwanza = £18.02 = \$33.76.

Exchange Rate
An official exchange rate of US \$1 = 29.62 kwanza was introduced in 1976 and remained in force until September 1990. In that month the kwanza was replaced, at par, by the new kwanza. At the same time, it was announced that the currency was to be devalued by more than 50%, with the exchange rate adjusted to \$1 = 60 new kwanza, with effect from 1 October 1990.

BUDGET (million kwanza)

Revenue	1983	1984	1985
State enterprises	10,126	9,896	12,154
Taxes	38,669	54,897	56,393
Other*	6,796	9,763	9,981
Total	55,591	74,556	78,528

* Excluding loans (million kwanza): 7,746 in 1984; 11,960 in 1985.

ANGOLA — Statistical Survey

Expenditure	1983	1984	1985
Economic development	17,907	21,961	23,465
Social services	14,838	16,754	18,780
Defence and security	23,295	31,943	34,306
Administration	9,159	8,787	9,874
Other	2,378	2,857	4,063
Total	67,577	82,302	90,488

Source: Instituto Nacional de Estatística, Angola.

NATIONAL ACCOUNTS
(estimates, million kwanza at current prices)

Composition of the Gross National Product

	1984	1985
Gross domestic product (GDP) at factor cost	129,214.2	137,209.3
Indirect taxes	21,502.1	21,668.2
Less Subsidies	9,146.1	14,130.9
GDP in purchasers' values	141,570.2	144,746.6
Net factor income from abroad	−1,716.0	−6,977.0
Gross national product	139,854.2	137,769.6

Gross Domestic Product by Economic Activity (at factor cost)

	1984	1985
Agriculture and livestock	13,470.2	11,526.9
Manufacturing and mining (excl. petroleum)	11,576.0	12,616.4
Fishing	2,604.1	2,783.7
Transport and communications	7,489.3	7,914.4
Construction	3,377.6	6,131.4
Extraction and refining of petroleum	41,417.5	44,601.1
Other energy	725.5	1,030.0
Trade and other productive sectors	14,000.0	14,656.0
Other services	34,554.0	35,949.4
Total	129,214.2	137,209.3

Source: Instituto Nacional de Estatística, Angola.

BALANCE OF PAYMENTS (million kwanza)

	1982	1983	1984
Trade balance	11,021	17,785	20,850
Services (net)	−19,007	−19,792	−23,613
Unrequited transfers	794	986	1,047
Current balance	−7,192	−1,021	−1,716
Long-term capital (net)	3,026	1,628	6,103
Short-term capital, errors and omissions	3,901	−466	−2,557
Changes in reserves	−265	141	1,830

Source: Banco Nacional de Angola.

External Trade

SELECTED COMMODITIES (million kwanza)

Imports	1983	1984	1985
Animal products	1,315	1,226	1,084
Vegetable products	2,158	3,099	2,284
Fats and oils	946	1,006	1,196
Food and beverages	2,400	1,949	1,892
Mineral products	317	130	127
Industrial chemical products	1,859	1,419	1,702
Plastic materials	431	704	454
Paper products	376	380	411
Textiles	1,612	1,816	1,451
Footwear and headgear	207	265	218
Base metals	1,985	3,730	2,385
Electrical equipment	3,296	2,879	2,571
Transport equipment	2,762	2,240	3,123
Masonry products	132	137	132
Optical instruments	220	192	271
Total (incl. others)	20,197	21,370	19,694

Exports	1984	1985
Animal products	188	670
Vegetable products	2,363	1,624
Mineral products	55,209	62,319
Pearls, gemstones, precious metals	2,837	2,204
Total (incl. others)	60,823	66,968

Source: Instituto Nacional de Estatística, Angola.

SELECTED TRADING PARTNERS (million kwanza)

Imports	1983	1984	1985
Argentina	n.a.	780	848
Brazil	1,639	1,611	2,116
France	2,449	2,080	2,208
Germany, Federal Republic	1,023	1,347	1,519
Italy	861	1,022	725
Netherlands	1,633	1,520	1,424
Portugal	3,282	3,027	2,607
Sweden	688	511	1,090
United Kingdom	955	785	968
USA	1,462	3,300	1,406

Exports	1983	1984	1985
Belgium and Luxembourg	897	802	1,016
Brazil	4,899	3,539	4,194
German Democratic Republic	1,079	1,446	950
Netherlands	5,650	4,724	2,417
Portugal	255	700	2,144
Spain	4,432	5,234	7,873
United Kingdom	5,674	9,868	6,937
USA	26,090	23,667	29,077

Source: Instituto Nacional de Estatística, Angola.

Transport

GOODS TRANSPORT ('000 metric tons)

	1983	1984	1985
Road	691.5	725	996
Railway	399.2	458	522
Shipping (inshore and offshore)	401.3	444	512
Air	21.5	33	43
Total	1,513.5	1,660	2,073

PASSENGER TRANSPORT ('000 journeys)

	1983	1984	1985
Road	75,956.5	35,165	29,797
Railway	8,007.6	7,105	7,201
Air	959.3	727	927
Total	84,923.4	42,997	37,925

Sources: Instituto Nacional de Estatística, Angola; Ministry of Transport and Communications, Luanda.

INTERNATIONAL SEA-BORNE SHIPPING
(estimated freight traffic, '000 metric tons)

	1984	1985	1986
Goods loaded	9,675	10,140	10,600
Goods unloaded	912	980	1,065

Source: UN Economic Commission for Africa, *African Statistical Yearbook*.

ANGOLA

CIVIL AVIATION (traffic on scheduled services)

	1983	1984	1985
Kilometres flown (million)	15.7	15.1	15.5
Passengers carried ('000)	952	690	724
Passenger-km (million)	980	917	975
Freight ton-km (million)	46.2	25.1	25.8

Source: UN, *Statistical Yearbook*.

Communications Media

	1981	1982	1983
Radio receivers ('000 in use)	138	150	163
Television receivers ('000 in use)	31	32	33
Telephones ('000 in use)	40	n.a.	n.a.

Radio receivers: 230,000 in 1985; 400,000 (estimate) in 1986; 450,000 in 1987.
Television receivers: 40,000 in 1986; 50,000 in 1987.
Book production: 57 titles (books 33, pamphlets 24) and 430,000 copies (books 239,000, pamphlets 191,000) in 1979; 47 titles (books 35, pamphlets 12) and 419,000 copies (books 338,000, pamphlets 81,000) in 1985; 14 titles (all books) and 130,000 copies in 1986.
Daily newspapers: 4 (estimated circulation 112,000) in 1984; 4 (estimated circulation 103,000) in 1986.
Sources: UNESCO, *Statistical Yearbook*; UN, *Statistical Yearbook*.

Education

1981

	Teachers	Pupils
Pre-primary*	40,027	342,316
Primary		1,258,858
Secondary:		
general	3,870	134,578
teacher-training	410	2,564
vocational		2,642
Higher	374	2,666

* Initiation classes in which pupils learn Portuguese.

1984 (pupils): Pre-primary 208,459 (provisional); Primary 870,410; Secondary: general 144,612, teacher-training 3,586, vocational 3,561; Higher 4,493.
Source: UNESCO, *Statistical Yearbook*.
1985 ('000 pupils): Pre-primary 217; Primary 930.
Source: Instituto Nacional de Estatística, Angola.

Directory

The Constitution

The MPLA regime adopted an independence constitution for Angola in November 1975. It was amended in October 1976 and September 1980. The main provisions of the Constitution are summarized below:

BASIC PRINCIPLES

The People's Republic of Angola shall be a sovereign, independent and democratic state. All sovereignty shall be vested in the Angolan people. The Movimento Popular de Libertação de Angola—Partido do Trabalho (MPLA—PT), their legitimate representative, shall be responsible for the political, economic and social leadership of the nation. The people shall be guaranteed broad effective participation in the exercise of political power through the development of people's power organizations.

The People's Republic of Angola shall be a unitary and indivisible state. Economic, social and cultural solidarity shall be promoted between all the Republic's regions for the common development of the entire nation and the elimination of regionalism and tribalism.

Defence

Under the leadership of the MPLA—PT and with its President as Commander-in-Chief, the People's Armed Forces for the Liberation of Angola (FAPLA) shall be institutionalized as the national army of the Republic. It shall be the responsibility of FAPLA to defend the country and to participate alongside the people in production and hence in national reconstruction. The Commander-in-Chief of FAPLA shall appoint and dismiss high-ranking officers.

Religion

The Republic shall be a secular state and there shall be complete separation of the State and religious institutions. All religions shall be respected.

The Economy

Agriculture shall be regarded as the base and industry as the decisive factor in the Republic's development. The Republic shall promote the establishment of just social relations in all sectors of production, furthering and developing the public sector and fostering co-operatives. It shall recognize, protect and guarantee private activities and property, including that of foreigners, provided that they are useful to the country's economy and in the interests of the Angolan people. The fiscal system shall be guided by the principle of graduated direct taxation.

Education

The Republic shall vigorously combat illiteracy and obscurantism and shall promote the development of education and of a true national culture.

FUNDAMENTAL RIGHTS AND DUTIES

The State shall respect and protect the human person and human dignity. All citizens shall be equal before the law. They shall be subject to the same duties, without any distinction based on colour, race, ethnic group, sex, place of birth, religion, level of education, or economic or social status.

It shall be the right and duty of every citizen to participate in the defence of the country and to defend and extend the revolution. All citizens over the age of 18 shall have the right and duty to take an active part in public life, to vote and be elected or appointed to any state organ. All elected citizens shall be accountable to the electorate, which shall at any given time have the right to revoke the mandate given.

There shall be freedom of expression, assembly and association provided that the basic objectives of the Republic are adhered to. Every citizen has the right to a defence. Individual freedoms are guaranteed. Freedom of conscience and belief shall be inviolable. Work shall be the right and duty of all citizens. The State guarantees medical and health care and the right to assistance in childhood, motherhood, disability, old age, etc. It also guarantees access to education and culture.

STATE ORGANS

President of the Republic

The President of the Republic shall be the President of the MPLA—PT. As Head of State the President shall represent the Angolan nation and shall have the following specific functions:

to swear in the Government appointed by the National People's Assembly on the recommendation of the MPLA—PT;

to preside over the Council of Ministers;

to declare war and make peace, following authorization by the National People's Assembly;

to nominate, swear in and dismiss the Provincial Commissioners;

to sign, promulgate and publish the laws of the National People's Assembly, government decrees and statutory decrees;

to direct national defence;

to decree a state of siege or state of emergency;

to pardon and commute sentences;

to indicate from among the members of the Political Bureau who shall deputize when the President is absent or temporarily prevented from exercising presidential functions;

to discharge all the other functions conferred on the President by the National People's Assembly.

In the case of the death, resignation or permanent incapacity of the President, the Central Committee shall designate from among its members the person who shall provisionally exercise the duties of the President of the Republic.

National People's Assembly

The National People's Assembly is the supreme state body, to which the Government is responsible. Members are elected by colleges composed of representatives chosen by all loyal citizens over 18 years old in their work- or living-places. Elections are held every five years. (Between sessions of the National People's Assembly, affairs are conducted by its Permanent Commission. Local People's Assemblies are currently being elected at municipal and provincial level, although the security situation has hindered this process, and such bodies are also to be established at village, neighbourhood and communal level.)

Government

The Government shall comprise the President of the Republic, the ministers and the secretaries of state, and other members whom the law shall indicate, and shall have the following functions:

to guarantee the safety of persons and property;

to draw up and implement the general state budget once it is approved by the National People's Assembly;

to follow guidelines laid down by the National People's Assembly.

The Government may exercise by decree the legislative functions delegated to it by the National People's Assembly.

Judiciary

The organization, composition and competence of the courts shall be established by law. Judges shall be independent in the discharge of their functions.

Local Administration

The People's Republic of Angola shall be administratively divided into provinces (províncias), municipalities (municipios), communes (comunas), neighbourhoods (bairros) and villages (povoações).

Local administration shall be guided by the combined principles of unity, decentralization and local initiative.

In a province, the Provincial Commissioner shall be the direct representative of the Government. The Government shall be represented in the district by the local commissioner, and in the commune by the Commune Commissioner, who shall be appointed on the recommendation of the MPLA—PT. The administrative bodies of the district, commune, neighbourhood and village shall be, respectively, the local commission, the commune commission, and the people's neighbourhood or village commission.

Eighteen provincial assemblies of 55–85 deputies are elected every three years by all loyal citizens over 18 years old.

The local authorities shall have legal personality and shall enjoy administrative and financial autonomy. The structure and jurisdiction of the administrative bodies and other organs of local administration shall be established by law.

FINAL PROVISIONS

An amendment to the Constitution is made by the National People's Assembly. Laws and regulations may be repealed or amended if they conflict with the spirit of the present law or the Angolan revolutionary process.

Note: In December 1990 the third Congress of the MPLA—PT endorsed proposals for constitutional reform, which would assist Angola to 'evolve towards a multi-party system'. The reform proposals were subject to ratification by the National People's Assembly.

The Government

HEAD OF STATE

President: José Eduardo dos Santos (assumed office 21 September 1979).

COUNCIL OF MINISTERS
(December 1990)

Chairman of the Council of Ministers, Minister of Defence and Minister of State for Economic and Social Affairs: José Eduardo dos Santos.

Minister of State for Inspection and Control and Minister of State Security: Kundi Paihama.

Minister of External Relations: Lt-Col Pedro de Castro dos Santos Van-Dúnem (Loy).

Minister of Planning: Fernando José França Van-Dúnem.

Minister of Justice: Lazaro Manuel Dias.

Minister of Health: Flávio João Fernandes.

Minister of the Interior: Lt-Col Francisco Magalhães Paiva (Nvunda).

Minister of Education: Augusto Lopes Teixeira (Tutu).

Minister of Finance: Aguinaldo Jaime.

Minister of Labour and Social Security: Diogo Jorge de Jesus.

Minister of Trade and Industry: António de Oliveira Silvestre.

Minister of Construction: João Henriques Garcia (Cabelo Branco).

Minister of Transport and Communications: Col António Paulo Kassoma.

Minister of Energy and Petroleum: Zeferino Cassa Yombo.

Minister of Fisheries: Francisco José Ramos da Cruz.

Minister of Agriculture: Fernando Faustino Muteka.

Minister of Youth and Sport: Marcolino José Carlos (Moço).

Minister of Information: Boaventura da Silva Cardoso.

Secretary of the Council of Ministers: José Leitão da Costa e Silva.

MINISTRIES

Office of the President: Luanda; telex 3072.

Ministry of Agriculture: Avda Norton de Matos 2, Luanda; telex 3322.

Ministry of Construction: Prédio da Mutamba, Luanda; telex 3067.

Ministry of Defence: Rua Silva Carvalho ex Quartel General, Luanda; telex 3138.

Ministry of Education: Avda Comandante Jika, Luanda.

Ministry of Energy and Petroleum: Avda 4 de Fevereiro 105, CP 1279, Luanda; tel. 372300; telex 3300.

Ministry of External Relations: Avda Comandante Jika, Luanda; telex 3127.

Ministry of Finance: Avda 4 de Fevereiro, Luanda; tel. 344628; telex 3363.

Ministry of Fisheries: Ilha do Cabo Cais do Carvão, Luanda; telex 3273.

Ministry of Health: Rua Diogo Cão, Luanda.

Ministry of Information: Luanda.

Ministry of the Interior: Avda 4 de Fevereiro, Luanda.

Ministry of Justice: Largo do Palácio, Luanda.

Ministry of Labour and Social Security: Largo do Palácio, Luanda.

Ministry of Planning: Largo do Palácio, Luanda; telex 3082.

Ministry of State Security: Luanda.

Ministry of Trade and Industry: Largo Kinaxixi 14, Luanda; tel. 344525; telex 3282.

Ministry of Transport and Communications: Avda 4 de Fevereiro 42, CP 1250-C, Luanda; tel. 370061; telex 3108.

PROVINCIAL COMMISSIONERS*

Bengo: Col Pedro Benga Lima (Foguetão).

Benguela: Paulo Teixeira Jorge.

Bié: Luís Paulino dos Santos.

Cabinda: Jorge Barros Tchimpuati.

Cunene: Pedro Mutinde.

Huambo: Lt-Col Osvaldo de Jesus Serra Van-Dúnem.

ANGOLA

Huíla: Dumilde das Chagas Simões Rangel.
Kuando-Kubango: Col Domingos Hungo (SKS).
Kwanza Norte: Francisco Vieira Dias.
Kwanza-Sul: Aurelio Segunda.
Luanda: Cristovão Francisco da Cunha.
Lunda Norte: Norberto Fernades dos Santos.
Lunda Sul: Garciano Mende.
Malanje: João Ernesto dos Santos (Liberdade).
Moxico: Jaime Baptista Ndonje.
Namibe: Domingos José.
Uije: Jeremias Dumbo.
Zaire: José Aníbal Lopes Rocha.

*All Provincial Commissioners are ex-officio members of the Government.

Legislature

NATIONAL PEOPLE'S ASSEMBLY

The National People's Assembly, established in November 1980, is the legislative body, and has 318 members (including 29 alternate members) who are chosen for a five-year term by electoral colleges, composed of representatives elected by all 'loyal' citizens. The most recent elections were held in 1986.

Political Organizations

Movimento Popular de Libertação de Angola—Partido do Trabalho (MPLA–PT) (People's Movement for the Liberation of Angola—Workers' Party): Luanda; telex 3369; f. 1956; in 1961–74, as MPLA, conducted guerrilla operations against Portuguese rule; governing party since 1975; reorg. as MPLA–PT in 1977; in Dec. 1990 replaced Marxist-Leninist ideology with commitment to 'democratic socialism'; cen. cttee of 90 mems (75 full and 15 alt. mems); political bureau, comprising a maximum of 13 full mems and two alt. mems, is overall policy-making body; cen. cttee secr. of eight depts; Chair. José Eduardo dos Santos.

Political Bureau

Members:
José Eduardo dos Santos (President).
Afonso Pedro Van-Dúnem (Mbinda).
Col António dos Santos França (Ndalu).
Lt-Col Francisco Magalhães Paiva (Nvunda).
Col Julião Mateus Paulo (Dino Matross).
Kundi Paihama.
Manuel Alexandre Duarte Rodrigues (Kito).
Pascoal Luvualu.
Lt-Col Pedro de Castro dos Santos Van-Dúnem (Loy).
Col Pedro Maria Tonha (Pedalé).
Maj. Roberto António Francisco Victor de Almeida.

Alternate Members:
António Jacinto do Amaral Martins.
Maria Mambo Café.

Central Committee Secretariat

Secretary for Cadres and Organization: José Eduardo dos Santos.
Secretary for Ideology: Maj. Roberto António Francisco Victor de Almeida.
Secretary for State and Judicial Bodies: Col Julião Mateus Paulo (Dino Matross).
Secretary for Youth, Mass and Social Organization: Maria Mambo Café.
Secretary for Economic and Social Affairs and Production: Paulo Miguel Júnior.
Secretary for Agrarian Policy: Santana André Pitra (Petroff).
Secretary for External Relations: Afonso Pedro Van-Dúnem (Mbinda).
Secretary for Administration and Finance: Jacinto Venancio (Chipopa).

The following groups are in conflict with the Government:

Frente de Libertação do Enclave de Cabinda (FLEC): f. 1963; comprises several factions seeking the secession of Cabinda province; estimated strength of 200–300; Pres. Henrique Tiaho N'zita.

União Nacional para a Independência Total de Angola (UNITA): f. 1966 to secure independence from Portugal; later received Portuguese support to oppose the MPLA; UNITA and the União das Populações de Angola Frente Nacional de Libertação de Angola (UPA/FNLA, f. 1962 but inactive since 1984) conducted military campaign against the MPLA Govt with aid from some Western nations, 1975–76; openly supported by South Africa until 1984 and in 1987–88; US aid was received from 1986; operates mainly in central and southern Angola, with an estimated strength of 28,000 regular soldiers and 37,000 militia; Pres. Dr Jonas Savimbi; Sec.-Gen. Miguel N'zau Puna.

Note: A cease-fire between UNITA and the Government took effect on 24 June 1989. UNITA renounced the cease-fire in August, but agreed in October to resume peace negotiations with the Government. These were proceeding in late 1990.

Diplomatic Representation

EMBASSIES IN ANGOLA

Algeria: Luanda; Ambassador: Hanafi Oussedik.
Belgium: CP 1203, Luanda; tel. 336437; telex 3356; Ambassador: Guido Vansina.
Brazil: CP 5428, Luanda; tel. 343275; telex 3365; Ambassador: Paulo Dyrceu Pinheiro.
Bulgaria: Luanda; telex 3375; Ambassador: Boyan Mihaylov.
Cape Verde: Luanda; telex 3247; Ambassador: (vacant).
China, People's Republic: Luanda; Ambassador: Hu Lipeng.
Congo: Luanda; Ambassador: Anatole Khondo.
Côte d'Ivoire: Rua Karl Marx 43, Luanda; Ambassador: Jean-Marie Kacou Gervais.
Cuba: Luanda; telex 3236; Ambassador: Narcisco Martín Mora.
Czechoslovakia: Rua Amílcar Cabral 5, Luanda; Ambassador: Miloslav Polansky.
Egypt: Luanda; telex 3380; Ambassador: Anwar Dakroury.
France: Luanda; Ambassador: Jacques Gasseau.
Gabon: Avda 4 de Fevereiro 95, Luanda; tel. 372614; telex 3263; Ambassador: Raphaël Nkassa-Nzogho.
Germany: CP 1295, Luanda; tel. 334516; telex 3372; Ambassador: Hans Helmut Freundt.
Ghana: Rua Vereador Castelo Branco 5, CP 1012, Luanda; telex 3331; Ambassador: Dr Keli Nordor.
Guinea: Luanda; telex 3177.
Holy See: Rua Luther King 123, CP 1030, Luanda (Apostolic Delegation); tel. 336289; fax 332378; Apostolic Delegate: Most Rev. Fortunato Baldelli, Titular Archbishop of Mevania (Bevagna).
Hungary: Rua Vereador Jaime de Amorim 22–28, Alvalade, CP 2977, Luanda; telex 3084; Ambassador: József Németh.
India: Hotel Turismo, Rua Rainha Ginga, Luanda; tel. 393681; telex 4098; Ambassador: Vaman Sardesai.
Italy: Luanda; tel. 393533; telex 3265; Ambassador: Francesco Lanata.
Korea, Democratic People's Republic: Luanda; Ambassador: Kim Chung Nam.
Netherlands: CP 3624, Luanda; telex 3051; Ambassador: Cornelis de Sroot.
Nigeria: CP 479, Luanda; tel. 340084; telex 3014; Ambassador: Gabriel Sam Akumafor.
Poland: CP 1340, Luanda; telex 3222; Ambassador: Jan Bojko.
Portugal: Rua Karl Marx 50, CP 1346, Luanda; tel. 333027; telex 3370; Ambassador: António d'Oliveira Pinto da França.
Romania: Rua 5 de Outubro 68, Luanda; tel. 336757; telex 3022; Ambassador: Marin Iliescu.
São Tomé and Príncipe: Luanda; Ambassador: Ariosto Castelo David.
Spain: CP 3061, Luanda; tel. 371952; telex 3526; Ambassador: Antonio Sánchez Jara.
Sweden: Luanda; telex 3126; Ambassador: Per Lindstrom.
Switzerland: CP 3163, Luanda; tel. 338314; telex 3172; Chargé d'affaires: Giambattista Mondada.
Tanzania: Luanda; Ambassador: Crispin Mbadila.
USSR: CP 3141, Luanda; tel. 345028; Ambassador: (vacant).
United Kingdom: Rua Diogo Cão 4, CP 1244, Luanda; tel. 334582; telex 3130; fax 333331; Ambassador: John Gerrard Flynn.
Viet-Nam: Luanda; telex 3226; Ambassador: Nguyen Huy Loi.
Yugoslavia: Luanda; telex 3234; Ambassador: Zivadin Jovanović.
Zaire: Luanda; Ambassador: Ilangwa-e-Yoka.

ANGOLA

Zambia: CP 1496, Luanda; tel. 331145; telex 3439; Ambassador: BONIFACE ZULU.

Zimbabwe: Luanda; Ambassador: NEVILLE NDONDO.

Judicial System

There is a Supreme Court and Court of Appeal in Luanda. There are also civil, criminal, military and revolutionary people's courts.

Religion

Much of the population follows traditional African beliefs.

CHRISTIANITY

Conselho Angolano de Igrejas Evangélicas (Angolan Council of Evangelical Churches): Rua Amílcar Cabral 182, 1° andar, CP 1659, Luanda; tel. 330415; telex 3255; f. 1977; 12 mem. churches; two assoc. mems; Pres. Rev. EMILIO J. M. DE CARVALHO (Evangelical Reformed Church of Angola); Gen. Sec. Rev. AUGUSTO CHIPESSE.

Protestant Churches

Evangelical Congregational Church in Angola (Igreja Evangélica Congregacional em Angola): CP 551, Huambo; tel. 3087; 100,000 mems; Gen. Sec. Rev. JÚLIO FRANCISCO.

Evangelical Pentecostal Church of Angola (Missão Evangélica Pentecostal de Angola): CP 219, Porto Amboim; 13,600 mems; Sec. Rev. JOSÉ DOMINGOS CAETANO.

United Evangelical Church of Angola (Igreja Evangélica Unida de Angola): CP 122, Uíge; 11,000 mems; Gen. Sec. Rev. A. L. DOMINGOS.

Other active denominations include the African Apostolic Church, the Church Full of the Word of God, the Church of Apostolic Faith in Angola, the Church of Our Lord Jesus Christ in the World, the Evangelical Baptist Church, the Evangelical Church in Angola, the Evangelical Church of the Apostles of Jerusalem, the Evangelical Reformed Church of Angola, the Kimbanguist Church in Angola and the United Methodist Church.

The Roman Catholic Church

Angola comprises three archdioceses and 11 dioceses. At 31 December 1988 there were an estimated 5.13m. adherents.

Bishops' Conference: Conferência Episcopal de Angola e São Tomé, CP 87, Luanda; tel. 334640; f. 1981; Pres. Most Rev. MANUEL FRANKLIN DA COSTA, Archbishop of Lubango.

Archbishop of Huambo: Most Rev. FRANCISCO VITI, Arcebispado, CP 10, Huambo; tel. 2371.

Archbishop of Luanda: Cardinal ALEXANDRE DO NASCIMENTO, Arcebispado, CP 87, 1230C, Luanda; tel. 334640.

Archbishop of Lubango: Most Rev. MANUEL FRANKLIN DA COSTA, Arcebispado, CP 231, Lubango; tel. 20405.

The Press

The press was nationalized in 1976.

DAILIES

Diário da República: CP 1306, Luanda; official govt news sheet.

O Jornal de Angola: CP 1312, Luanda; tel. 331623; telex 3341; f. 1923; Dir-Gen. ADELINO MARQUES DE ALMEIDA; mornings and Sunday; circ. 41,000.

Newspapers are also published in several regional towns.

PERIODICALS

Angola Norte: Malanje; weekly.

A Célula: Luanda; political journal of MPLA–PT; monthly.

Jornal de Benguela: CP 17, Benguela; 2 a week.

Lavra & Oficina: CP 2767-C, Luanda; tel. 322155; f. 1975; journal of the Union of Angolan Writers; monthly; circ. 5,000.

Noticia: Calçada G. Ferreira, Luanda; weekly.

Novembro: CP 3947, Luanda; tel. 331660; monthly; Dir ROBERTO DE ALMEIDA.

O Planalto: CP 96, Huambo; 2 a week.

A Voz do Trabalhador: CP 28, Luanda; journal of União Nacional de Trabalhadores Angolanos (National Union of Angolan Workers); monthly.

NEWS AGENCIES

ANGOP: Rua Rei Katiavala 120, Luanda; tel. 334595; telex 4162; Dir-Gen. and Editor-in-Chief AVELINO MIGUEL.

Foreign Bureaux

Agence France-Presse (AFP): Prédio Mutamba, CP 2357, Luanda; tel. 334939; telex 3334; Bureau Chief MANUELA TEIXEIRA.

Allgemeiner Deutscher Nachrichtendienst (ADN) (Germany): CP 3193, Luanda; telex 3323; Correspondent GUDRUN GROSS.

Informatsionnoye Agentsvo Novosti (IAN) (USSR): Luanda; Chief Officer VLADISLAV Z. KOMAROV.

Inter Press Service (IPS) (Italy): Rua Alberto Lemos 34, CP 3593, Luanda; tel. 338724; telex 3304; Correspondent JUAN PEZZUTO.

Prensa Latina (Cuba): Rua D. Miguel de Melo 92-2, Luanda; tel. 336804; telex 3253; Chief Correspondent LÁZARA RODRÍGUEZ.

Telegrafnoye Agentstvo Sovetskovo Soyuza (TASS) (USSR): Rua Marechal Tito 75, Luanda; telex 3244; Correspondent NIKOLAI SEMYONOV.

Xinhua (New China) News Agency (People's Republic of China): Rua Karl Marx 57-3, andar E, Bairro das Ingombotas, Zona 4, Luanda CP; tel. 332415; telex 4054; Correspondent ZHAO XIAOZHONG.

Publishers

Empresa Distribuidora Livreira (EDIL), UEE: Rua da Missão 107, CP 1245, Luanda; tel. 334034.

Neográfica, SARL: CP 6518, Luanda; publ. *Novembro*.

Nova Editorial Angolana, SARL: CP 1225, Luanda; f. 1935; general and educational; Man. Dir POMBO FERNANDES.

Offsetográfica Gráfica Industrial Lda: CP 911, Benguela; tel. 32568; f. 1966; Man. FERNANDO MARTINS.

Government Publishing House

Imprensa Nacional, UEE: CP 1306, Luanda; f. 1845; Gen. Man. Dr ANTÓNIO DUARTE DE ALMEIDA E CARMO.

Radio and Television

In 1987 there were an estimated 450,000 radio receivers and 50,000 television receivers in use.

RADIO

Rádio Nacional de Angola: Rua Comandante Jika, CP 1329, Luanda; tel. 321190; telex 3066; broadcasts in Portuguese, English, French, Spanish and vernacular languages (Chokwe, Kikongo, Kimbundu, Kwanyama, Fiote, Ngangela, Luvale, Songu, Umbundu); Dir-Gen. GUILHERME MOGAS.

TELEVISION

Televisão Popular de Angola (TPA): Rua Ho Chi Minh, CP 2604, Luanda; tel. 320025; telex 3238; fax 391091; f. 1975; state-controlled; Dir-Gen. OLIMPIO DE SOUSA E SILVA (acting).

Finance

(cap. = capital; dep. = deposits; res = reserves; m. = million; brs = branches; amounts in kwanza)

BANKING

All banks were nationalized in 1975.

Central Bank

Banco Nacional de Angola: Avda 4 de Fevereiro 151, CP 1298, Luanda; tel. 339141; telex 3005; fax 393179; f. 1976 to replace Banco de Angola; bank of issue; cap. and res 7,657m.; dep. 111,975m. (1983); Gov. FERNANDO ALBERTO DA GRAÇA TEIXEIRA; Dep. Gov. JOÃO BAPTISTA TORRES; 55 brs and agencies.

Commercial Banks

Banco de Crédito Comercial e Industrial: CP 1395, Luanda.

Banco Popular de Angola: Avda 4 de Fevereiro, Luanda; tel. 336598; telex 3367; dep. 17,102m. (1983); Dir-Gen. JOÃO ABEL DAS NEVES; brs throughout Angola.

Foreign Bank

Banque Paribas (France): CP 1385, Rua Dr Alfredo Trony, Edificio BPA, 18° andar, Luanda; tel. 390877; telex 4068; fax 392339; Rep. SERGIO COLLAVINI.

ANGOLA
Directory

INSURANCE

Empresa Nacional de Seguros e Resseguros de Angola (ENSA), UEE: Avda 4 de Fevereiro 93, CP 5778, Luanda; tel. 370169; telex 3087.

Trade and Industry

SUPERVISORY BODIES

National Planning Committee: Ministry of Planning, CP 1205, Luanda; tel. 339052; telex 3082; f. 1977; responsible for drafting and supervising the implementation of the National Plan and for co-ordinating economic policies and decisions; Chair. Minister of Planning.

National Supplies Commission: Luanda; f. 1977 to combat sabotage and negligence.

CHAMBER OF COMMERCE

Associação Comercial de Luanda: Edifício Palácio de Comércio, 1° andar, CP 1275, Luanda; tel. 322453.

STATE TRADING ORGANIZATIONS

Angomédica, UEE: Rua Dr Américo Boavida 85/87, CP 2698, Luanda; tel. 332945; telex 4195; f. 1981 to import pharmaceutical goods; Gen. Dir Dr A. PITRA.

Direcção dos Serviços de Comércio (Dept of Trade): Largo Diogo Cão, CP 1337, Luanda; f. 1970; brs throughout Angola.

Epmel, UEE: Rua Karl Marx 35–37, Luanda; tel. 330943; industrial agricultural machinery.

Exportang, UEE: Rua dos Enganos 1A, CP 1000, Luanda; tel. 332363; telex 3318; co-ordinates exports.

Importang, UEE: Calçada do Município 10, CP 1003, Luanda; tel. 337994; telex 3169; f. 1977; co-ordinates majority of imports; Dir-Gen. LOURENÇO M. NETO.

Maquimport, UEE: Rua Rainha Ginga 152, CP 2975, Luanda; tel. 339044; telex 4175; f. 1981 to import office equipment.

Mecanang, UEE: Rua dos Enganos, 1°–7° andar, CP 1347, Luanda; tel. 390644; telex 4021; f. 1981 to import agricultural and construction machinery, tools and spare parts.

STATE INDUSTRIAL ENTERPRISES

Companhia do Açúcar de Angola: 77 Rua Direita, Luanda; production of sugar.

Companhia Geral dos Algodões de Angola (COTONANG): Avda da Boavista, Luanda; production of cotton textiles.

Empresa Abastecimento Técnico Material (EMATEC), UEE: Largo Rainha Ginga 3, CP 2952, Luanda; tel. 338891; telex 3349; technical and material suppliers to the Ministry of Defence.

Empresa Açucareira Centro (OSUKA), UEE: Estrada Principal do Lobito, CP 37, Catumbela; tel. 24681; telex 08268; sugar industry.

Empresa Açucareira Norte (ACUNOR), UEE: Rua Robert Shilds, CP 225, Caxito, Bengo; tel. 71720; sugar production.

Empresa Angolana de Embalagens (METANGOL), UEE: Rua Estrada do Cacuaco, CP 151, Luanda; tel. 370680; production of non-specified metal goods.

Empresa de Cimento de Angola (CIMANGOLA-UEM): Avda 4 de Fevereiro 42, Luanda; tel. 371190; telex 3142; f. 1954; 69% state-owned; cement production; exports to several African countries.

Empresa de Construção de Edificações (CONSTROI), UEE: Rua Alexandre Peres, CP 2566, Luanda; tel. 333930; telex 3165; construction.

Empresa de Pesca de Angola (PESCANGOLA), UEE: Luanda; f. 1981; state fishing enterprise, responsible to Ministry of Fisheries.

Empresa de Rebenefício e Exportação do Café de Angola (CAFANGOL), UEE: Avda 4 de Fevereiro 107, CP 342, Luanda; tel. 337916; telex 3011; f. 1983; national coffee-processing and trade organization.

Empresa de Tecidos de Angola (TEXTANG), UEE: Rua N'gola Kiluanji-Kazenga, CP 5404, Luanda; tel. 381139; telex 4062; production of textiles.

Empresa Nacional de Cimento (ENCIME), UEE: CP 157, Lobito; tel. 2325; cement production.

Empresa Nacional de Comercialização e Distribuição de Produtos Agrícolas (ENCODIPA): Luanda; central marketing agency for agricultural produce; numerous brs throughout Angola.

Empresa Nacional de Construções Eléctricas (ENCEL), UEE: Rua Comandante Che Guevara 185/7, Luanda; tel. 391630; fax 331411; electric energy.

Empresa Nacional de Diamantes de Angola (ENDIAMA), UEE: Rua Rainha Ginga 74, 3° andar, Luanda; tel. 393336; telex 3046; fax 391586; f. 1981 to control diamond mining; commenced operations 1986; Dir-Gen. NOÉ BALTAZAR.

Empresa Nacional de Electricidade (ENE), UEE: Edifício Geominas, 6°–7° andar, CP 772, Luanda; tel. 323568; telex 3170; fax 323382; f. 1980; distribution of electricity; Dir-Gen. Eng. JOAQUIM QUECHAS MESQUITA MOTA.

Empresa Nacional de Ferro de Angola (FERRANGOL): Rua João de Barros 26, CP 2692, Luanda; tel. 373800; state-owned; iron production; Dir ARMANDO DE SOUSA (MACHADINHO).

Empresa Nacional de Manutenção (MANUTECNICA), UEE: Rua 7ª Avda do Cazenga 10L, CP 3508, Luanda; tel. 383646; assembly of machines and specialized equipment for industry.

Empresa Publica de Telecomunicações (EPTEL), UEE: Rua I Congresso 26, CP 625, Luanda; tel. 392285; telex 3012; international telecommunications.

Empresa Texteis de Angola (ENTEX), UEE: Avda Comandante Kima Kienda, CP 5720, Luanda; tel. 336182; telex 3086; weaving and tissue finishing.

Fina Petróleos de Angola SARL: CP 1320, Luanda; tel. 336855; telex 3246; fax 391031; f. 1957; petroleum production, refining and exploration; operates Luanda oil refinery, Petrangol, with capacity of 35,000 b/d; also operates Quinfuquena terminal; Man. Dir RENÉ THIERS.

Siderurgia Nacional, UEE: CP Zona Industrial do Forel das Lagostas, Luanda; tel. 373028; telex 3178; f. 1963, nationalized 1980; steelworks and rolling mill plant.

Sociedade Nacional de Combustíveis de Angola (SONANGOL): Rua I Congresso do MPLA, CP 1318, Luanda; tel. 331690; telex 3148; f. 1976 for exploration, production and refining of crude oil, and marketing and distribution of petroleum products; sole concessionary in Angola, supervises on- and offshore operations of foreign oil cos; holds majority interest in jt ventures with Cabinda Gulf Oil Co, Fina Petróleos de Angola and Texaco Petróleos de Angola; Dir-Gen. JOAQUIM DAVID.

Cabinda Gulf Oil Co: CP 2950, Luanda; tel. 392646; telex 3167; exploration and production of petroleum in Cabinda province; 51% owned by SONANGOL, 9.8% owned by AGIP; operated by Chevron Corpn (USA); Man. Dir R. K. CONNON.

Sociedade Unificada de Tabacos de Angola (SUT): Rua Deolinda Rodrigues 537, CP 1263, Luanda; tel. 360170; telex 3237; f. 1919; tobacco products; Gen. Man. A. CAMPOS.

TRADE UNION

União Nacional de Trabalhadores Angolanos (UNTA) (National Union of Angolan Workers): Avda 4 de Fevereiro 210, CP 28, Luanda; telex 3387; f. 1960; Sec.-Gen. PASCOAL LUVUALU; 600,000 mems.

Transport

In 1988 a US $340m. emergency programme was launched to rehabilitate the transport infrastructure, which has been severely disrupted by the civil war.

RAILWAYS

The total length of track operated was 2,952 km in 1987. There are plans to extend the Namibe line beyond Menongue and to construct north–south rail links. Under the emergency transport programme launched in 1988, $121m. was allocated to the rehabilitation of the Namibe (Moçamêdes) and Luanda railways.

Caminhos de Ferro de Angola: Avda 4 de Fevereiro 42, CP 1250-C, Luanda; tel. 370061; telex 3108; national network operating four fmrly independent systems; Nat. Dir A. DE S. E. SILVA; Dep. Dir (Tech.) Eng. R. M. DA C. JUNIOR.

Amboim Railway: Porto Amboim; f. 1945; 123 track-km; Dir A. V. FERREIRA.

Benguela Railway (Companhia do Caminho de Ferro de Benguela): Rua Praça 11 Novembro 3, CP 32, Lobito; tel. 2645; telex 8253; f. 1903; owned 90% by Tank Consolidated Investments (a subsidiary of Société Générale de Belgique), 10% by Govt of Angola; passenger and freight line running from the port of Lobito across Angola, via Huambo and Luena, to the Zaire border, where it connects with the Société Nationale des Chemins de Fer Zaïrois system, which, in turn, links with Zambia Railways, thus providing the shortest west coast route for central African trade; 1,394 track-km; guerrilla operations by UNITA suspended all international traffic from 1975, with only irregular services from Lobito to Huambo being maintained; a declaration of intent to reopen the cross-border lines, at a projected cost of US $200m., was signed in April 1987 by Angola, Zambia and Zaire, and the rehabilitation of the railway was a priority of a 10-year programme, planned by the SADCC, to develop the Lobito corridor; Vice-Pres. F. G. DE MAGALHÃES FALCÃO; Dir-Gen. CLEOFAS SILINGE.

Luanda Railway (Empresa de Caminho de Ferro de Luanda, UEE): CP 1250C, Luanda; tel. 370061; telex 3108; f. 1886; serves an iron, cotton and sisal-producing region between Luanda and Malanje; 536 track-km; Dir J. M. FERREIRA DO NASCIMENTO.

Namibe Railway: Namibe; f. 1905; main line from Namibe to Menongue, via Lubango; br. lines to Chibia and iron ore mines at Cassinga; 899 track-km; Dir L. DA M. G. CIPRIANO.

ROADS

In 1986 Angola had 72,400 km of roads, of which 18,600 km were main roads and 28,800 km were secondary roads. About 12% of roads were paved in 1986. A total of 180 bridges and pontoons that were destroyed in the civil war had been rebuilt by the end of 1979. Rehabilitation of roads was to receive US $142m. under the emergency transport programme initiated in 1988.

SHIPPING

The main harbours are at Lobito, Luanda and Namibe; the commercial port of Porto Amboim, in Kwanza-Sul province, has been closed for repairs since July 1984. The expansion of port facilities in Cabinda was planned. In May 1983 a regular shipping service began to operate between Luanda and Maputo (Mozambique). Under the emergency transport programme launched in 1988, refurbishment work was to be undertaken on the ports of Luanda and Namibe (Moçâmedes). The first phase of a 10-year SADCC programme to develop the Lobito corridor, for which funds were pledged in January 1989, was to include the rehabilitation of the ports of Lobito and Benguela.

Angonave—Linhas Marítimas de Angola: Rua Gov. Eduardo Costa 31, CP 5953, Luanda; tel. 330144; telex 3313; national shipping line; operates 7 vessels; Dir-Gen. FRANCISCO VENÂNCIO.

Cabotang-Cabotagem Nacional Angolana: Avda 4 de Fevereiro 83A, Luanda; tel. 373133; telex 3007; operates 6 vessels off the coasts of Angola and Mozambique; Dir-Gen. JOÃO OCTAVIO VAN-DUNEN.

Empresa Portuaria do Lobito, UEE: Avda da Independência, CP 16, Lobito; tel. 2710; telex 8233; long-distance sea transport.

Empresa Portuaria de Moçâmedes—Namibe, UEE: Rua Pedro Benje 10A and 10C, CP 49, Namibe; tel. 60643; long-distance sea transport; Dir HUMBERTO DE ATAIDE DIAS.

Secil Marítima SARL, UEE: Avda 4 de Fevereiro 42, 1° andar, Luanda; telex 3060; operates 7 vessels.

CIVIL AVIATION

TAAG—Linhas Aéreas de Angola: Rua da Missão 123, CP 79, Luanda; tel. 332990; telex 3285; f. 1939; internal services, and services from Luanda to Cape Verde, the Congo, Mozambique, Namibia, São Tomé, Zaire, Zambia, Brazil, Cuba, France, Germany, Italy, Portugal and the USSR; Dir-Gen. JOSÉ FERNANDES; fleet of 1 Boeing 707-320B, 5 Boeing 707-320C, 4 Boeing 737-200, 1 Boeing 737-200C, 1 Lockheed L100-20, 1 Fokker F27-100, 1 Fokker F27-400M, 1 Fokker F27-500, 3 Fokker F27-600, 2 Yakovlev Yak-40.

Tourism

National Tourist Agency: Palácio de Vidro, CP 1240, Luanda; tel. 372750.

ANTARCTICA

Source: British Antarctic Survey, High Cross, Madingley Rd, Cambridge, CB3 0ET, England; tel. (0223) 61188; telex 817725; fax 62616.

The Continent of Antarctica is estimated to cover 13,900,000 sq km. There are no indigenous inhabitants, but since 1944 a number of permanent research stations have been established.

Major Stations

(The following list includes major stations south of latitude 60° occupied during 1990.)

	Latitude	Longitude
ARGENTINA		
Belgrano II	77° 52′ S	34° 37′ W
Esperanza	63° 24′ S	56° 59′ W
Jubany	62° 14′ S	58° 40′ W
Marambio	64° 14′ S	56° 38′ W
Orcadas	60° 45′ S	44° 43′ W
San Martín	68° 08′ S	67° 04′ W
AUSTRALIA		
Casey	66° 17′ S	110° 32′ E
Davis	68° 35′ E	77° 58′ E
Mawson	67° 36′ S	62° 52′ E
BRAZIL		
Comandante Ferraz	62° 05′ S	58° 23′ W
CHILE		
Arturo Prat	62° 30′ S	59° 41′ W
Bernardo O'Higgins	63° 19′ S	57° 54′ W
Rodolfo Marsh	62° 12′ S	58° 54′ W
PEOPLE'S REPUBLIC OF CHINA		
Great Wall	60° 13′ S	58° 58′ W
FRANCE		
Dumont d'Urville	66° 40′ S	140° 01′ E

In February 1990 the French Government announced that it planned to construct a new research station, which was to be called Dome C and which, when completed, will be Antarctica's third largest station (after the US South Pole/Amundsen-Scott base and the Soviet Vostok base), in the Australian sector of the continent, about 1,000 km from the Dumont d'Urville base. The project was due to be completed by 1993 at a cost of 35m. French francs.

	Latitude	Longitude
GERMANY		
Georg von Neumayer	70° 37′ S	8° 22′ W
INDIA		
Dakshin Gangotri	70° 05′ S	12° 00′ E
JAPAN		
Mizuho	70° 42′ S	44° 20′ E
Syowa	69° 00′ S	39° 35′ E
NEW ZEALAND		
Scott	77° 51′ S	166° 46′ E
POLAND		
Arctowski	62° 09′ S	58° 28′ W
SOUTH AFRICA		
Sanae	70° 19′ S	2° 25′ W
USSR		
Bellingshausen	62° 12′ S	58° 54′ W
Leningradskaya	69° 30′ S	159° 23′ E
Mirny	66° 33′ S	93° 01′ E
Molodezhnaya	67° 40′ S	45° 51′ E
Novolazarevskaya	70° 46′ S	11° 50′ E
Russkaya	74° 46′ S	136° 52′ W
Vostok	78° 27′ S	106° 51′ E
UNITED KINGDOM		
Faraday	65° 15′ S	64° 16′ W
Halley V	75° 35′ S	26° 15′ W
Rothera	67° 34′ S	68° 08′ W
Signy	60° 43′ S	45° 36′ W

In May 1990 the UK built an airfield at the Rothera scientific station.

	Latitude	Longitude
USA		
McMurdo	77° 51′ S	166° 40′ W
Palmer	64° 46′ S	64° 03′ W
Siple	75° 56′ S	84° 15′ W
South Pole (Amundsen-Scott)	South Pole	
URUGUAY		
Artigas	62° 11′ S	58° 53′ W

Territorial Claims

Territory	Claimant State
Antártida Argentina	Argentina
Antártida Chilena	Chile
Australian Antarctic Territory	Australia
British Antarctic Territory	United Kingdom
Dronning Maud Land	Norway
Ross Dependency	New Zealand
Terre Adélie	France

These claims are not recognized by the USA or the USSR. No formal claims have been made in the sector of Antarctica between 90° W and 150° W.

See also Article 4 of the Antarctic Treaty below.

Research

Scientific Committee on Antarctic Research (SCAR) of the **International Council of Scientific Unions (ICSU):** Secretariat: Scott Polar Research Institute, Lensfield Rd, Cambridge, CB2 1ER, England; tel. (0223) 62061; fax 336549; f. 1958 to further the co-ordination of scientific activity in Antarctica, with a view to framing a scientific programme of circumpolar scope and significance; mems 25 countries; associated mems four countries.

President: Dr R. M. Laws (UK).

Vice-Presidents: Prof. W. F. Budd (Australia), Prof. C. R. Bentley (USA), Dr C. A. Rinaldi (Argentina).

Secretary: Dr A. C. Rocha Campos (Brazil).

Executive Secretary: Dr P. D. Clarkson.

The Antarctic Treaty

The Treaty (summarized below) was signed in Washington, DC, on 1 December 1959 by the 12 nations co-operating in the Antarctic during the International Geophysical Year, and entered into force on 23 June 1961. The initial 30-year term of the Treaty was due to expire in June 1991.

Article 1. Antarctica shall be used for peaceful purposes only.

Article 2. On freedom of scientific investigation and co-operation.

Article 3. On exchange of information and personnel.

Article 4. i. Nothing contained in the present Treaty shall be interpreted as:

(a) a renunciation by any Contracting Party of previously asserted rights of or claims to territorial sovereignty in Antarctica;

(b) a renunciation or diminution by any Contracting Party of any basis of claim to territorial sovereignty in Antarctica which it may have whether as a result of its activities or those of its nationals in Antarctica, or otherwise;

(c) prejudicing the position of any Contracting Party as regards its recognition or non-recognition of any other State's right of or claim or basis of claim to territorial sovereignty in Antarctica.

ii. No acts or activities taking place while the present Treaty is in force shall constitute a basis for asserting, supporting or denying a claim to territorial sovereignty in Antarctica or create any rights of sovereignty in Antarctica. No new claim, or enlargement of an existing claim, to territorial sovereignty in Antarctica shall be asserted while the present Treaty is in force.

Article 5. Any nuclear explosions in Antarctica and the disposal there of radioactive waste material shall be prohibited.

Article 6. On geographical limits and rights on high seas.

Article 7. On designation of observers and notification of stations and expeditions.

Article 8. On jurisdiction over observers and scientists.

Article 9. On consultative meetings.

Articles 10-14. On upholding, interpreting, amending, notifying and depositing the Treaty.

SIGNATORIES

Argentina	France	South Africa
Australia	Japan	USSR
Belgium	New Zealand	United Kingdom
Chile	Norway	USA

ACCEDING STATES

Austria, Brazil, Bulgaria, Canada, the People's Republic of China, Cuba, Czechoslovakia, Denmark, Ecuador, Finland, Germany, Greece, Hungary, India, Italy, the Democratic People's Republic of Korea, the Republic of Korea, the Netherlands, Papua New Guinea, Peru, Poland, Romania, Spain, Sweden, Uruguay.

Brazil, the People's Republic of China, Germany, India, Italy, Poland, Spain, Sweden and Uruguay have achieved consultative status under the Treaty, by virtue of their scientific activity in Antarctica.

ANTARCTIC TREATY CONSULTATIVE MEETINGS

Meetings of representatives from all the original signatory nations of the Antarctic Treaty and 10 acceding nations accorded consultative status are held periodically to discuss scientific and political matters. The 14th meeting was held in Rio de Janeiro (Brazil) in October 1987, and the 15th meeting was held in Paris (France) in October 1989. The 16th meeting was to be held in Germany in 1991. The representatives elect a Chairman and Secretary. Committees and Working Groups are established as required.

Among the numerous measures which have been agreed and implemented by the Consultative Parties are several designed to protect the Antarctic environment and wildlife. These include Agreed Measures for the Conservation of Antarctic Flora and Fauna, the designation of Specially Protected Areas and Sites of Special Scientific Interest, and a Convention for the Conservation of Antarctic Seals. A Convention on the Conservation of Antarctic Marine Living Resources, concluded at a diplomatic conference in May 1980, entered into force in April 1982. A Convention on the Regulation of Antarctic Mineral Resource Activities (the Wellington Convention) was adopted in June 1988 and was opened for signature on 25 November 1988. To enter into force, the Wellington Convention required the ratification of 16 of the 22 Consultative Parties (including the USSR, the USA and five countries with territorial claims). However, France and Australia opposed the Convention, which would permit mineral exploitation (under stringent international controls) in Antarctica, and proposed the creation of an Antarctic wilderness reserve. An agreement was reached at the October 1989 consultative meeting, whereby two extraordinary meetings were to be convened in Chile in November 1990, one to discuss the protection of the environment and the other to discuss the issue of liability for environmental damage within the framework of the Wellington Convention. In September 1990 the Government of New Zealand, which played a major role in drafting the Wellington Convention, reversed its policy, stating that it was no longer willing to ratify the Convention. At the same time, it introduced legislation in the New Zealand House of Representatives to ban all mining and prospecting activities from its territories in Antarctica. At the extraordinary meetings which were held in Chile in November-December the Consultative Parties failed to reach an agreement regarding the protection of Antarctica's environment. The 39 countries did, however, approve a draft protocol on environmental protection, which was to be the basis for a further meeting, to be held in Madrid, Spain, in April 1991.

ANTIGUA AND BARBUDA

Introductory Survey

Location, Climate, Language, Religion, Flag, Capital

The country comprises three islands: Antigua (280 sq km—108 sq miles), Barbuda (161 sq km—62 sq miles) and the uninhabited rocky islet of Redonda (1.6 sq km—0.6 sq mile). They lie along the outer edge of the Leeward Islands chain in the West Indies. Barbuda is the most northerly (40 km—25 miles north of Antigua), and Redonda is 40 km south-west of Antigua. The French island of Guadeloupe lies to the south of the country, the British dependency of Montserrat to the south-west and Saint Christopher and Nevis to the west. The climate is tropical, although tempered by constant sea breezes and the trade winds, and the mean annual rainfall of 1,000mm (40 inches) is slight for the region. The temperature averages 27°C (81°F) but can rise to 33°C (93°F) during the hot season between May and October. English is the official language but an English patois is commonly used. The majority of the inhabitants profess Christianity, and are mainly adherents of the Anglican Communion. The national flag consists of an inverted triangle centred on a red ground and divided horizontally into three bands, of black, blue and white, with the black stripe bearing a symbol of the rising sun in gold. The capital is St John's, on Antigua.

Recent History

Antigua was colonized by the British in the 17th century. The island of Barbuda, formerly a slave stud farm for the Codrington family, was annexed to the territory in 1860. Until December 1959 Antigua and other nearby British territories were administered, under a federal system, as the Leeward Islands. The first elections under universal adult suffrage were held in 1951. The colony participated in the West Indies Federation, which was formed in January 1958 but dissolved in May 1962.

Attempts to form a smaller East Caribbean Federation failed, and most of the eligible colonies subsequently became Associated States in an arrangement which gave them full internal self-government while the United Kingdom retained responsibility for defence and foreign affairs. Antigua attained associated status in February 1967. The Legislative Council was replaced by a House of Representatives, the Administrator became Governor and the Chief Minister was restyled Premier.

In the first general election under associated status, held in February 1971, the Progressive Labour Movement (PLM) ousted the Antigua Labour Party (ALP), which had held power since 1946, by winning 13 of the 17 seats in the House of Representatives. George Walter, leader of the PLM, replaced Vere C. Bird, Sr as Premier. However, a general election in February 1976 was won by the ALP, with 11 seats, while the seat representing Barbuda was won by an independent. Vere Bird, the ALP's leader, again became Premier, while Lester Bird, one of his sons, became Deputy Premier.

In 1975 the Associated States agreed that they would seek independence separately. In the 1976 elections the PLM campaigned for early independence while the ALP stood against it. In September 1978, however, the ALP Government declared that the economic foundation for independence had been laid, and a premature general election was held in April 1980, when the ALP won 13 of the 17 seats. There was strong opposition from Barbuda to independence as part of Antigua, and at local elections in March 1981 the Barbuda People's Movement (BPM), which continued to campaign for secession from Antigua, won all the seats on the Barbuda Council. However, the territory finally became independent, as Antigua and Barbuda, on 1 November 1981, remaining within the Commonwealth. The grievances of the Barbudans concerning control of land and devolution of power were unresolved, although the ALP Government had made concessions, yielding a certain degree of internal autonomy to the Barbuda Council. The Governor, Sir Wilfred Jacobs, became Governor-General, while the Premier, Vere Bird, became the country's first Prime Minister.

Following disagreements within the opposition PLM, George Walter, the former Premier, formed his own political party, the United People's Movement (UPM), in 1982. In April 1984 at the first general election since independence, divisions within the opposition allowed the ALP to win convincingly in all of the 16 seats that it contested. The remaining seat, representing Barbuda, was retained by an unopposed independent. In March 1985 the Organization for National Reconstruction (ONR), a Barbudan party advocating co-operation with the ALP Government in Antigua, won a majority on the Barbuda Council in local elections. A new opposition party, the National Democratic Party (NDP), was formed in Antigua in 1985. In April 1986 it merged with the UPM to form the United National Democratic Party (UNDP). George Walter declined to play any significant public role in the UNDP, and Dr Ivor Heath, who had led the NDP, was elected leader of the new party.

In November 1986 a political crisis arose over a rehabilitation scheme at the international airport on Antigua. In January 1987, after a cabinet reshuffle, the Government appointed a former Chief Justice of Grenada, Sir Archibald Nedd, to conduct an official inquiry into the contract conditions and cost of the US $11.5m. project (worth no more than $0.5m. by World Bank estimates), which had been negotiated by Vere Bird, Jr (a senior minister and the eldest son of the Prime Minister). The report, published in August, stated that, while there was no evidence of criminal activity, Bird, Jr had acted 'in a manner unbecoming a minister of government' by awarding part of the contract to a company of which he was both the Chairman and the Legal Adviser. The controversy divided the ALP, with eight Ministers (including Lester Bird, the Deputy Prime Minister) demanding the resignation of Vere Bird, Jr, and Prime Minister Bird refusing to dismiss him. The rifts within the ALP and the Bird family continued into 1988, when new allegations of corruption by government members were made, this time implicating Lester Bird. In early 1989, however, the ALP Cabinet effected a reconciliation while the main opposition parties, the UNDP and the Antigua Caribbean Liberation Movement (ACLM), failed to negotiate an electoral pact.

At a general election in March 1989 the ALP remained the ruling party by retaining 15 of the 16 seats that it had held in the previous House of Representatives. The UNDP won more than 30% of all the votes cast, but only one seat. The mainland Antiguan parties did not contest the Barbuda seat, where the incumbent Barbuda National Party was defeated by the BPM. The UNDP proceeded to challenge the results in seven constituencies, and instituted legal proceedings. In June the High Court declared the result in one of these constituencies to be invalid, owing to irregularities in the conduct of the poll. The remaining six ALP members whose election was disputed then resigned and prepared to contest by-elections in August. The UNDP, however, refused to contest the elections without a reform of the electoral system, and the ACLM announced that it was unable to finance a further campaign. The ALP candidates were therefore declared elected in August.

Divisions within the Government reappeared after the elections. The principal issues were the question of a successor to the ailing Prime Minister (disputed among Lester Bird, Vere Bird, Jr, and those who opposed the dominance of the Bird family) and the continuing allegations of corruption. Some public disquiet about the Government's regular resort to judicial processes against its critics was allayed by the outcome of a case against Tim Hector, the editor of the weekly *Outlet* newspaper and the chairman of the ACLM. In January 1990 Antigua and Barbuda's final court of appeal, the Judicial Committee of the Privy Council (based in the United Kingdom), acquitted Hector of 'undermining public confidence in the Government'. The court declared the law under which he had been charged, the Public Order Act, to be unconstitutional and in contravention of fundamental human rights. In February 1990 the churches organized a demonstration against the general decline in moral standards in the country. The march, in which both members of the Government and the opposition took part, attracted substantial public support. The Government consequently agreed to establish an inquiry into drug-trafficking and prostitution.

ANTIGUA AND BARBUDA

In April 1990 the Government of Antigua and Barbuda received a diplomatic note of protest from the Government of Colombia regarding the sale of weapons to a leading Colombian trader in illegal drugs. The weapons had originally been sold by Israel to Antigua and Barbuda but, contrary to regulation, were then immediately shipped on to Colombia in April 1989. It was assumed that this could have occurred only with official connivance. The communication from the Colombian Government implicated Vere Bird, Jr. The Government established a committee of inquiry, chaired by the Deputy Prime Minister, Lester Bird. He subsequently demanded a judicial inquiry, which would have greater powers to obtain evidence. The Prime Minister eventually agreed, and on 25 April 1990 Vere Bird, Jr, was granted leave of absence from his ministerial duties until the matter was resolved. The inquiry conducted its investigations between June and September 1990 amid some controversy (including the alleged lack of co-operation by Vere Bird, Jr). There were also protests that the government-controlled media were not reporting the progress of the inquiry fully, and there were further disputes within the Cabinet. In September, as a response to disclosures made during the course of the inquiry, the Government announced measures designed to limit unethical practices in the conduct of public affairs. The proposals included legislation to prevent corruption, the establishment of a rigorous system governing the appointment of special envoys and the compilation of an official register regarding the business interests of government members. The opposition alleged that the proposals did not command the full support of the Government, and questioned the political will to effect them. In October the Chamber of Commerce recommended the resignation of the Government. In November a news agency obtained a copy of the unpublished report of the judicial inquiry, which accused Antigua and Barbuda of having become 'engulfed in corruption'. In the same month the Government acted upon the recommendations of the report: Vere Bird, Jr, was dismissed and banned for life from holding office in the Government, and the head of the defence force, Col Clyde Walker, was also dismissed.

There was increasing dissatisfaction on Barbuda during 1987 and 1988 as a result of the lack of consultation by the central Government about projects involving the island. In March 1989 local people blockaded the port of Barbuda to prevent the landing of more than 200 Chilean llamas. The Government in St John's and US business interests had agreed to establish a wildlife park and a quarantine station (for animals in transit to the USA) on Barbuda. The BPM was prominent in the campaign against these projects and not only won the parliamentary seat in the general election in March 1989 but also, later in the same month, won all five local government seats being contested on the island, thus giving the party complete control of the nine-seat Barbuda Council. The BPM aims to achieve separate status for Barbuda, but in August the Attorney-General informed the Barbuda Council that the Government would not consider any constitutional amendments. The Government did, however, agree to hold discussions with the Council, and in October the BPM requested a review of the Constitution, to be conducted by the Commonwealth Secretariat.

In foreign relations, the ALP Government follows a policy of non-alignment, although the country has strong links with the USA, and actively assisted in the US military intervention in Grenada in October 1983 as a member of the Organization of Eastern Caribbean States (OECS, see p. 109). Antigua and Barbuda is also a member of CARICOM (see p. 108), but in 1988 proved to be one of the main opponents of closer political federation within either organization. The Government did, however, agree to the reduction of travel restrictions between OECS members (which took effect in January 1990). Since 1982, Antigua and Barbuda has intensified its programme of foreign relations, strengthening its links in Latin America and with Canada, the Republic of Korea and the People's Republic of China. In September 1989 it was agreed that the People's Republic of China would open an embassy in St John's. In January 1990 diplomatic relations were established with the USSR.

Relations with Trinidad and Tobago were disrupted in 1988, when Antigua and Barbuda allegedly reneged on an agreement that would have allowed BWIA, Trinidad and Tobago's national airline, access to the profitable London Heathrow–Antigua route. The two Governments placed each other's goods under trade licence, but in March 1988 Antigua and Barbuda agreed to seek 'fifth freedom' rights for BWIA to land *en route* to London, and all trade barriers between the two countries were removed. In 1989, together with several other countries of the region, Antigua and Barbuda agreed to designate BWIA as the region's official carrier on the route to the United Kingdom. There was reported to be some British opposition to this proposal.

Government

Antigua and Barbuda is a constitutional monarchy. Executive power is vested in the British sovereign, as Head of State, and exercised by the Governor-General, who represents the sovereign locally and is appointed on the advice of the Antiguan Prime Minister. Legislative power is vested in Parliament, comprising the sovereign, a 17-member Senate and a 17-member House of Representatives. Members of the House are elected from single-member constituencies for up to five years by universal adult suffrage. The Senate is composed of 11 members (of whom one must be an inhabitant of Barbuda) appointed on the advice of the Prime Minister, four appointed on the advice of the Leader of the Opposition, one appointed at the discretion of the Governor-General and one appointed on the advice of the Barbuda Council. Government is effectively by the Cabinet. The Governor-General appoints the Prime Minister and, on the latter's recommendation, selects the other Ministers. The Prime Minister must be able to command the support of a majority of the House, to which the Cabinet is responsible.

Defence

There is a small defence force of almost 100 men. The US Government finances two military bases on Antigua. Antigua and Barbuda participates in the US-sponsored Regional Security System. In the 1990/91 budget, military expenditure increased to EC $3.9m. (representing 1.4% of recurrent government expenditure).

Economic Affairs

In 1988, according to estimates by the World Bank, Antigua and Barbuda's gross national product (GNP), measured at average 1986–88 prices, was US $230m., equivalent to US $2,800 per head. During 1980–88, it was estimated, GNP increased, in real terms, at an average annual rate of 5.4%, and GNP per head by 4.0%. Gross domestic product (GDP), in real terms, increased at an average rate of 7.5% per year between 1983 and 1988 (7.6% in 1988). GDP was estimated to be EC $740.6m., at current prices, in 1988.

Agriculture (including forestry and fishing) contributed 4.7% of GDP in 1987. Agricultural output increased sufficiently for the export of cucumbers and pumpkins in 1988. The other principal crops are mangoes, coconuts, limes and the speciality 'Antigua Black' pineapple. The development of livestock farming was intended to make the country self-sufficient in meat by 1989. However, the sector was severely affected by Hurricane Hugo in September 1989 and by severe storms in 1990.

The manufacturing sector consists of some light industries producing rum, garments and household appliances, and the assembly of electrical components for export. Manufacturing contributed 3.7% of GDP in 1987, and the construction sector 11.7%.

Tourism is the main economic activity, and by 1981 this sector accounted for approximately 25% of employment, made a direct contribution to GDP of 12% and accounted for some 40% indirectly, through other services. In 1986 earnings from tourism were estimated at EC $283m., equivalent to more than 50% of GDP. In 1987 the sector directly contributed 15.4% of GDP. In 1988 visitor expenditure totalled US $215m. Stop-over arrivals by air increased by 11% and cruise-ship visitors by 29% in 1988, to total 375,490. Most tourists are from the USA (52.9% in 1987), while numerous arrivals also come from the United Kingdom and Canada.

In 1987 Antigua and Barbuda recorded a visible trade deficit of US $229.8m. and a deficit of US $83.3m. on the current account of the balance of payments. The USA is the principal source of imports (32% in 1987) and also the principal market for exports (mainly re-exports). Apart from countries in CARICOM (see p. 108), major trading partners are the United Kingdom and Canada.

In the financial year ending 31 March 1990 there was a recurrent budgetary deficit of EC $20.0m. In the proposals for that budget, some EC $54m. was designated for debt-servicing,

ANTIGUA AND BARBUDA

the total external debt having increased to about US $250m. by mid-1989. The average annual rate of inflation was 6.1% in 1980–87. An estimated 21% of the labour force were unemployed in 1984, but this percentage subsequently declined.

Antigua and Barbuda is a member of CARICOM, the OECS, the Organization of American States (see p. 194), and is a signatory of the Lomé Conventions with the EEC (see p. 151).

In the 1980s the Government sought to diversify the economy, which is dominated by tourism. Agricultural policy is primarily designed to reduce imports, but the revival of the production of sea-island cotton (formerly Antigua's main export) is being encouraged for export. Adverse weather conditions, particularly drought, are a problem. The development of tourism remains the Government's priority, but it was estimated that some 60% of earnings were remitted abroad. Antigua and Barbuda also has one of the highest debt-servicing commitments in the Caribbean, and a large public sector (government services contributed 15.5% of GDP in 1987). In 1990 there was some apprehension, in the business community particularly, that the political troubles would deter foreign investors.

Social Welfare

There are two state welfare schemes providing free health care, and a range of pensions, benefits and grants. Antigua has a 220-bed general hospital and 25 health centres and clinics. In 1987 there were 48 physicians and seven dentists working in the islands.

Education

Education is compulsory for 11 years between five and 16 years of age. Primary education begins at the age of five and normally lasts for six years. Secondary education, beginning at 11 years of age, lasts for five years, comprising a first cycle of three years and a second cycle of two years. In 1987 there were 43 primary and 15 secondary schools; the majority of schools are administered by the Government. In 1987/88, 9,097 primary school pupils and 4,413 secondary school pupils were enrolled. Teacher training and technical training are available at the State Island College. An extra-mural department of the University of the West Indies offers several foundation courses leading to higher study at branches elsewhere.

Public Holidays

1991: 1 January (New Year's Day), 29 March (Good Friday), 1 April (Easter Monday), 6 May (Labour Day), 19 May (Whit Monday), 8 June (Queen's Official Birthday), 5–6 August (Carnival), 1 November (Independence Day), 25–26 December (Christmas).

1992: 1 January (New Year's Day), 17 April (Good Friday), 20 April (Easter Monday), 4 May (Labour Day), 8 June (Whit Monday), 13 June (Queen's Official Birthday), 3–4 August (Carnival), 2 November (for Independence Day), 25–26 December (Christmas).

Weights and Measures

The imperial system is in use but a metrication programme is being introduced.

Statistical Survey

Source (unless otherwise stated): Ministry of Finance, Long St, St John's; tel. 462-1199.

AREA AND POPULATION

Area: 441.6 sq km (170.5 sq miles).

Population: 65,525 (males 31,054, females 34,471) at census of 7 April 1970; 78,400 (estimate, mid-1989).

Density (mid-1989): 177.5 per sq km.

Principal Town (estimate, 1986): St John's (capital), population 36,000.

Births and Deaths (1987): Birth rate 14.3 per 1,000; Death rate 5.1 per 1,000.

Economically Active Population (estimates, 1985): Employed 25,455 (males 14,257, females 11,198); Unemployed 6,799 (males 5,075, females 1,724); Total labour force 32,254.

AGRICULTURE, ETC.

Principal Crops (metric tons, 1986): Cucumbers 329.0, Aubergines 186.2, Pumpkins 176.7, Limes 188.8, Mangoes ('000 fruits) 1,001.4, Coconuts ('000) 514, Sugar cane 5,000 (FAO estimate).

Livestock (FAO estimates, '000 head, year ending September 1989): Horses and Asses 3, Cattle 18, Pigs 4, Sheep 13, Goats 13. Source: FAO, *Production Yearbook*.

Fishing (metric tons, live weight): Total catch 2,407 (Marine fishes 2,290, Caribbean spiny lobster 117) in 1985; 2,400 per year in 1986, 1987 and 1988 (FAO estimates). Source: FAO, *Yearbook of Fishery Statistics*.

INDUSTRY

Production (estimates, 1985): Rum and alcohol 2,776.8 hectolitres; Wines and vodka 380.4 hectolitres; Electric energy (1987) 90.6m. kWh.

FINANCE

Currency and Exchange Rates: 100 cents = 1 East Caribbean dollar (EC $). *Coins:* 1, 2, 5, 10, 25 and 50 cents, 1 dollar. *Notes:* 1, 5, 10, 20 and 100 dollars. *Sterling and US Dollar equivalents* (30 September 1990): £1 sterling = EC $5.058; US $1 = EC $2.700; EC $100 = £19.77 = US $37.04. *Exchange rate:* Fixed at US $1 = EC $2.700 since July 1976.

Budget (estimates, EC $ million, 1989): Recurrent expenditure 263.6; Recurrent revenue 236.7. *1990:* Recurrent expenditure 272.

International Reserves (US $ million at 31 December 1989): Foreign exchange 28.07; Total 28.07. Source: IMF, *International Financial Statistics*.

Money Supply (EC $ million at 31 December 1988): Currency outside banks 51.31; Demand deposits at deposit money banks 76.68; Total money 127.99. Source: IMF, *International Financial Statistics*.

Cost of Living (Consumer Price Index; base: 1980 = 100): 118.8 in 1983; 123.4 in 1984; 124.7 in 1985. Source: IMF, *International Financial Statistics*.

Gross Domestic Product by Economic Activity (EC $ million at current prices, 1986): Agriculture, hunting, forestry and fishing 24.6; Mining and quarrying 9.9; Manufacturing 21.5; Electricity, gas and water 19.9; Construction 50.6; Trade, restaurants and hotels 133.6; Transport, storage and communications 88.4; Finance, insurance, real estate and business services 85.0; Government services 89.7; Other community, social and personal services 43.9; *Sub-total* 567.1; *Less* Imputed bank service charges 30.0; *GDP at factor cost* 537.1; Indirect taxes, *less* subsidies 104.7; *GDP in purchasers' values* 641.8. Source: UN, *National Accounts Statistics*. Note: Revised figures estimated GDP in purchasers' values (EC $ million at current prices) to be: 525.5 in 1986; 616.1 in 1987; 740.6 in 1988. Source: IMF, *International Financial Statistics*.

Balance of Payments (US $ million, 1987): Merchandise exports f.o.b. 28.5; Merchandise imports f.o.b. −258.25; *Trade balance* −229.75; Exports of services 194.3; Imports of services −66.55; *Balance on goods and services* −102.0; Unrequited transfers (net) 18.7; *Current balance* −83.3; Direct capital investment (net) 29.2; Other long-term capital (net) 47.4; Other short-term capital (net) −6.4; Net errors and omissions 8.79; *Total (net monetary movements)* −4.31; Valuation changes (net) −2.76; Exceptional financing (net) 8.8; *Changes in reserves* 1.73. Source: IMF, *International Financial Statistics*.

EXTERNAL TRADE

Principal Commodities (EC $ million, 1984): *Imports:* Food and live animals 69.8; Beverages and tobacco 11.7; Mineral fuels, lubricants, etc. 89.1; Chemicals 22.7; Basic manufactures 44.7; Machinery and transport equipment 77.8; Miscellaneous manufactured articles 32.2; Total (incl. others) 356.1. *Exports:* Mineral fuels, lubricants, etc. 5.5; Chemicals 3.6; Basic manufactures 3.3; Machinery and transport equipment 14.3; Miscellaneous manufactured articles 18.0; Total (incl. others) 47.5. Source: UN, *International Trade Statistics Yearbook*.

Imports (EC $ million, c.i.f.): 301.80 in 1985, 560.23 in 1986, 600.09 in 1987, 608.79 in 1988. **Exports** (EC $ million, f.o.b.): 35.64 in 1985, 52.88 in 1986, 46.48 in 1987, 60.04 in 1988. Source: IMF, *International Financial Statistics*.

Principal Trading Partners (EC $ million): *Imports* (1984): Canada 12.0; United Kingdom 37.6; USA 134.7; Yugoslavia 13.7; Total (incl. others) 356.1. *Exports* (1984): Canada 0.8; Caribbean countries 18.1; South and Central America 10.0; United Kingdom 1.6; USA 8.4; Total (incl. others) 47.5. Source: UN, *International Trade Statistics Yearbook*.

TRANSPORT

Road Traffic (registered vehicles, 1986): Passenger motor cars 11,188; Motor cycles 834, Station wagons, vans, pick-ups, jeeps, lorries and buses 3,321.

Shipping (freight traffic, '000 metric tons, 1986): Goods loaded 15.6; Goods unloaded 346.6. *Arrivals* (vessels, 1987): 3,940.

Civil Aviation (aircraft landings, 1987): 23,409.

TOURISM

Foreign Tourist Arrivals: 249,871 in 1985; 281,301 in 1986; 324,541 (159,207 by air, 14,026 by sea, 153,308 cruise-ship passengers) in 1987. *1988:* 176,893 visitors by air; 198,597 cruise-ship passengers.

COMMUNICATIONS MEDIA

Weekly newspapers (1987): 4.

Radio Receivers (1987): 22,618 in use.

Television Receivers (1988): 27,000 in use.

Telephones (1988): 7,400 in use.

EDUCATION

Pre-primary (1983): 21 schools; 23 teachers; 677 pupils.

Primary (1987/88): 43 schools; 446 teachers; 9,097 students.

Secondary (1987/88): 15 schools; 319 teachers; 4,413 students.

Tertiary (1986): 2 colleges; 631 students.

Directory

The Constitution

The Constitution, which came into force at the independence of Antigua and Barbuda on 1 November 1981, states that Antigua and Barbuda is a 'unitary sovereign democratic state'. The main provisions of the Constitution are summarized below:

FUNDAMENTAL RIGHTS AND FREEDOMS

Regardless of race, place of origin, political opinion, colour, creed or sex, but subject to respect for the rights and freedoms of others and for the public interest, every person in Antigua and Barbuda is entitled to the rights of life, liberty, security of the person, the enjoyment of property and the protection of the law. Freedom of movement, of conscience, of expression (including freedom of the press), of peaceful assembly and association is guaranteed and the inviolability of family life, personal privacy, home and other property is maintained. Protection is afforded from discrimination on the grounds of race, sex, etc., and from slavery, forced labour, torture and inhuman treatment.

THE GOVERNOR-GENERAL

The British sovereign, as Monarch of Antigua and Barbuda, is the Head of State and is represented by a Governor-General of local citizenship.

PARLIAMENT

Parliament consists of the Monarch, a 17-member Senate and the House of Representatives composed of 17 elected members. Senators are appointed by the Governor-General: 11 on the advice of the Prime Minister (one of whom must be an inhabitant of Barbuda), four on the advice of the Leader of the Opposition, one at his own discretion and one on the advice of the Barbuda Council. The Barbuda Council is the principal organ of local government in that island, whose membership and functions are determined by Parliament. The life of Parliament is five years.

Each constituency returns one Representative to the House who is directly elected in accordance with the Constitution.

The Attorney-General, if not otherwise a member of the House, is an ex-officio member but does not have the right to vote.

Every citizen over the age of 18 is eligible to vote.

Parliament may alter any of the provisions of the Constitution.

THE EXECUTIVE

Executive authority is vested in the Monarch and exercisable by the Governor-General. The Governor-General appoints as Prime Minister that member of the House who, in the Governor-General's view, is best able to command the support of the majority of the members of the House, and other Ministers on the advice of the Prime Minister. The Governor-General may remove the Prime Minister from office if a resolution of no confidence is passed by the House and the Prime Minister does not either resign or advise the Governor-General to dissolve Parliament within seven days.

The Cabinet consists of the Prime Minister and other Ministers and the Attorney-General.

The Leader of the Opposition is appointed by the Governor-General as that member of the House who, in the Governor-General's view, is best able to command the support of a majority of members of the House who do not support the Government.

CITIZENSHIP

All persons born in Antigua and Barbuda before independence who, immediately prior to independence, were citizens of the United Kingdom and Colonies automatically become citizens of Antigua and Barbuda. All persons born outside the country with a parent or grandparent possessing citizenship of Antigua and Barbuda automatically acquire citizenship as do those born in the country after independence. Provision is made for the acquisition of citizenship by those to whom it would not automatically be granted.

The Government

Head of State: HM Queen ELIZABETH II (succeeded to the throne 6 February 1952).

Governor-General: Sir WILFRED EBENEZER JACOBS (took office 1 November 1981).

CABINET
(November 1990)

Prime Minister: VERE C. BIRD, Sr.

Deputy Prime Minister and Minister of Economic Development, External Affairs, Tourism and Energy: LESTER BRYANT BIRD.

Minister of Finance: JOHN E. ST LUCE.

Attorney-General and Minister of Legal Affairs: KEITH B. FORD.

Minister of Public Utilities and Aviation: ROBIN YEARWOOD.

Minister of Agriculture, Fisheries, Housing and Lands: HILLROY HUMPHRIES.

Minister of Home Affairs: CHRISTOPHER MANASSEH O'MARD.

Minister of Education, Culture and Youth Affairs: REUBEN H. HARRIS.

Minister of Labour and Health: ADOLPHUS ELEAZER FREELAND.

Minister of Public Works and Communications: EUSTACE COCHRANE.

Minister of Trade, Industry and Commerce: HUGH MARSHALL.

Minister without Portfolio and Leader of Government Business in the Senate: BERNARD S. PERCIVAL.

MINISTRIES

Office of the Prime Minister: Factory Rd, St John's; tel. 462-0773; telex 2127.

Ministry of Agriculture, Fisheries, Housing and Lands: Long St, St John's; tel. 462-1007.

Ministry of Education, Culture and Youth Affairs: Church St, St John's; tel. 462-0192.

ANTIGUA AND BARBUDA

Ministry of Economic Development, External Affairs, Tourism and Energy: Queen Elizabeth Highway, St John's; tel. 462-0092; telex 2122.

Ministry of Finance: Long St, St John's; tel. 462-1199.

Ministry of Labour and Health: Redcliffe St, St John's; tel. 462-0011.

Ministry of Legal Affairs: Hadeed Bldg, Redcliffe St, St John's; tel. 462-0017.

Ministry of Public Works and Communications: St John's St, St John's; tel. 462-0894.

Ministry of Trade, Industry and Commerce: St John's.

Legislature

PARLIAMENT

Senate

President: Bradley Carrot.
There are 17 nominated members.

House of Representatives

Speaker: Casford Murray.
Ex-Officio Member: The Attorney-General.
Clerk: L. Dowe.

General Election, 9 March 1989

Party	Votes cast	%	Seats
Antigua Labour Party	14,218	63.8	15*
United National Democratic Party	6,896	31.0	1
Antigua Caribbean Liberation Movement	434	1.9	—
Others†	723	3.2	1
Total	22,271	100.0	17

* The results in seven constituencies were challenged in court but, after resigning their seats in July, the seven successful candidates were returned unopposed on 5 August.

† There were six other candidates: three independent candidates for Antiguan seats, and three candidates in the constituency of Barbuda, which was won by the Barbuda People's Movement.

Political Organizations

Antigua Caribbean Liberation Movement (ACLM): POB 493, St John's; f. 1979; left-wing; Chair. Tim Hector.

Antigua Labour Party (ALP): St Mary's St, St John's; tel. 462-1059; f. 1968; Leader Vere C. Bird, Sr; Chair. Lester Bryant Bird; Sec. J. E. St Luce.

Barbuda Independence Movement: Codrington; f. 1983 as Organisation for National Reconstruction, re-formed 1988; advocates self-government for Barbuda; Leader Arthur Nibbs.

Barbuda National Party: Codrington; Leader Eric Burton.

Barbuda People's Movement (BPM): Codrington; campaigns for separate status for Barbuda; Parliamentary Leader Thomas Hilbourne Frank.

Progressive Labour Movement (PLM): St John's; f. 1970; Leader Robert Hall.

United National Democratic Party (UNDP): St John's; f. 1986 by merger of the United People's Movement (f. 1982) and the National Democratic Party (f. 1985); Chair. George Piggott; Leader Dr Ivor Heath; Parliamentary Leader Baldwin Spencer.

Diplomatic Representation

EMBASSIES AND HIGH COMMISSION IN ANTIGUA AND BARBUDA

China, People's Republic: St John's; Ambassador: Zhou Wenzhong.

United Kingdom: British High Commission Office, 38 St Mary's St, POB 483, St John's; tel. 462-0008; telex 2113; fax 462-2806; (High Commissioner resident in Barbados).

USA: Queen Elizabeth Highway, St John's; tel. 462-3505; telex 2140 Chargé d'affaires: Robert W. DuBose, Jr.

Venezuela: Cross and Redcliffe Sts, POB 1201, St John's; tel. 462-1570; telex 2161; fax 462-1570; Ambassador: Daniela Szokoloczi.

Judicial System

Justice is administered by the Eastern Caribbean Supreme Court, based in Saint Lucia, which consists of a High Court of Justice and a Court of Appeal. One of the Court's Puisne Judges is resident in and responsible for Antigua and Barbuda, and presides over the Court of Summary Jurisdiction on the islands. There are also Magistrate's Courts for lesser cases.

Religion

The majority of the inhabitants profess Christianity, and the largest denomination is the Church in the Province of the West Indies (Anglican Communion).

CHRISTIANITY

Antigua Christian Council: POB 863, St John's; tel. 462-0261; f. 1964; five mem. churches; Pres. Rev. Neville Brodie (Methodist Church); Exec. Sec. Miss Edris Roberts.

The Anglican Communion

Anglicans in Antigua and Barbuda are adherents of the Church in the Province of the West Indies. The diocese of the North Eastern Caribbean and Aruba comprises 12 islands: Antigua, Saint Christopher (St Kitts), Nevis, Anguilla, Barbuda, Montserrat, Dominica, Saba, St Maarten/St Martin, Aruba, St Bartholomew and St Eustatius; the total number of Anglicans is about 60,000. The See City and the headquarters of the Provincial Secretariat is St John's.

Bishop of the North Eastern Caribbean and Aruba and Archbishop of the West Indies: Most Rev. Orland U. Lindsay, Bishop's Lodge, POB 23, St John's; tel. 462-0151; fax 462-2090.

The Roman Catholic Church

The diocese of St John's-Basseterre, suffragan to the archdiocese of Castries (Saint Lucia), includes Anguilla, Antigua and Barbuda, the British Virgin Islands, Montserrat and Saint Christopher and Nevis. At 31 December 1988 there were an estimated 14,230 adherents in the diocese. The Bishop participates in the Antilles Episcopal Conference (currently based in Jamaica).

Bishop of St John's-Basseterre: Rt Rev. Donald J. Reece; Catholic Offices, POB 836, St John's; tel. 461-1135; fax 462-2383.

Other Christian Churches

Antigua Baptist Association: POB 277, St John's; tel. 462-1254; Pres. Ivor Charles.

Evangelical Lutheran Church: POB 968, St John's; tel. 462-2896; Pastors M. Henrich, D. Kehl.

Methodist Church: c/o POB 863, St John's; Superintendent Rev. Eloy Christopher.

There are also Pentecostal, Seventh-day Adventist, Moravian, Nazarene, Salvation Army and Wesleyan Holiness places of worship.

The Press

Business Expressions: POB 774, St John's; tel. 462-0743; monthly; organ of the Antigua Chamber of Commerce.

The Herald: 2nd Floor, Redcliffe House, Cross and Redcliffe Sts, St John's; tel. 462-3752; weekly; Editor Everton Barnes; circ. 2,500.

The Nation's Voice: Public Information Division, Church St and Independence Ave, POB 590, St John's; tel. 462-0090; weekly; Editor Robin Bascus; circ. 1,500.

The Outlet: Cross St and Tanner St, POB 493, St John's; tel. 462-4425; f. 1975; weekly; publ. by the Antigua Caribbean Liberation Movement; Editor Tim Hector; circ. 5,500.

Rappore: St John's; f. 1986; weekly; official organ of the United National Democratic Party.

The Worker's Voice: Emancipation House, 46 North St, POB 3, St John's; tel. 462-0090; f. 1943; weekly; official organ of the Antigua Labour Party and the Antigua Trades and Labour Union; Editor Noel Thomas; circ. 2,000.

FOREIGN NEWS AGENCY

Inter Press Service (IPS) (Italy): Old Parham Rd, St John's; tel. 462-3602; Correspondent Louis Daniel.

ANTIGUA AND BARBUDA

Publishers

Antigua Printing and Publishing Ltd: POB 670, St John's; tel. 462-1265.

Wadadli Productions Ltd: POB 571, St John's; tel. 462-4489.

Radio and Television

There were an estimated 22,618 radio receivers in use in 1987, and 27,000 television receivers in 1988.

Antigua and Barbuda Broadcasting Service (ABBS): Public Information Div., Office of the Prime Minister, POB 590, St John's; tel. 462-3602; Gen. Man. HOLLIS HENRY; comprises:

ABBS Radio: POB 590, St John's; tel. 462-3602; telex 2127; f. 1956; Prog. Man. (Radio) D. L. PAYNE.

ABBS Television: POB 1280, St John's; tel. 462-0821; f. 1964; Programme Man. (Television) F. LIBURD.

Caribbean Radio Lighthouse: POB 1057, St John's; tel. 462-1454; f. 1975; religious broadcasts; operated by Baptist Int. Mission Inc. (USA); Dir CURTIS L. WAITE.

CTV Entertainment Systems: 25 Long St, St John's; tel. 462-0346; fax 462-4211; cable television co; transmits 12 channels of US television 24 hours per day to subscribers; Prog. Dir J. COX.

Radio ZDK: Grenville Radio Ltd, POB 1100, St John's; tel. 462-1100; f. 1970; privately-owned; commercial; CEO Mrs L. BIRD; Man. IVOR BIRD.

There are also relay stations for US, British and German radio services.

Finance

(cap. = capital; brs = branches)

BANKING

The Eastern Caribbean Central Bank (see p. 109), based in Saint Christopher, is the central issuing and monetary authority for Antigua and Barbuda.

Antigua Commercial Bank: Corner of St Mary's and Thames Sts, POB 95, St John's; tel. 462-1217; telex 2175; f. 1955; auth. cap. $5m.; Man. JOHN BENJAMIN; 2 brs.

Antigua and Barbuda Development Bank: 27 St Mary's St, POB 1279, St John's; tel. 462-0838; f. 1974; Man. BERNARD S. PERCIVAL.

Bank of Antigua: Corner of High and Thames Sts, POB 315, St John's; tel. 462-4282; telex 2180; 1 br.

Fidelity Trust Bank Ltd: High St, St John's.

Foreign Banks

Bank of Nova Scotia (Canada): High St, POB 342, St John's; tel. 462-1104; telex 2118; Man. L. J. NELSON.

Barclays Bank PLC (UK): High St, POB 225, St John's; tel. 462-0334; telex 2135; Man. I. C. LAYNE; 2 brs.

Canadian Imperial Bank of Commerce: 28 High St, POB 28, St John's; tel. 462-0836; telex 2150; Man. G. R. HILTS.

Royal Bank of Canada: High St and Market St, POB 252, St John's; tel. 462-0325; telex 2120; offers a trustee service.

Swiss American National Bank: High St, POB 1302, St John's; tel. 462-4460; telex 2181; Chief Exec. JOHN GREAVES.

INSURANCE

Several foreign companies have offices in Antigua. Local insurance companies include the following:

Diamond Insurance Co Ltd: Camacho's Ave, POB 489, St John's; tel. 462-3474; telex 2173.

General Insurance Agency Co Ltd: Redcliffe St, POB 340, St John's; tel. 462-2346.

Sentinel Insurance Co Ltd: Antigua Mill Hotel, POB 207, St John's; tel. 462-0808.

State Insurance Corpn: Redcliffe St, POB 290, St John's; tel. 462-0110; telex 2177; fax 462-2649.

Trade and Industry

Antigua and Barbuda Manufacturers' Association: POB 1158, St John's; tel. 462-1536; fax 462-1523; Chair. PETER HARKER; Exec. Sec. BRIAN STUART-YOUNG.

Antigua Chamber of Commerce Ltd: Cross and Redcliffe Sts, POB 774, St John's; tel. 462-0743; telex 2105; f. 1944; 90 mems; Pres. EUSTACE FRANCIS; Exec. Dir LIONEL BOULOS.

Antigua Cotton Growers' Association: Dunbars, St John's; tel. 462-4962; telex 2122; Chair. FRANCIS HENRY; Sec. PETER BLANCHETTE.

Antigua Employers' Federation: 7 Redcliffe Quay, Redcliffe St, POB 298, St John's; tel. 462-0449; f. 1950; 94 mems; Chair. ARMALD DERRICK; Sec. HENDERSON BASS.

Antigua Fisheries Corpn: St John's; partly funded by the Antigua and Barbuda Development Bank; aims to help local fishermen.

Antigua Sugar Industry Corpn: Gunthorpes, POB 899, St George's; tel. 462-0653.

Private Sector Organization of Antigua and Barbuda: St John's.

DEVELOPMENT AGENCIES

Barbuda Development Agency: St John's; economic development projects for Barbuda; Chair. HAKIM AKBAR.

Industrial Development Board: Newgate St, St John's; tel. 462-1038; f. 1984 to stimulate investment in local industries.

St John's Development Corporation: c/o Ministry of Economic Development, Queen Elizabeth Highway, St John's; tel. 462-3925.

TRADE UNIONS

Antigua and Barbuda Public Service Association (ABPSA): POB 747, St John's; Pres. LINDBERG DOWE; Gen. Sec. ELLOY DE FREITAS; 500 mems.

Antigua Trades and Labour Union (ATLU): 46 North St, St John's; tel. 462-0090; f. 1939; affiliated to the Antigua Labour Party; Pres. WILLIAM ROBINSON; Gen. Sec. NOEL THOMAS; about 10,000 mems.

Antigua Workers' Union (AWU): Freedom Hall, Newgate St, St John's; tel. 462-2005; f. 1967 after a split with ATLU; not affiliated to any party; Pres. MALCOLM DANIEL; Gen. Sec. KEITHLYN SMITH; 10,000 mems.

National Assembly of Workers: Cross St, St John's; affiliated to the Antigua Caribbean Liberation Movement.

Transport

ROADS

There are 384 km (239 miles) of main roads and 781 km (485 miles) of secondary dry-weather roads.

SHIPPING

The main harbour is the St John's Deep Water Harbour. It is used by cruise ships and a number of foreign shipping lines. There are regular cargo and passenger services internationally and regionally. At Falmouth, on the south side of Antigua, is a former Royal Navy dockyard in English Harbour. The harbour is now used by yachts and private pleasure craft.

Caribbean Link: High St, St John's; tel. 462-3000; f. 1987; operates high-speed passenger and cargo ferry; scheduled services to 10 islands; Dirs DON MARSHALL, KEVIN BELIZAIRE; 2 vessels.

Vernon Edwards Shipping Co: Thames St, St John's; weekly cargo service to Dominica.

CIVIL AVIATION

Antigua's V.C. Bird (formerly Coolidge) International Airport, 11 km (4.5 miles) north-east of St John's, is modern and accommodates jet-engined aircraft. There is a small airstrip at Codrington on Barbuda. Antigua and Barbuda Airlines, a nominal company, controls international routes, but services to Europe and North America are operated by American Airlines, Pan Am (USA), Lufthansa (Germany), Air Canada and British Airways. Antigua and Barbuda is a shareholder in, and the headquarters of, the regional airline, LIAT. Other regional services are operated by BWIA (Trinidad and Tobago) and Air BVI (British Virgin Islands).

LIAT (1974) Ltd: POB 819, V.C. Bird International Airport; tel. 462-0700; telex 2124; fax 462-4765; f. 1956 as Leeward Islands Air Transport Services; shares are held by the Governments of Antigua and Barbuda, Montserrat, Grenada, Barbados, Trinidad and Tobago, Jamaica, Guyana, Dominica, Saint Lucia, Saint Vincent and the Grenadines and Saint Christopher and Nevis; scheduled passenger and cargo services to 25 destinations in the Caribbean; charter flights are also undertaken; Chair. PETER LOOK HONG; Man. Dir ARTHUR FOSTER; fleet of 5 BAe HS.748, 5 Dash 8-100, 6 Twin Otter, 2 BN Islander.

Four Island Air Services Ltd: wholly-owned subsidiary of LIAT; runs scheduled services between Antigua, Barbuda and Saint Christopher and Nevis.

Inter Island Air Services Ltd: wholly-owned subsidiary of LIAT; runs scheduled services between Saint Vincent and the Grenadines, Grenada and Saint Lucia.

Carib Aviation Ltd: V.C. Bird Int. Airport; tel. 462-3147; charter co; operates regional services.

Tourism

Tourism is the main industry. Antigua offers a reputed 365 beaches, the annual attractions of an international sailing regatta and Carnival week, and the historic Nelson's Dockyard in English Harbour (a national park since 1985). Barbuda is less developed but is noted for its beauty, wildlife and beaches of pink sand. In 1986 the Government established the St John's Development Corporation to oversee the redevelopment of the capital as a commercial duty-free centre, with extra cruise-ship facilities. In 1988 there were 176,893 stop-over visitors who arrived by air and 198,597 cruise-ship passengers, most of whom came from the USA, Canada, the United Kingdom and from other Caribbean countries. There were an estimated 42 hotels with a total of 4,256 beds in 1987.

Antigua Department of Tourism: Long and Thames Sts, POB 363, St John's; tel. 462-0029; telex 2122; Man. EDIE HILL-THIBOU.

Antigua Hotels and Tourist Association (AHTA): POB 454, St John's; tel. 462-0374; telex 2171; fax 462-3702; Pres. CHARLES HAWLEY.

In June 1989 the Caribbean Hotel Association (CHA), a regional organization based in Puerto Rico, announced that it intended to move its headquarters to Antigua. The CHA comprises 700 member-hotels and 400 allied members, and its President is Alfred Taylor.

ARGENTINA

Introductory Survey

Location, Climate, Language, Religion, Flag, Capital

The Argentine Republic occupies almost the whole of South America south of the Tropic of Capricorn and east of the Andes. It has a long Atlantic coastline stretching from Uruguay and the River Plate to Tierra del Fuego. To the west lie Chile and the Andes mountains, while to the north are Bolivia, Paraguay and Brazil. Argentina also claims the Falkland Islands (known in Argentina as the Islas Malvinas), South Georgia, the South Sandwich Islands and part of Antarctica. The climate varies from sub-tropical in the Chaco region of the north to sub-arctic in Patagonia, generally with moderate summer rainfall. Temperatures in Buenos Aires are generally between 5°C (41°F) and 29°C (84°F). The language is Spanish. The great majority of the population profess Christianity: more than 90% are Roman Catholics and about 2% Protestants. The national flag (proportions 2 by 1) has three equal horizontal stripes, of light blue, white and light blue. The state flag (proportions 3 by 2) has the same design with, in addition, a gold 'Sun of May' in the centre of the white stripe. The capital is Buenos Aires, but the transfer to a new capital at the twin towns of Viedma-Carmen de Patagones is expected to be completed by 1995.

Recent History

In 1916 Hipólito Yrigoyen, a member of the reformist Unión Cívica Radical (UCR), became Argentina's first President to be freely elected by direct popular vote. He remained in office until 1922, when another UCR politician became President. In 1928 Yrigoyen was elected for a second term, but in 1930 he was overthrown by an army coup, and the country's first military regime was established. Civilian rule was restored in 1932. Conservative politicians and landowners held power from then until June 1943, when another coup took place. Military rule was imposed until 1946.

A leading figure in the military regime was Col (later Lt-Gen.) Juan Domingo Perón Sosa, who became Secretary for Labour and Social Welfare in November 1943. In this post, he promoted labour reforms and encouraged unionization. Subsequently, Col Perón also became Vice-President and Minister of War, but in October 1945 he was forced to resign all his posts. This led to popular protests and demonstrations. Perón won a presidential election in February 1946, and took office in June. The new Government extended the franchise to women in 1947. President Perón founded the Peronista party in 1948, and was re-elected in November 1951. His position was greatly enhanced by the popularity, particularly among industrial workers and their families, of his second wife, Eva ('Evita') Duarte de Perón, who died, aged 33, in July 1952. As President, Gen. Perón pursued a policy of extreme nationalism and social improvement. In 1954, however, his measures of secularization and the legalization of divorce brought him into conflict with the Roman Catholic Church. In September 1955 President Perón was deposed by a revolt of the armed forces. He went into exile, eventually settling in Spain, from where he continued to direct the Peronist movement.

Following the overthrow of Gen. Perón, Argentina entered a lengthy period of political instability. A provisional government that took power after the coup was replaced in November 1955 by a military junta, with Gen. Pedro Aramburu, the Chief of General Staff, as President. Congressional and presidential elections were held in February 1958. The presidential election was won by Dr Arturo Frondizi, a left-wing Radical, who took office in May. His party, the UCR Intransigente (UCRI), won large majorities in both chambers of Congress. In March 1962, following Peronist successes in national and provincial elections, President Frondizi was deposed by a military coup. He was replaced by Dr José María Guido, hitherto the President of the Senate, who resigned from the UCRI as a result of criticism from party members. The next presidential election, in July 1963, was won by another Radical, Dr Arturo Illía, who took office in October. However, President Illía was overthrown by a coup in June 1966. Power was assumed by a military junta, led by Lt-Gen. Juan Carlos Onganía, a former Commander-in-Chief of the Army. The legislature was closed, and political parties were banned. In May 1970 Gen. Aramburu, the former President, was abducted by members of the Montoneros, a guerrilla group of left-wing Peronist sympathizers. In June he was killed by his captors. Later that month, President Onganía was deposed by his military colleagues, and a junta of the three armed forces' leaders took power. The junta appointed Brig.-Gen. Roberto Levingston, a former Minister of Defence, to be President. In March 1971, however, President Levingston was overthrown by the junta, which nominated one of its members, Lt-Gen. Alejandro Lanusse (Commander-in-Chief of the Army since October 1968), to be President. Urban guerrilla groups intensified their activities in 1971 and 1972.

Congressional and presidential elections were held in March 1973. The Frente Justicialista de Liberación, a Peronist coalition, won control of the National Congress, while the presidential election was won by the party's candidate, Dr Héctor Cámpora, who took office in May. However, President Cámpora resigned in July, to enable the holding of a fresh presidential election which Gen. Perón, who had returned to Argentina in June (after nearly 18 years in exile), would be eligible to contest. This election, in September 1973, returned the former President to power, with more than 60% of the votes. He took office in October, with his third wife, María Estela ('Isabelita') Martínez de Perón, as Vice-President.

General Perón died in July 1974 and was succeeded as President by his widow. The Government's economic austerity programme and the soaring rate of inflation caused widespread strikes and dissension among industrial workers. This increasingly chaotic situation resulted in demands for the resignation of President Perón. In March 1976 the armed forces, led by Lt-Gen. Jorge Videla (Commander of the Army), overthrew the President and installed a three-man junta: Gen. Videla was sworn in as President. The junta made substantial alterations to the Constitution, dissolved Congress, suspended all political and trade union activity and removed most government officials from their posts. Several hundred people were arrested, while Señora Perón was detained and later went into exile.

The new military regime launched a successful, although ferocious, offensive against left-wing guerrillas and opposition forces, and reintroduced the death penalty for abduction, subversion and terrorism. The imprisonment, torture and murder of many people who were suspected of left-wing political activity by the armed forces provoked protests over violations of human rights, from within Argentina and from abroad. The number of people who 'disappeared' after the coup was estimated to be between 6,000 and 15,000. Repression eased in 1978, after all armed opposition had been eliminated.

In May 1978 the junta confirmed President Videla in office until March 1981. In August 1978 he retired from the army and ceased to be part of the junta. In March 1981 Gen. Roberto Viola, a former member of the junta, succeeded President Videla and promised to extend the dialogue with the political parties as a prelude to an eventual return to democracy. After suffering a heart attack, he was replaced in December by Lt-Gen. Leopoldo Galtieri, the Commander-in-Chief of the Army, who attempted to cultivate popular support by continuing the process of political liberalization which had been initiated by his predecessor.

To distract attention from the unstable domestic situation, and following unsuccessful negotiations with the UK in February over Argentina's long-standing sovereignty claim, President Galtieri ordered the invasion of the Falkland Islands (Islas Malvinas) in April 1982 (see chapter on the Falkland

Islands, Vol. II). The UK recovered the islands after a short conflict, in the course of which about 750 Argentine lives were lost. Argentine forces surrendered in June 1982, but no formal cessation of hostilities was declared until October 1989. The defeat brought about the final humiliation of the armed forces: Galtieri was forced to resign, and the rest of the junta were replaced. The army, under the control of Lt-Gen. Cristino Nicolaides, installed a retired general, Reynaldo Bignone, as President in July 1982. The armed forces were held responsible for the disastrous economic situation, and, unable to resolve the crisis, were forced to move rapidly towards the transfer of power to a civilian government. Moreover, in 1983 a Military Commission of Inquiry into the war concluded in its report that the main responsibility for Argentina's defeat lay with members of the former junta, who were recommended for trial. Galtieri was given a prison sentence, while several other officers were put on trial for corruption, murder and insulting the honour of the armed forces. Meanwhile, in August 1983 the regime approved the Ley de Pacificación Nacional, an amnesty law which granted retrospective immunity to the police, the armed forces and others for political crimes that had been committed over the previous 10 years.

In February 1983 the Government announced that general and presidential elections would be held on 30 October. In April the ban on 'Isabelita' Perón and 25 former government and trade union officials was lifted. Señora Perón was retained as titular head of the Peronist party, the Partido Justicialista, but remained in Spain. The other main party, the UCR, which was supported by some socialist and some conservative groups, announced its candidate, Dr Raúl Alfonsín, in July. At the elections, the UCR succeeded in attracting the votes of many former Peronist supporters. It won 317 of the 600 seats in the presidential electoral college, and 129 of the 254 seats in the Chamber of Deputies, although the Peronists won a narrow majority of provincial governorships. Dr Alfonsín took office as President on 10 December.

Shortly after taking office, President Alfonsín announced a radical reform of the armed forces, which led to the immediate retirement of more than one-half of the military high command. In addition, he repealed the Ley de Pacificación Nacional and ordered the court martial of the first three military juntas to rule Argentina after the coup of 1976, for offences including abduction, torture and murder. Public opposition to the former military regime was strengthened by the discovery and exhumation of hundreds of bodies from unmarked graves throughout the country. It was believed that between 15,000 and 30,000 people had disappeared during the so-called 'dirty war' between the former military regime and its opponents from 1976 until 1983. In December the Government announced the formation of the National Commission on the Disappearance of Persons (CONADEP) to investigate the events of the 'dirty war'. A report by CONADEP, published in September 1984, gave details of 8,960 people who had disappeared during the 'dirty war' and implicated 1,300 officers of the armed forces in the campaign of repression and violence. In October President Alfonsín announced that the court martial of the former leaders would be transferred to the civilian Federal Court of Appeal.

The trial of the former leaders began in April 1985. Several hundred prosecution witnesses gave testimonies which revealed the systematic atrocities and the campaign of terror perpetrated by the former military leaders. The verdicts on the nine accused officers were announced in December 1985. Four of the accused were acquitted, but sentences were passed on the remaining five, including sentences of life imprisonment for two former junta members, Gen. Videla and Adm. Eduardo Massera.

The court martial of the members of the junta which had held power during the Falklands war was conducted concurrently with the trial of the former military leaders. In May 1986 all three members of that junta were found guilty of negligence and received prison sentences, including a term of 12 years for Galtieri. In July 1988 consideration of an appeal by Galtieri and five other military leaders against their sentences began at the civilian Federal Court of Appeals. In October 1988 the Court announced its decision to uphold the sentence against Galtieri, but in October 1989 he was pardoned, along with two other senior military leaders (see below).

Public approval of the Government's policies was reflected in the results of the national and local elections in November 1985. At the elections for one-half of the seats in the Chamber of Deputies, the UCR received 43.5% of the votes and increased its strength by one seat. In January 1986 President Alfonsín announced the formation of an 18-member advisory body, the Consejo para la Consolidación de la Democracia, which was to advise the Government on the proposed reform of the Constitution. In September 1988, however, Alfonsín reluctantly announced the postponement of such a measure, having failed to secure any consensus with the other political parties on this issue.

In May 1986 the President announced plans to transfer the capital of Argentina from Buenos Aires to the twin towns of Viedma-Carmen de Patagones, about 750 km south of the present capital. The announcement aroused considerable controversy, principally because such a move was expected to cost in excess of US $3,000m. A further conflict developed with the Roman Catholic Church over the administration's plans to legalize divorce, which had been overwhelmingly approved by the Chamber of Deputies in August. Following some amendment, the legislation was eventually approved in June 1987.

In late 1986 the Government sought approval for the Punto Final ('Full Stop') Law, whereby civil and military courts were to begin new judicial proceedings against members of the armed forces accused of violations of human rights within a 60-day period, ending on 22 February 1987. The legislation provoked widespread opposition but was, nevertheless, approved by the Senate in December. In early 1987 Adm. Ramón Arosa, the Navy Chief of Staff, warned the Government that more trials of military personnel would further undermine military morale. His warning was seemingly vindicated when, in April, a series of rebellions broke out at army garrisons throughout the country. The most serious insurrection occurred at the Campo Mayo base and involved more than 100 middle-ranking officers, who proclaimed their opposition to the Government's policy on the prosecution of members of the armed forces, and demanded a general amnesty and changes in the high command. Although the rebellions were resolved without incident, many observers considered that the President had made significant concessions to the rebel officers, a view supported by the Government's disclosure, in May, of new legislation governing violations of human rights, known as the Obediencia Debida ('Due Obedience') Law. Under the legislation, an amnesty was to be declared for all members of the armed forces below the rank of colonel. By June the legislation had been approved by the Senate and the Supreme Court, and had been extended to absolve all military and police officers holding the rank of Brigadier-General. Therefore, under the new law, of the 350–370 officers hitherto due to face prosecution for violations of human rights, only 30–50 senior officers were now to be tried.

The legislation provoked great controversy, and was a decisive factor in the ruling party's appeal to voters at the gubernatorial and legislative elections of 6 September 1987, when voting was held for 127 seats in the Chamber of Deputies, 22 provincial governorships, more than 700 provincial legislative seats and more than 10,000 municipal posts. The Partido Justicialista made significant gains, while the UCR suffered an unexpected and severe defeat, losing its overall majority in the lower house and five of the seven provincial governorships that it had previously held, including the key governorship of Buenos Aires province.

The UCR's defeat was also attributed to its imposition, in July 1987, of an unpopular programme of strict austerity measures. Following the elections, however, further stringent measures were introduced to reverse the economic decline, which immediately led to protests by the powerful trade union, the Confederación General del Trabajo (CGT). Since 1984 the CGT had held a series of general strikes in protest at the Government's economic policy, and two further strikes were organized in early November and December, leaving the Government's plans for a 'Pacto de Garantías', a new social and economic accord with the trade unions and Peronists, in jeopardy.

In January 1988 Lt-Col Aldo Rico, a prominent figure in the insurrection of April 1987 (see above), led a rebellion at the garrison town of Monte Caseros, and in December of the same year, at the Villa Martelli munitions depot near Buenos Aires, another revolt took place, under the leadership of a right-wing nationalist officer, Col Mohamed Alí Seineldín, with the support of some 850 followers. Both insurrections were swiftly suppressed. In both incidents, the rebel military factions demanded higher salaries for soldiers, an increase in the military budget and some form of amnesty for officers awaiting trial for violations of human rights during the 'dirty war'. The insurgents insisted that both public and governmental recognition of the justifiable necessity of certain military actions during the 'dirty war' was vital to the restoration of the honour and morale of the armed forces.

In January 1989 the army quickly repelled an attack by 40 left-wing activists on a military base at La Tablada, 25 km west of Buenos Aires, in which 39 lives were lost. Many of the guerrilla band were identified as members of the Movimiento Todos por la Patria. While Alfonsín publicly congratulated the military on its swift suppression of the uprising, opposition groups (including the Peronist presidential candidate, Carlos Saúl Menem of the Partido Justicialista) accused government and military bodies of having deliberately provoked the attack in an attempt to discredit all opposition factions. In January the National Security Council was established to co-ordinate 'a new fight against subversion', and in March the Internal Security Committee was established, providing for legal military intervention in domestic conflicts if police and security forces were overwhelmed.

In the campaign for the May 1989 elections, Menem headed the Frente Justicialista de Unidad Popular (FREJUPO) electoral alliance, comprising the Partido Justicialista, the Partido Demócrata Cristiano (PDC) and the Partido Intransigente (PI). He sought to attract the popular vote with his flamboyant style and the promise of a 'production revolution', to be based on wage increases and significant aid to industry. On 14 May the Peronists were guaranteed a return to power after a 13-year absence, having secured, together with the two other members of the FREJUPO alliance, 48.5% of the votes cast in the presidential election and 310 of the 600 seats in the electoral college. The Peronists were also victorious in the election for 127 seats (one-half of the total) in the Chamber of Deputies, winning 45% of the votes and 66 seats, in contrast to the 29% (41 seats) obtained by the UCR.

The breakdown of attempts by the retiring and incoming administrations to collaborate, and the reluctance of the Alfonsín administration to continue in office with the prospect of further economic embarrassment, left the nation in a political vacuum. Menem was due to take office on 10 December 1989, but the worsening economic situation which compelled Alfonsín to introduce a 'war economy', to appoint a crisis Cabinet and to declare a 30-day state of siege after several people were killed and 800 arrested during food riots, looting and bombings in several Argentine cities, forced him to resign five months earlier than scheduled. Menem took office on 8 July.

Rumours of a possible amnesty for imprisoned officers and others still awaiting trial, encouraged by suspicions that such an offer had been made to the armed forces in return for electoral support, led to the biggest ever demonstration for human rights in Argentina in September 1989, when more than 100,000 people gathered in Buenos Aires. In October, however, the Government issued Decrees 1003, 1004 and 1005, whereby 210 officers, NCOs and soldiers involved in the 'dirty war', the governing junta during the Falklands War and leaders of three recent military uprisings (including Lt-Col Aldo Rico and Col Mohamed Alí Seineldín) were pardoned.

Economic affairs dominated the latter half of 1989 and much of 1990. The Minister of the Economy, Nestór Rapanelli, introduced several measures, including the devaluation of the austral, but these failed to reverse the trend towards hyperinflation, and Rapanelli resigned in December 1989. His successor, Antonio Ermán González, introduced a comprehensive plan for economic readjustment, incorporating the expansion of existing plans for the transfer to private ownership of many state-owned companies (including ENTel, the state telecommunications company, and Aerolíneas Argentinas, a state-owned airline, both of which were acquired by consortia headed by Spanish companies in 1990), the rationalization of government-controlled bodies, and the restructuring of the nation's financial systems. Four further adjustments were made to González's economic programme during 1990. In each case, restrictions on government spending were intensified, and non-profit-making concerns were rationalized (often leading to forced retirement or temporary redundancy for thousands of employees) or offered for transfer to private ownership. Following the dismissal or resignation of a succession of Governors of the Central Bank, González appointed himself to the post and assumed almost total control of the country's financial structure. In an attempt to attain economic targets that the Treasury had guaranteed as a condition for securing disbursements from the IMF, the Government raised charges for public utilities, transport and fuel, so as to increase revenues.

Public disaffection with the Government's economic policy was widespread. Failure to contain the threat of hyperinflation led to a loss in purchasing power, and small-scale food riots and looting became more frequent. The Government's rationalization programme proved, predictably, unpopular with public-sector employees, and industrial action and demonstrations, organized from within the sector with the backing of trades unions, political opposition parties and human rights organizations, were well supported. Attempts to declare one-day general strikes, however, were only partially successful. In October 1990, following its failure to gain support as a congressional bill, legislation limiting the right to strike of workers employed in essential services was proclaimed as a presidential decree. Opposition to González's economic readjustment programme, however, was by no means universal. In response to a request from President Menem for a 'marcha del Sí' some 80,000 government supporters gathered in Buenos Aires in April 1990 to demonstrate their approval of government policy.

Despite attempts by President Menem to gain the support of dissident trade unionists by appointing them to newly-created government commissions, divisions within the CGT between supporters and opponents of the Government's economic policy in general, and wage restraint and potential unemployment in particular, were physically realized in 1990, when both factions (the pro-Government CGT-San Martín, headed by Guerino Andreoni, and the anti-Government CGT-Azopardo, headed by Saúl Ubaldini) received legal recognition.

Attempts by President Menem to consolidate the Government's position had failed earlier in 1990, and divisions within the Peronists themselves became increasingly apparent. Eight dissident Peronist deputies accused Menem of allying himself to traditional enemies of the Peronist movement, and published an alternative economic programme advocating a return to a system of state regulation of the market. Antonio Cafiero, Governor of the province of Buenos Aires and one of Menem's most vociferous critics, resigned from the post of chairman of the Partido Justicialista following the defeat of proposals for constitutional reform in the province, advocated by Cafiero, at a referendum held in August 1990. Although Menem had supported the proposals for constitutional reform, Cafiero's defeat allowed Menem to assume the chairmanship of the party and to gain a dominant position in a contest which had threatened to divide Peronist supporters into 'menemista' and 'cafierista' factions early in the year.

In August 1990, following a formal declaration by the PI and the PDC of their intention to leave the 1989 (FREJUPO) alliance, Menem announced his readiness to enter into electoral alliances with centre-right parties for congressional elections due to be held in 1991. It was also understood that the President planned to seek constitutional reform, at a national level, as part of the electoral campaign for 1991.

Widespread public concern at the apparent impunity of military personnel increased following President Menem's suggestion that a further military amnesty would be granted before the end of 1990, and was exacerbated by rumours of escalating military unrest (which were realized in December 1990 when 200–300 rebel soldiers staged a swiftly-suppressed uprising at the Patricios infantry garrison in Buenos Aires). Meanwhile, Menem sought to renew public confidence in the armed forces by encouraging military participation in the Independence Day parade and the unpopular decision to dispatch two warships and a small contingent of military personnel to the Persian Gulf to support the imposition of trade sanctions against Iraq, recommended by the UN following the forcible annexation of Kuwait by Iraq in August 1990.

In May 1985 a treaty was formally ratified by representatives of the Argentine and Chilean Governments, concluding the territorial dispute over three small islands in the Beagle Channel, south of Tierra del Fuego. The islands were awarded to Chile, while Argentine rights to petroleum and other minerals in the disputed waters were guaranteed.

Full diplomatic relations were restored with the UK in February 1990, following three days of high-level negotiations in Madrid. Trade and communications restrictions, which had been in force since the conflict over the Falkland Islands in 1982 (including the 150-mile military protection zone around the islands), were expected to be relaxed or removed com-

ARGENTINA

pletely during 1990. The question of sovereignty over the disputed islands, however, was not resolved. Following the improvement in relations between Argentina and the UK, the EEC signed a new five-year trade and co-operation agreement with Argentina in April 1990.

The Government hoped to continue the attempt to improve Argentina's international trading position, initiated by the Alfonsín administration, through integration and co-operation policies agreed with neighbouring Latin American countries in 1988–90, and a strengthening of trading links with the USSR, Peru, Canada and Syria in 1989.

Government

Argentina comprises a Federal District, 23 provinces and the National Territory of Tierra del Fuego.

Legislative power is vested in the bicameral Congress: the Chamber of Deputies has 254 members, elected by universal adult suffrage for a term of four years (with one-half of the seats renewable every two years), while the Senate has 46 members, nominated by provincial legislatures for a term of nine years (with one-third of the seats renewable every three years). Executive power is vested in the President, elected by an electoral college for a six-year term. Each province has its own elected Governor and legislature, concerned with all matters not delegated to the Federal Government.

Defence

A period of national service is compulsory for men between the ages of 18 and 45 years. The length of service is 6–12 months in the army, 12 months in the air force or 14 months in the navy; some conscripts may serve less. The total strength of the regular armed forces in June 1990 was 75,000 (including an estimated 16,000 conscripts), of which the army had 40,000 with a further 250,000 trained reservists, the navy had 20,000 and the air force 15,000 men. There were also paramilitary forces numbering 15,000 men. Defence expenditure for 1990 was estimated to be 381,534m. australes.

Economic Affairs

In 1988, according to estimates by the World Bank, Argentina's gross national product (GNP), measured at average 1986–88 prices, was US $83,040m., equivalent to $2,640 per head. During 1980–88, it was estimated, GNP decreased, in real terms, at an average annual rate of 0.3%, and GNP per head declined by 1.6% per year. Over the same period, Argentina's population increased by an annual average of 1.4%, while gross domestic product (GDP) decreased, in real terms, by an annual average of 0.2%.

Agriculture (including forestry and fishing) contributed 13% of GDP (at current prices) in 1987. About 11% of the labour force were employed in agriculture in 1987. The principal cash crops are wheat, maize, sorghum and soybeans. Beef production is also important. During 1980–88 agricultural production increased by an annual average of 1.4%.

Industry (including mining, manufacturing, construction and power) contributed 43% of GDP in 1987. During 1980–88 industrial production decreased by an annual average of 0.8%.

Mining contributed 2.4% of GDP in 1987, and employed 0.5% of the labour force in 1980. Argentina has substantial deposits of petroleum and natural gas, as well as steam coal and lignite.

Manufacturing contributed 31% of GDP in 1987, and employed 20% of the labour force in 1980. The most important sectors, measured by gross value of output, are food-processing, machinery and transport equipment, chemicals and textiles. During 1986–88 manufacturing output decreased by an annual average of 0.2%.

Energy is derived principally from hydroelectric power (43.8% in 1987) and coal. As much as 15% of Argentina's electricity can be produced by its two nuclear power stations. Imports of mineral fuels comprised 11.4% of the cost of total imports in 1987.

In 1989 Argentina recorded a visible trade surplus of US $5,709m., but there was a deficit of $1,292m. on the current account of the balance of payments. In 1987 the principal source of imports (16%) was the USA, which was also the principal market for exports (14%). Other major trading partners are Brazil and the USSR. The principal exports in 1987 were prepared animal fodder, cereals and fats and oils. The principal imports were machinery and chemical and mineral products.

In mid-1989 the projected budget deficit for that year was estimated to be equivalent to some 15% of GDP. Argentina's total external public debt was US $48,166m. at the end of 1988, and was expected to reach $64,000m. by the end of 1989. In 1988 the cost of debt-servicing exceeded 32% of revenue from exports of goods and services. The annual rate of inflation averaged 3,079% in 1989 and was 1,838% in the 12-month period to October 1990. An estimated 5.2% of the labour force were unemployed in 1987.

During 1986–90 Argentina signed a series of integration treaties with neighbouring Latin American countries, aimed at increasing bilateral trade and establishing the basis for a Latin American economic community. Argentina is a member of ALADI (see p. 172).

During the 1980s the cereal and beef sectors were adversely affected by intense competition from sales of subsidized produce by other countries. Massive external debt obligations and a scarcity of raw materials damaged industry. The temporary cessation of interest payments on foreign debts in April 1988, and the failure to fulfil economic stipulations attached to loans from the IMF and the World Bank, restricted Argentine access to further significant financial aid. In September 1989, however, the IMF, recognizing the success of the austerity measures, adopted under the new Menem administration, and approving the extensive privatization plans, signed a letter of intent to guarantee a stand-by loan of US $1,400m. By November 1990, however, disbursements had been suspended on three occasions, owing to the Government's failure to stem burgeoning inflation. In June 1990, following a 26-month moratorium, Argentina resumed interest payments on outstanding debt with a modest repayment plan of US $40m. per month.

Social Welfare

Social welfare benefits comprise three categories: retirement, disability and survivors' pensions; family allowances; and health insurance. The first is administered by the Subsecretaría de Seguridad Social (part of the Ministry of Labour and Social Security) and funded by compulsory contributions from all workers, employed and self-employed, over 18 years of age. The second is supervised by the Subsecretaría and funded by employers. The third is administered by means of public funds and may be provided only by authorized public institutions. Work insurance is the responsibility of the employer. Of total expenditure by the central Government in 1987, ₳754m. (2.1%) was for health services, and a further ₳11,257m. (31.2%) for social security and welfare. Government expenditure on social welfare in 1990 was expected to total ₳622,406m.

In September 1990, owing to persistently high inflation, the minimum monthly salary for employees was increased from ₳20,000 to ₳720,000.

In 1975 there were 48,693 physicians working in Argentina, equivalent to one for every 530 inhabitants: the best doctor-patient ratio of any country in Latin America.

Education

Education from pre-school to university level is available free of charge. Education is officially compulsory for all children at primary level, between the ages of six and 14 years. Secondary education lasts for between four and six years, depending on the type of course: the normal certificate of education (bachillerato) course lasts for five years, whereas a course leading to a commercial bachillerato may last for four or five years, and one leading to a technical or agricultural bachillerato lasts for six years. The total enrolment at primary and secondary schools in 1987 was equivalent to 96% of the school-age population. Non-university higher education, usually leading to a teaching qualification, is for three or four years, while university courses last for four years or more. There are 29 state universities and 23 private universities. Government expenditure on education and culture for 1990 was budgeted at ₳303,973m.

According to estimates by UNESCO, the average rate of adult illiteracy in 1985 was only 4.5%.

Public Holidays

1991: 1 January (New Year's Day), 29 March (Good Friday), 1 May (Labour Day), 25 May (Anniversary of the 1810 Revolution), 10 June (Occupation of the Islas Malvinas), 20 June (Flag Day), 10 July (Independence Day), 17 August (Death of Gen. José de San Martín), 12 October (Discovery of America), 25 December (Christmas).

ARGENTINA

1992: 1 January (New Year's Day), 17 April (Good Friday), 1 May (Labour Day), 25 May (Anniversary of the 1810 Revolution), 10 June (Occupation of the Islas Malvinas), 20 June (Flag Day), 10 July (Independence Day), 17 August (Death of Gen. José de San Martín), 12 October (Discovery of America), 25 December (Christmas).

Weights and Measures
The metric system is in force.

Statistical Survey

Sources (unless otherwise stated): Instituto Nacional de Estadística y Censos, Hipólito Yrigoyen 250, 12°, Of. 1210, 1310 Buenos Aires; tel. (1) 33-7872; telex 21952; and Banco Central de la República Argentina, Reconquista 266, 1003 Buenos Aires; tel. (1) 394-8111; telex 1137; fax (1) 334-5712.

Area and Population

AREA, POPULATION AND DENSITY

Area (sq km)	2,766,889*
Population (census results)†	
30 September 1970	23,362,204
22 October 1980	
Males	13,755,983
Females	14,191,463
Total	27,947,446
Population (official estimates at mid-year)	
1987	31,137,301
1988	31,534,098
1989	31,928,519
Density (per sq km) at mid-1989	11.5

* 1,068,302 sq miles. The figure excludes the Falkland Islands (Islas Malvinas) and Antarctic territory claimed by Argentina.
† Figures exclude adjustment for underenumeration, estimated to have been 1% at the 1980 census.

PROVINCES (estimates at mid-1989)

	Population	Capital
Buenos Aires—Federal District	2,900,794	
Buenos Aires—Province	12,604,018	La Plata
Catamarca	232,523	Catamarca
Córdoba	2,748,006	Córdoba
Corrientes	748,834	Corrientes
Chaco	824,447	Resistencia
Chubut	327,780	Rawson
Entre Ríos	1,005,885	Paraná
Formosa	354,512	Formosa
Jujuy	502,694	Jujuy
La Pampa	237,386	Santa Rosa
La Rioja	191,468	La Rioja
Mendoza	1,387,914	Mendoza
Misiones	723,839	Posadas
Neuquén	326,313	Neuquén
Río Negro	466,713	Viedma
Salta	822,378	Salta
San Juan	528,838	San Juan
San Luis	246,087	San Luis
Santa Cruz	147,928	Río Gallegos
Santa Fé	2,765,678	Santa Fé
Santiago del Estero	641,273	Santiago del Estero
Tucumán	1,134,309	San Miguel de Tucumán
Territory		
Tierra del Fuego	58,881	Ushuaia

Source: Ministerio de Salud y Acción Social.

PRINCIPAL TOWNS (estimated population at mid-1985)

Buenos Aires (capital)	10,728,000*		San Juan	324,000*
Córdoba	1,055,000*		Santa Fé	310,000
Rosario	1,016,000*		Salta	302,000
Mendoza	668,000*		Resistencia	262,000*
La Plata	611,000*		Bahía Blanca	242,000*
San Miguel de Tucumán	571,000*		Corrientes	197,000
			Posadas	191,000
Mar del Plata	448,000		Paraná	178,000
			Santiago del Estero	172,000

* Including suburbs.

Source: UN, *Demographic Yearbook*.

BIRTHS AND DEATHS

	Registered live births		Registered deaths	
	Number	Rate (per 1,000)	Number	Rate (per 1,000)
1982	663,429	22.8	233,071	8.0
1983	655,876	22.1	251,301	8.5
1984	635,323	21.2	255,591	8.5
1985	650,873	21.5	241,377	7.9
1986	n.a.	n.a.	n.a.	n.a.
1987	662,871	21.1	250,226	7.9
1988	653,576	20.7	263,655	8.4

Marriages: 177,010 (marriage rate 6.0 per 1,000) in 1983.

Source: UN, *Demographic Yearbook* and *Population and Vital Statistics Report*.

ECONOMICALLY ACTIVE POPULATION*
(persons aged 14 years and over, census of 22 October 1980)

	Males	Females	Total
Agriculture, hunting, forestry and fishing	1,123,138	77,854	1,200,992
Mining and quarrying	44,194	2,977	47,171
Manufacturing	1,566,028	429,967	1,985,995
Electricity, gas and water	94,789	8,467	103,256
Construction	981,251	21,924	1,003,175
Wholesale and retail trade, restaurants and hotels	1,221,063	481,017	1,702,080
Transport, storage and communication	424,671	35,805	460,476
Finance, insurance, real estate and business services	265,475	130,229	395,704
Community, social and personal services	1,044,416	1,354,623	2,399,039
Activities not adequately described	494,678	196,624	691,302
Total labour force	7,249,703	2,739,487	9,989,190

* Figures exclude persons seeking work for the first time, totalling 44,608 (males 28,331; females 16,277).

Source: ILO, *Year Book of Labour Statistics*.

Mid-1987 (official estimates): Total labour force 11,793,000 (males 8,609,000; females 3,184,000).

ARGENTINA

Agriculture

PRINCIPAL CROPS ('000 metric tons)

	1986	1987	1988
Wheat	8,700	9,000*	7,769*
Rice (paddy)	439	371	383
Barley	133	282	266
Maize	12,100	9,250	9,200
Rye	60	88	41
Oats	495	718	620
Millet	107	80	50
Sorghum	4,061	3,040	3,200
Potatoes	2,022	2,150†	2,190†
Sweet potatoes	409	415†	420†
Cassava (Manioc)†	157	160†	160†
Soybeans	7,100	7,000	9,830
Groundnuts (in shell)	379	500	443
Sunflower seed	4,340	2,250	2,915
Linseed	622	590	535
Seed cotton	377	323	849
Cotton Lint	120	100	282
Tomatoes	824	800†	780†
Onions (dry)†	290†	280†	280†
Grapes	2,411	3,689	3,304
Sugar cane	15,465	14,479	14,773
Tea (green)	41	45	32
Tobacco (leaves)	66	70*	74*

* Estimate. † FAO estimate.
Source: FAO, *Production Yearbook*.

LIVESTOCK ('000 head, year ending September)

	1986	1987	1988
Horses*	3,000	3,000	3,100†
Cattle*	53,480	51,683	50,782
Pigs*	4,000	4,100†	4,100†
Sheep*	29,243	28,998	29,202
Goats†	3,100	3,100	3,200

* Estimate. † FAO estimate.

Chickens (million, FAO estimates): 47 in 1986; 53 in 1987; 55 in 1988.
Ducks (million, FAO estimates): 2 in 1986; 2 in 1987; 2 in 1988.
Turkeys (million, FAO estimates): 3 in 1986; 3 in 1987; 3 in 1988.
Source: FAO, *Production Yearbook*.

LIVESTOCK PRODUCTS ('000 metric tons)

	1986	1987	1988
Beef and veal	2,779	2,680*	2,650*
Mutton and lamb*	90†	82	83
Goats' meat†	6	6	6
Pig meat†	210	220	224
Horse meat†	51	51	52
Poultry meat	382	424	434
Cows' milk	6,118	6,582*	6,450*
Butter	32	34	33*
Cheese	261	277	279
Hen eggs†	279	285	293
Wool:			
greasy*	138	136	138†
scoured*	92	91	92†
Cattle hides (fresh)†	414	384	360

* Estimate. † FAO estimate.
Source: FAO, *Production Yearbook*.

Forestry

ROUNDWOOD REMOVALS ('000 cubic metres, excl. bark)

	1984	1985	1986
Sawlogs, veneer logs and logs for sleepers	1,935	1,818	2,563
Pulpwood	3,043	3,168	3,584
Other industrial wood	436	314	340
Fuel wood	5,900	5,755	4,332
Total	11,314	11,055	10,819

1987–88: Annual output as in 1986 (FAO estimates).
Source: FAO, *Yearbook of Forest Products*.

SAWNWOOD PRODUCTION ('000 cubic metres, incl. boxboards)

	1984	1985	1986
Coniferous (soft wood)	175	146	150
Broadleaved (hard wood)	846	825	1,200
Total	1,021	971	1,350

Railway sleepers: 96,000 cubic metres per year in 1984–86.
1987–88: Annual production as in 1986 (FAO estimates).
Source: FAO, *Yearbook of Forest Products*.

Fishing

('000 metric tons, live weight)

	1985	1986	1987
Freshwater fishes	9.6	8.6	7.8
Argentine hake	259.3	270.6	314.2
Other marine fishes	102.8	119.4	181.0
Crustaceans	10.6	7.3	3.1
Argentine shortfin squid	21.5	12.5	51.1
Other molluscs	2.6	2.0	2.2
Total catch	406.4	420.4	559.4

Source: FAO, *Yearbook of Fishery Statistics*.

Mining

('000 metric tons, unless otherwise indicated)

	1985	1986	1987
Hard coal	400	365	373
Crude petroleum	23,607	22,283	21,999
Natural gas ('000 terajoules)	508.8	552.6	657.0
Iron ore*	389	514	360
Lead ore*	28.6	26.9	26.1
Zinc ore*	35.7	39.5	35.6
Tin concentrates (metric tons)*	451	379	186
Silver ore (metric tons)*	68	66	60
Uranium ore (metric tons)*	126	173	100

* Figures refer to the metal content of ores and concentrates.
Source: UN, mainly *Industrial Statistics Yearbook*.

1989: Crude petroleum 23.2m. metric tons; Natural gas 775,300 terajoules (Source: UN, *Monthly Bulletin of Statistics*).

ARGENTINA

Industry

SELECTED PRODUCTS
('000 metric tons, unless otherwise indicated)

	1985	1986	1987
Edible vegetable oils	1,435.5	1,565.1	1,169.3
Wheat flour	2,801.0	2,761.6	2,795.6
Sugar	1,099.2	1,052.3	n.a.
Beer and malt ('000 litres)	382,698	551,801	586,100
Cigarettes (metric tons)	31,092	32,112	29,745
Paper	690	799	817
Mechanical wood pulp	125	129	126
Chemical and semi-chemical pulp	458	501	504
Quebracho extract	62	n.a.	n.a.
Rayon and acetate continuous filaments (metric tons)	1,424	3,619	3,302
Non-cellulosic continuous filaments (metric tons)	20,106	33,644	30,550
Non-cellulosic discontinuous fibres (metric tons)	16,616	27,008	27,772
Sulphuric acid (metric tons)	235,454	250,840	253,046
Rubber tyres ('000)	5,664	7,489	7,222
Portland cement	4,693	5,558	6,302
Crude steel	2,775	3,147	n.a.
Ferro-alloys	59	n.a.	n.a.
Diesel oil ('000 cu metres)	1,031	962	991
Fuel oil ('000 cu metres)	6,126	5,736	5,047
Gas oil ('000 cu metres)	8,053	7,860	7,620
Kerosene ('000 cu metres)	518	514	398
Passenger motor vehicles (number)	119,733	147,063	157,120
Commercial motor vehicles (number)	21,365	28,835	39,782
Domestic sewing machines (number)	31,778*	n.a.	n.a.
Refrigerators and washing machines (number)	271,150	378,200	308,032
Television receivers (number)	599,255	800,975	695,187

* Provisional.

Finance

CURRENCY AND EXCHANGE RATES

Monetary Units:
100 centavos = 1 austral (₳).

Denominations:
Coins: 1, 5, 10 and 50 centavos.
Notes: 1, 5, 10, 50 and 100 australes.

Sterling and Dollar Equivalents (30 September 1990)
£1 sterling = 10,604.0 australes;
US $1 = 5,660.0 australes;
100,000 australes = £9.430 = $17.668.

Average Exchange Rate (australes per US $)
1987   2.14
1988   8.75
1989 423.34

Note: The austral was introduced on 15 June 1985, replacing the peso argentino at the rate of 1 austral = 1,000 pesos argentinos. The peso argentino, equal to 10,000 former pesos, had itself been introduced on 1 June 1983.

Statistical Survey

BUDGET (million australes)*

Revenue	1985	1986	1987
Taxation	7,484.5	13,756	29,584
Taxes on income, profits, etc.	406.0	945	2,762
Social security contributions	2,241.8	3,826	8,564
Taxes on property	403.1	1,022	2,176
Value-added tax	1,141.5	2,306	4,765
Excises	1,850.3	3,156	6,229
Other domestic taxes on goods and services	106.0	217	349
Import duties, etc.	328.6	817	2,207
Export duties	774.0	800	624
Foreign exchange conversion tax	51.7	87	207
Stamp duties	93.6	180	330
Other tax revenue	87.8	400	1,371
Property income	287.1	213	580
Administrative fees and charges, etc.	141.8	190	407
Other current revenue	371.7	1,017	1,860
Capital revenue	1.4	3	196
Total revenue	8,286.3	15,179	32,627

Expenditure†	1985	1986	1987
General public services	663.6‡	731	2,030
Defence	490.9	952	2,459
Public order and safety	n.a.‡	548	1,386
Education	566.3	965	2,458
Health	119.8	302	754
Social security and welfare	3,056.4	5,167	11,257
Housing and community amenities	39.4	65	113
Other community and social services	42.7	115	301
Economic services	1,730.4	2,902	6,275
General administration, regulation and research	226.9	148	189
Agriculture, forestry and fishing	65.7	150	456
Electricity, gas, steam and water	593.1	1,042	1,812
Roads	300.1	478	1,209
Inland and coastal waterways	27.8	67	177
Other transport and communications	451.1	700	1,629
Other purposes	2,333.1	4,512	9,100
Interest payments	1,076.8	1,246	2,862
Sub-total	9,042.5	16,259	36,133
Adjustment to cash basis	338.5	−264	−605
Total expenditure	9,381.0	15,995	35,528
Current	8,583.1	14,704	32,665
Capital	797.9	1,291	2,863

* Budget figures refer to the consolidated accounts of the central Government, including special accounts, government agencies and the national social security system. The budgets of provincial and municipal governments are excluded.
† Excluding net lending (million australes): 1,829.1 in 1985; 1,148 in 1986; 3,774 in 1987.
‡ For 1985, public order and safety are included in general public services.

Source: IMF, *Government Finance Statistics Yearbook*.

1988 (estimate, million australes): Revenue 83,050.4, Expenditure 116,052.9.

CENTRAL BANK RESERVES* (US $ million at 31 December)

	1987	1988	1989
Total	1,617	3,363	1,463

* Figures exclude reserves of gold, totalling 4,373,000 troy ounces in all three years. The national valuation of these gold reserves was US $1,421 million at 31 December each year.

Source: IMF, *International Financial Statistics*.

ARGENTINA

MONEY SUPPLY (million australes at 31 December)

	1986	1987	1988
Currency outside banks	3,989.6	9,261	43,186
Demand deposits at commercial banks	1,597.9	3,306	11,850

Source: IMF, *International Financial Statistics*.

COST OF LIVING
(Consumer Price Index for Buenos Aires. Base: 1974 = 100)

	1986	1987	1988
Food and drink	160,384,935	373,316,516	1,635,076,473
Clothing	61,744,792	128,392,652	544,209,115
Rent, fuel and light	123,690,853	283,004,584	1,300,319,174
Domestic goods	121,569,665	267,107,003	1,291,296,231
Medical services	241,943,993	560,741,029	2,098,193,589
Transport and communications	164,729,250	373,415,295	1,973,970,245
Education	172,298,388	400,644,832	1,632,529,439
Other goods and services	179,448,334	446,496,442	1,964,271,211
All items	149,510,306	345,863,652	1,532,020,416

NATIONAL ACCOUNTS (australes at constant 1970 prices)
Expenditure on the Gross Domestic Product

	1985	1986	1987
Final consumption expenditure	8,065	8,991	9,113
Increase in stocks	−124	−58	−20
Gross fixed capital formation	1,210	1,293	1,456
Total domestic expenditure	9,151	10,226	10,549
Exports of goods and services	1,671	1,536	1,509
Less Imports of goods and services	837	1,102	1,186
GDP in purchasers' values	9,986	10,660	10,872

Gross Domestic Product by Economic Activity (at factor cost)

	1985	1986	1987
Agriculture, forestry and fishing	1,407	1,379	1,423
Mining and quarrying	245	240	233
Manufacturing	2,035	2,297	2,265
Construction	308	309	357
Electricity, gas and water	418	449	476
Transport and communications	1,037	1,082	1,131
Trade, restaurants and hotels	1,128	1,370	1,392
Finance	693	741	768
Other services	1,579	1,575	1,587
Total	8,847	9,444	9,632

BALANCE OF PAYMENTS (US $ million)

	1987	1988	1989
Merchandise exports f.o.b.	6,360	9,134	9,573
Merchandise imports f.o.b.	−5,392	−4,900	−3,864
Trade balance	968	4,234	5,709
Exports of services	2,040	2,150	2,483
Imports of services	−7,239	−7,999	−9,492
Balance of goods and services	−4,231	−1,615	−1,300
Unrequited transfers (net)	−8	—	8
Current balance	−4,239	−1,615	−1,292
Direct capital investment (net)	−19	1,147	1,028
Other long-term capital (net)	199	−801	−2,527
Short-term capital (net)	−132	103	−4,784
Net errors and omissions	−217	−140	−313
Total (net monetary movements)	−4,408	−1,306	−7,888
Valuation changes	−297	64	26
Exceptional financing (net)	2,365	3,226	6,615
Official financing (net)	126	−62	−75
Changes in reserves	−2,213	1,922	−1,322

Source: IMF, *International Financial Statistics*.

External Trade

PRINCIPAL COMMODITIES (distribution by BTN, US $ '000)

Imports c.i.f.	1985	1986	1987
Vegetable products	124,229	245,402	176,275
Coffee, tea, maté, etc.	66,960	150,380	89,065
Mineral products	570,260	570,517	823,331
Metallurgical minerals, slag and cinder	85,735	105,514	112,931
Mineral fuels and oils, bituminous substances, etc.	460,430	423,416	664,812
Chemical products	798,876	1,036,154	1,040,014
Inorganic chemicals, compounds of precious metals, etc.	110,147	150,318	132,589
Organic chemicals and products	359,357	514,422	512,696
Artificial resins and plastics, natural and synthetic rubber, etc.	182,485	285,005	311,496
Artificial resins and plastics, cellulose, etc.	131,948	212,702	237,165
Paper-making material, paper and manufactures	74,748	123,231	141,815
Paper and paper products	50,218	85,480	103,402
Basic metals and manufactures	324,662	396,409	566,334
Iron and steel, and manufactures	228,680	254,967	388,884
Machinery and apparatus, incl. electrical	1,040,705	1,196,578	1,724,506
Boilers, machinery and mechanical appliances	693,546	701,356	1,055,760
Electrical machinery	347,159	495,222	668,746
Transport equipment	293,708	282,831	351,102
Land vehicles	239,388	272,288	319,327
Sea and river vehicles	27,356	3,189	19,260
Scientific and precision instruments, audiovisual equipment, etc.	157,333	224,408	287,992
Total (incl. others)	3,814,148	4,724,053	5,817,818

1988: Total imports US $5,321.6m.
1989: Total imports US $4,200.5m.

ARGENTINA

Exports f.o.b.	1985	1986	1987
Live animals and animal products	424,752	560,593	655,177
Meat and edible offal	223,834	285,509	336,858
Vegetable products	3,306,267	2,204,770	1,373,360
Edible fruits	137,387	138,247	168,147
Cereals	2,264,976	1,245,299	744,122
Oilseeds and nuts	725,205	646,882	334,207
Animal and vegetable fats and oils	992,825	656,425	546,111
Prepared foodstuffs, beverages and tobacco	855,126	1,169,047	1,336,714
Meat and fish preparations	162,807	180,897	265,513
Sugar and preserves	33,604	35,372	29,083
Residues and waste from food industry; prepared animal fodder	515,241	821,799	877,002
Chemical products	329,525	297,619	343,544
Hides, skins, furs, etc.	317,354	381,406	418,870
Hides and skins	288,945	340,715	358,178
Paper-making material, paper and manufactures	52,492	53,172	79,140
Textiles and manufactures	321,752	245,677	314,204
Wool and other animal hair	196,262	178,578	190,295
Cotton	108,923	36,039	76,312
Base metals and manufactures	508,117	474,163	532,083
Iron and steel and manufactures	357,770	343,234	377,160
Machinery and apparatus, incl. electrical	268,450	280,171	269,862
Boilers, machinery and mechanical appliances	211,324	231,289	223,535
Transport equipment	236,245	212,101	134,571
Land vehicles	94,802	122,221	119,133
Total (incl. others)	8,396,017	6,852,213	6,360,160

1988: Total exports US $9,134.8m.
1989: Total exports US $9,567.2m.

PRINCIPAL TRADING PARTNERS (US $ '000)

Imports c.i.f.	1985	1986	1987
Belgium	70,594	148,741	191,626
Bolivia	382,860	352,741	304,751
Brazil	611,521	691,298	819,234
Chile	84,409	148,585	152,501
Colombia	24,288	69,372	30,089
France	207,867	236,703	236,232
Germany, Federal Republic	404,001	523,375	765,655
Italy	233,880	239,469	371,533
Japan	265,580	336,618	441,470
Mexico	59,816	100,135	153,071
Netherlands	63,151	97,093	122,577
Paraguay	20,122	47,435	70,139
Peru	36,500	60,120	46,203
Spain	67,869	102,846	120,783
Sweden	35,956	51,133	73,088
Switzerland	103,307	92,221	112,850
USSR	41,876	59,170	90,471
USA	685,028	824,811	939,392
Uruguay	65,957	92,967	113,994
Total (incl. others)	3,814,148	4,724,053	5,817,818

Exports f.o.b.	1985	1986	1987
Algeria	28,031	84,503	21,614
Belgium	148,762	190,460	161,694
Bolivia	69,252	60,478	90,663
Brazil	496,297	698,070	539,335
Canada	58,752	53,852	76,545
Chile	111,050	136,780	145,916
China, People's Republic	311,004	252,053	265,575
Colombia	132,749	60,970	61,154
Cuba	283,408	181,784	133,641
Czechoslovakia	58,013	91,832	83,102
Egypt	143,675	90,843	38,239
France	122,179	102,924	128,126
Germany, Federal Republic	289,221	352,756	382,890
Iran	313,936	256,318	191,787
Italy	300,646	285,330	232,045
Japan	360,890	391,074	223,907
Mexico	255,472	158,356	37,285
Netherlands	856,348	735,825	617,912
Paraguay	72,236	67,443	60,883
Peru	161,968	189,125	139,094
Poland	98,197	100,749	18,543
Portugal	73,841	96,071	37,697
Spain	213,093	170,578	154,829
USSR	1,212,699	208,840	640,775
USA	1,003,560	677,917	897,624
Uruguay	99,017	129,322	168,419
Venezuela	72,846	44,804	56,816
Total (incl. others)	8,396,017	6,852,213	6,360,160

Transport

RAILWAYS (traffic)

	1985	1986	1987
Passengers carried (million)	300	359	352
Freight carried ('000 tons)	34,436	15,018	13,577
Passenger-km (million)	10,544	12,459	12,475
Freight ton-km (million)	18,981	8,761	7,952

ROAD TRAFFIC (motor vehicles in use at 31 December)

	1984	1985	1986
Passenger cars	3,685,000	3,773,600	3,898,000
Buses and coaches	56,000	57,300	59,700
Goods vehicles	1,332,000	1,338,700	1,375,000

Source: IRF, *World Road Statistics*.

SHIPPING (vessels entering Argentine ports)

	1986	1987	1988
Displacement ('000 net reg. tons)	31,026	17,844	29,912

Source: Administración General de Puertos.

CIVIL AVIATION (traffic)

	1985	1986	1987
Passengers carried ('000)	5,869	6,749	6,993
Freight carried (tons)	76,231	89,282	85,642
Kilometres flown ('000)	86,144	94,236	91,019

ARGENTINA

Tourism

FOREIGN VISITORS BY ORIGIN

	1986	1987	1988
North and South America	1,566,973	1,419,905	1,473,142
Europe	172,359	159,296	160,888
Asia, Africa and Oceania	36,151	45,078	46,136
Total	1,774,483	1,624,279	1,680,166

Source: Dirección Nacional de Migraciones.

Communications Media

	1983	1985	1987
Radio receivers ('000 in use)	16,000	20,000	20,500
Television receivers ('000 in use)	5,910	6,500	6,750
Telephones ('000 in use)*	2,518	2,580†	n.a.
Book production‡:			
Titles	4,216	n.a.	4,836
Copies ('000)	13,526	n.a.	n.a.
Daily newspapers	n.a.	188†	218§

* Source: Empresa Nacional de Telecomunicaciones.
† Figures refer to 1984.   ‡ Including pamphlets.
§ Figure refers to 1986.
1986: Book production 4,818 titles.
In 1989 there were an estimated 21.6m. radio receivers and 7.2m. television receivers in use.
Source: mainly UNESCO, *Statistical Yearbook*.

Education

(1985, provisional)

	Institutions	Students	Teachers
Pre-primary	8,015	693,259	36,287
Primary	26,275	4,811,736	254,970
Secondary	5,405	1,683,520	220,003
Universities*	462	664,200	44,038
Colleges of higher education*	912	181,945	26,661
Other	4,061	255,953	20,442

* Including faculties in other towns.
Source: Ministerio de Educación y Justicia.

Directory

Note: In June 1987 Congress approved a law to transfer the federal capital from Buenos Aires to the twin towns of Viedma-Carmen de Patagones. The transfer was expected to take place by 1995.

The Constitution

The return to civilian rule in 1983 represented a return to the principles of the 1853 Constitution, with some changes in electoral details. The Constitution is summarized below:

DECLARATIONS, RIGHTS AND GUARANTEES

Each province has the right to exercise its own administration of justice, municipal system and primary education. The Roman Catholic religion, being the faith of the majority of the nation, shall enjoy state protection; freedom of religious belief is guaranteed to all other denominations. All the inhabitants of the country have the right to work and exercise any legal trade; to petition the authorities; to leave or enter the Argentine territory; to use or dispose of their properties; to associate for a peaceable or useful purpose; to teach and acquire education, and to express freely their opinion in the press without censorship. The State does not admit any prerogative of blood, birth, privilege or titles of nobility. Equality is the basis of all duties and public offices. No citizens may be detained, except for reasons and in the manner prescribed by the law; or sentenced other than by virtue of a law existing prior to the offence and by decision of the competent tribunal after the hearing and defence of the person concerned. Private residence, property and correspondence are inviolable. No one may enter the home of a citizen or carry out any search in it without his consent, unless by a warrant from the competent authority; no one may suffer expropriation, except in case of public necessity and provided that the appropriate compensation has been paid in accordance with the provisions of the laws. In no case may the penalty of confiscation of property be imposed.

LEGISLATIVE POWER

Legislative power is vested in the bicameral Congress, comprising the Chamber of Deputies and the Senate. The Chamber of Deputies has 254 directly-elected members, chosen for four years and eligible for re-election; one-half of the membership of the Chamber shall be renewed every two years. The Senate has 46 members, chosen by provincial legislatures for a nine-year term, with one-third of the seats being renewed every three years.

The powers of Congress include regulating foreign trade; fixing import and export duties; levying taxes for a specified time whenever the defence, common safety or general welfare of the State so require; contracting loans on the nation's credit; regulating the internal and external debt and the currency system of the country; fixing the budget and providing for whatever is conducive to the prosperity and welfare of the nation. Congress also approves or rejects treaties, authorizes the Executive to declare war or make peace, and establishes the strength of the armed forces in peace and war.

EXECUTIVE POWER

Executive power is vested in the President, who is the supreme chief of the nation and handles the general administration of the country. The President issues the instructions and rulings necessary for the execution of the laws of the country, and himself takes part in drawing up and promulgating those laws. The President appoints, with the approval of the Senate, the judges of the Supreme Court and all other competent tribunals, ambassadors, civil servants, members of the judiciary and senior officers of the armed forces and bishops. The President may also appoint and remove, without reference to another body, his cabinet ministers. The President is Commander-in-Chief of all the armed forces.

JUDICIAL POWER

Judicial power is exercised by the Supreme Court and all other competent tribunals. The Supreme Court is responsible for the internal administration of all tribunals. In April 1990 the number of Supreme Court judges was increased from five to nine.

PROVINCIAL GOVERNMENT

The 22 provinces retain all the power not delegated to the Federal Government. They are governed by their own institutions and elect their own governors, legislators and officials.

ARGENTINA

The Government

HEAD OF STATE

President of the Republic: CARLOS SAÚL MENEM (took office 8 July 1989).

Vice-President: EDUARDO DUHALDE.

THE CABINET
(November 1990)

Minister of the Interior: JULIO MERA FIGUEROA.

Minister of Foreign Affairs and Worship: DOMINGO CAVALLO.

Minister of Education and Justice: ANTONIO FRANCISCO SALONIA.

Minister of National Defence: HUMBERTO ROMERO.

Minister of the Economy: ANTONIO ERMÁN GONZÁLEZ.

Minister of Labour and Social Security: ALBERTO JORGE TRIACA.

Minister of Public Health and Welfare: ALBERTO KOHAN.

Minister of Public Works and Services: JOSÉ ROBERTO DROMI.

Secretary-General to the Presidency: EDUARDO BAUZÁ.

MINISTRIES

General Secretariat to the Presidency: Balcarce 50, 1064 Buenos Aires; tel. (1) 46-9841.

Ministry of the Economy: Hipólito Yrigoyen 250, 1310 Buenos Aires; tel. (1) 34-6411; telex 21952.

Ministry of Education and Justice: Pizzurno 935, 1020 Buenos Aires; tel. (1) 42-4551; telex 22646.

Ministry of Foreign Affairs and Worship: Reconquista 1088, 1003 Buenos Aires; tel. (1) 311-0071; telex 21194.

Ministry of the Interior: Balcarce 24, 1064 Buenos Aires; tel. (1) 46-9841.

Ministry of Labour and Social Security: Avda Julio A. Roca 609, 1067 Buenos Aires; tel. (1) 33-7888; telex 18007.

Ministry of National Defence: Avda Paseo Colón 255, 1063 Buenos Aires; tel. (1) 30-1561; telex 22200.

Ministry of Public Health and Welfare: Defensa 120, 1345 Buenos Aires; tel. (1) 30-4322; telex 25064.

Ministry of Public Works and Services: Avda 9 de Julio 1925, 1332 Buenos Aires; tel. (1) 38-8911; telex 22577; fax (1) 331-9967.

President and Legislature

PRESIDENT

Election, 14 May 1989*

Candidates	Votes	%	Seats in electoral college
CARLOS SAÚL MENEM (Partido Justicialista—Peronists)	8,044,861	48.5	310
EDUARDO CÉSAR ANGELOZ (Unión Cívica Radical)	6,165,476	37.1	211
Others	2,390,100	14.4	79
Total	16,600,437	100.0	600

* The election on 14 May was for a 600-member presidential electoral college, which later met to elect the President.

CONGRESS

Cámara de Diputados
(Chamber of Deputies)

President: CÉSAR JAROSLAVSKY.

The Chamber has 254 members, who hold office for a four-year term, with one-half of the seats renewable every two years.

General Election, 6 September 1987*

	Seats
Unión Cívica Radical	117
Partido Justicialista	105
Unión del Centro Democrático	7
Partido Intransigente	5
Pacto Autonomista-Liberal	4
Partido Demócrata Cristiano	3
Partido Demócrata Progresista	2
Movimiento Popular Neuquino	2
Renovador de Salta	2
Others	7
Total	254

* The table indicates the distribution of the total number of seats, following the election for one-half of the membership.

In May 1989 elections for 127 seats gave the FREJUPO electoral alliance (comprising the Partido Justicialista, the Partido Demócrata Cristiano and the Partido Intransigente) 44.6% of the total votes cast (66 seats), the UCR 28.9% (41 seats) and the UCeDé 9.5% (9 seats). Other parties obtained a total of 17% (11 seats).

Senado
(Senate)

President: Dr VÍCTOR MARTÍNEZ.

The 46 members of the Senate are nominated by the legislative bodies of each province (two Senators for each), with the exception of Buenos Aires, which elects its Senators by means of a special Electoral College. The Senate's term of office is nine years, with one-third of the seats renewable every three years.

Political Organizations

Frente de Izquierda Popular: Buenos Aires; left-wing; Leader JORGE ABELARDO RAMOS.

Fuerza Republicana (FR): Buenos Aires; Leader Gen. DOMINGO BUSSI.

Grupo de 8: Buenos Aires; f. 1990; formed by dissident members of the Partido Justicialista; Leader LUIS BRUNATI.

Movimiento de Integración y Desarrollo (MID): Buenos Aires; f. 1963; Pres. ROGELIO FRIGERIO; 145,000 mems.

Movimiento al Socialismo (MAS): Leaders RUBÉN VISCONTI, LUIS ZAMORA; 55,000 mems.

Partido Comunista de Argentina: Buenos Aires; f. 1918; Leader PATRICIO ECHEGARAY; Sec.-Gen. ATHOS FAVA; 76,000 mems.

Partido Demócrata Cristiano (PDC): Buenos Aires; f. 1954; Leader ELIO SILVEIRA; 68,000 mems.

Partido Demócrata Progresista (PDP): Chile 1934, 1227 Buenos Aires; Leader RAFAEL MARTÍNEZ RAYMONDA; 85,000 mems.

Partido Intransigente: Buenos Aires; f. 1957; left-wing; Leaders Dr OSCAR ALENDE, LISANDRO VIALE; Sec. MARIANO LORENCES; 90,000 mems.

Partido Justicialista: Buenos Aires; Peronist party; f. 1945; 3m. mems; Pres. CARLOS SAÚL MENEM; three factions within party:

Frente Renovador, Justicia, Democracia y Participación—Frejudepa: f. 1985; reformist wing; Leaders CARLOS SAÚL MENEM, ANTONIO CAFIERO, CARLOS GROSSO.

Movimiento Nacional 17 de Octubre: Leader HERMINIO IGLESIAS.

Oficialistas: Leaders JOSÉ MARÍA VERNET, LORENZO MIGUEL.

Partido Nacional de Centro: Buenos Aires; f. July 1980; conservative; Leader RAÚL RIVANERA CARLES.

Partido Obrero: Ayacucho 444, Buenos Aires; tel. (1) 953-8433; f. 1982; Trotskyist; Leaders JORGE ALTAMIRA, CHRISTIAN RATH; 61,000 mems.

Partido Popular Cristiano: Leader JOSÉ ANTONIO ALLENDE.

Partido Socialista Democrático: Rivadavia 2307, 1034 Buenos Aires; Leader AMÉRICO GHIOLDI; 39,000 mems.

Partido Socialista Popular: f. 1982; Leaders GUILLERMO ESTÉVEZ BOERO, EDGARDO ROSSI; 60,500 mems.

Unión del Centro Democrático (UCeDé): Buenos Aires; f. Aug. 1980 as coalition of eight minor political organizations to challenge the 'domestic monopoly' of the populist movements; Leader ÁLVARO ALSOGARAY.

Unión Cívica Radical (UCR): Buenos Aires; tel. (1) 49-0036; telex 21326; moderate; f. 1890; Leader Dr RAÚL ALFONSÍN FOULKES; First Vice-Pres. CÉSAR JAROSLAVSKY; 1,410,000 mems.

ARGENTINA

Unión para la Nueva Mayoría: Buenos Aires; f. 1986; centre-right; Leader José Antonio Romero Feris.

Other parties and groupings include: Alianza Socialista, Confederación Socialista Argentina, Movimiento Línea Popular, Movimiento Patriótico de Liberación, Movimiento Popular Neuquino, Pacto Autonomista-Liberal, Partido Bloquista de San Juan, Partido Conservador Popular, Partido Izquierda Nacional, Partido Obrero Comunista Marxista-Leninista, Partido Socialista Auténtico, Partido Socialista Unificado and Renovador de Salta.

The following political parties and guerrilla groups are illegal:

Intransigencia y Movilización Peronista: Peronist faction; Leader Nilda Garres.

Movimiento Todos por la Patria (MTP): left-wing movement.

Partido Peronista Auténtico (PPA): f. 1975; Leaders Mario Firmenich, Óscar Bidegain, Ricardo Obregón Cano.

Partido Revolucionario de Trabajadores: political wing of the **Ejército Revolucionario del Pueblo (ERP)**; Leader Luis Mattini.

Triple A—Alianza Anticomunista Argentina: extreme right-wing; Leader Aníbal Gordon (in prison).

The dissolution of the Movimiento Peronista Montonero (MPM) was announced in December 1983. Mario Firmenich, the former leader of the MPM, was arrested in Brazil in 1983 and was transferred into the custody of the Argentine authorities in 1984. In mid-1990 the Government announced that Firmenich was to be released in a general amnesty which was expected to take place later that year.

Diplomatic Representation

EMBASSIES IN ARGENTINA

Albania: Olazábal 2060, 1428 Buenos Aires; tel. (1) 781-7740; telex 22658; Ambassador: Piro Andoni.

Algeria: Montevideo 1889, 1021 Buenos Aires; tel. (1) 22-1271; telex 22467; Ambassador: Abdallah Feddal.

Australia: Avda Santa Fé 846, 8°, 1059 Buenos Aires; tel. (1) 312-6841; telex 21946; Ambassador: Robert Henry Robertson.

Austria: French 3671, 1425 Buenos Aires; tel. (1) 802-7195; telex 18853; fax (1) 805-4016; Ambassador: Dr Gerhard Heible.

Belgium: Defensa 113, 8°, 1065 Buenos Aires; tel. (1) 331-0066; telex 22070; Ambassador: Thierry Muuls.

Bolivia: Corrientes 545, 2°, 1043 Buenos Aires; tel. (1) 394-6042; telex 24362; Ambassador: Agustín Saavedra Weise.

Brazil: Cerrito 1350, 1007 Buenos Aires; tel. (1) 812-0035; telex 21158; fax (1) 814-4085; Ambassador: Francisco Thompson-Flôres Netto.

Bulgaria: Manuel Obarrio 2967, 1425 Buenos Aires; tel. (1) 802-9251; telex 21314; Ambassador: Parvan Alexandrov Chernev.

Canada: Edif. Brunetta, 25°, Suipacha 1111, Casilla 1598, 1368 Buenos Aires; tel. (1) 312-9081; telex 21383; Ambassador: Clayton Bullis.

Chile: Tagle 2762, 1425 Buenos Aires; tel. (1) 802-7020; telex 21669; Ambassador: Carlos Figueroa Serrano.

China, People's Republic: Avda Crisólogo Larralde 5349, 1425 Buenos Aires; tel. (1) 543-8862; telex 22871; Ambassador: Li Guoxin.

Colombia: Avda Santa Fé 782, 1°, 1059 Buenos Aires; tel. (1) 325-0258; telex 22254; Ambassador: Hernando Pastrana Borrero.

Costa Rica: Lavalle 507, 4°, 1048 Buenos Aires; tel. (1) 325-6022; telex 21394; Ambassador: Fernando Salazar Navarrete.

Côte d'Ivoire: Ugarteche 3069, 1425 Buenos Aires; tel. (1) 802-3982; Ambassador: Gaston Ouassenan Kone.

Cuba: Virrey del Pino 1810, 1426 Buenos Aires; tel. (1) 782-9049; telex 22433; Ambassador: Santiago Díaz Paz.

Czechoslovakia: Figueroa Alcorta 3240, 1425 Buenos Aires; tel. (1) 801-3804; telex 22748; Ambassador: Jaroslav Pavlicek.

Denmark: Avda Leandro N. Alem 1074, 1001 Buenos Aires; tel. (1) 312-7680; telex 22173; Ambassador: Karl-Frederik Hasle.

Dominican Republic: Avda Santa Fé 1206, 2°, 1059 Buenos Aires; tel. (1) 41-4669; Ambassador: Jesús M. Hernández Sánchez.

Ecuador: Avda Pte Quintana 585, 8°/10°, Buenos Aires; tel. (1) 804-0073; Ambassador: Luis Valencia Rodríguez.

Egypt: Juez Tedín 2795, 1425 Buenos Aires; tel. (1) 801-6145; Ambassador: Hassan I. Abdel Hadi.

El Salvador: Avda Santa Fé 868, 12°, 1059 Buenos Aires; tel. (1) 394-7628; Ambassador: Horacio Trujillo.

Finland: Avda Santa Fé 846, 5°, 1059 Buenos Aires; tel. (1) 312-0600; telex 21702; fax (1) 312-0670; Ambassador: Pertti A. O. Karkkainen.

France: Cerrito 1399, 1010 Buenos Aires; tel. (1) 393-1071; telex 24300; Ambassador: Pierre Décamps.

Gabon: Avda Figueroa Alcorta 3221, 1425 Buenos Aires; tel. (1) 801-9840; telex 18577; Ambassador: J.-B. Eyi-Nkoumou.

Germany: Villanueva 1055, 1426 Buenos Aires; tel. (1) 771-5054; telex 21668; Ambassador: Herbert Limmer.

Greece: Avda Pte Roque Sáenz Peña 547, 4°, 1035 Buenos Aires; tel. (1) 34-4589; telex 22426; Ambassador: Apostolos Anninos.

Guatemala: Avda Santa Fé 830, 5°, 1059 Buenos Aires; tel. (1) 313-9180; fax (1) 313-9181; Ambassador: Leslie Mishaan de Kirkvoorde.

Haiti: Avda Figueroa Alcorta 3297, 1425 Buenos Aires; tel. (1) 802-0211; Ambassador: Frank Paul.

Holy See: Avda Alvear 1605, 1014 Buenos Aires; tel. (1) 42-9697; telex 17406; Apostolic Nuncio: Monsignor Ubaldo Calabresi.

Honduras: Avda Santa Fé 1385, 4°, 1059 Buenos Aires; tel. (1) 42-1643; telex 18008; Ambassador: Edgardo Paz Barnica.

Hungary: Coronel Díaz 1874, 1425 Buenos Aires; tel. (1) 824-5845; telex 22843; Ambassador: László Major.

India: Córdoba 950, 4°, 1054 Buenos Aires; tel. (1) 393-4001; telex 23413; fax (1) 112569; Ambassador: A. N. Ram.

Indonesia: M. Ramón Castilla 2901, 1425 Buenos Aires; tel. (1) 801-6622; telex 21781; Ambassador: Pudisanto Sadarjoen.

Iran: Figueroa Alcorta 3229, 1425 Buenos Aires; tel. (1) 802-1470; telex 21288; Ambassador: Hossein Tajgardon.

Iraq: Villanueva 1400, 1426 Buenos Aires; tel. (1) 771-5620; telex 17134; Ambassador: Sahib Hussain Tahir.

Ireland: 1059 Buenos Aires; tel. (1) 325-8588; telex 17654; Ambassador: Bernard Davenport.

Israel: Arroyo 916, 1007 Buenos Aires; tel. (1) 325-2502; telex 17106; Ambassador: Itshak Shefi.

Italy: Billinghurst 2577, 1425 Buenos Aires; tel. (1) 802-0071; telex 21961; Ambassador: Ludovico Incisa di Camerana.

Japan: Avda Paseo Colón 275, 1063 Buenos Aires; tel. (1) 30-2561; telex 22516; Ambassador: Agustin Yoshio Fujimoto.

Korea, Republic: Avda Libertador 2257, 1425 Buenos Aires; tel. (1) 802-9665; telex 22294; Ambassador: Sang Chin Lee.

Lebanon: Avda Libertador 2354, 1425 Buenos Aires; tel. (1) 802-4492; telex 22866; Ambassador: Jihad Mortada.

Libya: Alejandro M. de Aguado 2885, 1425 Buenos Aires; tel. (1) 801-7267; telex 22682; Ambassador: Gibreel Mansoury.

Malaysia: Sheraton Hotel, 20, San Martín 1225, 1104 Buenos Aires; tel. (1) 311-6311; Ambassador: Hee K. Hor.

Mexico: Larrea 1230, 1117 Buenos Aires; tel. (1) 826-2161; telex 21869; Ambassador: Jesús Puente Leyva.

Morocco: Calle Mariscal Ramón Castilla No. 2952, 1425 Buenos Aires; tel. (1) 801-8154; telex 18161; Ambassador: Mohammed Boucetta.

Netherlands: Edif. Holanda, 2°, Maipú 66, 1084 Buenos Aires; tel. (1) 331-6066; telex 21824; Ambassador: Schelto van Heemistar.

Nicaragua: Villanueva 1080, 1426 Buenos Aires; tel. (1) 772-2268; telex 23481; Ambassador: Ariel Ramón Granera Sacasa.

Nigeria: 11 de Setiembre 839, 1426 Buenos Aires; tel. (1) 771-6541; telex 23565; Ambassador: Okon Edet Uya.

Norway: Esmeralda 909, 3°, 1007 Buenos Aires; tel. (1) 312-2204; telex 22811; Chargé d'affaires: Dr Lars Vaagen.

Pakistan: 3 de Febrero 1326, 1084 Buenos Aires; tel. (1) 782-7663; Ambassador: Raja Tridiv Roy.

Panama: Avda Santa Fé 1461, 5°, 1019 Buenos Aires; tel. (1) 42-8543; Ambassador: María Esther Villalaz de Arias.

Paraguay: Las Heras 2545, 1425 Buenos Aires; tel. (1) 802-4948; telex 21687; Ambassador: Miguel Bestard.

Peru: Avda Libertador 1720, 1425 Buenos Aires; tel. (1) 802-6824; telex 17807; Ambassador: Alfonso Grados Bertorini.

Philippines: Juramento 1945, 1428 Buenos Aires; tel. (1) 781-4170; Ambassador: Sime D. Hidalgo.

Poland: Alejandro María de Aguado 2870, 1425 Buenos Aires; tel. (1) 802-9681; telex 22736; Ambassador: Janusz Bałewski.

Portugal: Córdoba 3151, 3°, 1054 Buenos Aires; tel. (1) 311-2586; telex 22736; Ambassador: António Baptista Martins.

Romania: Arroyo 962, 1007 Buenos Aires; tel. (1) 393-0883; telex 24301; Ambassador: Muntean Mihail.

Saudi Arabia: Alejandro María de Aguado 2881, 1425 Buenos Aires; tel. (1) 802-4735; telex 23291; Ambassador: Fuad A. Nazir.

ARGENTINA

Spain: Mariscal Ramón Castilla 2720, 1425 Buenos Aires; tel. (1) 802-6031; telex 21660; Ambassador: RAIMUNDO BASSOLS JACAS.

Sweden: Corrientes 330, 3°, 1378 Buenos Aires; tel. (1) 311-3088; telex 21340; Ambassador: ANDERS SANDSTRÖM.

Switzerland: Avda Santa Fé 846, 12°, 1059 Buenos Aires; tel. (1) 311-6491; telex 22418; fax (1) 313-2998; Ambassador: KARL FRITSCHI.

Syria: Calloa 956, 1023 Buenos Aires; tel. (1) 42-2113; Ambassador: ABDUL HASSIB ITSWANI.

Thailand: Virrey del Pino 2458, 6°, 1426 Buenos Aires; tel. (1) 785-6504; Ambassador: VICHIEN CHATSUWAN.

Turkey: Juez Tedín 2728, 1425 Buenos Aires; tel. (1) 802-3676; telex 21135; Ambassador: SEKIH BELEN.

USSR: Avda Rodríguez Peña 1741, 1021 Buenos Aires; tel. (1) 42-1552; telex 22147; Ambassador: VLADIMIR V. NIKITIN.

United Kingdom: Dr Luis Agote 2412/52, Casilla 2050, 1425 Buenos Aires; tel. (1) 803-7070; fax (1) 803-1731; Ambassador: HUMPHREY MAUD.

USA: Avda Colombia 4300, Palermo, 1425 Buenos Aires; tel. (1) 774-7611; telex 18156; fax (1) 775-4205; Ambassador: TERENCE TODMAN.

Uruguay: Avda Las Heras 1907, 1127 Buenos Aires; tel. (1) 803-6030; telex 25526; Ambassador: ADOLFO CASTELLS MENDIVIL.

Venezuela: Avda Santa Fé 1461, 2°, 1060 Buenos Aires; tel. (1) 42-0114; telex 21089; Ambassador: GUIDO GROOSCORS.

Yugoslavia: Marcelo T. de Alvear 1705, 1060 Buenos Aires; tel. (1) 41-2860; telex 21479; Ambassador: RUDOLF HAZURAN.

Zaire: Villanueva 1356, 2°, Casilla 5589, 1426 Buenos Aires; tel. (1) 771-0075; telex 22324; Ambassador: BADASSA-BAHADUKA.

Judicial System

SUPREME COURT

Corte Suprema: Talcahuano 550, 4°, 1013 Buenos Aires; tel. (1) 40-1540.

All members of the Supreme Court are appointed by the Executive, with the agreement of the Senate. Members are dismissed by impeachment. The number of members was increased from five to nine in May 1990.

President: ENRIQUE SANTIAGO PETRACCHI.

Justices: CARLOS SANTIAGO FAYT, AUGUSTO CÉSAR BELLUSCIO, ERNESTO CORBALÁN NANCLARES, JULIO OYHANARTE, RICARDO LIVENE, RODOLFO BARRA, MARIANO CAVAGNA MARTÍNEZ, JULIO NAZARENO.

Attorney-General: ANDRÉS D'ALESSIO.

OTHER COURTS

Judges of the lower, national or further lower courts are appointed by the President, with the agreement of the Senate, and are dismissed by impeachment.

The Federal Court of Appeal in Buenos Aires has three courts: civil and commercial, criminal, and administrative. There are six other courts of appeal in Buenos Aires: civil, commercial, criminal, peace, labour, and penal-economic. There are also federal appeal courts in: La Plata, Bahía Blanca, Paraná, Rosario, Córdoba, Mendoza, Tucumán and Resistencia.

The provincial courts each have their own Supreme Court and a system of subsidiary courts. They deal with cases originating within and confined to the provinces.

Religion

CHRISTIANITY

More than 90% of the population are Roman Catholics and about 2% are Protestants.

Federación Argentina de Iglesias Evangélicas (Argentine Federation of Evangelical Churches): José María Moreno 873, 1424 Buenos Aires; tel. (1) 922-5356; f. 1958; 29 mem. churches; Pres. Rev. RODOLFO ROBERTO REINICH (Evangelical Church of the River Plate); Exec. Sec. Rev. ENRIQUE LAVIGNE.

The Roman Catholic Church

Argentina comprises 13 archdioceses, 46 dioceses (including one for Catholics of the Ukrainian rite and one for Catholics of the Armenian rite) and three territorial prelatures. The Archbishop of Buenos Aires is also the Ordinary for Catholics of Oriental rites.

Bishops' Conference: Conferencia Episcopal Argentina, Calle Suipacha 1034, 1088 Buenos Aires; tel. (1) 311-0993; f. 1959; Pres. Cardinal RAÚL FRANCISCO PRIMATESTA, Archbishop of Córdoba.

Armenian Rite

Bishop of San Gregorio de Narek en Buenos Aires: VARTAN WALDIR BOGHOSSIAN (also Apostolic Exarch of Latin America), Charcas 3529, 1425 Buenos Aires; tel. (1) 824-1613.

Latin Rite

Archbishop of Bahía Blanca: JORGE MAYER, Avda Colón 164, 8000 Bahía Blanca; tel. (91) 22-070.

Archbishop of Buenos Aires: Cardinal JUAN CARLOS ARAMBURU, Arzobispado, Rivadavia 415, 1002 Buenos Aires; tel. (1) 30-3925.

Archbishop of Córdoba: Cardinal RAÚL FRANCISCO PRIMATESTA, Avda Hipólito Yrigoyen 98, 5000 Córdoba; tel. (51) 21015.

Archbishop of Corrientes: FORTUNATO ANTONIO ROSSI, 9 de Julio 1573, 3400 Corrientes; tel. (783) 22-436.

Archbishop of La Plata: ANTONIO QUARRACINO, Calle 14, No 1009, 1900 La Plata; tel. (21) 21-8286.

Archbishop of Mendoza: CÁNDIDO GENARO RUBIOLO, Catamarca 98, 5500 Mendoza; tel. (61) 233-862.

Archbishop of Paraná: ESTANISLAO ESTEBAN KARLIC, Monte Caseros 77, 3100 Paraná; tel. (43) 211-440.

Archbishop of Resistencia: JUAN JOSÉ IRIARTE, Bartolomé Mitre 363, Casilla 35, 3500 Resistencia; tel. (711) 26867.

Archbishop of Rosario: JORGE MANUEL LÓPEZ, Córdoba 1677, 2000 Rosario; tel. (41) 21-1207.

Archbishop of Salta: MOISÉS JULIO BLANCHOUD, España 596, 4400 Salta; tel. (87) 214-306.

Archbishop of San Juan de Cuyo: ITALO SEVERINO DI STEFANO, Bartolomé Mitre 240, Oeste, 5400 San Juan de Cuyo; tel. (64) 22-2578.

Archbishop of Santa Fé: EDGARDO GABRIEL STORNI, Avda General López 2720, 3000 Santa Fé; tel. (42) 35 791.

Archbishop of Tucumán: HORACIO ALBERTO BÓZZOLI, Avda Sarmiento 895, 4000 San Miguel de Tucumán; tel. (81) 31-0617.

Ukrainian Rite

Bishop of Santa María del Patrocinio en Buenos Aires: ANDRÉS SAPELAK, Ramón L. Falcón 3960, Casilla 28, 1407 Buenos Aires; tel. (1) 67-4192.

The Anglican Communion

The Iglesia Anglicana del Cono Sur de América (Anglican Church of the Southern Cone of America) was formally inaugurated in Buenos Aires in April 1983. The Church comprises six dioceses: Argentina, Northern Argentina, Chile, Paraguay, Peru with Bolivia, and Uruguay.

Bishop of Argentina: Rt Rev. DAVID LEAKE, 25 de Mayo 282, 1002 Buenos Aires; tel. (1) 34-4618.

Bishop of Northern Argentina: Rt Rev. MAURICE SINCLAIR, Casilla 187, 4400 Salta; tel. (54) 21-5554.

Protestant Churches

Baptist Evangelical Convention: Rivadavia 3476, 1203 Buenos Aires; tel. (1) 88-8924; Pres. Dr JORGE FERRARI.

Iglesia Evangélica Congregacionalista (Evangelical Congregational Church): Perón 525, 3100 Paraná; tel. (43) 21-6172; f. 1924; 100 congregations, 8,000 mems, 24,000 adherents; Supt Rev. GERARDO ARNDT.

Iglesia Evangélica Luterana Argentina: Ing. Silveyra 1639-41, 1607 Villa Adelina, Buenos Aires; tel. (1) 766-8560; f. 1905; 30,000 mems; Pres. ROBERTO M. KROEGER.

Iglesia Evangélica del Río de la Plata: Mariscal Sucre 2855, 1428 Buenos Aires; tel. (1) 784-1029; f. 1899; 50,000 mems; Pres. RODOLFO R. REINICH.

Iglesia Evangélica Metodista Argentina (Methodist Church of Argentina): Rivadavia 4044, 3°, 1205 Buenos Aires; tel. (1) 982-3712; f. 1836; 6,040 mems, 9,000 adherents, seven regional superintendents; Bishop ALDO M. ETCHEGOYEN; Exec. Sec. Gen. Board JORGE A. LEÓN TOLEDO.

JUDAISM

Delegación de Asociaciones Israelitas Argentinas—DAIA (Delegation of Argentine Jewish Associations): Pasteur 633, 5°, Buenos Aires; f. 1935; there are about 400,000 Jews, mostly in Buenos Aires; Pres. Dr DAVID GOLDBERG; Sec.-Gen. Dr HÉCTOR UMASCHI.

ARGENTINA

The Press

PRINCIPAL DAILIES

Buenos Aires

Ambito Financiero: Carabelas 241, 3°, 1009 Buenos Aires; tel. (1) 331-5528; telex 17721; fax (1) 331-4547; f. 1976; morning (Mon.–Fri.); business; Dir JULIO A. RAMOS; circ. 115,000.

Buenos Aires Herald: Azopardo 455, 1107 Buenos Aires; tel. (1) 34-8477; f. 1876; English; morning; independent; Editor RONALD HANSEN; circ. 20,000.

Boletín Oficial de la República Argentina: Suipacha 767, 1008 Buenos Aires; tel. (1) 322-4164; f. 1893; morning (Mon.–Fri.); official records publication; Dir HORACIO GASTIABURO.

Clarín: Piedras 1743, 1140 Buenos Aires; tel. (1) 27-0061; f. 1945; morning; independent; Dir Sra ERNESTINA LAURA HERRERA DE NOBLE; circ. 480,000 (daily), 750,000 (Sunday).

Crónica: Garay 130, 1063 Buenos Aires; tel. (1) 361-1001; f. 1963; morning and evening; Dir MARIO ALBERTO FERNÁNDEZ (morning), RICARDO GANGEME (evening); circ. 330,000 (morning), 190,000 (evening), 450,000 (Sunday).

El Cronista Comercial: Alsina 547, 1087 Buenos Aires; tel. (1) 33-3015; f. 1908; morning; Editor DANIEL DELLA COSTA; circ. 100,000.

Diario Popular: Beguerestain 182, 1870 Avellaneda, Buenos Aires; tel. (1) 204-6056; f. 1974; morning; Dir ALBERTO ALBERTENGO; circ. 145,000.

La Gaceta: Beguerestain 182, 1870 Avellaneda, Buenos Aires; Dir RICARDO WEST OCAMPO; circ. 35,000.

La Nación: Bouchard 557, 1106 Buenos Aires; tel. (1) 313-1003; telex 18558; f. 1870; morning; independent; Dir BARTOLOMÉ MITRE; circ. 210,648.

Página 12: Buenos Aires; f. 1987; morning; left-wing.

La Prensa: Avda de Mayo 567, 1319 Buenos Aires; tel. (1) 331-1001; f. 1869 by José C. Paz; morning; independent; Dir MÁXIMO GAINZA; circ. 65,000.

La Razón: Gral Hornos 690, 1272 Buenos Aires; tel. (1) 26-9051; f. 1905; morning and evening; Exec. Dir PATRICIO PERALTA RAMOS; circ. 180,000.

The Southern Cross: Medrano 107, 1178 Buenos Aires; tel. (1) 983-1371; f. 1875; Dir P. FEDERICO J. RICHARDS.

Sur: Buenos Aires; left-wing.

Tiempo Argentino: Lafayette 1910, 1286 Buenos Aires; tel. (1) 28-1929; telex 22276; Editor Dr TOMÁS LEONA; circ. 75,000.

La Voz: Tabaré 1641, 1437 Buenos Aires; tel. (1) 922-3800; Dir VICENTE LEÓNIDAS SAADI.

PRINCIPAL PROVINCIAL DAILIES

Bahía Blanca

La Nueva Provincia: Sarmiento 54/64, 8000 Bahía Blanca, Provincia de Buenos Aires; tel. (91) 20201; telex 81826; f. 1898; morning; independent; Dir DIANA JULIO DE MASSOT; circ. 36,000 (weekdays), 55,000 (Sunday).

Catamarca

El Sol: Esquiú 551, 4700 San Francisco del Valle de Catamarca; tel. (833) 23844; f. 1973; morning; Dir TOMÁS NICOLÁS ALVAREZ SAAVEDRA.

Comodoro Rivadavia

Crónica: Namuncurá 122, 9000 Comodoro Rivadavia, Provincia del Chubut; tel. (967) 31200; telex 86996; f. 1962; morning; Dir Dr DIEGO JOAQUÍN ZAMIT; circ. 10,000.

Concordia

El Heraldo: Quintana 46, 3200 Concordia; tel. (45) 215304; telex 46508; f. 1915; evening; Editor Dr CARLOS LIEBERMANN; circ. 10,000.

Córdoba

Comercio y Justicia: Mariano Moreno 378, 5000 Córdoba; tel. (51) 33788; telex 51563; f. 1939; morning; economic and legal news; Editor JORGE RAÚL EGUÍA; circ. 12,000.

Córdoba: Santa Rosa 167, 5000 Córdoba; tel. (51) 22072; f. 1928; evening; Dir GUSTAVO ALONSO OBIETA; circ. 25,000.

La Voz del Interior: Avellaneda 1661, 5000 Córdoba; tel. (51) 72-9535; f. 1904; morning; independent; Dir LUIS EDUARDO REMONDA; circ. 87,000.

Corrientes

El Liberal: 25 de Mayo 1345, 3400 Corrientes; tel. (783) 22069; f. 1909; evening; Dir JUAN FRANCISCO TORRENT.

Directory

El Litoral: H. Yrigoyen 990, 3400 Corrientes; tel. (783) 22264; f. 1960; morning; Dir GABRIEL FERIS; circ. 25,000.

La Plata

El Día: Avda Ameghino Diagonal 80, No 817/21, 1900 La Plata, Provincia de Buenos Aires; tel. (21) 21-0101; telex 31165; fax (21) 21-0101; f. 1884; morning; independent; Dir RAÚL E. KRAISELBURD; circ. 54,868.

Mar del Plata

El Atlántico: Bolívar 2975, 7600 Mar del Plata, Provincia de Buenos Aires; tel. (23) 35462; f. 1938; morning; Dir OSCAR ALBERTO GASTIARENA; circ. 20,000.

La Capital: Avda Champagnat 2551, 7600 Mar del Plata, Provincia de Buenos Aires; tel. (23) 77-1164; telex 39884; f. 1905; Dir TOMÁS R. STEGAGNINI; circ. 32,000.

Mendoza

Los Andes: San Martín 1049, 5500 Mendoza; tel. (61) 24-4500; f. 1882; morning; independent; Dir JORGE ENRIQUE OVIEDO; circ. 60,662.

Mendoza: San Martín 947, 5500 Mendoza; tel. (61) 24-1064; f. 1969; Dir ALFREDO ORTIZ BARILI; circ. 6,670.

Paraná

El Diario: Buenos Aires y Urquiza, 3100 Paraná, Entre Ríos; tel. (43) 21-0082; telex 45108; f. 1914; morning; democratic; Dir Dr LUIS F. ETCHEVEHERE; circ. 20,000.

Quilmes, B.A.

El Sol: H. Yrigoyen 122, Quilmes 1878; tel. (1) 253-4595; f. 1927; Dir JOSÉ MARÍA GHISANI; circ. 25,000.

Resistencia

El Territorio: Casilla 320, Carlos Pellegrini 211/231, 3500 Resistencia; f. 1919; morning; Dir RAÚL ANDRÉS AGUIRRE; circ. 15,000.

La Rioja

La Gaceta Riojana: 25 de Mayo 76, 5300 La Rioja; tel. (822) 26443; f. 1988; Editor RAÚL NICOLÁS CHACÓN.

Río Negro

Río Negro: Gral Roca (8332), Río Negro; tel. (941) 22021; f. 1912; morning; Editor JAMES NEILSON.

Rosario

La Capital: Sarmiento 763, 2000 Rosario, Santa Fé; tel. (43) 392-2193; f. 1867; morning; independent; Dir CARLOS OVIDIO LAGOS; circ. 93,920.

Salta

El Tribuno: Ruta 68, Km 1592, 4400 Salta; tel. (87) 24-0000; telex 65126; f. 1949; morning; Dir ROBERTO EDUARDO ROMERO; circ. 41,215.

San Juan

Diario de Cuyo: Mendoza 380 Sur, 5400 San Juan; tel. (64) 29680; f. 1947; morning; independent; Dir FRANCISCO MONTES; circ. 25,000.

Tribuna de la Tarde: Mitre 85 Oeste, 5400 San Juan; tel. (64) 40-0923; f. 1931; evening; Dir DANTE AMÉRICO MONTES.

Santa Fé

Hoy: 1° de Mayo 2820, 3000 Santa Fé; f. 1986; Dir ANDRÉS SAAVEDRA; circ. 30,000.

El Litoral: San Martín 2651-59, 3000 Santa Fé; tel. (42) 20101; f. 1918; morning; independent; Dir ENZO VITTORI; circ. 40,000.

Santiago del Estero

El Liberal: Libertad 263, 4200 Santiago del Estero; tel. (5484) 22-4400; telex 64114; f. 1898; morning; Editors Dr ALDO CLAUDIO CASTIGLIONE, Dr JULIO CÉSAR CASTIGLIONE; circ. 30,000.

Tucumán

La Gaceta: Mendoza 654, 4000 San Miguel de Tucumán; tel. (81) 21-9260; telex 61208; fax (81) 31-1597; f. 1912; morning; independent; Dir EDUARDO R. GARCÍA HAMILTON; circ. 80,552.

La Tarde: Mendoza 654, San Miguel de Tucumán 4000; tel. (81) 21-9260; telex 61208; fax (81) 31-1597; f. 1981; evening; Dir ENRIQUE R. GARCÍA HAMILTON.

WEEKLY NEWSPAPER

El Informador Público: Buenos Aires; right-wing; Editor JESÚS IGLESIAS ROUCO.

ARGENTINA

PERIODICALS

Aeroespacio: Casilla 37, Sucursal 12B, 1412 Buenos Aires; tel. (1) 322-2753; telex 39-21763; fax (81) 11-8125; f. 1931; aeronautics; Dir José Cándido D'Odorico; circ. 26,000.

Billiken: Azopardo 579, 1307 Buenos Aires; tel. (1) 30-7040; telex 21163; f. 1919; weekly; children's magazine; Dir Carlos Silveyra; circ. 240,000.

Canal TV: Azopardo 579, 1307 Buenos Aires; weekly; TV guide.

Casas y Jardines: Sarmiento 643, 1382 Buenos Aires; tel. (1) 45-1793; f. 1932; every 2 months; houses and gardens; publ. by Editorial Contémpora SRL; Dir Norberto M. Muzio.

Chacra & Campo Moderno: Editorial Atlántida SA, Azopardo 579, 1307 Buenos Aires; tel. (1) 333-4591; telex 21163; f. 1930; monthly; farm and country magazine; Dir Constancio C. Vigil; circ. 35,000.

Claudia: Avda Leandro N. Alem 896, 1001 Buenos Aires; tel. (1) 312-6010; telex 9229; f. 1957; monthly; women's magazine; Dir Mercedes Marques; circ. 17,100.

El Derecho: Tucumán 1436, 1050 Buenos Aires; tel. (1) 45-3302; law.

Desarrollo Económico-Revista de Ciencias Sociales: Aráoz 2838, 1425 Buenos Aires; tel. (1) 804-4949; every 3 months; publication of Instituto de Desarrollo Económico y Social; circ. 2,000.

El Economista: Avda Córdoba 632, 2°, 1054 Buenos Aires; tel. (1) 322-3308; telex 23542; fax (1) 322-8157; f. 1951; weekly; financial; Dir Dr D. Radonjic; circ. 37,800.

Gente: Azopardo 579, 3°, 1307 Buenos Aires; tel. (1) 33-4591; telex 21163; f. 1965; weekly; general; Dir Jorge de Luján Gutiérrez; circ. 133,000.

El Gráfico: Azopardo 579, 1307 Buenos Aires; tel. (1) 33-4591; telex 21163; f. 1919; weekly; sport; Dir Constancio C. Vigil; circ. 127,000.

Humor: Venezuela 842, 1095 Buenos Aires; tel. (1) 334-5400; telex 9072; fax (1) 11-2700; f. 1978; every 2 weeks; satirical revue; Editor Andrés Cascioli; circ. 140,000.

Jurisprudencia Argentina: Talcahuano 650, 1013 Buenos Aires; tel. (1) 40-7850; f. 1918; weekly; law; Dir Ricardo Estévez Boero; circ. 10,000.

Legislación Argentina: Talcahuano 650, 1013 Buenos Aires; tel. (1) 40-0528; f. 1958; Dir Ricardo Estévez Boero; circ. 15,000.

Mercado: Perú 263, 2°, 1067 Buenos Aires; tel. (1) 34-6713; fax (1) 805-3798; f. 1969; monthly; business; Dir Gerardo López Alonso.

Mundo Israelita: Lavalle 2615, 1°, 1052 Buenos Aires; tel. (1) 961-7999; f. 1923; weekly; Editor Dr José Kestelman; circ. 26,000.

Nuestra Arquitectura: Sarmiento 643, 5°, 1382 Buenos Aires; tel. (1) 45-1793; f. 1929; every 2 months; architecture; publ. by Editorial Contémpora SRL; Dir Norberto M. Muzio.

Nueva Presencia: Castelli 330, 1032 Buenos Aires; tel. (1) 89-2727; weekly; Editor Herman Schiller.

Para Ti: Azopardo 579, 1307 Buenos Aires; tel. (1) 33-4591; f. 1922; weekly; women's interest; Dir Aníbal C. Vigil; circ. 104,000.

Pensamiento Económico: Avda Leandro N. Alem 36, 1003 Buenos Aires; tel. (1) 331-8051; telex 18542; f. 1925; every 3 months; review of Cámara Argentina de Comercio; Dir Lic. Pedro Naón Argerich.

Perfil: Sarmiento 1113, 1041 Buenos Aires; tel. (1) 35-2552; telex 18213; Editor Daniel Pliner.

El Periodista: Buenos Aires; weekly; Dir Carlos Gabetta.

Política Obrera: Avda Belgrano 2608, Buenos Aires; tel. (1) 943-2439; every 2 months; publication of Partido Obrero; circ. 5,000.

La Prensa Médica Argentina: Junín 845, 1113 Buenos Aires; tel. (1) 961-9793; f. 1914; monthly; medical; Editor Dr P. A. López; circ. 8,000.

Prensa Obrera: Ayacucho 444, Buenos Aires; tel. (1) 953-8433; f. 1982; weekly; publication of Partido Obrero; circ. 16,000.

Review of the River Plate: Casilla de Correo 294, 1413 Buenos Aires; tel. (1) 982-4961; f. 1891; every 2 weeks; agricultural, financial, economic and shipping news and comment; Dir Archibald B. Norman; circ. 3,500.

La Semana: Sarmiento 1113, 1041 Buenos Aires; tel. (1) 35-2552; telex 18213; general; Editor Daniel Pliner.

La Semana Médica: Arenales 3574, 1425 Buenos Aires; tel. (1) 824-5673; f. 1894; monthly; Dir Dr Eduardo F. Mele; circ. 7,000.

Siete Días: Avda Leandro N. Alem 896, 1001 Buenos Aires; tel. (1) 32-6010; f. 1967; weekly; general; Dir Ricardo Cámara.

Somos: Azopardo 579, 1307 Buenos Aires; tel. (1) 331-4591; f. 1976; weekly; general; independent; Dir Raúl García; circ. 21,000.

Directory

Técnica e Industria: Rodríguez Peña 694, 5°, 1020 Buenos Aires; tel. (1) 46-3193; f. 1922; monthly; technology and industry; Dir E. R. Fedele; circ. 5,000.

Visión: Montevideo 496, 6°, 1019 Buenos Aires; tel. (1) 49-3652; telex 21926; f. 1950; every 2 weeks; Latin American affairs, politics; Dir Dr Mariano Grondona.

Vosotras: Avda Leandro N. Alem 896, 3°, 1001 Buenos Aires; tel. (1) 32-6010; f. 1935; women's weekly; Dir Abel Zanotto; circ. 33,000. **Monthly supplements: Labores:** circ. 130,000; **Modas:** circ. 70,000.

NEWS AGENCIES

Agencia TELAM SA: Bolívar 531, 1066 Buenos Aires; tel. (1) 34-2162; telex 21077; Pres. Hugo Heguy.

Diarios y Noticias (DYN): Chacabuco 314, 6°, 1069 Buenos Aires; tel. (1) 33-3971; telex 23058; Dir Jorge Carlos Brinsek.

Noticias Argentinas SA (NA): Chacabuco 314, 8°, 1069 Buenos Aires; tel. (1) 33-8688; telex 18363; f. 1973; Dir Raúl Eduardo García.

Foreign Bureaux

Agence France-Presse (AFP): Avda Corrientes 456, 6°, Of. 61/62, 1366 Buenos Aires; tel. (1) 394-8169; telex 24349; Bureau Chief Gilles Bertin.

Agencia EFE (Spain): Guido 1770, 1016 Buenos Aires; tel. (1) 41-0666; telex 17568; Bureau Chief Manuel M. Meseguer Sánchez.

Agenzia Nazionale Stampa Associata (ANSA) (Italy): Avda Eduardo Madero 940/942, 24°, 1106 Buenos Aires; tel. (1) 313-4449; telex 24214; fax (1) 313-0293; Bureau Chief Ricardo Benozzo.

Associated Press (AP) (USA): Bouchard 551, 5°, Casilla 1296, 1106 Buenos Aires; tel. (1) 311-0081; telex 121053; Bureau Chief William H. Heath.

Deutsche Presse-Agentur (dpa) (Germany): Avda Corrientes 456, 10°, Of. 104, 1366 Buenos Aires; tel. (1) 394-0990; Bureau Chief Hasso Ramspeck.

Inter Press Service (IPS) (Italy): Corrientes 456, 8°, Of. 87, Edif. Safico, 1068 Buenos Aires; tel. (1) 394-0829; telex 24712; Bureau Chief Ramón M. Gorriarán; Correspondent Gustavo Capdevilla.

Magyar Távirati Iroda (MTI) (Hungary): M.T. de Alvear 624, 3° 16, 1058 Buenos Aires; tel. (1) 312-9596; telex 17106; Correspondent Endre Simó.

Prensa Latina (Cuba): Corrientes 456, 2°, Of. 27, Buenos Aires; tel. (1) 394-0565; telex 24410; Correspondent Mario Hernández del Llano.

Reuters (UK): Avda Eduardo Madero 940, 25°, 1106 Buenos Aires; tel. (1) 313-2021; Chief Correspondent R. Jarvie.

Telegrafnoye Agentstvo Sovetskovo Soyuza (TASS) (USSR): Avda Córdoba 652, 11°'E', 1054 Buenos Aires; tel. (1) 392-2044; Dir Isidoro Gilbert.

United Press International (UPI) (USA): Casilla 796, Correo Central 1000, Avda Belgrano 271, 1092 Buenos Aires; tel. (1) 34-5501; telex 350-1225; fax (1) 334-1818; Dir Alberto J. Schazín.

Xinhua (New China) News Agency (People's Republic of China): Calle Tucumán 540, 14°, Apto D, 1049 Buenos Aires; tel. (1) 313-9755; telex 23643; Bureau Chief Ju Qingdong.

The following are also represented: Central News Agency (Taiwan), Interpress (Poland), Jiji Press (Japan).

PRESS ASSOCIATION

Asociación de Entidades Periodísticas Argentinas: Esmeralda 356, 1035 Buenos Aires.

Publishers

Editorial Abril, SA: Avda Belgrano 1580, 4°, 1093 Buenos Aires; tel. (1) 37-7355; telex 22630; f. 1961; fiction, non-fiction, children's books, textbooks; Dir Roberto M. Ares.

Editorial Acme SA: Santa Magdalena 632, 1277 Buenos Aires; tel. (1) 28-2014; f. 1949; general fiction, children's books, agriculture, textbooks; Man. Dir Emilio I. González.

Aguilar, Altea, Taurus, Alfaguara, SA de Ediciones: Beazley 3860, 1437 Buenos Aires; tel. (1) 91-411; telex 25248; fax (1) 953-3716; f. 1946; general, literature, children's books; Gen. Dir Esteban Fernández Rozado.

Editorial Albatros, SACI: Hipólito Yrigoyen 3920, 1208 Buenos Aires; tel. (1) 981-1161; telex 24787; fax (1) 334-3136; f. 1961; technical, non-fiction, social sciences, medicine and agriculture; Man. Andrea Inés Canevaro.

ARGENTINA

Amorrortu Editores, SA: Paraguay 1225, 7°, 1057 Buenos Aires; tel. (1) 393-8812; f. 1967; anthropology, religion, economics, sociology, philosophy, psychology, pschoanalysis, current affairs; Man. Dir HORACIO DE AMORRORTU.

Angel Estrada y Cía, SA: Bolívar 462, 1066 Buenos Aires; tel. (1) 331-6521; telex 17990; f. 1869; textbooks, children's books; Pres. PATRICIA DE ESTRADA.

El Ateneo, Librería—Editorial: Patagones 2463, 1282 Buenos Aires; tel. (1) 942-9002; telex 18522; fax (1) 11-2486; f. 1912; medicine, engineering, economics and general; Dirs PEDRO GARCÍA RUEDA, EUSTASIO A. GARCÍA.

Editorial Atlántida, SA: Azopardo 579, 1307 Buenos Aires; tel. (1) 331-4591; telex 21163; fax (1) 331-3272; f. 1918; fiction and non-fiction, children's books; Founder CONSTANCIO C. VIGIL; Man. Dir ALFREDO J. VERCELLI.

Ediciones La Aurora: Deán Funes 1823/25, 1244 Buenos Aires; tel. (1) 941-8940; f. 1925; general, religion, spirituality, theology, philosophy, psychology, history, semiology, linguistics; Dir Dr HUGO O. ORTEGA.

Editorial Bruguera: 648-650, 1086 Buenos Aires; tel. (1) 553-2885; Man. Dir JORGE MERLINI.

Centro Editor de América Latina, SA: Cangallo 1228, 2°D, 1038 Buenos Aires; tel. (1) 35-9449; f. 1967; literature, history; Man. Dir JOSÉ B. SPIVACOW.

Centro Nacional de Información Educativa: Ministerio de Educación y Justicia, Paraguay 1657, 1°, 1062 Buenos Aires; tel. (1) 41-5420; education, bibliography, directories, etc.; Dir LAUREANO GARCÍA ELORRIO.

Editorial Ciordia, SRL: Avda Belgrano 2271, 1094 Buenos Aires; tel. (1) 48-1681; f. 1938; general educational and fiction; Man. Dir EDUARDO B. CIORDIA.

Editorial Claretiana: Lima 1360, 1138 Buenos Aires; tel. (1) 27-9250/; f. 1956; Catholicism; Dir JOSÉ A. HERNANDO.

Editorial Claridad, SA: San José 1627, 1076 Buenos Aires; tel. (1) 23-5573; fax (1) 325-8265; f. 1922; literature, biographies, social science, politics; Pres. Dra ANA MARÍA CABANELLAS.

Club de Lectores: Avda de Mayo 624, 1084 Buenos Aires; tel. (1) 34-3955; f. 1938; non-fiction; Dir JUAN MANUEL FONTENLA.

Club de Poetas: Casilla 189, 1401 Buenos Aires; f. 1975; poetry and literature; Exec. Dir JUAN MANUEL FONTENLA.

Editorial Columba, SA: Sarmiento 1889, 5°, 1044 Buenos Aires; tel. (1) 45-4297; f. 1953; classics in translation, 20th century; Man. Dir CLAUDIO A. COLUMBA.

Editorial Contémpora, SRL: Sarmiento 643, 1382 Buenos Aires; tel. (1) 45-1793; architecture, town-planning, interior decoration and gardening; Dir NORBERTO M. MUZIO.

Cosmopolita, SRL: Piedras 744, 1070 Buenos Aires; tel. (1) 361-8049; f. 1940; science and technology; Man. Dir RUTH F. DE RAPP.

Ediciones Depalma SRL: Talcahuano 494, 1013 Buenos Aires; tel. (1) 46-1815; fax (1) 40-6913; f. 1944; periodicals and books covering law, politics, sociology, philosophy, history and economics; Dir ROBERTO SUARDIAZ.

Editorial Difusión, SA: Sarandi 1065-67, Buenos Aires; tel. (1) 941-0088; f. 1937; literature, philosophy, religion, education, textbooks, children's books; Dir DOMINGO PALOMBELLA.

Emecé Editores, SA: Alsina 2048, 1090 Buenos Aires; tel. (1) 953-4038; telex 21945; fax (1) 953-4200; f. 1939; fiction, non-fiction, biographies, history, art, poetry, essays; Pres. BONIFACIO DEL CARRIL; Editors JORGE NAVEIRO, BONIFACIO P. DEL CARRIL.

Espasa Calpe Argentina, SA: Tacuarí 328, 1071 Buenos Aires; tel. (1) 34-0073; f. 1937; literature, science, dictionaries; publ. *Colección Austral*; Dir RAFAEL OLARRA JIMÉNEZ.

EUDEBA—Editorial Universitaria de Buenos Aires: Rivadavia 1573, 1033 Buenos Aires; tel. (1) 37-2202; f. 1958; university text books and general interest publications; Gen. Man. GUILLERMO MINA.

Fabril Editora, SA: California 2098, 1289 Buenos Aires; tel. (1) 21-3601; f. 1958; non-fiction, science, arts, education and reference; Editorial Man. ANDRÉS ALFONSO BRAVO; Business Man. RÓMULO AYERZA.

Editorial Glem, SACIF: Avda Caseros 2056, 1264 Buenos Aires; tel. (1) 26-6641; f. 1933; psychology, technology; Pres. JOSÉ ALFREDO TUCCI.

Editorial Guadalupe: Mansilla 3865, 1425 Buenos Aires; tel. (1) 84-6066; fax (1) 805-4112; f. 1895; social sciences, religion, anthropology, children's books, and pedagogy; Man. Dir P. LUIS O. LIBERTI.

Editorial Hachette, SA: Rivadavia 739, 1002 Buenos Aires; tel. (1) 34-8481; telex 17479; fax (1) 814-4271; f. 1931; general non-fiction; Man. Dir J. A. MUSSET.

Editorial Heliasta, SRL: Viamonte 1730, 1°, 1055 Buenos Aires; tel. (1) 45-1843; telex 9900; fax (1) 325-8265; f. 1970; literature, biography, politics, social science; Pres. Dra ANA MARÍA CABANELLAS.

Editorial Hemisferio Sur, SA: Pasteur 743, 1028 Buenos Aires; tel. (1) 48-9825; telex 18522; fax (1) 334-2793; f.1966; agriculture, science; Man. Dirs JUAN ÁNGEL PERI, ADOLFO LUIS PEÑA.

Editorial Hispano-Americana, SA (HASA): Alsina 731, 1087 Buenos Aires; tel. (1) 331-5051; f. 1934; science and technology; Pres. Prof. HÉCTOR OSCAR ALGARRA.

Editorial Inter-Médica, SAICI: Junín 917, 1°, Casilla 4625, Buenos Aires; tel. (1) 961-9234; fax (1) 961-5572; f. 1959; science, medicine, dentistry, psychology, odontology, veterinary; Pres. JORGE MODYEIEVSKY.

Editorial Inter-Vet, SA: Avda de los Constituyentes 3141, Buenos Aires; tel. (1) 51-2382; f. 1987; veterinary; Pres. JORGE MODYEIEVSKY.

Editorial Kapelusz, SA: Moreno 372, 1091 Buenos Aires; tel. (1) 34-6451; telex 18342; f. 1905; textbooks, psychology, pedagogy, children's books; Man. Dir RICARDO PASCUAL ROBLES.

Editorial Kier, SACIFI: Avda Santa Fé 1260, 1059 Buenos Aires; tel. (1) 41-0507; f. 1907; Eastern doctrines and religions, astrology, parapsychology, tarot, I Ching, occultism, natural medicine; Pres. ALFONSO F. PIBERNUS.

Editorial Labor Argentina, SA (Spain): Venezuela 613, 1095 Buenos Aires; tel. (1) 33-4135; f. 1924; technology, science, art; Man. Dir PEDRO CLOTAS CIERCO.

Carlos Lohlé, SA: Tacuarí 1516, Casilla 3097, 1000 Buenos Aires; tel. (1) 27-9969; f. 1953; philosophy, religion, belles-lettres; Pres. CARLOS F. P. LOHLÉ; Dir FRANCISCO M. LOHLÉ.

Editorial Losada, SA: Moreno 3362/64, 1209 Buenos Aires; tel. (1) 88-8608; telex 27922; f. 1938; general; Pres. JOSÉ JUAN FERNÁNDEZ REGUERA.

Ediciones Macchi, SA: Alsina 1535 PB, 1088 Buenos Aires; tel. (1) 46-0594; f. 1947; economic sciences; Man. Dir RAÚL LUIS MACCHI.

Editorial Médica Panamericana, SA: Marcelo T. de Alvear 2143, 1122 Buenos Aires; tel. (1) 961-8815; telex 17666; fax (1) 11-1605; f. 1962; health sciences; Pres. ROBERTO BRIK; Vice-Pres. HUGO BRIK.

Editorial Nova, SACI: Buenos Aires; tel. (1) 34-8698; f. 1945; arts, philosophy, religion, medicine, textbooks, science and technology; Dir HORACIO D. ROLANDO.

Ediciones Nueva Visión, SAIC: Tucumán 3748, 1189 Buenos Aires; tel. (1) 89-5050; f. 1954; psychology, art, social sciences, architecture; Man. Dir HAYDÉE P. DE GIACONE.

Editorial Paidós: Defensa 599, 1°, 1065 Buenos Aires; tel. and fax (1) 331-2275; f. 1945; social sciences, medicine, philosophy, religion, history, literature, textbooks; Man. Dir MARITA GOTTHEIL.

Plaza y Janés, SA: Lambaré 893, Buenos Aires; tel. (1) 86-6769; popular fiction and non-fiction; Man. Dir JORGE PÉREZ.

Editorial Plus Ultra, SAI & C: Callao 572, 1022 Buenos Aires; tel. (1) 46-5092; f. 1964; literature, history, textbooks, law, economics, politics, sociology, pedagogy, children's books; Man. Editor CARLOS ALBERTO LOPRETE.

Schapire Editor, SRL: Uruguay 1249, 1016 Buenos Aires; tel. (1) 44-0765; f. 1941; music, art, theatre, sociology, history, fiction; Dir MIGUEL SCHAPIRE DALMAT.

Ediciones Siglo Veinte, SA: Maza 177, 1206 Buenos Aires; tel. (1) 88-2758; telex 22146; f. 1943; fiction and non-fiction; Man. Dir ISIDORO WAINER.

Editorial Sigmar, SACI: Belgrano 1580, 7°, 1093 Buenos Aires; tel. (1) 37-3045; telex 9073; fax (1) 11-2662; f. 1941; children's books; Man. Dir SIGFRIDO CHWAT.

Editorial Sopena Argentina, SACI e I: Moreno 957, 7°, Of. 2, Casilla 1075, 1091 Buenos Aires; tel. (1) 38-7182; f. 1918; dictionaries, classics, chess, health, politics, history, children's books; Exec. Pres. DANIEL CARLOS OLSEN.

Editorial Stella: Viamonte 1984, 1056 Buenos Aires; tel. (1) 46-0346; general non-fiction and textbooks; Propr Asociación Educacionista Argentina.

Editorial Sudamericana, SA: Humberto 531, 1°, 1103 Buenos Aires; tel. (1) 362-2128; telex 25644; f. 1939; general fiction and non-fiction; Gen. Man. JAIME RODRIGUÉ.

Editorial Troquel, SA: Bolívar 1721, 1141 Buenos Aires; tel. (1) 23-9350; fax (1) 34-5437; f. 1954; general literature, and textbooks; Pres. GUSTAVO A. RESSIA.

PUBLISHERS' ASSOCIATION

Cámara Argentina de Publicaciones: Reconquista 1011, 6°, 1003 Buenos Aires; tel. (1) 311-6855; f. 1970; Pres. AGUSTÍN DOS SANTOS; Man. LUIS FRANCISCO HOULIN.

ARGENTINA

Radio and Television

In 1989 there were an estimated 21.6m. radio receivers and 7.2m. television receivers in use.

Secretaría de Comunicaciones: Sarmiento 151, 4°, 1000 Buenos Aires; tel. (1) 331-1203; telex 21706; co-ordinates 30 stations and the international service; Sec. Ing. RAÚL JOSÉ OTERO.

Subsecretaría de Planificación y Gestión Tecnológica: Sarmiento 151, 4°, 1000 Buenos Aires; tel. (1) 311-5909; telex 21706; Under-Sec. Ing. LEONARDO JOSÉ LEIBSON.

Subsecretaría de Radiocomunicaciones: Sarmiento 151, 4°, 1000 Buenos Aires; tel. (1) 311-5909; telex 21706; Under-Sec. Ing. ALFREDO R. PARODI.

Subsecretaría de Telecomunicaciones: Sarmiento 151, 4°, 1000 Buenos Aires; tel. (1) 311-5909; telex 21706; Under-Sec. JULIO I. GUILLÁN.

Comité Federal de Radiodifusión (CFR): Suipacha 765, 1008 Buenos Aires; tel. (1) 394-4274; f. 1972; controls various technical aspects of broadcasting and transmission of programmes; Head LEÓN GUINSBURG.

RADIO

There are three privately-owned stations in Buenos Aires and 72 in the interior. There are also 37 state-controlled stations, four provincial, three municipal and three university stations. The principal ones are Radio El Mundo, Radio del Plata, Radio Nacional, Radio Rivadavia, Radio Belgrano, Radio Argentina, Radio Continental, Radio Mitre, Radio Antartida, Radio Excelsior, Radio Ciudad de Buenos Aires and Radio Splendid, all in Buenos Aires.

Servicio Oficial de Radiodifusión (SOR): Ayacucho 1556, 1112 Buenos Aires; tel. (1) 801-4804; Dir JULIO E. MAHARBIZ; controls:

Cadena Argentina de Radiodifusión (CAR): Avda Entre Ríos 149, 3°, 1079 Buenos Aires; tel. (1) 45-2113; groups all national state-owned commercial stations which are operated directly by the Subsecretaría Operativa.

LRA Radio Nacional: Ayacucho 1556, 1112 Buenos Aires; tel. (1) 803-5555; telex 21250; f. 1937; Supervisor JULIO E. MAHARBIZ.

Radiodifusión Argentina al Exterior (RAE): Ayacucho 1556, 1112 Buenos Aires; tel. (1) 803-2351; f. 1958; broadcasts in 8 languages to all areas of the world; Dir-Gen. Lic. LUIS ROMEO ROJAS.

Asociación de Radiodifusoras Privadas Argentinas (ARPA): Cangallo 1561, 8°, 1037 Buenos Aires; tel. (1) 35-4412; f. 1958; an association of all but 3 of the privately-owned commercial stations; Pres. EVARISTO R. E. ALONSO.

TELEVISION

There are four television channels in the federal capital of Buenos Aires, 26 in the province of Buenos Aires, 41 in the interior, and 117 relay stations. There are 28 private television channels, 14 state-supervised stations (both provincial and national) and two university channels. The national television network is controlled by the Secretariat of Culture (part of the Ministry of Education and Justice).

The following are some of the more important television stations in Argentina: Argentina Televisora Color LS82 Canal 7, LS83 Canal 9, LS84 Canal 11, LS85 Canal 13, Telenueva, Teledifusora Bahiense, Telecor, Dicor Difusión Córdoba, TV Universidad Nacional Córdoba, and TV Mar del Plata.

Asociación de Teleradiodifusoras Argentinas (ATA): Córdoba 323, 6°, 1054 Buenos Aires; tel. (1) 312-4219; telex 17253; fax (1) 312-4208; f. 1959; association of 23 private television channels; Pres. ALEJANDRO ENRIQUE MASSOT.

ATC—Argentina Televisora Color LS82 TV Canal 7: Avda Figueroa Alcorta 2977, 1425 Buenos Aires; tel. (1) 802-6001; fax (1) 802-9878; state-controlled channel; Dir RENÉ JOLIVET.

LS83 TV Canal 9: Gelly 3378, 1425 Buenos Aires; tel. (1) 801-3065; private channel; Dir ALEJANDRO RAMAY.

LS84 Canal 11: Pavón 2444, 1248 Buenos Aires; tel. (1) 941-0091; telex 22780; state-controlled channel; Dir-Gen. CARLOS M. NEGRI.

LS85 TV Canal 10: San Juan 1170, 1147 Buenos Aires; tel (1) 27-3661; telex 21762; f. 1960; state-controlled channel; Dir EDUARDO METZGER.

Finance

(cap. = capital; p.u. = paid up; res = reserves; dep. = deposits; m. = million; amounts in pesos argentinos or australes—₳)

BANKING

In 1986 there were 25 government-owned provincial banks, five government-owned municipal banks, 38 private commercial banks in the city of Buenos Aires and 90 private commercial banks in the rest of Argentina. There were also 31 foreign-owned banks operating in Argentina. In October 1986 the Government announced a reform of banking regulations, under which reserve requirements on deposits in Argentine banks were substantially reduced.

Central Bank

Banco Central de la República Argentina: Reconquista 266, 1003 Buenos Aires; tel. (1) 394-8411; telex 1137; f. 1935 as a central reserve bank; it has the right of note issue; all capital is held by the State; cap. and res 745,018m. (Dec. 1983); Gov. ANTONIO ERMÁN GONZÁLEZ; Pres. JAVIER GONZÁLEZ FRAGA.

Government-owned Commercial Banks

Banco de la Ciudad de Buenos Aires: Florida 302, 1313 Buenos Aires; tel. (1) 325-0726; telex 22365; fax (1) 325-2098; municipal bank; f. 1878; cap. and res ₳85,913.7m., dep. ₳458,450.8m. (Oct. 1989); Pres. SATURNINO MONTERO RUIZ; 32 brs.

Banco de Entre Ríos: San Martín 750, 3100 Paraná; tel. (43) 223700; telex 45115; f. 1935; provincial bank; cap. and res ₳10,718.6m., dep. ₳30,979.6m. (June 1989); Pres. Dr DARIO ALBERTO V. QUIROGA; 37 brs.

Banco de Mendoza: Gutiérrez 51, POB 19, 5500 Mendoza; tel. (061) 25-1200; telex 55204; f. 1934; provincial bank; cap. and res ₳807.8m., dep. ₳1,841.9m. (Jan. 1989); Pres. EDUARDO DEL AMOR; 77 brs.

Banco de la Nación Argentina: Bartolomé Mitre 326, 1036 Buenos Aires; tel. (1) 30-1011; telex 9190; fax (1) 112-067; f. 1891; national bank; cap. and res ₳22,017.2m., dep. ₳30,232.2m. (Jan. 1989); Pres. HUGO SANTILLI; 577 brs.

Banco de la Provincia de Buenos Aires: Avda San Martín 137, 1004 Buenos Aires; tel. (1) 331-3584; telex 18276; fax (1) 331-8375; f. 1822; provincial bank; cap. and res ₳389,520m. (Sept. 1989); dep. ₳20,261.5m. (Nov. 1988); Pres. EDUARDO P. AMADEO; 322 brs.

Banco del Chaco: Güemes 102, 3500 Resistencia; tel. (722) 24843; telex 71214; f. 1958; provincial bank; cap. and res ₳1,367.3, dep. ₳976.0m. (Jan. 1989); Pres. ANGEL CARLOS GIGLI; 27 brs.

Banco de la Provincia de Córdoba: San Jerónimo 166, 5000 Córdoba; tel. (51) 42001; telex 51756; f. 1873; provincial bank; cap. and res ₳2,043.7m., dep. ₳4,626.0m. (Jan. 1989); Pres. TITO MARCOS BATTISTEL; 157 brs.

Banco de la Provincia de Corrientes: 9 de Julio y San Juan, 3400 Corrientes; tel. (783) 65111; telex 74106; cap. and res ₳778.0m., dep. ₳967.4m. (Jan. 1989); Pres. RICARDO J. G. HARVEY; 33 brs.

Banco de la Provincia de Neuquén: Argentina 45, 8300 Neuquén; tel. (943) 31459; telex 84128; cap. and res ₳746.6m., dep. ₳1,247.4m. (Jan. 1989); Pres. OMAR SANTIAGO NEGRETTI; 21 brs.

Banco de la Provincia de Santa Fé: San Martín 715, 2000 Rosario, Santa Fé; tel. (41) 40151; telex 41751; f. 1874; provincial bank; cap. and res ₳1,214.3m., dep. ₳2,829.8m. (Jan. 1989); Pres. EMILIO SÁNCHEZ GARCÍA.

Private Commercial Banks

Banco Alas: Sarmiento 528/32, 1041 Buenos Aires; tel. (1) 313-3400; telex 9127; cap. and res ₳16.3m., dep. ₳57.5m. (March 1986); Govt Administrator LUIS PEDERNERA; 69 brs.

Banco Comercial del Norte: Reconquista 200, 4°, 1003 Buenos Aires; tel. (1) 394-8206; telex 9148; f. 1912; cap. and res ₳696.9m., dep. ₳1,544.8m. (Dec. 1988); Govt Administrator JOSÉ A. TOMÉ; 1 br.

Banco de Crédito Argentino SA: Reconquista 2, Buenos Aires; tel. (1) 334-1181; telex 18077; fax (1) 334-8980; f. 1887; cap. and res ₳1,758.8m., dep. ₳5,316.9m. (Jan. 1989); merged with Banco Financiero Argentino in 1987; Pres. Dr RICARDO CAIROLI; Exec. Dir FERNANDO DE SANTIBARES; 111 brs.

Banco Español del Río de la Plata Ltdo: Juan D. Perón 402, 1003 Buenos Aires; tel. (1) 331-2951; telex 21562; f. 1886; cap. and res ₳1,024.8m., dep. ₳627.6m. (Dec. 1988); Govt Administrator JOSÉ A. TOMÉ; 1 br.

Banco Francés del Río de la Plata: Reconquista 199, 1003 Buenos Aires; tel. (1) 331-7025; telex 9119; fax (1) 953-8009, f. 1886; cap. and res ₳997.9m., dep. ₳4,013.0m. (Jan. 1989); Pres. Dr LUIS MARÍA OTERO MONSEGUR; 53 brs.

Banco de Galicia y Buenos Aires: Juan D. Perón 407, Casilla 86, 1038 Buenos Aires; tel. (1) 394-7080; telex 9124; fax (1) 393-1603; f. 1905; cap. and res ₳18,390.1m., dep. ₳165,549.5m. (June 1989); Pres. EDUARDO J. ESCASANY; 175 brs.

Banco Mercantil Argentino: Avda Corrientes 629, 1324 Buenos Aires; tel. (1) 334-9999; telex 9122, fax (1) 11-1440, f. 1920; cap. and res ₳29,419.2m., dep. ₳78,061.0m. (Jan 1989); Pres. Dr WERTHEIN; 57 brs.

ARGENTINA

Banco Quilmes SA: Juan D. Perón 564, 2°, 1038 Buenos Aires; tel. (1) 331-8110; telex 17895; fax (1) 334-5235; f. 1907; cap. and res ₳1,012.2m., dep. ₳10,471.5m. (March 1989); Pres. Dr PEDRO O. FIORITO; 79 brs.

Banco Río de la Plata SA: Bartolomé Mitre 480, 1004 Buenos Aires; tel. (1) 331-8361; telex 9215; fax (1) 11-1225; f. 1908; cap. and res ₳113,403.7m., dep. ₳553,975.5m. (July 1989); Exec. Vice-Pres. ROQUE MACCARONE; 169 brs.

Banco Shaw SA: Sarmiento 355, 1041 Buenos Aires; tel. (1) 311-6271; telex 21226; fax (1) 312-4743; f. 1959; cap. and res ₳21,057.7m., dep. ₳184,094.8m. (Aug. 1989); Pres. Dr ALEJANDRO SHAW; 38 brs.

Other National Banks

Banco Hipotecario Nacional: Defensa 192, 1065 Buenos Aires; tel. (1) 34-2001; f. 1886; mortgage bank; cap. and res ₳1,018.8m., dep. ₳1,039.7m. (April 1988); Govt Administrator EDGARDO CIVIT; in 1990 the Government announced the closure of all 53 brs in preparation for total restructuring.

Banco Nacional de Desarrollo: 25 de Mayo 145, 1002 Buenos Aires; tel. (1) 331-2091; telex 9179; f. 1944; development bank; cap. and res ₳5,393.6m., dep. ₳3,366.0m. (Dec. 1988); Pres. ROBERTO L. ARANA.

Caja Nacional de Ahorro y Seguro: Hipólito Yrigoyen 1770, 1308 Buenos Aires; tel. (1) 45-5861; telex 22642; fax (1) 11-1568; f. 1915; savings bank and insurance institution; cap. and res ₳672.8m., dep. ₳8,806.5m. (Jan. 1989); Pres. JESÚS L. D'ALESSANDRO; 61 brs.

Foreign Banks

Banca Nazionale del Lavoro SA—BNL (Italy): Florida 32–36, 1005 Buenos Aires; tel. (1) 331-1580; telex 24028; cap. and res ₳1,613.6m., dep. ₳2,168.5m. (Jan. 1989); took over Banco de Italia y Río de la Plata in 1987; Pres. GIUSEPPE PASQUA.

Banco do Brasil SA (Brazil): Sarmiento 487, 1041 Buenos Aires; tel. (1) 325-6633; telex 24197; f. 1960; cap. and res ₳452.5m., dep. ₳50.7m. (Jan. 1989); Gen. Man. ANTONIO MACHADO DE MACEDO.

Banco Europeo para América Latina SA: Juan D. Perón 338, 1038 Buenos Aires; tel. (1) 331-6544; telex 9152; f. 1914; cap. and res ₳423.1m., dep. ₳758.9m. (Jan. 1989); Gen. Man. MARC LEFLOT; 17 brs.

Banco Holandés Unido (Netherlands): Florida 361, 1005 Buenos Aires; tel. (1) 394-1022; telex 9160; f. 1914; cap. and res ₳370.7m., dep. ₳726.2m. (Jan. 1989); Gen. Man. ROBERTO WESSELS.

Banco di Napoli (Italy): Bartolomé Mitre 699, 1036 Buenos Aires; tel. (1) 30-5555; f. 1930; cap. and res ₳547.4m., dep. ₳144.1m. (Jan. 1989); Gen. Man. PASCUAL FILOMENO.

Banco Popular Argentino: Florida 201 esq. Juan D. Perón, Casilla 3650, 1001 Buenos Aires; tel. (1) 331-6071; telex 9220; fax (1) 331-0482; f. 1887; cap. and res ₳761.7m., dep. ₳1,363.6m. (Jan. 1989); Pres. LUIS CORONEL DE PALMA; 28 brs.

Banco de Santander SA (Spain): Bartolomé Mitre 575, 1036 Buenos Aires; tel. (1) 331-0014; f. 1964; cap. and res ₳228.7m., dep. ₳576.6m. (Jan. 1989); Dir and Gen. Man. JOSÉ A. PARRA.

Banco Sudameris: Juan D. Perón 500, 1038 Buenos Aires; tel.(1) 331-4061; telex 9186; f. 1910; cap. and res ₳405.2m., dep. ₳2,227.6m. (Jan. 1989); Gen. Man. FRANCISCO CAPURRO.

Banco Supervielle Société Générale SA: Reconquista 330, 1003 Buenos Aires; tel. (1) 322-9354; telex 9108; fax (1) 11-1811; f. 1887; cap. and res ₳39,660m., dep. ₳64,712m. (Dec. 1989); Pres. and Gen. Man. GILBERT GREY.

Banco Tornquist SA: Bartolomé Mitre 531, 1036 Buenos Aires; tel. (1) 30-7841; telex 9193; f. 1960; cap. and res ₳897.7m., dep. ₳2,158.9m. (Jan. 1989); Pres. JACQUES GIRAULT; Vice-Pres. FRANCIS GANIER; 33 brs.

Bank of America NT & SA (USA): Juan D. Perón 525, Casilla 5393, 1038 Buenos Aires; tel. (1) 394-9009; telex 9145; f. 1940; cap. and res ₳308.9m., dep. ₳518.2m. (Jan. 1989); Pres. JAIME RIVERA.

Lloyds Bank (Bank of London and South America) Ltd (UK): Reconquista 101-51, Casilla 128, 1003 Buenos Aires; tel. (1) 331-3551; telex 21558; f. 1862; part of Lloyd's Bank Group; cap. and res ₳1,015.1m., dep. ₳587.1m. (Jan. 1989); Gen. Man. for Argentina MICHAEL KENT ATKINSON; 41 brs.

Bank of Tokyo Ltd (Japan): Corrientes 420, 1043 Buenos Aires; tel. (1) 322-7087; f. 1956; cap. and res ₳357.4m., dep. ₳366.5m. (Jan. 1989); Gen. Man. SCHINICHIRO KOBAYASHI.

Banque Nationale de Paris (France): 25 de Mayo 471, 1002 Buenos Aires; tel. (1) 311-4490; telex 23285; fax (1) 311-1368; f. 1981; cap. and res ₳384.6m., dep. ₳476.0m. (Jan. 1989); Gen. Man. PHILIPPE DE BOISSIEU.

Barclays Bank International PLC (UK): 25 de Mayo 555, 6°, 1002 Buenos Aires; tel. (1) 313-1638; telex 22080; fax (1) 313-1535; f. 1979; cap. and res ₳160.5m., dep. ₳4.2m. (Jan. 1989); Gen. Man. GABRIEL BUEDO.

Chase Manhattan Bank NA (USA): 25 de Mayo 140, 1002 Buenos Aires; tel. (1) 30-0400; telex 9138; f. 1904; cap. and res ₳503.0m., dep. ₳1,036.9m. (Jan 1989); Gen. Man. WILLIAM GAMBREL.

Citibank NA (USA): Bartolomé Mitre 530, 1036 Buenos Aires; tel. (1) 331-8281; telex 21583; f. 1914; cap. and res ₳1,399.9m., dep. ₳3,875.5m. (Jan. 1989); Pres. RICARDO HANDLEY; Vice-Pres. ALCIDES MIRÓ; 16 brs.

Deutsche Bank AG (Germany): Reconquista 134 y Bartolomé Mitre 401, Casilla 995, 1036 Buenos Aires; tel. (1) 30-2510; telex 9115; fax (1) 30-3536; f. 1960; cap. and res ₳910.4m., dep. ₳3,767.9m. (Jan. 1989); Dirs RAÚL G. STOCKER, KARL OSTENRIEDER, EKKEHARD WAGNER; 41 brs.

First National Bank of Boston (USA): Florida 99, 1005 Buenos Aires; tel. (1) 34-3051; f. 1784; cap. and res ₳21,783m., dep. ₳71,743m. (June 1989); Vice-Pres. and Gen. Man Ing. MANUEL SACERDOTE; 43 brs.

Royal Bank of Canada: Florida 202, Casilla 1899, 1005 Buenos Aires; tel. (1) 46-9851; telex 18613; fax (1) 40-4654; f. 1869; cap. and res ₳202.6m., dep. ₳388.2m. (Jan. 1989); Gen. Man. W. R. CAMERON; 2 brs.

Bankers' Associations

Asociación de Bancos Argentinos (ADEBA): San Martín 229, 10°, 1004 Buenos Aires; tel. (1) 394-1430; telex 23704; fax (1) 394-6340; f. 1972; Pres. ROQUE MACCARONE; Exec. Dir Dr NORBERTO C. PERUZZOTTI; 28 mems.

Asociación de Bancos de la República Argentina (ABRA): Reconquista 458, 2°, 1358 Buenos Aires; tel. (1) 394-1871; telex 28165; f. 1919; Pres. RICARDO HANDLEY; Exec. Dir ADALBERTO BARBOSA; 37 mems.

Asociación de Bancos de Provincia de la República Argentina (ABAPRA): Florida 470, 1°, 1005 Buenos Aires; tel. (1) 322-6321; telex 24015; f. 1959; Pres. Dr EDUARDO J. DEL AMOR; Man. ADRIÁN H. FERRARI; 34 mems.

Asociación de Bancos del Interior de la República Argentina (ABIRA): Corrientes 538, 4°, 1043 Buenos Aires; tel. (1) 394-3439; telex 28273; f. 1956; Pres. Dr JORGE FEDERICO CHRISTENSEN; Dir IGNACIO JOSÉ CARLOS PREMOLI; 30 mems.

Federación de Bancos Cooperativos de la República Argentina (FEBANCOOP): Maipú 374, 9°/10°, 1006 Buenos Aires; tel. (1) 394-9949; telex 23650; f. 1973; Pres. RAÚL MEILÁN SALGADO; Exec. Dir Lic. SAMUEL GLEMBOCKI; 35 mems.

STOCK EXCHANGES

Mercado de Valores de Buenos Aires, SA: 25 de Mayo 367, 9°, 1002 Buenos Aires; tel. (1) 313-4522; telex 17445; Pres. JUAN BAUTISTA PEÑA.

There are also stock exchanges at Córdoba, Rosario, Mendoza and La Plata.

INSURANCE

Superintendencia de Seguros de la Nación: Avda Julio A. Roca 721, 1067 Buenos Aires; tel. (1) 30-6653; f. 1938; Superintendent Lic. DIEGO PEDRO PELUFFO.

In June 1985 it was announced that all existing companies should have a minimum capital of ₳279,090 (australes) for all classes of insurance.

In June 1983 there were nearly 260 insurance companies operating in Argentina, of which 14 were foreign. The following is a list of those offering all classes or a specialized service.

La Agrícola SA: Corrientes 447, Buenos Aires; tel. (1) 394-5031; f. 1905; associated company La Regional; all classes; Pres. LUIS R. MARCO; First Vice-Pres. JUSTO J. DE CORRAL.

Aseguradora de Créditos y Garantías SA: San Martín 379, 6°, 1004 Buenos Aires; tel. (1) 394-1018; telex 24334; fax (1) 325-4970; f. 1965; Pres. ALEJANDRO E. FRERS; Man. CARLOS GUSTAVO KRIEGER.

Aseguradora de Río Negro y Neuquén: Avda Alem 503, Cipolletti, Río Negro; f. 1960; all classes; Gen. Man. ERNESTO LÓPEZ.

Aseguradores de Cauciones SA: Paraguay 580, 1057 Buenos Aires; tel. (1) 312-5321; telex 17321; f. 1969; all classes; Pres. Dr AGUSTÍN DE VEDIA.

Aseguradores Industriales SA: Juan D. Perón 650, 6°, 1038 Buenos Aires; tel. (1) 46-5425; f. 1961; all classes; Exec. Pres. Dir LUIS ESTEBAN LOFORTE.

La Austral: Juncal 1319, 1062 Buenos Aires; tel. (1) 42-9881; telex 21078; fax (1) 953-4459; f. 1942; all classes; Pres. RODOLFO H. TAYLOR.

ARGENTINA

Colón, Cía de Seguros Generales SA: San Martín 548–550, 1004 Buenos Aires; tel. (1) 393-5069; telex 23923; f. 1962; all classes; Gen. Man. L. D. STÜCK.

Columbia SA: Juan D. Perón 690, 1038 Buenos Aires; tel. (1) 46-1240; f. 1918; all classes; Pres. EUGENIO M. BLANCO.

El Comercio, Compañía de Seguros a Prima Fija SA: Maipú 53, 1084 Buenos Aires; tel. (1) 34-2181; f. 1889; all classes; Pres. FELIPE JOSÉ LUIS M. GAMBA; Man. PABLO DOMINGO F. LONGO.

Compañía Argentina de Seguro de Crédito a la Exportación SA: Corrientes 345, 7°, 1043 Buenos Aires; tel. (1) 313-2683; telex 24207; fax (1) 313-2919; f. 1967; covers credit and extraordinary and political risks for Argentine exports; Pres. LUIS ORCOYEN.

Compañía Aseguradora Argentina SA: Casilla 3398, Avda Roque S. Peña 555, 1035 Buenos Aires; tel. (1) 30-1571; telex 22876; fax (1) 30-5973; f. 1918; all classes; Man. GUIDO LUTTINI; Vice-Pres. ALBERTO FRAGUIO.

La Continental SA: Corrientes 655, 1043 Buenos Aires; tel. (1) 393-8051; telex 121832; f. 1912; all classes; Pres. RAÚL MASCARENHAS.

La Franco-Argentina SA: Hipólito Yrigoyen 476, 1086 Buenos Aires; tel. (1) 30-3091; telex 17291; f. 1896; all classes; Pres. Dr GUILLERMO MORENO HUEYO; Gen. Man. Dra HAYDÉE GUZIAN DE RAMÍREZ.

Hermes SA: Edif. Hermes, Bartolomé Mitre 754/60, 1034 Buenos Aires; tel. (1) 34-8441; f. 1926; all classes; Pres. CARLOS ANÍBAL PERALTA; Gen. Man. DIONISIO KATOPODIS.

Iguazú SA: San Martín 442, 1004 Buenos Aires; tel. (1) 394-6661; f. 1947; all classes; Pres. RAMÓN SANTAMARINA.

India SA: Avda Roque S. Peña 730, 1035 Buenos Aires; tel. (1) 30-6001; f. 1950; all classes; Pres. CARLOS DE ALZAGA; Vice-Pres. MATILDE DÍAZ VÉLEZ.

Instituto Italo-Argentino de Seguros Generales SA: Avda Roque S. Peña 890, 1035 Buenos Aires; tel. (1) 45-5814; f. 1920; all classes; Pres. LUIS GOTTHEIL.

La Meridonal SA: Juan D. Perón 646, 1038 Buenos Aires; tel. (1) 33-0941; f. 1949; life and general; Pres. G. G. LASCANO.

Plus Ultra, Cía Argentina de Seguros SA: San Martín 548–50, 1004 Buenos Aires; tel. (1) 393-5069; telex 23923; f. 1956; all classes; Gen. Man. L. D. STÜCK.

La Primera SA: Blvd Villegas y Oro, Trenque Lauquén, Prov. Buenos Aires; tel. (1) 393-8125; all classes; Pres. ENRIQUE RAÚL U. BOTTINI; Man. Dr RODOLFO RAÚL D'ONOFRIO.

La Rectora SA: Corrientes 848, 1043 Buenos Aires; tel. (1) 394-6081; f. 1951; all classes; Pres. PEDRO PASCUAL MEGNA; Gen. Man. ANTONIO LÓPEZ BUENO.

La República SA: San Martín 627/29, 1374 Buenos Aires; tel. (1) 393-9901; f. 1928; group life and general; Pres. ARTURO EDBROOKE; Man. RODNEY C. SMITH.

Sud América Terrestre y Marítima Cía de Seguros Generales SA: Avda Pdte R. S. Peña 530, 1035 Buenos Aires; tel. (1) 30-8570; telex 24256; f. 1919; all classes; Mans ALAIN HOMBREUX, JORGE O. SALVIDIO.

La Unión Gremial SA: Casilla 300, Gen. Mitre 665/99, 2000 Rosario, Santa Fé; tel. 47071; f. 1908; general; Pres. Cont. VÍCTOR MANUEL CABANELLAS; Gen. Man. Cont. EDUARDO IGNACIO LLOBET.

La Universal: Juncal 1319, 1062 Buenos Aires; tel. (1) 42-9881; telex 21078; fax (1) 953-4459; f. 1905; all classes; Pres. RODOLFO H. TAYLOR.

Reinsurance

Instituto Nacional de Reaseguros: Avda Pte Julio A. Roca 694, 1067 Buenos Aires; tel. (1) 34-0084; telex 2-1170; fax (1) 334-5588; f. 1947; reinsurance in all branches; Pres. and Man. REINALDO A. CASTRO.

Insurance Associations

Asociación Argentina de Compañías de Seguros: 25 de Mayo 565, 1002 Buenos Aires; tel. (1) 313-6974; telex 23837; fax (1) 312-6300; f. 1894; 137 mems; Pres. DANIEL R. SALAZAR.

Asociación de Aseguradores Extranjeros en la Argentina: San Martín 201, 7°, 1004 Buenos Aires; tel. (1) 394-3881; f. 1875; association of 11 foreign insurance companies operating in Argentina; Pres. ALEX MOCZARSKI; Sec. RICHARD MACGRATH.

Trade and Industry

CHAMBERS OF COMMERCE

Cámara Argentina de Comercio: Avda Leandro N. Alem 36, 1003 Buenos Aires; tel. (1) 331-8051; telex 18542; f. 1924; Pres. CARLOS R. DE LA VEGA.

Cámara de Comercio, Industria y Producción de la República Argentina: Florida 1, 4°, 1005 Buenos Aires; tel. (1) 331-0813; telex 18693; fax (1) 331-9116; f. 1913; Pres. JOSÉ CHEDIEK; Vice-Pres. Dr FAUSTINO S. DIÉGUEZ, Dr JORGE M. MAZALAN; 1,500 mems.

Cámara de Comercio Exterior de la Federación Gremial del Comercio e Industria: Avda Córdoba 1868, Rosario, Santa Fé; tel. (42) 21-3896; f. 1958; deals with imports and exports; Pres. EDUARDO C. SALVATIERRA; Vice-Pres. HUGO ULPIANO ARROYO; 120 mems.

Cámara de Exportadores de la República Argentina: Diag. Roque Sáenz Peña 740, 1°, 1035 Buenos Aires; f. 1943 to promote exports; Pres. Ing. DANIEL BRUNELLA; Vice-Pres. Ing. ALEJANDRO ACHAVAL; 700 mems.

Similar chambers are located in most of the larger centres and there are many foreign chambers of commerce.

GOVERNMENT REGULATORY AND SUPERVISORY BODIES

Consejo Federal de Inversiones: San Martín 871, 1004 Buenos Aires; tel. (1) 313-5557; telex 21180; fax (1) 313-4486; federal board to co-ordinate domestic and foreign investment and provide technological aid for the provinces; Sec.-Gen. Ing. JUAN JOSÉ CIÁCERA.

Instituto de Desarrollo Económico y Social (IDES): Araoz 2838, 1425 Buenos Aires; tel. (1) 804-4949; f. 1961; 700 mems; Pres. TORCUATO S. DITELLA; Sec. Dr CATALINA WAINERMAN.

Instituto Forestal Nacional (IFONA): Avda Pueyrredón 2446, 1119 Buenos Aires; tel. (1) 803-3728; telex 21535; national forestry commission; f. 1940; Principal Officer Ing. LEOPOLDO KUSCHNAROFF.

Junta Nacional de Carnes: San Martín 459, 1004 Buenos Aires; tel. (1) 394-6612; telex 24210; fax (1) 322-9357; f. 1933; national meat board; undertakes regulatory, promotional, advisory and administrative responsibilities on behalf of the meat and livestock industry; Pres. Lic. ROLANDO GARCIA LENZI.

Junta Nacional de Granos: Avda Paseo Colón 359, 1063 Buenos Aires; tel. (1) 30-0641; telex 21793; national grain board; supervises commercial practices and organizes the construction of farm silos and port elevators; Pres. JORGE CORT.

DEVELOPMENT ORGANIZATIONS

Instituto Argentino del Petróleo: Maipú 645, Buenos Aires; tel. (1) 392-3244; established to promote the development of petroleum exploration and exploitation.

Secretaría de Planificación: Hipólito Yrigoyen 250, 8°, Buenos Aires; tel. (1) 331-1722; f. 1961 to formulate national long-term development plans; Sec. Dr MOISES IKONICOFF.

Sociedad Rural Argentina: Florida 460, 1005 Buenos Aires; tel. (1) 322-2111; telex 23414; f. 1866; private organization to promote the development of agriculture; Pres. Dr EDUARDO A. C. DE ZAVALIA; 9,400 mems.

STATE ENTERPRISES

Directorio de Empresas Públicas (DEP): Lavalle 1429, Buenos Aires; tel. (1) 49-5414; f. 1986; holding company for state enterprises; Pres. Lic. HORACIO A. LOSOVIZ.

Sindicatura General de Empresas Públicas: Lavalle 1429, 1048 Buenos Aires; tel. (1) 40-5200; f. 1978; to exercise external control over wholly- or partly-owned public enterprises; Pres. MARIO J. TRUFFAT.

Agua y Energía Eléctrica Sociedad del Estado (AyEE): Avda Leandro N. Alem 1134, 1001 Buenos Aires; tel. (1) 311-6364; telex 22613; fax (1) 312-2236; f. 1947; state water and electricity board; Principal Officer CARLOS ALDERETTE.

Empresa Nacional de Correos y Telégrafos (ENCOTEL): Sarmiento 151, 1000 Buenos Aires; tel. (1) 311-5031; telex 22045; f. 1972; postal services; scheduled for transfer to private ownership in 1991; Principal Officer Dr RAÚL CARMELO VACCALLUZZO.

Empresa Nacional de Telecomunicaciones (ENTel): Defensa 143, 1065 Buenos Aires; tel. (1) 49-9684; telex 18003; f. 1949; state telecommunications corporation; transferred to private ownership in 1990; Supervisor Ing. MARÍA J. ALSOGARAY.

Gas del Estado: Alsina 1169, 1088 Buenos Aires; tel. (1) 37-2091; f. 1946; scheduled for transfer to private ownership in 1990 following merger with other state-owned energy companies; Principal Officer Ing. MIGUEL ANGEL MARIZZA.

Hidroeléctrica Norpatagónica SA (Hidronor): Avda Leandro N. Alem 1074, 1001 Buenos Aires; tel. (1) 312-6030; telex 18097; f. 1967; scheduled for transfer to private ownership in 1990 following merger with other state-owned energy companies; Principal Officer Dr CARLOS JOSÉ ANTONIO SERGNESE.

ARGENTINA

Obras Sanitarias de la Nación: Marcelo T. de Alvear 1840, Buenos Aires; tel. (1) 41-1081; f. 1973; sanitation; Principal Officer Ing. EDUARDO CEVALLO.

Petroquímica General Mosconi SAI y C: Perú 103, 1067 Buenos Aires; tel. (1) 33-5964; telex 22850; fax (1) 11-2394; f. 1970; state petrochemical industry; Pres. Dr ALFREDO JORGE CONNOLLI.

Servicios Eléctricos del Gran Buenos Aires SA (SEGBA): Balcarce 184, Buenos Aires; tel. (1) 33-1901; f. 1958; state electricity enterprise; due to be transferred to private ownership in 1990; Principal Officer Ing. ANTONIO FEDERICO.

Yacimientos Carboníferos Fiscales (YCF): Avda Roque S. Peña 1190, 1364 Buenos Aires; tel. (1) 35-4001; f. 1958; state coal-mining enterprise; due to be transferred to private ownership in 1991; Principal Officer HÉCTOR BUENO.

Yacimientos Mineros de Agua de Dionisio: Avda Julio A. Roca 710, 1067 Buenos Aires; tel. (1) 34-8024; f. 1958; state mining enterprise; Principal Officer EFRAÍN J. SAADI HERRERA.

Yacimientos Petrolíferos Fiscales Sociedad del Estado (YPF): Avda Roque S. Peña 777, 1364 Buenos Aires; tel. (1) 46-7270; telex 21999; f. 1922; public corporation authorized to formulate national petroleum policy and to develop, process and market hydrocarbon resources; in July 1987, as part of the deregulation of the petroleum industry, it was announced that YPF was to be separated into four operational divisions; due to be merged with other state-run energy companies and transferred to private ownership in 1990; Man. Dir JOSÉ ESTENSSORO.

TRADE ASSOCIATIONS

Asociación de Importadores y Exportadores de la República Argentina: Avda Belgrano 124, 1°, 1092 Buenos Aires; tel. (1) 34-0010; telex 25761; f. 1966; Pres. Lic. FERNANDO A. RAIMONDO; Man. ESTELIA D. DE AMATI.

Asociación de Industriales Textiles Argentinos: Uruguay 291, 4°, 1015 Buenos Aires; tel. (1) 49-2256; fax (1) 553-8370; f. 1945; textile industry; Pres. MANUEL CYWIN; 250 mems.

Asociación de Industrias Argentinas de Carnes: Avda Córdoba 991, 1°-A, 1054 Buenos Aires; tel. (1) 392-0587; telex 17304; meat industry; refrigerated and canned beef and mutton; Pres. JORGE BORSELLA.

Asociación Vitivinícola Argentina: Güemes 4464, 1425 Buenos Aires; tel. (1) 774-3370; f. 1904; wine industry; Pres. LUCIANO COTUMACCIO; Man. Lic. MARIO J. GIORDANO.

Cámara de Sociedades Anónimas: Sarmiento 299, Buenos Aires; tel. (1) 312-7434; Pres. Dr JORGE ENRIQUE RIVAROLA; Man. Dr ADALBERTO ZELMAR BARBOSA.

Centro de Exportadores de Cereales: Bouchard 454, 7°, 1106 Buenos Aires; tel. (1) 311-1697; telex 18644; fax (1) 312-6924; f. 1943; grain exporters; Pres. PEDRO E. GARCÍA OLIVER.

Confederación de Productores y Exportadores de la República Argentina: Bartolomé Mitre 2241, 1039 Buenos Aires; tel. (1) 48-6010; Pres. JACOBO RAIES.

Confederaciones Rurales Argentinas: México 682, 2°, 1097 Buenos Aires; tel. (1) 261-1501; Pres. Dr RAÚL ROMERO FERIS.

Federación Lanera Argentina: Paseo Colón 823, 5°, 1063 Buenos Aires; tel. (1) 361-4604; telex 28269; fax (1) 362-8650; f. 1929; wool industry; Pres. JORGE D. SRODEK; Sec. JOSÉ G. GALLIA; 119 mems.

EMPLOYERS' ORGANIZATION

Unión Industrial Argentina (UIA): Avda Leandro N. Alem 1067, 11°, 1001 Buenos Aires; tel. (1) 313-9399; telex 21749; fax (1) 313-2413; f. 1887; Argentine association of manufacturers representing 95% of industrial corporations; re-established in 1974 with the fusion of the Confederación Industrial Argentina (CINA) and the Confederación General de la Industria; following the dissolution of the CINA in 1977, the UIA was formed in 1979; Pres. GILBERTO MONTAGNA; Exec. Sec. JORGE GAIBISSO.

TRADE UNIONS

Confederación General del Trabajo—CGT (General Confederation of Labour): Buenos Aires; f. 1984; Peronist; Sec.-Gen. SAÚL EDOLVER UBALDINI; represents approximately 90% of Argentina's 1,100 trade unions and consists of three groups:

CGT: Buenos Aires.

Renovadores: Buenos Aires.

62 Organizaciones: Buenos Aires.

Note: In 1990 the CGT split into two legally recognized factions. See Recent History section, p. 356.

Transport

Ministerio de Obras y Servicios Públicos: Avda 9 de Julio 1925, 1322 Buenos Aires; tel. (1) 38-8911; telex 22577; fax (1) 331-9967; controls:

Directory

Secretaría de Transportes: Avda 9 de Julio 1925, 1332 Buenos Aires; tel. (1) 38-1435; Sec. (vacant).

  Subsecretaría de Transporte: Avda 9 de Julio 1925, 1332 Buenos Aires; tel. (1) 38-5838, ext. 407; Under-Sec. (vacant).

  Subsecretaría de Planificación del Transporte: Avda 9 de Julio 1925, 1322 Buenos Aires; tel. (1) 37-2571, ext. 465; Under-Sec. (vacant).

  Subsecretaría de Marina Mercante: Julio A. Roca 734, 1067 Buenos Aires; tel. (1) 30-2857; telex 21091; Under-Sec. (vacant).

  Dirección Nacional de Transporte Aerocomercial: Avda 9 de Julio 1925, 22°, 1332 Buenos Aires; tel. (1) 37-8365; telex 22577; Dir (vacant).

RAILWAYS

Lines: General Belgrano (narrow gauge), General Roca, General Bartolomé Mitre, General San Martín, Domingo Faustino Sarmiento (all wide gauge), General Urquiza (medium gauge) and Línea Metropolitana, which controls the railways of Buenos Aires and its suburbs. There are direct rail links with the Bolivian Railways network to Santa Cruz de la Sierra and La Paz; with Chile, through the Las Cuevas–Caracoles tunnel (across the Andes) and between Salta and Antofagasta; with Brazil, across the Paso de los Libres and Uruguayana bridge; with Paraguay (between Posadas and Encarnación by ferry-boat); and with Uruguay (between Concordia and Salto). In 1987 there were 34,509 km of tracks. In the Buenos Aires commuter area 270.4 km of wide gauge track and 52 km of medium gauge track are electrified. In mid-1988 work commenced on the construction of the 'Expreso del Sud' railway, linking Buenos Aires with the Bolivian capital, La Paz.

Ferrocarriles Argentinos (FA): Avda Ramos Mejía 1302, 1302 Buenos Aires; tel. (1) 312-1746; telex 22507; f. 1948 with the nationalization of all foreign property; autonomous body but policies are established by the Ministry of Public Works and Services through the Secretaría de Transportes; Supt (vacant).

Cámara de Industriales Ferroviarios: Alsina 1607, 1°, 1088 Buenos Aires; tel. (1) 40-5571; telex 21355; private organization to promote the development of Argentine railway industries; Pres. Ing. GUILLERMO NOTTAGE.

Buenos Aires also has an underground railway system:

Subterráneos de Buenos Aires: Bartolomé Mitre 3342, 1201 Buenos Aires; tel. (1) 89-0631; telex 18979; f. 1952; became completely state-owned in 1978; controlled by the Municipalidad de la Ciudad de Buenos Aires; five underground lines totalling 36 km, 63 stations, and a 14-km light rail line, which was opened in 1987; Pres. JOSÉ MARÍA GARCÍA ARECHA.

ROADS

In 1986 there were 211,369 km of roads, of which 378 km were motorways, 36,928 km were other main roads and 174,063 km were secondary roads. In 1990 the Government announced plans to transfer 9,800 km of main road to private ownership for conversion to a tolls system. In 1983 the network carried about 80% of all freight tonnage and 85% of all medium- and long-distance passengers. Four branches of the Pan-American highway run from Buenos Aires to the borders of Chile, Bolivia, Paraguay and Brazil.

Dirección Nacional de Vialidad: Comodoro Py 2002, 1104 Buenos Aires; tel. (1) 312-9021; telex 17879; controlled by the Secretaría de Transportes; Gen. Man. Ing. SAÚL MARTÍNEZ.

Asociación Argentina Empresarios Transporte Automotor (AAETA): Bernardo de Yrigoyen 330, 6°, 1072 Buenos Aires; Pres. LUIS CARRAL.

Federación Argentina de Entidades Empresarias de Autotransporte de Cargas (FADEAC): Avda de Mayo 1370, 3°, 1372 Buenos Aires; tel. (1) 37-3635; Pres. ROGELIO CAVALIERI IRIBARNE.

There are several international passenger and freight services including:

Autobuses Sudamericanos SA: Bernardo de Yrigoyen 1370, 1°, Casilla 40, 1401 Buenos Aires; tel. (1) 27-6591; telex 17870; fax (1) 311-4385; f. 1928; international bus services; car and bus rentals; charter bus services; Pres. ARMANDO SAMUEL SCHLEKER; Gen. Man. MARÍA ANTONIA APREA.

INLAND WATERWAYS

There is considerable traffic in coastal and river shipping, mainly carrying petroleum and its derivatives. In 1983 the total displacement of vessels entering Argentine ports for such transport was 28.2m. nrt.

Dirección Nacional de Construcciones Portuarias y Vías Navegables: Avda España 221, 4°, Buenos Aires; tel. (1) 361-5964; responsible for the maintenance and improvement of waterways and dredging operations; Dir Ing. ENRIQUE CASALS DE ALBA.

ARGENTINA

SHIPPING

There are more than 100 ports, of which the most important are Buenos Aires, Quequén, Rosario and Bahía Blanca. There are specialized terminals at Ensenada, Comodoro Rivadavia, San Lorenzo and Campana (petroleum); Bahía Blanca, Rosario, Santa Fé, Villa Concepción, Mar del Plata and Quequén (cereals); and San Nicolás and San Fernando/San Isidro (raw and construction materials). In May 1987 the World Bank allocated a loan of US $50m. to Argentina to help finance the rehabilitation of Bahía Blanca; and in 1988 Argentina received a loan of US $7.7m. for general improvements to port facilities from the Japanese Government. Argentina's merchant fleet totalled 2,066,661 grt in 1985; it comprised 64 cargo vessels, 26 bulk carriers, 58 tankers and 41 miscellaneous vessels.

Administración General de Puertos: Avda Julio A. Roca 734/42, 1067 Buenos Aires; tel. (1) 34-5621; telex 21879; f. 1956; state enterprise for direction, administration and exploitation of all national sea and river ports; scheduled for transfer to private ownership in 1991; Chair. (vacant).

Capitanía General del Puerto: Avda Julio A. Roca 734, 2°, 1067 Buenos Aires; tel. (1) 34-9784; f. 1967; co-ordination of port operations; Port Captain Capt. PEDRO TARAMASCO.

The chief state-owned shipping organizations are:

Empresa Líneas Marítimas Argentinas SA (ELMA): Avda Corrientes 389, 1043 Buenos Aires; tel. (1) 312-8111; telex 22317; f. 1941; state line operating 34 vessels (474,445 grt) to Northern Europe, Scandinavia, the Mediterranean, West and East Coasts of Canada and the USA, Gulf of Mexico, Caribbean ports, Brazil, Pacific ports of Central and South America, Far East, North and South Africa and the Near East; scheduled for transfer to private ownership in 1991; Pres. Dr L. A. J. OLAIZOLA.

Yacimientos Petrolíferos Fiscales (YPF): Avda Roque S. Peña 777, 1035 Buenos Aires; tel. (1) 46-7271; telex 21792; Pres. HÉCTOR J. FIORELI; fleet of 350,701 grt of cargo, tankers and tanker craft and motor launches.

Private shipping companies operating on coastal and overseas routes include:

Astra Compañía Argentina de Petróleo SA: Leandro N. Alem 621, 1001 Buenos Aires; tel. (1) 311-0091; telex 17478; Pres. Dr RICARDO GRUNEISEN; fleet of 52,969 grt of tankers and tanker craft.

Bottacchi SA de Navegación: Maipu 509, 1006 Buenos Aires; tel. (1) 392-7411; telex 22639; Pres. ANGEL L. M. BOTTACCHI; fleet of 79,696 grt of tankers and cargo craft.

Compañía Argentina de Transportes Marítimos SA: Avda Corrientes 327, 3°, 1043 Buenos Aires; tel. (1) 311-6300; telex 23524; Pres. JUAN L. MARTÍN; Vice-Pres. R. E. VÁSQUEZ; fleet of 54,153 grt.

CIVIL AVIATION

Argentina has 10 international airports (Aeroparque Jorge Newbery, Córdoba, Corrientes, El Plumerillo, Ezeiza, Jujuy, Resistencia, Río Gallegos, Salta and San Carlos de Bariloche). Ezeiza, 35 km from Buenos Aires, is one of the most important air terminals in Latin America.

Aerolíneas Argentinas: Paseo Colón 185, 1063 Buenos Aires; tel. (1) 30-2071; telex 22517; fax (1) 331-0356; f. 1950; transferred to private ownership (Iberia Airlines, Spain) in 1990; services to New York, Los Angeles, Miami, Mexico, Montreal and Europe; its South American services link Argentina with Bolivia, Chile, Colombia, Ecuador, Uruguay, Brazil, Peru, Venezuela and Paraguay; the internal network covers the whole country; passengers, mail and freight are carried; Pres. EDUARDO GONZÁLEZ DEL SOLAR; Vice-Pres. OSCAR CARBONE; fleet comprises 6 Boeing 747-200B, 1 747SP, 2 707-320B, 8 727-200, 9 737-200, 2 737-200C, 3 Fokker F.28-1000, 1 F.28-4000.

Aerolínea Federal Argentina (ALFA): Avda 9 de Julio 321, Resistencia; tel. (722) 4901; domestic passenger and cargo services from Resistencia; fleet comprises 2 Fairfield FH-227B.

Austral Líneas Aéreas (Cielos del Sur SA): Avda Corrientes 485, 1398 Buenos Aires; tel. (1) 325-0777; telex 9175; fax (1) 11-1295; f. 1971; taken over by the State in 1980 to prevent financial collapse; transferred to private ownership in Sept. 1987; domestic flights linking 20 cities in Argentina; Pres. Ing. AMEDEO RIVA ; fleet comprises 8 BAC 1-11 series 500, 1 MD-83, 2 MD-80.

Líneas Aéreas del Estado (LADE): Perú 710, Buenos Aires; tel. (1) 361-7174; telex 22040; f. 1940; controlled by the Air Ministry and operates through the Argentine Air Force; LADE operates from El Palomar Air Base, Buenos Aires, to 35 domestic points, all south of the capital; Dir OTTO A. RITONDALE; passenger fleet comprises 1 Fokker F.28-1000C, 2 F.27-600, 2 Twin Otter.

Tourism

Argentina's superb tourist attractions include the Andes mountains, the lake district centred on Bariloche (where there is a National Park), Patagonia, the Atlantic beaches and Mar del Plata, the Iguazú falls, the Pampas and Tierra del Fuego. Visitors to Argentina were estimated at 2,231,524 in 1988.

Secretaría de Turismo de la Nación: Calle Suipacha 1111, 21°, 1368 Buenos Aires; tel. (1) 312-5621; telex 24882; fax (1) 312-1638; Sec. JOSÉ OMAR FASSI LAVALLE.

Asociación Argentina de Agencias de Viajes y Turismo (AAAVYT): Viamonte 640, 10°, 1053 Buenos Aires; tel. (1) 322-2804; telex 25449; f. 1951; Pres. PEDRO BACHRACH; Gen. Man. HÉCTOR J. TESTONI.

Atomic Energy

Comisión Nacional de Energía Atómica (CNEA): Avda del Libertador 8250, 1429 Buenos Aires; tel. (1) 70-7711; telex 25392; fax (1) 786-9550; f. 1950; Pres. Dr MANUEL A. MONDINO.

Consejo Consultivo Nacional de Energía Atómica: Buenos Aires; f. 1987 to advise the CNEA's Pres. (see above) in the drawing-up of studies and projects concerned with the reorganization of nuclear activities.

Directorio de la CNEA: Avda del Libertador 8250, 1429 Buenos Aires; tel. (1) 70-7711; telex 25392; fax (1) 544-9252; f. 1989; Pres. Dr MANUEL A. MONDINO.

Argentina's first nuclear reactor, with a capacity of 335 MW, at Atucha, on the River Paraná de las Palmas, commenced operations in 1974. A second plant at Embalse (Córdoba), with an estimated capacity of 600 MW, came into operation in March 1983. A third plant, Atucha II, with an estimated capacity of 700 MW, was under construction in 1990, and was expected to begin operating in 1994. Argentina's first nuclear fuel production plant opened in April 1982, and a reprocessing plant began operations in early 1987. In recent years the development of the atomic energy sector has been severely hindered by lack of funds. In 1989 nuclear power supplied 13.9% of Argentina's total energy requirements.

Research reactors: The following research reactors are in operation:

RA-1 Centro Atómico Constituyentes: maximum thermal capacity 150 kW.

RA-2 Centro Atómico Constituyentes: maximum thermal capacity 30 MW.

RA-3 Centro Atómico Ezeiza: maximum thermal capacity 5 MW.

RA-6 Centro Atomico Bariloche: maximum thermal capacity 500 MW.

AUSTRALIA

Introductory Survey

Location, Climate, Language, Religion, Flag, Capital

The Commonwealth of Australia occupies the whole of the island continent of Australia, lying between the Indian and Pacific Oceans, and its offshore islands, principally Tasmania to the south-east. Australia's nearest neighbour is Papua New Guinea, to the north. In the summer (November–February) there are tropical monsoons in the northern part of the continent (except for the Queensland coast), but the winters (July–August) are dry. Both the north-west and north-east coasts are liable to experience tropical cyclones between December and April. In the southern half of the country, winter is the wet season; rainfall decreases rapidly inland. Very high temperatures, sometimes exceeding 50°C (122°F), are experienced during the summer months over the arid interior and for some distance to the south, as well as during the pre-monsoon months in the north. The official language is English. In 1986 some 73% of the population professed Christianity (24% Anglican, 26% Roman Catholics, 23% other denominations). The national flag (proportions 2 by 1) is blue, with a representation of the United Kingdom flag in the upper hoist, a large seven-pointed white star in the lower hoist and five smaller white stars, in the form of the Southern Cross constellation, in the fly. The capital, Canberra, lies in one of two enclaves of federal territory known as the Australian Capital Territory (ACT).

Recent History

Since the Second World War, Australia has played an important role in Asian affairs and has strengthened its political and economic ties with India, South-East Asia and Japan. The country co-operates more closely than formerly with the USA (see ANZUS, p. 235) and has given much aid to Asian countries.

In January 1966 Sir Robert Menzies resigned after 16 years as Prime Minister, and was succeeded by Harold Holt, who was returned to office at elections later that year. However, Holt died in December 1967. His successor, Senator John Gorton, took office in January 1968 but resigned, after losing a vote of confidence, in March 1971. William McMahon was Prime Minister from March 1971 until December 1972, when, after 23 years in office, the Liberal-Country Party coalition was defeated at a general election for the House of Representatives. The Australian Labor Party (ALP), led by Gough Whitlam, won 67 of the 125 seats in the House. Following a conflict between the Whitlam Government and the Senate, both Houses of Parliament were dissolved in April 1974, and a general election was held in May. The ALP was returned to power, although with a reduced majority in the House of Representatives. However, the Government failed to gain a majority in the Senate, and in October 1975 the Opposition in the Senate obstructed legislative approval of budget proposals. The Government was not willing to consent to a general election over the issue, but in November the Governor-General, Sir John Kerr, intervened and took the unprecedented step of dismissing the Government. A caretaker ministry was installed under Malcolm Fraser, the Liberal leader, who formed a coalition government with the Country Party. This coalition gained large majorities in both Houses of Parliament at a general election in December 1975, but the majorities were progressively reduced at general elections in December 1977 and October 1980.

Fraser's coalition Government was defeated by the ALP at a general election in March 1983. Robert Hawke, who had replaced William Hayden as Labor leader in the previous month, became the new Prime Minister and immediately organized a meeting of representatives of government, employers and trade unions to reach agreement on a prices and incomes policy (the 'Accord') that would allow economic recovery. Hawke called a general election for December 1984, 15 months earlier than necessary, and the ALP was returned to power with a reduced majority in the House of Representatives. The opposition coalition between the Liberal Party and the National Party (formerly known as the Country Party) collapsed in April 1987, when 12 National Party MPs withdrew from the agreement and formed the New National Party (led by the right-wing Sir Johannes Bjelke-Petersen, at that time the Premier of Queensland), while the remaining 14 National Party MPs continued to support their leader, Ian Sinclair, who wished to remain within the alliance. Both Houses of Parliament were dissolved in June, in preparation for an early general election in July. The election campaign was dominated by economic issues. The ALP was returned to office with an increased majority, securing 86 of the 148 seats in the House of Representatives. The Liberal and National Parties announced the renewal of the opposition alliance in August. Four months later, Bjelke-Petersen was forced to resign as Premier of Queensland, under pressure from National Party officials who blamed him for the sharp decline in support for the National Party in Queensland.

In early 1988 the Hawke Government suffered several defeats at by-elections, seemingly as a result of a decline in living standards and an unpopular policy of wage restraint. The ALP narrowly retained power in the state of Victoria, but was defeated in New South Wales, where it had held power for 12 years. In May 1989 the leader of the Liberal Party, John Howard, was replaced by Andrew Peacock, and Charles Blunt succeeded Ian Sinclair as leader of the National Party. In July a commission of inquiry into alleged corruption in Queensland published its report. The Fitzgerald report documented several instances of official corruption and electoral malpractice by the Queensland Government, particularly during the administration of Bjelke-Petersen (who was subsequently charged with corruption and perjury in October 1990). Following the publication of the report, support for the National Party within Queensland declined once more, and in December the ALP defeated the National Party in the state election (the first time that it had defeated the National Party in Queensland since 1957).

In August 1989 the popularity of the Hawke Government and, in particular, the personal reputation of the Prime Minister were further damaged by a dispute between the major domestic airlines and the airline pilots' federation, which, by October, had cost the Australian tourist industry some $A1,500m. The pilots had resigned *en masse* when both Ansett and Australian Airlines, with government approval, had rejected their claim (presented in July) for a 29.5% increase in wages, which would have contravened the Government's policy of pay restraint. Attempts by the Industrial Relations Commission to settle the dispute proved unsuccessful, and in September Hawke announced that the Government was to award substantial compensation to the airlines, which were estimated to be losing some $A30m. per week as a result of the dispute. In October the pilots' federation presented a reduced claim, linked to an increase in productivity, but this was also rejected. In November, with no solution to the dispute having been found, the airlines intensified recruitment initiatives in North America and western Europe, while maintaining a very limited service. By February 1990 the airlines claimed to have restored their operations through the recruitment of foreign pilots as well as former staff demoralized by the apparent failure of their action, and in March the remaining rebel pilots ended their strike.

In February 1990 Hawke announced that a general election for the Senate and the House of Representatives was to be held on 24 March. The Government's position in the period preceding the election had been strengthened by the ALP victory in Queensland in December 1989, the removal of an unpopular Labor leadership in Western Australia and its replacement by the first female Premier, Dr Carmen Lawrence, and by the support that it secured from environmental groups as a result of its espousal of 'green' issues. Although the opposition parties won the majority of the first-preference votes in the election for the House of Representatives, the endorsement of the environmental groups delivered a block of second-preference votes to the ALP, which was consequently returned to power, albeit with a reduced majority, gaining 78 of the 148 seats. Following its defeat, Peacock immediately resigned as leader of the Liberal Party and was replaced by Dr John Hewson; while Blunt lost his seat in the election and was succeeded as leader of the National Party by Tim Fischer.

In September 1990, at a meeting of senior ALP members, government proposals to initiate a controversial programme of privatization, including the sale of 49% of Qantas Airways and 100% of Australian Airlines, was endorsed, effectively ending almost 100 years of the ALP's stance against private ownership. Plans to end the State's monopoly of the telecommunications industry, through the transfer to private ownership of the government-owned and unprofitable satellite company, Aussat, were also approved. In November, however, the Government indicated that the privatization of the two state-owned airlines might be deferred until 1992, owing to the economic depression in the aviation industry. At a conference in Brisbane in late October, government plans for constitutional and structural reform were approved in principle by the leaders of the six state and two territory governments. The proposed reforms advocated the reduction or elimination of regional differences in regulations and services, and envisaged, in their place, the creation of national standards. They also proposed to alleviate the financial dependence of the states and territories on the Federal Government by according them greater responsibility in the levying of indirect taxes and in the disposal of revenue allocated by the Federal Government. These suggested reforms, however, encountered strong opposition from sections of the public services, the trade unions and the business community.

Owing to Australian opposition to French test explosions of nuclear weapons at Mururoa Atoll in the South Pacific Ocean, a ban on uranium sales was introduced. However, in August 1986 the Government announced its decision to resume uranium exports, claiming that the sanction had been ineffective and that the repeal of the ban would increase government revenue by $A66m., through the repayment of compensation that had been awarded to the mining industry. In December 1986 Australia ratified a treaty declaring the South Pacific area a nuclear-free zone. In May 1987 Australia and the United Kingdom began a joint operation to ascertain the extent of plutonium contamination resulting from British nuclear weapons testing at Maralinga between 1956 and 1967. Many Australians were highly critical of the UK's apparent disregard for the environmental consequences of the tests and of the British authorities' failure to make adequate arrangements to protect the local Aborigines, who were now campaigning for a thorough decontamination of their traditional lands.

The sensitive issue of Aboriginal land rights was addressed by the Government in August 1985, when it formulated proposals for legislation that would give Aborigines inalienable freehold title to national parks, vacant Crown land and former Aboriginal reserves, in spite of widespread opposition from state governments (which had formerly been responsible for their own land policies), from mining companies and from the Aborigines themselves, who were angered by the Government's withdrawal of its earlier support for the Aboriginal right to veto mineral exploitation. In October 1985 Ayers Rock, in the Northern Territory, was officially transferred to the Mutijulu Aboriginal community, on condition that continuing access to the rock (the main inland tourist attraction) be guaranteed. In 1986, however, the Government abandoned its pledge to impose such federal legislation on unwilling state governments, and this led to further protests from Aboriginal leaders. In September 1987 the Prime Minister proposed a treaty of understanding with the Aboriginal people, to coincide with the 200th anniversary, in 1988, of European settlement in Australia. However, by November 1990 no such treaty had been negotiated. In November 1987 an official commission of inquiry into the cause of the high death rate among Aboriginal prisoners recommended immediate government action, and in July 1988 it was announced that 108 cases remained to be investigated. In August 1988 a United Nations report accused Australia of violating international human rights in its treatment of the Aboriginal people. In November the Government announced an enquiry into its Aboriginal Affairs Department, following accusations, made by the opposition coalition, of nepotism and misuse of funds. The commission of inquiry published its first official report in February 1989. Following the report's recommendations, the Government announced the creation of a $A10m. programme to combat the high death rate among Aboriginal prisoners. In October an unofficial study indicated that Aborigines, although accounting for only 1% of the total population of Australia, comprised more than 20% of persons in prison.

In its foreign policy, the Hawke Government placed greater emphasis on links with South-East Asia. Australian relations with Indonesia, which had been strained since the Indonesian annexation of the former Portuguese colony of East Timor in 1976, improved in August 1985, when Hawke made a statement recognizing Indonesian sovereignty over the territory, but subsequently deteriorated, following the publication in a Sydney newspaper, in April 1986, of an article containing allegations of corruption against the Indonesian President, Gen. Suharto. Relations between Australia and Indonesia improved in December 1989, when they signed an accord regarding joint exploration for petroleum and gas reserves in the Timor Gap, an area of sea forming a disputed boundary between the two countries. In January 1989 Hawke proposed the creation of an Asia-Pacific Economic Co-operation Council (APEC) to facilitate the exchange of services, tourism and direct foreign investment in the region. In November, at the inaugural APEC conference in Canberra, the 12 Ministers of Foreign Affairs of the respective countries (the six ASEAN countries–see p. 103, Japan, the Republic of Korea, New Zealand, Australia, the USA and Canada) agreed to hold further talks in 1990 and 1991 'to advance the APEC concept' and committed themselves to increasing regional trade and investment.

The viability of the ANZUS military pact, which was signed in 1951, linking Australia, New Zealand and the USA, was disputed by the US Government following the New Zealand Government's declaration, in July 1984, that vessels which were believed to be powered by nuclear energy, or to be carrying nuclear weapons, would be barred from the country's ports. Hawke did not support the New Zealand initiative, and Australia continued to participate with the USA in joint military exercises from which New Zealand had been excluded. However, the Hawke Government declined directly to endorse US retaliation against New Zealand, and in 1986 stated that Australia regarded its 'obligations to New Zealand as constant and undiminishing'. In late 1988 Australia signed a 10-year agreement with the USA, extending its involvement in the management of US-staffed military bases in Australia. The pact was regarded as confirmation of Australia's continuing commitment to its alliance with the West. In response to growing Soviet influence in the Pacific region, the Government announced in early 1987 that Australia's defence ties with South Pacific nations were to be given the same priority as traditional links with South-East Asian countries. In March proposals for an ambitious new defence strategy were published, following the recommendations of a government-commissioned report advocating a comprehensive restructuring of the country's military forces, on the basis of greater self-reliance. The cost of the plan, however, was estimated at $A25,000m. over 15 years. In September 1990 Australia and New Zealand signed an agreement to establish a joint venture to construct as many as 12 naval frigates to patrol the South Pacific.

In August 1990, despite earlier statements that Australia's new security policy was based entirely on self-reliance, the Government dispatched two frigates and a support ship to the Gulf to participate in the UN-sanctioned blockade of Iraq, following its invasion and forcible annexation of Kuwait.

In March 1986 the last vestiges of Australia's constitutional links with the United Kingdom were finally severed by the Australia Act, which abolished the UK Parliament's residual legislative, executive and judicial controls over Australian state law.

Government

Australia comprises six states and two territories. Executive power is vested in the British monarch and exercised by the monarch's appointed representative, the Governor-General, who normally acts on the advice of the Federal Executive Council (the Ministry), led by the Prime Minister. The Governor-General appoints the Prime Minister and, on the latter's recommendation, other Ministers.

Legislative power is vested in the Federal Parliament. This consists of the monarch, represented by the Governor-General, and two chambers elected by universal adult suffrage (voting is compulsory). The Senate has 76 members (12 from each state and two from each of the territories), who are elected by a system of proportional representation for six years when representing a state, with half the seats renewable every three

AUSTRALIA

years, and for a term of three years when representing a territory. The House of Representatives has 148 members, elected for three years (subject to dissolution) from single-member constituencies. The Federal Executive Council is responsible to Parliament.

Each state has a Governor, representing the monarch, and its own legislative, executive and judicial system. The state governments are essentially autonomous, but certain powers are placed under the jurisdiction of the Federal Government. All except the Northern Territory, which acceded to self-governing status in 1978, and Queensland have an Upper House (the Legislative Council) and a Lower House (the Legislative Assembly or House of Assembly). The chief ministers of the states are known as Premiers, as distinct from the Federal Prime Minister.

Defence

Australia's defence policy is based on collective security and it is a member of the British Commonwealth Strategic Reserve and ANZUS, with New Zealand and the USA. In June 1990 Australia's armed forces numbered 68,100 (army 30,300, navy 15,650, air force 22,100). The defence budget for the financial year ending 30 June 1990 was $A8,330m. Service in the armed forces is voluntary.

Economic Affairs

In 1988, according to estimates by the World Bank, Australia's gross national product (GNP), measured at average 1986–88 prices, was US $204,446m., equivalent to $12,390 per head (comparable to the average levels in industrialized West European countries). It was estimated that Australia's GNP per head increased, in real terms, at an average rate of 1.7% per year between 1980 and 1988. Over the same period, the population increased by an average annual rate of 1.4%. The country's gross domestic product (GDP) increased, in real terms, by an annual average of 3.3% in 1980–88.

Agriculture (including forestry, hunting and fishing) contributed 4.0% of GDP in 1988, and engaged 5.3% of the employed labour force in 1989. During the mid-1980s the agricultural sector supplied an annual average of 37% of total export earnings. The principal cash crops are wheat, fruit, sugar and cotton, and Australia is the world's leading producer of wool (which provided 26.4% of the country's gross farm output in 1988/89). Beef production is also important, contributing 13.4% of the value of gross farm output in 1988/89. During 1980–86 agricultural production increased by an annual average of 6.1%.

Industry (comprising mining, manufacturing, construction and utilities) employed 26.6% of the working population in 1989 and provided about 32% of GDP in 1986/87. Industrial production increased at an average rate of 2.0% per year during 1980–86.

The mining sector employed 1.4% of the working population in 1988, and contributed 4.9% of GDP in 1987/88. Export earnings from the sector comprised 31.4% of total export receipts during the 12 months to March 1989. The principal minerals extracted are coal, iron ore, gold, silver, petroleum and natural gas. Bauxite, zinc, copper, titanium, nickel, tin, lead and zircon are also mined.

Manufacturing contributed 18% of GDP in 1987/88. The sector employed 16% of the working population in 1989. Measured by the value of output, the principal branches of manufacturing in the year ending 30 June 1985 were metal products (19.8%), food products (17.8%), transport equipment (9.7%), machinery (9%), chemicals and chemical products (7.9%), textiles and clothing, wood and paper products, and publishing.

Energy is derived principally from petroleum, natural gas and coal, which together provided 55% of the mining sector's output in 1986/87. Production of black coal totalled 167.7m. metric tons in 1987/88, when exports of coal were valued at more than $A4,800m.

In 1989 Australia recorded a visible trade deficit of US $4,169m., and there was a deficit of $16,861m. on the current account of the balance of payments. In the year ending 30 June 1989 the principal sources of imports were the USA (21.5%) and Japan (20.8%), which were also the principal markets for exports in that year (10.2% and 27.2% respectively). Other major trading partners are Germany, New Zealand and the United Kingdom. The principal exports in the year ending 30 June 1989 were metalliferous ores, textile fibres (mainly wool), coal, non-ferrous metals and cereals. The principal imports in that year were machinery and transport equipment, basic manufactures, and chemicals and related products.

Introductory Survey

In the 1989/90 financial year a budgetary surplus of $A8,036m. was projected. In March 1989 Australia's total external debt stood at $A128,600m. (equivalent to 39% of annual GDP), and by April 1990 it had risen to an estimated $A140,000m. An estimated 8.2% of the labour force were unemployed in November 1990. The annual rate of inflation averaged 8.2% in 1981–89, and stood at 7.7% for the year ending 30 June 1990.

Australia is a member of the South Pacific Forum (see p. 207) and the South Pacific Commission (see p. 205), and is a major financial contributor to the latter, as well as to the former's South Pacific Forum Secretariat (see p. 207). In 1989 Australia played a major role in the creation of the Asia-Pacific Economic Co-operation Council (APEC), which aimed to stimulate economic development in the region.

In 1982 Australia signed an agreement for a 'closer economic relationship' (CER) with New Zealand, aiming to eliminate trade barriers between the two countries. All barriers to bilateral trade were effectively removed in July 1990, following the completion of the CER accord, which stipulated the elimination of all remaining import restrictions and tariff quotas.

In the mid-1980s the Australian Government completed the deregulation of the financial sector and successfully pursued a policy of wage restraint to control the rate of inflation. In the late 1980s and the early 1990s, however, the economy was increasingly subject to inflationary pressure. Although there was a budget surplus in 1987/88 and 1988/89, several annual trade deficits and a substantial current account deficit were recorded. Interest rates rose sharply, reaching a record 18% in mid-1989, before falling back down to 13% in October 1990. In 1990 the Government announced a far-reaching programme of structural economic reforms. The proposals included the transfer to private ownership of the telecommunications and aviation industries, the devolution of economic power to the six state and two territory governments, the introduction of national standards in most areas, including transport (through the creation of a national rail freight corporation), and the co-ordination of expenditure on the infrastructure. The success of the Government's reforms, however, remained dependent on its ability to reduce the deficit on the current account of the balance of payments (which rose to a record $A21,157m. in the year ending 30 June 1990), a move that would stabilize Australia's external debt, and its ability to contain inflationary pressures without forcing the economy into severe recession.

Social Welfare

Australia provides old-age, invalid and widows' pensions, unemployment, sickness and supporting parents' benefits, family allowances and other welfare benefits and allowances. Reciprocal welfare agreements operate between Australia and New Zealand and the United Kingdom. In 1984 Australia had 3,535 hospital establishments, including nursing homes, with a total of 166,237 beds, equivalent to one for every 66 inhabitants. In 1984 there were 35,000 physicians registered in the country. The desert interior is served by the Royal Flying Doctor Service. Of total expenditure by the Federal Government and its agencies (excluding transfer to state governments) in the financial year ending 30 June 1987, $A7,372m. (11.8%) was for health services, while a further $A20,739m. (33.1%) was for social security and welfare. Expenditure on health by all levels of government in 1986/87 was $A14,587m. (14.5% of total government spending).

In February 1984 the Government introduced a system of universal health insurance, known as Medicare, whereby every Australian is protected against the costs of medical and hospital care. Where medical expenses are incurred, Medicare covers patients for 85% of the government-approved Schedule Fee for any service provided by a doctor in private practice. For hospital care, Medicare pays the full cost of shared-ward accommodation in public hospitals when treatment is provided by doctors employed by the hospital. Out-patient treatment is also free. Private health insurance is available to cover private hospital accommodation and the choice of doctor in a public hospital. The Medicare scheme is financed in part by a 1% levy on taxable incomes above a certain level.

Education

Education is the responsibility of each of the states and the Federal Government. It is compulsory, and available free of charge, for all children from the ages of six to 15 years. Primary education generally begins at six years of age and

AUSTRALIA

lasts for six years. Secondary education, beginning at the age of 12, usually lasts for five years. As a proportion of children in the relevant age-groups, the enrolment ratios in 1987 were 98% in primary schools and 87% in secondary schools. In 1989 there were 2,194,335 children enrolled in government primary and secondary schools, and 837,032 attending private schools. Special services have been developed to meet the needs of children living in the remote 'outback' areas, notably Schools of the Air, using two-way receiver sets. A system of one-teacher schools and correspondence schools also helps to satisfy these needs. Australia has 88 higher educational institutes (including 23 universities), with a total of 441,076 students in 1987. Expenditure on education by all levels of government in the financial year 1986/87 was $A14,100m. (14.0% of total government spending).

Public Holidays

1991: 1 January (New Year's Day), 26 January (Australia Day), 29 March–1 April (Easter), 25 April (Anzac Day), 10 June* (Queen's Official Birthday), 7 October‡ (Labour Day), 25 December (Christmas Day), 26 December (Boxing Day)†.

1992: 1 January (New Year's Day), 26 January (Australia Day), 17–20 April (Easter), 25 April (Anzac Day), 8 June* (Queen's Official Birthday), 5 October‡ (Labour Day), 25 December (Christmas Day), 26 December (Boxing Day)†.

* In Western Australia this holiday will be held on 30 September in 1991. No date has yet officially been announced for 1992.
† Boxing Day is not a public holiday in South Australia.
‡ In Western Australia this holiday will be held on 4 March in 1991 and on 2 March in 1992, in Victoria on 11 March in 1991 and on 9 March in 1992, and in Queensland on 6 May in 1991 and on 4 May in 1992.

There are also numerous state holidays.

Weights and Measures

The metric system is in force.

Statistical Survey

Source (unless otherwise stated): Australian Bureau of Statistics, POB 10, Belconnen, ACT 2616; tel. (06) 252-6627; telex 62020; fax (06) 251-6009.

Area and Population

AREA, POPULATION AND DENSITY

Area (sq km)	7,682,300*
Population (census results)†	
30 June 1976	14,033,100
30 June 1981	
Males	7,448,300
Females	7,475,000
Total	14,923,300
Population (official estimates at mid-year)†	
1987	16,263,319
1988	16,538,153
1989	16,806,700
Density (per sq km) at mid-1989	2.2

* 2,966,151 sq miles.
† Figures include Australian residents temporarily overseas. Census results also include an adjustment for underenumeration, estimated to have been 2.7% in 1976 and 1.9% in 1981. The enumerated totals were: 13,548,448 in 1976; 14,576,330 (males 7,267,076; females 7,309,254) in 1981.

STATES AND TERRITORIES (30 June 1988)

	Area (sq km)	Population	Density (per sq km)
New South Wales (NSW)	801,600	5,701,525	7.1
Victoria	227,600	4,261,945	18.7
Queensland	1,727,200	2,743,765	1.6
South Australia	984,000	1,408,255	1.4
Western Australia	2,525,500	1,544,806	0.6
Tasmania	67,800	448,457	6.6
Northern Territory	1,346,200	155,866	0.1
Australian Capital Territory	2,400	273,534	114.0
Total	**7,682,300**	**16,538,153**	**2.2**

PRINCIPAL TOWNS (estimated population at 30 June 1987)*

Canberra (national capital)	285,800†
Sydney (capital of NSW)	3,430,600
Melbourne (capital of Victoria)	2,931,900
Brisbane (capital of Queensland)	1,171,300
Perth (capital of W Australia)	1,025,300
Adelaide (capital of S Australia)	1,003,800
Newcastle	429,300
Wollongong	237,600
Gold Coast	219,300
Hobart (capital of Tasmania)	180,300
Geelong	145,900
Townsville	103,700

30 June 1988: Canberra 297,300†; Sydney 3,596,000; Melbourne 3,002,300; Brisbane 1,240,300; Perth 1,118,800; Adelaide 1,023,700.

* Figures refer to metropolitan areas, each of which normally comprises a municipality and contiguous urban areas.
† Including Queanbeyan, in NSW.

BIRTHS, MARRIAGES AND DEATHS*

	Registered live births		Registered marriages		Registered deaths	
	Number	Rate (per 1,000)	Number	Rate (per 1,000)	Number	Rate (per 1,000)
1981	235,842	15.8	113,905	7.6	109,003	7.3
1982	239,903	15.8	117,275	7.7	114,771	7.6
1983	242,570	15.8	114,860	7.5	110,084	7.2
1984	234,034	15.0	108,655	7.0	109,914	7.1
1985	247,348	15.7	115,493	7.3	118,808	7.5
1986	243,408	15.2	114,913	7.2	114,981	7.2
1987	244,347	15.0	114,074	7.0	117,441	7.2
1988	246,193	14.9	116,750†	7.1	119,866	7.2

* Data are tabulated by year of registration rather than by year of occurrence.
† Provisional.

1989 (rates per 1,000): Births 14.9; Deaths 7.3.

AUSTRALIA

PERMANENT AND LONG-TERM MIGRATION*

	1985	1986	1987
Arrivals			
Males	83,490	97,500	103,810
Females	79,760	88,890	100,650
Total	163,260	186,400	204,460
Departures			
Males	49,260	48,720	49,980
Females	45,990	43,750	45,340
Total	95,250	92,470	95,320
Net Increase	68,010	93,930	109,140

* Persons intending to stay for more than one year. Figures are rounded to the nearest 10.

ECONOMICALLY ACTIVE POPULATION ('000 persons aged 15 years and over, excluding armed forces, at August)

	1987	1988	1989
Agriculture and services to agriculture	404.0	431.0	406.2
Forestry, logging, fishing and hunting			
Mining and quarrying	99.4	96.7	105.4
Manufacturing	1,151.4	1,199.4	1,236.0
Electricity, gas and water	119.6	113.8	113.4
Construction	485.7	526.2	601.4
Wholesale and retail trade	1,408.0	1,496.1	1,606.9
Transport and storage	512.3	376.7	407.5
Communications		134.2	139.8
Financing, insurance, real estate and business services	766.7	801.1	875.2
Public administration and defence			324.0
Community services	2,126.1	2,154.8	1,356.9
Recreational, personal and defence			554.7
Total employed	7,073.2	7,730.2	7,727.6
Unemployed	601.9	538.8	469.4
Total labour force	7,675.1	7,869.0	8,197.0
Males	4,609.3	4,670.0	4,832.6
Females	3,065.8	3,199.0	3,364.4

Agriculture

PRINCIPAL CROPS ('000 metric tons)

	1986	1987	1988
Wheat	16,119	12,287	14,102
Rice (paddy)	716	693	740
Barley	3,548	3,417	3,270
Maize	278	206	208
Oats	1,584	1,698	1,815
Sorghum	1,416	1,419	1,633
Other cereals	331	276	313
Potatoes	965	1,015	1,060
Dry peas	241	511	485
Other pulses	614	970	995
Soybeans (Soya beans)	105	90	65
Sunflower seed	215	137	179
Rapeseed	76	66	59
Cottonseed	366	330	428
Cotton (lint)	258	214	276
Cabbages	79	83	83*
Tomatoes	266	277*	288*
Cauliflower	92	92*	92*
Pumpkins, squash and gourds	70	72*	74*
Onions (dry)	165	171*	178*
Green peas*	155	152	150

—continued	1986	1987	1988
Carrots	146	146	145*
Watermelons	90	96*	102*
Grapes	883	783	799
Sugar cane	24,720	25,390	27,697†
Apples	288	325	291
Pears	143	145	124
Peaches and nectarines	68	73†	75†
Oranges	523	475	465
Pineapples	142	128	154†
Bananas	158	147	159†

* FAO estimate(s).   † Unoffical estimate.
Source: FAO, *Production Yearbook*.

LIVESTOCK ('000 head at 31 March)

	1986	1987	1988
Horses	401	401*	401*
Cattle	23,436	21,915	23,500
Pigs	2,553	2,611	2,720
Sheep	155,561	149,157	164,000
Goats	509	548	600*

Chickens (million): 52 in 1986; 56† in 1987; 56* in 1988.
* FAO estimate.
† Unofficial estimate.
Source: FAO, *Production Yearbook*.

LIVESTOCK PRODUCTS ('000 metric tons)

	1986	1987	1988
Beef and veal	1,385	1,508	1,573
Mutton and lamb	578	583	584
Pig meat	271	282	284
Horse meat*	10	10	11
Poultry meat	367†	384	403
Cows' milk	6,205	6,333	6,298
Butter	124.5	124.2	114.6
Cheese	170.3	177.5	176.3
Hen eggs†	183.0	186.0	187.0
Other poultry eggs*	14.5	15.0	15.0
Honey	26.9	25.1†	29.0†
Wool:			
greasy	829.5	886.9	918.4
clean	505.0	516.0	540.0*
Cattle hides	148.0	158.0	158.0
Sheep skins*	160.3	161.3	160.2

* FAO estimate(s).   † Unofficial estimate(s).
Note: Figures for meat and milk refer to the 12 months ending 30 June of the year stated.
Source: FAO, *Production Yearbook*.

Forestry

ROUNDWOOD REMOVALS ('000 cubic metres)

	1986	1987*	1988*
Sawlogs, veneer logs and logs for sleepers	8,144	8,163	8,816
Pulpwood	7,859	7,859	7,859
Other industrial wood	1,116	1,116	1,116
Fuel wood	2,880*	2,880	2,886
Total	19,999*	20,018	20,677

* FAO estimate(s).
Source: FAO, *Yearbook of Forest Products*.

AUSTRALIA

SAWNWOOD PRODUCTION ('000 cubic metres)

	1986	1987	1988
Coniferous sawnwood	1,226	1,159	1,373
Broadleaved sawnwood	1,772	1,813	1,856
Sub-total	2,998	2,972	3,229
Railway sleepers	222	159	148
Total	3,220	3,131	3,377

Source: FAO, *Yearbook of Forest Products*.

Fishing

(FAO estimates, '000 metric tons, live weight, year ending 30 June)

	1984/85	1985/86	1986/87
Inland waters	2.3	2.5	2.5
Indian Ocean	97.4	106.8	116.8
Pacific Ocean	60.3	69.7	80.7
Total catch	160.0	179.0	200.0

Source: FAO, *Yearbook of Fishery Statistics*.

Mining*

(year ending 30 June, '000 metric tons, unless otherwise indicated)

	1985/86	1986/87	1987/88
Coal (black)	163,669	182,440	167,661
Coal, brown (lignite)[1]	33,312	39,712	41,525
Coal, brown (briquettes)	851	828	807
Bauxite	31,864	33,168	35,142
Zircon (metric tons)[2]	331,678	302,789	327,511
Iron ore	97,790	96,364	102,202
Lead	206	142	183
Zinc	297	300	305
Copper	163	171	186
Titanium[3]	1,024	954	1,458
Tin (metric tons)	2,208	784	501
Crude petroleum (million litres)[4]	31,669	30,205	31,297
Natural gas (million megajoules)	512,409	524,330	533,329
Gold (kg)	64,780	81,856	111,934
Silver (kg)	1,074,227	1,036,905	1,135,073
Nickel (metric tons)	80,528	74,509	72,231

* Figures for metallic minerals represent metal contents based on chemical assay, except figures for bauxite and iron ore, which are in terms of gross quantities produced. The estimated iron content of iron ore is 64%.
[1] Excludes coal used in making briquettes.
[2] In terms of zircon (ZrO_2) contained in zircon and rutile concentrates.
[3] In terms of TiO_2 contained in bauxite and mineral sands.
[4] Including condensate.

1988/89 ('000 metric tons, unless otherwise indicated): Lead 184; Zinc 303; Copper 211; Tin 377; Gold 169,653 kilograms.

Industry

SELECTED PRODUCTS (year ending 30 June, '000 metric tons, unless otherwise indicated)

	1986/87	1987/88	1988/89
Coke	3,253	3,727	3,889
Pig-iron	5,783	5,455	5,875
Steel (ingots)	6,387	6,093	6,651
Electric motors ('000)	2,523	2,844	3,077
Clay bricks (million)	2,002	2,032	2,326
Sulphuric acid	1,678	1,816	1,904
Nitric acid (metric tons)	203,484	203,547	n.a.
Television receivers ('000)	211	177	162
Refrigerators ('000)	289	386	380
Cotton yarn	21	21	20
Cotton cloth ('000 sq m)	38,237	39,415	36,243
Tinplate	292	307	n.a.
Electricity (million kWh)	130,122	136,869	144,854
Cement	5,920	6,158	6,901
Concrete—ready-mixed ('000 cu m)	13,810	15,093	17,030
Soap (metric tons)	27,361	30,365	26,764
Paper	1,209	1,235	1,269
Motor vehicles ('000)	323	338	360
Wheat flour	1,220	1,266	1,278
Margarine	151	157	151
Man-made fibres ('000 sq metres)	169,586	166,696	190,139
Lawn mowers ('000)	277	279	298
Synthetic resins and plastics	651	716	700
Domestic washing machines ('000)	400	394	397

Finance

CURRENCY AND EXCHANGE RATES

Monetary Units
100 cents = 1 Australian dollar ($A).

Denominations
Coins: 1, 2, 5, 10, 20 and 50 cents; 1 dollar.
Notes: 2, 5, 10, 20, 50 and 100 dollars.

Sterling and US Dollar Equivalents (30 September 1990)
£1 sterling = $A2.2650;
US $1 = $A1.2115;
$A100 = £44.15 = US $82.54.

Average Exchange Rate (US $ per Australian dollar)
1987 0.7009
1988 0.7842
1989 0.7925

COMMONWEALTH GOVERNMENT BUDGET
($A million, year ending 30 June)

Revenue	1986/87	1987/88	1988/89*
Tax revenue	66,354	74,897	82,318
Income tax on companies	7,888	10,348	11,900
Income tax on persons	38,074	41,886	47,580
Sales tax, customs and excise duties	18,920	20,898	20,872
Non-tax revenue			
Interest, rent, dividends, royalties, etc.	6,491	5,908	5,164
Total	72,845	80,805	87,482

* Provisional.
1989/90: Total estimated revenue, $A94,987m.

AUSTRALIA

Expenditure	1986/87	1987/88	1988/89*
Goods and services	14,071	14,735	15,277
Transfers	60,895	65,019	67,189
Personal benefit payments	24,082	26,819	28,510
Grants to states and Northern Territory	22,580	23,771	24,138
Grants to non-profit institutions	1,105	932	1,079
Interest paid	7,925	7,895	7,698
Overseas	812	844	918
Subsidies	1,333	1,378	1,311
Non-budget sector	2,753	3,028	3,161
Net Lending	524	67	248
Asset sales	—	−1,059	−700
Total	75,490	78,762	82,014

* Provisional.
1989/90: Total estimated expenditure $A86,951m.

STATE GOVERNMENT FINANCES*
($A million, year ending 30 June)

	Receipts		Expenditure	
	1983/84	1984/85	1983/84	1984/85
New South Wales	11,128	13,064	11,804	13,850
Victoria	9,805	10,941	10,174	11,436
Queensland	6,033	6,599	6,164	6,764
South Australia	3,193	3,459	3,270	3,604
Western Australia	3,920	4,155	4,052	4,305
Tasmania	1,372	1,550	1,389	1,582
Northern Territory	942	1,053	976	1,094

* Including all state government authorities.

OFFICIAL RESERVES (US $ million at 31 December)

	1987	1988	1989
Gold*	3,855	3,319	3,248
IMF special drawing rights	369	334	307
Reserve position in IMF	268	275	322
Foreign exchange	8,107	12,989	13,150
Total	12,599	16,917	17,027

* Valued at market-related prices.
Source: IMF, *International Financial Statistics*.

MONEY SUPPLY ($A million at 31 December)

	1987	1988	1989
Currency outside banks	10,841	12,267	13,018
Demand deposits at trading and savings banks	20,352	28,178	31,581

Source: IMF, *International Financial Statistics*.

COST OF LIVING (Consumer Price Index*. Base: 1980 = 100)

	1985	1986	1987
Food	145.1	158.1	166.8
Fuel and light	177.9	187.2	197.5
Clothing	138.0	151.2	164.4
Rent†	154.2	166.7	179.0
All items (incl. others)	148.9	162.4	176.3

1988: Food 180.0; All items (incl. others) 189.0.
1989: Food 195.8; All items (incl. others) 203.3.

* Weighted average of six state capitals.
† Including expenditure on maintenance and repairs of dwellings.
Source: International Labour Office, mainly *Year Book of Labour Statistics*.

NATIONAL ACCOUNTS
($A million at current prices, year ending 30 June)
National Income and Product

	1986/87	1987/88	1988/89
Compensation of employees	133,898	147,280	165,079
Operating surplus	55,209	66,573	80,339
Domestic factor incomes	189,107	213,853	245,418
Consumption of fixed capital	42,561	46,567	49,694
Gross domestic product (GDP) at factor cost	231,668	260,420	295,112
Indirect taxes, *less* subsidies	31,581	36,501	40,484
GDP in purchasers' values	263,249	296,921	335,596
Net factor income from abroad	−9,328	−10,560	−12,571
Gross national product	253,921	286,361	323,025
Less Consumption of fixed capital	42,561	46,567	49,694
National income in market prices	211,360	239,794	273,331

Expenditure on the Gross Domestic Product

	1986/87	1987/88	1988/89
Government final consumption expenditure	48,632	52,577	57,094
Private final consumption expenditure	155,895	172,625	191,331
Increase in stocks	−1,510	−561	3,349
Gross fixed capital formation	63,991	72,131	85,720
Statistical discrepancy	957	2,463	4,823
Total domestic expenditure	267,965	299,235	342,317
Exports of goods and services	43,328	50,382	54,024
Less Imports of goods and services	48,044	52,696	60,745
GDP in purchasers' values	263,249	296,921	335,596
GDP at constant 1984/85 prices	229,649	239,618	247,597

Gross Domestic Product by Economic Activity (at factor cost)

	1984/85	1985/86*	1986/87*
Agriculture, hunting, forestry and fishing	9,103	9,072	10,284
Mining and quarrying	8,999	10,662	10,855
Manufacturing	33,757	36,586	39,678
Electricity, gas and water	7,268	8,134	8,438
Construction	14,462	16,311	17,880
Wholesale and retail trade	25,333	28,775	31,361
Transport, storage and communications	16,881	18,841	21,157
Ownership of dwellings	16,024	18,235	20,753
Finance, insurance, real estate and business services	18,973	21,331	25,592
Public administration and defence	8,889	9,833	10,597
Other community, social and personal services (incl. restaurants and hotels)	32,572	35,913	39,930
Sub-total	192,261	213,693	236,525
Less Imputed bank service charge	−6,050	−6,372	−7,989
Total	186,211	207,321	228,536

* Figures are provisional.

AUSTRALIA

BALANCE OF PAYMENTS (US $ million)

	1987	1988	1989
Merchandise exports f.o.b.	26,270	32,778	36,173
Merchandise imports f.o.b.	−26,749	−33,892	−40,342
Trade balance	−480	−1,114	−4,169
Exports of services	8,646	11,185	12,609
Imports of services	−17,586	−21,781	−27,192
Balance on goods and services	−9,420	−11,710	−18,752
Private unrequited transfers (net)	1,196	1,706	2,073
Government unrequited transfers (net)	−178	−232	−182
Current balance	−8,402	−10,236	−16,861
Direct capital investment (net)	−2,099	1,568	3,762
Other long-term capital (net)	9,538	13,249	7,665
Short-term capital (net)	−636	−72	1,318
Net errors and omissions	1,970	741	4,743
Total (net monetary movements)	371	5,251	628
Valuation changes (net)	1,123	−424	−419
Official financing (net)	4	28	−28
Changes in reserves	1,497	4,855	181

Source: IMF, *International Financial Statistics*.

FOREIGN INVESTMENT ($A million, year ending 30 June)

Inflow	1982/83	1983/84	1984/85
EEC—United Kingdom	2,429	2,366	2,033
—Other	1,023	1,191	1,841
Switzerland	214	97	328
USA	328	925	2,052
Canada	30	91	192
Japan	3,239	1,226	3,153
ASEAN*	1,517	2,131	807
Other countries	1,174	1,290	2,183
Total	9,954	9,317	12,589

Outflow	1982/83	1983/84	1984/85
EEC—United Kingdom	133	111	66
—Other	4	14	13
New Zealand	126	150	154
USA	5	8	70
Papua New Guinea	33	77	31
ASEAN*	73	133	56
Other countries	73	67	72
Total	447	560	462

* Indonesia, Malaysia, the Philippines, Singapore and Thailand; also Brunei from 1 January 1984.

FOREIGN AID EXTENDED BY AUSTRALIA*
($A million, year ending 30 June)

	1983/84	1984/85	1985/86
Aid payments:			
Bilateral:			
Papua New Guinea	302	320	326
Other	395	438	422
Multilateral	216	235	259
Administration	19†	18†	24
Total	932	1,011	1,031

* Official only; excludes transfers by private persons and organizations to overseas recipients.
† Includes the cost of administration of overseas students by other government agencies.

Source: Statistical summary, Australian Official Development Assistance to Developing Countries.

External Trade

PRINCIPAL COMMODITIES ($A million, year ending 30 June)

Imports	1986/87	1987/88	1988/89
Food and live animals	1,611.6	1,688.8	1,832.9
Coffee, tea, cocoa and spices	404.9	378.6	352.5
Fish, crustaceans and molluscs	422.6	409.3	437.5
Beverages and tobacco	326.8	344.6	374.0
Crude materials (inedible) except fuels	1,083.2	1,321.5	1,608.3
Cork and wood	297.5	382.4	561.3
Mineral fuels, lubricants, etc.	1,749.4	2,050.1	2,014.8
Petroleum, petroleum products, etc.	1,742.3	2,040.2	2,000.3
Chemicals and related products	3,742.6	4,275.8	4,987.2
Organic chemicals	881.0	1,106.6	1,164.3
Basic manufactures	6,185.1	7,128.2	7,956.7
Paper, paperboard and manufactures	1,012.7	1,206.1	1,296.5
Textile yarn, fabrics, etc.	1,831.1	1,926.3	1,999.4
Machinery and transport equipment	15,389.5	16,368.5	20,634.3
Road vehicles and parts (excl. tyres, engines and electrical parts)	2,719.5	3,139.1	4,806.9
Miscellaneous manufactured articles	5,185.0	5,575.1	6,428.4
Total (incl. others)	36,988.1	40,596.6	47,064.2

Exports	1986/87	1987/88	1988/89
Food and live animals	8,017.8	8,099.9	8,331.0
Meat and meat preparations	2,248.9	2,558.8	2,249.3
Dairy products and birds' eggs	467.2	503.2	566.6
Cereals and cereal preparations	2,792.6	2,297.2	2,742.2
Sugar, sugar preparations and honey	715.9	719.8	925.1
Beverages and tobacco	151.4	248.4	248.8
Crude materials (inedible) except fuels	9,897.2	12,328.2	14,001.8
Textile fibres and waste*	3,870.1	5,600.3	6,254.1
Hides, skins and fur-skins (raw)	542.3	687.4	498.1
Metalliferous ores and metal scrap	4,849.7	5,284.6	6,345.2
Mineral fuels, lubricants, etc.†	7,308.8	7,036.8	6,369.4
Animal and vegetable oils, fats and waxes	123.9	138.1	121.3
Chemicals and related products	664.8	891.3	1,066.2
Basic manufactures	3,840.8	4,954.0	5,823.6
Machinery and transport equipment	2,611.8	2,731.8	2,696.6
Machinery	1,597.0	1,834.3	1,870.5
Transport equipment	1,014.8	897.5	826.1
Miscellaneous manufactured articles	853.6	1,026.0	1,045.8
Other commodities and transactions‡	n.a.	n.a.	3,752.7
Total	35,806.4	41,077.8	43,462.2

* Excluding wool tops.
† Excluding natural and manufactured gas.
‡ Including natural and manufactured gas.

AUSTRALIA

PRINCIPAL TRADING PARTNERS
($A million, year ending 30 June)

Imports	1986/87	1987/88	1988/89
Argentina	48.7	64.3	103.7
Belgium/Luxembourg	312.0	319.9	403.2
Brazil	219.5	298.5	430.4
Canada	750.5	863.3	1,066.7
China, People's Republic	588.8	850.7	1,026.7
Denmark	176.9	189.7	202.4
Finland	262.6	293.5	352.2
France	828.8	892.1	1,275.7
Germany, Federal Republic	2,780.9	2,918.1	2,950.8
Hong Kong	800.1	845.3	891.5
India	203.3	228.2	246.7
Indonesia	310.6	587.7	418.9
Ireland	184.2	201.6	171.5
Italy	1,110.3	1,329.8	1,375.1
Japan	7,709.7	7,816.5	9,766.5
Korea, Republic	891.3	1,020.3	1,262.0
Kuwait	162.6	121.0	89.7
Malaysia	409.7	590.7	687.1
Netherlands	486.6	595.9	601.0
New Zealand	1,431.2	1,732.5	1,970.5
Papua New Guinea	189.7	109.1	104.7
Philippines	113.4	127.0	165.4
Saudi Arabia	437.3	418.9	458.3
Singapore	755.8	899.0	1,090.0
South Africa	154.7	99.1	97.9
Spain	140.9	190.3	208.3
Sweden	655.4	776.6	840.4
Switzerland	489.9	543.8	496.3
Taiwan	1,517.4	1,743.9	1,919.9
Thailand	284.4	331.1	420.0
United Arab Emirates	175.8	215.8	396.3
United Kingdom	2,705.7	3,012.2	3,453.8
USA	8,118.5	8,532.0	10,129.4
Other countries	1,580.9	1,838.2	1,991.2
Total	36,988.1	40,596.6	47,064.2

Exports	1986/87	1987/88	1988/89
Argentina	77.1	74.9	95.9
Belgium/Luxembourg	297.7	368.3	366.7
Brazil	139.0	99.6	117.6
Canada	649.7	701.8	709.1
China, People's Republic	1,592.3	1,277.6	1,209.4
Egypt	362.5	316.7	423.2
Fiji	174.2	123.9	155.4
France	908.2	982.8	975.1
Germany, Federal Republic	1,100.7	1,066.7	1,071.5
Hong Kong	1,086.6	1,977.1	1,888.5
India	425.3	505.2	555.2
Indonesia	528.3	595.3	748.3
Iran	343.8	375.7	305.0
Iraq	194.8	178.4	311.0
Italy	823.2	1,093.0	1,017.5
Japan	9,083.3	10,684.1	11,840.5
Korea, Republic	1,503.8	1,782.4	2,182.7
Kuwait	98.0	81.1	77.7
Malaysia	591.6	655.9	742.4
Netherlands	598.4	626.7	660.6
New Zealand	1,777.0	2,181.5	2,219.2
Pakistan	100.6	101.4	144.0
Papua New Guinea	651.1	741.3	785.2
Philippines	259.0	257.5	410.7
Poland	107.4	199.5	182.7
Romania	114.8	123.4	100.3
Saudi Arabia	298.0	268.1	249.6
Singapore	729.4	1,166.1	1,481.0
South Africa	154.1	151.4	152.0
Spain	292.9	281.8	195.1
Sweden	120.8	120.6	142.7
Switzerland	365.1	307.7	348.7
Taiwan	1,228.9	1,386.5	1,566.5
Thailand	223.8	316.8	474.8
Turkey	116.7	191.1	79.9
USSR	687.7	630.3	1,012.9
United Arab Emirates	222.1	236.3	253.7
United Kingdom	1,374.5	1,771.6	1,522.5
USA	4,190.4	4,672.0	4,422.4
Other countries	2,163.6	2,405.7	2,265.0
Total	35,806.4	41,077.8	43,462.2

Transport

	1985/86	1986/87	1987/88
Railways:			
Passengers ('000)	n.a.	388,634	405,710
Goods and livestock ('000 metric tons)	171,841	174,530	173,421
Road traffic:			
Motor vehicles registered ('000)*	9,291	9,374	9,544
Overseas shipping:			
Vessels entered ('000 tons)†	307,406	300,348	n.a.
Vessels cleared ('000 tons)†	304,839	296,952	n.a.
Air transport, internal services:			
Kilometres flown ('000)	143,081	152,141	160,240
Passengers carried	12,099,813	12,506,706	13,647,756
Freight (metric tons)	150,470	135,572	143,324
Mail (metric tons)	18,056	18,726	20,793
Air transport, overseas services‡:			
Kilometres flown ('000)	79,050	91,874	98,999
Passengers carried	2,671,486	3,052,411	3,612,197
Freight (metric tons)	91,961	110,389	119,202
Mail (metric tons)	4,869	5,327	5,858

* Figures as at end of period.
† Figures are for deadweight tonnage of vessels.
‡ Refers only to services operated by Qantas Airways Ltd.

Tourism

('000 visitors*)

Country of origin	1986	1987	1988
Canada	47.0	52.7	66.7
Germany, Federal Republic	n.a.	53.3	65.9
Hong Kong	33.5	42.7	49.4
Indonesia	17.7	21.5	29.6
Japan	145.6	215.6	352.3
Malaysia	38.6	47.1	52.1
New Zealand	336.7	427.3	534.3
Papua New Guinea	31.9	32.8	37.8
Singapore	45.0	57.0	63.5
Sweden	14.2	21.9	n.a.
Switzerland	16.9	21.3	26.0
United Kingdom	176.0	198.9	260.3
USA	245.4	309.0	322.3
Total (incl. others)	1,429.4	1,784.9	2,249.3

* i.e. intending to stay for less than one year.

Communications Media

	1983	1984	1985
Telephones in use ('000 at 30 June)	8,267	8,329	8,727

Radio receivers (1987): 20,500,000 in use (estimate).
Television receivers (1987): 7,800,000 in use (estimate).
Book production (1986): 7,460 titles (including 2,511 pamphlets).
Newspapers (1986): 62 dailies (combined circulation 4,213,000); (1984): 465 non-dailies (circulation 15,208,000).
Source: mainly UNESCO, *Statistical Yearbook*.

Education

(1989)

	Institutions	Teaching staff	Students
Government schools	7,513	146,957	2,194,335
Non-government schools	2,523	51,611	837,032
Higher educational institutions	88	66,581	441,076

Directory

The Constitution

The Federal Constitution was adopted on 9 July 1900 and came into force on 1 January 1901. Its main provisions are summarized below:

PARLIAMENT

The legislative power of the Commonwealth of Australia is vested in a Federal Parliament, consisting of HM the Queen (represented by the Governor-General), a Senate, and a House of Representatives. The Governor-General may appoint such times for holding the sessions of the Parliament as he or she thinks fit, and may also from time to time, by proclamation or otherwise, prorogue the Parliament, and may in like manner dissolve the House of Representatives. By convention, these powers are exercised on the advice of the Prime Minister. After any general election Parliament must be summoned to meet not later than 30 days after the day appointed for the return of the writs.

THE SENATE

The Senate is composed of 12 senators from each state, two senators representing the Australian Capital Territory and two representing the Northern Territory. The senators are directly chosen by the people of the state or territory, voting in each case as one electorate, and are elected by proportional representation. Senators representing a state have a six-year term and retire by rotation, one-half from each state on 30 June of each third year. The term of a senator representing a territory is limited to three years. In the case of a state, if a senator vacates his or her seat before the expiration of the term of service, the houses of parliament of the state for which the senator was chosen shall, in joint session, choose a person to hold the place until the expiration of the term or until the election of a successor. If the state parliament is not in session, the Governor of the state, acting on the advice of the state's executive council, may appoint a senator to hold office until parliament reassembles, or until a new senator is elected.

The Senate may proceed to the dispatch of business notwithstanding the failure of any state to provide for its representation in the Senate.

THE HOUSE OF REPRESENTATIVES

In accordance with the Australian Constitution, the total number of members of the House of Representatives must be as nearly as practicable double that of the Senate. The number in each state is in proportion to population, but under the Constitution must be at least five. The House of Representatives is composed of 148 members, including two members for the Australian Capital Territory and one member for the Northern Territory.

Members are elected by universal adult suffrage and voting is compulsory. Only Australian citizens are eligible to vote in Australian elections. British subjects, if they are not Australian citizens or already on the rolls, have to take out Australian citizenship before they can enrol and before they can vote.

Members are chosen by the electors of their respective electorates by the preferential voting system.

The duration of the Parliament is limited to three years.

To be nominated for election to the House of Representatives, a candidate must be 18 years of age or over, an Australian citizen, and entitled to vote at the election or qualified to become an elector.

THE EXECUTIVE GOVERNMENT

The executive power of the Federal Government is vested in the Queen, and is exercisable by the Governor-General, advised by an Executive Council of Ministers of State, known as the Federal Executive Council. These ministers are, or must become within three months, members of the Federal Parliament.

The Australian Constitution is construed as subject to the principles of responsible government and the Governor-General acts on the advice of the ministers in relation to most matters.

THE JUDICIAL POWER

See Judicial System, p. 388.

THE STATES

The Australian Constitution safeguards the Constitution of each state by providing that it shall continue as at the establishment of the Commonwealth, except as altered in accordance with its own provisions. The legislative power of the Federal Parliament is limited in the main to those matters that are listed in section 51 of the Constitution, while the states possess, as well as concurrent powers in those matters, residual legislative powers enabling them to legislate in any way for 'the peace, order and good Government' of their respective territories. When a state law is inconsistent with a law of the Commonwealth, the latter prevails, and the former is invalid to the extent of the inconsistency.

The states may not, without the consent of the Commonwealth, raise or maintain naval or military forces, or impose taxes on any property belonging to the Commonwealth of Australia, nor may the Commonwealth tax state property. The states may not coin money.

The Federal Parliament may not enact any law for establishing any religion or for prohibiting the exercise of any religion, and no religious test may be imposed as a qualification for any office under the Commonwealth.

The Commonwealth of Australia is charged with protecting every state against invasion, and, on the application of a state executive government, against domestic violence.

Provision is made under the Constitution for the admission of new states and for the establishment of new states within the Commonwealth of Australia.

ALTERATION OF THE CONSTITUTION

Proposed laws for the amendment of the Constitution must be passed by an absolute majority in both Houses of the Federal Parliament, and not less than two or more than six months after its passage through both Houses the proposed law must be submitted in each state to the qualified electors.

In the event of one House twice refusing to pass a proposed amendment that has already received an absolute majority in the other House, the Governor-General may, notwithstanding such refusal, submit the proposed amendment to the electors. By convention, the Governor-General acts on the advice of the Prime Minister. If in a majority of the states a majority of the electors voting approve the proposed law and if a majority of all the electors voting also approve, it shall be presented to the Governor-General for Royal Assent.

No alteration diminishing the proportionate representation of any state in either House of the Federal Parliament, or the minimum number of representatives of a state in the House of Representatives, or increasing, diminishing or altering the limits of the state, or in any way affecting the provisions of the Constitution in relation thereto, shall become law unless the majority of the electors voting in that state approve the proposed law.

STATES AND TERRITORIES

New South Wales

The state's executive power is vested in the Governor, appointed by the Crown, who is assisted by a cabinet.

The state's legislative power is vested in a bicameral Parliament, composed of the Legislative Council and the Legislative Assembly. The Legislative Council, formerly consisting of 60 members, began, in late 1978, a process of reconstitution at the end of which it was to consist of 45 members directly elected for the duration of three parliaments, 15 members retiring every four years. The Legislative Assembly consists of 99 members and sits for four years.

Victoria

The state's legislative power is vested in a bicameral Parliament: the Upper House, or Legislative Council, of 44 members, elected for six years, and the Lower House, or Legislative Assembly, of 88 members, elected for four years. One-half of the members of the Council retires every three years.

In the exercise of the executive power the Governor is assisted by a cabinet of responsible ministers. Not more than five members of the Council and not more than 13 members of the Assembly may occupy salaried office at any one time.

The state has 88 electoral districts, each returning one member, and 22 electoral provinces, each returning two Council members.

Queensland

The state's legislative power is vested in a unicameral Parliament composed of 82 members who are elected from 82 districts for a term of three years.

South Australia

The state's Constitution vests the legislative power in a Parliament elected by the people and consisting of a Legislative Council and

AUSTRALIA

a House of Assembly. The Council is composed of 22 members, one-half of whom retires every three years. Their places are filled by new members elected under a system of proportional representation, with the whole state as a single electorate. The executive has no authority to dissolve this body, except in circumstances warranting a double dissolution.

The 47 members of the House of Assembly are elected for three years from 47 electoral districts.

The executive power is vested in a Governor, appointed by the Crown, and an Executive Council consisting of 13 responsible ministers.

Western Australia

The state's administration is vested in the Governor, a Legislative Council and a Legislative Assembly.

The Legislative Council consists of 34 members, each of the 17 provinces returning two members. Election is for a term of six years, one-half of the members retiring every three years.

The Legislative Assembly consists of 57 members, elected for three years, each representing one electorate.

Tasmania

The state's executive authority is vested in a Governor, appointed by the Crown, who acts upon the advice of his premier and ministers, who are elected members of either the Legislative Council or the House of Assembly. The Council consists of 19 members who sit for six years, retiring in rotation. The House of Assembly has 35 members elected for four years.

Northern Territory

On 1 July 1978, the Northern Territory was established as a body politic with executive authority for specified functions of government. Most functions of the Federal Government were transferred to the Territory Government in 1978 and 1979, major exceptions being Aboriginal affairs and uranium mining.

The Territory Parliament consists of a single house, the Legislative Assembly, with 25 members. The first Parliament stayed in office for three years. As from the election held in August 1980, members are elected for a term of four years.

The office of Administrator continues. The Northern Territory (Self-Government) Act provides for the appointment of an Administrator by the Governor-General charged with the duty of administering the Territory. In respect of matters transferred to the Territory Government, the Administrator acts with the advice of the Territory Executive Council; in respect of matters retained by the Commonwealth, the Administrator acts on Commonwealth advice.

Australian Capital Territory

On 29 November 1988 the Australian Capital Territory (ACT) was established as a body politic. The ACT Government has executive authority for specified functions, although a number of these were to be retained by the Federal Government for a brief period during which transfer arrangements were to be finalized.

The ACT Parliament consists of a single house, the Legislative Assembly, with 17 members. The first election was held in March 1989. Members are to be elected for a term of four years.

The Federal Government retains control of some of the land in the ACT for the purpose of maintaining the Seat of Government and the national capital plan.

The Government

Head of State: HM Queen ELIZABETH II.

Governor-General: WILLIAM GEORGE HAYDEN (took office 16 February 1989).

THE MINISTRY
(December 1990)

Prime Minister: ROBERT (BOB) J. L. HAWKE*.

Deputy Prime Minister, Treasurer and Minister Assisting the Prime Minister for Commonwealth–State Relations: PAUL J. KEATING.*

Minister for Justice and Consumer Affairs: Senator MICHAEL TATE.

Minister for Industry, Technology and Commerce: Senator JOHN N. BUTTON*.

Minister for Customs and Small Business: DAVID BEDALL.

Minister for Transport and Communications: KIM C. BEAZLEY.

Minister for Finance: RALPH WILLIS*.

Minister for Foreign Affairs and Trade: Senator GARETH J. EVANS*.

Attorney-General: MICHAEL J. DUFFY*.

Minister for Industrial Relations and Minister Assisting the Prime Minister for Public Service Matters: Senator PETER COOK*.

Minister for Employment, Education and Training: JOHN S. DAWKINS*.

Minister for Higher Education and Employment Services: PETER J. BALDWIN.

Minister for Science and Technology, Minister Assisting the Prime Minister for Science and Minister Assisting the Treasurer: SIMON CREAN.

Minister for Aboriginal Affairs: ROBERT TICKNER.

Minister for Defence: Senator ROBERT RAY*.

Minister for Primary Industries and Energy: JOHN C. KERIN*.

Minister for Resources: ALAN GRIFFITHS.

Minister for Social Security: Senator GRAHAM RICHARDSON*.

Minister for Administrative Services: Senator NICK BOLKUS*.

Minister for Community Services and Health and Minister Assisting the Prime Minister for Social Justice: BRIAN L. HOWE*.

Minister for the Aged, Family and Health Services: PETER STAPLES.

Minister for Veterans' Affairs: BENJAMIN C. HUMPHREYS.

Minister for the Arts, Sport, the Environment, Tourism and Territories: ROS KELLY*.

Minister for the Arts, Tourism and Territories: DAVID W. SIMMONS.

Minister for Immigration, Local Government and Ethnic Affairs and Minister Assisting the Prime Minister for Multicultural Affairs: GERALD L. HAND*.

Minister for Local Government and Minister Assisting the Prime Minister for the Status of Women: WENDY F. FATIN.

Minister for Land Transport: BOB BROWN.

Minister for Trade Negotiations, Minister Assisting the Minister for Industry, Technology and Commerce and Minister Assisting the Minister for Primary Industries and Energy: Dr NEAL BLEWETT.

Minister for Defence, Science and Personnel: GORDON N. BILNEY.

Minister for Shipping and Aviation Support and Minister Assisting the Prime Minister for Northern Australia: Senator BOB COLLINS.

* Denotes member of the Inner Cabinet.

DEPARTMENTS

Department of the Prime Minister and Cabinet: 3–5 National Circuit, Barton, ACT 2600; tel. (06) 271-5111; telex 61616; fax (06) 271-5415.

Department of Aboriginal Affairs: MLC Tower, Woden Town Centre, Phillip, ACT 2606; tel. (06) 289-1222; telex 62471.

Department of Administrative Services: POB 1920, Canberra City, ACT 2601; tel. (06) 275-3000; telex 62482.

Department of the Arts, Sport, the Environment, Tourism and Territories: POB 787, Canberra, ACT 2601; tel. (06) 274-1111; telex 62960; fax (06) 274-1123.

Attorney-General's Department: Robert Garran Offices, Barton, ACT 2600; tel. (06) 250-6666; telex 62002; fax (06) 250-5900.

Department of Community Services and Health: POB 9848, Canberra, ACT 2601; tel. (06) 289-1555; telex 62149.

Department of Defence: Russell Offices, Canberra, ACT 2600; tel. (06) 265-9111; telex 62053.

Department of Employment, Education and Training: GPO Box 9880, Canberra, ACT 2601; tel. (06) 276-8111; fax (06) 276-9226.

Department of Finance: Newlands St, Parkes, ACT 2600; tel. (06) 263-2222; telex 62639; fax (06) 273-3021.

Department of Foreign Affairs and Trade: Bag 8, Queen Victoria Terrace, Canberra, ACT 2600; tel. (06) 261-9111; telex 62007.

Department of Immigration, Local Government and Ethnic Affairs: Benjamin Offices, Chan St, Belconnen, ACT 2617; tel. (06) 264-1111; telex 62077; fax (06) 264-2364.

Department of Industrial Relations: POB 9879, Canberra, ACT 2601; tel. (06) 243-7333; fax (06) 243-7508.

Department of Industry, Technology and Commerce: 51 Allara St, Canberra, ACT 2601; tel. (06) 276-1000; telex 62654; fax (06) 276-1111.

Department of Primary Industries and Energy: GPO Box 858, Canberra, ACT 2601; tel. (06) 272-3933; telex 62188; fax (06) 272-5161.

AUSTRALIA

Department of Social Security: Juliana House, Bowes St, Phillip, ACT 2606; tel. (06) 284-4844; telex 62143.

Department of Transport and Communications: 74 Northbourne Ave, Canberra, ACT 2600; POB 594, Canberra, ACT 2601; tel. (06) 268-7111; telex 62065; fax (06) 257-2505.

Department of the Treasury: Parkes Place, Parkes, ACT 2600; tel. (06) 263-2111; telex 62010; fax (06) 273-2614.

Department of Veterans' Affairs: MLC Tower, Keltie St, Phillip, ACT 2606; tel. (06) 289-1111; telex 62706.

ADMINISTRATORS OF TERRITORIES
Northern Territory: JAMES H. MUIRHEAD.
Norfolk Island: H. B. MACDONALD.
Cocos (Keeling) Islands: A. D. LAWRIE.
Christmas Island: A. D. TAYLOR.

Legislature
FEDERAL PARLIAMENT
Senate
President: Senator KERRY WALTER SIBRAA (Lab.).
Chairman of Committees: Senator MALCOLM A. COLSTON (Lab.).
Leader of the Government in the Senate: Senator JOHN N. BUTTON (Lab.).
Leader of the Opposition in the Senate: Senator ROBERT HILL (Lib.).

Election, 24 March 1990

Party	Seats
Labor Party	32
Liberal Party	29
National Party	4
Australian Democrats	8
Independents and others	3
Total	76

House of Representatives
Speaker: LEO B. MCLEAY (Lab.).
Chairman of Committees: RONALD EDWARDS (Lab.).
Leader of the House: KIM C. BEAZLEY (Lab.).
Leader of the Opposition: Dr JOHN R. HEWSON (Lib.).

Election, 24 March 1990

Party	Seats
Labor Party	78
Liberal Party	55
National Party	14
Independent	1
Total	148

State Governments
NEW SOUTH WALES
Governor: Rear-Adm. PETER SINCLAIR.

Liberal-National Party Ministry
(December 1990)
Premier: NICK F. GREINER.

Legislature
Legislative Council: Pres. JOHN RICHARD JOHNSON; Chair. of Cttees Sir A. SOLOMONS.
Legislative Assembly: Speaker K. R. ROZZOLI; Chair. of Cttees Ms W. S. MACHIN.

VICTORIA
Governor: Rev. Dr JOHN DAVIS MCCAUGHEY.

Labor Ministry
(December 1990)
Premier: Mrs JOAN KIRNER.

Legislature
Legislative Council: Pres. ALAN JOHN HUNT; Chair. of Cttees KENNETH IRVING MACKENZIE; Clerk of the Council ALAN V. BRAY.
Legislative Assembly: Speaker KENNETH ALASTAIR COGHILL; Chair. of Cttees TERENCE RICHARD NORRIS; Clerk of the Assembly RAYMOND KEITH BOYES.

QUEENSLAND
Governor: Sir WALTER CAMPBELL.

Labor Ministry
(December 1990)
Premier: WAYNE GOSS.

Legislature
Legislative Assembly: Speaker D. FOURAS; Chair. of Cttees C. B. CAMPBELL; Clerk A. R. WOODWARD.

SOUTH AUSTRALIA
Governor: ROMA MITCHELL.

Labor Ministry
(December 1990)
Premier: JOHN CHARLES BANNON.

Legislature
Legislative Council: Pres. and Chair. of Cttees GORDON LINDSAY BRUCE; Clerk of the Council C. H. MERTIN.
House of Assembly: Speaker N. T. PETERSON; Chair. of Cttees M. G. EVANS; Clerk of the House G. D. MITCHELL.

WESTERN AUSTRALIA
Governor: FRANCIS BURT.

Labor Ministry
(December 1990)
Premier: Dr CARMEN LAWRENCE.

Legislature
Legislative Council: Pres. CLIVE EDWARD GRIFFITHS; Chair. of Cttees J. BROWN; Clerk of the Council LAURENCE BERNHARD MARQUET.
Legislative Assembly: Speaker MICHAEL BARNETT; Chair. of Cttees I. C. ALEXANDER; Clerk of the Assembly PETER JOHN MCHUGH.

TASMANIA
Governor: Gen. Sir PHILIP BENNETT.

Labor Ministry
(December 1990)
Premier: MICHAEL FIELD.

Legislature
Legislative Council: Pres. ALBERT JAMES BROADBY; Chair. of Cttees R. T. HOPE; Clerk of the Council ADRIAN JACK SHAW.
House of Assembly: Speaker R. CORNISH; Chair. of Cttees JOHN BEATTIE; Clerk of the House PAUL TREVOR MCKAY.

Territory Governments
NORTHERN TERRITORY
Administrator: JAMES H. MUIRHEAD.

Liberal-National Party Ministry
(December 1990)
Chief Minister: MARSHALL B. PERRON.

Legislature
Legislative Assembly: Speaker NICHOLAS DONDAS.

AUSTRALIAN CAPITAL TERRITORY
Labor Ministry
(December 1990)
Chief Minister: ROSEMARY FOLLETT.

Legislature
Legislative Assembly: Speaker DAVID PROWSE.

AUSTRALIA

Directory

Political Organizations

Australian Democratic Labor Party: 155–159 Castlereagh St, Sydney, NSW; f. 1956 following a split in the Australian Labor Party; Pres. P. J. KEOGH; Gen. Sec. JOHN KANE.

Australian Democrats Party: 71 Smith St, Fitzroy, Vic 3065; tel. (03) 419-5808; telex 39117; fax (03) 419-5697; f. 1977; comprises the fmr Liberal Movement and the Australia Party; Leader Senator JANET POWELL.

Australian Labor Party: John Curtin House, 22 Brisbane Ave, Barton, ACT 2600; tel. (06) 273-3133; fax (06) 273-2031; f. 1891; advocates the democratic socialization of industry, production, distribution and exchange, with the declared aim of eliminating exploitation and other anti-social features in these fields; Fed. Parl. Leader ROBERT J. L. HAWKE; Nat. Pres. JOHN BANNON; Nat. Sec. ROBERT HOGG.

Communist Party of Australia: 635 Harris St, Ultimo, NSW 2007; tel. (02) 281-2899; fax (02) 281-2897; f. 1920; advocates democratic socialism, human rights and liberation; independent of both Soviet and Chinese influence; decided in December 1989 to reduce its activities in favour of the newly-formed New Left Party and will decide in 1991 on its final dissolution; Nat. Exec.: B. AARONS, R. DURBRIDGE, P. RANALD, A. SHACKEY, M. EVANS, J. STEVENS.

Communist Party of Australia (Marxist-Leninist): f. 1967 following a split in Communist Party of Australia; Maoist; Chair. E. F. HILL.

Liberal Party of Australia: Federal Secretariat, Cnr Blackall and Macquarie Sts, Barton, ACT 2600; tel. (06) 273-2564; fax (06) 273-1534; f. 1944; advocates private enterprise, social justice, individual liberty and initiative; committed to national development, prosperity and security; Fed. Pres. JOHN D. ELLIOTT; Fed. Parl. Leader JOHN HEWSON.

National Party of Australia: John McEwen House, National Circuit, Barton, ACT 2600; tel. (06) 273-3822; fax (06) 273-1745; f. 1916 as the Country Party of Australia; adopted present name in 1982; advocates balanced national development based on free enterprise, with special emphasis on the needs of people outside the major metropolitan areas; Fed. Pres. STUART MCDONALD; Fed. Parl. Leader TIMOTHY FISCHER; Fed. Dir PAUL DAVEY.

New Left Party: f. 1989.

Socialist Party of Australia: 65 Campbell St, Surry Hills, NSW 2010; tel. (02) 212-6855; telex 126784; fax (02) 281-5795; f. 1971; advocates public ownership of the means of production, working-class political power; Pres. J. MCPHILLIPS; Gen. Sec. P. SYMON.

Other political parties include the **Farm and Town Party** and the **Green Party**.

Diplomatic Representation

EMBASSIES AND HIGH COMMISSIONS IN AUSTRALIA

Algeria: 13 Culgoa Circuit, O'Malley, ACT 2606; tel. (06) 286-1788; telex 61607; Ambassador: LAHCENE MOUSSAOUI.

Argentina: MLC Tower, Suite 102, 1st Floor, Woden, ACT 2606; POB 262, Woden, ACT 2606; tel. (06) 282-4855; telex 62195; fax (06) 285-3062; Ambassador: Dr JUAN CARLOS BELTRAMINO.

Austria: 12 Talbot St, Forrest, ACT 2603; tel. (06) 295-1533; telex 62726; fax (06) 239-6751; Ambassador: Dr WALTER HIETSCH.

Bangladesh: 11 Molineaux Place, Farrer, ACT 2607; POB 197, Mawson, ACT 2607; tel. (06) 286-3992; telex 61729; High Commissioner: Air Vice-Marshal Sultan MAHMUD.

Belgium: 19 Arkana St, Yarralumla, ACT 2600; tel. (06) 273-2501; telex 62601; fax (06) 273-3392; Ambassador: Dr WILFRIED DE PAUW.

Brazil: 19 Forster Crescent, Yarralumla, ACT 2600; GPO Box 1540, Canberra, ACT 2601; tel. (06) 273-2372; telex 62327; fax (06) 273-2375; Ambassador: MARCOS HENRIQUE CAMILLO CÔRTES.

Brunei: 16 Bulwarra Close, O'Malley, ACT 2606; tel. (06) 290-1801; High Commissioner: Dato PADUKA Haji ABDULLAH.

Canada: Commonwealth Ave, Canberra, ACT 2600; tel. (06) 273-3844; telex 62017; fax (06) 273-3285; High Commissioner: R. ALLEN KILPATRICK.

Chile: 10 Culgoa Circuit, O'Malley, ACT 2606; tel. (06) 286-2430; telex 62685; Chargé d'affaires: JORGE DUPOUY.

China, People's Republic: 14 Federal Highway, Watson, Canberra, ACT 2602; tel. (06) 241-2446; telex 62489; fax (06) 241-1530; Ambassador: ZHANG ZAI.

Colombia: 2nd Floor, 101 Northbourne Ave, Turner, ACT 2601; tel. (06) 257-2027; fax (06) 257-1448; Ambassador: Dr ANTONIO PUERTO.

Cyprus: 37 Endeavour St, Red Hill, ACT 2603; tel. (06) 295-2120; telex 62499; fax (06) 295-2892; High Commissioner: ANDREAS PIRISHIS.

Czechoslovakia: 47 Culgoa Circuit, O'Malley, ACT 2606; tel. (06) 290-1516; telex 61807; Ambassador: Dr PETR KADLEC.

Denmark: 15 Hunter St, Yarralumla, ACT 2600; tel. (06) 273-2195; telex 262661; fax (06) 273-3864; Ambassador: HANS JØRGEN ASSING.

Egypt: 1 Darwin Ave, Yarralumla, ACT 2600; tel. (06) 273-4437; telex 62497; Ambassador: NABIL MOHAMMED BADR.

Fiji: 9 Beagle St, Red Hill, ACT 2603; POB E159, Queen Victoria Terrace, ACT 2600; tel. (06) 295-9148; fax (06) 295-3283; Ambassador: Dr MESAKE BIUMAIWAI.

Finland: 10 Darwin Ave, Yarralumla, ACT 2600; tel. (06) 273-3800; telex 62713; fax (06) 273-3603; Ambassador: ULF-ERIK SLOTTE.

France: 6 Perth Ave, Yarralumla, ACT 2600; tel. (06) 270-5111; fax (06) 273-3193; Ambassador: ROGER DUZER.

Germany: 119 Empire Circuit, Yarralumla, ACT 2600; tel. (06) 270-1911; telex 62035; fax (06) 273-4836; Ambassador: Dr HANS SCHAUER.

Greece: 9 Turrana St, Yarralumla, ACT 2600; tel. (06) 273-3011; telex 62724; fax (06) 273-2620; Ambassador: EFTHYMIOS TZAPHERIS.

Holy See: 2 Vancouver St, Red Hill, ACT 2603 (Apostolic Nunciature); tel. (06) 295-3876; Apostolic Pro-Nuncio: Most Rev. FRANCO BRAMBILLA, Titular Archbishop of Viminacium.

Hungary: 79 Hopetoun Circuit, Yarralumla, ACT 2600; tel. (06) 282-3226; telex 62737; Ambassador: Dr ZOLTÁN JUHÁR.

India: 3–5 Moonah Place, Yarralumla, ACT 2600; tel. (06) 273-3999; telex 62362; fax (06) 273-3328; High Commissioner: SUDARSHAN KUMAR BHUTANI.

Indonesia: 8 Darwin Ave, Yarralumla, ACT 2600; tel. (06) 273-3222; telex 62525; fax (06) 273-3748; Ambassador: Air Vice-Marshal ROESMAN.

Iran: 14 Torrens St, Red Hill, ACT 2603; POB 3219, Manuka, ACT 2603; tel. (06) 295-2544; telex 62490; fax (06) 295-2882; Ambassador: MEHDI KHANDAGHABADI.

Iraq: 48 Culgoa Circuit, O'Malley, ACT 2606; tel. (06) 286-1333; telex 61520; Ambassador: AFIF ISSA AL-RAWI.

Ireland: 20 Arkana St, Yarralumla, ACT 2600; tel. (06) 273-3022; telex 62720; fax (06) 273-3741; Ambassador: MARTIN B. BURKE.

Israel: 6 Turrana St, Yarralumla, ACT 2600; tel. (06) 273-1309; fax (06) 273-4273; Ambassador: ZVI KEDAR.

Italy: 12 Grey St, Deakin, ACT 2601; POB 360, Canberra City, ACT 2601; tel. (06) 273-3333; telex 62028; fax (06) 273-4223; Ambassador: Dr FRANCESCO CARDI.

Japan: 112 Empire Circuit, Yarralumla, ACT 2600; tel. (06) 273-3244; telex 62034; fax (06) 273-1848; Ambassador: HIROMU FUKADA.

Jordan: 20 Roebuck St, Red Hill, ACT 2603; tel. (06) 295-9951; telex 62551; Ambassador: SAAD BATAINAH.

Kenya: QBE Bldg, 6th Floor, 33–35 Ainslie Ave, Canberra, ACT 2601; POB 1990, Canberra, ACT 2601; tel. (06) 247-4788; telex 61929; High Commissioner: Maj.-Gen. JOSEPH MBYATI MUSOMBA.

Korea, Republic: 113 Empire Circuit, Yarralumla, ACT 2600; tel. (06) 273-3044; Ambassador: CHANG SOO LEE.

Laos: 1 Dalman Crescent, O'Malley, ACT 2606; tel. (06) 286-4595; telex 61627; Ambassador: VANG RATTANAVONG.

Lebanon: 27 Endeavour St, Red Hill, ACT 2603; tel. (06) 295-7378; telex 61762; Ambassador: LATIF ABUL-HUSN.

Malaysia: 7 Perth Ave, Yarralumla, ACT 2600; tel. (06) 273-1543; High Commissioner: Datuk ABDUL KARIM MARZUKI.

Malta: 261 La Perouse St, Red Hill, ACT 2603; tel. (06) 295-1586; telex 62817; fax (06) 239-6084; High Commissioner: VICTOR J. GAUCI.

Mauritius: 43 Hampton Circuit, Yarralumla, ACT 2600; tel. (06) 281-1203; telex 62863; fax (06) 282-3235; High Commissioner: PARRWIZ CASSIM HOSSEN (acting).

Mexico: 14 Perth Ave, Yarralumla, ACT 2600; tel. (06) 273-3905; telex 62329; fax (06) 273-3488; Ambassador: ALEJANDRO MORALES.

Myanmar: 22 Arkana St, Yarralumla, ACT 2600; tel. (06) 273-3811; telex 61376; Ambassador: THANE MYINT.

Netherlands: 120 Empire Circuit, Yarralumla, ACT 2600; tel. (06) 273-3111; telex 62047; fax (06) 273-3206; Ambassador: JORIS MICHAEL VOS.

New Zealand: Commonwealth Ave, Canberra, ACT 2600; tel. (06) 273-3611; telex 62019; fax (06) 273-3194; High Commissioner: EDWARD A. WOODFIELD.

Nigeria: 7 Terrigal Crescent, O'Malley, ACT 2606; POB 241, Civic Square, ACT 2608; tel. (06) 286-1322; High Commissioner: GODFREY J. N. ANIEMENA.

AUSTRALIA

Norway: 17 Hunter St, Yarralumla, ACT 2600; tel. (06) 273-3444; telex 62569; fax (06) 273-3669; Ambassador: PER THELIN HAUGESTAD.

Pakistan: 59 Franklin St, Forrest, ACT 2603; POB 3198, Manuka, ACT 2603; tel. (06) 295-0021; fax (06) 295-2707; High Commissioner: BASHIR KHAN BABAR.

Papua New Guinea: Forster Crescent, Yarralumla, ACT 2600; POB 572, Manuka, ACT 2603; tel. (06) 273-3322; telex 62592; High Commissioner: PAUL BERNARD SONGO.

Peru: Qantas House, Suite 1, 9th Floor, 197 London Circuit, Canberra City, ACT 2601; POB 971, Civic Square, ACT 2608; tel. (06) 257-2953; telex 61664; fax (06) 257-5198; Ambassador: GONZALO BEDOYA.

Philippines: 1 Moonah Place, Yarralumla, ACT 2600; POB 3297, Manuka, ACT 2603; tel. (06) 273-2535; telex 62665; fax (06) 273-3984; Ambassador: RORA NAVARRO-TOLENTINO.

Poland: 7 Turrana St, Yarralumla, ACT 2600; tel. (06) 273-1208; telex 62584; Ambassador: ANTONI PIERZCHALA.

Portugal: 6 Campion St, 1st Floor, Deakin, ACT 2600; tel. (06) 285-2084; telex 62649; Ambassador: Dr JOSÉ LUIZ-GOMES.

Saudi Arabia: 12 Culgoa Circuit, O'Malley, ACT 2605; POB 63, Garran, ACT 2605; tel. (06) 286-2099; telex 61454; Ambassador: A. RAHMAN N. ALOHALY.

Singapore: 17 Forster Crescent, Yarralumla, ACT 2600; tel. (06) 273-3944; telex 62192; fax (06) 273-3260; High Commissioner: JOSEPH FRANCIS CONCEICAO.

South Africa: cnr State Circle and Rhodes Place, Yarralumla, ACT 2600; tel. (06) 273-2424; telex 62734; fax (06) 273-3543; Ambassador: F. D. TOTHILL.

Spain: 15 Arkana St, Yarralumla, ACT 2600; POB 76, Deakin, ACT 2600; tel. (06) 273-3555; telex 62485; fax (06) 273-3918; Ambassador: Dr JOSÉ LUIS PARDOS.

Sri Lanka: 35 Empire Circuit, Forrest, ACT 2603; tel. (06) 295-3521; telex 61620; High Commissioner: EDWIN LOKU BANDARA HURULLE.

Sweden: 5 Turrana St, Yarralumla, ACT 2600; tel. (06) 273-3033; telex 62303; fax (06) 273-3298; Ambassador: HANS BJÖRK.

Switzerland: 7 Melbourne Ave, Forrest, ACT 2603; tel. (06) 273-3977; telex 62275; fax (06) 273-3428; Ambassador: Dr ARNOLD HUGENTOBLER.

Thailand: 111 Empire Circuit, Yarralumla, ACT 2600; tel. (06) 285-2328; telex 62533; Ambassador: Dr CHAWAN CHAWANID.

Turkey: 60 Mugga Way, Red Hill, ACT 2603; tel. (06) 295-0227; telex 62764; fax (06) 239-6592; Ambassador: ERGÜN PELIT.

USSR: 78 Canberra Ave, Griffith, ACT 2603; tel. (06) 295-9033; telex 61365; fax (06) 295-1847; Ambassador: Dr YEVGENI M. SAMOTEIKIN.

United Kingdom: Commonwealth Ave, Canberra, ACT 2600; tel. (06) 270-6666; telex 62222; fax (06) 273-3236; High Commissioner: Sir JOHN COLES.

USA: Chancery, Yarralumla, ACT 2600; tel. (06) 270-5000; fax (06) 270-5970; Ambassador: MELVIN F. SEMBLER.

Uruguay: Bonner House, Suite 5, Woden, ACT 2606; POB 318, Woden, ACT 2606; tel. (06) 282-4418; telex 61486; Chargé d'affaires a.i.: JULIO GIAMBRUNO.

Venezuela: MLC Tower, Suite 106, 1st Floor, Woden, ACT 2606; POB 37, Woden, ACT 2606; tel. (06) 282-4827; telex 62110; fax (06) 281-1969; Ambassador: Dr EDUARDO MORREO.

Viet-Nam: 6 Timbarra Crescent, O'Malley, ACT 2606; tel. (06) 286-6059; fax (06) 286-4534; Ambassador: TRAN TUAN ANH.

Western Samoa: 33 Murray Crescent, Manuka, ACT 2603; tel. (06) 239-6996; fax (06) 239-6252; High Commissioner: FEESAGO SIAOSI FEPULEA'I.

Yugoslavia: 11 Nuyts St, Red Hill, ACT 2603; POB 3161, Manuka, ACT 2603; tel. (06) 295-1458; telex 62317; fax (06) 239-6178; Ambassador: Dr BORIS CIZELJ.

Zambia: 28 Guilfoyle St, Yarralumla, ACT 2600; tel. (06) 281-0111; telex 61796; High Commissioner: JASON C. MFULA.

Zimbabwe: 11 Culgoa Circuit, O'Malley, ACT 2606; tel. (06) 286-2700; telex 62211; High Commissioner: EUBERT P. T. MASHAIRE.

Judicial System

The judicial power of the Commonwealth of Australia is vested in the High Court of Australia, in such other Federal Courts as the Federal Parliament creates, and in such other courts as it invests with Federal jurisdiction.

The High Court consists of a Chief Justice and six other Justices, each of whom is appointed by the Governor-General in Council, and has both original and appellate jurisdiction.

The High Court's original jurisdiction extends to all matters arising under any treaty, affecting representatives of other countries, in which the Commonwealth of Australia or its representative is a party, between states or between residents of different states or between a state and a resident of another state, and in which a writ of mandamus, or prohibition, or an injunction is sought against an officer of the Commonwealth of Australia. It also extends to matters arising under the Australian Constitution or involving its interpretation, and to many matters arising under Commonwealth laws.

The High Court's appellate jurisdiction has, since June 1984, been discretionary. Appeals from the Federal Court, the Family Court and the Supreme Courts of the states and of the territories may now be brought only if special leave is granted, in the event of a legal question that is of general public importance being involved, or of there being differences of opinion between intermediate appellate courts as to the state of the law.

Legislation enacted by the Federal Parliament in 1976 substantially changed the exercise of Federal and Territory judicial power, and, by creating the Federal Court of Australia in February 1977, enabled the High Court of Australia to give greater attention to its primary function as interpreter of the Australian Constitution. The Federal Court of Australia has assumed, in two divisions, the jurisdiction previously exercised by the Australian Industrial Court and the Federal Court of Bankruptcy and has additionally been given jurisdiction in trade practices and in the developing field of administrative law. Jurisdiction has also been conferred on the Federal Court of Australia, subject to a number of exceptions, in matters in which a writ of mandamus, or prohibition, or an injunction is sought against an officer of the Commonwealth of Australia. The Court also hears appeals from the Court constituted by a single Judge, from the Supreme Courts of the territories, and in certain specific matters from State Courts, other than a Full Court of the Supreme Court of a state, exercising Federal jurisdiction.

In March 1986 all remaining categories of appeal from Australian courts to the Queen's Privy Council in the UK were abolished by the Australia Act.

FEDERAL COURTS

High Court of Australia

POB E435, Queen Victoria Terrace, Canberra, ACT 2600; tel. (06) 270-6862; telex 61430; fax (06) 273-3025.

Chief Justice: Sir ANTHONY FRANK MASON.

Justices: Sir FRANCIS GERARD BRENNAN, Sir WILLIAM PATRICK DEANE, Sir DARYL MICHAEL DAWSON, JOHN LESLIE TOOHEY, MARY GENEVIEVE GAUDRON, MICHAEL HUDSON McHUGH.

Federal Court of Australia

Chief Judge: Sir NIGEL HUBERT BOWEN.

There are more than 30 other Judges.

Family Court of Australia

Chief Judge: ALISTAIR BOTHWICK NICHOLSON.

There are more than 50 other Judges.

NEW SOUTH WALES
Supreme Court

Chief Justice: Sir LAURENCE WHISTLER STREET.
President of the Court of Appeal: MICHAEL DONALD KIRBY.
Chief Judge in Equity: MICHAEL MANIFOLD HELSHAM.
Chief Judge of Common Law: JOHN PATRICK SLATTERY.

VICTORIA
Supreme Court

Chief Justice: Sir JOHN McINTOSH YOUNG.

QUEENSLAND
Supreme Court

Southern District (Brisbane)
Chief Justice: D. G. ANDREWS.
Senior Puisne Judge: J. KELLY.

Central District (Rockhampton)
Puisne Judge: A. G. DEMACK.

Northern District (Townsville)
Puisne Judge: Sir GEORGE KNEIPP.

SOUTH AUSTRALIA
Supreme Court

Chief Justice: LEONARD JAMES KING.

AUSTRALIA   *Directory*

WESTERN AUSTRALIA
Supreme Court
Chief Justice: DAVID MALCOLM.

TASMANIA
Supreme Court
Chief Justice: Sir GUY STEPHEN MONTAGUE GREEN.

AUSTRALIAN CAPITAL TERRITORY
Supreme Court
Chief Justice: JEFFREY ALLAN MILES.

NORTHERN TERRITORY
Supreme Court
Chief Justice: K. J. A. ASCENE.

Religion

CHRISTIANITY

Australian Council of Churches: POB C199, Clarence St, Sydney, NSW 2000; tel. (02) 299-2215; telex 171715; fax (02) 262-4514; f. 1946; 13 mem. churches; Pres. Rt Rev. OLIVER S. HEYWARD; Gen. Sec. Rev. DAVID GILL.

The Anglican Communion

The constitution of the Church of England in Australia came into force in January 1962. The body was renamed the Anglican Church of Australia in August 1981. The Church comprises five provinces (together containing 23 dioceses) and the extra-provincial diocese of Tasmania. In 1988 there were an estimated 3,723,419 adherents.

National Office of the Anglican Church: General Synod Office, Box Q190, Queen Victoria PO, Sydney, NSW 2000; tel. (02) 265-1525; fax (02) 264-6552; Gen. Sec. JOHN G. DENTON.

Archbishop of Adelaide and Metropolitan of South Australia: (vacant), Bishop's Court, 45 Palmer Place, North Adelaide, South Australia 5006.

Archbishop of Brisbane and Metropolitan of Queensland: Most Rev. PETER J. HOLLINGWORTH, Bishopsbourne, Box 421, GPO, Brisbane, Queensland 4001.

Archbishop of Melbourne and Metropolitan of Victoria: Most Rev. KEITH RAYNOR, Bishopscourt, 120 Clarendon St, Melbourne, Victoria 3002.

Archbishop of Perth and Metropolitan of Western Australia: Most Rev. PETER F. CARNLEY, Bishop's House, 90 Mounts Bay Rd, Perth, Western Australia 6000; also has jurisdiction over Christmas Island and the Cocos (Keeling) Islands.

Archbishop of Sydney and Metropolitan of New South Wales: Most Rev. DONALD W. B. ROBINSON, Box Q190, Queen Victoria PO, Sydney, NSW 2000.

The Roman Catholic Church

Australia comprises seven archdioceses (including two directly responsible to the Holy See) and 25 dioceses (including one each for Catholics of the Maronite, Melkite and Ukrainian rites). At 31 December 1988 there were an estimated 4,350,732 adherents in the country.

Australian Catholic Bishops Conference: 63 Currong St, Braddon (POB 368, Canberra), ACT 2601; tel. (06) 247-2011; fax (06) 247-6083; f. 1979; Pres. Cardinal EDWARD BEDE CLANCY, Archbishop of Sydney.

Archbishop of Adelaide: Most Rev. LEONARD A. FAULKNER, Catholic Diocesan Centre, 39 Wakefield St, POB 1364, Adelaide, South Australia 5001; tel. (08) 210-8108; fax (08) 223-3880.

Archbishop of Brisbane: Most Rev. FRANCIS R. RUSH, Catholic Centre, 790 Brunswick St, Brisbane, Queensland 4005; tel. (07) 224-3361; fax (07) 358-1357.

Archbishop of Canberra and Goulburn: Most Rev. FRANCIS P. CARROLL, Archbishop's House, POB 89, Commonwealth Ave, Canberra, ACT 2601; tel. (06) 248-6411; fax (06) 247-9636.

Archbishop of Hobart: Most Rev. ERIC D'ARCY, Catholic Church Office, POB 62A, Hobart, Tasmania 7001; tel. (002) 345-688; fax (002) 253-865.

Archbishop of Melbourne: Most Rev. THOMAS F. LITTLE, Catholic Diocesan Centre, POB 146, 383 Albert St, East Melbourne, Victoria 3002; tel. (03) 667-0377; fax (03) 667-0313.

Archbishop of Perth: Most Rev. WILLIAM J. FOLEY, St Mary's Cathedral, 21 Victoria Sq., Perth, Western Australia 6000; tel. (09) 325-9177; fax (09) 221-1716.

Archbishop of Sydney: Cardinal EDWARD BEDE CLANCY, Archdiocesan Chancery, Polding House, 13th Floor, 276 Pitt St, Sydney, NSW 2000; tel. (02) 264-7211; fax (02) 261-8312.

Orthodox Churches

Greek Orthodox Archdiocese: 242 Cleveland St, Redfern, Sydney, NSW 2016; tel. (02) 698-5066; fax (02) 698-5368; f. 1924; 700,000 mems; offices in Melbourne, Adelaide, Brisbane and Perth; Primate His Eminence Archbishop STYLIANOS.

The Antiochian, Coptic, Romanian, Serbian and Syrian Orthodox Churches are also represented.

Other Christian Churches

Baptist Union of Australia: POB 377, Hawthorn, Vic 3122; tel. (03) 818-0341; fax (03) 818-2128; f. 1926; 61,728 mems; 768 churches; Nat. Pres. W. C. MCFARLANE; Nat. Sec. O. C. ABBOTT.

Churches of Christ in Australia: 52 La Trobe St, Melbourne, Vic. 3000; tel. (03) 662-2377; 35,500 mems; Pres. C. L. WARD; Sec. Mrs I. E. ALLSOP.

Lutheran Church of Australia: Lutheran Church House, 58 O'Connell St, North Adelaide, SA 5006; tel. (08) 267-4922; fax (08) 239-0173; f. 1966; 105,532 mems; Pres. Rev. Dr L. G. STEICKE; Sec. Rev. K. J. SCHMIDT.

Uniting Church in Australia: POB E266, St James, NSW 2000; tel. (02) 287-0900; fax (02) 287-0999; f. 1977 with the union of Methodist, Presbyterian and Congregational Churches; 1.1m. mems; Pres. Rev. Dr D'ARCY WOOD; Sec. Rev. GREGOR HENDERSON.

Other active denominations include the Armenian Apostolic Church, the Assyrian Church of the East and the Society of Friends (Quakers).

JUDAISM

Great Synagogue: 166 Castlereagh St, Sydney, NSW; tel. (02) 267-2477; fax (02) 264-8871; f. 1828; Sr Minister Rabbi RAYMOND APPLE.

The Press

The total circulation of Australia's daily newspapers is very high but in the remoter parts of the country weekly papers are even more popular. Most of Australia's newspapers are published in sparsely populated rural areas where the demand for local news is strong. The only newspapers that may fairly claim a national circulation are the dailies *The Australian* and *Australian Financial Review*, and the weeklies *The Bulletin*, the *National Times* and the *Nation Review*, the circulation of most newspapers being almost entirely confined to the state in which each is produced.

The trend in recent years towards the concentration of media ownership has led to the development of three principal groups of newspapers. Economic conditions have been conducive to the expansion of newspaper companies into magazine and book publishing, radio and television, etc. The principal groups are as follows:

The ASM Group: 6/5 Vuko Place, Warriewood, NSW 2102; tel. (02) 913-1444; fax (02) 913-2342; publishes *Focus on Photography*, *Stereo Buyer's Guide* and other magazines.

Australian Consolidated Press Ltd: 54-58 Park St, Sydney, NSW 2000; tel. (02) 282-8000; telex 120514; fax (02) 267-2150; publishes *Australian Women's Weekly*, *The Bulletin with Newsweek*, *Australian Business*, *Cleo*, *Cosmopolitan*, *Woman's Day*, *Dolly* and other magazines.

The Herald and Weekly Times Ltd: 44-74 Flinders St, Melbourne, Vic 3000; tel. (03) 652-1111; telex 30104; fax (03) 652-2112; acquired by News Ltd in 1987; Chair. JANET CALVERT-JONES; Man. Dir MALCOLM COLLESS; publs include *The Herald*, *The Sunday Herald*, *The Sun News-Pictorial*, *The Sunday Sun News-Pictorial*, *The Weekly Times*, *The Sporting Globe*, *The Bendigo Advertiser*, *The Geelong Advertiser*, *The Post Courier* (Papua New Guinea), *Fiji Times*.

The John Fairfax Group: 235 Jones St, Broadway, NSW 2007; POB 506, Sydney, NSW 2001; tel. (02) 282-2833; telex 23425; fax (02) 282-3133; f. 1987; went into receivership in Dec. 1990; Chair. KEITH HALKERSTON; CEO WARWICK FAIRFAX; controls *The Sydney Morning Herald*, *Australian Financial Review* and *Sun-Herald* (Sydney), *The Age*, *The Sunday Age* and *BRW Publications* (Melbourne), *Illawarra Mercury* (Wollongong), *The Newcastle Herald* (Newcastle).

News Corp: 2 Holt St, Surry Hills, Sydney, NSW 2010; tel. (02) 288-3000; telex 20124; Chair. RICHARD H. SEARBY; CEO K. RUPERT MURDOCH; controls *The Australian* (national), *Daily Telegraph Mirror*, *Sunday Telegraph* (Sydney), *The Herald-Sun* (Victoria), *Northern Territory News* (Darwin), *Sunday Times* (Perth), *Herald & Weekly Times* (Melbourne), *Townsville Bulletin*, *Courier Mail*,

AUSTRALIA

Sunday Mail (Queensland), *The Mercury, The Advertiser, Sunday Mail* (South Australia), *Progress Press* (Melbourne). Assoc. publs: *New Idea* and *TV Week* (National), *The Mercury* (Tasmania), *The Sun, News of the World, The Times* and *The Sunday Times* (London), *Boston Herald* (Boston), *Express-News* (San Antonio, Texas).

David Syme & Co Ltd: 250 Spencer St, Melbourne, Vic 3000; tel. (03) 600-4211; telex 30449; fax (03) 670-7514; f. 1834; wholly-owned by John Fairfax Group (see above); publishes *The Age* and other newspapers and magazines in Victoria; Man. Dir G. J. TAYLOR.

NEWSPAPERS
Australian Capital Territory

The Canberra Times: 9 Pirie St, Fyshwick 2609; tel. (06) 280-2122; telex 62069; fax (06) 280-7562; f. 1926; daily and Sun.; morning; Editor CRISPIN HULL; circ. 45,000.

New South Wales
Dailies

The Australian: News Ltd, 2 Holt St, Surry Hills 2010, POB 4245; tel. (02) 288-3000; telex 20124; f. 1964; edited in Sydney, simultaneous edns in Sydney, Melbourne, Perth, Townsville and Brisbane; Propr K. RUPERT MURDOCH; Editor DAVID ARMSTRONG; circ. 147,187.

Australian Financial Review: 235 Jones St, Broadway, POB 506, Sydney, NSW 2007; tel. (02) 282-2833; telex 24851; fax (02) 282-2484; f. 1951; Mon.-Fri.; distributed nationally; Editor-in-Chief PETER ROBINSON; circ. 74,000.

Daily Commercial News: POB 1552, Sydney 2001; tel. (02) 211-4055; telex 121874; f. 1891; Editor JOHN SPIERS.

Daily Telegraph Mirror: 46 Cooper St, Surry Hills, NSW 2010; tel. (02) 288-3000; telex 20124; fax (02) 288-2300; f. 1879 as Daily Telegraph, merged in 1990 with Daily Mirror (f. 1941); 24-hour broadsheet; CEO K. RUPERT MURDOCH.

The Manly Daily: 26 Sydney Rd, Manly 2095; tel. (02) 977-3333; fax (02) 977-1830; f. 1906; Tue.-Sat.; Man. JENNIFER STOKELD; circ. 83,136.

The Newcastle Herald: 28–30 Bolton St, Newcastle 2300; tel. (049) 263222; telex 28269; fax (049) 296407; f. 1858; morning; 6 a week; Editor B. W. POMFRETT; circ. 56,000.

The Sydney Morning Herald: 235 Jones St, Broadway, POB 506, Sydney 2001; tel. (02) 282-2833; telex 21717; f. 1831; morning; Editor-in-Chief J. H. ALEXANDER; circ. 266,000 (Mon.-Fri.), 400,000 (Sat.).

Weeklies

Bankstown Canterbury Torch: 398 Marion St, Bankstown 2200; tel. (02) 709-3433; f. 1920; Wed.; Publr J. P. ENGISCH; circ. 78,000.

Northern District Times: 116 Rowe St, Eastwood 2122; tel. (02) 858-1766; fax (02) 804-6901; f. 1921; Wed.; Man. R. JENKINS; Editor C. ZUILL; circ. 53,088.

The Parramatta Advertiser: 142 Macquarie St, Parramatta 2150; tel. (02) 689-5500; telex 72133; fax (02) 689-5353; Wed.; Editor S. STICKNEY; circ. 95,036.

Parramatta and District Mercury: 38 George St, 1st Floor, Parramatta 2150; f. 1977; Tues.; circ. 102,000.

St George and Sutherland Shire Leader: 172 Forest Rd, Hurstville 2220; tel. (02) 579-5033; f. 1960; Tues. and Thurs.; Man. IAN MUDDLE; Editor MICHAEL GARDNER; circ. 118,383.

Sun-Herald: 235 Jones St, Broadway, POB 506, Sydney 2001; tel. (02) 282-2822; telex 20121; f. 1953; Sunday; Editor DAVID HICKIE; circ. 671,000.

Sunday Telegraph: 46 Cooper St, Surry Hills, NSW 2010; tel. (02) 288-3000; telex 20124; fax (02) 288-2300; f. 1938; Editor IAN MOORE; circ. 562,000.

Northern Territory
Daily

Northern Territory News: 3 Printers Place, POB 1300, Darwin 0801; tel. (089) 828200; telex 85574; f. 1952; Mon.-Sat.; Man. Editor J. SWINSTEAD; circ. 19,000.

Weeklies

The Darwin Star: 31 Bishop St, POB 39330 Winnellie, Darwin 5789; f. 1976; Thur.; Man. Editor PATRICK CUSICK; circ. 13,000.

Sunday Territorian: Printers Place, POB 1300, Darwin 5794; tel. (089) 828200; telex 85574; Sun.; Editor G. SHIPWAY; circ. 21,000.

Queensland
Dailies

Courier-Mail: Campbell St, Bowen Hills, Brisbane 4000; tel. (07) 252-6011; telex 40101; fax (07) 252-6696; f. 1933; morning; Editor G. T. CHAMBERLIN; circ. 250,000.

The Sun: 367 Brunswick St, Fortitude Valley, Brisbane 4006; tel. (07) 253-3333; telex 40121; fax (07) 253-3103; f. 1988; Man. Dir F. MOORE; Editor-in-Chief M. QUIRK; circ. 125,326.

Weeklies

The Suburban: POB 10, 10 Aspinall St, Nundah 4012; tel. (07) 266-6666; five suburban edns; Publr Mrs HEATHER JEFFERY; combined circ. 117,000.

Sunday Mail: Campbell St, Bowen Hills, Brisbane 4006; tel. (07) 252-6011; telex 40110; fax (07) 252-6692; f. 1923; Editor BOB GORDON; circ. 345,000.

Sunday Sun: 367 Brunswick St, Fortitude Valley, Brisbane 4006; tel. (07) 253-3333; telex 40101; fax (07) 253-3103; f. 1971; Man. Dir F. MOORE; Editor T. SWEETMAN; circ. 382,921.

South Australia
Dailies

Advertiser: 121 King William St, Adelaide 5001; tel. (08) 218-9218; telex 82101; fax (08) 231-1147; f. 1858; morning; Editor P. AKERMAN; circ. 212,658.

News: 112 North Terrace, Adelaide 5001; tel. (08) 510351; telex 82131; f. 1923; evening; Mon.-Fri.; Man. Editor ROGER HOLDEN; circ. 129,819.

Weekly

Sunday Mail: 6th Floor, 121 King William St, Adelaide 5000; tel. (08) 218-9218; fax (08) 212-6264; f. 1912; Editor KERRY SULLIVAN; circ. 268,000.

Victoria
Dailies

The Age: 250 Spencer St (cnr Lonsdale St), Melbourne 3000; tel. (03) 600-4211; telex 30449; f. 1854; independent; morning; Man. Dir G. J. TAYLOR; Editor MICHAEL SMITH; circ. 232,690.

The Herald-Sun: 44–74 Flinders St, Melbourne, Vic 3000; tel. (03) 652-1111; telex 30104; fax (03) 654-3133; f. 1840 as The Herald, merged with the Sun-News Pictorial (f. 1922) in 1990; 24-hour broadsheet.

Weeklies

The Malvern Caulfield Progress: 92 Atherton Rd, Oakleigh 3166; tel. (03) 568-4644; f. 1960; publ. by Leader Group; Wed.; Editor ALLISON HICKS; circ. 54,000.

Sporting Globe: 44 Flinders St, Melbourne, Vic 3000; tel. (03) 652-1111; telex 30104; fax (03) 654-3133; f. 1922; Mon.; Editor NEVILLE WILLMOTT; circ. 43,049.

Sunday Age: GPO Box 257C, Melbourne, Vic 3000; tel. (03) 600-4211; fax (03) 602-1856; f. 1989; publ. by David Syme and Co Ltd; Editor STEVE HARRIS.

Sunday Herald: 61 Flinders Lane, Melbourne, Vic 3000; tel. (03) 652-1111; fax (03) 652-2020; f. 1989; publ. by Herald and Weekly Times Ltd; Editor ALAN FARRELLY; circ. 280,000.

Sunday Sun News-Pictorial: 44–74 Flinders St, Melbourne, Vic 3000; f. 1989; publ. by Herald and Weekly Times Ltd; Editor CHRIS DE KRETSEA.

Truth: 272 Rosslyn St, West Melbourne, Vic 3003; tel. (03) 329-0277; telex 30562; f. 1890; Mon. and Thur.; Editor C. SMITH; circ. 240,433.

Tasmania
Dailies

Advocate: POB 63, Burnie 7320; tel. (004) 301409; fax (004) 301461; f. 1890; morning; Editor H. M. CATCHPOLE; circ. 27,000.

Examiner: 71-75 Paterson St, POB 99A, Launceston 7250; tel. (003) 315-111; fax (003) 320-300; f. 1842; morning; independent; Editor M. C. P. COURTNEY; circ. 39,000.

Mercury: 91-93 Macquarie St, Hobart 7000; tel. (002) 300622; fax (002) 300711; f. 1854; morning; Editor I. MCCAUSLAND; circ. 54,446.

Weeklies

Advocate Weekender: POB 63, Burnie 7320; tel. (004) 301409; fax (004) 301461; f. 1968; Sat.; Editor H. M. CATCHPOLE; circ. 14,000.

Sunday Examiner: 71-75 Paterson St, Launceston 7250; tel. (003) 315-111; fax (003) 320-300; f. 1924; Editor M. C. P. COURTNEY; circ. 39,000.

Sunday Tasmanian: 91-93 Macquarie St, Hobart 7000; tel. (002) 300-622; fax (002) 300-711; f. 1984; morning; Editor IAN MCCAUSLAND; circ. 54,759.

The Tasmanian Mail: 130 Collins St, Hobart 7000; tel. (002) 211-211; telex 57150; f. 1978; Man. Editor W. A. J. HASWELL; circ. 131,000.

AUSTRALIA   Directory

Western Australia
Dailies

The West Australian: Bell Publishing Group Pty Ltd, Forrest Centre, 219 St George's Terrace, Perth 6000; POB D162, GPO Perth 6001; tel. (09) 482-3111; telex 92109; fax (09) 324-1416; f. 1833; morning; Editor P. R. MURRAY; circ. 253,788.

Weeklies

The Countryman: 219 St George's Terrace, GPO Box D162, Perth 6001; tel. (09) 482-3111; telex 94999; fax (09) 482-3317; f. 1885; Thur.; farming; Editor R. C. RAYMOND; circ. 15,000.

Sunday Times: 34–42 Stirling St, Perth 6000; tel. (09) 326-8326; telex 92015; fax (09) 221-1121; f. 1897; Gen. Man. MALCOLM NOAD; Man. Editor DON SMITH; circ. 313,000.

PRINCIPAL PERIODICALS
Weeklies and Fortnightlies

The Advocate: 196–200 Lygon St, Carlton, Vic 3053; tel. (03) 662-1100; fax (03) 662-1139; f. 1868; Thur.; Roman Catholic; Man. Editor PETER PHILP; circ. 18,000.

Australasian Post: 32 Walsh St, West Melbourne, Vic 3003; tel. (03) 320-7000; fax (03) 320-7410; f. 1946; factual, general interest, Australiana; Thur.; Editor TERRY CARROLL; circ. 204,693.

The Bulletin: 54 Park St, Sydney, NSW 2000; tel. (02) 282-8200; telex 120514; fax (02) 267-2150; f. 1880; Wed.; Editor DAVID DALE.

Business Review Weekly: Level 2, 469 La Trobe St, Melbourne, Vic 3000; tel. (03) 603-3888; telex 38995; fax (03) 670-4328; f. 1973; Chair. ROBERT COTTLIEBSEN; Editor DAVID UREN; circ. 77,084.

The Medical Journal of Australia: 1-5 Commercial Road, Kingsgrove, NSW 2208; tel. (02) 502-4899; fax (02) 502-3626; f. 1914; fortnightly; Editor Dr LAUREL THOMAS; circ. 23,000.

New Idea: 32 Walsh St, Melbourne, Vic 3001; tel. (03) 320-7000; fax (03) 320-7410; weekly; women's; Editor-in-Chief D. BOLING.

News Weekly: POB 66A, GPO Melbourne, Vic 3001; tel. (03) 326-5757; fax (03) 328-2877; f. 1943; publ. by National Civic Council; fortnightly; Sat.; political, social, educational and trade union affairs; Editor PETER WESTMORE; circ. 17,000.

People: 54 Park St, Sydney, NSW 2000; tel. (02) 282-8000; telex 25027; fax (02) 267-2105; weekly; Editor CHRIS BLACK; circ. 260,200.

Queensland Country Life: POB 586, Cleveland, Qld 4163; tel. (07) 286-5688; telex 42523; fax (07) 821-1226; f. 1935; Thurs.; Editor-in-Chief PETER OWEN; circ. 41,000.

The South Sea Digest: 46 Kippax St, 4th Floor, Surry Hills, NSW 2010; POB 4245, Sydney, NSW 2001; tel. (02) 288-3000; telex 20124; fax (02) 288-3322; f. 1981; fortnightly; business and politics in South Pacific; Editor JOHN CARTER.

Stock and Land: POB 1386, Collingwood, Vic 3066; tel. (03) 418-7900; telex 35668; fax (03) 418-7998; f. 1914; weekly; livestock, wool markets, crops, regional news journal; Man. Editor IAN L. MCPHEDRAN; circ. 26,000.

Time Australian Magazine: POB 3814, Sydney, NSW 2001; tel. (03) 603-3999; telex 38995; fax (03) 670-4238; Editor JEFF PENBERTHY; circ. 107,000.

TV Week: 32 Walsh St, Melbourne, Vic 3000; tel. (03) 320-7000; telex 30578; fax (03) 320-7410; f. 1957; Mon.; colour national; Editor-in-Chief JOHN HALL; circ. 780,000.

Video and Music Business: POB 1024, Richmond North, Vic 3121; tel. (03) 429-5599; telex 38225; fax (03) 427-0332; f. 1984; fortnightly; Editor GEOFFREY M. GOLD; circ. 3,000.

Weekly Times: Box 751F, GPO Melbourne, Vic 3001; tel. (03) 652-1111; telex 30104; fax (03) 652-2697; f. 1869; farming, gardening, country life and sport; Wed.; Editor MICHAEL PRAIN; circ. 90,000.

Woman's Day: 54 Park St, POB 5245, Sydney, NSW 2001; tel. (02) 282-8000; telex 120514; fax (02) 267-2150; weekly; circulates throughout Australia and NZ; Editor NENE KING; circ. 927,000.

Monthlies and Others

Archaeology in Oceania: University of Sydney, NSW 2006; tel. (02) 692-2666; telex 26169; fax (02) 692-4203; f. 1966; 3 a year; archaeology and physical anthropology; Editor J. PETER WHITE.

Architecture Media Australia Pty Ltd: 10A Beach St, Port Melbourne, Vic 3207; tel. (03) 646-4760; fax (03) 646-4918; f. 1904; 11 a year; Editor IAN MCDOUGALL; circ. 11,500.

Australian Business: 54 Park St, Sydney, NSW 2000; tel. (02) 282-8300; telex 120514; fax (02) 267-2150; f. 1980; business news and information; Publr RICHARD WALSH; Editor-in-Chief TREVOR SYKES; circ. 50,200.

Australian Asian and Pacific Electrical World: 9th Floor, 162 Goulbuth St, Darlinghurst, NSW 2010; tel. (02) 266-9711; telex 121417; fax (02) 267-1223; f. 1935; monthly; Editor DECLAN CULLEN; circ. 7,945.

Australian Cricket: POB 746, Darlinghurst, NSW 2010; tel. (02) 331-5006; telex 72964; fax (02) 360-5367; f. 1968; monthly during summer; Editor-in-Chief PHILIP MASON.

Australian Design Series: 54 Park St, Sydney, NSW 2000; tel. (02) 282-8450; telex 120514; fax (02) 267-2150; f. 1981; monthly; domestic and commercial design and interiors; Publr RICHARD WALSH; Editor STEPHANIE KING.

Australian Hi-Fi and Music Review Magazine: POB 341, Mona Vale, NSW 2103; tel. (02) 913-1444; fax (02) 913-2342; f. 1970; monthly; Editor GREG BORROWMAN; circ. 24,000.

Australian Historical Studies: Dept of History, Monash University, Clayton, Vic 3168; tel. (03) 565-2187; telex 32691; fax (03) 565-2210; f. 1940; 2 a year; Editor JOHN RICKARD; circ. 1,500.

Australian Home Beautiful: 32 Walsh St, West Melbourne, Vic 3003; telex 30578; fax (03) 320-7410; f. 1925; monthly; Editor-in-Chief TONY FAWCETT.

Australian House and Garden: 54 Park St, Sydney, NSW 2000; tel. (02) 282-8413; telex 20514; fax (02) 282-8116; f. 1948; monthly; building, furnishing, decorating, handicrafts, gardening, entertaining; Editor ROSE-MARIE HILLIER; circ. 110,200.

Australian Journal of Agricultural Research: CSIRO, 314 Albert St, POB 89, East Melbourne, Vic 3002; tel. (03) 418-7333; fax (03) 419-4046; f. 1950; 8 a year; Man. Editor M. J. SHARKEY.

Australian Journal of Marine and Freshwater Research: CSIRO, 314 Albert St, POB 89, East Melbourne, Vic 3002; tel. (03) 418-7333; telex 30236; fax (03) 419-4096; f. 1950; 6 a year; Man. Editor A. GRANT.

Australian Journal of Mining: POB 1024, Richmond North, Vic 3121; tel. (03) 429-5599; fax (03) 427-0332; f. 1986; monthly; Editor LIZ REID; circ. 9,032.

Australian Journal of Pharmacy: 40 Burwood Rd, Hawthorn, Vic 3122; tel. (03) 810-9800; fax (03) 819-1706; f. 1886; monthly; journal of the associated pharmaceutical orgs; Editor S. L. DICKSON; Man. G. E. SIMONSEN; circ. 7,600.

Australian Journal of Physics: CSIRO, 314 Albert St, POB 89, East Melbourne, Vic 3002; tel. (03) 418-7333; telex 30236; fax (03) 419-4096; f. 1953; 6 a year; Man. Editor R. P. ROBERTSON.

Australian Journal of Politics and History: University of Queensland, St Lucia, Qld 4072; tel. (07) 377-3136; telex 40315; fax (07) 371-5896; f. 1955; 3 a year; Editor J. A. MOSES; circ. 1,000.

Australian Law Journal: 44–50 Waterloo Rd, North Ryde, NSW 2113; tel. (02) 887-0177; telex 27995; fax (02) 888-9706; f. 1927; monthly; Gen. Editor J. G. STARKE; circ 7,000.

Australian Left Review: POB A247, South Sydney PO, NSW 2000; f. 1966; 6 a year.

Australian Photography: POB 606, Sydney, NSW 2001; tel. (02) 281-2333; telex 121887; fax (02) 281-2750; monthly; journal of the Australian Photographic Soc.; Editor MICHAEL RICHARDSON.

Australian Quarterly: 72 Bathurst St, Sydney, NSW 2000; tel. (02) 264-8923; f. 1929; quarterly; Editors HUGH PRICHARD, GERALDINE WALSH; circ. 1,500.

Australian Women's Weekly: 54 Park St, Sydney, NSW 2000; telex 120514; fax (02) 282-8116; f. 1933; monthly; Publr RICHARD WALSH; Editor JENNIFER ROWE; circ. 1,180,000.

The Australian Worker incorporating The Worker: 35 Regent St, 3rd Floor, Chippendale, NSW 2008; tel. (02) 698-7393; telex 73231; f. 1891; 6 a year; journal of the Australian Workers' Union; circ. 105,000.

Belle: 54 Park St, Sydney, NSW 2000; tel. (02) 282-8258; telex 32796; fax (02) 267-2150; f. 1975; every 2 months; Publr RICHARD WALSH; Editor MICHAELA DUNWORTH; circ. 49,400.

Camera Buyer's Guide: POB 341, Mona Vale, NSW 2103; annual; Editor DON NORRIS; circ. 23,000.

Cleo: 54 Park St, Sydney, NSW 2000; POB 4088, Sydney, NSW 2001; tel. (02) 282-8617; telex 120514; fax (02) 267-2150; f. 1972; women's monthly; Editor LISA WILKINSON; circ. 300,000.

Cosmopolitan: 54 Park St, Sydney, NSW 2000; tel. (02) 282-8496; telex 120514; fax (02) 267-2150; f. 1973; monthly; Publr RICHARD WALSH; Editor PAT WALSH; circ. 205,800.

Current Affairs Bulletin: 72 Bathurst St, Sydney, NSW 2000; tel. (02) 264-5726; fax (02) 267-7900; f. 1947; monthly; Man. S. PHILLIPS; Editor R. HOWARD; circ. 4,500.

Economic Record: Dept of Econometrics, University of Sydney, NSW 2006; tel. (02) 692-3069; fax (02) 552-3105; f. 1925; quarterly; journal of Economic Soc. of Australia; Jt Editors Prof. A. D. WOODLAND, Prof. G. BRENNAN.

Ecos: CSIRO, POB 225, Dickson, ACT 2602; tel. (06) 276-6584; telex 62003; fax (06) 276-6641; f. 1974; quarterly; reports of CSIRO

AUSTRALIA
Directory

environmental research findings for the non-specialist reader; Editor ROBERT LEHANE; circ. 8,000.

Electronics Australia: POB 199, Alexandria, NSW 2015; tel. (02) 693-6620; fax (02) 693-9935; f. 1922; monthly; technical, radio, television, microcomputers, hi-fi and electronics; Man. Editor JAMIESON ROWE.

Focus on Photography: POB 341, Mona Vale, NSW 2103; annual; Editor DON NORRIS; circ. 22,000.

Good Housekeeping: 54 Park St, Sydney, NSW 2000; tel. (02) 282-8000; telex 120514; fax (02) 267-2150; f. 1983; monthly; Publr R. WALSH; Editor J. SHEARD; circ. 90,300.

Industrial and Commercial Photography: POB 606, Sydney, NSW 2001; tel. (02) 281-2333; telex 121887; fax (02) 281-2750; every 2 months; journal of the Professional Photographers Assen of Australia, Australian Inst. of Medical and Biological Illustration and Photographic Industrial Marketing Assen of Australia; Publr MICHAEL RICHARDSON; Editor MIKE ELTON.

Journal of Pacific History: Research School of Pacific Studies, Australian National University, POB 4, Canberra, ACT 2601; tel. (06) 249-3145; f. 1966; 3 a year; Editors NIEL GUNSON, STEWART FIRTH.

Manufacturer's Monthly: 68–72 Wentworth Ave, Darlinghurst, NSW 2010; tel. (02) 211-4055; telex 23036; fax (02) 281-1763; f. 1961; circ. 12,339.

Modern Boating: The Federal Publishing Co Pty Ltd, 180 Bourke Rd, Alexandria, NSW 2015; tel. (02) 693-6666; fax (02) 693-9935; f. 1965; monthly; Editor MARK ROTHFIELD; circ. 14,700.

Modern Motor: 540 George St, Sydney, NSW 2000; tel. (02) 282-8350; telex 120514; fax (02) 282-8944; f. 1954; monthly; Editor DAVID ROBERTSON; circ. 50,000.

Nation Review: POB 1024, Richmond North, Vic 3121; tel. (03) 429-5599; fax (03) 427-0332; f. 1958; independent, progressive monthly; Editor-in-Chief GEOFFREY M. GOLD; circ. 46,000.

New Horizons in Education: 178 Hargreaves Ave, Chelmer, Qld 4068; tel. (07) 379-6207; fax (07) 366-2562; f. 1938; 2 a year; Editor Dr ELIZABETH M. CAMPBELL.

Oceania: The University of Sydney, Sydney, NSW 2006; tel. (02) 692-2666; telex 26169; fax (02) 692-4203; f. 1930; quarterly; social anthropology; Editors L. R. HIATT, F. MERLAN, J. R. BECKETT.

The Open Road: 151 Clarence St, Sydney, NSW 2000; tel. (02) 260-9222; fax (02) 260-8288; f. 1927; every 2 months; journal of National Roads and Motorists' Assen (NRMA); Editor BILL McKINNON; circ. 1,700,000.

Overland: POB 14146, Melbourne 3000; tel. (03) 380-1152; fax (03) 852-0527; f. 1954; quarterly; literary, social, political; Editor BARRETT REID; circ. 3,000.

Pacific Islands Monthly: 64–76 Kippax St, Surry Hills, NSW 2010; POB 4245, Sydney, NSW 2001; tel. (02) 288-3000; telex 20124; fax (02) 288-3322; f. 1930; political, economic and cultural affairs in the Pacific Islands; Editor JALE MOALA.

Panorama: 54 Park St, Sydney, NSW 2000; tel. (02) 868-2010; telex 120514; fax (02) 267-2150; f. 1958; monthly; business and travel; Publr RICHARD WALSH; Editor JANE RICH; circ. 81,642.

Personal Investment: 469 La Trobe St, Melbourne, Vic 3000; tel. (03) 603-3888; fax (03) 670-4328; monthly; Editor ROSS GREENWOOD; circ. 67,500.

Photo Traveller: POB 341, Mona Vale, NSW 2103; annual; Editor DON NORRIS; circ. 30,000.

Photoworld Magazine: POB 341, Mona Vale, NSW 2103; tel. (02) 913-1444; fax (02) 913-2342; f. 1978; monthly; photographic equipment and travel; Editor DON NORRIS; circ. 14,000.

Queensland Countrywoman: 89–95 Gregory Terrace, Brisbane, Qld; f. 1929; monthly; journal of the Qld Countrywomen's Assen; Editor BERYL SYMONS.

Reader's Digest: POB 4353, Sydney, NSW 2001; tel. (02) 690-6111; fax (02) 699-8165; monthly; Editor HUGH VAUGHAN-WILLIAMS; circ. 472,638.

Robotic Age: POB 1024, Richmond North, Vic 3121; tel. (03) 429-5599; fax (03) 427-0332; f. 1983; quarterly; Editor GEOFFREY M. GOLD; circ. 8,000.

Search—Science and Technology in Australia and New Zealand: POB 873, Sydney, NSW 2001; tel. (02) 552-1693; fax (02) 516-3229; f. 1970; 8 a year; journal of Australia and NZ Assen for the Advancement of Science; Editor Dr S. GARNETT; circ. 5,000.

Stereo Buyer's Guide: POB 341, Mona Vale, NSW 2103; tel. (02) 997-1188; fax (02) 997-4169; f. 1971; 5 a year; Editor DON NORRIS; circ. 20,000.

Street Machine: 54–50 Park St, Sydney, NSW 2000; tel. (02) 282-8000; telex 120514; fax (02) 267-2150; Editor ANGUS McKENZIE; circ. 111,500.

Today, The Environment Magazine: POB 341, Mona Vale, NSW 2103; every 2 months; Editor JUNE McGOWAN; circ. 40,000.

What's on Video and Cinema: POB 1024, Richmond North, Vic 3121; tel. (03) 429-5599; fax (03) 427-0332; f. 1981; monthly; Editor GEOFFREY GOLD; circ. 295,000.

Wildlife Australia: Level 4, 160 Edward St, Brisbane, Qld 4000; tel. (07) 221-0194; fax (07) 221-0701; quarterly; journal of the Wildlife Preservation Soc. of Qld; Editor ANTHONY BROWN.

Wildlife Research: CSIRO, 314 Albert St, POB 89, East Melbourne, Vic 3002; tel. (03) 418-7333; telex 30236; fax (03) 419-4096; f. 1974; 6 a year; Man. Editor D. W. MORTON.

World Review: c/o Australian Institute of International Affairs, POB E181, Queen Victoria Terrace, Canberra, ACT 2600; tel. (062) 822133; f. 1962; quarterly; Editor Dr GLEN ST J. BARCLAY.

Your Computer: 180 Bourke Rd, Alexandria, NSW 2015; tel. (02) 693-6666; telex 74488; fax (02) 693-9935; circ. 19,854.

Your Garden: 32 Walsh St, West Melbourne, Vic 3003; tel. (03) 320-7000; monthly; Editor-in-Chief TONY FAWCETT; circ. 90,000.

NEWS AGENCIES

Australian Associated Press: 364 Sussex St, Sydney, NSW 2000; POB 3888, Sydney 2001; tel. (02) 236-8800; telex 25510; fax (02) 236-8839; f. 1935; owned by major daily newspapers of Australia; Chair. E. J. L. TURNBULL; CEO C. L. CASEY.

Foreign Bureaux

Agence France-Presse (AFP): 4th Floor, 364 Sussex St, Sydney, NSW 2000; tel. (02) 264-1822; fax (02) 267-7362; Bureau Chief ROBERT HOLLOWAY.

Agencia EFE (Spain): 5 Erldunda Circuit, Hawker, Canberra, ACT 2614; tel. (06) 254-3732; Correspondent ANTONIO-JOSÉ ARJONILLA.

Agenzia Nazionale Stampa Associata (ANSA) (Italy): Angus and Coote House, 8th Floor, 500 George St, Sydney, NSW 2000; tel. (02) 264-8348; telex 71770; fax (02) 261-3155; Bureau Chief CLAUDIO MARCELLO.

Associated Press (AP) (USA): 4th Floor, 364 Sussex St, Sydney, NSW 2000; POB K378, Haymarket, NSW 2000; tel. (02) 267-2122; telex 121181; Bureau Chief PETER O'LOUGHLIN.

Deutsche Presse-Agentur (dpa) (Germany): 67 Kipling Ave, Mooroolbark, Melbourne, Vic 3138; tel. (03) 726-5551; telex 33131; Bureau Chief BORIS B. BEHRSING.

Jiji Press (Australia) Pty Ltd (Japan): Paxton House, 5th Floor, 90 Pitt St, Sydney, NSW 2000; tel. (02) 221-6148; telex 75974; Bureau Chief MASANORI GURI.

Kyodo News Service (Japan): 364 Sussex St, Sydney, NSW 2000; tel. (02) 264-7390; telex 75851; fax (02) 261-4039; Bureau Chief OSAMU WATANABE.

Reuters Australia Pty Ltd: 14th Floor, 10–16 Queen St, Melbourne, Vic 3000; tel. (03) 614-1766; telex 154925; fax (03) 614-5774.

Telegrafnoye Agentstvo Sovetskovo Soyuza (TASS) (USSR): 8 Elliott St, Campbell, Canberra, ACT 2601; Correspondent SERGEI SOLOVEV.

United Press International (UPI) (USA): News House, 2 Holt St, 3rd Floor, Sydney, NSW 2010; tel. (02) 954-9423; telex 20578; fax (02) 281-1771; Bureau Chief BRIAN DEWHURST.

Xinhua (New China) News Agency (People's Republic of China): 50 Russell St, Hackett, Canberra, ACT 2602; tel. (06) 248-6369; telex 61507; Correspondent JIN MINGYUAN.

The Central News Agency (Taiwan) and the New Zealand Press Association are represented in Sydney, and Antara (Indonesia) is represented in Canberra.

PRESS ASSOCIATIONS

Australian Newspapers Council: 44–74 Flinders St, Melbourne, Vic 3000; tel. (03) 652-1607; telex 30104; fax (03) 652-2112; f. 1958; 5 mems, confined to metropolitan daily or Sunday papers; Pres. G. J. TAYLOR; Sec. A. L. GREEN.

Country Press Association of New South Wales Inc: POB C599, Clarence St, Sydney, NSW 2000; tel. (02) 29-4658; fax (02) 29-1892; f. 1900; Exec. Dir D. J. SOMMERLAD; 75 mems.

Country Press Association of South Australia Incorporated: 130 Franklin St, Adelaide, SA 5000; tel. (08) 212-6646; f. 1912; represents South Australian country newspapers; Pres. J. PICK; Exec. Dir M. R. TOWNSEND.

Country Press Australia: POB C599, Clarence St, Sydney, NSW 2000; tel. (02) 29-4658; fax (02) 29-1892; f. 1906; Exec. Dir D. J. SOMMERLAD; 275 mems.

Queensland Country Press Association: POB 103, Paddington, Qld 4064; tel. (07) 356-0033; Pres. B. LEWIS; Sec. N. D. McLARY.

AUSTRALIA

Regional Dailies of Australia Ltd: 119 Market St, South Melbourne, Vic 3205; tel. (03) 696-0488; f. 1936; Chair. R. G. McLean; CEO R. W. Sinclair; 34 mems.

Tasmanian Press Association Pty Ltd: 71-75 Paterson St, Launceston, Tas; tel. (003) 31-5111; telex 58511; Sec. B. J. McKendrick.

Victoria Country Press Association Ltd: 33 Rathdowne St, Carlton, Vic 3053; tel. (03) 662-3244; fax (03) 663-7433; f. 1910; Pres. I. H. Thomas; Exec. Dir R. C. McDiarmid; 114 mems.

Publishers

ABC Enterprises: 20 Atchison St, Crows Nest, NSW 2065; tel. (02) 430-3999; fax (02) 430-3888; general; Gen. Man. Julie Steiner.

Addison-Wesley Publishing Co: 6 Byfield St, North Ryde, NSW 2113; tel. (02) 888-2733; fax (02) 888-9404; educational, scientific, technical, computer, general; Man. Dir Derek Hall.

Allen and Unwin Australia Pty Ltd: 12th Floor, NCR House, 8 Napier St, POB 764, North Sydney, NSW 2059; tel. (02) 955-3155; telex 24331; fax (02) 955-3155; fiction, trade, educational, children's; Man. Dir Patrick A. Gallagher.

Ashton Scholastic Pty Ltd: Railway Crescent, Lisarow, POB 579, Gosford, NSW 2250; tel. (043) 28-3555; telex 24881; fax (043) 23-3827; f. 1968; educational and children's; Chair. M. Sinclair; Man. Dir Ken Jolly.

Bacon Publishing Pty Ltd: 9 Kingston Town Close, POB 223, Oakleigh, Vic 3166; tel. (03) 563-1044; fax (03) 569-7211; f. 1938; theology and Christian education, educational; Chair. M. Bacon; Man. Dir J. R. Bacon.

Bay Books: Suite 501, Henry Lawson Business Centre, Drummoyne, NSW 2047; tel. (02) 819-6155; fax (02) 815-450; art, general, Australiana; CEO George Barber.

Butterworths Pty Ltd: 271-273 Lane Cove Rd, POB 345, North Ryde, NSW 2113; tel. (02) 887-3444; fax (02) 887-4555; f. 1910; law, medical, tax, technical, scientific, library and commercial; Chair. G. R. N. Cusworth; Man. Dir D. J. Jackson.

Cambridge University Press (Australia): 10 Stamford Road, Oakleigh, Melbourne, Vic 3166; tel. (03) 568-0322; fax (03) 563-1517; scholarly and educational; Dir Kim W. Harris.

Collins/Angus and Robertson Publishers Australia: 4 Eden Park, 31 Waterloo Rd, POB 290, North Ryde, NSW 2113; tel. (02) 888-4111; telex 26452; fax (02) 888-9972; f. 1886; fiction, non-fiction, reference, general and children's; CEO Terry Kitson.

Commonwealth Scientific and Industrial Research Organization (CSIRO): 314 Albert St, East Melbourne, Vic 3002; tel. (03) 418-7333; telex 30236; fax (03) 419-4096; f. 1948; scientific journals, books and indices; Man. Editorial Services P. W. Reekie.

Doubleday Australia Pty Ltd: 91 Mars Rd, Lane Cove, NSW 2066; tel. (02) 427-0377; fax (02) 427-6973; educational, trade, non-fiction, Australiana; Man. Dir David Harley.

Encyclopaedia Britannica (Australia) Inc: 22 Lambs Rd, Artarmon, NSW 2064; tel. (02) 438-4544; telex 23044; fax (02) 438-5516; reference, education, art, science and commerce; Pres. H. W. De Weese.

Golden Press Pty Ltd: 46 Egerton St, Silverwater, NSW 2141; tel. (02) 648-5697; telex 26070; fax (02) 648-5697; Gen. Man. Ross Alexander.

Gordon and Gotch Ltd: 25-37 Huntingdale Rd, POB 290, Burwood, Vic 3125; tel. (03) 805-1700; fax (03) 808-0437; general; Chair. and Man. Dir I. D. Golding.

Harcourt Brace Jovanovich Group (Australia) Pty Ltd: 30-52 Smidmore St, Marrickville, NSW 2204; tel. (02) 517-8999; fax (02) 517-2249; trade, educational, technical, scientific, medical; Man. Dir Anthony W. Craven.

Harper Collins Publishers (Australia) Pty Ltd: 15th Floor, 55 Clarence St, Sydney, NSW 2000; tel. (02) 819-7433; fax (02) 819-7575; Man. Dir T. J. Kitson.

Harper Educational Ltd: Unit 3B, Artarmon Industrial Estate, cnr Reserve Rd and Frederick St, POB 226, Artarmon, NSW 2064; tel. (02) 439-6155; telex 72598; fax (02) 438-2542; reference, educational, medical; Man. Dir Ms F. J. Gehring.

Hodder and Stoughton (Australia) Pty Ltd: 10-16 South St, Rydalmere, NSW 2116; tel. (02) 638-5299; telex 24858; fax (02) 684-4942; fiction, general, educational, technical, children's; Man. Dir Michael H. Duffett.

Horwitz Grahame Pty Ltd: 506 Miller St, POB 306, Cammeray, NSW 2062; tel. (02) 929-6144; fax (02) 957-1814; fiction, reference, educational, Australiana, general; Chief Exec. Peter D. L. Horwitz.

Houghton Mifflin Australia Pty Ltd: 112 Lewis Rd, Knoxfield, Vic 3180; tel. (03) 801-7333; fax (03) 801-9885; general; Man. Dir R. F. Makin.

Hyland House Publishing Pty Ltd: 23 Bray St, South Yarra, Vic 3141; tel. (03) 827-6336; telex 39476; fax (03) 826-6317; trade, general; Rep. Al Knight.

Jacaranda Wiley Ltd: 33 Park Rd, Milton, Qld 4064; POB 1226, Milton, Qld 4064; tel. (07) 369-9755; telex 41845; fax (07) 369-9155; f. 1954; educational, technical and cartographic; Publr Greg Browne.

The Law Book Co Ltd: 44-50 Waterloo Road, North Ryde, NSW 2113; tel. (02) 887-0177; telex 27995; fax (02) 888-9706; legal and professional; Man. Dir W. J. Mackarell.

Longman Cheshire Pty Ltd: Kings Gardens, 95 Coventry St, South Melbourne, Vic 3205; tel. (03) 697-0666; telex 33501; fax (03) 699-2041; f. 1957; incorporates Pitman Publishing Pty Ltd; mainly educational, legal, professional, some general; Man. Dir N. J. Ryan.

Lothian Books: 11 Munro St, Port Melbourne, Vic 3207; tel. (03) 645-1544; fax (03) 646-4882; f. 1888; general, gardening, health, juvenile; Man. Dir Peter Lothian.

McGraw-Hill Publishing Co Australia Pty Ltd: 4 Barcoo St, East Roseville, Sydney, NSW 2069; tel. (02) 417-4288; telex 120849; fax (02) 417-5687; educational and technical; Man. Dir Brian D. Wilder.

Majura Press: POB 25, Hackett, ACT 2602; tel. (06) 241-3329; f. 1984; non-fiction; Man. S. French.

Melbourne University Press: 268 Drummond St, Carlton South, Vic 3053; tel. (03) 347-3455; fax (03) 344-6214; f. 1923; academic, educational, Australiana, general except children's; Chair. Prof. J. R. V. Prescott; Dir John Iremonger.

Mills & Boon Pty Ltd: 72-74 Gibbes St, Chatswood, NSW 2067; tel. (02) 417-7333; fax (02) 416-5232; romantic fiction; Man. Dir Guy Hallowes.

Murdoch Books: 11th Floor, 213 Miller St, North Sydney, NSW 2060; tel. (02) 956-1000; fax (02) 956-1088; general non-fiction; Man. Dir Matt Handbury.

National Library of Australia: Canberra, ACT 2600; tel. (06) 262-1111; telex 62100; fax (06) 257-1703; f. 1961; national bibliographical and general interest pubs, facsimiles of materials in the library's collections; Dir-Gen. W. M. Horton.

Thomas Nelson Australia: 102 Dodds St, South Melbourne, Vic 3205; tel. (03) 685-4111; fax (03) 685-4199; educational, vocational, professional and specialized; Man. Dir B. D. Heer.

New South Wales University Press Ltd: POB 1, Kensington, NSW 2033; tel. (02) 398-8900; telex 26054; fax (02) 398-3408; f. 1961; general and educational; Man. Dir Douglas Howie.

Octopus Publishing Group Australia Pty Ltd: POB 460, Port Melbourne, Vic 3207; tel. (03) 646-6688; telex 35347; fax (03) 646-6925; educational and general; Chair. Nicholas Thompson; Man. Dir (General) Sandy Grant; Man. Dir (Educational) Paul Lewis.

Oxford University Press: 253 Normanby Rd, South Melbourne, Vic 3205; tel. (03) 646-4200; telex 35330; fax (03) 646-3251; f. 1908; general non-fiction and educational; Man. Dir Sandra McComb.

Pan/Macmillan Books (Australia) Pty Ltd: 63-71 Balfour St, Chippendale, NSW 2008; tel. (02) 318-0111; fax (02) 319-3438; general, educational, reference, children's; Chair. B. J. Davies.

Penguin Books Australia Ltd: 487/493 Maroondah Highway, POB 257, Ringwood, Vic 3134; tel. (03) 871-2400; fax (03) 870-9618; f. 1946; general; Man. Dir Peter Field; Publishing Dir Robert Sessions.

Pergamon—MCC Australia Group: 19A Boundary St, Rushcutter's Bay, NSW 2011; tel. (02) 331-5211; telex 27458; fax (02) 332-2304; f. 1949; educational, general, scientific; Chair. Ian R. Maxwell; Deputy Chair. Roderick McLeod.

Random Century Australia Pty Ltd: 20 Alfred St, Milsons Point, NSW 2061; tel. (02) 954-9966; fax (02) 954-4562; fiction, non-fiction, general and children's; Man. Dir Ernie F. Mason.

Reader's Digest (Australia) Pty Ltd: 26-32 Waterloo St, Surry Hills, NSW 2010; POB 4353, Sydney, NSW; tel. (02) 690-6111; fax (02) 699-8165; general; Man. Dir Martin J. Pearson.

Reed Books Pty Ltd: Suite 3, 470 Sydney Rd, Balgowlah, NSW 2093; tel. (02) 907-9966; fax (02) 907-9664; f. 1964; Australiana, general non-fiction; Publr W. A. Templeman; Gen. Man. D. A. Maclellan.

Rigby Education: POB 460, Port Melbourne, Vic 3207; tel. (03) 646-6677; telex 36521; educational; Man. Dir Paul Lewis.

Schwartz Publishing (Victoria) Pty Ltd: 45 Flinders Lane, Melbourne, Vic 3000; tel. (03) 654-2000; telex 30625; fax (03) 654-5418; fiction, non-fiction; Dir Morry Schwartz.

Simon and Schuster Australia: 20 Barcoo St, POB 507, East Roseville, NSW 2069; tel. (02) 417-3255; fax (02) 417-3188; educational, trade, reference and general; Gen. Man. Jon Attenborough.

AUSTRALIA

Thames and Hudson (Australia) Pty Ltd: 86 Stanley St, West Melbourne, Vic 3003; tel. (03) 329-8044; fax (03) 329-9359; art, history, archaeology, architecture and photography; Man. Dir RICHARD M. GILMOUR.

D. W. Thorpe: 18 Salmon St, POB 146, Port Melbourne, Vic 3207; tel. (03) 645-1511; telex 39476; fax (03) 645-3981; biographies, trade, paperbacks; Man. Dir M. WEBSTER.

Time Life Books (Australia) Pty Ltd: 6th Floor, ACC Building, 61 Lavender St, Milsons Point, NSW 2061; tel. (02) 929-0933; fax (02) 956-6184; general and educational; Man. Dir BONITA L. BOEZEMAN.

Transworld Publishers (Aust) Pty Ltd: 40 Yeo St, Neutral Bay, NSW 2089; tel. (02) 908-4366; fax (02) 953-8563; general, fiction, juvenile, education; Man. Dir GEOFFREY S. RUMPF.

University of Queensland Press: POB 42, St Lucia, Qld 4067; tel. (07) 365-2127; telex 40315; fax (07) 365-1988; f. 1948; scholarly and general cultural interest; Gen. Man. LAURIE MULLER.

University of Western Australia Press: c/o University of Western Australia, Nedlands, WA 6009; tel. (09) 380-3182; fax (09) 380-1027; f. 1954; educational, secondary and university, technical, scientific, scholarly, humanities; Man. M. M. CHESTERTON (acting).

Weldon International Pty Ltd: 372 Eastern Valley Way, Chatswood, NSW 2067; tel. (02) 406-9222; telex 121546; fax (02) 406-6919; general non-fiction, literature, Australiana; Chair. KEVIN WELDON.

Government Publishing House

Australian Government Publishing Service: POB 84, Canberra, ACT 2601; tel. (06) 295-4411; telex 62013; fax (06) 295-4455; f. 1970; Dir of Publishing F. W. THOMPSON.

PUBLISHERS' ASSOCIATION

Australian Book Publishers Association: 161 Clarence St, Sydney, NSW 2000; tel. (02) 29-5422; fax (02) 262-1631; f. 1949; c. 150 mems; Pres. LAURIE MULLER; Dir SUSAN BLACKWELL.

Radio and Television

The programmes for the National Broadcasting Service and National Television are provided by the non-commercial statutory corporation, the Australian Broadcasting Corporation (ABC).

The Corporation operates 131 medium-wave stations, 39 FM, 6 domestic and 10 overseas (Radio Australia) short-wave stations broadcasting in English, French, Indonesian, Japanese, Standard Chinese, Cantonese, Neo-Melanesian, Thai and Vietnamese. In 1983 the Government agreed to provide funds to establish a second regional radio network for the ABC, due to be completed by 1990.

There is one national television network of 11 stations with 471 transmitters and 233 translator stations.

Commercial radio and television services are provided by stations operated by companies under licences granted and renewed by the Australian Broadcasting Tribunal. They rely for their income on the broadcasting of advertisements. On 30 June 1990, there were 149 commercial radio stations in operation, and 45 commercial television stations.

In 1987 there were an estimated 20.5m. radio receivers and 7.8m. television receivers in use.

Australian Broadcasting Corporation (ABC): 150 William St, POB 9994, Sydney, NSW 2001; tel. (02) 339-0211 (radio), (02) 437-8000 (television); telex 26506 (corporate), 176464 (radio), 120432 (television); fax (02) 339-2603 (radio), (02) 950-3055 (television); f. 1932 as Australian Broadcasting Commission; Chair. ROBERT SOMERVAILLE; Man. Dir DAVID HILL.

RADIO

Federation of Australian Radio Broadcasters: POB 299, St Leonards, NSW 2065; tel. (02) 906-5944; telex 25161; fax (02) 906-5128; asscn of privately-owned stations; Fed. Dir M. J. HARTCHER.

Major Commercial Broadcasting Station Licensees

Associated Broadcasting Services Ltd: Walker St, Ballarat, Vic 3350; tel. (053) 31-3166; telex 32011; fax (053) 33-1598; f. 1957; operates three television stations; Chair. W. M. HARRISON; Exec. Dir MICHAEL J. FAULKNER.

Associated Communications Enterprises (Holdings) Pty Ltd: POB 4008, Melbourne, Vic 3001; tel. (03) 329-0277; fax (03) 328-1511; operates five stations.

Austereo Ltd: POB 404, Unley, SA 5061; tel. (08) 271-3688; fax (08) 271-1507; operates six stations; Dir B. BICKMORE.

Australian Broadcasting Company Pty Ltd: POB 1107, Neutral Bay, NSW 2089; tel. (02) 908-1900; fax (02) 908-2746; operates seven stations; Dir E. ALBERT.

Directory

Australian Radio Network: 9 Rangers Rd, POB 1107, Neutral Bay, NSW 2089; tel. (02) 908-1900; telex 22797; operates eight stations; CEO B. E. BYRNE.

AWA Ltd: 422 Lane Cove Rd, North Ryde, NSW 2113; tel. (02) 887-7111; telex 121515; fax (02) 805-0660; f. 1913; operates eight stations; Chair. and CEO J. A. ILIFFE.

Broadcast Operations Pty Ltd: POB 493, Griffiths, NSW 2680; tel. (069) 62-4500; fax (069) 62-6291; operates seven stations; Dir B. CARALIS.

Broadcasting Station 2SM Pty Ltd: 186 Blues Point Rd, North Sydney, NSW 2060; tel. (02) 922-1270; telex 25350; fax (02) 954-3117; f. 1931; main station 23M; CEO VINCE CONNELLY.

Carillon Development Ltd: POB 497, Tamworth, NSW 2340; tel. (067) 65-4500; fax (067) 65-0385; operates five stations; Chair. W. HARRINGTON.

Consolidated Broadcasting System (WA) Pty Ltd: Kalgoorlie St, 89 Egan, WA; fax (090) 91-2209; operates four stations; CEO R. BIGUM.

The Eagle Pty Ltd: POB 33, Tuart Hill, WA 6060; tel. (09) 344-1080; fax (09) 349-2111; radio station; Gen. Man. PETER SINCLAIR.

Grangeridge Nominees Pty Ltd: POB 121, West Perth, WA 6005; tel. (09) 324-1488; fax (09) 324-1848; operates four stations; Dir C. HOPKINS.

Harbour Radio Ltd: 364 Sussex St, Sydney, NSW 2000; POB 4290, Sydney, NSW 2001; tel. (02) 269-0646; fax (02) 287-2800; main station: 2GB, Sydney; Man. Dir HARRY LEDOWSKY.

Hoyts Media Ltd: 26th Floor, 500 Oxford St, Bondi Junction, NSW 2022; tel. (02) 389-9433; fax (02) 387-2268; operates nine stations; Chair. L. FINK.

KAFM Broadcasters Pty Ltd: 106 Currie St, Adelaide, SA 5000; tel. (08) 231-5511; fax (08) 231-0770; operates one station.

Nine Network Australia Ltd: POB 24, Willoughby, NSW 2068; tel. (02) 282-8585; fax (02) 267-2150; operates four stations; Chair. KERRY PACKER.

Southern State Broadcasters Pty Ltd: 121 King William St, Adelaide, SA 5000; POB 518, Adelaide, SA 5001; tel. (08) 211-7666; fax (08) 231-1891; operates two stations; Gen. Man. BRIAN NIELSEN.

Tamworth Radio Development Company Pty Ltd: POB 497, Tamworth, NSW 2340; tel. (067) 65-7055; telex 63166; fax (067) 65-2762; operates five stations; Man. E. C. WILKINSON.

Wesgo Communications Pty Ltd: POB 234, Seven Hills, NSW 2147; tel. (02) 671-2411; fax (02) 621-3729; operates 9 stations; CEO C. J. SMITH.

TELEVISION

Federation of Australian Commercial Television Stations: 44 Avenue Rd, Mosman, NSW 2088; tel. (02) 960-2622; fax (02) 969-3520; f. 1960; represents all commercial television stations; Chair. L. A. MAUGER; Fed. Dir JOHN CORMACK.

Commercial Television Station Licensees

Amalgamated Television Services Pty Ltd: Mobbs Lane, Epping, NSW 2121; tel. (02) 877-7777; telex 20250; fax (02) 858-7888; f. 1956; operates one station; Man. Dir A. S. TYSON.

Austarama Television Pty Ltd: tel. (03) 234-1010; telex 30628; f. 1964; operates one station at Melbourne; Station Man. C. O'CONNELL.

Australian Capital Television Pty Ltd: Private Bag 10, Dickson, ACT 2602; tel. (06) 241-1000; telex 62046; fax (06) 241-7230; f. 1962; operates three stations; Chief Exec. STAVROS PIPPOS.

Brisbane TV Ltd: POB 604, Brisbane, Qld 4001; tel. (07) 369-7777; telex 41653; fax (07) 368-2970; f. 1959; operates one station; Man. Dir C. J. CHAPMAN.

Broadcast Operations Ltd: POB 493, Griffith, NSW 2680; tel. (069) 62-4500; telex 169991; fax (069) 62-6921; f. 1965; operates one television station; Chief Exec. B. MEADLEY; Gen. Man. M. BISHOP.

Broken Hill Television Ltd: POB 472, Broken Hill, NSW 2880; tel. (080) 6013; telex 80874; f. 1968; operates one station; Chair. P. MARTIN; Man. Dir J. M. STURROCK.

Capital Television Holdings Ltd: Level 3, 55 Harrington St, Sydney, NSW 2000; tel. (02) 247-9459; fax (02) 252-4641; operates three stations; Dir C. CURRAN.

Country Television Services Ltd: POB 465, Orange, NSW 2800; tel. (063) 62-2144; telex 163012; fax (063) 63-1889; f. 1962; operates two radio stations; Man. Dir I. RIDLEY; Station Mans D. STURGISS (television); S. WARD (radio).

Darling Downs TV Ltd: POB 920, Coffs Harbour, NSW 2450; tel. (066) 52-2777; fax (066) 52-3034; f. 1962; operates four stations; Dir L. BARBER.

ENT Ltd: 37 Watchorn St, Launceston, Tas 7250; tel. (003) 349-9999; fax (003) 349-2110; operates three stations; Dir E. PRESSER.

AUSTRALIA
Directory

Far Northern Television Ltd: 101 Aumuller, Cairns, Qld 4870; tel. (070) 51-6322; telex 48401; fax (070) 51-1401; f. 1966; operates one station; Chair. JACK GLEESON; Gen. Man. DAVID ASTLEY.

General Television Corporation Pty Ltd: 22–46 Bendigo St, POB 100, Richmond, Vic 3121; tel. (03) 420-3111; telex 30189; fax (03) 429-9870; f. 1957; operates one station; Man. Dir D. LECKIE; Gen. Man. I. J. JOHNSON.

Geraldton Telecasters Pty Ltd: 7 Fore St, Perth, WA 6000; tel. (09) 328-9833; telex 94382; f. 1977; operates one station; Gen. Man. BRIAN HOPWOOD.

Golden West Network Ltd: POB 1062, West Perth, WA 6005; tel. (09) 481-0050; fax (09) 321-2470; f. 1967; operates three stations; CEO W. G. RAYNER.

HSV Channel 7 Pty Ltd: POB 407, South Melbourne, Vic 3205; tel. (03) 697-7777; telex 30707; f. 1956; operates one station; Chair. CHRISTOPHER C. SKASE; Man. Dir B. J. MALLON.

Mackay Television Ltd: 216 Victoria St, Mackay, Qld 4740; tel. (079) 57-6333; telex 48152; fax (079) 51-1063; f. 1968; operates one station; Gen. Man. RAY COX.

Mildura Television Pty Ltd: 18 Deakin Ave, Mildura, Vic 3500; tel. (050) 23-0204; telex 55304; f. 1965; Chair. KEITH HARDMAN; Man. Dir DAVID MCQUESTIN.

Mt Isa Television Pty Ltd: 110 Camooweal St, Mt Isa, Qld 4825; tel. (077) 43-8888; telex 49947; fax (077) 43-9803; f. 1971; operates one station; Chair. and Man. Dir J. GLEESON; Gen. Man. D. ASTLEY.

NBN Ltd: Mosbri Crescent, POB 750L, Newcastle, NSW 2300; tel. (049) 26-0321; telex 28039; fax (049) 26-3629; f. 1962; operates one station; CEO JOE SWEENEY.

Network Ten Australia Pty Ltd: 10, Lane Cove, NSW 2066; tel. (02) 887-0222; telex 75789; fax (02) 887-0458.

Nine Network Australia Ltd: POB 24, Willoughby, NSW 2068; tel. (02) 282-8585; fax (02) 267-2150; operates five stations; Chair. KERRY PACKER.

Northern Rivers Television Ltd: Peterson Rd, POB 920, Coffs Harbour, NSW 2450; tel. (066) 52-2777; fax (066) 52-3034; f. 1965; operates two stations; Gen. Man. RON LAWRENCE.

Northern Star Holdings Ltd: 303 Castlereagh St, Sydney, NSW 2000; tel. (02) 565-8222; fax (02) 565-8325; operates three stations; CEO G. RICE.

Northern Television (TNT9) Pty Ltd: Watchorn St, Launceston, Tas 7250; tel. (003) 44-0202; telex 58512; fax (003) 43-0340; f. 1962; operates one station; Gen. Man. DAVID W. WHITE.

NWS Channel 9: 202 Tynte St, North Adelaide 5006; tel. (08) 267-0111; fax (08) 267-3996; f. 1959; Man. Dir JOHN W. LAMB.

Prime Television Group: Level 13, 1 Pacific Highway, North Sydney, NSW 2060; tel. (02) 967-7900; fax (02) 967-7949; f. 1965; operates four stations; Chair. H. JOSEPH; Gen. Man. M. M. MORONEY.

Qintex Television Ltd: POB 77, Tuart Hill, WA 6060; tel. (09) 344-0777; fax (09) 344-1526; operates seven stations.

Queensland Television Ltd: POB 72, GPO Brisbane, Qld 4001; tel. (07) 369-9999; telex 42347; f. 1959; operates one station; Exec. Dir KERRY PACKER; Gen. Man. IAN R. MÜLLER.

Quoiba Ltd: POB 493, Griffith, NSW 2680; tel. (069) 62-4500; fax (069) 62-6921; operates one station; Dir J. BLOOD.

Regional Television Australia Pty Ltd: 82–84 Sydenham Rd, Marrickville, NSW 2204; POB 285, Sydney, NSW 2001; tel. (02) 516-1233; telex 120581; fax (02) 550-2338; CEO LLOYD D. BARWELL.

Riverina and North East Victoria TV Pty Ltd: POB 2, Kooringal via Wagga, NSW 2650; tel. (069) 21-1222; telex 69022; fax (069) 21-6142; f. 1964; Man. A. COOK.

Riverland Television Pty Ltd: Murray Bridge Rd, POB 471, Loxton, SA 5333; tel. (085) 84-6891; telex 80313; fax (085) 84-7378; f. 1976; operates one station; Exec. Chair. E. H. URLWIN; Gen. Man. W. L. MUDGE.

Rockhampton Television Ltd: Dean St, POB 568 Rockhampton, Qld 4700; tel. (079) 28-5222; telex 49008; fax (079) 28-7699; f. 1963; Gen. Man. TONY SHIELDS.

South Australian Telecasters Ltd: 45–49 Park Terrace, Gilberton, SA 5081; tel. (08) 269-7777; telex 82084; f. 1965; operates one station; Man. Dir D. EARL.

South East Telecasters Ltd: 51 John Watson Drive, Mount Gambier, SA 5290; tel. (087) 25-6366; telex 80013; fax (087) 25-0144; f. 1966; operates two stations; Chair. A. A. SCOTT; Man. Dir G. J. GILBERTSON.

Southern Cross Network: Lily St, POB 888, Bendigo, Vic 3550; tel. (054) 302-888; telex 32885; fax (054) 302-880; f. 1961; part of Tricom Corporation Ltd; operates seven stations; CEO GRAEME L. EDDY.

Southern Television Corporation Ltd: 202 Tynte St, North Adelaide, SA 5006; tel. (08) 267-0111; telex 82238; fax (08) 267-3996; f. 1958; operates one station; Gen. Man. TYRRELL TALBOT.

Spencer Gulf Telecasters Ltd: POB 305, Port Pirie, SA 5540; tel. (086) 32-2555; telex 80320; fax (086) 32-3750; f. 1968; operates two stations; Chair. P. STURROCK.

Swan Television and Radio Broadcasters Ltd: POB 99, Tuart Hill, WA 6060; tel. (09) 349-9999; telex 92142; fax (09) 349-2110; f. 1965; operates one station; Dir E. PRESSER.

Tasmanian Television Ltd: 52 New Town Rd, Hobart, Tas 7008; tel. (002) 78-0666; telex 58019; fax (002) 28-1835; f. 1959; operates one station; Exec. Dir D. ROUSE.

TCN Channel Nine Pty Ltd: 24 Artarmon Rd, POB 27, Willoughby, NSW 2068; tel. (02) 906-9999; telex 20689; fax (02) 906-9999; f. 1956; operates one station; Exec. and Man. Dir (Bond Media) SAMUEL CHISHOLM; Man. Dir (Bond Television) GARY RICE.

Telecasters North Queensland Ltd: 12 The Strand, POB 1016, Townsville, Qld 4810; tel. (077) 21-3377; telex 47023; fax (077) 21-1705; f. 1962; operates 7 stations; Chair. J. F. GLEESON; Gen. Man. DAVID ASTLEY.

Television Victoria Ltd: POB 666, Shepparton, Vic 3630; tel. (058) 329666; telex 30742; fax (056) 221948; f. 1961; operates three stations; Chair. W. HARRISON; Gen. Man. A. KENISON.

Television Wollongong Transmissions Ltd: Fort Drummond, Mt St Thomas, POB 1800, Wollongong, NSW 2500; tel. (042) 28-5444; telex 29029; fax (042) 27-3682; f. 1962; Chair. W. LEAN; Gen. Man. J. RUSHTON.

Territory Television Pty Ltd: POB 176, Darwin, NT 0801; tel. (089) 81-8888; telex 85138; fax (089) 81-6802; f. 1971; operates one station; Dir J. BELL.

Tricom Corporation Ltd: Lily St, POB 888, Bendigo, Vic 3550; tel. (054) 302-888; fax (054) 302-880; f. 1932; operates two stations; C.E.O. GRAEME L. EDDY.

TV Broadcasters Ltd: 125 Strangways Terrace, North Adelaide, SA 5006; tel. (08) 239-1010; telex 82141; fax (08) 239-0007; f. 1959; operates one station; Man. Dir S. PIPPOS.

TVW Enterprises Ltd: POB 77, Tuart Hill, Osborne Rd, WA 6060; tel. (09) 344-0777; fax (09) 344-1526; f. 1959; Chair. K. V. CAMPBELL.

TWT Holdings Ltd: POB 1800, Wollongong, NSW 2500; tel. (042) 28-5444; fax (042) 27-3682; operates two stations; Dir B. GORDON.

United Telecasters Sydney Ltd: POB 10, Sydney, NSW 2001; tel. (02) 565-8222; telex 121767; fax (02) 565-8325; f. 1965; operates three stations; CEO STEVE COSSER.

Wide Bay-Burnett Television Ltd: 187–189 Cambridge St, Maryborough, Qld 4650; tel. (071) 22-2288; telex 49702; fax (071) 22-2106; f. 1965; Man. Dir G. J. MCVEAN.

Finance

(cap. = capital; p.u. = paid up; res = reserves; dep. = deposits; m. = million; brs = branches; amounts in Australian dollars)

BANKING

Central Bank

Reserve Bank of Australia: 65 Martin Place, Sydney, NSW 2000; GPO Box 3947, Sydney, NSW 2001; tel. (02) 551-8111; telex 121636; fax (02) 551-8000; f. 1911; bank of issue; cap. and res 4,042.6m., dep. 5,195.0m. (June 1990); Gov. BERNIE FRASER; Dep. Gov. M. J. PHILLIPS.

Commonwealth Banks

Commonwealth Bank Group: POB 2719, Pitt St and Martin Place, Sydney, NSW 2001; tel. (02) 227-7111; telex 120345; fax (02) 232-6573; f. 1960; controlling body for three mem. banks; cap. and res 3,982.6m., dep. 34,237.3m. (June 1989); Chair. M. A. BESLEY; Man. Dir D. N. SANDERS; 1,261 brs.

Commonwealth Bank of Australia: Pitt St and Martin Place, Sydney, NSW 2000; POB 2719, Sydney, NSW 2001; tel. (02) 227-7111; telex 120345; f. 1912; cap. and res 4,027.8m., dep. 34,237.3m. (1989); Man. Dir D. N. SANDERS; Deputy Man. Dir I. K. PAYNE; more than 1,260 brs world-wide.

Commonwealth Development Bank of Australia: Prudential Bldg, 39 Martin Place, Sydney, NSW 2001; POB 2719, Sydney, NSW 2001; tel. (02) 227-7111; telex 120345; fax (02) 227-5588; f. 1960; cap. and res 261.7m., dep. 1,722.1m. (June 1989); Gen. Man. B. J. WRIGHT.

Commonwealth Savings Bank of Australia: Pitt St and Martin Place, Sydney, NSW 2001; POB 2719, Sydney, NSW 2001; tel. (02) 227-7111; telex 120267; fax (02) 232-6573; f. 1912; cap. and res

AUSTRALIA

979.4m., dep. 16,590.1m. (June 1989); Chief Gen. Man. H. L. SPENCER.

Development Banks

Australian Resources Development Bank Ltd: 40 Market St, POB 53, Melbourne, Vic 3000; tel. (03) 616-2800; telex 32078; fax (03) 616-2893; f. 1967 by major Australian trading banks, with support of Reserve Bank of Australia, to marshal funds from local and overseas sources for the financing of Australian participation in projects of national importance; acquired Australian Banks' Export Re-Finance Corpn in 1980; cap. and res 20.3m., dep. 267m. (Sept. 1989); Chair. W. H. HODGSON; Deputy Chair. B. A. POULTER.

Primary Industry Bank of Australia Ltd: 115 Pitt St, Sydney, NSW 2000; POB 4577, Sydney, NSW 2001; tel. (02) 231-5655; telex 123495; fax (02) 221-6218; f. 1978; cap. and res 45.7m., dep. 882m. (1990); Chair. Dr R. G. GARNAUT; Man. Dir B. H. WALTERS.

Trading Banks

Australia and New Zealand Banking Group Ltd: Collins Place, 55 Collins St, Melbourne, Vic 3000; POB 537 E, Melbourne, Vic 3001; tel. (03) 658-2955; telex 39920; fax (03) 658-2909; f. 1828; present name adopted in 1970; cap. and res 3,334.9m., dep. 49,560.3m. (Sept. 1989); over 2,200 points of representation in Australia, New Zealand and world-wide; Chair. MILTON BRIDGLAND; Deputy Chair. and CEO W. J. BAILEY.

Australian Bank Ltd: 17 O'Connell St, POB 1631, Sydney, NSW 2000; tel. (02) 264-8000; telex 72252; fax (02) 232-4208; f. 1981; cap. and res. 82.4m., dep. 163.1m. (June 1989); Chair. N. A. SMITH; Man. Dir ED CONDRAN; 2 brs.

Bank of Melbourne Ltd: 541 St Kilda Rd, Melbourne, Vic 3000; tel. (03) 520-0000; f. 1989; assets 3,700m.; Chair. and CEO CHRIS STEWART.

Bank of Queensland Ltd: 229 Elizabeth St, POB 898, Brisbane, Qld 4001; tel. (07) 231-0421; telex 41565; fax (07) 221-5869; f. 1874; cap. and res 88.8m., dep. 653.1m. (1990); Chair. HARRY BAYNES; Gen. Man. GRAHAM J. HART; 72 brs.

Macquarie Bank Ltd: Level 26, 20 Bond St, Sydney, NSW 2000; tel. (02) 237-3333; telex 122246; fax (02) 237-3350; f. 1969 as Hill Samuel Australia Ltd; present name adopted in 1985; cap. and res 148.2m., dep. 792.4m. (1989); Chair. DAVID S. CLARKE; Man. Dir ANTHONY R. BERG; 3 brs.

National Australia Bank Ltd: 500 Bourke St, Melbourne, Vic 3001; tel. (03) 641-3500; telex 30241; fax (03) 641-4916; f. 1981 by merger of Commercial Banking Co of Sydney with National Bank of Australasia; cap. and res 6,000.0m., dep. 46,200m. (Sept. 1989); Chair. Sir RUPERT CLARKE; Man. Dir D. R. ARGUS; 1,219 brs.

Rural and Industries Bank of Western Australia: 108 St George's Terrace, POB E237, Perth, WA 6001; tel. (09) 320-6206; telex 92417; fax (09) 320-6444; f. 1945; WA govt bank; cap. and res 621m., dep. 5,265m. (1989); Chair. Dr ROSS GARNAUT; Man. Dir WARWICK G. KENT; 109 brs.

State Bank of New South Wales Ltd: 52 Martin Place, POB 41, Sydney, NSW 2001; tel. (02) 226-8000; telex 74238; fax (02) 226-8588; f. 1933; cap. and res 1,289.7m., dep. 10,556.2m. (June 1989); Chair. D. S. GREATOREX; Man. Dir J. A. O'NEILL; 295 brs in Australia.

State Bank of South Australia: 91 King William St, Adelaide, SA 5000; POB 399, Adelaide, SA 5001; tel. (08) 210-4411; telex 82082; fax (08) 210-4758; f. 1984 by merger; cap. 1,381.3m., dep. 16,684.1m. (June 1990); Chair. DAVID SIMMONS; Group Man. Dir TIM MARCUS CLARK; 183 brs.

Westpac Banking Corporation: 60 Martin Place, Sydney, NSW 2001; tel. (02) 226-3311; telex 22891; fax (02) 226-4128; f. 1982 by merger; cap. p.u. 1,257.7m., dep. 62,931.8m. (1989); Chair. Sir ERIC NEAL; Man. Dir STUART FOWLER.

Savings Banks

Advance Bank Australia Ltd: POB R221, Royal Exchange, Sydney, NSW 2000; tel. (02) 964-5000; telex 73066; fax (02) 964-5111; Man. Dir JOHN THAME.

Civic Advance Bank Ltd: Advance Bank Centre, 60 Marcus Clarke St, Canberra City, ACT 2601; tel. (06) 243-5555; telex 62093; Chair. J. G. SERVICE; CEO G. B. MEYER.

SBT Bank (The Hobart Savings Bank): 39 Murray St, Hobart, Tas 7000; tel. (002) 30-4777; telex 58296; fax (002) 31-0278; f. 1845; cap. and res 30.7m., dep. 545.4m. (Aug. 1989); Chair. R. J. HARRIS; Gen. Man. P. W. KEMP; 31 brs.

State Bank of Victoria: 385 Bourke St, Melbourne, Vic 3000; POB 267D, Melbourne, Vic 3001; tel. (03) 678-7000; telex 32910; fax (03) 670-7042; f. 1842; cap. 787.4m., dep. 16,240.5m. (June 1990); Chair. C. R. WARD AMBLER; CEO P. J. RIZZO; 532 brs.

Tasmania Bank: 79 St John St, POB 288, Launceston, Tas 7250; tel. (003) 37-3444; telex 58579; fax (003) 34-2367; f. 1987 by the merger of the Launceston Bank for Savings (f. 1835) and Tasmanian Permanent Building Society; res 46.5m., dep. 748.1m. (Aug. 1989); Chair. ROBERT MATHER; Man. Dir DON ADAMS; 41 brs.

Westpac Savings Bank Ltd: 60 Martin Place, Sydney, NSW 2000; tel. (02) 226-3311; telex 22891; fax (02) 226-4128; f. 1956; cap. p.u. 90m., dep. 11,430.6m. (1989); Chair. Sir ERIC NEAL; Man. Dir S. A. FOWLER.

Foreign Banks

Bankers' Trust Australia Ltd (USA): POB H4, Australia Sq., Sydney, NSW 2000; tel. (02) 259-3555; telex 121821; fax (02) 235-2882; f. 1969; cap. 72.8m., res 22.3m., dep. 35.9m.; Chair. DAVID HOARE; Deputy Chair. RONALD DEANS.

Bank of America Australia Ltd (USA): 13th Floor, 167 Macquarie St, Sydney, NSW 2000; tel. (02) 221-1588; telex 24223; fax (02) 235-0485.

Bank of China (People's Republic of China): 65 York St, cnr of Barrack St, Sydney, NSW 2000; telex 177033.

Bank of New Zealand: 9th Floor, BNZ House, 333-339 George St, Sydney, NSW 2000; tel. (02) 290-6666; telex 22884; fax (02) 290-3414; Chair. M. G. KING; CEO H. L. SACK.

Bank of Singapore (Australia) Ltd: Bank of Singapore House, 99 Queen St, Melbourne, Vic 3000; tel. (03) 602-2700; telex 152696; fax (03) 670-9436; f. 1986; cap. 50m., res 1.7m., dep. 166.5m. (Dec. 1988); Exec. Dir and CEO J. BRUCE BRAWN; 5 brs.

Bank of Tokyo Australia Ltd (Japan): Level 15, State Bank Centre, 52 Martin Place, Sydney, NSW 2000; POB 4210, Sydney, NSW 2001; tel. (02) 225-9700; telex 73354; fax (02) 225-9870; f. 1985; cap. 50.0m., res 13.3m., dep. 766.4m. (Dec. 1989); Chair. and Man. Dir HIDEHIRO KIKUCHI.

Banque Nationale de Paris (France): 12 Castlereagh St, Sydney, NSW 2000; POB 269, Sydney, NSW 2001; tel. (02) 232-8733; telex 20132; fax (02) 221-8005; Gen.-Man. SERGE BASSET; 6 brs.

Barclays Bank (Australia) Ltd (UK): POB 3357, Sydney, NSW 2001; tel. (02) 238-4789; telex 22114; fax (02) 235-0235; cap. 114.6m., res 3.2m., dep. 821.9m.; Chair. and CEO RICHARD M. WEBB.

Chase AMP Bank Ltd (USA): 36th Floor, Qantas International Centre, 1 Jamison St, Sydney, NSW 2000; tel. (02) 250-4111; telex 176117; fax (02) 250-4664; f. 1985; cap. 267m., dep. 3,355.9m.; Chair. Sir JAMES BALDERSTONE; Man. Dir L. R. ANDERSON.

Citibank Ltd (USA): 7th Floor, Darwin Plaza, 41 The Mall, Darwin; tel. (089) 81-7733; telex 85275.

Deutsche Bank (Australia) Ltd (Germany): 1 Collins St, Melbourne, Vic 3000; tel. (03) 654-1277; telex 152314; fax (03) 650-6497; cap. 125m., dep. 854.9m. (1988); Man. Dir Dr HANS J. BECK.

Habib Finance (Australia) Ltd (Pakistan): 66th Level, MLC Centre, Martin Place, Sydney, NSW 2000; tel. (02) 233-5233; telex 121098; fax (02) 231-5162; f. 1987.

HongkongBank of Australia Ltd (Hong Kong): 99 William St, Melbourne, Vic 3000; tel. (03) 619-0338; telex 152117; fax (03) 629-6066; f. 1985; cap. and res 250.8m., dep. 1,942.9m. (Dec. 1989); CEO RICHARD ORGILL; Jt Man. Dirs K. C. D. ROXBURGH, J. S. DICKINSON.

IBJ Australia Bank Ltd: Chancery House, 37 St George's Terrace, Perth, WA 6000; tel. (09) 220-9777; telex 96993; fax (09) 221-1014; f. 1985; cap. 100m.; Chair. Sir HAROLD KNIGHT.

Lloyds Bank NZA PLC (New Zealand): Lloyds Bank House, 35 Pitt St, POB R220, Royal Exchange, Sydney, NSW 2000; tel. (02) 239-5555; telex 26115; fax (02) 251-7340; f. 1985; cap. 47.7m., res 16.2m., dep. 461.8m. (Dec. 1989); Chair. Sir JOHN MASON; CEO TONY DAVIES.

Mitsubishi Bank of Australia Ltd (Japan): Level 1, 255 George St, Sydney, NSW 2000; tel. (02) 250-1800; telex 27234; fax (02) 235-0883; f. 1985; cap. 53.4m.; Man. Dir SHUICHI TAKAHASHI.

NatWest Australia Bank Ltd: 39th Qantas International Centre, International Sq., Sydney, NSW 2000; tel. (02) 250-8500; telex 177326; fax (02) 251-2763; f. 1986; cap. and res. 258.4m., dep. 2,575.2m. (1989); Chair. J. K. BAIN.

Standard Chartered Bank Australia Ltd (UK): POB 2633, Adelaide, SA 5001; tel. (08) 218-0711; telex 87043; fax (08) 211-7801; f. 1986; cap. and res 99.1m., dep. 1,144.9m. (1989); Chair. Sir BRUCE MACKLIN; Group Man. Dir E. B. KNOX.

STOCK EXCHANGES

Australian Stock Exchange Ltd: Level 9, Plaza Bldg, Australia Sq., Sydney, NSW 2000; tel. (02) 227 0400; telex 24628; fax (02) 235-0056; f. 1987 by merger of the stock exchanges in the six capital cities (listed below), to replace the fmr Australian Associated Stock Exchange; Group Man. Dir J. GAVIN CAMPBELL; Deputy Group Man. Dir ROLAND L. COPPEL.

AUSTRALIA

Australian Stock Exchange (Adelaide) Ltd: 55 Exchange Place, Adelaide, SA; tel. (08) 212-3702; telex 82186; fax (08) 231-1740; f. 1887; Chair. B. H. PITTMAN; Man. Dir T. J. THURGARLAND.

Australian Stock Exchange (Brisbane) Ltd: 123 Eagle St, Brisbane, Qld 4000; POB 7055, Riverside Centre, Brisbane, Qld 4001; tel. (07) 831-1499; telex 40264; f. 1884; 38 mems; Chair. R. B. MCCRORY; Man. Dir G. P. CHAPMAN.

Australian Stock Exchange (Hobart) Ltd: 86 Collins St, Hobart, Tas 7000; tel. (002) 34-7333; telex 58111; fax (002) 34-2836; f. 1891.

Australian Stock Exchange (Melbourne) Ltd: 351 Collins St, Melbourne, Vic 3000; tel. (03) 617-8611; telex 30550; fax (03) 617-0303; f. 1884, inc. 1970; Chair. C. M. BATROUNEY; Man. Dir R. B. LEE.

Australian Stock Exchange (Perth) Ltd: Exchange House, 68 St George's Terrace, Perth, WA 6001; tel. (09) 327-0000; telex 92159; fax (09) 321-7670; f. 1889; 44 mems; Chair. J. H. POYNTON; Man. Dir CHRISTOPHER J. COLE.

Australian Stock Exchange (Sydney) Ltd: Exchange Centre, 20 Bond St, Australia Sq., POB H224, Sydney, NSW 2000; tel. (02) 225-6600; telex 20630; fax (02) 233-5836; f. 1871; 245 mems; Chair. KEVIN J. TROY; Man. Dir PETER W. MARSHMAN.

Supervisory Bodies

Australian Securities Commission: Canberra; f. 1990 to ensure the enforcement of company and securities' laws; Chair. TONY HARTNELL.

National Companies and Securities Commission: Melbourne, Vic; telex 33050; supervisory body; Chair. HENRY BOSCH.

PRINCIPAL INSURANCE COMPANIES

AMP General Insurance Ltd: 8 Loftus St, Sydney Cove, NSW 2000; tel. (02) 257-2500; telex 177001; fax (02) 257-2199; f. 1958; Chair. J. W. UTZ; Man. Dir J. K. STAVELEY.

Australian Guarantee Corpn Ltd: 130 Phillip St, Sydney, NSW 2000; tel. (02) 234-1122; telex 26612; fax (02) 234-1225; f. 1925; Chair. I. MATHIESON; Man. Dir P. C. WILSON.

Australian Natives' Association Insurance Co Ltd: 114–124 Albert Rd, South Melbourne, Vic 3205; tel. (03) 697-0218; fax (03) 696-1276; f. 1948; Chair. Mrs R. E. MITCHELL; Gen. Man. C. A. GAAL.

Australian Reinsurance Co Ltd: 31 Queen St, Melbourne, Vic 3000; tel. (03) 616-9200; telex 34201; fax (03) 614-3458; f. 1962; reinsurance; Chair. J. H. WINTER; Gen. Mans S. V. F. BRAIN, S. M. WESTWOOD.

Capita Financial Group Ltd: 9 Castlereagh St, Sydney, NSW 2000; tel. (02) 220-7000; telex 24086; f. 1878 as the City Mutual Life Assurance Society Ltd; present name adopted in 1986; life insurance, superannuation and financial services; Chair. GERALD WELLS; Man. Dir MONTY I. HILKOWITZ.

Catholic Church Insurances Ltd: 387 St Kilda Rd, Melbourne, Vic 3004; tel. (03) 267-5900; fax (03) 820-0370; f. 1911; Chair. Mgr P. H. JONES; Gen. Man. C. R. O'MALLEY.

The Chamber of Manufactures Insurance Ltd: 370 St Kilda Rd, Melbourne, Vic 3004; tel. (03) 699-4211; telex 39482; fax (03) 696-4683; f. 1914; Chair. W. D. MCPHERSON; Gen. Man. and CEO T. R. LONGES.

Colonial Mutual General Insurance Co Ltd: 330 Collins St, Melbourne, Vic 3000; tel. (03) 607-6111; telex 34059; fax (03) 605-4785; f. 1958; Chair. D. S. ADAM; Gen. Man. A. D. BOWLES.

The Colonial Mutual Life Assurance Society Ltd: 330 Collins St, Melbourne, Vic 3000; tel. (03) 607-6111; telex 34059; fax (03) 607-6294; f. 1873; Chair. D. S. ADAM; Man. Dir JOHN MILBURN-PYLE.

Commercial Union Assurance Co of Australia Ltd: Commercial Union Centre, 485 La Trobe St, Melbourne, Vic; tel. (03) 605-8222; telex 33100; fax (03) 605-8366; f. 1960; fire, accident, marine; Chair. J. A. HANCOCK; Man. Dir P. R. CLAIRS.

Copenhagen Reinsurance Co (Aust.) Ltd: 60 Margaret St, Sydney, NSW 2000; tel. (02) 247-7266; telex 26721; fax (02) 235-3320; f. 1961; reinsurance; Chair. DAVID BROWN; Gen. Man. PAUL ALLISON.

FAI Insurances Ltd: FAI Insurance Group, 185 Macquarie St, Sydney, NSW 2000; tel. (02) 221-1155; telex 21755; fax (02) 223-1776; f. 1956; Chair. JOHN LANDERER; CEO RODNEY ADLER.

The Federation Insurance Ltd: 342–348 Flinders St, Melbourne, Vic 3000; tel. (03) 620101; telex 30847; fax (03) 614-2905; f. 1926; Chair. R. L. M. SUMMERBELL; Gen. Man. A. J. KELL.

GRE Insurance Ltd: 604 St Kilda Rd, Melbourne, Vic 3004; tel. (03) 520-6233; telex 31259; fax (03) 521-2449; fire, accident, general; Man. Dir D. R. MELDRUM.

Directory

Manufacturers' Mutual Insurance Ltd: 2 Market St, Sydney, NSW 2000; tel. (02) 390-6222; telex 126666; f. 1914; workers' compensation; fire, general accident, motor and marine; Chair. C. W. LOVE; Man. Dir A. T. C. VENNING.

Mercantile & General Life Reinsurance Group of Australia Ltd: Royal Exchange Bldg, 56 Pitt St, Sydney, NSW 2000; tel. (02) 251-8000; telex 120318; fax (02) 251-1771; f. 1956; reinsurance; Chair. G. T. KRYGER; Man. Dir S. R. B. FRANCE.

Mercantile Mutual Holdings Ltd: 55 Clarence St, Sydney, NSW; tel. (02) 234-8111; telex 176577; f. 1878; Chair. J. B. STUDDY; Man. Dir P. R. SHIRRIFF.

MLC Insurance Ltd: 44 Martin Place, Sydney, NSW 2000; tel. (02) 957-8000; telex 74679; fax (02) 929-0971; f. 1958; Chair. R. C. GARROWAY; Gen. Man. D. A. WHIPP.

MLC Life Ltd: 105–153 Miller St, POB 200, North Sydney, NSW 2060; tel. (02) 957-8000; telex 121290; fax (02) 929-0971; f. 1886; Chair. V. E. MARTIN; Man. Dir I. K. CROW.

National & General Insurance Co Ltd: 5 Blue St, Sydney, NSW 2060; tel. (02) 922-3822; f. 1954; fire, marine, general; Chair. Sir ARVI PARBO; Gen. Man. A. J. SCOTT.

The National Mutual Life Association of Australasia Ltd: 447 Collins St, Melbourne, Vic 3000; tel. (03) 616-3911; telex 35654; fax (03) 614-7026; f. 1869; Chair. S. B. MYER; Group Man. Dir E. A. MAYER.

NRMA Insurance Ltd: 151 Clarence St, Sydney, NSW 2000; tel. (02) 260-9222; telex 22348; fax (02) 260-8472; f. 1926; associated with National Roads and Motorists' Asscn; Gen. Man. R. B. WILLING.

QBE Insurance Group Ltd: 82 Pitt St, Sydney, NSW 2000; tel. (02) 235-4444; telex 26914; fax (02) 235-3166; f. 1886; general insurance; Chair. J. D. O. BURNS; Man. Dir E. J. CLONEY.

Reinsurance Co of Australasia Ltd: 1 York St, Sydney, NSW 2000; tel. (02) 221-2144; telex 24504; fax (02) 251-1665; f. 1961; reinsurance, fire, accident, marine; Chair. M. T. SANDOW; Man. Dir P. J. MILLER.

Southern Pacific Insurance Co Ltd: 80 Alfred St, Milson's Point, NSW 2061; f. 1935; fire, accident, marine; Chair. C. H. V. CARPENTER; Chief Gen. Man. B. A. SELF.

Sun Alliance Australia Ltd: Sun Alliance Bldg, 22–34 Bridge St, Sydney, NSW 2000; fax (02) 233-9876; fire, accident and marine insurance; Gen. Man. J. J. MALLICK.

Wesfarmers Insurance Ltd: 184 Railway Parade, Bassendean, WA 6054; tel. (09) 279-0333; telex 96159; fax (09) 378-2172; Man. T. I. CORNFORD.

Westpac Life Ltd: 35 Pitt St, Sydney, NSW 2000; tel. (02) 220-4768; f. 1986; CEO DAVID WHITE.

Insurance Associations

Australian Insurance Association: Capital Centre, 4th Floor, 54 Marcus Clarke St, POB 2013, Canberra, ACT 2601; tel. (06) 249-7666; fax (06) 257-2560; f. 1968; Pres. C. R. O'MALLEY; Exec. Sec. D. L. CARRINGTON.

Australian Insurance Institute: 31 Queen St, Melbourne, Vic 3000; tel. (03) 629-4021; telex 139668; fax (03) 629-4204; f. 1919; Pres. W. K. ROBERTS; CEO A. V. SMYTHE; 8,972 mems.

Insurance Council of Australia Ltd: 31 Queen St, Melbourne, Vic 3000; tel. (03) 614-1077; fax (03) 614-7924; f. 1975; CEO G. C. BOND

Life Insurance Federation of Australia Inc: 31 Queen St, Melbourne, Vic 3000; tel. (03) 629-5751; fax (03) 614-4877; f. 1979; Chair. I. F. STANWELL; Exec. Dir D. A. PURCHASE; 49 mems.

Trade and Industry

CHAMBERS OF COMMERCE

International Chamber of Commerce: POB E118, Queen Victoria Terrace, Canberra, ACT 2600; tel. (06) 295-1961; fax (06) 295-0170; f. 1927; 65 mems; Chair. J. COLLINS; Sec.-Gen. H. C. GRANT.

Australian Chamber of Commerce: POB E139, Queen Victoria Terrace, ACT 2600; tel. (06) 273-2381; telex 62507; fax (06) 273-3646; f. 1901; mems include Chambers of Commerce in Sydney, Melbourne, Canberra, Brisbane, Adelaide, Perth, Hobart; Pres. J. COLLINS.

Chamber of Commerce and Industry SA, Inc: 136 Greenhill Road, Unley, SA 5061; tel. (08) 373-1422; telex 88370; fax (08) 272-9662; 3,100 mems; Gen. Man. L. M. THOMPSON.

Hobart Chamber of Commerce: 65 Murray St, Hobart, Tas 7000; POB 969K, Hobart, Tas 7001; tel. (002) 34-4325; fax (002) 31-1639; f. 1851; Dir V. J. BARRON.

Launceston Chamber of Commerce: 99 George St, Launceston, Tas 7250; POB 780, Launceston, Tas 7250; tel. (003) 318988; f. 1849; Sec. A. G. HART.

AUSTRALIA

State Chamber of Commerce and Industry: 93 York St, POB 4280, GPO Sydney, NSW 2001; tel. (02) 290-5400; telex 127113; fax (02) 290-3278; f. 1826; Dir DAVID J. G. TAYLOR.

State Chamber of Commerce and Industry (Qld): 243 Edward St, Brisbane, Qld 4000; POB 1390, Brisbane, Qld 4001; tel. (07) 221-1766; telex 145636; fax (07) 221-6872; f. 1868; Dir P. L. ROUBICEK.

State Chamber of Commerce and Industry (Victoria): Commerce House, World Trade Centre, cnr Flinders and Spencer Sts, Melbourne, Vic 3005; tel. (03) 611-2233; telex 31255; f. 1851; Exec. Dir D. LARKIN.

Western Australian Chamber of Commerce and Industry (Inc): 38 Parliament Place, West Perth, WA 6005; tel. (09) 322-2688; telex 93609; fax (09) 481-0980; f. 1890; 4,000 mems; Dir I. WHITAKER.

AGRICULTURAL AND INDUSTRIAL ORGANIZATIONS

AIDC Ltd: Level 33, AIDC Tower, 201 Kent St, Sydney, NSW 2000; tel. (02) 235-5155; telex 23107; fax (02) 235-5195; f. 1989 to take over the business of the Australian Industry Development Corporation (est. 1970); a Commonwealth statutory corpn providing finance and financial services, including the arrangement of project finance and equity participations, to promote the development of Australian industries and assist Australian participation in the ownership and control of industries and resources; brs in Sydney, Melbourne, Perth, Adelaide and Brisbane; cap. p.u. $A270m., total assets $A3,403m. (1990); Chair. Sir GORDON JACKSON; CEO ARTHUR W. O'SULLIVAN.

The Australian Agricultural Council: Dept of Primary Industries and Energy, Barton, Canberra, ACT 2600; tel. (06) 272-5220; telex 62188; fax (06) 272-4772; f. 1934 to provide means for consultation between individual states and the Commonwealth on agricultural production and marketing (excluding forestry and fisheries), to promote the welfare and standards of Australian agricultural industries and to foster the adoption of national policies in regard to these industries; nine mems comprising the state/territory ministers responsible for agriculture and the Commonwealth Minister for Primary Industries and Energy; Sec. A. J. FREE.

  Standing Committee on Agriculture: f. 1934; an advisory body to the Australian Agricultural Council; implements co-ordination of agricultural research and of quarantine measures relating to pests and diseases of plants and animals; comprises the state/territories Dirs of Agriculture and reps of Commonwealth Depts with an interest in agriculture; Sec. A. J. FREE.

Australian Dairy Corporation: 1601 Malvern Rd, Glen Iris, Vic 3146; tel. (03) 805-3777; telex 30503; fax (03) 885-5885; promotes local consumption and controls the export of dairy produce; Chair. JOHN C. FREARSON; Man. Dir JOHN L. GIBSON.

Australian Meat and Livestock Corporation: POB 4129, Sydney, NSW 2001; tel. (02) 260-3111; fax (02) 267-6620; statutory federal govt marketing authority assisting the Australian meat and livestock industries in domestic and international trade; Chair. R. AUSTEN.

Australian Trade Development Council: c/o Dept of Foreign Affairs and Trade, Canberra, ACT 2600; tel. (06) 261-2246; fax (06) 261-2696; f. 1958; advises the Minister for Foreign Affairs and Trade on all aspects of the development of overseas trade; Chair. Dr B. W. SCOTT.

Australian Wheat Board: Ceres House, 528 Lonsdale St, Melbourne, Vic 3000; tel. (03) 605-1555; telex 130196; fax (03) 670-2782; f. 1939; marketing authority for wheat on the export market; 11 mems; Chair. CLINTON CONDON.

Australian Wool Corporation: Wool House, 369 Royal Parade, Parkville, Vic 3052; tel. (03) 341-9111; telex 30548 (general), 34128 (sales); fax (03) 341-9273; f. 1973; responsible for wool marketing and research; Chair. HUGH S. BEGGS.

Department of Primary Industries and Energy: Edmund Barton Bldg, Broughton St, Barton, Canberra, ACT 2600; tel. (06) 272-3933; telex 62188; fax (06) 272-5161; f. 1987 to replace the fmr Depts of Primary Industry and of Resources and Energy; responsible for national resources and energy policy and for the promotion and development of primary industries; Chair. Minister for Primary Industries and Energy; Sec. GEOFF MILLER.

Wool Council of Australia: POB E10, Queen Victoria Terrace, Canberra, ACT 2600; tel. (06) 273-2531; telex 62683; comprises 20 mems; levies wool tax for research and development, promotion and market support; consults with Australian Wool Corpn on reserve prices; represents wool-growers to govt and industry; Chair. JOHN MCCRACKEN; Pres. K. M. SAWERS.

EMPLOYERS' ORGANIZATIONS

Australian Co-operative Foods Ltd: 55 Chandos St, St Leonard's, NSW 2065; tel. (02) 430-1222; telex 21438; fax (02) 438-3020, f. 1000; as Dairy Farmers Co-operative; Man. Dir D. S. KINNERSLEY.

Confederation of Australian Industry: 44th Level, Nauru House, 80 Collins St, Melbourne, Vic; tel. (03) 654-2788; telex 36663; fax (03) 650-1420; Pres. C. R. BERGLUND; CEO I. O. SPICER.

The Master Builders' Association of New South Wales: Forest Lodge, 52 Parramatta Rd, NSW 2007; tel. (02) 660-7188; telex 27308; fax (02) 660-4437; f. 1873; Exec. Dir R. L. ROCHER; 4,500 mems.

Meat and Allied Trades Federation of Australia: 25–27 Albany St, Crows Nest, NSW 2065; POB 1208, Crows Nest, NSW 2065; tel. (02) 438-5144; fax (02) 439-8494; f. 1928; Pres. A. J. MULLAN; Nat. Dir A. M. KING.

Metal Trades Industry Association of Australia: 51 Walker St, North Sydney, NSW 2060; tel. (02) 929-5566; telex 121257; fax (02) 929-8758; f. 1873; Nat. Pres. Dr W. W. J. UHLENBRUCH; CEO A. C. EVANS; 6,700 mems.

New South Wales Farmers' Association: 1 Bligh St, Sydney, NSW 2001; POB 1068, GPO Sydney, NSW 2001; tel. (02) 251-1700; telex 26638; fax (02) 221-6913; f. 1978 as The Livestock and Grain Producers' Asscn of NSW; CEO JOHN O. WHITE.

New South Wales Flour Millers' Council: POB 261, Glebe, NSW 2037; tel. (02) 552-2700; fax (02) 660-8747; Sec. K. G. WILLIAMS.

Screen Production Association of Australia: Suite 16, 40 Yeo St, Neutral Bay, NSW 2089; tel. (02) 953-0777; fax (02) 953-9894; Pres. PHIL GERLACH; Exec. Dir JOANNA SIMPSON.

Timber Trade Industrial Association: 155 Castlereagh St, Sydney, NSW 2000; f. 1940; 530 mems; Man. H. J. MCCARTHY.

MANUFACTURERS' ORGANIZATIONS

The Australian Chamber of Manufactures (NSW): Private Bag 938, North Sydney, NSW 2059; tel. (02) 957-5792; telex 122050; fax (02) 923-1166; f. 1885; CEO P. M. HOLT.

The Australian Chamber of Manufactures (Victoria): Industry House, 370 St Kilda Rd, POB 1469N, GPO Melbourne, Vic 3001; tel. (03) 698-4111; telex 32596; fax (03) 699-1729; f. 1877; 8,500 mems; Nat. CEO W. J. HENDERSON; Dir, Victoria Div. K. C. CROMPTON.

Australian Manufacturers' Export Council: MMI Bldg, POB 233, Civic Sq., Canberra, ACT 2608; tel. (06) 248-6477; fax (06) 248-6993; f. 1955; Exec. Officer G. J. CHALKER.

Business Council of Australia: 10 Queen's Rd, Melbourne, Vic 3004; POB 7225, Melbourne, Vic 3004; tel. (03) 867-6288; fax (03) 867-7861; public policy research and advocacy; governing council comprises chief execs of Australia's major cos; Pres. B. T. LOTON; Exec. Dir P. A. MCLAUGHLIN.

Confederation of Western Australian Industry, Inc: POB 6209, East Perth, WA 6004; tel. (09) 421-7555; telex 94124; fax (09) 325-6550; Exec. Dir L. G. ROWE.

Queensland Confederation of Industry: Industry House, 375 Wickham Terrace, Brisbane, Qld 4000; tel. (07) 831-1699; telex 41369; fax (07) 832-3195; f. 1976; 2,700 mems; Gen. Man. BARRY CANNON (acting).

Tasmanian Confederation of Industries: 242 Liverpool St, Hobart, Tas 7000; tel. (002) 345933; fax (002) 311278; f. 1898; Exec. Dir E. C. ILES.

PRINCIPAL TRADE UNIONS

Australian Council of Trade Unions (ACTU): 393–397 Swanston St, Melbourne, Vic 3000; tel. (03) 663-5266; telex 33943; fax (03) 663-4051; f. 1927; br. in each state, generally known as a Trades and Labour Council; 156 affiliated trade unions; Pres. MARTIN FERGUSON; Sec. WILLIAM J. KELTY.

Administrative and Clerical Officers' Association: 3rd Floor, 245 Castlereagh St, Sydney, NSW 2000; tel. (02) 267-3000; telex 26021; fax (02) 261-5668; Jt Nat. Secs PETER ROBSON, JOY PALMER; 82,655 mems.

Amalgamated Footwear and Textile Workers' Union of Australia: 132–138 Leicester St, Carlton, Vic 3053; tel. (03) 347-2766; f. 1919; Nat. Pres J. ROUGHLEY; 30,000 mems.

Amalgamated Metal Workers' Union: 136 Chalmers St, Surry Hills, NSW 2010; tel. (02) 690-1411; telex 23763; fax (02) 319-1061; 155,730 mems.

Australasian Meat Industry Employees' Union: 377 Sussex St, Sydney, NSW 2000; tel. (02) 264-2279; fax (02) 261-1970; Fed. Sec. J. O'TOOLE; 45,000 mems.

Australian Building Construction Employees' and Builders Labourers' Federation: 190 Sturt St, Adelaide, SA 5000; tel. (08) 211-8977; fax (08) 231-5098; Gen. Sec. N. L. GALLAGHER; 45,000 mems.

Australian Postal and Telecommunications Union: 139 Queensberry St, 1st Floor, Carlton, Vic 3053; tel. (03) 347-8022;

AUSTRALIA

fax (03) 348-1285; Pres. M. J. ANTHONY; Gen. Sec. P. WATSON; 48,000 mems.

Australian Public Service Federation: 139 Queensberry St, Carlton South, Vic 3053; POB 147, Carlton South, Vic 3053; tel. (03) 347-2488; fax (03) 347-0462; f. 1912; Pres. BILL HIGHAM; Sec. L. N. RICHES; 29,000 mems.

Australian Railways Union: 377 Sussex St, 6th Floor, Sydney, NSW 2000; tel. (02) 267-6116; fax (02) 264-2896; Nat. Sec. R. C. TAYLOR; 42,416 mems.

Australian Teachers' Union: POB 415, Carlton South, Vic 3053; tel. (03) 348-1700; telex 152486; fax (03) 347-6330; f. 1920; Pres. DI FOGGO; Gen. Sec. DAVID ROBSON; 174,000 mems.

Australian Telecommunications Employees' Association: 139 Queensberry St, Carlton, Vic 3053; tel. (03) 348-1022; telex 33677; fax (03) 347-3448; Pres. IAN MCLEAN; Sec. I. M. MUSUMECI; 25,200 mems.

Australian Workers' Union: 245 Chalmers St, Redfern, NSW 2016; tel. (02) 690-1022; telex 73231; fax (02) 690-1020; f. 1886; Pres. W. P. LUDWIG; Gen. Sec. E. R. HODDER; 122,000 mems.

Building Workers' Industrial Union of Australia: 361 Kent St, 4th Floor, Sydney, NSW 2000; tel. (02) 267-3929; telex 25836; fax (02) 262-1465; f. 1945; Pres. BILL ETHELL; Gen. Sec. TOM MCDONALD; 41,260 mems.

Electrical Trades Union of Australia: National Council, 302–306 Elizabeth St, Sydney, NSW 2010; tel. (02) 211-5888; telex 73372; f. 1919; Pres. R. C. LUCKMAN; Nat. Sec. T. A. JOHNSON; 88,569 mems.

Federal Clerks' Union of Australia: 53 Queen St, 2nd Floor, Melbourne, Vic 3000; tel. (03) 629-3801; fax (03) 614-3250; Nat. Pres. J. P. MAYNES; Nat. Sec. T. W. SULLIVAN; 100,000 mems.

Federated Ironworkers' Association of Australia: 51-65 Bathurst St, Sydney, NSW 2000; tel. (02) 264-2877; telex 176770; fax (02) 261-1701; f. 1911; Nat. Pres. R. REDMOND; Nat. Sec. STEVE HARRISON; 65,000 mems.

The Federated Miscellaneous Workers Union of Australia: 1st Floor, 365–375 Sussex St, Sydney, NSW 2000; tel. (02) 267-9681; telex 75879; fax (02) 267-3778; f. 1916; Pres. CHRIS RAPER; GEN. SEC. M. J. FERGUSON; 127,000 mems.

Federated Municipal and Shire Council Employees' Union of Australia: 1-3 O'Connell St, North Melbourne, Vic. 3051; tel. (03) 326-6001; fax (03) 326-5313; Pres. A. VEITCH; Sec. PAUL SLAPE; 49,158 mems.

Hospital Employees' Federation of Australia: POB 655, Carlton South, Vic 3053; tel. (03) 663-8224; fax (03) 663-8225; Nat. Sec. RAY COLLEY; 30,579 mems.

Printing and Kindred Industries Union: 594–596 Crown St, Surry Hills, NSW 2010; tel. (02) 690-1000; fax (02) 699-1061; f. 1916; Sec.-Treas. JOHN P. CAHILL; 48,000 mems.

Seamen's Union of Australia: 289 Sussex St, Sydney, NSW 2000; tel. (02) 267-3801; fax (02) 261-5897; Pres. JOHN BENSON; Sec. PATRICK GERAGHTY.

Transport Workers' Union of Australia: 2nd Floor, 18-20 Lincoln Sq., North Carlton, Vic 3053; tel. (03) 347-0099; fax (03) 347-2502; Pres. K. CYS; Sec. I. HODGSON; 94,499 mems.

Vehicle Builders Employees' Federation of Australia: 1st Floor, 61-65 Drummond St, Carlton South, Vic 3053; tel. (03) 663-5866; fax (03) 663-5685; Pres. W. A. TAYLOR; Gen. Sec. WAYNE BLAIR; 33,671 mems.

Waterside Workers' Federation of Australia: 365–375 Sussex St, Sydney, NSW 2000; tel. (02) 267-9134; fax (02) 261-3481; f. 1902; Pres. JIM BEGGS; Gen. Sec. T. I. BULL.

Transport

Australian Transport Advisory Council: POB 594, Canberra, ACT 2601; tel. (06) 268-7851; telex 62018; fax (06) 274-6775; f. 1946; Mems: Federal Minister for Transport and Communications, State and Territory Ministers of Transport, Roads and Marine and Ports; Observer: the New Zealand Minister of Transport; initiates discussion, and reports as necessary, on any matter which will tend to promote a better co-ordination of transport development, while encouraging modernization and innovation; promotes research; Sec. P. CAETJENS.

State Transit Authority of New South Wales: 100 Miller St, North Sydney, NSW 2000; tel. (02) 956-4777; fax (02) 956-4710; operates publicly-owned buses and ferries in Sydney and Newcastle; exercises broad policy control over privately operated public vehicles in the above areas; Chair. J. LANDELS; CEO J. R. BREW.

Directory

RAILWAYS

Before July 1975 there were seven government-owned railway systems in Australia. In July 1975 Australian National was formed to incorporate the Commonwealth Railways, non-metropolitan South Australian Railways and the Tasmanian Government Railways. In 1984 there were 40,807 km of railway in Australia.

Australian National: 1 Richmond Rd, Keswick, SA 5035; tel. (08) 217-4111; telex 88445; fax (08) 217-4544; f. 1975; a federal statutory authority operating 6,678 km of track (June 1990); Chair. Dr D. G. WILLIAMS; Man. Dir R. M. KING.

Queensland Railways: Railway Centre, 305 Edward St, Brisbane, Qld 4000; POB 1429, Brisbane, Qld 4001; tel. (07) 235-2222; telex 41514; fax (07) 235-1799; operates 10,094 km of track; Commr V. O'ROURKE.

State Rail Authority of New South Wales: 11–31 York St, Sydney, NSW 2000; POB 29, Sydney, NSW 2001; tel. (02) 219-8888; telex 25702; f. 1980; administers passenger and freight rail service in NSW over a track network of 9,917 km; Chair. and CEO R. SAYERS.

State Transport Authority (South Australia): 136 North Terrace, Adelaide, SA 5000; POB 2351, GPO Adelaide, SA 5001; tel. (08) 218-2200; f. 1978; operates metropolitan bus, train and tram services; Chair. J. D. RUMP; Gen. Man. J. V. BROWN.

State Transport Authority (Victoria): 14th Floor, Transport House, 589 Collins St, Melbourne, Vic 3000; tel. (03) 619-1111; telex 33801; fax (03) 619-4143; f. 1983; operates 5,809 km of track; Chair. J. KING; Man. Dir K. M. FITZMAURICE.

Western Australian Government Railways (Westrail): Westrail Centre, POB S1422, East Perth, Perth 6001, WA; tel. (09) 326-2222; telex 92879; fax (09) 326-2589; operates passenger and freight transport services mainly in the south of WA; 5,563 main line route-km of track; Commr Dr J. GILL.

ROADS

At 31 December 1985 there were 852,986 km of roads, including 787 km of motorways, 38,728 km of other main roads and 91,777 km of secondary roads.

SHIPPING

Commonwealth of Australia, Australian National Line: (ANL Ltd), 432 St Kilda Rd, Melbourne, Vic 3004; POB 2238T, Melbourne, Vic 3001; tel. (03) 869-5555; telex 130584; fax (03) 869-5319; f. 1956; shipping agents; coastal trade and coastal and overseas bulk shipping; container management services; overseas container services to Europe, Hong Kong, New Zealand, Taiwan, the Philippines, Korea, Singapore, Malaysia, Thailand, Indonesia and Japan; bulk services to Japan, India, Pakistan, Malaysia, Indonesia, New Zealand; Chair. W. BOLITHO; Man. Dir J. BICKNELL.

The Adelaide Steamship Co Ltd: 123 Greenhill Rd, Unley, SA 5061; tel. (08) 272-3077; telex 82133; fax (08) 272-3509; f. 1875; Man. Dir J. G. SPALVINS.

Ampol Ltd: 580 George St, Sydney, NSW 2000; tel. (02) 364-4444; telex 121325; f. 1936; bulk carriage of crude oil to Brisbane and Sydney, and carriage of refined products and black oils from the Brisbane refinery to Qld out-ports; Chair. Sir TRISTAN ANTICO; Man. Dir A. J. HURLSTONE; 2 vessels.

John Burke Shipping: 14-24 Macquarie St, New Farm, POB 509, Fortitude Valley, Qld 4006; tel. (07) 852-1701; telex 40483; fax (07) 852-4675; f. 1887; coastal services and trade with Papua New Guinea; Gen. Man. Capt. D. W. SIMS; 4 vessels.

Burns, Philp and Co Ltd: 7 Bridge St, Sydney, NSW; POB 543, Sydney, NSW 2001; tel. (02) 259-1111; telex 120290; fax (02) 251-1681; f. 1883; Chair. J. D. O. BURNS; CEO ANDREW TURNBULL.

Holyman W. and Sons Pty Ltd: Remount Rd, Mowbray, POB 70, Launceston, Tas; tel. (003) 26-3388; telex 58517; fax (003) 26-3337; coastal services; Chair. K. C. HOLYMAN.

Howard Smith Industries Pty Ltd: POB N364, Grosvenor Place, Sydney, NSW 2000; tel. (02) 230-1777; telex 20747; fax (02) 251-2702; ship and tug services; Chair. Sir NEIL CURRIE; CEO D. A. W. THOMSON.

McIlwraith McEacharn Ltd: 32 Walker St, Sydney 2060; tel. (02) 954-1445; telex 178116; 114 William St, Melbourne, Vic 3000; tel. (03) 602-2394; telex 30339; f. 1875; tug and launch owners and operators; ship management; mfrs of hyperbaric equipment, mining, mineral processing; investment; Chair. Sir IAN POTTER; Man. Dir A. B. LAWRANCE.

Mason Shipping: Tingira St, POB 840, Portsmith, Cairns, Qld 4870; tel. (070) 516933; telex 48405; a division of Portsmith Stevedoring Co Pty Ltd; coastal services and stevedoring; Man. D. W. SIMS; 4 vessels.

TNT Shipping and Development Ltd: TNT Plaza, Tower 1, Lawson Sq., POB 33, Redfern, NSW 2016; tel. (02) 698-9222; telex

399

AUSTRALIA

27343; fax (02) 318-1921; f. 1958; wholly owned subsidiary of TNT Ltd; shipowner and operator; charters vessels; Chair. F. W. MILLAR; Man. Dir Sir PETER ABELES.

Western Australian Coastal Shipping Commission (Stateships): Port Beach Rd, North Fremantle, WA 6160; POB 394, Fremantle, WA 6160; tel. (09) 430-0200; telex 92054; fax (09) 430-4506; Chair. and Gen. Man. D. F. WILSON.

CIVIL AVIATION

In the sparsely-populated areas of central and western Australia, air transport is extremely important, and Australia has pioneered services such as the Flying Doctor Service to overcome the problems of distance. The country is also well served by international airlines.

Air NSW: Level 4, 431 Glebe Point Rd, Glebe, Sydney, NSW 2020; tel. (02) 268-1678; telex 20143; fax (02) 556-1336; f. 1934; a division of Ansett Transport Industries (Operations) Pty Ltd; extensive services from Sydney throughout NSW and Qld's Sunshine Coast; Chair. Sir RODEN CUTLER; Gen. Man. JON HUTCHISON; fleet includes 2 Fokker F-28-1000, 5 Fokker F-28-4000, 5 Fokker F-50.

Ansett Airlines of Australia: 501 Swanston St, Melbourne, Vic 3000; tel. (03) 668-1211; telex 30085; fax (03) 668-3584; f. 1936; a division of Ansett Transport Industries (Operations) Pty Ltd; passenger and air cargo services throughout Australia; Chair. and Jt Man. Dirs K. RUPERT MURDOCH, Sir PETER ABELES; Gen. Man. G. J. MCMAHON; fleet includes 5 Boeing 767-200, 5 Boeing 727-200, 1 Boeing 727F, 16 Boeing 737-300, 8 A320, 3 Fokker F-50.

Ansett NT: 46 Smith St, Darwin, NT 0800; tel. (089) 819800; fax (089) 819256; f. 1981; a division of Ansett Transport Industries (Operations) Pty Ltd; services link Darwin with Katherine, Tennant Creek, Alice Springs, Gove, Ayers Rock, Groote Eylandt, Cairns; Gen. Man. PETER HILLAS; fleet includes 1 Fokker F-28-1000, 1 BAe 146-200.

Ansett WA: Perth Domestic Airport, Cloverdale, Perth, WA 6105; tel. (09) 478-9222; telex 92147; fax (09) 478-9286; f. 1934; a division of Ansett Transport Industries (Operations) Pty Ltd; services from Perth to Darwin via north-west ports and throughout Western Australia; Gen. Man. R. BUCKLEY; Admin. Man. R. SMITH; fleet of 3 Fokker F-28-1000, 2 Fokker F-28-4000, 5 BAe 146-200.

Australian Airlines: 50 Franklin St, POB 2806AA, Melbourne, Vic 3001; tel. (03) 665-1333; telex 30109; fax (03) 666-3881; f. 1946 as Trans-Australia Airlines (TAA); present name adopted in 1986; services to all states; in 1990 it was announced that the airline was to be transferred to private ownership; Chair. A. E. HARRIS; Man. Dir and CEO JOHN W. SCHAAP; fleet includes 4 Airbus A300B4, 16 Boeing 737-376, 7 Boeing 727-276, 7 Boeing 737-476, 2 Fokker F-27.

Compass Airlines: Melbourne; f. 1990; Chair. BRYAN GREY.

Eastern Australia Airlines: Sydney; telex 27231; domestic flights; fleet of 2 DHC-Dash 8-300, 3 BAe Jetstream Super 31.

Eastwest Airlines Ltd: Level 3, 431 Glebe Point Rd, Glebe, NSW 2037; fax (02) 552-8288; f. 1947; services to Queensland, NSW, Victoria, Tasmania and Northern Territory; Gen. Man. NEIL BERKETT; fleet includes 5 BAe 146-300, 3 Fokker F-28.

Qantas Airways Ltd: Qantas International Centre, International Sq., GPO Box 489, Sydney, NSW 2000; tel. (02) 236-3636; telex 20113; fax (02) 236-3277; f. 1920; govt-owned; services to 44 cities in 22 countries, including destinations in the UK, Europe, the USA, Canada, Japan, Asia, the Pacific, Africa, South America and New Zealand; Chair. W. L. DIX; CEO J. F. WARD; fleet includes 14 Boeing 747-200B, 6 Boeing 747-300, 5 Boeing 747-400, 2 Boeing 747-200 Combi, 2 747SP, 1 Boeing 747-200, 7 Boeing 767-200ER, 5 Boeing 767-300ER.

Sunstate Airlines: POB 186, Maryborough, Qld 4650; tel. (07) 860-4577; telex 140753; fax (07) 860-4578; 33.3% owned by Australian Airlines; operates passenger and cargo services from Brisbane.

Tourism

The main attractions are swimming and surfing on the Pacific beaches, sailing from Sydney and other harbours, skin-diving along the Great Barrier Reef, winter sports in the Australian Alps, notably the Snowy Mountains, and summer sports in the Blue Mountains. The town of Alice Springs and the sandstone monolith of Ayers Rock are among the attractions of the desert interior. Much of Australia's wildlife is unique to the country. Australia received an estimated 2,249,300 foreign tourist visitors in 1988. The majority of visitors come from the USA, New Zealand, the United Kingdom and Japan.

Australian Tourist Commission: 80 William St, Woolloomooloo, Sydney, NSW 2011; tel. (02) 360-1111; telex 22322; fax (02) 331-6469; f. 1967 for promotion of tourism; 12 offices, of which 11 are overseas; Chair. JOHN HADDAD; Man. Dir TONY THIRLWELL.

Australian Tourism Industry Association: Chair. Sir FRANK MOORE.

Atomic Energy

Australian Institute of Nuclear Science and Engineering: PMB 1, Menai, NSW 2234; tel. (02) 543-3376; fax (02) 543-9268; supports university research and training projects in all branches of nuclear science and engineering; mems comprise 21 academic institutions, ANSTO and CSIRO; Scientific Sec. Dr R. B. GAMMON.

Australian Nuclear Science and Technology Organisation (ANSTO): Lucas Heights Research Laboratories, New Illawarra Rd, Lucas Heights, NSW 2234; PMB 1, Menai, NSW 2234; tel. (02) 543-3111; telex 24562; fax (02) 543-5097; f. 1987 to replace the Australian Atomic Energy Commission (AAEC), which had been in existence since 1953; aims to bring the benefits of nuclear science and technology to industry, to medicine and to the community; Chair. Prof. R. E. COLLINS; Exec. Dir Dr DAVID J. COOK; 800 employees.

HIFAR: 10-MW thermal research reactor; critical 1958; for production of radioisotopes, studies of effects of high-intensity radiation on materials and of the use of neutrons to analyse crystal lattices, molecular structure, trace element concentrations and uranium in ores.

MOATA: 100-kW thermal research reactor; critical 1962; provides neutron radiography, fission and alpha track analyses, activation services and research in physical chemistry and materials.

ANSTO Training Centre: PMB 1, Menai, NSW 2233; tel. (02) 543-3111; telex 24562; fax (02) 543-9259; provides short courses for participants from Australia and overseas, covering radionuclides in medicine, radioisotope techniques, radiation protection, occupational health and safety; Dir PETER NIXON.

AUSTRALIAN EXTERNAL TERRITORIES

CHRISTMAS ISLAND

Introduction

Christmas Island lies 360 km south of Java Head (Indonesia) in the Indian Ocean. The nearest point on the Australian coast is North West Cape, 1,408 km to the south-east. The majority of the population are of ethnic Chinese origin (55%, according to the census of 1981), but there are large minorities of Malays and Europeans. A variety of languages are spoken, but English is the official language. The predominant religious affiliation is Buddhist (36% in 1981). The principal settlement is Flying Fish Cove.

Following annexation by the United Kingdom in 1888, Christmas Island was incorporated for administrative purposes with the Straits Settlements (now Singapore and part of Malaysia) in 1900. Japanese forces occupied the island from March 1942 until the end of the Second World War, and in 1946 Christmas Island became a dependency of Singapore. Administration was transferred to the United Kingdom on 1 January 1958, pending final transfer to Australia, effected on 1 October 1958. The Australian Government appointed Official Representatives to the Territory until 1968, when new legislation provided for an Administrator, appointed by the Governor-General. Responsibility for administration lies with the Minister of Territories. In 1980 an Advisory Council was established for the Administrator to consult. In 1984 the Christmas Island Services Corporation was created in order to perform those functions which are normally the responsibility of municipal government. This body was placed under the direction of the Christmas Island Assembly, the first elections to which took place on 28 September 1985. Nine members were elected for one-year terms. On 3 November 1987 the Assembly was dissolved, and the Administrator empowered to perform its functions.

Christmas Island has no indigenous population. In June 1989 the population was estimated at 1,230, comprising mainly Chinese and Malays and a small number of Indians, Europeans and Eurasians.

Since 1981, all residents of the island have been eligible to acquire Australian citizenship. In 1984 the Australian Government extended social security, health and education benefits to the island, and enfranchised Australian citizens resident there. Full income-tax liability was to be introduced progressively over four years from July 1985.

The economy has been based on the recovery of phosphates. During the year ending 30 June 1984 about 463,000 metric tons were exported to Australia, 332,000 tons to New Zealand and 341,000 tons to other countries. Reserves were estimated to be sufficient to enable production to be maintained until 1991. In November 1987, however, the Australian Government announced the closure of the phosphate mine, owing to industrial unrest. Mining activity ceased in December. The Government announced that it would consider proposals by private operators to recommence phosphate-mining, subject to certain conditions such as the preservation of the rain forest. Meanwhile, the Government provided resources for redundancy and relocation payments to former phosphate miners, and extended its training programmes. Efforts are to be made to develop the island's considerable potential for tourism. In April 1986 initial plans were announced for a hotel and casino complex.

Statistical Survey

AREA AND POPULATION

Area: 135 sq km (52 sq miles).

Population: 2,871 (males 1,918, females 953) at census of 30 June 1981; 1,230 (official estimate) at mid-1989. *Ethnic Groups* (1981): Chinese 1,587, Malay 693, European 336, Total (incl. others) 2,871. Source: UN, *Demographic Yearbook*.

Density (1989): 9.1 per sq km.

Births and Deaths (1985): Registered live births 36 (birth rate 15.8 per 1,000); Registered deaths 2.

MINING

Production (phosphate exports, '000 metric tons): 1,187 in 1985; 880 in 1986; 842 (estimate) in 1987. Source: US Bureau of Mines.

FINANCE

Currency and Exchange Rates: Australian currency is used (see p. 380).

EXTERNAL TRADE

Principal Trading Partners (phosphate exports, '000 metric tons, year ending 30 June 1984): Australia 463, New Zealand 332, Total (incl. others) 1,136. Most requirements are imported, the principal supplier being Australia.

Directory

The Government

An Administrator, appointed by the Governor-General of Australia and responsible to the Minister for Territories, is the senior government representative on the island.

Administrator: A. D. TAYLOR.

Administration Headquarters: Christmas Island 6798, Indian Ocean.

Christmas Island Assembly: f. 1985; dissolved, and suspended, 1987; nine members were elected by universal adult suffrage, on the basis of proportional representation, for a term of one year; most recent election 17 Oct. 1987; Assembly dissolved, and responsibilities assumed by Administrator, in Nov. 1987.

Judicial System

The judicial system comprises a Supreme Court, a District Court, a Magistrate's Court and a Children's Court.

Supreme Court: c/o Government Offices, Christmas Island 6798, Indian Ocean; tel. 8501; telex 78001; Judges (non-resident): ROBERT SHERATON FRENCH, MALCOLM CAMERON LEE.

Religion

According to the census of 1981, of the 2,871 residents of Christmas Island, 36%, or 1,036, were Buddhists, 25%, or 730, were Muslims, and 18%, or 514, were Christians. Within the Christian churches, Christmas Island lies in the jurisdiction of both the Anglican and Roman Catholic Archbishops of Perth, in Western Australia.

Radio and Television

There were an estimated 2,500 radio receivers in use in 1985.

Christmas Island Broadcasting: Christmas Island 6798, Indian Ocean; tel. 8316; telex 78002; f. 1967; owned and operated by the Christmas Island Services Corporation; daily broadcasting service by Radio VLU-2 on 1422 KHz, in English, Malay, Cantonese and Mandarin; Station Man. TERRY WHITE.

Christmas Island Television: Christmas Island 6798, Indian Ocean; tel. 8315; fax 8127; Station Man. BARRIE FULLARD.

Trade and Industry

Phosphate Mining Corporation of Christmas Island (PMCI), formerly the principal employer on the island, ceased mining activities at the end of 1987.

Christmas Island Services Corpn: Christmas Island 6798, Indian Ocean; f. 1984; statutory corpn; provides local govt services; Chair. The Administrator.

Christmas Island Workers' Union: Christmas Island 6798, Indian Ocean; formerly represented phosphate workers.

Transport

In 1987 railway lines, with a total length of 24 km, served the island's phosphate mines. There are good roads in the developed areas. Australian government charter aircraft operate a weekly service from Perth via the Cocos (Keeling) Islands. The Australian National Line operates ships to the Australian mainland. In 1987 the Phosphate Mining Corporation of Christmas Island operated a cargo-shipping service to Singapore and shipped phosphate to Australia and New Zealand, and to Malaysian and other Asian ports. It also operated weekly flights from Singapore to Christmas Island.

COCOS (KEELING) ISLANDS

Introduction

The Cocos (Keeling) Islands are 27 in number and lie 2,768 km north-west of Perth, in the Indian Ocean. The islands form two low-lying coral atolls, densely covered with coconut palms. The climate is equable, with temperatures varying from 19°C (68°F) to 31°C (88°F), and rainfall of 2,000 mm per year. In 1981 some 58% of the population were of the Cocos Malay community, and 26% were Europeans. The Cocos Malays are descendants of the people brought to the islands by Alexander Hare and of labourers who were subsequently introduced by the Clunies-Ross family (see below). English is the official language, but Cocos Malay and Malay are also widely spoken. Most of the inhabitants are Muslims (56.8% in 1981). Home Island is where the Cocos Malay community is based. The only other inhabited island is West Island, where most of the European community lives, the administration is based and the airport is located.

The islands were uninhabited when discovered by Capt. William Keeling of the British East India Company, in 1609, and the first settlement was not established until 1826, by Alexander Hare. The islands were declared a British possession in 1857 and came successively under the authority of the Governors of Ceylon (now Sri Lanka), from 1878, and the Straits Settlements (now Singapore and part of Malaysia), from 1886. Also in 1886 the British Crown granted all land on the islands above the high-water mark to John Clunies-Ross and his heirs and successors in perpetuity. In 1946, when the islands became a dependency of the Colony of Singapore, a resident Administrator, responsible to the Governor of Singapore, was appointed. Administration of the islands was transferred to the Commonwealth of Australia on 23 November 1955. The agent of the Australian Government was known as the Official Representative until 1975, when an Administrator was appointed. The Minister of Territories is responsible for the governance of the islands.

In June 1977 the Australian Government announced new policies concerning the islands, which resulted in its purchase from John Clunies-Ross of the whole of his interests in the islands, with the exception of his residence and associated buildings. The purchase took effect on 1 September 1978. An attempt by the Australian Government to acquire Clunies-Ross' remaining property was deemed by the Australian High Court in October 1984 to be unconstitutional.

In July 1979 the Cocos (Keeling) Islands Council was established, with a wide range of functions in the Home Island village area (which the Government has transferred to the Council on trust for the benefit of the Cocos Malay community) and, since September 1984, in the greater part of the rest of the Territory.

On 6 April 1984 a referendum to decide the future political status of the islands was held by the Australian Government, with United Nations observers present. A large majority voted in favour of integration with Australia. As a result, the islanders were to acquire the rights, privileges and obligations of all Australian citizens. The powers and functions of the Islands Council were to be expanded to give it greater responsibility, and the inhabitants of the Territory were to have full voting rights in elections to the Australian Parliament.

Although local fishing is good, some livestock is kept and domestic gardens provide vegetables, bananas and pawpaws, the islands are not self-sufficient, and other foodstuffs, fuels and consumer items are imported from mainland Australia. A Cocos postal service (including a philatelic bureau) came into operation in September 1979, and revenue from the service is used for the benefit of the community.

Coconuts, grown throughout the islands, are the sole cash crop: total output was an estimated 5,000 metric tons in 1984, and total exports in 1984/85 were 202 metric tons.

Primary education is provided at the schools on Home and West Islands. Secondary education is provided to the age of 10 years on West Island. A bursary scheme enables Cocos Malay children to continue their education on the Australian mainland.

Statistical Survey

AREA AND POPULATION

Area: 14.2 sq km (5.5 sq miles).
Population: 555 (males 298, females 257) at census of 30 June 1981; 665 (Home Island residents 414, West Island residents 218) at mid-1988. *Ethnic Groups* (1981): Cocos Malay 320, European 143, Total (incl. others) 555. Source: UN, *Demographic Yearbook*.
Density: (1988): 46.8 per sq km.
Births and Deaths (1986): Registered live births 12; Registered deaths 2.

AGRICULTURE

Production (estimate, metric tons, 1984): Coconuts 5,000.

FINANCE

Currency and Exchange Rates: Australian currency is used (see p. 380).

EXTERNAL TRADE

Principal Commodities (metric tons, year ending 30 June 1985): *Exports*: Coconuts 202. *Imports*: Most requirements come from Australia. The trade deficit is offset by philatelic sales and Australian federal grants and subsidies.

Directory

The Government

An Administrator, appointed by the Governor-General of Australia and responsible to the Minister for Territories, is the senior government representative in the islands.
Administrator: A. D. LAWRIE.
Administrative Headquarters: West Island, Cocos (Keeling) Islands 6799, Indian Ocean.
Chairman of the Cocos (Keeling) Islands Council: Parson BIN YAPAT.

Judicial System

Supreme Court, Cocos (Keeling) Islands: Cocos (Keeling) Islands 6799, Indian Ocean; tel. 6660; telex 67002; Judge: ROBERT SHERATON FRENCH; Additional Judge: MALCOLM CAMERON LEE.
Magistrates' Court, Cocos (Keeling) Islands: Special Magistrate: KEN MOORE (non-resident).

Religion

According to the census of 1981, of the 555 residents, some 57%, or 314, were Muslims and 22%, or 124, Christians. The Cocos Islands lie within both the Anglican and the Roman Catholic archdioceses of Perth (Western Australia).

Radio

There were an estimated 250 radio receivers in use in 1985. There is no television service.
Radio VKW Cocos: POB 70, Cocos Islands 6799, Indian Ocean; tel. 0000, non-commercial; daily broadcasting service in Cocos Malay and English; Station Man. D. WILLIAMS; Programme Man. R. F. CAREY.

AUSTRALIAN EXTERNAL TERRITORIES   Cocos (Keeling) Islands, Norfolk Island

Industry

Cocos Islands Co-operative Society Ltd: Home Island, Cocos Islands, Indian Ocean; tel. 7598; telex 67001; f. 1979; conducts the business enterprises of the Cocos Islanders; activities include boat construction and repairs, copra and coconut production, sail-making, stevedoring; owns and operates a supermarket and a hostel; Chair. MEDOUS BIN BYNIE.

Transport

Australian government charter aircraft from Perth provide a weekly service for passengers, supplies and mail to and from the airport on West Island. Cargo vessels from Perth deliver supplies, at intervals of six to eight weeks.

NORFOLK ISLAND

Introductory Survey

Location, Climate, Language, Religion, Capital

Norfolk Island lies off the eastern coast of Australia, about 1,400 km east of Brisbane, to the south of New Caledonia and 640 km north of New Zealand. The Territory also comprises uninhabited Phillip Island, 7 km south of the main island. Norfolk Island is hilly and fertile, with a coastline of cliffs and an area of 34.6 sq km. It is about 8 km long and 4.8 km wide. The climate is mild and subtropical, and the average annual rainfall is 1,350 mm. The population consists of 'islanders' (descendants of the mutineers from HMS *Bounty*, evacuated from Pitcairn Island) and 'mainlanders' (originally from Australia, New Zealand or the United Kingdom). English is the official language, but a local Polynesian dialect (related to Pitcairnese) is also spoken. Most of the population adhere to the Christian religion. The capital of the Territory is Kingston.

Recent History and Economic Affairs

The island was uninhabited when discovered in 1774 by a British expedition, led by Capt. James Cook. Norfolk Island was used as a penal settlement from 1788 to 1814 and again from 1825 to 1855, when it was abandoned. In 1856 it was resettled by 194 emigrants from Pitcairn Island, which had become overpopulated. Norfolk Island was administered as a separate colony until 1897, when it became a dependency of New South Wales. In 1913 control was transferred to the Australian Government. Norfolk Island has a continuing dispute with the Australian Government concerning the island's status as a territory of the Commonwealth of Australia. There have been successive assertions of Norfolk Island's right to self-determination, as a distinct colony.

Under the Norfolk Island Act 1979, Norfolk Island is progressing to responsible legislative and executive government, enabling the Territory to administer its own affairs to the greatest practicable extent. Wide powers are exercised by the nine-member Legislative Assembly and by an Executive Council comprising the executive members of the Legislative Assembly who have ministerial-type responsibilities. The Act preserves the Australian Government's responsibility for Norfolk Island as a Territory under its authority, with the Minister for Territories and Local Government as the responsible minister. The Act indicated that consideration would be given within five years to an extension of the powers of the Legislative Assembly and the political and administrative institutions of Norfolk Island. In 1985 legislative and executive responsibility was assumed by the Norfolk Island Government for public works and services, civil defence, betting and gaming, territorial archives and matters relating to the exercise of executive authority. In 1988 further amendments empowered the Legislative Assembly to select a Norfolk Island Government Auditor (territorial accounts were previously audited by the Commonwealth Auditor-General). The office of Chief Minister was replaced by that of the President of the Legislative Assembly. David Ernest Buffett was appointed to this post following the May 1989 general election to the fifth Legislative Assembly, in which 16 candidates contested the nine seats.

In 1985 the gross domestic product of Norfolk Island was estimated to be some $A4m. (about US $2.8m.), equivalent to $A2,105 per person. Despite the island's natural fertility, agriculture is no longer the principal economic activity. About 400 ha of land are arable. The main crops are Kentia palm seed, cereals, vegetables and fruit. Some flowers and plants are grown commercially. The administration is increasing the area devoted to Norfolk Island pine and hardwoods. Seed of the Norfolk Island pine is exported.

The authorities receive revenue from customs duties and the sale of postage stamps, but tourism is the island's main industry. In 1988/89 there were 28,891 tourist arrivals on the island. In 1985 and 1986 the Governments of Australia and Norfolk Island jointly established the 465-ha Norfolk Island National Park. This was to protect the remaining native forest, which is the habitat of several unique species of flora (including the largest fern in the world) and fauna (such as the Norfolk Island green parrot and the guavabird). Conservation efforts include the development of Phillip Island as a nature reserve.

Education

Education is free and compulsory for all children between the ages of six and 15. Pupils attend the government school from infant to secondary level. Students wishing to follow higher education in Australia are eligible for bursaries and scholarships. The budgetary allocation for education was $A983,200 in 1988/89.

Weights and Measures

The metric system is in force.

Statistical Survey

AREA AND POPULATION

Area: 34.6 sq km (13.3 sq miles).

Population (census results): 2,175 (males 1,067; females 1,108) at 30 June 1981; 2,367 (males 1,170; females 1,197), including 390 visitors, at 30 June 1986.

Density (resident population, 1986): 57.2 per sq km.

Births and Deaths (1986): Live births 25 (birth rate 10.6 per 1,000); Deaths 15 (death rate 6.3 per 1,000).

Economically Active Population (persons aged 10 years and over, 1981 census): 985 (males 583; females 402).

FINANCE

Currency and Exchange Rates: Australian currency is used (see p. 380).

Budget (year ending 30 June 1990): Revenue $A5,659,000 (Customs duties $A2,005,000); Expenditure $A5,650,000 (Recurrent expenditure $A5,008,898).

Gross Domestic Product (estimate, 1985): $A2,105 per head.

EXTERNAL TRADE

1988/89 (year ending 30 June): *Imports*: $A23,114,221, mainly from Australia. *Exports*: $A2,827,860.

TOURISM

Visitors (year ending 30 June): 29,085 in 1987; 28,192 in 1988; 28,891 in 1989.

Directory

The Constitution

The Norfolk Island Act 1979 constitutes the administration of the Territory as a body politic and provides for a responsible legislative and executive system, enabling it to administer its own affairs to the greatest practicable extent. The preamble of the Act states that it is the intention of the Australian Parliament to consider the further extension of powers.

The Act provides for an Administrator, appointed by the Australian Government, who shall administer the government of Norfolk Island as a Territory under the authority of the Commonwealth of Australia. The Administrator is required to act on the advice of the Executive Council or the responsible Commonwealth Minister in those matters specified as within their competence. Every proposed law passed by the Legislative Assembly must be effected

AUSTRALIAN EXTERNAL TERRITORIES

by the assent of the Administrator, who may grant or withhold that assent, reserve the proposed law for the Governor-General's pleasure or recommend amendments.

The Act provides for a Legislative Assembly and an Executive Council, comprising the executive members of the Assembly who have ministerial-type responsibilities. Both bodies are led by the President of the Legislative Assembly. The nine members of the Legislative Assembly are elected for a term of not more than three years under a cumulative method of voting: each elector is entitled to as many votes (all of equal value) as there are vacancies, but may not give more than four votes to any one candidate. The nine candidates who receive the most votes are declared elected.

The Government

The Administrator, who is the senior representative of the Commonwealth Government, is appointed by the Governor-General of Australia and is responsible to the Minister for Territories. A form of responsible legislative and executive government was extended to the island in 1979, as outlined above.

Administrator: H. B. MacDonald (assumed office in 1989).

EXECUTIVE COUNCIL
(November 1990)

President of the Legislative Assembly: David Ernest Buffett.
Deputy President: Rosemarie Gaye Evans.
Minister for Finance: Neville Charles Christian.
Minister for Immigration and Commerce: William Arthur Blucher.
Minister for Tourism: George Charles Smith.
Minister for Community Services: Ernest Christian.
Minister responsible for Health and Social Services: Alice Inez Buffett.

GOVERNMENT OFFICE

Administration of Norfolk Island: Administration Offices, Kingston, Norfolk Island 2899; tel. 2001; telex 30003; fax 3177; all govt depts; headed by Chief Administrative Officer.

Legislature
LEGISLATIVE ASSEMBLY

Nine candidates are elected for not more than three years. The most recent general election was held on 10 May 1989.

President: David Ernest Buffett.
Members: Rosemarie Gaye Evans (Deputy President), Neville Charles Christian, William Arthur Blucher, George Charles Smith, Alice Inez Buffett, Ernest Christian, John Terrence Brown, Cedric Newton Ion-Robinson.

Judicial System

Supreme Court of Norfolk Island: Kingston; appeals lie to the Federal Court of Australia.
Judges: Trevor Rees Morling (Chief Justice), Bryan Alan Beaumont.

Religion

The majority of the population professes Christianity (75%, according to the census of 1981), and most of the rest claim no religious adherence.

The Press

Norfolk Island Government Gazette: Kingston, Norfolk Island 2899; tel. 2001; telex 30003; fax 3177; weekly.

Norfolk Island

Norfolk Islander: 'Greenways Press', POB 150, Norfolk Island 2899; tel. 2159; f. 1965; weekly; Co-Editors Tom Lloyd, Tim Lloyd; circ. 1,300.

Radio and Television

There were an estimated 1,500 radio receivers and 900 television receivers in use in 1990.

Norfolk Island Broadcasting Service: New Cascade Rd, Norfolk Island 2899; tel. 2137; fax 2499; govt-owned; non-commercial; broadcasts 112 hours per week; Broadcasting Officer Kathy M. LeCren.

Norfolk Island Television Service: f. 1987; programmes of Australian Broadcasting Corpn, relayed by satellite.

Finance
BANKING

Commonwealth Banking Corpn (Australia): Kingston, Norfolk Island 2899; telex 32011.

Westpac Banking Corpn Savings Bank Ltd (Australia): Kingston, Norfolk Island 2899.

Trade

Norfolk Island Chamber of Commerce: POB 370, Norfolk Island 2899; f. 1966; affiliated to the Australian Chamber of Commerce; 60 mems; Pres. Ian Andersen; Sec. Ray Brennan.

Transport
ROADS

There are about 80 km of roads, including 53 km of sealed road.

SHIPPING

The Compagnie des Chargeurs Calédoniens operates cargo services from Sydney, Australia, and Auckland, New Zealand. A small tanker from Nouméa (New Caledonia) delivers petroleum products to the island and another from Australia delivers liquid propane gas. Sofrana Unilines and the South Pacific Shipping Co also operate vessels on these routes.

CIVIL AVIATION

Norfolk Island has one airport, with two runways (of 1,900 m and 1,550 m), capable of taking medium jet aircraft. Ansett NSW (Australia) resumed services between Norfolk Island and Australia in 1990, with five flights per week from Sydney and two per week from Brisbane.

Norfolk Airlines: National Bank House, cnr Adelaide and Creek Sts, POB 905, Brisbane, Qld 4001, Australia; tel. 229-5872; fax 229-1920; f. 1973; operates regular flights from Brisbane and Sydney to Lord Howe Island (a dependency of New South Wales) and Norfolk Island, and charters throughout Australia and the South Pacific; Man. Dir John Brown; Gen. Man. Judy Jarvis; fleet of 30 aircraft, including Beechcraft Super King Air 200s and 1 Boeing Dash-8.

Tourism

Norfolk Island Government Tourist Board: Burnt Pine, POB 211, Norfolk Island 2899; tel. 2147; telex 32010; fax 3109; Chair. K. Nobbs.

Norfolk Island Government Visitors' Information Bureau: Burnt Pine, POB 211, Norfolk Island 2899; tel. 2147; fax 3109; CEO Lisle Snell.

OTHER TERRITORIES

Ashmore and Cartier Islands

The Ashmore Islands (known as West, Middle and East Islands) and Cartier Island are situated in the Timor Sea, about 850 km and 790 km west of Darwin respectively. The islands are small and uninhabited, consisting of sand and coral, surrounded by shoals and reefs. Grass is the main vegetation. Maximum elevation is about 2.5 m above sea-level. The islands abound in sea-cucumbers (*bêches-de-mer*) and, seasonally, turtles.

The United Kingdom took formal possession of the Ashmore Islands in 1878, and Cartier Island was annexed in 1909. The islands were placed under the authority of the Commonwealth of Australia in 1931. They were annexed to, and deemed to form part of, the Northern Territory of Australia in 1938. On 1 July 1978 the Australian Government assumed direct responsibility for the administration of the islands, which rests with the Minister for Territories. Periodic visits are made to the islands by the Royal Australian Navy and aircraft of the Royal Australian Air Force, and the Civil Coastal Surveillance Service makes aerial surveys of the islands and neighbouring waters.

The area is thought to hold good prospects for petroleum exploration. In August 1983 Ashmore Reef was declared a national nature reserve, in recognition of its environmental significance. An agreement between Australia and Indonesia permits Indonesian traditional fishermen to continue fishing in these territorial waters and permits them to land on West Island for fresh water. In 1985 the Australian Government extended the laws of the Northern Territory to apply in Ashmore and Cartier, and decided to station caretakers there during the Indonesian fishing season (March–November), to monitor the fishermen and to perform other tasks.

Australian Antarctic Territory

The Australian Antarctic Territory was established by Order in Council in February 1933 and proclaimed in August 1936, subsequent to the Australian Antarctic Territory Acceptance Act (1933). It consists of the portion of Antarctica (divided by the French territory of Adélie Land) lying between 45°E and 136°E, and between 142°E and 160°E. The Australian National Antarctic Research Expeditions (ANARE) maintains three permanent scientific stations, Mawson, Davis and Casey, in the territory. The area of the territory is estimated to be 6,043,728 sq km (2,333,496 sq miles), and there are no permanent inhabitants, although there is a permanent presence of scientific personnel. The Minister of Territories is responsible. Australia is a signatory of the Antarctic Treaty (see p. 345).

Coral Sea Islands Territory

The Coral Sea Islands became a Territory of the Commonwealth of Australia under the Coral Sea Islands Act of 1969. It comprises several islands and reefs east of Queensland between the Great Barrier Reef and longitude 156° 06′E, and between latitude 12° and 24°S. The islands are composed largely of sand and coral, and have no permanent fresh water supply, but some have a cover of grass and scrub. The area has been known as a notorious hazard to shipping since the 19th century, the danger of the reefs being compounded by shifting sand cays and occasional tropical cyclones. The Coral Sea Islands have been acquired by Australia by numerous acts of sovereignty since the early years of the 20th century.

Spread over a sea area of approximately 780,000 sq km (300,000 sq miles), all the islands and reefs in the Territory are very small, totalling only a few sq km of land area. They include Cato Island, Chilcott Islet in the Coringa Group, and the Willis Group. A meteorological station, operated by the Commonwealth Bureau of Meteorology and with a staff of three, has provided a service on one of the Willis Group since 1921. The other islands are uninhabited. There are nine automatic weather stations and several navigation aids distributed throughout the Territory.

The Act constituting the Territory did not establish an administration on the islands but provides means of controlling the activities of those who visit them. The Lihou Reef and Coringa-Herald National Nature Reserves were established in 1982 to provide protection for the wide variety of terrestrial and marine wildlife, which include rare species of birds and sea turtles (one of which is the largest, and among the most endangered, of the world's species of sea turtle). The Australian Government has concluded agreements for the protection of endangered and migratory birds with Japan and the People's Republic of China. The increasing range and scope of international fishing enterprises made desirable an administrative framework and system of law. The Governor-General of Australia is empowered to make ordinances for the peace, order and good government of the Territory and, by ordinance, the laws of the Australian Capital Territory apply. The Supreme Court and Court of Petty Sessions of Norfolk Island have jurisdiction in relation to the Territory. The Minister for Territories is responsible for matters affecting the Territory, and the area is visited regularly by the Royal Australian Navy.

Heard Island and McDonald Islands

These islands are situated about 4,000 km (2,500 miles) south-west of Perth, Western Australia. The Territory consists of Heard Island, Shag Island (8 km north of Heard) and the McDonald Islands, is almost entirely covered in ice and has a total area of 417 sq km (161 sq miles). The Territory has been administered by the Australian Government since December 1947, when it established a scientific research station on Heard Island (which functioned until 1955) and the United Kingdom ceded its claim to sovereignty. There are no permanent inhabitants, but Australian expeditions visit from time to time. Heard Island is about 44 km (27 miles) long and 20 km (12 miles) wide. In January 1991 a US scientific project, centred on Heard Island, was scheduled to commence. The experiment involved the transmission of sound waves, beneath the surface of the ocean, in order to monitor any evidence of the 'greenhouse effect' (melting of polar ice and the rise in sea-level as a consequence of pollution). The pulses of sound, which travel at a speed largely influenced by temperature, will be received at various places around the world, with international co-operation. The McDonald Islands, with an area of about 1 sq km (0.4 sq mile), lie some 42 km (26 miles) west of Heard Island. The islands are administered by the Department of Science.

AUSTRIA

Introductory Survey

Location, Climate, Language, Religion, Flag, Capital

The Republic of Austria lies in central Europe, bordered by Switzerland and Liechtenstein to the west, by Germany and Czechoslovakia to the north, by Hungary to the east, and by Italy and Yugoslavia to the south. The climate varies sharply, owing to great differences in elevation. The mean annual temperature lies between 7° and 9°C (45° and 48°F). The population is 99% German-speaking, with small Croat and Slovene-speaking minorities. Almost all of the inhabitants profess Christianity: about 89% are Roman Catholics, while about 6% are Protestants. The national flag (proportions 3 by 2) consists of three equal horizontal stripes, of red, white and red. The state flag has, in addition, the coat of arms (a small shield, with horizontal stripes of red separated by a white stripe, superimposed on a black eagle, wearing a golden crown and holding a sickle and a hammer in its feet, with a broken chain between the legs) in the centre. The capital is Vienna (Wien).

Recent History

Austria was formerly the centre of the Austrian (later Austro-Hungarian) Empire, which comprised a large part of central Europe. The Empire, under the Habsburg dynasty, was dissolved in 1918, at the end of the First World War, and Austria proper became a republic. The first post-war Council of Ministers was a coalition led by Dr Karl Renner, who remained Chancellor until 1920, when a new constitution introduced a federal form of government. Most of Austria's inhabitants favoured union with Germany but this was forbidden by the post-war peace treaties. In March 1938, however, Austria was occupied by Nazi Germany's armed forces and incorporated into the German Reich.

After liberation by Allied forces, a provisional government, under Dr Renner, was established in April 1945. In July, following Germany's surrender, Austria was divided into four zones, occupied by forces of the USA, the USSR, the United Kingdom and France. These four approved the first post-war elections, held in November 1945, when the conservative Österreichische Volkspartei (ÖVP, Austrian People's Party) won 85, and the Sozialistische Partei Österreichs (SPÖ, Socialist Party of Austria) 76, of the 165 seats in the Nationalrat (National Council). These two parties formed a coalition government. In December Dr Renner became the first President of the second Austrian Republic, holding office until his death in December 1950. However, it was not until May 1955 that the four powers signed a State Treaty with Austria, ending the occupation and recognizing Austrian independence, effective from 27 July. Occupation forces left in October 1955.

More than 20 years of coalition government came to an end in April 1966 with the formation of a Council of Ministers by the ÖVP alone. Dr Josef Klaus, the Federal Chancellor since April 1964, remained in office. Dr Bruno Kreisky, a former Minister of Foreign Affairs, was elected leader of the SPÖ in 1967. The SPÖ achieved a relative majority in the March 1970 general election and formed a minority government, with Kreisky as Chancellor. In April 1971 the incumbent President, Franz Jonas of the SPÖ, was re-elected, defeating the ÖVP candidate, Dr Kurt Waldheim, a former Minister of Foreign Affairs (who subsequently served two five-year terms as UN Secretary-General, beginning in January 1972). The SPÖ won an absolute majority of seats in the Nationalrat at general elections in October 1971 and October 1975. Meanwhile, President Jonas died in April 1974. A presidential election, held in June, was won by Dr Rudolf Kirchschläger, who had been Minister of Foreign Affairs since 1970. He took office for a six-year term, and was re-elected in 1980.

In November 1978 the Government was defeated in a national referendum on whether to commission Austria's first nuclear power plant, and it was widely expected that Kreisky would resign. However, the SPÖ gave him its full support and he emerged in an apparently even stronger position. The possible use of nuclear power remains a controversial issue. At the general election in May 1979 the SPÖ increased its majority in the Nationalrat. In January 1981 Kreisky announced a government reshuffle, following the resignation of the Vice-Chancellor and Minister of Finance, Hannes Androsch, who had been criticized for his personal financial practices. (In January 1988 Androsch was found guilty of making false statements concerning his financial affairs, and was forced to resign from his post as director of a major bank.)

The general election of April 1983 marked the end of the 13-year era of one-party government, when the SPÖ lost its absolute majority in the Nationalrat, and Kreisky, unwilling to participate in a coalition government, resigned as Chancellor. The reduction in the SPÖ's representation was partly attributed to the emergence of two environmentalist 'Green' parties, both founded in 1982. The two parties together received more than 3% of the total votes, but failed to win any seats. Kreisky's successor, Dr Fred Sinowatz (the former Vice-Chancellor and Minister of Education), took office in May, leading a coalition of the SPÖ and the small liberal Freiheitliche Partei Österreichs (FPÖ, Freedom Party of Austria). The new Government continued the social welfare policy of its predecessor, also maintaining Austria's foreign policy of 'active neutrality'.

A presidential election was held in 1986, when Dr Kirchschläger retired after two six-year terms of office as Head of State. The SPÖ candidate for the election was Dr Kurt Steyrer (the Minister of Health and Environment), while Dr Waldheim, the former UN Secretary-General, stood as an independent candidate but with the support of the ÖVP. There were also two other candidates: Freda Meissner-Blau, an environmentalist, and Otto Scrinzi, a right-wing nationalist. The campaign was dominated by allegations that Waldheim, a former officer in the army of Nazi Germany, had been implicated in atrocities committed by the Nazis in the Balkans in 1942-45, provoking a bitter controversy which divided the country and brought unexpected international attention to the election. No candidate achieved the required 50% of the vote at the first ballot on 4 May (Waldheim received 49.65% of the votes cast, while Steyrer received 43.67%); a second 'run-off' ballot between the two principal candidates was therefore held on 8 June. Waldheim then won a clear victory, with 53.89% of the votes, compared with Steyrer's 46.11%. After the defeat of the SPÖ presidential candidate, Chancellor Sinowatz and four of his ministers resigned. Dr Franz Vranitzky, who had been Minister of Finance, became the new Chancellor, and replaced several ministers. In September the ruling coalition collapsed, when the FPÖ elected a new leader, Jörg Haider, who represented the right wing of his party. This precipitated the end of the partnership between the SPÖ and the FPÖ, and the general election for the Nationalrat, scheduled for April 1987, was brought forward to 23 November 1986. At the election no party won an absolute majority: the SPÖ won 80 seats, the ÖVP 77, the FPÖ 18 and the alliance of 'Green' parties 8. Dr Vranitzky tendered his resignation on 25 November, but was immediately requested by President Waldheim to initiate negotiations on the formation of a new coalition. The preceding Government remained in power while these negotiations took place. On 25 January 1987 the formation of a 'grand coalition' of the SPÖ and the ÖVP was announced.

The election to the presidency of Waldheim, who took office in July 1986, drew criticism from some foreign governments, and relations with Israel and the USA, in particular, were severely strained. Waldheim's presidency has remained controversial, both at home and abroad, and since his election he has been ostracized by large sections of the international community. In February 1988 a specially-appointed international commission of historians concluded that Waldheim must have been aware of the atrocities that had been committed, but the President refused to resign, despite a substantial decline in his popular support within the country. The issue inevitably provoked divisions within the ruling coalition, and ceremonies commemorating the 50th anniversary of the occupation by Nazi Germany, held in March 1988, brought renewed attention to the question. A report by the British Ministry of

Defence, published in October 1989, absolved Waldheim of any criminal involvement in the execution of seven British commandos in the Balkans in 1944. In July 1990 Waldheim's international standing was enhanced somewhat by a meeting, in Salzburg, with Presidents Havel and von Weizsäcker of Czechoslovakia and the Federal Republic of Germany, respectively. In late August Waldheim achieved considerable domestic success, following a visit to Iraq, where he secured the release of nearly 100 Austrians who had been stranded there as a result of Iraq's invasion and forced annexation of Kuwait.

In January 1989 the Minister of the Interior, Karl Blecha, and the President of the Nationalrat, Leopold Gratz, resigned in connection with the so-called 'Lucona affair'—an insurance fraud surrounding the sinking of a cargo ship in the Indian Ocean in 1977, which resulted in six deaths. A special parliamentary committee of inquiry established that Blecha had tried to obstruct investigations into the affair, while Gratz had helped to release from prison those responsible for the fraud. A further scandal arose in July 1989, when it was revealed that the state-owned weapons industry had sold armaments to Iran in 1984–86, thus infringing Austria's neutrality law which bans the sale of military equipment to countries at war. The Ministry of Justice ordered an inquiry to establish whether the former Federal Chancellor, Dr Sinowatz, Blecha and Gratz had been involved. In September 1990 it was announced that the three men were to be charged with abuse of office in connection with the illegal sales.

In April 1989, seemingly in response to its disappointing performance at regional elections in Kärnten, Salzburg and Tirol in the previous month, the ÖVP reshuffled several of its members of the Council of Ministers. In the same month Alois Mock resigned as Vice-Chancellor (while retaining his post of Minister of Foreign Affairs) and was replaced by Josef Riegler, formerly Minister of Agriculture and Forestry. In May Riegler was elected the new Chairman of the ÖVP, replacing Mock.

At the next general election, held in early October 1990, the SPÖ retained its majority, receiving 42.79% of the votes and increasing its number of seats in the Nationalrat by one, to 81 seats. The ÖVP, however, suffered a major electoral set-back: with 32.06% of the votes, it obtained 60 seats in the Nationalrat, a loss of 17. The FPÖ (which had made significant gains in regional elections during 1989 and early 1990) received 16.64% of the votes, increasing its representation in the Nationalrat by 15 seats, to 33. The FPÖ's success was attributed, in large part, to its support of restricted immigration, especially from Eastern Europe. The alliance of environmentalist parties, the Green Alternative List (GAL), increased its number of seats by one, to nine seats. The SPÖ and the ÖVP began discussions on the formation of a new coalition government; a new Council of Ministers was expected to be announced in December 1990.

Government

Austria is a federal republic, divided into nine provinces, each with its own provincial assembly and government. Legislative power is held by the bicameral Federal Assembly. The first chamber, the Nationalrat (National Council), has 183 members, elected by universal adult suffrage for four years (subject to dissolution) on the basis of proportional representation. The second chamber, the Bundesrat (Federal Council), has 63 members, elected for varying terms by the provincial assemblies. The Federal President, elected by popular vote for six years, is the Head of State, and normally acts on the advice of the Council of Ministers, led by the Federal Chancellor, which is responsible to the Nationalrat.

Defence

After the ratification of the State Treaty in 1955, Austria declared its permanent neutrality. To protect its independence, the armed forces were instituted. Military service is compulsory and consists of six months' initial training, followed by a maximum of 60 days' reservist training and 30 to 90 days' specialist training each year for 15 years. In June 1990 the total armed forces numbered 42,500 (including 22,300 conscripts), comprising an army of 38,000 (20,000 conscripts) and an air force of 4,500 (2,300 conscripts). Austrian air units are an integral part of the army. Total reserves are 242,000, of whom 80,000 undergo refresher training each year. The defence budget for 1990 amounted to 19,250m. Schilling.

Economic Affairs

In 1988, according to estimates by the World Bank, Austria's gross national product (GNP), measured at average 1986–88 prices, was US $117,644m., equivalent to $15,560 per head. Both overall GNP and GNP per head increased, in real terms, by an average of 1.7% per year between 1980 and 1988. Over the same period, the population increased by only 0.6%. Austria's gross domestic product (GDP) increased, in real terms, by an annual average of 1.7% in 1980–88 and by 3.8% in 1989.

The contribution of agriculture (including hunting, forestry and fishing) to GDP was 3.2% in 1989. In that year 7.8% of the labour force were employed in agriculture. Austrian farms produce more than 90% of the country's food requirements, and surplus dairy products are exported. The principal crops are wheat, barley, maize and sugar beet. During 1980–88 agricultural production increased by an annual average of 0.7%.

Industry (including mining and quarrying, manufacturing, construction and power) employed 37.0% of the labour force, and contributed 38.3% of GDP, in 1989. During 1980–88 industrial production increased by an annual average of 1.1%.

Mining and quarrying contributed 0.3% of GDP, and employed 0.4% of the labour force, in 1989. The most important indigenous mineral resource is iron ore (2.4m. metric tons, with an iron content of 31%, were mined in 1989). Austria also has deposits of petroleum, lignite, magnesite, lead and some copper.

Manufacturing contributed 27.8% of GDP, and employed 27.1% of the labour force, in 1989. Measured by the value of output, the principal branches of manufacturing in 1986 were machinery (accounting for 20.3% of the total), metals and metal products (14.7%), food products (12.7%), wood and paper products (10.0%) and chemical products (8.5%). Between 1980 and 1988 the manufacturing sector increased its production by an average annual rate of 1.6%.

Power supplies in Austria are provided by petroleum, natural gas, coal and hydroelectric plants. Hydroelectric power resources provide the major domestic source of energy, accounting for 71% of total electricity production in 1986. Austria is heavily dependent on imports of energy, mainly from the Eastern bloc.

In 1988, 13.5% of the labour force were employed in commerce (including storage), 6.3% in transport and communications, and 34.4% in other services. Tourism is a leading source of revenue, providing receipts of 120,200m. Schilling in 1988.

In 1989 Austria recorded a visible trade deficit of US $7,363m., while the current account of the balance of payments showed a deficit of $94m. Much of Austria's trade is conducted with member countries of the EEC (see p. 135), which accounted for 68.0% of Austria's imports and 64.0% of exports in 1988. In 1989 the principal source of imports (43.6%) was the Federal Republic of Germany (West Germany), which was also the principal market for exports (34.5%). Austria's level of trading with members of the Council for Mutual Economic Assistance (CMEA, see p. 125) is higher than that of most other Western countries (CMEA countries accounted for 6% of Austria's imports and 9% of exports in 1988).

The federal budget for 1989 envisaged revenue of 398,632m. Schilling and expenditure of 523,346m. Schilling. The average annual rate of inflation was 2.5% in 1989, when 5.0% of the labour force were unemployed.

Austria is a member of the European Free Trade Association (EFTA, see p. 154) and has a bilateral free trade agreement with the EEC. The Austrian Government recognized that, after the implementation of the EEC's single European market (planned for 1992), Austrian traders might suffer competitive disadvantages, and in 1989 it applied for full membership of the EEC. Negotiations for Austria's entry into the EEC were expected to begin before 1993.

During the 1980s the Government implemented a major restructuring of the state sector, permitting the sale of shares in some nationalized companies to private or foreign partners, although the ÖIAG, the state holding company (later restructured as Austrian Industries AG), was to maintain a controlling interest of at least 51%. The first partial privatization took place in 1987. In the late 1980s the Austrian economy showed strong growth. The increase in real GDP in 1988, at 4.2%, was the highest rate since 1979, and in 1989 the rate of growth of GDP decelerated only slightly, to 3.8%. Both increased exports and domestic demand contributed to this favourable trend.

Economic growth was also stimulated by the reform of the income-tax system in 1989. In the late 1980s the rates of inflation and unemployment were both below the European average.

Social Welfare

The social insurance system covers all wage-earners and salaried employees, agricultural and non-agricultural self-employed and dependants, regardless of nationality. The coverage is compulsory and provides earnings-related benefits in case of old age, invalidity, death, sickness, maternity and injuries at work. About 95% of the population are protected. There are separate programmes which provide unemployment insurance, family allowance, benefits for war victims, etc. In 1986 Austria had 79,083 hospital beds (one for every 96 inhabitants), and in 1987 there were 22,529 physicians working in the country. Of total expenditure by the central Government in 1988, about 79,860m. Schilling (12.8%) was for health services, while a further 279,720m. Schilling (44.8%) was for social security and welfare.

Education

The central controlling body is the Federal Ministry of Education, the Arts and Sport. Higher education and research are the responsibility of the Federal Ministry of Science and Research. Provincial boards (Landesschulräte) supervise school education in each of the nine federal provinces. Expenditure on education by the central Government in 1988 was about 58,120m. Schilling (9.3% of total spending).

Education is free and compulsory between the ages of six and 15 years. All children undergo four years' primary education at a Volksschule, after which they choose between two principal forms of secondary education. This may be a Hauptschule which, after four years, may be followed by one of a variety of schools offering technical, vocational and other specialized training, some of which provide a qualification for university. Alternatively, secondary education may be obtained in an Allgemeinbildende höhere Schule, which provides an eight-year general education covering a wide range of subjects, culminating in the Reifeprüfung or Matura. This gives access to all Austrian universities. Since 1977/78, however, all Austrian citizens over the age of 24, and with professional experience, may attend certain university courses in connection with their professional career or trade.

Opportunities for further education exist in six universities as well as 14 specialist colleges, all of which have university status, and schools of technology, art and music. Institutes of adult education (Volkshochschulen) are found in all provinces, as are other centres run by public authorities, church organizations and the Austrian Trade Union Federation.

Public Holidays

1991: 1 January (New Year's Day), 6 January (Epiphany), 1 April (Easter Monday), 1 May (Labour Day), 9 May (Ascension Day), 20 May (Whit Monday), 30 May (Corpus Christi), 15 August (Assumption), 26 October (National Holiday), 1 November (All Saints' Day), 8 December (Immaculate Conception), 25 December (Christmas Day), 26 December (St Stephen's Day).

1992: 1 January (New Year's Day), 6 January (Epiphany), 20 April (Easter Monday), 1 May (Labour Day), 28 May (Ascension Day), 8 June (Whit Monday), 18 June (Corpus Christi), 15 August (Assumption), 26 October (National Holiday), 1 November (All Saints' Day), 8 December (Immaculate Conception), 25 December (Christmas Day), 26 December (St Stephen's Day).

Weights and Measures

The metric system is in force.

Statistical Survey

Source (unless otherwise stated): Austrian Central Statistical Office, 1033 Vienna, Hintere Zollamtsstr. 2B; tel. (01) 711-28; telex 132600; fax (01) 711-28-77-28.

Area and Population

AREA, POPULATION AND DENSITY

Area (sq km)	83,857*
Population (census results)	
12 May 1971	7,491,526†
12 May 1981‡	
Males	3,572,426
Females	3,982,912
Total	7,555,338
Population (official estimates at mid-year)‡	
1987	7,564,668
1988	7,595,358
1989	7,617,779
Density (per sq km) at mid-1989	90.8

* 32,377 sq miles.
† Total includes foreign workers with families abroad.
‡ Figures include all foreign workers.

PROVINCES

	Area (sq km)	Population (1989 annual average)	Density (per sq km)	Provincial Capital (with 1981 population)
Burgenland	3,965.5	267,200	67.4	Eisenstadt (10,102)
Kärnten (Carinthia)	9,533.1	542,300	56.9	Klagenfurt (87,321)
Niederösterreich (Lower Austria)	19,173.7	1,430,200	74.9	Sankt Pölten (50,419)*
Oberösterreich (Upper Austria)	11,979.8	1,306,600	109.1	Linz (199,910)
Salzburg	7,154.3	468,400	65.5	Salzburg (139,426)
Steiermark (Styria)	16,387.2	1,180,400	72.0	Graz (243,166)
Tirol (Tyrol)	12,647.2	619,600	49.0	Innsbruck (117,287)
Vorarlberg	2,601.4	321,400	123.5	Bregenz (24,561)
Wien (Vienna)*	414.9	1,487,600	3,585.4	—
Total	**83,857.1**	**7,623,600**	**90.9**	—

* Vienna, the national capital, has separate provincial status. The area and population of the city are not included in the province of Lower Austria, which is also administered from Vienna, pending the completion of provincial government buildings at Sankt Pölten, which became the provincial capital on 10 July 1986.

AUSTRIA

PRINCIPAL TOWNS (population at 1981 census)

Vienna (capital) 1,531,346	Klagenfurt 87,321
Graz 243,166	Villach 52,692
Linz 199,910	Wels 51,060
Salzburg 139,426	Sankt Pölten 50,419
Innsbruck 117,287	Steyr 38,942

BIRTHS, MARRIAGES AND DEATHS

	Registered live births		Registered marriages		Registered deaths	
	Number	Rate (per 1,000)	Number	Rate (per 1,000)	Number	Rate (per 1,000)
1982	94,840	12.5	47,643	6.3	91,339	12.1
1983	90,118	11.9	56,171	7.4	93,041	12.3
1984	89,234	11.8	45,823	6.1	88,466	11.7
1985	87,440	11.6	44,867	5.9	89,578	11.9
1986	86,964	11.5	45,821	6.1	87,071	11.5
1987	86,503	11.4	76,205	10.1	84,907	11.2
1988	88,052	11.6	35,361	4.7	83,263	11.0
1989	88,759	11.6	42,523	5.6	83,407	10.9

Expectation of life at birth: Males 72.1 years; females 78.8 years (1989).

ECONOMICALLY ACTIVE POPULATION
('000 persons, 1989 average*)

	Males	Females	Total
Agriculture, forestry, hunting and fishing	142	126	268
Mining and quarrying	12	1	13
Manufacturing	683	253	936
Construction	269	21	290
Electricity, gas, water and sanitary services	35	7	42
Commerce (incl. storage)	197	269	466
Transport and communications	174	44	218
Services	525	664	1,189
Other activities (not adequately described)	11	22	33
Total	**2,048**	**1,407**	**3,455**

* Yearly average based on the results of quarterly sample surveys.

Agriculture

PRINCIPAL CROPS ('000 metric tons)

	1987	1988	1989
Wheat	1,450	1,560.0	1,363.0
Barley	1,179	1,366.4	1,421.6
Maize	1,685	1,700.4	1,491.3
Rye	309	355.9	381.2
Oats	245	273.1	249.1
Mixed grain	85	103.5	103.0
Potatoes	879	1,001.0	845.5
Sugar beet	2,128	1,933.7	2,640.8
Apples	264	413.0	321.3
Pears	106	189.4	133.3
Plums	51	85.9	81.7
Cherries	21	17.3	26.7
Currants	26	30.3	30.7

Grapes ('000 metric tons): 310 (unofficial estimate) in 1987; 480 (FAO estimate) in 1988; 280 (FAO estimate) in 1989 (Source: FAO, *Quarterly Bulletin of Statistics*).

LIVESTOCK ('000 head at December)

	1987	1988	1989
Horses	45.2	44.4	47.9
Cattle	2,590.0	2,541.4	2,562.4
Pigs	3,947.0	2,873.9	3,772.7
Sheep	261.0	255.6	288.9
Goats	33.5	32.3	36.4
Chickens	14,503.8	13,589.5	14,145.1
Ducks	130.0	130.9	115.3
Geese	25.2	21.2	26.4
Turkeys	377.0	407.5	484.8

LIVESTOCK PRODUCTS ('000 metric tons)

	1987	1988	1989
Milk	3,724.5	3,353.5	3,351.2
Butter	41.0	42.5	40.0
Cheese	78.0	84.5	88.0
Hen eggs*	1,817.5	1,757.0	1,695.3
Beef	220.0	208.5	198.5
Veal	17.5	16.0	14.5
Pig meats	361.5	398.5	403.5
Poultry meat	84.0	84.0	84.0

* Millions.

Forestry

ROUNDWOOD REMOVALS
('000 cubic metres, excluding bark)

	1987	1988	1989
Sawlogs, veneer logs and logs for sleepers	6,688	7,340	8,245
Pitprops (mine timber), pulpwood, and other industrial wood	2,568	2,702	2,901
Fuel wood	2,504	2,734	2,676
Total	**11,760**	**12,776**	**13,822**

SAWNWOOD PRODUCTION ('000 cubic metres)

	1987	1988	1989
Coniferous sawnwood*	5,686	6,211	6,634
Broadleaved sawnwood*	199	211	234
Sub-total	**5,885**	**6,422**	**6,868**
Railway sleepers	24	18	17
Total	**5,909**	**6,440**	**6,885**

* Including boxboards.

AUSTRIA

Mining

('000 metric tons, unless otherwise indicated)

	1987	1988	1989
Brown coal (incl. lignite)	2,790	2,129	2,066
Crude petroleum	1,063	1,175	1,158
Iron ore:			
gross weight	3,050	2,300	2,410
metal content	949	722	757
Magnesite (crude)	947	1,122	1,205
Salt (unrefined)	703	708	686
Antimony ore (metric tons)*	399	270	412
Lead ore (metric tons)*	6,437	3,315	2,345
Zinc ore (metric tons)*	16,983	19,134	16,139
Graphite (natural)	39	8	15
Gypsum (crude)	665	722	806
Kaolin	445	500	482
Talc	130	133	133
Natural gas (million cu metres)	1,167	1,265	1,323

* Figures refer to the metal content of ores.

Tungsten ore: 1,250 metric tons (estimated metal content) in 1987 (Source: UN, *Industrial Statistics Yearbook*).

Industry

SELECTED PRODUCTS

('000 metric tons, unless otherwise indicated)

	1987	1988	1989
Wheat flour	351	354	366
Raw sugar	359	327	423
Margarine (metric tons)	46,977	46,970	49,104
Wine ('000 hectolitres)	2,183.6	3,502.5	2,580.9
Beer ('000 hectolitres)	8,640	8,938	9,174
Cigarettes (million)	15,100	14,324	14,402
Cotton yarn—pure and mixed (metric tons)	18,362	16,743	15,736
Woven cotton fabrics—pure and mixed (metric tons)	14,299	13,693	13,855
Wool yarn—pure and mixed (metric tons)	7,367	7,340	7,740
Woven woollen fabrics—pure and mixed (metric tons)	3,652	3,236	2,684
Mechanical wood pulp	192	276	299
Chemical and semi-chemical wood pulp	1,141	1,180	1,204
Newsprint	246	252	255
Other printing and writing paper	989	1,204	1,268
Other paper	755	803	836
Paperboard	392	391	395
Nitrogenous fertilizers (metric tons)[1]	194,000	249,600	222,000
Phosphate fertilizers (metric tons)[1]	109,300	105,000	110,000
Plastics and resins	743	861	919
Liquefied petroleum gas	72	47	40
Motor spirit (petrol)[2]	2,325	2,379	2,386
Kerosene	4	9	13
Jet fuel	196	220	287
Distillate fuel oils	2,536	2,452	2,550
Residual fuel oils	1,864	1,806	1,584
Lubricating oils	185	n.a.	n.a.
Petroleum bitumen (asphalt)	228	235	245
Coke-oven coke	1,727	1,744	1,771
Cement	4,520	4,763	4,981
Pig-iron (excl. ferro-alloys)	3,451	3,665	3,823
Crude steel	4,301	4,560	4,718
Aluminium—unwrought (metric tons): primary	93,414	95,494	92,933
secondary[3]	62,731	70,359	76,051
Refined copper—unwrought (metric tons): primary	3,855	3,551	7,178
secondary	29,070	34,829	39,089
—continued	1987	1988	1989
Refined lead—unwrought (metric tons): primary	6,809	8,316	9,370
secondary	16,032	16,731	14,648
Refined zinc—unwrought (metric tons): primary	18,282	18,970	20,791
secondary	1,467	1,758	1,339
Passenger motor cars (number)	6,958	7,261	6,638
Motorcycles, etc. (number)	55,737	23,099	16,352
Construction: new dwellings completed (number)	38,494	39,226	37,947
Electric energy (million kWh)	50,518	49,013	50,167
Manufactured gas (million cu metres): from gasworks	37	37	36
from cokeries	712	720	748

[1] Estimated production during 12 months ending 30 June of the year stated. Figures for nitrogenous fertilizers are in terms of nitrogen, and those for phosphate fertilizers are in terms of phosphoric acid. Source: FAO, *Quarterly Bulletin of Statistics*.
[2] Including aviation gasoline.
[3] Secondary aluminium produced from old scrap and remelted aluminium.

Finance

CURRENCY AND EXCHANGE RATES

Monetary Units
100 Groschen = 1 Schilling.

Denominations
Coins: 2, 5, 10 and 50 Groschen; 1, 5, 10, 20, 25, 50, 500 and 1,000 Schilling.
Notes: 20, 50, 100, 500, 1,000 and 5,000 Schilling.

Sterling and Dollar Equivalents (30 September 1990)
£1 sterling = 20.605 Schilling;
US $1 = 11.0125 Schilling;
1,000 Schilling = £48.53 = $90.81.

Average Exchange Rate (Schilling per US $)
1987 12.643
1988 12.348
1989 13.231

FEDERAL BUDGET (million Schilling)*

Revenue	1987	1988	1989
Direct taxes on income and wealth	114,834	141,202	141,947
Social security contributions —unemployment insurance	20,747	24,805	26,181
Indirect taxes	143,111	148,109	157,661
Current transfers	19,324	14,248	17,338
Sales and charges	12,494	13,078	13,939
Interest, shares of profit and other income	16,636	16,570	22,798
Sales of assets	6,713	3,928	11,504
Repayments of loans granted	529	504	560
Capital transfers	733	837	797
Borrowing	113,090	117,561	124,714
Other revenue	4,866	5,573	5,907
Total	**453,077**	**486,415**	**523,346**

AUSTRIA

Expenditure	1987	1988	1989
Current expenditure on goods and services	98,957	101,132	105,614
Interest on public debt	46,778	49,830	58,451
Current transfers to:			
Regional and local authorities	34,675	35,386	36,295
Other public bodies	63,058	70,428	74,588
Households	82,013	80,978	81,898
Other	44,164	43,591	46,668
Deficits of government enterprises	10,650	8,816	9,172
Gross capital formation	10,466	9,776	9,660
Capital transfers	9,372	26,506	26,128
Acquisition of assets	2,913	2,344	2,231
Loans granted	711	725	590
Debt redemption	35,105	51,080	62,008
Other expenditure	6,006	5,823	10,043
Total	444,868	486,415	523,346

* Figures refer to federal government units covered by the general budget. The data exclude the operations of social insurance institutions and other units with their own budgets.

NATIONAL BANK RESERVES
(US $ million at 31 December)

	1987	1988	1989
Gold*	3,523	3,153	3,277
IMF special drawing rights	292	268	298
Reserve position in IMF	468	389	361
Foreign exchange	6,772	6,711	7,939
Total	11,055	10,521	11,875

* Valued at 60,000 Schilling per kilogram.

Source: IMF, *International Financial Statistics*.

MONEY SUPPLY ('000 million Schilling at 31 December)

	1987	1988	1989
Currency outside banks	93.0	98.7	102.6
Demand deposits at deposit money banks	120.5	133.5	139.5
Total money	213.5	232.2	242.1

Source: IMF, *International Financial Statistics*.

COST OF LIVING (Consumer Price Index; base: 1986 = 100)

	1987	1988	1989
Food and beverages	100.7	101.5	102.8
Rent (incl. maintenance and repairs)	102.8	105.3	108.4
Fuel and light	94.7	92.6	91.8
Clothing	101.5	104.3	107.8
Total (incl. others)	101.4	103.4	106.0

NATIONAL ACCOUNTS ('000 million Schilling at current prices)
National Income and Product

	1987	1988	1989
Compensation of employees	792.73	822.36	876.23
Operating surplus*	299.52	338.40	365.36
Domestic factor incomes	1,092.26	1,160.76	1,241.59
Consumption of fixed capital	183.87	194.11	205.63
Gross domestic product at factor cost	1,276.13	1,354.87	1,447.22
Indirect taxes	245.15	254.89	271.64
Less Subsidies	47.38	45.08	45.44
GDP in purchasers' values	1,473.90	1,564.68	1,673.43
Factor income received from abroad	57.36	66.63	91.23
Less Factor income paid abroad	70.27	80.33	104.33
Gross national product	1,461.00	1,550.98	1,660.33
Less Consumption of fixed capital	183.87	194.11	205.63
National income in market prices	1,277.13	1,356.87	1,454.70
Other current transfers from abroad	17.55	19.11	20.42
Less Other current transfers paid abroad	14.74	16.02	15.83
National disposable income	1,279.94	1,359.96	1,459.28

* Including a statistical discrepancy.

Expenditure on the Gross Domestic Product

	1987	1988	1989
Government final consumption expenditure	280.44	288.35	302.08
Private final consumption expenditure	835.46	875.30	927.93
Increase in stocks*	8.90	23.65	32.55
Gross fixed capital formation	341.75	370.68	402.19
Total domestic expenditure	1,466.54	1,557.98	1,664.75
Exports of goods and services	527.18	590.32	669.30
Less Imports of goods and services	519.83	583.62	660.62
GDP in purchasers' values	1,473.90	1,564.68	1,673.43
GDP at constant 1983 prices	1,287.10	1,336.82	1,390.03

* Including a statistical discrepancy.

AUSTRIA

Gross Domestic Product by Economic Activity

	1987	1988	1989
Agriculture, hunting, forestry and fishing	48.47	49.07	51.80
Mining and quarrying	5.85	5.49	5.34
Manufacturing	381.53	414.53	446.51
Electricity, gas and water	47.21	47.26	48.68
Construction	99.63	106.08	114.45
Wholesale and retail trade	178.75	190.34	203.65
Restaurants and hotels	53.62	58.36	64.96
Transport, storage and communications	86.15	93.53	99.51
Owner-occupied dwellings	100.34	105.25	110.63
Finance, insurance and real estate	136.71	151.19	165.37
Public administration and defence	205.91	210.53	220.86
Other community, social and personal services	55.17	59.25	63.73
Private non-profit services to households	10.60	10.73	11.12
Domestic services of households	0.66	0.62	0.59
Sub-total	1,410.59	1,502.23	1,607.20
Value-added tax	133.96	137.63	147.08
Import duties	9.86	10.63	11.51
Less Imputed bank service charges	80.51	85.81	92.36
Total*	1,473.90	1,564.68	1,673.43

* Including a statistical discrepancy.

BALANCE OF PAYMENTS (US $ million)

	1987	1988	1989
Merchandise exports f.o.b.	26,558	30,056	31,607
Merchandise imports f.o.b.	−31,702	−36,358	−38,970
Trade balance	−5,144	−6,301	−7,363
Exports of services	20,059	23,348	24,794
Imports of services	−15,263	−17,469	−17,547
Balance on goods and services	−348	−422	−116
Private unrequited transfers (net)	−10	38	93
Government unrequited transfers (net)	−71	−74	−72
Current balance	−429	−458	−94
Direct capital investment (net)	145	190	−75
Other long-term capital (net)	1,735	408	167
Short-term capital (net)	−1,403	552	703
Net errors and omissions	356	−297	295
Total (net monetary movements)	404	395	996
Monetization of gold	−86	−57	22
Valuation changes (net)	1,049	−505	140
Changes in reserves	1,367	−167	1,158

Source: IMF, *International Financial Statistics*.

External Trade

Note: Austria's customs territory excludes Mittelberg im Kleinen Walsertal (in Vorarlberg) and Jungholz (in Tyrol). The figures also exclude trade in silver specie and monetary gold.

PRINCIPAL COMMODITIES
(distribution by SITC, million Schilling)

Imports c.i.f.	1987	1988	1989
Food and live animals	21,962.0	22,789.1	24,830.5
Vegetables and fruit	8,219.0	8,194.7	8,645.2
Coffee, tea, cocoa and spices	4,556.8	4,670.8	5,232.6
Crude materials (inedible) except fuels	21,301.4	24,534.4	27,972.8
Metalliferous ores and metal scrap	4,257.0	5,724.5	7,053.0
Mineral fuels, lubricants, etc. (incl. electric current)	29,808.6	25,455.0	29,246.6
Coal, coke and briquettes	5,614.0	4,813.6	4,733.4
Petroleum, petroleum products, etc.	18,594.2	15,069.1	18,886.0
Crude petroleum oils, etc.	10,943.7	8,194.2	10,963.8
Refined petroleum products	6,687.1	5,953.0	6,933.2
Gas (natural and manufactured)	4,825.2	4,308.6	4,260.4
Petroleum gases, etc., in the gaseous state	4,488.2	4,018.1	3,939.2
Chemicals and related products	42,428.2	47,450.5	52,151.1
Organic chemicals	5,884.1	7,115.9	7,785.8
Medicinal and pharmaceutical products	7,920.3	8,145.1	9,082.3
Artificial resins, plastic materials, etc.	12,751.3	14,288.3	15,671.7
Basic manufactures	78.950.0	86,252.7	100,261.4
Paper, paperboard and manufactures	7,795.6	8,700.8	10,108.7
Textile yarn, fabrics, etc.	18,870.5	18,778.7	20,502.5
Non-metallic mineral manufactures	7,914.7	8,626.9	9,530.9
Iron and steel	10,953.9	13,142.8	16,915.7
Non-ferrous metals	8,681.6	11,908.7	14,506.4
Other metal manufactures	14,850.1	15,578.5	18,031.7
Machinery and transport equipment	143,082.2	165,784.9	190,964.8
Power-generating machinery and equipment	7,324.8	8,288.0	9,583.9
Machinery specialized for particular industries	16,904.4	17,480.4	20,305.5
General industrial machinery, equipment and parts	22,980.9	23,885.9	27,140.3
Office machines and automatic data processing equipment	11,606.1	14,909.2	18,339.5
Telecommunications and sound equipment	10,048.3	11,832.6	13,524.8
Other electrical machinery, apparatus, etc.	25,816.6	31,057.1	35,304.7
Road vehicles and parts*	40,477.1	49,479.9	55,626.2
Passenger motor cars (excl. buses)	23,969.9	30,894.9	35,368.1
Parts and accessories for cars, buses, lorries, etc.*	6,696.2	7,123.5	8,081.8
Miscellaneous manufactured articles	71,097.3	76,034.8	85,807.8
Furniture and parts	7,433.0	8,100.6	9,407.0
Clothing and accessories (excl. footwear)	21,579.6	21,213.7	22,867.3
Professional, scientific and controlling instruments, etc.	7,356.2	7,863.6	9,011.5
Photographic apparatus, etc., optical goods, watches and clocks	5,964.7	5,746.9	6,438.9
Total (incl. others)	411,858.8	451,441.8	514,686.4

* Excluding tyres, engines and electrical parts.

AUSTRIA

Statistical Survey

Exports f.o.b.	1987	1988	1989
Food and live animals	10,661.3	11,845.9	13,656.6
Crude materials (inedible) except fuels	18,222.0	20,596.6	23,400.7
Cork and wood	8,762.0	9,668.7	11,976.6
Simply worked wood and railway sleepers	7,888.0	8,799.7	10,842.2
Sawn coniferous wood	7,228.0	8,158.2	10,033.0
Chemicals and related products	30,765.3	37,206.3	39,791.1
Organic chemicals	4,984.0	5,868.9	6,349.3
Artificial resins, plastic materials, etc.	10,917.5	14,618.3	15,318.8
Basic manufactures	112,907.4	125,566.1	141,739.1
Paper, paperboard and manufactures	20,165.5	23,745.8	26,703.4
Paper and paperboard (not cut to size or shape)	14,822.4	17,246.0	19,055.3
Textile yarn, fabrics, etc.	18,350.3	19,342.4	21,726.8
Non-metallic mineral manufactures	11,476.4	11,770.6	13,140.7
Iron and steel	25,490.4	28,731.6	32,552.3
Tubes, pipes and fittings	5,517.5	7,285.8	8,891.5
Non-ferrous metals	8,021.0	10,346.7	11,998.0
Aluminium and aluminium alloys	5,300.0	6,714.3	7,578.9
Other metal manufactures	16,422.1	17,951.3	20,823.5
Machinery and transport equipment	114,530.2	130,834.8	147,755.7
Power-generating machinery and equipment	17,036.8	19,271.8	23,572.5
Internal combustion piston engines and parts	12,794.3	15,310.6	18,918.3
Engines for road vehicles, tractors, etc.	11,264.0	13,272.1	15,900.5
Machinery specialized for particular industries	20,302.9	20,773.0	24,058.0
General industrial machinery, equipment and parts	19,000.3	21,960.9	25,515.1
Telecommunications and sound equipment	11,325.9	12,698.0	14,707.4
Other electrical machinery, apparatus, etc.	23,944.7	28,351.4	28,022.0
Road vehicles and parts (excl. tyres, engines and electrical parts)	14,179.0	14,904.3	17,118.8
Miscellaneous manufactured articles	47,846.6	50,810.0	55,614.1
Clothing and accessories (excl. footwear)	12,075.5	11,754.6	12,173.2
Footwear	4,739.8	4,650.9	4,733.8
Total (incl. others)	342,433.4	383,212.6	429,309.5

PRINCIPAL TRADING PARTNERS (million Schilling)*

Imports c.i.f.	1987	1988	1989
Algeria	1,291.0	1,365.3	3,505.2
Belgium/Luxembourg	9,985.8	12,104.2	13,821.1
Brazil	2,007.1	2,473.5	2,757.4
Czechoslovakia	5,917.7	6,049.2	6,735.0
France	16,687.1	17,761.4	22,676.9
Germany, Federal Republic	181,950.9	200,942.7	224,519.6
Hungary	6,178.1	6,367.9	7,839.4
Italy	38,674.0	40,289.5	46,171.8
Japan	17,945.7	23,132.7	25,457.5
Libya	3,200.5	2,608.3	2,013.3
Netherlands	11,369.9	12,606.6	14,159.8
Poland	4,017.1	4,237.4	4,350.6
Sweden	7,234.7	8,291.8	9,151.6
Switzerland/Liechtenstein	19,401.1	19,890.1	21,298.0
USSR	8,501.4	8,633.1	8,522.3
United Kingdom	9,886.7	11,183.4	12,906.9
USA	14,236.7	15,311.3	18,610.6
Yugoslavia	3,929.0	4,681.4	6,001.2
Total (incl. others)	411,858.8	451,441.8	514,686.4

Exports f.o.b.	1987	1988	1989
Belgium/Luxembourg	8,130.0	9,145.5	9,983.2
Czechoslovakia	3,935.6	4,690.0	5,010.3
Denmark	3,811.8	3,842.1	3,997.5
France	15,349.3	17,665.7	20,031.6
German Democratic Republic	5,970.4	5,712.6	5,714.8
Germany, Federal Republic	119,271.2	134,235.6	148,173.1
Hungary	6,624.0	6,824.8	8,676.4
Iran	1,733.6	1,928.7	2,407.1
Iraq	1,211.6	2,021.1	2,027.3
Italy	35,492.3	39,905.6	45,251.4
Netherlands	9,214.0	9,942.0	12,705.4
Poland	2,985.8	3,721.8	5,238.2
Saudi Arabia	1,482.9	2,104.8	1,595.7
Spain	6,300.2	7,363.7	9,386.5
Sweden	6,672.5	7,707.8	8,344.0
Switzerland/Liechtenstein	25,385.6	27,620.4	31,057.3
USSR	8,503.1	11,022.2	11,473.4
United Kingdom	15,649.6	18,108.6	19,524.6
USA	12,185.2	13,496.7	14,926.1
Yugoslavia	6,780.8	7,787.2	9,201.1
Total (incl. others)	342,433.4	383,212.6	429,309.5

* Imports by country of production; exports by country of consumption.

Transport

RAILWAYS (Federal Railways only)

	1987	1988	1989
Passenger-km (millions)	7,434	7,783	8,445
Freight (net ton-km) (millions)	11,008	11,213	11,849
Freight tons carried ('000)	54,730	55,422	58,606

ROAD TRAFFIC (motor vehicles in use at 31 December)

	1987	1988	1989
Private cars	2,684,780	2,784,792	2,902,949
Buses and coaches	9,267	9,274	9,405
Goods vehicles	221,139	234,611	246,823
Motorcycles and scooters	87,980	99,445	104,840
Mopeds	522,115	501,845	484,609

SHIPPING (freight traffic in '000 metric tons)

	1987	1988	1989
Goods loaded	1,846	2,092	2,538
Goods unloaded	5,418	6,059	6,607

CIVIL AVIATION (Austrian Airlines, '000)

	1987	1988	1989
Kilometres flown	24,656	25,509	32,465
Passenger ton-km	152,184	157,129	217,919
Cargo ton-km	19,056	19,168	36,376
Mail ton-km	3,978	3,926	5,144

Tourism

FOREIGN TOURIST ARRIVALS (by country of origin)

	1987	1988	1989
Belgium/Luxembourg	348,000	378,080	422,431
France	692,000	701,455	778,415
Germany, Federal Republic	8,450,000	8,996,778	9,666,493
Italy	695,000	866,122	1,101,380
Netherlands	1,301,000	1,331,165	1,403,383
Switzerland	575,000	641,456	744,672
United Kingdom	762,000	753,230	863,534
USA	672,000	620,078	676,085
Total (incl. others)	15,761,400	16,571,289	18,201,763

Communications Media

	1987	1988	1989
Telephones in use	2,906,736	3,001,319	3,102,814
Radio licences issued	2,690,871	2,694,260	2,700,136
Television licences issued	2,483,846	2,486,968	2,494,355
Book titles produced		9,786	9,036	10,358

1989: Daily newspapers 29 (average circulation 2,775,214); Non-daily newspapers 145; Other periodicals 2,565.

Education

(1989/90)

	Institutions	Staff	Students
Primary	3,717	33,796	386,739
General secondary	1,684	52,214	419,162
Compulsory vocational	1,157	22,663	316,127
Teacher training:			
second level	35	1,034	10,416
third level	26	1,875	6,124
Universities and other higher schools	27	11,773	187,409

Directory

The Constitution

The Austrian Constitution of 1920, as amended in 1929, was restored on 1 May 1945. Its main provisions are summarized below:

Austria is a democratic republic, having a president (Bundespräsident), elected directly by the people, and a two-chamber legislature, the Federal Assembly. The republic is organized on the federal system, comprising the provinces (Länder) of Burgenland, Carinthia, Lower Austria, Upper Austria, Salzburg, Styria, Tyrol, Vorarlberg and Vienna. There is universal suffrage for men and women who are more than 19 years of age.

The Nationalrat (National Council) consists of 183 members, elected by universal direct suffrage, according to a system of proportional representation. It functions for a period of four years.

The Bundesrat (Federal Council) represents the federal provinces. Vienna sends 12 members, Lower Austria 12, Upper Austria 10, Styria 10, Carinthia 4, Tyrol 5, Salzburg 4, Burgenland and Vorarlberg 3 each, making 63 in all. The seats are divided between the parties according to the number of seats they hold in the provincial assemblies and are held during the life of the provincial government which they represent. Each province in turn provides the chairman for six months.

For certain matters of special importance the two chambers meet together; this is known as a Bundesversammlung.

The President, elected by popular vote, is the Head of State and holds office for six years. The President is eligible for re-election only once in succession. Although invested with special emergency powers, the President normally acts on the authority of the Government, and it is the Government which is responsible to the National Council for governmental policy.

The Government consists of the Chancellor, the Vice-Chancellor and the other ministers, who may vary in number. The Chancellor is chosen by the President, usually from the party with the strongest representation in the newly-elected National Council, and the other ministers are then chosen by the President on the advice of the Chancellor.

If the National Council passes an explicit vote of 'no confidence' in the Federal Government or individual members thereof, the Federal Government or the Federal Minister concerned shall be removed from office.

All new acts must be read and put to the vote in both houses. A new bill goes first to the National Council, where it usually has three readings, and secondly to the Federal Council, where it can be held up, but not vetoed.

The Constitution also provides for appeals by the Government to the electorate on specific points by means of referendum. There is further provision that if 200,000 or more electors present a petition to the Government, the Government must lay it before the National Council.

The Landtag (Provincial Assembly) exercises the same functions in each province as the National Council does in the State. The members of the Landtag elect a government (Landesregierung) consisting of a provincial governor (Landeshauptmann) and his councillors (Landesräte). They are responsible to the Landtag.

The spheres of legal and administrative competence of both national and provincial governments are clearly defined. The Constitution distinguishes four groups:

1. Law-making and administration are the responsibility of the State: e.g. foreign affairs, justice and finance.

2. Law-making is the responsibility of the State, administration is the responsibility of the provinces: e.g. elections, population matters and road traffic.

3. The State lays down the rudiments of the law, the provinces make the law and administer it: e.g. charity, rights of agricultural workers, land reform.

4. Law-making and administration are the responsibility of the provinces in all matters not expressly assigned to the State: e.g. municipal affairs, building theatres and cinemas.

The Government

HEAD OF STATE

Federal President: Dr KURT WALDHEIM (sworn in 8 July 1986).

COUNCIL OF MINISTERS

(November 1990)

A coalition of the Socialist Party of Austria (SPÖ) and the Austrian People's Party (ÖVP).

Federal Chancellor: Dr FRANZ VRANITZKY (SPÖ).
Vice-Chancellor and Minister of Federalism and Administrative Reform: Dipl.-Ing. JOSEF RIEGLER (ÖVP).

AUSTRIA   Directory

Minister of Economic Affairs: Dr WOLFGANG SCHÜSSEL (ÖVP).
Minister of Foreign Affairs: Dr ALOIS MOCK (ÖVP).
Minister of the Interior: Dr FRANZ LÖSCHNAK (SPÖ).
Minister of Agriculture and Forestry: Dipl.-Ing. Dr FRANZ FISCHLER (ÖVP).
Minister of the Public Sector and Transport: Dipl.-Ing. Dr RUDOLF STREICHER (SPÖ).
Minister of Justice: Dr EGMONT FOREGGER (Independent).
Minister of Employment and Social Affairs: Dr WALTER GEPPERT (SPÖ).
Minister of Finance: Dkfm. FERDINAND LACINA (SPÖ).
Minister of National Defence: Dr ROBERT LICHAL (ÖVP).
Minister of Science and Research: Dr ERHARD BUSEK (ÖVP).
Minister of Education, the Arts and Sport: Dr HILDE HAWLICEK (SPÖ).
Minister of Environment, Youth and Family: Dr MARILIES FLEMMING (ÖVP).
Minister of the Federal Chancellery (Health and Public Service): Ing. HARALD ETTL (SPÖ).
Secretary of State to the Federal Chancellery: JOHANNA DOHNAL (SPÖ).
Secretary of State in the Ministry of Finance: Dr GÜNTHER STUMMVOLL (ÖVP).

MINISTRIES

Office of the Federal Chancellor: 1014 Vienna, Ballhausplatz 2; tel. (01) 53-11-50; telex 1370900; fax (01) 531-15-28-80.
Ministry of Agriculture and Forestry: 1010 Vienna, Stubenring 1; tel. (01) 75-0-00; fax (01) 713-93-11.
Ministry of Economic Affairs: 1010 Vienna, Stubenring 1; tel. (01) 75-0-00; telex 111780; fax (01) 713-93-11.
Ministry of Education, the Arts and Sport: 1014 Vienna, Minoritenplatz 5; tel. (01) 53-1-20; fax (01) 531-20-43-35.
Ministry of Employment and Social Affairs: 1010 Vienna, Stubenring 1; tel. (01) 71-1-00; fax (01) 713-93-11.
Ministry of Environment, Youth and Family: 1031 Vienna, Radetzkystr. 2; tel. (01) 71-1-58; telex 3221371; fax (01) 711-58-42-21.
Ministry of Finance: 1010 Vienna, Himmelpfortgasse 4-8B; tel. (01) 51-4-33; telex 111688; fax (01) 514-33-19-38.
Ministry of Foreign Affairs: 1014 Vienna, Ballhausplatz 2; tel. (01) 53-1-15; telex 01371; fax (01) 535-45-30.
Ministry of the Interior: 1014 Vienna, Herrengasse 7; tel. (01) 66-2-60; fax (01) 531-26-39-10.
Ministry of Justice: 1016 Vienna, Museumstr. 7; tel. (01) 52-1-52-0; fax (01) 52-1-52-727.
Ministry of National Defence: 1030 Vienna, Dampfschiffstr. 2; tel. (01) 51-5-95; telex 112145.
Ministry of the Public Sector and Transport: 1031 Vienna, Radetzkystr. 2; tel. (0222) 711-62; telex 111800; fax (0222) 73-03-26.
Ministry of Science and Research: 1014 Vienna, Minoritenplatz 5; tel. (01) 53-1-20; telex 111157; fax (01) 531-20-43-35.

President and Legislature

PRESIDENT

Presidential Election, First Ballot, 4 May 1986

Candidates	Votes	%
Dr KURT WALDHEIM	2,343,387	49.65
Dr KURT STEYRER (SPÖ)	2,061,162	43.67
FREDA MEISSNER-BLAU	259,471	5.49
OTTO SCRINZI	55,940	1.18

Second Ballot, 8 June 1986

Candidates	Votes	%
Dr KURT WALDHEIM	2,460,203	53.89
Dr KURT STEYRER (SPÖ)	2,105,118	46.11

NATIONALRAT
(National Council)

President of the Nationalrat: ROBERT LICHAL.

General Election, 7 October 1990

	Votes	% of Total	Seats
Socialist Party (SPÖ)	2,012,463	42.79	81
People's Party (ÖVP)	1,508,226	32.06	60
Freedom Party (FPÖ)	782,610	16.64	33
Green/Alternative List (GAL)	224,941	4.78	9

Other parties together received about 3.7% of the votes but won no seats.

BUNDESRAT
(Federal Council)
(October 1990)

President of the Bundesrat: Ing. GEORG LUDESCHER (July–Dec. 1990).

Provinces	Total seats	SPÖ	ÖVP	FPÖ
Burgenland	3	2	1	—
Carinthia	4	2	1	1
Lower Austria	12	5	6	1
Upper Austria	10	4	6	—
Salzburg	4	1	2	1
Styria	10	4	6	—
Tyrol	5	1	3	1
Vorarlberg	3	1	2	—
Vienna	12	8	3	1
Total	**63**	**28**	**30**	**5**

Political Organizations

Freiheitliche Partei Österreichs (FPÖ) (Freedom Party of Austria): 1010 Vienna I, Kärntnerstr. 28; tel. (0222) 512-35-35; fax (0222) 513-88-58; f. 1955; Liberal party which partially succeeds the Verband der Unabhängigen (League of Independents), dissolved in 1956, and stands for moderate social reform, for the participation of workers in management, for European co-operation and for good relations with all the countries of Free Europe; Chair. Dr JÖRG HAIDER; Secs-Gen. Dr HEIDE SCHMIDT, Ing. MATHIAS REICHHOLD.

Die Grüne Alternative (Grüne) (The Green Alternative): 1070 Vienna, Stiftgasse 6; tel. (0222) 52-125-0; f. 1986; campaigns for environmental protection, peace and social justice; Chair. JOHANNES VOGGENHUBER, PIUS STROBL; Leader of Parliamentary Group ANDREAS WABL.

Kommunistische Partei Österreichs (KPÖ) (Communist Party of Austria): 1206 Vienna, Höchstädtplatz 3; tel. (01) 33-46-11; telex 114082; f. 1918; strongest in the industrial centres and trade unions; advocates a policy of strict neutrality and friendly relations with neighbouring states and with the USSR; Chair. Dr WALTER SILBERMAYR, Dr SUSANNE SOHN.

Österreichische Volkspartei (ÖVP) (Austrian People's Party): 1010 Vienna I, Kärntnerstr. 51; tel. (0222) 515-21; telex 111735; fax (0222) 513-27-58; f. 1945; Christian-Democratic party; the 'Salzburg programme' (1972) defines it as 'progressive centre party'; 760,000 mems; Chair. Dipl.-Ing. JOSEF RIEGLER; Sec.-Gen. HELMUT KUKACKA.

Sozialistische Partei Österreichs (SPÖ) (Socialist Party of Austria): 1014 Vienna I, Löwelstr. 18; tel. (01) 534-27-0; telex 114198; fax (01) 535-96-83; founded as the Social-Democratic Party in 1889; advocates democratic socialism and Austria's permanent neutrality; 700,000 mems; Chair. Dr FRANZ VRANITZKY; Secs JOSEF CAP, PETER MARIZZI.

Vereinte Grüne Österreichs (VGÖ) (United Green Party of Austria): 4020 Linz, Göthestr. 9; tel. (0732) 66-83-91; f. 1982; ecologist party; Chair. JOSEF BUCHNER; Gen. Sec. WOLFGANG PELIKAN.

Diplomatic Representation

EMBASSIES IN AUSTRIA

Afghanistan: 1010 Vienna, Doblhoffgasse 3/4; tel. (01) 43-24-01; telex 111891; Chargé d'affaires a.i.: ABDUL HABIB MAJID.

AUSTRIA

Albania: 1190 Vienna, Blaasstr. 24; tel. (01) 36-91-229; telex 133248; fax (01) 36-14-83; Ambassador: ENGJËLL KOLANECI.

Algeria: 1190 Vienna, Rudolfinergasse 18; tel. (01) 36-88-53; telex 134163; Ambassador: AHMED AMINE KHERBI.

Argentina: 1010 Vienna, Goldschmiedgasse 2/1; tel. (01) 533-85-77; telex 114512; fax (01) 63-87-97; Ambassador: Dr JORGE ALBERTO TAIANA.

Australia: 1040 Vienna, Mattiellistr. 2–4/III; tel. (01) 512-85-80; telex 114313; fax (01) 513-29-08; Ambassador: MICHAEL JOHN WILSON.

Belgium: 1040 Vienna, Operngasse 20B; tel. (01) 56-75-79; telex 133004; fax (01) 56-75-88; Ambassador: Vicomte GEORGES VILAIN XIIII.

Bolivia: 1010 Vienna, Bauernmarkt 6/6; tel. (01) 535-04-91; telex 135555; fax (01) 535-04-92; Ambassador: Dr A. GASTÓN PONCE CABALLERO.

Brazil: 1010 Vienna, Lugeck 1/V/15; tel. (01) 512-06-310; telex 111925; Ambassador: JOÃO TABAJARA DE OLIVEIRA.

Bulgaria: 1040 Vienna, Schwindgasse 8; tel. (0222) 505-64-44; telex 131794; fax (0222) 505-14-23; Ambassador: Dr TOSCHKO TOSCHKOV.

Canada: 1010 Vienna, Luegerring 10; tel. (01) 533-36-91; fax (01) 535-44-73; Ambassador: EDWARD LEE.

Chile: 1010 Vienna, Lugeck 1/III/10; tel. (01) 512-92-08; telex 115952; fax (01) 512-92-08-33; Ambassador: HERNÁN GUTIÉRREZ LEYTON.

China, People's Republic: 1030 Vienna, Metternichgasse 4; tel. (01) 75-31-49; telex 135794; fax (01) 713-68-16; Ambassador: HU BENYAO.

Colombia: 1010 Vienna, Stadiongasse 6–8; tel. (01) 42-42-49; telex 116798; fax (01) 48-83-03; Ambassador: Dr MARIO LASERNA PINZÓN.

Costa Rica: 1030 Vienna, Paulusgasse 13/1/5; tel. (01) 713-05-40; fax (01) 713-05-41; Ambassador: Prof. Dr MANUEL A. CONSTENLA.

Côte d'Ivoire: 1090 Vienna, Alser Str. 28/12; tel. (01) 408-37-23; telex 111108; Ambassador: ADONIT MANOUAN.

Cuba: 1130 Vienna, Eitelbergergasse 24; tel. (01) 82-81-98; telex 131398; Ambassador: GUSTAVO MAZORRA HERNÁNDEZ.

Czechoslovakia: 1140 Vienna, Penzinger Str. 11–13; tel. (01) 894-21-26; telex 131702; Ambassador: MAGDALÉNA VÁSÁRYOVÁ.

Denmark: 1010 Vienna, Führichgasse 6; tel. (01) 512-79-04; telex 113261; fax (01) 513-81-20; Ambassador: HENRIK MUNCK NETTERSTRØM.

Ecuador: 1010 Vienna, Goldschmiedgasse 10/II/24; tel. (01) 535-32-08; telex 134958; fax (01) 535-08-97; Ambassador: JORGE E. PAREJA CUCALÓN.

Egypt: 1190 Vienna, Gallmeyergasse 5; tel. (01) 36-11-34; telex 115623; fax (01) 36-63-21; Ambassador: MERVAT TALLAWY.

Finland: 1020 Vienna, Untere Donaustr. 13–15; tel. (01) 24-75-21; telex 135230; fax (01) 24-52-74; Ambassador: MATTI KALERVO KAHILUOTO.

France: 1040 Vienna, Technikerstr. 2; tel. (01) 505-47-47; telex 131333; fax (01) 505-63-92-91; Ambassador: JEAN FRANÇOIS NOIVILLE.

Germany: 1030 Vienna, Metternichgasse 3; tel. (01) 71-1-54; telex 134261; Ambassador: PHILIPP JENNINGER.

Greece: 1040 Vienna, Argentinierstr. 14; tel. (01) 505-57-91; telex 133176; fax (01) 505-62-17; Ambassador: ANTONIOS J. COUNDAKIS.

Guatemala: 1010 Vienna, Opernring I/R/4/407; tel. (01) 56-91-01; Ambassador: EDUARDO CASTILLO ARRIOLA.

Holy See: 1040 Vienna, Theresianumgasse 31; tel. (01) 505-13-27; Apostolic Nuncio: Most Rev. DONATO SQUICCIARINI, Titular Archbishop of Tiburnia.

Hungary: 1010 Vienna, Bankgasse 4–6; tel. (01) 533-26-31; telex 135546; Ambassador: JÁNOS NAGY.

India: 1015 Vienna, Kärntner Ring 2; tel. (01) 505-86-66; telex 113721; fax (01) 505-92-19; Ambassador: PETER L. SINAI.

Indonesia: 1180 Vienna, Gustav-Tschermak-Gasse 5–7; tel. (01) 34-25-34; telex 75579; Ambassador: JOHANNES PETRUS LOUHANAPESSY.

Iran: 1030 Vienna, Jaurèsgasse 9; tel. (01) 72-26-57; telex 131718; fax (01) 713-57-33; Ambassador: HOSSEIN NOGHREHKAR SHIRAZI.

Iraq: 1010 Vienna, Johannesgasse 26; tel. (01) 713-81-95; telex 135397; fax (01) 713-67-20; Ambassador: Dr RAHIM ABID ALKITAL.

Ireland: 1030 Vienna, Hilton Centre, 16th Floor, POB 139; tel. (01) 75-42-46; telex 136887; fax (01) 713-60-04; Ambassador: JOSEPH SMALL.

Israel: 1180 Vienna, Anton-Frank-Gasse 20; tel. (01) 31-15-06; telex 4005; fax (01) 31-70-09; Chargé d'affaires a.i. GIDEON YARDEN.

Italy: 1030 Vienna, Rennweg 27; tel. (01) 712-51-21; telex 132620; Ambassador: Dr ALESSANDRO QUARONI.

Japan: 1040 Vienna, Argentinierstr. 21; tel. (01) 501-71-0; telex 135810; fax (01) 505-45-37; Ambassador: KAZUTOSHI HASEGAWA.

Korea, Democratic People's Republic: 1140 Vienna, Beckmanngasse 10–12; tel. (01) 89-42-311; telex 131750; Ambassador: PAK SI UNG.

Korea, Republic: 1020 Vienna, Praterstr. 31; tel. (01) 21-63-441; telex 131252; Ambassador: LEE CHANG-CHOON.

Kuwait: 1010 Vienna, Universitätsstr. 5; tel. (01) 42-56-46; telex 135898; Ambassador: ABDUL-HAMID ABDULLAH AL-AWADHI.

Lebanon: 1010 Vienna, Schwedenplatz 2/15; tel. (01) 63-88-21; telex 115273; Chargé d'affaires: CHRISTIANE GEZRAWI-BASSILE.

Libya: 1170 Vienna, Dornbacherstr. 27; tel. (01) 45-36-11; telex 116267; Secretary of People's Bureau: ENBEIA MANSUR WADI.

Luxembourg: 1190 Vienna, Hofzeile 27; tel. (01) 36-21-86; telex 115276; Ambassador: JACQUES REUTER.

Malaysia: 1040 Vienna, Prinz Eugen-Str. 18; tel. (01) 505-10-42; telex 133830; fax (01) 505-79-42; Ambassador: ABDUL HALIM BIN ALI.

Mexico: 1040 Vienna, Renngasse 4; tel. (01) 535-17-76; telex 115660; fax (01) 535-17-76-19; Ambassador: EUGENIO ANGUIANO ROCH.

Morocco: 1020 Vienna, Untere Donaustr. 13–15; tel. (01) 24-25-68; fax (01) 216-79-84; Ambassador: TAOUFIK KABBAJ.

Netherlands: 1020 Vienna, Untere Donaustr. 13–15/VIII; tel. (01) 24-85-87; telex 135462; fax (01) 216-57-22; Ambassador: LODEWIJK H. J. B. VAN GORKOM.

New Zealand: 1010 Vienna, Lugeck 1; tel. (01) 512-66-36; telex 136582; fax 512-66-39; Ambassador: BARRY H. BROOKS.

Nigeria: 1030 Vienna, Rennweg 25; tel. (01) 72-66-85; telex 131583; Ambassador: TIMOTHY ANAELE MGBOKWERE.

Norway: 1030 Vienna, Bayerngasse 1/3; tel. (01) 715-66-92; telex 132768; fax (01) 72-65-52; Ambassador: KNUT HEDEMANN.

Oman: 1090 Vienna, Währingerstr. 2–4/24–25; tel. (01) 31-64-52; telex 116662; Chargé d'affaires: YAHYA S. H. AL-WAHAIBI.

Pakistan: 1190 Vienna, Hofzeile 13; tel. (0222) 36-73-81; telex 135634; fax (0222) 36-73-76; Ambassador: (vacant).

Panama: 1030 Vienna, Strohgasse 35/6; tel. (01) 713-46-33; Ambassador: ERNESTO KOREF.

Peru: 1030 Vienna, Gottfried-Keller-Gasse 2; tel. (01) 713-43-77; telex 135524; fax (01) 712-77-04; Ambassador: Dr ALEJANDRO SAN MARTÍN CARO.

Philippines: 1190 Vienna, Nedergasse 34; tel. (01) 36-84-48; telex 132740; Ambassador: NELSON D. LAVIÑA.

Poland: 1130 Vienna, Hletzinger Hauptstr. 42c; tel. (01) 82-74-44; fax (01) 82-92-68; Ambassador: STANISŁAW BEJGER.

Portugal: 1040 Vienna, Operngasse 20B; tel. (01) 56-75-36; telex 113237; fax (01) 587-58-39; Ambassador: CARLOS ARY-DOS-SANTOS.

Qatar: 1090 Vienna, Strudlhofgasse 10; tel. (01) 31-66-39; telex 131306; fax (01) 31-70-86; Ambassador: JASIM YOUSOF JAMAL.

Romania: 1040 Vienna, Prinz Eugen-Str. 60; tel. (01) 65-32-27; telex 133335; Ambassador: TRANDAFIR COCARLA.

San Marino: 1090 Vienna, Spitalgasse 17A; tel. (01) 42-42-47; telex 113792; fax (01) 48-76-13; Ambassador: GIOVANNI VITO MARCUCCI.

Saudi Arabia: 1190 Vienna, Formanekgasse 38; tel. (01) 36-23-16; telex 115757; Ambassador: ESSA A. AL-NOWAISER.

South Africa: 1190 Vienna, Sandgasse 33; tel. (01) 32-64-93; telex 116671; Ambassador: CECILIA JOHANNA SCHMIDT.

Spain: 1040 Vienna, Argentinierstr. 34; tel. (01) 505-57-80; telex 131545; fax (01) 65-09-059; Ambassador: Dr JESÚS NÚÑEZ.

Sudan: 1090 Vienna, Spittelauer Platz 4/1-4; tel. (01) 34-46-40; telex 114385; Ambassador: ALI YASSIN GAILI.

Sweden: 1025 Vienna, Obere Donaustr. 49–51; tel. (01) 33-45-45; telex 114720; fax (01) 35-75-82; Ambassador: CURT LIDGARD.

Switzerland: 1030 Vienna, Prinz-Eugen-Str. 7; tel. (01) 78-45-21; telex 132960; fax (01) 78-45-21-21; Ambassador: JEAN-PIERRE RITTER.

Thailand: 1180 Vienna, Weimarer-Str. 68; tel. (01) 310-16-30; telex 133893; fax (01) 310-39-35; Ambassador: SAWANIT KONGSIRI.

Tunisia: 1030 Vienna, Ghegastr. 3; tel. (01) 78-65-52; telex 111748; fax (01) 78-73-41; Ambassador: HABIB AMMAR.

Turkey: 1040 Vienna, Prinz-Eugen-Str. 40; tel. (01) 505-55-59; telex 131927; fax (01) 505-36-60; Ambassador: AYHAN KAMEL.

USSR: 1030 Vienna, Reisnerstr. 45–47; tel. (01) 712-12-29; telex 136278; fax (01) 72-33-88; Ambassador: VALERI N. POPOV.

United Arab Emirates: 1190 Vienna, Peter-Jordan-Str. 66; tel. (01) 36-14-55; telex 114106; Ambassador: ABDUL AZIZ AL-OWAIS.

United Kingdom: 1030 Vienna, Jaurèsgasse 12; tel. (0222) 713-15-75; telex 132810; fax (0222) 75-78-24; Ambassador: BRIAN L. CROWE.

AUSTRIA   *Directory*

USA: 1090 Vienna, Boltzmanngasse 16; tel. (01) 31-55-11; telex 114634; fax (01) 31-00-682; Ambassador: ROY M. HUFFINGTON.

Uruguay: 1010 Vienna, Krugerstr. 3/1/4–6; tel. (01) 513-22-40; telex 112589; Ambassador: JOSÉ D. LISSIDINI.

Venezuela: 1030 Vienna, Marokkanergasse 22; tel. (01) 75-32-19; telex 136219; fax (01) 72-26-38; Ambassador: Dr REINALDO PABÓN GARCÍA.

Yugoslavia: 1030 Vienna, Rennweg 3; tel. (01) 713-25-95; telex 135398; Ambassador: Dr IVAN BRNELIĆ.

Zaire: 1030 Vienna, Marokkanergasse 22/1/6; tel. (01) 713-88-75; telex 133565; Ambassador: BOKONGA EKANGA BOTOMBELE.

Judicial System

The Austrian legal system is based on the principle of a division between legislative, administrative and judicial power. There are three supreme courts (Verfassungsgerichtshof, Verwaltungsgerichtshof and Oberster Gerichtshof). The judicial courts are organized into about 200 local courts (Bezirksgerichte), 17 provincial and district courts (Landes- und Kreisgerichte), and 4 higher provincial courts (Oberlandesgerichte) in Vienna, Graz, Innsbruck and Linz.

SUPREME ADMINISTRATIVE COURTS

Verfassungsgerichtshof (Constitutional Court): Vienna I, Judenplatz 11; f. 1919; deals with matters affecting the Constitution, examines the legality of legislation and administration; Pres. Univ. Doz. Dr LUDWIG ADAMOVICH; Vice-Pres. Prof. Dr KURT RINGHOFER.

Verwaltungsgerichtshof (Administrative Court): Vienna I, Judenplatz 11; deals with matters affecting the legality of administration; Pres. Dr INGRID PETRIK; Vice-Pres. Mag. ALFRED KOBZINA.

SUPREME JUDICIAL COURT

Oberster Gerichtshof: Vienna I, Museumstr. 12; Pres. Dr WALTER MELNIZKY; Vice-Pres. Dr KARL PISKA.

Religion

CHRISTIANITY

Ökumenischer Rat der Kirchen in Österreich (Ecumenical Council of Churches in Austria): 1050 Vienna, Hamburgerstr. 3; tel. (01) 587-31-41; f. 1958; 13 mem. Churches, 11 observers; Hon. Pres. Superintendent Mag. WERNER HORN (Protestant Church of the Augsburg Confession); Vice-Pres. Bishop MICHAEL STAIKOS (Greek Orthodox Church); Sec. Superintendent HELMUT NAUSNER.

The Roman Catholic Church

The vast majority of Austrians belong to the Roman Catholic Church. Austria comprises two archdioceses, seven dioceses and the territorial abbacy of Wettingen-Mehrerau (directly responsible to the Holy See). The Archbishop of Vienna is also the Ordinary for Catholics of the Byzantine rite in Austria (totalling an estimated 3,500 at 31 December 1988).

Bishops' Conference: Österreichische Bischofskonferenz, 1010 Vienna, Rotenturmstrasse 2; tel. (01) 51-5-52; f. 1989; Pres. Cardinal Dr HANS HERMANN GROËR, Archbishop of Vienna; Sec. Dr ALFRED KOSTELECKY, Titular Bishop of Wiener Neustadt.

Archbishop of Salzburg: Dr GEORG EDER, 5010 Salzburg, Kapitelplatz 2, Postfach 62; tel. (0662) 42-5-91.

Archbishop of Vienna: Cardinal Dr HANS HERMANN GROËR, 1010 Vienna, Rotenturmstr. 2; tel. (01) 51-5-52.

Orthodox Churches

The Armenian Church and the Bulgarian, Coptic, Greek, Romanian, Russian, Serbian and Syrian Orthodox Churches are active in Austria.

The Anglican Communion

Within the Church of England, Austria forms part of the diocese of Gibraltar in Europe. The Bishop is resident in London.

Anglican Church: Christ Church, 1030 Vienna, Jaurèsgasse 17; tel. (01) 712-33-96; Chaplain Rev. Canon JEREMY PEAKE.

Protestant Churches

Baptist Union of Austria: 1160 Vienna, Mörikeweg 16/1; tel. (01) 94-84-465; Pres. Rev. AUGUST HIRNBÖCK.

Evangelische Kirche Augsburgischen Bekenntnisses in Österreich (Protestant Church of the Augsburgian Confession): 1180 Vienna, Severin-Schreiber-Gasse 3; tel. (01) 47-15-23; fax (01) 47-15-23-20; 352,585 mems; Bishop D. DIETER KNALL.

Evangelische Kirche HB (Helvetischen Bekenntnisses) (Protestant Church of the Helvetic Confession): 1010 Vienna, Dorotheergasse 16; tel. (01) 513-65-64; 15,863 mems; Landessuperintendent Pfr. Mag. PETER KARNER.

Evangelisch-methodistische Kirche (United Methodist Church): 1100 Vienna, Landgutgasse 39/7; tel. (01) 604-53-47; Superintendent HELMUT NAUSNER.

Other Christian Churches

Alt-Katholische Kirche Österreichs (Old Catholic Church in Austria): 1010 Vienna, Schottenring 17; tel. (01) 34-83-94-0; approx. 22,000 mems; Bishop NIKOLAUS HUMMEL.

JUDAISM

There are about 10,000 Jews in Austria.

Israelitische Kultusgemeinde (Jewish Community): 1010 Vienna, Seitenstettengasse 4; tel. (0222) 53-104-0; telex 136298; fax (0222) 533-15-77; Pres. PAUL GROSZ.

The Press

Austria's *Wiener Zeitung*, founded in 1703, is the oldest daily paper published in the world, and Austria's press history dates back to 1605, when its first newspaper was published. Article 13 of the 1867 Constitution gave citizens of the Austro-Hungarian Empire the right to express opinions freely and stated that the press could not be censored. Restrictions on this freedom of the press are permissible only within the framework of Article 10 (2) of the European Convention of Human Rights.

By the 1922 Press Law, any person who had been subject to an incorrect statement in the press was granted the right to publish a reply free of charge. This right of reply, which was unsatisfactory to the newspapers as well as to the person in question, was fundamentally reformed by the Media Law of 1982: the post of Verantwortlicher Redakteur (Responsible Editor—who had been penally liable if the newspaper refused to publish a reply) was abolished and the liability was removed. Now a newspaper may refuse to accept the reply if it is untrue.

Any person who feels himself to have been maligned by a newspaper has, in addition to the right of reply, the right to sue the author of the article. Furthermore, he may demand compensation of up to 100,000 Schilling from the publisher. This right is lost, however, if the newspaper can prove that the publication was true or that 'journalistic care' was taken.

In 1961 the Austrian Press Council (Presserat) was founded. It consists of representatives of the publishers and journalists and its principal duties are to watch over the freedom of the press and to ascertain grievances of the press. Although there is a strong press in some provinces, the country's press is centred in Vienna. The three highest circulation dailies are the *Neue Kronen-Zeitung*, the *Kurier*, and the *Kleine Zeitung* (Graz).

PRINCIPAL DAILIES

Bregenz

Neue Vorarlberger Tageszeitung: 6901 Bregenz, Kornmarktstr. 18; tel. (05574) 24-6-01; telex 57730; fax (05574) 25-5-69; f. 1972; morning; independent; Editor (vacant); circ. weekdays 38,465, Saturday 31,307.

Vorarlberger Nachrichten: Bregenz, Kirchstr. 35; tel. (05574) 512-0; telex 57710; fax (05574) 512-227; morning; Editor EUGEN A. RUSS; circ. weekdays 70,554, Saturday 73,407.

Graz

Kleine Zeitung: 8011 Graz, Schönaugasse 64; tel. (0316) 80-63-0; telex 311782; fax (0316) 80-63-476; f. 1904; independent; Editor Dr FRITZ CSOKLICH; circ. 268,283.

Neue Zeit: 8054 Graz, Ankerstr. 4; tel. (0316) 28-08-0; telex 115928; fax (0316) 28-08-325; f. 1945; morning; Editor JOSEF RIEDLER; circ. 72,786.

Innsbruck

Tiroler Tageszeitung: 6020 Innsbruck, Ing.-Etzel-Str. 30; tel. (0512) 5354-0; telex 534482; fax (0512) 57-59-24; morning; independent; Editor JOSEPH S. MOSER; circ. weekdays 97,570, Saturday 112,326.

Klagenfurt

Kärntner Tageszeitung: 9020 Klagenfurt, Viktringer Ring 28; tel. (04222) 58-66; telex 422415; fax (04222) 541-21; f. 1946; morning except Monday; Socialist; Editor Dr HELLWIG VALENTIN; circ. weekdays 65,200, Friday 68,200.

Kleine Zeitung: 9020 Klagenfurt, Funderstr. 1A; tel. (0463) 200-58-00; telex 422413; fax (04222) 570-64; independent; Editor HEINZ STRITZL; circ. weekdays and Sunday 96,887, Friday 117,718.

AUSTRIA

Linz

Neues Volksblatt: 4020 Linz, Hafenstr. 1–3; tel. (0732) 28-19-01; telex 21235; fax (0732) 27-92-42; f. 1869; Austrian People's Party; Editor Peter Klar; circ. weekdays 29,153, Friday 34,373.

Oberösterreichische Nachrichten: 4010 Linz, Promenade 23; tel. (0732) 280-50; fax (0732) 28-05-448; f. 1865; morning; independent; Editor Dr Hermann Polz; circ. weekdays 109,631, Saturday 142,122.

Oberösterreichisches Tagblatt: 4010 Linz, Landstr. 36; tel. (0732) 58-89-60; independent; Editor Gerald Höchtler; circ. weekdays 31,657, Friday 34,388.

Salzburg

Neues Salzburger Tagblatt: 5020 Salzburg, Auerspergstr. 42; tel. (0662) 72491; independent; Editor Dr Manfred Scheuch; circ. weekdays 8,727.

*Salzburger Nachrichten: 5021 Salzburg, Bergstr. 14; tel. (0662) 74-5-71; telex 633583; fax (0662) 775-91-348; f. 1945; morning; independent; Editor-in-Chief Prof. Dr Karl Heinz Ritschell; circ. weekdays 89,993, Saturday 123,826.

Salzburger Volkszeitung: 5020 Salzburg, Elisabethkai 58; tel. (06222) 79-49-10; telex 633627; fax (06222) 794-91-13; Austrian People's Party; Editor Willi Sauberer; circ. weekdays 12,095.

Sankt Pölten

Der gute Tag: 3100 St Pölten, Julius Raab Promenade 27; tel. (02742) 51-6-44; f. 1990; independent; Editor K. Stiefsohn.

Vienna

*Kurier: 1072 Vienna, Seidengasse 11; tel. (01) 96-2-10; telex 132631; fax (01) 96-78-50; f. 1954; independent; Editors Dr Franz Ferdinand Wolf, Dr Günther Wessig; circ. 442,651.

*Neue A-Z: 1060 Vienna, Windmühlgasse 26; tel. (01) 58-89-60; f. 1889; morning; independent; Editor Dr Peter Pelinka; circ. 138,119.

*Neue Kronen-Zeitung: 1190 Vienna, Muthgasse 2; tel. (01) 3601-0; telex 114327; fax (01) 36-56-64; f. 1900; independent; Editor Hans Dichand; circ. 1,074,743.

*Die Presse: 1015 Vienna, Parkring 12a; tel. (01) 51-4-14; telex 114110; fax (01) 514-14-251; f. 1848; morning; independent; Editor Dr Thomas Chorherr; circ. Mon.-Wed. 72,125, Thur.-Sat. 85,236.

*Der Standard: 1010 Vienna, Herrengasse 1; tel. (01) 53-1-70; f. 1988; independent; Editor-in-Chief Oscar Bronner; Circ. Mon.-Sat. 74,000.

*Volksstimme: 1206 Vienna, Höchstädtplatz 3; tel. 33-1-07; f. 1945; morning; Communist Party; Editor Mag. Michael Graber; circ. weekdays 34,965, Sunday 71,784.

*Wiener Zeitung: 1037 Vienna, Rennweg 12a; tel. (01) 78-76-31; telex 131805; fax (01) 78-76-31-433; f. 1703; morning; official government paper; Editor Heinz Fahnler; circ. 26,860.

* National newspapers.

PRINCIPAL WEEKLIES

Agrar Post: 1141 Vienna, Jenallgasse 4; tel. (01) 82-74-86; f. 1924; independent; agriculture.

Blickpunkt: 6410 Telfs, Blickpunkt-Verlagshaus; tel. (05262) 69-00; telex 534006; fax (05262) 69-00-24; Editor Norbert Walser; circ. 45,200.

Die Furche: 1010 Vienna, Singerstr. 7; tel. (01) 512-52-61; fax (01) 512-82-15; f. 1945; Catholic; Editor Hannes Schopf; circ. 20,150.

Die ganze Woche: 1160 Vienna, Odoakergasse 34–36; tel. (01) 46-26-91; telex 134008; fax (01) 450-16-81; circ. 820,000.

Die Industrie: 1010 Vienna, Bösendorferstr. 2/16; tel. (01) 505-72-15; Editor Milan Frühbauer; circ. 13,300.

IW-Internationale Wirtschaft: 1050 Vienna, Nikolsdorfer Gasse 7–11; tel. (01) 55-55-85; economics; Editor Nikolaus Gerstmayer; circ. 13,000.

Kärntner Nachrichten: 9013 Klagenfurt, Waagplatz 7; tel. (0463) 51-38-69; fax (0463) 56-404-24; Austrian Liberal Party; Editor Andreas Molzer.

Die neue Wirtschaft: 1051 Vienna, Nikolsdorfer Gasse 7–11; tel. (01) 55-55-85; telex 111669; economics; circ. 25,500.

Neue Wochenschau: 1070 Vienna, Kaiserstr. 10; tel. (0222) 523-56-46; fax (0222) 523-56-46; f. 1908; Editors Gerhard Leimer, Franz Weber; circ. 128,500.

NFZ—Neue Freie Zeitung: 1010 Vienna, Kärntner Str. 28; tel. (01) 512-94-52; telex 113610; Austrian Liberal Party; Editor Mag. Christian Wehrschütz; circ. 40,000.

Niederösterreichische Nachrichten: 3100 St Pölten, Gutenbergstr. 12; tel. (02742) 61-5-61; telex 15512; fax (02742) 61-5-61-464; Editor Hans Ströbitzer; circ. 134,400.

Oberösterreichische Rundschau: 4010 Linz, Hafenstr. 1–3; tel. (0732) 278-1-21; telex 02/1014; circ. 253,433.

Der Österreichische Bauernbündler: 1014 Vienna, Bankgasse 1–3; tel. (0222) 533-96-76; fax (0222) 533-96-76; Editor Ing. Paul Gruber; circ. 80,300.

Präsent: 6020 Innsbruck, Exlgasse 20; tel. (0512) 81-5-41; telex 533620; f. 1892; independent Catholic; Chief Editor Dr Hanns Humer.

Samstag: 1081 Vienna, Strozzigasse 8; tel. (01) 43-59-11; f. 1951; weekly; independent; Editor Dietmar Grieser; circ. 101,900.

Tiroler Bauernzeitung: 6021 Innsbruck, Brixner Str. 1; tel. (0512) 59-900-0; telex 33804; published by Tiroler Bauernbund; Chief Editor Georg Keuschnigg; circ. 23,000.

Vídeňské svobodné listy: 1050 Vienna, Margaretenplatz 7; weekly for Czech and Slovak communities in Austria; Editor Dr Jan Krupka.

Vorarlberger Volksbote: 6901 Bregenz, Anton-Schneider-Str. 32; tel. (05574) 23-6-71; fax (05574) 27-1-71; Editor Walter Zeiner; circ. 21,500.

Wochenpost: 8011 Graz, Parkstr. 1; tel. (0316) 77-5-11; independent; illustrated; non-political; Chief Editor Dr Margit Gratzer; circ. 13,500.

POPULAR PERIODICALS

Austria-Ski: 6020 Innsbruck, Olympiastr. 10; tel. (0512) 59501; telex 533876; 6 a year; official journal of Austrian Skiing Assen; Editor Mag. Josef Schmid.

auto touring: 3400 Klosterneuburg, Hölzlgasse 66; tel. (02243) 85600; fax (02243) 86671; monthly; official journal of the Austrian Automobile Organizations; Editor Otto Burghart; circ. 860,000.

Basta: 1050 Vienna, Krongasse 6; tel. (01) 588-91; fax (01) 587-29-15; monthly; Chief Editor Werner Schmid.

Bunte Österreich: 1010 Vienna, Karl Luegen Platz 2; tel. (01) 513-88-34; illustrated weekly; circ. 96,425.

Frauenblatt: 1081 Vienna, Strozzigasse 8; tel. (01) 43-59-11; women's weekly; Editor Gerlinde Kolanda; circ. 53,000.

Profil: 1010 Vienna, Marc-Aurel-Str. 12; tel. (01) 53-4-70; telex 136404; fax (01) 535-32-50; weekly; political general; independent; circ. 106,000.

RZ—Illustrierte Roman- und Rätselzeitung: 1072 Vienna, Kaiser Str. 10; tel. (0222) 523-56-46; fax (0222) 523-56-46-22; f. 1936; weekly illustrated; Editors Gerhard Leimer, Franz Weber; circ. 34,000.

Sport und Toto: 1080 Vienna, Piaristengasse 16; tel. (01) 43-34-63; fax (01) 42-55-89-27; weekly sports illustrated; Editor Ralph Zeilinger.

Sportfunk: 1010 Vienna, Ditscheinergasse 3/3/129; tel. (01) 75-56-55; telex 113191; sporting weekly.

Trend: 1010 Vienna, Marc-Aurel-Str. 12; tel. (01) 53-4-70; telex 136404; monthly; economics; circ. 93,000.

Welt der Frau: 4020 Linz, Lustenauerstr. 21; tel. (0732) 27-02-91; women's monthly magazine; circ. 81,800.

Wiener: 1060 Vienna, Lehargasse 11; tel. (01) 58-88-50; fax (01) 588-85-66; monthly; Chief Editor Gerd Leitgeb.

Wochenpresse: 1070 Vienna, Seidengasse 11; tel. (01) 96-21-0; telex 135869; fax (01) 96-21-22-21; f. 1946; independent; weekly news magazine; Chief Editor (vacant); circ. 46,472.

SPECIALIST PERIODICALS

Acta Chirurgica Austriaca: 1238 Vienna, Feldgasse 13; tel. (01) 889-36-46; fax (01) 889-36-47-24; 6 a year; journal of the Austrian Surgical Soc.; Editor Mag. Richard Hollinek.

Acta Mechanica: Springer Verlag, 1010 Vienna, Mölkerbastei 5; tel. (01) 533-96-14-0; f. 1965; irregular; Editors S. Leibovich (Ithaca, NY), H. Troger (Vienna), G. J. Weng (New Brunswick, NJ), F. Ziegler (Vienna), J. Zierep (Karlsruhe).

Acta Medica Austriaca: 1238 Vienna, Feldgasse 13; tel. (01) 889-36-46; fax (01) 889-36-47-24; 5 a year; journal of the Austrian Soc. for Internal Medicine and associated societies; Editor Mag. Richard Hollinek.

Forum: 1070 Vienna, Museumstr. 5; tel. (01) 93-27-33; fax (01) 93-83-68; f. 1954; every 2 months; international magazine for cultural freedom and political equality; Editor-in-Chief Gerhard Oberschlick; circ. 23,000.

itm praktiker: 1125 Vienna, Marschallplatz 23/1/21; technical hobbies; Chief Editor Gerhard K. Buchberger; circ. 18,800.

Juristische Blätter mit Beilage 'Wirtschaftsrechtliche Blätter': Springer Verlag, 1010 Vienna, Mölkerbastei 5; tel. (01) 533-96-14-0; f. 1872; monthly; Editors F. Bydlinski, H. R. Klecatsky, G. Wilhelm (Beilage 'Wirtschaftsrechtliche Blätter').

AUSTRIA

Die Landwirtschaft: 1011 Vienna, Seilergasse 6–8; tel. (01) 51-5-46; telex 111349; f. 1923; monthly; agriculture and forestry; owned and published by Österreichischer Agrarverlag; Editor Ing. Franz Gebhart; circ. 95,000.

Literatur und Kritik: Otto Müller Verlag, 5021 Salzburg, Ernest-Thun-Str. 11; tel. (0662) 88-19-76; fax (0662) 72-3-87; f. 1966; 5 a year; Austrian and East European literature and criticism; Editor Karl-Markus Gauss.

Monatshefte für Chemie: 1010 Vienna, Mölkerbastei 5; tel. (01) 533-96-14-0; f. 1880; monthly; chemistry; Man. Editor K. Schlögl.

Monatshefte für Mathematik: Springer Verlag, 1010 Vienna, Mölkerbastei 5; tel. (01) 533-96-14-0; f. 1890; irregular; Editor H. Reiter.

Österreichische Ärztezeitung: 1010 Vienna, Weihburggasse 10–12; tel. (01) 512-44-86; telex 112701; fax (01) 51-31-92-524; f. 1945; 6 a year; organ of the Austrian Medical Board; Editor Mag. Martin Stickler.

Österreichische Ingenieur-und Architekten-Zeitschrift: 1010 Vienna, Eschenbachgasse 9; tel. (01) 587-35-36; f. 1958; monthly; Editors W. Koenne, R. Mayr-Harting, G. Widtmann.

Österreichische Monatshefte: 1010 Vienna, Kärntnerstr. 51; tel. (01) 51-5-21; telex 01/1771; f. 1945; monthly; organ of Austrian People's Party; Editor Dr Alfred Grinschgl.

Österreichische Musikzeitschrift: 1010 Vienna, Hegelgasse 13/22; tel. (01) 512-68-69; f. 1946; monthly; Editors E. Lafite, Dr M. Diederichs-Lafite.

Pädiatrie und Pädologie: Springer Verlag, 1010 Vienna, Mölkerbastei 5; tel. (01) 533-96-14-0; f. 1965; irregular; Editor G. Weippl.

Reichsbund-Aktuell mit SPORT: 1010 Vienna, Ebendorferstr. 6/V; tel. (01) 42-54-06; f. 1917; monthly; Catholic; organ of Reichsbund, Bewegung für christliche Gesellschaftspolitik und Sport; Editor Kurt Hlawacek.

Reiseland Österreich: 1110 Vienna, Leberstr. 122; tel. (01) 74-15-95; telex 13/2312; f. 1928; monthly; Editor-in-Chief Ewald Schmitt; circ. 35,000.

Trotzdem: 1070 Vienna, Neustiftgasse 3; tel. (01) 523-41-23; monthly; organ of the Socialist Youth of Austria; Editor Martin Winkler.

Welt der Arbeit: 1030 Vienna, Viehmarktgasse 4; tel. (01) 79-02-0; socialist industrial journal; Editor Kurt Horak; circ 64,350.

Wiener klinische Wochenschrift: 1010 Vienna, Mölker Bastei 5; tel. (01) 533-96-14-0; telex 114506; fax (01) 63-81-58; f. 1888; medical bi-weekly; Editors O. Kraupp, H. Sinzinger.

Wiener Medizinische Wochenschrift: 1238 Vienna, Feldgasse 13; tel. (01) 889-36-46; fax (01) 889-36-47-24; 2 a month; journal of graduate medical education; Editor Mag. Richard Hollinek.

Zukunft: 1014 Vienna, Loewelstr. 18; tel. (01) 53-427-306; monthly; Socialist party; Editor Albrecht K. Konecny.

NEWS AGENCIES

APA (Austria Presse-Agentur): Internationales Pressezentrum (IPZ), 1199 Vienna, Gunoldstr. 14; tel. (01) 36-05-0; telex 114721; f. 1946; co-operative agency of the Austrian Newspapers and Broadcasting Co (private company); 37 mems; Man. Dir Dr Wolfgang Vyslozil; Chief Editor Josef Nowak.

Foreign Bureaux

Agence France-Presse (AFP): IPZ, 1199 Vienna, Gunoldstr. 14; tel. (01) 36-31-87; telex 115833; fax (01) 36-92-568; Correspondent Jean Burner.

Agenzia Nazionale Stampa Associata (ANSA) (Italy): IPZ, 1199 Vienna, Gunoldstr. 14; tel. (01) 36-13-00; telex 114891; fax (01) 36-79-35; Bureau Chief Flaminia Bussotti.

Associated Press (AP) (USA): IPZ, 1199 Vienna, Gunoldstr. 14; tel. (01) 36-41-56; telex 115930; fax (01) 36-91-558; Bureau Chief Alison Smale.

Československá tisková kancelář (ČTK) (Czechoslovakia): 1080 Vienna, Auerspergstr. 15; tel (01) 42-03-75; telex 114215.

Deutsche Presse-Agentur (dpa) (Germany): IPZ, 1199 Vienna, Gunoldstr. 14; tel. (01) 36-21-58; telex 114633; fax (01) 36-85-49; Correspondent Dr Gerd Kriwanek.

Inter Press Service (IPS) (Italy): IPZ, 1199 Vienna, PF 38, Gunoldstr. 14/910; tel. (01) 36-85-06; telex 136081; fax (01) 36-81-78; Dir Federico Nier-Fischer.

Jiji Tsushin-Sha (Japan): IPZ, 1199 Vienna, Gunoldstr. 14; tel. (0222) 36-91-797; telex 112056; fax (0222) 36-91-052; Bureau Chief Kazuya Kitagata.

Kyodo Tsushin (Japan): IPZ, 1199 Vienna, Gunoldstr. 14; tel. (01) 36-15-20; telex 135736; fax (01) 36-92-522; Bureau Chief Motohiro Miura.

Magyar Távirati Iroda (MTI) (Hungary): 1010 Vienna, Teinfaltstr. 4; tel. (01) 533-31-38; telex 115025; Correspondent József Pomazi.

Novinska Agencija Tanjug (Tanjug) (Yugoslavia): IPZ, 1190 Vienna, Gunoldstr. 14; tel. (01) 36-11-80.

Reuters (UK): 1010 Vienna 1, Börsegasse 11; tel. (01) 531-12-0; telex 114645; fax (01) 531-12-5; Chief Correspondent Colin A. McIntyre.

Telegrafnoye Agentstvo Sovetskovo Soyuza (TASS) (USSR): 1040 Vienna, Grosse Neugasse 28; tel. (01) 56-10-46; telex 113413; fax (01) 56-65-36.

United Press International (UPI) (USA): 1199 Vienna, Gunoldstr. 14/6; tel. (01) 369-12-58; telex 111662.

Xinhua (New China) News Agency (People's Republic of China): 1030 Vienna, Reisnerstr. 21; tel. (01) 73-41-40; telex 134384; Correspondent Li Chunguang.

Central News Agency (CNA) (Taiwan) is also represented.

PRESS ASSOCIATIONS

Österreichischer Zeitschriftenverband (Asscn of Periodical Publishers): 1090 Vienna, Hörlgasse 18/5; tel. (01) 31-70-01; f. 1945; 170 mems; Pres. Dr Rudolf Bohmann.

Verband Österreichischer Zeitungsherausgeber und Zeitungsverleger (Austrian Newspaper Publishers' Asscn): 1010 Vienna, Schreyvogelgasse 3; tel. (01) 533-61-78; fax (01) 533-61-78/22; f. 1945; all daily and most weekly papers are mems; Pres. Dir Herbert Binder; Sec.-Gen. Mag. Franz Ivan.

Publishers

Akademische Druck- und Verlagsanstalt: 8010 Graz, Schönaugasse 6, Postfach 598; tel. (0316) 81-34-60; telex 312234; fax (0316) 81-34-60-24; f. 1949; scholarly reprints and new works, facsimile editions of Codices; Dir Manfred Kramer.

Bergland Verlag GmbH: 1051 Vienna, Spengergasse 39; tel. (01) 55-56-41; fax (01) 55-56-41/66; f. 1937; belles-lettres, art, history, fiction; Owner and Dir Friedrich Geyer.

Betz, Annette, Verlag GmbH: 1091 Vienna, Alserstr. 24; tel. (01) 40-444-0; telex 114802; f. 1962; Dir Dr Oskar Mennel.

Blackwell MZV—Medizinische Zeitschriftengesellschaft: 1238 Vienna, Feldgasse 13; tel. (01) 889-36-46; fax (01) 889-36-47-24; f. 1989; medicine, medical journals; Dir Mag. Richard Hollinek.

Böhlau Verlag GmbH & Co KG: 1011 Vienna, Dr Karl Lueger-Ring 12; tel. (0222) 63-87-35; telex 114506; fax (0222) 63-81-58; f. 1947; history, law, philology, the arts, sociology; Dirs Dr Peter Rauch, Rudolf Siegle.

Bohmann Druck und Verlag GmbH & Co KG: 1110 Vienna, Leberstr. 122; tel. (01) 74-15-95; telex 132312; fax (01) 74-15-95-183; f. 1936; trade, technical and industrial books and periodicals; Dirs Dr Rudolf Bohmann, Heinz Keller.

Christian Brandstätter, Verlag und Edition: 1080 Vienna, Wickenburggasse 26; tel. (01) 408-38-14; f. 1982; art books; Chair. Christian Brandstätter.

Wilhelm Braumüller, GmbH: 1092 Vienna, Servitengasse 5; tel. (0222) 34-81-24; fax (0222) 310-28-05; f. 1783; sociology, politics, history, ethnology, linguistics, psychology and philosophy; university publrs; Dir Brigitte Pfeifer.

Franz Deuticke Verlagsgesellschaft mbH: 1011 Vienna, Helferstorferstr. 4; tel. (0222) 533-43-45; telex 753106; fax (0222) 533-23-47; f. 1878; science text books, school books; Dir Dr Scharetzer.

Ludwig Doblinger, KG: 1010 Vienna I, Dorotheergasse 10; tel. (01) 515-030; fax (01) 515-03-51; f. 1876; music; Dir Helmuth Pany.

Europa Verlag GmbH: 1232 Vienna, Altmannsdorfer Str. 154-156; tel. (01) 67-26-22; telex 131326; fax (01) 67-25-11-300; Dirs Ing. Friedrich Löw, Karin Unger.

Freytag-Berndt und Artaria KG Kartographische Anstalt: 1071 Vienna VII, Schottenfeldgasse 62; tel. (01) 93-95-01; telex 133526; f. 1879 (1920—Artaria); geography, maps and atlases; Chair. Harald Hochenegg.

Gerold & Co: 1011 Vienna, Graben 31; tel. (01) 533-50-14; telex 136157; fax (01) 512-47-31-29; f. 1867; philology, literature, Eastern Europe, sociology and philosophy; Dir Hans Neusser.

Globus Zeitungs-, Druck- und Verlagsanstalt GmbH: 1206 Vienna, Höchstädtplatz 3; tel. (01) 33-45-01; telex 114629; fax (01) 33-45-01-237; f. 1945; newspapers, political science, popular sciences, fiction; Gen. Man. Dr H. Zaslawski.

Herder & Co: 1011 Vienna, Wollzeile 33, Postfach 248; tel. (01) 512-14-13; telex 1046; fax (01) 512-14-13/50; f. 1886; religion, theology, history, juvenile; Dir Erich M. Wolf.

AUSTRIA

Herold Druck- und Verlagsgesellschaft mbH: 1080 Vienna, Strozzigasse 8; tel. (01) 43-15-51; telex 111760; fax (01) 40-150/115; f. 1947; art, history, politics, religion; Dirs FRANZ HÖRMANN, LEOPOLD KURZ.

Hölder-Pichler-Tempsky Verlag: 1096 Vienna, Frankgasse 4; tel. (01) 43-89-93; fax (01) 43-89-93-85; f. 1922; school text-books; Man. Dir GUSTAV GLÖCKLER.

Brüder Hollinek: 1238 Vienna, Feldgasse 13; tel. (01) 889-36-46; fax (01) 889-36-47-24; f. 1872; science, law and administration, dictionaries; Dir Mag. RICHARD HOLLINEK.

Jugend und Volk Verlagsgesellschaft mbH: 1153 Vienna, Anschützgasse 1; tel. (01) 812-05-17; telex 136103; fax (01) 812-05-17-27; f. 1921; pedagogics, art, literature, children's books; Dir Dr OTTO SCHIMPF.

Verlag Kremayr & Scheriau: 1121 Vienna, Niederhofstr. 37; tel. (01) 811-02; telex 31405; fax (01) 81102-4; f. 1951; non-fiction, history; Dir Dr PETER LIEGER.

Kunstverlag Wolfrum: 1010 Vienna, Augustinerstr. 10; tel. (01) 512-41-78; f. 1919; art; Dirs HUBERT WOLFRUM, MONIKA ENGEL.

Leykam Verlag: 8011 Graz, Stempfergasse 3; tel. (0316) 81-66-76; telex 32209; fax (0316) 81-66-76-39; art, literature, academic, law; Dir Dkfm. Mag. Dr K. OKTABETZ.

Manz'sche Verlags- und Universitätsbuchhandlung: 1014 Vienna, Kohlmarkt 16; tel. (01) 53-161; telex 75310631; fax (01) 53-161-81; f. 1849; law, political and economic sciences; textbooks and schoolbooks; Exec. Principals Dkfm. FRANZ STEIN, Dr ANTON C. HILSCHER.

Wilhelm Maudrich: 1097 Vienna, Lazarettgasse 1; tel. (01) 402-47-12; telex 135177; fax (01) 48-50-80; f. 1909; medical; Man. Dir Dr HEINZ PINKER.

Otto Müller Verlag: 5021 Salzburg, Ernest-Thun-Str. 11; tel. (0662) 88-19-74; fax (0662) 72-387; f. 1937; general; Man. ARNO KLEIBEL.

Paul Neff Verlag KG: 1140 Vienna, Hackingerstr. 52; tel. (01) 94-06-11; f. 1829; fiction, biographies, music, theatre, etc.

R. Oldenbourg KG: 1030 Vienna, Neulinggasse 26/12; tel. (01) 72-62-580; f. 1959; Dirs Dr KARL CORNIDES, Dr THOMAS CORNIDES.

Verlag Orac: 1010 Vienna, Graben 17; tel. (01) 55-16-21-0; telex 136365; fax (01) 55-16-21-78; f. 1946; Dir HELMUT HANUSCH.

Österreichischer Gewerbeverlag GmbH: 1014 Vienna, Herrengasse 10; tel. (01) 63-07-68; fax (01) 63-07-68-30; f. 1945; general; Man. F. SCHARETZER.

Pinguin Verlag Pawlowski KG: 6021 Innsbruck, Lindenbühelweg 2; tel. (0512) 81-1-83; illustrated books; Dirs OLAF PAWLOWSKI, HELLA PFLANZER.

Residenz Verlag GmbH: 5020 Salzburg, Gaisbergstr. 6; tel. (0662) 64-19-86; fax (0662) 64-35-48; f. 1956; Dir Dr JOCHEN JUNG.

Anton Schroll & Co: 1051 Vienna, Spengergasse 39; tel. (01) 55-56-41; fax (01) 55-56-41-66; f. 1884; also in Munich; art books; Man. F. GEYER.

Springer-Verlag KG: 1200 Vienna, Sachsenplatz 4–6; f. 1924; medicine, science, technology, law, sociology, economics, periodicals; Dirs Dr K. F. SPRINGER, C. MICHALETZ, Prof. Dr D. GÖTZE, Ing. WOLFRAM JOOS, R. SIEGLE.

Leopold Stocker Verlag: 8011 Graz, Hofgasse 5; tel. (0316) 82-16-36; fax (0316) 83-56-12; f. 1917; history, nature, hunting, fiction, poetry, textbooks; Dir Dr ILSE DVORAK-STOCKER.

Verlag Styria: 8011 Graz, Schönaugasse 64; tel. (0316) 8063-0; telex 312387; fax (0316) 80-63-204; f. 1869; literature, history, theology, philosophy; Gen. Dir Dr HANNS SASSMANN.

Verlagsanstalt Tyrolia GmbH: 6020 Innsbruck, Exlgasse 20; tel. (0512) 81-5-41; f. 1907; geography, history, science, religion, fiction; Chair. Dr GEORG SCHIEMER.

Carl Ueberreuter Verlag: 1091 Vienna, Alser Str. 24; tel. (01) 40-444-0; telex 114802; non-fiction, children's; Dir Dr OSKAR MENNEL.

Universal Edition: 1010 Vienna, Postfach 3, Karlsplatz 6; tel. (01) 505-86-95; telex 11397; fax (01) 505-27-20; f. 1901; music; Dir Dr J. JURANEK.

Urban & Schwarzenberg, KG: 1006 Vienna, Frankgasse 4; tel. (01) 42-27-31; f. 1866; science, medicine; Dir MICHAEL URBAN.

Paul Zsolnay Verlag GmbH: 1041 Vienna, Prinz Eugen-Str. 30 (also in Darmstadt); tel. (01) 505-76-61; telex 132279; fax (01) 505-76-61-10; f. 1923; fiction, non-fiction; Dir Dkfm. BRANDTNER.

Government Publishing Houses

Österreichische Staatsdruckerei (Austrian State Printing Office): 1037 Vienna, Rennweg 12A; tel. (01) 78-76-310; f. 1804; law, art reproductions; Dir ARIBERT SCHWARZMANN.

Österreichischer Bundesverlag GmbH: 1015 Vienna, Schwarzenbergstr. 5; tel. (01) 514-05; telex 131159; fax (01) 514-05-210; f. 1772 by Empress Maria Theresia; school textbooks, education, culture, travel guides, science, children's books; Dirs Mag. WALTER AMON, Dr ROBERT SEDLACZEK.

PUBLISHERS' ASSOCIATION

Hauptverband des österreichischen Buchhandels (Association of Austrian Publishers and Booksellers): 1010 Vienna I, Grünangergasse 4; tel. (01) 512-15-35; fax (01) 512-15-35-21; f. 1859; Pres. OTTO HAUSA; Gen. Sec. Dr WOLFGANG RAMJOUÉ; 670 mems.

Radio and Television

In January 1988 there were 619 radio transmitters in the provinces, broadcasting two national programmes (one for 18 hours and one for 24 hours), 10 local programmes and an overseas service on shortwave. At the same time there were 913 television transmitters. In 1989 there were 2,700,136 radio licences issued and 2,494,355 television licences issued.

Österreichischer Rundfunk (ORF) (Austrian Broadcasting Company): 1136 Vienna, Würzburggasse 30; tel. (01) 82-91-0; telex 133601; fax (01) 82-91/22-50; f. 1955; controls all radio and television in Austria; Dir-Gen. GERD BACHER; Dirs JOHANNES KUNZ, ERNST WOLFRAM MARBOE (Television Programmes), ERNST GRISSEMANN (Radio Programmes), HEINZ DOUCHA (Technology), Dr PETER RADEL (Finance and Administration).

Finance

(cap. = capital; p.u. = paid up; dep. = deposits; m. = million; brs = branches; amounts in Schilling)

BANKS

Banks in Austria, apart from the National Bank, belong to one of six categories. The first category comprises banks that are organized as corporations (i.e. joint-stock banks), and special-purpose credit institutions. In July 1990 these numbered, respectively, 52 and 83. The second category comprises private banks, which numbered three, and the third category comprises savings banks, which numbered 126. The fourth category comprises co-operative banks. These include rural credit co-operatives (Raiffeisenkassen), which numbered 865 in July 1990, and industrial credit co-operatives (Volksbanken), which numbered 100. The remaining two categories comprise the mortgage banks of the various Austrian 'Länder', which numbered 10 in July 1990, and the building societies, which numbered four in July 1990. The majority of Austrian banks (with the exception of the building societies) operate on the basis of universal banking, although certain categories have specialized. Banking operations are governed by the Banking Act of 1979 (Kreditwesengesetz–KWG), as amended in 1986.

Central Bank

Oesterreichische Nationalbank (Austrian National Bank): 1090 Vienna, Otto Wagner-Platz 3; tel. (0222) 404-20-0; telex 114669; fax (0222) 404-20-6714; f. 1922; cap. 150m., dep. 51,114m. (Dec. 1989); Pres. Dr MARIA SCHAUMAYER; Gen. Man. ADOLF WALA; 7 brs.

Commercial Banks

Adria Bank AG: 1011 Vienna, Tegetthoffstr. 1; tel. (01) 513-15-76; telex 134892; fax (01) 513-15-76-43; f. 1980; cap. 151.6m., reserves 261.2m., dep. 3,725.2m. (Dec. 1989); Mans Dipl. Oec. RUDOLF VRAČKO, Dr ALFRED SCHERHAMMER.

AVA–Bank GmbH: 1015 Vienna, Operngasse 2; tel. (01) 51-5-71; telex 111173; fax (01) 515-71-481; f. 1927; cap. 925m., dep. 9,803m. (1989); Gen. Man. Dr JOHANN BURGEMEISTER; 37 brs.

Banco do Brasil AG: 1010 Vienna, Tegetthoffstr. 4; tel. (01) 512-66-63; telex 111997; cap. 47m. (1989); Chair. NIVALDO VOIGT.

Bank der Österreichischen Postsparkasse AG: 1015 Vienna, Opernring 3–5; tel. (01) 588-09-0; telex 112268; fax (01) 588-09-127; cap. 645m., dep. 13,643m. (1989); Chair. and Man. Dkfm. Dr VIKTOR WOLF.

Bank für Arbeit und Wirtschaft AG: 1010 Vienna, Seitzergasse 2–4; tel. (0222) 53-4-53-0; telex 115311; fax (0222) 534-53-2840; f. 1947; cap. 7,616m., dep. 178,546m. (1989); Chair. and Gen. Man. Komm. Rat WALTER FLÖTTL; 129 brs.

Bank für Wirtschaft und Freie Berufe AG: 1072 Vienna, Zieglergasse 5; tel. (01) 96-15-46; telex 132346; fax (01) 96-15-46-57; f. 1914; cap. 106m., dep. 1,416m. (Dec. 1989); Mans PETER SCHLADOFSKY, PETER WENINGER, HANNES ROTTER.

Bank Gebrüd. Gutmann Nfg AG: 1011 Vienna, Schwarzenbergplatz 16; tel. (0222) 50220-0; telex 136506; fax (0222) 50220-249; f. 1922; cap. 70m.; Gen. Man. Dr HELMUTH E. FREY.

AUSTRIA

Bank Winter & Co AG: 1011 Vienna, Singerstr. 10; tel. (01) 51-50-40; telex 112462; fax (01) 515-04-213; f. 1959; cap. 1,438m., dep. 28,032m. (1989); Chair. SIMON MOSKOVICS; Man. Dirs THOMAS MOSKOVICS, ADA HAFNER; 1 br.

Bankhaus Feichtner & Co AG: 1011 Vienna, Wipplingerstr. 1; tel. (01) 533-16-06; telex 114260; fax (01) 533-16-02-222; f. 1878; cap. 298m., dep. 5,486m. (1989); Chair. Dr WOLFGANG WIPLER.

Bankhaus Rössler AG: 1015 Vienna, Kärntner Ring 17; tel. (01) 514-68; telex 131815; fax (01) 514-68/34; f. 1955; cap. 150m. (1989); Management Board HANNS CHRISTIAN, Dr GERHARD TANEW.

Bankhaus Schelhammer & Schattera AG: 1011 Vienna, Goldschmiedgasse 3; tel. (01) 53-4-34; telex 13206; fax (01) 53-4-34/64; f. 1832; cap. 272m., dep. 2,710m. (Dec. 1989); private bank; Gen. Dir Komm. Rat Dipl.-Ing. JOSEF MELCHART; Dir Dkfm. JOSEF LÖW; 8 brs.

Bankhaus C. A. Steinhäusser: 1014 Vienna, Kohlmarkt 1/10; tel. (01) 533-10-10; telex 133146; f. 1856; cap. 63m. (1989); Mans ERNST DEMUTH, HERBERT BÖHM.

Central Wechsel- und Creditbank AG: 1015 Vienna, Kärntner Str. 43; tel. (01) 515-66-0; telex 112387; fax (01) 515-66-9; cap. 435m. (1989); Gen. Man. Dr KÁLMÁN MÉSZÁROS.

Centro Internationale Handelsbank AG: 1015 Vienna, Tegetthoffstr. 1; tel. (01) 51-5-20-0; telex 136990; fax (01) 513-43-96; f. 1973; cap. 374m., dep. 6,363m. (Dec. 1989); Exec. Bd Dr GERHARD VOGT (Chair.), JERZY PLUSA, CHRISTIAN SPERK.

Chase Manhattan Bank (Austria) AG: 1011 Vienna, Parkring 12A, Postfach 582; tel. (01) 51-5-89; telex 112570; fax (01) 515-89-27; f. 1956 as Österreichische Privat- und Kommerzbank AG; present name adopted in 1974; cap. 148m., total resources 2,859m. (Dec. 1989); Chair. RICHARD MOUNCE; Gen. Man. ANDREAS TREICHL.

Citibank (Austria) AG: 1015 Vienna, Lothringer Str. 7; tel. (01) 71-71-70; telex 112105; fax (01) 713-92-06; f. 1959 as Internationale Investitions- und Finanzierungs Bank AG; present name adopted 1978; wholly-owned subsidiary of Citibank Overseas Investment Corpn; cap. 400m., dep. 9,235m.; Gen. Man. Dr OLAF NEUBERT.

Constantia Privatbank AG: 1010 Vienna, Opernring 17; tel. (01) 58875-0; fax (01) 58875-90; cap. 106m. (1989); Gen. Man. Dr CHRISTOPH KRAUS.

Creditanstalt-Bankverein: 1010 Vienna, Schottengasse 6; tel. (01) 531-31-0; telex 133030; fax (01) 531-31-75-66; f. 1855; cap. 3,600m., dep. 492,725m. (Dec. 1989); Chair. Dr G. SCHMIDT-CHIARI; 377 brs.

Deutsche Bank (Austria) AG: 1013 Vienna, Hohenstaufengasse 4; tel. (01) 5335621-0; fax (01) 51535-297; Mans Mag. STEPHAN HANDL, Dr WILHELM GORTON.

Donau-Bank AG: 1011 Vienna, Parkring 6; tel. (0222) 5-15-35; telex 116473; fax (0222) 515-35/297; f. 1974; jointly owned by the State Bank of the USSR and the Bank for Foreign Economic Affairs of the USSR; cap. 600m., dep. 17,612m. (1989); Chair. ANDREJ I. AKIMOV.

Elsässische Bank AG: 1015 Vienna, Schwarzenbergplatz 1; tel. (01) 712-51-03-0; telex 133766; fax (01) 712-51-03/35; f. 1972; wholly-owned subsidiary of Société Générale Alsacienne de Banque (France); cap. 204m., dep. 5,769m. (1989); Gen. Mans Dr ALBERT MÜRSCH (Strasbourg); Dr MANFRED KUNZE (Vienna).

Gara Real- und Personalkreditbank AG: 1061 Vienna, Theobaldgasse 19; tel. (01) 58823-0; fax (01) 58823-224; cap. 81m. (1989); Mans Dkfm. WERNER KRONFELLNER, ARTHUR SCHNEIDER, Dkfm. JOHANN ZWETTLER.

Internationale Bank für Aussenhandel AG: 1011 Vienna, Neuer Markt 1; tel. (0222) 51-5-56-0; telex 113564; fax (0222) 515-56-50; f. 1970; cap. 207m., dep. 4,721m. (1989); Gen. Mans Dkfm. Dr WALTER BEYER, Dkfm. HUBERT WIELEBNOWSKI.

Kathrein & Co Bank AG: 1013 Vienna, Wipplingerstr. 25; tel. (01) 53451; telex 14123; fax (01) 53451/274; f. 1924; Gen. Man. Dr WOLFGANG FENKART-FRÖSCHL; Mans STEFAN BREZOVICH, HEINZ HÖDL.

Länderbank-Exportbank AG: 1010 Vienna, Wallnerstr. 8; tel. (0222) 53-13-40; telex 133468; fax (0222) 53-13-45; f. 1973; present name adopted 1987; cap. 142m., dep. 7,426m. (Sept. 1989); Chair. HELMUT BOHUNOVSKY.

Meinl Bank AG: 1015 Vienna, Bauernmarkt 2; tel. (0222) 531-88; telex 132256; fax (0222) 531-88-44; f. 1922; cap. 332m., dep. 4,744m. (1989); Dirs JULIUS MEINL, WOLFGANG SAMESCH, ERNST WIMMER.

Mercurbank AG: 1015 Vienna, Kärntner Ring 8; tel. (01) 6 50132-0; telex 131439; cap. 312m., dep. 4,790m. (1989); Mans MANFRED KOPRIVA, Dr LEOPOLD RÖHREK, Dkfm. ROBERT SCHILDER; 31 brs.

Österreichische Konsumbank AG: 1061 Vienna, Theobaldgasse 19; tel. (01) 58822-0; cap. 192m. (1989); Mans Dr GERHARD PARTIK, Dkfm. KURT SAGMEISTER, Dkfm. WERNER KRONFELLNER.

Österreichische Länderbank AG: 1011 Vienna, Am Hof 2; tel. (01) 531-24-0; telex 115561; fax (01) 531-24-55; f. 1880; cap. 10,206m., dep. 204,800m. (Dec. 1989); Gen. Man. Dkfm. HANS GERHARD RANDA; 141 brs.

Österreichische Verkehrskreditbank AG: 1081 Vienna, Auerspergstr. 17; tel. (01) 42-76-48-0; telex 115965; fax (01) 42-76-48-18; cap. 112m. (1989); Chair. Dkfm. HERBERT WAGNER.

Österreichisches Credit-Institut AG: 1010 Vienna, Herrengasse 12; tel. (01) 531-30-0; telex 115260; fax (01) 531-30-299; f. 1896; subsidiary of Österreichische Länderbank AG; cap. 400m., dep. 25,007m. (1989); Gen. Man. Dr GEROLD PIRINGER; Man. FREIMUT DOBRETSBERGER; 44 brs.

Royal Trust Bank (Austria) AG: 1011 Vienna, Rathausstr. 20, Postfach 306; tel. (01) 43-61-61; telex 114911; fax (01) 42-81-42; f. 1890; present name adopted 1988; wholly-owned affiliate of Royal Trustco Ltd, Canada; cap. 112m., dep. 1,897m.; Chair. and Gen. Man. Dkfm. Dr ERICH STÖGER.

Sanpaolo Bank (Austria) AG: 1090 Vienna, Türkenstr. 9; tel. (0222) 31-330-0; telex 111715; fax (0222) 31-54-23; f. 1984; cap. 300m., dep. 4,000m. (1990); Gen. Man. SERGIO ZEME; 2 brs.

Schoeller & Co Bank AG: 1011 Vienna, Renngasse 1–3; tel. (01) 53471; telex 114219; f. 1833; cap. 992m., dep. 18,435m. (1989); Chair. and Gen. Man. Dr HERBERT SCHOELLER; 12 brs.

Westdeutsche Landesbank (Austria) AG: 1015 Vienna, Kärntner Ring 10; tel. (01) 5053394; telex 133608; fax (01) 5051070; f. 1984 as Standard Chartered Bank (Austria) AG; present name adopted 1990; cap. 192m. (1990); Mans Dkfm. JAN PROSKAR (Chair. Bd of Management), CHARLES KESTEMONT, Dr WOLFGANG HABERMAYER.

Regional Banks

Bank für Handel und Industrie AG: 8011 Graz, Herrengasse 28; tel. (0316) 821687-0; telex 31298; fax (0316) 82-16-87-17; f. 1956; cap. 88m. (1989); Pres. GOTTFRIED PENGG; Mans REINHARD FISCHER, ERHARD WRESSNIG; 3 brs.

Bank für Kärnten und Steiermark AG: 9010 Klagenfurt, Dr Arthur Lemisch-Platz 5; tel. (0463) 5858-0; telex 422454; fax (0463) 5858-454; f. 1922; cap. 1,549m., dep. 20,304m. (1989); Gen. Man. Konsul MAXIMILIAN MERAN; Dir Dr HEIMO PENKER; 28 brs.

Bank für Oberösterreich und Salzburg: 4010 Linz, Hauptplatz 10-11; tel. (0732) 2802/0; telex 21802; fax (0732) 2802-2183; f. 1869; cap. 3,075m., dep. 46,326m. (Dec. 1989); Chair. Dr HERMANN BELL; 75 brs.

Bank für Tirol und Vorarlberg AG: 6021 Innsbruck, Erlerstr. 5–9; tel. (0512) 5333-0; telex 533619; fax (0512) 5333-509; f. 1904; cap. 1,429m., dep. 22,186m. (1989); Gen. Man. Komm. Rat Dr GERHARD MOSER; Dirs Dr OTTO KASPAR, Dr JÜRGEN WAGENSONNER; 34 brs.

Bankhaus Krentschker & Co AG: 8011 Graz, Am Eisernen Tor 3; tel. (0316) 8030; telex 311411; fax (0316) 8030-22; f. 1924; Chair. Dr HEINZ HOFER; 3 brs.

Eisenstädter Bank AG: 7001 Eisenstadt, Hauptstr. 31; tel. (02682) 605-0; telex 17610; fax (02682) 61039; f. 1872; cap. 60m. (1989); Dirs MANFRED SCHNEIDER, ERNST GASSNER; 8 brs.

Privatinvest Bank AG: 5010 Salzburg, Griesgasse 11; tel. (0662) 8048-0; telex 633267; fax (0662) 8048-333; f. 1885 as Bankhaus Daghofer & Co; present name adopted 1990; cap. 80m. (1990); Dirs Dr HERMANN REIF, JOSEF TSCHELLING; 2 brs.

Salzburger Kredit- und Wechsel-Bank AG: 5024 Salzburg, Marktplatz 1; tel. (0662) 72516-0; telex 633625; fax (0662) 72516-21; f. 1921; cap. 288m.; Dirs KLAUS BÖNING, GEORG EBNER; 3 brs.

Steiermärkische Bank GmbH: 8011 Graz, Hauptplatz, Rathaus; tel. (0316) 8032-0; telex 311930; fax (0316) 80-32-407; f. 1922; cap. 457m. (1989); Gen. Man. Dr JAN OHMS; 12 brs.

Volkskreditbank AG: 4010 Linz, Rudigierstr. 5–7; tel. (0732) 278456-0; telex 02-2282; fax (0732) 278456-200; f. 1872; cap. 618m., dep. 10,472m. (Dec. 1989); Man. Dr GERNOT KRENNER.

Specialized Banks

Österreichische Investitionskredit AG: 1013 Vienna, Renngasse 10; tel. (01) 53135; telex 111619; fax (01) 53135-990; cap. 2,472m. (1989); Mans Dr HARALD LANG, Dkfm. ALFRED REITER.

Österreichische Kommunalkredit AG: 1011 Vienna, Renngasse 10; tel. (01) 533-26-77; cap. 175m. (1989).

Österreichische Kontrollbank AG: 1010 Vienna, Am Hof 4; tel. (01) 531-27-0; telex 132747; fax (01) 531-27-533; f. 1946; export financing, stock exchange clearing, money market operations; cap. 701m. (Dec. 1989); Chair. and Gen. Man. Komm. Rat HELMUT H. HASCHEK.

Österreichischer Exportfonds GmbH: 1031 Vienna, Gottfried-Keller-Gasse 1; tel. (01) 726151-0; fax (01) 726151-30; cap. 122m. (1989); Mans Dkfm. HERBERT ALLWINGER, HERBERT NIEMETZ.

Savings Banks

Girozentrale und Bank der Österreichischen Sparkassen AG (GZ) (Central Bank of the Austrian Savings Banks): 1011 Vienna, Schubertring 5; tel. (0222) 711-94-0; telex 132591; fax (0222) 713-18-05; f. 1937; central institution of savings banks; cap. 12,259m., dep. 258,361m. (1989); Chair. and Man. Dir Dr Hans Haumer.

Die Erste Österreichische Spar-Casse (First Austrian Savings Bank): 1010 Vienna, Graben 21; tel. (0222) 53100; telex 114012; fax (0222) 53100-448; f. 1819; cap. 6,967m., dep. 135,603m. (Dec. 1989); Chair. and CEO Dr Konrad Fuchs; 110 brs.

Österreichische Postsparkasse: 1018 Vienna, Georg-Coch Platz 2; tel. (0222) 51-40-00; telex 111663; fax (0222) 514-00-17-00; f. 1883; cap. 5,835m., dep. 169,862m. (1989); Gov. Dkfm. Kurt Nösslinger; Vice-Govs Dr V. Wolf, Dr. E. Hampel; 12 brs.

Zentralsparkasse und Kommerzialbank Wien (Z) (Savings Bank): 1030 Vienna, Vordere Zollamtsstr. 13; tel. (01) 7292-0; telex 133615; fax (01) 711-91-1796; f. 1905; cap. 7,691m., dep. 185,901m. (1987); Chair. Prof. Dr Helmut Zilk; 173 brs.

Co-operative Banks

Österreichische Volksbanken-AG: 1090 Vienna, Peregringasse 3; tel. (0222) 3134-0; telex 134206; fax (0222) 31340-3103; f. 1922; cap. 2,355m., dep. 58,233m. (1989); Chair. and CEO Robert Mädl.

Raiffeisen Zentralbank Österreich AG: 1031 Vienna, Am Stadtpark 9; tel. (01) 71707-0; telex 136989; fax (01) 71707-1715; f. 1927; cap. 7,731m., dep. 165,160m. (Dec. 1989); central institute of the Austrian Raiffeisen banking group; Pres. Dr Christian Konrad; Gen. Man. Dr Klaus Liebscher; 3 brs.

Bankers' Organization

Verband österreichischer Banken und Bankiers (Asscn of Austrian Banks and Bankers): 1013 Vienna, Börsegasse 11; tel. (01) 535-17-71; telex 132824; fax (01) 535-71-71/38; f. 1945; Pres. Dr Guido Schmidt-Chiari; Gen. Sec Dr Fritz Diwok; 55 mems.

STOCK EXCHANGE

Wiener Börsekammer (Vienna Stock Exchange): 1011 Vienna, Wipplingerstr. 34; tel. (0222) 53-4-99; telex 132447; fax (0222) 535-68-57; f. 1771; two sections: Stock Exchange, Commodity Exchange; Pres. Dkfm. Gerhard Wagner; Gen. Sec. Dr Kurt Neuteufel.

INSURANCE COMPANIES

In 1988 there were 69 insurance organizations in Austria. A selection of companies is given below.

Anglo-Elementar Versicherungs-AG: 1015 Vienna, Kärntner Ring 12; tel. (01) 501-67-0; telex 132355; fax (01) 505-40-08; Gen. Man. Erik Skreiner.

Austria Österreichische Versicherungs-AG: 1021 Vienna II, Untere Donaustr. 25; tel. (0222) 21-1-75; telex 135308; fax (0222) 751-1999; f. 1936; Gen. Man. Dipl. Ing. Herbert Schimetschek.

Donau Allgemeine Versicherungs-AG: 1010 Vienna, Schottenring 15; tel. (0222) 31-311; fax (0222) 34-65-87; f. 1867; all classes; Gen. Man. Dr Gerhard Puschmann.

EA-General Aktiengesellschaft: 1011 Vienna, Landskrongasse 1-3; tel. (01) 534-01; telex 114085; fax (01) 534-01/226; f. 1882 as Erste Allgemeine Versicherungs; Gen. Man. Dr Dietrich Karner.

Grazer Wechselseitige Versicherung: 8011 Graz, Herrengasse 18–20; tel. (0316) 8037-0; telex 31414; fax (0316) 80-37-414; f. 1828; all classes; Gen. Man. Dr Friedrich Fall.

Interunfall-RAS Versicherungs-Aktiengesellschaft: 1011 Vienna, Tegetthoffstr. 7; tel. (01) 51403-0; telex 112111; fax (01) 514-03/560; cap. 300,000m. (1990); all classes of insurance (including reinsurance); Man. Hellmuth Wandschneider.

Versicherungsanstalt der österreichischen Bundesländer Versicherungs-AG: 1021 Vienna, Praterstr. 1–7; tel. (01) 21111-0; telex 134800; fax (01) 211-11/552; Gen. Man. Dr Walter Petrak.

Wiener Allianz Versicherungs-AG: 1131 Vienna, Hietzinger Kai 101–105; tel. (01) 94-85-11-0; telex 134222; fax (01) 94-85-11/260; f. 1860; all classes except life insurance; Gen. Man. Dr Ernst Baumgartner.

Wiener Städtische Wechselseitige Versicherungsanstalt (Municipal Insurance Co of the City of Vienna): 1010 Vienna, Schottenring 30; tel. (01) 531-39-0; telex 135140; fax (01) 535-34-37; f. 1898; all classes; Chair. The Mayor of Vienna; Gen. Man. Dkfm. Dr Siegfried Sellitsch.

Zürich Kosmos Versicherungen AG: 1015 Vienna I, Schwarzenbergplatz 15; tel. (01) 501-25-0; telex 133375; fax (01) 505-04-85; f. 1910; all classes; Gen. Man. Dr Werner Faber.

Insurance Organization

Verband der Versicherungsunternehmungen Österreichs (Asscn of Austrian Insurance Companies): 1030 Vienna III, Schwarzenbergplatz 7; tel. (0222) 711-56-0; telex 133289; fax (0222) 711-56/270; f. 1945; Pres. Dr Walter Petrak; Gen. Sec. Dr Herbert Pflüger.

Trade and Industry

CHAMBERS OF COMMERCE

All Austrian enterprises must by law be members of the Economic Chambers. The Federal Economic Chamber promotes international contacts and represents the economic interest of trade and industry on a federal level. Its Foreign Trade Organization includes about 90 offices abroad.

Bundeskammer der gewerblichen Wirtschaft (Federal Economic Chamber): 1045 Vienna, Wiedner Hauptstr. 63; tel. (0222) 50105; telex 111871; fax (0222) 50206; f. 1946; six sections: Commerce, Industry, Small-scale Production, Banking and Insurance, Transport and Tourism; these divisions are subdivided into branch associations; Local Economic Chambers with divisions and branch associations in each of the nine Austrian provinces; Pres. Abg. z. Nationalrat Ing. Leopold Maderthaner; Sec.-Gen. D.Dr Karl Kehrer; 290,000 mems.

INDUSTRIAL ASSOCIATIONS

Bundeskammer der gewerblichen Wirtschaft—Bundessektion Industrie: 1045 Vienna I, Wiedner Hauptstr. 63; tel. (01) 501-05; telex 11871; fax (01) 502-06; f. 1896 as Zentralverband der Industrie Österreichs (Central Federation of Austrian Industry), merged into present organization 1947; Chair. Dipl. Volksw. Philipp Schoeller; Deputy Chair. Pres. Dr Christian Beurle; Dir Dr Friedrich Placek; comprises the following industrial federations:

Fachverband der Audiovisions- und Filmindustrie (Films): 1045 Vienna, Wiedner Hauptstr. 63; tel. (01) 501-05; telex 111871; fax (01) 50206/270; Chair. Prof. Walther K. Stoitzner, Dr Elmar A. Peterlunger; 1,300 mems.

Fachverband der Bauindustrie (Building): 1030 Vienna, Engelsberggasse 4; tel. (01) 713-65-04-0; telex 135284; fax (01) 713-65-04-19; Chair. Dipl.-Ing. Friedrich Fellerer; Dir Dr Johannes Schenk; 136 mems.

Fachverband der Bekleidungsindustrie (Clothing): 1030 Vienna III, Schwarzenbergplatz 4; tel. (01) 712-12-96; telex 134891; fax (01) 713-92-04; Chair. Dipl.-Ing. Konrad Wührer; Dir Christoph Haidinger; 606 mems.

Fachverband der Bergwerke und Eisenerzeugenden Industrie (Mining and Iron Producing): 1015 Vienna, Goethegasse 3, Postfach 300; tel. (01) 512-46-01-0; fax (01) 512-46-01/20; Chair. Dipl.-Ing. Dr-Ing. Friedrich Schmollgruber; Sec. Ing. Mag. Hermann Prinz; 112 mems.

Fachverband der Chemischen Industrie (Chemicals): 1045 Vienna 4, Wiedner Hauptstr. 63; tel. (01) 501-05; telex 111871; fax (01) 502-06-280; Chair. Gen. Dir Komm. Rat Dipl.-Ing Dr Wolfgang Unger; Dir Mag. Dr Harald Strassnitzky; 750 mems.

Fachverband der Eisen- und Metallwarenindustrie Österreichs (Iron and Metal Goods): 1045 Vienna 4, Wiedner Hauptstr. 63, Postfach 335; tel. (0222) 501-05; telex 111871; fax (0222) 505-09-28; f. 1908; Chair. Komm. Rat Hannes Folter; Dir Dipl. Kfm. Gottfried Taurer; 800 mems.

Fachverband der Elektro-und Elektronikindustrie (Electrical): 1010 Vienna, Rathausplatz 8; tel. (01) 42-55-97; fax (01) 408-53-13; Chair. Dipl. Ing. Alfred Mosbeck; Dir Dr Heinz Raschka; 558 mems.

Fachverband der Erdölindustrie (Oil): 1031 Vienna, Erdbergstr. 72; tel. (01) 713-23-48; telex 132138; fax (01) 713-05-10; f. 1947; Gen. Dir Dr Herbert Kaes; Gen. Sec. Dr Herbert Lang; 24 mems.

Fachverband der Fahrzeugindustrie (Vehicles): 1045 Vienna 4, Wiedner Hauptstr. 63; tel. (0222) 501-05; telex 111871; fax (0222) 502-06-289; Pres. Dipl.-Ing. Otto Voisard; Gen. Sec. Mag. Erik Baier; 160 mems.

Fachverband der Gas- und Wärmeversorgungsunternehmungen (Gas and Heating): 1010 Vienna, Schubertring 14; tel. (01) 513-15-88; fax (01) 513-15-88-25; Gen. Dir Dr Bruno Zidek; Dir Dkfm. Gerhard Janaczek; 115 mems.

Fachverband der Giessereiindustrie (Foundries): 1045 Vienna, Wiedner Hauptstr. 63, Postfach 339; tel. (01) 50105-3463; telex 111871; fax (01) 50206-273; Chair. Ing. Michael Zimmermann; Dir Dr Kurt Krenkel; 109 mems.

Fachverband der Glasindustrie (Glass): 1045 Vienna 4, Wiedner Hauptstr. 63, Postfach 328; tel. (01) 501-05; telex 111871; fax (01) 502-06/281; Chair. Dipl.-Ing. Raimund Crammer; Dir Dr Peter Schoepf; 65 mems.

AUSTRIA

Fachverband der Holzverarbeitenden Industrie (Wood Processing): 1037 Vienna III, Schwarzenbergplatz 4, Postfach 123; tel. (01) 712-26-01; telex 134891; fax (01) 713-03-09; f. 1946; Chair. Komm. Rat Hanno Weiss; Dir Dr Georg Penka; 613 mems.

Fachverband der Ledererzeugenden Industrie (Leather Producing): 1045 Vienna 4, Wiedner Hauptstr. 63, Postfach 312; tel. (01) 501-05; telex 111871; fax (01) 502-06/270; f. 1945; Chair. Komm. Rat Helmut Schmidt; Dir Dr Heinrich Leopold; 13 mems.

Fachverband der Lederverarbeitenden Industrie (Leather Processing): 1045 Vienna 4, Wiedner Hauptstr. 63, Postfach 313; tel. (01) 501-05; telex 111871; fax (01) 502-06/270; f. 1945; Chair. Gerhard Wallner; Dir Dr Heinrich Leopold; 72 mems.

Fachverband der Maschinen- und Stahlbauindustrie (Machinery and Steel Construction): 1045 Vienna 4, Wiedner Hauptstr. 63; tel. (01) 501-05; telex 111970; fax (01) 505-10-20; Pres. Dr Josef Bertsch; Dir Mag. Otto Neumayer; 800 mems.

Fachverband der Metallindustrie (Metals): 1045 Vienna 4, Wiedner Hauptstr. 63, Postfach 338; tel. (01) 501-05; telex 75312406; fax (01) 502-06/273; f. 1946; Chair. Komm. Rat Dr Othmar Rankl; Dir Dr Günter Greil; 69 mems.

Fachverband der Nahrungs- und Genussmittelindustrie (Provisions): Vienna III, Zaunergasse 1-3; tel. (01) 712-21-21; telex 131247; fax (01) 713-18-02; Chair. Ing. Martin Pecher; Dir Dr Klaus Smolka; 674 mems.

Fachverband der Papier und Pappe verarbeitenden Industrie (Paper and Board Processing): 1041 Vienna, Brucknerstr. 8; tel. (01) 505-53-82-0; fax (01) 505-90-18; Chair. Komm. Rat Gustav Glöckler; Mag. Rudolf Bergolth; 134 mems.

Fachverband der Papierindustrie (Paper): 1061 Vienna, Gumpendorferstr. 6; tel. (01) 58-886-0; telex 32213492; fax (01) 58-886-222; Chair. Dr Robert Launsky-Tieffenthal; Dir Dr Gerolf Ottawa; 63 mems.

Fachverband der Sägeindustrie (Sawmills): 1011 Vienna, Uraniastr. 4/1; tel. (0222) 75-76-25; fax (0222) 713-10-18; f. 1947; Chair. Dipl.-Ing. Herbert Kulterer; Dir Dr Gerhard Altrichter; 2,000 mems.

Fachverband der Stein- und keramischen Industrie (Stone and Ceramics): 1045 Vienna, Wiedner Hauptstr. 63, Postfach 329; tel (01) 501-05-3531; telex 111871; fax (01) 505-62-40; f. 1946; Chair. Dr Carl Hennrich; Pres. Sen. Ing. Leopold Helbich; 440 mems.

Fachverband der Textilindustrie (Textiles): 1013 Vienna I, Rudolfsplatz 12; tel. (01) 533-37-26-0; telex 114125; fax (01) 533-37-26-40; Pres. Dr Theodor Hladik; Dir Dr Helmut Huber; 400 mems.

TRADE UNIONS

The Trade Union Federation represents employees at all levels, except top managerial. By law all employees are subject to collective agreements which are negotiated annually by the Federation. About 60% of workers are members.

Österreichischer Gewerkschaftsbund (ÖGB) (Austrian Trade Union Federation): 1010 Vienna, Hohenstaufengasse 10-12; tel. (0222) 53-444; telex 114316; fax (0222) 533-52-93; non-party union organization with voluntary membership; f. 1945; organized in 15 trade unions, affiliated with ICFTU and ETUC; Pres. Friedrich Verzetnitsch; Exec. Secs Karl Drochter, Herbert Tumpel; 1,644,408 mems (1988).

Bundesfraktion Christlicher Gewerkschafter im Österreichischen Gewerkschaftsbund (Christian Trade Unionists' Section of the Austrian Trade Union Federation): 1010 Vienna, Hohenstaufengasse 12; tel. (0222) 53-444; organized in Christian Trade Unionists' Sections of the following 15 trade unions; affiliated with WCL; Sec.-Gen. Karl Klein.

Gewerkschaft der Bau- und Holzarbeiter (Building Workers and Woodworkers): 1010 Vienna I, Ebendorferstr. 7; tel. (01) 42-36-41; telex 114833; fax (01) 42-36-41-258; Chair. Josef Hesoun; 184,689 mems (1989).

Gewerkschaft der Chemiearbeiter (Chemical Workers): 1060 Vienna VI, Stumpergasse 60; tel. (01) 597-15-01; fax (01) 597-21-01-23; Chair. Erwin Holzerbauer; 58,523 mems (1989).

Gewerkschaft Druck und Papier (Printing and Paper Trade Workers): 1072 Vienna, Postfach 91, Seidengasse 15-17; tel. (01) 93-82-31; fax (01) 93-35-68-28; f. 1842; Chair. Herbert Bruna; 23,301 mems (1989).

Gewerkschaft der Eisenbahner (Railwaymen): 1051 Vienna V, Margaretenstr. 166; tel. (01) 55-46-41; Chair. Franz Hums; 114,251 mems (1989).

Gewerkschaft der Gemeindebediensteten (Municipal Employees): 1090 Vienna, Maria-Theresien-Str. 11; tel. (01) 34-36-00; fax (01) 34-36-00-275; Chair. Rudolf Pöder; 169,657 mems (1989).

Gewerkschaft Land-Forst-Garten (Agricultural and Forestry Workers): 1013 Vienna I, Wipplingerstr. 35; tel. (01) 53-444-480; f. 1906; Chair. Erich Dirngrabner; 18,549 mems (1989).

Gewerkschaft Handel, Transport, Verkehr (Workers in Commerce and Transport): 1010 Vienna, Teinfaltstr. 7; tel. (01) 53-4-54; fax (01) 53-4-54/325; f. 1904; Chair. Peter Schneider; 37,846 mems (1989).

Gewerkschaft Hotel, Gastgewerbe, Persönlicher Dienst (Hotel and Restaurant Workers): 1013 Vienna I, Hohenstaufengasse 10; tel. (01) 534-44; f. 1906; Chair. Franz Erwin Niemitz; 52,812 mems (1989).

Gewerkschaft Kunst, Medien, freie Berufe (Musicians, Actors, Artists, Journalists, etc.): 1090 Vienna IX, Maria-Theresien-Str. 11; tel. (01) 34-36-00; fax (01) 34-24-39; f. 1945; Chair. Ing. Stefan Müller; Sec.-Gen. Walter Bacher; 16,310 mems (1989).

Gewerkschaft der Lebens- und Genussmittelarbeiter (Food, Beverage and Tobacco Workers): 1080 Vienna, Albertgasse 35; tel. (01) 42-15-45; Chair. Dr Leopold Simperl; 40,113 mems (1989).

Gewerkschaft Metall-Bergbau-Energie (Metal Workers, Miners and Power Supply Workers): 1041 Vienna IV, Plösslgasse 15; tel. (01) 501-46; f. 1890; Chair. Rudolf Nürnberger; 240,185 mems (1989).

Gewerkschaft Öffentlicher Dienst (Public Employees): 1010 Vienna I, Teinfaltstr. 7; tel. (01) 53-4-54; telex 114402; fax (01) 53-4-54/326; f. 1945; Chair. Siegfried Dohr; Gen. Secs Alfred Stifter, Erich Bürger, Gerhard Neugebauer; 230,000 mems (1989).

Gewerkschaft der Post- und Fernmeldebediensteten (Postal and Telegraph Workers): 1010 Vienna, Biberstr. 5; tel. (01) 512-55-11; telex 112042; fax (01) 512-55-11/52; Chair. Norbert Tmej; 79,357 mems (1989).

Gewerkschaft der Privatangestellten (Commercial, Clerical and Technical Employees): 1013 Vienna, Deutschmeisterplatz 2; tel. (01) 34-35-20; telex 114114; fax (01) 34-35-20-388; Chair. Eleonora Hostasch; 340,348 mems (1989).

Gewerkschaft Textil, Bekleidung, Leder (Textile, Garment and Leather Workers): 1010 Vienna I, Hohenstaufengasse 10; tel. (01) 534-44; fax (01) 534-44-498; f. 1945; Chair. Harald Ettl; 38,580 mems (1989).

NATIONALIZED INDUSTRIES

After the Second World War, the Nationalrat adopted legislation which granted the State control of more than 70 industrial companies. In the following years these companies were supervised and administered by various ministries, as well as by organizations specifically created for this purpose. In 1967 the Österreichische Industrieverwaltungs-Gesellschaft mbH (ÖIG) was founded to administer the industrial companies as a trustee of the Republic of Austria. In 1970 the ÖIG was transformed into a joint-stock company, the Österreichische Industrieholding Aktiengesellschaft (ÖIAG), with the Republic of Austria as the only shareholder. In April 1986 the Nationalrat adopted the 'ÖIAG Act', whereby the ÖIAG was instructed to transform the existing group of diverse companies into a strong industrial conglomerate. In 1989 the ÖIAG was restructured as Austrian Industries AG, comprising five former sectoral holding groups of the ÖIAG. Austrian Industries AG is Austria's largest industrial group (with 79,200 employees) and ranks among the leading 50 in Europe. Its more than 150 production subsidiaries offer products and services in the fields of steel, aluminium, machinery construction, electrical engineering and electronics, engineering and contracting, petroleum, natural gas, petrochemicals and chemicals. In 1989 Austrian Industries AG contributed 12.6% of Austria's total exports of goods, and sales turnover amounted to 140,700m. Schilling (19.7% of which was generated outside Austria). In June 1990 Austrian Industries AG issued a 'going public' option bond; it also plans to issue shares in 1992.

Austrian Industries AG: 1015 Vienna, Kantgasse 1; tel. (0222) 71-114; telex 132047; fax (0222) 71-114-245; f. 1970 (see above); Chair. Board of Dirs Dr Hugo Michael Sekyra; Chair. Supervisory Board Dr Josef Staribacher; controls the following sectoral holding companies and their subsidiaries (as at 30 October 1990):

AMAG–Austria Metall AG: 5282 Braunau am Inn-Ranshofen; tel. (07722) 2341; telex 27745; fax (07722) 7741; f. 1939; non-ferrous metals, especially aluminium; Chair. Board of Dirs Dr Robert Ehrlich; Chair. Supervisory Board Dr Hugo Michael Sekyra; 8,000 employees.

Elektro- und Elektronik-Industrieholding AG: 1140 Vienna, Penzingerstr. 76; tel. (0222) 89-100-0; telex 112763; fax (0222) 89-46-468; f. 1988, following the conversion of various departments of the former Elin Union AG into independent companies; electrical engineering and electronics; Chair. Board of Dirs Dipl.-Ing.

GUIDO KLESTIL; Chair. Supervisory Board Dr HUGO MICHAEL SEKYRA; 9,500 employees.

Maschinen- und Anlagenbau Holding AG: 4031 Linz, Lunzerstr. 64; tel. (0732) 5986-0; fax (0732) 5980-9578; f. 1988; construction of industrial plants, energy and environmental technology, machine tools and systems technology, mining and tunnelling, traffic engineering, erection and assembly technology, stainless steel products; Chair. Board of Dirs Dipl.-Ing. OTHMAR PÜHRINGER; Chair. Supervisory Board Dr HUGO MICHAEL SEKYRA; 16,500 employees.

ÖMV–AG: 1090 Vienna, Otto-Wagner-Platz 5; tel. (01) 40-440; telex 114801; fax (01) 40-440-91; f. 1955 as Österreichische Mineralölverwaltung; partially privatized in 1987 (15%) and 1989 (10%); oil, natural gas, oil products, petrochemical and plastic products, chemicals; CEO Dr SIEGFRIED MEYSEL; Deputy CEO Dr RICHARD SCHENZ; 12,550 employees.

Voest-Alpine Stahl AG: 4031 Linz, Turmstr. 45; tel. (0732) 585; telex 2207450; fax (0732) 59-80-3181; f. 1988; production and processing of steel and special steel; Chair. Board of Dirs Dr LUDWIG VON BOGDANY; Chair. Supervisory Board Dr HUGO MICHAEL SEKYRA; 32,500 employees.

TRADE FAIRS

Trade Fairs play an important part in the economic life of Austria. The largest are held during the spring and autumn at Vienna, but there are also a number of important fairs held in the provinces.

Contact Fachmessen Salzburg GmbH & Co KG: 5021 Salzburg, Postfach 285; tel. (0662) 37551-0; telex 633131; fax (0662) 30115; twice yearly: fashion, sports equipment; every two years: garage equipment, glass, energy technology, plastics, furniture.

Dornbirner Messe GmbH: 6854 Dornbirn, Messestr. 4, Postfach 805; tel. (05572) 25-6-94; fax (05572) 25-6-94-11; annually (July); average number of visitors 200,000.

Grazer Messe International: 8011 Graz, Postfach 63; tel. (0316) 8088-0; telex 311511; fax (0316) 8088-244; f. 1906; twice yearly (May and October); exhibits of all categories, but special emphasis on agriculture, iron and steel, hotel and building equipment; average number of visitors 500,000; once yearly: Technova, international high-tech, innovation fair; Dir GERD NOVAK.

Innsbrucker Messe GmbH: 6020 Innsbruck, Falkstr. 2–4; tel. (0512) 58-59-11; fax (0512) 58-42-90; annually (April and September); mainly devoted to tourism and equipment for the tourist; average number of visitors 200,000.

Klagenfurter Messe: 9021 Klagenfurt, Postfach 380, Valentin-Leitgeb-Str. 11; tel. (0463) 56-800; telex 422268; fax (0463) 56-800-28; f. 1951; annually; Dir Dr HANS-JÖRG PAWLIK.

Praesenta, Werbe- und Ausstellungs GmbH: 1020 Vienna, Praterstr. 12/17; tel. (0222) 26-65-26; telex 135205; fax (0222) 26-65-29-22.

Rieder Messe: 4910 Ried im Innkreis, Postfach 61; tel. (07752) 4011-0; telex 027/720; fax (07752) 4011-44; holds International Agricultural Fair and Ried Spring Fair in alternate years, Ried Leisure Fair annually; over 1m. visitors.

Vienna Fairs and Congress Ltd: 1071 Vienna, Messeplatz 1, Postfach 124; tel. (01) 93-15-24; telex 133491; fax (01) 93-15-24/290; f. 1921; three annual general fairs (February, March and September), 22–26 specialized fairs per year at two sites; exhibits of all categories; average number of visitors 1,200,000; Pres. MANFRED MAUTNER MARKHOF; Dirs Dr REGINALD FÖLDY, GERD A. HOFFMANN.

Welser Messe: 4601 Wels, Messehaus; tel. (07242) 8-22-22; fax (07242) 66-8-40-74; every 2 years; agriculture, cattle-breeding, industry, trade; average number of visitors approx. 1m.

Transport

RAILWAYS

The Austrian Federal Railways operate 90% of all the railway routes in Austria. There are approximately 5,800 km of track and all main lines are electrified.

Österreichische Bundesbahnen (ÖBB) (Austrian Federal Railways): Head Office: 1010 Vienna, Elisabethstr. 9; tel. (01) 56-50-0; telex 1377; fax (01) 56-36-80; Dir-Gen. Dr HEINRICH ÜBLEIS.

Innsbruck Divisional Management: 6020 Innsbruck, Claudiastr. 2; fax (0512) 56-27-46; Pres. Dr A. SOLLATH.

Linz Divisional Management: 4020 Linz, Bahnhofstr. 3; tel. (0732) 56411; fax (0732) 56411-1833; Pres. HELMUT AFLENZER; Vice-Pres. Dipl.-Ing. KLAUS SEEBACHER.

Vienna Divisional Management: 1020 Vienna, Nordbahnstr. 50; fax (0222) 216-79-28; Pres. Dr ERWIN SEMMELRATH.

Villach Divisional Management: 9500 Villach, 10.-Oktober-Str. 20; fax (04242) 235-11-35-33; Pres. Dr RUDOLF REISP.

Other railway companies include: Achensee Railway, Graz–Köflach Railway, Györ–Sopron–Ebenfurt Railway, Montafon Railway, Salzburg-Lamprechtshausen, Stern and Hafferl Light Railways Co, Styrian Provincial Railways, Tirol Zugspitze Railway, Vienna Local Railways, Zillertal Railway (Jenbach–Mayrhofen).

ROADS

At 31 December 1989 Austria had 109,480 km of classified roads, of which 1,407 km were modern motorways, 287 km expressways, 10,098 km main roads, 25,689 km secondary roads and 70,000 km communal roads.

INLAND WATERWAYS

The Danube (Donau) is Austria's only navigable river. It enters Austria from Germany at Passau and flows into Czechoslovakia near Hainburg. The length of the Austrian section of the river is 351 km. Danube barges carry up to 1,800 tons, but loading depends on the water level, which varies considerably during the year. Cargoes are chiefly petroleum and derivatives, coal, coke, iron ore, iron, steel, timber and grain. A passenger service is maintained on the Upper Danube and between Vienna and the Black Sea. Passenger services are also provided on Bodensee (Lake Constance) and Wolfgangsee by Austrian Federal Railways, and on all the larger Austrian lakes.

Ministry of the Public Sector and Transport: 1031 Vienna, Radetzkystr. 2; tel. (0222) 711-62; telex 111800; fax (0222) 73-03-26; responsible for the administration of inland waterways.

Erste Donau-Dampfschiffahrts-Gesellschaft (First Danube Steamship Co): 1021 Vienna, Handelskai 265; tel. (01) 217-10-0; telex 131698; fax (01) 217-10-250; fleet consists of 12 passenger vessels, 9 towboats and pushers, 29 motor-cargoships, 106 cargo-barges and lighters, 9 motor tankships, 37 tank-barges and lighters.

CIVIL AVIATION

The main international airport is at Schwechat, near Vienna. There are also international flights from Innsbruck, Salzburg, Graz, Klagenfurt and Linz, and internal flights between these cities.

Österreichische Luftverkehrs AG (Austrian Airlines): 1107 Vienna, Fontanastr. 1; tel. (0222) 68-35-11; telex 131811; fax (0222) 68-65-26; f. 1957; 52% state-owned; serves 56 cities in 36 countries of Europe, North Africa, Asia and the USA, covering 100,358 km; external flights from Vienna, Graz, Linz, Klagenfurt and Salzburg to 55 cities on four continents; Chair. and Dir-Gen. OTTO BINDER; Pres. D.Dr A. HESCHGL; fleet of 2 Airbus A310, 11 MD-81, 2 MD-82, 4 Fokker 50; on order: 2 Airbus A310, 2 MD-83, 1 Fokker 50.

Tourism

Tourism plays an important part in the Austrian economy; receipts from tourism were estimated at 120,200m. Schilling in 1988, when Austria received 16.6m. foreign visitors. The country's mountain scenery attracts visitors in both summer and winter, while Vienna and Salzburg, where internationally-renowned art festivals are held, are important cultural centres.

Österreich Werbung (Austrian National Tourist Office): 1040 Vienna, Margaretenstr. 1; tel. (01) 588-66; telex 3222306; fax (01) 588-66-20.

Atomic Energy

Construction of Austria's first nuclear power station, at Zwentendorf on the Danube, was begun in 1971. A referendum was held in November 1978, when it was decided that the plant should not be put into operation, and public opinion remains divided on the issue. In March 1985 a formal decision to dismantle the plant was taken, in view of the high maintenance costs, and it seemed likely that parts of the installation would be sold.

Österreichisches Forschungszentrum Seibersdorf GmbH–ÖFZS (Austrian Research Centre, Seibersdorf): 2444 Seibersdorf; tel. (02254) 800; telex 014353; fax (02254) 80-2118; f. 1956; a limited company of which the capital is shared by the Austrian Government (51%), state industries (25%) and private enterprises (24%). Man. Dirs Prof. Dr PETER KOSS (Science and Technology), Dr WINFRIED SCHENK (Industry and Marketing); Chair. Dipl.-Ing. Dr ERICH STASKA.

THE BAHAMAS

Introductory Survey

Location, Climate, Language, Religion, Flag, Capital

The Commonwealth of the Bahamas consists of about 700 islands and more than 2,000 cays and rocks, extending from off the Florida coast of the USA to just north of Cuba and Haiti, in the West Indies. The main islands are New Providence, Grand Bahama, Andros, Eleuthera and Great Abaco. More than 60% of the population reside on the island of New Providence. The remaining members of the group are known as the 'Family Islands'. A total of 29 of the islands are inhabited. The climate is mild and sub-tropical, with average temperatures of about 30°C (86°F) in summer and 20°C (68°F) in winter. The average annual rainfall is about 1,000 mm (39 in). The official language is English. Most of the inhabitants profess Christianity, the largest denominations being the Anglican, Baptist, Roman Catholic and Methodist Churches. The national flag has three equal horizontal stripes, of blue, gold and blue, with a black triangle at the hoist, extending across one-half of the width. The capital is Nassau, on the island of New Providence.

Recent History

A former British colonial territory, the Bahamas attained internal self-government in January 1964, although the parliamentary system dates back to 1729. The first elections under universal adult suffrage were held in January 1967 for an enlarged House of Assembly. The Progressive Liberal Party (PLP), supported mainly by Bahamians of African origin and led by Lynden (later Sir Lynden) Pindling, won 18 of the 38 seats, as did the ruling United Bahamian Party (UBP), dominated by those of European origin. With the support of another member, the PLP formed a government and Pindling became Premier. At the next elections, in April 1968, the PLP won 29 seats and the UBP only seven.

Following a constitutional conference in September 1968, the Bahamas Government was given increased responsibility for internal security, external affairs and defence in May 1969. In the elections of September 1972, which were dominated by the issue of independence, the PLP maintained its majority. Following a constitutional conference in December 1972, the Bahamas became an independent nation, within the Commonwealth, on 10 July 1973. Pindling remained Prime Minister. The PLP increased its majority in the elections of July 1977 and was again returned to power in the June 1982 elections, with 32 of the 43 seats in the House of Assembly. The remaining 11 seats were won by the Free National Movement (FNM), which had reunited for the elections after splitting into several factions over the previous five years.

Trading in illicit drugs, mainly for the US market, has become a major problem for the country, since many of the small islands and cays are being used by drug traffickers in their smuggling activities. In 1983 allegations were made of widespread corruption, and the abuse of Bahamian bank secrecy laws by drug financiers and US tax evaders. These claims were denied by Sir Lynden Pindling, who announced, in November 1983, the appointment of a Royal Commission to investigate thoroughly all aspects of the drug trade in the Bahamas. The Commission's hearings revealed the extent to which money deriving from the drug trade had permeated Bahamian social and economic affairs. By November 1985 a total of 51 suspects had been indicted, including the assistant police commissioner, Howard Smith, who was charged with bribery and dismissed from the force. In October 1984 two cabinet ministers, implicated by the evidence presented to the Commission, resigned. The Commission also revealed that Sir Lynden had received several million dollars in gifts and loans from businessmen, although the Commission stated that there was no evidence that the payments were drug-related. After unsuccessfully demanding Sir Lynden's resignation, the Deputy Prime Minister, Arthur Hanna, resigned, and two further ministers were dismissed. The opposition FNM staged demonstrations, demanding Pindling's resignation, but the Prime Minister refused to accept any personal responsibility for corruption by public officials, and the PLP convention at the end of October unanimously endorsed Pindling as party leader.

An early general election was held on 19 June 1987. The issue of the illegal drug trade and of drug-related corruption within the Government dominated the campaign, but the PLP was returned to power for a fifth consecutive term, obtaining 53% of the total votes and winning 31 of the 49 seats in the enlarged House of Assembly. The FNM won 16 seats, while the remaining two seats were won by independents. The opposition later claimed that the election had been fraudulent, and in December the courts agreed to examine the allegations in nearly one-half of the constituencies.

Statistics relating to crime in 1987 indicated unprecedented levels of violent and drug-related offences, and in February 1988 new claims of official corruption were made at the trial in Florida, USA, of a leading Colombian drug-trafficker. Pindling and the Deputy Prime Minister were alleged to have accepted bribes, but this was vehemently denied. Furthermore, new measures were announced against the drug trade and corruption. The Judicial Committee of the Privy Council, in the United Kingdom, finally rejected accusations by the opposition, in May 1988, that Sir Lynden and Lady Pindling's financial affairs had not been sufficiently investigated. It also ruled, in September 1989, that conspiracy to import dangerous and illegal drugs into the USA was an extraditable offence.

In March 1990 the Minister of Agriculture, Trade and Industry, Ervin Knowles, resigned, following allegations of nepotism and the misuse of public funds. An independent Member of Parliament, Perry Christie (who was one of those dismissed from the Government in 1984), replaced him and rejoined the PLP. The other independent member, Hubert Ingraham, subsequently joined the FNM and became its leader in May, upon the death of Sir Cecil Wallace-Whitfield. In September there was a reallocation of cabinet portfolios.

The Bahamas' traditionally close relationship with the USA has been strained by the increasingly aggressive attitudes of the US Government towards the bank secrecy laws and the drug smuggling in the islands. In July 1988 the Bahamas led a protest of the CARICOM (see p. 108) nations at US attempts to impose its extraterritorial jurisdiction on small neighbours. Nevertheless, the USA and the Bahamas have collaborated in a series of operations to intercept drug smugglers; financial and institutional co-operation has increased; in June 1987 a legal assistance treaty was signed with the USA; and in May 1988 the Bahamas requested US naval co-operation. The US Senate then approved the certification of the Bahamas as 'fully co-operative' in the campaign against illicit drugs, and an attempt to reverse this decision was defeated in May 1989. There was a significant reduction in the amount of cocaine seized in Bahamian territory during 1990, and this was assumed to indicate that the islands were no longer so important as a route for drug-smuggling. Relations with the Bahamas' other neighbours, Haiti and Cuba, have been strained by the influx of large numbers of illegal Haitian immigrants, and the sinking of a Bahamian patrol boat by Cuba in 1980. In 1990 the Bahamian Government announced that it intended to improve relations with Cuba, and that agreement was to be sought on the delimitation of maritime boundaries.

Government

Legislative power is vested in the bicameral Parliament. The Senate has 16 members, of whom nine are appointed by the Governor-General on the advice of the Prime Minister, four by the Leader of the Opposition and three after consultation with the Prime Minister. The House of Assembly has 49 members, elected for five years (subject to dissolution) by universal adult suffrage. Executive power is vested in the British monarch, represented by a Governor-General, who is appointed on the Prime Minister's recommendation and who acts, in almost all matters, on the advice of the Cabinet. The Governor-General appoints the Prime Minister and, on the latter's recommendation, selects the other Ministers. The Cabinet is responsible to the House.

THE BAHAMAS

Defence

The Royal Bahamian Defence Force, a paramilitary coastguard, is the only security force in the Bahamas, and numbered 750 in June 1990. The defence budget in 1988 was a record B $77.7m. (including the allocation for the 2,000-strong police force), most of which was to finance the anti-drug trafficking campaign.

Economic Affairs

In 1988, according to estimates by the World Bank, the Bahamas' gross national product (GNP), measured at average 1986–88 prices, was US $2,611m., equivalent to US $10,570 per head (the highest level among Caribbean countries). It was estimated that GNP increased, in real terms, at an average rate of 4.5% per year between 1980 and 1988. GNP per head increased by an annual average of 2.4% over the same period, although no growth was recorded between 1986 and 1988. The population increased by an annual average of 2.0% between 1980 and 1988. Gross domestic product (GDP), measured at current prices, was B $2,116m. in 1987.

Agriculture and fishing, which together accounted for less than 5% of GDP in 1981 and employed 5% of the working population in 1986, have been developed by the Government to reduce dependence on imports (80% of food supplies were imported in the early 1980s). The increase in agricultural output has resulted in some exports, particularly of cucumbers, tomatoes, pineapples, papayas, avocados, mangoes, limes and other citrus fruits. The development of commercial fishing has concentrated on conches and crustaceans. There is also some exploitation of pine forests in the northern Bahamas.

Industry (comprising mining, manufacturing, construction and utilities) employed 15.3% of the working population in 1986. The manufacturing sector contributed some 10% of GDP in 1982, since when it has declined, owing to the reduced activity and subsequent closure, in 1985, of the petroleum refinery. The principal industrial products are now cement, beer and rum (production of rum was worth some B $15.5m. in 1987), and, despite decreasing production in the late 1980s, pharmaceuticals, salt and aragonite. Petroleum transhipment on Grand Bahama remains an important activity (mineral fuels accounted for some 74% of the cost of imports and 88% of export revenue in 1986), and the construction sector has, since 1986, experienced much activity owing to hotel-building and harbour developments.

Most of the energy requirements of the Bahamas are fulfilled by the petroleum that Venezuela and, particularly, Mexico provide under the San José Agreement (originally negotiated in 1980), which commits both the petroleum-producers to selling subsidized supplies, on favourable terms, to the developing countries of the region. There are hopes that exploration for local petroleum reserves will prove successful.

Service industries constitute the principal sectors of the economy. The Bahamas established its own shipping registry in 1976, and by 1983 had one of the largest 'open-registry' fleets in the world. The country is also a leading 'offshore' financial centre, and banking is the second most important economic activity (after tourism). Although relatively few local people are employed in the industry, operating fees payable by the banks are an important source of revenue. There are almost 400 banks in the Bahamas, which held at least US $100m. in deposits at the end of 1986.

Tourism is the predominant sector of the economy of the Bahamas, directly accounting for about 54% of GDP in 1985, and employing some 43% of the working population. About 90% of tourists are from the USA. Tourist arrivals increased at an average annual rate of 7.6% between 1983 and 1988, by which time the total had reached some 3.2m. Total tourist arrivals amounted to 3.4m. in 1989. Receipts from tourism were estimated at B $1,170.3m. in 1987. As well as considerable capital investment for the benefit of the sector, the Government increased expenditure on tourism by 17%, to B $34.2m., in the budget estimates for 1988 (almost 7% of total expenditure).

In 1989 the Bahamas recorded a visible trade deficit of US $895m., but receipts from services, worth US $1,443m., helped to offset this. A deficit of US $179m. was recorded on the current account of the balance of payments. The USA is the principal trading partner of the Bahamas. Excluding the trade in petroleum and its products, the principal exports in 1985 were chemical products, while the principal imports were foodstuffs.

In 1989 the budget deficit was almost B $43m., despite original estimates of B $3.8m. The total public debt of the Bahamas at the end of March 1990 was $581.7m., of which only 14.7% was owed abroad. The annual rate of inflation averaged 6.3% during 1980–87, falling to 4.2% in 1988 but rising again to 5.4% in 1989. It was estimated that more than 18% of the labour force were unemployed at mid-1987, although this level subsequently declined.

The Bahamas is a member of CARICOM (see p. 108) and the OAS (see p. 194), and is a signatory of the Lomé Conventions with the EEC (see p. 151).

Despite increasing competition, the Bahamas has maintained its position as the principal tourist destination of the Caribbean. The European market is being encouraged in order to reduce dependence on the USA, the problems of which were illustrated by a temporary, but significant, reduction in the number of arrivals in the aftermath of the severe decline in stock-market prices in October 1987. In 1990 the Prime Minister himself assumed the tourism portfolio and urged an improvement in the standard of service. Despite government criticism of the banking community and the doubling of bank operating fees in 1988, the Bahamas is committed to retaining its status as a tax haven. To broaden the economic base of the country, the development of the primary sector has been encouraged (mainly to supply the local market), and incentives have been offered to light industries. As yet, these attempts at economic diversification have achieved little success. It was hoped, however, that the purchase of the petroleum refinery on Grand Bahama in 1990, by a Venezuelan petroleum company, would result in renewed industrial activity there.

Social Welfare

The health service is centralized in Nassau at the government general hospital, which has 454 beds. In 1988 the Bahamas had six hospital establishments, with a total of 982 beds; there were 197 physicians working in the country in 1980. In the Family Islands there were 19 clinics with resident medical officers in 1988, and there are more than 50 other medical centres. A Flying Doctor Service supplies medical attention to islands that lack resident personnel. Flying Dental Services and nursing personnel from the Community Nursing Service are also provided. In 1988 the Government announced plans for expenditure of B $4.5m., over four years, on modernizations and on hospitals in Nassau and Grand Bahama. A National Insurance Scheme, established in 1972, provides a wide range of benefits, including sickness, maternity, retirement and widows' pensions as well as social assistance payments. In 1990 the Government proposed a national health insurance scheme, financed by compulsory contributions from earnings. An Industrial Injuries Scheme has been established. Expenditure by the central Government in 1987 included B $74.5m. on health (equivalent to about 17% of total expenditure).

Education

Education is compulsory between the ages of five and 14 years, and is provided free of charge in government schools. There is an extensive primary and secondary school system, with 122 schools in 1985. There are several private and denominational schools. Primary education begins at five years of age and lasts for six years. Secondary education, beginning at the age of 11, also lasts for six years and is divided into two equal cycles. The University of the West Indies has an extra-mural department in Nassau, offering degree courses in hotel management and tourism. A training college for the tourist and hotel industry was to be established by 1992. Technical, teacher-training and professional qualifications can be obtained at the two campuses of the College of the Bahamas, while the Universities of Miami and St John's, New York, also operate degree programmes. Government expenditure on education in 1987 was B $96.5m. (or about 22% of total government spending).

Public Holidays

1991: 1 January (New Year's Day), 29 March (Good Friday), 1 April (Easter Monday), 20 May (Whit Monday), 7 June (Labour Day), 10 July (Independence Day), 5 August (for Emancipation Day), 14 October (for Discovery Day/Columbus Day), 25–26 December (Christmas).

1992: 1 January (New Year's Day), 17 April (Good Friday), 20 April (Easter Monday), 5 June (Labour Day), 8 June (Whit Monday), 10 July (Independence Day), 3 August (for Emancipation Day), 12 October (Discovery Day/Columbus Day—Quincentenary), 25–26 December (Christmas).

Weights and Measures

The imperial system is used.

Statistical Survey

Source (unless otherwise stated): Central Bank of the Bahamas, Frederick St, POB N-4868, Nassau; tel. 322-2193; telex 20115; fax 322-4321.

AREA AND POPULATION

Area: 13,939 sq km (5,382 sq miles).

Population: 175,192 at census of 7 April 1970; 209,505 (males 101,774, females 107,731) at census of 12 May 1980; 249,000 (provisional official estimate) at mid-1989. *By island* (1980): New Providence 135,437 (including the capital, Nassau); Grand Bahama 33,102; Andros 8,397; Eleuthera 8,326.

Density (mid-1989): 17.9 per sq km.

Principal Town: Nassau (capital), estimated population 153,620 (1985).

Births, Marriages and Deaths (1987): Registered live births 4,331 (birth rate 18.0 per 1,000); Registered marriages 1,888 (marriage rate 7.6 per 1,000); Registered deaths 1,377 (death rate 5.7 per 1,000). *1988* (provisional): Births 4,943 (birth rate 20.2 per 1,000); Deaths 1,319 (death rate 5.4 per 1,000).

Economically Active Population (persons aged 15 years and over, 1986): Agriculture, hunting, forestry and fishing 4,905; Mining and quarrying 120; Manufacturing 4,945; Electricity, gas and water 1,705; Construction 8,125; Trade, restaurants and hotels 31,555; Transport, storage and communications 7,885; Financing, insurance, real estate and business services 7,990; Community, social and personal services 29,925; Activities not adequately defined 245; Total employed 97,400 (males 53,200, females 44,200); Total unemployed 13,500 (males 5,700, females 7,800); Total labour force 110,900 (males 58,900; females 52,000). Source: ILO, *Year Book of Labour Statistics*.

AGRICULTURE, ETC.

Principal Crops (FAO estimates, '000 metric tons, 1988): Sugar cane 240; Tomatoes 8; Bananas 9. Source: FAO, *Production Yearbook*.

Livestock (FAO estimates, '000 head, year ending September 1988): Cattle 5; Pigs 20; Sheep 40; Goats 19; Chickens 1,000. Source: FAO, *Production Yearbook*.

Forestry (FAO estimates, '000 cu m, 1988): Roundwood removals: Sawlogs and veneer logs 15, Pulpwood 100, Total 115. Sawnwood: Coniferous (softwood) 1. Source: FAO, *Yearbook of Forest Products*.

Fishing (metric tons, live weight): Total catch 5,893 in 1986; 7,091 in 1987; 7,236 (Caribbean spiny lobster 5,071) in 1988. Source: FAO, *Yearbook of Fishery Statistics*.

MINING AND INDUSTRY

Production (estimates, '000 metric tons, 1987): Unrefined salt 811 (Source: US Bureau of Mines); Cement (1984) 63; Electric energy 965m. kWh. Source: UN, *Industrial Statistics Yearbook*.

FINANCE

Currency and Exchange Rates: 100 cents = 1 Bahamian dollar (B $). *Coins:* 1, 5, 10, 15, 25 and 50 cents; 1, 2 and 5 dollars. *Notes:* 50 cents; 1, 3, 5, 10, 20, 50 and 100 dollars. *Sterling and dollar equivalents* (30 September 1990): £1 sterling = B $1.8735; US $1 = B $1.0000; B $100 = £53.38 = US $100.00. *Exchange rate:* Since February 1970 the official exchange rate, applicable to most transactions, has been US $1 = B $1, i.e. the Bahamian dollar has been at par with the US dollar. There is also an investment currency rate, applicable to certain capital transactions between residents and non-residents and to direct investments outside the Bahamas. The average of this exchange rate (B $ per US $) was: 1.199 in 1987; 1.225 in 1988; 1.225 in 1989.

Budget (B $ million, 1987): *Revenue:* Taxation 353.5 (import tax 246.3); Other receipts 45.1; Total 398.7. *Expenditure:* General public services 88.4; Defence 13.1; Education 96.5; Health 74.5; Social services 14.7; Housing 3.9; Other community services 4.0; Economic services 100.3 (transport 19.9, tourism 33.4, public works and water supply 36.3); Public debt interest 40.7; Total 436.0 (current 383.2; capital 52.8).
1988* (B $ million): Total revenue 432.6; Total expenditure 513.3.
1989* (B $ million): Total revenue 448.2; Total expenditure 561.6.
1990 (estimates, B $ million): Total expenditure 583.0 (current 462.1; capital 120.9).

* Source: IMF, *International Financial Statistics*.

International Reserves (US $ million at 31 December 1989): IMF special drawing rights 0.2; Reserve position in IMF 11.4; Foreign exchange 135.3; Total 146.6. Source: IMF, *International Financial Statistics*.

Money Supply (B $ million at 31 December 1989): Currency outside banks 79.5; Demand deposits at deposit money banks 218.8; Total money 298.3. Source: IMF, *International Financial Statistics*.

Cost of Living (consumer price index; base: 1985 = 100): 111.7 in 1987; 116.4 in 1988; 122.7 in 1989. Source: IMF, *International Financial Statistics*.

Gross Domestic Product (B $ million at current prices): 1,879.8 in 1985; 2,039.4 in 1986; 2,115.7 in 1987.

Balance of Payments (B $ million, 1989): Merchandise exports f.o.b. 259.2; Merchandise imports f.o.b. −1,151.9; *Trade balance* −892.7; Exports of services 1,443.0; Imports of services −730.7; *Balance on goods and services* −180.4; Private unrequited transfers (net) −17.9; Government unrequited transfers (net) 18.9; *Current balance* −179.4; Direct capital investment (net) 25.0; Other long-term capital (net) 1.1; Short-term capital (net) 50.0; Net errors and omissions 149.5; *Total (net monetary movements)* 46.2; Valuation changes (net) −71.4; *Changes in reserves* −25.2. Source: IMF, *International Financial Statistics*.

EXTERNAL TRADE

Principal Commodities (B $ million, 1985): *Imports c.i.f.:* Food and live animals 154.2; Crude petroleum 1,706.5; Petroleum products 557.6 (residual fuel oils 390.0); Chemicals 119.6; Basic manufactures 138.3; Machinery and transport equipment 199.2; Miscellaneous manufactured articles 150.5; Total (incl. others) 3,077.9. *Exports f.o.b.:* Crude petroleum 1,855.7; Petroleum products 548.7 (distillate fuels 157.4, residual fuel oils 351.9); Chemicals 238.0 (organic chemicals 192.1); Total (incl. others) 2,728.4. Source: UN, *International Trade Statistics Yearbook*. **1986** (B $ million): Imports c.i.f. 3,289; Exports f.o.b. 2,702. Source: UN, *Monthly Bulletin of Statistics*. **1987** (B $ million): Imports c.i.f. 3,233; Exports f.o.b. 2,545. Source: UN, *Monthly Bulletin of Statistics*.

Principal Trading Partners (B $ million 1985): *Imports:* Angola 148.9, Indonesia 89.0, Mexico 237.1, Netherlands Antilles 72.6, Nigeria 1,042.7, United Kingdom 131.2, USA and Puerto Rico 859.8; Total (incl. others) 3,077.9. *Exports:* United Kingdom 81.2, USA and Puerto Rico 2,395.4; Total (incl. others) 2,728.4. Source: UN, *International Trade Statistics Yearbook*.

TRANSPORT

Road Traffic (registered vehicles, 1987): 74,062.

Shipping: *Merchant fleet* (displacement, '000 grt at 30 June): 9,105 in 1987; 8,963 in 1988; 11,579 in 1989. Source: *Lloyd's Register of Shipping*. International sea-borne freight traffic (estimates, '000 metric tons, 1985): Goods loaded 9,325; Goods unloaded 8,710. Source: UN, *Monthly Bulletin of Statistics*.

TOURISM

Tourist Arrivals: 3,081,370 in 1987; 3,158,091 in 1988; 3,398,311 (1,908,305 by sea, 1,490,006 by air) in 1989.

COMMUNICATIONS MEDIA

Radio Receivers (1987): 124,407 in use.

Television Receivers (1987): 53,724 in use.

Telephones (1987): 119,061 in use.

Daily Newspapers (1988): 3 titles (total circulation 38,000 copies). Source: Ministry of Tourism.

EDUCATION*

Primary (1988): 101 schools, 24,050 students.

Junior/Senior High (1988): 39 schools, 23,293 students.

All-Age Schools (1988): 86 schools, 12,286 students.

Special Schools (1988): 8 schools, 280 students.

In August 1988 there were about 2,000 students registered at the College of the Bahamas.

* Source: Ministry of Tourism.

Directory

The Constitution

A new constitution for the Commonwealth of the Bahamas came into force at independence on 10 July 1973. The main provisions of the Constitution are summarized below:

Parliament consists of a Governor-General (representing the British monarch), a nominated Senate and an elected House of Assembly. The Governor-General appoints the Prime Minister and, on the latter's recommendation, the remainder of the Cabinet. Apart from the Prime Minister, the Cabinet has not fewer than eight other ministers, of whom one is the Attorney-General. The Governor-General also appoints a Leader of the Opposition.

The Senate (upper house) consists of 16 members, of whom nine are appointed by the Governor-General on the advice of the Prime Minister, four on the advice of the Opposition Leader, and three on the Prime Minister's advice after consultation with the Opposition Leader. The House of Assembly (lower house) has 49 members. A Constituencies Commission reviews numbers and boundaries at intervals of not more than five years and can recommend alterations for approval of the House. The life of Parliament is limited to a maximum of five years.

The Constitution provides for a Supreme Court and a Court of Appeal.

The Government

Head of State: HM Queen ELIZABETH II (succeeded to the throne 6 February 1952).

Governor-General: Sir HENRY MILTON TAYLOR (acting—took office 26 June 1988).

THE CABINET
(November 1990)

Prime Minister and Minister of Tourism: Sir LYNDEN OSCAR PINDLING.
Deputy Prime Minister and Minister of Foreign Affairs and Public Personnel: Sir CLEMENT T. MAYNARD.
Minister of Finance: PAUL L. ADDERLEY.
Minister of National Security: DARREL E. ROLLE.
Minister of Works and Lands: PHILIP M. BETHEL.
Minister of Employment and Immigration: ALFRED T. MAYCOCK.
Minister of Youth, Sports and Community Affairs: Dr NORMAN GAY.
Minister of Housing and National Insurance: GEORGE W. MACKEY.
Minister of Transport: Senator PETER J. BETHEL.
Minister of Education: BERNARD NOTTAGE.
Miniser of Health: E. CHARLES CARTER.
Attorney-General: Senator SEAN MCWEENEY.
Minister of Agriculture, Trade and Industry: PERRY G. CHRISTIE.
Minister of Consumer Affairs: VINCENT PEET.
Minister of Local Government: MARVIN PINDER.

MINISTRIES

Office of the Prime Minister: Rawson Sq., POB N-3733, Nassau; tel. 322-2805.
Ministry of Agriculture, Trade and Industry: East Bay St, POB N-3028, Nassau; tel. 323-1777.
Ministry of Consumer Affairs: POB N-3017, Nassau; tel. 328-1774.
Ministry of Education: Shirley St, POB N-3913, Nassau; tel. 322-8140.
Ministry of Employment and Immigration: Clarence Bain Bldg, POB N-3002, Nassau; tel. 322-8163.
Ministry of Finance: Rawson Sq., POB N-3017, Nassau; tel. 322-4151; telex 20255.
Ministry of Foreign Affairs: East Hill St, POB N-3746, Nassau; tel. 322-7624; telex 20264.
Ministry of Health: Post Office Bldg, East Hill St, POB N-3729, Nassau; tel. 322-7425; telex 20516; fax 322-7788.
Ministry of Housing and National Insurance: Boulevard Bldg, Thompson Blvd, POB N-2306, Nassau; tel. 322-4415; telex 20164.
Ministry of Local Government: Nassau.
Ministry of National Security: Clarence A. Bain Bldg, POB N-3002, Nassau; tel. 322-8163.
Ministry of Tourism: Bay St, POB N-3701, Nassau; tel. 322-7500; telex 20164.
Ministry of Transport: Post Office Bldg, East Hill St, POB N-3008, Nassau; tel. 323-7814; telex 20263.
Ministry of Works and Lands: J. F. Kennedy Drive, POB N-8156, Nassau; tel. 322-4380; fax 326-7344.
Ministry of Youth, Sports and Community Affairs: POB N-10114, Nassau; tel. 322-3140.

Legislature

PARLIAMENT

Houses of Parliament: Parliament Sq., Nassau.

Senate
President: EDWIN COLEBY.
There are 16 nominated members.

House of Assembly
Speaker: Sir CLIFFORD DARLING.
The House has 49 members.

General Election, 19 June 1987

Party	Seats
Progressive Liberal Party (PLP)	31
Free National Movement (FNM)	16
Independents	2*
Total	49

* In March 1990 one independent member joined the PLP upon his appointment to the Cabinet. In April the other independent joined the FNM and, in May, became its leader. The PLP, therefore, held 32 seats and the FNM 17.

Political Organizations

Free National Movement (FNM): POB N-8181, Nassau; tel. 325-0637; telex 20238; f. 1972; Leader HUBERT A. INGRAHAM; Senate Leader JOHN HENRY BOSTWICK.

People's Democratic Force (PDF): Nassau; f. 1989; Leader FRED MITCHELL.

Progressive Liberal Party (PLP): Nassau; tel. 325-2900; f. 1953; centrist party; Leader Sir LYNDEN PINDLING; Chair. ERRINGTON ISAACS (acting).

Vanguard Party: Nassau; socialist; Leader Dr JOHN MCCARTNEY.

Diplomatic Representation

EMBASSY AND HIGH COMMISSION IN THE BAHAMAS

United Kingdom: 3rd Floor, Bitco Bldg, East St, POB N-7516, Nassau; tel. 325-7471; telex 20112; fax 323-3871; High Commissioner: COLIN G. MAYS.

USA: Mosmar Bldg, Queen St, POB N-8197, Nassau; tel. 322-4733; telex 20138; Ambassador: JACOB (CHIC) HECHT.

Judicial System

The Judicial Committee of the Privy Council (based in the United Kingdom), the Bahamas Court of Appeal, the Supreme Court and the Magistrates' Courts are the main courts of the Bahamian judicial system.

All courts have both a criminal and civil jurisdiction. The Magistrates' Courts are presided over by professionally qualified Stipendiary and Circuit Magistrates in New Providence and Grand

Bahama, and by Commissioners sitting as Magistrates in the other Family Islands.

Whereas all magistrates are empowered to try offences which may be tried summarily, a Stipendiary and Circuit Magistrate may, with the consent of the accused, also try certain less serious indictable offences. The jurisdiction of magistrates is, however, limited by law.

The Supreme Court consists of the Chief Justice and not more than four and not less than two justices.

Appeals in almost all matters lie from the Supreme Court to the Court of Appeal with further appeal in certain instances to the Judicial Committee of the Privy Council.

Supreme Court of the Bahamas: Parliament Sq., POB N-8167, Nassau; Chief Justice J. C. GONSALVES SABOLA.

Court of Appeal: POB N-8167, Nassau; President KENNETH C. HENRY.

Magistrates' Courts: POB N-421, Nassau; eight magistrates and a circuit magistrate.

Registrar of the Supreme Court: JOSEPH C. STRACHAN, POB N-532, Nassau.

Attorney-General: Senator SEAN MCWEENEY.

Office of the Attorney-General: East Hill, POB N-3007, Nassau; tel. 322-1141; Dir of Legal Affairs RICARDO MARQUES; Solicitor-General BURTON HALL.

Religion

Most of the population profess Christianity, but there are also small communities of Jews and Muslims. Traditional beliefs in witchcraft and 'bush medicine' persist in some areas; these practices are known as voodoo or obeah.

CHRISTIANITY

According to the census of 1980, there were 42,091 Anglicans and Episcopalians (20.1% of the population), 39,397 Roman Catholics (18.8%) and 67,193 Baptists (32.1%). Other important denominations include the Church of God (5.7%) and the Methodists (6.1%).

Bahamas Christian Council: POB SS-5863, Nassau; tel. 393-2710; f. 1948; 10 mem. churches; Sec. Bishop HARCOURT PINDER.

The Roman Catholic Church

The Bahamas comprises the single diocese of Nassau, suffragan to the archdiocese of Kingston in Jamaica. At 31 December 1988 there were an estimated 42,461 adherents in the Bahamas. The Bishop participates in the Antilles Episcopal Conference (currently based in Kingston, Jamaica).

Bishop of Nassau: Rt Rev. LAWRENCE A. BURKE, West St, POB N-8187, Nassau; tel. 322-8919.

The Anglican Communion

Anglicans in the Bahamas are adherents of the Church in the Province of the West Indies (the metropolitan is based in St John's, Antigua and Barbuda). The diocese of Nassau and the Bahamas also includes the Turks and Caicos Islands.

Bishop of Nassau and the Bahamas: Rt Rev. MICHAEL ELDON, Addington House, POB N-7107, Nassau; tel. 322-3015; fax 322-7943.

Other Churches

Greek Orthodox Church: West St, Nassau; part of the Archdiocese of North and South America, based in New York (USA).

Methodist Church in the Bahamas: POB N-3702, Nassau; General Superintendent Rev. Dr KENNETH HUGGINS.

Other denominations include the Assemblies of Brethren, the Jehovah's Witnesses, the Salvation Army and the Seventh-day Adventist, Pentecostal, Presbyterian, Lutheran and Assembly of God churches.

OTHER RELIGIONS

Islam: The Mosque, Nassau; there is a small community of Muslims in the Bahamas.

Judaism: The Synagogue, Freeport; most of the Bahamian Jewish community are based on Grand Bahama. There were 204 Jews, according to the 1980 census.

The Press

NEWSPAPERS

Freeport News: POB F-7, Freeport; tel. 352-8321; f. 1961; daily; Dir DUDLEY N. BYFIELD; Editor RICHARDSON CAMPBELL; circ. 5,000.

Nassau Daily Tribune: Shirley St, POB N-3207, Nassau; tel. 322-2766; fax 328-2398; f. 1903; Publr/Editor EILEEN DUPUCH CARRON; circ. 12,000.

Nassau Guardian: Oakes Field, POB N-3011, Nassau; tel. 323-5654; telex 20100; f. 1844; daily; Publr/Gen. Man. KENNETH W. FRANCIS; Editor CHRISTOPHER SYMONETTE; circ. 11,044.

PERIODICALS

The Bahamas Financial Digest: POB N-4271, Nassau; tel. 322-1149; telex 20447; fax 328-1922; f. 1973; 4 a year; business and investment; Publr/Editor MICHAEL A. SYMONETTE.

Bahamas Tourist News: Bayparl Bldg, Parliament St, POB N-4855, Nassau; monthly; Editor PAUL BOWER; circ. 240,000 (annually).

Bahamian Review Magazine: Collins Ave, POB N-494, Nassau; tel. 322-8922; f. 1952; monthly; banking, finance, tourism; Editor WILLIAM CARTWRIGHT; circ. 55,000.

Nassau: POB N-1914 Nassau; tel. 322-1149; f. 1984; literature, current affairs, reviews; 4 a year; Publr MICHAEL A. SYMONETTE.

Official Gazette: c/o Cabinet Office, POB N-7147, Nassau; tel. 322-2805; weekly; publ. by the Cabinet Office.

Publishers

Bahama Publishers Ltd: Cedar St, POB F-7, Freeport; tel. 352-8321.

Bahamas International Publishing Co Ltd: Nassau Court, POB N-1914, Nassau; tel. 322-1149; fax 328-1922.

Commonwealth Publications Ltd: POB N-4826, Nassau; tel. 322-1038; telex 20275; f. 1979; publishes *Bahamas Business Guide* (a guide to doing business in the Bahamas and the Government's economic and financial policies) and *An Economic History of the Bahamas*.

Etienne Dupuch Jr Publications Ltd: Oakes Field, POB N-7513, Nassau; tel. 323-5665; fax 323-5728; publishes *Bahamas Handbook*, *What To Do* magazines, *Welcome Bahamas*, *Tadpole* (educational colouring book) series and *Dining and Entertainment Guide*; Dirs ETIENNE DUPUCH, Jr, S. P. DUPUCH.

Radio and Television

In 1987 there were reported to be 124,407 radio receivers and 53,724 television receivers in use.

Broadcasting Corporation of the Bahamas: POB N-1347, Centreville, New Providence; tel. 322-4623; telex 20253; fax 322-3924; f. 1936; government-owned; commercial; Gen. Man. CALSEY JOHNSON.

Radio Bahamas: f. 1950; broadcasts 24 hours per day on three stations: the main Radio Bahamas (ZNS1), Radio New Providence (ZNS2—both based in Nassau) and the Northern Service (ZNS3—Freeport; f. 1973; Station Man. A. ADDERLEY); Programme Dir A. FOSTER.

Bahamas Television: f. 1977; broadcasts for Nassau, New Providence and the Central Bahamas; transmitting power of 50,000 watts; full colour; Programme Dir R. SIMMONS (acting).

US television programmes and some satellite programmes can be received. Freeport, the second city, has a cable television network.

Finance

In recent years the Bahamas has developed into one of the world's foremost financial centres (there are no corporation, income, capital gains or withholding taxes or estate duty), and finance has become a significant feature of the economy. At 31 March 1990 there were 391 financial institutions in the Bahamas: 274 dealt with the general public while the remaining 117 were restricted, non-active or nominee institutions. There were 140 Bahamian-incorporated banks and/or trust companies: 106 were subsidiaries of foreign institutions and 34 were Bahamian-based.

In 1990 the Government announced that it intended to introduce legislation enabling the establishment of a stock exchange.

BANKING

(cap. = capital; dep. = deposits; res = reserves; m. = million; brs = branches; amounts in Bahamian dollars, unless otherwise stated)

Central Bank

The Central Bank of the Bahamas: Frederick St, POB N-4868, Nassau; tel. 322-2193; telex 20115; fax 322-4321; f. 1973; bank of issue; external res B $158.5m. (March 1990); Gov. JAMES H. SMITH.

THE BAHAMAS *Directory*

Development Bank
The Bahamas Development Bank: Bay St, POB N-3034, Nassau; tel. 322-8721; telex 20297; f. 1978 to fund approved projects and channel funds into appropriate investments; Chair. ISHMAEL LIGHTBOURNE.

Principal Bahamian-based Banks
Bahama Bank Ltd: POB N-272, Nassau; f. 1964.

Bank of the Bahamas Ltd: Euro Canadian Centre, George and Marlborough Sts, POB N-7118, Nassau; tel. 322-1690; telex 20141; f. 1970, name changed 1988, when Bank of Montreal Bahamas Ltd became jointly owned by Govt and European Canadian Bank; fully owned by Govt in 1990; cap. B $3.0m., dep. B $82.9m. (Oct. 1988); Chair. Lord PRITCHARD; Man. Dir T. R. KESSLER; 3 brs.

Bank of New Providence Ltd: Claughton House, Shirley and Charlotte Sts, POB N-4723, Nassau; tel. 322-3824; telex 20464; Gen. Man. BYRD OSBORNE.

Commonwealth Industrial Bank Ltd: 610 Bay St, POB SS-5541, Nassau; tel. 328-1854; f. 1960; Exec. Vice-Pres. JAMES D. COCKWELL; 8 brs.

Dominion Charter Bank Ltd: POB SS-5539, Nassau; tel. 393-8777; telex 20611; fax 393-0582; f. 1980.

Equator Bank Ltd: Norfolk House, Frederick St, POB N-9925, Nassau; tel. 322-2754; telex 20409; fax 326-5706; f. 1975; cap. US $1.0m., dep. US $184.4m. (Dec. 1989); CEO FRANKLIN H. KENNEDY.

Fidenas International Bank Ltd: Bolam House, George St, POB N-4816, Nassau; tel. 325-6052; telex 20278; fax 325-2592; f. 1979; cap. US $10.0m., dep. US $54.9m. (Dec. 1989); Chair. GEOFFREY P. JURICK; Pres. COLIN G. HONESS.

Finance Corpn of the Bahamas Ltd (FINCO): Frederick St, POB N-3038, Nassau; tel. 322-4822; fax 328-8848; f. 1953; Man. Dir PETER THOMPSON; 3 brs.

First Home Banking Centre Ltd: The Mall, POB F-2644, Freeport; tel. 352-6676; f. 1978; Pres. ALFRED STEWART.

Meridien International Bank Ltd: Meridien House, East Bay St, POB N-3209, Nassau; tel. 393-4857; telex 20386; fax 393-4974; f. 1981; cap. US $20.0m., res US $22.2m., dep. US $383.3m. (Sept. 1989); Pres. E. ROBERT SYDER; Chair. ANDREW S. SARDINAS.

People's Penny Savings Bank: Market St, POB N-1484, Nassau; tel. 322-4140; telex 20353; f. 1952; 3 brs.

Principal Foreign Banks
In 1983 there were more than 100 foreign banks with branches in the Bahamas, including 91 from the USA.

Banca della Svizzera Italiana (Overseas) Ltd (Italy): Norfolk House, Frederick St, POB N-7130, Nassau; tel. 323-8312; telex 20197.

Bank of Nova Scotia (Canada): Rawson Sq., POB N-7518, Nassau; tel. 322-1071; telex 20187; Man. GEORGE E. MARSHALL; Deputy Man. JAMES BRAMMER; 11 brs.

Barclays Bank PLC (UK): Bay St, POB N-8350, Nassau; tel. 322-4921; telex 20149; Man. H. G. SANDS.

Canadian Imperial Bank of Commerce: Shirley St, POB N-7125, Nassau; tel. 322-8455; telex 20169; Area Man. TERRY HILTS; 9 brs.

Charterhouse Japhet Bank and Trust International Ltd (UK): E. D. Sassoon Bldg, Parliament St, POB N-3045, Nassau; tel. 322-4643; telex 20142; Bahamas incorporated 1950; cap. B $2m.; Chair. and CEO RENO J. BROWN; Dir PETER F. JAKOBSEN.

Chase Manhattan Bank NA (USA): Shirley and Charlotte Sts, POB N-4921, Nassau; tel. 322-8792; telex 20140; Gen. Man. KEN BROWN; 4 brs.

Citibank NA (USA): Thompson Blvd, Oakes Field, POB N-8158, Nassau; tel. 322-4240; telex 20153; Gen. Man. PAUL D. MAJOR; 2 brs.

Lloyds Bank International (Bahamas) Ltd (UK): King and George Sts, POB N-1262, Nassau; tel. 322-8711; telex 20107; Gen. Man. ENRIQUE NYBORG-ANDERSEN; Asst Man. R. FUNES; 1 br.

The Royal Bank of Canada Ltd: POB N-7537, Nassau; tel. 322-4980; telex 20182; fax 323-3407; Man. Dir G. B. GREENSLAND; 16 brs.

Swiss Bank Corpn (Overseas) Ltd: 3rd Floor, Claughton House, Shirley St, POB N-7757, Nassau; tel. 322-7570; telex 20348; fax 323-8953.

Principal Bahamian Trust Companies
Bahamas International Trust Co Ltd (Bitco): Bitco Bldg, Bank Lane, POB N-7768, Nassau; tel. 322-1101, telex 20143; fax 326-5020; incorporated 1957; cap. B $1.0m., res B $4.9m., dep. B $00.0m. (Nov. 1988); Chair. L. B. JOHNSON; Man. Dir JAMES M. KNOTT.

Coutts and Co International (Bahamas) Ltd: West Bay St, POB N-7788, Nassau; tel. 326-0404; telex 20177; fax 326-6709; f. 1936; Swiss-registered subsid. of National Westminster Bank (UK); Chair. DONALD R. KESTER; Deputy Chair. J. D. FRIZELL.

Euro-Dutch Trust Co (Bahamas) Ltd: Charlotte House, POB N-9204, Nassau; f. 1975; tel. 325-1033; telex 20303.

Leadenhall Trust Co Ltd: 1 Cumberland Court, Cumberland St, POB N-1965, Nassau; tel. 325-5508; telex 20584; fax 326-6725; f. 1976; Man. Dir ROBERT A. MONTGOMERY.

Rawson Trust Co Ltd: Charlotte House, POB N-4465, Nassau; tel. 322-7461; telex 20172; f. 1969.

Bankers' Organizations
Association of International Banks and Trust Companies in the Bahamas: POB N-7880, Nassau; tel. 326-0041.

Bahamas Institute of Bankers: The Plaza, Mackey St, POB N-3202, Nassau; tel. 393-0456; fax 393-0456.

INSURANCE
The leading British and a number of US and Canadian companies have agents in Nassau and Freeport. Local insurance companies include the following:

Bahamas First General Insurance Co Ltd: Centreville House, Second Tce, West Collins Ave, POB N-1216, Nassau; tel. 326-5439; telex 20576.

Bahamas International Assurance Co: Palmdale Ave, POB SS-6201, Nassau; tel. 322-3196.

Bahamas Pioneer Insurance Co Ltd: East Shirley and Kemp Rd, POB SS-6207, Nassau; tel. 325-7468.

International Bahamian Insurance Co: Peek Bldg, POB N-10280, New Providence; tel. 322-2504.

Trade and Industry

Bahamas Chamber of Commerce: Shirley St, POB N-665, Nassau; tel. 322-2145; fax 322-4649; f. 1935 to promote, foster and protect trade, industry and commerce; Pres. CAREY G. LEONARD (until May 1991); Exec. Dir RUBY L. SWEETING; 900 mems.

Bahamas Agricultural and Industrial Corpn (BAIC): BAIC Bldg, East Bay St, POB N-4940, Nassau; tel. 322-3740; telex 20648; fax 322-2123; f. 1971 as Bahamas Development Corpn to promote investment in all sectors of the economy and to act as a clearance agency for all projects; name changed 1981; Chair. PERRY G. CHRISTIE (Minister of Agriculture, Trade and Industry).

Nassau/Cable Beach/Paradise Island Promotion Board: Dean's Lane, Fort Charlotte, POB N-7799, Nassau; tel. 322-8381; fax 326-5346; f. 1970; Chair. C. RICHARD COOK; Sec. MICHAEL C. RECKLEY; 30 mems.

EMPLOYERS' ASSOCIATIONS
Bahamas Association of Architects: Shirley St, POB N-1207, Nassau; tel. 325-6115; Pres. WINSTON JONES.

Bahamas Association of Land Surveyors: POB N-7782, Nassau; tel. 322-4569; Pres. ANDREW C. LAVILLE; Vice-Pres./Sec. SHERLYN W. HALL; 30 mems.

Bahamas Association of Shipping Agents: POB N-1451, Nassau.

Bahamas Boatmen's Association: f. 1974; POB ES-5212, Nassau; Pres. and Sec. FREDERICK GOMEZ.

Bahamas Contractors' Association: POB N-8049, Nassau; Pres. BRENDON C. WATSON; Sec. EMMANUEL ALEXIOU.

Bahamas Employers' Confederation: POB N-166, Nassau; tel. 328-1757; telex 20392; f. 1963; Pres. TYRONE D'ARVILLE.

Bahamas Hotel Employers' Association: Dean's Lane, Fort Charlotte, POB N-7799, Nassau; tel. 322-2262; telex 20392; f. 1958; Pres. J. BARRIE FARRINGTON; Exec. Dir MICHAEL C. RECKLEY; 26 mems.

Bahamas Institute of Chartered Accountants: POB N-7037, Nassau; Pres. WILLIAM WALLACE.

Bahamas Institute of Commerce: Robinson Rd, POB N-7917, New Providence; tel. 323-6117.

Bahamas Institute of Professional Engineers: Nassau; Pres. IVERN DAVIES.

Bahamas Motor Dealers' Association: POB N-4824, Nassau; tel. 322-1149; fax 328-1922; Pres. FREDDY ALBURY.

Bahamas Real Estate Association: Bahamas Chamber Bldg, POB N-8860, Nassau; tel. 325-4942; Pres. FRANK CAREY.

Nassau Association of Shipping Agents: Nassau.

Soft Drink Bottlers' Association: POB N-212, Nassau.

THE BAHAMAS

TRADE UNIONS

The Commonwealth of the Bahamas Trade Union Congress (CBTUC): POB N-4692, Nassau; all Bahamian unions are mems of the CBTUC; affiliated to the Caribbean Congress of Labour; Pres. ARLINGTON MILLER; 11,000 mems.

The main unions are as follows:

Bahamas Airport, Service and Industrial Workers' Union: Workers House, Balfour Ave, POB N-3364, Nassau; tel. 323-5030; f. 1958; Pres. HENRY DEAN; Gen. Sec. RAMON NEWBALL; 532 mems.

Bahamas Brewery, Distillers and Allied Workers' Union: POB N-299, Nassau; f. 1968; Pres. BRADICK CLEARE; Gen. Sec. DAVID KEMP; 140 mems.

Bahamas Communication and Public Officers' Union: East St, POB N-3190, Nassau; tel. 322-1537; f. 1973; Pres. KEITH E. ARCHER; Sec.-Gen. AUDLEY G. WILLIAMS; 1,611 mems.

Bahamas Doctors' Union: Nassau; Pres. Dr EUGENE NEWERY; Gen. Sec. GEORGE SHERMAN.

Bahamas Electrical Workers' Union: East West Highway, POB GT-2535, Nassau; tel. 323-1838; telex 2535; Pres. SAMUEL MITCHELL; Gen. Sec. JONATHAN CAMBRIDGE.

Bahamas Hotel Catering and Allied Workers' Union: POB GT-2514, Nassau; tel. 323-5933; f. 1958; Pres. THOMAS BASTIAN; Gen. Sec. LEONARD WILSON; 5,500 mems.

Bahamas Housekeepers' Union: POB 898, Nassau; f. 1973; Pres. MERLENE DECOSTA; Gen. Sec. MILLICENT MUNROE.

Bahamas Maritime Port and Allied Workers' Union: POB 10517, Nassau; Pres. JAMES BLATCH; Gen. Sec. ANTHONY WILLIAMS.

Bahamas Musicians' and Entertainers' Union: Horseshoe Drive, POB N-880, Nassau; tel. 322-3734; f. 1958; Pres. LEROY (DUKE) HANNA; Sec. RONALD SIMMS; 410 mems.

Bahamas Oil and Fuel Services Workers' Union: POB 10597, Nassau; f. 1956; Pres. VINCENT MUNROE.

Bahamas Public Services Union: Wulff Rd, POB N-4692, Nassau; tel. 325-0038; f. 1959; Pres. ARLINGTON MILLER; Sec.-Gen. ERIC DARVILLE; 4,247 mems.

Bahamas Taxi-Cab Union: POB N-1077, Nassau; tel. 323-5952; telex 20480; Pres. OSWALD NIXON; Gen. Sec. ROSCOE WEECH.

Bahamas Transport, Agricultural, Distributive and Allied Workers' Trade Union: Wulff Rd, POB N-7821, Nassau; tel. 323-4538; f. 1959; Pres. RANDOLF FAWKES; Gen. Sec. MAXWELL N. TAYLOR; 1,362 mems.

Bahamas Union of Teachers: 104 Bethel Ave, Stapledon Gdns, POB N-3482, Nassau; tel. 323-7085; f. 1945; Pres. DONALD SYMONETTE; Gen. Sec. LESLIE DEAN; 1,985 mems.

Bahamas Utilities Services and Allied Workers' Union: POB GT-2515, Nassau; Pres. DREXEL DEAN; Gen. Sec. HERMAN ROKER.

Bahamas Workers' Council International: POB MS-5337, Nassau; f. 1969; Chair. DUDLEY WILLIAMS.

Commonwealth Cement and Construction Workers' Union: POB N-8680, Nassau; Pres. AUDLEY HANNA; Gen. Sec. ERMA MUNROE.

Commonwealth Electrical Workers' Union: POB F-1983, Grand Bahama; Pres. OBED PINDER, Jr; Gen. Sec. CHRISTOPHER COOPER.

Commonwealth Transport Union: POB F-1983, Freeport; Pres. LEO DOUGLAS; Gen. Sec. KENITH CHRISTIE.

Commonwealth Union of Hotel Services and Allied Workers: White House of Labour, Cedar St, POB F-1983, Freeport; tel. 352-9361; Pres. HURIE BODIE; Gen. Sec. (vacant).

Commonwealth Wholesale, Retail and Allied Workers' Union: POB F-1983, Freeport; tel. 352-9361; Pres. MERLENE THOMAS; Gen. Sec. KIM SMITH.

Eastside Stevedores' Union: POB N-1176, Nassau; f. 1972; Pres. SALATHIEL MACKEY; Gen. Sec. CURTIS TURNQUEST.

Grand Bahama Commercial, Clerical and Allied Workers' Union: 33A Kipling Bldg, POB F-839, Freeport; tel. 352-7438; Pres. NEVILLE SIMMONS; Gen. Sec. LIVINGSTONE STUART.

Grand Bahama Construction, Refinery and Maintenance Workers' Union: 33A Kipling Bldg, POB F-839, Freeport; tel. 352-7438; f. 1971; Pres. JAMES TAYLOR; Gen. Sec. EPHRAIM BLACK.

Grand Bahama Entertainers' Union: POB F-2672, Freeport; Pres. CHARLES SMITH; Gen. Sec. IRMA THOMPSON.

Grand Bahama Telephone and Communications Union: POB F-2478, Freeport; Pres. NAAMAN ELLIS; Gen. Sec. DOROTHY CLARKE.

United Brotherhood of Longshoremen's Union: Wulff Rd, POB N-7317, Nassau; f. 1959; Pres. J. MCKINNEY; Gen. Sec. W. SWANN; 157 mems.

Transport

ROADS

There are about 966 km (600 miles) of roads in New Providence and 1,368 km (850 miles) in the Family Islands, mainly on Grand Bahama, Cat Island, Eleuthera, Exuma and Long Island.

SHIPPING

The principal seaport is at Nassau, on New Providence, which can accommodate the very largest cruise ships. The other main ports are at Freeport (Grand Bahama) and Matthew Town (Inagua). There are also modern berthing facilities for cruise ships at Potters Cay (New Providence), Governor's Harbour (Eleuthera), Morgan's Bluff (North Andros) and George Town (Exuma).

The Bahamas converted to free-flag status in 1976, and by 1983 possessed the world's third largest open-registry fleet. The fleet's displacement was 8.9m. grt in 1988.

The following are the chief shipping and cruise lines calling at Nassau: P & O, Pacific Steam Navigation Co, Tropical Shipping, Home Lines, Eastern Steamship Co, Norwegian-American Lines, Costa Lines, NCL Norwegian Caribbean Lines, Holland American Lines, and the Scandinavian World Cruises.

There is a weekly mail and passenger service to all the Family Islands.

Grand Bahama Port Authority: Pioneers' Way, East Mall, POB F-2666, Freeport; tel. 352-6711; telex 30020.

New Providence Port Authority: Prince George Wharf, POB N-1417, Nassau; tel. 322-8832; regulates principal port of the Bahamas.

Principal Shipping Companies

Cavalier Shipping: Crawford St, Oakes Field, POB N-8170, New Providence; tel. 323-3821.

R. R. Farrington & Sons: Union Dock, POB N-93, Nassau; tel. 322-2203; telex 20123.

Pioneer Shipping Ltd: Union Dock Bay, POB N-3044, Nassau; tel. 325-7889; telex 20350.

United Shipping Co Ltd: POB F-2552, Freeport; tel. 352-9315; telex 30048.

CIVIL AVIATION

Nassau International Airport (15 km (9 miles) outside the capital) and Freeport International Airport (5 km outside the city, on Grand Bahama) are the main terminals for international and internal services. There are also important airports at West End (Grand Bahama) and Rock Sound (Eleuthera) and some 50 smaller airports and landing strips throughout the islands.

Bahamasair: Windsor Field, POB N-4881, Nassau; tel. 327-8451; telex 20239; fax 327-7409; f. 1973; scheduled services between Nassau, Freeport, destinations within the USA, the Turks and Caicos Islands and 20 locations within the Family Islands; Exec. Chair. DARREL ROLLE; Exec. Dir DAVID L. JOHNSON; fleet of 4 de Havilland Dash-8, 2 Boeing 737-200, 3 Cessnas (for charter), 1 Beechercraft (for the use of the Prime Minister).

Tourism

The mild climate and beautiful beaches attract many tourists. In 1988 there were 187 hotels, with a total of 12,480 rooms and there were 3.1m. tourist arrivals (including 1.5m. cruise-ship passengers), mostly from the USA, Canada and the United Kingdom. Receipts from tourism reached an estimated B $1,149.5m. in that year. Tourist arrivals rose to 3.4m. in 1989.

Ministry of Tourism: Bay St, POB N-3701, Nassau; tel. 322-7500; telex 20164; Dir-Gen. BALTRON BETHEL.

Bahamas Hotel Association: Dele West Bay St, sub Dean's Lane, POB N-7799, Nassau; tel. 322-8381; telex 20392; fax 326-5346.

BAHRAIN

Introductory Survey

Location, Climate, Language, Religion, Flag, Capital

The State of Bahrain consists of a group of about 35 islands, situated midway along the Persian (Arabian) Gulf, about 24 km (15 miles) from the east coast of Saudi Arabia (to which it is linked by a causeway), and 28 km (17 miles) from the west coast of Qatar. There are six principal islands in the archipelago, and the largest of these is Bahrain itself, which is about 50 km (30 miles) long and between 13 km and 25 km (8 to 15 miles) wide. To the north-east of Bahrain island, and linked to it by a causeway and motor-road, lies Muharraq island, which is approximately 6 km (4 miles) long. Another causeway links Bahrain with Sitra island. The climate is temperate from December to the end of March, with temperatures ranging between 19°C (66°F) and 25°C (77°F), but becomes very hot and humid during the summer months. In August and September temperatures can rise to 40°C (104°F). The official language is Arabic, but English is also widely spoken. Almost all Bahraini citizens are Muslims, divided into two sects: Shi'ites (almost 60%) and Sunnis (over 40%). Non-Bahrainis, who comprise more than 30% of the total population, include Muslims, Christians and adherents of other religions. The national flag (proportions 5 by 3) is scarlet, with a vertical white stripe at the hoist, the two colours being separated by a serrated line. The capital is Manama.

Recent History

Bahrain, a traditional Arab monarchy, became a British Protected State in the 19th century. Under this arrangement, government was shared between the ruling sheikh and his British adviser. Following a series of territorial disputes in the 19th century, Persia (now Iran) made renewed claims to Bahrain in 1928. This disagreement remained unresolved until May 1970, when Iran accepted the findings of a report, commissioned by the UN, which showed that the inhabitants of Bahrain overwhelmingly favoured complete independence, rather than union with Iran.

During the reign of Sheikh Sulman bin Hamad al-Khalifa, who became ruler of Bahrain in 1942, social services and public works were considerably expanded. Sheikh Sulman died in November 1961 and was succeeded by his eldest son, Sheikh Isa bin Sulman al-Khalifa. Extensive administrative and political reforms came into effect in January 1970, when a 12-member Council of State was established. The formation of this new body, which became Bahrain's supreme executive authority, represented the first formal derogation of the ruler's powers. Sheikh Khalifa bin Sulman al-Khalifa, the ruler's eldest brother, became President of the Council.

Meanwhile, in January 1968 the United Kingdom had announced its intention to withdraw British military forces from the area by 1971. In March 1968 Bahrain joined the nearby territories of Qatar and the Trucial States (now the United Arab Emirates), which were also under British protection, in a Federation of Arab Emirates. It was intended that the Federation should become fully independent, but the interests of Bahrain and Qatar proved to be incompatible with those of the smaller sheikhdoms, and both seceded from the Federation. Bahrain thus became a separate independent state on 15 August 1971, when a new treaty of friendship was signed with the United Kingdom. Sheikh Isa took the title of Amir, while the Council of State became the Cabinet, with Sheikh Khalifa as Prime Minister. A Constituent Assembly, convened in December 1972, produced a new constitution, providing for a National Assembly which would contain cabinet ministers and 30 elected members. On 6 December 1973 the Constitution came into force, and on the following day elections were held for the new Assembly. In the absence of political parties, candidates stood in an individual capacity. In August 1975 the Prime Minister submitted his resignation, complaining of obstruction by the National Assembly. However, Sheikh Khalifa was reappointed and, at his request, the Assembly was dissolved by Amiri decree. New elections were promised, but by late 1990 there were no signs that the National Assembly would be reconvened. Without the Assembly, the ruling family has almost absolute powers.

Although major international territorial claims were brought to an end by the 1970 agreement with Iran, the Iranian revolution of 1979 led to uncertainty about possible future claims to Bahrain. There has also been evidence of tension between Shi'ite Muslims, who form a slender majority in Bahrain, and the dominant Sunni Muslims, the sect to which the ruling family belongs. In December 1981 more than 70 people, mainly Bahrainis, were arrested when a supposedly Iranian-backed plot to overthrow the Government was thwarted. In 1984 there were renewed fears of Iranian attempts to disrupt the country's stability when a cache of weapons was discovered in a Bahraini village, and in June 1985 six men were deported from the United Kingdom, following the discovery of a planned coup against the Bahraini Government.

In March 1981 Bahrain was one of the six founder-members of the Gulf Co-operation Council (GCC, see p. 123), which was established in order to co-ordinate defence strategy and to promote freer trading and co-operative economic protection among Gulf states. A number of joint industrial projects were initiated in the early 1980s. In 1986 the King Fahd Causeway between Bahrain and Saudi Arabia was opened, indicating Bahrain's commitment to closer links with other Gulf states.

In April 1986 the then US Vice-President, George Bush, visited Bahrain to reaffirm the USA's readiness to preserve Gulf security in the event of an escalation of the Iran-Iraq war, which began in September 1980. In January 1987 the USA announced its intention to sell 12 F-16 fighter aircraft to Bahrain as part of a contract, valued at US $400m., to provide military equipment. Bahrain would thereby become the first Gulf nation to receive any of these aircraft. Work began on the construction of an air-force base, in the south of the island, to accommodate the F-16 aircraft. Bahrain already provides an onshore 'facility' for the US forces, and there is a large US navy presence. In September the US Secretary of Defense, Caspar Weinberger, presented Sheikh Isa with a letter from President Reagan, expressing his gratitude to Bahrain for its assistance in enabling US warships to escort 'reflagged' Kuwaiti merchant vessels in Gulf waters. In December a controversial sale of 70 Stinger anti-aircraft missiles and 14 launchers, worth $7m., was agreed between Bahrain and the USA. The weapons were to be delivered as soon as possible. Conditions of sale included the stipulation that Bahrain sell back the weapons either when another US air defence system could be found for the country, or after 18 months.

In July 1987, as a result of the escalation of tension in the Gulf (exacerbated by the presence of US and Soviet naval forces), the UN Security Council adopted Resolution 598, urging an immediate cease-fire. Iraq agreed to observe a cease-fire if Iran would reciprocate, but Iran prevaricated, attaching conditions to its acceptance of the Resolution. In November 1987, at an extraordinary meeting of the League of Arab States in Amman, Jordan, representatives of the member states, including Bahrain, unanimously condemned Iran for prolonging the Gulf War, deplored its occupation of Arab (i.e. Iraqi) territory, and urged it to accept Resolution 598 without preconditions. (For more detailed coverage of the Gulf War and of the events that led to the cease-fire in August 1988, see the chapters on Iran and Iraq.) In February 1988 three Bahrainis were convicted by the security court for their involvement in an Iranian-supported plot, revealed in December 1987, to sabotage Bahrain's petroleum refinery.

In August 1990 Bahrain, in common with the whole Gulf area, seemed likely to be drawn into a conflict as a result of Iraq's invasion and forced annexation of Kuwait. Following the annexation, Bahrain firmly supported the implementation of UN economic sanctions against Iraq and permitted the stationing of US combat aircraft in Bahrain in support of US marine positions in the eastern part of Saudi Arabia.

In recent years Bahrain has acquired focal importance in the Gulf region. Its international airport is the centre of Gulf aviation, and the Arabian Gulf University is situated in Bah-

BAHRAIN

Introductory Survey

rain. A stock exchange opened in Bahrain in June 1989, trading in the shares of 29 local and joint-venture companies.

In April 1986 Qatari military forces raided the island of Fasht ad-Dibal, a coral reef situated midway between Bahrain and Qatar, over which both claim sovereignty. During the raid Qatar seized 29 foreign workers (most of whom were subsequently released), who were constructing a Bahraini coastguard station on the island. Officials of the GCC met representatives from both states in an attempt to reconcile them and avoid a split within the Council. Fasht ad-Dibal became the third area of dispute between the two countries, the others being Zubara, on mainland Qatar, and Hawar island. The dispute was referred to the GCC for settlement in early 1989.

In June 1988 Bahrain held its first official talks with the USSR, when the Amir of Bahrain met the Soviet Ambassador to Kuwait, to discuss ways of developing links between the two countries. In April 1989 Bahrain established diplomatic relations with the People's Republic of China. In December 1989 Bahrain and Iraq signed an agreement pledging non-interference in each other's internal affairs.

In October 1990 Bahrain established diplomatic relations with the USSR, a move which precipitated the establishing of diplomatic relations with Czechoslovakia shortly afterwards. In the same month the Minister of Foreign Affairs, Muhammad bin Mubarak bin Hamad al-Khalifa, visited Tehran, (the first such visit for a decade) to discuss the Gulf crisis and in an attempt to improve relations with Iran.

Government

Bahrain is ruled by an Amir through an appointed Cabinet. In August 1975 the National Assembly was dissolved.

Defence

Military service is voluntary. In June 1990 the Bahrain Defence Force consisted of 6,050 men (5,000 army, 600 navy, 450 air force). The defence budget for 1990 was BD 75.9m. In 1982 the GCC states pledged defence aid of some US $1,000m. for the modernization of equipment, and in 1984 this was followed by a further grant, for the same amount, to be shared between Bahrain and Oman.

Economic Affairs

In 1987, according to estimates by the World Bank, Bahrain's gross national product (GNP), measured at average 1985–87 prices, was US $3,027m., equivalent to $6,610 per head. During 1980–86, according to UN estimates, overall gross domestic product (GDP) increased at an average rate of 2.5% annually. GDP per head, however, decreased at an average annual rate of 0.3% over the same period. In 1988, according to the IMF, GDP, at current prices, totalled BD 1,262.9m. During 1981–88 the population increased by an annual average of 4.2%.

Agriculture and fishing employed 2.7% of the labour force in 1981 and contributed an estimated 1.5% of GDP in 1986. The principal crops are dates, tomatoes and melons. In 1988 the total production of vegetables and melons was an estimated 12,000 metric tons. Poultry production is also important, satisfying 51% of local demand by 1986. At mid-1989 about 75% of the country's fish resources remained unexploited. The total catch was 7,842 tons in 1987.

Industry (comprising mining, manufacturing, construction and utilities) employed 34.9% of the labour force in 1981 and provided an estimated 39.7% of GDP in 1986.

Mining and quarrying employed 3.5% of the labour force in 1981 and contributed an estimated 16.5% of GDP in 1986. The major mining activities are the exploitation of petroleum and natural gas. There are sufficient reserves of natural gas to maintain 1987 output levels (an average of 20m. cu m per day) until the year 2018.

Manufacturing employed 8.2% of the labour force in 1981 and provided an estimated 12.4% of GDP in 1986. Important industries include the petroleum refinery at Sitra, aluminium and aluminium-related enterprises, shipbuilding, iron and steel and chemicals. Light industries were being developed in the mid-1980s.

Total energy demand in 1987 was 630 MW, and this was expected to increase to 1,110 MW by 1997.

Banking is a major source of Bahrain's prosperity. In 1975 the Government decided to license 'offshore' banking units (OBUs) in Bahrain. OBUs are not involved in local banking, but serve to channel money from the petroleum-producing region back into world markets. In late 1990 there were 61 OBUs in Bahrain. In 1988 they announced record results, owing partly to a return to stability in the region, following the cease-fire in the Gulf War. However, in August 1990 Bahrain's role as an 'offshore' banking centre came under threat as a result of the crisis in the Gulf (see Recent History). A number of foreign institutions severed their lines of credit to the OBUs in Bahrain, and it was expected that some of the smaller units would be unable to maintain enough business to remain in operation.

In 1988 Bahrain recorded a visible trade surplus of US $77.4m., and there was a surplus of $189.9m. on the current account of the balance of payments. In that year the principal source of non-oil imports was the United Kingdom, while Saudi Arabia provided most of Bahrain's oil imports. Saudi Arabia and the United Arab Emirates were important markets for Bahraini exports. The principal exports in 1988 were petroleum, petroleum products and aluminium. Export revenues from petroleum and petroleum products represented 75.9% of total export earnings in 1988. The principal import was crude petroleum.

The 1990 budget envisaged a deficit of BD 100m., the same as that projected for 1989. Transfers and loan repayments were expected to decline by 41% in 1990, as a result of increased aid from Arab development funds. During 1980–88 consumer prices declined by an average annual rate of 1.3%. The annual rate of inflation averaged 1.5% in 1989, and was 1.0% in the year to July 1990.

Bahrain is a member of the Gulf Co-operation Council (GCC, see p. 123), which seeks to co-ordinate defence strategy and to promote freer trading and co-operative economic protection among Gulf states.

The opening of the King Fahd Causeway, linking Bahrain with Saudi Arabia, in 1986 and the cease-fire in the Gulf War in 1988 generated an economic recovery in the late 1980s (including the stabilization of oil prices by September 1989). However, the threat of open warfare in the Gulf, following Iraq's invasion and annexation of Kuwait in August 1990, disrupted the continued stability of Bahrain's economy. The immediate set-backs were, nevertheless, mostly overcome, owing to encouraging signs of economic strength in the first half of 1990, but the long-term effects could prove to be a detrimental factor in the future development of Bahrain's economy. It was projected that few foreign or private investors would be likely to embark on new projects in Bahrain until the crisis had been resolved, thus severely restricting the country's plans to diversify its industrial base.

Social Welfare

The state-administered medical service provides comprehensive treatment for all residents, including expatriates. There are also physicians, dentists and opticians in private practice. In 1983 Bahrain had six hospitals, 27 health centres and 16 child welfare centres. A Social Security Law covers pensions, industrial accidents, sickness, unemployment, maternity and family allowances. In 1982 there were 397 physicians working in the country. Of total projected expenditure (recurrent and development) by the central Government in 1990, BD 43.3m. (8%) was for health services.

Education

Education is not compulsory, but state education is available free of charge. Private and religious education are also available. There are five different types of schooling: primary and religious schooling (for children aged six to 11 years), intermediate (12–14 years), secondary or commercial streaming (15–17 years). The University of Bahrain, whose creation was proclaimed by Amiri decree in 1986, comprises four colleges: the College of Engineering, the College of Arts and Science, the College of Education and the College of Management and Business Administration. The first phase in the construction of the Arabian Gulf University (AGU) was completed in 1982, but lack of funding from the six Arab Governments sponsoring the project has delayed its completion. In 1989 there were only 58 students attending the AGU. In 1985 an estimated 94% of children aged six to 11 years (94.6% of boys; 93.8% of girls) attended primary schools, 52.4% of those aged 12 to 14 were enrolled at intermediate schools, and 41% of those aged 15–17 were enrolled at secondary schools. In 1986 there were 85,867 students attending the 139 primary, intermediate and secondary schools. In early 1988, according to the Ministry of

BAHRAIN

Introductory Survey, Statistical Survey

Education, more than 65% of teachers were native Bahrainis. The Government's 1990 budget (recurrent and development) allocated 10.1% of total expenditure (BD 54.8m.), to education. Plans have been formulated for the construction of 18 new schools, at a cost of BD 14.4m., by 1990. The 1989 building programme included BD 4m. for the construction of four new schools and a teacher-training complex. In 1981 the average rate of adult illiteracy among the indigenous Bahraini population was 31.3% (males 21.2%; females 41.4%). In 1985, according to UNESCO estimates, the illiteracy rate among all adults was 27.3% (males 20.7%; females 35.9%).

Public Holidays

1991: 1 January (New Year's Day), 12 February* (Leilat al-Meiraj, Ascension of the Prophet), 17 March* (Ramadan begins), 16 April* (Id al-Fitr, end of Ramadan), 23 June* (Id al-Adha, Feast of the Sacrifice), 13 July* (Muharram, Islamic New Year), 22 July* (Ashoura), 21 September* (Mouloud, Birth of the Prophet), 16 December (National Day).

1992: 1 January (New Year's Day), 1 February* (Leilat al-Meiraj, Ascension of the Prophet), 5 March* (Ramadan begins), 4 April* (Id al-Fitr, end of Ramadan), 11 June* (Id al-Adha, Feast of the Sacrifice), 2 July* (Muharram, Islamic New Year), 11 July* (Ashoura), 10 September* (Mouloud, Birth of the Prophet), 16 December (National Day).

* These holidays are dependent on the Islamic lunar calendar and may vary by one or two days from the dates given.

Weights and Measures

The metric system is being introduced.

Statistical Survey

Source (unless otherwise stated): Central Statistics Organization, POB 5835, Manama; tel. 242353; telex 8853.

AREA AND POPULATION

Area: 691.2 sq km (266.9 sq miles).

Population: 350,798 (males 204,793, females 146,005), comprising 238,420 Bahraini citizens (males 119,924, females 118,496) and 112,378 aliens (males 84,869, females 27,509), at census of 5 April 1981; 503,000: Bahraini citizens 336,000, aliens 167,000 (official estimate for May 1990).

Principal Towns (population at 1981 census): Manama (capital) 121,986; Muharraq Town 61,853.

Births and Deaths (UN estimates, 1985–90): Average annual birth rate 28.2 per 1,000; Death rate 3.8 per 1,000; Life expectancy at birth (1981): males 65.9 years, females 68.9 years.

Economically Active Population (1981 census): Agriculture, hunting, forestry and fishing 3,709; Mining and quarrying 4,778; Manufacturing 11,387; Electricity, gas and water 2,854; Construction 29,261; Trade, restaurants and hotels 18,507; Transport, storage and communications 13,181; Financing, insurance, real estate and business services 4,624; Community, social and personal services 47,608; Activities not adequately defined 2,244; *Total labour force* 138,153 (males 123,462; females 14,691. Figures exclude persons seeking work for the first time, totalling 4,231 (males 2,717; females 1,514), but include other unemployed persons, totalling 261 (males 241; females 20). Source: International Labour Office, *Year Book of Labour Statistics*.

AGRICULTURE, ETC.

Principal Crops (FAO estimates, '000 metric tons, 1988): Tomatoes 5; Other vegetables and melons 7; Dates 45 (Source: FAO, *Production Yearbook*).

Livestock (FAO estimates, '000 head, year ending September 1988): Cattle 6; Sheep 8; Goats 16 (Source: FAO, *Production Yearbook*).

Livestock Products (FAO estimates, '000 metric tons, 1988): Poultry meat 3; Cows' milk 6; Hen eggs 4.0 (Source: FAO, *Production Yearbook*).

Fishing ('000 metric tons, live weight): Total catch 7.8 in 1985; 8.1 in 1986; 7.8 in 1987 (Source: FAO, *Yearbook of Fishery Statistics*).

MINING

Production (1987): Crude petroleum 15,216,000 barrels; Natural gas 5,843 million cu metres.

INDUSTRY

Production ('000 barrels, 1987): Liquefied petroleum gas 296; Naphtha 12,785; Motor spirit (petrol) and aviation gasoline 19,418; Kerosene 2,681; Fuel oil 21,225; Diesel oil 42; Gas oil 28,029; Heavy lubricant distillate 1,161; Petroleum bitumen (asphalt) 967; Electric energy 2,996 million kWh; Aluminium (unwrought, '000 metric tons) 180.3.

FINANCE

Currency and Exchange Rates: 1,000 fils = 1 Bahrain dinar (BD). *Coins:* 1, 5, 10, 25, 50 and 100 fils. *Notes:* 500 fils; 1, 5, 10 and 20 dinars. *Sterling and Dollar Equivalents* (30 September 1990): £1 sterling = 704.4 fils; US $1 = 376.0 fils; 100 Bahrain dinars = £141.96 = $265.96. *Exchange Rate:* Fixed at US $1 = 376.0 fils (BD 1 = $2.6596) since November 1980.

Budget (estimates, BD million, 1990): Revenue 440 (Petroleum receipts 250, Fees and charges 146, Grants and loans 44); Expenditure 540 (Recurrent: Education 50.8, Health 36.9, Public works, power and water 44.9, Defence 72.9, Interior 67.4, Transfer and loan repayments 37.9, *Total* 415.0; Development: Power and water 37.0, Housing 20.0, Roads and sewage 27.0, Airport 8.0, Health 6.4, Education 4.0, Other 22.6, *Total* 125.0) (Source: Ministry of Finance and National Economy).

Development Plan (proposed expenditure, BD million, 1982–87*): Infrastructure 768 (Electricity 260, Water and Sewerage 192, Housing 182, Roads 72, Ports and Airport 37, Other 25); Social Services 86 (Education 37, Health 12, Other 37); Economic Services 34 (Agriculture 21, Industry 11, Other 2); Administrative Services 93 (Defence and Security 80, Other 13); Other sectors 41; Total 1,022 (Source: Statistical Bureau, Ministry of Finance and National Economy).

* In May 1983 the Five-Year Plan was extended for a further year.

International Reserves (US $ million at 31 December 1989): Gold (valued at cost of acquisition) 6.6; IMF special drawing rights 20.9; Reserve position in IMF 38.9; Foreign exchange 990.3; Total 1,056.7 (Source: IMF, *International Financial Statistics*).

Money Supply (BD million at 31 December 1989): Currency outside banks 84.77; Demand deposits at commercial banks 149.91; Total money 234.67 (Source: IMF, *International Financial Statistics*).

Cost of Living (Consumer Price Index for Bahraini nationals; base: 1985 = 100): 96.0 in 1987; 96.3 in 1988; 97.7 in 1989 (Source: IMF, *International Financial Statistics*).

Gross Domestic Product (BD million at current prices): 1,198.2 in 1986; 1,191.8 in 1987; 1,262.9 in 1988 (Source: IMF, *International Financial Statistics*).

Balance of Payments (US $ million, 1988): Merchandise exports f.o.b. 2,411.4; Merchandise imports f.o.b. −2,334.0; *Trade balance* 77.4; Exports of services 1,162.5; Imports of services −1,223.4; *Balance on goods and services* 16.5; Private unrequited transfers (net) −193.1; Government unrequited transfers (net) 366.5; *Current balance* 189.9; Long-term capital (net) 205.1; Short-term capital (net) −419.7; Net errors and omissions 112.8; *Total* (net monetary movements) 88.0; Valuation changes (net) 15.2; *Changes in reserves* 103.2 (Source: IMF, *International Financial Statistics*).

EXTERNAL TRADE

Principal Commodities (BD million, 1989): *Imports c.i.f.:* Crude petroleum 466.7; Total (incl. others) 1,054.0. *Exports f.o.b.:* Petroleum and petroleum products 800.5; Aluminium 76.5; Total (incl. others) 1,009.6 (Source: IMF, *International Financial Statistics*).

Principal Trading Partners (US $ million, 1982): *Imports c.i.f.:* Australia 196.7; Federal Republic of Germany 117.6; Japan 252.8; Republic of Korea 70.2; United Kingdom 253.3; USA 353.8; Total (incl. others) 1,774.7 (excl. crude petroleum 1,840.7, mainly from

Saudi Arabia). *Exports f.o.b.*: Hong Kong 110.3; India 127.7; Japan 256.8; Kuwait 125.5; Oman 168.9; Qatar 74.5; Saudi Arabia 115.1; Singapore 380.6; United Arab Emirates 432.1; Zambia 92.8; Total (incl. others) 3,582.8. Source: UN, *International Trade Statistics Yearbook*.

TRANSPORT

Road Traffic (registered motor vehicles, 1986): Private cars 81,872; Taxis 973; Vans and lorries 22,557; Private buses 2,394; Public buses 528; Motorcycles 1,658; Total 109,982.

Shipping (international sea-borne freight traffic, '000 dwt, 1986): *Goods loaded:* Dry cargo 1,954; Petroleum products 89,543,000 barrels. *Goods unloaded:* 1,109.

Civil Aviation (Bahrain International Airport, 1987): 20,398 aircraft arrived and departed.

COMMUNICATIONS MEDIA

Radio Receivers: 248,251 in use (1988).

Television Receivers: 185,952 in use (1988).

Telephones: 76,792 in use (1987).

Book Production: 46 titles (1983).

Daily Newspapers: 2; estimated circulation 19,000 (1986).

EDUCATION

Government Institutions (1986): *Primary:* 1,454 classes; 50,936 students. *Intermediate:* 566 classes; 19,838 students. *Secondary* (general): 256 classes, 7,815 students; (commercial): 145 classes, 4,534 students; (technical): 95 classes, 2,630 students. *Religious education:* 9 classes, 114 students.

Directory

The Constitution

A 108-article constitution was ratified in June 1973. It states that 'all citizens shall be equal before the law' and guarantees freedom of speech, of the press, of conscience and religious beliefs. Other provisions include the outlawing of the compulsory repatriation of political refugees. The Constitution also states that the country's financial comptroller should be responsible to the legislature and not to the Government, and allows for national trade unions 'for legally justified causes and on peaceful lines'. Compulsory free primary education and free medical care are also laid down in the Constitution. The Constitution, which came into force on 6 December 1973, also provided for a national assembly, composed of the members of the Cabinet and 30 members elected by popular vote, although this was dissolved in August 1975.

The Government

HEAD OF STATE

Amir: Sheikh ISA BIN SULMAN AL-KHALIFA (succeeded to the throne on 2 November 1961; took the title of Amir on 16 August 1971).

THE CABINET
(August 1990)

Prime Minister: Sheikh KHALIFA BIN SULMAN AL-KHALIFA.

Minister of Defence: Maj.-Gen. Sheikh KHALIFA BIN AHMAD AL-KHALIFA.

Minister of Finance and National Economy: IBRAHIM ABD AL-KARIM MUHAMMAD.

Minister of Foreign Affairs: Sheikh MUHAMMAD BIN MUBARAK BIN HAMAD AL-KHALIFA.

Minister of Education: Dr ALI MUHAMMAD FAKHRO.

Minister of Health: JAWAD SALIM AL-ARRAYEDH.

Minister of the Interior: Sheikh MUHAMMAD BIN KHALIFA BIN HAMAD AL-KHALIFA.

Minister of Information: TARIQ ABD AR-RAHMAN AL-MOAYED.

Minister of Justice and Islamic Affairs: Sheikh ABDULLAH BIN KHALID AL-KHALIFA.

Minister of Development and Industry and Acting Minister of State for Cabinet Affairs: YOUSUF AHMAD ASH-SHIRAWI.

Minister of Transport: IBRAHIM MUHAMMAD HUMAIDAN.

Minister of Labour and Social Affairs: Sheikh KHALIFA BIN SULMAN BIN MUHAMMAD AL-KHALIFA.

Minister of Housing: Sheikh KHALID BIN ABDULLAH BIN KHALID AL-KHALIFA.

Minister of Public Works, Power and Water: MAJID JAWAD AL-JISHI.

Minister of Commerce and Agriculture: HABIB AHMAD QASSIM.

Minister of State for Legal Affairs: Dr HUSSAIN MUHAMMAD AL-BAHARNA.

MINISTRIES

Amiri Court: POB 555, Riffa Palace, Manama; tel. 661451; telex 8666.

Office of the Prime Minister: POB 1000, Government House, Government Rd, Manama; tel. 262266; telex 9336.

Ministry of Commerce and Agriculture: POB 5479, Diplomatic Area, Manama; tel. 531531; telex 9171.

Ministry of Defence: POB 245, West Rifa'a; tel. 665599; telex 8429.

Ministry of Development and Industry: POB 1435, Manama; tel. 291511; telex 8344; fax 271468.

Ministry of Education: POB 43, Khalid bin al-Walid Rd, Qudhaibiya, Manama; tel. 258400; telex 9094.

Ministry of Finance and National Economy: POB 333, Government House, Government Rd, Manama; tel. 262400; telex 8933; fax 243655.

Ministry of Foreign Affairs: POB 547, Government House, Government Rd, Manama; tel. 258200; telex 8228.

Ministry of Health: POB 12, Sheikh Sulman Rd, Manama; tel. 250834; telex 8511.

Ministry of Housing: POB 802, Diplomatic Area, Manama; tel. 533000; telex 8599; fax 245368.

Ministry of Information: POB 253, Isa Town; tel. 681555; telex 8399; fax 682777.

Ministry of the Interior: POB 13, Police Fort Compound, Manama; tel. 254021; telex 8333.

Ministry of Justice and Islamic Affairs: POB 450, Diplomatic Area, Manama; tel. 531333.

Ministry of Labour and Social Affairs: POB 32333, Isa Town, Manama; tel. 687800; telex 9062.

Ministry of Public Works, Power and Water: POB 6000, Muharraq Causeway Rd, Manama; tel. 533133; telex 8515; fax 533027.

Ministry of State for Cabinet Affairs: POB 1000, Government House, Government Road, Manama; tel. 262266; telex 7424.

Ministry of State for Legal Affairs: POB 790, Al-Hidaya Bldg, Government Rd, Manama; tel. 259990.

Ministry of Transport: POB 10325, Diplomatic Area, Manama; tel. 232023; telex 8989.

Legislature

NATIONAL ASSEMBLY

In accordance with the 1973 Constitution, elections to a national assembly took place in December 1973. About 30,000 electors elected 30 members for a four-year term. Since political parties are not allowed, all 114 candidates stood as independents but, in practice, the National Assembly was divided almost equally between conservative, moderate and more radical members. In addition to the 30 elected members, the National Assembly contained the members of the Cabinet. In August 1975 the Prime Minister resigned because, he complained, the National Assembly was preventing the Government from carrying out its functions. The Amir invited the Prime Minister to form a new cabinet, and two days later the National Assembly was dissolved by Amiri decree. It has not been revived.

BAHRAIN

Diplomatic Representation

EMBASSIES IN BAHRAIN

Algeria: POB 26402, Adiliya 336, Villa 579, Rd 3622, Manama; tel. 713783; telex 2775; Ambassador: BELAID MOHAND OUSSAID.

Bangladesh: POB 26718, House 159, Rd 2004, Area 320, Hoora; tel. 293371; telex 7029; Chargé d'affaires: A. MOMEN CHOUDHURY.

Denmark: POB 45, Maersk Line, Manama; tel. 727896; telex 8676; Ambassador: B. DAN NIELSON.

Egypt: POB 818, Adiliya; tel. 720005; telex 8248; Ambassador: NABIL MUSTAFA IBRAHIM.

France: POB 11134, King Faisal Rd, Diplomatic Area, Manama; tel. 291734; telex 9281; Ambassador: PIERRE BOILLOT.

Germany: POB 10306, Diplomatic Area 317, Al-Hasan Bldg, Sheikh Hamad Causeway, Manama; tel. 530210; telex 7128; Ambassador: Dr BERND WULFFEN.

India: POB 26106, Bldg 182, Rd 2608, Qudhaibiya, Area 326, Adliya, Manama; tel. 712785; telex 9047; fax 715527; Ambassador: NATHU RAM VERMA.

Iran: POB 26477, Sheikh Isa Rd 2709, Manama; tel. 712151; telex 8238; Chargé d'affaires: HUSSAIN NARAQIAN.

Iraq: Ar-Raqeeb Bldg, No 17, Rd 2001, Comp 320, King Faisal Rd, Manama; tel. 290999; telex 9620; Ambassador: TAHA M. ALLAWI AL-QAISI.

Japan: POB 23720, House 403, Rd 915, Salmaniya, Manama; tel. 243364; Ambassador: TOSHIRO OGUSHI.

Jordan: POB 5242, Villa 43, Rd 1901, Al-Fatih Ave, Manama; tel. 291109; Ambassador: AMJAD AL-MAJALI.

Korea, Republic: POB 11700, King Faisal Rd, Manama; tel. 291629; telex 8736; Ambassador: MOON-KI WOO.

Kuwait: POB 786, Diplomatic Area, 76 Rd 1703, Manama; tel. 242330; telex 8830; Ambassador: FAISAL M. AL-HAJI.

Oman: POB 26414, Diplomatic Area, Bldg 37, Rd 1901, Manama; tel. 293663; telex 9332; Ambassador: GHALIB BIN ABDULLAH BIN JUBRAN.

Pakistan: POB 563, House 75, Rd 3403, Area 334, Mahooz, Manama; tel. 712470; Ambassador: MUHAMMAD KHAN JUNEJO.

Saudi Arabia: POB 1085, Bldg 1450, Rd 4043, Jufair, Manama; tel. 727223; Ambassador: Dr GHAZI ABD AR-RAHMAN AL-GOSAIBI.

Tunisia: POB 26911, al-Mahouz, Manama; tel. 721431; Ambassador: NOURREDDIN HAMDANE.

United Kingdom: POB 114, 21 Government Rd, Manama; tel. 534404; telex 8213; fax 531273; Ambassador: JOHN ALAN SHEPHERD.

USA: POB 26431, Off Sheikh Isa Rd, Manama; tel. 714151; telex 9398; fax 712554; Ambassador: CHARLES HOSTLER.

Judicial System

Since the termination of British legal jurisdiction in 1971, intensive work has been undertaken on the legislative requirements of Bahrain. The Criminal Law is at present contained in various Codes, Ordinances and Regulations. All nationalities are subject to the jurisdiction of the Bahrain courts which guarantee equality before the law irrespective of nationality or creed.

Directorate of Courts: POB 450, Government House, Government Rd, Manama; tel. 531333.

Religion

At the April 1981 census the population was 350,798, distributed as follows: Muslims 298,140; Christians 25,611; Others 27,033; No religion 14.

ISLAM

Muslims are divided between the Sunni and Shi'ite sects. The ruling family is Sunni, although the majority of the Muslim population (almost 60%) are Shi'ite.

CHRISTIANITY

The Anglican Communion

Within the Episcopal Church in Jerusalem and the Middle East, Bahrain forms part of the diocese of Cyprus and the Gulf. There are two Anglican churches in Bahrain, St Christopher's Cathedral in Manama and the Community Church in Awali, and the congregations are entirely expatriate. The Bishop in Cyprus and the Gulf is resident in Cyprus, while the Archdeacon in the Gulf is resident in the United Arab Emirates.

Provost: Very Rev. DEREK J. TAYLOR, St Christopher's Cathedral, POB 36, Al-Mutanabi Ave, Manama; tel. 253866.

The Press

DAILIES

Akhbar al-Khalij (Gulf News): POB 5300, Manama; tel. 620111; telex 8565; f. 1976; Arabic; Chair. IBRAHIM AL-MOAYED; Man. Dir ANWAR M. ABD AR-RAHMAN; Editor-in-Chief AHMAD KAMAL; circ. 22,000.

Al-Ayam (The Days): POB 3232, Manama; tel. 727111; fax 729009; f. 1989; publ. by Al Ayam Establishment for Press and Publications; Chair. and Editor-in-Chief NABIL YAQUB AL-HAMER; circ. 25,000.

BAPCO Daily News: Awali; tel. 755047; telex 8214; fax 752924; publ. by the Bahrain Petroleum Co BSC; English; Saturday to Wednesday inclusive; Editor SAMUEL KNIGHT; circ. 1,000.

Daily News Bulletin: POB 1062, Manama; tel. 251881.

Gulf Daily News: POB 5300, Manama; tel. 620222; telex 8565; fax 621566; f. 1978; English; Editor-in-Chief CLIVE JACQUES; Editor GEORGE WILLIAMS; circ. 11,500.

WEEKLIES

Al-Adhwaa' (Lights): POB 250, Manama; tel. 245251; telex 8564; fax 293166; f. 1965; Arabic; publ. by Arab Printing and Publishing House; Chair. RAID MAHMOUD AL-MARDI; Editor-in-Chief MUHAMMAD QASSIM SHIRAWI; circ. 7,000.

Akhbar BAPCO (BAPCO News): Bahrain Petroleum Co BSC, POB 25149, Awali; tel. 755055; telex 8214; fax 752924; f. 1981; formerly known as an-Najma al-Usbou' (The Weekly Star); Arabic; house journal; Editor KHALID F. MEHMAS; circ. 8,000.

Al-Bahrain: POB 26005, Isa Town; Arabic; tel. 683986; telex 8399; fax 685114; publ. by the Ministry of Information; Editor HAMAD AL-MANNAI; circ. 3,000.

Al-Jaridat ar-Rasmiya (The Official Gazette): POB 253, Isa Town; f. 1957; Arabic; publ. by the Ministry of Information.

Al-Masirah: POB 5981, Manama; tel. 258882; telex 7421; fax 276178; f. 1977; Arabic; politics; publ. by Al-Masirah Journalism, Printing and Publishing House; Chair. and Editor-in-Chief KHALIFA HASAN QASSIM.

Al-Mawakif (Attitudes): POB 1083, Manama; tel. 231231; fax 271720; f. 1973; Arabic; general interest; Editor MANSOOR RADHI; circ. 4,000.

Sada al-Usbou' (Weekly Echo): POB 549, Bahrain; tel. 290111; telex 8880; fax 290507; f. 1969; Arabic; Owner and Editor-in-Chief ALI SAYYAR; circ. 25,000 (in various Gulf states).

OTHER PERIODICALS

Afaq Amniya (Security Outlook): POB 13, Manama; f. 1983; monthly; Arabic; publ. by Ministry of the Interior.

Bahrain Medical Bulletin: POB 32159, Manama; tel. 279472; f. 1979; quarterly; English; Editor JAFFAR AL-IBRIQ; circ. 1,750.

Delmon: POB 5087, Manama; tel. 727895; f. 1973; English and Arabic; publ. by Bahrain Historical and Archaeological Society; Editor-in-Chief Dr MUHAMMAD KHOZAI; circ. 2,000.

Discover Bahrain: POB 10704, Manama; f. 1988; publ. by G. and B. Media Ltd; Publr and Editor ROBERT GRAHAM.

Gulf Construction: POB 224, Manama; monthly; English; publ. by Al-Hilal Publishing and Marketing Co; Editor TONY MORBIN; circ. 10,166.

Gulf Panorama: POB 1122, Manama; tel. 277677; monthly; Editor IBRAHIM BASHMI; circ. 15,000.

The Gulf Tourism Directory: POB 859, Manama; tel. 731224; fax 731067; f. 1990; English; Publr RASHID BIN MUHAMMAD AL-KHALIFA.

Al-Hayat at-Tijariya (Commerce Review): POB 248, Manama; tel. 233913; telex 8691; fax 241294; monthly; English and Arabic; publ. by Bahrain Chamber of Commerce and Industry; Editor KHALIL YOUSUF; circ. 3,500.

Al-Hidayah (Guidance): POB 450, Manama; tel. 522384; f. 1978; monthly; Arabic; publ. by Ministry of Justice and Islamic Affairs; Editor-in-Chief ABD AR-RAHMAN BIN MUHAMMAD RASHID AL-KHALIFA; circ. 5,000.

Inside Bahrain: POB 102435, Manama; tel. 291110; fax 294055; fortnightly; English; publ. by Inside Bahrain Promotions; Editor-in-Chief ISA BIN KHALIFA AL-KHALIFA; circ. 11,000.

BAHRAIN

Al-Muhami (The Lawyer): POB 5095, Manama; f. 1982; Arabic; publ. by Bahrain Lawyers Association.

Al-Muhandis (The Engineer): POB 835, Manama; f. 1975; quarterly; Arabic; publ. by Bahrain Association of Engineers; Editor JASSIM SHIRAWI.

Al-Murshid (The Guide): POB 553, Manama; monthly; English and Arabic; includes 'What's on in Bahrain'; publ. by Arab Printing and Publishing House; Editor M. SOLIMAN.

Al-Musafir al-Arabi (Arab Traveller): POB 5028, Manama; f. 1984; bi-monthly; Arabic; publ. by Falcon Publishing WLL; Editor-in-Chief MUHAMMAD AS-SAID.

Oil and Gas News: POB 224, Manama; tel. 231122; telex 8981; monthly; publ. by Al-Hilal Publishing and Marketing Co.

Al-Quwwa (The Force): POB 245, Manama; tel. 665599; telex 8429; f. 1977; monthly; Arabic; publ. by Bahrain Defence Forces; Editor-in-Chief Maj. AHMAD MAHMOUD AS-SUWAIDI.

Shipping and Transport News International: POB 224, Manama; fortnightly; English; publ. by Al-Hilal Publishing and Marketing Co; Editor SABY GANGULI; circ. 5,500.

This is Bahrain and What's On: POB 726, Manama; tel. 250014; telex 8494; fax 230025; f. 1975; quarterly; English; general interest; publ. by Gulf Advertising and Marketing Co; Editor FENELLA FLANAGAN; circ. 15,000.

Time Magazine: POB 30334, Manama; tel. 694571; telex 9952.

Travel and Tourism News International: POB 224, Manama; tel. 231122; telex 8981; fax 234175; fortnightly; travel trades; publ. by Al-Hilal Publishing and Marketing Co; Editor LINDSAY STONER; circ. 5,900.

Al-Wathiqa (The Document): POB 28882; tel. 661681; f. 1982; twice a year; publ. by Historical Documentation Centre; Editor ABDULLAH BIN KHALID AL-KHALIFA.

Az-Zira'a fi al-Alam al-Arabi (Agriculture in the Arab World): POB 5028, Manama; monthly; Arabic; publ. by Falcon Publishing WLL.

NEWS AGENCIES

Agence France-Presse (France): Direction Régionale pour le Golfe, POB 5890, Manama; tel. 259115; telex 8987; fax 277438; Regional Man. for the Gulf JEAN-PIERRE PERRIN.

Associated Press (AP) (USA): POB 11022, Al-Moosa Bldg, Manama; tel. 530101; telex 9470; fax 530249; Chief of Bureau ALI MAHMOUD.

Deutsche Presse-Agentur (dpa) (Germany): POB 26995, Rd 3435, Bldg 1464, Apt 2, Al-Mahouz, Manama; tel. 727523; telex 9542; Correspondent (vacant).

Gulf News Agency: POB 301, Manama; tel. 687272; telex 9030; fax 687008; Editor-in-Chief KHALID ZAYAN.

Inter Press Service (IPS) (Italy): c/o Gulf News Agency, POB 301, Manama; tel. 532235; fax 687008.

Iraqi News Agency: POB 26477, Manama; tel. 290999; fax 293124; Chief of Bureau SAMIR AZZAWI.

Press Trust of India: POB 2546, Manama; tel. 713431; telex 8482; Chief of Bureau SHAKIL AHMAD.

Reuters (UK): UGB Bldg, 5th Floor, Diplomatic Area, Manama; tel. 536111; telex 9402; fax 536193; Chief of Bureau CHARLES ROBERT HORROCKS.

Publishers

Arab Printing and Publishing House: POB 553, Manama; fax 293145.

Arab Communicators: POB 551, Manama; tel. 211006; telex 8263; fax 210931; publrs of annual Bahrain Business Directory; Dirs AHMAD A. FAKHRI, HAMAD A. ABUL.

Falcon Publishing WLL: POB 5028, Manama; tel. 253162; telex 8917; fax 259694; Chair and Man. Dir ABD AN-NABI ASH-SHO'ALA.

Gulf Advertising and Marketing Co: POB 726, Manama; tel. 250014; telex 8494; fax 230025.

Al-Hilal Publishing and Marketing Co: POB 224, Manama; tel. 293131; telex 8981; fax 293400; specialist magazines of commercial interest; Chair. A. M. ABD AR-RAHMAN; Man. Dir R. MIDDLETON.

Al-Masirah Journalism, Printing and Publishing House: POB 5981, Manama; tel. 258882; telex 7421.

Government Publishing House

Directorate of Publications: POB 26005, Manama; tel. 689077; Dir MUHAMMAD AL-KHOZAI.

Radio and Television

In 1989 there were 250,000 radio receivers and 185,952 television receivers in use. English language programmes, broadcast from Saudi Arabia by the US Air Force in Dhahran and by the Arabian-American Oil Co (Aramco), can be received in Bahrain, as can the television service provided by the latter.

Bahrain Broadcasting Station: POB 194, Manama; tel. 712278; telex 9259; f. 1955; state-owned and -operated enterprise; two 10 kW transmitters; programmes are in Arabic and English, and include news, plays and talks; Station Mans HASSAN SALMAN KAMAL (Arabic service), AHMAD M. SULAIMAN (English service).

Radio Bahrain: POB 702, Manama; tel. 629062; telex 8311; fax 780911; f. 1977; commercial radio station in English language; Man. AHMAD M. SULAIMAN.

Bahrain Television: POB 1075, Manama; tel. 681811; telex 8311; fax 681544; commenced colour broadcasting in 1973; second channel in English began broadcasting in October 1981; the station takes advertising; covers Bahrain, eastern Saudi Arabia, Qatar and the UAE; Dir HALA AL-UMRAN.

Finance

(cap. = capital; p.u. = paid up; dep. = deposits; m. = millions; res = reserves; brs = branches; amounts in Bahraini dinars unless otherwise stated)

BANKING
Central Bank

Bahrain Monetary Agency (BMA): POB 27, Manama; tel. 241241; telex 9144; f. 1973, in operation from January 1975; controls issue of currency, regulates exchange control and credit policy, organization and control of banking system and bank credit; cap. p.u. 20m., dep. 181.5m., res 115.3m., total assets 407.3m. (Dec. 1987); Governor ABDULLAH HASSAN SAIF; Chair. Sheikh KHALIFA BIN SALMAN AL-KHALIFA.

Locally Incorporated Commercial Banks

Al-Ahli Commercial Bank BSC: POB 5941, Manama; tel. 244333; telex 9130; fax 241301; f. 1977; full commercial bank; dep. 145.2m., total assets 168.2m. (Dec. 1989); Chair. MUHAMMAD YOUSUF JALAL; Gen. Man. QASIM M. QASIM.

Arlabank International EC: POB 5070, Manama Centre, Manama; tel. 232124; telex 9345; fax 246239; f. 1983; wholly owned subsidiaries: Arab-Latin American Bank (Banco Arabe Latinoamericano) in Peru, Alpha Lambda Investment and Securities Corpn in the British Virgin Islands; cap. p.u. US $183.7m., total assets US $1,314.6m. (Dec. 1989); Chair. ABDULLAH A. SAUDI; Gen. Man. CHRISTIAN RODRIGUEZ-CAMILLONI.

Bahrain Middle East Bank EC: POB 797, Manama; tel. 532345; telex 9706; fax 530526; f. 1982; owned by Burgan Bank (28%) and GCC nationals (72%); cap. US $139.9m., res US $4.1m., dep. US $476.7m., total assets US $642m. (Dec. 1989); Chair. ABDUL RAHMAN SALEM AL-ATEEQI; Gen. Man. and CEO K. J. A. KATCHADURIAN.

Bahraini Saudi Bank BSC (BSB): POB 1159, Government Rd, Manama; tel. 263111; telex 7010; fax 263048; f. 1983; commenced operations in early 1985; licensed as a full commercial bank; cap. 20.0m., res 0.7m., dep. 75.1m. (Dec. 1989); Chair. Sheikh IBRAHIM BIN HAMAD AL-KHALIFA; Gen. Man. MANSOOR AS-SAYED (acting).

Bank of Bahrain and Kuwait BSC (BBK): POB 597, Manama; tel. 253388; telex 8919; fax 275785; f. 1971; cap. 55m., dep. 611.8m., total assets 687.5m. (Dec. 1989); Chair. RASHID ABD AR-RAHMAN AZ-ZAYANI; Gen. Man. MURAD ALI MURAD; 18 local brs, 3 brs overseas.

Faysal Islamic Bank of Bahrain: Chamber of Commerce Bldg, POB 20492, King Faysal Rd, Manama; tel. 275040; telex 9411; fax 277305; f. 1982 as Massraf Faysal Al-Islami of Bahrain EC; renamed as above in 1987; cap. US $30m., res US $17.7m., dep. US $1,023.6m. (Dec. 1989); Chair. ABDULLAH AHMED ZAINAL ALIREZA; Gen. Man. IMTIAZ PERVEZ; 6 brs.

Gulf International Bank BSC (GIB): POB 1017, Ad-Dowali Bldg, 3 Palace Ave, Manama; tel. 534000; telex 8801; fax 522633; f. 1975; owned by Governments of Bahrain, Iraq, Kuwait, Oman, Qatar, Saudi Arabia and the UAE; cap. p.u. US $1,001.1, total assets US $9,893.0m. (Dec. 1989); Chair. ABDULLAH HASSAN SAIF; Gen. Man. GHAZI M. ABD AL-JAWAD; 3 brs, 2 rep. offices.

National Bank of Bahrain BSC (NBB): POB 106, Government Rd, Manama; tel. 258800; telex 8242; fax 263876; f. 1957; commercial bank with Government of Bahrain as major shareholder; total assets 680.3m. (1990); Chair. AHMAD ALI KANOO; Gen. Man. and CEO HUSSAIN ALI JUMA; 19 brs.

BAHRAIN

Directory

Foreign Commercial Banks

Algemene Bank Nederland NV (Netherlands): POB 350, Manama; tel. 255420; telex 8356; Regional Man. (Middle East and Africa) P. V. CALLENFELS.

Arab Bank Ltd (Jordan): POB 395, Manama Centre, Manama; tel. 256398; telex 8658; Senior Man. J. W. TAKCHI; 4 brs.

Bank Melli Iran: POB 785, Government Rd, Manama; tel. 259910; telex 8266; fax 270768; Gen. Man. MUHAMMAD HASSAN NAJIMI; 1 br.

Bank Saderat Iran: POB 825, Manama; tel. 255318; telex 8688; Man. Y. M. SHENOY; 2 brs.

Banque du Caire (Egypt): POB 815, Manama; tel. 254454; telex 8298; Man. MAHMOUD ABBAS ABU AL-KHAIR.

Banque Paribas FCB (France): POB 5241, Manama; tel. 253119; telex 8458; Gen. Man. M. APTHORPE.

British Bank of the Middle East (BBME) (Hong Kong): POB 57, Manama; tel. 242555; telex 8230; fax 256822; Area Man. ALAN D. WHYTE; 5 brs.

Chase Manhattan Bank NA (USA): POB 368, Manama; tel. 251401; telex 8286; Vice-Pres. and Man. STEVE FULLENKAMP; 1 br.

Citibank NA (USA): POB 548, Manama; tel. 257124; telex 8225; Vice-Pres. ROSS DI BACCO; 1 br.

Grindlays Bahrain Bank BSC: POB 793, Manama; tel. 250805; telex 8335; fax 272708; f. 1984 when Bahraini citizens acquired 60% of equity held by Grindlays Bank PLC (London); total assets 57.9m. (Dec. 1989); Chair. MUHAMMAD ABDULLAH AZ-ZAMIL; Gen. Man. JAMES MCNIE; 3 brs.

Habib Bank Ltd (Pakistan): POB 566, Manama Centre, Manama; tel. 271402; telex 9448; f. 1941; Sr Vice-Pres. and Gen. Man. ABD AL-HANNAN MIRZA.

Hongkong and Shanghai Banking Corpn Ltd (Hong Kong): POB 5497, Yateem Centre 2, 2nd Floor, Al-Khalifa Ave, Manama; tel. 255828; telex 8707; Man. PAUL STICKLAND.

National Bank of Abu Dhabi: POB 5247, Manama; tel. 250824; telex 8483; Man. ROGER C. V. BACKETT; 1 br.

Rafidain Bank (Iraq): POB 607, Manama; tel. 255456; telex 8332; fax 255656; f. 1979; Man. ABBAS HADI AL-BAYATI; 1 br.

Saudi National Commercial Bank: POB 20363, Manama; tel. 231182; telex 9298; Gen. Man. SAID CHAUDHRY.

Standard Chartered Bank (UK): POB 29, Manama; tel. 255946; telex 8229; f. in Bahrain 1920; Gen. Man. ROSS HOLDEN; 5 brs.

United Bank Ltd (Pakistan): POB 546, Government Rd, Manama; tel. 254032; telex 8247; Man. YOUSUF AHMAD AL-MADINI; 2 brs.

Specialized Financial Institutions

Arab Banking Corpn BSC: POB 5698, ABC Tower, Diplomatic Area, Manama; tel. 532235; telex 9433; fax 533163; f. 1980 by Amiri decree; jointly owned by Kuwait Ministry of Finance, Central Bank of Libya and Abu Dhabi Investment Authority; offers full range of commercial, merchant and investment banking services; cap. and res US $1,250m., total assets $21,730m. (Dec. 1989); Pres. and Chief Exec. ABDULLAH A. SAUDI; 6 brs.

Bahrain Housing Bank: POB 5370, Diplomatic Area, Manama; tel. 534443; telex 8599; f. 1979; fax 533437; provides finance for the construction industry; Chair. Sheikh KHALID BIN ABDULLAH BIN KHALID AL-KHALIFA; Gen. Man. ISA SULTAN ATH-THAWADI.

Bahrain Islamic Bank BSC: POB 5240, Government Rd, Manama; tel. 231402; telex 9388; f. 1979; cap. and res BD 6.6m., total assets BD 91.7m. (1989); Pres. and Gen. Man. ABD AL-LATIF A. RAHIM JANAHI.

'Offshore' Banking Units

Bahrain has been encouraging the establishment of 'offshore' banking units (OBUs) since October 1975. An OBU is not allowed to provide local banking services but is allowed to accept deposits from governments and large financial organizations in the area and make medium-term loans for local and regional capital projects. In late 1990 there were 61 OBUs in operation in Bahrain.

Operational OBUs

Algemene Bank Nederland NV (ABN BANK): POB 350; tel. 255420; telex 8356; fax 262241.

Allied Banking Corporation: POB 20493; tel. 246616; telex 9349.

ALUBAF Arab International Bank EC: POB 11529; tel. 531212; telex 9671.

American Express Bank Ltd: POB 93; tel. 531383; telex 8536.

ANZ Grindlays Bank PLC: POB 5793; tel. 233210; telex 8793.

Arab Asian Bank EC: POB 5619; tel. 233129; telex 8583.

Arab Bank Ltd: POB 395; tel. 555988; telex 8232.

Arab Banking Corporation: POB 5698; tel. 232235; telex 9432.

Arab International Bank: POB 1114; tel. 261611; telex 9489.

Arab Investment Company SAA (TAIC): POB 5559; tel. 271126; telex 8334.

Arab Malaysian Development Bank: POB 5619; tel. 257059; telex 9393.

Arab Saudi Bank: POB 10100; tel. 530011; telex 7218; fax 530788.

Arlabank International EC: POB 5070; tel. 232124; telex 9345.

Al-Bahrain Arab African Bank EC (Al-Baab): POB 20488; tel. 230491; telex 9380.

Bahrain International Bank EC: POB 5016; tel. 274545; telex 9832.

Banco de Vizcaya SA: POB 5307; tel. 253340; telex 9060.

Banco do Estado de São Paulo SA (BANESPA): POB 25615; tel. 232241; telex 9347.

Bank Bumiputra Malaysia Berhad: POB 20392; tel. 231073; telex 8884.

Bank Negara Indonesia 1946: POB 20715; tel. 277562; telex 8208.

Bank of Bahrain and Kuwait BSC: POB 597; tel. 253388; telex 8919.

Bank of Baroda: POB 1915; tel. 253681; telex 9449.

Bank of Credit and Commerce International SA: POB 569; tel. 256501; telex 8346.

Bank of Oman Ltd: POB 20654; tel. 232882; telex 9565.

Bank of Tokyo Ltd: POB 5850; tel. 26518; telex 9066.

Bank Saderat Iran: POB 825; tel. 255318; telex 8688.

Bankers' Trust Co: POB 5905; tel. 259841; telex 9020.

Banque Indosuez: POB 5410; tel. 257019; telex 8976; fax 531224.

Banque Nationale de Paris: POB 5253; tel. 250852; telex 8595.

Banque Paribas: POB 5993; tel. 259272; telex 9078.

Barclays Bank PLC: POB 5120; tel. 242024; telex 8747.

British Bank of the Middle East: POB 57; tel. 255933; telex 8230.

Chase Manhattan Bank NA: POB 368; tel. 251401; telex 8286.

Chemical Bank: POB 5492; tel. 252619; telex 8562.

Citibank NA: POB 548; tel. 257124; telex 8225.

Commercial Bank of Australia: POB 5467; tel. 254792; telex 8687.

Crédit Suisse: POB 5100; tel. 232123; telex 8422.

FRAB-Bank (Middle East) EC: POB 5290; tel. 259862; telex 9024.

Gulf International Bank BSC (GIB): POB 1017; tel. 534000; telex 8802; fax 222633.

Gulf Riyad Bank EC: POB 20220; tel. 232030; telex 9088; fax 250102.

Habib Bank Ltd: POB 566; tel. 271811; telex 8240.

Hanil Bank Ltd: POB 1151; tel. 243503; telex 7048; fax 271812.

Korea Exchange Bank: POB 5767; tel. 255418; telex 8846.

Kuwait Asia Bank EC: POB 10401; tel. 532111; telex 9611; fax 530831.

Manufacturers' Hanover Trust Co: POB 5471; tel. 254375; telex 8556.

Massraf Faysal al-Islami of Bahrain EC: POB 20492; tel. 275040; telex 9270.

National Bank of Abu Dhabi: POB 5886; tel. 255776; telex 8982.

National Bank of Bahrain: POB 106; tel. 258800; telex 8242.

National Bank of Pakistan: POB 775; tel. 244191; telex 9221.

Overseas Trust Bank Ltd: POB 5628; tel. 245145; telex 9238.

Al-Saudi Banque (Paris): POB 5820; tel 257319; telex 8969.

Saudi European Bank SA: POB 26380; tel. 232884; telex 8732; fax 270138.

Saudi National Commercial Bank: POB 20363; tel. 231182; telex 9298.

Security Pacific National Bank: POB 5589; tel. 259956; telex 9034.

Standard Chartered Bank PLC: POB 29; tel. 255946; telex 8229.

State Bank of India: POB 5466; tel. 253640; telex 8804; fax 230503.

Swiss Bank Corporation: POB 5560; tel. 257221; telex 9173.

Union de Banques Arabes et Françaises (UBAF): POB 5595; tel. 250985; telex 8840.

United Bank of Kuwait PLC: POB 5494; tel. 256774; telex 8649.

United Gulf Bank EC: POB 5964; tel. 533233; telex 9556.

Yamaichi International (Middle East) EC: POB 26894; tel. 253922; telex 9468.

Yapi ve Kredi Bankasi: POB 1104; tel. 270089; telex 9931.

Representative Offices

In January 1988 a total of 59 banks maintained representative offices in Bahrain.

Investment Banks

Investment banks operating in Bahrain include the following: Arab Financial Services Co EC, Arab Multinational Investment Co (AMICO), Bahrain International Investment Centre (BIIC), Bahrain Investment Bank BSC, Bahrain Islamic Investment Co BSC, Bahraini Kuwaiti Investment Group (BKIG), Al-Baraka Islamic Investment Bank BSC, Citicorp Investment Bank (CIB), Elders IXL, Gulf Investments Co, EF Hutton International Inc., InvestBank EC, Islamic Investment Company of the Gulf (Bahrain) EC, Merrill Lynch Int. Inc., National Bank of Pakistan, Nikko Investment Banking (Middle East) EC, Nomura Investment Banking (Middle East) EC, Okasan Int. (Middle East) EC, Robert Fleming Holdings Ltd, Sumitomo Finance (Middle East) EC,

BAHRAIN

Trans-Arabian Investment Bank EC (TAIB), United Gulf Investment Co, Yamaichi International (Middle East) EC, Az-Zayani Investments Ltd.

INSURANCE

Al-Ahlia Insurance Co BSC: POB 5282, Manama; tel. 258860; telex 8761; f. 1976; fax 245597; auth. cap. BD 5m.; Chair. QASSIM AHMAD FAKHRO.

Arab Insurance Group BSC (ARIG): POB 26992, Arig House, Diplomatic Area, Manama; tel. 531110; telex 9395; fax 530289; f. 1980; owned by Governments of Kuwait, Libya and Abu Dhabi; cap. p.u. US $150m. (June 1988); all non-life reinsurance; Chair. ABD AL-WAHAB A. AT-TAMMAR; Gen. Man. and CEO NOOR UD-DIN A. NOOR UD-DIN.

Arab International Insurance Co EC (AIIC): POB 10135, Manama; tel. 530087; telex 9226; fax 530122; f. 1981; cap. p.u. US $4m.; non-life reinsurance; Chair. and Man. Dir Sheikh KHALID J. AS-SABAH.

Bahrain Insurance Co BSC (BIC): POB 843, Suite 310, Sh. Mubarak Bldg, Government Ave, Manama; tel. 255641; telex 8463; f. 1969; all classes including life insurance; cap. BD 1.2m.; 66.66% Bahraini-owned; 33.33% Iraqi-owned; Gen. Man. MUNEM AL-KHAFAJI; 5 brs.

Bahrain Kuwait Insurance Co BSC: POB 10166, Diplomatic Area, Manama; tel. 532323; telex 8672; fax 530799; f. 1975; cap. p.u. US $3.2m.; Gen. Man. PETER L. ATKINSON.

National Insurance Co BSC (NIC): POB 1818, Unitag House, Government Rd, Manama; tel. 244181; telex 8908; fax 230228; f. 1982; cap. p.u. US $1.66m.; all classes of general insurance; Chair. J. A. WAFA; Pres. SAMIR AL-WAZZAN.

STOCK EXCHANGE

Bahrain Stock Exchange: c/o Bahrain Monetary Agency, Manama; f. 1989; 30 mems.

Trade and Industry

CHAMBER OF COMMERCE

Bahrain Chamber of Commerce and Industry: POB 248, Manama; tel. 233913; telex 8691; fax 241294; f. 1939; 4,200 mems; Pres. ALI BIN YOUSEF FAKHROO; Sec.-Gen. JASSIM MUHAMMAD ASH-SHATTI.

STATE ENTERPRISES

Aluminium Bahrain BSC (ALBA): POB 570, Manama; tel. 752222; telex 8253; fax 830083; f. 1971; operates a smelter owned by the Governments of Bahrain (74.9%) and Saudi Arabia (20%), the remainder being held by Breton Investments; 186,395 metric tons of aluminium produced in 1989; Chief Exec. GUDVIN K. TOFTE.

Bahrain Aluminium Extrusion Co BSC (BALEXCO): POB 1053, Manama; tel. 730221; telex 8634; fax 731678; f. 1976; supplies aluminium profiles in mill finish; 100% owned by the Government of Bahrain; capacity 6,000 metric tons per year (1990); Chair. Dr ABD AL-LATIF KANOO; Gen. Man. ABD AL-MONEM ASH-SHIRAWI.

Bahrain Atomizers International: POB 5328, Manama; tel. 830008; fax 830025; f. 1973; produces 7,000 metric tons of atomized aluminium powder per year; owned by the Government of Bahrain (51%) and Breton Investments (49%); Chair. Y. SHIRAWI.

Bahrain National Gas Co BSC (BANAGAS): POB 29099, Rifa'a; tel. 756222; telex 9317; fax 756991; f. 1979; responsible for extraction, processing and sale of hydrocarbon liquids from associated gas derived from onshore Bahrain fields; ownership is 75% Government of Bahrain, 12.5% Caltex and 12.5% Arab Petroleum Investments Corporation (APICORP); produced 153,750 metric tons of LPG and 136,244 tons of natural gasoline in 1989; Chair. Sheikh HAMAD BIN IBRAHIM AL-KHALIFA; Production Man. ALI A. GINDI.

Bahrain National Oil Co (BANOCO): POB 25504, Awali; tel. 754666; telex 8670; fax 753203; f. 1976; responsible for exploration, production, processing, transportation and storage of petroleum and petroleum products; distribution and sales of petroleum products (including natural gas), international marketing of crude petroleum and petroleum products, supply and sales of aviation fuels; produced 14.3m. barrels of crude petroleum, 1.3m. barrels of natural gas liquids and 227m. cu ft of natural gas in 1988; CEO MUHAMMAD SALEH SHEIKH ALI.

Bahrain Petroleum Co BSC (BAPCO): Awali; tel. 754444; telex 8214; fax 752924; f. 1980; a refining company owned by the Government of Bahrain (60%) and Caltex Bahrain (40%); refined 90.2m. barrels of crude petroleum in 1989; Chair. YOUSUF AHMAD ASH-SHIRAWI (Minister of Development and Industry); Chief Exec. DON F. HEPBURN.

Bahrain-Saudi Aluminium Marketing Co (BALCO): POB 20079, Manama; tel. 532626; telex 9110; fax 532727; f. 1976; to market ALBA products; owned by the Government of Bahrain (74.33%) and Saudi Basic Industries Corporation (25.67%); Gen. Man. MAHMOUD M. A. AS-SOUFI.

Bahrain Telecommunications Co BSC (BATELCO): POB 14, Manama; tel. 881881; telex 8201; fax 883451; f. 1981; operates all telecommunications services; cap. BD 60m.; 80% owned by Government of Bahrain, 20% by Cable and Wireless PLC (United Kingdom); Chair. IBRAHIM MUHAMMAD HASSAN HUMAIDAN; Gen. Man. BRIAN WOOD.

General Poultry Co: POB 5472, Bahrain; tel. 631001; telex 8678; fully-owned by Government of Bahrain; produces poultry feed and eggs; Chair. SIDDIQ AL-ALAWI.

Gulf Aluminium Rolling Mill Co (GARMCO): POB 20725, Manama; tel. 731000; telex 9786; fax 730542; f. 1980 as a joint venture between the Governments of Bahrain, Saudi Arabia, Kuwait, Iraq Oman and Qatar; produced 44,000 tons of rolled aluminium in 1989; Chair. and Man. Dir Sheikh IBRAHIM BIN KHALIFA AL-KHALIFA; Gen. Man. JOHN PATERSON (acting).

Gulf Industrial Investment Co (GIIC): POB 50177, Hidd; tel. 673311; telex 9993; fax 675258; f. 1988; owned by Kuwait Petroleum Corpn (KPC); manufactures iron ore pellets; Chair. AWWAD AL-KHALDI.

Gulf Petrochemical Industries Co BSC (GPIC): POB 26730, Sitra; tel. 731777; telex 9897; fax 731047; f. 1979 as a joint venture between the Governments of Bahrain, Kuwait and Saudi Arabia, each with one-third equity participation; cap. p.u. BD 60m.; a petrochemical complex at Sitra, inaugurated in 1981; produces 1,200 tons of both methanol and ammonia per day (1990); Chair. Sheikh ISA BIN ALI AL-KHALIFA; Gen. Man. MUSTAFA AS-SAYED.

TRADE UNIONS

There are no trade unions in Bahrain.

Transport

ROADS

Most inhabited areas of Bahrain are linked by bitumen-surfaced roads. By 1987 the number of private cars in Bahrain had risen to 115,000, compared with 20,000 in 1971. Public transport consists of taxis and privately-owned bus services. A national bus company provides public services throughout the country. A modern network of dual highways is being developed, and a 25-km causeway link with Saudi Arabia was opened in November 1986. In its first year of operation, more than 4.5m. people and more than 1.3m. vehicles used the King Fahd Causeway. A three-lane dual carriageway links the causeway to Manama. A joint Bahraini-Saudi bus company was formed in 1986, with capital of US $266,600, to operate along the causeway. A second causeway, linking Manama with Muharraq, was planned for construction between 1989 and 1992, at an estimated cost of US $53m.

Directorate of Roads and Sewerage: POB 5, Exhibition Rd, Hoora, Manama; tel. 291603; telex 9854; fax 292358; responsible for road maintenance and construction; Adviser JACK K. MCDADE.

SHIPPING

Numerous shipping services link Bahrain and the Gulf with Europe, the USA, Pakistan, India, the Far East and Australia.

The deep-water harbour of Mina Sulman was opened in April 1962; it has 14 conventional berths, two container terminals and a roll-on/roll-off berth. In the vicinity are two slipways able to take vessels of up to 1,016 tons and 73 m in length, with services available for ship repairs afloat. The second container terminal, which has a 400-m quay (permitting two 180-m container ships to be handled simultaneously), was opened in April 1979. Further development of Mina Sulman, to allow handling of larger quantities of container cargo, began in 1983. During 1989 Mina Sulman handled a total of 71,306 20-ft equivalent units. In 1989 plans were announced to build a new floating dry dock, with a capacity of 70,000 dwt. In 1990 it was announced that the first phase of an expansion programme at Mina Sulman was due to be completed in August 1992, at an estimated cost of US 55m. It was to include the construction of a graving dock for vessels of up to 180,000 dwt and a 350-m repair quay.

Directorate of Customs and Ports: POB 15, Manama; tel. 243533; telex 8642; responsible for customs activities and acts as port authority; President of Customs and Ports Sheikh DAIJ BIN KHALIFA AL-KHALIFA; Port Director EID ABDULLAH YOUSUF.

Arab Shipbuilding and Repair Yard Co (ASRY): POB 50110, Hidd; tel. 671111; telex 8455; fax 670236; f. 1974 by OAPEC members; 500,000-ton dry dock opened 1977; repaired 94 ships in 1989; Chair. Sheikh DAIJ BIN KHALIFA AL-KHALIFA; Gen. Man. ANTÓNIO J. MACHADO LOPES.

CIVIL AVIATION

Bahrain International Airport has a first-class runway, capable of taking the largest aircraft in use. In 1987 there were 20,398 flights to and from the airport.

Directorate of Civil Aviation: POB 586, Bahrain International Airport, Muharraq; tel. 321332; telex 9186; Asst Under-Sec. Sheikh HAMAD BIN ABDULLAH AL-KHALIFA.

Gulf Air Co GSC (Gulf Air): POB 138, Manama; tel. 322200; telex 8255; fax 530385; f. 1950; jointly owned by the Governments of Bahrain, Oman, Qatar and Abu Dhabi; network includes Abu Dhabi, Amman, Athens, Baghdad, Bahrain, Bangkok, Bombay, Cairo, Colombo, Damascus, Dar es Salaam, Delhi, Dhahran, Dhaka, Doha, Dubai, Frankfurt, Fujairah, Hong Kong, Istanbul, Jeddah, Karachi, Khartoum, Kuwait, Larnaca, London, Manila, Muscat, Nairobi, New York, Paris, Ras al-Khaimah, Riyadh, Salalah, San'a and Sharjah; Chair. ABDULLAH BIN NASSER AS-SUWEIDI (Bahrain); Pres. and Chief Exec. ALI IBRAHIM AL-MALKI (Qatar); fleet consists of 11 TriStar, 8 Boeing 737-200 and 6 Boeing 767-300.

Tourism

There are several archaeological sites of importance. Bahrain is the site of the ancient trading civilization of Dilmun. There is a wide selection of hotels and restaurants, and a new national museum opened in early 1989. In 1989 about 1.3m. tourists visited Bahrain, and revenue from tourism totalled BD 31.9m.

Bahrain Tourism Co (BTC): POB 5831, Manama; tel. 530530; telex 8929.

Directorate of Tourism and Archaeology: POB 26613, Manama; tel. 211199; telex 8311; fax 210969; Dir Dr KADHIM RAJAB; Asst Under-Sec. Sheikh RASHID BIN KHALIFA AL-KHALIFA.

BANGLADESH

Introductory Survey

Location, Climate, Language, Religion, Flag, Capital

The People's Republic of Bangladesh lies in southern Asia, surrounded by Indian territory except for a short south-eastern frontier with Myanmar (formerly Burma) and a southern coast fronting the Bay of Bengal. The country has a tropical monsoon climate and suffers from periodic cyclones. The average temperature is 19°C (67°F) from October to March, rising to 29°C (84°F) between May and September. The average annual rainfall in Dhaka is 188 cm (74 in), of which about three-quarters occurs between June and September. About 95% of the population speak Bengali, the state language, while the remainder mostly use tribal dialects. More than 85% of the people are Muslims, Islam being the state religion, and there are small minorities of Hindus, Buddhists and Christians. The national flag is green, with a red disc in the centre. The capital is Dhaka (Dacca).

Recent History

Present-day Bangladesh was formerly East Pakistan, one of the five provinces into which Pakistan was divided at its initial creation, when Britain's former Indian Empire was partitioned in August 1947. East Pakistan and the four western provinces were separated by about 1,000 miles (1,600 km) of Indian territory. East Pakistan was formed from the former Indian province of East Bengal and the Sylhet district of Assam. Although the East was more populous, government was based in West Pakistan. Dissatisfaction in East Pakistan at its dependence on a remote central government flared up in 1952, when Urdu was declared Pakistan's official language. Bengali, the main language of East Pakistan, was finally admitted as the joint official language in 1954, and in 1955 Pakistan was reorganized into two wings, east and west, with equal representation in the central legislative assembly. However, discontent continued in the eastern wing, particularly as the region was under-represented in the administration and armed forces, and received a disproportionately small share of Pakistan's development expenditure. The leading political party in East Pakistan was the Awami League, led by Sheikh Mujibur Rahman, who demanded autonomy for the East. General elections in December 1970 gave the Awami League an overwhelming victory in the East, and thus a majority in Pakistan's National Assembly; Sheikh Mujib should have become Prime Minister, but Pakistan's President, Gen. Yahya Khan, would not accept this, and negotiations on a possible constitutional compromise broke down. The convening of the new National Assembly was postponed indefinitely in March 1971, leading to violent protests in East Pakistan. The Awami League decided that the province should unilaterally secede from Pakistan, and on 26 March Mujib proclaimed the independence of the People's Republic of Bangladesh ('Bengal Nation').

Civil war immediately broke out. President Yahya Khan outlawed the Awami League and arrested its leaders. By April 1971 the Pakistan army dominated the eastern province. In August Sheikh Mujib was secretly put on trial in West Pakistan. Resistance continued, however, from the Liberation Army of East Bengal (the 'Mukhti Bahini'), a group of irregular fighters who launched a major offensive in November. As a result of the fighting, an estimated 9.5m. refugees crossed into India. On 4 December India declared war on Pakistan, with Indian forces intervening in support of the 'Mukhti Bahini'. Pakistan surrendered on 16 December and Bangladesh's independence became a reality. Pakistan was thus confined to its former western wing. In January 1972 Sheikh Mujib was freed by Pakistan's new President, Zulfiqar Ali Bhutto, and became Prime Minister of Bangladesh. Under a provisional constitution, Bangladesh was declared to be a secular state and a parliamentary democracy. The new nation quickly achieved international recognition, causing Pakistan to withdraw from the Commonwealth in January 1972. Bangladesh joined the Commonwealth in April. The members who had been elected from the former East Pakistan for the Pakistan National Assembly and the Provincial Assembly in December 1970 formed the Bangladesh Constituent Assembly. A new constitution was approved by this Assembly in November 1972 and came into effect in December. A general election for the country's first Jatiya Sangsad (Parliament) was held in March 1973. The Awami League received 73% of the total votes and won 292 of the 300 directly elective seats in the legislature. Bangladesh was finally recognized by Pakistan in February 1974. Stability was threatened by opposition groups which resorted to terrorism and included both political extremes. In December a state of emergency was declared and constitutional rights were suspended. In January 1975 parliamentary government was replaced by a presidential form of government. Sheikh Mujib became President, assuming absolute power, and created the Bangladesh Peasants' and Workers' Awami League. In February Bangladesh became a one-party state.

In August 1975 Sheikh Mujib and his family were assassinated in a right-wing coup, led by a group of Islamic army majors. Khandakar Mushtaq Ahmed, the former Minister of Commerce, was installed as President, declared martial law and banned political parties. A counter-coup on 3 November brought to power Brig. Khalid Musharaf, the pro-Indian commander of the Dhaka garrison, who was appointed Chief of Army Staff, but on 7 November a third coup overthrew Brig. Musharaf's four-day-old regime and power was assumed by the three service chiefs jointly, under a non-political President, Abusadet Mohammed Sayem, the Chief Justice of the Supreme Court. A neutral non-party government was formed, in which the reinstated Chief of Army Staff, Major-Gen. Ziaur Rahman (Gen. Zia), took precedence over his colleagues. Political parties were legalized again in July 1976.

An early return to representative government was promised, but in November 1976 elections were postponed indefinitely and, in a major shift of power, Gen. Zia took over the powers of Chief Martial Law Administrator from President Sayem, assuming the presidency also in April 1977. He amended the Constitution, making Islam, instead of secularism, its first basic principle. In a national referendum in May 1977, 99% of voters affirmed their confidence in President Zia's policies, and in June 1978 the country's first direct presidential election resulted in a clear victory for Zia, who formed a Council of Ministers to replace his Council of Advisers. Parliamentary elections followed in February 1979 and, in an attempt to persuade opposition parties to participate in the elections, President Zia met some of their demands by repealing 'all undemocratic provisions' of the 1974 constitutional amendment, releasing political prisoners and withdrawing press censorship. Consequently, 29 parties contested the elections, in which President Zia's Bangladesh Nationalist Party (BNP) received 49% of the total votes and won 207 of the 300 directly elective seats in the Jatiya Sangsad. In April a new Prime Minister was appointed, and martial law was repealed. The state of emergency was revoked in November.

Political instability recurred, however, when Gen. Zia was assassinated on 30 May 1981 during an attempted military coup, supposedly led by Maj.-Gen. Mohammad Abdul Manzur, an army divisional commander who was himself later killed in confused circumstances. The elderly Vice-President, Justice Abdus Sattar, assumed the role of acting President but was confronted by strikes and demonstrations in protest against the execution of several officers who had been involved in the coup, and pressure from opposition parties to have the date of the presidential election moved. As the only person acceptable to the different groups within the BNP, Sattar was nominated as the party's presidential candidate, gaining an overwhelming victory at the November election. President Sattar announced his intention of continuing the policies of the late Gen. Zia. He found it increasingly difficult, however, to retain civilian control over the country, and in January 1982 he formed a National Security Council, which included military personnel, led by the Army Chief of Staff, Lt-Gen. Hossain Mohammad Ershad. On 24 March Gen. Ershad seized power in a bloodless coup, claiming that political corruption and economic mismanagement had become intolerable. The country was placed under martial law, with Ershad as Chief Martial Law Administrator (in

October his title was changed to Prime Minister), aided by a mainly military Council of Advisers; a retired judge, Justice Abul Chowdhury, was nominated as President by Ershad. Political activities were banned. Later in the year, several former ministers were tried and imprisoned on charges of corruption.

Although the Government's economic policies achieved some success and gained a measure of popular support for Ershad, there were increasing demands in 1983 for a return to democratic government. The two principal opposition groups that emerged were an eight-party alliance, headed by a faction of the Awami League under Sheikh Hasina Wajed (daughter of the late Sheikh Mujib), and a seven-party group which was led by a faction of the BNP under the former President Sattar (who died in October 1985) and Begum Khalida Zia (widow of Gen. Zia). In September 1983 the two groups formed an alliance, the Movement for the Restoration of Democracy (MRD), and jointly issued demands for an end to martial law, for the release of political prisoners and for the holding of parliamentary elections before any others. In November permission was given for the resumption of political activity, and it was announced that a series of local elections between December 1983 and March 1984 were to precede a presidential election and parliamentary elections later in the year. A new political party, the Jana Dal (People's Party), was formed in November 1983 to support Ershad as a presidential candidate. Following demonstrations demanding civilian government, the ban on political activity was reimposed at the beginning of December, only two weeks after it had been rescinded, and leading political figures were detained. On 11 December Ershad declared himself President.

Bangladesh remained disturbed in 1984, with frequent strikes and political demonstrations. Local elections to *upazilla* (sub-district) councils, due to take place in March, were postponed, as the opposition objected to their being held before the presidential and parliamentary elections, on the grounds that Ershad was trying to improve his power-base. The presidential and parliamentary elections, scheduled for May, were also postponed, until December, because of persistent opposition demands for the repeal of martial law and for the formation of an interim neutral government to oversee a fair election. In October Ershad agreed to repeal martial law in three stages in November and December if the opposition would participate in these elections. They responded with an appeal for a campaign of civil disobedience, which led to the announcement in October that the elections were to be indefinitely postponed.

In January 1985 it was announced that parliamentary elections would be held in April, to be preceded by a relaxation of martial law in certain respects: the Constitution was to be fully restored after the elections. The announcement was followed by the formation of a new Council of Ministers, composed entirely of military officers and excluding all members of the Jana Dal, in response to demands by the opposition parties for a 'neutral' government during the pre-election period. Once more, the opposition threatened to boycott the elections, as President Ershad would not relinquish power to an interim government, and in March political activity was banned again. This was immediately followed by a referendum, held in support of the presidency, in which Ershad received 94% of the total votes. Local elections for *upazilla* councils in rural areas were held in May, without the participation of the opposition, and Ershad claimed that 85% of the elected council chairmen were his supporters, although not necessarily of his party. In September a new five-party political alliance, the National Front (comprising the Jana Dal, the United People's Party, the Gonotantrik Party, the Bangladesh Muslim League and a breakaway section of the BNP), was established to proclaim government policies.

In January 1986 the 10-month ban on political activity was ended. The five components of the National Front formally became a single pro-Government entity, named the Jatiya Dal (National Party). Further strikes and demonstrations were organized by opposition groups, who continued to demand the repeal of martial law before the holding of any parliamentary or presidential elections. In March President Ershad announced that parliamentary elections were to be held (under martial law) at the end of April. He relaxed martial law, however, by removing all army commanders from important civil posts and by abolishing more than 150 military courts and the martial law offices. These concessions fulfilled some of the opposition's demands and, as a result, candidates from the Awami League alliance (including Sheikh Hasina Wajed herself), the Jamaat-e-Islami Bangladesh and other smaller opposition parties participated in the parliamentary elections on 7 May (postponed from 26 April). However, the BNP alliance, led by Begum Khalida Zia, boycotted the polls. The elections were characterized by allegations of extensive fraud, violence and intimidation. The Jatiya Dal won 153 of the 300 directly elective seats in the Jatiya Sangsad. In addition, the 30 seats reserved for women in the legislature were filled by nominees of the Jatiya Dal.

In June 1986, while the Constitution remained suspended, the Awami League alliance again demanded the repeal of martial law, the resignation of Ershad and the restoration of a complete democratic system. At the beginning of July Ershad announced that martial law would be repealed only after a presidential election. Although the Awami League members had been sworn in as MPs, they refused to attend the inauguration of the Jatiya Sangsad. In late July the Jatiya Sangsad was prorogued for an indefinite period. A civilian Council of Ministers was sworn in. Mizanur Rahman Chowdhury, former General-Secretary of the Jatiya Dal, became Prime Minister.

In order to be eligible to stand as a candidate in the presidential election in October 1986, Ershad retired as Army Chief of Staff in August and appointed Maj.-Gen. M. Atiqur Rahman in his place, while remaining as Chief Martial Law Administrator and Commander-in-Chief of the Armed Forces. In early September Ershad joined the Jatiya Dal, being elected as chairman of the party and nominated as its presidential candidate. At the presidential election in mid-October, which was boycotted by both the BNP and the Awami League, Ershad won an overwhelming victory over his 11 opponents, receiving nearly 22m. votes, according to official results. Alleged malpractice was reportedly more discreet than in the May parliamentary elections.

In November 1986 Ershad summoned the Jatiya Sangsad, which approved indemnity legislation, legalizing the military regime's actions since March 1982. Ershad repealed martial law and restored the 1972 Constitution. The opposition alliances criticized the indemnity law, stating that they would continue to campaign for the dissolution of the Jatiya Sangsad and the overthrow of the Ershad Government. In December 1986, in an attempt to curb increasing dissension, President Ershad formed a new Council of Ministers, including four MPs from the Awami League. The Justice Minister, Justice A. K. M. Nurul Islam, was appointed Vice-President.

In 1987 the opposition groups continued to hold anti-Government strikes and demonstrations, often with the support of the trade unions and student groups, demanding the resignation of President Ershad and his Government, the installation of an interim neutral government, and the holding of fresh elections. The Government, in turn, continued to reject these demands. In July the Jatiya Sangsad approved the Zilla Parishad (District Council) Amendment Bill, enabling army representatives to participate in the 64 district councils, along with the elected representatives. The adoption of this controversial legislation led to widespread and often violent strikes and demonstrations, organized by the opposition groups, who claimed that the bill represented an attempt by the President to secure an entrenched military involvement in the governing of the country, despite the ending of martial law in November 1986. Owing to the intensity of public opposition, President Ershad was forced to withdraw the bill in August 1987 and return it to the Jatiya Sangsad for reconsideration. A major government reshuffle followed. Political events were overshadowed in August and September, however, when the most severe floods in Bangladesh for 40 years resulted in widespread devastation. In a renewed effort to oust President Ershad, the opposition groups combined forces and organized further protests in November. Thousands of activists were detained, but demonstrations, strikes and opposition rallies continued, leading to numerous clashes between police units and protesters. After 16 days of violent agitation, the Dhaka police chief imposed a 30-day ban on marches and rallies in the capital. The unrest had caused considerable economic dislocation, and the Government claimed that the country was losing US $50m. per day. As a result of this, and in an attempt to forestall another general strike being planned by opposition groups, President Ershad declared a nationwide state of emergency on 27 November, suspending political activity and civil rights, and banning all anti-Government protests, initially for 120 days. In spite of the imposition of curfews on the main towns, reports of disturbances continued, as the opposition maintained its campaign to force Ershad's resignation. In early December, when about 6,000 people were being detained in prison as a result of the unrest, opposition parties in the Jatiya Sangsad announced that their representatives would resign their seats. On 6 December, after 12 opposition members had resigned and the 73 Awami League members had agreed to do likewise, President Ershad dissolved the Jatiya Sangsad. Sheikh Hasina Wajed and Begum Khalida Zia were subsequently released, after being under house arrest for four weeks, but both women rejected President Ershad's offer of peace negotiations and pledged to continue the campaign for his resignation. In January 1988 the President announced that parliamentary elections would be held on 28 February, but leaders of the main opposition parties declared their intention to boycott the proposed poll while Ershad remained in office. As a result of the boycott campaign organized by the opposition, the elections were postponed until 3 March. In January, however, an alliance of 76 very minor political parties formed a government-approved 'Combined Opposition Group' (COG), led by the head of the left-wing Jatiya Samajtantrik Dal (R), A.S.M. Abdur Rab, to contest the parliamentary elections. Local elections to the Union Parishads, which were held throughout Bangladesh in February and which were not boycotted by the opposition, were marred by serious outbreaks of violence. The parliamentary elections were also characterized by widespread violence, as well as by alleged fraud and malpractice. The opposition's boycott campaign proved to be highly successful and the actual level of participation by the electorate appeared to have been considerably lower than the Government's estimate of 50%. As expected, the Jatiya Dal won a large majority of the seats.

In late March 1988 a radical reshuffle of the Council of Ministers included the appointment of a new Prime Minister, Moudud Ahmed, a long-time political ally of Ershad and hitherto the Minister of Industry and a Deputy Prime Minister, in place of Mizanur Rahman Chowdhury. Owing to an abatement in the opposition's anti-Government campaign, Ershad repealed the state of emergency in April. Despite strong condemnation by the opposition and sections of the public, legislation to amend the Constitution, establishing Islam as Bangladesh's state religion, was approved by an overall majority in the Jatiya Sangsad (and by Ershad a few days later) in June. The opposition movement suffered a serious set-back in July, when the Secretary-General of the BNP, A.K.M. Obaidur Rahman, was dismissed, together with several other senior party members, following internal disputes. He subsequently formed a rival faction, challenging the leadership of Begum Khalida Zia. By early September, however, political events had been completely overshadowed by a new wave of disastrous monsoon floods, which began in August and proved to be the most severe in the area's recorded history. Bangladesh suffered further flooding in December 1988 and January 1989, following a severe cyclone in late November. Such economic problems undoubtedly compounded the political unrest in Bangladesh. In late 1988 the Government established a national Disaster Prevention Council and urged the use of regional co-operation to evolve a comprehensive solution to the problem of flooding.

Further reshuffles of the Council of Ministers were implemented in December 1988 (occasioned by the resignation, following a customs scandal, of the Minister of Foreign Affairs, Humayan Rashid Chowdhury) and in March and July 1989. The Government claimed that it was reinforcing constitutionality and democracy when, in July 1989, the Jatiya Sangsad approved legislation limiting the tenure of the presidency to two electoral terms of five years each and creating the post of a directly-elected Vice-President (previously appointed by the President). In August Ershad appointed Moudud Ahmed, hitherto the Prime Minister, as Vice-President, to replace Justice A.K.M. Nurul Islam, who was dismissed following charges of inefficiency. Kazi Zafar Ahmed, formerly the Minister of Information and a Deputy Prime Minister, was promoted to the post of Prime Minister. Local elections were held in March 1990. These elections were officially boycotted by the opposition parties, but, in fact, many of their members participated on an individual basis. In April Ershad announced that he would present himself as a candidate in the presidential election, which was scheduled to be held in mid-1991. In the following month the President implemented an extensive ministerial reshuffle, following widespread allegations of governmental corruption.

In late 1990 the opposition groups, with the support of thousands of students, worked more closely together and increased the intensity of their anti-Government campaign of strikes and demonstrations. In October at least eight demonstrators were shot dead by riot police, more than 500 people were arrested and Ershad announced the closure of Dhaka University and other educational institutions. Violent incidents also occurred in Chittagong and in several other towns in southern and central Bangladesh. The Government's problems were compounded in late October, when communal violence broke out between Muslims and Hindus, following news that Hindu militants had attacked a mosque in Ayodhya in northern India (see India chapter). Curfews were consequently imposed on Dhaka and Chittagong. The communal violence was successfully curbed, but the anti-Government demonstrations and strikes showed no sign of abating. On 27 November President Ershad proclaimed a nationwide state of emergency for the second time in three years, suspending civil rights, imposing strict press censorship and enforced an indefinite curfew throughout the country. On the following day, however, army units were summoned to impose order in the capital when crowds of thousands defied the curfew and attacked police in protest at the imposition of the state of emergency. The death toll in resultant clashes between the troops and demonstrators was variously estimated at between 20 and 70. Under intensifying pressure from the opposition groups, President Ershad resigned on 4 December and declared that parliamentary elections would be held before the presidential election. At the same time, the state of emergency was revoked, and the Jatiya Sangsad was dissolved. Following his nomination by the three main opposition alliances, Justice Shahabuddin Ahmed, the Chief Justice of the Supreme Court, was appointed Vice-President. He assumed the responsibilities of acting President and was put at the head of a neutral caretaker government, pending fresh parliamentary elections. Shahabuddin Ahmed dismissed chiefs of financial institutions, purged local government, and ordered a massive reshuffle in the civil service to remove persons appointed by Ershad from important posts. The opposition parties welcomed all these dramatic political developments and abandoned their protest campaigns, while appealing for calm. They also demanded that Ershad should be tried for alleged corruption and abuse of power. In the week following his resignation, Ershad was put under house arrest and detained for 120 days, in accordance with a law that permits arrest without charges. In mid-December it was announced that parliamentary elections were to be held on 2 March 1991.

In foreign affairs, Bangladesh has maintained a policy of non-alignment. Relations with Pakistan improved in 1976: ambassadors were exchanged, and trade, postal and telecommunication links were resumed. Pakistan, however, refuses to accept the 250,000 Bihari Muslims (who supported Pakistan in Bangladesh's war of liberation in 1972) still remaining in refugee camps in Bangladesh, unless it does not have to bear the cost of absorbing them. Relations with India have been strained over the questions of cross-border terrorism (especially around the area of the Chittagong Hill Tracts, where Buddhist tribal rebels, the Shanti Bahini, have been waging guerrilla warfare against the Bangladeshi police and the Bengali settlers for several years) and of the Farrakka barrage, which has been constructed by India on the Ganga (Ganges) river, so depriving Bangladesh of water for irrigation and river transport during the dry season. In August 1985 Bangladesh and Burma (now Myanmar) completed work on the demarcation of their common border, in accordance with a May 1979 agreement.

In 1989 the Government attempted to suppress the continuing insurgency being waged by the Shanti Bahini in the Chittagong Hill Tracts, by introducing concessions providing limited autonomy to the region in the form of three new semi-autonomous hill districts. In June voting to elect councils for the new districts took place reasonably peacefully, despite attempts at disruption by the Shanti Bahini, who continued to demand total autonomy for the tribals. The powers vested in the councils were designed to give the tribals sufficient authority to regulate any further influx of Bengali settlers to the districts (the chief complaint of the tribals since Bengalis were settled in the Chittagong Hill Tracts, as plantation workers and clerks, by the British administration in the 19th century). Despite these concessions, the violence continued unabated in the latter half of 1989 and in 1990, and refugees continued to

BANGLADESH — Introductory Survey

flee across the border into India (there are about 60,000 refugees living in camps in Tripura).

Bangladesh is a member of the South Asian Association for Regional Co-operation (SAARC, see p. 225), formally constituted in December 1985, with Bhutan, India, Maldives, Nepal, Pakistan and Sri Lanka. Included in SAARC's newly-drafted charter were pledges of non-interference by members in each other's internal affairs and a joint effort to avoid 'contentious' issues whenever the association meets.

In early September 1990 Bangladesh sent a token military contingent (of about 2,300 men) to Saudi Arabia to join the multinational forces assembling there in support of a UN-sponsored embargo against Iraq, following Iraq's invasion and annexation of Kuwait in August. This move provoked much protest from the opposition parties in Bangladesh. By early October it was estimated that more than 55,000 Bangladeshi nationals had been repatriated from the Gulf region.

Government

With the ending of martial law, constitutional government was revived in November 1986 (having been suspended in March 1982). Bangladesh has a presidential form of government. The President is elected by universal suffrage for a five-year term and appoints his Council of Ministers from the 330-member Jatiya Sangsad (Parliament), 300 members of which are elected by universal suffrage. An additional 30 women members are appointed by the other members. The Jatiya Sangsad serves a five-year term, subject to dissolution. In 1983 a system of 493 local administrative sub-districts (*upazillas*), each containing an average of 260,000 people, was established as part of a plan to decentralize government. These *upazillas* are staffed by civil servants from Dhaka but headed by local chairmen, who hold office for five years. They have increased local involvement in development schemes, and development funds are allocated yearly to each of them.

Defence

Military service is voluntary. In June 1990 the armed forces numbered 103,500: an army of 90,000, a navy of 7,500 and an air force of 6,000. The paramilitary forces totalled 55,000, and included the Bangladesh Rifles (border guard) of 30,000. Budget expenditure on defence was estimated at 11,390m. taka for 1990.

Economic Affairs

In 1988, according to estimates by the World Bank, Bangladesh's gross national product (GNP), measured at average 1986–88 prices, was US $18,310m., equivalent to $170 per head. During 1980–88, it was estimated, GNP increased, in real terms, at an average annual rate of 3.6%, although GNP per head grew by only 0.8% per year. Over the same period, the population increased by an annual average of 2.8%. Bangladesh's gross domestic product (GDP), in purchasers' values, increased, in real terms, by an annual average of 3.7% in 1980–88.

Agriculture (including hunting, forestry and fishing) contributed 37.8% of total GDP in 1988/89. About 60% of the labour force were employed in agriculture in 1989. The principal sources of revenue in the agricultural sector are jute (which accounted for about 27.3% of total export earnings in 1988/89), fish and tea. During 1980–88 agricultural production increased by an annual average of 2.1%.

Industry (including mining, manufacturing, power and construction) employed 11.5% of the working population in 1984/85, and contributed 15.4% of total GDP in 1988/89. During 1980–88 industrial production increased by an annual average of 4.9%.

Mineral resources in Bangladesh are few. There are, however, large reserves of natural gas and smaller deposits of coal and petroleum.

Manufacturing contributed 8.5% of total GDP in 1988/89, and employed 9.3% of the working population in 1984/85. The most important sectors are the jute-based industries, cotton textiles, chemicals and sugar.

Energy is derived principally from natural gas and petroleum. Imports of mineral fuels comprised about 14.4% of the cost of total imports in 1987/88.

In 1989, according to the IMF, Bangladesh recorded a visible trade deficit of US $1,985.9m. and a deficit of $1,103.0m. on the current account of the balance of payments. In 1988/89 the principal source of imports (10.7%) was Japan, while the USA was the principal market for exports (26.2%). Other major trading partners are Singapore, India and the UK. The principal exports in 1988/89 were cotton textiles (Bangladesh's most important source of foreign exchange), jute and jute goods, fish and fish preparations, and hides, skins and leather goods. The principal imports were mineral products (including fuel), textiles and textile articles, base metals and base metal products, machinery and mechanical and electrical appliances, and wheat.

For 1990/91, taking into account both recurrent expenses and development spending, there was a projected budgetary deficit of about 54,052.2m. taka. Bangladesh's total external public debt, according to the World Bank, was US $9,330m. at the end of 1988. In that year the cost of debt-servicing exceeded 20% of the total revenue from exports of goods and services. The annual rate of inflation averaged 11.1% in 1980–88, and was 10.0% in 1989. About 1.8% of the total labour force were unemployed in 1984/85.

Bangladesh is a member of the South Asian Association for Regional Co-operation (SAARC, see p. 225), which seeks to improve regional co-operation, particularly in economic development.

The problems of developing Bangladesh are manifold, in view of the widespread poverty, malnutrition and underemployment superimposed on a rapidly increasing population and a poor resource base. There are grounds, however, for cautious optimism. Despite the frequency of natural disasters, food production has improved somewhat in recent years, and quite remarkable achievements have been made in the field of export-promotion, especially in non-traditional items (notably cotton garments). Bangladesh remains, however, heavily dependent on large amounts of foreign aid. Total pledges of aid by its main donor countries and agencies amounted to US $1,800m. for 1990/91. The economic situation in Bangladesh deteriorated rapidly in late 1990, as a result of the loss of remittances of convertible currency from Bangladeshi workers in the Persian (Arabian) Gulf region (which had become the country's largest source of foreign exchange revenue), the increase in the cost of petroleum imports, and the prospect of a large rise in unemployment (following the return of thousands of expatriate workers) and a fall in exports. The Government estimated that Bangladesh would lose about $1,400m. (including $100m.–$200m. in remittances) annually from direct and indirect consequences of the Gulf crisis. In an attempt to counter the adverse impact of the crisis on Bangladesh's fragile economy, the Government introduced a number of austerity measures, including restrictions on expenditure.

Social Welfare

The principal medical objective after independence was to prevent epidemics and widespread malnutrition, and to treat and rehabilitate war victims. Basic health services remain relatively undeveloped: in the early 1980s about 25% of all live-born children died before reaching five years of age. Health programmes give particular priority to the popularization of birth control. In 1981 Bangladesh had 504 hospital establishments, with a total of only 19,727 beds, equivalent to one for every 4,545 inhabitants: one of the lowest levels of health-care provision in the world. In 1981 there were 10,065 physicians working in the country. The Government's annual expenditure (recurrent and development) on health increased from 1,618m. taka in 1982/83 to 3,843m. taka in 1988/89.

In 1986 the Government adopted a policy of 'Health for All', and several programmes were incorporated in the third Five-Year Plan (1985–89) with the aim of achieving this objective: the number of health centres was to be increased (in 1985 a total of 355 *upazilla* health complexes were in operation), more people were to be given medical training, and the public education programme on family planning was to be expanded.

Education

Education is not compulsory but the Government provides free primary schooling for five years. Primary education begins at five years of age and lasts for five years. Secondary education, beginning at the age of 10, lasts for up to seven years, comprising a first cycle of five years and a second cycle of two further years. In 1988 an estimated 62% of children (67% of boys; 57% of girls) in the relevant age-group attended primary

BANGLADESH

schools, while the enrolment ratio at secondary schools was equivalent to 18% of children (24% of boys; 11% of girls) in the relevant age-group. Secondary schools and colleges in the private sector vastly outnumber government institutions: in 1976 government high schools comprised only about 2% of the country's total. There are seven universities, including one for agriculture, one for Islamic studies and one for engineering. Educational reform is designed to assist in satisfying the manpower needs of the country, and most importance is given to primary, technical and vocational education. In 1990 the Government initiated the Primary Education Sector Project, which aimed to help to achieve universal primary education and the eradication of illiteracy by the year 2000. In 1988 the rate of adult illiteracy was about 76%. Government budgetary expenditure (recurrent and development) on education increased from 3,346m. taka in 1982/83 to 11,809m. taka in 1988/89.

Public Holidays

1991: 1 January (New Year's Day), 21 February (National Mourning Day), 26 March (Independence Day), 29 March (Good Friday), 1 April (Easter Monday), 16 April* (Id al-Fitr, end of Ramadan), 1 May (May Day), May* (Buddha Purinama), 23 June* (Id al-Adha, Feast of the Sacrifice), 13 July* (Muharram, Islamic New Year), July* (Jamat Wida), August/September (Janmashtami), 21 September* (Birth of the Prophet), September* (Shab-i-Bharat), September* (Durga Puja), 7 November (National Revolution Day), 16 December (National Day), 25 December (Christmas), 26 December (Boxing Day).

1992: 1 January (New Year's Day), 21 February (National Mourning Day), 26 March (Independence Day), 4 April* (Id al-Fitr, end of Ramadan), 17 April (Good Friday), 20 April (Easter Monday), 1 May (May Day), May* (Buddha Purinama), 11 June* (Id al-Adha, Feast of the Sacrifice), 2 July* (Muharram, Islamic New Year), July* (Jamat Wida), August/September (Janmashtami), 10 September* (Birth of the Prophet), September* (Shab-i-Bharat), September* (Durga Puja), 7 November (National Revolution Day), 16 December (National Day), 25 December (Christmas), 26 December (Boxing Day).

* Dates of certain religious holidays are subject to the sighting of the moon, and there are also optional holidays for different religious groups.

Weights and Measures

The imperial system of measures is in force, pending the introduction of the metric system. The following local units of weight are also used:

1 maund = 82.28 lb (37.29 kg).
1 seer = 2.057 lb (932 grams).
1 tola = 180 grains (11.66 grams).

Statistical Survey

Source (unless otherwise stated): Bangladesh Bureau of Statistics, Industry, Trade, Labour Statistics and National Income Wing, 14/2 Topkhana Rd, Dhaka; tel. (2) 409871.

Area and Population

AREA, POPULATION AND DENSITY

Area (sq km)	143,998*
Population (census results)†	
1 March 1974	76,398,000
6 March 1981	
Males	46,295,000
Females	43,617,000
Total	89,912,000
Population (official estimates at mid-year)	
1987	102,563,000
1988	104,532,000
1989	106,507,000
Density (per sq km) at mid-1989	739.6

* 55,598 sq miles.
† Including adjustment for net underenumeration, estimated to have been 6.9% in 1974 and 3.2% in 1981. The enumerated totals were: 71,479,071 in 1974; 87,119,965 (males 44,919,191, females 42,200,774) in 1981.

POPULATION BY DIVISIONS

	1974 Census	1981 Census
Chittagong	19,914,000	23,322,000
Dhaka	22,780,000	27,091,000
Khulna	15,177,000	17,695,000
Rajshahi	18,527,000	21,804,000
Total	76,398,000	89,912,000

PRINCIPAL TOWNS (population at 1981 census)

Dhaka (capital)	3,430,312*	Barisal	172,905
Chittagong	1,391,877	Sylhet	168,371
Khulna	646,359	Rangpur	153,174
Rajshahi	253,740	Jessore	148,927
Comilla	184,132	Saidpur	126,608

* Including Narayanganj (population 270,680 in 1974).

BIRTHS AND DEATHS*

	Registered live births Rate (per 1,000)	Registered deaths Rate (per 1,000)
1984	34.8	12.3
1985	34.6	12.0
1986	34.4	11.9
1987	33.3	11.5
1988	33.2	11.3

* Registration is incomplete. According to UN estimates, the average annual rates per 1,000 were: Births 44.8 in 1980–85, 42.2 in 1985–90; Deaths 17.5 in 1980–85, 15.5 in 1985–90 (Source: UN, *World Population Prospects: 1988*).

BANGLADESH
Statistical Survey

ECONOMICALLY ACTIVE POPULATION*
(sample survey, '000 persons aged 10 years and over, 1984/85)

	Males	Females	Total
Agriculture, hunting, forestry and fishing	16,474	238	16,712
Mining and quarrying	3	—	3
Manufacturing	2,030	658	2,688
Electricity, gas and water	87	4	91
Construction	535	17	552
Trade, restaurants and hotels	3,485	125	3,610
Transport, storage and communications	1,160	10	1,171
Financing, insurance, real estate and business services	188	13	199
Community, social and personal services	2,180	370	2,550
Activities not adequately defined	288	1,114	1,402
Total employed	26,431	2,547	28,978
Unemployed	381	152	532
Total labour force	26,812	2,699	29,510

* All figures are rounded, so totals may not always be the sum of their component parts.

Source: ILO, *Year Book of Labour Statistics*.

Agriculture

PRINCIPAL CROPS (million long tons, year ending 30 June)

	1986/87	1987/88	1988/89
Rice (milled)	15.16	15.17	15.30
Wheat	1.07	1.03	1.01
Sugar cane	6.79	7.09	6.60
Potatoes	1.05	1.26	1.07
Sweet potatoes	0.54	0.55	0.54
Pulses	0.40	0.54	0.54
Oilseeds	0.43	0.44	0.44
Jute	1.21	0.84	0.79

Tobacco (production, '000 metric tons): 46 in 1986; 40 in 1987; 42 in 1988; 43 (unofficial estimate) in 1989 (Source: FAO, *Production Yearbook*).

Tea (production, '000 metric tons): 37.6 in 1986; 40.6 in 1987; 43.6 in 1988; 38.4 in 1989 (Source: International Tea Committee, *Annual Bulletin of Statistics*).

LIVESTOCK ('000 head at 30 June)

	1986/87	1987/88	1988/89
Cattle	22,567	22,789	23,015
Buffaloes	664	698	733
Sheep	770	803	837
Goats	17,034	18,274	19,604
Chickens	75,974	80,715	85,752
Ducks	13,525	13,673	13,823

LIVESTOCK PRODUCTS
(metric tons, unless otherwise indicated, year ending 30 June)

	1986/87	1987/88	1988/89
Beef and veal	135,823	137,166	138,547
Buffalo meat	2,463	2,613	2,762
Mutton and lamb	1,344	1,418	1,456
Goats' meat	59,607	63,936	68,602
Poultry meat	65,131	68,714	72,484
Edible offals ('000 pieces)	11,000	11,652	12,350
Cows' and buffalo milk	741,669	749,843	757,270
Sheep's milk*	18,000	18,000	18,000
Goats' milk*	216,000	224,000	228,000
Butter	560	560	560
Cheese	933	933	933
Hen eggs ('000)	875,232	929,837	987,869
Other poultry eggs ('000)	405,780	410,220	414,720
Wool:			
greasy*	1,400	1,400	1,400
clean*	820	830	840
Cattle and buffalo hides ('000)	2,878	2,908	2,940
Sheep and goat skins ('000)	9,778	10,482	11,237

* FAO estimates for 1987–89.

Forestry

ROUNDWOOD REMOVALS ('000 cubic metres)

	1986	1987*	1988*
Sawlogs, veneer logs and logs for sleepers	467*	467	467
Pulpwood	69	69	69
Other industrial wood*	311	320	328
Fuel wood*	27,016	27,751	28,504
Total	27,863	28,607	29,368

* FAO estimates.

Source: FAO, *Yearbook of Forest Products*.

SAWNWOOD PRODUCTION ('000 cubic metres)

	1984	1985	1986
Total (incl. boxboards)	148*	93	73

* FAO estimate.

Railway sleepers (FAO estimates, '000 cubic metres): 6 per year in 1984–86.

1987–88: Annual production as in 1986 (FAO estimates).

Source: FAO, *Yearbook of Forest Products*.

Fishing

('000 long tons, year ending 30 June)

	1986/87	1987/88	1988/89
Inland	588	600	590
Marine	215	223	229
Total catch	802	824	819

Source: Directorate of Fisheries.

Mining

	1987	1988	1989
Natural gas (million cu metres)	3,813	4,266	4,769

Industry

SELECTED PRODUCTS ('000 long tons, unless otherwise indicated, public sector only, year ending 30 June)

	1986/87	1987/88	1988/89
Jute textiles	530	518	501
Hessian	200	216	185
Sacking	244	225	237
Carpet backing	79	65	69
Others	7	12	10
Cotton cloth (million yards)	65	67	71
Cotton yarn (million lb)	100	103	108
Newsprint	47	49	43
Other paper	43	42	41
Cement	305	305	339
Steel ingots	81	69	85
Re-rolled steel products	34	32	29
Petroleum products	959	935	1,032
Urea fertilizer	833	1,266	1,424
Ammonium sulphate	9	6	9
Chemicals	24	22	21
Refined sugar	179	175	108
Wine and spirits ('000 liquid proof galls)	1,187	1,050	786
Tea (million lb)*	87	89	92
Edible oil and vegetable ghee	27	33	29
Cigarettes ('000 million)	15	14	14

* Including production in the private sector.

Finance

CURRENCY AND EXCHANGE RATES

Monetary Units
100 poisha = 1 taka.

Denominations
Coins: 1, 2, 5, 10, 25 and 50 poisha.
Notes: 1, 2, 5, 10, 20, 50, 100, 500 taka.

Sterling and Dollar Equivalents (30 September 1990)
£1 sterling = 66.865 taka;
US $1 = 35.690 taka;
1,000 taka = £14.955 = $28.019.

Average Exchange Rate (taka per US $)
1987 30.950
1988 31.733
1989 32.270

Note: The foregoing information refers to the official exchange rate, applicable to most transactions. Between November 1988 and March 1990 this rate was fixed at US $1 = 32.27 taka. There is also a secondary rate, determined by bidding for foreign exchange by importers in an auction market. At 30 September 1990 this auction market rate was US $1 = 36.40 taka.

BUDGET (estimates, million taka, year ending 30 June)

Revenue	1986/87	1987/88	1988/89
Customs duties	14,928	16,310	18,201
Excise duties	8,506	11,506	14,000
Sales tax	5,528	5,359	5,400
Stamps	1,668	1,507	1,700
Motor vehicle taxes	119	163	200
Income taxes	5,434	1,203	1,700
Land revenue	649	761	850
Interest receipts	1,702	2,235	2,200
Railways	1,322	1,531	1,503
Other revenue	6,329	10,944	12,468
Total	**46,185**	**51,519**	**58,222**

Expenditure	1986/87	1987/88	1988/89
General administration	13,599	16,359	27,250
Justice and police	3,852	4,503	4,979
Defence	7,259	8,162	10,161
Scientific departments	251	294	305
Education	7,436	8,820	9,492
Health	2,493	2,996	3,223
Social welfare	222	284	361
Agriculture	1,301	1,432	1,557
Manufacturing and construction	174	234	253
Transport and communication	1,214	1,594	1,500
Railways	2,924	3,263	3,233
Other expenditure	2,055	2,574	2,924
Total	**42,780**	**50,515**	**65,238**

Source: Ministry of Finance.

1989/90 (estimates, million taka): *Revenue* 71,805.5; *Expenditure*: Finance 10,094.2, Education 9,701.9, Health and population control 3,356.2, Domestic debt servicing 2,587.7, Foreign debt servicing 5,080.0, Unexpected expenditure 7,681.2; Total (incl. others) 69,000.
1990/91 (estimates, million taka): *Revenue* Official taxes 58,520, Unofficial taxes 4,480, Non-tax revenue 12,627.8; Total 75,627.8. *Expenditure* 73,000.

PUBLIC-SECTOR DEVELOPMENT EXPENDITURE
(estimates, million taka, year ending 30 June)

	1986/87	1987/88	1988/89
Agriculture	2,286	2,487	2,804
Rural development	624	807	992
Water and flood control	2,203	5,227	8,928
Industry	7,492	4,615	6,419
Power, scientific research and natural resources	15,194	14,197	9,597
Transport	5,052	5,207	7,095
Communication	394	1,208	2,299
Physical planning and housing	1,416	2,346	2,110
Education and training	2,053	2,376	2,317
Health	345	326	620
Population planning	1,057	1,375	1,839
Social welfare	205	178	395
Manpower and employment	73	20	28
Miscellaneous	105	103	146
Total development expenditure	**38,499**	**40,472**	**45,589**

Source: Ministry of Finance.

1989/90 (estimates, million taka): Agriculture 4,902.7, Water resources 7,436.3, Industry 4,059.7, Power 7,206.0, Transport 5,981.5, Education and religion 3,447.9, Health and family planning 300.0, Upazillas 2,300.0, Dhaka City Flood Control Project 1,500.0; Total development expenditure (incl. others) 58,030.2.
1990/91 (estimate): Total development expenditure 56,680m. taka.
Fourth Five-Year Plan (1990–95) (estimates, million taka): Public sector outlay 419,300; Private sector outlay 270,000; Total expenditure 689,300.

INTERNATIONAL RESERVES (US $ million at 31 December)

	1987	1988	1989
Gold*	22.8	24.0	21.4
IMF special drawing rights	53.3	54.0	3.0
Reserve position in IMF	31.8	30.1	29.4
Foreign exchange	758.1	961.9	469.0
Total	**866.0**	**1,070.0**	**522.8**

* Valued at market-related prices.

Source: IMF, *International Financial Statistics*.

BANGLADESH

Statistical Survey

MONEY SUPPLY (million taka at 31 December)

	1987	1988	1989
Currency outside banks	22,440	25,282	27,286
Demand deposits at deposit money banks*	28,510	27,883	32,718
Total money†	51,000	53,165	60,004

* Comprises the scheduled banks plus the agricultural and industrial development banks.
† Including private-sector deposits held by monetary authorities.
Source: IMF, *International Financial Statistics*.

COST OF LIVING (Consumer Price Index for middle-class families in Dhaka, year ending 30 June; base: 1973/74 = 100)

	1986/87	1987/88	1988/89
Food	483	535	566
Fuel and lighting	542	562	621
Housing and household requisites	551	648	723
Clothing and footwear	293	319	348
Miscellaneous	460	524	598
All items	481	536	579

NATIONAL ACCOUNTS
(million taka at current prices, year ending 30 June)

Expenditure on the Gross Domestic Product

	1986/87	1987/88	1988/89
Government final consumption expenditure	40,154	48,555	62,430
Private final consumption expenditure	481,269	530,579	581,037
Increase in stocks	5,990	6,502	14,722
Gross fixed capital formation	66,742	66,295	80,200
Total domestic expenditure	594,155	651,931	738,389
Exports of goods and services	32,292	n.a.	n.a.
Less Imports of goods and services	88,112	n.a.	n.a.
GDP in purchasers' values	538,335	594,423	656,402

* Provisional.

Gross Domestic Product by Economic Activity

	1986/87	1987/88	1988/89
Agriculture and hunting	181,197	185,521	198,954
Forestry and logging	20,544	24,402	26,579
Fishing	18,020	20,728	22,303
Mining and quarrying	4	3	4
Manufacturing	47,631	50,437	55,608
Electricity, gas and water	3,545	4,597	6,471
Construction	28,839	34,602	39,130
Wholesale and retail trade	45,017	48,655	52,202
Transport, storage and communications	61,901	65,945	70,856
Owner-occupied dwellings	40,988	49,982	59,866
Finance, insurance, real estate and business services	10,116	11,435	13,482
Public administration and defence	20,867	24,735	27,318
Other services	59,666	73,381	83,629
Total	538,335	594,423	656,402

BALANCE OF PAYMENTS (US $ million)

	1987	1988	1989
Merchandise exports f.o.b.	1,076.9	1,291.0	1,304.9
Merchandise imports f.o.b.	−2,445.6	−2,734.5	−3,290.8
Trade balance	−1,368.8	−1,443.4	−1,985.9
Exports of services	295.4	332.5	423.2
Imports of services	−666.7	−807.0	−930.6
Balance on goods and services	−1,740.1	−1,917.9	−2,493.3
Private unrequited transfers (net)	788.3	827.2	806.8
Government unrequited transfers (net)	713.9	804.4	583.6
Current balance	−237.9	−286.4	−1,103.0
Direct capital investment (net)	3.2	1.8	1.1
Other long-term capital (net)	593.2	619.4	845.1
Short-term capital (net)	−38.3	−232.6	−29.3
Net errors and omissions	−123.8	29.8	−29.2
Total (net monetary movements)	196.5	132.0	−315.2
Valuation changes (net)	−35.1	61.1	−52.0
Exceptional financing (net)	0.8	0.4	—
Official financing (net)	−41.5	—	−37.8
Changes in reserves	120.7	193.6	−405.1

Source: IMF, *International Financial Statistics*.

FOREIGN AID (US $ million, year ending 30 June)

Donor	1985/86	1986/87	1987/88
Canada	98	100	68
India	6	22	8
Japan	139	332	315
Netherlands/Belgium	43	37	63
Sweden	12	20	50
USSR	22	47	13
United Kingdom	42	46	37
USA	104	124	143
Total	466	728	697

Source: Ministry of Finance.

BANGLADESH

External Trade

PRINCIPAL COMMODITIES
(million taka, year ending 30 June)

Imports	1986/87	1987/88	1988/89
Live animals and animal products	2,188	2,424	3,372
Vegetables and vegetable products	8,956	16,001	11,813
Wheat	6,078	9,712	9,105
Rice	1,289	3,364	325
Animal and vegetable oils and fats	4,234	6,340	5,521
Prepared foodstuffs, beverages and tobacco	1,307	1,552	2,404
Mineral products (incl. fuel)	12,594	15,868	15,072
Chemicals and allied products	5,436	6,658	8,318
Plastics, rubber and articles thereof	1,804	3,486	3,573
Wood, wooden products and basketware	180	102	109
Wood pulp and paper	1,417	1,049	1,476
Textiles and textile articles	6,978	13,337	13,478
Stoneware, ceramic products and glass	280	390	415
Base metals and base metal products	7,497	7,667	10,504
Machinery, mechanical and electrical appliances	10,365	11,176	10,247
Vehicles, aircraft and transport equipment	3,726	3,650	7,040
Clocks and watches, musical instruments, photographic equipment, etc.	975	1,055	1,011
Miscellaneous manufactured articles, etc.	489	802	527
Total (incl. others)	68,496	91,588	95,075

Exports	1986/87	1987/88	1988/89
Raw jute and jute cuttings	2,754.2	2,485.8	2,812.8
Jute goods	8,944.9	9,423.5	8,853.2
Tea	903.2	1,292.8	1,208.3
Hides, skins and leather goods	3,652.5	4,582.7	4,514.1
Fish and fish preparations	4,442.0	5,063.7	5,240.5
Total (incl. others)	33,682.1	41,161.1	42,686.1

PRINCIPAL TRADING PARTNERS (million taka)

Imports c.i.f.	1986/87	1987/88	1988/89
Australia	1,135.5	1,843.4	2,291.7
Canada	3,315.2	2,985.9	2,666.0
China, People's Republic	3,150.8	3,475.8	3,939.3
France	1,184.3	3,529.5	2,190.3
Germany, Federal Republic	3,414.6	2,437.0	3,044.0
Hong Kong	1,267.7	4,271.4	3,473.4
India	3,632.8	4,106.1	5,428.4
Japan	9,052.4	10,097.8	10,219.2
Malaysia	1,022.3	1,806.3	1,801.7
Netherlands	1,569.0	2,018.8	1,903.6
Singapore	5,582.9	6,327.4	5,140.1
USSR	880.2	942.1	1,116.0
United Kingdom	2,928.6	4,196.7	4,040.0
USA	5,298.5	8,160.8	11,208.0

Exports f.o.b.	1986/87	1987/88	1988/89
Belgium	1,234.2	1,431.6	1,777.1
India	56.1	95.1	106.7
Italy	2,897.0	3,677.0	3,289.7
Japan	2,292.1	1,297.2	2,134.2
Singapore	1,577.6	1,666.7	2,701.9
USSR	986.8	1,250.4	1,032.4
United Kingdom	1,913.9	2,432.9	2,646.1
USA	10,478.5	12,044.5	11,200.0

Transport

RAILWAYS (year ending 30 June)

	1986/87	1987/88	1988/89
Passenger-kilometres (million)	6,027	5,365	4,841
Freight ton-kilometres (million)	512	696	628

Source: Bangladesh Railway.

ROAD TRAFFIC (motor vehicles in use, year ending 30 June)

	1986/87	1987/88	1988/89
Private motor cars	25,384	26,826	30,624
Taxis	1,288	1,379	1,628
Buses and minibuses	18,162	19,048	21,540
Trucks	25,736	26,517	29,707
Jeeps	5,757	6,071	6,917
Auto-rickshaws	17,940	19,766	23,052
Motor cycles	66,947	73,113	84,227
Others	4,306	4,469	5,099
Total	165,520	177,189	202,794

Source: Bangladesh Road Transport Authority.

INTERNATIONAL SEA-BORNE SHIPPING
(freight traffic, '000 long tons, year ending 30 June)

	1986/87	1987/88	1988/89
Chalna			
Goods loaded	730	626	637
Goods unloaded	1,557	2,228	1,882
Chittagong			
Goods loaded	402	632	835
Goods unloaded	5,836	7,108	7,122
Total goods loaded	1,132	1,258	1,472
Total goods unloaded	7,393	9,336	9,004

Tourism

	1987	1988	1989
Tourist arrivals	106,765	120,782	93,405

BANGLADESH

Communications Media

	1986	1987	1988
Radio receivers ('000 licensed)*	561	435	454
Television receivers ('000 in use)	369	426	420
Telephones ('000 in use)	164	174	188
Book production: titles	1,209	1,022	941
Daily newspapers:			
Number of titles	58	59	68
Average circulation ('000)	590	848	918

* In 1987 an estimated 4,250,000 radio receivers were in use (Source: UNESCO, *Statistical Yearbook*).

Education

(1987/88)

	Institutions	Students
Primary schools	44,202	11,755,000
Secondary schools	9,197	3,144,000
Technical colleges and institutes (government)*	140	24,360
Universities	7	41,382

* In addition to government-owned and managed institutes, there are many privately-administered vocational training centres.

Directory

The Constitution

The members who were returned from East Pakistan (now Bangladesh) for the Pakistan National Assembly and the Provincial Assembly in the December 1970 elections formed the Bangladesh Constituent Assembly. A new constitution for the People's Republic of Bangladesh was approved by this Assembly on 4 November 1972 and came into effect on 16 December 1972. The Constitution was amended in 1973, 1974, 1975, 1977, 1979, 1981, 1988 and 1989. Following the military coup of 24 March 1982, the Constitution was suspended, and the country was placed under martial law. On 10 November 1986 martial law was repealed and the suspended Constitution was revived.

SUMMARY

Fundamental Principles of State Policy

The Constitution was initially based on the fundamental principles of nationalism, socialism, democracy and secularism, but in 1977 an amendment replaced secularism with Islam. The amendment states that the country shall be guided by 'the principles of absolute trust and faith in the Almighty Allah, nationalism, democracy and socialism'. A further amendment in 1988 established Islam as the state religion. The Constitution aims to establish a society free from exploitation in which the rule of law, fundamental human rights and freedoms, justice and equality are to be secured for all citizens. A socialist economic system is to be established to ensure the attainment of a just and egalitarian society through state and co-operative ownership as well as private ownership within limits prescribed by law. A universal, free and compulsory system of education shall be established. In foreign policy the State shall endeavour to consolidate, preserve, and strengthen fraternal relations among Muslim countries based on Islamic solidarity.

Fundamental Rights

All citizens are equal before the law and have a right to its protection. Arbitrary arrest or detention, discrimination based on race, age, sex, birth, caste or religion, and forced labour are prohibited. Subject to law, public order and morality, every citizen has freedom of movement, of assembly and of association. Freedom of conscience, of speech, of the press and of religious worship are guaranteed.

GOVERNMENT

The President

The President is the constitutional Head of State and is elected for a term of five years. He is eligible for re-election. The supreme control of the armed forces is vested in the President. He appoints the Prime Minister and other Ministers as well as the Chief Justice and other judges. The President and Vice-President are elected by universal adult suffrage.

The Executive

Executive authority shall rest in the President and shall be exercised by him either directly or through officers subordinate to him in accordance with the Constitution.

There shall be a Council of Ministers to aid and advise the President. All ministers shall hold office during the pleasure of the President.

The Legislature

Parliament (Jatiya Sangsad) is a unicameral legislature. It comprises 300 members and an additional 30 women members elected by the other members. Members of Parliament, other than the 30 women members, are directly elected on the basis of universal adult franchise from single territorial constituencies. Persons aged 18 and over are entitled to vote. The parliamentary term lasts for five years unless Parliament is dissolved sooner by the President. War can be declared only with the assent of Parliament. In the case of actual or imminent invasion, the President may take whatever action he may consider appropriate.

THE JUDICIARY

The Judiciary comprises a Supreme Court with High Court and an Appellate Division. The Supreme Court consists of a Chief Justice and such other judges as may be appointed by the President. The High Court division has such original appellate and other jurisdiction and powers as are conferred on it by the Constitution and by other law. The Appellate Division has jurisdiction to determine appeals from decisions of the High Court division. Subordinate courts, in addition to the Supreme Court, have been established by law.

ELECTIONS

An Election Commission supervises elections for the Presidency and for Parliament, delimits constituencies and prepares electoral rolls. It consists of a Chief Election Commissioner and other Commissioners as may be appointed by the President. The Election Commission is independent in the exercise of its functions. Subject to the Constitution, Parliament may make provision as to elections where necessary.

The Government

HEAD OF STATE

Vice-President: Justice SHAHABUDDIN AHMED (assumed powers of acting President on 6 December 1990).

COUNCIL OF MINISTERS*
(November 1990)

President of the Council of Ministers and Minister of Defence and of Establishment and Reorganization: Lt-Gen. (retd) HOSSAIN MOHAMMAD ERSHAD.

Vice-President and Minister of Industries: MOUDUD AHMED.

Prime Minister and Minister of Education: KAZI ZAFAR AHMED.

Deputy Prime Minister and Minister of Food: SHAH MOAZZEM HOSSAIN.

Minister of Home Affairs: Maj.-Gen. (retd) M. MAHMUDUL HASAN.

Minister of Finance and Planning: Maj.-Gen. (retd) M. A. MUNIM.

Minister of Foreign Affairs: ANISUL ISLAM MAHMUD.

Minister of Social Affairs: MOHAMMAD REZWANUL HAQ CHOWDHURY.

Minister of Communications: ANWAR HUSSAIN MANZUR.

Minister of Women's Affairs: SYEDA RAZIA FAIZ.

Minister of Energy and Mineral Resources: ZIAUDDIN AHMED BABLU.

BANGLADESH
Directory

Minister of Fisheries and Livestock: Mustafa Jamal Haider.
Minister of Irrigation, Water Development and Flood Control: Dr Mizanur Rahman Shelley.
Minister of Health and Family Planning: Dr Azizur Rahman.
Minister of Jute: Sheikh Shahidul Islam.
Minister of Textiles: A. B. M. Ruhul Amin Howlader.
Minister of Ports, Shipping and Inland Water Transport: Mahmudur Rahman Chowdhury.
Minister of Labour and Manpower: Serajul Hossain Khan.
Minister of Law and Justice: Habibul Islam Bhuiyan.
Minister of Agriculture: Sardar Amzad Hossain.
Minister of Land Administration and Land Reform: Tajul Islam Chowdhury.
Minister of Information: A. B. M. Ghulam Mostafa.
Minister of Works: Abul Hasnat.
Minister of Commerce: Maj.-Gen. (retd) Shamsul Huq.
Minister of Relief and Rehabilitation: Monzur Quader.
Minister of Forests and the Environment: Zafar Imam.
Minister of Civil Aviation and Tourism: Lt-Col (retd) H. M. A. Gaffar.
Minister of Local Government, Rural Development and Co-operatives: Mohammad Naziur Rahman.
Minister of Post and Telecommunications: Kazi Feroj Rashid.
Minister of State for Cultural Affairs: Syed Deedar Bakht.
Minister of State for Youth and Sports: Nitai Roy Chowdhury.
Minister of State for Religious Affairs: Kazi Mufazzal Hossain Kaikobad.

* The Council of Ministers was dissolved in early December 1990, and a neutral interim Council of Ministers was appointed, pending the holding of a fresh general election on 2 March 1991.

MINISTRIES

Ministry of Agriculture: Bangladesh Secretariat, Bhaban 4, 2nd Storey, Dhaka.
Ministry of Commerce: Shilpa Bhaban, Motijheel C/A, Dhaka; telex 642201.
Ministry of Communications: Bangladesh Secretariat, Bhaban 7, 1st 9-Storey Bldg, 8th Floor, Dhaka; telex 65712.
Ministry of Cultural Affairs: Dhaka.
Ministry of Defence: Old High Court Bldg, Dhaka; tel. (2) 259082.
Ministry of Education: Bangladesh Secretariat, Bhaban 7, 2nd 9-Storey Bldg, 6th Floor, Dhaka.
Ministry of Energy and Mineral Resources: Bangladesh Secretariat, Bhaban 6, New Bldg, 2nd Floor, Dhaka.
Ministry of Finance and Planning: Bangladesh Secretariat, Bhaban 7, 1st 9-Storey Bldg, 3rd Floor, Dhaka; telex 65886.
Ministry of Food: Bangladesh Secretariat, Bhaban 4, 2nd 9-Storey Bldg, 3rd Floor, Dhaka; telex 65671.
Ministry of Foreign Affairs: Topkhana Rd, Dhaka: tel. (2) 236020; telex 642200; fax (2) 411281.
Ministry of Health and Family Planning: Bangladesh Secretariat, Main Bldg, 3rd Floor, Dhaka.
Ministry of Home Affairs: School Bldg, 2nd and 3rd Floors, Bangladesh Secretariat, Dhaka.
Ministry of Industries: Shilpa Bhaban, 91 Motijheel C/A, Dhaka 1000; telex 672830.
Ministry of Information: Bangladesh Secretariat, 2nd 9-Storey Bldg, 8th Floor, Dhaka; tel. (2) 235111.
Ministry of Irrigation, Water Development and Flood Control: Dhaka.
Ministry of Jute and Textiles: Dhaka.
Ministry of Labour and Manpower: Bangladesh Secretariat, 1st 9-Storey Bldg, 4th Floor, Dhaka.
Ministry of Land Administration and Land Reform: Bangladesh Secretariat, Bhaban 4, 2nd 9-Storey Bldg, 3rd Floor, Dhaka.
Ministry of Local Government: Bangladesh Secretariat, Bhaban 7, 1st 9-Storey Bldg, 6th Floor, Dhaka.
Ministry of Ports, Shipping and Inland Water Transport: Dhaka; tel. (2) 404345.
Ministry of Religious Affairs: Dhaka.
Ministry of Social Affairs and Women's Affairs: Bangladesh Secretariat, Bhaban 6, New Bldg, Dhaka.
Ministry of Works: Bangladesh Secretariat, Main Extension Bldg, 2nd Floor, Dhaka.

President and Legislature

PRESIDENT

A total of 12 candidates contested the presidential election held on 15 October 1986. According to official results, Lt-Gen. (retd) Hossain Mohammad Ershad won 21,795,337 votes (83.5% of the votes cast). His nearest rivals were Maulana M. H. Huzur (1,510,456 votes) and Lt-Col (retd) Said Faruq Rahman (1.17m. votes).

Ershad resigned on 4 December 1990, and Justice Shahabuddin Ahmed, in the capacity of Vice-President, assumed the powers of acting President.

JATIYA SANGSAD*
(Parliament)

Speaker: Shamsul Huda Chowdhury.
Deputy Speaker: M. Riazuddin Ahmed.

General Election, 3 March 1988

	Seats
Jatiya Dal	252
Combined Opposition Group (COG)	18
Jatiya Samajtantrik Dal (S)	3
Freedom Party	2
Independents	25
Total	**300**

In addition to the 300 directly-elected members, a further 30 seats are reserved for women members.

* The Jatiya Sangsad was dissolved in early December 1990. Fresh parliamentary elections were due to be held on 2 March 1991.

Political Organizations

Since August 1975, when all political parties were banned, political activity has been prohibited intermittently. Political activity was again prohibited from November 1987. Numerous groups oppose the Government of President Ershad. The principal opposition alliances are led by the Awami League and the Bangladesh National Party, and comprised eight and seven parties respectively in 1987. A third alliance, led by Rashed Khan Menon and Hasanul Huq Inu, comprises five Marxist-Leninist parties. The following parties are among the more influential of those currently active:

Awami League: 23 Bangabandhu Ave, Dhaka; f. 1949; supports parliamentary democracy; advocates socialist economy, but with private sector, and a secular state; pro-Soviet and pro-Indian; Pres. Sheikh Hasina Wajed; Gen.-Sec. Begum Sajeda Chowdhury; c. 1,025,000 mems.

Bangladesh Communist Party: Dhaka; f. 1948; pro-Soviet; allied to Awami League; Sec.-Gen. Saifuddin Ahmed Manik; c. 2,500 mems; banned November 1987.

Bangladesh Jatiya League: 500A Dhanmandi R/A, Rd 7, Dhaka; f. 1970 as Pakistan National League, renamed in 1972; supports parliamentary democracy; Leader Ataur Rahman Khan; c. 50,000 mems.

Bangladesh Jatiyatabadi Dal (Bangladesh Nationalist Party—BNP): Sattar House 19A, Rd 27 (Old) and 16 (New), Dhanmandi R/A, Dhaka; f. 1978 by merger of groups supporting Ziaur Rahman, including Jatiyatabadi Gonotantrik Dal (Jagodal—Nationalist Democratic Party); right of centre; favours democratic presidential system of govt; Chair. Begum Khaleda Zia; Vice-Chair. Prof. A. Q. M. Badruddoza Chaudhry; Sec.-Gen. Abdus Salam Talukdar; in July 1988 a group of dissidents, led by a fmr Sec.-Gen., A. K. M. Obaidur Rahman, formed a rival faction.

Bangladesh Khilafat Andolon: 314/2 Jagannath Saha Rd, Lalbagh Killar mor, Dhaka; tel. (2) 250500.

Bangladesh Krishak Sramik Party (Peasants' and Workers' Party): Sonargaon Bhavan, 99 South Kamalapur, Dhaka 17; f. 1914, renamed 1953; supports parliamentary democracy, non-aligned foreign policy and socialism; Pres. A. S. M. Sulaiman; Gen.-Sec. Muhammad Emdad Hussain; c. 125,000 mems.

Bangladesh People's League: Dhaka; f. 1976; supports parliamentary democracy; c. 75,000 mems.

Combined Opposition Group (COG): f. 1988; a govt-approved alliance of 76 minor political parties; Leader A. S. M. Abdur Rab.

Democratic League: 68 Jigatola, Dhaka 9; f. 1976; conservative; Leader Khandakar Mushtaq Ahmed.

Freedom Party: f. 1987; Islamic; opposed to Awami League; Co-Chair. Lt-Col (retd) Said Faruq Rahman, Lt-Col (retd) Khandakar Abdur Rashid.

BANGLADESH
Directory

Gonoazadi League: 30 Banagran Lane, Dhaka.

Islamic Democratic League: 84 Testari Bazar, Dhaka; Leader Maulana ABDUR RAHIM.

Jamaat-e-Islami Bangladesh: 505 Elephant Rd, Bara Maghbazar, Dhaka 1217; tel. (2) 401581; f. 1941; Islamic fundamentalist; Pres. ABBAS ALI KHAN (acting).

Jatiya Dal (National Party): Dhaka; f. 1983 as Jana Dal; reorg. 1986, when the National Front (f. 1985), a five-party alliance of the Jana Dal, the United People's Party, the Gonotantrik Dal, the Bangladesh Muslim League and a breakaway section of the Bangladesh Nationalist Party, formally converted itself into a single pro-govt grouping; advocates nationalism, democracy, Islamic ideals and progress; Chair. Lt-Gen. (retd) HOSSAIN MOHAMMAD ERSHAD; Sec.-Gen. SHAH MOAZZAM HOSSAIN.

Jatiya Samajtantrik Dal (R): breakaway faction of JSD; Leader A. S. M. ABDUR RAB.

Jatiya Samajtantrik Dal (JSD—(S)) (National Socialist Party): 23 DIT Ave, Malibagh Choudhury Para, Dhaka; f. 1972; left-wing; Leader SHAJAHAN SIRAJ; c. 5,000 mems.

Jatiyo Janata Party: Janata Bhaban, 47A Toyenbee Circular Rd, Dhaka 1203; tel. (2) 282689; f. 1976; social democratic; Convener NURUL ISLAM KHAN; Jt Conveners Syed ABUL HUSSAIN KHAJA (Rajshahi Div.), MUJIBUR RAHMAN HERU (Dhaka Div.), Alhaj AMJAD HUSSAIN (Khulna Div.), B. M. NOWAB JAKARIA (Chittagong Div.); c. 25,000 mems.

National Awami Party—Bhashani (NAP): 226 Outer Circular Rd, Dhaka; f. 1957; Maoist; Pres. ABU NASSER KHAN BHASHANI; Gen.-Sec. ABDUS SUBHANI.

National Awami Party—Muzaffar (NAP—M): 21 Dhanmandi Hawkers' Market, 1st Floor, Dhaka 5; f. 1957, reorg. 1967; pro-Soviet; c. 500,000 mems; Pres. MUZAFFAR AHMED; Sec.-Gen. PANKAJ BHATTACHARYA.

Samyabadi Dal: Dhaka; Maoist; Leader MOHAMMAD TOAHA.

Zaker Party: f. 1989; supports sovereignty and Islamic values; Leader Syed HASMATULLAH.

Diplomatic Representation

EMBASSIES AND HIGH COMMISSIONS IN BANGLADESH

Afghanistan: House CWN(C)-2A Gulshan Ave, Gulshan Model Town, Dhaka 12; tel. (2) 603232; Chargé d'affaires a.i.: ABDUL AHAD WOLASI.

Algeria: 4 CWN(C) Gulshan Ave, Gulshan Model Town, Dhaka 12; tel. (2) 605021; Ambassador: MUHAMMAD CHADLY.

Australia: 184 Gulshan Ave, Gulshan Model Town, Dhaka 12; tel. (2) 600091; telex 642317; High Commissioner: SUSAN J. D. BOYD.

Belgium: House 40, Rd 21, Block B, Banani, Dhaka; tel. (2) 600138; telex 642304; Ambassador: Baron OLIVIER GILLES.

Bhutan: House 58, Rd 3A, Dhanmandi R/A, POB 3141, Dhaka; tel. (2) 505418; Ambassador: D. K. CHHETRI.

Brazil: House 23, Rd 5, Baridhara Model Town, Dhaka 1212; tel. (2) 605390; telex 642334; Chargé d'affaires a.i.: BERNARDINO RAIMUNDO DA SILVA.

Canada: House 16A, Rd 48, Gulshan Model Town, POB 569, Dhaka 12; tel. (2) 607071; telex 642328; High Commissioner: EMILE GAUVREAU.

China, People's Republic: Plot NE(L)6, Rd 83, Gulshan Model Town, Dhaka 12; tel. (2) 601037; Ambassador: CHEN SONGLU.

Czechoslovakia: House 3A NE(O), Rd 90, Gulshan Model Town, Dhaka 12; tel. (2) 601673; telex 65730; Ambassador: JIŘÍ MAJSAJDR.

Denmark: House NW(H)1, Rd 51, Gulshan Model Town, POB 2056, Dhaka 12; tel. (2) 600108; telex 642320; Ambassador: JØRN KROGBECK.

Egypt: House NE(N)-9, Rd 90, Gulshan Model Town, Dhaka 12; tel. (2) 600158; Ambassador: MUHAMMAD MUSTAFA BADR.

France: POB 22, House 18, Rd 108, Gulshan Model Town, Dhaka 12; tel. (2) 607083; Ambassador: STANISLAS FILLIOL.

Germany: 178 Gulshan Ave, Gulshan Model Town, POB 108, Dhaka 12; tel. (2) 600166; telex 642331; Ambassador: KLAUS MAX FRANKE.

Holy See: Plot 1-2, Baridhara Model Town, POB 6003, Dhaka 1212 (Apostolic Nunciature); tel. (2) 882018; fax (2) 883574; Apostolic Pro-Nuncio: Most Rev. PIERO BIGGIO, Titular Archbishop of Otricoli.

Hungary: 80 Gulshan Ave, Gulshan Model Town, POB 6012, Dhaka 1212; tel. (2) 608101; telex 642314; Chargé d'affaires a.i.: I. B. BUDAY.

India: House 120, Rd 2, Dhanmandi R/A, Dhaka 1205; tel. (2) 503606; telex 642336; High Commissioner: K. SRINIVASAN.

Indonesia: 75 Gulshan Ave, Gulshan Model Town, Dhaka 12; tel. (2) 600131; telex 65639; Ambassador: MUHAMMAD ACHIRUL AEN.

Iran: CWN(A)-12 Kamal Ataturk Ave, Gulshan Model Town, Dhaka 12; tel. (2) 601432; telex 65714; Ambassador: MUHAMMAD GANJJIDOOST.

Iraq: 112 Gulshan Ave, Gulshan Model Town, Dhaka 12; tel. (2) 600298; telex 642307; Ambassador: ZUHAIR MUHAMMAD ALOMAR.

Italy: House NWD(4), Rd 58/62, Gulshan Model Town, Dhaka 12; tel. (2) 603161; telex 642313; Ambassador: Dr SANDRO MARIA SIGGIA.

Japan: Plot 110, Rd 27, Block A, Banani Model Town, Dhaka 13; tel. (2) 608191; telex 65872; Ambassador: TAKEO IGUCHI.

Korea, Democratic People's Republic: House 6, Rd 7, Baridhara Model Town, Dhaka; tel. (2) 601250; Ambassador: KANG TAL-SON.

Korea, Republic: House NW(E)17, Rd 55, Gulshan Model Town, Dhaka 12; tel. (2) 604921; Ambassador: MAN SOON CHANG.

Kuwait: Plot 39, Rd 23, Block J, Banani, Dhaka 13; tel. (2) 600233; telex 65600; Ambassador: AHMAD MURSHED AL-SULIMAN.

Libya: NE(D), 3A, Gulshan Ave (N), Gulshan Model Town, Dhaka 12; tel. (2) 600141; Secretary of People's Committee: MUSBAH ALI A. MAIMOON (acting).

Malaysia: House 4, Rd 118, Gulshan Model Town, Dhaka 12; tel. (2) 600291; High Commissioner: ZAINUDDIN A. RAHMAN.

Myanmar: 89(B), Rd 4, Banani, Dhaka; tel. (2) 601915; Ambassador: U SOE MYINT.

Nepal: United Nations Rd 2, Baridhara Model Town, Dhaka; tel. (2) 601790; telex 65643; Ambassador: Dr MOHAN PRASAD LOHANI.

Netherlands: House 49, Rd 90, Gulshan Model Town, Dhaka 12; tel. (2) 600278; Ambassador: J. H. J. JEURISSEN.

Pakistan: House NEC-2, Rd 71, Gulshan Model Town, Dhaka 12; tel. (2) 600276; High Commissioner: ANWAR KEMAL.

Philippines: House NE(L) 5, Rd 83, Gulshan Model Town, Dhaka 12; tel. (2) 605945; Ambassador: REYNALDO O. ARCHILLA.

Poland: 53 Gulshan Ave, Gulshan Model Town, Dhaka 12; tel. (2) 606098; telex 642316; Ambassador: EDWARD BARADZIEJ.

Qatar: House 23, Rd 108, Gulshan Model Town, Dhaka 12; tel. (2) 604477; Chargé d'affaires a.i.: ABDULLAH AL-MUTAWA.

Romania: House 33, Rd 74, Gulshan Model Town, Dhaka 12; tel. (2) 601467; telex 65739; Chargé d'affaires a.i.: ALEXANDRU VOINEA.

Saudi Arabia: House SW(A)-25, Rd 10, Gulshan Ave, Dhaka 12; tel. (2) 600221; telex 642305; Ambassador: ABDUL LATIF ABDULLAH IBRAHIM AL-MAIMANEE.

Sri Lanka: House 22 (NW), Rd 56, Gulshan Model Town, Dhaka 12; tel. (2) 604009; telex 642321; High Commissioner: A. K. DAVID.

Sweden: 73 Gulshan Ave, Gulshan Model Town, POB 304, Dhaka 12; tel. (2) 607061; telex 642303; Ambassador: EVA HECKSCHER.

Thailand: House NW (E) 12, Rd 59, Gulshan Model Town, Dhaka; tel. (2) 601475; Ambassador: CHAIYA CHINDAWONGSE.

Turkey: House 7, Rd 62, Gulshan Model Town, Dhaka 12; tel. (2) 602198; Ambassador: MUAMMER TUNCER.

USSR: NE(J) 9, Rd 79, Gulshan Model Town, Dhaka 12; tel. (2) 601050; Ambassador: VITALY STEPANOVICH SMIRNOV.

United Arab Emirates: House CEN(H)41, Rd 113, Gulshan Model Town, Dhaka 12; tel. (2) 604775; telex 642301; Ambassador: IBRAHIM JAWAD AL-RIDHA.

United Kingdom: Abu Bakr House, Plot 7, Rd 84, Gulshan Model Town, POB 6079, Dhaka 12; tel. (2) 600133; telex 671066; fax (2) 883437; High Commissioner: COLIN HENRY IMREY.

USA: Diplomatic Enclave, Madani Ave, Baridhara Model Town, Dhaka 1212; tel. (2) 884700; telex 642319; fax (2) 411648; Ambassador: WILLIAM B. MILAM.

Yugoslavia: House 10, Rd 62, Gulshan Model Town, Dhaka 12; tel. (2) 601505; Ambassador: KALMAN FEHER.

Judicial System

A judiciary, comprising a Supreme Court with High Court and Appellate Divisions, is in operation. See under Constitution.

Chief Justice: Dr F. K. M. A. MUNIM.

Attorney-General: M. NURULLAH.

Religion

Preliminary results of the 1981 census classified 86.6% of the population as Muslims, 12.1% as caste Hindus and scheduled castes, and the remainder as Buddhists, Christians and tribals.

BANGLADESH

Freedom of religious worship is guaranteed under the Constitution but, under the 1977 amendment to the Constitution, Islam was declared to be one of the nation's guiding principles and, under the 1988 amendment, Islam was established as the state religion.

BUDDHISM

World Federation of Buddhists Regional Centre: Buddhist Monastery, Kamalapur, Dhaka 14; Leader Ven. VISUDDHANANDA MAHATHERO.

CHRISTIANITY

Jatio Church Parishad (National Council of Churches): 395 New Eskaton Rd, Moghbazar, Dhaka 2; tel. (2) 402869; f. 1949 as East Pakistan Christian Council; four mem. churches; Pres. Dr SAJAL DEWAN; Gen. Sec. M. R. BISWAS.

Church of Bangladesh—United Church

After Bangladesh achieved independence, the Diocese of Dacca (Dhaka) of the Church of Pakistan (f. 1970 by the union of Anglicans, Methodists, Presbyterians and Lutherans) became the autonomous Church of Bangladesh. In 1986 the Church had an estimated 12,000 members.

Bishop of Dhaka: Rt Rev. BARNABAS DWIJEN MONDAL, St Thomas's Church, 54 Johnson Rd, Dhaka 1100; tel. (2) 236546.

The Roman Catholic Church

For ecclesiastical purposes, Bangladesh comprises one archdiocese and four dioceses. At 31 December 1988 there were an estimated 190,157 adherents in the country.

Catholic Bishops' Conference: Archbishop's House, POB 3, 1 Kakrail Rd, Dhaka 1000; tel. (2) 408879; f. 1978; Pres. Most Rev. MICHAEL ROZARIO, Archbishop of Dhaka.

Archbishop of Dhaka: Most Rev. MICHAEL ROZARIO, Archbishop's House, POB 3, 1 Kakrail Rd, Dhaka 1000; tel. (2) 408879.

Other Christian Churches

Bangladesh Baptist Sangha: 26/B Senpara Parbatta, Mirpur Section 10, Dhaka 1216; tel. (2) 380167; telex 632429; 26,500 mems (1985); Pres. M. S. ADHIKARI; Gen. Sec. Rev. PARITOSH BISWAS.

Among other denominations active in Bangladesh are the Bogra Christian Church, the Evangelical Christian Church (12,350 mems in 1985), the Garo Baptist Union (16,000 mems), the Reformed Church of Bangladesh and the Sylhet Presbyterian Synod (9,500 mems).

The Press

In 1989, 75 daily newspapers (with a total daily circulation of about 750,000 copies), 289 weekly periodicals, 33 fortnightlies, 120 monthlies, 50 quarterlies and 12 other periodicals were published in Bangladesh.

PRINCIPAL DAILIES

Bengali

Azad: 27K Dhakeshari Rd, Ramna, Dhaka 5; tel. (2) 502403; f. 1936; morning; Editor MD JAINUL ANAM KHAN; circ. 12,000.

Azadi: 9 C.D.A. C/A, Momin Rd, Chittagong; tel. (31) 224341; f. 1960; Editor Prof. MOHAMMAD KHALED; circ. 13,000.

Banglar Bani: 81 Motijheel C/A, Dhaka 1000; tel. (2) 237548; f. 1972; Editor Sheikh FAZLUL KARIM SALIM; circ. 20,000.

Dainik Bangla: 1 DIT Ave, Dhaka 1000; tel. (2) 235065; f. 1964; govt-owned; Editor AHMED HUMAYUN; circ. 50,000.

Dainik Barta: Natore Rd, Rajshahi; tel. 2424; f. 1976; morning; govt-owned; publication suspended in 1989; Editor MOSLEM ALI BISWAS; circ. 6,000.

Dainik Desh: 5 Segun Bagicha, Dhaka 1000; tel. (2) 244040; telex 235161; f. 1979; publ. of Quasem Publication Ltd; Editor ANWARUL ISLAM; circ. 30,000.

Dainik Inquilab: 2/1 Ramkrishna Mission Rd, Dhaka 1203; tel. (2) 240147; Editor A. M. M. BAHAUDDIN; circ. 42,000.

Dainik Ittefaq: 1 Ramkrishna Rd, Dhaka 1203; tel. (2) 256075; f. 1953; Editor AKTHER-UL-ALAM (acting); circ. 195,000.

Dainik Jahan: 3/B Shehra Rd, Mymensingh; tel. (91) 5677; f. 1980; Editor MUHAMMAD HABIBUR RAHMAN SHEIKH; circ. 4,000.

Dainik Janata: 24 Aminbagh, Shanti Nagar, Dhaka 1217; tel. (2) 400498; Editor SANAULLAH NOORI.

Dainik Janmobhumi: 36 Islampur Rd, Khulna; tel. (41) 21965; f. 1982; Editor HUMAYUN KABIR; circ. 6,000.

Directory

Dainik Khabar: 137 Shanti Nagar, Dhaka 1217; tel. (2) 406601; f. 1985; Editor MIZANUR RAHMAN MIZAN; circ. 18,000.

Dainik Millat: Dhaka; tel. (2) 242351; Editor CHOWDHURY MOHAMMAD FAROOQ.

Dainik Nava Avijan: Lalkuthi, North Brook Hall Rd, Dhaka; tel. (2) 257516; Editor A. S. M. REZAUL HAQUE; circ. 15,000.

Dainik Patrika: 85 Elephant Rd, Dhaka 17; tel. (2) 405057; Chief Editor MIA MUSA HOSSAIN.

Dainik Purbanchal: 38 Iqbal Nagar Mosque Lane, Khulna; tel. (41) 21944; fax (41) 21013; f. 1974; Editor LIAQUAT ALI; circ. 30,000.

Dainik Rupashi Bangla: Abdur Rashid Rd, Natun Chowdhury Para, Bagicha Gaon, Comilla 3500; tel. (81) 6689; f. 1971 (a weekly until 1979); Editor Prof. ABDUL WAHAB; circ. 4,000.

Dainik Samachar: 31/32 P.K. Roy Rd, Ispahani Bldg, Bangla Bazar, Dhaka 1100; tel. (2) 282480; f. 1964; Editor SEKANDAR HAYAT MAJUMDAR.

Dainik Sangram: 423 Elephant Rd, Bara Maghbazar, Dhaka 1217; tel. (2) 405279; Man. Dir MOHAMED SHAMSUR RAHMAN; Editor ABUL ASAD; circ. 19,000.

Dainik Shakti: 64/1 Purana Paltan, Dhaka 1000; tel. (2) 405535; Editor A. Q. M. ZAIN-UL-ABEDIN; circ. 4,000.

Dainik Sphulinga: Amin Villa, P-5 Housing Estate, Jessore 7401; tel. (421) 6433; f. 1971; Editor MIAN ABDUS SATTAR; circ. 14,000.

Dainik Uttara: Bahadur Bazar, Dinajpur Town, Dinajpur; tel. (531) 4326; f. 1974; Editor Prof. MUHAMMAD MOHSIN; circ. 8,500.

Ganakantha: 24C Tipu Sultan Rd, Dhaka 1203; tel. (2) 606784; telex 642696; f. 1979; morning; publication suspended in 1989; Editor JAHANGIR KABIR CHOWDHURY; Exec. Editor SAIYED RABIUL KARIM; circ. 15,000.

Janabarta: 5 Babu Khan Rd, Khulna; tel. (41) 21075; f. 1974; Editor SYED SOHRAB ALI; circ. 4,000.

Karatoa: Chandni Bazar, Bogra; tel. (51) 6111; f. 1976; Editor MOZAMMEL HAQUE LALU; circ. 3,000.

Naya Bangla: 101 Momin Rd, Chittagong; tel. (31) 206247; f. 1978; Editor ABDULLAH AL-SAGIR; circ. 12,000.

Probaho: 2 Raipara Cross Rd, Khulna; tel. (41) 23650; f. 1977; Editor ASHRAFUL HOQUE; circ. 3,000.

Protidin: Ganeshtola, Dinajpur; tel. (531) 4555; f. 1980; Editor KHAIRUL ANAM; circ. 3,000.

Runner: Pyari Mohan Das Rd, Bejpara, Jessore; tel. (421) 6943; f. 1980; Editor R. M. SAIFUL ALAM MUKUL; circ. 2,000.

Sangbad: 36 Purana Paltan, Dhaka 1000; tel. (2) 238147; telex 642454; fax (2) 865159; f. 1952; Editor AHMADUL KABIR; circ. 73,005.

Swadhinata: 99A Zamal Khan Lane, Chittagong; tel. (31) 209644; f. 1972; Editor ABDULLAH-AL-HARUN; circ. 4,000.

Zamana: Shahityik Mahbubul Alam Sarak Kazir Dewry, Chittagong; tel. (31) 226288; f. 1955; morning; Editor MOYEENUL ALAM; circ. 17,000.

English

Bangladesh Observer: Observer House, 33 Toyenbee Circular Rd, Motijheel C/A, Dhaka 1000; tel. (2) 235105; f. 1949; morning; Editor S. M. ALI; circ. 43,000.

Bangladesh Times: 1 Rajuk Ave, Dhaka 1000; tel. (2) 258840; f. 1949; morning; Editor SYED MAHBOOB ALAM CHOWDHURI; circ. 20,000.

Daily Capital News: Dhaka; tel. (2) 257985; f. 1982; Editor SEKANDER HAYAT MAJUMDER.

Daily Life: 27 Sadarghat Rd, Chittagong; tel. (31) 223171; f. 1977; Editor ANWARUL ISLAM BOBY; circ. 10,000.

Daily Tribune: 38 Iqbal Nagar Mosque Lane, Khulna; tel. (41) 21944; f. 1978; morning; Editor FERDOUS ALI; circ. 6,000.

Morning Post: 280 New Eskaton Rd, Dhaka 1000; tel. (2) 413256; f. 1969; Editor HABIBUL BASHAR; circ. 20,000.

New Nation: 1 Ramkrishna Mission Rd, Dhaka 1203; tel. (2) 256071; f. 1981; Editor FAZLE RASHID (acting); circ. 10,000.

People's View: 102 Siraj-ud-Daulla Rd, Chittagong; tel. (31) 227403; f. 1969; Editor SABBIR ISLAM; circ. 3,000.

PERIODICALS

Bengali

Aachal: 100B Malibagh Chowdhury Para, Dhaka 1219; tel. (2) 414043; weekly; Editor FERDOUSI BEGUM.

ADAB Sangbad: 1/3 Block F, Lalmatia, Dhaka 1207; tel. (2) 313318; telex 642940; f. 1974; monthly; publ. by the Assen of Devt Agencies in Bangladesh (ADAB); Exec. Editor MINAR MONSUR; circ. 7,000.

Ad-Dawat: Rajshahi Town; f. 1976; monthly; Editor MOHAMMAD ABUL QASEM.

BANGLADESH
Directory

Ahmadi: 4 Bakshi Bazar Rd, Dhaka 1211; f. 1925; fortnightly; Editor MAQBUL AHMAD KHAN.

Amod: Comilla Sadar, Comilla; tel. (81) 5193; f. 1955; weekly; Editor SHAMSUN NAHAR RABBI; circ. 6,000.

Ananda Bichitra: 1 DIT Ave, Dhaka; tel. (2) 241639; f. 1986; fortnightly; Editor SHAHADAT CHOWDHURY; circ. 32,000.

Ananda Chitra: 55 Inner Circular Rd, Shanti Nagar, Dhaka; Editor K. G. KARIM.

Ananda Patra: 188 Motijheel Circular Rd, Dhaka 1000; tel. (2) 406988; weekly; Editor MOSTAFA JABBAR.

Bangla Dak: 12 Avoy Das Lane, Dhaka; Editor SALEH AHMED; circ. 2,000.

Begum: 66 Loyal St, Dhaka 1; tel. (2) 233789; f. 1947; women's illustrated weekly; Editor NURJAHAN BEGUM; circ. 25,000.

Bichitra: Dainik Bangla Bhaban, 1 DIT Ave, Dhaka 1000; tel. (2) 232086; f. 1972; weekly; Editor SHAHADAT CHOWDHURY; circ. 42,000.

Biplav: 5 Shegunbagicha, Dhaka 2; f. 1982; weekly; Editor SIKDER AMINUL HUQUE.

Chakra: 242A Nakhalpara, POB 2682, Dhaka 1215; tel. (2) 604568; social welfare weekly; Editor HUSNEARA AZIZ.

Chitra Bangla: 137 Shanti Nagar, Dhaka; tel. (2) 407601; weekly; Editor FULLORA BEGUM FLORA; circ. 46,000.

Chitra Desh: 24 Ramkrishna Mission Rd, Dhaka 1203; weekly; Editor HENA AKHTAR CHOWDHURY.

Chitrakalpa: 12 Folder St, Dhaka 3; Editor ASIRUDDIN AHMED.

Chitrali: Observer House, 33 Toyenbee Circular Rd, Motijheel C/A, Dhaka 1000; tel. (2) 235105; f. 1963; film weekly; Editor AHMED ZAMAN CHOWDHURY; circ. 25,000.

Chutti: 87 Bijoy Nagar, Dhaka 1000; tel. (2) 241112; weekly; Editor JAWADUL KARIM; circ. 18,000.

Dhaka Digest: 34 Topkhana Rd, Dhaka; f. 1974; monthly; Editor RASHID CHOWDHURY; circ. 7,000.

Ekota: 15 Larmini St, Wari, Dhaka; tel. (2) 257854; f. 1970; weekly; Editor MATIUR RAHMAN; circ. 25,000.

Fashal: 28J Toyenbee Circular Rd, Motijheel C/A, Dhaka 1000; tel. (2) 233099; f. 1965; agricultural weekly; Chief Editor ERSHAD MAZUMDAR; circ. 8,000.

Ispat: Majampur, Kushtia; tel. (71) 3676; f. 1976; weekly; Editor WALIUR BARI CHOUDHURY; circ. 3,000.

Jahan-e-Nau: 13 Karkun Bari Lane, Dhaka; tel. (2) 252205; f. 1960; weekly; Editor MD HABIBIUR RAHMAN; circ. 9,000.

Janakatha: 130 DIT Extension Rd, Dhaka; Editor IBRAHIM RAHMAN.

Jhorna: 4/13 Block A, Lalmatia, Dhaka; tel. (2) 415239; Editor MUHAMMAD JAMIR ALI.

Jugabheri: Rasheedistan, Rai Hussain, Amberkhana, Sylhet; tel. (821) 5461; f. 1931; weekly; Editor FAHMEEDA RASHEED CHOUDHURY; circ. 6,000.

Kalantar: 87 Khanjahan Ali Rd, Khulna; tel. (41) 61424; f. 1971; weekly; Editor NOOR MOHAMMAD; circ. 12,000.

Kankan: Nawab Bari Rd, Bogra; tel. (51) 6424; f. 1974; weekly; Editor Mrs SUFIA KHATUN; circ. 6,000.

Kanak: 144 DIT Extension Rd, Dhaka; tel. (2) 415110; weekly; Editor AMIR HOSSAIN.

Kirajagat: National Sports Control Board, 62/63 Purana Paltan, Dhaka; f. 1977; weekly; Editor ALI MUZZAMAN CHOWDHURY; circ. 7,000.

Kishore Bangla: Observer House, Motijheel C/A, Dhaka 1000; juvenile weekly; f. 1976; Editor RAFIQUL HAQUE; circ. 5,000.

Krishi Katha: Dhaka; f. 1957; monthly; Editor NURJAHAN KORESHI; circ. 6,000.

Mallika: 51 Lalchan-Mokim Lane, Roth Khola, Dhaka; tel. (2) 251408; Editor Dr JHORNA DATTA.

Meghna: 55 Inner Circular Rd, Shanti Nagar, Dhaka 1217; tel. (2) 404983; weekly; Editor MOSTAFA AMIR FAISAL; circ. 16,000.

Moha Nagar: 4 Dilkusha C/A, Dhaka 1000; tel. (2) 255282; Editor SYED MOTIUR RAHMAN.

Moshal: 4 Dilkusha C/A, Dhaka 1000; tel. (2) 231092; Editor MUHAMMAD ABUL HASNAT; circ. 3,000

Muktibani: Toyenbee Circular Rd, Motijheel C/A, Dhaka 1000; tel. (2) 253712; telex 642474; f. 1972; weekly; Editor NIZAM UDDIN AHMED; circ. 35,000.

Natun Bangla: 44A Hatirpur, Sonargaont Rd, Dhaka 1205; tel. (2) 508102; weekly; Editor MUJIBUR RAHMAN.

Natun Katha: 31E Topkhana Rd, Dhaka; weekly; Editor HAJERA SULTANA; circ. 4,000.

Nayajug: 32 Purana Paltan, Dhaka; tel. (2) 283510; f. 1976; weekly; Editor KAZI ZAFAR AHMED; circ. 9,000.

Nipun: 520 Peyarabag, Magbazar, Dhaka 11007; tel. (2) 312156; monthly; Editor SHAJAHAN CHOWDHURY.

Parikrama: 65 Shanti Nagar, Dhaka; tel. (2) 415640; Editor MOMTAZ SULTANA.

Patuakhali Samachur: Patuakhali Town; f. 1970; fortnightly; Editor SHAMSUL HAQ KHAN.

Prohar: 35 Siddeswari Rd, Dhaka 1217; tel. (2) 404206; Editor MUJIBUL HUQ.

Protirodh: Dept of Answar and V.D.P. Khilgoan, Ministry of Home Affairs, School Bldg, 2nd and 3rd Floors, Bangladesh Secretariat, Dhaka; tel. (2) 405971; f. 1977; fortnightly; Editor ZAHANGIR HABIBULLAH; circ. 20,000.

Purbani: 1 Ramkrishna Mission Rd, Dhaka 1203; tel. (2) 256503; f. 1951; film weekly; Editor KHONDKER SHAHADAT HOSSAIN; circ. 22,000.

Reporter: 28J Toyenbee Circular Rd, Motijheel C/A, Dhaka; tel. (2) 257589; f. 1976; news weekly; Chief Editor ERSHAD MAZUMDAR; circ. 5,000.

Robbar: 1 Ramkrishna Mission Rd, Dhaka; tel. (2) 256071; f. 1978; weekly; publication suspended Dec. 1987; Editor ABDUL HAFIZ; circ. 20,000.

Rokshena: 13B Avoy Das Lane, Tiktuli, Dhaka; tel. (2) 255117; Editor SYEDA AFSANA.

Rupashi: 7 Segunbagicha, Dhaka; tel. (2) 239622; Editor GULSHAN AHMED.

Sachitra: 50F Inner Circular Rd, Naya Paltan, Dhaka; tel. (2) 403242; Editor KHALID MAHMOUD.

Sachitra Bangladesh: 112 Circuit House Rd, Dhaka 1000; tel. (2) 402129; f. 1979; fortnightly; Editor A. B. M. ABDUL MATIN; circ. 8,000.

Sachitra Sandhani: 68/2 Purana Paltan, Dhaka; tel. (2) 409680; f. 1978; weekly; Editor GAZI SHAHABUDDIN MAHMUD; circ. 13,000.

Sandip: 28/A/3 Toyenbee Circular Rd, Dhaka; tel. (2) 235542; weekly; Editor MOHSEN ARA RAHMAN.

Satodal: Dhaka; Editor A. L. ZAHIRUL HUQ KHAN.

Shishu: Bangladesh Shishu Academy, Old High Court Compound, Dhaka 1000; tel. (2) 238871; f. 1977; children's monthly; Editor GOLAM KIBRIA; circ. 9,000.

Sonar Bangla: 423 Elephant Rd, Mogh Bazar, Dhaka 1217; tel. (2) 400637; f. 1961; Editor MUHAMMED QAMARUZZAMAN; circ. 25,000.

Swadesh: 19 B.B. Ave, Dhaka; tel. (2) 256946; weekly; Editor ZAKIUDDIN AHMED; circ. 8,000.

Tarokalok: 8/3 Neelkhet, Babupura, Dhaka 1205; tel. (2) 507952; weekly; Editor SAJJAD KADIR.

Tide: 56/57 Motijheel C/A, Dhaka 1000; tel. (2) 259421; Editor ENAYET KARIM.

Tilotwoma: 14 Bangla Bazar, Dhaka; Editor ABDUL MANNAN.

English

ADAB News: 1/3, Block F, Lalmatia, Dhaka 1207; tel. (2) 327424; telex 642940; f. 1974; 6 a year; publ. by the Asscn of Devt Agencies in Bangladesh (ADAB); Editor-in-Chief AZFAR HUSSAIN; circ. 10,000.

Bangladesh: 112 Circuit House Rd, Dhaka 1000; tel. (2) 402013; fortnightly; Editor A. B. M. ABDUL MATIN.

Bangladesh Gazette: Bangladesh Government Press, Tejgaon, Dhaka; f. 1947, name changed 1972; weekly; official notices; Editor M. HUDA.

Bangladesh Illustrated Weekly: 31A Rankin St, Wari, Dhaka; tel. (2) 23358; Editor ATIQUZZAMAN KHAN; circ. 3,000.

Bangladesh Today: Dhaka; Editor SERAJUL ISLAM CHOWDHURY.

Cinema: 81 Motijheel C/A, Dhaka 1000; Editor SHEIKH FAZLUR RAHMAN MARUF; circ. 11,000.

Consumer-Economist: Yasmin Palace, Jubilee Rd, Chattagram; tel. (31) 204038; f. 1980; weekly; Editor MOYEENUL ALAM; circ. 16,000.

Detective: Polwell Bhaban, Naya Paltan, Dhaka 2; tel. (2) 402757; f. 1960; weekly; also publ. in Bengali; Editor SYED AMJAD HOSSAIN; circ. 3,000.

Dhaka Courier: 62/61 Purana Paltan, Dhaka; tel. (2) 238222; weekly; Editor ENAYET ULLAH KHAN; circ. 5,000.

Economic Times: 65/2 Laboratory Rd, Dhaka 1205; tel. (2) 413027; f. 1989; weekly; Editor and Publr MUNIRUL HUQ; circ. 5,000.

Friday: 17/1 Eskaton Gardon Rd, Dhaka; tel. (2) 409580; telex 642866; Editor SHAWFIKUL GHAANI SHAPAN.

Herald: 87 Bijoy Nagar, Dhaka; tel. (2) 231533; f. 1981; weekly; Editor JAQADUL KARIM; circ. 4,000.

Holiday: Holiday Bldg, 30 Tejgaon Industrial Area, Dhaka 1208; tel. (2) 329163; f. 1965; weekly; independent; Editor FAZAL M. KAMAL; circ. 19,000.

Karnaphuli Shipping News: 88 Ghat Farhadbag, Kazem Ali Rd, Chittagong 4000; tel. (31) 220366; telex 66483; f. 1977; twice a week; Editor F. KARIM; circ. 10,000.

Motherland: Khanjahan Ali Rd, Khulna; tel. (41) 61685; f. 1974; weekly; Editor M. N. KHAN.

Saturday Post: 280 New Eskaton Rd, Dhaka 1000; tel. (2) 413256; f. 1975; weekly; Man. Editor ZAKIR HOSSAIN; Editor HABIBUL BASHAR; circ. 15,000.

Sunday Star: 149/A DIT Extension Ave, Dhaka; tel. (2) 403980; f. 1981; weekly; Editor MOHIUDDIN AHMED.

Tide: 56/57 Motijheel C/A, Dhaka; tel. (2) 259421; Editor ENAYET KARIM.

Voice From the North: Dinajpur Town, Dinajpur; tel. (531) 3256; f. 1981; weekly; Editor Prof. MUHAMMAD MOHSIN; circ. 5,000.

NEWS AGENCIES

Bangladesh Sangbad Sangstha (BSS) (Bangladesh News Agency): 68/2 Purana Paltan, Dhaka 1000; tel. (2) 235036; telex 642202; Man. Dir and Chief Editor MAHBUBUL ALAM.

Eastern News Agency (ENA): 3/3C Purana Paltan, Dhaka 1000; tel. (2) 234206; telex 642410; f. 1970; Man. Dir and Chief Editor GOLAM RASUL MALLICK.

Foreign Bureaux

Agence France-Presse (AFP): Shilpa Bank, 5th Floor, 8 DIT Ave, nr Dhaka Stadium, Dhaka; tel. (2) 242234; telex 5526; Correspondent GOLAM TAHABOOR.

Associated Press (AP) (USA): 8/6 Segun Bagicha, Dhaka 1000; tel. (2) 253420; telex 642967; Representative HASAN SAEED.

Inter Press Service (IPS) (Italy): c/o Bangladesh Sangbad Sangstha, 68/2 Purana Paltan, Dhaka 1000; tel. (2) 235036; Correspondent A. K. M. TABIBUL ISLAM.

Reuters Ltd (UK): POB 3993, Dhaka; tel. (2) 506363; telex 642540; fax (2) 411063; Bureau Chief ATIQUL ALAM.

Telegrafnoye Agentstvo Sovetskovo Soyuza (TASS) (USSR): Dhaka; tel. (2) 316314.

United Press International (UPI) (USA): Dhaka; tel. (2) 233132; telex 642817.

Xinhua (New China) News Agency (People's Republic of China): 22 New Eskaton Rd, Dhaka 1000; tel. (2) 403167; Correspondent XUAN ZENGPEI.

PRESS ASSOCIATIONS

Bangladesh Council of Newspapers and News Agencies: Dhaka; tel. (2) 413256; Chair. MOINUL HOSSAIN; Sec.-Gen. HABIBUL BASHAR.

Bangladesh Federal Union of Journalists: National Press Club Bldg, 18 Topkhana Rd, Dhaka 1000; tel. (2) 254777; f. 1973; Pres. REAZUDDIN AHMED; Sec.-Gen. SYED ZAFAR AHMED.

Bangladesh Sangbadpatra Karmachari Federation (Newspaper Employees' Fed.): 47/3 Toyenbee Circular Rd, Bikrampur House, Dhaka 1000; tel. (2) 235065; f. 1972; Pres. RAFIQUL ISLAM; Sec.-Gen. MIR MOZAMMEL HOSSAIN.

Bangladesh Sangbadpatra Press Sramik Federation (Newspaper Press Workers' Federation): 1 Ramkrishna Mission Rd, Dhaka; f. 1960; Pres. M. ABDUL KARIM; Gen.-Sec. BELAYAT HOSSAIN.

Dhaka Union of Journalists: National Press Club, Dhaka; f. 1947; Pres. ABEL KHAIR; Gen.-Sec. ABDUL KALAM AZAD.

Overseas Correspondents' Association Bangladesh (OCAB): 18 Topkhana Rd, Dhaka 1000; f. 1979; Pres. GOLAM TAHABOOR; Gen. Sec. TAHMINA SAYEED; 51 mems.

Publishers

Adeyle Brothers: 60 Patuatuly, Dhaka 1.

Ahmed Publishing House: 7 Zindabahar 1st Lane, Dhaka 1; tel. (2) 36492; f. 1942; literature, history, science, religion, children's, maps and charts; Man. Dir KAMALUDDIN AHMED; Man. MESBAHUDDIN AHMED.

Ashrafia Library: 4 Hakim Habibur Rahman Rd, Chawk Bazar, Dhaka 1000; Islamic religious books, texts, and reference works of Islamic institutions.

Asiatic Society of Bangladesh: 5 Old Secretariat Rd, Ramna, Dhaka; tel. (2) 239390; f. 1951; periodicals on science and humanities; Pres. A. K. M. ZAKARIA; Sec. Prof. SERAJUL.

Bangla Academy: Burdwan House, Dhaka 1000; tel. (2) 500131; f. 1955; higher education textbooks in Bengali, research works in language, literature and culture, popular science, drama, encyclopaedias, translations of world classics, dictionaries; Dir-Gen. MAHMUD SHAH QURESHI.

Bangladesh Book Corporation: 73/74 Patuatuly, Dhaka.

Bangladesh Publishers: 45 Patuatuly, Dhaka.

Bangladesh Books International Ltd: Ittefaq Bhaban, 1 Ramkrishna Mission Rd, POB 377, Dhaka 3; tel. (2) 256071; f. 1975; reference, academic, research, literary, children's in Bengali and English; Chair. MOINUL HOSSEIN; Man. Dir ABDUL HAFIZ.

Barnamala Prakashani: 30 Bangla Bazar, Dhaka.

Boi Prakashani: 38A Bangla Bazar, Dhaka.

Boighar: 149 Government New Market, Dhaka.

Book Society: 38 Bangla Bazar, Dhaka.

Co-operative Book Society Ltd: Motijheel, Dhaka.

Didar Publishing House: 45 Johnson Rd, Dhaka.

Emdadia Library: Chawk Bazar, Dhaka.

Habibia Library: Chawk Bazar, Dhaka.

Islamic Foundation: Baitul Mukarram, Dhaka.

Jatiya Sahitya Prakashani: 51 Purana Paltan, Dhaka 1000; f. 1970; Prin. Officer MOFIDUL HOQUE.

Khan Brothers & Co: 67 Pyari Das Rd, Dhaka.

Liaquat Publications: 34 North Brook Hall Rd, Dhaka.

Model Publishing House: 34 Bangla Bazar, Dhaka.

Mofiz Book House: 37 Bangla Bazar, Dhaka.

Mowla Brothers: Bangla Bazar, Dhaka.

Muktadhara: 74 Farashganj, Dhaka 1100; tel. (2) 231374; f. 1971; educational, literary and general; Bengali and English; Man. Dir C. R. SAHA; Chief Editor S. P. LAHIRY.

Mullick Brothers: 3/1 Bangla Bazar, Dhaka; educational.

Osmania Book Depot: 42/43 North Brook Hall Rd, Dhaka 1.

Puthighar Ltd: 74 Farashganj, Dhaka 1100; tel. (2) 231374; f. 1951; educational; Bengali and English; Man. Dir C. R. SAHA; Chief Editor S. P. LAHIRY.

Puthipatra: 1/6 Shirish Das Lane, Banglabazar, Dhaka 1; f. 1952.

Rahman Brothers: 5/1 Gopinath Datta, Kabiraj St, Babu Bazar, Dhaka; tel. (2) 282633; educational.

Royal Library: Ispahani Bldg, 31/32 P. K. Roy Rd, Banglabazar, Dhaka 1; tel. (2) 250863.

Sahitya Kutir: Bogra.

Sahityika: 6 Bangla Bazar, Dhaka.

Samakal Prakashani: 36A Toyenbee Circular Rd, Dhaka 1000.

Standard Publishers Ltd: Dhaka Stadium, Dhaka 1.

Student Ways: 9 Bangla Bazar, Dhaka.

University Press Ltd: POB 2611, Red Cross Bldg, 114 Motijheel C/A, Dhaka 1000; tel. (2) 232950; f. 1975; educational, academic and general; Man. Dir MOHIUDDIN AHMED; Editor MAHBOOB HASSAN.

Government Publishing Houses

Bangladesh Bureau of Statistics: Bldg 8, Room 12, Bangladesh Secretariat, Dhaka 1000; tel. (2) 409571; f. 1971; statistical yearbooks, censuses, surveys, special reports and monthly bulletins; Dep. Dir Md. MOHIUDDIN AHMED; Sec. ABDUS SALAM.

Bangladesh Government Press: Tejgaon, Dhaka; tel. (2) 603897; f. 1972.

Department of Films and Publications: 112 Circuit House Rd, Dhaka 1000; tel. (2) 402263.

Press Information Department: Bhaban 6, Bangladesh Secretariat, Dhaka 1000; tel. (2) 400958; telex 65619.

PUBLISHERS' ASSOCIATIONS

Bangladesh Publishers' and Booksellers' Association: 3rd Floor, 3 Liaquat Ave, Dhaka 1; f. 1972; Pres. JANAB JAHANGIR MOHAMMED ADEL; 2,500 mems.

National Book Centre of Bangladesh: 67A Purana Paltan, Dhaka 1000; f. 1963 to promote the cause of 'more, better and cheaper books'; organizes book fairs, publs a monthly journal; Dir FAZLE RABBI.

Radio and Television

In 1987 there were an estimated 4,250,000 radio receivers in use. In 1988 the number of television receivers in use totalled 420,000.

BANGLADESH

Directory

National Broadcasting Authority (NBA): NBA House, Shahbag Ave, Dhaka; tel. (2) 500143; telex 642228; f. 1984 by merger of Radio Bangladesh and Bangladesh Television; Chair. SAIFUL BARI.

Radio Bangladesh: f. 1971; tel. (2) 506206; telex 642221; govt-controlled; regional stations at Chittagong, Dhaka, Khulna, Rajshahi, Rangpur and Sylhet broadcast a total of approximately 92 hours daily; transmitting centres at Lalmai and Thakurgaon broadcast 8 hours daily; external service broadcasts 9 transmissions daily in Arabic, Bengali, English, Hindi, Nepalese and Urdu; Chair. and Dir-Gen. SAIFUL BARI.

Bangladesh Television (BTV): POB 456, Rampura, Dhaka 1219; tel. (2) 400131; telex 65624; fax (2) 832927; f. 1971; govt-controlled; colour transmissions from 1980; daily broadcasts on one channel from Dhaka station for 7 hours; transmissions also from relay stations at Chittagong, Khulna, Mymensingh, Natore, Noakhali, Rangpur, Satkhira, Sylhet, Cox's Bazar and Rangamati; Chair. SAIFUL BARI; Gen. Man. MUSTAFIZUR RAHMAN.

Finance

(cap. = capital; p.u. = paid up; res = reserves; dep. = deposits; m. = million; brs = branches; amounts in taka, unless otherwise indicated)

BANKING

Central Bank

Bangladesh Bank: Motijheel C/A, POB 325, Dhaka 1000; tel. (2) 235000; telex 65657; fax (2) 412437; f. 1971; cap. p.u. 30m., dep. 43,040m., total assets 97,230m. (June 1990); Gov. and Chair. SHEGUFTA BAKHT CHAUDHURI; Dep. Govs MAHABUBUR RAHMAN KHAN, A. S. M. FAKHRUL AHSAN; 7 brs.

Nationalized Commercial Banks

Agrani Bank: 9D Dilkusha C/A, Motijheel, POB 531, Dhaka 1000; tel. (2) 257051; telex 642757; f. 1972; cap. p.u. 35m., res 81m., dep. 30,762m. (June 1990); Chair. IMAM UDDIN AHMAD CHOUDHURY; Man. Dir HUMAYUN HAMID; 874 brs.

Janata Bank: 110 Motijheel C/A, Motijheel, POB 468, Dhaka 1000; tel. (2) 240000; telex 675840; f. 1972; cap. p.u. 40.0m., res 184.5m., dep. 36,783.0m. (June 1990); Chair. Maj. (retd) HAFIZUDDIN AHMED; Man. Dir M. HAYATUR RAHMAN; 892 brs.

Rupali Bank Ltd: 34 Dilkusha C/A, POB 719, Dhaka 1000; tel. (2) 256021; telex 675635; f. 1972; cap. p.u. 272m., res 77m., dep. 16,672m. (June 1990); Chair. M. NURUL ISLAM MONI; Man. Dir A. K. S. M. TAIFUR HUSSAIN; 516 brs.

Sonali Bank: 35-44 Motijheel C/A, POB 3130, Dhaka 1000; tel. (2) 252990; telex 642644; f. 1972; cap. p.u. 55m., res 254m., dep. 48,104m. (June 1990); Chair. ABDUR RAHIM; Man. Dir M. AHSANUL HAQUE; 1,289 brs.

In 1985 the Government announced a phased divestment of 49% of the shares of the Agrani, Janata and Rupali Banks. The Sonali Bank has remained under full government ownership.

Private Commercial Banks

Al Baraka Bank Bangladesh Ltd: Kashfia Plaza, 35c Naya Paltan, VIP Rd, POB 3467, Dhaka 1000; tel. (2) 243061; telex 632118; fax (2) 834943; f. 1987 on Islamic banking principles; 70% owned by Al Baraka Group, Saudi Arabia, 12.5% by Bangladesh sponsors, 12.5% by local shareholders and 5% by Bangladesh Govt; cap. p.u. 150.0m., res 18.3m., dep. 3,515.6m. (June 1990); Chair. Dr HASSAN ABDULLAH KAMEL; Man. Dir A. N. HAMIDULLAH; 18 brs.

Arab Bangladesh Bank Ltd: BCIC Bhaban, 30-31 Dilkusha C/A, POB 3522, Dhaka 1000; tel. (2) 240312; telex 642520; f. 1982 as first jt-venture Bangladeshi private sector commercial bank; cap. p.u. 100.0m., res 80.4m., dep. 5,004.3m. (June 1990); Chair. M. MORSHED KHAN; Man. Dir A. K. M. GHAFFAR; 30 brs.

Bangladesh Commerce and Investment Ltd: 19 Rajuk Ave, Motijheel, POB 3797, Dhaka; tel. (2) 236195; telex 642415; f. 1986; cap. p.u. 50.0m., res 4.0m., dep. 2,146.5m. (June 1990); Chair. and Man. Dir MUSTAFIZUR RAHMAN; 24 brs.

City Bank: Tower Bldg, 10 Dilkusha C/A, POB 3381, Dhaka 1000; tel. (2) 235071; telex 642581; f. 1983; cap. p.u. 160.0m., res 93.4m., dep. 4,255.5m. (June 1990); Chair. IBRAHIM MIA; Man. Dir M. A. YOUSSUF KHAN; 51 brs.

International Finance Investment and Commerce Bank Ltd (IFICB): BSB Bldg, 17th-19th Floors, 8 Rajuk Ave, POB 2229, Dhaka 1000; tel. (2) 232400; telex 632404; fax (2) 833198; f. 1983; cap. p.u. 131.6m., res 136.0m., dep. 5,828.6m. (June 1990); Chair. JAHIRUL ISLAM; Man. Dir M. FAZLUR RAHMAN; 61 brs.

Islami Bank Bangladesh Ltd (IBB): 71 Dilkusha C/A, POB 233, Dhaka 1000; tel. (2) 234040; telex 642525; fax (2) 833632; f. 1983 on Islamic banking principles; cap. p.u. 160.0m., res 88.8m., dep. 3,634.3m. (June 1990); Chair. Cdre (retd) M. ATAUR RAHMAN; Man. Dir LUTFAR RAHMAN SARKER; 40 brs.

National Bank Ltd: 18 Dilkusha C/A, POB 3424, Dhaka 1000; tel. (2) 243081; telex 642791; fax (2) 833584; f. 1983; cap. p.u. 192.0m., res 132.8m., dep. 8,350.2m. (June 1990); Chair. Dr AZIZUR RAHMAN MALLICK; Man. Dir R. A. HOWLADER; 48 brs.

Pubali Bank Ltd: Pubali Bank Bhaban, 26 Dilkusha C/A, POB 853, Dhaka 1000; tel. (2) 259681; telex 65844; f. 1959 as Eastern Mercantile Bank Ltd; name changed to Pubali Bank in 1972; cap. and res 195.7m., dep. 9,751.2m. (Dec. 1988); Chair. EMADUDDIN AHMED CHOUDHURY; Man. Dir SHAIKH AMINUL ISLAM; 356 brs.

United Commercial Bank Ltd: Federation Bhaban, 60 Motijheel C/A, POB 2653, Dhaka 1000; tel. (2) 235075; telex 642733; f. 1983; cap. p.u. 120.0m., res 70.3m., dep. 3,974.1m. (June 1990); Chair. S. M. SHAFIUL AZAM; Man. Dir S. A. SHAKOOR; 54 brs.

Uttara Bank Ltd: 90-91 Motijheel C/A, POB 818 & 217, Dhaka 1000; tel. (2) 232114; telex 642915; fax (2) 833529; f. 1965 as Eastern Banking Corpn Ltd; name changed to Uttara Bank in 1972; cap. p.u. 94.3m., res 43.0m., dep. 8,570.3m. (June 1990); Chair. Dr SYEDA FEROZA BEGUM; Man. Dir Dr A. K. M. SYEDUR RAHMAN; 191 brs.

Foreign Banks

American Express Bank Ltd (USA): ALICO Bldg, 18-20 Motijheel C/A, POB 420, Dhaka 1000; tel. (2) 238351; telex 632305; f. 1966; res 907m., dep. 3,682m. (June 1990); Gen. Man. DENNIS J. REYNARD; 1 br.

ANZ Grindlays Bank PLC (UK): 2 Dilkusha C/A, POB 502, Dhaka 1000; tel. (2) 235024; telex 642597; fax (2) 833347; f. 1903 as Grindlays Bank; now part of Australia and New Zealand Banking Group; res 404.2m., dep. 2,365.2m. (June 1990); Gen. Man. BRIAN K. REITER; 12 brs.

Bank of Credit and Commerce International (Overseas) Ltd (BCCI) (Cayman Islands): Jiban Bima Bhaban, 10 Dilkusha C/A, POB 896, Dhaka 1000; tel. (2) 236360; telex 642482; f. 1976; cap. p.u. 213m., res 259m., dep. 6,069m. (June 1990); Gen. Man. MD QAMRUL HUDA; 4 brs.

Banque Indosuez (France): 47 Motijheel C/A, POB 3490, Dhaka 1000; tel. (2) 238285; telex 642438; fax (2) 833137; f. 1981; dep. 2,250m. (Dec. 1989); Man. (Bangladesh) MARC DUMETZ; Gen. Man. D. DAS GUPTA; 4 brs.

Habib Bank Ltd (Pakistan): 53 Motijheel C/A, POB 201, Dhaka 1000; tel. (2) 235091; telex 65772; f. 1976; Vice-Pres. and Man. HABIB H. MIRZA; 1 br.

Standard Chartered Bank (UK): ALICO Bldg, 18-20 Motijheel C/A, POB 536, Dhaka 1000; tel. (2) 236372; telex 65859; f. 1966; cap. and res 71.1m., dep. 769m. (Dec. 1987); Chair. and Man. Dir RODNEY GALPIN; 2 brs.

State Bank of India: 24-25 Dilkusha C/A, POB 981, Dhaka 1000; tel. (2) 253914; telex 642431; f. 1975; cap. p.u. 8m., dep. 97m. (Dec. 1987); Man. Dir P. GANGULY; 1 br.

DEVELOPMENT FINANCE ORGANIZATIONS

Bangladesh House Building Finance Corpn (BHBFC): HBFC Bldg, 22 Purana Paltan, POB 2167, Dhaka 1000; tel. (2) 241315; f. 1952; provides low-interest credit for house-building; cap. p.u. 98.3m., res 151.9m. (June 1990); Chair. Dr T. I. M. FAZLE RABBI CHOWDHURY; Man. Dir MOHAMMAD ISMAIL HOSSAIN; 19 brs.

Bangladesh Krishi Bank (BKB): 83-85 Motijheel C/A, POB 357, Dhaka 2; tel. (2) 233028; telex 642526; f. 1961; provides credit for agricultural and rural devt; cap. and res 953.7m., dep. 5,247.2m. (June 1988); Chair. Maj.-Gen. (retd) MAHABBAT JAN CHOWDHURY; Man. Dir Dr A. M. M. SHAWKAT ALI; 823 brs.

Bangladesh Samabaya Bank Ltd (BSBL): 'Samabaya Sadan', 9D Motijheel C/A, POB 505, Dhaka 1000; tel. (2) 231129; f. 1948; provides credit for agricultural co-operatives; cap. p.u. 30.0m., res 298.0m., dep. 23.9m. (June 1990); Chair. HABIBUR RAHMAN SARKER; Gen. Man. Z. A. DEWAN.

Bangladesh Shilpa Bank (BSB) (Industrial Development Bank): Shilpa Bank Bhaban, 8 DIT Ave, POB 975, Dhaka; tel. (2) 235151; telex 642950; f. 1972; fmrly Industrial Devt Bank; provides finance for industrial devt; cap. and res 1,707.1m., dep. 3,660.0m. (June 1988); Chair. K. M. RABBANI; Man. Dir Dr MUHIUDDIN KHAN ALAMGIR; 13 brs.

Bangladesh Shilpa Rin Sangstha (BSRS) (Industrial Loan Agency): BIWTA Bhaban, 5th Floor, 141-143 Motijheel C/A, POB 473, Dhaka 1000; tel. (2) 252016; fax (2) 833247; f. 1972; cap. p.u. 700.0m., res 688.2m. (June 1990); Chair. A. K. M. MOSHARRAF HUSSAIN; Man. Dir M. M. NURUL HAQUE; 4 brs.

Bank of Small Industries and Commerce Bangladesh Ltd (BASIC): 73 Motijheel C/A, Dhaka 1000; tel. (2) 243068; telex 632185; f. 1989; joint venture enterprise of the Government and

BANGLADESH

Directory

the BCC Foundation; provides development finance for small-scale and cottage industries; cap. p.u. 80.0m., res 0.8m., dep. 393.0m. (June 1990); Chair. A. K. M. Mosharraf Hossain; Man. Dir A. A. Qureshi; 4 brs.

Grameen Bank: Mirpur-2, Dhaka 1210; tel. (2) 383081; telex 642601; fax (2) 803559; f. 1976; provides credit for the landless rural poor; cap. p.u. 72.0m., res 25.7m., dep. 574.3m. (June 1990); Chair. Prof. Md. Kaiser Hossain; Man. Dir Dr Muhammad Yunus; 733 brs.

Investment Corpn of Bangladesh (ICB): BSB Bldg, 12th–14th Floors, 8 Rajuk Ave, POB 2058, Dhaka 1000; tel. (2) 254112; f. 1976; provides devt financing; cap. p.u. 200.0m., res 259.6m. (June 1990); Chair. Maj.-Gen. (retd) M. A. Matin; Man. Dir Shah Mohammad Afanoor; 4 brs.

National Credit Ltd: 7-8 Motijheel C/A, POB 2920, Dhaka; tel. (2) 239449; telex 642821; f. 1985; cap. p.u. 50.0m., res 3.8m., dep. 1,461.6m. (June 1990); Chair. and Man. Dir M. Haider Chowdhury; 16 brs.

Rajshahi Krishi Unnayan Bank: Shadharan Bima Bhaban, Kazihata, Greater Rd, Rajshahi 6000; tel. 5848; f. 1987; cap. p.u. 160.0m., res 60.2m., dep. 998.5m. (June 1990); Chair. Prof. Dr M. Solaiman Mandol; Man. Dir Nur Ahmad; 280 brs.

STOCK EXCHANGE

Dhaka Stock Exchange: Dhaka; f. 1960; 120 mems.

INSURANCE

Department of Insurance (attached to Ministry of Commerce): 74 Motijheel C/A, Dhaka 1000; state-owned; controls activities of all insurers, home and foreign; Controller of Insurance Shamsuddin Ahmad.

In 1973 the two corporations below were formed, one for life insurance and the other for general insurance.

Jiban Bima Corpn: 24 Motijheel C/A, Dhaka 1000; tel. (2) 232047; state-owned; comprises 36 national life insurance cos; life insurance; Man. Dir M. A. Rahim.

Sadharan Bima Corpn: 33 Dilkusha C/A, Dhaka 1000; tel. (2) 252026; state-owned; general insurance; Man. Dir M. Shamsul Alam.

Trade and Industry

In 1972 the Government took over all cotton, jute and other major industrial enterprises and the tea estates. Management Boards were appointed by the Government. During 1976 and 1977 many tea plantations and the smaller industrial units were returned to the private sector. Further privatization, particularly in the jute and textile industries, was carried out in 1982. By 1986 the proportion of the country's industrial assets under government ownership had fallen to 45% (from 85% in 1972).

Export Promotion Bureau: 122-124 Motijheel C/A, Dhaka 1000; tel. (2) 232245; telex 642204; fax (2) 833167; f. 1972; attached to Ministry of Commerce; regional offices in Chittagong, Khulna and Rajshahi; brs in Comilla, Sylhet, Bogra and Barisal; Vice-Chair. Abu Syeed Chowdhury.

Planning Commission: Planning Commission Secretariat, G.O. Hostel, Sher-e-Bangla Nagar, Dhaka; f. 1972; govt agency responsible for all aspects of economic planning and development including the preparation of the five-year plans and annual development programmes (in conjunction with appropriate govt ministries), promotion of savings and investment, compilation of statistics and evaluation of development schemes and projects.

GOVERNMENT-SPONSORED ORGANIZATIONS

Bangladesh Chemical Industries Corpn: BCIC Bhaban, 30-31 Dilkusha C/A, Dhaka; tel. (2) 259852; telex 65847; Chair. A. K. M. Mosharraf Hossain.

Bangladesh Export Processing Zones Authority: 222 New Eskaton Rd, Dhaka 1000; tel. (2) 405032; telex 642268; f. 1983 to operate and control export processing zones in Bangladesh; Chair. Brig. (retd) A. K. M. Azizul Islam.

Bangladesh Fisheries Development Corpn: 24/25 Dilkusha C/A, Motijheel, Dhaka 1000; tel. (2) 259190; telex 255518; f. 1964; Chair. Brig. (retd) Sirajul Haque.

Bangladesh Forest Industries Development Corpn: 186 Circular Rd, Motijheel C/A, Dhaka 1000; Chair. M. Atikullah.

Bangladesh Jute Mills Corpn: Adamjee Court (Annexe), 115-120 Motijheel C/A, Dhaka 1000; tel. (2) 238192; telex 675676; fax (2) 833329; f. 1972; operates 35 jute mills, incl. 2 carpet mills; world's largest manufacturer and exporter of jute goods; Chair. Muhammad Nefaur Rahman.

Bangladesh Mineral Exploration and Development Corpn: HBFC Bldg, 8th-9th Floors, 22 Purana Paltan, Dhaka 1000; telex 65737; Chair. M. W. Ali.

Bangladesh Oil, Gas and Mineral Corpn (Petrobangla): 122-124 Motijheel C/A, Chamber Bldg, Dhaka 1000; tel. (2) 253131; telex 725; Chair. Abdus Sattar (acting).

Bangladesh Small and Cottage Industries Corpn (BSCIC): 137/138 Motijheel C/A, Dhaka 1000; tel. (2) 233202; f. 1957; Chair. Muhammad Sirajuddin.

Bangladesh Steel and Engineering Corpn: Bangladesh Steel House, Airport Rd, Kawran Bazar, Dhaka; tel. (2) 315145; telex 642225; Chair. Nefaur Rahman.

Bangladesh Sugar and Food Industries Corpn: Shilpa Bhaban, Motijheel C/A, Dhaka 1000; tel. (2) 258084; telex 642210; f. 1972; Chair. M. Nefaur Rahman.

Bangladesh Textile Mills Corpn: Shadharan Bima Bhaban, 33 Dilkusha C/A, Dhaka 1000; tel. (2) 252504; telex 65703; f. 1972; Chair. M. Nurunnabi Chowdhury.

Trading Corpn of Bangladesh: HBFC Bldg, 22 Purana Paltan, Dhaka 1000; tel. (2) 325030; telex 642217; f. 1972; Chair. A. K. M. Azizul Islam.

CHAMBERS OF COMMERCE

Federation of Bangladesh Chambers of Commerce and Industry (FBCCI): Federation Bhaban, 60 Motijheel C/A, 4th Floor, POB 2079, Dhaka 1000; tel. (2) 250566; telex 642733; f. 1973; Pres. Akhtaruzzaman Chowdhury.

Agrabad Chamber of Commerce and Industry: Chamber Bldg, Bangabandhu Rd, POB 70, Chittagong; tel. (31) 501031; Pres. L. D. B. Bryceson.

Barisal Chamber of Commerce and Industry: Asad Mansion, 1st Floor, Sadar Rd, Barisal; tel. (431) 3984; Pres. Kazi Israil Hossain.

Bogra Chamber of Commerce and Industry: Chamber Bhaban, Jhautola, Bogra 5800; tel. (51) 6257; f. 1963; Pres. Taher Uddin Chowdhury.

Chittagong Chamber of Commerce and Industry: Chamber House, Agrabad C/A, POB 481, Chittagong; tel. (31) 502325; telex 66472; f. 1959; 3,516 mems; Pres. Amir Khosru Mahmud Chowdhury; Sec. M. H. Chowdhury.

Comilla Chamber of Commerce and Industry: Rammala Rd, Ranir Bazar, Comilla; tel. (81) 5444; Pres. Afzal Khan.

Dhaka Chamber of Commerce and Industry: Dhaka Chamber Bldg, 65-66 Motijheel C/A, POB 2641, Dhaka 1000; tel. (2) 234383; telex 642418; f. 1958; 4,000 mems; Pres. A. S. Mahmud; Sr Vice-Pres. A. M. Mubash-Shar.

Dinajpur Chamber of Commerce and Industry: Jail Rd, Dinajpur; tel. (531) 3189; Pres. Khairul Anam.

Faridpur Chamber of Commerce and Industry: Chamber House, Niltuly, Faridpur; tel. 3530; Pres. Khandoker Mohsin Ali.

Khulna Chamber of Commerce and Industry: 6 Lower Jessore Rd, Khulna; tel. (41) 24135; f. 1934; Pres. S. K. Zahoiul Islam.

Khustia Chamber of Commerce and Industry: 15, NS Rd, Kushtia; tel. (71) 3448; Pres. Din Mohammad.

Metropolitan Chamber of Commerce and Industry: Chamber Bldg, 4th Floor, 122-124 Motijheel C/A, Dhaka 1000; tel. (2) 235168; telex 642413; fax (2) 833075; f. 1904; 241 mems; Pres. Syed Manzur Elahi; Sec. C. K. Hyder.

Noakhali Chamber of Commerce and Industry: Noakhali Pourshara Bhaban, 2nd Floor, Maiydee Court, Noakhali; tel. 5229; Pres. Mohammad Nazibur Rahman.

Rajshahi Chamber of Commerce and Industry: Chamber Bldg, Station Rd, Ghoramara; tel. 2215; f. 1960; 48 mems; Pres. Mesbahuddin Ahmed.

Sylhet Chamber of Commerce and Industry: Chamber Bldg, Jail Rd, POB 97, Sylhet 3100; tel. (821) 4403; Pres. M. A. Mumin.

TRADE ASSOCIATIONS

Bangladeshiyo Cha Sangsad (Tea Assen of Bangladesh): 6 Jahan Bldg, 2nd Floor, 93 Agrabad C/A, POB 287, Chittagong; tel. (31) 501009; f. 1952; Chair. Faiz Ahmad; Sec. M. A. H. al-Azad.

Bangladesh Jute Association: BJA Bldg, 77 Motijheel C/A, Dhaka; tel. (2) 256558; Chair. M.A. Mannan; Sec. S. H. Prodhan.

Bangladesh Jute Goods Association: 3rd Floor, 150 Motijheel C/A, Dhaka 1000; tel. (2) 253640; f. 1979; 17 mems; Chair. M. A. Kashem, Haji Mohammad Ali.

BANGLADESH

Bangladesh Jute Mills Association: 8th Floor, Hadi Mansion, 2 Dilkusha C/A, Dhaka 1000; tel. (2) 253279; Chair. SYED MOHSEN ALI.

Bangladesh Jute Spinners Association: 55 Purana Paltan, 3rd Floor, Dhaka 1000; tel. (2) 231317; telex 642413; f. 1979; 33 mems; Chair. MUHAMMAD SHAMS-UL HAQUE; Sec. SHAHIDUL KARIM.

Bangladesh Tea Board: 111/113 Motijheel C/A, Dhaka 1000; tel. (2) 282141; telex 66304; Chair. Brig. AMIN AHMED CHOWDHURY.

Jute Marketing and Export Corporation: 14 Topkhana Rd, Dhaka; tel. (2) 236090; Chair. MUSTAFIZUR RAHMAN.

CO-OPERATIVES

Bangladesh Co-operative Marketing Society: 9D Motijheel C/A, Dhaka 1000.

Chattagram Bahini Kalyan Shamabaya Samity Ltd: 70 Agrabad C/A, Osman Court, Chittagong; f. 1972.

TRADE UNIONS

The ban on trade union activity was lifted in January 1986. Anti-Government strikes were banned in November 1987.

In 1986 only about 3% of the total labour force was unionized. There were 2,614 registered unions, organized mainly on a sectoral or occupational basis. There were about 17 national trade unions to represent workers at the national level.

Transport

RAILWAYS

Bangladesh Railway: Railway HQ, Chittagong; tel. (31) 500120; telex 66200; supervised by the Railway Division of the Ministry of Communications; divided into East and West zones, with HQ at Chittagong and Rajshahi (tel. 2576); total length of running track 4,439.8 km (June 1989); 502 stations; Dir-Gen. (Railway Div.) MANZUR-UL-KARIM; Gen. Man. (East Zone) A. K. M. ZAINUL ABEDIN; Gen. Man. (West Zone) M. LUTFUR RAHMAN; Gen. Man. (Projects) A. K. M. AMANUL ISLAM CHOWDHURY.

ROADS

Of the 6,240 km of road, about 3,840 km are metalled. More than 3,500 km of road and 250 bridges were destroyed in the disastrous monsoon floods in 1988.

Bangladesh Road Transport Corpn: Paribhaban, DIT Ave, Dhaka; f. 1961; transportation services including a truck division, transports govt foodgrain; 700 vehicles (1980).

INLAND WATERWAYS

In Bangladesh there are some 8,433 km of navigable waterways, which transport 70% of total domestic and foreign cargo traffic and on which are located the main river ports of Dhaka, Narayanganj, Chandpur, Barisal and Khulna. A river steamer service connects these ports several times a week. Vessels of up to 175-m overall length can be navigated on the Karnaphuli river.

Bangladesh Inland Water Transport Corpn: 5 Dilkusha C/A, Dhaka 1000; tel. (2) 257092; f. 1972; 273 vessels (1986).

SHIPPING

The chief ports are Chittagong, where the construction of a second dry-dock is planned, and Chalna. A modern seaport is being developed at Mangla.

Atlas Shipping Lines Ltd: Jiban Bima Bhaban, SK. Mujib Rd, Agrabad C/A, Chittagong 2; tel. (31) 504287; telex 66213; fax (31) 225520; Man. Dir S. U. CHOWDHURY.

Bangladesh Shipping Corpn: Pine View, 100 Agrabad C/A, POB 641, Chittagong; tel. (31) 501855; telex 66277; f. 1972; maritime shipping; 21 vessels, 270,153 tons capacity (1987); Chair. JANAB M. KORBAN ALI; Man. Dir TARECK ANIS AHMED.

Bangladesh Steam Navigation Co Ltd: Dhaka; coastal services; Chair. A. K. KHAN; Man. Dir A. M. Z. KHAN.

Chittagong Port Authority: POB 2013, Chittagong 4100; tel. (31) 505041; telex 66264; f. 1887; provides bunkering, ship repair, towage and lighterage facilities as well as provisions and drinking water supplies; Chair. MD SHAHADAT HUSSAIN.

United Shipping Corpn Ltd: Dhaka.

CIVIL AVIATION

There is an international airport at Dhaka (Zia International Airport) situated at Kurmitola and opened in 1980, with the capacity to handle 5m. passengers annually. There are also airports at all major towns.

Biman Bangladesh Airlines: Biman Bhaban, Motijheel C/A, Dhaka 1000; tel. (2) 240151; telex 642649; fax (2) 833005; f. 1972; 100% state-owned; internal services to all major towns; international services to Bahrain, Bhutan, France, Germany, Greece, India, Iraq, Italy, Kuwait, Libya, Malaysia, Myanmar, Nepal, the Netherlands, Oman, Pakistan, Qatar, Saudi Arabia, Singapore, Thailand, the UAE and the United Kingdom; Chair. Minister of Civil Aviation and Tourism; Man. Dir Group Capt. (retd) M. SHAWKAT-UL-ISLAM; fleet of 3 British Aerospace ATP, 2 F-28 and 4 DC 10-30.

Tourism

Tourist attractions include the cities of Dhaka and Chittagong, Cox's Bazar—which has the world's longest beach (120 km)—on the Bay of Bengal, and Teknaf, at the southernmost point of Bangladesh. Tourist arrivals totalled 93,405 in 1989. The majority of visitors are from India, Pakistan, Japan, the United Kingdom and the USA. Earnings from tourism increased from 230m. taka in 1981 to 900m. taka in 1985.

Bangladesh Parjatan Corpn (National Tourism Organization): 233 Old Airport Rd, Tejgaon, Dhaka 1215; tel. (2) 325155; telex 642206; there are four tourist information centres in Dhaka, and one each in Bogra, Chittagong, Cox's Bazar, Khulna, Rajshahi and Rangamati; Chair. HABIBUR RAHMAN; Gen. Man. (Information, Tours and Public Relations) GAZI SADEQ.

Atomic Energy

Bangladesh Atomic Energy Commission (BAEC): 4 Kazi Nazrul Islam Ave, POB 158, Dhaka 1000; tel. (2) 502600; telex 632203; f. 1964 as Atomic Energy Centre of the fmr Pakistan Atomic Energy Comm. in East Pakistan, reorg. 1973; operates an atomic energy research establishment and a 3-MW research nuclear reactor (inaugurated in January 1987) at Savar, an atomic energy centre at Dhaka, ten nuclear medicine centres, and a beach-sand exploitation centre at Cox's Bazar; nuclear power project involving the exploitation of uranium and thorium; gamma radiation sources for food preservation and industrial radiography; construction of a 320-MW nuclear power plant at Rooppur, with technical assistance from Germany, to begin operating in mid-1990s; Chair. Dr M. A. MANNAN; Sec. RAFIQUL ALAM.

BARBADOS

Introductory Survey

Location, Climate, Language, Religion, Flag, Capital

Barbados is the most easterly of the Caribbean islands, lying about 320 km (200 miles) north-east of Trinidad. There is a rainy season from July to November and the climate is cool during the rest of the year. The mean annual temperature is about 26°C (78°F). The language is English. Almost all of the inhabitants profess Christianity, but there are small groups of Hindus, Muslims and Jews. The largest denomination is the Anglican church, but about 90 other Christian sects are represented. The national flag (proportions 3 by 2) has three equal vertical stripes, of blue, gold and blue; superimposed on the centre of the gold band is the head of a black trident. The capital is Bridgetown.

Recent History

Barbados was formerly a British colony. The Barbados Labour Party (BLP) won a general election in 1951, when universal adult suffrage was introduced, and held office until 1961. Although the parliamentary system dates from 1639, ministerial government was not established until 1954, when the BLP's leader, Sir Grantley Adams, became the island's first Premier. He was subsequently Prime Minister of the West Indies Federation from January 1958 until its dissolution in May 1962.

Barbados achieved full internal self-government in October 1961. An election in December 1961 was won by the Democratic Labour Party (DLP), formed in 1955 by dissident members of the BLP. The DLP's leader, Errol Barrow, became Premier, succeeding Dr Hugh Cummins of the BLP. When Barbados achieved independence on 30 November 1966, Barrow became the island's first Prime Minister, having won another election earlier in the month.

The DLP retained power in 1971, but in the general election of September 1976 the BLP, led by J. M. G. M. ('Tom') Adams (Sir Grantley's son), ended Barrow's 15-year rule. The BLP successfully campaigned against alleged government corruption, winning a large majority over the DLP. Both parties were committed to retaining a system of free enterprise and alignment with the USA. At a general election in June 1981 the BLP was returned to office, owing mainly to its economic achievements in government, with 17 of the 27 seats in the newly enlarged House of Assembly. The remainder of the seats were won by the DLP. A cabinet reshuffle took place in early 1983, and in September the Minister of Health, Dr Donald Blackman, left the Cabinet following allegations that he had publicly criticized a fellow minister. There was also disagreement between the Government and the opposition concerning the amount spent on defence. Adams died suddenly in March 1985 and was succeeded as Prime Minister by his deputy, Bernard St John, a former leader of the BLP.

At a general election in May 1986 the DLP won a decisive victory, receiving 59.4% of the total votes and winning 24 of the 27 seats in the House of Assembly. Bernard St John and all except one of his cabinet ministers lost their seats, and Errol Barrow returned as Prime Minister after 10 years in opposition. The new Government later introduced a programme of tax reforms, which was intended to reduce expenditure and borrowing by the public sector. In June 1986 it was announced that Barrow was to review Barbados' participation in the US-supported Regional Security System (RSS), the defence force that had been established soon after the US invasion of Grenada in October 1983. Barbados, under Adams, was one of the countries whose troops supported the invasion. In November 1986 Barrow announced a halt in recruitment to the Barbados Defence Force. In June 1987 Barrow died suddenly. He was succeeded by L. Erskine Sandiford (hitherto the Deputy Prime Minister), who pledged to continue Barrow's economic and social policies.

In September 1987, however, the Minister of Finance, Dr Richard (Richie) Haynes, resigned, accusing Sandiford of failing to consult him over financial appointments. Sandiford assumed the financial portfolio, but acrimony over government policy continued to trouble the DLP into 1988. In February 1989 Haynes and three other Members of Parliament resigned from the DLP and announced the formation of the National Democratic Party (NDP). Haynes, who accused the Government of reneging on its election commitments by increasing taxation in 1988, was subsequently appointed as leader of the parliamentary opposition. This was recognition of the NDP's total of four seats in the House of Assembly, compared with the three of the BLP, although the latter party had won some 40% of the votes cast in the previous general election. Further disputes within the DLP during 1990, including the resignation of a government senator in October, increased speculation that an early general election was likely.

Relations with Trinidad and Tobago were strained between 1982 and 1985 by publicly-stated differences over the intervention in Grenada, and by Trinidad and Tobago's imposition of import restrictions (a compromise on this was reached in August 1986). In May 1988 talks were held with Trinidad and Tobago to resolve a fishing dispute, and in November 1990 the two Governments signed a bilateral fishing agreement, to take effect in January 1991. In mid-1989 it was agreed that Trinidad and Tobago's national airline, BWIA, was to be designated as the region's official carrier on the route to the United Kingdom. The Governments of Barbados, Trinidad and Tobago and several other eastern Caribbean countries agreed to adopt a common position in negotiations with the United Kingdom for a multilateral air transport agreement. Some success in this respect was achieved during 1990.

In 1988 relations with Jamaica were strained over the approach to events in Haiti, and the Barbadian pressure for closer integration within CARICOM (see p. 108). Moves towards a Caribbean internal market continued, despite political differences and trade tensions with the OECS (see p. 109) in late 1987. In June 1988 import duties were abolished for all but four CARICOM countries.

Government

Executive power is vested in the British monarch, represented by a Governor-General, who acts on the advice of the Cabinet. The Governor-General appoints the Prime Minister and, on the latter's recommendation, other members of the Cabinet. Legislative power is vested in the bicameral Parliament, comprising a Senate of 21 members, appointed by the Governor-General, and a House of Assembly with 27 members, elected by universal adult suffrage for five years (subject to dissolution) from single-member constituencies. During 1990 a new constituency was created, which would give the House of Assembly a total of 28 members after the next general election (scheduled to take place by June 1991). The Cabinet is responsible to Parliament. Elected local government bodies were abolished in 1969 in favour of a division into 11 parishes, all of which are administered by the central Government.

Defence

The Barbados Defence Force, established in April 1978, consists of 154 regular personnel. It is divided into regular defence units and a coastguard service with armed patrol boats; there is also a volunteer force and a reserve. Government spending on defence in the 1988/89 financial year was Bds $17.3m., representing 1.8% of total budget expenditure.

Economic Affairs

In 1988, according to estimates by the World Bank, the island's gross national product (GNP), measured at average 1986–88 prices, was US $1,530m., equivalent to US $5,990 per head. Between 1980 and 1988, it was estimated, GNP increased, in real terms, at an average annual rate of 1.7%, while GNP per head increased by 1.4% per year. Over the same period, the population increased by 0.3% per year. Between 1980 and 1987, Barbados' gross domestic product (GDP), at factor cost, increased, in real terms, by an annual average of 0.8%. In 1989 GDP increased, in real terms, by an estimated 3.7%. Real GDP growth was expected to be negligible during 1990.

Agriculture (excluding the sugar industry, but including forestry and fishing) contributed 4.0% of GDP in 1988, and 8.0% of the working population were employed in agriculture as a whole in 1987. The sugar sector of the economy (including refining) contributed 2.5% of GDP in 1988, and sugar remains the main commodity export, earning Bds $47.1m. (12.6% of total exports) in 1989. Sea-island cotton, once the island's main export crop, was revived in the mid-1980s and is again an important export. The other principal crops, primarily for local consumption, are sweet potatoes, carrots, yams and other vegetables and fruit. Fishing was also developed in the 1980s, and Barbados is now virtually self-sufficient. In 1988 there was a fleet of about 750 fishing vessels.

Industry (excluding sugar refining) accounted for 19.2% of GDP in 1988. Overall growth in industrial production between 1981 and 1987 was negligible. In 1988, however, it increased by almost 6%, compared with the previous year.

Owing to fluctuations in international prices, the production of crude petroleum declined by some 37% from its peak in 1985, to 427,100 barrels in 1988, or 30% of Barbados' requirements. Production of natural gas, however, increased to 35m. cu m in 1988. Mining, together with construction (an industry that contributed over 6% to GDP in 1988), employed 7.9% of the working population in 1987.

Manufacturing contributed 9.0% to GDP in 1988, and employed 12.6% of the working population in 1987. Real output in the sector increased by 5.4% in 1989, particularly on account of the production levels of chemicals and wooden furniture. Excluding sugar factories and refineries, the principal branches of manufacturing, measured by the value of output, in 1986 were food products (accounting for 26.1% of the total), chemical, petroleum, plastic and rubber products (22.8%) and beverages and tobacco (13.6%). Other important activities are the manufacture of garments and electrical components.

Service industries are the main sector of the economy. Finance, business and insurance services contributed 13.5% of GDP in 1988. The Government has encouraged the growth of 'offshore' financial facilities, particularly by the negotiation of double taxation agreements with other countries. By the end of 1988 there were some 650 companies registered in the 'offshore' sector, including 150 international business companies, 263 foreign sales corporations and 156 exempt insurance companies. One new 'offshore' bank was licensed in 1988, bringing the total of such banks to six. In the same year the sector contributed Bds $40m. in foreign earnings.

Tourism made a direct contribution of 11.8% to GDP in 1988. Tourism and trade employed 22.4% of the working population in 1987. Tourist expenditure almost doubled between 1980 and 1988, increasing by 21% in the latter year alone, to Bds $918.5m. Stop-over tourist arrivals increased by 2.2% in 1989, to 461,258, and cruise-ship passenger arrivals increased by about 16%, to some 337,100. In 1988 about 38% of stop-over arrivals were from the USA, 14% from Canada and 22% from the United Kingdom (a percentage that has almost doubled since 1986).

In 1989 Barbados recorded a visible trade deficit of US $373m., but receipts of US $658m. from services helped to restrict the total deficit on goods and services to US $20m. There was a small surplus of US $8m. on the current account of the balance of payments. In 1988 the principal source of imports (35%) was the USA, which was also the principal single market for exports (21%). Other major trading partners included the United Kingdom (11% of imports, 17% of exports) and the CARICOM nations (14% of imports, 27% of exports). Barbados' principal trading partner within CARICOM is Trinidad and Tobago, which accounted for 9% of total imports and 7% of exports in 1988. The principal commodity exports were provided by the sugar industry (sugar, molasses, syrup and rum). The principal imports were machinery, transport equipment and basic manufactures.

For the financial year ending 31 March 1991 there was a projected total budgetary deficit (including both current and capital expenditure) of Bds $212m., although the current budget itself was expected to record a surplus of Bds $16m.

At December 1989 the national debt of Barbados was Bds $1,695.1m., of which 48% was external debt. The average annual rate of inflation was 6.0% between 1980 and 1989, and 6.2% in 1989 alone. At the end of 1988, some 19% of the labour force remained unemployed.

Political stability and consensus have contributed to the economic strengths of Barbados. Successive Governments have attempted to broaden the economic base of the island. Services remain the principal sector of the economy and are dominated by tourism, but 'offshore' banking has been developed, particularly since the mid-1980s. Another successful 'offshore' industry that has been officially encouraged is data processing, mainly for US firms. Manufacturing is also an important sector, although it suffered from the closure of several electrical components firms in 1985 and 1986. Barbados aims for self-sufficiency in petroleum. The diversification of agriculture was expected to improve supply to the local market, while sugar remains the principal agricultural export. There was, however, concern that those industries which earned foreign exchange had not been major contributors to the growth in GDP of the late 1980s. The sugar industry and the tourist sector did not perform strongly in 1990, and no real growth in GDP was expected in that year.

Social Welfare

A social security scheme was established in 1967, and a National Drug Plan was introduced in 1980. Old-age pensions and unemployment insurance are available. The Government has also created a building scheme of group housing for lower-income families. In 1982 Barbados had 11 hospital establishments, with a total of 2,151 beds, and there were 221 physicians working on the island. Government expenditure on health services in the 1988/89 financial year was Bds $127.3m., which represented 13.1% of total budgetary spending, while social security and welfare received 9.8% of current expenditure.

Education

Education is compulsory for 11 years, between five and 16 years of age. Primary education begins at the age of five and lasts for six years. Secondary education, beginning at 11 years of age, also lasts for six years, divided into two equal cycles. Enrolment of children in the primary age-group was 99% in 1982. The ratio for secondary schoolchildren was 89% in 1984. Tuition at all government schools is free, and the State provides for approximately 86% of those eligible for primary and secondary education. The adult literacy rate was believed to be 98% in 1985. In 1986 there were 126 primary and secondary schools, six senior schools, a community college, a teacher training college, a theological college, a technical institute and a polytechnic. Degree courses in arts, law, education, natural sciences and social sciences are offered at the Barbados branch of the University of the West Indies. The faculty of medicine administers the East Caribbean Medical Scheme, while an in-service training programme for graduate teachers in secondary schools is provided by the School of Education. Government expenditure on education was Bds $185.6m., or 19.1% of total budgetary spending, in the 1988/89 financial year.

Public Holidays

1991: 1 January (New Year's Day), 21 January (Errol Barrow Day), 29 March (Good Friday), 1 April (Easter Monday), 1 May (Labour Day), 20 May (Whit Monday), 5 August (Kadooment Day), 7 October (United Nations Day), 30 November (Independence Day), 25–26 December (Christmas).

1992: 1 January (New Year's Day), 20 January (Errol Barrow Day), 17 April (Good Friday), 20 April (Easter Monday), 4 May (Labour Day), 8 June (Whit Monday), 3 August (Kadooment Day), 7 October (United Nations Day), 30 November (Independence Day), 25–26 December (Christmas).

Weights and Measures

The metric system is used.

BARBADOS

Statistical Survey

Sources (unless otherwise stated): Barbados Statistical Service, National Insurance Bldg, Fairchild St, Bridgetown; tel. 427-7841; Central Bank of Barbados, POB 1016, Bridgetown; tel. 436-6870.

AREA AND POPULATION

Area: 430 sq km (166 sq miles).

Population: 252,029 (males 119,665, females 132,364) at census of 12 May 1980; 256,000 (provisional official estimate) at mid-1989.

Density (mid-1989): 595.3 per sq km.

Ethnic Groups (*de jure* population, excl. persons resident in institutions 1980 census): Negro 224,565; Mixed race 6,362; White 7,953; Total (incl. others) 244,228. Source: UN, *Demographic Yearbook*.

Principal Town: Bridgetown (capital), population 7,466 at 1980 census. Source: UN, *Demographic Yearbook*.

Births, Marriages and Deaths (registrations): Live births 3,739 (birth rate 14.7 per 1,000) in 1988; Marriages 1,461 (marriage rate 5.8 per 1,000) in 1986; Deaths 2,198 (death rate 8.6 per 1,000) in 1988. Source: UN, *Demographic Yearbook*.

Economically Active Population (labour force sample survey, '000 persons, excluding institutional households, 1988): Agriculture, forestry and fishing 9.3; Manufacturing 15.5; Electricity, gas and water 1.5; Construction and quarrying 10.7; Trade, restaurants and hotels 28.5; Transport, storage and communications 4.7; Financing, insurance, real estate and business services 3.9; Government and other services 43.5; Total labour force 117.6 (males 61.8, females 55.8). Figures exclude 4,100 unemployed persons (1,100 males, 3,000 females) not previously employed, but include 17,100 other unemployed. Source: ILO, *Year Book of Labour Statistics*.

AGRICULTURE, ETC.

Principal Crops (FAO estimates, metric tons, 1989): Maize 2,000; Sweet potatoes 3,000; Yams 2,000; Other roots and tubers 1,000; Coconuts 2,000; Carrots 2,000; Other vegetables 4,000; Fruit 3,000; Sugar cane 675,000 (unofficial estimate). Source: FAO, *Production Yearbook*.

Livestock (FAO estimates, '000 head, year ending September 1989): Horses, mules and asses 5; Cattle 18; Pigs 49; Sheep 56; Goats 34; Chickens 1,000. Source: FAO, *Production Yearbook*.

Livestock Products (metric tons, 1988): Beef 390; Veal 8; Chicken and turkey meat 9,000; Mutton 23; Pig meat 1,176; Cows' milk 11,840; Hen eggs 1,584.

Fishing (metric tons, live weight): Total catch 4,227 in 1986; 3,702 in 1987; 9,097 (Flying fishes 6,269; Common dolphinfish 2,011) in 1988. Source: FAO, *Yearbook of Fishery Statistics*.

MINING

Production (1988): Natural gas 35.3 million cu m.; Crude petroleum 69,132,000 litres.

INDUSTRY

Production (1988, unless otherwise indicated): Raw sugar 69,300 metric tons (1990); Rum 3,329,000 litres; Beer 7,551,000 litres; Cigarettes 149 metric tons; Batteries 20,003; Electric energy 449m. kWh.

FINANCE

Currency and Exchange Rates: 100 cents = 1 Barbados dollar (Bds $). *Coins:* 1, 5, 10 and 25 cents; 1 dollar. *Notes:* 1, 2, 5, 10, 20 and 100 dollars. *Sterling and US Dollar equivalents* (30 September 1990): £1 sterling = Bds $3.768; US $1 = Bds $2.011; Bds $100 = £26.54 = US $49.72. *Exchange Rate:* Fixed at US $1 = Bds $2.0113 since August 1977.

Budget (Bds $ '000, year ending 31 March 1989): *Current Revenue:* Tax revenue 743,796 (Taxes on income and profit 222,708; Taxes on property 47,739; Taxes on goods and services 265,811; Import duties 119,830; Stamp duties 82,708); Non-tax revenue 138,587 (Government departments 67,117); Total 882,383. *Current Expenditure:* General public services 128,608; Defence 17,312; Education 170,599; Health 112,999; Social security and welfare 76,319; Housing and community amenities 36,822; Other community and social services 12,033; Economic services 116,509 (Agriculture 18,000; Roads and other transport 66,085); Debt charges 109,729; Total 780,930. *Capital expenditure:* Education 14,976; Health 14,252; Housing and community amenities 17,583; Economic services 87,467 (Agriculture 14,404; Roads and other transport 63,507); Total 191,478. *1989/90* (Bds $ million): Current revenue 905.1; Current expenditure 985.1; Capital expenditure 218.8. *1990/91* (estimates, Bds $ million): Current revenue 1,002.7; Current expenditure 987.2; Capital expenditure 227.8.

International Reserves (US $ million at 31 December 1989): Gold 3.11; Reserve position in IMF 2.86; Foreign exchange 106.60 (Monetary Authorities 92.73, Govt 13.87); Total 112.57. Source: IMF, *International Financial Statistics*.

Money Supply (Bds $ million at 31 December 1989): Currency outside banks 182.72; Demand deposits at commercial banks 260.32. Source: IMF, *International Financial Statistics*.

Cost of Living (retail price index; base: 1985 = 100): 104.7 in 1987; 109.8 in 1988; 116.6 in 1989.

Gross Domestic Product (Bds $ million in current purchasers' values): 2,646.0 in 1986; 2,847.6 in 1987; 3,097.0 in 1988.

Balance of Payments (US $ million, 1988): Merchandise exports f.o.b. 144.8; Merchandise imports f.o.b. −517.9; *Trade balance* −373.0; Exports of services 658.4; Imports of services −305.2; *Balance on goods and services* −19.8; Unrequited transfers (net) 28.2; *Current balance* 8.4; Direct capital investment (net) 10.5; Other long-term capital (net) 20.9; Short-term capital (net) 10.4; Net errors and omissions −12.2; *Total* (net monetary movements) 38.0; Valuation changes (net) 3.9; *Changes in reserves* 41.9. Source: IMF, *International Financial Statistics*.

EXTERNAL TRADE

Principal Commodities (Bds $ '000, 1988): *Imports:* Food and live animals 181,879; Beverages and tobacco 29,041; Crude materials (inedible) except fuels 36,215; Mineral fuels, lubricants, etc. 110,480; Animal and vegetable oils and fats 12,864; Chemicals 125,909; Basic manufactures 223,410; Machinery and transport equipment 269,317; Miscellaneous manufactured articles 137,141; Other commodities and transactions 37,625; Total 1,163,881. *Exports:* Sugar 62,950; Molasses and syrup 5,519; Rum 10,939; Semi-processed and other food products 14,649; Basic manufactures 86,007; Machinery and transport equipment 62,012; Chemicals 39,485; Mineral fuels, lubricants, etc. 57,903; Other items 14,729; Total 354,194. (*1989* (Bds $ million): Imports c.i.f. 1,354.0; Exports f.o.b. 374.46 (Sugar 47.06). Source: IMF, *International Financial Statistics*.

Principal Trading Partners (Bds $ '000, 1988): *Imports:* Canada 82,263; CARICOM countries 162,795 (Trinidad and Tobago 104,874); Japan 63,656; United Kingdom 133,687; USA 401,753; Total (incl. others) 1,163,881. *Exports:* Canada 12,243; CARICOM countries 94,701 (Trinidad and Tobago 25,047); Puerto Rico 11,124; United Kingdom 66,234; USA 75,645; Total (incl. others) 354,194.

TRANSPORT

Road Traffic (motor vehicles in use, 1988): Passenger cars (incl. hired cars and taxis) 37,459; Pick-ups, vans and station wagons 2,722; Lorries 1,817; Buses and minibuses 473; Tractors 644; Motor cycles 1,525.

International Shipping (estimated freight traffic, '000 metric tons, 1985): Goods loaded 211; Goods unloaded 460. Source: UN, *Monthly Bulletin of Statistics*.

Civil Aviation (1987): Aircraft movements 31,600; Freight loaded 4,054.9 metric tons; Freight unloaded 7,741.4 metric tons.

TOURISM

Tourist Arrivals: *Stop-overs:* 421,859 in 1987; 451,485 in 1988; 461,258 in 1989. *Cruise-ship passengers:* 224,778 in 1987; 290,993 in 1988; 337,100 (provisional) in 1989.

COMMUNICATIONS MEDIA

Radio Receivers (1988): 222,720 in use.

Television Receivers (1988): 65,792 in use.

Telephones (1987): 94,338 in use.

Book Production (1983): 87 titles (18 books, 69 pamphlets).

Daily Newspapers (1986): 2 (circulation 40,000). Source: UNESCO, *Statistical Yearbook*.

EDUCATION

Pre-primary (state education): 126 schools (1982); 132 teachers (1982); 3,602 pupils (1987).

Primary (1985/86): 105 schools; 28,235 pupils.

Secondary (1985/86): 21 schools; 21,501 pupils.

BARBADOS

Senior (1985/86): 6 schools; 1,050 students.
Technical (1985/86): 1 institution; 1,852 students.
Teacher Training (1985/86): 1 institution; 87 students.
Theological (1985/86): 1 institution; 20 students.
Community College (1985/86): 1 institution; 1,750 students.
University of the West Indies (1985/86): 1 institution; 1,932 students.

There are also 15 government-aided independent schools and 23 non-aided independent schools, with 4,311 and 3,586 students respectively in 1985/86.

Teachers (1984): Primary 1,421; Secondary (incl. senior schools) 1,449; Tertiary 544 (Source: UNESCO, *Statistical Yearbook*).

Directory

The Constitution

The parliamentary system has been established since the 17th century, when the first Assembly sat, in 1639, and the Charter of Barbados was granted, in 1652. A new constitution came into force on 30 November 1966, when Barbados became independent. Under its terms, protection is afforded to individuals from slavery and forced labour, from inhuman treatment, deprivation of property, arbitrary search and entry, and racial discrimination; freedom of conscience, of expression, assembly, and movement are guaranteed.

Executive power is nominally vested in the British monarch, as Head of State, represented in Barbados by a Governor-General, who appoints the Prime Minister and, on the advice of the Prime Minister, appoints other Ministers and some Senators.

The Cabinet consists of the Prime Minister, appointed by the Governor-General as being the person best able to command a majority in the House of Assembly, and not fewer than five other Ministers. Provision is also made for a Privy Council, presided over by the Governor-General.

Parliament consists of the Governor-General and a bicameral legislature, comprising the Senate and the House of Assembly. The Senate has 21 members: 12 appointed by the Governor-General on the advice of the Prime Minister, two on the advice of the Leader of the Opposition, and seven as representatives of such interests as the Governor-General considers appropriate. The House of Assembly has (since 1981) 27 members, elected by universal adult suffrage for a term of five years (subject to dissolution). The House of Assembly will have 28 members following the next general election, which is scheduled to take place in 1991. The minimum voting age is 18 years.

The Constitution also provides for the establishment of Service Commissions for the Judicial and Legal Service, the Public Service, the Police Service and the Statutory Boards Service. These Commissions are exempt from legal investigation; they have executive powers relating to appointments, dismissals and disciplinary control of the services for which they are responsible.

The Government

Head of State: HM Queen ELIZABETH II (succeeded to the throne 6 February 1952).

Governor-General: Dame NITA BARROW (took office 6 June 1990).

THE CABINET
(December 1990)

Prime Minister and Minister of the Civil Service, Finance and Economic Affairs: LLOYD ERSKINE SANDIFORD.

Deputy Prime Minister and Minister of International Transport, Telecommunications and Immigration: PHILIP M. GREAVES.

Minister of Foreign Affairs, Attorney-General and Minister of Legal Affairs: MAURICE A. KING.

Minister of Health: BRANDFORD M. TAITT.

Minister of Trade, Industry and Commerce: E. EVELYN GREAVES.

Minister of Housing and Lands: HAROLD A. BLACKMAN.

Minister of Agriculture, Food and Fisheries: WARWICK O. FRANKLYN.

Minister of Transport and Works: Dr DONALD BLACKMAN.

Minister of Tourism and Sports: WESLEY W. HALL.

Minister of Employment, Labour Relations and Community Development: N. KEITH SIMMONS.

Minister of Education and Culture: CYRIL V. WALKER.

Minister of State in the Ministry of Finance and Economic Affairs: Senator Dr CARL CLARKE.

Minister of State in the Office of the Prime Minister: Senator L. V. HARCOURT LEWIS.

MINISTRIES

Office of the Prime Minister: Government Headquarters, Bay St, St Michael; tel. 436-6435.

Ministry of Agriculture, Food and Fisheries: Graeme Hall, POB 505, Christ Church; tel. 428-4150.

Ministry of the Civil Service: Government Headquarters, Bay St, St Michael; tel. 429-8955.

Ministry of Education and Culture: Jemmot's Lane, St Michael; tel. 427-3272.

Ministry of Employment, Labour Relations and Community Development: Marine House, Hastings, Christ Church; tel. 427-5420.

Ministry of Finance and Economic Affairs: Government Headquarters, Bay St, St Michael; tel. 436-6435.

Ministry of Foreign Affairs: 1 Culloden Rd, St Michael; tel. 436-2990; telex 2222; fax 429-6652.

Ministry of Health: Jemmott's Lane, St Michael; tel. 426-5080; fax 426-5570.

Ministry of Housing and Lands: Marine House, Hastings, Christ Church; tel. 427-5420.

Ministry of International Transport, Telecommunications and Immigration: Herbert House, Reef Rd, Fontabelle, St Michael; tel. 427-5163.

Ministry of Legal Affairs: Marine House, Hastings, Christ Church; tel. 427-5420.

Ministry of Tourism and Sports: GPO Building, Cheapside, Bridgetown; tel. 436-4830; telex 2222; fax 436-9280.

Ministry of Trade, Industry and Commerce: Savannah Lodge, Garrison, St Michael; tel. 427-5270.

Ministry of Transport and Works: POB 25, Bridgetown; tel. 429-2191; telex 2203.

Legislature

PARLIAMENT

Senate

President: FRANK WALCOTT.

There are 20 other members.

House of Assembly

Speaker: LAWSON WEEKES.

Clerk of Parliament: GEORGE BRANCKER.

General Election, 28 May 1986

Party	Votes	%	Seats
Democratic Labour Party (DLP)	80,028	59.45	24*
Barbados Labour Party (BLP)	54,367	40.38	3
Others	227	0.17	—
Total	134,622	100.00	27

* In February 1989 four disaffected members of the ruling DLP formed a new opposition party, the National Democratic Party.

BARBADOS   *Directory*

Political Organizations

Barbados Labour Party: Grantley Adams House, 111 Roebuck St, Bridgetown; tel. 426-2274; f. 1938; moderate social democrat; Leader and Chair. HENRY FORDE; Gen. Sec. O'BRIEN TROTMAN.

Democratic Labour Party: George St, Belleville, St Michael; tel. 429-3104; f. 1955; Leader L. ERSKINE SANDIFORD; Gen. Sec. DAVID THOMPSON.

National Democratic Party: 'Sueños', 3 Sixth Ave, Belleville; tel. 429-6882; f. 1989 by split from Democratic Labour Party; Leader Dr RICHARD (RICHIE) HAYNES.

People's Pressures Movement: Bridgetown; f. 1979; Leader ERIC SEALY.

Workers' Party of Barbados: Bridgetown; tel. 425-1620; f. 1985; small left-wing organization; Gen. Sec. Dr GEORGE BELLE.

Diplomatic Representation

EMBASSIES AND HIGH COMMISSIONS IN BARBADOS

Brazil: Sunjet House, Independence Square, Bridgetown; tel. 427-1735; telex 2434; Ambassador: AMAURY BIER.

Canada: Bishops Court Hill, St Michael; tel. 429-3550; telex 2247; fax 429-3780; High Commissioner: JANET ZUKOWSKY.

China, People's Republic: 17 Golf View Terrace, Rockley, Christ Church; tel. 436-6042; telex 2363; Ambassador: LU ZONGQING.

Colombia: 'Rosemary', Dayrells Rd, Rockley, Christ Church; tel. 429-6821; telex 2499; Ambassador: LIGIA LONDOÑO (designate).

Costa Rica: 'Highbury House', Sandy Lane Estate, St James; tel. 432-1164; telex 2203; fax 429-4854; Chargé d'affaires a.i.: Dr LUIS CARLOS MORA CORRALES.

Trinidad and Tobago: Cockspur House, Nile St, Bridgetown; tel. 429-9600/1; telex 2326; High Commissioner: MAURICE ST JOHN.

United Kingdom: Lower Collymore Rock, POB 676, St Michael; tel. 436-6694; telex 2219; fax 426-7916; High Commissioner: EMRYS THOMAS DAVIES.

USA: Canadian Imperial Bank of Commerce Bldg, Broad St, POB 302, Bridgetown; tel. 436-4950; telex 2259; fax 429-5246; Ambassador: G. PHILLIP HUGHES.

Venezuela: El Sueño, Worthing, Christ Church; tel. 435-7619; telex 2339; Ambassador: ORESTES DI GIACOMO.

Judicial System

Justice is administered by the Supreme Court of Judicature, which consists of a High Court and a Court of Appeal. Final appeal lies with the Judicial Committee of the Privy Council, in the United Kingdom. There are Magistrates' Courts for lesser offences, with appeal to a Divisional Court of the High Court.

Supreme Court: Judiciary Office, Bridgetown; tel. 426-3461.

Chief Justice: Sir DENYS A. WILLIAMS.

Puisne Judges: CLIFFORD S. HUSBANDS, JOHN HUSBAND, ELLIOTT F. BELGRAVE, ERROL DACOSTA CHASE.

Registrar of the Supreme Court: MARIE MACCORMACK.

Chief Magistrate: FRANK KING.

Religion

More than 90 religious denominations and sects are represented in Barbados, but the vast majority of the population profess Christianity. According to the 1980 census, there were 96,894 Anglicans (or some 40% of the total population), while the Pentecostal (8%) and Methodist (7%) churches were next in importance. The regional Caribbean Conference of Churches (see p. 250) is based in Barbados. There are also small groups of Hindus, Muslims and Jews.

CHRISTIANITY

The Anglican Communion

Anglicans in Barbados are adherents of the Church in the Province of the West Indies, comprising eight dioceses. The Archbishop of the Province is the Bishop of the North Eastern Caribbean and Aruba, resident at St John's, Antigua. In Barbados there is a Provincial Office (St George's Church, St George) and an Anglican Theological College (Codrington College, St John).

Bishop of Barbados: Rt Rev. DREXEL GOMEZ, Diocesan Office, Mandeville House, Bridgetown; tel. 426-2761.

The Roman Catholic Church

Barbados comprises a single diocese (formed when the diocese of Bridgetown-Kingstown was divided in January 1990), which is suffragan to the archdiocese of Port of Spain (Trinidad and Tobago). In January 1990 there were an estimated 10,500 adherents in the diocese. The Bishop participates in the Antilles Episcopal Conference (currently based in Kingston, Jamaica).

Bishop of Bridgetown: Rt Rev. ANTHONY H. DICKSON, St Patrick's Cathedral, Jemmott's Lane, POB 1223, St Michael; tel. 426-2325.

Protestant Churches

Baptist Churches of Barbados: National Baptist Convention, President Kennedy Dr., Bridgetown; tel. 429-2697.

Church of God (Caribbean Atlantic Assembly): St Michael's Plaza, St Michael's Row, POB 1, Bridgetown; tel. 427-5770; Pres. Rev. VICTOR BABB.

Church of Jesus Christ of Latter-day Saints (Mormons)—West Indies Mission: Carleigh House, 3 Golf Club Rd, Bridgetown; tel. 435-7853; telex 2561; fax 435-8278.

Church of the Nazarene: District Office, Eagle Hall, Bridgetown; tel. 425-1067.

Methodist Church: Bethel Church Office, Bay St, Bridgetown; tel. 426-2223; Chair. Rev. LEONARD W. B. ROCK.

Moravian Church: Roebuck St, Bridgetown; tel. 426-2337; Superintendent Rev. RUDOLPH HOLDER.

Seventh-day Adventists (East Caribbean Conference): Brydens Ave, POB 223, Brittons Hill, St Michael; tel. 429-7234; fax 429-8055.

Wesleyan Holiness Church: General Headquarters, Bank Hall; tel. 429-4864.

Other denominations include the Apostolic Church, the Assemblies of Brethren, the Salvation Army, Presbyterian congregations, the African Methodist Episcopal Church, the Mt Olive United Holy Church of America and Jehovah's Witnesses.

ISLAM

Islamic Teaching Centre: Harts Gap, Hastings; tel. 427-0120; there were 773 Muslims, according to the census of 1980.

JUDAISM

Jewish Community: Barbados Synagogue, Synagogue Lane, Bridgetown; there were 255 Jews at the census of 1980.

HINDUISM

Hindu Community: Bridgetown; there were 411 Hindus at the census of 1980.

The Press

Barbados Advocate: Fontabelle, POB 230, St Michael; tel. 426-1210; telex 2613; fax 429-7045; f. 1895; daily; Man. Dir and Publr PATRICK HOYOS; Man. Editor ROBERT BEST; circ. 19,000.

The Beacon: 111 Roebuck St, Bridgetown; organ of the Barbados Labour Party; weekly; circ. 15,000.

Caribbean Week: Bridgetown; f. 1989; regional newspaper; weekly; Editor GARRY STECKLES.

The Nation: Nation House, Fontabelle, St Michael; tel. 436-6240; telex 2310; f. 1973; daily; Man. Dir HAROLD HOYTE; circ. 22,008 (weekday), 33,714 (weekend).

The New Bajan: Nation House, Fontabelle, St Michael; tel. 436-6240; f. 1953; fmrly *The Bajan and South Caribbean*; monthly; illustrated magazine; Man. Editor GLYNE MURRAY; circ. over 8,000.

Official Gazette: Government Printing Office, Bay St, St Michael; tel. 436-6776; Mon. and Thur.

Sunday Advocate (News): Fontabelle, POB 230, St Michael; tel. 426-1210; telex 2613; f. 1895; Man. Dir and Publr PATRICK HOYOS; Editor ULRIC RICE; circ. 30,308.

The Sunday Sun: Fontabelle, St Michael; tel. 436-6240; telex 2310; fax 427-6968; f. 1977; Dir HAROLD HOYTE; circ. 34,830.

NEWS AGENCIES

Caribbean News Agency (CANA): Culloden View, Beckles Road, St Michael; tel. 429-2903; telex 2228; fax 429-4355; f. 1976; public and private shareholders from English-speaking Caribbean; Gen. Man. RICHARD (DIK) A. HENDERSON.

Foreign Bureaux

Agencia EFE (Spain): 48 Gladioli Dr., Husbanos, St James; tel. 425-1542; Rep. YUSSUFF HANIFF.

BARBADOS

Inter Press Service (IPS) (Italy): POB 697, Bridgetown; tel. 426-4474; Correspondent MARVA COSSY.

United Press International (UPI) (USA): Bridgetown; tel. 436-0465; Correspondent RICKEY SINGH.

Xinhua (New China) News Agency (People's Republic of China): 29 Newton Terrace, POB 22A, Christ Church; telex 2458; Chief Correspondent DING BAOZHONG.

Publishers

Caribbean Contact Ltd: c/o Caribbean Conference of Churches, POB 616, Bridgetown; tel. 427-2681; telex 2335; religion, social sciences, children's books.

Caribbean Publishing Co Ltd: Nation House, Fontabelle, St Michael; tel. 436-5889.

Nation Publishing Co Ltd: Nation House, Fontabelle, St Michael; tel. 436-6240; telex 2310.

Radio and Television

In 1988 there were some 222,720 radio receivers and 65,792 television receivers in use.

Caribbean Broadcasting Corporation (CBC): Pine Hill, POB 900, Bridgetown; tel. 429-2041; telex 2560; fax 429-4795; f. 1963; Chair. Dr C. HOPE.

RADIO

Barbados Broadcasting Service Ltd: Astoria St G., Bridgetown; tel. 437-9550; f. 1981; FM station.

Barbados Rediffusion Service Ltd: River Rd, St Michael; tel. 426-0820; fax 429-8093; f. 1935; public company; Gen. Man. VIC FERNANDES; Programme Dir J. ROGERS.

Radiodiffusion Star Radio, at River Rd, St Michael, is a commercial wired service with island-wide coverage.

Voice of Barbados, at Boarded Hall, St George (f. 1981) is a commercial station covering Barbados and the Eastern Caribbean.

YESS Ten-Four FM, at Mt Misery, St George (f. 1988) is a commercial station.

CBC Radio: POB 900, Bridgetown; tel. 429-2041; telex 2560; fax 429-4795; f. 1963; commercial; Gen. Man. SAM TAITT; Programme Man. C. GRAHAM.

CBC Radio 900, f. 1963, broadcasts 20 hours daily.

Radio Liberty FM, f. 1984, broadcasts 13 hours Sun.–Thur., 18 hours Fri. and Sat.

TELEVISION

CBC TV: POB 900, Bridgetown; tel. 429-2041; telex 2560; fax 429-4795; f. 1964; Channel Nine is the main national service, broadcasting at least six hours daily; three cabled subscription channels are available; Programme Man. O. CUMBERBATCH.

Finance

(cap. = capital; auth. = authorized; dep. = deposits; res = reserves; brs = branches; m. = million)

BANKING
Central Bank

Central Bank of Barbados: Church Village, POB 1016, St Michael; tel. 436-6870; telex 2251; fax 427-9559; f. 1972; bank of issue; cap. Bds $2m., res Bds $10m., dep. Bds $126.3m. (Dec. 1989); Gov. Dr KURLEIGH KING; Gen. Man. CALVIN M. SPRINGER (acting).

National Development Bank

Barbados Development Bank: Level 7, Central Bank Bldg, Church Village, POB 50, St Michael; tel. 436-8870; telex 2295; f. 1969; auth. cap. Bds $60m.; Man. Dir CECIL H. CLARKE.

National Bank

Barbados National Bank: 11 James St, POB 1002, Bridgetown; tel. 427-5920; telex 2271; f. 1978 by the merger of the Barbados Savings Bank, Sugar Industry Agricultural Bank, Agricultural Credit Bank and The Public Officers Housing Loan Fund; cap. Bds $12.5m., res Bds $12.4m., dep. Bds $506.4m. (Dec. 1988); Chair. Sen. AMORY PHILLIPS; Man. Dir L. G. FRANCIS; 5 brs.

Foreign Banks

Bank of Nova Scotia (Canada): Broad St, POB 202, Bridgetown; tel. 426-0230; telex 2223; Man. Y. L. LESSARD; 7 brs.

Barclays Bank PLC (UK): Broad St, POB 301, Bridgetown; tel. 429-5151; telex 2348; fax 436-7957; f. 1837; Man. K. L. LEWIS; 12 brs.

Canadian Imperial Bank of Commerce: Broad St, POB 405, Bridgetown; tel. 426-0571; telex 2230; Man. T. MULLOY; 10 brs and 2 sub-brs.

Caribbean Commercial Bank (Trinidad and Tobago): Lower Broad St, Bridgetown; tel. 426-5022; telex 2289; f. 1984; Pres. MICHAEL WRIGHT.

Chase Manhattan Bank NA (USA): Lower Broad St, Bridgetown; tel. 436-6900; telex 2269.

Royal Bank of Canada: Trident House, Broad St, POB 68, Bridgetown; tel. 426-5200; telex 2634; f. 1911; Man. C. D. MALONEY; 7 brs.

Trust Companies

Bank of Commerce Trust Company Barbados Ltd: POB 503, Bridgetown; tel. 426-2740.

Bank of Nova Scotia Trust Co (Caribbean) Ltd: Bank of Nova Scotia Bldg, Broad St, POB 1003B, Bridgetown; tel. 426-5285; telex 2223.

Barclays Bank Trust Co: Roebuck St, POB 180, Bridgetown; tel. 426-1608.

Caribbean Commercial Trust Co Ltd: White Park Rd, Bridgetown; tel. 436-6910.

Royal Bank (Barbados) Financial Corporation: Royal Bank House, Bush Hill, Garrison, POB 48B, St Michael; tel. 436-6596; fax 436-9675; Man. N. L. SMITH.

STOCK EXCHANGE

Securities Exchange of Barbados (SEB): 6th Floor, Central Bank Bldg, Church Village, St Michael; tel. 436-9871; fax 429-8942; f. 1987; in 1989 the Governments of Barbados, Trinidad and Tobago and Jamaica agreed to combine their national exchanges into a regional stock exchange; cross-listings were scheduled to commence in January 1991; Gen. Man. ANTHONY K. JOHNSON.

INSURANCE

The leading British and a number of US and Canadian companies have agents in the territory. Local insurance companies include the following:

Barbados Commercial Insurance Co Ltd: Harrison's Bldg, 1 Broad St, Bridgetown; tel. 436-6560.

Barbados Fire & General Insurance Co: Beckwith Place, Broad St, POB 150, Bridgetown; tel. 426-4291; telex 2393; f. 1880.

Barbados Mutual Life Assurance Society: Collymore Rock, St Michael; tel. 436-6750; telex 2423; f. 1840; Chair. P. McG. PATTERSON; Man. D. W. ALLAN.

Insurance Corporation of Barbados: Roebuck St, Bridgetown; tel. 427-5590; telex 2317; f. 1978; cap. Bds $3m.; Chair. JOHN MAYERS; Gen. Man. DAVID DEANE.

Life of Barbados Ltd: Wildey, POB 69, St Michael; tel. 426-1060; telex 2389; fax 436-8835; f. 1971; Pres. CECIL F. DE CAIRES.

United Insurance Co Ltd: Cavan House, Lower Broad St, POB 1215, Bridgetown; tel. 436-1991; telex 2343; f. 1976; Dir G. M. CHALLENOR.

Trade and Industry

CHAMBERS OF COMMERCE

Barbados Chamber of Commerce Inc: 1st Floor, Nemwil House, Lower Collymore Rock, POB 189, St Michael; tel. 426-2056; fax 429-2907; f. 1825; 150 mem. firms, 260 reps; Pres. JOHN BELLAMY; Exec. Dir STANLEY L. TAYLOR.

Barbados Junior Chamber of Commerce: Bridgetown; Pres. AVRIL BREWSTER; Sec. VINCENT HAYNES.

DEVELOPMENT ORGANIZATIONS

Agricultural Venture Trust: Bridgetown; f. 1987; US-financial regional development org.; develops agriculture and agro-industries.

Barbados Agricultural Development Corpn: Fairy Valley, Christ Church; tel. 428-0001; f. 1965; programme of diversification and land reforms; Chair. E. R. S. CUMBERBATCH; Gen. Man. G. V. J. GARVEY; Sec. FRANK B. TAYLOR.

Barbados Export Promotion Corpn: Pelican Industrial Park, St Michael; tel. 427-5758; telex 2486; fax 427-5807; co-ordinates activities of Barbadian manufacturers; Chief Exec. PHILIP WILLIAMS.

BARBADOS

Barbados Industrial Development Corpn: Pelican House, Princess Alice Highway, POB 250, Bridgetown; tel. 427-5350; telex 2295; fax 426-7802; f. 1969; facilitates the devt of the industrial sector, especially in the areas of manufacturing and data-processing; offers free consultancy to investors; provides factory space; administers the Fiscal Incentives Legislation; Chair. A. L. KNIGHT; Gen. Man. ROY CLARKE.

Barbados Marketing Corpn: POB 703C, Bridgetown; tel. 427-5250; telex 2253; Chair. ROBERT MORRIS; Gen. Man. CLYDE KING.

British Development Division in the Caribbean: Collymore Rock, POB 167, St Michael; tel. 436-9873; telex 2236; fax 426-2194; Head MICHAEL G. BAWDEN.

STATE-OWNED COMPANIES

Arawak Cement Co Ltd: Checker Hall, St Lucy; tel. 439-9880; telex 2478; fax 439-7976; f. 1981; joint venture between Trinidad and Barbados; manufacture, marketing and export of cement to markets in the Caribbean; Chair TONY GIBBS.

Barbados National Oil Company Ltd (BNOCL): Woodbourne, St Philip; tel. 423-0918; telex 2334; fax 423-0166; f. 1982; exploration for crude petroleum and natural gas; Gen. Man. RONALD HEWITT.

Barbados Sugar Industry Ltd: POB 719C, Warrens, St Thomas; tel. 425-0010; telex 2418; fax 425-3505; Man. Dir ERRIE A. B. DEANE; Sec. D. H. A. JOHNSON.

ASSOCIATIONS

Barbados Agricultural Society: The Grotto, Culloden and Beckles Rd, St Michael; tel. 436-6680; Pres. PATRICK BETHELL.

Barbados Association of Medical Practitioners: Avondale, 16 George St, Belleville, St Michael; tel. 429-7569.

Barbados Association of Professional Engineers: Noranda, Lower Collymore Rock, St Michael; tel. 426-9123.

Barbados Builders' Association: Bridgetown; Pres. KEITH CODRINGTON.

Barbados Hotel Association: 4th Ave, Belleville, St Michael; tel. 426-5041; telex 2314; fax 429-2845; Pres. RALPH TAYLOR; Exec. Dir RUSSELL KELLMAN.

Barbados Manufacturers' Association: Prescod Blvd, Harbour Rd, St Michael; tel. 426-4474; fax 436-5182; f. 1964; Pres. RALPH JOHNSTON; Exec. Sec. RITA ALKINS; 109 mem. firms.

Barbados National Association of Co-operative Societies (BAR-NACS): James St, Bridgetown; tel. 436-2270; f. 1981; provides financial, educational and secretarial services for its members; Pres. LOUIS SEALY; Man. JAMES PAUL.

Barbados Small Business Association: Princess Alice Highway, Bridgetown; tel. 429-7849.

West Indian Sea Island Cotton Association (Inc): c/o Barbados Agricultural Development Corpn, Fairy Valley, Christ Church; tel. 428-0250; Pres. E. LeROY WARD; Sec. MICHAEL I. EDGHILL; 8 mem. associations.

EMPLOYERS' ORGANIZATION

Barbados Employers' Confederation: 1st Floor, Nemwil House, Lower Collymore Rock, St Michael; tel. 426-1574; fax 429-2907; f. 1956; Pres. ALLAN C. FIELDS; Exec. Dir JAMES A. WILLIAMS; 256 mems. (incl. associate mems).

TRADE UNIONS

Principal unions include:

Barbados Industrial and General Workers' Union: Bridgetown; f. 1981; Leader ROBERT CLARKE; Gen. Sec. LADEPOO SALANKEY; c. 2,000 mems.

Barbados Secondary Teachers' Union: Ryeburn, 8th Ave, Belleville, St Michael; tel. 429-7676; f. 1948; Pres. ALVIN PERRY; Sec. PATRICK FROST; 364 mems.

Barbados Union of Teachers: Welches, POB 58, St Michael; f. 1974; tel. 436-6139; Pres. RONALD DaC. JONES; Gen. Sec. HARRY HUSBANDS; 2,000 mems.

Barbados Workers' Union: Solidarity House, Harmony Hall, POB 172, St Michael; tel. 426-3492; telex 2527; f. 1941; operates a Labour College; Sec.-Gen. Sir FRANK WALCOTT; 20,000 mems.

Caribbean Association of Media Workers (Camwork): Bridgetown; f. 1986; regional; Pres. RICKEY SINGH.

National Union of Public Workers: Dalkeith Rd, POB 174, Bridgetown; tel. 426-1764; f. 1944; Pres. NIGEL O. HARPER; Gen. Sec. JOHN GODDARD; 6,000 mems.

National Union of Seamen: 34 Tudor St, Bridgetown; tel. 436-6137.

Transport

ROADS

Ministry of Transport and Works: The Pine, POB 25, St Michael; tel. 429-2191; telex 2203; maintains a network of about 1,642 km (1,020 miles) of roads, of which 1,300 km (808 miles) have an asphalt surface; Chief Technical Officer C. H. ARCHER.

SHIPPING

Inter-island traffic is catered for by a fortnightly service of one vessel of the West Indies Shipping Corpn (WISCO, the regional shipping company, based in Trinidad and Tobago, in which the Barbados Government is a shareholder) operating from Trinidad as far north as Jamaica. The CAROL container service consortium connects Bridgetown with West European ports and several foreign shipping lines call at the port. Bridgetown harbour has berths for eight ships and simultaneous bunkering facilities for five.

Shipping Association of Barbados: Carlisle House, Hincks St, Bridgetown; tel. 427-9860.

Barbados Shipping and Trading Co Ltd: Musson Bldg, Hincks St, POB 1227C, Bridgetown; tel. 436-6013; telex 2237; fax 427-4719.

DaCosta Ltd: Carlisle House, Hincks St, POB 103, Bridgetown; tel. 426-0850; telex 2328; shipping company.

Tore Torsteinson: Fairfield House, St Philip; tel. 423-6125; fax 423-4664; f. 1970; shipping company.

CIVIL AVIATION

The principal airport is Grantley Adams International Airport, at Seawell, 18 km (11 miles) from Bridgetown. The national airline, Caribbean Airways, ceased operating scheduled services from April 1987. Caribbean Air Cargo (CARICARGO), which was jointly owned by Barbados and Trinidad and Tobago, ceased operating scheduled services in 1990.

Aero Services: Grantley Adams International Airport, Seawell; charter co.

EC Air: f. 1990; jointly-owned by Air Martinique; daily services between Barbados, Martinique, Saint Lucia and Saint Vincent and the Grenadines; also to Dominica.

Tourism

The natural attractions of the island consist chiefly of the healthy climate and varied scenery. In addition, there are many facilities for outdoor sports of all kinds. Revenue from tourism increased from Bds $13m. in 1960 to over Bds $1,000m. in 1989. The number of stop-over tourist arrivals rose from 451,485 in 1988 to 461,258 in 1989, while the number of visiting cruise-ship passengers increased by some 16%, to 337,100.

Barbados Board of Tourism: Harbour Rd, POB 242, Bridgetown; tel. 427-2623; telex 2420; fax 426-4080; f. 1958; offices in London, New York, Montreal, Toronto, California and Frankfurt; Chair. CLEVEDON MAYERS; Dir of Tourism PATRICIA NEHAUL.

BELGIUM

Introductory Survey

Location, Climate, Language, Religion, Flag, Capital

The Kingdom of Belgium lies in north-western Europe, bounded to the north by the Netherlands, to the east by Luxembourg and Germany, to the south by France, and to the west by the North Sea. The climate is temperate. Temperatures in Brussels are generally between 0°C (32°F) and 23°C (73°F). Dutch, spoken in the north (Flanders), and French, spoken in the south (Wallonia), are the two main official languages. A 1963 law established four linguistic regions, the French, Dutch and German-speaking areas and Brussels, which is situated in the Flemish part but has bilingual status. Approximately 57% of the population are Dutch-speaking, 42% are French-speaking and 0.6% speak German. Almost all of the inhabitants profess Christianity, and the great majority are Roman Catholics. The national flag (proportions 15 by 13) consists of three equal vertical stripes, of black, yellow and red. The capital is Brussels.

Recent History

Since the Second World War, Belgium has become recognized as a leader of international co-operation in Europe. It is a founder member of many important international organizations, including the Council of Europe, the European Communities and the Benelux Economic Union.

In the post-war period linguistic divisions have been exacerbated by the political and economic polarization of Dutch-speaking Flanders in the north and francophone Wallonia in the south. The population of Flanders has traditionally supported the conservative Flemish Christian Social Party (CVP) and the nationalist Volksunie (VU), while Walloons have predominantly socialist political sympathies. Most major parties have both French and Flemish sections (although linguistic conflicts frequently override political considerations), as a result of the trend away from centralized administration towards greater regional control. Moderate constitutional reforms, introduced in July 1971, were the first steps towards regional autonomy; in 1972 further concessions were made, with the German-speaking community being represented in the Cabinet for the first time, and in 1973 linguistic parity was assured in central government. Provisional legislation, passed in 1974, established separate Regional Councils and Ministerial Committees. One of the main disputes concerned the status of Brussels: 85% of the city's inhabitants are francophone but the Flemish parties were, until the late 1980s, unwilling to grant the capital equal status with the other two regional bodies (see below).

In June 1977 Leo Tindemans formed a coalition composed of the Christian Social parties, the Socialists, the Front Démocratique des Francophones (FDF) and the VU. The Cabinet, in what became known as the Egmont Pact, proposed the abolition of the virtually defunct nine-province administration, and devolution of power from the central Government to create a federal Belgium, comprising three political and economic regions (Flanders, Wallonia and Brussels), and two linguistic communities. However, these proposals were not implemented. Tindemans resigned in October 1978 and the Minister of Defence, Paul Vanden Boeynants, was appointed Prime Minister in a transitional government. Legislative elections that were held in December resulted in little change in the distribution of seats in the Chamber of Representatives. Four successive Prime Ministers-designate failed to form a new government, the main obstacle again being the future status of Brussels. The six-month crisis was finally resolved when a new coalition government was formed in April 1979 under Dr Wilfried Martens, President of the CVP.

During 1980 the linguistic conflict worsened, sometimes involving violent incidents. Legislation was formulated, under the terms of which Flanders and Wallonia were to be administered by regional assemblies, with control of cultural matters, public health, roads, urban projects and 10% of the national budget, while Brussels was to retain its three-member executive.

Belgium suffered severe economic difficulties during the late 1970s and early 1980s, and internal disagreement over Martens' proposals for their resolution resulted in the formation of four successive coalition governments between April 1979 and October 1980. The announcement of austerity measures, including a 'freeze' on wages and reductions in public expenditure at a time of high unemployment, provoked demonstrations and lost Martens the support of the Socialist parties. Martens also encountered widespread criticism as a result of the proposed installation of NATO nuclear missiles in Belgium. In April 1981 a new government was formed, comprising a coalition of the Christian Social parties and the Socialist parties and led by Mark Eyskens (CVP), hitherto Minister of Finance. The composition of the Cabinet, which expressed its intention to promote investment and industrial development while cutting public spending, remained almost unchanged. Lack of parliamentary support for his policies led to Eyskens' resignation in September. In December Martens formed a new centre-right government, comprising the two Christian Social parties and the two Liberal parties. In 1982 Parliament granted special powers for the implementation of austerity measures; these were effective until 1984, and similar powers were approved in March 1986. Opposition to reductions in public spending was vigorous, with public-sector unions undertaking damaging strike action in November 1982, September 1983, May 1986 and November 1988. In October 1989 the inability of Liège city council to pay the salaries of public employees provoked a series of demonstrations and strikes.

The issue of the installation of 48 US 'cruise' nuclear missiles on Belgian territory prompted a two-day debate in the Chamber of Representatives in November 1983 and a deferral of the final decision until 1985. A series of bombings, directed against NATO-connected targets, was carried out during 1984, and included six explosions along an oil pipeline in December. Responsibility for the attacks was claimed by an extreme left-wing organization, the Cellules Communistes Combattantes (CCC), suspected of having close links with the French terrorist group, Action Directe. In March 1985 the Chamber finally carried a majority vote in favour of the cruise sitings, and 16 missiles were installed at Florennes. However, these missiles were removed in December 1988, under the terms of the Intermediate-range Nuclear Forces treaty concluded by the USA and the USSR in December 1987.

Following a riot in May 1985 at a football match between English and Italian clubs (in the final of the European Cup competition) at the Heysel Stadium in Brussels, which resulted in 39 deaths, demands were made for the resignation of the Minister of the Interior, Charles-Ferdinand Nothomb, over accusations of inefficient policing. In July the resignation (in connection with the issue) of six Liberal Cabinet members, including the Deputy Prime Minister, Jean Gol, precipitated the collapse of the coalition. Martens offered the resignation of his Government, but this was 'suspended' by King Baudouin: the Government took responsibility for a minimal programme, pending a general election, which was called for October. In the mean time, however, controversy regarding educational reform provoked a dispute between the two linguistic groups and caused the final dissolution of Parliament in September 1985. The general election returned the Christian Social-Liberal alliance to power, and in November Martens formed his sixth Cabinet.

The incidence of terrorist attacks gathered momentum in the weeks following the 1985 election. An extraordinary session of the new Cabinet was convened, following the violent deaths of 16 people in two armed attacks on supermarkets in the Brabant region and the bombing of four banks. Responsibility for the bank attacks was again claimed by the CCC. Further attacks, mainly centred on NATO targets, were carried out before a number of arrests were made. In January 1986 the Government announced new security legislation, which placed more stringent restrictions on the sale of weapons and ammunition. In October 1988 four members of the CCC were sentenced to life imprisonment, with hard labour, for their part in 21 attacks, perpetrated in 1984 and 1985, while two alleged members of an associated group, the Front Révolutionnaire d'Action Prolétarienne (FRAP), received five-year prison sentences, after having been convicted of acts of urban violence. The complicity of elements of the Belgian security forces in the Brabant killings of the mid-1980s has frequently been alleged. In mid-1990 the Martens Government proposed an extensive reorganization of the police forces, apparently in response to the findings of a parliamentary commission that had criticized the manner in which the attacks had been investigated.

In 1983 the election of a francophone mayor, José Happart, in the Flemish commune of Voeren (known in French as Les Fourons), which had been transferred from the French-speaking Liège province to Dutch-speaking Limburg in 1963, caused a linguistic conflict that split the Cabinet. A compromise solution failed to prevent the re-emergence of the problem in October 1986, when Happart was dismissed from his post for refusing to prove his fluency in Dutch. The incident provoked another bitter conflict between the two linguistic groups in the coalition, leading Nothomb to resign the Interior portfolio, and causing Martens to tender his resignation as Prime Minister. This was, however, refused by King Baudouin. The issue continued to generate tension between the coalition parties during 1987, as Happart was repeatedly re-elected as acting mayor despite the Limburg authorities' frequent attempts to remove him from office, and finally caused the Government to collapse in October, when its resignation was accepted by King Baudouin. At a general election in December, the CVP sustained significant losses in Flanders, while the French-speaking Socialist Party (PS) gained seats in Wallonia, and the Socialists became the largest overall grouping in the Chamber of Representatives. However, no party had a clear mandate for power, and the ensuing negotiations for a new coalition lasted 146 days. During this time, Martens assumed a 'caretaker' role, pending the formation of a new government, and a series of mediators, appointed by King Baudouin, attempted to reach a compromise. In May 1988 Martens was sworn in at the head of his eighth administration, after agreement was finally reached by the French- and Dutch-speaking wings of both the Christian Social and Socialist parties and by the VU.

The five-party coalition agreement committed the new Government to a programme of further austerity measures, together with tax reforms and increased federalization. In August 1988 Parliament approved the first phase of the federalization plan, intended ultimately to lead to a constitutional amendment, whereby increased autonomy would be granted to the country's Communities and Regions in several areas of jurisdiction, including education and socio-economic policy. Agreement was also reached by which Brussels was to have its own regional Council, with an Executive responsible to it, giving the city equal status with Flanders and Wallonia. In an attempt to end linguistic conflicts such as that generated by Happart, it was announced that officials in communes such as Voeren would have to demonstrate proficiency in both French and Dutch. Despite his success in municipal elections, held in October, Happart agreed, in December, not to seek reappointment as mayor of Voeren.

In January 1989 Parliament approved the second phase of the federalization programme, allocating the public funds necessary to give effect to the regional autonomy that had been approved in principle in August 1988, providing for the creation of a regional authority for Brussels, and establishing a body whose purpose was to consider conflicts of a constitutional nature that might arise during the period of transition to a federal system of government. The federal constitution formally came into effect in July 1989. However, coal-miners in Limburg province had already been involved in violent clashes with the gendarmerie in June, following protests against a decision by the Flanders Executive to override an earlier resolution, made by the central Government, not to close the region's two remaining major coal-mines until 1996. Protracted industrial action by francophone schoolteachers, which began in April 1990, indicated that the new federal system might, in fact, exemplify the economic disparity between French- and Dutch-speaking regions: in spite of an obvious discrepancy between the salaries of the francophone teachers and those of their Flemish counterparts, the budget allocated to the French Community by the central Government was insufficient to meet the teachers' demands for parity.

A brief constitutional crisis in 1990 provoked widespread demands for a review of the powers of the Monarch, as defined by the Constitution. In late March proposals for the legalization of abortion (in strictly-controlled circumstances) completed their passage through the Belgian Parliament. However, King Baudouin had previously stated that his religious convictions would render him unable to give royal assent to any such legislation. A compromise solution was reached in early April, whereby Article 82 of the Constitution, which makes provision for the Monarch's 'incapacity to rule', was invoked. Baudouin thus abdicated for 36 hours, during which time the new legislation was promulgated. A joint session of Parliament was then convened to declare the resumption of Baudouin's reign. However, the incident prompted considerable alarm within Belgium: Article 82 had hitherto been interpreted as a provision for a monarch's physical, mental or material incapacity to rule, rather than a moral incapacity. Concern was expressed that Baudouin, who was known to oppose the federalization of the Belgian political system, might refuse to give his assent to the further devolution of political competence.

Divisions within the coalition impeded the successful formulation and execution of Belgium's foreign and defence policies. In November 1988 the Socialist Minister of National Defence, Guy Coëme, refused to endorse a communiqué, drafted at a session of the NATO Nuclear Planning Group, regarding the modernization of short-range nuclear missiles deployed in Western Europe. Coëme's insistence that NATO should make a formal commitment to a policy of disarmament and détente, before any modernization of existing tactical missiles could be considered, was criticized by some members of the CVP and PSC, who feared that such a policy would isolate Belgium within NATO. Reductions in the deployment of Belgian army personnel and in expenditure on weapons systems were announced in February 1989. Disagreements regarding defence policy continued when, in January 1990, the Minister of Foreign Affairs, Mark Eyskens, condemned as premature an announcement by Coëme that 25,000 Belgian troops were to be withdrawn from the Federal Republic of Germany (West Germany). Eyskens warned that the Belgian Government should not anticipate the outcome of multilateral negotiations regarding the reduction of conventional forces in Europe.

Beginning in late 1988 Belgium's hitherto cordial relations with its former colonies underwent considerable strain. Proposals, made by Martens in November 1988, regarding the relief of public and commercial debts owed to Belgium by Zaire (formerly the Belgian Congo) were opposed by the Socialist parties, and provoked allegations, in certain Belgian newspapers, of corruption within the Zairean Government and of the misappropriation of development aid to the former colony. President Mobutu Sese Seko of Zaire responded by ordering the withdrawal of all Zairean state-owned businesses from Belgium and by demanding that all Zairean nationals resident in Belgium remove their assets from, and leave, their host country. In January 1989 Mobutu announced the unilateral abrogation of two treaties of friendship and co-operation between the two countries, and imposed a moratorium on debt-servicing payments to Belgium. In addition, the number of flights made by the Belgian national air carrier to Zaire was reduced, and it was announced that Zairean blister copper would, henceforth, be refined elsewhere in Europe. Martens retaliated by stating that Belgium would finance no new development projects in Zaire, and that his Government would seek legal recourse for Zaire's alleged violation of bilateral air-transport agreements. The situation was apparently resolved in July, following meetings between Martens and Mobutu. A draft agreement was subsequently formulated by Mark Eyskens, who had recently replaced Leo Tindemans as Minister of Foreign Affairs, and his Zairean counterpart, Nguza Karl-I-Bond, which stated that Zaire's public debt to Belgium, together with one-third of the country's commercial debt to Belgium, would be cancelled. The remainder of the commercial debt was to be rescheduled, while the interest accrued thereon was to be reinvested in development projects. However, the Martens Government demonstrated a less conciliatory approach when, in May 1990, the Mobutu regime refused to accede to demands for an international inquiry into the alleged massacre of as many as 150 students by the Zairean security forces. Belgium announced an immediate moratorium on official aid transfers to Zaire, together with the suspension of preparations for a session of the two countries' joint co-operation commission that was to have been convened in June. Mobutu accused Belgium of interfering in his country's internal affairs, and ordered the expulsion from Zaire of some 700 Belgian technical workers, together with the closure of three of Belgium's four consular offices; restrictions were again imposed on flights to Zaire by the Belgian national carrier. Moreover, the Zairean Government announced that it would not comply with the debt-relief agreement that had been formulated in July 1989.

In October 1990 the Martens Government dispatched 600 troops to Rwanda (part of the former Belgian territory of Ruanda-Urundi) to protect the interests of some 1,600 Belgian nationals resident in Rwanda, when that country was invaded by opponents of the incumbent regime who had been living in exile. The Belgian Government insisted that the deployment was a purely humanitarian action, and stated that it would not agree to a request from the Rwandan Government for military assistance in repelling the opposition forces, citing unacceptable violations of human rights by the Rwanda authorities. Martens, Coëme and Eyskens participated in negotiations that resulted in the entry into force of a cease-fire agreement in late October; Belgian forces were withdrawn from Rwanda in early November.

Government

Belgium is a constitutional and hereditary monarchy, comprising nine provinces. Legislative power is vested in the King and the bicameral Parliament (the Senate and the Chamber of Representatives). The Senate has 182 members, including 106 directly elected by universal adult suffrage, 50 elected by provincial councils, 25 co-opted by the elected members and one Senator by right, the heir to the throne. The Chamber has 212 members, all directly elected by popular vote, on the basis of proportional representation. Members of both Houses serve for up to four years. Executive power, nominally vested in the King, is exercised by the Cabinet. The King appoints the Prime Minister and, on the latter's advice, other Ministers. The Cabinet is responsible to Parliament. The Flemish, French and German-speaking Communities and the Flemish, Walloon and Brussels Regions each have a legislative Council, an Executive and a civil service. The Brussels Region comprises French, Flemish and Joint Communal Commissions. In practice, the Councils and Executives of the Region and Community of Flanders are organized and administered as a single entity.

The Communities are, in most cases, empowered to formulate legislation regarding education, cultural affairs and health and social aid, while the Regions are responsible for the formulation of socio-economic policies. All other powers are vested in the central Government.

Defence

Belgium is a member of NATO. In June 1990 the total strength of the armed forces was 92,000 (of whom 36,200 were conscripts), comprising army 68,700, navy 4,500 and air force 18,800. The defence budget for 1991 was estimated at 100,000m. Belgian francs. The duration of military service, hitherto 10 months for postings to Germany and one year for conscripts serving in Belgium, was expected to be reduced in 1991.

Economic Affairs

In 1988, according to estimates by the World Bank, Belgium's gross national product (GNP), measured at average 1986–88 prices, was US $143,560m., equivalent to $14,550 per head. During 1980–88, it was estimated, total GNP and GNP per head both increased, in real terms, at an average annual rate of 1.4%. Over the same period, the population increased by only 0.4%. The country's gross domestic product (GDP) increased, in real terms, by an annual average of 1.4% in 1980–88.

Agriculture (including forestry and fishing) contributed 2.1% of GDP in 1989. An estimated 2.8% of the employed labour force were engaged in the sector in 1988. The principal agricultural products are sugar beet, cereals and potatoes. Pig meat, beef and dairy products are also important. Exports of food, livestock and livestock products accounted for 8.5% of total export revenue in 1989 (according to provisional figures). During 1980–87 agricultural production increased by an average of 2.5% annually.

Industry (including mining and quarrying, manufacturing, power and construction) contributed 30.7% of GDP in 1989. An estimated 28% of the employed labour force were engaged in industry in 1988. During 1980–87, industrial production increased by an annual average of 1.1%.

Apart from coal, Belgium has few mineral resources. In 1989 extractive activities accounted for 0.3% of GDP. An estimated 0.4% of the employed labour force worked in the sector in 1988.

Manufacturing contributed 21.9% of GDP in 1988. The sector accounted for an estimated 20.9% of the employed labour force in 1988. Imported raw materials are processed and exported as semi-finished goods, such as plastics and chemicals. The metallurgical (especially iron and steel), engineering, gem-diamond, food-processing and textiles industries are also significant.

Belgium's seven nuclear reactors accounted for about 65% of total electricity generation in the late 1980s. However, the country's dependence on imported petroleum and natural gas was likely to increase, following the announcement by the Government, in late 1988, of the indefinite suspension of its nuclear programme and of the construction of a gas-powered generator. Imports of mineral fuels comprised 7.7% of the value of total imports in 1989.

Finance, insurance, real estate and business services contributed 17.4% of GDP in 1989. An estimated 8.2% of the employed labour force were engaged in these activities in 1988. A computerized dealing system and other measures aimed at reforming trading practices in Belgium's four stock exchanges came into effect during 1989. The presence in Belgium of the offices of many international organizations and businesses is a significant source of revenue.

In 1989 the Belgo-Luxembourg Economic Union (BLEU) recorded a visible trade surplus of US $967m. while there was a surplus of $3,197m. on the current account of the balance of payments. In 1989 Belgium's three major trading partners (the Federal Republic of Germany (West Germany), France and the Netherlands) together accounted for 54.5% of the BLEU's total external trade (56.0% of imports, 53.0% of exports). The principal exports in 1989 were basic manufactures (including gem diamonds and iron and steel), machinery and transport equipment, chemicals and related products, food and live animals and miscellaneous manufactured articles. The principal imports in that year were basic manufactures, machinery and transport equipment, chemicals and related products, miscellaneous manufactured articles and food and live animals.

In 1989 there was a budget deficit of BF 397,200m. (equivalent to 6.6% of annual GNP). The annual rate of inflation averaged 4.8% in 1980–88. Consumer prices increased by an annual average of 3.1% in 1989, and by 3.3% in the year to August 1990. An estimated 8.2% of the labour force were unemployed in July 1990.

Belgium is a member of the European Communities (see p. 135), including the European Monetary System (EMS, see p. 148), and of the Benelux Economic Union (see p. 222). The dual exchange rate that had been operated by the single customs region of the BLEU was abolished in March 1990, in compliance with plans to remove all capital controls within the EEC.

During the late 1980s Belgium enjoyed strong and sustained economic growth that was characterized by real GNP growth of an estimated 4.4% in 1989, a relatively low rate of inflation and a buoyant balance-of-payments position. The Government is strongly committed to further European economic integration, and has initiated measures to ensure a prominent role for the Belgian economy during the 1990s. However, severe structural weaknesses remain, notably the chronic public-sector deficit, which had accumulated to some BF 7,179,000m. by the end of 1989 (equivalent to about 130% of annual GNP). Attempts to reduce the budget deficit have had considerable success, but remain impeded by the need for a reform of the taxation system, and by a cumbersome public sector. The high level of unemployment also needs to be considerably lowered. The Belgian economy is dependent on external trade, and is thus vulnerable to fluctuations in international prices and in demand for goods and services. Moreover, economic prosperity in Flanders will continue to be offset by industrial decline in Wallonia.

Social Welfare

Social welfare is administered mainly by the National Office for Social Security. Contributions are paid by employers and employees towards family allowances, health insurance, unemployment benefit and pensions. Most allowances and pensions are periodically adjusted in accordance with changes to the consumer price index. Workers and employees are entitled to four weeks' holiday for every 12-month period of work. They are insured against accidents occurring on the work premises or on the way to and from work. Medical care is free to widows, pensioners, orphans and the disabled. Ordinary and

BELGIUM

supplementary family allowances are the entitlement of all families. Social welfare is also administered at a local level by Public Assistance Commissions which have been set up in every municipality. In 1982 Belgium had 531 hospital establishments, with a total of 92,686 beds (one for every 106 inhabitants), and there were 26,593 physicians working in the country. Of total expenditure by the central Government in 1987, about 51,000m. francs (1.8%) was for health, and 1,124,600m. francs (40.8%) was for social security and welfare.

Education

Legislation granting increased autonomy in the formulation of education policy to the Flemish, French and German-speaking Communities, as part of the Government's federalization programme, came into effect in 1989. Education may be provided by the Communities, by public authorities or by private interests. All educational establishments, whether official or 'free' (privately-organized), receive most of their funding from the Communities. Roman Catholic schools constitute the greatest number of 'free' establishments.

Full-time education in Belgium is compulsory from the ages of six to 16 years. Thereafter, pupils must remain in part-time education for a further two-year period. In accordance with the 1963 Language of Instruction Act, teaching is given in the language of the region: in the Brussels district teaching is in the mother language of the pupil. In June 1986 it was announced that the study of Dutch as a second language in Wallonian schools was to be introduced, and was eventually to become compulsory.

About 90% of infants attend state-financed nursery schools. Elementary education begins at six years of age and consists of three courses of two years each. Secondary education, beginning at the age of 12, lasts for six years and is divided into three two-year cycles or, in a few cases, two three-year cycles.

The requirement for university entrance is a pass in the 'examination of maturity', taken after the completion of secondary studies. Courses are divided into 2–3 years of general preparation followed by 2–3 years of specialization. The French Community controls four universities, while the Flemish Community controls three such institutions; in addition, there are 11 university centres or faculties (6 French, 5 Flemish). A total of 17,769 Belgian students graduated from the country's university-level establishments in 1988. Non-university institutions of higher education provide arts education, technical training and teacher training. A National Study Fund provides grants where necessary and almost 20% of students receive scholarships.

Expenditure on education and culture by the central Government was budgeted at 295,584m. francs (15.1% of total expenditure) for 1989.

Public Holidays

1991: 1 January (New Year's Day), 1 April (Easter Monday), 1 May (Labour Day), 9 May (Ascension Day), 20 May (Whit Monday), 21 July (National Day), 15 August (Assumption), 1 November (All Saints' Day), 11 November (Armistice Day), 25 December (Christmas Day).

1992: 1 January (New Year's Day), 20 April (Easter Monday), 1 May (Labour Day), 28 May (Ascension Day), 8 June (Whit Monday), 21 July (National Day), 15 August (Assumption), 1 November (All Saints' Day), 11 November (Armistice Day), 25 December (Christmas Day).

Weights and Measures

The metric system is in force.

Statistical Survey

Source: mainly Institut National de Statistique, 44 rue de Louvain, 1000 Brussels; tel. (02) 513-96-50; fax (02) 513-86-80.

Area and Population

AREA, POPULATION AND DENSITY

Area (sq km)	30,519*
Population (census results)†	
31 December 1970	9,650,944
1 March 1981	
Males	4,810,349
Females	5,038,298
Total	9,848,647
Population (official estimates at 31 December)†	
1986	9,867,751
1987	9,875,716
1988	9,927,612
Density (per sq km) at 31 December 1988	325.3

* 11,783 sq miles.   † Population is *de jure*.

PROVINCES (population at 31 December 1988)

	Population	Capital (with population)
Antwerp	1,592,437	Antwerp (473,082*)
Brabant	2,240,926	Brussels (970,501*)
Flanders (East)	1,329,830	Ghent (230,822)
Flanders (West)	1,099,384	Bruges (117,653)
Hainaut	1,278,255	Mons (91,650)
Liège	997,364	Liège (199,020)
Limburg	740,974	Hasselt (65,861)
Luxembourg	229,587	Arlon (23,213)
Namur	418,855	Namur (103,131)

* Including suburbs.

PRINCIPAL TOWNS (population at 31 December 1988)

Bruxelles (Brussel, Brussels)	970,501*
Antwerpen (Anvers, Antwerp)	473,082†
Gent (Gand, Ghent)	230,822
Charleroi	208,021
Liège (Luik)	199,020
Brugge (Bruges)	117,653
Namur (Namen)	103,131
Mons (Bergen)	91,650
Kortrijk (Courtrai)	76,279
Mechelen (Malines)	75,514
Oostende (Ostend)	68,370
Hasselt	65,861

* Including Schaerbeek, Anderlecht and other suburbs.
† Including Deurne and other suburbs.

BELGIUM

Statistical Survey

BIRTHS, MARRIAGES AND DEATHS

	Registered live births		Registered marriages*		Registered deaths†	
	Number	Rate (per 1,000)	Number	Rate (per 1,000)	Number	Rate (per 1,000)
1982	120,382	12.2	62,423	6.3	112,506	11.4
1983	117,395	11.9	59,652	6.1	114,814	11.6
1984	115,790	11.8	58,989	6.0	110,577	11.2
1985	114,283	11.6	57,630	6.0	112,691	11.4
1986	117,271	11.9	56,657	5.7	111,671	11.3
1987	117,448	11.9	56,588	5.7	105,840	10.7
1988	119,456	12.1	59,093	6.0	104,552	10.6
1989	121,117	12.2	63,528	6.4	106,949	10.8

* Including marriages among Belgian armed forces stationed outside the country and alien armed forces in Belgium, unless performed by local foreign authority.
† Including Belgian armed forces stationed outside the country but excluding alien armed forces stationed in Belgium.

ECONOMICALLY ACTIVE POPULATION (ISIC Major Divisions, estimates, '000 persons at 30 June each year)

	1986	1987	1988‡
Agriculture, forestry and fishing	103.2	100.4	102.3
Mining and quarrying	22.6	20.9	13.0
Manufacturing	799.1	781.8	764.8
Electricity, gas and water	31.7	31.7	31.6
Construction	204.6	205.5	212.1
Trade, restaurants and hotels	712.7	730.1	671.8
Transport, storage and communications	260.5	257.4	253.3
Finance, insurance, real estate and business services	301.5	321.5	301.3
Community, social and personal services*	1,262.0	1,262.4	1,303.1
Total in home employment	3,697.9	3,711.7	3,653.3
Persons working abroad	35.8	38.9	48.7
Total in employment	3,733.7	3,750.6	3,702.0
Unemployed†	477.9	466.1	424.5
Total labour force	4,211.6	4,216.8	4,126.5
Males	2,514.0	2,500.8	2,425.3
Females	1,697.7	1,716.0	1,701.2

* Including members of the armed forces ('000): 89.3 in 1986; 90.7 in 1987; 92.2 in 1988.
† Figures exclude older unemployed persons not seeking employment ('000): 59.0 in 1986; 65.8 in 1987; 70.7 in 1988.
‡ Figures for 1988 are based on a revised series of estimates, and are not, therefore, strictly comparable with those for earlier years.

Agriculture

PRINCIPAL CROPS ('000 metric tons)

	1987	1988	1989
Wheat	1,046.5	1,251.8	1,402.1
Spelt	36.5	36.8	41.8
Barley	678.1	737.8	647.0
Maize	40.3	54.0	53.7
Rye	16.7	14.3	12.5
Oats	60.4	69.7	44.7
Potatoes	1,620.3	1,613.7	1,442.7
Linseed	6.7	7.9	8.2
Flax fibre	13	14	11
Sugar beet	5,425.2	6,108.6	6,061.3

LIVESTOCK ('000 head at 1 December)

	1987	1988	1989
Horses	23.1	22.1	21.9
Cattle	2,950.2	2,966.8	3,049.3
Pigs	5,880.8	6,233.4	6,439.9
Sheep	133.1	129.0	131.6
Goats	7.8	8.3	9.3
Chickens	31,830	29,877	25.5
Ducks	65	69	65
Turkeys	215	183	192

LIVESTOCK PRODUCTS ('000 metric tons)

	1987	1988	1989
Beef and veal	317	309	298
Pig meat	779	805	822
Milk	3,777	3,637	3,632
Butter	86	73	83
Cheese	56	59	62
Hen eggs	174	167	163

Fishing*

('000 metric tons)

	1986	1987	1988
Marine fishes	28.2	29.2	29.3
Crustaceans and molluscs	2.3	2.2	2.1
Total catch	30.5	31.4	31.4

* Figures refer to marketable quantities landed in Belgium, which may be less than the live weight of the catch. The total catch (in '000 metric tons) was: 31.3 in 1986; 32.9 in 1987; 32.2 in 1988.

Mining

	1986	1987	1988
Hard coal ('000 metric tons)	5,589	4,356	2,487
Natural gas* (million cu metres)	37	38	24

1989: Hard coal ('000 metric tons) 1,893.
* From coal mines.

Industry

SELECTED PRODUCTS
('000 metric tons, unless otherwise indicated)

	1987	1988	1989
Wheat flour[1]	931.8	896.0	990.0*
Raw sugar	915	910	1,312
Margarine	184.4	184.0	185.7
Beer ('000 hectolitres)	13,987.7	13,792.0	13,163.6
Cigarettes (million)	28,953.1	29,056.2	27,879.3
Cotton yarn—pure and mixed (metric tons)	55,869	45,291	48,655
Woven cotton fabrics—pure and mixed (metric tons)[2]	53,945	48,792	56,591
Flax yarn (metric tons)[3]	7,689	8,856	8,069
Jute yarn (metric tons)	10,917	7,150	7,065
Other vegetable textile yarns (metric tons)	7,867	8,836	6,445

BELGIUM

SELECTED PRODUCTS—continued
('000 metric tons, unless otherwise indicated)

	1987	1988	1989
Wool yarn—pure and mixed (metric tons)	84,846	90,199	97,422
Woven woollen fabrics—pure and mixed (metric tons)[2]	33,858	35,778	36,541
Rayon continuous filaments (metric tons)	4,491	5,995	7,558
Woven rayon and acetate fabrics—pure and mixed (metric tons)[4]	29,783	29,744	39,080
Mechanical wood pulp	168	210	217
Chemical and semi-chemical wood pulp	270	271	287
Newsprint	110.7	113.4	112.3
Other paper and paperboard	1,003.7	1,114.5	1,153.8
Ethyl alcohol—Ethanol ('000 hectolitres)	117.9	120.9	125.3
Sulphuric acid (100%)	2,069.4	2,135.5	1,956.4
Nitric acid (100%)	1,469.5	1,344.9	1,328.7
Nitrogenous fertilizers[5]	795	760	700
Phosphate fertilizers[6]	389	368	325
Liquefied petroleum gas	533	516	506
Naphtha	1,421	1,380	1,603
Motor spirit (petrol)	4,857	4,923	5,333
Aviation gasoline	139.7	15.6	12.7
Kerosene	35	81	58
White spirit	327.7	347.7	360.4
Jet fuel	1,243.1	1,476.1	1,661.8
Distillate fuel oils	9,073.3	9,171.0	9,745.6
Residual fuel oil	7,773.4	6,568.4	5,746.1
Lubricating oils	2	3	5
Petroleum bitumen (asphalt)	652.3	733.9	762.9
Coke-oven coke	5,226	5,549	5,459
Cement	5,689	6,451	6,720
Pig-iron	8,242.4	9,146.9	8,862.7
Crude steel	9,786.4	11,220.4	10,952.8
Refined copper—unwrought (metric tons)[7]	475,906	504,620	563,323
Refined lead—unwrought (metric tons)[8]	108,030	126,561	109,442
Tin: primary (metric tons)	3,904	4,972	5,978
Zinc—unwrought (metric tons)[9]	308,580	323,758	306,022
Radio receivers ('000)[10]	1,165	836	859
Television receivers ('000)[10]	917	946	979
Merchant vessels launched ('000 gross reg. tons)[11]	52	27	46
Passenger motor cars ('000)[12]	1,140.6	1,161.1	1,170.4
Commercial motor vehicles ('000)[12]	54.4	69.4	75.5
Electric energy (million kWh)	63,367.0	65,348.9	67,481.4
Manufactured gas (million cu metres)	2,237	2,309	2,252

* Provisional figure.
[1] Industrial production only. [2] Including blankets.
[3] Including yarn made from tow.
[4] Including fabrics of natural silk and blankets and carpets of cellulosic fibres.
[5] Estimated production in Belgium and Luxembourg during 12 months ending 30 June of the year stated. Figures are in terms of nitrogen. Source: FAO, *Quarterly Bulletin of Statistics*.
[6] Estimated production in Belgium and Luxembourg during 12 months ending 30 April of the year stated. Figures are in terms of phosphoric acid. Source: FAO, *Quarterly Bulletin of Statistics*.
[7] Including alloys and the processing of refined copper imported from Zaire.
[8] Primary and secondary production, including alloys and remelted lead.
[9] Including alloys and remelted zinc.
[10] Factory shipments.
[11] Source: *Lloyd's Register of Shipping*.
[12] Assembled wholly or mainly from imported parts.

Finance

CURRENCY AND EXCHANGE RATES

Monetary Units
100 centimes (centiemen) = 1 franc belge (frank) or Belgian franc (BF).

Denominations
Coins: 50 centimes; 1, 5, 20 and 50 francs.
Notes: 100, 500, 1,000 and 5,000 francs.

Sterling and Dollar Equivalents (30 September 1990)
£1 sterling = 60.40 francs;
US $1 = 32.25 francs;
1,000 Belgian francs = £16.556 = $31.008.

Average Exchange Rate (francs per US $)
1987   37.334
1988   36.768
1989   39.404

Note: The information on the exchange rate refers to the official market rate, used for most current transactions. There is also a free exchange market rate, applicable to most capital transactions. The average of this latter rate (francs per US dollar) was: 37.57 in 1987; 37.01 in 1988; 39.51 in 1989.

BUDGET (million Belgian francs)

Revenue	1988*	1989†
Direct taxation	925,189	947,395
Customs and excise	109,355	121,301
VAT, stamp, registration and similar duties	409,965	433,356
Other current revenue	48,703	54,677
Capital revenues	4,831	6,843
Total	1,498,043	1,563,572

Expenditure	1988*	1989†
Government departments	796,104	790,533
Public debt	400,278	423,885
Pensions	194,866	198,507
Education and cultural services	285,615	295,584
Defence	102,423	99,000
Other expenditure	173,556	155,706
Total	1,952,842	1,963,215

* Provisional.   † Official estimates.

NATIONAL BANK RESERVES (US $ million at 31 December)*

	1987	1988	1989
Gold	1,421	1,421	1,277
IMF special drawing rights	700	563	556
Reserve position in IMF	557	464	449
Foreign exchange	8,363	8,306	9,760
Total	11,041	10,754	12,042

* Figures for gold and foreign exchange refer to the monetary association between Belgium and Luxembourg. Gold is valued at $42.22 per troy ounce. Figures exclude deposits made with the European Monetary Co-operation Fund.

MONEY SUPPLY ('000 million Belgian francs at 31 December)

	1987	1988	1989
Currency outside banks	410.7	415.0	422.6
Demand deposits at commercial banks	502.6	515.6	575.1
Monetary liabilities of other monetary institutions	180.3	192.4	215.0

BELGIUM

Statistical Survey

COST OF LIVING (Consumer Price Index. Base: 1981 = 100)

	1985	1986	1987
Food	132.1	134.5	133.66
Fuel and light	138.8	115.1	104.47
Clothing	128.0	137.7	145.23
All items (incl. others)	129.9	131.6	133.60

NATIONAL ACCOUNTS
('000 million Belgian francs at current prices)

National Income and Product

	1987	1988	1989
Compensation of employees	2,850.8	2,963.6	3,120.9
Operating surplus	1,448.0	1,617.8	1,852.7
Domestic factor incomes	4,298.8	4,581.4	4,973.6
Consumption of fixed capital	494.2	518.1	553.8
Gross domestic product (GDP) at factor cost	4,793.0	5,099.5	5,527.4
Indirect taxes	617.3	658.0	722.6
Less Subsidies	59.6	72.9	69.9
GDP in purchasers' values	5,350.7	5,684.6	6,180.1
Factor income from abroad	612.5	721.0	1,054.1
Less Factor income paid abroad	652.1	768.2	1,111.9
Gross national product (GNP)	5,311.1	5,637.4	6,122.3
Less Consumption of fixed capital	494.2	518.1	553.8
National income in market prices	4,816.9	5,119.3	5,568.5
Other current transfers from abroad	54.2	57.5	65.2
Less Other current transfers paid abroad	90.9	110.2	122.8
National disposable income	4,780.2	5,066.6	5,510.9

Expenditure on the Gross Domestic Product

	1987	1988	1989
Government final consumption expenditure	893.3	899.8	930.1
Private final consumption expenditure*	3,463.9	3,608.8	3,874.8
Increase in stocks†	14.5	26.4	43.5
Gross fixed capital formation	836.4	969.1	1,154.1
Total domestic expenditure	5,208.1	5,504.1	6,002.5
Exports of goods and services	3,476.7	3,899.9	4,498.0
Less Imports of goods and services	3,334.1	3,719.4	4,320.4
GDP in purchasers' values	5,350.7	5,684.6	6,180.1
GDP at constant 1985 prices	5,050.7	5,282.3	5,495.5

* Including statistical discrepancy ('000 million francs): 7.0 in 1987; 3.0 in 1988; 11.4 in 1989.
† Including adjustment in connection with gross fixed capital ('000 million francs): 1.7 in 1987; 0.8 in 1988; 3.5 in 1989.

Gross Domestic Product by Economic Activity

	1987	1988	1989
Agriculture and livestock	99.2	104.8	123.6
Forestry and logging	6.7	6.7	7.0
Fishing	2.5	2.2	2.3
Mining and quarrying	15.6	17.0	18.6
Manufacturing[1]	1,204.2	1,296.1	1,408.8
Electricity, gas and water	175.7	178.7	192.6
Construction	273.0	309.2	351.2
Wholesale and retail trade[2]	917.0	969.6	1,042.2
Distribution of petroleum products[2]	209.6	212.7	230.0
Transport, storage and communications	407.8	444.4	454.6
Finance and insurance	356.0	374.1	414.2
Real estate[3]	314.8	335.6	357.1
Business services	257.2	287.3	345.6
Public administration and defence	418.0	429.2	450.3
Education	294.3	297.7	313.1
Health services	149.2	160.6	172.4
Other community, social and personal services[4]	399.9	436.8	486.5
Domestic service of households	50.6	50.6	50.7
Sub-total	5,551.3	5,913.3	6,420.8
Imputed bank service charge	−93.0	−88.9	−94.5
Value-added tax deductible from capital formation	−102.6	−120.8	−146.6
Statistical discrepancy[5]	−5.0	−19.0	0.4
Total	5,350.7	5,684.6	6,180.1

[1] Including garages.　[2] Including import duties.
[3] Including imputed rent of owner-occupied dwellings.
[4] Including restaurants and hotels.
[5] Including a correction to compensate for the exclusion of certain own-account capital investments ('000 million francs): 7.6 in 1987; 8.9 in 1988; 10.1 in 1989.

BALANCE OF PAYMENTS (US $ million)*

	1987	1988	1989
Merchandise exports f.o.b.	76,088	85,496	89,988
Merchandise imports f.o.b.	−76,268	−84,273	−89,020
Trade balance	−180	1,223	967
Exports of services	48,264	56,112	71,850
Imports of services	−43,864	−51,986	−67,902
Balance on goods and services	4,220	5,349	4,915
Private unrequited transfers (net)	−114	41	47
Government unrequited transfers (net)	−1,313	−1,796	−1,765
Current balance	2,794	3,594	3,197
Direct capital investment (net)	−427	1,428	245
Other long-term capital (net)	−1,532	−5,174	−2,682
Short-term capital (net)	1,450	−1,209	−2,767
Net errors and omissions	−11	1,255	−311
Total (net monetary movements)	2,273	−104	−2,319
Monetization of gold (net)	−287	—	—
Valuation changes (net)	1,665	−1,155	1,437
Official financing (net)	161	965	2,320
Changes in reserves	3,812	−294	1,439

* Including Luxembourg.
Source: IMF, *International Financial Statistics*.

BELGIUM

External Trade of Belgium and Luxembourg

Note: Figures exclude trade in monetary gold, non-commercial military goods and silver specie.
Exports include stores and bunkers for foreign ships and aircraft.

PRINCIPAL COMMODITIES
(distribution by SITC, million Belgian francs)

Imports c.i.f.	1987	1988	1989*
Food and live animals	273,444	294,076	312,404
Dairy products and birds' eggs	40,540	46,869	52,296
Cereals and cereal preparations	50,498	55,894	49,117
Vegetables and fruit	56,113	58,445	66,021
Coffee, tea, cocoa and spices	28,939	27,506	27,371
Animal feeding-stuff (excl. cereals)	27,210	32,185	35,235
Beverages and tobacco	38,340	38,247	40,180
Crude materials (inedible) except fuels[1]	194,564	226,298	262,243
Oil seeds and oleaginous fruit	26,731	27,423	28,056
Textile fibres and waste[2]	28,792	31,669	35,138
Metalliferous ores and metal scrap[1]	59,841	79,472	98,345
Non-ferrous base metal waste and scrap	22,433	30,506	37,345
Mineral fuels, lubricants, etc. (incl. electric current)	283,757	243,518	297,216
Coal, coke and briquettes	34,619	37,425	41,135
Coal, lignite and peat	25,499	25,334	28,638
Petroleum, petroleum products, etc.	205,013	168,942	213,761
Crude petroleum oils, etc.	117,585	93,724	123,571
Refined petroleum products	82,796	71,296	85,595
Gas oils (distillate fuels)	26,056	21,153	28,319
Residual fuel oils	30,327	24,915	35,876
Gas (natural and manufactured)	38,593	30,448	—
Petroleum gases, etc., in the gaseous state	30,596	n.a.†	n.a.†
Animal and vegetable oils, fats and waxes	10,289	12,659	14,907
Chemicals and related products[2]	323,528	389,643	448,110
Organic chemicals[2]	99,738	131,684	149,321
Hydrocarbons and their derivatives[2]	43,208	61,592	69,560
Artificial resins, plastic materials, etc.[2]	78,947	25,307	31,034
Products of polymerization, etc.[2]	51,475	53,654	65,005
Basic manufactures[1,2]	670,222	805,270	953,396
Paper, paperboard and manufactures[2]	73,969	79,871	88,055
Paper and paperboard (not cut to size or shape)[2]	52,030	55,918	61,257
Textile yarn, fabrics, etc.	99,572	105,076	113,672
Textile yarn	41,036	41,871	43,701
Non-metallic mineral manufactures	219,045	267,602	337,663
Pearls, precious and semi-precious stones	176,912	217,330	281,746
Non-industrial diamonds (unset)	175,805	215,956	279,752
Sorted diamonds (rough or simply worked)	112,172	117,138	151,405
Cut diamonds (unmounted)	61,588	80,019	101,559
Iron and steel	90,473	114,830	131,873
Non-ferrous metals[1,2]	77,329	105,696	133,105
Copper and copper alloys[1]	31,772	42,379	62,266
Unwrought copper and alloys[1]	26,080	10,261	15,174
Aluminium and aluminium alloys	31,702	27,988	31,660
Other metal manufactures	68,396	81,560	93,974

Imports c.i.f.—continued	1987	1988	1989*
Machinery and transport equipment	920,910	809,973	941,204
Power generating machinery and equipment	73,285	51,874	54,698
Internal combustion piston engines (incl. parts)	56,853	35,941	34,263
Machinery specialized for particular industries	70,951	86,170	101,200
General industrial machinery, equipment and parts	86,778	105,535	122,665
Office machines and automatic data processing equipment	72,006	66,192	78,063
Automatic data processing machines, etc.	44,186	39,157	47,579
Electrical machinery, apparatus, etc.	136,042	158,123	178,710
Road vehicles and parts[3]	420,105	293,638	341,300
Passenger motor cars (excl. buses)	137,198	148,093	173,769
Parts and accessories for cars, buses, lorries, etc.	236,914	93,924	101,659
Miscellaneous manufactured articles	315,936	343,909	379,498
Clothing and accessories (excl. footwear)[2]	94,446	97,758	104,828
Other commodities and transactions	79,101	229,965	230,240
Non-monetary gold (excl. gold ores and concentrates)	23,309	31,288	13,148
Unwrought or semi-manufactured gold (excl. rolled gold)	23,213	31,045	12,981
Confidential transactions	48,523	28,843	30,456
Total	3,110,090	3,393,558	3,879,401

* Provisional.
† Beginning in 1988, revised SITC classifications have been used. The values of certain transactions are not, therefore, strictly comparable with those in earlier years.
[1] Copper matte, usually classified with metal ores and concentrates (under 'crude materials'), is included in non-ferrous metals (under 'basic manufactures').
[2] Figures exclude the value of certain confidential transactions, included in the last item of the table.
[3] Excluding tyres, engines and electrical parts.

Exports f.o.b.	1987	1988	1989*
Food and live animals[1]	279,056	283,899	333,873
Meat and meat preparations	55,250	59,464	72,921
Fresh, chilled or frozen meat	40,750	44,895	56,548
Dairy products and birds' eggs	48,671	54,179	61,496
Cereals and cereal preparations	40,461	38,734	39,218
Vegetables and fruit	44,518	45,996	56,892
Beverages and tobacco	25,563	24,516	26,879
Crude materials (inedible) except fuels[1,2]	77,351	94,216	110,026
Mineral fuels, lubricants, etc. (incl. electric current)	118,296	117,106	135,618
Petroleum, petroleum products, etc.	105,235	103,032	120,076
Refined petroleum products	98,780	96,381	112,798
Motor spirit (petrol) and other light oils	27,918	29,515	35,675
Motor spirit (incl. aviation spirit)	15,185	18,241	24,983
Gas oils (distillate fuels)	17,126	17,371	17,507
Residual fuel oils	31,244	27,845	34,425
Animal and vegetable oils, fats and waxes[1]	12,542	14,765	18,574
Chemicals and related products[1]	388,791	475,678	540,422
Organic chemicals[1]	61,910	93,147	106,204
Medicinal and pharmaceutical products[1]	40,320	10,629	12,176
Artificial resins, plastic materials, etc.	147,614	175,768	199,065
Products of polymerization, etc.[1]	101,944	88,095	98,517

BELGIUM   Statistical Survey

Exports f.o.b.—continued	1987	1988	1989*
Basic manufactures[1]	909,592	1,083,107	1,295,988
Paper, paperboard and manufactures	50,811	58,704	67,620
Textile yarn, fabrics, etc.[1]	174,416	181,447	206,126
Textile yarn	37,093	33,255	35,086
Floor coverings, etc.[1]	56,371	61,498	71,170
Carpets, carpeting, rugs, mats, etc.	55,584	60,744	70,268
Non-metallic mineral manufactures[1]	250,476	300,902	374,010
Pearls, precious and semi-precious stones	180,767	225,259	287,020
Non-industrial diamonds (unset)	179,854	224,243	285,271
Sorted diamonds (rough or simply worked)	93,151	119,641	155,814
Cut diamonds (unmounted)	86,656	104,510	129,404
Iron and steel[1]	224,348	293,413	339,417
Ingots and other primary forms	45,964	13,192	16,918
Bars, rods, angles, shapes, etc.	39,499	121,195†	130,445†
Universals, plates and sheets	102,084	43,595†	51,637†
Thin sheets and plates (rolled but not further worked)	42,100	n.a.†	n.a.†
Non-ferrous metals[1,2]	92,707	123,790	166,838
Copper and copper alloys[1,2]	38,865	53,992	78,452
Aluminium and aluminium alloys	31,957	42,793	51,088
Other metal manufactures	66,509	70,263	80,705
Machinery and transport equipment[1]	836,943	869,958	998,517
Power generating machinery and equipment[1]	19,862	19,696	21,147
Machinery specialized for particular industries[1]	82,424	86,310	100,872
General industrial machinery, equipment and parts[1]	53,905	60,464	72,421
Telecommunications and sound equipment	67,224	62,044	66,230
Other electrical machinery, apparatus, etc.	71,634	81,008	93,519
Road vehicles and parts[1,3]	464,788	491,993	554,580
Passenger motor cars (excl. buses)	356,483	357,257	397,533
Parts and accessories for cars, buses, lorries, etc.[3]	50,636	57,693	63,746
Miscellaneous manufactured articles[1]	251,343	261,933	294,363
Furniture and parts	35,584	37,529	41,272
Clothing and accessories (excl. footwear)	51,021	50,431	57,079
Photographic apparatus, etc., optical goods, watches and clocks[1]	46,396	47,392	51,512
Photographic and cinematographic supplies	41,886	42,293	44,746
Photographic film, plates and paper	37,626	37,592	40,202
Other commodities and transactions	200,673	157,151	185,819
Confidential transactions	184,688	138,670	163,401
Total	3,100,149	3,382,328	3,940,077

* Provisional.
† Beginning in 1988, revised SITC classifications have been used. The values of certain transactions are not, therefore, strictly comparable with those in earlier years.
[1] Figures exclude the value of certain confidential transactions, included in the last item of the table.
[2] Copper matte, usually classified with metal ores and concentrates (under 'crude materials'), is included in non-ferrous metals (under 'basic manufactures').
[3] Excluding tyres, engines and electrical parts.

PRINCIPAL TRADING PARTNERS* (million Belgian francs)

Imports c.i.f.	1987	1988	1989†
Austria	23,928	26,274	30,557
Brazil	17,524	19,032	22,858
Canada	21,624	23,267	25,824
France	487,807	522,176	578,609
Germany, Federal Republic	755,713	829,256	912,441
Iraq	11,881	6,599	11,602
Italy	132,440	144,410	164,463
Japan	82,960	77,087	88,152
Libya	13,662	7,977	7,458
Netherlands	533,407	602,458	682,276
Norway	19,349	19,469	31,719
Saudi Arabia	16,701	19,179	16,740
South Africa and Namibia	14,362	20,688	28,828
Spain (excl. Canary Is.)	37,124	51,323	55,048
Sweden	70,544	73,304	81,856
Switzerland	60,520	61,252	63,210
USSR	48,008	45,928	46,543
United Kingdom	244,250	259,002	305,983
USA	147,643	150,464	178,778
Zaire	23,934	31,287	34,298
All countries (incl. others)	3,097,558	3,391,395	3,877,161
Not distributed	12,532	2,163	2,240
Total	3,110,090	3,393,558	3,879,401

Exports f.o.b.	1987	1988	1989†
Austria	29,155	35,437	41,000
Canada	15,070	17,205	19,045
Denmark	32,847	32,107	35,023
France	633,880	675,507	804,065
Germany, Federal Republic	614,626	657,305	744,525
India	38,463	50,785	63,956
Israel	46,645	52,621	60,271
Italy	197,523	210,375	251,028
Japan	31,671	39,827	51,530
Netherlands	465,961	497,965	540,272
Norway	21,982	19,433	21,910
Saudi Arabia	15,075	15,851	16,898
Spain (excl. Canary Is.)	57,104	72,859	91,958
Sweden	44,461	51,729	60,143
Switzerland	70,898	76,985	89,595
USSR	18,352	19,328	21,229
United Kingdom	261,012	315,520	370,114
USA	161,264	168,304	189,721
All countries (incl. others)	3,076,890	3,359,922	3,910,971
Not distributed	23,259	22,406	29,106
Total	3,100,149	3,382,328	3,940,077

* Imports by country of production; exports by country of last consignment.
† Provisional.

Transport

RAILWAYS (traffic)

	1987	1988	1989
Passenger-km (million)	6,270	6,348	6,400
Freight ton-km (million)	7,266	7,694	8,049

ROAD TRAFFIC (motor vehicles in use at 1 August)

	1988	1989	1990
Private cars	3,613,571	3,736,317	3,864,159
Buses and coaches	15,811	15,831	15,644
Goods vehicles	309,972	326,681	343,241
Tractors (non-agricultural)	32,936	35,198	37,138

BELGIUM

SHIPPING

Fleet (at 30 June)

	1988	1989	1990
Merchant shipping:			
Steamships:			
number	1	1	1
displacement*	78.5	78.5	78.5
Motor vessels:			
number	77	74	68
displacement*	1,960.9	1,936.4	1,836.0
Inland waterways:			
Powered craft:			
number	1,828	1,796	1,769
displacement*	1,095.7	1,092.6	1,090.8
Non-powered craft:			
number	167	151	164
displacement*	334.0	329.5	365.9

* '000 gross registered tons.

Freight Traffic ('000 metric tons)

	1987	1988	1989
Sea-borne shipping:			
Goods loaded	45,648	49,440	n.a.
Goods unloaded	81,652	87,221	n.a.
Inland waterways:			
Goods loaded	50,843	50,556	48,433
Goods unloaded	62,692	67,562	67,269

CIVIL AVIATION (traffic)

	1987	1988	1989
Kilometres flown ('000)	57,910	64,332	72,035
Passenger-km ('000)	5,976,593	6,528,322	6,759,997
Ton-km ('000)	538,148	587,549	608,000
Mail ton-km ('000)	22,549	24,826	25,000

Figures refer to SABENA.

Tourism

	1987	1988	1989
Number of tourist nights*	10,064,504	10,577,065	12,168,303

* Foreign visitors only.

Communications Media

	1987	1988	1989
Telephones in use	4,719,273	4,941,110	5,138,000
Television receivers in use	3,172,636	3,258,127	3,274,236
Radio receivers in use	4,608,000	n.a.	n.a.

Newspapers (1989): 35 general interest dailies (combined circulation 2,120,887).

Book titles (production, 1985): 8,327, of which 7,392 were first editions.

Source: partly UNESCO, *Statistical Yearbook*, and Association Belge des Editeurs de Journaux.

Education

(1988/89)

	Institutions		Students	
	French and German	Dutch	French and German	Dutch
Pre-primary	2,034	2,155	155,589	213,735
Primary	2,165	2,443	320,631	434,998
Secondary	884	1,239	366,697	459,223
Non-university higher education	204	253	50,542	79,721
University level	10	8	51,196	53,069

Source: Ministerie van Onderwijs, *Educational Developments in Belgium 1988-1990*.

Teachers: Pre-primary 19,793 in 1985; Primary 71,064 in 1987; Secondary 114,628 in 1987; Non-university higher education 14,548 in 1987; University level 5,349 in 1986.

Directory

The Constitution

The Belgian Constitution has been considerably modified by amendments since its origin in 1831. Belgium is a constitutional monarchy. The central legislature consists of a Chamber of Representatives and a Senate. The Chamber of Representatives consists of 212 members, who are elected for four years unless the Chamber is dissolved before that time has elapsed. The existence of French, Flemish and German-speaking Communities, and of regional authorities for Flanders, Wallonia and Brussels, was envisaged in the constitutional revision of 24 December 1970. (The Flemish and Walloon Regions became operational following the enactment of legislation in August 1980.) The establishment of a regional body for Brussels, and the transfer of certain competences and public funds from the central Government to the Communities, was effected by a series of modifications to the Constitution that were approved by the legislature in 1988-89.

ELECTORAL SYSTEM

Members must be 25 years of age, and they are elected by secret ballot according to a system of proportional representation. Suffrage is universal for citizens of 18 years or over, and voting is compulsory.

The Senate, or Second Chamber, is chosen in the following manner. It is composed of:

(1) Half as many members as the Chamber of Representatives, elected directly by the same electors.

(2) Members chosen by the Provincial Councillors, in the proportion of one for every 200,000 population.

(3) Members co-opted by groups (1) and (2), up to half the number of group (2).

(4) One Senator by right, the heir to the throne.

There are now 182 Senators.

All Senators must be over 40, with the exception of a small number of members of the royal family, who become Senators by right at the age of 18. Members are elected for four years.

THE CROWN

The King has the right to veto legislation, but, in practice, he does not exercise it. The king is nominally the supreme head of the executive, but, in fact, he exercises his control through the Cabinet, which is responsible for all acts of government to the Chamber of

BELGIUM

Representatives. According to the Constitution, the King appoints his own ministers, but in practice, since they are responsible to the Chamber of Representatives and need its confidence, they are generally the choice of the Representatives. Similarly, the royal initiative is in the control of the ministry.

LEGISLATION

Legislation is introduced either by the Government or the members in the two Houses, and as the party complexion of both Houses is generally almost the same, measures passed by the Chamber of Representatives are usually passed by the Senate. Each House elects its own President at the beginning of the session, who acts as an impartial Speaker, although he is a party nominee. The Houses elect their own committees, through which all legislation passes. They are so well organized that through them the Legislature has considerable power of control over the Cabinet. Nevertheless, according to the Constitution (Article 68), certain treaties must be communicated to the Chamber only as soon as the 'interest and safety of the State permit'. Further, the Government possesses an important power of dissolution which it uses; a most unusual feature is that it may be applied to either House separately or to both together (Article 71).

Revision of the Constitution is to be first settled by an ordinary majority vote of both Houses, specifying the article to be amended. The Houses are then automatically dissolved. The new Chambers then determine the amendments to be made, with the provision that in each House the presence of two-thirds of the members is necessary for a quorum, and a two-thirds majority of those voting is required.

LOCAL ADMINISTRATION

The system of local government conforms to the general European practice of being based on a combination of central officials as the executive agent and locally elected councillors as the deliberating body. The areas are the provinces and the communes, and the latter are empowered by Article 108 of the Constitution to associate for the purposes of better government.

The Government

HEAD OF STATE

King of the Belgians: HM King BAUDOUIN (BOUDEWIJN) (took the oath 17 July 1951).

THE CABINET
(November 1990)

(CVP) and (PSC) Christian Social Party; (PS) Parti Socialiste; (SP) Socialistische Partij; (VU) Volksunie.

Prime Minister: Dr WILFRIED MARTENS (CVP).
Deputy Prime Minister, Minister for the Brussels Region and of Institutional Reforms (French Sector): PHILIPPE MOUREAUX (PS).
Deputy Prime Minister, Minister of Economic Affairs and Planning and National Education (Flemish Sector): WILLY CLAES (SP).
Deputy Prime Minister, Minister of Communications and Institutional Reforms (Flemish Sector): JEAN-LUC DEHAENE (CVP).
Deputy Prime Minister, Minister of Justice and the Middle Classes: MELCHIOR WATHELET (PSC).
Deputy Prime Minister, Minister of the Budget and Scientific Policy: HUGO SCHLTZ (VU).
Minister of Foreign Affairs: MARK EYSKENS (CVP).
Minister of Finance: PHILIPPE MAYSTADT (PSC).
Minister of Foreign Trade: ROBERT URBAIN (PS).
Minister of the Civil Service: RAYMOND LANGENDRIES (PSC).
Minister of Posts and Telecommunications: FREDDY WILLOCKX (SP).
Minister of Social Affairs: PHILIPPE BUSQUIN (PS).
Minister of National Defence: GUY COËME (PS).
Minister of Public Works: PAULA D'HONDT-VAN OPDENBOSCH (CVP).
Minister of the Interior and for the Modernization of the Civil Service and National Scientific and Cultural Institutions: LOUIS TOBBACK (SP).
Minister of National Education (French Sector): YVAN YLIEFF (SP).
Minister of Development Co-operation: ANDRÉ GEENS (VU).
Minister of Pensions: ALAIN VAN DER BIEST (PS).
Minister of Employment and Labour: LUC VAN DEN BRANDE (CVP).

There are 13 Secretaries of State.

MINISTRIES

Office of the Prime Minister: 16 rue de la Loi, 1000 Brussels; tel. (02) 513-80-20; telex 62400.
Ministry for the Brussels Region: 21–23 blvd du Régent, 1000 Brussels; tel. (02) 513-82-00; telex 25190.
Ministry of the Budget and Scientific Policy: 26 rue de la Loi, 1040 Brussels; tel. (02) 237-93-11; telex 22292; fax (02) 237-93-64.
Ministry of the Civil Service: Lynton Building, 31 rue du Commerce, 1040 Brussels; tel. (02) 513-88-40.
Ministry of Communications and Institutional Reforms (Flemish Sector): 65 rue de la Loi, 1040 Brussels; tel. (02) 237-67-11; telex 25183; fax (02) 230-18-24.
Ministry of Development Co-operation: WTC Tower 2, 162 blvd Emile Jacqmain, BP 44, 1210 Brussels; tel. (02) 210-19-11; telex 20832; fax (02) 217-33-28.
Ministry of Economic Affairs and Planning: 23 square de Meeûs, 1040 Brussels; tel. (02) 511-19-30; telex 21062; fax (02) 514-03-89.
Ministry of Education and Scientific Research (French Sector): 68A rue du Commerce, 1040 Brussels; tel. (02) 511-72-60; telex 24619; fax (02) 511-94-07.
Ministry of Employment and Labour: 51 rue Belliard, 1040 Brussels; tel. (02) 233-41-11; telex 22937; fax (02) 233-44-88.
Ministry of Finance: 12 rue de la Loi, 1000 Brussels; tel. (02) 233-81-11.
Ministry of Foreign Affairs: 2 rue des Quatre Bras, 1000 Brussels; tel. (02) 516-81-11; telex 23979; fax (02) 514-30-67.
Ministry of Foreign Trade: 2 rue des Quatre Bras, 1000 Brussels; tel. (02) 516-83-11; fax (02) 512-72-21.
Ministry of Institutional Reforms (French Sector): 21–23 blvd du Régent, 1000 Brussels; tel. (02) 513-82-00.
Ministry of the Interior and for the Modernization of Public Services and National Scientific and Cultural Institutions: 94 rue Royale, 1000 Brussels; tel. (02) 210-84-11; fax (02) 217-81-26.
Ministry of Justice: 4 place Poelaert, 1000 Brussels; tel. (02) 513-67-88; telex 62440; fax (02) 514-15-75.
Ministry of the Middle Classes: 61 rue de la Régence, 1000 Brussels; tel. (02) 511-19-48.
Ministry of National Defence: 8 rue Lambermont, 1000 Brussels; tel. (02) 512-16-10; telex 61104.
Ministry of National Education (Flemish Sector): 3 rue Ducale, 1000 Brussels; tel. (02) 513-28-90; telex 26750.
Ministry of Pensions: 31 rue du Commerce, 1040 Brussels; tel. (02) 513-63-70.
Ministry of Posts and Telecommunications: 56 rue de la Loi, 1040 Brussels; tel. (02) 230-13-30; telex 22681; fax (02) 230-57-02.
Ministry of Public Works: 155 rue de la Loi (9e étage), 1040 Brussels; tel. (02) 734-91-07; telex 63477; fax (02) 230-99-12.
Ministry of Social Affairs: 66 rue de la Loi, 1040 Brussels; tel. (02) 238-28-11; fax (02) 230-38-95.

Legislature

CHAMBRE DES REPRÉSENTANTS/KAMER VAN VOLKSVERTEGENWOORDIGERS
(Chamber of Representatives)

General Election, 13 December 1987

	Votes	%	Seats
CVP	1,194,687	19.45	43
PS	961,429	15.66	40
SP	913,975	14.88	32
PVV	709,137	11.55	25
PRL	577,897	9.41	23
PSC	491,839	8.01	19
VU	494,229	8.05	16
Agalev	275,307	4.48	6
Ecolo	157,985	2.57	3
FDF	71,340	1.16	3
Vlaams Blok	116,410	1.90	2
PCB/KPB	51,074	0.83	0
PvdA/PTB	45,102	0.74	0
Others	80,741	1.31	0
Total	**6,141,212**	**100.00**	**212**

SÉNAT/SENAAT
General Election, 13 December 1987

	Votes	%	Seats
CVP	1,169,539	19.20	22
PS	958,760	15.74	20
SP	896,114	14.71	17
PRL	564,221	9.26	12
PVV	686,608	11.27	11
PSC	474,708	7.79	9
VU	494,432	8.12	8
Agalev	299,051	4.91	3
Ecolo	168,381	2.76	2
Vlaams Blok	122,925	2.02	1
FDF	77,596	1.27	1
PCB/KPB	52,322	0.86	0
PvdA/PTB	43,381	0.71	0
Others	84,522	1.39	0
Total	6,092,560	100.00	106

In addition, the Senate has 50 members elected by provincial councils, a further 25 co-opted by the elected members and one Senator by right, the heir to the throne.

Political Organizations

Anders Gaan Leven (Agalev) (Ecologist Party—Dutch-speaking): 78 Twee Kerkenstraat, 1040 Brussels; tel. (02) 230-66-66; f. 1982; Pres. LÉO COX.

Ecolo (Ecologist Party—French-speaking): 28 rue Basse-Marcelle, 5000 Namur; tel. (081) 22-78-71; fax (081) 28-06-03; Federal Secs JACKY MORAEL, MARCEL CHERON, CLAUDE ADRIAEN, DIDIER PATERNOTTE, SALVATORE MIRAGLIA..

Front Démocratique des Bruxellois Francophones (FDF) (French-speaking Democratic Front): 127 chaussée de Charleroi, 1060 Brussels; tel. (02) 538-83-20; f. 1964; aims at the preservation of the French character of Brussels and the establishment of a federal state; Pres. GEORGES CLERFAYT; Sec.-Gen. JEAN-PIERRE CORNELISSEN.

Front National: f. 1988; extreme right-wing nationalist party; Leader WERNER VAN STEEN.

Partei der Deutschsprachigen Belgier (PDB) (German-speaking Party): 6 Kaperberg, 4700 Eupen; f. 1971; aims at equality of rights for the German-speaking minority as recognized in the national constitution; Pres. ALFRED KEUTGEN (Eupen).

Parti Féministe Humaniste: 35 ave des Phalènes, BP 14, 1050 Ixelles, Région bruxelloise; tel. (02) 648-87-38; f. 1972 as Parti Féministe Unifié, name changed 1990; aims at the creation of a humanistic, self-governing, egalitarian and pacific republic where the fundamental rights of the individual and of society are respected.

Parti de la Liberté du Citoyen (PLC): 46 ave de Scheut, 1070 Brussels; tel. (02) 524-39-66; Pres. LUC EYKERMAN.

Parti Réformateur Libéral (PRL) (Liberal Party—French-speaking wing): Centre International Rogier, 26e étage, BP 570, 1210 Brussels; tel. (02) 219-43-30; fax (02) 217-65-48; f. 1979 as Parti des Réformes et de la Liberté en Wallonie; Pres. ANTOINE DUQUESNE; Vice-Pres. DANIEL DUCARME; 60,000 mems.

Parti Social Chrétien (PSC)/Christelijke Volkspartij (CVP) (Christian Social Party): 41 rue des deux Eglises, 1040 Brussels; tel. (02) 238-01-11; fax (02) 238-01-29 (PSC); tel. (02) 230-60-70 (CVP); f. 1945; Pres. (PSC) GÉRARD DEPREZ; Pres. (CVP) HERMAN VAN ROMPUY; 186,000 mems.

Parti Socialiste (PS) (Socialist Party—French-speaking wing): Maison du PS, 13 blvd de l'Empereur, 1000 Brussels; tel. (02) 513-82-70; fax (02) 513-23-92; f. in 1885 as the Parti Ouvrier Belge; split from the Flemish wing in 1979; Pres. GUY SPITAELS; Sec. ROGER GAILLIEZ.

Parti Wallon (PW) (Walloon Party): 2 rue Maurice Lange, 1381 Quenast; f. 1985 by amalgamation of the Rassemblement Wallon (f. 1968), the Rassemblement Populaire Wallon and the Front Indépendantiste Wallon; left-wing socialist party advocating an independent Walloon state; Pres. JEAN-CLAUDE PICCIN.

Partij van de Arbeid van België (PvdA)/Parti du Travail de Belgique (PTB) (Belgian Labour Party): f. 1979; Marxist-Leninist; Leader LUDO MARTENS.

Partij voor Vrijheid en Vooruitgang (PVV) (Liberal Party—Dutch-speaking wing): 34 Melsensstraat, 1000 Brussels; tel. (02) 512-78-70; f. 1961; succeeded the former Liberal Party; Pres. GUY VERHOFSTADT.

Socialistische Partij (SP) (Socialist Party—Flemish wing): 13 blvd de l'Empereur, 1000 Brussels; tel. (02) 513-28-78; fax (02) 511-12-90; f. 1885; Pres. FRANK VANDENBROUCKE; Sec. CARLA GALLE.

Union des Communistes de Belgique–Unie van Kommunisten van België (PCB-KPB) (Communist Party): 18–20 ave de Stalingrad, 1000 Brussels; tel. (02) 514-54-64; fax (02) 512-23-84; f. 1921 as Parti Communiste de Belgique–Kommunistische Partij van België, name changed 1990; Pres. LOUIS VAN GEYT; Vice-Pres. MARCEL LEVAUX; 7,000 mems.

Vlaams Blok (Flemish Nationalist Party): 8 Madouplein, bus 9, 1030 Brussels; tel. (02) 219-60-09; fax (02) 217-52-75; f. 1979; Chair. KAREL DILLEN.

Volksunie (VU) (People's Union): 12 Barrikadenplein, 1000 Brussels; tel. (02) 219-49-30; fax (02) 217-35-10; f. 1954; 60,000 mems; Flemish nationalist party aiming at federal structure for the country; Pres. JAAK GABRIELS; Sec. P. VAN GREMBERGEN.

Terrorist organizations include the extreme left-wing Cellules Communistes Combattantes (CCC) and the associated Front Révolutionnaire d'Action Prolétarienne (FRAP), and the extreme right-wing Westland New Post (WNP).

Diplomatic Representation

EMBASSIES IN BELGIUM

Algeria: 209 ave Molière, 1060 Brussels; tel. (02) 343-50-78; telex 64142; Ambassador: NOURREDINE KERROUM.

Angola: 182 rue Franz Merjay, 1180 Brussels; tel. (02) 344-49-80; telex 63170; Ambassador: EMÍLIO CARVALHO GUERRA.

Argentina: 225 ave Louise, BP 6, 1050 Brussels; tel. (02) 647-78-12; Ambassador: Dr VICTOR MASSUH.

Australia: 6–8 rue Guimard, 1040 Brussels; tel. (02) 231-05-00; telex 21834; fax (02) 230-68-02; Ambassador: PETER CAMPBELL JOHN CURTIS.

Austria: 47 rue de l'Abbaye, 1050 Brussels; tel. (02) 649-91-70; telex 22463; Ambassador: HEINZ WEINBERGER.

Bangladesh: 29–31 rue Jacques Jordaens, 1050 Brussels; tel. (02) 640-55-00; telex 63189; Ambassador: A. K. M. KAMALUDDIN CHOUDHURY.

Barbados: 162 ave Louise (1e étage), 1050 Brussels; tel. (02) 648-13-58; telex 63926; fax (02) 646-23-97; Ambassador: RASHID ORLANDO MARVILLE.

Benin: 5 ave de l'Observatoire, 1180 Brussels; tel. (02) 374-91-92; telex 24568; Ambassador: TAIRON DJAOUGA-MAMADOU.

Bolivia: 176 ave Louise, BP 6, 1050 Brussels; tel. (02) 647-27-18; telex 63494; fax (02) 647-47-82; Ambassador: EDUARDO RUÍZ GARCÍA.

Botswana: 169 ave de Tervueren, 1040 Brussels; tel. (02) 735-20-70; telex 22849; fax (02) 735-63-18; Ambassador: ERNEST SIPHO MPOFU.

Brazil: 350 ave Louise, BP 5, 1050 Brussels; tel. (02) 640-20-15; telex 26758; fax (02) 640-81-34; Ambassador: MARCO CÉSAR MEIRA NASLAUSKY.

Bulgaria: 58 ave Hamoir, 1180 Brussels; tel. (02) 374-59-63; telex 22473; Ambassador: ATANAS GUEORGUIEV GUINEV.

Burkina Faso: 16 place Guy d'Arezzo, 1060 Brussels; tel. (02) 345-99-12; telex 22252; Ambassador: AMADÉ OUEDRAOGO.

Burundi: 46 square Marie-Louise, 1040 Brussels; tel. (02) 230-45-35; telex 23572; fax (02) 230-78-83; Ambassador: JULIEN NAHAYO.

Cameroon: 131 ave Brugmann, 1060 Brussels; tel. (02) 345-18-70; telex 24117; Ambassador: ISABELLE BASSONG-AKOUMBA-MONNEYANG.

Canada: 2 ave de Tervueren, 1040 Brussels; tel. (02) 735-60-40; telex 21613; fax (02) 735-33-83; Ambassador: JACQUES J. A. ASSELIN.

Central African Republic: 416 blvd Lambermont, 1030 Brussels; tel. (02) 242-28-80; telex 22493; Ambassador: JOSÉ-MARIA W. PEHOUA.

Chad: 52 blvd Lambermont, 1030 Brussels; tel. (02) 215-19-75; Ambassador: ABDOULAYE LAMANA.

Chile: 17 rue Montoyer, 1040 Brussels; tel. (02) 512-46-00; telex 61955; Ambassador: JUAN LUIS GONZÁLEZ REYES.

China, People's Republic: 443–445 ave de Tervueren, 1150 Brussels; tel. (02) 771-33-09; Ambassador: XIA DAOSHENG.

Colombia: 44 rue Van Eyck, BP 5–6, 1050 Brussels; tel. (02) 649-56-79; telex 25254; fax (02) 649-42-39; Ambassador: MANUEL JOSÉ CÁRDENAS.

Congo: 16-18 ave F. D. Roosevelt, 1050 Brussels; tel. (02) 648-38-56; telex 23677; Ambassador: AMBROISE GAMBOUELE.

BELGIUM
Directory

Costa Rica: 489 ave Louise, 1050 Brussels; tel. (02) 640-55-41; fax (02) 648-31-92; Ambassador: Daniel Ratton Thiery.

Côte d'Ivoire: 234 ave F. D. Roosevelt, 1050 Brussels; tel. (02) 672-23-57; telex 21993; Ambassador: Charles Valy Tuho.

Cuba: 77 rue Roberts-Jones, 1180 Brussels; tel. (02) 343-00-20; telex 21945; fax (02) 344-96-91; Ambassador: Teresita Averhoff Purón.

Cyprus: 83 rue de la Loi (4e étage), 1040 Brussels; tel. (02) 230-12-95; telex 25172; Ambassador: Nicos Agathocleous.

Czechoslovakia: 152 ave Adolphe Buyl, 1050 Brussels; tel. (02) 647-68-09; telex 64565; fax (02) 647-71-26; Ambassador: Karel Lukas.

Denmark: 221 ave Louise, BP 7, 1050 Brussels; tel. (02) 648-25-25; telex 22591; fax (02) 647-07-09; Ambassador: Carl Ernst Wilhelm Ulrichsen.

Djibouti: 24 ave F. D. Roosevelt, 1050 Brussels; tel. (02) 646-29-99; Ambassador: Hassan Idriss Ahmed.

Dominica: 12 rue des Bollandistes, 1040 Brussels; tel. (02) 733-43-28; Ambassador: Charles Angelo Savarin.

Dominican Republic: 106A ave Louise, 1050 Brussels; tel. (02) 646-08-40; Chargé d'affaires a.i.: Renso Herrera Franco.

Ecuador: 70 chaussée de Charleroi, 1060 Brussels; tel. (02) 537-91-30; telex 63292; fax (02) 537-90-66; Ambassador: Xavier Pérez Martínez.

Egypt: 44 ave Léo Errera, 1180 Brussels; tel. (02) 345-52-53; telex 23716; fax (02) 343-65-33; Ambassador: Hussein el-Kamel.

Ethiopia: 32 blvd St Michel, 1040 Brussels; tel. (02) 733-98-18; telex 62285; fax (02) 732-18-51; Ambassador: Hailu Wolde Amanuel.

Fiji: 66–68 ave de Cortenberg (7e étage), BP 7, 1040 Brussels; tel. (02) 736-90-50; telex 26934; fax (02) 736-14-58; Ambassador: Kaliopate Tavola.

Finland: 489 ave Louise (5e étage), 1050 Brussels; tel. (02) 648-84-84; telex 23099; Ambassador: Ensio Helaniemi.

France: 65 rue Ducale, 1000 Brussels; tel. (02) 512-17-15; telex 21478; Ambassador: Comte Xavier du Cauzé de Nazelle.

Gabon: 112 ave W. Churchill, 1180 Brussels; tel. (02) 343-00-55; telex 23383; Ambassador: Michel Leslie Taele.

Gambia: 126 ave F. D. Roosevelt, 1050 Brussels; tel. (02) 640-10-49; telex 24344; Ambassador: Mamadu Kalifo Bojang.

Germany: 190 ave de Tervueren, 1150 Brussels; tel. (02) 770-58-30; telex 21382; fax (02) 772-36-92; Ambassador: Renate Finke-Osiander.

Ghana: 44 rue Gachard, 1050 Brussels; tel. (02) 649-01-63; telex 22572; Ambassador: H. O. Quashie.

Greece: 430 ave Louise (3e étage), 1050 Brussels; tel. (02) 648-33-02; telex 25521; Ambassador: Constantin Eliopoulos.

Grenada: 24 ave des Arts (7e étage), BP 2, 1040 Brussels; tel. (02) 230-62-65; telex 64015; fax (02) 230-39-63; Chargé d'affaires a.i.: Samuel Orgias.

Guatemala: 53 blvd Général Wahis, 1030 Brussels; tel. (02) 736-03-40; telex 25130; Ambassador: Carlos Humberto Jiménez Licona.

Guinea: 75 ave Roger Vandendriessche, 1150 Brussels; tel. (02) 771-01-26; telex 64731; Ambassador: Mamadou Bobo Camara.

Guinea-Bissau: 70 ave F. D. Roosevelt, 1050 Brussels; tel. (02) 647-08-90; telex 63631; fax (02) 640-43-12; Ambassador: Bubacar Turé.

Guyana: 21–22 ave des Arts, 1040 Brussels; tel. (02) 230-60-65; telex 26180; Ambassador: James Henry Edward Matheson.

Haiti: 160A ave Louise, BP 25, 1050 Brussels; tel. (02) 649-73-81; fax (02) 649-62-47; Chargé d'affaires a.i.: Maryse Penette.

Holy See: 5–9 ave des Franciscains, 1150 Brussels (Apostolic Nunciature); tel. (02) 762-20-05; Apostolic Nuncio: Most Rev. Giovanni Moretti, Titular Archbishop of Vartana.

Honduras: 3 ave des Gaulois (5e étage), 1040 Brussels; tel. (02) 734-00-00; telex 63175; Chargé d'affaires a.i.: Edith Glynn.

Hungary: 41 rue Edmond Picard, 1180 Brussels; tel. (02) 343-67-90; telex 21428; Ambassador: György Granasztói.

Iceland: 5 rue Archimède (8e étage), 1040 Brussels; tel. (02) 231-03-95; telex 29459; fax (02) 230-81-46; Ambassador: Einar Benediktsson.

India: 217 chaussée de Vleurgat, 1050 Brussels; tel. (02) 640-91-40; telex 22510; fax (02) 648-96-30; Ambassador: G. V. Ramakrishna.

Indonesia: 294 ave de Tervueren, 1150 Brussels; tel. (02) 771-20-14; telex 21200; Ambassador: Atmono Suryo.

Iran: 415 ave de Tervueren, 1150 Brussels; tel. (02) 762-37-45; telex 24000; Ambassador: Mohammad Reza Bakhtiari.

Iraq: 131 ave de la Floride, 1180 Brussels; tel. (02) 374-59-92; telex 26414; Ambassador: Zaïd Hwaishan Haidar.

Ireland: 19 rue du Luxembourg (3e étage), 1040 Brussels; tel. (02) 513-66-33; telex 24598; Ambassador: Gearoid Ó Clerich.

Israel: 40 ave de l'Observatoire, 1180 Brussels; tel. (02) 374-90-80; telex 24290; fax (02) 374-98-20; Ambassador: Avraham Primor.

Italy: 28 rue Emile Claus, 1050 Brussels; tel. (02) 649-97-00; telex 23950; fax (02) 648-54-85; Ambassador: Giovanni Saragat.

Jamaica: 83–85 rue de la Loi (5e étage), 1040 Brussels; tel. (02) 230-11-70; telex 26644; Ambassador: Leslie Wilson.

Japan: 58 ave des Arts (7e étage), 1040 Brussels; tel. (02) 513-92-00; telex 22174; Ambassador: Atsuhiko Yatabe.

Jordan: 104 ave F. D. Roosevelt, 1050 Brussels; tel. (02) 640-77-55; telex 62513; Chargé d'affaires a.i.: Nabil Masarweh.

Kenya: 1–5 ave de la Joyeuse Entrée, 1040 Brussels; tel. (02) 230-30-65; telex 62568; Ambassador: Francis Kirimi Muthaura.

Korea, Republic: 3 ave Hamoir, 1180 Brussels; tel. (02) 375-39-80; telex 26256; Ambassador: Chung Woo Young.

Kuwait: 43 ave F. D. Roosevelt, 1050 Brussels; tel. (02) 647-79-50; telex 62904; fax (02) 646-12-98; Ambassador: Ahmad A. Al-Ebrahim.

Lebanon: 2 rue Guillaume Stocq, 1050 Brussels; tel. (02) 649-94-60; telex 22547; Ambassador: Dr Saïd al-Assaad.

Lesotho: 66 ave de Cortenbergh, BP 5, 1040 Brussels; tel. (02) 736-39-76; telex 25852; Ambassador: Mabotse Lerotholi.

Liberia: 55 ave F. D. Roosevelt, 1050 Brussels; tel. (02) 648-13-49; telex 61384; Chargé d'affaires a.i.: Jarjar Kamara.

Libya: 28 ave Victoria, 1050 Brussels; tel. (02) 649-21-12; Sec. of People's Bureau: Dr Mohamed Saraf Edin Alfaituri.

Luxembourg: 211 rue du Noyer, 1040 Brussels; tel. (02) 733-99-77; Ambassador: Guy de Muyser.

Madagascar: 276 ave de Tervueren, 1150 Brussels; tel. (02) 770-17-26; telex 61197; Ambassador: Christian Rémi Richard.

Malawi: 13 rue de la Loi, 1040 Brussels; tel. (02) 231-09-80; telex 24128; Ambassador: Lawrence P. Anthony.

Malaysia: 414A ave de Tervueren, 1150 Brussels; tel. (02) 762-67-67; telex 26396; fax (02) 762-50-49; Ambassador: Dato Dali M. Hashim.

Mali: 487 ave Molière, 1060 Brussels; tel. (02) 345-74-32; telex 22508; fax (02) 344-57-00; Ambassador: Lamine Keïta.

Malta: 44 rue Jules Lejeune, 1060 Brussels; tel. (02) 343-01-95; telex 26616; fax (02) 343-01-06; Ambassador: Dr Joseph Licari.

Mauritania: 127 ave Gustave Demey, 1160 Brussels; tel. (02) 672-47-47; Ambassador: Ely Ould Allaf.

Mauritius: 68 rue des Bollandistes, 1040 Brussels; tel. (02) 733-99-88; telex 23114; fax (02) 734-40-21; Ambassador: Raymond Chasle.

Mexico: 164 chaussée de la Hulpe, 1170 Brussels; tel. (02) 676-07-11; telex 22355; fax (02) 672-93-12; Ambassador: Adolfo Hegewisch.

Monaco: 17 place Guy d'Arezzo, BP 7, 1060 Brussels; tel. (02) 347-49-87; fax (02) 343-49-20; Ambassador: François Giraudon.

Morocco: 29 blvd St Michel, 1040 Brussels; tel. (02) 736-11-00; telex 21233; fax (02) 734-64-68; Ambassador: Abdallah Lahlou.

Mozambique: 97 blvd Saint-Michel, 1040 Brussels; tel. (02) 736-25-64; telex 65478; fax (02) 735-62-07; Ambassador: Frances Victoria Velho Rodrigues.

Netherlands: 35 rue de la Science, 1040 Brussels; tel. (02) 230-30-20; telex 21311; Ambassador: Hubert Joseph Marie van Nispen tot Sevenaer.

New Zealand: 47–48 blvd du Régent, 1000 Brussels; tel. (02) 512-10-40; fax (02) 513-48-56; Ambassador: David Lepreu Gamble.

Nicaragua: 55 ave de Wolvendael, 1180 Brussels; tel. (02) 375-65-00; telex 63553; fax (02) 375-71-88; Ambassador: Sergio Mario Blandon Lanzas.

Niger: 78 ave F. D. Roosevelt, 1050 Brussels; tel. (02) 648-61-40; telex 22857; Ambassador: Adamou Zada.

Nigeria: 288 ave de Tervueren, 1150 Brussels; tel. (02) 762-98-31; telex 22435; Ambassador: Maurice B. Ekpang.

Norway: 130A ave Louise, 1050 Brussels; tel. (02) 646-07-80; telex 62563; Ambassador: Knut Sverre.

Pakistan: 57 ave Delleur, 1170 Brussels; tel. (02) 673-80-07; telex 61816; fax (02) 675-31-37; Ambassador: Munir Akram.

Panama: 8 blvd Brand Whitlock, 1750 Brussels; tel. (02) 733-90-89; telex 25169; fax (02) 733-77-79; Ambassador: Roberto Alemán.

Papua New Guinea: 17–19 rue Montoyer, 1040 Brussels; tel. (02) 512-31-27; fax (02) 512-86-43; Ambassador: Brown Bai.

Paraguay: 42 ave de Saturne, 1180 Brussels; tel. (02) 374-87-48; telex 20535; Ambassador: Dido Florentín-Bogado.

Peru: 179 ave de Tervueren, 1150 Brussels; tel. (02) 733-33-19; telex 24577; Ambassador: Julio Ego-Aguirre Alvarez.

BELGIUM

Philippines: 299 ave Molière, 1060 Brussels; tel. (02) 343-68-32; telex 23631; Ambassador: ROBERTO R. ROMULO.

Poland: 29 ave des Gaulois, 1040 Brussels; tel. (02) 735-72-12; telex 21562; Ambassador: TADEUSZ OLECHOWSKI.

Portugal: 115 rue Defacqz (5e étage), 1050 Brussels; tel. (02) 539-38-50; telex 24570; Ambassador: ANTÓNIO AUGUSTO DE MEDEIROS PATRICIO.

Qatar: 71 ave F. D. Roosevelt, 1050 Brussels; tel. (02) 640-74-06; telex 63754; fax (02) 648-40-78; Chargé d'affaires a.i.: ALI HASSAN AL-HAMADI.

Romania: 105 rue Gabrielle, 1180 Brussels; tel. (02) 345-26-80; telex 21859; Ambassador: OVIDIU POPESCU.

Rwanda: 1 ave des Fleurs, 1150 Brussels; tel. (02) 763-07-05; telex 26653; Ambassador: FRANÇOIS NGARUKIYINTWALI.

San Marino: 44 ave Brugman, BP 6, 1060 Brussels; tel. (02) 344-60-67; fax (02) 347-17-08; Ambassador: GIAN NICOLA FILIPPI BALESTRA.

São Tomé and Príncipe: 42 ave Brugman, 1060 Brussels; tel. (02) 347-53-75; telex 65313; Chargé d'affaires a.i.: CARLOS GUSTAVO DOS ANJO.

Saudi Arabia: 45 ave F. D. Roosevelt, 1050 Brussels; tel. (02) 649-57-25; telex 64626; Chargé d'affaires a.i.: OMAR BAMANIE.

Senegal: 196 ave F. D. Roosevelt, 1050 Brussels; tel. (02) 673-08-87; telex 63951; Ambassador: FALILOU KANE.

Sierra Leone: 410 ave de Tervueren, 1150 Brussels; tel. (02) 771-11-80; telex 63624; Ambassador: MARIAN JUDITH TANNER KAMARA.

Singapore: 198 ave F. D. Roosevelt, 1050 Brussels; tel. (02) 660-30-98; telex 26731; Ambassador: JAYALEKSHIMI MOHIDEEN.

Somalia: 66 ave F. D. Roosevelt, 1050 Brussels; tel. (02) 640-16-69; telex 24807; Ambassador: ALI HASSAN ALI.

South Africa: 26 rue de la Loi, BP 7 & 8, 1040 Brussels; tel. (02) 230-68-45; telex 23495; Ambassador: MARINUS LEONARD TE WATER NAUDÉ.

Spain: 19 rue de la Science, 1040 Brussels; tel. (02) 230-03-40; telex 22092; Ambassador: NICOLÁS MARTÍNEZ-FRESNO Y PAVIA.

Sri Lanka: 21–22 ave des Arts, 1040 Brussels; tel. (02) 230-48-90; telex 26927; Ambassador: TYRREL DERRIC SAMUEL ALARIC DISSANAYAKA.

Sudan: 124 ave F. D. Roosevelt, 1050 Brussels; tel. (02) 647-94-94; telex 24370; Ambassador: SAEED SAAD MAHGOUB SAAD.

Suriname: 379 ave Louise, BP 20, 1050 Brussels; tel. (02) 640-11-72; telex 62680; Ambassador: DONALD ALOYSIUS MCLEOD.

Swaziland: 71 rue Joseph II (5e étage), BP 8, 1040 Brussels; tel. (02) 230-00-44; telex 26254; fax (02) 230-50-83; Ambassador: J. B. J. S. DHLAMINI.

Sweden: 148 ave Louise, 1050 Brussels; tel. (02) 641-66-11; telex 21148; fax (02) 641-66-20; Ambassador: HENRIK LILJEGREN.

Switzerland: 26 rue de la Loi, BP 9, 1040 Brussels; tel. (02) 230-61-45; telex 63711; Ambassador: GASPARD BODMER.

Syria: 3 ave F. D. Roosevelt, 1050 Brussels; tel. (02) 648-01-35; telex 26669; Ambassador: SIBA NASSER.

Tanzania: 363 ave Louise (7e étage), 1050 Brussels; tel. (02) 640-65-00; telex 63616; Ambassador: Prof. ABDI HASSAN MASANGAMA.

Thailand: 2 square du Val de la Cambre, 1050 Brussels; tel. (02) 640-68-10; telex 63510; Ambassador: DANAI TULALAMBA.

Togo: 264 ave de Tervueren, 1150 Brussels; tel. (02) 770-17-91; telex 25093; Ambassador: ASSIONGBON AGBENOU.

Trinidad and Tobago: 14 ave de la Faisanderie, 1150 Brussels; tel. (02) 762-94-00; fax (02) 772-27-83; Ambassador: TERRENCE BADEN-SEMPER.

Tunisia: 278 ave de Tervueren, 1150 Brussels; tel. (02) 771-73-95; telex 22078; Ambassador: RACHID SFAR.

Turkey: 4 rue Montoyer, 1040 Brussels; tel. (02) 513-40-93; telex 24677; fax (02) 514-07-48; Ambassador: ECMEL BARUTÇU.

Uganda: 317 ave de Tervueren, 1150 Brussels; tel. (02) 762-58-25; telex 62814; Ambassador: CHARLES KAKURU KATUNGI.

USSR: 66 ave de Fré, 1180 Brussels; tel. (02) 374-34-06; telex 65272; Ambassador: NIKOLAI N. AFANASYEVSKY.

United Arab Emirates: 73 ave F. D. Roosevelt, 1050 Brussels; tel. (02) 640-60-00; telex 26559; Ambassador: SALEM RACHED SALEM AL-AGROOBI.

United Kingdom: Britannia House, 28 rue Joseph II, 1040 Brussels; tel. (02) 217-90-00; telex 22703; fax (02) 217-67-63; Ambassador: ROBERT JAMES O'NEILL.

USA: 27 blvd du Régent, 1000 Brussels; tel. (02) 513-38-30; telex 21336; fax (02) 511-27-25; Ambassador: MAYNARD WAYNE GLITMAN.

Uruguay: 437 ave Louise, 1050 Brussels; tel. (02) 640-11-69; telex 24663; fax (02) 648-29-09; Ambassador: JOSÉ MARIA ARANEO.

Venezuela: 6 rue P. E. Jonson, 1050 Brussels; Ambassador: JÚLIO CÉSAR GIL.

Western Samoa: 95 ave F. D. Roosevelt, 1050 Brussels; tel. (02) 660-84-54; Ambassador: AFAMASAGA FA'AMATALA TOLEAFOA.

Yugoslavia: 11 ave Emile de Mot, 1050 Brussels; tel. (02) 647-26-52; telex 26156; Ambassador: KUZMAN DIMCEVSKI.

Zaire: 30 rue Marie de Bourgogne, 1040 Brussels; tel. (02) 513-66-10; telex 21983; Ambassador: KIMBULU MOYANSO WA LOKWA.

Zambia: 469 ave Molière, BP 2, 1060 Brussels; tel. (02) 343-56-49; Ambassador: KAPEMBE N'SINGO.

Zimbabwe: 21–22 ave des Arts, BP 2/3, 1040 Brussels; tel. (02) 230-85-35; telex 24133; Ambassador: Dr ANDREW H. MTETWA.

Judicial System

The independence of the judiciary is based on the constitutional division of power between the legislative, executive and judicial bodies, each of which acts independently. Judges are appointed by the crown for life, and cannot be removed except by judicial sentence. The law of 1967, in force since 1970, unified civil procedure in the district courts, and reorganized the courts' areas of competence. Each of Belgium's nine provinces is divided into judicial districts, and these, in turn, into judicial cantons. The judiciary is organized on four levels, from the judicial canton to the district, regional and national courts. The lowest courts are those of the Justices of the Peace, of which there are 222, and the 20 Police Tribunals; each type of district court numbers 27, one in each district, including the Tribunals of the First Instance, Tribunals of Commerce, and Labour Tribunals. There are five regional Courts of Appeal, five regional Labour Courts, and one Court of Assizes in each province. The highest courts are the five civil and criminal Courts of Appeal, the five Labour Courts and the supreme Court of Cassation. The Military Court of Appeal is in Brussels.

COUR DE CASSATION/HOF VAN CASSATIE (SUPREME COURT OF JUSTICE)

First President: R. SOETAERT.

President: O. STRANARD.

Counsellors: H. D. BAETE-SWINNEN, G. DE BAETS, Y. BELLE-JEANMART, E. BOON, C. CAENEPEEL, M. CHARLIER, F. FISCHER, E. FORRIER, P. GHISLAIN, J. D'HAENENS, D. HOLSTERS, M. LAHOUSSE, P. MARCHAL, J. MATTHIJS, C. PARMENTIER, J. DE PEUTER, Y. RAPPE, J. RAUWS, J. SACE, A. SIMONET, T. VERHEYDEN, I. VEROUGSTRAETE, L. WILLEMS.

General Prosecutor: (vacant).

First Attorney-General: J. VELU.

Attorneys-General: G. D'HOORE, B. JANSSENS DE BISTHOVEN, J. DU JARDIN, J. F. LECLERCQ, H. LENAERTS, E. LIEKENDAEL, J. M. PIRET, A. TILLEKAERTS.

COURS D'APPEL/HOVEN VAN BEROEP (CIVIL AND CRIMINAL HIGH COURTS)

Antwerp: fax (03) 216-41-27; First Pres. A DE MAN; Gen. Prosecutor R. VAN CAMP.

Brussels: fax (02) 508-63-50; First Pres. J. VERDOODT; Gen. Prosecutor A. VAN OUDENHOVE.

Ghent: fax (091) 24-02-54; First Pres. M. COUCKUYT; Gen. Prosecutor N. BAUWENS.

Liège: fax (041) 22-91-22; First Pres. R. LAURENT; Gen. Prosecutor L. GIET.

Mons: fax (065) 31-89-16; First Pres. P. GUERITTE; Gen. Prosecutor G. DEMANET.

Religion

CHRISTIANITY

The Roman Catholic Church

Belgium comprises one archdiocese and seven dioceses. At 31 December 1988 there were 8,498,161 adherents (about 86.4% of the total population).

Bishops' Conference: Bisschoppenconferentie van België/Conférence Episcopale de Belgique, 15 Wollemarkt, 2800 Mechelen; tel. (015) 21-65-01; fax (015) 20-94-85; f. 1981; Pres. Cardinal GODFRIED DANNEELS, Archbishop of Mechelen-Brussels.

Archbishop of Mechelen-Brussels: Cardinal GODFRIED DANNEELS, Aartsbisdom, 15 Wollemarkt, 2800 Mechelen; tel. (015) 21-65-01; fax (015) 20-94-85.

BELGIUM — Directory

Protestant Churches

Belgian Evangelical Lutheran Church: 26 rue du Major René Dubreucq, 1050 Brussels; tel. (02) 511-92-47; f. 1950; 425 mems; Pres C. J. HOBUS.

Church of England: 29 rue Capitaine Crespel, 1050 Brussels; tel. (02) 511-71-83; Ven. JOHN LEWIS, Archdeacon of North-West Europe (Diocese of Gibraltar in Europe) and Chancellor of the Pro-Cathedral of the Holy Trinity, Brussels.

Eglise Protestante Unie de Belgique: 5 rue du Champ de Mars, 1050 Brussels; tel. (02) 511-44-71; 35,000 mems; Pres. Rev. M. J. BEUKENHORST; Sec. Mme R. FRAISSE-LHEUREUX.

Mission Evangélique Belge: 158 blvd Lambermont, 1030 Brussels; tel. (02) 241-30-15; f. 1918; about 2,000 mems.

Union of Baptists in Belgium (UBB): 35 rue Laplace, 4100 Seraing; tel. (041) 37-31-15; f. 1922 as Union of Evangelical Baptist Churches; Pres. HENRY BENS; Sec. GASTON WATHIEU.

ISLAM

There are some 250,000 Muslims in Belgium.

Leader of the Islamic Community: Imam Prof. SALMAN AL-RAHDI.

JUDAISM

There are about 35,000 Jews in Belgium.

Consistoire Central Israélite de Belgique (Central Council of the Jewish Communities of Belgium): 2 rue Joseph Dupont, 1000 Brussels; tel. (02) 512-35-78; f. 1808; Chair. M. GEORGES SCHNEK.

The Press

Article 18 of the Belgian Constitution states: 'The Press is free; no form of censorship may ever be instituted; no cautionary deposit may be demanded from writers, publishers or printers. When the author is known and is resident in Belgium, the publisher, printer or distributor may not be prosecuted.'

There are 35 general information dailies (19 French-language, 15 Dutch, one German), 15 of which are autonomous. Some of the remainder are, under a different title, regional editions of a larger paper. In 1989 the combined circulation of all daily newspapers averaged 2,120,887 copies per issue.

There is a trend towards concentration. The 'Le Soir' group consists of five dailies. Other significant groupings are the 'De Standaard' and 'Vers l'Avenir' groups. The former consists of three Catholic newspapers, while the latter links five titles.

There are few official political organs, but nearly all the Belgian dailies have political or trade union leanings. It is not, however, possible to establish a parallel between the supporters of the parties and the readership of the dailies.

There is no easy division of the daily newspapers into popular and serious press, but most newspapers strive to give a serious news coverage. The most widely-circulating dailies in French in 1989 were: *Le Soir* (199,825), *La Meuse/La Lanterne* (130,361), *La Libre Belgique/La Libre Belgique—Gazette du Liège* (86,105) and *La Dernière Heure/Les Sports* (91,412); the total circulation of those newspapers in the 'Vers l'Avenir' group was 146,474. The corresponding figures for Dutch-language dailies were: *Het Laatste Nieuws/De Nieuwe Gazet* (291,092), *De Standaard/Nieuwsblad/De Gentenaar* (382,424), *Het Volk/De Nieuwe Gids* (189,366) and *Gazet van Antwerpen/Gazet van Mechelen* (190,810). The major weeklies include *De Bond* (337,350), *Flair* (315,762), *Humo* (264,441), *Télémoustique* (223,091) and *Le Soir Illustré* (107,000), the latter associated with the daily *Le Soir*, and the cultural periodicals *Pourquoi Pas?/L'Express*, *Le Vif/L'Express* (109,000) and *Knack* (125,000). The popular women's periodical *Femmes d'Aujourd'hui* (160,000) also has considerable sales in France. Some periodicals are printed in French and in Dutch.

PRINCIPAL DAILIES

Antwerp

De Antwerpse Morgen: 38–40 Broederminstraat, 2018 Antwerp; tel. (03) 216-49-30; fax (03) 237-79-73; f. 1983; independent; Dir-Gen. EGBERT HANS; Chief Editor PAUL GOOSSENS.

De Financieel Ekonomische Tijd: 5 Brouwersvliet, bus 3, 2000 Antwerp; tel. (03) 231-57-56; telex 32614; fax (03) 234-36-41; f. 1968; economic and financial; Gen. Man. J. LAMERS; Chief Editor JERRY VAN WATERSCHOOT; circ. 34,530.

Gazet van Antwerpen: 2 Katwijgweg, 2050 Antwerp; tel. (03) 210-02-10; telex 31385; fax (03) 219-41-65; f. 1891; Christian Democrat; Dir-Gen. R. VAN TONGERLOO; Editor L. DE CLERCK; circ. 190,810 (with *Gazet van Mechelen*).

Le Lloyd: 23 Eiermarkt, 2000 Antwerp; tel. (03) 234-05-50; telex 31446; fax (03) 219-41-65; f. 1858; French and Dutch edns, with supplements in English; shipping transport, commerce, industry, finance; Dir G. DUBOIS; circ. 10,250.

De Nieuwe Gazet: 10 Leopoldstraat, 2000 Antwerp; tel. (03) 231-96-80; fax (03) 232-64-12; f. 1897; Liberal; Editor FRANS STRIELEMAN; circ. 291,092 (with *Het Laatste Nieuws*).

Arlon

L'Avenir du Luxembourg: 38 rue des Déportés, 6700 Arlon; tel. (063) 22-03-49; fax (063) 22-05-16; f. 1897; Catholic; Editor JO MOTTET.

Brussels

La Côte Libre: 131 rue de Birmingham, 1070 Brussels; tel. (02) 526-56-66; f. 1868; financial; Editor O. DE BEAUFORT; circ. 7,500.

Courrier de la Bourse: 131 rue de Birmingham, 1070 Brussels; tel. (02) 526-56-66; f. 1896; financial, economic, industrial and political; Admin. Dir O. DE BEAUFORT; circ. 9,500.

La Dernière Heure/Les Sports: 127 blvd Emile Jacqmain, 1000 Brussels; tel. (02) 211-28-88; telex 21448; fax (02) 211-28-70; f. 1906; independent Liberal; Dir P. LE HODEY; Chief Editor DANIEL VAN WYLICK; circ. 91,412.

Le Drapeau Rouge: 33 rue de la Caserne, 1000 Brussels; tel. (02) 512-51-98; fax (02) 514-34-23; f. 1921; Communist; Editor PIERRE BEAUVOIS; Man. R. DUSSART; circ. 15,000.

L'Echo: 131 rue de Birmingham, 1070 Brussels; tel. (02) 526-55-11; telex 23396; fax (02) 526-55-26; f. 1881; economic and financial; Dir R. WATSON; Editor F. MELAET; circ. 29,668.

Het Laatste Nieuws: 105 Emile Jacqmainlaan, 1000 Brussels; tel. (02) 220-22-11; telex 21495; fax (02) 217-98-46; f. 1888; Dutch; independent; Dir CHR. VAN THILLO; Editors R. ADAMS, M. WILMET; circ. 291,092 (with *De Nieuwe Gazet*).

La Lanterne: 134 rue Royale, 1000 Brussels; tel. (02) 218-21-08; fax (02) 217-68-56; f. 1944; independent; Gen. Man. M. FROMONT; Chief Editor A. OBER; circ. 130,361 (with *La Meuse*).

La Libre Belgique: 127 blvd Emile Jacqmain, 1000 Brussels; tel. (02) 211-27-77; telex 21550; fax (02) 211-23-32; f. 1884; Catholic; independent; Dir P. LE HODEY; Chief Editor J. FRANCK; circ. 86,105.

De Morgen (group combining **De Morgen, Vooruit, De Antwerpse Morgen**): 54 Brogniezstraat, 1070 Brussels; tel. (02) 527-00-30; telex 63428; fax (02) 520-41-92; Dir-Gen. EGBERT HANS; circ. 46,884.

De Morgen: 54 Brogniezstraat, 1070 Brussels; tel. (02) 527-00-30; telex 63428; fax (02) 520-35-15; f. 1978; Dir-Gen. EGBERT HANS; Chief Editor PAUL GOOSSENS.

De Nieuwe Gids: 105 Koningsstraat, 1000 Brussels; tel. (02) 218-56-05; telex 21891; fax (02) 218-59-06; f. 1944; Dutch; Dir-Gen. ANTOON VAN MELKEBEEX; Chief Editor PAUL DE BAERE; circ. 189,366 (with *Het Volk*).

Het Nieuwsblad: 28 Gossetlaan, 1702 Groot Bijgaarden; tel. (02) 467-22-11; telex 23039; fax (02) 466-30-93; f. 1923; Dir-Gen. G. VERDEYEN; Chief Editor ROGER SCHOEMANS.

Le Soir: 21 place de Louvain, 1000 Brussels; tel. (02) 217-77-50; telex 24298; fax (02) 219-08-36; f. 1887; independent; Dir-Gen. ANDRÉ DE BETHUNE; Chief Editor GUY DUPLAT; circ. 199,825.

Krantengroep De Standaard (group combining **De Standaard, Het Nieuwsblad, De Gentenaar**): published by Vlaamse Uitgeversmaatschappij NV, 30 Gossetlaan, 1702 Groot Bijgaarden; tel. (02) 467-22-11; fax (02) 466-30-93; Christian Socialist; Dir G. VERDEYEN; circ. 382,424.

De Standaard: 28 Gossetlaan, 1702 Groot Bijgaarden; tel. (02) 467-22-11; telex 23039; fax (02) 466-30-93; f. 1914; Dir-Gen. G. VERDEYEN; Chief Editor LODE BOSTOEN.

Charleroi

Le Journal & Indépendance/Le Peuple: 18 rue du Collège, 6000 Charleroi; tel. (071) 31-01-90; fax (071) 33-16-50; f. 1837; Gen. Man. C RENARD; Editor JEAN GUY; circ. 111,123 (with *La Nouvelle Gazette; La Province*).

La Nouvelle Gazette (Charleroi, La Louvière, Philippeville, Namur, Nivelles); La Province (Mons): 2 quai de Flandre, 6000 Charleroi; tel. (071) 27-64-11; telex 51218; fax (071) 27-65-67; f. 1878; Man. Dir MICHEL FROMONT; Editor J.-P. VANDERMEUSE; circ. 111,123 (with *Le Journal & Indépendance/Le Peuple*).

Le Rappel: 24 rue de Montigny, 6000 Charleroi; tel. (071) 31-22-80; fax (071) 31-43-61; f. 1900; Dir-Gen. JACQUES DE THYSEBAERT; Chief Editor JEAN-CLAUDE BAFFREY.

Eupen

Grenz-Echo: 8 Marktplatz, 4700 Eupen; tel. (087) 55-47-05; fax (087) 74-38-20; f. 1927; German; independent Catholic; Dir A. KÜCHENBERG; Editor HEINZ WARNY; circ. 13,500.

BELGIUM

Ghent

De Gentenaar: 30 Gouvernementstraat, 9000 Ghent; tel. (091) 23-95-30; telex 11244; fax (091) 23-09-56; f. 1879; Catholic; Man. G. VERDEYEN; Chief Editor LODE BOSTOEN.

Het Volk: 22 Forelstraat, 9000 Ghent; tel. (091) 25-57-01; telex 11228; fax (091) 25-35-27; f. 1891; Catholic; Dir ANTOON VAN MELKEBEEK; Editor PAUL DE BAERE; circ. 189,366 (with *De Nieuwe Gids*).

Vooruit: 65A St-Kwintensberg, 9000 Ghent; tel. (091) 33-27-91; fax (091) 24-02-63; f. 1884; independent; Dir-Gen. EGBERT HANS; Editor PAUL GOOSSENS.

Hasselt

Het Belang van Limburg: 10 Herckenrodesingel, 3500 Hasselt; tel. (011) 29-42-11; telex 39034; fax (011) 25-18-54; f. 1879; Christian Social; Editor PETER BAERT; circ. 103,812.

Liège

La Libre Belgique—Gazette du Liège: 26–28 blvd d'Avnoy, 4000 Liège; tel. (041) 23-19-33; telex 41297; f. 1840; Dir LILY PORTUGAELS; circ. 86,105 (with *La Libre Belgique*—Brussels).

La Meuse: 8-12 blvd de la Sauvenière, 4000 Liège; tel. (041) 20-08-11; telex 41521; fax (041) 20-08-40; f. 1855; independent; Gen. Man. M. FROMONT; Editor W. MEURENS; circ. 130,361 (with *La Lanterne*).

La Wallonie: 55 rue de la Régence, 4000 Liège; tel. (041) 20-18-11; telex 41143; fax (041) 23-31-17; f. 1919; progressive; Dir C. GLUZA; Editor J. DUBOIS; circ. 48,200.

Mechelen

Gazet van Mechelen: 13 Befferstraat, 2800 Mechelen; tel. (015) 20-83-83; f. 1896; Christian Democrat; Gen. Man. R. VAN TONGERLOO; Editor L. DE CLERCK; circ. 190,810 (with *Gazet van Antwerpen*).

Namur

Vers l'Avenir: 12 blvd Ernest Mélot, 5000 Namur; tel. (081) 24-88-11; telex 59121; fax (081) 22-60-24; f. 1918; Christian Democrat; Editor JEAN-CLAUDE BAFFREY; circ. 67,631.

Tournai

Le Courrier de l'Escaut: 24 rue du Curé Notre-Dame, 7500 Tournai; tel. (069) 22-81-43; telex 57147; fax (069) 23-20-34; f. 1829; Christian Social; Dir MARC LESTIENNE.

Verviers

Le Jour/Le Courrier: 14 rue du Brou, 4800 Verviers; tel. (087) 31-33-61; fax (087) 31-33-61; f. 1894; independent; Dir J. DE THYSEBAERT; Chief Editor R. MONAMI.

WEEKLIES

La Cité: 26 rue St Laurent, 1000 Brussels; tel. (02) 217-23-90; fax (02) 217-69-95; f. 1950 as daily, weekly 1988; Christian Democrat; Editor JOS SCHOONBROODT; circ. 20,000.

De Boer en de Tuinder: 8 Minderbroedersstraat, 3000 Louvain; tel. (016) 24-21-60; telex 24166; fax (016) 24-21-68; f. 1891; agriculture and horticulture; circ. 52,000.

De Bond: 170 Langestraat, 1150 Brussels; tel. (02) 782-00-00; fax (02) 782-16-16; f. 1921; general interest; circ. 337,350.

Brugsch Handelsblad: 4 Eekhoutstraat, 8000 Bruges; tel. (050) 33-06-61; telex 81222; fax (050) 33-46-33; f. 1906; local, national and international news; Dirs RIK DE NOLF, LEO CLAEYS; Editor J. HERREBOUDT; circ. 40,000.

Dag Allemaal: 7 Luchthavenlei, 2100 Antwerp; tel. (03) 218-76-40; telex 33451; fax (03) 218-77-03; f. 1984; general interest; circ. 104,031.

Femmes d'Aujourd'hui: 9 ave Frans van Kalken, 1070 Brussels; tel. (02) 526-84-11; telex 25104; fax (02) 526-85-60; f. 1933; women's magazine; Dir L. HIERGENS; Chief Editor Y. MIGNOLET; circ. 160,000.

Flair: 7 Jan Blockxstraat, 2018 Antwerp; tel. (03) 247-45-11; telex 32979; fax (03) 237-95-11; Dutch and French; women's magazine; Dir K. HUYSMANS; Chief Editor C. VAN WACKERBARTH; circ. (in Belgium) 239,858.

Humo: 46 De Jonckerstraat, 1060 Brussels; tel. (02) 537-08-00; telex 23291; fax ((02) 537-45-63; general weekly and TV and radio guide in Dutch; Chief Editor GUY MORTIER; circ. 264,441.

L'Instant: Brussels; f. 1990; current affairs; circ. 55,000.

Joepie: 7 Luchthavenlei, 2100 Antwerp; tel. (03) 218-76-40; telex 33451; fax (03) 218-77-03; f. 1973; teenagers' interest; Chief Editor GUIDO VAN LIEFFERINGE; circ. 144,841.

Kerk en Leven: 92 Halewijnlaan, 2050 Antwerp; tel. (03) 219-38-00; fax (03) 219-79-12; religious; circ. 800,000.

Knack: 153 Tervurenlaan, 1150 Brussels; tel. (02) 736-60-40; fax (02) 736-48-22; independent news magazine; Dir FRANS VERLEYEN; Chief Editors HUBERT VAN HUMBEECK, FRANK DE MOOR; circ. 125,000.

Kwik: 105-107 Emile Jacqmainlaan, 1000 Brussels; tel. (02) 220-22-11; telex 21495; fax (02) 219-63-57; f. 1962; Dir RIK DUYCK; Editor K. VANDER MIJNSBRUGGE; circ. 78,294.

Landbouwleven: 92 ave Léon Grosjean, 1140 Brussels; tel. (02) 736-59-80; fax (02) 736-04-14; agriculture; circ. 45,489.

Libelle: 7 Jan Blockxstraat, 2018 Antwerp; tel. (03) 247-45-11; telex 32979; fax (03) 216-17-67; f. 1945; Dutch and French; women's magazine; Dir K. HUYSMANS; Chief Editor M. DE BORGER; circ. 192, 842 (Dutch), 66,981 (French).

Panorama/De Post: 7 Jan Blockxstraat, 2018 Antwerp; tel. (03) 247-45-11; telex 32979; fax (03) 247-47-98; f. 1956; Dutch; general interest; Dir K. HUYSMANS; Chief Editor K. ANTHIERENS; circ. 115,000.

Pourquoi Pas?/L'Express: 33 place Jamblinne de Meux, 1040 Brussels; tel. (02) 736-79-00; fax (02) 734-30-40; f. 1910; news; Dir GERALD JACOBY; Chief Editor CHR. LAURENT; circ. 130,000 (with *Le Vif/L'Express*).

Het Rijk der Vrouw: 9 Frans van Kalkenlaan, 1070 Brussels; tel. (02) 526-84-11; telex 25104; fax (02) 526-85-60; f. 1932; women's interest; Dir L. HIERGENS; Chief Editor Y. MIGNOLET; circ. 187,571.

Le Sillon Belge: 92 ave Léon Grosjean, 1140 Brussels; tel. (02) 736-59-80; fax (02) 736-04-14; f. 1952; agriculture; Dir JOHAN VAN OYEN; Chief Editor ANDRÉ DE MOL; circ. 45,463.

Le Soir Illustré: 21 place de Louvain, 1000 Brussels; tel. (02) 217-77-50; fax (02) 219-08-36; f. 1928; independent illustrated; Dir A. DECLERQ; circ. 116,766.

Spirou/Robbedoes: 637 chemin de Waterloo, 1060 Brussels; tel. (02) 344-13-60; children's interest; circ. 63,000.

Sport '90: 95 Emile Jacqmainlaan, 1000 Brussels; tel. (02) 219-32-90; telex 21495; fax (02) 217-98-46; sport; circ. 80,000.

Story: 7 Jan Blockxstraat, 2018 Antwerp; tel. (03) 247-45-11; telex 32979; fax (03) 216-17-67; f. 1975; Dutch; women's interest; Dir K. HUYSMANS; Chief Editor L. VAN RAAK; circ. 175,111.

TeVe-Blad: 18 Kammenstraat, 2000 Antwerp; tel. (03) 231-47-90; telex 33134; fax (03) 234-34-66; f. 1981; illustrated; Dir J. MERCKX; Chief Editor ROB JANS; circ. 248,811.

Télémoustique: 46 De Jonckerstraat, 1060 Brussels; tel. (02) 537-08-00; telex 23291; fax ((02) 537-45-63; f. 1924; radio and TV; Dir LOUIS CROONEN; Editor ALAIN DE KUYSSCHE; circ. 226,982.

TV Ekspres: 18 Kammenstraat, 2000 Antwerp; tel. (03) 231-47-90; telex 33134; fax (03) 234-34-66; Dir JAN MERCKX; Chief Editor ROB JANS; circ. 227, 208 (with *TV Strip*, *ZIE Magazine*).

TV Strip: 18 Kammenstraat, 2000 Antwerp; tel. (03) 231-47-90; telex 33134; fax (03) 234-34-66; circ. 227,208 (with *TV Ekpress*, *ZIE Magazine*).

Le Vif/L'Express: 33 place Jamblinne de Meux, 1040 Brussels; tel. (02) 736-79-00; fax ((02) 734-30-40; Dir GÉRALD JACOBY; Chief Editor JEAN-PIERRE STROOBANTS; circ. 130,000 (with *Pourquoi Pas?/L'Express*).

Het Wekelijks Nieuws: 5 Nijverheidslaan, 8970 Poperinge; tel. (057) 33-67-21; fax (057) 33-40-18; Christian news magazine; Dirs HERMAN and LUC SANSEN; Editor HERMAN SANSEN; circ. 56,000.

ZIE-Magazine: 18 Kammenstraat, 2000 Antwerp; tel. (03) 231-47-90; telex 33134; fax (03) 234-34-66; f. 1930; illustrated; Dir JAN MERCKX; Chief Editor ROB JANS; circ. 227,208 (with *TV Ekpress*, *TV Strip*).

Zondag Nieuws: 105 Emile Jacqmainlaan, 1000 Brussels; tel. (02) 220-22-11; telex 21495; fax (02) 217-98-46; f. 1958; general interest; Dir RIK DUYCK; Chief Editor LUC VANDRIESSCHE; circ. 113,567.

Zondagsblad: 22 Forelstraat, 9000 Ghent; tel. (091) 25-57-01; fax (091) 24-23-07; f. 1949; Catholic; Dir A. VAN MELKEBEEK; Editor JEF NIJS; circ. 68,894.

SELECTED OTHER PERIODICALS

Belgian Business Magazine: 42 ave du Houx, 1170 Brussels; tel. (02) 673-81-70; telex 23830; monthly; management; circ. 65,700.

Het Beste uit Reader's Digest: 12A Grote Markt, 1000 Brussels; monthly; general; Dir-Gen. JOE H. BEAUDUIN; circ. 100,000.

Eigen Aard: 170 Langestraat, 1150 Brussels; tel. (02) 782-00-00; fax (02) 782-16-16; f. 1911; monthly; women's interest; circ. 155,091.

International Equipment News: 216 Groenstraat, 1030 Brussels; tel. (02) 242-29-92; business; Dir H. BRIELS.

Jet Limburg: 21 Bedrijfsstraat, 3500 Hasselt; tel. (011) 22-58-77; fax (011) 24-12-66; fortnightly; general interest; circ. 242,000.

BELGIUM

Directory

Marie Claire: 68 ave Winston Churchill, 1180 Brussels; tel. (02) 345-99-20; fax (02) 344-28-27; monthly; women's interest; circ. 80,000.

Le Moniteur de l'Automobile: 181 chaussée de la Hulpe, BP 2, 1170 Brussels; tel. (02) 660-19-20; telex 26379; fortnightly; motoring; Editor ÉTIENNE VISART; circ. 85,000.

The Office: 81 ave Franklin Roosevelt, 1050 Brussels; tel. (02) 640-69-80; telex 64028; fax (02) 648-39-77; f. 1935; English; monthly; Editor WILLIAM R. SCHULHOF; circ. 160,000.

Santé: 17 rue Karel Gilson, 1610 Ruisbroek; tel. (02) 331-00-22; fax (02) 331-02-51; monthly; popular medicine; circ. 130,000.

Sphere: 140B blvd Lambermont, 1030 Brussels; 6 a year; travel; circ. 77,000.

Vie Féminine: 170 Langestraat, 1150 Brussels; tel. (02) 782-00-00; fax (02) 782-16-16; f. 1917; monthly; women's interest; circ. 81,291.

Vrouw & Wereld: 170 Langestraat, 1150 Brussels; tel. (02) 782-00-00; fax (02) 782-16-16; f. 1920; monthly; women's interest; circ. 321,923.

NEWS AGENCIES

Agence Belga (Agence Télégraphique Belge de Presse SA)—Agentschap Belga (Belgisch Pers-telegraafagentschap NV): 1 blvd Charlemagne, BP 51, 1041 Brussels; tel. (02) 230-50-55; telex 21408; fax (02) 230-99-52; f. 1920; largely owned by daily papers; Chair. G. VERDEYEN; Gen. Man. R. DE CEUSTER.

Agence Europe: 10 blvd St Lazare, 1210 Brussels; tel. (02) 219-02-56; telex 21108; f. 1952; daily bulletin on EEC activities.

Centre d'Information de Presse (CIP): 1 chemin de Maecht, 1030 Brussels; f. 1946; Chair LOUIS MEERTS.

Foreign Bureaux

Agence France-Presse (AFP): 1 blvd Charlemagne, BP 3, 1041 Brussels; tel. (02) 230-83-94; telex 24889; fax (02) 230-23-04; Dir CHARLES SCHIFFMANN.

Agencia EFE (Spain): 1 blvd Charlemagne, BP 20, 1041 Brussels; tel. (02) 230-45-68; telex 23185; Dir RAMÓN CASTILLO MESEGUER.

Agenzia Nazionale Stampa Associata (ANSA) (Italy): 1 blvd Charlemagne, BP 7, 1040 Brussels; tel. (02) 230-81-92; telex 63717; fax (02) 230-60-82; Dir CORRADO SELLAROLI.

Algemeen Nederlands Persbureau (ANP) (Netherlands): 1 blvd Charlemagne, 1041 Brussels; tel. (02) 230-85-27; Correspondents MARTINUS VAN DIJK, RIK WINKEL.

Allgemeiner Deutscher Nachrichtendienst (ADN) (Germany): 47 ave des Cattleyas, 1150 Brussels; tel. (02) 734-59-57; telex 23731; fax (02) 736-27-11; Correspondents BARBARA SCHUR, ULLRICH SCHUR.

Associated Press (AP) (USA): 1 blvd Charlemagne, BP 49, 1041 Brussels; tel. (02) 230-52-49; telex 21741; Dir ROBERT WIELAARD.

Československá tisková kancelář (ČTK) (Czechoslovakia): 2 rue des Egyptiens, BP 6, 1050 Brussels; tel. (02) 648-01-33; telex 23092; fax (02) 648-01-33; Correspondent J. PRUSEK.

Deutsche Presse-Agentur (dpa) (Germany): 1 blvd Charlemagne, BP 17, 1041 Brussels; tel. (02) 230-36-91; telex 22356; fax (02) 230-98-96; Dir HARTWIG NATHE.

Informatsionnoye Agentstvo Novosti (IAN) (USSR): 22 rue Général Lotz, 1180 Brussels; tel. (02) 343-26-58; telex 23798; fax (02) 343-38-65; Dir IGOR ROUJENSTEV.

Inter Press Service (IPS) (Italy): (French-speaking) 35 rue du Framboisier, 1180 Brussels; tel. (02) 374-77-18; Correspondent JACQUES ELIAS; (Dutch-speaking) 21 Inquisitiestraat, 1040 Brussels; tel. (02) 736-18-31; fax (02) 736-82-00; Dir DIRK PEETERS.

Jiji Press (Japan): 1 blvd Charlemagne, BP 26, 1041 Brussels; tel. (02) 238-09-48; telex 25029; fax ((02) 230-14-50; Dir MAHITO TSUCHIYAMA.

Kyodo Tsushin (Japan): 1 blvd Charlemagne, BP 37, 1041 Brussels; tel. (02) 238-09-10; fax ((02) 230-53-34; Dir AKIHIRO ONODA.

Magyar Távirati Iroda (MTI) (Hungary): 41 rue Jean Chapelie, 1060 Brussels; tel. and fax (02) 343-75-35; telex 24455; Dir DÉNES BARACS.

Reuters (UK): 61 rue de Trèves, 1040 Brussels; tel. (02) 230-92-15; telex 21633; fax (02) 230-77-10; Chief Correspondent SIMON ALTERMAN.

United Press International (UPI) (USA): 17 rue Philippe le Bon, 1040 Brussels; tel. (02) 230-43-30; telex 26997; fax (02) 230-43-81; Correspondent CHARLES GOLDSMITH.

Xinhua (New China) News Agency (People's Republic of China): 32 square Ambiorix, Résidence le Pavois, BP 4, 1040 Brussels; tel. (02) 230-32-54; telex 26555; Chief Correspondent LE ZUDE.

Novinska Agencija Tanjug (Yugoslavia) and TASS (USSR) also have bureaux in Brussels.

PRESS ASSOCIATIONS

Association belge des Editeurs de Journaux/Belgische Vereniging van de Dagbladuitgevers: 20 rue Belliard, BP 5, 1040 Brussels; tel. (02) 512-17-32; telex 26854; fax (02) 511-99-69; f. 1964; 23 mems; Pres ANDRÉ DE BÉTHUNE; Sec.-Gen. JEAN HOET.

Association générale des Journalistes professionnels de Belgique/Algemene Vereniging van de Beroeps-journalisten in België: International Press Center, 1 blvd Charlemagne, BP 54, 1041 Brussels; tel. (02) 238-08-11; f. 1979 on merger of Association Générale de la Presse Belge (f. 1885) and Union Professionnelle de la Presse Belge (f. 1914); 1,630 mems (1989); affiliated to IFJ (International Federation of Journalists); Pres MARCEL BAUWENS; Sec.-Gen. JOSEPH VANDEN HOECK.

Fédération de la Presse Périodique de Belgique/Federatie van de periodieke pers van België (FPPB): 54 rue Charles Martel, 1040 Brussels; tel. (02) 230-09-99; fax (02) 231-14-59; f. 1891; Pres. MICHEL DAMANET; Sec.-Gen. RENÉ VAN HOOF.

Principal Publishers

Acco CV: 134-136 Tiensestraat, 3000 Louvain; tel. (016) 23-35-20; telex 62547; fax (016) 20-73-89; f. 1960; general reference, schoolbooks, periodicals; Dir CEES STAVENUITER.

Altiora NV (Publishing Dept): 1 Abdijstraat, BP 54, 3271 Averbode; tel. (013) 78-02-02; telex 39104; fax (013) 77-68-37; f. 1934; general, fiction, juvenile and religious (Roman Catholic); weekly children's periodicals; Dir T. G. SECUIANU.

Atlen NV: 4 G. Rodenbachstraat, 1030 Brussels; tel. (02) 242-39-00; telex 63698; f. 1978; reference; Dir J. THURMAN.

De Boeck Wesmael SA: 203 ave Louise, BP 1, 1050 Brussels; tel. (02) 640-72-72; telex 65701; fax (02) 641-92-84; f. 1795; school, technical and university textbooks, youth, nature and documentaries; Dirs CHR. DE BOECK, G. HOYOS.

Brepols IGP NV: 8 Baron Frans du Fourstraat, 2300 Turnhout; tel. (014) 41-54-51; telex 34182; fax (014) 42-89-19; f. 1975; religion, history; Man. Dir LAURENT BOLS.

Casterman SA: 28 rue des Soeurs Noires, 7500 Tournai; tel. (069) 25-42-11; telex 57328; fax (069) 25-42-29; f. 1780; fiction, encyclopaedias, education, history, fine arts, periodicals, comic books and children's books; Man. Dir R. VANGENEBERG.

Davidsfonds vzw: 79 Blijde Inkomststraat, 3000 Louvain; tel. (016) 22-18-01; fax (016) 22-25-32; f. 1875; general, reference, textbooks; Dir N. D'HULST.

Didier Hatier SA: 18 rue Antoine Labarre, 1050 Brussels; tel. (02) 649-99-45; fax (02) 646-06-48; f. 1979; school books, general literature; Dir M. MARCHAL.

Die Keure NV: 108 Oude Gentweg, 8000 Bruges; tel. (050) 33-12-35; telex 81411; fax (050) 34-37-68; f. 1948; textbooks, law, political and social sciences; Dirs J. P. STEEVENS (textbooks), R. CARTON (law, political and social sciences).

Editions Duculot SA: 65 ave de Lauzelle, 1348 Louvain-la-Neuve; tel. (10) 47-19-11; fax (10) 47-19-25; f. 1919; literature, art, religion, juveniles, linguistics, general science, school and university textbooks, guides, regional literature; Gen. Man. JEAN VEROUGSTRAETE.

Editions Dupuis SA: 7 blvd Tirou, 6000 Charleroi; tel. (071) 32-44-47; telex 51370; fax (071) 33-03-97; f. 1898; children's fiction, periodicals and comic books for children and adults; Dir JEAN DENEUMOSTIER.

Etablissements Emile Bruylant: 67 rue de la Régence, 1000 Brussels; tel. (02) 512-98-45; fax (02) 511-72-02; f. 1838; law; Chief Man. Dir J. VANDEVELD; Gen. Man. Mme A. VAN SPRENGEL.

Hadewijch NV: 33 Vrijheidstraat, 2000 Antwerp; tel. (03) 238-12-96; f. 1983; Dir W. HAZEU.

Halewijn NV: 92 Halewijnlaan, 2050 Antwerp; tel. (03) 219-38-00; fax (03) 219-79-12; f. 1953; general, periodicals; Dir-Gen. J. CORNILLE.

Editions Hemma SA: 106 rue de Chevron, 4987 Chevron; tel. (086) 43-36-36; telex 41507; fax (086) 43-36-40; f. 1956; juveniles, educational books and materials; Dir J. HEMMERLIN.

Kluwer Algemene Uitgeverijen België (KAUB): 21-23 Santvoortbeeklaan, 2100 Deurne; tel. (03) 360-02-11; telex 33649; fax (03) 360-04-66; f. 1986; fiction and popular non-fiction, general reference books; Dir C. VAN BAELEN.

Kritak NV: 249 Diestsestraat, 3000 Louvain; tel. (016) 23-12-64; fax (016) 22-33-10; f. 1976; art, law, social sciences, education, humanities, literature, periodicals; Dir ANDRÉ VAN HALEWIJCK.

Editions Labor-Nathan: 156-158 chaussée de Haecht, 1030 Brussels; tel. (02) 216-81-50; fax (02) 216-34-47; f. 1925; general; *L'Ecole 2000* (periodical); Gen. Man. JACQUES FAUCONNIER.

BELGIUM   *Directory*

Lannoo NV: 97 Kasteelstraat, 8700 Tielt; tel. (051) 42-42-11; telex 81555; fax (051) 40-11-52; f. 1909; general, reference; Dirs GODFRIED LANNOO, LUC DEMEESTER.

Maison Ferdinand Larcier SA: 39 rue des Minimes, 1000 Brussels; tel. (02) 512-47-12; f. 1839; legal publications; Dir J. M. RYCKMANS.

Editions du Lombard SA: 1–11 ave Paul-Henri Spaak, 1070 Brussels; tel. (02) 526-68-11; telex 23097; f. 1946; juveniles, games, education, geography, history, religion; Man. Dir ROB HARREU.

Imprimerie Robert Louis Editions: 35–43 rue Borrens, 1050 Brussels; tel. (02) 640-10-40; fax (02) 640-07-39; f. 1952; science and technical; Man. PIERRE LOUIS.

Manteau NV: 12 Beeldhouwersstraat, 2000 Antwerp; tel. (03) 237-17-92; f. 1932; literature, periodicals; Dir L. DEFLO.

Mercatorfonds: 85 Meir, 2000 Antwerp; tel. (03) 231-38-40; telex 71876; f. 1965; art, ethnography, literature, music, geography and history; Dirs JAN MARTENS, R. DE VOCHT.

Nouvelles Editions Marabout SA: 30 ave de l'Energie, 4430 Alleur; tel. (041) 61-18-63; telex 42072; f. 1977; paperbacks; Man. Dir SERGE MARTIANO; Dir JEAN-PAUL MICHAUD.

Peeters pvba: 153 Bondgenotenlaan, 3000 Louvain; tel. (016) 23-51-70; fax (016) 22-85-00; f. 1970; general, reference; Dir M. PEETERS-LISMOND.

Pelckmans NV: 222 Kapelsestraat, 2080 Kapellen; tel. (03) 664-53-20; telex 32242; fax (03) 655-02-63; f. 1893 as De Nederlandsche Boekhandel, name changed 1988; school books, scientific, general; Dirs J. and R. PELCKMANS.

Reader's Digest SA: 12A Grand' Place, 1000 Brussels; tel. (02) 423-25-11; telex 21876; f. 1967; education, sport, games, geography, history, travel, periodicals; Dir-Gen. JOE H. BEAUDUIN.

Roularta NV: 217 Amerikalei, 2000 Antwerp; f. 1954; Man. Dirs P. VAN DEN HEUVEL, R. DE NOLF.

De Sikkel: 8 Nijverheidsstraat, 2390 Malle; tel. (03) 312-47-61; fax (03) 311-77-39; f. 1919; education, literature, art, history of art, technical, sciences, sports, school magazines, trade papers and journals; Dir K. DE BOCK.

Snoeck-Ducaju en Zoon NV: 464 Begijnhoflaan, 9000 Ghent; tel. (091) 23-48-97; fax (091) 24-01-60; f. 1948; art books, holiday guides; Pres. SERGE SNOECK.

Société Belgo-Française de Presse et de Promotion (SBPP) SA: 68 ave Winston Churchill, 1180 Brussels; tel. (02) 345-99-20; fax (02) 344-28-27; periodicals; Dir CLAUDE CUVELIER.

Standaard Uitgeverij NV: 147A Belgiëlei, 2018 Antwerp; tel. (03) 239-59-00; telex 31421; fax (03) 230-85-50; f. 1924; general, reference, periodicals; Dir M. VAN TREECK.

Wolters Leuven: 50 Blijde-Inkomststraat, 3000 Louvain; tel. (016) 20-81-91; fax (016) 22-66-90; f. 1959; education; Dir JACQUES GERMONPREZ.

Zuidnederlandse Uitgeverij NV: 7 Vluchtenburgstraat, 2630 Aartselaar; tel. (03) 887-83-00; telex 31739; fax (03) 887-10-11; f. 1956; general fiction and non-fiction, children's books; Dir J. VANDE VELDEN.

PUBLISHERS' ASSOCIATIONS

Association des Editeurs Belges (ADEB): 140 blvd Lambermont, 1030 Brussels; tel. (02) 241-65-80; fax (02) 216-71-31; f. 1922; assen of French-language book publishers; Dir BERNARD GÉRARD.

Cercle Belge de la Librairie: 35 rue de la Chasse Royale, 1160 Brussels; tel. (02) 640-52-41; f. 1883; assen of Belgian booksellers and publishers; 205 mems; Pres. M. DESTREBECQ.

Vereniging van Uitgevers van Nederlandstalige Boeken: 93 Frankrijklei, 2000 Antwerp; tel. (03) 232-46-84; fax (03) 231-74-60; assen of Dutch-language book publishers; Sec. WIM DE MONT.

Radio and Television

In 1989 there were 3,274,236 television receivers in use. In 1986 there were an estimated 4.6m. radio receivers in use.

STATE BROADCASTING ORGANIZATIONS

French

Radio-Télévision Belge de la Communauté Culturelle Française (RTBF): 52 blvd Auguste Reyers, 1040 Brussels; tel. (02) 737-21-11; telex 21437; fax (02) 736-95-66; Chair. M. VAN CAMPENHOUDT; Admin-Gen. ROBERT STEPHANE; Dir of Radio Programmes PHILIPPE DASNOY; Dir of Television Programmes GEORGES KONEN; Dir of Information Service (Radio and Television) (vacant).

Dutch

Belgische Radio en Televisie: Instituut der Nederlandse Uitzendingen, 52 August Reyerslaan, 1040 Brussels; tel. (02) 737-31-11; telex 24216; fax (02) 735-37-04; Chair. ELS WITTE; Admin.-Gen. CASIMIR GOOSSENS; Dir of Radio Programmes PIET VAN ROE; Dir of Television Programmes JAN CEULEERS; Dir of News Department MARC GEVAERT; Dir Educational Broadcasting LEA MARTEL; Dir Technical Department MICHEL GEWILLIG.

German

Belgisches Rundfunk- und Fernsehzentrum der Deutschsprachigen Gemeinschaft (BRT): 82 Herbesthaler Str., 4700 Eupen; tel. (087) 59-44-11; telex 49427; fax (087) 59-45-99; Pres. K. KLEIN; Dir H. ENGELS.

COMMERCIAL, CABLE AND PRIVATE BROADCASTING

Many private radio stations operate in Belgium. Television broadcasts, including foreign transmissions, are received either directly or via cable. Belgium's first subscription-funded channel, Canal Plus Belgique, came into operation in mid-1989.

Canal Plus Belgique: 656 chaussée de Louvain, Schaerbeek; fax (02) 732-18-48; f. 1989; 33.3% owned by Canal Plus France, 33.3% by RTBF; broadcasts to Brussels region and Wallonia.

Télévision Indépendante (TVI): 67 ave Franklin Roosevelt; 1050 Brussels; tel. (02) 640-51-50; telex 64430; commercial station; broadcasts in French.

Vlaamse Televisie Maatschappij: 22 Luchthavenlaan, Vilvoorde; fax (02) 252-37-87; commercial station; broadcasts in Dutch; Man. Dir J. MERCKX.

Finance

(cap. = capital; m. = million; res = reserves;
dep. = deposits; brs = branches; frs = Belgian francs)

BANKING

Commission Bancaire: 99 ave Louise, 1050 Brussels; tel. (02) 535-22-11; telex 62107; fax (02) 535-23-23; f. 1935 to supervise the application of the law relating to the legal status of banks and bankers and to the public issue of securities; also the application of the legal status of common trust funds (1957), of certain non-banking financial enterprises (1964), of holding companies (1967) and of the private savings banks (1976); Pres. JEAN-LOUIS DUPLAT; Man. Dirs P. DUBOIS, G. GELDERS, M. MAES, J. VERTENEUIL.

Central Bank

Banque Nationale de Belgique: 5 blvd de Berlaimont, 1000 Brussels; tel. (02) 221-21-11; telex 21355; fax (02) 221-31-01; f. 1850; bank of issue; cap. 400m. frs, res 30,123m. frs, dep. 20,659m. frs (Dec. 1989); Gov. ALFONS VERPLAETSE; Vice Gov. W. FRAEYS; Exec. Dirs F. JUNIUS, J.-P. PAUWELS, G. QUADEN, J.-J. REY; 2 brs.

Development Banks

Gewestelijke Investeringsmaatschappij voor Vlaanderen: 37 Karel Oomstraat, 2018 Antwerp; tel. (03) 248-23-21; telex 34167; fax (03) 238-41-93; f. 1980; promotes creation, restructuring and extension of private enterprises, stimulation of public initiatives, implementation of the industrial policy of state and regions; cap. 3,174m. frs; Pres. R. VAN OUTRYVE D'YDEWALLE; CEO G. VAN ACKER.

Institut de Réescompte et de Garantie (IRG)/Herdiscontering-en Waarborginstituut (HWI): 78 rue du Commerce, 1040 Brussels; tel. (02) 511-73-30; fax (02) 514-34-50; f. 1935; deals with banks, public credit institutions, private savings banks and other financial intermediaries (money-market dealer and administrator of a deposit protection scheme); cap. and res 2,506.3m. frs; Chair. WILLIAM FRAEYS (acting); Gen. Man. FERNAND VANBEVER.

Nationale Investeringsmaatschappij (NIM)/Société Nationale d'Investissement (SNI): 63–67 rue Montoyer, 1040 Brussels; tel. (02) 237-06-11; telex 25744; f. 1962; reconstituted in 1976 as a 100% state-owned holding company; cap. 14,000m. frs; wide cash-raising powers to muster equity capital; private sector representation on governing body and investment committee; Pres. P. WILMES.

Société Régional d'Investissement de Wallonie: 19 place Joséphine-Charlotte, BP1, 5100 Jambes; tel. (081) 32-22-11; telex 59415; fax (081) 30-64-24; f. 1979; shareholding company; promotion of creation, restructuring and extension of private enterprises; stimulation of the industrial policy of state and provinces; cap. 11,899m. frs; Pres. JEAN-CLAUDE DEHOVRE.

Major state-owned Banks

Caisse Nationale de Crédit Professionnel/Nationale Kas voor Beroepskrediet: 16 blvd de Waterloo, 1000 Brussels; tel. (02) 513-64-80; telex 22026; f. 1929; res 2,158m. frs; Gen. Man. D. PONLOT.

Crédit Communal SA/Gemeentekrediet NV: 44 blvd Pachéco, 1000 Brussels; tel. (02) 222-41-11; telex 26354; fax (02) 222-55-04; f.

BELGIUM

1860; 'public credit institution', retail and savings bank; cap. 3,500m. frs, res 35,780m. frs, dep. 1,511,996m. frs (Dec. 1989); Chair. F. SWAELEN; Man. Dir FRANÇOIS NARMON; 1,281 brs.

Institut National de Crédit Agricole/Nationaal Instituut voor Landbouwkrediet: 56 rue Joseph II, 1040 Brussels; tel. (02) 234-12-11; telex 26863; f. 1937; agricultural credits; credits granted to agricultural associations; financing of agricultural products and foodstuffs; Pres. J. DETRY.

Société Nationale de Crédit à l'Industrie (SNCI)/Nationale Maatschappij voor Krediet aan de Nijverheid (NMKN): 14 ave de l'Astronomie, 1030 Brussels; tel. (02) 214-12-11; telex 25996; fax (02) 218-04-78; f. 1919; 'public credit institution'; share capital 50% state-owned, 50% by private interests; extends long-, medium- and short-term credits to industrial and commercial enterprises; cap. 410m. frs, res 11,142m. frs, dep. 411,815m. frs (Dec. 1989); Chair. K. DIERCKX; Gen. Man. ALFRED RAMPEN; 18 brs.

Major Commercial Banks

Algemene Bank Nederland (België) NV: 53 Regentlaan, 1000 Brussels; tel. (02) 518-02-11; telex 27040; fax (02) 513-27-65; f. 1960 as Internationale Handels- en Diamantbank NV, name changed 1984; cap. 900m. frs, res 1,036m. frs, dep. 12,756m. frs (Dec. 1989); Chair. P. J. PISTOR; Man. Dirs J. H. O. VAN DEN BOSCH, H. GOOSSENS; 5 brs.

Antwerpse Diamantbank NV/Banque Diamantaire Anversoise SA: 54 Pelikaanstraat, 2018 Antwerp; tel. (03) 233-90-80; telex 31673; fax (03) 233-90-95; f. 1934; cap. 1,386m. frs, res 910m. frs, dep. 18,997m. frs (March 1989); Chair. HENRI FAYT; Dir, Gen. Man. and Chair. of Exec. Cttee PAUL M. DE GROOTE.

Antwerpse Hypotheekkas/Caisse Hypothécaire Anversoise (AN–HYP): 214 Grotesteenweg, 2600 Antwerp; tel. (03) 218-21-11; telex 33100; fax (03) 218-24-07; f. 1881; savings bank; cap. 868m. frs, res 12,641m. frs, dep. 204,691m. frs (Dec. 1989); Chair. Baron PHILIPPE VANDERLINDEN; Gen. Man. JOZEF VAN RIET; 67 brs.

ASLK–CGER Bank (Algemene Spaar-en Lijfrentekas/Caisse Générale d'Epargne et de Retraite): 48 Wolvengracht, 1000 Brussels; tel. (02) 213-89-06; telex 26860; fax (02) 213-67-99; f. 1865; res 31,681m. frs, dep 1,343,436m. frs (Dec. 1989); Chair. LUC AERTS; 1,169 brs.

BACOB SC: 25 Trierstraat, 1040 Brussels; tel. (02) 237-82-11; telex 62199; fax (02) 230-71-78; f. 1924; savings bank; cap. 7,650m. frs, res 13,302m. frs, dep. 487,314m. frs (Dec. 1989); Chair. H. DETREMMERIE; 540 brs.

Banco Hispano Americano (Benelux) SA: 227 rue de la Loi, 1040 Brussels; tel. (02) 230-61-06; telex 21219; fax (02) 230-09-40; f. 1914, name changed 1970 and 1988; cap. 650m. frs, res 764m. frs, dep. 24,596m. frs (Dec. 1989); Chair. LEOPOLDO CALVO SOTELO Y BUSTELO; Man. Dir LEONARDO CABALLERO ALCÓN.

Banco di Roma (Belgio) SA: 24 rue Joseph II, 1040 Brussels; tel. (02) 219-36-60; telex 21573; fax (02) 218-83-91; f. 1947; cap. 600m. frs, res 608m. frs, dep. 59,343m. frs (June 1989); Chair. Comte A. D'ALCANTARA; Dir and Gen. Man. MANLIO DI MASE; 4 brs.

Bank J. van Breda & Co GCV: 295 Plantin & Moretuslei, 2200 Antwerp; tel. (03) 217-51-11; telex 31788; fax (03) 217-00-18; f. 1930; cap. 100m. frs, res 869m. frs, dep. 23,310m. frs (Dec. 1988); Mans RUDOLF D'HOORE, VAAST LEYSEN, MARK LEYSEN; 31 brs.

Bank of Yokohama (Europe) SA: 287 ave Louise, BP 1, 1050 Brussels; tel. (02) 648-82-85; telex 21709; fax (02) 648-31-48; f. 1983; cap. 875m. frs, res 48m. frs, dep. 18,675m. frs (March 1989); Man. Dir MASAHIRO TAKANO.

Bank van Roeselare NV: 38 Noordstraat, 8800 Roeselare; tel. (051) 23-52-11; telex 81734; fax (051) 21-12-97; f. 1924, name changed 1935, 1955 and 1986; commercial and savings bank; cap. 2,100m. frs, res 925m. frs, dep. 58,981m. frs (Dec. 1989); Chair. LAURENT SCHATTEMAN; Man. Dirs GERARD TYVAERT, AIME DECAT; 73 brs.

Banque Bruxelles Lambert SA: 24 ave Marnix, 1050 Brussels; tel. (02) 517-21-11; telex 21421; fax (02) 517-38-44; f. 1975 by merger; cap. 18,401m. frs, res 24,619m. frs, dep. 1,922,674m. frs (Sept. 1989); Chair. JACQUES THIERRY; 985 brs.

Banque Européenne pour l'Amérique Latine SA: 59 rue de l'Association, 1000 Brussels; tel. (02) 219-00-15; telex 22431; fax (02) 217-67-57; f. 1974; cap. 1,800m. frs, res 1,391m. frs, dep. 48,129m. frs (Dec. 1989); Chair. MICHEL BERGES; Man. Dir MARC GEDOPT.

Banque Indosuez Belgique SA: 9–13 Grote Markt, 2000 Antwerp; tel. (03) 225-07-80; telex 31730; fax (03) 231-98-75; f. 1954, present name from Oct. 1986; cap. 1,025m. frs, res 1,537m. frs, dep. 82,665m. frs (Dec. 1988); Chair. JO HOLVOET; 5 brs.

Banque Nagelmackers 1747 SA: 18 place de la Cathédrale, 4000 Liège; tel. (041) 20-02-11; telex 41271; fax (041) 20-02-63; f. 1747; cap. 1,169m. frs, res 1,435m. frs, dep. 31,855m. frs (Sept. 1989); Exec. Cttee GÉRARD FIEVET, BAUDOUIN NAGELMACKERS, ANDRÉ PAQUOT; 45 brs.

Banque Paribas Belgique SA/Paribas Bank België NV: 162 blvd E. Jacqmain, BP 2, 1210 Brussels; tel. (02) 220-41-11; telex 21349; fax (02) 218-51-42; f. 1968; cap. 3,600m. frs, res 5,856m. frs, dep. 308,849m. frs (Dec. 1989); Chair. F. ROBERT VANES; 58 brs.

Belgolaise SA: 1 Cantersteen, BP 807, 1000 Brussels; tel. (02) 518-72-11; telex 21375; fax (02) 518-75-15; f. 1960 as Banque Belgo-Congolaise SA, name changed 1972; cap. 1,000m. frs, res 2,119m. frs, dep. 57,038m. frs (Dec. 1988); Pres. JACQUES VERDICKT; Man. Dir MICHEL ISRALSON.

CC-Banque Belgique SA: 32 rue du Fossé-aux-Loups, 1000 Brussels; tel. (02) 211-32-11; telex 21670; fax (02) 217-97-99; f. 1896, name changed 1919 and 1989; cap. 1,135m. frs, res 19m. frs, dep. 25,995m. frs (Dec. 1989); Man. Dir and Chair. Exec. Cttee PEDRO M. GUIJARRO; 23 brs.

CERA: 52 Parijsstraat, 3000 Leuven; tel. (016) 24-49-99; telex 24166; fax (016) 24-49-32; f. 1935 as Centrale Raiffeisenkas CV/Centrale des Caisses Rurales; central organization of co-operative banks; cap. 13,123m. frs, res 26,351m. frs, dep. 510,319m. frs (Dec. 1989); Chair. of Board of Dirs R. EECKLOO; Chair. of Exec. Cttee W. DANCKAERT; 1,032 brs.

Crédit Général SA de Banque: 5 Grand'Place, 1000 Brussels; tel. (02) 516-12-11; telex 21903; fax (02) 516-13-12; f. 1958; cap. 2,000m. frs, res 1,074m. frs, dep. 102,686m. frs (Dec. 1988); Chair. JAN HUYGHEBAERT.

Crédit Lyonnais Belgium SA: 17 ave Marnix, 1050 Brussels; tel. (02) 516-95-11; telex 20227; fax (02) 511-24-58; f. 1893 as Banque de Commerce SA (Handelsbank NV), name changed 1985 and 1989; cap. 2,000m. frs, res 786m. frs, dep. 50,853m. frs (Dec. 1989); Chair. BERNARD THIOLON; Chief Exec. ALFRED BOUCKAERT; 33 brs.

Generale Bank NV/Générale de Banque SA: 3 Montagne du Parc, 1000 Brussels; tel. (02) 518-21-11; telex 21283; fax (02) 516-42-20; f. 1965 as Société Générale de Banque SA/Generale Bankmaatschappij NV, name changed 1985; cap. 19,893m. frs, res 60,743m. frs, dep. 2,303,463m. frs (Dec. 1989); Chair. of Board of Man. Dirs Baron PAUL-EMMANUEL JANSSEN; Chair. of Board of Dirs JACQUES GROOTHAERT; 1,154 brs.

Générale de Banque Belge pour l'Etranger: 3 Montagne du Parc, 1000 Brussels; tel. (02) 511-26-31; f. 1935, name changed 1972 and 1985; cap. 1,100m. frs, res 366m. frs, dep. 60,163m. frs (Dec. 1989); Chair. HENRI FAYT.

Ippa Bank NV/SA: 23 Vorstlaan, 1170 Brussels; tel. (02) 676-12-11; telex 25635; fax (02) 676-12-13; f. 1969; cap. 3,500m. frs, res 1,476m. frs, dep. 183,135m. frs (Dec. 1989); Chair. P. VAN DER MEERSCH; Man. Dir ALBERT VAN HOUTTE; 39 brs.

Kredietbank NV: 7 Arenbergstraat, 1000 Brussels; tel. (02) 517-41-11; telex 21207; f. 1935; cap. 7,799m. frs, res 41,952m. frs, dep. 1,490,242m. frs (March 1990); Chair. JAN HUYGHEBAERT; Man. Dirs JOZEF LAMBRECHTS, MARCEL COCKAERTS, WILFRIED JANSSENS, REMI VERMEIREN.

Lloyds Bank (Belgium) SA: 2 ave de Tervueren, 1040 Brussels; tel. (02) 739-58-11; telex 64359; fax (02) 733-11-07; f. 1953; cap. 153m. frs, res 134m. frs, dep. 13,015m. frs (Dec. 1989); Man. Dir R. C. SEAMER; 2 brs.

The Long-Term Credit Bank of Japan (Europe) SA: 40 blvd du Régent, BP 4, 1000 Brussels; tel. (02) 513-90-20; telex 61393; fax (02) 512-73-20; f. 1976 as Nippon European Bank SA, name changed 1988; cap. 840m. frs, res 494m. frs, dep. 42,502m. frs (Mar. 1989); Chair. KOICHI INAMURA; Man. Dir YOICHI HAGINO.

Metropolitan Bank NV: 191–197 blvd du Souverain, 1160 Brussels; tel. (02) 673-80-01; telex 24036; fax (02) 673-75-19; f. 1935, name changed 1966; cap. 830m. frs, res 48m. frs, dep. 22,438m. frs (Dec. 1989); Chair. RAYMOND LAUWYCK; Pres. of Exec. Cttee G. WERBROUCK.

Mitsubishi Bank (Europe) SA: 39 ave des Arts, 1040 Brussels; tel. (02) 513-97-70; telex 24168; fax (02) 513-28-51; f. 1974; cap. 1,970m. frs, res 219m. frs, dep. 89,806m. frs (Dec. 1988); Chair. HAJIME YAMADA; Man. Dirs HIDENARI HIROTA, MASAMI YASHIMA.

Mitsui Trust Bank (Europe) SA: 287 ave Louise, BP 5, 1050 Brussels; tel. (02) 640-88-50; telex 64720; fax (02) 640-73-29; f. 1980; cap. 710m. frs, res 2,045m. frs, dep. 44,912m. frs (Dec. 1989); Chair. SHOHEI YAMADA; Man. Dir KATSUJI SUZUKI.

NMB Bank (Belgium) SA: 1 rue de Ligne, 1000 Brussels; tel. (02) 217-40-40; telex 21780; fax (02) 217-04-91; f. 1934, name changed 1983 and 1989; wholly-owned subsidiary of NMB Bank (Netherlands); cap. 540m. frs, res 910m. frs, dep. 31,632m. frs (Dec. 1989); Man. Dir W. PIJPERS.

Saitama Bank (Europe) SA: 27 ave des Arts, BP 4, 1040 Brussels; tel. (02) 230-81-00; telex 24368; fax (02) 230-29-52; f. 1980; cap. 1,450m. frs, res 200m. frs, dep. 22,353m. frs (Dec. 1989); Chair. SHOICHI KAMIO; Gen. Man. SHIGEYUKI TORII.

Takugin International Bank (Europe) SA: 40 rue Montoyer, 1040 Brussels; tel. (02) 230-07-14; telex 23568; fax (02) 231-18-99; f. 1981;

BELGIUM
Directory

cap. 1,735m. frs, res 57m. frs, dep. 22,835m. frs (Dec. 1989); Chair. Hiroji Nakamura; Man. Dir M. Otobe.

Banking Associations

Association Belge des Banques/Belgische Vereniging van Banken: 36 rue Ravenstein, BP 5, 1000 Brussels; tel. (02) 507-68-11; telex 25575; fax (02) 511-19-51; f. 1936; represents all commercial banks; 86 mems; affiliated to Fédération des Entreprises de Belgique; Pres. Henri Fayt; Dir-Gen. Michel de Smet; Ombudsman Jan van Nuland.

Groupement Belge des Banques d'Epargne (GBE) (Savings Banks): 34–35 place Jamblinne de Meux, 1040 Brussels; tel. (02) 736-99-20; fax (02) 736-99-26; f. 1961; affiliated to Fédération des Entreprises de Belgique; Chair. August van Put; Gen. Man. Chris de Noose.

STOCK EXCHANGE

La Bourse de Fonds Publics de Bruxelles et la Commission de la Bourse (Stock Exchange): 2 rue Henri Maus, 1000 Brussels; tel. (02) 509-12-11; telex 21374; fax (02) 511-95-00; Pres. Jean Peterbroeck; Man. Dir Luc de Brabandere.

There are also stock exchanges in Antwerp, Ghent and Liège. The Belgian Futures and Options Exchange (BELFOX) was expected to begin operations in early 1991.

INSURANCE COMPANIES

Abeille-Paix, Société Anonyme Belge d'Assurances: 80 rue de la Loi, 1040 Brussels; telex 21819; fire, accident, general; Chair. M. J. Arvis; Gen. Man. M. P. Meyerson.

Abeille-Paix Vie, Société Anonyme Belge d'Assurances: 80 rue de la Loi, 1040 Brussels; tel. (02) 230-40-20; telex 21819; fax (02) 230-94-73; life; Chair. M. M. Garnier; Gen. Man. M. P. Meyerson.

Amev/AG: 53 blvd Emile Jacqmain, 1000 Brussels; tel. (02) 220-81-11; telex 22766; f. 1990, following merger of Groupe AG (Belgium) and AMEV NV (Netherlands).

Assubel-Vie: Brussels; Pres. Pierre Schoier.

Assurances Groupe Josi SA: 11 rue des Colonies, 1000 Brussels; tel. (02) 515-12-11; telex 21463; fax (02) 513-70-84; f. 1955; accident, fire, marine, general, life; Pres. and Dir-Gen. J. P. Laurent Josi.

Aviabel, Compagnie Belge d'Assurances Aviation, SA: 10 ave Brugmann, 1060 Brussels; tel. (02) 349-12-11; telex 21928; fax (02) 349-12-99; f. 1935; aviation, insurance, reinsurance; Chair. G. Cambron; Gen. Man. J. Verwilghen.

Belgamar, Compagnie Belge d'Assurances Maritimes SA: 54 St-Katelijnevest, Bus 39/40, 2000 Antwerp; tel. (03) 231-56-62; telex 33411; f. 1945; marine reinsurance; Chair. P. van der Meersch; Dir-Man. A. Thièry.

La Belgique, Compagnie d'Assurances SA: 1000 Brussels; tel. (02) 511-38-40; telex 63869; f. 1855; cap. 400m. frs; Chair. Hervé Nagelmackers; Gen. Man. P. Rousselle.

Compagnie d'Assurance de l'Escaut: 10 rue de la Bourse, Antwerp; f. 1821; fire, accident, life, burglary, reinsurance; Man E. Diercxsens.

Compagnie Belge d'Assurance-Crédit SA (COBAC): 15 rue Montoyer, 1040 Brussels; tel. (02) 513-89-30; telex 22337; f. 1929; Chair. R. Lamy; Man. Dir A. Stas de Richelle.

Compagnie Financière et de Réassurance du Groupe AG: 53 blvd Emile Jacqmain, 1000 Brussels; tel. (02) 220-81-11; f. 1824; all forms of reinsurance world-wide; Chair. and Man. Dir M. Lippens; Gen. Man. V. Croes.

Generali Belgium SA: 149 ave Louise, 1050 Brussels; tel. (02) 536-72-11; telex 21772; fire, accident, marine, life, reinsurance; Pres. Baron Lambert; Dir-Gen. C. Dendal.

Groupe Eagle-Star-Compagnie de Bruxelles 1821 SA d'Assurances: 62 rue de la Loi, 1040 Brussels; tel. (02) 237-12-11; telex 24443; fax (02) 237-12-16; f. 1821; fire, life, general; Pres. G. H. Lockwood; Man. Dir Antoine Meyer.

Les Patrons Réunis SA: 60 Chaussée de Charleroi, 1060 Brussels; tel. (02) 537-30-50; telex 64654; f. 1887; fire, life, accident; Chair. H. Liekens; Gen. Man. R. Nicolas.

Royale Belge: 25 blvd Souverain, 1170 Brussels; tel. (02) 661-61-11; telex 23000; fax (02) 661-93-40; f. 1853; life, accident, fire, theft, reinsurance, and all other risks; Pres. Pierre van den Meersch; Vice-Pres Jean Peyrelevade, Albert Frère; Man. Dirs Jean-Pierre Gerard, Pierre Labadie, Jean-Marie de Munter.

Société Mutuelle des Administrations Publiques: 24 rue des Croisiers, 4000 Liège; tel. (041) 20-31-11; telex 41216; institutions, civil service employees, public administration and enterprises.

Urbaine UAP Compagnie Belge d'Assurances et de Réassurances SA: 32 rue Belliard, 1040 Brussels; tel. (02) 238-51-11; telex 62060; fax (02) 230-59-15; f. 1900; all risks; Chair. J. P. de Launoit; Man. Dir J. Vanderhulst.

Insurance Associations

Fédération des Producteurs d'Assurances de Belgique (FEPRABEL): 40 ave Albert-Elisabeth, 1200 Brussels; tel (02) 733-35-22; fax (02) 735-44-58; f. 1934; Pres. Carlo Claeskens; Dir Jean Schouterden; 700 mems.

Union Professionnelle des Entreprises d'Assurances Belges et Etrangères Opérant en Belgique—Beroepsvereniging der Belgische en Buitenlandse Verzekeringsondernemingen: 29 square de Meeûs, 1040 Brussels; tel. (02) 513-68-45; telex 63652; fax (02) 514-24-69; f. 1921; affiliated to Fédération des Entreprises de Belgique; Pres. Valère Croes; Man. Dir Michel Baecker; 181 mems.

Trade and Industry

PRINCIPAL CHAMBERS OF COMMERCE

There are chambers of commerce and industry in all major towns and industrial areas.

Kamer van Koophandel en Nijverheid van Antwerpen: 12 Markgravestraat, 2000 Antwerp; tel. (03) 232-22-19; telex 71536; fax (03) 233-64-42; f. 1969; Gen. Man. M. Verboven.

Chambre de Commerce et d'Industrie de Bruxelles: 500 ave Louise, 1050 Brussels; tel. (02) 648-50-02; telex 22082; fax (02) 640-92-28; f. 1875.

TRADE AND INDUSTRIAL ASSOCIATIONS

Fédération des Entreprises de Belgique (Belgian Business Federation): 4 rue Ravenstein, 1000 Brussels; tel. (02) 515-08-11; telex 26576; fax (02) 515-09-99; f. 1895; federates all the main industrial and non-industrial associations; Pres. Philippe Bodson; Man. Dir Raymond Pulinckx.

Association Belge des Entreprises d'Alimentation à Succursales (ABEAS) (Food Chain Stores): 60 rue St Bernard, 1060 Brussels; tel. (02) 537-30-60; fax (02) 539-40-26; f. 1941; Pres. Guy Beckers; Dir-Gen. Alphonse de Vadder.

Association des Entreprises Exportatrices de l'Industrie Alimentaire Belge/Vereniging van de uitvoerende Bedrijven van de Belgische Voedingsindustrie—VITABEL (Exporting Food Manufacturers): 172 ave de Cortenbergh, BP 7, 1040 Brussels; tel. (02) 735-81-70; telex 26246; fax (02) 733-94-26; f. 1984; Pres. A. Beaumont; Dir Y. Neuckens.

Association des Exploitants de Carrières de Porphyre (Porphyry): 64 rue de Belle-Vue, 1050 Brussels; tel. (02) 648-68-60; f. 1967; Pres. Philippe Notté; Dir Georges Hansen.

Association des Fabricants de Pâtes, Papiers et Cartons de Belgique (COBELPA) (Paper): 39–41 rue d'Arlon, BP 9, 1040 Brussels; tel. (02) 230-70-20; telex 22713; fax (02) 230-11-46; f. 1940; co-operative asscn; Pres. Fred van dem Keybus; Dir Alfred Rose.

Association des Groupements et Entreprises de Distribution de Belgique (AGED) (Distribution): 3 rue de la Science, 1040 Brussels; tel. (02) 537-30-60; f. 1946; Pres. Michel Buisseret; Dir-Gen. Alfons de Vedder.

Association des Industries des Carrières (AIC) (Federation of Quarrying Industries): 64 rue de Belle-Vue, 1050 Brussels; tel. (02) 648-68-60; f. 1975; Pres. Philippe Notté; Dir Georges Hansen.

Confédération des Brasseries de Belgique (Breweries): Maison des Brasseurs, 10 Grand' Place, 1000 Brussels; tel. (02) 511-49-87; fax (02) 511-32-59; f. 1971; Pres. Jean Martens; Dir Michel Brichet.

Confédération Nationale de la Construction (CNC) (Civil Engineering, Road and Building Contractors and Auxiliary Trades): 34–42 rue du Lombard, 1000 Brussels; tel. (02) 510-46-11; telex 64956; fax (02) 513-30-04; f. 1946; 15,000 mems; Pres. Roland Maes; Man. Dir Freddy Feys, Admin. Dir Edwin Jacobs.

Confédération Professionnelle du Sucre et de ses Dérivés (Sugar): 182 ave de Tervueren, 1150 Brussels; tel. (02) 771-01-30; fax (02) 772-46-57; f. 1938; mems 10 groups, 66 firms; Pres. Oswald Adriaensen; Dir-Gen. Jules Beauduin.

Fédération Belge du Commerce Alimentaire (FEBECA) (Foodstuffs Trade): 60 rue St-Bernard, 1060 Brussels; tel. (02) 537-30-60; fax (02) 539-40-26; f. 1941; Pres. Georges de Meyere; Dir-Gen. J. Degrave.

Fédération Belge des Dragueurs de Gravier et de Sable (BELBAG-DRAGBEL) (Dredging): 12 ave Hippocrate, BP 19, 1932 Woluwé-Saint-Etienne; tel. (02) 736-02-15; f. 1967; Pres. Daniel de Groote.

Fédération Belge des Entreprises de Distribution (FEDIS): 60 rue St-Bernard, 1060 Brussels; tel. (02) 537-30-60; fax (02) 539-40-26; Man. Dir Robert van Assche.

BELGIUM

Fédération Belge des Entreprises de la Transformation du Bois (FEBELBOIS) (Wood): Maison du Bois, 109–111 rue Royale, 1000 Brussels; tel. (02) 217-63-65; telex 64143; fax (02) 217-59-04; Gen. Pres. GUSTAAF NEYT; Man. Dir HUBERT FONDERIE.

Fédération Belge de la Fourrure ASBL (Furs and Skins): 102 ave de la Constitution, 1090 Brussels: tel. (02) 420-19-43; fax (02) 420-08-74; f. 1947; Pres. G. VERGEYLEN; Sec.-Gen. C. KOHNER.

Fédération Belge des Industries Graphiques (FEBELGRA) (Graphic Industries): 20 rue Belliard, BP 16, 1040 Brussels; tel. (02) 512-36-38; telex 26854; fax (02) 513-56-76; f. 1978; 1,000 mems; Pres. POL VERWAEST; Sec.-Gen. JOS ROSSIE.

Fédération Belge des Industries de l'Habillement (Clothing and Outfitting): 24 rue Montoyer, BP 11, 1040 Brussels; tel. (02) 230-88-90; telex 61055; fax (02) 230-47-00; f. 1946; Pres. ANDRÉ DELFOSSE; Dir ROBERT DE MÛELENAERE.

Fédération Belge de L'Industrie de la Chaussure (FEBIC) (Footwear): 53 rue François Bossaerts, 1030 Brussels; tel. (02) 735-27-01; telex 65625; fax (02) 736-12-76; f. 1968; Pres. ROELAND SMETS.

Fédération Belgo-Luxembourgeoise des Industries du Tabac (FEDETAB) (Tobacco): 480 ave Louise, BP 14, 1050 Brussels; tel. (02) 646-04-20; fax (02) 646-22-13; f. 1947; Pres. EMMANUEL VAN OUTRYVE D'YDEWALLE; Chief Exec. GUY DEMOULIN; Sec.-Gen. D. VUIJLSTEKE.

Fédération Charbonnière de Belgique (Coal): 21 ave des Arts, 1040 Brussels; tel. (02) 230-37-40; fax (02) 230-88-50; f. 1909; Pres. YVES SLEUWAEGEN; Dir GUY VAN BRUYSTEGEM.

Fédération des Carrières de Petit Granit (Granite): 245 rue de Cognebeau, 7400 Soignies; tel. (067) 33-41-21; fax (067) 33-00-59; f. 1948; Pres. ERIC LEMAIGRE.

Fédération des Entreprises de l'Industrie des Fabrications Métalliques, Mécaniques, Electriques, Electroniques et de la Transformation des Matières Plastiques (FABRIMETAL) (Metalwork, Engineering, Electrics, Electronics and Plastic Processing): 21 rue des Drapiers, 1050 Brussels; tel. (02) 510-23-11; telex 21078; fax (02) 510-23-01; f. 1946; Pres. RICHARD GANDIBLEUX; CEO PHILIPPE DE BUCK VAN OVERSTRAETEN.

Fédération des Entreprises de Métaux non Ferreux (Nonferrous Metals): 47 rue Montoyer, 1040 Brussels; tel. (02) 506-41-11; fax (02) 511-75-53; f. 1918; 40 mems; Pres. LEANDRO ALIMENTI; Dir JACQUES HENNEVAUX.

Fédération des Industries Agricoles et Alimentaires/Verbond der Landbouw en Voedingsnijverheid (Food and Agricultural Industries): 172 Kortenberglaan, bus 7, 1040 Brussels; tel. (02) 735-81-70; telex 26246; fax (02) 733-94-26; f. 1937; Pres. PIERRE GODFROID; Dir-Gen. PAUL VERHAEGHE.

Fédération de l'Industrie du Béton (FeBe) (Precast Concrete): 207–209 blvd August Reyers, 1040 Brussels; tel. (02) 735-80-15; fax (02) 734-77-95; f. 1936; Pres. RAF BULCKE; Dir WILLY SIMONS.

Fédération des Industries Céramiques de Belgique et du Luxembourg (FEDICER) (Ceramics): 4 ave Gouverneur Cornez, 7000 Mons; tel. (065) 34-80-00; telex 57865; fax (065) 34-80-05; f. 1919; Pres. C. Y. DUMOLIN; Dir P. DE BRUYCKER.

Fédération des Industries Chimiques de Belgique (Chemical Industries): 49 square Marie-Louise, 1040 Brussels; tel. (02) 238-97-11; telex 23167; fax (02) 231-13-01; f. 1919; Pres. GEORGES JACOBS; Man. Dir PAUL-F. SMETS.

Fédération de l'Industrie Cimentière (Cement): 46 rue César Franck, 1050 Brussels; tel. (02) 645-52-11; fax (02) 640-06-70; f. 1949; Pres. ANDRÉAS PESTALOZZI; Dir-Gen. JEAN-PIERRE LATTEUR.

Fédération des Industries Extractives et Transformatrices de Roches non-Combustibles SC (Extraction and processing of non-fuel rocks): 61 rue du Trône, 1050 Brussels; tel. (02) 511-61-73; f. 1942 as Union des Producteurs Belges de Chaux, Calcaires, Dolomies et Produits Connexes, name changed 1990; co-operative society; Pres. CHARLES MOREAU DE MELEN; Dir EMILE WOUTERS.

Fédération de l'Industrie du Gaz (FIGAZ) (Gas): 4 ave Palmerston, 1040 Brussels; tel. (02) 237-11-11; fax (02) 230-44-80; f. 1946; Pres. JEAN FREROT; Sec.-Gen. LIEVEN BLOM.

Fédération de l'Industrie Textile Belge (FEBELTEX) (Textiles): 24 rue Montoyer, 1040 Brussels; tel. (02) 230-93-30; fax (02) 230-65-85; f. 1945; Pres. LUC SANTENS; Dir-Gen. F. BLEECKX; 900 mems.

Fédération des Industries Transformatrices de Papier et Carton (FETRA) (Paper and Cardboard): 715 chaussée de Waterloo, BP 25, 1180 Brussels; tel. (02) 344-19-62; fax (02) 344-86-61; f. 1947; Pres. PHILIPPE DE SOMER; Dir PHILIPPE DELLA FAILLE DE LEVERGHEM; 300 mems.

Fédération de l'Industrie du Verre (Glass): 47 rue Montoyer, 1040 Brussels; tel. (02) 509-15-20; fax (02) 514-23-45; f. 1947; Pres. GÉRY LIVREMONT; Dir PIERRE VAN DE PUTTE.

Fédération Patronale des Ports Belges (Port Employers): 33 Brouwersvliet, bus 7, 2000 Antwerp; tel. (03) 232-19-27; fax (03) 232-38-26; f. 1937; Pres. EDUARD FOERTS; Secs WALTER BAGUE, FRANS GIELEN.

Fédération Pétrolière Belge (Petroleum): 4 rue de la Science, 1040 Brussels; tel. (02) 512-30-03; telex 26930; fax (02) 512-30-03; f. 1926; Pres. GEORGES DE GRAEVE.

Groupement National de l'Industrie de la Terre Cuite (Bricks): 13 rue des Poissonniers, BP 22, 1000 Brussels; tel. (02) 511-25-81; fax (02) 513-26-40; f. 1947; Pres. MODEST HEYLEN; Dir GIOVANNI PEIRS.

Groupement Patronal des Bureaux Commerciaux et Maritimes (Employers' Association of Trade and Shipping Offices): 33 Brouwersvliet, bus 7, 2000 Antwerp; tel. (03) 232-19-27; fax (03) 232-38-26; f. 1937; Pres. EDUARD FOERTS; Sec. FRANS GIELEN.

Groupement des Sablières (Sand and Gravel): 49 Quellinstraat, 2018 Antwerp; tel. (03) 223-66-83; f. 1937; Pres. ALFRED PAULUS; Sec. PAUL DE NIE.

Groupement de la Sidérurgie (Iron and Steel): 47 rue Montoyer, 1040 Brussels; tel. (02) 509-14-11; telex 21287; fax (02) 509-14-00; f. 1982; Pres. and Dir-Gen. CHRISTIAN OURY.

Union des Armateurs Belges (Shipowners): 9 Lijnwaadmarkt, 2000 Antwerp; tel. (03) 232-72-31; fax (03) 225-28-36; Chair. JACQUES SAVERYS; Man. R. VAN HERCK.

Union des Carrières et Scieries de Marbres de Belgique (UCSMB) (Marble): 40 rue Bosquet, 1060 Brussels; tel. (02) 538-46-61; telex 24235; fax (02) 537-35-59; Pres. J. VAN DEN WILDENBERG; Vice-Pres. P. STONE.

Union des Exploitations Electriques et Gazières en Belgique (UEGB) (Electricity and Gas): 4 galerie Ravenstein, BP 6, 1000 Brussels; tel. (02) 511-19-70; telex 62409; fax (02) 511-29-38; f. 1911; Pres. Baron ANDRÉ ROLIN; Sec.-Gen. MICHEL LONCOUR.

Industrie des Huiles Minérales de Belgique (IHMB—IMOB) (Mineral Oils): 49 square Marie-Louise, 1040 Brussels; tel. (02) 238-97-11; telex 23167; fax (02) 231-13-01; f. 1921; Pres. R. VANDATTE; Sec. M. DONCKERWOLCKE; 90 mems.

Union Professionnelle des Producteurs de Fibres-Ciment (Asbestos-Cement): World Trade Centre, 162 blvd Emile Jacqmain, BP 37, 1210 Brussels; tel. (02) 211-04-11; telex 21696; fax (02) 219-69-08; f. 1941; Pres. ETIENNE VAN DER REST; Sec. PAUL VAN REETH.

Union de la Tannerie et de la Mégisserie Belges (UNITAN) (Tanning and Tawing): 161 rue Th. de Cuyper, BP 32, 1200 Brussels; tel. and fax (02) 771-32-06; f. 1962; Pres. MARC WAMWELDEN; Sec. JACQUES FELDHEIM; 13 mems.

TRADE UNIONS AND PROFESSIONAL ORGANIZATIONS

Fédération Générale du Travail de Belgique (FGTB)/Algemeen Belgisch Vakverbond (ABVV): 42 rue Haute, 1000 Brussels; tel. (02) 506-82-11; telex 24620; fax (02) 513-47-21; f. 1899; affiliated to ICFTU; Pres. FRANÇOIS JANSSENS; Gen. Sec. MIA DE VITS; has 12 affiliated unions with an estimated total membership of 1,036,028 (1986). Affiliated unions:

La Centrale Générale/De Algemene Centrale (Central Union, building, timber, glass, paper, chemicals and petroleum industries): 26–28 rue Haute, 1000 Brussels; tel. (02) 513-06-25; telex 62559; fax (02) 514-16-91; Pres. JUAN FERNANDEZ; Sec.-Gen. HENRI LORENT; Nat. Secs MAURICE CORBISIER, ERIC GOETHALS, MICHEL NOLLET, ALFONS VAN NOOTEN, HANS RAES; 250,000 mems (1988).

Centrale Générale des Services Publics/Algemene Centrale der Openbare Diensten (Public Service Workers): Maison des Huit Heures, 9–11 place Fontainas, 1000 Brussels; tel. (02) 508-58-11; telex 22563; fax (02) 508-59-02; f. 1945; Pres. R. PITON; Gen. Secs F. FERMON, G. LONNOY, G. SERET, K. STESSENS; 253,000 mems (1989).

Centrale de l'Industrie du Livre et du Papier/Centrale der Boek- en Papiernijverheid (Graphical and Paper Workers): galerie du Centre, bloc 2, 17 rue des Fripiers, 1000 Brussels; tel. (02) 511-09-66; f. 1945; Secs ROBERT LELOUP, ROGER SAGON; 11,918 mems (1987).

Centrale du Vêtement et Parties Similaires de Belgique/Centrale der Kleding en Aanverwante Vakken van België (Clothing Workers): 32 Ommeganckstraat, 2018 Antwerp; tel. (03) 233-56-72; fax (03) 226-01-09; f. 1898; Pres. JEF HUYMANS; Gen. Sec. RENÉ STABEL; 27,450 mems (1989).

Centrale des Métallurgistes de Belgique/Centrale der Metaalbewerkers van België (Metal Workers): 17 rue Jacques Jordaens,

BELGIUM

1050 Brussels; tel. (02) 647-83-14; fax (02) 647-83-92; f. 1887; Sec.-Gen. MICHEL COSSAER; 172,896 mems (1990).

La Centrale des Ouvriers Textiles de Belgique/Textielarbeiderscentrale van België (Textile Workers): 143 Opvoedingsstraat, 9000 Ghent; tel. (091) 21-75-11; fax (091) 21-08-93; f. 1898; Nat. Pres. DONALD WITTEVRONGEL; Nat. Sec. LUC VANNESTE; 38,389 mems (1986).

Centrale Syndicale des Travailleurs des Mines de Belgique/Belgische Mijnwerkerscentrale (Miners): 8 J. Stevensstraat, bus 4, 1000 Brussels; tel. (02) 511-96-45; f. 1889; Pres. J. OLYSLAEGERS; 19,142 mems (1987).

Centrale des Travailleurs de l'Alimentation et de l'Hôtellerie/Centrale der Voeding en Hotelarbeiders (Catering and Hotel Workers): 18 rue des Alexiens, 1000 Brussels; tel. (02) 512-97-00; f. 1912; Pres. ARTHUR LADRILLE; Nat. Sec. EDUARD PEPERMANS; 57,380 mems.

Syndicat des Employés, Techniciens et Cadres de Belgique/Bond der Bedienden, Technici en Kaders van België (Employees, Technicians and Administrative Workers): 42 rue Haute, 1000 Brussels; tel. (02) 513-18-91; f. 1891; Pres. KAREL BOEYKENS; Gen. Sec. GILBERT CLAJOT; 174,528 mems (1986).

Le Syndicat des Ouvriers Diamantaires/Belgische Diamantbewerkersbond (Diamond Workers): 57 Lange Kievitstraat, bus 1, 2018 Antwerp; tel. (03) 232-48-60; f. 1896; Pres. C. DENISSE; 3,672 mems (1986).

Union Belge des Ouvriers du Transport/Belgische Transportarbeidersbond (Belgian Transport Workers): 66 Paardenmarkt, 2000 Antwerp; tel. (03) 224-34-11; telex 73080; fax (03) 234-01-49; f. 1913; Pres. REMI VAN CANT; 24,000 mems (1989).

Les Cadets, an organization for students and school pupils, is also affiliated to the FGTB/ABVV.

Confédération des Syndicats Chrétiens (CSC): 121 rue de la Loi, 1040 Brussels; tel. (02) 233-34-11; telex 61770; Pres. WILLY PEIRENS; has 18 affiliated unions with an estimated total membership of 1,336,000 (1987). Affiliated unions:

Centrale Chrétienne de l'Alimentation et des Services (Food and Service Industries): 27 rue de l'Association, 1000 Brussels; tel. (02) 218-21-71; f. 1919; Pres. W. VIJVERMAN; Sec.-Gen. F. BOCKLANDT; 111,049 mems (1982).

Centrale Chrétienne des Métallurgistes de Belgique (Metal Workers): 127 rue de Heembeek, 1120 Brussels; tel. (02) 215-88-40; fax (02) 241-48-27; Pres. T. JANSSEN; 232,000 mems.

Centrale Chrétienne des Ouvriers des Industries des Mines, de l'Energie, de la Chimie, du Cuir et Diverses (Mines, Power, Chemical, Leather, etc., Workers): 26–32 ave d'Auderghem, 1040 Brussels; tel. (02) 238-73-32; f. 1912; Pres. A. VAN GENECHTEN; Nat. Sec. A. CUYVERS; Gen. Sec. M. SOMMEREYNS; 77,651 mems (1987).

Centrale Chrétienne des Ouvriers du Textile et du Vêtement de Belgique (Textile and Clothing Workers): 27 Koning Albertlaan, 9000 Ghent; tel. (091) 22-57-01; fax (091) 20-45-59; f. 1886; Pres. A. DUQUET; Gen. Sec. L. MEULEMAN; 120,000 mems (1987).

Centrale Chrétienne des Ouvriers du Transport et des Ouvriers Diamantaires (Transport and Diamond Workers): 12–14 Entrepotplaats, 2000 Antwerp; tel. (03) 231-47-85; fax (03) 231-47-81; Pres. JOHN JANSSENS.

Centrale Chrétienne du Personnel de l'Enseignement Moyen et Normal Libre (Lay Teachers in Secondary and Teacher-Training Institutions): 26–32 ave d'Auderghem, 1040 Brussels; tel. (02) 231-00-90; f. 1924; f. 1950; Pres. ROGER DENIS; 18,000 mems (1987).

Centrale Chrétienne du Personnel de l'Enseignement Technique (Teachers in Technical Education): 26 ave d'Auderghem, 1040 Brussels; tel. (02) 238-74-67; f. 1924; Pres. JEAN LUC MASUY; Sec.-Gen. JEAN PIERRE LECLERCQ; 8,000 mems (1990).

Centrale Chrétienne des Services Publics—Christelijke Centrale van de Openbare Diensten (Public Service Workers): 26 ave d'Auderghem, 1040 Brussels; tel. (02) 231-00-90; f. 1921; Pres. FILIP WIEERS; Sec.-Gen. GUY RASNEUR; 93,000 mems (1976).

Centrale Chrétienne des Travailleurs du Bois et du Bâtiment (Wood and Building Workers): 31 rue de Trèves, 1040 Brussels; tel. (02) 230-85-70; Pres. A. DESLOOVERE; Sec.-Gen. BERNARD BAERT; 188,300 mems (1987).

Centrale Chrétienne des Travailleurs de la Pierre, du Ciment, de la Céramique et du Verre (Stone, Cement, Ceramic and Glass Workers): 26–32 ave d'Auderghem, 1040 Brussels; tel. (02) 231-00-90; Pres. AUGUST DE DECKER; Secs LÉO DUSOLEIL, RAYMOND GROETEMBRIL; 26,000 mems (1981).

Centrale des Francs Mineurs (Miners' Union): 26 ave d'Auderghem, 1040 Brussels; Pres. ANDRÉ DAEMEN; Sec. FRANS VANDERLINDEN; 31,725 mems (1976).

Centrale Nationale des Employés/Landelijke Bedienden Centrale (Employees): (Northern Region) 1 Beggaardenstraat, 2000 Antwerp; tel. (03) 234-15-00; (Southern Region) 33–35 ave d'Auderghem, 1040 Brussels; tel. (02) 230-65-73; f. 1912; Secs-Gen. L. STRAGIER (Northern), JOSÉ ROISIN (Southern); 240,000 mems (1979).

Christelijke Centrale van Diverse Industrieen (Miscellaneous): Oudergemselaan 26–32, 1040 Brussels; tel. (02) 231-00-90; Pres. LEO DUSOLEIL; National Secs RAYMOND GROETEMBRIL, LEON VAN HAUDT.

Christen Onderwijzersverbond van België (School teachers): 203 Koningstraat, 1210 Brussels; tel. (02) 217-40-50; fax (02) 219-47-61; f. 1893; Pres. G. BOURDEAUD'HUI; Sec.-Gen. L. VAN BENEDEN; 39,500 mems (1990).

Fédération des Instituteurs Chrétiens de Belgique (Schoolteachers): 20 rue de la Victoire, 1060 Brussels; f. 1893; Sec.-Gen. R. DOHOGNE; 11,100 mems (1988).

Service Syndical Sports (Sport): 7 Poel, 9000 Ghent; tel. (091) 24-00-42; Pres. E. LAENEN; Sec. M. LIPPENS.

Syndicat Chrétien des Communications et de la Culture (Christian Trade Unions of Railway, Post and Telecommunications, Shipping, Civil Aviation, Radio, TV and Cultural Workers): 26 ave d'Auderghem, 1040 Brussels; tel. (02) 238-72-11; fax (02) 231-14-44; f. 1919; Pres. M. BOVY; Vice-Pres. P. BERTIN; Secs L. VAN DEN BERGH, P. VAN DEN DOOREN, R. FRIPPIAT, J. HINNEKENS; 60,000 mems (1987).

Union Chrétienne des Membres du Personnel de l'Enseignement Officiel: 26 ave d'Auderghem, 1040 Brussels; tel. (02) 231-00-90; Pres. A. POLLET; Secs E. BODSON, J. LUYTEN.

Centrale Générale des Syndicats Libéraux de Belgique (CGSLB) (General Federation of Liberal Trade Unions of Belgium): 2 rue Brederode, 1000 Brussels; tel. (02) 511-15-95; f. 1889; National Pres. WILLY WALDACK; 250,000 mems.

Fédération Nationale des Unions Professionnelles Agricoles de Belgique: 94–96 rue Antoine Dansaert, 1000 Brussels; tel. (02) 511-07-37; f. 1919; Pres. L. ERNOUX; Sec.-Gen. J. P. CHAMPAGNE.

Nationale Unie der Openbare Diensten (NUOD)/Union Nationale des Services Publics (UNSP): 54 Paviljoenstraat, 1210 Brussels; tel. (02) 215-66-70; fax (02) 242-87-82; f. 1983; Pres. GERALD VAN ACKER; Sec.-Gen. FREDDY MALFROOID.

TRADE FAIRS

Foire Internationale de Bruxelles (Brussels International Trade Fair): Parc des Expositions, 1020 Brussels; tel. (02) 477-04-77; fax (02) 477-03-90; f. 1919; holds more than 25 fairs and trade shows each year, as well as 60 congresses and technical exhibitions; Gen. Man. J. ISAAC CASTIAU.

International Fair of Flanders: Congrescentrum (5th floor), 9000 Ghent; tel. (091) 22-40-22; telex 12666; fax (091) 20-10-81; f. 1946; holds several fairs annually.

Transport

RAILWAYS

The Belgian railway network is one of the densest in the world. The main lines are operated by the SNCB under lease from the State Transport Administration. In 1989 the SNCB approved plans for the Belgian section of a proposed high-speed railway network for northern Europe that would eventually link Belgium, France, the Netherlands, the United Kingdom and Germany. The existing system is complemented by the SNCV bus and light railway network for local traffic. Six regional companies run trams, rapid transit systems and metros.

Société Nationale des Chemins de Fer Belges (SNCB)/Nationale Maatschappij der Belgische Spoorwegen (NMBS): 85 rue de France, 1070 Brussels; tel. (02) 525-21-11; telex 62925; fax (02) 525-40-45; f. 1926; 143.1m. passengers were carried in 1988; directed by a board of 16 members; 3,554 km of lines, of which 2,264 km are electrified; Gen. Man. E. SCHOUPPE.

ROADS

At 31 December 1988 there were 1,593 km of motorways, 12,902 km of other main or national roads and 13,850 km of secondary or regional roads. In addition, there are about 100,000 km of minor roads.

Société Nationale des Chemins de Fer Vicinaux (SNCV) (Light railways, buses and trams): 14 rue de la Science, 1040 Brussels; tel. (02) 237-62-11; fax (02) 237-63-98; f. 1884; operates all public bus and tram services; Pres. R. Denison; Dir-Gen. Hugo van Wesemael.

INLAND WATERWAYS

There are over 1,500 km of inland waterways in Belgium, of which 654 km are navigable rivers and 860 km are canals. In 1988 an estimated 99,159,000 metric tons of cargo were carried on the inland waterways. Under the Investment Plan that was inaugurated in 1957 canals and rivers have been modified to accommodate more traffic.

Ministerie van Openbare Werken: Hoofdbestuur der Waterwegen, Residence Palace, Wetstraat 155, 1040 Brussels; tel. (02) 733-96-70; telex 63477; fax (02) 230-32-70; Dir-Gen. Ir. J. Demoen.

SHIPPING

The modernized port of Antwerp is the second biggest in Europe and handles 80% of Belgian foreign trade by sea and inland waterways. It is also the largest railway port and has one of the largest petroleum refining complexes in Europe. It has 98 km of quayside and 17 dry docks, and is currently accessible to vessels of up to 75,000 tons: extensions are being carried out which will increase this limit to 125,000 tons. The port receives some 19,000 vessels and handled 90 million tons of cargo in 1986. Other ports include Zeebrugge, Ostend, Ghent, Liège and Brussels.

Ahlers Lines NV: 139 Noorderlaan, 2030 Antwerp; tel. (03) 543-72-11; telex 72154; fax (03) 541-23-09; services to Finland, Poland, USSR, Morocco; Dirs H. Coppieters, J. Gelens, H. Knoche.

Belfranline NV: 24–29 Meir, 2000 Antwerp; tel. (03) 234-84-11; telex 34115; fax (03) 231-36-70; f. 1957; liner services to Venezuela, Dominican Republic, Haiti, Netherlands Antilles, Trinidad and Tobago, Barbados and Jamaica; also to Central America (East Coast); Pres. J. E. Sasse; Man. Dir E. J. Sasse.

CMB SA/NV: (Reg. Office) 61 St Katelijnevest, 2000 Antwerp; (Commercial Office) 1 Meir, 2000 Antwerp; tel. (03) 223-21-11; telex 72304; fax (03) 223-24-88; f. 1895, fmrly known as Compagnie Maritime Belge (Lloyd Royal) SA, merged with Methania SA/NV in 1985; European service and lines to North and South America, Africa, Middle East and Indian sub-continent; Chair. E. Davignon; Dir-Gen. J. Saverijs; 41 freight vessels (conventional, container, bulk).

De Keyser Thornton: 38 Huidevettersstraat, 2000 Antwerp; tel. (03) 233-01-05; telex 72511; fax (03) 234-27-86; f. 1983; shipping agency, forwarding and warehousing services; Man. Dir M. P. Ingham.

ESSO Belgium: Antwerp; tel. (03) 543-31-11; telex 35600; fax (03) 543-34-95; refining and marketing of petroleum products; Pres. R. Dahan; Dirs J. Hook, A. Spoor.

North Sea Ferries (Belgium) NV: Leopold II Dam, 13, 8380 Zeebrugge; tel. (050) 54-34-11; telex 81469; fax (050) 54-68-35; operated in conjunction with North Sea Ferries Ltd, UK; roll-on/roll-off ferry services between Zeebrugge and Hull and Middlesbrough; Dirs M. L. van Leeuwen, R. D. Peters, M. Storme.

Northern Shipping Service NV: 54 St Katelijnevest, 2000 Antwerp; tel. (03) 233-99-85; telex 32315; fax (03) 231-30-51; forwarding, customs clearance, liner and tramp agencies, chartering, Rhine and inland barging, multi-purpose bulk/bags fertilizer terminal; Pres. L. M. Heintz.

Petrofina SA: 52 rue de l'Industrie, 1040 Brussels; tel. (02) 233-91-11; telex 21556; fax (02) 233-34-45; integrated oil company active in exploration and production, transportation and oil refining, petrochemicals, etc., marketing of petroleum products and research; Pres. and Man. Dir François Cornelis.

Regie voor Maritiem Transport (Belgian Maritime Transport Authority): 30 rue Belliard, 1040 Brussels; tel. (02) 230-01-80; telex 23851; fax (02) 231-14-80; Gen. Man. P. Muyldermans; Ostend–Dover lines; 2 jetfoils and 5 multi-purpose vessels.

Société Belge de Navigation Maritime/Navibel SA: 54 St Katelijnevest, 2000 Antwerp; tel. (03) 233-99-85; telex 32315; tramp, European and Mediterranean cargo services; Pres. R. de Vlaminck.

Ubem NV/SA: 368 Graandok, Antwerp; tel. (03) 237-29-50; telex 32515; fax (03) 541-84-53; bulk carriers and car ferry services; Man. Dir E. de Laet.

CIVIL AVIATION

The main international airport is at Brussels, with a direct train service from the air terminal. A major programme of expansion that would double the airport's passenger-handling capacity by 2010, at a cost of some US $375m., began in 1989. There are also international airports at Antwerp, Liège, Charleroi and Ostend.

SABENA World Airlines (Société anonyme belge d'exploitation de la navigation aérienne): Air Terminal, 35 rue Cardinal Mercier, 1000 Brussels; tel. (02) 723-31-11; telex 21322; fax (02) 509-23-99; f. 1923, present name since 1989; 54% state-owned, 20% by British Airways, 20% by KLM (the Netherlands); services to most parts of the world; Pres. Pierre Godfroid; Vice-Pres. André Pahaut; fleet of 3 Boeing 747, 19 Boeing 737, 3 Airbus A310, 5 DC-10-30 CF, 2 Cessna, 8 SF-260, 5 EMB 121 Xingu.

Delta Air Transport (DAT) NV: Deurne Airport, BP 4, 2100 Antwerp; tel. (03) 239-58-35; telex 32602; fax (03) 218-76-53; f. 1966; 49% owned by SABENA, 33% by KLM (the Netherlands); scheduled and charter services from Antwerp and Brussels to many European destinations; Pres. Carlos van Rafelghem; Gen. Man. Tony Vangrieken; fleet of 4 BA 146/200, 2 F28, 7 EMB 120.

Sobelair (Société Belge de Transports par Air) NV: 131 ave Frans Courtens, 1030 Brussels; tel. (02) 216-21-75; telex 22095; fax (02) 216-18-67; f. 1946; subsidiary of Sabena, operating charter and inclusive-tour flights; Man. Dir P. Jonnart; Dir R. Minet; Man. J. Edom; fleet of 2 Boeing 737-200, 1 Boeing 737-300, 1 Boeing 737-400.

Trans European Airways (TEA): Bldg 117, Melsbroek Airport, 1910 Melsbroek; tel. (02) 752-05-11; telex 21886; fax (02) 752-06-06; f. 1970; charter and inclusive-tour flights; Man. Dir G. P. Gutelman; fleet of 1 Airbus A300B1, 5 Boeing 737-300, 1 Gulfstream III.

Tourism

Belgium has several towns of rich historic and cultural interest, such as Bruges, Ghent, Antwerp, Liège, Tournai, Namur and Durbuy. The country's seaside towns attract many visitors. The forest-covered Ardennes region is excellent hill-walking country. Belgium is also renowned for its cuisine.

Office de Promotion du Tourisme de la Communauté Française: 61 rue Marché-aux-Herbes, 1000 Brussels; tel. (02) 513-90-90; telex 63245; fax (02) 513-69-50; f. 1981; promotion of tourism in French-speaking Belgium; Dir José Clossen.

Tourist Information Brussels (TIB): Hôtel de Ville, Grand-Place, 1000 Brussels; tel. (02) 513-89-40; telex 65206; fax (02) 514-45-38; Pres. Jean Leroy; Dir E. Puttaert.

Tourist Office for Flanders: 61 Grasmarkt, 1000 Brussels; tel. (02) 513-90-90; telex 63245; fax (02) 513-88-03; f. 1985; official promotion and policy body for tourism in Flemish part of Belgium; Gen. Commissioner Urbain Claeys.

Atomic Energy

In the late 1980s about 65% of Belgium's electricity was produced by nuclear power. There were seven reactors in all, with a total capacity of 5,500 MW. In late 1988 the Government announced the indefinite suspension of its nuclear programme. Accordingly, the construction of a planned eighth reactor was cancelled.

Commissariat à l'Energie Atomique (Atomic Energy Commission): Administration de l'Energie, Ministère des Affaires Economiques, 30 rue de Mot, 1040 Brussels; tel. (02) 233-61-11; telex 23509; f. 1950; deals with nuclear matters falling within the competence of the Ministry of Economic Affairs and Planning.

Institut Interuniversitaire des Sciences Nucléaires/Interuniversitair Instituut voor Kernwetenschappen: 5 rue d'Egmont, 1050 Brussels; tel. (02) 513-61-11; f. 1947 to promote research in nuclear science and solid state physics in advanced teaching and research establishments, including departments in the universities and centres at the State University (formerly Polytechnic Institute) of Mons and the Royal Military School at Brussels; 170 scientific researchers; Pres. R. Dillemans; Sec.-Gen. P. Levaux, dr.sc.

Organisme National de Déchets Radioactifs et des Matières fissiles (ONDRAF/NIRAS): 1 place Madou, 1030 Brussels; tel. (02) 212-10-11; telex 65784; fax (02) 218-51-65; f. 1981; management of radioactive waste; Gen. Man. E. Detilleux.

Studiecentrum voor Kernenergie (SCK)/Centre d'Etude de l'Energie Nucléaire (CEN): 1 rue Charles Lemaire, 1160 Brussels; tel. (02) 661-08-11; telex 22718; laboratories: 200 Boeretang, 2400 Mol; tel. (014) 31-18-01; telex 31922; f. 1952; currently engaged in basic research, contract and service activities in a number of sectors; staff of 900 including 300 senior scientists; Pres. I. van Vaerenbergh; Man. Dir R. van Geen.

BELIZE

Introductory Survey

Location, Climate, Language, Religion, Flag, Capital

Belize lies on the Caribbean coast of Central America, with Mexico to the north-west and Guatemala to the south-west. The climate is sub-tropical, tempered by trade winds. The temperature averages 24°C (75°F) from November to January, and 27°C (81°F) from May to September. Annual rainfall ranges from 1,290 mm (51 inches) in the north to 4,450 mm (175 inches) in the south. The average annual rainfall in Belize City is 1,650 mm (65 inches). Belize is ethnically diverse, the population (according to the 1980 census) consisting of 40% Creoles (those of predominantly African descent), 33% Mestizos (Maya–Spanish), 8% Garifuna ('Black Caribs', descendants of those deported from the island of Saint Vincent in 1797), 7% Amerindian (mainy Maya) and communities of Asians, Portuguese, German Mennonites and others of European descent. English is the official language and an English Creole is widely understood. Spanish is the mother-tongue of some 15% of the population but is spoken by many others. There are also speakers of Garifuna (Carib), Maya and Ketchi, while the Mennonites speak a German dialect. Most of the population profess Christianity, with some 60% being Roman Catholics. The national flag is dark blue, with narrow horizontal red stripes at the upper and lower edges; at the centre is a white disc containing the state coat of arms, bordered by an olive wreath. The capital is Belmopan.

Recent History

Belize, known as British Honduras until June 1973, was first colonized by British settlers (the 'Baymen') in the 17th century, but was not recognized as a British colony until 1862. In 1954 a new constitution granted universal adult suffrage and provided for the creation of a legislative assembly. The territory's first general election, in April 1954, was won by the only party then organized, the People's United Party (PUP), led by George Price. The PUP won all subsequent elections until 1984. In 1961 Price was appointed First Minister under a new ministerial system of government. The colony was granted internal self-government in 1964, with the United Kingdom retaining responsibility for defence, external affairs and internal security. Following an election in 1965, Price became Premier and a bicameral legislature was introduced. In 1970 the capital of the territory was moved from Belize City to the newly built town of Belmopan.

Much of the recent history of Belize has been dominated by the territorial dispute with Guatemala, particularly in the years prior to Belize's independence (see below). This was achieved on 21 September 1981, within the Commonwealth, and with George Price becoming Prime Minister. However, the failure of the 1981 draft treaty with Guatemala, and the clash of opposing wings within the ruling party, undermined the dominance of the PUP. Internal disputes within the PUP intensified during 1983, although Price succeeded in keeping the factions together. However, at the general election held in December 1984 the PUP's 30 years of rule ended when the United Democratic Party (UDP) received 53% of the total votes and won 21 of the 28 seats in the enlarged House of Representatives. The remaining seven seats were won by the PUP, with 44% of the votes, but Price and several of his ministers lost their seats. The UDP's leader, Manuel Esquivel, was appointed Prime Minister. The new Government pledged itself to reviving Belize's economy through increased foreign investment.

In 1988, however, the UDP suffered from internal dissension, following municipal elections in March, when the opposition won control of four out of seven Town Boards. The PUP had been able to take advantage of the controversy surrounding the Government's creation of a Security and Intelligence Service (SIS), a body intended to operate covertly against the illegal drugs trade, but also responsible for scrutinizing appointments to the civil service. The SIS was established through legislation, including a constitutional amendment, during 1988. The UDP Government was also accused of attempting to suppress the expression of opposition by a series of court actions against the PUP's newspaper, *The Belize Times*, the limiting of opposition broadcasts, and the dismissals of some senior public officials. Despite this acrimony, there was a bipartisan consensus on negotiations with Guatemala in 1988.

A general election was held in September 1989. The UDP underwent a damaging selection process for candidates to contest the election, and encountered criticism that its economic successes had benefited only foreign investors and a limited number of Belizeans. The PUP campaigned for a more liberal broadcasting policy, including the establishment of a broadcasting corporation independent of direct government control, and against the sale of citizenship, of which many Hong Kong Chinese had taken advantage. At the election the PUP obtained almost 51% of the total valid votes cast, and won 15 seats in the 28-member House of Representatives. The UDP received 49% of the votes and retained 13 seats, although one of their members subsequently joined the PUP. George Price was again appointed Prime Minister, and his new Government immediately began moves to end the issue of citizenship bonds and to disband the SIS.

The frontier with Guatemala was agreed by a convention in 1859 but this was declared invalid by Guatemala in 1940. Guatemalan claims to sovereignty of Belize date back to the middle of the 19th century and were written into Guatemala's Constitution in 1945. In November 1975 and July 1977 British troops and aircraft were sent to protect Belize from the threat of Guatemalan invasion, and a battalion of troops and a detachment of fighter aircraft remained in the territory. Negotiations between the United Kingdom and Guatemala began in 1977. In 1980 Britain warned that it might unilaterally grant independence to Belize if no settlement with Guatemala were forthcoming, and later that year the British Government finally excluded the possibility of any cession of land to Guatemala, although offering economic and financial concessions. In November the UN General Assembly overwhelmingly approved a resolution urging that Belize be granted independence (similar resolutions having been adopted in 1978 and 1979), and the United Kingdom decided to proceed with a schedule for independence. A tripartite conference in March 1981 appeared to produce a sound basis for a final settlement, with Guatemala accepting Belizean independence in exchange for access to the Caribbean Sea through Belize and the use of certain offshore cayes and their surrounding waters. A state of emergency was declared for three weeks in April, following strikes and serious rioting, apparently organized by the opposition in protest at the preliminary 'Heads of Agreement' which had been reached in the previous month. A constitutional conference nevertheless went ahead in April. However, further tripartite talks in May and July collapsed as a result of renewed claims by Guatemala to Belizean land. With Belizean independence imminent, Guatemala made an unsuccessful appeal to the UN Security Council to intervene, severing diplomatic relations with the United Kingdom and sealing its border with Belize on 7 September. However, on 21 September, as scheduled, Belize achieved independence. Guatemala alone refused to recognize Belize's new status, and during 1982 requested the reopening of negotiations with the United Kingdom, alleging that Belize was not legally independent. Tripartite talks in January 1983 collapsed when Belize rejected Guatemala's proposal that Belize should cede the southern part of the country. This claim was subsequently suspended. Belize is a member of CARICOM (see p. 108), whose summit conferences have consistently expressed support for Belize's territorial integrity against claims by Guatemala, most recently in 1989.

At independence the United Kingdom had agreed to leave troops as protection and for training of Belizean defence forces 'for an appropriate time'. In 1984 Prime Minister Esquivel was given renewed assurances from the British Government as regards its commitment to keep British troops in Belize until the resolution of the territorial dispute with Guatemala. Discussions with Guatemala resumed in February 1985, with greater optimism shown by all three parties. In July the new draft Guatemalan Constitution omitted the previous unconditional claim to Belize, while Esquivel had previously acknowledged Guatemala's right of access to the Caribbean Sea, but no settlement was forthcoming. In January 1986 Dr Marco Vinicio Cerezo was inaugurated as the elected President of Guatemala, representing a change from a military to a civilian government. In August the United Kingdom and Guatemala renewed diplomatic relations at consular level, and in December the restoration of full diplomatic relations was announced. Meanwhile, a six-member select committee of the Belize House of Representatives was established in June 1986, to examine information on Guatemala's claim to Belize. In March 1987 the first Guatemalan trade delegation since independence visited Belize. In April 1987 renewed discussions were held between Guatemala, the United Kingdom and Belize (although Belize was still regarded by Guatemala as being only an observer). Tripartite negotiations continued, and in May 1988 the formation of a permanent Joint Commission (which, in effect, entailed a recognition of the Belizean state by Guatemala) was announced. This body, which established three committees to examine the political, economic and security issues, was to attempt to draft a treaty that would be validated by referendums in both Guatemala and Belize. The agreement was sanctioned by Florencio Marin, parliamentary Leader of the Opposition, despite the tension between the PUP and the ruling UDP over other matters.

In November 1988 there was a minor incident in the disputed waters of the Gulf of Honduras, when a Guatemalan gunboat fired on an unarmed British naval vessel. This issue was resolved by further meetings of the Joint Commission in 1989. In April it was agreed that discussions of the outstanding issues should resume as soon as possible. The United Kingdom announced that it would extend economic aid to both countries if a settlement were reached. The PUP Government, elected in September 1989, committed itself to continuing all-party negotiations with Guatemala through the Joint Commission. In May 1990 there was a clash between Belizeans and a group of Guatemalans who had crossed the border into the Toledo district to farm. Nevertheless, there was considerable progress in negotiations, and the Belizean delegation which met the UN Secretary-General in October seemed optimistic about the prospect of a settlement with Guatemala. Despite the uncertainty of the Guatemalan election results, reports from Belize indicated that the main outstanding issues were now economic and not territorial. In November the British Government again gave reassurances that its forces would remain in Belize as requested.

In 1989 Belize established diplomatic relations at ambassadorial level with Spain and Taiwan. The latter move caused the People's Republic of China to sever diplomatic relations with Belize.

Government

Belize is a constitutional monarchy, with the British sovereign as Head of State. Executive authority is vested in the sovereign and is exercised by the Governor-General, who is appointed on the advice of the Prime Minister, must be of Belizean nationality, and acts in almost all matters on the advice of the Cabinet. The Governor-General is also advised by an appointed Belize Advisory Council. Legislative power is vested in the bicameral National Assembly, comprising a Senate (eight members appointed by the Governor-General) and a House of Representatives (28 members elected by universal adult suffrage for five years, subject to dissolution). The Governor-General appoints the Prime Minister and, on the latter's recommendation, other Ministers. The Cabinet is responsible to the House.

Defence

The Belize Defence Force was formed in 1978 and was based on a combination of the existing Police Special Force and the Belize Volunteer Guard. Military service is voluntary. Provision has been made for the establishment of National Service if necessary to supplement normal recruitment. In June 1990 the regular armed forces totalled 760 (including 50 in the maritime wing and 15 in the air wing), with some 500 militia reserves, and there were also approximately 1,500 British troops (including about 300 air force personnel) in Belize. The estimated defence budget for 1989 was BZ $19.9m.

Economic Affairs

In 1988, according to estimates by the World Bank, the country's gross national product (GNP), measured at average 1986-88 prices, was US $264m., equivalent to $1,460 per head. Between 1980 and 1988, it was estimated, GNP increased in real terms, at an average annual rate of 3.6%, while GNP per head grew by only 0.7% per year. Over this period, Belize's population increased by 2.8% per year. In 1987 gross domestic product (GDP), at constant 1984 factor cost, amounted to BZ $400.4m.

Although 40% of the country is considered suitable for agriculture, only 5% of total land area was used for agricultural purposes in 1987. Nevertheless, agriculture, forestry and fishing employed 37% of the working population in 1980, and contributed 18.4% of GDP in 1987. The principal cash crops are sugar cane (sugar accounted for some 39% of total domestic exports in 1988), citrus fruits (citrus products accounted for 19%) and bananas (9%). Rice, red kidney beans and maize are the principal domestic food crops, and the development of other crops, such as cocoa, coconuts and soybeans (soya beans), is being encouraged. Dairy-farming, livestock and bee-keeping are also being fostered. Belize has considerable timber reserves, particularly of tropical hardwoods, and the forestry sector is being developed. In 1988 fishing provided export earnings of BZ $16m. in 1988, of which some 70% were derived from lobster sales.

Industry (including mining, manufacturing, construction, water and electricity) employed 16.5% of the working population in 1980, and contributed 21.1% of GDP in 1987. Manufacturing alone, particularly of clothing, accounted for 12.1% of GDP in 1987, and the sector employed 10.4% of the working population in 1980. The processing of agricultural products is important, particularly sugar cane (for sugar and ethanol). During 1980–87 industrial production increased by an annual average of 0.6%, mainly after 1984. In 1988, however, industrial production increased by 40.3%, principally because of the rise in output of flour.

Belize has no indigenous energy resources other than wood. Imports of petroleum accounted for some 11% of total import costs in 1988. However, following the implementation of a feasibility study in 1990, it was hoped that a proposed hydroelectric project on the Macal River would provide 70% of the country's energy requirements in the future.

Trade, restaurants and hotels employed 14.2% of the working population in 1980, and contributed 18.0% of GDP in 1987. Tourist development is concentrated on promoting 'eco-tourism', based on the attraction of Belize's natural environment, particularly its rain forests and the barrier reef, the second largest in the world. Tourist arrivals increased to 144,210 in 1988, and revenue from the tourism sector totalled some BZ $56m.

In 1989, according to the IMF, Belize recorded a visible trade deficit of US $64.1m., and a deficit of US $19.1m. on the current account of the balance of payments. In 1988 the principal source of imports was the USA (53%), which was also the principal market for exports (45%). The United Kingdom is another important trading partner (accounting for 9% of imports and 37% of exports), as is Mexico, and the Netherlands and its Caribbean dependencies. The principal exports are agricultural products.

For the financial year ending 31 March 1991 there was a projected surplus of BZ $21m. on the recurrent budget. Belize's total public external debt was BZ $248.3m. at the end of 1988. The annual rate of inflation averaged only 1.1% in 1980-87, rising to 3.1% in 1988. The average rate in 1989 was 1.5%. In June 1984 an estimated 13.6% of the labour force were unemployed. Many Belizeans, however, work abroad, and remittances to the country from such workers are an important source of income. Emigration, mainly to the USA, is offset by the number of immigrants and refugees from other Central American countries, particularly El Salvador.

Belize is a member of CARICOM (see p. 108), and since November 1989 has had observer status at the OAS (see p. 194).

Agriculture is the dominant sector of the Belizean economy, although the country can be susceptible to adverse weather conditions. The Government has encouraged diversification, mainly to satisfy domestic demands, around the three main crops. The development of tourism and the availability of foreign investment have been hindered by the uncertainties of the dispute with Guatemala and the unfavourable publicity regarding the problems resulting from drug-trafficking. The cultivation of hemp (marijuana) and the trade in illicit drugs has proved to be an increasing problem for the Government.

BELIZE

In the mid-1980s it was estimated that enough of the marijuana crop survived attempts to destroy it, by spraying the plantations with herbicides, to provide an annual income of US $55m., equivalent to one-third of Belize's GDP. Continuing efforts by the authorities, however, have reduced the prevalence of the drug trade. Belize receives international aid for this policy, including the assistance of the British garrison (which itself, it was estimated in 1988, contributed at least 15% to GDP). The Government is also attempting to develop service industries, establishing an international shipping register in 1989 and introducing legislation on 'offshore' financial services in 1990.

Social Welfare

There were eight urban and 23 rural health centres in 1988; pre-natal and child welfare clinics are sponsored by the Ministry of Health. In 1989 there were 583 hospital beds and 88 registered physicians. The infant mortality rate declined from 51 per 1,000 live births in 1970 to 21 per 1,000 in 1988. Of total estimated budgetary expenditure by the central Government in the financial year 1987/88, BZ $17.1m. (6.8%) was for health.

Education

Education is compulsory for all children between the ages of six and 14 years. Primary education, beginning at six years of age and lasting for eight years, is provided free of charge, principally through subsidized denominational schools under government control. There were 40,287 pupils enrolled at 226 primary schools in 1988. Secondary education, beginning at the age of 14, lasts for four or five years. There were 7,376 students enrolled in 27 general secondary schools in 1988, and the Government contributed up to 70% of the schools' operational costs. In 1988 the total enrolment at primary and secondary schools was equivalent to between 85% and 90% of the school-age population.

In 1988 there were 1,170 students enrolled in eight other educational institutions, which included technical, vocational and teacher-training colleges. The University College of Belize was established in 1986 and there is also an extra-mural branch of the University of the West Indies in Belize. Estimated budgetary expenditure on education in the financial year 1987/88 was BZ $29.6m., representing 11.8% of total spending by the central Government. The estimated adult literacy rate is more than 90%.

Public Holidays

1991: 1 January (New Year's Day), 4 March (Baron Bliss Day/Commonwealth Day), 29 March-1 April (Easter), 1 May (Labour Day), 10 June (Queen's Official Birthday), 10 September (St George's Caye Day), 21 September (Independence Day), 14 October (for Columbus Day, anniversary of the discovery of America), 19 November (Garifuna Settlement Day), 25-26 December (Christmas).

1992: 1 January (New Year's Day), 12 March (Baron Bliss Day/Commonwealth Day), 17-20 April (Easter), 30 April (for Labour Day), 11 June (Queen's Official Birthday), 10 September (St George's Caye Day), 21 September (Independence Day), 12 October (Columbus Day, anniversary of the discovery of America), 19 November (Garifuna Settlement Day), 25-26 December (Christmas).

Weights and Measures

Imperial weights and measures are used, but petrol and paraffin are measured in terms of the US gallon (3.785 litres).

Statistical Survey

Source (unless otherwise stated): Statistical Office of the Department of Economic Development, Belmopan; tel. (8) 22207.

AREA AND POPULATION

Area: 22,965 sq km (8,867 sq miles).

Population: 144,857 (males 73,213, females 71,644) at census of 12 May 1980; 179,814 (official estimate, mid-1988).

Density (1988): 7.8 per sq km.

Principal Towns (estimated population, 1988): Belmopan (capital) 3,694; Belize City (former capital) 49,671; Orange Walk 10,468; Corozal 8,518; Dangriga (formerly Stann Creek) 8,107.

Births, Marriages and Deaths (1988): Registered live births 6,701 (birth rate 37.3 per 1,000); Registered marriages 1,072 (marriage rate 6.0 per 1,000); Registered deaths 738 (death rate 4.1 per 1,000).

Economically Active Population (1980 census): Agriculture, hunting, forestry and fishing 14,745; Mining and quarrying 32; Manufacturing 4,142; Electricity, gas and water 604; Construction 1,772; Trade, restaurants and hotels 5,646; Transport, storage and communications 1,725; Financing, insurance, real estate and business services 360; Community, social and personal services 8,956; Activities not adequately defined 1,791; Total employed 39,773 (males 31,749, females 8,024); Unemployed 7,554 (males 4,836, females 2,718); Total labour force 47,327 (males 36,585, females 10,742) Source: ILO, *Year Book of Labour Statistics*.

AGRICULTURE, ETC.

Principal Crops (1989): Sugar cane 867,276 long tons, Red kidney beans 4.9 million lb; (estimates from the FAO, *Production Yearbook*, '000 metric tons: Maize 24, Rice (paddy) 6; Roots and tubers 4, Pulses (dry beans) 2, Coconuts 3, Vegetables and melons 5, Oranges 52, Grapefruit and pomelo 31, Bananas 35, Other fruit 4.

Livestock (official estimates, '000 head, 1989): Horses 5*; Mules 4*; Cattle 51; Pigs 25; Sheep 1; Goats 1*; Chickens 1.

*Estimates from the FAO, *Production Yearbook* (year ending September 1989).

Livestock Products (FAO estimates, '000 metric tons, 1989): Meat 7; Cows' milk 4; Hen eggs 1.4; Honey 0.3. Source: FAO, *Production Yearbook*.

Forestry ('000 cu m): *Roundwood removals* (1987): Industrial wood (Sawlogs) 62, Fuel wood 126 (FAO estimate), Total 188 (FAO estimated 1988 production as in 1987). *Sawnwood* (1986): 14 (FAO estimated 1987 and 1988 production as in 1986). Source: FAO, *Yearbook of Forest Products*.

Fishing (metric tons, live weight): Total catch 1,434 in 1986; 1,501 in 1987; 1,492 (Caribbean spiny lobster 581) in 1988. Source: FAO, *Yearbook of Fishery Statistics*.

INDUSTRY

Production (1988): Raw sugar (1989) 90,934 long tons; Molasses 23,138 long tons; Cigarettes 94.4 million; Beer 640,000 gallons; Batteries 8,835; Flour 8,839 long tons; Fertilizers 8,578 short tons; Garments 3,696,000 items; Citrus concentrate 1,653,000 gallons; Soft drinks 734,000 cases.

FINANCE

Currency and Exchange Rates: 100 cents = 1 Belizean dollar (BZ $). *Coins:* 1, 5, 10, 25 and 50 cents; 1 dollar. *Notes:* 1, 2, 5, 10, 20, 50 and 100 dollars. *Sterling and US Dollar equivalents:* (30 September 1990): £1 sterling = BZ $3.747; US $1 = BZ $2.000; BZ $100 = £26.69 = US $50.00. *Exchange rate:* Fixed at US $1 = BZ $2.000 since May 1976.

Budget (BZ $ million, year ending 31 March 1988): *Revenue:* Taxation 112.2 (Import duties 62.5); Other current revenue 11.7; Capital revenue 0.3; Total 124.2 (excl. grants 2.5). *Expenditure:* General public services 52.4 (Administration 34.4); Law, order and defence 17.9; Community and social services 64.0 (Education 29.6; Health 17.1; Housing and community development 5.8; Water and sanitation 7.6; Other social services 3.9); Economic services 82.7 (Agriculture, lands, forestry and fisheries 26.8; Energy and resources development 0.6; Roads and bridges 31.0; Other transport and communications 23.0; Other economic services 1.3); Debt-servicing 34.9; Total 251.9. *1990/91* (estimates, BZ $ million): Total revenue 286.8 (Current revenue 174.8, Capital receipts 5, Foreign borrowing 68.4, Domestic borrowing 38.6); Total expenditure 265.9 (Current 153.9; Capital 112.0).

BELIZE

Statistical Survey, Directory

International Reserves (US $ million at 31 December 1989): Reserve position in the IMF 2.51; Foreign exchange 57.37; Total 59.88. Source: IMF, *International Financial Statistics*.

Money Supply (BZ $ million at 31 December 1989): Currency outside banks 40.44; Demand deposits at commercial banks 56.58. Source: IMF, *International Financial Statistics*.

Cost of Living (retail price index for May each year; base: February 1980 = 100): 147.6 in 1987; 153.0 in 1988; 155.9 in 1989.

Gross Domestic Product (BZ $ million at constant 1984 factor cost): 347.3 in 1985; 357.0 in 1986; 400.4 in 1987. Source: Central Bank of Belize.

Balance of Payments (US $ million, 1989): Merchandise exports f.o.b. 124.4; Merchandise imports f.o.b. −188.5; *Trade balance* −64.1; Exports of services 95.6; Imports of services −81.6; *Balance on goods and services* −50.1; Private unrequited transfers (net) 20.7; Government unrequited transfers (net) 10.4; *Current balance* −19.1; Direct capital investment (net) 18.7; Other long-term capital (net) 11.3; Short-term capital (net) −4.4; Net errors and omissions 9.1; *Total* (net monetary movements) 15.5; Valuation changes (net) −2.8; *Changes in reserves* 12.7. Source: IMF, *International Financial Statistics*.

EXTERNAL TRADE

Principal Commodities (BZ $ million, 1988): *Imports:* Total 361.9. *Exports:* Sugar 70.0; Molasses 1.0; Bananas 17.2; Citrus products 34.6; Fish products 16.1; Timber (sawn wood) 5.4; Garments 37.3; Total 181.6 (excl. re-exports 47.9).

Principal Trading Partners (US $ million, 1988): *Imports:* Guatemala 2.5; Japan 2.3; Mexico 12.5; Netherlands 8.0; Netherlands Antilles 1.5; United Kingdom 16.0; USA 96.7; Total (incl. others) 180.9; *Exports:* Mexico 2.5; United Kingdom 35.0; USA 42.9; Total (incl. others) 95.1.

TRANSPORT

Road Traffic (motor vehicles licensed, 1988): 14,014.

International Shipping (sea-borne freight traffic, '000 metric tons, 1988): Goods loaded 124; Goods unloaded 120.

Civil Aviation (1988): Passenger movements 401,082.

TOURISM

Tourist arrivals (1988): 144,210.

COMMUNICATIONS MEDIA

Radio Receivers (1988): 110,000 in use.

Television Receivers (estimate, 1987): 12,000 in use.

Telephones (1988): 14,000 in use.

Newspapers (1988): There are no daily newspapers, but five newspapers are published weekly.

EDUCATION

Primary (1988): 226 schools, 1,575 teachers, 40,287 students.

Secondary (1988): 30 schools, 572 teachers, 7,376 students.

Higher (1988): 8 institutions, 37 teachers, 1,170 students.

Directory

The Constitution

The Constitution came into effect at the independence of Belize on 21 September 1981. Its main provisions are summarized below:

FUNDAMENTAL RIGHTS AND FREEDOMS

Regardless of race, place of origin, political opinions, colour, creed or sex, but subject to respect for the rights and freedoms of others and for the public interest, every person in Belize is entitled to the rights of life, liberty, security of the person, and the protection of the law. Freedom of movement, of conscience, of expression, of assembly and association and the right to work are guaranteed and the inviolability of family life, personal privacy, home and other property and of human dignity is upheld. Protection is afforded from discrimination on the grounds of race, sex, etc, and from slavery, forced labour and inhuman treatment.

CITIZENSHIP

All persons born in Belize before independence who, immediately prior to independence, were citizens of the United Kingdom and Colonies automatically become citizens of Belize. All persons born outside the country having a husband, parent or grandparent in possession of Belizean citizenship automatically acquire citizenship, as do those born in the country after independence. Provision is made which permits persons who do not automatically become citizens of Belize to be registered as such. (Belizean citizenship was also offered, under the Belize Loans Act 1986, in exchange for interest-free loans of US $25,000 with a 10-year maturity.)

THE GOVERNOR-GENERAL

The British monarch, as Head of State, is represented in Belize by a Governor-General, a Belizean national.

Belize Advisory Council

The Council consists of not less than six people 'of integrity and high national standing', appointed by the Governor-General for up to 10 years upon the advice of the Prime Minister. The Leader of the Opposition must concur with the appointment of two members and be consulted about the remainder. The Council exists to advise the Governor-General, particularly in the exercise of the prerogative of mercy, and to convene as a tribunal to consider the removal from office of certain senior public servants and judges.

THE EXECUTIVE

Executive authority is vested in the British monarch and exercised by the Governor-General. The Governor-General appoints as Prime Minister that member of the House of Representatives who, in the Governor-General's view, is best able to command the support of the majority of the members of the House, and appoints a Deputy Prime Minister and other Ministers on the advice of the Prime Minister. The Governor-General may remove the Prime Minister from office if a resolution of 'no confidence' is passed by the House and the Prime Minister does not, within seven days, either resign or advise the Governor-General to dissolve the National Assembly. The Cabinet consists of the Prime Minister and other Ministers.

The Leader of the Opposition is appointed by the Governor-General as that member of the House who, in the Governor-General's view, is best able to command the support of a majority of the members of the House who do not support the Government.

THE LEGISLATURE

The Legislature consists of a National Assembly comprising two chambers: the Senate, with eight nominated members; and the House of Representatives, with (since 1984) 28 elected members. The Assembly's normal term is five years. Senators are appointed by the Governor-General: five on the advice of the Prime Minister; two on the advice of the Leader of the Opposition or on the advice of persons selected by the Governor-General; and one after consultation with the Belize Advisory Council. If any person who is not a Senator is elected to be President of the Senate, he or she shall be an ex-officio Senator in addition to the eight nominees.

Each constituency returns one Representative to the House, who is directly elected in accordance with the Constitution.

If a person who is not a member of the House is elected to be Speaker of the House, he or she shall be an ex-officio member in addition to the 28 members directly elected. Every citizen older than 18 years is eligible to vote. The National Assembly may alter any of the provisions of the Constitution.

The Government

Head of State: HM Queen ELIZABETH II (succeeded to the throne 6 February 1952).

Governor-General: Dame ELMIRA MINITA GORDON (assumed office 21 September 1981).

THE CABINET
(December 1990)

Prime Minister and Minister of Finance, Home Affairs, Defence and Trade and Commerce: GEORGE PRICE.

BELIZE

Directory

Deputy Prime Minister and Minister of Natural Resources: FLORENCIO MARIN.

Minister of Foreign Affairs, Economic Development and Education: SAID MUSA.

Minister of Housing, Co-operatives and Industry: LEOPOLDO BRICEÑO.

Minister of Works: SAMUEL WAIGHT.

Minister of Health and Urban Development: Dr THEODORE ARANDA.

Attorney-General and Minister of Tourism and the Environment: GLENN GODFREY.

Minister of Social Services and Community Development: REMIJIO MONTEJO.

Minister of Agriculture and Fisheries: MICHAEL ESPAT.

Minister of Labour, Public Service and Local Government: VALDEMAR CASTILLO.

Minister of Energy and Communications: CARLOS DIAZ.

Ministers of State

Ministry of Finance, Home Affairs, Defence and Trade and Commerce: Senator RALPH FONSECA, DANIEL SILVA, Jr.

Ministry of Natural Resources: GUADALUPE PECH.

Ministry of Foreign Affairs, Economic Development and Education: VILDO MARIN.

Ministry of Energy and Communications: MIGUEL RUIZ.

MINISTRIES

Office of the Prime Minister: Belmopan; tel. (8) 2346; telex 102; fax (8) 23323.

Ministry of Foreign Affairs: POB 174, Belmopan; tel. (8) 22322; telex 102.

All other Ministries are also situated in Belmopan.

Legislature

NATIONAL ASSEMBLY
The Senate

President: JANE USHER.

There are eight nominated members.

House of Representatives

Speaker: ROBERT SWIFT.

Clerk: A. E. JOHNSON.

General Election, 4 September 1989

	Votes cast	% of total	Seats*
People's United Party (PUP)	29,986	50.87	15
United Democratic Party (UDP)	28,900	49.02	13
Independent	65	0.11	—
Total	58,951	100.00	28

* Four days after the election, one UDP member joined the PUP instead, increasing the ruling party's parliamentary representation to 16 seats.

Political Organizations

People's United Party (PUP): Belize City; tel. (2) 45886; fax (2) 31940; f. 1950; based on organized labour; merged with Christian Democratic Party in 1988; Leader GEORGE PRICE; Chair. SAID MUSA.

United Democratic Party (UDP): 19 King St, Belize City; tel. (2) 72576; fax (2) 31004; f. 1974 by merger of People's Development Movement, Liberal Party and National Independence Party; conservative; Leader MANUEL ESQUIVEL; Chair. ALFREDO MARTINEZ.

Diplomatic Representation

EMBASSIES AND HIGH COMMISSION IN BELIZE

Belgium: Belize City; Ambassador: WILLY VERRIEST.

China (Taiwan): 7 Cork St, POB 1020, Belize City; tel. (2) 78744; fax (2) 31890; Ambassador: DAVID HONG.

Costa Rica: POB 922, Belize City; tel. (2) 45635; telex 1154; Ambassador: ROBERTO FRANCISCO ANGLEDA SOLER.

Germany: Belize City; Ambassador: Dr NILS GRÜBER.

Honduras: 91 North Front St, POB 285, Belize City; tel. (2) 45889; telex 103; Chargé d'affaires: GUSTAVO MILLA BERMÚDEZ.

Mexico: 20 North Park St, Belize City; tel. (2) 44301; telex 277; Ambassador: FEDERICO URUCHUA.

Panama: 79 Unity Blvd, Belmopan; tel. (8) 22714; Chargé d'affaires: JOSÉ DE LA CRUZ PAREDES.

United Kingdom: Embassy Sq., POB 91, Belmopan; tel. (8) 22146; telex 284; fax (8) 22761; High Commissioner: DAVID MACKILLIGIN (designate).

USA: Gabourel Lane and Hutson St, Belize City; tel. (2) 77161; fax (2) 30802; Ambassador: ROBERT G. RICH, Jr.

Venezuela: 18–20 Unity Blvd, POB 49, Belmopan; tel. (8) 22384; telex 249; Ambassador: Dr JOSÉ TINEO FARILLAS.

Judicial System

Summary Jurisdiction Courts (criminal jurisdiction) and District Courts (civil jurisdiction), presided over by magistrates, are established in each of the six judicial districts. Summary Jurisdiction Courts have a wide jurisdiction in summary offences and a limited jurisdiction in indictable matters. Appeals lie to the Supreme Court, which has jurisdiction corresponding to the English High Court of Justice and where a jury system is in operation. From the Supreme Court further appeals lie to a Court of Appeal, established in 1968, which holds an average of four sessions per year. Final appeals are made to the Judicial Committee of the Privy Council in the United Kingdom.

Court of Appeal: K. SAINT L. HENRY (President), Dr NICHOLAS LIVERPOOL, Sir DENNIS MALONE.

Chief Justice: TAUFIK S. COTRAN.

Supreme Court: Supreme Court Bldg, Belize City; tel. (2) 72754; Registrar HECTOR KNIGHT.

Chief Magistrate: TRAODIO GONZALEZ, Paslow Bldg, Belize City; tel. (2) 77164.

Religion

CHRISTIANITY

Most of the population are Christian, the largest denomination being the Roman Catholic Church (62% of the population, according to the census of 1980). The other main groups were the Anglican (12% in 1980), Methodist (6%), Mennonite (4%), Seventh-day Adventist (3%) and Pentecostal (2%) churches.

Belize Council of Churches: POB 508, 149 Allenby St, Belize City; tel. (2) 77077; f. 1957 as Church World Service Committee, present name adopted 1984; eight mem. Churches, four assoc. bodies; Pres. Maj. ERROL ROBATEAU (Salvation Army); Gen. Sec. SADIE VERNON.

The Roman Catholic Church

Belize comprises the single diocese of Belize City-Belmopan, suffragan to the archdiocese of Kingston in Jamaica. In December 1989 it was estimated that there were 115,650 adherents in the diocese. The Bishop participates in the Antilles Episcopal Conference (currently based in Jamaica).

Bishop of Belize City-Belmopan: OSMOND PETER MARTIN, POB 616, Bishop's House, 144 North Front St, Belize City; tel. (2) 72122.

The Anglican Communion

Anglicans in Belize belong to the Church in the Province of the West Indies, comprising eight dioceses. The Archbishop of the Province is the Bishop of the North Eastern Caribbean and Aruba, resident at St John's, Antigua.

Bishop of Belize: Rt Rev. DESMOND SMITH, POB 535, Bishopthorpe, Southern Foreshore, Belize City; tel. (2) 73380.

Protestant Churches

Methodist Church (Belize/Honduras District): POB 212, Belize City; c. 2,334 mems; Chair. and General Superintendent Rev. OTTO WADE.

Mennonite Congregations in Belize: c/o Mennonite Church, Spanish Lookout; three main Mennonite settlements: at Spanish Lookout, Shipyard and Blue Creek.

BELIZE
Directory

Other denominations active in the country include the Seventh-day Adventists, Pentecostals, Presbyterians, Baptists, Moravians, Jehovah's Witnesses, the Church of God, the Assemblies of Brethren and the Salvation Army.

OTHER RELIGIONS

There are also small communities of Hindus (106, according to the census of 1980), Muslims (110 in 1980), Jews (92 in 1980) and Bahá'ís.

The Press

Amandala: Amandala Press, POB 15, 3304 Partridge St, Belize City; tel. (2) 77276; fax (2) 75934; f. 1969; weekly; independent; Editor EVAN X. HYDE; circ. 10,000.

The Beacon: 7 Church St, Belize City; f. 1969; weekly; supports UDP; Publr and Editor MICHAEL FINNIGAN; circ. 4,200; publication suspended Sept. 1989.

The Belize Times: POB 506, 3 Queen St, Belize City; tel. (2) 45757; f. 1956; weekly; party political paper of People's United Party; Editor AMALIA MAI; circ. 5,000.

Belize Today: Government Information Service, POB 60, Belmopan; tel. (8) 22159; fax (8) 23242; monthly; official; Editor M. A. ROMERO; circ. 14,000.

Government Gazette: Government Printery, Power Lane, Belmopan; tel. (8) 22127; official; weekly.

People's Pulse: 7 Church St, Belize City; f. 1988; weekly; organ of the United Democratic Party; Editor ZELMA JEX; circ. 5,000.

The Reporter: 147 Allenby St, corner with West St, POB 707, Belize City; tel. (2) 72503; f. 1968; weekly; Editor HARRY LAWRENCE; circ. 6,500.

NEWS AGENCY

Agencia EFE (Spain): c/o POB 506, Belize City; tel. (2) 45757; Correspondent AMALIA MAI.

Radio and Television

In 1988 it was estimated that there were about 110,000 radio receivers and 12,000 television receivers in use.

RADIO

Belize Broadcasting Network (BBN): Albert Cattouse Bldg, POB 89, Belize City; tel. (2) 77246; telex 157; fax (2) 75040; f. 1937; govt-operated semi-commercial service; broadcasts in English (75%) and Spanish; Dir RENÉ R. VILLANUEVA.

Belize Radio One broadcasts for about 168 hours per week on AM.

Friends FM broadcasts for about 133 hours per week on FM.

British Forces Broadcasting Service also operates a radio station for Belize.

TELEVISION

In August 1986 the Belize Broadcasting Authority issued licences to eight television operators for 14 channels, which mainly retransmit US satellite programmes, thus placing television in Belize on a fully legal basis for the first time. In June 1988 zoning regulations were issued for Belize City also.

BBN Teleproductions: POB 89, Belize City; govt-owned; video production unit; local programmes for broadcasting.

CTV (Channel 9): 27 Bayman Ave, Belize City; tel. (2) 44400; commercial; Man. MARIE HOARE.

Tropical Vision (Channel 7): 73 Albert St, Belize City; tel. (2) 72825; commercial; Man. NESTOR VASQUEZ.

Finance

(cap. = capital; brs = branches)

BANKING
Central Bank

Central Bank of Belize: Treasury Lane, POB 852, Belize City; tel. (2) 77216; telex 225; fax (2) 77106; f. 1982; cap. BZ $10m. (1988); Gov. Sir EDNEY CAIN.

Development Bank

Development Finance Corporation: Bliss Parade, Belmopan; tel. (8) 22350; telex 248; fax (8) 23096; issued cap. BZ $10m.; Chair. HERBERT MASSON, Sr; Gen. Man. DORLA GILL LESLIE; 5 brs.

Other Banks

Atlantic Bank Ltd (USA): 6 Albert St, POB 481, Belize City; tel. (2) 77301; telex 216; fax (2) 77736; f. 1971; Gen. Man. SANDRA BEDRAN; 1 br.

Banca Serfín, SNC (Mexico): Belize City; f. 1990; 1 br.

Bank of Nova Scotia (Canada): Albert St, POB 708, Belize City; tel. (2) 77028; telex 218; Man. JOSÉ R. ROSADO; 5 brs.

Barclays Bank PLC (UK): 21 Albert St, POB 363, Belize City; tel. (2) 77211; telex 217; fax (2) 78572; Man. GEOFFREY M. HART; 3 brs.

Belize Bank: 60 Market Sq., POB 364, Belize City; tel. (2) 77132; telex 158; fax (2) 72712; Chair. MICHAEL ASHCROFT; Senior Vice-Pres. and Gen. Man. LOUIS ANTHONY SWASEY.

There is also a Government Savings Bank.

INSURANCE

General insurance is provided by local companies, and British, American and Jamaican companies are also represented.

Trade and Industry

Belize Chamber of Commerce: 7 Cork St, POB 291, Belize City; telex 121; f. 1918; Pres. WILLIAM MUSA; Man. DAVID USHER; 300 mems.

Belize Export and Investment Promotion Unit: 7 Cork St, POB 291, Belize City; tel. (2) 44913; telex 121; fax (2) 30755; f. 1986; joint government and private-sector institution to encourage export and investment; Gen. Man. HUGH FULLER.

Department of Economic Development: Ministry of Foreign Affairs, Economic Development and Education, Belmopan; administration of public and private sector investment; statistics agency; Head SHARMAN YVONNE HYDE.

STATUTORY BODIES

Banana Control Board: c/o Dept of Agriculture, West Block, Belmopan; management of banana industry; in 1989 it was decided to make it responsible to growers, not an independent executive.

Belize Beef Corporation: c/o Dept of Agriculture, West Block, Belmopan; f. 1978; placed in receivership in 1990; semi-governmental organization to aid development of cattle-rearing industry.

Citrus Control Board: c/o Dept of Agriculture, West Block, Belmopan; tel. (8) 22199; f. 1966; determines basic quota for each producer, fixes annual price of citrus; Chair. C. SOSA.

Marketing Board: POB 479, Belize City; tel. (2) 77402; f. 1948 to encourage the growing of staple food crops; purchases crops at guaranteed prices, supervises processing, storing and marketing; Chair. SANTIAGO PERDOMO.

Belize Sugar Board: 2nd St South, Corozal Town; tel. (4) 22005; fax (4) 22672; f. 1960 to control the sugar industry and cane production; includes representatives of the Government, sugar manufacturers, cane farmers and the public sector; Chair. D. A. K. GIBSON; Exec. Sec. S. O. BOBADILLA.

DEVELOPMENT ORGANIZATION

Belize Reconstruction and Development Corporation: 1 Bliss Promenade, POB 92, Belize City; (2) 77424; Chair. SAMUEL WAIGHT; Gen. Man. A. BRYAN CARD.

EMPLOYERS' ASSOCIATIONS

Cane Farmers' Association: San Antonio Rd, Orange Walk; tel. (3) 22005; f. 1959 to assist cane farmers and negotiate with the Sugar Board and manufacturers on their behalf; Chair. PABLO TUN; 16 district brs.

Citrus Growers' Association: POB 7, Dangriga; tel. (5) 22442; f. 1966; citrus crop farmers' asscn; Chair. LEROY DIAZ; Gen. Man. CLINTON HERNÁNDEZ.

Livestock Producers' Association: National Agricultural and Trade Show Grounds, POB 183, Belmopan; tel. (8) 23202; Chair. JOHN CARR.

TRADE UNIONS

National Trades Union Congress of Belize (NTUCB): Belize City; Pres. EDBERT HIGINIO.

Principal Unions

United General Workers' Union: 1259 Lakeland City, Dangriga; tel (5) 22105; f. 1979 by amalgamation of the Belize General Development Workers' Union and the Southern Christian Union;

BELIZE

three branch unions affiliated to the central body; affiliated to ICFTU; Pres. FRANCIS SABAL; Gen. Sec. CONRAD SAMBULA.

Belize National Teachers' Union: POB 382, Belize City; tel. (2) 72857; Pres. HELEN STUART; Sec. MIGUEL WONG; 1,000 mems.

Christian Workers' Union: 23 George St, Belize City; tel. (2) 72150; f. 1962; general; Pres. DESMOND VAUGHN; 2,000 mems.

Democratic Independent Union: POB 695, Belize City; Pres. CYRIL DAVIS; 1,250 mems.

Public Service Union of Belize: 3 Kut Avenue, Belize City; tel. (2) 72318; f. 1922; public workers; Pres. GODWIN SUTHERLAND; Sec.-Gen. CARL SMITH; 1,150 mems.

CO-OPERATIVES

In 1988 there were 40 Credit Unions, 78 Agricultural, Producer and Marketing Co-operatives, 13 Fishing Co-operatives, seven Bee-Keepers' Co-operatives, five Housing Co-operatives, three Transport Co-operatives, three Consumer Co-operatives, one Arts and Craft Co-operative and one Women's Co-operative.

There were also five co-operative societies, including the Belize Credit Union League (25 mems), the Fishing Co-operative Association (five mems) and the Honey Producers Federation (five mems).

Transport

RAILWAYS

There are no railways in Belize.

ROADS

There are about 1,600 km (1,000 miles) of all-weather main and feeder roads and about 400 km (250 miles) of cart roads and bush trails. A number of logging and forest tracks are usable by heavy-duty vehicles in the dry season.

SHIPPING

A new deep-water port at Belize City was opened to traffic in 1980. There is a second port at Commerce Bight near Dangriga (formerly Stann Creek), to the south of Belize City. A port for the export of bananas was completed at Big Creek in 1990. Nine major shipping lines operate vessels calling at Belize City, including the Carol Line (consisting of Harrison, Hapag-Lloyd, Nedlloyd and CGM).

CIVIL AVIATION

Philip S. W. Goldson International Airport, 14 km (9 miles) from Belize City, can accommodate medium-sized jet-engined aircraft, and a new terminal was completed in 1990. There are airstrips for light aircraft on internal flights near the major towns and offshore islands.

Belize Trans Air: Philip S.W. Goldson Int. Airport, Belize City; f. 1990; services to USA; Pres. DEREK AIKMAN.

Maya Airways Ltd: 6 Fort St, POB 458, Belize City; tel. (2) 77215; telex 280; f. 1961; privately owned; division of Maya Corpn; internal services, centred on Belize City; Chair. D. COURTENAY; Dir GORDON A. ROE; fleet of 3 BN-2A Islander.

Tropic Air: Philip S.W. Goldson International Airport, Belize City; operates services to Mexico.

Western Caribbean Airlines: Philip S.W. Goldson International Airport, Belize City; Belizean-owned; services to Honduras, daily, and Mexico.

Tourism

The main tourist attractions are the beaches and the barrier reef, hunting and fishing, and remains of the Mayan civilization. There are eight major wildlife reserves (including the world's only reserves for the jaguar and for the red-footed booby), and government policy is to develop 'eco-tourism', based on the attractions of an unspoilt environment and Belize's natural history. There were 188 hotels in Belize and 144,210 tourist arrivals in 1988, and income from tourism was estimated at BZ $56m

Belize Tourist Board: 53 Regent St, POB 325, Belize City; tel. (2) 77213; f. 1964; fmrly Belize Tourist Bureau; six mems; Chair. ALLAN FORMAN.

BENIN

Introductory Survey

Location, Climate, Language, Religion, Flag, Capital

The Republic of Benin (known as the People's Republic of Benin between 1975 and 1990) is a narrow stretch of territory in West Africa. The country has an Atlantic coastline of about 100 km (60 miles), flanked by Nigeria to the east and Togo to the west; its northern borders are with Burkina Faso and Niger. The climate is tropical in the north, with one rainy season and a maximum temperature of 46°C (115°F), and equatorial in the south, with average temperatures of 20°–34°C (68°–93°F) and two rainy seasons. French is the official language, but each of the indigenous ethnic groups has its own language. Bariba and Fulani are the major languages in the north, while Fon and Yoruba are widely spoken in the south. The majority of the people follow traditional beliefs and customs. About 15% of the inhabitants are Christians, mainly Roman Catholics, and about 13% are Muslims. The national flag (proportions 3 by 2) is green, with a five-pointed red star in the upper hoist. The capital is Porto-Novo, but most government offices and other state bodies are in Cotonou.

Recent History

Benin, called Dahomey until 1975, was formerly part of French West Africa. It became a self-governing republic within the French Community in December 1958, and an independent state on 1 August 1960. The country's history from independence until 1972 was marked by chronic political instability, with five successful coups involving the army.

Elections in December 1960 were won by the Parti dahoméen de l'unité, whose leader, Hubert Maga (a northerner), became the country's first President. In October 1963, following riots by workers and students, President Maga was deposed by a military coup, led by Col (later Gen.) Christophe Soglo, Chief of Staff of the Army. Soglo served as interim Head of State until the election in January 1964 of a government headed by Sourou-Migan Apithy, a southerner who had been Vice-President under Maga. Another southerner, Justin Ahomadegbé, became Prime Minister. This regime was resented in the north, where rioting occurred. In November 1965, following a series of political crises, Gen. Soglo forced Apithy and Ahomadegbé to resign. A provisional government was formed but the army intervened again in December, when Gen. Soglo assumed power at the head of a military regime. In December 1967 industrial unrest, following a ban on trade union activity, led to another coup, this time by younger officers, led by Maj. (later Lt-Col) Maurice Kouandété. An interim regime was established, with Lt-Col Alphonse Alley, formerly Chief of Staff, as Head of State and Kouandété as Prime Minister.

A return to civilian rule was attempted in 1968. A referendum in March approved a new constitution, based on a strong presidency, and a presidential election was held in May. However, leading politicians, including all former Presidents, were banned from participation in the presidential poll and called on their supporters to boycott the election. As a result, only about 26% of the electorate voted, with the abstention rate reaching 99% in the north. The election was declared void, and in June the military regime nominated Dr Emile-Derlin Zinsou, formerly Minister of Foreign Affairs, as President; he was confirmed in office by referendum in the following month. In December 1969 Zinsou was deposed by Lt-Col Kouandété, then Commander-in-Chief of the Army, and a Military Directorate, led by Lt-Col Paul-Emile de Souza, assumed power.

In March 1970 a presidential election was held amid violent incidents and widespread claims of irregularities. The poll was abandoned when counting revealed roughly equal support for the three main candidates, Ahomadegbé, Apithy and Maga. In May, however, the Directorate handed over power to a Presidential Council comprising these three veteran politicians. It was agreed that each member of the triumvirate would act as Head of State, in rotation, for a two-year period. As a concession to the north, Maga became the first to hold this office, being succeeded in May 1972 by Ahomadegbé. In late October, however, the collective civilian leadership was deposed by Maj. (later Brig.-Gen.) Mathieu Kerekou, Deputy Chief of Staff of the armed forces. Kerekou established a military regime, which, he maintained, would be based on equal representation between northern, central and southern regions. In September 1973 a National Council of the Revolution (CNR) was established.

Under Kerekou, a policy of 'scientific socialism', based on Marxism-Leninism, was to be pursued. The vital sectors of the economy, including the banks and the distribution of petroleum products, were taken over by the State. In February 1975 the country's co-operation agreements with France were renegotiated. Between 1974 and 1978 a decentralized local administration was set up, the education system taken over and the legal system put under review. The army and the gendarmerie were merged to form a National Defence Force, following an unsuccessful attempt (in January 1975), by the Minister of Public Administration and Labour and elements of the paramilitary forces, to overthrow the Government. A further plot to depose Kerekou, initiated by former President Zinsou, was disclosed in October. In November the Parti de la révolution populaire du Bénin (PRPB) was established as the 'highest expression of the political will of the people of Benin', and in December the country's name was changed from Dahomey to the People's Republic of Benin.

In January 1977 an airborne mercenary attack on Cotonou, led by a French national, Col Robert Denard, was repelled by the armed forces. In August the CNR adopted a *Loi Fondamentale* which decreed new structures in government. Under its terms, a National Revolutionary Assembly (ANR) was instituted as the supreme authority of the State, following an election, held in November 1979, for the 336 members of the Assembly: a single list of candidates was presented and approved by 97.5% of the voters. The CNR was disbanded and a National Executive Committee (CEN) was established. At the first Ordinary Congress of the PRPB, held in December, it was decided that Kerekou would be the sole candidate for President of the Republic; the ANR unanimously elected him to this office in February 1980. In April 1981 it was announced that the three members of the former Presidential Council, who had been imprisoned following the coup of 1972, had been released from house arrest. A gradual moderation in Benin's domestic policies followed, and ministerial changes in April and December 1982 reflected the Government's campaign against corruption and inefficiency. Members of an extreme left-wing faction ('Les Ligueurs') lost influence, as did the army, whose officers were, for the first time, in a minority in the Government.

In February 1984 the ANR amended the *Loi Fondamentale*, thus increasing the mandates of assembly members (People's Commissioners) and of the President from three years to five years. Moreover, the number of People's Commissioners was reduced from 336 to 196. At legislative elections, held in June, 97.96% of voters approved the single list of candidates for the ANR. In July that body re-elected Kerekou, the sole candidate, as President. The membership of the CEN was subsequently reduced, by seven, to 15. Upon his re-election, Kerekou announced an amnesty for several political prisoners, including Alphonse Alley, the former Head of State.

Following a boycott of classes by students, in April 1985, riots broke out in May at the University of Benin and in schools; the Government responded by closing all educational establishments until the beginning of June. Several students were detained following the riots, and, in an ensuing reorganization of the Government, the Ministers of Secondary and Higher Education and of Culture, Youth and Sports were replaced. In November about 100 people, including teachers, engineers and prominent public officials, were arrested on suspicion of belonging to the banned Parti communiste dahoméen (PCD). Although Kerekou ordered the release of 50 of those implicated in the 1985 student riots in September 1986, it was subsequently claimed by the human rights organization, Amnesty International, that at least 88 detainees were still being held, without charge, in unhealthy conditions. Further student unrest occurred in 1987 and 1988. In April 1989 it was

BENIN

announced that 50 of those who had been detained since 1985 were to be released.

In January 1987 Kerekou resigned from the army to become a civilian Head of State. Growing concern among army officers at widespread corruption within Kerekou's civilian Government, together with opposition to the proposed establishment of a Court of State Security, culminated in a coup attempt in March 1988. Almost 150 officers, including members of the presidential guard, were reported to have been arrested following the incident. It was subsequently reported that a further attempt to overthrow the Government had taken place in June, while President Kerekou had been attending a 'summit' meeting of the Economic Community of West African States (ECOWAS) in Togo. In August Amnesty International reported that many of those who had been arrested in the aftermath of the two incidents were being detained without charge. The organization also claimed that a large number of Benin's detainees could be classified as prisoners of conscience, and revealed that political prisoners were being tortured. In the same year, it was alleged that Benin had agreed to accept shipments of toxic waste from several Western countries. In November it was reported that one of the alleged instigators of the March coup attempt, Capt. Hountoundji, had died in detention, possibly as a result of torture (however, he was subsequently said to be among the defendants at trials of those who had been implicated in the incident), while another of the alleged perpetrators, Lt-Col François Kouyami, was among four prisoners who had escaped before they could be brought to trial. In June 1989 Kerekou commissioned an inquiry into allegations of the detention of civil offenders at the Guezo military camp in Cotonou. It was subsequently announced that some detainees would be transferred to civilian prisons, while those convicted of attacks on state security would continue to be held at the base.

In February 1989 Capt. Abdourrhamane Amadou (like Hountoundji, a former member of the presidential guard) and Ahmed Kadi Youba (a Mauritanian national) were sentenced to 20 years' imprisonment by the Court of State Security, after having been convicted for involvement in the June 1988 coup attempt. Two other defendants received lesser custodial sentences. In July Gbandamassi Moudachirou was condemned (*in absentia*) to life imprisonment for his part in the incident. In the same month, however, the trial of those who had been charged with involvement in the attempt to overthrow the Kerekou Government in March 1988 was postponed, pending clarification of certain legal issues.

Elections to the ANR were held in June 1989. It was reported that the single list of candidates was approved by 89.6% of the votes cast. The increase in opposition to the official list, compared with the result that was recorded at the 1984 legislative election, was attributed to popular dissatisfaction with the country's persistent economic difficulties. On 2 August, none the less, the ANR re-elected Kerekou (the sole candidate) to the office of President of the Republic. An extensive reallocation of ministerial portfolios followed, as a result of which Robert Dossou (who had, in the previous month, advocated greater openness in the Beninois political system, together with the establishment of a multi-party system) was appointed to the post of Minister Delegate to the Presidency in charge of Planning and Statistics. One of Kerekou's closest associates, Daniel Tawema, was nominated Minister of Foreign Affairs and Co-operation, while Rafiatou Karimou, who assumed the Public Health portfolio, became the first female member of the CEN. In late August an amnesty was announced for 192 prisoners: among those pardoned was the exiled former President Zinsou.

In 1986 the Beninois Government began a series of negotiations with the IMF and the World Bank, in order to facilitate a rescheduling of the country's external debt and the granting of new credits. In July 1988 five ministers were dismissed, accused of economic incompetence, and the Ministry of Finance and Economy was replaced by two ministries, with responsibility for finance and for industry and energy.

The Government's attempts to reach accommodation with external creditors provoked considerable disquiet within Benin. In January 1989 public-sector employees, including civil servants, schoolteachers and lecturers at the University of Cotonou, staged strikes in Porto-Novo and Cotonou, in protest at delays in the payment of salaries. At the same time, students, who were demanding the disbursement of grants and scholarships, boycotted classes. Troops were deployed, with authorization to open fire on demonstrators. Later in the same month, the payment of salaries was authorized. However, arrears again accumulated, and the proposal, in March, of substantial reductions in remuneration (as part of the 1989 austerity budget) provoked further industrial action. In June economic adjustment measures were agreed with the IMF and the World Bank. None the less, the unrest escalated in July, when civil servants at 10 government ministries withdrew their labour; teaching staff were suspended, and the 1988/89 academic year was declared invalid in all institutions where strikes had taken place. In September the Government promised partial payment, to teaching staff, of outstanding salaries, following pledges of financial assistance from multilateral and bilateral creditors. Classes resumed in late October. In the same month the Union nationale des syndicats des travailleurs du Bénin (UNSTB), hitherto the sole officially-recognized trade union, announced that it was to sever its ties with the PRPB, and demanded the payment of salary arrears to 47,000 civil servants, together with a commitment, by the Government, to make future payments on a regular basis (in July the Syndicat national de l'enseignement supérieur, the trade union representing teaching staff in higher-education establishments, had withdrawn from the UNSTB, owing to that organization's close links with the ruling party). In December further disruption was precipitated by the Kerekou administration's failure to fulfil its earlier commitments to public-sector employees. The Government then yielded to domestic pressure and to demands made by Benin's external creditors (notably France), and instituted radical political changes. It was announced that Marxism-Leninism would no longer be the official ideology of the State, and a national conference was planned for early 1990, at which the drafting of a new constitution was to be initiated. Foreign donors agreed to contribute towards the payment of outstanding salaries, and the Government warned that employees who did not return to work in January would not be entitled to this remuneration (a ruling that was not, however, enforced). None the less, demonstrations that had been organized by the PCD were reportedly attended by 40,000 people, thus prompting the Government to impose a temporary ban on all public gatherings.

In accordance with the announcements of December 1989, a national conference of what were termed the 'active forces of the nation' was convened in Cotonou in February 1990. The sessions were attended by 488 delegates, representing more than 50 political organizations. (The PCD, however, declined to attend the conference.) Delegates voted to abolish the 1977 *Loi Fondamentale*, and all resolutions adopted by the conference were to be incorporated in a 'national charter' that was to form the basis of a new constitution. An interim Haut conseil de la République (HCR) was appointed to assume the functions of the ANR, which was to be dissolved. Among the 27 members of the HCR were former Presidents Ahomadegbé, Maga and Zinsou, all of whom had recently returned to Benin as the leaders of opposition parties. Presidential and legislative elections were scheduled for early 1991. Both elections were to be on the basis of universal suffrage, with the President of the Republic being elected for a five-year term, renewable only once. A former official of the World Bank, Nicéphore Soglo, was designated Prime Minister; Kerekou, who reluctantly acceded to the conference's decisions, subsequently relinquished the defence portfolio to Soglo. Delegates also voted to change the country's name to the Republic of Benin. In early March an interim Council of Ministers announced an amnesty for all political dissidents. The HCR was inaugurated, and Soglo appointed a transitional government. This civilian administration comprised 15 members, all of whom were new to ministerial office. (Of the previous Council of Ministers, therefore, only Kerekou remained in government.) The Soglo Government undertook to honour all financial commitments to public-sector employees and students, and all those detained during the unrest of late 1989 were released.

In May 1990 the incumbent prefects of Benin's six provinces, all of whom were military officers, were replaced by civilian administrators. In the following month the Government effected an extensive restructuring of the armed forces (see Defence).

The impending dissolution of the PRPB was announced in April 1990. Accordingly, a new political organization, the Union des forces du progrès (UFP), was established in the following month to replace the former ruling party. In August the Government promulgated a law permitting the registration of political parties: in mid-October it was announced that 24 parties had been accorded official status (it was believed that at least 16 other parties remained unofficial at that time).

The draft Constitution, which was published in May 1990, was originally due to be submitted for approval in a national referendum in August of that year. However, delays were encountered, and, after having been postponed on several occasions, the referendum was eventually conducted on 2 December. Voters were asked to choose between two versions of the Constitution, one of which incorporated a clause stipulating upper and lower age-limits for presidential candidates. It was reported that 95.8% of those who voted gave their approval to one or other of the versions, with 79.7% of voters favouring the document in its entirety. (Several opposition parties had campaigned vigorously against the imposition of an upper age-limit, which effectively prevented ex-presidents Ahomadegbé, Maga and Zinsou from contesting the presidency.) The new document envisaged that executive authority would be counterbalanced by several institutions, including a multi-party legislative body, an independent judiciary, an economic and social council and a broadcasting authority.

Under the transitional Government, attempts were instigated to alleviate the bankrupt country's chronic economic difficulties. It was announced that corrupt officials would be prosecuted and required to reimburse embezzled funds, and a restructuring of the state sector was undertaken. In July 1990 it was announced that Mamadou Cissé (who had, until mid-1989, been a close associate of Kerekou, and who had been sought by both the Beninois and French authorities in connection with fraudulent activities) had been arrested in Côte d'Ivoire, whence he was later extradited to Benin. However, some popular dissatisfaction at the failure of the transitional administration to bring about immediate economic recovery was apparent, notably among students.

Benin's international reputation was enhanced with the relaxation of Kerekou's regime during the 1980s. Relations with France, Benin's main trading partner and supplier of aid, deteriorated sharply in 1977, following the mercenary attack on Cotonou. Dialogue between the two countries resumed in full in 1978, and France was among the most prominent advocates of Benin's transition to multi-party democracy in December 1989.

In 1988 relations with the USA deteriorated when that country accused Benin of allowing Libyan agents to use its territory as a base for terrorist activities. None the less, Kerekou ordered the head of the Libyan diplomatic mission in Cotonou, who had allegedly been involved in the transfer of explosives, to leave the country, and closed the offices of a Libyan-supported import-export agency that was implicated in the affair. New restrictions on the entry of Libyan nationals into the country and the rejection of a Libyan offer of economic aid were perceived to be further indications of Benin's wish to restrict its relations with the Qaddafi regime. Moreover, defendants at the February 1989 coup trial suggested the involvement of Libyan interests in attempts to destabilize the Kerekou Government.

In 1990 Soglo and other members of the transitional Government travelled extensively abroad, in an attempt to promote harmonious trading and diplomatic relations with external creditors. In November of that year the Togolese Government accused the Beninois media of reporting recent disturbances within Togo in a manner that was injurious to the Eyadéma administration, and banned the sale of all Beninois newspapers in Togo.

Government

In February 1990 the *Loi Fondamentale* that had been adopted in 1977 was repealed, and the drafting of a new constitution providing for a separation of the powers of the executive, legislature and judiciary, in the context of a multi-party system, was initiated. The new Constitution was approved in a national referendum on 2 December 1990 (see Recent History).

For the purposes of local administration, Benin is divided into six provinces, within which there is a total of 78 districts. Civilian prefects were appointed to the provinces (which had hitherto been governed by military administrators) in May 1990.

Defence

A major restructuring of the armed forces was effected in June 1990. The Beninois Armed Forces (hitherto the People's Armed Forces of Benin) thus comprised the land army, air force, army and a national gendarmerie. An increase in the strength and equipment of the gendarmerie was envisaged. The people's militia was disbanded. At the time of the reorganization the army numbered 3,800, the air force 350, the navy 200 and the gendarmerie 2,000. In 1989 the estimated defence budget was 9,125m. francs CFA (8.8% of consolidated budget expenditure).

Economic Affairs

In 1988, according to estimates by the World Bank, Benin's gross national product (GNP) per head, measured at average 1986–88 prices, was US $390. During 1965–88, it was estimated, GNP per head increased at an average annual rate of only 0.1%. Over the period 1980–88, the population was estimated to have increased by an annual average of 3.2%. Benin's gross domestic product (GDP) increased, in real terms, by an annual average of 2.4% during the same period.

Agriculture (including forestry and fishing) contributed 40% of GDP in 1988. About 62.3% of the labour force were employed in agriculture in 1989. The principal cash crops are cotton (exports of cottonseed and raw cotton accounting for about 21% of export earnings in 1984), oil palm, groundnuts and shea nuts (karité nuts). The principal subsistence crops are cassava, yams and maize. During 1980–86 agricultural production increased by an annual average of 4.2%.

Industry (including mining, manufacturing, construction and power) contributed 13% of GDP in 1988. Only about 6.6% of the labour force were engaged in industrial activities in 1980. During 1980–88 industrial production increased by an annual average of 5.8%.

Mining and manufacturing together contributed 6% of GDP in 1986. Petroleum, marble, limestone and gold are exploited (gold by artisans). However, it was believed that Benin's reserves of petroleum could be exhausted by 1991. The existence of deposits of phosphates, iron ore, kaolin, silica sand and chromium has been confirmed.

Manufacturing is based on the processing of primary products (such as cotton-ginning and oil-palm processsing). A cement factory and a sugar complex are operated in co-operation with Nigerian interests, while a private US investor has established a wire and steel complex. The inauguration of a petroleum refinery is also envisaged.

The completion, in 1988, of a hydroelectric power installation, constructed in co-operation with Togo, was expected to reduce Benin's dependence on imported energy. Imports of fuel products comprised 31% of the value of merchandise imports in 1988.

In 1988, according to provisional figures, Benin recorded a visible trade deficit of 56,400m. francs CFA, and there was a deficit of 14,800m. francs CFA on the current account of the balance of payments. In 1984 the principal source of imports (24.8%) was France; other major suppliers were the United Kingdom, the Netherlands, the People's Republic of China and the USA. In the same year the principal market for exports (35.2%) was the Netherlands; other important purchasers were the USA, Spain and the Federal Republic of Germany (West Germany). The principal exports in 1984 were fuel products, ginned cotton, cocoa beans and palm products. The principal imports were foodstuffs (particularly cereals), beverages and tobacco, machinery and transport equipment and refined petroleum products.

Consolidated budget estimates for 1989 envisaged a deficit of 28,380m. francs CFA. Benin's total external public debt was US $904m. at the end of 1988. In that year the cost of debt-servicing was equivalent to 5.4% of revenue from exports of goods and services. Annual inflation averaged 8.0% in 1980–88.

Benin is a member of the Communauté Economique de l'Afrique de l'Ouest (CEAO, see p. 120), of the Conseil de l'Entente (see p. 122), of the Economic Community of West African States (ECOWAS, see p. 133) and of the West African organs of the Franc Zone (see p. 156).

In 1986 the Kerekou Government began negotiations with the IMF and the World Bank, in an attempt to reduce the country's chronic budgetary and balance-of-payments problems, which had been exacerbated by the effects of drought on Benin's major cash crops, the two-year closure of the border with Nigeria, and the decline in international prices for cotton. In mid 1989 those agencies agreed to provide funding in support of a three-year (1989–92) programme of economic adjustment. The programme emphasized the restructuring of the

BENIN
Introductory Survey, Statistical Survey

banking and taxation systems and of the state bureaucracy, the promotion of private enterprise and the rehabilitation of unprofitable state-owned organizations. None the less, the inability of the Kerekou administration to discharge its domestic financial obligations contributed to demands for political change during 1989 (see Recent History). The transitional administration demonstrated its commitment to the economic reforms that had been advocated by Benin's external creditors. Adherence to these reforms was expected to facilitate debt-relief concessions from foreign donors; however, the Beninois economy remained fragile in late 1990.

Social Welfare

In 1980 Benin had 204 physicians (one for every 17,000 inhabitants). In 1982 there were six hospitals, 31 health centres, 186 dispensaries and 65 maternity clinics. Two further hospitals were opened at Abomey and Natitingou in 1985 and 1986 respectively, and it was announced in 1989 that a hospital was to be built in northern Benin, with assistance from the Democratic People's Republic of Korea. In 1989 the World Bank approved a credit of SDR 14.1m., in support of a programme to improve fundamental health-care facilities. There is a minimum hourly wage for workers. Consolidated budget estimates for 1989 allocated 2,531m. francs CFA (2.4% of total expenditure by the central Government) to health and 4,987m. francs CFA (4.8%) to social welfare.

Education

Following legislation in 1975, the State took control of all education, which is public, secular and provided free of charge. Education is officially compulsory for five years between the ages of six and 11 years. Primary education begins at six years of age and lasts for six years. Secondary education, beginning at 12 years of age, lasts for up to seven years, comprising a first cycle of four years and a second of three years. In 1987 and estimated 50% of children in the relevant age-group were enrolled at primary schools (66% of boys; 34% of girls). In 1986 the comparable ratio for secondary enrolment was only 13% (18% of boys; 7% of girls). In 1985, according to UNESCO estimates, the average rate of adult illiteracy was 74.1% (males 63.3%; females 84.3%).

The University of Benin was founded at Cotonou in 1970, and teacher-training colleges were opened at Lokossa, Natitingou and Parakou in September 1987. A major education project, launched in 1986 with funding from UNESCO, aimed to construct 67 new primary schools in the northern provinces of Atacora and Borgou and in the southern province of Mono.

In 1989, according to consolidated budget estimates, 16,116m. francs CFA was allocated to the education sector (15.5% of total expenditure by the central Government).

Public Holidays

1991: 1 January (New Year's Day), 16 January (Martyrs' Day, anniversary of mercenary attack on Cotonou), 29 March (Good Friday), 1 April (Youth Day, Easter Monday), 16 April* (Id al-Fitr, end of Ramadan), 1 May (Workers' Day), 9 May (Ascension Day), 20 May (Whit Monday), 23 June* (Id al-Adha, Feast of the Sacrifice), 15 August (Assumption), 26 October (Armed Forces Day), 1 November (All Saints' Day), 30 November (National Day), 25 December (Christmas Day), 31 December (Harvest Day).

1992: 1 January (New Year's Day), 16 January (Martyrs' Day, anniversary of mercenary attack on Cotonou), 1 April (Youth Day), 4 April* (Id al-Fitr, end of Ramadam), 17 April (Good Friday), 20 April (Easter Monday), 1 May (Workers' Day), 28 May (Ascension Day), 8 June (Whit Monday), 11 June* (Id al-Adha, Feast of the Sacrifice), 15 August (Assumption), 26 October (Armed Forces Day), 1 November (All Saints' Day), 30 November (National Day), 25 December (Christmas Day), 31 December (Harvest Day).

* These holidays are dependent on the Islamic lunar calendar and may vary by one or two days from the dates given.

Weights and Measures

The metric system is in force.

Statistical Survey

Source (unless otherwise stated): Institut National de la Statistique et de l'Analyse Economique, BP 323, Cotonou; tel. 31-40-81.

Area and Population

AREA, POPULATION AND DENSITY

Area (sq km)	112,622*
Population (census of 20–30 March 1979)	
Males	1,596,939
Females	1,734,271
Total	3,331,210
Population (official estimates at mid-year)	
1987	4,304,000
1988	4,446,000
1989	4,591,000
Density (per sq km) at mid-1989	40.8

* 43,484 sq miles.

ETHNIC GROUPS

1979 census (percentages): Fon 39.2; Yoruba 11.9; Adja 11.0; Bariba 8.5; Houeda 8.5; Peulh 5.6; Djougou 3.0; Dendi 2.1; Non-Africans 6.5; Others 1.2; Unknown 2.4.

POPULATION BY PROVINCE (1979 census)

Atakora	479,604
Atlantique	686,258
Borgou	490,669
Mono	477,378
Ouémé	626,868
Zou	570,433
Total	3,331,210

PRINCIPAL TOWNS

(estimated population at 1 July 1981)
Cotonou 383,250; Porto-Novo (capital) 144,000.

BIRTHS AND DEATHS (UN estimates, annual averages)

	1975–80	1980–85	1985–90
Birth rate (per 1,000)	51.1	50.7	50.5
Death rate (per 1,000)	24.6	21.2	19.0

Source: UN, *World Population Prospects: 1988.*

BENIN

ECONOMICALLY ACTIVE POPULATION
(ILO estimates, '000 persons at mid-1980)

	Males	Females	Total
Agriculture, etc.	598	648	1,246
Industry	91	28	118
Services	218	193	410
Total	906	869	1,775

Source: ILO, *Economically Active Population Estimates and Projections, 1950–2025*.

Mid-1989 (estimates in '000): Agriculture, etc. 1,337; Total 2,146 (Source: FAO, *Production Yearbook*).

Agriculture

PRINCIPAL CROPS ('000 metric tons)

	1987	1988	1989
Rice (paddy)	8	10	9
Maize	267	430	455
Millet	20	23	21†
Sorghum	95	97	110
Sweet potatoes	31	41	24
Cassava (Manioc)	570	780	1,002
Yams	835	922	1,049
Taro (Coco yam)	2	3	2*
Dry beans	35	44	48
Groundnuts (in shell)	53	72	70
Cottonseed*	40	60	60
Cotton (lint)†	27	43	40
Coconuts*	20	20	20
Palm kernels	20	25†	20*
Tomatoes	49	70	72
Chillies and peppers (green)*	21	21	21
Oranges*	12	12	12
Mangoes*	12	12	12
Bananas*	13	13	13
Pineapples*	3	3	3
Coffee (green)	4†	5*	5*

* FAO estimate(s).   † Unofficial estimate(s).
Source: FAO, *Production Yearbook*.

LIVESTOCK ('000 head, year ending September)

	1987	1988	1989
Horses*	6	6	6
Asses*	1	1	1
Cattle	896	914	932
Pigs	617	648	680
Sheep*	831	860	890
Goats	928	960	994

Poultry (million)*: 23 in 1987; 23 in 1988; 24 in 1989.
* FAO estimates.
Source: FAO, *Production Yearbook*.

LIVESTOCK PRODUCTS (FAO estimates, '000 metric tons)

	1987	1988	1989
Beef and veal	13	13	14
Mutton and lamb	3	3	3
Goats' meat	3	3	3
Pig meat	7	7	8
Poultry meat	27	27	29
Other meat	5	6	5
Cows' milk	15	15	15
Goats' milk	5	5	5
Hen eggs	17.1	17.1	18.0

Source: FAO, *Production Yearbook*.

Forestry

ROUNDWOOD REMOVALS ('000 cubic metres, excluding bark)

	1986*	1987	1988*
Sawlogs, veneer logs and logs for sleepers	20	32	32
Other industrial wood*	209	215	222
Fuel wood*	4,308	4,443	4,519
Total	4,537	4,690	4,845

* FAO estimates.
Source: FAO, *Yearbook of Forest Products*.

SAWNWOOD PRODUCTION ('000 cubic metres)

	1984	1985	1986
Total	5	8	11

1987–88: Annual production as in 1986 (FAO estimate).
Source: FAO, *Yearbook of Forest Products*.

Fishing

('000 metric tons, live weight)

	1986	1987	1988
Inland waters	30.0*	32.0	28.6
Atlantic Ocean	8.7	9.9	9.7*
Total catch	38.7*	41.9	38.3*

* FAO estimate.
Source: FAO, *Yearbook of Fishery Statistics*.

Mining

(provisional or estimated figures, '000 metric tons)

	1985	1986	1987
Crude petroleum	325	365	350

Source: UN, *Industrial Statistics Yearbook*.

Industry

SELECTED PRODUCTS
('000 metric tons, unless otherwise indicated)

	1985	1986	1987
Palm oil and palm kernel oil*	37	38	38
Salted, dried or smoked fish*	2	2	2
Cement†	300	300*	300*
Electric energy (million kWh)	5	5	5

* Provisional or estimated figures.
† Source: US Bureau of Mines.
Source: UN, *Industrial Statistics Yearbook*.

BENIN

Statistical Survey

Finance

CURRENCY AND EXCHANGE RATES

Monetary Units
100 centimes = 1 franc de la Communauté financière africaine (CFA).

Denominations
Coins: 1, 2, 5, 10, 25, 50, 100 and 500 francs CFA.
Notes: 50, 100, 500, 1,000 and 5,000 francs CFA.

French Franc, Sterling and Dollar Equivalents (30 September 1990)
1 French franc = 50 francs CFA;
£1 sterling = 491.1 francs CFA;
US $1 = 262.1 francs CFA;
1,000 francs CFA = £2.036 = $3.815.

Average Exchange Rate (francs CFA per US $)
1987 300.54
1988 297.85
1989 319.01

BUDGET (million francs CFA)

Revenue	1987*	1988*	1989†
Fiscal receipts	43,407	42,943	37,179
Taxes on income and profits	9,393	10,140	6,030
Taxes on goods and services	6,456	4,825	4,314
Taxes on international trade and transactions	20,593	21,010	24,417
Other current receipts	6,616	8,961	10,870
Capital receipts	30	25	17
Aid, grants and subsidies	—	—	14,700
Loans	—	—	12,500
Total	50,053	51,929	75,266

Expenditure	1987*	1988*	1989†
General public services	8,079	8,212	6,295
Defence	10,656	11,039	9,125
Public order and security	1,581	1,376	1,105
Education	17,072	15,701	16,116
Health	4,047	3,304	2,531
Social security and welfare	606	574	4,987
Other community and social services	715	655	711
Economic services	6,039	4,918	6,075
Agriculture, forestry and fishing	3,817	3,289	3,286
Transport and communications	1,883	1,332	2,255
Other economic services	339	297	258
Other purposes	7,135	7,958	56,700
Debt-servicing	600	600	17,248
Total	55,930	53,737	103,646

* Administrative budget. † Consolidated budget.
Note: Figures for 1988 and 1989 are estimates.
Source: Banque Centrale des Etats de l'Afrique de l'Ouest.

1990 (administrative budget estimates, million francs CFA): Revenue 39,000; Expenditure 67,000.

Investment Budget (estimates, million francs CFA): 50,800 in 1987; 54,100 in 1988; 54,848 in 1989; 52,000 in 1990.

DEVELOPMENT PLAN, 1981–90
(planned public investment, '000 million francs CFA)

Agriculture	55.6
Industry/Mining	44.5
Infrastructure	297.2
Railways	188.3
Ports	30.1
Water/Dams	42.7
Roads	14.2
Total (identified)	397.3
Total (planned)	958.8

Source: *Bulletin de l'Afrique Noire*, December 1981.

CENTRAL BANK RESERVES (US $ million at 31 December)

	1987	1988	1989
Gold*	5.2	4.6	4.3
IMF special drawing rights	0.1	0.1	—
Reserve position in IMF	2.9	2.7	2.7
Foreign exchange	0.6	1.4	0.7
Total	8.8	8.8	7.7

* Valued at market-related prices.
Source: IMF, *International Financial Statistics*.

MONEY SUPPLY ('000 million francs CFA at 31 December)

	1987	1988	1989
Currency outside banks	19.61	23.69	36.39
Demand deposit at deposit money banks	38.90	42.30	39.90
Checking deposits at post office	3.00	3.41	3.47
Total money (incl. others)	61.84	71.95	84.37

Source: IMF, *International Financial Statistics*.

NATIONAL ACCOUNTS (million francs CFA at current prices)
National Income and Product

	1984	1985	1986
Compensation of employees	98,961	109,618	110,886
Operating surplus	296,500	312,177	311,239
Domestic factor incomes	395,461	421,795	422,125
Consumption of fixed capital	48,565	51,102	53,773
Gross domestic product (GDP) at factor cost	444,026	472,897	475,898
Indirect taxes, *less* subsidies	22,175	26,951	26,768
GDP in purchasers' values	466,201	499,848	502,666
Net factor income from abroad	−38,827	−20,119	−8,020
Gross national product	427,374	479,729	494,646
Less Consumption of fixed capital	48,565	51,102	53,773
National income in market prices	378,809	428,627	440,873
Other current transfers from abroad (net)	48,010	30,200	40,000
National disposable income	426,819	458,827	480,873

BENIN

Expenditure on the Gross Domestic Product

	1984	1985	1986
Government final consumption expenditure	41,824	42,168	43,585
Private final consumption expenditure	385,069	404,322	435,261
Increase in stocks	5,200	-1,604	13,600
Gross fixed capital formation	60,472	77,462	82,820
Total domestic expenditure	492,565	522,348	575,266
Exports of goods and services	91,945	106,700	78,000
Less Imports of goods and services	118,309	129,200	150,600
GDP in purchasers' values	466,201	499,848	502,666
GDP at constant 1978 prices	265,371	271,911	263,210

Gross Domestic Product by Economic Activity

	1984	1985	1986
Agriculture, hunting, forestry and fishing	177,798	179,571	200,183
Mining and quarrying } Manufacturing	42,403	46,699	28,335
Electricity, gas and water	3,584	3,556	4,282
Construction	17,045	23,423	24,564
Trade, restaurants and hotels	86,632	96,500	96,637
Transport, storage and communications	43,280	46,014	48,100
Finance, insurance, real estate and business services*	34,813	38,293	34,476
Public administration and defence	38,471	38,841	39,321
GDP at factor cost	444,026	472,897	475,898
Indirect taxes, *less* subsidies	22,175	26,951	26,768
GDP in purchasers' values	466,201	499,848	502,666

* Including community, social and personal services (other than government services).

Source: UN, *National Accounts Statistics*.

BALANCE OF PAYMENTS (million francs CFA)

	1987*	1988†	1989†
Merchandise exports f.o.b.	44,800	39,900	45,600
Merchandise imports f.o.b.	-108,700	-113,100	-102,000
Trade balance	-63,900	-73,200	-56,400
Services (net)	-17,900	-16,100	-9,400
Balance on goods and services	-81,800	-89,300	-65,800
Private unrequited transfers (net)	22,800	24,300	19,000
Government unrequited transfers (net)	16,800	21,600	32,000
Current balance	-42,200	-43,400	-14,800
Long-term capital (net)	13,100	32,900	25,000
Short-term capital (net)	5,500	11,900	16,300
Net errors and ommissions	-200	100	4,000
Total (net monetary movements)	-23,800	1,500	30,500

* Provisional figures. † Estimated figures.
Source: Banque Centrale des Etats de l'Afrique de l'Ouest.

External Trade

Source: Banque Centrale des Etats de l'Afrique de l'Ouest.

PRINCIPAL COMMODITIES (million francs CFA)

Imports c.i.f.	1982	1983	1984
Food products of animal origin	2,963	3,297	3,158
Cereals	6,727	8,510	8,619
Sugar and sugar preparations	216	330	3,671
Beverages and tobacco	20,858	16,320	18,584
Refined petroleum products	5,930	1,484	13,834
Non-electrical machinery	13,263	8,955	5,844
Electrical machinery	11,920	8,238	7,253
Road transport equipment	9,352	7,544	4,398
Chemicals	9,378	7,891	9,286
Miscellaneous manufactured articles	60,178	35,432	37,607
Cotton yarn and fabrics	24,060	14,113	10,336
Total (incl. others)	152,553	112,032	125,903

Exports f.o.b.	1982	1983	1984
Coffee	932	661	2,385
Cocoa beans	282	1,740	9,594
Palm products	1,886	2,701	5,834
Shea (karité) butter	238	557	2,267
Fuels	551	13,584	32,557
Cottonseed	49	176	852
Cotton (ginned)	1,465	4,938	14,522
Machinery and transport equipment	518	90	864
Miscellaneous manufactured articles	479	101	2,280
Cotton yarn and fabrics	132	16	1,945
Total (incl. others)	7,837	25,351	72,822

PRINCIPAL TRADING PARTNERS (million francs CFA)

Imports	1982	1983	1984
Austria	1,629.0	1,212.7	2,967.7
Belgium and Luxembourg	6,713.6	1,819.1	4,978.7
Brazil	1,340.9	116.1	4,055.8
China, People's Republic	9,385.0	6,950.6	6,768.6
Côte d'Ivoire	1,444.3	1,153.1	2,736.7
France	37,530.4	29,976.6	31,183.5
Germany, Federal Republic	8,566.9	5,389.2	2,962.4
Ghana	1,545.9	2,936.4	2,665.5
India	6,762.3	2,462.2	1,723.1
Italy	5,618.6	5,028.9	3,487.0
Japan	8,540.1	4,759.7	5,038.7
Netherlands	11,704.2	7,188.8	8,472.3
Nigeria	3,831.8	1,711.3	5,215.3
Senegal	1,887.3	1,207.9	1,595.9
Spain	1,400.4	2,052.8	2,286.0
Taiwan	2,022.7	1,535.9	1,394.6
USSR	1,375.9	1,148.4	450.7
United Kingdom	18,758.1	13,704.6	15,058.4
USA	8,030.3	4,888.6	6,321.9
Total (incl. others)	152,552.5	112,032.4	125,902.6

BENIN   Statistical Survey

Exports	1982	1983	1984
Belgium and Luxembourg	24.3	438.7	1,419.2
China, People's Republic	n.a.	n.a.	1,749.0
France	1,130.9	1,644.8	3,625.7
Germany, Federal Republic	604.1	321.9	5,460.9
Greece	n.a.	140.0	706.2
Italy	46.0	127.7	1,412.9
Japan	969.3	2,507.2	1,354.5
Netherlands	1,723.4	5,727.1	25,608.9
Niger	797.5	944.0	265.7
Nigeria	867.8	420.6	965.6
Portugal	n.a.	n.a.	3,216.5
Spain	n.a.	n.a.	8,267.4
Togo	146.8	304.7	2,010.8
United Kingdom	545.7	481.5	2,387.2
USA	n.a.	10,636.0	12,834.1
Total (incl. others)	7,837.5	25,351.1	72,822.0

Transport

RAILWAYS (traffic)

	1985	1986	1987
Passenger-km (million)	150	167	120
Freight ton-km (million)	179	186	191

Source: UN Economic Commission for Africa, *African Statistical Yearbook*.

ROAD TRAFFIC ('000 motor vehicles in use at 31 December)

	1985	1986	1987
Passenger cars	25	25	26
Commercial vehicles	12	12	13

Source: UN Economic Commission for Africa, *African Statistical Yearbook*.

INTERNATIONAL SEA-BORNE SHIPPING
(freight traffic at Cotonou, '000 metric tons)

	1986	1987	1988
Goods loaded	137.1	172.7	95.2
Goods unloaded	1,030.1	1,094.7	1,094.1

Source: Banque Centrale des Etats de l'Afrique de l'Ouest.

CIVIL AVIATION (traffic on scheduled services)*

	1983	1984	1985
Kilometres flown (million)	2.0	1.9	2.1
Passengers carried ('000)	80	80	86
Passenger-km (million)	211	211	235
Freight ton-km (million)	18.7	17.4	18.4

* Including an apportionment of the traffic of Air Afrique.
Source: UN, *Statistical Yearbook*.

Tourism

	1985	1986	1987
Estimated tourist arrivals ('000)	48	48	48

Source: UN Economic Commission for Africa, *African Statistical Yearbook*.

Communications Media

	1985	1986	1987
Radio receivers ('000 in use)	300	310	325
Television receivers ('000 in use)	15	16	17
Daily newspapers			
Number	n.a.	1	n.a.
Circulation ('000 copies)	n.a.	1	n.a.

Telephones (1987): 23,000 in use.
Books (1978): 13 titles (18,000 copies) produced.
Source: mainly UNESCO, *Statistical Yearbook*.

Education

(1987/88)

	Schools	Teachers	Pupils		
			Males	Females	Total
Pre-primary	334	722	7,513	5,937	13,450
Primary	2,850	15,319	312,650	158,366	471,016
Secondary:					
general	151	2,711	64,863	25,321	90,184
vocational	33	687	4,196	2,683	6,879
Higher	13	1,110	8,519	1,593	10,112

Source: Ministère des Enseignements Moyens et Supérieur, Cotonou.

Directory

The Constitution

On 25 February 1990 a national conference of the 'Active Forces of the Nation' voted to repeal the *Loi Fondamentale* that was adopted in August 1977. A new constitution was approved in a national referendum on 2 December 1990.

The Constitution of the Republic of Benin guarantees the basic rights and freedoms of citizens. The functions of the principal organs of state are delineated therein.

The principle of a ruling party was abolished. The President of the Republic was to be elected, by direct universal suffrage, for a period of five years, renewable only once. The Executive was to be responsible to the Legislature, which was, similarly, to be directly elected. The principle of an independent judiciary was established.

The Government

HEAD OF STATE

President: MATHIEU KEREKOU (assumed office 27 October 1972; elected President 5 February 1980; re-elected 31 July 1984 and 2 August 1989).

TRANSITIONAL GOVERNMENT
(December 1990)

Prime Minister and Minister of Defence: NICÉPHORE SOGLO.
Minister of Finance: IDELPHONSE LEMON.
Minister of Foreign Affairs and Co-operation: THÉOPHILE NATA.
Minister of the Interior, Public Security and Territorial Administration: FLORENTIN FELIHO.
Minister of Justice and Legislation: YVES YEHOUESSI.
Minister of National Education: PAULIN HOUNTONDJI.
Minister of Public Health: VÉRONIQUE LAWSON.
Minister of Labour and Social Affairs: VÉRONIQUE AHOYO.
Minister of Planning and Statistics: PAUL DOSSOU.
Minister of Equipment and Transport: EUSTACHE SARRE.
Minister of Information and Communications: TOUSSAINT TCHITCHI.
Minister of Industry, Energy and Public Enterprises: FATIOU ADEKOUNTE.
Minister of Trade, Crafts and Tourism: RICHARD ADJAHO.
Minister of Rural Development and Co-operative Action: ADAMOU N'DIAYE.
Minister of Culture, Youth and Sports: KARIM DRAMANE.

MINISTRIES

Office of the President: BP 2028, Cotonou; tel. 30-00-90; telex 5222.
Office of the Prime Minister: Cotonou.
Ministry of Culture, Youth and Sports: BP 65, Porto-Novo; tel. 21-24-30.
Ministry of Defence: BP 2028, Cotonou; tel. 30-00-90; telex 5222.
Ministry of Equipment and Transport: Cotonou; tel. 31-46-64.
Ministry of Finance: BP 302, Cotonou; tel. 31-40-53; telex 5009.
Ministry of Foreign Affairs and Co-operation: BP 318, Cotonou; tel. 30-04-00; telex 5200.
Ministry of Industry, Energy and Public Enterprises: Cotonou.
Ministry of Information and Communications: BP 180, Cotonou; tel. 31-43-34; telex 5208.
Ministry of the Interior, Public Security and Territorial Administration: Cotonou; tel. 30-11-06.
Ministry of Justice and Legislation: BP 967, Cotonou; tel. 31-31-46.
Ministry of Labour and Social Affairs: BP 907, Cotonou; tel. 31-31-12.
Ministry of National Education: Cotonou; tel. 30-06-81.
Ministry of Planning and Statistics: BP 342, Cotonou; tel. 30-05-41; telex 5252.
Ministry of Public Health: BP 882, Cotonou; tel. 31-26-70.
Ministry of Rural Development and Co-operative Action: BP 34, Porto-Novo; tel. 21-30-53.
Ministry of Trade, Crafts and Tourism: BP 2037, Cotonou; tel. 31-52-58.

Legislature

HAUT CONSEIL DE LA RÉPUBLIQUE

In March 1990 an interim, 27-member Haut conseil de la République (HCR) assumed the functions of the Assemblé nationale révolutionnaire, whose dissolution had been decreed in February by the national conference of the 'Active Forces of the Nation'. A new legislative body was to be elected, by direct universal suffrage, in early 1991.

President of the Haut conseil de la République: Rt Rev. ISIDORE DE SOUZA.

Political Organizations

Beginning in early 1990, a number of opposition leaders, exiled since the time of Kerekou's accession to power, returned to Benin. In April of that year the political bureau of the ruling Parti de la révolution populaire du Bénin (PRPB) voted to dissolve the party. A law was promulgated in August 1990 that allowed for the registration of opposition parties. Accordingly, by October of that year 24 organizations had been accorded official status. It was believed that at least 16 other opposition movements had declined to apply for, or had been refused, official status. Among the first parties to be established in Benin in the aftermath of the December 1989 political changes were:

Union des forces du progrès (UFP): Cotonou; f. May 1990 to succeed the PRPB; Sec.-Gen. GUISSOU MATIOVI.

Rassemblement des forces démocratiques (RFD): f. 1990 as a united front comprising the following parties:

  Mouvement républicain démocratique (MRD): Leader JOSEPH KÉKÉ.

  Parti républicain du Dahomey (PRD)*.

  Rassemblement démocratique dahoméen (RDD)*: Leader HUBERT MAGA.

  Union démocratique du Dahomey (UDD)*: Leader JUSTIN AHOMADEGBÉ.

  Union national pour la démocratie et le progrès (UNDP)*: Leader Dr EMILE-DERLIN ZINSOU.

* Founder member of the RFD.

In late 1990 the Parti communiste dahoméen (PCD), led by FIDEL QUENUM, remained in official exile in Paris; representatives of the PCD were, however, resident in Benin at that time.

Diplomatic Representation

EMBASSIES IN BENIN

Algeria: Les Cocotiers, BP 1809, Cotonou; tel. 30-04-54; telex 5030; Ambassador: HANAFI OUSSEDIK.
Bulgaria: BP 7058, Cotonou; tel. 30-03-66; telex 1110; Chargé d'affaires a.i.: PETUR JORDANOV KRASTEV.
Chad: BP 080359, Cotonou; tel. 33-08-51; Chargé d'affaires a.i.: DARKOU AHMAT KALABASSOU.
China, People's Republic: BP 196, Cotonou; tel. 30-12-92; Ambassador: ZHU YOURONG.
Cuba: BP 948, Cotonou; tel. 31-47-92; telex 5277; Ambassador: JOSÉ FELIPE SUÁREZ GÓMEZ.
Egypt: BP 1215, Cotonou; tel. 30-08-42; telex 5274; Ambassador: MOHSEN AMIN KHALIFA.
France: route de l'Aviation, BP 966, Cotonou; tel. 30-08-24; telex 5209; Ambassador: GUY AZAÏS.
Germany: 7 route Inter-Etats, BP 504, Cotonou; tel. 31-29-67; telex 5224; Ambassador: FRITZ HERMANN FLIMM.
Ghana: Les Cocotiers, BP 488, Cotonou; tel. 30-07-46; Ambassador: CHRISTIAN. T. K. QUARSHIE.
Korea, Democratic People's Republic: BP 317, Cotonou; Ambassador: AN GUI-BOK.
Libya: Les Cocotiers, BP 405, Cotonou; tel. 30-04-52; telex 5254; People's Bureau Representative: ALI SAHLI.

BENIN

Niger: derrière Hôtel de la Plage, BP 352, Cotonou; tel. 31-40-30; telex 5005; Ambassador: SALOU YAROH.
Nigeria: blvd de France Marina, BP 2019, Cotonou; tel. 30-11-42; telex 5247; Ambassador: PHILIP B. KOROYE.
USSR: BP 2013, Cotonou; tel. 31-28-34; Ambassador: VALENTIN PAVLOV.
USA: rue Caporal Anani Bernard, BP 2012, Cotonou; tel. 30-17-92; fax 30-19-74; Ambassador: HARRIET WINSAR.
Zaire: BP 130, Cotonou; tel. 30-19-83; Ambassador: (vacant).

Judicial System

The Constitution of December 1990 states that the Judiciary is an organ of state whose authority may counterbalance that of the Executive and of the Legislature. The document provides for a Constitutional Court, a High Court of Justice and a Supreme Court.

President of the Supreme Court: FRÉDÉRIC NOUTAI HOUNDETON.

Religion

According to the 1961 census, 65% of the population held animist beliefs, 15% were Christians (Roman Catholic 12%, Protestant 3%) and 13% Muslims. Since 1975, religious and spiritual cults have been discouraged.

CHRISTIANITY

The Roman Catholic Church

Benin comprises one archdiocese and five dioceses. At 31 December 1988 there were an estimated 760,941 Roman Catholics (about 16.5% of the population), mainly in the south of the country.

Bishops' Conference: Conférence Episcopale du Bénin, Archevêché, BP 491, Cotonou; tel. 30-01-45; Pres. Mgr CHRISTOPHE ADIMOU, Archbishop of Cotonou.

Archbishop of Cotonou: Mgr CHRISTOPHE ADIMOU, Archevêché, BP 491, Cotonou; tel. 30-01-45.

Protestant Church

There are 257 Protestant mission centres with a personnel of about 120.

Eglise protestante méthodiste en République populaire du Bénin: 54 ave Sékou Touré, Carré 206, BP 34, Cotonou; tel. 31-25-20; f. 1843; 62,000 mems (1985); Pres. Rev. HARRY Y. HENRY; Sec. Rev. SAMUEL J. DOSSOU.

The Press

L'Aube Nouvelle: Cotonou; daily.
Bénin-Magazine: BP 1210, Cotonou; monthly; social and economic affairs; circ. 5,000.
Bénin-Presse Information: BP 72, Cotonou; tel. 31-26-55; publ. by Agence Bénin-Presse; weekly.
Bulletin de l'Agence Bénin-Presse: BP 72, Cotonou; tel. 31-26-55; publ. by Agence Bénin-Presse; daily.
La Croix du Bénin: BP 105, Cotonou; tel. 32-11-19; f. 1946; Roman Catholic; fortnightly; Dir BARTHÉLEMY CAKPO ASSOGBA.
La Gazette du Golfe: Carré 961 'J' Etoile Rouge, BP 03-1624, Cotonou; tel. 31-35-58; telex 5053; fax 30-01-99; f. 1987; fortnightly; independent; Dir ISMAËL Y. SOUMANOU; circ. national edn 18,000, international edn 15,000.
Journal Officiel de la République Populaire du Bénin: Porto-Novo; official govt bulletin; fortnightly.
La Nation: BP 1210, Cotonou; tel. 30-08-75; f. 1990, to replace *Ehuzu* as official newspaper; daily; Dir MAURICE CHABI.
Tam Tam-Express: BP 2302, Cotonou; tel. 30-00-11; telex 5324; fax 31-38-09; f. 1988; weekly; independent; Dir DENIS HODONOU; circ. 15,000.

NEWS AGENCIES

Agence Bénin-Presse (ABP): BP 72, Cotonou; tel. 31-26-55; telex 5221; f. 1961; national news agency; section of the Ministry of Information and Communications; Dir BONIFACE AGUEH.

Foreign Bureaux

Informatsionnoye Agentstvo Novosti (IAN) (USSR): 'Les Cocotiers', Lot F-12, BP 968, Cotonou; tel. 30-10-23; Dir V. MIKHAILOV.

Telegrafnoye Agentstvo Sovetskovo Soyuza (TASS) (USSR): Lot 186, Patte d'Oie, BP 928, Cotonou 6; tel. 30-01-33; telex 5204; Correspondent ALEKSANDR PROSVETOV.

Publishers

Imprimerie Industrielle Nouvelle Presse: BP 2572, Cotonou; tel. 33-10-09; telex 1110.

Government Publishing House

Office National d'Edition, de Presse et d'Imprimerie (ONEPI): BP 1210, Cotonou; tel. 30-08-75; f. 1975; Dir-Gen. BONI ZIMÉ MAKO.

Radio and Television

According to UNESCO, there were an estimated 325,000 radio sets and 17,000 television receivers in use in 1987.

Office de Radiodiffusion et de Télévision du Bénin: BP 366, Cotonou; tel. 31-20-41; telex 5132; state-owned; radio programmes in French, English and 18 local languages; TV transmissions 25 hours weekly; Dir-Gen. NICOLAS BENON; Dir of Radio MARIE-CONSTANCE EGBO-GLELE; Dir of TV MICHÈLE BADAROU.

Finance

(cap. = capital; res = reserves; m. = million; br. = branch; amounts in francs CFA)

BANKING

Central Bank

Banque Centrale des Etats de l'Afrique de l'Ouest (BCEAO): route de Lomé, BP 325, Cotonou; tel. 31-24-66; telex 5211; fax 31-24-65; br. in Parakou; headquarters in Dakar, Senegal; f. 1955; bank of issue for the seven states of the Union monétaire ouest-africaine (UMOA), comprising Benin, Burkina Faso, Côte d'Ivoire, Mali, Niger, Senegal and Togo; cap. and res 217,441m. (Sept. 1989); Gov. (vacant); Dir in Benin GILBERT MEDJE; br. at Parakou.

Two state-owned banks, Banque Béninoise pour le Développement and Banque Commerciale du Bénin, entered receivership in 1989.

Commercial Banks

Bank of Africa–Benin: blvd de France, BP 8, Cotonou; tel. 31-32-28; telex 5079; f. 1990; cap. 1,000m.; Pres. GATIEN HOUNGBEDJI; Dir-Gen. PAUL DERREUMAUX.
Banque Internationale du Bénin: Cotonou; f. 1989 by private Beninois and Nigerian interests; cap. 1,000m.
Ecobank-Bénin: BP 1280, Cotonou; f. 1989; subsidiary of Ecobank Transnational Inc (see ECOWAS, p. 133); Dir-Gen. PETER GRAHAM BATES.
Financial Bank: rue du Commandant Decoeur, BP 2700, Cotonou; tel. 31-31-00; telex 5280; fax 31-31-02; f. 1988; cap. 1,000m.; Pres. CHARLES BAYSSET; Dir-Gen. REMY BAYSSET.

INSURANCE

Société Nationale d'Assurances et de Réassurance (SONAR): Lot 11, Les Cocotiers, BP 2030, Cotonou; tel. 30-16-49; telex 5231; fax 30-09-84; f. 1974; state-owned; cap. 300m.; Pres. ANTOINE URSULE CAKPO; Dir-Gen. MATHIEU-AIMÉ LAWSON.

Trade and Industry

DEVELOPMENT ORGANIZATIONS

Caisse Centrale de Coopération Economique (CCCE): blvd de France, BP 38, Cotonou; tel. 31-35-80; telex 5082; fax 31-20-18; Dir HENRI PHILIPPE DE CLERCQ.

Mission de Coopération et d'Action Culturelle (Mission Française d'Aide et de Coopération): BP 476, Cotonou; tel. 30-08-24; telex 5209; centre for administering bilateral aid from France according to the co-operation agreement signed in Feb. 1975; Dir BERNARD HADJADJ.

MARKETING BOARDS

Office National du Bois (ONAB): BP 1238, Cotonou; tel. 33-16-32; telex 5160; f. 1983; forest development and marketing of wood products; cap. 300m. francs CFA; Man. Dir GABRIEL LOKOUN.

Société Béninoise des Matériaux de Construction (SOBEMAC): BP 1209, Cotonou; tel. 31-25-93; telex 5262; f. 1975; cap. 100m.

francs CFA; state-owned; monopoly of cement marketing; Pres. MAMOUD MOUSTAPHA SOULE; Man. Dir RENÉ DOSSA MEGNIHO.

Société Nationale de Commercialisation et d'Exportation du Bénin (SONACEB): BP 933, Cotonou; tel. 31-28-22; telex 5248; f. 1972; monopoly of internal marketing of all agricultural produce except palm products, cotton and tobacco; monopoly of cement exports; Pres. ARMAND ALAPINI; Man. Dir POLYCARPE AGOSSA.

Société Nationale de Commercialisation des Produits Pétroliers (SONACOP): ave d'Ornano, BP 245, Cotonou; tel. 31-22-90; telex 5245; f. 1974; cap. 1,500m. francs CFA; state-owned; importer and distributor of petroleum products; Pres. RICHARD ADJAHO; Man. Dir EDMOND-PIERRE AMOUSSOU.

Société Nationale pour le Développement des Fruits et Légumes (SONAFEL): BP 2040, Cotonou; tel. 31-52-34; telex 5031; headquarters at Bohicon; f. 1975; cap. 50m. francs CFA; state-owned; monopoly of export of fruit and vegetable produce; Man. Dir JOACHIM PHILIPPE D'ALMEIDA.

Société Nationale pour la Promotion Agricole (SONAPRA): BP 933, Cotonou; tel. 33-08-20; telex 5248; f. 1983; cap. 500m. francs CFA; state-owned; distribution of fertilizers, marketing of agricultural products; Pres. VALENTIN AGBO; Dir-Gen. PATRICE DOFONSOU GBEGBELEGBE.

Société Nationale d'Equipement (SONAE): BP 2042, Cotonou; tel. 31-31-26; telex 5201; f. 1975; cap. 300m. francs CFA; state-owned; import and export of capital goods; Pres. CÉLESTIN ZEKPA; Man. Dir NICOLAS ADAGBE.

CHAMBER OF COMMERCE

Chambre de Commerce, d'Agriculture et d'Industrie de la République Populaire du Bénin (CCIB): ave du Général de Gaulle, BP 31, Cotonou; tel. 31-32-99; Pres. RAFFET LOKO; Vice-Pres. J.-V. ADJOVI, M. T. LALEYE; Sec.-Gen. N. A. VIADENOU.

EMPLOYERS' ORGANIZATIONS

Association des Syndicats du Bénin (ASYNBA): Cotonou; Pres. PIERRE FOURN.

Groupement Interprofessionnel des Entreprises du Bénin (GIBA): BP 6, Cotonou; Pres. A. JEUKENS.

Syndicat des Commerçants Importateurs et Exportateurs du Bénin: BP 6, Cotonou; Pres. M. BENCHIMOL.

Syndicat Interprofessionnel des Entreprises Industrielles du Bénin: Cotonou; Pres. M. DOUCET.

Syndicat National des Commerçants et Industriels Africains du Bénin (SYNACIB): BP 367, Cotonou; Pres. URBAIN DA SILVA.

Syndicat des Transporteurs Routiers du Bénin: Cotonou; Pres. PASCAL ZENON.

STATE ENTERPRISES

In 1987, under a programme to rationalize the public sector, studies began on the future of 11 state-owned enterprises, including ONPB, AGB, La Béninoise and a number of transport organizations, with a view to their rehabilitation or liquidation.

Société Agro-Animale Bénino-Arabe-Libyenne (SABLI): BP 03-1200, Cotonou; tel. 31-19-50; telex 5353; f. 1979; cap. 1,112m. francs CFA; 51% state-owned, 49% by Libya; poultry and poultry products; Man. Dir SALÉ IMOROU.

Société d'Alimentation Générale du Bénin (AGB): 21 route de Porto-Novo, BP 53, Cotonou; tel. 33-07-28; telex 5062; f. 1978; cap. 300m. francs CFA; 100% state-owned; monopoly importer and distributor of basic foodstuffs, drink and tobacco; chain of 23 supermarkets and 3 wholesale stores; Man. Dir CHRISTOPHE YEBE SEMAKO.

Société Bénino-Arabe-Libyenne des Mines (BELIMINES): BP 1913, Cotonou; tel. 31-59-24; telex 5128; f. 1979; cap. US $2m.; 51% state-owned, 49% owned by Govt of Libya; mining, processing and marketing of marble; Pres. ANDRÉ YORO; Man. Dir HASSAN A. RAGHI.

Société Bénino-Arabe-Libyenne de Pêche Maritime (BELI-PECHE): BP 1516, Cotonou; tel. 31-51-36; f. 1977; cap. US $5m.; 51% state-owned, 49% owned by Govt. of Libya; fish and fish products; Pres. LAURENT FAGBOHOUN; Dir SALEH AREIBI.

Société Béninoise d'Electricité et d'Eau (SBEE): BP 123, Cotonou; tel. 31-24-10; telex 5207; fax 31-30-70; f. 1973; cap. 3,000m. francs CFA; 100% state-owned; production and distribution of electricity and water; Man. Dir EMILE LOUIS PARAÏSO.

Société Béninoise de Palmier à Huile (SOBEPALH): ave Victor Regis, BP 12, Porto-Novo; tel. 21-29-03; f. 1961, nationalized 1975; cap. 425m. francs CFA; 100% state-owned; production of palm oil and cottonseed oil; refineries at Mono, Hinvy and Agonvy; Man. Dir MARIUS KOKOU QUENUM.

Société des Ciments d'Onigbolo (SCO): Onigbolo; f. 1975; cap. 6,000m. francs CFA; 51% state-owned, 43% owned by Govt of Nigeria; production and marketing of cement; Pres. JUSTIN GNIDEHOU; Man. Dir R. J. K. FRYMANN.

Société de Fabrication des Portes Isolantes (SFPI): route Inter-Etats, quartier Agbocodji, Godomey, BP 2420, Cotonou; f. 1984; cap. 125m. francs CFA; 51% state-owned; Pres. RODOLPHE DAIZO; Man. Dir JACQUES LEDUE.

Société Nationale de Boissons (La Béninoise): route de Porto-Novo, BP 135, Cotonou; tel. 33-10-61; telex 5275; fax 33-01-48; f. 1957, nationalized 1975; cap. 3,200m. francs CFA; production and marketing of beer, soft drinks and ice; Pres. BARNABÉ BIDOUZO; Dir-Gen. MANASSÉ AYAYI.

Société Nationale de Construction et de Travaux Publics (SONACOTRAP): BP 286, Cotonou; tel. 30-15-35; f. 1976; cap. 200m. francs CFA; Dir-Gen. THÉODORE AHOUSSOU.

Société Nationale d'Irrigation et d'Aménagement Hydro-Agricole (SONIAH): BP 312, Porto-Novo; tel. 21-34-20; f. 1972; cap. 350m. francs CFA; development of irrigation and rice-growing projects; Dir-Gen. YENAKPONDJI CAPOCHICHI; Sec.-Gen. TOSSA JÉRÔME TONI.

Société Nationale pour l'Industrie des Corps Gras (SONICOG): BP 312, Cotonou; tel. 33-06-41; telex 5205; f. 1962; cap. 2,555m. francs CFA; 100% state-owned; production of palm oil, palm kernel and groundnut oils and cakes, shea (karité) butter and soaps; Dir-Gen. BENJAMIN K. SOUDE.

TRADE UNIONS

Union Nationale des Syndicats des Travailleurs du Bénin (UNSTB): BP 69, Cotonou; tel. 31-56-13; telex 5200; f. 1974 as the sole officially-recognized trade union, incorporating all pre-existing trade union organizations; announced plans in Oct. 1989 to sever all links with the PRPB; Sec.-Gen. AMIDOU LAWANI.

Syndicat National de l'Enseignement Supérieur (SNES): Cotonou; withdrew from UNSTB in Aug. 1989; Sec.-Gen. LÉOPOLD DOSSOU.

Transport

RAILWAYS

In 1987 the network handled 444,000 metric tons of goods. Plans for a 650-km extension, linking Parakou to Niamey (Niger), via Gaya, were postponed in the late 1980s, owing to lack of finance.

Organisation Commune Bénin-Niger des Chemins de Fer et des Transports (OCBN): BP 16, Cotonou; tel. 31-33-80; telex 5210; fax 31-41-50; f. 1959; 50% owned by Govt of Benin, 50% by Govt of Niger; total of 579 track-km; main line runs for 438 km from Cotonou to Parakou in the interior; br. line runs westward via Ouidah to Sègboroué (34 km); also line of 107 km from Cotonou via Porto-Novo to Pobè near the Nigerian border; Dir-Gen. A. TAMOU-TABE.

ROADS

In 1985 there were 7,445 km of classified roads, including 3,359 km of main roads and 596 km of secondary roads. About 11% of the network was paved. The roads along the coast and those from Cotonou to Bohicon and from Parakou to Malanville, a total of 700 km, are bitumen-surfaced. A major highways rehabilitation project was announced in May 1987 as part of a wider transport infrastructure programme. Construction of a road linking Parakou with Djougou and Natitingou, with financial aid from multilateral agencies, was to begin in 1991. The road is the first phase of a highway that is intended ultimately to link Benin with Burkina Faso and Togo.

Compagnie de Transit et de Consignation du Bénin (CTCB Express): route de l'Aéroport, BP 7079, Cotonou; f. 1986; cap. 100m. francs CFA; Pres. SOULÉMAN KOURA ZOUMAROU.

Société des Transports Routiers du Bénin (TRANS-BENIN): BP 703, Cotonou; tel. 31-32-28; f. 1977; cap. 300m. francs CFA; 49% state-owned; passenger and goods transport; Man. Dir PROSPER DJIDJOHO.

SHIPPING

The main port is at Cotonou. In 1987 the port handled 1,267,400 metric tons of goods, of which 296,500 tons were from Niger, 18,300 tons from Mali and 5,500 tons from Burkina Faso. A total of 1,189,300 tons was handled in 1988.

Capacity was 2m. metric tons in 1986. Further improvements were to be carried out under the transport infrastructure rehabilitation project announced in May 1987, with finance from France and multilateral agencies and with a loan from the Islamic Development Bank, announced in March 1988.

Association des Professionnels Agréés en Douanes du Bénin (APRAD): BP 2141, Cotonou; tel. 31-55-05; telex 5355; Chair. GATIEN HOUNGBEDJI.

Cie Béninoise de Navigation Maritime (COBENAM): BP 2032, Cotonou; tel. 31-27-96; telex 5225; f. 1974; cap. 500m. francs CFA; 51% state-owned, 49% by Algeria; Pres. ABDER KADER ALLAL; Man. Dir ADAMOU LAFIA.

Delmas—Bénin: place des Martyrs, BP 213, Cotonou; tel. 30-07-69; telex 5308; fax 30-06-90; f. 1986; cap. 100m. francs CFA; Pres. PATRICE VIELJEUX; Dir ALEXIS AHOUANSOU.

Office Béninois des Manutentions Portuaires (OBEMAP): place des Martyrs, BP 35, Cotonou; tel. 31-39-83; telex 5135; cap. 500m. francs CFA; state-owned; Pres. GEORGES SEKLOKA; Man. Dir PAULIN DJAKPO.

Port Autonome de Cotonou: BP 927, Cotonou; tel. 31-28-90; telex 5004; f. 1965; cap. 16,577m. francs CFA; state-owned; Man. Dir ODON BRICE HOUNCANRIN.

CIVIL AVIATION

The international airport at Cotonou has a 2.4-km runway, and there are secondary airports at Parakou, Natitingou, Kandi and Abomey. There were 86,000 passengers at Cotonou in 1985.

Air Afrique: ave du Gouverneur Ballot, BP 200, Cotonou; tel. 31-21-07; fax 31-53-41; see under Côte d'Ivoire; Dir in Benin JOSEPH KANZA.

Tourism

Benin's national parks and game reserves are its principal tourist attractions. About 48,000 tourists visited Benin in 1987.

Office National du Tourisme et de l'Hôtellerie (ONATHO): BP 89, Cotonou; tel. 31-26-87; telex 5032; f. 1974; state tourist agency; Dir CLÉMENT LOKOSSOU.

Société Béninoise pour la Promotion du Tourisme (SBPT): BP 1508, Cotonou; tel. 30-05-84; telex 5143; f. 1986.

BHUTAN

Introductory Survey

Location, Climate, Language, Religion, Flag, Capital

The Kingdom of Bhutan lies in the Himalaya range of mountains, with the People's Republic of China to the north and India to the south. Average monthly temperature ranges from 4.4°C (40°F) in January to 17°C (62°F) in July. Rainfall is heavy, ranging from 150 cm (60 inches) to 300 cm (120 inches) per year. The official language is Dzongkha, spoken mainly in western Bhutan. Written Dzongkha is based on the Tibetan script. The state religion is Mahayana Buddhism, mainly the Drukpa school of the Kagyupa sect, although Nepali settlers, who comprise about one-quarter of the country's total population, practise Hinduism. The Nepali-speaking Hindus dominate southern Bhutan and are referred to as southern Bhutanese. The national flag (proportions 5 by 4) is divided diagonally from the lower hoist to the upper fly, so forming two triangles, one orange and the other maroon, with a white dragon superimposed in the centre. The capital is Thimphu.

Recent History

The first hereditary King of Bhutan was installed on 17 December 1907. An Anglo-Bhutanese Treaty, signed in 1910, placed Bhutan's foreign relations under the supervision of the Government of British India. After India became independent, that treaty was replaced in August 1949 by the Indo-Bhutan Treaty of Friendship, whereby Bhutan agrees to seek the advice of the Government of India with regard to its foreign relations, but remains free to decide whether or not to accept such advice. King Jigme Dorji Wangchuk, installed in 1952, established the National Assembly (Tshogdu) in 1953 and a Royal Advisory Council in 1965. He formed the country's first Cabinet in May 1968. He died in July 1972 and was succeeded by the Western-educated 16-year-old Crown Prince, Jigme Singye Wangchuk. The new King stated his wish to maintain the Indo-Bhutan Treaty and further to strengthen friendship with India. In 1979, however, during the Non-Aligned Conference and later at the UN General Assembly, Bhutan voted in opposition to India, in favour of Chinese policy. In December 1983 India and Bhutan made a new trade agreement concerning overland trade with Bangladesh and Nepal. India raised no objection to Bhutan's decision to negotiate directly with the People's Republic of China over the Bhutan-China border, and discussions were begun in April 1984. At the seventh round of negotiations, held in Thimphu in August 1990, further progress was made when the two sides, having agreed on the 'guiding principles' towards the demarcation of the border during the fifth round in 1988, expressed their sincere hopes that the border issue would be peaceably settled in the near future.

When Chinese authority was established in Tibet (Xizang) in 1959, Bhutan granted asylum to more than 6,000 Tibetan refugees. As a result of the discovery that many refugees were engaged in spying and subversive activities, the Bhutan Government decided in 1976 to disperse them in small groups, introducing a number of Bhutanese families into each settlement. In early 1978 discussions with the Dalai Lama, the spiritual leader of Tibet, collapsed after four years. In June 1979 the National Assembly approved a directive establishing the end of the year as a time-limit for the refugees to decide whether to acquire Bhutanese citizenship or accept repatriation to Tibet. In October India announced that it would not be able to accept refugees who refused Bhutanese nationality as there were still about 10,000 Tibetans in India who were awaiting rehabilitation. By September 1985, however, most of the Tibetans had chosen Bhutanese citizenship, and the remainder were to be accepted by India. A revised Citizenship Act, adopted by the National Assembly in 1985, set residence in Bhutan in 1958 as a fundamental basis for automatic citizenship, but this was to be flexibly interpreted.

In mid-1988, in an apparent reversal of his earlier policy of ethnic integration, the King initiated a programme of Driglam Namza, a revival of Bhutanese (Drukpa) identity and culture, which was to be applied to both Nepali and Drukpa alike. The programme included enforcing the wearing of traditional garb by all Bhutanese when they appear in public, forbidding the teaching of Nepali in schools, limiting the number of foreign visitors, making certain holy places inaccessible to tourists, discontinuing the admission of television broadcasts from India, and stopping the issuing of work permits for non-nationals. Those who failed to comply would be subject to a fine and imprisonment for a month. This programme was strongly opposed by Bhutan's population of Nepali-speaking Hindus, who have been migrating from Nepal to Bhutan's fertile lowlands since the late 19th century (although immigration from Nepal has been banned since 1958, it has, nevertheless, continued unabated). In 1990 ethnic unrest became apparent when a group of Nepali students founded the outlawed Bhutan People's Party (BPP), which, because of its illegal status, was based in Kathmandu in Nepal. In September the BPP, with the support of thousands of southern Bhutanese villagers and Nepalese who marched in from across the Indian border, organized demonstrations in at least nine border towns in southern Bhutan to protest against domination by the indigenous Buddhist Drukpa and to demand the introduction of a multi-party democracy, basic freedoms, a greater role in the country's political and economic life, and a change to a constitutional (rather than absolute) monarchy. The BPP claimed that more than 300 protestors had been killed by the security forces, but was unable to substantiate its claim. The Bhutanese authorities, on the other hand, announced that only one person had been killed, and accused the BPP of being a terrorist organization and its supporters of being 'anti-nationals'. Two other illegal pro-democracy groups that were established in 1989–90 (with their bases also in Kathmandu) were the People's Forum for Human Rights and the United Liberation People's Front. Schools and bridges have become principal targets for arson and looting in the anti-Government campaign of intimidation and violence, directed by the disaffected ethnic Nepalese in Bhutan. All of the schools in southern Bhutan were closed indefinitely from the end of September, in response to threats to the lives of teachers and students' families.

Bhutan has asserted itself as a fully sovereign, independent state, becoming a member of the UN in 1971 and of the Non-Aligned Movement in 1973. By 1990 Bhutan had established diplomatic relations with 16 countries, and maintained diplomatic missions at the UN in New York and Geneva, in New Delhi, Dhaka and Kuwait (the last-mentioned mission was closed in August 1990, following Iraq's invasion of Kuwait).

In 1983 Bhutan was an enthusiastic founder-member of the South Asian Regional Co-operation (SARC) organization, with Bangladesh, India, Maldives, Nepal, Pakistan and Sri Lanka. In May 1985 Bhutan was host to the first meeting of ministers of foreign affairs from SARC member countries, which agreed to give their grouping the formal title of South Asian Association for Regional Co-operation (SAARC, see p. 225).

Government

Bhutan is an absolute monarchy, without a written constitution. The system of government is unusual in that power is shared by the monarchy (assisted by the Royal Advisory Council), the Council of Ministers, the National Assembly (Tshogdu) and the Head Abbot (Je Khempo) of Bhutan's 3,000–4,000 Buddhist monks. The National Assembly, which serves a three-year term, has 151 members, including 106 directly elected by adult suffrage. Ten seats in the Assembly are reserved for religious bodies, while the remainder are occupied by officials, ministers and members of the Royal Advisory Council.

Defence

The strength of the Royal Bhutanese Army, which is under the direct command of the King, is 5,000. Army training facilities are provided by an Indian military training team. Although India is not directly responsible for the country's defence, the Indian Government has indicated that any act of aggression against Bhutan would be regarded as an act of aggression against India. Part-time militia training for senior school pupils and government officials was instituted in 1989.

BHUTAN

Economic Affairs

In terms of average income, Bhutan is one of the poorest countries in the world. In 1987, according to estimates by the World Bank, the kingdom's gross national product (GNP), measured at average 1985–87 prices, was US $202m., equivalent to about $150 per head. It was, however, estimated that GNP per head increased, in real terms, by 10.6% in 1987, one of the highest growth rates in the world. During 1980–88, the population increased by an annual average of 2.1%. The average annual increase of gross domestic product (GDP), in real terms, was estimated at 6.4% during the period of the Fifth Development Plan (1981–86).

Agriculture (including livestock and forestry) contributed 44.2% of GDP in 1988. More than 90% of the labour force were employed in agriculture in 1989. The principal sources of revenue in the agricultural sector in 1987 were fruit products, oranges, rosin and cardamom. Timber production is also important.

Industry (including mining, manufacturing, electricity and construction) employed only about 1% of the labour force in 1981/82, but contributed 24.4% of GDP in 1988. The production of low-cost electricity by the Chukha hydroelectric project (see below) was expected to help to stimulate growth in the industrial sector.

Mining contributed only 0.8% of GDP in 1988. Talc powder was the major mineral export in 1983. Gypsum, coal, limestone, slate and dolomite are also mined.

Manufacturing contributed 5.7% of GDP in 1988. The most important sector is cement production. Commercial production began at a calcium carbide plant at Pasakha, near Phuntsholing, in June 1988. Bhutan also has some small-scale manufacturers, producing, for example, textiles, soap, matches, candles and carpets.

Energy is derived principally from hydroelectric power. The Chukha hydroelectric project, with a generating capacity of about 338 MW, was formally inaugurated in October 1988. In 1983 the cost of imports of diesel fuel was more than US $4m.

In the financial year ending 30 June 1989 Bhutan recorded a visible trade deficit of an estimated Nu 744.3m., and there was a deficit of an estimated Nu 967.4m. on the current account of the balance of payments. In 1986 the principal source of imports (86%) was India, which was also the principal market for exports (99%). The principal exports in 1983 were cement, talc powder and fruit products. Exports of electric energy to India commenced in 1988, with the inauguration of the Chukha hydroelectric project. The principal imports in 1983 were aircraft, diesel fuel and rice.

In 1988/89 there was an estimated budgetary surplus of Nu 163.5m. Bhutan's total outstanding foreign debt was US $73.6m. at the beginning of July 1990. Debt-service repayments amounted to $6.8m. in 1989/90. For 1988/89, grants from the Government of India provided 23.3% of total budgetary revenue, and direct grants from international agencies amounted to 8.3%.

Bhutan is a member of the South Asian Association for Regional Co-operation (SAARC, see p. 225), which seeks to improve regional co-operation, particularly in economic development.

Nine major policy objectives were declared in the Sixth Development Plan (1987–92): the strengthening of government administration (including the continued campaign against corruption and nepotism), the preservation and promotion of national identity, the mobilization of internal resources, the enhancement of rural incomes, the improvement of rural housing and resettlement, the consolidation and improvement of services, the development of human resources, the promotion of popular participation in the formulation and execution of development plans and strategies, and the promotion of national self reliance. Considerable emphasis was also placed on the formulation of a strategy for the rapid expansion of export-oriented industries.

Social Welfare

At the end of 1988 there were 28 hospitals (including five leprosy hospitals), with a total of 932 beds (one for every 1,480 inhabitants), and there were 142 doctors (one for every 9,700 inhabitants) and 674 paramedics working in the country. Because of a shortage of medical personnel and a lack of funds, local dispensaries are being converted into basic health units (of which there were 69 in 1988), providing basic medical services. Malaria and tuberculosis are still widespread. The budget for the financial year 1990/91 allocated Nu 78.6m. (3.5% of total projected expenditure) to health.

Education

Education is not compulsory. Primary education begins at six years of age and lasts for six years. Secondary education, beginning at the age of 12, lasts for a further five years, comprising a first cycle of three years and a second cycle of two years. Free education is available, but there are insufficient facilities to accommodate all school-age children. In 1987 a 'shift' system of extended classrooms (ECRs—early primary classes) was introduced as a temporary measure in some primary schools in Thimphu, to accommodate additional children. In 1985 the total enrolment at primary schools was equivalent to an estimated 26% of children in the relevant age-group (31% of boys, 20% of girls), while the comparable ratio for secondary schools was only 5% (boys 7%, girls 2%). All schools are co-educational. English is the language of instruction. Bhutan has no mission or private schools, and all schools are subsidized by the Government. Many Indian teachers are employed. In April 1990 the total number of enrolled pupils was 70,354, and the total number of teachers was 2,625. In 1990 there were more than 200 educational institutions under the supervision of the Department of Education, including 156 primary schools, 21 junior high schools, 10 high schools, one junior college, one degree college, six technical schools, 22 schools for Buddhist studies and monastic schools, two teacher-training institutes and four schools for Tibetan refugees. A number of Bhutanese students were receiving higher education abroad. The 1990/91 budget allocated Nu 157.7m. (7.1% of total projected expenditure) to education. In 1988 the rate of adult illiteracy in Bhutan was about 85%.

Public Holidays

1991 and 1992: The usual Buddhist holidays are observed, as well as the Birthday of HM Jigme Singye Wangchuk (11 November), the movable Hindu feast of Dussehra and the National Day of Bhutan (17 December).

Weights and Measures

The metric system is in operation.

Statistical Survey

Source (unless otherwise stated): Royal Government of Bhutan, Thimphu.

Area and Population

AREA, POPULATION AND DENSITY

Area (sq km)	46,500*
Population (Dec. 1980 census)	931,514†
Population (official estimates at mid-year)	
1986	1,312,700
1987	1,343,600
1988	1,375,400
Density (per sq km) at mid-1988	29.6

* 17,954 sq miles.
† Excluding adjustment for underenumeration.
Capital: Thimphu (estimated population 15,000 at 1 July 1987).

POPULATION OF DISTRICTS*
(mid-1985 estimates, based on 1980 census)

Bumthang	23,842
Chirang	108,807
Dagana	28,352
Gasa†	16,907
Gaylegphug	111,283
Haa	16,715
Lhuntshi	39,635
Mongar	73,239
Paro	46,615
Pema Gatshel	37,141
Punakha†	16,700
Samchi	172,109
Samdrup Jongkhar	73,044
Shemgang	44,516
Tashigang	177,718
Thimphu	58,660
Tongsa	26,017
Wangdiphodrang	47,152
Total rural population	1,119,452
Total urban population	167,823
Total	1,286,275

* The above figures are approximate, and predate the creation of a new district, Chukha, in August 1987. Chukha has an estimated total population of about 13,372 (based on the figure of 3,343 households, with an estimated average of four persons per household), who were formerly included in Samchi, Paro or Thimphu districts.
† Gasa and Punakha were merged into a single district in August 1987.

BIRTHS AND DEATHS (UN estimates, annual averages)

	1975–80	1980–85	1985–90
Birth rate (per 1,000)	40.0	39.0	38.3
Death rate (per 1,000)	19.8	18.1	16.8

Source: UN, *World Population Prospects: 1988*.
Official estimates (Demographic Sample Survey, 1984): Birth rate 39.1 per 1,000; Death rate 19.3 per 1,000.

LIFE EXPECTANCY
45.6 years at birth (1985 estimate).

ECONOMICALLY ACTIVE POPULATION
(estimates, '000 persons, 1981/82)

Agriculture, etc.	613
Industry	6
Trade	9
Public services	22
Total	650

Agriculture

PRINCIPAL CROPS ('000 metric tons)

	1987	1988*	1989*
Rice (paddy)	85	80	83
Wheat	19	16	16
Barley	4	4	4
Maize	85	81	81
Millet	7†	7	8
Other cereals	5	6	6
Potatoes	50	50	53
Other roots and tubers	19	19	20
Pulses	4†	4	4
Vegetables	11†	10	10
Citrus fruit	53	51	55
Other fruits	5	5	5

* FAO estimates.   † Unofficial figure.
Source: FAO, *Production Yearbook*.

LIVESTOCK (FAO estimates, '000 head, year ending September)

	1987	1988	1989
Horses	16	16	16
Mules	9	9	9
Asses	18	18	18
Cattle	395	409	424
Buffaloes	7	7	7
Pigs	62	63	64
Sheep	25	27	30
Goats	30	32	34

Source: FAO, *Production Yearbook*.
1986 ('000 head): Yaks 36; Poultry 211.

LIVESTOCK PRODUCTS (FAO estimates, '000 metric tons)

	1987	1988	1989
Beef and veal	5	5	6
Pigmeat	1	1	1
Other meat	1	1	—
Cows' milk	28	28	28
Buffaloes' milk	2	3	3
Cheese	1.9	1.9	2.0
Butter and ghee	0.5	0.5	0.5
Hens eggs	0.2	0.3	0.3
Cattle and buffalo hides	1.1	1.2	1.2

Source: FAO, *Production Yearbook*.

Forestry

ROUNDWOOD REMOVALS
(FAO estimates, '000 cubic metres, excl. bark)

	1979	1980	1981
Sawlogs, veneer logs and logs for sleepers	240*	240	240
Other industrial wood	38*	38	38
Fuel wood	2,814	2,884	2,946
Total	3,092	3,162	3,224

* Unofficial figure.

1982–88: Annual output as in 1981 (FAO estimates).

Sawnwood production ('000 cubic metres): 5 in 1981; 5 per year (FAO estimates) in 1982–88.

Source: FAO, *Yearbook of Forest Products*.

Logging ('000 cubic metres, year ending 31 March): 149.0 in 1986/87; 135.5 in 1987/88; 77.6 in 1988/89.

Source: Department of Forestry, Ministry of Agriculture.

Fishing

Total catch 1,500 metric tons of freshwater fishes per year.

Mining

	1985	1986	1987
Gypsum (metric tons)	12,000	24,833	15,900
Coal ('000 metric tons)*	30	30	n.a.
Limestone ('000 metric tons)	144	172	n.a.
Slate (sq ft)	540,000	614,152	370,625
Dolomite (metric tons)	162,014	238,533	242,399

* The coal industry was nationalized in 1984.

1988: Slate 300,000 sq ft; Dolomite 196,689 metric tons.

Source: Department of Industries and Mines, Royal Government of Bhutan.

Industry

SELECTED PRODUCTS (year ending 31 March)

	1981/82	1982/83	1983/84
Minerals (metric tons)	136,010	33,188	37,988
Cement (metric tons)	99,008	88,688	169,624
Electric energy (million kWh)	22	24	26

Source: Department of Industries and Mines, Royal Government of Bhutan.

Finance

CURRENCY AND EXCHANGE RATES

Monetary Units
100 chetrum (Ch) = 1 ngultrum (Nu).

Denominations
Coins: 5, 10, 25 and 50 chetrum; 1 ngultrum.
Notes: 1, 2, 5, 10, 20, 50 and 100 ngultrum.

Sterling and Dollar Equivalents (30 September 1990)
£1 sterling = 33.850 ngultrum;
US $1 = 18.068 ngultrum;
1,000 ngultrum = £29.54 = $55.35.

Average Exchange Rate (ngultrum per US $)
1987 12.962
1988 13.917
1989 16.226

Note: The ngultrum is at par with the Indian rupee.

BUDGET (estimates, million ngultrum, year ending 30 June)

Revenue	1988/89	1989/90	1990/91
Internal revenue	805.0	1,188.0	1,211.0
tax	232.0	251.0	250.6
non-tax	480.0	566.0	640.7
Grants from Government of India	564.0	348.0	440.6
Grants from UN and other international agencies	227.0	367.0	466.8
Total	1,596.0	1,903.0	2,118.5

Expenditure	1986/87*†	1987/88‡	1988/89
Public works department (incl. urban development)	163,046	281,485	228,995
Power (excl. Chukha hydroelectric project)	205,218	272,872	145,340
Agriculture and irrigation (incl. Food Corpn of Bhutan)	108,079	123,360	106,880
Education (incl. Royal Institute of Management)	86,436	183,788	125,109
Ministry of Finance	175,555	108,834	138,348
Health	45,910	77,779	75,173
Trade and industry	188,164	328,185	299,680
Geology and mining	1,155	5,009	7,237
Forestry	40,426	57,543	91,593
District administration	106,666	61,339	n.a.
Post and telecommunications	21,923	81,423	63,967
Animal husbandry	15,414	65,547	48,343
Foreign affairs	27,184	44,838	39,281
Police (incl. jail dept)	18,599	25,130	35,085
Planning commission (incl. statistics)	8,707	15,478	4,009
Home affairs (excl. police and dzongkhag administration)	16,141	20,747	19,465
Administration of justice	5,718	9,838	12,376
Civil aviation	1,717	24,641	18,426
Information and broadcasting	70,570	34,888	18,675
Communications and tourism policy unit	906	1,580	n.a.
Special Commission	7,491	13,641	13,114
Central monastic affairs	13,350	21,712	30,144
Other departments	147,810	159,910	n.a.
Total	1,496,005	2,019,567	1,994,274

Revised expenditure figures (million ngultrum): 1,740 (current 775, capital 965) in 1987/88‡; 1,978 (current 909, capital 1,069) in 1988/89; 2,075 (current 1,096, capital 979) in 1989/90; 2,229 (current 1,094, capital 1,135) in 1990/91

1990/91 expenditure by sector (million ngultrum): Finance 195.8, Education 157.7, Housing and works 145.1, Agriculture 181.4, Power 301.1, Roads 199.1, District administration 237.3.

* Revised budget.
† Year ending 31 March.
‡ Figures refer to the 15 months from 1 April 1987 to 30 June 1988.

Source: Budget Bureau, Royal Government of Bhutan.

BHUTAN

Statistical Survey

SIXTH DEVELOPMENT PLAN (1987–92)*
(revised, sectoral allocation of proposed expenditure, million ngultrum)

	Total	% of total
Agriculture and irrigation	880.4	9.2
Food Corpn of Bhutan	106.5	1.1
Animal husbandry	331.0	3.5
Forestry	418.2	4.4
Trade and industry	1,276.1	13.3
Geological Survey of Bhutan	35.3	0.4
Public works	887.2	9.3
Power	1,247.9	13.1
Road transport and aviation	48.8	0.5
Telephones	133.8	1.4
Postal, telegraph and radio services	68.1	0.7
Information and broadcasting	95.9	1.0
Education	778.8	8.1
Health	339.1	3.5
Urban Development Corpn	248.7	2.6
General development	1,973.0	20.6
Druk-Air Corpn	391.0	4.1
Districts (Dzongkhags)	238.5	2.5
Total (incl. others)	**9,559.2**	**100.0**

* All figures are rounded, so totals may not always be the sum of their component parts.

Source: Planning Commission, Royal Government of Bhutan.

FOREIGN EXCHANGE RESERVES (year ending 31 March)

	1986/87	1987/88	1988/89
Indian rupee reserves (million Indian rupees)	446.9	689.0	776.9
Royal Monetary Authority	10.7	12.3	81.1
Bank of Bhutan	436.2	676.9	695.8
Convertible currency reserves (US $ million)	28.1	40.2	50.1
Royal Monetary Authority*	26.9	37.9	47.6
Bank of Bhutan	1.1	2.3	2.5

* Includes tranche position in the International Monetary Fund.

Source: Royal Monetary Authority of Bhutan.

MONEY SUPPLY (million ngultrum at 31 December)

	1987	1988	1989
Currency outside banks*	103.5	149.1	188.1
Demand deposits	213.3	263.0	358.2
Total money	**316.8**	**412.0**	**546.3**

* Including an estimate for Indian rupees.

Source: Royal Monetary Authority of Bhutan.

COST OF LIVING
(Consumer Price Index at 31 December; base: 1979 = 100)

	1987	1988	1989
All items	196.4	215.3	233.6

Source: Central Statistical Office of the Planning Commission.

NATIONAL ACCOUNTS (million ngultrum at current prices)
Gross Domestic Product by Economic Activity

	1986	1987	1988
Agriculture, forestry and livestock	1,399.2	1,623.5	1,746.3
Mining and quarrying	37.4	37.0	33.4
Manufacturing	137.1	204.7	226.5
Electricity*	96.6	377.1	394.6
Construction	267.5	349.9	309.0
Trade, restaurants and hotels	234.1	248.2	258.5
Transport, storage and communications	114.2	126.0	180.6
Finance, insurance and real estate	170.7	210.5	295.1
Community, social and personal services	350.8	416.0	507.8
Sub-total	**2,807.6**	**3,592.8**	**3,951.8**
Less Imputed bank service charges	49.0	62.0	93.7
GDP in purchasers' values	**2,758.6**	**3,530.8**	**3,858.1**
GDP at constant 1983 prices	**1,674.5**	**1,973.1**	**2,038.3**

* Including electricity generated by the Chukha hydroelectric project, which started production in September 1986.

BALANCE OF PAYMENTS (million ngultrum)

	1986/87	1987/88*	1988/89†
Merchandise exports f.o.b.	427.1	711.9	1,072.6
Merchandise imports c.i.f.	−1,205.4	−1,124.2	−1,817.0
Trade balance	**−778.3**	**−412.3**	**−744.3**
Services and transfers:			
Receipts	314.7	288.3	412.2
Payments	−616.0	−511.4	−635.2
Current balance	**−1,079.6**	**−635.3**	**−967.4**
Foreign aid	1,268.8	1,046.6	1,086.3
Net errors and omissions	−3.9	−5.6	229.4
Total (net monetary movements)	**185.3**	**405.7**	**348.3**

* Figures refer to the 15 months from 1 April 1987 to 30 June 1988.
† Preliminary estimates. New fiscal year ending 30 June.

Source: Royal Monetary Authority of Bhutan.

External Trade

SELECTED COMMODITIES (US $'000)

Imports c.i.f.	1982	1983
Aircraft	—	4,219
Diesel fuel	4,041	4,039
Rice	1,743	1,344
Motor cars	1,151	1,100
Metal containers	n.a.	959
Soya-fortified bulgar	n.a.	792

Exports f.o.b.	1982	1983
Cement	3,809	3,516
Talc powder	459	1,428
Fruit products	980	1,095
Rosin	808	870
Cardamom	1,274	798
Sawn timber, coniferous	703	575
Potatoes	943	508

Trade with India (US $'000, 1987): *Imports* Rice 4,020, Iron rods 3,790, Diesel oil 3,470, Tyres and tubes 2,310, Truck chassis 1,800, Machinery parts 1,630; *Exports* Cement 7,940, Timber 9,320, Block boards 2,250, Cardamom 1,700; Fruit products 1,710, Potatoes 1,780.

BHUTAN

PRINCIPAL TRADING PARTNERS
(US $'000, year ending 31 March)

Imports c.i.f.	1986/87	1987/88*	1988/89†
India	70,083	64,633	71,682
Other countries	22,639	16,127	40,268

Exports f.o.b.	1986/87	1987/88*	1988/89†
India	32,642	50,459	61,562
Other countries	209	682	4,526

* Figures refer to the 15 months from 1 April 1987 to 30 June 1988.
† Preliminary estimates. New fiscal year ending 30 June.
Source: Trade Information Bureau, Royal Government of Bhutan.

Transport

ROAD TRAFFIC
In 1988 there were 7,002 registered vehicles, including 4,567 private cars, jeeps or scooters, 250 taxis (mainly four-wheel drive), 71 diplomatic vehicles and 1,370 heavy vehicles.

CIVIL AVIATION (traffic, year ending 30 June)

	1985	1986	1987
Kilometres flown ('000)	152	201	n.a.
Passengers	5,928	7,776	8,700
Passenger-km ('000)	3,349	4,381	n.a.

Source: Central Statistical Office, Planning Commission.

Tourism

Arrivals: 2,524 in 1987; 2,197 in 1988; 1,480 in 1989.
Receipts (US $ million): 2.4 in 1987; 2.0 in 1988; 2.0 in 1989.
Source: Bhutan Tourism Corpn.

Communications Media

In 1985 there were 8,121 registered radio receivers and 200 television receivers. In 1987 there were 1,945 telephones in use. There are no television transmission stations in Bhutan, but broadcasts from Bangladesh and India can be received in Phuntsholing. In 1989, however, the Government ordered the dismantling of all existing television aerials, claiming that it wanted to protect Bhutan's national culture.

Education

(at 30 April 1990)

Extended classrooms (ECRs—early primary classes)	46
Primary schools	156
Junior high schools	21
High schools	10
Teachers' training institutes	2
Schools for Buddhist studies and monastic schools	22
Sanskrit Pathsalas	5
Junior college	1
Degree college*	1
Technical schools	6
Schools for Tibetan refugees	4
Total pupils	70,354
Total teachers	2,625

* Affiliated to the University of Delhi.
Source: Department of Education, Royal Government of Bhutan.

Directory

The Constitution

The Kingdom of Bhutan has no formal constitution. However, the state system is a modified form of constitutional monarchy. Written rules, which are changed periodically, govern procedures for the election of members of the Royal Advisory Council and the Legislature, and define the duties and powers of those bodies.

The Government

Head of State: HM Druk Gyalpo ('Dragon King') JIGME SINGYE WANGCHUCK (succeeded to the throne in July 1972).

LODOI TSOKDE
(Royal Advisory Council)
(December 1990)

The Royal Advisory Council (Lodoi Tsokde), established in 1965, comprises nine members: two monks representing the Central and District Monastic Bodies (Rabdeys), six people's representatives and a Chairman (Kalyon), nominated by the King. The people's representatives have their names endorsed at village assemblies, forwarded by district Dzongdas (local administrative officials) and voted on by all members of the Tshogdu (National Assembly). The Council's principal task is to advise the King, as head of government, and to supervise all aspects of administration. The Council is in permanent session, virtually as a government department, and acts as the *de facto* Standing Committee of the Tshogdu. Members serve for five years and may be re-elected.

Chairman: KUNZANG TANGBI.
Councillors: Dasho KUNZANG WANGDI (Lhuntshi)*, Lam JAMBEY (Tongsa Rabdey)†, Dasho TSHEWANG DORJI (Shemgang)*, Lop TSHEWANG NIDUP (Dratshang)†, Dasho DEVAN TAMANG (Chirang)*, Dasho BHIM BAHADUR RAI (Samchi)*, Dasho DORJI TSHERING (Paro)*, Dasho NAMGAY RINCHEN (Thimphu)*.

* To October 1992.
† To March/April 1991.

LHENGYE SHUNGTSOG
(Council of Ministers)
(December 1990)

Chairman: HM Druk Gyalpo JIGME SINGYE WANGCHUCK.
Minister of Finance: Lyonpo DORJI TSHERING.
Representative of His Majesty in the Ministry of Agriculture and in the Ministry of Communications: HRH Ashi (Princess) DECHAN WANGMO WANGCHUCK DORJI.
Minister of Trade and Industry: Lyonpo OM PRADHAN.
Minister of Home Affairs: HRH NAMGYEL WANGCHUCK.
Minister of Foreign Affairs and Secretary of the Council of Ministers: Lyonpo DAWA TSERING.
Minister of Social Services and of Communications: Lyonpo Dr T. TOBGYAL.
Deputy Minister of Defence: Maj.-Gen. LAM DORJI.
Chairman of the Special Commission on Customs and Traditions: (vacant).

MINISTRIES

All Ministries are in Thimphu.

Ministry of Finance: Thimphu; telex 890201.
Ministry of Foreign Affairs: Tashichhodzong, Thimphu; telex 890214.

BHUTAN *Directory*

Ministry of Social Services: Thimphu; telex 890203.
Ministry of Trade and Industry: Thimphu; telex 890215.
Office of the Royal Advisory Council: POB 200, Tashichhodzong, Thimphu; tel. 22816.

Legislature

TSHOGDU

A National Assembly (Tshogdu) was established in 1953. The Assembly has a three-year term and meets twice yearly, in spring (May–June) and autumn (October–November). The size of the membership is based, in part, on the population of the districts, and is subject to periodic revision. In 1990 the Assembly had 150 members, of whom 105 were directly elected by the public. Ten seats were reserved for religious bodies, one was assigned to a representative of industry (elected by the Bhutan Chamber of Commerce and Industry), and the remainder were occupied by officials nominated by the Government (including the 18 Dzongdas). The Assembly elects its own Speaker from among its members. It enacts laws, advises on constitutional and political matters and debates all important issues. Both the Royal Advisory Council and the Council of Ministers are responsible to the Assembly.

Speaker: Lyonpo SANGYE PENJOR.
Deputy Speaker: Dasho PASANG DORJI.

LOCAL ADMINISTRATION

There are 18 districts (dzongkhags), each headed by a Dzongda (in charge of administration and law and order) and a Thrimpon (in charge of judicial matters). Dzongdas were previously appointed by the King, but are now appointed by the Royal Civil Service Commission, established in 1982. The Dzongdas are responsible to the Royal Civil Service Commission and the Ministry of Home Affairs, while the Thrimpons are responsible to the High Court. The principal officers under the Dzongda are the Dzongda Wongma and the Dzongrab, responsible for locally administered development projects and fiscal matters respectively. Seven of the districts are further sub-divided into sub-districts (dungkhags), and the lowest administrative unit in all districts is the bloc (gewog) of several villages.

Under provisions of the 1981–87 Plan, with the introduction of decentralization, Punakha and Thimphu were merged as one district for a few years in the early 1980s. However, this did not prove successful, and by 1985 they were once more administered separately. In August 1987 Gasa and Punakha were amalgamated into a single district, and a new district, named Chukha, was created from portions of three existing districts in western Bhutan. There are two municipal corporations (in Thimphu and Phuntsholing), each of which is headed by a Thrompon (mayor) and is composed of government officials.

Political Organizations

There are no political parties in Bhutan. There are, however, three outlawed opposition groups composed of Nepali-speaking Hindus, which are based in Kathmandu, Nepal:

Bhutan People's Party (BPP): f. 1990; advocates unconditional release of all political prisoners, change from absolute monarchy to constitutional monarchy, judicial reform, freedom of religious practices, linguistic freedom, freedom of press, speech and expression, and equal rights for all ethnic groups; Pres. R. K. BUDATHOKI; Gen. Sec. D. K. RAI.

People's Forum for Human Rights: f. 1989; Leaders VIKAY THAPA, GOPAL SHARMA.

United Liberation People's Front: f. 1990; Leader BALARAM POUDYAL.

Diplomatic Representation

EMBASSIES IN BHUTAN

Bangladesh: POB 178, Thorilam, Thimphu; tel. 22539; Ambassador: (vacant).

India: India House Estate, Lungtenzampa, Thimphu; tel. 22162; telex 890211; Ambassador: VINOD KUMAR CHANDRANARAIN KHANNA.

Judicial System

Bhutan has Civil and Criminal Codes, which are based on those laid down by the Shabdrung Ngawang Namgyal in the 17th century. Law was mostly administered at the district level until 1968. Existing laws were consolidated in 1982.

Appeal Court: The Supreme Court of Appeal is the King.
High Court (Thrimkhang Gongma): Established 1968 to review appeals from Lower Courts, although some cases are heard at the first instance; eight Judges (six nominated by the King and two elected by the Tshogdu, who serve for a five-year period), headed by the Chief Justice. Three judges form a quorum. The judges are assisted by seven senior Ramjams (judges in training).

Chief Justice: (vacant).

Magistrates' Courts (Dzongkhag Thrimkhang): Each district has a court, headed by the Thrimpon (magistrate) and aided by a junior Ramjam, which tries most cases. Appeals are made to the High Court, and less serious civil disputes may be settled by a Gup or Mandal (village headman) through written undertakings.

All citizens have the right to make informal appeal for redress of grievances directly to the King, through the office of the Gyalpoi Zimpon (court chamberlain).

Religion

The state religion is Mahayana Buddhism, but the southern Bhutanese are predominantly followers of Hinduism. Buddhism was introduced into Bhutan in the eighth century AD by the Indian saint Padmasambhava, known in Bhutan as Guru Rimpoche. In the 13th century Phajo Drugom Shigpo made the Drukpa school of Kagyupa Buddhism pre-eminent in Bhutan, and this sect is still supported by the dominant ethnic group, the Drukpas. The main monastic group, the Central Monastic Body (comprising 1,160 monks), is led by an elected Head Abbot (Je Khenpo), is directly supported by the state and spends six months of the year at Tashichhodzong and at Punakha respectively. A further 2,120 monks, who are members of the District Monastic Bodies, are sustained by the lay population. The Council for Ecclesiastical Affairs oversees all religious bodies. Monasteries (Gompas) and shrines (Lhakhangs) are numerous.

Council for Ecclesiastical Affairs (Dratshang Lhentshog): established in 1984, as the Central Monastic Secretariat, to oversee all Buddhist meditational centres and schools of Buddhist studies, as well as the Central and District Monastic Bodies; renamed 1989; Chair. His Holiness the Je Khenpo GEDUEN RINCHEN; Sec. Dasho RIGZIN DORJI.

The Press

Kuensel: Dept of Information, Ministry of Communications, POB 204, Thimphu; tel. 22134; telex 890212; f. 1965 as a news bulletin; reorg. as a national weekly newspaper in 1986; in English, Dzongkha and Nepali; Editors R. N. MISHRA (Nepali), KINLEY DORJI (English), GOEMBO DORJI (Dzongkha); circ. 253 (Nepali), 6,023 (English), 1,441 (Dzongkha).

Radio

There are 36 radio stations for administrative communications. Of these, 34 are for internal communications (to which the public has access), and two are external stations serving the Bhutanese diplomatic missions in India and Bangladesh. A further eight stations are for hydrological and meteorological purposes. In 1985 there were an estimated 15,000 radio receivers in use, of which 8,121 were registered.

Bhutan Broadcasting Service (BBS): Dept of Information, POB 101, Thimphu; tel. 22533; telex 890212; f. 1973 as Radio National Youth Association of Bhutan (NYAB); present name adopted 1986; short-wave radio station broadcasting 30 hours per week in Dzongkha, Sharchopkha, Lhotsam and English; a daily FM programme (for Thimphu only) began in 1987; Jt Dir LOUISE DORJI; Programme Officer TASHI DORJI.

Finance

(cap. = capital; auth. = authorized; p.u. = paid up;
res = reserves; dep. = deposits; m. = million; brs = branches;
amounts in ngultrum)

BANKING

Central Bank

Royal Monetary Authority (RMA): POB 154, Thimphu; tel. 22540; telex 890206; f. 1982; bank of issue; frames and implements official monetary policy, co-ordinates the activities of financial institutions and holds foreign-exchange deposits on behalf of the Govt; cap. 1.5m.; Chair. HRH Ashi Sonam Chhoden Wangchuck; Man. Dir Bap Kesang.

Commercial Bank

Bank of Bhutan: POB 75, Phuntsholing; tel. 225; telex 890304; f. 1968; 20%-owned by the State Bank of India and 80% by the Govt of Bhutan; auth cap. 40m., cap. p.u. 10m., res (with Royal Monetary Authority of Bhutan) 596.7m., dep. (incl. foreign liabilities) 1,450.3m. (31 March 1990); Dirs nominated by the Bhutan Govt: Chair. Lyonpo Dorji Tshering; Dirs Dasho Pema Wangchuck, Dasho Chenkyab Dorji, Yeshey Zimba, Bap Kesang; Dirs nominated by the State Bank of India: P. K. Pain, V. S. Yadava; Man. Dir Ram Nath; 25 brs.

Development Bank

Bhutan Development Finance Corporation (BDFC): POB 256, Thimphu; tel. 22579; telex 890223; f. 1988; provides long-term development loans and shorter-term agricultural credit; auth. cap. 100m., cap. p.u. 12.5m.; Chair. Lyonpo D. Tshering; Man. Dir Pema Tenzin.

Savings Institution

Unit Trust of Bhutan: POB 96, Phuntsholing; tel. 502; telex 890305; offers various forms of investment in unit trusts (mutual funds) guaranteed by the Govt; Gen. Man. Sangay Dorji.

INSURANCE

Royal Insurance Corporation of Bhutan: POB 77, Phuntsholing; tel. 309; telex 890305; f. 1975; cap. 12.0m., total investments 443.0m. (1988); Chair. HRH Ashi Sonam Chhoden Wangchuck; Man. Dir Dasho U. Dorji.

Trade and Industry

CHAMBER OF COMMERCE

Bhutan Chamber of Commerce and Industry: POB 147, Thimphu; tel. 22742; telex 890229; f. 1980; reorg. 1988; 40 gen. mems and 25 exec. mems; Pres. Dasho Ugen Dorji; Gen. Sec. Thinley Penjor.

GOVERNMENT ORGANIZATIONS

Food Corporation of Bhutan (FCB): Phuntsholing; tel. 241; f. 1974; activities include retailing, marketing, storage, import and export of agricultural products and establishment of regulated market yards and horticultural processing units in the country; operates a rural finance scheme, receiving loans from the Bank of Bhutan and the Royal Insurance Corpn, to assist farmers; Man. Dir Hadi Ali.

National Commission for Trade and Industry: Thimphu; tel. 22403; fmrly Industrial Development Corpn; regulates the type, quality and quantity of proposed industrial projects; Chair. HM Druk Gyalpo Jigme Singye Wangchuck.

State Trading Corpn of Bhutan (STCB): POB 76, Phuntsholing; tel. 286; telex 890301; manages imports and exports on behalf of the Govt; Man. Dir R. B. Basnet; brs in Thimphu (tel. 22953) and Calcutta, India.

TRADE UNIONS

Trade union activity is illegal in Bhutan.

Transport

ROADS AND TRACKS

In June 1989 there were more than 2,280 km of roads (1,761 km of which were surfaced). In addition, surfaced roads link the important border towns of Phuntsholing, Gaylegphug, Sarbhang and Samdrup Jongkhar in southern Bhutan to towns in West Bengal and Assam in India. Under the Sixth Development Plan (1987–92), the Government proposed to construct and upgrade about 1,000 km of roads to provide vital links to the national road network. There is a shortage of road transport. Yaks, ponies and mules are still the chief means of transport on the rough mountain tracks. By April 1990 most of the previously government-operated transport facilities on major and subsidiary routes had been transferred to private operators on the basis of seven-year contracts.

Bhutan Government Transport Service (BGTS): Phuntsholing; tel. Thimphu 22345; f. 1962; operates a fleet of 111 buses; services include a twice-daily minibus service between Thimphu and Phuntsholing; Man. Dir Lhendup Dorji; brs in most towns.

Transport Corpn of Bhutan: POB 7, Phuntsholing; tel. 476; telex 890305; f. 1982; subsidiary of Royal Insurance Corpn of Bhutan; operates direct coach service between Phuntsholing and Calcutta.

Other operators are Barma Travels, Dawa Transport, Gyamtsho Transport, Guring Transport Service and Sonam Rinchen Travels.

Lorries for transporting goods are operated by the private sector.

CIVIL AVIATION

There is an international airport at Paro. There are also numerous helicopter landing pads.

Druk-Air Corpn (Royal Bhutan Airlines): POB 209, Lower Market, Thimphu; tel. 22215; telex 890219; fax 873-1443342; national airline; f. 1981; became fully operational in February 1983; services from Paro to New Delhi, Calcutta, Kathmandu, Bangkok and Dhaka; charter services also undertaken; operates a minibus service between Paro and Thimphu; Chair. Lyonpo Dr T. Tobgyal; Man. Dir Tshering Wangdi; fleet of 1 BAe 146-100.

Tourism

Bhutan was opened to tourism in 1974, and the tourist seasons are from March to June and September to December. From 1974 to 1982 all tourists arrived by road via India. In 1983 Druk-Air began regular flights between Calcutta and Paro. In 1986 Druk-Air began daily flights between Calcutta and Paro. By March 1989 there were also weekly services between Dhaka and Paro, Bangkok and Paro, and between Kathmandu and Paro. In addition a twice-weekly service between Delhi and Paro began operations in 1989. In 1989 the total number of foreign visitors was 1,480 and receipts from tourism totalled US $1.95m. Tourists travel in organized 'package' or trekking tours, or individually, accompanied by government-appointed guides. Hotels have been constructed by the Department of Tourism and Communications at Phuntsholing, Paro and Thimphu, with lodges at Tongsa, Bumthang and Manas. Government-operated guest-houses are maintained in the principal towns. There are also many small privately-operated hotels and guest-houses. The first mountaineering expedition took place in 1983, to Mt Jichudrake. In early 1987 Mt Gangar Phunsum, one of the world's highest unclimbed mountains, was forbidden to climbers, to respect the wishes of the local people. Central Bhutan was opened for trekkers and coach tours in 1982. Eastern Bhutan was officially opened to tourists in late 1989, although individual groups had visited the region on a limited scale for many years. The Government exercises close control over the development of tourism. In July 1987 the National Assembly resolved that all monasteries, mountains and other holy places should be inaccessible to tourists from 1988, and in 1989 it was decided that the number of foreign visitors should be strictly regulated and limited.

Bhutan Tourism Corpn (BTC): POB 159, Thimphu; tel. 22647; telex 890217; transferred to private ownership in mid-1990; operates two hotels for tourists and govt and state guests; also operates three tourist lodges and many tourist rest houses throughout the kingdom; Man. Dir Jigme Tshultim; Dir (Sales and Promotion) Dominic Sitling.

BOLIVIA

Introductory Survey

Location, Climate, Language, Religion, Flag, Capital

The Republic of Bolivia is a land-locked state in South America, bordered by Chile and Peru to the west, by Brazil to the north and east, and by Paraguay and Argentina to the south. The climate varies, according to altitude, from humid tropical conditions in the northern and eastern lowlands, which are less than 500 m (1,640 ft) above sea-level, to the cool and cold zones at altitudes of more than 3,500 m (about 11,500 ft) in the Andes mountains. The official languages are Spanish, Quechua and Aymará. Almost all of the inhabitants profess Christianity, and the great majority are adherents of the Roman Catholic Church. The national flag (proportions 3 by 2) has three equal horizontal stripes, of red, yellow and green. The state flag has, in addition, the national emblem (an oval cartouche enclosing a mountain, an alpaca, a breadfruit tree and a sheaf of grain, all surmounted by a condor and superimposed on crossed cannons, rifles and national banners) in the centre of the yellow stripe. The legal capital is Sucre. The administrative capital and seat of government is La Paz.

Recent History

The Incas of Bolivia were conquered by Spain in 1538 and, although there were many revolts against Spanish rule, independence was not achieved until 1825. Bolivian history has been characterized by recurrent internal strife, resulting in a succession of presidents, and frequent territorial disputes with its neighbours, including the 1879–83 War of the Pacific between Bolivia, Peru and Chile, and the Chaco Wars of 1928–30 and 1933–35 against Paraguay.

At a presidential election in May 1951 the largest share of the vote was won by Dr Víctor Paz Estenssoro, the candidate of the Movimiento Nacionalista Revolucionario (MNR), who had been living in Argentina since 1946. He was denied permission to return to Bolivia and contested the election *in absentia*. However, he failed to gain an absolute majority, and the incumbent President transferred power to a junta of army officers. This regime was itself overthrown in April 1952, when a popular uprising, supported by the MNR and a section of the armed forces, enabled Dr Paz Estenssoro to return from exile and assume the presidency. His government, a coalition of the MNR and the Labour Party, committed itself to profound social revolution. It nationalized the tin mines and introduced universal suffrage (the franchise had previously been limited to literate adults) and land reform. Dr Hernán Siles Zuazo, a leading figure in the 1952 revolution, was elected President for the 1956–60 term, and Dr Paz Estenssoro was again elected President in 1960. However, the powerful trade unions came into conflict with the Government, and in November 1964, following widespread strikes and disorder, President Paz Estenssoro was overthrown by the Vice-President, Gen. René Barrientos Ortuño, who was supported by the army. After serving with Gen. Alfredo Ovando Candía as Co-President under a military junta, Gen. Barrientos resigned in January 1966 to campaign for the presidency. He was elected in July 1966.

President Barrientos met strong opposition from left-wing groups, including mineworkers' unions. There was also a guerrilla uprising in south-eastern Bolivia, led by Dr Ernesto ('Che') Guevara, the Argentine-born revolutionary who had played a leading role in the Castro regime in Cuba. However, the insurgency was suppressed by government troops, with the help of US advisers, and guerrilla warfare ended in October 1967, when Guevara was captured and killed. In April 1969 President Barrientos was killed in an air crash and Dr Luis Adolfo Siles Salinas, the Vice-President, succeeded to the presidency. In September 1969, however, President Siles Salinas was deposed by the armed forces, who installed Gen. Ovando in power again. He was forced to resign in October 1970, when, after a power struggle between right-wing and left-wing army officers, Gen. Juan José Torres González, who had support from leftists, emerged as President, pledging support for agrarian reform and worker participation in management. A 'People's Assembly', formed by Marxist politicians, radical students and leaders of trade unions, was allowed to meet and demanded the introduction of extreme socialist measures, causing disquiet in right-wing circles. President Torres was deposed in August 1971 by Col (later Gen.) Hugo Bánzer Suárez, who drew support from the right-wing Falange Socialista Boliviana and a section of the MNR, as well as from the army. In June 1973 President Bánzer announced an imminent return to constitutional government, but elections were later postponed to June 1974. The MNR withdrew its support and entered into active opposition.

Following an attempted military coup in June 1974, the Cabinet was replaced by an all-military one. After an attempt to overthrow him in November 1974, President Bánzer declared that elections had been postponed indefinitely and that his military regime would retain power until at least 1980. All political and union activity was banned. Political and industrial unrest in 1976, however, led President Bánzer to announce that elections would be held in July 1978. Allegations of fraud rendered the elections void but Gen. Juan Pereda Asbún, the armed forces candidate in the elections, staged a successful military coup. In November 1978 his right-wing government was overthrown in another coup, led by Gen. David Padilla Aranciba, Commander-in-Chief of the Army, with the support of national left-wing elements.

Elections were held in July 1979 for a President and a bicameral Congress. The presidential poll resulted in almost equal support for two ex-Presidents, Dr Siles Zuazo (with 36.0% of the vote) and Dr Paz Estenssoro (with 35.9%), who were now leading rival factions of the MNR. Congress, which was convened in August to resolve the issue, failed to give a majority to either candidate. An interim government was formed under Walter Guevara Arce, President of the Senate, but this administration was overthrown on 1 November by a right-wing army officer, Col Alberto Natusch Busch. He withdrew 15 days later after failing to gain the support of Congress, which elected Dra Lidia Gueiler Tejada, President of the Chamber of Deputies, as interim Head of State pending presidential and legislative elections scheduled for June 1980.

The 1980 presidential election also yielded no clear winner, and in July, before Congress could meet to decide between the two main contenders (again Dr Siles Zuazo and Dr Paz Estenssoro), a military junta led by the army commander, Gen. Luis García Meza, staged a coup—the 189th in Bolivia's 154 years of independence. In August 1981 a military uprising forced Gen. García to resign. In September the junta transferred power to the army commander, Gen. Celso Torrelio Villa, who declared his intention to fight official corruption and to return the country to democracy within three years. Labour unrest, provoked by Bolivia's severe economic crisis, was appeased by restitution of trade union and political rights, and a mainly civilian cabinet was appointed in April 1982. Elections were scheduled for April 1983. The political liberalization disturbed the armed forces, who attempted to create a climate of violence, and President Torrelio resigned in July 1982, amid rumours of an impending coup. The junta installed the less moderate Gen. Guido Vildoso Calderón, the Army Chief of Staff, as President. Unable to resolve the worsening economic crisis or to control a general strike, the military regime announced in September 1982 that power would be handed over in October to the Congress which had originally been elected in 1980. Dr Siles Zuazo, who had obtained most votes in both 1979 and 1980, was duly elected President by Congress, and was sworn in for a four-year term in October 1982.

President Siles Zuazo appointed a coalition cabinet consisting of members of his own party, the Movimiento Nacionalista Revolucionario de Izquierda (MNRI), the Movimiento de la Izquierda Revolucionaria (MIR) and the Partido Comunista de Bolivia (PCB). Economic aid from the USA and Europe was resumed but the Government found itself unable to fulfil the expectations that had been created by the return to democratic rule. The entire Cabinet resigned in August 1983, and the President appointed a cabinet in which the number of portfolios that were held by the right-wing of the MNRI, the Partido Demócrata Cristiano (PDC) and independents was increased. The MIR joined forces with the MNR and with business interests in rejecting the Government's policy of complying with IMF conditions for assistance, which involved harsh economic measures. The Government lost its majority in Congress and faced strikes and mass labour demonstrations. In November the opposition-dominated Senate approved an increase of 100% in the minimum wage, in defiance of the Government's austerity measures. Following a 48-hour general strike, the whole Cabinet resigned once again on 14 December, in anticipation of an opposition motion of censure; the ministers accused the Senate of planning a 'constitutional coup' and called for the formation of a government of national unity. In January 1984 President Siles Zuazo appointed a new coalition cabinet, including 13 members of the previous Government.

The new Cabinet's main priority was to tackle Bolivia's grave economic decline. However, constant industrial agitation by the trade union confederation, the Central Obrera Boliviana (COB), coupled with rumours of an imminent coup, seriously undermined public confidence in the President. The subsequent introduction of austerity measures resulted in widespread protests. The Government, therefore, agreed to a series of economic concessions, including a moratorium on Bolivia's foreign debt to commercial banks. In June, however, the country was again thrown into turmoil by the temporary abduction of President Siles Zuazo. Two former cabinet ministers and some 100 right-wing army officers were arrested in connection with the kidnapping, which was believed to have been supported by leading drug dealers.

In September 1984 the Government faced another crisis, following the discovery of a plot by extreme right-wing groups to overthrow the President. Following the disclosure that Congress had ordered an enquiry into suspected links between the Government and cocaine dealers, President Siles Zuazo undertook a five-day hunger strike in a bid to secure national unity and stability. In November another general strike was held, and the President announced that he would leave office a year early, in August 1985, after a general election, which was to be held in June. In January 1985 a new cabinet was formed, comprising only members of the MNRI and independents. In the same month it was announced that an attempted coup by former military officers had been thwarted.

In March 1985, following the Government's decision to introduce a new series of austerity measures, the COB called a general strike, which lasted for 16 days. The Government's offer to form a 'co-administrative' joint government with the trade unions was rejected by the COB, whose leaders advocated a revolution as the only solution to the crisis. The strike was eventually halted when a majority of union leaders accepted the Government's offer of a pay increase of more than 300%.

The principal consequence of the general strike was the Government's decision to postpone the general election until July 1985. At the election, amid reports of electoral malpractice and poor organization, the right-wing Acción Democrática Nacionalista (ADN), whose presidential candidate was Gen. Hugo Bánzer Suárez (the former dictator), received 28.6% of the votes cast, and the MNR obtained 26.4%, while the MIR was the leading left-wing party. At a further round of voting in Congress in August, an alliance between the MNR and the leading left-wing groups, including the MIR, enabled Dr Víctor Paz Estenssoro of the MNR to secure the presidency (which he had previously held in 1952–56 and 1960–64). The armed forces pledged their support for the new Government.

On taking office in August 1985, the new Government immediately introduced a very strict economic programme, designed to reduce inflation, which was estimated to have reached 14,173% in the year to August. The COB rejected the programme and called an indefinite general strike in September. The Government responded by declaring the strike illegal and by ordering a 90-day state of siege throughout Bolivia. Leading trade unionists were detained or banished, and thousands of strikers were arrested. The strike was called off in October, when union leaders agreed to hold talks with the Government. The conclusion of the strike was regarded as a considerable success for the new administration which, in spite of having achieved office with the assistance of left-wing parties, had subsequently found a greater ally in the right-wing ADN. The alliance between the MNR and the ADN was consolidated by the signing of a 'pacto por la democracia' in October. The collapse of the world tin market in late 1985 had a catastrophic impact on the Bolivian economy. In January 1986 the Cabinet resigned to enable the President to modify government policies, but Paz Estenssoro remained fully committed to the economic programme.

In July 1986 the Government was strongly criticized by opposition groups and trade unions when 160 US soldiers arrived in Bolivia to participate in a joint campaign with the Bolivian armed forces to eradicate illegal coca plantations. The Government was accused of having contravened the Constitution and of compromising national sovereignty. The allocation of US aid, however, was to be conditional upon the elimination of Bolivia's illegal cocaine trade. In October the US administration agreed to provide more than US $100m. in aid to continue the drug eradication campaign, and US troops were withdrawn, so that the Bolivian authorities could assume responsibility for the campaign. However, within a few months of the troops' withdrawal, cocaine production was once again flourishing; the price of coca leaves recovered, and workshops for the conversion of coca paste into cocaine had resumed operations.

Throughout 1986, demonstrations and strikes were held by the COB in protest at the Government's austerity measures. Following a 48-hour general strike in August, the Government imposed a state of siege for 90 days. Opposition politicians and trade unionists were detained, while a strike by miners, protesting at reductions in tin production, continued until union leaders were released in exchange for a promise to return to work. However, social unrest persisted in 1987, and President Paz Estenssoro threatened to reimpose the state of siege. Several ministers were replaced in a cabinet reshuffle in February 1987.

Discontent with the Government's austerity policies was demonstrated by the results of the municipal elections of December 1987. The ADN and MIR emerged as the two major parties. Nevertheless, the 'pacto por la democracia' between the MNR and the ADN remained in force, as the ADN had lost a considerable amount of its support to the MIR. After the elections, the Government entered into negotiations with the COB, in an attempt to avert further social unrest. In February 1988 discussions were halted, after the price of petrol was raised again. Widescale unrest followed, culminating in April with a national hunger strike, called by the COB, to protest against the Government's plans for the decentralization of the health and education services and against the continuing austerity measures. These problems led to the resignation of the Cabinet, following the MNR party congress in August, although all except four ministers were reappointed.

Presidential and legislative elections were scheduled to be held in May 1989. In September 1988 Gonzalo Sánchez de Losada, hitherto Minister of Planning, was confirmed as the MNR's presidential candidate. The candidates for the ADN and the MIR were Gen. Bánzer Suárez (as in 1985) and Jaime Paz Zamora respectively. Regarding major issues, a consensus existed in the electoral manifestos of the three main candidates, which included a broad endorsement of the economic austerity measures of the MNR Government and a commitment to campaigning against drug-trafficking and to finding alternative employment and crops for coca-growers. About two-thirds of the total eligible electorate registered to vote in the elections, which took place on 7 May 1989. Of the votes cast in the presidential election, Sánchez obtained 23.07%, Bánzer 22.70%, and Paz Zamora 19.64%. As no candidate had gained the requisite absolute majority, responsibility for the choice of President passed to the newly-elected Congress, which was to convene on 4 August. Political uncertainty prevailed in the interim, and this led, in turn, to economic stagnation. Initially, a power-sharing agreement between the MNR and the MIR appeared to be the most likely outcome, as animosity between Sánchez and Bánzer precluded a renewal of the MNR-ADN pact. However, shortly before the second stage of the election, Bánzer withdrew his candidacy in order to support his former adversary, Paz Zamora. The 46 ADN and 41 MIR seats in Congress were sufficient to assure a majority vote for Paz Zamora. On 6 August he assumed the presidency for a four-year term. A coalition government of 'national unity' was then formed, with an even distribution of ministerial posts between the ADN and the MIR, although ADN members occupied the important Ministries of Finance, Defence and Foreign Affairs. Luis Ossio Sanjines of the PDC became Vice-President. At the same time, a joint political council (with undefined powers), headed by Gen. Bánzer, was established.

In his inaugural speech, President Paz Zamora gave assurances that fiscal discipline would be maintained, that savings in US dollars would be guaranteed, and that market forces would determine interest rates, prices and the single exchange rate, in order to assuage fears in the business community, which, in the period prior to his election, had provoked a loss of confidence in the banks, including withdrawals totalling US $70m. Moreover, the new Minister of Finance, David Blanco Zavala, threatened to resign if attempts to increase public spending were made without first increasing government revenues. He foresaw a gradual increase in taxes and commodity prices and reductions in the number of public service employees.

Meanwhile, further measures to reduce the production of coca were taken during 1988. An anti-narcotics department was established in April. The drug control troops, Unidad Móvil de Patrullaje Rural (UMOPAR), were provided with greater resources and were further supported by a coca limitation law (adopted by the Bolivian Congress in July), restricting to 12,000 ha the land allowed for coca production (the leaves to be used for 'traditional' purposes only). In the same month, Roberto Suárez, Bolivia's leading cocaine-trafficker, was arrested and imprisoned for trading in illicit drugs. Suárez's arrest led to the exposure of drug-trading involving leading members of the ADN, and was linked to a bomb attack on US Secretary of State George Shultz's motorcade in La Paz in August, during a visit to show support for the campaign against coca production.

By mid-1989, however, the Government had failed to attain the targets of its coca eradication programme, having encountered staunch opposition from the powerful coca-growers' organizations. Clashes between UMOPAR and drug-traffickers had become increasingly violent, especially in the coca-processing region of northern Beni. Consequently, the US Government withheld US $5.8m. of a total aid programme of $24.5m. At a 'summit' conference to discuss the problem of drugs, held in Cartagena, Colombia, in February 1990, and attended by the Presidents of Bolivia, Peru, Colombia and the USA, President Paz Zamora criticized the militaristic approach of the USA to coca-eradication and emphasized the need for economic and social support. In May, however, he accepted US $35m. in military aid from the USA. In response to accusations that he was succumbing to US pressure, Paz Zamora declared that no foreign troops would be involved in the campaign against drug-trafficking in Bolivia while he remained in power. In June the US President, George Bush, announced that he would be seeking $150m. in economic aid for Bolivia from the US Congress for 1991. In the following month the Bolivian Minister of the Interior, Migration and Justice, Guillermo Capobianco, stated that more than 5,000 ha of coca had been eradicated in the first half of 1990, a figure exceeding targets initially set for the period. In late 1990 reaction to US involvement in Bolivia became increasingly violent. The left-wing Nestor Paz Zamora guerrilla group claimed responsibility for several bomb attacks, one of which, at a US marine base, resulted in the death of a Bolivian policeman. The group declared that its actions were in response to the violation of Bolivia's political and territorial sovereignty by the USA. The issue of combating drug-trafficking while maintaining austerity measures presented the greatest challenge to the new Government. In effect, the cocaine industry sustained a thriving 'black' economy which mitigated the effects of government economic policy, notably widespread unemployment.

A state of siege, banning strikes, was imposed in November 1989, since, according to the Government, teachers striking over the issue of bonuses presented a threat to the anti-inflation austerity policy. Municipal elections were held in December, despite the state of siege, which was eventually repealed in February 1990.

The long-standing issue of possible Bolivian access to the Pacific Ocean was finally resolved in mid-1990, when the international highway from Tambo Quemado, Bolivia, to Arica, on the Pacific coast of Chile, was completed and plans were announced for the construction of a new road, at a projected cost of US $90.9m., linking Tambo Quemado with Patacamaya, south of La Paz.

In December 1989 a serious institutional conflict arose when the Government allowed a former Minister of the Interior, Migration and Justice, Col Luis Arce Gómez, to be taken to Miami, Florida, to be tried on drug-trafficking charges, despite the absence of a formal extradition treaty between Bolivia and the USA. Arce Gómez had been on trial in Bolivia since 1986, accused of violating human rights. His extradition, therefore, constituted a contravention of Bolivian law, which states that a Bolivian cannot be extradited while undergoing trial in Bolivia. The Supreme Court accused the President of an assault on judicial power. In response, the Minister of the Interior, Migration and Justice, Guillermo Capobianco, accused the judges of corruption, claiming that extradition was the only way to ensure an appropriate sentence for Arce Gómez. In January 1990 the Government threatened to initiate impeachment proceedings in Congress unless the members of the Supreme Court resigned. In November 1990 Congress temporarily suspended eight of the 12 Supreme Court judges two weeks after the judges had ruled that a beer tax authorized by Congress was illegal. In retaliation the court threatened to annul the 1989 elections.

In September 1990, following the completion of a 32-day, 650-km march of protest by 700 indigenous Indians from the town of Trinidad, in Beni, to the capital, La Paz, the Government issued four decrees in an unprecedented act of recognition of Indian land rights. Besides acknowledging as Indian territory more than 1.6m. ha of tropical rainforest in northern Bolivia, a multiparty commission, comprising government and indigenous Indian representatives, was to be established in order to draft a new Law for Indigenous Indians of the East and Amazonia. In addition, it was established that timber merchants in the central Chimanes forest had to cease operations by the end of October 1990.

Government

Legislative power is held by the bicameral Congress, comprising a Senate (27 members) and a Chamber of Deputies (130 members). Both houses are elected for a four-year term by universal adult suffrage. Executive power is vested in the President and the Cabinet, which the President appoints. The President is also directly elected for four years. If no candidate gains an absolute majority of votes, the President is chosen by Congress. The country is divided, for administrative purposes, into nine departments, each of which is governed by a prefect, appointed by the President.

Defence

Military service, for one year, is selective. In June 1990 the armed forces numbered 28,000 men, of whom the army had 20,200 (including 15,000 conscripts), the air force 4,000, and the navy 3,800. The defence budget for 1988 was 204.01m. bolivianos.

Economic Affairs

In 1988, according to World Bank estimates, Bolivia's gross national product (GNP) measured at average 1986–88 prices, totalled US $3,930m., equivalent to $570 per head. In the period 1980–88 GNP decreased, in real terms, at an average annual rate of 1.7%, while GNP per head declined by 4.3% per year. During the same period the population increased by an annual average of 2.7%. Bolivia's gross domestic product (GDP) decreased, in real terms, by an annual average of 1.6% in 1980–88.

Agriculture (including forestry and fishing) contributed 22.6% of GDP in 1988. In 1987 47.4% of the working population were employed in agriculture. Wood accounted for 4.2% of export earnings in 1988. The principal cash crops are coffee, sugar and soybeans. Beef and hides are also important exports. In the period 1980–88 agricultural GDP increased at an average annual rate of 2.1%.

Industry (including mining, manufacturing, construction and power) provided 27.6% of GDP in 1988. In 1987 12.8% of the working population were employed in industry. During the period 1980–88 industrial production declined at an average annual rate of 5.7%. Mining (including petroleum exploration) contributed 13.0% of GDP in 1988. The sector employed 2.5% of the working population in 1987. Tin, zinc, gold, silver and antimony were the major mineral exports in 1988. Tungsten and lead continued to be mined. Minerals accounted for 45.5% of legal exports in 1988.

In 1988 manufacturing accounted for 10.9% of GDP. In 1987 7.1% of the working population were employed in manufacturing. The output of this sector declined during 1980–88 at an average annual rate of 5.6%. Measured by the value of output, the principal branches of manufacturing in 1986 were petroleum refineries (providing 31.3% of the total), food products (24.9%), beverages, leather and products, and non-ferrous metals.

Energy is derived principally from petroleum and natural gas. In 1989 production of crude petroleum averaged about 23,000 barrels per day, all of which was consumed domestically. Petroleum reserves at mid-1986 were estimated to be 151m. barrels. Exports of natural gas accounted for 35.8% of total export earnings in 1988. Energy production declined during the period 1980–88 at an average annual rate of 0.2%. In 1988 fuel imports were equivalent to only 3% of the revenue from Bolivia's total merchandise exports.

The services sector accounted for 49.8% of GDP in 1988. During the period 1980–88 the output of this sector declined at an average annual rate of 0.2%.

In 1989 Bolivia recorded a visible trade deficit of US $6.0m., and there was a deficit of $264.2m. on the current account of the balance of payments. In 1987 the main sources of imports were Brazil (22.6%), the USA (19.4%) and Argentina (14.0%). Argentina was the major recipient of Bolivian exports in 1988 (37.9%), followed by the USA (17.0%) and the United Kingdom (11.8%). The principal imports in 1987 included industrial materials and machinery, transport equipment and consumer goods. The principal legal exports in 1988 were metallic minerals, natural gas, wood and soybeans. In 1990 government sources estimated that around US $600m. (almost equivalent to annual earnings from official exports) were absorbed annually into the economy as a result of the illegal trade in coca and its derivatives (mainly cocaine).

In 1988 Bolivia's budget deficit amounted to 45m. bolivianos. Bolivia's total external public debt in 1988 was US $4,451m., and debt-servicing in that year was equivalent to almost 33% of revenue from exports of goods and services. In 1989 the average annual rate of inflation was 15.2% (compared with 11,750% in 1985). In 1988 an estimated 20% of the labour force were unemployed.

Bolivia is a signatory of the Andean Pact (see p. 93), and in 1989 the Andean Social Development Fund was established. The country is also a member of ALADI (see p. 172). Bolivia became the 97th contracting party to GATT (see p. 58) in 1989.

The coalition Government that President Jaime Paz Zamora formed in August 1989 undertook to continue restrictive fiscal and monetary policies. In 1989 the IDB granted a series of loans to Bolivia, worth more than US $130m., and pledged to invest a further $1,000m., over four years, in projects relating to a 25-year contract to supply electricity to Brazil, which was signed in August 1989 and was due to take effect in 1992. At a World Bank Consultative Group meeting held in Paris in October 1989, member countries and multilateral agencies pledged a total of US $2,175m. in aid for Bolivia to fund a three-year development plan commencing in 1990. Negotiations between the Bolivian Government and creditors, which commenced in 1988, have led to a considerable easing of the burden of debt-servicing. By September 1990 Bolivia had repurchased $500m. of its debt to commercial banks at 11% of its nominal value, and, according to government reports, was expected to repurchase its remaining debt of $200m., at a similar rate, by the end of the year, using funds provided by the Netherlands, Sweden, the USA and the World Bank. In September 1989 an important bilateral debt settlement was reached with Argentina, which since 1986 had defaulted on its payments to Bolivia for supplies of natural gas, thus accumulating a debt of around US $300m. Bolivia's debt to Argentina totalled some $800m. Bolivia's bilateral debt was further reduced in 1990 through an agreement with Brazil, allowing Bolivia to repurchase $300m. of foreign bank debt, at 25% of its nominal value, on the secondary market. A meeting of the 'Paris Club' (Western creditor governments) in March 1990 led to a rescheduling of Bolivia's bilateral debt, enabling the Government to revise forecasts of debt-servicing costs from $283m. to $15.3m. for the two years 1990 and 1991.

In April 1990 the Government announced plans to undertake a major programme of privatization, whereby 100 of the country's 157 state-owned companies would be sold to private interests, over a period of five years, in an attempt to give a much required stimulus to the economy. Bolivia's need to secure more foreign investment was reflected by a new law, enacted in September, offering guarantees to foreign investors. However, government plans encountered strong resistance from opposition parties and from trade unions, which were opposed to overseas ownership and to any relaxation of state control over major sectors of the economy, such as the mining industry.

Social Welfare

There are benefits for unemployment, accident, sickness, old age and death. In 1978 the Government established a social security and health scheme covering 1.66m. rural workers. In 1978 there were 1,158 hospitals, clinics and medical posts, with 3,410 physicians. In 1984 there were 1,540 inhabitants per physician. Of total expenditure by the central Government in 1986, about 19.1m. bolivianos (1.9%) was for health, and a further 250.2m. bolivianos (24.8%) for social security and welfare.

Education

Primary education, beginning at six years of age and lasting for eight years, is officially compulsory and is available free of charge. Secondary education, which is not compulsory, begins at 14 years of age and lasts for up to four years. In 1987 the total enrolment at primary and secondary schools was equivalent to 76% of the school-age population (81% of boys; 70% of girls). In that year an estimated 83% of children in the relevant age-group (88% of boys; 78% of girls) attended primary schools, while the comparable ratio for secondary enrolment was only 27% (28% of boys; 25% of girls). There are eight state universities and two private universities. In 1985, according to UNESCO estimates, the rate of adult illiteracy stood at 25.8% (males 16.2%; females 34.9%). Expenditure on education by the central Government in 1986 was about 185.5m. bolivianos, representing 18.4% of total spending.

Public Holidays

1991: 1 January (New Year), 10 February (Oruro only), 29 March (Good Friday), 15 April (Tarija only), 1 May (Labour Day), 25 May (Sucre only), 30 May (Corpus Christi), 16 July (La Paz only), 6 August (Independence), 14 September (Cochabamba only), 24 September (Santa Cruz), 1 October (Pando only), 1 November (All Saints' Day and Potosí), 18 November (Beni only), 25 December (Christmas).

1992: 1 January (New Year), 10 February (Oruro only), 15 April (Tarija only), 17 April (Good Friday), 1 May (Labour Day), 25 May (Sucre only), 18 June (Corpus Christi), 16 July (La Paz only), 6 August (Independence), 14 September (Cochabamba only), 24 September (Santa Cruz only), 1 October (Pando only), 1 November (All Saints' Day and Potosí), 18 November (Beni only), 25 December (Christmas).

Weights and Measures

The metric system is officially in force, but various old Spanish measures are also used.

Statistical Survey

Sources (unless otherwise indicated): Instituto Nacional de Estadística, Plaza Mario Guzmán Aspiazu No. 1, Casilla 6129, La Paz; tel. (2) 367-443; Banco Central de Bolivia, Ayacucho esq. Mercado, Casilla 3118, La Paz; tel. (2) 350-726; telex 2286.

Area and Population

AREA, POPULATION AND DENSITY

Area (sq km)	
Land	1,084,391
Inland water	14,190
Total	1,098,581*
Population (census results)†	
5 September 1950	2,704,165
29 September 1976	
Males	2,276,029
Females	2,337,457
Total	4,613,486
Population (official estimates at mid-year)	
1987	6,797,359
1988	6,993,344
1989‡	7,193,000
Density (per sq km) at mid-1989	6.5

* 424,164 sq miles.
† Figures exclude adjustment for underenumeration. This was estimated at 8.4% in 1950 and 6.99% in 1976. The adjusted total for 1950 is 3,019,031, including an estimate of 87,000 for the tribal Indian population.
‡ Provisional.

DEPARTMENTS (estimated population at mid-1988)*

	Population	Capital
Beni	282,631	Trinidad
Chuquisaca	496,781	Sucre
Cochabamba	1,073,539	Cochabamba
La Paz	2,134,008	La Paz
Oruro	437,324	Oruro
Pando	55,251	Cobija
Potosí	841,156	Potosí
Santa Cruz	1,314,585	Santa Cruz de la Sierra
Tarija	293,224	Tarija
Total	6,928,499	

* Figures are provisional. The revised total is 6,993,344.

PRINCIPAL TOWNS (estimated population at mid-1988)

La Paz (administrative capital)	1,049,800
Santa Cruz de la Sierra	615,122
Cochabamba	377,259
Oruro	195,239
Potosí	114,092
Sucre (legal capital)	95,635
Tarija	68,493

BIRTHS AND DEATHS (UN estimates, annual averages)

	1975–80	1980–85	1985–90
Birth rate (per 1,000)	44.8	44.0	42.8
Death rate (per 1,000)	17.5	15.9	14,1

Source: UN, *World Population Prospects: 1988*.

ECONOMICALLY ACTIVE POPULATION
(mid-year estimates, '000 persons aged 10 years and over)

	1985	1986	1987
Agriculture, hunting, forestry and fishing	799.6	788.0	791.3
Mining and quarrying	68.5	42.3	42.4
Manufacturing	147.1	117.1	118.1
Electricity, gas and water	8.2	8.1	8.1
Construction	46.3	43.6	45.8
Trade, restaurants and hotels	127.8	135.9	136.1
Transport, storage and communications	96.8	121.9	122.8
Financing, insurance, real estate and business services	14.5	14.0	14.3
Community, social and personal services	377.0	390.4	391.4
Total employed	1,685.8	1,661.4	1,670.3
Unemployed	370.9	415.4	430.7
Total labour force	2,056.7	2,076.8	2,101.1
Males	1,577.4	1,590.0	1,605.6
Females	479.2	486.8	495.4

Source: International Labour Office, *Year Book of Labour Statistics*.

Agriculture

PRINCIPAL CROPS ('000 metric tons)

	1986	1987	1988
Wheat	81.2	65.8	63.8
Rice (paddy)	137.0	164.4	161.2
Barley	78.0	67.0	68.9
Maize	457.2	430.0	396.0
Sorghum	59.3	60.0	57.1
Potatoes	697	598	598
Cassava (Manioc)	420	425	425
Other roots and tubers	88.7	94.8	n.a.
Soya beans	80.9	140.0	141.0
Groundnuts (in shell)	15	15	15
Cottonseed	n.a.	6.4	n.a.
Cotton (lint)	4.7	5.5	5.3
Sugar cane	2,870	2,730	2,670
Oranges	40.0	69.0	70.7
Bananas and plantains	396.0	450.0	462.6
Coffee (green)	23.7	25.2	25.5
Natural rubber*	5	5	5

* FAO estimates. Source: FAO, *Production Yearbook*.
Source: Departamento de Estadísticas, Ministerio de Asuntos Campesinos y Agropecuarios (MACA).

BOLIVIA

LIVESTOCK ('000 head, year ending September)

	1986	1987	1988
Horses	385.0	388.0	n.a.
Mules*	80†	80†	80†
Asses*	600†	610†	620†
Cattle	5,300.0	5,380.0	5,401.6
Pigs	1,650.0	1,690.0	2,019.9
Sheep	8,115.0	8,440.0	7,505.5
Goats	2,360.0	2,290.0	n.a.
Poultry (million)	9†	11‡	12†

* Source: FAO, *Production Yearbook*.
† FAO estimate.   ‡ Unofficial estimate.
Source: Departamento de Estadísticas, Ministerio de Asuntos Campesinos y Agropecuarios.

LIVESTOCK PRODUCTS ('000 metric tons)

	1986	1987	1988
Beef and veal	123	125	128*
Mutton and lamb*	22	22	23
Goats' meat*	5	5	5
Pig meat	37	38	40*
Poultry meat*	13	19	26
Cows' milk	95*	103†	105*
Sheep's milk	30	30	31
Goats' milk*	11	11	11
Cheese*	7.0	6.9	7.2
Hens eggs*	26.4	28.0	30.0
Wool: greasy*	9.5	9.5	9.6
scoured*	4.8	5.0	5.1
Cattle hides (fresh)*	14.3	14.5	14.9
Sheepskins (fresh)*	6.0	6.0	6.2

* FAO estimates.   † Unofficial estimate.
Source: FAO, *Production Yearbook*.

Forestry

ROUNDWOOD REMOVALS
(FAO estimates, '000 cubic metres, excluding bark)

	1986	1987	1988
Sawlogs, veneer logs and logs for sleepers*	136	136	136
Other industrial wood†	13	13	13
Fuel wood	1,199	1,230	1,268
Total	1,348	1,379	1,417

* Assumed to be unchanged since 1983.
† Assumed to be unchanged since 1982.
Source: FAO, *Yearbook of Forest Products*.

SAWNWOOD PRODUCTION ('000 cubic metres)

	1986	1987	1988
Broadleaved sawnwood	86	91	91*
Railway sleepers*	4	4	4
Total	90	95	95

* FAO estimate(s).
Source: FAO, *Yearbook of Forest Products*.

Fishing
('000 metric tons, live weight)

	1985	1986	1987
Total catch	4.7	4.8*	4.8*

* FAO estimate.
Source: FAO, *Yearbook of Fishery Statistics*.

Mining*
(metric tons, unless otherwise indicated)

	1986	1987	1988
Tin	10,396	8,128	10,504
Lead	3,121	9,118	12,531
Zinc	33,472	39,292	56,957
Copper	297	9	153
Tungsten (Wolfram)	1,380	804	1,165
Antimony	10,243	10,635	9,943
Silver	95	142	232
Gold	0.7	2.7	5.0
Petroleum (million barrels)	6.4	6.9	7.0
Natural gas ('000 million cu ft)	160.8	161.2	169.9

* Figures for metallic minerals refer to the metal content of ores.
Sources: Ministerio de Minería y Metalurgia; Yacimientos Petrolíferos Fiscales Bolivianos.

Industry

SELECTED PRODUCTS (metric tons, unless otherwise indicated)

	1986	1987	1988
Flour	292,898	184,362	99,564
Cement	293,816	382,225	448,194
Refined sugar	173,475	169,533	175,389
Coffee	23,630	26,200	25,450
Alcohol ('000 litres)	20,329	17,851	n.a.
Electric energy (million kWh)	1,717	1,723	1,878

Finance

CURRENCY AND EXCHANGE RATES
Monetary Units
 100 centavos = 1 boliviano (B).

Denominations
 Coins: 2, 5, 10, 20 and 50 centavos; 1 boliviano.
 Notes: 2, 5, 10, 20, 50, 100 and 200 bolivianos.

Sterling and Dollar Equivalents (30 September 1990)
 £1 sterling = 6.108 bolivianos;
 US $1 = 3.260 bolivianos;
 100 bolivianos = £16.373 = $30.675.

Average Exchange Rate (bolivianos per US $)
 1987   2.055
 1988   2.350
 1989   2.692

Note: In January 1987 the Bolivian peso was replaced by a new currency, the boliviano, with a value equivalent to 1,000,000 former pesos. Some figures in this Survey are still expressed in terms of pesos.

BOLIVIA

Statistical Survey

BUDGET (million bolivianos)*

Revenue†	1984‡	1985	1986
Taxation	572.5	217.9	750.2
Taxes on income, profits and capital gains	45.6	6.2	14.5
Social security contributions	156.0	22.4	139.8
Taxes on property	6.1	1.4	12.5
Sales taxes	30.7	13.6	28.8
Excises	88.7	122.7	326.1
Other domestic taxes on goods and services	10.1	2.4	4.7
Import duties	146.5	30.2	114.2
Export duties	0.1	11.4	11.4
Exchange taxes and profits	72.4	6.2	—
Taxes on international transport	4.3	—	—
Stamp taxes	9.4	0.8	1.9
Other taxes	5.4	0.6	96.3
Adjustment to tax revenue	−2.8	—	—
Property income	166.9	12.2	242.4
Administrative fees, charges, etc.	4.6	0.9	4.7
Fines and forfeits	0.4	0.1	0.2
Other current revenue	0.3	1.4	3.0
Total revenue	**744.7**	**232.5**	**1,000.5**

Expenditure§	1983‡	1984‡	1986
General public services	33.0	4,591.6	159.2
Public order and safety	n.a.	n.a.	61.3
Defence	17.1	372.1	146.6
Education	42.7	843.1	185.5
Health	4.9	102.2	19.1
Social security and welfare	27.9	359.3	250.2
Housing and community amenities	0.7	13.8	8.4
Other community and social services	0.3	7.2	0.6
Economic services	20.6	364.5	172.7
Agriculture, forestry and fishing	2.1	36.3	n.a.
Mining, manufacturing and construction	0.6	10.2	n.a.
Roads	} 4.1 {	110.6	n.a.
Other transport		142.2	n.a.
Communications		15.3	n.a.
Other purposes	11.7	237.4	67.7
Total expenditure	**158.9**	**6,891.2**	**1,010.0**
Current‖	148.2	6,761.1	910.5
Capital	10.7	130.1	99.5

* Figures refer to the transactions of central government units covered by the General Budget, plus the operations of other units (government agencies and 32 social security institutions) with their own budgets.
† Excluding grants received ('000 million pesos): 47.2 in 1984; 12.7 (million bolivianos) in 1986.
‡ Figures are in '000 million pesos bolivianos.
§ Excluding net lending ('000 million pesos): 0.5 in 1983; 16.0 in 1984; 8.7 (million bolivianos) in 1986. Figures for 1985 are not available.
‖ Including interest payments ('000 million pesos): 9.3 in 1983; 150.0 in 1984; 50.9 (million bolivianos) in 1986.

Source: IMF, *Government Finance Statistics Yearbook*.

INTERNATIONAL RESERVES (US $ million at 31 December)*

	1987	1988	1989
Foreign exchange	97.3	105.8	204.9

* Figures exclude gold reserves, totalling 894,000 troy ounces in each year 1985–89. These reserves were valued at US $37.8 million at 31 December 1986.

Source: IMF, *International Financial Statistics*.

MONEY SUPPLY (million bolivianos at 31 December)

	1986	1987	1988
Currency outside banks	294	397	526
Private sector deposits at Central Bank	6	2	2
Demand deposits at commercial banks	69	105	135
Total money	**369**	**504**	**663**

Source: IMF, *International Financial Statistics*.

COST OF LIVING (Consumer Price Index; Base: 1966 = 100)

	1986	1987	1988
Food	60,176,942	66,345,504	73,934,650
Housing	22,717,098	26,308,338	32,633,070
Clothes	32,644,777	40,628,938	46,610,490
Various	43,223,610	55,669,564	73,710,930
All items	**47,742,001**	**54,702,175**	**63,455,600**

NATIONAL ACCOUNTS (estimates, million pesos at 1980 prices)
Gross Domestic Product by Economic Activity

	1986	1987	1988
Agriculture, forestry and fishing	25,534	25,483	25,204
Mining (incl. petroleum exploration)	12,062	12,255	14,448
Manufacturing	11,038	11,423	12,142
Electricity	987	926	978
Construction	2,918	2,895	3,134
Transport and fuel	7,557	7,971	8,410
Commerce and finance	27,867	28,597	28,575
Services and rent	3,356	3,354	3,365
Public administration	14,646	15,171	15,027
Sub-total	**105,965**	**108,075**	**111,283**
Taxes on international trade	1,246	1,404	1,270
Total	**107,211**	**109,479**	**112,553**

BALANCE OF PAYMENTS (US $ million)

	1987	1988	1989
Merchandise exports f.o.b.	518.7	542.5	723.5
Merchandise imports f.o.b.	−646.3	−590.9	−729.5
Trade balance	**−127.6**	**−48.4**	**−6.0**
Exports of services	147.7	146.5	167.2
Imports of services	−564.1	−537.8	−581.2
Balance on goods and services	**−544.0**	**−439.7**	**−420.0**
Private unrequited transfers (net)	18.0	12.7	20.6
Government unrequited transfers (net)	99.2	123.9	135.2
Current balance	**−426.8**	**−303.1**	**−264.2**
Direct capital investment (net)	36.4	−12.0	−25.4
Other long-term capital (net)	−74.2	97.6	103.0
Short-term capital (net)	−103.9	−110.3	−181.0
Net errors and omissions	174.6	46.6	−32.1
Total (net monetary movements)	**−393.9**	**−281.2**	**−399.7**
Valuation changes (net)	−26.8	7.3	−21.8
Exceptional financing (net)	389.0	250.2	199.2
Official financing (net)	−43.5	−12.4	95.7
Changes in reserves	**−75.2**	**−36.0**	**−126.6**

Source: IMF, *International Financial Statistics*.

BOLIVIA

External Trade

PRINCIPAL COMMODITIES (US $ million)

Imports	1985	1986	1987
Consumer goods	132.5	174.3	124.8
Non-durable	26.6	42.6	52.0
Durable	69.9	70.6	72.8
Raw materials	182.1	248.8	314.1
Materials for agriculture	14.6	21.6	21.8
Materials for industry	184.6	200.2	245.3
Capital goods	231.8	283	322.5
Construction	21.0	34	43.7
Agriculture	21.8	44.7	37.6
Industry	109.2	172.7	180.2
Transport equipment	71.1	112.9	104.7
Total (incl. others)	551.9	711.5	776.0

Exports	1986	1987	1988
Metallic minerals	196.8	207.2	273.1
Natural gas	328.6	248.6	214.9
Coffee	13.2	11.5	16.9
Sugar	4.9	8.6	6.3
Wood	22.7	30.9	25.5
Rubber	3.8	1.9	2.0
Chestnuts	3.5	6.7	5.6
Hides	6.2	8.1	19.5
Cattle	13.4	6.8	0.5
Soybeans	18.7	19.2	20.2
Total (incl. others)	637.8	569.5	600.2

Source: Ministerio de Industria, Comercio y Turismo.

EXPORTS OF MINING PRODUCTS (US $ '000)

	1986	1987	1988
Tin	104,100	68,873	76,899
Tungsten	6,649	5,050	5,300
Antimony	14,499	22,768	17,357
Lead	5,000	4,259	5,919
Zinc	28,010	32,796	60,113
Copper	777	12*	112
Silver	27,293	33,349	45,057
Gold	7,200	37,500	59,800

* Source: Instituto Nacional de Estadística; Departamento Comercio Exterior.
Source: Ministerio de Minería y Metalurgia.

PRINCIPAL TRADING PARTNERS (US $ '000)

Imports	1985*	1986	1987
Argentina	82,800	75,610	45,689
Belgium	4,400	16,416	4,863
Brazil	115,900	124,405	73,990
Canada	4,900	4,697	3,974
Chile	27,600	34,301	23,252
France	9,900	6,239	2,269
Germany, Federal Republic	39,700	45,873	20,428
Italy	4,400	5,497	2,482
Japan	38,600	65,333	30,598
Netherlands	9,400	5,783	2,752
Peru	27,600	14,890	5,716
Sweden	3,900	8,719	4,309
Switzerland	5,000	4,826	3,519
United Kingdom	11,000	31,009	2,652
USA	121,400	150,052	63,476
Total (incl. others)	551,900	674,033	327,165

* Estimates.

Exports	1986	1987	1988
Argentina	340,744	259,886	227,536
Belgium	10,933	17,725	35,981
Brazil	26,037	19,479	11,280
Chile	19,913	16,640	29,505
Colombia	1,873	4,071	3,913
France	5,629	5,232	7,520
Germany, Federal Republic	37,902	33,416	34,418
Netherlands	674	192	2,149
Peru	22,263	24,036	22,658
Switzerland	7,502	6,956	9,725
United Kingdom	50,863	61,004	71,010
USA	97,072	96,077	102,215
Total (incl. others)	640,338	569,793	600,215

Transport

RAILWAYS (traffic)

	1986	1987	1988
Passengers carried	1,885,338	1,392,621	1,050,798
Passenger-kilometres	657,121	500,388	368,886
Freight carried (metric tons)	923,432	981,812	872,416
Freight ton-kilometres	463,617	504,753	423,850

Source: Dirección General de Ferrocarriles.

ROAD TRAFFIC (motor vehicles in use)

	1986	1987	1988
Cars	69,269	78,208	83,741
Buses	11,271	11,982	12,395
Trucks	38,329	41,325	43,118
Lorries	36,639	40,265	42,648
Vans	27,050	29,944	32,629
Jeeps	17,918	19,232	20,108
Motor cycles	47,379	47,816	51,813

CIVIL AVIATION (traffic on scheduled services)

	1983	1984	1985
Kilometres flown (million)	9.7	11.0	11.3
Passengers carried ('000)	1,299	1,359	1,343
Passenger-km (million)	787	877	894
Freight ton-km (million)	17.2	38.0	41.5

Source: United Nations, *Statistical Yearbook*.

Tourism

	1982	1983	1984
Arrivals at hotels	150,142	175,903	163,183

Education

(1986)

	Institutions*	Teachers†	Students
Primary and elementary	9,093	51,038	1,355,338
Pre-basic	1,065	1,954	137,018
Basic	6,633	40,104	947,291
Intermediate	1,395	8,980	271,029
Middle	909	7,970	206,405
Other	—	2,405	18,551
Total	10,002	62,413	1,580,294

* 1984 figures. † 1985 figures.

Directory

The Constitution

Bolivia became an independent republic in 1825 and received its first constitution in November 1826. Since that date a number of new constitutions have been promulgated. Following the *coup d'état* of November 1964, the Constitution of 1947 was revived. Under its provisions, executive power is vested in the President. According to the revised Constitution, the President is elected by direct suffrage for a four-year term and is not eligible for immediate re-election. In the event of the President's death or failure to assume office, the Vice-President or, failing the Vice-President, the President of the Senate becomes interim Head of State.

The President has power to appoint members of the Cabinet, diplomatic representatives, and archbishops and bishops from a panel proposed by the Senate. The President is responsible for the conduct of foreign affairs and is also empowered to issue decrees, and initiate legislation by special messages to Congress.

Congress consists of a Senate (27 members) and a Chamber of Deputies (130 members). Congress meets annually and its ordinary sessions last only 90 working days, which may be extended to 120. Each of the nine departments (La Paz, Chuquisaca, Oruro, Beni, Santa Cruz, Potosí, Tarija, Cochabamba and Pando), into which the country is divided for administrative purposes, elects three senators. Members of both houses are elected for four years.

The supreme administrative, political and military authority in each department is vested in a prefect appointed by the President. The sub-divisions of each department, known as provinces, are administered by sub-prefects. The provinces are further divided into cantons. There are 94 provinces and some 1,000 cantons. The capital of each department has its autonomous municipal council and controls its own revenue and expenditure.

Public order, education and roads are under national control.

A decree issued in July 1952 conferred the franchise on all persons who had reached the age of 21 years, whether literate or illiterate. Previously the franchise had been restricted to literate persons. (The voting age for married persons was lowered to 18 years at the 1989 elections.)

The death penalty was restored in October 1971 for terrorism, kidnapping and crimes against government and security personnel. In 1981 its scope was extended to drug trafficking.

The Government

HEAD OF STATE

President: Jaime Paz Zamora (MIR) (took office 6 August 1989).
Vice-President: Luis Ossio Sanjines (PDC).

THE CABINET
(November 1990)

Minister of Foreign Affairs and Worship: Carlos Iturralde Ballivián (ADN).
Minister of Finance: David Blanco Zavala (ADN).
Minister of Planning and Co-ordination: Enrique García Rodríguez (ADN).
Minister of Education and Culture: Mariano Baptista Gumucio (MIR).
Minister of Labour: Oscar Zamora Medinacelli (MIR).
Minister of Urban Affairs: Elena Velasco (ADN).
Minister of the Interior, Migration and Justice: Guillermo Capobianco Rivera (MIR).
Minister of Defence: Héctor Ormachea Peñaranda (ADN).
Minister of Industry, Trade and Tourism: Guido Céspedes Argandoña (MIR).
Minister of Transport and Communications: Willy Vargas Vacaflor (ADN).
Minister of Public Health and Social Security: Mario Paz Zamora (MIR).
Minister of Mining and Metallurgy: Walter Soriana Lea Plaza (ADN).
Minister of Agriculture: Mauro Bertero Gutiérrez (ADN).
Minister of Energy: Angel Bánzer Ojaros (MIR).
Minister of Aviation: Luis González Quintanilla (MIR).
Minister of Information: Manfredo Kempff Suárez (ADN).
Minister of the Presidency: Gustavo Fernández Saavedra (MIR).
Minister without Portfolio: Guillermo Fortún Suárez (ADN).

MINISTRIES

Office of the President: Palacio de Gobierno, Plaza Murillo, La Paz; tel. (2) 37-1317; telex 5242.
Ministry of Agriculture: Avda Camacho 1407, La Paz; tel. (2) 37-4260; telex 5242.
Ministry of Aviation: Avda Arce 2579, Casilla 6176, La Paz; tel. (2) 37-4142; telex 3413.
Ministry of Defence: Plaza Abaroa esq. 20 de Octubre, La Paz; tel. (2) 37-7130; telex 5242.
Ministry of Education and Culture: Avda Arce 2408, La Paz; tel. (2) 37-3260; telex 3373.
Ministry of Energy: Avda Mariscal Santa Cruz 1322, La Paz; tel. (2) 37-4050; telex 5366.
Ministry of Finance: Calle Bolívar, La Paz; tel. (2) 37-9240; telex 2617.
Ministry of Foreign Affairs and Worship: Edif. BCB, 6° piso, La Paz; tel. (2) 37-1152; telex 5242.
Ministry of Industry, Trade and Tourism: Avda Camacho esq. Bueno, Casilla 1372, La Paz; tel. (2) 37-2044; telex 3259.
Ministry of Information: La Paz; tel. (2) 37-6350.
Ministry of the Interior, Migration and Justice: Avda Arce, La Paz; tel. (2) 37-0460; telex 5437.
Ministry of Labour: Calle Yanacocha esq. Calle Mercado, La Paz; tel. (2) 37-4351; telex 5242.
Ministry of Mining and Metallurgy: Avda 16 de Julio 1769, La Paz; tel. (2) 37-9310; telex 5564.
Ministry of Planning and Co-ordination: Avda Arce 2147, La Paz; tel. (2) 37-2060; telex 5321.
Ministry of Public Health and Social Security: Plaza del Estudiante, La Paz; tel. (2) 37-5460; telex 5242.
Ministry of Transport and Communications: Edif. La Urbana, Avda Camacho, La Paz; tel. (2) 37-7220; telex 2648.
Ministry of Urban Affairs: Avda 20 de Octubre esq. F. Guachalla, Casilla 5926, La Paz; tel. (2) 37-2240; telex 5242.

President and Legislature

PRESIDENT

At the presidential election that took place on 7 May 1989, the three principal candidates were Gonzalo Sánchez de Lozada of the ruling Movimiento Nacionalista Revolucionario (MNR), who obtained 363,113 votes (23.07%), Gen. (retd) Hugo Bánzer Suárez of Acción Democrática Nacionalista (ADN), who won 357,298 votes (22.70%), and Jaime Paz Zamora of the Movimiento de la Izquierda Revolucionaria (MIR), who received 309,033 votes (19.64%). As no candidate obtained the requisite absolute majority, responsibility for the selection of the President passed to the new National Congress, and on 6 August Jaime Paz Zamora was duly elected for a four-year term, taking office on the same day.

CONGRESO NACIONAL

President: Julio Garrett.

General election, 7 May 1989

Party	Seats Chamber of Deputies	Senate
Movimiento Nacionalista Revolucionario (Histórico) (MNR)	40	9
Acción Democrática Nacionalista (ADN)	38	8
Movimiento de la Izquierda Revolucionaria (MIR)	33	8
Conciencia de Patria (Condepa)	9	2
Izquierda Unida (IU)	10	—
Total	**130**	**27**

BOLIVIA

Political Organizations

Acción Democrática Nacionalista (ADN): La Paz; f. 1979; right-wing; Leader Gen. HUGO BÁNZER SUÁREZ; Sec.-Gen. GUILLERMO FORTÚN.

Alianza Patriótica (AP): La Paz; left-wing; absorbed MIR—Masas (breakaway faction of MIR, f. 1985); Leader WALTER DELGADILLO.

Alternativa Revolucionaria del Pueblo (ARP): La Paz; Leader JUAN LECHÍN OQUENDO.

Centro Nacionalista (CEN): Héroes del Arce 1746, Of. La Voz del Pueblo, La Paz; right-wing; Leader Dr ROBERTO ZAPATA DE LA BARRA.

Conciencia de Patria (Condepa): La Paz; f. 1988; populist party; Leader CARLOS PALENQUE.

Falange Socialista Boliviano (FSB): La Paz; f. 1937; right-wing; Leaders DAVID AÑEZ, REMY SOLARES; divided into two factions:
  Gutiérrez: Sánchez Lima 2278, La Paz; f. 1937; Leader Dr MARIO GUTIÉRREZ.
  Moreira: Canoniga Ayllón esq. Boquerón 597, Casilla 4937, La Paz; Leader GASTÓN MOREIRA OSTRÍA; Sec.-Gen. Dr AUGUSTO MENDIZÁBAL; 100,000 mems.

Falange Socialista Boliviana de la Izquierda (FSBI): Casilla 1649, La Paz; f. 1970; Leader Dr ENRIQUE RIVEROS ALIAGA; 150,000 mems.

Frente del Pueblo Unido (FPU): left-wing; comprising dissident members of the PRIN, the MIR and the PCB (see below).

Frente Revolucionario de Izquierda (FRI): Mercado 996, 2°, Of. 2, La Paz; left-wing; Leader Dr MANUEL MORALES DÁVILA.

Mandato de Acción y Unidad Nacional (MAN): Comercio 1057, 3°, Casilla 2169, La Paz; f. 1972; Leader Dr GONZALO ROMERO ALVAREZ GARCÍA; Sec. Dr FERNANDO OBLITAS MENDOZA; 2,000 mems.

Movimiento Agrario Revolucionario del Campesinado Boliviano (MARC): Yanacocha 448, Of. 17, La Paz; f. 1978; nationalist movement; Pres. Gen. (retd) RENÉ BERNAL ESCALANTE; Exec. Sec. Dr JOSÉ ZEGARRA CERRUTO.

Movimiento Bolivia Libre (MBL): Calle Batallón Victoria esq. Armentia 807, Casilla 10382, La Paz; tel. (2) 34-0257; f. 1985; left-wing; breakaway faction of MIR; allied to FPU (see above); Leader ANTONIO ARANÍBAR QUIROGA.

Movimiento de la Izquierda Nacional (MIN): La Paz; left-wing; Leader Dr LUIS SANDOVAL MORÓN.

Movimiento de la Izquierda Revolucionaria (MIR): Avda América 119, 2°, La Paz; telex 3210; f. 1971; split into several factions in 1985; left-wing; Leader JAIME PAZ ZAMORA; Sec.-Gen. OSCAR EID FRANCO.

Movimiento Nacionalista Revolucionario (Histórico)—MNR: Genaro Sanjines 541, Pasaje Kuljis, La Paz; formerly part of the Movimiento Nacionalista Revolucionario (MNR, f. 1942); centre-right; Leader (vacant); Sec.-Gen. JOSÉ LUIS HARB; 700,000 mems.

Movimiento Nacionalista Revolucionario de Izquierda (MNRI): La Paz; f. 1979; formerly part of the Movimiento Nacionalista Revolucionario (MNR, f. 1942); left of centre; Leader Dr HERNÁN SILES ZUAZO; Sec.-Gen. FEDERICO ALVAREZ PLATA.

Movimiento Nacionalista Revolucionario (MNR)—Julio: Claudio Pinilla 1648, La Paz; formerly part of the Movimiento Nacionalista Revolucionario (MNR, f. 1942); Leader RUBÉN JULIO CASTRO.

Movimiento Nacionalista Revolucionario del Pueblo (MNRP): Casilla 3030, La Paz; f. 1965; nationalist movement; Leader JAIME ARELLANO CASTEÑADA; 50,000 mems.

Movimiento Revolucionario Tupac Katarí (MRTK): Linares esq. Sagáruaga 901, Casilla 3636, La Paz; f. 1978; peasant party; Pres. JUAN CONDORI URUCHI; Leader GENARO FLORES SANTOS; 80,000 mems.

Ofensiva de la Izquierda Democrática (OID): Edif. Herrmann 11°, Plaza Venezuela 1440, La Paz; f. 1979; Leader LUIS ADOLFO SILES SALINAS.

Organización de Unidad Revolucionaria (OUR): Comercio 979, 1°, Of. 14, La Paz; f. 1977; Sec.-Gen. Dr MARIO LANZA SUÁREZ; 5,000 mems.

Partido Comunista de Bolivia (PCB): La Paz; f. 1950; follows Moscow line; First Sec. SIMÓN REYES RIVERA.

Partido Comunista Marxista Leninista de Bolivia: c/o Palacio Legislativo, Palacio Murillo, La Paz; f. 1965; formerly part of the PCB.

Partido Demócrata Cristiano (PDC): Casilla 4345, La Paz; telex 2532; f. 1954; Pres. Dr JORGE AGREDA VALDERRAMA; Sec. ANTONIO CANELAS-GALATOIRE; 50,000 mems.

Partido Indio: La Paz.

Directory

Partido Obrero Revolucionario (POR): Correo Central, La Paz; f. 1935; Trotskyist; Leader GUILLERMO LORA.

Partido de la Revolución Nacional (PRN): Saavedra 1026, Casilla 8466, La Paz; f. 1966; left-wing; Leader RUBÉN ARIAS ALVIS; Sec.-Gen. LUIS JIMÉNEZ ESPINOZA; 50,000 mems.

Partido Revolucionario Auténtico (PRA): Yanacocha 448, Of. 2, La Paz; f. 1960; formerly part of the Movimiento Nacionalista Revolucionario (MNR, f. 1942); Leader Dr WALTER GUEVARA ARCE.

Partido Revolucionario de la Izquierda Nacional Gueiler (PRING): Mercado 996, 2°, La Paz; Leader Dra LIDIA GUEILER TEJADA.

Partido Revolucionario de la Izquierda Nacionalista (PRIN): Colón 693, La Paz; f. 1964; left-wing.

Partido Social Demócrata (PSD): Edif. Barrosquira 6°, La Paz; f. 1945; Leader Dr ANTONIO CHIQIE DIPP.

Partido Socialista-Uno (PS-1): La Paz; Leader ROGER CÓRTEZ.

Partido Socialista-Uno—Marcelo Quiroga: La Paz; Leader JOSÉ MARÍA PALACIOS.

Partido Unión Boliviana (PUB): Pichincha 729 esq. Indaburo, La Paz; Leader WALTER GONZALES VALDA.

Partido de la Unión Socialista Republicana (PURS): Casilla 3724, La Paz; f. 1945; left-wing; Leader Dr CONSTANTINO CARRIÓN V.; Sec.-Gen. PEDRO MONTAÑO; 30,000 mems.

Partido de Vanguardia Obrera: Plaza Venezuela 1452, La Paz; Leader FILEMÓN ESCOBAR.

Vanguardia Revolucionaria 9 de Abril: Casilla 5810, La Paz; tel. (2) 32-0311; telex 2613; Leader Dr CARLOS SERRATE REICH.

In September 1988 the formation of **Izquierda Unida (IU)**, an electoral alliance of eight left-wing parties, was announced. Members included the MBL, PCB, AP and PS-1 (1989 Presidential Candidate: ANTONIO ARANÍBAR QUIROGA). The MBL left the alliance in February 1990.

Diplomatic Representation

EMBASSIES IN BOLIVIA

Argentina: Calle Aspiazu 497, La Paz; tel. (2) 32-2172; telex 3300; fax (2) 39-1083; Ambassador: EDUARDO HÉCTOR IGLESIAS.

Belgium: Avda Hernando Siles 5290, Casilla 2433, La Paz; tel. (2) 78-4925; telex 3274; Ambassador: PHILIPPE JOTTARD.

Brazil: Fernando Guachalla 494, Casilla 429, La Paz; tel. (2) 35-0718; telex 2494; Ambassador: JOÃO TABAJARA DE OLIVEIRA.

China, People's Republic: La Paz; telex 5558; Ambassador: XIE RUMAO.

Colombia: Calle 20 de Octubre 2427, Casilla 1418, La Paz; tel. (2) 35-9658; telex 3593; Ambassador: CARLOS EDUARDO LOZANO TOVAR.

Costa Rica: Avda Vera 6870, Casilla 2780, La Paz; Ambassador: GUILLERMO GAGO PÉREZ.

Cuba: Avda Arequipa 8037, Calacoto, La Paz; tel. (2) 79-2616; telex 2447; Ambassador: GUSTAVO BRUGUÉS-PÉREZ.

Czechoslovakia: Urb. Las Colinas, Calle 24, No 6, Calacoto, Casilla 2780, La Paz; telex 2530; Ambassador: STANISLAV NOVOTNÝ.

Ecuador: Edif. Herrman 14°, Plaza Venezuela, Casilla 406, La Paz; tel. (2) 32-1208; telex 3388; Ambassador: OLMEDO MONTEVERDE PAZ.

Egypt: Avda Ballivián 599, Casilla 2956, La Paz; tel. (2) 78-6511; telex 2612; Ambassador: Dr GABER SABRA.

France: Avda Hernando Silés 5390, esq. calle 8, Obrajes, Casilla 824, La Paz; tel. (2) 78-6114; telex 2484; Ambassador: PIERRE MUTTER.

Germany: Avda Arce 2395, Casilla 5265, La Paz; tel. (2) 39-0850; telex 3303; fax (2) 39-1297; Ambassador: Dr HERMANN SAUMWEBER.

Holy See: Avda Arce 2990, Casilla 136, La Paz; tel. (2) 37-5007; telex 2393; Apostolic Nuncio: Most Rev. GIOVANNI TONUCCI, Titular Archbishop of Torcello.

Israel: Edif. Esperanza 10°, Avda Mariscal Santa Cruz, Casilla 1309, La Paz; tel. (2) 32-5463; telex 3297; Ambassador: BERL ZERUBAVEL.

Italy: Avda 6 de Agosto 2575, Casilla 626, La Paz; tel. (2) 32-7329; telex 2654; Ambassador: Dr GIOVANNI MINGAZZINI.

Japan: Calle Rosendo Gutiérrez 497, Casilla 2725, La Paz; tel. (2) 37-3152; telex 2548; Ambassador: (vacant).

Korea, Democratic People's Republic: La Paz; Ambassador: KIM CHAN SIK.

BOLIVIA

Korea, Republic: Avda 6 de Agosto 2592, Casilla 1559, La Paz; tel. (2) 36-4485; telex 3262; Ambassador: CHO KAB-DONG.
Mexico: Avda 6 de Agosto 2652, POB 430, La Paz; tel. (2) 32-9505; telex 3316; Ambassador: Lic. MARCELO VARGAS CAMPOS.
Panama: Calle Potosí 1270, Casilla 678, La Paz; tel. (2) 37-1277; telex 2314; Chargé d'affaires a.i.: Lic. JOSÉ RODRIGO DE LA ROSA.
Paraguay: Edif. Venus, Avda Arce esq. Montevideo, Casilla 882, La Paz; tel. (2) 32-2018; Ambassador: Gen. RAMÓN DUARTE VERA.
Peru: Calle Rosendo Gutiérrez 113 esq. Capitán Ravelo, Casilla 668, La Paz; tel. (2) 35-3550; telex 2475; Ambassador: JAIME CACHO SOUSA.
Romania: Calle Capitán Ravelo (Pasaje Isaac G. Eduardo) 2173, Casilla 20879, La Paz; tel. (2) 37-8632; telex 3260; Ambassador: ION FLORES.
South Africa: Calle 22, Calacoto No. 7810, Casilla 6018, La Paz; tel. (2) 79-2101; telex 3279; Ambassador: (vacant).
Spain: Avda 6 de Agosto 2860, Casilla 282, La Paz; tel. (2) 34-3518; telex 3304; Ambassador: CARMELO ANGULO BARTUREN.
Switzerland: Edif. Petrolero, Avda 16 de Julio 1616, Casilla 657, La Paz; tel. (2) 35-3091; telex 2325; Ambassador: (vacant).
USSR: Avda Arequipa 8128, Casilla 5494, La Paz; tel. (2) 79-2048; telex 2480; Ambassador: TAKHIR BYASHIMOVICH DURDIYEV.
United Kingdom: Avda Arce 2732-2754, Casilla 694, La Paz; tel. (2) 32-9401; telex 2341; fax (2) 39-1063; Ambassador: MICHAEL DALY.
USA: Edif. Banco Popular del Perú, Calle Colón 290, Casilla 425, La Paz; tel. (2) 35-0120; telex 3268; fax (2) 35-9875; Ambassador: ROBERT SIDNEY GELBARD.
Uruguay: Avda Arce 2985, Casilla 441, La Paz; tel. (2) 35-3857; telex 2378; Ambassador: JOSÉ M. ALVAREZ.
Venezuela: Calle Méndez Arcos 117, Casilla 960, La Paz; tel. (2) 32-0872; telex 2383; Ambassador: EDUARDO MORREO BUSTAMANTE.
Yugoslavia: Benito Juárez 315, La Florida, Casilla 1717, La Paz; tel. (2) 79-2148; Chargé d'affaires: SVETISLAV RAJEVIĆ.

Judicial System

SUPREME COURT

Corte Suprema: Calle Yanacocha 417, La Paz; tel. (2) 37-7032; telex 2320.

Judicial power is vested in the Supreme Court. There are 12 members, appointed by Congress for a term of 10 years. The court is divided into four chambers of three justices each. Two chambers deal with civil cases, the third deals with criminal cases and the fourth deals with administrative, social and mining cases. The President of the Supreme Court presides over joint sessions of the courts and attends the joint sessions for cassation cases.

President of the Supreme Court: Dir EDGAR OBLITAS FERNÁNDEZ.

DISTRICT COURTS

There is a District Court sitting in each Department, and additional provincial and local courts to try minor cases.

ATTORNEY-GENERAL

In addition to the Attorney-General at Sucre (appointed by the President on the proposal of the Senate), there is a District Attorney in each Department as well as circuit judges.

Attorney-General: Dr JOSÉ HUGO VILAR TUFINO.

Religion

The majority of the population are Roman Catholics; there were an estimated 2.1m. adherents in 1989. Religious freedom is guaranteed. There is a small Jewish community, as well as various Protestant denominations, in Bolivia.

CHRISTIANITY

The Roman Catholic Church

Bolivia comprises four archdioceses, four dioceses, two Territorial Prelatures and six Apostolic Vicariates.

Bishops' Conference: Conferencia Episcopal de Bolivia, Calle Potosí 814, Casilla 2309, La Paz; tel. (2) 32-1254; fax (2) 31 0601; f. 1972; Pres. Rt Rev. JULIO TERRAZAS SANDOVAL, Bishop of Oruro.
Archbishop of Cochabamba: Most Rev. RENÉ FERNÁNDEZ APAZA, Calle Calama E. 0169, Casilla 129, Cochabamba; tel. (42) 22984.

Archbishop of La Paz: Most Rev. LUIS SÁINZ HINOJOSA, Calle Ballivián 1277, Casilla 259, La Paz; tel. (2) 34-1920.
Archbishop of Santa Cruz de la Sierra: Most Rev. LUIS ANÍBAL RODRÍGUEZ PARDO, Casilla 25, Ingavi 49, Santa Cruz de la Sierra; tel. (33) 24286.
Archbishop of Sucre: Most Rev. JESÚS GERVASIO PÉREZ RODRÍGUEZ, Calle Bolívar 702, Casilla 205, Sucre; tel. (64) 21703.

The Anglican Communion

Within the Iglesia Anglicana del Cono Sur de América (Anglican Church of the Southern Cone of America), Bolivia forms part of the diocese of Peru. The Bishop is resident in Lima, Peru.

Protestant Churches

Baptist Convention of Bolivia: Casilla 3147, Santa Cruz; tel. (33) 40717; f. 1947; Pres. FÉLIX VARGAS G.
Baptist Union of Bolivia: Casilla 1408, La Paz; Pres. Rev. AUGUSTO CHUIJO.
Iglesia Evangélica Metodista en Bolivia (Evangelical Methodist Church in Bolivia): Casilla 356, La Paz; tel. (2) 34-2702; autonomous since 1969; 5,000 mems; Bishop Rt Rev. ROLANDO VILLENA VILLEGAS.

BAHÁ'Í FAITH

National Spiritual Assembly of the Bahá'ís of Bolivia: Casilla 1613, La Paz; tel. (2) 78-5058; mems resident in 5,867 localities.

The Press

DAILY NEWSPAPERS

Cochabamba

Los Tiempos: Santiváñez 4110, Casilla 525, Cochabamba; tel. (42) 28586; f. 1943; morning; independent; right-wing; Dir CARLOS CANELAS; circ. 18,000.

La Paz

El Diario: Loayza 118, Casilla 5, La Paz; tel. (2) 35-6835; telex 5530; f. 1904; morning; conservative; Dir JORGE CARRASCO VILLALOBOS; circ. 45,000.
Hoy: Avda 6 de Agosto 2170, Casilla 477, La Paz; tel. (2) 32-6683; telex 2613; f. 1968; morning and midday editions; independent; Dir Dr CARLOS SERRATE REICH; circ. 45,000.
Jornada: Junín 608, Casilla 1628, La Paz; tel. (2) 35-3844; f. 1964; evening; independent; Dir JAIME RÍOS CHACÓN; circ. 11,500.
Presencia: Avda Mariscal Santa Cruz 1295, Casilla 1451, La Paz; tel. (2) 37-2344; telex 2659; f. 1952; morning and evening; Catholic; Dir Lic. ARMANDO MARIACA V.; Man. Lic. FELICÍSIMO TARILONTE P.; circ. 90,000.
Ultima Hora: Avda Camacho 309, Casilla 5920, La Paz; tel. (2) 37-0416; f. 1939; evening; independent; Dir JORGE SILES SALINAS; Editor JORGE CANELAS; circ. 35,000.

Oruro

El Expreso: Potosí 319 esq. Oblitas, Oruro; f. 1973; morning; independent; right-wing; Dir GENARO FRONTANILLA VISTAS; circ. 1,000.
La Patria: Avda Camacho 1892, Casilla 48, Oruro; tel. (52) 50761; f. 1919; morning; independent; Dir ENRIQUE MIRALLES; circ. 5,000.

Potosí

El Siglo: Calle Linares 99, Casilla 389, Potosí; f. 1975; morning; Dir WILSON MENDIETA PACHECO; circ. 1,500.

Santa Cruz

El Deber: Suárez Arana 264, Casilla 2144, Santa Cruz; tel. (33) 23588; f. 1965; morning; independent; Dir PEDRO RIVERO MERCADO; circ. 8,000.
El Mundo: Calle Beni 169, Santa Cruz; tel. (33) 34770; f. 1979; morning; owned by Santa Cruz Industrialists' Association; Dir SIXTO NELSON FLEIG; circ. 20,000.

Tarija

La Verdad: Tarija; Dir JOSÉ LANZA; circ. 3,000.

Trinidad

La Razón: Avda Bolívar 295, Casilla 166, Trinidad; tel. (2) 1377; f. 1972; Dir CARLOS VÉLEZ.

PERIODICALS

Actualidad Boliviana Confidencial: Fernando Guachalla 969, Casilla 648, La Paz; f. 1966; weekly; Dir HUGO GONZÁLEZ RIOJA; circ. 6,000.

BOLIVIA

Aquí: Casilla 10937, La Paz; tel. (2) 34-3524; f. 1979; weekly; circ. 10,000.

Bolivia Libre: Edif. Esperanza 5°, Avda Mariscal Santa Cruz 2150, Casilla 6500, La Paz; fortnightly; published by the Ministry of Information.

Carta Cruceña de Integración: Casilla 3531, Santa Cruz de la Sierra; weekly; Dirs HERNÁN LLANOVARCED A., JOHNNY LAZARTE J.

Comentarios Económicos de Actualidad (CEA): Casilla 12097, La Paz; tel. (2) 35-4520; fortnightly; articles and economic analyses.

Extra: Oruro; weekly; Dir JORGE LAZO.

Información Política y Económica (IPE): Calle Comercio, Casilla 2484, La Paz; weekly; Dir GONZALO LÓPEZ MUÑOZ.

Informe R: La Paz; weekly; Editor SARA MONROY.

Notas: Casilla 5782, La Paz; tel. (2) 37-3773; telex 3236; weekly; political and economic analysis; Editor JOSÉ GRAMUNT DE MORAGAS.

El Noticiero: Sucre; weekly; Dir DAVID CABEZAS; circ. 1,500.

Servicio de Información Confidencial (SIC): Elías Sagárnaga 274, Casilla 5035, La Paz; weekly; publ. by Asociación Nacional de Prensa; Dir JOSÉ CARRANZA.

Siglo XXI: La Paz; weekly.

Unión: Sucre; weekly; Dir JAIME MERILES.

PRESS ASSOCIATIONS

Asociación Nacional de Periodistas: Avda 6 de Agosto 2170, Casilla 477, La Paz; Pres. ALBERTO ZUAZO NATHES.

Asociación Nacional de Prensa: Comercio 1048, Casilla 3089, La Paz; Pres. Dr CARLOS SERRATE REICH.

Asociación de Periodistas de La Paz: Comercio 1048, Casilla 3089, La Paz; tel. (2) 36-9916; Pres. HUMBERTO VACAFLOR GANAM.

NEWS AGENCIES

Agencia de Noticias Fides (ANF): Edif. Mariscal de Ayacucho, 6°, Of. 601, Calle Loayza, Casilla 5782, La Paz; tel. (2) 36-5152; telex 3236; fax (2) 36-5153; owned by Catholic Church; Dir JOSÉ GRAMUNT DE MORAGAS.

Foreign Bureaux

Agencia EFE (Spain): Edif. Esperanza, Avda Mariscal Santa Cruz 2150, Casilla 7403, La Paz; tel. (2) 36-7205; telex 2535; fax (2) 39-1441; Bureau Chief AGUSTÍN DE GRACIA.

Agenzia Nazionale Stampa Associata (ANSA) (Italy): Edif. Cosmos, 12°, Avda 16 de Julio 1800, La Paz; tel. (2) 35-5521; telex 3410; fax (2) 36-8221; Correspondent ERIC UKROW.

Associated Press (AP) (USA): Edif. Mariscal de Ayacucho, Of. 1209, Calle Loayza, Casilla 9569, La Paz; tel. (2) 37-0128; telex 3283; Correspondent PETER J. McFARREN.

Deutsche Presse-Agentur (dpa) (Germany): Plaza Venezuela 1456, 1°, Of. F, Casilla 135, La Paz; tel. (2) 35-2684; telex 2601; Correspondent GONZALO RUÍZ TOVAR.

Informatsionnoye Agentstvo Novosti (IAN) (USSR): Edif. Mariscal Ballivián, Of. 401, Calle Mercado, La Paz; tel. (2) 37-3857; telex 3285; Correspondent VLADIMIR RAMÍREZ.

Inter Press Service (IPS) (Italy): Edif. Esperanza 6°, Of. 6, Casilla 4313, La Paz; tel. (2) 36-1227; Correspondent RONALD GREBE LÓPEZ.

Prensa Latina (Cuba): Edif. Mariscal de Ayacucho, Of. 905, 9°, Calle Loaya, La Paz; tel. (2) 32-3479; telex 2525; Correspondent MANUEL ROBLES SOSA.

Reuters (UK): Calle Loayza, 11°, Of. 1112-3, Casilla 4057, La Paz; tel. (2) 35-1106; telex 2573; Correspondent JUAN JAVIER ZEBALLOS.

Telegrafnoye Agentstvo Sovetskovo Soyuza (TASS) (USSR): Casilla 6839, San Miguel, Bloque 0-33, Casa 958, La Paz; tel. (2) 79-2108; Correspondent ELDAR ABDULLAEV.

United Press International (UPI) (USA): Plaza Venezuela 1456, 1°, Of. B, Casilla 1219, La Paz; tel. (2) 37-1278; telex 2453; Correspondent ALBERTO ZUAZO NATHES.

Agence France-Presse and Telam (Argentina) are also represented.

Publishers

Editora Khana Cruz SRL: Avda Camacho 1372, Casilla 5920, La Paz; tel. (2) 37-0263; Dir GLADIS ANDRADE.

Editora Lux: Edif. Esperanza, Avda Mariscal Santa Cruz, Casilla 1566, La Paz; tel. (2) 32-9102; f. 1952; Dir FELICISIMO TARILONTE PÉREZ.

Editorial los Amigos del Libro: Avda Heroínas E-0311, Casilla 450, Cochabamba; tel. (42) 22920; f. 1945; general; Man. Dir WERNER GUTTENTAG.

Editorial Bruño: Casilla 4809, Calle Mercado esq. Loayza, La Paz; tel. (2) 32-0198; f. 1964; Dir IRINEO LOMAS.

Editorial Difusión: Avda 16 de Julio 1601, Casilla 1510, La Paz; tel. (2) 32-8126; f. 1960; literature, history, politics, social studies; Man. Dir JORGE F. CATALANO.

Editorial Don Bosco: Avda 16 de Julio 1899, Casilla 4458, La Paz; tel. (2) 37-1149; social sciences, literature and the cinema; Dir JULIAN BELLOMO MUSCI.

Editorial Icthus: Avda 16 de Julio 1800, Casilla 8353, La Paz; tel. (2) 35-4007; f. 1967; general and textbooks; Man. Dir DANIEL AQUIZE.

Editorial y Librería Juventud: Plaza Murillo 519, Casilla 1489, La Paz; tel. (2) 34-1694; f. 1946; textbooks and general; Dirs RAFAEL URQUIZO, GUSTAVO URQUIZO.

Editorial Popular: Plaza Pérez Velasco 787, Casilla 4171, La Paz; tel. (2) 35-0701; f. 1935; textbooks, postcards, tourist guides, etc; Man. Dir GERMÁN VILLAMOR.

Editorial Puerta del Sol: Edif. Litoral Sub Suelo, Avda Mariscal Santa Cruz, La Paz; tel. (2) 36-0746; f. 1965; Man. Dir OSCAR CRESPO.

Empresa Editora Proinsa: Calle Ballivián 1279, Casilla 7181, La Paz; tel. (2) 35-7781; Dirs FLOREN SANABRIA G., CARLOS SANABRIA G.

Gisbert y Cía, SA: Comercio 1270, Casilla 195, La Paz; tel. (2) 37-2961; f. 1907; textbooks, history, law and general; Pres. JAVIER GISBERT; Dirs CARMEN G. DE SCHULCZEWSKI, ARMANDO PAGANO.

Ivar American: Calle Potosí 1375, Casilla 6016, La Paz; tel. (2) 36-1519; Man. Dir HÉCTOR IBÁÑEZ.

Librería El Ateneo SRL: Calle Ballivián 1275, Casilla 7917, La Paz; tel. (2) 36-9925; Dirs JUAN CHIRVECHES D., MIRIAN C. DE CHIRVECHES.

Librería Dismo Ltda: Comercio 806, Casilla 806, La Paz; tel. (2) 35-3119; Dir TERESA GONZÁLEZ DE ALVAREZ.

Librería La Paz: Colón 618, Casilla 539, La Paz; tel. (2) 35-3323; f. 1900; Dirs CARLOS BURGOS R., CARLOS BURGOS M.

Librería La Universal SRL: Calle Genaro Sanjines 538, Casilla 2888, La Paz; tel. (2) 34-2961; f. 1958; Man. Dir ROLANDO CONDORI.

Librería San Pablo: Calle Colón 627, Casilla 3152, La Paz; tel. (2) 32-6084; f. 1967; Man. Dir MARÍA DE JESÚS VALERIANO.

PUBLISHERS' ASSOCIATION

Cámara Boliviana del Libro: Edif. Las Palmas, Avda 20 de Octubre 2005, Casilla 682, La Paz; tel. (2) 32-7039; Pres. NANCY C. DE MONTOYA (acting).

Radio and Television

In 1987 there were an estimated 3.6m. radio receivers and 520,000 television receivers in use.

Dirección General de Telecomunicaciones: Edif. Guerrero, Mercado 1115, Casilla 4475, La Paz; tel. (2) 36-8788; telex 2595; government-controlled broadcasting authority; Dir-Gen. Ing. FREDDY CANAVIRE PARDO.

RADIO

There were 158 radio stations in 1985, the majority of which were commercial. Broadcasts are in Spanish, Aymará and Quechua.

Asociación Boliviana de Radiodifusoras (ASBORA): Potosí 920, Casilla 7958, La Paz; tel. (2) 32-8513; broadcasting authority; Pres. MIGUEL A. DUERI; Vice-Pres. ENRIQUE COSTAS.

TELEVISION

Empresa Nacional de Televisión: Ayacucho 467, Casilla 900, La Paz; tel. (2) 37-6356; telex 2312; f. 1969; government network operating stations in La Paz, Oruro, Cochabamba, Potosí, Sucre, Pando, Beni, Tarija and Santa Cruz; Dir-Gen. J. BARRAGÁN; Gen. Man. RAÚL NOVILLO ALARCÓN.

Televisión Universitaria—Canal 13: Av. 6 de Agosto 2170, Edif. 'Hoy', Pisos 12 y 13, La Paz; tel. (2) 35-9297; telex 3438; fax (2) 35-9491; f. 1980; educational programmes; stations in Oruro, Cochabamba, Potosí, Sucre, Tarija, Beni and Santa Cruz; Dir CARLOS SORIA GALVARRO.

BOLIVIA
Directory

Finance

(cap. = capital; p.u. = paid up; res = reserves;
dep. = deposits; m. = million; brs = branches; amounts are in
bolivianos unless otherwise stated)

BANKING

Supervisory Authority

Superintendencia de Bancos: Calle Loayza 155, Casilla 3118, La Paz; tel. (2) 35-8169; fax (2) 37-0102; f. 1928; Man. Lic. LUIS DEL RÍO CHÁVEZ.

State Banks

Banco Central de Bolivia: Ayacucho esq. Mercado, Casilla 3118, La Paz; tel. (2) 37-4151; telex 3403; fax (2) 37-1009; f. 1928; bank of issue; cap. and res 336.1m. (Dec. 1989); Pres. Lic. RAÚL BOADA RODRIGUEZ; Gen. Man. Lic. JAVIER PANTOJA ROMERO.

Banco del Estado: Calle Colón esq. Mercado, Casilla 1401, La Paz; tel. (2) 35-2868; telex 3267; fax (2) 39-1682; f. 1970; state bank incorporating banking department of Banco Central de Bolivia; cap. and res 51.1m., dep. 92.5m. (June 1990); Pres. Lic. RAMÓN RADA VELASCO; Gen. Man. JUAN LUIS PACHECO RAMÍREZ; 55 brs.

Banco Agrícola de Bolivia: Avda Mariscal Santa Cruz esq. Almirante Grau, Casilla 1179, La Paz; tel. (2) 36-5876; telex 3278; fax (2) 35-5940; f. 1942; cap. and res 100.4m. (June 1990); Pres. Lic. WALTER NÚÑEZ R.; Gen. Man. Lic. JUAN CARLOS PEREDO P.

Banco Minero de Bolivia: Calle Comercio 1290, Casilla 1410, La Paz; tel. (2) 35-2168; telex 2568; fax (2) 36-8870; f. 1936; finances private mining industry; cap. and res 44.6m. (June 1990); Pres. Ing. JAIME ASCARRUNZ E.; Gen. Man. Ing. RENÉ SANZ M.

Banco de la Vivienda: Avda Camacho 1336, Casilla 8155, La Paz; tel. (2) 34-3510; telex 2295; f. 1964; to encourage and finance housing developments; 51% state participation; initial cap. 100m. Bolivian pesos; Pres. (vacant); Gen. Man. Lic. JOSÉ RAMÍREZ MONTALVA.

Commercial Banks

Banco Boliviano Americano: Avda Camacho esq. Loayza, Casilla 478, La Paz; tel. (2) 36-1101; telex 2279; fax (2) 35-3984; f. 1957; cap. and res 30.0m., dep. 279.6m. (June 1990); Pres. LUIS EDUARDO SILES; Exec. Vice-Pres. JOSÉ A. ARIAS; 13 brs.

Banco de Cochabamba, SA: Warnes 40, Casilla 4107, Santa Cruz; tel. (33) 51036; telex 4265; cap. and res 20.8m., dep. 128.8m. (June 1990); Exec. Pres. GUILLERMO GUTIÉRREZ SOSA; Gen. Man. EDGAR DICK NOYA; 5 brs.

Banco de Financiamiento Industrial, SA: Plaza 10 de Febrero acera Adolfo Mier esq. La Plata, Casilla 51, Oruro; tel. (52) 53759; telex 2234; f. 1974 to encourage and finance industrial development; cap. p.u. 2.6m. Bolivian pesos, dep. 1.1m. Bolivian pesos; Pres. Lic. HUGO CAMPOS; Man. FRANCISCO BERMÚDEZ.

Banco Industrial, SA: Avda 16 de Julio 1628, 8°, Casilla 1290, La Paz; tel. (2) 35-9471; telex 2584; fax (2) 39-2013; f. 1963; industrial credit bank; cap. and res 35.3m., dep. 53.3m. (June 1990); Pres. JULIO LEÓN PRADO; Gen. Man. JUAN OTERO S.; 1 br.

Banco Industrial y Ganadero del Beni, SA: Edif. Bigbeni, Avda 6 de Agosto, Casilla 54, Trinidad; tel. (46) 21476; telex 6320; cap. and res 22.4m., dep. 121.8m. (June 1990); Pres. Dr ISAAC SHIRIQUI V.; 11 brs.

Banco de Inversión Boliviano, SA: Avda 16 de Julio 1571, Casilla 8639, La Paz; tel. (2) 35-4233; telex 2465; fax (2) 32-6536; f. 1977; cap. and res 10.1m., dep. 57.4m. (June 1990); Pres. JAIME GUTIÉRREZ MOSCOSO; Gen. Man. RAMIRO ALVAREZ RUÍZ.

Banco de La Paz SA: Avda 16 de Julio 1473, Casilla 6826, La Paz; tel. (2) 36-4142; telex 2423; fax (2) 35-7135; f. 1975; cap. and res 17.7m.; dep. 140.0m. (June 1990); Exec. Pres. Lic. GUIDO E. HINOJOSA; Man. Lic. RUBÉN ROMERO DEL C.; 11 brs.

Banco Mercantil SA: Ayacucho esq. Mercado, Casilla 423, La Paz; tel. (2) 35-6902; telex 2270; fax (2) 39-1442; f. 1905; cap. and res 30.5m., dep. 207.2m. (June 1990); Pres. JAVIER ZUAZO CHÁVEZ; Exec. Vice-Pres. EMILIO UNZUETA ZEGARRA; 6 brs.

Banco Nacional de Bolivia: Avda Camacho esq. Colón, Casilla 360, La Paz; tel. (2) 37-9989; telex 2583; fax (2) 37-1279; f. 1872; cap. and res 27.1m., dep. 243.1m. (June 1990); Pres. Dr FERNANDO CALVO UNZUETA; Gen. Man. Lic. EDUARDO ALVAREZ L.; 10 brs.

Banco de Santa Cruz de la Sierra, SA: Calle Junín esq. 21 de Mayo, Casilla 865, Santa Cruz; tel. (33) 39911; telex 5611; fax (33) 50114; f. 1966; cap. and res 44.2m., dep. 315.4m. (June 1990); Pres. Ing. LÍDERS PAREJA EGUEZ; Gen. Man. Ing. LUIS FERNANDO SAAVEDRA BRUNO; 10 brs.

Banco de la Unión SA: Calle Rene Moreno esq. Republiquetas, No 418, Casilla 4057, Santa Cruz; tel. (33) 46869; telex 4285; fax (33) 40684; f. 1982; cap. and res 23.6m., dep. 165.1m. (June 1990); Pres. Arq. CRISTÓBAL RODA DAZA; Gen. Man. Ing. JORGE ARIAS LAZCANO; 3 brs.

BHN Multibanco SA: Avda 16 de Julio 1630, Casilla 4824, La Paz; tel. (2) 35-9351; telex 2290; fax (2) 39-1358; f. 1890; fmrly known as Banco Hipotecario Nacional; cap. and res 26.5m., dep. 173.2m. (June 1990); Pres. FERNANDO ROMERO M.; Exec. Vice-Pres. Lic. CARLOS H. FERNÁNDEZ M.

Caja Central de Ahorro y Préstamo para la Vivienda: Avda Mariscal Santa Cruz 1364, 20°, Casilla 4808, La Paz; tel. (2) 37-1280; telex 5611; f. 1967; assets US $28m. (1983); Gen. Man. Dr GASTÓN MUJÍA T.

Foreign Banks

Banco do Brasil SA: Avda Camacho 1448, Casilla 1650, La Paz; tel. (2) 34-3007; telex 2316; fax (2) 39-1036; f. 1960; Man. MARIO JOSÉ SOARES ESTEVES; 3 brs.

Banco de la Nación Argentina: Avda 16 de Julio 1486, Casilla 4312, La Paz; tel. (2) 35-9211; telex 2282; Man. RICARDO M. CABRERA; 3 brs.

Banco Popular del Perú: Mercado esq. Colón, Casilla 6014, La Paz; tel. (2) 35-5023; telex 2344; fax (2) 35-5023; f. 1942; Central Man. MANUEL BARRETO; 6 brs.

Banco Real SA: Avda Camacho 1355, Casilla 20270, La Paz; tel. (2) 36-6603; telex 2396; fax (2) 39-1413; Gen. Man. CARLOS ALBERTO R. COUTINHO.

Citibank N.A. (USA): Plaza Venezuela 1434, Casilla 260, La Paz; tel. (2) 32-1742; telex 2546; fax (2) 32-1743; Vice-Pres. JOSÉ MARÍA LASA.

Deutsch-Südamerikanische Bank AG (Banco Germánico de la América del Sud) and Dresdner Bank AG (Germany): Joint representation: Avda Mariscal Santa Cruz, esq. Yanacocha, Edif. Hansa 4°, Casilla 1077, La Paz; tel. (2) 37-4450; telex 2311; fax (2) 39-1060; Rep. CARLOS A. MARTINS.

Banking Association

Asociación de Bancos e Instituciones Financieras de Bolivia (ASOBAN): Edif. Cámara Nacional de Comercio, 15°, Avda Mariscal Santa Cruz esq. Colombia 1392, Casilla 5822, La Paz; tel. (2) 32-1379; telex 2439; fax (2) 39-1093; f. 1957; Pres. Dr FERNANDO CALVO UNZUETA; Exec. Sec. Lic. GUIDO ANTEZANA V.; 22 mems.

INSURANCE

Supervisory Authority

Superintendencia Nacional de Seguros y Reaseguros: Calle Batallón Colorados 162, 3° y 4°, Casilla 6118, La Paz; tel. (2) 37-4137; fax (2) 39-1819; f. 1975; Superintendent EDUARDO SALINAS BALDIVIEZO; Man. Lic. ORLANDO NOGALES NOGALES.

National Companies

(p.i. = premium income; amounts in Bolivian pesos, $bs, unless otherwise stated)

Argos, Cía de Seguros, SA: Edif. Argos, Calle Potosí esq. Colón, Casilla 277, La Paz; tel. (2) 34-0029; telex 2297; f. 1962; all classes except life; p.i. 38.3m. (1982); Pres. JOSÉ T. KAWAI; Gen. Man. ABSALÓN OMOYA.

Bolívar SA de Seguros: Edif. Bolivar, Avda Mariscal Santa Cruz 1287, Casilla 1459, La Paz; tel. (2) 35-1441; telex 3292; fax (2) 39-1248; f. 1952; all classes; p.i. 3.8m. (1989); Pres. Lic. FREDDY OPORTO MÉNDEZ; Gen. Man. MARIO OPORTO M.

Cía Americana de Seguros y Reaseguros, SA: Edif. Sáenz 3°, Avda Camacho 1377, Casilla 6180, La Paz; tel. (2) 32-9374; telex 2589; f. 1970; all classes; p.i. 27.1m. (1982); Pres. MARIO PATIÑO MILÁN; Gen. Man. JULIO BUTRÓN MENDOZA.

Cía Andina de Seguros y Reaseguros, SA: Edif. Alborada 2°, Mercado esq. Loayza, Casilla 4723, La Paz; tel. (2) 37-4371; telex 4723; f. 1974; all classes; p.i. 96.7m. (1982); Pres. Lic. LUIS ADOLFO DE UGARTE; Dir RAMÓN ESCÓBAR AGUILAR.

Cía de Seguros y Reaseguros Santa Cruz, SA: Edif. CIACRUZ, Calle Pari No 28, Casilla 2233, Santa Cruz; tel. (33) 42319; telex 4257; f. 1980; all classes; p.i. US $620m. (1981); Pres. JUAN MANUEL PARADA PERDRIEL; Gen. Man. ANTONIO OLEA BAUDOIN.

Cooperativa de Seguros Cruceña Ltda: Calle Junín 363, Casilla 297, Santa Cruz; tel. (33) 43254; telex 4326; Pres. ADALBERTO TERCEROS BANZER; Man. MARIO ANTELO BURELA.

Credinform International SA de Seguros: Edif. Credinform, Potosí esq. Ayacucho, Casilla 1724, La Paz; tel. (2) 35-6931; telex 2304; f. 1954; all classes; p.i. 4,709m.; Pres. Dr RODÍN BARRAGÁN PELAEZ; Gen. Man. MIGUEL ANGEL BARRAGÁN IDANQUIBI.

Delta Insurance Co, SA: 25 de Mayo, Casilla 920, Cochabamba; tel. (42) 26006; f. 1965; all classes except life; Pres. JUAN JOSÉ GALINDO B.; Gen. Man. CARLOS CHRISTIE J.

BOLIVIA
Directory

Fénix Boliviana SA de Seguros y Reaseguros: Edif. Naira, Of. 5, Potosí esq. Loayza, Casilla 4409, La Paz; tel. (2) 37-0271; telex 3470; f. 1978; all classes; p.i. 40m. (1982); Pres. Lic. WALTER SÁNCHEZ; Gen. Man. Lic. ORLANDO NOGALES.

La Boliviana de Seguros y Reaseguros SA: Colón 288, Casilla 628, La Paz; tel. (2) 37-9438; telex 2562; fax (2) 39-1309; f.1946; cap. and res US $5m. (1989); Pres. GONZALO BEDOYA H.; Gen. Man. Lic. ALFONSO IBÁÑEZ.

La Mercantil de Seguros y Reaseguros, SA: Mercado 1121, Casilla 2727, La Paz; tel. (2) 35-5893; telex 3313; f. 1957; all classes; p.i. 50m. (1982); Pres. Dr HUGO ECHEVERRÍA; Gen. Man. ASTENIO AVERANGA.

Nacional de Seguros y Reaseguros SA: Avda 20 de Octubre 2095, Casilla 14, La Paz; tel. (2) 32-1217; telex 3235; f. 1977; fmrly known as Condor, SA de Seguros y Reaseguros; p.i. US $350m.; Pres. JOSÉ DEL CASTILLO; Gen. Man. DAVID ALCOREZA MARCHETTI.

Real Bolivia de Seguros, SA: Edif. Litoral, Colón 150, Casilla 1847, La Paz; tel. (2) 32-8823; telex 2431; f. 1980; all classes; p.i. 30.7m.; Pres. SEBASTIAO BERNARDES RENGEL; Gen. Man. FRANCISCO FREITAS.

Seguros Illimani, SA: Edif. Mariscal de Ayacucho 10°, Calle Loayza, Casilla 133, La Paz; tel. (2) 37-1090; telex 3261; f. 1979; all classes; p.i. 66.8m.; Pres. Dr OVIDIO SUÁREZ; Gen. Man. FERNANDO ARCE G.

Union Insurance Company, SA (Cía Union de Seguros): Edif. El Condor, Piso 16°, Calle Batallón Colorados, Casilla 2922, La Paz; tel. (2) 32-2991; telex 2315; all classes; Pres. Dr JORGE RENGEL SILLERICO; Man. PABLO SCHNEID.

There are also three foreign-owned insurance companies operating in Bolivia: American Life Insurance Co, American Home Assurance Co and United States Fire Insurance Co.

Insurance Association

Asociación Boliviana de Aseguradores: Edif. Castilla 5°, Of. 506, Loayza 250, Casilla 4804, La Paz; tel. (2) 32-8804; f. 1962; Pres. Lic. GONZALO BEDOYA HERRERA; Exec. Sec. BLANCA M. DE OTERMÍN.

Trade and Industry

CHAMBERS OF COMMERCE

Cámara Nacional de Comercio: Edif. Cámara Nacional de Comercio, Avda Mariscal Santa Cruz 1392, Casilla 7, La Paz; tel. (2) 35-4255; telex 2305; fax (2) 39-1004; f. 1890; 30 brs and special brs; Pres. DANIEL PAZ PACHECO; Gen. Man. RENÉ CANDÍA NAVARRO.

Cámara Departamental de Industria y Comercio de Santa Cruz: Avda Suárez de Figueroa 127, 3° y 4°, Casilla 180, Santa Cruz; tel. (33) 34183; telex 4298; fax (33) 42353; f. 1915; Pres. JOSÉ LUIS CAMACHO; Dir-Gen. Ing. JUSTO YÉPEZ KAKUDA.

Cámara Departamental de Comercio de Cochabamba: Calle Sucre E-0336, Casilla 493, Cochabamba; tel. (42) 22905; telex 6380; fax (42) 25590; f. 1922; Pres. OSCAR BAKIR HANDAL; Dir-Gen. EDUARDO REYES BELLOT.

Cámara Departamental de Comercio de Oruro: Pasaje Guachalla, Casilla 148, Oruro; tel. (52) 50606; telex 2230; fax (52) 50606; f. 1895; Pres. JOSÉ FERNÁNDEZ FUENTES; Gen. Man. LUIS CAMACHO VARGAS.

Cámara Departamental de Comercio de Potosí: Casilla 159, Potosí; tel. (62) 22641; telex 2266; Pres. NÉSTOR ZAMORA MUÑOZ; Gen. Man. WALTER ZABALA AYLLON.

Cámara Departamental de Industria y Comercio de Chuquisaca: Casilla 3, Sucre; tel. (64) 21320; telex 2292; fax (64) 21850; Pres. ANTONIO SANTA CRUZ; Gen. Man. ANTONIO LANDÍVAR.

Cámara Nacional de Exportadores: Avda Arce 2017, esq. Goitia, Casilla 12145, La Paz; tel. (2) 34-1220; telex 2471; fax (2) 36-1491; f. 1970; Pres. JAVIER CASTELLANOS HOCHKOFLER; Gen. Man. JORGE ADRIAZOLA REIMERS.

STATE INSTITUTES AND DEVELOPMENT ORGANIZATIONS

Cámara Agropecuaria del Oriente: 3 anillo interno entre Pirai y Roca Coronado, Casilla 116, Santa Cruz; tel. (33) 23164; telex 4438; fax (33) 22621; f. 1964; agriculture and livestock association for eastern Bolivia; Pres. Ing. OSMAN LANDÍVAR; Gen. Man. Ing. JUAN CARLOS VELARDE.

Cámara Agropecuaria de La Paz: Calle Santa Cruz 266, Casilla 6297, La Paz; tel. (2) 32-6854; Pres. FERNANDO PALACIOS; Gen. Man. HÉCTOR ELÍAS AYOROA.

Cámara Nacional Forestal: Calle Manuel Ignacio Salvatierra 1055, Casilla 346, Santa Cruz; tel. (33) 23996; telex 4330; fax (33) 31456; f. 1971; represents the interests of the Bolivian timber industry; Pres. EDGAR LANDÍVAR LANDÍVAR; Man. Lic. ARTURO BOWLES OLHAGARY.

Cámara Nacional de Industria: Edif. Cámara Nacional de Comercio 14°, Avda Mariscal Santa Cruz 1392, Casilla 611, La Paz; tel. (2) 37-4478; telex 3533; f. 1931; Pres. HUGO CASTELLANOS; Gen. Man. Dr ALFREDO ARANA RUCK.

Cámara Nacional de Minería: Pasaje Bernardo Trigo 429, Casilla 2022, La Paz; tel. (2) 35-0623; f. 1953; mining institute; Pres. Ing. LUIS PRADO BARRIENTOS; Sec.-Gen. GERMÁN GORDILLO S.

Comité Boliviano de Productores de Antimonio: Pasaje Bernardo Trigo 429, Casilla 2022, La Paz; tel. (2) 32-5140; f. 1978; controls the marketing, pricing and promotion policies of the antimony industry; Pres. MARIO MERCADO VACA GUZMÁN; Vice-Pres. ALBERTO BARRIOS MORALES.

Comité Boliviano del Café (COBOLCA): Avda Villazón 1970, Casilla 9770, La Paz; tel. (2) 36-2561; telex 3504; controls the export, marketing and growing policies of the coffee industry; Gen. Man. JUAN CARLOS CONCHA URQUIZO.

Consejo Nacional de Planificación (CONEPLAN): Edif. Banco Central de Bolivia 26°, La Paz; tel. (2) 37-7115; f. 1985; under the direction of the Ministry of Planning and Co-ordination.

Corporación de las Fuerzas Armadas para el Desarrollo Nacional (Cofadena): Avda 6 de Agosto 2649, Casilla 1015, La Paz; tel. (2) 37-7305; telex 3286; fax (2) 36-0900; f. 1972; industrial, agricultural and mining holding company and development organization owned by the Bolivian armed forces; Gen. Man. AUGUSTO SÁNCHEZ VALLE.

Corporación Minera de Bolivia (COMIBOL): Avda Mariscal Santa Cruz 1092, Casilla 349, La Paz; tel. (2) 35-7979; telex 2420; fax (2) 36-7483; f. 1952; state mining corporation; taken over by FSTMB (miners' union) in April 1983; owns both mines and processing plants; Gen. Man. Ing. ALBERTO OÑO VILLEGAS.

Corporación Regional de Desarrollo de La Paz (Cordepaz): Edif. Santa Isabel, 2°, Bloque A, Avda Arce esq. Pinilla, Casilla 6102, La Paz; tel. (2) 34-2325; telex 3256; f. 1972; decentralized government institution to foster the development of the La Paz area; Pres. Lic. RICARDO PAZ BALLIVIÁN; Gen. Man. Ing. JUAN G. CARRASCO R.

Empresa Metalúrgica Vinto (EMV): Casilla 612, Oruro; tel. (52) 52857; telex 2255; fax (52) 50458; f. 1966; state company for the smelting of non-ferrous minerals and special alloys; Pres. Ing. GONZALO MARTÍNEZ; Gen. Man. Ing. ALVARO REJAS.

Empresa Nacional de Electricidad, SA (ENDE): Colombia No 655, esq. Falsuri, Casilla 565, Cochabamba; tel. (42) 46322; telex 6251; fax (42) 42700; f. 1962; state electricity company; Pres. ANGEL ZANNIER CLAROS (Minister of Energy); Gen. Man. GONZALO RICO CALDERÓN.

Empresa Nacional de Telecomunicaciones (ENTEL): Edif. Palacio de Comunicaciones, Avda Mcal. Santa Cruz esq. calle Oruro, Casilla 4450, La Paz; tel. (2) 35-5908; telex 3202; f. 1965; Gen. Man. Ing. JUAN JOSÉ PERALTA C.

Instituto Nacional de Inversiones (INI): Edif. Cristal 10°, Calle Yanacocha, Casilla 4393, La Paz; tel. (2) 37-5730; fax (2) 36-7297; f. 1971; state institution for the promotion of new investments and the application of the Investment Law; Exec. Dir Ing. JOSÉ MARIO FERNÁNDEZ IRAHOLA.

Yacimientos Petrolíferos Fiscales Bolivianos (YPFB): Calle Bueno 185, Casilla 401, La Paz; tel. (2) 35-6540; telex 2376; fax (2) 39-1048; f. 1936; state petroleum enterprise; Pres. Ing. RAFAEL PEÑA PARADA; Vice-Pres. for Operations Ing. MARIO ARENAS VISCARRA; Vice-Pres. for Administration and Finance Dr MANUEL OLAVE SARMIENTO.

EMPLOYERS' ASSOCIATIONS

Asociación Nacional de Mineros Medianos: Calle Pedro Salazar 600 esq. Presbítero Medina, Casilla 6094, La Paz; tel. (2) 37-1112; telex 3377; f. 1939; association of the 20 private medium-sized mining companies; Pres. Lic. ALFREDO ROJAS; Sec.-Gen. ROLANDO JORDÁN POZO.

Confederación de Empresarios Privados de Bolivia (CEPB): Edif. Cámara Nacional de Comercio, 7°, Avda Mariscal Santa Cruz 1392, Casilla 20439, La Paz; tel. (2) 35-6831; telex 2305; largest national employers' organization; Pres. Lic. CARLOS CALVO GALINDO; Exec. Sec. Lic. JOHNNY NOGALES VIRUEZ.

There are also employers' federations in Santa Cruz, Cochabamba, Oruro, Potosí, Beni and Tarija.

TRADE UNIONS

Central Obrera Boliviana (COB): Edif. Confederación de Ferroviarios, Calle Ayacucho 286, Casilla 6552, La Paz; tel. (2) 35-2426; f. 1952; main union confederation; 500,000 mems; Exec. Sec. VÍCTOR LÓPEZ ARIAS; Sec.-Gen. DANIEL SANTALLA.

BOLIVIA

Affiliated unions:

Central Obrera Departamental de La Paz: Estación Central 284, La Paz; tel. (2) 35-2898; Exec. Sec. Flavio Clavijo.

Confederación Sindical Unica de los Trabajadores Campesinos de Bolivia (CSUTCB): Calle Sucre esq. Yanacocha, La Paz; tel. (2) 36-9433; f. 1979; peasant farmers' union; Exec. Sec. Juan de la Cruz Villca.

Federación de Empleados de Industria Fabril: Edif. Fabril, Plaza de San Francisco 5°, La Paz; tel. (2) 37-2759; Exec. Sec. Carlos Solari.

Federación Sindical de Trabajadores Mineros Bolivianos (FSTMB): Plaza Venezuela 1470, La Paz; tel. (2) 35-9656; mineworkers' union; Exec. Sec. Víctor López Arias; 27,000 mems.

Federación Sindical de Trabajadores Petroleros de Bolivia: Calle México 1504, La Paz; tel. (2) 35-1748; Exec. Sec. Neftaly Mendoza Durán.

Confederación General de Trabajadores de Bolivia (CGTB): f. 1985; Sec. Francisco Chambi Mangula.

Transport

RAILWAYS

Empresa Nacional de Ferrocarriles (ENFE): Estación Central de Ferrocarriles, Plaza Zalles, Casilla 428, La Paz; tel. (2) 32-7401; telex 2405; f. 1964; administers most of the railways in Bolivia. Total networks: 3,655km (1990); Western Network: Total 2,275 km; Eastern Network: Total 1,380 km; Gen. Man. Ing. Rafael Echazú Brown.

A former private railway, Machacamarca–Uncia, owned by Corporación Minera de Bolivia (105 km), merged with the Western network of ENFE in February 1987. There are plans to construct a railway line with Brazilian assistance, to link Cochabamba and Santa Cruz.

ROADS

In 1984 Bolivia had 40,987 km of roads, of which 1,538 km were paved and 9,268 km were all-weather roads. Almost the entire road network is concentrated in the *altiplano* region and the Andes valleys. A 560-km highway runs from Santa Cruz to Cochabamba, serving a colonization scheme on virgin lands around Santa Cruz. The Pan-American highway, linking Argentina and Peru, crosses Bolivia from south to north-west. In March 1989 the International Development Association granted credit of US $37m. for improvements on these two highways and for the transport system in general. In 1990 plans were announced for the construction of a US $90.9m. highway linking Patacamaya, south of La Paz, to the existing highway, completed in the same year, which links Tambo Quemado, in Bolivia, with Arica, on the Pacific coast of Chile. The project is to be financed jointly by Japan and the Inter-American Development Bank.

INLAND WATERWAYS

By agreement with Paraguay in 1938 (confirmed in 1939), Bolivia has an outlet on the River Paraguay. This arrangement, together with navigation rights on the Paraná, gives Bolivia access to the River Plate and the sea. The River Paraguay is navigable for vessels of 12-ft draught for 288 km beyond Asunción in Paraguay and for smaller boats another 960 km to Corumbá in Brazil.

In 1974 Bolivia was granted free duty access to the Brazilian coastal ports of Belém and Santos and the inland ports of Corumbá and Port Velho. In 1976 Argentina granted Bolivia free port facilities at Rosario on the River Paraná. Most of Bolivia's foreign trade is handled through the ports of Matarani (Peru), Antofagasta and Arica (Chile), Rosario and Buenos Aires (Argentina) and Santos (Brazil).

Bolivia has over 14,000 km of navigable rivers which connect most of Bolivia with the Amazon basin.

Bolivian River Navigation Company: f. 1958; services from Puerto Suárez to Buenos Aires (Argentina).

OCEAN SHIPPING

Líneas Navieras Bolivianas (LINABOL): Edif. Hansa 16°, Avda Mariscal Santa Cruz, Apdo 8695, La Paz; tel. (2) 37-9459; telex 2411; fax (2) 39-1079; Pres. Luis Azurduy Z; Vice-Pres. Wolfgang Apt S.

CIVIL AVIATION

Bolivia has 30 airports including the two international airports at La Paz (El Alto) and Santa Cruz (Viru-Viru).

Lloyd Aéreo Boliviano, SAM (LAB): Casilla 132, Aeropuerto 'Jorge Wilstermann', Cochabamba; tel. (42) 5900; telex 6290; fax (42) 29207; f. 1925; 99.98% government-owned; due to be privatized in 1990; operates a network of scheduled services to 21 cities within Bolivia and to 15 international destinations, namely, Buenos Aires, Asunción, São Paulo, Arica, Lima, Santiago, Manaus, Caracas, Cuzco, Panamá, Salta, Rio de Janeiro, Belo Horizonte, Montevideo, and Miami; Pres. Gonzalo Campero Paz; Gen. Man. Lic. Fernando Vargas; fleet: 2 Boeing 727-100, 3 Boeing 727-200, 1 Fokker F.27-600, 1 F.27-200, 2 Boeing 707-323C (passenger), 1 Boeing 727-100C.

Transportes Aéreos Militares: Avda Panamericana Alto, La Paz; tel. (2) 38-9433; internal passenger and cargo services; Dir-Gen. Col J. M. Coquis; fleet: 1 DC-54, 4 CV-440, 20 C-47, 1 C-46, 6 IAI Arava.

Tourism

Lake Titicaca, at 3,810 m (12,500 ft) above sea-level, offers excellent fishing and the 'reed' island of Suriqui, while on its shore stands the famous Roman Catholic sanctuary of Copacabana. There are pre-Incan ruins at Tiwanaku. The Andes peaks include Chacaltaya, which has the highest ski-run in the world. In 1984 about 163,000 foreign visitors arrived at Bolivian hotels and similar establishments. In 1985 receipts from tourism totalled US $30m. Tourists come mainly from the USA, Europe and South American countries.

Instituto Boliviano de Turismo: Calle Mercado 1328, Casilla 1868, La Paz; tel. (2) 36-7463; telex 2534; f. 1977; Exec. Dir Hortensia Romero de Vallotón.

Asociación Boliviana de Agencias de Viajes y Turismo: Edif. Litoral, Mariscal Santa Cruz 1351, POB 3967, La Paz; f. 1984; Pres. Eugenio Monroy Vélez.

Atomic Energy

Instituto Boliviano de Ciencia y Tecnología Nuclear (IBTEN): Avda 6 de Agosto 2905, Casilla 4821, La Paz; tel. (2) 35-6877; telex 2220; f. 1983; main activities include: nuclear engineering, agricultural and industrial application of radio-isotopes, radiochemical analysis, neutron generating, nuclear physics and dosimetry; Exec. Dir Ing. Juan Carlos Méndez Ferry (acting).

BOTSWANA

Introductory Survey

Location, Climate, Language, Religion, Flag, Capital

The Republic of Botswana is a land-locked country in southern Africa, with South Africa to the south and east, Zimbabwe to the north-east and Namibia to the west and north. A short section of the northern frontier adjoins Zambia. The climate is generally sub-tropical, with hot summers. Annual rainfall averages about 457 mm (18 in), varying from 635 mm (25 in) in the north to 228 mm (9 in) or less in the western Kalahari desert. The country is largely near-desert, and most of its inhabitants live along the eastern border, close to the main railway line. English is the official language, and Setswana the national language. Most of the population follow African religions, but several Christian churches are also represented. The national flag (proportions 3 by 2) consists of a central horizontal stripe of black, edged with white, between two blue stripes. The capital is Gaborone.

Recent History

Botswana was formerly Bechuanaland, which became a British protectorate, at the request of the local rulers, in 1885. It was administered as one of the High Commission Territories in southern Africa, the others being the colony of Basutoland (now Lesotho) and the protectorate of Swaziland. The British Act of Parliament that established the Union of South Africa in 1910 also allowed for the inclusion in South Africa of the three High Commission Territories, on condition that the local inhabitants were consulted. Until 1960, successive South African governments asked for the transfer of the three territories, but the native chiefs always objected to such a scheme.

Within Bechuanaland, gradual progress was made towards self-government, mainly through nominated advisory bodies. A new constitution was introduced in December 1960, and a Legislative Council (partly elected, partly appointed) first met in June 1961. Bechuanaland was made independent of High Commission rule in September 1963, and the office of High Commissioner was abolished in August 1964. The seat of government was transferred from Mafeking (now Mafikeng), in South Africa, to Gaberones (now Gaborone) in February 1965. On 1 March 1965 internal self-government was achieved, and the territory's first direct election, for a Legislative Assembly, was held on the basis of universal adult suffrage. Of the Assembly's 31 seats, 28 were won by the Bechuanaland Democratic Party (BDP or Domkrag), founded in 1962. The leader of the BDP, Seretse Khama, was sworn in as the territory's first Prime Minister. Bechuanaland became the independent Republic of Botswana, within the Commonwealth, on 30 September 1966, with Sir Seretse Khama (as he had just become) taking office as the country's first President. The BDP, restyled the Botswana Democratic Party at independence, won elections to the National Assembly, with little opposition, in 1969, 1974 and 1979. Sir Seretse, a liberal conservative, consolidated his leadership of the country while pursuing a national programme of democracy, development, self-reliance and unity.

Sir Seretse Khama died in July 1980. His successor to the presidency was Dr Quett Masire, previously Vice-President and Minister of Finance. Dr Masire's presidency was renewed in September 1984, when, in a general election to the National Assembly, the ruling BDP again achieved a decisive victory. Although the BDP's success in the general election consolidated its position, some discontent among the population at the country's high level of unemployment was reflected in the outcome of the simultaneous elections to local government offices, in which the BDP lost control of all the town councils except that of Selebi-Phikwe. The elections to the leadership of the BDP, held in July 1985, resulted in a number of changes in the membership of the party's Central Committee, although the principal officers of the party retained their posts.

During 1987 there was growing tension between the BDP and the main opposition party, the Botswana National Front (BNF). In March an unprecedented outbreak of rioting was attributed by observers to popular dissatisfaction with the Government as a result of increasing unemployment. The BNF was subsequently accused of provoking the unrest. Several members of the BDP suggested that BNF youths were being trained by Libya and the USSR in order to overthrow the Government. In a letter to President Masire, Dr Kenneth Koma, the leader of the BNF, protested against the allegations and urged the President not to ban the BNF. At five parliamentary by-elections held in August 1987, four seats were held by the BDP, while the BNF retained the fifth. In the following month a referendum was held on constitutional amendments concerning the electoral system; a large majority reportedly voted in favour of endorsing the reforms, although the BNF boycotted the referendum. During 1989 widespread labour unrest occurred, involving bank employees, mineworkers and school teachers. Nevertheless, in October the BDP received 65% of the votes cast at a general election to the National Assembly, winning 27 of the 30 elective seats (the remaining three seats were won by the BNF). The new National Assembly re-elected Dr Masire for a third five-year term as President. From mid-1990 discussions took place between representatives of the BNF and two other opposition parties, the Botswana People's Party and the Botswana Progressive Union, on the issue of a proposed merger of the three parties.

Botswana occupies a delicate position in southern African politics. Although, as one of the 'front-line states', Botswana does not have diplomatic links with South Africa and is openly critical of apartheid, it depends heavily on its neighbour for trade and communications. In April 1980 Sir Seretse chaired the Lusaka summit meeting which established the Southern African Development Co-ordination Conference (SADCC), an economic union of southern African states committed to reducing their dependence on South Africa. In July 1981 the SADCC decided to establish a permanent secretariat in Gaborone (see p. 209).

From independence, it was the Botswana Government's stated policy not to permit any guerrilla groups to operate from Botswanan territory. Relations with South Africa deteriorated in May 1984, when President Masire accused South Africa of exerting pressure on Botswana to sign a non-aggression pact, aimed at preventing the alleged use of Botswana's territory by guerrilla forces of the African National Congress of South Africa (ANC), a South African opposition organization which was banned in that country during 1960-90. In June 1985 and May 1986 South African forces launched raids on alleged ANC bases in Botswana, causing several deaths. Owing to Botswana's vulnerable position, however, the Government did not commit itself to the imposition of economic sanctions against South Africa when this was recommended by the SADCC in August 1986. In early 1987, with the approach of the South African whites-only general election in May, tension mounted as South Africa warned that it would launch attacks against Botswana in order to pre-empt disruption of the election by the ANC. In April four people were killed in a bomb explosion in Gaborone; South African involvement was strongly suspected.

During 1988 there was speculation that South Africa was again attempting to coerce the Botswana Government into signing a security accord. In March South Africa openly admitted responsibility for a commando raid on a house in Gaborone, in which four alleged members of the ANC were killed. In June President Masire reported the arrest of two members of a South African Defence Force unit which had allegedly opened fire on Botswana security forces near Gaborone while attempting to conduct a commando raid. South Africa claimed that the unit had been on a mission only to gather information, and that the members of the unit had been fired on by the Botswanans before opening fire themselves. Following an abortive attempt to rescue the two South African gunmen from prison in September, they were both sentenced in December to 10 years' imprisonment for inflicting grievous bodily harm. In mid-December two people were killed in a raid, reportedly by South African commandos, on a Botswanan village near the Botswana-South Africa border. A further alleged South African intrusion occurred towards the end of December, when a bomb exploded in Gaborone, killing one person.

During early 1989 the Botswana Government reaffirmed that it did not permit Botswanan territory to be used as a base for terrorist attacks. In late March nine South Africans were expelled from the country for 'security reasons'. In May five members of the ANC were arrested by troops of the Botswana Defence Force and charged with the illegal possession of firearms and ammunition; the guerrillas were sentenced to five years' imprisonment in July. It was reported in the following month that the South African army had erected an electrified fence along a 24-km section of the South Africa-Botswana border, in order to halt the reputed threat of guerrilla infiltration into South Africa via Botswana.

In early 1990 relations between Botswana and South Africa appeared to improve, owing to political developments in the latter country (see chapter on South Africa).

In 1983, following allegations that armed dissidents from Zimbabwe were being sheltered among Zimbabwean refugees encamped in Botswana, the Botswana Government agreed to impose stricter restrictions on the refugees. In May 1983 Botswana and Zimbabwe established full diplomatic relations. The first meeting of the Botswana-Zimbabwe joint commission for co-operation was held in October 1984. A new influx of refugees, following the Zimbabwe general election in July 1985, threatened to strain relations between the two countries. In May 1988, however, President Masire expressed confidence that the Zimbabwean refugees would return to their country as a result of an apparent improvement in the political climate in Zimbabwe. Nevertheless, in April 1989 about 600 Zimbabwean refugees remained in Botswana; at the end of that month the Botswana Government announced that refugee status for Zimbabwean nationals was to be revoked; by September almost all former Zimbabwean refugees had reportedly left Botswana.

In August 1987 Botswana and Mozambique agreed to establish a permanent joint commission to develop and strengthen political, economic and cultural links. In July 1990 it was announced that a joint commission for co-operation was to be established by Botswana and Namibia.

Government

Legislative power is vested in the National Assembly, with 36 members holding office for five years, including 30 elected by universal adult suffrage and four appointed by the President. Executive power is vested in the President, elected by the Assembly for its duration. He appoints and leads a Cabinet, which is responsible to the Assembly. The President has powers to delay implementation of legislation for six months, and certain matters also have to be referred to the 15-member House of Chiefs for approval, although this body has no power of veto. Local government is effected through nine district councils and four town councils.

Defence

Military service is voluntary. Botswana established a permanent Defence Force in 1977. In June 1990 its total strength was 4,500. In addition, there was a paramilitary police force of 1,000. Defence was allocated about 8% of recurrent expenditure in the budget for 1990/91.

Economic Affairs

In 1988, according to estimates by the World Bank, Botswana's gross national product (GNP) per head, measured at average 1986–88 prices, was US $1,010. During 1980–88, it was estimated, overall GNP increased, in real terms, by 10.2%, while GNP per head increased by an annual average of 6.7%. Over the same period, the population increased by an average of 3.3% per year. Botswana's gross domestic product (GDP) increased, in real terms, by an annual average of 11.4% in 1980–88, one of the highest growth rates in the world. Real GDP rose by 13.5% in the year ending 30 June 1989.

Agriculture (including hunting, forestry and fishing) contributed 2.9% of GDP in 1988/89. About 65% of the labour force were employed in the agricultural sector in 1988. The principal agricultural activity is beef production. Other livestock farming is also important. The main subsistence crops are sorghum, maize and pulses. During 1980-88 agricultural production decreased by an annual average of 5.9%.

Industry (including mining, manufacturing, construction and power) employed 10.6% of the working population in 1984–85,
but contributed an estimated 59.3% of GDP in 1988/89. During 1980–88 industrial production increased by an annual average of 15.1%.

Mining contributed an estimated 50.1% of GDP in 1988/89, although the sector employed only 3.3% of the working population in 1984–85. Diamonds (which accounted for an estimated 77% of export earnings in 1988) and copper-nickel matte are the major mineral exports. Coal and gold are also mined. In addition, Botswana has reserves of soda ash, salt, plutonium, asbestos, chromite, fluorspar, iron, manganese, potash, silver, talc and uranium.

Manufacturing contributed an estimated 4.1% of GDP in 1988/89, and employed 3.3% of the working population in 1984–85. Measured by the value of output, the main branches of the sector in 1984/85 were food products (accounting for 39% of the total) and beverages (21%). Other manufactured products include textiles, chemicals, paper, plastics and electrical goods. The output of the manufacturing sector increased at an average rate of 5.0% per year during 1980–88.

Energy is derived principally from fuelwood and coal. Imports of mineral fuels comprised an estimated 7.3% of the value of total imports in 1987.

In 1989 Botswana recorded a visible trade surplus of US $751m., and there was a surplus of $402.3m. on the current account of the balance of payments. In 1987 the principal source of imports (an estimated 79%) was the Southern African Customs Union (see below). The principal market for exports (an estimated 91%) was Europe. The principal exports in 1987 were diamonds, copper-nickel matte and meat and meat products. The principal imports were food, beverages, machinery, electrical goods and transport equipment.

In the financial year to 31 March 1990 there was an estimated budgetary surplus of P57.6m. Botswana's total external public debt was US $494m. in 1988. The cost of debt-servicing was equivalent to 4.0% of export earnings in that year. The average annual rate of inflation was 10.0% in 1980–88. The rate averaged more than 11% in 1989, and was 10.6% in the year to July 1990. An estimated 25% of the labour force were unemployed in mid-1989.

Botswana is both a member of the Southern African Development Co-ordination Conference (see p. 209), which seeks to reduce the economic dependence of southern African states on South Africa, and a member (with Lesotho, Namibia, South Africa and Swaziland) of the Southern African Customs Union.

During the 1980s Botswana's mineral wealth generated large reserves of foreign exchange. However, the agricultural sector was adversely affected by prolonged drought, while the manufacturing sector remained underdeveloped. The high level of unemployment required the Government to encourage private enterprise and to offer incentives to attract foreign investment, in order to diversify the economy. The Sixth National Development Plan (1985–91) aimed to expand employment opportunities in manufacturing, trade and agriculture, to develop rural areas and to improve Botswana's infrastructure and education system. Throughout the 1980s Botswana was dependent on South African transport routes.

Social Welfare

Health services are being developed, and in 1980 there were 13 general hospitals, one mental hospital, 103 clinics (32 with maternity wards), 215 health posts and 341 mobile health stops. There were 111 registered physicians, 10 dentists and 1,071 nurses. The construction at Francistown of a new hospital, the largest in the country, was due to be completed in the late 1980s. Medical treatment for children under 11 years of age is provided free of charge. Health was allocated 2.5% of total budgetary expenditure in 1989/90.

Education

Education is not compulsory. Primary education, which is provided free of charge, begins at seven years of age and lasts for up to seven years. Secondary education, beginning at the age of 14, lasts for a further five years, comprising a first cycle of two years and a second of three years. As a proportion of the school-age population, the total enrolment at primary and secondary schools increased from 52% (boys 47%; girls 56%) in 1975 to 69% in 1988. The Government aims to provide universal access to nine years of basic education by the year 2000. Under the sixth National Development Plan, P315m. was spent on education, including the construction of primary and secondary schools and the expansion of technical education and

BOTSWANA   Introductory Survey, Statistical Survey

of teacher-training facilities. Botswana continues to rely heavily on expatriate secondary school teachers.

Enrolment at primary schools in 1988 included 92.4% of children in the relevant age-group. In 1986 secondary schools were attended by only 25% of children in the relevant age-group (boys 23%; girls 26%). In 1988 there were 261,352 pupils in primary schools, 40,357 secondary students, 1,631 technical students, and 2,837 students at the University of Botswana. In addition, there were 1,111 students at brigades, which are small, semi-autonomous units providing craft and practical training. There were also 1,841 students enrolled at teacher-training colleges. In 1985 there were two teacher-training colleges for the secondary level.

Adult illiteracy averaged 59% (males 63%; females 56%) in 1971, but, according to estimates by UNESCO, the rate had declined to 29.2% (males 27.4%; females 30.5%) by 1985. A National Literacy Programme was initiated in 1980, and 26,200 people were enrolled under the programme in 1988. Education was allocated P265m. (19.5%) of recurrent expenditure in the 1990/91 budget.

Public Holidays

1991: 1-2 January (New Year), 29 March-1 April (Easter), 9 May (Ascension Day), 15-16 July (for President's Day), 30 September-1 October (for Botswana Day), 25-26 December (Christmas).

1992: 1-2 January (New Year), 17-20 April (Easter), 28 May (Ascension Day), 15-16 July (for President's Day), 30 September-1 October (for Botswana Day), 25-26 December (Christmas).

Weights and Measures

The metric system is in use.

Statistical Survey

Source (unless otherwise stated): Central Statistics Office, Private Bag 0024, Gaborone; tel. 50000.

Area and Population

AREA, POPULATION AND DENSITY

Area (sq km)	582,000*
Population (census results)	
31 August 1971	574,094†
12-26 August 1981‡	
Males	443,104
Females	497,923
Total	941,027
Population (official estimates at mid-year)	
1987	1,169,000
1988	1,211,816
1989	1,255,749
Density (per sq km) at mid-1989	2.2

* 224,711 sq miles.
† Excluding 10,550 nomads and 10,861 non-citizens.
‡ Excluding 42,069 citizens absent from the country during enumeration.

Sources: Central Statistics Office, Gaborone; Bank of Botswana.

POPULATION BY CENSUS DISTRICT
(mid-1989 estimates)

Barolong	19,868		Kweneng		154,733
Central	373,667		Lobatse		26,841
Chobe	10,794		Ngamiland		81,184
Francistown	52,725		Ngwaketse		127,180
Gaborone	120,239		North-East		45,645
Ghanzi	24,825		Orapa		8,894
Jwaneng	13,895		Selebi-Phikwe		49,542
Kgalagadi	31,662		South-East		32,448
Kgatleng	52,918				

PRINCIPAL TOWNS (mid 1988 estimates)

Gaborone (capital)	110,973		Kanye	26,300
Francistown	49,396		Mahalapye	26,239
Selebi-Phikwe	46,490		Lobatse	25,689
Molepolole	29,212		Maun	18,470
Serowe	28,267		Ramotswa	17,961
Mochudi	26,320			

Mid-1989 (estimates): Gaborone 120,239; Francistown 52,725; Selibe-Phikwe 49,542; Lobatse 26,841.

Source: Bank of Botswana, Gaborone.

BIRTHS AND DEATHS
(UN estimates, annual averages)

	1975-80	1980-85	1985-90
Birth rate (per 1,000)	50.5	49.2	47.3
Death rate (per 1,000)	15.5	14.3	11.7

Source: UN, *World Population Prospects: 1988*.

ECONOMICALLY ACTIVE POPULATION
(persons aged 12 years and over, 1984-85 sample survey*)

	Males	Females	Total
Agriculture, hunting, forestry and fishing	77,148	81,986	159,134
Mining and quarrying	8,280	719	8,999
Manufacturing	5,033	3,921	8,954
Electricity, gas and water	1,876	112	1,988
Construction	8,810	470	9,280
Trade, restaurants and hotels	6,624	9,046	15,670
Transport, storage and communications	2,140	433	2,573
Financing, insurance, real estate and business services	1,759	1,279	3,038
Community, social and personal services	27,707	37,446	65,153
Activities not adequately defined	32	32	64
Total employed	139,409	135,444	274,853
Unemployed	33,354	59,942	93,096
Total labour force	172,763	195,186	367,949

* Excluding institutional households and members of the armed forces.

Mid-1988 (estimates in '000): Agriculture, etc. 260; Total labour force 403. Source: FAO, *Production Yearbook*.

BOTSWANA

CIVILIAN EMPLOYMENT
(formal sector only; March each year)

	1987	1988	1989
Agriculture	5,100	6,600	8,400
Mining and quarrying	7,200	7,300	7,600
Manufacturing	12,900	15,300	17,900
Electricity and water	2,100	2,200	2,200
Construction	14,600	20,700	24,700
Trade, restaurants and hotels	24,500	26,300	27,300
Transport and communications	6,400	7,100	7,800
Finance and business services	8,800	10,100	11,900
Community, social and personal services	58,500	65,200	74,400
Total	140,200	160,900	182,200

The number of Batswana employed in South African mines was: 20,112 in 1987; 19,320 in 1988; 17,874 in 1989.
Source: Bank of Botswana, Gaborone.

Agriculture

PRINCIPAL CROPS ('000 metric tons)

	1986	1987	1988
Maize	1	3*	12
Millet	1*	1*	3
Sorghum	16	18	40†
Roots and tubers*	7	7	7
Pulses*	14	14	14
Groundnuts (in shell)*	1	1	1
Sunflower seed*	1	1	1
Cottonseed*	2	2	2
Cotton (lint)*	1	1	1
Vegetables*	16	16	16
Fruit*	11	11	11

* FAO estimates.
† Unofficial estimate.
Source: FAO, *Production Yearbook*.

LIVESTOCK ('000 head, year ending September)

	1986	1987*	1988*
Cattle*	2,400	2,300	2,350
Horses	24	25	25
Donkeys*	143	144	145
Sheep	210	215	220
Goats*	1,000	1,050	1,100
Pigs*	9	9	9

* FAO estimates.
Source: FAO, *Production Yearbook*.

LIVESTOCK PRODUCTS (FAO estimates, '000 metric tons)

	1986	1987	1988
Beef and veal	33	34	36
Goats' meat	3	3	3
Other meat	9	9	9
Cows' milk	98	100	101
Goats' milk	3	3	3
Cheese	1.2	1.2	1.3
Butter and ghee	1.4	1.4	1.5
Hen eggs	0.7	0.7	0.7
Cattle hides	4.4	4.5	4.6

Source: FAO, *Production Yearbook*.

Forestry

ROUNDWOOD REMOVALS
(FAO estimates, '000 cubic metres)

	1986	1987	1988
Industrial wood	73	76	79
Fuel wood	1,116	1,156	1,197
Total	1,189	1,232	1,276

Source: FAO, *Yearbook of Forest Products*.

Fishing

	1985	1986	1987
Total catch (metric tons)	1,500	1,700	1,900

Source: FAO, *Yearbook of Fishery Statistics*.

Mining
(metric tons, unless otherwise indicated)

	1987	1988	1989
Coal	579,409	612,873	663,045
Copper ore*	18,465	24,428	21,709
Nickel ore*	16,997	22,533	19,759
Diamonds ('000 carats)	13,324	15,229	15,201

* Figures refer to the metal content of ores.
Source: Bank of Botswana, Gaborone.

Industry

SELECTED PRODUCTS

	1982	1983	1984
Beer ('000 litres)	58,600	63,600	63,800
Electric energy (million kWh)	604	622	661

1985: Electric energy 701 million kWh.
1986: Electric energy 575 million kWh.
1987: Electric energy 891 million kWh.
1988: Electric energy 1,052 million kWh.

Sources: Central Statistics Office, Gaborone; Bank of Botswana, Gaborone.

Finance

CURRENCY AND EXCHANGE RATES
Monetary Units
  100 thebe = 1 pula (P).

Denominations
  Coins: 1, 2, 5, 10, 25 and 50 thebe; 1 pula.
  Notes: 1, 2, 5, 10, 20 and 50 pula.

Sterling and Dollar Equivalents (30 September 1990)
  £1 sterling = 3.5362 pula;
  US $1 = 1.8875 pula;
  100 pula = £28.28 = $52.98.

Average Exchange Rate (US $ per pula)
  1987   0.5960
  1988   0.5507
  1989   0.4969

BOTSWANA

BUDGET ('000 pula, year ending 31 March)

Revenue	1987/88	1988/89	1989/90*
Taxation	1,423,590	1,989,040	2,194,940
Mineral revenues	1,034,470	1,508,060	1,550,900
Customs pool revenues	234,130	292,590	374,000
Non-mineral income tax	129,610	164,760	240,800
Other current revenue	291,110	450,230	407,230
Interest	47,220	94,120	52,250
Other property income	202,280	321,060	327,430
Fees, charges, etc.	41,610	35,050	27,550
Sales of fixed assets and land	4,410	7,090	2,040
Total (incl. others)	1,719,110	2,446,360	2,604,210

* Estimates.

Expenditure	1987/88	1988/89	1989/90*
Office of the President	85,970	115,540	154,560
Finance and development planning	52,260	50,420	91,880
Labour and home affairs	15,480	20,820	24,690
Agriculture	50,330	64,970	79,230
Education	135,490	182,810	236,050
Commerce and industry	7,470	9,870	14,810
Local government and lands	97,840	137,340	181,260
Works and communications	105,160	125,760	166,360
Mineral resources and water affairs	16,820	22,470	29,570
Health	42,120	53,320	63,180
External affairs	8,030	11,190	15,110
Appropriations from revenue	709,300	1,026,280	1,354,980
Public debt interest	73,480	104,350	90,980
Total (incl. others)	1,433,010	1,960,030	2,546,630

* Estimates.

Source: Bank of Botswana, Gaborone.

NATIONAL DEVELOPMENT PLAN, 1985–91
(projected expenditure in million pula)

Office of the President	72.5
Finance and development planning	19.8
Home affairs	15.3
Agriculture	52.8
Education	198.0
Commerce and industry	19.3
Local government and lands	133.4
Works and communications	322.9
Mineral resources and water affairs	93.8
Health	69.8
Non-allocated expenditures	240.0
Total	1,222.3

Source: Ministry of Finance and Development Planning, Gaborone.

INTERNATIONAL RESERVES (US $ million at 31 December)

	1987	1988	1989
IMF special drawing rights	21.82	22.59	24.85
Reserve position in IMF	22.32	18.36	25.26
Foreign exchange	2,012.95	2,217.14	2,791.00
Total	2,057.08	2,258.09	2,841.11

Source: IMF, *International Financial Statistics*.

MONEY SUPPLY (million pula at 31 December)

	1987	1988	1989
Currency outside banks	68.6	95.8	117.6
Demand deposits at commercial banks	243.6	310.7	388.9
Total money	312.1	406.5	506.5

Source: IMF, *International Financial Statistics*.

COST OF LIVING (Consumer Price Index; base: 1985 = 100)

	1987	1988	1989
Food	120.0	132.0	144.8
Clothing	129.6	153.5	170.4
All items (incl. others)	120.6	133.1	148.2

Source: Bank of Botswana, Gaborone.

NATIONAL ACCOUNTS
(million pula at current prices, year ending 30 June)

National Income and Product

	1983/84	1984/85	1985/86
Compensation of employees	476.4	553.6	650.2
Operating surplus	416.6	673.7	1,081.9
Domestic factor incomes	893.0	1,227.3	1,732.1
Consumption of fixed capital	243.7	278.4	349.8
Gross domestic product (GDP) at factor cost	1,136.7	1,505.7	2,081.9
Indirect taxes	166.1	160.4	160.4
Less subsidies	0.7	5.4	7.0
GDP in purchasers' values	1,302.1	1,660.7	2,235.3
Factor income received from abroad	91.6	118.0	305.6
Less Factor income paid abroad	196.5	313.2	
Gross national product	1,197.2	1,465.5	1,929.7
Less Consumption of fixed capital	243.7	278.4	349.8
National income in market prices	953.5	1,187.1	1,579.9
Other current transfers from abroad	29.4	26.4	21.3
Less Other current transfers paid abroad	5.9	5.0	
National disposable income	977.0	1,208.5	1,601.2

Source: Bank of Botswana, Gaborone.

Expenditure on the Gross Domestic Product

	1983/84	1984/85	1985/86
Government final consumption expenditure	362.8	443.1	531.8
Private final consumption expenditure	629.3	746.3	840.1
Increase in stocks	−19.8	15.2	−12.2
Gross fixed capital formation	337.6	484.0	411.9
Total domestic expenditure	1,309.9	1,688.6	1,771.6
Exports*	772.3	970.3	1,591.6
Less Imports†	780.1	998.2	1,127.9
GDP in purchasers' values	1,302.1	1,660.7	2,235.3
GDP at constant 1979/80 prices	1,120.1	1,211.5	1,308.2

* Exports of goods only.
† Imports of goods plus net imports of services.

Sources: Central Statistics Office, Gaborone; Bank of Botswana, Gaborone.

BOTSWANA   Statistical Survey

Gross Domestic Product by Economic Activity

	1986/87	1987/88	1988/89
Agriculture, hunting, forestry and fishing	107.0	136.2	149.1
Mining and quarrying	1,089.7	1,478.5	2,542.1
Manufacturing	161.9	166.8	209.4
Electricity, gas and water	72.2	81.2	92.9
Construction	81.8	110.4	165.6
Trade, restaurants and hotels	485.0	594.8	818.3
Transport, storage and communication	56.6	67.8	81.6
Finance, insurance, real estate and business services	164.6	206.9	262.9
Government services	403.9	524.2	638.1
Other services	81.5	102.3	118.4
Sub-total	2,704.2	3,469.1	5,078.4
Less Imputed bank service charge	56.7	71.2	90.5
GDP in purchasers' values	2,647.5	3,397.9	4,987.9

Source: Bank of Botswana, Gaborone.

BALANCE OF PAYMENTS (US $ million)

	1987	1988	1989
Merchandise exports f.o.b.	1,586.6	1,468.9	1,816.9
Merchandise imports f.o.b.	−803.9	−986.9	−1,065.9
Trade balance	782.7	482.0	751.0
Exports of services	296.9	330.4	357.0
Imports of services	−589.6	−791.9	−886.6
Balance on goods and services	490.0	20.5	221.9
Private unrequited transfers (net)	6.8	−17.5	−15.6
Government unrequited transfers (net)	166.7	184.6	196.0
Current balance	663.5	187.6	402.3
Direct capital investment (net)	113.6	39.9	135.7
Short-term capital (net)	−5.5	−65.2	20.2
Net errors and omissions	−12.2	220.0	20.2
Total (net monetary movements)	561.5	382.3	578.4
Valuation changes (net)	297.9	−181.3	4.7
Changes in reserves	859.4	201.0	583.0

Source: IMF, *International Financial Statistics*.

External Trade

PRINCIPAL COMMODITIES ('000 UA*)

Imports	1986	1987†	1988†
Food, beverages and tobacco	269,684	318,100	383,000
Fuel	135,945	139,100	168,000
Chemicals and rubber	151,599	187,300	226,000
Wood and paper	61,980	85,100	103,000
Textiles and footwear	126,990	169,000	204,000
Metal and metal products	148,816	178,000	215,000
Machinery and electrical goods	266,541	309,600	373,000
Vehicles and transport equipment	270,299	299,000	360,000
Other commodities	186,369	202,300	270,000
Total	1,618,232	1,905,700	2,302,000

Exports	1985	1986	1987†
Meat and meat products	113,696	146,896	125,692
Diamonds	1,237,227	1,455,606	2,728,626
Copper-nickel matte	140,604	147,117	143,542
Textiles	37,730	52,509	68,800
Hides and skins	21,852	12,402	9,400
Other commodities	80,091	148,498	153,640
Total	1,631,200	1,963,078	3,229,700

* Figures are in terms of the Unit of Account (UA) used by the Southern African Customs Union. This is equivalent to the South African rand. Its average value was: 0.858 pula in 1985; 0.822 pula in 1986; 0.825 pula in 1987; 0.805 pula in 1988.
† Preliminary estimates.

1988 (million pula): *Imports c.i.f.*: Total 1,871.8; *Exports f.o.b.*: Meat 116.4; Diamonds 1,976.5; Copper-nickel matte 370.2; Total (incl. others) 2,575.8 (Source: IMF, *International Financial Statistics*).

PRINCIPAL TRADING PARTNERS ('000 UA)

Imports	1985	1986	1987†
SACU*	966,229	1,241,938	1,502,600
Other Africa	100,962	122,896	145,800
United Kingdom	58,955	39,865	42,400
Other Europe	96,095	99,854	137,000
USA	35,146	46,057	38,600
Others	17,018	67,713	39,200
Total	1,274,405	1,618,323	1,905,700

Exports	1985	1986	1987†
SACU*	95,021	110,782	141,300
Other Africa	59,746	118,011	143,800
United Kingdom	83,550	73,016	44,800
Other Europe	1,269,153	1,646,236	2,878,300
USA	115,856	4,472	10,700
Others	7,854	10,561	10,800
Total	1,631,180	1,963,078	3,229,700

* Southern African Customs Union, of which Botswana is a member; also including Lesotho, Namibia, South Africa and Swaziland.
† Estimates.

Transport

RAILWAYS (year ending 30 June)

	1985/86	1986/87	1987/88
Passenger journeys*	526,956	489,952	428,725
Freight (net ton-km)	1,328,106	1,400,565	769,872

* Internal traffic only.
Source: Bank of Botswana, Gaborone.

ROAD TRAFFIC

	1986	1987	1988
Vehicles registered*	50,127	52,811	58,357

* Excluding government vehicles.
Source: Bank of Botswana, Gaborone.

BOTSWANA

CIVIL AVIATION (traffic)

	1986	1987	1988
Passenger journeys	172,506	226,615	224,463
Freight (metric tons)	453	381	477
Mail (metric tons)	118	94	109

Source: Bank of Botswana, Gaborone.

Tourism

	1986	1987	1988
Tourist arrivals ('000)	849	881	897
Tourist receipts (million pula)	71	71	63

Source: Bank of Botswana, Gaborone.

Communications Media

	1981	1982	1983
Radio receivers ('000 in use)	80	100	120

Radio receivers ('000 in use): 140 in 1986; 150 in 1987.
Book production (1987): 289 titles (books 134; pamphlets 155).
Daily newspapers (1986): 1 title (estimated circulation 18,000 copies).
Telephones in use: 19,109 in 1985; 21,000 in 1986; 22,000 in 1987.
Sources: UNESCO, *Statistical Yearbook*; Central Statistics Office, Gaborone.

Education

(1988)

	Institutions	Teachers	Students
Primary	559	8,102	261,352
Secondary	91	2,004	40,357
Brigades	24	171	1,111
Teacher training	5	157	1,841
Technical education	6	714	1,631
University	1	205	2,837

1984: There were 218 Batswana studying abroad.

Source: Ministry of Education, Gaborone.

Directory

The Constitution

The Constitution of the Republic of Botswana took effect at independence on 30 September 1966.

EXECUTIVE

President

Executive power lies with the President of Botswana, who is also Commander-in-Chief of the armed forces. Election for the office of President is linked with the election of members of the National Assembly. Presidential candidates must be over 30 years of age and receive at least 1,000 nominations. If there is more than one candidate for the Presidency, each candidate for office in the Assembly must declare support for a presidential candidate. The candidate for President who commands the votes of more than half the elected members of the Assembly will be declared President. If the Presidency falls vacant the members of the National Assembly will themselves elect a new President. The President will hold office for the duration of Parliament. After the 1974 elections the President became an ex officio member of the Assembly. The President chooses four members of the National Assembly.

Cabinet

There is also a Vice-President, whose office is ministerial. The Vice-President is appointed by the President and deputizes in the absence of the President. The Cabinet consists of the President, the Vice-President and 10 other Ministers appointed by the President. The Cabinet is responsible to the National Assembly.

LEGISLATURE

Legislative power is vested in Parliament, consisting of the President and the National Assembly, acting after consultation in certain cases with the House of Chiefs. The President may withhold assent to a Bill passed by the National Assembly. If the same Bill is again presented after six months, the President is required to assent to it or to dissolve Parliament within 21 days.

House of Chiefs

The House of Chiefs comprises the Chiefs of the eight principal tribes of Botswana as ex-officio members, four members elected by sub-chiefs from their own number, and three members elected by the other 12 members of the House. Bills and motions relating to chieftaincy matters and alterations of the Constitution must be referred to the House, which may also deliberate and make representations on any matter.

National Assembly

The National Assembly consists of the Speaker, the Attorney-General, who does not have a vote, 30 members elected by universal adult suffrage and four specially elected members chosen by the President. The life of the Assembly is five years.

The Constitution contains a code of human rights, enforceable by the High Court.

The Government

HEAD OF STATE

President: Dr QUETT KETUMILE JONI MASIRE (took office 18 July 1980; re-elected 10 September 1984 and 7 October 1989).

CABINET
(November 1990)

President: Dr QUETT KETUMILE JONI MASIRE.
Vice-President and Minister of Local Government and Lands: PETER S. MMUSI.
Minister of Health: KEBATHLAMANG PITSEYOSI MORAKE.
Minister of Agriculture: DANIEL K. KWELAGOBI.
Minister of External Affairs: Dr GAOSITWE K. T. CHIEPE.
Minister of Mineral Resources and Water Affairs: ARCHIE MOGWE.

BOTSWANA

Minister of Commerce and Industry: PONATSHENGO H. K. KEDIKILWE.
Minister of Works, Transport and Communications: CHAPSON J. BUTALE.
Minister of Finance and Development Planning: FESTUS G. MOGAE.
Minister of Presidential Affairs and Public Administration: Lt-Gen. MOMPATE MERAFE.
Minister of Education: RAY MOLOMO.
Minister of Labour and Home Affairs: PATRICK K. BALOPI.
Assistant Minister of Agriculture: GEOFFREY M. OTENG.
Assistant Ministers of Local Government and Lands: MICHAEL R. TSHIPINARE, RONALD SEBEGO.
Assistant Minister of Finance and Development Planning: D. N. MAGANG.

MINISTRIES

Office of the President: Private Bag 001, Gaborone; tel. 355434; telex 2414.
Ministry of Agriculture: Private Bag 003, Gaborone; tel. 350581; telex 2543.
Ministry of Commerce and Industry: Private Bag 004, Gaborone; tel. 353881; telex 2674; fax 371539.
Ministry of Education: Private Bag 005, Gaborone; tel. 355294; telex 2944.
Ministry of Finance and Development Planning: Private Bag 008, Gaborone; tel. 355272; telex 2401.
Ministry of Health: Private Bag 0038, Gaborone; tel. 355557.
Ministry of Home Affairs: Private Bag 002, Gaborone; tel. 355212.
Ministry of Local Government and Lands: Private Bag 006, Gaborone; tel. 352091.
Ministry of Mineral Resources and Water Affairs: Private Bag 0018, Gaborone; tel. 352454; telex 2503.
Ministry of Works, Transport and Communications: Private Bag 007, Gaborone; tel. 355303; telex 2743; fax 313303.

Legislature

NATIONAL ASSEMBLY

Speaker: JAMES G. HASKINS.

General Election, 7 October 1989

Party	Votes	%	Seats
Botswana Democratic Party	157,824	65.0	31*
Botswana National Front	67,317	27.7	3
Botswana People's Party	9,699	4.0	—
Botswana Independence Party	4,393	1.8	—
Botswana Progressive Union	2,186	0.9	—
Botswana Freedom Party	1,363	0.6	—
Total	242,782	100.0	34†

* Of the 31 members of the BDP in the National Assembly, four were specially elected by the President.
† There are two additional members of the Assembly: the Speaker and the Attorney-General. The President is an ex-officio member.

HOUSE OF CHIEFS

The House has a total of 15 members.
Chairman: Chief SEEPAPITSO.

Political Organizations

Botswana Democratic Party (BDP): POB 31, Gaborone; f. 1962; Pres. Dr QUETT MASIRE; Chair. PETER S. MMUSI; Sec.-Gen. DANIEL K. KWELAGOBE.
Botswana Freedom Party (BFP): f. 1989; Pres. LEACH TLHOMELANG.
Botswana Independence Party (BIP): POB 3, Maun; f. 1962; Pres. MOTSAMAI K. MPHO; Sec.-Gen. EMMANUEL R. MOKOBI.
Botswana Labour Party: f. 1989; Pres. LENYELETSE KOMA.
Botswana Liberal Party (BLP): POB 250, Francistown, f. 1988; Pres. MARTIN CHAKALISA.
Botswana National Front (BNF): POB 42, Mahalapye; f. 1967; Pres. Dr KENNETH KOMA; Sec.-Gen. JAMES PILANE.

Botswana People's Party (BPP): POB 159, Francistown; f. 1960; Pres. Dr KNIGHT MARIPE; Chair. KENNETH MKHWA; Sec.-Gen. JOHN MOSOJANE.
Botswana Progressive Union (BPU): POB 10229, Francistown; f. 1982; Pres. D. K. KWELE; Chair. G. G. BAGWASI; Sec.-Gen. R. K. MONYATSIWA.

Diplomatic Representation

EMBASSIES AND HIGH COMMISSIONS IN BOTSWANA

Angola: Private Bag 111, Gaborone; tel. 352599; Ambassador: AGNELO DA CONCEIÇÃO PEREIRA DE SILVA.
China, People's Republic: POB 1031, Gaborone; tel. 352209; telex 2428; Ambassador: ZHI CHENGXUN.
Germany: POB 315, Gaborone; tel. 353143; telex 2225; Ambassador: EGON KATZKI.
India: Tirelo House, 4th Floor, The Mall, Private Bag 249, Gaborone; tel. 372676; telex 2622; fax 374636; High Commissioner: (vacant).
Libya: POB 180, Gaborone; tel. 352481; telex 2501; Secretary of People's Bureau: (vacant).
Nigeria: POB 274, Gaborone; tel. 313561; telex 2415; High Commissioner: M. ZUBAIRU.
Poland: Private Bag 00209, Gaborone; tel. 352501; Chargé d'affaires: Dr JAN RUDKOWSKI.
Sweden: Private Bag 0017, Gaborone; tel. 353912; telex 2421; fax 353942; Ambassador: FOLKE LÖFGREN.
USSR: POB 81, Gaborone; tel. 353389; telex 2595; Ambassador: VIKTOR G. KRIVDA.
United Kingdom: Private Bag 0023, Gaborone; tel. 352841; telex 2370; fax 356105; High Commissioner: BRIAN SMITH.
USA: POB 90, Gaborone; tel. 353982; telex 2554; fax 356947; Ambassador: DAVID PASSAGE.
Zambia: POB 362, Gaborone; tel. 351951; telex 2416; High Commissioner: KASONDE P. KASUTO.
Zimbabwe: POB 1232, Gaborone; tel. 314495; telex 2701; High Commissioner: Dr N. G. MAKURA.

Judicial System

There is a High Court at Lobatse and a branch at Francistown, and Magistrates' Courts in each district. Appeals lie to the Court of Appeal of Botswana.

Chief Justice: EBEN LIVESEYLUKE.
President of the Court of Appeal: A. N. E. AMMISSAH.
Justices of Appeal: T. A. AGUDA, G. BIZOS, W. H. R. SCHREINER, D. R. DOYLE.
Puisne Judges: I. R. ABOADYE, K. J. GYEKE-DAKO.
Registrar and Master of the High Court: K. YOGANATHAS.
Chief Magistrates: G. RWELENGA, F. B. SWANNIKER.
Senior Magistrates: K. OBENG, Y. D. PETKAR, K. B. MOESI, E. T. GALAFOROWE, I. M. I. NGITAMI, V. JEGASOTHY, N. Z. BOPA, S. N. NTOMIWA.
Attorney-General: MOLELEKI D. MOKAMA.

Religion

The majority of the population hold animist beliefs; an estimated 30% are thought to be Christians. There are Islamic mosques in Gaborone and Lobatse. The Bahá'í Faith is also represented.

CHRISTIANITY

Lekgotla la Sekeresete la Botswana (Botswana Christian Council): POB 355, Gaborone; tel. 315191; f. 1966; comprises 20 churches and seven other organizations; Chair. Rev. JACOB T. LIPHOKO; Gen. Sec. NATHANIEL T. K. MMONO.

The Anglican Communion

Anglicans are adherents of the Church of the Province of Central Africa, comprising 10 dioceses and covering Botswana, Malawi, Zambia and Zimbabwe. The Province was inaugurated in 1955 and the diocese of Botswana was formed in 1972.

Archbishop of the Province of Central Africa and Bishop of Botswana: Most Rev. WALTER PAUL KHOTSO MAKHULU, POB 769, Gaborone; fax 313015.

BOTSWANA

Protestant Churches

African Methodist Episcopal Church: POB 141, Lobatse; Rev. L. M. Mbulawa.

Evangelical Lutheran Church in Botswana: POB 1976, Gaborone; tel. 352227; fax 313966; Bishop Rev. Philip Robinson; 16,305 mems.

Evangelical Lutheran Church in Southern Africa (Botswana Diocese): POB 400, Gaborone; tel. 353976; Bishop Rev. M. Ntuping.

Methodist Church in Botswana: POB 260, Gaborone; Dist. Supt Rev. Z. S. M. Mosai.

United Congregational Church of Southern Africa: POB 1263, Gaborone; tel. 352491; autonomous since 1980; Chair. Rev. S. R. Pheto (designate); Sec. Rev. K. F. Mokobi; 14,000 mems.

Other denominations active in Botswana include the Church of God in Christ, the Dutch Reformed Church and the United Methodist Church.

The Roman Catholic Church

Botswana comprises a single diocese. The metropolitan see is Bloemfontein, South Africa. The church was established in Botswana in 1928, and had an estimated 45,050 adherents in the country at 31 December 1988. The Bishop participates in the Southern African Catholic Bishops' Conference, based in Pretoria, South Africa.

Bishop of Gaborone: Rt Rev. Boniface Tshosa Setlalekgosi, Bishop's House, POB 218, Gaborone; tel. 312958.

The Press

DAILY NEWSPAPER

Dikgang Tsa Gompieno (Botswana Daily News): Private Bag 0060, Gaborone; tel. 352541; telex 2409; f. 1964; publ. by Dept of Information and Broadcasting; Setswana and English; Mon.–Fri.; circ. 35,000.

PERIODICALS

Agrinews: Private Bag 003, Gaborone; f. 1971; monthly; technical journal on agriculture and rural development; circ. 6,000.

Botswana Advertiser: 5647 Nakedi Rd, POB 130, Broadhurst, Gaborone; tel. 312844; telex 2351; weekly.

Botswana Guardian: POB 1641, Gaborone; tel. 314937; telex 2692; fax 374381; weekly; Editor (vacant); circ. 16,500.

The Gazette: POB 1605, Gaborone; tel. 312833; telex 2631; weekly; circ. 16,000.

Government Gazette: Private Bag 0081, Gaborone; tel. 314441; telex 2414.

Kutlwano: Private Bag 0060, Gaborone; tel. 352541; telex 2409; monthly; Setswana and English; publ. by Dept of Information and Broadcasting; circ. 18,000.

Mmegi: Private Bag BR50, Gaborone; tel. 374784; telex 2753; fax 314311; f. 1984; weekly; Setswana and English; publ. by Mmegi Publishing Trust; circ. 15,000.

News Link: Private Bag 40063, Gaborone; tel. 372852; fax 374558; weekly.

Northern Advertiser: POB 402, Francistown; tel. 212265; fax 213769; f. 1985; weekly; advertisements, local interest, sport.

The Reporter: Gaborone; weekly.

The Sun: POB 40063, Gaborone; tel. 372852; fax 374558.

The Zebra's Voice: Private Bag 00114, Gaborone; f. 1982; quarterly; cultural magazine; publ. by the National Museum, Monuments and Art Gallery; circ. 4,000.

NEWS AGENCIES

Botswana Press Agency (BOPA): Private Bag 060, Gaborone; tel. 313601; telex 2284; f. 1981.

Foreign Bureaux

Inter Press Service (IPS) (Italy): POB 1605, Gaborone; tel. 312833; telex 2631.

Xinhua (New China) News Agency (People's Republic of China): Plot 5379, President's Drive, POB 1031, Gaborone; tel. 353434; telex 2428; Correspondent Chen Guowei.

Publishers

A.C. Braby (Botswana) (Pty) Ltd: POB 1549, Gaborone; telex 2371; telephone directories.

Department of Information and Broadcasting: Private Bag 0060, Gaborone; tel. 352541; telex 2409; publs include *Dikgang Tsa Gompieno* and *Kutlwano*.

Longman Botswana (Pty) Ltd: POB 1083, Gaborone; tel. 313969; fax 374682; f. 1981.

Macmillan Botswana Publishing Co (Pty) Ltd: POB 1155, Gaborone; tel. 314379; telex 2841; fax 374326.

Magnum Press (Pty) Ltd: Private Bag 40063, Gaborone; tel. 372852; fax 374558.

Printing and Publishing Co (Botswana) (Pty) Ltd: 5647 Nakedi Rd, POB 130, Broadhurst, Gaborone; tel. 312844; telex 2351; publr of *Botswana Advertiser*.

Government Publishing House

Department of Government Printing and Publishing Services: Private Bag 0081, Gaborone; tel. 314441; telex 2414.

Radio and Television

RADIO

There were an estimated 150,000 radio receivers in use in 1987. The introduction of a commercial radio network is under consideration.

Radio Botswana: Private Bag 0060, Gaborone; tel. 352541; telex 2633; broadcasts in Setswana and English; f. 1965; Dir Mrs M. Nasha.

TELEVISION

TV Association of Botswana: Gaborone; two transmitters relaying SABC-TV and BOP-TV programmes from South Africa; plans for a national TV service are under consideration.

Finance

(cap. = capital; dep. = deposits; res = reserves; m. = million; brs = branches; amounts in pula)

BANKING

Central Bank

Bank of Botswana: POB 712, Gaborone; tel. 351911; telex 2405; fax 372984; f. 1975; bank of issue; cap. and res 503.2m., dep. 4,206.4m., (Dec. 1989); Gov. H. C. L. Hermans; Dir of Operations G. G. O. Hobona (acting).

Commercial Banks

Bank of Credit and Commerce (Botswana) Ltd: BCC House, 884 Khama Crescent, POB 1552, Gaborone; tel. 374369; telex 2520; fax 372949; f. 1982; cap. and res 11.1m., dep. 96.0m. (Aug. 1990); Chair. E. A. Garda; Man. Y. H. Patel; 5 brs.

Barclays Bank of Botswana Ltd: Barclays House, Government Enclave, POB 478, Gaborone; tel. 352041; telex 2417; fax 313672; f. 1975; cap. and res 47.3m., dep. 568.2m. (Aug. 1990); Chair. Louis G. Nchindo; Man. Dir Eric Clark; 17 brs.

Standard Chartered Bank Botswana Ltd: Standard House, 5th Floor, The Mall, POB 496, Gaborone; tel. 353111; telex 2422; fax 372933; f. 1975; cap. and res 46.2m., dep. 330.5m. (Aug. 1990); Chair. J. G. Haskins; Man. Dir C. J. Mallard; 15 brs.

Zimbank Botswana Ltd: Zimbank House, The Mall, Private Bag B052, Gaborone; tel. 312622; telex 2985; fax 312596; f. 1990; cap. and res 7.0m., dep. 3.7m. (Aug. 1990); Chair. L. L. Tsumba; Man. Dir A. O'Dwyer; 2 brs.

Other Banks

Botswana Co-operative Bank Ltd: Co-operative Bank House, Broadhurst Mall, POB 40106, Gaborone; tel. 371398; telex 2298; f. 1974; cap. and res 0.3m., loans 5.9m. (1987); central source of credit for registered co-operative societies; Pres. M. L. Setlhare; Gen. Man. Dr Harry Tlale.

National Development Bank: Development House, The Mall, POB 225, Gaborone; tel. 352801; telex 2553; fax 372086; f. 1964; cap. and res 7.7m., dep. 50.1m. (March 1986); priority given to agricultural credit for Botswana farmers, and co-operative credit and loans for local business ventures; Chair. G. F. Stoneham; Gen. Man. B. I. Gasennelwe; 18 brs.

INSURANCE

Associated Insurance Brokers of Botswana (Pty) Ltd: Standard House, POB 624, Gaborone; tel. 351481; telex 2539; fax 314608; f. 1982 by merger; Man. Dir C. P. M. Cowper.

Botswana Eagle Insurance Co Ltd: 501 Botsalano House, POB 1221, Gaborone; telex 2259; fax 373274.

BOTSWANA
Directory

Botswana Insurance Co (Pty) Ltd: BIC House, POB 336, Gaborone; tel. 351791; telex 2359; fax 313290; Gen. Man. P. B. SUMMER.

ECB Insurance Brokers (Botswana) (Pty) Ltd: Botsalano House, POB 1195, Gaborone.

IGI Botswana (Pty) Ltd: IGI House, POB 715, Gaborone; tel. 351521; telex 2430; Gen. Man. P. S. DENNISS.

Trade and Industry

PUBLIC CORPORATIONS

Botswana Housing Corporation: POB 412, Gaborone; tel. 353341; telex 2729; fax 352070; provides housing for central govt and local authority needs and assists with private-sector housing schemes; Chair. the Perm. Sec., Ministry of Local Govt and Lands; Gen. Man. J. M. O. LETSHOLO; 900 employees.

Botswana Meat Commission (BMC): Private Bag 4, Lobatse; tel. 330321; telex 2420; f. 1966; slaughter of livestock, exports of hides and skins, carcasses, frozen and chilled boneless beef; operates tannery and beef products cannery; Exec. Chair. DAVID W. FINLAY; Gen. Man. F. BOAKGOMO.

Botswana Power Corporation: Motlakase House, Macheng Way, POB 48, Gaborone; tel. 352211; telex 2431; fax 373563; Chair. the Dep. Perm. Sec., Ministry of Mineral Resources and Water Affairs; CEO COLM O'DUINN.

Botswana Telecommunications Corporation: POB 700, Gaborone; tel. 353611; telex 2252; f. 1980; CEO M. T. CURRY.

Water Utilities Corporation: Private Bag 00276, Gaborone; tel. 352521; telex 2545; f. 1970; public water supply undertaking for principal townships; Chair. the Perm. Sec., Ministry of Mineral Resources and Water Affairs; CEO T. WATERS.

CHAMBER OF COMMERCE

Botswana National Chamber of Commerce and Industry: POB 20344, Gaborone; tel. 52677.

MARKETING BOARD

Botswana Agricultural Marketing Board: Private Bag 0053, Gaborone; tel. 351341; telex 2530; cap. P4.2m.; Chair. the Perm. Sec., Ministry of Agriculture; Gen. Man. P. R. J. MULLIGAN.

DEVELOPMENT ORGANIZATIONS

Botswana Development Corporation Ltd: Madirelo House, Mmanaka Rd, POB 438, Gaborone; tel. 351811; telex 2251; fax 373539; f. 1985/86; cap. p.u. P29.0m. (June 1988); Chair. the Perm. Sec., Ministry of Finance and Development Planning; Gen. Man. M. O. MOLEFANE.

Botswana Livestock Development Corporation (Pty) Ltd: POB 455, Gaborone; tel. 351949; telex 2543; f.1977; cap. P2.1m. (1988); Chair. M. M. MANNATHOKO; Gen. Man. S. M. R. BURNETT.

Department of Trade and Investment Promotion (TIPA), Ministry of Commerce and Industry: Private Bag 004, Gaborone; tel. 353881; telex 2674; fax 371539; promotes industrial and commercial investment, diversification and expansion, offers consultancy, liaison and information services; participates in int. trade fairs and trade and investment missions; Dir Mrs D. T. TIBONE.

Financial Services Co of Botswana (Pty) Ltd: Plot 170, Emang Close, POB 1129, Gaborone; tel. 351363; telex 2207; fax 357815; f. 1974; cap. and res P1.9m.; hire purchase, mortgages and industrial leasing; Chair. M. E. HOPKINS; Gen. Man. R. A. PAWSON.

Integrated Field Services: Ministry of Commerce and Industry, Private Bag 004, Gaborone; tel. 353881; telex 2674; promotes industrialization and rural development; Dir B. T. TIBONE.

EMPLOYERS' ASSOCIATION

Botswana Confederation of Commerce, Industry and Manpower: Botsalano House, POB 432, Gaborone; f. 1971; Chair. R. MANNATHOKO; Sec.-Gen. MODIRE J. MBAAKANYI; 600 affiliated mems.

TRADE UNIONS

Botswana Federation of Trade Unions: POB 440, Gaborone; tel. 352534; f. 1977; Gen. Sec. RONALD DUST BAIPIDI.

Affiliated Unions

Air Botswana Employees' Union: POB 92, Gaborone; Gen. Sec. JOYCE MOTHUPI.

Botswana Bank Employees' Union: POB 338, Selebi-Phikwe; Gen. Sec. KEOLOPILE GABORONE.

Botswana Commercial and General Workers' Union: POB 62, Gaborone; Gen. Sec. CYNTHIA MOGAMI.

Botswana Construction Workers' Union: POB 1508, Gaborone; Gen. Sec. J. MOLAPISI.

Botswana Diamond Sorters-Valuators' Union: POB 1186, Gaborone; Gen. Sec. FELIX T. LESETEDI.

Botswana Housing Corporation Staff Union: POB 412, Gaborone; Gen. Sec. MAXWELL G. K. MOTOWANE.

Botswana Meat Industry Workers' Union: POB 181, Lobatse; Gen. Sec. RUSSIA SESINYE.

Botswana Mining Workers' Union: POB 14, Selebi-Phikwe; Gen. Sec. BALEKAMANG GABOSIANE.

Botswana Railways Senior Staff Union: POB 494, Gaborone; Gen. Sec. L. LETSWELETSE.

Botswana Railways Staff and Artisan Employees' Union: POB 1486, Gaborone; Gen. Sec. P. MOGOWE.

Botswana Railways Workers' Union: POB 181, Gaborone; Gen. Sec. ERNEST T. G. MOHUTSIWA.

Central Bank Union: POB 712, Gaborone; Gen. Sec. G. A. SHAGWA.

Insurance Employees' Union of Botswana: POB 1863, Gaborone; Gen. Sec. G. T. MMATLI.

National Development Bank Staff Union: POB 225, Gaborone; Gen. Sec. M. LEBOTSE.

National Amalgamated Local and Central Government, Parastatal, Statutory Body and Manual Workers' Union: POB 374, Gaborone; Gen. Sec. ALLISON T. MANGENA.

CO-OPERATIVES

Department of Co-operative Development: POB 86, Gaborone; f. 1964; promotes marketing and supply, consumer, dairy, horticultural and fisheries co-operatives, thrift and loan societies, credit societies, a co-operative union and a co-operative bank.

Botswana Co-operative Union: Gaborone; telex 2298; f. 1970; Dir AARON RAMOSAKO.

Transport

RAILWAYS

In 1989 there were 712 km of 1,067-mm-gauge track within Botswana, including two spurs serving the Selebi-Phikwe mining complex (56 km) and the Morupule colliery (16 km). The entire main railway line in Botswana is to be rehabilitated under an SADCC project, estimated to cost US $114m. Feasibility studies were undertaken in 1984 for the construction of a trans-Kalahari rail link, about 875 km in length, which would provide Botswana with an outlet to the Atlantic Ocean on the coast of Namibia. A 175-km rail link between the Sua Pan soda ash deposits and Francistown was due for completion by May 1991. The 960-km railway line from Mafikeng, South Africa, to Bulawayo, Zimbabwe, passes through Botswana.

Botswana Railways: Private Bag 00125, Gaborone; tel. 373185; telex 2980; fax 312305; fmrly owned and operated by National Railways of Zimbabwe; ownership was transferred to Botswana Railways in January 1987; Gen. Man. FRANK MARKHAM.

ROADS

In 1989 there were some 13,500 km of roads, of which about 2,400 km were bituminized (including a main road from Gaborone, via Francistown, to Kazungula, where the borders of Botswana, Namibia, Zambia and Zimbabwe meet). The Government aims to construct several main roads and to extend the networks of both feeder and rural roads serving the remoter areas. In 1990 the construction of a 340-km road between Nata and Maun was under way, and plans to build a trans-Kalahari road from Jwaneng to Sekoma (on the border with Namibia) were being considered. There is a ferry service from Kazungula across the Zambezi river into Zambia.

CIVIL AVIATION

The international airport is at Gaborone. A second major airport, at Kasane in the Chobe area of northern Botswana, is due to come into operation in 1991. There are airfields at Francistown, Maun

BOTSWANA

and at other population centres, and there are numerous airstrips throughout the country. Scheduled services of Air Botswana are supplemented by an active charter and business sector which carries 40% of the total passengers. In addition, most regional airlines operate services to Gaborone. In early 1988 it was announced that Botswana was planning to assume control of its airspace from South Africa.

Air Botswana: POB 92, Gaborone; tel. 352812; telex 2413; fax 374802; f. 1988; govt-owned; domestic services between Gaborone, Maun, Francistown, Selebi-Phikwe, Kasane and Gantsi, connecting with regional services to most countries in eastern and southern Africa; fleet of 1 BAe 146; 1 Dornier 228; 2 ATR-42; Gen. Man. Capt. B. L. R. POCOCK.

Tourism

There are five game reserves and three national parks, including Chobe, near Victoria Falls, on the Zambia-Zimbabwe border. Efforts to expand the tourist industry include plans for the construction of new hotels and the rehabilitation of existing hotel facilities. In 1988 an estimated 897,000 tourists visited Botswana, and earnings from tourism were estimated at P63m.

Department of Wildlife and National Parks: POB 131, Gaborone; tel. 351461; Dir. K. T. NGWAMOTSOKO.

Tourism Development Unit, Ministry of Commerce and Industry: Private Bag 0047, Gaborone; tel. 353024; telex 2414; f. 1973 to promote tourism in Botswana; Dir CHAWA BOGOSI.

BRAZIL

Introductory Survey

Location, Climate, Language, Religion, Flag, Capital

The Federative Republic of Brazil, the fifth largest country in the world, lies in central and north-eastern South America. To the north are Venezuela, Colombia, Guyana, Suriname and French Guiana, to the west Peru and Bolivia, and to the south Paraguay, Argentina and Uruguay. Brazil has a very long coastline on the Atlantic Ocean. Climatic conditions vary from hot and wet in the tropical rain forest of the Amazon basin to temperate in the savannah grasslands of the central and southern uplands, which have warm summers and mild winters. In Rio de Janeiro temperatures are generally between 17°C (63°F) and 29°C (85°F). The language is Portuguese. Almost all of the inhabitants profess Christianity, and about 90% are adherents of the Roman Catholic Church. The national flag (proportions 10 by 7) is green, bearing, at the centre, a yellow diamond containing a blue celestial globe with 23 white five-pointed stars (one for each of Brazil's original states), arranged in the pattern of the southern firmament, and an equatorial scroll with the motto 'Ordem e Progresso' ('Order and Progress'). The capital is Brasília, although some administrative offices still remain in Rio de Janeiro, which was the capital of Brazil until 1960.

Recent History

Formerly a Portuguese possession, Brazil became an independent monarchy in 1822, and a republic in 1889. A federal constitution for the United States of Brazil was adopted in 1891. Following social unrest in the 1920s, the economic crisis of 1930 resulted in a major revolt, led by Dr Getúlio Vargas, who was installed as President. He governed the country as a benevolent dictator until forced to resign by the armed forces in December 1945. During Vargas's populist rule, Brazil enjoyed internal stability and steady economic progress. He established a strongly authoritarian corporate state, similar to fascist regimes in Europe, but in 1942 Brazil entered the Second World War on the side of the Allies. Brazil was the first South American country to dispatch fighting troops to Europe, sending an expeditionary force to Italy in 1944.

In 1946 Gen. Eurico Dutra was elected President and a new constitution was adopted. Vargas was re-elected President in 1950, but failed to create the necessary stability; he committed suicide in August 1954. The next President was Dr Juscelino Kubitschek, who took office in 1956. Brazil's capital was moved in 1960 from Rio de Janeiro to the newly-constructed city of Brasília, sited on a previously uninhabited jungle plateau about 1,000 km (600 miles) inland. President Kubitschek was succeeded by Dr Jânio Quadros, who was elected in October 1960 and took office in January 1961. President Quadros resigned after only seven months in office, and in September 1961 the Vice-President, João Goulart, was sworn in as President.

Military leaders suspected Goulart, the leader of the Partido Trabalhista Brasileiro (PTB), of communist sympathies, and they were reluctant to let him succeed to the presidency. As a compromise, the Constitution was amended to restrict the powers of the President and to provide for a Prime Minister. Upon taking office, President Goulart appointed Dr Tancredo de Almeida Neves, a member of the Partido Social Democrático (PSD) and a former Minister of Justice, to be Prime Minister. However, Dr Neves and most of his Cabinet resigned in June 1962. He was succeeded by Dr Francisco Brochada da Rocha, also of the PSD, who was Prime Minister from July to September 1962. His successor was Dr Hermes Lima of the PTB, hitherto Minister of Labour, but a referendum in January 1963 approved a return to the presidential system of government, whereupon President Goulart formed his own Cabinet.

Following a period of rapid inflation and allegations of official corruption, the left-wing regime of President Goulart was overthrown by a bloodless army revolution on 31 March–1 April 1964. The leader of this right-wing military coup was Gen. (later Marshal) Humberto Castelo Branco, the Army Chief of Staff, who was elected President by Congress. In October 1965 President Castelo Branco assumed dictatorial powers, and all of Brazil's 13 existing political parties were banned. In December, however, two artificially-created parties, the pro-Government Aliança Renovadora Nacional (ARENA) and the opposition Movimento Democrático Brasileiro (MDB), were granted official recognition. President Castelo Branco nominated as his successor the Minister of War, Marshal Artur da Costa e Silva, who was elected President in October 1966 and took office in March 1967. At the same time, a new constitution, changing the country's name to the Federative Republic of Brazil, was introduced. The ailing President da Costa e Silva was forced to resign in September 1969 and was replaced by a triumvirate of military leaders.

During its early years the military regime promulgated a series of Institutional Acts which granted the President wide-ranging powers to rule by decree. On 20 October 1969 the ruling junta introduced a revised constitution, vesting executive authority in an indirectly-elected President. Congress, suspended since December 1968, was recalled and elected Gen. Emílio Garrastazú Médici, who took office as President on 30 October 1969. Urban guerrilla activity was widespread during 1970 but was largely eliminated by stern security measures. The next President was Gen. Ernesto Geisel, chosen by an electoral college, who took office in March 1974. Despite President Geisel's more liberal outlook, the MDB made sweeping gains in the congressional elections of November 1974, and calls were made for an end to military government.

In January 1978 President Geisel's choice of Gen. João Baptista de Figueiredo as his successor was endorsed by the national convention of the ARENA. General Figueiredo was duly elected President by an electoral college in October 1978 and took office in March 1979, promising to continue the *abertura*, or opening to democratization, begun by President Geisel. In the face of growing political agitation, Congress approved various reforms that had been proposed by President Geisel. In November 1979 Congress approved legislation to end the controlled two-party system. The new parties that were subsequently formed included the first independent labour party, the Partido dos Trabalhadores (PT).

President Figueiredo suffered a heart attack in September 1981 and was temporarily replaced by Vice-President Antônio Aureliano Chaves de Mendonça, the first civilian to hold presidential office since 1964. Congressional, state and municipal elections were held in November 1982. The government-sponsored Partido Democrático Social (PDS) gained a majority of seats in the Senate, but failed to win an absolute majority in the Chamber of Deputies, and was also defeated in elections for the governorships of 10 states and in municipal elections in more than 75% of the main towns. The pre-election legislative measures ensured, however, that the PDS would have a majority in the presidential electoral college, due to choose a successor to Gen. Figueiredo in 1985.

In February 1983, to limit the strength of the opposition, the President issued a decree which reduced the authority of the state governors before they had even taken office, and the regime introduced other measures which concentrated political power in Brasília. Lacking a working majority in the Chamber of Deputies, the President ruled by decree laws until May 1983, when he was able to form an alliance of the PDS with the small Partido Trabalhista Brasileiro (PTB, unrelated to the former PTB, banned in 1965), thereby obtaining 248 out of 479 seats. In August 1983 the PTB withdrew from its pact with the PDS, and in October a 60-day state of emergency was declared in Brasília. In December 1983, responding to opposition demands for direct voting in the presidential election, President Figueiredo confirmed that the system of indirect election, through an electoral college, would be retained.

Throughout 1984 Brazil's political life was dominated by the issue of succession. In February the four opposition parties announced the formation of the Free Elections Movement and proposed a constitutional amendment to provide for an immediate return to direct presidential elections. In an attempt to regain the political initiative, President Figueiredo presented his own draft amendment, which proposed the return of Brazil to full democracy (including the holding of direct presidential elections) by 1988, a reduction in the presidential term of office from six to four years and the curtailment of the President's exceptional powers. In April Congress voted on the opposition's amendment; in spite of considerable backing from members of the PDS, the opposition narrowly failed to obtain the two-thirds majority that was required.

In July 1984 Vice-President Chaves de Mendonça and the influential Marco de Oliveira Maciel, a former Governor of Pernambuco State, announced the formation of an alliance of liberal PDS members with members of the Partido do Movimento Democrático Brasileiro (PMDB). This offered the opposition a genuine opportunity to defeat the PDS in the electoral college. In August Senator Tancredo Neves, the Governor of Minas Gerais State (who had been Prime Minister in 1961–62), was named presidential candidate for the liberal alliance, while the former President of the PDS, José Sarney, was declared vice-presidential candidate. In December the liberal alliance formed an official political party, the Partido Frente Liberal (PFL). At the presidential election, held in January 1985, Neves was elected as Brazil's first civilian President for 21 years, winning 480 of the 686 votes in the electoral college. Prior to the inauguration ceremony in March 1985, however, Neves was taken ill, and in April, following a series of operations, he died. José Sarney, who had assumed the role of Acting President in Neves' absence, took office as President in April. President Sarney made no alterations to the Cabinet selected by Neves, and he affirmed his commitment to fulfilling the objectives of the late President-designate. In May Congress approved a constitutional amendment restoring direct elections by universal suffrage. The right to vote was also extended to illiterate adults. The first direct elections took place in November, when municipal elections were held in 31 cities.

The introduction in February 1986 of an anti-inflation programme, the Cruzado Plan, proved, initially, to be a considerable success for the Government and boosted the personal popularity of President Sarney. The Government hoped to capitalize on its popularity at elections for the National Congress, to act as the Constitutional Assembly, in November 1986, when an electorate of some 69m. Brazilians were eligible to vote for 49 senators and 487 federal deputies. Gubernatorial elections were held concurrently with the congressional elections. At the elections the PMDB emerged as the leading party within the ruling coalition: its representatives secured a majority in the Constitutional Assembly and more than 20 state governorships. The Constitutional Assembly was to draft a new constitution and determine the length of the presidential term of office.

A programme of agrarian reform, based on the confiscation and redistribution of 40.2m. ha of land to 1.4m. landless families, proved to be unsuccessful, serving only to exacerbate the already tense relations between landowners and peasants. The Ministry for Land Reform was abolished in 1989.

The Constitutional Assembly was installed in February 1987, and it was soon apparent that the constitutional debate was to be dominated by the issue of the length of the presidential mandate. The issue caused serious divisions within not only the Assembly but also the PMDB. In May President Sarney attempted to take the initiative in the debate by offering to reduce his term of office from six to five years, and to step down in March 1990. The President's difficulties with the Assembly and the decline in his popularity were compounded by the failure of the Cruzado Plan in early 1987. In February Brazil declared a unilateral moratorium on the repayment of $68,000m. of debt to commercial banks; this decision had serious repercussions for Brazil's overall debt-restructuring programme, but the Government was unable to devote its attention to the problem of the country's foreign debt until the question of the new Constitution had been resolved.

At an extraordinary convention of the PMDB, in July 1987, a majority of the PMDB's members refused to endorse Sarney's offer to relinquish office in 1990, asserting that the Constitutional Assembly was the only appropriate forum to resolve such an issue. In November the Systematization Committee of the Constitutional Assembly voted to reduce the presidential mandate to four years and to introduce a parliamentary form of government. The Committee's vote represented a humiliating blow for the President, who subsequently announced that he would not contest the Assembly's decision, and that he would act as an 'independent arbitrator' at the forthcoming presidential election.

In March 1988, however, President Sarney's administration was bolstered by the Constitutional Assembly's vote in favour of maintaining a presidential system of government. President Sarney was reported to have threatened to resign if the Assembly voted for the introduction of a parliamentary form of government, and his stance on the issue was reported to have caused a serious division within the PMDB. In June the Constitutional Assembly reversed the earlier decision by the Systematization Committee, and approved a presidential mandate of five years. The first round of voting for the presidential election was provisionally set for 15 November 1989, thereby enabling Sarney to remain in office until March 1990. This *de facto* victory for the President precipitated a series of resignations from the PMDB by some of its leading members, who subsequently formed a new centre-left party, the Partido da Social Democracia Brasileira (PSDB). In July 1988 the Assembly began the process of drafting the definitive version of the new Constitution. The President's views on the content of the new Constitution brought him into direct conflict with the President of the Assembly, Ulysses Guimarães, and led to the resignation of three Ministers opposed to the President's interference in the matter. In spite of last-minute disagreements, the Constitution was approved by the National Congress on 22 September 1988, and was promulgated on 5 October. Among its 245 articles were provisions transferring many hitherto presidential powers to the National Congress. In addition, censorship was abolished; the National Security Law, whereby many political dissidents had been detained, was abolished; the minimum voting age was lowered to 16 years; and the principle of habeas corpus was recognized. However, the Constitution offered no guarantees of land reform, and was thought by many to be nationalistic and protectionist.

The other main issue confronting the administration throughout 1988 was that of economic policy. Following the appointment of three new Ministers of Finance within only nine months, the Government eventually revealed its commitment to drastic reductions in planned public-sector expenditure, primarily based on a 'freeze' on salary increases for state employees. The adoption of such an unpopular policy led to widespread strikes in the state sector, and in June 1988 both the Head of the General Staff of the Armed Forces and the President of Petrobrás, the state petroleum company, left office, following their public criticism of the Government's economic programme. Despite the announcement, in November, of the formation of a tripartite social pact (composed of the Government and representatives of trade unions and the business sector), protests occurred throughout Brazil, following violent clashes at a state-controlled steel mill at Volta Redonda, near Rio de Janeiro, in the course of which government troops shot dead at least three protesters. The combination of industrial unrest and social tension was thought to have been a decisive factor in the generally poor results that the PMDB obtained at municipal elections held on 15 November, when the centre-left Partido Democrático Trabalhista (PDT) and the left-wing PT made important gains at the expense of the ruling party.

Environmental issues dominated the latter part of 1988 and much of 1989. The murder of Francisco (Chico) Mendes, the leader of the rubber-tappers' union and a pioneering ecologist, in December 1988 brought Brazil's environmental problems to international attention. The first official meeting of some 20 Amazonian tribes, at a five-day conference in Altamira, demonstrated their united opposition to the proposed construction, in 1993, of the Caraoa dam in Kayapó territory. International concern was expressed that development projects of this kind, together with the 'slash-and-burn' farming techniques of cattle ranchers, peasant smallholders and loggers, and the release of large amounts of mercury into the environment by an estimated 60,000 gold prospectors (or *garimpeiros*) in the Amazon region, presented a serious threat to the survival of both the indigenous Indians and the rain forest. A proposal by several US senators to purchase part of Brazil's vast foreign debt, in exchange for the guaranteed protection of the Amazonian rain forest, provoked strong nationalist reaction. At a meeting of the Amazon Pact in March 1989, the eight member nations firmly denounced any international interference in the Amazon region, and in May they signed the Declaration of Manaus in affirmation of this stance. In April President Sarney had announced Brazil's first major plan to protect the environment. Implementation of the plan, entitled 'Our Nature', was expected to cost US $178m. in its first year. The plan included such measures as the suspension of government subsidies for cattle ranchers in the Amazon, the establishment of a national fund for environmental protection, the Instituto Brasileiro do Meio Ambiente e Recursos Naturais Renováveis (IBAMA), to replace the Instituto Brasileiro do Desenvolvimento Florestal (abolished earlier in the year), and the creation of several new parks and reserves. Despite the imposition of curbs on the use of mercury and the announcement of plans to establish a 2,000-strong National Environmental Guard later in 1989, the Government's measures to protect the Amazon region were considered to be inadequate by many international environmental organizations.

Economic problems continued into 1989, and early in the year the Government presented Congress with further emergency measures in an attempt to halt the drift towards hyperinflation. The 'Summer Plan' proposed the imposition of an indefinite 'freeze' on prices, an end to inflation-linked wage increases, an increase in interest rates, the creation of a new currency (the novo cruzado, equivalent to 1,000 old cruzados), the abolition of five ministries and the dismissal of as many as 60,000 civil servants. Although not all the proposals were agreed by Congress, the Summer Plan was unpopular with Brazil's two largest trade union organizations, the Central Unica dos Trabalhadores and the Confederação General dos Trabalhadores, and in March a general strike was held. Further strikes in April in the ports, schools, banks and motor industry, in support of demands for pay increases to compensate for an alleged 80% loss in purchasing power since the introduction of the Summer Plan, forced the Government to reassess the right to strike, as specified in the new Constitution, and regulatory proposals were sent to Congress. The Summer Plan was finally abandoned in June, with a return to daily currency indexing.

In the latter part of 1989 Brazil was unable to make payments due to foreign creditors and appeared to be heading toward an undeclared moratorium on interest payments. Concerned at the low levels of its currency reserves, the Government submitted legislation to Congress in August to prepare for the 'privatization' of 17 state-owned companies.

Brazil's first presidential election by direct voting since 1960 was held on 15 November 1989. The main contenders were a young conservative, Fernando Collor de Mello of the newly-formed Partido de Reconstrução Nacional (PRN); Luís Inácio (Lula) da Silva, the President of the PT; and Leonel Brizola, the President of the PDT. Since no candidate received the required overall majority, a second round of voting was held on 17 December, contested by Collor de Mello and da Silva, who were first and second, respectively, in the November poll. Collor de Mello was declared the winner, with 53% of the votes cast. The critical condition of the economy continued to dominate political affairs in 1990 and, following his inauguration as President on 15 March, Collor de Mello announced an ambitious programme of economic reform, with the principal aim of reducing inflation, which had reached a monthly rate of more than 80%. Among the extraordinary provisions of the programme entitled 'New Brazil' (or, more commonly, the 'Collor Plan') was the immediate sequestration of an estimated US $115,000m. in personal savings and corporate assets for an 18-month period, limiting withdrawals from interest-bearing money market accounts to 20%, and those from savings and current accounts to around US $1,000 until September 1991. The new economic plan (which was subject to ratification by Congress) also introduced a new currency, the cruzeiro (to replace, at par, the novo cruzado), a 30-day 'freeze' on prices and wage increases (with controls to be applied to future increases), the expansion of the taxation system, a relaxation of controls on trade and foreign currency transactions, a comprehensive divestment programme (which was initiated in September 1990 with the sale of the São Paulo state-owned airline, VASP) and a comprehensive rationalization of the public sector, entailing the abolition of 21 government agencies, including the Sugar and Alcohol Institute (IAA) and the Brazilian Coffee Institute (IBC), and a reduction in the number of government ministries to 13. Most of the proposed measures were eventually approved by Congress, although strong opposition to the President's insistence that the ending of inflation-linked wage increases was essential to combat the threat of hyperinflation continued until August.

The decision to rationalize the public sector, and the large number of redundancies implicit in such a measure, encountered almost immediate opposition from trade union organizations, giving rise to widespread labour unrest and the recurrent threat of a general strike. In May 1990 President Collor de Mello announced that some 20%–25% of the Government's estimated 1.6m. employees would be made redundant in an attempt to accelerate the programme of administrative reform. By the end of June, however, only 90,000 had been dismissed (many on reduced pay) and the eventual total was not expected to exceed 120,000.

Despite an initial fall in monthly inflation rates (the rate was less than 5% in April 1990), the impact of the new economic measures dissipated swiftly, as businesses found means of evading the Government's 'liquidity squeeze' and the price of petroleum increased, following the Iraqi invasion of Kuwait in August. By September the monthly rate of inflation again exceeded 10%. The Minister of the Economy, Zélia Cardoso de Mello, blamed unscrupulous business practices for the apparent failure of the programme and openly criticized Luíz Octávio da Motta Veiga, the President of PETROBRÁS (the state-owned petroleum company), for granting high wage increases and exhibiting 'excessive corporatism'. Motta Veiga later resigned, complaining that government directives to maintain low petroleum prices had forced the company to operate at a loss.

Failure to reduce inflation significantly, coupled with predictions of the worst recession in 50 years, forced the Government to extend its moratorium on interest payments on foreign debt indefinitely and reduced the likelihood of further credits from international financial organizations.

Elections on 3 October 1990 for 31 senators, 503 seats in the Chamber of Deputies and 27 state governors led to widespread concern at the high level of apathy among voters, when some 20% of registered voters failed to cast a vote and a similar proportion cast blank or spoiled votes. The election results were interpreted as a rejection of extreme left- and right-wing parties in favour of familiar candidates from small, centre-right parties. It was expected that the Government would strengthen its position in Congress as a result, and would continue to secure the necessary support to pursue its programme of economic reform. A second round of voting was held on 25 November to elect governors in more than one-half of the States, candidates having failed to receive more than 50% of the valid votes cast on 3 October.

Despite the appointment of internationally-acclaimed ecologist José Lutzemberger as Collor de Mello's Minister of the Environment, the dynamiting of illegal airstrips in an attempt to solve the problem of unauthorized gold prospecting in the Amazon region, and the introduction of a new environmental programme entitled 'Operation Amazonia', international criticism of the Government's poor response to the threat to the environment persisted throughout 1990. Of particular concern to many international observers was the plight of the Yanomami Indian tribe in Roraima. It was estimated that, since the arrival of the *garimpeiros* to the region, some 10%–15% of the Yanomami's total population had been exterminated as a result of pollution and disease, introduced to the area by the gold prospectors. The National Indian Foundation (FUNAI) was heavily criticized for its role in the affair and was accused of failing to provide effective protection and support for Brazil's Indian population.

In 1990 a series of bilateral trade agreements were signed with Argentina, in a development widely believed to signify the first stage in a process leading to the eventual establishment of a Southern Cone common market (Mercosur), also to include Paraguay and Uruguay. A further agreement between Brazil and Argentina in the same year expressed the commitment of the two nations to dedicate their nuclear programmes to exclusively peaceful uses. The agreement followed revelations by President Collor de Mello that previous Brazilian administrations had been involved in clandestine projects to develop a nuclear capability for possible military use.

In 1988 the Uruguayan Government announced its intention to seek discussions with Brazil on some 22,000 ha of Brazilian land claimed by Uruguay, and the sovereignty of a Brazilian island in the Quarai river.

Government

Under the 1988 Constitution, the country is a federal republic comprising 26 States and a Federal District (Brasília). Legislative power is exercised by the bicameral National Congress, comprising the Chamber of Deputies (members elected by a system of proportional representation for four years) and the

BRAZIL

Federal Senate (members elected by the majority principle in rotation for eight years). The number of deputies is based on the size of the population. Election is by universal adult suffrage (the franchise was extended to illiterate adults in 1985). Executive power is exercised by the President, elected by direct ballot for five years. (At the presidential election in January 1985, the President was chosen by an electoral college.) The President appoints and leads the Cabinet. Each State has a directly elected Governor and an elected legislature. For the purposes of local government, the States are divided into municipalities.

Defence

Military service, lasting 12 months, is compulsory for men between 18 and 45 years of age. In June 1990 the armed forces comprised 324,200 men (including 145,200 conscripts): army 223,000 (143,000 conscripts), navy 50,500 and air force 50,700. Public security forces number about 243,000 men. Defence expenditure for 1988 was estimated at 317m. new cruzados. In 1989 an estimated 6% of the national budget was allocated to the armed forces. The percentage was expected to decrease to 2.2% in 1990.

Economic Affairs

In 1988, according to estimates by the World Bank, Brazil's gross national product (GNP), measured at average 1986–88 prices, was US $328,860m., equivalent to $2,280 per head. During 1980–88, it was estimated, GNP increased, in real terms, at an average annual rate of 3.4%, while GNP per head increased by 1.2% per year. Over the same period, the population increased by an annual average of 2.2%. Brazil's gross domestic product (GDP) increased, in real terms, by an annual average of 2.9% in 1980–88.

Agriculture (including forestry and fishing) employed 24.6% of the working population in 1987 and contributed 7.7% of GDP in the same year. The principal cash crops are soybeans (soybean products accounted for about 9% of export earnings in 1988), coffee, tobacco, sugar cane and cocoa beans. Beef and poultry production are also important. During 1980–88 agricultural production increased by an annual average of 3.5%.

Industry (including mining, manufacturing, construction and power) employed 23.8% of the working population in 1987 and provided 38.6% of GDP in the same year. During 1980–88 industrial production increased by an annual average of 2.6%.

Mining contributed 2.0% of GDP in 1987. Iron ore (haematite) and tin are the major mineral exports. Gold, phosphates, platinum, bauxite, uranium, manganese, copper and coal are also mined. In 1990 deposits of niobium, thought to be the world's largest, were discovered in the state of Amazonas. Brazil's largest state-run company, PETROBRÁS, is one of the world's leading oil-producing companies.

Manufacturing contributed 26.5% of GDP in 1987. With mining, the sector employed 15.7% of the working population in that year. The most important industries, measured by gross value of output, are machinery and transport equipment, food-processing, textiles and clothing and chemicals.

In 1986, 31.8% of total energy was derived from electricity (90% of which was hydroelectric), 30.2% from petroleum, 17.6% from wood and charcoal and 12.3% from fuel alcohol. Other energy sources, including coal and natural gas, accounted for 8.1%.

In 1988 Brazil recorded a visible trade surplus of US $19,168m., and there was a surplus of $4,159m. on the current account of the balance of payments. In that year the principal source of imports (21.4%) was the USA, which was also the principal market for exports (25.8%). Other major trading partners were the Federal Republic of Germany, Japan, Iraq, the Netherlands and the United Kingdom. The principal exports were steel products, transport equipment, soybean products, coffee and metallic minerals. The principal imports were mineral products, machinery and mechanical appliances, and chemical products.

In 1988 there was a budget deficit equivalent to 6% of GDP. Brazil's total external public debt was US $89,841m. at the end of 1988. In that year the cost of debt-servicing exceeded 35% of revenue from exports of goods and services. In 1989 the cost of debt-servicing was forecast at 4% of GDP. The annual rate of inflation averaged 166.3% in 1980–87, rising to 682.3% in 1988 and 1,287% in 1989. The rate reached 6,407% in the 12 months ending April 1990. An estimated 3.6% of the labour force were unemployed in 1987.

Brazil is a member of ALADI (see. p.172).

The 'economic miracle' of the 1960s and early 1970s in Brazil (with GDP expanding, in real terms, by an annual average of 11.3% between 1967 and 1974) gradually subsided in the 1980s, when economic affairs were dominated by Brazil's position as the developing world's largest debtor. Brazil dominated the world coffee market in the 1980s, but the International Coffee Organization's suspension of export quotas from July 1989 created a free market. Consequently Brazil's share of world coffee exports declined by 3.3% in the 12-month period to July 1990. Industrial expansion has been hindered by resistance from overseas markets, and many power development projects have suffered from conflict with environmentalists. An ambitious programme of economic reform, introduced by the Collor de Mello administration in March 1990, seemed likely to fail in its attempt to reduce inflation significantly, and predictions of a contraction in real GDP of 3%–5% for 1990 gave rise to fears that the country was entering a period of serious recession.

Social Welfare

The social security system, in existence since 1923, was rationalized in 1960, and the Instituto Nacional de Previdência Social (INPS) was formed in 1966. All social welfare programmes were consolidated in 1977 under the National System of Social Insurance and Assistance (SINPAS). The INPS administers benefits to urban and rural employees and their dependants. Employers and employees contribute 53.19%, the Federal Union 8.23% and other sources 36.37%. SINPAS revenue for 1983 was estimated at CR$6,636,898m. equal to 5.48% of GNP. Benefits include sickness benefit, invalidity, old age, length of service and widows' pensions, maternity and family allowances and grants. There are three government agencies: the Instituto de Administração Financeira da Previdência e Assistência Social collects contributions and revenue and supplies funds, the Instituto Nacional de Assistência Médica da Previdência Social is responsible for medical care, and CEME (Central Medicines) supplies medicines at a low price.

In 1982 there were 171,585 physicians in Brazil's hospitals; in 1984 the country had 12,175 hospital establishments, with a total of 538,721 beds. The private medical sector controls 90% of Brazil's hospitals. In response to a highly critical report on the health services, made in 1981, the Government introduced a health and welfare programme, Prevsaúde. This has been replaced by the Plan for the Reorientation of Health Aid, which proposes to adapt available resources to the requirements of the public. The plan has been co-ordinated by the Ministries of Social Welfare, Education and Health and by the State and Municipal Secretaries for Health. Expenditure by the central Government in 1987 included NCZ $273.2m. on health services and NCZ $680.8m. on social security and welfare (equivalent to 8.8% and 21.8% of total expenditure, respectively). In early 1988, however, the World Bank strongly criticized the misallocation of funds in the health sector, of which only 15% were assigned to preventative health care, such as immunization programmes and child health.

The welfare of the dwindling population of indigenous American Indians is the responsibility of the Fundação Nacional do Indio (FUNAI), which was formed to assign homelands to the Indians, most of whom are landless and threatened by the exploitation of the Amazon forest.

Education

Education is free in official pre-primary schools and is compulsory between the ages of seven and 14 years. Primary education begins at seven years of age and lasts for eight years. Secondary education, beginning at 15 years of age, lasts for four years and is also free in official schools. In 1987 a total of 26,208,051 children were enrolled at primary schools, but only 15% of those aged 15 to 17 were enrolled at secondary schools. The Federal Government is responsible for higher education, and in 1989 there were 74 universities, of which almost 50 were state-administered. There are a large number of private institutions in all levels of education. Expenditure on education by the central Government in 1987 was NCZ $137.3m., representing 4.4% of total expenditure.

Despite an anti-illiteracy campaign, initiated in 1971, the adult illiteracy rate in 1985 averaged 22.2% (males 20.9%; females 23.4%).

BRAZIL   *Introductory Survey, Statistical Survey*

Public Holidays

1991: 1 January (New Year's Day), 21 April (Tiradentes Day), 1 May (Labour Day), 9 May (Ascension Day), 30 May (Corpus Christi), 7 September (Independence Day), 12 October (Our Lady Aparecida, patroness of Brazil), 2 November (All Souls' Day), 15 November (Proclamation of the Republic), 25 December (Christmas Day).

1992: 1 January (New Year's Day), 21 April (Tiradentes Day), 1 May (Labour Day), 28 May (Ascension Day), 18 June (Corpus Christi), 7 September (Independence Day), 12 October (Our Lady Aparecida, patroness of Brazil), 2 November (All Souls' Day), 15 November (Proclamation of the Republic), 25 December (Christmas Day).

Other local holidays include 20 January (Foundation of Rio de Janeiro) and 25 January (Foundation of São Paulo).

Weights and Measures

The metric system is in force.

Statistical Survey

Sources (unless otherwise stated): Banco Central do Brasil, Brasília, DF; tel. (61) 224-1453; telex (61) 1702; Fundação Instituto Brasileiro de Geografia e Estatística (FIBGE), Av. Franklin Roosevelt 166, 20.021 Rio de Janeiro, RJ; tel. (21) 252-3501; telex (21) 30939.

Area and Population

AREA, POPULATION AND DENSITY

Area (sq km)	8,511,965*
Population (census results)†	
1 September 1970	93,139,037
1 September 1980	
Males	60,298,897
Females	60,849,685
Total	121,148,582
Population (official estimates at mid-year)†	
1987	141,452,000
1988	144,428,000
1989	147,404,000
Density (per sq km) at mid-1989	17.3

* 3,286,488 sq miles.
† Excluding Indian jungle population, numbering 45,429 in 1950. Census results also exclude an adjustment for underenumeration.

ADMINISTRATIVE DIVISIONS (mid-1989, official estimates)

State	Population ('000)*	Capital
Acre (AC)	412	Rio Branco
Alagoas (AL)	2,409	Maceió
Amapá (AP)	258	Macapá
Amazonas (AM)	2,141	Manaus
Bahia (BA)	11,625	Salvador
Ceará (CE)	6,401	Fortaleza
Espírito Santo (ES)	2,499	Vitória
Goiás (GO)	4,082	Goiânia
Maranhão (MA)	5,131	São Luís
Mato Grosso (MT)	1,931	Cuiabá
Mato Grosso do Sul (MS)	1,775	Campo Grande
Minas Gerais (MG)	16,063	Belo Horizonte
Pará (PA)	4,997	Belém
Paraíba (PB)	3,282	João Pessoa
Paraná (PR)	9,168	Curitiba
Pernambuco (PE)	7,303	Recife
Piauí (PI)	2,657	Teresina
Rio de Janeiro (RJ)	13,880	Rio de Janeiro
Rio Grande do Norte (RN)	2,336	Natal
Rio Grande do Sul (RS)	9,265	Porto Alegre
Rondônia (RO)	1,021	Porto Velho
Roraima (RR)	130	Boa Vista
Santa Catarina (SC)	4,402	Florianópolis
São Paulo (SP)	32,684	São Paulo
Sergipe (SE)	1,429	Aracajú
Tocantins (TO)	966	Miracema do Tocantins
Distrito Federal (DF)	1,803	Brasília
Total	**150,052**	

* Figures are provisional. The revised total is 147,404,000.

PRINCIPAL TOWNS* (estimated population at mid-1989)

Brasília (capital)	1,803,478		Maceió	527,220
São Paulo	10,997,472		São João de	
Rio de Janeiro	6,011,181		Meriti	504,631
Belo Horizonte	2,339,039		Santos	483,314
Salvador	2,000,387		Niterói	477,120
Fortaleza	1,763,546		Jaboatão	470,220
Nova Iguaçu	1,498,227		Contagem	454,550
Curitiba	1,390,967		João Pessoa	440,279
Porto Alegre	1,371,313		Campo Grande	435,448
Recife	1,352,024		São José dos	
Belém	1,190,017		Campos	423,207
Manaus	1,089,962		Ribeirão Preto	421,562
Goiânia	1,038,187		Aracaju	398,183
Campinas	946,035		Feira de Santana	396,471
Guarulhos	821,224		Juíz de Fora	378,533
São Gonçalo	818,447		Londrina	377,326
Duque de Caxias	734,322		Olinda	374,946
Santo André	683,964		Diadema	374,660
Osasco	661,218		Campos dos	
São Bernardo do			Goytacazes	367,162
Campo	643,949		Sorocaba	361,738
São Luís	624,321		Uberlândia	360,557
Natal	578,487		Jundiaí	346,293
Teresina	533,678		Joinville	343,632

* Figures refer to *municípias*, which may contain rural districts.

BIRTHS AND DEATHS (UN estimates, annual averages)

	1975–80	1980–85	1985–90
Birth rate (per 1,000)	32.0	30.6	28.6
Death rate (per 1,000)	8.9	8.4	7.9

Source: UN, *World Population Prospects: 1988*.

BRAZIL   Statistical Survey

ECONOMICALLY ACTIVE POPULATION
(household surveys, '000 persons aged 10 years and over)*

	1985	1986	1987
Agriculture, hunting, forestry and fishing	15,190.4	14,330.6	14,116.2
Mining and quarrying	} 7,847.3	8,986.4	9,005.1
Manufacturing			
Electricity, gas and water	839.3	820.6	856.3
Construction	3,097.4	3,588.7	3,813.4
Wholesale and retail trade	5,814.7	6,252.1	6,655.3
Transport and communications	1,916.0	1,988.7	2,161.4
Community, social and personal services (incl. restaurants and hotels)	15,351.8	16,337.5	17,439.6
Financing, insurance, real estate and business services	} 3,180.1	1,569.2	1,654.1
Activities not adequately defined		1,562.1	1,708.5
Total employed	53,236.9	55,436.0	57,410.0
Unemployed	1,861.6	1,380.2	2,133.0
Total labour force	55,098.5	56,816.2	59,543.0
Males	36,625.4	37,596.6	38,874.0
Females	18,473.1	19,219.6	20,669.0

* Figures exclude aborigines, non-resident foreigners and the rural population of the northern region. Also excluded are members of the armed forces in barracks.

Source: mainly International Labour Office, *Year Book of Labour Statistics*.

Agriculture

PRINCIPAL CROPS ('000 metric tons)

	1987	1988	1989
Wheat	6,035	5,751	5,407
Rice (paddy)	10,419	11,806	11,107
Barley	197	126	223
Maize	26,803	24,750	26,508
Oats	176	136	170†
Sorghum	438	296	254
Potatoes	2,331	2,299	2,104
Sweet potatoes	757	760*	750*
Cassava (Manioc)	23,464	21,612	23,247
Yams*	210	200	210
Dry beans	2,007	2,901	2,491
Soybeans (Soya beans)	16,969	18,021	24,044
Groundnuts (in shell)	196	170	156
Castor beans	104	145	148
Cottonseed	1,070	1,620	1,131
Coconuts	603	695	686
Babassu kernels*	205	202	205
Tomatoes	2,049	2,407	2,387
Onions (dry)	854	756	785
Other vegetables	1,977	2,006	1,960
Water-melons	415	430*	420*
Sugar cane	268,741	258,449	262,792
Grapes	566	765	706
Apples	334	433	470
Peaches and nectarines	108	100*	105*
Oranges	14,714	15,110	16,807
Tangerines, mandarins, clementines and satsumas	672	650†	650*
Lemons and limes	394	360*	370*
Avocados	115	110*	113*
Mangoes	422	400*	410*

PRINCIPAL CROPS ('000 metric tons)—continued

	1987	1988	1989
Pineapples	957	1,012	855
Bananas	5,131	5,156	5,588
Papayas	1,517	1,600*	1,650*
Other fruits and berries	1,469	1,518*	1,575*
Cashew nuts	75†	143	178
Coffee beans (green)‡	2,203	1,352	1,510
Cocoa beans	329	375	397
Tobacco (leaves)	397	430	445
Jute and allied fibres	66	69	49
Sisal	191	190	227
Cotton (lint)†	552	837	756
Other fibre crops*	72	70	72
Natural rubber	30	33†	36†

* FAO estimate(s).
† Unofficial figure(s).
‡ Official figures, reported in terms of dry cherries, have been converted into green coffee beans at 50%.

Source: FAO, *Production Yearbook*.

LIVESTOCK ('000 head, year ending September)

	1987	1988	1989
Cattle	135,726	134,133	136,814
Buffaloes	1,082	1,100*	1,150*
Horses	5,855	5,850*	5,850*
Asses	1,295	1,310*	1,320*
Mules	1,952	1,980*	2,000*
Pigs	32,480	32,700†	33,200†
Sheep	19,860	20,000*	20,500*
Goats	10,792	11,000*	11,000*

Chickens (million): 515 in 1987; 550* in 1988; 600* in 1989.
Ducks (million): 6 in 1987; 6* in 1988; 6* in 1989.
Turkeys (million): 4 in 1987; 4* in 1988; 5* in 1989.

* FAO estimate.   † Unofficial figure.

Source: FAO, *Production Yearbook*.

LIVESTOCK PRODUCTS ('000 metric tons)

	1987	1988	1989
Beef and veal	2,262	2,581	2,478*
Mutton and lamb†	32	35	37
Goats' meat†	27	27	27
Pig meat	990†	1,100*	1,000*
Horse meat	6	5	5†
Poultry meat	1,855	2,004	2,140
Edible offals†	656	748	717
Cows' milk	13,399	13,609*	13,609*
Goats' milk†	108	111	111
Butter*	77	79	80
Cheese†	59	60	60
Dried milk*	122	130	130
Hen eggs	1,235	1,191*	1,100*
Other poultry eggs†	9	9	9
Honey	14	16†	16†
Wool:			
greasy	31	32*	32†
scoured†	19	20	20
Cattle hides (fresh)	300†	390*	380*

* Unofficial estimate(s).   † FAO estimate(s).

Source: FAO, mainly *Production Yearbook*.

BRAZIL

Forestry

ROUNDWOOD REMOVALS
(FAO estimates, '000 cubic metres, excluding bark)

	1986	1987	1988
Sawlogs, veneer logs and logs for sleepers	39,983	39,983	40,263
Pulpwood*	20,900	20,900	20,900
Other industrial wood	5,248	5,360	5,473
Fuel wood	171,753	175,426	179,115
Total	237,884	241,669	245,751

* Assumed to be unchanged since 1980.
Source: FAO, *Yearbook of Forest Products*.

SAWNWOOD PRODUCTION
(FAO estimates, '000 cubic metres)

	1986	1987	1988
Coniferous (softwood)*	8,384	8,384	8,384
Broadleaved (hardwood)	9,679	9,679	9,795
Total	18,063	18,063	18,179

* Assumed to be unchanged since 1984.
Source: FAO, *Yearbook of Forest Products*.

Fishing

(metric tons, live weight)

	1986	1987	1988*
Inland waters	223,573	232,179	220,000
Atlantic Ocean	570,666	500,703	530,000
Total catch	794,239	732,882	750,000

* FAO estimates.
Source: FAO, *Yearbook of Fishery Statistics*.

Mining

	1985	1986	1987
Bauxite ('000 metric tons)	9,963	8,981	10,319
Coal ('000 metric tons)	24,414	22,574	18,627
Iron ore ('000 metric tons)*	167,232	175,725	182,745
Manganese ore ('000 metric tons)*	3,516	3,475	3,046
Lead ('000 metric tons)*	316	258	180
Dolomite ('000 metric tons)	2,208	2,816	3,317
Sea salt ('000 metric tons)	1,734	1,600	3,600
Gold (kilograms)	29,673	23,361	34,996
Silver (kilograms)	48,891	59,514	61,095
Crude petroleum ('000 cu metres)	31,669	33,200	32,629
Natural gas (million cu metres)	5,466	5,686	5,786

* Figures refer to the gross weight of ores. The metal content (in '000 metric tons) was: Iron 127,730 in 1985, 129,405 in 1986, 134,100 in 1987; Manganese 2,320 in 1985, 2,499 in 1986, 1,945 in 1987; Lead 28.5 in 1985, 23.1 in 1986, 20.5 in 1987.

1988: Crude petroleum 32,237,000 cu metres; Natural gas 5,844 million cu metres.

Source: *Anuário Mineral Brasileiro*, Ministério das Minas e Energia.

Other ores (metal content, metric tons): Copper 49,700 in 1985, 46,400 in 1986, 37,800* in 1987; Nickel 16,473 in 1985, 21,103 in 1986, 13,340* in 1987; Zinc 152,000 in 1985, 177,800 in 1986; 119,400* in 1987; Tin 26,514 in 1985, 26,405 in 1986, 30,405 in 1987, 44,020 in 1988, 50,161 in 1989; Chromium 131,000 in 1985, 126,000 in 1986, 59,000* in 1987; Tungsten 2,050 in 1985, 1,502 in 1986, 672 in 1987; Uranium 84 in 1985, 31 in 1986, 50 in 1987.

* Estimate (Source: UN, *Industrial Statistics Yearbook*).

Industry

SELECTED PRODUCTS
('000 metric tons, unless otherwise indicated; data for final quarters are estimates)

	1986	1987	1988
Asphalt	1,375	1,275	1,276
Electric power (million kWh)	201,810	208,999	221,747
Coke	7,344	7,474	7,973
Pig iron	20,249	20,944	23,454
Crude steel	21,233	22,228	24,657
Cement*	25,257	25,470	25,329
Tyres ('000 units)	27,046	25,341	30,026
Synthetic rubber (metric tons)	270,817	251,547	289,276
Passenger cars (units)	815,976	683,485	782,407
Commercial vehicles (units)	241,281	236,723	286,447
Tractors (units)	61,065	54,743	44,802
Sugar	7,548	8,757	7,894
Newsprint	213	232	247
Other paper and board	4,272	4,480	4,392

* Portland cement only.

BRAZIL

Finance

CURRENCY AND EXCHANGE RATES

Monetary Units
100 centavos = 1 cruzeiro (CR $).

Sterling and Dollar Equivalents (30 September 1990)
£1 sterling = 156.91 cruzeiros;
US $1 = 83.75 cruzeiros;
1,000 cruzeiros = £6.373 = $11.940.

Average Exchange Rates (new cruzados per US $)
1987 0.03923
1988 0.26238
1989 2.83392

Note: In March 1986 the cruzeiro (CR $) was replaced by a new currency unit, the cruzado (CZ $), equivalent to 1,000 cruzeiros. In January 1989 the cruzado was, in turn, replaced by the new cruzado (NCZ $), equivalent to CZ $1,000 and initially at par with the US dollar. In March 1990 the new cruzado was replaced by the cruzeiro (CR $), at an exchange rate of one new cruzado for one cruzeiro. Some figures in this Survey continue to be in terms of old or new cruzados.

GENERAL BUDGET (estimates, NCZ $ '000)

Revenue	1987	1988	1989
Taxes	306,600.0	2,471,000.0	33,915,739.8
Patrimonial revenue	1,811.7	12,000.0	1,171,998.0
Industrial revenue	69.2	395.2	14,914.6
Currency transfers	460.9	1,500.0	7,508.5
Miscellaneous	245,358.2	2,044,499.9	36,531,209.0
Other revenue	2,353.0	15,767.7	6,204,025.9
National Treasury total	556,653.0	4,545,162.8	77,845,395.8
Official credit operations	—	—	13,991,755.4
Federal administration funds	—	—	25,189,207.3
Indirect administration funds	35,192.0	122,801.0	2,718,926.8
General total	591,845.0	4,667,963.8	119,745,285.3

Expenditure	1987	1988	1989
Legislative and auxiliary	4,450.6	22,602.0	770,632.0
Judiciary	6,166.9	30,422.4	1,667,439.0
Executive	546,035.5	4,492,138.4	75,407,324.8
Presidency (including Planning Secretariat)	14,888.8	85,453.2	1,903,203.7
Air	23,853.0	118,759.3	1,615,698.9
Agriculture	11,949.7	66,582.5	931,770.8
Communications	7,906.5	6,991.6	38,582.6
Education and culture	39,732.6	215,795.8	5,531,799.3
Army	14,911.0	74,692.1	2,051,648.5
Finance	7,249.7	34,846.3	891,490.6
Industry and commerce	17,251.7	103,192.0	1,323,647.1
Interior	14,339.6	52,129.1	961,493.1
Justice	2,609.4	12,982.0	321,309.9
Marine	15,386.4	81,546.4	1,656,954.5
Mines and power	2,237.8	73,287.8	872,512.4
Foreign affairs	3,357.4	16,388.6	315,372.3
Health	14,506.6	75,769.8	2,232,751.0
Work and social welfare	9,619.2	17,535.0	3,901,210.1
Transport	60,768.4	224,481.9	2,690,162.8
Unspecified items	285,468.6	3,231,705.3	48,167,418.0
National Treasury Total	556,653.0	4,545,162.8	77,845,395.8
Official credit operations	—	—	13,991,755.4
Federal administration funds	—	—	25,189,207.3
Indirect administration funds	35,192.0	122,801.0	2,718,926.8
General total	591,845.0	4,667,963.8	119,745,285.3

CENTRAL BANK RESERVES (US $ million at 31 December)

	1987	1988	1989
Gold	1,159	1,144	1,194
Foreign exchange	6,299	6,971	7,535
Total	7,458	8,115	8,729

MONEY SUPPLY (CR $ million at 31 December)

	1985	1986	1987
Currency outside banks	23.8	n.a.	n.a.
Demand deposits at deposit money banks	70.8	345.1*	730.1*

* Beginning in 1986, the figure consolidates the accounts of commercial banks and the Bank of Brazil. For earlier years, the total comprised commercial banks only.

Source: IMF, *International Financial Statistics*.

COST OF LIVING (Consumer Price Index, Rio de Janeiro; annual averages; base: March 1986 = 100)

	1986	1987	1988
Foodstuffs	102.5	322.9	2,717.6
Clothing	105.0	311.2	2,395.0
Housing	102.7	283.3	1,852.9
Household articles	101.1	300.0	2,187.3
Medicines and hygiene products	102.4	398.3	3,118.2
Personal services	101.2	364.7	2,578.7
Utilities and urban transport	100.9	400.8	3,471.5
All items	102.0	338.2	2,646.1

NATIONAL ACCOUNTS (CZ $ million at current prices)
Composition of the Gross National Product

	1985	1986	1987
Gross domestic product (GDP) at factor cost	1,289,405	3,295,240	10,682,465
Indirect taxes	146,167	466,853	1,398,284
Less Subsidies	21,780	53,897	196,015
GDP in purchasers' values	1,413,792	3,708,196	11,884,734
Factor income received from abroad	12,701	18,592	39,031
Less Factor income paid abroad	86,361	181,981	475,200
Gross national product	1,340,132	3,544,807	11,448,565

Expenditure on the Gross Domestic Product

	1985	1986	1987
Government final consumption expenditure	136,591	390,867	1,462,089
Private final consumption expenditure	965,933	2,514,132	7,401,647
Increase in stocks			
Gross fixed capital formation	240,031	713,042	2,644,070
Total domestic expenditure	1,342,555	3,618,041	11,507,806
Exports of goods and services	169,331	322,848	1,091,348
Less Imports of goods and services	98,094	232,693	714,420
GDP in purchasers' values	1,413,792	3,708,196	11,884,734
GDP at constant 1980 prices	13,114	14,109	14,618

BRAZIL

Gross Domestic Product by Economic Activity (at factor cost)

	1985	1986	1987
Agriculture, hunting, forestry and fishing	131,718	330,534	948,896
Mining and quarrying	51,554	105,375	239,404
Manufacturing	402,703	992,231	3,247,646
Electricity, gas and water	29,800	78,457	345,334
Construction	78,257	240,304	900,298
Trade, restaurants and hotels	135,416	337,467	1,034,694
Transport, storage and communications	66,423	159,747	511,610
Finance, insurance, real estate and business services	160,060	269,856	1,614,872
Government services	95,975	267,338	887,375
Other community, social and personal services	300,632	770,629	2,543,425
Sub-total	1,452,538	3,551,938	12,273,554
Less Imputed bank service charge	163,133	256,697	1,591,089
Total	1,289,405	3,295,241	10,682,465

BALANCE OF PAYMENTS (US $ million)

	1986	1987	1988
Merchandise exports f.o.b.	22,348	26,210	33,773
Merchandise imports f.o.b.	−14,044	−15,052	−14,605
Trade balance	8,304	11,158	19,168
Exports of services	2,783	2,520	3,050
Imports of services	−16,478	−15,198	−18,153
Balance on goods and services	−5,391	−1,520	4,065
Private unrequited transfers (net)	89	113	107
Government unrequited transfers (net)	−2	−43	−13
Current balance	−5,304	−1,450	4,159
Direct capital investment (net)	177	1,087	2,794
Other long-term capital (net)	−9,609	−11,653	−14,577
Short-term capital (net)	847	284	2,593
Net errors and omissions	66	−802	−847
Total (net monetary movements)	−13,823	−12,534	−5,878
Monetization of gold	135	293	223
Valuation changes (net)	−2,276	−658	181
Exceptional financing (net)	10,195	14,174	7,516
Official financing (net)	396	525	73
Changes in reserves	−5,372	1,800	2,115

OVERSEAS INVESTMENT IN BRAZIL (1988, US $ '000)

Countries of origin	Investments	Reinvestments	Total
Belgium	229,442	173,475	402,917
Canada	1,002,460	416,666	1,419,126
France	619,678	690,984	1,310,662
Germany, Federal Republic	3,159,353	1,553,090	4,712,443
Japan	2,415,692	542,787	2,958,479
Luxembourg	374,167	124,282	498,449
Netherlands	527,708	350,531	878,239
Netherlands Dependencies	233,218	18,910	252,128
Panama	525,615	408,184	933,799
Sweden	330,638	217,133	547,771
Switzerland	1,666,384	1,141,581	2,807,965
United Kingdom	1,046,954	868,711	1,915,665
USA	5,940,194	2,959,913	8,900,107
Others	2,771,952	393,370	3,165,322
Total	20,843,455	9,859,617	30,703,072

External Trade

PRINCIPAL COMMODITIES (US $ '000)

Imports f.o.b.	1986	1987	1988
Vegetable products	1,195,248	722,246	535,715
Mineral products	3,873,910	5,077,298	4,594,636
Products of the chemical and allied industries	2,126,747	2,212,983	2,347,476
Plastic materials, resins and rubber	417,171	475,517	535,016
Paper-making materials, paper	192,470	269,101	268,567
Base metals and articles of base metal	636,653	706,026	619,083
Machinery and mechanical appliances, electrical equipment	2,714,276	3,011,282	3,670,128
Transport equipment	749,644	946,736	524,755
Optical, photographic and measuring instruments, clocks and watches	586,949	520,950	643,883
Total (incl. others)	14,044,304	15,051,864	14,605,254

Exports f.o.b.	1986	1987	1988
Live animals and animal products	603,438	677,234	903,052
Vegetable products	2,594,040	2,901,827	3,081,128
Coffee	2,347,400	2,185,270	2,230,422
Animal and vegetable oils and fats	267,096	446,727	459,366
Food, beverages, vinegar and tobacco	4,337,018	4,500,650	5,567,742
Cocoa beans	273,322	265,587	215,495
Sugar	381,397	324,612	345,084
Tobacco leaf	394,520	405,497	522,785
Mineral products	2,540,715	2,777,843	3,114,433
Haematite	1,615,310	1,615,395	1,891,853
Products of chemical and allied industries	964,656	1,165,642	1,572,408
Hides and skins	247,166	265,373	414,439
Wood, charcoal and cork	311,111	400,113	512,394
Textiles and textile articles	890,099	1,202,007	1,299,979
Cotton (raw)	16,756	160,179	31,297
Machinery and mechanical appliances, electrical equipment	2,239,973	2,519,628	3,261,304
Transport equipment	1,568,887	2,774,916	3,054,218
Total (incl. others)	22,348,603	26,225,115	33,786,532

PRINCIPAL TRADING PARTNERS (US $ '000 f.o.b.)

Imports	1986	1987	1988
Argentina	736,988	580,063	707,105
Belgium-Luxembourg	102,515	128,235	128,888
Canada	433,559	409,233	418,859
Chile	278,393	353,098	348,584
France	568,934	601,036	574,311
Germany, Federal Republic	1,285,123	1,448,937	1,435,276
Iraq	960,220	1,436,352	1,160,852
Italy	348,641	333,409	289,457
Japan	881,584	843,377	959,972
Netherlands	253,013	287,152	243,991
Poland	180,949	155,052	162,258
Saudi Arabia	879,818	861,485	925,892
Sweden	136,453	161,184	193,732
Switzerland	350,430	345,839	403,404
USSR	44,811	70,197	26,553
United Kingdom	346,153	378,987	402,575
USA	3,186,733	3,142,781	3,121,108
Venezuela	95,583	157,058	139,207
Total (incl. others)	14,044,304	15,051,864	14,605,254

BRAZIL

Exports	1986	1987	1988
Argentina	678,336	831,782	979,047
Belgium-Luxembourg	484,486	611,388	934,543
Canada	436,057	561,551	893,942
Chile	246,074	354,824	542,066
Denmark	108,505	94,367	102,653
France	717,635	678,153	886,300
Germany, Federal Republic	1,099,200	1,228,522	1,513,600
Italy	910,439	1,269,706	1,429,689
Japan	1,513,585	1,676,476	2,326,382
Mexico	155,981	171,342	274,148
Netherlands	1,298,558	1,607,786	2,610,031
Nigeria	247,106	216,672	141,145
Norway	89,782	76,978	84,824
Peru	156,442	215,752	192,979
Poland	223,910	292,680	306,731
Saudi Arabia	211,752	481,181	314,952
Spain	447,035	444,428	775,360
Sweden	193,348	138,311	177,633
Switzerland	185,480	230,998	191,376
USSR	265,721	379,062	246,054
United Kingdom	646,217	755,740	1,086,039
USA	6,174,415	7,191,844	8,799,674
Venezuela	348,383	374,074	503,358
Total (incl. others)	22,348,603	26,225,115	33,788,376

Transport

RAILWAYS

	1985	1986	1987
Passengers ('000)	650,408	630,531	653,289
Passenger-km (million)	16,362	15,782	15,273
Passenger revenue ('000 cruzados)	280,637	614,455	2,633,076
Freight ('000 metric tons)	208,257	213,105	215,414
Freight ton-km (million)	99,863	103,860	109,421
Freight revenue ('000 cruzados)	6,300,159	11,786,160	39,382,109

ROAD TRAFFIC (motor vehicles in use at 31 December)

	1986	1987	1988
Passenger cars	12,306,570	12,782,646	14,995,837
Buses and coaches	158,563	165,098	193,683
Goods vehicles	1,162,129	1,207,086	1,416,081
Motorcycles and mopeds	1,367,563	1,420,467	1,666,407

Source: IRF, *World Road Statistics*.

SHIPPING

	1983	1984	1985
Brazilian fleet (vessels)	1,890	2,135	2,193
Capacity ('000 dwt)	2,344	10,001	10,462
Freight traffic ('000 metric tons):			
Goods loaded*	118,790	141,737	146,364
Goods unloaded*	55,056	53,970	48,864

* International sea-borne traffic only.

Source: Sunamam.

CIVIL AVIATION (embarked passengers, mail and cargo)

	1985	1986	1987
Number of passengers ('000)	13,182	16,285	16,144
Freight (metric tons)	1,038,826	1,225,884	1,215,797
Mail (metric tons)	22,161	20,167	18,325

Source: Departamento de Aviação Civil (DAC).

Tourism

	1986	1987	1988
Arrivals	1,934,091	1,929,053	1,742,939

Education

(1988)

	Institutions	Teachers	Students*
Pre-primary	n.a.	n.a.	3,930,579
Primary	201,541	1,119,907	25,691,090
Secondary†	10,174	229,183	3,290,021
Higher	871	138,016	1,493,742

* Figures refer to 1987.
† Including teacher-training and vocational education.

Directory

The Constitution

A new constitution was promulgated on 5 October 1988. The following is a summary of the main provisions:

The Federative Republic of Brazil, formed by the indissoluble union of the States, the Municipalities and the Federal District, is constituted as a democratic state. All power emanates from the people. The Federative Republic of Brazil seeks the economic, political, social and cultural integration of the peoples of Latin America.

All are equal before the law. The inviolability of the right to life, freedom, equality, security and property is guaranteed. No one shall be subjected to torture. Freedom of thought, conscience, religious belief and expression are guaranteed, as is privacy. The principles of habeas corpus and 'habeas data' (the latter giving citizens access to personal information held in government data banks) are granted. There is freedom of association, and the right to strike is guaranteed.

There is universal suffrage by direct secret ballot. Voting is compulsory for literate persons between 18 and 69 years of age, and optional for those who are illiterate, those over 70 years of age and those aged 16 and 17.

Brasília is the federal capital. The Union's competence includes maintaining relations with foreign states, and taking part in international organizations; declaring war and making peace; guaranteeing national defence; decreeing a state of siege; issuing currency; supervising credits, etc.; formulating and implementing plans for economic and social development; maintaining national services, including communications, energy, the judiciary and the police; legislating on civil, commercial, penal, procedural, electoral, agrarian, maritime, aeronautical, spatial and labour law, etc. The Union, States, Federal District and Municipalities must protect the Constitution, laws and democratic institutions, and preserve national heritage.

The States are responsible for electing their Governors by universal suffrage and direct secret ballot for a four-year term. The

LEGISLATIVE POWER

The legislative power is exercised by the National Congress, which is composed of the Chamber of Deputies and the Federal Senate. Elections for deputies and senators take place simultaneously throughout the country; candidates for Congress must be Brazilian by birth and have full exercise of their political rights. They must be at least 21 years of age in the case of deputies and at least 35 years of age in the case of senators. Congress meets twice a year in ordinary sessions, and extraordinary sessions may be convened by the President of the Republic, the Presidents of the Chamber of Deputies and the Federal Senate, or at the request of the majority of the members of either house.

The Chamber of Deputies is made up of representatives of the people, elected by a system of proportional representation in each State, Territory and the Federal District for a period of four years. The total number of deputies representing the States and the Federal District will be established in proportion to the population; each Territory will elect four deputies.

The Federal Senate is composed of representatives of the States and the Federal District, elected according to the principle of majority. Each State and the Federal District will elect three senators with a mandate of eight years, with elections after four years for one-third of the members and after another four years for the remaining two-thirds. Each Senator is elected with two substitutes. The Senate approves, by secret ballot, the choice of Magistrates, when required by the Constitution; of the Attorney-General of the Republic, of the Ministers of the Accounts Tribunal, of the Territorial Governors, of the president and directors of the central bank and of the permanent heads of diplomatic missions.

The National Congress is responsible for deciding on all matters within the competence of the Union, especially fiscal and budgetary arrangements, national, regional and local plans and programmes, the strength of the armed forces and territorial limits. It is also responsible for making definitive resolutions on international treaties, and for authorizing the President to declare war.

The powers of the Chamber of Deputies include authorizing the instigation of legal proceedings against the President and Vice-President of the Republic and Ministers of State. The Federal Senate may indict and impose sentence on the President and Vice-President of the Republic and Ministers of State.

Constitutional amendments may be proposed by at least one-third of the members of either house, by the President or by more than one-half of the legislative assemblies of the units of the Federation. Amendments must be ratified by three-fifths of the members of each house. The Constitution may not be amended during times of national emergency, such as a state of siege.

EXECUTIVE POWER

Executive power is exercised by the President of the Republic, aided by the Ministers of State. Candidates for the Presidency and Vice-Presidency must be Brazilian-born, be in full exercise of their political rights and be over 35 years of age. The candidate who obtains an absolute majority of votes will be elected President. If no candidate attains an absolute majority, the two candidates who have received the most votes proceed to a second round of voting, at which the candidate obtaining the majority of valid votes will be elected President. The President holds office for a term of five years and is not eligible for re-election.

The Ministers of State are chosen by the President and their duties include countersigning acts and decrees signed by the President, expediting instructions for the enactment of laws, decrees and regulations, and presentation to the President of an annual report of their activities.

The Council of the Republic is the higher consultative organ of the President of the Republic. It comprises the Vice-President of the Republic, the Presidents of the Chamber of Deputies and Federal Senate, the leaders of the majority and of the minority in each house, the Minister of Justice, two members appointed by the President of the Republic, two elected by the Federal Senate and two elected by the Chamber of Deputies, the latter six having a mandate of three years.

The National Defence Council advises the President on matters relating to national sovereignty and defence. It comprises the Vice-President of the Republic, the Presidents of the Chamber of Deputies and Federal Senate, the Minister of Justice, military Ministers and the Ministers of Foreign Affairs and of Planning.

JUDICIAL POWER

Judicial power in the Union is exercised by the Supreme Federal Tribunal; the Higher Tribunal of Justice; the Regional Federal Tribunals and federal judges; Labour Tribunals and judges; Electoral Tribunals and judges; Military Tribunals and judges; and the States' Tribunals and judges. Judges are appointed for life; they may not undertake any other employment. The Tribunals elect their own controlling organs and organize their own internal structure.

The Supreme Federal Tribunal, situated in the Union capital, has jurisdiction over the whole national territory and is composed of 11 Ministers. The Ministers are nominated by the President after approval by the Senate, from Brazilian-born citizens, between the ages of 35 and 65 years, of proved judicial knowledge and experience.

The Government

HEAD OF STATE

President: FERNANDO COLLOR DE MELLO (took office 15 March 1990).

Vice-President: ITAMAR AUGUSTO CANTIERO FRANCO.

CABINET
(December 1990)

Minister of Justice: Col (retd) JARBAS PASSARINHO.
Minister of Foreign Affairs: FRANCISCO REZEK.
Minister of the Economy: ZÉLIA CARDOSO DE MELLO.
Minister of Agriculture: ANTÔNIO CABRERA FILHO.
Minister of Education: CARLOS CHIARELLI.
Minister of the Environment: JOSÉ LUTZEMBERGER.
Minister of Labour: ANTÔNIO ROGÉRIO MAGRI.
Minister of Health: ALCENI GUERRA.
Minister of Infrastructure: Ing. OZIRES SILVA.
Minister of Social Action: MARGARIDA MAIA PROCÓPIO.
Minister of the Navy: Adm. MÁRIO CÉSAR FLORES.
Minister of the Army: Gen. CARLOS TINOCO RIBEIRO GOMES.
Minister of the Air Force: Brig. SÓCRATES DA COSTA MONTEIRO.

MINISTRIES

Office of the President: Palácio do Planalto, Praça dos Três Poderes, 70.150 Brasília, DF; tel. (61) 223-2714; telex (61) 1451.

Ministry of the Air Force: Esplanada dos Ministérios, Bloco M, 8°, 70.045 Brasília, DF; tel. (61) 223-0409; telex (61) 1152; fax (61) 223-0930.

Ministry of Agriculture: Esplanada dos Ministérios, Bloco D, 8°, 70.043 Brasília, DF; tel. (61) 218-2800; telex (61) 1138.

Ministry of the Army: Esplanada dos Ministérios, Bloco 4, 70.042 Brasília, DF; tel. (61) 224-6797; telex (61) 1094.

Ministry of the Economy: Esplanada dos Ministérios, Bloco P, 5°, 70.048 Brasília, DF: tel. (61) 223-2729; telex (61) 1142.

Ministry of Education: Esplanada dos Ministérios, Bloco L, 70.047 Brasília, DF; tel. (61) 223-7306; telex (61) 9105.

Ministry of Foreign Affairs: Palácio do Itamaraty, Esplanada dos Ministérios, 70.040 Brasília, DF; tel. (61) 226-1762; telex (61) 1319.

Ministry of Health: Esplanada dos Ministérios, Bloco 11, 70.058 Brasília, DF; tel. (61) 223-8158; telex (61) 1752.

Ministry of Infrastructure: Esplanada dos Ministérios, Bloco R, 70.044 Brasília, DF; tel. (61) 223-4992; telex (61) 1994; fax (61) 224-5969; replaced Ministries of Communications, Mines and Energy, and Transport in March 1989.

Ministry of Justice: Esplanada dos Ministérios, Bloco T, 70.064 Brasília, DF; tel. (61) 224-2964; telex (61) 1088.

Ministry of Labour: Esplanada dos Ministérios, Bloco F, 10°, 70.050 Brasília, DF; tel. (61) 224-6864; telex (61) 1158.

Ministry of the Navy: Esplanada dos Ministérios, Bloco 3, 70.055 Brasília, DF; tel. (61) 224-3489; telex (61) 1392.

Ministry of Social Action: Brasília.

BRAZIL   *Directory*

President and Legislature

PRESIDENT

Elections of 15 November and 17 December 1989

Candidate	First ballot	Second ballot
Fernando Collor de Mello (PRN)	20,611,011	35,089,998
Luís Inácio (Lula) da Silva (PT)	11,622,673	31,076,364
Leonel Brizola (PDT)	11,168,228	–
Mário Covas (PSDB)	7,790,392	–
Paulo Maluf (PDS)	5,989,575	–
Others	10,449,133	–
Total	67,631,012	66,166,362*

* In addition, there were 4,024,339 blank or spoiled votes.

CONGRESSO NACIONAL
(National Congress)

President of the Federal Senate: Senator Nelson Carneiro.
President of the Chamber of Deputies: Paes de Andrade.

General Election, 15 November 1986

Party	Federal Senate*	Chamber of Deputies
Partido do Movimento DemocráticoBrasileiro (PMDB)	44	259
Partido da Frente Liberal (PFL)	16	115
Partido Democrático Social (PDS)	5	36
Partido Democrático Trabalhista (PDT)	2	24
Partido dos Trabalhadores (PT)	–	19
Partido Trabalhista Brasileiro (PDB)	1	19
Partido Liberal (PL)	1	7
Partido Democrata Cristão (PDC)	1	3
Partido Comunista Brasileiro (PCB)	–	2
Partido Comunista do Brasil (PC do B)	–	2
Partido Socialista Brasileiro (PSB)	2	1
Total	72	487

* Elections for 49 Senate seats were held on 15 November 1986.

Note: This National Congress also acted as the Constitutional Assembly. The Assembly was installed in February 1987, and was responsible for drafting the 1988 Constitution.

Gubernatorial and legislative elections were held on 3 October 1990, but full results were not available.

Governors*

STATES

Acre: Flaviano Baptista de Melo (PMDB).
Alagoas: Moacir L. de Andrade.
Amapá: Jorge Nova da Costa.
Amazonas: Gilberto Mestrinho (PMDB).†
Bahia: Antônio C. Magalhães (PFL).†
Ceará: Ciro Gomes (PSDB).†
Espírito Santo: Max Freitas Mauro (PMDB).
Goias: Iris Rezende (PMDB).†
Maranhão: Epitácio Cafeteira Afonso Pereira (PMDB).
Mato Grosso: Jaime Campos (PFL).†
Mato Grosso do Sul: Pedro Pedrossian (PTB).†
Minas Gerais: Newton Cardoso (PMDB).
Pará: Hélio Mota Gueiros (PMDB).
Paraíba: Tarcísio de Miranda Burity (PMDB).
Paraná: Alvaro Fernandes Dias (PMDB).
Pernambuco: Joaquim Francisco (PFL).
Piauí: Alberto Tavares Silva (PMDB).
Rio de Janeiro: Leonel Brizola (PDT).†
Rio Grande do Norte: Geraldo Ferreira de Melo (PMDB).
Rio Grande do Sul: Pedro Jorge Simon (PMDB).
Rondônia: Jerônimo Garcia de Santana (PMDB).
Roraima: Romero Jucá Filho.
Santa Catarina: Vilson Kleinubing (PFL).†
São Paulo: Orestes Quércia (PMDB).
Sergipe: João Alves (PFL).†
Tocantins: José W. Siqueira Campos.

FEDERAL DISTRICT

Brasília: Joaquim Roriz.
Note: The Governor of Brasília is a federal government nominee.
* Pending full results of gubernatorial elections held on 25 November 1990 (see Late Information).
† Elected on 3 October 1990.

Political Organizations

In May 1985 the National Congress approved a constitutional amendment providing for the free formation of political parties. The following parties are represented in Congress:

Partido Comunista Brasileiro (PCB): Brasília, DF; f. 1922; pro-Moscow; Leader Roberto Freire; Sec.-Gen. Salomão Malina.

Partido Comunista do Brasil (PC do B): Brasília, DF; f. 1962; pro-Albanian; Leader Haroldo Lima; Sec.-Gen. João Amazonas; 5,000 mems.

Partido Democrata Cristão (PDC): Brasília, DF; Pres. Mauro Borges; Leader Roberto Balestra.

Partido Democrático Social (PDS): Senado Federal Anexo II, Presidência do PDS, 70.000 Brasília, DF; telex (61) 2402; f. 1980; Pres. Antônio Delfim Netto; Sec.-Gen. Amaral Neto.

Partido Democrático Trabalhista (PDT): Rua 7 de Setembro 141, 4°, 20.050 Rio de Janeiro, RJ; f. 1980; formerly the PTB (Partido Trabalhista Brasileiro), renamed 1980 when that name was awarded to a dissident group following controversial judicial proceedings; Pres. Leonel Brizola; Gen. Sec. Dr Carmen Cynira.

Partido da Frente Liberal (PFL): Brasília, DF; f. 1984 by moderate members of the PDS and PMDB; Pres. Aureliano de Mendonça Chaves; Gen. Sec. Saulo Queiroz.

Partido Liberal (PL): Brasília, DF; Pres. Álvaro Valle; Leader Adolfo Oliveira.

Partido do Movimento Democrático Brasileiro (PMDB): f. 1980; moderate elements of former MDB; merged with Partido Popular February 1982; Pres. Ulysses Guimarães; Gen.-Sec. Tarcísio Delgado; factions include: the **Históricos** and the **Movimento da Unidade Progressiva (MUP)**.

Partido de Reconstrução Nacional (PRN): Brasília; f. 1988; right-wing; Leader Fernando Collor de Mello.

Partido da Social Democracia Brasileira (PSDB): Brasília, DF; f. 1988; centre-left; formed by dissident members of the PMDB (incl. Históricos), PFL, PDS, PDT, PSB and PTB; Pres. Mário Covas; Leader Euclides Scalco.

Partido Socialista Brasileiro (PSB): Brasília, DF; Pres. Jamil Hadad; Leader João Herrman Neto.

Partido dos Trabalhadores (PT): Congresso Nacional, 70.160, Brasília, DF; tel. (61) 224-1699; f. 1980; first independent labour party; associated with the *autêntico* branch of the trade union movement; 350,000 mems; Pres. Luís Inácio (Lula) da Silva; Vice-Pres. Jacó Bittar; Sec.-Gen. José Luís Fevereiro.

Partido Trabalhista Brasileiro (PTB): Brasília, DF; f. 1980; Pres. Luís Gonzaga de Paiva Muniz; Gen. Sec. José Correia Pedroso Filho.

Diplomatic Representation

EMBASSIES IN BRAZIL

Algeria: SHIS, Q1 09, Conj. 13, Casa 01, Lago Sul, 71.600 Brasília, DF; tel. (61) 248-4039; telex (61) 1278; Ambassador: Abdelouahab Keramane.

Angola: SHIS, Q1 09, Conj. 16, Casa 23, Brasília, DF; tel. (61) 248-3362; telex (61) 4971; Ambassador: Francisco Romão de Oliveira e Silva.

Argentina: SEPN, Av. W-3 Quadra 513, Bloco D, Edif. Imperador, 4° andar, 70.442 Brasília, DF; tel. (61) 273-3737; telex (61) 1013; Ambassador: Héctor Alberto Subiza.

Australia: SHIS, QI 09 Conj. 16, Casa 01, Lago Sul, 70.469 Brasília, DF; tel. (61) 248-5523; telex (61) 1025; Ambassador: Warwick Robinson Pearson.

Austria: SES, Av. das Nações, Lote 40, CP 07-1215, Brasília, DF; tel. (61) 243-3111; telex (61) 1202; Ambassador: Dr Nikolaus Horn.

BRAZIL

Bangladesh: SHIS, QL 10, Conj. 01, Casa 17, 70.468 Brasília, DF; tel. (61) 248-4609; Ambassador: MUJIB-UR RAHMAN.

Belgium: Av. das Nações, Lote 32, 70.422 Brasília, DF; tel. (61) 243-1133; telex (61) 1261; fax (61) 243-1219; Ambassador: CHRISTIAN DE SAINT HUBERT.

Bolivia: SHIS, QL 20, Conj. 05, Casa 17, Lago Sul, 70.470 Brasília, DF; tel. (61) 366-1441; telex (61) 1946; Ambassador: JAIME BALCAZAR ARANIBAR.

Bulgaria: SEN, Av. das Nações, Lote 8, 70.432 Brasília, DF; tel. (61) 223-5193; telex (61) 1305; Ambassador: GEORGI JEKOV GEUROV.

Cameroon: QI 3, Conj. 5, Casa 2, Lago Sul, 71.600 Brasília, DF; tel. (61) 248-4433; telex (61) 2235; Ambassador: MARTIN NGUELE MBARGA.

Canada: SES, Av. das Nações, Lote 16, CP 07-0961, 70.410 Brasília, DF; tel. (61) 223-7515; telex (61) 1296; fax (61) 225-5233; Ambassador: JOHN PETER BELL.

Chile: SES, Av. das Nações, Lote 11, 70.407 Brasília, DF; tel. (61) 226-5545; telex (61) 1075; Ambassador: RAÚL SCHMIDT DUSSAILLANT.

China, People's Republic: SES, Av. das Nações, Lote 51, 70.443 Brasília, DF; tel. (61) 244-8695; telex (61) 1300; Ambassador: SHEN YUNAO.

Colombia: SES, Av. das Nações, Lote 10, 70.444 Brasília, DF; tel. (61) 226-8902; telex (61) 1458; Ambassador: GERMÁN RODRÍGUEZ FONNEGRO.

Costa Rica: SCS, Edif. Ceará 501/502, CP 13-2058, 70.303 Brasília, DF; tel. (61) 226-7212; telex (61) 1690; Ambassador: MIGUEL ANGEL CAMPOS SANDI.

Côte d'Ivoire: SEN, Av. das Nações, Lote 09, 70.473 Brasília, DF; tel. (61) 321-4656; telex (61) 1095; Ambassador: Gen. BERTIN ZEZE BAROAN.

Cuba: QI 05, Conj. 18, Casa 01, Lago Sul, 71.600 Brasília, DF; tel. (61) 248-2018; Ambassador: RENÉ RODRÍGUEZ.

Czechoslovakia: SES, Av. das Nações, Lote 21, 70.414 Brasília, DF; tel. (61) 243-1263; telex (61) 1073; Ambassador VLADIMIR GULLA.

Denmark: SES, Av. das Nações, Lote 26, CP 07-0484, 70.416 Brasília, DF; tel. (61) 242-8188; telex (61) 1494; Ambassador: ERIK LYRTOFT-PETERSEN.

Dominican Republic: QI 17, Conj. 03, Casa 13, Lago Sul, 70.440 Brasília, DF; tel. (61) 248-1405; Ambassador: OSCAR HAZIM SUBERO.

Ecuador: QI 11, Conj. 09, Casa 24, 71.600 Brasília, DF; tel. (61) 248-5560; telex (61) 1290; Ambassador: JERNÁN VEINTIMILLA S.

Egypt: SEN, Av. das Nações, Lote 12, 70.435 Brasília, DF; tel. (61) 225-8517; telex (61) 1387; Ambassador: MEDHAT IBRAHIM TEWFIK.

El Salvador: QI 5, Bloco F 130, Sala 110, 71.600 Brasília, DF; tel. (61) 248-6409; telex (61) 2763; fax (61) 248-6409; Ambassador: MAURICIO CASTRO ARAGON.

Finland: SES, Av. das Nações, Lote 27, 70.417 Brasília, DF; tel. (61) 242-8555; telex (61) 1155; Ambassador: RISTO KAUPPI.

France: SES, Av. das Nações, Lote 4, 70.404 Brasília, DF; tel. (61) 321-5354; telex (61) 1078; Ambassador: JEAN-BERNARD OUVRIEU.

Germany: CP 07-0752, SES, Av. das Nações, Lote 25, 70.415 Brasília, DF; tel. (61) 243-7466; telex (61) 1198; fax (61) 244-6063; Ambassador: HEINZ DITTMANN.

Ghana: SHIS QL 10, Conj. 08, Casa 02, CP 07-0456, 71.600 Brasília, DF; tel. (61) 248-6047; Ambassador: (vacant).

Greece: SHIS, QL 04, Conj. 1, Casa 18, 70.461 Brasília, DF; tel. (61) 248-1127; telex (61) 1843; Ambassador: STEFANOS POTAMIANOS.

Guatemala: SHIS, QL 08, Conj. 05, Casa 11, 70.460 Brasília, DF; tel. (61) 248-3318; fax (61) 248-4383; Ambassador: CARLOS ALBERTO PRERA.

Guyana: Edif. Venâncio III, salas 410–414, 70.438 Brasília, DF; tel. (61) 224-9229; Ambassador: HUBERT O. JACK.

Haiti: SHIS, QI 7, Conj. 16, Casa 13, Lago Sul, 70.465 Brasília, DF; tel. (61) 248-6860; Ambassador: RAYMOND MATHIEU.

Holy See: SES, Av. das Nações, Lote 1, CP 070153, 70.401 Brasília, DF (Apostolic Nunciature); tel. (61) 223-0794; telex (61) 2125; Apostolic Nuncio: Most Rev. CARLO FURNO, Titular Archbishop of Abari.

Honduras: SBN, Edif. Eng. Paulo Mauricio Sampaio, 12°, sala 1209, CEP 70.040, Brasília, DF; tel. (61) 223-2773; telex (61) 3736; Ambassador: ROBERTO ARITA QUIÑÓÑEZ.

Hungary: SES, Av. das Nações, Lote 19, 70.413 Brasília, DF; tel. (61) 243-0822; telex (61) 1285; fax (61) 244-3426; Ambassador: GABOR SUTO.

India: SCS, Edif. Denasa, 13° andar, CP 1-1097, Brasília, DF; tel. (61) 226-1585; telex (61) 1245; Ambassador: AVADUTH RAOJI KAKODKAR.

Indonesia: SES, Av. das Nações, Lote 20, Q. 805, 70.200 Brasília, DF; tel. (61) 243-0102; telex (61) 2541; Ambassador: ALEX RUMAMBY.

Iran: SES, Av. das Nações, Lote 31, 70.421 Brasília, DF; tel. (61) 242-5733; telex (61) 1347; Ambassador: MAHMOUD MOVAHEDI.

Iraq: SES, Av. das Nações, Lote 64, Brasília, DF; tel. (61) 243-1804; telex (61) 1331; Ambassador: OAIS TAWFIG ALMUKHFAR.

Israel: SES, Av. das Nações, Lote 38, 70.424 Brasília, DF; tel. (61) 244-7675; telex (61) 1093; Ambassador: ITZHAK SARFATY.

Italy: SES, Av. das Nações, Lote 30, 70.420 Brasília, DF; tel. (61) 244-0044; telex (61) 1488; Ambassador: ANTONIO CIARRAPICO.

Japan: SES, Av. das Nações, Lote 39, 70.425, Brasília, DF; tel. (61) 242-6866; telex (61) 1376; Ambassador: HARUNORY KAYA.

Korea, Republic: SEN Av. das Nações, Lote 14, 70.436, Brasília, DF; tel. (61) 223-3466; telex (61) 1085; Ambassador: TAE WOONG KWON.

Kuwait: SHI-Sul, QI 5, Ch. 30, 70.467 Brasília, DF; tel. (61) 248-1634; telex (61) 1367; Ambassador: FAISAL RASHED AL-GLAIS.

Lebanon: SES, Av. das Nações, Q.805, Lote 17, 70.411 Brasília, DF; tel. (61) 242-4801; telex (61) 1295; Ambassador: SAMIR HOBEICA.

Libya: SHIS, QI 15, Chácara 26, CP 3505, 71.462 Brasília, DF; tel. (61) 248-6710; telex (61) 1099; Ambassador: ALI SULEIMAN AL-AUJALI.

Malaysia: SHIS, QI 05, Chácara 62, Lago Sul, 70.477 Brasília, DF; tel. (61) 248-5008; telex (61) 3666; Ambassador: M. M. SATHIAH.

Mexico: SES, Av. das Nações, Lote 18, 70.359 Brasília, DF; tel. (61) 244-1011; telex (61) 1101; Ambassador: JESÚS CABRERA MUÑOZ-LEDO.

Morocco: SHIS, QI 11, Conj. 05, Casa 13, Lago Sul, 71.600 Brasília, DF; Ambassador: MOHAMED LARBI MESSARI.

Netherlands: SES Av. das Nações, Lote 05, 70.405, Brasília, DF; POB 07-0098, 70.000; tel. (61) 223-20-25; telex (61) 1492; Ambassador: Jonkheer HUBERT VAN NISPEN.

Nicaragua: SCS, Edif. Venâncio da Silva 1301/1310, 70.302 Brasília, DF; tel. (61) 225-0283; telex (61) 2495; Ambassador: (vacant).

Nigeria: SEN, Av. das Nações, Lote 05, CP 11-1190, 70.432 Brasília, DF; tel. (61) 226-1717; telex (61) 1315; fax (61) 224-9830; Ambassador: Dr PATRICK DELE COLE.

Norway: SES, Av. das Nações, Lote 28, CP 07-0670, 70.351 Brasília, DF; tel. (61) 243-8720; telex (61) 1265; fax (61) 242-7989; Ambassador: SIGURD ENDRESEN.

Pakistan: SCS, Edif. Central, 5°, 70.458 Brasília, DF; tel. (61) 224-2922; telex (61) 2252; Ambassador: TARIQ KHAN AFRIDI.

Panama: SCS, Edif. JK, 13° andar, 132/133, CP 13-2334, 70.449 Brasília, DF; tel. (61) 225-0859; Ambassador: VÍCTOR MANUEL BARLETA MILLÁN.

Paraguay: SES, Av. das Nações, Lote 42, CP 14-2314, 70.427 Brasília, DF; tel. (61) 242-3723; telex (61) 1845; Ambassador: JUAN ESTEBAN AGUIRRE.

Peru: SES, Av. das Nações, Lote 43, 70.428 Brasília, DF; tel. (61) 242-9435; telex (61) 1108; Ambassador: HUGO PALMA VALDERRAMA.

Philippines: SEN, Av. das Nações, Lote 1, 70.431 Brasília, DF; tel. (61) 223-5143; telex (61) 1420; Ambassador: LAURO L. BAJA, Jr.

Poland: SES, Av. das Nações, Lote 33, 70.423 Brasília, DF; tel. (61) 243-3438; telex (61) 1165; Ambassador: STANISŁAW PAWLISZEWSKI.

Portugal: SES, Av. das Nações, Lote 2, 70.402 Brasília, DF; tel. (61) 321-3434; telex (61) 1033; Ambassador: ADRIANO DE CARVALHO.

Romania: SEN, Av. das Nações, Lote 6, 70.456 Brasília, DF; tel. (61) 226-0746; telex (61) 1283; Ambassador: CONSTANTIN DUMITRESCU.

Saudi Arabia: SHI-Sul, QL 10, Conj. 9, Casa 20, 70.471 Brasília, DF; tel. (61) 248-3523; telex (61) 1656; Ambassador: ABDULLAH SALEH HABABI.

Senegal: SEN, Av. das Nações, Lote 18, 70.437 Brasília, DF; tel. (61) 226-4405; telex (61) 1377; Ambassador: El Hadj DIOUF.

South Africa: SES, Av. das Nações, Lote 6, CP 11-1170, 70.406 Brasília, DF; tel. (61) 223-4873; telex (61) 1683; Ambassador: JOHAN RIENK VON GERNET.

Spain: SES, Av. das Nações, Lote 44, 70.429 Brasília, DF; tel. (61) 242-1074; telex (61) 1313; Ambassador: JOSÉ LUIS CRESPO DE VEGA.

Suriname: SCS, Edif. OK, 9° andar, 70.000 Brasília, DF; tel. (61) 321-8122; telex (61) 1414; Ambassador: Dr SIEGFRIED EDMUND WERNERS.

Sweden: SES, Av. das Nações, Lote 29, 70.419 Brasília, DF; tel. (61) 243-1444; telex (61) 1225; Ambassador: KRISTER KUMLIN.

BRAZIL
Directory

Switzerland: SES, Av. das Nações, Lote 41, 70.448, Brasília, DF; tel. (61) 244-5500; telex (61) 1135; fax (61) 244-5711; Ambassador: CHARLES HENRY BRUGGMANN.

Syria: SEN, Av. das Nações, Lote 11, 70.434 Brasília, DF; tel. (61) 226-0970; telex (61) 1721; Ambassador: GHASSOUB RIFAI.

Thailand: SEN, Av. das Nações Norte, Lote 10, 70.433 Brasília, DF; tel. (61) 224-6943; telex (61) 3763; Ambassador: PRADEEP SOCHIRATNA.

Togo: SHIS QI 11, Conj. 9, Casa 10, CP 13-1998, 71.259 Brasília, DF; tel. (61) 248-4752; telex (61) 1837; Ambassador: LAMBANA TCHAOU.

Trinidad and Tobago: SHIS, QL 8, Conj. 4, Casa 5, 71.600 Brasília, DF; tel. (61) 248-1922; telex (61) 1844; Ambassador: BABOORAM RAMBISSOON.

Turkey: SES, Av. das Nações, Lote 23, 70.452 Brasília, DF; tel. (61) 242-1850; telex (61) 1663; Ambassador: METIN KUSTALOGLU.

USSR: SES, Av. das Nações, Lote A, 70.476 Brasília, DF; tel. (61) 223-3094; telex (61) 1273; Ambassador: LEONID FILIPPOVICH KUZMIN.

United Kingdom: SES, Quadra 801, Conj. K, CP 07-0586, 70.408 Brasília, DF; tel. (61) 225-2710; telex (61) 1360; fax (61) 225-1777; Ambassador: MICHAEL J. NEWINGTON.

USA: SES, Av. das Nações, Lote 3, 70.403 Brasília, DF; tel. (61) 321-7272; telex (61) 41167; Ambassador: RICHARD MELTON.

Uruguay: SES, Av. das Nações, Lote 14, 70.450 Brasília, DF; tel. (61) 224-2415; telex (61) 1173; Ambassador: Dr ROBERTO VIVO BONOMI.

Venezuela: SES, Av. das Nações, Lote 13, Q-803, 70.451 Brasília, DF; tel. (61) 223-9325; telex (61) 1325; Ambassador: FERNANDO GERBASI.

Yemen: Brasília, DF; Ambassador: (vacant).

Yugoslavia: SES, Av. das Nações, Q-803, Lote 15, CP 07-1240, 70.409 Brasília, DF; tel. (61) 223-7272; telex (61) 2053; Ambassador: BRANKO TRPENOVSKI.

Zaire: SHIS, QI 9, Conj. 8, Casa 20, Lago Sul, CP 07-0041, 71.600 Brasília, DF; tel. (61) 248-3348; telex (61) 1435; Ambassador: NGOIE KAMPENG KAMAKANGA.

Judicial System

The judiciary powers of the State are held by the following: the Supreme Federal Tribunal, the Higher Tribunal of Justice, the Regional Federal Tribunals and federal judges, the Labour, Electoral and Military Tribunals and judges, and the Tribunals and judges of the states, of the Federal District and of the Territories.

The Supreme Federal Tribunal comprises 11 ministers, nominated by the President and approved by the Senate. It judges offences committed by persons such as the President, the Vice-President, members of the National Congress, Ministers of State, its own members, judges of other courts, and heads of permanent diplomatic missions. It also judges cases of litigation between the Union and the states, between the states, or between foreign nations and the Union or the states; disputes as to jurisdiction between justices and/or tribunals of the different states, including the Federal District; in cases involving the extradition of criminals, in certain special cases involving the principle of habeas corpus and habeas data, and in other cases.

The Higher Tribunal of Justice comprises at least 33 members, appointed by the President and approved by the Senate. Its jurisdiction includes the judgment of offences committed by State Governors. The Regional Federal Tribunals comprise at least seven judges, recruited when possible in the respective region and appointed by the President of the Republic. The Higher Labour Tribunal comprises 27 members, appointed by the President and approved by the Senate. The judges of the Regional Labour Tribunals are also appointed by the President. The Higher Electoral Tribunal comprises at least seven members: three judges from among those of the Supreme Federal Tribunal, two from the Higher Tribunal of Justice (elected by secret ballot) and two appointed by the President. The Regional Electoral Tribunals are also composed of seven members. The Higher Military Tribunal comprises 15 life members, appointed by the President and approved by the Senate; three from the navy, four from the army, three from the air force and five civilian members. The states are responsible for the administration of their own justice, according to the principles established by the Constitution.

THE SUPREME FEDERAL TRIBUNAL

Supreme Federal Tribunal: Praça dos Três Poderes, 70.175 Brasília, DF; tel. (61) 224-7179; telex (61) 1473.

President: JOSÉ NÉRI DA SILVEIRA.

Vice-President: ALDIR G. PASSARINHO.

Justices: JOSÉ CARLOS MOREIRA ALVES, JOSÉ FRANCISCO REZEK, SIDNEY SANCHES, LUÍS OCTÁVIO PIRES E ALBUQUERQUE GALLOTI, CARLOS ALBERTO MADEIRA, CÉLIO DE OLIVEIRA BORJA, PAULO BROSSARD DE SOUZA PINTO, JOSÉ PAULO SEPÚLVEDA PERTENCE, JOSÉ CELSO DE MELLO FILHO.

Procurator-General: ARISTIDES JUNQUEIRA DE ALVARENGA.

Director-General (Secretariat): MAURÍCIO MARANHÃO AGUIAR.

Religion

CHRISTIANITY

Conselho Nacional de Igrejas Cristãs do Brasil—CONIC (National Council of Christian Churches in Brazil): Rua Senhor dos Passos 202, CP 2876, 90.020 Porto Alegre, RS; tel. (512) 24-5010; telex (51) 2332; f. 1982; six mem. churches; Pres. Pastor Dr GOTTFRIED BRAKEMEIER (Pres. of Igreja Evangélica de Confissão Luterana no Brasil); Exec. Sec. Rev. GODOFREDO G. BOLL.

The Roman Catholic Church

Brazil comprises 36 archdioceses, 197 dioceses (including one each for Catholics of the Maronite, Melkite and Ukrainian Rites), 14 territorial prelatures and two territorial abbacies. The Archbishop of São Sebastião do Rio de Janeiro is also the Ordinary for Catholics of other Oriental Rites in Brazil (estimated at 9,000 in 1988). The great majority of Brazil's population are adherents of the Roman Catholic Church (around 106m. at the time of the 1980 census), although a report published by the Brazilian weekly, *Veja*, in July 1989 concluded that since 1950 the membership of non-Catholic Christian Churches had risen from 3% to 6% of the total population, while membership of the Roman Catholic Church had fallen from 93% to 89% of Brazilians.

Bishops' Conference: Conferência Nacional dos Bispos do Brasil, SE/Sul Quadra 801, Conj. B, CP 13-2067, 70.401 Brasília, DF; tel. (61) 225-2955; telex (61) 1104; f. 1980 (statutes approved 1986); Pres. Mgr LUCIANO P. MENDES DE ALMEIDA, Archbishop of Mariana, MG.

Latin Rite

Archbishop of São Salvador da Bahia, BA: Cardinal LUCAS MOREIRA NEVES, Primate of Brazil, Palácio da Sé, Praça da Sé 1, 40.020 Salvador, BA; tel. (71) 243-5411.

Archbishop of Aparecida, SP: GERALDO MARIA DE MORAIS PENIDO.

Archbishop of Aracajú, SE: LUCIANO JOSÉ CABRAL DUARTE.

Archbishop of Belém do Pará, PA: ALBERTO GAUDÊNCIO RAMOS.

Archbishop of Belo Horizonte, MG: SERAFIM FERNANDES DE ARAÚJO.

Archbishop of Botucatú, SP: ANTÔNIO MARÍA MUCCIOLO.

Archbishop of Brasília, DF: Cardinal JOSÉ FREIRE FALCÃO.

Archbishop of Campinas, SP: GILBERTO PEREIRA LOPES.

Archbishop of Campo Grande, MS: VITÓRIO PAVANELLO.

Archbishop of Cascavel, PR: ARMANDO CIRIO.

Archbishop of Cuiabá, MT: BONIFÁCIO PICCININI.

Archbishop of Curitiba, PR: PEDRO ANTÔNIO MARCHETTI FEDALTO.

Archbishop of Diamantina, MG: GERALDO MAJELA REIS.

Archbishop of Florianópolis, SC: ALFONSO NIEHUES.

Archbishop of Fortaleza, CE: Cardinal ALOISIO LORSCHEIDER.

Archbishop of Goiânia, GO: ANTÔNIO RIBEIRO DE OLIVEIRA.

Archbishop of Juiz de Fora, MG: JUVENAL RORIZ.

Archbishop of Londrina, PR: GERALDO MAJELLA AGNELO.

Archbishop of Maceió, AL: EDVALDO GONÇALVES AMARAL.

Archbishop of Manaus, AM: CLÓVIS FRAINER.

Archbishop of Mariana, MG: LUCIANO P. MENDES DE ALMEIDA.

Archbishop of Maringá, PR: JAIME LUÍS COELHO.

Archbishop of Natal, RN: ALAÍR VILAR FERNANDES DE MELO.

Archbishop of Niterói, RJ: JOSÉ GONÇALVES DA COSTA.

Archbishop of Olinda e Recife, PE: JOSÉ CARDOSO SOBRINHO.

Archbishop of Paraíba, PB: JOSÉ MARIA PIRES.

Archbishop of Porto Alegre, RS: JOÃO CLÁUDIO COLLING.

Archbishop of Porto Velho, RO: JOSÉ MARTINS DA SILVA.

Archbishop of Pouso Alegre, MG: JOSÉ D'ANGELO NETO.

Archbishop of Ribeirão Prêto, SP: ARNALDO RIBEIRO.

Archbishop of São Luís do Maranhão, MA: PAULO EDUARDO DE ANDRADE PONTE.

BRAZIL
Directory

Archbishop of São Paulo, SP: Cardinal PAULO EVARISTO ARNS.
Archbishop of São Sebastião do Rio de Janeiro, RJ: Cardinal EUGÊNIO DE ARAÚJO SALES.
Archbishop of Teresina, PI: MIGUEL FENELON CÂMARA FILHO.
Archbishop of Uberaba, MG: BENEDITO DE ULHÔA VIEIRA.
Archbishop of Vitória, ES: SILVESTRE LUÍS SCANDIAN.

Maronite Rite
Bishop of Nossa Senhora do Libano em São Paulo, SP: JOÃO CHEDID.

Melkite Rite
Bishop of Nossa Senhora do Paraíso em São Paulo, SP: SPIRIDON MATTAR.

Ukrainian Rite
Bishop of São João Batista em Curitiba, PR: EFREM BASÍLIO KREVEY.

The Anglican Communion
Anglicans form the Episcopal Church of Brazil (Igreja Episcopal do Brasil), comprising seven dioceses.

Igreja Episcopal do Brasil: POB 11.510, 90.641 Porto Alegre, RS; tel. (512) 360651; f. 1890; 70,000 mems (1989); Primate: Rt Rev. OLAVO VENTURA LUIZ, Bishop of Southwestern Brazil; Sec. Rev. Canon JUBAL P. NEVES.

Protestant Churches
Igreja Cristã Reformada do Brasil: CP 2808, 01.000 São Paulo, SP; Pres. Rev. JANOS APOSTOL.

Igreja Evangélica de Confissão Luterana no Brasil (IECLB): Rua Senhor dos Passos 202, 2° andar, CP 2876, 90.020 Porto Alegre, RS; tel. (512) 21-3433; telex (51) 2332; fax (61) 225-7244; f. 1949; 870,000 mems; Pres. Pastor Dr GOTTFRIED BRAKEMEIER.

Igreja Evangélica Congregacional do Brasil: CP 414, 98.700 Ijuí, RS; tel. (55) 332-4656; f. 1942; 41,000 mems, 310 congregations; Pres. Rev. H. HARTMUT W. HACHTMANN.

Igreja Evangélica Luterana do Brasil: Rua Cel. Lucas de Oliveira 894, CP 1076, 90.001 Porto Alegre, RS; tel. (512) 322-111; telex (51) 515741; 200,000 mems; Pres. LEOPOLDO HEIMANN.

Igreja Metodista do Brasil: General Communication Secretariat, Rua Artur Azevedo 1192, Apdo 81, Pinheiros, 05.404 São Paulo, SP; Exec. Sec. Dr ONÉSIMO DE OLIVEIRA CARDOSO.

Igreja Presbiteriana Unida do Brasil (IPU): Caixa Postal 2368, 29001 Vitória, ES; tel. (5527) 222-8024; f. 1978.

BAHÁ'Í FAITH
Bahá'í Community of Brazil: SHIS, QL 08, conj. 08, c/05, 71.500 Brasília, DF, POB 7035; tel. (61) 248-4718; fax (61) 248-4321; f. 1921.

National Spiritual Assembly: Rua Eng. Gama Lobo 267, Vila Isabel, 20.551 Rio de Janeiro, RJ; tel. (21) 288-9846; mems resident in 1,250 localities.

BUDDHISM
Federação das Seitas Budistas do Brasil: Av. Paulo Ferreira 1133, Piqueri, São Paulo, SP.

Sociedade Budista do Brasil (Rio Buddhist Vihara): Dom Joaquim Mamede 45, Santa Tereza, 20.241 Rio de Janeiro, RJ; tel. (21) 220-7486; f. 1972; Pres. JOÃO REIS MARQUES.

The Press

The most striking feature of the Brazilian press is the relatively small circulation of newspapers in comparison with the size of the population. The newspapers with the largest circulations are *O Dia* (207,000), *O Globo* (350,000), *Fôlha de São Paulo* (211,900), and *O Estado de São Paulo* (230,000). The low circulation is mainly due to high costs resulting from distribution difficulties. In consequence there are no national newspapers. In 1988 a total of 288 newspaper titles were published in Brazil. The last remaining censorship on books and newspapers was abolished in July 1985.

DAILY NEWSPAPERS

Belém, PA
O Liberal: Rua Gaspar Viana 253, Belém, PA, 66.000; tel. (91) 222-0466; telex (91) 1026; f. 1946; Pres. LUCIDEA MAIORANA; circ. 20,000.

Belo Horizonte, MG
Diário da Tarde: Rua Goitacás 71, 30.190 Belo Horizonte, MG; tel. (31) 226-2322; telex (31) 1253; fax (31) 273-2322; f. 1930; evening; Dir PEDRO AGUINALDO FULGÊNCIO; total circ. 150,000.

Diário de Minas: Rua Francisco Salles 536, 30.150 Belo Horizonte, MG; tel. (31) 222-1305; telex (31) 1264; f. 1949; Pres. JOSÉ NUNES; circ. 50,000.

Diário do Comércio: Av. Américo Vespúcio 1660; 31-230 Belo Horizonte, MG; tel. (31) 469-1011; telex (31) 1509; f. 1932; Pres. JOSÉ COSTA.

Estado de Minas: Rua Goiás 36, 30.190 Belo Horizonte, MG; tel. (31) 262-2322; telex (31) 1164; f. 1928; morning; independent; Dir PEDRO AGNALDO FULGÊNCIO; circ. 65,000.

Blumenau, SC
Jornal de Santa Catarina: Rua São Paulo 1120, 89.010 Blumenau, SC; tel. (473) 22-6400; telex (473) 343; f. 1971; Dir. SANTO SILVEIRA; circ. 25,000.

Brasília, DF
Correio Braziliense: SIG, Q2, Lote 340, 70.610 Brasília, DF; tel. (61) 321-1314; telex (61) 1727; f. 1960; Dir-Gen. PAULO C. DE ARAÚJO; circ. 30,000.

Jornal de Brasília: SIG Trecho 1, Lotes 585/645, 70.610 Brasília, DF; tel. (61) 225-2515; telex (61) 1208; f. 1972; Dir JAIME CÂMARA JÚNIOR; circ. 25,000.

Campinas, SP
Correio Popular: Rua Conceição 124, 13.015 Campinas, SP; tel (19) 31-8588; telex (19) 2477; f. 1927; Pres. SYLVINO DE GODOY NETO; circ. 15,000.

Curitiba, PR
O Estado do Paraná: Rua João Tschannerl 800, CP 868, 80.520 Curitiba, PR; tel. (41) 233-8811; telex (41) 5388; fax (41) 233-6983; f. 1951; Pres. PAULO CRUZ PIMENTEL; circ. 15,000.

Gazeta do Povo: Praça Carlos Gomes 04, 80.010 Curitiba, PR; tel. (41) 224-0522; telex (41) 6520; f. 1919; Pres. FRANCISCO CUNHA PEREIRA, Filho; circ. 40,000.

Tribuna do Paraná: Rua João Tschannerl 800, 80.520 Curitiba PR; tel. (41) 233-8811; telex (41) 5388; fax (41) 233-6983; f. 1956; Pres. PAULO CRUZ PIMENTEL; circ. 15,000.

Florianópolis, SC
O Estado: Rodovia SC-401, Km 3, 88.030 Florianópolis, SC; tel. (482) 33-5555; telex (482) 177; f. 1915; Pres. JOSÉ MATUSALÉM COMELLI; circ. 20,000.

Fortaleza, CE
O Povo: Av. Aguanambi 40, 60.055 Fortaleza, CE; tel. (85) 211-9666; telex (85) 1107; f. 1928; evening; Pres. DEMÓCRITO ROCHA DUMMAR; circ. 20,000.

Tribuna do Ceará: Av. Desemb. Moreira 2470, 60.170 Fortaleza, CE; tel. (85) 224-3101; telex (85) 1207; f. 1957; Dir J. TAMER SANCHO; circ. 12,000.

Goiânia, GO
Diário da Manhã: Av. 24 de Outubro 1240, 74.000 Goiânia, GO; tel. (62) 233-5013; telex (62) 1055; f. 1980; Pres. JULIO NASSER CUSTÓDIO DOS SANTOS; circ. 16,000.

O Popular: Rua Thómas Edson Q7, Sector Serrinha, 74.510 Goiânia, GO; tel. (62) 241-5533; telex (62) 2110; f. 1938; Pres. JAIME CÂMARA, Jr; circ. 20,000.

Londrina, PR
Fôlha de Londrina: Rua Piauí 241, 86.010 Londrina PR; tel. (432) 24-2020; telex (432) 123; f. 1947; Pres. JOÃO MILANEZ; circ. 35,000.

Manaus, AM
A Critica: Rua Lobo D'Almada 278, 69.007 Manaus; tel. (92) 232-2525; telex (92) 2820; f. 1949; Dir UMBERTO CADERARO, Filho; circ. 19,000.

Niterói, RJ
O Fluminense: Rua Visconde de Itaboraí 184, 24.030 Niterói, RJ; tel. (21) 719-3311; telex (21) 32054; f. 1978; Dir ALBERTO FRANCISCO TORRES; circ. 80,000.

A Tribuna: Rua Barão do Amazonas 31, 24.030 Niterói, RJ; tel. (21) 719-1886; f. 1926; Dir-Gen. MARIA MADALENA A. TANURA; circ. 18,000.

Porto Alegre, RS
Zero Hora: Av. Ipiranga 1075, 90,069 Porto Alegre, RS; tel. (512) 23-1110; telex (512) 4100; f. 1964; Pres. JAYME SIROTSKY; circ. 110,000 (Mon.), 115,000 weekdays, 250,000 Sunday.

Recife, PE

Diário de Pernambuco: Praça da Independência 12, 2° andar, 50.018 Recife, PE; tel. (81) 231-6222; telex (81) 1057; f. 1825; morning; independent; Pres. ANTÔNIO C. DA COSTA; circ. 31,000.

Ribeirão Preto, SP

Diário da Manhã: Rua Duque de Caxias 179, 14.015 Ribeirão Preto, SP; tel. (16) 634-0909; f. 1898; Dir PAULO M. SANT'ANNA; circ. 17,000.

Rio de Janeiro, RJ

Brazil Herald: Rua do Rezende 65, 20.231 Rio de Janeiro, RJ; tel. (21) 221-2772; f. 1946; daily, except Mondays; morning; only English language daily in Brazil; Dir MAURO SALLES; circ. 18,000.

O Dia: Rua Riachuelo 359, 20.235 Rio de Janeiro, RJ; tel. (21) 292-2020; telex (21) 22385; f. 1951; morning; popular labour; Pres. ANTÔNIO ARY DE CARVALHO; circ. 207,000 weekdays, 400,000 Sundays.

O Globo: POB 1090, Rua Irineu Marinho 35, 20.233 Rio de Janeiro, RJ; tel. (21) 272-2000; telex (21) 22595; f. 1925; morning; Dir FRANCISCO GRAELL; circ. 350,000 weekdays, 520,000 Sundays.

Jornal do Brasil: Av. Brasil 500, São Cristovão, 20.949 Rio de Janeiro, RJ; tel. (21) 585-4422; telex (21) 23690; f. 1891; morning; Catholic, liberal; Pres. M. F. DO NASCIMENTO BRITO; circ. 200,000 weekdays, 325,000 Sundays.

Jornal do Comércio: Rua do Livramento 189, 20.225 Rio de Janeiro, RJ; tel. (21) 252-1682; telex (21) 22165; f. 1827; morning; Pres. AUSTREGÉSILO DE ATHAYDE; circ. 31,000 weekdays.

Jornal dos Sports: Rua Tenente Possolo 15/25, Cruz Vermelha, 20.230 Rio de Janeiro, RJ; tel. (21) 232-8010; telex (21) 23093; f. 1931; morning; sporting daily; Dir VENÂNCIO P. VELLOSO, Filho; circ. 38,000.

Ultima Hora: Rua Equador 702, 20.220 Rio de Janeiro, RJ; tel. (21) 223-2444; telex (21) 22551; f. 1951; evening; Dir-Gen. JOSÉ CARLOS DE ANDRADE; circ. 56,000.

Salvador, BA

Correio da Bahia: Av. Luis Viana Filho s/n, 40.100 Salvador, BA; tel. (71) 231-2811; telex (71) 1594; f. 1979; Pres. ARMANDO GONÇALVES.

Jornal da Bahia: Rua Djalma Dutra 121, 40.255 Salvador, BA; tel. (71) 233-7428; telex (71) 1296; f. 1958; Pres. CARLOS EDUARDO V. BARRAL; circ. 20,000.

A Tarde: Av. Tancredo Neves 1092, 41.820 Salvador, BA; tel. (71) 231-0077; telex (71) 1299; f. 1912; evening; Pres. REGINA SIMÕES DE MELLO LEITÃO; circ. 54,000.

Santo André, SP

Diário do Grande ABC: Rua Catequese 562, 09.090 Santo André, SP; tel. (11) 449-5533; telex (11) 44034; fax (11) 449-5472; f. 1958; Pres. EDSON DANILLO DOTTO; circ. 98,000.

Santos, SP

A Tribuna: Rua General Câmara 90/94, 11.010 Santos, SP; tel. (13) 232-7711; telex (13) 1058; f. 1984; Pres. GIUSFREDO SANTINI; circ. 35,000.

São Luís, MA

O Imparcial: Rua Afonso Pena 46, 65.000 São Luís, MA; tel. (98) 222-5120; telex (98) 2106; f. 1926; Dir-Gen. PEDRO BATISTA FREIRE.

São Paulo, SP

DCI Comércio e Indústria: Rua Alvaro de Carvalho 354, 01.050 São Paulo, SP; tel. (11) 256-5011; telex (11) 21436; f. 1933; morning; Pres. WALDEMAR DOS SANTOS; circ. 50,000.

Diário Popular: Rua Major Quedinho 28, 1°-6°, 01.050 São Paulo, SP; tel. (11) 258-2133; telex (11) 21213; f. 1884; evening; independent; Pres. ANTÔNIO ARY DE CARVALHO; circ. 90,000.

O Estado de São Paulo: Av. Eng. Caetano Álvares 55, 02.550 São Paulo, SP; tel. (11) 856-2122; telex (11) 23511; f. 1875; morning; independent; Dir FRANCISCO MESQUITA NETO; circ. 230,000 weekdays, 460,000 Sundays.

Fôlha de São Paulo: Alameda Barão de Limeira 425, Campos Elísios, 01.202 São Paulo, SP; tel. (11) 874-2192; telex (11) 22930; f. 1945; morning; Editorial Dir RENATO CASTANHARI; circ. 211,900 weekdays, 314,830 Sundays.

Gazeta Mercantil: Rua Major Quedinho 90, 5°, 01.050 São Paulo, SP; tel. (11) 256-3133; telex (11) 37802; f. 1920; business paper; Pres. LUIZ FERREIRA LEVY; circ. 80,000.

Jornal da Tarde: Av. Eng. Caetano Álvares 55, 02.550 São Paulo, SP; tel. (11) 856-2122; telex (11) 23511; f. 1966; evening; independent; Pres. JOSÉ V. C. MESQUITA; circ. 120,000, 180,000 Mondays.

Notícias Populares: Alameda Barão de Limeira 425, 01.202 São Paulo, SP; tel. (11) 874-2222; telex (11) 22930; f. 1963; Dir: see *Fôlha de São Paulo*, above; circ. 150,000.

Vitória, ES

A Gazeta: Rua Charif Murad 902, 29.050 Vitória, ES; tel. (27) 222-8333; telex (27) 2273; f. 1928; Pres. EUGÊNIO PACHECO DE QUEIROZ; circ. 19,000.

PERIODICALS

Rio de Janeiro, RJ

Amiga: Rua do Russell 766/804, 22.214 Rio de Janeiro, RJ; tel. (21) 265-2012; telex (21) 21525; weekly; women's interest; Pres. ADOLPHO BLOCH; circ. 83,000.

Antenna-Eletrônica Popular: Av. Marechal Floriano 143, CP 1131, 20.060 Rio de Janeiro, RJ; tel. (21) 223-2442; f. 1926; monthly; telecommunications and electronics, radio, TV, hi-fi, amateur and CB radio; Dir GILBERTO AFFONSO PENNA; circ. 24,000.

Carícia: Av. Marquês de São Vicente 1771, 01.139 Rio de Janeiro, RJ; tel. (11) 826-6777; telex (11) 26070; monthly; women's interest; Dir ANGELO ROSSI; circ. 210,000.

Carinho: Rua do Russell 766/804, 22.214 Rio de Janeiro, RJ; tel. (21) 265-2012; telex (21) 21525; monthly; women's interest; Pres. ADOLPHO BLOCH; circ. 65,000.

Casa e Jardim: Rua Felizbelo Freire 671, 20.071 Rio de Janeiro, RJ; tel. (21) 270-6262; f. 1953; monthly; homes and gardens, illustrated; Editor MILTON MADEIRA; circ. 80,000.

Conjuntura Econômica: Praia de Botafogo 190, 22.253 Rio de Janeiro, RJ; tel. (21) 551-0698; f. 1947; monthly; economics and finance; published by Fundação Getúlio Vargas; Pres. LUÍZ SIMÕES LOPES; circ. 22,000.

Criativa: Rua Itapiri 1209, 21.251 Rio de Janeiro, RJ; tel. (21) 273-5522; telex (21) 23365; monthly; women's interest; Pres. OSCAR D. NEVES; circ. 121,000.

Desfile: Rua do Russell 766/804, 22.214 Rio de Janeiro, RJ; tel. (21) 265-2012; telex (21) 21525; f. 1969; monthly; women's interest; Dir ADOLPHO BLOCH; circ. 120,000.

Ele Ela: Rua do Russell 766/804, 22.214 Rio de Janeiro RJ; tel. (21) 265-2012; telex (21) 21525; fax (21) 205-4999; f. 1969; monthly; men's interest; Dir ADOLPHO BLOCH; circ. 150,000.

Fatos e Fotos: Rua do Russell 766/804, 20.210 Rio de Janeiro, RJ; tel. (21) 285-0033; telex (21) 21525; illustrated weekly; general interest; Pres. ADOLPHO BLOCH; circ. 110,000.

Manchete: Rua do Russell 766/804, 20.214 Rio de Janeiro, RJ; tel. (21) 265-2012; telex (21) 22214; f. 1952; weekly; general; Dir ADOLPHO BLOCH; circ. 110,000.

São Paulo, SP

Capricho: Rua Geraldo Flausino Gomes 61, 04.575 São Paulo, SP; tel. (11) 545-8122; telex (11) 24134; monthly; women's interest; Dir VICTOR CIVITA; circ. 167,000.

Claudia: Rua Geraldo Flausino Gomes 61, 04.575 São Paulo, SP, CP 2372; tel. (11) 545-8122; telex (11) 54563; fax (11) 534-5638; f. 1962; monthly; women's magazine; Dir VICTOR CIVITA; circ. 420,000.

Digesto Econômico: Associação Comercial de São Paulo, Rua Boa Vista 51, 01.014 São Paulo, SP; tel. (11) 234-3322; telex (11) 33355; fax (11) 239-0067; every 2 months; Pres. ROMEU TRUSSARDI FILHO.

Dirigente Rural: Rua Afonso Celso 243, 04.119 São Paulo, SP; tel. (11) 549-4344; telex (11) 23552; monthly; agriculture; Dir HENRY MAKSOUD; Editor ISAAC JORDANOVSKI; circ. 64,577.

Disney Especial: Rua Bela Cintra 299, 01.415 São Paulo, SP; tel. (11) 257-0999; every 2 months; children's magazine; Dir VICTOR CIVITA; circ. 211,600.

Exame: Av. Octaviano Alves de Lima, 4400, 02909 São Paulo, SP; tel. (11) 877-1322; telex (11) 22115; fax (11) 877-1640; fortnightly; business; Dir ANTONIO MACHADO DE BARROS; circ. 101,000.

Iris: Rua Jacucaim 67, Brooklin, 04.563 São Paulo, SP; tel. (11) 531-1299; fax (11) 531-1627; f. 1947; monthly; photography, video; Dirs BEATRIZ AZEVEDO MARQUES, SILVIA HELENA DE AZEVEDO MARQUES PILZ; circ. 98,000.

Manequim: Rua Geraldo Flausino Gomes 61, 04.575 São Paulo, SP; tel. (11) 545-8122; telex (11) 24134; monthly; fashion; Dir VICTOR CIVITA; circ. 300,000.

Máquinas e Metais: Rua Dona Elisa 167, 01.155 São Paulo, SP; (11) 826-4511; fax (11) 66-9585; f. 1964; monthly; machine and metal industries; Editor JOSÉ ROBERTO GONÇALVES; circ. 20,000.

Margarida: Rua Bela Cintra 299, 01.415 São Paulo, SP; tel. (11) 257-0999; every 2 weeks; children's magazine; Dir VICTOR CIVITA; circ. 80,000.

BRAZIL   *Directory*

Mickey: Rua Bela Cintra 299, 01.415 São Paulo, SP; tel. (11) 257-0999; telex (11) 70522; monthly; children's magazine; Dir VICTOR CIVITA; circ. 76,000.

Micromundo-Computerworld do Brasil: Rua Caçapava 79, 01.408 São Paulo, SP; tel. (11) 881-6844; telex (11) 32017; monthly; computers; Gen. Dir ERIC HIPPEAU; circ. 38,000.

Mundo Elétrico: Rua Consórcio 59, 04.535 São Paulo, SP; tel. (11) 280-9411; telex (11) 30410; fax (11) 883-2831; f. 1959; monthly; electricity; Pres. MANFREDO GRUENWALD.

Nova: Rua Geraldo Flausino Gomes 61, 04.575 São Paulo, SP; tel. (11) 545-8122; telex (11) 24134; f. 1973; monthly; women's interest; Dir VICTOR CIVITA; circ. 156,000.

Pato Donald: Rua Bela Cintra 299, 01.415 São Paulo, SP; tel. (11) 257-0999; telex (11) 70522; every 2 weeks; children's magazine; Dir VICTOR CIVITA; circ. 120,000.

Placar: Rua Geraldo Flausino Gomes 61, 04.575 São Paulo, SP; tel. (11) 545-8299; telex (11) 24134; fax (11) 522-1504; f. 1970; weekly; sports magazine; Dir JUCA KFOURI; circ. 127,000.

Quatro Rodas: Rua Geraldo Flausino Gomes 61, Brooklin, 04.575 São Paulo, SP; tel. (11) 545-8122; telex (11) 24134; fax (11) 522-1504; f. 1960; monthly; motoring; Pres. VICTOR CIVITA; circ. 250,000.

Revista O Carreteiro: Rua Palacete das Águias 284, 04.635 São Paulo, SP; tel. (11) 533-5237; monthly; transport; Dir JOSÉ A. DE CASTRO; circ. 160,000.

Saúde: Av. Nações Unidas 5777, 05477 São Paulo, SP; tel. (11) 211-7675; telex (11) 83178; fax (11) 813-9115; monthly; health; Dir ANGELO ROSSI; circ. 180,000.

Veja: Av. Otaviano Alves de Lima 4400, 02.909 São Paulo, SP; tel. (11) 877-1322; telex (11) 22115; fax (11) 877-1640; f. 1968; news weekly; Dirs JOSÉ ROBERTO GUZZO, TALES ALVARENGA, MÁRIO SERGIO CONTI; circ. 800,000.

Video Business: Rua Iraci 102/112, Brooklin, 01.457 São Paulo, SP; tel. (11) 211-8499; f. 1987; monthly; video; Dirs BEATRIZ A. MARQUES, SILVIA H. A. MARQUES PILZ; circ. 80,000.

Visão: Rua Afonso Celso 243, 01.419 São Paulo, SP; tel. (11) 549-4344; telex (11) 23552; f. 1952; weekly; news magazine; Editor HENRY MAKSOUD; circ. 148,822.

NEWS AGENCIES

Editora Abril, SA: Av. Otaviano Alves de Lima 4400, CP 2372, 02.909 São Paulo, SP; tel. (11) 877-1322; telex (11) 2215; fax (11) 877-1640; Pres. VICTOR CIVITA.

Agência ANDA: Edif. Correio Braziliense, Setor das Indústrias Gráficas 300/350, Brasília, DF; Dir EDILSON VARELA.

Agência o Estado de São Paulo: Av. Eng. Caetano Alvares 55, 02.550 São Paulo, SP; tel. (11) 856-2122; telex (11) 22700; Rep. SAMUEL DIRCEU F. BUENO.

Agência Fôlha de São Paulo: Alameda Barão de Limeira 425, Campos Elísios, 01.290 São Paulo; tel. (11) 243-6428; Dir TARSIO NITRINI.

Agência Globo: Rua Irineu Marinho 35, 2° andar, Centro, 20.030 Rio de Janeiro, RJ; tel. (21) 292-2000; telex (21) 31614; fax (21) 292-2000; Dir CARLOS LEMOS.

Agência Jornal do Brasil: Av. Brasil 500, 8° andar, São Cristovão, 20.949 Rio de Janeiro, RJ; tel. (21) 580-9944; telex 21160; fax (21) 585-4428; Dir SÉRGIO BUARQUE DE GUSMÃO.

Foreign Bureaux

Agence France-Presse (AFP) (France): CP 2575-ZC-00, Rua México 21, 7° andar, 20.031 Rio de Janeiro, RJ; tel. (21) 240-6634; telex (21) 22494; Bureau Chief JEAN-FRANÇOIS LE MOUNIER; Rua Sete de Abril 230, 11° andar, Bloco B, 01.044 São Paulo, SP; tel. (11) 255-2566; telex (11) 21454; Bureau Chief RICARDO UZTARROZ; SDS, Edif. Venâncio IV, sala 307, Brasília, DF; tel. (61) 224-3576; telex (61) 1291; Bureau Chief MICHEL GALAN.

Agencia EFE (Spain): Av. Rio Branco 25, 13° andar, 20.090 Rio de Janeiro, RJ; tel. (21) 253-4465; telex (21) 30073; Bureau Chief ZOILO G. MARTÍNEZ DE LA VEGA; SCS, QI Bl.M. Edif. Gilberto Salamão, sala 508, 70.305 Brasília, DF, tel. (61) 225-9183; Bureau Chief RICARDO PALMÁS.

Agenzia Nazionale Stampa Associata (ANSA) (Italy): Av. Pres. Antônio Carlos 40, Cobertura, CP 16095, Rio de Janeiro, RJ; tel. (21) 220-5528; telex (21) 22296; Bureau Chief MANUEL HORACIO PALLAVIDINI; Av. São Luís 258, 13° andar, Of. 1302, São Paulo, SP; tel. (11) 256-5835; telex (11) 21421; Bureau Chief RICCARDO CARUCCI; c/o Correio Brasiliense 300/350, 70.610 Brasília, DF; tel. (61) 226-1755; telex (61) 2211; Bureau Chief HUMBERTO ANTONIO GIMINIII, Rua Barão do Rio Branco 596, Curitiba, PA; tel. (41) 24 5000; Bureau Chief ELOIN DANTÉ ALBERTI.

Associated Press (AP) (USA): Av. Brasil 500, sala 847, CP 72-ZC-00, 20.001 Rio de Janeiro, RJ; tel. (21) 580-4422; telex (21) 21888; Bureau Chief BRUCE HANDLER; Rua Major Quedinho 28, 6° andar, CP 3815, 01.050 São Paulo, SP; tel. (11) 256-0520; telex (11) 21595; Correspondent STAN LEHMAN; a/c Sucursal Folha de São Paulo, CLS 104 Bloco C Loja 41, CP 14-2260, 70.343 Brasília, DF; tel. (61) 223-9492; telex (61) 1454; Correspondent JORGE MEDEROS.

Deutsche Presse-Agentur (dpa) (Germany): Abade Ramos 65, 22.461 Rio de Janeiro, RJ; tel. (21) 248-9156; telex (21) 22550; fax (21) 286-0349; Bureau Chief SIEGFRIED NIEBUHR.

Inter Press Service (IPS) (Italy): Rua do Russell 450/602, 22.210 Rio de Janeiro; tel. (21) 285-7982; telex (21) 34845; Correspondent MARIO CHIZUO OSAVA.

Jiji Tsushin-Sha (Japan): Av. Pailista 854, 7° andar, Bela Vista, 01.310 São Paulo, SP; tel. (11) 287-9526; telex (11) 24594; fax (11) 285-3816; Chief Correspondent TSUTOMU MARUMOTO.

Kyodo Tsushin (Japan): Praia do Flamengo 168-701, Flamengo, 22.210 Rio de Janeiro, RJ; tel. (21) 285-2412; telex (21) 33653; Bureau Chief TAKAYOSHI MAKITA.

Prensa Latina (Cuba): Marechal Mascarenhas de Moraes 121, Apto 203, Copacabana, 22.030 Rio de Janeiro, RJ; tel. (21) 256-7259; telex (21) 36510; Correspondent SERGIO PINEDA.

Reuters (UK): SCS, Edif. Gilberto Salomão, 8° andar, salas 807-810, 70.300 Brasília, DF; tel. (61) 223-5918; telex (61) 1982; Rua Líbero Badaró 377, 21°, 01.009 São Paulo, SP; tel. (11) 35-1046; telex (11) 23796; fax (11) 37-8253; Av. Rio Branco 25, 12°, Conj. C/D, CP 266, 20.090 Rio de Janeiro, RJ; tel. (21) 233-5430; telex (21) 23222; fax (21) 263-8187; Chief Correspondent STEPHEN POWELL.

Telegrafnoye Agentstvo Sovetskovo Soyuza (TASS) (USSR): Rua General Barbosa 34, Apto 802, Rio de Janeiro, RJ; Correspondent ALEKSANDR MAKSIMOV; Av. das Naçoes, Lote A, 70.000 Brasília, DF; Correspondent YURIY BESPALCO.

United Press International (UPI) (USA): Rua Uruguaina 94, 18°, Centro, 20.050 Rio de Janeiro, RJ; tel. (21) 224-4194; telex (21) 22680; fax (21) 232-8293; Rua Sete de Abril 230, Bloco A, 816/817, 01.044 São Paulo, SP; tel. (11) 258-6869; telex (11) 22235; Edif. Gilberto Salamão, Sala 805/806, 70.305 Brasília, DF; tel. (61) 224-6413; telex (61) 1507; Gen. Man. ANTÔNIO PRAXEDES; Chief Correspondent H. E. COYA HONORES.

Xinhua (New China) News Agency (People's Republic of China): SHI/S QI 15, Conj. 16, Casa 14, CP 7089; 71.600 Brasília, DF; tel. (61) 248-5489; telex (61) 2788; Chief Correspondent WANG ZHIGEN.

Central News Agency (Taiwan) and Informatsionnoye Agentstvo Novosti (IAN) (USSR) are also represented in Brazil.

PRESS ASSOCIATIONS

Associação Brasileira de Imprensa: Rua Araújo Pôrto Alegre 71, Castelo, 20.030 Rio de Janeiro, RJ; f. 1908; 4,000 mems; Pres. BARBOSA LIMA SOBRINHO; Sec. JOSUÉ ALMEIDA.

Federação Nacional dos Jornalistas—FENAJ: CRS 502, Bloco A, Entrada 51, 1°-2°, 70.330, Brasília, DF; tel. (61) 223-7002; telex (61) 1792; f. 1946; represents 29 regional unions; Pres. ARMANDO SOBRAL ROLLEMBERG.

Publishers

There are nearly 500 publishers in Brazil. The following is a list of the most important by virtue of volume of production.

Rio de Janeiro, RJ

Bloch Editores, SA: Rua do Russell 766/804, Glória, 22.214 Rio de Janeiro, RJ; tel. (21) 265-2012; telex (21) 21525; f. 1966; general; Pres. ADOLPHO BLOCH.

Distribuidora Record de Serviços de Imprensa, SA: Rua Argentina 171, São Cristóvão, CP 884, 20.921 Rio de Janeiro, RJ; tel. (21) 580-3668; telex (21) 30501; fax (21) 580-4911; f. 1941; general fiction and non-fiction, education, textbooks, fine arts; Pres. ALFREDO C. MACHADO.

Ebid-Editora Páginas Amarelas, Ltda: Av. Pres. Wilson 165, 3° andar, 20.080 Rio de Janeiro, RJ; tel. (21) 292-6116; telex (21) 21678; commercial directories.

Editora Artenova, SA: Rua Pref. Olímpio de Mello 1774, Benfica, 20.000 Rio de Janeiro, RJ; tel. (21) 264-9198; f. 1971; sociology, psychology, occultism, cinema, literature, politics and history; Man. Dir ALVARO PACHECO.

Editora Brasil-América (EBAL), SA: Rua Gen. Almérico de Moura 302/320, São Cristóvão, 20.921 Rio de Janeiro, RJ; tel. (21) 580-0303; telex (21) 21293; f. 1945; children's books; Dir ADOLFO AIZEN.

Editora Delta, SA: Av. Almirante Barroso 63, 26° andar, CP 2226, 20.031 Rio de Janeiro, RJ; tel. (21) 240-0072; f. 1958; reference books.

Editora Globo, SA: Rua Itapiru 1209, Rio Comprido, 20.251 Rio de Janeiro, RJ; tel. (21) 273-5522; telex (21) 23365; fax (21) 273-8329; f. 1957; general; Gen. Man. OSCAR NEVES.

Editora e Gráfica Miguel Couto, SA: Rua da Passagem 78, Loja A, Botafogo, 22.290 Rio de Janeiro, RJ; tel. (21) 541-5145; f. 1969; engineering; Dir PAULO KOBLER PINTO LOPES SAMPAIO.

Editora Monterrey, Ltda: Rio de Janeiro, RJ; f.1963; fiction; Dir J. GUEIROS.

Editora Nova Fronteira, SA: Rua Bambina 25, Botafogo, 22.251 Rio de Janeiro, RJ; tel. (21) 286-7822; telex (21) 34695; fax (21) 286-6755; f. 1965; fiction, psychology, history, politics, science fiction, poetry, leisure, reference; Pres. SÉRGIO C. A. LACERDA.

Editora Tecnoprint, SA: Rua Nova Jerusalém 345, CP 1880, 21.040 Rio de Janeiro, RJ; tel. (21) 260-6122; f. 1939; general.

Editora Vecchi, SA: Rua do Rezende 144, Esplanada do Senado, 20.231 Rio de Janeiro, RJ; tel. (21) 221-0822; telex (21) 32756; f. 1913; general literature, juvenile, reference, cookery, magazines; Dir DELMAN BONATTO.

Editora Vozes, Ltda: Rua Frei Luís 100, CP 90023, 25.600 Petrópolis, RJ; tel. (21) 43-5112; f. 1901; Catholic publishers; management, theology, anthropology, fine arts, history, linguistics, science, fiction, education, data processing, etc.; Dir Dr MIGUEL GOMES MOURÃO DE CASTRO.

Exped—Espansão Editorial, Ltda: Estrada dos Bandeirantes 1700, Bloco H, Jacarapeguá, 22.700 Rio de Janeiro, RJ; tel. (21) 342-0669; telex (21) 33280; f. 1967; textbooks, literature, reference; Gen. Man. FERDINANDO BASTOS DE SOUZA.

Fundação de Assistência ao Estudante (FAE): Rua Miguel Ângelo 96, Maria da Graça, 20.781 Rio de Janeiro, RJ; tel. (21) 261-7750; f. 1967; education; Man. Dir RUBENS JOSÉ DE CASTRO.

Gráfica Editora Primor, Ltda: Rodv. Pres. Dutra 2611, 21.530 Rio de Janeiro, RJ; tel. (21) 371-6622; telex (21) 22150; f. 1968.

Livraria Francisco Alves Editora, SA: Rua 7 de Setembro 177, 20.050 Rio de Janeiro, RJ; tel. (21) 221-3198; f. 1854; textbooks, fiction, non-fiction; Dir Supt LEO MAGARINOS DE SOUZA LEÃO.

Livraria José Olympio Editora, SA: Rua Marquês de Olinda 12, CP 9018, Botafogo, 22.252 Rio de Janeiro, RJ; tel. (21) 551-0642; telex (21) 21327; f. 1931; juvenile, science, history, philosophy, psychology, sociology, fiction; Dir LUIZ OCTÁVIO DO ESPÍRITO SANTO.

Ao Livro Técnico SA Indústria e Comércio: Rua Sá Freire 40, São Cristóvão, 20.930 Rio de Janeiro, RJ; tel. (21) 580-1168; telex (21) 30472; f. 1933; technical, scientific, children's, languages, textbooks; Man. Dir REYNALDO MAX PAUL BLUHM.

Otto Pierre Editores, Ltda: Rua Dr Nunes 1225, Olaria, 21.021 Rio de Janeiro, RJ.

Tesla Publicações, Ltda: Rua da Quitanda 49, 1° andar, salas 110/12, 20.011 Rio de Janeiro, RJ; tel. (21) 242-0135; f. 1960; children's books.

São Paulo, SP

Atual Editora, Ltda: Rua José Antônio Coelho 785, Vila Mariana, 04.011 São Paulo, SP; tel. (11) 575-1544; f. 1973; school books, literature; Dirs GELSON IEZZI, OSVALDO DOLCE.

Cedibra Editora Brasileiro, Ltda: Rua Papa Paulo VI, 856 Campinas, 13.100 São Paulo, SP; tel. (192) 83626; fax (192) 21112; literature and children's books; Man. Dir JAN RAIS.

Cia Editora Nacional: Rua Joli 294, Brás, CP 5312, 03.016 São Paulo, SP; tel. (11) 291-2355; f. 1925; textbooks, history, science, social sciences, philosophy, fiction, juvenile; Dirs JORGE YUNES, PAULO C. MARTI.

Cia Melhoramentos de São Paulo, Indústrias de Papel: Rua Tito 479, 05.051 São Paulo, SP; tel. (11) 262-6866; telex (11) 23151; f. 1890; history, science, juvenile education, history; Gen. Man. RAINER OELLERS.

Editora Abril, SA: Av. Octaviano Alves de Lima 4400, CP 02909, São Paulo, SP; tel. (11) 877-1322; telex (11) 22115; fax (11) 877-1640; f. 1950; Pres. VICTOR CIVITA.

Editora Atica, SA: Rua Barão de Iguape 110, CP 8656, 01.507 São Paulo, SP; tel. (11) 278-9322; telex (11) 32969; f. 1965; textbooks, Brazilian and African literature; Pres. ANDERSON FERNANDES DIAS.

Editora Atlas, SA: Rua Conselheiro Nébias 1384, Campos Elíseos, CP 7186, 01.203 São Paulo, SP; tel. 221-9144; fax (11) 220-7830; f. 1944; business administration, data-processing, economics, accounting, law, education, social sciences; Pres. LUIZ HERRMANN.

Editora Brasiliense, SA: Rua Gal. Jardim 160, 01.223 São Paulo, SP; tel. (11) 231-1422; f. 1943; education, sociology, history, administration, psychology, literature, children's books; Mans CAIO GRACO DA SILVA PRADO, THEOPHILO ISIDORE DE ALMEIDA, Filho.

Editora do Brasil, SA: Rua Conselheiro Nébias 887, Campos Elíseos, CP 4986, 01.203 São Paulo, SP; tel. (11) 222-0211; f. 1943; commerce, education, history, psychology and sociology.

Editora Caminho Suave, Ltda: Rua Fagundes 157, Liberdade, 01.508 São Paulo, SP; tel. (11) 278-5840; f. 1965; textbooks.

Editora e Encadernadora Formar, Ltda: Rua dos Trilhos 1126, Mooca, CP 13250, 03.168 São Paulo, SP; tel. (11) 93-5133; f. 1962; general.

Editora F.T.D., SA: Rua do Lavapés 1023, CP 30402, 01.519 São Paulo, SP; tel. (11) 278-8264; f. 1897; textbooks; Pres. JOÃO TISSI.

Editora Luzeiro, Ltda: Rua Almirante Barroso 730, Brás, 03.025 São Paulo, SP; tel. (11) 292-3188; f. 1973; folklore and literature.

Editora Moderna, Ltda: Rua Afonso Brás 431, Ibirapuera, CP 45364, 04.511 São Paulo, SP; tel. (11) 531-5099; f. 1969; education and children's books; Man. Dir Prof. RICARDO FELTRE.

Editora Nova Cultural, Ltda: Av. Brigadeiro Faria Lima 2000, Torre Norte, 3°/4°/5° andares, 01.452 São Paulo, SP; tel. (11) 815-8055; telex (11) 83765; f. 1965; general encyclopaedias, pocket books, children's activities manuals, elementary educational books; Man. Dir FLAVIO BARROS PINTO.

Editora Revista dos Tribunais, Ltda: Rua Conde do Pinhal 78, CP 8153, 01.501 São Paulo, SP; tel. (11) 37-8689; f. 1955; law and jurisprudence, administration, economics and social sciences; Man. Dir NELSON PALMA TRAVASSOS.

Editora Rideel, Ltda: Alameda Afonso Schmidt 877, Santa Terezinha, 02.450 São Paulo, SP; tel. (11) 267-8344; f. 1971; general; Dir ITALO AMADIO.

Editora Scipione, Ltda: Praça Carlos Gomes 46, 01.501 São Paulo, SP; tel. (11) 37-4151; f. 1983; textbooks, mathematics; Dir MAURÍCIO FERNANDES DIAS.

Encyclopaedia Britannica do Brasil Publicações, Ltda: Rua Rego Freitas 192, Vila Buarque, CP 31027, 01.220 São Paulo, SP; tel. (11) 221-7122; telex (11) 21460; f. 1951; reference books.

Ênio Matheus Guazzelli & Cia, Ltda (Livraria Pioneira Editora): Praça Dirceu de Lima 313, Casa Verde, 02.515 São Paulo, SP; tel. (11) 858-3199; f. 1964; architecture, political and social sciences, business studies, languages, children's books; Dir ÊNIO MATHEUS GUAZZELLI.

Gráfica-Editora Michalany, SA: Rua Biobedas 321, Saúde, CP 12933, 04.302 São Paulo, SP; tel. (11) 275-9716; f. 1965; biographies, economics, textbooks, geography, history, religion, maps; Dir DOUGLAS MICHALANY.

Instituto Brasileiro de Edições Pedagógicas, Ltda: Rua Joli 294, Brás, CP 5321, 03.016 São Paulo, SP; tel. (11) 291-2355; f. 1972; textbooks, foreign languages, reference books and chemistry.

Lex Editora, SA: Rua Machado de Assis 47/57, Vila Mariana, CP 12888, 04.106 São Paulo, SP; tel. (11) 549-0122; f. 1937; legislation and jurisprudence; Dir AFFONSO VITALE SOBRINHO.

Saraiva SA Livreiros Editores: Av. Marquês de São Vicente 1697, CP 2362, 01.139 São Paulo, SP; tel. (11) 826-8422; telex 26789; f. 1914; education, textbooks, law, economics; Pres. PAULINO SARAIVA.

Belo Horizonte, MG

Editora Lê, SA: Av. D. Pedro II, 4550 Jardin Montanhês, CP 2585, 30.730 Belo Horizonte, MG; tel. (31) 462-6262; telex (31) 3340; f. 1967; textbooks.

Editora Lemi, SA: Av. Nossa Senhora de Fátima 1945, CP 1890, 30.000 Belo Horizonte, MG; tel. (31) 201-8044; f. 1967; administration, accounting, law, ecology, economics, textbooks, children's books and reference books.

Editora Vigília, Ltda: Rua Felipe dos Santos 508, Bairro de Lourdes, CP 2468, 30.180 Belo Horizonte, MG; tel. (31) 337-2744; telex (31) 3728; f. 1960; general.

Curitiba, PR

Editora Educacional Brasileira, SA: Rua XV de Novembro 178, salas 101/04, CP 7498, 80.000 Curitiba, PR; tel. (41) 223-5012; f. 1963; biology, textbooks and reference books.

PUBLISHERS' ASSOCIATIONS

Associação Brasileira do Livro: Av. 13 de Maio 23, 16°, 20.031 Rio de Janeiro, RJ; tel. (21) 240-9115; Pres. ERNESTO ZAHAR.

Câmara Brasileira do Livro: Av. Ipiranga 1267, 10°, 01.039 São Paulo, SP; tel. (11) 229-7855; telex (11) 24788; fax (11) 229-7463; f. 1946; Pres. ARY K. BENCLOWICZ.

Sindicato Nacional dos Editores de Livros: Av. Rio Branco 37, 15°, 20.097 Rio de Janeiro, RJ; tel. (21) 233-6481 ; telex (21) 37063; 200 mems; Pres. REGINA BILAC PINTO; Exec. Sec. SIMONE PATRICIA KATZ.

There are also regional publishers' associations.

BRAZIL
Directory

Radio and Television

In 1989 there were an estimated 59m. radio receivers and 36m. television receivers in use. In 1988, as part of the Government's proposals to transfer state-controlled enterprises to private ownership, plans were announced to privatize 14 radio stations and one television station.

Departamento Nacional de Telecomunicações (Dentel) (National Telecommunications Council): Via N2, Anexo do Ministério das Comunicações, Esplanada dos Ministérios, Bloco R, 70.044 Brasília, DF; tel. (61) 223-3229; telex (61) 1175; Dir-Gen. Dr RUBENS BUSSACOS.

Empresa Brasileira de Comunicação, SA (Radiobrás) (Brazilian Communications Company): CP 04/0340, 70.323 Brasília, DF; tel. (61) 224-3949; telex (61) 1682; fax (61) 321-7602; f. 1988 following merger of Empresa Brasileira de Radiodifusão and Empresa Brasileira de Notícias; Pres. MARCELO AMORIM NETTO.

RADIO

In 1989 there were 2,789 radio stations in Brazil, including 20 in Brasília, 38 in Rio de Janeiro, 32 in São Paulo, 24 in Curitiba, 24 in Porto Alegre and 23 in Belo Horizonte.

The main broadcasting stations in Rio de Janeiro are: Rádio Nacional, Rádio Globo, Rádio Eldorado, Rádio Jornal do Brasil, Rádio Tupi and Rádio Mundial. In São Paulo the main stations are Rádio Bandeirantes, Rádio Mulher, Rádio Eldorado, Rádio Gazeta and Rádio Excelsior; and in Brasília: Rádio Nacional, Rádio Alvorada, Rádio Planalto and Rádio Capital.

TELEVISION

In 1989 there were 235 television stations in Brazil, of which 118 were in the state capitals and six in Brasília. PAL-M colour television was adopted in 1972 and the Brazilian system is connected with the rest of the world by satellite.

The main television networks are:

TV Bandeirantes—Canal 13: Rádio e Televisão Bandeirantes, SA, Rua Radiantes 13, Morumbí, CP 372, 05.699 São Paulo, SP; tel. (11) 842-3011; telex (11) 56375; 23 television networks throughout Brazil; Pres. JOÃO JORGE SAAD.

RBS TV—Canal 12: Rua Radio y TV Gaúcha 189, 90.650 Porto Alegre, RS; tel. (512) 235-5000; telex (51) 4118; Dir JAIME SIROTSKY.

TV Globo—Canal 4: Rua Lopes Quintas 303, Jardim Botanico, 22.463 Rio de Janeiro, RJ; tel. (21) 529-2000; telex (21) 22795; fax (21) 294-2042; f. 1965; 8 stations; national network; Pres. ROBERTO MARINHO.

TV Manchete-Canal 6: Rua do Russel 766, 20.000 Rio de Janeiro, RJ; tel. (21) 265-2012; telex (21) 21525; Dir-Gen. R. FURTADO.

TV Record—Canal 7: Av. Miruna 713, Aeroporto, 01.000 São Paulo, SP; tel. (11) 542-9000; telex (11) 22245; fax (11) 532-0894; Dir-Supt AILTON TREVISON.

TVSBT—Canal 4 de São Paulo, SA: Rua Dona Santa Veloso 535, Vila Guilherme, 02.050 São Paulo, SP; tel. (11) 292-9044; telex (11) 22126; fax (11) 264-6004; Vice-Pres. GUILHERME STOLIAR.

BROADCASTING ASSOCIATIONS

Associação Brasileira de Emissoras de Rádio e Televisão (ABERT): Mezanino do Hotel Nacional, salas 5 a 8, CP 40280, 70.322 Brasília, DF; tel. (61) 224-4600; telex (61) 2001; f. 1962; mems: 32 shortwave, 643 FM, 1,294 medium-wave and 84 tropical-wave radio stations and 177 television stations (mid-1986); Pres. JOAQUIM MENDONÇA; Exec. Dir ANTÔNIO ABELIN.

There are regional associations for Bahia, Ceará, Goiás, Minas Gerais, Paraná, Pernambuco, Rio de Janeiro and Espírito Santo (combined), Rio Grande do Sul, Santa Catarina, São Paulo, Amazonas, Distrito Federal, Mato Grosso and Mato Grosso do Sul (combined) and Sergipe.

Finance

(cap. = capital; p.u. = paid up; dep. = deposits; res = reserves; m. = million; brs = branches; amounts in old cruzados, unless otherwise stated)

BANKING

In September 1988 the Conselho Monétario Nacional approved legislation to allow foreign banks to hold up to 33% of the voting stock and 50% of the total capital of local financial institutions.

Conselho Monetário Nacional: SBS, Edif. Banco do Brasil, 9° andar, Brasília, DF; f. 1964 to formulate monetary policy and to supervise the banking system; Pres. Minister of the Economy.

Central Bank

Banco Central do Brasil: SBS, Edif. Sede, Conj. 7, Bloco A, 70.074 Brasília, DF; tel. (61) 224-1453; telex (61) 2113; fax (61) 223-1983; f. 1965 to execute the decisions of the Conselho Monetário Nacional; bank of issue; total assets 38,939,538.1m. (May 1988); Pres. ELMO DE ARAÚJO CAMÕES.

State Commercial Banks

Banco do Brasil, SA: Setor Bancário Sul, Lote 32, Bloco C, Edif. Sede III, CP 562, Brasília, DF; tel. (61) 212-2465; telex (61) 2107; fax (61) 223-0156; f. 1808; cap. 3,199m., res 59,301m., dep. 326,044m. (Dec. 1989); Pres. ALBERTO POLICARO; 4,755 brs.

Banco do Estado da Bahia, SA: Av. Estados Unidos 26, CP 68, 40.010 Salvador, BA; tel. (71) 243-6944; telex (71) 3149; f. 1936; cap. NCZ $33.8m., res NCZ $693.4m., dep. NCZ $1,058.1m. (Dec. 1989); Pres. JOSÉ VIEIRA DE SANTANA NETO; 224 brs.

Banco do Estado de Minas Gerais, SA: Rua Rio de Janeiro 471, CP 300, 30.160 Belo Horizonte, MG; tel. (31) 239-1252; telex (31) 2134; fax (31) 201-1977; f. 1967; cap. 3,995m., res 39,101m., dep. 158,816m. (June 1988); Pres. JOSÉ LUIS ROCHA; 238 brs.

Banco do Estado do Paraná, SA: Rua Máximo João Kopp 274, CP 3331, 80.000 Curitiba, PR; tel. (41) 251-8250; telex (41) 30004; fax (41) 253-8383; f. 1928; cap. NCZ $113m., res NCZ $1,615m., dep. NCZ $4,722m. (Dec. 1989); Pres. CARLOS ANTÔNIO DE ALMEIDA FERREIRA; 310 brs.

Banco do Estado de Pernambuco, SA: Cais do Apolo 222, 8 andar, 50.038 Recife, PE; tel. (81) 224-5276; telex (81) 2164; f. 1938; cap. NCZ $25.5m., res NCZ $589.7m., dep. NCZ $1,945.9m. (Dec. 1989); Pres. JOSÉ SOARES NUTO.

Banco do Estado do Rio Grande do Sul, SA: Rua Capitão Montanha 177, CP 505, 90.010 Porto Alegre, RS; tel. (512) 21-5023; telex (512) 474; fax (512) 28-6473; f. 1928; cap. NCZ $790.9m., res NCZ $1,199.6m., dep. NCZ $760m. (Dec. 1989); Pres. RICARDO RUSSOWSKY; 302 brs.

Banco do Estado do Rio de Janeiro, SA (BANERJ): Av. Nilo Peçanha 175, 17° andar, CP 21090, 20.020 Rio de Janeiro, RJ; tel. (21) 224-7679; telex (21) 23290; fax (21) 533-1118; f. 1976; cap. and res 1,833,952m., dep. 11,095,895m. (Dec. 1989); Pres. MÁRCIO FORTES; 2 brs.

Banco do Estado de Santa Catarina, SA: Praça XV de Novembro 1, 88.000 Florianópolis, SC; tel. (48) 22-8000; telex (48) 2163; f. 1962; Pres. CARLOS PASSONI FILHO; 204 brs.

Banco do Estado de São Paulo, SA (Banespa): Praça Antônio Prado 6, 6° andar, 01.062 São Paulo, SP; tel. (11) 239-6622; telex (11) 37692; fax (11) 34-8523; f. 1926; cap. US $1,066.6m., dep. US $6,770.7m. (Dec. 1989); Chair. WADICO WALDIR BUCCHI; 1,400 brs.

Banco Meridional do Brasil, SA: Rua 7 de Setembro 1028, CP 26, 90.010 Porto Alegre, RS; tel. (512) 25-6088; telex (512) 513250; fax (512) 21-5033; f. 1985, formerly Banco Sulbrasileiro, SA; taken over by the Government in Feb. 1985; cap. NCZ $179.7m., res NCZ $2,470.1m., dep. NCZ $3,526.2 m. (Dec. 1989); Pres. CARLOS TADEU AGRIFOGLIO VIANNA; 321 brs.

Banco do Nordeste do Brasil, SA: Praça Murilo Borges 1, Edif. Raul Barbosa, CP 628, 60.035 Fortaleza, CE; tel. (85) 211-3333; telex (85) 3901; fax (85) 211-3359; f. 1954; cap. NCZ $2,267m., res NCZ $935.3m., dep. NCZ $12,345.8m. (Dec. 1989); Pres. JORGE LINS FREIRE; 180 brs.

Private Banks

Banco América do Sul, SA: Av. Brig. Luís Antônio 2020, CP 8075, 01.318 São Paulo, SP; tel. (11) 288-4933; telex (11) 21892; fax (11) 285-4564; f. 1940; cap. NCZ $70.9m., res NCZ $150.5m., dep. NCZ $621.8m. (June 1989); Pres. YOSUKE YOSHIDA; 121 brs.

Banco Bamerindus do Brasil, SA: Av. Presidente Kennedy, 3080 Curitiba, PR; tel. (41) 242-7411; telex (41) 5303; fax (41) 223-0320; f. 1952; cap. and res 51.5m., dep. 93.7m. (May 1988); Pres. JAIR JACOB MOCELIN; Dir OTTORINO MARINI; 825 brs.

Banco Bandeirantes, SA: Rua Boa Vista 150, 7° andar, CP 8260, 01.014 São Paulo, SP; tel. (11) 823-1122; telex (11) 21915; fax (11) 36-0633; f. 1944; cap. 1,500m., res 27,950.3m., dep. 129,433.1m. (Dec. 1988); Pres. Dr GILBERTO DE ANDRADE FARIA; 146 brs.

Banco BHM, SA: Rua Líbero Badaró 425, 9°, 01.009 São Paulo, SP; tel. (11) 258-9322; telex (11) 34517; fax (11) 36-5176.

Banco Boavista, SA: Praça Pio X 118, CP 1560, 20.092 Rio de Janeiro, RJ; tel. (21) 211-1661; telex (21) 21858; fax (21) 253-1579; f. 1924; cap. NCZ $19.0m., dep. NCZ $1,203.4m. (Dec. 1989); Pres. LINNEO DE PAULA MACHADO; 25 brs.

Banco Bozano, Simonsen, SA: Av. Rio Branco 138, 20.057 Rio de Janeiro, RJ; tel. (21) 271-8000; telex (21) 31956; fax (21) 271-8053; f. 1967; cap. NCZ $16.4m., res NCZ $607.9m., dep. NCZ $2,510.7m. (Dec. 1989); Pres. JÚLIO RAFAEL DE ARAGÃO BOZANO; 16 brs.

BRAZIL
Directory

Banco Bradesco, SA: Cidade de Deus, Vila Yara, 06.000 Osasco, SP; tel. (11) 704-3311; telex (11) 74001; fax (11) 704-4630; f. 1943; fmrly Banco Brasileiro de Descontos; cap. and res NCZ $18,683.8m., dep. NCZ $71,032.5m. (Dec. 1989); Chair. AMADOR AGUIAR; 1,767 brs.

Banco Chase Manhattan, SA: Praia de Botafogo 374, CP 221, Rio de Janeiro, RJ; tel. (21) 286-5232; telex (21) 31692; f. 1925; fmrly Banco Lar Brasileiro, SA; cap. 5,090.0m., res 4,586.1m., dep. 269,259.1m. (Dec. 1988); Pres. ALFREDO SALAZAR FILHO; Exec. Vice-Pres. MILTON TESSEROLLI; 44 brs.

Banco Cidade: Praça Dom José Gaspar 106, CP 30735, 01.047 São Paulo, SP; tel. (11) 231-6433; telex (11) 36194; f. 1965; cap. and res 7,361.3m., dep. 20,829.6m (May 1988); Pres. EDMUNDO SAFDIE; 25 brs.

Banco de Crédito Nacional, SA (BCN): Rua Boa Vista 228, CP 30-243, 01.014 São Paulo, SP; tel. (11) 235-1118; telex (11) 21284; fax (11) 35-6892; f. 1924; cap. and res NCZ $1,814.9m., dep. NCZ $32,333.9m. (Dec. 1989); Pres. PEDRO CONDE; 105 brs.

Banco de Crédito Real de Minas Gerais, SA: Rua Espírito Santo 485, CP 90, 30.310 Belo Horizonte, MG; tel. (31) 222-2058; telex (31) 3356; f. 1889; cap. NCZ $33.9m., res NCZ $515.9m., dep. NCZ $623.1m. (Dec. 1989); Pres. SERGIO MURTA MACHADO; 179 brs.

Banco Econômico, SA: Rua Miguel Calmon 285, Edif. Goes Calmon, 40.000 Salvador, BA; tel. (71) 254-1834; telex (71) 1197; fax (71) 241-0621; f. 1834; cap. and res 222.2m., dep. 406,189.0m. (Dec. 1988); Pres. ANGELO CALMON DE SA; 280 brs.

Banco Europeu para a América Latina (BEAL), SA: Rua Bela Cintra 952, 01.415 São Paulo, SP; tel. (11) 231-9969; telex (11) 23985; fax (11) 255-3478; f. 1911; formerly Banco Ítalo-Belga; cap. and res 3,038.1m., dep. 15,610.4m. (May 1988); Gen. Man. F. W. VISSER'THOOFT; 8 brs.

Banco Francês e Brasileiro, SA: Av. Paulista 1318, 01.310 São Paulo, SP; tel. (11) 251-4522; telex (11) 23340; fax (11) 284-3081; f. 1948; affiliated with Crédit Lyonnais; cap. and res NCZ $304.9m., dep. NCZ $1,264.8m. (Dec. 1989); Chair. JOÃO PEDRO GOUVEA VIEIRA; 63 brs.

Banco Hispano Americano: Alameda Santos 960, 01.418 São Paulo, SP; tel. (11) 284-9355; telex (11) 35596; f. 1981; cap. and res 888.7m., dep. 208.4m. (May 1988); Dir RAMÓN JARABA TELLO.

Banco Holandês Unido, SA: Rua do Ouvidor 107, 20.040 Rio de Janeiro, RJ; tel. (21) 297-2055; telex (21) 23663; fax (21) 221-0225; f. 1917; cap. and res 881.8m., dep. 2,703.6m. (June 1987); Gen. Man. DENIS ZIENGS; 10 brs.

Banco Itaú, SA: Rua XV de Novembro 306, 10°, 01013 São Paulo, SP; tel. (11) 239-8000; telex (11) 13044; fax (11) 34-8652; f. 1944; cap. NCZ $5,538.5m., res NCZ $9,700.6m., dep. NCZ $43,826.5m. (Dec. 1989); Chair. OLAVO EGYDIO SETUBAL; 886 brs.

Banco Mercantil de São Paulo, SA: Av. Paulista 1450, CP 4077, 01.310 São Paulo, SP; tel. (11) 252-2121; telex (11) 37701; fax (11) 284-3312; f. 1938; cap. NCZ $107.9m., res NCZ $5,467.0m., dep. NCZ $10,245.3m. (Dec. 1989); Pres. GASTÃO AUGUSTO DE BUENO VIDIGAL; 209 brs.

Banco Mercantil do Brasil, SA: Rua Rio de Janeiro 680, CP 836, 30.000 Belo Horizonte, MG; tel. (31) 239-6122; telex (31) 1341; f. 1943; cap. and res 17,731.8m., dep. 17,991.8m. (May 1988); Pres. OSWALDO DE ARAÚJO; 224 brs.

Banco Mitsubishi Brasileiro: Rua Líbero Badaró 641, CP 30179, 01.009 São Paulo, SP; tel. (11) 239-5244; telex (11) 21854; fax (11) 36-2060; f. 1933; cap. 1,800.0m., res 28,487.5m., dep. 412,961.5m. (Dec. 1988); Pres. HIROSHI NAGAI; 18 brs.

Banco Nacional, SA: Rio Branco 123, 2° andar, 20.040 Rio de Janeiro, RJ; tel. (21) 533-2863; telex (21) 21265; fax (21) 296-7722; f. 1944; cap. NCZ $275.6m., res NCZ $2,456.7m., dep. NCZ $29,664.7m. (Dec. 1989); Pres. MARCOS DE MAGALHÃES PINTO; 430 brs.

Banco Noroeste, SA: Rua Alvares Penteado 216, CP 8119, 01.012 São Paulo, SP; tel. (11) 35-1674; telex (11) 36991; fax (11) 35-4811; f. 1923; cap. NCZ $40.0m., res NCZ $115.7m., dep. NCZ $2,021.3m. (Dec. 1989); Pres. JORGE WALLACE SIMONSEN; 78 brs.

Banco Real, SA: Av. Paulista 1374, POB 5766, 01.310 São Paulo, SP; tel. (11) 251-9655; telex (11) 12610; fax (11) 283-2020; f. 1925; cap. NCZ $94.9m., res NCZ $3,837.3m., dep. NCZ $25,655.1m. (Dec. 1989); Pres. Dr ALOYSIO DE ANDRADE FARIA; 544 brs.

Banco Royal do Canada, SA: Rua XV de Novembro 240, 01.013 São Paulo, SP; tel. (11) 239-4533; telex (11) 23351; f. 1984; fmrly Banco Internacional, SA; cap. and res 1,800.1m., dep. 3,762m. (May 1988); Pres. ROBERT WAWN BRYDON; 4 brs.

Banco Safra, SA: Av. Paulista 2100, 16° andar, 01.310 São Paulo, SP; tel. (11) 251-7575; telex (11) 37742; fax (11) 251-7413; f. 1940; cap. and res 87,965.3m., dep. 1,779,359.1m. (May 1988); Pres. CARLOS ALBERTO VIEIRA; 54 brs.

Banco Sudameris Brasil, SA: Av. Paulista 1000, 01.310 São Paulo, SP; tel. (11) 283-9633; telex (11) 30397; fax (11) 289-1239; f. 1910; cap. and res NCZ $1,554.2m., dep. NCZ $6,853.3m. (Dec. 1989); Chair. HENRIQUE DE BOTTON; 17 brs.

Banco Sumitomo Brasileiro: Av. Paulista 949, CP 7961, 01.311 São Paulo, SP; tel. (11) 289-5044; telex (11) 70801; fax (11) 289-6996; f. 1958; cap. and res NCZ $419.2m., dep. NCZ $3,517.3m. (Dec. 1989); Pres. YOSHIAKA UEDA; 4 brs.

Banco de Tokyo, SA: Av. Paulista 1274, 01.310 São Paulo, SP; tel. (11) 285-6011; telex (11) 21192; f. 1972; cap. and res 42,670.0m., dep. 356,509.6m. (Dec. 1988); Pres. TOSHIRO KOBAYASHI; 5 brs.

Transcontinental Bank: Av. Ipiranga 952, 4° andar, 01.040 São Paulo; tel. (11) 222-9226; fax (11) 842-9991; f. 1990; Chairs WILLIAM SIMON, RAOUL GARDINI.

UNIBANCO—União de Bancos Brasileiros, SA: Avda Eusébio Matoso 891, 22° andar, CP 8185, 01.000 São Paulo, SP; tel. (11) 817-4322; telex (11) 80893; fax (11) 210-4518; f. 1924; cap. and res NCZ $6,447.7m., dep. NCZ $43,315.3 m. (Dec. 1989); Chair. WALTHER MOREIRA SALLES; 635 brs.

Development Banks

Banco de Desenvolvimento de Minas Gerais, SA—BDMG: Rua da Bahia 1600, Belo Horizonte, MG; tel. (31) 219-8000; telex (31) 1343; fax (31) 273-5084; f. 1962; long-term credit operations; cap. and res CR $7,570.7m., dep. CR $3,023.6m. (March 1990); Pres. CARLOS ALBERTO TEIXEIRA DE OLIVEIRA.

Banco de Desenvolvimento do Espírito Santo, SA: Av. Princesa Isabel 54, CP 1168, 29.000 Vitoria, ES; tel. (27) 223-8333; telex (27) 2131; cap. CR $2.3m. (1984); Pres. ODILON BORGES JÚNIOR.

Banco de Desenvolvimento do Estado da Bahia, SA: Av. Tancredo Neves 776, 40.000 Salvador, BA; tel. (71) 359-2322; telex (71) 1665; f. 1966; cap. 3,977.6m., res 43,619.5m., dep. 10,179.0m. (Dec. 1988); Pres. JOSÉ VIEIRA DE SANTANA NETO.

Banco de Desenvolvimento do Estado de São Paulo, SA (BADESP): Av. Paulista 1776, 01.310 São Paulo, SP; tel. (11) 289-2233; telex (11) 22763; Pres. JOSÉ ANTONIO MACHADO DE CAMPOS.

Banco de Desenvolvimento do Estado do Rio Grande do Sul, SA (BADESUL): Rua 7 de Setembro 666, 90.010 Porto Alegre, RS; tel. (512) 28-9455; telex (512) 1159; fax (512) 27-2221; f. 1975; cap. NCZ $115.0m., dep. NCZ $2,547.5m. (Dec. 1989); Pres. JAMES GIACOMONI.

Banco de Desenvolvimento do Paraná, SA: Av. Vicente Machado 445, CP 6042, 80.420 Curitiba, PR; tel. (41) 224-9711; telex (41) 5083; fax (41) 224-9763; f. 1962; cap. NCZ $33.6m., res NCZ $542.4m., dep. NCZ $1,100.8m. (Dec. 1989); Pres. CELSO DA COSTA SABÓIA.

Banco Nacional de Crédito Cooperativo, SA: SBN, Q.01-BL.C-2° and s/n Edif. Palácio do Desenvolvimento-Asa Norte, 70.057 Brasília, DF; tel. (61) 224-5575; telex (61) 1370; established in association with the Ministry of Agriculture and guaranteed by the Federal Government to provide co-operative credit; cap. and res 22.1m., dep. 3,832.0m. (May 1987); Pres. ESUPÉRIO S. DE CAMPOS AGUILAR (acting); 39 brs.

Banco Nacional do Desenvolvimento Econômico e Social (BNDES): Av. República do Chile 100, 20.031 Rio de Janeiro, RJ; tel. (21) 291-4442; telex (21) 22466; fax (21) 220-9786; f. 1952 to act as main instrument for financing of development schemes sponsored by the Government and to support programmes for the development of the national economy; cap. and res 57,209.3m., dep. 263,503.1m. (Dec. 1986); disbursements 48,774.5m. (1986); Pres. EDUARDO MODIANO.

Banco Regional de Desenvolvimento do Extremo Sul (BRDE): Rua Uruguai 155, POB 139, 90.010 Porto Alegre, RS; tel. (51) 221-9200; telex (51) 1229; f. 1961; cap. and res 25,644.6m., dep. 99,213.5m. (May 1988); development bank for the states of Paraná, Rio Grande do Sul and Santa Catarina; acts as agent for numerous federal financing agencies and co-operates with IBRD and Eximbank; finances small- and medium-sized enterprises; Dir-Pres. WALDEMAR ALLEGRETTI; 3 brs.

Investment Banks

Banco Finasa de Investimento, SA: Av. Paulista 1450, 01.310 São Paulo, SP; tel. (11) 258-1411; telex (11) 21785; f. 1965; medium- and long-term financing for industrial and commercial activities; underwriting shares and debentures; investment advisers; cap. and res 3,013.8m., dep. 3,074.6m. (June 1987); Pres. GASTÃO AUGUSTO DE BUENO VIDIGAL; 7 brs.

Banco de Montreal Investimento, SA (Montrealbank): Travessa Ouvidor 4, 20.149 Rio de Janeiro, RJ; tel. (21) 291-1122; telex (21) 21956; cap. and res 6,850.6m., dep. 73,974.3m. (May 1988); Pres. PEDRO LEITÃO DA CUNHA; 8 brs.

BRAZIL
Directory

Foreign Banks

Banca Commerciale Italiana (Italy): Av. Paulista 407, CP 30461, 01.311 São Paulo, SP; tel. (11) 289-4666; telex (11) 23679; cap. and res 1,575.3m., dep. 901.2m. (May 1988); Man. ANTÔNIO RAMPONE; 2 brs.

Banco de la Nación Argentina: Av. Rio Branco 134-A, 20.040 Rio de Janeiro, RJ; tel. (21) 252-2029; telex (21) 23673; fax (21) 232-8604; f. 1891; cap. and res 113,991m., dep. 7,498m. (March 1990); Dir-Gen. GUSTAVO GASTAUD; 2 brs.

Banco Unión (Venezuela): Av. Paulista 1708, 01.310 São Paulo, SP; tel. (11) 283-3722; telex (11) 30476; fax (11) 283-2434; f.1892; cap. and res 1,681.9m., dep. 3,253.9m. (May 1988); Dir-Gen. DONALDISON MARQUES DA SILVA; 151 brs.

Citibank NA (USA): Av. Nilo Pecanha 50, 22° andar, Rio de Janeiro, RJ; tel. (21) 296-1222; telex (21) 22907; fax (21) 276-3287; f. 1812; cap. and res 20,909.2m., dep. 137,064.3m. (May 1988); Dir ARNOLDO SOUZA DE OLIVEIRA; 13 brs.

Deutsche Bank AG (Germany): Rua Alexandre Dumas 2200, 04717 São Paulo, SP; tel. (11) 523-7599; telex (11) 53256; fax (11) 524-2793; f. 1969; cap. and res NCZ $30m. dep. NCZ $235.8m. (June 1989); Man. MANFRED HAMBURGER; brs in Campinas and Porte Alegre.

The First National Bank of Boston (USA): Rua Líbero Badaró 487, 01.009 São Paulo, SP; tel. (11) 234-5622; telex (11) 22285; cap. and res 6,474.3m., dep. 40,197.1m. (May 1988); Pres. DONALD W. MCDARBY; 8 brs.

The International Finance Corporation: São Paulo; private sector arm of the World Bank; office opened in July 1990.

Lloyds Bank PLC (UK): Rua XV de Novembro, 165 São Paulo, SP; tel. (11) 814-1488; telex (11) 83099; fax (11) 239-0322; cap. and res CR $13,614.9m., dep. CR $65,191.9m. (May 1990); Gen. Man. FREDERICK H. CIBBS; 17 brs.

Unión de Bancos del Uruguay: Rua 7 de Setembro 64, 20.050 Rio de Janeiro, RJ; tel. (21) 252-8070; telex (21) 31571; cap. and res 354.6m., dep. 54.1m. (May 1988); Man. NELSON VAZ MOREIRA.

Banking Associations

Federação Nacional dos Bancos: Rua Líbero Badaró 425, 17° andar, 01.009 São Paulo, SP; tel. (11) 239-3000; telex (11) 24710; f. 1966; Pres. ANTÔNIO DE PÁDUA ROCHA DINIZ; Vice-Pres PEDRO CONDE, THEÓPHILO AZEREDO SANTOS.

Sindicato dos Bancos dos Estados do Rio de Janeiro e Espírito Santo: Av. Rio Branco 81, 19° andar, Rio de Janeiro, RJ; Pres. THEÓPHILO DE AZEREDO SANTOS; Vice-Pres. Dr NELSON MUFARREJ.

Sindicato dos Bancos dos Estados de São Paulo, Paraná, Mato Grosso e Mato Grosso do Sul: Rua Líbero Badaró 293, 13° andar, 01.905 São Paulo, SP; f. 1924; Pres. PAULO DE QUEIROZ.

There are eight other banking associations in Maceió, Salvador, Fortaleza, Belo Horizonte, João Pessoa, Recife, Rio de Janeiro and Porto Alegre.

STOCK EXCHANGES

Comissão de Valores Mobiliários CVM: Rua 7 de Setembro 111, 32° andar, 20.050 Rio de Janeiro, RJ; tel. (21) 292-5117; telex (21) 21549; fax (21) 224-0679; f. 1977 to supervise the operations of the stock exchanges and develop the Brazilian securities market; Chair. MARTIN WINNER.

Bolsa de Valores do Rio de Janeiro: Praça 15 de Novembro 20, 20.010 Rio de Janeiro, RJ; tel. (21) 271-1001; telex (21) 35100; fax (21) 232-2796; f. 1843; 700 stocks quoted; Pres. Dr FRANCISCO BORGES DE SOUZA DANTAS; Vice-Pres. Dr CESAR MANDEL DE SOUZA.

Bolsa de Valores de São Paulo (BOVESPA): Alvares Peuteado 151, São Paulo, SP; tel. (11) 258-7222; fax (11) 258-7222; 500 stocks quoted; Pres. FERNANDO NABUCO.

There are commodity exchanges at Porto Alegre, Vitória, Recife, Santos and São Paulo.

INSURANCE
Supervisory Authorities

Superintendência de Seguros Privados (SUSEP): Rua Buenos Aires 256, 4° andar, 20.061 Rio de Janeiro, RJ; tel. (21) 232-4929; telex (21) 36149; f. 1966; within Ministry of the Economy; Superintendent JOÃO RÉGIS RICARDO DOS SANTOS.

Conselho Nacional de Seguros Privados (CNSP): 20.061 Rio de Janeiro, RJ; tel. (21) 297-4415; f. 1966; Sec. WALTER J. BARROS GRANEIRO

Instituto de Resseguros do Brasil (IRB): Av. Marechal Câmara 171, 20.023 Rio de Janeiro, RJ; tel. (21) 297-1212; telex (21) 21237; fax (21) 240-3923; f. 1939; reinsurance; Pres. LUIZ QUATTRONI.

Principal National Companies

The following is a list of the 23 principal national insurance companies, selected on the basis of premium income.

Rio de Janeiro, RJ

Bradesco Seguros, SA: Rua Barão de Itapagipe 225, 20.261 Rio de Janeiro, RJ; tel. (21) 264-0101; telex (21) 22055; f. 1935; general; Pres. ARARINO SALLUM DE OLIVEIRA.

Cia Internacional de Seguros: Rua Ibituruna 81, Maracanã, CP 1137, 20.271 Rio de Janeiro, RJ; tel. (21) 284-1222; f. 1920; property, life and risk; Pres. Dr MAURICE ALBERT BERCOFF.

Generali do Brasil, Cia Nacional de Seguros: Av. Rio Branco 128, 7° andar, Rio de Janeiro, RJ; tel. (21) 292-0144; telex (21) 22846; fax (21) 242-5181; f. 1945; general; Pres. CLÁUDIO BIETOLINI.

Nacional, Cia de Seguros: Av. Pres. Vargas 850, 20.091 Rio de Janeiro, RJ; tel. (21) 296-2112; telex (21) 30881; f. 1946; life and risk; Pres. VICTOR ARTHUR RENAULT.

Sasse, Cia Nacional de Seguros Gerais: Av. Rio Branco 125, 4°-5° andares, 20.031 Rio de Janeiro, RJ; tel. (21) 275-4022; f. 1967; general; Pres. OYAMA PEREIRA.

Sul América, Cia Nacional de Seguros: Rua da Quitanda 86, 20.091 Rio de Janeiro, RJ; tel. (21) 276-8585; telex (21) 30407; fax (21) 252-4559; f. 1895; life and risk; Pres. RONY CASTRO DE OLIVEIRA LYRIO; offices in São Paulo, Porto Alegre, Belo Horizonte and Recife.

Sul América Terrestres, Marítimos e Acidentes Cia de Seguros: Rua da Quitanda 86, sala 770, Rio de Janeiro, RJ; tel. (21) 291-2020; telex (21) 30677; f. 1914; general; Pres. RONY CASTRO DE OLIVEIRA LYRIO.

Yorkshire-Corcovado Cia de Seguros: Av. Almirante Barroso 52, 24° andar, 20.031 Rio de Janeiro, RJ; tel. (21) 292-1125; telex (21) 22343; f. 1943; life and risk; Pres. MANOEL PIO CORRÊA, Filho.

São Paulo, SP

Brasil, Cia de Seguros Gerais: Rua Luiz Coelho 26, 01.309 São Paulo, SP; tel. (11) 285-1533; telex (11) 21401; fax (11) 285-4813; f. 1904; general; Pres. JEAN-MARIE MONTEIL.

Cia Paulista de Seguros: Rua Líbero Badaró 158, CP 709, 01.008 São Paulo, SP; tel. (11) 229-0811; telex (11) 37787; f. 1906; general; Pres. ROBERTO PEREIRA DE ALMEIDA, Filho.

Cia Real Brasileira de Seguros: Av. Paulista 1374, 6° andar, 01.310 São Paulo, SP; tel. (11) 285-0255; telex (11) 24744; fax (11) 211-9222; f. 1965; Pres. ALOYSIO DE ANDRADE FARIA.

Cia de Seguros do Estado de São Paulo: Rua Pamplona 227, 01.405 São Paulo, SP; tel. (11) 284-4888; telex (11) 21999; f. 1967; life and risk; Pres. HERBERT JÚLIO NOGUEIRA.

Iochpe Seguradora, SA: Rua Dr Miguel Couto 58, 5° andar, 01.008 São Paulo, SP; tel. (11) 239-1822; telex (11) 37776; fax (11) 369-557; f. 1964; life and risk; Pres. FERNANDO A. SODRÉ FARIA.

Itaú Seguros, SA: Praça Alfredo Egydio de Souza Aranha 100, Bloco A, 04.390 São Paulo, SP; tel. (11) 582-3322; telex (11) 56212; fax (11) 577-6058; f. 1921; all classes; Gen. Dir LUIZ DE CAMPOS SALLES.

Porto Seguro Cia de Seguros Gerais: Av. Rio Branco 1489, 01.311 São Paulo, SP; tel. (11) 223-0022; telex (11) 32613; f. 1945; life and risk; Pres. ROSA GARFINKEL.

Skandia-BRADESCO Cia Brasileira de Seguros: Av. Paulista 1415, 01.311 São Paulo, SP; tel. (11) 287-4710; f. 1914; Man. Dir SVEN SCHÉLE.

Sul América Bandeirante Seguros, SA: Rua Anchieta 35, 01.016 São Paulo, SP; tel. (11) 259-3555; telex (11) 24021; f. 1944; life and risk; Pres. RONY CASTRO DE OLIVEIRA LYRIO.

Sul América Unibanco Seguradora, SA: Rua Líbero Badaró 293, 32° andar, 01.009 São Paulo, SP; tel. (11) 235-5000; telex (11) 34826; f. 1866; Pres. RONY CASTRO DE OLIVEIRA LYRIO.

Vera Cruz Seguradora, SA: Av. Maria Coelho Aguiar 215, Bloco D, 2° andar, 05.804 São Paulo, SP; tel. (11) 545-4944; f. 1955; general; Pres. HORÁCIO IVES FREYRE.

Provincial Companies

The following is a list of the principal provincial insurance companies, selected on the basis of premium income.

Bamerindus Cia de Seguros: Rua Marechal Floriano Peixoto 5500, Curitiba, PR; tel. (41) 221-2121; telex (41) 5672; f. 1938; all classes; Pres. HAMILCAR PIZZATTO.

Cia de Seguros Aliança da Bahia: Rua Pinto Martins 11, 9° andar, 40.000 Salvador, BA; tel. 242-1065; f. 1870; general; Pres. PAULO S. FREIRE DE CARVALHO.

BRAZIL

Directory

Cia de Seguros Minas-Brasil: Rua dos Caetés 745, 30.120 Belo Horizonte, MG; tel. (31) 219-3000; telex (31) 1506; fax (31) 219-3820; f. 1938; life and risk; Pres. JOSÉ CARNEIRO DE ARAÚJO.

Cia União de Seguros Gerais: Av. Borges de Medeiros 261, 90.020 Porto Alegre, RS; tel. (512) 26-7933; telex (512) 2530; f. 1891; Pres. ATTILA SÁ D'OLIVEIRA.

Trade and Industry

GOVERNMENT ADVISORY BODIES

Comissão de Fusão e Incorporação de Empresa (COFIE): Ministério da Fazenda, Edif. Sede, Ala B, 1° andar, Esplanada dos Ministérios, Brasília, DF; tel. (61) 225-3405; telex (61) 1539; mergers commission; Pres. SEBASTIÃO MARCOS VITAL; Exec. Sec. EDGAR BEZERRA LEITE, Filho.

Conselho de Desenvolvimento Comercial (CDC): Ministry of Infrastructure, Bloco R, Esplanada dos Ministérios, 70.044 Brasília, DF; tel. (61) 223-0308; telex (61) 2537; commercial development council; Exec. Sec. Dr RUY COUTINHO DO NASCIMENTO.

Conselho de Desenvolvimento Econômico (CDE): Bloco K, 7° andar, Esplanada dos Ministérios, 70.063 Brasília, DF; tel. (61) 215-4100; f. 1974; economic development council; Gen. Sec. JOÃO BATISTA DE ABREU.

Conselho de Desenvolvimento Social (CDS): Bloco K, 3° andar, 382, Esplanada dos Ministérios, 70.063 Brasília, DF; tel. (61) 215-4477; social development council; Exec. Sec. JOÃO A. TELES.

Conselho Federal de Desestacização: f. 1988; responsible for proposed privatization of some 70 state companies; Dir EDUARDO MODIANI.

Conselho Interministerial de Preços (CIP): Av. Pres. Antônio Carlos 375, 10° andar, 20.020 Rio de Janeiro, RJ; tel. (21) 224-7949; telex (21) 33314; prices commission; Exec. Sec. EDGAR DE ABREU CARDOSO.

Conselho Nacional do Comércio Exterior (CONCEX): Fazenda, 5° andar, Gabinete do Ministro, Bloco 6, Esplanada dos Ministérios, 70.048 Brasília, DF; tel. (61) 223-4856; telex (61) 1142; f. 1966; responsible for foreign exchange and trade policies and for the control of export activities; Exec. Sec. NAMIR SALEK.

Conselho Nacional de Desenvolvimento Científico e Tecnológico (CNPq): Av. W-3 Norte, Quadra 507, Bloco B, 70.740 Brasília, DF; tel. (61) 274-1155; telex (61) 1089; f. 1951; scientific and technological development council; Pres. Dr CRODOVALDO PAVAN.

Conselho Nacional de Desenvolvimento Pecuário (CONDEPE): to promote livestock development.

Conselho de Não-Ferrosos e de Siderurgia (CONSIDER): Ministério da Indústria e do Comércio, Esplanada dos Ministérios, Bloco 6, 5° andar, 70.053 Brasília, DF; tel. (61) 224-6039; telex (61) 1012; f. 1973; exercises a supervisory role over development policy in the non-ferrous and iron and steel industries; Exec. Sec. WILLIAM ROCHA CANTAL.

Conselho Nacional do Petróleo (CNP): SGA Norte, Quadra 603, Módulos H, I, J, 70.830 Brasília, DF; tel. (61) 226-0403; telex (61) 1673; f. 1938; directs national policy on petroleum; Pres. Gen. ROBERTO FRANCO DOMINGUES.

Fundação Instituto Brasileiro de Geografia e Estatística (IBGE): Av. Franklin Roosevelt 166, Castelo, 20.021 Rio de Janeiro, RJ; tel. (21) 220-6671; telex (21) 30939; f. 1936; produces and analyses statistical, geographical, cartographic, geodetic, demographic and socio-economic information; Pres. CHARLES CURT MUELLER; Dir-Gen. DAVID WU TAI.

Instituto Nacional de Metrologia, Normalização e Qualidade Industrial (INMETRO): SCS, Edif. Chams, 2° andar, 70.330 Brasília, DF; tel. (61) 224-2315; telex (61) 1834; in 1981 INMETRO absorbed the Instituto Nacional de Pesos e Medidas (INPM), the weights and measures institute; Pres. Dr MASAO ITO.

Instituto de Planejamento Econômico e Social (IPEA): SBS, Edif. BNDE, 6° andar, 70.076 Brasília, DF; tel. (61) 225-4350; telex (61) 01979; planning institute; Pres. RICARDO SANTIAGO.

Secretaria Especial de Desenvolvimento Industrial: Ministério do Desenvolvimento da Indústria e Comércio, SAS, Q2, Lotes 2/5–2/8, Bloco G, 8° andar, 70.070 Brasília, DF; tel. (61) 225-7556; telex (61) 2225; f. 1969; industrial development council; offers fiscal incentives for selected industries and for producers of manufactured goods under the Special Export Programme; Exec. Sec. Dr ERNESTO CARRARA FILHO.

Superintendência do Desenvolvimento da Pesca (SUDEPE): Edif. da Pesca, Av. W-3 Norte, Quadra 506, Bloco C, 70.040 Brasília, DF; tel. (61) 272-3229; telex (61) 1179; attached to the Ministry of Agriculture; assists development of fishing industry; Superintendent AÉCIO MOURA DA SILVA.

REGIONAL DEVELOPMENT ORGANIZATIONS

Companhia de Desenvolvimento do Vale do São Francisco (CODEVASF): SGAN, Q 601, Lote 1, Edif. Sede, 70.830 Brasília, DF; tel. (61) 223-2797; telex (61) 1057; fax (61) 226-2468; f. 1974; Pres. ELISEU ROBERTO DE ANDRADE ALVES.

Superintendência do Desenvolvimento da Amazônia (SUDAM): Av. Almirante Barroso 426, Bairro do Marco, 66.000 Belém, PA; tel. (91) 226-0044; telex (91) 1117; f. 1966 to develop the Amazon regions of Brazil; attached to the Ministry of Social Action; supervises industrial, cattle breeding and basic services projects; Superintendent Eng. HENRY CHECRALLA KAYATH.

Superintendência do Desenvolvimento do Nordeste (SUDENE): Praça Supt João Gonçalves de Souza, Cidade Universitária, 50.000 Recife, PE; tel. (81) 271-1044; telex (81) 1245; f. 1959; attached to the Ministry of Social Action; assists development of north-east Brazil; Superintendent PAULO GANEM SOUTO.

Superintendência do Desenvolvimento da Região Centro Oeste (SUDECO): SAS, Quadra 1, Bloco A, Lotes 9/10, 70.070 Brasília, DF; tel. (61) 225-6111; telex (61) 1616; f. 1967 to co-ordinate development projects in the states of Goiás, Mato Grosso, Mato Grosso do Sul, Rondônia and Distrito Federal; Superintendent RAMEZ TEBET.

Superintendência da Zona Franca de Manaus (SUFRAMA): Rua Ministro João Gonçalves de Souza, Cidade Universitária, Distrito Industrial, 69.000 Manaus, AM; tel. (92) 237-3288; telex (92) 2146; to assist in the development of the Manaus Free Zone; Superintendent JADYR CARVALHEDO MAGALHÃES.

Other regional development organizations include Poloamazônia (agricultural and agro-mineral nuclei in the Amazon Region), Polocentro (woodland savannah in Central Brazil), Poloeste (agricultural and agro-mineral nuclei in the Centre-West), Polonordeste (integrated areas in the North-East), Procacau (expansion of cocoa industry), Prodoeste (development of the Centre-South), Proterra (land distribution and promotion of agricultural industries in the North and North-East), Provale (development of the São Francisco basin).

COMMERCIAL, AGRICULTURAL AND INDUSTRIAL ORGANIZATIONS

ABRASSUCOS: São Paulo, SP; association of orange juice industry; Pres. MÁRIO BRANCO PERES.

Associação do Comércio Exterior do Brasil: Av. General Justo 335, Rio de Janeiro, RJ; tel. (21) 240-5048; exporters' association; Pres. NORBERTO INGO ZABROZNY.

Companhia Vale do Rio Doce, SA (CVRD): Av. Graça Aranha 26, Bairro Castelo, 20.005 Rio de Janeiro, RJ; tel. (21) 272-4477; telex (21) 23162; f. 1942; state-owned mining company; owns and operates the Vitória–Minas railway, the port of Tubarão and the Carajás iron ore project; also involved in forestry and pulp production; Pres. AGRIPINO ABRANCHES VIANA.

Confederação das Associações Comerciais do Brasil: Brasília, DF; confederation of chambers of commerce in each state; Pres. AMAURY TENPORAL.

Confederação Nacional da Agricultura (CNA): Brasília, DF; tel. (61) 225-3150; national agricultural confederation; Pres. ALYSSON PAULINELLI.

Confederação Nacional do Comércio (CNC): SCS, Edif. Presidente Dutra, 4° andar, Quadra 11, 70.327 Brasília, DF; tel. (61) 223-0578; national confederation comprising 35 affiliated federations of commerce; Pres. ANTÔNIO JOSÉ DOMINGUES DE OLIVEIRA SANTOS.

Confederação Nacional da Indústria (CNI): SBN, Edif. Roberto Simonsen, 16° andar, 70.040 Brasília, DF; tel. (61) 224-1328; f. 1938; national confederation of industry comprising the 21 state industrial federations; Pres. Dr ALBANO DO PRADO FRANCO; Vice-Pres. EDGAR ARP.

Confederação Nacional dos Transportes Terrestres (CNTT): Edif. Sofia, 2° andar, Setor Comercial Sul, Brasília, DF; tel. (61) 223-2300; confederation of land transport federations; Pres. CAMILO COLA.

Departamento Nacional da Produção Mineral (DNPM): SAN, Quadra 1, Bloco B, 3° andar, 70.040 Brasília, DF; tel. (61) 224-2670; telex (61) 1116; f. 1934; attached to the Ministry of Infrastructure; responsible for geological studies and control of exploration of mineral resources; Dir ELMER PRATA SALOMÃO.

Federação das Indústrias do Estado de São Paulo (FIESP): Av. Paulista 1313, 01.311 São Paulo, SP; tel. (11) 251-3522; telex (11) 22130; fax (11) 284-3971; regional manufacturers' association; Pres. MÁRIO AMATO; Vice-Pres. RICARDO SEMLER.

Instituto Brasileiro do Meio Ambiente e Recursos Naturais Renováveis (IBAMA): Setor de Áreas Isoladas, L4 Norte, 70.800 Brasília, DF; tel. (61) 321-2324; telex (61) 1711; f. 1967; responsible for the annual formulation of national and regional forest plans;

BRAZIL	*Directory*

merged with SEMA (National Environmental Agency) in 1988 and replaced the IBDF in 1989; Pres. FERNANDO CÉSAR DE MOREIRA MESQUITA.

Instituto Brasileiro do Mineração (IBRAM): Brasília, DF; Pres. JOÃO SÉRGIO MARINHO NUNES.

Instituto Nacional da Propriedade Industrial (INPI): Praça Mauá 7, 18° andar, 20.081 Rio de Janeiro, RJ; tel. (21) 223-4182; telex (21) 22992; f. 1970; Pres. PAULO AFONSO PEREIRA.

Instituto Nacional de Tecnologia (INT): Av. Venezuela 82, 8°, 20.081 Rio de Janeiro, RJ; tel. (21) 223-1320; telex (21) 30056; f. 1921; co-operates in national industrial development; Dir PAULO ROBERTO KRAHE.

União Democrática Ruralista (UDR): f. 1986; landowners' organization; Pres. RONALDO CAIADO.

PRINCIPAL STATE ENTERPRISES

In May 1990 the Government announced a policy of large-scale privatization of state-run enterprises over a period of 1–2 years. More than 40 enterprises were due to be transferred to private ownership by 1992.

Centrais Elétricas Brasileiras, SA (ELETROBRÁS): Av. Pres. Vargas 642, 20.071 Rio de Janeiro, RJ; tel. (21) 291-1222; telex (21) 22395; fax (21) 233-3248; f. 1962; government holding company (6 subsidiary and 23 associated electricity companies) responsible for planning, financing and managing Brazil's electrical energy programme; Pres. MARIO PENNA BHERING.

Companhia Siderúrgica Nacional, SA (CSN): Av. 13 de Maio 13, 8° andar, Centro, 20.031 Rio de Janeiro, RJ; tel. (21) 297-7177; telex (21) 23025; f. 1941; iron and steel; Pres. JUVENAL OSÓRIO GOMES.

Empresa de Assistência Técnica e Extensão Rural (EMATER): SAIN, Parque Rural, Edif. Sede EMATER, CP 04.235, 70.770 Brasília, DF; tel. (61) 274-9315; telex (61) 4669; Pres. MANOEL OLÍMPIO DE VASCONCELOS NETO.

Empresa Brasileira de Aeronáutica, SA (EMBRAER): Av. Brigadeiro Faria Lima 2170, CP 343, 12.225 São José dos Campos, SP; tel. (123) 25-1000; telex (123) 3589; fax (123) 21-8466; f. 1969; aeronautics industry; Chief Executive Officer (vacant).

Empresa Brasileira de Correios e Telégrafos (ECT): SBN, Edif. Sede, 19° andar, Conj. 3, Bloco A, 70.002 Brasília, DF; tel. (61) 224-9262; telex (61) 1119; fax (61) 223-4066; f. 1969; posts and telegraph; Pres. JOEL MARCIANO RAUBER.

Empresa Brasileira de Pesquisa Agropecuária (EMBRAPA): SAIN, Parque Rural, W/3 Norte, 70.770 Brasília, DF; tel. (61) 273-6215; telex (61) 1620; f. 1973; attached to the Ministry of Agriculture; agricultural research; Pres. CARLOS MAGNO CAMPOS DA ROCHA.

Empresa Brasileira de Telecomunicações, SA (EMBRATEL): Av. Pres. Vargas 1012, CP 2586, 20.071 Rio de Janeiro, RJ; tel. (21) 216-7400; telex (21) 22021; f. 1965; operates national and international telecommunications system; Pres. JOSÉ EUGÊNIO GUISARD FERRAZ.

Petróleo Brasileiro, SA (PETROBRÁS): Av. República do Chile 65, 20.035 Rio de Janeiro, RJ; tel. (21) 534-4477; telex (21) 23335; f. 1953; has monopoly on development and production of petroleum and petroleum products; 59,210 employees; Pres. EDUARDO DE FREITAS TEIXEIRA.

Petrobrás Distribuidora, SA: Praça 22 de Abril 36, 8° andar, Castelo, 20.021 Rio de Janeiro, RJ; tel. (21) 217-8066; telex (21) 21222; f. 1971; marketing of all petroleum by-products; Pres. MAXIMIANO FONSECA; Vice-Pres. LUIGI DALLOLIO.

Petrobrás Fertilizantes, SA (PETROFÉRTIL): Praça Mahatma Gandhi 14, 9°/13° andares, 20.031 Rio de Janeiro, RJ; tel. (21) 217-5335; telex (21) 23880; f. 1976; Pres. ROBERTO VILLA; Vice-Pres. AURÍLIO FERNANDES LIMA.

Petrobrás Internacional, SA (BRASPETRO): Praça Pio X 119, 20.040 Rio de Janeiro, RJ; tel. (21) 297-0102; telex (21) 21889; f. 1972; international division with operations in Algeria, Angola, People's Republic of China, Colombia, the Congo, Ghana, Guatemala, Libya, Norway, Trinidad and Tobago, Uruguay and Yemen; Pres. WAGNER FREIRE; Vice-Pres. ANTÔNIO SEABRA MOGGI.

Petrobrás Mineraçao, SA (Petromisa): Av. Pres. Vargas 583, 20.076 Rio de Janeiro, RJ; tel. (21) 224-7805; telex (21) 32509; potassium exploration and non-petroleum mining; Pres. JOSÉ EDILSON DE MELO TÁVORA; Exec. Vice-Pres. RUBEN LAHYR SCHNEIDER.

Petrobrás Química, SA (PETROQUISA): Rua Buenos Aires 40, 20.070 Rio de Janeiro, RJ; tel. (21) 297-6677; telex (21) 21496; f. 1968; petrochemicals industry; controls 27 affiliated companies and 4 subsidiaries; Pres. PAULO VIEIRA BELOTTI; Vice-Pres. TARCISIO DE VASCONCELOS MAIA.

Other state enterprises include Companhia Coque e Álcool de Madeira (COALBRA), Companhia Ferro e Aço de Vitória, Companhia Nacional de Alcalis, SA, Companhia Siderúrgica de Mogi das Cruzes, and Companhia Siderúrgica Paulista, SA.

TRADE UNIONS

Following the return to civilian government in March 1985, the ban on trade union associations, which had been in force under military rule, was repealed.

Central Unica dos Trabalhadores (CUT): Rua Ouvidor Peleja, 112 Bosque da Saúde, 04.123 São Paulo, SP; tel. (11) 577-4833; telex (11) 54282; f. 1983; central union confederation; left-wing; Pres. JAIR MENEGUELLI; Gen. Sec. AVELINO GANZER.

Confederação General dos Trabalhadores (CGT): São Paulo, SP; f. 1986; fmrly Coordenação Nacional das Classes Trabalhadoras; represents 1,258 labour organizations linked to PMDB; Pres. LUÍS ANTÔNIO MEDEIROS.

Confederação Nacional dos Metalúrgicos (Metal Workers): f. 1985; Pres. JOAQUIM DOS SANTOS ANDRADE.

Confederação Nacional das Profissões Liberais (CNPL) (Liberal Professions): SCS, Edif. Gilberto Salomão, Gr. 1.306/1.312, 70.305 Brasília, DF; tel. (61) 223-1683; telex (61) 3883; f. 1953; confederation of liberal professions; Pres. Dr JOSÉ AUGUSTO DE CARVALHO.

Confederação Nacional dos Trabalhadores na Indústria (CNTI) (Industrial Workers): Av. W 3 Norte, Quadra 505, Lote 01, 70.730 Brasília, DF; tel. (61) 274-4150; telex (61) 4230; f. 1946; Pres. JOSÉ CALIXTO RAMOS.

Confederação Nacional dos Trabalhadores no Comércio (CNTC) (Commercial Workers): Av. W/5 Sul, Quadra 902, Bloco C, 70.390 Brasília, DF; tel. (61) 224-3511; f. 1946; Pres. ANTÔNIO DE OLIVEIRA SANTOS.

Confederação Nacional dos Trabalhadores em Transportes Marítimos, Fluviais e Aéreos (CONTTMAF) (Maritime, River and Air Transport Workers): Av. Pres. Vargas 446, gr. 2205, 20.071 Rio de Janeiro, RJ; tel. (21) 233-8329; f. 1957; Pres. MAURÍCIO MONTEIRO SANT'ANNA.

Confederação Nacional dos Trabalhadores em Transportes Terrestres (CNTTT) (Land Transport Workers): SBS Edif. Seguradoras, 11° andar, 70.072 Brasília, DF; tel. (61) 224-5011; telex (61) 1593; f. 1952; 300,000 mems; Pres. ORLANDO COUTINHO.

Confederação Nacional dos Trabalhadores em Comunicações e Publicidade (CONTCOP) (Communications and Advertising Workers): SCS, Edif. Serra Dourada, 7° andar, Gr. 705/708, Quadra 11, 70.365 Brasília, DF; tel. (61) 224-7926; f. 1964; Pres. JOSÉ ALCEU PORTOCARRERO.

Confederação Nacional dos Trabalhadores nas Empresas de Crédito (CONTEC) (Workers in Credit Institutions): SEP-SUL, Av. W4, EQ 707/907 Lote E, 70.351 Brasília, DF; tel. (61) 244-5833; telex (61) 2745; f. 1958; 814,532 mems (1988); Pres. LOURENÇO FERREIRA DO PRADO.

Confederação Nacional dos Trabalhadores em Estabelecimentos de Educação e Cultura (CNTEEC) (Workers in Education and Culture): SAS, Quadra 4, Bloco B, 70.302 Brasília, DF; tel. (61) 226-2988; f. 1967; Pres. MIGUEL ABRAHÃO.

Confederação Nacional dos Trabalhadores na Agricultura (CONTAG) (Agricultural Workers): MSPW, Conjunto 502, Lote 2, Núcleo Bandeirante, 70.750 Brasília, DF; tel. (61) 552-0259; f. 1964; Pres. JOSÉ FRANCISCO DA SILVA.

Transport

Conselho Nacional de Transportes: Ministry of Infrastructure, Esplanada dos Ministérios, Bloco R, 70.044 Brasília, DF; tel. (61) 321-8886; telex (61) 1096; f. 1961 to study, co-ordinate and execute government transport policy and reorganize railway, road and ports and waterways councils; Pres. JOSÉ REINALDO CARNEIRO TAVARES; Exec. Sec. JOSÉ ROBERTO DE ALMEIDA NEVES.

Empresa Brasileira de Planejamento de Transportes (GEIPOT): SAN, Quadra 3, Blocos N/O, Edif. Núcleo dos Transportes, 70.040 Brasília, DF; tel. (61) 226-7335; telex (61) 1354; f. 1973; agency for the promotion of an integrated modern transport system; advises the Minister of Infrastructure on transport policy; Pres. MARIO ANTONIO GARCIA PICANÇO.

Empresa Brasileira dos Transportes Urbanos (EBTU): SAN, Quadra 3, Lote A, 3° andar, 70.040 Brasília, DF; tel. (61) 226-7335; telex (61) 1604; f. 1975 to administer resources for national urban transportation programmes; Pres. WALTER LUIZ DO REGO LUNA.

RAILWAYS

Of a total network of 29,901 km, 2,094 km of track has been electrified. In 1987 the Government announced controversial plans

BRAZIL

to construct a 1,600 km north–south railway, at an estimated cost of US $2,600m., to link the city of Açailândia, in the state of Marahão, with Brasília. The first 163 km was officially inaugurated in 1989.

Rêde Ferroviária Federal, SA (RFFSA) (Federal Railway Corporation): Praça Procópio Ferreira 86, 20.221 Rio de Janeiro, RJ; tel. (21) 223-5795; telex (21) 21372; fax (21) 263-3128; f. 1957; holding company for 18 railways grouped into 12 regional networks, with a total of 22,300 km in 1989; a mixed company in which the Government holds the majority of the shares; Pres. MARTINIANO LAURO AMARAL DE OLIVEIRA; Vice-Pres. PAULO CESAR CHIARELLI FONSECA.

There are also railways owned by state governments and several privately-owned railways:

Companhia Brasileira de Trens Urbanos (CBTU): Velha da Tijuca 77, Usina, 20.531 Rio de Janeiro, RJ; tel. (21) 288-1992; telex (21) 22793; a subsidiary of RFFSA responsible for suburban networks and metro systems throughout Brazil. In 1988 CBTU was proposed for transfer to local state government control. Pres. E. IBRAHIM.

Companhia Vale de Rio Doce (Vitória–Minas Railway): Av. Graça Aranha 26, Castelo, 20.005 Rio de Janeiro, RJ; tel. (21) 272-4477; telex (21) 23162; f. 1942; state-owned; transportation of iron ore, general cargo, passengers; Estrada de Ferro Carajás (902 km) and Estrada de Ferro Vitória Minas (815 km); Pres. AGRIPINO ABRANCHES VIANA.

Estrada de Ferro do Amapá: Porto de Santana, Santana, 68.925 Amapá; tel. (96) 632-6160; fax (96) 632-6825; opened 1957; 194 km open in 1985; operated by Indústria e Comércio de Minérios, SA; Pres. MARCIO VON KRUGER.

Ferrovia Paulista, SA (FEPASA): Praça Julio Prestes 148, 01.218 São Paulo, SP; tel. (11) 223-7211; telex (11) 22724; fax (11) 223-7211; formed in 1971 by merger of five railways operated by São Paulo State; 5,072 km open in 1987; Pres. ANTÔNIO CARLOS RIOS CORRAL.

Other privately-owned mineral lines are: Estrada de Ferro Campos do Jordão (47 km open in 1985), Estrada de Ferro Perus–Pirapora (33 km open in 1985), Estrada de Ferro Votorantim (15 km open in 1985) and Estrada de Ferro Trombetas (f. 1984; 35 km open in 1985). In 1988 a private company, Companhia Ferroviária Paraná-Oeste (Ferroeste), was set up to build a 420-km railway to serve the grain production regions in Paraná and Mato Grosso do Sul.

ROADS

In 1989 there were 1,663,987 km of roads in Brazil, of which 8% were paved. Brasília has been a focal point for inter-regional development, and paved roads link the capital with every region of Brazil. The building of completely new roads has taken place predominantly in the north. Roads are the principal mode of transport, accounting for 70% of freight and 97% of passenger traffic, including long-distance bus services, in 1979. Major projects include the 5,000-km Trans-Amazonian Highway, running from Recife and Cabedelo to the Peruvian border, the 4,138-km Cuibá–Santarém highway, which will run in a north–south direction, and the 3,555-km Trans-Brasiliana project which will link Marabá, on the Trans-Amazonian highway, with Aceguá on the Uruguayan frontier. In 1990 the Government announced plans to privatize many of Brazil's major roads and transfer others from federal to state jurisdiction.

Departamento Nacional de Estradas de Rodagem (DNER) (National Roads Development): Av. Pres. Vargas 522/534, 20.071 Rio de Janeiro, RJ; tel. (21) 233-2493; telex (21) 23535; f. 1945 to plan and execute federal road policy and to supervise state and municipal roads with the aim of integrating them into the national network; Dir ANTÔNIO ALBERTO CANABRAVA.

INLAND WATERWAYS

River transport plays only a minor part in the movement of goods, although total freight carried increased from 4.7m. tons in 1980 to 6.9m. tons in 1985. There are three major river systems, the Amazon, Paraná and the São Francisco. The Amazon is navigable for 3,680 km, as far as Iquitos in Peru, and ocean-going ships can reach Manaus, 1,600 km upstream. Plans have been drawn up to improve the inland waterway system and one plan is to link the Amazon and Upper Paraná to provide a navigable waterway across the centre of the country.

Companhia Docas do Pará: Av. Pres. Vargas 41, 2° andar, 66.000 Belém, PA; tel. (91) 223-2055; telex (91) 2320; f. 1967; administers the port of Belém; Dir-Pres. AFFONSO LOPES FREIRE.

Empresa de Navegação da Amazônia, SA (ENASA): Av. Pres. Vargas 41, CP 1068, 66.000 Belém, PA; tel. (91) 223-3011; telex (91) 1311; f. 1967; cargo and passenger services on the Amazon river and its principal tributaries, connecting the port of Belém with Marajó, Santarém, Parintins, Manaus and other river ports; Pres. VICENTE DE PAULA QUEIROZ; fleet of 10 vessels amounting to 8,564 grt.

SHIPPING

There are 36 deep-water ports in Brazil, five of which, including the port of Santos which handles 30% of all cargo, are privately owned. The largest ports are Santos, Rio de Janeiro, Paranaguá, Recife and Vitória. Tubarão, an iron ore port, and Santana (Amapá) on the Amazon, from where manganese is exported, are among the ports already equipped with automated facilities. Both ports are being expanded, as are Recife and Maceió, the sugar ports, and Ilheus, the cocoa port, on the eastern seaboard. The two main oil terminals, at São Sebastião (São Paulo) and Madre de Jesus (Bahia), are being expanded. Port expansion plans also include the building of terminals at Areia Branca, Paranaguá and Rio Grande. A new iron ore terminal is under construction at Sepetiba, and a sugar terminal is to be built in São Paulo State. All ports will be deepened to accommodate vessels of over 40,000 tons. In 1988 the World Bank allocated a loan of US $20m. to Brazil for a project to increase the efficiency of the country's ports. Brazil's merchant fleet is the largest in Latin America. In 1984 it comprised 1,636 vessels (10m. tons), of which 150 were oil tankers and 1,486 were cargo vessels. In 1984 Brazil reached agreement with Bolivia on the construction of a port on the Caceres lagoon and the dredging of the Tamengo channel.

Secretaria de Transportes Aquaviários: Av. Rio Branco 115, 14° andar, 20.040 Rio de Janeiro, RJ; tel. (21) 221-4015; telex (21) 21652; f. 1941; supervisory board of the merchant marine; Gen. Sec. Dr CLAUDIO R. F. DECOURT.

Companhia de Navegação Lloyd Brasileiro: Rua do Rosario 1, CP 1501, 20.041 Rio de Janeiro, RJ; tel. (21) 291-0077; telex (21) 23364; fax (21) 253-4867; f. 1890; partly government-owned; operates between Brazil, the USA, Northern Europe, Scandinavia, the Mediterranean, East and West Africa, the Far East, the Arabian Gulf, Japan, Australia and New Zealand, and around the South American coast through the associated company Lloyd-Libra. Operates with pelletized, containerized and frozen cargoes, as well as with general and bulk cargoes; Pres. MIGUEL MASELLA; 24 vessels.

Companhia de Navegação Marítima (NETUMAR): Av. Presidente Vargas 482, 22° andar, 20.000 Rio de Janeiro, RJ; tel. (21) 203-1272; telex (21) 22732; f. 1959; coastal traffic including Amazon region, foreign trade to USA and Canada, east coast and Great Lakes ports, Argentina and Uruguay; Dir JOSÉ CARLOS LEAL; 7 vessels.

Companhia de Navegação do Norte (CONAN): Av. Rio Branco 45, 23° e 25° andares, Rio de Janeiro, RJ; tel. (21) 223-4155; telex (21) 33154; fax (21) 253-7128; f. 1965; services to Brazil, Argentina, Uruguay and inland waterways; Chair. J. R. RIBEIRO SALOMÃO; 8 vessels.

Empresa de Navegação Aliança, SA: Av. Pasteur 110, Botafogo, 22.290 Rio de Janeiro, RJ; tel. (21) 546-1122; telex (21) 23778; f. 1950; cargo services to Argentina, Europe, Baltic, Atlantic and North Sea ports; Pres. CARLOS G. E. FISCHER; 14 vessels.

Empresa de Navegação Amazônica, SA: Av. Presidente Vargas 41, CP 199, Belém, PA; tel. (91) 223-3234; telex (91) 1311; cargo services between the Amazon region, Mexico, the Caribbean, the US Gulf ports, the east coast of the USA and Northern Europe; Pres. E. M. FRAZÃO; 8 vessels.

Empresa de Navegação Mercantil, SA: Rua da Assembléia 100, 8° andar, 20.011 Rio de Janeiro, RJ; tel. (21) 224-9232; telex (21) 34729; f. 1976 for the carriage of liquid and solid bulk cargoes; Pres. JOSÉ CELSO MACEDO SOARES GUIMARÃES; 8 vessels amounting to 255,863 grt.

Frota Oceânica Brasileira, SA: Av. Venezuela 110, CP 21-020, 20.081 Rio de Janeiro, RJ; tel. (21) 291-5153; telex (21) 23564; fax (21) 263-1439; f. 1947; Pres. JOSÉ CARLOS FRAGOSO PIRES; Vice-Pres. P. MORAND; 14 vessels.

Linhas Brasileiras de Navegação, SA (LIBRA): Av. Rio Branco 25, 15° andar, 20.090 Rio de Janeiro, RJ; tel. (21) 223-2017; telex (21) 21382; Pres. W. PENHA BORGES; 9 cargo vessels.

Petróleo Brasileiro, SA (Petrobrás) (Departamento de Transportes—DETRAN): Avda República do Chile 65, 12 andar, 20.035 Rio de Janeiro, RJ; tel. (21) 212-4477; telex (21) 21486; Pres. S. UEKI; tanker fleet of 81 vessels.

Vale do Rio Doce Navegação, SA (DOCENAVE): Rua Voluntários da Pátria 143, Botafogo, 20.000 Rio de Janeiro, RJ; tel. (21) 536-8002; telex (21) 22142; fax (21) 266-3592; bulk carrier to Japan, Arabian Gulf, Europe, North America and Argentina; Dir CARLOS AUTO DE ANDRADE; 17 vessels.

CIVIL AVIATION

There are about 1,500 airports and airstrips. Of the 48 principal airports 21 are international, although most international traffic is

BRAZIL

handled by the two airports at Rio de Janeiro and two at São Paulo. A new international airport was opened at Guarulhos, near São Paulo, in January 1985.

Serviços Aéreos Cruzeiro do Sul, SA: Av. Almirante Sílvio de Noronha 365, CP 190, 200.21 Rio de Janeiro, RJ; tel. (21) 297-5141; telex (21) 21765; fax (21) 240-6859; f. 1927; in 1975 VARIG purchased an 86% participation in the company; network routes: Brazil, Argentina, Barbados, Bolivia, Colombia, French Guiana, Suriname, Trinidad and Tobago, Uruguay; Pres. Dr AGUINALDO DE MELO JUNQUEIRA; fleet: 6 Boeing 727-100, 6 Boeing 737-200, 2 Airbus A-300 B4.

Transbrasil SA Linhas Aéreas: Aeroporto Internacional de Brasília, CEP, 71.600 Brasília; tel. (61) 1115; telex (61) 1115; fax (61) 224-9033; f. 1955 as Sadia, renamed 1972; scheduled passenger and cargo services to major Brazilian cities and Orlando; cargo charter flights to the USA; Chair. Dr OMAR FONTANA; fleet: 3 Boeing 707-320C, 3 Boeing 767-200, 11 Boeing 737-300, 8 Boeing 727-100, 1 Boeing 727-100C.

VARIG, SA (Viação Aérea Rio Grandense): Edif. Varig., Av. Almte Sílvio Noronha 365, 20.021 Rio de Janeiro, RJ; tel. (21) 297-5141; telex (21) 22363; f. 1927; international services; Argentina, Chile, Colombia, Costa Rica, Ecuador, Panama, Paraguay, Peru, Uruguay, Venezuela, Mexico, Canada, the USA, Angola, Côte d'Ivoire, Japan, Nigeria, Mozambique, South Africa and Western Europe; domestic services to major Brazilian cities; cargo services; Chair. and Pres. RUBEL THOMAS; fleet: 5 Boeing 707-320-C, 6 Boeing 727-100, 4 Boeing 727-100C, 12 Boeing 737-200, 3 Boeing 747-200B, 2 747-300 Combi, 4 Boeing 737-300, 3 Boeing 747-300, 6 Boeing 767-200ER, 2 Airbus A-300B4, 2 DC10-30F, 10 DC10-30, 14 Lockheed 188 Electra.

VASP, SA (Viação Aérea São Paulo): 04695 Edif. VASP, Aeroporto Congonhas, São Paulo, SP; tel. (11) 533-7011; telex (11) 56575; fax (11) 533-7011; f. 1933; privatized in Sept. 1990; international services to Aruba, Argentina, the Netherlands Antilles and the USA; domestic services covering all Brazil; Chair. and Pres. ANTONIO ANGARITA DE SILVA; fleet: 2 Boeing 727-200, 20 Boeing 737-200 Super Advanced, 6 Boeing 737-300, 3 Airbus A-300 B2.

In addition to the airlines listed above, there are a number of others operating regional services.

Tourism

In 1988 about 1.7m. tourists visited Brazil. Rio de Janeiro, with its famous beaches, is the centre of the tourist trade. Like Salvador, Recife and other towns, it has excellent examples of Portuguese colonial and modern architecture. The modern capital, Brasília, incorporates a new concept of city planning and is the nation's show-piece. Other attractions are the Iguaçu Falls, the seventh largest (by volume) in the world, and the tropical forests of the Amazon basin.

Centro Brasileiro de Informação Turística (CEBITUR): Rua Mariz e Barros 13, 6° andar, Praça da Bandeira, 20.270 Rio de Janeiro, RJ; tel. (21) 293-1313; telex (21) 21066; Pres. RICARDO MESQUITA DE FARIA.

Conselho Nacional de Turismo (CNTUR) (National Tourism Office): Ministry of Infrastructure, Rua Mariz e Barros 13, 5° andar, 20.270 Rio de Janeiro, RJ; tel. (21) 273-0691; f. 1966; Pres. JOSÉ EDUARDO GUINLER; Exec. Sec. JOSÉ E. CÁSSIO TEIXEIRA.

Divisão de Feiras e Turismo/Departamento de Promoção Comercial: Ministério das Relações Exteriores, Esplanada dos Ministérios, 2° andar, 70.170 Brasília, DF; tel. (61) 211-6644; f. 1977; organizes Brazil's participation in trade fairs and commercial exhibitions abroad; Sec. EDSON MARINHO DUARTE MONTEIRO.

Empresa Brasileira de Turismo—EMBRATUR: Rua Mariz e Barros 13, 12° andar, 20.270 Rio de Janeiro, RJ; tel. (21) 273-2212; telex (21) 21066; f. 1966; Pres. PEDRO GROSSI FILHO.

Atomic Energy

Brazil's first nuclear power station, at Angra dos Reis, RJ, commenced commercial operation (power of 626 MW) in early 1985, after design deficiencies had caused delays. Following an agreement between Brazil and the Federal Republic of Germany (West Germany), two other plants, of 1,300 MW (Angra II and III), were to be constructed at the same site, with Brazilian participation, and were originally expected to become operational in 1992 and 1995 respectively. Work on two further planned plants was postponed in 1983 owing to lack of available finance. In September 1985 construction of the Angra III plant and of two further plants, Iguape I and II, was postponed indefinitely. The construction of the Angra II plant was to be completed by 1995. Development within the sector has been severely hampered by government spending cuts in recent years. In 1987 the Angra I plant was closed for several months because of generating difficulties. A plant for enriching uranium was under construction at Iperó.

In 1988 the Government announced an extensive reorganization of the nuclear power sector, including the creation of the Conselho Superior de Política Nuclear and the dissolution of Nucleares Brasileiras (NUCLEBRÁS). In addition, the management and development of nuclear power plants was transferred to the electricity sector, principally to ELETROBRÁS.

In 1989 about 0.7% of Brazil's total production of electricity was generated by the Agra I plant.

Research reactors: The following research reactors are in operation:

(CDTN-RI) CDTN-NUCLEBRÁS, Belo Horizonte, MG; thermal power 250 kW.

(IPEN-RI) IPEN, São Paulo, SP; thermal power 5 MW.

(IEN-RI) IEN-CNEN, Rio de Janeiro, RJ; thermal power 10 kW.

(URANIE) CDTN-NUCLEBRÁS, Belo Horizonte, MG (subcritical).

(RESUCO) DEN-UFPe, Recife, Pe (subcritical).

(NC-9000) CTA, São José dos Campos, SP (subcritical).

(CAPITU) CDTN-NUCLEBRÁS, Belo Horizonte, MG (subcritical).

(SUBLIME) IME, Rio de Janeiro, RJ (planned).

Conselho Superior de Política Nuclear (CSPN): f. 1988; to determine and supervise the implementation of Brazil's nuclear power programme.

Comissão Nacional de Energia Nuclear (CNEN): Rua General Severiano 90, Botafogo, 22.294 Rio de Janeiro, RJ; tel. (21) 295-2232; telex (21) 21280; f. 1956; controlling organization for: Centro de Desenvolvimento da Tecnologia Nuclear—CDTN (nuclear research); Instituto de Engenharia Nuclear—IEN (nuclear engineering); Instituto de Radioproteção e Dosimetria—IRD (radiation protection and dosimetry) and Instituto de Pesquisas Energéticas e Nucleares—IPEN (energetics and nuclear research); in 1988 assumed responsibility for management of nuclear power programme; 1988 budget estimate: CZ $10,000m.; Pres. REX NAZARÉ ÁLVES.

Indústrias Nucleares do Brasil: f. 1988 to replace NUCLEBRÁS; responsible for construction and financing of nuclear power plants; Pres. JOHN FOREMAN.

Urânio do Brasil: f. 1988 to replace NUCLEBRÁS; responsible for fuel-cycle (from extraction of uranium to processing stage).

As a result of the agreement that Brazil and the Federal Republic of Germany (West Germany) signed in July 1975, four joint ventures between NUCLEBRÁS and West German firms were established: NUCLAM (mining), NUCLEI (enrichment by the nozzle method), NUCLEN (engineering) and NUCLEP (heavy equipment) and NUSTEP (in West Germany). In accordance with the Government's reorganization of the sector, announced in 1988, NUCLAM and NUSTEP were closed down; NUCLEI's activities were transferred to Urânio do Brasil; NUCLEN became a subsidiary of ELETROBRÁS; and NUCLEP was to be privatized.

BRUNEI

Introductory Survey

Location, Climate, Language, Religion, Flag, Capital

The Sultanate of Brunei (Negara Brunei Darussalam) lies in South-East Asia, on the north-west coast of the island of Kalimantan (Borneo, most of which is Indonesian territory). It is surrounded and bisected on the landward side by Sarawak, one of the two eastern states of Malaysia. The country has a tropical climate, characterized by consistent temperature and humidity. Average annual rainfall ranges from about 2,400 mm (95 in) in lowland areas to about 4,000 mm (158 in) in the interior. Temperatures are high, with the annual extreme range being 23°C (73°F) to 35.8°C (96.4°F). The principal language is Malay, although Chinese is also spoken and English is widely used. At the 1981 census 63.4% of the population were adherents of Islam, the official religion, while 14.0% were Buddhists and 9.7% Christians. The Malay population (68.8% of the total in 1989) are mainly Sunni Muslims. Most of the Chinese in Brunei are Buddhists, and some are also adherents of Confucianism and Daoism. Europeans and Eurasians are predominantly Christians. The flag (proportions 2 by 1) is yellow, with two diagonal stripes, of white and black, running from the upper hoist to the lower fly; superimposed in the centre is the state emblem (in red, with yellow Arabic inscriptions). The capital is Bandar Seri Begawan (formerly called Brunei Town).

Recent History

Brunei, a traditional Islamic monarchy, formerly included most of the coastal regions of North Borneo (now Sabah) and Sarawak, which later became states of Malaysia. During the 19th century the rulers of Brunei ceded large parts of their territory to the United Kingdom, reducing the sultanate to its present size. In 1888, when North Borneo became a British protectorate, Brunei became a British Protected State. In accordance with an agreement made in 1906, a British Resident was appointed to the court of the ruling Sultan as an adviser on administration. Under this arrangement, a form of government that included an advisory State Council emerged.

Brunei was invaded by Japanese forces in December 1941, but reverted to its former status in 1945, when the Second World War ended. The British-appointed Governor of Sarawak was High Commissioner for Brunei from 1948 until the territory's first written constitution was promulgated in September 1959, when a further agreement was made between the Sultan and the British Government. The United Kingdom continued to be responsible for Brunei's defence and external affairs until the Sultanate's declaration of independence in 1984.

In December 1962 a large-scale revolt broke out in Brunei and in parts of Sarawak and North Borneo. The rebellion was undertaken by the 'North Borneo Liberation Army', an organization linked with the Parti Rakyat Brunei (PRB—Brunei People's Party), led by Sheikh Ahmad Azahari, which was strongly opposed to the planned entry of Brunei into the Federation of Malaysia. The rebels proclaimed the 'revolutionary State of North Kalimantan', but the revolt was suppressed, after 10 days' fighting, with the aid of British forces from Singapore. A state of emergency was declared, the PRB was banned, and Azahari was given asylum in Malaya. In the event, the Sultan of Brunei, Sir Omar Ali Saifuddin III, decided in 1963 against joining the Federation. From 1962 he ruled by decree, and the state of emergency remained in force. In October 1967 Saifuddin, who had been Sultan since 1950, abdicated in favour of his son, Hassanal Bolkiah, who was then 21 years of age. Under an agreement signed in November 1971, Brunei was granted full internal self-government.

In December 1975 the UN General Assembly adopted a resolution advocating British withdrawal from Brunei, the return of political exiles and the holding of a general election. Negotiations in 1978, following assurances by Malaysia and Indonesia that they would respect Brunei's sovereignty, resulted in an agreement (signed in January 1979) that Brunei would become fully independent within five years. Independence was duly proclaimed on 1 January 1984, and the Sultan took office as Prime Minister and Minister of Finance and of Home Affairs, presiding over a cabinet of six other ministers (including two of the Sultan's brothers and his father, the former Sultan).

The future of the Chinese population, who controlled much of Brunei's private commercial sector but had become stateless since independence, appeared threatened in 1985, when the Sultan indicated that Brunei would become an Islamic state in which the indigenous, mainly Malay, inhabitants, known as *bumiputras* ('sons of the soil'), would receive preferential treatment. Several Hong Kong and Taiwan Chinese, who were not permanent Brunei residents, were repatriated.

In May 1985 a new political party, the Brunei National Democratic Party (BNDP), was formed. The new party, which comprised businessmen loyal to the Sultan, based its policies on Islam and a form of liberal nationalism. However, the Sultan forbade employees of the Government (about 40% of the country's working population) to join the party. Persons belonging to the Chinese community were also excluded from membership. Divisions within the new party led to the formation of a second group, the Brunei National United Party, in February 1986. This party, which also received the Sultan's official approval, placed greater emphasis on co-operation with the Government, and was open to both Muslim and non-Muslim ethnic groups.

Although the Sultan was not expected to allow any relaxation of restrictions on radical political activities, it became clear during 1985 and 1986 that a more progressive style of government was being adopted. The death of Sir Omar Ali Saifuddin, the Sultan's father, in September 1986 was expected to hasten modernization. In October the Cabinet was enlarged to 11 members when the Sultan carried out a government reshuffle, in which commoners and aristocrats were assigned portfolios that had previously been given to members of the royal family. In February 1988, however, the BNDP was dissolved by the authorities after it had demanded the resignation of the Sultan as Head of Government (although not as Head of State), an end to the 26-year state of emergency and the holding of democratic elections. The official reason for the dissolution of the party was its connections with a foreign organization, the Pacific Democratic Union. The leaders of the BNDP, Abdul Latif Hamid and Abdul Latif Chuchu, were arrested, under provisions of the Internal Security Act, and detained until March 1990. Abdul Latif Hamid died in May. In January of that year the Government ordered the release of six political prisoners, who had been detained soon after the revolt in 1962.

In 1990 the Government encouraged the population to embrace *Melayu Islam Beraja* (Malay Islamic Monarchy) as the state ideology. This affirmation of traditional Bruneian values for Malay Muslims was widely believed to be a response to an increase in social problems, which constituted a potential threat to national security.

Relations with the United Kingdom had become strained during 1983, following the Brunei Government's decision, in August, to transfer the management of its investment portfolio from the British Crown Agents to the newly-created Brunei Investment Agency. However, normal relations were restored in September, when the British Government agreed that a battalion of Gurkha troops, stationed in Brunei since 1971, should remain in Brunei after independence, at the Sultanate's expense, specifically to guard the oil and gas fields. This arrangement could, however, be under threat, owing to British uncertainty concerning the future of Gurkha forces after 1997, when Hong Kong (the site of the main Gurkha base) reverts to Chinese rule. The level of co-operation between Brunei and the United Kingdom was demonstrated by the extensive joint military exercise which took place in August 1988.

Brunei has developed close relations with the members of ASEAN (see p. 103), in particular Singapore, and became a full member of the organization immediately after independence. Royal visits were made to Thailand and Indonesia in 1984, and diplomatic relations with Japan were established in the same year. Brunei also joined the UN, the Commonwealth and the Organization of the Islamic Conference in 1984. A meeting of ASEAN Ministers of Foreign Affairs took place in Bandar Seri Begawan in July 1989.

In early 1987 the Brunei Government was highly embarrassed by the disclosure that the Sultan had arranged a contribution of US $10m. in 'humanitarian' aid to Nicaraguan 'Contra' rebels, and that this donation (made in response to a request by US officials at a time when all aid to the Contras from the USA had been prohibited by the US Congress) had been mistakenly deposited in a Swiss businessman's bank account. In July 1990, in response to the uncertainty over the future of US bases in the Philippines (see chapter on the Philippines, Vol. II), Brunei joined Singapore in offering the USA the option of operating its forces from Brunei.

In March 1987 Brunei showed interest in joining the Five-Power Defence Agreement, linking the United Kingdom, Malaysia, Singapore, Australia and New Zealand. Brunei's relations with Malaysia improved considerably in early 1987, when Malaysia offered to help Brunei with the establishment of an army reserve force, and in March, when the Malaysian Prime Minister, Datuk Seri Dr Mahathir Mohamad, visited Brunei for discussions. In September the two countries announced possible future co-operation in the production of defence equipment. In October 1989 Brunei signed a memorandum of understanding with the British Government for the purchase of fighter aircraft, patrol vessels and other military equipment, worth £250m.

In September 1987 the Sultan offered Indonesia a $100m. interest-free loan for industrial and transport projects, repayable over 25 years with a seven-year grace period.

Government

The 1959 Constitution confers supreme executive authority on the Sultan. He is assisted and advised by four Constitutional Councils: the Religious Council, the Privy Council, the Council of Cabinet Ministers and the Council of Succession. Since the rebellion of 1962, certain provisions of the Constitution have been suspended, and the Sultan has ruled by decree.

Defence

In June 1990 the Royal Brunei Malay Regiment numbered 4,200 (including 250 women): army 3,400; navy 500; air force 300. Military service is voluntary. Paramilitary forces comprised 1,750 Royal Brunei Police. The defence budget for 1988 was estimated at B $490.8m. A Gurkha battalion of the British army, comprising about 900 men has been stationed in Brunei since 1971. There are also about 500 troops from Singapore, operating a training school in Brunei.

Economic Affairs

In 1987, according to estimates by the World Bank, Brunei's gross domestic product (GDP), measured at average 1985–87 prices, was US $3,317m., equivalent to US $14,120 per head. Over the period 1980–87, it was estimated, GDP declined, in real terms, at an average annual rate of 0.7%, while real GDP per head declined at an average rate of 4.0% per year. During 1980–88 the population increased by 3.4% annually.

Agriculture (including forestry and fishing) employed 5.0% of the working population in 1981 and provided only 1.3% of GDP (provisional) in 1985. About 15% of the total land area is cultivated; the principal crops include rice, cassava, bananas and pineapples. The total fishing catch in 1987 was 2,652 metric tons, providing about 65% of domestic consumption. In 1985 Brunei imported 80% of its total food requirements.

Industry (comprising mining, manufacturing, construction and utilities) employed 31.2% of the working population in 1981 and contributed 67.8% of GDP (provisional) in 1985.

Brunei's economy depends almost entirely on its petroleum and natural gas resources. The mining sector employed only 5.7% of the working population in 1981 but it provided 53.6% of GDP (provisional) in 1985. Production of crude petroleum from the six offshore and two onshore fields averaged 150,000 barrels per day in 1989. Output of natural gas averaged 877m. cu ft (24.8m. cu m) per day in that year. Petroleum and natural gas together accounted for 96.3% of total export earnings in 1989. Reserves of petroleum were estimated at 1,686.3m. barrels in 1986, and those of natural gas at 225,000m. cu m in 1988. About 1.0% of petroleum production is used for domestic energy requirements.

Manufacturing is dominated by petroleum refining. The sector employed 4.1% of the working population in 1981 and contributed 10.3% of GDP (provisional) in 1985. By the late 1980s, several brickworks were in operation, and it was hoped that industries such as microchips, textiles, furniture, foodstuffs and concrete could be developed.

In 1989 imports amounted to an estimated B $2,359.5m., and revenue from exports an estimated B $3,693.5m., resulting in a trade surplus of B $1,334m. In 1986 Japan was Brunei's major trading partner, accounting for 66.9% of total exports (mainly natural gas on a long-term contract). Other major trading partners include Thailand, the Republic of Korea, Singapore and the USA. Principal imports comprised basic manufactures, machinery and transport equipment, food and live animals and chemicals; principal exports were crude petroleum and natural gas.

In 1988 government revenue, excluding investment income (unofficially estimated at between US $1,500m. and US $2,500m. in 1987), totalled B $2,486.7m., and expenditure B $2,721.4m., resulting in a budgetary deficit of B $234.7m. Brunei has no external public debt. International reserves totalled an estimated US $25,000m. in 1988. During 1980–88 consumer prices declined at an average rate of 4.4% per year, but in 1989 the annual rate of inflation averaged 1.3%. Foreign workers, principally from Malaysia and the Philippines, have helped to ease the labour shortage resulting from the small size of the population, and comprised about one-third of the labour force in 1985.

Brunei is a member of the Association of South East Asian Nations (see p. 103), and the UN Economic and Social Commission for Asia and the Pacific (see p. 25), which aim to accelerate economic progress in the region.

Brunei recognizes a need to diversify its economy. The Government's fifth Development Plan (1986–90) aimed to reduce dependence on income from petroleum and natural gas and to achieve self-sufficiency in food production. New emphasis was placed on the development of the private sector, and plans were announced for the conversion of Brunei into a regional centre for banking and finance. In the late 1980s unemployment began to rise (from 3.6% of the labour force in 1988 to 6% in 1989), owing to a shortage of non-manual jobs for the well-educated Bruneians. Since Brunei lacks the technology and marketing expertise to diversify on its own, it hoped to attract 2,000 new ventures by 1995, which were expected to provide 20,000–30,000 jobs.

Social Welfare

Free medical services are provided by the Government. In 1989 there were 171 physicians working in the country and 893 hospital beds. The main 550-bed central referral hospital is in Bandar Seri Begawan, but there are three other hospitals (in Kuala Belait, Tutong and Temburong), as well as private facilities provided by Brunei Shell. For medical care not available in Brunei, citizens are sent abroad at the Government's expense. There is a 'flying doctor' service, as well as various clinics, travelling dispensaries and dental clinics. A non-contributory state pensions scheme for elderly and disabled persons came into operation in 1955. The State also provides financial assistance to the poor, the destitute and widows. Under the 1986–90 Development Plan, B $756.9m. was allocated to health and social services. National pension schemes were to be introduced by the Government under the 1986–90 Plan.

Education

Education is free, and Islamic studies form an integral part of the school curriculum. Pupils who are Brunei citizens and live more than 8 km (5 miles) from their schools are entitled to free accommodation in hostels, free transport or a subsistence allowance. Schools are classified according to the language of instruction, i.e. Malay, English or Chinese (Mandarin). In 1989 total enrolment in primary schools was 40,611, while in general secondary schools and sixth-form centres enrolment was 19,761. In 1989 there was one teacher-training college, five colleges for vocational and technical education, one institute of higher education and one university. The University of Brunei Darussalam was formally established in 1985, but many students continue to be sent to universities abroad, at government expense. In 1989 935 students were enrolled at the four faculties. A new campus was scheduled to be completed in 1992, and intake was to be expanded to 2,000 students. In 1980 the estimated literacy rates for males and females aged nine years and above were 91.7% and 81.9% respectively. The 1985 budget allocated B $231m. to education.

BRUNEI

Public Holidays

1991: 1 January (New Year's Day), 12 February† (Isra Meraj, Ascension of the Prophet Muhammad), 15-17 February* (Chinese New Year), 23 February (National Day), 17 March† (First Day of Ramadan), 2 April† (Anniversary of the Revelation of the Koran), 16 April† (Hari Raya Puasa, end of Ramadan), 1 May (Anniversary of the Royal Brunei Malay Regiment), 23 June† (Hari Raya Haji, Feast of the Sacrifice), 13 July† (Hizrah, Islamic New Year), 15 July (Sultan's Birthday), 21 September† (Hari Mouloud, Birth of the Prophet), 25 December (Christmas).

1992: 1 January (New Year's Day), 1 February† (Isra Meraj, Ascension of the Prophet), 4-6 February* (Chinese New Year), 23 February (National Day), 5 March† (First Day of Ramadan), 21 March† (Anniversary of the Revelation of the Koran), 4 April† (Hari Raya Puasa, end of Ramadan), 1 May (Anniversary of the Royal Brunei Malay Regiment), 11 June† (Hari Raya Haji, Feast of the Sacrifice), 2 July† (Hizrah, Islamic New Year), 15 July (Sultan's Birthday), 10 September† (Hari Mouloud, Birth of the Prophet), 25 December (Christmas).

* From the first to the third day of the first moon of the lunar calendar.
† These holidays are dependent on the Islamic lunar calendar and may vary by one or two days from the dates given.

Weights and Measures

The imperial system is in operation but local measures of weight and capacity are used. These include the gantang (1 gallon), the tahil (1⅓ oz) and the kati (1⅓ lb).

Statistical Survey

Source (unless otherwise stated): Economic Planning Unit, Ministry of Finance, Bandar Seri Begawan 2012; tel. (02) 241991; telex 2676; fax (02) 226132.

AREA, POPULATION AND DENSITY

Area: 5,765 sq km (2,226 sq miles); *by district:* Brunei/Muara 570 sq km (220 sq miles), Seria/Belait 2,725 sq km (1,052 sq miles), Tutong 1,165 sq km (450 sq miles), Temburong 1,305 sq km (504 sq miles).

Population (excluding transients afloat): 192,832 (males 102,942, females 89,890) at census of 25 August 1981; 249,000 (males 128,600, females 120,400) at mid-1989 (official estimates). *By district* (1981 census): Brunei/Muara 114,231; Seria/Belait 50,768; Tutong 21,615; Temburong 6,218.

Principal Town: Bandar Seri Begawan (capital), population 50,500 (1986 estimate).

Density (mid-1989): 43.2 per sq km.

Ethnic Groups (mid-1989): Malay 171,300, Chinese 44,400, Other indigenous 13,100, Others 20,200, Total 249,000.

Births, Marriages and Deaths: Live births (registrations) 6,881 in 1988 (birth rate 28.5 per 1,000); Marriages 1,783 (Islamic 1,411, Others 372) in 1989; Deaths (registrations) 777 in 1988 (death rate 3.2 per 1,000).

Economically Active Population (1981 census): Agriculture, hunting, forestry and fishing 3,435; Mining and quarrying 3,863; Manufacturing 2,783; Electricity, gas and water 1,961; Construction 12,644; Trade, restaurants and hotels 7,363; Transport, storage and communications 4,529; Financing, insurance, real estate and business services 2,010; Community, social and personal services 29,282; Activities not adequately defined 258; Total employed 68,128 (males 52,737; females 15,391); Unemployed 2,562 (males 1,122; females 1,440); Total labour force 70,690 (males 53,859; females 16,831).

1986: Total labour force 86,400 (males 59,900; females 26,500): employed 81,100; unemployed 5,300.

AGRICULTURE, ETC.
(Source: FAO)

Principal Crops (FAO estimates, '000 metric tons, 1989): Rice (paddy) 1, Cassava (Manioc) 1, Vegetables (incl. melons) 9, Fruit 5 (Pineapples 1, Bananas 1).

Livestock (FAO estimates, '000 head, year ending September 1989): Cattle 1, Buffaloes 10, Pigs 23, Goats 1, Poultry 3,000.

Livestock Products (FAO estimates, metric tons, 1989): Poultry meat 5,000; Hen eggs 3,000.

Forestry (FAO estimates, '000 cu m, 1989): *Roundwood removals:* Sawlogs, veneer logs and logs for sleepers 206; Other industrial wood 9; Fuel wood 79; Total 294. *Sawnwood production:* Total (incl. boxboards) 90.

Fishing (metric tons, live weight, 1988): Inland waters 1,214 (common carp 570, other freshwater fishes 608, Giant river prawn 36); Pacific Ocean 2,062 (Marine fishes 1,622, Crustaceans and molluscs 440); Total catch 3,276.

MINING

Production (1989): Crude petroleum 150,000 barrels per day; Casing head petroleum spirit 718,000 metric tons (1987); Natural gas 877m. cu ft per day.

INDUSTRY

Production ('000 metric tons, 1987): Motor spirit (petrol) 125.4; Distillate fuel oils 77.0; Kerosene 29.7; Naphthas 6.8 (1985); Electric energy (million kWh) 1,114.1 (1988).

FINANCE

Currency and Exchange Rates: 100 sen (cents) = 1 Brunei dollar (B $). *Coins:* 1, 5, 10, and 50 cents. *Notes:* 1, 5, 10, 50, 100, 500 and 1,000 dollars. *Sterling and US Dollar Equivalents* (30 September 1990): £1 sterling = B $3.3010; US $1 = B $1.7645; B $100 = £30.29 = US $56.67. *Average Exchange Rate* (Brunei dollars per US $): 2.1060 in 1987; 2.0124 in 1988; 1.9503 in 1989. Note: The Brunei dollar is at par with the Singapore dollar.

Budget (estimates, B $ million, 1984): *Revenue:* Total 6,500; *Expenditure:* Royal Brunei Malay Regiment 340.2, Public works 231.3, Education 216.2, Transfer to Development Fund 950, Total (incl. others) 2,651. **1988** (estimates, B $ million): Revenue 2,486.7, Expenditure 2,721.4.

Cost of Living (Consumer Price Index; base: 1977 = 100): 150.9 in 1987; 152.7 in 1988; 154.7 in 1989.

Gross Domestic Product (B $ million in current purchasers' values): 5,858.4 in 1987; 5,915.8 in 1988; 6,440.5 in 1989.

EXTERNAL TRADE

Principal Commodities (B $ million, 1986): *Imports:* Food and live animals 209.1, Beverages and tobacco 84.9, Crude materials (inedible) except fuels 17.4, Mineral fuels, lubricants, etc. 14.6, Animal and vegetable oils and fats 5.5, Chemicals 101.5, Basic manufactures 305.7, Machinery and transport equipment 550.8, Miscellaneous manufactured articles 160.0, Total (incl. others) 1,450.4. *Exports:* Crude petroleum 1,619.9, Petroleum products 146.7, Natural gas 2,110.7, Total (incl. others) 3,990.1.
1989 (B $ million, estimates) *Imports:* Total 2,359.5. *Exports:* Crude petroleum 1,732.9, Natural gas 1,645.9, Casing head petroleum spirit 179.5, Total (incl. others) 3,693.5.

Principal Trading Partners (B $ million, 1985): *Imports:* Australia 37.2, China, People's Republic 27.4, Germany, Federal Republic 87.7, Japan 256.5, Malaysia (Peninsular) 75.5, Netherlands 48.4, Singapore 373.6, Taiwan 34.2, Thailand 45.2, United Kingdom 114.7, USA 177.2. *Exports:* Australia 33.3, Japan 2,667.9, Korea, Republic 293.6, Malaysia (Sarawak) 40.5, Singapore 266.7, Taiwan 67.1, Thailand 323.9, USA 243.2.

TRANSPORT

Road Traffic (registered vehicles, 1989): Private cars 99,997, Motor-cycles and scooters 3,924, Goods vehicles 11,450, Other vehicles 2,742, Total 118,113.

International Sea-borne Shipping (1986): *Vessels* ('000 net registered tons): Entered 11,458.9, Cleared 9,271.9. *Goods* ('000 metric tons): Loaded 18,627.0, Unloaded 671.7.

Civil Aviation (1989): Aircraft landings 4,806, aircraft take-offs 4,806 (1987); passenger arrivals 232,700, passenger departures

BRUNEI

226,100; freight loaded 7,028 metric tons, freight unloaded 1,437 metric tons.

TOURISM

Tourist Arrivals: 6,600 in 1986; 9,000 in 1987; 9,000 in 1988.

COMMUNICATIONS MEDIA

Radio receivers (1989): 92,000 in use.
Television receivers (1989, estimate): 63,000 in use.
Telephones (1989): 49,000 in use.
Book Production (1986): 15 titles; 38,000 copies.
Newspapers (1986): 2 (estimated combined circulation 70,000 copies per issue).
Other Periodicals (1986): 10 (estimated combined circulation 195,000 copies per issue).

Source: mainly UNESCO, *Statistical Yearbook*.

EDUCATION

1989:
Pre-primary: 157* schools; 428* teachers; 8,664 pupils.
Primary: 145* schools; 1,813* teachers; 40,611 pupils.
General Secondary: 27* schools; 1,713 teachers; 19,761 pupils.
Teacher Training: 1 college; 31 teachers; 278 pupils.
Vocational: 5 colleges; 295 teachers; 1,287 pupils.
Higher Education: 2 institutes; 214 teachers; 1,145 pupils.

* 1987 figures.

Directory

The Constitution

Note: Certain sections of the Constitution have been in abeyance since 1962.

A new constitution was promulgated on 29 September 1959. Under its provisions, sovereign authority is vested in the Sultan and Yang Di-Pertuan, who is assisted and advised by four Councils:

THE RELIGIOUS COUNCIL

In his capacity as head of the Islamic faith in Brunei, the Sultan and Yang Di-Pertuan is advised on all Islamic matters by the Religious Council, whose members are appointed by the Sultan and Yang Di-Pertuan.

THE PRIVY COUNCIL

This Council, presided over by the Sultan and Yang Di-Pertuan, is to advise the Sultan on matters concerning the Royal prerogative of mercy, the amendment of the Constitution and the conferment of ranks, titles and honours.

THE COUNCIL OF CABINET MINISTERS

Presided over by the Sultan and Yang Di-Pertuan, the Council of Cabinet Ministers considers all executive matters.

THE COUNCIL OF SUCCESSION

Subject to the Constitution, this Council is to determine the succession to the throne, should the need arise.

The State is divided into four administrative districts, in each of which is a District Officer responsible to the Prime Minister and Minister of Home Affairs.

The Government

HEAD OF STATE

Sultan and Yang Di-Pertuan: HM Sir MUDA HASSANAL BOLKIAH MU'IZZADDIN WADDAULAH (succeeded 4 October 1967; crowned 1 August 1968).

COUNCIL OF CABINET MINISTERS
(November 1990)

Prime Minister and Minister of Defence: The Sultan and Yang Di-Pertuan, HM Sir MUDA HASSANAL BOLKIAH MU'IZZADDIN WADDAULAH.
Minister of Home Affairs and Special Adviser to the Prime Minister: Pehin Dato' Haji ISA.
Minister of Foreign Affairs: Pengiran Perdana Wazir Pengiran MUDA MOHAMAD BOLKIAH.
Minister of Finance: Pengiran Di-Gadong MUDA JEFRI BOLKIAH.
Minister of Industry and Primary Resources: Pehin Dato' Haji ABDUL RAHMAN BIN TAIB.
Minister of Law: Pengiran BAHRIN BIN Pengiran Haji ABAS.
Minister of Education: Pehin Dato' Haji ABDUL AZIZ.
Minister of Development: Pengiran Dato' Di Haji ISMAIL.
Minister of Communications: Dato' Haji AWANG ZAKARIA BIN Haji SULEIMAN.
Minister of Religious Affairs: Pehin Dato' Dr Haji MOHD ZAIN.
Minister of Culture, Youth and Sports: Pehin Dato' Haji HUSSEIN.
Minister of Health: Dato' Dr Haji JOHAR.

MINISTRIES

Office of the Prime Minister: Istana Nurul Iman, Bandar Seri Begawan; tel. (02) 229988; telex 2727.
Ministry of Communications: Old Airport, Bandar Seri Begawan 1150; tel. (02) 242526; telex 2682; fax (02) 220127.
Ministry of Culture, Youth and Sports: Jalan Residency, Bandar Seri Begawan; tel. (02) 240585; telex 2642; fax (02) 241620.
Ministry of Defence: Bolkiah Garrison, Bandar Seri Begawan 1110; tel. (02) 230130; telex 2840; fax 230110.
Ministry of Development: Old Airport, Berakas, Bandar Seri Begawan; tel. (02) 241911; telex 2722.
Ministry of Education: Old Airport, Berakas, Bandar Seri Begawan 1170; tel. (02) 244233; telex 2602; fax (02) 240250.
Ministry of Finance: Bandar Seri Begawan; tel. (02) 242405; telex 2674.
Ministry of Foreign Affairs: Jalan Subok, Bandar Seri Begawan; tel. (02) 241177; telex 2292.
Ministry of Health: Old Airport, Bandar Seri Begawan 1210; tel. 226640; telex 2421; fax (02) 240980.
Ministry of Home Affairs: Bandar Seri Begawan; tel. (02) 223225.
Ministry of Industry and Primary Resources: Bandar Seri Begawan.
Ministry of Law: Bandar Seri Begawan; tel. (02) 244872.
Ministry of Religious Affairs: Bandar Seri Begawan.

Political Organizations

Partai Perpaduan Kebangsaan Brunei—PPKB (Brunei National United Party—BNUP): Bandar Seri Begawan; f. 1986 after split in BNDP (see below); pro-Govt party; Sec.-Gen. AWANG HATTA Haji ZAINAL ABIDDIN.

There were formerly four other political organizations: **Parti Rakyat Brunei** (PRB, Brunei People's Party), which is banned and whose leaders are all in exile; **Barisan Kemerdeka'an Rakyat** (BAKER, People's Independence Front), f. 1966 but no longer active; **Parti Perpaduan Kebangsaan Rakyat Brunei** (PERKARA, Brunei People's National United Party), f. 1968 but no longer active, and **Parti Kebangsaan Demokratik Brunei—PKDB** (Brunei National Democratic Party—BNDP), f. 1985 and dissolved by government order in 1988.

Diplomatic Representation

EMBASSIES AND HIGH COMMISSIONS IN BRUNEI

Australia: 4th Floor, Teck Guan Plaza, cnr Jalan Sultan and Jalan McArthur, Bandar Seri Begawan; tel. (02) 229435; telex 3582; High Commissioner: PHILIP MOULTON KNIGHT.
France: POB 3027, Bandar Seri Begawan; Ambassador: PATRICK AMIOT.

BRUNEI

Germany: 49–50 Jalan Sultan, POB 3050, Bandar Seri Begawan; tel. (02) 225547; telex 2742; Ambassador: FRIEDRICH KREKELER.
Indonesia: LB 711, Jalan Kumbang Pasang, Bandar Seri Begawan; tel. (02) 221852; Ambassador: ZUWIR DJAMAL.
Japan: LB 16464 Kampong Mabohai, Jalan Kebangsaan, POB 3001; tel. (02) 229265; telex 2564; Chargé d'affaires: YUTAKA SHIMOMOTO.
Korea, Republic of: No. 9, Lot 21652, Kampong Beribi, Jalan Gadong, Bandar Seri Begawan; tel. (02) 650471; telex 2615; fax (02) 650299; Ambassador: HUH SE-LIN.
Malaysia: 6th Floor, Darussalam Bldg, Jalan Sultan, Bandar Seri Begawan; tel. (02) 228410; telex 2401; High Commissioner: ZAINAL ABIDIN BIN MOKHTAR.
Pakistan: LB 277, Kampong Telanai, Mile 3, Jalan Tutong; tel. (02) 651623; High Commissioner: SAQUIB MAWAZ-KHAN.
Philippines: 4th–5th Floors, Badi-ah Bldg, Mile 1, Jalan Tutong, Bandar Seri Begawan 1930; tel. (02) 228241; telex 2673; Ambassador: EUSEBIO A. ABAQUIN.
Singapore: 5th Floor, RBA Plaza, Jalan Sultan, Bandar Seri Begawan; tel. (02) 227583; telex 2385; High Commissioner: TAN KENG JIN.
Thailand: LB 241, Jalan Elia Fatimah, Kampong Kiarong, POB 2989, Bandar Seri Begawan 1929; tel. (02) 229653; telex 2607; Ambassador: SOMCHIT INSINGHA.
United Kingdom: 3rd Floor, Hongkong and Shanghai Bank Chambers, Jalan Pemancha, POB 2197, Bandar Seri Begawan; tel. (02) 222231; telex 2211; High Commissioner: ROGER WESTBROOK.
USA: 3rd Floor, Teck Guan Plaza, cnr Jalan Sultan and Jalan McArthur, Bandar Seri Begawan; tel. (02) 229670; telex 2609; Ambassador: THOMAS C. FERGUSON.

Judicial System

SUPREME COURT

The Supreme Court consists of the Court of Appeal and the High Court.
Chief Registrar, Supreme Court: AWANG KIFRAWI BIN Dato' PADUKA KIFLI (acting).
The Court of Appeal: POB 2231, Bandar Seri Begawan 1922; tel. (02) 225853; fax (02) 241984; composed of the President and two Commissioners appointed by the Sultan. The Court of Appeal considers criminal and civil appeals against the decisions of the High Court. **President:** Dato' Seri Paduka Sir TI-LIANG YANG.
The High Court: composed of the Chief Justice and such Commissioners as the Sultan may appoint. In its appellate jurisdiction, the High Court considers appeals in criminal and civil matters against the decisions of the Subordinate Courts. The High Court has unlimited original jurisdiction in criminal and civil matters.
Chief Justice: Dato' Sir DENYS ROBERTS.

OTHER COURTS

The Subordinate Courts: presided over by the Chief Magistrate and magistrates, with limited original jurisdiction in civil and criminal matters.
The Courts of Kathis: deal solely with questions concerning Islamic religion, marriage and divorce. Appeals lie from these courts to the Sultan in the Religious Council. **Chief Kathi:** Pehin Haji ABDUL HAMID BIN BAKAL.
Attorney-General: Pengiran Haji BAHRAIN.

Religion

The official religion of Brunei is Islam, and the Sultan is head of the Islamic population. The majority of the Malay population are Muslims of the Sunni sect. The Chinese population is either Buddhist, Confucianist, Daoist or Christian. Large numbers of the indigenous ethnic groups are animists of various types. The remainder of the population are mostly Christians, generally Roman Catholics, Anglicans or members of the American Methodist Church of Southern Asia.

CHRISTIANITY

The Anglican Communion

Brunei is within the jurisdiction of the Anglican diocese of Kuching (Malaysia).

The Roman Catholic Church

Brunei is within the jurisdiction of the Roman Catholic archdiocese of Kuching (Malaysia).

The Press

NEWSPAPERS

Borneo Bulletin: 74 Jalan Sungei, POB 69, Kuala Belait; tel. (03) 334344; telex 3336; f. 1953; daily; English; independent; Editor HAN J. LING; circ. 30,000.
Brunei Darussalam Newsletter: Information Section, Broadcasting and Information Dept, Prime Minister's Office, Istana Nurul Iman, Bandar Seri Begawan; monthly; English; circ. 14,000.
Pelita Brunei: Information Section, Broadcasting and Information Dept, Prime Minister's Office, Istana Nurul Iman, Bandar Seri Begawan; f. 1956; weekly (Wed.); Malay; govt newspaper; distributed free; circ. 45,000.
Salam: c/o Brunei Shell Petroleum Co Sdn Bhd, Seria 7082; tel. (037) 8624; fax (037) 8494; f. 1953; monthly; Malay and English; distributed free to employees of the Brunei Shell Petroleum Co Sdn Bhd; circ. 9,000.

Publishers

Borneo Printers & Trading Sdn Bhd: POB 2211, Bandar Seri Begawan 1922; tel. (02) 224856; fax (02) 243407.
The Brunei Press: POB 69, Kuala Belait; tel. (03) 334344; telex 3336; fax (03) 334400; f. 1959; Dir DANNY SIM.
Capital Trading & Printing Pte Ltd: POB 1089; tel. (02) 244541.
Eastern Printers & Trading Co Ltd: POB 2304; tel. (02) 220434.
Leong Bros: 52 Jalan Bunga Kuning, POB 164, Seria; tel. (03) 222381.
Offset Printing House: POB 1111; tel. (02) 224477.
The Star Press: Bandar Seri Begawan; f. 1963; Man. F. W. ZIMMERMAN.

Government Publishing House

Government Printer: Government Printing Office, Old Airport, Berakas, Bandar Seri Begawan; tel. (02) 244541.

Radio and Television

In 1989 there were an estimated 92,000 radio receivers and 63,000 television receivers in use.

Radio Television Brunei: Dept of Broadcasting and Information, Bandar Seri Begawan 2042; tel. (02) 243111; telex 2311; fax (02) 241882; f. 1957; two radio networks, one broadcasting in Malay, the other in English and Chinese (Mandarin); a colour television service transmits programmes in Malay and English; Dir Pehin Dato' Paduka Haji AWANG BADARUDDIN BIN Pengiran Haji OTHMAN.

Finance

BANKING

The Treasury Department performs most of the functions of a central bank.

Commercial Bank

International Bank of Brunei: Bangunan IBB, Lot 155, Jalan Roberts, POB 2725, Bandar Seri Begawan; tel. (02) 220686; telex 2320; f. 1981 as Island Development Bank; Man. Dir AZIZ BIN ABDUL RAHMAN; 25 brs.

Foreign Banks

Citibank NA (USA): 147 Jalan Pemancha, Bandar Seri Begawan 2085; tel. (02) 243983; telex 2224; Country Corporate Officer DAVID CONNER; 2 brs.
The Hongkong and Shanghai Banking Corpn (Hong Kong): cnr Jalan Sultan and Jalan Pemancha, POB 59, Bandar Seri Begawan; tel. (02) 242305; telex 2273; fax (02) 241316; f. 1947; acquired assets of National Bank of Brunei in 1986; Man. I. C. A. KING-HOLFORD; 9 brs.
Malayan Banking Bhd (Malaysia): 148 Jalan Pemancha, POB 167, Bandar Seri Begawan 2085; tel. (02) 242494; telex 2316; f. 1960; Man. WAN MOHD DEN WAN MOHD ZIN; 2 brs.
Overseas Union Bank Ltd (Singapore): Unit G5, RBA Plaza, Jalan Sultan, Bandar Seri Begawan 2085; tel. (02) 225477; telex 2256; fax (02) 240792; f. 1973; Man. LAU KUIN SAM; 2 brs.
Standard Chartered Bank (UK): 51–55 Jalan Sultan, POB 186, Bandar Seri Begawan 1901; tel. (02) 242386; telex 2223; fax (02) 242390; f. 1958; Man. K. S. WESTON; 8 brs.

BRUNEI

United Malayan Banking Corpn Bhd (Malaysia): 141 Jalan Pemancha, POB 435, Bandar Seri Begawan 2085; tel. (02) 222516; telex 2207; f. 1963; Man. LIOW CHEE HWA; 1 br.

INSURANCE

There are several locally-incorporated insurance companies and a number of international insurance companies.

Trade and Industry

Trade in Brunei is largely conducted by Malay and Chinese agency houses and merchants.

CHAMBERS OF COMMERCE

Brunei State Chamber of Commerce: POB 2246, Bandar Seri Begawan 1922; tel. (02) 28533; telex 2203; Chair. DAVID P. CONNER; Sec. SHAZALI BIN Dato Paduka SULAIMAN; 91 mems.

Chinese Chamber of Commerce: POB 281, 9 Jalan Pretty, Bandar Seri Begawan; tel. (02) 224374; Chair. LIM ENG MING.

Indian Chamber of Commerce: POB 974, Bandar Seri Begawan; tel. (02) 223886; Pres. BIKRAMJIT BHALLA.

Malay Chamber of Commerce: POB 1099, Suite 301, 2nd Floor, Bangunan Guru-Guru Melayu Brunei, Jalan Kianggeh, Bandar Seri Begawan; tel. (02) 227297; telex 2445; f. 1964; Chair. A. A. HAPIZ LAKSAMANA; 200 mems.

TRADE UNIONS

Total membership of the four trade unions was c. 4,000 in 1983.

Brunei Government Junior Officers' Union: Bandar Seri Begawan; Pres. Haji ALI BIN Haji NASAR; Gen. Sec. Haji OMARALI BIN Haji MOHIDDIN.

Brunei Government Medical and Health Workers' Union: POB 459, Bandar Seri Begawan; Pres. Pengiran Haji MOHIDDIN BIN Pengiran TAJUDDIN; Gen. Sec. HANAFI BIN ANAI.

Brunei Oilfield Workers' Union: POB 175, Seria; f. 1961; 505 mems; Pres. SEMITH BIN SABLI; Vice-Pres. MOHD ALI Haji YUSOF; Sec.-Gen. ABDUL WAHAB JUNAIDI.

Royal Brunei Custom Department Staff Union: Custom Dept, Kuala Belait; f. 1972; Pres. HASSAN BIN BAKAR; Gen. Sec. ABDUL ADIS BIN TARIP.

Transport

RAILWAYS

There are no public railways in Brunei. The Brunei Shell Petroleum Co Sdn Bhd maintains a 19.3-km section of light railway between Seria and Badas.

ROADS

In 1988 there were an estimated 2,199.1 km of roads in Brunei, comprising 1,093.0 km with a bituminous or concrete surface, 512.4 km surfaced with gravel and 593.6 km passable only in dry conditions. The main highway connects Bandar Seri Begawan, Tutong and Kuala Belait. A 59-km coastal road links Muara and Tutong. Bus services operate between Brunei/Muara, Tutong and Belait districts.

Land Transport Department: Ministry of Communications, Km 4, Jalan Gadong, Bandar Seri Begawan; tel. (02) 224775; fax (02) 224775; Dir Pengiran RAKAWI BIN Pengiran Haji SABLI.

SHIPPING

Most sea traffic is handled by a deep-water port at Muara, 27 km from the capital. The original, smaller port at Bandar Seri Begawan itself is mainly used for local river-going vessels. There is a port at Kuala Belait which takes shallow-draught vessels and serves mainly the Shell oil field and Seria. Owing to Brunei's shallow waters at Seria, tankers are unable to come up to the shore to load and crude petroleum from the oil terminal is pumped through an underwater loading line to a single buoy mooring, to which the tankers are moored. At Lumut there is a 4.5-km jetty for liquefied natural gas (LNG) carriers.

Rivers are the principal means of communication in the interior and boats or water taxis the main form of transport for most residents of the water villages. Larger water taxis operate daily to Temburong district.

Bee Seng Shipping Co: 1½ Miles Jalan Tutong, POB 92, Bandar Seri Begawan; telex 2219.

Brunei Shell Tankers Sdn Bhd: Seria 7082; tel. (03) 773999; telex 3313; f. 1986; vessels operated by Shell Tankers UK; 7 vessels; Man. Dir G. INNES.

CIVIL AVIATION

There is an international airport near Bandar Seri Begawan. Substantial upgrading work was completed in 1987. The Brunei Shell Petroleum Co Sdn Bhd operates a private airfield at Anduki for helicopter services.

Directorate of Civil Aviation: Brunei International Airport, Bandar Seri Begawan 2015; tel. (02) 330142; telex 2267; Dir Dato' JOB LIM.

Royal Brunei Airlines Ltd: RBA Plaza, POB 737, Bandar Seri Begawan 1907; tel. (02) 240500; telex 2737; fax (02) 244737; f. 1974; operates services to Bangkok, Darwin, Dubai, Frankfurt, Hong Kong, Jakarta, Kota Kinabalu, Kuala Lumpur, Kuching, London, Manila, Perth, Singapore and Taiwan; Chair. Pengiran Di-Gadong JEFRI BOLKIAH (Minister of Finance); Man. Dir Pengiran TENGAH METASSIM; fleet of 1 B737-200, 3 B757-200, 1 B767-300 and 1 B767-200.

Tourism

Tourism is relatively underdeveloped: in 1988 only 9,000 tourists visited Brunei.

Information Bureau: Information Section, Broadcasting and Information Dept, Prime Minister's Office, Bandar Seri Begawan 2041; tel. (02) 240400; telex 2614; fax (02) 244104.

BULGARIA

Introductory Survey

Location, Climate, Language, Religion, Flag, Capital

The Republic of Bulgaria (known as the People's Republic of Bulgaria between 1947 and 1990) lies in the eastern Balkans, in south-eastern Europe. It is bounded by Romania to the north, by Turkey and Greece to the south and by Yugoslavia to the west. The country has an eastern coastline on the Black Sea. The climate is one of fairly sharp contrasts between winter and summer. Temperatures in Sofia are generally between −5°C (23°F) and 28°C (82°F). The official language is Bulgarian, a member of the Slavonic group, written in the Cyrillic alphabet. Minority languages include Turkish and Macedonian. Most Christians adhere to the Bulgarian Orthodox Church, while there is a substantial minority of Muslims. The national flag (proportions 3 by 2) has three equal horizontal stripes, of white, green and red (between 1947 and 1990 the flag also included the state emblem in the upper hoist). The capital is Sofia.

Recent History

Formerly a monarchy, Bulgaria allied with Nazi Germany in the Second World War and joined in the occupation of Yugoslavia in 1941. King Boris died in 1943 and was succeeded by his young son, Simeon II. In September 1944 the Fatherland Front, a left-wing alliance formed in 1942, seized power, with help from the USSR, and installed a government led by Kimon Georgiyev. In September 1946 the monarchy was abolished by popular referendum, and a republic was proclaimed. The first post-war election was held in October, when the Fatherland Front received 70.8% of the votes and won 364 seats, of which 277 were held by the Bulgarian Communist Party (BCP), in the 465-member National Assembly. In November Georgi Dimitrov, the First Secretary of the BCP and a veteran international revolutionary, became Chairman of the Council of Ministers (Prime Minister) in a government formed from members of the Fatherland Front. All opposition parties were abolished, and a new constitution, based on the Soviet model, was adopted in December 1947, when Bulgaria was designated a People's Republic. Dimitrov was replaced as Chairman of the Council of Ministers by Vasil Kolarov in March 1949, but remained leader of the BCP until his death in July. His successor as party leader, Vulko Chervenkov, also became Chairman of the Council of Ministers in February 1950. Political trials and executions became less frequent after the death in 1953 of Iosif Stalin, the Soviet leader, and the rehabilitation of those who had been disgraced began in 1956.

Todor Zhivkov succeeded Chervenkov as leader of the BCP in March 1954, although the latter remained Chairman of the Council of Ministers until April 1956, when he was replaced by Anton Yugov. Following an ideological struggle within the BCP, Zhivkov also became Chairman of the Council of Ministers in November 1962. In April 1965 an attempted coup against the Government was discovered. In May 1971 a new constitution was adopted, and in July Zhivkov relinquished his position as Chairman of the Council of Ministers to become the first President of the newly-formed State Council. He was re-elected in 1976, in 1981 and in 1986. In September 1978 a purge of BCP members commenced. At the twelfth BCP Congress, held in March and April 1981, the party's leader was restyled General Secretary. In June, following elections to the National Assembly, a new government was formed, headed by Grisha Filipov, a member of the BCP's Political Bureau, in succession to Stanko Todorov, who had been Chairman of the Council of Ministers since 1971. A far-reaching reshuffle, affecting senior posts in the BCP and the Government, was announced in January 1984. In 1985 the BCP leadership initiated a campaign against corruption and inefficiency, resulting in the dismissal and replacement of a number of ministers and senior officials. In 1986 the Council of Ministers underwent extensive reorganization, including the restructuring of several ministries and state committees. In March Georgi Atanasov, a former Vice-President of the State Council, replaced Filipov as Chairman of the Council of Ministers.

In August 1987 the National Assembly approved further structural reforms and personnel changes in the Council of Ministers. It also approved extensive administrative reform, aimed at increased efficiency and the promotion of the principles of self-government. The reforms included the creation of nine administrative regions to replace the existing 28 districts and involved the relocation of nearly 100,000 government employees. Amendments to the Constitution were also placed under consideration.

Proposals to restrict the tenure of office by high-ranking officials of the BCP to two five-year terms were approved, in principle, at a BCP conference in January 1988. This was followed in March by local elections, for which the authorities permitted, for the first time, the nomination of candidates other than those endorsed by the BCP, and in which candidates who had been presented by independent public organizations and workers' collectives obtained about one-quarter of the total votes cast. However, much of the Soviet-style programme of reform (*preustroistvo*), advocated at the 1987 session of the National Assembly, was not implemented in 1988. At a plenum of the BCP, held in July 1988, several prominent proponents of reform, including one member of the party's Political Bureau, were dismissed from office. The leading campaigners of an environmental pressure group, which had been established earlier in the year without official sanction, were expelled from the BCP at the same plenum.

In January 1985 reports were received in the West that Bulgaria had begun a campaign of forced assimilation of its ethnic Turkish minority (which constituted nearly 10% of Bulgaria's total population), in which they were forced to adopt Slavic names in advance of the next census, and were banned from practising Muslim religious rites. The Bulgarian Government denied that coercion was being used in a programme in which, so it claimed, the ethnic Turks were participating voluntarily. Following the population census (held in December 1985), Bulgaria was condemned by the Turkish Government for 'seeking to eliminate all statistical evidence of its ethnic Turks'. In 1986 the Bulgarian Government continued to refute allegations, made by Amnesty International, that more than 250 ethnic Turks had been arrested or imprisoned for refusing to accept new identity cards, and that many more had been forced to resettle away from their homes, in other regions of the country. In September 1987 Bulgaria's decision to declare 3 March a public holiday, to commemorate the establishment (in 1878) of the first Bulgarian state after 500 years of Turkish occupation, was criticized by the Turkish Government as further evidence of Bulgarian determination forcibly to assimilate its ethnic Turkish population. In February 1988, on the eve of a conference of Ministers of Foreign Affairs of the six Balkan nations, Bulgaria and Turkey signed a protocol to further bilateral economic and social relations. However, the situation worsened in May 1989, when Bulgarian militia violently suppressed demonstrations by an estimated 30,000 ethnic Turks in eastern Bulgaria against the continued assimilation campaign. The Bulgarian authorities claimed that seven people had been killed, while unofficial sources estimated that there had been as many as 30 deaths. More than 200 Turks, many of whom were activists for the rights of the Turkish minority, were deported to Turkey following the 'riots'. In June more than 80,000 ethnic Turks were expelled from Bulgaria, although the Bulgarian authorities claimed that the Turks had left voluntarily, following a relaxation in passport regulations to ease foreign travel. Furthermore, the Ministry of the Interior stated that it had received 250,000 applications for permission to travel to Turkey. In response, the Turkish Government opened the border and declared its commitment to accepting all the ethnic Turks as refugees from Bulgaria. By mid-August an estimated 310,000 Bulgarian Turks had crossed into Turkey. In late August the Turkish Government, alarmed by the continued influx of refugees, closed the border with Bulgaria, stating that all entrants from Bulgaria would henceforth require visas issued by Turkish consular offices in Bulgaria. In September a substantial number of the Bulgarian Turks, disillusioned with conditions in Turkey, began to return to Bulgaria (more than 100,000 had returned by February 1990).

The Turkish Government repeatedly proposed discussions with the Bulgarian Government, to be held under the auspices of the UN High Commissioner for Refugees (UNHCR), to establish the rights of the Bulgarian Turks and to formulate a clear immigration policy. Finally, Bulgaria agreed to negotiations, and in late October 1989 discussions were held in Kuwait between delegations of the two countries, led respectively by the Turkish Minister of Foreign Affairs and Georgi Yordanov, a Deputy Chairman of the Bulgarian Council of Ministers. The talks were described as 'encouraging', and the two sides agreed to meet again in Kuwait in November. In mid-December about 6,000 members of Bulgaria's Pomak community, a Muslim minority numbering about 300,000 people, held demonstrations to demand religious and cultural freedoms, as well as an official inquiry into alleged atrocities against Pomaks during Zhivkov's tenure of office. In January 1990 anti-Turkish demonstrations were held in the Kurdzhali district of southern Bulgaria, in protest at the Government's declared intention to restore civil and religious rights to the ethnic Turkish minority. Despite continuing demonstrations by Bulgarian nationalist protesters (including the holding of mass rallies in Sofia and strikes in several towns in Bulgaria), the National Assembly approved legislation, in March, permitting ethnic Turks and Pomaks to use their original Islamic names. This development was welcomed by the Turkish Government. Nevertheless, inter-ethnic disturbances continued, particularly in the Kurdzhali region, during 1990.

In the late 1980s a small number of opposition groups began to emerge. In October 1989, several unofficial groups took advantage of the holding in Sofia of an international environmental forum, organized by the Conference on Security and Co-operation in Europe (CSCE), to stage anti-Government demonstrations. The Independent Association for Human Rights in Bulgaria held its first rally since its foundation in January 1988, at which it appealed publicly for the respect of human rights and the release of Kotsi Ivanov, a prisoner of conscience; there was no intervention by the police. In the same month Bulgaria's principal religious opposition group, the Committee for the Protection of Religious Rights and Freedoms, organized a service in a church in Sofia to express solidarity with the country's opposition movement. In late October about 20 members of an unofficial environmentalist group, the Ecoglasnost Independent Association (more commonly referred to as, simply, Ecoglasnost), were attacked and arrested by security forces while preparing to collect signatures for a petition regarding environmental issues (all were released later). The authorities subsequently expressed regret over the incident and admitted that the security forces had acted with undue violence. Furthermore, several human rights campaigners, who had been deported to the provinces to prevent their activity during the CSCE meeting, were permitted to return to Sofia, following protests by participants in the conference. In early November more than 4,000 people took part in a march, organized by Ecoglasnost, to the National Assembly building, where the petition concerning environmental issues was handed to government officials. The march was tolerated by the authorities.

On 10 November 1989, at a plenary session of the Central Committee of the BCP, Zhivkov was unexpectedly relieved of his posts of General Secretary of the BCP (which he had held for 35 years) and member of the Political Bureau. He was replaced as General Secretary by Petur Mladenov, who had been the Minister of Foreign Affairs since 1971 and a member of the BCP's Political Bureau since 1977, and who was widely regarded as a liberal figure. In the following week Mladenov also replaced Zhivkov as President of the State Council, while resigning as Minister of Foreign Affairs. After his election as General Secretary, Mladenov pledged to introduce comprehensive political and economic reforms, and to give greater attention to environmental issues. He also invited 11 prominent intellectuals, who had been expelled from the BCP for their criticism of the Zhivkov Government, to rejoin the party. In mid-November 10 senior BCP officials, including three full members of the Political Bureau (Grisha Filipov, Milko Balev and Dimitur Stoyanov), were dismissed from the party. All had been closely associated with Zhivkov, and Balev and Stoyanov had played a leading part in organizing the campaign to assimilate ethnic Turks. On the following day, the National Assembly adopted proposals to dismiss several members of both the State Council and the Council of Ministers. The Assembly also voted for the abolition of part of the penal code prohibiting 'anti-State propaganda', and for the granting of an amnesty to those who had been convicted under it. On the same day, an estimated 100,000 people demonstrated in Sofia, in support of demands for democratic reform and the holding of free elections. Zhivkov was subsequently denounced by the BCP and divested of his party membership, and an investigation into the extent of corruption during his tenure of power was begun. (In early 1990 Zhivkov was arrested on charges of abuse of power, embezzlement of state funds and incitement to racial hatred; in November it was announced that he would stand trial on these charges.)

Following the appointment, in early December 1989, of Angel Dimitrov as the new leader of the Bulgarian Agrarian People's Union (BAPU, the sole legal political party apart from the BCP, with which it was originally allied), the BAPU was reformed as an independent opposition party. Also in early December, there was a further reshuffle of members of the BCP's Political Bureau and Central Committee. At a meeting of the Central Committee in mid-December it was proposed that the National Assembly make amendments to the Constitution, and that it adopt a new electoral law which would permit free and democratic elections to be held in the second quarter of 1990. In January 1990 the National Assembly voted overwhelmingly to remove from the Constitution the article guaranteeing the BCP's leading role in society. It also approved legislation permitting citizens to form independent groups and to hold demonstrations. (In mid-December 1989, in anticipation of the new law, Ecoglasnost had become the first independent organization to be legally registered.)

In early January 1990 a series of round-table discussions, covering political and economic reforms, was initiated between the BCP, the BAPU and the Union of Democratic Forces (UDF), a co-ordinating organization (established in December 1989) embracing several dissident and independent groups, including Ecoglasnost and the Podkrepa (Support) Independent Trade Union Federation. An extraordinary Congress of the BCP was held from late January to early February, at which the delegates adopted a new manifesto pledging the party's commitment to extensive political and economic reforms, the separation of party and state, and the introduction of a multi-party system. It was stressed, however, that the BCP would retain its Marxist orientation. The party's Central Committee was replaced by a 153-member Supreme Council (later reduced to 151 members), in which the great majority of the members were new. Aleksandur Lilov, who was formerly head of the BCP's ideology department and who had been expelled from the party in 1983 for criticism of Zhivkov, was elected Chairman of the Supreme Council. The Political Bureau and Secretariat of the Central Committee were replaced by the Presidium of the Supreme Council, also with Lilov as Chairman. Mladenov (who remained as President of the State Council) proposed the formation of an interim coalition government until the holding of elections to the National Assembly (later determined for June 1990). The UDF and the BAPU, however, rejected Mladenov's invitation to participate in such a coalition. Accordingly the new Council of Ministers, which was appointed on 8 February (following the resignation of the preceding Government), was comprised solely of BCP members. Andrei Lukanov, who was a former Minister of Foreign Economic Relations and was regarded as an advocate of reform, became Chairman of the Council of Ministers, replacing Georgi Atanasov.

There was further unrest in mid-February 1990, when an estimated 200,000 supporters of the UDF gathered in Sofia to demand the ending of BCP rule. The rally was reportedly the largest public demonstration ever held in the capital. In the same month, at a congress of the Central Council of Bulgarian Trade Unions, it was agreed to end the Council's affiliation to the BCP and to re-form it as the Confederation of Independent Bulgarian Trade Unions. After a suspension of the round-table talks (owing to a disagreement between the BCP and the UDF over the election of the new President), discussions resumed in late March, with the participation of the BAPU and other political and public organizations. It was finally agreed to re-elect Mladenov as President, although he was to be replaced following elections to the National Assembly in June and the subsequent approval of a new constitution. The participants in the talks also decided to dissolve the State Council, considering it to be an 'unnecessary institution'. In early April the National

Assembly adopted three laws: an electoral law, a constitutional amendment law and a political parties law. Under the latter, political pluralism was legalized, and the right of citizens to form political parties was guaranteed. The National Assembly then terminated its powers, although it was to continue to operate *ad interim*, pending the election of the new Grand National Assembly. Also in early April, the Supreme Council of the BCP voted overwhelmingly to rename the party the Bulgarian Socialist Party (BSP), to symbolize a 'clean break with the dictatorship which existed before 10 November 1989'. The BSP pledged to continue traditional ties with the USSR and to remain a member of the Warsaw Pact (see p. 211). At the same time, it expressed support for an accelerated but state-controlled transition to a market economy. At an extraordinary congress of the Fatherland Front (the former mass organization embracing the BCP and the BAPU), the delegates condemned the organization as having been 'transformed into an appendage of totalitarian power', and agreed to re-form as the Fatherland Union.

Following an election campaign that was marred by acts of intimidation and violence (including the deaths of five supporters of the UDF in separate incidents), elections to the Grand National Assembly were held in two stages, on 10 and 17 June 1990. About 91% of the electorate in the first round of voting, and about 84% in the second round, voted for candidates from 38 political parties, movements and coalitions in the 28 districts of Bulgaria. Under the recently adopted electoral law, 200 of the 400 members of the Grand National Assembly were elected directly to represent single-member constituencies, while the remaining 200 seats were filled according to a system of proportional representation of parties. The BSP emerged with 211 seats, thus securing an absolute majority in the legislature (in conspicuous contrast to the substantial losses suffered in legislative elections during 1990 by the communist parties of other Eastern European countries). The BSP's success was attributed to the continued strength of its local organizations in rural areas, and also to the opposition's lack of political experience. However, the BSP failed to gain the two-thirds majority of seats in the legislature necessary to secure support for the approval of constitutional and economic reforms. The UDF, which won the majority of votes in urban areas, obtained a total of 144 seats in the Assembly. The Movement for Rights and Freedoms (MRF), which had been established earlier in 1990 to represent the country's Muslim minority, won a large percentage of the votes in areas populated by ethnic Turks, and secured a total of 23 seats. The BAPU won 16 seats in the legislature, considerably fewer than had been expected. This was attributed to a split which had occurred within the party in late 1989 and the subsequent defection to the UDF of the breakaway Nikola Petkov Bulgarian Agrarian People's Union. Other parties and groups won a total of six seats in the Assembly (the Fatherland Union two, independents two, and the Bulgarian Social Democratic Party (non-Marxist—BSDP) and the Fatherland Party of Labour one seat each). Despite some irregularities reported during the second round of voting, the election was declared to have been fair and free by the more than 50 foreign observers invited to monitor the proceedings. The UDF, after initial protests against alleged electoral fraud, accepted the validity of the result. However, it again rejected the BSP's invitation to join a coalition government. In mid-July Nikolai Todorov, a member of the BSP and a former diplomat, was elected to the post of Chairman of the Grand National Assembly.

Disturbances broke out anew in mid-June and early July 1990, as students led a campaign of protests and strikes, in support of demands for the resignation of Mladenov as President. The unrest had been prompted by the UDF's disclosure of a video recording, made in December 1989 at a mass demonstration in Sofia, in which Mladenov could be heard advocating the deployment of tanks to suppress the demonstrators. Despite Mladenov's protestation that the tape was a 'slanderous montage', it was later proved to be authentic, and on 6 July 1990 Mladenov announced his resignation. In late July the Grand National Assembly convened to elect a new President. However, in four rounds of voting, none of the three candidates, representing the BSP, the UDF and the BAPU—Chavdar Kyuranov (a former dissident), Petur Dertliev (the leader of the BSDP—United) and Viktor Vulkov (Chairman of the BAPU), respectively—received the required two-thirds majority of the vote. On 1 August, following an agreement between the BSP and the UDF, Zhelyu Zhelev, the Chairman of the UDF, was elected President, and Col-Gen. Atanas Semerdzhiev, a BSP member and a former Minister of Internal Affairs, was elected Vice-President. Zhelev was subsequently replaced as Chairman of the UDF by Petur Beron, hitherto the Union's Secretary. Following Beron's resignation in December, Filip Dimitrov, a lawyer and Vice-President of the Green Party, was elected Chairman of the UDF.

Anti-Government demonstrations continued in late 1990, prompted, in particular, by the severe deterioration in the state of the economy, which had resulted in widespread shortages of food and fuel and the rationing of many basic commodities. In an attempt to prevent economic collapse, Lukanov proposed that the Grand National Assembly approve a programme of drastic economic reforms, including the privatization of small and medium-sized companies, the restructuring of the banking system and the liberalization of price controls. He also threatened to resign if the programme did not receive the support of two-thirds of the members of the Assembly, necessary for its approval. The UDF (which held more than one-third of the seats in the legislature) refused to support the reforms, although it proposed entering a coalition government, on condition that its representatives form the majority in the Council of Ministers and that the post of Chairman be occupied by a UDF member. The UDF proceeded to organize rallies in many parts of Bulgaria to demand the resignation of Lukanov's Government. The UDF's campaign was supported by student organizations, which staged sit-in strikes throughout the country, while the Podkrepa trade union federation recommended that a general strike be held if the UDF's demands were not satisfied. Public opinion polls, conducted in mid-October and late November, indicated that support for the UDF had increased substantially in the months following the general election, and exceeded support for the BSP by a wide margin.

A growing division between conservative and reformist elements within the BSP became manifest in early November 1990, when 16 BSP delegates to the Grand National Assembly declared their decision to form a separate parliamentary group, called the National Representatives for National Consensus. Although, it was stressed, the delegates would remain members of the BSP, the result of their decision was that the party's absolute majority in the legislature was no longer guaranteed. The political crisis deepened when, at a session of the Grand National Assembly in late November, the UDF proposed a vote expressing 'no confidence' in the Government, following which scuffles broke out in the Assembly building between rival deputies. In the event, the opposition's motion of no confidence was defeated by 201 votes to 159. However, on 29 November, following a four-day general strike organized by the Podkrepa trade union federation (in which, according to claims by Podkrepa, about 830,000 workers participated), Lukanov announced his resignation. On the following day the Government also resigned. Discussions were then initiated between representatives of all the political forces in the Grand National Assembly, aimed at the formation of a new 'government of national consensus'. This was announced in mid-December, and comprised members of the BSP, the UDF, the BAPU and four independents. Dimitur Popov, a lawyer with no party affiliation, had been elected in early December to chair the new Council of Ministers (which was to operate until the holding of fresh legislative elections, provisionally scheduled for May 1991).

In mid-November 1990 the Grand National Assembly voted to rename the country the Republic of Bulgaria (since 1947 it had been known as the People's Republic of Bulgaria). The Assembly also voted to remove from the national flag the state emblem, which included communist symbols (sheaves of grain and a five-pointed red star). A new state emblem was under discussion in late November.

Bulgaria has traditionally maintained close links with other Eastern European countries through is membership of the Warsaw Pact (see p. 211) and of the CMEA (see p. 125). Following the political upheavals which took place in Eastern Europe in 1989 and 1990, radical changes in the structure and activities of both the Warsaw Pact and the CMEA were expected to be made. In November 1990 it was announced that, following the dismantling of its military structure by mid-1991, the Warsaw Pact would be abolished, in its entirety, by early 1992. Likewise, the CMEA was to be replaced by a new co-operative organization based on market economy principles. Relations with Western states have steadily improved, and co-

BULGARIA

operation in economic and technical fields was expected to increase substantially in the 1990s. In 1990 Bulgaria re-established diplomatic relations with Israel and Chile. Diplomatic relations were also established with the Republic of Korea, the Holy See and Qatar.

Government

The supreme organ of state power is the unicameral Grand National Assembly, with 400 members elected for five years by universal adult suffrage. The Assembly, in turn, elects the President (an office created in April 1990, replacing the largely ceremonial State Council) and the Council of Ministers, the highest organ of state administration. Until December 1989 political power was held by the Bulgarian Communist Party. For local administration, Bulgaria comprises 28 districts (divided into a total of 273 municipalities).

Defence

Military service is for 18 months in the army, two years in the air force, and three years in the navy. According to Western estimates, the total strength of the armed forces in June 1990 was 129,000 (including 86,000 conscripts), comprising an army of 97,000, an air force of 22,000 and a navy of 10,000. Paramilitary forces include 13,000 border troops and 5,000 security police. There is a voluntary People's Militia of 150,000. Defence expenditure for 1990 was estimated at 1,656m. leva. Bulgaria is a member of the Warsaw Pact (which body was due to be completely abolished by early 1992, following the dismantling of its military structure by mid-1991).

Economic Affairs

In 1988, according to official government estimates, net material product (NMP) was 29,422.6m. leva, equivalent to 3,276 leva per head. In 1980–87 NMP increased, in real terms, at an average annual rate of 4.1%. In 1988 NMP increased by 6.2%, compared with the previous year. During 1980–88 the population increased by an annual average of 0.2%.

Agriculture (including forestry) contributed 13.0% of NMP in 1988. In that year the sector employed 19.3% of the labour force in state-controlled enterprises (excluding agricultural co-operatives). In 1990 private farming was legalized. The principal crops are wheat, maize, barley, sugar beet, grapes and tobacco. Tobacco accounts for about 20% of the value of all agricultural production. Viticulture has been developed extensively in recent years; in 1989 Bulgaria was the world's fourth largest exporter of wine. There is a large exportable surplus of processed agricultural products. In 1989 agricultural production decreased by 0.4%, compared with 1988.

Industry (including mining, manufacturing and utilities) contributed 58.1% of NMP in 1988. In that year the industrial sector employed 35.6% of the labour force in state-controlled enterprises. In 1989 industrial production increased by 1.1%, compared with the previous year.

Coal, iron ore, copper, lead and zinc are mined, while petroleum is extracted on the Black Sea coast. Compared with the previous year, the total output of coal (including brown coal) increased by 4.5% in 1987, to reach 36.8m. metric tons. In 1988, however, coal production declined by about 7%, to 34.1m. tons. In 1986 the construction of a gas pipeline, linking Bulgaria to the USSR, was completed. In the late 1980s the USSR supplied Bulgaria with 5,500m. cu m of gas per year.

In the manufacturing sector, food, beverages and tobacco products are the most important items, accounting for about 24% of total output in 1987. The engineering and electronics sectors, in particular, have been greatly developed (with production increasing by 11% in 1987), as have the chemical fertilizer and metallurgical industries.

Bulgaria produces less than one-third of its energy needs. The country's sole nuclear power station, at Kozlodui, provided 42% of electric energy in 1989. Production of electricity increased by 4.0% in 1987, and by 2.2% in 1988. It declined by 0.2% in 1989.

In 1987 Bulgaria recorded a visible trade deficit of US $306m. In that year 81.5% of foreign trade was conducted with socialist countries, and 80.3% with members of the CMEA. The USSR is Bulgaria's principal trading partner, accounting for 58.1% of total trade in 1989. The principal exports in 1989 were machines and equipment for industrial purposes (accounting for 59.8% of overall exports). The principal imports were machinery and equipment (accounting for 43.3% of total imports) and fuels, minerals and metals (34.5%). Bulgaria recorded a trade surplus of $640m. in 1988.

Introductory Survey

The budget for 1990 envisaged revenue of 24,894m. leva and expenditure of 25,851m. leva. In mid-1990 Bulgaria's total external debt was estimated at US $10,400m. The annual rate of inflation averaged 0.9% in 1980–85, increasing to 3.5% in 1986. However, the rate was only 0.1% in 1987, rising to 1.2% in 1988. In October 1990 an estimated 41,000 people were unemployed.

Bulgaria is a member of the CMEA (see p. 125, due to be replaced in the early 1990s by a co-operative organization operating on market economy principles), the International Bank for Economic Co-operation (see p. 160) and the UN Economic Commission for Europe (see p. 24). In September 1990 Bulgaria became a member of the IMF. Earlier in 1990 Bulgaria and the EEC signed an agreement covering trade and economic co-operation, under which the two parties were to enjoy the status of 'most-favoured nation'.

In the late 1980s the Bulgarian economy entered a severe decline: in 1989 national income decreased by 0.4%, compared with 1988, foreign trade declined by over 8%, and the total external debt exceeded US $10,000m. By October 1990 an estimated 41,000 people were unemployed, and it was expected that the total would increase. Moreover, retail prices had increased at an alarming rate, and in late 1990 the rationing of many basic commodities was introduced, as shortages of food and fuel became widespread. In September 1990 the Government was obliged to impose a ban on all exports of food until the end of March 1991. In an effort to revitalize the economy, the Government declared its support for a transition to a market-oriented system. To this end, it proposed a far-reaching programme of denationalization and privatization, as well as the reform of the monetary, credit and banking systems.

Social Welfare

State social insurance is directed by the Department of Public Insurance and the Pensions Directorate. For 1990, 5,100m. leva (19.7% of the state budget) were allotted to social security. Workers are paid compensation during sick leave. Women are entitled to full paid leave before and after childbirth. All pensions are non-contributory. Retirement pensions consist of a basic sum plus up to 12% allowance for additional service, over the minimum requirement. The basic pension is related to the average monthly pay in three of the last 15 years of service. Retirement age varies from 45 to 60 years, depending on the job. Women retire five years earlier than men.

Since 1951 all medical services and treatment have been provided free for the whole population. In 1988 there were 88,000 hospital beds and 22,000 beds in sanatoriums and health spas. In 1983 there were 24,000 physicians. All medical treatment establishments and medical schools, training colleges and research institutes are controlled by the Ministry of National Health. Departments of Public Health in the regional People's Councils supervise medical work, together with the Bulgarian Red Cross. In November 1989 the Government legalized private medical and dental practice, which had been banned since 1972.

In 1989 the authorities initiated a programme to test all the residents of Sofia between 16 and 65 years of age for AIDS. By October a total of 2.5m. people (including foreigners) had been tested for AIDS in Bulgaria; 81 Bulgarian citizens had been diagnosed as HIV carriers. At the same time, the Government intensified its publicity campaign to prevent the spread of the disease.

Education

Education in Bulgaria is provided free of charge and is compulsory between the ages of six and 16 years. It is administered by the Ministry of National Education, although direct organization of kindergartens and schools is exercised by specialized organs of local People's Councils. Semi-higher and higher educational institutions are administered by the Ministry of Science and Higher Education. In 1988 kindergartens were attended by 79.1% of all children between the ages of three and six years. In the late 1980s plans were being discussed to make attendance at kindergartens compulsory from the age of five. In the 1981/82 school year a thorough reform of the secondary educational system was undertaken. Unified secondary polytechnical schools, offering an 11-year course of training, were introduced, in which students obtain not only a general secondary education, but also vocational qualifications. There are two types of secondary vocational schools: secondary vocational-technical schools, which train executive cadres, and

BULGARIA

technical colleges (tekhnikums), which offer secondary training for specialists in industry, construction, agriculture, transport, trade and public health. After completing secondary education, students are entitled to continue their training in semi-higher institutes or in higher educational institutions. In the 1988/89 school year 339,891 pupils attended kindergartens, 1,234,851 attended unified secondary polytechnical schools, and 138,341 students took courses at semi-higher and higher educational institutions. In the 1987/88 school year 55% of all students received scholarships. At the same time, there were 4,395 Bulgarians studying abroad and 6,889 foreigners studying in Bulgaria.

Public Holidays

1991: 1 January (New Year), 3 March (National Day), 1 April (Easter Monday), 1 May (Labour Day), 24 May (Education Day), 9 September (Day of Freedom), 25 December (Christmas).

1992: 1 January (New Year), 3 March (National Day), 20 April (Easter Monday), 1 May (Labour Day), 24 May (Education Day), 9 September (Day of Freedom), 25 December (Christmas).

Weights and Measures
The metric system is in force.

Statistical Survey

Source (unless otherwise stated): Central Statistical Office at the Council of Ministers, Sofia, Panayot Volov St 2; tel. 46-01; telex 22001.

Area and Population

AREA, POPULATION AND DENSITY

Area (sq km)*	110,994†
Population (census results)	
2 December 1975	8,727,771
4 December 1985	
Males	4,433,302
Females	4,515,347
Total	8,948,649
Population (official estimates at 31 December)	
1986	8,966,500
1987	8,976,255
1988	8,986,636
Density (per sq km) at 31 December 1988	81.0

* Including territorial waters of frontier rivers (261.4 sq km).
† 42,855 sq miles.

ADMINISTRATIVE REGIONS (31 December 1988)*

	Area (sq km)	Estimated population	Density (per sq km)
Sofia (capital)†	1,310.8	1,217,024	928.5
Burgas	14,656.7	876,089	59.8
Khaskovo	13,891.6	1,050,860	75.6
Lovech	15,150.0	1,061,403	70.1
Mikhailovgrad	10,606.9	661,933	62.4
Plovdiv	13,628.1	1,270,454	93.2
Razgrad	10,842.4	850,724	78.5
Sofia†	18,978.5	1,015,741	53.5
Varna	11,928.6	982,408	82.4
Total	110,993.6	8,986,636	81.0

* In August 1987 the State Council issued a decree reorganizing Bulgaria's 28 administrative districts (*okruzhi*) into nine regions (*oblasti*). This decree was repealed by the National Assembly in January 1990.
† The city of Sofia, the national capital, had separate regional status. The area and population of the capital region were not included in the neighbouring Sofia region.

PRINCIPAL TOWNS
(estimated population at 31 December 1988)

Sofia (capital)	1,136,875	Stara Zagora	158,151
Plovdiv	364,162	Pleven	136,287
Varna	306,300	Tolbukhin*	112,582
Burgas (Bourgas)	200,464	Sliven	109,432
Ruse (Roussé)	190,720	Shumen	107,973

* The town's former name, Dobrich, was restored in September 1990.

BIRTHS, MARRIAGES AND DEATHS

	Registered live births		Registered marriages*		Registered deaths	
	Number	Rate (per 1,000)	Number	Rate (per 1,000)	Number	Rate (per 1,000)
1981	124,372	14.0	66,539	7.5	95,441	10.7
1982	124,166	13.9	67,154	7.5	100,293	11.2
1983	122,993	13.8	67,032	7.5	102,182	11.4
1984	122,303	13.6	65,361	7.3	101,419	11.3
1985	118,955	13.3	66,682	7.4	107,485	12.0
1986	120,078	13.4	64,965	7.3	104,039	11.6
1987	116,672	13.0	64,429	7.2	107,213	12.0
1988	117,440	13.1	62,617	7.0	107,385	12.0

* Including marriages of Bulgarian nationals outside the country but excluding those of aliens in Bulgaria.

Expectation of Life (years at birth, 1978–80): Males 68.35; Females 73.55.

ECONOMICALLY ACTIVE POPULATION
(persons aged 14 years and over, 1985 census)

	Males	Females	Total
Agriculture and hunting	392,781	379,081	771,862
Forestry and fishing			
Mining and quarrying			
Manufacturing	949,740	828,019	1,777,759
Electricity, gas and water			
Construction	328,076	78,643	406,719
Trade, restaurants and hotels	120,624	276,807	397,431
Transport, storage and communications	234,637	79,870	314,507
Financing, insurance, real estate and business services	5,285	19,411	24,696
Community, social and personal services	419,797	572,814	992,611
Activities not adequately defined	231	324	555
Total labour force	2,451,171	2,234,969	4,686,140

Source: International Labour Office, *Year Book of Labour Statistics*.

BULGARIA

ECONOMICALLY ACTIVE POPULATION
(persons aged 14 years and over, 1985 census)

	Males	Females	Total
Agriculture and hunting	392,781	379,081	771,862
Forestry and fishing			
Mining and quarrying			
Manufacturing	949,740	828,019	1,777,759
Electricity, gas and water			
Construction	328,076	78,643	406,719
Trade, restaurants and hotels	120,624	276,807	397,431
Transport, storage and communications	234,637	79,870	314,507
Financing, insurance, real estate and business services	5,285	19,411	24,696
Community, social and personal services	419,797	572,814	992,611
Activities not adequately defined	231	324	555
Total labour force	2,451,171	2,234,969	4,686,140

Source: International Labour Office, *Year Book of Labour Statistics*.

EMPLOYEES IN THE 'SOCIALIZED' SECTOR*
(annual averages, '000)

	1986	1987	1988
Agriculture*	848.1	824.3	787.8
Forestry	24.3	25.8	26.8
Industry†	1,403.0	1,437.5	1,451.0
Construction	359.2	362.9	354.3
Commerce	360.7	367.7	358.6
Transport and storage	263.2	260.4	255.7
Communications	43.1	43.7	44.2
Finance and insurance services	22.4	23.2	25.2
Education and culture	317.2	315.6	318.7
Public health, welfare and sports	201.8	206.9	210.7
Administration	54.3	57.9	55.3
Science and scientific institutes	83.0	84.6	89.9
Housing and community services‡	56.7	58.5	62.3
Total (incl. others)	4,076.5	4,108.5	4,077.6

* Excluding agricultural co-operatives (employing more than 280,000 people in 1975) but including state farms and machine-tractor stations.
† Mining, manufacturing and electricity.
‡ Including water supply.

Agriculture

PRINCIPAL CROPS ('000 metric tons)

	1987	1988	1989
Wheat	4,149	4,743	5,402
Rice (paddy)	53	46	50
Barley	1,091	1,313	1,568
Maize	1,858	1,557	2,421
Rye	49	61	51
Oats	41	53	104
Potatoes	316	358	538
Dry beans	30	29	46
Dry peas	35	46	46
Soybeans	33	17	23
Sunflower seed	410	374	447
Seed cotton	20	13	13
Cabbages	117	126	135
Tomatoes	828	806	850
Pumpkins, squash and gourds	66	69	61
Cucumbers and gherkins	165	155	127
Green chillies and peppers	235	245	197
Dry onions	81	96	110
Green beans	17	15	17
Green peas	18	20	21
Water-melons	362	318	79
Grapes	943	922	754
Apples	339	334	398
Pears	74	73	73
Plums	103	139	139
Peaches and nectarines	58	63	97
Apricots	18	35	44
Strawberries	13	15	17
Sugar beets	736	626	912
Tobacco leaves	133	116	125*

* Unofficial figure.
Source: FAO, *Production Yearbook*.

LIVESTOCK ('000 head at 1 January each year)

	1987	1988	1989
Horses	121	123	122
Asses	341	333	329
Cattle	1,678	1,649	1,613
Pigs	4,050	4,034	4,119
Sheep	9,563	8,886	8,609
Goats	441	428	434
Buffaloes	26	24	23
Poultry	39,735	41,424	41,000*

* FAO estimate.

BULGARIA

LIVESTOCK PRODUCTS (metric tons)

	1987	1988	1989
Beef and veal	127,000	120,000	121,000
Buffalo meat	2,000	2,000	2,000
Mutton and lamb	74,000	65,000	72,000
Goats' meat	6,000	5,000	6,000
Pigmeat	372,000	394,000	413,000
Poultry meat	169,000	183,000	198,000*
Edible offals	106,000	107,000	112,000
Cow milk	2,181,000	2,168,000	2,126,000
Buffalo milk	19,000	18,000	17,000
Sheep milk	309,000	305,000	285,000
Goat milk	81,000	79,000	64,000
Butter	26,257	23,691	21,420
Cheese (all kinds)	186,594	195,134	192,300
Hen eggs	158,403	153,420	150,000†
Other poultry eggs	2,696	1,156	1,120†
Honey	10,463	10,553	8,645
Raw silk	184	165†	160†
Wool:			
greasy	31,550	30,654	27,258
scoured	15,332	14,900	13,200
Cattle and buffalo hides†	20,200	19,100	20,900
Sheep skins†	35,800	25,500	26,000

* Unofficial figure.   † FAO estimates.
Source: FAO, mainly *Production Yearbook*.

Forestry

ROUNDWOOD REMOVALS
('000 cubic metres, state forests only)

	1986	1987	1988
Sawlogs, veneer logs and logs for sleepers	1,056	1,040	1,101
Pulpwood	553	575	625
Other industrial wood	1,108	1,059	935
Fuel wood	1,749	1,764	1,810
Total	4,466	4,438	4,471

Source: FAO, *Yearbook of Forest Products*.

SAWNWOOD PRODUCTION ('000 cubic metres, incl. boxboards)

	1986	1987	1988
Coniferous (soft wood)	974	1,097	1,003
Broadleaved (hard wood)	396	372	315
Total	1,370	1,469	1,318

Railway sleepers ('000 cubic metres): 23 in 1986; 21 in 1987; 24 in 1988.
Source: FAO, *Yearbook of Forest Products*.

Fishing

('000 metric tons, live weight)

	1986	1987	1988
Common carp	10.4	10.0	9.5
Southern blue whiting	10.7	7.8	2.2
Patagonian grenadier	0.8	9.6	33.6
Beaked redfish	11.4	12.3	8.8
Cape horse mackerel	48.5	49.4	43.8
European sprat	11.7	11.0	6.2
Other fishes (incl. unspecified)	8.3	7.2	9.0
Total fish	101.7	107.3	113.1
Crustaceans and molluscs	7.6	3.4	4.0
Total catch	109.3	110.7	117.1
Inland waters	14.1	12.9	12.2
Mediterranean and Black Seas	13.0	12.2	8.2
Atlantic Ocean	82.2	85.7	96.6

Source: FAO, *Yearbook of Fishery Statistics*.

Mining

('000 metric tons, unless otherwise indicated)

	1985	1986	1987
Anthracite	83	80	71
Other hard coal	140	127	127
Lignite	25,272	29,896	31,401
Other brown coal	5,385	5,119	5,220
Iron ore*	607	661	559
Copper ore*†	78	80	80
Lead ore*†	97	97	95
Zinc ore*†	68	70‡	68‡
Manganese ore*	11.3	11.2	10.9
Salt (refined)	89	91	92
Crude petroleum‡	300	300	290
Natural gas ('000 terajoules)	5	4	5

* Figures relate to the metal content of ores.
† Source: Metallgesellschaft Aktiengesellschaft (Frankfurt am Main).
‡ UN estimate(s).
Sources: UN, *Industrial Statistics Yearbook*; Committee for Social Information at the Council of Ministers, Sofia.

1988 ('000 metric tons): Anthracite 65; Lignite 29,189; Other brown coal 4,762; Iron ore (metal content) 528; Manganese ore (gross weight) 35; Salt (refined) 103. Source: *Bulgarian Statistical Yearbook 1989*.

Industry

SELECTED PRODUCTS
('000 metric tons, unless otherwise indicated)

	1986	1987	1988
Refined sugar	356	416	361
Wine ('000 hectolitres)	3,898	3,909	n.a.
Beer ('000 hectolitres)	6,023.5	6,212.0	6,331.6
Cigarettes and cigars (metric tons)	89,963	90,326	89,219
Cotton yarn (metric tons)[1]	85,078	88,094	85,717
Woven cotton fabrics ('000 metres)[2]	349,476	353,418	361,384
Flax and hemp yarn (metric tons)	8,465	8,185	8,225
Wool yarn (metric tons)[1]	35,241	41,002	38,205
Woven woollen fabrics ('000 metres)[2]	47,145	43,773	34,417
Woven fabrics of man-made fibres ('000 metres)[3]	37,177	38,062	32,024
Leather footwear ('000 pairs)	24,314	25,041	26,437
Rubber footwear ('000 pairs)	8,682	8,725	8,606
Chemical wood pulp	162.0	158.3	190.8
Paper	337.2	366.6	395.9
Paperboard	68.7	68.2	70.9
Rubber tyres ('000)[4]	1,667.9	1,856.6	1,693.4
Sulphuric acid (100%)	806.6	688.5	839.9
Caustic soda (96%)	143.6	108.6	134.2
Soda ash (98%)	1,054.2	1,070.2	1,100.0
Nitrogenous fertilizers (metric tons)[5]	817,929	804,992	956,270
Phosphate fertilizers (metric tons)[5]	132,377	127,962	178,550
Soap (metric tons)	25,760	28,901	26,470
Coke (gas and coke-oven)	1,156	1,314	1,457
Unworked glass—rectangles ('000 sq metres)	19,525	20,273	18,400
Clay building bricks (million)	1,145	1,051	1,049
Cement	5,702	5,494	5,535
Pig-iron and ferro-alloys	1,651	1,706	1,484
Crude steel	2,965	3,045	2,875
Tractors—10 h.p. and over (number)	5,094	4,751	5,309
Metal-working lathes (number)	5,912	4,886	4,953
Cranes (number)	1,340	1,351	1,456
Fork-lift trucks (number)[6]	84,864	85,110	82,485
Refrigerators—household (number)	117,964	110,530	110,570
Washing machines—household (number)	159,237	171,728	168,923
Radio receivers (number)	38,039	56,090	30,471
Television receivers (number)	153,687	198,592	181,165
Construction: dwellings completed (number)[7]	55,965	63,640	62,926
Electric energy (million kWh)	41,817	43,470	45,036

[1] Pure and mixed yarn. Figures for wool include yarn of man-made staple.
[2] Pure and mixed fabrics, after undergoing finishing processes.
[3] Finished fabrics, including fabrics of natural silk.
[4] Tyres for road motor vehicles (passenger cars and commercial vehicles).
[5] Figures for nitrogenous fertilizers are in terms of nitrogen, and for phosphate fertilizers in terms of phosphoric acid. Data for nitrogenous fertilizers include urea.
[6] Including hoisting gears.
[7] Including restorations and conversions.

Finance

CURRENCY AND EXCHANGE RATES

Monetary Units
100 stotinki (singular: stotinka) = 1 lev (plural: leva).

Denominations
Coins: 1, 2, 5, 10, 20 and 50 stotinki; 1, 2 and 5 leva.
Notes: 1, 2, 5, 10 and 20 leva.

Sterling and Dollar Equivalents (31 July 1990)
£1 sterling = 5.524 leva;
US $1 = 2.970 leva;
100 leva = £18.10 = $33.67.

Note: The foregoing information refers to non-commercial exchange rates, applicable to tourism. For the purposes of external trade, the average value of the lev was: US $1.1524 in 1987; US $1.1999 in 1988.

STATE BUDGET (million leva)

Revenue	1986	1987*	1988*
National economy	20,384.8	19,011.8	21,109.0
Other receipts	1,622.7	1,661.0	1,843.0
Total	22,007.5	20,672.8	22,952.0

Expenditure	1986	1987*	1988*
National economy	11,377.6	9,590.1	10,842.0
Education, health, science, art and culture	3,736.8	3,884.1	4,304.0
Social security†	3,631.7	3,726.9	3,914.0
Administration	3,163.6	336.9	355.0
Other expenditure		3,124.8	3,537.0
Total	21,909.7	20,662.8	22,952.0

* Approved budget proposals.
† Including the pension fund for agricultural co-operatives.

1989 (forecasts, million leva): Revenue 24,287.8; Expenditure 24,286.3.
1990 (forecasts, million leva): Revenue 24,894; Expenditure 25,851.

COST OF LIVING
(Consumer Price Index; base: 1980 = 100)

	1986	1987	1988
Food	112.4	112.4	114.0
Others	105.3	105.4	106.5
All items	108.3	108.4	109.7

NATIONAL ACCOUNTS

Net Material Product* (million leva at current market prices)

Activities of the Material Sphere	1986	1987	1988
Agriculture and livestock	3,957.2	3,712.1	3,712.0
Forestry†	104.9	107.9	108.2
Industry‡	16,676.8	16,649.7	17,088.3
Construction	2,564.3	2,674.7	2,780.3
Trade, restaurants, etc.§	1,227.0	2,499.8	2,471.2
Transport and storage	1,309.8	1,567.6	2,069.1
Communications	442.4	490.6	527.3
Other activities†	569.0	635.6	666.2
Total	26,851.4	28,338.0	29,422.6

* Defined as the total net value of goods and 'productive' services, including turnover taxes, produced by the economy. This excludes economic activities not contributing directly to material production, such as public administration, defence and personal and professional services.
† Beginning in 1986, forestry includes non-organized hunting and fishing, previously included in other activities.
‡ Principally manufacturing, mining, electricity, gas and water supply. The figures also include the value of hunting, fishing and logging when these activities are organized.
§ Includes material and technical supply.

BULGARIA

External Trade

PRINCIPAL COMMODITIES (million foreign exchange leva)

Imports f.o.b.	1986	1987	1988
Machinery and equipment	5,371.3	5,582.5	5,794.7
Power and electro-technical machinery	689.0	542.0	478.4
Mining, metallurgical and oil-drilling equipment	314.6	436.5	291.4
Tractors and agricultural machinery	334.8	378.3	441.4
Fuels, mineral raw materials and metals	6,306.7	5,701.0	5,108.2
Solid fuels	489.4	445.6	374.4
Ferrous metals	911.3	896.0	854.7
Chemicals, fertilizers and rubber	647.1	704.3	755.1
Chemicals	297.9	351.6	399.3
Agricultural crop and livestock crude materials (except foods)	635.0	663.5	748.7
Timber, cellulose and paper products	231.7	236.8	225.7
Textile raw materials and semi-manufactures	180.9	183.3	248.3
Raw materials for food production	471.6	412.4	431.0
Other industrial goods for consumption	580.2	656.4	709.3
Commodities for cultural purposes	165.9	153.9	155.4
Total (incl. others)	14,353.3	14,067.3	13,928.0

1989 (million leva): Machinery and equipment 5,436.6; Fuels, mineral raw materials and metals 4,335.9; Chemicals, fertilizers and rubber 627.9; Agricultural crop and livestock crude materials (except foods) 649.9; Raw materials for food production 510.7; Other industrial goods for consumption 644.4; Total (incl. others) 12,551.7.

Exports f.o.b.*	1986	1987	1988
Machinery and equipment	7,719.8	8,359.6	8,723.7
Power and electro-technical machinery	620.2	659.9	627.5
Hoisting and hauling equipment	1,361.3	1,449.8	1,436.6
Agricultural machinery	273.0	269.7	244.5
Fuels, mineral raw materials and metals	1,071.3	980.8	1,010.2
Ferrous metals	353.6	367.9	463.7
Chemicals, fertilizers and rubber	443.8	420.5	492.8
Chemicals	278.7	248.8	341.6
Building materials and components	271.0	258.2	273.3
Agricultural crop and livestock crude materials (except foods)	181.9	211.5	234.1
Raw materials for food production (incl. tobacco)	334.0	346.8	349.2
Foodstuffs, beverages and tobacco products	1,759.7	1,674.6	1,688.6
Meat and dairy products, animal fats and eggs	249.0	229.5	251.1
Wine, brandy and spirits	306.3	293.5	301.7
Cigarettes	670.8	673.6	672.4
Other industrial goods for consumption	1,434.7	1,460.2	1,541.7
Clothing and underwear	313.3	301.4	310.0
Total (incl. others)	13,350.5	13,802.0	14,417.4

* Figures include foreign aid and loans, and exports of ships' stores and bunkers for foreign vessels.

1989 (million leva): Machinery and equipment 8,071.1; Fuels, mineral raw materials and metals 939.5; Chemicals, fertilizers and rubber 471.0; Building materials and components 272.4; Agricultural crop and livestock crude materials (except foods) 243.9; Raw materials for food production (incl. tobacco) 303.2; Foodstuffs, beverages and tobacco products 1,592.5; Other industrial goods for consumption 1,513.8; Total (incl. others) 13,506.3.

PRINCIPAL TRADING PARTNERS*
(million foreign exchange leva)

Imports f.o.b.	1987	1988	1989
Austria	218.4	219.5	187.6
Cuba	252.3	172.3	220.0
Czechoslovakia	697.1	751.7	626.8
France	98.7	94.8	129.5
German Democratic Republic	804.2	818.0	734.2
Germany, Federal Republic	694.9	686.1	617.9
Hungary	285.3	265.3	170.8
Italy	164.6	156.3	181.1
Japan	145.1	156.7	159.9
Libya	135.7	92.9	72.1
Poland	669.9	691.6	605.6
Romania	306.5	288.6	238.4
Switzerland	192.7	192.3	207.2
USSR	8,056.1	7,453.8	6,731.3
United Kingdom	161.6	134.8	145.5
USA	91.8	123.8	189.0
Yugoslavia	105.0	136.6	106.7
Total (incl. others)	14,067.3	13,928.0	12,551.7

Exports f.o.b.	1987	1988	1989
Cuba	199.1	258.5	194.7
Czechoslovakia	673.4	665.6	594.8
German Democratic Republic	756.9	749.9	752.4
Germany, Federal Republic	159.7	142.4	150.7
Greece	140.3	136.3	175.6
Hungary	254.0	295.2	187.4
Iraq	394.8	396.2	135.4
Italy	82.5	103.5	n.a.
Libya	469.1	328.1	174.8
Poland	598.1	593.0	524.7
Romania	287.5	294.8	276.9
Switzerland	131.8	113.6	94.5
USSR	8,437.3	9,006.5	8,882.1
United Kingdom	75.9	97.4	99.7
Total (incl. others)	13,802.0	14,417.4	13,506.3

* Imports by country of purchase; exports by country of sale.

Transport

RAILWAYS (traffic)

	1986	1987	1988
Passenger-kilometres (million)	8,004	8,075	8,143
Freight ton-kilometres (million)	18,327	17,842	17,585

INLAND WATERWAYS (traffic)

	1986	1987	1988
Passenger-kilometres (million)	14	17	12
Freight ton-kilometres (million)	2,425	1,971	2,162

SEA-BORNE SHIPPING
(international and coastal traffic)

	1986	1987	1988
Passengers carried ('000)	527	460	464
Freight ('000 metric tons)	24,795	25,888	24,001

CIVIL AVIATION (traffic)

	1986	1987	1988
Passenger-kilometres (million)	2,961	3,578	3,897
Freight ton-kilometres (million)	43	42	45

BULGARIA
Statistical Survey, Directory

Tourism

VISITORS TO BULGARIA BY COUNTRY OF ORIGIN

	1986	1987	1988
Austria*	48,253	53,828	56,082
Czechoslovakia	383,682	398,053	425,934
France	27,252	32,872	34,857
German Democratic Republic	260,231	283,329	309,833
Germany, Federal Republic*	225,958	267,891	276,458
Greece	76,305	149,888	155,313
Hungary	213,432	243,163	246,561
Iran*	36,255	42,887	43,197
Italy	18,396	23,624	25,041
Poland	527,715	746,644	922,352
Romania	181,512	193,034	221,928
Sweden	16,969	28,185	27,549
Turkey*	2,897,168	2,949,674	3,230,528
USSR	303,613	384,054	471,560
United Kingdom	45,996	74,897	89,521
Yugoslavia	1,916,036	1,436,384	1,454,812
Total (incl. others)	7,567,062	7,593,637	8,294,985

* Mainly visitors in transit, totalling 4,327,575 (of whom 3,217,067 came from Turkey) in 1988.

Communications Media

	1986	1987	1988
Telephone subscribers	2,078,820	2,228,681	2,386,462
Radio licences	1,997,355	1,982,929	1,965,117
Television licences	1,692,744	1,692,411	1,679,777
Book production:			
Titles*	4,924	4,583	4,379
Copies ('000)*	58,985	60,078	58,943

* Figures include pamphlets (818 titles and 7,460,000 copies in 1986; 797 titles and 9,897,000 copies in 1987; 689 titles and 7,197,000 copies in 1988).

1984: Daily newspapers 12 (average circulation 2,298,000 copies); Non-daily newspapers 37 (average circulation 1,092,000 copies); Other periodicals 1,758 (average circulation 10,211,000 copies).

Education

(1988/89)

	Institutions	Teachers	Students
Kindergartens	4,666	28,897	339,891
Unified secondary polytechnical	3,516	73,794	1,234,851
Special	129	2,404	16,587
Vocational technical	3	50	1,586
Secondary vocational technical	262	7,101	107,964
Technical colleges and schools of arts	265	11,138	124,953
Technical colleges after secondary level	10	512	7,120
Semi-higher institutes (teacher training)	16	868	11,377
Higher educational	30	17,759	126,964

Source: Ministry of Education, Sofia.

Directory

The Constitution

Bulgaria was formerly a monarchy but on 15 September 1946 King Simeon was deposed and Bulgaria was declared a Republic. The Constitution of 1947 was replaced by a new constitution, which was adopted by a referendum held on 16 May 1971, and proclaimed by the Fifth National Assembly on 18 May. The following are among its main provisions:

The People's Republic of Bulgaria is a socialist state of the working people of towns and villages, headed by the working class. The Bulgarian Communist Party is the leading force in society and in the State. It guides the construction of a developed socialist society in the country in close fraternal co-operation with the Bulgarian Agrarian Union.*

The State serves the people. It defends their interests and socialist acquisitions; directs the country's socio-economic development according to a plan; creates conditions for the constant improvement of the welfare, education and health services of the people, as well as for the all-round development of science and culture; ensures the free development of man, guarantees his rights and protects his dignity; organizes the defence of national independence, state sovereignty and the country's territorial integrity; develops and consolidates the friendship, co-operation and mutual assistance with the Union of Soviet Socialist Republics and the other socialist countries; conducts a policy of peace and understanding with all countries and peoples.

In the People's Republic of Bulgaria all power comes from the people and belongs to the people. It is realized by the people through the freely elected representative organs—the National Assembly and the People's Councils—or directly. The representative organs are elected on the basis of a general, equal and direct right to vote by secret ballot.

All the citizens of the People's Republic of Bulgaria who are 18 years of age, irrespective of sex, nationality, race, religion, education, profession, official, public or property status, excluding those under restraint, are eligible to vote and to be elected.

The People's Republic of Bulgaria is governed strictly in accordance with the Constitution and the country's laws. It belongs to the world socialist community, which is one of the main conditions for its independence and all-round development.

THE NATIONAL ASSEMBLY

The National Assembly is the supreme representative organ which expresses the will of the people and their sovereignty. As a supreme organ of state power it combines the legislative and executive activities of the State and exercises supreme control. The term of its mandate is five years. It is composed of 400 people's representatives who are elected in constituencies with an equal number of inhabitants.† The people's representatives are responsible and account to their electorate. They may be recalled before the expiry of the term for which they have been elected. Their recall is effected by decision of the electorate in a manner laid down by law. The Assembly is convened to sessions by the State Council at least three times a year.

The National Assembly is the only legislative organ of the People's Republic of Bulgaria and the supreme organizer of the planned management of social development. It realizes the supreme leadership of the home and foreign policy of the State; approves and amends the Constitution; determines which questions should be decided by referendum, and in what manner; passes, amends and revokes laws; passes the unified plans for the social-economic

BULGARIA

development of the country and the reports on their fulfilment and the State Budget and the report of the Government on its realization the preceding year; establishes taxes and fixes their rate; grants amnesty; decides the questions of declaring war and concluding peace; appoints and relieves of his duties the Commander-in-Chief of the Armed Forces; may set up state-public organs with the status of ministries; elects and relieves of their duties the State Council‡, the Council of Ministers, the Supreme Court and the Chief Prosecutor of the People's Republic; passes laws, decisions, declarations and appeals.

Legislative initiative belongs to the State Council‡, the Council of Ministers, the permanent commissions of the National Assembly, the people's representatives, the Supreme Court and the Chief Prosecutor. The right of legislative initiative belongs also to public organizations in the person of the National Council of the Fatherland Front, the Central Council of Bulgarian Trade Unions, the Central Committee of the Dimitrov Young Communist League§ and the Executive Council of the Central Co-operative Council on questions referring to their activity.

THE COUNCIL OF MINISTERS

The Council of Ministers (the Government) is a supreme executive and administrative organ of the State Power. The Council effects its activities under the leadership and control of the National Assembly, and—when the latter is not in session—under the leadership and control of the State Council.§

The Council of Ministers is responsible for the conducting of the internal and external policy of the State. It exercises the right of legislative initiative and secures conditions for carrying through the rights and freedoms of citizens. It also ensures public order and the country's security. It is responsible for the general leadership of the Armed Forces and concludes international agreements. It directly guides, co-ordinates and controls the activities of the ministries and other departments. The Council organizes both the implementation of the acts of the National Assembly, and of the State Council.‡ It guides and controls the activities of the executive committees of the people's councils. It adopts decrees, instructions and decisions.

LOCAL GOVERNMENT

The territory of the Republic is divided for administrative purposes into nine regions‖ (each comprising several municipalities), which are governed by Regional People's Councils, elected by the local population. Their function is to implement all economic, social and cultural undertakings of local significance in conformity with the laws of the country. They prepare local economic plans and budgets within the framework of the State Economic Plan and the State Budget, and direct its execution. They are responsible for the correct administration of state property and economic enterprises in their areas, and for the maintenance of law and order. These councils report at least once a year to their electors on their activities.

JUSTICE

The judicial authorities apply the law. Justice is independent and subject only to the law. Lay judges (Assessors) also take part in the dispensation of justice. Judges of all ranks and assessors are elected except in special cases fixed by law. Supreme judicial control over every kind of court is exercised by the Supreme Court of the People's Republic, which is elected by the National Assembly for a term of five years.

Citizens whose rights have been violated by government organs may appeal against such violations before higher-ranking organs and courts, in accordance with the Law of Administrative Procedure, 1970.

The Chief Prosecutor, who is also elected by the National Assembly for five years, and is answerable to it alone, has supreme supervision over the correct observance of the law by Government organs, officials, and all citizens. It is his particular duty to attend to the prosecution and punishment of crimes that are detrimental to the national and economic interests of the Republic or affect its independence.

THE RIGHTS AND DUTIES OF CITIZENS

All citizens are equal before the law. No privileges or restrictions in rights based on nationality, origin, religion, sex, race, education or property are recognized. All preaching of racial, national or religious hatred is punishable by law.

Women have equal rights with men in all spheres, including equal pay for equal work. The State pays special attention to the needs of mothers and children. Marriage and the family are under state protection, although only civil marriage is legally valid. Children born out of wedlock have equal rights with legitimate offspring.

All citizens have the right to free medical treatment in hospitals.

Directory

Labour is recognized as the basic factor of public and economic life. All citizens have the right to work, and it is their duty to engage in socially useful labour, according to their abilities. Holidays, limited working hours, pensions and medical treatment are guaranteed.

All citizens have the right to free education, which is secular and democratic. Elementary education is compulsory. National minorities have the right to be educated in their own tongue, and to develop their national culture, although the study of Bulgarian is compulsory.

The Church is separate from the State. Citizens have freedom of religion and conscience. However, misuse of the Church and religion for political ends and the formation of religious organizations with a political basis is prohibited.

Citizens are guaranteed freedom of speech and of the Press, secrecy of correspondence, inviolability of persons and dwellings, and the right of meetings and rallies.

Military service is compulsory for all male citizens.

* Following the decision taken by the BCP in December 1989 to renounce its role as the 'leading force in society and in the State', the National Assembly voted in January 1990 to delete Paragraphs 2 and 3 of Article 1 from the Constitution. In April 1990 Paragraph 1 of Article 1 was amended to read: 'The People's Republic of Bulgaria is a democratic, parliamentary and law-abiding state'. (The country was subsequently renamed the Republic of Bulgaria.)
† The electoral procedure was altered prior to the general election, held in June 1990 (see Recent History).
‡ Dissolved in March 1990, and replaced by the office of President.
§ Renamed, respectively, the Fatherland Union, the Confederation of Independent Bulgarian Trade Unions, and the Bulgarian Democratic Youth Organization, in 1990.
‖ The decree replacing 28 administrative districts by nine regions was repealed in January 1990.

A new constitution was expected to be drafted by the end of 1991.

The Government
(January 1991)

HEAD OF STATE

President: ZHELYU ZHELEV (elected 1 August 1990).
Vice-President: Col.-Gen. ATANAS SEMERDZHIEV.

COUNCIL OF MINISTERS

The Council of Ministers is composed of members of the Bulgarian Socialist Party (BSP), the Union of Democratic Forces (UDF), the Bulgarian Agrarian People's Union (BAPU) and Independents.

Chairman: DIMITUR POPOV (Independent).
Deputy Chairmen: ALEKSANDUR TOMOV (BSP), DIMITUR LUDZHEV (UDF).
Deputy Chairman and Minister of Foreign Affairs: VIKTOR VULKOV (BAPU).
Minister of Finance: IVAN KOSTOV (UDF).
Minister of Industry, Trade and Services: IVAN PUSHKAROV (UDF).
Minister of Foreign Economic Relations: ATANAS PAPARIZOV (BSP).
Minister of Transport: VESELIN PAVLOV (BSP).
Minister of Justice: PENCHO PENEV (BSP).
Minister of Defence: YORDAN MUTAFCHIEV (BSP).
Minister of Internal Affairs: KHRISTO DANOV (Independent).
Minister of Agriculture: BORIS SPIROV (BAPU).
Minister of the Environment: DIMITUR VODENICHAROV (Independent).
Minister of Employment and Social Welfare: EMILIYA MASLAROVA (BSP).
Minister of Health: IVAN CHERNOZEMSKI (BSP).
Minister of Education: MATEI MATEEV (BSP).
Minister of Science and Higher Education: GEORGI FOTEV (UDF).
Minister of Culture: DIMO DIMOV (Independent).

MINISTRIES

Council of Ministers: 1000 Sofia, Blvd Dondukov 1; tel. 86-91.
Ministry of Agriculture: Sofia, Blvd Botev 55.
Ministry of Defence: Sofia, Levsky St.
Ministry of Education: 1000 Sofia, Blvd A. Stamboliiski 18; tel. 84-81; telex 22384; fax 87-12-89.

BULGARIA

Directory

Ministry of Employment and Social Welfare: 1000 Sofia, pl. Sveta Nedelya 5; tel. 86-31; telex 22430.

Ministry of Foreign Affairs: 1000 Sofia, 2 Al. Zhendov St; telex 22530.

Ministry of Foreign Economic Relations: 1000 Sofia, Sofiiska Komuna St 12.

Ministry of Internal Affairs: Sofia, ul. Shesti Septemvri.

Ministry of Justice: Sofia; telex 22933.

Ministry of Transport: 1000 Sofia, Levsky St 9-11; tel. 88-12-30; telex 23200; fax 88-50-94.

Legislature

VELIKO NARODNO SOBRANIYE
(Grand National Assembly)

Chairman: Acad. NIKOLAI TODOROV.

Deputy Chairmen: IVAN GLUSHKOV, GINYO GANEV, NIKODIM POPOV.

General election, 10 and 17 June 1990

Parties and Groups	% of votes*	Seats by proportional representation	Constituency seats	Total seats
Bulgarian Socialist Party (BSP)	47.15	97	114	211
Union of Democratic Forces (UDF)	37.84	75	69	144
Bulgarian Agrarian People's Union (BAPU)	8.03	16	0	16
Movement for Rights and Freedoms (MRF)	6.03	12	11	23
Fatherland Union†	—	0	2	2
Bulgarian Social Democratic Party (non-Marxist—BSDP)	0.05	0	1	1
Fatherland Party of Labour†	—	0	1	1
Independents†	—	0	2	2
Others	0.90	0	0	0
Total	100.00	200	200	400

* Percentage of votes won according to a system of proportional representation of parties.

† Did not contest the elections held according to a system of proportional representation of parties.

Political Organizations

Bulgarian Agrarian People's Union—BAPU (Bulgarski Zemedelski Naroden Soyuz—BZNS): Sofia, Yanko Zabunov St 1; tel. 88-19-51; telex 23302; fax 80-09-91; f. 1899; in opposition after Nov. 1989; 150,000 mems.; Chair. VIKTOR VULKOV.

Bulgarian Social Democratic Party (non-Marxist)—BSDP: Sofia; f. 1989 as the Bulgarian Socialist Party, renamed as above in 1990; c. 20,000 mems; Chair. IVAN VELKOV.

Bulgarian Socialist Party—BSP (Bulgarska Sotsialisticheska Partiya—BSP): Sofia, Blvd Dondukov 1; tel. 84-01; fax 87-12-92; f. 1891 as the Bulgarian Social Democratic Party (BSDP); renamed the Bulgarian Communist Party (BCP) in 1919; absorbed the remaining BSDP in 1947; renamed as above in April 1990; 260,000 mems (1990); Chair. of Supreme Council ALEKSANDUR LILOV; Deputy Chair. ALEKSANDUR TOMOV, CHAVDAR KYURANOV, DIMITUR YONCHEV, LYUBOMIR KUCHUKOV; Pres. of the All-Party Control Commission DEYAN RIZOV.

Christian Republican Party: Sofia; f. 1989; Chair. KONSTANTIN ADZHAROV.

Democratic Monarchist Party: Sofia, Rakovski St; f. 1990; campaigns for the restoration of civil rights to the former King Simeon II.

Fatherland Party of Labour: Kurdzhali; nationalist; Leader DIMITUR ARNAUDOV.

Fatherland Union: Sofia, Blvd Vitosha 18; tel. 88-12-21; telex 22783; f. 1942 as the Fatherland Front (a mass organization unifying the BAPU, the Bulgarian Communist Party (now the BSP) and social organizations); succeeded in 1990 by the Fatherland Union; a socio-political organization of individuals belonging to different political parties and independents; Chair. GINYO GANEV.

Movement for Rights and Freedoms (MRF): f. 1990; represents Muslim minority in Bulgaria; 140,000 mems; Pres. AKHMED DOGAN.

Republican Party: Sofia; f. 1990; Chair. Prof. ALEKSANDUR POPOV.

Union of Democratic Forces—UDF (Soyuz na Demokratichnite Sili): Sofia, Rakovski St 134; f. 1989; opposition alliance of six parties and 10 organizations and movements; Chair. of Co-ordination Council FILIP DIMITROV.

> **Alternative Socialist Party:** breakaway faction of BCP (later BSP); joined UDF in 1990; Chair. NIKOLAI VASILEV.
>
> **Bulgarian Social Democratic Party (United—BSDP):** Sofia; Chair. Dr PETUR DERTLIEV.
>
> **Citizens' Initiative Movement:** Leader LYUBOMIR SOBAZHIYEV.
>
> **Club for the Support of Glasnost and Perestroika:** f. 1988; Chair. Assoc. Prof. PETKO SIMEONOV.
>
> **Club of Persons Illegally Repressed After 1945:** f. 1989; Chair. DIMITUR BAKALOV.
>
> **Democratic Party:** reformed 1990; Chair. of Provisional Operational Bureau DIMITUR DIAMANDIEV.
>
> **Ecoglasnost Independent Association:** f. 1989; is represented in more than 50 clubs and organizations in Bulgaria; Chair. PETUR SLABAKOV; Chief Sec. GEORGI AVRAMOV.
>
> **Green Party:** f. 1989; environmentalist; 10,000 mems; Pres. ALEKSANDUR KARAKACHANOV.
>
> **New Social Democratic Party:** f. 1990; Chair. PETUR MARKOV.
>
> **Nikola Petkov Bulgarian Agrarian People's Union:** reformed 1989; Chief Sec. MILAN DRENCHEV.
>
> **Podkrepa (Support) Independent Trade Union Federation:** f. 1989; 400,000 mems; Chair. Dr KONSTANTIN TRENCHEV.
>
> **Radical Democratic Party:** Chair. Dr ELKA KONSTANTINOVA.
>
> The UDF also embraces the Committee for the Protection of Religious Rights and Freedoms, the Democratic Centre Association, the Independent Association for Human Rights in Bulgaria, and the Independent Student League.

Union of Free Democrats: Sofia; f. 1989; Chair. Asst Prof. KHRISTO STANULOV.

Diplomatic Representation

EMBASSIES IN BULGARIA

Afghanistan: Sofia, L. Karavelov St 34; tel. 66-12-45; Ambassador: MEHRABUDDIN PAKTIAWAL.

Albania: Sofia, Dimitur Polyanov St 10; tel. 44-33-81; Ambassador: BASHKIM RAMA.

Algeria: Sofia, Slavyanska St 16; tel. 87-56-83; telex 22519; Ambassador: ZINE EL-ABIDINE HACHICHI.

Argentina: Sofia, Blvd Klement Gottwald 42; tel. 44-38-21; Ambassador: RAÚL MEDINA MUÑOZ.

Austria: 1000 Sofia, Ruski St 13; tel. 52-28-07; telex 22566; Ambassador: Dr MANFRED KIEPACH.

Belgium: Sofia, ul. Frédéric Joliot-Curie 19; tel. 72-35-27; telex 22455; Ambassador: MICHAEL DOOMS.

Brazil: Sofia, Blvd Rusky 27; tel. 44-36-55; telex 22099; Chargé d'affaires a.i.: SONJA MARIA DE CASTRO.

Cambodia: Sofia, Mladost 1, Blvd S. Aliende Res. 2; tel. 75-51-35 Chargé d'affaires a.i.: SIM SUONG.

China, People's Republic: Sofia, Blvd Rusky 18; tel. 87-87-24; telex 22545; Ambassador: LI FENLIN.

Colombia: Sofia, Vasil Aprilov 17; tel. 44-61-77; telex 23393; Ambassador: EVELIO RAMÍREZ MARTÍNEZ.

Congo: Sofia, Blvd Klement Gottwald 54; tel. 44-65-18; telex 23828; Chargé d'affaires a.i.: PIERRE ADOUA.

Cuba: Sofia, Mladezhka St 1; tel. 72-09-96; telex 22428; Ambassador: MANUEL PÉREZ HERNÁNDEZ.

Czechoslovakia: Sofia, Blvd Vladimir Zaimov 9; tel. 44-62-81; Ambassador: VÁCLAV JANOUŠEK.

Denmark: 1000 Sofia, Blvd Rusky 10, POB 1393; tel. 88-04-55; telex 22099; Ambassador: S. G. MELLBIN.

Egypt: Sofia, ul. Shesti Septemvri 5; tel. 87-02-15; telex 22270; Ambassador: MOHAMED EL-ETREBY.

Ethiopia: Sofia, Vasil Kolarov St 28; tel. 88-39-24; Chargé d'affaires a.i.: AYELLE MAKONEN.

BULGARIA

Finland: Sofia, Volokamsko St 57; tel. 68-33-26; telex 23148; Ambassador: Pekka Artturi Oinonen.

France: Sofia, Oborishte St 29; tel. 44-11-71; telex 22336; Ambassador: Jacques Rummelhardt.

Germany: 1113 Sofia, Henri Barbusse St 7; tel. 72-21-27; telex 22590; fax 71-80-41; Ambassador: Karl Walter Lewalter.

Ghana: 1113 Sofia, Pierre Degeyter St 9, Apt 37-38; tel. 70-65-09; Ambassador: Coffi Akuwa-Harrison.

Greece: Sofia, Blvd Klement Gottwald 68; tel. 44-37-70; telex 22458; Ambassador: Georgios Christoyannis.

Hungary: Sofia, ul. Shesti Septemvri 57; tel. 66-20-21; telex 22459; Ambassador: Sándor Simics.

India: Sofia, Blvd Patriyarkh Evtimii 31; tel. 87-39-44; telex 22954; Ambassador: Girish Dhume.

Indonesia: 1504 Sofia, Veliko Turnovo St 32; tel. 44-23-49; telex 22358; Ambassador: Abdel Kobir Sasradipoera.

Iran: Sofia, Blvd Klement Gottwald 70; tel. 44-10-13; telex 22303; Ambassador: Sayyed Homayun Amir-Khalili.

Iraq: Sofia, Anton Chekhov St 21; tel. 87-00-13; telex 22307; Ambassador: Fawsi Dakir al-Ani.

Italy: Sofia, Shipka St 2; tel. 88-17-06; telex 22173; Ambassador: Paolo Taroni.

Japan: Sofia, Lyulyakova Gradina St 14; tel. 72-39-84; telex 22397; fax 72-25-15; Ambassador: Takashi Tajima.

Korea, Democratic People's Republic: Sofia, Mladost 1, Blvd S. Aliende Res. 4; tel. 77-53-48; Ambassador: Kim Pyong Il.

Korea, Republic: Sofia, Blvd Anton Ivmon; tel. 624-51; Ambassador: Kim Choe-Su.

Kuwait: Sofia, Blvd Klement Gottwald 47; tel. 44-19-92; telex 23586; Ambassador: Talib Jalal ad-Din al-Naqib.

Laos: Sofia, Ovcha Kupel, Buket St 80; tel. 56-55-08; Ambassador: Thaleune Warrintrasak.

Lebanon: Sofia, ul. Frédéric Joliot-Curie 19; tel. 72-04-31; telex 23140; Ambassador: Hussein Moussawi.

Libya: Sofia, Oborishte St 10; tel. 44-19-21; telex 22180; Secretary of People's Bureau: Omar Muftah Dallal.

Mexico: Sofia, Todor Strashimirov St 1; tel. 44-32-82; telex 22087; Ambassador: Jaime Fernández-MacGregor.

Mongolia: Sofia, ul. Frédéric Joliot-Curie 52; tel. 65-84-03; telex 22274; Ambassador: Lhamyn Tserendondog.

Morocco: Sofia, Blvd Klement Gottwald 44; tel. 44-27-94; telex 23515; Ambassador: Abdelhamid Bennani.

Mozambique: Sofia; Ambassador: Gonçalves Rafael Sengo.

Netherlands: Sofia, Denkoglu St 19a; tel. 87-41-86; telex 22686; Ambassador: Vivian H. Meertins.

Nicaragua: Sofia, Mladost 1, Blvd Aliende, Res. 1; tel. 75-41-57; Ambassador: Roger Vásquez Barrios.

Peru: Sofia, ul. Frédéric Joliot-Curie 19, Apt. 20; tel. 70-32-63; telex 23182; Chargé d'affaires: Julio Vega Erausquín.

Poland: Sofia, Khan Krum St 46; tel. 88-51-66; telex 22595; Ambassador: Wiesław Bek.

Portugal: Sofia, Ivats Voivoda St 6; tel. 44-35-48; telex 22082; Ambassador: Luiz Gonzaga Ferreira.

Romania: Sofia, Sitnyakovo St 4; tel. 70-70-47; telex 22321; Ambassador: Vasile Pungan.

Spain: Sofia, Oborishte St 47; tel. 43-00-17; telex 22308; Ambassador: Joaquín Pérez Gómez.

Sweden: Sofia, pl. Veltchova Zavera 1; tel. 65-10-02; telex 22373; Ambassador: Ake Berg.

Switzerland: 1000 Sofia, Shipka St 33; tel. 44-31-98; telex 22792; fax 44-39-47; Ambassador: Harald Borner.

Syria: Sofia, Hristo Georgiev 10; tel. 44-15-85; telex 23464; Chargé d'affaires: Ahmad Omran.

Turkey: Sofia, Blvd Tolbukhin 23; tel. 87-23-06; telex 22199; Ambassador: Yalçin Oral.

USSR: Sofia, Blvd Bulgaro-savetska druzhba 28; tel. 66-88-19; Ambassador: Viktor Vasilevich Sharapov.

United Kingdom: Sofia, Blvd Tolbukhin 65–67; tel. 87-95-75; telex 22363; fax 65-60-22; Ambassador: Richard Thomas.

USA: Sofia, Blvd A. Stamboliiski 1; tel. 88-48-01; telex 22690; fax 88-48-06; Ambassador: H. Kenneth Hill.

Uruguay: Sofia, Tsar Ivan Asen II St 91, POB 213; tel. 44-19-57; telex 23087; Ambassador: Guido M. Yerlas.

Venezuela: Sofia, ul. Frédéric Joliot-Curie 17; tel. 72-39-77; telex 23495; Ambassador: José Gregorio González Rodríguez.

Viet-Nam: Sofia, Ilya Petrov St 1; tel. 72-08-79; telex 22717; Ambassador: Nguyen Tien Thong.

Yemen: Sofia, Blvd S. Aliende, Res. 3; tel. 75-61-63; Ambassador: Ali Munassar Muhammad.

Yugoslavia: Sofia, G. Gheorghiu-Dej St 3; tel. 44-32-37; telex 23537; Ambassador: Milenko Stefanović.

Judicial System

Justice in the Republic of Bulgaria is administered by the district, regional and military courts and by the Supreme Court. All labour disputes are considered by the conciliation committees of the enterprises and by the regional courts. Civil law disputes among state enterprises, offices and co-operative and public organizations are adjudicated by the State Court of Arbitration, and disputes connected with international trade by the Foreign Trade Court of Arbitration at the Bulgarian Chamber of Commerce and Industry.

The district court judges and assessors are elected by the district people's councils for a term of five years. Judges and assessors of the Supreme Court are elected for a term of five years by the National Assembly. Judicial control over the activities of all courts is exercised by the Supreme Court. Control for the correct observance of the law by local government authorities and officials, and by the citizens, is exercised by the Chief Prosecutor of the Republic, who is elected by the National Assembly for a term of five years. All other prosecutors of courts are appointed and discharged by the Chief Prosecutor. All courts and prisons are under the Ministry of Justice. All lawyers are organized in consultation offices and citizens have the right to choose their own legal representatives from among the members of any such group. State enterprises may employ their own legal adviser.

President of the Supreme Court: Dimitur Lozanchev.

Chief Prosecutor: Evtim Stoichkov.

Religion

Committee for Affairs of the Bulgarian Orthodox Church and the Religious Denominations: Sofia, Al. Zhendov St 2; deals with relations between religious organizations and the Government; Chair. Lyubomir Popov.

CHRISTIANITY

The Orthodox Churches

Armenian-Apostolic-Orthodox Church: Sofia, Naicho Tzanov St 31; tel. 88-02-08; 20,000 adherents (1985); administered by Bishop Dirayr Mardikiyan (resident in Bucharest); Chair. of the Diocesan Council in Bulgaria Garo Dermesrobiyan.

Bulgarian Orthodox Church: 1090 Sofia, Synod Palace, 4 Oborishte St; tel. 87-56-11; f. 865; administered by the Bulgarian Patriarchy; there are 11 dioceses in Bulgaria and two foreign dioceses, each under a Metropolitan; adherents in Bulgaria comprise 80% of the church-going population; His Holiness Patriarch Maxim.

The Roman Catholic Church

Bulgarian Catholics may be adherents of either the Latin or the Bulgarian (Byzantine-Slav) Rite. The country comprises two dioceses, both directly responsible to the Holy See.

Latin Rite

Bishop of Nikopol: Samuil Serafimov Dzhundrin, 7000 Ruse, Rost. Blaskov St 14; tel. 2-81-88; 20,000 adherents (Dec. 1987).

Diocese of Sofia and Plovdiv: Georgi Ivanov Yovchev (Apostolic Administrator) 4000 Plovdiv, Lilyana Dimitrova St 3; tel. 22-84-30; 35,000 adherents (Dec. 1988).

Bulgarian Rite

Apostolic Exarch of Sofia: Metodi Dimitrov Stratiyev (Titular Bishop of Diocletianopolis in Thrace), 1606 Sofia, ul. Pashovi 10/B; tel. 52-02-97; 15,000 adherents (Dec. 1988).

The Protestant Churches

Bulgarian Evangelical Methodist Church: Sofia, Rakovski St 86; tel. 87-33-58; Gen. Superintendent Rev. Zdravko Bezlov.

Union of the Churches of the Seventh-day Adventists: Sofia, Vasil Kolarov St 10; tel. 88-12-18; Head Pastor Agop Tachmissjan.

Union of the Evangelical Baptist Churches: Varna, Georgi Dimitrov St 100; tel. 45-64-22; Head Pastor Georgi Todorov.

Union of the Evangelical Congregational Churches: Sofia, Vasil Kolarov St 49; tel. 88-05-93; Head Pastor Pavel Ivanov.

Union of the Evangelical Pentecostal Churches: 1557 Sofia, Bacho Kiro St 21; tel. 83-22-33; f. 1928; Head Pastor Dinko Jelev.

BULGARIA

ISLAM

Supreme Muslim Theological Council: Sofia, Bratya Miladinovi St 27; tel. 87-73-20; adherents estimated at 14% of the actively religious population, with an estimated 500 acting regional imams; Chief Mufti of the Turkish Muslims in Bulgaria NEDYO GEDZHEV; Mufti of the Bulgarian Muslims CHAVDAR ILIYEV, Smolyan.

JUDAISM

Central Jewish Theological Council: 1000 Sofia, Eksarkh Yosif St 16; tel. 83-12-73; 5,000 adherents; Head YOSSIF LEVI.

The Press

Prior to the political upheavals which began in late 1989, the press in Bulgaria was largely controlled by the Communist Party (later renamed the Bulgarian Socialist Party, BSP) and by organizations attached to the Fatherland Front. In 1990 the press laws were liberalized, and many publications, hitherto banned, became freely available. Of the new independent dailies established in 1990, the most important was *Demokratsiya*, published by the opposition Union of Democratic Forces, with a circulation of 197,000. At October 1990 the BSP daily *Duma* (formerly *Rabotnichesko Delo*) had the largest circulation (720,000), while *Trud*, the daily of the Confederation of Independent Trade Unions, ranked second, with a circulation of 280,000. The weekly publications with the largest circulation were *Pogled*, the organ of the Union of Bulgarian Journalists (380,000), and *Sturshel*, a satirical periodical (344,000).

PRINCIPAL DAILIES

Chernomorsky Far (Black Sea Lighthouse): 8000 Burgas, Milin Kamak 9; tel. 42-248; telex 83464; fax 40-178; f. 1950 as organ of the district committees of the Communist Party, the Fatherland Front and the District People's Council; publ. since 1988 as Burgas district daily; Editor-in-Chief MLADEN KARPULSKY; circ. 60,000.

Demokratsiya (Democracy): Sofia; f. 1990; publ. by the Union of Democratic Forces; Editor-in-Chief RUMYANA UZUNOVA; circ. 197,000.

Duma: Sofia, Blvd Lenin 47; f. 1927; formerly Rabotnichesko Delo; organ of the Bulgarian Socialist Party; Editor-in-Chief STEFAN PRODEV; circ. 720,000.

Dunavska Pravda (Danubian Truth): Ruse; f.1944 as organ of the district committees of the Communist Party, the Fatherland Front and the District People's Council; Editor-in-Chief TSVYATKO TSVETKOV; circ. 27,500.

Kooperativno Selo (Co-operative Farming): Sofia, 11 August St 18; tel. 83-50-33; telex 23174; f. 1951; organ of the Ministry of Agriculture; Editor-in-Chief GEORGI AVRAMOV; circ. 195,000.

Narodna Armiya (People's Army): Sofia, Ivan Vasov St 12; f. 1944; organ of the Ministry of Defence; Editor-in-Chief Col RANGEL ZLATKOV; circ. 68,000.

Mladezh (Youth): 1080 Sofia, Blvd Lenin 47; tel. 46-34-35; telex 22280; fax 44-12-87; f. 1944; formerly *Narodna Mladezh*; publ. by the Bulgarian Democratic Youth Organization; Editor-in-Chief VALENTIN KOLEV; circ. 130,000.

Narodno Delo (People's Cause): 9000 Varna, Khristo Botev St 3; tel. 22-24-37; telex 77377; fax 23-10-24; independent; 5 days a week; f. 1944; Editor-in-Chief SLAVCHO APOSTOLOV; circ. 100,000.

Otechestven Front (Fatherland Front): Sofia, Blvd Lenin 47; f. 1942 as organ of the National Council of the Fatherland Front; morning and evening editions; Editor-in-Chief GENCHO BUCHVAROV; total circ. 280,000.

Otechestven Glas (The Voice of the Fatherland): 4000 Plovdiv, Krakra St 9; tel. 22-67-40; telex 44506; f. 1943 as organ of the district committees of the Communist Party, the Fatherland Front and the District People's Council; Editor-in-Chief MIKHAIL MILCHEV; circ. 90,000.

Pirinsko Delo (Pirin's Cause): Blagoevrad, Assen Khristov St 19; organ of the district people's council, the district committees of the Bulgarian Socialist Party and the Fatherland Union; Editor-in-Chief ILYA SARIN; circ. 33,000.

Trud (Labour): Sofia, Blvd Dondukov 82; tel. 87-25-01; telex 22427; f. 1923; organ of the Confederation of Independent Trade Unions; Editor-in-Chief GEORGI TAMBUEV; circ. 280,000.

Vecherny Novini (Evening News): Sofia, Blvd Lenin 47; tel. 44-14-69; telex 22324; fax 46-50-65; f. 1951; publ. by the Vest Publishing House; Editor-in-Chief VASIL GADJANOV.

Zemedelsko Zname (Agrarian Banner): Sofia, Yanko Zabunov St 23; f. 1902; organ of the Bulgarian Agrarian People's Union; Editor-in-Chief Prof. DIMITUR DIMITROV; circ. 178,000.

PRINCIPAL PERIODICALS

Anteni (Antennae): Sofia, Khan Krum St 12; weekly on politics and culture; Editor-in-Chief VESELIN YOSIFOV; circ. 165,000.

Bulgaria: Sofia, Levsky St 1; monthly; Russian, German and Spanish; illustrated magazine; Editor-in-Chief (vacant); circ. 157,000.

Bulgaria Today: Sofia, Levsky St 1; monthly; French, English and Italian; Editor-in-Chief NIKOLA ZAKHARIYEV; total circ. 25,000.

Bulgarian Films: 1000 Sofia, Rakovski St 96; tel. 87-66-11; telex 22447; f. 1960; 8 a year; magazine in English, French and Russian; cinema; Editor-in-Chief IVAN STOYANOVICH; circ. 21,000.

Bulgarian Foreign Trade: Sofia, Parchvich 42; tel. 8-51-51; telex 23318; fax 87-32-09; f. 1952; fortnightly; French, German, English and Russian; organ of the Bulgarian Chamber of Commerce and Industry; Editor-in-Chief VENTSESLAV DIMITROV; circ. 13,000.

Bulgaro-Suvetska Druzhba: Sofia, Blvd Klement Gottwald 4; organ of the All-National Committee for Bulgarian-Soviet Friendship; Editor-in-Chief BORIS PETKOV; circ. 68,000.

Bulgarsky Voin (Bulgarian Soldier): Sofia, 11 August St 6; monthly organ of the Chief Political Department of the People's Army; literature and arts; Editor-in-Chief ORLIN ORLINOV; circ. 23,000.

Chitalishte (Reading Room): Sofia, Sofiiska Komuna St 4; monthly; organ of the Committee for Art and Culture; Editor-in-Chief BOYAN BALABANOV; circ. 5,000.

Computer for You: 1000 Sofia, Blvd Tolbukhin 51A; tel. 87-09-14; f. 1985; monthly; hardware and software; Editor-in-Chief GEORGI BALANSKY; circ. 30,000.

Darzhaven Vestnik (State Newspaper): 1123 Sofia; 2 a week; publishes the laws, decrees, etc., of the Grand National Assembly; Editor-in-Chief EMIL MITEV; circ. 63,587.

Discover Bulgaria: 1000 Sofia, pl. Sveta Nedelya. 1; tel. 88-49-61; f. 1958; every 2 months; French, English, German, Russian and Bulgarian; Editor-in-Chief LILIYA GERASIMOVA; circ. 47,000.

Do It Yourself: 1000 Sofia, Blvd Tolbukhin 51A; tel. 87-50-45; f. 1981; monthly; circ. 180,000.

Economic News of Bulgaria: Sofia, Blvd A. Stamboliiski 11A; monthly; English, French, German, Spanish and Russian; published by the Bulgarian Chamber of Commerce and Industry; Editor-in-Chief LYUBEN MIKHAILOV; circ. 15,000.

Ekopolitika: Sofia; f. 1990; weekly publication of the Green Party.

Fakel (The Torch): 1000 Sofia, Angel Kanchev St 5; tel. 88-00-31; f. 1981; every 2 months; translations of Soviet literature; published by the Committee for Culture, the Bulgarian Writers' Union and the Union of Translators; Editor-in-Chief GEORGI BORISOV; circ. 20,000.

Ikonomicheska Misal (Thoughts on Economics): Sofia, Aksakov 3; 12 a year; organ of the Institute of Economics of the Bulgarian Academy of Sciences; Editor-in-Chief PENKA POPOVA; circ. 7,000.

Ikonomika (Economics): Sofia, Blvd Dondukov 21; f. 1946 as *Planovo Stopanstvo* (Planning of the Economy); present name adopted in 1985; monthly; organ of the State Planning Commission, Ministry of Finance, Bulgarian National Bank and Central Statistical Office; Editor-in-Chief ZVETAN MARINOV; circ. 5,000.

Izkustvo (Art): 1504 Sofia, ul. Shipka 18; 1404 Sofia, POB 139; tel. 43-01-92; f. 1951; 10 a year; organ of the Committee for Art and Culture, and of the Union of Bulgarian Artists; Editor-in-Chief Prof. IVAN MARAZOV; circ. 5,200.

Kinoizkustvo (Cinematic Art): Sofia, pl. Slaveikov 11; f. 1946; monthly; cinema; Editor-in-Chief EMIL PETROV; circ. 9,000.

Kontakti (Contacts): 1000 Sofia, pl. Narodno Sobraniye 12; tel. 87-23-08; monthly magazine for Bulgarians living abroad; Editor-in-Chief EVTIM EVTIMOV; circ. 30,000.

Letopisy (Annals): 1000 Sofia, pl. Slaveikov 2a; tel. 87-48-86; monthly; publ. by the Union of Bulgarian Writers; literary; Editor-in-Chief TONCHO ZHECHEV; circ. 15,000.

LIK: Sofia, Blvd Lenin 49; weekly publication of the Bulgarian Telegraph Agency; literature, art and culture; Editor-in-Chief SIRMA VELEVA; circ. 19,000.

Literaturen Front: (Literary Front): Sofia, Angel Kanchev St 5; f. 1944; organ of the Union of Bulgarian Writers; Editor-in-Chief MARKO GANCHEV; circ. 32,000.

Lov i Ribolov (Hunting and Fishing): 1000 Sofia, Blvd Vitosha 31-33; tel. 88-42-20; telex 23024; f. 1895; monthly organ of the Hunting and Angling Union; Editor-in-Chief DONTCHO TSONCHEV; circ. 58,000.

Mladezh (Youth): Sofia, Blvd Khristo Botev 48; f. 1945; monthly; publ. by the Bulgarian Democratic Youth Organization; Editor-in-Chief LYUBOMIR STOIKOV; circ. 95,000.

Narodna Kultura (National Culture): 1040 Sofia, Sofiiska Komuna St 4; tel. 88-33-22; organ of the Committee for Culture; Editor-in-Chief STEFAN PRODEV; circ. 50,000.

BULGARIA

Narodna Prosveta (National Education): Sofia, Blvd Lenin 125; monthly organ of Ministry of Education and the Union of Bulgarian Teachers; Editor DIMITUR TSVETKOV; circ. 12,125.

Nasha Rodina (Our Country): Sofia, Blvd Lenin 47; monthly; socio-political and literary; illustrated; Editor-in-Chief DIMITUR METODIYEV; circ. 35,500.

Novo Vreme (New Time): Sofia, Blvd Lenin 47; f. 1897; monthly theoretical organ of the Supreme Council of the Bulgarian Socialist Party; Editor-in-Charge NIKOLAI IRIBADZHAKOV; circ. 32,000.

Obshestvo i Pravo (Society and Law): Sofia, Blvd Vitosha 2; monthly of the Ministry of Justice and of the Union of Bulgarian Jurists; Editor-in-Chief Prof. BORIS SPASOV; circ. 103,000.

Orbita: 1000 Sofia, Tsar Kaloyan St 8; tel. 88-51-68; f. 1969; weekly science and technology; Editor-in-Chief Dr DIMITUR PEEV; circ. 150,000.

Otechestvo (Fatherland): Sofia, Blvd Vitosha 18; fortnightly illustrated publication of the National Council of the Fatherland Union; Editor-in-Chief SERAFIM SEVERNYAK; circ. 90,000.

Paralleli: Sofia, Blvd Lenin 49; weekly illustrated publication of the Bulgarian Telegraph Agency; Editor-in-Chief VENELIN MITEV; circ. 210,000.

Plamak (Flame): Sofia, Angel Kanchev 5; f. 1924; monthly; literature, art and publishing; organ of the Union of Bulgarian Writers; Editor-in-Chief GEORGI KONSTANTINOV; circ. 13,000.

Pogled (Review): Sofia, 11 August St 6; weekly; organ of the Union of Bulgarian Journalists; Editor-in-Chief EVGENI STANCHEV; circ. 380,000.

Science and Technology: Sofia, Blvd Lenin 49; tel. 84-61; f. 1964; weekly of the Bulgarian Telegraph Agency; Editor-in-Chief VESELIN SEIKOV; circ. 18,000.

Septemvriiche (Septembrist): Sofia, Blvd Lenin 47; 2 a week; publ. by the Bulgarian Democratic Youth Organization; Editor-in-Chief NIKOLAI ZIDAROV; circ. 300,000.

Slavyani (Slavs): Sofia, Tsar Kaloyan St 1; monthly organ of the Slav committee in Bulgaria; Editor-in-Chief KATYA GEORGIYEVA; circ. 20,000.

Sofiiska Pravda (Sofia Truth): Sofia, Tsar Kaloyan St 3; f. 1955; 3 a week; organ of the District People's Council and the district committees of the Bulgarian Socialist Party and the Fatherland Union; Editor-in-Chief VASIL MILUSHEV; circ. 13,000.

Sport: Sofia, Blvd Lenin 113A; tel. 77-83-78; telex 22594; fax 77-04-90; f. 1927; 3 a week; independent; Editor-in-Chief NIKOLAI ANDONOV; circ. 270,000.

Start: Sofia, Vasil Levsky Stadium, POB 797; weekly publication of the Central Council of the Bulgarian Union for Physical Culture and Sports; circ. 110,000.

Sturshel (Hornet): 1504 Sofia, Blvd Lenin 47; tel. 44-35-50; f. 1946; weekly; humour and satire; Editor-in-Chief JORDAN POPOV; circ. 344,000.

Suvremenen Pokazatel (Contemporary Index): Sofia; f. 1990; weekly organ of the Supreme Council of the Bulgarian Socialist Party; Editor-in-Chief LALYU DIMITROV.

Teater (Theatre): Sofia, Blvd Dondukov 82; monthly organ of the Committee of Culture and Art, Bulgarian Writers' Union and Union of Actors; Editor-in-Chief Prof. YULIYAN VUCHKOV; circ. 6,100.

Televiziya i Radio: Sofia, ul. Shishman 30; organ of the Committee for Television and Radio; Editor-in-Chief KHRISTO CHAVDAROV; circ. 100,000.

Turist: Sofia, Blvd D. Blagoev 24; tel. 51-16-41; f. 1902; monthly organ of the Bulgarian Tourist Union; Editor-in-Chief KHRISTO GEORGIYEV; circ. 25,000.

Uchitelsko Delo (Teachers' Cause): Sofia, Blvd Lenin 125, Studentski Obshtezhitiya, Block G; f. 1905; organ of the Ministry of Education and the Central Cttee of the Bulgarian Teachers' Union; Editor-in-Chief PENCHO KOVACHEV; circ. 80,000.

Vanshna Targoviya (Foreign Trade): Sofia, Tsar Kaloyan 8; monthly; Editor-in-Chief ALEXANDUR CHICHOVSKY; circ. 3,000.

The World Over: 1000 Sofia, Blvd Lenin 39; telex 22821; f. 1964; weekly publication of the Bulgarian Telegraph Agency; international politics; Editor-in-Chief YOSSIF DAVIDOV.

Zdrave (Health): Sofia, Byalo More St 8; published by Bulgarian Red Cross; Editor-in-Chief MARIYA NIKOLOVA; circ. 200,000.

Zhenata Dnes (Women Today): Sofia, pl. Narodno Sabranie 12; monthly organ of the Women's Democratic Union; also in Russian; Editor-in-Chief ELEONORA TURLAKOVA.

NEWS AGENCIES

Bulgarska Telegrafna Agentsia (BTA): (Bulgarian Telegraph Agency): 1040 Sofia, Blvd Lenin 49; tel. 84-61; telex 22821; f. 1898; the official news agency, having agreements with the leading foreign agencies and correspondents in all major capitals; publishes weekly surveys of science and technology, international affairs, literature and art; Dir-Gen. IVO INDZHEV.

Sofia-Press Agency: 1040 Sofia, Slavyanska St 29; tel. 88-58-31; telex 22622; fax 88-34-55; f. 1967 by the Union of Bulgarian Writers, the Union of Bulgarian Journalists, the Union of Bulgarian Artists and the Union of Bulgarian Composers; publishes socio-political and scientific literature, fiction, children's and tourist literature, publications on the arts, a newspaper, magazines and bulletins in foreign languages; Dir-Gen. VENTSEL RAICHEV.

Foreign Bureaux

Agence France-Presse (AFP): 1000 Sofia, Blvd Tolbukhin 16; tel. 88-44-94; telex 22572; Correspondent VESSELA SERGEVA-PETROVA.

Allgemeiner Deutscher Nachrichtendienst (ADN) (Germany): 1000 Sofia, Moskovska 27A; tel. 87-82-73; Correspondent HEIDEMARIE DREISNER.

Československá tisková kancelář (ČTK) (Czechoslovakia): 1113 Sofia, ul. Gagarin, blok 154A, Apt 19; tel. 70-91-36; telex 22537; Correspondent VĚRA IVANOVIČOVÁ.

Informatsionnoye Agentstvo Novosti (IAN) (USSR): Sofia, 11 Avgust St 1, Apt 3; tel. 88-13-81; Bureau Man. YEVGENI VOROBYOV.

Magyar Távirati Iroda (MTI) (Hungary): Sofia, ul. Frédéric Joliot-Curie 15, blok 156/3, Apt 28; tel. 70-18-12; telex 22549; Correspondent KÁROLY NAGY.

Novinska Agencija Tanjug (Yugoslavia): 1000 Sofia, L. Koshut St 33; tel. 71-90-57; Correspondent PERO RAKOSEVIĆ.

Prensa Latina (Cuba): 1113 Sofia, ul. Yuri Gagarin 22, blok 154B, Apt 22; tel. 71-91-90; telex 22407; Correspondent SUSANA UGARTE SOLER.

Telegrafnoye Agentstvo Sovetskovo Soyuza (TASS) (USSR): 1000 Sofia, ul. A. Gendov 1, Apt 29; Correspondent ALEKSANDR STEPANENKO.

Xinhua (New China) News Agency (People's Republic of China): Sofia, pl. Narodno Sobraniye 3, 2nd Floor; tel. 88-49-41; telex 22539; Correspondent LI FUPIN.

The following agencies are also represented: PAP (Poland) and Reuters (UK).

PRESS ASSOCIATION

Union of Bulgarian Journalists: Sofia, Graf Ignatiyev St 4; tel. 87-27-73; telex 22635; f. 1955; Pres. STEFAN PRODEV; Gen.-Sec. ALEKSANDUR ANGELOV; 4,800 mems.

Publishers

Darzhavno Izdatelstvo 'Khristo G. Danov': Plovdiv, ul. Petko Karavelov 17; tel. 22-52-32; f. 1855; fiction, poetry, literary criticism; Dir PETUR ANASTASSOV.

Darzhavno Izdatelstvo Meditsina i Fizkultura: 1080 Sofia, pl. Slaveikov 11; tel. 87-13-08; medicine, physical culture and tourism; Dir PETUR GOGOV.

Darzhavno Izdatelstvo 'Narodna Kultura': Sofia, ul. Gavril Genov 4; tel. 87-80-63; f. 1944; foreign fiction and poetry in translation; Dir VERA GANCHEVA.

Darzhavno Izdatelstvo 'Narodna Prosveta': Sofia, ul. Vasil Drumev 37; educational publishing house; Dir SVYATKO GAGOV.

Darzhavno Izdatelstvo 'Nauka i Izkustvo': 1080 Sofia, Blvd Rusky 6; tel. 87-57-01; f. 1948; general publishers; Dir ANELIA VASSILEVA.

Darzhavno Izdatelstvo 'Tekhnika': 1000 Sofia, Blvd Rusky 6; tel. 87-57-01; f. 1958; textbooks for technical and higher education and technical literature; Dir PETRANA WURGOVA.

Darzhavno Izdatelstvo 'Zemizdat': 1504 Sofia, Blvd Lenin 47; tel. 46-31; f. 1949; specializes in works on agriculture, shooting, fishing, forestry, livestock-breeding, veterinary medicine and popular scientific literature and textbooks; Dir PETUR ANGELOV.

Darzhavno Voyenno Izdatelstvo: Sofia, ul. Ivan Vazov 12; military publishing house; Head Col GEORGI GEORGIYEV.

Izdatelstvo na Bulgarskata Akademiya na Naukite (Publishing House of the Bulgarian Academy of Sciences): 1113 Sofia, Acad. Georgi Bonchev St, blok 6; tel. 72-09-22; telex 23132; f. 1869; scientific works and periodicals of the Bulgarian Academy of Sciences; Dir TODOR RANGELOV.

Izdatelstvo 'Bulgarsky Khudozhnik': 1504 Sofia, Asen Zlatarov St 1; tel. 87-66-57; fax 88-47-49; f. 1952; art books, children's books; Dir STEFAN KURTEV.

BULGARIA

Izdatelstvo 'Bulgarsky Pisatel': Sofia, ul. Shesti Septemvri 35; publishing house of the Union of Bulgarian Writers; Bulgarian fiction and poetry, criticism; Dir SIMEON SULTANOV.

Izdatelstvo 'Khristo Botev': 1080 Sofia, Blvd Lenin 47; tel. 43-431; f. 1944; fmrly the Publishing House of the Bulgarian Communist Party; renamed as above 1990; Dir IVAN DINKOV.

Izdatelstvo na CC na DKMS 'Narodna Mladezh' (People's Youth Publishing House): Sofia, ul. Kaloyan 10; politics, history, original and translated fiction, and original and translated poetry for children; Dir ROSEN BOSEV.

Izdatelstvo na Natsionalniya Savet na Otechestveniya Front (Publishing House of the National Council of the Fatherland Front): Sofia, Blvd Dondukov 32; Dir (vacant).

Izdatelstvo 'Profizdat' (Publishing House of the Central Council of Bulgarian Trade Unions): Sofia, Blvd Dondukov 82; specialized literature and fiction; Dir STOYAN POPOV.

Knigoizdatelstvo 'Galaktika': 9000 Varna, pl. Deveti Septemvri 6; tel. 22-50-77; fax 22-50-77; f. 1960; popular science, science fiction, economics, Bulgarian and foreign literature; Dir PANKO ANCHEV.

Sinodalno Izdatelstvo: Sofia; religious publishing house; Dir KIRIL BOINOV.

STATE ORGANIZATION

Jusautor: 1463 Sofia, Ernst Thälmann Ave 17; tel. 87-28-71; telex 23042; fax 87-37-40; Bulgarian copyright agency; represents Bulgarian authors of literary, scientific, dramatic and musical works, and deals with all formalities connected with the grant of options, authorization for translations, drawing up of contracts for the use of their works by foreign publishers and producers; negotiates for the use of foreign works in Bulgaria; controls the application of copyright legislation; Dir-Gen. YANA MARKOVA.

WRITERS' UNION

Union of Bulgarian Writers: Sofia, Angel Kanchev 5; f. 1913; 370 mems; Chair. KOLYU GEORGIYEV; 400 mems.

Radio and Television

Radio and television are supervised by the Committee for Television and Radio of the Committee for Culture of the Council of Ministers.

There were an estimated 2,007,000 radio receivers in use and about 2,100,000 television receivers in use in 1988. Colour television was introduced in 1977.

Bulgarian Committee for Television and Radio: 1504 Sofia, San Stefano St 29; tel. 46-81; telex 22581; Chair. (vacant).

RADIO

Bulgarsko Radio: 1421 Sofia, Blvd Dragan Tsankov 4; tel. 85-41; telex 22557; there are four Home Service programmes and local stations at Blagoevgrad, Plovdiv, Shumen, Stara Zagora and Varna. The Foreign Service broadcasts in Bulgarian, Turkish, Greek, Serbo-Croat, French, Italian, German, English, Portuguese, Spanish, Albanian and Arabic.

TELEVISION

Bulgarska Televiziya: 1504 Sofia, ul. San Stefano 29; tel. 46-31; telex 22581; programmes are transmitted daily; there are two channels.

Finance

(cap. = capital; dep. = deposits; res = reserves; m. = million; amounts in leva)

BANKING

A major restructuring of the banking system began in 1987. Since then, many commercial banks have been established as self-managing shareholders' societies, legally responsible for their financial dealings. In October 1990 a new monetary, credit and banking system was proposed, as part of a comprehensive reform of the entire economic system.

National Bank

Bulgarska Narodna Banka (National Bank of Bulgaria): 1000 Sofia, Sofiiska Komuna St 2; tel. 85-51; telex 22392; f. c. 1879; issuing bank; Pres. IVAN DRAGNEVSKI; First Deputy Pres. T. CHAVDAROV.

Other Banks

Avtotekhnika (Motor and Engineering Bank): f. 1987.

Bank for Economic Projects (Mineralbank): 1000 Sofia, Legué St 17, POB 589; tel. 80-17-37; telex 23390; f. 1980, reorganized 1987; cap. 140m., dep. 1,105m., res 124m. (Dec. 1988); Pres. RUMEN GEORGIYEV.

Biochim (Commercial Bank): 1040 Sofia, Ivan Vazov St 1; tel. 54-11-21; telex 23862; fax 54-13-78; f. 1987; cap. 80m., res 27m., dep. 1,498m. (Dec. 1989); Pres. BORIS MITEV; Chair. IVAN DRAGNEVSKI

Bulgarian Foreign Trade Bank: 1040 Sofia, Sofiiska Komuna St 2; tel. 85-51; telex 22031; fax 88-56-81; f. 1964; commercial bank with major shareholders: National Bank of Bulgaria, Ministry of Foreign Economic Relations; cap. 320m.; res 484.5m. (Dec. 1989); Pres. VESSELIN RANKOV.

Economic Bank: Sofia; telex 23910; fax 65-51-52; f. 1987; Chair. ZVETAN PETKOV.

Electronica (Commercial Bank Electronica): 1574 Sofia, Chapaev St 55; tel. 70-74-47; telex 23745; fax 88-54-67; f. 1987; cap. 70m., dep. 379m. (1989); Pres. V. KARADJOV; 4 brs..

State Savings Bank: Sofia, Moskovska 19; f. 1951; provides general individual banking services; dep. 16,000m. (1986).

Stroybank Ltd: 1202 Sofia, Dunav Str. 46, POB 112; tel. 8-38-41; telex 23887; f. 1987; cap. 30m., dep. 661m. (June 1988); Pres. CHRISTOMIR YORDANOV.

Transportna Banka (Transport Bank): 9000 Varna, 5 Shipka St; tel. 22-30-73; telex 77293; fax 23-19-64; f. 1987; Pres. TODOR DIMITROV; Vice-Pres. IVAN KONSTANTINOV.

Zemedelska i kooperativna (Agricultural and Co-operative Bank): 4018 Plovdiv, G. Dimitrov Blvd 37; tel. 23-18-76; telex 44324; fax 22-39-64; f. 1987; supplies credit for reconstruction and modernization, technology transfer and quality improvement; cap. 72.8m. (Dec. 1989); Chair. YANKO MUSURLIEV; 11 brs.

INSURANCE

State Insurance Institute: Sofia, Rakovski St 102; all insurance firms were nationalized during 1947, and were reorganized into one single state insurance company; Chair. TOMA TOMOV.

Bulstrad (Bulgarian Foreign Insurance and Reinsurance Co, Ltd): 1000 Sofia, Dunav St 5; POB 627; tel. 8-51-91; telex 22564; f. 1961; deals with all foreign insurance and reinsurance; Chair. S. DARVINGOV.

Trade and Industry

INTERNATIONAL FREE ZONE

Ruse International Free Zone: 7000 Ruse, Blagoev St 5, POB 107; tel. 722-47; telex 62285; fax 700-84.

CHAMBER OF COMMERCE

Bulgarian Chamber of Commerce and Industry: 1040 Sofia, Blvd A. Stamboliiski 11A; tel. 87-26-31; telex 22374; fax 87-32-09; promotes economic relations and business contacts between Bulgarian and foreign companies and organizations; organizes official participation in international fairs and exhibitions and manages the international fairs in Plovdiv; publishes economic publications in Bulgarian and foreign languages; patents inventions and registers trade marks and industrial designs; organizes foreign trade advertising and publicity; provides legal and economic consultations etc.; Pres. VLADIMIR LAMBREV.

FOREIGN TRADE ORGANIZATIONS

Until 1989, foreign trade was a state monopoly in Bulgaria, and was conducted through foreign trade organizations and various state enterprises and corporations. However, following the enactment, in 1989, of Decree 56 on economic activity, the 'firma' (firm, company) was introduced as a basic structural unit of the economy. The 'firma' is a separate proprietary and organizational participant in the economy, with its own cost-benefit account. Under Decree 56, the following types of firm may be established: state, municipal, co-operative, private and mixed (in terms of ownership basis); and firms, stock firms, and limited liability companies (in terms of legal status).

According to the provisions of Decree 56, foreign, natural and legal persons may perform economic activities in Bulgaria independently, through a subsidiary which is a legal entity and is registered at the district court, as well as through a firm. To establish a bank subsidiary, a minimum statutory capital of 10m. leva is required. The procedures for the establishment of joint companies with foreign participation have been substantially simplified. Thus, when a foreign partner's share is up to 20%, in the case of stock

BULGARIA

companies, and no more than 49%, in the case of limited companies, no permission is required from the state authorities.

Principal organizations include:

Agrocommerce: 1000 Sofia, Blvd Dondukov 86; tel. 80-33-12; telex 23223; fax 87-28-69; export of agricultural products; import and maintenance of industrial equipment; import of consumer products and utilization of waste products; Dir-Gen. GEORGI GEORGIYEV.

Agromachinaimpex: 1040 Sofia, Stoyan Lepoyev St 1; tel. 20-03-91; telex 22563; export and import, maintenance and repair of agricultural equipment; Dir-Gen. TODOR TSONEV.

Balkancarimpex: 1040 Sofia, Kliment Okhridsky Blvd 18; tel. 7-53-01; telex 23431; export of trucks, lorries and other vehicles; construction of vehicle parts; Dir-Gen. ANDREI BUSSEV.

Banimpex: 1113 Sofia, G. Bonchev St 4, POB 98; tel. 70-04-11; telex 23688; fax 71-01-97; import of scientific equipment, electronic components and chemicals; export of scientific equipment and chemicals.

Bulgarcoop: 1000 Sofia, Rakovski St 99; tel. 84-41; telex 23429; export of live snails, live game and game meat; honey and bee products; nuts, pulses, medicinal plants, rose hips and rose-hip shells, fruit and vegetables (fresh and processed), essential oil seeds, etc.; onions and mushrooms; natural mineral water; consumer goods; Gen. Man. NENKO LECHEV.

Bulgariafilm: 1000 Sofia, Rakovski St 96; tel. 87-66-11; telex 22447; fax 88-24-31; export and import of films; participation in international film events; film services; Dir ZDRAVKO VATEV.

Bulgarplodexport: 1040 Sofia, Blvd A. Stamboliiski 7; tel. 88-59-51; telex 23297; fax 88-48-77; f. 1947; import and export of fresh and preserved fruit and vegetables; Dir-Gen. ALEKSANDUR MIRTCHEV.

Bulgartabac: 1000 Sofia, Blvd A. Stamboliiski 14; POB 96; tel. 87-52-11; telex 23288; covers manufacture, import and export of raw and manufactured tobacco; Dir-Gen. DIMITER YADKOV.

Chimimport: 1000 Sofia, Sofiiska Komuna St 1; tel. 88-38-11; telex 22521; import and export of chemicals, fertilizer, plant protection preparations, tyres, synthetic rubber and rubber wares, photographic paper, aniline dyes, crude petroleum and oil products, paraffins, petrochemicals, plastic and plastic products, fuels, etc.; Dir-Gen. BELO BELOV.

Corecom: 1000 Sofia, Tsar Kaloyan St 8; tel. 85-131; telex 22476; import and retail sale of imported and local goods for convertible currency; Dir-Gen. ORLIN MILEV.

Electroimpex: 1000 Sofia, George Washington St 17; tel. 8-61-81; telex 22075; fax 80-33-09; f. 1960; covers the export and import of electrical and power equipment and components for the electrical engineering industry; Gen. Man. EMIL UZUNOV.

Energoimpex: 1463 Sofia, Ernst Thaelmann Blvd 17A; tel. 51-88-67; telex 22669; fax 52-17-58; import and export of coal, electric power; delivery of machines and power equipment; Dir-Gen. DIMITAR ARNAUDOV.

Hemus: 1000 Sofia, Levsky St 7; tel. 80-30-00; telex 22267; import and export of books, periodicals, numismatic items, antique objects, philatelic items, art products, musical instruments, gramophone records, cinematographic equipment and souvenirs; Gen. Man. IVAN ABADZHIYEV.

Hranexport: 1080 Sofia, Alabin St 56; tel. 88-22-51; telex 22525; fax 87-74-53; f. 1949; import and export of grain, cocoa, sugar, oils, feed, pulses, vegetable oils, mixtures, etc.; Gen. Dir DIMITAR DJAMBAZOV.

Industrialimport: 1040 Sofia, Pozitano St 3; tel. 87-30-21; telex 22092; fax 66-53-29; import and export of cotton, woollen and silk ready-made garments, knitwear, cotton, woollen and silk textiles, leather goods, china and glassware, sports equipment; Gen. Man. NEDKO NEDKOV.

Inflot: 1504 Sofia, Blvd Vl. Zaimov 88; 1000 Sofia, POB 634; tel. 87-25-34; telex 22376; agency for foreign and Bulgarian shipping, inland and maritime; Dir-Gen. DIMITUR BOTZEV.

Intercommerce: 1040 Sofia, pl. Sveta Nedelya 16; POB 676; tel. 87-93-64; telex 22067; fax 87-45-29; all kinds of multilateral, compensation and barter deals, import and export, participation in foreign firms; Dir-Gen. IVAN DEEV.

Interpred: 1057 Sofia, Blvd Bulgarosavetska Druzhba 16; tel. 71-46-46-46; telex 23284; fax 70-00-06; agency for the representation of foreign firms in Bulgaria; Chair. KHARALAMBI LAMBEV.

Isotimpex: 1113 Sofia, Chapayev St 51; tel. 70-72-41; telex 22731; fax 70-65-86; import and export of computing and office equipment, electronic components; Pres. LYUBOMIR VITANOV.

Kintex: 1407 Sofia, Blvd Anton Ivanov 66; tel. 67-71-65; telex 22471; fax 65-71-65; import and export of complete plants and equipment, explosives, cords, detonators for industrial and mining pruposes; sports and hunting accessories; Dir-Gen. ANTON SALDJIISKI.

Koraboimpex Co Ltd: 9000 Varna, D. Blagoev Blvd 128; tel. 22-81-60; telex 77550; fax 82-33-86; imports and exports ships, marine and port equipment; Dir-Gen. NIKOLAI PARASHKEVOV.

Lessoimpex: 1303 Sofia, Antim I St 17; tel. 8-61-71; telex 23407; import and export of timber, furniture and wooden products; Dir-Gen. ANGEL ANGELOV.

Machinoexport: 1000 Sofia, Aksakov St 5; tel. 88-53-21; telex 23425; fax 87-56-75; export of metal-cutting and wood-working machines, industrial robots, hydraulic and pneumatic products and other equipment, tools and spare parts; Gen. Dir HRISTO ATZEV.

Maimex: 1431 Sofia, D. Nestorov St 15; tel. 59-61-75; telex 22712; fax 59-81-16; import and export of specialized medical equipment, consumables and pharmaceutical products; Dir TSONCHO TSONCHEV.

Metal Technology: 1574 Sofia, Chapaev St 53; tel. 7-14-21; telex 22903; export and import of machinery and industrial equipment.

Mineralimpex: 1156 Sofia, Blvd Kliment Okhridsky 44, Bl. 1A; tel. 77-95-06; telex 22973; export of mineral raw materials, drilling tools and products; import of machinery, minerals and diamond tools; Dir-Gen. SLAVCHO NAIDENOV.

Mladost: Sofia, Blvd A. Stamboliiski 45; tel. 87-95-52; telex 22168; production of and trade in footwear, sportswear and ready-made dresses; Dir-Gen. A. DIONISIEV.

Pharmachim: 1220 Sofia, Iliyensko chaussée 16; tel. 38-501; telex 22097; fax 38-81-71; import and export of drugs, pharmaceutical, microbiological and veterinary products, essential oils, cosmetics and dental materials; Dir-Gen. KHRISTO DRASHANSKI.

Pirin State Company: 1303 Sofia, Blvd A. Stamboliiski 125-2; tel. 20-67-11; telex 22761; f. 1965; production, export and import of footwear and leather goods; Dir-Gen. D. ENEV.

Raznoiznos: 1040 Sofia, Tsar Assen St 1; tel. 88-02-11; telex 23244; export and import of industrial and craftsmen's products, timber products, paper products, glassware, kitchen utensils, furniture, carpets, toys, sports equipment, musical instruments, etc.; Dir-Gen. IVAN NIKOLOV.

Ribno Stopanstvo: 1000 Sofia, Parchevich St 42; tel. 80-10-01; telex 22796; import and export of fish and fish products; Dir YULIAN YORDANOV.

Rodopaimpex: 1000 Sofia, Gavril Genov St 2; tel. 88-26-61; telex 22541; export of cattle, sheep, breeding animals, meat, meat products; dairy products, poultry, eggs; import of meat, breeding animals, tallow, artificial casing and equipment for the meat industry; Dir-Gen. ALEKSANDUR GORANOV.

Rudmetal: 1000 Sofia, Dobrudzha St 1; tel. 88-12-71; telex 22027; f. 1952; export and import of metal and metal products, lead, zinc, copper, pure lead, ores, coal, etc.; Dir-Gen. YOSIF YOSIFOV.

SO MAT: 1738 Sofia, Gorubliane; tel. 77-31-26; telex 22356; fax 75-80-15; international cargo road transport; Dir-Gen. YORDAN ASSENOV.

SPS-Software Products and Systems: Sofia, P. Volov St 3; tel. 43-401; telex 23149; fax 46-71-68; production, import and export of information systems, software products and system-engineering services; Dir-Gen. RASHKO ANGELINOV.

Stroyimpex: 1000 Sofia, Triyaditsa St 5; tel. 80-30-47; telex 22385; export of cement, lime, cement slabs, floor tiles, prefabricated wooden houses; etc.; import of building materials, machines and equipment; Dir-Gen. ATANAS VLAKHOV.

Technoexportstroy: 1303 Sofia, Antim I St 11; tel. 87-85-11; telex 22128; design and construction abroad of all types of public, utility, industrial and infrastructural projects; supply of machines and technical assistance; Gen. Man. MARIN DZHERMANOV.

Technika: 1113 Sofia, Blvd Lenin 125, block 2; tel. 733-91; telex 23468; fax 70-02-28; import and export of patents and licenses; Dir-Gen. IVAN CHORBADJIEV.

Technoimpex: 1000 Sofia, Tsar Kaloyan St 8, POB 932; tel. 88-15-71; telex 23783; fax 88-34-15; scientific and technological assistance abroad in the fields of industry, architecture, construction, transport and communications and education; Dir-Gen. DIMITAR ZDRAKOV.

Techno-import-export: 1113 Sofia, ul. Frédéric Joliot-Curie 20, POB 541; tel. 639-91; telex 22193; fax 65-81-47; import and export of machines and complete plants in the fields of power generation, metallurgy, mining, construction, plastic-processing industries and crane-building; Dir-Gen. STOYAN DRANDAROV.

Telecom: 1309 Sofia, Kiril Pchelinsky St 2; tel. 2-13-01; telex 22077; export and import of radioelectronic equipment and technology for the communications industry; Dir-Gen. NIKOLA MONOV.

Transimpex: 1606 Sofia, Skobelev Blvd 65; tel. 52-23-21; telex 22123; import and export of railway equipment, wagons, locomotives, boats and shipping parts.

BULGARIA

Directory

Vinimpex: 1080 Sofia, Lavele St 19; tel. 80-32-39; telex 224667; fax 80-12-99; import and export of wine and spirits and equipment and spares for the wine industry; Man. Dir MARGARIT TODOROV.

TRADE UNIONS AND CO-OPERATIVES

Confederation of Independent Bulgarian Trade Unions: Sofia, pl. D. Blagoev 1; tel. 86-61; telex 22446; f. 1904; the central trade union organization; Chair. Prof. Dr KRUSTYU PETKOV; Sec. MILADIN STOYNOV; total mems 3,600,000.

Podkrepa (Support) Independent Trade Union Federation: Sofia; f. 1989; affiliated to the opposition Union of Democratic Forces; Chair. Dr KONSTANTIN TRENCHEV; 400,000 mems.

Trade Unions

Federation of Independent Agricultural Trade Unions: 1606 Sofia, ul. Dimo Hadzhidimov 29; tel. 516-51; Pres. LYUBEN KHARALAMPIEV; 700,000 mems.

Federation of Trade Union Organizations of Biotechnical and Chemical Industry Workers: Sofia, ul. Alabin 3; Pres. IVAN SIMOV; 101,855 mems.

Federation of Trade Union Organizations of Communications Workers: 1000 Sofia, G. Genov St 1; tel. 88-93-65; f. 1904; Chair. VIOLETA STOYANOVA; 50,000 mems.

Federation of Trade Union Organizations of Construction and Building Industry Workers: Sofia, pl. Sveta Nedelya 4; Chair. IVAN TODOROV; 274,500 mems.

Federation of Trade Union Organizations of Workers in Electronics: Sofia, pl. Sveta Nedelya 4; tel. 87-81-73; f. 1987; Chair. NEDYALKO NEDYALKOV; 160,000 mems.

Federation of Trade Union Organizations of Forestry and Timber Industry Workers: 1606 Sofia, ul. Dimo Hadzhidimov 29; Pres. NIKOLA ABADJIEV; 111,000 mems.

Federation of Trade Union Organizations of Light Industry Workers: Sofia, ul. Shesti Septemvri 4; Chair. PETUR PETROV; 215,000 mems.

Federation of Trade Union Organizations of Machine-Building Workers: Sofia, pl. Sveta Nedelya 4; Chair. DOYCHO DINEV; 300,000 mems.

Federation of Independent Trade Unions of Miners, Metallurgists, Power Workers and Geologists: 1000 Sofia, pl. Sveta Nedelya 4; tel. 87-80-83; f. 1909; Pres. YORDAN RUSKOV; 230,000 mems.

Federation of Trade Union Organizations of Transport Workers: Sofia, Blvd Georgi Dimitrov 106; tel. 31-51-24; f. 1911; Chair. ATANAS STANEV; 330,000 mems.

Independent Trade Union of Beer Industry Workers: Sofia, 'Bulgarsko pivo', Kvartal Gorubliane; tel. 78-12-01; Pres. KRASIMIR PACHTRAPANSKY; 7,500 mems.

Independent Trade Union of Food Industry Workers: 1606 Sofia, ul. Dimo Hadzhidimov 29; tel. 516-51; Pres. SLAVCHO PETROV; 112,000 mems.

Independent Trade Union of Meat Industry Workers: Sofia, G. Genov St 21; tel. 88-26-01; Pres. DIMITUR ZLATINOV; 17,000 mems.

Independent Trade Union of Tobacco Industry Workers: Sofia, Blvd Stamboliiski 14; tel. 87-52-11; Pres. RADA SALUEVA; 22,000 mems.

Trade Union of Workers in Administration and Social Organization: Sofia, ul. Alabin 52; Chair. STOYAN CHOBANOV; 147,000 mems.

Trade Union of Health Service Workers: Sofia, pl. Sveta Nedelya 4; Chair. Dr IVAN SECHANOV; 157,000 mems.

Trade Union of Workers in the Polygraphic Industry and Cultural Institutions: Sofia, Zdanov St 7; Pres. BOICHO PAVLOV; 49,300 mems.

Trade Union of Trade Workers: Sofia, ul. Shesti Septemvri 4; Chair. PETUR TSEKOV; 520,000 mems.

Union of Bulgarian Actors: 1000 Sofia, ul. Pope Andrei 1; tel. 87-71-96; f. 1919; Chair. STEFAN ILIEV; 4,000 mems.

Union of Bulgarian Artists: Pres. KHRISTO NEYKOV.

Union of Bulgarian Cinematographers: Chair. LYUDMIL STAYKOV.

Union of Bulgarian Teachers: Sofia, pl. Sveta Nedelya 4; tel. 88-10-07; f. 1905; Chair. PANKA BABUKOVA; 238,000 mems.

Union of Musicians in Bulgaria: Sofia, ul. Alabin 52; Chair. Prof. GEORGI ROBEV; 6,000 mems.

Union of Scientific Workers in Bulgaria: Chair. ALEKSANDUR YANKOV; 11,000 mems.

Union of Workers' Productive Co-operatives: 1000 Sofia, Rakovski St 99, POB 55; tel. 87-19-70; telex 23229; f. 1988; umbrella organization of 164 workers' productive co-operatives; Pres. PAVEL TSVETANSKY; 75,000 mems.

Co-operatives

Central Co-operative Union: 1000 Sofia, Rakovski 99, POB 55; tel. 84-41; telex 23229; f. 1947; umbrella organization of 29 regional co-operative unions, 540 consumers' co-operatives, 98 producers' co-operatives and 87 school, students' and other co-operatives; about 1.9m. mems are affiliated to the Central Union; Pres. PANCHO IVANOV.

TRADE FAIR

Plovdiv International Fair: 4018 Plovdiv, Blvd G. Dimitrov 37; tel. 55-31-46; telex 44432; fax 26-54-32; f. 1933; organized by Bulgarian Chamber of Commerce and Industry; Dir-Gen. KIRIL ASPARUKHOV.

Transport

Ministry of Transport and Communications: 1080 Sofia, ul. Levsky 9; tel. 88-12-30; telex 23200; fax 88-50-94; directs the state rail, road, water and air transport organizations.

Despred: 1000 Sofia, Slavyanska St 2; tel. 87-60-16; telex 23306; fax 80-14-37; state firm; Dir-Gen. TRAIKO VARGOV.

RAILWAYS

There were 4,586 km of track in Bulgaria in 1989, of which more than 2,600 km were electrified. In June 1986 the new Sofia–Gorna Oryakhovitsa–Varna main-line railway was opened. Construction of an underground railway in Sofia began in 1979, and was still in progress in 1989. The system was to have a total length of 112 km.

Bulgarian State Railways (BDZ): 1080 Sofia, Ivan Vazov St 3; tel. 87-30-45; telex 22423; owns and controls all railway transport; Chair. VESELIN PAVLOV.

ROADS

There were 36,897 km of roads in Bulgaria at the beginning of 1989, including 258 km of motorways, 6,733 km of main roads and 29,906 km of secondary roads. A major motorway runs from Sofia to the coast.

General Road Administration: 1606 Sofia, Blvd D. Blagoev 3; tel. 52-17-66; telex 22679; f. 1965; Pres. DIMITAR DIMOV.

SHIPPING AND INLAND WATERWAYS

The Danube river is the main waterway. External services link Black sea ports to the USSR, the Mediterranean and Western Europe.

Bulgarian River Shipping Corporation: 7000 Ruse, pl. Otets Paisi 2; tel. 700-93; telex 62403; fax 701-61; f. 1935; shipment of cargo and passengers on the Danube; storage, handling and forwarding of cargo; Dir-Gen. TSONYO UZUNOV.

Navigation Maritime Bulgare: 9000 Varna, Blvd Chervenoarmeiska 1; tel. 22-24-74; telex 77351; f. 1892; sole enterprise in Bulgaria employed in sea transport; owns tankers, bulk carriers and container, ferry and passenger vessels with a displacement of more than 1,800,000 dwt; Dir-Gen. Capt. ATANAS YONKOV.

Shipping Corporation: Varna, Panagyurishte St 17; tel. 22-63-16; telex 077524; organization of sea and river transport; carriage of goods and passengers on waterways; controls all aspects of shipping and shipbuilding, also engages in research, design and personnel training; Dir-Gen. NIKOLAI YOVCHEV.

CIVIL AVIATION

Balkan Bulgarian Airlines: 1540 Sofia, Sofia Airport; pl. Narodno Sobraniye 12 (Head Office); tel. 66-16-90; telex 22342; f. 1947; state economic internal passenger and cargo services to Varna, Burgas, Ruse, Plovdiv, Kurdzhali, Targovishte, Silistra, Vidin and Gorna Oriakhovitsa; external services to Abu Dhabi, Algiers, Amsterdam, Ankara, Athens, Baghdad, Barcelona, Beirut, Belgrade, Berlin, Bratislava, Brussels, Bucharest, Budapest, Cairo, Casablanca, Copenhagen, Damascus, Dresden, Frankfurt am Main, Geneva, Harare, Helsinki, Istanbul, Khartoum, Kiev, Kuwait, Lagos, Leipzig, Leningrad, London, Luanda, Luxembourg, Madrid, Milan, Moscow, Nicosia, Paris, Prague, Rome, Stockholm, Tripoli, Tunis, Valletta, Vienna, Warsaw, Zürich; also agricultural aviation services; carried about 2.8m. passengers in 1987; fleet of 9 TU-134, 21 TU-154, 22 AN-24, 2 Il-18, 11 Yak-40 and 4 AN-12; Dir-Gen. KOSTADIN BOTEV.

Tourism

Bulgaria's tourist attractions include the resorts on the Black Sea coast and the mountain scenery. There were 8,294,985 foreign visitor arrivals in 1988, of which nearly half were from other socialist countries. In 1989 tourism accounted for 10% of total income in convertible currency.

Balkantourist: 1040 Sofia, Blvd Vitosha 1; tel. 4-33-31; telex 22568; f. 1948; the state tourist enterprise; Dir-Gen. A. SPASSOV.

Atomic Energy

A heterogeneous swimming-pool reactor, with a thermal capacity of 2,000 kW, came into operation near Sofia in 1961. The reactor, supplied under a bilateral agreement by the USSR, is used for the production of radioactive isotopes as well as for experimental work.

Bulgaria's first nuclear power station at Kozlodui, which opened in 1974 with an initial generating capacity of 440 MW, was expanded to provide a capacity of 2,585 MW by 1988. The construction, at Belene, of a second nuclear power station, rated at 6,000 MW, was suspended in 1990. In 1989 the Kozlodui station was producing 42% of the country's electricity.

Institute for Nuclear Research and Nuclear Energy of the Bulgarian Academy of Sciences: 1784 Sofia, Blvd Lenin 72; tel. 75-80-32; telex 23561; f. 1973; Dir Acad. KHR. KHRISTOV.

BURKINA FASO

Introductory Survey

Location, Climate, Language, Religion, Flag, Capital

Burkina Faso (formerly the Republic of Upper Volta) is a landlocked state in West Africa, bordered by Mali to the west and north, by Niger to the east, and by Benin, Togo, Ghana and Côte d'Ivoire to the south. The climate is hot and mainly dry, with an average annual temperature of 28°C (82°F). Humidity reaches 80% in the south during the rainy season, which occurs between June and October but is often very short. The official language is French, and there are numerous indigenous languages (principally Mossi), with many dialects. The majority of the population follow animist beliefs, about 30% are Muslims and fewer than 10% Christians, mainly Roman Catholics. The national flag (proportions 3 by 2) has two equal horizontal stripes, of red and green, with a five-pointed gold star in the centre. The capital is Ouagadougou.

Recent History

Burkina Faso (known as Upper Volta until August 1984) was formerly a province of French West Africa. It became a self-governing republic within the French Community in December 1958 and achieved full independence on 5 August 1960, with Maurice Yaméogo as President. In January 1966 President Yaméogo was deposed in a military coup, led by Lt-Col (later Gen.) Sangoulé Lamizana, the Army Chief of Staff, who took office as President and Prime Minister. The military regime dissolved the National Assembly, suspended the Constitution and established a Supreme Council of the Armed Forces. Political activities were suspended between September 1966 and November 1969. A new constitution, approved by popular referendum in June 1970, provided for a return to civilian rule after a four-year transitional regime of joint military and civilian administration. Elections for a national assembly were held in December, and the Union démocratique voltaïque (UDV) won 37 of the 57 seats. In January 1971 the President appointed the UDV leader, Gérard Ouedraogo, as Prime Minister. He took office in February at the head of a mixed civilian and military Council of Ministers.

In late 1973 conflicts between the Government and the National Assembly led to deadlock, and in February 1974 President Lamizana announced that the army had assumed power again. He dismissed the Prime Minister and dissolved the National Assembly. The Constitution and political activity were suspended, and the President assumed the functions of the premiership. In May the new military regime banned political parties. The Assembly was replaced by a National Consultative Council for Renewal, formed in July 1974, with 65 members nominated by the President.

Political parties were allowed to resume their activities from October 1977. A referendum in November approved a draft constitution which provided for a return to civilian rule. Seven parties contested elections for a new national assembly in April 1978. The UDV won 28 of the 57 seats, while the newly-formed Union nationale pour la défense de la démocratie (UNDD) secured 13 seats. Gen. Lamizana was elected President in May, and the seven parties grouped themselves into three alliances in the Assembly, as required by the Constitution. The main opposition front was formed by the UNDD and the Union progressiste voltaïque (UPV). In July the Assembly elected the President's nominee, Dr Joseph Conombo (a leading member of the UDV), to be Prime Minister.

The Conombo Government's attempts to accommodate the various groups and to improve the economy were impeded by the tacit hostility of the army and trade unions, and by the divisions in the National Assembly. Largely as a result of the deteriorating economic situation, the country suffered severe industrial unrest during 1979 and 1980. In November 1980 President Lamizana was overthrown in a bloodless coup, led by Col Saye Zerbo, who had been Minister of Foreign Affairs during the previous period of military rule. A 31-member Comité militaire de redressement pour le progres national (CMRPN) was established, and in December the new regime formed a Government of National Recovery, comprising both army officers and civilians. The Constitution was suspended, and the National Assembly was dissolved. Political parties and activities were banned, and a curfew was imposed. During 1981 Col Zerbo faced increasing opposition from the trade unions, a conflict which culminated, between November 1981 and February 1982, in the suspension of one of the union associations and the revocation of the right to strike. In November 1982 Col Zerbo was deposed in a military coup, led by non-commissioned army officers, in which five people were killed. Maj. Jean-Baptiste Ouedraogo emerged as leader of the new military regime, setting up the Conseil de salut du peuple (CSP). The CMRPN was dissolved, and a predominantly civilian government was formed. In February 1983 several soldiers and opposition figures were arrested, following the discovery of an alleged plot to reinstate the Zerbo regime. A power struggle within the CSP became apparent with the arrest, in May 1983, of radical left-wing elements within the Government, including the recently-appointed Prime Minister, Capt. Thomas Sankara. Maj. Ouedraogo announced the withdrawal of the armed forces from political life and disbanded the CSP. Sankara and his supporters were released after two weeks' detention, following a rebellion by pro-Sankara commandos at Pô, near the border with Ghana, under the leadership of Capt. Blaise Compaoré.

In August 1983 Sankara seized power in a coup, in which an estimated 15 people were killed. Opposition politicians were placed under house arrest, a strict curfew was imposed and a Conseil national révolutionnaire (CNR) set up. Capt. Compaoré, as Minister of State to the presidency, became the regime's second-in-command. Citizens were encouraged to join local administrative committees, Comités pour la défense de la révolution (CDRs), in an attempt to mobilize popular support for the regime. In September ex-President Zerbo was formally arrested, after his supporters attempted to overthrow the new Government. Administrative, judicial and military reforms were announced, and Tribunaux populaires révolutionnaires (TPRs) were inaugurated to consider cases of alleged corruption. Several former politicians, including Zerbo, appeared before these tribunals and were subsequently imprisoned.

In March 1984 a prominent teachers' union staged a 48-hour strike in protest at the arrest of three of its leaders. In June seven people were executed, convicted of plotting to overthrow the Government. Sankara accused an outlawed political group, the Front progressiste voltaïque (FPV, which comprised members of the former UPV and other left-wing groups), of complicity in the plot, alleging that it had been supported by France and other foreign powers: the French Government vigorously denied any involvement, and relations between the two countries underwent some strain. In August 1984, on the first anniversary of the coup that had brought him to power, Sankara announced that Upper Volta would henceforth be known as Burkina Faso ('Land of the Incorruptible Men'). Later that month, following signs of growing factionalism within the CNR, Sankara reorganized the Government, reducing the influence of the Ligue patriotique pour le développement (LIPAD), a Marxist faction which had begun to oppose Sankara's populist rhetoric.

During 1985 the Sankara regime again encountered opposition from trade unions. The Secretary-General of the LIPAD-affiliated Confédération syndicale burkinabè, Soumane Touré, was arrested in January, after having accused members of the CNR of embezzling public funds; in February a total of 20 union leaders were detained, following a brief 'leaflet war', organized in protest against the introduction of austerity measures. In rural districts, however, it had begun to appear that the extended role of the CDRs in imposing government policy and organizing local affairs had consolidated both the revolution and Sankara's position as leader. In August the Government repealed the curfew that had been in force since August 1983.

The intensification, during 1986, of measures aimed at furthering the development of the rural economy exacerbated tensions between the Government and the trade unions, despite the announcement, in October of that year, of an amnesty for all political prisoners. In early 1987 it was announced that austerity measures were to be introduced and that the public sector and the tax system were to undergo reform: a major tax-recovery operation was carried out in May and June, which reportedly led to the closure of many small businesses. In late May several influential trade-union activists, including Soumane Touré (who had been released under the October 1986 amnesty), were detained on charges of 'counter-revolutionary activities'.

Growing disharmony within the CNR itself became evident when several members of a leading left-wing faction, the Union des luttes communistes reconstruite (ULCR), were removed from ministerial office. On 15 October 1987 a 'Popular Front' (FP), under the leadership of Capt. Blaise Compaoré (Sankara's second-in-command), took power in a violent coup, in which Sankara and 13 of his close associates were killed. The CNR was dissolved, a curfew was imposed, and Burkina's land and air borders were closed for two weeks (the curfew remained in force until January 1988). The former President was denounced as an 'autocrat' and as a 'revolutionary gone astray'. The new regime pledged a continuation of the revolutionary process begun in August 1983, but stated that only by the instigation of a 'rectification process', principally in the area of economic policy, would popular confidence in the revolution be restored. The new 27-member Council of Ministers, announced on 31 October 1987, included only seven members of the previous Government and four military representatives. Compaoré became Head of State, assuming the title of Chairman of the Popular Front. A brief rebellion at the Koudougou garrison was rapidly quelled, and its instigator, Capt. Boukary Kaboré, fled to Ghana. However, Sankara's death continued to be mourned widely, and in November a clandestine movement of resistance to the new regime, the Rassemblement démocratique et populaire—Thomas Sankara, was formed in Ouagadougou.

Many of Sankara's close associates, including former ministers and members of his family, were arrested and detained without trial in the months following the coup. In January 1988 the FP denied allegations, made by the human rights organization, Amnesty International, that some detainees had been tortured. Soumane Touré was released from detention shortly after the coup, but LIPAD declined an invitation to participate in the FP.

In March 1988 it was announced that the CDRs were to be disarmed and replaced by Comités révolutionnaires (CRs), under Capt. Arsène Yè Bognessan; the powers of the TPRs were also to be curtailed. In August a reshuffle of the Council of Ministers consolidated Compaoré's position at the head of the new regime, with the appointment of a number of civilian ministers to oversee the implementation of the FP's economic programme.

By mid-1988, most of those who had been detained in the aftermath of the 1987 coup had been released. In December 1988 seven army officers (who were allegedly supporters of Kaboré) were executed, following their conviction for the murder of the officer who had quelled the Koudougou rebellion in October 1987. In January 1989 the deaths of five further Sankara loyalists were reported.

In April 1989 a new political grouping, the Organisation pour la démocratie populaire/Mouvement du travail (ODP/MT), was established, under the leadership of Clément Oumarou Ouedraogo, the former leader of the Union des communistes burkinabè (UCB), which, together with a faction of the Union des luttes communistes (ULC), had declared its affiliation to the new administration. The potential status of the ODP/MT was suggested by the dismissal from ministerial office, in the same month, of the Secretary-General of the Groupe communiste burkinabè (GCB), Jean-Marc Palm, and of the leader of the ULC, Alain Zougba (both of whom declined to join the new party). At the same time, Ouedraogo was appointed to the newly-created position of Minister Delegate to the Co-ordinating Committee of the FP.

In August 1989 an amnesty was announced for all political prisoners (including a number of close associates of Sankara), and the sentences of common-law offenders were reduced. However, an international human rights organization claimed that political prisoners, many of whom had been condemned by summary trials following the 1987 coup, were still being detained.

In September 1989 it was announced that the Commander-in-Chief of the Armed Forces and Minister of Popular Defence and Security, Maj. Jean-Baptiste Boukary Lingani, and the Minister of Economic Promotion, Capt. Henri Zongo (both of whom had been prominent at the time of the 1983 and 1987 coups), had been executed, together with two others, following the discovery of a plot to overthrow Compaoré on his return from the Far East. It was widely believed that Boukary Lingani and Zongo had opposed Compaoré's policy of 'rectification', notably the promotion of private enterprise and the commencement, in 1988, of negotiations with the IMF and the World Bank. Compaoré subsequently assumed the popular defence and security portfolio in a further reallocation of ministerial posts. In late December 1989 it was announced that a further attempt to overthrow the Compaoré Government had been thwarted. In November of the following year 19 people who had been detained in the aftermath of the incident were presented to the media; among those awaiting trial was Raymond Poda, a former Minister of Justice and Keeper of the Seals under Sankara.

Representatives of seven political tendencies attended the first congress of the FP, which was convened in March 1990. Delegates sanctioned the establishment of a commission whose task would be to draft a new constitution that would define a process of 'democratization'.

In April 1990 Clément Ouedraogo was dismissed from prominent posts within the FP, the ODP/MT and the Council of Ministers. He was replaced as Secretary for Political Affairs of the FP and as Secretary-General of the ODP/MT by Christian Roch Kaboré, hitherto Minister of Transport and Communications and, unlike Ouedraogo, a known supporter of Compaoré's ideals. In September Kaboré was appointed Minister of State, as part of a minor reorganization of the Government.

In May 1990 official reports cited the need to reinforce discipline within the army as the reason for the dismissal of Capt. Laurent Sedego from the Ministry of Peasant Affairs (Sedego and five other officers were also dismissed from the army).

The presentation of the draft Constitution to Compaoré, in October 1990, coincided with the third anniversary of the revolution that had brought the FP to power. Among the main provisions of the new document, which envisaged the creation of a 'revolutionary, democratic, unitary and secular State', was a clause denying legitimacy to any regime that might take power as the result of a *coup d'état*. The division of power between an executive, a legislature and an independent judiciary was envisaged. Presidential and legislative elections were anticipated: the seven-year mandate of the Head of State (who was to be elected by universal suffrage) would be renewable only once, while elections to a multi-party Assemblée des députés populaires would be held every four years. The draft Constitution was to be submitted for approval in a national referendum during 1991. Meanwhile, legislation permitting the registration of political parties that had been formed since the coup of October 1987 was to be promulgated. (By November 1990 the Compaoré Government acknowledged the existence of 11 political organizations, seven of which were affiliated to the FP; however, many other unofficial and clandestine movements were believed to be in existence.)

In December 1985 a long-standing border dispute with Mali erupted into a six-day war which left some 50 people dead. The conflict centred on an area known as the Agacher strip, reputed to contain significant deposits of minerals. Political tension between the two Governments had been rising since mid-1985, when the Malian Secretary-General of the Communauté économique de l'Afrique de l'Ouest (CEAO) was expelled from Burkina for criticizing austerity measures that had been imposed on the CEAO by Sankara. Following the cease-fire, which was arranged by the CEAO's defence grouping ANAD (Accord de non-agression et d'assistance en matière de défense), and as a result of the interim decision on the dispute that the International Court of Justice (ICJ) delivered in January 1986, troops were withdrawn from the Agacher area. Ambassadors were exchanged in June, and the ICJ's ruling, made in December, that the territory be divided equally between the two countries (with Burkina gaining sovereignty over the eastern district of Beli) was formally accepted by both countries.

Under the Sankara regime, Burkina established close links with neighbouring Ghana: a series of co-operation and security agreements were consolidated in 1984, and preliminary proposals for the eventual political and economic integration of the two countries were announced in August 1986. Summit

BURKINA FASO

meetings of leaders from Burkina and Ghana, together with Benin and Libya, were held regularly to demonstrate 'revolutionary solidarity'. In September 1986 both Burkina and Ghana were implicated by the Togolese Government in an alleged coup attempt in Lomé, and relations with Togo remained strained for several months.

In the months following his accession to power, Compaoré and other members of the FP visited neighbouring countries, in an attempt to rally support for the new regime. Among the first West African states to support Compaoré were Togo and Côte d'Ivoire, although suggestions that the latter country had assisted in the overthrow of Sankara were denied. The Libyan leader, Col Qaddafi, also expressed a desire to maintain close links with the FP. Those countries that had enjoyed particularly cordial contacts with Sankara, notably Ghana, Gabon and the Congo, condemned the coup, although relations with Ghana improved following meetings between the leaders of the two nations in early 1988. Compaoré continued to travel widely during the late 1980s. However, his international reputation was undermined as a result of the harsh repression of the September 1989 coup attempt. Burkina's relations with France (the country's major trading partner) and Ghana underwent some strain, following allegations, by the Burkinabè state-owned media, of the complicity of those countries in the incident. Despite Burkina's generally cordial relations with the Qaddafi regime, Libyan involvement in the coup attempt of December 1989 was widely alleged.

Relations with some members of the Economic Community of West African States (ECOWAS) deteriorated during 1990, owing to the Compaoré Government's overt support for Charles Taylor's rebel National Patriotic Forces of Liberia and the FP's refusal to participate in the military intervention by ECOWAS in Liberia.

Government

The draft Constitution that was to be submitted for approval in a national referendum during 1991 envisaged that the power of the Executive would be counterbalanced by a multi-party Assemblée des députés populaires (ADP) and by an independent Judiciary. Presidential and legislative elections were to be conducted by universal suffrage, with the President being elected for a seven-year term, renewable only once, and delegates to the new legislative body being elected for a four-year term. The President would be empowered to appoint a prime minister; however, the ADP would have the right to veto any such appointment. Both the Government and the Legislature would be competent to initiate legislation.

For administrative purposes, Burkina is divided into 250 departments, districts and villages. Local government is exercised by Comités révolutionnaires (CRs).

Defence

National service is voluntary, and lasts for two years on a part-time basis. In June 1990 the armed forces numbered 8,700 (army 7,000, air force 200, gendarmerie 1,500). Other units include a 'security company' of 250 and a part-time people's militia of 45,000. Defence expenditure for 1989 was estimated at 18,112m. francs CFA (16.9% of total budget expenditure).

Economic Affairs

In 1988, according to estimates by the World Bank, Burkina Faso's gross national product (GNP), measured at average 1986–88 prices, was US $1,960m., equivalent to $230 per head. During 1980–88, it was estimated, GNP increased, in real terms, at an average annual rate of 5.1%, while GNP per head increased by an annual average of 2.4%. During 1980–88 the population increased by an average of 2.6% annually. Over the same period, Burkina's gross domestic product (GDP) increased, in real terms, by an annual average of 5.5%.

Agriculture (including forestry and fishing) contributed 39% of GDP in 1988. About 84.6% of the labour force were employed in agriculture in 1989. The principal cash crop is cotton (exports of ginned cotton accounted for about 45.3% of the value of merchandise exports in 1988). The principal subsistence crops are millet, sorghum and maize. Livestock-rearing is also of some significance. During 1980–88 agricultural production increased by an annual average of 6.4%.

Industry (including mining, manufacturing, construction and power) contributed 29% of GDP in 1988, and employed 10% of the labour force in 1980. During 1980–88 industrial production increased by an annual average of 3.7%.

Although Burkina has considerable mineral resources, extractive activities contributed less than 0.1% of GDP in 1985. Reserves of gold, antimony and marble are exploited; exports of unworked gold contributed 29.3% of the value of merchandise exports in 1988. The extension of the railway network was expected to facilitate the exploitation of important deposits of manganese at Tambao. In addition, Burkina has reserves of phosphates, zinc, silver, lead, nickel and limestone.

The manufacturing sector, which contributed 13% of GDP in 1988, is based predominantly on the processing of primary products. Thus, the major activities are cotton-ginning, the production of textiles, food-processing (including milling and sugar-refining) and brewing.

The generation of electricity was, until the late 1980s, derived entirely from thermal power stations, and was therefore wholly dependent on imported fuel products. However, a hydroelectric power installation was inaugurated in early 1989. A second scheme was under development in that year, while there were plans for the construction of a third installation. Imports of refined petroleum products comprised 7.3% of the value of merchandise imports in 1988.

In 1989 Burkina recorded a visible trade deficit of US $298.1m., while there was a surplus of $66.5m. on the current account of the balance of payments. In 1987 the principal source of imports (31.2%) was France; other major suppliers of imports were Côte d'Ivoire, the USA and Japan. France was also the principal market for exports (34.4%) in that year; other important purchasers were Taiwan and Côte d'Ivoire. The principal exports in 1988 were ginned cotton, miscellaneous manufactured articles, unworked gold and livestock and livestock products (including hides and skins). In the same year the principal imports were machinery and transport equipment, miscellaneous manufactured articles, food products (including cereals), chemicals and refined petroleum products.

Revised budget estimates for 1990 envisaged a deficit of 8,300m. francs CFA. Burkina's total external public debt was US $805m. at the end of 1988. In that year the cost of debt-servicing was equivalent to 11.9% of the value of exports of goods and services. The annual rate of inflation averaged 3.2% in 1980–88. Consumer prices, which declined in 1986 and 1987, increased by an annual average of 4.4% in 1988 but declined again, by 0.5% in 1989.

Burkina Faso is a member of the Communauté Economique de l'Afrique de l'Ouest (CEAO, see p. 120), of the Conseil de l'Entente (see p. 122), of the Economic Community of West African States (ECOWAS, see p. 133) and of the West African organs of the Franc Zone (see p.156).

Burkina Faso's economic development has been impeded by its land-locked position, by the slow development of the mining and industrial sectors (and the consequent dependence on imported goods) and by its vulnerability to adverse climatic conditions and to fluctuations in international prices for its major export commodities. In 1988 the Compaoré Government began negotiations with the IMF and the World Bank, in an attempt to secure guarantees of financial support from those bodies for the country's adjustment efforts. An economic revival programme, announced in October 1989, aimed to achieve real annual GDP growth of 6% by 1992, by stimulating growth in the business, agriculture and energy sectors, and by promoting investment in the education, environment and health sectors.

Social Welfare

The Government provides hospitals and rural medical services. A special medical service for schools is in operation. In 1980 there were five main hospitals, with a total of 2,042 beds. There were also 254 dispensaries, 11 medical centres and 65 regional clinics. A new hospital, built with aid from the People's Republic of China, was inaugurated at Koudougou in 1988. In 1981 only 127 physicians were employed in official medical services (one per 55,858 inhabitants). By 1987, however, every village had its own elected health committee and a primary health centre, and there was one physician per 40,000 inhabitants. In addition, a major vaccination programme, involving 2.5m. Burkinabè children, had been implemented. An old-age and veterans' pension system was introduced in 1960, and extended workers' insurance schemes have been in operation since 1967. Of total planned budgetary expenditure by the central Government in 1989, 7,426m. francs CFA (6.9%) was for health, and a further 130m. francs CFA (0.1%) was for

BURKINA FASO

Introductory Survey, Statistical Survey

social security and welfare. Further payments (3,168m. francs CFA in 1985) are made from social security funds.

Education

Education is provided free of charge, and is officially compulsory for six years between the ages of seven and 14. Primary education begins at seven years of age and lasts for six years. Secondary education, beginning at the age of 13, lasts for a further seven years, comprising a first cycle of four years and a second of three years. It was estimated that in 1987 about 27% of children in the relevant age-group were enrolled at primary schools (34% of boys; 20% of girls). In the same year, however, total secondary school enrolment was equivalent to only 6% (boys 8%; girls 4%). The number of students in higher education increased, however, from 1,067 in 1975 to 3,869 in 1986. There is a university in Ouagadougou, and government grants are available for higher education in European and African universities. A rural radio service has been established to further general and technical education in rural areas. Adult 'functional literacy' programmes in national languages were introduced in 1983. In 1985, according to UNESCO estimates, adult illiteracy averaged 86.8% (males 79.3%; females 93.9%). Expenditure on education by the central Government in 1989 was budgeted at 19,747m. francs CFA, representing about 18.4% of total government spending.

Public Holidays

1991: 1 January (New Year's Day), 1 April (Easter Monday), 16 April* (Id al-Fitr, end of Ramadan), 1 May (Labour Day), 9 May (Ascension Day), 20 May (Whit Monday), 23 June* (Id al-Adha, Feast of the Sacrifice), 4 August (National Day), 15 August (Assumption), 21 September* (Mouloud, Birth of the Prophet), 1 November (All Saints' Day), 25 December (Christmas).

1992: 1 January (New Year's Day), 4 April* (Id al-Fitr, end of Ramadan), 20 April (Easter Monday), 1 May (Labour Day), 28 May (Ascension Day), 8 June (Whit Monday), 11 June* (Id al-Adha, Feast of the Sacrifice), 4 August (National Day), 15 August (Assumption), 10 September* (Mouloud, Birth of the Prophet), 1 November (All Saints' Day), 25 December (Christmas).

* These holidays are dependent on the Islamic lunar calendar and may vary by one or two days from the dates given.

Weights and Measures

The metric system is in force.

Statistical Survey

Source (except where otherwise stated): Institut National de la Statistique et de la Démographie, BP 374, Ouagadougou; tel. 33-55-37.

Area and Population

AREA, POPULATION AND DENSITY

Area (sq km)	274,200*
Population (census results)	
1–7 December 1975	5,638,203
10–20 December 1985	
Males	3,833,237
Females	4,131,468
Total	7,964,705
Population (official estimates at mid-year)	
1987	8,310,000
1988	8,540,000
1989	8,770,000
Density (per sq km) at mid-1989	32.0

* 105,870 sq miles.

PRINCIPAL TOWNS (population at 1985 census)

Ouagadougou (capital)	441,514	Ouahigouya	38,902
Bobo-Dioulasso	228,668	Banfora	35,319
Koudougou	51,926	Kaya	25,814

BIRTHS AND DEATHS (UN estimates, annual averages)

	1975–80	1980–85	1985–90
Birth rate (per 1,000)	47.3	47.1	47.2
Death rate (per 1,000)	21.5	19.9	18.5

Source: UN, *World Population Prospects: 1988*.

ECONOMICALLY ACTIVE POPULATION
(ILO estimates, '000 persons at mid-1980)

	Males	Females	Total
Agriculture, etc.	1,550	1,414	2,964
Industry	89	57	146
Services	145	165	310
Total	**1,784**	**1,637**	**3,421**

Source: ILO, *Economically Active Population Estimates and Projections, 1950–2025*.

1985 census (provisional): Total labour force 4,051,409 (males 2,060,410; females 1,990,999).

Mid-1989 (estimates in '000): Agriculture, etc. 3,944; Total 4,660 (Source: FAO, *Production Yearbook*).

Agriculture

PRINCIPAL CROPS ('000 metric tons)

	1987	1988	1989
Maize	131	227	257
Millet	632	817	649
Sorghum	848	1,009	991
Rice (paddy)	22	39	42
Sweet potatoes	25	39	24
Cassava (Manioc)	7*	8	32*
Yams	88	78	51
Vegetables*	128	128	128
Fruit*	70	70	70
Pulses	180	174	185
Groundnuts (in shell)	146	161	131
Cottonseed*	110	110	110
Cotton (lint)	59	59†	68†
Sesame seed	11	9	11*
Tobacco (leaves)*	1	1	1
Sugar cane*	330	340	340

* FAO estimate(s). † Unofficial figures.

Source: FAO, *Production Yearbook*.

BURKINA FASO

Statistical Survey

LIVESTOCK ('000 head, year ending September)

	1987	1988	1989
Cattle	2,754	2,809	2,850*
Sheep	2,885	2,972	3,050*
Goats	5,047	5,198	5,350*
Pigs	500	500	496
Horses*	70	70	70
Asses	270*	330*	403
Camels	5	5	5*

Poultry (million): 21 in 1987; 21 in 1988; 22* in 1989.
* FAO estimate(s).
Source: FAO, *Production Yearbook*.

LIVESTOCK PRODUCTS (FAO estimates, '000 metric tons)

	1987	1988	1989
Beef and veal	25	26	28
Mutton and lamb	5	5	6
Goats' meat	12	13	13
Pigs' meat	11	11	11
Horse meat	1	1	1
Poultry meat	22	23	24
Cows' milk	79	81	81
Goats' milk	15	16	16
Butter	0.6	0.6	0.6
Hen eggs	14.7	15.1	15.1
Cattle hides	4.3	4.4	4.5
Sheep skins	1.5	1.5	1.5
Goat skins	3.7	3.8	3.9

Source: FAO, *Production Yearbook*.

Forestry

ROUNDWOOD REMOVALS
(FAO estimates, '000 cubic metres, excluding bark)

	1986	1987	1988
Sawlogs, veneer logs and logs for sleepers	1	1	1
Other industrial wood	355	364	374
Fuel wood	7,514	7,711	7,923
Total	7,870	8,076	8,298

Source: FAO, *Yearbook of Forest Products*.

Fishing

('000 metric tons, live weight)

	1980	1981	1982
Total catch	6.5	7.5	7.0

1983–88: Annual catch as in 1982 (FAO estimate).
Source: FAO, *Yearbook of Fishery Statistics*.

Industry

SELECTED PRODUCTS (metric tons, unless otherwise indicated)

	1984	1985	1986
Flour	17,677	25,682	25,518
Raw sugar	26,773	27,939	10,000*†
Soap	11,971	13,456	10,100†
Cottonseed oil (refined)	4,116	5,945	6,000†
Beer (hectolitres)	623,160	623,000†	389,269
Soft drinks (hectolitres)	122,611	123,000†	128,644
Cigarettes ('000 packets)	33,569	33,569	25,492
Footwear ('000 pairs)	911	1,318	890
Cotton yarn	393	392	238
Bicycles, motor cycles and scooters ('000)	26.5	32.3	52.8
Bicycle and motor cycle tyres ('000)	714.4	994.6	526.1
Electric power ('000 kWh)	123,191	123,306	130,567

1987 ('000 metric tons, unless otherwise indicated)†: Wheat flour 21; Raw sugar 25*; Soap 13.3; Cottonseed oil (refined) 8; Beer ('000 hectolitres) 274; Soft drinks ('000 hectolitres) 124; Cigarettes (million) 430; Footwear ('000 pairs) 667; Bicycles, motor cycles and scooters ('000) 62; Bicycle and motor cycle tyres, including inner tubes ('000) 3,256; Electric power (million kWh) 125.

* Provisional or estimated figures.
† Source: UN, *Industrial Statistics Yearbook*.

Finance

CURRENCY AND EXCHANGE RATES

Monetary Units
100 centimes = 1 franc de la Communauté financière africaine (CFA).

Denominations
Coins: 1, 2, 5, 10, 25, 50, 100 and 500 francs CFA.
Notes: 50, 100, 500, 1,000, 5,000 and 10,000 francs CFA.

French Franc, Sterling and Dollar Equivalents (30 September 1990)
1 French franc = 50 francs CFA;
£1 sterling = 491.1 francs CFA;
US $1 = 262.1 francs CFA;
1,000 francs CFA = £2.036 = $3.815.

Average Exchange Rate (francs CFA per US $)
1987 300.54
1988 297.85
1989 319.01

BUDGET (million francs CFA)

Revenue	1987	1988*	1989*
Fiscal receipts	76,245	81,131	98,903
Taxes on income and profits	18,383	21,909	22,966
Individual taxes	9,033	10,655	13,046
Corporate and business taxes	5,128	8,900	8,000
Taxes on goods and services	20,048	29,955	32,907
Turnover taxes	5,900	16,432	17,480
Consumption taxes	8,103	10,775	10,889
Taxes on fiscal monopolies	4,041	940	2,600
Taxes on international trade and transactions	35,733	27,219	32,938
Import duties	32,238	25,040	30,684
Non-fiscal receipts	8,812	8,367	8,000
Administrative fees, charges and non-industrial sales	1,771	3,116	2,511
Capital receipts	971	798	1,630
Total	86,028	90,296	100,533

BURKINA FASO

Expenditure	1987	1988*	1989*
General public services	8,896	11,830	10,327
Defence	15,337	13,669	18,112
Public order and security	3,760	3,754	4,367
Education	16,065	17,523	19,747
Health	5,128	6,450	7,426
Social security and welfare	712	135	130
Housing and community amenities	327	735	357
Other community and social services	1,491	2,747	3,016
Economic services	10,674	15,296	19,277
Agriculture, forestry and fishing	4,153	6,201	5,708
Mining, manufacturing and construction	233	1,389	2,671
Transport and communications	4,352	6,596	9,010
Other economic services	1,936	1,110	1,888
Other purposes	36,204	24,147	24,455
Debt-repayment	18,570	15,557	17,150
Total	98,594	96,286	107,214

* Estimates.

Source: Banque Centrale des Etats de l'Afrique de l'Ouest.

1990 (Revised budget estimates, million francs CFA): Revenue 96,970; Expenditure 105,270.

CENTRAL BANK RESERVES (US $ million at 31 December)

	1987	1988	1989
Gold*	5.2	4.6	4.3
IMF special drawing rights	8.0	7.6	7.4
Reserve position in IMF	10.7	10.1	9.9
Foreign exchange	303.9	303.1	248.2
Total	327.8	325.5	269.8

* Valued at market-related prices.

Source: IMF, *International Financial Statistics*.

MONEY SUPPLY ('000 million francs CFA at 31 December)

	1987	1988	1989
Currency outside banks	43.71	49.31	53.28
Demand deposits at deposit money banks*	44.09	47.25	48.47
Checking deposits at post office	2.79	1.75	2.21

* Excluding the deposits of public establishments of an administrative or social nature.

Source: IMF, *International Financial Statistics*.

COST OF LIVING (Consumer Price Index for Africans in Ouagadougou; base: 1985 = 100)

	1987	1988	1989
All items	94.6	98.8	98.3

Source: IMF, *International Financial Statistics*.

NATIONAL ACCOUNTS
(million francs CFA at current prices)

Composition of the Gross National Product

	1983	1984	1985
Gross domestic product (GDP) at factor cost	357,929	368,035	427,384
Indirect taxes, *less* subsidies	24,084	22,530	28,496
GDP in purchasers' values	381,013	390,565	455,882
Factor income received from abroad	3,986	4,162	4,241
Less Factor income paid abroad	5,636	5,884	5,996
Gross national product	379,362	388,845	454,126

Source: UN, *National Accounts Statistics*.

Expenditure on the Gross Domestic Product

	1983	1984	1985
Government final consumption expenditure	78,795	76,922	72,602
Private final consumption expenditure	327,566	308,282	398,469
Increase in stocks	2,633	3,277	15,501
Gross fixed capital formation	90,354	90,828	113,491
Total domestic expenditure	499,348	479,309	600,063
Exports of goods and services	55,853	88,094	79,155
Less imports of goods and services	174,188	176,837	223,336
GDP in purchasers' values	381,013	390,565	455,882
GDP at constant 1979 prices	270,747	275,134	311,077

Source: UN, *National Accounts Statistics*.

Gross Domestic Product by Economic Activity

	1983	1984	1985
Agriculture, hunting, forestry and fishing	152,052	164,205	213,968
Mining and quarrying	77	304	294
Manufacturing	48,053	47,457	50,901
Electricity, gas and water	4,055	4,246	3,192
Construction	7,749	4,934	5,333
Trade, restaurants and hotels	46,344	42,187	45,418
Transport, storage and communications	24,211	29,011	30,913
Finance, insurance, real estate and business services	14,009	14,510	15,488
Government services	67,556	67,455	67,405
Other community, social and personal services	1,877	1,771	2,026
Other services	3,675	5,788	6,552
Sub-total	369,658	381,868	441,490
Import duties	18,131	16,219	21,151
Less Imputed bank service charge	6,778	7,523	6,758
GDP in purchasers' values	381,013	390,565	455,882

Source: UN, *National Accounts Statistics*.

BURKINA FASO

BALANCE OF PAYMENTS (US $ million)

	1987	1988	1989
Merchandise exports f.o.b.	229.9	249.1	214.4
Merchandise imports f.o.b.	−475.2	−486.8	−512.5
Trade balance	−245.2	−237.7	−298.1
Services (net)	−158.7	−182.0	−184.6
Balance on goods and services	−403.9	−419.7	−482.7
Private unrequited transfers (net)	164.0	165.2	144.2
Government unrequited transfers (net)	194.7	195.1	405.0
Current balance	−45.3	−59.4	66.5
Long-term capital (net)	81.9	63.1	−197.8
Short-term capital (net)	−5.8	17.4	69.1
Net errors and omissions	58.9	−18.7	9.2
Total (net monetary movements)	89.8	2.4	−53.1
Valuation changes (net)	1.6	−0.7	−0.3
Changes in reserves	91.4	1.7	−53.4

Source: IMF, *International Financial Statistics*.

External Trade

Source: Banque Centrale des Etats de l'Afrique de l'Ouest.

PRINCIPAL COMMODITIES (million francs CFA)

Imports c.i.f.	1986	1987	1988
Dairy products	5,331	4,976	5,275
Cereals	7,753	7,501	12,372
Beverages and tobacco	3,522	3,441	2,577
Refined petroleum products	15,413	10,073	9,836
Other raw materials	3,823	3,615	3,515
Fats and oils	3,295	1,782	1,338
Non-electrical machinery	15,121	15,006	14,750
Electrical machinery	5,265	6,126	7,826
Road transport equipment	17,703	13,691	14,823
Chemicals	15,749	17,583	15,867
Miscellaneous manufactured articles	33,564	34,109	35,814
Hydraulic cement	4,052	5,957	6,656
Total (incl. others)	139,640	130,527	134,944

Exports f.o.b.	1986	1987	1988
Livestock and livestock products	2,725	2,537	1,702
Vegetables	595	840	679
Hides and skins	1,408	1,654	2,205
Cotton (ginned)	10,633	20,138	19,011
Machinery and transport equipment	1,684	4,501	2,525
Miscellaneous manufactured articles	9,214	14,767	14,153
Unworked gold	7,666	13,059	12,307
Total (incl. others)	28,665	46,593	41,947

PRINCIPAL TRADING PARTNERS (million francs CFA)

Imports	1985	1986	1987
Algeria	2,700.5	16.6	22.8
Belgium/Luxembourg	1,595.0	1,759.6	2,634.2
Canada	1,116.6	2,304.6	695.7
China, People's Republic	3,618.4	1,603.0	1,680.6
Côte d'Ivoire	33,269.4	29,971.3	21,329.3
France	34,568.1	41,124.0	40,747.8
Germany, Federal Republic	6,962.6	5,108.1	5,356.8
Ghana	2,563.4	1,426.6	1,291.7
Italy	3,138.9	6,893.3	5,227.5
Japan	4,309.1	6,067.0	6,579.0
Netherlands	5,977.9	6,921.6	5,792.8
Nigeria	1,549.3	1,928.3	1,825.3
Senegal	1,143.6	1,732.6	784.8
Spain	1,161.7	2,001.0	1,745.0
Taiwan	1,275.5	1,126.4	1,307.9
Thailand	2,147.6	1,313.6	4,342.3
Togo	1,844.1	2,729.1	4,779.6
United Kingdom	2,920.5	2,467.9	3,219.8
USA	21,940.7	12,553.0	8,408.6
Total (incl. others)	146,243.3	139,639.9	130,526.6

Exports	1985	1986	1987
Belgium/Luxembourg	519.8	151.2	104.8
China, People's Republic	1,374.1	164.9	192.3
Côte d'Ivoire	4,680.6	4,336.9	6,777.2
Denmark	577.5	403.8	192.5
France	9,046.4	7,571.5	16,019.4
Germany, Federal Republic	438.7	606.4	987.7
Ghana	372.1	133.6	841.9
Italy	1,409.9	888.1	1,184.3
Japan	635.4	281.2	881.5
Morocco	929.2	0.4	1,115.1
Portugal	n.a.	277.4	1,016.1
Spain	338.1	904.7	1,106.3
Switzerland	2,205.1	2,191.8	2,046.4
Taiwan	5,278.8	7,166.0	7,257.6
Togo	342.9	252.5	2,266.8
United Kingdom	693.6	693.8	451.5
Total (incl. others)	31,157.0	28,664.7	46,593.1

Transport

RAILWAYS (traffic)

	1980	1981	1982
Passenger journeys ('000)	3,646	3,277	2,867
Passenger-km (million)	1,250	988	856
Freight ton-km (million)	600	634	668

Passengers carried: 2.4 million in 1985; 1.5 million in 1986.
Freight: 233,009 metric tons in 1985; 227,870 metric tons in 1986.

ROAD TRAFFIC ('000 motor vehicles in use)

	1985	1986	1987
Passenger cars	14	14	15
Commercial vehicles	13	13	13

Source: UN Economic Commission for Africa, *African Statistical Yearbook*.

BURKINA FASO

CIVIL AVIATION (traffic on scheduled services)*

	1983	1984	1985
Kilometres flown (million)	2.3	2.2	2.4
Passengers carried ('000)	93	93	100
Passenger-km (million)	222	222	246
Freight ton-km (million)	18.8	17.4	18.4
Mail ton-km (million)	0.8	0.8	0.7
Total ton-km (million)	40	38	41

* Including an apportionment of the traffic of Air Afrique.
Source: UN, *Statistical Yearbook*.

Tourism

	1985	1986	1987
Number of tourist arrivals	44,375	60,704	68,308

Receipts from tourism (million francs CFA): 2,193 in 1985; 2,212 in 1986; 2,300 in 1987.
Source: Division du Tourisme et de l'Hôtellerie, Ouagadougou.

Communications Media

	1985	1986	1987
Radio receivers ('000 in use)	145	170	200
Television receivers ('000 in use)	36	38	40

Telephones (1987, estimate): 15,000 in use.
Book production (1985): 9 titles.
Daily newspapers (1986): 1 (average circulation 3,000 copies).
Source: mainly UNESCO, *Statistical Yearbook*.

Education

(1986)

	Institutions	Teachers	Pupils Males	Pupils Females	Total
Primary	1,758	6,091	221,969	129,838	351,807
Secondary					
General	107	1,519	33,208	15,667	48,875
Vocational	18	421	2,601	2,207	4,808
Teacher training	1	n.a.	231	116	347
Higher	1	325	2,955	914	3,869

Source: Ministère de l'Education nationale, Ouagadougou.

1987: Primary Teachers 6,359, Pupils 411,907 (males 258,654, females 153,253); Secondary Pupils: General 67,271 (males 45,983, females 21,288), Vocational 4,586 (males 2,428, females 2,158), Teacher training 350 (Source: UNESCO, *Statistical Yearbook*).

Directory

The Constitution

The 1977 Constitution was suspended following the military coup of 25 November 1980. A commission was inaugurated in May 1990 to draft a new Constitution. The draft document, which was completed in October 1990, was to be submitted for approval in a national referendum during 1991. The following are the main provisions of the draft Constitution:

The Constitution of the 'revolutionary, democratic, unitary and secular' State of Burkina Faso guaranteed the collective and individual political and social rights of Burkinabè citizens, and delineated, the powers of the Executive, Legislature and Judiciary.

Executive power was to be vested in the President, who is Head of State, and in the Government, which was to be appointed by the President. The President was to be elected, by universal suffrage, for a seven-year term, renewable only once.

Legislative power was to be exercised by a multi-party Assemblée des députés populaires (ADP). Delegates to the ADP were to be elected, by universal suffrage, for a four-year term.

Both the Government and the Legislature were to be competent to initiate legislation.

The Judiciary was to be independent. Judges were to be accountable to a Higher Council, which was to be chaired by the Head of State.

The Constitution denied legitimacy to any regime that might take power as the result of a *coup d'état*.

The Government

HEAD OF STATE

Chairman of the Popular Front: Capt. BLAISE COMPAORÉ (assumed power 15 October 1987).

COUNCIL OF MINISTERS
(December 1990)

Chairman of the Popular Front, Head of Government and Minister of Popular Defence and Security: Capt. BLAISE COMPAORÉ.
Minister of State: CHRISTIAN ROCH KABORÉ.
Minister of Peasant Affairs: (vacant).
Minister of the Environment and Tourism: MAURICE DIEUDONNÉ BONANE.
Minister of Health and Social Action: KANIDOUA NABOMO.
Minister of Information and Culture: BÉATRICE DAMIBA.
Minister of External Relations: PROSPER VOKOUMA.
Minister of Sports: Lt KILIMITÉ HIEN.
Minister of Labour, Social Security and the Public Service: SALIF SAMPEBOGO.
Minister of Territorial Administration: JEAN-LÉONARD COMPAORÉ.
Minister of Finance: BINTOU SANOGO.
Minister of Economic Promotion: THOMAS SANOU.
Minister of Planning and Co-operation: FRÉDÉRIC ASSOMPTION KORSAGA.
Minister of Trade and Popular Supply: TOU NÉOLIE KONE.
Minister of Agriculture and Livestock: ALBERT DJIDMA.
Minister of Equipment: Capt. DAPROU KAMBOU.
Minister of Transport and Communications: JACQUES OUEDRAOGO.
Minister of Primary Education and Mass Literacy: ALICE TIENDRÉBÉOGO.
Minister of Secondary and Higher Education and Scientific Research: MOUHOUSSINE NACRO.
Minister of Justice and Keeper of the Seals: ANTOINE KOMI SAMBO.
Minister of Water Resources: SABNÉ KOANDA.
Secretary of State for Finance in charge of the Budget: CÉLESTIN TIENDRÉBÉOGO.
Secretary of State for Housing and Urban Affairs: JOSEPH KABORÉ.
Secretary of State for Culture: ALIMATA SALEMBÉRÉ.
Secretary of State for Social Action: ELIE SARÉ.
Secretary of State for Livestock: AMADOU MAURICE GUIAO.

BURKINA FASO

Secretary of State for Mines: ABOUBACAR YAHYA DIALLO.
Secretary-General of the Revolutionary Committees: Capt. ARSÈNE YÈ BOGNESSAN.
Secretary of State at the Presidency of the Republic: DIALLO SALIF.

MINISTRIES

Chairman's Office: Ouagadougou.
Ministry of Agriculture and Livestock: BP 7005, Ouagadougou.
Ministry of Economic Promotion: Ouagadougou.
Ministry of the Environment and Tourism: BP 7044, Ouagadougou; tel. 33-41-65; telex 5555.
Ministry of Equipment: BP 7011, Ouagadougou.
Ministry of External Relations: BP 7038, Ouagadougou; telex 5222.
Ministry of Finance: BP 7008, Ouagadougou; tel. 33-40-74; telex 5256.
Ministry of Health and Social Action: BP 7009, Ouagadougou.
Ministry of Information and Culture: BP 7045, Ouagadougou; tel. 33-44-67; telex 5285.
Ministry of Justice: BP 526, Ouagadougou.
Ministry of Labour, Social Security and the Public Service: BP 7006, Ouagadougou.
Ministry of Peasant Affairs: Ouagadougou.
Ministry of Planning and Co-operation: BP 7050, Ouagadougou; telex 5319.
Ministry of Popular Defence and Security: BP 496, Ouagadougou; telex 5297.
Ministry of Primary Education and Mass Literary: BP 7032, Ouagadougou; telex 5555.
Ministry of Secondary and Higher Education and Scientific Research: BP 7130, Ouagadougou.
Ministry of Sports: BP 7035, Ouagadougou.
Ministry of State: Ouagadougou.
Ministry of Territorial Administration: BP 7034, Ouagadougou.
Ministry of Trade and Popular Supply: BP 365, Ouagadougou.
Ministry of Transport and Communications: BP 7701, Ouagadougou.
Ministry of Water Resources: Ouagadougou.
Office of the Secretary-General: BP 7030, Ouagadougou.

Legislature

ASSEMBLÉE DES DÉPUTÉS POPULAIRES

The draft Constitution that was to be submitted for approval in a national referendum during 1991 provided for the establishment of a legislative body, the Assemblée des députés populaires (ADP), which was to be elected by direct universal suffrage.

Political Organizations

Legislation authorizing the registration of political parties was to be promulgated during 1991.

Front populaire (FP): Ouagadougou; f. Oct. 1987; Chair. of Exec. Cttee Capt. BLAISE COMPAORÉ; Sec. for Political Affairs CHRISTIAN ROCH KABORÉ; comprises seven political groupings:

Convention nationale des patriotes progressistes—Parti social-démocrate (CNPP—PSD).

Groupement des démocrates et patriotes (GDP).

Groupement des démocrates révolutionnaires (GDR).

Mouvement des démocrates et patriotes.

Organisation pour la démocratie populaire/Mouvement du travail (ODP/MT): f. 1989; fusion of Union des communistes burkinabe and a dissident faction of the Union des luttes communistes; Sec.-Gen. CHRISTIAN ROCH KABORÉ.

Union des démocrates et patriotes burkinabè (UDPB).

Union des sociaux-démocrates (USD): f. 1990; Leader ALAIN YODA.

Political organizations outside the FP in late 1990 included:

Groupe communiste burkinabè (GCB): Ouagadougou; Marxist-Leninist; Sec.-Gen. JEAN-MARC PALM.

Ligue patriotique pour le développement (LIPAD): Ouagadougou; f. 1970; Marxist, pro-Soviet; Pres. HAMIDOU COULIBALY.

Mouvement des démocrates progressistes (orthodoxe): Leader HERMAN YAMÉOGO.

Mouvement des démocrates progressistes (réformateur): f. 1990, following split with 'orthodoxe' faction (see above); Sec.-Gen. LASSANE OUANGRAWA.

Mouvement pour le progrès et la tolérance (MPT): f. 1990; Sec.-Gen. EMMANUEL NAYABTIGOUNGOU CONGO KABORÉ.

Parti africain de l'indépendance (PAI).

Parti communiste révolutionnaire voltaïque (PCRV).

Rassemblement démocratique et populaire—Thomas Sankara: f. 1987; clandestine resistance movement; Leader VINCENT OUEDRAOGO.

Union des luttes communistes (ULC): Ouagadougou; f. 1987; Leader ALAIN ZOUGBA.

Opposition movements in exile in 1990 included:

Front progressiste voltaïque (FPV): Sec.-Gen. Prof. JOSEPH KI-ZERBO.

Union des luttes communistes reconstruite (ULCR): f. 1984, in exile since 1987; Leaders VALERE SOMÉ, BASILE GUISSOU.

Diplomatic Representation

EMBASSIES IN BURKINA FASO

Algeria: BP 3893, Ouagadougou; telex 5359.
China, People's Republic: quartier Rotonde, BP 538, Ouagadougou; Ambassador: WU JIASEN.
Cuba: BP 3422, Ouagadougou; telex 5360; Ambassador: REME REMIGIO RUIZ.
Egypt: BP 668, Ouagadougou; telex 5289; Ambassador: Dr MOHAMAD ALEY EL-KORDY.
France: 902 ave de l'Indépendance, BP 504, Ouagadougou; tel. 33-38-92; telex 5211; Ambassador: ALAIN DESCHAMPS.
Germany: 01 BP 600, Ouagadougou 01; tel. 30-67-31; telex 5217; Ambassador: JÜRGEN DRÖGE.
Ghana: BP 212, Ouagadougou; tel. 33-28-75; Ambassador: (vacant).
Korea, Democratic People's Republic: BP 370, Ouagadougou; Ambassador: KIM SUN-CHE.
Libya: BP 1601, Ouagadougou; telex 5311; Secretary of People's Bureau: (vacant).
Netherlands: BP 1302, Ouagadougou; telex 5303; Ambassador: P. R. BROUWER.
Nigeria: BP 132, Ouagadougou; tel. 33-42-41; telex 5236; Chargé d'affaires a.i.: A. K. ALLI ASSAYOUTI.
USSR: BP 7041, Ouagadougou; Ambassador: YEVGENI NIKOLAYEVICH KORENDYASOV.
USA: 01 BP 35, Ouagadougou 01; tel. 30-67-23; telex 5290; Ambassador: EDWARD P. BRYNN.

Judicial System

The draft Constitution that was to be submitted for approval in a national referendum during 1991 provided for the independence of the Judiciary. Judges were to be accountable to a Higher Council, which was to be chaired by the Head of State.

Religion

More than 50% of the population follow animist beliefs.

ISLAM

At 31 December 1986 there were an estimated 2,514,261 Muslims in Burkina Faso.

CHRISTIANITY

Protestant Churches

At 31 December 1986 there were an estimated 106,467 adherents.

The Roman Catholic Church

Burkina comprises one archdiocese and eight dioceses. At 31 December 1988 there were an estimated 758,551 adherents (about 9.3% of the total population).

Bishops' Conference: Conférence des Evêques du Burkina Faso et du Niger, BP 1195, Ouagadougou; tel. 30-60-20; f. 1000, legally recognized 1978; Pres. Rt Rev. JEAN MARIE COMPAORÉ, Bishop of Fada N'Gourma.

Archbishop of Ouagadougou: Cardinal PAUL ZOUNGRANA, BP 1472, Ouagadougou; tel. 30-67-04.

BURKINA FASO

Directory

The Press

Direction de la presse écrite: Ouagadougou; official govt body responsible for media direction.

DAILIES

Bulletin Quotidien d'Information: BP 507, Ouagadougou; tel. 30-61-14; f. 1959; publ. by the Direction de la presse écrite; simultaneous edn publ. in Bobo-Dioulasso; Dir-Gen. HUBERT BAZIÉ; Editor PIERRE-CLAVIER TASSEMBEDO; circ. 1,500.

Dunia: Ouagadougou.

Jamaa (Voice of the Masses): Ouagadougou; f. 1988; organ of the Front populaire.

Lolowulein (Red Star): Ouagadougou; f. 1985; state-owned.

Notre Combat: BP 507, Ouagadougou.

Sidwaya (Truth): Ouagadougou; f. 1984; state-owned; Dir PIERRE WAONGO; circ. 7,000.

PERIODICALS

Armée du Peuple: Ouagadougou; f. 1982; monthly; armed forces and defence information; Editor-in-Chief Lt SEYDOU NIANG.

Bulletin Economique et Fiscal: BP 502, Ouagadougou; tel. 30-61-14; telex 5268; fax 30-61-16; f. 1971; monthly; legislative and statutory notices; distributed by the Chambre de Commerce, d'Industrie et d'Artisanat du Burkina; circ. 350.

Bulletin Mensuel de Statistique: BP 374, Ouagadougou; tel. 33-55-37; monthly; economic and demographic statistics; publ. by National Statistics Office.

Carrefour Africain: BP 507, Ouagadougou; f. 1960; monthly; state-owned; Dir-Gen. BABOU PAULIN BAMOUNI; circ. 6,000.

Courrier Consulaire du Burkina: BP 502, Ouagadougou; tel. 30-61-14; telex 5268; fax 30-61-16; f. 1960; monthly; legislative and statutory notices; publ. by the Chambre de Commerce, d'Industrie et d'Artisanat du Burkina; circ. 350.

L'Intrus: Ouagadougou; f. 1986; weekly; satirical humour.

Journal Officiel du Burkina: BP 568, Ouagadougou; weekly.

Manegda: Mooré; weekly.

NEWS AGENCIES

Agence Burkinabè de Presse: BP 2507, Ouagadougou; tel. 33-28-20; telex 5327; f. 1963; state-controlled.

Foreign Bureaux

Agence France-Presse (AFP): BP 391, Ouagadougou; tel. 33-56-56; telex 5204; Bureau Chief KIDA TAPSOBA.

TASS (USSR) also has a bureau in Ouagadougou.

Publishers

Imprimerie Nouvelle du Centre: Ouagadougou; social sciences.

Presses Africaines SA: BP 1471, Ouagadougou; tel. 33-43-07; telex 5344; general fiction, religion, primary and secondary textbooks; Man. Dir A. WININGA.

Société Nationale d'Edition et de Presse (SONEPRESS): BP 810, Ouagadougou; f. 1972; general, periodicals; Pres. MARTIAL OUEDRAOGO.

Government Publishing House

Imprimerie Nationale du Burkina Faso (INBF): route de l'Hôpital Yalgado, BP 7040, Ouagadougou; tel. 33-52-92; f. 1963; Dir LATY SOULEYMANE TRAORÉ.

Radio and Television

There were an estimated 200,000 radio receivers and 40,000 television receivers in use in 1987.

RADIO

Radiodiffusion-Télévision Burkina: BP 7029, Ouagadougou; tel. 33-68-05; telex 5132; f. 1959; services in French and 16 vernacular languages; Dir BAYER BALAWO.

Horizon FM: BP 2714, Ouagadougou; tel. 30-63-52; private commercial station; broadcasts in French, English and eight vernacular languages; Dir MUSTAPHA LAABLI THIOMBIANO.

Radio Bobo-Dioulasso: BP 392, Bobo-Dioulasso; tel. 99-11-58; daily programmes in French and vernacular languages.

Radio Tapoa: Diapaga; f. 1989; broadcasts to Tapoa province.

REP: Ouagadougou; f. 1987; private commercial station; Dir JEAN-HUBERT BAZIE.

TELEVISION

Télévision Nationale du Burkina: 29 blvd de la Révolution, 01 BP 2530, Ouagadougou; tel. 31-01-35; telex 5327; f. 1963; Dir SEYDOU AZAD SAWADOGO.

Finance

(cap. = capital; res = reserves; m. = million; brs = branches; amounts in francs CFA)

BANKING

Central Bank

Banque Centrale des Etats de l'Afrique de l'Ouest (BCEAO): ave Gamal-Abdel-Nasser, BP 356, Ouagadougou; tel. 30-60-15; telex 5205; fax 31-01-22; headquarters in Dakar, Senegal; f. 1955; bank of issue for the seven states of the Union monétaire ouest-africaine (UMOA), comprising Benin, Burkina Faso, Côte d'Ivoire, Mali, Niger, Senegal and Togo; cap. and res 217,441m. (Sept. 1989); Gov. (vacant); Dir in Burkina Faso MOUSSA KONÉ; br. in Bobo-Dioulasso.

State Banks

Banque Arabe-Libyenne-Burkinabè pour le Commerce et le Développement (BALIB): ave Nelson Mandela, 01 BP 1336, Ouagadougou 01; tel. 30-78-78; telex 5501; f. 1987, operations commenced 1989; 50% state-owned, 50% Libyan-owned; cap. 800m.; Pres. LUCAIN SOMÉ; Dir-Gen. ALI SALEH SAKKAH.

Banque pour le Financement du Commerce et des Investissements du Burkina (BFCIB): 4 rue du Marché, 01 BP 585, Ouagadougou 01; tel. 30-60-35; telex 5269; f. 1973; 79% state-owned; cap. and res 14,201m. (Sept. 1987); Pres. M. N'GOLO CHRISTOPHE KONÉ; Dir-Gen. JEAN-BAPTISTE CONFÉ.

Banque Internationale du Burkina SA (BIB): rue de la Chance angle rue Patrice Lumumba, 01 BP 362, Ouagadougou 01; tel. 31-01-00; telex 5210; fax 31-00-90; f. 1974; 53% state-owned, 40% owned by BIAO (France); cap. 1,638m. (Sept. 1989); Pres. DAOUDA BAYILI; Gen. Man. GASPARD OUEDRAOGO; 13 brs.

Banque Internationale pour le Commerce, l'Industrie et l'Agriculture du Burkina SA (BICIB): ave Dr Nkwamé N'Kruma, 01 BP 8, Ouagadougou 01; tel. 30-62-26; telex 5203; f. 1973; 51% state-owned; cap. 1,750m. (Sept. 1989); Man. Dir AUGUSTIN DER SOMDA; 11 brs.

Banque Nationale de Développement du Burkina (BNDB): place de la Révolution, 01 BP 148, Ouagadougou 01; tel. 30-60-82; telex 5225; f. 1962; 92% state-owned; cap. 2,510m. (Sept. 1988); Pres. BISSIRI JOSEPH SIRIMA; Man. Dir BOUKARY OUEDRAOGO; 6 brs.

Caisse Nationale de Crédit Agricole du Burkina (CNCAB): ave Kdiogo, 01 BP 1644, Ouagadougou 01; tel. 30-21-62; telex 5443; f. 1979; 54% state-owned; cap. 1,300m. (Sept. 1987); Pres. THÉODORE SAWADOGO; Dir-Gen. NOËL KABORÉ; 4 brs.

Union Révolutionnaire des Banques (UREBA): 2 ave Nelson Mandela, 01 BP 4414, Ouagadougou 01; tel. 30-61-17; telex 5458; f. 1984; 51% owned by govt and provinces; cap. 2,000m. (1990); Pres. GUÉBRILA OUEDRAOGO; Dir-Gen. OUMAR CHEIKH SONNY.

Financial Institution

Caisse Autonome d'Amortissement du Burkina: BP 1309, Ouagadougou; tel. 33-51-37; manages state funds; Dir-Gen. DOUAMBA TINGA DIDACE.

INSURANCE

Société Nationale d'Assurances et de Réassurances (SONAR): 01 BP 406, Ouagadougou 01; tel. 30-62-43; telex 5294; f. 1973; 51% state-owned, 21% owned by GFA (France); cap. 240m.; Man. Dir AUGUSTIN N. TRAORÉ.

Trade and Industry

ADVISORY BODY

Conseil Révolutionnaire Economique et Social: Ouagadougou; f. 1985; 38 mems; Pres. KADER CISSÉ.

GOVERNMENT REGULATORY BODIES

Autorité des Aménagements des Vallées des Voltas (AVV): BP 524, Ouagadougou; tel. 30-61-10; telex 5401; f. 1974; integrated rural development, including economic and social planning; Man. Dir EMMANUEL NIKIEMA.

BURKINA FASO

Bureau des Mines et de la Géologie du Burkina (BUMIGEB): 01 BP 601, Ouagadougou 01; tel. 30-02-27; telex 5340; f. 1978; cap. 818m. francs CFA; research into geological and mineral resources; Pres. ALY SEYE; Man. Dir KASSOUM JOSEPH KABORÉ.

Caisse de Stabilisation des Prix des Produits Agricoles (CSPPA): BP 1453, Ouagadougou; tel. 30-62-17; telex 5202; f. 1964; cap. 25m.; responsible for stabilization of agricultural prices; supervises trade and export; Pres. BOUREIMA TIEN; Dir EMMANUEL ANDRÉ YAMÉOGO; br. at Bobo-Dioulasso.

Office National des Céréales (OFNACER): BP 53, Ouagadougou; tel. 33-67-38; telex 5317; responsible for stabilization of the supply and price of cereals; Dir GOAMA HENRI KABORÉ.

Office National du Commerce Exterieur (ONAC): ave Léo Frobénius, BP 389, Ouagadougou; tel. 33-62-25; telex 5258; f. 1974; promotes and supervises external trade; Man. Dir SYLVIE KABORÉ.

Office National de l'Eau et de l'Assainissement (ONEA): 01 BP 170, Ouagadougou 01; tel. 30-60-73; telex 5226; f. 1977; cap. 3,087m. francs CFA; storage, purification and distribution of water; Dir ALI CONGO.

Office National de l'Exploitation des Ressources Animales: BP 7058, Ouagadougou; tel. 33-68-41; telex 5312; Dir-Gen. ROGER MOUSSA TALL.

CHAMBER OF COMMERCE

Chambre de Commerce, d'Industrie et d'Artisanat du Burkina: BP 502, Ouagadougou; tel. 30-61-14; telex 5268; fax 30-61-16; Pres. PAUL BALKOUMA; Sec.-Gen. SYLVIE KABORÉ; br. in Bobo-Dioulasso.

DEVELOPMENT AGENCIES

Caisse Centrale de Coopération Economique (CCCE): ave Binger, BP 529, Ouagadougou; tel. 33-60-76; telex 5271; Dir FRANÇOIS PEYREDIEU DU CHARLAT.

Mission Française de Coopération: 01 BP 510, Ouagadougou 01; tel. 30-67-71; telex 5211; centre for administering bilateral aid from France under co-operation agreements signed in 1961; Dir FERNAND CORNIL.

EMPLOYERS' ORGANIZATIONS

Association Professionnelle des Banques et Établissements Financiers (APBEF): Ouagadougou; Pres. JEAN-BAPTISTE CONFÉ.

Conseil National du Patronat Burkinabè: Ouagadougou.

Groupement Professionnel des Industriels: BP 810, Ouagadougou; tel. 33-28-81; f. 1974; Pres. MARTIAL OUEDRAOGO.

Syndicat des Commerçants Importateurs et Exportateurs (SCIMPEX): 01 BP 552, Ouagadougou 01; tel. 31-18-70; Pres. JEAN-FRANÇOIS MEUNIER.

Syndicat des Entrepreneurs et Industriels: Ouagadougou.

CO-OPERATIVES

Groupement Coopératif de Ventes Internationales des Produits du Burkina (Cooproduits): BP 91, Ouagadougou; telex 5224; cap. 30m. francs CFA; agricultural co-operative; exports seeds, nuts and gum arabic; Chair. and Man. Dir KÉOULÉ NACOULIMA.

Société de Commercialisation du Burkina 'Faso Yaar': ave du Loudun, BP 531, Ouagadougou; tel. 30-61-28; telex 5274; BP 375, Bobo-Dioulasso; tel. 98-18-31; f. 1967; cap. 2,209m. francs CFA; 99% state-owned; marketing organization with 30 retail outlets; Pres. Minister of Trade and Popular Supply; Man. Dir MAMADOU DIAWARA.

Union des Coopératives Agricoles et Maraîchères du Burkina (UCOBAM): BP 277, Ouagadougou; tel. 30-65-27; telex 5287; f. 1968; cap. 128m. francs CFA; comprises 8 regional co-operative unions (20,000 mems); production and marketing of fruit and vegetables; Dir-Gen. ISSAKA DERME; Commercial Dir ANDRÉ BICABA.

TRADE UNIONS

There are more than 20 autonomous trade unions. The five trade union syndicates are:

Confédération Générale du Travail Burkinabè (CGTB): Ouagadougou; f. 1988; confederation of several autonomous trade unions.

Confédération Nationale des Travailleurs Burkinabè (CNTB): BP 445, Ouagadougou; f. 1972; Leader of Governing Directorate ABDOULAYE BÂ.

Confédération Syndicale Burkinabè (CSB): BP 299, Ouagadougou; f. 1974; affiliated to Ligue patriotique pour le développement (LIPAD); mainly public service unions; Sec.-Gen. YACINTHE OUEDRAOGO.

Organisation Nationale des Syndicats Libres (ONSL): BP 99, Ouagadougou; f. 1960; Sec.-Gen. (vacant); 6,000 mems (1983).

Union Syndicale des Travailleurs Burkinabè (USTB): BP 381, Ouagadougou; f. 1958; Sec.-Gen. BONIFACE SOMDAH; 35,000 mems in 45 affiliated orgs.

Transport

RAILWAY

In 1990 there were some 622 km of track in Burkina Faso. A 77-km extension from Donsin to Kaya was inaugurated in August 1989. Plans exist for the construction of a 210-km extension to the manganese deposits at Tambao. In 1989 the cost of the project was estimated at 6,250m. francs CFA.

La Société des Chemins de Fer du Burkina SCFB: BP 192, Ouagadougou; tel. 30-60-50; telex 5433; fax 30-77-49; f. 1989 to operate the Burkinabè railway network that was fmrly managed by the Régie du Chemin de Fer Abidjan–Niger; length of railway: 622 km; Dir-Gen. GRÉGOIRE BABORÉ BADO.

ROADS

At 31 December 1986 there were 11,231 km of roads, including 4,576 km of main roads and 4,108 km of secondary roads. The Ghana-Burkina Faso Road Transport Commission, based in Accra, was established to implement the 1968 agreement on improving communications between the two countries.

In 1986 plans were announced for a 133-km tarred road, to connect Bobo-Dioulasso to the Mali border via Orodara, and in 1989 the upgrading of the 149-km road from Fada N'Gourma to the border with Benin was announced. The project (whose cost was estimated at $42.8m.) was to be funded by international donors, including the Arab Bank for Economic Development in Africa (BADEA) and the Islamic Development Bank (IDB).

Régie X9: 01 BP 2991, Ouagadougou 01; tel. 30-42-96; telex 5313; f. 1984; urban, national and international public transport co; Dir NEBAMA KERE.

CIVIL AVIATION

There are international airports at Ouagadougou and Bobo-Dioulasso, 49 small airfields and 13 private airstrips. The renovation and expansion of the airport at Ouagadougou, including the extension of the runway from 2,500 m to 3,000 m, was completed in early 1989. The runway at Bobo-Dioulasso was also extended, from 2,050 m to 2,500 m, in the late 1980s.

Air Afrique: see under Côte d'Ivoire.

Air Burkina: rue Binger, BP 1459, Ouagadougou; tel. 33-61-55; telex 203; f. 1967 as Air Volta, name changed 1984; 66% state-owned national airline; operates domestic services and flights to Bamako (Mali), Lomé (Togo), Cotonou (Benin), Niamey (Niger), Accra (Ghana), Bouaké and Abidjan (Côte d'Ivoire); Man. Dir (vacant); fleet of 1 DHG6 Twin Otter, 1 EMB 110 P2 Bandeirante, 1 Fokker F28.

Tourism

The principal tourist attraction is big game hunting in the east and south-west, and along the banks of the Mouhoun (Black Volta) river. There is a wide variety of wild animals in the game reserves. In 1987 there were 68,308 tourist arrivals at hotels, and receipts from tourism totalled 2,300m. francs CFA.

Direction Générale du Tourisme et de l'Hôtellerie: BP 624, Ouagadougou; tel. 30-63-96; telex 5555; Dir-Gen. ABDOULAYE SANKARA.

Faso Tours: BP 1318, Ouagadougou; tel. 30-66-71; telex 5377.

BURUNDI

Introductory Survey

Location, Climate, Language, Religion, Flag, Capital

The Republic of Burundi is a land-locked country lying on the eastern shore of Lake Tanganyika, in central Africa, a little south of the Equator. It is bordered by Rwanda to the north, by Tanzania to the south and east, and by Zaire to the west. The climate is tropical (hot and humid) in the lowlands, and cool in the highlands, with an irregular rainfall. The population is composed of three ethnic groups: Hutus (85%), Tutsis (14%) and Twas (1%). The official languages are French and Kirundi, while Swahili is used, in addition to French, in commercial circles. More than 60% of the inhabitants profess Christianity, with the great majority of the Christians being Roman Catholics. A large minority still adhere to traditional animist beliefs. The national flag (proportions 3 by 2) consists of a white diagonal cross on a background of red (above and below) and green (left and right), with a white circle, containing three green-edged red stars, in the centre. The capital is Bujumbura.

Recent History

Burundi (formerly Urundi) became part of German East Africa in 1899. In 1916, during the First World War, the territory was occupied by Belgian forces from the Congo (now Zaire). Subsequently, as part of Ruanda-Urundi, it was administered by Belgium under a League of Nations mandate and later as a UN Trust Territory. Elections in September 1961, held under UN supervision, were won by the Union pour le progrès national (UPRONA), which had been formed in 1958 by Ganwa (Prince) Louis Rwagasore, son of the reigning Mwami (King), Mwambutsa IV. Prince Rwagasore became Prime Minister, but was assassinated after only two weeks in office. He was succeeded by his brother-in-law, André Muhirwa. Internal self-government was granted in January 1962 and full independence on 1 July 1962, when the two parts of the Trust Territory became separate states, as Burundi and Rwanda. Tensions between Burundi's two main ethnic groups, the Tutsis (traditionally the dominant tribe, despite forming a minority of the overall population) and the Hutus, escalated during 1965. Following an unsuccessful attempt by the Hutus to overthrow the Tutsi-dominated Government in October 1965, virtually the entire Hutu political élite was executed, ending any significant participation by the Hutus in Burundi's political life until the late 1980s (see below). In July 1966 the Mwami was deposed, after a reign of over 50 years, by his son Charles and the Constitution was suspended. In November 1966 Charles, now Mwami Ntare V, was himself deposed by his Prime Minister, Capt. (later Lt-Gen.) Michel Micombero, who declared Burundi a republic.

Several alleged plots against the Government in 1969 and 1971 were followed in 1972 by an abortive coup during which Ntare V was killed. The Hutus were held responsible for the attempted coup and this served as a pretext for the Tutsis to conduct a series of large-scale massacres of the rival tribe, with the final death toll being estimated at around 100,000. Many Hutus fled to neighbouring countries.

In 1972 Micombero began a prolonged restructuring of the executive, which resulted in 1973 in an appointed seven-member Presidential Bureau, with Micombero holding the dual office of President and Prime Minister. In July 1974 the Government introduced a new republican constitution which vested sovereignty in UPRONA, the sole legal political party in Burundi. The President was elected Secretary-General of the party and re-elected for a seven-year presidential term.

On 1 November 1976 an army coup deposed Micombero, who died in exile in July 1983. The leader of the coup, Lt-Col (later Col) Jean-Baptiste Bagaza, was appointed President by the Supreme Revolutionary Council (composed of army officers), and a new council of ministers was formed. The new military Government declared that one of its fundamental aims was the elimination of corruption in the administration. In October 1978 President Bagaza announced a ministerial reshuffle in which he abolished the post of Prime Minister. The first national congress of UPRONA was held in December 1979, and a party Central Committee, headed by President Bagaza, was elected to take over the functions of the Supreme Revolutionary Council in January 1980. A new constitution, adopted by national referendum in November 1981, provided for the establishment of a national assembly, to be elected by universal adult suffrage. The first elections were held in October 1982. Having been re-elected President of UPRONA at the party's second national congress in July 1984, Bagaza was elected President of Burundi by direct suffrage for the first time in August, winning 99.63% of the votes cast; he was the only candidate for either election.

In 1985 relations between the Government and religious authorities in Burundi were affected by the arrest of several priests and the Roman Catholic Archbishop of Gitega, as well as by the expulsion of many foreign missionaries. The dispute was investigated by Amnesty International, which alleged that 20 priests were being detained without trial. An official government statement acknowledged that arrests had been made, but declared that those priests who had 'admitted their mistakes' had subsequently been released. In late 1986 the Government assumed responsibility for the organization and administration of all lower- and intermediate-level Roman Catholic seminaries, a measure that was regarded as one of retaliation against the Roman Catholic Church, which was alleged by the Government to have been 'disseminating tendentious information abroad'. Relations between the Government and church authorities deteriorated further in 1987, when restrictions were imposed upon Roman Catholic activities. However, in June, in a conciliatory gesture to the Church, the Government announced that all Catholic priests in custody were to be released.

On 3 September 1987 a military coup deposed President Bagaza while he was attending a conference in Canada. The coup was led by Major Pierre Buyoya, who accused Bagaza of corruption and immediately formed a Military Committee for National Salvation (CMSN) to administer the country, pending the appointment of a new President. The Constitution was suspended, and the National Assembly was dissolved. On 2 October Buyoya was sworn in as President of the Third Republic. Several hundred political prisoners were promptly released, and many of the restrictions that the previous regime had imposed on the Church were also repealed, leading to speculation that discontent at Bagaza's treatment of Catholic priests had been a major factor in the coup. The new Council of Ministers comprised civilians, but retained no minister from the previous regime. It was not expected, however, that conditions would improve for the Hutu people, as political power had, in effect, merely been transferred from one Tutsi clan to another. Tutsi domination of the army, where tribal members comprised 99.7% of soldiers, and of the administration, where Tutsis comprised 94% of party cadres and 95% of magistrates, was expected to continue.

In August 1988 tribal tensions flared in the north of the country when groups of Hutus, claiming Tutsi provocation, slaughtered hundreds of Tutsis in the towns of Ntega and Marangara. The Tutsi-dominated army was immediately dispatched to the region to restore order, and during that month large-scale tribal massacres, similar to those of 1972, occurred. More than 60,000 refugees fled to neighbouring Rwanda, as the death toll rose to an estimated 20,000. (Most of the refugees had been resettled in Burundi by mid-1989.) In the aftermath of the killings, a group of Hutu intellectuals were arrested for writing a letter of protest at the army's actions and for demanding the establishment of an independent commission of inquiry into the massacres. In October, however, Buyoya announced changes to the Council of Ministers, including the appointment of a Hutu to the newly-restored post of Prime Minister. The Council included, for the first time, a majority of Hutu representatives. Buyoya subsequently established a Committee for National Unity (comprising an equal number of Tutsis and Hutus) to investigate the massacres and to make recommendations for national reconciliation. Following the publication of the Committee's report, Buyoya announced plans to combat all forms of discrimination against the Hutus and to introduce new regulations to ensure equal opportunities in education, employment and in the armed forces. Notwithstanding Buyoya's efforts to achieve ethnic reconciliation, political tension remained at a high level in 1989. In May 1990 President Buyoya announced plans to introduce a 'democratic constitution under a one-party government' in place of military rule, and to hold a referendum on a charter aimed at unifying the Tutsis and Hutus. During mid-1990, however, anti-Government literature was reportedly disseminated in Bujumbura by PALIPEHUTU, a small, illegal Hutu opposition group which was based in Tanzania, and in mid-August three Burundi soldiers were killed by Hutu guerrillas. Later in that month the Government announced an amnesty for all political prisoners. In early September Pope John Paul II visited Burundi, demonstrating that relations between the Catholic Church and the Government had improved substantially under President Buyoya's rule.

Burundi is the largest recipient per caput of low-interest loans from the World Bank, and, under Buyoya, the country has satisfied several criteria imposed by the Bank, namely the devaluation of its currency, the elimination of import restrictions and the abolition of passbook laws, which prevented Hutus from moving to different areas of the country.

In 1985 Burundi and its neighbour, Rwanda, signed an accord of co-operation covering political, economic, commercial, technical, scientific, social and cultural affairs. In May 1983 Burundi signed a technical and economic agreement with Libya. Relations between the two countries flourished during the Bagaza Government's tenure of office. In April 1989, however, links with Libya were effectively terminated with the expulsion from Burundi of all Libyan diplomats and other nationals, following accusations of collusion with supporters of ex-President Bagaza to overthrow the Buyoya Government.

Government

The 1981 Constitution, which provided for the election by universal adult suffrage of a President for a five-year term, and of 52 representatives to a National Assembly for a similar period (a further 13 representatives being appointed by the President), was suspended in September 1987. Executive and legislative powers were assumed by a Military Committee for National Salvation (CMSN). The CMSN elected its Chairman as President of the Republic. A civilian Council of Ministers was appointed. UPRONA is the only authorized political party. For the purposes of local government, Burundi comprises 15 provinces, administered by civilian governors, each of which is divided into districts and further subdivided into communes.

Defence

The army was merged with the police force in 1967. The total strength of the armed forces in June 1990 was 7,200, comprising an army of 5,500, a navy of 50, an air force of 150, and a paramilitary force of 1,500 gendarmes. Defence expenditure in 1987 totalled an estimated 3,910m. Burundi francs.

Economic Affairs

In 1988, according to estimates by the World Bank, Burundi's gross national product (GNP), per head, measured at average 1986–88 prices, was US $240. During 1980–88, it was estimated, total GNP increased, in real terms, at an average annual rate of 2.9%, although GNP per head increased by only 0.1% per year. Over the same period, the population increased by an annual average of 2.9%. Burundi's gross domestic product (GDP) increased, in real terms, by an annual average of 4.3% in 1980–88.

Agriculture (including forestry and fishing) contributed 57.7% of GDP in 1988, when about 92% of the labour force were employed in the sector. The principal cash crops are coffee (which accounted for about 82% of export earnings in 1989), tea and cotton. The main subsistence crops are cassava and sweet potatoes. During 1980–88 agricultural production increased by an annual average of 3.1%.

Industry (comprising mining, manufacturing, construction and utilities) employed only 2.3% of the labour force in 1979, but contributed 11.9% of GDP in 1988. During 1980–88 industrial production increased by an annual average of 5.8%.

Mining and power employed 0.1% of the labour force in 1979 and contributed 1.1% of GDP in 1988. Gold, tungsten and columbo-tantalite are mined in small quantities. Burundi has important deposits of vanadium, uranium and also of nickel (estimated at 5% of world reserves). In addition, petroleum deposits have been detected.

Manufacturing employed 1.5% of the labour force in 1979 and contributed 6.2% of GDP in 1988. The sector consists largely of the processing of agricultural products. A native textile industry has been developed. During 1980–88 production increased by an annual average of 6.1%.

Energy is derived principally from hydroelectric power. A large hydroelectric power station, developed jointly with Rwanda and Zaire, came into operation in 1990. Peat is also exploited as an additional source of energy.

In 1989 Burundi recorded a visible trade deficit of US $58.9m., and there was a deficit of $29.1m. on the current account of the balance of payments. The EEC countries, in particular Belgium, France and Germany, are among Burundi's main trading partners, accounting for 46.8% of import costs in 1989. The principal exports in 1989 were coffee, tea and cotton.

In 1989 there was a budgetary deficit of 158.1m. Burundi francs. Burundi's total external public debt at the end of 1988 was US $749m. In that year the cost of debt-servicing was equivalent to 25.1% of revenue from the export of goods and services, representing 3.3% of Burundi's GNP. The annual rate of inflation averaged 4.0% in 1980–88. However, the rate increased to 11.6% in 1989.

Burundi maintains economic co-operation agreements with its neighbours Rwanda and Zaire through the Economic Community of the Great Lakes Countries (see p. 223). Burundi is also a member of the Preferential Trade Area for Eastern and Southern African States (see p. 224), and of the International Coffee Organization (see p. 228).

In terms of average income, Burundi is one of the poorest countries in the world, and its economic performance is heavily dependent on world prices for coffee. All sectors of Burundi's economy are supported by various development organizations, notably the IDA (see p. 66), the UNDP (see p. 39), the European Development Fund, and the Arab Bank for Economic Development in Africa (see p. 95). Burundi is expected to remain dependent on foreign assistance for some time, not only for capital projects but also for budgetary support. The main bilateral donors of aid and technical assistance are Belgium, France, Japan and Germany.

Social Welfare

Wage-earners are protected by insurance against accidents and occupational diseases and can draw on a pension fund. Medical facilities are, however, limited. In 1978 there were 22 hospitals, nine maternity units and 100 dispensaries. In 1981 Burundi had one hospital bed for every 286 inhabitants. In 1986 Burundi and the People's Republic of China signed a protocol whereby the latter undertook to provide Burundi with medical aid in the form of drugs and equipment, and by sending a team of 12 specialists to Burundi for two years.

Education

Education is provided free of charge. Kirundi is the language of instruction in primary schools, while French is used in secondary schools. Primary education, which is officially compulsory, begins at seven years of age and lasts for six years. Secondary education, which is not compulsory, begins at the age of 13 and lasts for up to seven years, comprising a first cycle of four years and a second of three years. In 1988 the total enrolment at primary and secondary schools was equivalent to 33% of the school-age population (males 39%; females 28%), whereas in 1980 the proportion had been only 16%. Enrolment at primary schools increased from 175,856 in 1980 to 560,095 in 1988. Enrolment at secondary schools, including pupils receiving vocational instruction and teacher training, rose from 19,013 in 1980 to 30,751 in 1988. However, the latter total was equivalent to only 4% of the population in the secondary age-group. There is one university, in Bujumbura, which was attended by 2,749 students in 1988. According to official estimates, the average rate of illiteracy among the population aged 10 years and over was 66.2% (males 57.2%; females 74.3%) in 1982. In 1988 the International Development Association (IDA) granted Burundi a credit of SDR 23m. to further the development of primary and general secondary education, and to make primary education universally accessible by the 1995/96 school year. Education was allocated about 16% of total government expenditure in the budget for 1989.

Public Holidays

1991: 1 January (New Year's Day), 1 April (Easter Monday), 1 May (Labour Day), 9 May (Ascension Day), 1 July (Indepen-

BURUNDI

dence Day), 15 August (Assumption), 18 September (Victory of UPRONA Party), 1 November (All Saints' Day), 25 December (Christmas).

1992: 1 January (New Year's Day), 20 April (Easter Monday), 1 May (Labour Day), 28 May (Ascension Day), 1 July (Independence Day), 15 August (Assumption), 18 September (Victory of UPRONA Party), 1 November (All Saints' Day), 25 December (Christmas).

Weights and Measures

The metric system is in force.

Statistical Survey

Area and Population

AREA, POPULATION AND DENSITY

Area (sq km)	27,834*
Population (census of 15–16 August 1979)	
Males	1,946,145
Females	2,082,325
Total	4,028,470
Population (official estimates at mid-year)	
1987	5,001,124
1988	5,149,158
1989	5,302,000
Density (per sq km) at mid-1989	190.5

* 10,747 sq miles.

PRINCIPAL TOWNS

Bujumbura (capital), population 215,243 (estimate, 1 January 1987); Gitega 15,943 (1978).

Source: Banque de la République du Burundi.

BIRTHS AND DEATHS (UN estimates, annual averages)

	1975–80	1980–85	1985–90
Birth rate (per 1,000)	48.2	47.2	45.7
Death rate (per 1,000)	20.5	19.0	17.0

Source: UN, *World Population Prospects: 1988*.

ECONOMICALLY ACTIVE POPULATION
(1983 estimates)

Traditional agriculture	2,319,595
Fishing	5,481
Traditional trades	22,820
Private sector (modern)	37,884
Public sector	95,061
Total labour force	**2,480,841**

1979 census: Total labour force 2,418,029 (males 1,137,042; females 1,280,987).

Sources: *Revue des statistiques du travail* and Centre de recherche et de formation en population.

1986 estimate: Total labour force 2,653,951 (males 1,254,041; females 1,399,910). Source: ILO, *Year Book of Labour Statistics*.
Mid-1988 estimates ('000): Agriculture etc. 2,469; Total labour force 2,697. **Mid-1989 estimates** ('000): Agriculture etc. 2,521; Total labour force 2,759. Source: FAO, *Production Yearbook*.

Agriculture

PRINCIPAL CROPS ('000 metric tons)

	1987	1988	1989
Wheat	9	9†	8†
Maize	174	206	190†
Millet	13	13	10
Sorghum	63	113	88
Rice	28	27	25†
Potatoes	43	43	19
Sweet potatoes	626	619	426
Cassava (Manioc)	579	567	600*
Yams	8	8	8*
Taro (Coco yam)	127	125	125*
Dry beans	327	320	187
Dry peas	34	34	34*
Palm kernels*	2.5	2.7	2.8
Groundnuts (in shell)*	80	85	86
Cottonseed†	4	5	5
Cotton (lint)†	2	3	3
Sugar cane	8	8	8*
Coffee (green)†	37	33	39
Tea (made)	4†	5†	5*
Tobacco (leaves)*	4	4	4
Bananas and plantains	1,440*	1,480†	1,490*

* FAO estimate(s). † Unofficial estimate(s).
Source: FAO, *Production Yearbook*.

LIVESTOCK ('000 head, year ending September)

	1987	1988	1989*
Cattle	479	340†	345
Sheep	329	350*	370
Goats	723	750*	770
Pigs	77	80*	84

* FAO estimate(s). † Unofficial estimate.
Poultry (FAO estimates, million): 4 in 1987; 4 in 1988; 4 in 1989.
Source: FAO, *Production Yearbook*.

LIVESTOCK PRODUCTS (FAO estimates, '000 metric tons)

	1987	1988	1989
Beef and veal	6	5	5
Mutton and lamb	1	1	1
Goats' meat	3	3	3
Pig meat	5	5	5
Cows' milk	21	21	21
Goats' milk	8	8	8
Hen eggs	2.9	3.0	3.1

Source: FAO, *Production Yearbook*.

BURUNDI

Forestry

ROUNDWOOD REMOVALS ('000 cubic metres)

	1986	1987*	1988
Sawlogs, veneer logs and logs for sleepers	6	6	6
Other industrial wood*	39	41	42
Fuel wood*	3,702	3,810	3,918
Total	3,747	3,857	3,966

* FAO estimates.

Source: FAO, *Yearbook of Forest Products*.

Fishing

('000 metric tons, live weight)

	1986	1987	1988
Dagaas	5.5	3.4	5.2
Freshwater perches	1.2	1.5	1.4
Others	0.1	0.1	0.1
Total catch	6.8	5.0	6.7

Source: FAO, *Yearbook of Fishery Statistics*.

Mining*

	1985	1986†	1987†
Gold (kilograms)	26	30	31
Peat ('000 metric tons)	10	13	13

* Estimates by the US Bureau of Mines.
† Provisional.

Source: UN, *Industrial Statistics Yearbook*.

Industry

SELECTED PRODUCTS

	1987	1988	1989
Beer ('000 hectolitres)	938	953	919
Soft drinks ('000 hectolitres)	130	126	139
Cigarettes (million)	271	285	333
Blankets ('000)	342	305	280
Footwear ('000 pairs)	398	149	289

Source: Banque de la République du Burundi.

Finance

CURRENCY AND EXCHANGE RATES

Monetary Units
100 centimes = 1 Burundi franc.

Denominations
Coins: 1, 5 and 10 francs.
Notes: 10, 20, 50, 100, 500, 1,000 and 5,000 francs.

Sterling and Dollar Equivalents (30 September 1990)
£1 sterling = 312.54 francs;
US $1 = 166.82 francs;
1,000 Burundi francs = £3.1996 = $5.9945.

Average Exchange Rate (Burundi francs per US dollar)
1987   123.56
1988   140.40
1989   158.67

Note: Between May 1976 and November 1983 the rate was fixed at US $1 = 90.0 Burundi francs. Since November 1983 the Burundi franc has been linked to the IMF's special drawing right (SDR), with the mid-point exchange rate initially fixed at SDR 1 = 122.7 francs. This remained in force until July 1986, since when the rate has been frequently adjusted. A rate of SDR 1 = 232.14 francs was established in December 1989.

BUDGET (million Burundi francs)

Revenue	1987	1988	1989
Income tax	4,159.8	5,047.7	5,003.7
Property tax	107.0	118.5	141.8
Customs duties	3,976.1	8,024.6	9,188.1
Excise duties	2,480.1	3,134.3	3,222.0
Other indirect taxes	5,098.7	5,291.0	7,579.7
Administrative receipts	2,007.4	2,267.7	6,362.6
Total revenue	17,829.1	23,883.8	31,497.9

Expenditure	1987	1988	1989
Goods and services	11,684.3	14,043.5	17,100.3
Subsidies and transfers	4,890.1	6,231.7	6,825.4
Net loans	161.5	13.1	26.7
Other	3,571.8	6,930.0	7,387.4
Total expenditure	20,307.7	27,218.3	31,339.8

Source: Banque de la République du Burundi.

CENTRAL BANK RESERVES (US $ million at 31 December)

	1987	1988	1989
Gold*	8.53	7.14	7.02
IMF special drawing rights	0.06	0.11	0.01
Reserve position in IMF	12.99	12.33	12.04
Foreign exchange	47.68	56.95	87.57
Total	69.26	76.52	106.64

* Valued at market-related prices.

Source: Banque de la République du Burundi.

MONEY SUPPLY (million Burundi francs at 31 December)

	1987	1988	1989
Currency outside banks	8,734	9,605	9,868
Official entities' deposits at Central Bank	1,199	1,287	1,377
Demand deposits at commercial banks	8,304	7,881	8,400
Demand deposits at other monetary institutions	986	821	696
Total money	19,223	19,594	20,341

Source: Banque de la République du Burundi.

BURUNDI

COST OF LIVING (Consumer Price Index for Bujumbura; base: January 1980 = 100)

	1987	1988	1989
Food	141.6	152.3	180.9
Clothing	166.1	168.4	182.0
Rent, fuel and light	149.3	156.4	171.3
All items (incl. others)	167.9	175.5	195.9

Source: Banque de la République du Burundi.

NATIONAL ACCOUNTS (million Burundi francs at current prices)
Expenditure on the Gross Domestic Product

	1986	1987	1988
Government final consumption expenditure	24,252	28,570	28,900
Private final consumption expenditure	104,340	107,015	117,433
Increase in stocks	3,247	3,762	2,376
Gross fixed capital formation	18,860	21,114	19,070
Total domestic expenditure	150,699	160,461	167,779
Exports of goods and services	15,625	13,015	17,981
Less Imports of goods and services	25,482	29,886	32,742
GDP in purchasers' values	140,842	143,590	153,018
GDP at constant 1980 prices	112,916	117,539	124,004

Source: Banque de la République du Burundi.
1989 (million Burundi francs at current prices): GDP 173,981.

Gross Domestic Product by Economic Activity*

	1986	1987	1988
Agriculture, hunting, forestry and fishing	72,057	70,680	73,981
Mining and quarrying	906	1,458	1,376
Electricity, gas and water			
Manufacturing	6,140	7,222	7,940
Construction	4,942	5,698	5,953
Trade, restaurants and hotels	11,072	11,011	10,778
Transport, storage and communications	3,540	3,719	4,024
Other commercial services	1,851	2,217	2,918
Government services	17,456	18,191	20,751
Non-profit services to households	500	466	497
GDP at factor cost	118,464	120,662	130,690†
Indirect taxes, *less* subsidies	17,725	15,638	14,198
GDP in purchasers' values	136,189	136,300	144,888

* Excluding GDP of the artisan branch (million francs): 4,653 in 1986; 7,290 in 1987; 8,130 in 1988.
† Including statistical discrepancy (2,472 million Burundi francs).
Source: Banque de la République du Burundi.

BALANCE OF PAYMENTS (US $ million)

	1987	1988	1989
Merchandise exports f.o.b.	98.3	124.4	93.2
Merchandise imports f.o.b.	−159.2	−166.1	−152.2
Trade balance	−60.8	−41.7	−58.9
Exports of services	14.8	14.8	21.7
Imports of services	−163.4	−141.3	−132.1
Balance on goods and services	−209.4	−168.2	−169.3
Private unrequited transfers (net)	7.2	10.0	8.6
Government unrequited transfers (net)	105.7	87.2	131.6
Current balance	−96.5	−71.0	−29.1
Direct capital investment (net)	1.4	1.2	0.6
Other long-term capital (net)	114.5	78.1	62.9
Short-term capital (net)	15.2	4.9	0.4
Net errors and omissions	−41.3	−16.8	−10.2
Total (net monetary movements)	−6.6	−3.6	24.6
Valuation changes (net)	7.2	3.8	−2.9
Changes in reserves	0.5	0.2	21.7

Source: IMF, *International Financial Statistics*.

External Trade

PRINCIPAL COMMODITIES (million Burundi francs)

Imports c.i.f.	1987	1988	1989
Intermediate goods	9,495.7	10,715.8	10,885.0
Capital goods	9,053.4	9,798.7	10,375.1
Consumer goods	6,916.2	8,370.0	8,649.6
Total	25,465.3	28,884.5	29,909.7

Exports f.o.b.	1987	1988	1989
Coffee	7,891.1	16,009.5	9,501.7
Cotton	502.3	110.1	31.3
Hides and skins	181.8	295.5	509.3
Tea	556.8	734.7	992.3
Minerals	1.5	21.5	39.0
Other products	395.7	397.4	553.9
Total	9,529.2	17,568.7	11,627.5

Source: Banque de la République du Burundi.

PRINCIPAL TRADING PARTNERS (million Burundi francs)

Imports	1987	1988	1989
Belgium-Luxembourg	4,823.0	4,852.0	4,630.1
France	2,112.6	3,563.6	3,036.1
Germany, Federal Republic	3,324.0	2,795.2	4,059.5
Italy	909.9	1,206.4	1,185.7
Japan	2,080.7	2,913.9	2,427.9
Kenya	658.6	805.2	893.6
Netherlands	1,382.4	610.6	488.8
Tanzania	115.9	210.6	354.9
United Kingdom	521.8	667.1	602.7
USA	468.2	531.6	365.8
Zaire	119.4	280.4	320.0
Others	8,948.8	10,447.9	11,544.6
Total	25,465.3	28,884.5	29,909.7

BURUNDI

Exports	1987	1988	1989
Belgium-Luxembourg	1,068.9	525.1	177.0
France	742.2	567.8	790.0
Germany, Federal Republic	3,337.8	5,006.4	1,873.4
Italy	260.6	305.9	275.0
Netherlands	756.9	342.7	119.6
United Kingdom	725.5	464.4	280.0
USA	790.8	11.1	887.7
Others	3,434.2	11,365.8	7,886.8
Total	11,116.9	18,589.2	12,289.5

Source: Banque de la République du Burundi.

Transport

ROAD TRAFFIC (motor vehicles in use)

	1986	1987	1988
Passenger cars	8,977	9,892	10,407
Vans	2,821	3,077	3,262
Lorries	1,607	1,753	1,848
All other vehicles	2,914	3,284	3,546
Total	16,319	18,006	19,063

Source: Banque de la République du Burundi.

LAKE TRAFFIC (Bujumbura—'000 metric tons)

	1987	1988	1989
Goods:			
Arrivals	157.2	141.3	150.4
Departures	31.4	38.4	33.0

Source: Banque de la République du Burundi.

CIVIL AVIATION (Bujumbura Airport)

	1987	1988	1989
Passengers:			
Arrivals	23,711	28,415	30,685
Departures	24,947	29,331	30,116
Freight (metric tons):			
Arrivals	4,228	4,103	4,198
Departures	2,168	1,616	1,868

Source: Banque de la République du Burundi.

Tourism

	1985	1986	1987
Tourist arrivals ('000)	54	66	80

Source: UN Economic Commission for Africa, *African Statistical Yearbook*.

Communications Media

	1985	1986	1987
Radio receivers ('000 in use)	250	280	285
Television receivers ('000 in use)	0.3	1	1
Telephones ('000 in use)	9	9	9
Book production*: titles	146	54	n.a.
copies ('000)	n.a.	448	n.a.
Daily newspapers	n.a.	2	n.a.

* Including pamphlets (17 titles and 174,000 copies in 1986).

Sources: UNESCO, *Statistical Yearbook*, and UN Economic Commission for Africa, *African Statistical Yearbook*.

Education

(1988/89)

	Teachers	Pupils
Pre-primary	40	2,087
Primary	8,126	560,095
Secondary:		
General	822	18,360
Vocational	325	3,598
Higher:		
University	239	2,749

Source: Ministry of Primary and Secondary Education.

Directory

The Constitution

Following the coup of September 1987, the Constitution of November 1981 was suspended. Its main provisions were as follows:

UPRONA (Union pour le progrès national) is the sole legal political party. It determines national political orientation and state policy, and supervises the action of the Government. The Head of State and the National Assembly, which holds legislative power and meets twice a year, are elected for a term of five years by direct universal adult suffrage. The sole candidate for the position of Head of State is the President of UPRONA.

The Government

HEAD OF STATE

President: Maj. PIERRE BUYOYA (assumed office 2 October 1987).

MILITARY COMMITTEE FOR NATIONAL SALVATION (CMSN)
(December 1990)

The CMSN comprises 30 members.

Executive Committee:
Maj. PIERRE BUYOYA (Chairman)
Lt-Col GERVAIS NDIKUMAGENGE
Lt-Col GEDEON FYIROKO
Lt-Col JEAN-CLAUDE NDIYO
Lt-Col JEAN-BAPTISTE MBONYINGINGO
Lt-Col ALOYS KADOYI
Maj. MICHEL MIBARURWA
Maj. GERARD CISHAHAYO
Maj. SIMON RUSUKU
Maj. ETIENNE SINDIHEBURA

COUNCIL OF MINISTERS
(December 1990)

President and Minister of National Defence: Maj. PIERRE BUYOYA.
Prime Minister and Minister of Planning: ADRIEN SIBOMANA.
Minister of Justice: EVARISTE NIYONKURU.
Minister of Internal Affairs: Lt-Col ALOYS KADOYI.
Minister of Foreign Relations and Co-operation: CYPRIEN MBONIMPA.
Minister of Finance: GÉRARD NIYIBIGIRA.
Minister of Rural Development and Handicrafts: GABRIEL TOYI.
Minister of Agriculture and Animal Husbandry: JUMAINE HUSSEIN.
Minister of Industry and Trade: BONAVENTURE KIDWINGIRA.
Minister of Transport, Posts and Telecommunications: Maj. SIMON RUSUKU.
Minister of Public Works and Urban Development: EVARISTE SIMBARAKIYE.
Minister of Energy and Mines: GILBERT MIDENDE.
Minister of Public Health: Dr NORBERT NGENDABANYIKWA.
Minister for Family and Women's Development Affairs: PIA NDAYIRAGIJE.
Minister for Social Affairs: JULIE NGIRIYE.
Minister of Labour and Professional Training: CHARLES KARIKURUBU.
Minister of Youth, Sport and Culture: ADOLPHE NAHAYO.
Minister of Information: FRÉDÉRIC NGENZEBUHORO.
Minister of the Public Service: DIDACE RUDARAGI.
Minister of Development, Tourism and the Environment: BASILE SINDAHARAYE.
Minister of Higher Education and Scientific Research: NICOLAS MAYUGI.
Minister of Primary and Secondary Education: GAMARIEL NDARUZANIYE.
Secretary of State in charge of Government Planning: SALVATOR SAHINGUVU.
Secretary of State in charge of International Co-operation: FRIDOLIN HATUNGIMANA.

MINISTRIES

Office of the President and Minister of National Defence: Bujumbura; tel. 6063; telex 5049.
Ministry of Agriculture and Animal Husbandry: Bujumbura; tel. 2087.
Ministry of Energy and Mines: Bujumbura.
Ministry of Family and Women's Development Affairs: Bujumbura; tel. 5561.
Ministry of Finance: BP 1830, Bujumbura; tel. 23988; telex 5135.
Ministry of Foreign Relations and Co-operation: Bujumbura; tel. 2150; telex 5065.
Ministry of Industry and Trade: Bujumbura; tel. 5330.
Ministry of Information: BP 4080, Bujumbura; tel. 4666; telex 56.
Ministry of Internal Affairs: Bujumbura; tel. 4242.
Ministry of Justice: Bujumbura; tel. 2148.
Ministry of Labour and Professional Training: BP 2830, Bujumbura; tel. 25058.
Ministry of Public Health: Bujumbura; tel. 6020.
Ministry of the Public Service: Bujumbura; tel. 3514.
Ministry of Public Works and Urban Development: BP 1860, Bujumbura; tel. 6841; telex 5048.
Ministry of Rural Development and Handicrafts: Bujumbura; tel. 5267.
Ministry of Social Affairs: Bujumbura; tel. 5039.
Ministry of Transport, Posts and Telecommunications: Bujumbura; tel. 2923; telex 5103.
Ministry of Youth, Sport and Culture: Bujumbura; tel. 6822.

Legislature

ASSEMBLÉE NATIONALE

The 65-member National Assembly was dissolved following the coup of September 1987. The new Government envisaged the restoration of the National Assembly within two years. By late 1990, however, the legislature had not been revived.

Political Organizations

Following the coup of September 1987, the Central Committee of the ruling UPRONA party was temporarily suspended. The party resumed operations in 1989.

Union pour le progrès national (UPRONA): BP 1810, Bujumbura; tel. 25028; telex 5057; f. 1958; following the 1961 elections, the many small parties which had been defeated subsequently merged with UPRONA, which became the sole legal political party in 1966; c. 1.2m. mems (1989); Sec.-Gen. LIBÈRE BARARUNYERETSE.

There is one small opposition group, in exile in Tanzania:

PALIPEHUTU: f. 1980; aims to liberate the Hutu tribe from domination by Burundi's Tutsi minority.

Diplomatic Representation

EMBASSIES IN BURUNDI

Belgium: 9 ave de l'Industrie, BP 1920, Bujumbura; tel. 3676; telex 5033; Ambassador: DENIS BANNEEL.
China, People's Republic: BP 2550, Bujumbura; tel. 24307; Ambassador: WANG JIANBANG.
Egypt: 31 ave de la Liberté, BP 1520, Bujumbura; tel. 3161; telex 5040; Ambassador: MUHAMMAD MOUSA.
France: 60 ave de l'UPRONA, BP 1740, Bujumbura; tel. 26464; telex 5044; Ambassador: ROBERT RIGOUZZO.
Germany: 22 rue 18 septembre, BP 480, Bujumbura; tel. 26412; telex 5068; Ambassador: KARL FLITTNER.
Holy See: 46 chaussée Prince Louis-Rwagasore, BP 1068, Bujumbura (Apostolic Nunciature); tel. 22326; fax 23176; Apostolic Pro-Nuncio: Most Rev. PIETRO SAMBI, Titular Archbishop of Belcastro.
Korea, Democratic People's Republic: BP 1620, Bujumbura; tel. 22881; Ambassador: AHN JAE BU.

BURUNDI

Romania: rue Pierre Ngendandumwe, BP 2770, Bujumbura; tel. 24135; Chargé d'affaires a.i.: ALEXANDRA ANDREI.
Rwanda: 24 ave du Zaïre, BP 400, Bujumbura; tel. 3140; telex 5032; Ambassador: EMMANUEL RUZINDANA.
Tanzania: BP 1653, Bujumbura; Ambassador: NICHOLAS J. MARO.
USSR: 9 ave de l'UPRONA, BP 1034, Bujumbura; tel. 26098, 22984; Ambassador: VSEVOLOD SOFINSKY.
USA: ave des Etats-Unis, BP 1720, Bujumbura; tel. 23454; fax 22926; Ambassador: CYNTHIA SHEPARD PERRY.
Zaire: 5 ave Olsen, BP 872, Bujumbura; tel. 3492; Ambassador: IKOLO MBOLOKO.

Judicial System

The Constitution prescribes a judicial system wherein the judges are subject to the decisions of UPRONA made in the light of the revolutionary concept of the law. No appeal is provided for in the case of decisions of the Supreme Court. A programme of legal reform was announced in December 1986, under which provincial courts were to be replaced by a dual system of courts of civil and criminal jurisdiction. A network of mediation and conciliation courts was to be established to arbitrate in minor disputes arising among the rural population.

Supreme Court: Bujumbura; tel. 5442. Four chambers: ordinary, cassation, constitutional and administrative.
Courts of Appeal: Bujumbura, Gitega and Ngozi.
Tribunals of First Instance: There are 15 provincial tribunals and 122 smaller resident tribunals in other areas.
Tribunal of Trade: Bujumbura.
Tribunals of Labour: Bujumbura and Gitega.
Administrative Courts: Bujumbura and Gitega.

Religion

More than 60% of the population are Christians, mostly Roman Catholics. Anglicans number about 60,000. There are about 200,000 Protestants, of whom some 160,000 are Pentecostalists. Fewer than 40% of the population adhere to traditional beliefs, which include the worship of the God 'Imana'. About 1% of the population are Muslims. The Bahá'í Faith is also active in Burundi.

CHRISTIANITY

Alliance des Eglises protestantes du Burundi: BP 17, Bujumbura; tel. 24216; f. 1970; five mem. churches; Pres. Bishop JEAN-ALFRED NDORICIMPA; Gen. Sec. Rev. NOÉ NZEYIMANA.

The Anglican Communion

Anglicans in Burundi form part of the Church of the Province of Burundi, Rwanda and Zaire, inaugurated in May 1980. The Church comprises 11 dioceses, including four in Burundi, where it incorporates the Eglise épiscopale du Burundi. Since 1987 the Archbishop of the Province has been the Most Rev. SAMUEL SINDAMUKA, who was the Bishop of Bujumbura until August 1990, when a new diocese of Matana, headed by Archbishop SINDAMUKA, was created.

Bishop of Matana and Archbishop of Burundi, Rwanda and Zaire: Most Rev. SAMUEL SINDAMUKA, BP 1300, Bujumbura; tel. 24389; telex 5127.
Bishop of Bujumbura: Rt Rev. PIÉ NTUKAMAZINA, BP 1300, Bujumbura; tel. 22641.
Bishop of Buye: Rt Rev. SAMUEL NDAYISENGA, BP 94, Ngozi.
Bishop of Gitega: Rt Rev. JEAN NDUWAYO, BP 23, Gitega.

The Roman Catholic Church

Burundi comprises one archdiocese and six dioceses. At 31 December 1988 there were an estimated 3,059,145 adherents.

Bishops' Conference: Conférence des Evêques catholiques du Burundi, BP 1390, Bujumbura; tel. 23263; f. 1980; Pres. Rt Rev. BERNARD BUDUDIRA, Bishop of Bururi.
Archbishop of Gitega: Most Rev. JOACHIM RUHUNA, Archevêché, BP 118, Gitega; tel. 2160.

Other Christian Churches

Union of Baptist Churches of Burundi: Rubura, DS 117, Bujumbura 1; Pres. PAUL BARUHENAMWO; Exec. Sec. OSIAS HABINGABWA.

Other denominations active in the country include the Evangelical Christian Brotherhood of Burundi, the Free Methodist Church of Burundi and the United Methodist Church of Burundi.

BAHÁ'Í FAITH

National Spiritual Assembly: BP 1578, Bujumbura.

The Press

All publications are strictly controlled by the Government.

NEWSPAPERS

Burundi chrétien: BP 232, Bujumbura; Roman Catholic weekly; French.
Le Renouveau du Burundi: BP 2870, Bujumbura; f. 1978; publ. by UPRONA; daily; French; circ. 20,000.
Ubumwe: BP 1400, Bujumbura; tel. 3929; f. 1971; weekly; Kirundi; circ. 20,000.

PERIODICALS

Bulletin économique et financier: BP 482, Bujumbura; bi-monthly.
Bulletin officiel du Burundi: Bujumbura; monthly.
Le Burundi en Images: BP 1400, Bujumbura; f. 1979; monthly.
Culture et Sociétés: BP 1400, Bujumbura; f. 1978; quarterly.
Ndongozi Yaburundi: Catholic Mission, BP 49, Gitega; fortnightly; Kirundi.

NEWS AGENCY

Agence burundaise de Presse (ABP): 6 ave de la Poste, BP 2870, Bujumbura; tel. 5417; telex 5056; publ. daily bulletin.

Publishers

Imprimerie du Parti: BP 1810, Bujumbura.
Les Presses Lavigerie: BP 1640, Bujumbura.

Government Publishing House

Imprimerie nationale du Burundi (INABU): BP 991, Bujumbura; tel. 4046; telex 80.

Radio and Television

In 1988 there were 276,000 radio receivers and about 4,500 television receivers in use. Colour television transmissions began in 1985.

Voix de la Révolution/La Radiodiffusion et Télévision Nationale du Burundi (RTNB): BP 1900, Bujumbura; tel. 23742; telex 5041; f. 1960; govt-controlled; daily radio programmes in Kirundi, Swahili, French and English; Dir-Gen. ALEXIS NTAVYO; Dirs (Radio) CHRISTINE NTAHE, ANTOINE NTAMIKEVYO; Dir (Television) J. NZOBONIMPA.

Finance

(cap. = capital; res = reserves; dep. = deposits; m. = million; brs = branches; amounts in Burundi francs)

BANKING

Central Bank

Banque de la République du Burundi (BRB): BP 705, Bujumbura; tel. 25142; telex 5071; f. 1964 as Banque du Royaume du Burundi; renamed as above in 1966; State-owned; cap. 100m., dep. 7,493m. (Dec. 1988); Gov. ISAAC BUDABUDA; Vice-Gov. EVARISTE NIBASUMBA; Dir PASCAL NTAMASHIMIKIRO.

Commercial Banks

Banque Commerciale du Burundi SARL (BANCOBU): chaussée Prince Louis-Rwagasore, BP 990, Bujumbura; tel. 22317; telex 5051; fax 226014; f. 1960; reorg. 1988, following merger with Banque Belgo-Africaine du Burundi; 51% state-owned; cap. and res 7,393m., dep. 7,393m. (May 1990); Chair. JUVÉNAL MANIRAMBONA; Man. Dir LIBÈRE NDABAKWAJE; 7 brs.
Banque de Crédit de Bujumbura SARL (BCB): ave Patrice Emery Lumumba, BP 300, Bujumbura; tel. 22091; telex 5063; fax 223007; f. 1964; cap. and res 709m., dep. 6,966m. (Dec. 1989); Chair. EDMOND BIZABIGOMBA; Man. Dir PAUL PEETERS; 6 brs.
Caisse d'Epargne du Burundi (CADEBU): BP 615, Bujumbura; tel. 22348; telex 71; f. 1964; state-owned; cap. 90m.; Chair. PASTEUR BUDEYI; Man. Dir BONIFACE BAGORIKUNDA.

BURUNDI

Development Banks

Banque Nationale pour le Développement Economique du Burundi (BNDE): BP 1620, Bujumbura; tel. 22888; telex 5091; f. 1966; cap. and res 1,154m. (Dec. 1988); Pres. Bonus Kemwenubusa; Man. Dir François Barwendere.

Caisse Centrale de Mobilisation et de Financement (CAMOFI): 4 ave de la JRR, BP 8, Bujumbura; tel. 25642; telex 5082; f. 1979; 50% state-owned; finances public-sector development projects; cap. 100m. (Sept. 1987); Dir-Gen. Evariste Minani.

Holding Arabe Libyen Burundais (HALB): BP 1892, Bujumbura; tel. 26635; telex 5090; f. 1975; cap. 1,036.1m. (Sept. 1987); Chair. Jean Berchmans Nsabiyumva.

Meridien Bank Burundi: Bujumbura; f. 1988; 25% owned by Meridien International Bank.

Société Burundaise de Financement (SBF): BP 270, 13-14 rue de l'Amitié, Bujumbura; tel. 22126; telex 5080; f. 1981; cap. 860m. (1988); Chair. Mathias Sinamenye.

INSURANCE

Société d'Assurances du Burundi (SOCABU): BP 2440, 14-18 rue de l'Amitié, Bujumbura; tel. 26803; telex 5113; fax 226803; f. 1977; partly state-owned; cap. 180m.; Man. Athanase Gahungu.

Union Commerciale d'Assurances et de Réassurance (UCAR): BP 3012, Bujumbura; tel. 23638; telex 5162; fax 223695; f. 1986; cap. 150m. (June 1990); Chair. Lt-Col Edouard Nzambimana; Man. Dir Henry Tarmo.

Trade and Industry

STATE TRADE ORGANIZATION

Office National du Commerce (ONC): Bujumbura; f. 1973; supervises international commercial operations between the Govt of Burundi and other states or private orgs; also ensures the import of essential materials; brs in each province.

DEVELOPMENT ORGANIZATIONS

Comité de Gérance de la Reserve Cotonnière (COGERCO): Bujumbura; develops the cotton industry.

Fonds de Promotion Economique: PB 270, Bujumbura; tel. 5562; telex 80; f. 1981 to finance and promote industrial, agricultural and commercial activities; Man. Dir Bonaventure Kidwingira.

Institut des Sciences Agronomiques du Burundi (ISABU): BP 795, Bujumbura; tel. 3384; f. 1962 for the scientific development of agriculture and livestock.

Office de la Tourbe du Burundi (ONATOUR): BP 2360, Bujumbura; tel. 6480; telex 48; f. 1977 to promote the exploitation of peat bogs.

Office des Cultures Industrielles du Burundi (OCIBU): BP 450, Bujumbura; tel. 2631; supervises coffee plantations and coffee exports.

Office du Thé du Burundi (OTB): Bujumbura; telex 5069; f. 1979 to develop the tea industry.

Office National du Bois (ONB): BP 1492, Bujumbura; tel. 4416; f. 1980 to exploit local timber resources and import foreign timber; Dir Lazare Runesa.

Office National du Logement (ONL): BP 2480, Bujumbura; tel. 6074; telex 48; f. 1974 to supervise housing construction.

Société d'Economie Mixte pour l'Exploitation du Quinquina au Burundi (SOKINABU): BP 1783, Bujumbura; tel. 23469; telex 81; f. 1975 to develop and exploit cinchona trees, the source of quinine; Man. Raphël Remezo.

Société de Stockage et de Commercialisation des Produits Vivriers (SOBECOV): Bujumbura; f. 1977 to stock and sell agricultural products in Burundi.

Société Mixte, Minière et Industrielle Roumano-Burundaise (SOMIBUROM): Bujumbura; f. 1977 to exploit and market mineral and industrial products.

Société Sucrière du Moso (SOSUMO): BP 835, Bujumbura; tel. 6576; telex 35; f. 1982 to develop and manage sugar cane plantations.

CHAMBER OF COMMERCE

Chambre de Commerce et de l'Industrie du Burundi: BP 313, Bujumbura; tel. 2280; f. 1923; Pres. M. R. Leclere; Hon. Sec. M. T. Pojer; 130 mems.

TRADE UNION

Union des Travailleurs du Burundi (UTB): BP 1340, Bujumbura; tel. 3884; telex 57; f. 1967 by merger of all previous unions; closely allied with UPRONA; sole authorized trade union, with 18 affiliated nat. professional feds; Sec.-Gen. Marius Rurahenye.

Transport

RAILWAYS

There are no railways in Burundi, but in 1987 plans were finalized for the construction of a line passing through Uganda, Rwanda and Burundi, to connect with the Kigoma–Dar es Salaam line in Tanzania, which would improve Burundi's isolated trade position.

ROADS

The road network is very dense and in 1981 there was a total of 5,144 km of roads, of which 1,710 km were national highways and 1,274 km secondary roads. In 1985 a contract was awarded to construct a 133-km road linking Rugombo and Kayanza, a town on the Rwandan border. In 1986 finance was obtained from international sources for the completion of the Makamba–Butembera road, providing improved access to agricultural areas bordering Tanzania.

INLAND WATERWAYS

Bujumbura is the principal port for both passenger and freight traffic on Lake Tanganyika, and the greater part of Burundi's external trade is dependent on the shipping services between Bujumbura and lake ports in Tanzania, Zambia and Zaire.

CIVIL AVIATION

There is an international airport at Bujumbura, equipped to take large jet-engined aircraft.

Air Burundi: BP 2460, 40 ave du Commerce, Bujumbura; tel. 3460; telex 80; f. 1971 as Société de Transports Aériens du Burundi, adopted present name in 1975; operates services to Entebbe (Uganda), Kigali (Rwanda), Kalémié, Bukavu and Goma (Zaire), and internally from Bujumbura to Kirundo; Man. Dir Gérard Mugabo; fleet of 1 Caravelle 3, 2 Twin Otter 300.

Tourism

Tourism is relatively undeveloped. Tourist arrivals totalled an estimated 80,000 in 1987.

Office National du Tourisme: BP 902, Bujumbura; tel. 22202; telex 5030; f. 1972; responsible for the promotion and supervision of the tourism sector; Dir André Ndayiragije.

CAMBODIA

Introductory Survey

Location, Climate, Language, Religion, Flag, Capital

The State of Cambodia occupies part of the Indochinese peninsula in South-East Asia. It is bordered by Thailand and Laos to the north, by Viet-Nam to the east and by the Gulf of Thailand to the south. The climate is tropical and humid. There is a rainy season from June to November, with the heaviest rainfall in September. The temperature is generally between 20°C and 36°C (68°F to 97°F), and the annual average in Phnom-Penh is 27°C (81°F). The official language is Khmer, which is spoken by everybody except the Vietnamese and Chinese minorities. The principal religion is Theravada Buddhism. The national flag (proportions 3 by 2) consists of two horizontal stripes, red above blue, with a stylized representation (in yellow) of the temple of Angkor Wat, with five towers, in the centre. The capital is Phnom-Penh.

Recent History

The Kingdom of Cambodia became a French protectorate in the 19th century and was incorporated into French Indo-China. In April 1941 Norodom Sihanouk, then aged 18, succeeded his grandfather as King. In May 1947 he promulgated a constitution which provided for a bicameral parliament, including an elected national assembly. Cambodia became an Associate State of the French Union in November 1949 and attained independence on 9 November 1953. In order to become a political leader, King Sihanouk abdicated in March 1955 in favour of his father, Norodom Suramarit, and became known as Prince Sihanouk: he founded a mass movement, the Sangkum Reastr Niyum (Popular Socialist Community), which won all the seats in elections to the National Assembly in 1955, 1958, 1962 and 1966. King Suramarit died in April 1960, and in June Parliament elected Prince Sihanouk as Head of State.

Prince Sihanouk's Government developed good relations with the People's Republic of China and with North Viet-Nam, but it was highly critical of the USA's role in Asia. From 1964, however, the Government was confronted by a pro-Communist insurgency movement, the Khmer Rouge, while it also became increasingly difficult to isolate Cambodia from the war in Viet-Nam.

In March 1970 Prince Sihanouk was deposed by a right-wing coup, led by the Prime Minister, Lt-Gen. (later Marshal) Lon Nol. The new Government pledged itself to the removal of foreign Communist forces and appealed to the USA for military aid. Sihanouk went into exile and formed the Royal Government of National Union of Cambodia (GRUNC), supported by the Khmer Rouge. Sihanoukists and the Khmer Rouge formed the National United Front of Cambodia (FUNC). Their combined forces, aided by South Viet-Nam's National Liberation Front and North Vietnamese troops, posed a serious threat to the new regime, but in October 1970 Marshal Lon Nol proclaimed the Khmer Republic. In June 1972 he was elected the first President.

During 1973 several foreign states recognized GRUNC as the rightful government of Cambodia. In 1974 the republican regime's control was limited to a few urban enclaves, besieged by GRUNC forces, mainly Khmer Rouge, who gained control of Phnom-Penh on 17 April 1975. Prince Sihanouk became Head of State again but did not return from exile until September. The country was subjected to a pre-arranged programme of radical social change immediately after the Khmer Rouge's assumption of power. The towns were largely evacuated, and their inhabitants put to work in rural areas. Many hundreds of thousands died as a result of ill-treatment, hunger and disease.

A new constitution, promulgated in January 1976, renamed the country Democratic Kampuchea, and established a republican form of government; elections for a 250-member People's Representative Assembly were held in March 1976. In April Prince Sihanouk resigned as Head of State and GRUNC was dissolved. The Assembly elected Khieu Samphan, formerly Deputy Prime Minister, to be President of the State Presidium (Head of State). The little-known Pol Pot became Prime Minister. In September 1977 it was officially disclosed that the ruling organization was the Communist Party of Kampuchea (CPK), with Pol Pot as the Secretary of its Central Committee.

After 1975 close links with the People's Republic of China developed, while relations with Viet-Nam deteriorated. In 1978, following a two-year campaign of raids across the Vietnamese border by the Khmer Rouge, the Vietnamese army launched a series of offensives into Kampuchean territory. In December the establishment of the Kampuchean National United Front for National Salvation (KNUFNS, renamed Kampuchean United Front for National Construction and Defence—KUFNCD—in December 1981, and United Front for the Construction and Defence of the Kampuchean Fatherland—UFCDKF—in 1989), a Communist-led movement opposed to Pol Pot and supported by Viet-Nam, was announced. Later in the month, Viet-Nam invaded Kampuchea, supported by the KNUFNS.

On 7 January 1979 Phnom-Penh was captured by Vietnamese forces, and three days later the People's Republic of Kampuchea was proclaimed. A People's Revolutionary Council was established, with Heng Samrin, leader of the KNUFNS, as President. It pledged to restore freedom of movement, freedom of association and of religion, and to restore the family unit. The CPK was replaced as the governing party by the Kampuchean People's Revolutionary Party (KPRP). The Khmer Rouge forces, however, remained active in the western provinces, near the border with Thailand, and conducted sporadic guerrilla activities elsewhere in the country. Several groups opposing both the Khmer Rouge and the Heng Samrin regime were established, including the Khmer People's National Liberation Front (KPNLF), headed by a former Prime Minister, Son Sann.

In July 1979, claiming that Pol Pot's regime had been responsible for 3m. deaths, the KPRP administration sentenced Pol Pot and his former Minister of Foreign Affairs, Ieng Sary, to death *in absentia*. In January 1980 Khieu Samphan assumed the premiership of the deposed Khmer Rouge regime, while Pol Pot became Commander-in-Chief of the armed forces.

During the first few years of the KPRP regime starvation and disease were prevalent, and thousands of Kampucheans crossed the border into Thailand. In December 1981 Pen Sovan was replaced as General Secretary of the KPRP by Heng Samrin. In December 1984 Chan Si, Chairman of the Council of Ministers, died in the USSR, and in January 1985 Hun Sen, a Vice-Chairman and Minister of Foreign Affairs, was appointed to replace him as Chairman.

After long negotiations between anti-Vietnamese resistance groups, an agreement was reached in June 1982 to form a coalition government-in-exile of Democratic Kampuchea, with the aim of securing the withdrawal of Vietnamese forces from Kampuchea. Prince Sihanouk, the former Head of State, became President, Khieu Samphan (Khmer Rouge) Vice-President and Son Sann (KPNLF) Prime Minister. The inclusion of the Khmer Rouge, despite its reputation for brutality, reflected its position as the resistance groups' principal source of military strength. The coalition gained the support of the People's Republic of China and of ASEAN member states (see p. 103) and retained the Kampuchean seat in the UN General Assembly. The KPRP Government received substantial support from the USSR.

After its invasion of Kampuchea in 1979, Viet-Nam launched regular major offensives during the annual dry season, between December and April, against the united armed forces of Democratic Kampuchea on the Thai–Kampuchean border. The offensive in 1984-85 resulted in particularly intense fighting, and many (possibly 230,000) refugees crossed the border into Thailand. The Vietnamese subsequently gained control over most of the border area, including the base camps of all three groups in the coalition. Large numbers of Vietnamese civilians had settled on Kampuchean territory; the KPRP administration stated in November 1986 that there were 57,000 such settlers, although the Government-in-exile claimed that the figure was as high as 700,000. In January 1986 a joint military command was formed by the KPNLF and Prince Sihanouk's Armée Nationale Sihanoukiste (ANS).

From 1982 onwards, Viet-Nam carried out annual mid-year public withdrawals of some 10,000 troops from Kampuchea (but these were widely suspected to be merely troop rotations), and in 1985 Viet-Nam announced that all its troops would be withdrawn by 1990. In July 1985 ASEAN proposed 'proximity' (indirect) talks between the Democratic Kampuchean coalition and a Vietnamese delegation, which would include representatives of the Heng Samrin Government, but this was rejected by Viet-Nam. A further proposal, an eight-point peace plan presented by the coalition in March 1986 (and supported by ASEAN and the People's Republic of China), was also rejected by Viet-Nam and the Heng Samrin Government. The plan suggested the withdrawal of Vietnamese forces in two phases (following a cease-fire, to be supervised by a UN observer group), and proposed that the KPRP and the Democratic Kampuchean coalition should establish a quadripartite administration (with Sihanouk as President and Son Sann as Prime Minister, and including members of the KPRP—a condition that the Khmer Rouge had previously refused to accept); subsequently, free elections would be held under the supervision of UN observers. Despite the announcement, in September 1985, that Pol Pot had retired as Commander-in-Chief of the Khmer Rouge armed forces, mistrust of the Khmer Rouge and suspicion of Pol Pot's continuing influence appeared to be an important factor in the Heng Samrin Government's rejection of the proposals.

In March 1987 Eduard Shevardnadze, the USSR's Minister of Foreign Affairs, toured six South-East Asian countries, including Kampuchea and Viet-Nam, and expressed the Soviet Government's desire to seek a solution to the conflict in Kampuchea. Viet-Nam and the Heng Samrin Government subsequently announced their willingness to include the People's Republic of China, ASEAN member states and Democratic Kampuchean groups in future peace talks; Viet-Nam also announced that it would withdraw up to 20,000 troops from Kampuchea in November 1987. In April the Democratic Kampuchean coalition insisted that Viet-Nam should be included in any peace talks from the outset, refusing proposals to participate in talks with the Heng Samrin Government alone, on the grounds that this would imply that the Kampuchean conflict was a purely internal affair, rather than the result of Vietnamese aggression.

In May 1987 Prince Sihanouk announced that he was to take one year's leave of absence as President of the Democratic Kampuchean Government-in-exile, in protest at violations of human rights, and attacks on his own forces, by the Khmer Rouge. Prince Norodom Rannarit, Prince Sihanouk's son and the Commander-in-Chief of the ANS, was appointed to be the President's official spokesman during his absence.

In September 1987 the Government of the People's Republic of China, the principal source of assistance for the Democratic Kampuchean forces, stated that it would accept a Kampuchean 'government of national reconciliation' under Prince Sihanouk, but that the presence of Vietnamese troops in Kampuchea remained a major obstacle. In the same month the USSR declared that it was 'prepared to facilitate a political settlement' in Kampuchea. Although Democratic Kampuchea announced its willingness to begin negotiations with Viet-Nam at any time, it emphasized that the complete withdrawal of foreign troops from Kampuchea was essential if a peaceful solution was to be reached. In late September the Heng Samrin Government announced that it was prepared to hold talks with some Khmer Rouge leaders (but not with Pol Pot or his close associates). In October it offered Prince Sihanouk a government post, and issued peace proposals suggesting the complete withdrawal of Vietnamese troops, internationally-observed elections, the formation of a coalition government, and a conference involving Viet-Nam, the USA, the USSR and the People's Republic of China.

Progress appeared to have been made in December 1987, when Prince Sihanouk and Hun Sen, the Chairman of the Council of Ministers in the Heng Samrin Government, met in France for private discussions (the first such meeting between leaders of the two opposing Kampuchean governments since the Vietnamese invasion in 1979). The two leaders issued a joint statement saying that the conflict in Kampuchea must be settled politically, by negotiations among all the Kampuchean parties, and that any resulting agreement should be guaranteed by an international conference. In December Son Sann, leader of the KPNLF, declared that he would participate in the talks, on condition that Viet-Nam was also represented or made a pledge to withdraw its troops from Kampuchea as soon as possible. In January 1988, after a second meeting with Hun Sen, Prince Sihanouk, who was still officially on one year's leave of absence from the presidency of the Democratic Kampuchean Government-in-exile, announced his permanent resignation from this position. In February, however, he retracted his resignation.

In May 1988 Viet-Nam announced that it would repatriate 50,000 of its troops from Kampuchea in 1988, and undertook to withdraw its troops in Kampuchea to a distance of 30 km from the Thai–Kampuchean border. The Vietnamese Government, under increasing pressure from the USSR (which perceived the Kampuchean problem as the principal obstacle to an improvement in Sino-Soviet relations), agreed in June to participate in informal discussions in Indonesia, which had originally been proposed in July 1987 by the Indonesian Minister of Foreign Affairs, Dr Mochtar Kusumaatmadja. (The Vietnamese Government had originally withdrawn its assent when ASEAN insisted that the talks should be based on the eight-point peace proposals put forward by Democratic Kampuchea in March 1986.) The Thai Government also attempted to advance the conciliation process in unofficial discussions with the USSR in May, and with Viet-Nam in June.

In early July 1988 Prince Sihanouk again resigned as President of the Democratic Kampuchean Government-in-exile. In the same month the Chinese Government issued a policy statement on Kampuchea, containing a modification of its support for the Khmer Rouge. The statement contained a provision that each faction's candidates for the proposed coalition administration in Kampuchea should be agreeable to the other three parties, thus effectively excluding Pol Pot and his closest colleagues. Viet-Nam intensified the urgency of the need to achieve a political settlement at the meeting by advancing its deadline for a complete withdrawal of troops to late 1989 or early 1990. The 'informal meeting', held in Indonesia in mid-July 1988, was attended by representatives of the four Kampuchean factions, Viet-Nam, Laos and the six ASEAN members, but was boycotted by Prince Sihanouk himself, who was, nevertheless, in Jakarta as a guest of President Suharto of Indonesia. A seven-point peace plan, proposed by Hun Sen, envisaged the establishment of a 'national reconciliation council', headed by Prince Sihanouk, to organize free elections (while the present Phnom-Penh regime remained in power) and of an international commission to supervise the withdrawal of Vietnamese troops; this was rejected by the members of the coalition. In his response, Prince Sihanouk relaxed his demands for the formation of an international peace-keeping force but insisted on the dissolution of the Heng Samrin Government and the installation of a quadripartite interim government, with armed forces comprising all four factions. Owing to the intransigence of the Khmer Rouge, no joint communiqué was issued. It was agreed, however, to establish a working group which was to report in December.

During August 1988 a reshuffle took place within the Heng Samrin Government: the Ministers of Defence and of the Interior were among those replaced, and a new Chief of General Staff of the Army was also appointed.

In August 1988 the Khmer Rouge issued a conciliatory statement (endorsed by the People's Republic of China), supporting the creation of international guarantees to prevent future domination of the other factions by the Khmer Rouge, and offered to reduce its armed forces to the level of those of the other Kampuchean factions. This statement, however, followed an offensive launched by the Khmer Rouge before the 'informal meeting' to regain areas close to the Thai border, and the forcible resettlement of refugees from camps inside Thailand to sites in Kampuchea that had been left vacant by the redeployment of Vietnamese troops. The Heng Samrin Government, supported by the Vietnamese, retaliated, driving the Khmer Rouge back to the borders. The Khmer Rouge, however, were reported to have forced civilians to transport an estimated two-year supply of weapons, provided by the People's Republic of China, into Kampuchea.

In October 1988 a meeting was held in Jakarta, which was attended by ASEAN, Viet-Nam, Laos, the Heng Samrin Government, the KPNLF and the Sihanoukists. The Khmer Rouge failed to attend and no progress was made. However, Khieu Samphan subsequently announced Khmer Rouge support for the creation of an international peace-keeping force as part of a future settlement. For nine consecutive years (1979–87), the UN General Assembly adopted an annual resolution urging the withdrawal of Vietnamese forces from Kampuchea. However, in 1988, owing to the increased co-operation of the Vietnamese, the threat of a return to power for the Khmer Rouge was perceived as being intensified, and in November the General Assembly adopted a modified resolution, still demanding a complete Vietnamese withdrawal but including a clause seeking to prevent a return to 'universally condemned policies and practices'.

In November 1988 Prince Sihanouk, Hun Sen and Son Sann conferred in Paris. The Khmer Rouge was, again, not represented at the discussions, and achievements were limited to the establishment of a working group which the Khmer Rouge was invited to join. In December the withdrawal of a further 18,000 Vietnamese troops was announced; the Vietnamese claimed that this would leave only 50,000 troops in Kampuchea, compared with Western estimates of 70,000 to 90,000. Following an unproductive meeting, attended by all four Kampuchean factions, in December, the Chinese Minister of Foreign Affairs visited Moscow. The People's Republic of China subsequently declared itself willing to reduce its support for the Khmer Rouge progressively, parallel with the Vietnamese withdrawal. The departure of the Vietnamese had previously been regarded by the Chinese as a prerequisite to the conclusion of any form of agreement.

In early January 1989 Heng Samrin pledged that all Vietnamese troops would be repatriated by September, if a political settlement could be achieved. Owing to the conciliatory attitudes of the People's Republic of China and the USSR, diplomatic activity intensified in January: the Thai Minister of Foreign Affairs met Vietnamese officials in Hanoi; the Vietnamese and Chinese Deputy Ministers of Foreign Affairs met in Beijing (the highest-level meeting between the two Governments since 1979); and Thailand abandoned its policy (and that of ASEAN) of isolating the Heng Samrin Government, and invited Hun Sen (in his capacity as the leader of one of the four Kampuchean factions) to hold private discussions with the Thai Prime Minister. An agreement was concluded on the repatriation of the estimated 300,000 Kampuchean refugees in Thailand over a period of three years from September, following the withdrawal of the Vietnamese troops. In early February discussions between the Chinese and Soviet Ministers of Foreign Affairs in Beijing resulted in agreements on a withdrawal of Vietnamese troops by September, an effective control mechanism to supervise this, the termination of foreign military aid and the holding of free elections. Prince Sihanouk subsequently resumed the leadership of the Democratic Kampuchean Government-in-exile, but refused to attend the second 'informal meeting' in Jakarta, as a protest against Thailand's reception of Hun Sen. The meeting, held in mid-February, was again attended by representatives of the four Kampuchean factions, ASEAN, Viet-Nam and Laos. The discussions, however, failed to resolve the two outstanding areas of contention—the nature of the international force to oversee troop withdrawals and the composition of an interim government before elections—and ended in an impasse.

In March 1989 it was announced that the Khmer Rouge, the KPNLF and the ANS had agreed to establish a unified military command. Prince Sihanouk was appointed as Supreme Commander of the resultant High Council for National Defence. The existence of this command structure was, however, subsequently subject to doubt.

In April 1989 an extraordinary session of the National Assembly in Phnom-Penh was convened to ratify several amendments to the Constitution, drafted by a 27-member commission, which had been appointed in March. Under the provisions of the amendments, the name of the country was changed to the State of Cambodia, a new national flag, emblem and anthem were introduced, Buddhism was reinstated as the state religion, and the death penalty was abolished. These amendments were made as a concessionary gesture prior to a meeting between Hun Sen and Prince Sihanouk, which was held in Jakarta in early May. Following this meeting, Hun Sen proposed the establishment of a quadripartite supreme council to prepare for a general election in Cambodia. This proposal was rejected by Prince Sihanouk, who reiterated his claim for a quadripartite government to organize the election, although he relinquished his demand for the complete dismantling of the Heng Samrin administration.

In May 1989, following a meeting with Hun Sen in Bangkok, the Thai Prime Minister, Gen. Chatichai Choonhavan, appealed to the four Cambodian factions to observe a cease-fire. His plea was rejected by the Khmer Rouge, who, together with the other members of the resistance forces, attempted to weaken the negotiating position of the Heng Samrin regime through military gains. In late July Hun Sen and Prince Sihanouk met in Paris, which was to be the venue of an international conference on Cambodia a few days later. The principal achievement of the opening session of this conference was an agreement to send a UN reconnaissance party to Cambodia to study the prospects for a cease-fire and the installation of a peace-keeping force. The conference, however, ended in failure at the end of August, when discussions were suspended, owing to continuing disagreements over the organization of a cease-fire, the role of the Khmer Rouge, the composition of an interim administration and the possible UN supervision of the Vietnamese withdrawal. Shortly before the closing session of the conference, Prince Sihanouk resigned from the leadership of his faction, the United National Front for an Independent, Neutral, Peaceful and Co-operative Cambodia (FUNCINPEC).

In September 1989 the withdrawal of the Vietnamese forces was completed on schedule, although, owing to the failure of the negotiations in Paris, it took place without UN or Western monitoring. Hun Sen subsequently invited the UN Secretary-General to send a mission to confirm the Vietnamese withdrawal and to support the termination of military aid to all factions. Gen. Chatichai continued his attempts at mediation, urging an immediate cease-fire, verification of the withdrawal and the dispatch of an international control commission to Cambodia to monitor the rival factions and to prepare for fresh negotiations.

Following the withdrawal of the Vietnamese troops, the resistance forces adopted more conventional fighting tactics and made greater incursions into Cambodia. The Khmer Rouge forces were particularly effective in combat, although it was difficult to monitor the extent of their victories, as independent confirmation of conflicting government and rebel claims proved to be almost impossible.

In November 1989, despite the Vietnamese withdrawal, there was increased pressure for the Cambodian seat at the UN to be vacated pending a general election. Following substantial military gains by the Khmer Rouge, the UN General Assembly also adopted a resolution supporting the formation of an interim government in Cambodia, which would include members of the Khmer Rouge. The resolution cast doubt on the Vietnamese withdrawal (since it was not monitored by the UN) and condemned 'demographic changes imposed in Cambodia' (a reference to the alleged presence of 1m. Vietnamese settlers in Cambodia), but retained the clause, introduced in 1988, indirectly relating to past atrocities perpetrated by the Khmer Rouge.

In January 1990 the five permanent members of the UN Security Council (the USA, the USSR, the People's Republic of China, the UK and France) unanimously approved an Australian peace initiative, which had been proposed in November 1989. The plan included a UN-monitored cease-fire, the UN Secretary-General's temporary assumption of executive powers in Cambodia, the formation of a supreme national council, and the holding of internationally-supervised national elections.

In January 1990 Prince Sihanouk announced his resignation from the posts of Supreme Commander of the High Council for National Defence and leader of the resistance coalition, but retained his position as the President of Democratic Kampuchea. At the beginning of February Prince Sihanouk declared that the coalition Government-in-exile of Democratic Kampuchea would henceforth be known as the National Government of Cambodia and would restore the traditional flag and national anthem. This was widely regarded as an attempt to distance the coalition from association with the former Democratic Kampuchean regime of the Khmer Rouge.

In February 1990 Hun Sen and Prince Sihanouk signed a joint communiqué emphasizing the need for participation by the UN in restoring peace to Cambodia. In the same month the four Cambodian factions were represented at the third 'informal meeting' in Jakarta, which was also attended by representatives of ASEAN, Laos, Viet-Nam, France and Australia. Disagreements about peripheral issues led to the premature termination of the talks. However, there appeared to be few serious objections to the main principles of the UN plan.

In March and April 1990 the Heng Samrin regime launched a series of successful offensives, reclaiming territory previously held by the resistance forces. At the end of April Prince Sihanouk announced that the ANS would henceforth be known as the National Army of Independent Cambodia. In May, following arbitration by Thailand's Minister of Foreign Affairs, the four Cambodian factions informally accepted broad plans for a future cease-fire. In June Prince Sihanouk, who had resumed the presidency of the resistance coalition in May, and Hun Sen signed a conditional cease-fire agreement in Bangkok. The agreement envisaged the formation of a supreme national council comprising equal numbers of representatives from the two rival Governments. In June a meeting in Tokyo, sponsored by the Japanese and Thai Governments, was attended by representatives from all four Cambodian factions, including both Hun Sen and Prince Sihanouk. The discussions collapsed, however, when the Khmer Rouge refused to sign a cease-fire agreement and proposed that each of the four Cambodian factions should have equal representation on a supreme national council. Despite his previous accord with Hun Sen, Prince Sihanouk offered his support for the Khmer Rouge proposal.

In June and July 1990 several of Hun Sen's 'reformist' political allies were dismissed or arrested for alleged attempts to establish a new party. They were replaced with supporters of the President of the National Assembly, Chea Sim, who was regarded as a 'conservative'.

In July 1990 the USA withdrew its support for the National Government of Cambodia's occupation of Cambodia's seat at the UN. The USA also announced its willingness to provide humanitarian assistance to the Phnom-Penh regime and to negotiate directly with Viet-Nam in an attempt to solve the Cambodian problem. The first formal bilateral talks between the USA and Viet-Nam took place at the UN in early August.

In late August 1990 the UN Security Council endorsed the framework for a comprehensive settlement in Cambodia. The agreement provided for UN supervision of an interim government, military arrangements for the transitional period, free elections and guarantees for the future neutrality of Cambodia. Under the plan, a special representative of the Secretary-General of the UN would control the proposed 'United Nations Transitional Authority in Cambodia'. The UN would also assume control of the Ministries of Foreign Affairs, National Defence, Finance, the Interior and Information, Press and Culture. China and the USSR subsequently pledged to cease supplies of military equipment to their respective allies, the Khmer Rouge and the Phnom-Penh regime. The USA later, in a reversal of previous policy, announced that it would hold direct talks with the Phnom-Penh regime. This was followed by a Soviet declaration that the USSR would hold talks with Prince Sihanouk, whose importance it had previously refused to recognize.

At an 'informal meeting' in Jakarta in September 1990 the four Cambodian factions accepted the UN proposals. They also agreed to the formation of the Supreme National Council (SNC), with six representatives from the Phnom-Penh regime and six from the National Government of Cambodia. The agreement also included a clause, proposed by Prince Sihanouk, that the SNC had the authority to elect a 13th member as its chairman. SNC decisions were to be taken by consensus, effectively allowing each faction the power of veto, and the SNC was to occupy the Cambodian seat at the UN General Assembly. Prior to the 'informal meeting', secret talks had been held between the Chinese and the Vietnamese, following which the Vietnamese endorsed the UN plan. It was widely assumed that the Chinese had promised an improvement in Sino-Vietnamese relations in return for Vietnamese approval of the plan.

The 12 members of the SNC met for the first time in mid-September 1990, in Bangkok, Thailand. Discussions were abandoned following the SNC's failure to reach agreement on the election of a chairman. Hun Sen demanded the vice-chairmanship of the SNC and the allocation of one extra seat to the State of Cambodia to compensate for the election of Prince Sihanouk to the chairmanship of the Council. Prince Sihanouk, the Khmer Rouge and the KPNLF subsequently agreed, in principle, to the nomination of a seventh delegate for the State of Cambodia, which would bring the total number of representatives to 14, but refused to endorse the appointment of Hun Sen as vice-chairman of the SNC.

In September 1990 Hor Nam Hong, previously the Minister Assistant to the Chairman of the Council of Ministers responsible for foreign and judicial affairs, was appointed Minister of Foreign Affairs, in place of Hun Sen, and Nhim Vanda, the Vice-Minister of National Defence, replaced Tang Saroem as Minister of Foreign Trade.

Following the impasse reached by the SNC in September 1990, fighting in Cambodia continued, with the Khmer Rouge intensifying military action in the northern provinces. The dry season, which facilitates the use of heavy artillery, was approaching, and there were reports in October that the Khmer Rouge had acquired tanks from China. Towards the end of November the UN Security Council completed the final draft of the Cambodian peace plan. In December, however, the Phnom-Penh regime reiterated its previous opposition to the principal provisions of the plan. It rejected any dismantling of the Phnom-Penh Government and remained opposed to the disarming of all four Cambodian factions, on the grounds that only government forces could be easily and effectively monitored. Another session of the Paris Conference on Cambodia, attended by all 12 members of the SNC, took place later in December. Some progress was reported, with all factions endorsing most aspects of the UN plan. The French co-chairman of the meeting announced that he hoped to convene a 19-nation conference to ratify a peace treaty in early 1991.

Government

Legislative power is vested in the National Assembly, which initially had 117 members, elected for five years by universal adult suffrage. The original Assembly's term expired in 1986, but was renewed for a further five years. In June 1987, however, supplementary elections were held in six provinces, increasing the Assembly's membership to 123. The Assembly elects the Council of State from among its members. Executive power is exercised by the Council of Ministers, which is appointed by, and responsible to, the National Assembly. Local administration is the responsibility of Local People's Committees.

Defence

The total strength of Cambodia's armed forces was estimated to be 112,300 in June 1990, comprising an army of some 55,500, a navy of about 1,000, an air force of 800, provincial forces of 22,500 and district forces of about 32,500. A system of conscription is in force, for those aged between 18 and 35, for five years. The total strength of the armed forces of the coalition National Government of Cambodia is unknown, but it is believed that the Khmer Rouge has 30,000 men, the KPNLF some 10,000–12,000, and Prince Sihanouk's National Army of Independent Cambodia (formerly the Armée Nationale Sihanoukiste—ANS) about 15,000–18,000.

Economic Affairs

In 1986, according to estimates by the UN Statistical Office, Cambodia's gross domestic product (GDP), measured at current prices, was US $585m., equivalent to only $78 per head. During 1980–86, it was estimated, total GDP declined, in real terms, at an average rate of 3.2% annually, while real GDP per head decreased by 4.8% annually. Over the same period, the population increased at an average rate of 2.7% per year.

Agriculture (including forestry and fishing) employed an estimated 70% of the total labour force in 1989. An estimated 2.5m. metric tons of the staple crop, rice, were harvested in 1989. However, a shortfall of about 300,000 tons of rice was projected for the 1990/91 harvest. Other principal crops include maize, sugar cane, cassava and bananas. The two most important export commodities in 1988 were rubber and timber: 42,000 ha of rubber trees produced an estimated 31,000 tons of latex, while timber production reached 280,000 cu m. In 1988 the total fishing catch was reported to be 82,000 tons.

Industry (including mining, manufacturing, construction and power) contributed 5% of GDP in 1988, and employed 6.7% of the labour force in 1980.

Cambodia has limited mineral resources, including phosphates, iron ore, gem stones, bauxite, silicon and manganese ore, of which only phosphates are, at present, being exploited.

The manufacturing sector is dominated by about 1,500 rice mills and about 80 state-owned factories, which produce, *inter alia*, household goods, textiles, tyres and pharmaceutical products.

CAMBODIA

In 1988 Cambodia recorded a trade deficit of US $115m. (imports $32m., exports $147m.). The USSR and other Eastern bloc countries accounted for about 80% of total trade. There was also a substantial amount of undeclared trade with Thailand and Singapore. The principal imports in 1988 were petroleum and petroleum products, machinery, irrigation equipment and consumer goods. The principal exports were rubber and timber (valued at $24m. and $5m. respectively), which together contributed 90% of total export revenue.

In 1986 Cambodia's gross long-term debt was US $622m., of which 61% was owed to the USSR and other members of the Council for Mutual Economic Assistance (CMEA, see p. 125), and 38% to members of the Organisation for Economic Co-operation and Development (OECD, see p. 186).

Cambodia's essentially agricultural economy was totally disrupted by war during the period 1970–75. After April 1975, urban residents were forced into the countryside to work on the land. All sectors of the economy were nationalized, and agriculture was collectivized. The country recovered from severe food shortages following the Vietnamese invasion in December 1978, but economic recovery since then has been hampered by embargoes on long-term development aid by Western countries and the UN, owing to the political situation. During the 1980s collectivization and state ownership were recognized as disincentives to production, and in 1986 private enterprise was legitimized by a constitutional amendment. Further economic reforms, which were aimed at promoting private-sector participation and encouraging the provision of foreign investment and aid, were subsequently implemented. In 1989 the National Assembly was considering a draft law on foreign investment, which, if approved, would permit the establishment of 100%-foreign-owned ventures in Cambodia. Foreign investment was particularly needed, since the USSR and Eastern European countries decided that, as from January 1991, Cambodia would have to begin paying commercial rates for financial assistance and imports. However, the USA announced in mid-1990 that it would provide humanitarian assistance to Cambodia. The continuing fighting in 1990 contributed to the rapid depletion of the country's food supply, resulted in an increase in the rate of inflation (which, in turn, led to several devaluations of the currency in that year), and caused labour shortages, owing to the increased rate of conscription into the armed forces.

Social Welfare

In 1985 there were 34 hospitals in the country, with 506 physicians and public health officers under the Ministry of Health. There were also 1,349 commune infirmaries. There was a total of 17,856 beds and a total staff of more than 13,000.

Education

The KPRP regime is attempting to re-establish a full educational system. The school system lasts for 10 years, with an emphasis on practical subjects such as agriculture. In the academic year 1988/89 the total enrolment in general education was 1.7m. pupils, while enrolment in secondary, vocational and higher education was 20,000 students. In 1980 the faculty of medicine of the former Phnom-Penh University and the teacher-training college were reopened. An agricultural college was opened in 1985. In 1988/89 about 6,000 students were sent abroad for further education.

Weights and Measures

The metric system is in force.

Public Holidays

1991: 7 January (National Day), April (New Year), 17 April (Victory over American Imperialism Day), 1 May (Labour Day), 20 May (Day of Hatred), 22 September (Feast of the Ancestors).

1992: 7 January (National Day), April (New Year), 17 April (Victory over American Imperialism Day), 1 May (Labour Day), 20 May (Day of Hatred), 22 September (Feast of the Ancestors).

Statistical Survey

Note: Some of the statistics below represent only sectors of the economy controlled by the Government of the former Khmer Republic. During the years 1970–75 no figures were available for areas controlled by the Khmer Rouge. Almost no official figures are available for the period since April 1975.

Area and Population

AREA, POPULATION AND DENSITY

Area (sq km)	181,035*
Population (census results)	
17 April 1962	5,728,771
Prior to elections of 1 May 1981	6,682,000
Population (UN estimates at mid-year)†	
1987	7,683,000
1988	7,869,000
1989	8,055,000
Density (per sq km) at mid-1989	44.5

* 69,898 sq miles.

† Source: UN, *World Population Prospects: 1988*.

Capital: Phnom-Penh, population 393,995 in 1962; 400,000 in 1981 (estimate); 700,000 in 1986 (estimate); 800,000 in 1989 (estimate).

BIRTHS AND DEATHS (UN estimates, annual averages)

	1975–80	1980–85	1985–90
Birth rate (per 1,000)	30.0	45.5	41.4
Death rate (per 1,000)	40.0	19.7	16.6

Source: UN, *World Population Prospects: 1988*.

ECONOMICALLY ACTIVE POPULATION
(ILO estimates, '000 persons at mid-1980)

	Males	Females	Total
Agriculture, etc.	1,346	1,107	2,454
Industry	130	90	220
Services	439	187	625
Total	**1,915**	**1,384**	**3,299**

Source: ILO, *Economically Active Population Estimates and Projections, 1950–2025*.

Mid-1989 (estimates in '000): Agriculture, etc. 2,632; Total 3,736 (Source: FAO, *Production Yearbook*).

CAMBODIA
Statistical Survey

Agriculture

PRINCIPAL CROPS ('000 metric tons)

	1987	1988	1989
Rice (paddy)	1,855	2,300*	2,100†
Maize†	95	100	115
Sweet potatoes†	40	42	43
Cassava (Manioc)†	112	115	110
Dry beans†	40	36	41
Groundnuts (in shell)†	10	12	13
Sesame seed†	6	7	8
Coconuts†	42	44	46
Copra†	7	7	8
Sugar cane†	205	210	220
Tobacco (leaves)†	10	11	12
Natural rubber	25*	27*	27†
Vegetables and melons†	466	470	470
Oranges†	40	41	42
Mangoes†	19	20	21
Pineapples†	10	10	11
Bananas†	106	110	112

* Unofficial estimate. † FAO estimate(s).
Source: FAO, *Production Yearbook*.

LIVESTOCK ('000 head, year ending September)

	1987	1988*	1989*
Horses*	14	15	16
Cattle	1,837	1,950	2,000
Buffaloes	687	700	730
Pigs	1,434	1,500	1,550

* FAO estimates.
Chickens (FAO estimates, million): 6 in 1987; 7 in 1988; 7 in 1989.
Ducks (FAO estimates, million): 3 in 1987; 3 in 1988; 3 in 1989.
Source: FAO, *Production Yearbook*.

LIVESTOCK PRODUCTS (FAO estimates, '000 metric tons)

	1987	1988	1989
Beef and veal	17	17	18
Buffalo meat	9	10	10
Pig meat	24	24	25
Poultry meat	21	22	23
Cows' milk	17	17	17
Hen eggs	10.5	11.5	12.0
Other poultry eggs	2.5	2.6	2.6
Cattle and buffalo hides	5.4	5.5	5.9

Source: FAO, *Production Yearbook*.

Forestry

ROUNDWOOD REMOVALS
(FAO estimates, '000 cu m, excl. bark)

	1986	1987	1988
Sawlogs, veneer logs and logs for sleepers*	110	110	110
Other industrial wood†	457	457	457
Fuel wood	4,859	4,983	5,110
Total	5,426	5,550	5,677

* Assumed to be unchanged since 1972.
† Assumed to be unchanged since 1979.
Source: FAO, *Yearbook of Forest Products*.

SAWNWOOD PRODUCTION
(FAO estimates, '000 cu m, all non-coniferous)

	1970	1971	1972
Sawnwood (incl. boxboards)	32	38	43
Railway sleepers	3	3	—
Total	35	41	43

1973–88: Annual production as in 1972 (FAO estimates).
Source: FAO, *Yearbook of Forest Products*.

Fishing

(FAO estimates, '000 metric tons, live weight)

	1984	1985	1986
Inland waters	59.5	62.0	63.5
Pacific Ocean	5.5	6.0	6.5
Total	65.0	68.0	70.0

1987–88: Annual catch as in 1986 (FAO estimate).
Source: FAO, *Yearbook of Fishery Statistics*.

Mining

('000 metric tons)

	1981	1982	1983
Salt (unrefined)*	37	38	41

1984–87: Annual production as in 1983*.
* Estimates by US Bureau of Mines.
Source: UN, *Industrial Statistics Yearbook*.

Industry

SELECTED PRODUCTS
('000 metric tons, unless otherwise indicated)

	1971	1972	1973
Distilled alcoholic beverages ('000 hectolitres)	45	55	36
Beer ('000 hectolitres)	26	23	18
Soft drinks ('000 hectolitres)	25	25*	25*
Cigarettes (million)	3,413	2,510	2,622
Cotton yarn—pure and mixed (metric tons)	1,068	1,094	415
Bicycle tyres and tubes ('000)	208	200*	200*
Rubber footwear ('000 pairs)	1,292	1,000*	1,000*
Soap (metric tons)	469	400*	400*
Motor spirit (petrol)	2	—	—
Distillate fuel oils	11	—	—
Residual fuel oils	14	—	—
Cement	44	53	78
Electric energy (million kWh)†	148	166	150

* Estimate. † Production by public utilities only.
Cigarettes (million): 1976–84 annual production 4,100 (estimates by US Department of Agriculture).
Cement ('000 metric tons): 50 in 1976; 50 in 1977; 10 in 1978 (estimates by US Bureau of Mines).
Electric energy (million kWh): 70 in 1985; 70 in 1986; 70 in 1987.
Source: UN, *Industrial Statistics Yearbook*.

CAMBODIA   *Statistical Survey*

Finance

CURRENCY AND EXCHANGE RATES

Monetary Units
100 sen = 1 new riel.

Denominations
Coin: 5 sen.
Notes: 10, 20 and 50 sen; 1, 5, 10, 20, 50 and 100 riels.

Sterling and Dollar Equivalents (30 September 1990)
£1 sterling = 955.5 riels;
US $1 = 510.0 riels;
1,000 new riels = £1.047 = $1.961.

Exchange Rate
Note: Some figures in this chapter are in terms of the old riel, whose value fluctuated. The average exchange rate (old riels per US dollar) was: 162.3 in 1972; 244.9 in 1973. The new riel, initially valued at 1 kg of rice, was introduced in 1980. The exchange rate was fixed at US $1 = 150 new riels between October 1988 and November 1989. A revised rate of $1 = 218 new riels was introduced in November 1989, but this was later adjusted.

External Trade

PRINCIPAL COMMODITIES (US $'000)

Trade with the USSR

Imports	1983	1984	1985
Petroleum and petroleum products	28,792	33,768	35,487
Cotton yarn	2,960	2,745	2,751
Woven cotton fabrics	2,691	3,958	4,215
Synthetic fabrics	3,094	2,831	2,938
Machinery, electrical equipment and road vehicles	36,595	34,338	40,085
Lorries	9,956	9,867	11,354
Total (incl. others)	91,219	93,887	109,546

Source: Statistisches Bundesamt, Wiesbaden, Federal Republic of Germany (West Germany).

Exports	1983	1984	1985
Crude rubber	5,398	6,393	10,241
Total (incl. others)	5,398	6,418	10,897

Source: Statistisches Bundesamt, Wiesbaden.

Trade with OECD countries

Imports	1983	1984	1985
Food and live animals	4,204	3,727	378
Cereals and cereal preparations	3,946	3,411	77
Beverages and tobacco	64	114	413
Crude materials (inedible) except fuels	61	565	81
Mineral fuels, lubricants, etc.	1	n.a.	13
Animal and vegetable oils, fats and waxes	2,209	1,006	4
Chemicals and related products	659	698	1,465
Organic chemicals	48	34	548
Medicinal and pharmaceutical products	462	154	638
Basic manufactures	973	1,536	1,724
Iron and steel	107	32	747
Machinery and transport equipment	1,803	2,224	3,385
Machinery specialized for particular industries	625	614	585
Road vehicles and parts (excl. tyres, engines and electrical parts)	334	912	1,414
Miscellaneous manufactured articles	692	626	327
Total (incl. others)	11,169	12,063	8,123

Source: Statistisches Bundesamt, Wiesbaden.

Exports	1983	1984	1985
Food and live animals	35	25	76
Beverages and tobacco	10	n.a.	43
Crude materials (inedible) except fuels	447	213	293
Chemicals and related products	81	21	n.a.
Basic manufactures	49	130	629
Leather, leather manufactures, dressed fur, etc.	n.a.	89	n.a.
Iron and steel	n.a.	n.a.	593
Machinery and transport equipment	206	268	145
Office machines and automatic data processing equipment / Telecommunications and sound equipment	95	121	n.a.
Other electrical machinery, apparatus, etc.	55	50	109
Road vehicles and parts (excl. tyres, engines and electrical parts)	45	n.a.	n.a.
Miscellaneous manufactured articles	192	242	368
Clothing and accessories (excl. footwear)	149	41	241
Total (incl. others)	1,022	908	1,617

Source: Statistisches Bundesamt, Wiesbaden.

SELECTED TRADING PARTNERS (US $'000)

Imports	1983	1984	1985
EEC states	3,620	3,488	3,543
Federal Republic of Germany	234	129	175
France	1,585	806	1,342
United Kingdom	1,251	852	608
Italy	163	1,250	421
USSR	91,219	93,887	109,546
Sweden	148	239	569
USA	2,485	1,126	13
Japan	3,475	5,207	1,748
Australia	967	1,145	1,237
New Zealand	331	717	520
Total	102,151	105,000	117,176

Source: Statistisches Bundesamt, Wiesbaden.

CAMBODIA
Statistical Survey, Directory

Exports	1983	1984	1985
EEC states	447	173	104
Federal Republic of Germany	2	n.a.	n.a.
United Kingdom	278	97	99
Italy	119	59	n.a.
Spain	46	16	n.a.
USSR	5,398	6,418	10,897
Turkey	50	224	593
Sweden	6	61	17
USA	80	125	358
Japan	423	273	364
Australia	11	33	22
Total	6,415	7,307	12,355

Source: Statistisches Bundesamt, Wiesbaden.

Transport

RAILWAYS (traffic)

	1971	1972	1973
Passenger-kilometres (million)	91	56	54
Freight ton-kilometres (million)	10	10	10

ROAD TRAFFIC (motor vehicles in use*)

	1971	1972	1973
Passenger cars	26,400	27,200	n.a.
Commercial vehicles†	11,100	11,100	11,000

* Including vehicles no longer in circulation.
† Excluding tractors and semi-trailer combinations.
Passenger cars: 700 in 1981.
Commercial vehicles: 1,800 in 1981.

INTERNATIONAL SEA-BORNE SHIPPING
(estimated freight traffic, '000 metric tons)

	1983	1984	1985
Goods loaded	10	10	10
Goods unloaded	100	100	100

Source: UN, *Monthly Bulletin of Statistics*.

CIVIL AVIATION (traffic on scheduled services)

	1975	1976	1977
Passenger-kilometres (million)	42	42	42
Freight ton-kilometres ('000)	400	400	400

Source: Statistisches Bundesamt, Wiesbaden.

Communications Media

	1985	1986	1987
Radio receivers ('000 in use)	800	800	815
Television receivers ('000 in use)	52	55	58

Source: UNESCO, *Statistical Yearbook*.

Education

(1983/84)

	Schools	Teachers	Pupils
Kindergarten	598	1,394	35,495
First level (primary)	n.a.	36,520	1,504,840
Second level (junior secondary)	207	4,494	145,730
Third level (senior secondary)	13	278	7,334

Source: Ministry of Education.

Directory

The Constitution

A new constitution was approved by the National Assembly on 27 June 1981. It consists of a Preamble and 10 Chapters, divided into 93 Articles. On 30 April 1989 the National Assembly unanimously endorsed several constitutional amendments, including the provision that the official name of the country should change from the People's Republic of Kampuchea to the State of Cambodia. The main Articles of the amended Constitution are summarized below:

POLITICAL SYSTEM

Article 1. The State of Cambodia is an independent, sovereign, peaceful, democratic, neutral and non-aligned state.
Article 2. All power belongs to the people. The people exercise power through the National Assembly and various other state bodies elected by the people and responsible to the people.
Article 4. The Kampuchean People's Revolutionary Party is the leading force of Cambodian society, and the core of national solidarity.
Article 6. Buddhism is the religion of the State.
Article 9. The State of Cambodia implements the principle that the entire people should take part in the defence and construction of the motherland.

Article 10. The foreign policy of the State of Cambodia is that of independence, peace, neutrality and non-alignment. It adheres to the principles of peaceful co-existence and extends friendly diplomatic relations with all countries, regardless of their political regimes.

ECONOMIC REGIME AND CULTURAL AND SOCIAL POLICIES

Article 11. The national economy is under the State's leadership.

Article 12. The national economy is composed of five sectors: the state economy, the joint state-private economy, the collective economy, the family economy and the private economy.

Article 15. Cambodian citizens have full rights to own and use land and to inherit land granted by the State.

Article 19. Trade inside the State should be expanded to increase activities of exchange. Citizens or production units are permitted to sell their products. Foreign trade is under state administration.

Article 29. The State provides social security for workers and employees who are no longer able to work, owing to sickness, old age or disability incurred through work. The State provides assistance to the unsupported aged, disabled, widows and orphans.

CAMBODIA

Directory

RIGHTS AND DUTIES OF CITIZENS

Article 30. The State of Cambodia recognizes and respects human rights. Cambodian citizens are equal before the law and have the same rights, freedoms and duties, regardless of their sex, beliefs, religion, race or social standing.

Article 31. Cambodian citizens of both sexes, who are at least 18 years of age, have the right to vote. Those above 21 years of age may seek election.

Article 37. Citizens have freedom of speech, of the press and of assembly. No one can abuse these rights to the detriment of other people's honour, public social order and national security.

NATIONAL ASSEMBLY

The National Assembly is the supreme organ of state power and the sole legislative organ. Its deputies are elected by the principle of universal secret ballot and its term of office is five years. It has the power to adopt and revise the Constitution and laws, to control their implementation, to adopt economic policies and the state budget, to elect or remove the Chairman, Vice-Chairman or Secretary from the National Assembly, the Council of State and the Council of Ministers, and to control the activities of the Council of State and the Council of Ministers.

COUNCIL OF STATE

The Council of State is the representative organ of the country and a standing organ of the National Assembly. Its members are elected from the National Assembly deputies. The Chairman of the Council of State is the Head of State of the State of Cambodia, Supreme Commander of the Armed Forces and Chairman of the National Defence Council, to be set up when necessary. Its duties include promulgating laws, deciding on the appointment or removal of members of the Council of Ministers, creating and abolishing ministries, and ratifying or rejecting international treaties except when it is deemed necessary to refer them to the National Assembly.

COUNCIL OF MINISTERS

The Council of Ministers is the governing body and organ of direct management of society, responsible to the National Assembly.

LOCAL PEOPLE'S COMMITTEES

The territory of Cambodia is divided into provinces and municipalities, under the direct administration of central authority. People's Committees are established in all provinces, municipalities, districts, communes and wards, and are responsible for local administration, public security and social order.

JUDICIARY AND COURTS

The judicial organs of Cambodia are the People's Courts and Military Tribunals.

The Government
(December 1990)

COUNCIL OF STATE

President of the Council: HENG SAMRIN.
Vice-President: SAY PHOUTHANG.
Secretary-General: CHAN VEN.
Members of the Council: MEN CHAN, KHAM LEN, HENG TEAV, CHEM SNGUON, Mrs PUNG PENG CHENG.

COUNCIL OF MINISTERS

Chairman: HUN SEN.
First Vice-Chairman: SAY CHHUM.
Vice-Chairman and Chairman of the Central Control Committee: SAY PHOUTHANG.
Minister of Foreign Affairs: HOR NAM HONG.
Minister Assistant to the Chairman of the Council of Ministers: Mrs PUNG PENG CHENG.
Vice-Chairman and Director of the Cabinet of the Council of Ministers: KONG SAM-OL.
Vice-Chairman and Minister of National Defence: TEA BANH.
Vice-Chairmen: CHEA SOTH, BOU THANG.
Minister of Agriculture: NGUON NHEL.
Minister of the Interior: SIN SONG.
Minister of Industry: HO HON.
Minister of Communications, Transport and Posts: ROS CHHUN.
Minister of Finance: CHHAY THAN.
Minister of Justice: OUK BUN CHOEUN.
Minister of Planning: CHEA CHANTO.
Chairman of the State Organization Committee: SAR KHENG.
Minister of Education: YOS SON.
Minister of Health: YIM CHHAILI.
Minister of Information, Press and Culture: HANG CHUON.
Minister of Foreign Trade: NHIM VANDA.
Minister of Social Affairs and War Invalids: KOY BUNTHA.
Director of State Affairs Inspectorate: KONG KORM.
Minister attached to Council of Ministers: KHUN CHHY.
Director of the General Department for Rubber Plantations: SAM SARIT.
Director of General Directorate for Tourism: CHEAM YIEP.
Chairman of the National Bank of Cambodia: CHA RIENG.
Attorney-General: CHAN MIN.
Deputy Minister of Defence and Chief of Staff: POL SAROEUN.

Vice-Ministers

Vice-Ministers of Foreign Affairs: DITH MOUNTY, SOK AN, LONG VISALO.
Vice-Ministers of National Defence: KE KIMYAN, SOY KEO, POL SAROEUN, NUON SOK, PHUONG SIPHAN, PENG PAT, NHIM VANDA.
Vice-Minister of Social Affairs: DOUANG CHOUM.
Vice-Ministers of Health: CHEA THANG, Mme CHEY KANH NHA.
Vice-Ministers of Education: SAR KAPON, EK SAM-OL.
Vice-Ministers of the Interior: KIM PHON, LOY SOPHAT, SIN SEN, SAM NEAT, HONG CHAN.
Vice-Ministers of Communications, Transport and Posts: CHHIM SENG, TRAM IEV-TOEK.
Vice-Ministers of Trade: PHANG SARET, TOP SAM, UK RABUN.
Vice-Ministers of Industry: SOK EISAN, KHLOT VANDHI.
Vice-Ministers of Agriculture: SO KHUN, PEN PANH-NHA.
Vice-Minister of Agriculture (Fisheries): MAU PHAUK.
Vice-Ministers of Planning: TI YAV, KEO SAMUT.
Vice-Ministers of Information, Press and Culture: HIM CHHEM, THONG KHON.
Vice-Minister of Finance: BUN SAM.
Vice-Minister of Justice: (vacant).
Vice-Ministers of the Council of Ministers' Cabinet: BIN UY, CHAM PRASIT.
Vice-Ministers of State Affairs Inspectorate: KHOEM CHEASAOPHOAN, NUON SARET.

MINISTRIES

All Ministries are in Phnom-Penh.

The following Government has been formed by groups opposed to the Government in Phnom-Penh (listed above):

NATIONAL GOVERNMENT OF CAMBODIA

(coalition Government-in-exile, formed, as the Government of Democratic Kampuchea, 22 June 1982, renamed in February 1990)
(December 1990)

President: Prince NORODOM SIHANOUK.
Official Spokesman for the President: Prince NORODOM RANNARIT (Sihanoukist/FUNCINPEC).
Vice-President in charge of Foreign Affairs: KHIEU SAMPHAN (Khmer Rouge).
Prime Minister: SON SANN (KPNLF).
Members of the Co-ordination Committees:
Defence: SON SEN (Khmer Rouge), IM CHHOUDETH (KPNLF), Prince NORODOM RANNARIT (Sihanoukist/FUNCINPEC).
Finance and Economy: IENG SARY (Khmer Rouge), BUON SAY (KPNLF), BUOR HELL (Sihanoukist/FUNCINPEC).
Education and Culture: THUON RUN (Khmer Rouge), CHAN SAROEUN (Sihanoukist/FUNCINPEC), CHHOY VU (KPNLF).
Health and Social Affairs: Dr THIOUNN THIOEUNN (Khmer Rouge), KHEK VANDY (Sihanoukist/FUNCINPEC), Dr BOU KHENG (KPNLF).

CAMBODIA

The United Nations recognizes the following coalition body as representing Cambodia:

SUPREME NATIONAL COUNCIL
(formed on 11 September 1990)

State of Cambodia
HUN SEN
TEA BANH
SIN SONG
KONG SAM-OL
CHEM SNGUON
HOR NAM HONG

National Government of Cambodia
KHIEU SAMPHAN (Khmer Rouge)
SON SEN (Khmer Rouge)
SON SANN (KPNLF)
IENG MULI (KPNLF)
Prince NORODOM RANNARIT (FUNCINPEC)
CHAU SEN KOSAL (FUNCINPEC)

Legislature

NATIONAL ASSEMBLY

Members of the Assembly serve a five-year term. A general election was held on 1 May 1981, the 117 seats being contested by 148 candidates. In February 1986 it was decided to prolong the Assembly's first term for another five years. In June 1987 supplementary elections took place in six provinces, increasing the number of members in the Assembly to 123. In April 1989 Hun Sen, the Chairman of the Council of Ministers, announced that a general election would be held in November 1989, following the withdrawal of Vietnamese troops in September of that year. The election was postponed, however, owing to increased military activity, which occurred as a result of the failure of all sides to reach any conclusive political settlement.

Chairman: CHEA SIM.

Vice-Chairmen: Ven. TEP VONG, NU BENG, MAT LY.

Secretary-General: PHLEK PIROUN.

Political Organizations

Kampuchean People's Revolutionary Party (KPRP): Phnom-Penh; f. 1951 (known as the Communist Party of Kampuchea 1960–79); pro-USSR; politburo of 12 full mems and three cand. mems; Cen. Cttee of 57 full mems and 17 cand. mems; Gen. Sec. of Cen. Cttee HENG SAMRIN; Pres. of Organizing Cttee (Control Comm.) SAY PHOUTHANG; Vice-Pres MAT LY, NEY PENA.

Politburo:
Full members:
HENG SAMRIN
CHEA SIM
HUN SEN
SAY PHOUTHANG
BOU THANG
SAR KHENG
TEA BANH
CHEA SOTH
MAT LY
NEY PENA
NGUON NHEL
SAY CHHUM

Candidate members:
SIM KA
SIN SONG
POL SAROEUN

United Front for the Construction and Defence of the Kampuchean Fatherland (UFCDKF): Phnom-Penh; f. 1978 as the Kampuchean National United Front for National Salvation (KNUFNS), renamed Kampuchean United Front for National Construction and Defence (KUFNCD) in 1981, present name adopted in 1989; mass organization supporting policies of the KPRP; an 89-mem. Nat Council and a seven-mem. hon. Presidium; Chair. of Nat. Council CHEA SIM; Sec.-Gen. ROS CHHUN; Chair. of Presidium HENG SAMRIN.

The following organizations constitute the coalition Government-in-exile, the National Government of Cambodia (formed in 1982 as the Government of Democratic Kampuchea):

Khmer People's National Liberation Front (KPNLF): f. March 1979 in France and formally est. in Cambodia in October 1979; Pres. SON SANN.

Party of Democratic Kampuchea (Khmer Rouge): f. 1960, known as the Communist Party of Kampuchea until dissolved in December 1981; Pres. KHIEU SAMPHAN; Vice-Pres. SON SEN.

United National Front for an Independent, Neutral, Peaceful and Co-operative Cambodia (FUNCINPEC): Leader Prince NORODOM RANNARIT; Vice-Pres Princess MONIQUE, NHIEK TIOULONG. FUNCINPEC's main military wing is the National Army of Independent Cambodia (formerly the Armée Nationale Sihanoukiste—ANS); Supreme Commander Prince NORODOM RANNARIT. FUNCINPEC remains under the influence of its former leader; Prince NORODOM SIHANOUK.

Diplomatic Representation

EMBASSIES IN CAMBODIA

Afghanistan: Phnom-Penh; Ambassador: MOHAMMED ISMAIL MAHSHOOK.

Bulgaria: 177 blvd Tou Samouth, Phnom-Penh; tel. 23181; Ambassador: L. Y. BEHARA.

Cuba: 98 Voi 2140 Router 214, Phnom-Penh; tel. 24181; Ambassador: VIRIATO MORA IAZ.

Czechoslovakia: 102 rue Tou Samouth, Phnom-Penh; tel. 23781; Ambassador: (vacant).

Hungary: 771-773 blvd Song Ngoc Minh, Phnom-Penh; tel. 22781; Ambassador: LAJOS TAMÁS.

India: Villa No. 177, blvd Achar Mean, Phnom-Penh; Chargé d'affaires: RINZING WANGDI.

Laos: 19 rue Tito, Phnom-Penh; tel. 25182; Ambassador: PHUONSAVAT THONGSOUKKHOUN.

Mongolia: Phnom-Penh; Ambassador: GELEGIYN ADIYA.

Nicaragua: Phnom-Penh; Ambassador: OLGA AILES LÓPEZ.

Poland: 767 blvd Achar Mean, Song Ngoc Minh, Phnom-Penh; tel. 23582; Ambassador: JÓZEF KOBIALKA.

USSR: Phnom-Penh; Ambassador: YURIY MYAKOTNYKH.

Viet-Nam: blvd Achar Mean, Phnom-Penh; tel. 25482; Ambassador: NGO DIEN.

Yemen: Phnom-Penh; Ambassador: I. ABDULLA SAIDI.

Several countries, including Bangladesh, the People's Republic of China, Egypt, the Democratic People's Republic of Korea, Malaysia, Mauritania, Pakistan, Senegal, Sierra Leone, Thailand and Yugoslavia, have accredited ambassadors to the National Government of Cambodia (formerly Democratic Kampuchea).

Judicial System

The judicial system comprises People's Courts and Military Tribunals. People's Assessors participate in judgment, and have the same rights as judges. The establishment of a Supreme People's Court and Supreme Public Prosecutor's Department was provided for in a law approved by the National Assembly in 1985.

President, Supreme People's Court: KHANG SARIN.

Religion

BUDDHISM

The principal religion of Cambodia is Theravada Buddhism (Buddhism of the 'Tradition of the Elders'), the sacred language of which is Pali. Before a ban imposed on all religious activity in 1975, there were more than 2,500 monasteries and nearly 20,000 Bonzes (Buddhist priests); in 1986 there were about 6,000 Bonzes. By a constitutional amendment, which was adopted in April 1989, Buddhism was reinstated as the national religion.

Patriotic Kampuchean Buddhists' Association: Phnom-Penh; mem. of UFCDKF; Pres. LONG SIM.

CHRISTIANITY

The Roman Catholic Church

Cambodia comprises the Apostolic Vicariate of Phnom-Penh and the Apostolic Prefectures of Battambang and Kompong-Cham. In 1974 there were an estimated 14,000 adherents in the country. An Episcopal Conference of Laos and Kampuchea was established in 1971. In 1975 the Government of Democratic Kampuchea banned all religious practice in Cambodia, and the right of Christians to meet to worship was not restored until 1990.

Vicar Apostolic of Phnom-Penh: (vacant), Evêché, 69 blvd Prachea Thippatei, Phnom-Penh; tel. 24904.

ISLAM

Islam is practised by a minority in Cambodia. Islamic worship was also banned in 1975, but it was legalized in 1979, following the defeat of the Democratic Kampuchean regime.

The Press

Although the KPRP has actively encouraged the news media, there was still no daily newspaper in 1990. The difficulties of newspaper distribution pose a major problem.

NEWSPAPERS

Kampuchea: 158 Tou Samouth, Phnom-Penh; tel. 25559; f. 1979; weekly; Chief Editor KEO PRASAT; circ. 55,000.

Kaset Kangtoap Padivoat (Kampuchean Revolutionary Army): Phnom-Penh; f. 1979; army newspaper; Editor ROS SOVAN.

Moha Samakki Kraom Tong Ranakse (Great Solidarity Under the Front Banner): Phnom-Penh.

Pracheachon (The People): 101 blvd Tou Samouth, Phnom-Penh; f. 1985; 2 a week; organ of the KPRP; Editor-in-Chief SOM KIMSUOR; circ. 50,000.

NEWS AGENCIES

Saporamean Kampuchea (SPK) (Kampuchea Information Agency): f. 1978; controlled by the UFCDKF; Dir-Gen. EM SAM AN.

Foreign Bureau

Telegrafnoye Agentstvo Sovetskovo Soyuza (TASS) (USSR): 755 Song Ngoc Minh, Phnom-Penh; tel. 25859; Correspondent ALEKSANDR SMELYAKOV.

ASSOCIATION

Association of Kampuchean Journalists: 101 blvd Tou Samouth, Phnom-Penh; tel. 25459; f. 1979; mem. of UFCDKF; Pres. SOM KIMSUOR; Vice-Pres KHIEU KANHARITH, EM SAM AN, VANN SENG LY.

Radio and Television

There were an estimated 58,000 television receivers and 815,000 radio receivers in use in 1987.

RADIO

Samleng Pracheachon Kampuchea (Voice of the Kampuchean People): 28 ave Sandech Choun Nath, Phnom-Penh; f. 1978; controlled by the UFCDKF; home service in Khmer; daily external services in English, French, Lao, Vietnamese and Thai; Dir-Gen. KIM YIN; Dep. Dir-Gen. VANN SENG LY.

In January 1984 the Sihanoukists and the KPNLF announced the establishment of a joint radio station, Samleng Khmer (Voice of the Khmers), broadcasting three times a day in Khmer.

TELEVISION

The main television station was established with assistance from the Vietnamese. In December 1988 there were two hours of broadcasts per night in the Phnom-Penh area; colour transmissions began in July 1988. A satellite ground station, built at Phnom-Penh with Soviet assistance, enabled the reception of Soviet television programmes from November 1988.

Democratic Kampuchean Television (TVK): 19 rue 242, Donpenh, Phnom-Penh; tel. 22349; opened 1984; controlled by the UFCDKF; broadcasts for 2 hours per day in Khmer; Chair. KIM YIN; Dep. Chair. VANN SUN HENG.

Finance

BANKING

The former Government of Pol Pot abolished banks and withdrew all currency from circulation. The regime installed in January 1979 established a new national bank. In March 1980 currency was reintroduced and the National Bank of Kampuchea (now National Bank of Cambodia) announced the establishment of a Foreign Trade Bank to expand trade, to provide international loans and to assist in foreign exchange control.

National Bank of Cambodia: 26 Song Ngoc Minh, Phnom-Penh; f. 1980; Chair. CHA RIENG.

Trade and Industry

All means of production were nationalized after 1975. By 1988 a total of 69 state factories had resumed activities. In 1986 there were 182,000 industrial workers, of whom only 4% were skilled. In 1986 private enterprise was legitimized by a constitutional amendment.

TRADE ORGANIZATIONS

KAMPEXIM: Phnom-Penh; f. 1979; handles Cambodia's imports and exports and the receipt of foreign aid.

National Trade Commission: Pres. (vacant).

TRADE UNIONS

A directive issued by the KPRP Central Committee in 1983 provided for the establishment of Marxist-Leninist trade unions on central, regional and local levels. By late 1985, 102,259 workers belonged to trade unions.

Kampuchean Federation of Trade Unions (KFTU): Phnom-Penh; f. 1979; affiliated to WFTU; Chair. MEN SAM-AN; Vice-Chair. LAY SAMON.

Transport

Much of Cambodia's transport and communications system was destroyed or disrupted during the period 1970–78.

RAILWAYS

Chemins de Fer du Cambodge: Moha Vithei Pracheathippatay, Phnom-Penh; tel. 25156; prior to April 1975 the total length of railway track was 1,370 km; lines linked Phnom-Penh with the Thai border, via Battambang, and with Kompong-Som; a new line between Samrong Station and Kompong Speu was constructed in 1978; by November 1979 the 260-km Phnom-Penh–Kompong-Som line, and by February 1980 the Phnom-Penh–Battambang line, had been restored. Discussions took place in June 1989 concerning the proposed reopening of the rail link between Poipet and Thailand's Aranyaprathet province. In 1988 a total of 900,000 passengers and 200,000 tons of freight were transported.

ROADS

In 1981 there were 13,351 km of motorable roads and tracks, of which 2,670 km were asphalted. In 1981 a newly-repaired section of the National Highway One, which runs from the Vietnamese border to Phnom-Penh, was formally opened.

INLAND WATERWAYS

The major routes are along the Mekong river, and up the Tonlé Sap river into the Tonlé Sap (Great Lake), covering in all about 1,400 km. The inland ports of Neak Luong, Kompong Cham and Prek Kdam have been supplied with motor ferries and the ferry crossings have been improved.

SHIPPING

The main port is Kompong-Som, on the Gulf of Thailand, which can handle vessels up to 10,000 tons; the total number of berths was raised to 10 in 1970. In 1984 the port was reportedly enlarged by the addition of another berth. Phnom-Penh port lies some distance inland. Steamers of up to 4,000 tons can be accommodated. In early 1985 a new river port, at Kratié, was commissioned to transport goods to Phnom-Penh and north-east Cambodia.

CIVIL AVIATION

There is an international airport at Pochentong, near Phnom-Penh.

Air Kampuchea: Phnom-Penh; f. 1982; operates routes from Phnom-Penh to Moscow, Ho Chi Minh City (Viet-Nam) and Vientiane (Laos), and flies charter tours to Angkor Wat: fleet of 1 Antonov-24.

Tourism

A limited number of tourists are permitted to take part in official tours, visiting the Angkor Wat temples, in north-western Cambodia, and the Toul Sleng Museum of Genocide. A state directorate for tourism was established in 1988. Tourist arrivals reached nearly 2,000 in 1989.

General Directorate for Tourism: Phnom-Penh; f. 1988; Dir CHEAM YIEP.

CAMEROON

Introductory Survey

Location, Climate, Language, Religion, Flag, Capital

The Republic of Cameroon lies on the west coast of Africa, with Nigeria to the west, Chad and the Central African Republic to the east, and the Congo, Equatorial Guinea and Gabon to the south. The climate is hot and humid in the south and west, with average temperatures of 26°C (80°F). The north is drier, with more extreme temperatures. The official languages are French and English, and many local languages are also spoken. Approximately 39% of Cameroonians follow traditional religious beliefs. About 40% are Christians, and about 21%, mostly in the north, are Muslims. The national flag (proportions 3 by 2) has three equal vertical stripes, of green, red and yellow, with a five-pointed gold star in the centre of the red stripe. The capital is Yaoundé.

Recent History

In 1884 a German protectorate was established in Cameroon (Kamerun). In 1916, during the First World War, the German administration was overthrown by invading British and French forces. Under an agreement made between the occupying powers in 1919, Cameroon was divided into two zones: a French-ruled area, in the east and south, and a smaller British-administered area in the west. In 1922 both zones became subject to mandates of the League of Nations, with France and the United Kingdom as the administering powers. In 1946 the zones were transformed into UN Trust Territories, with British and French rule continuing in their respective areas.

French Cameroons became an autonomous state, within the French Community, in 1957. Under the leadership of Ahmadou Ahidjo, a northerner who became Prime Minister in 1958, the territory became independent, as the Republic of Cameroon, on 1 January 1960. The first election for the country's National Assembly, held in April 1960, was won by Ahidjo's party, the Union camerounaise. In May the new Assembly elected Ahidjo to be the country's first President.

British Cameroons, comprising a northern and a southern region, was attached to neighbouring Nigeria, for administrative purposes, prior to Nigeria's independence in October 1960. Plebiscites were held, under UN auspices, in the two regions of British Cameroons in February 1961. The northern area voted to merge with Nigeria (becoming the province of Sardauna), while the south voted for union with the Republic of Cameroon, which took place on 1 October 1961.

The enlarged country was named the Federal Republic of Cameroon, with French and English as joint official languages. It comprised two states: the former French zone became East Cameroon, while the ex-British portion became West Cameroon. John Ngu Foncha, Prime Minister of West Cameroon and leader of the Kamerun National Democratic Party, became Vice-President of the Federal Republic. Under the continuing leadership of Ahidjo, who was re-elected President in May 1965, the two states became increasingly integrated, despite Cameroon's ethnic and cultural diversity. In September 1966 a one-party regime was established when the two governing parties and several opposition groups combined to form a single party, the Union nationale camerounaise (UNC). The party expanded to embrace almost all the country's political, cultural, professional and social organizations. The only significant opposition party, the extreme left-wing Union des populations camerounaises (UPC), was finally crushed in 1971, although the leaders continued activities in exile in Paris. Meanwhile, President Ahidjo was re-elected in March 1970, when Solomon Muna (who had replaced Foncha as Prime Minister of West Cameroon in 1968) became Vice-President.

In June 1972, after approval by referendum of a new constitution, the federal system was ended and the country became the United Republic of Cameroon. The office of Vice-President was abolished. A fully centralized political and administrative system was rapidly introduced, and in May 1973 a new National Assembly was elected for a five-year term. After the re-election of Ahidjo as President in April 1975, the Constitution was revised, and a Prime Minister, Paul Biya (a bilingual Christian southerner), was appointed in June. Despite opposition from anglophone intellectuals who desired a return to the federal system of government, Ahidjo was unanimously re-elected for a fifth five-year term of office in April 1980.

President Ahidjo announced his resignation in November 1982 and named Paul Biya, the Prime Minister, as his successor. No official reasons for the resignation were given. Bello Bouba Maigari, a northerner, was appointed Prime Minister. Ahidjo retained the presidency of the UNC and his political influence continued. In cabinet reshuffles in April and June 1983, Biya introduced more technocrats into the Government and gradually removed supporters of the former President. On 22 August 1983 Biya announced the discovery of a plot to overthrow his Government, and simultaneously dismissed the Prime Minister and the Minister of the Armed Forces, both northern Muslims. On 27 August former President Ahidjo resigned as President of the UNC and strongly criticized the regime of President Biya. In September Biya was elected President of the ruling party, and in January 1984 he was re-elected as President of the Republic, reportedly gaining 99.98% of the votes cast. In a subsequent cabinet reshuffle, the post of Prime Minister was abolished, and it was announced that the country's name was to revert from the United Republic of Cameroon to the Republic of Cameroon.

In February 1984 Ahidjo (who remained in exile in France and Senegal until his death in November 1989) and two of his close military advisers were tried for their alleged complicity in the coup plot of August 1983. All three men received death sentences which were, however, commuted to life imprisonment two weeks later. On 6 April 1984 rebel elements in the presidential guard, led by Col Saleh Ibrahim, a northerner, attempted to seize power and overthrow the Biya Government. After three days of heavy fighting, in which hundreds were reported to have been killed, the rebellion was crushed by forces loyal to the President. Trials of those implicated in the coup were held in May and November 1984, with a total of 51 defendants receiving death sentences. It was reported, following the May trials, that 46 executions had been carried out within hours of the announcement of the verdict. Following extensive changes within the military hierarchy, the UNC central committee and the leadership of state-controlled companies, in which supporters of the former President were dismissed, Biya reshuffled his Government in July and introduced more stringent press censorship.

At the party congress in March 1985, the UNC was renamed the Rassemblement démocratique du peuple camerounais (RDPC). In August 10 ministers were replaced as part of an extensive reorganization of the Cabinet. In January 1986 members of the exiled UPC movement claimed that between 200 and 300 opponents of the Biya Government (most of whom were anglophones or members of clandestine opposition movements) had been arrested in the preceding months, and that some of those in detention were being subjected to torture. A number of detainees were subsequently released.

Comprehensive changes in the internal structure of the RDPC occurred as a result of elections held between January and March 1986, with more than one-half of the party's 49 section presidents being replaced. Many of the posts were contested by more than one candidate. In November 1986, following a reorganization of the President's office, Biya again carried out a reshuffle of the Cabinet, appointing a total of four new ministers.

In January 1987 the Minister of Foreign Affairs, William Eteki Mboumoua, was abruptly dismissed from his post after having signed an agreement to restore diplomatic relations with Hungary, supposedly without the President's knowledge. Several journalists, including the two principal officials of the government-owned daily newspaper, were detained during early 1987 for the alleged publication of secret or politically sensitive material. The composition of the staff at the state-owned publishing concerns subsequently underwent extensive changes. In July the National Assembly approved a new electoral code providing for multiple candidacy in public elections, and in October voters in more than 40% of communes had a choice of RDPC-approved candidates in elections for seats on the 196 municipal councils.

Popular opposition to the austerity measures that the Government introduced in June 1987 became evident in December, when about 300 students were arrested, following a riot at the University of Yaoundé in protest at delays in the payment of grants. Unconfirmed sources also reported that a coup attempt, led by the Commander-in-Chief of the Air Force, Gen. Nganso, had taken place in the same month.

Ostensibly for reasons of economy, the presidential election, originally scheduled for January 1989, was brought forward to coincide with elections to the National Assembly, in April 1988. (Constitutional amendments, enabling the Head of State to call a presidential election before the end of his term of office, as well as increasing the number of seats in the National Assembly from 150 to 180, had been approved by the legislature in March.) President Biya was re-elected unopposed, securing 98.75% of the votes cast. Reflecting the fact that the electorate had, for the first time in a legislative election, been presented with a choice of RDPC-approved candidates, 153 of those elected to the National Assembly were new members. In May Biya announced a cabinet reshuffle and a streamlining of administrative structures. Several ministries were merged or abolished, and the posts of Secretary-General of the Government and Director of the Presidential Cabinet were replaced by a single Secretary-General at the Presidency. A campaign against corruption led to the arrest of more than 100 ministerial officials and executives of the country's state-owned industries, in connection with the misappropriation of public funds.

In spite of the electoral successes of Biya and the RDPC, the formation, in February 1989, of a special police unit to combat terrorism and organized crime, and the subsequent appointment of three reputedly authoritarian generals to prominent security posts, indicated that the Government would continue to repress dissent. In August the human rights organization, Amnesty International, expressed concern about living conditions in prisons in Yaoundé and Douala, and in March 1990 the same organization appealed for an inquiry into the deaths (allegedly from torture), in December 1989, of two prisoners who had been held in detention since April 1984. In early 1989 lawyers staged strikes, in protest at what they perceived to be the erosion of the rule of law in Cameroon.

A further reallocation of ministerial portfolios, in April 1989, reflected the Government's efforts to secure financial support from external creditors for its economic adjustment efforts. A prominent banker, Edouard Akame Mfoumou, was designated Secretary-General at the Presidency, while an additional Secretary of State for Finance was appointed. In June Biya eased restrictions on the disclosure, by government offices, of 'non-confidential' information to the media.

In February 1990, 11 people, including the former President of the Cameroonian Bar Association, Yondo Black, were arrested, as a result of their alleged involvement in an unofficial opposition organization, the Social Democratic Front (SDF). In April Yondo Black was sentenced to three years' imprisonment on charges of 'subversion'. Later in the same month, however, President Biya announced that all the prisoners who had been detained in connection with the 1984 coup attempt were to be released. In May a demonstration organized by the SDF was violently suppressed by security forces, and six deaths were subsequently reported. In the same month the Government suspended the publication of an independent newspaper, the *Cameroon Post*, which had implied support for the SDF.

In late June 1990 the congress of the RDPC re-elected Biya as President of the party and implemented a major reorganization of the central committee. During the meeting of the congress Biya stated that he envisaged the future adoption of a multi-party system, and announced a series of reforms, including the abolition of laws governing subversion, the revision of the law on political associations, and the reinforcement of press freedom. In the same month a committee for the revision of legislation on the rights of the individual was established. In August the release of several political prisoners, including Yondo Black, represented a further move towards political liberalization.

In early September Biya announced an extensive cabinet reshuffle, in which a new ministry to implement the Government's economic stabilization programme was created. In the same month the Vice-President of the RDPC, John Ngu Foncha, resigned in protest at alleged corruption and human rights violations on the part of the Government. In late November draft legislation, which provided for the establishment of a multi-party system, was proposed and later approved by the National Assembly. On 5 December Cameroon officially became a multi-party state. Under the new legislation the Government was required to provide an official response within three months to any political organization seeking legal recognition. However, the recruitment of party activists on an ethnic or regional basis, and the finance of political parties from external sources, remained illegal.

In July 1973 President Ahidjo announced his country's impending withdrawal from the Organisation commune africaine, malgache et mauricienne (OCAM), a grouping of mainly French-speaking African states, then based in Yaoundé. Cameroon also negotiated a revision of its co-operation agreements with France in 1974. The independent foreign policy that was pursued under President Ahidjo has been continued by his successor. In August 1986 Cameroon was forced to appeal for international emergency aid when an explosion of underwater volcanic gases at Lake Nyos, in the north-west of the country, led to an estimated 1,700 deaths and caused widespread suffering. The disaster coincided with a much-publicized visit to Cameroon by Shimon Peres, the Prime Minister of Israel, during which the two countries renewed diplomatic links, following a 13-year suspension of relations as a result of the Arab–Israeli war in 1973. Relations with France have generally remained close, although Cameroon has sought to resist overdependence: France currently accounts for more than one-third of the country's foreign trade transactions. The close relationship between the two countries was confirmed in 1988, when President Biya made a state visit to France in order to discuss economic co-operation. In recent years, however, Cameroon has become increasingly anxious to attract investment from other countries, notably the Federal Republic of Germany, whose Chancellor, Dr Helmut Kohl, visited the country in 1987. Relations with Nigeria, which had come under some strain as a result of a series of border disputes, showed signs of improvement following a state visit by President Babangida of that country in late 1987, when it was announced that joint border controls were to be established. In 1989 President Biya held negotiations with the Heads of State of the Congo and Gabon, as a result of which the three countries issued joint appeals, to their external creditors, for the formulation of a programme of debt relief. In July 1990 Biya met the French President, François Mitterrand, in Paris to discuss bilateral economic co-operation. In the same month Cameroon established diplomatic relations with Namibia.

Government

Under the amended 1972 Constitution, executive power is vested in the President, as Head of State, while legislative power is held by the unicameral National Assembly. Both the President and the Assembly are elected for five years by universal adult suffrage. In 1988 the number of deputies to the National Assembly was increased, from 150 to 180, to take account of the increase in population. The Cabinet is appointed by the President. In May 1988 the Secretariat-General of the Government and Cabinet of the President were merged to form a single Secretariat-General at the Presidency. Local administration is based on 10 provinces, each with a Governor who is appointed by the President.

Defence

In June 1990 Cameroon had an army of 6,600 and there were 4,000 men in paramilitary forces. The navy numbered 700 and the air force had 300 men. France has a bilateral defence agreement with Cameroon. The defence budget for 1989/90 was 52,000m. francs CFA (8.7% of total projected expenditure).

Economic Affairs

In 1988, according to estimates by the World Bank, Cameroon's gross national product (GNP), measured at average 1986–88 prices, was US $11,270m., equivalent to $1,010 per head. During 1980–88, it was estimated, GNP increased, in real terms, at an average annual rate of 6.4%, and GNP per head by 3.0%. Over the same period, the population increased by an annual average of 3.2%. Cameroon's gross domestic product (GDP) increased, in real terms, by an annual average of 5.4% in 1980–88.

Agriculture (including forestry and fishing) contributed 26% of GDP in 1988. About 62.0% of the labour force were employed in agriculture in 1989. The principal cash crops are coffee

CAMEROON

(which accounted for 21.5% of export earnings in 1986), cocoa and cotton. The principal subsistence crops are roots and tubers, plantains and millet and sorghum. About one-half of the country is covered by forest, but an inadequate transport infrastructure has impeded the development of the forestry sector. Livestock-rearing makes a significant contribution to the food supply. During 1980–88 agricultural production increased by an annual average of 2.4%.

Industry (including mining, manufacturing, construction and power) employed 6.7% of the working population in 1985, and contributed 30% of GDP in 1988. During 1980–88 industrial production increased by an annual average of 7.8%.

Mining contributed 12.4% of GDP in 1987, but employed only 0.05% of Cameroon's working population in 1985. Receipts from the exploitation of petroleum reserves constitute a principal source of government revenue. Deposits of limestone are also quarried. Significant reserves of natural gas, bauxite, iron ore, uranium and tin remain undeveloped.

Manufacturing contributed 13% of GDP in 1988, and employed 4.7% of the working population in 1985. The sector is based on the processing of both indigenous primary products (petroleum-refining, agro-industrial activities) and of imported raw materials (an aluminium-smelter uses alumina imported from Guinea). Manufacturing output increased by an average of 6.2% per year in 1980–88.

In the late 1980s about 95% of Cameroon's energy was derived from hydroelectric power installations. Imports of fuel products accounted for only 1% of the value of total imports in 1987.

In 1987 Cameroon recorded a visible trade surplus of US $254m. In the same year, however, there was a deficit of $893m. on the current account of the balance of payments. In 1986 the principal source of imports (42.2%) was France, while the principal market for exports (27.5%) was the Netherlands. Other major trading partners are Germany, Japan, Italy and the USA. The principal exports in 1986 were crude petroleum (which accounted for 35.6% of total export earnings), coffee and cocoa. The principal imports were road transport equipment, electrical, telegraphic and telephone appliances and machinery and iron and steel.

In the financial year ending June 1989 there was a budget deficit of about 70,000m. francs CFA (equivalent to some 2.5% of GDP). Cameroon's total external public debt was US $2,939m. at the end of 1988. In that year the cost of debt-servicing was equivalent to 11.9% of revenue from exports of goods and services. The annual rate of inflation averaged 7.0% in 1980–88. An estimated 5.8% of the labour force were unemployed in mid-1985.

Cameroon is a member of the Central African organs of the Franc Zone (see p. 156) and of the Communauté économique des Etats de l'Afrique centrale (CEEAC, see p. 223).

The decline, beginning in the mid-1980s, of international prices for Cameroon's major export commodities, in conjunction with the cost of maintaining a cumbersome bureaucracy, has undermined the country's hitherto buoyant economy. Funding agreements have been concluded with the IMF and the World Bank. Under the terms of the latter arrangement (which was announced in June 1989), the Biya Government undertook to reduce the dependence of the economy on the petroleum sector, to restructure the ailing banking system, and to rehabilitate, transfer to private ownership or liquidate unprofitable state-owned enterprises. The official prices payable to producers of coffee, cocoa and cotton were subsequently reduced, in an attempt to stimulate international demand for these commodities.

Social Welfare

The Government and Christian missions maintain hospitals and medical centres. In 1986 Cameroon had 26,872 hospital beds in 251 hospitals and health centres and 1,534 dispensaries. There were 790 physicians working in the country. The 1989/90 budget allocated 26,000m. francs CFA to public health (4.3% of total projected expenditure). A campaign aiming at 'Health for all by the year 2000' is being undertaken, with the emphasis on the development of preventive medicine. The 1986–91 Plan envisaged the development of a system of social security suitable to the country's needs.

Education

Since independence, Cameroon has achieved one of the highest rates of school attendance in Africa, but provision of educational facilities varies according to region. Education is provided by the Government, missionary societies and private concerns. Education in state schools is available free of charge, and the Government provides financial assistance for other schools. Bilingual teaching was introduced for the first time in primary schools in 1972, and school curricula were standardized in 1977.

Primary education begins at six years of age. It lasts for six years in Eastern Cameroon (where it is officially compulsory), and for seven years in Western Cameroon. Secondary education, beginning at the age of 12 or 13, lasts for a further seven years. In 1986 the total enrolment at primary and secondary schools was equivalent to 70% of the school-age population (77% of boys; 62% of girls): attendance at schools in the northern region, which had been as low as 32% in 1981, was estimated at 55% in 1986. In 1985, according to estimates by UNESCO, the average rate of adult illiteracy was 43.8% (males 31.6%; females 55.3%). The State University at Yaoundé, founded in 1962, has been decentralized, and consists of five regional campuses, each being devoted to a different field of study. Budgets in recent years have given high priority to education, with an allocation of 67,000m. francs CFA (11.2% of total projected expenditure) in 1989/90.

Public Holidays

1991: 1 January (New Year), 11 February (Youth Day), 29 March (Good Friday), 1 April (Easter Monday), 16 April* (Djoulde Soumae, end of Ramadan), 1 May (Labour Day), 9 May (Ascension Day), 20 May (National Day), 23 June* (Festival of Sheep), 10 December (Reunification Day), 25 December (Christmas).

1992: 1 January (New Year), 11 February (Youth Day), 4 April* (Djoulde Soumae, end of Ramadan), 17 April (Good Friday), 20 April (Easter Monday), 1 May (Labour Day), 20 May (National Day), 28 May (Ascension Day), 11 June* (Festival of Sheep), 10 December (Reunification Day), 25 December (Christmas).

* These holidays are dependent on the Islamic lunar calendar and may vary by one or two days from the dates given.

Weights and Measures

The metric system is in force.

CAMEROON   Statistical Survey

Statistical Survey

Source (unless otherwise stated): Direction de la Statistique et de la Comptabilité Nationale,
BP 25, Yaoundé; tel. 22-07-88; telex 8203.

Area and Population

AREA, POPULATION AND DENSITY

Area (sq km)	475,442*
Population (census of 9 April 1976)†	
Males	3,754,991
Females	3,908,255
Total	7,663,246
Population (official estimates at mid-year)	
1986	10,460,000
1987	10,821,746
1989‡	11,540,000
Density (per sq km) at mid-1989	24.3

* 183,569 sq miles.
† Including an adjustment for underenumeration, estimated at 7.4%. The enumerated total was 7,090,115 (males 3,472,786; females 3,617,329).
‡ Figure for 1988 is not available.

PROVINCES (population at 1976 census)

	Urban	Rural	Total
Centre-South	498,290	993,655	1,491,945
Littoral	702,578	232,588	935,166
West	232,315	803,282	1,035,597
South-West	200,322	420,193	620,515
North-West	146,327	834,204	980,531
North	328,925	1,904,332	2,233,257
East	75,458	290,750	366,235
Total	2,184,242	5,479,004	7,663,246

Note: In August 1983 the number of provinces was increased to 10. Centre-South province became two separate provinces, Centre and South. The northern province was split into three: Far North, North and Adamoua.

PRINCIPAL TOWNS

1976 (population at census): Douala 458,426, Yaoundé (capital) 313,706, Nkongsamba 71,298, Maroua 67,187, Garoua 63,900, Bafoussam 62,239, Bamenda 48,111, Kumba 44,175, Limbe (formerly Victoria) 27,016.
Mid-1986 (estimated population): Douala 1,029,731, Yaoundé 653,670, Nkongsamba (and environs) 123,149, Maroua (and environs) 103,653.

BIRTHS AND DEATHS (UN estimates, annual averages)

	1975-80	1980-85	1985-90
Birth rate (per 1,000)	46.3	44.3	41.6
Death rate (per 1,000)	18.9	17.3	15.6

Source: UN, *World Population Prospects: 1988.*

ECONOMICALLY ACTIVE POPULATION
(official estimates, persons aged six years and over, mid-1985)

	Males	Females	Total
Agriculture, hunting, forestry and fishing	1,574,946	1,325,925	2,900,871
Mining and quarrying	1,693	100	1,793
Manufacturing	137,671	36,827	174,498
Electricity, gas and water	3,373	149	3,522
Construction	65,666	1,018	66,684
Trade, restaurants and hotels	115,269	38,745	154,014
Transport, storage and communications	50,664	1,024	51,688
Financing, insurance, real estate and business services	7,447	562	8,009
Community, social and personal services	255,076	37,846	292,922
Activities not adequately defined	18,515	17,444	35,959
Total in employment	2,230,320	1,459,640	3,689,960
Unemployed	180,016	47,659	227,675
Total labour force	2,410,336	1,507,299	3,917,635

Source: International Labour Office, *Year Book of Labour Statistics.*

Mid-1988 (estimates in '000): Agriculture, etc. 2,637; Total 4,190 (Source: FAO, *Production Yearbook*).

Agriculture

PRINCIPAL CROPS ('000 metric tons)

	1987	1988	1989
Rice (paddy)*	70	85	90
Maize*	410	420	430
Millet and sorghum*	300	310	340
Potatoes*	172	174	180
Sweet potatoes*	150	152	154
Cassava (Manioc)*	1,500	1,500	1,530
Yams*	230	230	230
Other roots and tubers*	330	330	330
Dry beans*	114	115	117
Groundnuts (in shell)†	140	145	140
Sesame seed*	13	14	14
Cottonseed	62*	62†	63†
Cotton lint†	45	50	56
Palm kernels	21	27	30
Sugar cane*	1,260	1,280	1,300
Vegetables*	434	439	445
Avocados*	32	33	34
Pineapples*	34	34	34
Bananas*	68	68	68
Plantains*	1,000	1,100	1,150
Coffee (green)	96	138	80*
Cocoa beans	131	124†	120†
Tobacco (leaves)†	3	2	2
Natural rubber	26	33	34†

* FAO estimate(s).   † Unofficial estimate(s).
Source: FAO, *Production Yearbook.*

CAMEROON

LIVESTOCK ('000 head, year ending September)

	1987	1988	1989
Cattle	4,362	4,471	4,582
Pigs	1,178	1,237	1,299
Sheep	2,597	2,897	3,170
Goats	2,679	2,906	3,213

Poultry (million): 14 in 1987; 16 in 1988; 16 (FAO estimate) in 1989
Source: FAO, *Production Yearbook*.

LIVESTOCK PRODUCTS (FAO estimates, '000 metric tons)

	1987	1988	1989
Beef and veal	72	74	76
Mutton and lamb	11	12	13
Goats' meat	9	10	11
Pigmeat	14	15	16
Poultry meat	11	13	13
Other meat	8	6	4
Cows' milk	48	49	49
Hen eggs	10.8	11.2	11.6
Cattle hides	9.6	9.8	10.1
Sheepskins	1.8	2.0	2.2
Goatskins	0.9	1.0	1.1

Source: FAO, *Production Yearbook*.

Forestry

ROUNDWOOD REMOVALS ('000 cubic metres)

	1986	1987	1988
Sawlogs, veneer logs and logs for sleepers	2,088	2,091	1,969
Other industrial wood*	683	701	720
Fuel wood*	9,378	9,630	9,885
Total	12,149	12,422	12,574

* FAO estimates.
Source: FAO, *Yearbook of Forest Products*.

SAWNWOOD PRODUCTION ('000 cubic metres)

	1986	1987	1988
Total (incl. boxboards)	565*	565*	568

* FAO estimates.
Railway sleepers (FAO estimates, '000 cubic metres): 85 in 1986; 85 in 1987; 85 in 1988.
Source: FAO, *Yearbook of Forest Products*.

Fishing

('000 metric tons, live weight)

	1985	1986	1987
Freshwater fishes	20.0	20.0	20.0
Bigeye grunt	3.6	2.7	3.3
Croakers and drums	5.2	4.8	4.0
Threadfins and tasselfishes	4.0	3.5	1.7
Sardinellas	18.0	18.0	18.0
Bonga shad	18.0	18.0	18.0
Other marine fishes (incl. unspecified)	4.4	4.1	4.7
Total fish	73.3	71.1	69.7
Crustaceans and molluscs	12.7	12.9	12.8
Total catch	86.0	84.0	82.5

1988: Catch as in 1987 (FAO estimates).
Source: FAO, *Yearbook of Fishery Statistics*.

Mining

('000 metric tons, unless otherwise indicated)

	1985	1986	1987
Crude petroleum*	9,170	8,976	8,602
Tin (metric tons)†	24*	0	0
Limestone flux and calcareous stone	97	78	80*

* Provisional or estimated figure(s).
† Estimated metal content of ore (Source: International Tin Council).
Source: UN, *Industrial Statistics Yearbook*.

Crude petroleum ('000 metric tons): 8,690 in 1988 (Source: UN, *Monthly Bulletin of Statistics*).

Industry

SELECTED PRODUCTS
('000 metric tons, unless otherwise indicated)

	1985	1986	1987
Palm oil (crude)	66	85*	98*
Raw sugar*	74	75	70
Cocoa butter (exports)	3.5	5.2	7.5
Beer ('000 hectolitres)	4,904	5,615	5,622
Soft drinks ('000 hectolitres)	1,397	1,613	1,808
Cigarettes (million)	2,128	3,800*	1,202
Soap	26.1	28.4	39.1
Jet fuels	95	97	95
Motor spirit (petrol)	415	410	401
Kerosene	310	313	295
Distillate fuel oils	450	455	435
Residual fuel oils	593	650	610
Lubricating oils	115	113	110
Cement	785	779	707
Aluminium (unwrought)†	81.8	51.0	79.0
Radio receivers ('000)	16	n.a.	n.a.
Footwear ('000 pairs)	3,964	2,415	1,725
Electric energy (million kWh)	2,413	2,385	2,392

* Provisional or estimated figure(s).
† Using alumina imported from Guinea.
Source: UN, *Industrial Statistics Yearbook*.

CAMEROON

Statistical Survey

Finance

CURRENCY AND EXCHANGE RATES

Monetary Units
100 centimes = 1 franc de la Coopération financière en Afrique central (CFA).

Denominations
Coins: 1, 2, 5, 10, 25, 50, 100 and 500 francs CFA.
Notes: 100, 500, 1,000, 5,000 and 10,000 francs CFA.

French Franc, Sterling and Dollar Equivalents (30 September 1990)
1 French franc = 50 francs CFA;
£1 sterling = 491.1 francs CFA;
US $1 = 262.1 francs CFA;
1,000 francs CFA = £2.036 = $3.815.

Average Exchange Rate (francs CFA per US $)
1987   300.54
1988   297.85
1989   319.01

BUDGET ESTIMATES (million francs CFA, year ending 30 June)

Revenue	1987/88	1988/89	1989/90
Fiscal receipts	435,000	401,500	388,630
Indirect taxes	203,000	191,600	198,500
Registration and stamp duty	30,000	35,700	29,000
Customs and miscellaneous duties	202,000	174,200	161,130
Non-fiscal receipts	215,000	198,500	211,370
Property income	2,000	2,300	
Miscellaneous products and services	49,000	23,660	27,570
Petroleum royalties	150,000	150,000	150,000
Other non-fiscal receipts	14,000	22,540	33,800
Total revenue	650,000	600,000	600,000

Expenditure	1987/88	1988/89	1989/90
Current budget	400,000	375,000	425,000
Internal debt	12,000	12,000	12,000
Public authorities	320,200	300,190	342,230
Territorial administration	18,800	19,810	24,270
State intervention	49,000	43,000	46,500
Investment budget	250,000	225,000	175,000
Development expenditure	100,000	55,000	55,000
Investment-related debt	150,000	170,000	97,000
Counterpart funds	—	—	23,000
Total expenditure	650,000	600,000	600,000

Source: *La Zone Franc—Rapport 1989*.

CENTRAL BANK RESERVES (US $ million at 31 December)

	1987	1988	1989
Gold*	14.45	12.17	n.a.
IMF special drawing rights	0.26	0.03	0.29
Reserve position in IMF	0.28	0.30	0.29
Foreign exchange	63.22	150.17	79.33
Total	78.21	162.67	n.a.

* Valued at market-related prices.
Source: IMF, *International Financial Statistics*.

MONEY SUPPLY ('000 million francs CFA at 31 December)

	1987	1988	1989
Currency outside banks	171.11	161.66	162.85
Demand deposits at deposit money banks	214.80	222.96	281.20
Checking deposits at post office	1.10	3.48	n.a.
Total money	387.01	388.10	n.a.

Source: IMF, *International Financial Statistics*.

COST OF LIVING (Consumer Price Index for Africans in Yaoundé. Base: 1980 = 100)

	1985	1986	1987
Food	160.4	162.4	171.7
Clothing	257.1	284.4	374.4
All items (incl. others)	180.5	194.5	220.0

Source: ILO, *Year Book of Labour Statistics*.

NATIONAL ACCOUNTS
('000 million francs CFA at current prices)

National Income and Product (year ending 30 June)

	1982/83	1983/84	1984/85
Compensation of employees	747.4	875.5	989.5
Operating surplus	1,363.7	1,737.5	2,181.7
Domestic factor incomes	2,111.1	2,613.0	3,171.2
Consumption of fixed capital	158.1	165.2	194.7
Gross domestic product (GDP) at factor cost	2,269.2	2,778.3	3,365.9
Indirect taxes	355.0	434.1	485.4
Less Subsidies	6.1	17.4	12.4
GDP in purchasers' values	2,618.0	3,195.0	3,838.9
Factor income received from abroad	11.7	14.1	23.6
Less Factor income paid abroad	71.5	76.2	121.8
Gross national product	2,558.3	3,132.9	3,740.7
Less Consumption of fixed capital	158.1	165.2	194.7
National income in market prices	2,400.2	2,967.7	3,546.0
Other current transfers received from abroad	17.4	18.3	14.5
Less Other current transfers paid abroad	22.5	23.8	13.5
National disposable income	2,395.1	2,962.2	3,547.0

Expenditure on the Gross Domestic Product

	1985	1986	1987
Government final consumption expenditure	358	457	472*
Private final consumption expenditure	2,453	2,932	3,045*
Increase in stocks	16	22	25*
Gross fixed capital formation	939	1,210	1,213
Total domestic expenditure	3,766	4,621	4,755*
Exports of goods and services	710	692	710*
Less Imports of goods and services	638	785	848*
GDP in purchasers' values	3,839	4,528	4,617*

* Provisional or estimated figure.
Source: UN Economic Commission for Africa, *African Statistical Yearbook*.

CAMEROON

Gross Domestic Product by Economic Activity

	1985	1986	1987*
Agriculture, hunting, forestry and fishing	833	1,045	1,096
Mining and quarrying	574	513	515
Manufacturing	368	494	510
Electricity, gas and water	41	52	52
Construction	213	270	275
Wholesale and retail trade, restaurants and hotels	392	483	508
Transport and communications	172	211	210
Finance, insurance, real estate and business services	443	546	554
Public administration and defence	254	317	318
Other community, social and personal services	88	109	104
Sub-total	3,378	4,040	4,142
Less Statistical adjustment	42	52	55
GDP at factor cost	3,336	3,988	4,087
Indirect taxes, *less* subsidies	503	540	530
GDP in purchasers' values	3,839	4,528	4,617

* Provisional or estimated figures.

Source: UN Economic Commission for Africa, *African Statistical Yearbook*.

BALANCE OF PAYMENTS (US $ million)

	1985	1986	1987
Merchandise exports f.o.b.	1,679.3	2,090.0	1,689.1
Merchandise imports f.o.b.	−1,163.9	−1,650.1	−1,435.2
Trade balance	515.5	440.0	254.0
Exports of services	550.4	521.7	424.0
Imports of services	−1,633.8	−1,431.6	−1,471.8
Balance on goods and services	−568.0	−470.0	−793.9
Private unrequited transfers (net)	−102.1	−124.0	−125.7
Government unrequited transfers (net)	84.1	30.4	26.6
Current balance	−586.0	−563.5	−893.0
Direct capital investment (net)	317.5	4.8	0.4
Other long-term capital (net)	153.3	89.7	429.7
Short-term capital (net)	57.1	397.0	376.1
Net errors and omissions	190.8	−26.8	88.2
Total (net monetary movements)	132.7	−98.9	1.4
Valuation changes (net)	−53.8	30.9	9.8
Exceptional financing (net)	—	0.1	—
Official financing (net)	0.6	—	—
Changes in reserves	79.5	−68.0	11.2

Source: IMF, *International Financial Statistics*.

External Trade

PRINCIPAL COMMODITIES (million francs CFA)

Imports c.i.f.	1984	1985	1986
Tyres	6,373	7,856	5,181
Textiles	21,067	18,031	20,827
Malt	8,895	6,380	15,029
Cement	6,630	9,667	5,575
Alumina	15,373	14,804	9,593
Lubricants	3,614	3,438	3,917
Medicine	4,583	22,404	24,460
Books and newspapers	4,363	9,369	10,733
Iron and steel pipes	7,781	4,011	1,470
Paper and allied products	8,894	8,436	16,612
Drilling equipment	12,372	4,180	7,472
Footwear	3,549	4,300	5,143
Iron and steel	48,077	38,217	35,210
Cutting machinery	5,205	8,204	7,404
Generating machinery	5,004	8,919	6,971
Road transport equipment	57,995	65,566	66,940
Air transport equipment	1,397	6,758	10,797
Maritime transport equipment	10,077	1,636	1,996
Electrical, telegraphic, telephone appliances and machinery	30,709	46,108	56,112
Fertilizers	7,395	10,452	8,223
Total (incl. others)	484,646	513,898	590,439

Exports f.o.b.	1984	1985	1986
Cocoa	100,397	85,473	87,223
Coffee (arabica)	32,706	26,038	28,330
Coffee (robusta)	61,049	87,206	88,281
Bananas	6,663	6,764	5,670
Rubber	6,843	5,991	4,319
Tobacco	3,702	5,256	4,429
Cotton fibre	10,272	5,360	12,326
Cotton fabrics	9,403	5,923	3,984
Palm nuts and kernels	1,284	511	161
Palm oil	591	336	1,567
Cocoa pulp	6,437	8,717	5,533
Cocoa butter	7,857	7,844	8,661
Logs	14,324	27,971	18,488
Sawnwood and sleepers	4,018	5,690	2,712
Aluminium	29,794	22,083	16,914
Aluminium products	5,637	6,975	5,184
Crude petroleum	478,864	445,680	192,709
Total (incl. others)	822,041	816,912	541,728

PRINCIPAL TRADING PARTNERS (million francs CFA)

Imports c.i.f.	1984	1985	1986
Belgium/Luxembourg	14,342	14,999	20,432
France	207,536	219,709	248,932
Germany, Federal Republic	32,245	36,378	53,800
Italy	22,086	25,279	27,939
Japan	34,449	37,606	45,041
Netherlands	8,470	11,221	15,691
Spain	12,192	13,101	14,663
UDEAC*	9,809	5,172	2,181
UMOA†	8,495	n.a.	n.a.
United Kingdom	16,828	20,296	21,710
USA	49,619	37,241	29,116
Total (incl. others)	484,646	513,898	590,439

CAMEROON

Statistical Survey

Exports f.o.b.	1984	1985	1986
Belgium/Luxembourg	36,225	23,600	12,213
France	179,889	288,229	111,857
Germany, Federal Republic	34,713	49,095	39,647
Italy	50,739	52,105	29,658
Japan	3,882	n.a.	n.a.
Netherlands	138,212	120,728	148,924
Nigeria	8,264	9,870	14,533
Spain	8,559	49,785	27,669
UDEAC*	29,808	33,568	28,221
UMOA†	2,715	n.a.	n.a.
USSR	7,000	16,166	9,313
United Kingdom	3,498	n.a.	n.a.
USA	266,917	110,543	88,772
Total (incl. others)	822,041	816,912	541,728

* Union douanière et économique de l'Afrique centrale (Customs and Economic Union of Central Africa), comprising Cameroon, the Central African Republic, Chad (since December 1984), the Congo, Equatorial Guinea (since January 1985) and Gabon.

† Union monétaire ouest-africaine (West African Monetary Union), comprising Benin, Burkina Faso, Côte d'Ivoire, Mali (since February 1984), Niger, Senegal and Togo.

Source: Chambre de Commerce, d'Industrie et des Mines, Douala.

Transport

RAILWAYS (traffic, year ending 30 June)

	1985/86	1986/87	1987/88
Passengers carried ('000)	2,079	2,267	2,413
Passenger-km (million)	412	444	469
Freight carried ('000 tons)	1,791	1,411	1,375
Freight ton-km (million)	871	675	594

Source: Ministère des Travaux Publics et des Transports, Yaoundé.

ROAD TRAFFIC (motor vehicles in use at 31 December)

	1984	1985	1986
Passenger cars	72,449	77,105	80,757
Commercial vehicles	41,301	43,510	44,875
Tractors and trailers	2,045	2,473	2,709
Motorcycles and scooters	41,579	41,807	40,961

1987: Passenger cars 98,000; Commercial vehicles 33,000; Tractors and trailers 6,000; Motorcycles and scooters 63,000 (Source: Ministère des Travaux Publics et des Transports, Yaoundé).

INTERNATIONAL SEA-BORNE SHIPPING (Douala)

	1986	1987	1988
Vessels entered	1,366	1,260	1,122
Freight loaded ('000 metric tons)	1,179	1,119	1,210
Freight unloaded ('000 metric tons)	3,189	2,715	2,558

Source: Ministère des Travaux Publics et des Transports, Yaoundé.

CIVIL AVIATION (traffic on scheduled services)

	1983	1984	1985
Kilometres flown (million)	6.1	6.0	6.3
Passengers carried ('000)	631	677	718
Passenger-km (million)	568	540	580
Freight ton-km (million)	43.5	55.5	56.9

Source: UN, *Statistical Yearbook*.

Tourism

(foreign visitors staying at least two nights)

	1986	1987	1988
Tourist arrivals	130,803	117,536	100,121

Source: Ministère du Tourisme, Yaoundé.

Communications Media

	1985	1986	1987
Radio receivers ('000 in use)	940	1,250	1,300
Television receivers ('000 in use)	n.a.	n.a.	120

Telephones (1984): 49,000 in use.
Book production (first editions only, 1979): 22 titles (94,000 copies), excluding pamphlets.
Daily newspapers (1986): 1 (average circulation 35,000 copies).
Non-daily newspapers (1984): 3 (average circulation 35,000 copies).
Source: mainly UNESCO, *Statistical Yearbook*.

Education

(1986/87)

	Institutions	Pupils	Teachers
Pre-primary	626	83,963	2,952
Primary	5,941	1,795,254	35,728
Post-primary	122	9,111	927
Secondary	388	291,842	9,017
Technical	183	90,666	3,714
Teacher training	33	4,259	411
Higher*	5	19,586	975

* 1985/86 figures.

Source: Ministère de l'Education Nationale, Yaoundé.

Directory

The Constitution

The Constitution of the United Republic of Cameroon was promulgated on 2 June 1972, after approval by a referendum on 21 May 1972. It was revised on 9 May 1975.

In January 1984 the National Assembly approved a constitutional amendment, restoring the country's original name, the Republic of Cameroon. At the same time, the Assembly adopted further constitutional reforms, abolishing the post of Prime Minister and providing that the President of the Republic would be succeeded, in the event of death or incapacity, by the President of the National Assembly. Further constitutional amendments, agreed in March 1988, made provision for the holding of a presidential election before the expiry of the incumbent President's mandate, and increased the number of members in the Assembly from 150 to 180, effective from the general election of April 1988. In December 1990 the National Assembly adopted a constitutional amendment, which provided for the establishment of a multi-party system. Under new legislation, the Government is required to provide an official response within three months to any political organization seeking legal recognition. However, the formation of political parties on a tribal or regional basis is prohibited.

The main provisions of the 1972 Constitution, as amended, are summarized below:

The Constitution declares that the human being, without distinction as to race, religion, sex or belief, possesses inalienable and sacred rights. It affirms its attachment to the fundamental freedoms embodied in the Universal Declaration of Human Rights and the UN Charter. The State guarantees to all citizens of either sex the rights and freedoms set out in the preamble of the Constitution.

SOVEREIGNTY

1. The Republic of Cameroon shall be one and indivisible, democratic, secular and dedicated to social service. It shall ensure the equality before the law of all its citizens. Provisions that the official languages be French and English, for the motto, flag, national anthem and seal, that the capital be Yaoundé.

2-3. Sovereignty shall be vested in the people who shall exercise it either through the President of the Republic and the members returned by it to the National Assembly or by means of referendum. Elections are by universal suffrage, direct or indirect, by every citizen aged 21 or over in a secret ballot. Political parties or groups may take part in elections subject to the law and the principles of democracy and of national sovereignty and unity.

4. State authority shall be exercised by the President of the Republic and the National Assembly.

THE PRESIDENT OF THE REPUBLIC

5. The President of the Republic, as Head of State and Head of the Government, shall be responsible for the conduct of the affairs of the Republic. He shall define national policy and may charge the members of the Government with the implementation of this policy in certain spheres.

6-7. Candidates for the office of President must hold civic and political rights and be at least 35 years old, and may not hold any other elective office or professional activity. The President is elected for five years, by a majority of votes cast by the people, and may be re-elected. A presidential election may take place before the expiry of the five-year term, if the incumbent President so decides. Provisions are made for the continuity of office in the case of the President's resignation.

8-9. The Ministers and Vice-Ministers are appointed by the President to whom they are responsible, and they may hold no other appointment. The President is also head of the armed forces, he negotiates and ratifies treaties, may exercise clemency after consultation with the Higher Judicial Council, promulgates and is responsible for the enforcement of laws, is responsible for internal and external security, makes civil and military appointments, provides for necessary administrative services.

10. The President, by reference to the Supreme Court, ensures that all laws passed are constitutional.

11. Provisions whereby the President may declare a state of emergency or state of siege.

THE NATIONAL ASSEMBLY

12. The National Assembly shall be renewed every five years, though it may at the instance of the President of the Republic legislate to extend or shorten its term of office. It shall be composed of 180 members elected by universal suffrage.

13-14. Laws shall normally be passed by a simple majority of those present, but if a bill is read a second time at the request of the President of the Republic a majority of the National Assembly as a whole is required.

15-16. The National Assembly shall meet twice a year, each session to last not more than 30 days; in one session it shall approve the budget. It may be recalled to an extraordinary session of not more than 15 days.

17-18. Elections and suitability of candidates and sitting members shall be governed by law.

RELATIONS BETWEEN THE EXECUTIVE AND THE LEGISLATURE

19. Bills may be introduced either by the President of the Republic or by any member of the National Assembly.

20. Reserved to the legislature are: the fundamental rights and duties of the citizen; the law of persons and property; the political, administrative and judicial system in respect of elections to the National Assembly, general regulation of national defence, authorization of penalties and criminal and civil procedure etc., and the organization of the local authorities; currency, the budget, dues and taxes, legislation on public property; economic and social policy; the education system.

21. The National Assembly may empower the President of the Republic to legislate by way of ordinance for a limited period and for given purposes.

22-26. Other matters of procedure, including the right of the President of the Republic to address the Assembly and of the Ministers and Vice-Ministers to take part in debates.

27-29. The composition and conduct of the Assembly's programme of business. Provisions whereby the Assembly may inquire into governmental activity. The obligation of the President of the Republic to promulgate laws, which shall be published in both languages of the Republic.

30. Provisions whereby the President of the Republic, after consultation with the National Assembly, may submit to referendum certain reform bills liable to have profound repercussions on the future of the nation and national institutions.

THE JUDICIARY

31. Justice is administered in the name of the people. The President of the Republic shall ensure the independence of the judiciary and shall make appointments with the assistance of the Higher Judicial Council.

THE SUPREME COURT

32-33. The Supreme Court has powers to uphold the Constitution in such cases as the death or incapacity of the President and the admissibility of laws, to give final judgments on appeals on the Judgment of the Court of Appeal and to decide complaints against administrative acts. It may be assisted by experts appointed by the President of the Republic.

IMPEACHMENT

34. There shall be a Court of Impeachment with jurisdiction to try the President of the Republic for high treason and the Ministers and Vice-Ministers for conspiracy against the security of the State.

THE ECONOMIC AND SOCIAL COUNCIL

35. There shall be an Economic and Social Council, regulated by the law.

AMENDMENT OF THE CONSTITUTION

36-37. Bills to amend the Constitution may be introduced either by the President of the Republic or the National Assembly. The President may decide to submit any amendment to the people by way of a referendum. No procedure to amend the Constitution may be accepted if it tends to impair the republican character, unity or territorial integrity of the State, or the democratic principles by which the Republic is governed.

The Government

HEAD OF STATE

President: PAUL BIYA (took office 6 November 1982; elected 14 January 1984 for a five-year term; re-elected 24 April 1988).

CAMEROON

CABINET
(January 1991)

Secretary-General at the Presidency: SADOU HAYATOU.
Minister Delegate at the Presidency in charge of Defence: EDOUARD AKAME MFOUMOU.
Ministers at the Presidency in charge of Missions: OGORK EBOT NTUI, TITUS EDZOA.
Minister of Justice and Keeper of the Seals: ADOLPHE MOUDIKI.
Minister of External Relations: JACQUES-ROGER BOOH-BOOH.
Minister of Youth and Sports: IBRAHIM MBOMBO NJOYA.
Minister of Territorial Administration: GILBERT ANDZE TSOUNGUI.
Minister of Finance: SIMON BASSILEKEN.
Minister of National Education: JOSEPH MBOUI.
Minister of Labour and Social Welfare: JEAN BAPTISTE BOKAM.
Minister of Public Health: Prof. JOSEPH MBEDE.
Minister of Agriculture: JOHN NIBA NGU.
Minister of Planning and Territorial Development: MARCEL NIAT NJIFENJI.
Minister of Industrial and Commercial Development and Trade: RENÉ OWONA.
Minister of Social Affairs and Women's Affairs: AISSATOU YAOU.
Minister of Posts and Telecommunications: OUMAROU SANDA.
Minister of Mines, Water and Energy: FRANCIS WAINCHOM NKWAIN.
Minister of Housing and Town Planning: HENRI EYEBE AYISSI.
Minister of Public Works and Transport: PAUL TESSA.
Minister of Information and Culture: AUGUSTIN KONTCHOU KOUOMEGNI.
Minister of the Public Service and State Control: GARGA HAMAN ADJI.
Minister of Higher Education, Scientific Research and Computer Sciences: JOSEPH OWONA.
Minister of Livestock, Fisheries and Animal Husbandry: HAMADJODA ADJOUDJI.
Minister of Tourism: BENJAMIN ITOE.
Minister Delegate for National Security: FRANÇOIS ROGER N'NANG.
Minister Delegate for Stabilization of Public Finances, Planning and Economic Recovery: ROGER TCHOUNGUI.
Director of the Office of the President: LAURENT ESSO.

Secretaries of State:
Agriculture: TIKELA KEMONNE.
Planning and Territorial Development: NDANGA NDINGA BADEL.
Industrial and Commercial Development: LOUIS ABOGO NKONO.
Finance: URBAIN OLANGUEMA AWONO.
Education: JOSEPH YUNGA TEGHEN.
Defence: AMADOU ALI.

MINISTRIES

Correspondence to ministries not holding post boxes should generally be addressed c/o the Central Post Office, Yaoundé.

Office of the President: Yaoundé; tel. 23-40-25; telex 8207.
Ministry of Agriculture: Yaoundé; tel. 23-40-85; telex 8325.
Ministry of Defence: Yaoundé; tel. 23-40-55; telex 8261.
Ministry of External Relations: Yaoundé; tel. 22-01-33; telex 8252.
Ministry of Finance: BP 18, Yaoundé; tel. 23-40-00; telex 8260.
Ministry of Higher Education, Scientific Research and Computer Sciences: Yaoundé; telex 8418.
Ministry of Housing and Town Planning: Yaoundé; tel. 23-22-82; telex 8560.
Ministry of Industrial and Commercial Development and Trade: Yaoundé.
Ministry of Information and Culture: BP 1588, Yaoundé; tel. 22-31-55; telex 8215.
Ministry of Justice: Yaoundé; tel. 22-01-97; telex 8566.
Ministry of Labour and Social Welfare: Yaoundé; tel. 22-01-86.
Ministry of Livestock, Fisheries and Animal Husbandry: Yaoundé; tel. 22-33-11.
Ministry of Mines, Water and Energy: Yaoundé; tel. 23-34-04; telex 8504.
Ministry of National Education: Yaoundé; tel. 23-40-50; telex 8551.
Ministry of National Security: Yaoundé.
Ministry of Planning and Territorial Development: Yaoundé; telex 8268.
Ministry of Posts and Telecommunications: Yaoundé; tel. 23-40-16; telex 8582; fax 22-34-97.
Ministry of Public Health: Yaoundé; tel. 22-29-01; telex 8565.
Ministry of the Public Service and State Control: Yaoundé; telex 8597.
Ministry of Public Works and Transport: Yaoundé; tel. 22-16-22; telex 8653.
Ministry of Social Affairs and Women's Affairs: Yaoundé; tel. 22-41-48.
Ministry for Stabilization of Public Finances, Planning and Economic Recovery: Yaoundé.
Ministry of Territorial Administration: Yaoundé; tel. 23-40-90; telex 8503.
Ministry of Tourism: BP 266, Yaoundé; tel. 22-44-11; telex 8318.
Ministry of Youth and Sports: Yaoundé; tel. 23-32-57; telex 8568.

Legislature
ASSEMBLÉE NATIONALE

The number of seats in the Assemblée Nationale was increased from 150 to 180, following a constitutional amendment agreed in March 1988. Elections to the enlarged Assembly were held on 24 April 1988. A total of 324 candidates, all approved by the RDPC, contested the 180 seats.

President: LAWRENCE SHANG FONKA.
Secretary-General: EFOUA MBOZO'O.

Political Organizations

Rassemblement démocratique du peuple camerounais (RDPC): BP 867, Yaoundé; tel. 23-27-40; telex 8624; f. 1966 as Union nationale camerounaise (UNC) by merger of the Union camerounaise, the Kamerun National Democratic Party and four opposition parties; renamed in March 1985; comprises a congress which meets every five years, a 12-mem. political bureau and a cen. cttee of 76 mems and 20 alt. mems; there are two ancillary organs: Organisation des femmes du RDPC and Jeunesse du RDPC; Pres. PAUL BIYA; Political Sec. EBÉNÉZER NJOH MOUELLE.

The following organizations were illegal in mid-1990:

Cameroon Democratic Front (CDF): f. 1987 by the merger of a number of exiled opposition movements, including several factions of the Union des populations camerounaises (f. 1948); Leader NDEH NTUMAZA.

Social Democratic Front (SDF): Bamenda; f. 1990; Leader JOHN FRU NDI.

Diplomatic Representation
EMBASSIES IN CAMEROON

Algeria: BP 1619, Yaoundé; tel. 23-06-65; telex 8517; Ambassador: MISSOUM SBIH.
Belgium: BP 816, Yaoundé; tel. 22-27-88; telex 8314; Ambassador: FRANZ MICHILS.
Brazil: BP 348, Yaoundé; tel. 23-19-57; telex 8587; Ambassador: ANNUNCIATA SALGADO DOS SANTOS.
Canada: Immeuble Stamatiades, BP 572, Yaoundé; tel. 23-02-03; telex 8209; Ambassador: ANNE LEAHY.
Central African Republic: BP 396, Yaoundé; tel. 22-51-55; Ambassador: BASILE AKELELO.
Chad: BP 506, Yaoundé; tel. 22-06-24; telex 8352; Ambassador: NEATOBEI BIDI.
China, People's Republic: BP 1307, Yaoundé; tel. 23-00-83; Ambassador: SHEN LIANRUI.
Congo: BP 1422, Yaoundé; tel. 23-24-58; telex 8379; Ambassador: BERNADETTE BAYONNE.
Côte d'Ivoire: Immeuble Ndende, quartier Bastos, BP 203, Yaoundé; tel. 22-09-69; telex 8388; Ambassador: ANTOINE KONAN KOFFI.
Egypt: BP 809, Yaoundé; tel. 22-39-22; telex 8360; Ambassador: MOHAMED AL-KHAZINDAR.

CAMEROON

Equatorial Guinea: BP 277, Yaoundé; tel. 22-41-49; Ambassador: ALFREDO ABESO MVENO ONGUENE.
France: Plateau Atémengué, BP 1631, Yaoundé; tel. 22-02-33; telex 8233; Ambassador: YVON OMNÈS.
Gabon: BP 4130, Yaoundé; tel. 22-29-66; telex 8265; Ambassador: YVES ONGOLLO.
Germany: BP 1160, Yaoundé; tel. 23-05-66; telex 8238; Ambassador: EBERHARD NOLDEKE.
Greece: BP 82, Yaoundé; tel. 22-39-36; telex 8364; Chargé d'affaires a.i. DIMITRI KARABALIS.
Holy See: rue du Vatican, BP 210, Yaoundé (Apostolic Nunciature); tel. 22-04-75; telex 8382; Apostolic Pro-Nuncio: Most Rev. SANTOS ABRIL Y CASTELLÓ, Titular Archbishop of Tamada.
Israel: BP 5934, Yaoundé; tel. 22-16-44; telex 8632; Ambassador: YAACOV KEINAN.
Italy: Quartier Bastos, BP 827, Yaoundé; tel. 22-33-76; telex 8305; Ambassador: MARGHERITA COSTA.
Japan: Yaoundé; Ambassador HIDEO KAKINUMA.
Korea, Democratic People's Republic: Yaoundé; Ambassador KIL-MOUN YEUNG.
Korea, Republic: BP 301, Yaoundé; tel. 23-32-23; telex 8241; Ambassador: NAM-CHA HWANG.
Liberia: Ekoudou, Quartier Bastos, BP 1185, Yaoundé; tel. 23-12-96; telex 8227; Ambassador: CARLTON ALEXWYN KARPEH.
Libya: BP 1980, Yaoundé; telex 8272; Head of People's Bureau: HAMDI FANNOUSH.
Morocco: BP 1629, Yaoundé; tel. 22-50-92; telex 8347; Ambassador: MIMOUN MEHDI.
Namibia: Yaoundé.
Netherlands: BP 310, Yaoundé; tel. 22-05-44; telex 8237; Ambassador: GEORGES-ALBERT WEHRY.
Nigeria: BP 448, Yaoundé; tel. 22-34-55; telex 8267; Ambassador: MOHAMMED H. SAIDU.
Saudi Arabia: BP 1602, Yaoundé; tel. 22-39-22; telex 8336; Ambassador: HAMAD AL-TOAIMI.
Senegal: Plateau 'Bastos', BP 1716, Yaoundé; tel. 22-03-08; telex 8303; Ambassador: SALOUM KANDE.
Spain: BP 877, Yaoundé; tel. 22-41-89; telex 8287; Ambassador: MANUEL PIÑEIRO-SOUTO.
Switzerland: BP 1169, Yaoundé; tel. 23-28-96; telex 8316; Ambassador: JURG STREULI.
Tunisia: rue de Rotary, BP 6074, Yaoundé; tel. 22-33-68; telex 8370; Ambassador: HÉDI DRISSI.
USSR: BP 488, Yaoundé; tel. 22-17-14; Ambassador: VLADIMIR FEDEROV.
United Kingdom: ave Winston Churchill, BP 547, Yaoundé; tel. 22-05-45; telex 8200; fax 22-33-47; Ambassador: MARTIN REITH.
USA: rue Nachtigal, BP 817, Yaoundé; tel. 23-40-14; telex 8223; Ambassador: FRANCES COOK.
Zaire: BP 632, Yaoundé; tel. 22-51-03; telex 8317; Ambassador: KUTENDAKANA BUMBULU.

Judicial System

Supreme Court: Yaoundé; consists of a President, nine titular and substitute judges, a Procureur Général, an Avocat Général, deputies to the Procureur Général, a Registrar and clerks.

President of the Supreme Court: REMY-JEAN MBAYA.

High Court of Justice: Yaoundé; consists of 9 titular judges and 6 substitute judges, all elected by the National Assembly.

Attorney-General: ALEXIS DIPANDA MOUELLE.

Religion

It is estimated that 39% of the population follow traditional animist beliefs, 21% are Muslims and 40% Christians, mainly Roman Catholics.

CHRISTIANITY
Protestant Churches

There are about 1m. Protestants in Cameroon, with about 3,000 church and mission workers, and four theological schools.

Fédération des Eglises et missions évangéliques du Cameroun (FEMEC): BP 491, Yaoundé; tel. 22-30-78; f. 1968; 10 mem. churches; Pres. Rev. Dr JEAN KOTTO (Evangelical Church of Cameroon); Admin. Sec. Rev. Dr GRÉGOIRE AMBADIANG DE MENDENG (Presbyterian Church of Cameroon).

Eglise évangélique du Cameroun (Evangelical Church of Cameroon): BP 89, Douala; tel. 42-36-11; independent since 1957; 500,000 mems (1985); Sec. Rev. CHARLES E. NJIKE.

Eglise presbytérienne camerounaise (Presbyterian Church of Cameroon): BP 519, Yaoundé; tel. 32-42-36; independent since 1957; comprises four synods and 16 presbyteries; 200,000 mems (1985); Gen. Sec. Rev. GRÉGOIRE AMBADIANG DE MENDENG.

Eglise protestante africaine (African Protestant Church): BP 26, Lolodorf; active among the Ngumba people; 8,400 mems (1985); Dir-Gen. Rev. ANTOINE NTER.

Presbyterian Church in Cameroon: BP 19, Buéa; tel. 32-23-36; telex 5613; 184,257 mems (1987); 224 ministers; Moderator Rev. HENRY ANYE AWASOM.

Union des Eglises baptistes au Cameroun (Union of Baptist Churches of Cameroon): BP 6007, New Bell, Douala; tel. 42-41-06; autonomous since 1957; 37,000 mems (1985); Gen. Sec. Rev. EMMANUEL MBENDA.

Among other denominations active in the country are the Cameroon Baptist Church, the Cameroon Baptist Convention, the Church of the Lutheran Brethren of Cameroon, the Evangelical Lutheran Church of Cameroon, the Presbyterian Church in West Cameroon and the Union of Evangelical Churches of North Cameroon.

The Roman Catholic Church

Cameroon comprises four archdioceses and 13 dioceses. At 31 December 1988 there were an estimated 3,066,469 adherents (about 28% of the total population). There are several active missionary orders, and four major seminaries for African priests.

Bishops' Conference: Conférence Episcopale Nationale du Cameroun, BP 272, Garoua; tel. 27-13-53; f. 1981; Pres. Cardinal CHRISTIAN WIYGHAN TUMI, Archbishop of Garoua.

Archbishop of Bamenda: Mgr PAUL VERDZEKOV, Archbishop's House, BP 82, Bamenda; tel. 36-12-41.

Archbishop of Douala: Mgr SIMON TONYÉ, Archevêché, BP 179, Douala; tel. 42-37-14.

Archbishop of Garoua: Cardinal CHRISTIAN WIYGHAN TUMI, Archevêché, BP 272, Garoua; tel. 27-13-53.

Archbishop of Yaoundé: Mgr JEAN ZOA, Archevêché, BP 207, Yaoundé; tel. 23-04-83; telex 8681.

BAHÁ'Í FAITH

National Spiritual Assembly: BP 145, Limbe; tel. 33-21-46; mems in 1,744 localities.

The Press

The press in Cameroon has suffered from the problems of high production costs, low advertising revenue and a limited readership. Censorship controls have been in force since 1966.

DAILY

Cameroon Tribune: BP 1218, Yaoundé; tel. 22-27-00; telex 8311; f. 1974; govt-controlled; French; also weekly edn in English; Dir NDEMBY YEMBE; Editor-in-Chief ABUI MAMA ELOUNDOU; circ. 66,000 (daily), 25,000 (weekly).

PERIODICALS

Afrique en Dossiers: BP 1715; Yaoundé; f. 1970; French and English; Dir EBONGUE SOELLE.

Le Bamiléké: BP 329, Nkongsamba; monthly.

Bulletin de la Chambre de Commerce, d'Industrie et des Mines du Cameroun: BP 4011, Douala; tel. 42-28-88; telex 5616; monthly.

Bulletin Mensuel de la Statistique: BP 660, Yaoundé; monthly.

Cameroon Information: Yaoundé; fortnightly; French and English; circ. 5,000.

Cameroon—Magazine: 6 a year; independent; Editor-in-Chief FRANCIS EMILE MBOUNJA.

Cameroon Outlook: BP 124, Limbe; f. 1969; 3 a week; independent; English; Editor JEROME F. GWELLEM; circ. 20,000.

Cameroon Panorama: BP 46, Buéa; tel. 32-22-40; f. 1962; monthly; English; Roman Catholic; Editor Sister MERCY HORGAN; circ. 4,000.

Cameroon Post: Yaoundé; weekly; English; independent; Editor A. Y. NGALIM; circ. 20,000; publication suspended in May 1990.

Cameroon Times: BP 200, Limbe; f. 1960; 3 a week; English; Editor-in-Chief JEROME F. GWELLEM; circ. 12,000.

CAMEROON

Le Combattant: Yaoundé; weekly; independent; Editor BENYIMBE JOSEPH; circ. 21,000.

Courrier Sportif du Bénin: BP 17, Douala; weekly; Dir HENRI JONG.

Essor des Jeunes: BP 363, Nkongsamba; monthly; Roman Catholic; Editor Abbé JEAN-BOCO TCHAPE; circ. 3,000.

La Gazette: BP 5485, Douala; 2 a week; Editor ABODEL KARIMOU; circ. 35,000.

The Gazette: BP 408, Limbe; tel. 33-25-67; weekly; English edn of *La Gazette*; Editor JEROME F. GWELLEM; circ. 70,000.

Journal Officiel de la République du Cameroun: BP 1603, Yaoundé; tel. 23-12-77; telex 8403; fortnightly; official govt notices; circ. 4,000.

Le Libéral: Yaoundé; fortnightly.

Le Messager: Bafoussam; fortnightly; independent; Editor PUIS NJAWE; circ. 19,000.

Nleb Bekristen: Imprimerie Saint-Paul, BP 763, Yaoundé; f. 1935; fortnightly; Ewondo; Dir PASCAL BAYLON MVOE; circ. 6,000.

Les Nouvelles du Mungo: BP 1, Nkongsamba; monthly; circ. 3,000.

Le Patriote: Yaoundé.

Presbyterian Newsletter: BP 19, Buéa; telex 5613; quarterly.

Recherches et Études Camerounaises: BP 193, Yaoundé; monthly; publ. by Office National de Recherches Scientifiques du Cameroun.

Le Républicain: Yaoundé.

Revue d'Informations et d'Etudes Economiques et Financières: BP 1630, Yaoundé; quarterly.

Le Serviteur: BP 1405, Yaoundé; monthly; Protestant; Dir Pastor DANIEL AKO'O; circ. 3,000.

Le Travailleur/The Worker: BP 1610, Yaoundé; f. 1972; monthly; French and English; journal of Organisation des Syndicats des Travailleurs Camerounais; circ. 15,000.

L'Unité: BP 867, Yaoundé; weekly; French and English.

NEWS AGENCIES

CAMNEWS: c/o SOPECAM, BP 1218, Yaoundé; Dir JEAN NGANDJEU.

Foreign Bureaux

Agence France-Presse (AFP): Villa Kamdem-Kamga, BP 229, Elig-Essono, Yaoundé; telex 8218; Correspondent RENÉ-JACQUES LIGUE.

Agencia EFE (Spain): BP 11776, Yaoundé; Correspondent ANDREU CLARET.

Xinhua (New China) News Agency (People's Republic of China): ave Joseph Omgba, BP 1583, Yaoundé; tel. 22-25-72; telex 8294; Chief Correspondent LIANG GUIHE.

Reuters (UK) and TASS (USSR) are also represented in Cameroon.

Publishers

Centre d'Edition et de Production pour l'Enseignement et la Recherche (CEPER): BP 808, Yaoundé; tel. 22-13-23; telex 8338; f. 1977; general non-fiction, science and technology, tertiary, secondary and primary textbooks; Man. Dir JEAN CLAUDE FOUTH.

Editions Buma Kor: BP 727, Yaoundé; tel. 23-29-03; telex 8438; fax 22-48-99; f. 1977; general, children's, educational and Christian; English and French; Man. Dir B. D. BUMA KOR.

Editions Clé: BP 1501, Yaoundé; tel. 22-35-54; telex 8438; f. 1963; African and Christian literature and studies; school textbooks; Gen. Man. HENDRIK J. VAN DIJK.

Editions Le Flambeau: BP 113, Yaoundé; tel. 22-36-72; f. 1977; general; Man. Dir JOSEPH NDZIE.

Editions Semences Africaines: BP 5329, Yaoundé-Nlongkak; f. 1974; fiction, history, religion, textbooks; Man. Dir PHILIPPE-LOUIS OMBEDE.

Gwellem Publications: Presbook Compound (Down Beach), BP 408, Limbe; tel. 33-25-67; f. 1983; periodicals, books and pamphlets; Dir and Editor-in-Chief JEROME F. GWELLEM.

Imprimerie Saint-Paul: ave Monseigneur Vogt, BP 763, Yaoundé; education, medicine, philosophy, politics, religion and fiction.

Société Camerounaise de Publications (SCP): BP 20, Yaoundé; tel. 22-27-00; f. 1974; Man. Dir ENGELBERT NGOH HOP.

Société Kenkoson d'Etudes Africaines: BP 4064, Yaoundé; f. 1975; law, academic; CEO M. SALOMÉ.

Government Publishing Houses

Imprimerie Nationale: BP 1603, Yaoundé; tel. 23-12-77; telex 8403; Dir AMADOU VAMOULKE.

Société de Presse et d'Editions du Cameroun (SOPECAM): BP 1218, Yaoundé; tel. 23-40-12; telex 8311; f. 1977; under the supervision of the Ministry of Information and Culture; publr of the *Cameroon Tribune;* Dir-Gen. JOSEPH CHARLES DOUMBA; Editorial Dir ABUI MAMA ELOUNDOU.

Radio and Television

In 1987 there were an estimated 1.3m. radio receivers in use. In March 1985 a national television network, Cameroon Television (CTV), was inaugurated: there were an estimated 120,000 television receivers in use in 1987. In that year the two broadcasting companies, Radiodiffusion Nationale du Cameroun and CTV, were merged to form the Office de Radiodiffusion-Télévision Camerounaise (CRTV). By 1989 a total of 32 television transmitters were in service. Television programmes from France were to be broadcast by CRTV from early 1990.

Office de Radiodiffusion-Télévision Camerounaise (CRTV): BP 1634, Yaoundé; tel. 23-40-88; telex 8888; f. 1987 by merger; broadcasts in French and English; Pres. HENRI BANDOLO; Dir-Gen. GERVAIS MENDO ZE.

Radio Buéa: PMB, Buéa; tel. 32-25-25; programmes in English, French and 28 other local languages; Man. PETERSON CHIA YUH; Head of Station GIDEON TAKA.

Radio Douala: BP 986, Douala; tel. 42-60-60; programmes in French, English, Douala, Bassa, Ewondo, Bakoko and Bamiléké; Dir BRUNO DJEM; Head of Station LINUS ONANA MVONDO.

Radio Garoua: BP 103, Garoua; tel. 27-11-67; programmes in French, Hausa, English, Foulfouldé, Arabic and Choa; Dir BELLO MALGANA; Head of Station MOUSSA EPOPA.

There are also provincial radio stations at Abong Mbang, Bafoussam, Bamenda, Bertoua, Ebolowa, Maroua and Ngaoundéré, and there is a local radio station serving Yaoundé.

Finance

(cap. = capital; res = reserves; dep. = deposits; m. = million; brs = branches; amounts in francs CFA)

BANKING
Central Bank

Banque des Etats de l'Afrique Centrale (BEAC): rue Monseigneur Vogt, BP 1917, Yaoundé; tel. 23-40-30; telex 8343; fax 23-34-68; f. 1973 as the central bank of issue for mem. states of the Customs and Economic Union of Central Africa (UDEAC), comprising Cameroon, the Central African Republic, Chad, the Congo, Equatorial Guinea and Gabon; 6 brs in Cameroon; cap. and res 188,144m. (Dec. 1989); Gov. JEAN-FÉLIX MAMALEPOT; Commercial branch: BP 83, Yaoundé; Dir in Cameroon (vacant).

Commercial Banks

A major restructuring programme for the commercial banking sector was announced in 1989.

Bank of Credit and Commerce Cameroon SA (BCCC): Kennedy Bldg, ave John F. Kennedy, BP 1188, Yaoundé; tel. 22-29-86; telex 8558; fax 23-00-15; f. 1981; 35% state-owned, 65% by BCCI Holdings (Luxembourg) SA; cap. 1,350m. (June 1989); Pres. JEAN KANGA ZAMB; Man. Dir ENOW TANJONG; 3 brs.

Banque Internationale pour le Commerce et l'Industrie du Cameroun (BICIC): ave du Président Ahidjo, Yaoundé; tel. 23-40-07; telex 8202; f. 1962; 39% state-owned, 13% by Barclays Bank (UK), 11.5% by Banque Nationale de Paris; cap. and res 9,544m., dep. 334,654m. (June 1988); Pres. RAYMOND MALOUMA; Dir-Gen. ETIENNE NTSAMA; 34 brs.

Banque Unie de Crédit (BUC): place Elig Essono, BP 122, Yaoundé; tel. 23-15-72; telex 8879; f. 1976; state-owned; cap. 400m. (Dec. 1987); Pres. and Man. Dir GUSTAVE LELE.

BIAO—Cameroun: ave du Général de Gaulle, BP 4001, Douala; tel. 42-80-11; telex 5218; fax 42-67-86; f. 1974; cap. 4,095m., res 2,661.1m., dep. 197,734.8m. (June 1988); undergoing reorganization in 1990; Pres. ABDOULAYE SOUAIBOU; Gen. Man. FRANÇOIS MPONDO MBONGUE; 42 brs.

International Bank of Africa Cameroon SA: blvd de la Liberté, BP 3300, Douala; tel. 42-84-22; telex 5734; f. 1982; 35% state-owned; cap. 3,000m.; took over activities of Bank of America Cameroon SA; Pres. THOMAS EBONGALAME; Gen. Man. MAROUN W. KHALIFE.

CAMEROON

Meridien Bank Cameroon SA: 83 blvd de la Liberté, BP 1132, Douala; tel. 42-98-05; telex 5580; fax 42-25-48; f. 1988; 25% state-owned, 65% owned by Meridien International Bank (Zambia); took over activities of Chase Manhattan Overseas Banking Corpn; cap. 1,000m. (June 1989); Pres. DAVID T. ATOGHO; Gen. Man. EMMANUEL EDING; 4 brs.

Société Commerciale de Banque Crédit Lyonnais—Cameroun (SCBCL–C): rue Monseigneur Vogt, BP 700, Yaoundé; tel. 23-40-05; telex 8213; fax 22-41-32; f. 1989, following liquidation of Société Camerounaise de Banque; 35% state-owned, 65% by Crédit Lyonnais (France); cap. 6,000m.; Pres. MOÏSE FERDINAND BEKE BIHEGE; Dir-Gen. RAOUL FERREIN; 19 brs.

Société Générale de Banques au Cameroun (SGBC): ave Monseigneur Vogt, POB 244, Yaoundé; tel. 23-40-06; telex 8211; f. 1963; 30% state-owned, 37.8% by Société Générale (France); cap. 4,500m. (June 1989); Pres. AMADOU MOULIOM NJIFENJOU; Gen. Man. GASTON NGUENTI; 29 brs.

Standard Chartered Bank Cameroon SA: 57 blvd de la Liberté, BP 1784, Douala; tel. 42-36-12; telex 5858; fax 42-27-89; f. 1981; 66% owned by Standard Chartered Bank; cap. 1,000m. (June 1988); Chair. HERMAN MISSE; Gen. Man. N. A. SUMMERSALL; 2 brs.

Development Banks

Crédit Agricole du Cameroun: BP 11801, Yaoundé; tel. 23-19-09; fax 23-19-09; f. 1987 to take over activities of Fonds National de Développement Rural; 41% state-owned; cap. 4,850m. francs CFA; agricultural development bank; Chair. (vacant); Dir-Gen. AXEL VOLK.

Crédit Foncier du Cameroun (CFC): BP 1531, Yaoundé; tel. 22-03-73; telex 8368; f. 1977; 70% state-owned; cap. 6,000m. (June 1988); provides financial assistance for low-cost housing; Chair. EDOUARD KOULLA; Man. Dir ANDRÉ GIANNECHINI.

Crédit Industriel et Commercial: BP 1591, Yaoundé; tel. 23-16-90; telex 8395; fax 23-12-21; f. 1987, to assume activities of Fonds d'Aide et de Garantie des Crédits aux Petites et Moyennes Entreprises; industrial development bank.

Société Nationale d'Investissement du Cameroun (SNI): place de la Poste, BP 423, Yaoundé; tel. 22-44-22; telex 8205; fax 22-39-64; f. 1964; state-owned investment and credit agency; cap. 7,000m. (June 1986); Chair. VICTOR AYISSI MVODO; Man. Dir SIMON NGANN YONN.

Finance Institutions

Caisse Autonome d'Amortissement du Cameroun: BP 7167, Yaoundé; tel. 22-01-87; telex 8858; Dir-Gen. ISAAC NJIEMOUN.

Caisse Commune d'Epargne et d'Investissement (CCEI): BP 11834, Yaoundé; tel. 22-37-34; telex 8907; fax 22-17-85; Pres. PAUL KAMMOGNE FOKAM.

Fonds d'Aide et de Garantie des Crédits aux Petites et Moyennes Entreprises (FOGAPE): BP 1591, Yaoundé; tel. 23-38-59; telex 8395; fax 23-12-21; Pres. BERNARD BIDIAS NGON.

INSURANCE

Assurances Mutuelles Agricoles du Cameroun (AMACAM): BP 962, Yaoundé; tel. 22-49-66; telex 8300; f. 1965; cap. 100m.; Pres. JÉRÉMIE OBAM MFOU'OU; Man. Dir RAYMOND EKOUMOU.

Caisse Nationale de Réassurances (CNR): ave Foch, BP 4180, Yaoundé; tel. 22-37-99; telex 8262; fax 23-36-80; f. 1965; all classes of reinsurance; cap. 1,000m.; Man. Dir ANTOINE NTSIMI; Asst Man. Dir JOACHIM FOUNGTCHO.

Compagnie Camerounaise d'Assurances et de Réassurances (CCAR): rue Franqueville, BP 4068, Douala; tel. 42-62-71; telex 5341; f. 1974; cap. 499.5m.; Pres. YVETTE CHASSAGNE; Dir FABIEN ATANGANA.

Compagnie Nationale d'Assurances (CNA): BP 12125, Douala; tel. 42-16-28; telex 5100; fax 42-47-27; f. 1986; all classes of insurance; cap. 600m.; Chair. THÉODORE EBOBO; Man. Dir PROTAIS AYANGMA AMANG.

General and Equitable Assurance Cameroon Ltd (GEACAM): 56 blvd de la Liberté, BP 426, Douala; tel. 42-53-65; telex 5690; fax 42-71-03; fmrly Guardian Royal Exchange Assurance (Cameroon) Ltd; cap. 300m.; Pres. V. A. NGU; Man. Dir J. CHEBAUT.

Société Camerounaise d'Assurances (SOCAR): 86 blvd de la Liberté, BP 280, Douala; tel. 42-44-34; telex 5504; f. 1973; cap. 800m.; Chair. JEAN NKUETE; Man. Dir PAUL TSALA.

Société Nouvelle d'Assurances du Cameroun (SNAC): rue Manga Bell, BP 105, Douala; tel. 42-92-03; telex 5745; f. 1974; all classes of insurance; cap. 700m.; Man. Dir JEAN-CHARLES SUZEAU.

Trade and Industry

ADVISORY BODY

Economic and Social Council: BP 1058, Yaoundé; tel. 22-25-97; telex 8275; advises the govt on economic and social problems; comprises 85 mems, a perm. secretariat and a president; mems are nominated for a five-year term; Pres. LUC AYANG; Sec.-Gen. Dr JOSEPH SIMON EPALE.

PRINCIPAL DEVELOPMENT ORGANIZATIONS

Caisse Centrale de Coopération Economique (CCCE): BP 46, Yaoundé; tel. 22-23-24; telex 8301; Dir PIERRE MARSET.

Cameroon Development Corporation (CAMDEV): Bota, Limbe; tel. 33-22-51; telex 5242; f. 1947, reorg. 1982; cap. 12,242m. francs CFA; 91.7% state-owned; statutory agricultural corpn established to acquire and develop plantations of tropical crops, fmrly in German ownership; operates in four of 10 provinces, and is the second largest employer of labour; leases 98,000 ha from Govt, of which 40,000 ha are planted; operates two oil mills, four banana packing stations, three tea and seven rubber factories; a smallholders' scheme involves 432 farmers, cultivating 1,294 ha of rubber and oil palm; Chair. JOHN EBONG NGOLE; Gen. Man. PETER MAFANY MUSONGE.

Centre National d'Assistance aux Petites et Moyennes Entreprises (CAPME): BP 1377, Douala; tel. 42-58-58; telex 5590; f. 1970 by Cameroon Govt and UNDP; development centre for small and medium-sized businesses; advises on industrial techniques and training and undertakes market research; Pres. DIEUDONNÉ TSANGA ATANGANA; Dir M. BOUBA ARDO.

Centre National de Développement des Entreprises Co-operatives (CENADEC): BP 120, Yaoundé; f. 1975; state-owned; Dir-Gen. JACQUES SANGUE.

Centre National de Développement des Forêts (CENADEFOR): BP 369, Yaoundé; tel. 22-51-93; telex 8561; f. 1981; state-owned; development and protection of forests; Dir-Gen. SAMUEL MAKON WEHIONG.

Direction Générale des Grands Travaux du Cameroon (DGTC): Yaoundé; f. 1988; commissioning, implementation and supervision of public works contracts; Chair. JEAN FOUMAN AKAME; Man. Dir MICHEL KOWALZICK.

Hévéa-Cameroun (HEVECAM): BP 1298, Douala and BP 174, Kribi; tel. 46-19-19; telex 5970; fax 46-18-30; f. 1975; cap. 16,518m. francs CFA; state-owned; development of 15,000 ha rubber plantation; 4,500 employees; rehabilitation programme announced 1989; Pres. MAIDADI SADOU; Man. Dir JEAN REMY.

Mission d'Aménagement et d'Equipement des Terrains Urbains et Ruraux (MAETUR): BP 1248, Yaoundé; tel. 22-31-13; telex 8571; f. 1977; Pres. FERDINANG LÉOPOLD OYONO; Dir HERVÉ GABRIEL BLANDIN.

Mission de Développement des Cultures Vivrières (MIDEVIV): BP 1682, Yaoundé; tel. 22-38-29; f. 1973; development and improvement of seeds and planting materials; production and distribution of foodstuffs for urban centres; Pres. MAXIALE MAHI; Dir JEAN-BERNARD ABONG.

Mission Française de Coopération: BP 1616, Yaoundé; tel. 22-44-43; telex 8392; administers bilateral aid from France; Dir JEAN BOULOGNE.

Mission de Développement de la Province du Nord-Ouest (MIDENO): BP 442, Bamenda; telex 5842.

Office Céréalier dans la Province du Nord: BP 298, Garoua; tel. 27-14-38; telex 7603; f. 1975 to combat effects of drought in northern Cameroon and stabilize cereal prices; Pres. FON FOSSI YAKUM TAW; Dir-Gen. GILBERT GOURLEMOND.

Office National de Commercialisation des Produits de Base (ONCPB): BP 378, Douala; tel. 42-67-76; telex 5260; f. 1978; has monopoly of marketing cocoa, coffee, cotton, groundnuts and palm products; is responsible for the internal prices for the planters, the quality of the produce and development of production; rehabilitation programme announced 1989; holds 8.3% share in CAMDEV (q.v.); Pres. LUC AYANG; Man. Dir CYRILLE ETOUNDI ATANGANA.

Société de Développement du Cacao (SODECAO): BP 1651, Yaoundé; tel. 22-09-91; telex 8574; f. 1974, reorg. 1980; cap. 425m. francs CFA; development of cocoa, coffee and food crop production in the Centre-Sud province; Pres. JOSEPH-CHARLES DOUMBA; Dir-Gen. FÉLIX TONYE MBOG.

Société de Développement de l'Elevage (SODEVA): BP 50, Kousseri; cap. 50m. francs CFA; Dir Alhadji OUMAROU BAKARY.

Société de Développement et d'Exploitation des Productions Animales (SODEPA): BP 1410, Yaoundé; tel. 22-24-28; f. 1974; cap. 375m. francs CFA; development of livestock and livestock products; Man. Dir ETIENNE ENGUELEGUELE.

CAMEROON
Directory

Société de Développement de la Haute-Vallée du Noun (UNVDA): BP 25, N'Dop and BP 43, Bamenda; f. 1978; cap. 895m. francs CFA; rice cultivation; Dir-Gen. G. A. NIBA.

Société de Développement de la Riziculture dans la Plaine des Mbo (SODERIM): BP 146, Melong; f. 1977; cap. 1,535m. francs CFA; cultivation and processing of rice and other agricultural products; Pres. S. ETAME MASSOMA; Man. Dir JEAN-BAPTISTE YONKE.

Société d'Expansion et de Modernisation de la Riziculture de Yagoua (SEMRY): BP 46, Yagoua; tel. 29-62-03; f. 1971; cap. 4,580m. francs CFA; commercialization of rice products and expansion of rice-growing in areas where irrigation is possible; rehabilitation programme announced 1989; Pres. ALBERT EKONO NNA; Dir-Gen. TORI LIMANGANA.

Société Immobilière du Cameroun (SIC): BP 387, Yaoundé; tel. 23-34-11; telex 8577; f. 1952; cap. 1,000m. francs CFA; housing construction and development; Pres. GABRIEL LOUIS DJEUDJANG; Man. Dir ANDRÉ LEVY.

CHAMBERS OF COMMERCE

Chambre d'Agriculture, d'Elevage et des Forêts du Cameroun: Parc Repiquet, BP 287, Yaoundé; tel. 22-38-85; telex 8243; f. 1955; 44 mems; Pres. RENE GOBÉ; Sec.-Gen. SOLOMON NFOR GWEI; other delegations at Yaoundé, Bafoussam, Bamenda, Douala and Garoua.

Chambre de Commerce, d'Industrie et des Mines du Cameroun: BP 4011, Douala; tel. 42-28-88; telex 5616; f. 1963; branches: BP 12206, Douala; BP 36, Yaoundé; BP 211, Limbe; BP 59, Garoua; BP 944, Bafoussam; BP 551, Bamenda; 138 mems; Pres. PIERRE TCHANQUÉ; Sec.-Gen. SAÏDOU ABDOULAYE BOBBOY.

EMPLOYERS' ASSOCIATIONS

Groupement des Femmes d'Affaires du Cameroun (GFAC): BP 1940, Douala; tel. 42-4-64; telex 6100; Pres. FRANÇOISE FONING.

Groupement Interprofessionnel pour l'Etude et la Co-ordination des Intérêts Economiques au Cameroun (GICAM): ave Konrad Adenauer, BP 1134, Yaoundé; tel. 22-27-22; also at BP 829, Douala; tel. 42-31-41; f. 1957; Pres. CLAUDE MAÎTRE HENRY.

Syndicat Professionnel des Entreprises du Bâtiment, des Travaux Publics et des Activités Annexes: BP 1134, Yaoundé; br. at BP 660, Douala; telex 8286; Pres. PAUL SOPPO-PRISO.

Syndicat des Commerçants Importateurs-Exportateurs du Cameroun (SCIEC): 16 rue Quillien, BP 562, Douala; tel. 42-60-04; Sec.-Gen. G. TOSCANO.

Syndicat des Industriels du Cameroun (SYNINDUSTRICAM): BP 673, Douala; tel. 42-30-58; telex 5342; f. 1953; Pres. SAMUEL KONDO EBELLE; Sec.-Gen. Mme NSOMO.

Syndicat des Producteurs et Exportateurs de Bois du Cameroun: BP 570, Yaoundé; tel. 22-27-22; telex 8286; Pres. SAMUEL DUCLAIR FANDJO.

Syndicat des Transporteurs Routiers du Cameroun: BP 834, Douala; tel. 42-55-21.

Syndicats Professionnels Forestiers et Activités connexes du Cameroun: BP 100, Douala.

Union des Syndicats Professionnels du Cameroun (USPC): BP 829, Douala; Pres. MOUKOKO KINGUE.

West Cameroon Employers' Association (WCEA): BP 97, Tiko.

PRINCIPAL CO-OPERATIVE ORGANIZATIONS

Bakweri Co-operative Union of Farmers Ltd: Dibanda, Tiko; produce marketing co-operative for bananas, cocoa and coffee; 14 societies, 2,000 mems; Pres. Dr E. M. L. ENDELEY.

Cameroon Co-operative Exporters Ltd: BP 19, Kumba; f. 1953; mems: 8 socs; central agency for marketing of mems' coffee, cocoa and palm kernels; Man. A. B. ENYONG; Sec. M. M. EYOH (acting).

Centre National de Développement des Entreprises Coopératives (CENADEC): BP 120, Yaoundé; f. 1970; promotes and organizes the co-operative movement; bureaux at BP 43, Kumba and BP 26, Bamenda; Dir JACQUES SANGUE.

North-West Co-operative Association Ltd (NWCA): BP 41, Bamenda; tel. 36-12-12; telex 5842; Pres. MARTIN CHI AKUMA; Gen. Man. POLYCARP NDIBOTI NGWAYI.

Union Centrale des Coopératives Agricoles de l'Ouest (UCCAO): ave Samuel Wonko, BP 1002, Bafoussam; tel. 44-14-39; telex 7005; f. 1959; marketing of cocoa and coffee; 85,000 mems; Pres. ETIENNE POUPONG; Man. Dir HENRI FANKAM.

West Cameroon Co-operative Association Ltd: BP 135, Kumba; founded as central financing body of the co-operative movement; provides short-term credits and agricultural services to mem. socs; policy-making body for the co-operative movement in West Cameroon; 142 mem. unions and socs with total membership of c. 45,000; Pres. Chief T. E. NJEA; Sec. M. M. QUAN.

There are 83 co-operatives for the harvesting and sale of bananas and coffee and for providing mutual credit.

TRADE UNIONS

National Union of Private Journalists (NUPJ): Yaoundé; f. 1984; Pres. DOMINIQUE SIMI FOUDA; Vice-Pres. PADDY TAMBE JOHN, DAVID ACHIDI NDIFANG.

Organisation des Syndicats des Travailleurs Camerounais/Organization of Cameroon Workers' Unions (OSTC): BP 1610, Yaoundé; tel. 23-00-47; f. 1985; fmrly the Union National des Travailleurs du Cameroun (UNTC); Pres. DOMINIQUE FOUDA IMAH.

Transport

RAILWAYS

There are some 1,104 km of track, the West Line running from Douala to Nkongsamba (166 km) with a branch line leading south-west from Mbanga to Kumba (29 km), and the Transcameroon railway which runs from Douala to Ngaoundéré (885 km), with a branch line from Ngoumou to Mbalmayo (30 km). The section from Yaoundé to Ngaoundéré (622 km) was opened in 1974. An extension of its western branch is projected from Mbalmayo to Bangui, in the Central African Republic. Improvements to the line between Douala and Yaoundé were begun in 1974; those on the section between Yaoundé and Maloumé were completed in 1978, and those between Douala and Edéa in 1981. Improvements to the section between Edéa and Eseka, which cut the 90 km line to 71 km, were completed in 1982. The final section, between Eseka and Maloumé, was opened in May 1987.

Régie Nationale des Chemins de Fer du Cameroun (REGIFERCAM): BP 304, Douala; tel. 42-60-45; telex 5607; fax 42-32-05; f. 1947; rehabilitation programme announced 1989; Chair. SAMUEL EBOUA; Man. Dir SAMUEL MINKO.

Office du Chemin de Fer Transcamerounais: BP 625, Yaoundé; tel. 22-44-33; telex 8293; supervises the laying of new railway lines and improvements to existing lines, and undertakes relevant research; Dir-Gen. LUC TOWA FOTSO.

ROADS

At 30 June 1987 there were 52,214 km of roads, (including 7,548 km of main roads and 13,666 km of secondary roads), of which about 3,133 km were paved. A fast metalled road between Douala and Yaoundé was opened in August 1985. The 1986–91 Plan envisaged the construction of a further 3,000 km of tarred roads. However, improvements to Cameroon's road network, including the rehabilitation of the road from Mbalmayo to Ebolowa, as well as the construction of the Bamenda 'ring road', were likely to be delayed, following the announcement, in 1988, of a reduction in planned public expenditure.

SHIPPING

There are seaports at Kribi and Limbe/Tiko, a river port at Garoua, and an estuary port at Douala-Bonabéri, the principal port and main outlet. It has 2,510 m of quays and a minimum depth of 5.8 m in the channels, 8.5 m at the quays. In 1988 the port handled 3.8m. metric tons of cargo. Total handling capacity is 7m. metric tons annually. The port has been modernized and extended, and provides a storage zone for the use of land-locked central African countries. Facilities for ship-repair have also been provided, and there is a logistic area for oil research facilities. Plans are under way to increase the annual capacity of the container terminal from 1.5m. tons to 2m. tons.

Office National des Ports/National Ports Authority: 5 blvd Leclerc, BP 4020, Douala; tel. 42-01-33; telex 5270; cap. 12,040m. francs CFA; Chair. ANDRÉ-BOSCO CHEUOUA; Gen. Man. SIEGFRIED DIBONG.

CAMATRANS (Delmas-Vieljeux Cameroun): rue Kitchener, BP 263, Douala; tel. 42-10-36; telex 5222; f. 1977; cap. 1,000m. francs CFA; Pres. PATRICE VIELJEUX.

Cameroon Shipping Lines SA (CAMSHIPLINES): Centre des Affaires Maritimes, 18 rue Joffre, BP 4054, Douala; tel. 42-00-38; telex 5615; f. 1975; cap. 4,365m. francs CFA; 67% state-owned; 6 vessels trading with western Europe, USA, Far East and Africa; Chair. FRANÇOIS SENGAT KUO; Man. Dir RENÉ MBAYEN.

Conseil National des Chargeurs du Cameroun (CNCC): BP 1588, Douala; tel. 42-32-06; telex 5669; fax 42-89-01; f. 1986; cap. 800m. francs CFA; promotion of the maritime sector; Gen. Man. GUSTAVE TCHETGEN.

Fako Transport Shipping Lines (FTSC): Douala; f. 1985; joint-venture with USA.

Société Africaine de Transit et d'Affrètement (SATA): Vallée Tokoto, BP 546, Douala; tel. 42-82-09; telex 5239; f. 1950; cap. 625m. francs CFA; Man. Dir RAYMOND PARIZOT.

Société Agence Maritime de l'Ouest Africain Cameroun (SAMOA): place du Gouvernement, BP 1127, Douala; tel. 42-16-80; telex 5256; f. 1953; cap. 24m. francs CFA; agents for Lloyd Triestino, Armada Shipping, Black Star Line, Gold Star Line, Nigerian Star Line, OT Africa Line, Spliethoff, Jeco Shipping, Van Uden; Dir JEAN-PIERRE ALLAIN.

Société Camerounaise de Manutention et d'Acconage (SOCA-MAC): BP 284, Douala; tel. 42-40-51; telex 5537; f. 1976; cap. 1,013m. francs CFA; freight handling; Pres. MOHAMADOU TALBA; Dir-Gen. HARRY J. GHOOS.

Société Camerounaise de Transport et d'Affrètement (SCTA): BP 974, Douala; tel. 42-17-24; telex 6181; f. 1951; cap. 100m. francs CFA; Pres. JACQUES VIAULT; Dir-Gen. GONTRAN FRAUCIEL.

Société Ouest-Africaine d'Entreprises Maritimes—Cameroun (SOAEM—Cameroun): 5 blvd de la Liberté, BP 320, Douala; tel. 42-02-88; f. 1959; cap. 850m. francs CFA; Pres. RÉNÉ KOLOWSKI; Man. Dir JEAN-LOUIS GRECIET.

Société de Transports Urbains du Cameroun (SOTUC): BP 1697, Yaoundé; tel. 23-38-07; telex 8330; f. 1973; cap. 400m. francs CFA; 58% owned by Société Nationale d'Investissement du Cameroun; operates urban transport services in Yaoundé and Douala; rehabilitation programme announced 1989; Dir-Gen. MARCEL YONDO; Mans JEAN-VICTOR OUM (Yaoundé), GABRIEL VASSEUR (Douala).

SOCOPAO (Cameroun): BP 215, Douala; tel. 42-64-64; telex 5252; f. 1951; cap. 1,440m. francs CFA; agents for Palm/Elder/Hoegh Lines, Bank Line, CNAN, CNN, Comanav, Comasersa, Dafra Line, Grand Pale, Marasia SA, Maritima del Norte, Navcoma, Nigerian Shipping Line, Niven Line, Splosna Plovba, Rossis Maritime, SSSIM, Veb Deutsche Seereederei, Polish Ocean Lines, Westwind Africa Line, Nautilus Keller Line, Estonian Shipping Co, AGTI Paris, K-Line Tokyo; Pres. VINCENT BOLLORE; Man. Dir E. DUPUY.

Transcap Cameroun: BP 4059, Douala; tel. 42-72-14; telex 5247; f. 1960; cap. 342m. francs CFA; Pres. RÉNÉ DUPRAZ; Man. Dir MICHEL BARDOU.

CIVIL AVIATION

There are international airports at Douala and Garoua. Construction of a further international airport, at Yaoundé, began in 1988: completion of the project is scheduled for mid-1991. An international airport is also under construction at Bafoussam. There are 39 smaller airports and aerodromes.

Cameroon Airlines (Cam-Air): 3 ave du Général de Gaulle, BP 4092, Douala; tel. 42-25-25; telex 5345; f. 1971; 75% govt-owned and 25% by Air France; services to Benin, Burundi, CAR, Chad, Congo, Côte d'Ivoire, Equatorial Guinea, France, Gabon, Germany, Italy, Kenya, Nigeria, Rwanda, Switzerland, the United Kingdom and Zaire and domestic flights; fleet of 3 Boeing 737, 1 Boeing 747-200-B and 2 Hawker Siddeley 748; rehabilitation programme announced 1989; Chair. SAMUEL EBOUA; Dir-Gen. CLAUDE KIENZ.

Tourism

Tourists are attracted by the cultural diversity of local customs, and by the national parks, game reserves and sandy beaches. The tourist trade is being expanded, and in 1988 there were 100,121 foreign visitors. In January of that year there were 150 classified hotels, with a total of 8,000 rooms and 12,000 beds. A Ministry of Tourism was established in 1989. The 1986/87 budget allotted 1,544m. francs CFA to tourism.

Société Camerounaise de Tourisme (SOCATOUR): BP 7138, Yaoundé; tel. 23-32-19; telex 8766.

CANADA

Introductory Survey

Location, Climate, Language, Religion, Flag, Capital

Canada occupies the northern part of North America (excluding Alaska and Greenland) and is the second largest country in the world, after the USSR. It extends from the Atlantic Ocean to the Pacific. Except for the boundary with Alaska in the north-west, Canada's frontier with the USA follows the upper St Lawrence Seaway and the Great Lakes, continuing west along latitude 49°N. The climate is an extreme one, particularly inland. Winter temperatures drop well below freezing but summers are generally hot. Rainfall varies from moderate to light and there are heavy falls of snow. The two official languages are English and French, the mother tongues of 62.7% and 25.4%, respectively, at the general census in 1986. More than 98% of Canadians can speak English or French. About 45% of the population are Roman Catholics. The main Protestant churches are the United Church of Canada and the Anglican Church of Canada. Numerous other religious denominations are represented. The national flag (proportions 2 by 1) consists of a red maple leaf on a white field, flanked by red panels. The capital is Ottawa.

Recent History

The Liberals, led by Pierre Trudeau, were returned to office at general elections in 1968, 1972, 1974, and again in 1980 after a short-lived minority Progressive Conservative (PC) administration. Foreign relations altered significantly under the Liberals, with less emphasis on traditional links with Western Europe and the USA, and a fostering of relations with the Far East, Africa and Latin America.

The effects of international economic recession in the mid-1970s led to a steady erosion of the Government's popularity, and led to the Liberals' defeat at general elections held in May 1979, although the PC administration, led by Joe Clark, lacked an overall majority. In November, Trudeau announced that he was resigning as Liberal leader, but in the following month the Government was defeated on its budget proposals. Trudeau postponed his retirement, and at general elections in February 1980 the Liberals were returned with a strong majority. Popular support for the new Government, however, declined rapidly with the persistence of adverse economic conditions, while the PC party gained substantially in popularity under the leadership of Brian Mulroney, a Québec labour lawyer and businessman with no previous political experience, who replaced Clark in June 1983.

Trudeau, who had earlier indicated that he would relinquish the party leadership before the general elections due in 1985, resigned in June 1984 and was succeeded as Liberal leader and Prime Minister by John Turner, a former Minister of Finance. Shortly after taking office, Turner called general elections for September. The Liberals entered the pre-election period with revived popular support, but criticism of Turner's exercise of political patronage and of his general conduct of the election campaign eroded the Liberals' following. Mulroney, an able bilingual public speaker, led the PC party to the largest electoral majority in Canadian history.

During 1986, however, the resignations in discordant circumstances of five cabinet ministers, together with the persistence of high rates of unemployment, led to a fall in the Government's popularity. Further cabinet changes were carried out in 1987 in an effort to retrieve support for the Government, which continued, none the less, to decline amid further ministerial resignations, a controversial incident concerning the operations of the Canadian Security Intelligence Service, and criticism by the Liberals and the New Democratic Party (NDP) of the Government's negotiation of a new US-Canadian trade treaty, which the Liberals and the NDP viewed as overly advantageous to US business interests and potentially damaging to Canada's national identity. Controversy over the proposed agreement gained momentum during the early months of 1988, and led to a further decline in the popularity of the PC administration. The trade agreement was, however, approved in August by the House of Commons. In September Mulroney carried out an extensive reconstruction of the Cabinet, and in October, following indications that the PC proposals were gaining public support in the free trade debate, he called general elections for November. The PC party was re-elected, although with a reduced majority, and Senate approval of the trade agreement followed in December. Many Canadians, however, continued to express disquiet at the longer-term implications of the treaty for Canada's continued political and cultural autonomy. In February 1990 the Government opened negotiations with Mexico, with the aim of reducing trade barriers, and in September it was announced that Canada had begun preliminary discussions with the US and Mexican Governments to assess the feasibility of creating a free trade zone encompassing the whole of North America.

In the province of Québec, where four-fifths of the population speak French as a first language and which maintains its own cultural identity, the question of political self-determination has long been a sensitive issue. At provincial elections in 1976 the separatist Parti Québécois (PQ), led by René Lévesque, came to power, and in 1977 made French the official language of education, business and government in Québec. Certain sections of this legislation were subsequently invalidated by the Supreme Court of Canada. During 1977 the PQ administration reiterated its aim of sovereignty for Québec; however in 1978 Lévesque denied that unilateral separation was contemplated and stated that a 'sovereignty-association', with a monetary and customs union, would be sought. At a Québec provincial referendum held in May 1980, these proposals were rejected by an electoral margin of 59.5% to 40.5%. The PQ was re-elected at provincial general elections held in April 1981, but its electoral popularity subsequently declined, and in December 1985 it was replaced as the governing party in Québec by the Liberals. The Liberals retained power at the subsequent general elections held in September 1989, although a resurgence of support for greater provincial sovereignty was reflected in the achievement by the PQ of 40% of the popular vote. Additionally, a newly-formed anglophone party, seeking the repeal of legislation establishing French as the province's official language, obtained four seats in the provincial legislature.

In 1982 the UK Parliament transferred to Canada authority over all matters contained in British statutes relating to Canada, opening the way for the reform of central institutions and the redistribution of legislative powers between Parliament and the provincial legislatures. Following two years of negotiations between Trudeau and the provincial premiers, all the provinces except Québec had accepted constitutional provisions which included a charter of rights and a formula for constitutional amendments, whereby such amendments would require the support of at least seven provinces representing more than 50% of the population. Québec, however, maintained that its legislature could exercise the right to veto constitutional provisions.

Following the return to power in 1985 of the Liberals in Québec, the Federal Government adopted new initiatives to include Québec in the constitutional arrangements. In April 1987 Mulroney and the provincial premiers met at Meech Lake, Québec, to negotiate a constitutional accommodation for Québec. The resultant agreement, the Meech Lake Accord, was finalized in June. It recognized Québec as a 'distinct society' within the Canadian federation, and granted each of the provinces important new powers in the areas of federal parliamentary reform, judicial appointments and the creation of new provinces. The Accord was subject to ratification, not later than June 1990, by the Federal Parliament and all provincial legislatures. By early 1990 the Federal Parliament and each of the 10 provincial legislatures, except for New Brunswick and Manitoba, had approved the Accord.

Opposition to the Meech Lake arrangements, on the grounds that they afforded too much influence to Québec and failed to provide Inuit and Indian minorities with the same measure of protection as francophone groups, began to emerge in March 1990, when the Newfoundland legislature rescinded its earlier endorsement of the Accord. Following a meeting in June

CANADA

Introductory Survey

between Mulroney and the provincial premiers (at which a number of compromise amendments were adopted), the New Brunswick legislature agreed to accept the Accord, but the provinces of Manitoba and Newfoundland upheld their opposition. The Meech Lake Accord duly lapsed on 23 June, and the Québec government, which had opposed any changes to the earlier terms of the Accord, responded by refusing to participate in future provincial conferences, and by appointing a commission to make recommendations regarding the province's political future. In October Mulroney appointed a consultative panel to ascertain public opinion both on constitutional reform and on the wider issue of Canada's national future. The panel, which was to conduct public hearings country-wide, was to publish its report in July 1991.

Meanwhile, within the Federal Parliament itself, a split developed in francophone support for the Government. In May 1990, led by a former member of Mulroney's Cabinet, seven PC members representing Québec constituencies formed an independent Bloc Québécois (which later expanded, inclusive of disaffected Liberal support, to nine members) with the object of acting in the interests of a 'sovereign Québec'.

In September 1990 a constitutional debate arose over the conduct of business in the Federal Senate, an appointive body in which the Liberals had long held a majority, and in which there were 15 vacant seats left unfilled pending the eventual implementation of senate reform provisions in the Meech Lake Accord. With the demise of the Accord, however, the Senate's refusal to approve controversial legislation implementing a Goods and Services Tax (GST) prompted Mulroney to fill the existing vacancies with PC appointees, and to invoke a constitutional provision allowing the Government temporarily to enlarge the Senate by creating eight additional seats. The validity of these appointments was the subject of legal challenge by opposition groups in late 1990.

The question of land treaty claims by Canada's indigenous peoples assumed considerable prominence during 1990, when disputes over land rights arose in Ontario, Manitoba and, most notably, Québec, where armed confrontations took place between the civil authorities and militant Indian groups. The Northwest Territories (NWT), which form one-third of Canada's land mass but contain a population of only 52,000 (of which Inuit and Indians comprise about one-half), may eventually secure a new constitutional status. In November 1982 the Federal Government agreed in principle to implement the decision of a territorial referendum held in April, in which 56% of the voters approved a division of the NWT into two parts. In April 1985 the Federal Government stated that, subject to the eventual agreement of the provincial premiers and of Indian and Inuit organizations, it would incorporate into the Constitution the right to self-government of Canada's 500,000 indigenous peoples. Arrangements to divide the NWT into two self-governing units, Nunavut (to the east of a proposed boundary running northwards from the Saskatchewan-Manitoba border) and Denendeh (to the west), were approved by the NWT legislature in January 1987, subject to their eventual endorsement by a plebiscite among NWT residents, and approval by the Federal Government. In September 1988, following 13 years of negotiations, the Federal Government formally transferred to indigenous ownership an area covering 673,000 sq km in the NWT. Arrangements to transfer more than 181,000 sq km of land in the western NWT, together with a 352,000 sq km tract in the eastern NWT, which includes most of Canada's Arctic islands, were pending in late 1990. A similar process is under way in the Yukon Territory, where, in April 1990, an area of 41,000 sq km (representing 8.6% of the Territory's land) was transferred to indigenous control.

During his period in office, Mulroney has sought to re-establish Canada's traditional 'special relationship' with the USA, which had operated until the Trudeau period. Little progress was made during the late 1980s, however, in realizing Canada's wish to secure effective US government control of the emission of gases from industrial plants, which move northwards into Canada to produce environmentally destructive 'acid rain'. In 1985 President Reagan agreed to the formation of a joint governmental commission to examine this problem. In 1986 the commission recommended the implementation of a US $5,000m. anti-pollution programme, to be financed jointly by the US Government and the relevant industries, although no specific arrangements were set out for funding. This matter was further pursued by Mulroney at meetings held with President Reagan in April 1988 and with President Bush in July 1990, following the passage of clean-air legislation by the US Senate. The Canadian Government, meanwhile, has proceeded with a programme costing an estimated C $128,000m. to achieve the reduction by 20% of acid-pollution emissions from domestic sources by the year 2005. These aims were extended by a new environmental programme announced in December 1990, under which the Government was to spend a total of C $3,000m. on a range of environmental improvement measures. These sought to reduce air pollution by 40% over a 10-year period, while stabilizing carbon dioxide emissions at 1990 levels by the end of the century. In addition, work was to be undertaken to eliminate industrial pollution from the Great Lakes and other waterways. Financial provision was also made for contributions to projects seeking to stem global warming.

Relations between the USA and Canada came under strain in August and September 1985, when a US coastguard ice-breaker traversed the Northwest Passage without seeking prior permission from Canada, in assertion of long-standing US claims that the channels within this 1.6m. sq km tract of ice-bound islands are international waters. The Canadian Government declared sovereignty of this area as from 1 January 1986, and in January 1988 the USA recognized Canadian jurisdiction over the Arctic islands (but not over their waters) and undertook to notify the Canadian Government in advance of all Arctic passages by US surface vessels. Canada has also pursued a disagreement with France concerning the boundary of disputed waters near the French-controlled islands of St Pierre and Miquelon, off the coast of Newfoundland.

Government

Canada is a federal parliamentary state. Under the Constitution Act 1982, executive power is vested in the British monarch, as Head of State, and exercisable by her representative, the Governor-General, whom she appoints on the advice of the Canadian Prime Minister. The Federal Parliament comprises the Head of State, a nominated Senate (a maximum of 112 members, appointed on a regional basis) and a House of Commons (295 members elected by universal adult suffrage for single-member constituencies). A Parliament may last no longer than five years. The Governor-General appoints the Prime Minister and, on the latter's recommendation, other ministers to form the Cabinet. The Prime Minister should have the confidence of the House of Commons, to which the Cabinet is responsible. Canada comprises 10 provinces (each with a Lieutenant-Governor and a legislature, which may last no longer than five years, from which a premier is chosen), and two territories constituted by Act of Parliament.

Defence

Canada co-operates with the USA in the defence of North America and is a member of NATO. Military service is voluntary. In June 1990 the armed forces numbered 90,000: army 23,500, navy 17,100, air force 24,200 and 25,200 not identified by service. Defence expenditure for 1989/90 was estimated at C $11,454m. In 1987 the Government announced plans to modernize and expand the defence forces. Proposals to create a fleet of 10-12 nuclear submarines, however, were withdrawn for budgetary reasons in April 1989.

Economic Affairs

In 1988, according to estimates by the World Bank, Canada's gross national product (GNP), measured at average 1986-88 prices, was US $437,471m., equivalent to US $16,760 per head. Between 1980 and 1988, it was estimated, GNP increased, in real terms, by an annual average rate of 3.4%, while GNP per head increased at an average rate of 1.9% per year. Over the same period, the population increased by an annual average of 1.0%. Canada's gross domestic product (GDP) increased, in real terms, at an average rate of 3.3% per year in 1980-88.

Agriculture (including forestry and fishing) contributed about 4% of GDP in 1988, and about 4% of the labour force were employed in this sector in 1989. The principal crops are wheat, barley and other cereals, which, together with livestock production (chiefly cattle and pigs) and timber, provide an important source of export earnings. In 1989 Canada was the world's largest exporter (in terms of value) of fish and seafood. Production of furs is also important. During 1980-88 agricultural production increased by an annual average of 2.7%.

Industry (including mining, manufacturing, construction and power) employed 25.4% of the working population, and provided some 40% of GDP, in 1988. During 1980–88 industrial production increased at an average annual rate of 3.0%.

Mining provided 5.8% of GDP in 1986, but employed only 1.5% of the working population in 1989. Canada is the world's largest producer of zinc, and the second largest producer of asbestos, nickel, potash, uranium, gypsum, elemental sulphur and titanium concentrates. Gold, silver, iron, copper, cobalt and lead are also exploited. There are considerable reserves of petroleum and natural gas in Alberta, off the Atlantic coast, and in the Canadian Arctic islands.

Manufacturing contributed some 23% of GDP in 1988, and employed 18.4% of the labour force in 1989. The most important branches of manufacturing in 1986, measured by the value of output, were transport equipment (accounting for 20.1% of the total), food products (13.8%), paper, paper products, printing and publishing (10.7%), machinery (9.9%), chemical products, base metals, wood products and petroleum refineries. Manufacturing output increased at an average rate of 3.0% per year in 1980–88.

Energy is derived principally from hydroelectric power (which provided 67% of the electricity supply in 1985) and from coal-fired and nuclear power stations. Canada is an important source of US energy requirements, accounting in 1989 for 7% of the USA's requirements of natural gas and for 5% of its petroleum imports.

In 1989 Canada recorded a visible trade surplus of US $6,856m.; there was a deficit of US $14,091m. on the current account of the balance of payments. In 1989 the USA accounted for 73.3% of Canada's total exports and 65.2% of total imports; the EEC and Japan were also important trading partners. The principal exports in that year were motor vehicles and parts, lumber, wood pulp and paper, wheat and mineral fuels. The principal imports were foodstuffs, crude petroleum, chemicals, machinery, motor vehicles and computers. In January 1989 a free trade agreement with the USA entered into force, whereby virtually all remaining trade tariffs imposed between the two countries were to be eliminated over a 10-year period.

In the financial year ending 31 March 1990 there was an estimated budget deficit of C $28,942m. The annual rate of inflation averaged 5.0% in 1980–87, and stood at 4.0% in 1988, 5.4% in 1989 and 4.1% in the year ending July 1990. The rate of unemployment averaged 7.5% of the labour force in 1989.

Following the international recession of the mid-1970s, Canada's economy experienced inflationary pressures and, despite anti-inflationary measures (including the imposition of high interest rates), the average annual rate of inflation remained above 4% throughout the 1980s. Budgetary deficits in 1989 and 1990 were attributed largely to high interest rates. The rate of growth in real GDP exceeded 3.0% in 1989, but with the maintenance of high interest rates, was expected to decline to 1.8% in 1990 and to 1.1% in 1991.

Many sectors of Canadian industry rely heavily on foreign investment. Foreign control of Canadian corporations has been declining, however, since the mid-1970s, mainly as a result of government and private-sector acquisitions. In 1987 the share of total assets held by foreign-controlled corporations in Canadian industries was 18.2%: corporations classified as US-controlled accounted for 55.8% of these assets, and this proportion was expected to increase with the implementation, from 1989, of the US-Canada trade agreement. Canada is, however, a net capital exporter, largely as a result of massive flows of investment capital to the USA.

Social Welfare

Almost 39% of the 1989/90 federal budget was allocated to health and social welfare. The Federal Government administers family allowances, unemployment insurance and pensions. Other services are provided by the provinces. A federal medical care insurance programme covers all Canadians against medical expenses, and a federal-provincial hospital insurance programme covers over 99% of the insurable population.

Education

Education policy is a provincial responsibility, and the period of compulsory school attendance varies. French-speaking students are entitled by law, in some provinces, to instruction in French. Primary education is from the age of five or six years to 13–14, followed by three to five years at secondary or high school. In 1987 an estimated 97% of children aged six to 11 attended primary schools, while 92% of those aged 12 to 17 were enrolled at secondary schools. There are 69 universities and 201 other institutions of higher education.

Public Holidays

1991: 1 January (New Year), 29 March (Good Friday), 1 April (Easter Monday), 20 May (Victoria Day), 1 July (Canada Day), 2 September (Labour Day), 14 October (Thanksgiving), 11 November (Remembrance Day), 25 December (Christmas Day), 26 December (Boxing Day).

1992: 1 January (New Year), 17 April (Good Friday), 20 April (Easter Monday), 18 May (Victoria Day), 1 July (Canada Day), 7 September (Labour Day), 12 October (Thanksgiving), 11 November (Remembrance Day), 25 December (Christmas Day), 26 December (Boxing Day).

Weights and Measures

The metric system is in force.

CANADA — *Statistical Survey*

Statistical Survey

Source (unless otherwise stated): Statistics Canada, Ottawa K1A 0T6; tel. (613) 990-8116; telex 053-3585.

Area and Population

AREA, POPULATION AND DENSITY

Area (sq km)	
Land	9,215,430
Inland water	755,180
Total	9,970,610*
Population (census results)	
3 June 1981	24,343,180
3 June 1986†	
Males	12,485,650
Females	12,823,680
Total	25,309,330
Population (official estimates at 1 June)	
1988	25,909,200
1989	26,223,200
1990	26,584,000
Density (per sq km) at 1 June 1990	2.7

* 3,849,674 sq miles.
† Excluding census data for one or more incompletely enumerated Indian reserves or Indian settlements.

PROVINCES AND TERRITORIES
(census results, 3 June 1986)

	Land area (sq km)	Population*	Capital
Provinces:			
Alberta	644,390	2,365,825	Edmonton
British Columbia	929,730	2,883,367	Victoria
Manitoba	548,360	1,063,016	Winnipeg
New Brunswick	72,090	709,442	Fredericton
Newfoundland	371,690	568,349	St John's
Nova Scotia	52,840	873,176	Halifax
Ontario	891,190	9,101,694	Toronto
Prince Edward Island	5,660	126,646	Charlottetown
Québec	1,356,790	6,532,461	Québec
Saskatchewan	570,700	1,009,613	Regina
Territories:			
Northwest Territories	3,293,020	52,238	Yellowknife
Yukon Territory	478,970	23,504	Whitehorse
Total	9,215,430	25,309,331	—

* Excluding census data for one or more incompletely enumerated Indian reserves or Indian settlements.

PRINCIPAL TOWNS (census results, 3 June 1986)*

Ottawa (capital)	819,263†	St Catharines-Niagara	343,258
Toronto	3,427,168	London	342,302
Montréal‡	2,921,357	Kitchener	311,195
Vancouver	1,380,729	Halifax	295,990
Edmonton	785,465	Victoria	255,547
Calgary	671,326	Windsor	253,988
Winnipeg	625,304	Oshawa	203,543
Québec	603,267	Saskatoon	200,665
Hamilton	557,029		

* Including Canadian residents temporarily in the USA, but excluding US residents temporarily in Canada.
† Including Hull.
‡ Excluding census data for one or more incompletely enumerated Indian reserves or Indian settlements.

BIRTHS, MARRIAGES AND DEATHS

	Registered live births*		Registered marriages		Registered deaths*	
	Number	Rate (per 1,000)	Number	Rate (per 1,000)	Number	Rate (per 1,000)
1981	371,346	15.3	190,082	7.8	171,029	7.0
1982	373,082	15.1	188,360	7.6	174,413	7.1
1983	373,689	15.0	184,675	7.4	174,484	7.0
1984	377,031	15.0	185,597	7.4	175,727	7.0
1985	375,730	14.8	184,110	7.3	181,330	7.2
1986	372,913	14.7	175,518	6.9	184,224	7.3
1987	369,742	14.4	182,151	7.1	184,953	7.2
1988	376,795	14.5	187,728	7.2	190,011	7.3

* Including Canadian residents temporarily in the USA but excluding US residents temporarily in Canada.

IMMIGRATION

Country of Origin	1987	1988	1989*
United Kingdom	8,547	8,684	7,616
USA	7,967	6,518	6,916
Other	135,584	144,941	177,013
Total	**152,098**	**160,143**	**191,545**

* Preliminary.

ECONOMICALLY ACTIVE POPULATION*
('000 persons aged 15 years and over)

	1987	1988	1989
Agriculture	494	473	454
Fishing and trapping	44	48	46
Mines, quarries and oil wells	197	197	192
Manufacturing	2,202	2,271	2,294
Construction	790	834	876
Logging and forestry	88	89	87
Transport, communications and other utilities	956	960	1,011
Trade	2,271	2,328	2,346
Finance, insurance and real estate	731	755	764
Public administration	875	870	907
Other services	905	910	914
Total employed	**11,861**	**12,245**	**12,486**
Unemployed	1,150	1,030	1,018
Total labour force	**13,011**	**13,275**	**13,503**

* Figures exclude military personnel, inmates of institutions, residents of the Yukon and Northwest Territories, and Indian reserves.

CANADA *Statistical Survey*

Agriculture

PRINCIPAL CROPS ('000 metric tons)

	1987	1988	1989*
Wheat	25,950.2	15,996.1	24,382.9
Oats	2,995.2	2,993.4	3,548.9
Barley	13,957.1	10,212.3	11,672.4
Rye	436.7	267.9	835.4
Maize (Corn)	7,014.8	5,369.2	6,400.4
Buckwheat	44.1	30.7	32.2
Soybeans	1,269.8	1,152.6	1,219.0
Linseed	729.0	372.9	530.6
Rapeseed (Canola)	3,846.5	4,311.0	3,057.6
Beans	115.7	63.5	77.1
Tame hay	30,840.0	29,025.6	30,836.7

* Preliminary.
Potatoes ('000 metric tons): 3,033 in 1987; 2,778 in 1988; 2,754 in 1989.

LIVESTOCK ('000 head at 1 July)

	1988	1989	1990
Milch cows	1,429	1,421	1,379
Other cattle	12,060	12,199	12,287
Sheep	697	728	759
Pigs	10,890	10,635	10,532

DAIRY PRODUCE

	1987	1988	1989*
Milk (kilolitres)†	7,377,865	7,601,946	7,341,343
Creamery butter (metric tons)	94,208	104,324	98,531
Cheddar cheese (metric tons)	117,618	117,618	114,820
Ice-cream mix (kilolitres)	163,037	166,252	163,760
Eggs ('000 dozen)	475,450	476,902	476,950

* Preliminary.
† Farm sales of milk and cream.

Forestry

LUMBER PRODUCTION (1986, cubic metres)

	Softwoods	Hardwoods	Total
Newfoundland	37,171	14,880	52,051
Prince Edward Island	13,722	—	13,722
Nova Scotia	435,999	30,139	466,138
New Brunswick	1,427,504	49,493	1,476,997
Québec	10,757,338	551,496	11,308,834
Ontario	4,581,517	538,749	5,121,266
Manitoba	215,278	8,217	223,495
Saskatchewan	456,678	—	456,678
Alberta	2,943,725	—	2,943,725
British Columbia	30,990,299	6,175	30,996,474
Total	51,860,231	1,199,149	53,059,380

Fur Industry

NUMBER OF PELTS PRODUCED*

	1986/87	1987/88	1988/89
Newfoundland[1]	42,022	44,221	30,103
Prince Edward Island[2]	42,745	40,416	52,880
Nova Scotia[3]	345,689	298,252	339,974
New Brunswick	85,877	84,985	85,147
Québec	690,671	660,873	401,086
Ontario	1,555,869	1,515,967	1,115,739
Manitoba	409,789	440,939	165,650
Saskatchewan	412,265	490,449	148,128
Alberta	544,377	569,604	273,026
British Columbia	330,945	322,567	318,300
Northwest Territories[4]	178,071	150,985	69,788
Yukon[5]	26,265	25,858	19,837
Total[6]	4,664,585	4,645,119	3,019,658

* Including ranch-raised.
[1] Includes lynx from Nova Scotia.
[2] Excludes coyote (prairie wolf) and skunk, which is included in Nova Scotia.
[3] Includes coyote (prairie wolf) and skunk from Prince Edward Island, but excludes lynx, which is included in Newfoundland.
[4] Includes fisher (pekan or wood-shock) from the Yukon and white bear and coyote (prairie wolf) from the Northwest Territories for 1987/88, but excludes ermine (weasel).
[5] Includes ermine (weasel) and coyote (prairie wolf) from the Northwest Territories for 1988/89, but excludes white bear and white fox from the Yukon for 1987/88 and fisher (pekan or wood-shock) from the Yukon.
[6] Excludes hair seal.

Sea Fisheries

LANDINGS (metric tons, live weight)

	1987	1988	1989*
Atlantic total	1,265,913	1,326,828	1,285,202
Cod	458,051	467,834	422,163
Crab	28,798	31,284	24,109
Small flatfishes	90,629	73,945	70,194
Haddock	28,071	30,954	26,004
Halibut	2,417	2,566	2,317
Pollock	50,223	44,353	44,464
Redfish	79,016	78,112	75,567
Herring	248,744	266,484	221,952
Salmon	1,541	1,064	913
Lobsters	39,431	40,424	43,256
Scallops	73,813	77,800	91,987
Tuna	222	558	736
Pacific total	251,440	265,847	265,441
Halibut	7,240	7,802	5,142
Herring	37,615	31,601	40,107
Salmon	66,695	87,445	87,488
Canada total†	1,587,867	1,644,675	1,600,643

* Preliminary. † All sea fish.

CANADA

Mining

('000 metric tons, unless otherwise indicated)

	1987	1988	1989*
Metallic			
Bismuth (metric tons)	165	181	164
Cadmium (metric tons)	1,481	1,664	1,692
Cobalt (metric tons)	2,490	2,398	2,337
Copper (metric tons)	794,149	758,478	706,117
Gold (kilograms)	115,818	134,813	158,440
Iron ore	37,702	39,934	40,773
Lead (metric tons)	373,215	351,148	275,800
Molybdenum (metric tons)	14,771	13,535	13,716
Nickel (metric tons)	189,086	198,744	196,133
Platinum group (kilograms)	10,930	12,541	10,375
Selenium (metric tons)	430	321	363
Silver (metric tons)	1,375	1,443	1,262
Uranium oxide—U_3O_8 (metric tons)	13,612	12,066	11,564
Zinc (metric tons)	1,157,936	1,370,000	1,315,274
Non-metallic			
Asbestos	665	710	691
Gypsum	9,094	9,512	8,457
Nepheline syenite	506	540	626
Potash (K_2O)	7,668	8,154	7,036
Salt	10,129	10,687	11,350
Sulphur, in smelter gas	723	856	831
Sulphur, elemental	5,809	5,981	5,183
Fuels			
Coal	61,211	70,644	71,000
Natural gas (million cubic metres)†	78,267	90,911	92,837
Natural gas by-products ('000 cubic metres)‡	21,560	22,556	23,144
Petroleum, crude ('000 cubic metres)	89,140	93,806	90,427
Structural materials			
Cement	12,603	12,350	12,550
Sand and gravel	278,546	289,763	277,122
Stone	113,291	122,030	116,657

* Preliminary.
† Net withdrawals less processing and reprocessing shrinkage.
‡ Excludes sulphur.

Industry

VALUE OF SHIPMENTS (C $ million)

	1987	1988	1989*
Food industries	36,042	37,474	37,254
Beverage industries	5,324	5,659	5,574
Tobacco products industries	1,707	1,696	1,705
Rubber products industries	2,510	2,362	2,586
Plastic products industries	5,063	5,898	6,126
Leather and allied products industries	1,318	1,348	1,391
Primary textile industries	3,123	3,197	3,138
Textiles products industries	3,253	3,521	3,520
Clothing industries	6,457	6,532	6,817
Wood industries	14,611	14,906	15,178
Furniture and fixture industries	4,389	4,668	4,911
Paper and allied products industries	23,073	25,404	26,578
Printing, publishing and allied industries	11,180	12,227	12,890
Primary metal industries	19,154	22,168	22,048
Fabricated metal products industries	16,883	18,006	18,699
Machinery industries	8,725	9,808	10,062
Transportation equipment industries	43,334	50,509	53,529
Electrical and electronic products industries	16,069	18,271	19,599
Non-metallic mineral products industries	7,444	7,840	7,807

VALUE OF SHIPMENTS (C $ million)—*continued*

	1987	1988	1989*
Refined petroleum and coal products industries	16,494	14,089	14,401
Chemical and chemical products industries	20,248	22,741	23,051
Other manufacturing industries	5,635	6,112	6,321
Total	272,037	294,436	303,184

Electric Energy (net production, million kWh): 483,665 in 1987; 489,046 in 1988; 482,158 in 1989.

* Preliminary.

Finance

CURRENCY AND EXCHANGE RATES

Monetary Units
100 cents = 1 Canadian dollar (C $).

Denominations
Coins: 1, 5, 10, 25 and 50 cents; 1 dollar.
Notes: 2, 5, 10, 20, 50, 100 and 1,000 dollars.

Sterling and US Dollar Equivalents (30 September 1990)
£1 sterling = C $2.1625;
US $1 = C $1.1565;
C $100 = £46.24 = US $86.47.

Average Exchange Rate (C $ per US $)
1987 1.3260
1988 1.2307
1989 1.1840

FEDERAL BUDGET (C $ million, year ending 31 March)

Revenue	1988/89*	1989/90†
Personal income tax	46,026	51,895
Corporate income tax	11,730	13,021
Unemployment insurance contributions	11,268	10,738
Non-resident tax	1,578	1,361
Sales tax	15,645	17,671
Customs import duties	4,521	4,592
Energy taxes	2,646	2,471
Other excise taxes and duties	2,959	3,421
Other tax revenue	265	226
Non-tax revenue: return on investments	5,509	5,839
Other non-tax revenue	1,851	2,480
Total budgetary revenue	103,998	113,715

Expenditure	1988/89*	1989/90†
Major transfer and subsidy payments to persons	30,392	32,210
Old age security benefits, guaranteed income supplements and spouses' allowances	15,202	16,154
Unemployment insurance benefits	10,972	11,694
Family allowances	2,606	2,654
Veterans' benefits	1,612	1,708
Transfers to other levels of government	21,588	22,768
Fiscal arrangements	8,127	8,933
Insurance and medical care services	6,678	6,663
Canada Assistance Plan	4,556	5,006
Education support	2,227	2,166
Other programme expenditures	47,564	48,843
Defence	11,025	11,454
External affairs and aid	3,557	3,786
All other departments and agencies	32,982	33,603
Public debt charges	33,169	38,836
Total expenditure	132,713	142,657

1990/91: Operating surplus estimated at C $14,000m.; Budgetary deficit estimated at C $29,500m.–C $30,000m..

* Based on preliminary financial statements for the fiscal year ending 31 March 1989.
† Based on preliminary financial statements for the fiscal year ending 31 March 1990.

CANADA

GOLD RESERVES AND CURRENCY IN CIRCULATION
(C $ million at 31 December)

	1987	1988	1989
Gold holdings*	919.5	807.2	740.6
US dollar holdings*	6,163.0	12,608.3	11,489.3
Notes in circulation	19,447.0	21,032.0	22,093.0

* US $ million.

COST OF LIVING (Consumer Price Index. Base: 1986 = 100)

	1987	1988	1989
Food	104.4	107.2	111.1
Housing	104.0	108.6	114.3
Clothing	104.2	109.6	114.1
Transport	103.6	105.6	111.1
Health and personal care	105.0	109.6	114.4
Recreation, education and reading	105.4	111.3	116.2
Tobacco and alcohol	108.5	117.3	138.2
All items	104.4	108.6	114.0

NATIONAL ACCOUNTS (C $ million at current prices)
National Income and Product

	1987	1988	1989*
Compensation of employees	298,850	328,562	358,355
Operating surplus	128,336	142,763	149,245
Domestic factor incomes	427,186	471,325	570,600
Consumption of fixed capital	64,066	67,813	72,915
Gross domestic product at factor cost	491,252	539,138	580,515
Indirect taxes, less subsidies	58,432	65,205	73,133
Statistical discrepancy	1,652	−987	−2,032
GDP at market prices	551,336	603,356	651,616
Factor income from abroad†	8,056	11,319	8,499
Less Factor income paid abroad†	24,226	30,201	30,651
Gross national product	535,166	584,474	629,464
Less Consumption of fixed capital	64,066	67,813	72,915
Statistical discrepancy	−1,652	987	2,032
National income at market prices	469,448	517,648	558,581
Other current transfers from abroad‡	2,035	2,512	2,400
Less Other current transfers paid abroad‡	2,926	3,243	3,180
National disposable income	468,557	516,917	557,801

*Preliminary.
† Remitted profits, dividends and interest only.
‡ Transfers to and from persons and governments.

Expenditure on the Gross Domestic Product

	1987	1988	1989*
Government final consumption expenditure	106,099	113,295	121,242
Private final consumption expenditure	323,104	350,624	380,907
Increase in stocks	2,719	2,483	3,754
Gross fixed capital formation	116,177	131,536	143,352
Exports of goods and services	144,755	158,731	162,852
Less Imports of goods and services	139,867	154,299	162,523
Statistical discrepancy	−1,651	986	2,032
GDP at market prices	551,336	603,356	651,616
GDP at constant 1986 prices	526,123	549,237	565,657

* Preliminary.

BALANCE OF PAYMENTS (US $ million)

	1987	1988	1989
Merchandise exports f.o.b.	97,967	115,775	123,215
Merchandise imports f.o.b.	−89,092	−106,637	−116,359
Trade balance	8,875	9,139	6,856
Exports of services	17,317	22,497	21,507
Imports of services	−34,703	−43,340	−46,788
Balance on goods and services	−8,511	−11,704	−18,425
Private unrequited transfers (net)	2,044	3,834	4,703
Government unrequited transfers (net)	−451	−330	−368
Current balance	−6,917	−8,200	−14,091
Direct capital investment (net)	−3,150	−2,311	−985
Other long-term capital (net)	10,430	11,929	20,708
Short-term capital (net)	4,770	9,530	−771
Net errors and omissions	−2,354	−3,390	−4,567
Total (net monetary movements)	2,778	7,558	293
Valuation changes (net)	149	−38	−29
Exceptional financing (net)	564	—	—
Changes in reserves	3,491	7,521	264

Source: IMF, *International Financial Statistics*.

External Trade

PRINCIPAL COMMODITIES (C $ million)

Imports	1988	1989
Live animals	118.1	140.0
Food, feed, beverages and tobacco	7,024.3	7,412.0
Meat, fresh, chilled or frozen	1,282.2	1,377.8
Fish and marine animals	694.8	738.8
Fruit and vegetables	2,636.0	2,730.0
Raw sugar	210.9	203.8
Coffee	432.5	388.7
Distilled alcoholic beverages	160.2	204.1
Other beverages	350.3	461.4
Crude materials (inedible)	6,965.6	7,974.9
Fur skins (undressed)	152.4	103.1
Rubber and allied gums	133.4	120.3
Iron ores and concentrates	221.7	233.7
Aluminium ores, concentrates and scrap	225.2	204.6
Other metal ores, concentrates and scrap	924.0	1,119.0
Coal	728.2	685.3
Crude petroleum	2,820.8	3,602.4
Fabricated materials (inedible)	25,175.7	26,243.3
Wood and paper	2,282.4	2,391.1
Textiles	2,161.3	2,236.9
Chemicals	7,579.2	8,142.2
Iron and steel	3,032.1	2,584.5
Non-ferrous metals	2,911.1	2,832.1
End products (inedible)	89,716.5	90,529.1
General purpose machinery	4,828.7	5,156.3
Special industrial machinery	6,624.0	6,455.1
Agricultural machinery and tractors	1,672.6	1,885.5
Passenger automobiles and chassis	12,223.9	11,762.1
Trucks, truck tractors and chassis	3,033.1	2,608.3
Motor vehicle parts (excl. engines)	14,363.3	13,591.5
Televisions, radios and phonographs	996.4	1,097.7
Other telecommunication and related equipment	3,144.4	3,428.6
Miscellaneous electrical lighting distribution equipment	708.9	705.1
Miscellaneous measuring and laboratory equipment	1,158.6	1,308.8
Furniture and fixtures	904.6	1,113.0
Hand tools and cutlery	655.1	678.3
Electronic computers	5,747.4	5,989.6
Miscellaneous office machines and equipment	298.9	303.1
Miscellaneous equipment and tools	1,646.1	1,847.6
Special transactions, trade	2,663.7	2,835.7
Total	131,663.9	135,134.9

CANADA

Exports	1988	1989
Live animals	612.6	563.3
Food, feed, beverages and tobacco	11,113.0	9,300.9
Meat, fresh, chilled or frozen	884.7	885.6
Fish, fresh or frozen	746.9	686.6
Fish, fresh or frozen, whole	555.3	521.3
Barley	283.1	573.1
Wheat	4,442.8	2,579.0
Vegetables	443.6	471.1
Whisky	272.8	243.5
Crude materials (inedible)	17,248.1	18,027.0
Rapeseed	607.4	624.0
Iron ores and concentrates	968.0	943.2
Copper ores, concentrates and scrap	936.6	1,102.4
Nickel ores, concentrates and scrap	692.3	843.7
Crude petroleum	4,038.2	4,415.3
Natural gas	2,954.5	2,935.4
Coal and other bituminous substances	1,944.0	2,081.7
Asbestos (unmanufactured)	389.8	444.4
Fabricated materials (inedible)	47,526.1	47,111.4
Lumber, softwood	5,233.6	5,361.6
Wood pulp and similar pulp	6,495.8	6,945.1
Newsprint paper	7,299.2	6,447.8
Organic chemicals	1,880.6	1,824.9
Fertilizers and fertilizer material	1,663.4	1,464.4
Petroleum and coal products	2,359.6	2,315.8
Aluminium and alloys	3,487.9	3,281.0
Copper and alloys	1,020.1	1,229.9
Nickel and alloys	960.2	966.1
Precious metals and alloys	2,465.5	2,568.7
Electricity	893.8	662.8
End products (inedible)	57,318.3	58,051.6
Industrial machinery	3,730.7	3,964.3
Agricultural machinery and tractors	702.9	885.0
Passenger automobiles and chassis	17,127.2	16,470.4
Trucks, truck tractors and chassis	7,294.1	7,354.4
Motor vehicle engines and parts	2,324.7	2,259.3
Motor vehicle parts (excl. engines)	8,000.7	7,918.7
Office machines and equipment	2,476.1	2,291.5
Special transactions, trade	691.0	706.3
Total	134,509.1	133,760.5

PRINCIPAL TRADING PARTNERS (C $ million)

Imports	1988	1989
Australia	672	618
Austria	284	376
Belgium	587	540
Brazil	1,192	1,129
China, People's Repub.	955	1,182
Denmark	258	254
Finland	343	372
France	2,884	2,019
Germany, Fed. Repub.	3,841	3,709
Hong Kong	1,152	1,160
Italy	1,954	2,015
Japan	9,267	9,571
Korea, Repub.	2,270	2,441
Malaysia	323	320
Mexico	1,327	1,704
Netherlands	762	822
Nigeria	310	505
Norway	494	784
Puerto Rico	246	340
Saudi Arabia	95	253
Singapore	466	502
Spain	713	565
Sweden	932	939
Switzerland	698	599
Taiwan	2,255	2,351
Thailand	343	419
United Kingdom	4,629	4,562
USA	86,020	88,017
Venezuela	459	596
Total (incl. others)	131,171	135,033

Exports	1988	1989
Algeria	289	298
Australia	893	1,101
Belgium	1,168	1,425
Brazil	516	529
China, People's Repub.	2,606	1,145
France	1,227	1,318
Germany, Fed. Repub.	1,775	1,871
Hong Kong	1,004	1,076
India	391	311
Indonesia	318	311
Iran	1,034	1,128
Iraq	142	299
Italy	191	377
Korea, Repub.	1,210	1,655
Mexico	499	622
Netherlands	1,437	1,590
Norway	489	642
Philippines	133	221
Saudi Arabia	207	340
Singapore	294	265
Spain	245	404
Sweden	328	337
Switzerland	712	737
Taiwan	1,038	973
Thailand	269	345
USSR	1,152	688
United Kingdom	3,562	3,551
USA	100,321	101,411
Total (incl. others)	137,550	138,339

Transport

RAILWAYS (revenue traffic)*

	1987	1988	1989
Passenger-km (million)	1,854	2,142	2,226
Freight ton-km (million)	261,663	263,635	240,519

* Seven major rail carriers only.

ROAD TRAFFIC ('000 vehicles registered at 31 December)

	1986	1987	1988
Passenger cars (incl. taxis and for car hire)	11,586	11,686	12,086
Truck and truck tractors (commercial and non-commercial)	3,156	3,157	3,706
Buses (school and other)	56	59	60
Motorcycles	430	414	370
Other (ambulances, fire trucks, etc.)	72	83	84

INLAND WATER TRAFFIC
(St Lawrence Seaway, '000 metric tons)

	1987	1988	1989
Montréal–Lake Ontario	39,969	40,558	37,070
Welland Canal	42,725	43,536	39,909

Source: St Lawrence Seaway Authority.

CANADA

INTERNATIONAL SEA-BORNE SHIPPING

	1986	1987	1988
Goods ('000 metric tons)			
Loaded	144,561	158,994	171,064
Unloaded	62,012	68,025	78,912
Vessels (number)			
Arrived	28,086	29,404	31,011
Departed	28,061	29,666	30,038

CIVIL AVIATION (Canadian carriers—revenue traffic, '000)*

	1986	1987	1988
Passengers	26,099	26,791	30,180
Km flown	465,269	491,779	n.a.
Passenger-km	40,034,760	41,643,839	48,737,030
Goods ton-km	1,202,882	1,239,422	1,374,160

* Unit toll services.

Tourism

	1987	1988	1989
Travellers from the United States:			
Number ('000)	36,953	36,147	34,705
Expenditure (C $ million)	4,160	4,267	4,194
Travellers from other countries:			
Number ('000)	2,643	3,106	3,277
Expenditure (C $ million)	2,139	2,627	2,897

Communications Media

('000)

	1987	1988	1989
Total households	9,082	9,244	9,477
Homes with radio	8,977	9,124	9,377
Homes with television	8,942	9,112	9,355
Homes with telephone	8,944	9,099	9,351

Daily newspapers in French and English 107 (1988); total circulation 5,993,000.

Education

(1989/90)

	Institutions	Teachers*	Pupils*
Primary and secondary	15,440	283,068†	5,074,654
Post secondary non-university	201	25,890	321,190
Universities and colleges	69	37,680	315,130‡

* Full-time only.
† Estimate.
‡ Regular winter session only.

Directory

The Constitution

Constitutional development has been based mainly upon five important acts of the British Parliament: the Quebec Act of 1774, the Constitutional Act of 1791, the Act of Union of 1840, the British North America Act of 1867, and the Canada Act of 1982. The British North America Act 1867 provided that the Constitution of Canada should be 'similar in principle to that of the United Kingdom'; that the executive authority be vested in the Sovereign, and carried on in her name by a Governor-General and Privy Council; and that legislative power be exercised by a Parliament of two Houses, the Senate and the House of Commons. The enactment of the Canada Act of 1982 was the final act of the United Kingdom Parliament in Canadian constitutional development. The Act gave to Canada the power to amend the Constitution according to procedures determined by the Constitution Act 1982, which was proclaimed in force by the Queen on 17 April 1982. The Constitution Act 1982 added to the Canadian Constitution a Charter of Rights and Freedoms, and provisions which recognize the nation's multicultural heritage, affirm the existing rights of native peoples, confirm the principle of equalization of benefits among the provinces and strengthen provincial ownership of natural resources.

THE GOVERNMENT

The national government operates through three main agencies. There is Parliament (consisting of the Sovereign as represented by the Governor-General, the Senate and the House of Commons) which makes the laws; the Executive (the Cabinet or Ministry) which applies the laws; and the Judiciary which interprets the laws.

Particular features similar to the British system of government are the close relation which exists between the Executive and Legislative branches, and the doctrine of cabinet responsibility which has become crystallized in the course of time. The Prime Minister is appointed by the Governor-General and is habitually the leader of the political party commanding the confidence of the House of Commons. He chooses the members of his Cabinet from members of his party in Parliament, principally from those in the House of Commons. Each Minister or member of the Cabinet is usually responsible for the administration of a department, although there may be Ministers without portfolio whose experience and counsel are drawn upon to strengthen the Cabinet, but who are not at the head of departments. Each Minister of a department is responsible to Parliament for that department, and the Cabinet is collectively responsible before Parliament for government policy and administration generally.

Meetings of the Cabinet are presided over by the Prime Minister. From the Cabinet signed orders and recommendations go to the Governor-General for his or her approval, and the Crown acts only on the advice of its responsible Ministers. The Cabinet takes the responsibility for its advice being in accordance with the support of Parliament and is held strictly accountable.

THE FEDERAL PARLIAMENT

Parliament must meet at least once a year, so that twelve months do not elapse between the last meeting in one session and the first meeting in the next. The duration of Parliament may not be longer than five years from the date of election of a House of Commons. Senators (normally a maximum of 104 in number) are appointed until age 75 by the Governor-General in Council. They must be at least 30 years of age, residents of the province they represent and in possession of C $4,000 of real property over and above their liabilities. Members of the House of Commons are elected by universal adult suffrage for the duration of a Parliament.

Under the Constitution, the Federal Parliament has exclusive legislative authority in all matters relating to public debt and property; regulation of trade and commerce; raising of money by any mode of taxation; borrowing of money on the public credit; postal service, census and statistics; militia, military and naval service and defence; fixing and providing for salaries and allowances of the officers of the Government; beacons, buoys and lighthouses; navigation and shipping; quarantine and the establishment and maintenance of marine hospitals; sea-coast and inland fisheries; ferries on an international or interprovincial frontier;

CANADA

currency and coinage; banking, incorporation of banks, and issue of paper money; savings banks; weights and measures; bills of exchange and promissory notes; interest; legal tender; bankruptcy and insolvency; patents of invention and discovery; copyrights; Indians and lands reserved for Indians; naturalization and aliens; marriage and divorce; the criminal law, except the constitution of courts of criminal jurisdiction but including the procedure in criminal matters; the establishment, maintenance and management of penitentiaries; such classes of subjects as are expressly excepted in the enumeration of the classes of subjects exclusively assigned to the Legislatures of the provinces by the Act. Judicial interpretation and later amendment have, in certain cases, modified or clearly defined the respective powers of the Federal Government and provincial governments.

Both the Parliament of Canada and the legislatures of the provinces may legislate with respect to agriculture and immigration, but provincial legislation shall have effect in and for the provinces as long and as far only as it is not repugnant to any Act of Parliament. Both Parliament and the provincial legislatures may legislate with respect to old age pensions and supplementary benefits, but no federal law shall affect the operation of any present or future law of a province in relation to these matters.

PROVINCIAL AND MUNICIPAL GOVERNMENT

In each of the ten provinces the Sovereign is represented by a Lieutenant-Governor, appointed by the Governor-General in Council, and acting on the advice of the Ministry or Executive Council, which is responsible to the Legislature and resigns office when it ceases to enjoy the confidence of that body. The Legislatures are unicameral, consisting of an elected Legislative Assembly and the Lieutenant-Governor. The duration of a Legislature may not exceed five years from the date of the election of its members.

The Legislature in each province may exclusively make laws in relation to: amendment of the constitution of the province, except as regards the Lieutenant-Governor; direct taxation within the province; borrowing of money on the credit of the province; establishment and tenure of provincial offices and appointment and payment of provincial officers; the management and sale of public lands belonging to the province and of the timber and wood thereon; the establishment, maintenance and management of public and reformatory prisons in and for the province; the establishment, maintenance and management of hospitals, asylums, charities and charitable institutions in and for the province other than marine hospitals; municipal institutions in the province; shop, saloon, tavern, auctioneer and other licences issued for the raising of provincial or municipal revenue; local works and undertakings other than interprovincial or international lines of ships, railways, canals, telegraphs, etc., or works which, though wholly situtated within the province are declared by the Federal Parliament to be for the general advantage either of Canada or two or more provinces; the incorporation of companies with provincial objects; the solemnization of marriage in the province; property and civil rights in the province; the administration of justice in the province, including the constitution, maintenance and organization of provincial courts both in civil and criminal jurisdiction, and including procedure in civil matters in these courts; the imposition of punishment by fine, penalty or imprisonment for enforcing any law of the province relating to any of the aforesaid subjects; generally all matters of a merely local or private nature in the province. Further, provincial Legislatures may exclusively make laws in relation to education, subject to the protection of religious minorities; and to non-renewable natural resources, forestry resources and electrical energy, including their export from one province to another, and to the right to impose any mode or system of taxation thereon, subject in both cases to such laws not being discriminatory.

Under the Constitution Act, the municipalities are the creations of the provincial governments. Their bases of organization and the extent of their authority vary in different provinces, but almost everywhere they have very considerable powers of local self-government.

The Government

Head of State: HM Queen ELIZABETH II (succeeded to the throne 6 February 1952).

Governor-General: RAMON JOHN HNATYSHYN (took office 29 January 1990).

FEDERAL MINISTRY
(January 1991)

Prime Minister: (MARTIN) BRIAN MULRONEY.
Secretary of State for External Affairs: (CHARLES) JOSEPH CLARK.
Minister for International Trade: JOHN CARNELL CROSBIE.
Deputy Prime Minister, President of the Queen's Privy Council for Canada and Minister of Agriculture: DONALD FRANK MAZANKOWSKI.
Minister of Public Works and Minister for the purposes of the Atlantic Canada Opportunities Agency Act: ELMER MACINTOSH MACKAY.
Minister of Energy, Mines and Resources: ARTHUR JACOB EPP.
Minister of the Environment: ROBERT R. DE COTRET.
Minister of National Health and Welfare: HENRY PERRIN BEATTY.
Minister of Finance: MICHAEL HOLCOMBE WILSON.
Minister of State and Leader of the Government in the House of Commons: HARVIE ANDRE.
Minister of National Revenue: OTTO JOHN JELINEK.
Minister of Indian Affairs and Northern Development: THOMAS EDWARD SIDDON.
Minister of Western Economic Diversification and Minister of State (Grains and Oilseeds): CHARLES JAMES MAYER.
Minister of National Defence: WILLIAM HUNTER McKNIGHT.
Minister of Industry, Science and Technology: BENOÎT BOUCHARD.
Minister of Communications: MARCEL MASSE.
Minister of Employment and Immigration: BARBARA JEAN McDOUGALL.
Minister of Veterans' Affairs: GERALD STAIRS MERRITHEW.
Minister of State (Employment and Immigration) and Minister of State (Senior Citizens): MONIQUE VÉZINA.
Minister of Forestry: FRANK OBERLE.
Leader of the Government in the Senate and Minister of State (Federal-Provincial Relations): LOWELL MURRAY.
Minister of Supply and Services: PAUL WYATT DICK.
Solicitor-General of Canada: PIERRE H. CADIEUX.
Minister of State (Small Businesses and Tourism): THOMAS HOCKIN.
Minister for External Relations: MONIQUE LANDRY.
Minister of Fisheries and Oceans: BERANARD VALCOURT.
Secretary of State of Canada and Minister of State (Multiculturalism and Citizenship): GERRY WEINER.
Minister of Transport: DOUGLAS GRINSLADE LEWIS.
Minister of Consumer and Corporate Affairs and Minister of State (Agriculture): PIERRE BLAIS.
Minister of State (Privatization and Regulatory Affairs): JOHN HORTON McDERMID.
Minister of State (Indian Affairs and Northern Development): SHIRLEY MARTIN.
Associate Minister of National Defence and Minister responsible for the Status of Women: MARY COLLINS.
Minister of State (Housing): ALAN REDWAY.
Minister for Science: WILLIAM CHARLES WINEGARD.
Minister of Justice and Attorney-General of Canada: KIM CAMPBELL.
Minister of Labour and Minister of State (Transport): JEAN CORBEIL.
President of the Treasury Board and Minister of State (Finance): GILLES LOISELLE.
Minister of State (Youth), Minister of State (Fitness and Amateur Sport) and Deputy Leader of the Government in the House of Commons: MARCEL DANIS.

MINISTRIES

Office of the Prime Minister: Langevin Block, Parliament Bldgs, Ottawa K1A 0A2; tel. (613) 992-4211; telex 053-3208; fax (613) 995-0101.

Agriculture Canada: Sir John Carling Bldg, 930 Carling Ave, Ottawa K1A 0C5; tel. (613) 995-5222; telex 053-3283 fax (613) 996-9564.

Department of Communications: Journal North Tower, 300 Slater St, Ottawa K1A 0C8; tel. (613) 990-6886; telex 053-3342; fax (613) 952-2429.

Department of Consumer and Corporate Affairs: place du Portage, Ottawa-Hull K1A 0C9; tel. (819) 997-2938; telex 053-3694; fax (819) 997-2721.

Employment and Immigration Canada: 140 promenade du Portage, Ottawa-Hull K1A 0J9; tel. (819) 994-6313; fax (819) 994-0116.

CANADA   Directory

Department of Energy, Mines and Resources: 580 Booth St, Ottawa K1A 0E4; tel. (613) 995-3065; telex 053-3117; fax (613) 996-9094.

Environment Canada: Les Terrasses de la Chaudière, Ottawa K1A 0H3; tel. (819) 997-2800; telex 053-3608; fax (819) 953-6789.

Department of External Affairs: Lester B. Pearson Bldg, 125 Sussex Drive, Ottawa K1A 0G2; tel. (613) 995-1851; telex 053-3745; fax (613) 996-9288.

Department of Finance: 140 O'Connor St, Ottawa K1A 0G5; tel. (613) 992-1575; telex 053-3336; fax (613) 996-2690.

Department of Fisheries and Oceans: 200 Kent St, Ottawa K1A 0E6; tel. (613) 993-0600; telex 053-4228.

Department of Indian Affairs and Northern Development: Les Terrasses de la Chaudière, 10 Wellington St, Ottawa K1A 0H4; tel. (613) 995-5586; telex 053-3711; fax (613) 997-1587.

Department of Industry, Science and Technology: 235 Queen St, Ottawa K1A 0H5; tel. (613) 992-4292; telex 053-4123; fax (613) 954-1894.

Department of Justice: Justice Bldg, Kent and Wellington Sts, Ottawa K1A 0H8; tel. (613) 957-4222; telex 053-3603; fax (613) 954-0811.

Department of Labour: Labour Canada, Ottawa K1A 0J2; tel. (613) 997-2617; fax (819) 953-0176.

Department of National Defence: 101 Colonel By Drive, Ottawa K1A 0K2; tel. (613) 996-4450; telex 053-4218.

Department of National Health and Welfare: Brooke Claxton Bldg, Tunney's Pasture, Ottawa K1A 0K9; tel. (613) 957-2991; telex 053-3270; fax (613) 952-7266.

Department of Public Works: Sir Charles Tupper Bldg, Confederation Heights, Riverside Drive, Ottawa K1A 0M2; tel. (613) 736-2400; telex 053-4235; fax (613) 736-2344.

Department of Regional Industrial Expansion: 235 Queen St, Ottawa K1A 0H5; tel. (613) 995-9001; telex 053-4124.

Revenue Canada (Customs and Excise): Connaught Bldg, 2nd Floor, Sussex Drive, Ottawa K1A 0L5; tel. (613) 957-9192; telex 053-3330.

Revenue Canada (Taxation): Headquarters Bldg, 875 Heron Rd, Ottawa K1A 0L8; tel. (613) 995-2960; telex 053-4974.

Secretary of State of Canada: Ottawa K1A 0M5; tel. (819) 997-0055; fax (819) 953-5382.

Solicitor-General: Sir Wilfrid Laurier Bldg, 340 Laurier Ave West, Ottawa K1A 0P8; tel. (613) 991-2857; telex 053-3768.

Department of Supply and Services: 11 Laurier St, Ottawa-Hull K1A 0S5; tel. (819) 956-2304; fax (819) 994-8404.

Department of Transport: Place de Ville, Transport Canada Bldg, 330 Sparks St, Ottawa K1A 0N5; tel. (613) 990-2309; telex 053-3130; fax (613) 996-9622.

Treasury Board: 140 O'Connor St, Ottawa K1A 0R5; tel. (613) 996-2690; telex 053-3336; fax (613) 957-2400.

Department of Veterans' Affairs: POB 7700, Charlottetown, PEI C1A 8M9; tel. (902) 566-8888; telex 014-44228.

Department of Western Economic Diversification: Centennial Towers, 200 Kent St, 8th Floor, POB 2128, Station D, Ottawa K1P 5W3.

Federal Legislature

THE SENATE
Speaker: GUY CHARBONNEAU.

Seats at December 1990

Progressive Conservative	54
Liberal	52
Independent	4
Independent Liberal	1
Reform Party	1
Total	112*

* Includes eight supplementary seats created in September 1990. The total is to revert to 104 seats with retirements or resignations of incumbent members.

HOUSE OF COMMONS
Speaker: JOHN A. FRASER.

General Election, 21 November 1988

	Seats at election	Seats at Dec. 1990
Progressive Conservative	170	159
Liberal	82	80
New Democratic Party	43	44
Independent	—	11
Reform Party	—	1
Total	295	295

Provincial Legislatures

ALBERTA
Lieutenant-Governor: HELEN HUNLEY (until 21 January 1991).
Premier: DONALD GETTY.

Election, April 1989

	Seats at election	Seats at Nov. 1990
Progressive Conservative	59	59
New Democratic Party	16	16
Liberal	8	8
Total	83	83

BRITISH COLUMBIA
Lieutenant-Governor: DAVID LAM.
Premier: WILLIAM VANDER ZALM.

Election, October 1986

	Seats at election	Seats at Nov. 1990
Social Credit	47	43
New Democratic Party	22	26
Total	69	69

MANITOBA
Lieutenant-Governor: Dr GEORGE JOHNSON.
Premier: GARY FILMON.

Election, September 1990

	Seats at election
Progressive Conservative	30
New Democratic Party	20
Liberal	7
Total	57

NEW BRUNSWICK
Lieutenant-Governor: GILBERT FINN.
Premier: FRANK MCKENNA.

Election, October 1987

	Seats at election	Seats at Nov. 1990
Liberal	58	58
Progressive Conservative	—	—
New Democratic Party	—	—
Total	58	58

NEWFOUNDLAND AND LABRADOR
Lieutenant-Governor: JAMES A. MCGRATH.
Premier: CLYDE KIRBY WELLS.

CANADA

Election, April 1989

	Seats at election	Seats at Nov. 1990
Liberal	31	31
Progressive Conservative	21	18
Independent	—	2
Vacant	—	1
Total	**52**	**52**

NOVA SCOTIA
Lieutenant-Governor: LLOYD R. CROUSE.
Premier: ROGER S. BACON (acting).

Election, September 1988

	Seats at election	Seats at Nov. 1990
Progressive Conservative	28	28
Liberal	21	22
New Democratic Party	2	2
Independent	1	—
Total	**52**	**52**

ONTARIO
Lieutenant-Governor: LINCOLN M. ALEXANDER.
Premier: ROBERT K. RAE.

Election, September 1990

	Seats at election
New Democratic Party	74
Liberal	36
Progressive Conservative	20
Total	**130**

PRINCE EDWARD ISLAND
Lieutenant-Governor: MARION L. REID.
Premier: JOSEPH A. GHIZ.

Election, May 1989

	Seats at election	Seats at Nov. 1990
Liberal	30	29
Progressive Conservative	2	2
Vacant	—	1
Total	**32**	**32**

QUÉBEC
Lieutenant-Governor: MARTIAL ASSELIN.
Premier: ROBERT BOURASSA.

Election, September 1989

	Seats at election	Seats at Nov. 1990
Liberal	92	92
Parti Québécois	29	29
Equality Party	4	4
Total	**125**	**125**

SASKATCHEWAN
Lieutenant-Governor: SYLVIA FEDORUK.
Premier: GRANT DEVINE.

Election, October 1986

	Seats at election	Seats at Nov. 1990
Progressive Conservative	38	34
New Democratic Party	25	26
Liberal	1	—
Vacant	—	4
Total	**64**	**64**

Territorial Legislatures

NORTHWEST TERRITORIES
Commissioner: DAN NORRIS.
Government Leader and Minister of the Executive Department: DENNIS PATTERSON.

The Legislative Assembly, elected in October 1987, consists of 24 independent members without formal party affiliation.

YUKON TERRITORY
Commissioner: J. KENNETH MCKINNON.
Government Leader and Minister of the Executive Council Office: TONY PENIKETT.

Election, February 1989

	Seats at election	Seats at Nov. 1990
New Democratic Party	9	9
Progressive Conservative	7	6
Vacant	—	1
Total	**16**	**16**

Political Organizations

British Columbia Social Credit Party: 10711 Cambie Rd, Suite 236, Richmond, BC V6X 3G5; tel. (604) 270-4040; fax (604) 270-4726; conservative; governing party of British Columbia 1952–72 and since 1975; Leader WILLIAM VANDER ZALM; Pres. HOPE WOTHERSPOON.

Communist Party of Canada: 24 Cecil St, Toronto, Ont M5T 1N2; tel. (416) 979-2109; f. 1921; Chair. WILLIAM KASHTAN; Gen. Sec. GEORGE HEWISON.

Equality Party: 5473 ave Royalmount, Montréal, Qué H4P 1J3; tel. (514) 485-1060; f. 1989; represents interests of anglophone population of Québec; secured four seats in provincial legislative elections in Sept. 1989; Leader RICHARD HOLDEN.

Green Party of Canada/Canadian Greens: 831 Commercial Drive, Vancouver, BC V5L 3W6; tel. (604) 254-8165; fax (604) 254-8166; f. 1983; environmentalist.

Liberal Party of Canada: 200 Laurier Ave West, Suite 200, Ottawa K1P 6M8; tel. (613) 237-0740; fax (613) 235-7208; supports Canadian autonomy, comprehensive social security, freer trade within the North Atlantic Community; Leader JEAN CHRÉTIEN; Pres. DONALD J. JOHNSTON; Sec.-Gen. SHEILA GERVAIS.

New Democratic Party: 280 Albert St, Ottawa K1P 5G8; tel. (613) 236-3613; fax (613) 230-9950; f. 1961; social democratic; Leader AUDREY MCLAUGHLIN; Pres. SANDRA MITCHELL; Sec. DICK PROCTOR; 400,000 mems. (1990).

Parti Indépendantiste: 5933 rue Waverly, Montréal, Qué H2T 2Y4; tel. (514) 272-4654; f. 1984 by breakaway faction of Parti Québécois; seeks full independence for Québec; Dir-Gen. RAYMOND VILLENEUVE.

Parti Québécois: 7370 rue St-Hubert, Montréal, Qué H2R 2N3; tel. (514) 270-5400; fax (514) 270-2865; f. 1968; social democratic; seeks political sovereignty for Québec in an economic association with Canada; governing party of Québec 1976–85; Pres. JACQUES PARIZEAU; Chair. Nat. Exec. BERNARD LANDRY; 136,000 mems (1990).

Progressive Conservative Party: 161 Laurier Ave West, Suite 200, Ottawa K1P 5J2; tel. (613) 238-6111; fax (613) 563-7892; f. 1854; advocates individualism and free enterprise and continued Canadian participation in NATO; Leader (MARTIN) BRIAN MULRONEY; Pres. JERRY ST GERMAIN; Nat. Dir JEAN-CAROL PELLETIER.

Reform Party of Canada: 10053 111th St, Suite 501, Edmonton, Alta T5K 2H8; tel. (403) 482-5768; fax (403) 488-0242; f. 1987; seeks increased influence for western provinces at fed. parl. level; Leader PRESTON MANNING; Chief Admin. WESLEY MACLEOD.

Diplomatic Representation

EMBASSIES AND HIGH COMMISSIONS IN CANADA

Algeria: 435 Daly Ave, Ottawa K1N 6H3; tel. (613) 232-9453; telex 053-3625; fax (613) 232-9099; Ambassador: MOHAMMED GHOUALMI.

Antigua and Barbuda: Place de Ville, Tower B, 112 Kent St, Suite 205, Ottawa K1P 5P2; tel. (613) 234-9143; fax (613) 232-0539; High Commissioner: CONRAD F. RICHARDS.

CANADA
Directory

Argentina: 90 Sparks St, Suite 620, Ottawa K1P 5B4; tel. (613) 236-2351; telex 053-4293; fax (613) 235-2659; Ambassador: OSCAR FERNÁNDEZ.

Australia: 50 O'Connor St, Ottawa K1P 6L2; tel. (613) 236-0841; telex 053-3391; High Commissioner: JIM HUMPHREYS.

Austria: 445 Wilbrod St, Ottawa K1N 6M7; tel. (613) 563-1444; telex 053-3290; fax (613) 563-0038; Ambassador: Dr KURT HERNDL.

Bahamas: 360 Albert St, Suite 1020, Ottawa K1R 7X7; tel. (613) 232-1724; telex 053-3793; fax (613) 232-0097; High Commissioner: IDRIS REID.

Bangladesh: 85 Range Rd, Suite 402, Ottawa K1N 8J6; tel. (613) 236-0138; telex 053-4283; High Commissioner: A. N. M. NURUZZAMAN.

Barbados: 151 Slater St, Suite 210, Ottawa K1P 5H3; tel. (613) 236-9517; telex 053-3375; fax (613) 230-4362; High Commissioner: Sir JAMES TUDOR.

Belgium: 85 Range Rd, Suites 601–604, Ottawa K1N 8J6; tel. (613) 236-7267; telex 053-3568; fax (613) 236-7882; Ambassador: JEAN-FRANÇOIS DE LIEDEKERKE.

Belize: Ottawa; High Commissioner: RUDOLPH I. CASTILLO.

Benin: 58 Glebe Ave, Ottawa K1S 2C3; tel. (613) 233-4429; telex 053-3630; Ambassador: Mme BERNARDINE DE RÉGO.

Bolivia: 77 Metcalfe St, Suite 608, Ottawa K1P 5L6; tel. (613) 236-8237; Ambassador: LUIS PELÁEZ RIOJA.

Brazil: 255 Albert St, Suite 900, Ottawa K1P 6A9; tel. (613) 237-1090; telex 053-4222; fax (613) 237-6144; ; Ambassador: PAULO PIRES DO RIO.

Bulgaria: 325 Stewart St, Ottawa K1N 6K5; tel. (613) 232-3215; telex 053-4386; Ambassador: (vacant).

Burkina Faso: 48 Range Rd, Ottawa K1N 8J4; tel. (613) 238-4796; telex 053-4413; Ambassador: LÉANDRE B. BASSOLE.

Burundi: 151 Slater St, Suite 800, Ottawa K1P 5H3; tel. (613) 236-8483; telex 053-3393; fax (613) 563-1827; Ambassador: PHILIPPE KANONKO.

Cameroon: 170 Clemow Ave, Ottawa K1S 2B4; tel. (613) 236-1522; telex 053-3736; Ambassador: PHILÉMON YANG YUNJI.

Chile: 151 Slater St, Suite 605, Ottawa K1P 5H3; tel. (613) 235-4402; telex 053-3774; fax (613) 235-1176; Ambassador: FRANCISCO RIVAS.

China, People's Republic: 511-515 St Patrick St, Ottawa K1N 5H3; tel. (613) 234-2706; telex 053-3770; fax (613) 230-9794; Ambassador: WEN YEZHAN.

Colombia: 150 Kent St, Suite 404, Ottawa K1P 5P4; tel. (613) 230-3760; telex 053-3786; Ambassador: JAIME VIDAL PERDOMO.

Costa Rica: 150 Argyle Ave, Suite 115, Ottawa K2P 1B7; tel. (613) 234-5762; telex 053-4398; fax (613) 230-2656; Ambassador: CARLOS E. MIRANDA.

Côte d'Ivoire: 9 Marlborough Ave, Ottawa K1N 8E6; tel. (613) 236-9919; telex 053-3794; fax (613) 563-8287; Ambassador: JULIEN KACOU.

Cuba: 388 Main St, Ottawa K1S 1E3; tel. (613) 563-0141; telex 053-3135; fax (613) 563-0068; Ambassador: CARLOS CASTILLO.

Czechoslovakia: 50 Rideau Terrace, Ottawa K1M 2A1; tel. (613) 749-4442; telex 053-4224; fax (613) 749-4989; Ambassador: JÁN JANOVIČ.

Denmark: 85 Range Rd, Suite 702, Ottawa K1N 8J6; tel. (613) 234-0704; telex 053-3114; fax (613) 234-7368; Ambassador: BJØRN OLSEN.

Dominica, Grenada, Saint Christopher and Nevis, Saint Lucia and Saint Vincent and the Grenadines: Place de Ville, Tower B, 112 Kent St, Suite 1050, Ottawa K1P 5P2; tel. (613) 236-8952; telex 053-4476; fax (613) 236-3042; High Commissioner: Dr J. BERNARD YANKEY.

Ecuador: 50 O'Connor St, Suite 1311, Ottawa K1N 6L2; tel. (613) 563-8206; fax (613) 235-5776; Ambassador: Dr ALFONSO BARRERA.

Egypt: 454 Laurier Ave East, Ottawa K1N 6R3; tel. (613) 234-4931; telex 053-3340; fax (613) 234-9347; Ambassador: MOHAMED ADEL AL-SAFTY.

Finland: 55 Metcalfe St, Suite 850, Ottawa K1P 6L5; tel. (613) 236-2389; telex 053-4462; fax (613) 238-1474; Ambassador: ERKKI MÄENTAKANEN.

France: 42 Sussex Drive, Ottawa K1M 2C9; tel. (613) 232-1795; fax (613) 232-4302; Ambassador: FRANÇOIS BUJON DE L'ESTANG.

Gabon: 4 Range Rd, Ottawa K1N 8J5; tel. (613) 232-5301; telex 053-4295; fax (613) 232-6916; Ambassador: SIMON OMBEGUE.

Germany: 1 Waverley St, Ottawa K2P 0T8, tel. (613) 232-1101; telex 053-4226; fax (613) 594-9330; Ambassador: WOLFGANG BEHRENDS.

Ghana: 1 Clemow Ave, Ottawa K1S 2A9; tel. (613) 236-0871; telex 053-4276; fax (613) 236-0874; High Commissioner: DANIEL O. AGYEKUM.

Greece: 80 MacLaren St, Ottawa K2P 0K6; tel. (613) 238-6271; telex 053-3852; fax (613) 238-6273; Ambassador: LEONIDAS MAVROMICHALIS.

Guatemala: 294 Albert St, Suite 500, Ottawa K1P 6E6; tel. (613) 237-3941; telex 053-3065; fax (613) 237-0492; Ambassador: FEDERICO URRUELA-PRADO.

Guinea: 483 Wilbrod St, Ottawa K1N 6N1; tel. (613) 232-1133; Ambassador: THOMAS CURTIS.

Guyana: 151 Slater St, Suite 309, Ottawa K1P 5H3; tel. (613) 235-7249; telex 053-3684; fax (613) 235-1447; High Commissioner: HUBERT O. JACK.

Haiti: Place de Ville, Tower B, 112 Kent St, Suite 1308, Ottawa K1P 5P2; tel. (613) 238-1628; telex 053-3688; fax (613) 238-2986; Chargé d'affaires a.i.: JEAN GATEAU.

Holy See: Apostolic Nunciature, 724 Manor Ave, Rockcliffe Park, Ottawa K1M 0E3; tel. (613) 746-4914; telex 053-3380; Pro-Nuncio: Most Rev. CARLO CURIS, Titular Archbishop of Medeli.

Honduras: 151 Slater St, Suite 300A, Ottawa K1P 5H3; tel. (613) 233-8900; telex 053-4528; Ambassador: JUAN RAMÓN MOLINA CISNEROS.

Hungary: 7 Delaware Ave, Ottawa K2P 0Z2; tel. (613) 232-1711; telex 053-3251; fax (613) 232-5620; Ambassador: (vacant).

India: 10 Springfield Rd, Ottawa K1M 1C9; tel. (613) 744-3751; telex 053-4172; fax (613) 744-0913; High Commissioner: SURBIR JIT SINGH CHHATWAL.

Indonesia: 287 MacLaren St, Ottawa K2P 0L9; tel. (613) 236-7403; telex 053-3119; fax (613) 563-2858; Ambassador: (vacant).

Iran: 411 Roosevelt Ave, 4th Floor, Ottawa K2A 3X9; tel. (613) 729-0902; telex 053-4229; fax (613) 729-0075; Ambassador: HOSSEIN LAVASANI.

Iraq: 215 McLeod St, Ottawa K2P 0Z8; tel. (613) 236-9177; telex 053-4310; fax (613) 567-1101; Ambassador: HISHAM AL-SHAWI.

Ireland: 170 Metcalfe St, Ottawa K2P 1P3; tel. (613) 233-6281; telex 053-4240; fax (613) 233-5835; Ambassador: DECLAN M. KELLY.

Israel: 410 Laurier Ave West, Suite 601, Ottawa K1R 7T3; tel. (613) 237-6450; telex 053-4858; fax (613) 237-8865; Ambassador: ISRAEL GUR-ARIEH.

Italy: 275 Slater St, 21st Floor, Ottawa K1P 5H9; tel. (613) 232-2401; telex 053-3278; fax (613) 233-1484; Ambassador: SERGIO SILVIO BALANZINO.

Jamaica: 275 Slater St, Suite 402, Ottawa K1P 5H9; tel. (613) 233-9311; telex 053-3287; fax (613) 233-0611; High Commissioner: H. DALE ANDERSON.

Japan: 255 Sussex Drive, Ottawa K1N 9E6; tel. (613) 236-8541; telex 053-4220; fax (613) 563-9047; Ambassador: HIROSHI KITAMURA.

Jordan: 100 Bronson Ave, Suite 701, Ottawa K1N 6R4; tel. (613) 238-8090; telex 053-4538; Ambassador: HANI KHALIFEH.

Kenya: 415 Laurier Ave East, Ottawa K1N 6R4; tel. (613) 563-1773; telex 053-4873; fax (613) 233-6599; High Commissioner: PETER M. NYAMWEYA.

Korea, Republic: 151 Slater St, 5th Floor, Ottawa K1P 5H3; tel. (613) 232-1715; fax (613) 232-0928; Ambassador: SOO GIL PARK.

Lebanon: 640 Lyon St, Ottawa K1S 3Z5; tel. (613) 236-5825; telex 053-3571; fax (613) 232-1609; Ambassador: Dr ASSEM JABER.

Lesotho: 202 Clemow Ave, Ottawa K1S 2B4; tel. (613) 236-9449; telex 053-4563; High Commissioner: RAPHAEL RAMALIEHE KALI.

Malawi: 7 Clemow Ave, Ottawa K1S 2A9; tel. (613) 236-8931; telex 053-3365; fax (613) 236-1054; High Commissioner: M. W. MACHINJILI.

Malaysia: 60 Boteler St, Ottawa K1N 8Y7; tel. (613) 237-5182; telex 053-3064; fax (613) 237-4852; High Commissioner: Tan Sri Datuk THOMAS JAYASURIA.

Mali: 50 Goulburn Ave, Ottawa K1N 8C8; tel. (613) 232-1501; telex 053-3361; Ambassador: OUSMANE DEMBELE.

Mexico: 130 Albert St, Suite 1800, Ottawa K1P 5G4; tel. (613) 233-8988; telex 053-4520; Ambassador: ALFREDO PHILLIPS O.

Morocco: 38 Range Rd, Ottawa K1N 8J4; tel. (613) 236-7391; telex 053-3683; fax (613) 236-6164; Ambassador: MAATI JORIO.

Myanmar: 85 Range Rd, Suite 902, Ottawa K1N 8J6; tel. (613) 232-6434; telex 053-3334; fax (613) 232-6435; Chargé d'affairs a.i.: U HLA PE THAN.

Netherlands: 275 Slater St, 3rd Floor, Ottawa K1P 5H9; tel. (613) 237-5030; telex 053-3109; fax (613) 237-6471; Ambassador: J. F. E. BREMAN.

New Zealand: Metropolitan House, 99 Bank St, Suite 727, Ottawa K1P 6G3; tel. (613) 238-5991; telex 053-4282; fax (613) 238-5707; High Commissioner: BRUCE BROWN.

CANADA

Nicaragua: 170 Laurier Ave West, Suite 908, Ottawa, K1P 5V5; tel. (613) 234-9361; telex 053-4338; fax (613) 238-7666; Ambassador: Sergio Lacayo.

Niger: 38 Blackburn Ave, Ottawa K1N 8A2; tel. (613) 232-4291; telex 053-3757; fax (613) 230-9808; Ambassador: Abdubacar Abdou.

Nigeria: 295 Metcalfe St, Ottawa K2P 1R9; tel. (613) 236-0521; telex 053-3285; fax (613) 236-0529; High Commissioner: G. O. George.

Norway: 90 Sparks St, Suite 532, Ottawa K1P 5B4; tel. (613) 238-6571; telex 053-4239; fax (613) 238-2765; Ambassador: Jan E. Nyheim.

Pakistan: 151 Slater St, Suite 608, Ottawa K1P 5H3; tel. (613) 238-7881; telex 053-4428; fax (613) 238-7296; High Commissioner: S. M. A. Khairi.

Peru: 170 Laurier Ave West, Suite 1007, Ottawa K1P 5V5; tel. (613) 238-1777; telex 053-3754; fax (613) 232-3062; Ambassador: Jorge Gordillo.

Philippines: 130 Albert St, Suite 606, Ottawa K1P 5G4; tel. (613) 233-1121; telex 053-4537; fax (613) 233-4165; Ambassador: Ramón A. Diaz.

Poland: 443 Daly Ave, Ottawa K1N 6H3; tel. (613) 236-0468; telex 053-3133; fax (613) 232-3463; Ambassador: Alojzy Bartoszek.

Portugal: 645 Island Park Drive, Ottawa K1Y 0B8; tel. (613) 729-0883; telex 053-3756; Ambassador: João Uva de Matos Proença.

Romania: 655 Rideau St, Ottawa K1N 6A3; tel. (613) 232-5345; telex 053-3101; Ambassador: Dr Emilian Rodean.

Rwanda: 121 Sherwood Drive, Ottawa K1Y 3V1; tel. (613) 722-5835; telex 053-4522; fax (613) 729-3291; Ambassador: (vacant).

Saudi Arabia: 99 Bank St, Suite 901, Ottawa K1P 6B9; tel. (613) 237-4100; telex 053-4285; fax (613) 237-0567; Chargé d'affairs a.i.: Redha M. A. Mokhtar.

Senegal: 57 Marlborough Ave, Ottawa K1N 8E8; tel. (613) 238-6392; telex 053-4531; Ambassador: (vacant).

Somalia: 130 Slater St, Suite 1000, Ottawa K1P 6E2; tel. (613) 563-4541; telex 053-4739; Ambassador: Abdikarim Ali Omar.

South Africa: 15 Sussex Drive, Ottawa K1M 1M8; tel. (613) 744-0330; telex 053-4185; fax (613) 741-1639; Ambassador: Hendrik de Klerk.

Spain: 350 Sparks St, Suite 802, Ottawa K1R 7S8; tel. (613) 237-2193; telex 053-4510; Ambassador: Antonio José Fournier.

Sri Lanka: 85 Range Rd, Suites 102–104, Ottawa K1N 8J6; tel. (613) 233-8449; telex 053-3668; fax (613) 238-8448; High Commissioner: Walter G. Rupesinghe.

Sudan: 457 Laurier Ave East, Ottawa K1N 6R4; tel. (613) 235-4000; Ambassador: Nuri Khalil Siddiq.

Sweden: Mercury Court, 377 Dalhousie St, Ottawa K1N 9N8; tel. (613) 236-8553; telex 053-3331; fax (613) 236-5720; Ambassador: Håkan Berggren.

Switzerland: 5 Marlborough Ave, Ottawa K1N 8E6; tel. (613) 235-1837; telex 053-3648; fax (613) 563-1394; Ambassador: (vacant).

Tanzania: 50 Range Rd, Ottawa K1N 8J4; tel. (613) 232-1509; telex 053-3569; High Commissioner: Dr P. K. Palangyo.

Thailand: 180 Island Park Drive, Ottawa K1Y 0A2; tel. (613) 722-4444; telex 053-3975; fax (613) 722-6624; Ambassador: Chawat Arthayukti.

Togo: 12 Range Rd, Ottawa K1N 8J3; tel. (613) 238-5916; telex 053-4564; telex 053-4564; fax (613) 235-6425; Ambassador: Kossi Osseyi.

Trinidad and Tobago: 75 Albert St, Suite 508, Ottawa K1P 5E7; tel. (613) 232-2418; telex 053-4343; fax (613) 234-4349; High Commissioner: Laila Valere.

Tunisia: 515 O'Connor St, Ottawa K1S 3P8; tel. (613) 237-0330; telex 053-4161; fax (613) 237-7939; Ambassador: Sadok Bouzayen.

Turkey: 197 Wurtemburg St, Ottawa K1N 8L9; tel. (613) 232-1577; telex 053-4716; fax (613) 232-5498; Ambassador: Ali Tuygan.

Uganda: 231 Cobourg St, Ottawa K1N 8J2; tel. (613) 233-7797; telex 053-4469; fax (613) 232-6689; High Commissioner: Joseph Tomusange.

USSR: 285 Charlotte St, Ottawa K1N 8L5; tel. (613) 235-4341; telex 053-3332; fax (613) 236-6342; Ambassador: Aleksei Rodionov.

United Kingdom: 80 Elgin St, Ottawa K1P 5K7; tel. (613) 237-1530; telex 053-3318; fax (613) 237-7980; High Commissioner: Brian J. P. Fall.

USA: 100 Wellington St, Ottawa K1P 5T1; tel. (613) 238-5335; telex 053-3582; fax (613) 238-8750; Ambassador: Edward N. Ney.

Uruguay: 130 Albert St, Suite 1905, Ottawa K1P 5G4; tel. (613) 234-2727; Chargé d'affaires a.i.: Dr Zulma Guelmán.

Venezuela: 32 Range Rd, Ottawa K1N 8J4; tel. (613) 235-5151; telex 053-4729; fax (613) 235-3205; Ambassador: Santiago Ochoa Antich.

Yugoslavia: 17 Blackburn Ave, Ottawa K1N 8A2; tel. (613) 233-6289; telex 053-4203; fax (613) 233-7850; Ambassador: Goran Kapetanović.

Zaire: 18 Range Rd, Ottawa K1N 8J3; tel. (613) 236-7103; telex 053-4314; Ambassador: K. Bukasa-Muteba.

Zambia: 130 Albert St, Suite 1610, Ottawa K1P 5G4; tel. (613) 563-0712; telex 053-4418; fax (613) 235-0430; High Commissioner: Kebby S. K. Musokotwane.

Zimbabwe: 332 Somerset St West, Ottawa K2P 0J9; tel. (613) 237-4388; telex 053-4221; High Commissioner: M. S. Kajese.

Judicial System

FEDERAL COURTS

The Supreme Court of Canada: Supreme Court Bldg, Wellington St, Ottawa K1A 0J1; tel. (613) 995-4330; fax (613) 996-3063; ultimate court of appeal in both civil and criminal cases throughout Canada. The Supreme Court is also required to advise on questions referred to it by the Governor in Council. Important questions concerning the interpretation of the Constitution Act, the constitutionality or interpretation of any federal or provincial law, the powers of Parliament or of the provincial legislatures, among other matters, may be referred by the Government to the Supreme Court for consideration.

In civil cases, appeals may be brought from any final judgment of the highest court of last resort in a province. The Supreme Court will grant permission to appeal if it is of the opinion that a question of public importance is involved, one that transcends the immediate concerns of the parties to the litigation. In criminal cases, the Court will hear appeals as of right concerning indictable offences where an acquittal has been set aside or where there has been a dissenting judgment on a point of law in a provincial court of appeal. The Supreme Court may, in addition, hear appeals on questions of law concerning both summary conviction and all other indictable offences if permission to appeal is first granted by the Court.

Chief Justice of Canada: Antonio Lamer.

Puisne Judges: Bertha Wilson, Gérard V. La Forest, Claire L'Heureux-Dubé, John Sopinka, Charles Doherty Gonthier, Peter de Carteret Cory, Beverley McLachlin, William Stevenson.

The Federal Court of Canada: Supreme Court Bldg, Wellington St, Ottawa K1A 0H9; tel. (613) 992-4238; the Trial Division of the Federal Court has jurisdiction in claims against the Crown, claims by the Crown, miscellaneous cases involving the Crown, claims against or concerning crown officers and servants, relief against Federal Boards, Commissions, and other tribunals, interprovincial and federal-provincial disputes, industrial or industrial property matters, admiralty, income tax and estate tax appeals, citizenship appeals, aeronautics, interprovincial works and undertakings, residuary jurisdiction for relief if there is no other Canadian court that has such jurisdiction, jurisdiction in specific matters conferred by federal statutes.

The Federal Court of Appeal: Supreme Court Bldg, Wellington St, Ottawa K1A 0H9; tel. (613) 996-6795; has jurisdiction on appeals from the Trial Division, appeals from Federal Tribunals, review of decisions of Federal Boards and Commissions, appeals from Tribunals and Reviews under Section 28 of the Federal Court Act, and references by Federal Boards and Commissions. The Court has one central registry and consists of the principal office in Ottawa and local offices in major centres throughout Canada.

Chief Justice: Frank Iacobucci.

Associate Chief Justice: James A. Jerome.

Court of Appeal Judges: Louis Pratte, Darrel V. Heald, John J. Urie, Patrick M. Mahoney, Louis Marceau, James K. Hugessen, Arthur J. Stone, Mark R. MacGuigan, Alice Desjardins, Robert Decary, Allen M. Linden.

Trial Division Judges: George A. Addy, J.-E. Dubé, Paul U. C. Rouleau, Francis C. Muldoon, Barry L. Strayer, John C. McNair, Barbara J. Reed, Pierre Denault, Yvon Pinard, L. Marcel Joyal, Bud Cullen, Leonard A. Martin, Max M. Teitelbaum, William Andrew MacKay.

PROVINCIAL COURTS

Alberta

Court of Appeal

Chief Justice of Alberta: J. H. Laycraft.

Court of Queen's Bench

Chief Justice: W. K. Moore.

Associate Chief Justice: T. H. Miller.

CANADA

British Columbia
Court of Appeal
Chief Justice of British Columbia: A. McEachern.

Supreme Court
Chief Justice: W. A. Esson.
Associate Chief Justice: D. H. Campbell.

Manitoba
Court of Appeal
Chief Justice of Manitoba: R. J. Scott.

Court of Queen's Bench
Chief Justice: B. Hewak.
Associate Chief Justice: A. C. Hamilton.

New Brunswick
Court of Appeal
Chief Justice of New Brunswick: S. G. Stratton.

Court of Queen's Bench
Chief Justice: G. A. Richard.

Newfoundland
Supreme Court—Court of Appeal
Chief Justice: Noel H. A. Goodridge.

Trial Division
Chief Justice: T. A. Hickman.

Nova Scotia
Supreme Court—Appeal Division
Chief Justice of Nova Scotia: L. O. Clarke.

Trial Division
Chief Justice: C. R. Glube.

Ontario
Supreme Court—Court of Appeal
Chief Justice of Ontario: C. L. Dubin.
Associate Chief Justice of Ontario: J. W. Morden.

High Court of Justice
Chief Justice: F. W. Callaghan.
Associate Chief Justice: (vacant).

Prince Edward Island
Supreme Court—Appeal Division
Chief Justice: N. H. Carruthers.

Supreme Court—Trial Division
Chief Justice: K. R. MacDonald.

Québec
Court of Appeal
Chief Justice of Québec: C. Bisson.

Superior Court
Chief Justice: Alan B. Gold.
Senior Associate Chief Justice: Pierre Côté.
Associate Chief Justice: L. A. Poitras.

Saskatchewan
Court of Appeal
Chief Justice of Saskatchewan: E. D. Bayda.

Court of Queen's Bench
Chief Justice: D. K. MacPherson.

Northwest Territories
Supreme Court
Judges of the Supreme Court: M. M. de Weerdt, T. D. Marshall.

Court of Appeal
Chief Justice: J. H. Laycraft (Alberta).

Yukon Territory
Supreme Court
Judge of the Supreme Court: H. C. B. Maddison.

Court of Appeal
Chief Justice: A. McEachern (British Columbia).

Religion

CHRISTIANITY

About 75% of the population belong to the three main Christian churches: Roman Catholic, United and Anglican. Numerous other religious denominations are represented.

Canadian Council of Churches/Conseil canadien des Eglises: 40 St Clair Ave East, Toronto, Ont M4T 1M9; tel. (416) 921-4152; telex 065-24128; fax (416) 921-7478; f. 1944; 15 mem. churches, one assoc. mem.; Pres. Bishop Donald Sjoberg; Gen. Sec. Dr Stuart E. Brown.

The Anglican Communion

The Anglican Church of Canada (L'église épiscopale du Canada) comprises four ecclesiastical provinces (each with a Metropolitan archbishop), containing a total of 30 dioceses. The Church had 810,140 members in 1987.

General Synod of the Anglican Church of Canada: Church House, 600 Jarvis St, Toronto, Ont M4Y 2J6; tel. (416) 924-9192; fax (416) 924-0211; Gen. Sec. Archdeacon David Woeller.

Primate of the Anglican Church of Canada: Archbishop Michael Geoffrey Peers.

Archbishop of British Columbia: Douglas Walter Hambidge, Bishop of New Westminster.

Archbishop of Canada: Reginald Hollis, Bishop of Montréal.

Archbishop of Ontario: John Charles Bothwell, Bishop of Niagara.

Archbishop of Rupert's Land: Walter Heath Jones, Bishop of Rupert's Land.

The Orthodox Churches

Greek Orthodox Church: 40 Donlands Ave, Toronto, Ont M4J 3N6; tel. (416) 462-0833; 230,000 mems; Bishop of Toronto His Grace Sotirios.

Ukrainian Greek Orthodox Church: 9 St John's Ave, Winnipeg, Man R2W 1G8; tel. (204) 586-3093; fax (204) 582-5241; f. 1918; 280 parishes; 150,000 mems; Metropolitan of Winnipeg and of all Canada Most Rev. Wasyly (Fedak); Chair. Exec. Cttee of Consistory Very Rev. William Makarenko.

The Romanian, Serbian, Coptic, Antiochian, Armenian and Byelorussian Churches are also represented in Canada.

The Roman Catholic Church

For Catholics of the Latin rite, Canada comprises 17 archdioceses (including one directly responsible to the Holy See), 47 dioceses and one territorial abbacy. There are also one archdiocese and four dioceses of the Ukrainian rite. In addition, the Maronite, Melkite and Slovak rites are each represented by one diocese (all directly responsible to the Holy See). In 1989 the Roman Catholic Church had 11,402,605 adherents in Canada.

Canadian Conference of Catholic Bishops/Conférence des évêques catholiques du Canada: 90 Parent Ave, Ottawa K1N 7B1; tel. (613) 236-9461; Pres. Rt Rev. Robert Lebel, Bishop of Valleyfield, Qué; Vice-Pres. Rt Rev. Thomas B. Fulton, Bishop of St Catharines, Ont.

Latin Rite
Archbishop of Edmonton: Joseph N. MacNeil.
Archbishop of Grouard-McLennan: Henri Légaré.
Archbishop of Halifax: James M. Hayes.
Archbishop of Keewatin-Le Pas: Peter Alfred Sutton.
Archbishop of Kingston: Francis Spence.
Archbishop of Moncton: Donat Chiasson.
Archbishop of Montréal: Jean-Claude Turcotte.
Archbishop of Ottawa: Marcel Gervais.
Archbishop of Québec: Maurice Couture.
Archbishop of Regina: Charles A. Halpin.
Archbishop of Rimouski: Gilles Ouellet.
Archbishop of St Boniface: Maurice Antoine Hacault.
Archbishop of St John's, Nfld: Alphonsus L. Penney.
Archbishop of Sherbrooke: Jean-Marie Fortier.
Archbishop of Toronto: Aloysius Ambrozic.
Archbishop of Vancouver: James Francis Carney.
Archbishop of Winnipeg: Adam Exner.

CANADA

Ukrainian Rite

Ukrainian Catholic Church in Canada: 233 Scotia St, Winnipeg, Man R2V 1V7; tel. (204) 338-7801; fax (204) 339-4006; 190,585 mems (1981 census); Archeparch-Metropolitan of Winnipeg Most Rev. MAXIM HERMANIUK.

The United Church of Canada

The United Church of Canada (L'église unie du Canada) was founded in 1925 with the union of Methodist, Congregational and Presbyterian churches in Canada. The Evangelical United Brethren of Canada joined in 1968. In 1988 there were 2,420 pastoral charges, 4,175 congregations, 3,897 ministers and 863,910 mems.

Moderator: Rt Rev. WALTER FARQUHARSON.

General Secretary: Rev. HOWARD M. MILLS, The United Church House, 85 St Clair Ave East, Toronto, Ont M4T 1M8; tel. (416) 925-5931; telex 065-28224; fax (416) 925-3394.

Other Christian Churches

Canadian Baptist Federation: 7185 Millcreek Drive, Mississauga, Ont L5N 5R4; tel. (416) 826-0191; fax (416) 826-3441; 1,200 churches; 131,472 mems (1986); Pres. ROBERT MACQUADE; Gen. Sec. Dr RICHARD C. COFFIN.

Christian Reformed Church in North America: 3475 Mainway, POB 5070, Burlington, Ont L7R 3Y8; tel. (416) 336-2920; fax (416) 336-8344; f. 1857.

Church of Jesus Christ of Latter-day Saints (Mormon): 7181 Woodbine Ave, Suite 234, Markham, Ont L3R 1A3; tel. (416) 477-8595; 371 congregations; 118,500 mems; Area Pres R. C. REEVE, L. C. DUNN, J. K. CARMACK.

Lutheran Church—Canada: 59 Academy Rd, Winnipeg, Man R3M 0E2; tel. (204) 452-2747; fax (204) 452-3591; f. 1988; 325 congregations fmrly associated with the Lutheran Church Missouri Synod (USA); Pres. Rev. EDWIN LEHMAN.

Lutheran Council in Canada: 25 Old York Mills Rd, Willowdale, Ont M2P 1B5; f. 1967; tel. (416) 488-9430; co-ordinating agency for Evangelical Lutheran Church in Canada and Lutheran Church Canada; 1,165 ministers; 1,002 congregations; 296,888 mems (1988); Exec. Dir LAWRENCE R. LIKNESS.

Mennonite Central Committee Canada: 134 Plaza Drive, Winnipeg, Man R3T 5K9; tel. (204) 261-6381; telex 075-7525; f. 1963; 114,000 mems in 600 congregations; Exec. Dir DANIEL ZEHR.

Pentecostal Assemblies of Canada: 6745 Century Ave, Mississauga, Ont L5N 6P7; tel. (416) 542-7400; fax (416) 542-7313; 192,706 mems; Gen. Supt Rev. J. M. MACKNIGHT; Gen. Sec. Rev. CHARLES YATES.

Presbyterian Church in Canada: 50 Wynford Drive, Don Mills, Ont M3C 1J7; tel. (416) 441-1111; fax (416) 441-2825; f. 1875; 1,194 ministers, 1,014 congregations; 157,044 mems (1989); Moderator Rev. JOHN ALLAN; Prin. Clerk Dr E. F. ROBERTS.

Religious Society of Friends: 91A Fourth Ave, Ottawa K1S 2L1; tel. (613) 235-8553; Clerk of Canadian Yearly Meeting EDWARD S. BELL.

Seventh-day Adventists: 1148 King St East, Oshawa, Ont L1H 1H8; tel. (416) 433-0011; fax (416) 723-1903; org. 1901; 289 churches; 35,992 mems; Pres. D. D. DEVNICH; Sec. O. PARCHMENT.

BAHÁ'Í FAITH

Bahá'í Community of Canada: 7200 Leslie St, Thornhill, Ont L3T 6L8; tel. (416) 889-8168; fax (416) 889-8184; f. 1902; 21,000 mems; Sec. M. E. MUTTART.

BUDDHISM

Buddhist Churches of Canada: 918 Bathurst St, Toronto, Ont M5R 3G5; tel. (416) 534-4302; Jodo Shinshu of Mahayana Buddhism; Bishop Rev. TOSHIO MURAKAMI.

ISLAM

There are an estimated 350,000 Muslims in Canada.

Council of Muslim Communities of Canada: 1521 Trinity Drive, Unit 16, Mississauga, Ont L5T 1P6; tel. (416) 672-1566; co-ordinating agency; Pres. Dr MIR IQBAL ALI.

JUDAISM

The Jews of Canada are estimated to number 310,000.

Canadian Jewish Congress: 1590 ave Dr Penfield, Montréal, Qué H3G 1C5; tel. (514) 931-7531; fax (514) 931-0548; f. 1919; regional offices in Halifax, Ottawa, Willowdale, Ont, Winnipeg, Saskatoon and Vancouver; Exec. Vice-Pres. ALAN ROSE.

Directory

SIKHISM

There are an estimated 250,000 Sikhs in Canada.

Federation of Sikh Societies of Canada: POB 91, Station B, Ottawa K1P 6C3; tel. (613) 521-2566; Pres. MOHINDER SINGH GOSAL.

The Press

The daily press in Canada is essentially local in coverage, influence and distribution. Through the use of satellite transmission, a national edition of the Toronto *Globe and Mail*, established in 1981, is available coast to coast, and in 1988 the *Financial Post* began publication of a national edition, also using satellite transmission.

Independently-owned daily newspapers accounted for 17.3% of the circulation of Canadian dailies in early 1990. Chain ownership is predominant: almost 48% of daily newspaper circulation is represented by two major groups: Thomson Newspapers Ltd (20.5% of daily newspaper circulation) and Southam Inc (27.1%). In 1990 the Québécor Group accounted for 8.5% of the total circulation, while the Sun Publishing Group had 11%. There are also seven smaller groups.

In September 1980 a royal commission was appointed to investigate the effects of concentration of ownership in the newspaper industry. In August 1981 the commission reported that the existing concentration constituted a threat to press freedom, and recommended that some groups should be compelled to sell some of their newspaper interests in areas where there was extreme ownership concentration. The Government has subsequently continued to restrict cross-media ownership of newspapers, radio and television, and to prohibit non-media companies from owning daily newspapers.

In early 1990 there were 108 daily newspapers with a combined circulation of over 5.8m., representing 60.8% of the country's households. About 1,100 weekly and twice-weekly community newspapers reached an estimated 5.2m. people, mainly in the more remote areas of the country. A significant feature of the Canadian press is the number of newspapers catering for ethnic groups: there are over 80 of these daily and weekly publications appearing in over 20 languages.

There are numerous periodicals for business, trade, professional, recreational and special interest readership, although periodical publishing, particularly, suffers from substantial competition from publications originating in the USA. Among periodicals, the only one which can be regarded as national in its readership and coverage is *Maclean's Canada's Weekly Newsmagazine*.

The following are among the principal newspaper publishing groups:

Southam Newspaper Group: 150 Bloor St West, Suite 910, Toronto, Ont M5S 2Y9; tel. (416) 927-1877; Pres. RUSS MILLS.

Sterling Newspapers Ltd: 1827 West Fifth Ave, 2nd Floor, Vancouver, BC V6J 1P5; tel. (604) 732-4443; Pres. F. DAVID RADLER; Vice-Pres. and Gen. Man. STEEN O. JORGENSEN.

Thomson Newspapers Corpn: 65 Queen St West, Toronto, Ont M5H 2M8; tel. (416) 864-1710; fax (416) 864-0109; Pres. and CEO MICHAEL W. JOHNSTON.

PRINCIPAL DAILY NEWSPAPERS

(D = all day; E = evening; M = morning; S = Sunday)

Alberta

Calgary Herald: 215 16th St, SE, Calgary T2P 0W8; tel. (403) 235-7100; telex 038-22793; fax (403) 235-8668; f. 1883; Publr KEVIN PETERSON; Man. Editor GILLIAN STEWARD; circ. 135,000 (M); 123,000 (S).

Calgary Sun: 2615 12th St, NE, Calgary T2E 7W9; tel. (403) 250-4200; telex 038-22734; fax (403) 291-4242; f. 1980; Publr KENNETH M. KING; Editor-in-Chief ROBERT POOLE; circ. 71,000 (M), 98,000 (S).

Daily Herald-Tribune: 10604 100th St, Grande Prairie T8V 2M5; tel. (403) 532-1110; fax (403) 532-2120; f. 1964; Publr B. WAYNE JOBB; Man. Editor BILL SCOTT; circ. 8,000 (E).

Edmonton Journal: POB 2421, Edmonton T5J 2S6; tel. (403) 429-5100; telex 037-3492; fax (403) 429-5479; f. 1903; Publr DONALD BABICK; Editor LINDA HUGHES; circ. 159,000 (M), 146,000 (S).

Edmonton Sun: 4990 92nd Ave, Suite 250, Edmonton T6B 3A1; tel. (403) 468-0227; fax (403) 468-0128; f. 1978; Publr PATRICK A. HARDEN; Editor-in-Chief DAVID BAILEY; circ. 97,000 (M), 132,000 (S).

Lethbridge Herald: 504 Seventh St South, POB 670, Lethbridge T1J 3Z7; tel. (403) 328-4411; telex 038-49220; fax (403) 328-4536; f.

CANADA

1907; Publr and Gen. Man. DONALD R. DORAM; Man. Editor JIM HASKETT; circ. 26,000 (E).

Medicine Hat News: 3257 Dunmore Rd, SE, POB 10, Medicine Hat T1A 7E6; tel. (403) 527-1101; telex 038-48191; fax (403) 527-6029; f. 1910; Publr GEORGE S. WILLCOCKS; Editor PETER MOSSEY; circ. 14,000 (E).

Red Deer Advocate: 2950 Bremner Ave, POB 5200, Red Deer T4N 5G3; tel. (403) 343-2400; fax (403) 342-4051; f. 1901; Publr HOWARD D. JANZEN; Man. Editor JOE MCLAUGHLIN; circ. 23,000 (E).

British Columbia

Alberini Valley Times: 4918 Napier St, POB 400, Port Alberini V9Y 7N1; tel. (604) 723-8171; fax (604) 723-0586; Publr NIGEL E. HANNAFORD; Editor RON DIOTTE; circ. 7,000 (E).

Daily Courier: 550 Doyle Ave, Kelowna V1Y 7N4; tel. (604) 762-4445; fax (604) 762-3866; f. 1904; Publr DANIEL F. DOUCETTE; Man. Editor DAVE HENSHAW; circ. 17,000 (E).

Daily Free Press: 223 Commercial St, POB 69, Nanaimo V9R 5K5; tel. (604) 753-3451; fax (604) 753-8730; f. 1874; Publr CLYDE T. WICKS; Man. Editor WAYNE CAMPBELL; circ. 10,000 (E).

Daily News: 3309 31st Ave, Vernon V1T 6N8; tel. (604) 545-0671; fax (604) 545-7193; Publr ROBERT MCKENZIE; circ. 8,000 (E).

Kamloops Daily News: 63 West Victoria St, Suite 106, Kamloops V2C 6J6; tel. (604) 372-2331; fax (604) 374-3884; f. 1982; Publr GERALD HASLAM; Editor MEL ROTHENBURGER; circ. 20,000 (E).

Nelson Daily News: 266 Baker St, Nelson V1L 4H3; tel. (604) 352-3552; fax (604) 352-2418; f. 1902; Publr VERNE SHAULL; Man. Editor RYON GUEDES; circ. 5,000 (M).

Penticton Herald: 186 Nanaimo Ave West, Penticton V2A 1N4; tel. (604) 492-4002; fax (604) 492-2403; Publr EDWIN A. CLINE; Editor MIKE INGRAHAM; circ. 8,000 (E).

Prince George Citizen: 150 Brunswick St, POB 5700, Prince George V2L 5K9; tel. (604) 562-2441; fax (604) 562-7453; f. 1957; Publr ALASTAIR J. MCNAIR; Editor ROY K. NAGEL; circ. 22,000 (E).

The Province: 2250 Granville St, Vancouver V6H 3G2; tel. (604) 732-2513; fax (604) 732-2704; f. 1898; Publr and Editor-in-Chief IAN HAYSOM; circ. 184,000 (M), 224,000 (S).

The Vancouver Sun: 2250 Granville St, Vancouver V6H 3G2; tel. (604) 732-2513; telex 045-5695; fax (604) 732-2704; f. 1886; Publr NICK HILLS; Editor BRUCE LARSEN; circ. 222,000 (E).

Times-Colonist: 2621 Douglas St, POB 300, Victoria V8W 2N4; tel. (604) 380-5211; telex 049-7288; fax (604) 380-5255; f. 1858; Publr COLIN D. MCCULLOUGH; Man. Editor GORDON R. BELL; circ. 82,000 (M), 80,000 (S).

Manitoba

Brandon Sun: 501 Rosser Ave, Brandon R7A 5Z6; tel. (204) 727-2451; fax (204) 725-0976; f. 1882; Publr ROB FORBES; Man. Editor JACK GIBSON; circ. 19,000 (E).

Daily Graphic: 1941 Saskatchewan Ave West, POB 130, Portage La Prairie R1N 3B4; tel. (204) 857-3427; fax (204) 239-1270; Publr HUGH A. MCTAGGART; circ. 5,000 (E).

Flin Flon Reminder: 38 Main St, POB 727, Flin Flon R8A 1N5; tel. (204) 687-3454; fax (204) 687-4473; f. 1946; Publr RICH BILLY; Man. Editor RON DOBSON; circ. 4,000 (E).

Winnipeg Free Press: 300 Carlton St, Winnipeg R3C 3C1; tel. (204) 943-9331; fax (204) 947-6984; f. 1874; Publr BRUCE L. RUDD; Man. Editor DAVID C. LEE; circ. 169,000 (E), 231,000 (Sat.).

Winnipeg Sun: 1700 Church Ave, Winnipeg R2X 2W9; tel. (204) 632-2766; fax (204) 632-8709; f. 1980; Publr AL DAVIES; Editor-in-Chief BRIAN DUNLOP; circ. 50,000 (M), 57,000 (S).

New Brunswick

L'Acadie Nouvelle: 217 ouest, blvd St-Pierre, CP 100, Caraquet E0B 1K0; tel. (506) 727-4444; fax (506) 727-7620; f. 1984; Publr GILLES HACHÉ; Editor MICHEL DOUCET; circ. 10,000 (M).

Daily Gleaner: 12 Prospect St South, POB 3370, Fredericton E3B 5A2; tel. (506) 452-6671; fax (506) 452-7405; f. 1880; Publr TOM CROWTHER; Editor-in-Chief HAL P. WOOD; circ. 29,000 (E).

Telegraph-Journal and **Evening Times-Globe:** 210 Crown St, POB 2350, Saint John E2L 3V8; tel. (506) 632-8888; fax (506) 648-2652; Publr ARTHUR T. DOYLE; Editor-in-Chief FRED HAZEL; circ. 64,000 (E).

The Times-Transcript: 939 Main St, POB 1001, Moncton E1C 8P3; tel. (506) 859-4900; fax (506) 859-4899; Publr JAMES D. NICHOL; Man. Editor MIKE BEMBRIDGE; circ. 44,000 (E).

Newfoundland

Telegram: Columbus Drive, POB 5970, St John's A1C 5X7; tel. (709) 364-6300; fax (709) 364-9333; f. 1879; Publr S. R. HERDER; Editor W. R. CALLAHAN; circ. 40,000 (E), 57,000 (Sat.).

Western Star: 106 West St, POB 460, Corner Brook A2H 6E7; tel. (709) 634-4348; fax (709) 634-9824; f. 1900; Publr ROBERT C. MARSHALL; Editor-in-Chief RICHARD G. WILLIAMS; circ. 11,000 (E).

Nova Scotia

Amherst Daily News: 10 Lawrence St, POB 280, Amherst B4H 3Z2; tel. (902) 667-5102; fax (902) 667-0419; f. 1893; Publr EARL J. GOUCHIE; Editor JOHN CONRAD; circ. 4,000 (M).

Cape Breton Post: 255 George St, POB 1500, Sydney B1P 6K6; tel. (902) 564-5451; fax (902) 562-7077; f. 1900; Publr W. LEITH ORR; Man. Editor ANGUS MACDONALD; circ. 32,000 (E).

Chronicle-Herald and **Mail-Star:** 1650 Argyle St, POB 610, Halifax B3J 2T2; tel. (902) 426-2811; telex 019-21874; fax (902) 426-2800; Publr GRAHAM W. DENNIS; Man. Editor KEN FORAN; circ. 150,000 (D).

Daily News: POB 8330, Station A, Halifax; tel. (902) 468-1222; fax (902) 468-2645; f. 1974; Gen. Man. MARK RICHARDSON; Editor-in-Chief DOUGLAS MACKAY; circ. 25,000 (E), 33,000 (S).

Evening News: 352 East River Rd, New Glasgow B2H 5E2; tel. (902) 752-3000; fax (902) 752-1945; f. 1910; Publr DON BRANDER; Man. Editor DOUG MACNEILL; circ. 11,000 (E).

Truro Daily News: 6 Louise St, POB 220, Truro B2N 5C3; tel. (902) 893-9405; fax (902) 893-0518; f. 1891; Publr TERRENCE W. HONEY; Man. Editor ROBERT PAXTON; circ. 9,000 (E).

Ontario

Barrie Examiner: 16 Bayfield St, Barrie L4M 4T6; tel. (705) 726-6537; fax (705) 726-7245; f. 1864; Publr PETER KAPYRKA; Man. Editor MARK FURLONG; circ. 14,000 (E).

Beacon Herald: POB 430, Stratford N5A 6T6; tel. (519) 271-2220; fax (519) 271-1026; f. 1854; Co-Publr and Gen. Man. CHARLES W. DINGMAN; Co-Publr and Editor STANFORD H. DINGMAN; circ. 14,000 (E).

Brampton Times: 33 Queen St West, Brampton L6Y 1M1; tel. (416) 451-2020; fax (416) 451-4898; f. 1885; Publr STEVE RHODES; Man. Editor (vacant); circ. 9,000 (E).

Cambridge Reporter: 26 Ainslie St South, Cambridge N1R 3K1; tel. (519) 621-3810; fax (519) 621-8239; f. 1846; Publr JON BUTLER; Man. Editor ROSS FREAKE; circ. 14,000 (E).

Chatham Daily News: 45 Fourth St, POB 2007, Chatham N7M 2G4; tel. (519) 354-2000; fax (519) 436-0949; f. 1862; Publr F. IAN RUTHERFORD; Man. Editor STEVE ZAK; circ. 16,000 (E).

Cobourg Daily Star: POB 400, Cobourg K9A 4L1; tel. (416) 372-0131; fax (416) 372-4966; Publr BILL POIRIER; Editorial Dir JIM GROSSMITH; circ. 6,000 (E).

Daily Mercury: 8–14 Macdonnell St, Guelph N1H 6P7; tel. (519) 822-4310; fax (519) 767-1681; f. 1854; Publr J. PETER KOHL; Editor-in-Chief BOB BOXALL; circ. 19,000 (E).

Daily Press: 187 Cedar St South, POB 560, Timmins P4N 2G9; tel. (705) 268-5050; fax (705) 268-7373; f. 1933; Publr R. L. ETHELSTON; Editor J. HORNYAK; circ. 14,000 (E).

Le Droit: 47 Clarence St, Suite 222, Ottawa K1G 3J9; tel. (613) 560-2500; fax (613) 560-2572; f. 1913; French; Publr GILBERT LACASSE; Editor-in-Chief PIERRE ALLARD; circ. 34,000 (E).

Evening Guide: POB 296, Port Hope L1A 3W4; tel. (416) 885-2471; fax (416) 885-7442; Publr BILL POIRIER; Editorial Dir JIM GROSSMITH; circ. 4,000 (E).

Expositor: POB 965, Brantford N3T 5S8; tel. (519) 756-2020; fax (519) 756-4911; f. 1852; Publr WILLIAM FINDLAY; Editor K. J. STRACHAN; circ. 33,000 (E).

Financial Post: 777 Bay St, 6th Floor, Toronto M5G 2E4; tel. (416) 596-5649; telex 062-19547; fax (416) 596-5300; f. 1988; Publr NEVILLE J. NANKIVELL; Editor JOHN F. GODFREY; circ. 57,000 (M).

The Globe and Mail: 444 Front St West, Toronto M5V 2S9; tel. (416) 585-5000; telex 062-19721; fax (416) 585-5085; f. 1844; Publr A. ROY MEGARRY; Editor-in-Chief WILLIAM THORSELL; circ. 320,000 (M).

Hamilton Spectator: POB 300, Hamilton L8N 3G3; tel. (416) 526-3333; fax (416) 522-1696; f. 1846; Publr GORDON BULLOCK; Editor ALEX M. BEER; circ. 142,000 (E).

Intelligencer: POB 5600, Belleville K8N 5C7; tel. (613) 962-9171; fax (613) 962-9652; f. 1870; Publr and Gen. Man. H. MYLES MORTON; Man. Editor LEE BALLANTYNE; circ. 19,000 (E).

Kitchener-Waterloo Record: 225 Fairway Rd South, Kitchener N2G 4E5; tel. (519) 894-2231; fax (519) 894-3912; f. 1878; Publr K. A. BAIRD; Man. Editor WAYNE MACDONALD; circ. 81,000 (E).

Lindsay Daily Post: 15 William St North, Lindsay K9V 3Z8; tel. (705) 324-2113; fax (705) 324-0174; Publr BILL MACKIE; circ. 6,000 (E).

CANADA

Directory

London Free Press: POB 2280, London N6A 4G1; tel. (519) 679-1111; fax (519) 667-4530; f. 1849; Publr MARTHA G. BLACKBURN; Editor PHILIP R. MCLEOD; circ. 126,000 (M).

Niagara Falls Review: POB 270, Niagara Falls L2E 6T6; tel. (416) 358-5711; fax (416) 356-0785; f. 1879; Publr ROBERT MCKENZIE; Man. Editor DONALD W. MULLAN; circ. 25,000 (M).

Northern Daily News: 8 Duncan Ave, Kirkland Lake P2N 3L4; tel. (705) 567-5321; fax (705) 567-6162; f. 1922; Publr COLIN BRUCE; Editor AL HOGAN; circ. 6,000 (E).

The Nugget: POB 570, North Bay P1B 8J6; tel. (705) 472-3200; fax (705) 472-1438; f. 1909; Publr JACK R. OWENS; Editor COLIN P. VEZINA; circ. 24,000 (E).

Observer: 186 Alexander St, Pembroke K8A 4L9; tel. (613) 732-3691; f. 1855; Publr and Man. Editor W. H. HIGGINSON; circ. 7,000 (E).

Orillia Daily Packet and Times: 31 Colborne St East, Orillia L3V 1T4; tel. (705) 325-1355; fax (705) 325-7691; f. 1953; Publr J. C. MARSHALL; Man. Editor MARK FURLONG; circ. 11,000 (E).

Oshawa Times: 44 Richmond St West, Oshawa L1G 1C8; tel. (416) 723-3474; fax (416) 723-4366; f. 1871; Publr GARNET COWSILL; Man. Editor D. JAMES PALMATEER; circ. 22,000 (E).

Ottawa Citizen: POB 5020, Ottawa K2C 3M4; tel. (613) 829-9100; telex 053-4779; fax (613) 829-5032; f. 1843; Publr CLARK DAVEY; Editor GORDON FISHER; circ. 192,000 (D), 244,000 (Sat.), 167,000 (S).

Ottawa Sun: 380 Hunt Club Rd, Ottawa K1G 5H7; tel. (613) 739-7000; fax (613) 739-8043; Publr HARTLEY STEWARD; Editor DON HAWKES; circ. 29,000 (M), 32,000 (S).

Peterborough Examiner: POB 389, Peterborough K9J 6Z4; tel. (705) 745-4641; fax (705) 743-4581; f. 1884; Publr and Gen. Man. BRUCE L. RUDD; Man. Editor ED ARNOLD; circ. 28,000 (E).

Recorder and Times: 23 King St West, Brockville K6V 5T8; tel. (613) 342-4441; fax (613) 342-4456; f. 1821; Co-Publr H. S. GRANT; Co-Publr and Editor-in-Chief Mrs PERRY S. BEVERLEY; circ. 17,000 (E).

St Thomas Times-Journal: 16 Hincks St, St Thomas N5P 3W6; tel. (519) 631-2790; fax (519) 631-5653; f. 1882; Publr and Gen. Man. L. J. BEAVIS; Man. Editor JAMES BLAKE; circ. 10,000 (E).

Sarnia Observer: POB 3009, Sarnia N7T 7M8; tel. (519) 344-3641; fax (519) 332-2951; f. 1917; Publr and Gen. Man. TERENCE J. HOGAN; Man. Editor TERRY SHAW; circ. 25,000 (E).

Sault Star: POB 460, Sault Ste Marie P6A 5M5; tel. (705) 759-3030; fax (705) 942-8690; f. 1912; Publr E. PAUL WILSON; Editor DOUG MILLROY; circ. 27,000 (E).

Sentinel-Review: POB 1000, Woodstock N4S 8A5; tel. (519) 537-2341; fax (519) 537-3049; f. 1886; Publr PAUL J. TAYLOR; Man. Editor GARY MANNING; circ. 11,000 (E).

Simcoe Reformer: POB 370, Simcoe N3Y 4L2; tel. (519) 426-5710; fax (519) 426-9255; f. 1858; Publr JOHN COWLARD; Man. Editor RON KOWALSKY; circ. 10,000 (E).

Standard: 17 Queen St, St Catharines L2R 5G5; tel. (416) 684-7251; fax (416) 684-6670; f. 1891; Pres. and Publr HENRY B. BURGOYNE; Man. Editor MURRAY O. G. THOMSON; circ. 43,000 (E).

Standard-Freeholder: 44 Pitt St, Cornwall K6J 3P3; tel. (613) 933-3160; fax (613) 933-7521; Publr DON H. TOMCHICK; Editor JOAN NETTLE; circ. 18,000 (E).

Sudbury Star: 33 MacKenzie St, Sudbury P3C 4Y1; tel. (705) 674-5271; fax (705) 674-0624; f. 1909; Publr MAURICE H. SWITZER; Man. Editor JOHN A. FARRINGTON; circ. 30,000 (E).

Sun Times: POB 200, Owen Sound N4K 5P2; tel. (519) 376-2250; fax (519) 376-7190; f. 1853; Publr J. E. DOHERTY; Editor ROBERT HULL; circ. 24,000 (E).

Times-News and Chronicle-Journal: 75 Cumberland St South, Thunder Bay P7B 1A3; tel. (807) 344-3535; fax (807) 345-5991; Publr J. P. MILN; Man. Editor MICHAEL GRIEVE; circ. 38,000 (D).

Toronto Star: One Yonge St, Toronto M5E 1E6; tel. (416) 367-2000; telex 065-24387; fax (416) 869-4416; f. 1892; Publr DAVID R. JOLLEY; Editor JOHN HONDERICH; circ. 508,000 (D), 762,000 (Sat.), 533,000 (S).

Toronto Sun: 333 King St East, Toronto M5A 3X5; tel. (416) 947-2333; telex 062-17688; fax (416) 947-3139; f. 1971; Publr PAUL V. GODFREY; Editor JOHN DOWNING; circ. 296,000 (M), 465,000 (S).

Welland-Port Colborne Evening Tribune: POB 278, Welland L3B 5P5; tel. (416) 732-2411; fax (416) 732-4883; f. 1863; Publr JOHN W. VANKOOTEN; Editor JAMES R. MIDDLETON; circ. 17,000 (E).

Whig-Standard: 306 King St East, Kingston K7L 4Z7; tel. (613) 544-5000; fax (613) 544-6994; f. 1834; Publr MICHAEL L. DAVIES; Editor NEIL REYNOLDS; circ. 36,000 (E).

Windsor Star: 167 Ferry St, Windsor N9A 4M5; tel. (519) 255-5787; fax (519) 255-5778; f. 1918; Publr J. S. THOMSON; Editor CARL MORGAN; circ. 86,000 (E).

Prince Edward Island

Guardian and Patriot: 165 Prince St, POB 760, Charlottetown C1A 4R7; tel. (902) 894-8506; fax (902) 566-3808; f. 1887; Publr KEN SIMS; Man. Editor WALTER MACINTYRE; circ. 24,000 (D).

Journal-Pioneer: POB 2480, Summerside C1N 4K5; tel. (902) 436-2121; fax (902) 436-3027; f. 1865; Publr RALPH HECKBERT; Editor RON ENGLAND; circ. 12,000 (E).

Québec

Le Devoir: 211 rue St-Sacrement, Montréal H2Y 1X1; tel. (514) 844-3361; fax (514) 286-9255; f. 1910; Dir LISE BISSONNETTE; Editor-in-Chief BERNARD DESCÔTEAUX; circ. 28,000 (M).

The Gazette: 250 ouest, rue St-Antoine, Montréal H2Y 3R7; tel. (514) 282-2750; telex 055-61767; fax (514) 282-2342; f. 1778; Publr DAVID PERKS; Editor NORMAN WEBSTER; circ. 179,000 (M), 258,000 (Sat.), 160,000 (S).

Le Journal de Montréal: 4545 rue Frontenac, Montréal H2H 2R7; tel. (514) 521-4545; fax (514) 525-5442; f. 1964; Publr JACQUES GIRARD; Editor NORMAND GIRARD; circ. 324,000 (M), 350,000 (Sat.), 339,000 (S).

Le Journal de Québec: 450 ave Béchard, CP 2158, Ville de Vanier G1M 2E9; tel. (418) 683-1573; fax (418) 683-1027; f. 1967; Gen. Man. JEAN-CLAUDE L'ABBÉE; Chief Editor SERGE CÔTÉ; circ. 108,000 (M), 110,000 (Sat.), 99,000 (S).

Le Nouvelliste: 1850 rue Bellefeuille, Trois Rivières G9A 3Y2; tel. (819) 376-2501; fax (819) 376-0946; f. 1920; Publr CLAUDETTE TOUGAS; Man. Editor BERNARD CHAMPOUX; circ. 58,000 (M).

La Presse: 7 rue St-Jacques, Montréal H2Y 1K9; tel. (514) 285-7306; telex 052-4110; fax (514) 845-8129; f. 1884; Publr ROGER D. LANDRY; circ. 207,000 (M), 330,000 (Sat.), 195,000 (S).

Le Quotidien: 1051 blvd Talbot, Chicoutimi G7H 5C1; tel. (418) 545-4474; fax (418) 545-9854; f. 1973; Publr DENIS CLICHE; Newsroom Dir BERTRAND GENEST; circ. 34,000 (M).

The Record: 2850 rue Delorme, Sherbrooke J1K 1A1; tel. (819) 569-9525; fax (819) 569-3945; f. 1837; Publr RANDY KINNEAR; Editor CHARLES BURY; circ. 6,000 (M).

Le Soleil: 390 est, rue St Vallier, Québec G1K 7J6; tel. (418) 647-3233; telex 051-3755; fax (418) 647-3347; f. 1896; Pres. and Gen. Man. ROBERT NORMAND; Editor-in-Chief J.-JACQUES SAMSON; circ. 115,000 (M), 145,000 (Sat.), 94,000 (S).

La Tribune: 1950 rue Roy, Sherbrooke J1K 2X8; tel. (819) 564-5450; fax (819) 564-5455; f. 1910; Publr JEAN-GUY DUBUC; Editor JEAN VIGNEAULT; circ. 41,000 (M).

La Voix de L'Est: 76 rue Dufferin, Granby J2G 9L4; tel. (514) 375-6850; fax (514) 777-4865; f. 1945; Gen. Man. JACQUES BOUCHARD; Man. Editor RÉAL MARCHESSEAULT; circ. 16,000 (M).

Saskatchewan

Leader-Post: POB 2020, Regina S4P 3G4; tel. (306) 565-8211; telex 071-3131; fax (306) 565-2588; f. 1883; Pres. MICHAEL G. SIFTON; Editor JOHN SWAN; circ. 72,000 (E).

Moose Jaw Times-Herald: 44 Fairford St West, Moose Jaw S6H 1V1; tel. (306) 692-6441; fax (306) 692-2101; f. 1889; Publr DALE BRIN; Man. Editor JOHN STRAUSS; circ. 10,000 (E).

Prince Albert Herald: 30 10th St East, Prince Albert S6V 5R9; tel. (306) 764-4276; fax (306) 763-3331; f. 1917; Publr and Gen. Man. R. W. GIBB; Man. Editor W. ROZNOWSKY; circ. 10,000 (M).

Star-Phoenix: 204 Fifth Ave North, Saskatoon S7K 2P1; tel. (306) 644-8340; telex 074-2428; fax (306) 664-8208; f. 1902; Publr DICK THOMPSON; Exec. Editor BILL PETERSON; circ. 67,000 (E).

Yukon Territory

Whitehorse Star: 2149 Second Ave, Whitehorse, Yukon Y1A 1C5; tel. (403) 668-2063; f. 1985; Publr ROBERT ERLAM; Man. Editor JACKIE PIERCE; circ. 4,000.

SELECTED PERIODICALS

(W = weekly; F = fortnightly; M = monthly; Q = quarterly)

Alberta

Alberta Business: 333 11th Ave, SW, Calgary T2R 1L9; tel. (403) 262-4150; fax (403) 266-2465; f. 1984; Editor JOHN DODD; circ. 13,000; 10 a year.

Alberta Farm and Ranch Magazine: 4000 19th St, NE, Calgary T2E 6P8; tel. (403) 250-6633; fax (403) 291-0502; f. 1983; Editor JOY GREGORY; circ. 96,000 (M).

Alberta Report/Western Report: 17327 106th Ave, Edmonton T5S 1M7; tel. (403) 484-8884; fax (403) 489-3280; f. 1979; news magazine; Editor STEPHEN HOPKINS; circ. 52,000 (W).

CANADA

Ukrainski Visti (Ukrainian News): 10967 97th St, Edmonton T5H 2M8; tel. (403) 423-6985; f. 1929; Ukrainian and English; Editor K. Sherman; circ. 3,000 (w).

British Columbia

BC Business: 4180 Lougheed Hwy, Suite 401, Burnaby, V5C 6A7; tel. (604) 299-7311; fax (604) 299-9188; f. 1973; Editor Bonnie Irving; circ. 22,000 (M).

BC Outdoors: 1132 Hamilton St, Suite 202, Vancouver V6B 2S2; tel. (604) 687-1581; fax (604) 687-1925; f. 1945; Editor George Will; circ. 39,000; 7 a year.

Easy Living: 214 Sixth St, New Westminster V3L 3A2; tel. (604) 521-5103; fax (604) 521-3013; f. 1979; Editor Ann Brennan; circ. 350,000 (M).

Pacific Yachting: 1132 Hamilton St, Suite 202, Vancouver V6B 2S2; tel. (604) 687-1581; fax (604) 687-1925; f. 1968; Editor John Shinnick; circ. 17,000 (M).

Vancouver Magazine: 555 West 12th Ave, SE Tower, Suite 300, Vancouver V5Z 4L4; tel. (604) 877-7732; fax (604) 877-4848; f. 1957; Editor Malcolm Parry; circ. 76,000 (M).

Western Living: SE Tower, Suite 300, 555 West 12th Ave, Vancouver V5Z 4L4; tel. (604) 877-7732; fax (604) 877-4848; f. 1971; Editor Paula Brook; circ. 273,000 (M).

WestWorld Magazine: 4180 Lougheed Hwy, Suite 401, Burnaby V5C 6A7; tel. (604) 299-7311; fax (604) 299-9188; Editor Robin Roberts; circ. 731,000 (Q).

Manitoba

The Beaver: Exploring Canada's History: 450 Portage Ave, Winnipeg R3C 0E7; tel. (204) 786-7048; f. 1920; Canadian social history; Editor Christopher Dafoe; circ. 35,000; 6 a year.

Cattlemen: 1760 Ellice Ave, Winnipeg R3H 0B6; tel. (204) 784-0300; fax (204) 775-9052; f. 1938; animal husbandry; Editor Gren Winslow; circ. 39,000 (M).

Country Guide: 1760 Ellice Ave, Winnipeg R3H 0B6; tel. (204) 784-0317; f. 1882; agriculture; Editor David Wreford; circ. 176,000 (M).

Kanada Kurier: 955 Alexander Ave, POB 1054, Winnipeg R3C 2X8; tel. (204) 774-1883; fax (204) 783-5740; f. 1889; German; Editor Ralf Neuendorff; circ. 20,000 (w).

The Manitoba Co-operator: 220 Portage Ave, 4th Floor, POB 9800, Winnipeg R3C 3K7; tel. (204) 934-0401; fax (204) 934-0480; f. 1925; agricultural; Editor John W. Morriss; circ. 45,000 (w).

Motor in Canada: 1077 St James St, POB 6900, Winnipeg R3C 3B1; tel. (204) 775-0201; fax (204) 783-7488; f. 1915; Editor Dan Proudley; circ. 12,000 (M).

Trade and Commerce: 1077 St James St, POB 6900, Winnipeg R3C 3B1; tel. (204) 775-0201; fax (204) 783-7488; f. 1905; Editor George Mitchell; circ. 13,000 (M).

New Brunswick

Atlantic Advocate: POB 3370, Fredericton E3B 5A2; tel. (506) 452-6671; fax (506) 452-7405; f. 1956; Editor Marilee Little; circ. 28,000 (M).

Brunswick Business Journal: 83 Gordon St, Moncton E1C 1M3; tel. (506) 857-9696; fax (506) 859-7395; f. 1984; Editor Joanne Cadogan; circ. 9,000 (M).

Newfoundland

Newfoundland Lifestyle: 197 Water St, POB 2356, St John's A1C 6E7; tel. (709) 726-9300; Man. Editor Edwina Hutton; circ. 30,000; 6 a year.

Northwest Territories

L'Aquillon: POB 1325, Yellowknife X1A 2N9; tel. (403) 873-6603; fax (403) 873-2158; f. 1985; circ. 2,000 (w).

The Drum: POB 2719, Inuvik X0E 0T0; tel. (403) 979-4545; f. 1966; English; Editor Dan Holman; circ. 2,000 (w).

The Hub: POB 1250, Hay River X0E 0R0; tel. (403) 874-6577; circ. 2,000 (w).

Native Press: POB 1919, Yellowknife X1A 2P4; tel. (403) 873-2661; circ. 5,000 (w).

News/North: POB 2820, Yellowknife X1A 2R1; tel. (403) 873-2661; f. 1945; Man. Editor Craig Harper; circ. 9,000 (w).

Nunatsiaq News: POB 8, Iqaluit X0A 0H0; tel. (819) 979-5357; fax (819) 974-4763; f. 1972; English and Inuktitut; circ. 7,000 (w).

Slave River Journal: POB 990, Fort Smith X0E 0P0; tel. (403) 872-2704; fax (403) 872-2190; circ. 2,000 (w).

Yellowknifer: POB 2820, Yellowknife X1A 2R1; tel. (403) 873-4031; Editor Brian Jones; circ. 6,000 (w).

Nova Scotia

Atlantic Fisherman: 11 George St, POB 1000, Pictou B0K 1H0; tel. (902) 485-8014; fax (902) 752-4816; f. 1984; Editor Heather Richards; circ. 15,000 (M).

Atlantic Insight: 5502 Atlantic St, Halifax B3H 1G4; tel. (902) 421-1214; Editor Sharon Fraser; circ. 34,000 (M).

The Canadian Forum: 5502 Atlantic St, Halifax B3H 1G4; tel. (902) 421-1214; fax (902) 425-0166; f. 1920; political, literary and economic; Editor Duncan Cameron; circ. 10,000; 10 a year.

The Dalhousie Review: Dalhousie University Press, Sir James Dunn Science Bldg, Halifax B3H 3J5; tel. (902) 494-2541; f. 1921; literary and general; Editor Dr Alan Andrews; (Q).

Ontario

Canada Gazette: Canadian Government Publishing Centre, Supply and Services Canada, Ottawa K1A 0S9; tel. (819) 997-1988; fax (819) 956-5134; f. 1867; official bulletin of the Govt of Canada; Chief Beate Alaoui; (w).

Canada & the World: POB 7004, Oakville L6J 6L5; tel. (416) 338-3394; f. 1937; Editor Rupert J. Taylor; circ. 24,000; 9 a year.

Canadian Aeronautics and Space Journal: 222 Somerset St West, Suite 601, Ottawa K2P 2G3; tel. (613) 234-0191; fax (613) 234-9039; f. 1954; Chair. of Editorial Bd Dr G. F. Marsters; circ. 3,000 (M).

Canadian Architect: 1450 Don Mills Rd, Don Mills M3B 2X7; (416) 445-6641; telex 069-66612; fax (416) 442-2077; f. 1955; Publr and Man. Editor Robert Gretton; circ. 10,000 (M).

Canadian Bar Review: Canadian Bar Foundation, 50 O'Connor St, Suite 902, Ottawa K1P 6L2; tel. (613) 237-2925; fax (613) 237-0185; f. 1923; Editor A. J. McClean; circ. 34,000 (Q).

Canadian Boating: 5805 Whittle Rd, Suite 208, Mississauga L4Z 2J1; tel. (416) 568-4131; fax (416) 568-4133; f. 1925; Editor Gary Arthurs; circ. 17,000; 9 a year.

Canadian Chemical News: 130 Slater St, Suite 550, Ottawa K1P 6E2; tel. (613) 232-6252; fax (613) 232-5862; f. 1949; Editor Sandra Hollingshead; circ. 10,000; 10 a year.

Canadian Dental Association Journal: 1815 Alta Vista Drive, Ottawa K1G 3Y6; tel. (613) 523-1770; fax (416) 523-7736; f. 1935; Editor Dr Ralph Crawford; Scientific Editors Dr Robert Turnbull, Dr Pierre Desautels; (M).

Canadian Doctor: 625 Cochrane Drive, Suite 701, Markham L3R 9R9; tel. (416) 940-0136; fax (416) 940-1888; f. 1935; Editor Marc J. Charette; circ. 29,000 (M).

Canadian Geographic: 39 McArthur Ave, Vanier K1L 8L7; tel. (613) 745-4629; fax (613) 744-0947; f. 1930; publ. by the Royal Canadian Geographical Soc.; Editor Ian Darragh; circ. 225,000; 6 a year.

Canadian Labour: 2841 Riverside Drive, Ottawa K1V 8X7; tel. (613) 521-3400; telex 053-4750; f. 1956; publ. by the Canadian Labour Congress; Editors D. Hodgson, M. Walsh.

Canadian Medical Association Journal: 1867 Alta Vista Drive, Ottawa K1G 3Y6; tel. (613) 731-9331; telex 053-3152; fax (613) 523-0937; f. 1911; Editor-in-Chief Dr Bruce P. Squires; circ. 56,000 (F).

Canadian Nurse/L'infirmière canadienne: 50 The Driveway, Ottawa K2P 1E2; tel. (613) 237-2133; fax (613) 237-3520; f. 1908; journal of the Canadian Nurses Asscn; Editor Judith A. Banning; circ. 109,000 (M).

Canadian Pharmaceutical Journal: 1785 Alta Vista Drive, Ottawa K1G 3Y6; tel. (613) 523-7877; fax (613) 523-0445; f. 1869; Editor Jane Dewar; circ. 13,000 (M).

Canadian Public Policy—Analyse de Politiques: MacKinnon Bldg, Room 039, University of Guelph, Guelph N1G 2W1; tel. (519) 824-4120; fax (519) 824-9457; Editor Kenneth Norrie; circ. 2,000 (Q).

Canadian Sportsman: 25 Old Plank Rd, POB 129, Straffordville N0J 1Y0; tel. (519) 866-5558; fax (519) 866-5596; f. 1870; equestrian; Editor Gary Foerster; w (May–Oct.), f (Oct.–May).

Canadian Workshop: 130 Spy Court, Markham L3R 5H6; tel. (416) 475-8440; f. 1977; do-it-yourself; Editor Erina Kelly; circ. 130,000 (M).

CAR (Canadian Auto Review): 1450 Don Mills Rd, Don Mills M3B 2X7; tel. (416) 442-2000; fax (416) 442-2077; f. 1984; Editor Brian Harper; circ. 4,000 (M).

Electronics & Technology Today: 1300 Don Mills Rd, Don Mills M3B 3M8; tel. (416) 445-5600; fax (416) 445-8149; f. 1977; Editor Bill Markwick; circ. 8,000 (M).

Equinox: 7 Queen Victoria Rd, Camden East K0K 1J0; tel. (613) 378-6661; f. 1981; circ. 168,000; 6 a year.

Hockey News: 85 Cawardale Rd, Suite 100, Don Mills M3B 2R2; tel. (416) 445-5702; fax (416) 445-0753; f. 1947; Editor-in-Chief Bob McKenzie; circ. 114,000 (w).

CANADA

Holstein Journal: 333 Lesmill Rd, Don Mills M3B 2V1; tel. (416) 441-3030; fax (416) 441-3038; f. 1938; Editor BONNIE E. COOPER; circ. 11,000 (M).

Legion Magazine: 359 Kent St, Suite 504, Ottawa K2P 0R6; tel. (613) 235-8741; fax (613) 233-7159; f. 1926; Editor MAC JOHNSTON; circ. 526,000; 10 a year.

Magyar Élet (Hungarian Life): 221 Burbank Ave, Willowdale M2K 1P5; tel. (416) 733-4345; fax (416) 229-1606; f. 1948; Hungarian; Publr LASZLO SCHNEE; circ. 8,000 (W).

Modern Medicine of Canada: 1450 Don Mills Rd, Don Mills M3B 2X7; tel. (416) 445-6641; fax (416) 442-2201; f. 1946; Exec. Editor ODILE BROADBENT; English and French; circ. 35,000 (M).

Ontario Milk Producer: 6780 Campobello Rd, Mississauga L5N 2L8; tel. (416) 821-8970; fax (416) 821-3160; f. 1925; Editor BILL DIMMICK; circ. 14,000.

Oral Health: 1450 Don Mills Rd, Don Mills M3B 2X7; tel. (416) 445-6641; telex 069-66612; fax (416) 442-2077; f. 1911; dentistry; Man. Editor JANET BONELLIE; circ. 15,000 (M).

Photo Life: 130 Spy Court, Markham L3R 5H6; tel. (416) 475-8440; fax (416) 475-9246; circ. 60,000; 10 a year.

Style: 85 Scarsdale Rd, Suite 300, Don Mills M3B 2R2; tel. (416) 444-8407; telex 069-86391; fax (416) 444-5308; f. 1888; Editor MARSHA ROSS; circ. 15,000; 16 a year.

Teviskes Ziburiai (Lights of Homeland): 2185 Stavebank Rd, Mississauga L5C 1T3; tel. (416) 275-4672; fax (416) 275-1336; f. 1949; Lithuanian; Editor Rev. Dr PR. GAIDA; circ. 6,000 (W).

Toronto

Anglican Journal: 600 Jarvis St, Toronto M4Y 2J6; tel. (416) 924-9192; telex 065-24128; fax (416) 921-4452; f. 1871; official publ. of the Anglican Church of Canada; Editor (vacant); circ. 273,000 (M).

Arab News International (Akhbar El-Arab Al Dawlia): 511 Queen St East, Toronto M5A 1V1; tel. (416) 362-0304; telex 065-2629; fax (416) 861-0238; f. 1978; Arabic and English; Editor SALAH ALLAM; circ. 6,000 (W).

Books in Canada: 366 Adelaide St East, 4th Floor, Toronto M5A 3X9; tel. (416) 363-5426; f. 1971; Editor PAUL STUEWE; circ. 12,000; 9 a year.

CA magazine: The Canadian Institute of Chartered Accountants, 150 Bloor St West, Toronto M5S 2Y2; tel. (416) 962-1242; telex 062-22835; fax (416) 962-3375; f. 1911; Editor NELSON LUSCOMBE; circ. 64,000 (M).

The Campus Network: Youthstream Canada Ltd, 1541 Avenue Rd, Suite 203, Toronto M5M 3X4; tel. (416) 787-4911; fax (416) 787-4681; 30 campus edns; Pres. CAMERON KILLORAN; circ. 263,000.

Canadian Author & Bookman: 121 Avenue Rd, Suite 104, Toronto M5R 2G3; tel. (416) 926-8084; f. 1919; publ. by the Canadian Authors Asscn; Editor GORDON E. SYMONS; circ. 5,000 (Q).

Canadian Business: 70 The Esplanade, 2nd Floor, Toronto M5E 1R2; tel. (416) 364-4266; fax (416) 364-2783; f. 1927; Editor WAYNE GOODING; circ. 81,000 (M).

Canadian Defence Quarterly: 310 Dupont St, Toronto M5R 1V9; tel. (416) 968-7252; telex 065-28085; fax (416) 968-2377; Editor JOHN MARTEINSON; circ. 10,000 (Q).

Canadian Journal of Economics: c/o University of Toronto Press, Front Campus, Toronto M5S 1A6; tel. (416) 978-6739; f. 1968; Editor ROBIN BOADWAY; circ. 3,000 (Q).

Canadian Living: 50 Holly St, Toronto M4S 3B3; tel. (416) 482-8600; fax (416) 482-8153; f. 1975; Editor-in-Chief BONNIE COWAN; circ. 372,000 (M).

Canadian Musician: 3284 Yonge St, Toronto M4N 3M7; tel. (416) 485-8284; fax (416) 485-8924; f. 1979; Editor DAVID HENMAN; circ. 26,000; 6 a year.

Canadian Travel Press Weekly: 310 Dupont St, Toronto M5R 1V9; tel. (416) 968-7252; telex 065-28085; fax (416) 968-2377; Editor-in-Chief EDITH BAXTER; circ. 19,000.

Engineering Digest: 111 Peter St, Suite 411, Toronto M5V 2W2; tel. (416) 596-1624; f. 1954; Editor RONALD M. FARRELL; circ. 66,000; 6 a year.

Farm and Country: 950 Yonge St, 7th Floor, Toronto M4W 2J4; tel. (416) 924-6209; fax (416) 924-9951; f. 1936; Publr and Editor-in-Chief JOHN PHILLIPS; circ. 68,000; 18 a year.

Financial Times of Canada: 1231 Yonge St, Suite 300, Toronto M4T 2Z1; tel. (416) 922-1133; f. 1912; Publr DAVID TAFLER; circ. 105,000 (W).

Music Express: 47 Jefferson Ave, Toronto M6K 1Y3; tel. (416) 538-7500; fax (416) 538-7503; f. 1976; Editor KEITH SHARP; circ. 195,000 (M).

New Equipment News: 111 Peter St, Suite 411, Toronto M5V 2W2; tel. (416) 596-1624; f. 1940; Editor D. B. LEHMAN; circ. 32,000 (M).

Northern Miner: 7 Labatt Ave, Toronto M5A 3P2; tel. (416) 368-3481; fax (416) 367-4036; f. 1915; Editor J. S. BORLAND; circ. 28,000 (W).

Ontario Medical Review: 250 Bloor St East, Suite 600, Toronto M4W 3P8; tel. (416) 963-9383; fax (416) 963-8819; f. 1922; Editor R. DAVID FLETCHER; circ. 18,000 (M).

Quill and Quire: 70 The Esplanade, 4th Floor, Toronto M5E 1R2; tel. (416) 360-0044; fax (416) 941-9038; f. 1935; book-publishing industry; Editor TED MUMFORD; circ. 7,000 (M).

Saturday Night: 36 Toronto St, Suite 1160, Toronto M5C 2C5; tel. (416) 368-7237; fax (416) 368-7261; f. 1887; Editor JOHN FRASER; circ. 110,000 (M).

Select Homes & Food: 50 Holly St, Toronto M4S 3B3; tel. (416) 482-8260; fax (416) 482-1239; Publr DAVID TITCOMBE; circ. 138,000; 8 a year.

Time (Canada edn): 175 Bloor St East, North Tower, Suite 602, Toronto M4W 3R8; tel. (416) 929-1115; fax (416) 929-0019; f. 1943; Man. Dir SANDRA F. BERRY; circ. 351,000 (W).

Toronto Life Magazine: 59 Front St East, 3rd Floor, Toronto M5E 1B3; tel. (416) 364-3333; fax (416) 585-5275; f. 1966; Editor MARQ DE VILLIERS; circ. 96,000 (M).

TV Guide: 50 Holly St, Toronto M4S 3B3; tel. (416) 482-8600; fax (416) 485-1093; f. 1976; Editor JOHN KEYES; circ. 820,000 (W).

The following are all published by Maclean Hunter Ltd, 777 Bay St, Toronto M5W 1A7; tel. (416) 596-5000; telex 062-19547.

Aviation & Aerospace: tel. (416) 596-5789; fax (416) 596-5810; f. 1928; Editor AL DITTER; circ. 18,000 (M).

Canadian Building: tel. (416) 596-5760; fax (416) 596-5810; f. 1951; Editor AL ZABAS; circ. 19,000 (M).

Canadian Electronics Engineering: tel. (416) 596-5731; telex 062-19547; fax (416) 596-5526; f. 1957; Editor PETER J. THORNE; circ. 20,000 (M).

Canadian Grocer: tel. (416) 596-5772; telex 062-19547; fax (416) 593-3162; f. 1886; Editor GEORGE H. CONDON; circ. 18,000 (M).

Canadian Hotel & Restaurant: tel. (416) 596-5813; telex 062-19547; f. 1923; Editor JERRY TUTUNJIAN; circ. 37,000 (M).

Chatelaine: tel. (416) 596-5425; telex 062-19547; fax (416) 593-3197; f. 1928; women's journal; Editor MILDRED ISTONA; circ. 966,000 (M).

Civic Public Works: tel. (416) 596-5953; telex 062-19547; fax (416) 593-3193; f. 1949; Editor CLIFF ALLUM; circ. 13,000 (M).

Design Engineering: tel. (416) 596-5833; telex 062-19547; fax (416) 593-3193; f. 1955; Editor STEVE PURWITSKY; circ. 18,000 (M).

Flare: tel. (416) 596-5453; telex 062-19547; fax (416) 596-5526; f. 1984; Editor SHELLEY M. BLACK; circ. 206,000 (M).

Floor Covering News: tel. (416) 596-5940; telex 062-19547; fax (416) 593-3189; f. 1976; Editor MICHAEL J. KNELL; circ. 7,000; 10 a year.

Heavy Construction News: tel. (416) 596-5844; fax (416) 593-3193; f. 1956; Editor RUSSELL B. NOBLE; circ. 25,000 (F).

Maclean's Canada's Weekly Newsmazagine: tel. (416) 596-5311; telex 065-24196; fax (416) 596-6001; f. 1905; Editor KEVIN DOYLE; circ. 601,000 (W).

Marketing: tel. (416) 596-5835; telex 062-19547; f. 1906; Editor COLIN MUNCIE; circ. 12,000 (W).

Medical Post: tel. (416) 596-5770; telex 062-19547; f. 1965; Editor DEREK CASSELS; circ. 37,000 (F).

Office Equipment and Methods: tel. (416) 596-5920; telex 062-19547; f. 1954; Editor TOM KELLY; circ. 60,000 (M).

Québec

A + Le magazine Affaires: 465 rue St-Jean, 9e étage, Montréal H2Y 3S4; tel. (514) 842-6491; telex 055-61971; fax (514) 842-3032; f. 1978; Publr MICHEL LORD; circ. 99,000; 10 a year.

L'Actualité: 1001 ouest, blvd de Maisonneuve, Montréal, H3A 3E1; tel. (514) 845-2543; fax (514) 845-4393; f. 1976; general interest; Editor JEAN PARÉ; circ. 264,000 (M).

Le Bulletin des Agriculteurs: 110 ouest, blvd Crémazie, Bureau 422, Montréal H2P 1B9; tel. (514) 382-4350; fax (514) 382-4356; f. 1918; Editor MARC-ALAIN SOUCY; circ. 61,000 (M).

Canadian Forest Industries: 3300 Côte Vertu, Bureau 410, St-Laurent, Qué H4R 2B7; tel. (514) 339-1399; fax (514) 339-1396; f. 1880; Editor TIM TOLTON; circ. 21,000 (M).

Châtelaine: 1001 ouest, blvd de Maisonneuve, Montréal H3A 3E1; tel. (514) 843-2503; telex 055-60604; f. 1960; Editor MICHELINE LACHANCE; circ. 243,000 (M).

CIM Bulletin: 3400 ouest, blvd de Maisonneuve, Bureau 1210, Montréal H3Z 3B8; tel. (514) 939-2710; fax (514) 939-2714; publ. by

CANADA

the Canadian Inst. of Mining and Metallurgy; Editor PERLA GANTZ; circ. 11,000 (M).

Cinema Canada: 7383 rue de la Roche, Montréal H2R 2T4; tel. (514) 272-5354; fax (514) 270-5068; Editor CONNIE TADROS; circ. 10,000.

Il Cittadino Canadese: 6274 est, Jean-Talon, Montréal H1S 1M8; tel. (514) 253-2332; fax (514) 253-6574; f. 1941; Italian; Editor BASILIO GIORDANO; circ. 50,000 (W).

Clin d'Oeil: 7 chemin Bates, Outremont H2V 1A6; tel. (514) 270-1100; fax (514) 270-6900; Editor-in-Chief JEAN LESSARD; circ. 67,000 (M).

Coup de Pouce: 2001 rue Université, Bureau 900, Montréal H3A 2A6; tel. (514) 499-0561; fax (514) 499-1844; f. 1984; Publr JEAN DUROCHER; circ. 147,000 (M).

Decormag: 5148 blvd St-Laurent, Montréal H2T 1R8; tel. (514) 273-9773; fax (514) 273-9034; f. 1973; Editor CLAUDE GERVAIS; circ. 65,000; 10 a year.

Echos-Vedettes: 801 est, rue Sherbrooke, 2e étage, Montréal H2L 4X9; tel. (514) 521-3887; fax (514) 521-9621; f. 1963; Editor MARC CHATELLE; circ. 170,000 (W).

L'Essentiel: 7 chemin Bates, Outremont H2V 1A6; tel. (514) 270-1100; fax (514) 270-6900; Publr SYLVIE BERGERON; circ. 113,000 (M).

Femme Plus: 7 chemin Bates, Outremont H2V 1A6; tel. (514) 270-1100; fax (514) 270-6900; Publr SYLVIE BERGERON; circ. 77,000 (M).

Le Lundi: 7 chemin Bates, Outremont H2V 1A6; tel. (514) 270-1100; fax (514) 270-6900; f. 1976; Editor MICHEL CHOINIÈRE; circ. 106,000 (W).

Montréal Magazine: 1310 ave Greene, Bureau 920, Westmount H3Z 2B5; tel. (514) 933-2555; fax (514) 933-7327; f. 1971; Editor ANN HAMILTON; circ. 62,000; 10 a year.

Photo Sélection: 850 blvd Pierre-Bertrand, Bureau 440, Ville de Vanier G1M 3K8; tel. (418) 687-3550; f. 1980; Chief Editor JACQUES THIBAULT; circ. 18,000; 8 a year.

Le Producteur de Lait Québécois: 555 blvd Roland-Thérrien, Longueuil J4H 3Y9; tel. (514) 679-0530; fax (514) 679-5436; f. 1980; dairy farming; Dir HUGUES BELZILE; circ. 18,000 (M).

Progrès-Dimanche: 1051 blvd Talbot, Chicoutimi G7H 5C1; tel. (418) 545-4474; fax (418) 545-9854; f. 1964; Pres. DENIS CLICHE; circ. 52,000 (W).

Le Québec Industriel: 1001 ouest, blvd de Maisonneuve, Bureau 1000, Montréal H3A 3E1; tel. (514) 845-5141; fax (514) 845-4393; f. 1946; Editor BERTRAND DIONNE; circ. 17,000 (M).

Québec Science: 2875 blvd Laurier, Ste-Foy G1V 2M3; tel. (418) 657-3551; telex 051-31623; fax (418) 657-2096; f. 1969; Editor JACKI DALLAIRE; circ. 20,000 (M).

Reader's Digest/Selection du Reader's Digest: 215 ave Redfern, Westmount H3Z 2V9; tel. (514) 934-0751; fax (514) 920-6571; f. 1948; Editor DENISE SUPRENANT; circ. 1,706,000 (M).

Rénovation Bricolage: 7 chemin Bates, Outremont H2V 1A6; tel. (514) 270-1100; fax (514) 270-6900; f. 1976; Editor-in-Chief ANDRÉ VILDER; circ. 35,000 (M); 11 a year.

Revue Commerce: 465 rue St-Jean, 9e étage, Montréal H2Y 2R6; tel. (514) 844-1511; fax (514) 842-3032; f. 1898; Editor JEAN-PAUL LEJEUNE; circ. 38,000 (M).

La Terre de Chez Nous: 555 blvd Roland-Thérrien, Longueuil J4H 3Y9; tel. (514) 679-0530; fax (514) 679-5436; f. 1929; agriculture and forestry; French; Editor-in-Chief ANDRÉ CHARBONNEAU; circ. 44,000 (W).

TV Hebdo/TV Plus: 2001 rue Université, Bureau 900, Montréal H3A 2A6; tel. (514) 499-0561; fax (514) 843-3529; f. 1960; Publr MICHEL TRUDEAU; circ. 327,000 (W).

Saskatchewan

Farm Light & Power: 2330 15th Ave, Regina S4P 1A2; tel. (306) 525-3305; fax (306) 757-1810; f. 1959; Editor PAT REDIGER; circ. 176,000; 10 a year.

Western Producer: 2310 Millar Ave, POB 2500, Saskatoon S7K 2C4; tel. (306) 665-3500; fax (306) 653-1255; f. 1923; world and agricultural news; Editor R. KEITH DRYDEN; circ. 129,000 (W).

Western Sportsman: POB 737, Regina S4P 3A8; tel. (306) 352-2773; fax (306) 565-2440; f. 1968; Editor ROGER FRANCIS; circ. 29,000; 6 a year.

Yukon Territory

L'Aurore Boréal: POB 5025, Whitehorse Y1A 4Z1; tel. (403) 873-4031; circ. 1,000 (M).

Dannzha News: 22 Nisutlin Drive, Whitehorse Y1A 3S5; tel. (403) 667-6923; fax (403) 668-6577; f. 1973; Editor DORIS BILL; circ. 6,000; 6 a year.

Yukon News: 211 Wood St, Whitehorse Y1A 2E4; tel. (403) 667-6285; f. 1960; Editor PATRICIA LIVING; circ. 8,000; 2 a week.

NEWS AGENCIES

The Canadian Press: 36 King St East, Toronto, Ont M5C 2L9; tel. (416) 364-0321; fax (416) 364-0207; f. 1917; 109 daily newspaper mems; national news co-operative; Chair. DAVID JOLLEY; Pres. KEITH KINCAID.

Foreign Bureaux

Agence France-Presse (AFP): 1255 rue Université, Bureau 1418, Montréal, Qué H3B 3X1; tel. (514) 875-8877; fax (514) 393-1815; Bureau Chief EMMANUEL ANGLEYS; also office in Ottawa.

Agencia EFE (Spain): 165 Sparks St, Suite 502, Ottawa K1P 5B9; tel. (613) 230-2282.

Agenzia Nazionale Stampa Associata (ANSA) (Italy): 150 Wellington St, Press Gallery, Room 703, Ottawa K1P 5A4; tel. (613) 235-4248; telex 053-4392; Representative TITO W. MANZELLA.

Associated Press (USA): 36 King St East, Toronto, Ont M5C 2L9; tel. (416) 368-1388.

Deutsche Presse-Agentur (dpa) (Germany): 702 National Press Bldg, 150 Wellington St, Ottawa K1P 5A4; tel. (613) 234-6024; telex 0253-4812; Correspondent BARBARA HALSIG.

Jiji Tsushin-Sha (Japan): 372 Bay St, Suite 605, Toronto, Ont M5H 2W9; tel. (416) 368-8037; fax (416) 368-2905; Bureau Chief KENZO TANIAI; also office in Ottawa.

Prensa Latina (Cuba): 221 rue du St-Sacrement, Bureau 40, Montréal, Qué H2Y 1X1; tel. (514) 844-2975; Correspondent R. RAMOS.

Reuters (UK): 2020 rue Université, Bureau 1020, Montréal, Qué H3A 2A5; tel. (514) 282-0744; fax (514) 844-2327; also office in Vancouver.

Telegrafnoye Agentstvo Sovetskovo Soyuza (TASS) (USSR): 200 Rideau Terrace, Suite 1305, Ottawa; tel. (613) 745-4310; telex 053-4504; Correspondent ARTEM MELIKIAN.

Xinhua (New China) News Agency: (People's Republic of China: 406 Daly Ave, Ottawa K1N 6H2; tel. (613) 234-8424; telex 053-4362; Chief Corresp. YUAN RONGSHENG.

United Press International (USA) and Central News Agency (Taiwan) are also represented.

PRESS ASSOCIATIONS

Canadian Business Press: 100 University Ave, Suite 508, Toronto, Ont M5J 1V6; tel. (416) 593-5497; Chair. JAMES O. HALL; Pres. CY SUMMERFIELD; 138 mems.

Canadian Community Newspapers' Association: 88 University Ave, Suite 705, Toronto, Ont M5J 1T6; tel. (416) 598-4277; fax (416) 598-4410; f. 1919; Pres. BILL PRATT; Exec. Dir MICHAEL ANDERSON; 680 mems.

Canadian Daily Newspaper Publishers Association: 890 Yonge St, Suite 1100, Toronto, Ont M4W 3P4; tel. (416) 923-3567; fax (416) 923-7206; f. 1919; Chair. PAUL WILSON; Pres. JOHN E. FOY; 83 mems.

Canadian Magazine Publishers' Association: 2 Stewart St, Toronto, Ont M5V 1H6; tel. (416) 362-2546; fax (416) 362-2547; f. 1973; Exec. Dir CATHERINE KEACHIE.

Magazines Canada (The Magazine Asscn of Canada): 777 Bay St, 7th Floor, Toronto, Ont M5W 1A7; tel. (416) 596-2644; Chair. JAMES WARRILLOW.

Publishers

Addison-Wesley Publishers Ltd: 26 Prince Andrew Place, POB 580, Don Mills, Ont M3C 2T8; tel. (416) 447-5101; telex 069-86743; fax (416) 443-0948; f. 1966; mathematics, science, language, business and social sciences textbooks, trade, juvenile; CEO ANTHONY J. VANDER WOUDE.

Thomas Allen and Son Ltd: 390 Steelcase Rd East, Markham, Ont L3R 1G2; tel. (416) 475-9126; fax (416) 475-6747; f. 1916; Pres. JOHN D. ALLEN.

Annick Press Ltd: 15 Patricia Ave, Willowdale, Ont M2M 1H9; tel. (416) 221-4802; telex 069-86766; fax (416) 221-8400; f. 1976; children's; Co-Dirs RICK WILKS, ANNE W. MILLYARD.

Arsenal Pulp Press: POB 3868, Main PO, Vancouver, BC V6B 3Z3; tel. (604) 687-4233; telex 045-08338; f. 1972; literary, native, educational.

Avon Books of Canada: 2061 McCowan Rd, Suite 201, Scarborough, Ont M1S 0Y6; tel. (416) 293-9404; Pres. PETER AUSTIN.

Black Rose Books Ltd: CP 1950, succursale place du Parc, Montréal, Qué H2W 2R3; tel. (514) 844-4076; f. 1970; social studies; Pres. JACQUES ROUX.

CANADA

Les Editions du Boréal: 4447 rue St-Denis, Montréal, Qué H2J 2L2; tel. (514) 287-7401; fax (514) 287-7664; f. 1963; history, biography, fiction, politics, economics, educational, children's; Dirs PASCAL ASSATHIANY, RAYMOND PLANTE.

Borealis Press Ltd: 9 Ashburn Drive, Ottawa K2E 6N4; tel. (613) 224-6837; f. 1972; Canadian fiction and non-fiction, drama, juveniles.

Breakwater Books Ltd: 277 Duckworth St, POB 2188, St John's, Nfld A1C 6E6; tel. (709) 722-6680; f. 1973; fiction, general, children's, educational, folklore; Pres. CLYDE ROSE.

Butterworths: 75 Clegg Rd, Markham, Ont L3R 9Y6; tel. (416) 479-2665; fax (416) 479-2826; f. 1912; legal, professional, academic; Pres. S. G. CORBETT.

Canada Law Book Inc: 240 Edward St, Aurora, Ont L4G 3S9; tel. (416) 773-6300; f. 1855; law reports, law journals, legal textbooks, etc.; Pres. S. G. CORBETT.

Centre Educatif et Culturel: 8101 blvd Métropolitain, Anjou, Montréal, Qué H1J 1J9; tel. (514) 351-6010; telex 055-62172; fax (514) 351-3534; f. 1956; textbooks; Pres. and Dir-Gen. ANDRÉ ROUSSEAU.

The Coach House Press: 401 Huron St (rear), Toronto, Ont M5S 2G5; tel. (416) 979-2217; telex 055-62172; f. 1965; fiction, poetry; Owner STAN BEVINGTON.

Collier Macmillan Canada Inc: 1200 Eglinton Ave East, Suite 200, Don Mills, Ont M3C 3N1; tel. (416) 449-6030; telex 069-59372; f. 1958; trade, textbooks, reference; Pres. RAY LEE.

Copp Clark Pitman: 2775 Matheson Blvd East, Toronto, Ont M5V 1E9; tel. (416) 593-9911; fax (416) 238-6075; f. 1841; textbooks and reference material; Pres. and CEO STEPHEN MILLS.

Doubleday Canada Ltd: 105 Bond St, Toronto, Ont M5B 1Y3; tel. (416) 340-0777; fax (416) 977-8488; f. 1944; general, trade, textbooks, mass market; Pres. DAVID KENT.

Douglas and McIntyre: 1615 Venables St, Vancouver, BC V5L 2H1; tel. (604) 254-7191; fax (604) 254-9099; f. 1964; general non-fiction, juvenile; Pres. SCOTT MCINTYRE.

Editions Beauchemin Ltée: 3281 ave Jean-Béraud, Laval, Qué H7T 2S2; tel. (514) 334-5912; fax (514) 688-6269; f. 1842; textbooks and general; Pres. GUY FRENETTE.

Editions Bellarmin: 8100 blvd St-Laurent, Montréal, Qué H2P 2L9; tel. (514) 387-2541; fax (514) 387-0206; f. 1891; religious, educational, politics, sociology, ethnography, history, sport, leisure; Pres. and Gen. Man. ANDRÉ BEAUCHAMP.

Les Editions Fides: 5710 ave Decelles, Montréal, Qué H3S 2C5; tel. (514) 735-6406; fax (514) 735-4985; f. 1937; juvenile, history, theology, textbooks and literature; Dir-Gen. MICHELINE TREMBLAY.

Les Editions Françaises Inc: 1411 rue Ampère, CP 395, Boucherville, Qué J4B 5W2; tel. (514) 641-0514; telex 052-5107; f. 1951; textbooks; Pres. PIERRE LESPÉRANCE.

Editions France-Québec Inc: 955 rue Amherst, Montréal, Qué H2L 3K4; tel. (514) 323-1182; telex 052-4667; f. 1965; Editor BERNARD PRÉVOST.

Editions Héritage: 300 ave Arran, St-Lambert, Qué J4R 1K5; tel. (514) 875-0327; fax (514) 672-1481; f. 1968; history, biography, sport, juveniles; Pres. JACQUES PAYETTE.

Editions de l'Hexagone: 900 est, rue Ontario, Montréal, Qué H2L 1P4; tel (514) 525-2811; f. 1953; literature; Dir-Gen. ALAIN HORIC.

Editions Hurtubise HMH: 7360 blvd Newman, Ville LaSalle, Qué H8N 1X2; tel. (514) 364-0323; telex 055-67167; fax (514) 364-7435; f. 1960; general academic; Pres. and Dir-Gen. HERVÉ FOULON.

Editions du Renouveau Pédagogique Inc: 8925 blvd St-Laurent, Montréal, Qué H2N 1M5; tel. (514) 384-2690; fax (514) 384-0955; f. 1965; textbooks; Pres. FRANÇOIS TISSEYRE.

Editions du Richelieu: CP 142, Saint-Jean, Qué G3B 5W3; f. 1935; general fiction and non-fiction, Roman Catholic school religious texts; Pres. FELICIEN MESSIER.

Editions du Septentrion: 1300 ave Maguire, Sillery, Qué G1T 2R8; tel. (418) 688-3556; fax (418) 527-4978; f. 1956; history, essays, general; Man. DENIS VAUGEOIS.

Encyclopaedia Britannica Publications Ltd: 175 Holiday Drive, POB 2249, Cambridge, Ont N3C 3N4; tel. (519) 658-4621; fax (519) 658-8181; f. 1937; Pres. DAVID DURNAN.

Fitzhenry & Whiteside Ltd: 195 Allstate Pkwy, Markham, Ont L3R 4T8; tel. (416) 477-0030; f. 1966; textbooks, trade, educational; Pres. ROBERT I. FITZHENRY.

Gage Educational Publishing Co: 164 Commander Blvd, Agincourt, Ont M1S 3C7; tel. (416) 293-8141; telex 065-25374; fax (416) 293-9009; f. 1844; Pres. and CEO STANLEY J. REID.

Ginn and Co: 3771 Victoria Park Ave, Scarborough, Ont M1W 2P9; tel. (416) 497-4600; f. 1929; textbooks; Pres. RICHARD H. LEE.

GLC Publishers Ltd: 115 Nugget Ave, Agincourt, Ont M1S 3B1; tel. (416) 291-2926; Pres. NELSON PRISKE.

Grolier Ltd: 16 Overlea Blvd, Toronto, Ont M4H 1A6; tel. (416) 425-1924; fax (416) 425-4015; f. 1912; reference; Pres. J. H. RADFORD.

Harcourt Brace Jovanovich Canada: 55 Horner Ave, Toronto, Ont M8Z 4X6; tel. (416) 255-4491; fax (416) 255-4046; f. 1922; general, medical, educational, scholarly; Pres. ANTHONY W. CRAVEN.

Harlequin Books: 225 Duncan Mill Rd, Don Mills, Ont M3B 3K9; tel. (416) 445-5860; f. 1949; fiction, paperbacks; Pres. BRIAN E. HICKEY.

HarperCollins Canada Ltd: 1995 Markham Rd, Scarborough, Ont M1B 5M8; tel. (416) 321-2241; fax (416) 321-3033; f. 1932; trade, reference, bibles, dictionaries, juvenile, paperbacks; Pres. STANLEY COLBERT.

Harvest House Ltd: 1200 ave Atwater, Bureau 1, Montréal, Qué H3Z 1X4; tel. (514) 932-0666; fax (514) 489-4287; f. 1960; history, biography, environment, natural and social sciences; Dir MAYNARD GERTLER.

D. C. Heath Canada Ltd: 100 Adelaide St West, Suite 1600, Toronto, Ont M5H 1S9; tel. (416) 362-6483; fax (416) 362-7942; Pres. ROBERT H. ROSS.

Holt, Rinehart and Winston of Canada Ltd: 55 Horner Ave, Toronto, Ont M8Z 4X6; tel. (416) 255-4491; fax (416) 255-4046; f. 1904; educational, college, reference; Pres. ANTHONY W. CRAVEN.

Houghton Mifflin Canada Ltd: 150 Steelcase Rd West, Markham, Ont L3R 3J9; tel. (416) 475-1755; fax (416) 475-5290; educational; Pres. JOHN E. CHAMP.

Hurtig Publishers: 1302 Oxford Tower, 10235 101st St, Edmonton, Alta T5J 3G1; tel. (403) 426-2359; fax (403) 429-5996; f. 1961; non-fiction, politics, Canadiana; Pres. MEL HURTIG.

Institut de Recherches Psychologiques, Inc/Institute of Psychological Research Inc: 34 ouest, rue Fleury, Montréal, Qué H3L 1S9; tel. (514) 382-3000; fax (514) 382-3007; f. 1964; educational and psychological tests; Pres. Dr JEAN-MARC CHEVRIER.

IPI Publishing Ltd: 44 Charles St West, Suite 2704, Toronto, Ont M4Y 1R7; tel. (416) 964-6662; Pres. Dr DANIEL J. BAUM.

Irwin Publishing Inc: 1800 Steeles Ave West, Concord, Ont L4K 2P3; tel. (416) 660-0611; fax (416) 660-0676; f. 1945; educational; Pres. BRIAN O'DONNELL.

Key Porter Books: 70 The Esplanade, 3rd Floor, Toronto, Ont M5E 1R2; tel. (416) 862-7777; telex 062-18092; fax (416) 862-2304; f. 1980; general trade; Pres. ANNA PORTER.

Lancelot Press Ltd: POB 425, Hantsport, NS B0P 1P0; tel. (902) 684-9129; f. 1966; non-fiction, regional; Pres. WILLIAM POPE.

Leméac Editeur: 3575 blvd St-Laurent, Bureau 902, Montréal, Qué H2X 2T7; tel. (514) 848-1096; fax (514) 848-9906; f. 1957; literary, academic, general; Pres. JULES BRILLANT.

Lester & Orpen Dennys Ltd: 78 Sullivan St, Toronto, Ont M5T 1C1; tel. (416) 593-9602; fax (416) 593-4781; f. 1973; fiction, non-fiction, history, young adult, politics, social issues; Pres. MALCOLM LESTER.

Lidec Inc: CP 5000, succursale C, Montréal, Qué H2X 3M1; tel. (514) 843-5991; fax (514) 843-5252; f. 1965; educational, textbooks; Pres. and Dir-Gen. MARC-AIMÉ GUÉRIN.

James Lorimer & Co Ltd: 35 Britain St, Toronto, Ont M5A 1R7; tel. (416) 362-4762; fax (416) 363-4029; f. 1971; urban and labour studies, children's, general non-fiction.

McClelland and Stewart Inc: 481 University Ave, Suite 900, Toronto, Ont M5G 2E9; tel. (416) 598-1114; telex 062-18603; fax (416) 598-7764; f. 1906; trade, illustrated and educational; Chair. and Pres. AVIE BENNETT.

McGill-Queen's University Press: 3430 rue McTavish, Montréal, Qué H3A 1X9; tel. (514) 398-3750; fax (514) 398-4333; f. 1960; scholarly and general interest; Exec. Dir PHILIP J. CERCONE.

McGraw-Hill Ryerson Ltd: 330 Progress Ave, Scarborough, Ont M1P 2Z5; tel. (416) 293-1911; telex 065-25169; fax (416) 293-0827; f. 1944; general; Pres. and CEO MICHAEL G. RICHARDSON.

Merrill Publishing: 230 Barmac Drive, Weston, Ont M9L 2X5; tel. (416) 747-4626; telex 065-27166; fax (416) 746-7890; Gen. Man. LINDA MILNE.

Methuen Publications: 2330 Midland Ave, Scarborough, Ont M1S 1P7; f. 1965; trade, textbooks, professional; Gen. Man. FRED D. WARDLE.

Mosaic Press: 1252 Speers Rd, Unit 2, POB 1032, Oakville, Ont L6J 5E9; tel. (416) 825-2130; fax (416) 825-2130; f. 1974; literary, scholarly and cultural; Dir of Operations HOWARD ASTER.

Nelson Canada: 1120 Birchmount Rd, Scarborough, Ont M1K 5G4; tel. (416) 752-9100; telex 069-63813; f. 1914; school and university textbooks; Pres. A. G. COBHAM.

Oberon Press: 350 Sparks St, Suite 401A, Ottawa K1R 7S8; tel. (613) 238-3275; f. 1966; poetry, children's, fiction and general non-fiction; Pres. MICHAEL MACKLEM.

OISE Publishing: Ontario Institute for Studies in Education, 252 Bloor St West, Toronto, Ont M5S 1V6; tel. (416) 923-6641, ext. 2531; telex 062-17720; fax (416) 926-4725; f. 1965; educational texts, guidance and test materials and scholarly publications; Publr IAN WINCHESTER (acting).

Oxford University Press: 70 Wynford Drive, Don Mills, Ont M3C 1J9; tel. (416) 441-2941; fax (416) 444-0427; f. 1904; general, education, religious, juvenile, Canadiana; Man. Dir MICHAEL A. MORROW.

PaperJacks Ltd: 330 Steelcase Rd East, Markham, Ont L3R 2M1; tel. (416) 475-1261; fax (416) 475-7139; f. 1971; general paperbacks; Pres. SUSAN STODDART.

Penguin Books Canada Ltd: 2801 John St, Markham, Ont L3R 1B4; tel. (416) 475-1571; telex 069-86803; fax (416) 479-1705; f. 1974; Pres. SANDRA HARGREAVES.

Pippin Publishing Ltd: 1361 Huntingwood Drive, Unit 7, Agincourt, Ont M1S 3J1; tel. (416) 291-5857; fax (416) 291-1556; f. 1990; educational; Pres. STANLEY STARKMAN.

Pontifical Institute of Mediaeval Studies: 59 Queen's Park Crescent East, Toronto, Ont M5S 2C4; tel. (416) 926-7144; fax (416) 926-7276; f. 1939; scholarly pubs concerning the middle ages; Dir of Publs RON B. THOMSON.

Prentice Hall Canada Inc: 1870 Birchmount Rd, Scarborough, Ont M1P 2J7; tel. (416) 293-3621; telex 065-25184; fax (416) 299-2529; f. 1960; trade, textbooks; Pres. ROSS M. INKPEN.

Les Presses de l'Université Laval: CP 2447, Québec, Qué G1K 7R4; tel. (418) 656-3001; f. 1950; scholarly books and periodicals; Dir CLAUDE FRÉMONT.

Les Presses de l'Université de Montréal: CP 6128, succursale A, Montréal, Qué H3C 3J7; tel. (514) 343-6168; f. 1962; scholarly and general; Dir MARIE-CLAIRE BORGO.

Les Presses de l'Université du Québec: CP 250, Sillery, Qué G1T 2R1; tel. (418) 657-3551; telex 051-31623; f. 1969; scholarly and general; Dir-Gen. JACKI DALLAIRE.

Random House of Canada Ltd: 1265 Aerowood Drive, Mississauga, Ont L4W 1B9; tel. (416) 624-0672; f. 1944; Pres. GORDON BAIN.

The Reader's Digest Association (Canada) Ltd: 215 ave Redfern, Montréal, Qué H3Z 2V9; tel. (514) 934-0751; telex 052-5800; fax (514) 935-4463; Pres. and CEO RALPH HANCOX.

W. B. Saunders Co Canada Ltd: 35 Horner Ave, Toronto, Ont M8Z 4X6; tel. (416) 255-4491; telex 069-67890; fax (416) 255-4046; Vice-Pres. PAUL S. WOLFORD.

Scholastic Canada Ltd: 123 Newkirk Rd, Richmond Hill, Ont L4C 3G5; tel. (416) 883-5300; fax (416) 883-4113; Pres. F. LARRY MULLER.

Simon & Pierre Publishing Co Ltd: POB 280, Adelaide St Postal Station, Toronto, Ont M5C 2J4; tel. (416) 463-0313; fax (416) 463-4155; f. 1972; drama and performing arts, fiction and non-fiction; Pres. and Editor-in-Chief MARIAN M. WILSON.

Sogides Ltée: 955 rue Amherst, Montréal, Qué H2L 3K4; tel. (514) 523-1182; fax (514) 597-0370; f. 1958; general interest, fiction, psychology, biography; Pres. PIERRE LESPÉRANCE.

Stoddart Publishing Co Ltd: 34 Lesmill Rd, Don Mills, Ont M3B 2T6; tel. (416) 445-3333; fax (416) 445-5967; f. 1984; general fiction and non-fiction, textbooks, children's; Pres. JACK E. STODDART.

Talon Books Ltd: 201–1019 East Cordova St, Vancouver, BC V6A 1M8; tel. (604) 253-5261; f. 1967; fiction and non-fiction, poetry, drama; Pres. and Gen. Man. KARL SIEGLER.

Turnstone Press Ltd: 100 Arthur St, Suite 607, Winnipeg, Man R3B 1H3; tel. (204) 947-1555; fax (204) 942-1555; f. 1976; literary, regional; Man. Editor MARILYN MORTON.

University of Alberta Press: 141 Athabasca Hall, Edmonton, Alta T6G 2E8; tel. (403) 492-3662; telex 037-2979; fax (403) 492-7219; f. 1969; scholarly, general non-fiction.

University of British Columbia Press: 6344 Memorial Rd, Vancouver, BC V6T 1W5; tel. (604) 228-3259; fax (604) 228-6083; f. 1971; humanities, science, social science and scholarly journals; Dir R. PETER MILROY.

University of Manitoba Press: 106 Curry Place, Suite 244, University of Manitoba, Winnipeg, Man R3T 2N2; tel. (204) 474-9495; fax (204) 269-6629; scholarly; Dir PATRICIA A. DOWDALL.

University of Ottawa Press/Les Presses de l'Université d'Ottawa: 603 ave Cumberland, Ottawa K1N 6N5; tel. (613) 564-2270; fax (613) 564-9100; f. 1936; university texts, scholarly works in English and French, general; Dir TOIVO ROHT.

University of Toronto Press: 10 St Mary St, Suite 700, Toronto, Ont M4Y 2W8; tel. (416) 978-2239; fax (416) 978-4738; f. 1901; academic and general university texts and journals; Dir H. C. VAN IERSSEL (acting).

Western Legal Publications: 1 Alexander St, Suite 301, Vancouver, BC V6A 1B2; tel. (604) 687-5671; f. 1972; legal decisions, digests, manuals, texts and summaries; Gen. Man. PHILLIP W. GEORGE.

Western Producer Prairie Books: POB 2500, Saskatoon, Sask S7K 2C4; tel. (306) 665-3548; fax (306) 653-1255; f. 1954; history, biography, photography, natural history, young adult, regional interest; Publishing Dir ELIZABETH MUNROE.

John Wiley and Sons Canada Ltd: 22 Worcester Rd, Rexdale, Ont M9W 1L1; tel. (416) 675-3580; telex 069-89189; fax (416) 675-6599; Pres. JOHN DILL.

Government Publishing House

Canadian Government Publishing Centre: Ottawa K1A 0S9; tel. (819) 997-2560; telex 053-4296; fax (819) 994-1498; f. 1876; books and periodicals on numerous subjects, incl. agriculture, economics, environment, geology, history and sociology; Dir PATRICIA HORNER.

ORGANIZATIONS AND ASSOCIATIONS

Association of Canadian Publishers: 260 King St East, Toronto, Ont M5A 1K3; tel. (416) 361-1408; fax (416) 361-0643; f. 1976; 136 mems; trade asscn of Canadian-owned English-language book publrs; represents Canadian publishing internationally; Pres. PHILIP CERCONE; Exec. Dir WAYNE GILPIN.

Canadian Book Publishers' Council: 250 Merton St, Suite 203, Toronto, Ont M4S 1B1; tel. (416) 322-7011; fax (416) 322-6999; f. 1910; 42 mems; trade asscn of Canadian-owned publrs and Canadian-incorporated subsidiaries of UK and USA publrs; Pres. STEPHEN MILLS; Exec. Dir JACQUELINE HUSHION.

Société de Développement du Livre et du Périodique: 1151 rue Alexandre-De Sève, Montréal, Qué H2L 2T7; tel. (514) 524-7528; f. 1961; rue Dir-Gen. LOUISE ROCHON; seven constituent assens.

Radio and Television

The 1968 Broadcasting Act set out the broadcasting policy of Canada, established the Canadian Broadcasting Corporation (CBC) as the national, publicly-owned, broadcasting service and created the Canadian Radio-Television and Telecommunications Commission (CRTC) as the agency regulating radio, television and cable television. The CBC is financed mainly by public funds supplemented by revenue from television advertising. Programming policy is to use predominantly Canadian creative and other resources. Services are operated in both English and French.

Radio and television service is available to over 99% of the population: 78% of Canadian homes subscribe to cable television and existing wiring makes this service, which is provided by 1,797 cable television systems, immediately available to 88% of Canadian homes. Most television programming is in colour and 93% of homes have colour TV sets.

Many privately-owned television and radio stations have affiliation agreements with the CBC and help to distribute the national services. The major private television networks which also have affiliates are CTV, TVA (which serves the province of Ontario) and Quatre Saisons (which also serves the province of Québec) and Global (serving the province of Ontario), as well as the educational networks.

Canadian Broadcasting Corporation (CBC): 1500 Bronson Ave, POB 8478, Ottawa K1G 3J5; tel. (613) 724-1200; telex 053-4260; fax (613) 738-6843; f. 1936; financed mainly by public funds, with supplementary revenue from commercial advertising on CBC television; Pres. W. T. ARMSTRONG; Sr Vice-Pres. A. MANERA.

Canadian Radio-Television and Telecommunications Commission (CRTC): Ottawa K1A 0N2; tel. (819) 997-0313 (Information); telex 053-4253; fax (819) 994-0218; f. 1968; regional offices in Montréal, Halifax, Winnipeg and Vancouver; Chair. KEITH SPICER; Vice-Chair. LOUIS R. SHERMAN (Telecommunications), MONIQUE COUPAL (Broadcasting).

RADIO

The CBC operates two AM and two FM networks, one each in English and French. The CBC's Northern Service provides both national network programming in English and French, and special local and short-wave programmes, some of which are broadcast in the languages of the Indian and Inuit peoples. In March 1989 there were 760 outlets for CBC radio (70 CBC-owned stations, 044 CBC-owned relay transmitters, 40 private affiliates and rebroadcasters). CBC radio service, which is virtually free of commercial advertising, is within reach of 99.5% of the population. Radio Canada

CANADA

International, the CBC's overseas short-wave service, broadcasts daily in 11 languages and distributes recorded programmes free for use world-wide.

TELEVISION

The CBC operates two television networks, one in English and one in French. CBC's Northern Service provides both radio and television service to 98% of the 90,000 inhabitants of northern Québec, the Northwest Territories and the Yukon. Almost 41% of these inhabitants are native Canadians, and programming is provided in Dene and Inuktitut languages as well as English and French. As of March 1989, CBC television was carried on 837 outlets (30 CBC-owned stations, 612 CBC-owned rebroadcasters, 33 private affiliates and 162 private rebroadcasters). CBC television is available to over 98% of the population.

In 1972 Canada became the first country in the world to establish a domestic communications satellite system. Canada's commercial communications satellites are owned and operated by Telesat Canada. Canadian Satellite Communication Inc (Cancom) of Toronto, operates a multi-channel television and radio broadcasting service via satellite for the distribution of CTV, TVA and independent television and radio programmes (one AM and nine FM radio stations) to serve remote and under-served communities.

Canadian pay television has been in operation since 1983. These services include general interest, sports, music, children's and youth programming, religious broadcasts and news. In 1987-88, discretionary pay and speciality services accounted for 3% of all television viewing.

Canadian Satellite Communications Inc: 275 Slater St, Suite 1501, Ottawa K1P 5H9; tel. (613) 232-4814; Chair. J. R. PETERS; Pres. and CEO P. L. MORRISSETTE.

CTV Television Network: 42 Charles St East, Toronto, Ont M4Y 1T5; tel. (416) 928-6000; telex 062-2080; fax (416) 928-0907; 24 privately-owned affiliated stations from coast to coast, with 247 rebroadcasters; covers 99% of Canadian TV households; Pres. and CEO MURRAY CHERCOVER.

Global Television Network: 81 Barber Greene Rd, Don Mills, Ont M3C 2A2; tel. (416) 446-5311; telex 069-66767; fax (416) 446-5371; one station and eight rebroadcasters serving southern Ontario; Pres. DAVID MINTZ.

Réseau de télévision (TVA): 1600 est, blvd de Maisonneuve, CP 368, succursale C, Montréal, Qué H2L 4P2; tel. (514) 526-0476; telex 055-60626; f. 1971; French-language network, with 10 stations in Québec and 19 rebroadcasters serving 98% of the province and francophone communities in Ontario and New Brunswick; Pres. and Gen. Man. MICHEL HÉROUX.

Réseau de télévision Quatre-Saisons (TQS): 405 ave Ogilvy, Montréal, Qué H3N 2Y4; tel. (514) 271-3535; telex 058-25698; fax (514) 271-6231; f. 1986; French-language; 2 stations, 6 rebroadcasters and 2 retransmitters serving 98% of the province of Québec.

Telesat Canada: 333 River Rd, Ottawa, Ont K1L 8B9; tel. (613) 746-5920; telex 053-4184; f. 1969; Chair. D. A. GOLDEN; Pres. and CEO ELDON D. THOMPSON.

ASSOCIATION

Canadian Association of Broadcasters: 350 Sparks St, POB 627, Station B, Ottawa K1P 5S2; tel. (613) 233-4035; telex 053-3127; fax (613) 233-6961; Pres. and CEO MICHAEL MCCABE; 510 mems.

Finance

(cap. = capital; res = reserves; dep. = deposits; m. = million; brs = branches; amounts in Canadian dollars)

BANKING

The first Canadian commercial bank was founded in 1817. A further 34 banks were established over the next 50 years, and, following Confederation in 1867, the Bank Act of 1871 gave the Federal Government regulatory powers over banking operations throughout Canada.

The Bank Act of 1980 reorganized the banking structure by creating two categories of banking institution: 'Schedule I' banks, comprising the widely-held domestic chartered banks; and 'Schedule II' banks, which are either subsidiaries of foreign banks (whose total Canadian assets, excluding those held by US banks, which are exempt under the Canada-USA free trade agreement of 1989, cannot exceed 16% of those of the banking system in total), or Canadian-owned banks under private or semi-private ownership. The Act, which is subject to review at 10-year intervals to allow for changes in government policy and economic conditions, strictly limits the range of permitted operations outside the banking sphere, in order to curtail competition betweeen banks and commercial enterprises. In September 1990 there were eight 'Schedule I' banks (of which no individual shareholder may control more than 10%) and 59 'Schedule II' banks.

The Bank of Canada, established as the central bank in 1934 and controlled by the Federal Government, implements government monetary and credit policies through the commercial banks. It controls the banks' clearing system and also holds the banks' primary and secondary reserves. Direct regulatory inspections of the commercial banks are carried out by the Superintendent of Financial Institutions, who reports to the Minister of Finance, and a federal agency insures individual deposits up to a limit of C $60,000 per person per institution.

At the end of 1989, there were 7,307 commercial bank branches holding deposits totalling C $274,635m. The banks' combined assets totalled C $550,939m., of which 31% were represented by foreign currency assets, reflecting the importance of international business in Canadian banking.

Trust and loan companies, which were originally formed to provide mortgage finance and private customer loans, now occupy an important place in the financial system, offering current account facilities and providing access to money transfer services.

Central Bank

Bank of Canada: 234 Wellington St, Ottawa K1A 0G9; tel. (613) 782-8111; telex 053-4241; f. 1934; cap. and res 30m., dep. 2,434.3m. (Dec. 1989); Gov. JOHN W. CROW; Sr Dep. Gov. GORDON G. THIESSEN.

Principal Commercial Banks
Schedule 'I' Banks

Bank of Montréal: 129 ouest, rue St-Jacques, CP 6002, Montréal, Qué H3C 3B1; tel. (514) 877-7110; telex 052-67661; f. 1817; cap. and res 3,814.6m., dep. 70,116.3m. (July 1990); Chair. and CEO MATTHEW W. BARRETT; Pres. and Chief Operating Officer F. ANTHONY COMPER; 1,190 brs.

Bank of Nova Scotia (Scotiabank): Scotia Plaza, 44 King St West, Toronto, Ont M5H 1H1; tel. (416) 866-6161; telex 062-2106; f. 1832; cap. and res 3,971m., dep. 65,000m. (Oct. 1990); Chair. and CEO C. E. RITCHIE; Pres. J. A. G. BELL; 1,024 brs.

Canadian Imperial Bank of Commerce: Commerce Court, Toronto, Ont M5L 1A2; tel. (416) 980-2211; telex 065-24116; f. 1961; cap. and res 5,717m., dep. 87,041m. (July 1990); Chair., Pres. and CEO R. DONALD FULLERTON; 1,488 brs.

Canadian Western Bank: 10040 104th St, Edmonton, Alta T5J 3X6; tel. (403) 423-8888; telex 037-43148; fax (403) 423-8897; f. 1988 by merger; cap. and res 39.6m., dep. 343m. (July 1990); Chair. JACK DONALD; Pres. and CEO LARRY M. POLLOCK; 8 brs.

Laurentian Bank of Canada: 1981 ave Collège McGill, Montréal, Qué H3A 3K3; tel. (514) 284-3931; telex 052-4217; fax (514) 284-7519; f. 1846; cap. and res 273.5m., dep. 5,364.8m. (July 1990); Chair. C. CLAUDE CASTONGUAY; Pres. and CEO DOMINIC D'ALESSANDRO.

National Bank of Canada: 600 ouest, rue de la Gauchetière, Montréal, Qué H3B 4L2; tel. (514) 394-4000; telex 052-5181; f. 1979; cap. and res 1,713m., dep. 29,628m. (July 1990); Pres. and CEO ANDRÉ BÉRARD; 637 brs.

Royal Bank of Canada: 1 place Ville Marie, CP 6001, Montréal, Qué H3C 3A9; tel. (514) 874-2110; telex 055-61086; f. 1869; cap. and res 6,320.4m., dep. 98,570.6m. (July 1990); Chair. and CEO ALLAN TAYLOR; Pres. JOHN E. CLEGHORN; 1,559 brs.

Toronto-Dominion Bank: Toronto-Dominion Centre, POB 1, Toronto, Ont M5K 1A2; tel. (416) 982-8222; telex 065-24267; f. 1855; cap. and res 4,656m., dep. 52,648m. (July 1990); Chair. and CEO RICHARD M. THOMSON; Pres. ROBERT W. KORTHALS; 948 brs.

Schedule 'II' Banks

Banque Nationale de Paris (Canada): BNP Tower, 1981 ave Collège McGill, Montréal, Qué H3A 2W8; tel. (514) 285-6000; cap. and res 90m., dep. 1,540.7m. (1990); Pres. and CEO F. JONATHAN.

Barclays Bank of Canada: Commerce Court West, Suite 3500, POB 377, Toronto, Ont M5L 1G2; tel. (416) 862-0594; cap. and res 125.6m., dep. 1,894.6m. (1990); Pres. and CEO G. D. FARRAR.

Citibank Canada: University Place, 123 Front St West, Suite 1900, Toronto, Ont M5J 2M3; tel. (416) 947-5500; cap. and res 419.4m., dep. 2,880.3m. (1990); Pres. and CEO FREDERICK C. COPELAND.

Hongkong Bank of Canada: 885 West Georgia St, Suite 300, Vancouver, BC V6C 3E9; tel. (604) 685-1000; telex 045-07750; fax (604) 641-1849; f. 1981; cap. and res 379.3m., dep. 6,600.4m. (1990); Chair. JOHN R. BOND; Pres. and CEO JAMES H. CLEAVE; 61 brs.

Swiss Bank Corporation (Canada): 207 Queen's Quay West, Suite 780, POB 103, Toronto, Ont M5J 1A7; tel. (416) 865-0190; fax (416) 864-7505; cap. and res 106.4m., dep. 2,298.5m. (1990); Pres. K. FREI.

CANADA — *Directory*

Development Bank
Federal Business Development Bank: Tour de la Bourse, 800 place Victoria, CP 335, Montréal, Qué H4Z 1L4; tel. (514) 283-5904; f. 1975; auth. cap. 512.6m. (1988); Pres. G. A. LAVIGUEUR.

Principal Trust and Loan Companies
Canada Trustco Mortgage Co and The Canada Trust Co: 320 Bay St, Suite 1300, Toronto, Ont M5H 2P6; tel. (416) 361-8000; fax (416) 361-8178; f. 1855; total assets 67,400m. (1988); Chair. and CEO M. L. LAHN.

Central Guaranty Trust Co Ltd (Central Trust Co): 6 King St, Toronto, Ont M5H 1C3; tel. (416) 368-5911; fax (416) 345-4850; f. 1925; total assets 3,680m. (1986); Pres. and CEO W. T. HODGSON.

Montréal Trust: 1 place Montréal Trust, 1800 ave Collège McGill, Montréal, Qué H3A 2K9; tel. (514) 982-7000; telex 055-61286; fax (514) 982-7069; f. 1889; total assets 11,564m. (1990); Chair. J. V. RAYMOND CYR; Pres. and CEO JOHN D. THOMPSON.

National Trust Co Ltd: 21 King St East, Toronto, Ont M5C 1B3; tel. (416) 361-3611; telex 062-18674; f. 1898; total assets 2,787m. (1982); Chair. and CEO J. L. A. COLHOUN.

Royal Trustco Ltd: Royal Trust Tower, Toronto, Ont M5W 1P9; tel. (416) 981-7000; fax (416) 864-9021; f. 1892; total assets 140,000m. (1990); Chair. HARTLAND M. MACDOUGALL; Pres. and CEO MICHAEL A. CORNELISSEN.

Trust Général du Canada: 1100 rue Université, Montréal, Qué H3B 2G7; tel. (514) 871-7100; telex 055-61407; fax (514) 871-8525; f. 1928; cap. and res 94m., total assets 3,038m. (1985); Pres. and CEO MAURICE MYRAND.

Savings Institutions with Provincial Charters
Province of Alberta Treasury Branches: 9925-109 St, POB 1440, Edmonton, Alta T5J 2N6; tel. (403) 493-7307; telex 037-43122; f. 1938; assets 6,700m. (March 1989); Supt A. O. BRAY; 132 brs.

Province of Ontario Savings Office: 33 King St West, 6th Floor, Oshawa, Ont L1H 8H5; tel. (416) 433-5785; fax (416) 433-6519; f. 1921; assets 1,073m. (1988); Exec. Dir J. S. PURDON; Dir J. L. ALLEN; 21 brs.

Bankers' Organizations
The Canadian Bankers' Association: 2 First Canadian Place, POB 348, Toronto, Ont M5X 1E1; tel. (416) 362-6092; telex 062-3402; fax (416) 362-7705; f. 1891; Chair. PETER C. GODSOE; Pres. HELEN K. SINCLAIR; 65 mems.

Trust Companies Association of Canada Inc: 50 O'Connor St, Suite 720, Ottawa K1P 6L2; tel. (613) 563-3205; fax (613) 235-3111; Pres. and CEO JOHN L. EVANS; 35 corporate mems.

STOCK EXCHANGES
Alberta Stock Exchange: 300 Fifth Ave SW, 21st Floor, Calgary, Alta T2P 3C4; tel. (403) 262-7791; telex 038-21793; fax (403) 237-0450; f. 1914; 38 mems; Pres. T. A. CUMMING.

Montréal Exchange/Bourse de Montréal: Tour de la Bourse, 800 place Victoria, CP 61, Montréal, Qué H4Z 1A9; tel. (514) 871-2424; fax (514) 871-3533; f. 1874; 76 mems; Pres. and CEO BRUNO RIVERIN.

Toronto Stock Exchange: The Exchange Tower, 2 First Canadian Place, Toronto, Ont M5X 1J2; tel. (416) 947-4700; telex 062-17759; fax (416) 947-4585; f. 1852; 73 mems; Pres. and CEO J. P. BUNTING.

Vancouver Stock Exchange: Stock Exchange Tower, 609 Granville St, POB 10333, Vancouver, BC V7Y 1H1; tel. (604) 689-3334; fax (604) 688-6051; f. 1907; 49 mems; Pres. DONALD J. HUDSON.

Winnipeg Stock Exchange: One Lombard Place, Suite 2901, Winnipeg, Man R3B 0Y2; tel. (204) 942-8431; fax (204) 947-9536; 18 mems; Pres. VINCENT W. CATALANO.

INSURANCE
Principal Companies
Abbey Life Insurance Co of Canada: 3027 Harvester Rd, Burlington, Ont L7N 3G9; Pres. MARK SYLVIA.

Assurance—vie Desjardins inc: 200 ave des Commandeurs, Lévis-Lauzon, Qué G6V 6R2; tel. (418) 835-2462; fax (418) 835-9171; f. 1901; Pres. and Dir-Gen. CLAUDE GRAVEL.

Blue Cross Life Insurance Co of Canada: POB 220, Moncton, NB E1C 8L3; tel. (506) 853-1811; telex 014-2233; fax (506) 853-4651; Sec. I. M. RICHARD.

Canada Life Assurance Co: 330 University Ave, Toronto, Ont M5G 1R8; f. 1847; Pres. DAVID A. NIELD.

Canadian General Insurance Co: 2206 Eglinton Ave East, Suite 500, Scarborough, Ont M1L 4S8; tel. (416) 288-1800; fax (416) 288-5888; f. 1907; Pres. R. L. DUNN.

Canadian Home Assurance Co: 465 ouest, blvd René-Lévesque, Montréal, Qué H2Z 1A8; tel. (514) 866-6531; telex 052-5169; fax (514) 866-4857; f. 1928; Pres. J. P. LUSSIER.

Canadian Indemnity Co: 1981 ave Collège McGill, Montréal, Qué H3A 2N4; tel. (514) 288-1502; fax (514) 288-3864; f. 1912; Pres. D. A. WAUGH.

The Canadian Surety Co: Canada Sq., 2180 Yonge St, Toronto, Ont M4S 2C2; tel. (416) 487-7195; fax (416) 482-6176; Pres. and CEO J. ROBERTSON.

Le Groupe Commerce, compagnie d'assurances: 2450 ouest, blvd Girouard, St-Hyacinthe, Qué J2S 3B3; tel. (514) 773-9701; fax (514) 773-4892; f. 1907; Pres. and CEO GUY ST-GERMAIN.

Confederation Life Insurance Co: 321 Bloor St East, Toronto, Ont M4W 1H1; tel. (416) 323-8161; fax (416) 323-4191; f. 1871; Pres. P. D. BURNS.

Groupe Coopérants, inc, et Les Coopérants, société mutuelle d'assurance-vie: Maison des Coopérants, 600 ouest, blvd de Maisonneuve, Montréal, Qué H3A 3J9; tel. (514) 287-6600; fax (514) 287-6514; f. 1876; Pres. PAUL DOLAN; CEO PIERRE SHOONER.

Crown Life Insurance Co: 120 Bloor St East, Suite 100, Toronto, Ont M4W 1B8; tel. (416) 928-4604; telex 062-2741; fax (416) 928-7889; f. 1900; Chair. H. M. BURNS; Pres. and CEO R. F. RICHARDSON.

Dominion of Canada General Insurance Co: 777 Eighth Ave, SW, Suite 1700, Calgary, Alta T2P 3R5; tel. (403) 269-5501; fax (403) 263-8193; f. 1887; Pres. D. A. WAUGH.

Federation Insurance Co of Canada: 1080 côte du Beaver Hall, 20e étage, Montréal, Qué H2Z 1S8; tel. (514) 875-5790; telex 055-61701; fax (514) 875-9769; f. 1947; Pres. W. J. GREEN.

General Accident Assurance Co of Canada: The Exchange Tower, Suite 2600, 2 First Canadian Place, POB 410, Toronto, Ont M5X 1J1; tel. (416) 368-4733; telex 065-24272; f. 1906; Pres. LEONARD G. LATHAM.

Gerling Global General Insurance Co: 480 University Ave, Suite 1600, Toronto, Ont M5G 1V6; tel. (416) 598-4651; telex 065-24108; fax (416) 598-9507; f. 1955; Pres. Dr R. R. KERN.

Gore Mutual Insurance Co: 252 Dundas St, Cambridge, Ont N1R 5T3; tel. (519) 623-1910; fax (519) 623-4411; f. 1839; Sec. J. M. GRAY.

The Great-West Life Assurance Co: 100 Osborne St North, Winnipeg, Man R3C 3A5; tel. (204) 946-1190; telex 075-7519; fax (204) 946-7838; f. 1891; Pres. and CEO K. P. KAVANAGH.

Guardian Insurance Co of Canada: 181 University Ave, Toronto, Ont M5H 3M7; tel. (416) 941-5050; fax (416) 941-9791; f. 1911; Chair. GEORGE ALEXANDER; Pres. N. CURTIS.

Halifax Insurance Co: 75 Eglinton Ave East, Suite 400, Toronto, Ont M4P 3A3; tel. (416) 440-1000; telex 062-2264; fax (416) 440-0799; f. 1809; Pres. and CEO J. N. MCCARTHY.

Imperial Life Assurance Co of Canada: 95 St Clair Ave West, Toronto, Ont M4V 1N7; tel. (416) 926-2600; fax (416) 923-1599; f. 1896; Chair., Pres. and CEO CLAUDE BRUNEAU.

Kings Mutual Insurance Co: POB 10, Berwick, NS B0P 1E0; tel. (902) 538-3187; fax (902) 538-7172; f. 1904; Pres. M. VISSERS; Man. D. C. COOK.

Laurentian General Insurance Co Inc: 1100 ouest, blvd René-Lévesque, Montréal, Qué H3B 4P4; tel. (514) 392-6000; telex 055-62067; fax (514) 392-6328; Pres. JEAN BOUCHARD.

Le Groupe La Laurentienne: 500 est, Grande-Allée, Québec, Qué G1R 2J7; comprises 18 operating companies; Chair. and CEO CLAUDE CASTONGUAY.

London Life Insurance Co: 255 Dufferin Ave, London, Ont N6A 4K1; tel. (519) 432-5281; fax (519) 679-3518; f. 1874; Pres. GORDON R. CUNNINGHAM; Chair. EARL H. ORSER.

Manufacturers Life Insurance Co: 200 Bloor St East, Toronto, Ont M4W 1E5; tel. (416) 926-0100; fax (416) 926-5454; f. 1887; Chair., Pres. and CEO THOMAS A. DIGIACOMO.

Mercantile and General Reinsurance Co of Canada: 123 Front St West, Toronto, Ont M5J 2M7; tel. (416) 947-3800; telex 065-24320; fax (416) 947-1386; f. 1951; Pres. D. M. BATTEN.

Mutual Life of Canada: 3300 Bloor St West, Suite 650, Toronto, Ont M8X 2X2; tel. (416) 239-2981; fax (416) 239-0301; f. 1870; Chair. J. H. PANABAKER; Pres. and CEO JACK V. MASTERMAN.

The National Life Assurance Co of Canada: 522 University Ave, Toronto, Ont M5G 1Y7; tel. (416) 598-2122; fax (416) 598-2142; f. 1897; Pres. VINCENT TONNA.

North American Life Assurance Co: 5650 Yonge St, Toronto, Ont M2M 4G4; tel. (416) 229-4515; telex 062-2400; fax (416) 229-6594; f. 1881; Chair. D. G. PAYNE; Pres HAROLD THOMPSON.

Portage La Prairie Mutual Insurance Co: Portage La Prairie, Man R1N 3B8; tel. (204) 857-3415; f. 1884; Pres. and Gen. Man. H. G. OWENS.

CANADA

Directory

Québec Assurance Co: 10 Wellington St East, Toronto, Ont M5E 1L5; tel. (416) 366-7511; telex 065-24124; fax (416) 367-9869; f. 1818; Pres. ROBERT J. GUNN.

Saskatchewan Government Insurance: 2260 11th Ave, Regina, Sask S4P 0J9; tel. (306) 565-1200; telex 071-2417; fax (306) 525-6040; f. 1945; Pres. ALEX G. WILDE.

Seaboard Life Insurance Co: 2165 West Broadway, Vancouver, BC V6K 4N5; tel. (604) 737-9300; fax (604) 734-8221; f. 1953; Pres. J. S. M. CUNNINGHAM.

Société Nationale d'Assurances: 425 ouest, blvd de Maisonneuve, Bureau 1500, Montréal, Qué H3A 3G5; tel. (514) 288-8711; fax (514) 288-8269; f. 1940; Pres. HENRI JOLI-COEUR; Dir-Gen. PIERRE RENAUD.

Sovereign General Assurance Co: 520 Fifth Ave, SW Calgary, Alta T2P 3R7; tel. (403) 298-4290; fax (403) 298-4289; f. 1894; Pres. J. ROYER.

Sun Life Assurance Co of Canada: POB 4150, Station A, Toronto, Ont M5W 2C9; tel. (416) 979-9966; fax (416) 585-9546; f. 1865; Chair. and CEO JOHN D. MCNEIL; Pres. JOHN R. GARDNER.

Toronto Mutual Life Insurance Co: 112 St Clair Ave West, Toronto, Ont M4V 2Y3; tel. (416) 960-3463; fax (416) 960-0531; Pres. JOHN T. ENGLISH; Chair. WALTER B. THOMPSON.

United Canadian Shares Ltd: 1601 Church Ave, Winnipeg, Man R2X 1G9; tel. (204) 633-7042; fax (204) 632-6779; f. 1951; Chair. R. H. JONES; Pres. C. S. RILEY, Jr.

Wawanesa Mutual Insurance Co: 191 Broadway, Winnipeg, Man R3C 3P1; tel. (204) 985-3811; fax (204) 947-5192; f. 1896; Pres. I. M. MONTGOMERY.

Western Assurance Co: 10 Wellington St East, Toronto, Ont M5E 1L5; tel. (416) 366-7511; fax (416) 367-9869; f. 1851; Pres. ROBERT J. GUNN.

Zurich Life Insurance Co of Canada: 375 University Ave, Toronto, Ont M5G 2J7; tel. (416) 593-4444; fax (416) 593-0479; Pres. and CEO P. D. MCGARRY.

Insurance Organizations

Canadian Life and Health Insurance Association: 20 Queen St West, Suite 2500, Toronto, Ont M5H 3S2; tel. (416) 977-2221; fax (416) 977-1895; f. 1894; Pres. M. R. DANIELS; 108 mem. cos.

Insurance Brokers Association of Canada: 141 Adelaide St West, Suite 801, Toronto, Ont M5H 3L5; tel. (416) 367-1831; fax (416) 367-3687; f. 1921; Gen. Man. BASIL N. STEGGLES; 11 mem. asscns.

Insurance Bureau of Canada: 181 University Ave, Suite 1300, Toronto, Ont M5H 3M7; tel. (416) 362-2031; telex 062-3502; fax (416) 361-5952; Pres. and CEO J. L. LYNDON; 180 corporate mems.

Insurance Institute of Canada: 481 University Ave, 6th Floor, Toronto, Ont M5G 2E9; tel. (416) 591-1572; fax (416) 591-1678; f. 1952; Chair. J. PHELAN; Pres. J. C. RHIND; 26,000 mems.

Insurers' Advisory Organization Inc: 180 Dundas St West, Toronto, Ont M5G 1Z9; tel. (416) 597-1200; fax (416) 597-2180; f. 1855; Pres. and CEO G. A. CHELLEW; 65 mems.

Life Insurance Institute of Canada: 20 Queen St, Suite 2500, Toronto, Ont M5H 3S2; tel. (416) 977-2221; fax (416) 977-1895; Exec. Dir DEBBIE COLE-GAUER.

Life Underwriters' Association of Canada: 41 Lesmill Rd, Don Mills, Ont M3B 2T3; tel. (416) 444-5251; f. 1906; Exec. Vice-Pres. GORD WATT; 21,000 mems.

Trade and Industry

CHAMBER OF COMMERCE

The Canadian Chamber of Commerce: 55 Metcalfe St, Suite 1160, Ottawa K1P 6N4; tel. (613) 238-4000; telex 053-3360; fax (613) 238-7643; f. 1925; mems: 500 community chambers of commerce and boards of trade, 80 nat. trade asscns and 4,000 business corpns; affiliated with all provincial chambers of commerce and with International Chamber and other bilateral orgs; Pres. TIMOTHY E. REID.

INDUSTRIAL ASSOCIATIONS

There are about 2,000 trades associations in Canada.

The Canadian Manufacturers' Association: One Yonge St, Suite 1400, Toronto, Ont M5E 1J9; tel. (416) 363-7261; telex 065-24693; fax (416) 363-3779; f. 1871; the nat. organization of mfrs of Canada; 8,000 mems; Pres. and Exec. Dir J. LAURENT THIBAULT.

Agriculture and Horticulture

Agricultural Institute of Canada: 151 Slater St, Suite 907, Ottawa K1P 5H4; tel. (613) 232-9459; fax (613) 594-5190; f. 1920; 36 brs; 9 provincial sections; 8 affiliated societies; Gen. Man. Y. JACQUES.

Alberta Wheat Pool: 505 2nd St, SW, POB 2700, Calgary, Alta T2P 2P5; tel. (403) 290-4910; telex 038-21643; fax (403) 290-5528; Pres. R. C. SCHMITT; 60,900 mems.

Canada Grains Council: 760-360 Main St, Winnipeg, Man R3C 3Z3; tel. (204) 942-2254; f. 1969; Pres. Dr DONALD A. DEVER.

Canadian Federation of Agriculture: 75 Albert St, Suite 1101, Ottawa K1P 5E7; tel. (613) 236-3633; fax (613) 236-5749; f. 1935; 19 mems (8 provincial feds); Pres. D. A. KNOERR; Exec. Dir ANTHONY P. POLLARD.

Canadian Horticultural Council: 1101 Prince of Wales Drive, Suite 310, Ottawa K2C 3W7; tel. (613) 226-4187; fax (613) 226-2984; f. 1922; Exec. Vice-Pres. D. DEMPSTER.

Canadian Nursery Trades Association: 1293 Matheson Blvd, Mississauga, Ont L4W 1R1; tel. (416) 629-1367; fax (416) 629-4438; Exec. Dir CHRIS D. ANDREWS.

Canadian Seed Growers' Association: POB 8455, Ottawa K1G 3T1; tel. (613) 236-0497; fax (613) 563-7855; f. 1904; Exec. Dir W. K. ROBERTSON; 5,000 mems.

Dairy Farmers of Canada: 75 Albert St, Suite 1101, Ottawa K1P 5E7; tel. (613) 236-9997; fax (613) 236-5749; f. 1934; Exec. Dir RICHARD DOYLE; 18 mem. asscns.

National Dairy Council of Canada: 141 Laurier Ave West, Suite 704, Ottawa K1P 5J3; tel. (613) 238-4116; telex 053-3952; fax (613) 238-6247; Pres. KEMPTON L. MATTE; 250 mems.

National Farmers Union: 250c 2nd Ave South, Saskatoon, Sask S7K 2M1; tel. (306) 652-9465; fax (306) 664-6226; f. 1969; 6 regional offices; Exec. Sec. STUART THIESSON.

L'Union des producteurs agricoles: 555 blvd Roland-Thérrien, Longueuil, Qué J4H 3Y9; tel. (514) 679-0530; fax (514) 679-5436; f. 1924; Pres. JACQUES PROULX; Sec.-Gen. SERGE DESCHAMPS; 42,000 mems.

Building and Construction

Canadian Construction Association: 85 Albert St, Ottawa K1P 6A4; tel. (613) 236-9455; fax (613) 236-9526; f. 1918; Chair. ROBERT HUNTER; Pres. JOHN HALLIWELL; over 20,000 mems.

Canadian Institute of Steel Construction: 201 Consumers Rd, Suite 300, Willowdale, Ont M2J 4G8; tel. (416) 491-4552; telex 069-86547; Pres. H. A. KRENTZ; 50 mems.

Canadian Paint and Coatings Association: 9900 blvd Cavendish, Bureau 103, St-Laurent, Qué H4M 2V2; tel. (514) 745-2611; fax (514) 745-2031; f. 1913; Pres. R. W. MURRY; 130 mems.

Canadian Prestressed Concrete Institute: 196 Bronson Ave, Suite 100, Ottawa K1R 6H4; tel. (613) 232-2619; fax (613) 238-6124; Pres. J. R. FOWLER; 240 mems.

Construction Specifications Canada: 1 St Clair Ave West, Suite 1206, Toronto, Ont M4V 1K6; tel. (416) 922-3159; fax (416) 922-1694; f. 1954; Exec. Dir H. JAMES DUNCAN; 1,600 mems.

National Concrete Producers' Association: 1013 Wilson Ave, Suite 101, Downsview, Ont M3K 1G1; tel. (416) 635-7179; fax (416) 630-1916; Pres. R. GRIMM; Exec. Dir MARK PATAMIA; 55 mems.

Ontario Painting Contractors Association: 211 Consumers Rd, Suite 305, Willowdale, Ont M2J 4G8; tel. (416) 498-1897; fax (416) 498-6757; Exec. Dir MAUREEN MARQUARDT.

Clothing and Textiles

Apparel Manufacturers' Association of Ontario: 789 Don Mills Rd, Suite 700, Don Mills, Ont M3C 3L6; tel. (416) 429-7184; fax (416) 429-0153; f. 1970; Exec. Dir F. J. BRYAN; 79 mems.

Canadian Allied Textile Trades Association: 49 Front St East, Toronto, Ont M5E 1B3; tel. (416) 363-4266; Sec.-Treas. ALEX HARDIE.

Canadian Carpet Institute: 275 Slater St, Suite 1607, Ottawa K1P 5H9; tel. (613) 232-7183; fax (613) 232-3072; f. 1961; Pres. D. S. EDWARDS.

Canadian Textiles Institute: 280 Albert St, Suite 502, Ottawa K1P 5G8; tel. (613) 232-7195; fax (613) 232-8722; Pres. E. L. BARRY.

Tanners Association of Canada: 50 River St, Toronto, Ont M5A 3N9; tel. (416) 364-2134; fax (416) 360-6990; Exec. Vice-Pres. IAN C. KENNEDY; 8 mems.

Electrical and Electronics

Canadian Electrical Association: 1 place Westmount, Bureau 500, Montréal, Qué H3Z 2P9; tel. (514) 937-6181; fax (514) 937-6498; f. 1891; Pres. WALLACE S. READ; c. 2,500 mems.

Canadian Electrical Contractors' Association: 161 Eglinton Ave East, Suite 605, Toronto, Ont M4P 1J5; tel. (416) 486-1290; fax (416) 486-4431; Exec. Sec. ERYL M. ROBERTS.

Electrical and Electronic Manufacturers Association of Canada: 10 Carlson Court, Suite 500, Rexdale, Ont M9W 6L2; tel. (416) 674-7410; fax (416) 674-7412; Pres. NORMAN ASPIN; 220 mems.

Fisheries

Canadian Association of Fish Exporters: 77 Metcalfe St, Suite 200, Ottawa K1P 5L6; tel. (613) 232-6325; fax (613) 238-3542; f. 1978; Pres. NILO CACHERO.

Fisheries Council of Canada: 77 Metcalfe St, Suite 505, Ottawa K1P 5L6; tel. (613) 238-7751; fax (613) 238-3542; Pres. R. W. BULMER; 6 mem. asscns, 192 mem. cos, 90 assoc. mem. cos.

Food and Beverages

Bakery Council of Canada: 1185 Eglinton Ave East, Suite 101, Don Mills, Ont M3C 3C6; tel. (416) 423-0262; Pres. LINDA J. NAGEL; 650 mems.

Brewers Association of Canada: 155 Queen St, Suite 1200, Ottawa K1P 6L1; tel. (613) 232-9601; fax (613) 232-2283; f. 1943; Pres. R. A. MORRISON; Sec. Mrs F. T. BAMFORD.

Canadian Council of Grocery Distributors: place du Parc, CP 1082, Montréal, Qué H2W 2P4; tel. (514) 982-0267; fax (514) 849-3021; f. 1919; Pres. JACQUES G. AUGER; 60 mems.

Canadian Food Brokers Association: 50 River St, Toronto, Ont M5A 3N9; tel. (416) 368-5921; fax (416) 360-6990; Pres. IAN C. KENNEDY; 241 mems.

Canadian Meat Council: 5233 Dundas St West, Islington, Ont M9B 1A6; tel. (416) 239-8411; fax (416) 239-2416; f. 1919; Gen. Man. D. M. ADAMS; 83 mems.

Canadian National Millers' Association: 155 Queen St, Suite 1101, Ottawa K1P 6L1; tel. (613) 238-2293; telex 053-3964; fax (613) 234-5210; f. 1920; Exec. Sec. STEPHEN P. MARKEY; 19 mems.

Canadian Pork Council: 75 Albert St, Suite 1101, Ottawa K1P 5E7; tel. (613) 236-9239; fax (613) 236-5749; Pres. T. SMITH; Exec. Sec. MARTIN RICE; 10 mem. asscns.

Chilled and Frozen Food Association of Canada: 1306 Wellington St, Suite 303, Ottawa K1Y 3B2; tel. (613) 728-6306; fax (613) 728-4394; Exec. Dir CHRISTOPHER J. KYTE; 500 individual and 175 corporate mems.

Confectionery Manufacturers Association of Canada: 1185 Eglinton Ave East, Don Mills, Ont M3C 3C6; tel. (416) 429-1046; fax (416) 429-1940; f. 1919; Pres. CAROL HOCHU; mems: 22 active, 52 associate.

Grocery Products Manufacturers of Canada: 1185 Eglinton Ave East, Suite 101, Don Mills, Ont M3C 3C6; tel. (416) 429-4444; fax (416) 429-1940; Pres. GEORGE FLEISCHMANN; 140 corporate mems.

Forestry, Lumber and Allied Industries

Canadian Forestry Association: 185 Somerset St West, Ottawa K2P 0J2; tel. (613) 232-1815; fax (613) 232-4210; f. 1900; Pres. J. WALTER GILES; Exec. Dir GLEN BLOUIN.

Canadian Lumber Standards: 1055 West Hastings St, Suite 260, Vancouver, BC V6E 2E9; tel. (604) 687-2171; fax (604) 687-8036; Exec. Dir NILS LARSSON.

Canadian Lumbermen's Association: 27 Goulburn Ave, Ottawa K1N 8C7; tel. (613) 233-6205; telex 053-4519; fax (613) 233-1929; f. 1908; Exec. Dir J. F. MCCRACKEN; 300 mems.

Canadian Pulp and Paper Association: Sun Life Bldg, 19e étage, 1155 rue Metcalfe, Montréal, Qué H3B 4T6; tel. (514) 866-6621; telex 055-60690; fax (514) 866-3035; f. 1913; Pres. HOWARD HART; Exec. Vice-Pres. GORDON MINNES; 62 mems.

Ontario Forest Industries Association: 130 Adelaide St West, Suite 1700, Toronto, Ont M5H 3P5; tel. (416) 368-6188; fax (416) 368-5445; f. 1943; Pres. I. D. BIRD; Man. R. M. RAUTER; 24 mems.

Québec Forest Industries Association Ltd: 1200 ave Germain-des-Prés, Bureau 102, Ste-Foy, Qué G1V 3M7; tel. (418) 651-9352; fax (418) 651-4622; f. 1924; Pres. and Dir-Gen. ANDRÉ DUCHESNE; 28 mems.

Hotels and Catering

Canadian Restaurant and Foodservices Association: Nu-West Center, 80 Bloor St West, Suite 1201, Toronto, Ont M5S 2V1; tel. (416) 923-8416; fax (416) 923-1450; f. 1944; Exec. Vice-Pres. D. C. NEEDHAM; 8,500 mems.

Hotel Association of Canada Inc: 155 Carlton St, Suite 1505, Winnipeg, Man R3C 3H8; tel. (204) 942-0671; fax (204) 942-6719; JOHN D. REED.

Mining

Canadian Gas Association: 55 Scarsdale Rd, Don Mills, Ont M3B 2R3; tel. (416) 447-6465; telex 069-66824; fax (416) 447-7067; Pres. IAN C. MACNABB.

Canadian Petroleum Association: 150 Sixth Ave SW, Suite 3800, Calgary, Alta T2P 3Y7; tel. (403) 269-6721; fax (403) 261-4622; Pres. IAN R. SMYTH.

Mining Association of Canada: 350 Sparks St, Suite 809, Ottawa K1R 7S8; tel. (613) 233-9391; fax (613) 233-8897; f. 1935; Pres. C. GEORGE MILLER.

Northwest Territories Chamber of Mines: POB 2818, Yellowknife, NWT X1A 2R1; tel. (403) 873-5281; fax (403) 920-2145; f. 1967; Pres. MIKE MAGRUM; Gen. Man. TOM HOEFER; 150 mems.

Ontario Mining Association: 111 Richmond St West, Suite 1114, Toronto, Ont M5H 2G4; tel. (416) 364-9301; fax (416) 364-5986; f. 1920; Chair. A. C. RICKABY; Pres. T. P. REID; 44 mems.

Yukon Chamber of Mines: POB 4427, Whitehorse, Yukon Y1A 3T5; tel. (403) 667-2090; fax (403) 668-7127; Sec. (vacant); 210 individual mems, 65 corporate mems.

Pharmaceutical

Canadian Drug Manufacturers Association: 1120 Finch Ave West, Suite 604, Downsview, Ont M3J 3H7; tel. (416) 663-2362; fax (416) 663-9829; Chair. BRENDA DRINKWALTER; Exec. Dir NICHOLAS G. LELUK.

Pharmaceutical Manufacturers Association of Canada: 1111 Prince of Wales Drive, Suite 302, Ottawa K2C 3T2; tel. (613) 727-1380; fax (613) 727-1407; f. 1914; Pres. J. A. EROLA; 69 mems.

Retailing

Retail Council of Canada: 210 Dundas St West, Suite 600, Toronto, Ont M5G 2E8; tel. (416) 598-4684; fax (416) 598-3707; f. 1963; Pres. A. J. MCKICHAN; 6,000 mems.

Retail Merchants' Association of Canada Inc: 1780 Birchmount Rd, Scarborough, Ont M1P 2H8; tel. (416) 291-7903; f. 1896; Pres. and CEO JOHN GILLESPIE; 10,000 mems.

Transport

Air Transport Association of Canada: see Transport—Civil Aviation.

Canadian Institute of Traffic and Transportation: 573 King St East, Toronto, Ont M5A 1M5; tel. (416) 363-5696; fax (416) 363-5698; Exec. Vice-Pres. VICTOR S. DEYGLIO; 2,000 mems.

The Canadian Shippers' Council: see Transport—Shipping.

Canadian Trucking Association: Varette Bldg, 130 Albert St, Suite 300, Ottawa K1P 5G4; tel. (613) 236-9426; fax (613) 563-2701; f. 1937; Gen. Man. L. P. TARDIF.

Motor Vehicle Manufacturers' Association: 25 Adelaide St East, Suite 1602, Toronto, Ont M5C 1Y7; tel. (416) 364-9333; fax (416) 367-3221; f. 1926; Pres. N. A. CLARK; 8 mems.

The Railway Association of Canada: see Transport—Railways.

The Shipping Federation of Canada: see Transport—Shipping.

Wholesale Trade

Canadian Exporters Association: 99 Bank St, Suite 250, Ottawa K1P 6B9; tel. (613) 238-8888; fax (613) 563-9218; telex 053-4888; f. 1943; Pres. L. JAMES TAYLOR; 600 mems.

Canadian Importers Association, Inc: 210 Dundas St West, Suite 700, Toronto, Ont M5G 2E8; tel. (416) 595-5333; telex 065-24115; fax (416) 595-8226; f. 1932; CEO PETER J. DAWES; 650 mems.

Canadian Warehousing Association: 161 Holmcrest Trail, Westhill, Ont M1C 1W2; tel. (416) 282-2757; f. 1917; Exec. Dir DAVID I. KENTISH; 46 corporate mems.

Miscellaneous

Canadian Maritime Industries Association: POB 1429, Station B, Ottawa K1P 5R4; tel. (613) 232-7127; telex 053-4848; fax (613) 232-2490; f. 1944; Pres. J. Y. CLARKE; mems: 20 shipyards and ship repairing firms, 87 allied industries, 3 assoc./govt.

Canadian Tobacco Manufacturers' Council: 99 Bank St, Suite 701, Ottawa K1P 6B9; tel. (613) 238-2799; fax (613) 238-4463; Pres. WILLIAM H. NEVILLE.

Council of Printing Industries of Canada: 7 King St West, Suite 1908, Toronto, Ont M5C 1A2; tel. (416) 867-1520; fax (416) 867-1168; Gen. Man. FRANKLYN R. SMITH.

TRADE UNIONS

At the beginning of 1990 there were 4,031,000 union members in Canada, representing 29.9% of the civilian labour force. Of these, 37.6% belonged to unions with headquarters in the USA.

In 1990 unions affiliated to the Canadian Labour Congress represented 58.6% of total union membership.

Canadian Labour Congress: 2841 Riverside Drive, Ottawa K1V 8X7; tel. (613) 521-3400; telex 053-4750; fax (613) 521-4655; f. 1956; 2,360,656 mems (1990); Pres. SHIRLEY G. E. CARR; Sec.-Treas. RICHARD MERCIER.

Affiliated unions with over 15,000 members:

CANADA

Amalgamated Clothing and Textile Workers Union: 15 Gervais Drive, Suite 601, Don Mills, Ont M3C 1Y8; tel. (416) 441-1806; fax (416) 441-9680; Canadian Dir JOHN ALLERUZZO; 30,000 mems (1990).

Amalgamated Transit Union: 15 Gervais Drive, Suite 606, Don Mills, Ont M3C 1Y8; tel. (416) 445-6204; fax (416) 445-6208; Gen. Exec. Sec. in Canada KEN FOSTER; 25,000 mems (1990).

American Federation of Musicians of the United States and Canada: 75 The Donway West, Suite 1010, Don Mills, Ont M3C 2E9; tel. (416) 391-5161; fax (416) 391-5165; Vice-Pres. from Canada J. ALAN WOOD; 26,000 mems (1990).

Canadian Brotherhood of Railway, Transport and General Workers: 2300 Carling Ave, Ottawa K2B 7G1; tel. (613) 829-8764; f. 1908; Pres. J. D. HUNTER; 40,000 mems (1990).

Canadian Paperworkers Union: 255 rue St-Jacques, Montréal, Qué H2Y 1M6; tel. (514) 842-8931; fax (514) 843-5712; Pres. DONALD HOLDER; 69,000 mems (1990).

Canadian Union of Postal Workers: 280 Metcalfe St, Ottawa K2P 1R7; tel. (613) 236-7238; fax (613) 563-7861; f. 1965; Pres. JEAN-CLAUDE PARROT; 46,000 mems (1990).

Canadian Union of Public Employees: 21 Florence St, Ottawa K2P 0W6; tel. (613) 237-1590; fax (613) 237-5508; Nat. Pres. JEFF ROSE; 377,000 mems (1990).

Communications and Electrical Workers of Canada: 350 Sparks St, Suite 307, Ottawa K1R 7S8; tel. (613) 236-6083; fax (613) 236-0287; Pres. FRED W. POMEROY; 40,000 mems (1990).

Energy and Chemical Workers' Union: 9940 106th St, Suite 202, Edmonton, Alta T5K 2N2; tel. (403) 422-7932; fax (403) 424-2505; Pres. REGINALD C. BASKEN; 35,000 mems (1990).

Fraternité nationale des charpentiers-menuisiers, forestiers et travailleurs d'usine: 3750 est, blvd Crémazie, Bureau 310, Montréal, Qué H2A 1B6; tel. (514) 374-0952; fax (514) 374-2140; Pres. LOUIS-MARIE CLOUTIER; 16,000 mems (1990).

Graphic Communications International Union: 1110 Finch Ave West, Suite 600, Downsview, Ont M3J 2T2; tel. (416) 661-9761; Int. Vice-Pres. LÉONARD R. PAQUETTE; 23,000 mems (1990).

Hospital Employees Union, Local 180: 2006 West 10th Ave, Vancouver, BC V6J 4P5; tel. (604) 734-3431; fax (604) 734-3163; Prov. Pres. BILL MACDONALD; 28,000 mems (1989).

Hotel Employees and Restaurant Employees International Union: 1140 est, blvd de Maisonneuve, Bureau 500, Montréal, Qué H3A 1M8; tel. (514) 844-4167; fax (514) 844-1536; Vice-Pres JAMES STAMOS (Montréal), RON BONAR (Vancouver); 32,000 mems (1990).

International Association of Machinists and Aerospace Workers: 100 Metcalfe St, Suite 300, Ottawa K1P 5M1; tel. (613) 236-9761; fax (613) 563-7830; Gen. Vice-Pres. VALÉRIE E. BOURGEOIS; 61,000 mems (1990).

International Woodworkers Association of Canada (IWA—Canada): 1285 Pender St, Suite 500, Vancouver, BC V6E 4B2; tel. (604) 683-1117; fax (604) 688-6416; f. 1937; Pres. J. J. MUNRO; 50,000 mems (1990).

National Automobile, Aerospace and Agricultural Implement Workers Union of Canada (CAW-Canada): 205 Placer Court, North York, Willowdale, Ont M2H 3H9; tel. (416) 497-4110; telex 069-86509; fax (416) 495-6559; Pres. ROBERT WHITE; 170,000 mems (1990).

National Union of Provincial Government Employees: 2841 Riverside Drive, Suite 204, Ottawa K1V 8N4; tel. (613) 526-1663; fax (613) 526-0477; Pres. JAMES CLANCY; 301,000 mems (1990).

Office and Professional Employees' International Union: 1290 rue St-Denis, 5e étage, Montréal, Qué H6X 3J7; tel. (514) 288-6511; Canadian Dir and Int. Vice-Pres. ANNE HARVEY; 30,000 mems (1990).

Public Service Alliance of Canada: 233 Gilmour St, Ottawa K2P 0P1; tel. (613) 560-4200; fax (613) 563-3492; f. 1966; Pres. DARYL T. BEAN; 165,000 mems (1990).

Retail, Wholesale and Department Store Union: 15 Gervais Drive, Suite 310, Don Mills, Ont M3C 1Y8; tel. (416) 441-1414; Vice-Pres. and Dir in Canada THOMAS E. COLLINS; 28,000 mems (1990).

Service Employees International Union: 1 Credit Union Drive, Toronto, Ont M4A 2S6; tel. (416) 752-4073; fax (416) 752-1966; Vice-Pres S. E. (TED) ROSCOE, LOUIS DUVAL; 75,000 mems (1990).

United Brotherhood of Carpenters and Joiners of America: 5799 Yonge St, Suite 807, Willowdale, Ont M2M 3V3; tel. (416) 225-8885; fax (416) 225-5390; Officials in Canada EDWARD RYAN, PATRICK MATTEI; 62,000 mems (1990).

United Food and Commercial Workers International Union: 61 International Blvd, Suite 300, Rexdale, Ont M9W 6K4; tel. (416) 675-1104; fax (416) 675-6919; f. 1979; Vice-Pres. and Canadian Dir CLIFFORD EVANS; 170,000 mems (1990).

United Steelworkers of America: 234 Eglinton Ave East, 7th Floor, Toronto, Ont M4P 1K7; tel. (416) 487-1571; fax (416) 482-5548; Nat. Dir in Canada GÉRARD DOCQUIER; 160,000 mems (1990).

Other Central Congresses

Canadian Federation of Labour: 107 Sparks St, Suite 300, Ottawa K1P 5B5; tel. (613) 234-4141; fax (613) 234-5188; f. 1982; Pres. JAMES A. MCCAMBLY; 14 affiliated unions representing 225,000 mems (1990).

Affiliated unions with over 15,000 members:

International Brotherhood of Electrical Workers: 45 Sheppard Ave East, Suite 401, Willowdale, Ont M2N 5Y1; tel. (416) 226-5155; fax (416) 226-1492; Int.Vice-Pres. KEN J. WOOD; 66,000 mems (1990).

International Brotherhood of Painters and Allied Trades: 12 Morgan Ave, Thornhill, Ont L3T 1R1; tel. (416) 882-6412; Gen. Vice-Pres. ARMANDO COLAFRANCESCHI; 17,000 mems (1990).

International Union of Operating Engineers: 4211 Kingsway, Suite 401, Burnaby, BC V5H 1Z6; tel. (604) 438-1615; fax (604) 439-2459; Canadian Dir and Gen. Vice-Pres. J. V. BIDDLE; 36,000 mems (1990).

United Association of Journeymen and Apprentices of the Plumbing and Pipe Fitting Industry of the United States and Canada: 310 Broadway Ave, Suite 702, Winnipeg, Man R3C 0S6; tel. (204) 942-0836; fax (204) 943-8552; Vice-Pres. and Canadian Dir J. RUSS ST ELOI; 40,000 mems (1990).

Canadian National Federation of Independent Unions: 331 Major St, Welland, Ont L3B 3T7; tel. (416) 735-0531; f. 1980; Pres. VINCE VOCAL.

Centrale de l'enseignement du Québec: 9405 est, rue Sherbrooke, Montréal, Qué H1L 6P3; tel. (514) 356-8888; Pres. LORRAINE PAGÉ; 12 affiliated unions representing over 1120,000 mems (1990).

Affiliated union with over 15,000 members:

Fédération des enseignantes et des enseignants de commissions scolaires: 2336 chemin Ste-Foy, CP 5800, Sainte-Foy, Qué G1V 4E5; tel. (418) 658-5711; fax (418) 658-6057; Pres. LUC SAVARD; 75,000 mems (1990).

Centrale des syndicats démocratiques: 1259 rue Berri, Bureau 600, Montréal, Qué H2L 4C7; tel. (514) 842-3801; fax (514) 842-0518; f. 1972; Pres. CLAUDE GINGRAS; 3 federated and 341 non-federated unions representing 61,000 mems (1990).

Confederation of Canadian Unions: 1331½A St Clair Ave West, Toronto, Ont M6E 1C3; tel. (416) 651-5627; f. 1969; Pres. GARRY WORTH; 14 affiliated unions representing 32,000 mems (1990).

Confédération des syndicats nationaux: 1601 ave de Lorimier, Montréal, Qué H2K 4M5; fax (514) 598-2052; f. 1921; Pres. GÉRALD LAROSE; 2,075 affiliated locals representing 245,000 mems (1990).

Affiliated unions with over 15,000 members:

Fédération des employées et employés de services publics inc: 1601 ave de Lorimier, Montréal, Qué H2K 4M5; tel. (514) 598-2231; fax (514) 598-2398; Pres. GINETTE GUÉRIN; 28,000 mems (1990).

Fédération des affaires sociales inc: 1601 ave de Lorimier, Montréal, Qué H2K 4M5; tel. (514) 598-2210; Pres. CATHERINE LOUMÈDE; 95,000 mems (1990).

Fédération du commerce inc: 1601 ave de Lorimier, Bureau 122, Montréal, Qué H2K 4M5; tel. (514) 598-2181; fax (514) 598-2089; Pres. LISE POULIN; 30,000 mems (1990).

Fédération de la métallurgie: 1601 ave de Lorimier, Montréal, Qué H2K 4M5; tel. (514) 598-2136; fax (514) 598-2298; Pres. BENOÎT CAPISTRAN; 19,000 mems (1990).

Fédération des travailleurs du papier et de la forêt: 155 est, blvd Charest, Québec, Qué G1K 3G6; tel. (418) 647-5775; Pres. CLAUDE PLAMONDON; 16,000 mems (1990).

Federation nationale des enseignants et enseignantes du Québec: 1601 ave de Lorimier, Montréal, Qué H2K 4M5; tel. (514) 598-2241; fax (514) 598-2089; Pres. DENIS CHOINIÈRE; 17,000 mems (1990).

The American Federation of Labor and Congress of Industrial Organizations (AFL-CIO), with headquarters in Washington, DC, USA, represented 177,568 members, or 4.4% of the total union membership in Canada, at the beginning of 1990. Affiliated unions with over 15,000 members:

International Association of Bridge, Structural and Ornamental Iron Workers: 284 King St West, Suite 501, Toronto, Ont M5V

1J1; tel. (416) 593-7155; fax (416) 593-9844; Gen. Vice-Pres. DONALD W. O'REILLY; 20,000 mems (1990).

International Brotherhood of Teamsters, Chauffeurs, Warehousemen and Helpers of America: 8000 blvd Langelier, Bureau 404, St-Léonard, Qué H1P 3K2; tel. (514) 328-8926; fax (514) 328-1485; International Dir LOUIS LACROIX; 100,000 mems (1990).

Laborers' International Union of North America: 1177 Belanger Ave, Suite 101, Ottawa K1H 8N7; tel. (613) 738-3184; fax (416) 225-5390; Dir NELLO SCIPIONI; 57,000 mems (1990).

Principal Unaffiliated Unions

Alberta Teachers' Association: 11010 142nd St, Edmonton, Alta T5N 2R1; tel. (403) 453-2411; fax (403) 455-6481; Exec. Sec. J. S. BUSKI; 43,000 mems (1990).

British Columbia Nurses' Union: 4259 Canada Way, Suite 100, Burnaby, BC V5G 1H1; tel. (604) 433-2268; fax (604) 433-7945; Pres. PAT SAVAGE; 22,000 mems (1990).

British Columbia Teachers' Federation: 2235 Burrard St, Vancouver, BC V6J 3H9; tel. (604) 731-8121; fax (604) 731-4891; Pres. KEN NOVAKOWSKI; 37,000 mems (1990).

Canadian Telephone Employees' Association: place du Canada, Bureau 360; Montréal, Qué H3B 2N2; tel. (514) 861-9963; Pres. JUDITH KING; 20,000 mems (1990).

Fédération des infirmières et infirmiers du Québec: 175 rue St-Jean, 4e étage, Québec, Qué G1R 1N4; tel. (418) 647-1102; fax (418) 647-5985; Pres. DIANE LAVALLÉE; 42,000 mems (1990).

Federation of Women Teachers' Associations of Ontario: 1260 Bay St, Toronto, Ont M5R 2B8; tel. (416) 964-1232; fax (416) 964-0512; Pres. ANNE WILSON; 38,000 mems (1990).

Ontario English Catholic Teachers' Association: 65 St Clair Ave East, Suite 400, Toronto, Ont M4T 2Y8; tel. (416) 925-2493; fax (416) 925-7764; Pres. MICHAEL CÔTE; 30,000 mems (1990).

Ontario Nurses' Association: 85 Grenville St, Suite 600, Toronto, Ont M5B 2E7; tel. (416) 964-8833; fax (416) 964-8864; Pres. LESLEY BELL; 54,000 mems (1990).

Ontario Public School Teachers' Federation: 1260 Bay St, Toronto, Ont M5R 2B7; tel. (416) 928-1128; fax (416) 928-0179; Pres. BILL MARTIN; 25,000 mems (1990).

Ontario Secondary School Teachers Federation: 60 Mobile Drive, Toronto, Ont M4A 2P3; tel. (416) 751-8300; Pres. JIM HEAD; 43,000 mems (1990).

Professional Institute of the Public Service of Canada: 53 Auriga Drive, Nepean, Ont K2E 8C3; tel. (613) 228-6310; fax (613) 228-9048; Pres. IRIS CRAIG; 24,000 mems (1990).

Syndicat des fonctionnaires provinciaux du Québec: 5100 Des Gradins, Québec, Qué G2J 1N4; tel. (418) 623-2424; fax (418) 623-6109; Pres. JEAN-LOUIS HARGUINDEGUY; 40,000 mems (1990).

Transport

Owing to the size of the country, Canada's economy is particularly dependent upon an efficient system of transport. The St Lawrence Seaway allows ocean-going ships to reach the Great Lakes. There are almost 194,000 km (120,000 miles) of railway track, and the country's rail and canal system is being increasingly augmented by roads, air services and petroleum pipelines. The Trans-Canada Highway is one of the main features of a network of 392,000 km (243,600 miles) of roads and highways. In 1977 the Canadian Government extended its coastal jurisdiction to 370 km (200 nautical miles).

RAILWAYS

Algoma Central Corpn: POB 7000, Sault Ste Marie, Ont P6A 5P6; tel. (705) 949-2113; telex 067-77146; f. 1899; diversified transportation co moving cargo by rail and water; also has interests in commercial property development; Chair. HENRY N. R. JACKMAN; Pres. P. R. CRESSWELL.

BC Rail: POB 8770, Vancouver, BC V6B 4X6; tel. (604) 986-2012; telex 043-52752; f. 1912; 2,608 km; Pres. and CEO P. J. MCELLIGOTT.

CN Rail: 935 ouest, rue de la Gauchetière, CP 8100, Montréal, Qué H3C 3N4; tel. (514) 399-5430; telex 055-60519; f. 1923; 45,000 km; Chair. BRIAN SMITH; Pres. and CEO RONALD E. LAWLESS.

Canadian Pacific Ltd: CP 6042, succursale A, Montréal, Qué H3C 3E4; tel. (514) 395-5151; f. 1881; provides rail and other surface transport services; Chair. and CEO W. W. STINSON; Pres. J. F. HANKINSON.

Ontario Northland Transportation Commission: 555 Oak St East, North Bay, Ont P1B 8L3; tel. (705) 472-4500; telex 067-76103; fax (705) 476-5598; an agency of the govt of Ontario; operates rail services over 919.1 km of track; Chair. M. D. SINCLAIR; Pres. and CEO P. A. DYMENT.

VIA Rail Canada Inc: 2 place Ville-Marie, 4e étage, Montréal, Qué H3B 2G6; tel. (514) 871-6000; telex 052-68530; f. 1977; federal govt corpn; operates passenger services over existing rail routes throughout Canada; Chair. L. HANIGAN; Pres. and CEO RONALD E. LAWLESS.

Association

The Railway Association of Canada: 1117 ouest, rue Ste-Catherine, Bureau 721, Montréal, Qué H3B 1H9; tel. (514) 849-4274; fax (514) 849-2861; f. 1917; Pres. R. H. BALLANTYNE; 12 full mems and 9 associates.

ROADS

Provincial governments are responsible for roads within their boundaries. The Federal Government is responsible for major roads in the Yukon and Northwest Territories and in National Parks. In 1987 there were 844,386 km of roads (including 24,459 km of motorways and highways), of which 29% were paved.

The Trans-Canada Highway extends from St John's, Newfoundland, to Victoria, British Columbia.

INLAND WATERWAYS

The St Lawrence River and the Great Lakes provide Canada and the USA with a system of inland waterways extending from the Atlantic Ocean to the western end of Lake Superior, a distance of 3,769 km (2,342 miles). There is a 10.7-m (35-foot) navigation channel from Montréal to the sea and an 8.25-m (27-foot) channel from Montréal to Lake Erie. The St Lawrence Seaway, which was opened in 1959, was initiated partly to provide a deep waterway and partly to satisfy the increasing demand for electric power. Power development has been undertaken by the provinces of Québec and Ontario, and by New York State. In 1989 cargo traffic through the Seaway totalled 48.4m. metric tons. The navigation facilities and conditions are within the jurisdiction of the federal Governments of the USA and Canada.

St Lawrence River and Great Lakes Shipping

St Lawrence Seaway Authority: 360 Albert St, Ottawa K1R 7X7; tel. (613) 598-4600; telex 053-3322; fax (613) 598-4620; opened 1959 to admit ocean-going vessels to the Great Lakes of North America; operated jtly with the USA; Pres. GLENDON STEWART.

Canada Steamship Lines Inc: 759 Victoria Sq., Montréal, Qué H2Y 2K3; tel. (514) 288-0231; telex 052-5380; fax (514) 982-3803; f. 1913; Chair. JAMES R. ELDER; Pres. J. FREDERIC PITRE; 34 vessels; 750,000 grt.

Paterson, N. M., and Sons Ltd: POB 664, Thunder Bay, Ont P7C 4W6; tel. (807) 577-8421; telex 073-4566; bulk carriers; Vice-Pres. and Dir ROBERT J. PATERSON; 12 vessels; 95,536 grt.

Misener Shipping: 63 Church St, POB 100, St Catharines, Ont L2R 6S1; tel. (416) 688-3500; telex 061-5155; bulk cargo; Pres. DAVID K. GARDNER; 11 vessels; 200,000 grt.

ULS Corporation: 49 Jackes Ave, Toronto, Ont M4T 1E2; tel. (416) 920-7610; telex 065-24157; fax (416) 920-5785; Chair. and Dir J. D. LEITCH; Pres. and CEO D. MAXWELL; bulk carriers; 20 vessels; 417,604 grt.

SHIPPING

British Columbia Ferry Corporation: 1112 Fort St, Victoria, BC V8W 4V2; tel. (604) 381-1401; telex 049-7483; fax (604) 381-5452; passenger and car ferries; Gen. Man. ROD MORRISON; 38 ferries.

Esso Petroleum Canada: External Supply and Transportation Division, 55 St Clair Ave West, Toronto, Ont M5W 2J8; tel. (416) 968-5309; telex 065-28049; coastal, Great Lakes and St Lawrence River, South American, Caribbean and Gulf ports to Canadian east and US Atlantic ports; Pres. G. H. THOMSON; Man. (Marine Div.) H. M. WESTLAKE; 11 vessels; 41,836 grt.

Fednav Ltd: 600 ouest, rue de la Gauchetière, Bureau 2600, Montréal, Qué H3B 4M3; tel. (514) 878-6500; telex 055-60637; fax (514) 878-6642; f. 1944; shipowners, operators, contractors, terminal operators; Pres. L. G. PATHY; owned and chartered fleet of 68 vessels.

Marine Atlantic Inc: 100 Cameron St, Moncton, NB E1C 5Y6; tel. (506) 851-3600; telex 014-2833; fax (506) 851-3615; Pres. and CEO T. W. IVANY; serves Atlantic coast of Canada; 16 vessels, incl. passenger, roll-on/roll-off and freight ferries.

Papachristidis (Canada) Inc: 1350 ouest, rue Sherbrooke, Penthouse, Montréal, Qué H3G 1J1; tel. (514) 844-8404; telex 052-68780; Pres. NIKY PAPACHRISTIDIS; world-wide services; 4 vessels owned and managed; 52,309 grt.

CANADA

Seaboard Shipping Co Ltd: 171 West Esplanade, Suite 500, North Vancouver, BC V7M 1A1; services to UK-Continent, Japan, Australia, Mediterranean, Puerto Rico, US Atlantic Coast; Pres. C. D. G. ROBERTS.

Soconav Inc: 1801 ave Collège McGill, Bureau 830A, Montréal, Qué H3A 2N4; tel. (514) 284-9535; telex 052-67671; Great Lakes, St Lawrence River and Gulf, Atlantic Coast, Arctic and NWT; Chair. MICHEL GAUCHER; Pres. LOUIS ROCHETTE; Vice-Pres. (Operations) GUY BAZINET; 13 tankers, 76,476 grt.

Associations

The Canadian Shippers' Council: c/o Canadian Exporters' Association, 99 Bank St, Suite 250, Ottawa K1P 6B9; tel. (613) 238-8888; telex 053-4888; fax (613) 563-2918; Sec. J. D. MOORE.

The Shipping Federation of Canada: 300 rue St-Sacrement, Bureau 326, Montréal, Qué H2Y 1X4; tel. (514) 849-2325; telex 055-61042; fax (514) 849-6992; f. 1903; Pres. F. C. NICHOL; 69 mems.

CIVIL AVIATION
Principal Scheduled Companies

Air Canada: place Air Canada, Montréal, Qué H2Z 1X5; tel. (514) 879-7000; telex 062-17537; fax (514) 879-7990; f. 1937; investor-owned; Chair., Pres. and CEO CLAUDE I. TAYLOR; operates services throughout Canada and to the USA; also to the UK, Paris, Zürich, Geneva, Frankfurt, Düsseldorf, Munich, Vienna, Bombay, Singapore, Antigua, Bermuda, Barbados, Bahamas, Trinidad, Guadeloupe, Martinique, Cuba, Jamaica, Saint Lucia, the Dominican Republic and Haiti; fleet of 33 Boeing 727, 6 Boeing 747, 21 Boeing 767, 35 DC-9, 6 DC-8-73F, 14 L-1011.

Canadian Airlines International: 700 Second St SW, Suite 2800, Calgary, Alta T2P 2W2; tel. (403) 294-2000; telex 043-55610; f. 1988 by merger; Chair., Pres. and CEO RHYS T. EYTON; passenger and cargo charters and scheduled services to 50 destinations in North America and 22 international destinations; fleet of 58 Boeing 737, 12 Boeing 767, 11 DC-10-30, 8 Airbus 310.

Intair: Montréal International Airport, CP 750, Pointe-Claire Dorval, Qué H4Y 1B5; tel. (514) 631-9802; telex 058-22584; f. 1946; regional carrier and charter services; Chair. MARC RACICOT; Pres. and CEO MICHEL LEBLANC; fleet of 7 Fokker-100, 9 ATR-42.

Nationair Canada: Nationair Bldg, Cargo Rd A-1, Montréal International Airport (Mirabel), Mirabel, Qué J7N 1A5; tel. (514) 476-3318; telex 056-7513; fax (514) 476-1281; f. 1984; scheduled and charter services to the USA, Europe and South America; Pres. R. OBADIA; fleet of 4 DC-8-61, 2 DC-8-62, 2 DC-8-63, 3 Boeing 747, 2 Boeing 757.

Association

Air Transport Association of Canada: 99 Bank St, Suite 747, Ottawa K1P 6B9; tel. (613) 233-7727; fax (613) 230-8648; f. 1934; Pres. and CEO G. M. SINCLAIR; 200 mems.

Tourism

Most tourist visitors (34.7m. of a total 38.0m. in 1989) are from the USA. Expenditure by tourists in 1989 amounted to C $6,904m.

Tourism Canada: Federal Dept of Industry, Science and Technology, 235 Queen St, 4th Floor East, Ottawa K1A 0H6; tel. (613) 954-3851; telex 053-4123.

Tourism Industry Association of Canada: 130 Albert St, Suite 1016, Ottawa K1P 5G4; tel. (613) 238-3883; fax (613) 238-3878; f. 1931; private-sector asscn; encourages travel to and within Canada; promotes development of travel services and facilities; Exec. Dir JOHN LAWSON.

Atomic Energy

Atomic Energy of Canada Ltd: 344 Slater St, Ottawa K1A 0S4; tel. (613) 237-3270; telex 053-4867; fax (613) 563-9499; f. 1952; federal govt agency for nuclear research and development, production of radioactive isotopes and design, development and marketing of power reactors; four operational research reactors at Chalk River, Ont, and one at Whiteshell Laboratories, Pinawa, Man; isotope production facility at Chalk River; nuclear designer for CANDU (Canadian deuterium uranium) reactors: 17 commercial units now in service at four stations, providing a total capacity of 12,051 MW, representing 16.1% of Canada's total electricity generation; four others under construction in Canada; two units in service in India, one each in Pakistan, the Republic of Korea and Argentina, three units under construction in Romania and one in the Republic of Korea; Pres. and CEO STANLEY HATCHER.

Atomic Energy Control Board: POB 1046, Ottawa K1P 5S9; tel. (613) 995-5894; telex 053-3771; fax (613) 995-5086; f. 1946; responsible for all nuclear regulatory matters; Pres. R. J. A. LÉVESQUE; Sec. J. G. MCMANUS.

CAPE VERDE

Introductory Survey

Location, Climate, Language, Religion, Flag, Capital

The Republic of Cape Verde is an archipelago of 10 islands and five islets in the North Atlantic Ocean, about 500 km (300 miles) west of Dakar, Senegal. The country lies in a semi-arid belt, with little rain and an average annual temperature of 24°C (76°F). The official language is Portuguese, of which the locally spoken form is Creole (Crioulo). Virtually all of the inhabitants profess Christianity, and 98% are Roman Catholics. The national flag (proportions 3 by 2) comprises a vertical red stripe, at the hoist, and two equal horizontal stripes, of yellow and green. The red stripe bears, in the upper hoist, a five-pointed black star and a clamshell enclosed by a wreath of palms. The capital is Cidade de Praia.

Recent History

The Cape Verde Islands were colonized by the Portuguese in the 15th century. From the 1950s, liberation movements in Portugal's African colonies were campaigning for independence, and, in this context, the archipelago was linked with the mainland territory of Portuguese Guinea (now Guinea-Bissau) under one nationalist movement, the Partido Africano da Independência do Guiné e Cabo Verde (PAIGC). The independence of Guinea-Bissau was recognized by Portugal in September 1974, but the PAIGC leadership in the Cape Verde Islands decided to pursue its independence claims separately, rather than enter into an immediate federation with Guinea-Bissau. In December 1974 a transitional government, comprising representatives of the Portuguese Government and the PAIGC, was formed; members of other political parties were excluded. On 30 June 1975 elections for a National People's Assembly were held, in which only PAIGC candidates were allowed to participate. Independence was granted on 5 July 1975, with Aristides Pereira, Secretary-General of the PAIGC, becoming Cape Verde's first President. The country's first constitution was approved in September 1980.

Although Cape Verde and Guinea-Bissau remained constitutionally separate, the PAIGC supervised the activities of both states. Progress towards the ultimate goal of unification was halted by the November 1980 coup in Guinea-Bissau (during which the President, who was himself a Cape Verdean, was placed under house arrest). The Cape Verde Government condemned the coup, and in January 1981 the Cape Verde wing of the PAIGC was renamed the Partido Africano da Independência de Cabo Verde (PAICV). In February Pereira was re-elected as President by the National Assembly, and all articles concerning an eventual union with Guinea-Bissau were removed from the Constitution. Discussions concerning reconciliation were held in June 1982, however, after the release of Luis Cabral, formerly the Head of State in Guinea-Bissau, and diplomatic relations between the two countries were subsequently normalized.

A new National Assembly was elected in December 1985. The 83 candidates on the PAICV-approved list, of whom some were not members of the PAICV, obtained 94.5% of the votes cast. In January 1986 President Pereira was re-elected for a further five-year term by the National Assembly. In the new Government several ministerial functions were redistributed: in particular, all aspects of economic management were centralized in the office of the Prime Minister, Gen. Pedro Pires. In July 1987 Lisbon radio reported disturbances in Mindelo, São Vicente, after the National Assembly approved legislation decriminalizing abortion, as part of a policy to promote birth control during the course of the second Development Plan for 1986–90; 16 people were arrested, following demonstrations over the dismissal of a journalist from the opposition Catholic newspaper, Terra Nova, and one detainee was sentenced to three months' imprisonment. Further demonstrations against abortion and for greater political freedom were held in January 1988, but Pereira dismissed them as insignificant and not indicative of any general discontent. In September José Araujo, the Minister of Justice, resigned, owing to ill health, and the Prime Minister assumed temporary control of the justice portfolio. In October the state-controlled newspaper, Voz do Povo, published a manifesto, signed by 24 jurists, accusing the Government of failing to respect human rights. Later in October, Voz do Povo published a refutation of the jurists' manifesto, signed by 29 judges.

At the PAICV congress in November 1988, Pereira and Pires were re-elected Secretary-General and Deputy Secretary-General, respectively, of the party. The Political Commission, the executive body of the PAICV, was reshuffled in December, and three new members were appointed: Col Silvino Manuel da Luz, André Corsino Tolentino and Commdt Carlos N. Fernandes dos Reis. In June 1989 Corsino Fortes, former ambassador to Angola, was named as Minister of Justice. In September the Government declared three days' mourning, following the murder of the Secretary of State for Public Administration, Dr Renato de Silas Cardoso. A government communiqué stated that the killing was a common law crime, unconnected with Cardoso's position in the Government. In November two political commissions were established, to regulate legislative elections and to consider proposals for constitutional changes. In the same month it was announced that, although elections to the National People's Assembly were to be held (as scheduled) in 1990, local elections were to be deferred until 1991. The postponement was criticized by the Catholic newspaper, Terra Nova, which accused the Government of perpetuating its monopoly of power. In February 1990, in an apparent response to increasing pressure from church and academic circles, the PAICV announced the convening of an emergency congress to discuss the possible abolition of Article 4 of the Constitution, which guaranteed the supremacy of the PAICV. In April a newly-formed political organization, the Movimento para Democracia (MPD), issued a manifesto in Paris, which advocated the immediate introduction of a multi-party system. Pereira subsequently announced that the next presidential election, which was planned for December 1990, would be held, for the first time, on the basis of universal suffrage.

In July 1990 President Pereira implemented an extensive ministerial reshuffle, in which seven new state secretariats were created. In the same month a special congress of the PAICV reviewed proposals for new party statutes and the abolition of Article 4 of the Constitution. Pereira also announced his resignation as Secretary-General of the PAICV, and was later replaced by the Prime Minister, Gen. Pedro Pires. On 28 September Cape Verde officially became a multi-party state, with the endorsement of the constitutional amendment (abolishing the PAICV's monopoly of power) by the National Assembly (see Government, p. 669). The legislative elections were rescheduled for 20 January 1991. The MPD subsequently received official recognition as a political party. In late November 1990 the MPD announced its support for an independent candidate, Mascarenhas Monteiro (a former judge), in the presidential election, due to be held on 17 February 1991.

Cape Verde professes a non-aligned stance in foreign affairs and maintains relations with virtually all the power blocs. Cape Verde's reputation for political independence led to its selection as the venue for several important international conferences. In July 1988 the military commanders of Angola, Cuba and South Africa met in Cape Verde to pursue peace negotiations, under the auspices of the USA. In August the South African Deputy Minister of Foreign Affairs conferred with the Cape Verdean Minister of Foreign Affairs in Praia. In 1987 Cape Verde banned Saint Lucia Airways from the Amílcar Cabral international airport, following indications that the airline was using Cape Verde as a staging point in the transport of military equipment for the anti-Government rebels of UNITA in Angola. Cape Verde's relations with Guinea-Bissau showed further signs of improvement in 1988, when the two countries signed an agreement on bilateral co-operation. In the same year Mozambique and Cape Verde pledged solidarity with each other, during a visit to the islands by the Mozambican Prime Minister, Mário Machungo.

In 1985 Cape Verde agreed to accommodate up to eight members of the Basque separatist movement, ETA, who were being deported from Spain for terrorist activities. Following negotiations in June 1986 with the Spanish Minister of the Interior, Cape Verde agreed to accept more members of ETA. In July 1987, however, an enquiry was initiated when three of the four ETA members being accommodated on Cape Verde escaped from São Vicente Island.

In 1988 Cape Verde signed a two-year co-operation agreement with Portugal, covering education, military training and the rescheduling of debts owed to Portugal. Co-operation agreements were also signed with the USSR, Ghana and Nigeria. During a five-day visit to Portugal in July 1989, Pereira met Portugal's President Soares and the Prime Minister, Aníbal Cavaco Silva, to discuss bilateral relations and the situation in southern Africa. In September Pereira and Senegal's President Abdou Diouf met for private talks on Sal Island. In the same month, Cape Verde acted as a mediator in disputes between ECOWAS member-states. These efforts were commended by Nigeria's President Ibrahim Babangida, and served to consolidate relations between Cape Verde and Nigeria. In October a 'summit' meeting between the five Portuguese-speaking nations was held in Luanda, Angola. In a communiqué, the Heads of State of Angola, Mozambique, Cape Verde, Guinea-Bissau and São Tomé and Príncipe emphasized their support for the Angolan Government's peace plan, and for the peace initiative taken by the Government of Mozambique. During a two-day official visit to Angola in October 1990, Pereira met the Angolan President, José Eduardo dos Santos, to discuss bilateral relations.

Government

Under the 1980 Constitution (with modifications adopted by the National Assembly in September 1990), Cape Verde is a multi-party state, although the formation of parties on a religious or geographical basis is prohibited. Legislative power is vested in the National People's Assembly, which comprises 83 deputies, elected by universal adult suffrage for a five-year term. The Head of State is the President of the Republic, who governs with the assistance of an appointed Council of Ministers, led by the Prime Minister. Under electoral legislation endorsed by the National People's Assembly in September 1990, the President is elected by universal suffrage, and must obtain two-thirds of the votes cast to win in the first round. Voting is conducted by secret ballot. If no candidate secures the requisite majority, a new election is to be held within 21 days and contested by the two candidates who received the highest number of votes in the first round. The Prime Minister, who is appointed by the President, is elected by the deputies of the National Assembly.

Defence

The Popular Revolutionary Armed Forces were formed from ex-combatants in the liberation wars, and numbered less than 1,300 (army 1,000, navy 200, air force less than 100) in June 1990. There is also a police force and paramilitary People's Militia. National service is by selective conscription. Estimated defence expenditure in 1981 was US $3.5m. In 1988 Portugal agreed to provide military training and to allow Cape Verde to purchase light military equipment. In 1989 it was announced that the size of the armed forces was to be reduced.

Economic Affairs

In 1988, according to estimates from the World Bank, Cape Verde's gross national product (GNP) per head, measured at average 1986–88 prices, was US $680m. During 1980–87, it was estimated, GNP increased, in real terms, at an annual average rate of 3.3%, and GNP per head increased by 1.2% per year. During 1980–88 the population increased by an annual average of 2.2%.

Agriculture (including forestry and fishing) contributed about 15% of GDP, and employed an estimated 45% of the labour force, in 1988. The sector accounted for 33.2% of paid employment in 1980. The staple crops are maize and beans; potatoes, cassava, coconuts, dates, sugar cane and bananas are also cultivated. Fish and fish products accounted for an estimated 83% of export earnings in 1985. However, the total catch declined from 14,730 metric tons in 1981 to 5,372 tons in 1988. Lobster and tuna are among the most important exports.

Industry (including mining, manufacturing, construction and power) contributed an estimated 28.6% of GDP in 1987. At mid-1980 an estimated 22.7% of the labour force were employed in industry. In 1980 the sector provided 32.5% of total paid employment.

Mining accounted for 0.8% of paid employment in 1980 and contributed an estimated 0.3% of GDP in 1987. Salt and pozzolana, a volcanic ash used in cement manufacture, are the main non-fuel minerals produced.

Manufacturing contributed 5.4% of GDP in 1987 and provided 2.8% of paid employment in 1980. The most important branches, other than fish-processing, are machinery and electrical equipment, transport equipment, chemicals and textiles.

There are about 700,000 Cape Verdeans living outside the country, principally in the USA, the Netherlands, Portugal and Italy. In 1987 remittances from emigrants provided US $28m. (15% of Cape Verde's GDP). The Government has attempted to attract emigrants' capital into the light industry and fishing sectors in Cape Verde by offering favourable tax conditions to investors.

Energy is derived principally from hydroelectric power and gas. Imports of mineral fuels, comprised 12.7% of the value of total imports in 1984.

In 1988 Cape Verde recorded a trade deficit of 7,415m. escudos (compared with total export revenue of 237m. escudos). In 1987 there was a deficit of $1.65m. on the current account of the balance of payments. In 1984 the principal source of imports was Portugal, which accounted for 22.9% of the total value of imports. Other major trading partners were the Netherlands, France and Spain. The principal exports in 1987 were fish (38.5%) and bananas (18.3%). The major imports in 1987 were basic manufactures (53.3%), foodstuffs (32.6%) and petroleum (13.9%).

In 1984 there was an estimated budgetary deficit of 504.5m. escudos. Cape Verde's total external debt was US $133m. at the end of 1988. The cost of debt-servicing exceeded 8% of export earnings in 1987. The annual rate of inflation averaged 8.9% in 1980–88, and was 8.6% in the year to September 1989. An estimated 25% of the labour force were unemployed in 1988.

Cape Verde is a member of ECOWAS (see p. 133), which promotes trade and co-operation in West Africa, and is a signatory to the Lomé Convention (see p. 151). Since the late 1960s, Cape Verde's agricultural economy has been severely affected by drought; approximately 90% of the country's total food requirements are imported. Cape Verde has received considerable foreign aid towards the financing of agricultural development programmes, and the expansion of the country's network of transport and communication systems. External assistance (including food aid) in 1987 totalled US $84m., and accounted for 46% of GDP. A four-year Development Plan (1986–90) aimed to increase GDP by 4.5% per year and to expand the sectors of agriculture, tourism and industry. Plans to establish Cape Verde as an international centre of trade, based on transhipping and 'offshore' banking and financial services, were initiated in 1990.

Social Welfare

Medical facilities are limited and there is a severe shortage of staff and buildings, although plans for a national health service are being implemented. In 1980 Cape Verde had 21 hospital establishments, with a total of 632 beds, and there were 51 physicians working in government service. In 1987 Nigeria signed an agreement to construct a 200-bed hospital, as part of a technical aid programme. Development plans include the construction of more than 300 small local health units.

Education

Compulsory education is divided into Instrução Primária (for children aged seven to 12) and Escola Preparatória (for children aged 12 to 14). From the age of 14, children may attend one of the four liceus, which provide a three-year general course or a two-year pre-university course. In 1986/87 there were also three teacher-training units and one industrial and commercial school. In 1987 Nigeria agreed to construct a polytechnic, as part of a technical aid programme. In 1986 the total enrolment at primary and secondary schools was equivalent to 68% of all school-age children (70% of boys; 65% of girls). In 1986/87 there were 4,523 children enrolled at pre-primary schools, 60,226 at primary schools, and 5,026 at general secondary schools. Primary enrolment in 1986 included 88% of children in the relevant age-group (90% of boys; 86% of girls), but the comparable ratio for secondary enrolment was only 9%.

CAPE VERDE

A project to upgrade primary education was initiated in 1987, with the aims of reducing the high drop-out rate and of improving basic skills. The project proposed to replace the current two-cycle primary education system with a single six-year cycle, to improve teacher training and to provide better equipment. The project was to cost US $5.3m., of which $4.2m. was to be provided by a loan from the IDA. In the same year Cape Verde received a Swiss loan to finance a four-year adult literacy programme. In 1980, according to official estimates, the average rate of illiteracy among the population aged 14 years and over was 52.6% (males 38.6%; females 61.4%).

Public Holidays

1991: 1 January (New Year), 20 January (National Heroes' Day), 8 March (Women's Day), 1 May (Labour Day), 1 June (Children's Day), 5 July (Independence Day), 12 September (Day of the Nation), 25 December (Christmas Day).

1992: 1 January (New Year), 20 January (National Heroes' Day), 8 March (Women's Day), 1 May (Labour Day), 1 June (Children's Day), 5 July (Independence Day), 12 September (Day of the Nation), 25 December (Christmas Day).

Weights and Measures

The metric system is in force.

Statistical Survey

Source (unless otherwise stated): Statistical Service, Banco de Cabo Verde, Av. Amílcar Cabral, São Tiago; tel. 341; telex 99350.

AREA AND POPULATION

Area: 4,033 sq km (1,557 sq miles).

Population: 272,571 at census of 15 December 1970; 295,703 (males 135,695, females 160,008) at census of 2 June 1980; 347,000 (official estimate) at 31 December 1987. *By island* (1980 census): Boa Vista 3,397, Brava 6,984, Fogo 31,115, Maio 4,103, Sal 6,006, Santo Antão 43,198, São Nicolau 13,575, São Tiago 145,923, São Vicente 41,792.

Principal Town: Cidade de Praia (capital), population 57,748 at 1980 census.

Births and Deaths: Registered live births (1988) 12,443 (birth rate 34.8 per 1,000); Registered deaths (1985) 2,735 (death rate 8.4 per 1,000). Source: UN, *Population and Vital Statistics Report*.

Economically Active Population (persons aged 10 years and over, excluding unpaid family workers, 1980 census): Agriculture, hunting, forestry and fishing 22,144; Mining and quarrying 535; Manufacturing 1,871; Electricity, gas and water 336; Construction 18,873; Trade, restaurants and hotels 3,930; Transport, storage and communications 3,411; Financing, insurance, real estate and business services 226; Community, social and personal services 15,284; Total labour force 66,610 (males 46,281, females 20,329). Source: International Labour Office, *Year Book of Labour Statistics*. **Mid-1980** (ILO estimates, '000 persons). Agriculture, etc. 53; Industry 23; Services 26; Total 102 (males 74, females 28). Source: ILO, *Economically Active Population Estimates and Projections, 1950-2025*.

AGRICULTURE, ETC.

Principal Crops ('000 metric tons, 1989): Maize 7*, Potatoes 3†, Cassava 4†, Sweet potatoes 6†, Pulses 7†, Coconuts 10†, Dates 2†, Sugar cane 16†, Bananas 5†. Source: FAO, *Production Yearbook*.

Livestock ('000 head, year ending September 1989): Cattle 12†, Pigs 70†, Sheep 3†, Goats 80†, Asses 6†. Source: FAO, *Production Yearbook*.

Fishing ('000 metric tons, live weight): Total catch 6.4 in 1986; 6.9 in 1987; 5.4 in 1988. Source: FAO, *Yearbook of Fishery Statistics*.

* Unofficial estimate.
† FAO estimate.

MINING

Production (metric tons): Salt (unrefined) 5,000 (1986); Pozzolana 10,000 (estimate by US Bureau of Mines, 1987). Source: UN, *Industrial Statistics Yearbook*.

INDUSTRY

Production (metric tons, unless otherwise indicated, 1987): Biscuits 400, Bread 3,000, Canned fish 300, Frozen fish 2,300 (preliminary), Manufactured tobacco 104, Alcoholic beverages 200,000 litres, Soft drinks 200,000 litres, Electric energy 27m. kWh. Source: UN, *Industrial Statistics Yearbook*.

FINANCE

Currency and Exchange Rates: 100 centavos = 1 Cape Verde escudo; 1,000 escudos are known as a conto. *Coins:* 20 and 50 centavos; 1, 2½, 10, 20 and 50 escudos. *Notes:* 100, 500 and 1,000 escudos. *Sterling and Dollar Equivalents* (30 September 1990). £1 sterling = 127.988 escudos; US $1 = 68.315 escudos, 1,000 Cape Verde escudos = £7.813 = $14.638. *Average Exchange Rate* (escudos per US dollar): 58.29 in 1982; 71.69 in 1983; 84.88 in 1984.

Budget (estimates, million escudos, 1984): Revenue 1,630; Expenditure 2,134.5.
Source: *Marchés Tropicaux et Méditerranéens*.

Currency in Circulation ('000 escudos, 1976): Notes 465,609, Coins 8,415.

Cost of Living (Consumer Price Index for Praia, excluding rent; base: 1983 = 100): 130 in 1986; 135 in 1987; 141.3 in 1988. Source: UN, *Monthly Bulletin of Statistics*.

Gross Domestic Product by Economic Activity (estimates, million escudos at current factor cost, 1987): Agriculture, forestry and fishing 2,466; Mining and quarrying 32; Manufacturing 637; Electricity, gas and water 327; Construction 2,345; Trade, restaurants and hotels 2,868; Transport and communications 1,438; Finance, insurance, real estate and business services 434; Public administration and defence 1,031; Other services 113; *GDP at factor cost* 11,691; Indirect taxes, *less* subsidies 1,212; *GDP in purchasers' values* 12,903. Source: UN Economic Commission for Africa, *African Statistical Yearbook*.

Balance of Payments (million escudos, 1981): Merchandise trade (net) −3,880; Net services 15, *Balance on Goods and Services* −3,865; Private transfers 1,760; Other income 25; *Current Balance* −2,080; Public transfers 1,940; Net errors and omissions 170; Total (net monetary movements) 30. Source: Centro de Estudos Economia e Sociedade, Lisbon.

EXTERNAL TRADE

Principal Commodities (million escudos, 1984): *Imports:* Food and live animals 1,584 (fresh and preserved milk 182.6, rice 206.7, maize 314.6, sugar 171.6): Beverages and tobacco 319; Mineral fuels, lubricants, etc. 758 (gas oils 399.7); Chemicals 376; Basic manufactures 1,129 (cement 341.0); Machinery and transport equipment 1,224; Miscellaneous manufactured articles 323; Total (incl. others) 5,987. *Exports:* Food and live animals 186 (fresh and frozen fish 108.4, bananas 16.7); Total (incl. others) 222. Source: UN Economic Commission for Africa, *African Statistical Yearbook*.

Total Trade (million escudos, 1988): Imports 7,652, Exports 237. Source: UN, *Monthly Bulletin of Statistics*.

Principal Trading Partners (US $ million, 1984): *Imports:* Portugal 19.7, Netherlands 18.5, France 8.5, Spain 7.2, Belgium 4.7, Germany, Federal Republic 4.3, Brazil 3.5, Argentina 2.9, Italy 2.0, UK 1.7; Total (incl. others) 85.8. Source: IMF, *Direction of Trade Statistics Yearbook 1985*.

TRANSPORT

Road Traffic (motor vehicles in use, 1984): Passenger cars 3,000, Commercial vehicles 700.

Shipping (international freight traffic, estimates, 1985): Vessels entered 3,539; goods loaded 108,000 metric tons; goods unloaded 286,000 metric tons (Source: mainly UN, *Monthly Bulletin of Statistics*); (1981): Passengers embarked 97,746; passengers disembarked 97,746. Source: mainly Direcção Geral de Estatística, Praia, São Tiago.

Civil Aviation (Amílcar Cabral airport, 1982): Freight loaded 104.7 metric tons; freight unloaded 615.3 metric tons; passengers embarked 23,106; passengers disembarked 21,200. Source: Direcção Geral de Estatística, Praia, São Tiago.

CAPE VERDE

COMMUNICATIONS MEDIA

Radio receivers (1987): 53,000 in use. Source: UNESCO, *Statistical Yearbook*.

Television receivers (1987): 5,000 in use.

Telephones (estimate, 1987): 6,000 in use.

Book production (1985): 10 titles; 13,000 copies. Source: UNESCO, *Statistical Yearbook*.

EDUCATION

Pre-primary (1986/87): 58 schools, 4,523 pupils, 136 teachers.
Primary (1986/87): 545 schools, 60,226 pupils, 1,791 teachers.
Secondary (1986/87): 4 schools, 5,026 pupils, 170 teachers.
Teacher training (1986/87): 3 units, 211 pupils, 53 teachers.
Industrial school (1986/87): 1 school, 531 pupils, 52 teachers.
Source: Ministério da Educação e Cultura, CP 111, Praia, São Tiago.

Directory

The Constitution

The Constitution of the Republic of Cape Verde, the first since the country's independence in 1975, was approved on 7 September 1980. It was amended significantly in September 1990. The Constitution defines Cape Verde as 'a sovereign, democratic, unitary, anti-colonialist and anti-imperialist republic'. The Head of State is the President of the Republic, who is elected by universal adult suffrage and has a mandate of five years, as do the Assembly deputies, also elected by universal adult suffrage. The Prime Minister is nominated by the same Assembly, to which he is responsible. The President of the National Assembly may act as interim Head of State if necessary. He is not a member of the Government.

The Constitution abolishes both the death sentence and life imprisonment. Citizens have equality of rights and duties, without sexual, social, intellectual, religious or philosophical distinction. This extends to all Cape Verde emigrants throughout the world. Citizens also have freedom of thought, expression, association, demonstration, religion, rights and duties and the right to health care, culture and education.

On 12 February 1981 all articles concerning plans for eventual union with Guinea-Bissau were revoked, and an amendment was inserted to provide for the creation of the Partido Africano da Independência de Cabo Verde (PAICV) to replace the Cape Verde section of the PAIGC (defined in the Constitution as 'the leading force of society').

Constitutional reforms, which included the institution of a multi-party political system, were approved in September 1990.

The Government

HEAD OF STATE

President: ARISTIDES MARIA PEREIRA (took office 5 July 1975; re-elected February 1981 and January 1986).

COUNCIL OF MINISTERS
(November 1990)

Prime Minister, with responsibility for Defence: Gen. PEDRO VERONA RODRIGUES PIRES.
Minister of Foreign Affairs: Col SILVINO MANUEL DA LUZ.
Minister of Rural Development, Fisheries and Internal Administration: Commdt JOÃO PEREIRA SILVA.
Minister of Education: ANDRÉ CORSINO TOLENTINO.
Minister of Information, Culture and Sport: Dr DAVID HOPFER ALMADA.
Minister of Planning and Co-operation: JOSÉ BRITO.
Minister of Finance: Dr ARNALDO VASCONCELLOS FRANCA.
Minister of Transport, Commerce and Tourism: OMAR LIMA.
Minister of Industry and Energy: ADÃO SILVA ROCHA.
Minister of Health, Labour and Welfare: Dr IRENEU GOMES.
Minister of Justice: CORSINO FORTES.
Minister of Public Works: ADRIANO DE OLIVEIRA LIMA.
Deputy to the Prime Minister: AGUINALDO LISBOA RAMOS.
Secretary of State for Foreign Affairs and Immigration: ANTÓNIO BARRETO LIMA.
Secretary of State for Local Information: EURICO MONTEIRO.
Secretary of State for the Interior: ARMANDO SILVA.
Secretary of State for Rural Development: HELDOR SANTOS.
Secretary of State for Fisheries: ALEXANDRE PINA.
Deputy Secretary of State to the Minister of Finance: VIRGILIO FERNANDES.
Secretary of State for the Merchant Navy: HUMBERTO F. MORAIS.
Secretary of State for Commerce and Tourism: (vacant).
Secretary of State for the Armed Forces: Maj. ALVARO TAVARES.
Deputy Secretary of State to the Prime Minister: JOÃO MAXIMIANO.
Secretary of State for Public Administration: EDUARDO RODRIGUES.
Secretary of State for Youth: CLAUDIO FURTADO.

MINISTRIES

Office of the President: Presidência da República, Praia, São Tiago; tel. 61-26-69; telex 6051.
Office of the Prime Minister: Praça 12 de Setembro, CP 16, Praia, São Tiago; tel. 61-33-22; telex 6052.
Ministry of Agriculture and Fisheries: Rua António Pussich, Praia, São Tiago; tel. 335; telex 6072.
Ministry of the Armed Forces and Security: Avda Unidade Guiné, Praia, São Tiago; tel. 448; telex 6077.
Ministry of Education: Avda Amílcar Cabral, CP 111, Praia, São Tiago; tel. 345; telex 6057.
Ministry of Finance: 107 Avda Amílcar Cabral, CP 30, Praia, São Tiago; tel. 329; telex 6058.
Ministry of Foreign Affairs: Praça 10 de Mayo, CP 60, Praia, São Tiago; tel. 310; telex 6070.
Ministry of Health and Social Affairs: Praça 12 de Setembro, CP 47, Praia, São Tiago; tel. 422; telex 6059.
Ministry of Industry and Energy: Unidade de Promoção Industrial, POB 145, Praia, São Tiago; tel. 61-39-49; telex 6035.
Ministry of Information, Culture and Sport: Rua Massacre de Pidjiguiti, Praia; tel. 61-38-43; telex 6030; fax 61-43-69.
Ministry of the Interior: Rua Guerra Mendes, Praia, São Tiago; tel. 255; telex 6062.
Ministry of Justice: Praça 12 de Setembro, Praia, São Tiago; tel. 336; telex 6025.
Ministry of Transport, Trade and Tourism: Rua Guerra Mendes, CP 15, Praia, São Tiago; tel. 601; telex 6060.

Legislature

ASSEMBLÉIA NACIONAL POPULAR

The National People's Assembly consists of 83 deputies, elected for a term of five years by universal adult suffrage. The most recent general election was held on 7 December 1985, when 94.5% of the votes endorsed the single list of candidates presented by the PAICV. Following the adoption of new electoral legislation in September 1990 (see Government, p. 669), the number of deputies was to be reduced by between 10 and 20.

President: ABÍLIO AUGUSTO MONTEIRO DUARTE.

Political Organizations

Until 1990 the PAICV was the only authorized political party in Cape Verde. Amendments to the Constitution, which were approved in September 1990, permitted the formation of other political associations.

Movimento parce Democracia (MPD): Praia; f. 1990; leadership comprises a national council of 45 mems, a national commission of 15 mems, and a legal council; advocates administrative decentralization; Chair. CARLOS VEIGA.

CAPE VERDE
Directory

Partido Africano da Independência de Cabo Verde (PAICV): CP 22, São Tiago; telex 6022; f. 1956 as the Partido Africano da Independência do Guiné e Cabo Verde (PAIGC); name changed in 1981, following the Nov. 1980 coup in Guinea-Bissau, which the Cape Verde govt had opposed, having previously favoured an eventual union with Guinea-Bissau; sole authorized political party until 1990; Sec.-Gen. Gen. PEDRO VERONA RODRIGUES PIRES.

Political Commission

ARISTIDES MARIA PEREIRA.
Gen. PEDRO VERONA RODRIGUES PIRES.
ABÍLIO AUGUSTO MONTEIRO DUARTE.
OLÍVIO PIRES.
Col SILVINO MANUEL DA LUZ.
Col JÚLIO CÉSAR DE CARVALHO.
ANDRÉ CORSINO TOLENTINO.
Commdt CARLOS N. FERNANDES DOS REIS.

União Caboverdiana Independente e Democrática (UCID): based in Boston, USA; f. ???? by emigrants opposed to the PAICV; supports the MPD in the 1991 legislative elections; leader JOHN WAHNON.

Diplomatic Representation

EMBASSIES IN CAPE VERDE

Brazil: Rua Guerra Menoes, CP 93, Praia, São Tiago; tel. 385; telex 6075; Ambassador: FERNANDO BUARQUE FRANCO NETTE.

China, People's Republic: Praia, São Tiago; Ambassador: XIE ZHENLIY (resident in Dakar, Senegal).

Cuba: Público CV, Praia, São Tiago; tel. 465; telex 6087; Ambassador: GILBERTO GARCÍA ALONSO.

France: CP 192, Praia, São Tiago; tel. 290; telex 6064; Ambassador: CLAUDE THULLIER.

Portugal: Achada de Santo António, CP 160, Praia, São Tiago; tel. 408; telex 6055; Ambassador: Dr ANTÓNIO BAPTISTA MARTINS.

Senegal: Praia, São Tiago; Ambassador: OMAR BEN KHATAB SOKHNA.

USSR: CP 31, Praia, São Tiago; tel. 61-21-32; telex 6016; Ambassador: PAVEL MIKHAILOVICH SHMELKOV.

USA: Rua Hoji Ya Yenna 81, CP 201, Praia, São Tiago; tel. 61-43-63; telex 6068; fax 61-13-55; Ambassador: FRANCIS TERRY MCNAMARA.

Judicial System

Supremo Tribunal de Justiça: Praça 12 de Setembro, CP 117, Praia, São Tiago; tel. 61-23-69; telex 6025; established 1975; the highest court.

There is a network of tribunais populares at the local level.

Religion

CHRISTIANITY

At 31 December 1988 there were an estimated 327,546 adherents of the Roman Catholic Church, representing 99% of the total population. Protestant churches, among which the Church of the Nazarene is prominent, represent about 1% of the population.

The Roman Catholic Church

Cape Verde comprises the single diocese of Santiago de Cabo Verde, directly responsible to the Holy See. The Bishop participates in the Episcopal Conference of Senegal, Mauritania and Cape Verde, based in Senegal.

Bishop of Santiago de Cabo Verde: Mgr PAULINO DO LIVRAMENTO EVORA, CP 46, Praia, São Tiago; tel. 61-11-19.

The Anglican Communion

Cape Verde forms part of the diocese of The Gambia, within the Church of the Province of West Africa. The Bishop is resident in Banjul, The Gambia.

The Press

Boletim Informativo: CP 126, Praia, São Tiago; f. 1976; weekly; publ. by the Ministry of Foreign Affairs; circ. 1,500.

Boletim Oficial da República de Cabo Verde: Imprensa Nacional, CP 113, Praia, São Tiago; weekly; official.

Raízes: CP 98, Praia, São Tiago; tel. 319; f. 1977; quarterly; cultural review; Editor ARNALDO FRANÇA; circ. 1,500.

Terra Nova: Ilha do Fogo; weekly; Roman Catholic.

Unidade e Luta: Praia, São Tiago; organ of the PAICV.

Voz do Povo: CP 118, Praia, São Tiago; 3 a week; publ. by govt information service; Editor ALFREDO SIMÃO CARVALHO SANTOS; circ. 3,000.

NEWS AGENCIES

Agence France-Presse (AFP): CP 26/118 Praia, São Tiago; tel. 61-38-89; telex 52; Rep. Mme FATIMA AZEVADO.

Inter Press Service (IPS) (Italy): CP 14, Mindelo, São Vicente; tel. 31-45-50; Rep. JUAN A. COLOMA.

Publisher

Government Publishing House

Imprensa Nacional: CP 113, Praia, São Tiago.

Radio and Television

In 1987 there were an estimated 53,000 radio receivers and 5,000 television receivers in use. In March 1988 France agreed to provide aid for Cape Verdean radio and television, and in October a French company agreed to install a powerful short-wave relay station on Cape Verde, which would broadcast to Latin America and Africa.

RADIO

Rádio Nacional de Cabo Verde: Praça 12 de Setembro, CP 26, Praia, São Tiago; tel. 61-37-29; govt-controlled; five transmitters and five solar relay transmitters; FM transmission only; broadcasts in Portuguese and Creole for 18 hours daily; Dir CARLOS GONÇALVES.

Voz de São Vicente: CP 29, Mindelo, São Vicente; f. 1974; govt-controlled; Dir FRANCISCO TOMAR.

TELEVISION

Televisão Experimental de Cabo Verde (TEVEC): Achada de Santo António, CP 2, Praia, São Tiago; tel. 61-40-80; one transmitter and seven relay transmitters; broadcasts in Portuguese and Creole for three hours daily; Dir MARIA MANUELA AZEVEDO GRAÇA.

Finance

(cap. = capital; res = reserves; dep. = deposits; m. = million; brs = branches; amounts in Cape Verde escudos)

BANKING

Banco de Cabo Verde: 117 Avda Amílcar Cabral, CP 101, Praia, São Tiago; tel. 61-31-53; telex 99350; f. 1976; central bank; cap. and res 1,796.2m., dep. 3,790.4m. (1984); Gov. AMARO ALEXANDRE DA LUZ; 8 brs.

The **Fundo de Solidariedade Nacional** is the main savings institution; the **Fundo de Desenvolvimento Nacional** channels public investment resources; and the **Instituto Caboverdiano** administers international aid.

Trade and Industry

CHAMBERS OF COMMERCE

Associação Comercial Barlavento: CP 62, Mindelo, São Vicente; tel. 31-32-81.

Associação Comercial e Agricola de Sotavento: CP 78, Praia; tel. 61-29-91.

STATE INDUSTRIAL ENTERPRISES

Empresa Caboverdeana de Pescas (PESCAVE): CP 59, Mindelo, São Vicente; tel. 2434; telex 99384; f. 1987; co-ordinates and equips the fishing industry; manages the harbour, incl. cold-storage facilities (capacity 9,000 metric tons); operates ice supply and shipping agency.

CAPE VERDE

Empresa de Comercialização de Produtos do Mar—INTERBASE, EP: CP 59, Mindelo, São Vicente; tel. 31-23-49; telex 3084; supervises marketing of fish; shipping agency and ship chandler.

Empresa Nacional de Aeropuertos e Segurança Aerea: Aeroporto Amílcar Cabral, Ilha do Sal; tel. 41-13-94; telex 4036; airports and aircraft security.

Empresa Nacional de Avicultura, EP (ENAVI): CP 135, Praia, São Tiago; tel. 61-18-59; telex 6072; f. 1979; state enterprise for poultry farming.

Empresa Nacional de Combustíveis, EP: CP 1, Mindelo, São Vicente; f. 1979; state enterprise supervising import and distribution of petroleum; Dir RUI S. LOPES DOS SANTOS.

Empresa Nacional de Produtos Farmacêuticos (EMPROFAC): CP 59, Praia, São Tiago; tel. 61-14-94; telex 6024; fax 61-37-18; f. 1979; state pharmaceuticals enterprise holding monopoly of local production and medical imports.

Empresa Pública de Abastecimentos (EMPA): CP 107, Praia, São Tiago; tel. 61-11-54; telex 6054; f. 1975; state provisioning enterprise, supervising imports, exports and domestic distribution; Dir-Gen. ORLANDO JOSÉ MASCARENHAS.

Instituto Nacional de Cooperativas: Praia, São Tiago; central co-operative organization.

Secretaria de Estado das Pescas (SEP): CP 30, Praia, São Tiago; tel. 61-10-91; telex 6058; f. 1983; oversees the development of the fishing industry; Dir-Gen. VICENTE ANDRADE GOMES.

Sociedade de Comercialização e Apoio à Pesca Artesanal (SCAPA): Praia, São Tiago; state-controlled; co-ordinates small-scale fishing enterprises and promotes modern techniques.

TRADE UNION

União Nacional dos Trabalhadores de Cabo Verde—Central Sindical (UNTC—CS): Praia, São Tiago; f. 1978; Chair. ADOLINO MANUEL SILVA.

Transport

ROADS

In 1981 there were about 2,250 km of roads, of which 660 km were paved. In 1986 a loan of US $7.5m. from the People's Republic of China was used partly to finance new road-building projects.

SHIPPING

Cargo-passenger ships call regularly at Mindelo, on São Vicente, and Praia, on São Tiago. Praia and Porto Grande ports are being considerably enlarged, with the help of a US $7.2m. grant from the International Development Association, and a shipyard has been built at Mindelo. Work started in 1982 on a port at Palmeira, on Sal island. New ports are also being constructed at Sal-Rei, on Boa Vista, and at Tarrafal, on São Nicolau, with financial and technical assistance from the USSR.

Comissão de Gestão dos Transportes Marítimos de Cabo Verde: CP 153, São Vicente; tel. 31-49-79; telex 3031; fax 31-20-55; 3,199 grt.

Companhia Nacional de Navegação Arca Verde: 5 de Julho, CP 41, Praia, São Tiago; tel. 61-10-60; telex 6067; fax 61-28-24; f. 1975; 4,851 grt.

Companhia de Navegação Estrella Negra: Avda 5 de Julho 17, CP 91, São Vicente; tel. 31-54-23; telex 3030; 2,098 grt.

Companhia Nacional de Navegação Portuguesa: Agent in São Tiago: João Beneliel de Carvalho, Lda, CP 56, Praia, São Tiago.

Companhia Portuguesa de Transportes Marítimos: Agent in São Tiago: João Beneliel de Carvalho, Lda, CP 56, Praia, São Tiago.

Transportes Marítimos de Cabo Verde: Avda Kwame Nkrumah, CP 153, Mindelo, São Vicente; serves Portugal, Cádiz, Antwerp, Rotterdam, Hamburg, Ipswich, Felixstowe, Udvalla, Abidjan and Tema.

CIVIL AVIATION

The Amílcar Cabral international airport is at Espargos, on Sal Island, with capacity for aircraft of up to 50 tons. It can handle 1m. passengers per year. Expansion of the airport's facilities began in 1987, with EEC and Italian aid. There is also a small airport on each of the other main islands, except Brava.

Transportes Aéreos de Cabo Verde (TACV): 11-13 Rua Guerra Mendes, CP 1, Praia, São Tiago; tel. 339; telex 99365; f. 1955; connects Santiago-Praia, Maio, Fogo, São Vicente, Ilha do Sal, São Nicolau, Boa Vista and Santo Antão; also operates weekly services to Lisbon (Portugal) and Boston (USA); Gen. Man. VALDEMAR FORTES DE SOUSA LOBO; fleet: 2 BAe 748 Avro, 2 DHC Twin Otter, 1 Boeing 737-300 (on order).

Tourism

The islands of São Tiago, Santo Antão, Fogo and Brava offer a combination of mountain scenery and extensive beaches. In 1980 the Government initiated a tourist development scheme, and by 1987 there were two international hotels on Sal Island and a tourist complex in Praia. An estimated 2,000 tourists, mostly French and Italian, visit Cape Verde annually.

Secretaria de Estado de Comércio e Turismo: CP 105, Praia, São Tiago; tel. 573; telex 6058.

THE CENTRAL AFRICAN REPUBLIC

Introductory Survey

Location, Climate, Language, Religion, Flag, Capital

The Central African Republic is a land-locked country in the heart of equatorial Africa. It is bounded by Chad to the north, by Sudan to the east, by the Congo and Zaire to the south and by Cameroon to the west. The climate is tropical, with an average annual temperature of 26°C (79°F) and heavy rains in the south-western forest areas. The national language is Sango, but French is the official language. Many of the population hold animist beliefs, but about one-third are Christians. The national flag (proportions 5 by 3) has four horizontal stripes, of blue, white, green and yellow, divided vertically by a central red stripe, with a five-pointed yellow star and crescent in the upper hoist. The capital is Bangui.

Recent History

The former territory of Ubangi-Shari (Oubangui-Chari), within French Equatorial Africa, became the Central African Republic (CAR) on achieving self-government in December 1958. Full independence was attained on 13 August 1960. Barthélemy Boganda, founder of the Mouvement d'évolution sociale de l'Afrique noire (MESAN) and a principal figure in the campaign for self-government, became the country's first Prime Minister. However, he was killed in an air crash in March 1959. He was succeeded by his nephew, David Dacko, who led the country to independence and in 1962 established a one-party state, with MESAN as the sole authorized party. President Dacko was overthrown on 31 December 1965 by a military coup which brought to power his cousin, Col (later Marshal) Jean-Bédel Bokassa, Commander-in-Chief of the armed forces.

In January 1966 Bokassa formed a new government, rescinded the Constitution and dissolved the National Assembly. Bokassa, who became Life President in March 1972 and Marshal of the Republic in May 1974, forestalled several alleged coup attempts and employed increasingly repressive measures against dissidents. On two occasions, close associates of the President were implicated in plots to overthrow the regime. In April 1969 Lt-Col Alexandre Banza, the Minister of Public Health, was arrested and executed, after having been convicted of attempting to organize a coup against Bokassa. In April 1973 Auguste M'Bongo, hitherto Minister of State for Housing and Transport, was dismissed from the Government; he was subsequently accused of attempting to instigate another coup, and of having been a supporter of the 1969 plot. A government reorganization in January 1975 included the appointment of Élisabeth Domitien, the vice-president of MESAN, to the newly-created post of Prime Minister. She thus became the first woman to hold this position in any African country, but she was dismissed in April 1976, when President Bokassa assumed the premiership.

In September 1976 the Council of Ministers was replaced by the Council for the Central African Revolution, and ex-President Dacko was appointed personal adviser to the President. In December the Republic was renamed the Central African Empire (CAE), and a new constitution was instituted. Bokassa was proclaimed the first Emperor, and Dacko became his Personal Counsellor. The Imperial Constitution provided for the establishment of a national assembly, but no elections were held.

The elaborate preparations for Bokassa's coronation in December 1977 were estimated to have consumed about one-quarter of the country's income. In May 1978 Bokassa reshuffled the army leadership and strengthened its powers. In July he appointed a new Council of Ministers, headed by an erstwhile Deputy Prime Minister, Henri Maidou. In January 1979 violent protests, led by students, were suppressed, reportedly with the help of Zairean troops. Following a protest by schoolchildren against compulsory school uniforms (made by a company that was owned by the Bokassa family), many children were arrested in April. About 100 of them were killed in prison, and Bokassa himself allegedly participated in the massacre. In May the Emperor's ambassador in Paris, Gen. Sylvestre Bangui, resigned in protest, and in September he became the leader of a newly-formed government-in-exile, comprising four opposition groups. On 20 September 1979, while Bokassa was in Libya, David Dacko deposed him in a bloodless coup, which received considerable support from France, and resumed power as President. The country was again designated a republic, with Dacko as its President and Henri Maidou as Vice-President.

President Dacko's principal concern was to establish order and economic stability in the CAR, but his Government encountered opposition, particularly from students who objected to the continuation in office of CAE Ministers. In August 1980 Dacko accepted demands for the dismissal of both Maidou and the Prime Minister, Bernard Christian Ayandho. The new Council of Ministers was led by Jean-Pierre Lebouder, formerly Minister of Planning. Bokassa, at that time in exile in Côte d'Ivoire (and subsequently in Paris), was sentenced to death *in absentia* in December 1980.

In February 1981 a new constitution, providing for a multi-party system, was approved by referendum and promulgated by President Dacko. He won a presidential election in March and was sworn in for a six-year term in April. Electoral malpractice was alleged, and rioting broke out, prompting the declaration of a state of siege in Bangui. Political tension increased after a bomb attack on a Bangui cinema in July, in which three people died. The Mouvement centrafricain pour la libération nationale claimed responsibility and was subsequently banned. A state of siege was again declared, and the Government summoned assistance from army units to maintain order. The Chief of Staff of the armed forces, Gen. André Kolingba, deposed President Dacko in a bloodless coup on 1 September, citing 'gross violations of democracy' as reasons for the military take-over, and suspending all political activity. Power was assumed by a 23-member Comité militaire pour le redressement national (CMRN), and an all-military government was formed.

In March 1982 the exiled leader of the banned Mouvement pour la libération du peuple centrafricain (MLPC), Ange Patasse, returned to Bangui and was implicated in an unsuccessful coup attempt. Patasse, who had been the Prime Minister under Bokassa in 1976–78 and who had contested the March 1981 presidential election, sought asylum in the French embassy in Bangui, from where he was transported to exile in Togo. French support for Patasse strained the military regime's relations with France, but a visit by President Mitterrand of that country to the CAR in October 1982 normalized relations. Some former government ministers were also implicated in the coup attempt, and in August 1984 two of the accused ex-ministers, Gaston Ouédane and Jérôme Allan, were sentenced to 10 years' imprisonment.

Opposition to Gen. Kolingba's regime continued, despite the suspension of all political activity in September 1981. In August 1983 a clandestine opposition movement was formed, uniting the three main opposition parties. In September 1984 Gen. Kolingba announced an amnesty for the leaders of banned political parties, who had been under house arrest since January, and reduced the sentences of the ex-ministers who had been imprisoned for involvement in the 1982 coup attempt. Shortly afterwards, in December 1984, President Mitterrand paid a further visit to the country. A total of 89 political prisoners were released in December 1985. Several students were arrested during anti-French demonstrations in Bangui in March 1986, following the death of 35 civilians, including many schoolchildren, as a result of the crash of a French military aircraft. Shortly afterwards, a bomb exploded on the road leading to Bangui-Mpoko airport. Two Libyan diplomats were expelled from the CAR, suspected of complicity in the bomb attack. The students were released in September, along with a further, unspecified number of political prisoners (including Ouédane and Allan).

The appointment of several civilians as high commissioners (attached to the Council of Ministers, with responsibilities for various departments) in January 1984 was followed in September 1985 by the dissolution of the CMRN and the introduction, for the first time since Gen. Kolingba's assumption of power, of civilians into the Council of Ministers itself. In early 1986 a specially-convened commission drafted a new constitution, which provided for the creation of a sole legal political party, the Rassemblement démocratique centrafricain (RDC), and conferred strong executive powers on the President, while defining a predominantly advisory role for the legislature. In November the draft constitution was approved by 91.17% of the electorate in a referendum, as a result of which Kolingba was also elected to serve a further six-year term as President. The Council of Ministers was reorganized in December to include a majority of civilians, while Kolingba assumed the defence portfolio.

The RDC was officially established in February 1987, with Kolingba as founding president, and elections to the new National Assembly took place in July, at which 142 candidates, all nominated by the RDC, contested the 52 seats. It was estimated that only 50% of the electorate participated in the legislative elections. The new National Assembly held its first sitting in October. In December, following reports of student unrest, the Ministers of National Education and of Higher Education and Scientific Research were dismissed, and the two portfolios were merged to form a single ministry, as part of a government reshuffle. A further reallocation of ministerial posts took place in July 1988.

In October 1986 Bokassa returned unexpectedly to the CAR, and was immediately arrested. His new trial, on a total of 14 charges, opened in November, and continued until June 1987, when the former Emperor was sentenced to death, after having been convicted on charges of murder, conspiracy to murder, the illegal detention of prisoners and embezzlement. An appeal for a retrial was rejected by the Supreme Court in November. In February 1988, however, President Kolingba commuted the sentence to one of life imprisonment with hard labour. (In practice, hard labour is not exacted of prisoners in the CAR.) It was widely believed that this act of clemency resulted not only from Kolingba's desire to be regarded as a moderate and humane leader, but also from a fear of unrest among Bokassa's supporters in the event of the former Emperor's execution.

The appointment, during 1988, of former associates of Bokassa, Dacko and Patasse to prominent public offices (including the designation of Henri Maidou as President of the Union Bancaire en Afrique Centrale) was widely perceived to be an indication of Kolingba's attempts to consolidate national unity. A reallocation of ministerial portfolios occurred in January 1989, as a result of which Jean Bengue (a government minister at the time of the second Dacko presidency) and Hugues Debozeindi (formerly an influential member of the MLPC) were appointed to the Council of Ministers. A further government reshuffle occurred in June. In August, however, 12 opponents of the Kolingba regime, including members of the Front patriotique oubanguien-Parti du travail (FPO-PT) and the leader of the Rassemblement populaire pour la reconstruction de la Centrafrique (RPRC), Brig.-Gen. François Bozize, were arrested in Benin, where they had been living in exile. (During 1988 it was reported that President Kolingba had invited Bozize, one of the alleged perpetrators of the 1982 coup attempt, to return to the CAR.) In October 1989 the Government confirmed that the dissidents were being detained in the CAR, following their extradition from Benin.

During 1990 demands for higher salaries and improved working conditions resulted in unrest among teachers, university staff, students, hospital workers and civil servants, which escalated into a general strike in late November. In addition, pressure was exerted on the Government to introduce a multi-party political system: in May more than 250 civil servants and intellectuals petitioned the Government to convene a national conference on the future of the country. During that month an advisory committee of the RDC suggested that restrictions on the freedom of expression had contributed to the proliferation of tracts hostile to the Kolingba regime: it therefore advised a policy of greater 'openness' in government, together with increased freedom of speech. None the less, the RDC ruled that the establishment of a multi-party system in the CAR would be 'incompatible' with the country's political and economic development. In the aftermath of the advisory committee's report, Kolingba carried out a comprehensive reorganization of the Council of Ministers in June, relinquishing the defence portfolio and replacing the Ministers of Foreign Affairs and of Higher Education. In September Hugues Debozeindi was dismissed from the Ministry of Justice. In mid-October violent demonstrations by anti-Government protestors were suppressed by the security forces. Later in that month, at the first congress of the RDC, the possibility of the introduction of a multi-party system was again rejected. In December, however, the Executive Council of the RDC recommended a review of the Constitution.

Following his accession to power, Kolingba was anxious to secure international support for his regime, notably from France, which remains the country's principal source of budgetary and bilateral development aid. French military forces stationed in the CAR were used in support operations for the Government of Chad during that country's conflict with Libya. Kolingba visited France and the Federal Republic of Germany in 1988. In the same year it was announced that diplomatic relations with the USSR, which had been suspended in 1980, were to be resumed.

In January 1989, following the CAR's recognition of the declaration, by the Palestine Liberation Organization, of an independent State of Palestine, it was announced that the Kolingba Government was to re-establish diplomatic relations with Israel (which had been severed in 1973). In May 1989 diplomatic relations with Sudan were suspended, and the border with that country closed, when Sudan, in accordance with the boycott by the Arab states of all links with Israel, refused to allow the aircraft in which Kolingba was travelling, on an official visit to Israel, to cross its airspace. Kolingba's visit was postponed until July, when he travelled to Israel via Zaire and Europe. The CAR and Sudan restored diplomatic relations in September of that year.

Government

Under the terms of the November 1986 Constitution, executive power is vested in the President of the Republic, and legislative power in the bicameral Congress. This consists of a 52-seat National Assembly, whose sessions are held at the summons of the President, and an Economic and Regional Council, one-half of the members of which are elected by the Assembly and one-half appointed by the President. Both the President and the Assembly are elected by direct universal suffrage, the former for a six-year term and the latter for a five-year term. The Rassemblement démocratique centrafricain (RDC), officially founded in February 1987, is the sole legal political party, and its president is the President of the Republic. All 142 candidates in the July 1987 elections to the National Assembly were members of the RDC. Members of the Council of Ministers are appointed by the President. For administrative purposes, the country is divided into 16 prefectures and 52 sub-prefectures. At community level there are 18 communes de plein exercice, 39 communes de moyen exercice and 113 communes rurales.

Defence

In June 1990 the armed forces numbered about 3,800 men (army 3,500; air force 300), with a further 2,700 men in paramilitary forces. Military service is selective and lasts for two years. France maintains a force of 1,200 troops in the CAR. Estimated defence expenditure in 1987 was 5,610m. francs CFA.

Economic Affairs

In 1988, according to estimates by the World Bank, the CAR's gross national product (GNP), measured at average 1986-88 prices, was US $1,080m., equivalent to $390 per head. During 1980-88, it was estimated, GNP increased, in real terms, at an average annual rate of 1.8%, although GNP per head declined by 0.7% per year. Over the same period, the population increased by an average of 2.5%, and the country's gross domestic product (GDP) increased, in real terms, by an annual average of 2.1%.

Agriculture (including forestry and fishing) contributed 44% of GDP in 1988. About 63.7% of the working population were employed in the sector in 1989. The principal cash crops are coffee (which accounted for 22.6% of export earnings in 1986) and cotton. The major subsistence crops are cassava (manioc) and yams. In spite of attempts by the Government to encourage the development of the livestock sector, the CAR remains dependent on imports of meat. The exploitation of the country's large forest resources represents a significant source of export revenue (wood exports accounting for 17.7% of the total in 1986); however, the full potential of this sector has yet to be realized, owing to the inadequacy of the transport infrastructure. During 1980-88 agricultural production increased by an annual average of 2.6%.

THE CENTRAL AFRICAN REPUBLIC

Introductory Survey, Statistical Survey

Industry (including mining, manufacturing, construction and power) contributed 13% of GDP in 1987. About 6.3% of the labour force were employed in the sector in 1980. During 1980–88 industrial production increased by an annual average of 2.0%.

Mining contributed 2.5% of GDP in 1985. The principal activity is the extraction of diamonds (exports of which contributed 27% of total export revenue in 1986). Deposits of gold are also exploited. The development of uranium resources awaits an increase in international prices for this commodity. Deposits of iron ore, copper and manganese have also been located.

The manufacturing sector, which contributed 8% of GDP in 1987, is based upon the processing of primary products. In 1986 the major activities, measured by gross value of output, were the processing of foods, beverages and tobacco, furniture, fixtures and paper and textiles.

In the late 1980s almost 80% of electrical energy generated within the CAR was derived from the country's two hydroelectric power installations. Imports of fuel products comprised 8% of the value of merchandise imports in 1988.

In 1987 the CAR recorded a visible trade deficit of US $70.6m., and there was a deficit of $75.2m. on the current account of the balance of payments. In 1982 the principal source of imports (53.3%) was France, which was also the principal market for exports (44.1%). Other major trading partners in that year were the Belgo-Luxembourg Economic Union, Zaire and Israel. By the early 1990s Germany had become established as a major trading partner. The principal exports in 1988 were diamonds, coffee, wood and cotton. The principal imports in 1980 were machinery and transport equipment, basic manufactures, food and live animals, chemicals and related products and beverages and tobacco.

A budget deficit of 54,100m. francs CFA was recorded in 1989. Budget estimates for 1990 envisaged a deficit of 48,500m. francs CFA. The CAR's total external public debt was US $584m. at the end of 1988. In that year the total cost of debt-servicing was equivalent to 5.9% of export earnings. The annual rate of inflation averaged 6.7% in 1980–88. Consumer prices declined at an average annual rate of 4.0% in 1988, but increased by an average of 0.7% in 1989.

The CAR is a member of the Central African organs of the Franc Zone (see p. 156) and of the Communauté Economique des Etats de l'Afrique Centrale (CEEAC, see p. 223).

The CAR's land-locked position, together with the inadequacy of the transport infrastructure and the country's vulnerability to adverse climatic conditions and to fluctuations in international prices for coffee and cotton, has impeded sustained economic growth. Since the mid-1980s, adjustment efforts (that have been implemented with financial assistance from the IMF and the World Bank) have sought to promote growth and diversification in the agricultural sector; retrenchment measures have been undertaken in the public sector, while the participation in the economy of private enterprise has been encouraged.

Social Welfare

An Employment Code guarantees a minimum wage for 60,000 employees and provides for the payment of benefits to compensate for accidents at work. In 1984 there were 7,023 hospital beds in the CAR (one per 371 inhabitants), but only 112 physicians were working in the country.

Education

Education is officially compulsory for eight years between six and 14 years of age. Primary education begins at the age of six and lasts for six years. Secondary education begins at the age of 12 and lasts for up to seven years, comprising a first cycle of four years and a second of three years. In 1987 an estimated 49% of children in the relevant age-group (59% of boys; 39% of girls) attended primary schools, while secondary enrolment was equivalent to only 12% (boys 17%; girls 6%). According to estimates by UNESCO, the adult illiteracy rate in 1985 averaged 59.8% (males 46.7%; females 71.4%). In January 1986 a three-year project, aimed at improving educational facilities in rural areas, was initiated, with the African Development Fund providing US $7.6m. in finance. In 1987 the Government announced a six-year project aiming to improve the quality of primary education and the management of educational resources. The project also envisaged a scholarship system for higher education and a development plan for the University of Bangui. The International Development Association (IDA) was to assist the $20.7m. plan with a credit of $18m. French aid to the education sector totalled more than 1,000m. francs CFA in 1988/89.

Public Holidays

1991: 1 January (New Year), 29 March (Anniversary of death of Barthélemy Boganda), 1 April (Easter Monday), 1 May (May Day), 9 May (Ascension Day), 20 May (Whit Monday), 30 June (National Day of Prayer), 13 August (Independence Day), 15 August (Assumption), 1 November (All Saints' Day), 1 December (National Day), 25 December (Christmas).

1992: 1 January (New Year), 29 March (Anniversary of death of Barthélemy Boganda), 20 April (Easter Monday), 1 May (May Day), 28 May (Ascension Day), 8 June (Whit Monday), 30 June (National Day of Prayer), 13 August (Independence Day), 15 August (Assumption), 1 November (All Saints' Day), 1 December (National Day), 25 December (Christmas).

Weights and Measures

The metric system is officially in force.

Statistical Survey

Source (unless otherwise stated): Direction de la Statistique Générale et des Etudes Economiques, BP 696, Bangui; tel. 61-45-74.

Area and Population

AREA, POPULATION AND DENSITY

Area (sq km)	622,984*
Population (census of 8–22 December 1975)	
Males	985,224
Females	1,069,386
Total	2,054,610
Population (official estimates)	
1982 (31 December)	2,442,000
1984 (31 December)	2,607,626
1986 (mid-year)	2,710,000
Density (per sq km) at mid-1986	4.4

* 240,535 sq miles.

PRINCIPAL TOWNS

Bangui (capital), population 473,817 (Dec. 1984 estimate); Berbérati 100,000, Bouar 55,000 (1982 estimates).

BIRTHS AND DEATHS (UN estimates, annual averages)

	1975–80	1980–85	1985–90
Birth rate (per 1,000)	44.9	44.6	44.3
Death rate (per 1,000)	23.5	21.8	19.7

Source: UN, *World Population Prospects: 1988.*

THE CENTRAL AFRICAN REPUBLIC

ECONOMICALLY ACTIVE POPULATION
(ILO estimates, '000 persons at mid-1980)

	Males	Females	Total
Agriculture, etc.	436	432	868
Industry	56	20	76
Services	131	124	255
Total	623	576	1,200

Source: ILO, *Economically Active Population Estimates and Projections, 1950–2025*.

Mid-1989 (estimates in '000): Agriculture, etc. 868; Total 1,363 (Source: FAO, *Production Yearbook*).

Agriculture

PRINCIPAL CROPS ('000 metric tons)

	1987	1988	1989
Rice (paddy)	11	14	10*
Maize	66	70	70*
Millet and sorghum	49*	59†	65*
Cassava (Manioc)	529	533	540*
Yams*	220	230	230
Taro (Coco yam)*	59	60	61
Groundnuts (in shell)	88	97	100*
Sesame seed	16	18	20*
Cottonseed	19	16	15*
Pumpkins, squash and gourds	12	13	14*
Oranges*	14	14	14
Mangoes*	6	7	7
Bananas*	84	86	87
Plantains*	65	66	67
Coffee (green)	21	25	25*
Tobacco (leaves)	1	1*	1*
Cotton (lint)	8	11	11†

* FAO estimate(s).   † Unofficial estimates.
Source: FAO, *Production Yearbook*.

LIVESTOCK ('000 head, year ending September)

	1987	1988	1989
Cattle	2,306	2,390	2,495
Goats	1,135	1,159	1,200
Sheep	117	120	130
Pigs	371	382	397

Chickens (million): 3 in 1987; 3* in 1988; 3* in 1989.
* FAO estimates.
Source: FAO, *Production Yearbook*.

LIVESTOCK PRODUCTS (FAO estimates, metric tons)

	1987	1988	1989
Beef and veal	40,000	42,000	43,000
Mutton and lamb	1,000	1,000	1,000
Goats' meat	3,000	4,000	4,000
Pig meat	13,000	14,000	14,000
Poultry meat	2,000	2,000	2,000
Other meat	8,000	7,000	8,000
Cows' milk	5,000	5,000	5,000
Cattle hides (fresh)	5,871	6,094	6,292
Sheep skins (fresh)	20,440	21,280	22,400
Hen eggs	990	1,008	1,026
Honey	7,300	7,400	7,600

Source: FAO, *Production Yearbook*.

Forestry

ROUNDWOOD REMOVALS ('000 cubic metres, excluding bark)

	1986	1987	1988*
Sawlogs, veneer logs and logs for sleepers	198	154	154
Other industrial wood*	229	234	240
Fuel wood	2,990*	3,055	3,055
Total	3,417	3,443	3,449

*FAO estimates.
Source: FAO, *Yearbook of Forest Products*.

SAWNWOOD PRODUCTION ('000 cubic metres)

	1986	1987	1988*
Total (incl. boxboards)	54	52	52

* FAO estimate.
Source: FAO, *Yearbook of Forest Products*.

Fishing

('000 metric tons, live weight)

	1986	1987	1988
Total catch (freshwater fish)	13	13	13

Source: FAO, *Yearbook of Fishery Statistics*.

Mining

	1984	1985	1986
Gold (kg)*	216	188	186
Gem diamonds ('000 carats)	236	245†	245†
Industrial diamonds ('000 carats)	101	105	165

* Metal content of ore (Source: US Bureau of Mines).
† Provisional or estimated figures.
Source: Direction Générale des Mines et de la Géologie.

1987: Gold (kg, metal content of ore) 224; Gem diamonds ('000 carats) 304; Industrial diamonds ('000 carats) 109 (Source: UN, *Industrial Statistics Yearbook*).

THE CENTRAL AFRICAN REPUBLIC

Industry

SELECTED PRODUCTS

	1983	1984	1985
Beer (hectolitres)	210,715	217,771	275,560
Soft drinks (hectolitres)	56,691	46,204	49,758
Cigarettes and cigars (million)	436	447	572
Woven cotton fabrics ('000 sq metres)*	4,000	4,000	n.a.
Footwear ('000 pairs)	266	582	611
Motor cycles (number)	5,610	4,020	4,515
Bicycles (number)	2,939	3,045	3,103
Electric energy (million kWh)	69	74	78

* UN estimates.

1986: Beer ('000 hectolitres) 280; Soft drinks ('000 hectolitres) 59; Cigarettes and cigars (million) 440; Footwear ('000 pairs) 544; Motor cycles (number) 3,000; Bicycles (number) 3,000; Electric energy (million kWh) 94.

1987: Beer ('000 hectolitres) 299; Soft drinks ('000 hectolitres) 68; Cigarettes and cigars (million) 476; Footwear ('000 pairs) 159; Motor cycles (number) 3,000; Bicycles (number) 1,000; Electric energy (million kWh) 92.

Source: UN, *Industrial Statistics Yearbook*.

Finance

CURRENCY AND EXCHANGE RATES

Monetary Units
100 centimes = 1 franc de la Coopération financière en Afrique centrale (CFA).

Denominations
Coins: 1, 2, 5, 10, 25, 50 and 100 francs CFA.
Notes: 100, 500, 1,000, 5,000 and 10,000 francs CFA.

French Franc, Sterling and Dollar Equivalents
(30 September 1990)
1 French franc = 50 francs CFA;
£1 sterling = 491.1 francs CFA;
US $1 = 262.1 francs CFA;
1,000 francs CFA = £2.036 = $3.815.

Average Exchange Rate (francs CFA per US $)
1987 300.54
1988 297.85
1989 319.01

BUDGET (million francs CFA)

Revenue	1988	1989	1990*
Fiscal receipts	35,200	35,900	40,600
Non-fiscal receipts	5,000	7,800	6,200
Total	40,200	43,700	46,800

Expenditure	1988	1989	1990*
Current expenditure	43,700	42,600	49,600
Capital expenditure	26,800	38,000	45,800
Extra-budgetary expenditure	800	—	—
Net lending	9,400	17,200	—
Total	80,700	97,800	95,300

* Budget estimates.
Source: *La Zone Franc—Rapport 1989*.

CENTRAL BANK RESERVES (US $ million at 31 December)

	1987	1988	1989
Gold*	5.37	4.52	n.a.
IMF special drawing rights	6.99	12.31	n.a.
Reserve position in IMF	0.16	0.15	0.14
Foreign exchange	89.58	96.01	113.08
Total	102.10	112.99	n.a.

* Valued at market-related prices.
Source: IMF, *International Financial Statistics*.

MONEY SUPPLY ('000 million francs CFA at 31 December)

	1987	1988	1989
Currency outside banks	41.46	41.58	42.24
Demand deposits at commercial and development banks	11.78	10.85	14.42
Checking deposits at post office	0.31	0.31	n.a.
Total money	53.55	52.74	56.66

Source: IMF, *International Financial Statistics*.

NATIONAL ACCOUNTS (million francs CFA at current prices)
Gross Domestic Product by Economic Activity

	1983	1984	1985
Agriculture, hunting, forestry and fishing	99,372	109,275	130,927
Mining and quarrying	6,155	7,622	7,822
Manufacturing	19,065	21,691	23,149
Electricity, gas and water	1,285	2,399	2,557
Construction	5,074	7,297	7,946
Trade, restaurants and hotels	51,581	58,291	68,015
Transport, storage and communications	10,230	11,497	12,982
Finance, insurance, real estate and business services	8,962	9,756	10,806
Government services	30,289	28,443	30,372
Other community, social and personal services	11,337	12,454	13,973
Sub-total	243,350	268,725	308,549
Import duties	13,220	15,842	16,710
Less Imputed bank service charge	5,515	5,840	6,582
GDP in purchasers' values	251,055	278,727	318,677
GDP at constant 1982 prices	230,969	247,657	256,074

Source: UN, *National Accounts Statistics*.

THE CENTRAL AFRICAN REPUBLIC

Statistical Survey

BALANCE OF PAYMENTS (US $ million)

	1985	1986	1987
Merchandise exports f.o.b.	131.0	129.5	127.1
Merchandise imports f.o.b.	−167.7	−201.0	−197.7
Trade balance	−36.7	−71.5	−70.6
Exports of services	53.4	58.8	70.6
Imports of services	−122.1	−156.8	−176.4
Balance on goods and services	−105.4	−169.5	−176.4
Private unrequited transfers (net)	−11.8	−19.5	−23.7
Government unrequited transfers (net)	68.5	102.4	124.8
Current balance	−48.6	−86.6	−75.2
Direct capital investment (net)	2.4	6.9	9.3
Other long-term capital (net)	43.1	78.6	70.9
Short-term capital (net)	−13.9	−9.2	−16.8
Net errors and omissions	−8.1	7.2	0.1
Total (net monetary movements)	−25.1	−3.0	−11.6
Valuation changes (net)	10.8	6.6	10.3
Exceptional financing (net)	6.7	9.7	22.7
Official financing (net)	—	−0.3	—
Changes in reserves	−7.6	13.1	21.4

Source: IMF, *International Financial Statistics*.

External Trade

Note: The data exclude trade with other countries in the Customs and Economic Union of Central Africa (UDEAC): Cameroon, Chad (since December 1984), the Congo, Equatorial Guinea (since January 1985) and Gabon.

PRINCIPAL COMMODITIES (distribution by SITC, US $'000)

Imports c.i.f.	1978	1979	1980
Food and live animals	5,346	8,148	11,244
Cereals and cereal preparations	1,755	4,166	5,400
Wheat flour	803	2,653	3,603
Beverages and tobacco	3,734	2,591	5,135
Beverages	3,213	2,192	4,396
Alcoholic beverages	3,056	2,039	4,109
Chemicals and related products	5,070	9,393	9,490
Medicinal and pharmaceutical products	1,884	3,200	4,588
Medicaments	1,710	3,040	4,364
Pesticides, disinfectants, etc.	405	3,331	1,497
Basic manufactures	11,802	11,448	15,393
Non-metallic mineral manufactures	2,233	2,375	3,418
Machinery and transport equipment	21,609	27,407	27,243
Power generating machinery and equipment	1,326	4,954	1,873
Internal combustion piston engines and parts	911	4,184	1,245
Machinery specialized for particular industries	1,604	3,167	2,957
General industrial machinery, equipment and parts	3,483	5,341	3,970
Electrical machinery, apparatus, etc.	3,187	2,974	4,707

Imports c.i.f.—continued	1978	1979	1980
Road vehicles and parts (excl. tyres, engines and electrical parts)	11,182	9,745	13,120
Motor vehicles for goods transport and special purposes	5,022	4,417	4,409
Goods vehicles (lorries and trucks)	4,983	4,128	3,989
Miscellaneous manufactured articles	6,601	4,938	8,008
Total (incl. others)	56,662	66,530	80,461

Source: UN, *International Trade Statistics Yearbook*.

Total imports (million francs CFA): 25,646 in 1981; 41,306 in 1982; 25,951 in 1983; 38,193 in 1984; 50,686 in 1985; 87,190 in 1986 (Source: IMF, *International Financial Statistics*).

Exports f.o.b.	1978	1979	1980
Food and live animals	20,957	20,447	31,766
Coffee, tea, cocoa and spices	20,956	20,358	31,759
Coffee (green and roasted)	20,830	20,265	31,611
Crude materials (inedible) except fuels	21,441	20,893	47,678
Cork and wood	11,687	9,787	33,212
Sawlogs and veneer logs	6,547	6,777	27,407
Sawn lumber	5,140	3,010	5,805
Textile fibres and waste	4,426	5,364	8,645
Cotton	4,426	5,364	8,644
Bones, ivory, horns, etc.	3,856	4,594	4,277
Basic manufactures	26,924	35,296	28,945
Non-metallic mineral manufactures	26,860	35,019	28,908
Diamonds (non-industrial)	26,860	35,019	28,898
Gold (non-monetary)	—	—	4,163
Total (incl. others)	71,717	79,547	115,400

Source: UN, *International Trade Statistics Yearbook*.

1981 (million francs CFA): Coffee 7,263; Wood 9,642; Cotton 5,294; Diamonds 9,035; Total (incl. others) 21,323.
1982 (million francs CFA): Coffee 9,927; Wood 7,833; Cotton 2,738; Diamonds 9,046; Total (incl. others) 35,461.
1983 (million francs CFA): Coffee 14,674; Wood 8,414; Cotton 5,628; Diamonds 8,114; Total (incl. others) 28,405.
1984 (million francs CFA): Coffee 10,553; Wood 9,053; Cotton 8,988; Diamonds 13,524; Total (incl. others) 37,022.
1985 (million francs CFA): Coffee 18,469; Wood 9,025; Cotton 6,789; Diamonds 14,173; Total (incl. others) 41,217.
1986 (million francs CFA): Coffee 10,285; Wood 8,064; Cotton 4,391; Diamonds 12,273; Total (incl. others) 45,480.
1987 (million francs CFA): Coffee 5,180; Wood 5,976; Cotton 2,742; Diamonds 15,056.
1988 (million francs CFA): Coffee 7,469; Wood 4,760; Cotton 2,355; Diamonds 14,316.
1989 (million francs CFA): Coffee 8,745.

Source: IMF, *International Financial Statistics*.

PRINCIPAL TRADING PARTNERS (US $'000)

Imports c.i.f.	1979	1980	1982*
Belgium/Luxembourg	1,100	1,298	1,290
Chad	226	260	1,160
Côte d'Ivoire	1,359	541	480
France	42,209	48,851	65,750
Germany, Federal Republic	2,261	2,441	3,410
Guinea-Bissau	402	1,015	n.a.
Italy	720	1,314	1,970
Japan	2,897	5,815	5,840
Netherlands	1,659	2,895	3,330
Nigeria	236	1,157	1,250
Spain	1,819	1,831	1,640
United Kingdom	2,176	2,221	1,670
USA	3,070	2,779	5,290
Zaire	952	2,145	11,130
Total (incl. others)	66,523	80,461	123,380

* **1981** (US $'000): Total imports 95,000.

THE CENTRAL AFRICAN REPUBLIC

Exports f.o.b.	1979	1980	1982†
Belgium/Luxembourg	16,993	16,550	24,720
Chad	527	466	1,780
Denmark	876	1,741	1,100
France	36,285	59,434	47,320
Germany, Federal Republic	154	470	2,040
Israel	9,113	8,990	9,600
Italy	1,359	2,827	970
Netherlands	1,530	1,051	260
Portugal	42	159	2,370
Romania	1,221	738	n.a.
Spain	678	3,046	690
Sudan	175	377	2,240
Switzerland	596	1,103	3,660
United Kingdom	1,669	2,873	2,300
USA	6,512	4,745	5,280
Yugoslavia	263	4,728	1,670
Total (incl. others)	79,547	111,237	107,320

† **1981** (US $'000): Total exports 79,000.

Source: UN, *International Trade Statistics Yearbook*.

Transport

ROAD TRAFFIC (motor vehicles in use at 31 December)

	1981	1982	1983
Passenger cars	23,750	38,930	41,321
Buses and coaches	79	103	118
Goods vehicles	3,060	3,190	3,720
Motorcycles and scooters	170	278	397
Mopeds	62,518	71,421	79,952

Source: IRF, *World Road Statistics*.

1987: 46,000 passenger cars and 5,000 commercial vehicles (Source: UN Economic Commission for Africa, *African Statistical Yearbook*).

INLAND WATERWAYS TRAFFIC—INTERNATIONAL SHIPPING (metric tons)

	1983	1984	1985
Freight unloaded at Bangui	105,900	89,000	115,500
Freight loaded at Bangui	38,100	49,200	44,300
Total	144,000	138,200	159,800

CIVIL AVIATION (traffic on scheduled services)*

	1983	1984	1985
Kilometres flown (million)	2.4	2.4	2.6
Passengers carried ('000)	114	118	123
Passenger-km (million)	219	220	243
Freight ton-km (million)	18.8	17.5	18.5

*Including an apportionment of the traffic of Air Afrique.
Source: UN, *Statistical Yearbook*.

Tourism

	1985	1986	1987
Foreign tourist arrivals	7,000	4,000	4,000

Source: UN Economic Commission for Africa, *African Statistical Yearbook*.

Communications Media

	1985	1986	1987
Radio receivers	150,000	158,000	163,000
Television receivers	4,500	5,000	6,000

Source: UNESCO, *Statistical Yearbook*.

Telephones: 13,000 in use in 1987 (Source: UN Economic Commission for Africa, *African Statistical Yearbook*).

Education

(1986)

	Institutions	Teachers	Pupils Males	Pupils Females	Pupils Total
Pre-primary	164	360	6,947	4,503	11,450
Primary	1,004	4,544	169,148	105,031	274,179
Secondary General	n.a.	1,013	34,857	13,701	48,558
Teacher-training	n.a.	22	68	4	72
Vocational	n.a.	111	1,145	915	2,060
Higher*	n.a.	489	2,102	272	2,374

* 1985 figures.

1987: Primary 1,014 institutions, 4,563 teachers, 286,422 pupils (males 177,194; females 109,228); Secondary general 1,013 teachers, 44,250 pupils (males 32,267; females 11,983), teacher-training 45 pupils (males 44; females 1), vocational 121 teachers, 1,963 pupils (males 1,077; females 886); Higher 2,754 pupils (males 2,383; females 371).

Source: UNESCO, *Statistical Yearbook*.

Directory

The Constitution

The Constitution that had been promulgated on 6 February 1981 was suspended following the coup of 1 September 1981. All legislative and executive powers were assumed by the Military Committee for National Recovery (Comité militaire pour le redressement national—CMRN). The CMRN was dissolved on 21 September 1985, and a 22-member Council of Ministers was appointed. The present Constitution of the Central African Republic was adopted following its approval by referendum on 21 November 1986.

PREAMBLE

Affirms the adoption by the Central African people of the principles of liberty and equality before the law of all citizens, regardless of sex, race and culture; of freedom of education and equality of access to the organs of justice; of freedom of expression, movement and assembly, and of the inalienable status of the individual.

SOVEREIGNTY

The Central African Republic is one and indivisible. It is a sovereign and democratic state. The national language is Sango, and the official language is French. National sovereignty belongs to the people, who exercise it through their representative or through referenda. Suffrage is universal, equal and secret. The Rassemblement Démocratique Centrafricain is the sole political party.

THE PRESIDENCY

The President of the Republic is Head of State and Commander-in-Chief of the national armed forces. He conducts the nation's policies, negotiates and ratifies treaties, promulgates laws, has power to make regulations and is responsible for civilian and military appointments. The President is elected for a six-year term by direct universal suffrage. He is elected by an absolute majority of votes cast. If such is not obtained at the first ballot, a second ballot is to take place within two weeks of the first, contested by the two candidates gaining the largest number of votes in the first ballot. The election of the new President is to take place not less than 20 days and not more than 40 days before the expiration of the mandate of the President in office. However, the President may choose to hold a referendum to determine whether or not his mandate is to be renewed. Should the electorate reject the proposal, the President is to resign and a new presidential election is to be held two weeks after the publication of the results of the referendum. The Presidency is to become vacant only in the event of the President's death, resignation, condemnation by the High Court of Justice (see below) or permanent physical incapacitation, as certified by a Special Committee comprising the presidents of the National Assembly, the Economic and Regional Council and the Supreme Court (see below). The election of a new President must take place not less than 20 days and not more than 40 days following the occurrence of a vacancy, during which time the president of the National Assembly is to act as interim President, with limited powers.

The President appoints and dismisses ministers, who are permitted to hold no other office, and presides over the Council of Ministers. He promulgates laws adopted by the National Assembly or by the Congress, and may call referenda on proposed legislation. Laws are promulgated within two weeks of their adoption by Parliament or by referendum. The President has the power to dissolve the National Assembly, in which event legislative elections must take place not less than 20 and not more than 40 days following its dissolution. Provisions are made for the short-term implementation of decrees adopted by the Council of Ministers and for the introduction of emergency measures in the event of a serious threat to national unity.

PARLIAMENT

This is composed of the National Assembly and the Economic and Regional Council, which, when sitting together, are to be known as the Congress. The primary function of the Congress is to pass organic laws in implementation of the Constitution, whenever these are not submitted to a referendum.

The National Assembly

The National Assembly is composed of deputies elected by direct universal suffrage for a five-year term. Its formation and functioning are determined by an organic law. Its president is designated by, and from within, its bureau. Legislation may be introduced either by the President of the Republic or by a consensus of one-third of the members of the Assembly. Provisions are made for the rendering inadmissible of any law providing for the execution of projects carrying a financial cost to the State which exceeds their potential value. The National Assembly holds two ordinary sessions per year of 60 days each, at the summons of the President of the Republic, who may also summon it to hold extraordinary sessions with a pre-determined agenda. Sessions of the National Assembly are opened and closed by presidential decree.

The Economic and Regional Council

The Economic and Regional Council is composed of representatives from the principal sectors of economic and social activity. One-half of its members are appointed by the President, and the remaining half are elected by the National Assembly on the nomination of that body's president. Its formation and functioning are determined by an organic law. It acts as an advisory body in matters referred to it by the President, as well as in all legislative proposals of an economic and social nature.

The Congress

The Congress has the same president and bureau as the National Assembly. An absolute majority of its members is needed to pass organic laws, as well as laws pertaining to the amendment of the Constitution which have not been submitted to a referendum. It defines development priorities and may meet, at the summons of the President, to ratify treaties or to determine the existence of a state of war.

THE JUDICIARY

The Supreme Court

Members are appointed by the President and may hold no other office. The organization and functioning of the Supreme Court, as well as its areas of responsibility, are determined by an organic law.

The High Court of Justice

The High Court of Justice is composed of nine judges, of whom one-third are appointed by the President of the Republic, one-third by the president of the Congress and one-third by the president of the Supreme Court. Its president is appointed by the President of the Republic and has the casting vote. The High Court of Justice has the power to try ministers, members of the Congress and all persons guilty of breaching state security. Its organization and functioning are determined by an organic law. The President of the Republic may be judged by the High Court of Justice only if he is indicted on a charge of high treason by a three-quarters majority of members of the Congress.

Additional clauses deal with the administration of the CAR's 'collectivités territoriales' and with the procedure for constitutional amendments.

The Government

HEAD OF STATE

President: Gen. ANDRÉ KOLINGBA (assumed power 1 September 1981; elected 21 November 1986 for a six-year term).

COUNCIL OF MINISTERS
(December 1990)

Prime Minister: Gen. ANDRÉ KOLINGBA.

Minister of State at the Presidency, in charge of the Cabinet Secretariat and of Relations with the National Assembly: EDOUARD FRANCK.

Minister of State at the Presidency, in charge of Economy and Finance, Planning and International Co-operation: DIEUDONNÉ WAZOUA.

Minister of Defence and Justice and Keeper of the Seals: Lt-Col CHRISTOPHE GRELOMBE.

Minister of the Interior and Territorial Administration: THOMAS MATOUKA.

Minister of Foreign Affairs: LAURENT GOMINA-PAMPALI.

Minister of Primary, Secondary and Technical Education: JOSEPH MABINGUI.

Minister of Higher Education: JEAN-MARIE BASSIA.

THE CENTRAL AFRICAN REPUBLIC   *Directory*

Minister of Transport and Civil Aviation: Pierre Gonifei-Ngaibonanou.

Minister of the Civil Service, Labour, Social Security and Professional Training: Gaston Azibolo.

Minister of Public Health and Social Affairs: Geneviève Lombilo.

Minister of Rural Development: Casimir Amakpio.

Minister of Posts and Telecommunications: Jean Tchombego.

Minister of Public Works and Territorial Development: Dieudonné Nana.

Minister of Energy, Mines, Geology and Water Resources: Dieudonné Padoudji-Yadjoua.

Minister of Water, Forests, Wildlife, Fisheries and Tourism: Raymond Mbitikon.

Minister of Trade, Industry and Small- and Medium-scale Enterprises: Timothée Marboua.

Minister of Communications, Arts and Culture: Tony da Silva.

Secretary of State for Economy and Finance in charge of Budget and Debt Management: Patrice Endjingboma.

Secretary of State for Planning, Statistics and International Co-operation: Thierry Bingaba.

Secretary of State for the Interior and Territorial Administration: Augustin Mbanda.

Secretary of State for Energy, Mines, Geology and Water Resources: Octave Kossi Oudegbe.

Secretary of State for Foreign Affairs: Jules Kouale-Yabro.

Secretary of State for the Cabinet Secretariat: Christian Yamale.

Secretary of State for Social Affairs: Antoinette Teguedere.

MINISTRIES

Office of the President: Palais de la Renaissance, Bangui; tel. 61-03-23; telex 5253.

Ministry of the Civil Service, Labour, Social Security and Professional Training: Bangui; tel. 61-01-44.

Ministry of Communications, Arts and Culture: BP 1290, Bangui; telex 5301.

Ministry of Defence: Bangui; tel. 61-46-11; telex 5298.

Ministry of Economy and Finance, Planning and International Co-operation: Bangui; tel. 61-08-11; telex 5280.

Ministry of Energy, Mines, Geology and Water Resources: Bangui; telex 5243.

Ministry of Foreign Affairs: Bangui; tel. 61-15-74; telex 5213.

Ministry of the Interior and Territorial Administration: tel. 61-44-77.

Ministry of Justice: Bangui; tel. 61-16-44.

Ministry of National and Higher Education: BP 791, Bangui; telex 5333.

Ministry of Posts and Telecommunications: Bangui; tel. 61-29-46; telex 5304.

Ministry of Public Health and Social Affairs: Bangui; tel. 61-29-01.

Ministry of Public Works and Territorial Development: Bangui; tel. 61-28-00.

Ministry of Rural Development: Bangui; tel. 61-28-00.

Ministry of Trade, Industry and Small- and Medium-scale Enterprises: Bangui; tel. 61-44-88; telex 5215.

Ministry of Transport and Civil Aviation: Bangui; tel. 61-23-07; telex 5335.

Ministry of Water, Forests, Wildlife, Fisheries and Tourism: Bangui.

Legislature

According to the November 1986 Constitution, legislative power is vested in a bicameral Congress, comprising a National Assembly and an Economic and Regional Council.

ASSEMBLÉE NATIONALE

A National Assembly comprising 52 seats was elected on 31 July 1987 for a five-year term. All 142 candidates were members of the Rassemblement démocratique centrafricain (RDC).

President: Michel Docko.

Secretary-General: Émile Nicaise Mbari.

CONSEIL ÉCONOMIQUE ET RÉGIONAL

The November 1986 Constitution provides for the establishment of an Economic and Regional Council, an advisory body.

Political Organizations

Rassemblement démocratique centrafricain (RDC): Bangui; f. 1987 as sole legal political party; to be led by a congress which will meet every three years, a political bureau and a 7-mem. exec. council; a 44-mem. provisional council was appointed to oversee activities until above bodies were elected; Pres. Gen. André Kolingba; Exec. Sec. Jean-Paul Ngoupande.

In 1983 the main active opposition groups formed the **Parti révolutionnaire centrafricain (PRC)**, which, in late 1990, comprised:

Front patriotique oubanguien–Parti du travail (FPO–PT): f. 1979 as FPO; Leader Abel Goumba.

Mouvement centrafricain pour la libération nationale (MCLN): Leader Dr Iddi Lala.

Mouvement pour la libération du peuple centrafricain (MLPC): f. 1979; Leader Ange Patasse.

Rassemblement populaire pour la reconstruction de la Centrafrique (RPRC): Leader Brig.-Gen. François Bozize.

In December 1984 several opposition leaders formed a Provisional Government for National Salvation (in exile), under the aegis of the provisional executive council of the MLPC. The President of the Provisional Government is (former Brig.-Gen.) Alphonse Mbaikoua. In July 1986 the MLPC and the FPO–PT formed the **Front Uni**, which seeks the restoration of the 1981 Constitution and the re-establishment of a multi-party political system.

Diplomatic Representation

EMBASSIES IN THE CENTRAL AFRICAN REPUBLIC

Cameroon: BP 935, Bangui; telex 5249; Ambassador: Christopher Nsahlai.

Chad: BP 461, Bangui; telex 5220; Ambassador: El Hadj Mouli Seid.

China, People's Republic: BP 1430, Bangui; Ambassador: Zhou Xianjue.

Congo: BP 1414, Bangui; telex 5292; Chargé d'affaires: Antoine Delica.

Côte d'Ivoire: BP 930, Bangui; telex 5279; Ambassador: Jean-Marie Agnini Bile Malan.

Egypt: BP 1422, Bangui; telex 5284; Ambassador: Sameh Samy Darwiche.

France: blvd du Général de Gaulle, BP 884, Bangui; tel. 61-30-00; telex 5218; Ambassador: Antoine Frasseto.

Gabon: BP 1570, Bangui; tel. 61-29-97; telex 5234; Ambassador: François de Paule Moulengui.

Germany: ave G. A. Nasser, BP 901, Bangui; tel. 61-07-46; telex 5219; Ambassador: Ulrich Dreesen.

Holy See: ave Boganda, BP 1447, Bangui; tel. 61-26-54; Apostolic Pro-Nuncio: Most Rev. Beniamino Stella, Titular Archbishop of Midila.

Iraq: Bangui; telex 5287; Chargé d'affaires: Abdul Karim Aswad.

Japan: BP 1367, Bangui; tel. 61-06-68; telex 5204; Chargé d'affaires: Kiyoji Yamakawa.

Korea, Democratic People's Republic: BP 1816, Bangui; Ambassador: Y. Yong-hak.

Libya: BP 1732, Bangui; telex 5317; Head of Mission: El-Senuse Abdallah.

Nigeria: BP 1010, Bangui; tel. 61-39-00; telex 5269; Chargé d'affaires: T. A. O. Odegbile.

Romania: BP 1435, Bangui; Chargé d'affaires a.i.: Mihai Gaftoniuc.

USA: blvd David Dacko, BP 924, Bangui; tel. 61-02-00; fax 61-44-94; Ambassador: Daniel H. Simpson.

Yugoslavia: BP 1049, Bangui; Chargé d'affaires: Spiridon Petrović; temporarily closed February 1988.

Zaire: BP 989, Bangui; telex 5232; Ambassador: Embe Isea Mbambe.

Judicial System

Supreme Court: BP 926, Bangui; tel. 61-41-33; highest judicial organ; acts as a Court of Cassation in civil and penal cases and as

THE CENTRAL AFRICAN REPUBLIC

Court of Appeal in administrative cases; made up of four chambers: constitutional, judicial, administrative and financial.

President of the Supreme Court: ANTOINE GROTHE.

There is also a Court of Appeal, a Criminal Court, 16 tribunaux de grande instance, 37 tribunaux d'instance, six labour tribunals and a permanent military tribunal. A High Court of Justice was established following the adoption of the November 1986 Constitution, and is competent to try all cases of crimes against state security, including high treason by the President of the Republic.

Religion

An estimated 60% of the population hold animist beliefs, 5% are Muslims and 35% Christians; Roman Catholics comprise about 20% of the total population.

CHRISTIANITY
The Roman Catholic Church

The Central African Republic comprises one archdiocese and five dioceses. There were an estimated 500,000 adherents at 31 December 1989.

Bishops' Conference: Conférence Episcopale Centrafricaine, BP 1518, Bangui; tel. 61-00-02; fax 61-46-92; f. 1982; Pres. Mgr JOACHIM N'DAYEN, Archbishop of Bangui.

Archbishop of Bangui: Mgr JOACHIM N'DAYEN, Archevêché, BP 798, Bangui; tel. 61-08-98.

Protestant Church
Eglise Protestante de Bangui: Bangui.

The Press

DAILY
E Le Songo: Bangui; Sango; circ. 200.

PERIODICALS
Bangui Match: Bangui; monthly.

Le Courrier Rural: BP 850, Bangui; publ. by Chambre d'Agriculture.

Journal Officiel de la République Centrafricaine: BP 739, Bangui; f. 1974; fortnightly; economic data; Dir-Gen. GABRIEL AGBA.

Renouveau Centrafricain: Bangui; weekly.

Ta Tene (The Truth): BP 1290, Bangui; monthly.

Terre Africaine: Bangui; weekly.

NEWS AGENCIES
Agence Centrafricaine de Presse (ACAP): BP 40, Bangui; tel. 61-10-88; telex 5299; f. 1974 following nationalization of the Bangui branch of Agence France-Presse; Gen. Man. VICTOR DETO TETEYA.

TASS (USSR) is the only foreign press agency represented in the CAR.

Publisher

Government Publishing House
Imprimerie Centrafricain: BP 329, Bangui; tel. 61-00-33; f. 1974; Dir-Gen. PIERRE SALAMATE-KOILET.

Radio and Television

There were an estimated 163,000 radio receivers in use in 1987. A 100-kW transmitter came into service at Bimbo in 1970, and two 50-kW transmitters were introduced in 1984. Television broadcasting began in December 1983. There were an estimated 6,000 television receivers in use in 1987.

Radiodiffusion-Télévision Centrafrique: BP 940, Bangui; telex 2355; f. 1958 as Radiodiffusion Nationale Centrafricaine; govt-controlled; radio programmes in French and Sango; Dir F. P. ZEMONIAKO.

Finance

(cap. = capital; res = reserves; dep. = deposits; m. = million; amounts in francs CFA)

BANKING
Central Bank
Banque des Etats de l'Afrique Centrale (BEAC): BP 851, Bangui; tel. 61-24-00; telex 5236; headquarters in Yaoundé, Cameroon; f. 1973 as the central bank of issue for mem. states of the Customs and Economic Union of Central Africa (UDEAC), comprising Cameroon, the Central African Republic, Chad, the Congo, Equatorial Guinea and Gabon; cap. 36,000m., res 162,037m. (June 1989); Gov. JEAN-FÉLIX MAMALEPOT; Dir in CAR ALPHONSE KOYAMBA.

Commercial Banks
Banque de Crédit Agricole et de Développement (BCAD): 1 place de la République, BP 801, Bangui; tel. 61-32-00; telex 5207; f. 1984; 50% owned by Banque de Participation et de Placement (Switzerland), 33% state-owned; cap. 600m. (Dec. 1987); Pres. MICHEL CHAUTARD.

BIAO-Centrafrique: place de la République, BP 910, Bangui; tel. 61-46-33; telex 5233; fax 61-61-36; f. 1980; undergoing reorganization in 1990; cap. 700m. (Dec. 1988); Pres. BERTRAND LE BAIL; Dir-Gen. FRANÇOIS EPAYE.

Union Bancaire en Afrique Centrale: rue de Brazza, BP 59, Bangui; tel. 61-29-90; telex 5225; f. 1962; 60% state-owned; cap. 1,000m. (Dec. 1988); Pres. HENRI MAIDOU; Gen. Man. JOSEPH KOYAGBELE.

Investment Bank
Banque Centrafricaine d'Investissement (BCI): BP 933, Bangui; tel. 61-00-64; telex 5317; f. 1976; 34.8% state-owned; cap. 1,000m.; Pres. ALPHONSE KONGOLO; Man. Dir GÉRARD SAMBO.

Financial Institution
Caisse Autonome d'Amortissement de la République Centrafricaine: Bangui; management of state funds; Dir-Gen. Dr C. GOUYOMGBIA-KONGBA-ZEZE.

Development Agencies
Caisse Centrale de Coopération Economique: BP 817, Bangui; tel. 61-36-34; telex 5291; Dir NILS ROBIN.

Mission Française de Coopération: BP 784, Bangui; tel. 61-30-00; telex 5218; administers bilateral aid from France; Dir MICHEL LANDRY.

INSURANCE
Agence Centrafricaine d'Assurances (ACA): BP 512, Bangui; tel. 61-06-23; f. 1956; cap. 3.8m.; Dir Mme R. CERBELLAUD.

Assureurs Conseils Centrafricains Faugère et Jutheau: rue de la Kouanga, BP 743, Bangui; tel. 61-19-33; f. 1968; cap. 1m.; Dir JEAN-YVES DEBOUDÉ.

Entreprise d'Etat d'Assurances et de Réassurances (SIRIRI): ave du Président Mobutu, BP 852, Bangui; tel. 61-36-55; telex 5306; f. 1972; general; cap. 100m.; Pres. EMMANUEL DOKOUNA; Dir-Gen. JEAN-MARIE YOLLOT.

Legendre, A. & Cie: rue de la Victoire, BP 896, Bangui; cap. 1m.; Pres. and Dir-Gen. ANDRÉ LEGENDRE.

Trade and Industry

CHAMBERS OF COMMERCE
Chambre d'Agriculture, d'Elevage, des Eaux, Forêts, Chasses, Pêches et Tourisme: BP 850, Bangui; Pres. MAURICE METHOT; Sec.-Gen. ANATOLE POSSITI.

Chambre de Commerce, d'Industrie, des Mines et de l'Artisanat (CCIMA): BP 813, Bangui; tel. 61-42-55; telex 5261; Pres. BERNARD-CHRISTIAN AYANDHO; Sec.-Gen. JEAN-LOUIS GIACOMETTI (acting).

PRINCIPAL DEVELOPMENT ORGANIZATIONS
Agence de Développement de la Zone Caféière (ADECAF): BP 1935, Bangui; tel. 61-47-30; coffee producers' asscn; assists coffee marketing co-operatives; Dir-Gen. J. J. NIMIZIAMBI.

Caisse de Stabilisation et de Péréquation des Produits Agricoles (CAISTAB): BP 76, Bangui; tel. 61-08-00; telex 5278; supervises pricing and marketing of agricultural products; Dir-Gen. M. BOUNANDELE-KOUMBA.

Comptoir National du Diamant (CND): blvd B. Boganda, BP 1011, Bangui; tel. 61-07-02; telex 5262; f. 1964; cap. 195m. francs CFA; 50% state-owned, 50% owned by Diamond Distributors (USA); extraction and marketing of diamonds; Dir-Gen. M. VASSOS.

Office National des Forêts (ONF): BP 915, Bangui; tel. 61-38-27; f. 1969; reafforestation, development of forest resources; Dir-Gen. C. D. SONGUET.

Société Centrafricaine de Développement Agricole (SOCADA): ave David Dacko, BP 997, Bangui; tel. 61-30-33; telex 5212; f. 1964; reorg. 1980; cap. 1,000m. francs CFA; 75% state-owned, 25% Cie

THE CENTRAL AFRICAN REPUBLIC

française pour le développement des fibres textiles (France); cotton ginning at 20 plants, production of cotton oil (at two refineries) and groundnut oil; Pres. MAURICE METHOT; Man. Dir PATRICE ENDJINGBOMA.

Société Centrafricaine de Palmiers à Huile (CENTRAPALM): BP 1355, Bangui; tel. 61-49-40; telex 5271; fax 61-38-75; f. 1975; cap. 2,125m. francs CFA; state-owned; development of palm products; operates the Bossongo agro-industrial complex (inaugurated 1986); Pres. ANDRÉ GOMBAKO; Gen. Man. JEAN-PRIVAT MBAYE.

TRADE UNION

All trade union activities were suspended in September 1981.

Transport

A five-year programme for the modernization of the CAR's transport infrastructure, at a total projected cost of US $139m. (to be funded by bilateral and multilateral creditors), was announced in mid-1990.

RAILWAYS

There are no railways at present. There are long-term plans to connect Bangui to the Transcameroon railway. A line linking Sudan's Darfur region with the CAR's Vakaga province is also planned.

ROADS

At 31 December 1986 there were about 20,278 km of roads, including 5,044 km of main roads and 3,934 km of secondary roads. Only about 2.2% of the total network is paved. Eight main routes serve Bangui, and those that are surfaced are toll roads. Both the total road length and the condition of the roads are currently inadequate for traffic requirements. The Government has initiated a major project of road rehabilitation and construction. The CAR is linked with Cameroon by the Transafrican Lagos–Mombasa highway.

Bureau d'Affrètement Routier Centrafricain (BARC): BP 523, Bangui; tel. 61-20-55; telex 5336; Dir-Gen. J. M. LAGUEREMA-YADINGUIN.

Compagnie Nationale des Transports Routiers (CNTR): BP 330, Bangui; tel. 61-46-44; cap. 35.5m. francs CFA; state-owned; Dir-Gen. GEORGES YABADA.

Compagnie de Transports Routiers de l'Oubangui Degrain & Cie (CTRO): BP 119, Bangui; f. 1940; cap. 100m. francs CFA; Man. Mme NICOLE DEGRAIN.

INLAND WATERWAYS

There are two navigable waterways. The first, formed by the Congo and Oubangui rivers, is open all the year, except in the dry season, and can accommodate convoys of barges (of up to 800 tons load) between Bangui, Brazzaville and Pointe-Noire. The second is the river Sangha, a tributary of the Oubangui, on which traffic is also seasonal. There are two ports, at Bangui and Salo, on the rivers Oubangui and Sangha respectively. Efforts are being made to develop the stretch of river upstream from Salo to increase the transportation of timber from this area, and to develop Nola as a timber port. The 1990–95 transport development programme aims to improve the navigability of the Oubangui river.

Agence Centrafricaine des Communications Fluviales (ACCF): BP 822, Bangui; tel. 61-02-11; telex 5256; f. 1969; state-owned; development of inland waterways transport system; Man. Dir JUSTIN NDJAPOU.

Société Centrafricaine de Transports Fluviaux (SOCATRAF): BP 1445, Bangui; telex 5256; f. 1980; cap. 400m. francs CFA; 51% owned by ACCF; Man. Dir FRANÇOIS TOUSSAINT.

CIVIL AVIATION

The international airport is at Bangui-Mpoko. There are also 37 small airports for domestic services.

Air Afrique: BP 875, Bangui; tel. 61-46-60; telex 5281; see under Côte d'Ivoire; Dir in Bangui ALBERT BAGNERES.

Inter-RCA: BP 1413, Bangui; telex 5239; f. 1980 to replace Air Centrafrique; 52% state-owned, 24% by Air Afrique; extensive internal services; Man. Dir JULES BERNARD OUANDE; fleet of 1 Caravelle and 1 DC-4.

Tourism

The main tourist attractions are the waterfalls, the forests and many varieties of wild animals. There are excellent hunting and fishing opportunities. There were an estimated 4,000 tourist arrivals in 1987. In 1983 tourist receipts were about US $4m.

Office National Centrafricain du Tourisme (OCATOUR): BP 655, Bangui; tel. 61-45-66.

CHAD

Introductory Survey

Location, Climate, Language, Religion, Flag, Capital

The Republic of Chad is a land-locked country in north central Africa, bordered to the north by Libya, to the south by the Central African Republic, to the west by Niger and Cameroon and to the east by Sudan. The climate is hot and arid in the northern desert regions of the Sahara but very wet (annual rainfall 500 cm) in the south. The official languages are French and Arabic, and various African languages are also widely spoken. Almost one-half of the population are Muslims, living in the north, while most of the remainder follow animistic beliefs. About 6% are Christians. The national flag (proportions 3 by 2) has three equal vertical stripes, of blue, yellow and red. The capital is N'Djamena (formerly called Fort-Lamy).

Recent History

Formerly a province of French Equatorial Africa, Chad became an autonomous state within the French Community in November 1958. François (later Ngarta) Tombalbaye, a southerner and leader of the Parti progressiste tchadien (PPT), became Prime Minister in March 1959. Chad achieved independence on 11 August 1960, with Tombalbaye as President. In 1962 Tombalbaye banned all opposition parties, and Chad became a single-party state. Civil disturbances began in 1963, with riots in the capital, and a full-scale rebellion broke out in 1965, concentrated mainly in the north, which had until that year remained under French military control. The Muslims of northern Chad have traditionally been in conflict with their black southern compatriots, who are generally animists or Christians. The banned Front de libération nationale du Tchad (FROLINAT, founded in Sudan in 1966) assumed leadership of the revolt, which was quelled in 1968 with French military intervention. In 1973 several leading figures of the regime, including the Army Chief of Staff, Gen. Félix Malloum, were imprisoned on conspiracy charges. The PPT was replaced by a new political party, the Mouvement national pour la révolution culturelle et sociale (MNRCS).

In April 1975 Tombalbaye was killed in a military coup. Gen. Malloum was released and became President at the head of a Supreme Military Council. The provisional Government dissolved the MNRCS and appealed for national reconciliation. Some rebel leaders rallied to the regime, but FROLINAT remained in opposition, receiving clandestine support from Libya, which since 1973 had occupied the 'Aozou strip' of northern Chad. This region covers about 114,000 sq km (44,000 sq miles), and is believed to contain significant deposits of uranium. The Libyan claim to sovereignty over the Aozou region was based upon an unratified treaty signed by Vichy France and Italy in 1943.

In early 1978 FROLINAT unified its command under a Revolutionary Council (led by Goukouni Oueddei), and gained large areas of territory before its advance was halted following the arrival of French reinforcements. In August a former leader of FROLINAT, Hissène Habré, was appointed Prime Minister. However, central authority was soon undermined by disagreements between Habré and Malloum, and fighting between government forces and troops loyal to Habré broke out in February 1979. Habré's Forces armées du nord (FAN) took control of most of the capital, and in March Malloum resigned and fled the country, leaving governmental responsibility with the commander of the gendarmerie, Lt-Col (later Col) Wadal Abdelkader Kamougue. French troops were sent to Chad, and a cease-fire was agreed.

In April 1979, following the failure of reconciliation conferences held in Nigeria, a provisional government was formed, comprising members of FROLINAT, FAN, the Mouvement populaire pour la libération du Tchad (MPLT), also known as the 'Troisième armée') and the government armed forces (Forces armées tchadiennes—FAT). Lol Mahamat Shawwa of the MPLT was appointed President, while Goukouni Oueddei became Minister of the Interior and Habré Minister of Defence. This regime, which excluded the extreme factions of the south (now led by Kamougue) was denounced both by dissatisfied Chadian factions and by several neighbouring countries.

Sporadic fighting continued, and disagreements between Goukouni and Habré were evident. In August 1979, at a conference held in Nigeria, 11 Chadian factions agreed to form a Gouvernement d'union nationale de transition (GUNT) under the presidency of Goukouni, with Lt-Col Kamougue as Vice-President. A Council of Ministers, representing the various factions, was appointed in November.

Goukouni's authority was undermined by continual disagreements with Habré, and in March 1980 fighting resumed in the capital. Numerous attempts at mediation failed; in May all French troops withdrew from Chad, and in June a treaty of friendship was signed between Col Muammar al-Qaddafi of Libya and a representative of President Goukouni, without the prior consent of the GUNT. During October 1980 Libyan forces intervened directly in the hostilities, resulting in the defeat of Habré and the retreat of the FAN from N'Djamena. A Libyan force of 15,000 men was established in the country.

In January 1981 proposals were made for a gradual merger of Chad and Libya, but the Libyan presence in Chad was unpopular, and guerrilla warfare continued. Habré and other FAN leaders were sentenced to death *in absentia* in June. By September President Goukouni had finally renounced the proposed merger, and in November Libyan troops were withdrawn at Goukouni's request. An inter-African peace-keeping force was installed under the auspices of the OAU, which drafted proposals for a cease-fire and for elections.

In early 1982, however, these proposals were abandoned, as President Goukouni refused to negotiate with Habré. In an attempt to strengthen the GUNT, weakened by internal conflicts, Goukouni formed a Conseil d'Etat, appointed a Prime Minister and reorganized the Council of Ministers in May. However, fighting intensified, and N'Djamena fell to Habré's forces on 7 June. The formation of a new Conseil d'Etat, with Habré as Head of State, was announced on 19 June. By the end of that month the OAU force had withdrawn fully from Chad. A provisional constitution, the *acte fondamental*, was promulgated in September, and in October Habré took the oath as President and formed a new government. Goukouni, who had fled to Cameroon and thence to Algeria, continued to contest Habré's leadership. With Libyan support, his troops regained control over parts of northern Chad, and in October a rival 'government of national salvation' was formed by GUNT supporters in Bardai. Habré's regime succeeded in obtaining international recognition, having gained the support of the majority of African states by mid-1983.

In January 1983 some members of Kamougue's FAT joined the ranks of the FAN to form the Forces armées nationales tchadiennes (FANT). In June Goukouni's rebel forces, with Libyan support, captured the northern administrative centre of Faya-Largeau. Habré secured US $10m. of military aid from the USA, as well as a contingent of Zairean paratroopers and increased logistical aid from France. Government troops repossessed Faya-Largeau at the end of July, but, after prolonged bombing by Libyan aircraft, the town again fell to the rebel forces in August. In response to Habré's renewed appeals, France intervened with *Opération Manta*, sending 3,000 troops to Chad. President Mitterrand of France proposed the establishment of a federation as a solution to the dispute, but this was rejected by a spokesman for Goukouni Oueddei. An 'interdiction line' separating the warring factions was imposed by France along latitude 15°N, and in mid-September it was announced that fighting had ceased.

In January 1984 a meeting of representatives from all factions, held in Addis Ababa under the aegis of the OAU ended in failure, following a disagreement over protocol and representation. Renewed fighting in January led to the shooting-down of a French aircraft and the death of its pilot. France subsequently extended the limit of the defensive zone 100 km northwards, to latitude 16°N. In an attempt to consolidate his political power, Habré dissolved his FROLINAT-FAN faction in June, created a new official political party, the Union nationale pour l'indépendance et la révolution (UNIR). The Government was reorganized in July. Major dissension among anti-Habré forces became increasingly evident during 1984 with the formation, by GUNT factions, of new 'splinter groups' and an anti-Goukouni movement.

In May 1984 Col Qaddafi proposed the simultaneous withdrawal of Libyan 'support elements' and French troops; a Franco-Libyan agreement was reached in September for the joint evacuation of both countries' military forces, and in mid-November it was announced that the troops had been withdrawn. None the less, US and Chadian intelligence reports maintained that 3,000 Libyan troops were still in the country, in contravention of the agreement. At the Franco-African 'summit' in December, President Mitterrand declared that France would not use force to repulse Libyans from northern Chad, but would intervene if Libyan forces moved south of the 16th parallel.

The civil war in southern Chad between Habré's forces and various guerrilla commandos ('codos') escalated in October and November 1984, with the Government reportedly conducting summary executions in an attempt to reassert its authority in the area. To escape the increasing violence, more than 50,000 Chadians were estimated to have fled to Sudan, the Central African Republic (CAR) and Cameroon. In an attempt to ease unrest in the south, Habré made several tours of the area in early 1985: calm finally returned at the end of that year, when 1,200 'codos' responded to financial inducements and rallied to the government side.

At a meeting of factions loyal to Goukouni, held in Benin in August 1985, a Conseil suprême de la révolution (CSR), comprising members of seven leading anti-Government groupings, was established. Subsequent to the realignment of the 'codos', a number of former opposition factions also declared support for the Habré regime, including the Front démocratique du Tchad (FDT), a grouping of four factions hostile to both Habré and Goukouni, which had been founded in March 1985 under the leadership of Gen. Djibril Négué Djogo, and the Comité d'action et de concertation (CAC-CDR), which had split from the pro-Goukouni Conseil Démocratique Révolutionnaire (CDR) early in 1985. In response, Habré announced the release of 122 political prisoners in January 1986.

In February 1986 hostilities resumed with Libyan-supported attacks by GUNT forces on government positions to the south of the French interdiction line. Habré appealed to France for increased military assistance, and a few days later French military aircraft, operating from the CAR, bombed a Libyan-built airstrip at Ouadi Doum, north-east of Faya-Largeau. A retaliatory strike on N'Djamena airport caused minor damage, and France established a defensive air-strike force in the capital, an intervention which was codenamed *Opération Epervier*. Further rebel incursions across the interdiction line in March were, however, contained by the FANT. The USA provided US $10m. in supplementary military aid to the Habré regime during the period of hostilities, which ceased temporarily following the destruction in mid-March, by the FANT, of a rebel base at Chicha, north of latitude 16°N. OAU-convened reconciliation talks, scheduled to take place in the Congo at the end of March, failed to materialize when Goukouni refused to attend. In the same month Habré appointed several former opponents to the Council of Ministers.

Goukouni's failure to attend the negotiations prompted the resignation, in June 1986, of GUNT vice-president Col Wadal Abdelkader Kamougue, who rallied to Habré in February 1987 and joined the Government in August of that year. In August 1986 Acheikh Ibn Oumar's CDR withdrew its support from Goukouni. In October, following the onset of armed clashes in the Tibesti region between the CDR (with Libyan backing) and his own Forces armées populaires (FAP), Goukouni declared himself willing to seek a reconciliation with Habré. In November he was replaced as president of a reconstituted GUNT (comprising seven of the original 11 factions, and also known as the néo-GUNT) by Acheikh Ibn Oumar.

In December 1986 clashes began in the Tibesti region between Libyan forces and the now pro-Habré FAP. FANT troops moved into northern Chad, and both France and the USA increased their logistical support, with French aircraft crossing the 16th parallel to parachute arms and supplies to besieged government troops. By the end of January 1987, the FANT had recaptured a number of strategic targets in the north of the country, while France had responded to a Libyan military incursion in southern Chad by launching a second retaliatory air attack on Ouadi Doum. In early February France announced that it had 'redeployed' a number of troops to positions just south of the 16th parallel, and in March the Ouadi Doum airbase fell to Habré's troops. Faya-Largeau was subsequently evacuated by the retreating Libyan army, and in May it was announced that Libya was transferring control of its remaining positions south of the Aozou strip to the FAP. France subsequently extended its logistical and humanitarian aid to cover most of northern Chad, while maintaining a reduced defensive force in the south of the country.

During June and July 1987 Habré made official visits to both the USA and France. Both countries pledged further military and financial assistance, and Chad subsequently received deliveries of anti-aircraft missiles and anti-tank weapons from the USA. However, France advised caution regarding the resolution of the dispute with Libya about the sovereignty of the Aozou region by military means, urging that the issue be submitted to international arbitration. In early August Habré's forces attacked and occupied the town of Aozou, the administrative centre of the disputed region. Twenty days later, following a series of Libyan air raids on Chadian targets, Col Qaddafi's forces recaptured the town, and the FANT withdrew to positions in the Tibesti. The attempt to gain control of Aozou was followed, in early September, by an incursion by Habré's forces into southern Libya, where they attacked the airbase of Maaten-es-Sarra, claimed to be an important operating point for Libyan raids into Chad. A Libyan military aircraft was subsequently shot down over N'Djamena by the French defensive force, and French positions at Abéché were bombed. In protest at this offensive, the French Government suspended supplies of arms to Chad until December, when President Mitterrand renewed his support for the Habré regime.

Efforts at mediation by the OAU intensified as the conflict escalated, and on 11 September 1987 a cease-fire took effect. In November, however, Chad claimed that FANT troops had clashed with members of what it claimed to be a Libyan-supported 'Islamic Legion' near the Sudanese border. (The alleged presence of 'Islamic Legion' troops in the Darfur region of Sudan led to a deterioration of relations between that country and Chad in 1987 and 1988.) It was also claimed that Libyan aircraft were repeatedly violating Chadian airspace. Further engagements took place in November, near Goz Beïda, and to the east of Ennedi in March 1988.

In November 1987 the UN General Assembly refused to debate the question of the sovereignty of the Aozou region, concluding that the resolution of the dispute was the responsibility of the OAU. A meeting between the Heads of State of Chad and Libya, proposed by the OAU *ad hoc* committee on the dispute, was scheduled for 24 May 1988, after having been postponed several times. On the eve of the 'summit', it was announced that Col Qaddafi would not be attending, in protest at Chad's treatment of Libyan prisoners of war. On 25 May, however, the Libyan leader announced his willingness to recognize the Habré regime. Qaddafi also invited Habré and Goukouni Oueddei to hold reconciliation talks in Libya, and offered to provide financial aid for the reconstruction of bombed towns in northern Chad. Habré reacted with caution to these proposals, but announced that Chad was prepared to restore diplomatic relations with Libya, which had been severed in 1982. Negotiations between the Ministers of Foreign Affairs of the two countries, held in Gabon in July 1988, were largely inconclusive, although agreement was reached, in principle, regarding the re-establishment of diplomatic relations; however, the questions of the sovereignty of the Aozou region, the fate of Libyan prisoners of war in Chad and the future security of common borders remained unresolved. In October of that year the two countries issued a joint communiqué, in which they expressed their willingness to seek a peaceful solution to the territorial dispute, and to co-operate with the OAU committee appointed for that purpose. The September 1987 cease-fire agreement was reaffirmed, and diplomatic relations were resumed (ambassadors were exchanged in November 1988). None the less, Chad continued to accuse Libya of violating the cease-fire agreement. In November a Libyan aircraft that had allegedly entered Chadian airspace was shot down by the FANT, and in December it was announced that a military engagement had taken place between Chadian and pro-Libyan forces near the border with Sudan.

In July 1987 reconciliation talks between UNIR and Goukouni Oueddei, who in April had appealed for the universal recognition of Habré as Chad's legitimate Head of State, were reported to have failed. The cohesion of the GUNT was further undermined in 1988 by a dispute between Goukouni and Acheikh Ibn Oumar regarding the leadership of the movement. Several former opposition parties announced their support for the Habré regime, while the GUNT was reconstituted under Goukouni. In November, following the conclusion of a peace agreement with UNIR, Acheikh Ibn Oumar and his supporters returned to Chad.

Relations between Chad and Libya deteriorated further in June 1989, when the Habré Government accused Qaddafi of preparing (with the complicity of the al-Mahdi Government in Sudan) a further military offensive against Chad. Habré warned that the possibility could not be discounted of a pre-emptive strike by the FANT into the Darfur region, where, it was alleged, Sudanese and Libyan troops were gathering in preparation for an assault. In the same month a session of the OAU *ad hoc* committee was suspended, following the failure of the representatives of Chad and Libya to agree on an agenda. In July Habré and Qaddafi met for the first time in Mali. Although their meeting was reported to have been cordial, negotiations between the two leaders were inconclusive, owing to Habré's rejection of proposals made by President Chadli of Algeria, which envisaged the withdrawal of the French *Epervier* force from Chad, and which were thus deemed to be too favourable to Libyan interests. On 31 August, however, Acheikh Ibn Oumar (who had been appointed Minister of Foreign Affairs in March) and his Libyan counterpart, Jadallah Azouz at-Tali, met in Algeria, where they signed an outline peace accord. The *accord cadre* envisaged the peaceful resolution of the dispute: if such a political settlement were not achieved within one year, the issue would be submitted to the International Court of Justice (ICJ) for arbitration. Provision was made for the withdrawal of all forces from the Aozou region, under the supervision of non-partisan African observers, and for the release of all prisoners of war. The two countries reaffirmed their mutual commitment to the principles of the September 1987 cease-fire agreement. A policy of mutual non-interference in each other's internal affairs was declared, under the terms of which hostile radio broadcasts and financial and military support for dissidents were to cease. A joint commission was to be established to oversee the implementation of the accord. In September the Chadian Government was reported to have released an unspecified number of Libyan prisoners of war. In spite of the 1989 agreement, military engagements between FANT personnel and pro-Libyan forces were reported in October and November of the same year.

Attempts to resolve the conflict with Libya coincided with a period of apparent political unity within Chad, which was exemplified, in March 1989, by Acheikh Ibn Oumar's inclusion in the Council of Ministers. In early April, however, the Minister of the Interior and Territorial Administration, Mahamat Itno (who had been prominent at the time of the return of Oumar and his supporters to N'Djamena), was arrested, following the discovery of a coup attempt. Meanwhile, the Commander-in-Chief of the Armed Forces, Hassan Djamous, and his predecessor in that post, Idriss Deby, both of whom were implicated in the plot, fled to Sudan. It was subsequently announced that Djamous had died as a result of wounds sustained during conflict with forces loyal to Habré. In June a new opposition movement, the Action du 1 avril, was formed in Sudan, with Deby as its leader. (The movement was among those which were reported to have been involved in clashes with the FANT in late 1989.) The unity of the GUNT was undermined in July, when elements of its member-groupings announced their withdrawal from the exiled coalition. Other opposition factions pledged their allegiance to UNIR during 1989.

A reorganization of the Chadian Council of Ministers occurred in October 1989, following the death, in the previous month, of the Minister of Planning and Co-operation, Soumaila Mahamat. (Mahamat was among 171 people who were killed when a French airliner exploded over Niger, shortly after leaving N'Djamena.)

In July 1988 a presidential decree established a committee to draft a new constitution. The document, which gave wider powers to the President, was approved in a national referendum on 10 December 1989 (reportedly receiving the support of 99.94% of those who voted). In endorsing the Constitution, the electorate also confirmed Habré in the office of President for a further seven-year term. The new Constitution upheld the principle of a sole ruling party, and envisaged the creation of a legislative body, the Assemblée nationale, which was to be elected, with a five-year mandate, by direct universal suffrage. Accordingly, legislative elections were held in July 1990, at which 436 candidates contested 123 seats (five of which were reserved for women). Most of the candidates were members of UNIR, although several prominent members of the ruling party failed to secure seats in the new chamber.

Meanwhile, attempts to achieve a diplomatic resolution to the dispute with Libya continued to be undermined by mutual recriminations regarding each side's commitment to the negotiation process. In late March 1990 discussions between representatives of Chad and Libya were immediately preceded by Chadian accusations that the Governments of Libya and Sudan were supporting a rebellion, led by Idriss Deby, in the Biltine district of eastern Chad (see below). In May further negotiations were compromised by the seizure, by Chadian forces, of Libyan vehicles on Sudanese territory (an action which prompted Libya to protest to the UN and the OAU at this offensive against what were claimed to be civilian vehicles). In late July an emergency session of the Executive Bureau of UNIR issued a communiqué in which it was alleged that Libya and Sudan were massing forces in Sudan's Darfur region, in preparation for a 'total war' against Chad. Subsequent discussions between Chadian and Libyan delegates failed. Thus, as it became increasingly unlikely that, despite six sessions of the Chad-Libya joint commission (that had been envisaged in the *accord cadre* of August 1989), the issue of the sovereignty of the Aozou strip would be resolved by diplomatic means, Habré and Qaddafi held apparently cordial discussions in Morocco in late August 1990, shortly before the expiry of the deadline for a negotiated settlement that had been stipulated in the accord. On 31 August Libya announced that it was to refer the dispute unilaterally to the ICJ; a similar concession was made by Chad on 3 September.

In October 1990 the Rassemblement pour la démocratie et le progrès, an opposition movement based in the Congo, alleged that several senior Chadian public officials and military officers had been arrested during September. All those detained, some of whom were subsequently executed, had advocated the immediate introduction of a multi-party system in Chad. In October Col Wadal Abdelkader Kamougue was transferred from the Ministry of Justice to the Ministry of Trade and Industry. (The previous incumbent in the latter post, Amoussa Raoulengar, was among those who were dismissed in a reallocation of portfolios in February.)

In late March 1990 Idriss Deby and his supporters, the Forces patriotiques du salut (subsequently known as the Mouvement patriotique du salut, MPS), invaded Chad from bases in Sudan and occupied or destroyed many villages in the east of the country. The FANT suffered heavy losses in the ensuing conflict: many troops were killed or injured, while others deserted or joined Deby. France sent military personnel and equipment to reinforce the *Epervier* contingent at Abéché; however, French forces did not participate in the military engagements. Both Libya and Sudan refuted Habré's accusations of their complicity in the invasion.

On 10 November 1990 forces led by Deby again invaded Chad from Sudan and launched an attack on Chadian positions at Tiné, to the north-east of Abéché. The Chadian Government again claimed that Libya and Sudan had supported the incursion, an allegation that was denied by the Governments of both countries and by Deby himself. Qaddafi reiterated his country's commitment to the 1989 *accord cadre*, and stated that the hostilities between the forces of Habré and Deby represented a 'civil war' between the two leaders' tribes (the Gorane and the Azakawa, respectively). After 24 hours of fighting, the FANT forced some 2,000 rebels to retreat, 'in disarray', into Sudan. However, attacks were quickly resumed, and by mid-November Deby's MPS claimed to have taken control of Tiné. By the time when the French Government had agreed to transfer troops from N'Djamena to Abéché, the rebels claimed to have captured the border-towns of Iriba and Guéréda; again, however, French forces did not assist the FANT in repelling the MPS. While the Habré Government claimed successes in checking the advance of the MPS, Deby's forces continued to consolidate their position in eastern Chad, and it was reported that many FANT units were transferring their allegiance to Deby. Negotiations regarding the sovereignty of the Aozou region, that had been scheduled to be held in N'Djamena in late November, were cancelled by Qaddafi, who claimed that recent Chadian allegations of Libyan complicity in the rebel invasion had not been conducive to 'favourable conditions' for the discussions. The US Government pledged its full support for Habré; however, France reiterated its policy of non-interference in Chad's internal affairs.

On 29 November 1990 the MPS captured Abéché. It was reported that Deby's forces encountered no resistance, and, for their part, had not attacked the *Epervier* contingent. Deby's subsequent progress from Abéché to N'Djamena (a distance of some 800 km) was largely unchecked, and on 30 November it was reported that Habré, together with members of his family and of the Council of Ministers, had fled to Maroua, in eastern Cameroon. Deby arrived in N'Djamena two days later. A curfew was immediately imposed, in an attempt to quell the rioting and looting that had followed Habré's flight from the capital. Deby announced his commitment to the installation of a multi-party system in Chad, and stated that new presidential and legislative elections would be held at a future date. On 3 December the National Assembly was dissolved and the Constitution suspended. It was subsequently announced that a provisional Conseil d'Etat was to assume power, and that its Chairman (Deby) was to be Head of State. The political programme that had been adopted by the MPS upon its foundation in Libya in March 1990 was to become supreme law until democratic institutions could be established. In an attempt to unify the country, diverse ethnic groups were represented in the Conseil d'Etat; among the members of the new Government were several former prominent officials under the Habré administation, including Dr Jean Alingue Bawoyeu (the Speaker of the dissolved National Assembly) and Kotiga Guerina. Acheikh Ibn Oumar was reported to have fled initially to Cameroon; however, the former Minister of Foreign Affairs was subsequently appointed special adviser to the new Head of State. Deby accused Habré of violations of human rights and of embezzling state funds, and appealed for the extradition of the former President from Senegal (where he had been granted political asylum), in order that he might be brought before a special criminal court.

In the aftermath of Deby's accession to power, many political organizations that had opposed Habré announced their support for the MPS. Goukouni Oueddei announced his willingness to open a dialogue with the new Government, and denied persistent reports that he was massing forces in northern Chad. Some representatives of UNIR, based in northern Nigeria, appealed for a national conference to be convened to consider Chad's future.

In mid-December 1990 the human rights organization, Amnesty International, alleged that more than 300 political detainees had been executed by the Chadian Presidential Guard shortly before Habré's downfall. This report followed earlier claims by the same organization that large numbers of military personnel and civilians had been executed by the FANT in the border-region with Sudan in March and April 1990.

Following his accession to power, Deby thanked the French Government for having maintained a neutral position during the overthrow of Habré. It was subsequently announced that aid and co-operation agreeements that had been signed by the Mitterrand and Habré Governments would be honoured, and that new accords would be formulated. Moreover, the *Epervier* force would continue to be deployed in Chad. It was widely believed that France's lack of support for the incumbent regime at the time of the MPS invasion reflected Habré's failure to initiate a transition towards multi-party democracy. The USA adopted a more ambivalent attitude to the new administration, affirming its commitment to existing aid agreements while condemning Deby's allegedly close links with Libya. The Libyan and Sudanese Governments welcomed the overthrow of Habré, and expressed a desire to establish cordial relations with the MPS. Both countries undertook not to allow forces hostile to Deby to operate in their territory. Shortly after Deby's arrival in N'Djamena, it was reported that as many as 500 Libyan prisoners of war had been repatriated. However, Qaddafi protested at the airlift, that was apparently overseen by the USA and France, of several hundred Libyan detainees, who had allegedly been trained by the USA to mount military offensives against the Libyan leader, from Chad to Nigeria and Zaire.

Beginning in mid-December 1990, representatives of the new Government travelled to other countries in the region, in an attempt to secure guarantees of support for the MPS. These missions were largely successful. In late December, however, it was reported that one envoy, whose mission had been to persuade exiles in Cameroon to return to Chad, had been murdered in Maroua.

In January 1989 it was announced that the French-operated radar facility at Moussoro, to the north-east of N'Djamena, was to be withdrawn, while the number of French troops deployed in Chad was to be reduced, by 200, to 1,500 (a further reduction, also of 200 troops, was announced in September of that year). In February 1990 the *Epervier* force was reduced to 1,000, with most of the contingent being withdrawn from Abéché. However, the French Government consistently expressed its support for Chad's efforts to maintain its territorial integrity.

Government

Following the accession to power of the Mouvement patriotique du salut (MPS) in December 1990, the Constitution that had been promulgated in December 1989 was suspended, and the National Assembly that had been elected in July 1990, in accordance with the Constitution, was dissolved. The MPS announced that new presidential and legislative elections were to be held, in the context of a multi-party system. Pending these elections, the President of the MPS became Head of State, and a provisional Conseil d'Etat assumed governmental responsibility.

For administrative purposes, Chad is divided into 14 prefectures.

Defence

In June 1990 the total strength of the Forces armées nationales tchadiennes (FANT) was estimated to be some 17,200 (army approximately 17,000, air force 200). In addition, there were paramilitary forces of as many as 5,700. The size and structure of the new government force was unknown in early 1991. Under defence agreements with France, the army receives technical and other aid: France maintained about 1,000 troops in Chad in late 1990. Contributions for the upkeep of the armed forces, that had been compulsory under the Habré Government, were to be abolished by Idriss Deby's Mouvement patriotique du salut. Defence expenditure (excluding French and US subventions) in 1989 was an estimated 18,000m. francs CFA.

Economic Affairs

In 1988, according to estimates by the World Bank, Chad's gross national product (GNP), measured at average 1986–88 prices, was US $850m., equivalent to $160 per head (one of the lowest per caput levels in the world). During 1980–87, it was estimated, GNP increased, in real terms, at an average annual rate of 4.9%. GNP per head declined by an annual average of 0.2% in 1965–88. Between 1980 and 1988 the gross domestic product (GDP) increased by an average of 3.9% per year. Over the same period the population increased by an annual average of 2.4%.

Agriculture (including forestry and fishing) contributed 47% of GDP in 1988. About 75.6% of the labour force were employed in the sector in 1989. Most agricultural activity is concentrated in the south of the country. The principal cash crop is cotton (which is the major export commodity, accounting for about 70% of export earnings in the late 1980s). The principal subsistence crops are millet, sorghum and groundnuts. Livestock-rearing makes an important contribution both to the domestic food supply and to export earnings, although a significant proportion of the output is smuggled out of the country. During 1980–88 agricultural production increased by an annual average of 2.6%.

Industry (including mining, manufacturing, construction and power) contributed 18% of GDP in 1988. About 4.6% of the population were employed in the sector in 1980. During 1980–88 industrial production increased by an annual average of 7.7%.

The mining sector contributed only 0.4% of GDP in 1987: the only significant activity is the extraction of natron. The commercial development of petroleum resources has been impeded by the uncertain political situation, in addition to the low international prices for this commodity. However, it seemed probable that important reserves of petroleum in the Lake Chad area would be exploited during the 1990s. Deposits of tungsten, cassiterite (tin ore), bauxite, gold, iron ore, titanium, limestone and kaolin have been located, but their exploitation is minimal. The Aozou region, which has been the subject of a protracted territorial dispute with Libya, is believed to contain valuable resources of uranium.

The manufacturing sector, which contributed 15% of GDP in 1988, operates mainly in the south of the country, and is dominated by agro-industrial activities, notably the processing of the cotton crop by the Société Cotonnière du Tchad (COTONTCHAD, the state-owned cotton monopoly). A sugar-refining complex is also in operation.

Chad is heavily dependent on imports of mineral fuels (principally from Cameroon and Nigeria) for the generation of electricity. Imports of petroleum products comprised 16.8% of the value of total imports in 1983. The use of wood-based fuel products by most households has contributed to the severe depletion of Chad's forest resources.

In 1989 Chad recorded a visible trade deficit of US $89.4m., while there was a surplus of $19.5m. on the current account of the balance of payments. In 1986 Chad's principal source of imports (37%) was France; other major suppliers were Cameroon, the USA and Nigeria. The principal market for exports in that year was Cameroon (which received 50% of Chadian export commodities); France was also a significant purchaser. The principal export is cotton. Exports of raw cotton contributed 91.1% of total export earnings in 1983; by the late 1980s, however, the decline in international prices for this commodity had resulted in a significant reduction in export revenue. The principal imports in 1983 were petroleum products, cereals, pharmaceuticals, chemicals, machinery and transport and electrical equipment.

Chad recorded an administrative-budget deficit of 6,197m. francs CFA in 1988. Chad's total external public debt was US $300m. at the end of 1988. In that year the cost of debt-servicing was equivalent to about 2.7% of earnings from exports of goods and services (the low ratio reflecting the highly concessional nature of most of the country's aid inflows). The average level of consumer prices declined in 1986 and 1987; consumer prices increased by an annual average of 15.5% in 1988, but declined again, by 4.9%, in 1989.

Chad is a member of the Central African organs of the Franc Zone (see p. 156) and of the Communauté Économique des Etats de l'Afrique Centrale (CEEAC, see p. 223).

Chad's protracted civil war and the prolonged conflict with Libya, together with the lack of diversification in the agricultural sector (which has resulted in vulnerability to adverse climatic conditions and to fluctuations in international prices for cotton), the paucity of exploitable mineral resources and the inadequacy of the transport infrastructure, have inhibited sustained economic growth. The achievement of self-sufficiency in foodstuffs remains a major priority. A programme to restructure COTONTCHAD has, none the less, had some success. During the late 1980s the Habré Government's adjustment efforts, which aimed to achieve real GDP growth by reducing both the rate of inflation and the external current account deficit, received the support of external creditors. Existing co-operation agreements between Chad and bilateral and multilateral creditors were expected to be honoured following the accession to power of the Mouvement patriotique du salut (MPS) in late 1990. However, the long-term economic policy of the MPS remained unclear in early 1991.

Social Welfare

An Employment Code guarantees a minimum wage and other rights for employees. There are four hospitals, 28 medical centres and several hundred dispensaries. In 1978 there were 3,373 beds in government-administered hospital establishments (one per 1,278 inhabitants), while only 90 physicians were employed in official medical services. A development programme was inaugurated in 1986 by UNICEF, at an estimated cost of US $30m.

Education

Education is officially compulsory for eight years between six and 14 years of age. Primary education begins at the age of six and lasts for six years. Secondary education, from the age of 12, lasts for seven years, comprising a first cycle of four years and a second of three years. In 1987, 38% of children in the relevant age group were enrolled in primary schools (52% of boys; 23% of girls), while the comparable ratio for secondary enrolment was equivalent to only 6% (10% of boys; 2% of girls). The Université du Tchad was opened at N'Djamena in 1971. In addition, there are several technical colleges. In 1985, according to estimates by UNESCO, the average rate of adult illiteracy was 74.7% (males 59.5%; females 89.1%). In 1988 the International Development Association (IDA) gave US $22m., in support of a programme to reconstruct schools in areas affected by the conflict with Libya, and to provide improved teacher-training facilities. In the following year the African Development Bank (ADB) approved a loan of more than 3,500m. francs CFA for the construction of 40 primary schools.

Public Holidays

1991: 1 January (New Year), 1 April (Easter Monday), 16 April* (Id al-Fitr, end of Ramadan), 1 May (Labour Day), 20 May (Whit Monday), 25 May ('Liberation of Africa', anniversary of the OAU's foundation), 23 June* (Id al-Adha, Feast of the Sacrifice), 11 August (Independence Day), 15 August (Assumption), 21 September* (Maloud, Birth of the Prophet), 1 November (All Saints' Day), 28 November (Proclamation of the Republic), 25 December (Christmas).

1992: 1 January (New Year), 4 April* (Id al-Fitr, end of Ramadan), 20 April (Easter Monday), 1 May (Labour Day), 25 May ('Liberation of Africa', anniversary of the OAU's foundation), 8 June (Whit Monday), 11 June* (Id al-Adha, Feast of the Sacrifice), 11 August (Independence Day), 15 August (Assumption), 10 September* (Maloud, Birth of the Prophet), 1 November (All Saints' Day), 28 November (Proclamation of the Republic), 25 December (Christmas).

* These holidays are dependent on the Islamic lunar calendar and may vary by one or two days from the dates given.

Weights and Measures

The metric system is officially in force.

Statistical Survey

Source (unless otherwise stated): Direction de la Statistique, des Etudes Economiques et Démographiques, BP 453, N'Djamena.

Area and Population

AREA, POPULATION AND DENSITY

Area (sq km)	
Land	1,259,200
Inland waters	24,800
Total	1,284,000*
Population (sample survey)	
December 1963–August 1964	3,254,000†
Population (official estimate at mid-year)	
1988	5,428,000
Density (per sq km) at mid-1988	4.2

* 495,800 sq miles.
† Including areas not covered by the survey.

PREFECTURES (official estimates, 1988)

	Area (sq km)	Population	Density (per sq km)
Batha	88,800	431,000	4.9
Biltine	46,850	216,000	4.6
Borkou-Ennedi-Tibesti (BET)	600,350	109,000	0.2
Chari-Baguirmi	82,910	844,000	10.2
Guéra	58,950	254,000	4.3
Kanem	114,520	245,000	2.1
Lac	22,320	165,000	7.4
Logone Occidental	8,695	365,000	42.0
Logone Oriental	28,035	377,000	13.4
Mayo-Kebbi	30,105	852,000	28.3
Moyen Chari	45,180	646,000	14.3
Ouadaï	76,240	422,000	5.5
Salamat	63,000	131,000	2.1
Tandjilé	18,045	371,000	20.6
Total	**1,284,000**	**5,428,000**	**4.2**

PRINCIPAL TOWNS (officially-estimated population in 1988)

N'Djamena (capital)	594,000	Moundou	102,000
Sarh	113,400	Abéché	83,000

BIRTHS AND DEATHS (UN estimates, annual averages)

	1975–80	1980–85	1985–90
Birth rate (per 1,000)	44.1	44.2	44.2
Death rate (per 1,000)	23.1	21.4	19.5

Source: UN, *World Population Prospects: 1988*.

ECONOMICALLY ACTIVE POPULATION
(ILO estimates, '000 persons at mid-1980)

	Males	Females	Total
Agriculture, etc.	1,043	318	1,361
Industry	72	4	76
Services	154	44	197
Total	**1,269**	**366**	**1,635**

Source: ILO, *Economically Active Population Estimates and Projections, 1950–2025*.

Mid-1989 (estimates in '000): Agriculture 1,462; Total 1,934 (Source: FAO, *Production Yearbook*).

Agriculture

PRINCIPAL CROPS ('000 metric tons)

	1987	1988	1989
Wheat	3*	2†	2†
Rice (paddy)	42†	74†	57*
Maize†	34	34	16
Millet and sorghum	518	697†	546†
Other cereals†	28	40	56
Potatoes*	15	18	18
Sweet potatoes*	44	46	46
Cassava (Manioc)	305†	330*	330*
Yams*	230	240	240
Taro (Coco yam)*	9	9	9
Dry beans*	42	42	42
Other pulses*	18	18	18
Groundnuts (in shell)	96	79	80†
Sesame seed	10	8	12*
Cottonseed*	75	80	70
Cotton (lint)	48	53†	51†
Dry onions*	14	14	14
Other vegetables*	60	60	60
Dates*	32	32	32
Mangoes*	32	32	32
Other fruit*	50	52	52
Sugar cane*	290	290	290

* FAO estimate(s). † Unofficial figure(s).
Source: FAO, *Production Yearbook*.

LIVESTOCK ('000 head, year ending September)

	1987	1988	1989
Cattle	3,980	4,076	4,115*
Goats*	2,160	2,225	2,310
Sheep*	2,160	2,225	2,310
Pigs	12	12	13
Horses	186	189	195*
Asses	234	239	245*
Camels	503	518	516

Poultry* (million): 4 in 1987; 4 in 1988; 4 in 1989.
* FAO estimate(s).
Source: FAO, *Production Yearbook*.

LIVESTOCK PRODUCTS (FAO estimates, '000 metric tons)

	1987	1988	1989
Total meat	63	64	67
Beef and veal	38	39	41
Mutton and lamb	9	9	10
Goats' meat	8	8	8
Poultry meat	4	4	4
Cows' milk	108	111	111
Sheep's milk	8	8	9
Goats' milk	13	13	14
Butter	0.3	0.3	0.3
Hen eggs	3.2	3.2	3.4
Cattle hides	7.0	7.2	7.3
Sheep skins	1.8	1.9	1.9
Goat skins	1.5	1.5	1.5

Source: FAO, *Production Yearbook*.

CHAD

Statistical Survey

Forestry

ROUNDWOOD REMOVALS
(FAO estimates, '000 cubic metres, excluding bark)

	1986	1987	1988
Sawlogs, etc.	2	2	2
Other industrial wood	514	527	540
Fuel wood	3,136	3,211	3,292
Total	3,652	3,740	3,834

Source: FAO, *Yearbook of Forest Products*.

Fishing

('000 metric tons, live weight)

	1986	1987	1988
Total catch (freshwater fishes)	110	110	110

Source: FAO, *Yearbook of Fishery Statistics*.

Industry

SELECTED PRODUCTS
('000 metric tons, unless otherwise indicated)

	1985	1986	1987
Salted, dried or smoked fish*	19	19	19
Raw sugar†	8	10	20
Electric energy (million kWh)	51	51	51

* Provisional or estimated figures.
† Source: International Sugar Organization.
Source: UN, *Industrial Statistics Yearbook*.

Finance

CURRENCY AND EXCHANGE RATES

Monetary Units
100 centimes = 1 franc de la Coopération financière en Afrique centrale (CFA).

Denominations
Coins: 1, 5, 10, 25, 50, 100 and 500 francs CFA.
Notes: 500, 1,000, 5,000 and 10,000 francs CFA.

French Franc, Sterling and Dollar Equivalents (30 September 1990)
1 French franc = 50 francs CFA;
£1 sterling = 491.1 francs CFA;
US $1 = 262.1 francs CFA;
1,000 francs CFA = £2.036 = $3.815.

Average Exchange Rate (francs CFA per US $)
1987   300.54
1988   297.85
1989   319.01

ADMINISTRATIVE BUDGET (million francs CFA)

Revenue	1986	1987	1988
Fiscal receipts	15,250	17,854	23,455
Taxes on income and profits	3,339	3,494	4,544
Taxes on goods and services	3,019	3,223	6,002
Taxes on international trade and transactions	6,164	5,092	6,227
Receipts from Caisse autonome d'amortissement	1,500	4,060	4,789
Other fiscal receipts	1,229	1,985	1,893
Non-fiscal receipts	2,497	1,617	1,320
Total	17,748	19,471	24,775

Expenditure	1986	1987	1988
Personnel	9,583	11,325	12,363
Equipment	4,071	3,886	4,014
Interest due	1,129	875	896
Transfers	1,320	2,058	1,199
Other expenditure	8,908	9,568	12,500
Total	25,011	27,712	30,972

1990: Proposed recurrent revenue 29,300 million francs CFA; Proposed recurrent expenditure 41,300 million francs CFA.
1991: Proposed recurrent expenditure 43,854 million francs CFA; Proposed equipment, investment and capital expenditure 96,859 million francs CFA.

CENTRAL BANK RESERVES (US $ million at 31 December)

	1986	1987	1988
Gold*	4.36	5.37	4.52
IMF special drawing rights	2.07	9.01	7.70
Reserve position in IMF	0.32	0.37	0.35
Foreign exchange	13.52	42.73	53.06
Total	20.27	57.48	65.63

* Valued at market-related prices.
1989: IMF special drawing rights 1.76; Reserve position in IMF 0.34; Foreign exchange 126.84.
Source: IMF, *International Financial Statistics*.

MONEY SUPPLY ('000 million francs CFA at 31 December)

	1986	1987	1988
Currency outside banks	46.67	46.70	42.01
Demand deposits at commercial and development banks	22.34	23.68	22.47
Checking deposits at post office	0.13	0.22	0.21
Total money	69.14	70.60	64.68

1989: Currency outside banks 43.09; Demand deposits at commercial and development banks 23.35; Total money 66.44.
Source: IMF, *International Financial Statistics*.

COST OF LIVING (Consumer price index for African households in N'Djamena; base: 1985 = 100)

	1987	1988	1989
All items	81.7	94.4	89.8

Source: IMF, *International Financial Statistics*.

CHAD

NATIONAL ACCOUNTS
(estimates, million francs CFA at current prices)
Expenditure on the Gross Domestic Product

	1985	1986	1987
Government final consumption expenditure	60,050	68,870	72,382
Private final consumption expenditure	227,290	252,900	272,904
Gross fixed capital formation	19,130	20,980	21,420
Total domestic expenditure	306,470	342,750	366,706
Exports of goods and services	65,240	62,590	67,597
Less Imports of goods and services	83,680	88,830	92,738
GDP in purchasers' values	288,030	316,510	341,565
GDP at constant 1980 prices	169,842	178,675	182,020

Source: UN Economic Commission for Africa, *African Statistical Yearbook*.

Gross Domestic Product by Economic Activity

	1985	1986	1987
Agriculture, hunting, forestry and fishing	123,700	133,880	141,228
Mining and quarrying	1,400	1,350	1,384
Manufacturing	22,600	25,220	26,472
Electricity, gas and water	1,240	1,370	1,445
Construction	4,440	4,870	5,326
Trade, restaurants and hotels	68,640	75,270	83,122
Transport, storage and communications	5,020	5,570	6,143
Finance, insurance, real estate and business services	1,770	1,940	2,168
Public administration and defence	33,470	38,380	43,404
Other services	2,650	2,940	3,308
GDP at factor cost	264,930	290,790	314,000
Indirect taxes, *less* subsidies	23,100	25,720	27,565
GDP in purchasers' values	288,030	316,510	341,565

Source: UN Economic Commission for Africa, *African Statistical Yearbook*.

BALANCE OF PAYMENTS (US $ million)

	1987	1988	1989
Merchandise exports f.o.b.	109.4	145.9	146.0
Merchandise imports f.o.b.	−225.9	−228.4	−235.4
Trade balance	−116.5	−82.5	−89.4
Exports of services	73.3	80.9	78.7
Imports of services	−211.0	−233.4	−229.7
Balance on goods and services	−254.2	−235.0	−240.4
Private unrequited transfers (net)	−9.8	−17.1	−3.4
Government unrequited transfers (net)	238.5	277.7	263.4
Current balance	−25.5	25.5	19.5
Direct capital investment (net)	0.2	−12.6	—
Other long-term capital (net)	40.9	63.1	80.4
Short-term capital (net)	−32.4	−26.2	−22.6
Net errors and omissions	16.5	−83.7	−25.2
Total (net monetary movements)	−0.3	−33.8	52.2
Valuation changes (net)	8.9	24.6	8.6
Exceptional financing (net)	18.3	21.3	—
Official financing (net)	0.3	—	—
Changes in reserves	27.3	12.1	60.8

Source: IMF, *International Financial Statistics*.

External Trade

PRINCIPAL COMMODITIES (million francs CFA)

Imports	1983
Beverages	71.7
Cereal products	2,272.1
Sugar, confectionery, chocolate	292.7
Petroleum products	2,280.5
Textiles, clothing, etc.	392.1
Pharmaceuticals, chemicals	1,561.9
Minerals and metals	311.2
Machinery	843.2
Transport equipment	987.6
Electrical equipment	773.3
Total (incl. others)	13,539.6

Total imports (million francs CFA): 79,272 in 1984; 107,985 in 1985; 99,708 in 1986; 110,026 (estimate) in 1987 (Source: UN Economic Commission for Africa, *African Statistical Yearbook*).

Exports	1983
Live cattle	49.5
Meat	23.5
Fish	2.0
Oil-cake	8.1
Natron	8.1
Gums and resins	0.4
Hides and skins	16.6
Raw cotton	3,753.7
Total (incl. others)	4,120.0

Total exports (million francs CFA): 57,384 in 1984; 39,381 in 1985; 34,145 in 1986; 33,224 (estimate) in 1987 (Source: UN Economic Commission for Africa, *African Statistical Yearbook*).

PRINCIPAL TRADING PARTNERS (million francs CFA)

Imports	1984	1985	1986
Belgium/Luxembourg	435	520	1,712
Cameroon	3,461	12,371	8,777
China, People's Republic	n.a.	39	896
Congo	417	519	395
France	22,132	14,439	21,772
Germany, Fed. Republic	1,322	1,562	2,876
Italy	3,133	2,874	3,263
Netherlands	777	1,950	2,017
Nigeria	4,817	4,368	5,673
USA	4,095	9,247	7,670
Total (incl. others)	45,759	51,520	58,831

Exports	1984	1985	1986
Cameroon	929	1,711	2,661
Central African Republic	64	1,219	321
France	6,950	1,432	1,774
Nigeria	113	1,981	425
Sudan	8	47	101
Zaire	125	5	n.a.
Total (incl. others)	8,231	6,446	5,374

CHAD
Statistical Survey, Directory

Transport

ROAD TRAFFIC (motor vehicles in use)

	1985
Private cars	2,741
Buses, lorries and coaches	4,000
Tractors	711
Scooters and motorcycles	3,442
Trailers	977
Total	**11,871**

Source: Ministère des Transports et de l'Aviation Civile.

CIVIL AVIATION (traffic on scheduled services*)

	1983	1984	1985
Kilometres flown ('000)	2,400	2,000	2,200
Passenger-km ('000)	219,000	218,000	241,000
Freight ton-km ('000)	18,800	17,500	18,600
Mail ton-km ('000)	900	900	900

* Including an apportionment of the traffic of Air Afrique.
Source: UN, Statistical Yearbook.

Tourism

	1985	1986	1987
Foreign tourist arrivals	11,000	25,000	27,000

Source: UN Economic Commission for Africa, African Statistical Yearbook.

Communications Media

	1985	1986	1987
Radio receivers ('000 in use)	1,100	1,200	1,250
Television receivers ('000 in use)	n.a.	n.a.	5*

* Provisional or estimated figure.
Daily newspapers: 1 in 1986 (average circulation 1,000).
Telephones: 9,000 in 1987.
Sources: UNESCO, Statistical Yearbook, and UN Economic Commission for Africa, African Statistical Yearbook.

Education

(1987)

	Institutions	Teachers	Pupils
Primary	1,139	4,288	300,110
Secondary:			
General	48	1,204	42,066
Teacher training	18	94	2,896
Vocational	7	55	1,080
Higher	4	26	2,038

Source: Ministère de l'Education Nationale.

Directory

The Constitution

Upon the accession to power of the Mouvement patriotique du salut, in December 1990, the Constitution of 20 December 1989 was suspended.

The Government

HEAD OF STATE

Chairman of the Council of State: IDRISS DEBY (took office 4 December 1990).

COUNCIL OF STATE
(January 1991)

Chairman: IDRISS DEBY.
Vice-Chairman: MALDOUM BABA ABBAS.
Commissioner for External Relations: SOUNGUI AHMAD.
Commissioner for the Interior and Security: MAHAMAT SALEH ADOUM.
Commissioner for Agriculture: JEAN ALINGUE BAWOYEU.
Commissioner for Justice: ABAKAR MALLAH.
Commissioner for Defence: DJIBRINE DASSERT.
Commissioner for Finance and Equipment: MOHIADDINE SALAH.
Commissioner for Planning and Co-operation: HASSAN FADOUL KITTIR.
Commissioner for National Education: ABDERAMANE KOKO.
Commissioner for Public Health: HASSAN MAHAMAT HASSAN.
Commissioner for Trade and Industry: MBAILAMDANA NGARNAYAL.
Commissioner for Public Works and Transport: MAHAMOUT HISSEIN MAHAMOUT.
Commissioner for Mines and Energy: ALI GADAYE.
Commissioner for Livestock and Animal Resources: HABIB DOUTOUM.
Commissioner for Higher Education and Research: NGALI NGATA.
Commissioner for Information and Culture: NADJITA BEASSOUMAL.
Commissioner for the Civil Service and Labour: MUSTAPHA ALI ALIPHEI.
Commissioner for Tourism and the Environment: KOTIGA GUERINA.
Commissioner for Women and Social Affairs: ACHTA TONE GOSSINGAR.
Commissioner for Posts and Telecommunications: DJIDI BICHARA.
Commissioner for Food Supplies: BRAHIM SEID.
Commissioner-delegate to the Head of State, with responsibility for Water Resources: ADOUM DIAR.
Commissioner-delegate to the Head of State, with responsibility for the General Inspectorate and State Control: CHEMI KOGRI.
Secretary-General of the Council of State: OUSMANE NGAM.
In addition, there are 10 Deputy Commissioners.

OFFICES OF STATE

Office of the Head of State: N'Djamena; tel. 51-44-37; telex 5201.
Commission for Agriculture: N'Djamena; tel. 51-37-52.
Commission for the Civil Service and Labour: N'Djamena; tel. 51-56-56.
Commission for Defence: N'Djamena; tel. 51-58-89.
Commission for External Relations: N'Djamena; tel. 51-50-82; telex 5238.

CHAD

Commission for Finance and Equipment: N'Djamena; tel. 51-55-53; telex 5257.

Commission for Food Supplies: N'Djamena; tel. 51-36-38.

Commission for Information and Culture: BP 748, N'Djamena; tel. 51-56-56; telex 5240.

Commission for the Interior and Security: N'Djamena; tel. 51-46-59.

Commission for Justice: N'Djamena; tel. 51-56-56.

Commission for Livestock and Animal Resources: N'Djamena; tel. 51-59-07.

Commission for Mines and Energy: N'Djamena; tel. 51-20-96.

Commission for National and Higher Education and Research: BP 731, N'Djamena; tel. 51-44-76.

Commission for Planning and Co-operation: N'Djamena; tel. 51-58-98.

Commission for Posts and Telecommunications: N'Djamena; tel. 51-42-64; telex 5254.

Commission for Public Health: N'Djamena; tel. 51-39-60.

Commission for Public Works and Transport: N'Djamena; tel. 51-20-96.

Commission for Tourism and the Environment: N'Djamena; tel. 51-56-56.

Commission for Trade and Industry: BP 453, N'Djamena; tel. 51-56-56.

Commission for Water Resources: N'Djamena.

Commission for Women and Social Affairs: N'Djamena; tel. 51-56-56.

Office of the Commissioner-delegate to the Head of State, with responsibility for the General Inspectorate and State Control: N'Djamena; tel. 51-56-56.

Legislature

Upon the accession to power of the Mouvement patriotique du salut in December 1990, the National Assembly that had been elected in July 1990 was dissolved. Elections to a new legislative body, in the context of a multi-party political system, were envisaged.

Political Organizations

Mouvement patriotique du salut (MPS): N'Djamena; f. 1990 in Libya, as an opposition grouping embracing several movements, including the Action du 1 avril, the Mouvement pour le salut national du Tchad and the Forces armées tchadiennes; further opposition parties rallied to the MPS during the November 1990 offensive against the Government of Hissène Habré, and others announced their support for the movement following its accession to power in December of that year; Chair. IDRISS DEBY.

In early 1991 it remained unclear how many of the organizations that had opposed the Habré regime supported the Government of the MPS. However, it was known that elements of the **Union nationale pour l'indépendance et la révolution (UNIR)**, the former ruling party, were active in eastern Cameroon and in northern Nigeria. Former President Goukouni Oueddei, who claimed to be the leader of a faction of the **Front de libération nationale du Tchad (FROLINAT)**, announced his willingness to negotiate with the MPS; however, some reports stated that he was massing opposition forces in northern Chad.

Diplomatic Representation

EMBASSIES IN CHAD

Algeria: N'Djamena; tel. 51-38-15; telex 5216; Ambassador: MAMI ABDERRAHMANE.

Central African Republic: BP 115, N'Djamena; tel. 51-32-06; Ambassador: MARTIN KOYOU-KOUMBELE.

China, People's Republic: ave Président Blanchart, BP 1133, N'Djamena; tel. 51-37-72; telex 5235; Ambassador: ZHOU ZHENDONG.

Egypt: BP 1094, N'Djamena; tel. 51-36-60; telex 5216; Ambassador: AZIZ M. NOUR EL-DIN.

France: BP 431, N'Djamena; tel. 51-25-75; telex 5202; Ambassador: FRANÇOIS GENDREAU.

Germany: ave Félix Eboué, BP 893, N'Djamena; tel. 51-30-90; telex 5246; Ambassador: Dr AXEL WEISHAUPT.

Iraq: N'Djamena; tel. 51-22-57; telex 5339; Chargé d'affaires: ALI MAHMOUD HASHIM.

Libya: N'Djamena; Ambassador: GAITH SALEM AN-NASSER.

Nigeria: 35 ave Charles de Gaulle, BP 752, N'Djamena; tel. 51-24-98; telex 5242; Chargé d'affaires: A. M. ALIYU BIU.

Sudan: BP 45, N'Djamena; tel. 51-34-97; telex 5235; Ambassador: TAHA MAKKAWI.

USA: ave Félix Eboué, BP 413, N'Djamena; tel. 51-40-09; telex 5203; fax 51-33-72; Ambassador: RICHARD W. BOGOSIAN.

Zaire: ave du 20 août, BP 910, N'Djamena; tel. 51-59-35; telex 5322; Ambassador: Gen. MALU-MALU DHANDA.

Judicial System

The Supreme Court was abolished after the coup of April 1975. Under the Government of Hissène Habré, there was a Court of Appeal at N'Djamena. Criminal courts sat at N'Djamena, Sarh, Moundou and Abéché, and elsewhere as necessary, and each of these four major towns had a magistrates' court. In October 1976 a permanent Court of State Security was established, comprising eight civilian or military members.

Religion

It is estimated that some 50% of the population are Muslims and about 7% Christians, mainly Roman Catholics. Most of the remainder follow animistic beliefs.

ISLAM

Comité Islamique du Tchad: N'Djamena; tel. 51-51-80.

Head of the Islamic Community: Imam MOUSSA IBRAHIM.

CHRISTIANITY

The Roman Catholic Church

Chad comprises one archdiocese and four dioceses. There were an estimated 328,018 adherents at 31 December 1988.

Bishops' Conference: Conférence Episcopale du Tchad, BP 456, N'Djamena; tel. 51-44-43; telex 5360; Pres. Most Rev. CHARLES VANDAME, Archbishop of N'Djamena.

Archbishop of N'Djamena: Most Rev. CHARLES VANDAME, Archevêché, BP 456, N'Djamena; tel. 51-44-43; telex 5360.

Protestant Church

Eglise évangélique du Tchad: BP 127, N'Djamena; tel. 51-48-18; a fellowship of churches and missions working in Chad; includes Eglise évangélique au Tchad, Assemblées Chrétiennes, Eglise fraternelle Luthérienne and Eglise évangélique des frères.

BAHÁ'Í FAITH

National Spiritual Assembly: BP 181, N'Djamena; tel. 51-47-05; mems in 1,125 localities.

The Press

Al-Watan: BP 407, N'Djamena; tel. 51-57-96; weekly; Editor-in-Chief MOUSSA NDORKOÏ.

Bulletin Mensuel de Statistiques du Tchad: BP 453, N'Djamena; monthly.

Comnat: BP 731, N'Djamena; tel. 29-68; publ. by UNESCO National Commission.

Contact: N'Djamena; f. 1989; independent; current affairs; Dir KOULAMALO SOURADJ.

Info-Tchad: BP 670, N'Djamena; daily news bulletin issued by Agence Tchadienne de Presse; French.

Informations Economiques: BP 458, N'Djamena; publ. by the Chambre de Commerce, d'Agriculture et d'Industrie; weekly.

Journal Officiel de la République du Tchad: N'Djamena.

NEWS AGENCIES

Agence Tchadienne de Presse (ATP): BP 670, N'Djamena; tel. 51-58-67; telex 5240.

Foreign Bureaux

Agence France-Presse (AFP): BP 83, N'Djamena; tel. 51-54-71; telex 5248; Correspondent ALDOM NADJI TITO.

CHAD

Reuters (United Kingdom): N'Djamena; tel. 51-56-57; Correspondent ABAKAR ASSIDIC.

Publisher

Government Publishing House: BP 453, N'Djamena.

Radio and Television

RADIO
There were an estimated 1.25m. radio receivers in use in 1987.

Radiodiffusion Nationale Tchadienne: BP 892, N'Djamena; tel. 51-60-71; govt station; programmes in French, Arabic and eight vernacular languages; there are four transmitters; Dir-Gen. MOUSSA DAGO.

Radio Sarh: BP 270, Sarh; daily programmes in French and Sara; Dir DOKOIMBAYE TIMIDE.

Radio Moundou: BP 122, Moundou; tel. 322; daily programmes in French, Sara and Arabic; Dir DIMANANGAR DJAÏNTA.

TELEVISION
In 1987, according to estimates by UNESCO, there were some 5,000 television sets in use.

Télé-Chad: Commission for Information and Culture, BP 748, N'Djamena; tel. 51-26-22; govt station; broadcasts c. 12 hours per week in French and Arabic.

Finance

(cap. = capital; res = reserves; br. = branch; m. = million; amounts in francs CFA)

BANKING

Central Bank

Banque des Etats de l'Afrique Centrale (BEAC): BP 50, N'Djamena; tel. 51-41-76; telex 5220; headquarters in Yaoundé, Cameroon; f. 1973 as central bank of issue for mem. states of the Customs and Economic Union of Central Africa (UDEAC), comprising Cameroon, the Central African Republic, Chad, the Congo, Equatorial Guinea and Gabon; cap. 36,000m., res 162,037m. (June 1989); Gov. JEAN-FÉLIX MAMALEPOT; Dir in Chad ADAM MADJI; 2 brs.

Other Banks

Banque de Développement du Tchad (BDT): rue Capitaine Ohrel, BP 19, N'Djamena; tel. 51-28-29; telex 5375; f. 1962; 58.4% state-owned; cap. 520m.; Man. Dir JACQUES SAVARY (acting).

BIAT: BP 87, N'Djamena; tel. 51-43-14; telex 5228; fax 51-23-45; f. 1980; 35% state-owned; cap. 600m. (Dec. 1988); Pres. ALAIN LAVELLE; Dir-Gen. PHILIPPE BLANCARD.

Banque Internationale pour le Commerce et l'Industrie du Tchad (BICIT): 15 ave Charles de Gaulle, BP 38, N'Djamena; telex 5233; 40% state-owned, 30.6% by Société Financière pour les Pays d'Outre-Mer (France), 29.4% by Banque Nationale de Paris; Man. Dir HISSEINE LAMINE; activities temporarily suspended.

Banque Tchadienne de Crédit et de Dépôts (BTCD): 2-6 rue Robert Lévy, BP 461, N'Djamena; tel. 51-41-90; telex 5212; f. 1963; 40% state-owned, 34% owned by Crédit Lyonnais (France); cap. 440m. (Dec. 1988); Pres. MADENGAR BÉRÉMADJI; Man. Dir MAHAMAT FARRIS; br. at Moundou.

Bankers' Organizations

Association Professionnelle des Banques au Tchad: N'Djamena.

Conseil National de Crédit: N'Djamena; f. 1965 to formulate a national credit policy and to organize the banking profession.

INSURANCE

Assureurs Conseils Tchadiens Faugère et Jutheau et Cie: BP 139, N'Djamena; tel. 51-21-15; telex 5235; Dir PHILIPPE GARDYE.

Société de Représentation d'Assurances et de Réassurances Africaines (SORARAF): N'Djamena; Dir Mme FOURNIER.

Société Tchadienne d'Assurances et de Réassurances (STAR): BP 914, N'Djamena; tel. 51-56-77; telex 5268; Dir PHILIPPE SABIT.

Directory

Trade and Industry

CHAMBER OF COMMERCE

Chambre Consulaire: BP 458, N'Djamena; tel. 51-52-64; f. 1938; Pres. ELIE ROMBA; Sec.-Gen. SALEH MAHAMAT RAHMA; brs at Sarh, Moundou, Bol and Abéché.

DEVELOPMENT ORGANIZATIONS

Caisse Centrale de Coopération Economique: BP 478, N'Djamena; tel. 51-40-71; Dir FRANÇOIS VINCENT.

Mission Française de Coopération et d'Action Culturelle: BP 898, N'Djamena; tel. 51-42-87; telex 5340; administers bilateral aid from France; Dir JACQUES COMPAGNON.

Office National de Développement Rural (ONDR): BP 896, N'Djamena; tel. 51-48-64; f. 1968; Dir MICKAEL DJIBRAEL.

Société pour le Développement de la Région du Lac (SODELAC): BP 782, N'Djamena; tel. 51-35-03; telex 5248; f. 1967; cap. 180m. francs CFA; Pres. CHERIF ABDELWAHAB; Dir-Gen. MAHAMAT MOCTAR ALI.

TRADE

Office National des Céréales (ONC): BP 21, N'Djamena; tel. 51-37-31; f. 1978; production and marketing of cereals; Dir YBRAHIM MAHAMAT TIDEI; 11 regional offices.

Société Nationale de Commercialisation du Tchad (SONACOT): N'Djamena; telex 5227; f. 1965; cap. 150m. francs CFA; 76% state-owned; national marketing, distribution and import-export company; has monopoly of purchase and sale of gum arabic in Chad; Man. Dir MARBROUCK NATROUD.

TRADE UNION

Union Nationale des Syndicats du Tchad (UNST): N'Djamena; f. 1988, following a merger of the Confédération Syndicale du Tchad (CST) and the Union Nationale des Travailleurs du Tchad (UNATRAT).

Transport

RAILWAYS
In 1962 Chad signed an agreement with Cameroon to extend the Transcameroon railway from N'Gaoundéré to Sarh, a distance of 500 km. Although the Transcameroon reached N'Gaoundéré in 1974, the proposed extension into Chad has been indefinitely postponed. Other possibilities of extending Sudanese and Nigerian lines into Chad are being explored.

ROADS
In 1976 there were 30,725 km of roads, of which 4,628 km were national roads and 3,512 km were secondary roads. There are also some 20,000 km of tracks suitable for motor traffic during the October–July dry season. In July 1986 the World Bank provided a loan of US $21m. towards a major programme to rehabilitate 2,000 km of roads, with the aim of improving the movement of goods within the country. In 1988 the International Development Association (IDA) granted $47m. to support the final stage of the programme: the rehabilitation of the 30-km N'Djamena–Djermaya road and the 146-km N'Djamena–Guelengdeng road. In the following year the IDA approved a further credit of $60m. for the rehabilitation of more than 1,800 km of main roads. The EEC is helping to fund the construction of a highway leading from N'Djamena to Sarh and Lere, on the Cameroon border. In 1989 the World Bank estimated that at least $300m. was required, in order to fund urgent road repairs, and in 1990 that organization was formulating a major road construction programme, thought to involve 1,800 km of roads.

Coopérative des Transportateurs Tchadiens (CTT): BP 336, N'Djamena; tel. 51-43-55; telex 5225; road haulage; Pres. SALEH KHALIFA; brs at Sarh, Moundou, Bangui (CAR), Douala and N'Gaoundéré (Cameroon).

INLAND WATERWAYS
There is a certain amount of traffic on the Chari and Logone rivers which meet just south of N'Djamena. Both routes, from Sarh to N'Djamena on the Chari and from Bongor and Moundou to N'Djamena on the Logone, are open only during the wet season, August–December, and provide a convenient alternative when roads become impassable.

CIVIL AVIATION
The international airport at N'Djamena has been in use since 1967: an improvement programme was completed in 1987. The renewal

CHAD

of the runway at Abéché, with French aid, began in 1988, and the upgrading of facilities at Faya-Largeau, also with assistance from France, was due to begin in 1990. There are more than 40 smaller airfields.

Air Afrique: BP 466, N'Djamena; tel. 51-40-20; see under Côte d'Ivoire.

Air Tchad: 27 ave du Président Tombalbaye, BP 168, N'Djamena; tel. 51-45-64; telex 5345; f. 1966; govt majority holding with 2% UTA interest; international charters and regular passenger, freight and charter services within Chad; Dir-Gen. MAHAMAT NOURI; fleet of 1 Fokker F. 27-500, 2 Twin Otter, 1 Cessna 310.

Tourism

Chad's potential attractions for tourists include a variety of scenery from the dense forests of the south to the deserts of the north. Wild animals abound, especially in the two national parks and five game reserves. An estimated 27,000 foreign visitors arrived in 1987.

Direction du Tourisme, des Parcs Nationaux et Réserves de Faune: BP 86, N'Djamena; tel. 51-45-26; also Délégation Régionale au Tourisme at BP 88, Sarh; tel. 274; f. 1962; Dir DABOULAYE BAN-YMARY.

Société Hôtelière et Touristique: BP 478, N'Djamena; Dir ANTOINE ABTOUR.

CHILE

Introductory Survey

Location, Climate, Language, Religion, Flag, Capital

The Republic of Chile is a long, narrow country lying along the Pacific coast of South America, extending from Peru and Bolivia in the north to Cape Horn in the far south. Isla de Pascua (Easter Island), about 3,780 km (2,350 miles) off shore, and several other small islands form part of Chile. To the east, Chile is separated from Argentina by the high Andes mountains. Both the mountains and the cold Humboldt Current influence the climate; between Arica in the north and Punta Arenas in the extreme south, a distance of about 4,000 km (2,500 miles), the average maximum temperature varies by no more than 13°C. Rainfall varies widely between the arid desert in the north and the rainy south. The language is Spanish. There is no state religion but the great majority of the inhabitants profess Christianity, and more than 85% are adherents of the Roman Catholic Church. The national flag (proportions 3 by 2) is divided horizontally: the lower half is red, while the upper half has a five-pointed white star on a blue square, at the hoist, with the remainder white. The capital is Santiago.

Recent History

Chile was ruled by Spain from the 16th century until its independence in 1818. For most of the 19th century it was governed by a small oligarchy of land-owners. Chile won the War of the Pacific (1879–83) against Peru and Bolivia. Most of the present century has been characterized by the struggle for power between right- and left-wing forces.

In September 1970 Dr Salvador Allende Gossens, the Marxist candidate of Unidad Popular (a coalition of five left-wing parties, including the Partido Comunista de Chile), was elected to succeed Eduardo Frei Montalva, a Christian Democrat who was President between 1964 and 1970. Allende promised to transform Chilean society by constitutional means, and imposed an extensive programme of nationalization. The Government failed to obtain a congressional majority in the elections of March 1973 and was faced with a deteriorating economic situation as well as an intensification of violent opposition to its policies. Accelerated inflation led to food shortages and there were repeated clashes between pro- and anti-Government activists. The armed forces finally intervened in September 1973, claiming that a military take-over was necessary because of the increasingly anarchic situation and economic breakdown. President Allende died during the coup.

Congress was dissolved, all political activity banned and strict censorship introduced. The military Junta dedicated itself to the eradication of Marxism and the reconstruction of Chile, and its leader, Gen. Augusto Pinochet Ugarte, became Supreme Chief of State in June and President in December 1974. The Junta was widely criticized abroad for its repressive policies and violations of human rights. Critics of the regime were tortured and imprisoned, and several thousand disappeared. Some of those who had been imprisoned were released, as a result of international pressure, and sent into exile.

In September 1976 three constitutional acts were promulgated with the aim of creating an 'authoritarian democracy'. All political parties were banned in March 1977, when the state of siege was extended. Following a UN General Assembly resolution in December 1977, condemning the Government for violating human rights, President Pinochet called a referendum in January 1978 to endorse the regime's policies. As more than 75% of the voters supported the President in his defence of Chile 'in the face of international aggression', the state of siege (in force since 1973) was lifted and was replaced by a state of emergency.

A plebiscite in September 1980 showed a 67% vote in favour of a new constitution which had been drawn up by the Government, although dubious electoral practices were allegedly employed. The new Constitution was described as providing a 'transition to democracy' but, although President Pinochet ceased to be head of the armed forces, additional clauses allowed him to maintain his firm hold on power until 1989. Political parties, which were still officially outlawed, began to re-emerge, and in July 1983 five moderate parties formed a coalition, the 'Alianza Democrática', demanding a return to democratic rule within 18 months. A left-wing coalition was also created.

An anti-Government campaign of bombings, begun in late 1983 and directed principally against electricity installations, continued throughout 1984. In response, in January 1984 the Government announced new anti-terrorist legislation and extensive security measures. Relations between the Roman Catholic Church and the State began to deteriorate after anti-Government demonstrations at Punta Arenas in February, for which the Government blamed the Church. The first May Day rally in Santiago since 1973 was attended by 150,000 people, and public protests were held throughout the country. Two days of violent clashes between police and demonstrators in September resulted in nine deaths, including that of a French priest. Following the demonstrations, the opposition called a general strike in October. During the two days of protests accompanying the strike, a further nine people were killed.

Despite the Government's strenuous attempts to eradicate internal opposition, the campaign of bombings and public protests continued throughout 1985. In September 10 people were killed and several hundred were arrested during two days of anti-Government demonstrations. Opposition leaders and trade unionists were also detained and sent into internal exile. During an anti-Government protest in November, four people were killed and hundreds were arrested by the security forces. In the same month President Pinochet appointed a new army representative to the Junta, in what was widely regarded as a move to consolidate support for his presidency within the ruling body.

Throughout 1986 President Pinochet's regime came under increasing attack from opposition groups, the Roman Catholic Church, guerrilla organizations (principally the Frente Patriótico Manuel Rodríguez—FPMR) and international critics including the US administration, which had previously refrained from condemning the regime's notorious record of violations of human rights. A bombing campaign by the FPMR continued intermittently: 267 acts of terrorism were recorded in the first half of 1986. In April leading trade union, professional and community groups, many of whom had previously been passive critics of the Government, formed the Asamblea de la Civilidad, an organization whose aim was to seek a peaceful transition to democracy. However, during a two-day general strike called by the Asamblea in July, eight people were killed and several hundred were detained. The death of an American resident, who was reported to have been deliberately set alight by a group of soldiers, provoked international condemnation and brought renewed criticism from the USA.

In September 1986 the FPMR made an unsuccessful attempt to assassinate President Pinochet. The regime's immediate response was to impose a state of siege throughout Chile, under which leading members of the opposition were detained and strict censorship was introduced. One consequence of the state of siege was the reappearance of right-wing death squads, who were implicated in a series of murders which followed the assassination attempt.

In February 1984 the Council of State, a government-appointed consultative body, began drafting a law to legalize political parties and to prepare for elections in 1989. In March 1984 President Pinochet confirmed that a plebiscite would be held at an unspecified time to decide on a timetable for the elections. In September, however, President Pinochet firmly rejected any possibility of a return to civilian rule before 1989. In August 1985 the Roman Catholic Church sponsored talks between 11 opposition groups, which resulted in the drafting of an Acuerdo Nacional para la Transición a la Plena Democracia (National Accord for the Transition to Full Democracy). President Pinochet rejected the opposition's proposals.

In 1986 reports that President Pinochet intended to extend his term of office until the late 1990s, by seeking the presidential candidacy for the plebiscite due to be held in either 1988 or 1989, caused considerable dismay among opposition groups, and gave rise to speculation that the Junta and the Government were divided over the issue of a return to full democracy after 1989. In February 1987 the registration of voters opened for the presidential plebiscite. In March the Government promulgated a law under which non-Marxist political parties were to be permitted to register officially. The opposition parties, however, were divided over the question of registration, with several left-wing groups refusing to register. By mid-1987 President Pinochet had clearly indicated his intention to remain in office beyond 1989 by securing the presidential candidacy; a cabinet reshuffle in July enabled him to appoint confirmed supporters of his policies.

Following anti-Government protests during Pope John Paul II's visit to Chile in April 1987, further demonstrations against the regime (resulting in the deaths of two people) occurred in October, during a general strike which was called by a leading trade union organization. In November some 150,000–200,000 people participated in a demonstration in Santiago, organized by the Asamblea de la Civilidad and the trade unions, in support of demands for the ending of military rule and for the holding of free elections. The opposition's cause was boosted, in December, by the US Congress's vote to donate US $1m. to its campaign for open elections. However, Congress's decision precipitated a further deterioration in relations between Chile and the USA, as the Chilean Government protested strongly at US 'interference' in Chile's internal affairs.

In January 1988 the Government confirmed that the plebiscite would be held between 11 September and 12 December 1988. In February 13 political parties and opposition groups, including the Izquierda Cristiana and leading factions of the Partido Radical, Partido Socialista and the Movimiento de Acción Popular Unitario (but excluding the Partido Comunista de Chile), signed a pact to form a united front to oppose the government candidate. By May a further three organizations had joined the front, which assumed the title of El Comando por el No. The front's principal function was to co-ordinate the campaign for the anti-Government vote at the forthcoming referendum.

In July 1988 the Junta announced that the selection of the government candidate would take place on 30 August. Mounting public interest in the plebiscite was demonstrated by the number of people registering to vote, which greatly exceeded both the Government's and the opposition's expectations. When the registration closed, at the end of August, some 7.4m. people, out of a potential electorate of approximately 8m., had registered. The opposition campaign was vastly overshadowed by official propaganda for the plebiscite, but in August the Junta agreed to give opposition parties access to television broadcasts for the first time since 1973. Moreover, on 24 August the Government announced the repeal of the states of exception, comprising the state of emergency and the state of threat to domestic order, which had been in force almost continuously since 1973. As a result of the Government's decision, the opposition was able to hold public rallies, and it was hoped that tension surrounding the forthcoming plebiscite would be dispelled.

On 30 August 1988 President Pinochet was named by the Junta as the single candidate at the plebiscite scheduled for 5 October. The Junta's decision provoked widespread protests by the opposition, and led to disturbances in Santiago, resulting in three deaths. In September the Government announced that all Chileans in political exile, who were believed to number 430, were henceforth permitted to return to Chile (although the cases of 177 exiles would be subject to review by the courts). The opposition's campaign concluded in early October with a mass rally in Santiago, attended by almost 1m. people.

Prior to the plebiscite on 5 October 1988, President Pinochet gave public assurances that the result would be respected by his administration. Despite some reports of electoral malpractice, the plebiscite took place without major incident. The official result gave the anti-Pinochet campaign 54.7% of the votes cast, and President Pinochet 43.1%. The opposition's victory precipitated widespread public celebrations and, subsequently, clashes between government forces and opposition supporters, during which two people were killed. The cabinet members tendered their resignations, but these were initially refused by President Pinochet.

Following the plebiscite, the opposition made repeated demands for changes to the Constitution, in order to accelerate the democratic process, and sought to initiate discussions with the armed forces. However, President Pinochet rejected the opposition's proposals, and affirmed his intention to remain in office until March 1990. Moreover, pro-Government supporters attempted to construe the result of the referendum as a testimony to President Pinochet's personal popularity, and it was suggested that he would contest the presidential election due to be held in December 1989.

In late October 1988 President Pinochet announced a cabinet reshuffle, and in November he authorized the retirement of 13 generals, in the most radical revision of the army High Command since 1973. Moreover, in the same month Gen. Santiago Sinclair Oyaneder, a firm supporter of President Pinochet, was appointed the army's representative in the Junta.

The settlement of leadership disputes and of certain ideological differences in mid-1989 led to the emergence of Patricio Aylwin Azócar, a lawyer and former senator who had been a vociferous supporter of the 'no' vote in the October 1988 plebiscite, as the sole presidential candidate for the centre-left Concertación de los Partidos por la Democracia (CPD, formerly the Comando por el No), an alliance of 17 parties, including the Partido Demócrata Cristiano (PDC), of which Aylwin had hitherto been president, and several socialist parties.

Throughout 1989 the election campaign was dominated by demands from both the CPD and right-wing parties for constitutional reform, and by the ensuing lengthy negotiations with Carlos Cáceres Contreras, the Minister of the Interior. A draft document, proffered by the Government, was initially rejected by the CPD, on the grounds that it contained inadequate provisions for comprehensive constitutional amendment in the future, for controls over the composition and function of the National Security Council and for greater freedom in the creation and composition of Congress. A later proposal, expanded to 54 amendments (including the legalization of Marxist political parties) and ratified by the Junta, was finally accepted by the opposition, with some reservations, and the constitutional reforms (see p. 705) were approved by 85.7% of voters in a national referendum in July 1989.

In early 1989 journalists on trial for publishing anti-Government material were pardoned; later in the year, union leaders Manuel Bustos and Arturo Martínez were released from internal exile, after pressure from the Roman Catholic Church and the leader of the Polish Solidarity movement, Lech Wałęsa. Despite these initial indications that a peaceful transition to democratically-elected government was possible, the electoral campaign was accompanied by intermittent outbursts of political violence and government intervention. In the three months to October 1989 there were more than 1,000 arrests for alleged political violations and 23 attacks against political offices. Jécar Cristi, spokesman of the Movimiento de la Izquierda Revolucionaria (MIR), was shot dead in September; an unknown right-wing organization was thought to be responsible for the killing. Union leaders and members of the Partido Comunista de Chile and other left-wing parties were arrested on suspicion of participating in subversive activities, including a partially successful one-day general strike in April 1989, during which at least two people were killed and hundreds were detained when police and demonstrators clashed violently. Many party leaders were later released on bail.

Uncertainty regarding President Pinochet's own intentions concerning the forthcoming elections was finally dispelled in mid-1989, when he dismissed the possibility of his candidacy as unconstitutional, but reiterated his intention to continue as Commander-in-Chief of the Army for at least four years. Opposition leaders interpreted subsequent actions by the Government (including the proposal of a law providing for the autonomy of the Banco Central de Chile (implemented in early December), the appointment of directors to state-owned companies with mandates of up to 10 years and curbs on the Government's power to remove state officials from their posts) as an attempt by the President to retain some power beyond his term of office.

The presidential and congressional elections were held on 14 December 1989. Patricio Aylwin Azócar of the centre-left CPD secured 55.2% of the valid votes cast in the presidential election, thus achieving a clear victory over the former Minister of Finance, Hernán Büchi Buc, who was supported by the Government and who won 29.4%. Francisco Javier Errázuriz, also of the right wing, received 15.4% of the votes. In January 1990 President-Elect Aylwin announced the composition of his Cabinet, and asked two members of the outgoing Junta to remain as commanders of the air force and police. The transfer of power took place on 11 March 1990 at the newly-constructed Congress building in Valparaíso.

Having failed to obtain the support of the two-thirds majority in Congress necessary to amend the 1980 Constitution significantly (owing partly to an electoral system weighted heavily in favour of pro-regime candidates and the power of the outgoing Junta to nominate almost one-fifth of the Senate), Aylwin's new CPD administration was forced to reconcile attempts to fulfil campaign promises as quickly as possible with the need to adopt a conciliatory approach towards more right-wing parties in Congress, whose support was essential for the enactment of new legislation. Agreement was reached almost immediately, however, on a series of modifications to the tax laws, which were expected to generate sufficient surplus revenue for the implementation of several new initiatives for social welfare. Attempts to amend existing articles of law considered repressive by the new administration (including the death penalty and provisions for the censorship of the press) were less successful. In October 1990 military courts were continuing to initiate proceedings against journalists for alleged defamation of the armed forces, and in November a draft law proposing the abolition of the death penalty was finally defeated in the Senate, the sentence being retained for some 30 offences.

In April 1990 the Government created the Commission for Truth and Reconciliation to document and investigate alleged violations of human rights during the previous administration. Although Pinochet had, before leaving office, provided for the impunity of the former military Junta with regard to abuses of human rights, it was suggested by human rights organizations that such safeguards might be circumvented by indicting known perpetrators of atrocities on charges of 'crimes against humanity', a provision which gained considerable public support following the discovery, during 1990, of a number of mass graves containing the remains of political opponents of the 1973–90 military regime. The army High Command openly condemned the Commission for undermining the prestige of the armed forces and attempting to contravene the terms of a comprehensive amnesty declared in 1978. Although a new accord between military leaders and the Government-Elect had been negotiated in January 1990 (whereby the Junta of Commanders-in-Chief was abolished and the role of the armed forces redefined as essentially subservient to the Ministry of Defence), relations between the new Government and the army High Command remained tense throughout the year.

Escalating public and political antagonism towards the former military leadership was fuelled by further revelations of human rights abuses and financial corruption connected with the state secret police (CNI), officially disbanded in early 1990, and gave rise to renewed political violence (including the assassination of a former chief of police intelligence and the attempted assassination of an ex-air force chief). Gen. Pinochet, who had warned, in early 1990, that attempted reprisals against members of the armed forces would constitute a serious threat to a peaceful transition to democracy, became the focus for widespread disaffection with the army High Command but resisted repeated demands for his resignation, reiterating his intention to continue as Commander-in-Chief of the Army until 1997.

In September 1990 the body of former President Allende (see above) was exhumed from an unmarked grave in Viña del Mar, where it had been interred without ceremony following the 1973 military coup, and was reburied in Santiago with massive popular tribute. Some days later, mourners visiting the grave, on the 17th anniversary of Allende's death, clashed violently with security forces, and several arrests were made.

In December 1990 President Aylwin attempted to restore public confidence in the supremacy of the Government over the armed forces by publicly challenging Pinochet's authority and vetoing two army promotions recommended by the General, while transferring authority for the police force from the Ministry of Defence to the Ministry of the Interior.

In 1985 the Chilean Government was strongly criticized by opposition groups and the inhabitants of Isla de Pascua (Easter Island) for its decision to extend and improve the island's Mataveri airstrip for use by the US National Aeronautics and Space Administration (NASA). The improved airstrip was opened in August 1987.

Chile has had border disputes: to the north with Bolivia and to the south with Argentina. In 1978 Bolivia severed diplomatic relations with Chile on the grounds that the Chilean Government had not shown sufficient flexibility over the question of Bolivia's access to the Pacific Ocean. In 1987 the dispute was revived, following Chile's refusal to consider a new attempt by Bolivia to obtain a sovereign seaport. The issue of Bolivian access to the coast was finally resolved in mid-1990, when the international highway from Tambo Quemado, Bolivia, to Arica, on the Pacific coast of Chile, was completed, and plans were announced for the construction of a new road, at a projected cost of US $90.9m., linking Tambo Quemado with Patacamaya, south of the Bolivian administrative capital of La Paz. Chile's dispute with Argentina concerned three small islands in the Beagle Channel, south of Tierra del Fuego. The issue of sovereignty over these islands has, on occasions, brought the two countries to the verge of war. In December 1978 the case was referred to papal mediation, and in December 1980 the resultant proposals were presented to the two Governments. In October 1984 it was announced that total agreement had been reached. Under the terms of the settlement, Chile was awarded 12 islands and islets to the south of the Beagle Channel, including Lennox, Picton and Nueva. The agreement was formally approved by the ruling Junta in April 1985, and was ratified in May by representatives of the Argentine and Chilean Governments.

In 1990, following the successful transition to democratically-elected government, diplomatic relations were restored with Algeria, Czechoslovakia, Hungary, Mexico, Poland, the USSR and Yugoslavia.

Government

Chile is a republic, divided into 12 regions and a metropolitan area. Under a new constitution, which was promulgated in March 1981 and took full effect from 1989 (see Constitution), executive power is vested in the President, who is directly elected for a four-year term. The President is assisted by a cabinet. Legislative power is vested in the bicameral National Congress, comprising the 47-member Senate and the 120-member Chamber of Deputies.

Defence

Military service lasts two years and is compulsory for men at 19 years of age. In June 1990 the army had a strength of 54,000, the navy 29,000 and the air force 12,800. Paramilitary security forces number about 27,000 carabineros. Defence expenditure for 1990 was expected to total 165,160m. pesos.

Economic Affairs

In 1988, according to estimates by the World Bank, Chile's gross national product (GNP), measured at average 1986–88 prices was US $19,220m., equivalent to $1,510 per head. During 1980–88, it was estimated, GNP increased, in real terms, at an average annual rate of 1.6%, while GNP per head declined by 0.1% per year. Over the same period, the population increased by an annual average of 1.7%. Chile's gross domestic product (GDP) increased by an annual average of 1.9% in 1980–88.

Agriculture (including forestry and fishing) contributed 9.4% of GDP in 1988. About 20.3% of the working population were employed in this sector in 1988. Chile is a major exporter of fruit and vegetables (fruit alone accounted for 12% of total exports in 1987). Wood and wood products are also important. During 1980–88 agricultural production increased by an annual average of 3.8%.

Industry (including mining, manufacturing, construction and power) contributed about 37% of GDP and employed 24.8% of the working population in 1988. During 1980–88 industrial production increased by an annual average of 2.2%.

Mining contributed 7.7% of GDP and employed 2.0% of the working population in 1988. Chile is the world's largest producer and exporter of copper. Copper accounted for 87.5% of Chile's total export earnings in 1970, but the proportion decreased to an annual average of 44.1% in the period 1984–88. Gold, silver, iron ore, saltpetre, molybdenum and iodine are also mined. Petroleum and natural gas have been located in the south.

Manufacturing contributed 21% of GDP and employed 15.7% of the working population in 1988. The most important sectors, measured by gross value of output, are food-processing, wood and paper products, textiles, rubber and chemicals. Manufacturing output increased by an average of 2.0% per year in 1980–88.

Energy is derived principally from petroleum and natural gas (some 60%), hydroelectric power (24%) and coal (15%).

In 1989 Chile recorded a visible trade surplus of US $1,578m., but there was a deficit of $905m. on the current account of the balance of payments. In 1989 the principal source of imports (20.0%) was the USA, which was also the principal market for exports (17.8%). Other major trading partners were Brazil, the

CHILE

Federal Republic of Germany and Japan. The principal exports in 1988 were copper (47.9% of total export revenue), fruit and vegetables (9.1%), meat and fish meal fodder (6.5%) and wood pulp (4.4%). The principal imports in that year were technical and electrical equipment, mineral products, chemicals and transport equipment.

In 1988 there was a budgetary surplus of 198,684m. pesos. Chile's total external debt was US $16,248m. at the end of 1989. The annual rate of inflation averaged 20.8% in 1980–88, declining to 17.0% in 1989. An estimated 6.5% of the labour force were unemployed in mid-1990.

Chile is a member of ALADI (see p. 172) and was admitted to the Group of Río (see p. 236) in 1990.

Owing to the relaxation of import duties in the early 1980s, Chile's potential in the agricultural and manufacturing sectors was stifled by cheaper imported goods. Exports of fruit, seafoods and wines, however, have expanded considerably. Chile imports some 85% of its petroleum requirements. The rise in world petroleum prices, following the Iraqi invasion and annexation of Kuwait in August 1990, was expected to prove a serious obstacle to future economic growth. A development project to expand the output of wood and pulp was expected to cost US $1,900m. during 1987–92. Chile's successful debt-reduction programme (having reduced debt with commercial banks by more than 40% during 1983–88) has received praise from the World Bank and the IMF, and has afforded Chile eligibility for debt relief under the Brady Plan, proposed by the USA.

Social Welfare

Employees, including agricultural workers, may receive benefits for sickness, unemployment, accidents at work, maternity and retirement, and there are dependants' allowances, including family allowances. In May 1981 the management of social security was transferred to the private sector, and operated by the Administradoras de Fondo de Pensiones. A National Health Service was established in 1952. There were 5,671 physicians working in official medical services in 1979. Chile had 300 hospital establishments, with a total of 37,971 beds, in 1980. Of total expenditure by the central Government in 1987, about 76,820m. pesos (6.3%) was for health services, and a further 419,470m. pesos (34.4%) for social security and welfare.

Education

Pre-primary education is widely available for all children up to the age of six years. Primary education is officially compulsory, and is provided free of charge, for eight years, beginning at six or seven years of age. It is divided into two cycles: the first lasts for four years and provides a general education; the second cycle offers more specialized schooling. Secondary education, beginning at 13 or 14 years of age, is divided into the humanities-science programme (lasting for four years), with the emphasis on general education and possible entrance to university, and the technical-professional programme (lasting for between four and six years), designed to fulfil the requirements of specialist training. In 1988 the total enrolment at primary schools included an estimated 90% of children in the relevant age-group, while the comparable ratio for secondary enrolment was 56%. Higher education is provided by three kinds of institution: universities, professional institutes and centres of technical formation. An intensive national literacy campaign, launched in 1980, reduced the rate of adult illiteracy from 11% in 1970 to an estimated 5.6% in 1983. The university law of January 1981 banned all political activity in universities, reduced the number of degree courses from 33 to 12, halved future government funding and encouraged the establishment of private specialized universities. In recent years the Government has initiated new programmes specifically designed for adult education. Expenditure on education by all levels of government in 1987 was about 180,740m. pesos (13.7% of total public spending).

Public Holidays

1991: 1 January (New Year's Day), 29–30 March (Good Friday and Easter Saturday), 1 May (Labour Day), 21 May (Battle of Iquique), 15 August (Assumption), 18 September (Independence Day), 12 October (Day of the Race, anniversary of the discovery of America), 1 November (All Saints' Day), 8 December (Immaculate Conception), 25 December (Christmas Day), 31 December (New Year's Eve).

1992: 1 January (New Year's Day), 17–18 April (Good Friday and Easter Saturday), 1 May (Labour Day), 21 May (Battle of Iquique), 15 August (Assumption), 18 September (Independence Day), 12 October (Day of the Race, anniversary of the discovery of America), 1 November (All Saints' Day), 8 December (Immaculate Conception), 25 December (Christmas Day), 31 December (New Year's Eve).

Weights and Measures

The metric system is officially in force.

Statistical Survey

Source (unless otherwise stated): Instituto Nacional de Estadísticas, Avda Bulnes 418, Casilla 498-3, Correo 3, Santiago; tel. (2) 699-1441.

Area and Population

AREA, POPULATION AND DENSITY*

Area (sq km)	756,626†
Population (census results)‡	
22 April 1970	8,884,786
21 April 1982	
Males	5,553,409
Females	5,776,327
Total	11,329,736
Population (official estimates at mid-year)	
1988	12,748,207
1989	12,961,032
1990	13,173,347
Density (per sq km) at mid-1990	17.4

* Excluding Chilean Antarctic Territory.
† 292,135 sq miles.
‡ Excluding adjustment for underenumeration, estimated at 5.12% in 1970.

REGIONS*

		Area (sq km)	Population (30 June 1990)	Capital
I	De Tarapacá	58,698	358,088	Iquique
II	De Antofagasta	126,444	389,547	Antofagasta
III	De Atacama	75,573	197,842	Copiapó
IV	De Coquimbo	40,656	486,493	La Serena
V	De Valparaíso	16,396	1,381,948	Valparaíso
VI	Del Libertador Gen. Bernardo O'Higgins	16,365	649,764	Rancagua
VII	Del Maule	30,302	840,457	Talca
VIII	Del Bío-Bío	36,929	1,674,243	Concepción
IX	De la Araucanía	31,858	795,932	Temuco
X	De Los Lagos	66,997	922,543	Puerto Montt
XI	Aisén del Gen. Carlos Ibáñez del Campo	109,025	80,278	Coihaique
XII	De Magallanes y Antártida Chilena	132,034	159,885	Punta Arenas
	Metropolitan Region (Santiago)	15,349	5,236,321	—

* Before 1975 the country was divided into 25 provinces. With the new administrative system, the 13 regions are sub-divided into 50 new provinces and the metropolitan area of Santiago.

CHILE

PRINCIPAL TOWNS (population at 15 June 1990)

Gran Santiago (capital)	4,385,481	Arica	177,330
Concepción	306,464	Talca	164,492
Viña del Mar	281,063	Iquique	148,511
Valparaíso	276,756	Chillán	145,972
Talcahuano	246,853	Punta Arenas	120,030
Antofagasta	218,754	Osorno	117,444
Temuco	211,693	Valdivia	113,512
Rancagua	190,379	Quilpué	107,396
San Bernardo	188,156	Puerto Montt	106,528
Puente Alto	187,368	La Serena	105,594

* Including suburbs.

BIRTHS, MARRIAGES AND DEATHS

	Registered live births*		Registered marriages		Registered deaths	
	Number	Rate (per 1,000)	Number	Rate (per 1,000)	Number	Rate (per 1,000)
1982	274,335	23.9	80,115	7.0	69,887	6.1
1983	260,655	22.2	82,483	7.1	74,296	6.4
1984	265,016	22.2	87,261	7.3	74,669	6.3
1985	261,978	21.6	91,099	7.5	73,534	6.1
1986	272,997	22.1	93,995	7.6	72,209	5.9
1987	279,712	22.3	95,531	7.6	70,559	5.6
1988	296,581	23.3	103,484	8.1	74,435	5.8

* Figures include adjustment for underenumeration, estimated at 6.5% for 1982-83 and 5% for 1984-88.

ECONOMICALLY ACTIVE POPULATION*
('000 persons aged 15 years and over, October-December)

	1987	1988	1989
Agriculture, hunting, forestry and fishing	837.4	865.2	857.4
Mining and quarrying	82.2	88.2	103.1
Manufacturing	607.3	670.5	746.0
Electricity, gas and water	25.1	25.4	23.8
Construction	209.0	276.1	298.9
Trade, restaurants and hotels	690.5	731.8	756.2
Transport, storage and communications	253.4	275.0	301.4
Financing, insurance, real estate and business services	177.2	182.1	192.3
Community, social and personal services	1,126.6	1,150.6	1,145.1
Activities not adequately defined	0.9	1.0	0.4
Total employed	4,010.6	4,266.0	4,424.7
Unemployed	343.4	286.1	250.0
Total labour force	4,354.0	4,552.2	4,674.7
Males	3,048.7	3,157.1	3,236.2
Females	1,305.3	1,395.0	1,438.5

* Figures are based on sample surveys, covering 36,000 households, and exclude members of the armed forces.

Agriculture

PRINCIPAL CROPS ('000 metric tons)

	1987	1988	1989
Wheat	1,874	1,734	1,766
Rice (paddy)	147	162	185
Barley	48	82	85
Oats	128	157	165
Rye	5	4	9
Maize	617	661	938
Dry beans	81	100	73
Lentils	25	20	8
Potatoes	727	928	882
Sunflower seed	40	49	32
Sugar beet	2,650	2,487	2,810
Rapeseed	95	123	113
Tomatoes	396	414	410*
Pumpkins, etc.	132	153	155*
Onions (dry)	228	255	250*
Water melons	93	86	88*
Melons	82	79	90*
Grapes	963†	999†	1,100*
Apples	580	630	680
Peaches and nectarines	147	151	163
Dry peas	5	5	6
Chick-peas	15	8	4

* FAO estimate. † Unofficial estimate.
Source: FAO, *Production Yearbook*.

LIVESTOCK ('000 head, year ending September)

	1987	1988	1989
Horses*	490	490	490
Cattle	3,371	3,468	3,500
Pigs	1,300	1,360	1,400
Sheep	6,470	6,429	6,600
Goats	600*	600	600*

* FAO estimate(s).
Source: FAO, *Production Yearbook*.

LIVESTOCK PRODUCTS ('000 metric tons)

	1987	1988	1989
Beef and veal	175	197	200
Mutton and lamb	14	14	16
Pig meat	88	100	110
Horse meat	9	8	9
Poultry meat	100	112	110
Cows' milk	1,128	1,149	1,290†
Butter	5.0	4.9	5.0*
Cheese	23.0	25.5	24.7*
Hen eggs	83.7	81.9	83.0*
Wool:			
greasy	20.1	19.6	23.0†
clean	10.0	9.8	11.5†

* FAO estimate. † Unofficial estimate.
Source: FAO, *Production Yearbook*.

CHILE
Statistical Survey

Forestry

ROUNDWOOD REMOVALS ('000 cubic metres, excluding bark)

	1986	1987	1988
Sawlogs, veneer logs and logs for sleepers	5,751	5,568	5,665*
Pulpwood	3,922	4,106	4,106
Other industrial wood*	553	553	553
Fuel wood*	6,222	6,329	6,437
Total	16,448	16,556	16,761

* FAO estimate(s).
Source: FAO, *Yearbook of Forest Products*.

SAWNWOOD PRODUCTION ('000 cubic metres, incl. boxboards)

	1986*	1987	1988
Coniferous (soft wood)	1,734	2,309	2,381
Broadleaved (hard wood)	291	368	324
Total	2,025	2,677	2,705

* Source: FAO, *Yearbook of Forest Products*.
Source: Corporación de Fomento de la Producción (CORFO).
Railway sleepers ('000 cubic metres): 3 per year (1981–88). Source: FAO, *Yearbook of Forest Products*.

Fishing*

('000 metric tons, live weight)

	1986	1987	1988
Chilean hake	29.7	30.9	50.1
Patagonian hake	38.5	56.6	69.3
Chilean jack mackerel	1,184.3	1,710.0	2,138.3
Chilean sprat	22.9	31.8	18.1
Chilean pilchard (sardine)	2,585.2	2,234.3	1,525.8
Anchoveta (Peruvian anchovy)	1,463.4	335.9	911.7
Chub mackerel	1.6	32.8	26.4
Other marine fishes (incl. unspecified)	89.3	154.8	288.0
Total fish	5,414.9	4,647.1	5,027.7
Crustaceans	26.5	30.5	33.4
Clams	37.2	35.0	43.8
Other molluscs	63.2	72.9	77.0
Other aquatic animals	29.9	28.8	26.8
Total catch	5,571.7	4,814.3	5,208.7

* Excluding aquatic plants but including quantities landed by foreign fishing craft in Chilean ports.

Mining

('000 metric tons, unless otherwise indicated)

	1987	1988	1989*
Copper (metal content)	1,412.9	1,472	1,621
Coal	1,749.9	2,485.1	2,100.4
Iron ore†	6,690	7,865	9,206
Calcium carbonate	2,428.8	2,896.7	3,046
Sodium sulphate—hydrous (metric tons)	12,406	15,879	10,245
Molybdenum—metal content (metric tons)	16,941	15,527	16,665
Manganese (metric tons)‡	31,803	43,655	43,814
Gold (kilograms)	17,035	20,614	19,981
Silver (kilograms)	499,761	506,501	490,549
Petroleum (cubic metres)	1,736,398	1,420,393	1,281,282
Natural gas ('000 cubic metres)	4,352,554	4,278,447	4,236,137

* Provisional.
† Gross weight. The estimated iron content is 61%.
‡ Gross weight. The estimated metal content is 32%.

Industry

SELECTED PRODUCTS
('000 metric tons, unless otherwise indicated)

	1986	1987	1988
Sugar	384	348	365
Cement	1,441	1,500	1,885
Beer (million litres)	205	255	265
Gasoline*	916	1,018	1,140
Kerosene and jet fuels*	302	346	355
Distillate fuel oils*	1,313	1,358	1,614
Residual fuel oil*	1,085	1,046	1,205
Tyres ('000)	862	1,221	1,347
Cigarettes (million)†	8,296	8,183	n.a.
Glass sheets ('000 sq metres)	3,134	2,310	2,792

* Source: UN, *Monthly Bulletin of Statistics*.
† Source: UN, *Industrial Statistics Yearbook*.
1989 ('000 metric tons, unless otherwise indicated): Sugar 353; Cement 2,010; Beer (million litres) 277; Tyres ('000) 1,562; Glass sheets ('000 sq metres) 5,677.

Finance

CURRENCY AND EXCHANGE RATES
Monetary Units
  100 centavos = 1 Chilean peso.

Denominations
  Coins: 1, 5, 10, 50 and 100 pesos.
  Notes: 500, 1,000, 5,000 and 10,000 pesos.

Sterling and Dollar Equivalents (30 September 1990)
  £1 sterling = 575.7 pesos;
  US $1 = 307.3 pesos;
  1,000 Chilean pesos = £1.737 = $3.254.

Average Exchange Rate (pesos per US $)
  1987 219.54
  1988 245.05
  1989 267.16

BUDGET (million pesos)

Revenue	1986	1987	1988
Income from taxes	671,077	887,089	1,086,889
Non-tax revenue	1,266,469	1,455,649	1,909,464
Total current revenue	1,937,546	2,342,738	2,996,353

CHILE

Statistical Survey

Expenditure	1986	1987	1988
Remunerations	161,078	181,244	219,318
Purchase of goods and services	77,721	104,825	110,282
Transfers	753,013	896,259	1,047,030
Mortgage services	—	—	612
Real investment	90,058	106,818	146,239
Amortizations	64,246	88,238	88,895
Capital transfers	28,509	45,871	126,208
Interest on the public debt	111,165	143,245	227,446
Past operational expenditure	6,053	5,381	6,385
Commitments pending	1,403	2,058	1,410
Free fiscal contribution	570,764	679,749	823,844
Total	**1,864,010**	**2,253,688**	**2,797,669**

CENTRAL BANK RESERVES (US $ million at 31 December)

	1986	1987	1988
IMF special drawing rights	0.2	40.8	44.3
Foreign exchange	2,351.1	2,463.0	3,116.2
Total*	**2,351.3**	**2,503.8**	**3,160.5**

* Excluding gold (1,529,000 troy oz in each year).
1989 (US $ million at 31 December): IMF special drawing rights 24.4.
Source: IMF, *International Financial Statistics*.

MONEY SUPPLY (million pesos at 31 December)

	1986	1987	1988
Currency outside banks	108,560	135,698	181,536
Demand deposits at commercial banks	73,164	63,900	182,490
Total money	**181,724**	**199,598**	**364,026**

COST OF LIVING
(Consumer Price Index, annual averages. Base: April 1989 = 100)

	1986	1987	1988
Food	69.44	85.72	97.35
Housing	68.56	83.83	94.57
Clothing	66.78	82.02	95.63
Miscellaneous	72.61	85.88	95.10
All items	**70.10**	**85.13**	**95.93**

NATIONAL ACCOUNTS (million pesos at current prices)
Expenditure on the Gross Domestic Product

	1987*	1988*	1989*
Government final consumption expenditure	475,087	568,466	667,006
Private final consumption expenditure	2,811,039	3,534,776	4,520,375
Increase in stocks	36,335	36,062	128,400
Gross fixed capital formation	666,763	882,657	1,249,918
Total domestic expenditure	**3,989,224**	**5,021,961**	**6,565,699**
Exports of goods and services	1,394,265	2,022,033	2,533,794
Less Imports of goods and services	1,223,727	1,632,969	2,320,050
GDP in purchasers' values	**4,159,762**	**5,411,025**	**6,779,443**
GDP at constant 1977 prices	**398,230**	**427,530**	**470,243**

* Provisional.

Gross Domestic Product by Economic Activity
(million pesos at constant 1977 prices)

	1986	1987	1988
Agriculture, forestry and fishing	37,107	38,308	40,398
Mining and quarrying	31,523	31,525	32,853
Manufacturing	78,507	82,804	89,997
Electricity, gas and water	9,744	10,117	11,060
Construction	20,852	23,056	24,454
Wholesale and retail trade	62,919	67,635	74,235
Transport, storage and communications	21,571	23,755	26,485
Other services	114,404	121,030	128,048
GDP in purchasers' values	**376,627**	**398,230**	**427,530**

BALANCE OF PAYMENTS (US $ million)

	1987	1988	1989
Merchandise exports f.o.b.	5,224	7,052	8,080
Merchandise imports f.o.b.	−3,994	−4,833	−6,502
Trade balance	**1,230**	**2,219**	**1,578**
Exports of services	1,268	1,399	1,638
Imports of services	−3,432	−3,962	−4,361
Balance on goods and services	**−934**	**−344**	**−1,145**
Private unrequited transfers (net)	65	63	58
Government unrequited transfers (net)	61	114	182
Current balance	**−808**	**−167**	**−905**
Direct capital investment (net)	97	109	259
Other long-term capital (net)	−1,003	1,088	396
Short-term capital (net)	−130	−76	724
Net errors and omissions	−78	−109	−51
Total (net monetary movements)	**−1,922**	**845**	**423**
Monetization of gold	7	5	3
Valuation changes (net)	−116	−27	9
Exceptional financing (net)	1,980	−112	17
Official financing (net)	77	93	130
Changes in reserves	**26**	**804**	**581**

Source: IMF, *International Financial Statistics*.

External Trade

PRINCIPAL COMMODITIES (US $ million)

Imports c.i.f.	1987	1988	1989
Consumer goods	584.1	788.7	1,142.0
Agricultural products	13.0	15.3	16.5
Manufactured foodstuffs	50.3	78.2	82.6
Other manufactured products	435.6	554.0	730.4
Drugs and medicaments	50.2	61.1	68.5
Machinery	38.2	44.0	57.6
Others	347.2	448.9	604.3
Automobiles	85.2	141.2	313.1
Capital goods	981.5	1,258.3	1,826.0
Industrial machinery	718.3	877.7	1,268.1
Transport equipment	259.5	375.7	551.8
Livestock	3.7	4.9	6.1
Intermediate goods	2,227.7	2,683.8	3,527.2
Primary agricultural goods	83.9	112.1	78.6
Foodstuffs	39.5	61.2	26.6
Others	44.4	50.9	52.0
Primary industrial products	740.1	871.7	1,043.3
Foodstuffs	70.7	84.6	94.6

Imports c.i.f.—continued	1987	1988	1989
Others	669.4	787.1	948.7
Intermediate industrial products	576.3	651.0	967.3
Spare parts	277.9	352.6	468.9
Industrial plant	229.7	298.4	399.7
Transport equipment	48.2	54.2	69.2
Oil and combustibles	460.1	571.5	796.5
Crude petroleum	378.9	457.4	572.6
Others	81.2	114.1	223.9
Car assembly machinery	89.4	124.9	172.6
Sub-total	3,793.3	4,730.8	6,495.8
Free trade zones	230.0	193.2	238.4
Total	4,023.3	4,924.0	6,734.2

Exports f.o.b.	1987	1988	1989
Minerals	2,745.8	4,100.1	4,840.7
Agricultural and fish products	743.0	861.2	851.9
Agricultural products	605.1	683.8	710.4
Cattle	54.2	55.7	48.8
Forestry	71.0	108.7	78.2
Fish products	12.7	13.0	14.5
Industrial goods	1,613.1	2,087.0	2,497.8
Foodstuffs	739.9	953.4	1,099.3
Wine, liquor and other drinks	33.5	38.3	52.8
Wood	151.5	210.3	276.7
Paper, cellulose and derivatives	364.9	417.1	422.3
Chemicals and petroleum products	103.2	174.8	298.5
Base metals	87.3	117.8	119.6
Wood, metal and electrical products	26.8	27.6	34.0
Transport materials	32.2	34.8	36.5
Other manufactured goods	73.8	112.9	158.1
Total	5,101.9	7,048.3	8,190.4

PRINCIPAL TRADING PARTNERS (US $ million)

Imports	1987	1988	1989
Argentina	159.0	278.6	398.8
Brazil	380.0	554.9	703.1
Canada	66.4	110.7	106.7
Ecuador	37.2	55.5	39.2
France	129.3	149.6	223.3
Germany, Federal Republic	335.1	365.1	482.9
Italy	95.8	120.3	153.2
Japan	387.2	341.8	737.0
Korea, Republic	82.2	107.5	164.6
Nigeria	75.0	100.8	140.8
Peru	27.9	33.0	63.2
Spain	116.6	117.9	157.2
Switzerland	55.5	84.9	77.3
United Kingdom	128.3	123.3	151.5
USA	773.1	1,002.1	1,347.9
Venezuela	143.7	165.0	166.8
Total (incl. others)	4,023.3	4,924.0	6,734.2

Exports	1987	1988	1989
Argentina	174.9	168.1	110.1
Belgium	58.6	118.2	179.1
Brazil	348.2	341.7	522.6
Canada	71.1	48.2	65.4
China, People's Republic	78.7	99.1	104.1
Colombia	51.0	57.8	81.9
France	178.6	353.7	392.9
Germany, Federal Republic	483.4	817.9	914.3
Italy	273.8	452.5	409.9
Japan	561.3	881.3	1,120.5
Korea, Republic	109.0	146.1	257.5
Netherlands	164.2	247.4	265.9
Peru	85.8	63.0	54.9
Spain	146.8	178.4	222.5
Taiwan	129.6	245.3	399.8
United Kingdom	317.8	365.6	499.0
USA	1,140.5	1,393.2	1,456.0
Venezuela	71.2	105.0	33.2
Total (incl. others)	5,101.9	7,048.3	8,190.4

Transport

PRINCIPAL RAILWAYS* ('000)

	1986	1987	1988
Passengers (number)	6,243	7,239	6,773
Passenger/km	1,274,457	1,176,437	998,433
Freight (tons)	23,844	15,667	19,418

* Includes all international cargo of Ferrocarril Transandino.

ROAD TRAFFIC (motor vehicles in use)

	1986	1987	1988
Cars	590,719	618,496	669,097
Buses and coaches	21,559	23,487	24,748
Lorries	220,492	244,447	272,271
Motor cycles	22,661	23,076	23,606

INTERNATIONAL SEA-BORNE SHIPPING
(freight traffic, '000 metric tons)

	1986	1987	1988
Goods loaded	13,448	15,149	17,698
Goods unloaded	5,001	5,947	7,434

CIVIL AVIATION

	1986	1987	1988
Kilometres flown ('000)*	27,522	32,439	38,146
Passengers (number)	875,156	990,976	1,139,110
Freight ('000 ton-km)	316,304	379,584	465,394

* Includes airline taxis.

Tourism

	1987	1988	1989
Arrivals	575,221	623,853	797,396

Communications Media

	1985	1986	1987
Radio receivers ('000 in use)	4,000	4,100	4,200
Television receivers ('000 in use)	1,750	n.a.	2,050
Telephones ('000 in use)	711	786	807
Book production: titles	1,638	1,499	1,654
Daily newspapers	40	n.a.	74

1988: 868,000 telephones in use.
Source: mainly UNESCO, *Statistical Yearbook*.

Education

(Number of pupils)

	1987	1988	1989
Kindergarten	228,117	217,100	223,106
Basic	2,038,775	2,036,231	2,020,815
Middle	695,863	735,701	742,010
Higher (incl. universities)	224,338	233,148	n.a.

Source: Ministerio de Educación.

Directory

The Constitution

Note: From 1973 government was based on the three Constitutional Acts (see below). In accordance with the new Constitution approved by a plebiscite in 1980, the previous 1925 Constitution was abolished and the new Fundamental Law came into effect in March 1981. Provisions concerning the National Congress were to be fully effective from 1989.

The three Constitutional Acts of 1976 provided for a 'new democratic structure' for Chilean society based on the family and rejecting class struggle. The following rights are guaranteed: the right to life and personal integrity, to a defence, to personal liberty and individual security; the right to reside in, cross or leave the country; the right of assembly, petition, association and free expression and the right to work. Men and women are accorded equal rights; no-one shall be obliged to join any association; any group considered to be contrary to morality, public order or state security shall be prohibited; the courts shall be able to prohibit any publication or broadcast considered to be contrary to public morality, order, national security or individual privacy.

The 1981 Constitution, described as a 'transition to democracy', separated the presidency from the junta and provided for presidential elections and for the re-establishment of the bicameral legislature, consisting of an upper chamber of both elected and appointed senators, who are to serve an eight-year term, and a lower chamber of 120 deputies elected for a four-year term. All former Presidents are to be senators for life. There is a National Security Council consisting of the President, the heads of the armed forces and the police, and the presidents of the Supreme Court and the Senate.

In July 1989 a national referendum approved 54 reforms to the Constitution, including 47 proposed by the Government and seven by the Military Junta. Among provisions made within the articles were an increase in the number of directly-elected senators from 26 to 38, the abolition of the need for the approval of two successive Congresses for constitutional amendments (the support of two-thirds of the Chamber of Deputies and the Senate being sufficient), the reduction in term of office for the President to be elected in 1989 from eight to four years, with no immediate re-election possible, and the redrafting of the provision that outlawed Marxist groups so as to ensure 'true and responsible political pluralism'. The President's right to dismiss Congress and sentence to internal exile were eliminated.

The Government

HEAD OF STATE

President: PATRICIO AYLWIN AZÓCAR (took office 11 March 1990).

THE CABINET
(January 1991)

Minister of the Interior: ENRIQUE KRAUSS RUSQUE (PDC).
Minister of Foreign Affairs: ENRIQUE SILVA CIMMA (PR).
Minister of Labour and Social Security: RENÉ CORTÁZAR SANZ (PDC).
Minister of Finance: ALEJANDRO FOXLEY RIOSECO (PDC).
Minister of Economy, Development and Reconstruction: CARLOS OMINAMI PASCUAL (PPD/PS de C).
Minister of Public Education: RICARDO LAGOS ESCOBAR (PPD/PS de C).
Minister of Justice: FRANCISCO CUMPLIDO CERECEDA (PDC).
Minister of National Defence: PATRICIO ROJAS SAAVEDRA (PDC).
Minister of Public Works: CARLOS HURTADO RUIZ-TAGLE (PAC).
Minister of Transport and Telecommunications: GERMÁN CORREA DÍAZ (PS de C—Almeyda).
Minister of Agriculture: JUAN AGUSTÍN FIGUEROA (PR).
Minister of National Property: LUIS ALVARADO (PPD/PS de C).
Minister of National Planning and Co-ordination: SERGIO MOLINA SILVA (PDC).
Minister of Mines: JUAN HAMILTON DEPASSIER (PDC).
Minister of Energy: JAIME TOHÁ GONZÁLEZ (PPD/IC).
Minister of Public Health: JORGE JIMÉNEZ DE LA JARA (PDC).
Minister of Housing and Urban Development: ALBERTO ETCHEGARAY AUBRY (pro-PDC).
Minister of Production Development (Vice-President of CORFO): RENÉ ABELIUK MANASEVICH (PSD).
Minister Secretary-General of Government: ENRIQUE CORREA DÍAZ (PPD/MAPU).
Secretary-General of the Presidency: EDGARDO BOENINGER KAUSEL (PDC).

MINISTRIES

Ministry of Agriculture: Teatinos 40, Santiago; tel. (2) 71-7436; telex 240745.
Ministry of Economy, Development and Reconstruction: Teatinos 120, Santiago; tel. (2) 72-5522; telex 240558.
Ministry of Energy: Teatinos 120, 7°, Casilla 14, Correo 21, Santiago; tel. (2) 698-1757; telex 240948; fax (2) 698-1757.
Ministry of Finance: Teatinos 120, 12°, Santiago; tel. (2) 698-2051; telex 241334.
Ministry of Foreign Affairs: Palacio de la Moneda, Santiago; tel. (2) 698-2501; telex 40595.
Ministry of Housing and Urban Development: Serrano 15, 4°, Santiago; tel. (2) 33-1624; telex 240124.
Ministry of the Interior: Palacio de la Moneda, Santiago; tel. (2) 71-4103; telex 240273; fax (2) 696-8740.
Ministry of Justice: Compañía 1111, Santiago; tel. (2) 696-8151; telex 241316.
Ministry of Labour and Social Security: Huérfanos 1273, 6°, Santiago; tel. (2) 715-1333; telex 242559; fax (2) 71-6539.
Ministry of Mines: Teatinos 120, 9°, Santiago; tel. (2) 696-5872; telex 240948.
Ministry of National Defence: Plaza Bulnes s/n, 4°, Santiago; tel. (2) 696-5271; telex 40537.
Ministry of National Planning and Co-ordination: Ahumada 48, Casilla 9140, Santiago; tel. (2) 72-2033; telex 341400.
Ministry of National Property: Avda Libertador B. O'Higgins 280, Santiago; tel. (2) 222-4669.
Ministry of Production Development (CORFO): Moneda 921, Casilla 3886, Santiago; tel. (2) 38-0521; telex 240421.
Ministry of Public Education: Avda Libertador B. O'Higgins 1371, Santiago; tel. (2) 698-3351; telex 240567; fax 698-7831.
Ministry of Public Health: Enrique McIver 541, 1°, Santiago; tel. (2) 39-4001; telex 240136.

CHILE — Directory

Ministry of Public Works: Dirección de Vialidad, Morandé 59, 2°, Santiago; tel. (2) 696-4839; telex 240777.

Ministry of Transport and Telecommunications: Amunátegui 139, Santiago; tel. (2) 72-6503; telex 240200.

Office of the Comptroller of the Republic: Teatinos 56, 9°, Santiago; tel. (2) 72-4212; telex 240281.

Office of the Minister Secretary-General of Government: Palacio de la Moneda, Santiago; tel. (2) 71-4103; telex 240142; fax (2) 699-1657.

President and Legislature

PRESIDENT

Election, 14 December 1989

	Votes cast	Percentage of votes cast
Patricio Aylwin Azócar	3,849,584	55.2
Hernán Büchi Buc	2,051,674	29.4
Francisco Javier Errázuriz	1,076,825	15.4
Total	6,978,083*	100.0

* In addition, there were 178,403 blank or spoiled votes.

CONGRESO NACIONAL

President (Senate): Gabriel Valdés (PDC).
President (Chamber of Deputies): José Antonio Viera Gallo (PS de C).

General election, 14 December 1989

	Senate	Chamber of Deputies
Partido Demócrata Cristiano (PDC)	13	38
Renovación Nacional (RN)	11	29
Partido por la Democracia (PPD)	4	17
Unión Demócrata Independiente (UDI)	2	11
Independents of the Centre-Right	3	8
Partido Socialista de Chile (PS de C—Almeyda*)	1	6
Partido Radical (PR)	2	5
Others	2	6
Total	38†	120

* Following the election, the Almeyda faction rejoined the PS de C.

† A further nine senators were appointed by the outgoing Government and the Supreme Court, bringing the total to 47.

Political Organizations

In March 1987 a law to legalize political parties, with the exception of Marxist organizations, was promulgated. Under a constitutional amendment, approved by referendum in July 1989, the ban on Marxist parties was revoked.

The most prominent political organizations are:

Avanzada Nacional: Santiago; tel. (2) 698-3588; right-wing; Pres. Col (retd) Alvaro Corvalán.

Intransigencia Democrática: Santiago; tel. (2) 72-4164; f. 1985; centre-left alliance; Pres. Manuel Sanhueza Cruz.

Izquierda Cristiana (IC): Christian left; Sec.-Gen. Luis Maira.

Movimiento de Acción Popular Unitaria (MAPU): Marxist; Leader Oscar Garretón; joined PS de C in Dec. 1989.

Movimiento de Izquierda Revolucionaria (MIR): revolutionary left; Leader Andrés Pascal Allende.

Movimiento Social Cristiano: Santiago; tel. (2) 696-1961; f. 1984; right-wing party; Pres. Juan de Dios Carmona; Sec.-Gen. Manuel Rodríguez.

Pacto de Alianza de Centro (PAC): Santiago; centre; Leader Germán Riesco.

Partido Comunista de Chile (PCCh): Santiago; tel. (2) 72-4164; achieved legal status in October 1990; Sec.-Gen. Volodia Teitelboim.

Partido por la Democracia (PPD): Padre Luis de Valdivia 333, Santiago; tel. (2) 33-0296; fax (2) 39-2389; Pres. Eric Schnake.

Partido Democracia Social: San Antonio 220, Of. 604, Santiago; tel. (2) 39-4244; democratic socialist party; Pres. Luis Angel Santibáñez; Sec.-Gen. Jaime Carmona Donoso.

Partido Demócrata Cristiano (PDC): Carmen 8, 6°, Santiago; tel. (2) 33-8535; telex 242397; f. 1957; Pres. Andrés Zaldívar; Sec.-Gen. Gutenberg Martínez Ocamica.

Partido Humanista: Las Urbinas 145, Depto 20, Santiago; tel. (2) 231-9089; f. 1987; humanist party; Pres. José Tomás Sáenz.

Partido Liberal: San Antonio 418, Of. 803, Santiago; tel. (2) 48-0738; liberal party; Pres. Guillermo Toro Albornoz; Vice-Pres. Olga Reyes.

Partido Nacional de Democracia Centrista: Santiago; f. 1990, following the merger of the Partido Democracia Radical, the Partido Nacional and the Partido Nacional Vanguardista; centre-right; Pres. Julio Durán.

Partido Radical (PR): Avda Santa María 281, Santiago; tel. (2) 77-9903; f. 1863; social democratic; mem. of Socialist International; Pres. Enrique Silva Cimma; Sec.-Gen. Ricardo Navarrete.

Partido Republicano: Sótero del Río 492, 3°, Santiago; tel. (2) 698-4167; f. 1983; centre-right party; Pres. (vacant); Sec.-Gen. Gabriel León Echaiz.

Partido Socialdemocracia (PSD): París 815, Casilla 50.220, Correo Central, Santiago; tel. (2) 39-9064; f. 1973; Pres. Arturo Venegas Gutiérrez; Sec.-Gen. Levián Muñoz Pellicer.

Partido Socialista de Chile—PS de C: Santiago; left-wing; split into several factions; reunited Dec. 1989; Pres. Dr Clodomiro Almeyda Medina; Sec.-Gen. Jorge Arrate.

Partido Tercera República (PTR): Santiago; f. 1990; Pres. Francisco Javier Iturriaga Aste.

Renovación Nacional (RN): Santiago; f. 1987; right-wing; Pres. Sergio Onofre Jarpa; Sec.-Gen. Andrés Allamand; comprises:

  Frente Nacional del Trabajo: Dr Barros Borgoño 21, Santiago; tel. (2) 41923; Sec.-Gen. Angel Fantuzzi.

  Unión Nacional: Ricardo Matte Pérez 0140, Santiago; tel. (2) 744-9915; centre-right party; Pres. Andrés Allamand Zavala.

Unión Demócrata Independiente (UDI): Suecia 286, Santiago; tel. (2) 232-2686; right-wing; Leader Jaime Guzmán Errázuriz.

Unión Socialista Popular: Teatinos 251, Of. 809, Santiago; tel. (2) 698-4269; left-wing party; Sec.-Gen. Ramón Silva Ulloa.

Los Verdes (The Greens): Santiago; f. 1987; environmentalist party; Pres. Andrés R. Koryzma.

In early 1988, 16 political parties and opposition groups, including the Izquierda Cristiana, the Partido Humanista, Partido Demócrata Cristiana and factions of the Partido Radical, Partido Socialista de Chile and the Movimiento de Acción Popular Unitaria, united to form the **Comando por el No,** an opposition front to campaign against the government candidate in the plebiscite of 5 October 1988. Following the plebiscite, the Comando por el No (expanded to a total of 17 parties) assumed the title of **Concertación de los Partidos de la Democracia (CPD),** and presented a single candidate, Patricio Aylwin Azócar, the former president of the PDC, to contest the presidential election of 14 December 1989.

However, other political alliances reported to have formed since the plebiscite include:

Partido Amplio de Izquierda Socialista (PAIS): Santiago; f. 1988; Marxist; Pres. Luis Maira; comprises:

  Izquierda Cristiana (see above).

  Partido Comunista de Chile (see above).

  Partido Radical Socialista Democrático.

Guerrilla groups:

Acción Chilena Anticomunista (ACHA): right-wing; Pres. Juan Serrano.

Frente Patriótico Manuel Rodríguez (FPMR): f. 1983; Communist; Leader Commdr Daniel Huerta.

Frente de Resistencia Nacionalista (FRN): right-wing.

Frente Revolucionario Nacionalista—FREN: left-wing.

Diplomatic Representation

EMBASSIES IN CHILE

Argentina: Miraflores 285, Santiago; tel. (2) 33-1076; telex 240280; Ambassador: José María Alvarez de Toledo.

Australia: Gertrudis Echeñique 420, Casilla 33, Correo 10, Las Condes, Santiago; tel. (2) 228-5065; telex 240855; Ambassador: Malcolm J. Dan.

Austria: Barrique Fumouria 1068, 2°, Casilla 16106, Santiago; tel. (2) 223-4774; telex 240528; Ambassador: Harald Kreid.

Belgium: Avda Providencia 2653, 11°, Of. 1104, Santiago; tel. (2) 232-1070; telex 440088; Chargé d'affaires: Michel Godfrind.

CHILE
Directory

Brazil: Alonso Ovalle 1665, Santiago; tel. (2) 698-2486; telex 340350; Ambassador: RONALDO COSTA.

Canada: Ahumada 11, 10°, Casilla 427, Santiago; tel. (2) 696-2256; Ambassador: MICHEL DE GOUMOIS.

China, People's Republic: Pedro de Valdivia 550, Santiago; tel. (2) 25-0755; telex 240863; Ambassador: HUANG SHIKANG.

Colombia: Darío Urzúa 2080, Santiago; tel. (2) 74-7570; telex 340401; Ambassador: JORGE E. RODRÍGUEZ.

Costa Rica: Barcelona 2070, Santiago; tel. (2) 231-8915; Ambassador: FABIO CRUZ BRICEÑO.

Denmark: Avda Santa María 0182, Casilla 13430, Santiago; tel. (2) 37-6056; telex 440032; Chargé d'affaires: BENT ROLL.

Dominican Republic: Mariscal Petain 125, Santiago; tel. (2) 228-8083; Ambassador: RAFAEL VÁLDEZ HICARIO.

Ecuador: Avda Providencia 1979, 5°, Santiago; tel. (2) 23-5742; telex 240717; Ambassador: CÉSAR VALDIVIESO CHIRIBOGA.

Egypt: Roberto del Río 1871, Santiago; tel. (2) 274-8881; telex 440156; Ambassador: ADEL AHMAD EL SAMAWI.

El Salvador: Calle Noruega 6595, Las Condes, Santiago; tel. (2) 25-1096; Ambassador: Dr JOSÉ HORACIO TRUJILLO.

France: Avda Condell 65, Casilla 38-D, Santiago; tel. (2) 225-1030; telex 240535; Ambassador: DANIEL LEQUERTIER.

Germany: Agustinas 785, 7° y 8°, Santiago; tel. (2) 33-5031; telex 240583; fax (2) 33-6119; Ambassador: Dr WIEGAND PABSCH.

Guatemala: Los Españoles 2155, Pedro de Valdivia Norte, Providencia, Santiago; tel. (2) 231-7367; fax (2) 232-4494; Ambassador: JULIO GÁNDARA VALENZUELA.

Haiti: Avda 11 de Septiembre 2155, Of. 801, Torre B, Santiago; tel. (2) 231-8233; Ambassador: MAX JADOTTE.

Holy See: Calle Nuncio Sotero Sanz 200, Casilla 507, Santiago (Apostolic Nunciature); tel. (2) 231-2020; telex 241035; Nuncio: Excmo Rev. Mgr ANGELO SODANO.

Honduras: Avda 11 de Septiembre 2155, Of. 303, Santiago; tel. (2) 231-4161; telex 440456; Ambassador: CARLOS H. REYES.

India: Triana 871, Casilla 10433, Santiago; tel. (2) 223-1548; telex 340046; Ambassador: SARV KUMAR KATHPALIA.

Israel: San Sebastián 2812, 5°, Casilla 1224, Santiago; tel. (2) 246-1570; telex 240627; Ambassador: DANIEL MOKADY.

Italy: Clemente Fabres 1050, Santiago; tel. (2) 225-9029; telex 440321; Chargé d'affaires: ARMANDO SANGUINI.

Japan: Avda Providencia 2653, 19°, Casilla 2877, Santiago; tel. (2) 232-1807; telex 440132; Ambassador: SHUICHI NOMIYAMA.

Jordan: Los Militares 4280, Las Condes, Casilla 10431, Santiago; tel. (2) 228-8989; telex 346196; Ambassador: WAEL D. TUQAN.

Korea, Republic: Alcántara 74, Casilla 1301, Santiago; tel. (2) 228-4214; telex 340380; Ambassador: SUH KYUNG-SUK.

Lebanon: Isidoro Goyenechea 3607, Casilla 3667, Santiago; tel. (2) 232-5027; telex 440118; Ambassador: IBRAHIM KRAIDY.

Netherlands: Las Violetas 2368, Casilla 56-D, Santiago; tel. (2) 223-6825; telex 340381; Ambassador: ROBERT FRUIN.

New Zealand: Avda Isidora Goyenechea 3516, Casilla 112, Las Condes, Santiago; tel. (2) 231-4204; telex 3440066; Ambassador: PAUL J. A. TIPPING.

Norway: Américo Vespucio Norte 548, Casilla 2431, Santiago; tel. (2) 228-1024; telex 440150; Ambassador: HELGE VINDENES.

Panama: Bustos 2199, Correo 9892, Santiago; tel. (2) 225-0147; Ambassador: RICARDO MORENO VILLALAZ.

Paraguay: Huérfanos 886, 5°, Ofs 514-515, Santiago; tel. (2) 39-4640; telex 645357; Ambassador: Dr FABIO RIVAS ARAUJO.

Peru: Avda Andrés Bello 1751, Providencia, Santiago 9, Casilla 16277, Santiago; tel. (2) 223-8883; telex 440095; Ambassador: LUIS MARCHAND STENS.

Philippines: San Crecente 551, esq. Presidente Errázuriz, Las Condes, Santiago; tel. (2) 228-6135; Ambassador: RODOLFO A. ARIZALA.

Romania: Benjamín 2955, Casilla 290, Santiago; tel. (2) 231-1893; telex 440378; Chargé d'affaires a.i.: GHEORGHE PETRE.

South Africa: Avda 11 de Septiembre 2353, 16°, Torre San Ramón, Santiago; tel. (2) 231-2860; telex 341522; Ambassador: Lt-Gen. PIETER W. VAN DER WESTHUIZEN.

Spain: Avda Andrés Bello 1895, Casilla 16456, Santiago; tel. (2) 74-2021; telex 340253; Ambassador: PEDRO BREMEJO MARÍN.

Sweden: Santiago; tel. (2) 232-3981; telex 440153; fax (2) 232-4188; Ambassador: STAFFAN WRIGSTAD.

Switzerland: Avda Providencia 2653, Of. 1602, Casilla 3875, Santiago; tel. (2) 232-2693; telex 340870; Ambassador: PAUL WIPFLI.

Syria: Carmencita 111, Casilla 12, Correo 10, Santiago; tel. (2) 232-7471; telex 240095; Ambassador: HISHAM HALLAJ.

Turkey: N. Sótero Sanz 136, Casilla 16182-9, Providencia, Santiago; tel. (2) 231-8952; telex 340278; Ambassador: NURETTIN KARAKÖYLÜ.

USSR: Santiago; Ambassador: YURI I. PAVLOV.

United Kingdom: La Concepción 177, Casilla 72 D, Santiago; tel. (2) 223-9166; telex 340483; fax (2) 223-1917; Ambassador: RICHARD NEILSON.

USA: Agustinas 1343, 5°, Santiago; tel. (2) 71-0133; telex 240062; Ambassador: CHARLES GILLESPIE.

Uruguay: Avda Pedro de Valdivia 711, Casilla 2636, Santiago; tel. (2) 74-3569; telex 340371; Ambassador: ALFREDO BIANCHI PALAZZO.

Venezuela: Mar del Plata 2055, Casilla 16577, Santiago; tel. (2) 225-0021; telex 440170; Ambassador: HÉCTOR VARGAS ACOSTA.

Yugoslavia: Santiago; Ambassador: FRANC KRNIC.

Note: Following the transition to democratically-elected government on 11 March 1990, it was reported that full diplomatic relations had been resumed with Algeria, Czechoslovakia, Hungary, Mexico and Poland.

Judicial System

The following are the main tribunals:

The Supreme Court, consisting of 17 members, appointed for life by the President of the Republic from a list of five names submitted by the Supreme Court when vacancies arise. The President of the Supreme Court is elected by the 17 members of the Court.

There are 17 Courts of Appeal (in the cities or departments of Arica, Iquique, Antofagasta, Copiapó, La Serena, Valparaíso, Santiago, Presidente Aguirre Cerda, Rancagua, Talca, Chillán, Concepción, Temuco, Valdivia, Puerto Montt, Coyhaique and Punta Arenas) whose members are appointed for life from a list submitted to the President by the Supreme Court. The number of members of each court varies. Judges of the lower courts are appointed in a similar manner from lists submitted by the Court of Appeal of the district in which the vacancy arises.

Corte Suprema: Plaza Montt Varas, Santiago; tel. (2) 698-0561.

President of the Supreme Court: LUIS MALDONADO BOGGIANO.

Ministers of the Supreme Court:
OSVALDO FAÚNDEZ VALLEJOS
ROBERTO DAVILA DÍAZ
RAFAEL RETAMAL LÓPEZ
LIONEL BERAUD POBLETE
ARNALDO TORO LEIVA
ENRIQUE CORREA LABRA
EFREN ARAYA VERGARA
EMILIO ULLOA MUÑOZ
MARCOS ABURTO OCHOA
MARCO AURELIO PERALES MARTÍNEZ
GERMÁN VALENZUELA ERAZO
HERNÁN ALVÁREZ GARCÍA
HERNÁN CERECEDA BRAVO
SERGIO MERY BRAVO
SERVANDO JORDÁN LÓPEZ
ENRIQUE ZURITA CAMPS

Attorney-General: RENÉ PICA URRUTIA.

Secretary of the President: CÉSAR DERAMOND RUBIO.

Secretary of the Court: CARLOS A. MENESES PIZARRO.

Comisión Nacional de Verdad y Reconciliación: f. 1990; Pres. RAÚL RETTIG; established to investigate violations of human rights committed during the period of military dictatorship.

Religion

CHRISTIANITY

The Roman Catholic Church

Chile comprises five archdioceses, 16 dioceses, two territorial prelatures and two Apostolic Prefectures.

Bishops' Conference: Conferencia Episcopal de Chile, Cienfuegos 47, Casilla 13191, Correo 21, Santiago; tel. (2) 71-7733; telex 343066; fax (2) 698-1416; f. 1982; Pres. CARLOS GONZÁLEZ CRUCHAGA, Bishop of Talca.

Archbishop of Antofagasta: (vacant), Casilla E, San Martín 2628, Antofagasta; tel. (83) 22-1164.

Archbishop of Concepción: ANTONIO MORENO CASAMITJANA, Calle Barros Araña 544, Casilla 65-C, Concepción; tel. (41) 23-5779.

Archbishop of La Serena: BERNARDINO PIÑERA CARVALLO, Los Carrera 450, Casilla 613, La Serena; tel. (51) 21-1324.

CHILE

Archbishop of Puerto Montt: BERNARDO CAZZARO BERTOLLO, Calle Benavente 385, Casilla 17, Puerto Montt; tel. (65) 25-2215.

Archbishop of Santiago de Chile: CARLOS OVIEDO CAVADA, Erasmo Escala 1822, Casilla 30-D, Santiago; tel. (2) 696-3275.

The Anglican Communion

Anglicans in Chile come within the Diocese of Chile, which forms part of the Anglican Church of the Southern Cone of America, covering Argentina, Bolivia, Chile, Paraguay, Peru and Uruguay.

Bishop of Chile and Primate of the Province of the Southern Cone of America: Right Rev. COLIN FREDERICK BAZLEY, Iglesia Anglicana, Casilla 50675, Santiago; tel. (2) 38-3009; fax (2) 39-4581.

Other Christian Churches

Baptist Evangelical Convention: Casilla 1055-22, Santiago; tel. (2) 222-4085; Gen. Sec. FAUSTINO AGUILERA C.; Pres. ESTEBAN JOFRE C.

Evangelical Lutheran Church: Alonso de Camargo 8040, Casilla 15167, Santiago; tel. (2) 229-7437; f. 1937 as German Evangelical Church in Chile; present name adopted in 1959; Pres. Rev. WILLIAM E. GORSKI; 2,500 mems.

Methodist Church: Sargento Aldea 1041, Casilla 67, Santiago; tel. (2) 56-6074; autonomous since 1969; 6,000 mems; Bishop ISAIAS GUTIÉRREZ V.

Pentecostal Church: Calle Pena 1103, Casilla de Correo 2, Curicó; tel. (75) 1035; f. 1945; 90,000 mems; Bishop ENRIQUE CHÁVEZ CAMPOS.

Pentecostal Mission Church: Avda Pedro Montt 1473, Casilla 5391, Santiago 3; tel. (2) 56-8657; f. 1952; Sec. Rev. ARTURO PALMA CHER; Pres. Rev. NARCISO SEPÚLVEDA BARRA; 12,000 mems.

BAHÁ'Í FAITH

National Spiritual Assembly: Casilla 3731, Darío Urzúa 1588, Providencia, Santiago; tel. (2) 225-5326; telex 340436.

The Press

Most newspapers of nationwide circulation in Chile are published in Santiago. According to official sources, there are 128 newspapers which appear more than twice a week, with a combined circulation of more than 900,000 copies per issue.

DAILIES
Santiago

Circulation figures listed below are supplied mainly by the Asociación Nacional de la Prensa. Other sources give much lower figures.

Diario Oficial de la República de Chile: Agustinas 1269, Santiago; tel. (2) 698-3969; Dir ENRIQUE MENCHACA SALGADO; circ. 15,000.

La Época: Olivares 1229, 5°, 6° y 9°, Santiago; tel. (2) 699-0067; telex 240990; f. 1987; morning; centre; independent; Gen. Editor ASCANIO CAVALLO; circ. 50,000.

Fortín Diario: Agustinas 1849, Santiago; tel. (2) 699-0376; f. 1984; opposition; independent; Dir EDUARDO TRABUCCO PONCE.

El Mercurio: Avda Santa María 5542, Casilla 13-D, Santiago; tel. (2) 228-8147; f. 1827; morning; conservative; Man. Dir AGUSTÍN EDWARDS; circ. 120,000 (weekdays), 250,000 (Sundays).

La Nación: Agustinas 1269, Santiago; tel. (2) 698-2222; f. 1980 to replace government-subsidized *El Cronista*; morning; financial; Propr Sociedad Periodística La Nación; Dir Editor ANDRÉS SÁNCHEZ ARRIAGADA; circ. 20,000.

La Segunda: Avda Santa María 5542, Santiago; tel. (2) 228-7048; f. 1931; evening; Dir CRISTIÁN ZEGERS ARIZTÍA; circ. 40,000.

La Tercera de la Hora: Vicuña Mackenna 1870, Santiago; tel. (2) 51-7067; f. 1950; morning; Dir ARTURO ROMÁN HERRERA; circ. 170,000.

Las Ultimas Noticias: Avda Santa María 5542, Santiago; tel. (2) 228-7048; f. 1902; morning; Man. Dir HÉCTOR OLAVE VALLEJOS; owned by the Proprs of *El Mercurio*; circ. 150,000 (except Saturdays and Sundays).

Antofagasta

La Estrella del Norte: Calle Matta 2112, Antofagasta; tel. (83) 22-2847; f. 1966; evening; Dir ROBERTO RETAMAL PACHECO; circ. 10,000.

El Mercurio: Manuel Antonio Matta 2112, Antofagasta; tel. (83) 22-3406; f. 1906; morning; conservative independent; Proprs Soc. Chilena de Publicaciones; Dir DARÍO CANUT DE BON URRUTIA; circ. 20,000.

Arica

La Estrella de Arica: San Marcos 580, Arica; tel. (80) 23-1834; fax (80) 25-2890; f. 1976; Dir DARÍO CANUT DE BON URRUTIA; circ. 11,600.

Calama

La Estrella del Loa: Abaroa 1929, Calama; tel. (82) 21-2535; f. 1969; Propr Soc. Chilena de Publicaciones; Dir ROBERTO RETAMAL PACHECO; circ. 4,000 (weekdays), 7,000 (Sundays).

El Mercurio: Abaroa 1929, Calama; tel. (82) 21-1604; f. 1968; Propr Soc. Chilena de Publicaciones; Dir DARÍO CANUT DE BON; circ. 4,500 (weekdays), 7,000 (Sundays).

Chillán

La Discusión de Chillán: Casilla 14-D, Calle 18 de Septiembre 721, Chillán; tel. (42) 22-2651; f. 1870; morning; independent; Propr Universidad de Concepción; Dir TITO CASTILLO PERALTA; circ. 8,500.

Concepción

El Sur: Casilla 8-C, Calle Freire 799, Concepción; tel. (41) 23-5825; f. 1882; morning; independent; Editor HERNÁN ALVEZ C. TIRADA; circ. 38,000.

Copiapó

Atacama: Manuel Rodríguez 740, Copiapó; tel. (52) 2255; morning; independent; Dir SAMUEL SALGADO; circ. 6,500.

Curicó

La Prensa: Casilla 6-D, Merced 373, Curicó; tel. (75) 31-0453; f. 1898; morning; right-wing; Man. Dir MANUEL MASSA MAUTINO; circ. 4,000.

Iquique

La Estrella de Iquique: Luis Uribe 452, Iquique; tel. (81) 22401; telex 223134; f. 1966; evening; Dir ARCADIO CASTILLO ORTIZ; circ. 8,500.

La Serena

El Día: Casilla 13-D, Brasil 395, La Serena; tel. (51) 21-1284; f. 1944; morning; Dir ANTONIO PUGA RODRÍGUEZ; circ. 10,800.

Los Angeles

La Tribuna: Casilla 15-D, Calle Colo Colo 464, Los Angeles; tel. (43) 32-1928; independent; Dir CIRILO GUZMÁN DE LA FUENTE; circ. 10,000.

Osorno

El Diario Austral: Plazuela Yungay 581, Osorno; tel. (642) 5191; telex 373014; Dir ENRIQUE JORQUERA MÁRQUEZ; circ. 6,350.

Diario 24 Horas: Osorno; tel. (642) 2300; Dir ROBERTO SILVA BAJIT.

Puerto Montt

El Llanquihue: Antonio Varas 167, Puerto Montt; tel. (65) 2578; f. 1885; morning; independent; Dir MIGUEL ESTEBAN VEYL BETANZO; circ. 6,000.

Punta Arenas

La Prensa Austral: Waldo Seguel 636, Casilla 9-D, Punta Arenas; tel. (61) 22-1976; telex 380029; fax (61) 22-7406; f. 1941; morning; independent; Dir PABLO CRUZ NOCETI; circ. 10,000, Sunday (*El Magallanes*; f. 1894) 12,000.

Rancagua

El Rancagüino: O'Carroll 518, Rancagua; tel. (72) 21729; f. 1915; independent; Dir HÉCTOR GONZÁLEZ; circ. 10,000.

Talca

La Mañana de Talca: 1 Norte 911, Casilla 7-D, Talca; tel. (71) 32520; Dir JUAN C. BRAVO; circ. 5,000.

Temuco

El Diario Austral: Bulnes 699, Casilla 1-D, Temuco; tel. (45) 23-2233; f. 1916; morning; commercial, industrial and agricultural interests; Dir MARCO ANTONIO PINTO ZEPEDA; Propr Soc. Periodística Araucanía, SA; circ. 26,000.

Tocopilla

La Prensa: Matta 2112, Antofagasta, Casilla 2099, Tocopilla; tel. (83) 22-2847; f. 1924; morning; independent; Dir ROBERTO RETAMAL; circ. 8,000.

Valdivia

El Correo de Valdivia: Yungay 758, Casilla 15-D, Valdivia; f. 1895; morning; non-party; Dir PATRICIO GÓMEZ COUCHOT; circ. 12,000.

CHILE

El Diario Austral: Yungay 499, Valdivia; tel. (21) 3353; telex 371011; fax (21) 2236; f. 1982; Editor GUSTAVO SERRANO COTAPOS; circ. 5,000.

Valparaíso

La Estrella: Esmeralda 1002, Casilla 57-V, Valparaíso; tel. (32) 25-8011; telex 230531; f. 1921; evening; independent; Dir ALFONSO CASTAGNETO; owned by the Proprs of *El Mercurio*; circ. 25,000, 30,000 (Saturdays).

El Mercurio: Esmeralda 1002, Casilla 57-V, Valparaíso; tel. (32) 25-8011; telex 330445; fax (32) 25-6438; f. 1827; morning; Dir ENRIQUE SCHRÖDER VICUÑA; owned by the Proprs of *El Mercurio* in Santiago; circ. 65,000.

Victoria

Las Noticias: Casilla 240, Confederación Suiza 895, Victoria; tel. (45) 84-1543; f. 1910; morning; independent; Dir TRÁNSITO BUSTAMENTE MOLINA; circ. 8,000.

El Pehuén de Curacautín: Casilla 92, Avda Central 895, Victoria; morning; independent; Dir GINO BUSTAMENTE BARRÍA; circ. 3,000.

PERIODICALS
Santiago

Análisis: Manuel Montt 425, Santiago; tel. (2) 223-4386; f. 1977; weekly; political, economic and social affairs; published by Emisión Ltda; Dir JUAN PABLO CÁRDENAS; circ. 30,000.

Apsi: Gen. Alberto Reyes 032, Providencia, Casilla 9896, Santiago; tel. (2) 77-5450; f. 1976; fortnightly; Dir MARCELO CONTRERAS NIETO; circ. 30,000.

La Bicicleta: José Fagnano 614, Santiago; tel. (2) 222-3969; satirical; Dir ANTONIO DE LA FUENTE.

CA Revista Oficial del Colegio de Arquitectos de Chile AG: Manuel Montt 515, Santiago; tel. (2) 44734; f. 1964; 4 a year; architects' magazine; Editor Arq. JAIME MÁRQUEZ ROJAS; circ. 3,000.

El Campesino: Tenderini 187, Casilla 40-D, Santiago; tel. (2) 39-6710; telex 240760; f. 1838; monthly; farming; Dir PATRICIO MONTT; circ. 5,000.

Carola: San Francisco 116, Casilla 1858, Santiago; tel. (2) 33-6433; telex 240656; fortnightly; women's magazine; published by Editorial Antártica, SA; Dir ISABEL MARGARITA AGUIRRE DE MAINO.

Cauce: Huérfanos 713, Of. 604–60, Santiago; tel. (2) 38-2304; fortnightly; political, economic and cultural affairs; Dir ANGEL FLISFICH; circ. 10,000.

Chile Agrícola: Casilla 2, Correo 13, Teresa Vial 1172, Santiago; tel. (2) 551-6039; f. 1976; monthly; farming; Dir Ing. Agr. RAÚL GONZÁLEZ VALENZUELA; circ. 10,000.

Chile Filatélico: Almirante Simpson 75, Casilla 13245, Santiago; tel. (2) 222-8036; f. 1929; quarterly; Editor RICARDO BOIZARD G.

Chile Forestal: Avda Bulnes 259, Of. 706, Santiago; tel. (2) 696-6724; telex 240001; fax (2) 71-5881; f. 1974; monthly; technical information and features on forestry sector; Dir Ing. MARIO ALVARADO EVA; circ. 5,600.

Cosas: Almirante Pastene 329, Providencia, Santiago; tel. (2) 225-8630; telex 340905; fax (2) 225-7799; f. 1976; fortnightly; international affairs; Editor MÓNICA COMANDARI KAISER; circ. 25,000.

Creces: Manuel Montt 1922, Santiago; tel. (2) 223-4337; telex 341011; monthly; science and technology; Dir SERGIO PRENAFETA; circ. 12,000.

Deporte Total: Luis Thayer Ojeda 1626, Casilla 3092, Providencia, Santiago; tel. (2) 74-9421; telex 341194; f. 1981; weekly; sport, illustrated; Dir DARÍO ROJAS MORALES; circ. 25,000.

Economía y Sociedad: MacIver 125, 10°, Santiago; tel. (2) 33-1034; telex 340656; Dir JOSÉ PIÑERA; circ. 10,000.

Ercilla: Las Hortensias 2340, Casilla 63-D, Santiago; tel. (2) 225-5055; f. 1936; weekly; general interest; Dir MANFREDO MAYOL DURÁN; circ. 146,000.

Estanquero 11: Santiago; tel. (2) 223-3065; f. 1985; monthly; politics; published by Sociedad Periodística Estanquero Once Ltda; Dir GASTÓN ACUÑA MACLEAN; circ. 6,000.

Estrategia: Rafael Cañas 114, Casilla 16845, Correo 9, Santiago; tel. (2) 49-1526; telex 34036; fax (2) 274-5494; f. 1975; monthly; business, economic and financial affairs; Dir VÍCTOR MANUEL OJEDA MÉNDEZ; circ. 15,000.

Gestión: Rafael Cañas 114, Santiago; tel. (2) 274-5494; telex 440001; fax (2) 274-5494; f. 1975; monthly; business matters; Dir VÍCTOR MANUEL OJEDA MÉNDEZ; circ. 15,000.

Hoy: Mons. Miller 74, Clasificador 654, Correo Central, Santiago; tel. (2) 223-6102; fax (2) 249-5000; f. 1977; weekly; general interest; Dir ABRAHAM SANTIBAÑEZ; circ. 30,000.

Jurídica del Trabajo: Avda Bulnes 180, Of. 80, Casilla 9447, Santiago; tel. (2) 696-7474; Editor MARIO SOTO VENEGAS.

Mensaje: Almirante Barroso 24, Casilla 10445, Santiago; tel. (2) 696-0653; f. 1951; monthly; national, church and international affairs; Dir JOSE ARTEAGA; circ. 8,000.

Microbyte: Portugal 28, Torre 4, Dpto 33, Santiago; tel. (2) 222-0750; telex 243259; f. 1984; monthly; computer science; Dir JOSÉ KAFFMAN; circ. 8,000.

Paula: Triana 851, Santiago; tel. (2) 225-3447; fortnightly; women's magazine; Dir ANDREA ELUCHANS; circ. 20,000.

¿Qué Pasa?: Darío Urzua 2109, Casilla 13279, Santiago; tel. (2) 251-6352; telex 341029; fax (2) 225-3201; f. 1971; weekly; general interest; Dir ROBERTO PULIDO ESPINOSA; circ. 30,000.

El Siglo: Santiago; f. 1989; fortnightly; published by the Communist Party (PCCh); Dir JUAN ANDRÉS LAGOS.

Super Rock: Luis Thayer Ojeda 1626, Casilla 3092, Providencia, Santiago; tel. (2) 74-8231; telex 341194; f. 1985; weekly; Latin and European rock music, illustrated; Dir DARÍO ROJAS MORALES; circ. 40,000.

Vea: Luis Thayer Ojeda 1626, Casilla 3092, Providencia, Santiago; tel. (2) 74-9421; telex 341194; f. 1939; weekly; general interest, illustrated; Dir DARÍO ROJAS MORALES; circ. 150,000.

PRESS ASSOCIATION

Asociación Nacional de la Prensa: Bandera 84, Of. 411, Santiago; tel. (2) 696-6431; Pres. CARLOS PAÚL LAMAS; Sec. JAIME MARTÍNEZ WILLIAMS.

NEWS AGENCIES

Orbe Servicios Informativos, SA: Phillips 56, 6°, Of. 66, Santiago; tel. (2) 39-4774; Dir ALFREDO STEINMEYER FARIÑA.

Foreign Bureaux

Agence France-Presse (France): Avda O'Higgins 1316, 9°, Apt. 92, Santiago; tel. (2) 696-0559; telex 440074; Correspondent HUMBERTO ZUMARÁN ARAYA.

Agencia EFE (Spain): Coronel Santiago Bueras 188, Santiago; tel. (2) 38-0179; telex 240075; fax (2) 33-6130; f. 1966; Bureau Chief RAMIRO GAVILANES GRANJA.

Agenzia Nazionale Stampa Associata (ANSA) (Italy): Moneda 1040, Of. 702, Santiago; tel. (2) 698-5811; telex 741353; f. 1945; Bureau Chief GIORGIO BAGONI BETTOLLINI.

Associated Press (AP) (USA): Tenderini 85, 10°, Of. 100, Casilla 2653, Santiago; tel. (2) 33-5015; telex 645493; Bureau Chief KEVIN NOBLET.

Deutsche Presse-Agentur (dpa) (Germany): San Antonio 427, Of. 306, Santiago; tel. (2) 39-3633; Correspondent CARLOS DORAT.

Inter Press Service (IPS) (Italy): Phillips 40, Of. 68, Santiago; tel. (2) 39-7091; Dir and Correspondent GUSTAVO GONZÁLEZ RODRÍGUEZ.

Prensa Latina (Cuba): Bombero Ossa 1010, Of. 1104, Santiago; tel. (2) 22-6848; telex 441545; Correspondent JOSÉ BODES GÓMEZ.

Reuters (UK): Neuva York 33, 11°, Casilla 4248, Santiago; tel. (2) 72-8800; telex 240584; fax (2) 696-0161; Correspondent RICHARD WADDINGTON.

United Press International (UPI) (USA): Nataniel 47, 9°, Casilla 71-D, Santiago; tel. (2) 696-0162; telex 240570; Bureau Chief TOM HARVEY.

Xinhua (New China) News Agency (People's Republic of China): Biarritz 1981, Providencia, Santiago; tel. (2) 25-5033; telex 94293; Correspondent SUN KUOGUOWEIN.

Publishers

Ediciones Paulinas: Vicuña MacKenna 10777, Casilla 3746, Santiago; tel. (2) 698-9145; fax (2) 71-6884; Catholic texts.

Ediciones Universitarias de Valparaíso: Universidad Católica de Valparaíso, Avenido Brasil 2890, 11°, Casilla 1415, Valparaíso; tel. (32) 25-2900; telex 230389; fax (32) 21-2746; also Moneda 673, 8°, Santiago; tel. (2) 33-2230; f. 1970; general literature, social sciences, engineering, education, music, arts, textbooks; Gen. Man. KARLHEINZ LAAGE II.

Editora Nacional Gabriel Mistral Ltda: Santiago; tel. (2) 77-9522; literature, history, philosophy, religion, art, education; government-owned; Man. Dir JOSÉ HARRISON DE LA BARRA.

Editorial Andrés Bello/Jurídica de Chile: Avda Ricardo Lyon 946, Casilla 4256, Santiago; tel. (2) 40436; telex 240901; fax (2) 225-3600; f. 1947; history, arts, literature, philosophy, politics, economics, agriculture, textbooks, law and social science; Gen. Man. WILLIAM THAYER.

Editorial El Sembrador: Sargento Aldea 1041, Casilla 2037, Santiago; tel. (2) 556-9454; Dir ISAÍAS GUTIÉRREZ.

Editorial Nascimento, SA: Chiloé 1433, Casilla 2298, Santiago; tel. (2) 555-0254; f. 1898; general; Man. Dir CARLOS GEORGE NASCIMENTO MÁRQUEZ.

Editorial Universitaria, SA: María Luisa Santander 0447, Casilla 10220, Santiago; tel. (2) 223-4555; fax (2) 49-9455; f. 1947; general literature, social science, technical, textbooks; Man. Dir GABRIELA MATTE ALESSANDRI.

Empresa Editora Zig-Zag SA: Avda Holanda 1543, Santiago; tel. (2) 223-4675; telex 340455; fax (2) 223-5766; general publishers of literary works, reference books and magazines; Pres. SERGIO MÚJICA L.; Gen. Man. RODRIGO CASTRO C.

ASSOCIATION

Cámara Chilena del Libro AG: Ahumada 312, Of. 806, Casilla 13526, Santiago; tel. (2) 698-9519; telex 241330; fax (2) 698-1474; Pres. EDUARDO CASTILLO; Exec. Sec. CARLOS FRANZ.

Radio and Television

In 1987 there were an estimated 4.2m. radio receivers and 2.1m. television receivers in use. There were six short-wave, 155 medium-wave and 215 FM stations.

RADIO

Asociación de Radiodifusores de Chile (ARCHI): Pasaje Matte 956, Of. 801, Casilla 10476, Santiago; tel. (2) 39-8755; f. 1936; 340 broadcasting stations; Pres. OSCAR PIZARRO ROMERO; Sec.-Gen. NELSON ENCINA GÓMEZ.

Radio Nacional de Chile: San Antonio 220, 2°, Casilla 244-V, Correo 21, Santiago; tel. (2) 33-9071; government station; domestic service; Dir JOSÉ LUIS CORDOVA.

TELEVISION

In November 1988 the Government announced that Televisión Nacional de Chile—Canal 7 was to become a *Sociedad Anónima*, prior to its eventual privatization. Canal 4 and Canal 11 (see below) were also included in the Government's long-term proposals for privatization. In 1989 the National Television Council was established to approve concessions for private television stations and the sale of existing stations.

Televisión Nacional de Chile—Canal 7: Bellavista 0990, Casilla 16104, Santiago; tel. (2) 77-4552; telex 241375; fax (2) 35-3000; government network; 122 stations; Dir-Gen. Col ALEJANDRO BRIONES LEA-PLAZA.

Corporación de Televisión de la Universidad Católica de Chile—Canal 13: Inés Matte Urrejola 0848, Casilla 14600, Santiago; tel. (2) 51-4000; telex 440182; f. 1959; non-commercial; Exec. Dir ELEODORO RODRÍGUEZ MATTE.

Corporación de Televisión de la Universidad Católica de Valparaíso—Canal 4: Agua Santa 2455, Viña del Mar; Casilla 4059, Valparaíso; tel. (32) 66-3132; f. 1957; Dir CAMILO LOBOS LEIVA.

Universidad de Chile—Canal 11: Inés Matte Urrejola 0825, Casilla 16457, Correo 9, Providencia, Santiago; tel. (2) 77-6273; telex 340492; f. 1960; educational; Vice-Pres. JUAN PABLO O'RYAN GUERRERO.

Universidad del Norte—Red Telenorte de Televisión: Carrera 1625, Casilla 1045, Antofagasta; tel. (83) 22-6725; telex 325142; f. 1981; operates Canal 11-Arica, Canal 12-Iquique and Canal 3-Antofagasta; Dir JOSÉ MANUEL FERNÁNDEZ SOLAR.

Empresa Nacional de Telecomunicaciones, SA—ENTEL CHILE, SA: Santa Lucía 360, Casilla 4254, Santiago; tel. (2) 690-2121; telex 240683; f. 1964; operates the Chilean land satellite stations of Longovilo, Punta Arenas and Coihaique, linked to INTELSAT system; Gen. Man. Lt-Col IVÁN VAN DE WYNGARD MELLADO.

Finance

(cap. = capital; p.u. = paid up; dep. = deposits; res = reserves; m. = million; amounts in pesos unless otherwise specified)

BANKING

In 1980 the law referring to banks was amended to eliminate the categories of commercial and provincial banks. New banking legislation, designed to limit new loans by banks to 5% of their capital, was introduced in November 1986. In December 1988 President Pinochet presented new legislation under which the Banco Central became an autonomous body in December 1989.

Supervisory Authority

Superintendencia de Bancos e Instituciones Financieras: Moneda 1123, 6°, Santiago; tel. (2) 699-0072; fax (2) 71-1654; f. 1925; run by Ministry of Finance; Superintendent GUILLERMO RAMÍREZ VILARDELL.

Central Bank

Banco Central de Chile: Agustinas 1180, Santiago; tel. (2) 696-2281; telex 240658; fax (2) 698-4847; f. 1926; under Ministry of Finance until Dec. 1989, when autonomy was granted; bank of issue; cap. 500,000m. (Dec. 1989); res 292,292.9m., dep. 5,032,968.6m. (Dec. 1988); Pres. ANDRÉS BIANCHI; Vice-Pres. ROBERTO ZAHLER; 7 brs.

State Bank

Banco del Estado de Chile: Avda B. O'Higgins 1111, Casilla 24, Santiago; tel. (2) 71-6001; telex 240536; fax (2) 698-3299; f. 1953; state bank; cap. and res 80,820.4m., dep. 358,190.2m. (Dec. 1989); Pres. ANDRES SANFUENTES; Exec. Gen. Man. ARTURO MORENO; 179 brs.

National Banks

Banco de A. Edwards: Huérfanos 740, Santiago; tel. (2) 38-4641; telex 340428; fax (2) 38-0904; f. 1851; cap. and res 13,399.6m., dep. 181,517.2m. (Dec. 1989); Chair. AGUSTÍN EDWARDS DEL RÍO; Gen. Man. JULIO JARAQUEMADA LEDOUX; 34 brs.

Banco Bice: Teatinos 220, Santiago; tel. (2) 698-2931; telex 645197; fax (2) 696-5324; f. 1979; cap. and res 7,178.2m., dep. 140,329.6m. (Dec. 1989); Pres. JORGE SCHNEIDER HERNÁNDEZ; Gen. Man. GONZALO VALDÉS BUDGE; 5 brs.

Banco de Chile: Ahumada 251, Casilla 151-D, Santiago; tel. (2) 38-3044; telex 520176; fax (2) 72-1459; f. 1894; cap. and res 75,804.4m. (July 1989); Chair. ADOLFO ROJAS GANDULFO; Gen. Man. SEGISMUNDO SCHULIN-ZEUTHEN SERRANO; 102 brs.

Banco Concepción: Huérfanos 1072, Casilla 80-D, Santiago; tel. (2) 698-2741; telex 240556; fax (2) 698-3891; f. 1871; cap. and res 12,779.9m. (July 1989); Pres. MANUEL FELIÚ JUSTINIANO; Gen. Man. JORGE DÍAZ VIAL; 34 brs.

Banco Continental—Crédit Lyonnais: Huérfanos 1219, Casilla 10492, Santiago; tel. (2) 696-8201; telex 645347; fax (2) 71-3307; f. 1958; cap. and res 5,318.4m. (July 1989); bought by Crédit Lyonnais in Sept. 1987; Pres. NICOLÁS YARUR LOLAS; Gen. Man. PIERRE JEAN EYMERY; 1 br.

Banco de Crédito e Inversiones: Huérfanos 1134, Casilla 136-D, Santiago; tel. (2) 696-6633; telex 340373; fax (2) 699-0729; f. 1937; cap. and res 24,712.7m., dep. 398,867.4m. (Dec. 1989); Pres. JORGE YARUR BANNA; Gen. Man. LUIS ENRIQUE YARUR REY; 95 brs.

Banco del Desarrollo: Avda B. O'Higgins 949, 3°, Casilla 320-V, Correo 21, Santiago; tel. (2) 698-2901; telex 340654; f. 1983; cap. and res 3,804.4m. (July 1989); Pres. DOMINGO SANTA MARÍA SANTA CRUZ; Gen. Man. VICENTE CARUZ MIDDLETON.

Banco Español-Chile: Agustinas 920, Casilla 76-D, Santiago; tel. (2) 38-1501; telex 340298; fax (2) 33-4476; f. 1926; cap. and res 15,849.3m. (July 1989), dep. 207,565.9m. (Dec. 1988); subsidiary of Banco de Santander, Spain; Pres. EMILIO BOTÍN SANZ DE SAUTUOLA Y GARCÍA DE LOS RÍOS; Gen. Man. JOSÉ ANTONIO CAMBA FERNÁNDEZ; 53 brs.

Banco Exterior, SA: MacIver 225, Casilla 324-V, Santiago; tel. (2) 39-4731; telex 340462; cap. and res 5,313.0m. (July 1989); Pres. CALIXTO RÍOS PÉREZ; Gen. Man. PERE CAMPISTOL SIRERA.

Banco Hipotecario Internacional Financiero: Huérfanos 1234, Casilla 517, Santiago; tel. 698-1842; telex 340269; fax (2) 698-5640; f. 1883; cap. and res 9,546.5m. (July 1989); Pres. IGNACIO COUSIÑO ARAGÓN; Gen. Man. RICARDO BACARREZA RODRÍGUEZ; 10 brs.

Banco Internacional: San Antonio 76, Casilla 135-D, Santiago; tel. (2) 698-1722; telex 341066; fax (2) 33-9134; f. 1944; cap. and res 4,269.4m. (Aug. 1989), dep. US $ 72.5m. (Dec. 1989); placed under state control Jan. 1983 but returned to the private sector in May 1986; Pres BORIS SUBELMAN; Gen. Man. CÉSAR BESIO; 9 brs.

Banco Nacional: Bandera 287, Casilla 131-D, Santiago; tel. (2) 698-2091; telex 340830; f. 1906; cap. and res 6,977.1m. (July 1989); Pres. FRANCISCO ERRÁZURIZ TALAVERA; Gen. Man. ALFREDO Neut Blanco; 31 brs.

Banco O'Higgins: Bandera 201, Casilla 51-D, Santiago; tel. (2) 696-3153; telex 341186; fax (2) 71-7152; f. 1956; cap. and res 16,478.5m., dep. 262,606.5m. (Dec. 1989); Pres. ANDRÓNICO LUKSIC CRAIG; Gen. Man. GONZALO MENÉNDEZ DUQUE; 37 brs.

Banco Osorno y La Unión: Bandera 102, Casilla 57-D, Santiago; tel. (2) 696-0414; telex 240407; fax (2) 699-7842; f. 1908; cap. and res US $85,100m. (Dec. 1989); incorporated the Banco del Trabajo in 1989; Pres. CARLOS ABUMOHOR TOUMA; Gen. Man. JUAN CARLOS MARTINO GONZÁLEZ; 70 brs.

Banco del Pacífico: Moneda 1096, Casilla 458-V, Santiago; tel. (2) 698-1873; telex 340466; cap. and res 4,802.4m. (Dec. 1989); Pres. CARLOS CARDOEN; Gen. Man. EMILIANO FIGUEROA; 10 brs.

Banco de Santiago: Bandera 172, Casilla 14437, Santiago; tel. (2) 72-8072; telex 340140; f. 1977; cap. and res 73,598.6m. (Dec. 1989), dep. 583,144.5m. (Dec. 1989); merged with Banco Colocadora Nacional de Valores in 1986; Pres. JULIO BARRIGA SILVA; Chair. and Gen. Man. HÉCTOR VALDÉS RUÍZ; 32 brs.

Banco Security Pacific: Agustinas 621, Santiago; tel. (2) 38-1620; telex 340791; fax (2) 33-2156; f. 1981; fmrly Banco Urquijo de Chile; cap. and res US $27.4m., dep. US $93.6m. (June 1988); Pres. FRANCISCO SILVA S.; Gen. Man. RENATO PEÑAFIEL M; 1 br.

Banco Sud Americano: Morandé 226, Casilla 90-D, Santiago; tel. (2) 698-2391; telex 340436; fax (2) 698-2391; f. 1944; cap. 13,293.4m., res 2,128.2m., dep. 291,602.2m. (Dec. 1989); Pres. JOSÉ BORDA ARETXABALA; Gen. Man. JUAN LUIS KÖSTNER MANRÍQUEZ; 28 brs.

NMB Bank Chile: Moneda 970, 13°, Casilla 500-V, Santiago; tel. (2) 72-1037; telex 341244; fax (2) 699-1113; cap. and res. 2,146.8m. (July 1989); Pres. GERRIT JAN TAMMES; Gen. Man. LORENZO STEFANO RONCARI; 1 br.

Foreign Banks

Foreign banks that have opened branches in Chile include the following:
American Express International Banking Corporation (USA), Banco do Brasil, Banco de Colombia, Banco do Estado de São Paulo (Brazil), Banco de la Nación Argentina, Banco Real (Brazil), Banco Sudameris (France), Bank of America NT & SA (USA), Bank of Tokyo (Japan), Centrobanco, Chase Manhattan Bank (USA), Chicago Continental Bank (USA), Citibank NA (USA), Hongkong and Shanghai Banking Corporation (Hong Kong), First National Bank of Boston (USA), Manufacturers Hanover Bank, Republic National Bank of New York (USA).

Association

Asociación de Bancos e Instituciones Financieras de Chile AG: Agustinas 1476, 10°, Santiago; tel. (2) 71-7149; telex 340958; fax (2) 699-3634; f. 1946; Pres. ADOLFO ROJAS GANDULFO; Gen. Man. ARTURO TAGLE QUIROZ.

STOCK EXCHANGES

Bolsa de Comercio de Santiago: La Bolsa 64, Casilla 123-D, Santiago; tel. and fax (2) 698-2001; telex 340531; f. 1893; 35 mems; Pres. PABLO YRARRÁZAVAL VALDÉS; Man. ENRIQUE GOLDFARB SKLAR.

Bolsa de Corredores y Valores de Chile: Santiago; f. 1989; 32 mems; Gen. Man. EDUARDO SANGUESA.

Bolsa de Corredores y Valores de Valparaíso: Prat 798, Casilla 218-V, Valparaíso; tel. (32) 25-0677; f. 1905; Pres. CARLOS F. MARÍN ORREGO; Man. ARIE JOEL GELFENSTEIN FREUNDLICH.

INSURANCE

In May 1990 there were 23 general insurance, 25 life insurance and three reinsurance companies operating in Chile.

Supervisory Authority

Superintendencia de Valores y Seguros: Teatinos 120, 6°, Santiago; tel. (2) 696-2194; telex 340260; fax (2) 698-7425; f. 1931; under Ministry of Finance; Supt HUGO LAVADOS MONTES.

Principal Companies

Cía de Seguros Generales Aetna Chile, SA: Coyancura 2270, 11°, Santiago; tel. (2) 231-4566; telex 241295; fax (2) 231-0989; f. 1900; general; Pres. SERGIO BAEZA VALDÉS.

Cía de Seguros Generales Consorcio Nacional de Seguros, SA: Bandera 236, 6°, Santiago; tel. (2) 71-8232; telex 240466; fax (2) 698-9089; f. 1920; general; Pres. CARLOS EUGENIO LAVÍN GARCÍA-HUIDOBRO.

Cía de Seguros Generales Cruz del Sur, SA: Ahumada 370, 4°, Casilla 2682, Santiago; tel. (2) 72-7572; telex 340030; fax (2) 698-9126; f. 1974; general; Pres. JOSÉ TOMÁS GUZMÁN DUMAS.

Cía de Seguros Generales Euroamérica, SA: Agustinas 1127, 2°, Santiago; tel. (2) 72-7242; fax (2) 696-4086; f. 1986; general; Pres. BENJAMÍN DAVIS CLARKE.

Aetna Chile Seguros de Vida, SA: Coyancura 2270, 10°, Of. 1020, Santiago; tel. (2) 233-4566; telex 341624; fax (2) 232-6731; f. 1981; life; Pres. SERGIO BAEZA VALDÉS.

Cía de Seguros de Vida Consorcio Nacional de Seguros, SA: Bandera 236, 8°, Santiago; tel. (2) 72-1511; telex 240947; fax (2) 72-4252; f. 1916; life; Pres. RICHARD J. BENTLEY.

Cía de Seguros de Vida La Construcción, SA: Marchant Pereira 10, 19-20°, Providencia, Santiago; tel. (2) 233-1363; telex 725881; fax (2) 231-0966; f. 1985; life; Pres. SERGIO ORELLANA SALCEDO.

Cía de Seguros de Vida El Roble, SA: Teatinos 333, 9°, Santiago; tel. (2) 72-4351; telex 242122; f. 1981; life; Pres. JOSÉ TOMÁS GUZMÁN DUMAS.

Cía de Seguros de Vida Santander, SA: Agustinas 785, 2°, Santiago; tel. (2) 632-1222; fax (2) 632-1875; f. 1989; life; Pres. CARLOS GARCÍA RODRÍGUEZ.

Instituto de Seguros del Estado (ISE): Moneda 1025, 7°, Santiago; tel. (2) 696-4271; telex 240204; fax (2) 696-5732; f. 1888; general; Pres. GUSTAVO DUPUIS PINILLOS.

La Interamericana Compañía de Seguros de Vida: Miraflores 178, 9°, Santiago; tel. (2) 33-7663; telex 440295; fax (2) 33-3606; f. 1980; life; Pres. RICARDO PERALTA VALENZUELA.

Renta Nacional Compañía de Seguros de Vida, SA: Dr Sótero del Río 326, 3°, Santiago; tel. (2) 699-1050; telex 241136; fax (2) 698-0173; f. 1982; life; Pres. FRANCISCO JAVIER ERRÁZURIZ TALAVERA.

Reinsurance

Caja Reaseguradora de Chile, SA (Generales): Bandera 84, 6°, Santiago; tel. (2) 698-2941; telex 340276; fax (2) 698-9730; f. 1927; general; Pres. GUSTAVO DUPUIS PINILLOS.

Caja Reaseguradora de Chile, SA: Bandera 84, 6°, Santiago; tel. (2) 698-2941; telex 340276; fax (2) 698-9730; f. 1980; life; Pres. GUSTAVO DUPUIS PINILLOS.

Cía de Reaseguros de Vida Soince, SA: Agustinas 785, 2°, Santiago; tel. (2) 632-1222; f. 1990; life; Pres. CARLOS GARCÍA RODRÍGUEZ.

Cía Reaseguradora Bernardo O'Higgins (American Reinsurance Company): Huérfanos 1189, 5°, Santiago; tel. (2) 696-7929; telex 242155; fax (2) 72-3169; f. 1981; general; Pres. MAHMOUD ABDALLAH.

Insurance Association

Asociación de Aseguradores de Chile: Moneda 920, Of. 1002, Casilla 2630, Santiago; tel. (2) 696-7431; fax (2) 698-4820; f. 1931; Pres. JOSÉ GANDARILLAS CHADWICK; Gen. Man. JORGE CAÑAS SUÁREZ.

Trade and Industry

CHAMBER OF COMMERCE

Cámara de Comercio de Santiago de Chile, AG: Santa Lucía 302, 3°, Casilla 1297, Santiago; tel. (2) 33-0962; telex 240868; f. 1919; 1,100 mems; Pres. LUIS CORREA PRIETO; Man. HARALD WEINREICH TASSO.

There are Chambers of Commerce in all major towns.

STATE ECONOMIC AND DEVELOPMENT ORGANIZATIONS

In 1980 the Government began a policy of denationalization, comprising three stages, and by early 1981 over 500 state companies had been sold. Only those concerns considered to be of strategic importance continue in the state sector and each must show an annual profit of 10% of its capital. In 1985 the Government launched the third stage of the privatization programme, under which 26 state concerns were to be partially or completely sold to private interests.

Comisión Nacional de Energía: Teatinos 120, 7°, Casilla 14, Correo 21, Santiago; tel. (2) 698-1757; telex 240948; fax (2) 698-1758; f. 1978 to determine Chile's energy policy and approve investments in energy-related projects; Pres. Min. of Energy JAIME TOHA GONZÁLEZ; Exec. Sec. SEBASTIÁN BERNSTEIN LETELIER.

Corporación de Fomento de la Producción—CORFO: Moneda 921, Casilla 3886, Santiago; tel. (2) 38-0521; telex 240421; fax (2) 71-1058; f. 1939; holding group of principal state enterprises; under Ministry of Economy, Development and Reconstruction; grants loans and guarantees to private sector; responsible for sale of non-strategic state enterprises; Vice-Pres. RENÉ ABELIUK MANASEVICH; Gen. Man. Col EUGENIO LAVÍN HOLLUB; controls:

Cía de Acero del Pacífico, SA: Casilla 167-D, Santiago; telex 240288; f. 1946; cap. US $427.1m.; iron and steel production; Gen. Man. ROBERTO DE ANDRACA BARBAS; 6,767 employees.

Complejo Forestal y Maderero Panguipulli Ltda: Agustinas 785, Of. 560, Santiago; tel. (2) 39-7054; telex 346093; fax (2) 698-4127; Gen. Man. MANUEL F. IZQUIERDO FERNÁNDEZ.

Distribuidora Chilectra Metropolitana: Santo Domingo 789, Casilla 1557, Santiago; tel. (2) 38-2000; telex (2) 40645; fax (2) 39-

3280; f. 1921; transmission and distribution of electrical energy; Gen. Man. José Yuraszek T.

Empresa Minera de Aysén Ltda: Calle 21, De Mayo 466, 3°, Coyhaique; zinc and lead mining; Gen. Man. Sergio Araneda Valdivieso.

Empresa Nacional del Carbón—ENACAR: Avda Libertador Bernardo O'Higgins 396, Casilla 271, Concepción; tel. (41) 71-7201; telex 240522; in charge of coal production; Gen. Man. Col Eudoro Quiñones Silva.

Empresa Nacional de Computación e Informática, SA—ECOM: Apoquindo 3063, Santiago; tel. (2) 231-3466; fax (2) 231-8049; f. 1968; Pres. Gustavo Ramdohr Vargas.

Empresa Nacional de Electricidad, SA—ENDESA: Santa Rosa 76, Casilla 1392, Santiago; tel. (2) 222-9080; fax (2) 222-6328; f. 1943; cap. p.u. 433,615m.; installed capacity 1,828 MW; Chair. Rodrigo Manubens Molteado; Gen. Man. Jaime Bauzá Bauzá.

Empresa Nacional de Explosivos, SA—ENAEX: Agustinas 1350, 3°, Casilla 255-V, Santiago; tel. (2) 698-2148; telex 440069; fax (2) 698-2326; Gen. Man. Oscar Jadue Salvador.

Industria Azucarera Nacional—IANSA: Avda Bustamente 26, Casilla 6099, Correo 22, Santiago; tel. (2) 225-8077; telex 240670; f. 1953; cap. US $82.04m.; 1987 production: 410,000 metric tons sugar, 100,000 metric tons beet pulp pellets; factories in Curicó, Linares, Rapaco, Los Angeles and Ñuble; 75% owned by private sector; Gen. Man. M. Verónica González Gil.

Sociedad Química y Minera de Chile—SOQUIMICH: Moneda 970, 15°, Santiago; tel. (2) 71-1121; telex 240762; nitrate mining and exploration; Exec. Gen. Man. Eduardo Bobenrieth Giglio.

Corporación Nacional del Cobre de Chile (CODELCO—Chile): Huérfanos 1270; POB 150-D, Santiago; tel. (2) 698-8801; telex 240672; f. 1976 as a state-owned enterprise with four copper-producing operational divisions at Chuquicamata, Salvador, Andina and El Teniente; attached to Ministry of Mines; Exec. Pres. Alejandro Noemi.

Corporación Nacional Forestal—CONAF: Avda Bulnes 285, Of. 501, Santiago; tel. (2) 72-2724; telex 440138; f. 1972 to centralize forestry activities, to enforce forestry law, to promote afforestation, to administer subsidies for afforestation projects and to increase and preserve forest resources; manages 13.3m. ha designated as National Parks, Natural Monuments and National Reserves; under Ministry of Agriculture; Exec. Dir Iván Castro Poblete.

Empresa Nacional de Minería—ENAMI: MacIver 459, 2°, Casilla 100-D, Santiago; tel. (2) 39-6061; telex 240574; fax (2) 38-4094; promotes the development of the small- and medium-sized mines; attached to Ministry of Mines; Exec. Vice-Pres. Sergio Pérez Hormazábal.

Empresa Nacional de Petróleo—ENAP: Ahumada 341, 3°, Casilla 3556, Santiago; tel. (2) 38-1845; telex 240447; fax (2) 39-1093; f. 1950; development, exploitation and refining of Chilean petroleum resources; attached to Ministry of Mines; CEO Juan Pedrals G.

Oficina de Planificación Nacional—ODEPLAN: Ahumada 48, 7°, Casilla 9140, Santiago; tel. (2) 72-2033; telex 341400; fax (2) 72-1879; f. 1967 to assist the President of the Republic in all matters relating to social and economic planning; Dir Minister of National Planning Sergio Molina Silva.

PROCHILE (Dirección General de Relaciones Económicas Internacionales): Teatinos 120, 2°, POB 16587, Correo 9, Santiago; tel. (2) 696-0043; telex 240836; fax (2) 696-0639; f. 1974; bureau of international economic affairs; Dir Juan Manuel Casanueva Préndez.

Servicio Agrícola y Ganadero (SAG): Avda Bulnes 140, 8°, Santiago; tel. (2) 698-2244; telex 242745; fax (2) 72-1812; under Ministry of Agriculture; Exec. Dir Alejandro Marchant Baeza.

Sociedad Agrícola y Servicios Isla de Pascua: Alfredo Lecannellier 1940, Providencia, Santiago; tel. (2) 232-7497; telex 240690; fax (2) 71-1058; administers agriculture and public services on Easter Island; Gen. Man. Fernando Maira Palma.

Subsecretaría de Pesca: Bellavista 168, 16-18°, Valparaíso; tel. (32) 21-2187; telex 230355; fax (32) 21-2790; f. 1976; controls and promotes fishing industry; Sub-Sec. Andrés Couve Rioseco.

EMPLOYERS' ORGANIZATIONS

Confederación de la Producción y del Comercio: Estado 337, Of. 507, Casilla 9984, Santiago; tel. (2) 33-3690; f. 1936; Pres. Manuel Feliú J.; Gen. Man. José Francisco Aguirre O.
Affiliated organizations:

Asociación de Bancos e Instituciones Financieras de Chile (q.v.).

Cámara Chilena de la Construcción: Marchant Pereira 10, 3°, Providencia, Casilla Clasificador 679, Santiago; tel. (2) 233-1131; fax (2) 232-7600; f. 1951; Pres. José Antonio Guzmán Matta; Gen. Man. Blas Bellolio; 3,000 mems.

Cámara Nacional de Comercio de Chile: Santa Lucía 302, 4°, Casilla 1015, Santiago; tel. (2) 39-7694; telex 340110; fax (2) 38-0234; f. 1858; Pres. Daniel Platovsky Turek; Gen. Sec. José Manuel Melero Abaroa; 120 mems.

Sociedad de Fomento Fabril—SOFOFA: Agustinas 1357, 11°-12°, Casilla 44-D, Santiago; tel. (2) 698-2646; telex 34035; f. 1883; largest employers' organization; Pres. Fernando Aguero Garcés; 2,000 mems.

Sociedad Nacional de Agricultura—Federación Gremial (SNA): Tenderini 187, 2°, Casilla 40-D, Santiago; tel. (2) 39-6710; telex 240760; f. 1838; landowners' association; controls Radio Stations CB 57 and XQB8 (FM) in Santiago, CB-97 in Valparaíso, CD-120 in Los Angeles, CA-144 in La Serena, CD-127 in Temuco; Pres. Jorge Prado Aránguiz; Gen. Sec. Raúl García Astaburuaga.

Sociedad Nacional de Minería—SONAMI: Teatinos 20, 3°, Of. 33, Casilla 1807, Santiago; tel. (2) 81696; f. 1883; Pres. Manuel Feliú J.; Man. Alfredo Araya Muñoz.

Confederación de Asociaciones Gremiales y Federaciones de Agricultores de Chile: Lautaro 218, Los Angeles; registered with Ministry of Economic Affairs in 1981; Pres. Domingo Durán Neumann.

Confederación del Comercio Detallista de Chile: Merced 380, 8°, Santiago; tel. (2) 38-0338; f. 1938; retail trade; registered with Ministry of Economic Affairs in 1980; Pres. Elías Brugére L.; Vice-Pres. Ivonne Betbeder A.

Confederación Gremial Nacional Unida de la Mediana y Pequeña Industria, Servicios y Artesanado—CONUPIA: Santiago; registered with Ministry of Economic Affairs in 1980; small- and medium-sized industries and crafts; Pres. Roberto Parraque Bonet.

There are many federations of private industrialists, organized by industry and region.

TRADE UNIONS

In September 1973 the Central Única de Trabajadores de Chile (CUT) was outlawed as it was deemed to be a political organ of the Communist Party. Trade union activities were severely curtailed under the Pinochet regime, and in 1978 seven trade union federations, representing 529 trade unions and some 400,000 workers, were banned, as they were deemed to be Marxist, and their property was confiscated. However, the CUT was revived in August 1988.

New labour legislation, introduced in 1979 and embodied in the 1981 Constitution, included: the right of association; that unions are to be organized only on a company basis; that the Government's right to control union budgets is to be abolished; that union representatives must not engage in any political activity; that strikes involving stoppages to essential public services or which endanger national security are to be prohibited and that strikes may last no longer than 60 days.

There are more than 20 national labour federations and unions. The confederations include:

Confederación de la Construcción: Serrano 444, Santiago; tel. (2) 39-7472; trade union for workers in construction industry; Pres. Sergio Troncoso; Sec.-Gen. Claudina García.

Confederación de Empleados Particulares de Chile—CEPCH: Teatinos 727, 3°, Santiago; tel. (2) 72-2093; trade union for workers in private sector; Pres. Edmundo Lillo; Sec.-Gen. Federico Mujica.

Confederación General de Trabajadores (CGT): Santa Lucia 162, Santiago; tel. (2) 38-2354; pro-Govt; Pres. Manuel Contreras.

Confederación Marítima de Chile—COMACH: Eleuterio Ramírez 476, 8°, Valparaíso; tel. (32) 25-7656; f. 1985; Leader Eduardo Ríos; Sec.-Gen. Sergio Correa; 5,000 mems.

Confederación de Trabajadores del Cobre (CTC): MacIver 283, 5°, Casilla 9094, Santiago; tel. (2) 38-0835; Pres. Darwin Bustamente; Sec.-Gen. Roberto Carvajal; 20,000 mems.

Frente Nacional de Trabajadores Demócratas Cristianas (FNT-DC): Carmen 8, 8°, Santiago; Christian Democratic trade union organization; Pres. Luis Sepúlveda Gutiérrez; Sec.-Gen. Mario Pereda Sandoval.

Grupo de los Diez: Christian Democratic trade union organization.

Unión Democrática de Trabajadores (UDT): f. 1981; 49 affiliated organizations; set up under auspices of Grupo de los Diez; Leader Hernol Flores; c. 780,000 mems.

The trade unions include:

Central Democrática de Trabajadores (CDT): Erasmo Escala 2170, Santiago; tel. (2) 71-5338; 27 affiliated organizations; Pres. Eduardo Ríos Arias.

CHILE *Directory*

Central Unitaria de Trabajadores de Chile (CUT–Chile): Santa Mónica 2015, Santiago; tel. (2) 698-9770; fax (2) 696-1943; f. 1988; 2 associations, 27 confederations, 49 federations; Pres. MANUEL BUSTOS; Sec.-Gen. NICANOR ARAYA; 411,000 mems.

Coordinadora Nacional Sindical (CNS): Abdón Cifuentes 67, Santiago; tel. (2) 698-5586; national co-ordinating body; 13 affiliated organizations; Pres. (vacant); Sec.-Gen. MOISÉS LABRAÑA; c. 700,000 mems.

Frente Nacional de Organizaciones Autónomas—FRENAO: Santa Lucía 162, Santiago; tel. (2) 38-2354; Pres. MANUEL CONTRERAS LOYOLA.

Frente Unitario de Trabajadores (FUT): Compañía 3127, Santiago; tel. (2) 96-114; five affiliated organizations; Pres. CARLOS ROJAS; Sec.-Gen. HUMBERTO SOTO.

Transport

Ministerio de Transportes y Telecomunicaciones: Amunátegui 139, Santiago; tel. (2) 72-6503; telex 240200.

RAILWAYS

The total length of the railway system in 1990 was 8,185 km, of which almost 90% was state-owned. The privately-owned lines are in the north. There are also four international railways, two to Bolivia, one to Argentina and one to Peru.

In 1983 management of the State Railways system was decentralized and divided into three autonomous operating regions, consisting of Northern (re-organized as a *Sociedad Anónima* in 1989, see below), Southern and the Arica–La Paz railways. Further decentralization, in 1987, included the Metro Regional de Valparaíso. Future expansion of the Santiago underground transport system is to be carried out by private enterprise.

State Railways

Empresa de los Ferrocarriles del Estado: Avda Bernardo O'Higgins 3322, 3°, Casilla 134-D, Santiago; tel. (2) 79-0707; telex 242290; fax (2) 76-2609; f. 1851; 4,727 km of track (1990). The State Railways are divided between the Ferrocarril Regional de Arica (formerly Ferrocarril Arica–La Paz), Metro Regional de Valparaíso (passenger service only) and the Ferrocarril del Sur (Southern Railway); Dir Gen. IGNACIO ECHEVARRÍA ARANEDA.

Parastatal Railways

Ferrocarril del Norte (FERRONOR), SA: Avda Bulnes 79, 9, Of. 90, Santiago; tel. (2) 696-1769; telex 401067; established as a public/private concern, following the transfer of the Ferrocarril Regional del Norte de Chile to the Ministry of Economy, Development and Reconstruction as a *Sociedad Anónima* in 1989; operates cargo services only; Gen. Man. Ing. FERNANDO KAISER OETTINGER.

Metro de Santiago: Red de Transporte Colectivo Independiente, Dirección General del Metro, Avda Libertador B. O'Higgins 1426, Santiago; tel. (2) 698-8218; telex 240777; started operations Sept. 1975; 27.25 km open in Sept. 1987; 2 lines; Gen. Man. LUDOLF LAUSEN KUHLMANN.

Private Railways

Antofagasta (Chili) & Bolivia Railway PLC: Bolívar 255, Casilla S-T, Antofagasta; tel. (83) 25-1700; telex 325002; fax (83) 22-1206; f. 1888; British-owned; Chair. ANDRÓNICO LUKSIC ABAROA; Gen. Man. FRANCISCO J. COURBIS GREZ. Operates an international railway to Bolivia and Argentina; cargo forwarding services; total track length 728 km.

Ferrocarril Codelco-Chile: Barquito, III region, Atacama; Gen. Man. B. BEHNT.

   Diego de Almagro a Potrerillos: transport of forest products, minerals and manufactures; 99 km.

   Ferrocarril Rancagua-Teniente: transport of forest products, livestock, minerals and manufactures; 68 km.

Ferrocarril Tocopilla–Toco: Calle Arturo Prat 1060, Casilla 2098, Santiago; tel. and fax (83) 81-1011; telex 325601; owned by Sociedad Química y Minera de Chile, SA; 116 km; Gen. Man. SEGISFREDO HURTADO GUERRERO.

ROADS

Ministerio de Obras Públicas: Dirección de Vialidad, Morandé 59, 2°, Santiago; tel. (2) 696-4839; telex 240777; fax (2) 72-6609; the authority responsible for roads; the total length of roads in Chile in 1990 was 79,130 km, of which 11,000 km were paved. The road system includes the completely paved Pan American Highway extending 3,455 km from north to south. Toll gates exist on major motorways and charge approximately US $2.5 per vehicle. Important projects include the resurfacing of sections of the Pan American Highway and the construction of the Southern Highway Network; a four-year rehabilitation, maintenance and upgrading programme launched in 1986, at a total cost of US $850m.; and investment of US $183m. annually. A three-year maintenance programme for secondary roads and two-lane highways was due to begin in 1990 at an estimated cost of $907m. and was expected to increase the total length of paved roads by 1,000 km; Dir Ing. ARMANDO SÁNCHEZ ARAYA.

SHIPPING

As a consequence of Chile's difficult topography, maritime transport is of particular importance. The principal ports are Valparaíso, Talcahuano, Antofagasta, San Antonio and Punta Arenas.

Chile's merchant fleet had a total capacity of 1,166,465 dwt in 1983.

Supervisory Authorities

Asociación Nacional de Armadores: Blanco 869, Valparaíso; tel. (32) 21257; also Teatinos 20, Of. 91, 9°, Santiago; tel. (2) 71-0126; shipowners' association; Pres. BELTRÁN URENDA ZEGERS; Man. SERGIO NÚÑEZ RAMÍREZ.

Cámara Marítima de Chile: Blanco 869, Valparaíso; tel. (32) 25-3443; telex 230491; fax (32) 25-0231; Pres. RALPH DELAVAL.

Dirección General de Territorio Marítimo y Marina Mercante: Errázuriz 537, 4°, Valparaíso; tel. (32) 25-8061; telex 230662; fax (32) 25-2539; maritime admin. of the coast and national waters, control of the merchant navy; Dir Rear Adm. FERNANDO LAZCANO.

Empresa Portuaria de Chile—EMPORCHI: Blanco 839, Valparaíso; tel. (32) 25-7167; telex 230313; fax (32) 25-9937; also Huérfanos 1055, Of. 804, Santiago; tel. (2) 698-2232; telex 240624; fax (2) 698-9441; Dir RAUL URZUA MARAMBIO.

Santiago

Cía Marítima Isla de Pascua, SA (COMAIPA): MacIver 225, Of. 2001, 20°, Santiago; tel. (2) 38-3036; telex 240646; Pres. FEDERICO BARRAZA; Gen. Man. ALEJANDRO BARRAZA BARRY.

Marítima Antares, SA: MacIver 225, Of. 2001, 2°, Santiago; tel. (2) 38-3036; telex 340464; Pres. ALFONSO GARCÍA-MIÑAUR G.; Gen. Man. LUIS BEDRIÑANA RODRÍGUEZ.

Valparaíso

A. J. Broom y Cía, SAC: Blanco 951, POB 910, Valparaíso and Agustinas 853, 6°, POB 448, Santiago; f. 1920; Pres. Capt. JENS SORENSEN; Gen. Man. MARCELO VARGAS MUÑOZ.

Cía Chilena de Navegación Interoceánica, SA: Avda Libertador B. O'Higgins 949, 22°, Casilla 4246; Santiago; tel. (2) 72-3006; telex 240486; fax (2) 698-4542; also Plaza de la Justicia 59, Casilla 1410, Valparaíso; tel. (32) 25-9001; telex 230386; fax (32) 25-5949; f. 1930; regular sailings to Japan, Republic of Korea, Taiwan, Hong Kong, USA, South Pacific, South Africa and Europe; bulk and dry cargo services; Pres. ANTONIO JABAT ALONSO; Gen. Man. PATRICIO LABBÉ CASTRO.

Cía Sud-Americana de Vapores: Blanco 895, Casilla 49-V, Valparaíso; tel. (32) 25-9061; telex 230001; fax (32) 21-8724; also Moneda 970, 10° y 11°, Santiago; tel. (2) 696-4181; telex 240480; fax (2) 698-9441; f. 1872; 15 cargo vessels; regular service between Chile and US/Canadian East Coast ports, US Gulf ports, North European, Mediterranean, Scandinavian and Far East ports; bulk carriers, tramp and reefer services; Pres. RICARDO CLARO VALDÉS; Man. PATRICIO FALCONE SCHIAVETTI.

Empresa Marítima, SA (Empremar Chile): Almirante Gómez Carreño 49, POB 105-V, Valparaíso; tel. (32) 25-8061; telex 230382; fax (32) 21-3904; f. 1953; 14 vessels; international and coastal services; Exec. Pres. GASTON ROJAS PAREDES.

Naviera Chilena del Pacífico, SA: Errázuriz 556, Casilla 370, Valparaíso; tel. (32) 25-0551; telex 230357; fax (32) 25-3869; also Serrano 14, Of. 502, Santiago; tel. (2) 33-3063; telex 240457; fax (2) 39-2069; cargo; 3 vessels; Pres. ARTURO FERNÁNDEZ; Gen. Man. PABLO SIMIAN.

Naviera Interoceangas, SA: Miraflores 178, 11–12°, POB 2829, Santiago; tel. (2) 696-3211; telex 341234; fax (2) 33-1871; Gen. Man. FRANCISCO SAHLI CRUZ.

Pacific Steam Navigation Co: Blanco 625, 6°, Casilla 24-V, Valparaíso; tel. (32) 21-3191; telex 230384; also Moneda 970, 9°, Casilla 4087, Santiago; brs in Antofagasta and San Antonio; Man. DAVID KIMBER SMITH.

Sociedad Anónima de Navegación Petrolera (SONAP): Errázuriz 471, 3°, Casilla 1870, Valparaíso; tel. (32) 25-9476; telex 230392; fax (32) 25-1325; f. 1953; tanker services; 4 vessels; Pres. LUIS E. GUBLER ESCOBAR.

Transmares Naviera Chilena Ltda: Moneda 970, 19°, Casilla 193-D, Santiago; tel. (2) 72-2686; telex 240440; fax (2) 698-3205; also

CHILE

Cochrane 813, 8°, Valparaíso; tel. (32) 25-9051; telex 230383; fax (32) 25-6607; f. 1969; dry cargo service Chile–Uruguay–Brazil; Gen. Man. ERICH STRELOW.

Several foreign shipping companies operate services to Valparaíso.

Ancúd

Sociedad Transporte Marítimo Chiloé-Aysén Ltda: Casilla 387, Ancúd; tel. (656) 317; Deputy Man. PEDRO HERNÁNDEZ LEHMAN.

Puerto Montt

Naviera Magallanes, SA (NAVIMAG): Avda Suiza 248, Cerrillos, POB 2829, Santiago; tel. (2) 683-2344; telex 340885; f. 1979; Gen. Man. PATRICIO LATORRE SEPÚLVEDA; Man. FRANCISCO SAHLI CRUZ.

Punta Arenas

Cía Marítima de Punta Arenas, SA: Casilla 337, Punta Arenas; tel. (61) 38-0041; telex 380041; also Casilla 2829, Santiago; tel. (2) 696-3211; telex 341234; f. 1949; shipping agents and owners operating in the Magellan Straits; Dir ROBERTO IZQUIERDO MENÉNDEZ.

San Antonio

Naviera Aysén Ltda: San Antonio; tel. (35) 32578; telex 238603; also Huérfanos 1147, Of. 542, Santiago; tel. (2) 698-8680; telex 240982; Man. RAÚL QUINTANA A.

Naviera Paschold Ltda: Centenario 9, San Antonio; tel. (35) 31654; telex 238603; also Huérfanos 1147, Santiago; tel. (2) 698-8680; telex 240982; Gen. Man. FERNANDO MARTÍNEZ M.

CIVIL AVIATION

There are 325 airfields in the country, of which eight have long runways. Arturo Merino Benítez, 20 km north-east of Santiago, and Chacalluta, 14 km north-east of Arica, are the principal international airports.

Fast Air Carrier: Cargo Terminal, Comodoro A. Merino Benítez International Airport, Santiago; tel. (2) 71-9430; telex 719430; f. 1978; operates international, scheduled and charter cargo services to Bogotá, Frankfurt, Miami, New York, Panamá and São Paulo; Chair. and Pres. JUAN CUETO S.; fleet 1 Boeing 707-320C.

Línea Aérea Nacional de Chile (LAN-Chile): Estado 10, Santiago; tel. (2) 39-4411; telex 441061; fax (2) 38-1729; f. 1929; operates scheduled domestic passenger and cargo services, also Santiago–Easter Island; international services to Bolivia, Brazil, Canada, French Polynesia, Panama, Argentina, Peru, Spain, the USA, Uruguay and Venezuela; under the Govt's privatization programme, a 51% interest in LAN-Chile was sold to private interests in 1989; Pres. JOSÉ LUIS MOURE; fleet: 2 Boeing 767-200ER, 2 Boeing 707-320, 1 Boeing 707-320F, 3 Boeing 737-200, 1 Boeing 737-200C, 2 BAe 146-200.

Línea Aérea del Cobre SA—LADECO: Victoria Subercaseaux 381, POB 13740, Santiago; tel. (2) 39-5053; telex 240116; fax (2) 39-7277; f. 1958; internal passenger and cargo services; international passenger and cargo services to Argentina, Brazil, Colombia, Ecuador, Paraguay and the USA; Chair. JOSÉ-LUIS IBÁÑEZ; CEO ERNESTO SILVA BAFALLUY; fleet of 4 Boeing 727-100, 2 727-100C, 1 Boeing 707-320C, 2 Fokker F27-500.

Tourism

Chile has a wide variety of attractions for the tourist, including fine beaches, ski resorts in the Andes, lakes and rivers. There are many opportunities for hunting and fishing in the southern archipelago, where there are plans to make an integrated tourist area with Argentina, requiring investment of US $120m. Isla de Pascua (Easter Island) may also be visited by tourists.

Servicio Nacional de Turismo—SERNATUR: Avda Providencia 1550, Casilla 14082, Santiago; tel. (2) 696-0474; telex 240137; fax (2) 696-0981; f. 1975; Dir EUGENIO YUNIS AHUES.

Asociación Chilena de Empresas de Turismo—ACHET: Moneda 973, Of. 674, Casilla 3402, Santiago; tel. (2) 696-5677; telex 340843; fax (2) 699-4245; f. 1946; 205 mems; Pres. RODOLFO GARCÍA SIR.

Atomic Energy

Comisión Chilena de Energía Nuclear: Amunátegui 95, Casilla 188-D, Santiago; tel. (2) 699-0070; telex 340468; fax (2) 699-1618; f. 1965; government body to develop peaceful uses of atomic energy; autonomous organization that concentrates, regulates and controls all matters related to nuclear energy; Exec. Dir Dr Ing. FRANCISCO BRIEVA RODRÍGUEZ.

In 1980 the Government decided to postpone the building of a nuclear power station until the end of the century on grounds of commercial viability.

THE PEOPLE'S REPUBLIC OF CHINA

Note: The Pinyin system of transliteration has replaced the Wade-Giles system.

Introductory Survey

Location, Climate, Language, Religion, Flag, Capital

The People's Republic of China covers a vast area of eastern Asia, with Mongolia to the north, the USSR to the north and west, Afghanistan and Pakistan to the west, and India, Nepal, Bhutan, Myanmar (formerly Burma), Laos and Viet-Nam to the south. The country borders the Democratic People's Republic of Korea in the north-east, and has a long coastline on the Pacific Ocean. The climate ranges from sub-tropical in the far south to an annual average temperature of below 10°C (50°F) in the north, and from the monsoon climate of eastern China to the aridity of the north-west. The principal language is Northern Chinese (Mandarin); in the south and south-east local dialects are spoken. The Xizangzu (Tibetans), Wei Wuer (Uighurs), Menggus (Mongols) and other groups have their own languages. The traditional religions and philosophies of life are Confucianism, Buddhism and Daoism. There are also small Muslim and Christian minorities. The national flag (proportions 3 by 2) is plain red, with one large five-pointed gold star and four similar but smaller stars, arranged in an arc, in the upper hoist. The capital is Beijing (Peking).

Recent History

The People's Republic of China was proclaimed on 1 October 1949, following the victory of Communist forces over the Kuomintang government, which fled to the island province of Taiwan. The new Communist regime received widespread international recognition, but it was not until 1971 that the People's Republic was admitted to the United Nations, in place of the Kuomintang regime, as the representative of China. Most other countries now recognize the People's Republic.

With the establishment of the People's Republic, the leading figure in China's political affairs was Mao Zedong, who was Chairman of the Chinese Communist Party (CCP) from 1935 until his death in 1976. Chairman Mao, as he was known, also became Head of State in October 1949, but he relinquished this post in December 1958. His successor was Liu Shaoqi, First Vice-Chairman of the CCP, who was elected Head of State in April 1959. Liu was dismissed in October 1968, during the Cultural Revolution (see below), and died in prison in 1969. The post of Head of State was left vacant, and was formally abolished in January 1975, when a new constitution was adopted. The first Premier (Head of Government) of the People's Republic was Zhou Enlai, who held this office from October 1949 until his death in 1976. Zhou was also Minister of Foreign Affairs from 1949 to 1958, and subsequently remained largely responsible for China's international relations.

The economic progress which was achieved during the early years of Communist rule enabled China to withstand the effects of the industrialization programmes of the late 1950s (called the 'Great Leap Forward'), the drought of 1960–62 and the withdrawal of Soviet aid in 1960. To prevent the establishment of a ruling class, Chairman Mao launched the Great Proletarian Cultural Revolution in 1966. The ensuing excesses of the Red Guards caused the army to intervene; Liu Shaoqi, Head of State, and Deng Xiaoping, General Secretary of the CCP, were disgraced. In 1971 an attempted coup by the Defence Minister, Marshal Lin Biao, was unsuccessful, and by 1973 it was apparent that Chairman Mao and Premier Zhou Enlai had retained power. In 1975 Deng Xiaoping re-emerged as first Vice-Premier and Chief of the General Staff. Zhou Enlai died in January 1976. Hua Guofeng, hitherto Minister of Public Security, was appointed Premier, and Deng was dismissed. Mao died in September 1976. His widow, Jiang Qing, tried unsuccessfully to seize power, with the help of three radical members of the CCP's Politburo. The 'gang of four' and six associates of Lin Biao were tried in November 1980. All were found guilty. The 10th anniversary of Mao's death was marked in September 1986 by an official reassessment of his life; while his accomplishments were praised, it was now acknowledged that he had made mistakes, although most of the criticism was directed at the 'gang of four'.

In October 1976 Hua Guofeng succeeded Mao as Chairman of the CCP and Commander-in-Chief of the People's Liberation Army. The 11th Congress of the CCP, held in August 1977, restored Deng Xiaoping to his former posts. In September 1980 Hua Guofeng resigned as Premier but retained his chairmanship of the CCP. The appointment of Zhao Ziyang, a Deputy Premier since April 1980, to succeed Hua as Premier confirmed the dominance of the moderate faction of Deng Xiaoping. In June 1981 Hua Guofeng was replaced as Chairman of the CCP by Hu Yaobang, former Secretary-General of the Politburo, and as Chairman of the party's Central Military Commission by Deng Xiaoping. A sustained campaign by Deng to purge the Politburo of leftist elements led to Hua's demotion to a Vice-Chairman of the CCP and, in September 1982, to his exclusion from the Politburo.

In September 1982 the CCP was reorganized and the post of Party Chairman abolished. Hu Yaobang became, instead, General Secretary of the CCP. A year later a 'rectification' (purge) of the CCP was launched, aimed at expelling 'Maoists', who had risen to power during the Cultural Revolution, and those opposed to the pragmatic policies of Deng. China's new Constitution, adopted in December 1982, restored the office of Head of State, and in June 1983 Li Xiannian, a former Minister of Finance, became President of China.

In 1983–84 several moves were made to consolidate the authority of the Government: following the announcement of a major anti-crime drive in late 1983, thousands of people were reported to have been executed, while at the same time a campaign was launched against 'spiritual pollution'; stricter censorship was introduced to limit the effects of Western cultural influences. The reorganization of the CCP and of the Government continued. During 1984–85 a programme of modernization for the armed forces was undertaken. In September 1986 the sixth plenary session of the CCP Central Committee adopted a detailed resolution on the 'guiding principles for building a socialist society', which redefined the general ideology of the CCP, to provide a theoretical basis for the programme of modernization and the 'open door' policy of economic reform.

In January 1986 a high-level 'anti-corruption' campaign was launched, to investigate reports that many officials had exploited the programme of economic reform for their own gain. In the field of culture and the arts, however, there was a significant liberalization in 1986, with a revival of the 'Hundred Flowers' movement of 1956–57, which had encouraged the development of intellectual debate. However, a wave of student demonstrations in major cities in late 1986 was regarded by China's leaders as an indication of excessive 'bourgeois liberalization', and in the ensuing government clamp-down, in January 1987, Hu Yaobang unexpectedly resigned as CCP General Secretary, being accused of 'mistakes on major issues of political principles'. Zhao Ziyang became acting General Secretary.

The campaign against 'bourgeois liberalization' was widely regarded as part of a broader, ideological struggle between those Chinese leaders who sought to extend Deng's reforms and those, generally elderly, 'conservative' leaders who opposed the reforms and the 'open door' policy. At the 13th National Congress of the CCP, which opened in October 1987, it became clear that the 'reformist' faction within the Chinese leadership had prevailed. The 'work report', delivered to the Congress by Zhao Ziyang, emphasized the need for further reform and the extension of the 'open door' policy. Deng Xiaoping retired from the Central Committee, but amendments to the Constitution of the CCP permitted him to retain the influential position of Chairman of the Central Military Commission. He was thus believed to have achieved his principal aim of resigning from some posts within the CCP, while retaining overall control of Chinese affairs.

The composition of the new Politburo, appointed by the Central Committee in November 1987, represented the fulfilment of another of Deng's goals: the promotion of his supporters within the CCP. The majority of its 18 members were relatively young officials, including the mayors, or party secretaries, of China's major industrial cities, which had been at the forefront of the urban reform programme. The membership of the new Politburo also indicated a decline in military influence in Chinese politics. The newly-appointed Standing Committee of the Politburo was regarded, on balance, as being 'pro-reform'. In late November Li Peng was appointed Acting Premier of the State Council, in place of Zhao Ziyang. At the first session of the Seventh National People's Congress (NPC), held over the period 25 March–13 April 1988, Li Peng was confirmed as Premier, and Yang Shangkun (a member of the CCP Politburo) was elected President.

The death of Hu Yaobang, in Beijing on 15 April 1989, served as a catalyst for the most serious student demonstrations ever seen in the People's Republic of China. The students' demands were addressed mainly at the alleged prevalence of corruption and nepotism within the Government and sought a limited degree of Soviet-style *glasnost* in public life. The protests were initially tolerated by the Government, but, when they persisted beyond Hu's funeral ceremony, Deng authorized the inclusion of an editorial in the *People's Daily* newspaper condemning the students' actions. On the following day, the demonstrations resumed in Beijing, and, after negotiations between government officials and the students' leaders had failed to satisfy the protesters' demands, workers from various professions joined the demonstrations in Tian An Men Square, which had now become the focal point of the protests. At one stage more than 1m. people congregated in the Square, as demonstrations spread to more than 20 other Chinese cities. As May progressed, the Government became increasingly anxious to terminate the protests, in view of the imminent arrival of President Gorbachev of the USSR, who was to attend a 'summit' meeting with Deng (see below). On 13 May, however, some 3,000 students began a hunger strike in Tian An Men Square, while protesters demanded the resignation of both Deng Xiaoping and Li Peng, and invited President Gorbachev to address them. Gorbachev arrived on 15 May, but his visit was largely overshadowed by the events in Tian An Men Square. The students ended their hunger strike some four days later, at the request of Zhao Ziyang, who was generally regarded as being sympathetic to the students' demands and had argued within the Politburo for serious discussions with the students' leaders. On 20 May a state of martial law was declared in Beijing. This was widely interpreted as an indication that known 'hard-liners' in the leadership (principally President Yang, Li Peng and, latterly, Deng) had prevailed in a political struggle against the reformist faction, led by Zhao. Within days, some 300,000 troops had assembled around Beijing, but the progress of troop convoys towards Tian An Men Square was halted by crowds of people acting in support of the students. At the end of May the students erected a 30m high replica of the US Statue of Liberty in the Square, entitled the Goddess of Democracy and Freedom. On 3 June a further unsuccessful attempt was made to dislodge the demonstrators, but on the following day troops of the 27th army of the People's Liberation Army attacked protesters on and around the Square, killing an unspecified number of people. Television evidence and eye-witness accounts estimated the total dead at somewhere between 1,000 and 5,000, although the Government immediately rejected these figures and claimed, furthermore, that the larger part of the casualties had been soldiers.

Following the armed suppression of the demonstrations (which had now become collectively known as the Pro-Democracy Movement), the Government initiated a large-scale propaganda campaign, alleging that a counter-revolutionary rebellion had been taking place and portraying the army as innocent victims. A wave of arrests and executions ensued, although some student leaders eluded capture and fled to Hong Kong, and those involved in the protests were compelled to undergo televised self-criticism. At the fourth plenary session of the Central Committee on 23 June, Zhao Ziyang was dismissed from all his party posts and replaced as General Secretary of the CCP by Jiang Zemin, hitherto the secretary of the Shanghai municipal party committee. Zhao was described as a proponent of 'bourgeois liberalization' and accused of participating in a political conspiracy to overthrow the CCP and to establish a bourgeois republic in China. Zhao had not been seen in public since the declaration of martial law and was apparently under house arrest. In November Deng resigned as Chairman of the CCP Central Military Commission, his sole remaining party position, and was succeeded by Jiang Zemin. A personality cult was immediately fostered around Jiang, who was hailed as the first of China's 'third generation' of communist leaders (Mao being representative of the first, and Deng of the second). However, despite Deng's assertion that he would no longer interfere in political affairs, it was conjectured that he would retain effective power.

In January 1990 martial law was lifted in Beijing, and it was announced that a total of 573 prisoners, detained following the pro-democracy demonstrations, had been released. Further groups of detainees were released during the course of the year. In June Fang Lizhi, the prominent astrophysicist and dissident (who, although required to stand trial on charges of participation in the pro-democracy protests, had been granted refuge in the US embassy in Beijing), was permitted to leave the country for the United Kingdom. In October Wang Ruowang, the eminent writer and dissident, was released from prison after 13 months in detention. In late 1990, however, human rights organizations estimated that hundreds of pro-democracy activists remained in prison. Furthermore, the authorities were proceeding with the prosecution of prominent dissidents. In January 1991 seven received short prison sentences.

Meanwhile, in March 1990 Deng Xiaoping resigned from his last official post, that of Chairman of the State Central Military Commission, being succeeded by Jiang Zemin. During April and May an extensive military reshuffle was carried out. The changes included the replacement of six of the country's seven regional commanders. In September Premier Li Peng resigned from the position of Minister in Charge of the State Commission for Restructuring the Economy.

Tibet (now Xizang), a semi-independent region of western China, was occupied in 1950 by Chinese Communist forces. In March 1959 there was an unsuccessful armed uprising by Tibetans opposed to Chinese rule. As a result, the Dalai Lama, the head of Tibet's Buddhist clergy and thus the region's spiritual leader, fled with some 100,000 supporters to northern India, where a government-in-exile was established. The Chinese ended the former dominance of the lamas (Buddhist monks) and destroyed many monasteries. Tibet became an 'Autonomous Region' of China in September 1965, but the majority of Tibetans have continued to regard the Dalai Lama as their 'god-king', and to resent the Chinese presence. In October 1987, shortly before the 37th anniversary of China's occupation of Tibet, violent clashes occurred in Lhasa (the regional capital) between the Chinese authorities and Tibetans seeking independence. Further demonstrations during a religious festival in March 1988 resulted in a riot and several deaths, and a number of Tibetan separatists were arrested and detained without trial. The Dalai Lama has, however, renounced demands for independence, and in 1988 proposed that Tibet become a self-governing Chinese territory, in all respects except foreign affairs. In December 1988 an offer from the Dalai Lama to meet Chinese representatives in Geneva was rejected, and later that month two more demonstrators were killed by security forces during a march to commemorate the 40th anniversary of the UN General Assembly's adoption of the Universal Declaration of Human Rights. On 7 March 1989 martial law was imposed in Lhasa for the first time since 1959, after further violent clashes between separatists and the Chinese police. The violence ensued when a pro-independence demonstration was dispersed by police, resulting in the deaths of 16 protesters. In October the Chinese Government condemned as an interference in its internal affairs the award of the Nobel Peace Prize to the Dalai Lama. In November 1989 several Tibetan Buddhist nuns claimed to have been severely tortured for their part in the demonstrations in March of that year. In early May 1990 martial law was lifted in Lhasa. At the end of the month, following the resignation of Doje Cering, Gyaincain Norbu became Chairman of the Xizang Autonomous Region. Human rights groups claimed that during the last six months of the period of martial law as many as 2,000 persons had been executed. Furthermore, political and religious repression and torture were reported to be continuing throughout 1990. In December, renouncing his insistence on complete separation, the Dalai Lama proposed a 'loose confederation' for Tibet.

In the Xinjiang Uygur Autonomous Region anti-Chinese sentiment continued to increase. Unrest intensified in early 1990, and in April as many as 60 people were reported to have been killed when government troops opened fire on Muslim protesters. Following the uprising, the Communist authorities initiated a new campaign to repress the Islamic separatist movement.

In the early years of the People's Republic, China was dependent on the USSR for economic and military aid, and Chinese planning was based on the Soviet model, with highly centralized control. From 1955 onwards, however, Mao Zedong set out to develop a distinctively Chinese form of socialism. As a result of increasingly strained relations between Chinese and Soviet leaders, caused partly by ideological differences, the USSR withdrew all technical aid to China in August 1960. Chinese hostility to the USSR increased, and was aggravated by territorial disputes between the two countries, and by the Soviet invasion of Afghanistan and the Soviet-backed Vietnamese invasion of Cambodia. Sino-Soviet relations remained strained until 1987, when representatives of the two countries signed a partial agreement concerning the exact demarcation of the disputed Sino-Soviet border at the Amur river. The withdrawal of Soviet troops from Afghanistan (completed in February 1989) and Viet-Nam's assurance that it would end its military presence in Cambodia by September 1989 resulted in a further *rapprochement*. In May 1989 the Soviet President, Mikhail Gorbachev, attended a full 'summit' meeting with Deng Xiaoping in Beijing, at which state and party relations between the two countries were formally normalized. However, the massacre in Tian An Men Square in June 1989 limited subsequent Sino-Soviet contacts, although Gorbachev proposed the creation of joint economic zones on the Sino-Soviet border. In April 1990 Li Peng paid an official visit to the USSR, the first by a Chinese Premier for 26 years.

During the 1970s Sino-Soviet friction was accompanied by an improvement in China's relations with Japan and the West. Almost all Western countries had recognized the Government of the People's Republic as the sole legitimate government of China, and had consequently withdrawn recognition from the 'Republic of China', which had been confined to Taiwan since 1949. The People's Republic claimed Taiwan as an integral part of its territory, although the island remained to be 'liberated'. For many years, however, the USA refused to recognize the People's Republic but, instead, regarded the Taiwan administration as the legitimate Chinese government. In February 1972 President Richard Nixon of the USA visited the People's Republic and acknowledged that 'Taiwan is a part of China'. In January 1979 the USA recognized the People's Republic and severed diplomatic relations with Taiwan. For its part, Taiwan has repeatedly rejected China's proposals for reunification, whereby Taiwan would become a 'special administrative region', and has sought reunification under its own terms. China has threatened military intervention, in the event that Taiwan should declare itself independent of the mainland. Trade and reciprocal visits greatly increased in 1988, as relations improved. Reconciliation initiatives were abruptly halted, however, by the violent suppression of the Pro-Democracy Movement in June 1989. The actions of the Chinese Government were strongly condemned by Taiwan, although it was indicated that there would be no consequent change in official policy towards China. In May 1990 President Lee of Taiwan suggested the opening of direct dialogue on a government-to-government basis with the People's Republic. Beijing, however, rejected the proposal, maintaining that it would negotiate only on a party-to-party basis with the Kuomintang.

China will re-establish sovereignty over Hong Kong when the existing lease on most of the territory expires in 1997. In September 1984, following protracted negotiations, China reached agreement with the British Government over the terms of Chinese administration of the territory after that date. In 1985 a Basic Law Drafting Committee (BLDC), including 25 representatives from Hong Kong, was established in Beijing to prepare a new Basic Law (Constitution) for Hong Kong. Consultations on the Committee's second draft were temporarily suspended in 1989, following the student massacre in Tian An Men Square. The armed suppression of the Pro-Democracy Movement had a profoundly disturbing impact on local confidence in Hong Kong, where as many as 1m. people demonstrated in protest against the actions of the Chinese Government. China accused several Hong Kong citizens of financially supporting the Pro-Democracy Movement and blamed the United Kingdom for the unsettled nature of the territory. The Basic Law for Hong Kong was approved by the NPC in April 1990. In July a Minister of State at the Foreign and Commonwealth Office of the United Kingdom visited Beijing for consultations on the future of Hong Kong.

In June 1986 China and Portugal opened formal negotiations for the return of the Portuguese overseas territory of Macau to full Chinese sovereignty. In January 1987 the Portuguese Council of State agreed that withdrawal from Macau should take place in 1999. The agreement is based upon the 'one country, two systems' principle, which formed the basis of China's negotiated settlement regarding the return of Hong Kong.

China condemned Viet-Nam's invasion of Kampuchea (now Cambodia) in December 1978, and launched a punitive attack into northern Viet-Nam in February 1979. Armed clashes across the border continued, and negotiations between the two countries failed to resolve the dispute. China continued to give sustained financial and military support to Cambodian resistance organizations, notably the communist Khmer Rouge, despite the Vietnamese troop withdrawal (completed in September 1989), as it refused to accept Viet-Nam's assurance that its military presence in Cambodia had ended. However, in November 1990, following an improvement in Sino-Vietnamese relations, China announced that it had ceased supplying weapons to the Khmer Rouge.

China's relations with the USA improved steadily throughout the 1980s, but were seriously impaired by the student massacre in 1989. In 1984 Premier Zhao Ziyang visited Washington, and in the same year President Ronald Reagan visited Beijing, where a bilateral agreement on industrial and technological co-operation was signed. Following the suppression of the Pro-Democracy Movement, however, the new US President, George Bush, suspended all high-level government exchanges and banned the export of weapons to China. In November 1989, at a meeting in Beijing with the former US President, Richard Nixon, Deng accused the USA of being deeply involved in the 'counter-revolutionary rebellion' in June, and indicated that the USA, and not China, was responsible for the deterioration in relations between the two countries. In the same month the US Congress approved a proposal to extend the sanctions that President Bush had imposed in June. In December representatives of the US Government conferred with Deng in Beijing, and it was revealed that secret Sino-US negotiations had taken place in July of that year. In November 1990 President Bush received the Chinese Minister of Foreign Affairs in Washington, thereby resuming contact at the most senior level. Another obstacle to good relations between China and the USA is the question of Taiwan, and, in particular, the continued sale of US armaments to Taiwan.

China's relations with Japan, a major trading partner, began to deteriorate in 1982, after China complained that passages in Japanese school textbooks sought to justify the Japanese invasion of China in 1937. Since 1985 China has expressed dissatisfaction at the level of its trade deficit with Japan, and at the low inflow of Japanese investment into China. Chinese leaders have also criticized the rising level of Japan's defence spending and its close commercial relations with Taiwan. In June 1989 the Japanese Government criticized the Chinese Government's suppression of the Pro-Democracy Movement and suspended (until late 1990) a five-year aid programme to China.

The long-standing border dispute with India, which gave rise to a short military conflict in 1962, remained unresolved in 1990 (see chapter on India). Diplomatic relations with Indonesia, broken off in 1967, were formally restored in August 1990, and in October diplomatic relations between China and Singapore were established.

In July 1990 Saudi Arabia transferred its recognition from Taiwan to the People's Republic, and in September, as the Gulf crisis continued, China expressed its support for Saudi Arabia in its defence against Iraq. In November, hoping to secure a peaceful solution, the Chinese Minister of Foreign Affairs (the most senior representative of the five permanent members of the UN Security Council to visit Iraq since the onset of the crisis) travelled to Baghdad in an attempt to persuade Saddam Hussein to withdraw his forces from Kuwait.

Government

China is a unitary state. Directly under the Central Government there are 22 provinces, five autonomous regions, including Xizang (Tibet), and three municipalities (Beijing, Shanghai and Tianjin). The highest organ of state power is the National

THE PEOPLE'S REPUBLIC OF CHINA

People's Congress (NPC). In March 1988, when the first session of the Seventh NPC was convened, the legislature had 2,970 deputies, indirectly elected for five years by the people's congresses of the provinces, autonomous regions, municipalities directly under the Central Government, and the People's Liberation Army. The NPC elects a Standing Committee to be its permanent organ. The current Constitution, adopted by the NPC in December 1982, was China's fourth since 1949. It restored the office of Head of State (President of the Republic). Executive power is exercised by the State Council (Cabinet), comprising the Premier, Vice-Premiers and other Ministers heading ministries and commissions. The State Council is appointed by, and accountable to, the NPC.

Political power is held by the Chinese Communist Party (CCP). The CCP's highest authority is the Party Congress, convened every five years. In October 1987 the CCP's 13th National Congress elected a Central Committee of 175 full members and 110 alternate members. To direct policy, the Central Committee elected an 18-member Politburo. This was reduced to 15 members at the fourth plenum of the Central Committee in June 1989.

Local people's congresses are the local organs of state power. Local revolutionary committees, created during the Cultural Revolution, were abolished in January 1980 and replaced by local people's governments.

Defence

China is divided into seven major military units. All armed services are grouped in the People's Liberation Army (PLA). In June 1990, according to Western estimates, the regular forces totalled 3,030,000: the army numbered 2,300,000, the navy 260,000 (including a naval air force of 25,000), and the air force 470,000 (including 220,000 air defence personnel). There are also strategic rocket forces of 90,000 and more than 1.2m. reserves and about 12m. in paramilitary forces. Military service is by selective conscription, and lasts for three years in the army and marines, and for four years in the air force and navy. Defence expenditure for 1990 was budgeted at 28,970m. yuan.

Economic Affairs

In 1988, according to estimates by the World Bank, China's gross national product (GNP), measured at average 1986–88 prices, was US $356,490m., equivalent to some $330 per head. During 1980–88, it was estimated, GNP increased in real terms at an average annual rate of 10.5%, one of the highest growth rates in the world. Over the same period the population grew by an average annual rate of 1.2% In real terms compared with the previous year, GNP grew by 3.9% in 1989 and was expected to increase by 4.5% in 1990. China's gross domestic product (GDP) grew, in real terms, by an average annual rate of 10.3% in 1980–88.

Agriculture (including forestry and fishing) contributed 32% of GNP in 1988. Agricultural production increased by an average annual rate of 6.8% in 1980–88. In 1989 (when the value of agricultural output reached 655,000m. yuan) output value rose by 3.3% compared with the previous year. Almost 60% of the labour force were employed in agriculture in 1988. China's principal crops are rice (which accounted for 34.5% of the total world harvest in 1988), sweet potatoes, wheat, maize, soybeans, sugar cane, tobacco, cotton and jute. The harvest of grain (cereals, pulses, soybeans and tubers in 'grain equivalent') increased from 394m. metric tons in 1988 to 407m. tons in 1989. The 1990 harvest was expected to total 425m. tons.

Industry (including mining, manufacturing, construction and power) contributed 46% of GNP in 1988. Industrial output increased by an average annual rate of 12.4% in 1980–88. In 1989 (when the value of industrial production totalled 2,188,000m. yuan) output value rose by 8.3% compared with the previous year, and was expected to expand by 6% in 1990. China is the world's largest producer of coal and natural graphite, with output in 1988 reaching 980m. metric tons and 300,000 tons respectively. Coal output reached 1,040m. tons in 1989. Other important minerals include tungsten, molybdenum, antimony, tin, lead, mercury, bauxite, phosphate rock, iron ore and manganese. China is also the world's largest producer of raw cotton, woven textile fabrics and cement, with output in 1989 totalling 3.8m. metric tons, 18,600m. m and 207m. metric tons respectively.

Energy is derived principally from coal (76.1% in 1988), petroleum (17.1%) and hydroelectric power (4.7%). In 1989 crude petroleum output totalled 137.65m. tons.

Introductory Survey

In 1989 China recorded a trade deficit of US $5,620m., and there was a deficit of $4,317m. on the current account of the balance of payments. In the same year the principal trading partners were Hong Kong (which provided 21% of imports and received 42% of exports), Japan (18% of imports and 16% of exports) and the USA (13% of imports and 8% of exports). The principal imports in 1989 were machinery and transport equipment, basic manufactures and chemicals and related products. The principal exports were basic manufactures, miscellaneous manufactured articles and food and live animals. In an effort to increase exports, China devalued its currency by 21.2% and 9.6% against the US dollar in December 1989 and November 1990 respectively.

In 1990 there was a projected budget deficit of 8,893m. yuan. China's total external public debt at the end of 1988 was estimated to be US $32,196m. In that year the cost of debt-servicing was equivalent to 6.9% of revenue from exports of goods and services. External debt reached $41,300m. in December 1989, rising to $45,400m. in mid-1990. The annual rate of inflation averaged 4.9% in 1980–88, reaching 18.5% in 1988. The rate in 1989 was 17.8%. In the year to October 1990, however, the cost of living for urban residents rose by only 3.6%. An estimated 3% of the labour force were unemployed in 1990.

The Chinese economy has, since 1953, been subject to central control within the framework of five-year plans. Details of the Eighth Five-Year Plan (1991–1995) awaited confirmation in late 1990. In 1978 a process of economic reform, known as the 'open door' policy, was introduced to decentralize the economic system and to attract overseas investment to China. The state monopoly on foreign trade was gradually relinquished, commercial links were diversified, and by the late 1980s six 'special economic zones' had been established. The result of the reforms was a rapid growth in industrial production and a consequent increased demand for imports, which, in turn, resulted in high inflation. Measures to reduce inflation, in the form of an austerity programme, were introduced in September 1988. These were designed to limit annual growth of real GNP for the remaining years of the 1986–90 Plan and included the reassertion of central economic controls. Following the political developments of mid-1989 (during which several prominent economic reformers were discredited), much overseas aid was temporarily halted, and the austerity programme was extended. The 'open door' policy of economic reform was under review in 1990.

Social Welfare

Western and traditional Chinese medical attention is available in the cities and, to a lesser degree, in rural areas. A fee is charged. In 1989 there were 1.72m. doctors (one per 647 people) and in 1990 there were 208,000 health establishments. About 1.3m. 'barefoot doctors', semi-professional peasant physicians, assist with simple cures, treatment and the distribution of contraceptives. There were 2.6m. hospital beds in 1990. Large factories and other enterprises provide social services for their employees. Industrial wage-earners qualify for pensions. It was announced in 1986 that China was to introduce a social security system to meet the needs of retired people and unemployed contract workers, as part of the planned reform in the labour system.

Education

The education system expanded rapidly after 1949. Fees are charged at all levels. Much importance is attached to kindergartens. Primary education begins for most children at seven years of age and lasts for five years. Secondary education usually begins at 12 years of age and lasts for a further five years, comprising a first cycle of three years and a second cycle of two years. Free higher education was abolished in 1985; instead, college students have to compete for scholarships, which are awarded according to academic ability. As a result of the student disturbances in May and June 1989, college students are required to complete one year's political education, prior to entering college. In November 1989 it was announced that post-graduate students were to be selected on the basis of assessments of moral and physical fitness, as well as academic ability. Since 1978 education has been included as one of the main priorities for modernization. The whole educational system was to be reformed, with the aim of introducing nine-year compulsory education in 75% of the country by 1995. As a proportion of the total school-age population, enrolment at primary and secondary schools declined from 95% in 1978 to 73% in 1982, but rose to 80% (boys 88%; girls 73%) in 1986. In that year primary enrolment included an estimated 95% of children in the relevant age-group (boys 99%; girls 91%). The average rate of adult illiteracy in 1982 was 34.5% (males 20.8%; females 48.9%). In 1989 there were about 123.7m. pupils enrolled at primary schools. In 1988 about 47.6m. students were at general secondary schools and 2,066,000 received higher education. The 1990 state budget allocated 48,406m. yuan to education.

Public Holidays

1991: 15–17 February* (Lunar New Year), 8 March (International Women's Day), 1 May (Labour Day), 1 August (Army Day), 1–2 October (National Days).

1992: 4–6 February* (Lunar New Year), 8 March (International Women's Day), 1 May (Labour Day), 1 August (Army Day), 1–2 October (National Days).

* From the first to the third day of the first moon of the lunar calendar.

Weights and Measures

The metric system is officially in force, but some traditional Chinese units are still used.

THE PEOPLE'S REPUBLIC OF CHINA

Statistical Survey

Source (unless otherwise stated): State Statistical Bureau, Sanlihe, Beijing; tel. (01) 868521.

Note: Wherever possible, figures in this Survey exclude Taiwan province. In the case of unofficial estimates for China, it is not always clear if Taiwan is included or excluded. Where a Taiwan component is known, either it has been deducted from the all-China figure or its inclusion is noted.

Area and Population

AREA, POPULATION AND DENSITY

Area (sq km)	9,571,300*
Population (census results)	
1 July 1982	1,008,180,738
1 July 1990	
Males	584,949,922
Females	548,732,579
Total	1,133,682,501
Density (per sq km) at 1 July 1990	118.4

* 3,695,500 sq miles.

BIRTHS AND DEATHS (sample surveys)

	1987	1988	1989
Birth rate (per 1,000)	21.04	20.78	20.83
Death rate (per 1,000)	6.65	6.58	6.50

LIFE EXPECTANCY (years at birth)
Males 61.8 in 1970–75, 66.0 in 1975–80; Females 64.6 in 1970–75, 68.6 in 1975–80 (UN estimates, including Taiwan).
1981 (official estimates): 67.88 (Males 66.43; Females 69.35).

ADMINISTRATIVE DIVISIONS (previous spelling given in brackets)

	Area ('000 sq km)	Population (official estimates at 31 Dec. 1988)* Total ('000)	Density (per sq km)	Capital of province or region	Estimated population ('000) at 31 Dec. 1988†
Provinces					
Sichuan (Szechwan)	567	105,760	187	Chengdu (Chengtu)	2,740
Shandong (Shantung)	153	80,610	527	Jinan (Tsinan)	2,180
Henan (Honan)	167	80,940	485	Zhengzhou (Chengchow)	1,630
Jiangsu (Kiangsu)	103	64,380	625	Nanjing (Nanking)	2,430
Hebei (Hopei)	188	57,950	308	Shijiazhuang (Shihkiachwang)	1,260
Guangdong (Kwangtung)‡	212	65,560	309	Guangzhou (Canton)	3,490
Hunan (Hunan)	210	58,900	280	Changsha (Changsha)	1,260
Anhui (Anhwei)	139	53,770	387	Hefei (Hofei)	950
Hubei (Hupeh)	186	51,850	279	Wuhan (Wuhan)	3,640
Zhejiang (Chekiang)	102	41,700	409	Hangzhou (Hangchow)	1,310
Liaoning (Liaoning)	146	38,200	262	Shenyang (Shenyang)	4,440
Yunnan (Yunnan)	394	35,940	91	Kunming (Kunming)	1,480
Jiangxi (Kiangsi)	169	36,090	214	Nanchang (Nanchang)	1,290
Shaanxi (Shensi)	206	31,350	152	Xian (Sian)	2,650
Heilongjiang (Heilungkiang)	469	34,660	74	Harbin (Harbin)	2,930
Shanxi (Shansi)	156	27,550	177	Taiyuan (Taiyuan)	2,010
Guizhou (Kweichow)	176	31,270	178	Guiyang (Kweiyang)	1,460
Fujian (Fukien)	121	28,450§	235	Fuzhou (Foochow)	1,250
Jilin (Kirin)	187	23,730	127	Changchun (Changchun)	2,020
Gansu (Kansu)	454	21,360	47	Lanzhou (Lanchow)	1,450
Qinghai (Tsinghai)	721	4,340	6	Xining (Hsining)	630
Autonomous regions					
Guangxi Zhuang (Kwangsi Chuang)	236	40,880	173	Nanning (Nanning)	1,030
Nei Monggol (Inner Mongolia)	1,183	20,940	18	Hohhot (Huhehot)	850
Xinjiang Uygur (Sinkiang Uighur)	1,600	14,260	9	Urumqi (Urumchi)	1,070
Ningxia Hui (Ninghsia Hui)	66	4,450	67	Yinchuan (Yinchuen)	576‖
Xizang (Tibet)	1,228	2,120	2	Lhasa (Lhasa)	105‖
Municipalities					
Beijing (Peking)	17	10,810	635	—	6,800
Shanghai (Shanghai)	6	12,620	2,103	—	7,330
Tianjin (Tientsin)	11	8,430	766	—	5,620
Total	9,571	1,088,870	114		

* Figures exclude armed forces.
† Excluding population in counties under cities' administration.
‡ Including Hainan Island (population 6,280,000 at 31 Dec. 1988), which became a separate province in 1988.
§ Excluding islands administered by Taiwan, mainly Jinmen (Quemoy) and Mazu (Matsu), with 57,847 inhabitants at 31 May 1982.
‖ 1982 figures.

1 July 1990: Populations of municipalities at census: Beijing 10,819,407; Shanghai 13,341,896; Tianjin 8,785,402.

THE PEOPLE'S REPUBLIC OF CHINA

PRINCIPAL TOWNS
(Wade-Giles or other spellings in brackets)
Population at 31 December 1988 (official estimates in '000)*

Shanghai (Shang-hai)	7,330
Beijing (Pei-ching or Peking, the capital)	6,800
Tianjin (T'ien-chin or Tientsin)	5,620
Shenyang (Shen-yang or Mukden)	4,440
Wuhan (Wu-han or Hankow)	3,640
Guangzhou (Kuang-chou or Canton)	3,490
Harbin (Ha-erh-pin)	2,930
Chongqing (Ch'ung-ch'ing or Chungking)	2,750
Chengdu (Ch'eng-tu)	2,740
Xian (Hsi-an or Sian)	2,650
Nanjing (Nan-ching or Nanking)	2,430
Zibo (Tzu-po or Tzepo)	2,400
Dalian (Ta-lien or Dairen)	2,330
Jinan (Chi-nan or Tsinan)	2,180
Changchun (Ch'ang-ch'un)	2,020
Qingdao (Ch'ing-tao or Tsingtao)	2,010
Taiyuan (T'ai-yüan)	2,010
Zhengzhou (Cheng-chou or Chengchow)	1,630
Kunming (K'un-ming)	1,480
Guiyang (Kuei-yang or Kweiyang)	1,460
Tangshan (T'ang-shan)	1,460
Lanzhou (Lan-chou or Lanchow)	1,450
Anshan (An-shan)	1,350
Qiqihar (Ch'i-ch'i-ha-erh or Tsitsihar)	1,350
Fushun (F'u-shun)	1,320
Hangzhou (Hang-chou or Hangchow)	1,310
Nanchang (Nan-ch'ang)	1,290
Changsha (Chang-sha)	1,260
Shijiazhuang (Shih-chia-chuang or Shihkiachwang)	1,260
Fuzhou (Fu-chou or Foochow)	1,250
Jilin (Chi-lin or Kirin)	1,230
Baotau (Pao-t'ou or Paotow)	1,160
Huainan (Huai-nan or Hwainan)	1,140
Luoyang (Lo-yang)	1,130
Urumqi (Urumchi)	1,070
Datong (Ta-t'ung or Tatung)	1,060
Handan (Han-tan)	1,060
Ningbo (Ning-po)	1,060
Nanning (Nan-ning)	1,030

* Data refer to municipalities, which may include large rural areas as well as an urban centre. The listed towns comprise those with a total population of more than 1,000,000 and a non-agricultural population of more than 500,000.

CIVILIAN EMPLOYMENT
(official estimates, '000 persons at 31 December)

	1986	1987	1988
Industry*	89,804	93,429	96,608
Construction and resources prospecting	23,760	25,266	25,267
Agriculture, forestry, water conservancy and meteorology	313,106	317,201	323,083
Transport, posts and telecommunications	13,050	13,734	14,346
Commerce, catering trade, service trade and supply and marketing of materials	24,844	26,552	28,287
Scientific research, culture, education, public health and social welfare	19,584	20,288	20,725
Government agencies and people's organizations	8,736	9,250	9,711
Others	19,938	22,111	25,309
Total	512,822	527,833	543,336

* Mining, manufacturing, electricity, gas and water.
1989: Total 553.29 million.

Agriculture

PRINCIPAL CROPS
(FAO estimates, unless otherwise indicated; '000 metric tons)

	1987	1988	1989
Wheat	85,902†	85,432†	91,000
Rice (paddy)	174,262†	169,107†	176,980‡
Barley	2,800	3,000	3,200
Maize	79,241†	77,351†	75,510‡
Rye	1,000	1,000	1,000
Oats	500	600	600
Millet	4,537†	4,412†	5,700
Sorghum	5,426†	5,594†	6,000
Potatoes	28,000	28,000	30,000
Sweet potatoes	113,445	108,135	113,750
Cassava (Manioc)	3,300	3,250	3,160
Taro (Coco yam)*	1,277	1,179	1,140
Dry beans	1,500	1,450	1,500
Dry broad beans	2,400	2,100	2,200
Dry peas	1,500	1,320	1,325
Chick-peas	200	180	175
Lentils	100	100	100
Soybeans (Soyabeans)	12,465†	11,645†	10,800‡
Groundnuts (in shell)	6,171†	5,693†	5,330‡
Castor beans‡	330	280	275
Sunflower seed	1,241†	1,180†	980‡
Rapeseed†	6,605	5,044	5,440
Sesame seed	526†	404†	500
Linseed	138‡	137‡	165
Flax fibre and tow	320†	200	220
Cottonseed†	8,490	8,298	7,580
Cotton (lint)†	4,245	4,149	3,790
Coconuts	80	83	85
Vegetables and melons*	109,963	112,655	114,337
Grapes	641†	792†	
Apples	4,264†	4,344†	
Pears	2,489†	2,721†	18,370†
Citrus fruits	3,224†	2,560†	
Bananas	2,030†	1,830†	
Other fruits (excl. melons)	4,031†	4,414†	
Tree nuts*	447	458	440
Sugar cane†	47,363	49,064	48,570
Sugar beet†	8,140	12,810	9,360
Tea (made)†	508.0	545.4	534.9
Tobacco (leaves)	1,943†	2,734†	2,850‡
Jute and jute substitutes‡	569	539	665
Natural rubber†	237.6	239.8	240

* Including Taiwan.   † Official estimate(s).
‡ Unofficial estimate(s).
Source: mainly FAO, *Production Yearbook*, and State Statistical Bureau, *China Statistical Yearbook*.

LIVESTOCK ('000 head at 31 December)

	1986	1987	1988
Horses	10,988	10,691	10,540
Mules	5,113	5,248	5,366
Asses	10,689	10,846	11,052
Cattle	71,230	73,827	97,948
Buffaloes	20,823	20,824	
Camels	504	475	472
Pigs	337,191	327,733	342,218
Sheep	99,009	102,655	110,571
Goats	67,220	77,687	90,956

Chickens (FAO estimates, million, year ending September): 1,730 in 1987; 1,780 in 1988; 1,903 in 1989 (Source: FAO, *Production Yearbook*).
Ducks (FAO estimates, million, year ending September): 305 in 1987; 312 in 1988; 321 in 1989 (Source: FAO, *Production Yearbook*).
1989 ('000 head at 31 December): Pigs 352,000; Sheep and goats 211,000.

THE PEOPLE'S REPUBLIC OF CHINA

LIVESTOCK PRODUCTS
(FAO estimates, unless otherwise indicated; '000 metric tons)

	1987	1988	1989
Beef and veal*	613‡	642	662
Buffalo meat*	183‡	203	223
Mutton and lamb*	350‡	400	420
Goat's meat*	370‡	381	401
Pig meat*	19,287†	20,134†	22,070‡
Horse meat*	50	50	52
Poultry meat*	2,564	2,656	2,767
Other meat*	546	564	583
Edible offals*	2,214	2,303	2,399
Cows' milk†	3,301	3,660	3,800
Buffaloes' milk	1,800	1,850	1,900
Sheep's milk	558	567	570
Goats' milk	173	180	185
Butter*	57.4	59.6	63.3
Cheese*	134.4	137.0	141.8
Hen eggs	5,902†	6,955†	6,600
Other poultry eggs†	26.1	23.4	23.4
Honey	204†	195†	176‡
Raw silk (incl. waste)	40.9†	42.0	42.0
Wool:			
greasy†	208.9	221.7	238.0
clean	124.8†	112.0‡	n.a.
Cattle and buffalo hides*	207.2	214.6	221.0
Sheep skins*	91.6	104.7	109.9
Goat skins*	80.1	81.8	86.0

* Including Taiwan.   † Official estimate(s).
‡ Unofficial estimate.

Source: mainly FAO, *Production Yearbook* and *Quarterly Bulletin of Statistics*.

Other official estimates ('000 metric tons): Beef, buffalo meat, mutton, goats' meat and pig meat 19,860 (beef and buffalo meat 792, mutton and goats' meat 719, pig meat 18,349) in 1987, 21,936 (beef and buffalo meat 958, mutton and goats' meat 802, pig meat 20,176) in 1988, 23,280 in 1989.

Forestry

ROUNDWOOD REMOVALS*
(FAO estimates, '000 cubic metres)

	1986	1987	1988
Sawlogs, veneer logs and logs for sleepers	54,592	54,517	53,770
Pulpwood	6,921	6,888	7,178
Other industrial wood	35,734	37,503	37,503
Fuel wood	174,129	177,610	177,610
Total	271,376	276,518	276,061

* Including Taiwan.

Source: FAO, *Yearbook of Forest Products*.

Timber production (official estimates, '000 cubic metres): 65,024 in 1986; 64,079 in 1987; 62,176 in 1988; 61,000 in 1989.

SAWNWOOD PRODUCTION*
(FAO estimates, '000 cubic metres)

	1986	1987	1988
Coniferous sawnwood	17,117	17,806	17,046
Broadleaved sawnwood	9,208	9,192	9,170
Total	26,325	26,278	26,216

Railway sleepers (FAO estimates, '000 cubic metres): 66 per year in 1980-88.
* Including Taiwan.
Source: FAO, *Yearbook of Forest Products*.

Fishing
('000 metric tons, live weight)

	1986	1987	1988
Fishes	6,291.2	7,197.1	7,773.4
Crustaceans	817.0	951.5	1,118.4
Molluscs	872.3	1,139.0	1,434.7
Other aquatic animals	19.6	58.7	32.1
Total catch	8,000.1	9,346.2	10,358.7
Inland waters	3,481.7	4,071.5	4,551.9
Atlantic Ocean	5.0	7.4	7.4
Pacific Ocean	4,513.3	5,267.3	5,799.3

Aquatic plants ('000 metric tons, wet weight): 1,540.4 in 1986; 1,354.2 in 1987; 1,645.0 in 1988.
Source: FAO, *Yearbook of Fishery Statistics*.

Aquatic products (official estimates, '000 metric tons): 8,235.6 (marine 4,753.7, freshwater 3,481.9) in 1986; 9,553.5 (marine 5,481.6, freshwater 4,071.9) in 1987; 10,609.2 (marine 6,057.0, freshwater 4,552.2) in 1988; 11,480 in 1989. Figures include aquatic plants on a dry-weight basis ('000 metric tons): 233.1 in 1986; 236.7 in 1987; 251.1 in 1988.

Mining
('000 metric tons, unless otherwise indicated; unofficial estimates)

	1985	1986	1987
Coal (incl. lignite)*	872,284	894,039	927,965
Crude petroleum*	124,895	130,688	134,140
Iron ore*†	69,095	73,755	80,715
Bauxite	1,650	1,650	2,400
Copper ore†	190	200	300
Lead ore†	175	185	252
Magnesite	2,000	2,000*	2,000
Manganese ore†	480	480	480
Zinc ore†	300	396	425
Salt (unrefined)*	14,789	17,612	17,645
Phosphate rock	6,970	6,700	9,000
Potash‡	40	40	40
Sulphur (native)	300	300	300
Natural graphite	185	270.5*	296.6*
Antimony ore (metric tons)†	15,000	15,000	15,000
Mercury (metric tons)	700	700	700
Molybdenum ore (metric tons)†	2,000	2,000	2,000
Silver (metric tons)†	78	93	93
Tin concentrates (metric tons)†	20,000	25,000	28,000
Tungsten concentrates (metric tons)†	17,000*	17,000*	18,000
Gold (kg)†	59,097	65,317	71,538
Natural gas (million cu m)*	12,927	13,764	13,894

* Official estimate(s). Figures for petroleum include oil from shale and coal.
† Figures refer to the metal content of ores and concentrates.
‡ Potassium oxide (K_2O) content of potash salts mined.

Sources for unofficial estimates: For tin, Metallgesellschaft Aktiengesellschaft (Frankfurt am Main, Germany); for all other minerals, US Bureau of Mines.

Source: mainly UN, *Industrial Statistics Yearbook*.

Official estimates ('000 metric tons, unless otherwise indicated): Coal (incl. brown coal and waste) 979,877 in 1988, 1,040,000 in 1989; Crude petroleum 137,046 in 1988, 137,000 in 1989; Salt 22,637 in 1988, 28,020 in 1989; Natural gas 14,264 million cu m in 1988.

Industry

SELECTED PRODUCTS
Unofficial Estimates
('000 metric tons, unless otherwise indicated)

	1985	1986	1987
Palm oil (crude)[1]	192	195	200
Tung oil[1]	58	61	66
Rayon continuous filaments[2]	50.0	60.0	70.0
Rayon discontinuous fibres[2]	130.0	130.0	140.0
Non-cellulosic continuous filaments[2]	134.9	207.4	269.0
Non-cellulosic discontinuous fibres[2]	597.1	593.6	641.0
Plywood ('000 cu m)[1,3]	1,389	1,511	1,583
Mechanical wood pulp[1,3]	402	402	384
Chemical wood pulp[1,3]	1,199	1,256	1,325
Other fibre pulp[1,3]	5,467	5,685	6,272
Newsprint	425	414	366
Other printing and writing paper[1,3]	2,899	3,116	3,406
Other paper and paperboard[1,3]	7,779	8,205	8,957
Synthetic rubber[4]	181.1	188.4	218.7
Sulphur[5,6] (a)	400	300	300
(b)	2,200	2,500	2,500
Motor spirit (petrol)[4]	14,719	16,848	17,370
Kerosene[4]	4,053	4,164	4,183
Distillate fuel oils[4]	20,232	22,305	23,657
Residual fuel oil[4]	28,358	29,862	31,306
Lubricating oils[4]	1,700	1,700	1,700
Paraffin wax[4]	520	525	530
Petroleum coke[4]	966	975	1,000
Petroleum bitumen (asphalt)[4]	2,100	2,200	2,200
Liquefied petroleum gas[4]	1,597	2,020	2,153
Aluminium (unwrought)[5]	480	510	540
Refined copper (unwrought)[5]	400	400	400
Lead (unwrought)[5]	210	240	240
Tin (unwrought)[7]	19.0	20.0	25.0
Zinc (unwrought)[5]	275	336	375

[1] Source: FAO.
[2] Source: Textile Economics Bureau Inc, New York, USA.
[3] Including Taiwan.
[4] Source: UN, *Industrial Statistics Yearbook*.
[5] Source: US Bureau of Mines.
[6] Figures refer to (a) sulphur recovered as a by-product in the purification of coal-gas, in petroleum refineries, gas plants and from copper, lead and zinc sulphide ores; and (b) the sulphur content of iron and copper pyrites, including pyrite concentrates obtained from copper, lead and zinc ores.
[7] Source: Metallgesellschaft Aktiengesellschaft, Frankfurt am Main, Germany.

1988 (FAO estimates, '000 metric tons): Palm oil 205; Tung oil 67; Mechanical wood pulp 403; Chemical wood pulp 1,375. Data on pulp include Taiwan.
1989 (FAO estimates, '000 metric tons): Palm oil 209.5; Tung oil 69.

Official Estimates ('000 metric tons, unless otherwise indicated)

	1986	1987	1988
Raw sugar	5,246.4	5,055.8	4,611.6
Beer	4,130.1	5,404.3	6,564.3
Cotton yarn (pure and mixed)	3,977.9	4,368.1	4,657.3
Woven cotton fabrics—pure and mixed (million metres)	16,473	17,305	18,786
Woollen fabrics ('000 metres)	251,870	265,378	286,086
Silk fabrics (million metres)	1,499.5	1,602.2	n.a.
Chemical fibres	1,017.3	1,175.0	1,301.2
Paper and paperboard	9,986.3	11,410.7	12,702.6
Rubber tyres ('000)	19,243.2	23,331.9	29,910.5
Ethylene (Ethene)	695.2	937.2	1,232.1
Sulphuric acid	7,631.1	9,832.9	11,113.0
Caustic soda (Sodium hydroxide)	2,518.0	2,739.1	3,004.6
Soda ash (Sodium carbonate)	2,146.3	2,363.1	2,608.5
Insecticides	203.3	161.2	179.1
Nitrogenous fertilizers (a)*	11,592	13,423	13,656
Phosphate fertilizers (b)*	2,340	3,259	3,692
Potash fertilizers (c)*	25	40	54
Plastics	1,320.8	1,526.3	1,904.1
Coke-oven coke	40,927	43,748	45,424
Cement	166,062	186,249	210,136
Pig-iron	50,638	55,032	57,040
Crude steel	52,197	56,275	59,431
Internal combustion engines ('000 horse-power)†	36,079.5	43,358.4	58,320.8
Tractors—over 20 horse-power (number)	28,641	37,123	47,186
Sewing machines ('000)	9,894.1	9,699.7	9,832.3
Railway locomotives—diesel (number)	818	909	844
Railway freight wagons (number)	20,592	21,639	23,323
Road motor vehicles ('000)	369.8	471.8	644.7
Bicycles ('000)	35,682.6	41,166.8	41,401.2
Watches ('000)	73,319.9	61,593.6	67,888.5
Radio receivers ('000)‡	15,895.2	17,638.2	15,489.4
Television receivers ('000)	14,594.0	19,343.7	25,050.7
Cameras ('000)	2,025.4	2,567.0	3,122.6
Electric energy (million kWh)	449,536	497,266	545,208

* Production in terms of (a) nitrogen; (b) phosphoric acid; or (c) potassium oxide.
† Sales. ‡ Portable battery sets only.

1989 (official estimates, '000 metric tons, unless otherwise indicated): Raw sugar 4,960; Cotton yarn (pure and mixed) 4,740; Paper and paperboard 12,800; Sulphuric acid 11,410; Soda ash 2,980; Insecticides 223.7; Chemical fertilizers 18,550; Cement 207,000; Crude steel 61,240; Tractors 43,300 units; Railway locomotives 679 units; Road motor vehicles 573,700 units; Bicycles 36.7m. units; Television receivers 27.0m. units; Cameras 2.3m. units; Electric energy 582,000m. kWh.

Finance

CURRENCY AND EXCHANGE RATES

Monetary Units
100 fen (cents) = 1 jiao (chiao) = 1 renminbiao (People's Bank Dollar), usually called a yuan.

Denominations
Coins: 1, 2 and 5 fen.
Notes: 10, 20 and 50 fen; 1, 2, 5 and 10 yuan.

Sterling and Dollar Equivalents (30 September 1990)
£1 sterling = 8.847 yuan;
US $1 = 4.722 yuan;
100 yuan = £11.30 = $21.18.

Average Exchange Rate (yuan per US $)
1987   3.7221
1988   3.7221
1989   3.7651

Note: Between November 1986 and December 1989 the official mid-point exchange rate was US $1 = 3.7221 yuan. In December 1989 the yuan was devalued by 21.2%, with the mid-point exchange rate adjusted to $1 = 4.7221 yuan. This rate remained in force until November 1990.

THE PEOPLE'S REPUBLIC OF CHINA

STATE BUDGET (million yuan)

Revenue	1985	1986	1987*
Tax receipts	204,079	206,450	219,398
Funds for projects	14,679	16,000	17,700
State treasury bonds	6,061	6,200	6,000
Receipts from enterprises	4,375	3,571 }	16,203
Other domestic receipts	5,224	14,185 }	
Sub-total	234,418	246,406	259,301
Less Subsidies	50,702	32,246	35,972
Total domestic receipts	183,716	214,160	223,329
Foreign loans	2,924	7,870	14,600
Total	186,640	222,030	237,929

* Figures are provisional. The revised total (in million yuan) is 234,663 (tax receipts 213,482).
1988 (million yuan): Revenue 258,780.
1989 (million yuan): Total revenue 291,920 (estimate).
1990 (million yuan): Total revenue 323,653 (estimate).

Expenditure	1988	1989*	1990*
Capital construction	61,949	62,792	65,945
Subsidies to enterprises	31,695	40,965	40,558
Agriculture and rural communes	15,510	17,398	21,481
Education, science and health services	47,907	51,388	59,745
National defence	21,796	24,550	28,970
Administrative expenses†	22,107	22,664	27,234
Total (incl. others)	266,831	293,080	332,546

* Planned expenditure.
† Including expenditure on armed police.

SEVENTH FIVE-YEAR PLAN, 1986–90
(proposed investment in fixed assets, '000m. yuan)

State enterprises and institutions	896
Capital construction	500
by central departments	375
by local authorities	112.5
Special Economic Zones	12.5
Technological transformation and equipment renewal	276
Other projects	120
Collective enterprises	160
Private enterprises in towns and counties	240
Total	1,296

INTERNATIONAL RESERVES (US $ million at 31 December)

	1987	1988	1989
Gold*	629	594	587
IMF special drawing rights	640	586	540
Reserve position in IMF	429	407	398
Foreign exchange	15,236	17,548	17,022
Total	16,934	19,135	18,547

* Valued at 35 SDR per troy ounce.
Source: IMF, *International Financial Statistics*.

MONEY SUPPLY (million yuan at 31 December)

	1987	1988	1989
Currency outside banks	145,450	213,260	234,210
Deposits at People's Bank of China	45,310	39,720	48,760
Demand deposits at specialized banks	244,690	270,010	274,710
Demand deposits at rural credit co-operatives	21,950	25,750	25,740
Total money	457,400	548,740	583,420

Source: IMF, *International Financial Statistics*.

COST OF LIVING
(General Retail Price Index; base = 1985 = 100)

	1987	1988	1989
All items	116.4	140.5	163.4

Source: IMF, *International Financial Statistics*.

NATIONAL ACCOUNTS
Net Material Product* (million yuan at current prices)

	1986	1987	1988
Agriculture	272,000	315,400	381,800
Industry	357,300	426,200	543,200
Construction	51,400	63,700	78,300
Transport	32,000	36,500	43,800
Commerce	77,200	94,300	129,900
Total	789,900	936,100	1,177,000

* Defined as the total net value of goods and 'productive' services, including turnover taxes, produced by the economy. This excludes economic activities not contributing directly to material production, such as public administration, defence and personal and professional services.

BALANCE OF PAYMENTS (US $ million)

	1987	1988	1989
Merchandise exports f.o.b.	34,734	41,054	43,220
Merchandise imports f.o.b.	−36,395	−46,369	−48,840
Trade balance	−1,661	−5,315	−5,620
Exports of services	5,413	6,327	6,497
Imports of services	−3,676	−5,233	−5,575
Balance on goods and services	76	−4,221	−4,698
Private unrequited transfers	249	416	238
Government unrequited transfers	−25	3	143
Current balance	300	−3,802	−4,317
Long-term capital (net)	5,752	7,139	5,240
Short-term capital (net)	212	58	−1,518
Net errors and omissions	−1,481	−1,021	117
Total (net monetary movements)	4,783	2,374	−478
Valuation changes (net)	−14	5	2
Changes in reserves	4,768	2,379	−476

Source: IMF, *International Financial Statistics*.

External Trade

COMMODITY GROUPS (US $ million)

Imports c.i.f.	1987	1988	1989
Food and live animals	2,443.3	3,475.9	4,192.7
Beverages and tobacco	263.1	345.9	201.5
Crude materials (inedible) except fuels	3,320.4	5,089.6	4,835.1
Mineral fuels, lubricants, etc.	539.1	787.5	1,650.2
Animal and vegetable oils, fats and waxes	349.1	368.9	875.3
Chemicals and related products	5,008.2	9,139.1	7,556.2
Basic manufactures	9,729.7	10,409.7	12,335.1
Machinery and transport equipment	14,607.1	16,689.9	18,207.6
Miscellaneous manufactured articles	1,877.3	1,982.6	2,072.9
Other commodities and transactions	5,078.3	6,070.2	7,215.2
Total	43,215.6	55,268.3	59,141.8

THE PEOPLE'S REPUBLIC OF CHINA

Exports f.o.b.	1987	1988	1989
Food and live animals	4,780.7	5,889.8	6,144.7
Beverages and tobacco	174.7	235.5	313.7
Crude materials (inedible) except fuels	3,650.4	4,257.1	4,211.5
Mineral fuels, lubricants, etc.	4,543.8	3,949.6	4,269.6
Animal and vegetable oils, fats and waxes	81.3	74.3	86.1
Chemicals and related products	2,234.6	2,896.8	3,201.1
Basic manufactures	8,570.2	10,489.1	10,896.9
Machinery and transport equipment	1,740.8	2,769.4	3,874.0
Miscellaneous manufactured articles	6,273.4	8,267.7	10,754.8
Other commodities and transactions	7,387.2	8,686.6	8,737.9
Total	39,437.0	47,515.8	52,485.9

PRINCIPAL TRADING PARTNERS (US $ million)

Imports c.i.f.	1987	1988	1989
Argentina	332.2	414.3	567.1
Australia	1,322.4	1,107.8	1,471.9
Brazil	452.0	798.1	940.0
Canada	1,398.4	1,855.8	1,077.9
Czechoslovakia	316.9	471.4	521.5
France	899.1	986.9	1,420.3
Germany, Federal Republic	3,131.1	3,433.6	3,379.1
Hong Kong	8,437.2	11,973.3	12,541.7
Indonesia	591.1	681.5	582.3
Italy	1,237.9	1,549.0	1,835.4
Japan	10,074.8	11,057.1	10,534.5
Malaysia	302.2	568.9	692.4
New Zealand	216.3	407.4	304.4
Poland	458.9	333.4	365.1
Romania	443.5	580.0	473.1
Singapore	617.9	1,018.4	1,498.9
Switzerland	503.9	491.3	526.1
Thailand	404.6	632.6	756.3
USSR	1,271.6	1,782.1	2,147.3
United Kingdom	899.7	898.3	1,083.5
USA	4,831.0	6,631.1	7,868.4
Total (including others)	43,215.6	55,250.7	59,141.6

Exports f.o.b.	1987	1988	1989
Canada	408.7	389.9	411.7
France	436.4	515.2	527.4
Germany, Federal Republic	1,224.2	1,484.5	1,608.7
Hong Kong	13,777.4	18,268.6	21,915.9
Italy	555.8	745.8	714.7
Japan	6,398.3	7,922.1	8,362.5
Jordan	1,341.3	725.0	319.2
Macau	427.3	442.0	469.0
Netherlands	607.7	749.1	759.4
Poland	402.7	371.3	382.8
Singapore	1,327.5	1,485.1	1,692.8
USSR	1,247.1	1,476.0	1,849.3
United Kingdom	531.9	659.0	635.1
USA	3,037.5	3,380.0	4,391.0
Zaire	707.3	976.9	53.9
Total (including others)	39,437.0	47,540.3	52,485.9

Transport

	1987	1988	1989
Freight (million ton-km):			
Railways	947,100	987,800	1,039,100
Roads	240,900	322,000	332,900
Inland waterways	939,700	1,007,000	1,115,100
Air	660	730	700
Passenger-km (million):			
Railways	284,300	326,000	303,700
Roads	212,900	252,800	252,100
Inland waterways	19,200	20,400	19,000
Air	18,600	21,400	18,000

SEA-BORNE SHIPPING (freight traffic, '000 metric tons)

	1986	1987	1988
Goods loaded and unloaded	377,980	396,250	438,140

Tourism

FOREIGN VISITORS ('000)

Country of origin	1986	1987	1988
Hong Kong, Macau and Taiwan	21,269.0	25,087.4	29,773.3
Japan	483.5	577.7	591.9
USA	291.8	315.3	300.9
Total (incl. others)	22,819.4	26,902.3	31,694.8

Communications Media

(million copies)

	1986	1987	1988
Newspapers	19,390	20,600	20,720
Magazines	2,400	2,590	2,560
Books	5,200	6,250	6,220

Radio receivers: 150m. in use in 1986.
Television receivers: 10.5m. in use in 1986.

Education

(1988)

	Institutions	Full-time Teachers ('000)	Students ('000)
Kindergartens	171,845	670	18,545
Primary schools	793,261	5,501	125,358
General secondary schools	91,492	2,960	47,615
Secondary technical schools	2,957	168	1,368
Teacher training schools	1,065	57	684
Agricultural and vocational schools	8,954	203	2,794
Special schools	446	9	45
Higher education	1,075	393	2,066

1989: Primary school students 123,730,000.

Directory

The Constitution

A new constitution was adopted on 4 December 1982 by the Fifth Session of the Fifth National People's Congress. Its principal provisions are detailed below. The Preamble, which is not included here, states that 'Taiwan is part of the sacred territory of the People's Republic of China'.

GENERAL PRINCIPLES

Article 1: The People's Republic of China is a socialist state under the people's democratic dictatorship led by the working class and based on the alliance of workers and peasants.

The socialist system is the basic system of the People's Republic of China. Sabotage of the socialist system by any organization or individual is prohibited.

Article 2: All power in the People's Republic of China belongs to the people.

The organs through which the people exercise state power are the National People's Congress and the local people's congresses at different levels.

The people administer state affairs and manage economic, cultural and social affairs through various channels and in various ways in accordance with the law.

Article 3: The state organs of the People's Republic of China apply the principle of democratic centralism.

The National People's Congress and the local people's congresses at different levels are instituted through democratic election. They are responsible to the people and subject to their supervision.

All administrative, judicial and procuratorial organs of the State are created by the people's congresses to which they are responsible and under whose supervision they operate.

The division of functions and powers between the central and local state organs is guided by the principle of giving full play to the initiative and enthusiasm of the local authorities under the unified leadership of the central authorities.

Article 4: All nationalities in the People's Republic of China are equal. The State protects the lawful rights and interests of the minority nationalities and upholds and develops the relationship of equality, unity and mutual assistance among all of China's nationalities. Discrimination against and oppression of any nationality are prohibited; any acts that undermine the unity of the nationalities or instigate their secession are prohibited.

The State helps the areas inhabited by minority nationalities speed up their economic and cultural development in accordance with the peculiarities and needs of the different minority nationalities.

Regional autonomy is practised in areas where people of minority nationalities live in compact communities; in these areas organs of self-government are established for the exercise of the right of autonomy. All the national autonomous areas are inalienable parts of the People's Republic of China.

The people of all nationalities have the freedom to use and develop their own spoken and written languages, and to preserve or reform their own ways and customs.

Article 5: The State upholds the uniformity and dignity of the socialist legal system.

No law or administrative or local rules and regulations shall contravene the Constitution.

All state organs, the armed forces, all political parties and public organizations and all enterprises and undertakings must abide by the Constitution and the law. All acts in violation of the Constitution and the law must be looked into.

No organization or individual may enjoy the privilege of being above the Constitution and the law.

Article 6: The basis of the socialist economic system of the People's Republic of China is socialist public ownership of the means of production, namely, ownership by the whole people and collective ownership by the working people.

The system of socialist public ownership supersedes the system of exploitation of man by man; it applies the principle of 'from each according to his ability, to each according to his work.'

Article 7: The state economy is the sector of socialist economy under ownership by the whole people; it is the leading force in the national economy. The State ensures the consolidation and growth of the state economy.

Article 8: Rural people's communes, agricultural producers' co-operatives, and other forms of co-operative economy such as producers', supply and marketing, credit and consumers' co-operatives, belong to the sector of socialist economy under collective ownership by the working people. Working people who are members of rural economic collectives have the right, within the limits prescribed by law, to farm private plots of cropland and hilly land, engage in household sideline production and raise privately-owned livestock.

The various forms of co-operative economy in the cities and towns, such as those in the handicraft, industrial, building, transport, commercial and service trades, all belong to the sector of socialist economy under collective ownership by the working people.

The State protects the lawful rights and interests of the urban and rural economic collectives and encourages, guides and helps the growth of the collective economy.

Article 9: Mineral resources, waters, forests, mountains, grassland, unreclaimed land, beaches and other natural resources are owned by the State, that is, by the whole people, with the exception of the forests, mountains, grassland, unreclaimed land and beaches that are owned by collectives in accordance with the law.

The State ensures the rational use of natural resources and protects rare animals and plants. The appropriation or damage of natural resources by any organization or individual by whatever means is prohibited.

Article 10: Land in the cities is owned by the State.

Land in the rural and suburban areas is owned by collectives except for those portions which belong to the state in accordance with the law; house sites and private plots of cropland and hilly land are also owned by collectives.

The State may in the public interest take over land for its use in accordance with the law.

No organization or individual may appropriate, buy, sell or lease land, or unlawfully transfer land in other ways.

All organizations and individuals who use land must make rational use of the land.

Article 11: The individual economy of urban and rural working people, operated within the limits prescribed by law, is a complement to the socialist public economy. The State protects the lawful rights and interests of the individual economy.

The State guides, helps and supervises the individual economy by exercising administrative control.

Article 12: Socialist public property is sacred and inviolable.

The State protects socialist public property. Appropriation or damage of state or collective property by any organization or individual by whatever means is prohibited.

Article 13: The State protects the right of citizens to own lawfully earned income, savings, houses and other lawful property.

The State protects by law the right of citizens to inherit private property.

Article 14: The State continuously raises labour productivity, improves economic results and develops the productive forces by enhancing the enthusiasm of the working people, raising the level of their technical skill, disseminating advanced science and technology, improving the systems of economic administration and enterprise operation and management, instituting the socialist system of responsibility in various forms and improving organization of work.

The State practises strict economy and combats waste.

The State properly apportions accumulation and consumption, pays attention to the interests of the collective and the individual as well as of the State and, on the basis of expanded production, gradually improves the material and cultural life of the people.

Article 15: The State practises economic planning on the basis of socialist public ownership. It ensures the proportionate and co-ordinated growth of the national economy through overall balancing by economic planning and the supplementary role of regulation by the market.

Disturbance of the orderly functioning of the social economy or disruption of the state economic plan by any organization or individual is prohibited.

Article 16: State enterprises have decision-making power in operation and management within the limits prescribed by law, on condition that they submit to unified leadership by the State and fulfil all their obligations under the state plan.

State enterprises practise democratic management through congresses of workers and staff and in other ways in accordance with the law.

Article 17: Collective economic organizations have decision-making power in conducting independent economic activities, on condition that they accept the guidance of the state plan and abide by the relevant laws.

Collective economic organizations practise democratic management in accordance with the law, with the entire body of their workers electing or removing their managerial personnel and deciding on major issues concerning operation and management.

Article 18: The People's Republic of China permits foreign enterprises, other foreign economic organizations and individual foreigners to invest in China and to enter into various forms of economic co-operation with Chinese enterprises and other economic organizations in accordance with the law of the People's Republic of China.

All foreign enterprises and other foreign economic organizations in China, as well as joint ventures with Chinese and foreign investment located in China, shall abide by the law of the People's Republic of China. Their lawful rights and interests are protected by the law of the People's Republic of China.

Article 19: The State develops socialist educational undertakings and works to raise the scientific and cultural level of the whole nation.

The State runs schools of various types, makes primary education compulsory and universal, develops secondary, vocational and higher education and promotes pre-school education.

The State develops educational facilities of various types in order to wipe out illiteracy and provide political, cultural, scientific, technical and professional education for workers, peasants, state functionaries and other working people. It encourages people to become educated through self-study.

The State encourages the collective economic organizations, state enterprises and undertakings and other social forces to set up educational institutions of various types in accordance with the law.

The State promotes the nationwide use of Putonghua (common speech based on Beijing pronunciation).

Article 20: The State promotes the development of the natural and social sciences, disseminates scientific and technical knowledge, and commends and rewards achievements in scientific research as well as technological discoveries and inventions.

Article 21: The State develops medical and health services, promotes modern medicine and traditional Chinese medicine, encourages and supports the setting up of various medical and health facilities by the rural economic collectives, state enterprises and undertakings and neighbourhood organizations, and promotes sanitation activities of a mass character, all to protect the people's health.

The State develops physical culture and promotes mass sports activities to build up the people's physique.

Article 22: The State promotes the development of literature and art, the press, broadcasting and television undertakings, publishing and distribution services, libraries, museums, cultural centres and other cultural undertakings, that serve the people and socialism, and sponsors mass cultural activities.

The State protects places of scenic and historical interest, valuable cultural monuments and relics and other important items of China's historical and cultural heritage.

Article 23: The State trains specialized personnel in all fields who serve socialism, increases the number of intellectuals and creates conditions to give full scope to their role in socialist modernization.

Article 24: The State strengthens the building of socialist spiritual civilization through spreading education in high ideals and morality, general education and education in discipline and the legal system, and through promoting the formulation and observance of rules of conduct and common pledges by different sections of the people in urban and rural areas.

The State advocates the civic virtues of love for the motherland, for the people, for labour, for science and for socialism; it educates the people in patriotism, collectivism, internationalism and communism and in dialectical and historical materialism; it combats capitalist, feudalist and other decadent ideas.

Article 25: The State promotes family planning so that population growth may fit the plans for economic and social development.

Article 26: The State protects and improves the living environment and the ecological environment, and prevents and remedies pollution and other public hazards.

The State organizes and encourages afforestation and the protection of forests.

Article 27: All state organs carry out the principle of simple and efficient administration, the system of responsibility for work and the system of training functionaries and appraising their work in order constantly to improve quality of work and efficiency and combat bureaucratism.

All state organs and functionaries must rely on the support of the people, keep in close touch with them, heed their opinions and suggestions, accept their supervision and work hard to serve them.

Article 28: The State maintains public order and suppresses treasonable and other counter-revolutionary activities; it penalizes actions that endanger public security and disrupt the socialist economy and other criminal activities, and punishes and reforms criminals.

Article 29: The armed forces of the People's Republic of China belong to the people. Their tasks are to strengthen national defence, resist aggression, defend the motherland, safeguard the people's peaceful labour, participate in national reconstruction, and work hard to serve the people.

The State strengthens the revolutionization, modernization and regularization of the armed forces in order to increase the national defence capability.

Article 30: The administrative division of the People's Republic of China is as follows:

(1) The country is divided into provinces, autonomous regions and municipalities directly under the central government;

(2) Provinces and autonomous regions are divided into autonomous prefectures, counties, autonomous counties and cities;

(3) Counties and autonomous counties are divided into townships, nationality townships and towns.

Municipalities directly under the central government and other large cities are divided into districts and counties. Autonomous prefectures are divided into counties, autonomous counties, and cities.

All autonomous regions, autonomous prefectures and autonomous counties are national autonomous areas.

Article 31: The State may establish special administrative regions when necessary. The systems to be instituted in special administrative regions shall be prescribed by law enacted by the National People's Congress in the light of the specific conditions.

Article 32: The People's Republic of China protects the lawful rights and interests of foreigners within Chinese territory, and while on Chinese territory foreigners must abide by the law of the People's Republic of China.

The People's Republic of China may grant asylum to foreigners who request it for political reasons.

FUNDAMENTAL RIGHTS AND DUTIES OF CITIZENS

Article 33: All persons holding the nationality of the People's Republic of China are citizens of the People's Republic of China.

All citizens of the People's Republic of China are equal before the law.

Every citizen enjoys the rights and at the same time must perform the duties prescribed by the Constitution and the law.

Article 34: All citizens of the People's Republic of China who have reached the age of 18 have the right to vote and stand for election, regardless of nationality, race, sex, occupation, family background, religious belief, education, property status, or length of residence, except persons deprived of political rights according to law.

Article 35: Citizens of the People's Republic of China enjoy freedom of speech, of the press, of assembly, of association, of procession and of demonstration.

Article 36: Citizens of the People's Republic of China enjoy freedom of religious belief.

No state organ, public organization or individual may compel citizens to believe in, or not to believe in, any religion; nor may they discriminate against citizens who believe in, or do not believe in, any religion.

The State protects normal religious activities. No one may make use of religion to engage in activities that disrupt public order, impair the health of citizens or interfere with the educational system of the state.

Religious bodies and religious affairs are not subject to any foreign domination.

Article 37: The freedom of person of citizens of the People's Republic of China is inviolable.

No citizen may be arrested except with the approval or by decision of a people's procuratorate or by decision of a people's court, and arrests must be made by a public security organ.

Unlawful deprivation or restriction of citizens' freedom of person by detention or other means is prohibited; and unlawful search of the person of citizens is prohibited.

Article 38: The personal dignity of citizens of the People's Republic of China is inviolable. Insult, libel, false charge or frame-up directed against citizens by any means is prohibited.

Article 39: The home of citizens of the People's Republic of China is inviolable. Unlawful search of, or intrusion into, a citizen's home is prohibited.

Article 40: The freedom and privacy of correspondence of citizens of the People's Republic of China are protected by law. No organization or individual may, on any ground, infringe upon the freedom and privacy of citizens' correspondence except in cases where, to meet the needs of state security or of investigation into criminal offences, public security or procuratorial organs are permitted to censor correspondence in accordance with procedures prescribed by law.

Article 41: Citizens of the People's Republic of China have the right to criticize and make suggestions to any state organ or functionary. Citizens have the right to make to relevant state organs complaints and charges against, or exposures of, violation of the law or dereliction of duty by any state organ or functionary; but fabrication or distortion of facts with the intention of libel or frame-up is prohibited.

In case of complaints, charges or exposures made by citizens, the state organ concerned must deal with them in a responsible manner after ascertaining the facts. No one may suppress such complaints, charges and exposures, or retaliate against the citizen making them.

Citizens who have suffered losses through infringement of their civic rights by any state organ or functionary have the right to compensation in accordance with the law.

Article 42: Citizens of the People's Republic of China have the right as well as the duty to work.

Using various channels, the State creates conditions for employment, strengthens labour protection, improves working conditions and, on the basis of expanded production, increases remuneration for work and social benefits.

Work is the glorious duty of every able-bodied citizen. All working people in state enterprises and in urban and rural economic collectives should perform their tasks with an attitude consonant with their status as masters of the country. The State promotes socialist labour emulation, and commends and rewards model and advanced workers. The State encourages citizens to take part in voluntary labour.

The State provides necessary vocational training to citizens before they are employed.

Article 43: Working people in the People's Republic of China have the right to rest.

The State expands facilities for rest and recuperation of working people, and prescribes working hours and vacations for workers and staff.

Article 44: The State prescribes by law the system of retirement for workers and staff in enterprises and undertakings and for functionaries of organs of state. The livelihood of retired personnel is ensured by the State and society.

Article 45: Citizens of the People's Republic of China have the right to material assistance from the State and society when they are old, ill or disabled. The State develops the social insurance, social relief and medical and health services that are required to enable citizens to enjoy this right.

The State and society ensure the livelihood of disabled members of the armed forces, provide pensions to the families of martyrs and give preferential treatment to the families of military personnel.

The State and society help make arrangements for the work, livelihood and education of the blind, deaf-mute and other handicapped citizens.

Article 46: Citizens of the People's Republic of China have the duty as well as the right to receive education.

The State promotes the all-round moral, intellectual and physical development of children and young people.

Article 47: Citizens of the People's Republic of China have the freedom to engage in scientific research, literary and artistic creation and other cultural pursuits. The State encourages and assists creative endeavours conducive to the interests of the people that are made by citizens engaged in education, science, technology, literature, art and other cultural work.

Article 48: Women in the People's Republic of China enjoy equal rights with men in all spheres of life, political, economic, cultural and social, including family life.

The State protects the rights and interests of women, applies the principle of equal pay for equal work for men and women alike and trains and selects cadres from among women.

Article 49: Marriage, the family and mother and child are protected by the State.

Both husband and wife have the duty to practise family planning.

Parents have the duty to rear and educate their minor children, and children who have come of age have the duty to support and assist their parents.

Violation of the freedom of marriage is prohibited. Maltreatment of old people, women and children is prohibited.

Article 50: The People's Republic of China protects the legitimate rights and interests of Chinese nationals residing abroad and protects the lawful rights and interests of returned overseas Chinese and of the family members of Chinese nationals residing abroad.

Article 51: The exercise by citizens of the People's Republic of China of their freedoms and rights may not infringe upon the interests of the State, of society and of the collective, or upon the lawful freedoms and rights of other citizens.

Article 52: It is the duty of citizens of the People's Republic of China to safeguard the unity of the country and the unity of all its nationalities.

Article 53: Citizens of the People's Republic of China must abide by the Constitution and the law, keep state secrets, protect public property and observe labour discipline and public order and respect social ethics.

Article 54: It is the duty of citizens of the People's Republic of China to safeguard the security, honour and interests of the motherland; they must not commit acts detrimental to the security, honour and interests of the motherland.

Article 55: It is the sacred obligation of every citizen of the People's Republic of China to defend the motherland and resist aggression.

It is the honourable duty of citizens of the People's Republic of China to perform military service and join the militia in accordance with the law.

Article 56: It is the duty of citizens of the People's Republic of China to pay taxes in accordance with the law.

STRUCTURE OF THE STATE

The National People's Congress

Article 57: The National People's Congress of the People's Republic of China is the highest organ of state power. Its permanent body is the Standing Committee of the National People's Congress.

Article 58: The National People's Congress and its Standing Committee exercise the legislative power of the state.

Article 59: The National People's Congress is composed of deputies elected by the provinces, autonomous regions and municipalities directly under the Central Government, and by the armed forces. All the minority nationalities are entitled to appropriate representation.

Election of deputies to the National People's Congress is conducted by the Standing Committee of the National People's Congress.

The number of deputies to the National People's Congress and the manner of their election are prescribed by law.

Article 60: The National People's Congress is elected for a term of five years.

Two months before the expiration of the term of office of a National People's Congress, its Standing Committee must ensure that the election of deputies to the succeeding National People's Congress is completed. Should exceptional circumstances prevent such an election, it may be postponed by decision of a majority vote of more than two-thirds of all those on the Standing Committee of the incumbent National People's Congress, and the term of office of the incumbent National People's Congress may be extended. The election of deputies to the succeeding National People's Congress must be completed within one year after the termination of such exceptional circumstances.

Article 61: The National People's Congress meets in session once a year and is convened by its Standing Committee. A session of the National People's Congress may be convened at any time the Standing Committee deems this necessary, or when more than one-fifth of the deputies to the National People's Congress so propose.

When the National People's Congress meets, it elects a presidium to conduct its session.

Article 62: The National People's Congress exercises the following functions and powers:

(1) to amend the Constitution;

(2) to supervise the enforcement of the Constitution;

(3) to enact and amend basic statutes concerning criminal offences, civil affairs, the state organs and other matters;

(4) to elect the President and the Vice-President of the People's Republic of China;

(5) to decide on the choice of the Premier of the State Council upon nomination by the President of the People's Republic of China, and to decide on the choice of the Vice-Premiers, State Councillors, Ministers in charge of Ministries or Commissions and the Auditor-General and the Secretary-General of the State Council upon nomination by the Premier;

(6) to elect the Chairman of the Central Military Commission and, upon his nomination, to decide on the choice of all the others on the Central Military Commission;

(7) to elect the President of the Supreme People's Court;

(8) to elect the Procurator-General of the Supreme People's Procuratorate;

(9) to examine and approve the plan for national economic and social development and the reports on its implementation;

THE PEOPLE'S REPUBLIC OF CHINA

(10) to examine and approve the state budget and the report on its implementation;

(11) to alter or annul inappropriate decisions of the Standing Committee of the National People's Congress;

(12) to approve the establishment of provinces, autonomous regions, and municipalities directly under the Central Government;

(13) to decide on the establishment of special administrative regions and the systems to be instituted there;

(14) to decide on questions of war and peace; and

(15) to exercise such other functions and powers as the highest organ of state power should exercise.

Article 63: The National People's Congress has the power to recall or remove from office the following persons:

(1) the President and the Vice-President of the People's Republic of China;

(2) the Premier, Vice-Premiers, State Councillors, Ministers in charge of Ministries or Commissions and the Auditor-General and the Secretary-General of the State Council;

(3) the Chairman of the Central Military Commission and others on the Commission;

(4) the President of the Supreme People's Court; and

(5) the Procurator-General of the Supreme People's Procuratorate.

Article 64: Amendments to the Constitution are to be proposed by the Standing Committee of the National People's Congress or by more than one-fifth of the deputies to the National People's Congress and adopted by a majority vote of more than two-thirds of all the deputies to the Congress.

Statutes and resolutions are adopted by a majority vote of more than one half of all the deputies to the National People's Congress.

Article 65: The Standing Committee of the National People's Congress is composed of the following:

the Chairman;

the Vice-Chairmen;

the Secretary-General; and

members.

Minority nationalities are entitled to appropriate representation on the Standing Committee of the National People's Congress.

The National People's Congress elects, and has the power to recall, all those on its Standing Committee.

No one on the Standing Committee of the National People's Congress shall hold any post in any of the administrative, judicial or procuratorial organs of the state.

Article 66: The Standing Committee of the National People's Congress is elected for the same term as the National People's Congress; it exercises its functions and powers until a new Standing Committee is elected by the succeeding National People's Congress.

The Chairman and Vice-Chairmen of the Standing Committee shall serve no more than two consecutive terms.

Article 67: The Standing Committee of the National People's Congress exercises the following functions and powers:

(1) to interpret the Constitution and supervise its enforcement;

(2) to enact and amend statutes with the exception of those which should be enacted by the National People's Congress;

(3) to enact, when the National People's Congress is not in session, partial supplements and amendments to statutes enacted by the National People's Congress provided that they do not contravene the basic principles of these statutes;

(4) to interpret statutes;

(5) to examine and approve, when the National People's Congress is not in session, partial adjustments to the plan for national economic and social development and to the state budget that prove necessary in the course of their implementation;

(6) to supervise the work of the State Council, the Central Military Commission, the Supreme People's Court and the Supreme People's Procuratorate;

(7) to annul those administrative rules and regulations, decisions or orders of the State Council that contravene the Constitution or the statutes;

(8) to annul those local regulations or decisions of the organs of state power of provinces, autonomous regions and municipalities directly under the Central Government that contravene the Constitution, the statutes or the administrative rules and regulations;

(9) to decide, when the National People's Congress is not in session, on the choice of Ministers in charge of Ministries or Commissions or the Auditor-General and the Secretary-General of the State Council upon nomination by the Premier of the State Council;

(10) to decide, upon nomination by the Chairman of the Central Military Commission, on the choice of others on the Commission, when the National People's Congress is not in session;

(11) to appoint and remove the Vice-Presidents and judges of the Supreme People's Court, members of its Judicial Committee and the President of the Military Court at the suggestion of the President of the Supreme People's Court;

(12) to appoint and remove the Deputy Procurators-General and Procurators of the Supreme People's Procuratorate, members of its Procuratorial Committee and the Chief Procurator of the Military Procuratorate at the request of the Procurator-General of the Supreme People's Procuratorate, and to approve the appointment and removal of the Chief Procurators of the People's Procuratorates of provinces, autonomous regions and municipalities directly under the Central Government;

(13) to decide on the appointment and recall of plenipotentiary representatives abroad;

(14) to decide on the ratification and abrogation of treaties and important agreements concluded with foreign states;

(15) to institute systems of titles and ranks for military and diplomatic personnel and of other specific titles and ranks;

(16) to institute state medals and titles of honour and decide on their conferment;

(17) to decide on the granting of special pardons;

(18) to decide, when the National People's Congress is not in session, on the proclamation of a state of war in the event of an armed attack on the country or in fulfilment of international treaty obligations concerning common defence against aggression;

(19) to decide on general mobilization or partial mobilization;

(20) to decide on the enforcement of martial law throughout the country or in particular provinces, autonomous regions or municipalities directly under the Central Government; and

(21) to exercise such other functions and powers as the National People's Congress may assign to it.

Article 68: The Chairman of the Standing Committee of the National People's Congress presides over the work of the Standing Committee and convenes its meetings. The Vice-Chairmen and the Secretary-General assist the Chairman in his work.

Chairmanship meetings with the participation of the Chairman, Vice-Chairmen and Secretary-General handle the important day-to-day work of the Standing Committee of the National People's Congress.

Article 69: The Standing Committee of the National People's Congress is responsible to the National People's Congress and reports on its work to the Congress.

Article 70: The National People's Congress establishes a Nationalities Committee, a Law Committee, a Finance and Economic Committee, an Education, Science, Culture and Public Health Committee, a Foreign Affairs Committee, an Overseas Chinese Committee and such other special committees as are necessary. These special committees work under the direction of the Standing Committee of the National People's Congress when the Congress is not in session.

The special committees examine, discuss and draw up relevant bills and draft resolutions under the direction of the National People's Congress and its Standing Committee.

Article 71: The National People's Congress and its Standing Committee may, when they deem it necessary, appoint committees of inquiry into specific questions and adopt relevant resolutions in the light of their reports.

All organs of state, public organizations and citizens concerned are obliged to supply the necessary information to those committees of inquiry when they conduct investigations.

Article 72: Deputies to the National People's Congress and all those on its Standing Committee have the right, in accordance with procedures prescribed by law, to submit bills and proposals within the scope of the respective functions and powers of the National People's Congress and its Standing Committee.

Article 73: Deputies to the National People's Congress during its sessions, and all those on its Standing Committee during its meetings, have the right to address questions, in accordance with procedures prescribed by law, to the State Council or the Ministries and Commissions under the State Council, which must answer the questions in a responsible manner.

Article 74: No deputy to the National People's Congress may be arrested or placed on criminal trial without the consent of the presidium of the current session of the National People's Congress or, when the National People's Congress is not in session, without the consent of its Standing Committee.

Article 75: Deputies to the National People's Congress may not be called to legal account for their speeches or votes at its meetings.

Article 76: Deputies to the National People's Congress must play an exemplary role in abiding by the Constitution and the law and keeping state secrets and, in production and other work and their public activities, assist in the enforcement of the Constitution and the law.

Deputies to the National People's Congress should maintain close contact with the units which elected them and with the people, listen to and convey the opinions and demands of the people and work hard to serve them.

Article 77: Deputies to the National People's Congress are subject to the supervision of the units which elected them. The electoral units have the power, through procedures prescribed by law, to recall the deputies whom they elected.

Article 78: The organization and working procedures of the National People's Congress and its Standing Committee are prescribed by law.

The President of the People's Republic of China

Article 79: The President and Vice-President of the People's Republic of China are elected by the National People's Congress.

Citizens of the People's Republic of China who have the right to vote and to stand for election and who have reached the age of 45 are eligible for election as President or Vice-President of the People's Republic of China.

The term of office of the President and Vice-President of the People's Republic of China is the same as that of the National People's Congress, and they shall serve no more than two consecutive terms.

Article 80: The President of the People's Republic of China, in pursuance of decisions of the National People's Congress and its Standing Committee, promulgates statutes; appoints and removes the Premier, Vice-Premiers, State Councillors, Ministers in charge of Ministries or Commissions, and the Auditor-General and the Secretary-General of the State Council; confers state medals and titles of honour; issues orders of special pardons; proclaims martial law; proclaims a state of war; and issues mobilization orders.

Article 81: The President of the People's Republic of China receives foreign diplomatic representatives on behalf of the People's Republic of China and, in pursuance of decisions of the Standing Committee of the National People's Congress, appoints and recalls plenipotentiary representatives abroad, and ratifies and abrogates treaties and important agreements concluded with foreign states.

Article 82: The Vice-President of the People's Republic of China assists the President in his work.

The Vice-President of the People's Republic of China may exercise such parts of the functions and powers of the President as the President may entrust to him.

Article 83: The President and Vice-President of the People's Republic of China exercise their functions and powers until the new President and Vice-President elected by the succeeding National People's Congress assume office.

Article 84: In case the office of the President of the People's Republic of China falls vacant, the Vice-President succeeds to the office of President.

In case the office of the Vice-President of the People's Republic of China falls vacant, the National People's Congress shall elect a new Vice-President to fill the vacancy.

In the event that the offices of both the President and the Vice-President of the People's Republic of China fall vacant, the National People's Congress shall elect a new President and a new Vice-President. Prior to such election, the Chairman of the Standing Committee of the National People's Congress shall temporarily act as the President of the People's Republic of China.

The State Council

Article 85: The State Council, that is, the Central People's Government, of the People's Republic of China is the executive body of the highest organ of state power; it is the highest organ of state administration.

Article 86: The State Council is composed of the following: the Premier; the Vice-Premiers; the State Councillors; the Ministers in charge of ministries; the Ministers in charge of commissions; the Auditor-General; and the Secretary-General.

The Premier has overall responsibility for the State Council. The Ministers have overall responsibility for the respective ministries or commissions under their charge.

The organization of the State Council is prescribed by law.

Article 87: The term of office of the State Council is the same as that of the National People's Congress.

The Premier, Vice-Premiers and State Councillors shall serve no more than two consecutive terms.

Article 88: The Premier directs the work of the State Council. The Vice-Premiers and State Councillors assist the Premier in his work.

Executive meetings of the State Council are composed of the Premier, the Vice-Premiers, the State Councillors and the Secretary-General of the State Council.

The Premier convenes and presides over the executive meetings and plenary meetings of the State Council.

Article 89: The State Council exercises the following functions and powers:

(1) to adopt administrative measures, enact administrative rules and regulations and issue decisions and orders in accordance with the Constitution and the statutes;

(2) to submit proposals to the National People's Congress or its Standing Committee;

(3) to lay down the tasks and responsibilities of the ministries and commissions of the State Council, to exercise unified leadership over the work of the ministries and commissions and to direct all other administrative work of a national character that does not fall within the jurisdiction of the ministries and commissions;

(4) to exercise unified leadership over the work of local organs of state administration at different levels throughout the country, and to lay down the detailed division of functions and powers between the Central Government and the organs of state administration of provinces, autonomous regions and municipalities directly under the Central Government;

(5) to draw up and implement the plan for national economic and social development and the state budget;

(6) to direct and administer economic work and urban and rural development;

(7) to direct and administer the work concerning education, science, culture, public health, physical culture and family planning;

(8) to direct and administer the work concerning civil affairs, public security, judicial administration, supervision and other related matters;

(9) to conduct foreign affairs and conclude treaties and agreements with foreign states;

(10) to direct and administer the building of national defence;

(11) to direct and administer affairs concerning the nationalities, and to safeguard the equal rights of minority nationalities and the right of autonomy of the national autonomous areas;

(12) to protect the legitimate rights and interests of Chinese nationals residing abroad and protect the lawful rights and interests of returned overseas Chinese and of the family members of Chinese nationals residing abroad;

(13) to alter or annul inappropriate orders, directives and regulations issued by the ministries or commissions;

(14) to alter or annul inappropriate decisions and orders issued by local organs of state administration at different levels;

(15) to approve the geographic division of provinces, autonomous regions and municipalities directly under the Central Government, and to approve the establishment and geographic division of autonomous prefectures, counties, autonomous counties and cities;

(16) to decide on the enforcement of martial law in parts of provinces, autonomous regions and municipalities directly under the Central Government;

(17) to examine and decide on the size of administrative organs and, in accordance with the law, to appoint, remove and train administrative officers, appraise their work and reward or punish them; and

(18) to exercise such other functions and powers as the National People's Congress or its Standing Committee may assign it.

Article 90: The Ministers in charge of ministries or commissions of the State Council are responsible for the work of their respective departments and convene and preside over their ministerial meetings or commission meetings that discuss and decide on major issues in the work of their respective departments.

The ministries and commissions issue orders, directives and regulations within the jurisdiction of their respective departments and in accordance with the statutes and the administrative rules and regulations, decisions and orders issued by the State Council.

Article 91: The State Council establishes an auditing body to supervise through auditing the revenue and expenditure of all departments under the State Council and of the local government at different levels, and those of the state financial and monetary organizations and of enterprises and undertakings.

Under the direction of the Premier of the State Council, the auditing body independently exercises its power to supervise through auditing in accordance with the law, subject to no interference by any other administrative organ or any public organization or individual.

Article 92: The State Council is responsible, and reports on its work, to the National People's Congress or, when the National People's Congress is not in session, to its Standing Committee.

The Central Military Commission

Article 93: The Central Military Commission of the People's Republic of China directs the armed forces of the country.

The Central Military Commission is composed of the following: the Chairman; the Vice-Chairmen; and members.

The Chairman of the Central Military Commission has overall responsibility for the Commission.

The term of office of the Central Military Commission is the same as that of the National People's Congress.

Article 94: The Chairman of the Central Military Commission is responsible to the National People's Congress and its Standing Committee.

(Two further sections, not included here, deal with the Local People's Congresses and Government and with the Organs of Self-Government of National Autonomous Areas respectively.)

The People's Courts and the People's Procuratorates

Article 123: The people's courts in the People's Republic of China are the judicial organs of the state.

Article 124: The People's Republic of China establishes the Supreme People's Court and the local people's courts at different levels, military courts and other special people's courts.

The term of office of the President of the Supreme People's Court is the same as that of the National People's Congress; he shall serve no more than two consecutive terms.

The organization of people's courts is prescribed by law.

Article 125: All cases handled by the people's courts, except for those involving special circumstances as specified by law, shall be heard in public. The accused has the right of defence.

Article 126: The people's courts shall, in accordance with the law, exercise judicial power independently and are not subject to interference by administrative organs, public organizations or individuals.

Article 127: The Supreme People's Court is the highest judicial organ.

The Supreme People's Court supervises the administration of justice by the local people's courts at different levels and by the special people's courts; people's courts at higher levels supervise the administration of justice by those at lower levels.

Article 128: The Supreme People's Court is responsible to the National People's Congress and its Standing Committee. Local people's courts at different levels are responsible to the organs of state power which created them.

Article 129: The people's procuratorates of the People's Republic of China are state organs for legal supervision.

Article 130: The People's Republic of China establishes the Supreme People's Procuratorate and the local people's procuratorates at different levels, military procuratorates and other special people's procuratorates.

The term of office of the Procurator-General of the Supreme People's Procuratorate is the same as that of the National People's Congress; he shall serve no more than two consecutive terms.

The organization of people's procuratorates is prescribed by law.

Article 131: People's procuratorates shall, in accordance with the law, exercise procuratorial power independently and are not subject to interference by administrative organs, public organizations or individuals.

Article 132: The Supreme People's Procuratorate is the highest procuratorial organ.

The Supreme People's Procuratorate directs the work of the local people's procuratorates at different levels and of the special people's procuratorates; people's procuratorates at higher levels direct the work of those at lower levels.

Article 133: The Supreme People's Procuratorate is responsible to the National People's Congress and its Standing Committee. Local people's procuratorates at different levels are responsible to the organs of state power at the corresponding levels which created them and to the people's procuratorates at the higher level.

Article 134: Citizens of all nationalities have the right to use the spoken and written languages of their own nationalities in court proceedings. The people's courts and people's procuratorates should provide translation for any party to the court proceedings who is not familiar with the spoken or written languages in common use in the locality.

In an area where people of a minority nationality live in a compact community or where a number of nationalities live together, hearings should be conducted in the language or languages in common use in the locality; indictments, judgements, notices and other documents should be written, according to actual needs, in the language or languages in common use in the locality.

Article 135: The people's courts, people's procuratorates and public security organs shall, in handling criminal cases, divide their functions, each taking responsibility for its own work, and they shall co-ordinate their efforts and check each other to ensure correct and effective enforcement of law.

THE NATIONAL FLAG, THE NATIONAL EMBLEM AND THE CAPITAL

Article 136: The national flag of the People's Republic of China is a red flag with five stars.

Article 137: The national emblem of the People's Republic of China is the Tian An Men (Gate of Heavenly Peace) in the centre, illuminated by five stars and encircled by ears of grain and a cogwheel.

Article 138: The capital of the People's Republic of China is Beijing (Peking).

The Government

HEAD OF STATE

President: YANG SHANGKUN (elected by the Seventh National People's Congress on 8 April 1988).

Vice-President: WANG ZHEN.

STATE COUNCIL
(December 1990)

Premier: LI PENG.

Vice-Premiers: YAO YILIN, TIAN JIYUN, WU XUEQIAN.

State Councillors:

CHEN XITONG
LI GUIXIAN
LI TIEYING
WANG BINGQIAN
WANG FANG

QIN JIWEI
SONG JIAN
ZOU JIAHUA
CHEN JUNSHENG

Secretary-General: LUO GAN.

Minister of Foreign Affairs: QIAN QICHEN.

Minister of National Defence: QIN JIWEI.

Minister in Charge of the State Planning Commission: ZOU JIAHUA.

Minister in Charge of the State Commission for Restructuring the Economy: CHEN JINHUA.

Minister in Charge of the State Education Commission: LI TIEYING.

Minister in Charge of the State Science and Technology Commission: SONG JIAN.

Minister in Charge of the Commission of Science, Technology and Industry for National Defence: DING HENGGAO.

Minister in Charge of the State Nationalities Affairs Commission: ISMAIL AMAT.

Minister of Machine-Building and Electronics Industry: HE GUANGYUAN.

Minister of Public Security: TAO SIJU.

Minister of State Security: JIA CHUNWANG.

Minister of Civil Affairs: CUI NAIFU.

Minister of Justice: CAI CHENG.

Minister of Supervision: WEI JIANXING.

Minister of Finance: WANG BINGQIAN.

Minister of Commerce: HU PING.

Minister of Foreign Economic Relations and Trade: LI LANQING.

Minister of Agriculture: LIU ZHONGYI.

Minister of Forestry: GAO DEZHAN.

Minister of Energy Resources: HUANG YICHENG.

Minister of Water Resources: YANG ZHENHUAI.

Minister of Construction: LIN HANXIONG.

Minister of Geology and Mineral Resources: ZHU XUN.

Minister of Metallurgical Industry: QI YUANJING.

Minister of Aeronautics and Astronautics Industry: LIN ZONGTANG.

Minister of Chemical Industry: MS GU XIULIAN.

Minister of Textile Industry: MS WU WENYING.

Minister of Light Industry: ZENG XIANLIN.
Minister of Materials: LIU SUINIAN.
Minister of Railways: LI SENMAO.
Minister of Communications: QIAN YONGCHANG.
Minister of Posts and Telecommunications: YANG TAIFANG.
Minister of Personnel: ZHAO DONGWAN.
Minister of Labour: RUAN CHONGWU.
Minister of Culture: HE JINGZHI (acting).
Minister of Radio, Film and Television: AI ZHISHENG.
Minister of Public Health: CHEN MINZHANG.
Minister in Charge of the State Physical Culture and Sports Commission: WU SHAOZU.
Minister in Charge of the State Family Planning Commission: MS PENG PEIYUN.
Governor of the People's Bank of China: LI GUIXIAN.
Auditor-General: LU PEIJIAN.

MINISTRIES

Ministry of Aeronautics and Astronautics Industry: Beijing.
Ministry of Agriculture: Hepingli, Dongcheng Qu, Beijing; tel. (01) 463061; fax (01) 5002448.
Ministry of Chemical Industry: Liupukang, Deshengmenwai, Beijing; tel. (01) 446561; fax (01) 4215982.
Ministry of Civil Affairs: 147 Donganmen, Beijing; tel. (01) 551731.
Ministry of Commerce: 45 Fuxingmenwai Jie, POB 100801, Beijing; tel. (01) 668581; telex 20032.
Ministry of Communications: 10 Fuxing Lu, Beijing; tel. (01) 8642371; telex 22462.
Ministry of Construction: Baiwanzhuang Jie, Beijing; tel. (01) 8992833; telex 222302.
Ministry of Culture: Donganmen Bei Jie, Beijing; tel. (01) 442131.
Ministry of Energy: Beijing.
Ministry of Finance: Sanlihe Nan Jie, Fuxingmenwai, Beijing; tel. (01) 868731; telex 222308.
Ministry of Foreign Affairs: 225 Chaoyangmennei Jie, Dongsi, Beijing; tel. (01) 553831.
Ministry of Foreign Economic Relations and Trade: 2 Dongchangan Jie, Beijing 100731; tel. (01) 553031; telex 22168.
Ministry of Forestry: Hepingli, Dongchang Qu, Beijing; tel. (01) 463061; telex 22237.
Ministry of Geology and Mineral Resources: Xisi Yangshi Jie, Beijing; tel. (01) 668741; telex 22531.
Ministry of Justice: 2 Nan Shun Cheng Jie, Xi Zhi Men, Beijing; tel. (01) 668971.
Ministry of Labour: Beijing.
Ministry of Light Industry: Fuchengmenwai Jie, Beijing; tel. (01) 890751; telex 22465.
Ministry of Machine-Building Industry: Beijing.
Ministry of Materials: Beijing; telex 200155.
Ministry of Metallurgical Industry: 46 Xi Dongsi Jie, Beijing; tel. (01) 557431.
Ministry of National Defence: Beijing; tel. (01) 667343.
Ministry of Personnel: Beijing.
Ministry of Posts and Telecommunications: 13 Changan Xi Jie, Beijing 100804; tel. (01) 660540; telex 222187.
Ministry of Public Health: 44 Houhaibeiyan, Beijing; tel. (01) 440531; telex 22193.
Ministry of Public Security: Dongchangan Jie, Beijing; tel. (01) 553871.
Ministry of Radio, Film and Television: Fu Xing Men Wai Jie 2, POB 4501, Beijing; tel. (01) 862753; telex 22236; fax (01) 8012174.
Ministry of Railways: 10 Fuxing Jie, Beijing; tel. (01) 864061; telex 22483.
Ministry of State Security: Dongchangan Jie, Beijing; tel. (01) 553871.
Ministry of Supervision: Beijing 100083; tel. (01) 2016113.
Ministry of Textile Industry: 12 Dongchangan Jie, Beijing; tel. (01) 5129542; telex 22661.
Ministry of Water Resources: 1 Xiang, Baiguang Jie, Guanganmen, Beijing; tel. (01) 365563; telex 22466.

STATE COMMISSIONS AND CORPORATIONS

State Education Commission: 37 Damucang Hutong, Xicheng Qu, Beijing; tel. (01) 658731.
State Family Planning Commission: Xizhimen Shuncheng Nan Jie, Beijing; tel. (01) 668971.
State Nationalities Affairs Commission: 252 Taipingqiao Jie, Beijing; tel. (01) 666931.
State Physical Culture and Sports Commission: 9 Tiyuguan Lu, 100061 Beijing; tel. (01) 5112233; telex 22323.
State Commission for Restructuring the Economy: Beijing.
State Science and Technology Commission: 54 Sanlihe, Fuxingmenwai, 100862 Beijing; tel. (01) 8012594; telex 22349; fax (01) 8012594.
State Commission of Science, Technology and Industry for National Defence: Beijing.

Legislature

QUANGUO RENMIN DIABIAO DAHUI
(National People's Congress)

The National People's Congress (NPC) is the highest organ of state power, and is indirectly elected for a five-year term. The third plenary session of the Seventh NPC was convened in Beijing in March 1990, and was attended by about 3,000 deputies. The third session of the Seventh National Committee of the Chinese People's Political Consultative Conference (CPPCC, Chair. LI XIANNIAN), a revolutionary united front organization led by the Communist Party, took place simultaneously. The CPPCC holds discussions and consultations on the important affairs in the nation's political life. Members of the CPPCC National Committee or of its Standing Committee may be invited to attend the NPC or its Standing Committee as observers.

Standing Committee

In March 1988, 135 members were elected to the Standing Committee. In mid-1990 the Committee had 155 members. The 15th session of the Seventh NPC Standing Committee was convened in August 1990.

Chairman: WAN LI.

Vice-Chairmen:

XI ZHONGXUN	YE FEI
PENG CHONG	LIAO HANSHENG
ZHU XUEFAN	NI ZHIFU
NGAPOI NGAWANG JIGME	CHEN MUHUA
Gen. SEYPIDIN AZE	FEI XIAOTONG
ZHOU GUCHENG	SUN QIMENG
YAN JICI	LEI JIEQIONG
RONG YIREN	WANG HANBIN

Secretary-General: PENG CHONG.

Local People's Congresses

Province	Chairman of Standing Committee of People's Congress
Anhui	WANG GUANGYU
Fujian	CHENG XU
Gansu	XU FEIQING
Guangdong	LIN RUO
Guizhou	ZHANG YUHUAN
Hainan Island	XU SHIJIE
Hebei	GUO ZHI
Heilongjiang	SUN WEIBEN
Henan	YANG XIZONG
Hubei	HUANG ZHIZHEN
Hunan	LIU FUSHENG
Jiangsu	HAN PEIXIN
Jiangxi	XU QIN
Jilin	HUO MINGGUANG
Liaoning	WANG GUANGZHONG
Qinghai	HUANJUE CAILANG
Shaanxi	LI XIPU
Shandong	LI ZHEN
Shanxi	WANG TINGDONG
Sichuan	HE HAOJU
Yunnan	Miss LI GUIYING
Zhejiang	CHEN ANYU

THE PEOPLE'S REPUBLIC OF CHINA

Special Municipalities
Beijing	Zhao Pengfei
Shanghai	Ye Gongqi
Tianjin	Wu Zhen

Autonomous Regions
Guangxi Zhuang	Gan Ku
Nei Monggol	Batu Bagen
Ningxia Hui	Ma Sizhong
Xinjiang Uygur	Amudun Niyaz
Xizang	Ngapoi Ngawang Jigme

People's Governments

Province	Governor
Anhui	Fu Xishou
Fujian	Jia Qinglin (acting)
Gansu	Jia Zhijie
Guangdong	Ye Xuanping
Guizhou	Wang Chaowen
Hainan Island	Liu Jianfeng
Hebei	Cheng Weigao
Heilongjiang	Shao Qihui
Henan	Li Changchun (acting)
Hubei	Guo Shuyan
Hunan	Chen Bangzhu
Jiangsu	Chen Huanyou
Jiangxi	Wu Guanzheng
Jilin	Wang Zhongyu
Liaoning	Yue Qifeng (acting)
Qinghai	Jin Jipeng
Shaanxi	Bai Qingcai
Shandong	Zhao Zhihao
Shanxi	Wang Senhao
Sichuan	Zhang Haoruo
Yunnan	He Zhiqiang
Zhejiang	Ge Hongsheng (acting)

Special Municipalities	Mayor
Beijing	Chen Xitong
Shanghai	Zhu Rongji
Tianjin	Nie Bichu

Autonomous Regions	Chairman
Guangxi Zhuang	Cheng Kejie
Nei Monggol	Bu He
Ningxia Hui	Bai Lichen
Xinjiang Uygur	Tomur Dawamat
Xizang	Gyaincain Norbu

Political Organizations

COMMUNIST PARTY

Zhongguo Gongchan Dang (Chinese Communist Party—CCP): Beijing; f. 1921; 48m. mems in 1989. At the 13th Nat. Congress of the CCP, in October 1987, a new Cen. Cttee of 175 full mems and 110 alternate mems was elected. At its first plenary session in November, the 13th Cen. Cttee appointed a new Politburo of 17 full mems and one alternate mem. Two members, Zhao Ziyang and Hu Qili, were removed from the Standing Cttee at the fourth plenary session of the Cen. Cttee in June 1989, following the suppression of the Pro-Democracy Movt, for which the death of a third member, Hu Yaobang, had acted as a catalyst. The sixth plenary session was held in March 1990.

Thirteenth Central Committee
General Secretary: Jiang Zemin.

Politburo
Members of the Standing Committee:
Jiang Zemin	Yao Yilin
Li Peng	Song Ping
Qiao Shi	Li Ruihuan

Other Full Members:
Wan Li	Yang Rudai
Tian Jiyun	Yang Shangkun
Li Tieying	Wu Xueqian
Li Ximing	Qin Jiwei

Alternate Member: Ding Guangen.

Secretariat
Full Members:
Qiao Shi	Ding Guangen
Li Ruihuan	Yang Baibing

Alternate Member: Wen Jiabao.
Chairman of Central Advisory Committee: Chen Yun.
Vice-Chairmen: Bo Yibo, Song Renqiong.

OTHER POLITICAL ORGANIZATIONS

China Association for Promoting Democracy: Beijing; tel. (01) 447128; f. 1945; mems drawn mainly from literary, cultural and educational circles; Chair. Lei Jieqiong; Sec.-Gen. Chen Yiqun.

China Democratic League: 1 Beixing Dongchang Hutong, Beijing 100006; tel. (01) 550495; telex 211246; fax (01) 5125090; f. 1941; formed from reorganization of League of Democratic Parties and Organizations of China; mems mainly intellectuals active in education, science and culture; Chair. Fei Xiaotong; Sec.-Gen. Wu Xiuping.

China National Democratic Construction Association: 93 Beiheyan Dajie, 100006 Beijing; tel. (01) 5136677; telex 22044; f. 1945; mems mainly industrialists and businessmen; Chair. Sun Qimeng; Sec.-Gen. Feng Kexu.

China Zhi Gong Dang: Beijing; f. 1925; reorg. 1947; party for public interests; mems are mainly returned overseas Chinese; Chair. Dong Yinchu.

Chinese Communist Youth League: Beijing; tel. (01) 757201; fax (01) 754481; f. 1922; 56m. mems; First Sec. of Cen. Cttee Song Defu.

Chinese Peasants' and Workers' Democratic Party: f. 1930 as the Provisional Action Cttee of the Kuomintang; took present name in 1947; 46,000 mems, active mainly in public health and medicine; Chair. Lu Jiaxi.

Guomindang (Kuomintang) Revolutionary Committee: tel. (01) 550388; f. 1948; mainly fmr Kuomintang mems, and those in cultural, educational, health and financial fields; Chair. Zhu Xuefan.

Jiu San (3 September) Society: f. 1946; fmrly Democratic and Science Soc.; mems mainly scientists and technologists; Chair. Zhou Peiyuan; Sec.-Gen. Zhao Weizhi.

Taiwan Democratic Self-Government League: f. 1947; recruits Taiwanese living on the mainland; Chair. Cai Zimin; Sec.-Gen. Pan Yuanjing.

Diplomatic Representation

EMBASSIES IN THE PEOPLE'S REPUBLIC OF CHINA

Afghanistan: 8 Dong Zhi Men Wai Dajie, Chao Yang Qu, Beijing; tel. (01) 5321582; Ambassador: (vacant).

Albania: 28 Guang Hua Lu, Beijing; tel. (01) 5321120; Ambassador: Justin Niko Papajorgji.

Algeria: Dong Zhi Men Wai Dajie, 7 San Li Tun, Beijing; tel. (01) 5321231; telex 22437; Ambassador: Mourad Bencheikh.

Argentina: Bldg 11, 5 Dong Jie, San Li Tun, Beijing; tel. (01) 5322090; telex 22269; Ambassador: Arturo Enrique Ossorio Arana.

Australia: 15 Dong Zhi Men Wai Dajie, Beijing; tel. (01) 5322331; telex 22263; fax (01) 5324605; Ambassador: David Sadleir.

Austria: 5 Xiu Shui Nan Jie, Jian Guo Men Wai, Beijing; tel. (01) 5322061; telex 22258; Ambassador: (vacant).

Bangladesh: 42 Guang Hua Lu, Beijing; tel. (01) 5321819; telex 22143; fax (01) 5324346; Ambassador: Farooq Sobhan.

Belgium: 6 San Li Tun Lu, Beijing; tel. (01) 5321736; telex 22260; Ambassador: (vacant).

Benin: 38 Guang Hua Lu, Beijing; tel. (01) 5322741; telex 22599; Ambassador: Auguste Alavo.

Bolivia: Ta Yuan Diplomatic Office Bldg, 14 Liang Ma He Nan Lu, Beijing; tel. (01) 523074; Ambassador: (vacant).

Brazil: 27 Guang Hua Lu, Beijing; tel. (01) 5322881; telex 22117; fax (01) 5322751; Ambassador: Roberto Abdenur.

Bulgaria: 4 Xiu Shui Bei Jie, Jian Guo Men Wai, Beijing; tel. (01) 5322231; Ambassador: Filip Markov.

Burkina Faso: 52 Dong Liu Jie, San Li Tun, Beijing; telex 22666; Ambassador: Hama Arba Diallo.

Burundi: 25 Guang Hua Lu, Beijing; tel. (01) 5322328; telex 22271; Ambassador: (vacant).

Cameroon: 7 San Li Tun, Dong Wu Jie, Beijing; tel. (01) 5321771; telex 22256; Ambassador: Eleih Elle Etian.

Canada: 10 San Li Tun Lu, Chao Yang Qu, Beijing; tel. (01) 5323536; telex 22717; fax (01) 5324072; Ambassador: Fred Bild.

THE PEOPLE'S REPUBLIC OF CHINA

Central African Republic: 1 Dong San Jie, San Li Tun, Beijing; tel. (01) 5322867; telex 22142; Ambassador: FERDINAND PIERRE POUNZI.
Chad: 21 Guang Hua Lu, Jianguo Men Wai, Beijing; telex 22287; Ambassador: ISSA ABBAS ALI.
Chile: 1 San Li Tun, Dong Si Jie, Beijing; tel. (01) 5321641; telex 22252; fax (01) 5323170; Ambassador: EDUARDO BRAVO.
Colombia: 34 Guang Hua Lu, Beijing; tel. (01) 5323166; telex 22460; fax (01) 5321969; Ambassador: (vacant).
Congo: 7 San Li Tun, Dong Si Jie, Beijing; tel. (01) 5321644; telex 20428; Ambassador: GABRIEL EMOUENGUE.
Côte d'Ivoire: Beijing; tel. (01) 5321482; telex 22723; Ambassador: AMOAKON EJAMPAN THIEMELE.
Cuba: 1 Xiu Shui Nan Jie, Jian Guo Men Wai, Beijing; tel. (01) 5321714; telex 22249; Ambassador: JOSÉ ARMANDO GUERRA MENCHERO.
Cyprus: 2-13-2, Tayuan Diplomatic Office Bldg, Liang Ma He Nan Lu, Chao Yang Qu, Beijing 100600; tel. (01) 5325057; fax (01) 5325060; Ambassador: SOTIRIOS C. ZACHEOS.
Czechoslovakia: Ri Tan Lu, Jian Guo Men Wai, Beijing; tel. (01) 5321531; telex 222553; Ambassador: BORIVOJ CUDA.
Denmark: 1 Dong Wu Jie, San Li Tun, Beijing; tel. (01) 5322431; telex 22255; Ambassador: ARNE BELLING.
Ecuador: 2–41 San Li Tun, Beijing; telex 22710; Ambassador: Dr RODRIGO VÁLDEZ BAQUERO.
Egypt: 2 Ri Tan Dong Lu, Beijing; tel. (01) 5322541; telex 22134; Ambassador: BADR HAMMAM.
Equatorial Guinea: 2 Dong Si Jie, San Li Tun, Beijing; tel. (01) 5323709; Ambassador: LINO-SIMA EKUA AVOMO.
Ethiopia: 3 Xiu Shui Nan Jie, Jian Guo Men Wai, Beijing; telex 22306; Ambassador: PHILIPPOS WOLDE-MARIAM.
Finland: Tayuan Diplomatic Office Bldg, 1-10-1, Beijing; tel. (01) 5321806; telex 22129; fax (01) 5321884; Ambassador: ARTO MANSALA.
France: 3 Dong San Jie, San Li Tun, Beijing; tel. (01) 5321331; telex 22183; Ambassador: CLAUDE MARTIN.
Gabon: 36 Guang Hua Lu, Beijing; tel. (01) 5322810; telex 22110; Ambassador: HUBERT OKOUMA.
Germany: 5 Dong Zhi Men Wai Dajie, Beijing 100600; tel. (01) 5322161; telex 22259; Ambassador: Dr HANNSPETER HELLBECK.
Ghana: 8 San Li Tun Lu, Beijing; tel. (01) 5322288; Ambassador: JONAS AWUKU AFARI.
Greece: 19 Guang Hua Lu, Beijing; tel. (01) 5321317; telex 22267; Ambassador: EMMANUEL E. MEGALOKONOMOS.
Guinea: 7 Dong San Jie, San Li Tun, Beijing; tel. (01) 5323649; telex 22706; Ambassador: ABOU CAMARA.
Guyana: 1 Xiu Shui Dong Jie, Jian Guo Men Wai, Beijing; tel. (01) 5321601; telex 22295; Ambassador: PETER W. DENNY.
Hungary: 10 Dong Zhi Men Wai Dajie, Beijing; tel. (01) 5321683; telex 22679; Ambassador: IVAN NÉMETH.
Iceland: Beijing; Ambassador BENEDIKT GRÖNDAL.
India: 1 Ri Tan Dong Lu, Beijing; tel. (01) 5321927; telex 22126; Ambassador: CHETPUT VENKATASUBBAN RANGANATHAN.
Indonesia: Beijing; Ambassador: ABDURRAHMAN GUNADIRDJA.
Iran: Dong Liu Ji, San Li Tun, Beijing; tel. (01) 5322040; telex 22253; Ambassador: ALA ED-DIN BROUJERDI.
Iraq: 3 Ri Tan Dong Lu, Chao Yang Qu, Beijing; tel. (01) 5321950; telex 22288; Ambassador: MOHAMED AMIN AHMED AL-JAF.
Ireland: 3 Ri Tan Dong Lu, Beijing; tel. (01) 5322691; telex 22425; Ambassador: GEAROID O'BROIN.
Italy: 2 Dong Er Jie, San Li Tun, Beijing 100600; tel. (01) 5322131; telex 22414; fax (01) 5324676; Ambassador: OLIVIERO ROSSI.
Japan: 7 Ri Tan Lu, Jian Guo Men Wai, Beijing; tel. (01) 5322361; telex 22275; Ambassador: HIROSHI HASHIMOTO.
Jordan: 54 Dong Liu Jie, San Li Tun, Beijing; tel. (01) 5323906; telex 22651; Ambassador: WALID AL-SADD AL-BATAYNEH.
Kenya: 4 Xi Liu Jie, San Li Tun, Beijing; tel. (01) 5323381; telex 22311; Ambassador: JELANI HABIB.
Korea, Democratic People's Republic: Ri Tan Bei Lu, Jian Guo Men Wai, Beijing; telex 20448; Ambassador: (vacant).
Kuwait: 23 Guang Hua Lu, Beijing; tel. (01) 5322216; telex 22127; Ambassador: (vacant).
Laos: 11 Dong Jie, San Li Tun, Chao Yang Qu, Beijing 100600; tel. (01) 5321244; telex 22144; Ambassador: PHONGSAVATH BOUPHA.
Lebanon: 51 Dong Liu Jie, San Li Tun, Beijing; tel. (01) 5322770; telex 22113; Ambassador: FARID SAMAHA.

Libya: 55 Dong Liu Jie, San Li Tun, Beijing; telex 22310; Secretary of the People's Bureau: ABD AL-HAMID AL-ZINTANI.
Luxembourg: 21 Nei Wu Bu Jie, Beijing; tel. (01) 556175; telex 22638; Ambassador: PAUL SCHULLER.
Madagascar: 3 Dong Jie, San Li Tun, Beijing; tel. (01) 5321353; telex 22140; Ambassador: JEAN-JACQUES MAURICE.
Malaysia: 13 Dong Zhi Men Wai Dajie, San Li Tun, Beijing; tel. (01) 5322531; telex 22122; Ambassador: Dato NOOR ADLAN YAHAYAUDDIN.
Mali: 8 Dong Si Jie, San Li Tun, Beijing; tel. (01) 5321704; telex 22257; Ambassador: NAKOUNTE DIAKITÉ.
Malta: 2-2-71 Jian Guo Men Wai, Beijing; tel. (01) 5323114; telex 22670; Ambassador: RICHARD LAPIRA.
Mauritania: 9 Dong San Jie, San Li Tun, Beijing; tel. (01) 5321346; telex 22514; Ambassador: TAKI OULD SIDI.
Mexico: 5 Dong Wu Jie, San Li Tun, Beijing; tel. (01) 5322122; telex 22262; Ambassador: JORGE EDUARDO NAVARRETE.
Mongolia: 2 Xiu Shui Bei Jie, Jian Guo Men Wai, Beijing; tel. (01) 5321203; telex 22262; Ambassador: (vacant).
Morocco: 16 San Li Tun Lu, Beijing; tel. (01) 5321489; telex 22268; Ambassador: ABDERRAHIM BOUCHAARA.
Mozambique: San Li Tun, Entrance No. L, 8th Floor, Beijing; tel. (01) 523664; telex 22705; Ambassador: DANIEL BANZE.
Myanmar: 6 Dong Zhi Men Wai Dajie, Chao Yang Qu, Beijing; tel. (01) 5321584; telex 10416; Ambassador: U TIN AUNG TUN.
Nepal: 1 San Li Tun Xiliujie, Beijing; tel. (01) 5321795; telex 210408; Ambassador: NAYAN BAHADUR KHATRI.
Netherlands: 1-15-2 Tayuan Diplomatic Office Bldg, 14 Liang Ma He Nan Lu, Beijing; tel. (01) 5321131; telex 22277; Ambassador: Dr ROLAND VAN DEN BERG.
New Zealand: 1 Ri Tan, Dong Er Jie, Chaoyang Qu, Beijing 100600; tel. (01) 5322731; telex 22124; fax (01) 5324317; Ambassador: MICHAEL J. POWLES.
Niger: 50 Dong Liu Jie, San Li Tun, Beijing; tel. (01) 5321616; telex 22133; Ambassador: ISSOUFOU MAYAKI.
Nigeria: 2 Dong Wu Jie, San Li Tun, Beijing; telex 22274; Ambassador: E. N. OBA.
Norway: 1 San Li Tun, Dong Yi Jie, Beijing; tel. (01) 5322261; telex 22266; fax (01) 5322392; Ambassador: JAN TORE HOLVIK.
Oman: 6 Liang Ma He Nan Lu, San Li Tun, Beijing; tel. (01) 5323956; telex 22192; Ambassador: MUSHTAQ BIN ABDULLAH BIN JAFFER AL-SALEH.
Pakistan: 1 Dong Zhi Men Wai Dajie, Beijing; tel. (01) 5322504; Ambassador: AKRAM ZAKI.
Peru: 2–82 San Li Tun, Beijing; tel. (01) 5324658; telex 22278; fax (01) 5322178; Ambassador: ROBERTO VILLARÁN KOECHLIN.
Philippines: 23 Xiu Shui Bei Jie, Jian Guo Men Wai, Beijing; tel. (01) 5323420; telex 22132; Ambassador: FELIPE MABILANGAN.
Poland: 1 Ri Tan Lu, Jian Guo Men Wai, Beijing; tel. (01) 5321235; Ambassador: ZBIGNIEW DEMBOWSKI.
Portugal: 2–72 San Li Tun, Beijing; tel. (01) 5323220; telex 22326; fax (01) 5324637; Ambassador: JOSÉ MANUEL VILLAS-BOAS.
Qatar: Beijing; Ambassador: MOHAMED SAAD AL-FAHID.
Romania: Jian Guo Men Wai, Xiushui, Beijing; tel. (01) 5323255; telex 22250; Ambassador: ANGELO MICULESCU.
Rwanda: 30 Xiu Shui Bei Jie, Beijing; tel. (01) 5322193; telex 22104; Ambassador: KARAMAGE AUGUSTIN.
Saudi Arabia: Beijing; Ambassador: TAWFIQ AL-ALAMDAR.
Senegal: 1 Ri Tan Dong Yi Jie, Jian Guo Men Wai, Beijing; tel. (01) 5322576; telex 22100; Ambassador: MADY NDAO.
Sierra Leone: 7 Dong Zhi Men Wai Dajie, Beijing; tel. (01) 5321222; telex 22166; Ambassador: SHEKU BADARA BASTRU DUMBUYA.
Singapore: 4 Liang Ma He Nan Lu, San Li Tun, Beijing 100600; tel. (01) 5323926; Ambassador: (to be appointed).
Somalia: 2 San Li Tun Lu, Beijing; tel. (01) 5321752; telex 22121; Ambassador: MOHAMED HASSAN SAID.
Spain: 9 San Li Tun Lu, Beijing; tel. (01) 5323742; telex 22108; fax (01) 5323401; Ambassador: EUGENIO BREGOLAT Y OBIOLS.
Sri Lanka: 3 Jian Hua Lu, Jian Guo Men Wai, Beijing 100600; tel. (01) 5321861; telex 22136; Ambassador: SUHITA GAUTAMADASA.
Sudan: 1 Dong Er Jie, San Li Tun, Beijing; telex 22116; Ambassador: ANMAR EL-HADI ABDEL RAHMAN.
Sweden: 3 Dong Zhi Men Wai Dajie, Beijing; tel. (01) 5323331; telex 22261; Ambassador: BJÖRN INGVAR SKALA.
Switzerland: 3 Dong Wu Jie, San Li Tun, Beijing 100600; tel. (01) 5322736; telex 22251; fax (01) 5324353; Ambassador: Dr ERWIN SCHURTENBERGER.

THE PEOPLE'S REPUBLIC OF CHINA

Syria: 6 Dong Si Jie, San Li Tun, Beijing; telex 22138; Ambassador: LOUTOF ALLAH HAYDAR.
Tanzania: 53 Dong Liu Jie, San Li Tun, Beijing; tel. (01) 5321408; telex 22749; Ambassador: FERDINAND K. RUHINDA.
Thailand: 40 Guang Hua Lu, Beijing; tel. (01) 5321903; telex 22145; fax (01) 5323986; Ambassador: TEJ BUNNAG.
Togo: 11 Dong Zhi Men Wai Dajie, Beijing; tel. (01) 5322202; telex 22130; Ambassador: YAO BLOUA AGBO.
Tunisia: 1 Dong Jie, San Li Tun, Beijing; tel. (01) 5322435; telex 22103; Ambassador: SALAH JEBALI.
Turkey: 9 Dong Wu Jie, San Li Tun, Beijing; tel. (01) 5322650; telex 210168; fax (01) 5323268; Ambassador: BILAL SIMSIR.
Uganda: 5 Dong Jie, San Li Tun, Beijing; tel. (01) 5322370; telex 22272; fax (01) 5322242; Ambassador: WILLIAM WYCLIFFE RWETSIBA.
USSR: 4 Dong Zhi Men Wai Zhong Jie, Beijing; telex 22247; Ambassador: NIKOLAI N. SOLOVYEV.
United Kingdom: 11 Guang Hua Lu, Jian Guo Men Wai, Beijing; tel. (01) 5321961; telex 211216; fax (01) 5321961; Ambassador: Sir ALAN EWEN DONALD.
USA: 3 Xiu Shui Bei Jie, Beijing 100600; tel. (01) 5323831; telex 22701; fax (01) 5323178; Ambassador: JAMES RODERICK LILLEY.
Uruguay: 2-7-2 Tayuan Bldg, Beijing; tel. (01) 5324445; telex 211237; fax (01) 5324357; Ambassador: GUILLERMO VALLES GALMES.
Venezuela: 14 San Li Tun Lu, Beijing; tel. (01) 5321295; telex 22137; Ambassador: (vacant).
Viet-Nam: 32 Guang Hua Lu, Jian Guo Men Wai, Beijing; Ambassador: DANG NGHIEM HOANH.
Yemen Arab Republic: 4 Dongzhi Men Wai Dajie, Beijing; tel. (01) 5323346; Ambassador: GHALEB SAEED AL-ADOOFI.*
Yemen, People's Democratic Republic: 5 Dong San Jie, San Li Tun, Beijing; telex 22279; fax (01) 5324305; Ambassador: IBRAHIM ABDULLA SAIDI.*
Yugoslavia: 1 Dong Liu Jie, San Li Tun, Beijing; tel. (01) 5323516; telex 22403; Ambassador: ILIJA DJUKIĆ.
Zaire: 6 Dong Wu Jie, San Li Tun, Beijing; tel. (01) 421966; telex 22273; Ambassador: LOMBO LO MANGAMANGA.
Zambia: 5 Dong Si Jie, San Li Tun, Beijing; tel. (01) 5321554; telex 22388; Ambassador: PETER LESA KASANDA.
Zimbabwe: 7 Dong San Jie, Beijing; tel. (01) 5321652; telex 22671; Ambassador: NICHOLAS TASUNUNGURWA GOCHE.

* Merged in May 1990.

Judicial System

The general principles of the Chinese judicial system are laid down in Articles 123–135 of the December 1982 constitution (q.v.).

PEOPLE'S COURTS

Supreme People's Court: Dongjiaomin Xiang, Beijing; tel. (01) 550131; f. 1949; the highest judicial organ of the state; directs and supervises work of lower courts (few cases are tried directly by the Supreme Court); its judgments and rulings are final; Pres. REN JIANXIN (five-year term of office coincides with that of National People's Congress, by which the President is elected).
Local People's Courts: comprise higher courts, intermediate courts and 'grass root' courts.
Special People's Courts: include military tribunals, maritime courts and railway transport courts.

PEOPLE'S PROCURATORATES

Supreme People's Procuratorate: Donganmen Beiheyan, Beijing; tel. (01) 550831; acts for the National People's Congress in examining govt depts, civil servants and citizens, to ensure observance of the law; prosecutes in criminal cases. Procurator-Gen. LIU FUZHI (elected by the National People's Congress for five years).
Local People's Procuratorates: undertake the same duties at the local level. Ensure that the judicial activities of the people's courts, the execution of sentences in criminal cases, and the activities of departments in charge of reform through labour, conform to the law; institute, or intervene in, important civil cases which affect the interest of the state and the people.

Religion

During the 'Cultural Revolution' places of worship were closed. After 1977 the Government adopted a policy of religious tolerance, and the 1982 Constitution states that citizens enjoy freedom of religious belief, and that legitimate religious activities are protected. Many temples, churches and mosques have reopened.
Bureau of Religious Affairs: 22 Xianmen Dajie, 100017 Beijing; tel. (01) 652625; Dir REN WUZHI.

ANCESTOR WORSHIP

Ancestor worship is believed to have originated with the deification and worship of all important natural phenomena. The divine and human were not clearly defined; all the dead became gods and were worshipped by their descendants. The practice has no code or dogma and the ritual is limited to sacrifices made during festivals and on birth and death anniversaries.

BUDDHISM

Buddhism was introduced into China from India in AD 67, and flourished during the Sui and Tang dynasties (6th–8th century) when eight sects were established. The Chan and Pure Land sects are the most popular. There were 100m. believers in 1990.
Buddhist Association of China (BAC): f. 1953; Pres. ZHAO PUCHU; Sec.-Gen. ZHOU SHAOLIANG.
14th Dalai Lama: His Holiness TENZIN GYATSO, Thekchen Choeling, McLeod Ganj 176219, Dharamsala, Himachal Pradesh, India; spiritual leader of Tibet; fled to India after Tibetan uprising in 1959.
Tibetan Institute of Lamaism: Pres. BUMI JANGBALUOCHU; Vice-Pres. CEMOLIN DANZENGCHILIE.

CHRISTIANITY

During the 19th century and the first half of the 20th century, large numbers of foreign Christian missionaries worked in China. According to official sources, there were 5m. Protestants and 4m. Catholics in China in 1990, although unofficial sources estimate that the total is several times greater. In December 1989 a Catholic church was permitted to reopen in Beijing, bringing the total number of functioning Catholic churches there to five. Beijing had an estimated 40,000 Catholics in late 1989.
Three-Self Patriotic Movement Committee of Protestant Churches of China: Chair. DING GUANGXUN; Sec.-Gen. SHEN DERONG.
China Christian Council: 169 Yuan Ming Yuan Lu, Shanghai 200002; tel. (021) 3213396; f. 1980; comprises provincial Christian councils; Pres. Bishop DING GUANGXUN; Gen. Sec. Bishop ZHENG JIANYE.
Anglican Church: 169 Yuan Ming Yuan Lu, Shanghai; tel. (021) 3210806; Chair. of Council Bishop DING GUANGXUN.
The Roman Catholic Church: Catholic Mission, Si-She-Ku, Beijing; Bishop of Beijing (vacant).
Chinese Patriotic Catholic Association: Chair. Mgr ZONG HUAIDE; Sec.-Gen. ZHU SHICHANG; c. 3m. mems (1988).

CONFUCIANISM

Confucianism is a philosophy and a system of ethics, without ritual or priesthood. The respects that adherents accord to Confucius are not bestowed on a prophet or god, but on a great sage whose teachings promote peace and good order in society and whose philosophy encourages moral living.

DAOISM

Daoism was founded by Zhang Daoling during the Eastern Han dynasty (AD 125–144). Lao Zi, a philosopher of the Zhou dynasty (born 604 BC), is its principal inspiration, and is honoured as Lord the Most High by Daoists.
China Daoist Association: Temple of the White Cloud, Xi Bian Men, 100045 Beijing; tel. (01) 367179; f. 1957; Chair. LI YUHANG; Sec.-Gen. LI WENCHENG.

ISLAM

According to Muslim history, Islam was introduced into China in AD 651. There were almost 20m. adherents in China in 1990, chiefly among the Wei Wuer (Uighur) and Hui people.
Beijing Islamic Association: Dongsi Mosque, Beijing; f. 1979; Chair. Imam Al-Hadji SALAH AN SHIWEI.
China Islamic Association: Beijing; f. 1953; Pres. Al-Hodji ILYAS SHEN XIAXI; Sec.-Gen. MA XIAN.

The Press

In 1988 China had 2,191 newspaper titles and 5,865 magazine titles. Each province publishes its own daily. Only the major newspapers

THE PEOPLE'S REPUBLIC OF CHINA   Directory

and periodicals are listed below, and only a restricted number are allowed abroad.

PRINCIPAL NEWSPAPERS

Beijing Ribao (Beijing Daily): 34 Xi Biaobei Hutong, Dongdan, Beijing; tel. (01) 553431; f. 1952; organ of the Beijing municipal cttee of the CCP; Dir MAN YUNLAI; Editor-in-Chief LIU HUSHAN; circ. 1m.

Beijing Wanbao (Beijing Evening News): 34 Xi Biaobei Hutong, Dongdan, Beijing; tel. (01) 553431; telex 283642; f. 1958; Editor GU XING; circ. 500,000.

Can Kao Xiao Xi (Reference News): Beijing; reprints from foreign newspapers; publ. by Xinhua (New China) News Agency; circ. 3.6m.

China Daily: 15 Huixin Dongjie, Chaoyang District, Beijing 100029; tel. (01) 4220955; telex 22022; fax (01) 4220922; f. 1981; English; coverage: China's political, economic and cultural developments; world, financial and sports news; Editor-in-Chief CHEN LI; circ. 150,000.

Dazhong Ribao (Masses Daily): 99 Lishan Lu, Jinan, Shandong Province; tel. 47951; telex 9993; f. 1939; circ. 600,000; Editor-in-Chief LIU HONGXI.

Fujian Ribao (Fujian Daily): Hualin Lu, Fuzhou, Fujian Province; tel. 57756; daily; Editor-in-Chief LIN ZHENXIA.

Gongren Ribao (Workers' Daily): Liupukeng, Andingmen Wai, Beijing; tel. (01) 4211561; telex 210423; fax (01) 4214890; f. 1949; trade union activities and workers' lives; also major home and overseas news; Editor-in-Chief LI JI; circ. 2.5m.

Guangming Ribao (Guangming Daily): 106 Yongan Lu, 100050 Beijing; tel. (01) 338561; telex 20021; f. 1949; literature, art, science, education, history, economics, philosophy; Editor-in-Chief ZHANG CHANGHAI; circ. 1.5m.

Guangzhou Ribao (Canton Daily): 10 Dongle Lu, Renmin Zhonglu, Guangzhou, Guangdong Province; tel. 85812; f. 1952; daily; economic and current affairs; Editor-in-Chief HUANG YONGZHAN.

Guizhou Ribao (Guizhou Daily): Guiying, Guizhou Province; circ. 300,000; Editor-in-Chief LIU XUEZHU.

Hebei Ribao (Hebei Daily): Yuhua Lu, Shijiazhuang 050013, Hebei Province; tel. 48901; f. 1949; Editor-in-Chief YE ZHEN.

Hubei Ribao (Hubei Daily): 4 Dongting 2 Lu, Wuhan 430077, Hubei Province; tel. 814531; telex 5590; f. 1949; Chief Officer ZHOU CHUANREN; circ. 800,000.

Jiangxi Ribao (Jiangxi Daily): Nanchang, Jiangxi Province; f. 1949; Editor-in-Chief JIANG HUINENG.

Jiefang Ribao (Liberation Daily): 274 Han Kou Lu, Shanghai; tel. (021) 3221300; telex 6078; f. 1949; Chief Editor CHEN NIANYUN; circ. 1m.

Jiefangjun Bao (Liberation Army Daily): Beijing; f. 1956; official organ of the Central Military Comm.; Dir LU LIANG; Editor-in-Chief WU ZHIFEI; circ. 800,000.

Jingji Ribao (Economic Daily): 9 Xi Huangchengen Nanjie, Beijing; tel. (01) 652018; fax (01) 5125015; f. 1983; financial affairs, domestic and foreign trade; Editor-in-Chief FAN JINGYI; circ. 1.59m.

Nanfang Ribao (Nanfang Daily): Dongfeng Donglu, Guangzhou, Guangdong Province; tel. 77022; f. 1949; Dir DING XILING; Editor-in-Chief ZHANG CONG; circ. 1m.

Nongmin Ribao (Peasants' Daily): Shilipu Beili, Chao Yang Men Wai, Beijing; tel. (01) 583431; telex 6592; f. 1980; 6 a week; circulates in rural areas nation-wide; Editor-in-Chief ZHANG GUANGYOU; circ. 1m.

Qingdao Ribao (Qingdao Daily): 33 Taiping Lu, Qingdao, Shandong Province; tel. 86237; f. 1949; daily; circ. 2.6m.

Renmin Ribao (People's Daily): 2 Jin Tai Xi Lu, Beijing; tel. (01) 5092121; telex 22320; fax (01) 5091982; f. 1948; organ of the CCP; also publishes overseas edn; Dir GAO DI; Editor-in-Chief SHAO HUAZE; circ. 5m.

Shanxi Ribao (Shanxi Daily): Shuangtasi, Taiyuan, Shanxi Province; tel. 24835; Dir WANG XIYI; Editor-in-Chief CHEN MOZHANG.

Shenzhen Tequ Bao (Shenzhen Special Zone Daily): 1 Shennan Zhonglu, Shenzhen; tel. 22840; f. 1982; reports on special economic zones, as well as Hong Kong and Macau; Editor-in-Chief LUO MIAO.

Sichuan Ribao (Sichuan Daily): 70 Hongxing Zhonglu, Chengdu, Sichuan Province; tel. 22911; f. 1952; circ. 1.35m.; Editor-in-Chief YAO ZHINENG.

Tianjin Ribao (Tianjin Daily): 66 An Shan Lu, Heping Qu, Tianjin; tel. 25803; f. 1949; Editor-in-Chief LU SI; circ. 600,000.

Wenhui Bao: 149 Yuanmingyuan Lu, Shanghai; tel. (021) 3211410; telex 33080; f. 1938; Editor-in-Chief MA DA; circ. 1.7m.

Xin Min Wan Bao (Xin Min Evening News): Jiujianlu 41, Shanghai; tel. (021) 3217307; f. 1946; Dir ZHAO CHAOGOU; circ. 1,365,768.

Xinhua Ribao (New China Daily): 55 Zhongshan Lu, Nanjing, Jiangsu Province; tel. 42638; circ. 900,000.

Yangcheng Wanbao (Yangcheng Evening Post): 733 Dongfeng Donglu, Guangzhou, Guangdong Province; tel. 776211; f. 1957; circ. 1.66m.

Zhongguo Qingnian Bao (China Youth News): 2 Haiyuncang, Dongzhimen Nei, Beijing; tel. (01) 446581; f. 1951; 4 a week; aimed at 14–25 age-group; Dir LI ZHILUN; Editor-in-Chief XU ZHUQING; circ. 3m.

SELECTED PERIODICALS

Ban Yue Tan (Fortnightly Review): Beijing; tel. (01) 668521; f. 1980; in Chinese and Wei Wuer (Uighur); Editor-in-Chief MIN FANLU; circ. 5.3m.

Beijing Review: 24 Baiwanzhuang Lu, Beijing 100037; tel. (01) 8314318; telex 222374; fax (01) 8314318; weekly; edns in English, French, Spanish, Japanese and German; also **Chinafrica** (monthly in English); Editor-in-Chief GENG YUXIN (acting).

Chinese Literature Press: 24 Baiwanzhuang Lu, Beijing 100037; tel. (01) 892554; telex 222374; f. 1951; quarterly; in English and French; contemporary and classical writing, poetry, literary criticism and arts; Editor-in-Chief WANG MENG.

Chinese Science Abstracts: Science Press, 16 Donghuangchenggen Beijie, Beijing 100707; tel. (01) 4018833; telex 210247; fax (01) 4012180; f. 1982; monthly in English; science and technology; Chief Editor YAN MINGWEN.

Dianying Xinzuo (New Films): 796 Huaihai Zhonglu, Shanghai; tel. (021) 4379710; f. 1979; bi-monthly; introduces new films.

Dianzi yu Diannao (Electronics and Computers): Beijing; f. 1985; popularized information on computers and microcomputers.

Feitian (Fly Skywards): 50 Donggan Xilu, Lanzhou, Gansu; tel. 25803; f. 1961; monthly.

Guoji Xin Jishu (New International Technology): Zhanwang Publishing House, Beijing; f. 1984; also publ. in Hong Kong; international technology, scientific and technical information.

Guowai Keji Dongtai (Scientific and Technical Trends Abroad): Institute of Scientific and Technical Information of China, 15 Fuxing Lu, Beijing 100038; tel. (01) 8015544; telex 20079; fax (01) 8014025; f. 1969; scientific journal.

Hai Xia (The Strait): 27 De Gui Xiang, Fuzhou, Fujian Province; tel. (01) 33656; f. 1981; quarterly; literary journal; Prin. Officers YANG YU, JWO JONG LIN.

Huasheng Bao (Voice of Overseas Chinese): 12 Bai Wan Zhuang Nan Jie, Beijing 100037; tel. (01) 8315039; f. 1983; 2 a week; intended mainly for overseas Chinese and Chinese nationals resident abroad; Pres. and Editor-in-Chief ZHOU TI.

Jianzhu (Construction): Baiwanzhuang, Beijing; tel. (01) 8992849; f. 1956; monthly; Editor FANG YUEGUANG; circ. 500,000.

Jinri Zhongguo (China Today): 24 Baiwanzhuang Lu, Beijing 100037; tel. (01) 892190; fax (01) 8022338; f. 1952; fmrly *China Reconstructs*; monthly; edns in English, Spanish, French, Arabic, Portuguese, Chinese and German; economic, social and cultural affairs; illustrated; Dir and Editor-in-Chief MENG JIQING.

Liaowang (Outlook): 57 Xuanwumen Xijie, Beijing; tel. (01) 3073049; f. 1981; weekly; current affairs; Gen. Man. FENG LI; Editor CHEN DABIN; circ. 500,000.

Luxingjia (Traveller): 23A Dong Jiaomin Xiang, Beijing; tel. (01) 552631; f. 1955; monthly; Chinese scenery, customs, culture.

Meishu Zhi You (Friends of Art): 32 Beizongbu Hutong, East City Region, Beijing; tel. (01) 5122583; telex 5019; f. 1982; every 2 months; art review journal, also providing information on fine arts publs in China and abroad; Editors PENG SHEN, BAOLUN WU.

Nianqingren (Young People): 169 Mayuanlin, Changsha, Hunan Province; tel. 23610; f. 1981; monthly; general interest for young people.

Nongye Zhishi (Agricultural Knowledge): 7 Shimuyuan Dongjie, Jinan, Shandong; tel. 42238; f. 1950; fortnightly; popular agricultural science; Dir YIANG XIANFEN; circ. 400,000.

Qiushi (Seeking Truth): 2 Shatan Beijie, Beijing 100727; tel. (01) 4011155; telex 1219; f. 1988 to succeed *Hong Qi* (Red Flag); every 2 months; theoretical journal of the CCP; Editor-in-Chief YOU LIN; circ. 1.83m.

Renmin Huabao (China Pictorial): Huayuancun, West Suburbs, Beijing 100044; tel. (01) 8411144; f. 1950; monthly; edns: 2 in Chinese, 4 in minority languages and 15 in foreign languages; Dir and Editor-in-Chief FING YAN.

Shichang Zhoubao (Market Weekly): 2 Duan, Sanhao Jie, Heping Qu, Shenyang, Liaoning Province; tel. 482983; f. 1979; weekly in

Chinese; trade, commodities and financial and economic affairs; circ. 1m.

Shufa (Calligraphy): 83 Kangping Lu, Shanghai; tel. (021) 4377711; telex 5928; f. 1977; every 2 months; journal on ancient and modern calligraphy; Chief Editor CAI DATUAN.

Tiyu Kexue (Sports Science): 8 Tiyuguan Lu, Beijing; tel. (01) 757161; f. 1981; sponsored by the China Sports Science Soc.; quarterly; in Chinese; circ. 20,000.

Wenxue Qingnian (Youth Literature Journal): Mu Tse Fang 27, Wenzhou, Zhejiang Province; tel. 3578; f. 1981; monthly; Editor-in-Chief CHEN YUSHEN; circ. 80,000.

Xian Dai Faxue (Modern Law Science): Chongqing 630031, Sichuan Province; tel. 661671; f. 1979; bi-monthly; theoretical law journal, with summaries in English; Dirs LI GUOZHI, XU JINGCUN.

Yinyue Aihaozhe (Music Lovers): 74 Shaoxing Lu, Shanghai 200020; tel. (021) 4372608; telex 33384; fax (021) 4332452; f. 1979; every 2 months; popular music knowledge; illustrated; Editor-in-Chief CHEN XUEYA; circ. 50,000.

Zhongguo Duiwai Maoyi (China's Foreign Trade): 1 Fu Xing Men Wai Jie, Beijing; tel. (01) 863790; telex 22315; fax (01) 8011370; f. 1956; monthly; edns in Chinese, English, French and Spanish; carries information about Chinese imports and exports and explains foreign trade and economic policies; Editor-in-Chief LIU DEYU.

Zhongguo Ertong (Chinese Children): 21, Xiang 12, Dongsi, Beijing; tel. (01) 444761; telex 4357; f. 1980; monthly; illustrated journal for elementary school pupils.

Zhongguo Funu (Women of China): 24A Shijia Hutong, Beijing; tel. (01) 551765; f. 1956; monthly; women's rights and status, marriage and family, education, family planning, arts, cookery, etc.; Editor-in-Chief Ms WANG XIULIN.

Zhongguo Guanggao Bao (China's Advertising): Editorial Dept, Beijing Exhibition Hall, Xizhimen Wai, Beijing; tel. (01) 890661; f. 1984; weekly; all aspects of advertising and marketing; offers advertising services for domestic and foreign commodities.

Zhongguo Guangbo Dianshi (China Radio and Television): 12 Fucheng Lu, Beijing; tel. (01) 896217; f. 1982; monthly; sponsored by Ministry of Radio, Film and Television; reports and comments.

Zhongguo Sheying (Chinese Photography): 61 Hongxing Hutong, Dongdan, Beijing 100005; tel. (01) 552277; f. 1957; every 2 months; photographs and comments; Editor LIU BANG.

Zhongguo Xinwen (China News): 12 Baiwanzhuang Nanjie, Beijing; tel. (01) 8315012; f. 1952; daily; current affairs.

Zhongguo Zhenjiu (Chinese Acupuncture and Moxibustion): China Academy of Traditional Chinese Medicine, Dongzhimen Nei, Beijing 100700; tel. (01) 4014411; telex 210340; f. 1981; 2 a month; publ. by Chinese Soc. of Acupuncture and Moxibustion; partly in English; Editor-in-Chief Prof. WANG BENXIAN.

NEWS AGENCIES

Xinhua (New China) News Agency: 57 Xuanwumen Xidajie, Beijing 100803; tel. (01) 3073767; telex 22316; f. 1931; offices in all Chinese provincial capitals, and about 95 overseas bureaux; news service in Chinese, English, French, Spanish, Arabic and Russian, feature and photographic services; Pres. MU QING; Editor-in-Chief NAN ZHENZHONG.

Zhongguo Xinwen She (China News Agency): POB 1114, Beijing; f. 1952; office in Hong Kong; supplies news features, special articles and photographs for newspapers and magazines in Chinese printed overseas; services in Chinese; Dir WANG SHIGU.

Foreign Bureaux

Agence France-Presse (AFP) (France): 11-11 Jian Guo Men Wai, Beijing; tel. (01) 5322371; Bureau Chief DENIS HIAULT.

Agencia EFE (Spain): 2-2-132 Jian Guo Men Wai, Beijing 100600; tel. (01) 5323449; telex 22167; fax (01) 5323688; Rep. ENRIQUE IBÁÑEZ.

Agenzia Nazionale Stampa Associata (ANSA) (Italy): 2-81 Ban Gong Lu, 2-81 San Li Tun, Beijing; tel. (01) 5321954; fax (01) 5323651; telex 22290; Correspondent BARBARA ALIGHIERO ANIMALI.

Allgemeiner Deutscher Nachrichtendienst (ADN) (Germany): Jian Guo Men Wai, Qi Jia Yuan Gong Yu 7-2-61, Beijing; telex 22109; Correspondent OTTO MANN.

Associated Press (AP) (USA): 7-2-52 Qi Jia Yuan, Diplomatic Quarters, Beijing; tel. (01) 5323419; telex 22196; Bureau Chief JAMES ABRAMS.

Bulgarska Telegrafna Agentsia (BTA) (Bulgaria): 1-4-13 Jian Guo Men Wai, Beijing; tel. (01) 5321226; telex 22128; Bureau Chief YEVGENI DRAGOMIROV DONCHEV.

Československá tisková kancelář (ČTK) (Czechoslovakia): 3-1-4 Qi Jia Yuan, Beijing 100600; tel. (01) 5321831, Ext. 348; telex 22105.

Deutsche Presse-Agentur (dpa) (Germany): Ban Gong Lu, San Li Tun, Apt 1-31, Beijing 100600; tel. (01) 5321473; telex 22297; fax (01) 5321615; Bureau Chief EDGAR BAUER.

Inter Press Service (IPS) (Italy): c/o ISTIC, Room 209, n. 15, Fu Xing Lu, POB 3811, Beijing; tel. (01) 863326; telex 20079; Dir WANG LIANHAI.

Jiji Tsushin-Sha (Japan): 9-1-13 Jian Guo Men Wai, Beijing; tel. (01) 5322924; telex 22381; fax (01) 5323413; Correspondent KENZO SHIDA.

Kyodo Tsushin (Japan): 3-91 Jian Guo Men Wai, Beijing; tel. (01) 522680; telex 8522324; Bureau Chief SHIGEYOSHI FUSE.

Magyar Távirati Iroda (MTI) (Hungary): 1-42 Ban Gong Lu, San Li Tun, Beijing; tel. (01) 5321744; telex 22106; Correspondent GÉZA FARKAS.

Prensa Latina (Cuba): 6 Wai Jiao Da Lu, Beijing; tel. (01) 521831; telex 22284; Correspondent JOSÉ LUIS ROBAINA.

Reuters (UK): 1-11 Ban Gong Lou, San Li Tun, Beijing; tel. (01) 5321921; telex 22702; fax 5324978; Chief Representative G. V. BERGER.

Telegrafnoye Agentstvo Sovetskovo Soyuza (TASS) (USSR): Jian Guo Men Wai, Qi Jia Yuan Gong Yu, Beijing; telex 22115; Correspondent GRIGORIY ARSLANOV.

United Press International (UPI) (USA): 7-1-11 Qi Jia Yuan, Beijing; tel. (01) 5323456; telex 22197; Correspondents DAVID R. SCHWEISBERG, SCOTT SAVITT.

The following are also represented: Agerpres (Romania), Korean Central News Agency (Democratic People's Republic of Korea), Tanjug (Yugoslavia) and VNA (Viet-Nam).

PRESS ASSOCIATIONS

All China Journalists' Association: Xijiaominxiang, Beijing; tel. (01) 657170; telex 222719; fax (01) 6014658; Exec. Chair. WU LENGXI; Exec. Vice-Chair. QIN CHUAN.

Association of Newspaper Industry: Beijing; Pres. BAO YUJUN.

Publishers

In 1988 there were 502 publishing houses in China, including a regional 'People's Publishing House' for each province. A total of 62,962 titles were published in that year.

The Press and Publication Administration of The People's Republic of China: Beijing; administers publishing, printing and distribution under the State Council; Dir SONG MUWEN.

Beijing Chubanshe (Beijing Publishing House): 6 Bei Sanhuan Dong Lu, Beijing; tel. (01) 2012339; f. 1956; political theory, history, philosophy, economics, geography, etc.

Beijing Daxue Chubanshe (Beijing University Press): Beijing University, Haidian District, 100871 Beijing; tel. (01) 2561166; telex 22239; f. 1979; academic and general.

Dianzi Gongye Chubanshe (Publishing House of the Electronics Industry): 27 Wanshou Lu, 100036 Beijing; tel. (01) 815245; f. 1982; natural sciences; Dir LIANG XIANGFENG; Editor-in-Chief ZHANG DIANGE.

Dolphin Books: 24 Baiwanzhuang Lu, Beijing 100037; tel. (01) 8311325; telex 22475; fax (01) 8317390; f. 1986; children's books in Chinese and foreign languages; Dir JIANG CHENGAN.

Falü Chubanshe (Law Publishing House): POB 111, 100036 Beijing; tel. (01) 815325; f. 1980; current laws and decrees, legal textbooks, translations of important foreign legal works; Dir LAN MINGLIANG.

Gaodeng Jiaoyu Chubanshe (Higher Education Press): 55 Shatan Houjie, Beijing 100009; tel. (01) 4014043; fax (01) 4014048; f. 1954; academic; Pres. ZU ZHENQUAN; Editor-in-Chief YANG LINGKANG.

Gongren Chubanshe (Workers' Press): Liupukeng, Andingmen Wai, Beijing; tel. (01) 4215278; f. 1949; labour movement, trade unions, science and technology related to industrial production.

Guangdong Keji Chubanshe (Guangdong Scientific and Technical Press): 11 Shuiyin Lu, Huanshidong Lu, Guangzhou 510075, Guangdong; tel. 768688; f. 1978; natural sciences, technology, agriculture, medicine; Dir OU YANGLIAN.

Guoji Shudian (China International Book Trading Corporation): POB 399, Chegongzhuang Xilu 21, Beijing; tel. (01) 891203; telex 22466; f. 1949; foreign trade org. specializing in pubs, including books, periodicals, art and crafts, microfilms, etc.; import and export distributors; Pres. LIU CHUANWEI.

Heilongjiang Kexue Jishu Chubanshe (Heilongjiang Scientific and Technical Publishing House): 28 Fenbu Jie, Nangang Qu, Harbin, Heilongjiang; tel. 35613; f. 1979; industrial and agricultural technology, natural sciences.

THE PEOPLE'S REPUBLIC OF CHINA

Huashan Wenyi Chubanshe (Huashan Literature and Art Publishing House): 45 Bei Malu, Shijiazhuang, Hebei; tel. 22501; f. 1982; novels, poetry, drama, etc.

Kexue Chubanshe (Science Press): 16 Donghuangchenggen Beijie, Beijing 100707; tel. (01) 441815; telex 210247; fax (01) 4012180; f. 1954; science and technology.

Lingnan Meishu Chubanshe (Lingnan Art Publishing House): 11 Shuiyin Lu, Guangzhou 510075, Guangdong; tel. 861251; f. 1981; works on classical and modern painting, picture albums, photographic, painting techniques; Editor-in-Chief HUANG SHUDE.

Minzu Chubanshe (Nationalities Publishing House): Hepingli Dong Lu, Beijie 14, 100013 Beijing; tel. (01) 4211261; f. 1953; books and periodicals in minority languages, e.g. Mongolian, Tibetan, Uigur, Korean, Kazakh, etc.; Editor-in-Chief ZHU YINGWU.

Qunzhong Chubanshe (Masses Publishing House): 14 Dongchangan Jie, Beijing 100741; tel. (01) 5121672; telex 2831; f. 1956; politics, law, judicial affairs, criminology, public security, etc.

Renmin Chubanshe (People's Publishing House): Dir XUE DEZHEN; Editor-in-Chief ZHANG HUIQING.

Renmin Jiaoyu Chubanshe (People's Education Press): 55 Shatan Hou Jie, Beijing 100009; tel. (01) 4010370; fax (01) 4010370; f. 1950; school textbooks, guidebooks, teaching materials, etc.

Renmin Meishu Chubanshe (People's Fine Arts Publishing House): 32 Beizongbu Hutong, 100735 Beijing; tel. (01) 5122371; fax (01) 5122370; f. 1951; works by Chinese and foreign painters, picture albums, photographic, painting techniques; Dir MENG WEIZAI; Editor-in-Chief LIU YUSHAN.

Renmin Weisheng Chubanshe (People's Medical Publishing House): 10 Tiantan Xi Li, Beijing 100050; tel. (01) 755431; f. 1953; medicine (Western and traditional Chinese), pharmacology, dentistry, public health; Pres. DONG MIANGUO.

Renmin Wenxue Chubanshe (People's Literature Publishing House): 166 Chaoyangmen Nei Dajie, Beijing 100705; tel. (01) 5138394; telex 2192; f. 1951; largest publr of literary works and translations into Chinese; Dir and Editor-in-Chief CHEN ZAOCHUN.

Shanghai Guji Chubanshe (Shanghai Classics Publishing House): 272 Ruijin Erlu, Shanghai; tel. (021) 4370013; f. 1978; classical Chinese literature.

Shanghai Jiaoyu Chubanshe (Shanghai Educational Publishing House): 123 Yongfu Lu, Shanghai; tel. (021) 4377165; telex 3413; f. 1958; academic.

Shanghai Yiwen Chubanshe (Shanghai Translation Publishing House): 14 Xiang 955, Yanan Zhonglu, Shanghai 200040; tel. (021) 4311890; f. 1978; translations of foreign classic and modern literature; philosophy, social sciences, dictionaries.

Shangwu Yinshuguan (Commercial Press): 36 Wangfujing Dajie, Beijing; tel. (01) 552026; f. 1897; dictionaries and reference books in Chinese and foreign languages, translations of foreign works on social sciences; Gen. Man. LIN ERWEI.

Shaonian Ertong Chubanshe (Juvenile and Children's Publishing House): 1538 Yanan Xi Lu, Shanghai; tel. (021) 2522519; telex 5801; f. 1952; Editor-in-Chief CHEN XIANGMING; children's educational and literary works, teaching aids and periodicals.

Waiwen Chubanshe (Foreign Language Press): 24 Baiwanzhuang Lu, Beijing 100037; tel. (01) 8317385; telex 222475; fax (01) 8317390; f. 1952; books in foreign languages reflecting political, economic and cultural progress in People's Republic of China; Dirs SHEN XIFEI, XU MINGQIANG.

Wenwu Chubanshe (Cultural Relics Publishing House): 29 Wusi Dajie, Beijing; tel. (01) 441761; f. 1956; books and catalogues of Chinese relics in museums and those recently discovered; Dir WANG DAIWEN.

World Culture Publishing House: Dir ZHU LIE.

Wuhan Daxue Chubanshe (Wuhan University Press): Wuhan University, Wuchang, Hubei; tel. 75941; f. 1952; academic.

Xiandai Chubanshe (Modern Press): 504 Anhua Li, Andingmenwai, Beijing; tel. (01) 4216251; telex 210215; f. 1981; directories, reference books, etc.

Xinhua Publishing House: Beijing; Dir XU BANG.

Xuelin Chubanshe (Scholar Books Publishers): 120 Wenmiao Lu, Shanghai; tel. (021) 3777108; f. 1981; academic, including personal academic works at authors' own expense; Dir LEI QUNMING; Editor-in-Chief LIU ZHAORUI.

Youyi Chubanshe (Friendship Publishing House): Editor-in-Chief HUO BAOZHEN.

Zhongguo Caizheng Jingji Chubanshe (China Financial and Economic Publishing House): 8 Dafosi Dongjie, Dongcheng District, Beijing; tel. (01) 4011805; f. 1961; finance, economics, commerce and accounting.

Zhongguo Dabaike Quanshu Chubanshe (Encyclopaedia of China Publishing House): 17 Fuchengmen Bei Dajie, Beijing 100037; tel. (01) 8315610; f. 1978; specializes in encyclopaedias; Dir MEI YI.

Zhongguo Ditu Chubanshe (China Cartographic Publishing House): 3 Baizhifang Xijie, Beijing 100054; tel. (01) 330808; f. 1954; cartographic publr; Dir ZHANG XUELIANG.

Zhongguo Funü Chubanshe (China Women's Publishing House): 24A Shijia Hutong, 100010 Beijing; tel. (01) 5126986; f. 1981; women's movement, marriage and family, child-care, etc.; Dir LI ZHONGXIU.

Zhongguo Qingnian Chubanshe (China Youth Publishing House): 21 Dongsi Shiertiao Hutong, Beijing 100708; tel. (01) 444761; telex 4357; f. 1950; literature, ethics, social and natural sciences, youth work, autobiography; also periodicals; Dir CAI YUN.

Zhongguo Shehui Kexue Chubanshe (China Social Sciences Publishing House): 158A Gulou Xidajie, Beijing; tel. (01) 441531; f. 1978; Dir YU SHUNYAO.

Zhongguo Xiju Chubanshe (China Theatrical Publishing House): 52 Dongsi Batiao Hutong, Beijing; tel. (01) 4015815; telex 0489; f. 1957; traditional and modern Chinese drama.

Zhonghua Shuju (Chung Hwa Book Co): 36 Wangfujing Dajie, Beijing; tel. (01) 554504; f. 1912; general; Gen. Man. WANG CHUNG.

PUBLISHERS' ASSOCIATION

Publishers' Association of China: Beijing; f. 1979; arranges academic exchanges with foreign publrs; Chair. WANG ZIYE; Sec.-Gen. SONG MUWEN.

Radio and Television

In 1987 there were 215 radio broadcasting stations and in 1984 575 transmitting and relay stations. In 1978, 63% of households in the countryside had loudspeakers connected to the radio rediffusion system. There were an estimated 150m. radio receivers in use in 1986.

There were 202 television stations and 2,050 transmitting and relay stations equipped with transmitters in 1989. There were an estimated 75m. television receivers in use.

Ministry of Radio, Film and Television: Fu Xing Men Wai Jie 2, POB 4501, Beijing; tel. (01) 862753; telex 22236; fax (01) 8012174; controls the Central People's Broadcasting Station, the Central TV Station, Radio Beijing, China Record Co., Beijing Broadcasting Institute, Broadcasting Research Institute, the China Broadcasting Art Troupe, etc.; Minister of Radio, Film and Television AI ZHISHENG.

RADIO

Central People's Broadcasting Station: Fu Xing Men Wai Jie 2, Beijing; domestic service in Chinese, Guanghua (Cantonese), Zang Wen (Tibetan), Chaozhou, Min Nan Hua (Amoy), Ke Jia (Hakka), Fuzhou Hua (Foochow dialect), Hasaka (Kazakh), Wei Wuer (Uygur), Menggu Hua (Mongolian) and Chaoxian (Korean); Dir YANG ZHENGQUAN.

Radio Beijing: 2 Fu Xing Men Wai Dajie, Beijing 100866; tel. (01) 862691; telex 222271; fax (01) 8013176; f. 1947; foreign service in 38 languages incl. Arabic, Burmese, Czech, English, Esperanto, French, German, Indonesian, Italian, Japanese, Lao, Polish, Portuguese, Russian, Spanish, Turkish and Vietnamese; Dir CUI YULIN.

TELEVISION

China Central Television Station: Bureau of Broadcasting Affairs of the State Council, Beijing; f. 1958; operates three channels; Dir HUANG HUIQUN.

Finance

BANKING

(cap. = capital; auth. = authorized; p.u. = paid up; res = reserves; dep. = deposits; m. = million; amounts in yuan)

Central Bank

People's Bank of China: Sanlihe, West City, Beijing; tel. (01) 863907; telex 22612; f. 1948; bank of issue; Gov. LI GUIXIAN; Deputy Gov. GUO ZHENGQIAN; 2,204 brs.

Other Banks

Agricultural Bank of China: 23 Fuxing Lu, Beijing; tel. (01) 011024, telex 22017, f. 1903, functions directly under the State Council and handles state agricultural investments; dep. 6,200m. (Aug. 1979); Pres. MA YONGWEI.

THE PEOPLE'S REPUBLIC OF CHINA

Bank of China: Bank of China Bldg, 410 Fuchengmen Nei Dajie, Beijing; tel. (01) 6016688; telex 22254; fax (01) 2015523; f. 1912; handles foreign exchange and international settlements; cap. p.u. 15,000m., dep. 451,304m. (Dec. 1989); Chair. and Pres. WANG DEYAN; 522 brs, 46 abroad.

Bank of Communications of China: 200 Jiang Xi Zhong Lu, Shanghai 200002; tel. (021) 3255900; telex 30247; fax (021) 3290566; f. 1908; commercial bank; cap. 2,499m., res 567m., dep. 104,569m. (Dec. 1988); Chair. LI XIANGREI; Pres. DAI XIANGLONG.

China and South Sea Bank Ltd: 17 Xi Jiao Min Xiang, Beijing; f. 1921; cap. 400m., res 361m., dep. 9,353m. (Dec. 1988); Chair. CUI PING.

China International Trust and Investment Corporation (CITIC): 19 Jianguomenwai Jie, 100004 Beijing; tel. (01) 5002255; telex 22305; fax (01) 5001525; f. 1979; economic and technological co-operation; assists foreign investors in establishing joint ventures or their solely-owned enterprises in China; registered; cap. 3,000m.; Chair. RONG YIREN; Pres. WEI MINGYI.

China Investment Bank: 27-B Wanshou Lu, Beijing; tel. (01) 863027; telex 22537; f. 1981; specializes in raising foreign funds for domestic investment and credit; Chair. ZHOU DAOJIONG; Pres. LU XIANLIN.

China Merchants Bank: I/F, China Merchants Bldg, Zhaoshang Lu, Shekou, Shenzhen; tel. 692988; telex 420818; f. 1987; cap. 421m., dep. 2,137m. (Dec. 1989); Pres. and Gen. Man. WANG SHIZHEN; Chair. YUAN GENG.

China State Bank Ltd: 17 Xi Jiao Min Xiang, Beijing; cap. 400m., res 235m., dep. 7,239m. (Dec. 1988); Gen. Man. LI PINZHOU.

Guangdong Provincial Bank: 17 Xi Jiao Min Xiang, Beijing; cap. and res 466m. (1983); Gen. Man. CHENG KEDONG.

Industrial and Commercial Bank of China: 13 Cuiwei Lu, Haidianqu, Beijing 100036; tel. (01) 8217925; telex 22770; fax (01) 8217920; f. 1984; handles industrial and commercial credits and international business; Pres. ZHANG XIAO.

Kincheng Banking Corporation: 17 Xi Jiao Min Xiang, Beijing; f. 1917; cap. 500m., res 565m., dep. 15,926m. (Dec. 1988). Gen. Man. XIANG KEFANG.

National Commercial Bank Ltd: 17 Xi Jiao Min Xiang, Beijing; f. 1907; cap. 400m., res 380m., dep. 10,167m. (Dec. 1988); Gen. Man. WANG WEICAI.

People's Construction Bank of China: 12 Fuxing Lu, Beijing 100810; tel. (01) 8014488; telex 222977; fax (01) 8015328; f. 1954; state-owned specialized bank; finances medium- and long-term projects; engaged in government investment management and credit banking; both domestic and international activities; total assets 407,493m., capital funds 28,103m., dep. 115,157m. (Dec. 1989); Pres. ZHOU DAOJIONG; 4,000 brs and sub-brs.

Sin Hua Trust, Savings and Commercial Bank Ltd: 17 Xi Jiao Min Xiang, Beijing; cap. 500m., res 581m., dep. 16,434m. (Dec. 1988); Gen. Man. CUI YANXU; 39 brs.

Yien Yieh Commercial Bank Ltd: 17 Xi Jiao Min Xiang, Beijing; cap. 400m., res 474m., dep. 8,344m. (Dec. 1988); Gen. Man. PAN JAW LING.

Foreign Banks

Barclays Bank (UK): Beijing; tel. (01) 552417; telex 22589; fax (01) 5127889; Rep. W. H. SPEIRS.

First National Bank of Chicago (USA): CITIC Bldg, Room 1604, Jian Guo Men Wai, Beijing; tel. (01) 5003281; telex 22433; fax (01) 5003166; Chief Rep. ANNIE WONG.

Hongkong and Shanghai Banking Corporation (Hong Kong): 185 Yuan Ming Yuan Lu, POB 151, Shanghai 200002; tel. (021) 3218383; telex 33058; fax (021) 3291659; f. 1865; Man. D. K. S. CHEUNG.

Midland Bank Group (UK): CITIC Bldg, Room 1103, Jian Guo Men Wai, 100004 Beijing; tel. (01) 5004410; telex 22594; fax (01) 5004825; Sr Group Rep. LANCE BROWNE.

Oversea-Chinese Banking Corporation Ltd (Singapore): brs in Xiamen (Amoy): tel. 59234441, telex 93067, fax 59235182, Man. LOW BOON WAH; and Shanghai: tel. (021) 3233888, telex 33541, fax (021) 3290888, Man. LEE YEOH NGUAN.

Standard Chartered Bank (UK): Union Bldg, 9th Floor, 100 Yanan Dong Lu, Shanghai; tel. (021) 3218253; telex 33067; f. 1853; Rep. TIM HOOPER.

The following foreign banks also have offices in Beijing: Banca Commerciale Italiana, Bank of Brazil, Bank of Nova Scotia, Bank of Tokyo, Banque Nationale de Paris, Banque de l'Union Européenne, Banque Indosuez, Banque Paribas, Chase Manhattan, Commerzbank, Crédit Lyonnais, Deutsche Bank, Dresdner Bank, National Bank of Pakistan, National Commercial Banking Corporation of Australia, Royal Bank of Canada, Société Générale de Banque.

In late 1990 a total of 33 branches of foreign banks were in existence in Shenzhen, Xiamen, Zhuhai, Shanghai and Haikou.

STOCK EXCHANGES

There were five stock exchanges in the process of development in late 1990.

Stock Exchange Executive Council (SEEC): Beijing; f. 1989 to oversee the development of financial markets in China; mems comprise leading non-bank financial institutions authorized to handle securities; Vice-Pres. WANG BOMING.

Shanghai Securities Exchange: Pujiang Hotel, Shanghai; f. 1990; trade in 30 issues; Pres. LI XIANGREI.

INSURANCE

China Insurance Co Ltd: 22 Xi Jiao Min Xiang, POB 20, Beijing; tel. (01) 654231; telex 22102; fax (01) 6011869; f. 1931; cargo, hull, freight, fire, life, personal accident, industrial injury, motor insurance, reinsurance, etc.; Man. SONG GUO HUA.

The People's Insurance Co of China (PICC): 410 Fuchengmen Nei Dajie, Beijing; tel. (01) 6016688; telex 22532; fax (01) 6011869; f. 1949; hull, marine cargo, aviation, motor, life, fire, accident, liability and reinsurance, etc.; Chair. and Pres. QIN DAOFU; Vice-Chair. FAN HUA, SONG GUOHUA.

Tai Ping Insurance Co Ltd: 410 Fu Cheng Men Nei Dajie, Beijing; tel. (01) 6016688; telex 42001; fax (01) 6011869; marine freight, hull, cargo, fire, personal accident, industrial injury, motor insurance, reinsurance, etc.; Pres. LI PINZHOU.

Trade and Industry

EXTERNAL TRADE

All-China Federation of Industry and Commerce: 93 Beiheyan Dajie, Beijing 100006; tel. (01) 554231; telex 22044; fax (01) 5122631; f. 1953; promotes overseas trade relations; Chair. RONG YIREN.

China Council for the Promotion of International Trade (CCPIT): 1 Fu Xing Men Wai Jie, Beijing 100860; tel. (01) 8013344; telex 22315; fax (01) 8011370; f. 1952; encourages foreign trade and economic co-operation; sponsors and arranges Chinese exhbns abroad and foreign exhbns in China; helps foreigners to apply for patent rights and trade-mark registration in China; promotes foreign investment and organizes tech. exchanges with other countries; provides legal services; publishes trade periodicals; Chair. ZHENG HONGYE; Sec.-Gen. LIU FUGUI.

Ministry of Foreign Economic Relations and Trade: (see under Ministries).

Export and Import Corporations

Beijing Foreign Trade Corporation: Bldg 12, Yong An Dong Li, Jian Guo Men Wai, Beijing 100022; tel. (01) 5001315; telex 210064; fax (01) 5001668; controls import-export trade, foreign trade transportation, export commodity packaging and advertising for Beijing; Dir WU YUTIAN.

China International Book Trading Corporation: (see under Guoji Shudian in Publishers Section).

China International Water and Electric Corporation: Block 1, Liupukang, Beijing 100011; tel. (01) 4015511; telex 22485; fax (01) 4014075; f. 1956 as China Water and Electric International Corpn, name changed 1983; exports equipment for projects in the field of water and electrical engineering, and undertakes such projects; Pres. ZHU JINGDE.

China Metallurgical Import and Export Corporation (CMIEC): 46 Dongsi Xidajie, Beijing 100711; tel. (01) 555714; telex 22461; fax (01) 5123792; f. 1980; imports ores, spare parts, automation and control systems, etc.; exports metallurgical products, technology and equipment; establishes joint ventures and trade with foreign companies; Pres. BAI BAOHUA.

China National Aerotechnology Import and Export Corporation: 5 Liangguochang Dongcheng Qu, Beijing 100010; tel. (01) 4017722; telex 22318; fax (01) 4015381; exports signal flares, electric detonators, tachometers, parachutes, general purpose aircraft, etc.; Pres. SUN ZHAOQING; Chair. MO WENXIANG.

China National Animal Breeding Stock Import and Export Corporation: 10A Yangli Xiang, Dong Qu, Beijing 100020; tel. (01) 464344; telex 210101; fax (01) 5128694; sole agency for import and export of stud animals including cattle, sheep, goats, swine, horses, donkeys, camels, rabbits, poultry, etc., as well as pasture seeds and feed additives; Pres. YANG QING.

China National Arts and Crafts Import and Export Corporation: 82 Donganmen Jie, Beijing 100747; tel. (01) 552187; telex 22155; fax (01) 5123204; deals in jewellery, ceramics, handicrafts, embroidery, pottery, wicker, bamboo, etc.; Pres. YU ZHITING.

China National Cereals, Oils and Foodstuffs Import and Export Corporation: 82 Donganmen Jie, Beijing 100747; tel. (01) 555180; telex 22281; fax (01) 551488; imports and exports cereals, sugar,

THE PEOPLE'S REPUBLIC OF CHINA

vegetable oils, meat, eggs, fruit, dairy produce, vegetables, wines and spirits, canned foods and aquatic products, etc.; Pres. CHEN FAXIAN.

China National Chartering Corporation (SINOCHART): Import Bldg, Erligou, Xijiao, Beijing 100044; tel. (01) 8317733; telex 222508; fax (01) 8314002; f. 1950; functions under Ministry of Foreign Economic Relations and Trade; agents for SINOTRANS (see below); arranges chartering of ships; reservation of space, managing and operating chartered vessels; Pres. PING JIAN.

China National Chemicals Import and Export Corporation (SINOCHEM): Erligou, Xijiao, Beijing 100044; tel. (01) 8311106; telex 22243; fax (01) 8313680; deals in rubber, crude petroleum, petroleum products, paints, fertilizers, inks, dyestuffs, chemicals and drugs; Pres. ZHENG DUNXUN; Chair. ZHU DAZHI.

China National Coal Import and Export Corporation (CNCIEC): 8 Xiaguangli, Chaoyangmen, Beijing 100006; tel. (01) 4082244; telex 211273; fax (01) 4081035; imports and exports coal and tech. equipment for coal industry, joint coal development and compensation trade; Pres. WEI GUOFU; Chair. HONG SHANGQING.

China National Electronics Import and Export Corporation: 49 Fuxing Lu, Beijing 100036; tel. (01) 8022711; telex 22475; fax (01) 8314387; Pres. QU YANG.

China National Foreign Trade Transportation Corporation (SINOTRANS): Import Bldg, Erligou, Xijiao, Beijing 100044; tel. (01) 8317733; telex 22153; fax (01) 8311070; f. 1950; functions under Ministry of Foreign Economic Relations and Trade; agents for Ministry's import and export corpns; arranges customs clearance, deliveries, forwarding and insurance for sea, land and air transportation; Chair. PING JIAN; Pres. LIU FULIN.

China National Import and Export Commodities Inspection Corporation: 12 Jianguomenwai Jie, Beijing 100022; tel. (01) 5004626; telex 210076; fax (01) 5004625; inspects, tests and surveys import and export commodities for overseas trade, transport, insurance and manufacturing firms; Pres. LIANG JIE.

China National Instruments Import and Export Corporation (CNIIEC): Erligou, Xijiao, Beijing 100044; POB 1818, Beijing; tel. (01) 8317733; telex 22304; fax (01) 8315925; imports and exports computers, communication and broadcasting equipment, audio and video systems, scientific instruments, etc.; Pres. ZHANG BAOHE.

China National Light Industrial Products Import and Export Corporation: 82 Donganmen Jie, Beijing 100747; tel. (01) 5123763; telex 22282; fax (01) 5123763; imports and exports household electrical appliances, audio equipment, photographic equipment, films, paper goods, building materials, bicycles, sewing machines, enamelware, glassware, stainless steel goods, footwear, leather goods, watches and clocks, cosmetics, stationery, sporting goods, etc.; Pres. LI WENZHI.

China National Machine Tool Corporation: 19 Fang Jia Xiaoxiang, An Nei Jie, Beijing 100007; tel. (01) 4015657; telex 210088; fax (01) 4015657; f. 1979; imports and exports machine tools and tool products, components and equipment; supplies apparatus for machine building industry; Pres. QUAN YILU.

China National Machinery and Equipment Import and Export Corporation: 16 Fuxing Menwai Jie, Beijing 100045; tel. (01) 8013460; telex 22186; fax (01) 362375; f. 1978; imports and exports machine tools, all kinds of machinery, automobiles, hoisting and transport equipment, electric motors, photographic equipment, etc.; Pres. YAO MINGWEI; Chair. WANG ZIYI.

China National Machinery Import and Export Corporation: Erligou, Xijiao, POB 49, Beijing 100044; tel. (01) 8317733; telex 22242; fax (01) 8314143; imports and exports machine tools, diesel engines and boilers and all kinds of machinery; imports aeroplanes, ships, etc.; Pres. LI GUANGYUAN.

China National Medicines and Health Products Import and Export Corporation: Bldg 12, Jianguomenwai Jie, Beijing 100022; tel. (01) 5002673; telex 210103; fax (01) 5014182; Pres. ZHENG YISHAN.

China National Metallurgical Products Import and Export Corporation: 46 Dongsi Jie, Beijing 100711; tel. (01) 555714; telex 22461; fax (01) 5123792; Pres. BAI BAOHUA; Chair. LIN HUA.

China National Metals and Minerals Import and Export Corporation: Erligou, Xijiao, Beijing 100044; tel. (01) 8317733; telex 22241; fax (01) 8315079; f. 1950; principal imports and exports include steel, antimony, tungsten concentrates and ferrotungsten, zinc ingots, tin, mercury, pig iron, cement, etc.; Pres. WANG YAN.

China National Native Produce and Animal By-Products Import and Export Corporation (TUHSU): 82 Donganmen Dajie, Beijing 100747; tel. (01) 5124370; telex 22283; fax (01) 5121626; imports and exports tea, coffee, cocoa, fibres, etc.; 11 subsidiary enterprises, 18 tea hrs; 18 overseas subsidiaries; Gen. Man. WANG ZHIYIN.

China National Non-ferrous Metals Import and Export Corporation (CNIEC): 12B Fuxing Lu, Beijing 100814; tel. (01) 8014419; telex 22086; fax (01) 8015368; Pres. ZHENG RUGUI.

Directory

China National Offshore Oil Corporation (CNOOC): Nansidaokou Lu, Dazhongsi, Beijing 100086; tel. (01) 2014650; telex 22611; fax (01) 2014650; Pres. ZHONG YIMING.

China National Packaging Import and Export Corporation: 28 Donghouxiang, Andingmenwai, Beijing 100731; tel. (01) 4214058; telex 22490; fax (01) 4212124; handles import and export of packaging materials, containers, machines and tools; contracts for the processing and converting of packaging machines and materials using raw materials supplied by foreign customers; Pres. XU JIANGUO.

China National Petro-Chemical Corporation (SINOPEC): 24 Xiaoguan Jie, Andingmenwai, Beijing 100013; tel. (01) 4216731; telex 22655; fax (01) 4216972; f. 1983; under direct control of the State Council; petroleum refining, petrochemicals, synthetic fibres, etc.; 61 subordinate enterprises; approx. 500,000 employees; Pres. SHENG HUAREN; Chair. LI RENJUN.

China National Petroleum and Natural Gas Corporation: Liupukang, Beijing; tel. (01) 2015544; telex 22312; Pres. WANG TAO.

China National Publications Import and Export Corporation: 137 Chaoyangmennei Jie, Beijing 100011; tel. (01) 440731; telex 22313; fax (01) 4015664; imports principally foreign books, newspapers and periodicals, records, etc., exports principally Chinese scientific and technical journals published in foreign languages; Pres. CHEN WEIJIANG.

China National Publishing Industry Trading Corporation: POB 782, 504 An Hui Li, An Ding Men Wai, Beijing 100011; tel. (01) 4215031; telex 210215; fax (01) 4214540; imports and exports books, journals, paintings, woodcuts, watercolour prints and rubbings; holds book fairs abroad; undertakes joint publication; Pres. LOU MING.

China National Seed Corporation: 31 Min Feng Hu Tong, Xidan, Beijing 100032; tel. (01) 652592; telex 22598; fax (01) 6012808; imports and exports crop seeds, including cereals, cotton, oil-bearing crops, teas, flowers and vegetables; seed production for foreign seed companies etc.; Pres. HU QINLING.

China National Silk Import and Export Corporation: 105 Bei He Yan Jie, Beijing; tel. (01) 5125125; telex 22652; fax (01) 5136838; Pres. HUANG JIANMO.

China National Technical Import and Export Corporation: Erligou, Xijiao, Beijing 100044; tel. (01) 8317733; telex 22244; fax (01) 8313584; f. 1952; imports all kinds of complete plant and equipment, acquires modern technology and expertise from abroad, undertakes co-production and jt-ventures, and technical consultation and updating of existing enterprises; Pres. XU DEEN; Chair. CHEN XIAN.

China National Textiles Import and Export Corporation: 82 Donganmen Jie, Beijing 100747; tel. (01) 558831; telex 22280; fax (01) 5124711; imports synthetic fibres, raw cotton, wool, garment accessories, etc.; exports cotton yarn, cotton fabric, knitwear, woven garments, etc.; Pres. ZHONG QUANSHENG.

China North Industries Group: 7A Yuetan Nan Jie, Beijing 100823; tel. (01) 868441; telex 22339; fax (01) 867092; exports mechanical products, light industrial products, chemical products, opto-electronic products, military products, etc.; Chair. ZOU JIAHUA; Pres. LAI JINLIE.

China Nuclear Energy Industry Corporation (CNEIC): 21 Nanlishi Lu, Beijing 100045; tel. (01) 867717; telex 22240; fax (01) 8012393; exports air filters, vacuum valves, dosimeters, radioactive detection elements and optical instruments; Pres. ZHANG XINDUO.

China Road and Bridge Group: 3 Waiguan Jie, An Ding Men Wai, Beijing 100011; tel. (01) 4213378; telex 22336; fax (01) 4217849; overseas building of highways, urban roads, bridges, tunnels, industrial and residential buildings, airport runways and parking areas; contracts to do all surveying, designing, pipe-laying, water supply and sewerage, building, etc., and/or to provide technical or labour services; Gen. Man. ZHU ZHENLIANG.

Shanghai Foreign Trade Corporation: 27 Zhongshan Dong Yi Lu, Shanghai; tel. (021) 3217350; telex 33034; handles import-export trade, foreign trade transportation, chartering, export commodity packaging, storage and advertising for Shanghai municipality.

Shanghai International Trust Trading Corporation: 521 Henan Lu, POB 002-066, Shanghai 200001; tel. (021) 3226650; telex 33627; fax (021) 3207412; f. 1979, present name adopted 1988; handles import and export business, international mail orders, processing, assembling, compensation trade etc.

INTERNAL TRADE

State Administration for Industry and Commerce: 8 Sanlihe Dong Lu, Xichengqu, Beijing 100820; tel. (01) 8013300; telex 222431; fax (01) 862771; functions under the direct supervision of the State Council; Dir LIU MINXUE.

TRADE UNIONS

All-China Federation of Trade Unions: 10 Fu Xing Men Wai Jie, Beijing 100865; tel. (01) 8012200; telex 222290; fax (01) 8012922;

THE PEOPLE'S REPUBLIC OF CHINA

f. 1925; organized on an industrial basis; 15 affiliated national industrial unions, 30 affiliated local trade union councils; membership is voluntary; trade unionists enjoy extensive benefits; in late 1988 there were about 100m. members; Pres. NI ZHIFU; First Sec. YU HONGEN.

Principal affiliated unions:

All-China Federation of Railway Workers' Union: Chair. WU CHU.

Architectural Workers' Trade Union: Sec. SONG ANRU.

China Self-Employed Workers' Association: Pres. REN ZHONGLIN.

Light Industrial Workers' Trade Union: Chair. LI SHUYING.

Machinery Metallurgical Workers' Union: Chair. ZHANG CUNEN.

Postal and Telecommunications Workers' Trade Union of China: Chair. LUO SHUZHEN.

Seamen's Trade Union of China: Chair. QIU JIN.

Workers' Autonomous Federation (WAF): f. 1989; aims to create new trade union movement in China, independent of the All-China Federation of Trade Unions.

TRADE FAIRS

Chinese Export Commodities Fair (CECF): Guangzhou Foreign Trade Centre, 117 Lui Hua Lu, Guangzhou; tel. 677000; telex 44465; f. 1957; organized by the Ministry of Foreign Economic Relations and Trade; 2 trade fairs a year: 15–30 April; 15–30 October.

Chinese Technology and Products Fair: Guangzhou; f. 1989; 1 trade fair a year: 8–14 November.

Transport

RAILWAYS

Ministry of Railways: 10 Fuxing Lu, Beijing; tel. (01) 363875; telex 22483; controls all railways through regional divisions. The railway network has been extended to all provinces and regions except Xizang, where construction is in progress. Total length measured 54,000 km in 1989, of which 6,185 km or 11.5% was electrified. The major routes include Beijing–Guangzhou, Tianjin–Shanghai, Manzhouli–Vladivostok, Jiaozuo–Zhicheng and Lanzhou–Badou. In addition, special railways serve factories and mines. There is an extensive development programme to improve the rail network.

There is an underground system serving Beijing. Its total length was 23 km in 1984, and further lines are under construction. In 1984 Tianjin city opened an underground line.

ROADS

In 1989 China had 1.01m. km of highways. Four major highways link Lhasa with Sichuan, Xinjiang, Qinghai Hu and Kathmandu (Nepal). There were plans to build 11 motorways by 1990, with a total length of 2,000 km. The 375-km Shenyang to Dalian expressway opened in 1990.

WATER TRANSPORT

Bureau of Water Transportation: Controls rivers and coastal traffic. In 1986 there were 109,400 km of navigable inland waterways in China. The main rivers are the Huanghe (Yellow River), Changjiang (Yangtze River) and Zhu. The Changjiang is navigable by vessels of 10,000 tons as far as Wuhan, more than 1,000 km from the coast. Vessels of 1,000 tons can continue to Chongqing upstream. More than one-third of internal freight traffic is carried by water.

SHIPPING

In 1989 China had a network of about 600 ports of which 44 were open to foreign vessels. The greater part of its shipping is handled in nine of these: Dalian, Qinhuangdao, Xingang, Qingdao, Lianyungang, Shanghai, Huangpu (Whampoa), Guangzhou and Zhanjiang. Three-quarters of the handling facilities are mechanical, and harbour improvement schemes are constantly in progress. In 1985 China's merchant fleet ranked ninth in the world in terms of tonnage: including chartered ships, the merchant navy had a total capacity of 14.4m. dwt.

China Ocean Shipping Co (COSCO): 6 Dongchangan Jie, Beijing; tel. (01) 5121188; telex 22264; fax (01) 5122408; br. offices: Shanghai, Guangzhou, Tianjin, Qingdao, Dalian; merchant fleet of 614 vessels of various types with a dwt of 13m. tons; serves China/Japan, China/SE Asia, China/Australia, China/Gulf, China/Europe and China/N. America; Pres. LIU SONGJIN.

China Ocean Shipping Agency: 6 Dongchangan Jie, Beijing; tel. (01) 5121188; telex 211208; fax (01) 5121924; f. 1953; br. offices at Chinese foreign trade ports; the largest shipping agency which undertakes business for ocean-going vessels calling at Chinese ports; arranges sea passage, booking space, transhipment of cargoes; attends to chartering, purchase or sale of ships etc; Pres LIU SONGJIN, CHEN ZHONGBIAO.

Minsheng Shipping Co: 35 Shan Xi Lu, Chongqing; tel. 45695; telex 62241; f. 1984; 66 river boats, 4 ocean-going ships, totalling 90,000 dwt; Gen. Man. LU GUOJI.

CIVIL AVIATION

New international airports were opened at Beijing in 1980 and Xiamen in 1983. The construction of international airports at other major centres is planned, while other airports (e.g. at Shanghai and Chengdu) are being expanded. Chinese airlines carried a total of 12m. passengers in 1989.

Civil Aviation Administration of China (CAAC): 155 Dongxi Jie, Beijing; tel. (01) 550626; telex 22101; f. 1949; controls all civil aviation activities, including a domestic network of 269 routes, with a total length of over 332,500 km and with services to all provinces and autonomous regions except Taiwan; in 1988 CAAC was restructured as a purely supervisory agency, and its operational functions were transferred to new airlines (see below; also China United Airlines and China Capital Helicopter Service); external services are operated by Air China from Beijing to Addis Ababa, Baghdad, Bangkok, Belgrade, Bucharest, Frankfurt, Hong Kong, Istanbul, Karachi, Kuwait, London, Los Angeles, Manila, Melbourne, Moscow, Nagasaki, New York, Osaka, Paris, Pyongyang, Rome, San Francisco, Sharjah, Singapore, Stockholm, Sydney, Tokyo, Toronto, Vancouver, Yangon and Zürich; Dir-Gen. HU YIZHOU; fleet of 4 Boeing 747SP, 2 747-200B Combi, 1 747-200, 5 757-200, 3 Airbus A310-200, 2 A310-300, 5 767-200ER, 10 707-320B/C, 13 737-200, 3 737-200C, 10 737-300, 8 MD-82, 21 Trident 2E, 2 Trident 3B, at least 13 Tu-154M, at least 20 Il-18, at least 50 Antonov An-24, at least 50 Il-14, 10 BAe 146-100, at least 5 An-26, at least 5 An-12, 15 Xian Y-7, Lisunov Li-2, 7 Shorts 360 and a number of smaller aircraft and helicopters; on order: 3 B747-400, 3 757-200, 1 767-200ER, 40 Y-7-100, 22 MD-82, 2 Dash 8-300.

Air China: Beijing International Airport, Beijing; Pres. XU BAILING.

China Eastern Airways: Shanghai International Airport, Shanghai; Gen. Man. YUAN TAOYUAN.

China Northeastern Airways: Shenyang.

China Northern Airways.

China Northwestern Airways: Xian.

China Southern Airways: Guangzhou.

China Southwestern Airways: Chengdu.

In addition, there are a number of provincial airlines.

Shanghai Air Lines: 191 Changle Lu, Shanghai; Chair. HE PENGNIAN.

Tourism

China has enormous potential for tourism, and the sector is developing rapidly. Attractions include dramatic scenery and places of historical interest such as the Great Wall, the Ming Tombs, the Temple of Heaven and the Forbidden City in Beijing, and the terracotta warriors at Xian. Xizang (Tibet), with its monasteries and temples, has also been opened to tourists. Tours of China are organized for groups of visitors, and Western-style hotels have been built in many areas: by the end of 1985 there were more than 700 tourist hotels, with 242,000 beds. A total of 31.7m. tourists visited China in 1988 (an increase of 17.8% on the total for 1987), including many from Hong Kong and Macau. The tourist industry generated revenue of US $2,220m. in foreign exchange in 1988, an increase of 19.2% on 1987. However, revenue from tourism declined dramatically in 1989, to an estimated $1,800m., following the suppression of the Pro-Democracy Movement in Beijing in June of that year. Overseas tourist arrivals fell to 24.5m. in 1989.

China International Travel Service (CITS): 6 Dongchangan Dajie, Beijing; tel. (01) 5121122; telex 22350; fax (01) 5122068; makes travel arrangements for foreign tourists; Gen. Man. WANG ERKANG; general agency in Hong Kong, business offices in London, Paris, New York, Los Angeles, Frankfurt, Sydney and Tokyo.

Chinese People's Association for Friendship with Foreign Countries: 1 Tai Ji Chang Jie, 100740 Beijing; tel. (01) 5122474; telex 210368; fax (01) 5128354; f. 1954; Pres. HAN XU; Sec.-Gen. XU QUN.

National Tourism Administration: 6 Dongchangan Dajie, Beijing; tel. (01) 5121122; telex 22350; Dir LIU YI.

THE PEOPLE'S REPUBLIC OF CHINA

Atomic Energy

China's first (300,000-kW) nuclear power station at Qinshan in Zhejiang Province was to begin operating in late 1990. A second plant, with two 900,000-kW units, at Daya Bay in Shenzhen Special Economic Zone, Guangdong Province, was scheduled to begin operations in 1992. A third station is proposed for Liaoning Province. China expects to have nuclear power plants with a combined generating power of 6,000 MW by the end of the century. In October 1983 China was admitted to the International Atomic Energy Agency (IAEA).

China Institute of Atomic Energy: POB 275, Beijing; tel. (01) 868221; telex 222373; f. 1958; research and development in the field of nuclear physics, radiochemistry and nuclear chemical engineering, reactor engineering, accelerator engineering, nuclear instrumentation, preparation of isotopes, environmental and radiation protection, radiometrology, etc.; promotion of a non-nuclear application and development for the national economy; Pres. Prof. SUN ZUXUN.

Atomic Research Centre: Tarim Pendi, Xingjiang; f. 1953; Dir WANG GANZHANG.

Military Scientific Council: Beijing; Dir Dr JIAN XUESAN.

State Committee for Nuclear Safety: Beijing; Chair. ZHOU PING.

CHINA (TAIWAN)

Introductory Survey

Location, Climate, Language, Religion, Flag, Capital

The Republic of China has, since 1949, been confined mainly to the province of Taiwan (comprising one large island and several much smaller ones), which lies off the south-east coast of the Chinese mainland. The territory under the Republic's effective jurisdiction consists of the island of Taiwan (also known as Formosa) and nearby islands, including the P'enghu (Pescadores) group, together with a few other islands which lie just off the mainland and form part of the province of Fujian (Fukien), west of Taiwan. The largest of these is Chinmen (Jinmen), also known as Quemoy, which (with three smaller islands) is about 10 km from the port of Xiamen (Amoy), while five other islands under Taiwan's control, mainly Matsu (Mazu), lie further north, near Fuzhou. Taiwan itself is separated from the mainland by the Taiwan (Formosa) Strait, which is about 145 km (90 miles) wide at its narrowest point. The island's climate is one of rainy summers and mild winters. Average temperatures are about 15°C (59°F) in the winter and 26°C (79°F) in the summer. The average annual rainfall is 2,565 mm (101 in). The official language is Northern Chinese (Mandarin). The predominant religion is Buddhism but there are also Muslims, Daoists and Christians (Roman Catholics and Protestants). The philosophy of Confucianism has a large following. The national flag (proportions 3 by 2) is red, with a dark blue rectangular canton, containing a white sun, in the upper hoist. The capital of Taiwan is Taipei.

Recent History

China ceded Taiwan to Japan in 1895. The island remained under Japanese rule until 1945, when the Second World War ended. As a result of Japan's defeat in the war, Taiwan was returned to Chinese control, becoming a province of the Republic of China, then ruled by the Kuomintang (KMT, Nationalist Party). The leader of the KMT was Gen. Chiang Kai-shek, President of the Republic since 1928.

The KMT Government's forces were defeated in 1949 by the Communist revolution in China. President Chiang and many of his supporters withdrew from the Chinese mainland and established themselves on Taiwan, where they set up a KMT regime in succession to their previous all-China administration. This regime continued to assert that it was the rightful Chinese Government, in opposition to the People's Republic of China, which had been proclaimed by the victorious Communists in 1949. Since establishing their base in Taiwan, the Nationalists have successfully resisted attacks by their Communist rivals and have, in turn, declared that they intend to recover control of mainland China from the Communists.

Although its effective control was limited to Taiwan, the KMT regime continued to be dominated by politicians who had formerly been in power on the mainland. In support of the regime's claim to be the legitimate government of all China, Taiwan's legislative bodies were filled mainly by surviving mainland members, and the representatives of the island's native Taiwanese majority occupied only a minority of seats. Unable to replenish their mainland representation, the National Assembly (last elected fully in 1947) and other organs extended their terms of office indefinitely, although fewer than half of the original members were alive on Taiwan in the 1980s. While it has promised eventually to reconquer the mainland, the KMT regime has been largely preoccupied with ensuring its own survival, and promoting economic development, on Taiwan. The political domination of the island by immigrants from the mainland has caused some resentment among Taiwanese, and has led to demands for increased democratization and for the recognition of Taiwan as a state independent of China. The KMT has, however, consistently rejected demands for independence, constantly restating the party's long-standing policy of seeking political reunification, although under KMT terms, with the mainland.

In 1954 the USA, which had refused to recognize the People's Republic of China, signed a mutual security treaty with the KMT Government, pledging to protect Taiwan and the Pescadores. In 1955 the islands of Quemoy and Matsu, lying just offshore from the mainland, were included in the protected area.

In spite of being confined to Taiwan, the KMT regime continued to represent China at the United Nations (and as a permanent member of the UN Security Council) until 1971, when it was replaced by the People's Republic. Nationalist China was subsequently expelled from several other international organizations. In August 1990 Saudi Arabia withdrew recognition from Taiwan and established diplomatic relations with the People's Republic of China. Conversely, in November, Nicaragua transferred its recognition from the People's Republic to Taiwan. Thus, in late 1990 the Taiwan regime was recognized by only 28 countries.

In 1973 the Taiwan Government rejected an offer from the People's Republic to hold secret discussions on the reunification of China, and this policy has since been strongly reaffirmed. In October 1981 Taiwan rejected China's suggested terms for reunification, whereby Taiwan would become a 'special administrative region' and would have a substantial degree of autonomy, including the retention of its own armed forces and its relatively high standard of living. In 1983 China renewed its offer of autonomy for Taiwan, including a guarantee to maintain the status quo in Taiwan for 100 years if the province agreed to reunification. In 1984, following the agreement between the People's Republic of China and the United Kingdom that China would regain sovereignty over the British colony of Hong Kong in 1997, Chinese leaders urged Taiwan to accept similar proposals for reunification on the basis of 'one country—two systems'. The Taipei Government insisted that Taiwan would never negotiate with Beijing until the mainland regime renounced communism. In May 1986, however, the Government was forced to make direct contact with the Beijing Government for the first time, over the issue of a Taiwanese pilot who had defected to the mainland with his aircraft, and whose fellow crew-members wished to return. In March 1987 Taiwan declared the agreement that had been concluded between the People's Republic of China and Portugal, regarding the return of the Portuguese Overseas Territory of Macau to Chinese sovereignty in 1999, to be null and void. In October the Government announced the repeal of the 38-year ban on visits to the mainland by Taiwanese citizens, with the exception of civil servants and military personnel, but insisted that visits were permitted solely for 'humanitarian reasons', to allow Taiwanese of mainland descent to visit relatives 'by blood or marriage'. In late 1988 permission was extended to include visits to Taiwan by mainland Chinese, also for humanitarian purposes.

In March 1989 the President of Taiwan paid a state visit to Singapore, the first official visit overseas by a Taiwanese head of state for 12 years. The trip signalled the advent of a more pragmatic approach by the Taiwan Government to its foreign policy. In a further attempt to end Taiwan's diplomatic isolation, the President stated that he was willing to visit any foreign country, even if it maintained diplomatic relations with Beijing. In April the Government announced that it was considering a 'one China, two governments' formula for its future relationship with the mainland, whereby China would be a single country under two administrations, one in Beijing and one in Taipei. In May a high-level delegation, led by the Minister of Finance, attended a meeting of the Asian Development Bank (ADB) in Beijing, as representatives of 'Taipei, China'. Although the Taiwan Government stressed that the delegation would not be allowed to confer with Chinese government officials, the visit, together with one made by a party of Taiwanese gymnasts a month earlier, represented a considerable relaxation in Taiwan's attitude to relations with mainland China.

Reconciliation initiatives were abruptly halted, however, by the violent suppression of the Pro-Democracy Movement in Beijing in June 1989 (see p. 716). The actions of the Chinese Government were strongly condemned by Taiwan, although it was indicated that there would be no consequent change in official policy towards the mainland. In May 1990 the President of Taiwan suggested the opening of direct dialogue on a government-to-government basis with the People's Republic. The proposal, however, was rejected by Beijing, which continued to maintain that it would negotiate only on a party-to-party basis with the KMT. In December Taiwan announced that the state of war with the People's Republic would be formally ended by May 1991.

Meanwhile, legislative elections were held in December 1972, for the first time in 24 years, to fill 53 seats in the National Assembly. The new members, elected for a fixed term of six years, joined 1,376 surviving 'life-term' members of the Assembly. President Chiang Kai-shek remained in office until his death in April 1975. He was succeeded as leader of the ruling KMT by his son, Gen. Chiang Ching-kuo, who had been Prime Minister since May 1972. The new President was Dr Yen Chia-kan, Vice-President since 1966. In May 1978 President Yen retired and was succeeded by Gen. Chiang, who appointed Sun Yun-suan, hitherto Minister of Economic Affairs, to be Prime Minister. At elections for 71 seats in the Legislative Yuan in December 1983, the KMT won an overwhelming victory, confirming its dominance over the independent 'Tangwai' (non-party) candidates. In March 1984 President Chiang was re-elected for a second six-year term, and Lee Teng-hui, a former Mayor of Taipei and a native Taiwanese, became Vice-President. In May a major government reshuffle took place, and Yu Kuo-hwa, formerly the Governor of the Central Bank, replaced Sun Yun-suan as Prime Minister. President Chiang died in January 1988 and was succeeded by Lee Teng-hui who, under the Constitution, was legally entitled to serve the remainder of President Chiang's term of office.

In September 1986 135 leading opposition politicians formed the Democratic Progressive Party (DPP), in defiance of the KMT's ban on the formation of new political parties. In response, the KMT announced that it would henceforth allow the establishment of new parties (although subject to approval of their policies), and that martial law (in force since 1949) would be replaced by a new national security law. During 1987 and 1988 four new political parties were formed. Elections for 84 seats in the National Assembly and 73 seats in the Legislative Yuan were held in December 1986. The KMT achieved a decisive victory, winning 68 seats in the National Assembly and 59 in the Legislative Yuan, but the DPP received about one-quarter of the total votes, and won 11 seats in the Assembly and 12 in the Legislative Yuan, thus more than doubling the non-KMT representation. In February 1987 the KMT began to implement a programme of political reform. The most significant change was the replacement of martial law by the new National Security Law in July. Under the terms of the new legislation, political parties other than the KMT were permitted, and civilians were removed from the jurisdiction of military courts. However, the DPP remained opposed to the conditions with which opposition groups had to comply in order to gain legal recognition. The KMT also attempted to rejuvenate Taiwan's ageing leadership. Younger members of the party, who supported the reform programme, were promoted to positions of influence, and in April they secured seven major posts in a reshuffle of the Executive Yuan.

In February 1988 a plan to restructure the legislative bodies was approved by the Central Standing Committee of the KMT. Under the provisions of the plan, voluntary resignations were to be sought from 'life-term' members of the Legislative Yuan and National Assembly. In addition, seats were no longer to be reserved for representatives of mainland constituencies. In December it was announced that, subject to approval by the Legislative Yuan, members who accepted voluntary retirement would receive around NT $3.7m. in severance pay.

In November 1987 the second annual Congress of the DPP approved a resolution declaring that Taiwanese citizens had the right to advocate independence for Taiwan. In January 1988, however, two opposition activists were imprisoned, on charges of sedition, for voicing such demands. At the third annual Congress of the DPP, held in October 1988, Huang Hsin-chieh replaced Yao Chia-wen as Chairman of the party, and it was thought likely that he would be a less vigorous proponent of Taiwanese independence.

The 13th national Congress of the KMT was held in July 1988. In an attempt to accelerate the process of reform, the Congress decided that, for the first time, free elections would be held for two-thirds of the members of the KMT's Central Committee. In the ensuing ballot, numerous new members were elected, and the proportion of native Taiwanese increased sharply. The Central Standing Committee was similarly affected, with several of its members being replaced by younger, liberal members of the KMT. A reshuffle of the Executive Yuan, later in the month, resulted in a government comprising younger members, who were expected to hasten the programme of reform. At the same time, President Lee promoted three draft legislative measures: a revision of regulations concerning the registration of political parties; a retirement plan for those members of the three legislative assemblies who had been elected by mainland constituencies in 1947; and a new law aiming to give greater autonomy to the Taiwan Provincial Government and its assembly. In January 1989 the three measures were enacted, and in the following month the KMT became the first political party to register under the new legislation. However, the new laws were severely criticized by the DPP, which protested at the size of the retirement pensions being offered and at the terms of the Civic Organizations Law, which required that, in order to register, political parties undertook to reject communism and any notion of official political independence for Taiwan. Despite these objections, the DPP applied for official registration in April. In May Yu Kuo-hwa resigned as Premier of the Executive Yuan and was replaced by Lee Huan, the Secretary-General of the KMT.

Partial elections to the Legislative Yuan and the Taiwan Provincial Assembly were held on 2 December 1989. A total of 101 seats in the Legislative Yuan were contested by the KMT, the DPP and several independent candidates. The result of the elections, in which the KMT obtained 72 seats and the DPP won 21, was variously interpreted. However, by virtue of achieving more than 20 seats, the DPP secured the prerogative to propose legislation in the Legislative Yuan. Following the elections, a spokesman for the KMT affirmed that the party would continue to introduce a greater degree of democracy in Taiwan. In late December 2,000 demonstrators, demanding swifter political reforms, marched through Taipei.

In February 1990 the opening of the National Assembly's 35-day plenary session, convened every six years to elect the country's President, was disrupted by DPP members' violent action in a protest against the continuing domination of the Assembly by elderly KMT politicians, who had been elected on the Chinese mainland prior to 1949 and who had never been obliged to seek re-election. At the Legislative Yuan, demonstrators attempted to prevent senior KMT members from entering the building, and the election of a KMT veteran as president of the legislature had to be postponed, when opposition members deliberately delayed the procedure. More than 80 people were injured during the ensuing street clashes between riot police and demonstrators.

In March 1990 DPP members were barred from the National Assembly for refusing to swear allegiance to 'The Republic of China', attempting instead to substitute 'Taiwan' upon taking the oath. A number of amendments to the Temporary Provisions, which for more than 40 years had permitted the effective suspension of the Constitution, were approved by the National Assembly in mid-March. Revisions included measures to strengthen the position of the mainland-elected KMT members, who were granted new powers to initiate and veto legislation, and also an amendment to permit the National Assembly to meet annually. The revisions were opposed not only by the DPP but also by more moderate members of the KMT, and led to a large protest rally in Taipei, which attracted an estimated 10,000 demonstrators, who continued to demand the abolition of the National Assembly and the holding of direct presidential elections. Nevertheless, President Lee was duly re-elected, unopposed, by the National Assembly for a six-year term, two rival KMT candidates having withdrawn from the contest. Immediately after his re-election, President Lee held a meeting with student representatives, as a result of which a sit-in protest by students at a public square in the centre of the capital was ended peacefully; however, the students pledged to continue their campaign for full democracy. In April President Lee and the Chairman of the DPP met for discussions. At this unprecedented meeting the subjects of constitutional and political reforms, and also the question of relations with the People's Republic of China, were discussed, in preparation for a forthcoming national conference.

There was renewed unrest in May 1990, however, following President Lee's unexpected appointment as the new Prime Minister of Gen. (retd) Hau Pei-tsun, the former Chief of the General Staff and, since December 1989, the Minister of

CHINA (TAIWAN)

Defence. Outraged opposition members prevented Hau from addressing the National Assembly, which was unable to approve his nomination until the session was reconvened a few days later, police being summoned to the Assembly to restore order. Angry demonstrators, fearing a reversal of the process of democratic reform, again clashed with riot police on the streets of Taipei. During the disturbances at least 40 people were hurt, and several government buildings were set on fire following petrol bomb attacks. The new Executive Yuan, announced at the end of the month, included a civilian as Minister of Defence. New Ministers of Foreign Affairs and of Finance were appointed, but the majority of ministers retained their previous portfolios.

The National Affairs Conference (NAC), convened in late June 1990, was attended by 150 delegates from various sections of society. At the historic meeting, proposals for reform were presented for discussion. A Constitutional Reform Planning Group was subsequently established. The NAC also reached consensus on the issue of direct presidential elections, which would permit the citizens of Taiwan, rather than the ageing members of the National Assembly, to select the Head of State.

Meanwhile, the Council of Grand Justices had ruled that elderly members of the National Assembly and of the Legislative Yuan should step down by the end of 1991. Upon the resignation of a 95-year-old member of the Legislative Yuan in August 1990, for the first time Taiwan-elected delegates to the legislature outnumbered those elected on the mainland more than 40 years previously. In late September the opening session of the legislature was once again disrupted by opposition members.

In October 1990 a National Unification Council, chaired by President Lee, was formed, and a Council of Mainland Affairs was established. The DPP urged the Government to renounce its claim to sovereignty over mainland China and also Mongolia.

With the announcement, in December 1990, of Taiwan's intention formally to end the state of war with the People's Republic of China, the declaration of emergency (in force in Taiwan since 1949) was to be rescinded by May 1991, thus opening the way to improved relations with Beijing and to further democratic reform in Taiwan. Nevertheless, about 10,000 protesters took part in a march in Taipei to demand even swifter reform.

In January 1979 Taiwan suffered a serious set-back when the USA established full diplomatic relations with the People's Republic and severed relations with Taiwan. The USA also terminated the mutual security treaty with Taiwan. Commercial links are still maintained, however, under the terms of the USA's Taiwan Relations Act of March 1979. Taiwan's purchase of armaments from the USA has remained a controversial issue and has caused increased tension with mainland China. In August 1982 Taiwan's morale was further damaged when a joint Sino-US communiqué was published, in which the USA pledged to reduce gradually its sale of armaments to Taiwan. Despite this, substantial sales of weapons have continued. In April 1984 the US President, Ronald Reagan, gave an assurance that he would continue to support Taiwan, despite the improved relations between the USA and the People's Republic, which had provoked uncertainty in Taiwan.

Government

Under the provisions of the 1947 Constitution, the Head of State is the President, who is elected for a term of six years by the National Assembly. There are five Yuans (governing bodies), the highest legislative organ being the Legislative Yuan, to which the Executive Yuan (the Council of Ministers) is responsible. In mid-1990 the Legislative Yuan comprised 267 members, many of whom were life members. Elections for supplementary seats are held every three years. There are also Control, Judicial and Examination Yuans. Their respective functions are: to investigate the work of the executive; to interpret the Constitution and national laws; and to supervise examinations for entry into public offices. The Legislative Yuan submits proposals to the National Assembly. Elections to the Assembly are by universal adult suffrage every six years, but in 1990 many of the Assembly seats continued to be held by life members who formerly represented mainland constituencies. In mid-1990 the Assembly had 691 members. Martial law was declared in 1949, and remained in force until July 1987, when it was replaced by a new National Security Law.

Defence

In June 1990 the armed forces totalled 370,000: army 270,000, air force 70,000, navy 30,000. Military service lasts for two years. Defence expenditure for 1990 was projected at NT $233,400m.

Economic Affairs

In 1989 Taiwan's gross national product (GNP), at current prices, was US $150,300m., having increased, in real terms, by 7.3% compared with 1988. GNP per head stood at US $7,512 in 1989. Real GNP was expected to grow by 5.2% in 1990. In 1989 gross domestic product (GDP) increased by 7.6%, in real terms, to total NT $3,878,547m. at current prices. Between 1982 and 1988, real GDP expanded at an average annual rate of 9.2%.

Agriculture (including forestry and fishing) contributed 4.8% of GDP, at current prices, and employed 12.9% of the working population, in 1989. The principal crops are rice, sugar cane, maize and sweet potatoes. Agricultural production declined by 0.6% in 1988.

Industry (comprising mining, manufacturing, construction and utilities) employed 42.2% of the working population, and provided 42.4% of GDP, in 1989. Industrial production increased at an average rate of 9.2% per year between 1982 and 1988.

Mining contributed only 0.4% of GDP, and employed less than 0.3% of the working population, in 1989. Coal, copper, marble and dolomite are the principal minerals extracted, although gold and silver are also mined.

Manufacturing contributed 34.6% of GDP, and employed 33.9% of the working population, in 1989. In 1987, 85.4% of export revenue was derived from manufacturing. The most important branches, measured by gross value of output, are electronics, plastic goods, synthetic yarns and the motor vehicle industry.

Energy is derived principally from imported petroleum (some 80% in 1987). Imports of petroleum accounted for almost 5.0% of total import expenditure in 1989. In 1987 nuclear power supplied 48% of Taiwan's electricity requirements, thermal power 41% and hydroelectric power 11%.

For many years, banking in Taiwan was rigidly regulated by the Government, which owned all licensed banking institutions. In July 1989, however, a revised banking law was introduced, authorizing the establishment of private banks and the partial 'privatization' of three prominent state-owned commercial banks. In May 1984 the first 'offshore' banking licences were issued, as the initial move towards an eventual liberalization of Taiwan's stringent controls on the availability of foreign exchange. The controls were further eased in 1987.

In 1989 Taiwan recorded a trade surplus of US $16,350m., and there was a surplus of US $11,145m. on the current account of the balance of payments. In 1989 the principal sources of imports were Japan (31%) and the USA (23%). The principal markets for exports were the USA (36%), Japan (14%) and Hong Kong (11%). The principal imports in 1989 were machinery and transport equipment, basic manufactures and chemicals. The principal exports were miscellaneous manufactured articles, machinery and transport equipment and basic manufactures.

In the financial year ending 30 June 1990 there was a projected budgetary deficit of NT $40m. Taiwan's total external debt was US $1,150m. (the lowest for 14 years) at the end of 1989, when the cost of debt-servicing amounted to 0.7% of total export earnings. The annual rate of inflation averaged 3.0% during the period 1980–87. The rate was 1.2% in 1988, rising to 4.4% in 1989, and to 6.5% in the year to September 1990, the highest level for nine years. Less than 1.7% of the labour force were unemployed in June 1990.

Taiwan's economic growth since the Second World War has been substantial, the economy proving to be more resilient in response to the world recession of the early 1980s than that of virtually any other country. In the late 1980s, however, the economy began to experience particular problems, the most prominent of which was the size of Taiwan's continuing trade surplus with the USA. The surplus was sharply reduced in 1988, when trade was diversified and imports liberalized, but the possibility of future trade restrictions by the USA remains. As a result of its repeated trade surpluses, Taiwan possesses the world's second largest reserves of foreign exchange (after Japan). A high rate of GNP growth was expected to be maintained in 1990. Owing to higher international petroleum

CHINA (TAIWAN)

prices and to the increase in inflation, however, the anticipated rate of GNP growth in 1990 was revised downwards from 7% to 5.2%.

Social Welfare
In June 1990 the Labour Insurance programme covered around 6,612,000 workers, providing benefits for injury, disability, birth, death and old age. At the same time, about 1,075,000 government employees and their dependants were covered by a separate scheme. In 1978 a system of supplementary benefits for those with low incomes was introduced. In 1989 Taiwan had a total of 12,267 medical institutions, hospitals and clinics, with a total of 86,639 beds. There were 20,835 physicians (including Chinese herb doctors) and 5,005 dentists working in the country. Of total government expenditure in 1987, NT $4,829m. (1.4%) was for health, and a further NT $62,784m. (17.7%) for social security and welfare.

Education
Education at primary schools and junior high schools is free and compulsory between the ages of six and 15 years. Secondary schools consist of junior and senior middle schools, normal schools for teacher-training and vocational schools. There are also a number of private schools. Higher education is provided in universities, colleges, junior colleges and graduate schools. Government expenditure on education, science and culture in 1989/90 totalled NT $103,337m. In 1989/90 there were almost 2.4m. pupils enrolled in state primary schools and more than 1.7m. in secondary schools. There are 16 universities and 11 independent colleges.

Public Holidays
1991: 1 January (Founding of the Republic), 15–17 February (Chinese New Year), 29 March (Youth Day), 5 April (Ching Ming), 16 June (Dragon Boat Festival), 22 September (Mid-Autumn Moon Festival), 28 September (Teachers' Day—Birthday of Confucius), 10 October (Double Tenth Day, anniversary of 1911 revolution), 25 October (Retrocession Day, anniversary of end of Japanese occupation), 31 October (Birthday of Chiang Kai-shek), 12 November (Birthday of Sun Yat-sen), 25 December (Constitution Day).

1992: 1 January (Founding of the Republic), 4–6 February (Chinese New Year), 29 March (Youth Day), 5 April (Ching Ming), 5 June (Dragon Boat Festival), 11 September (Mid-Autumn Moon Festival), 28 September (Teachers' Day—Birthday of Confucius), 10 October (Double Tenth Day, anniversary of 1911 revolution), 25 October (Retrocession Day, anniversary of end of Japanese occupation), 31 October (Birthday of Chiang Kai-shek), 12 November (Birthday of Sun Yat-sen), 25 December (Constitution Day).

Weights and Measures
The metric system is officially in force, but some traditional Chinese units are still used.

Statistical Survey

Source (unless otherwise stated): Directorate-General of Budget, Accounting and Statistics, Executive Yuan, 2 Kwang Chow St, Taipei; tel. (02) 3117147.

Area and Population

AREA, POPULATION AND DENSITY

Area (sq km)	36,000*
Population (census results)	
16 December 1975	16,191,609
28 December 1980	
Males	9,362,026
Females	8,587,082
Total	17,949,108
Population (official estimates at 31 December)	
1987	19,672,612
1988	19,903,812
1989	20,107,440
Density (per sq km) at 31 December 1989	558.5

Population (official estimate at 30 June 1990): 20,217,487.
* 13,900 sq miles.

PRINCIPAL TOWNS
(estimated population at 31 December 1989)

Taipei (capital)	2,702,678	Hsinchuang	287,645
Kaohsiung	1,374,231	Fengshan	285,853
Taichung	746,780	Chungli	262,653
Tainan	675,685	Chiayi	256,165
Panchiao	531,065	Yungho	247,939
Shanchung	370,957	Taoyuan	235,521
Chungho	365,224	Hsintien	216,757
Keelung	350,283	Changhwa	212,311
Hsinchu	319,197	Pingtung	207,970

BIRTHS, MARRIAGES AND DEATHS

	Live births		Marriages		Deaths	
	Number	Rate (per 1,000)	Number	Rate (per 1,000)	Number	Rate (per 1,000)
1985	345,053	18.03	153,565	8.03	92,011	4.81
1986	308,187	15.92	145,592	7.52	94,712	4.89
1987	313,062	16.00	146,075	7.47	96,033	4.91
1988	341,054	17.24	155,321	7.85	101,786	5.14
1989	314,553	15.72	158,015	7.90	102,975	5.15

ECONOMICALLY ACTIVE POPULATION
(annual averages, '000 persons aged 15 years and over*)

	1987	1988	1989
Agriculture, forestry and fishing	1,226	1,112	1,065
Mining and quarrying	31	28	24
Manufacturing	2,810	2,798	2,803
Construction	554	588	625
Electricity, gas and water	35	35	35
Commerce	1,435	1,539	1,613
Transport, storage and communications	429	431	450
Finance and insurance	229	269	310
Other services	1,275	1,308	1,332
Total in employment	8,022	8,108	8,258
Unemployed	161	139	132
Total labour force	8,183	8,247	8,390

* Excluding members of the armed forces and persons in institutional households.

CHINA (TAIWAN)

Agriculture

PRINCIPAL CROPS ('000 metric tons)

	1987	1988	1989
Rice*	1,900.5	1,844.8	1,864.6
Sweet potatoes	344.8	254.8	206.0
Asparagus	40.1	32.9	25.1
Soybeans	18.0	14.6	11.0
Maize	306.9	321.2	328.5
Tea	25.6	23.6	22.1
Tobacco	24.0	20.2	18.5
Groundnuts	111.7	83.3	64.8
Cassava (Manioc)	39.4	27.3	20.1
Sugar cane	5,162.9	6,767.5	6,627.8
Bananas	204.5	228.7	198.4
Pineapples	193.3	228.1	230.7
Citrus fruit	522.9	559.5	568.7
Vegetables	3,283.5	3,094.5	2,954.6
Mushrooms	50.3	37.0	30.9

* Figures are in terms of brown rice. The equivalent in paddy rice is approximately 31% greater (1 metric ton of paddy rice = 763.66 kg of brown rice).

LIVESTOCK ('000 head at 31 December)

	1987	1988	1989
Cattle	136.3	142.1	138.3
Buffaloes	35.5	34.2	26.8
Pigs	7,129.0	6,954.3	7,783.3
Sheep and goats	207.6	196.2	179.4
Chickens	68,978	77,651	84,259
Ducks	12,915	12,229	13,125
Geese	1,959	1,948	2,062
Turkeys	529	464	395

LIVESTOCK PRODUCTS

	1987	1988	1989
Beef (metric tons)	4,171	4,727	6,058
Pig meat (metric tons)	1,137,918	1,105,731	1,112,590
Goat meat (metric tons)	677	844	961
Chickens ('000 head)*	174,400	193,018	215,940
Ducks ('000 head)*	39,745	37,717	39,952
Geese ('000 head)*	3,923	3,942	4,140
Turkeys ('000 head)*	1,111	920	899
Milk (metric tons)	144,390	173,407	182,421
Duck eggs ('000)	450,752	404,249	393,907
Hen eggs ('000)	3,546,186	3,432,113	3,844,170

* Figures refer to numbers slaughtered.

Forestry

ROUNDWOOD REMOVALS ('000 cu m)

	1987	1988	1989
Industrial wood	422.6	253.3	157.3
Fuel wood	67.6	57.1	33.9
Total	490.2	310.4	191.2

Fishing

('000 metric tons, live weight)

	1987	1988	1989
Total catch	1,236.2	1,360.9	1,371

Mining

(metric tons, unless otherwise indicated)

	1987	1988	1989
Coal	1,499,240	1,225,487	784,400
Gold (kg)	536.0	237.0	269.1
Silver (kg)	9,855.7	8,388.0	649.0
Electrolytic copper	46,961	43,333	43,233
Crude petroleum ('000 litres)	148,407	139,816	135,120
Natural gas ('000 cu m)	1,056,916	1,157,495	1,157,870
Salt	99,943	111,341	169,980
Gypsum	1,378	2,438	3,904
Sulphur	89,082	86,541	76,060
Marble	10,633,023	11,213,317	12,115,470
Talc	22,102	21,603	22,559
Dolomite	339,880	447,510	418,716

Industry

SELECTED PRODUCTS
('000 metric tons, unless otherwise indicated)

	1987	1988	1989
Wheat flour	619.4	620.5	619.3
Refined sugar	538.5	567.3	490.9
Alcoholic beverages—excl. beer ('000 hectolitres)	2,248.3	2,295.1	2,409.3
Cigarettes (million)	28,037	28,420	29,849
Cotton yarn	246.4	252.5	266.2
Paper	799.7	893.8	879.8
Sulphuric acid	741.8	663.8	767.9
Spun yarn	247.2	239.7	383.3
Motor spirit—petrol (million litres)	3,544.5	4,211.5	4,294.6
Diesel oil (million litres)	4,066.8	3,678.0	4,295.4
Cement	15,663.4	17,280.8	18,043.2
Pig iron	87.2	25.1	29.9
Steel ingots	2,081.2	2,533.9	2,728.6
Radio receivers ('000 units)	11,599.7	11,143.9	7,902.1
Television receivers ('000 units)	6,442	5,031	5,172
Ships ('000 dwt)*	564.3	662.5	201.5
Electric energy (million kWh)	65,514	71,643	76,912
Liquefied petroleum gas	446.7	346.0	361.2

* Excluding motor yachts.

Finance

CURRENCY AND EXCHANGE RATES

Monetary Units
100 cents = 1 New Taiwan dollar (NT $).

Denominations
Coins: 50 cents; 1, 5 and 10 dollars.
Notes: 10, 50, 100, 500 and 1,000 dollars.

Sterling and US Dollar Equivalents (30 September 1990)
£1 sterling = NT $51.85;
US $1 = NT $27.725;
NT $1,000 = £19.29 = US $36.07.

Average Exchange Rate (NT $ per US $)
1987   31.845
1988   28.589
1989   26.407

CHINA (TAIWAN)

Statistical Survey

BUDGET (estimates, NT $ million, year ending 30 June)

Revenue	1987/88	1988/89	1989/90
Taxes	301,599	381,989	400,000
Monopoly profits	30,166	30,915	32,445
Non-tax revenue from other sources	207,988	199,940	247,999
Total	539,753	612,844	680,424

Expenditure	1987/88	1988/89	1989/90
General administration	31,664	45,965	57,212
National defence	160,375	187,942	212,480
Education, science and culture	59,115	75,748	103,337
Economic development	n.a.	91,782	108,553
Social security	88,760	100,160	125,981
Obligations	23,151	30,384	49,377
Trust account	4,230	—	—
Subsidies to provincial and municipal governments	17,518	12,254	12,453
Other expenditure	1,842	5,731	11,281
Total	470,255	549,932	680,464

INTERNATIONAL RESERVES (US $ million at 31 December)

	1987	1988	1989
Gold*	2,698	5,395	5,828
Foreign exchange	76,748	73,897	73,334
Total	79,446	79,292	79,652

* National valuation.

MONEY SUPPLY (NT $ million at 31 December)

	1987	1988	1989
Currency outside banks	284,964	320,624	348,416
Demand deposits at deposit money banks	1,283,261	1,629,849	1,720,343
Total	1,568,225	1,950,473	2,068,759

COST OF LIVING
(Consumer Price Index; base: 1986 = 100)

	1987	1988	1989
Food	101.27	102.73	109.12
Clothing	98.23	99.65	98.99
Housing	100.52	101.21	105.70
Transport and communications	98.22	96.81	97.51
Medicines and medical care	100.63	100.97	106.60
Education and entertainment	101.92	107.61	112.65
All items (incl. others)	100.52	101.81	106.30

NATIONAL ACCOUNTS (NT $ million in current prices)
National Income and Product

	1987	1988	1989
Compensation of employees	1,575,009	1,743,912	2,062,956
Operating surplus	1,026,431	1,055,766	1,016,167
Domestic factor incomes	2,601,440	2,799,678	3,079,123
Consumption of fixed capital	280,557	302,782	335,147
Gross domestic product (GDP) at factor cost	2,881,997	3,102,460	3,414,270
Indirect taxes	344,424	397,719	460,195
Less Subsidies	3,428	3,228	3,716
GDP in purchasers' values	3,222,993	3,496,951	3,870,749
Factor income from abroad	123,001	154,007	178,000
Less Factor income paid abroad	57,021	65,664	87,001
Gross national product (GNP)	3,288,973	3,585,294	3,961,748
Less Consumption of fixed capital	280,557	302,782	335,147
National income in market prices	3,008,416	3,282,512	3,626,601
Other current transfers from abroad	15,774	27,385	40,879
Less Other current transfers paid abroad	37,964	82,426	82,803
National disposable income	2,986,226	3,227,471	3,584,677

Expenditure on the Gross Domestic Product

	1987	1988	1989
Government final consumption expenditure	463,920	529,926	619,439
Private final consumption expenditure	1,537,782	1,765,247	2,060,300
Increase in stocks	39,750	91,148	32,892
Gross fixed capital formation	620,098	724,904	838,009
Total domestic expenditure	2,661,550	3,111,225	3,550,640
Exports of goods and services	1,855,409	1,914,488	1,934,971
Less Imports of goods and services	1,293,966	1,528,762	1,614,862
GDP in purchasers' values	3,222,993	3,496,951	3,870,749
GDP at constant 1986 prices	3,207,382	3,442,826	3,697,581

Gross Domestic Product by Economic Activity

	1987	1988	1989
Agriculture and livestock	122,648	126,473	144,228
Forestry and logging	4,251	4,730	2,957
Fishing	44,335	44,421	44,455
Mining and quarrying	15,163	16,285	16,973
Manufacturing	1,272,324	1,321,705	1,376,699
Construction	126,146	148,733	176,831
Electricity, gas and water	115,081	110,734	115,270
Transport, storage and communications	197,314	217,830	240,231
Trade, restaurants and hotels	452,332	500,871	576,695
Finance, insurance and real estate	268,045	338,141	432,361
Housing services*	181,740	210,582	237,971
Government services	292,026	333,991	388,180
Other services	173,659	194,246	221,316
Sub-total	3,265,064	3,568,742	3,974,167
Import duties	105,115	117,238	129,217
Less Imputed bank service charge	147,186	189,029	232,635
GDP in purchasers' values	3,222,993	3,496,951	3,870,749

*Including imputed rents of owner-occupied dwellings.

CHINA (TAIWAN)

BALANCE OF PAYMENTS (US $ million)

	1987	1988	1989
Merchandise exports f.o.b.	53,298	60,319	65,904
Merchandise imports f.o.b.	−33,012	−46,485	−49,554
Trade balance	20,286	13,834	16,350
Exports of services	8,179	11,246	13,662
Imports of services	−9,770	−12,979	16,763
Balance on goods and services	18,695	12,101	13,249
Private unrequited transfers (net)	−704	−1,921	−2,096
Government unrequited transfers (net)	8	−3	−8
Current balance	17,999	10,177	11,145
Direct capital investment (net)	11	−3,161	−5,374
Other long-term capital (net)	−2,596	−3,112	−2,414
Short-term capital (net)	12,982	−5,182	−4,368
Net errors and omissions	−305	−114	239
Total (net monetary movements)	28,091	−1,392	−745
Monetization of gold (net)	992	2,629	18
Valuation changes (net)	2,739	−1,390	522
Changes in reserves	31,822	−153	−205

External Trade

SELECTED COMMODITIES (NT $ million)

Imports c.i.f.	1987	1988	1989
Wheat (unmilled)	3,854.7	4,586.9	4,657.8
Maize (unmilled)	11,259.5	15,706.1	16,201.9
Soybeans	13,690.8	15,809.1	14,417.8
Logs	12,884.8	12,455.7	13,433.9
Natural rubber	3,272.7	6,865.2	2,581.5
Crude petroleum	80,527.5	63,395.4	68,996.1
Raw cotton	16,804.7	13,739.2	11,172.9
Yarn from synthetic fibres	3,039.7	3,227.1	6,765.9
Distillate fuels	4,742.4	9,186.9	10,521.1
Thin iron and steel sheets	6,832.8	6,803.4	10,220.4
Thermoplastic resins	15,465.0	19,600.2	8,247.4
Iron and steel scrap	6,058.5	7,441.8	8,613.5
Spinning, extruding machines	13,466.2	12,060.8	10,745.9
Television receivers	1,410.3	3,338.0	5,475.9
Internal combustion engines other than for aircraft	7,088.0	7,066.5	2,699.1
Ships for breaking	11,170.7	6,004.2	1,011.8
Total (incl. others)	1,113,104.9	1,422,614.1	1,385,273.2

Exports f.o.b.	1987	1988	1989
Fresh bananas	1,716.9	1,264.1	1,182.2
Canned mushrooms	1,896.6	780.0	317.3
Canned asparagus	861.8	582.4	179.8
Raw sugar	195.3	189.9	291.5
Cotton fabrics	3,855.5	3,038.0	5,962.6
Yarn from synthetic fibres	16,108.6	16,191.2	21,245.7
Synthetic fabrics	33,048.3	33,034.1	23,498.4
Plywood	9,711.4	9,001.1	6,006.9
Clothing (incl. knitted and crocheted fabrics)	150,971.5	125,967.8	83,190.4
Thermionic articles, valves, tubes, photocells, transistors etc.	50,097.5	62,867.8	31,389.5
Calculating machines	125,320.1	153,346.2	103,948.0
Television receivers	21,455.8	17,360.6	35,512.8
Radio receivers	20,846.9	16,741.9	19,802.0
Plastic articles	148,090.8	142,796.5	101,047.8
Dolls and toys	29,028.8	19,233.2	11,749.7
Total (incl. others)	1,705,649.7	1,729,465.8	1,745,104.2

PRINCIPAL TRADING PARTNERS (US $ '000)

Imports c.i.f.	1987	1988	1989
Australia	999,923	1,336,207	1,631,027
Canada	651,747	953,279	995,999
Germany, Federal Republic	1,633,504	2,132,075	2,593,483
Hong Kong	753,784	1,921,692	2,304,796
Indonesia	567,248	613,433	706,117
Italy	442,181	650,238	789,094
Japan	11,840,527	14,824,174	16,026,943
Korea, Republic	532,702	900,067	1,238,880
Kuwait	730,154	489,447	434,461
Malaysia	729,044	943,332	887,441
Philippines	194,435	242,293	238,466
Saudi Arabia	1,075,312	1,237,018	1,375,481
Singapore	522,145	740,042	888,973
Thailand	200,413	341,880	389,996
United Kingdom	789,184	1,111,513	926,677
USA	7,629,488	13,002,029	11,995,093
Total (incl. others)	34,957,239	49,655,819	52,248,568

Exports f.o.b.	1987	1988	1989
Australia	1,100,839	1,356,882	1,576,328
Canada	1,558,862	1,581,990	1,356,760
Germany, Federal Republic	1,986,840	2,338,115	2,561,257
Hong Kong	4,117,621	5,579,666	7,029,566
Indonesia	444,452	631,110	733,149
Italy	655,067	834,230	868,467
Japan	6,978,195	8,762,068	9,051,101
Korea, Republic	637,209	917,087	1,132,245
Kuwait	150,267	166,384	138,120
Malaysia	271,855	450,646	693,454
Philippines	458,174	599,876	776,587
Saudi Arabia	703,472	629,011	555,614
Singapore	1,348,839	1,680,007	1,973,474
Thailand	424,114	752,877	1,106,382
United Kingdom	1,547,242	1,904,945	2,099,032
USA	23,660,225	23,430,965	23,996,237
Total (incl. others)	53,611,697	60,585,422	66,201,101

Transport

RAILWAYS (traffic)

	1987	1988	1989
Passengers ('000)	134,367	132,315	127,973
Passenger-km ('000)	8,458,514	8,233,044	8,144,909
Freight ('000 metric tons)	31,211	30,399	30,867
Freight ton-km ('000)	2,490,214	2,278,043	2,111,502

ROAD TRAFFIC (motor vehicles in use at 31 December)

	1987	1988	1989
Passenger cars	1,254,955	1,579,121	1,969,291
Buses and coaches	21,608	21,955	21,852
Goods vehicles	451,100	502,189	573,576
Motorcycles and scooters	5,958,754	6,810,540	7,619,038

INTERNATIONAL SEA-BORNE SHIPPING
(freight traffic, '000 metric tons)

	1987	1988	1989
Goods loaded	103,194	108,865	113,470
Goods unloaded	157,326	174,329	182,840

CHINA (TAIWAN)

CIVIL AVIATION (traffic on scheduled services)

	1987	1988	1989
Passengers carried ('000)	12,361.3	14,742.7	17,207.0
Passenger-km (million)	14,498.2	17,609.5	20,797.4
Freight carried ('000 metric tons)	510.7	542.8	608.6
Freight ton-km (million)	2,944.6	3,218.5	3,727.0

Communications Media

	1987	1988	1989
Telephones	6,548,733	7,159,213	7,834,910

Education

(1989/90)

	Schools	Full-time teachers	Pupils/Students
Pre-school	2,556	13,244	242,785
Primary	2,484	80,849	2,384,801
Secondary (incl. vocational)	1,073	81,986	1,767,835
Higher	116	25,581	535,064
Special	11	750	3,163
Supplementary	499	3,720	262,951
Total (incl. others)	6,740	206,172	5,212,521

Directory

The Constitution

On 1 January 1947 a new constitution was promulgated for the Republic of China (confined to Taiwan since 1949). The form of government that was incorporated in the Constitution is based on a five-power system and has the major features of both cabinet and presidential government. The following are the principal organs of government:

NATIONAL ASSEMBLY

The Assembly, composed of elected delegates, meets to elect or recall the President and Vice-President, to amend the Constitution, or to vote on proposed constitutional amendments that have been submitted by the Legislative Yuan. Since the removal of the Republic of China from the mainland to Taiwan, full National Assembly elections have not been held. Many of the seats are held by 'life-term' members, originally elected to represent mainland constituencies. On 21 June 1990 the Council of Grand Justices, which is responsible for interpreting the Constitution, ruled that members of the nation's three central elective bodies who last faced election in mainland China more than 40 years ago, should step down by the end of 1991.

PRESIDENT

Elected by the National Assembly for a term of six years, and may be re-elected for a second term (the two-term restriction is at present suspended). Represents country at all state functions, including foreign relations; commands land, sea and air forces, promulgates laws, issues mandates, concludes treaties, declares war, makes peace, declares martial law, grants amnesties, appoints and removes civil and military officers, and confers honours and decorations. He also convenes the National Assembly, and subject to certain limitations, may issue emergency orders to deal with national calamities and ensure national security.

EXECUTIVE YUAN

Is the highest administrative organ of the nation and is responsible to the Legislative Yuan; has three categories of subordinate organization:

Executive Yuan Council (policy-making organization)
Ministries and Commissions (executive organization)
Subordinate organization (19 bodies, including the Secretariat, Government Information Office, Directorate-General of Budget, Accounting and Statistics, Council for Economic Planning and Development, and Environmental Protection Administration).

LEGISLATIVE YUAN

Is the highest legislative organ of the state, composed of elected members; holds two sessions a year, is empowered to hear administrative reports of the Executive Yuan, and to change government policy. Like the National Assembly, many of its seats are held by 'life-term' members, who are due to step down by the end of 1991.

JUDICIAL YUAN

Is the highest judicial organ of state and has charge of civil, criminal and administrative cases, and of cases concerning disciplinary measures against public functionaries (see Judicial System).

EXAMINATION YUAN

Supervises examinations for entry into public offices, and deals with personnel questions of the civil service.

CONTROL YUAN

Is a body elected by local councils to impeach or investigate the work of the Executive Yuan and the Ministries and Executives; meets once a month, and has a subordinate body, the Ministry of Audit.

The Government

HEAD OF STATE

President: LEE TENG-HUI (took office 13 January 1988, re-elected by the National Assembly 20 March 1990).
Vice-President: LI YUAN-ZU.
Secretary-General: TSIANG YIEN-SI.

THE EXECUTIVE YUAN
(December 1990)

Premier: Gen. (retd) HAU PEI-TSUN.
Vice-Premier: SHIH CHI-YANG.
Secretary-General: WANG CHOU-MING.
Minister of the Interior: HSU SHUI-TEH.
Minister of Foreign Affairs: FREDERICK F. CHIEN.
Minister of National Defence: CHEN LI-AN.
Minister of Finance: WANG CHIEN-SHIEN.
Minister of Education: MAO KAO-WEN.
Minister of Justice: LU YOU-WEN.
Minister of Economic Affairs: VINCENT S. SIEW.
Minister of Communications: CLEMENT C. P. CHANG.
Ministers of State: HUANG KUN-HUI, KUO NAN-HUNG, CHANG CHIEN-HAN, HUANG SHIEH-CHEN, WANG CHOU-MING, SHIRLEY W. Y. KUO, WU PO-HSIUNG.
Director-General of Council for Economic Planning and Development: SHIRLEY W. Y. KUO.
Chairman of the Overseas Chinese Affairs Commission: TSENG KWANG-SHUN.
Chairman of the Mongolian and Tibetan Affairs Commission: WU HUA-PENG.
Director-General of the Government Information Office: SHAW YU MING.
Director-General of Directorate-General of Budget, Accounting and Statistics: YU CHIEN-MIN.

CHINA (TAIWAN)

Director-General of Central Personnel Administration: PU TA-HAI.
Director-General of Department of Health: CHANG PO-YA.
Director-General of Environmental Protection Administration: EUGENE Y. H. CHIEN.
Chairman of National Council of Science: HSIA HAN-MIN.
Chairman of Council of Agriculture: YU YU-HSIEN.
Chairman of Council of Cultural Planning and Development: KUO WEI-FAN.
Chairman of Research, Development and Evaluation Commission: MA YING-JEOU.

MINISTRIES AND COMMISSIONS

Office of the President: Chiehshou Hall, Chungking South Rd, Taipei.
Ministry of Communications: 2 Changsha St, Sec. 1, Taipei; tel. (02) 3112661.
Ministry of Economic Affairs: 15 Foochow St, Taipei; tel. (02) 3517271; telex 19884.
Ministry of Education: 5 Chungshan South Rd, Taipei 10040; tel. (02) 3513111; telex 10894.
Ministry of Finance: 2 Aikuo West Rd, Taipei; tel. (02) 3228000; telex 11840.
Ministry of Foreign Affairs: 2 Chiehshou Rd, Taipei 10016; tel. (02) 3119292; telex 11299.
Ministry of the Interior: 107 Roosevelt Rd, Sec. 4, Taipei; tel. (02) 3415241.
Ministry of Justice: 130 Chungching South Rd, Sec. 1, Taipei 10036; tel. (02) 3146871.
Ministry of National Defence: Chiehshou Hall, Chungking South Rd, Taipei 10016; tel. (02) 3117001.
Office of the Director-General of Budget, Accounting and Statistics: 1 Chung Hsiao East Rd, Sec. 1, Taipei; tel. (02) 3915231.
Mongolian and Tibetan Affairs Commission: 109 Roosevelt Rd, Sec. 4, Taipei; tel. (02) 3513131.
Overseas Chinese Affairs Commission: 30 Kungyuan Rd, Taipei; tel. (02) 3810039.

Note: The creation of four new Ministries (the Ministries of Social Welfare, of Culture, of Labour and of Agriculture) was approved by the Legislative Yuan in October 1989. In late 1990, however, the Ministries had yet to be inaugurated.

Legislature

KUO-MIN TA-HUI
(National Assembly)

Many of the seats in the Assembly are held by members who were originally elected to represent constituencies on the Chinese mainland. Since the removal of the Republic from the mainland to Taiwan in 1949, these members hold office for an indefinite period, as full elections have not been possible. The most recent election for additional members was held on 6 December 1986, when 84 new members (68 KMT, 11 DPP, four independents and one CDSP) were elected. In June 1990 the National Assembly had 691 members. Elections for 375 of the seats were to be held by the end of 1991. Delegates meet to elect or recall the President and Vice-President, to amend the Constitution or to vote on proposed constitutional amendments submitted by the Legislative Yuan.

LI-FA YUAN
(Legislative Yuan)

The Legislative Yuan is the highest legislative organ of state. As in the National Assembly, many of the seats are held by life members, originally elected on the Chinese mainland. The chamber also includes members appointed by the President, representing overseas Chinese communities. Other members are elected by universal suffrage for a term of three years and are eligible for re-election. Elections were held on 2 December 1989 for 101 seats, of which 72 were won by the KMT, 21 by the DPP and eight by independents. In June 1990 there were 267 members, comprising 227 KMT members, 21 DPP members, seven members of the Young China Party, three members of the China Democratic Socialist Party and nine independents.
President: LIANG SU-YUNG.
Vice-President: LIU SUNG-FAN.

CONTROL YUAN

The 49-member Control Yuan exercises powers of investigation, impeachment and censure, and powers of consent in the appointment of the President, Vice-President and the grand justices of the Judicial Yuan, and the president, vice-president and the members of the Examination Yuan, and power of audit over central and local government finances (see the Constitution).
President: HUANG TZUEN-CHIOU.
Vice-President: MA KUNG-CHUN.

Political Organizations

China Democratic Socialist Party (CDSP): 6 Lane 357, Hoping East Rd, Sec. 2, Taipei; tel. (02) 7074636; f. 1932 by merger of National Socialists and Democratic Constitutionalists; aims to promote democracy, to protect fundamental freedoms, and to improve public welfare and social security; 30,000 mems; Chair. WANG SHIH-HSIEN; Sec.-Gen. WONG HOU-SEN.

China Socialist Democratic Party: 3 Tsing-tao East Rd, 4th Floor, Taipei; tel. (02) 3938446; f. 1990 by breakaway faction of DPP; Leader CHU KAO-CHENG.

Chinese Freedom Party (CFP): Taipei; f. 1987; advocates the holding of free elections, liberalization of relations with mainland China and improved measures to combat corruption.

Chinese Republican Party (CRP): Taipei; f. 1988; advocates peaceful struggle for the salvation of China and the promotion of world peace; 1,746 mems; Chair. WANG YING-CHUN.

Democratic Liberal Party (DLP): Taipei; f. 1987; aims to promote political democracy and economic liberty for the people of Taiwan.

Democratic Progressive Party (DPP): 115 Chien Kuo North Rd, 7th Floor, Sec. 2, Taipei 10479; tel. (02) 5051115; fax (02) 5055539; f. 1986; advocates full elections to remove parliamentarians still holding the majority votes and their parliamentary posts since 1947, and 'self-determination' for the people of Taiwan; 20,000 mems; Chair. HUANG HSIN-CHIEH; Sec.-Gen. CHANG CHUN-HUNG.

Kungtang (KT) (Labour Party): 300 Roosevelt Rd, 5th Floor, Sec. 3, Taipei; tel. (02) 3121472; f. 1987; aims to become the main political movement of Taiwan's industrial work-force; 4,500 mems; Chair. WANG YI-HSIUNG; Sec.-Gen. YAU-NAN WANG.

Kuomintang (KMT) (Nationalist Party of China): 11 Chung Shan South Rd, Taipei; tel. (02) 3417211; fax (02) 3973896; f. 1894; ruling party; aims to supplant communist rule in mainland China; advocates constitutional government and the unification of China under the 'Three Principles of the People'; aims to promote market economy and equitable distribution of wealth; c. 2.4m. mems; Chair. LEE TENG-HUI; Sec.-Gen. JAMES C. Y. SOONG; Dep. Secs-Gen. KAO MING-HUEY, CHENG SHIN-HSIUNG, HSU LI-TEH.

New State, New Constitution Alliance: Taipei; f. 1989; advocates independent sovereignty for Taiwan and seeks to promulgate a new constitution.

Workers' Party: 181 Fu-hsing South Rd, 2nd Floor, Sec. 2, Taipei; tel. (02) 7555868; f. 1989 by breakaway faction of the Kungtang; radical; Leader LOU MEIWEN.

Young China Party: 256 King Hwa St, Taipei; tel. (02) 3413842; f. 1923; aims to recover sovereignty over mainland China, to safeguard the Constitution and democracy, and to foster understanding between Taiwan and the non-communist world; Chair. LI HUANG.

Diplomatic Representation

EMBASSIES IN THE REPUBLIC OF CHINA

Costa Rica: Tulip Bldg, 1st Floor, 108 Chung Cheng Rd, Sec. 2, Taipei; tel. (02) 8712422; Ambassador: FRANCISCO TACSAN LAM.
Dominican Republic: 110 Chung Cheng Rd, 1st Floor, Sec. 2, Tien Mou, Taipei; tel. (02) 8717938; telex 19873; Ambassador: JOSÉ MANUEL LÓPEZ BALAGUER.
El Salvador: 15 Lane 34, Ku Kung Rd, Shih Lin 11102, Taipei; tel. (02) 8819887; fax (02) 8817995; Ambassador: FRANCISCO RICARDO SANTANA BERRIOS.
Guatemala: 6 Lane 88, Chien Kuo North Rd, Sec. 1, Taipei; tel. (02) 5077043; fax (02) 5060577; Ambassador: CARLOS ORIOL JIMÉNEZ QUIROA.
Haiti: 246 Chungshan North Rd, 3rd Floor, Sec. 6, Taipei; tel. (02) 8317086; Ambassador: RAYMOND PERODIN.
Holy See: 87 Ai Kuo East Rd, Taipei 10605 (Apostolic Nunciature); tel. (02) 3216847; fax (02) 23911926; Chargé d'affaires a.i.: Mgr ADRIANO BERNARDINI.
Honduras: 142 Chung Hsiao East Rd, Room 701, Sec. 4, Taipei; tel. (02) 7518737; telex 14224; Ambassador: AGRIPINO FLORES AGUILAR.
Korea, Republic: 345 Chung Hsiao East Rd, Sec. 4, Taipei; tel. (02) 7619363; Ambassador: HAN CHUL-SOO.

CHINA (TAIWAN)

Panama: 13 Te Huei St, 5th Floor, Taipei; tel. (02) 5968563; Ambassador: CARLOS YAP CHONG.

Paraguay: 20 Lane 38 Tien Yee St, 2nd Floor, Tien Mou, Taipei; tel. (02) 8728932; telex 13744; Ambassador: ANGEL JUAN SOUTO HERNÁNDEZ.

South Africa: Bank Tower, 13th Floor, 205 Tun Hua North Rd, Taipei; tel. (02) 7153251; telex 21954; Ambassador: ALAN MCALLISTER HARVEY.

Judicial System

The interpretative powers of the Judicial Yuan are exercised by the Council of Grand Justices nominated and appointed for nine years by the President of the Republic of China with the consent of the Control Yuan. The President of the Judicial Yuan also presides over the Council of Grand Justices.

The Judicial Yuan has jurisdiction over the high courts and district courts. The Ministry of Justice is under the jurisdiction of the Executive Yuan.

Judicial Yuan: 124 Chungking South Rd, Sec. 1, Taipei; Pres. LIN YANG-KANG; Vice-Pres. WANG TAO-YUAN; Sec.-Gen. WANG CHIA-YI; the highest judicial organ, and the interpreter of the constitution and national laws and ordinances. Other judicial powers are exercised by:

Supreme Court: Court of third and final instance for civil and criminal cases; President CHU CHIEN-HUNG.

High Courts: Courts of second instance for appeals of civil and criminal cases.

District Courts: Courts of first instance in civil, criminal and non-contentious cases.

Administrative Court: Court of final resort in cases brought against govt agencies; President WANG JUI-LIN.

Committee on the Discipline of Public Functionaries: sentences persons impeached by the Control Yuan; Chair. FAN KUEI-SHU.

Religion

BUDDHISM

Buddhists belong to the Mahayana and Theravada schools. Leader PAN SHENG. The Buddhist Association of Taiwan has 1,462 group members and more than 4.09m. adherents.

CHRISTIANITY

The Roman Catholic Church

Taiwan comprises one archdiocese, six dioceses and two apostolic administrative areas. In 1988 there were approximately 300,000 adherents, of whom 69,258 resided in the archdiocese of Taipei.

Bishops' Conference: Regional Episcopal Conference of China, POB 36603, 34 Lane 32, Kuangfu South Rd, Taipei 10552; tel. (02) 7711295; f. 1978; Pres. Rt Rev. PAUL SHAN KUO-HSI, Bishop of Hualien.

Archbishop of Taipei: Most Rev. JOSEPH TI-KANG, Archbishop's House, 94 Loli Rd, Taipei 10668; tel. (02) 7371311.

The Anglican Communion

Anglicans in Taiwan are adherents of the Protestant Episcopal Church. In 1989 the Church had about 2,500 members.

Bishop of Taiwan: Rt Rev. JOHN CHIH-TSUNG CHIEN, 7 Lane 105, Hangchow South Rd, Sec. 1, Taipei 10044; tel. (02) 3411265; fax (02) 3962014.

Presbyterian Church

Tai-oan Ki-tok Tiu-Lo Kau-Hoe (Presbyterian Church in Taiwan): 3 Lane 269, Roosevelt Rd, Sec. 3, 10763 Taipei; tel. (02) 3625282; telex 20588; fax (02) 3628096; f. 1865; Gen. Sec. Rev. C. S. YANG; 211,531 mems (1989).

DAOISM (TAOISM)

There are about 2.35m. adherents.

ISLAM

Leader DAWUD FU HSU; 58,660 adherents.

The Press

An official ban on the registration of new newspapers was in force between 1951 and January 1988, when a limit on the maximum number of pages per issue was raised from 12 to 32. The liberalization of press restrictions has stimulated the launching of new publications, and by mid-1990 the number of newspapers had increased from 31 to 212, although only 59 newspapers were publishing on a regular basis. Most newspapers are based in western Taiwan, particularly Taipei, but their readership is island-wide. The majority of newspapers are privately owned, although one is controlled by the Government, three by the Kuomintang party and five by the Ministry of National Defence. The total circulation of all daily newspapers was approximately 5.7m. in mid-1990.

PRINCIPAL DAILIES

Taipei

Central Daily News: 260 Pa Teh Rd, Sec. 2, Taipei; tel. (02) 7213710; telex 24884; fax (02) 7775835; f. 1928; morning; Chinese; official Kuomintang organ; Publr SHIH YUNG-KUEI; Editor-in-Chief SHEH TSE-DIN; circ. 600,000.

China News: 277 Hsinyi Rd, Sec. 2, POB 1-23, Taipei; tel. (02) 3210882; fax (02) 3945543; f. 1949; morning; English; Publr SIMON WEI; Man. Editor MONANAN KUPPUSAMY; circ. 15,000.

China Post: 8 Fu Shun St, Taipei 10453; tel. (02) 5969971; telex 24059; fax (02) 5957962; f. 1952; morning; English; Publr NANCY HUANG; Editor JACK HUANG; circ. 150,000.

China Times: 132 Da Li St, Taipei; tel. (02) 3087111; telex 26464; fax (02) 3048138; f. 1950; morning; Chinese; Chair. YU CHI-CHUNG; Publr YU CHIEN-HSIN; Editor HUANG CHAO-SONG; circ. 1.2m.

China Times Express: 132 Da Li St, Taipei; tel. (02) 3082221; telex 26464; fax (02) 3048138; f. 1988; evening; Chinese; Publr ALICE YU; circ. 400,000.

Chung Cheng Pao: 100 Li-hsing Rd, Shing-den, Taipei; f. 1948; morning; armed forces; Publr HUANG CHIA-CHIN; Editor HSIAO CHIEN-MIN.

Commercial Times: 132 Da Li St, Taipei; tel. (02) 3087111; telex 26464; fax (02) 3048138; f. 1978; morning; Chinese; Publr YU FAN-YING; Editor-in-Chief CHENG IOU; circ. 250,000.

Economic Daily News: 555 Chung Hsiao East Rd, Sec. 4, Taipei; tel. (02) 7681234; telex 27710; f. 1967; morning; Publr WANG PI-LY; Editor LIN TUNG-SHIH.

Hsin Sheng Pao: 12-F Yenping South Rd, Taipei; tel. (02) 3110873; fax (02) 3115319; f. 1945; morning; Chinese; also southern edn publ. in Kaohsiung; Publr SHEN YUEH; Editor HSU CHANG; circ. 460,000.

Independence Evening Post: 15 Chinan Rd, Sec. 2, Taipei; tel. (02) 3519621; fax (02) 3419054; f. 1947; afternoon; Chinese; Publr Dr WU SHUH-MIN; Editor HU YUAN-HUI; circ. 180,000.

Independence Morning Post: 15 Chinan Rd, Taipei; tel. (02) 3519621; fax (02) 3514219; f. 1988; Chinese; Publr Dr WU SHUH-MIN; Editor WU GE-CHING; circ. 230,000.

Mandarin Daily News: 4 Fuchow St, Taipei; tel. (02) 3216765; f. 1948; morning; Publr HSIA CHENG-YING; Editor YANG RU DER.

Min Sheng Pao: 555 Chung Hsiao East Rd, Sec. 4, Taipei; tel. (02) 7681234; telex 27710; fax (02) 7560455; f. 1978; sport and leisure; Publr WANG SHAW-LAN; Editor SHIH PIN; circ. 457,000.

United Daily News: 555 Chung Hsiao East Rd, Sec. 4, Taipei; tel. (02) 7681234; fax (02) 7672129; f. 1951; morning; Publr WANG PI-CHENG; Editor CHANG TSO-CHIN; circ. 1.2m.

Youth Daily News: 3 Hsinyi Rd, Sec. 1, Taipei; tel. (02) 3212788; f. 1984; morning; Chinese; armed forces; Publr CHEN CHI; Editor NIEN CHEN-YU.

Provincial

Chien Kuo Daily News: 36 Min Sheng Rd, Makung, Chen, Penghu; tel. 272675; f. 1949; morning; Editor WANG LIEN-CHERNG; circ. 15,000.

China Daily News (Southern Edn): 57 Hsi Hwa St, Tainan; tel. 2202691; f. 1946; morning; Publr CHAN TIEN-HSING; Editor CHENG CHI-LING; circ. 260,000.

China Evening News: 243 Hsinleh St, Kaohsiung; tel. 3332203; f. 1955; afternoon; Publr LIU HEN-HSIU; Editor YANG NIEN-TSU; circ. 70,000.

Keng Sheng Daily News: 36 Wuchuan St, Hualien; tel. (038) 340131; f. 1947; morning; Publr HSIEH YING-YI; Editor CHEN HSING; circ. 5,000.

Kinmen Daily News: Chin Hu Village, Kinmen; tel. 2374; f. 1965; morning; Publr LEE JUI-HWA; Editor GUU HWA-CHING; circ. 5,000.

Matsu Daily News: Matsu; tel. 2276; f. 1957; morning; Publr WU TUNG-LUNG; Editor YU CHANG-CHAO.

Min Chung Daily News: 410 Chung Shan 2 Rd, Kaohsiung; tel. 3353131; f. 1950; morning; Publr LEE JUI PIAO; Editor HSU SU-HUNG; circ. 148,000.

CHINA (TAIWAN) *Directory*

Shin Wen Evening News: 249 Chungcheng 4 Rd, Kaohsiung; tel. (07) 2212858; f. 1985; afternoon; Publr YEH CHIEN-LI; Dir YEH CHIEN-LI; Editor LIU TII-CHANG; circ. 12,000.

Taiwan Daily News: 361 Wen Shin Rd, Sec. 3, Taichung; tel. (04) 2958511; f. 1964; morning; Chair. HSU HENG; Publr CHEN MAO-PANG; Editor CHANG CHIA-HSIANG; circ. 250,000.

Taiwan Hsin Wen Daily News: 249 Chung Cheng 4 Rd, Kaohsiung; tel. 2212154; f. 1949; morning; southern edn of *Hsin Sheng Pao*; Publr YEH CHIEN-LI; Editor HSIEH TSUNG-MIN.

Taiwan Times: 110 Chungshan 1 Rd, Kaohsiung; tel. (07) 7258111; f. 1971; Publr YU TSANG-CHOW; Editor YAO CHIH-HAI; circ. 148,000.

SELECTED PERIODICALS

Agri-week: 14 Wenchow St, Taipei; tel. (02) 3628148; fax (02) 3636724; f. 1975; weekly; Editor JAMES H. LEE; Publr Dr YU YU-HSIEN.

Artist Magazine: 147 Chung Ching South Rd, 6th Floor, Sec. 1, Taipei; tel. (02) 3719692; fax (02) 3317096; f. 1975; monthly; Publr HO CHENG KWANG; circ. 28,000.

Biographical Literature: 230 Hsinyi Rd, 4th Floor, Sec. 2, Taipei; tel. (02) 3410213; Publr LIU TSUNG-HSIANG.

China Times Weekly: 132 Da Li St, Taipei; tel. (02) 3087111; telex 26464; fax (02) 3020983; f. 1978; weekly; Chinese; Editor WU KUO-TUNG; Publr CHIEN CHIH-HSIN; circ. 180,000.

Continent Magazine: 11-6 Foochow St, Taipei; tel. (02) 3518310; f. 1950; monthly; archaeology, history and literature; Publr WAN SHAO-CHANG.

Crown: 50 Lane 120, Tun Hwa North Rd, Taipei; tel. (02) 7168888; fax (02) 7133422; f. 1954; monthly; literature and arts; Publr PING SIN TAO.

Evergreen Monthly: 2 Pa Teh Rd, 11th Floor, Sec. 3, Taipei; tel. (02) 7731665; fax (02) 7416838; f. 1983; health care knowledge; Publr WALTER C. H. WANG; circ. 140,000.

Families Monthly: 2 Pa Teh Rd, 11th Floor, Sec. 3, Taipei; tel. (02) 7731665; fax (02) 7416838; f. 1976; family life; Publr WALTER C. H. WANG; circ. 155,000.

Free China Review: 2 Tientsin St, Taipei 10023; tel. (02) 3516419; telex 11636; fax (02) 3516227; f. 1951; monthly; English; illustrated; Publr SHAW YU-MING; Deputy Editor-in-Chief BETTY WANG.

Free China Journal: 2 Tientsin St, Taipei 10023; tel. (02) 3718201; telex 11636; fax (02) 3416252; f. 1964; English; news review; Publr SHAW YU-MING; Editor LEE MING-LIANG.

The Gleaner: Kaohsiung Refinery, 2 Hung-i 1 Rd, Nantz, Kaohsiung; tel. 3621367; Publr CHIN KAI-YIN.

Harvest Farm Magazine: 14 Wenchow St, Taipei; tel. (02) 3628148; fax (02) 3636724; f. 1951; every 2 weeks; Publr Dr YU YU-HSIEN; Editor JAMES H. LI.

Information and Computer: 116 Nanking East Rd, Sec. 2, Taipei; tel. (02) 5422540; fax (02) 5310760; f. 1980; monthly; Chinese; Publr FANG HSIEN-CHI; Editor LEE MING-FENG; circ. 28,000.

Issues and Studies: Institute of International Relations, 64 Wan Shou Rd, Mucha, Taipei 11625; tel. (02) 9394921; fax (02) 9382133; f. 1965; monthly; English; Chinese studies and international affairs; Publr LIN BIH-JAW; Editor DAVID S. CHOU.

Jade Biweekly Magazine: 11-F-4, 103 Fuh Hsing South Rd, Taipei; tel. (02) 7771343; fax (02) 7772279; f. 1982; economics, social affairs, leisure; Vice-Pres. ERIC WU; circ. 98,000.

Management Magazine: 166 Fu Hsing Rd, 9th Floor, Taipei; tel. (02) 7150471; fax (02) 7135701; monthly; Chinese; Publr and Editor FRANK L. HUNG; circ. 340,000.

Music and Audiophile: 271 Hsinyi Rd, 6th Floor, Sec. 2, Taipei; tel. (02) 3937201; f. 1973; Publr ADAM CHANG.

National Palace Museum Bulletin: Wai Shuang Hsi, Shih Lin, Taipei 11102; tel. (02) 8812021; fax (02) 8821440; f. 1966; every 2 months; Chinese art history research in English; Publr and Dir CHIN HSIAO-YI; Editor-in-Chief WU PING; Editor SU TU-JEN; circ. 1,000.

National Palace Museum Monthly of Chinese Art: Wai Shuang Hsi, Shih Lin, Taipei; tel. (02) 8821230; fax (02) 8821440; f. 1983; monthly in Chinese; Publr CHIN HSIAO-YI; Editor-in-Chief LIN PO-TING; circ. 10,000.

Reader's Digest (Chinese Edn): 872 Min Sheng East Rd, 3rd Floor, Taipei; tel. (02) 7637206; telex 20954; monthly; Editor-in-Chief CHENG CHIEN-NUO.

Sinorama: 2 Tientsin St, Taipei 10047; tel. (02) 3123342; telex 11636; fax (02) 3615734; f. 1976; monthly; cultural; bilingual magazine with edns in Chinese with Japanese, Spanish and English; Publr SHAW YU-MING; Editor-in-Chief SUNNY HSIAO; circ. 100,000.

Sinwen Tienti (Newsdom): 207 Fuh Hsing North Rd, 10th Floor, Taipei; tel. (02) 7139668; fax (02) 7131763; f. 1945; weekly; Chinese; Dir PU SHAO-FU; Editor LI CHI-LIU.

Taiwan Pictorial: 20 Chungking South Rd, Sec. 2, Taipei 10741; tel. (02) 3115586; fax (02) 3115586; f. 1954; monthly; Chinese; general illustrated; Publr LO SEN-TUNG; Editor LIN KUO-CHIN.

Tien Sia (Commonwealth Monthly): 87 Song Chiang Rd, 4th Floor, Taipei; tel. (02) 5518627; monthly; business; Pres. CHARLES H. C. KAO; Publr and Editor DIANE YING.

Times Newsweekly: 132 Da Li St, Taipei; tel. (02) 3087111; f. 1986; weekly; Chinese; Publr ALBERT C. YU; circ. 30,000.

TV Weekly: 2 Pa Teh Rd, 11th Floor, Taipei; tel. (02) 7731665; fax (02) 7416838; f. 1962; Publr WALTER H. WANG; circ. 160,000.

Unitas: 180 Keelung Rd, 7th Floor, Sec. 1, Taipei; tel. (02) 7666759; monthly; Chinese; literary journal; Publr CHANG PAO-CHING; Editor CHU AN-MIN.

Woman ABC Magazine: Apollo Bldg, 13th Floor, 218-4 Chung Hsiao East Rd, Sec. 4, Taipei; tel. (02) 7314625; fax (02) 7314328; f. 1982; monthly; Publr ANNIE CHEN; circ. 72,000.

The Woman: 3 Lane 52, Nanking East Rd, Sec. 4, Taipei; tel. (02) 7524425; telex 11887; fax (02) 7814308; f. 1968; monthly; Publr CHANG CHIN; Editor-in-Chief C. Y. CHANG; circ. 80,000.

NEWS AGENCIES

Central News Agency Inc. (CNA): 209 Sungkiang Rd, Taipei; tel. (02) 5611181; telex 11548; f. 1924; Pres. HWANG TIEN-TSAI; Editor-in-Chief CONRAD K. Y. LU.

Chiao Kwang News Agency: 28 Tsinan Rd, 4th Floor, Sec. 2, Taipei; tel. (02) 3214803; Publr MING CHUN-HWA; Dir HUANG HO.

Foreign Bureaux

Agence France-Presse (AFP): 209 Sungkiang Rd, 6th Floor, Room 616, Taipei; tel. (02) 5106395; Correspondents YANG HSIN-HSIN, CHEN MEI-HUI.

Associated Press (AP) (USA): 209 Sungkiang Rd, 6th Floor, Room 630, Taipei; tel. (02) 5015109; telex 21835; Correspondents PAN YUEH-KAN, ANNIE HUANG, YANG CHI-HSIEN, SHIRLEY LAI.

Reuters (UK): SN Bldg, 10th Floor, 381 Minsheng East Rd, Taipei; tel. (02) 5033034; telex 22360; fax (02) 5031793; Chief Representative RICHARD PASCOE; Correspondents DAVID SCHLESINGER, C. K. CHEN, ANDREW QUINN.

United Press International (UPI) (USA): 209 Sungkiang Rd, 6th Floor, Room 624, Taipei; tel. (02) 5052549; Correspondent KATHERINE CHEN.

PRESS ASSOCIATION

Taipei Journalists Association: 555 Chung Hsiao East Rd, Sec. 4, Taipei; tel. (02) 7681234; c. 3,080 mems representing editorial and business executives of newspapers and broadcasting stations.

Publishers

Art Book Co: 18 Lane 283, 4th Floor, Roosevelt Rd, Sec. 3, Taipei; tel. (02) 3210578; Publr HO KUNG SHANG.

Buffalo Publishing Co: 135 Chin Shan South Rd, 2nd Floor, Sec. 1, Taipei; Publr PENG CHUNG HANG.

Cheng Chung Book Co: 20 Hengyang Rd, Taipei; humanities, social sciences, medicine, fine arts; Publr HUANG CHAO-HENG.

Cheng Wen Publishing Co: POB 22605, Taipei; tel. (02) 3628032; telex 13542; fax (02) 3925428; Publr HUANG CHENG CHU.

China Times Publishing Co Ltd: 132 Darli St, 4th Floor, Taipei; tel. (02) 3087111; Publr CHANG YUAN-HO.

Chinese Culture University Press: Hua Kang, Yangmingshan, Taipei; tel. (02) 8611861; Publr LEE FU-CHEN.

Chung Hwa Book Co Ltd: 94 Chungking South Rd, Sec. 1, Taipei; tel. (02) 3113541; humanities, social sciences, medicine, fine arts, school books; Gen. Man. HSIUNG DUN SENG.

The Commercial Press Ltd: 37 Chungking S. Rd, Sec. 1, Taipei; tel. (02) 3116118; Publr CHU CHIEN-MIN.

Crown Publishing Co: 50 Lane 120, Tunhua S. Rd, Taipei; tel. (02) 7168888; Publr PHILIP PING.

The Eastern Publishing Co Ltd: 121 Chungking South Rd, Sec. 1, Taipei; tel. (02) 3114514; Publr CHENG LI-TSU.

Elite Publishing Co: 33-1 Lane 113, 1st Floor, Hsiamen St, Taipei; tel. (02) 3211021; Publr KO CHING-HWA.

Far East Book Co: 66-1 Chungking South Rd, 10th Floor, Sec. 1, Taipei; tel. (02) 3118740; art, education, history, physics, mathematics, law, literature, dictionaries; Publr GEORGE C. L. PU.

Hilit Publishing Co Ltd: 1 Hsinyi Rd, 3rd Floor, Sec. 4, Taipei 10656; tel. (02) 7049633; telex 26229; fax (02) 7019311; Publr DIXON D. S. SUNG.

CHINA (TAIWAN) *Directory*

Hua Hsin Culture and Publications Center: 133 Kuang Fu North Rd, 2nd Floor, Taipei; tel. (02) 7658848; f. 1960; Dir JAMES K. CHENG.

International Cultural Enterprises: 25 Po Ai Rd, 6th Floor, Taipei; tel. (02) 3318080; Publr HU TZE-DAN.

Kwang Fu Book Co Ltd: 38 Fuhsing North Rd, 6th Floor, Taipei; tel. (02) 7716622; telex 19565; fax (02) 7315982; Publr LIN CHUN-HUI.

Kwang Hwa Publishing Co: 2 Tientsin St, Taipei 10041; tel. (02) 322888; fax (02) 3416252; Publr SHAW YU-MING.

Li-Ming Cultural Enterprise Co: 3 Hsin Yi Rd, 10th Floor, Sec. 1, Taipei; tel. (02) 3952500; telex 27377; Publr LIU YEN-SHENG; Gen. Man. CHANG MING HONG.

Linking Publishing Co Ltd: 555 Chunghsiao East Rd, Sec. 4, Taipei; tel. (02) 7631000; Publr WANG PI-CHENG.

San Min Book Co: 61 Chungking South Rd, Sec. 1, Taipei 10036; tel. (02) 3617511; f. 1953; literature, history, philosophy, social sciences; Publr LIU CHEN-CHIANG.

Sitak Publishing & Book Corpn: 35 Lane 639, Minsheng E. Rd, Taipei; tel. (02) 7135272; Publr CHU PAO-LOUNG.

Taiwan Kaiming Book Co: 77 Chung Shan North Rd, Sec. 1, Taipei; tel. (02) 5415369; Publr CHAO LIU CHING-TI.

Tung Hua Book Co Ltd: 105 Ermei St, Taipei; tel. (02) 3611464; Publr CHARLES CHOH.

The World Book Co: 99 Chungking South Rd, Sec. 1, Taipei; tel. (02) 3311616; f. 1921; literature, textbooks; Chair. CHEN SHEH WOO; Publr YEN FENG-CHANG.

Youth Cultural Enterprise Co Ltd: 66–1 Chungking South Rd, 3rd Floor, Sec. 1, Taipei; Publr LEE CHUNG-KUEI; Gen. Man. CHENG SUNG-NIEN.

Yuan Liou Publishing Co Ltd: 7F/5, 782 Ding Chou Rd, Taipei 10714; tel. (02) 3923707; f.1975; fiction, non-fiction, children's; Publr WANG JUNG-WEN; Pres. JAN HUNG-TZE.

Radio and Television

In 1988 there were an estimated 16m. radio receivers, and 5.2m. television sets. Broadcasting stations are mostly commercial. The Ministry of Communications determines power and frequencies, and the Government Information Office supervises the operation of all stations, whether private or governmental.

RADIO

In 1988 there were 33 radio broadcasting corporations (with 186 stations and 388 transmitters), of which the following are the most important:

Broadcasting Corpn of China (BCC): 53 Jen Ai Rd, Sec. 3, Taipei; tel. (02) 7710150; telex 27498; fax (02) 7410066; f. 1928; domestic (8 networks) and external services in 15 languages and dialects; 9 local stations, 120 transmitters; Pres. P. P. TANG; Chair. JOHN KUAN.

Cheng Sheng Broadcasting Corpn Ltd: 66–1 Chungking South Rd, 6th–8th Floors, Sec. 1, Taipei; tel. (02) 3617231; f. 1950; 6 stations, 9 relay stations; Chair. CHANG CHIEN-JEN; Pres. YUN-HAN KAO.

Fu Hsing Broadcasting Corpn: 5, Lane 280, Sec. 5, Chung Shan N. Rd, Taipei; 27 stations; Dir LIN LU-TSEN.

TELEVISION

Taiwan Television Enterprise (TTV): 10 Pa Teh Rd, Sec. 3, Taipei; tel. (02) 7711515; telex 25714; fax (02) 7762757; f. 1962; Chair. HSU CHIN-TEH; Pres. WANG CHIA-HUA.

China Television Co (CTV): 120 Chung Yang Rd, Nan Kang District, Taipei; tel. (02) 7838308; telex 25080; f. 1969; Pres. CHU TZUNG-KE; Chair. KAN YU-JEN.

Chinese Television Service (CTS): 100 Kuang Fu South Rd, Taipei; tel. (02) 7510321; telex 24195; f. 1971; cultural and educational; Chair. YEE CHIEN-CHIU; Pres. WU SHIH-SUNG.

Finance

(cap. = capital; p.u. = paid up; dep. = deposits; m. = million; brs = branches; amounts in New Taiwan dollars)

BANKING
Central Bank

Central Bank of China: 2 Roosevelt Rd, Sec. 1, Taipei 10757; tel. (02) 3936161; telex 21532; fax (02) 3223223; f. 1928; bank of issue; cap. 23,000m., dep. 2,192,770m. (June 1989); Gov. S. C. SHIEH; Dep. Govs CHEN S. YU, PAUL C. H. CHIU.

Domestic Banks

Bank of Communications: 91 Heng Yang Rd, Taipei 10003; tel. (02) 3613000; telex 11341; fax (02) 3612046; f. 1907; cap. 10,000m., dep. 168,412m. (June 1989); Chair. KUO-SHU LIANG; Pres. C. Y. LEE; 20 brs, incl. 2 overseas.

Bank of Taiwan: 120 Chungking South Rd, Sec. 1, Taipei 10036; tel. (02) 3147377; telex 11201; fax (02) 3812284; f. 1946; cap. 8,000m., dep. 633,179m. (Dec. 1989); Chair. Dr I-SHUAN SUN; Pres. PU CHEN-MING; 70 brs.

Co-operative Bank of Taiwan: 77 Kuan Chien Rd, Taipei 10038; tel. (02) 7400628; telex 17176; fax (02) 7400546; f. 1946; acts as central bank for co-operatives, and as major agricultural credit institution; cap. 3,000m., dep. 660,300m. (June 1989); Chair. HUBERT M. F. HSU; Pres. H. P. LIAO; 118 brs.

Export-Import Bank: 3 Nan Hai Rd, 8th Floor, Taipei; tel. (02) 3210511; telex 26044; fax (02) 3940630; f. 1979; cap. 9,000m., dep. 3,593m. (June 1989); Chair. P. Y. PAI; Pres. C. S. LO; 1 br.

Farmers Bank of China: 85 Nanking East Rd, Sec. 2, Taipei 10408; tel. (02) 5517141; telex 21610; fax (02) 5515438; f. 1933; cap. 4,435m., dep. 150,133m. (June 1989); Chair. HONG-AO LEE; Pres. RICHARD M. C. TSAI; 35 brs.

International Commercial Bank of China: 100 Chi Lin Rd, Taipei 10424; tel. (02) 5633156; telex 11300; fax (02) 5632614; f. 1912; cap. 7,404m., dep. 130,028m. (Dec. 1989); Chair. C. D. WANG; Pres. THEODORE S. S. CHENG; 32 brs.

Land Bank of Taiwan: 46 Kuan Chien Rd, Taipei 10038; tel. (02) 3613020; telex 14564; fax (02) 3812066; f. 1946; cap. 12,000m., dep. 420,445m. (June 1990); Chair. J. D. SHYU; Pres. T. L. LIN; 61 brs.

Commercial Banks

Bank of Kaohsiung: 21 Wu Fu 3rd Rd, Kaohsiung; tel. 2413051; telex 73266; fax (07) 2826462; f. 1982; cap. 850m., dep. 26,921m. (June 1989); Chair. J. S. HSIEH; Pres. CHUN CHUNG-HUANG; 8 brs.

Central Trust of China: 49 Wu Chang St, Sec. 1, Taipei 10006; tel. (02) 3111511; telex 11377; fax (02) 3822010; f. 1935; cap. 5,000m., dep. 30,662m. (June 1990); Chair. W. S. KING; Pres. T. Y. CHU; 5 brs.

Chang Hwa Commercial Bank Ltd: 38 Tsuyu Rd, Sec. 2, Taichung 40010; tel. (04) 2222001; telex 51248; fax (04) 2231170; f. 1905; 51% govt-owned; transfer to private sector ownership pending in 1990; cap. 4,500m., dep. 462,900m. (June 1989); Chair. LIANG KUO-SHU; Pres. K. H. YEH; 107 brs.

City Bank of Taipei: 50, Sec. 2, Chungshan North Rd, Taipei 10419; tel. (02) 5425656; telex 11722; fax (02) 5231235; f. 1969; cap. 6,000m., dep. 192,669m. (June 1989); Chair. W. K. WU; Pres. S. C. WANG; 34 brs.

First Commercial Bank: POB 395, 15 Chungking South Rd, Sec. 1, Taipei; tel. (02) 3111111; telex 11310; fax (02) 3610036; f. 1899; 74% govt-owned; transfer to private sector ownership pending in 1990; cap. 4,896m., dep. 413,299m. (June 1989); Chair. H. A. CHEN; Pres. KENNETH B. K. TSAN; 137 brs.

Hua Nan Commercial Bank Ltd: 38 Chungking South Rd, Sec. 1, Taipei; tel. (02) 3713111; telex 11307; fax (02) 3817491; f. 1919; 51% govt-owned; transfer to private sector ownership pending in 1990; cap. 4,536m., dep. 506,539m. (June 1989); Chair. KENNETH K. H. LO; Pres. JAMES CHI TANG-LO; 98 brs.

Overseas Chinese Commercial Banking Corpn: 8 Hsiang Yang Rd, Taipei; tel. (02) 3715181; telex 21571; fax (02) 3814056; f. 1961; general banking and foreign exchange; cap. p.u. 2,563m., dep. 445,466m. (June 1989); Chair. CHUA SIAO HUA; Pres. L. S. LIN; 14 brs.

Shanghai Commercial and Savings Bank Ltd: 16 Jen Ai Rd, Sec. 2, POB 1648, Taipei 10018; tel. (02) 3933111; telex 22507; fax (02) 3934773; f. 1915; cap. p.u. 1,000m., dep. 34,671m. (Dec. 1989); Chair. JU-TANG CHU; Pres. RICHARD J. R. YEN; 17 brs.

United World Chinese Commercial Bank: 65 Kuan Chien Rd, POB 1670, Taipei 10038; tel. (02) 3125555; telex 21378; fax (02) 3318263; f. 1975; cap. 2,430m. (April 1989), dep. 176,476m. (Dec. 1989); Chair. SNIT VIRAVAN; Pres. GREGORY K. H. WANG; 8 brs.

There are also a number of Medium Business Banks throughout the country.

Foreign Banks

American Express Bank Ltd (USA): 214 Tung Hua North Rd, 4th Floor, Taipei; tel. (02) 7151581; telex 11349; fax (02) 7130263; Vice-Pres. JAMES D. VAUGHN.

Bangkok Bank Ltd (Thailand): 121 Sung Chiang Rd, 1st–3rd Floors, POB 22419, Taipei; tel. (02) 5073275; telex 11289; fax (02) 5064625; Vice-Pres. and Man. PHALLOBH SOPITPONGSTORN.

CHINA (TAIWAN)

Bank of America NT and SA (USA): 205 Tun Hua North Rd, Taipei; tel. (02) 7154111; telex 11610; fax (02) 7132850; Vice-Pres. and Man. WILLIAM D. CRAWFORD.

Chase Manhattan Bank NA (USA): 673 Ming Sheng East Rd, 8th Floor, POB 3996, Taipei; tel. (02) 5141234; telex 21823; fax (02) 5141299; Vice-Pres. and Gen. Man. J. MICHAEL CLATTERBUCK.

Chemical Bank (USA): Worldwide House, 7th Floor, 683-5 Ming Sheng East Rd, POB 48-11, Taipei; tel. (02) 7121181; telex 22411; fax (02) 7121450; Vice-Pres. and Gen. Man. HANK W. PENG.

Citibank NA (USA): 742 Min Sheng East Rd, POB 3343, Taipei; tel. (02) 7155931; telex 23547; fax (02) 7127388; Vice-Pres. THOMAS M. MCKEON.

Dai-Ichi Kangyo Bank Ltd (Japan): 137 Nanking East Rd, Sec. 2, Taipei; tel. (02) 5064371; telex 11220; fax (02) 5074388; Pres. MASAJI TAMURA.

First Interstate Bank of California (USA): 675 Ming Sheng East Rd, 6th Floor, Taipei; tel. (02) 7153572; telex 11830; fax (02) 7160388; Vice-Pres. and Gen. Man. H. SCOTT STEVENSON.

Hongkong and Shanghai Banking Corpn (Hong Kong): 333 Keelung Rd, 13th–14th Floors, Sec.1, Taipei; tel. (02) 7380088; telex 10934; fax (02) 7576333; Branch Man. IAN CAMERON MANZIES.

International Bank of Singapore: 178 Nanking East Rd, Taipei; tel. (02) 5810531; telex 25530; fax (02) 7576090; Vice-Pres. and Branch Man. NA WU-BENG.

Irving Trust Co (USA): 437 Tun Hua South Rd, 4th Floor, Taipei; tel. (02) 7716612; telex 21710; Vice-Pres. EDWARD J. MORIARTY.

Metropolitan Bank and Trust Co (Philippines): 107 Chung Hsiao East Rd, Sec. 4, Taipei 10646; tel. (02) 7766355; telex 21688; fax (02) 7211497; Vice-Pres. and Gen. Man. HENRY SO UY.

Société Générale (France): 629 Ming Shen East Rd, 7th Floor, Taipei 10446; tel. (02) 7155050; telex 23904; fax (02) 7152781; Gen. Man. GUY PASTURAUD.

Standard Chartered Bank (UK): 337 Fu Hsing North Rd, Taipei 10483; tel. (02) 7163858; telex 12133; fax (02) 7174563; Man. JOHNSON C. FU.

Toronto Dominion Bank (Canada): 337 Fu Hsing North Rd, 2nd Floor, Taipei 10483; tel. (02) 7162162; telex 22503; fax (02) 7134816; Man. RAYMOND H. D. GUNN.

The following foreign banks also have branches in Taiwan: Amsterdam-Rotterdam Bank (Netherlands), American Express Bank (USA), Bank of Tokyo, Bankers Trust Co (USA), Banque Indosuez (France), Banque Nationale de Paris (France), Banque Paribas (France), Citibank NA (USA), Crédit Lyonnais SA (France), Deutsche Bank (Germany), Development Bank of Singapore, First National Bank of Boston (USA), ANZ Grindlays Bank (UK), Hollandsche Bank-Unie NV (Netherlands), Lloyds Bank PLC (UK), Manufacturers' Hanover Trust Co (USA), Rainier National Bank (USA), Royal Bank of Canada, Security Pacific National Bank (USA), Standard Bank of South Africa Ltd, Westpac Banking Corpn (Australia).

DEVELOPMENT CORPORATION

China Development Corpn: CDC Tower, 125 Nanking East Rd, Sec. 5, Taipei 10572; tel. (02) 7638800; telex 23147; fax (02) 7686060; f. 1959 as privately-owned development finance co to assist in creation, modernization and expansion of private industrial enterprises in Taiwan; encourages participation of private capital in such enterprises; cap. 3,000m. (1990); Chair. YUNG-LIANG LIN; Pres. W. L. KIANG.

STOCK EXCHANGE

Taiwan Stock Exchange Corpn: City Bldg, 10th Floor, 85 Yen-Ping South Rd, Taipei 10034; tel. (02) 3114020; telex 22914; fax (02) 3114004; f. 1962; Chair. CHI-FANG WU.

INSURANCE

Cathay Insurance Co Ltd: 237 Chien Kuo South Rd, Sec. 1, Taipei; tel. (02) 7067890; telex 11143; fax (02) 7042915; f. 1961; Chair. TSAI WAN-TSAI; Gen. Man. SHIH-YEN LIAO.

Cathay Life Insurance Co Ltd: 296 Jen Ai Rd, Sec. 4, Taipei; tel. (02) 7551399; telex 24994; fax (02) 7042915; f. 1962; Chair. TSAI WAN-LIN; Gen. Man. F. J. TU.

Central Insurance Co Ltd: 6 Chung Hsiao East Rd, Sec. 1, Taipei; tel. (02) 3819910; telex 22871; fax (02) 3116901; f. 1962; Chair. T. C. SU; Gen. Man. THOMAS T. L. LIN.

Central Reinsurance Corpn: 53 Nanking East Rd, Sec. 2, Taipei; tel. (02) 5115211; telex 11471; fax (02) 5235350; f. 1968; Chair. C. C. YANG; Gen. Man. C. K. LIU.

Central Trust of China, Life Insurance Dept: 76 Poai Rd, 5th–7th Floors, Taipei; tel. (02) 3144327; telex 21154; fax (02) 3140542; f. 1941; life insurance; Pres. TSENG-YU CHU; Man. SHIH-PIN WANG.

Directory

China Mariners' Assurance Corpn Ltd: 62 Hsin Sheng South Rd, Sec. 1, Taipei; tel. (02) 3913201; telex 21748; fax (02) 3915945; f. 1948; Chair VICTOR D. F. FAN; Gen. Man. K. T. FAN.

Chung Kuo Insurance Co Ltd: ICBC Bldg, 10th–12th Floors, 100 Chilin Rd, Taipei 10424; tel. (02) 5513345; telex 21573; fax (02) 5414046; f. 1931; fmrly China Insurance Co Ltd; Chair. PETER K. H. CHENG; Pres. C. F. HSU.

CITC Life Insurance Co Ltd: 122 Tun Hua North Rd, 6th Floor, Taipei; tel. (02) 7134511; fax (02) 7125966; f. 1963; Chair. L. S. KU; Gen. Man. C. Y. KU.

The First Insurance Co Ltd: 54 Chung Hsiao East Rd, Sec. 1, Taipei; tel. (02) 3913271; telex 28971; fax (02) 3412864; f. 1962; Chair. Z. T. LEE; Gen. Man. C. H. LEE.

The First Life Insurance Co Ltd: 550 Chung Hsiao East Rd, 12th Floor, Sec. 4, Taipei; tel. (02) 7582727; telex 12277; fax (02) 7586758; f. 1962; Chair. C. C. CHUNG; Gen. Man. ROBERT KUO.

Kuo Hua Insurance Co Ltd: 166 Chang An East Rd, Sec. 2, Taipei; tel. (02) 7514225; telex 22554; fax (02) 7817801; f. 1962; Chair. J. B. WANG; Gen. Man. C. H. CHAN.

Kuo Hua Life Insurance Co Ltd: 42 Chung Shan North Rd, Sec. 2, Taipei; tel. (02) 5621101; telex 22486; fax (02) 5313241; f. 1963; Chair. E. M. OUNG; Gen. Man. DANIEL I. M. OUNG.

Mingtai Fire and Marine Insurance Co Ltd: 156-1 Sung Chiang Rd, Taipei; tel. (02) 5711231; telex 22792; fax (02) 5367714; f. 1961; Chair. P. C. LIN; Gen. Man. H. T. CHEN.

Nan Shan Life Insurance Co Ltd: 302 Min Chuan East Rd, Taipei 10461; tel. (02) 5013333; telex 11868; fax (02) 5012555; f. 1963; Chair. K. K. TSE; Pres. and Man. Dir W. T. KOAY.

Shin Kong Fire and Marine Insurance Co Ltd: 13 Chien Kuo North Rd, 9th–12th Floors, Taipei; tel. (02) 5415335; telex 11393; f. 1963; Chair. ANTHONY T. S. WU; Gen. Man. Y. H. CHANG.

Shin Kong Life Insurance Co Ltd: 123 Nanking East Rd, Sec. 2, Taipei; tel. (02) 7753535; telex 21471; f. 1963; Chair. EUGENE T. C. WU; Gen. Man. WU CHIA-LU.

South China Insurance Co Ltd: 560 Chung Hsiao East Rd, 5th Floor, Sec. 4, Taipei; tel. (02) 7038418; telex 21977; f. 1963; Chair. C. F. LIAO; Gen. Man. CHIA-LU WU.

Tai Ping Insurance Co Ltd: 550 Chung Hsiao East Rd, 3rd–5th Floors, Sec. 4, Taipei; tel. (02) 7002700; telex 21641; fax (02) 7045681; f. 1929; Chair. GEORGE Y. L. WU; Gen. Man. C. C. CHEN.

Taian Insurance Co Ltd: 59 Kuan Tsien Rd, Taipei; tel. (02) 3819678; telex 21735; fax (02) 3816057; f. 1961; total gross premium income NT $2,468m. (1989); Chair. LIN KUN-CHUNG; Pres. CHEN LANG-HWA.

Taiwan Fire and Marine Insurance Co Ltd: 49 Kuan Chien Rd, Taipei; tel. (02) 3317261; telex 21694; fax (02) 3145287; f. 1946; Chair. L. F. TSAI; Gen. Man. K. Y. LU.

Taiwan Life Insurance Co Ltd: 17 Hsu Chang St, 18th Floor, Taipei; tel. (02) 3116411; fax (02) 3611344; f. 1947; Chair. YUEH-AY WU; Pres. L. C. HUNG.

Union Insurance Co Ltd: 219 Chung Hsiao East Rd, 2nd Floor, Sec. 4, Taipei; tel. (02) 7765587; telex 27616; fax (02) 7718601; f. 1963; Chair. Y. T. WANG; Gen. Man. FRANK S. WANG.

Trade and Industry

CHAMBER OF COMMERCE

General Chamber of Commerce of the Republic of China: 390 Fu Hsing South Rd, 6th Floor, Sec. 1, Taipei; tel. (02) 7012671; telex 11396; fax (02) 7542107; f. 1946; 33 mems, incl. 8 nat. feds of trade asscns, 31 dist. export asscns and 3 dist. chambers of commerce; Chair. CHUNG-SAN CHAO; Sec.-Gen. CHAO-HSIN CHIOU.

TRADE AND INDUSTRIAL ORGANIZATIONS

China External Trade Development Council: 333 Keelung Rd, 4th–8th Floors, Sec. 1, Taipei 10548; tel. (02) 7382345; telex 21676; fax (02) 7576653; trade promotion body; Sec.-Gen. AGUSTIN TING-TSU LIU.

China Productivity Centre: 340 Tun Hua North Rd, 2nd Floor, Taipei 10592; tel. (02) 7137731; telex 22954; fax (02) 7120650; f. 1955; industrial management and technical consultants; Pres. CASPER T. Y. SHIH.

Chinese National Association of Industry and Commerce: 390 Fu Hsing South Rd, 13th Floor, Sec. 1, Taipei; tel. (02) 7070111; telex 10774; Chair. KOO CHEN-FU; Sec.-Gen. C. CHAO.

Chinese National Federation of Industries (CNFI): 390 Fu Hsing South Rd, 12th Floor, Sec. 1, Taipei; tel. (02) 7033500; telex 14565; fax (02) 7033982; f. 1948; 134 mem. asscns; Chair. HSUI SHENG-FA; Sec.-Gen. HO CHUN-YIH.

CHINA (TAIWAN)

Industrial Development and Investment Centre: Ministry of Economic Affairs, 7 Roosevelt Rd, 10th Floor, Sec. 1, Taipei 10757; tel. (02) 3947213; telex 10634; fax (02) 3926835; f.1959 to assist investment and planning; Dir JOHN C. I. NI.

Taiwan Handicraft Promotion Centre: 1 Hsu Chow Rd, Taipei; tel. (02) 3217233; fax (02) 3937330; f. 1956; Chair. PHILLIP P. C. LIU; Sec.-Gen. Y. C. WANG.

Trading Department of Central Trust of China: 49 Wuchang St, Sec. 1, Taipei 10006; tel. (02) 3111511; telex 26254; fax (02) 3821047; f. 1935; export and import agent for private and govt-owned enterprises.

CO-OPERATIVES

In December 1989 there were 4,863 co-operatives, with a total membership of 5,127,764 people and total capital of NT $16,357.55m. Of the specialized co-operatives the most important was the consumers' co-operative (4,086 co-ops; 3,189,683 mems; cap. NT $346.91m.).

The centre of co-operative financing is the Co-operative Bank of Taiwan (see Finance section), owned jointly by the Taiwan Government and 284 co-operative units. The Co-operative Institute (f. 1918) and the Co-operative League (f. 1940), which has 430 institutional and 4,516 individual members, exist to further the co-operative movement's national and international interests; departments of co-operative business have been set up on three university campuses.

RURAL RECONSTRUCTION

Council of Agriculture (COA): 37 Nanhai Rd, Taipei 10728; tel. (02) 3317541; fax (02) 3310341; f. 1984 to replace the Council for Agricultural Planning and Development (CAPD), and the Bureau of Agriculture (BOA); govt agency directly under the Executive Yuan, with ministerial status; administration of all affairs related to food, crops, forestry, fisheries and the animal industry; promotes technology and provides external assistance; Chair. Y. H. YU; Vice-Chair. M. Y. TJIU, S. N. LING; Sec.-Gen. H. Y. CHEN.

TRADE UNIONS

Chinese Federation of Labour: 201-18 Tun Hua North Rd, 11th Floor, Taipei; tel. (02) 7135111; f. 1948; mems: c. 3,336 unions representing 2,187,074 workers; Pres. HSIEH SHEN-SAN; Gen. Sec. CHIU CHING-HWUI.

National Federations

Chinese Federation of Postal Workers: 45 Chungking South Rd, 9th Floor, Sec. 2, Taipei 107; tel. (02) 3921380; f. 1930; 23,916 mems; Pres. KO YU-CHIN.

Chinese National Federation of Railway Workers: 107 Chengchou Rd, Taipei; tel. (02) 5119090; f. 1947; 21,296 mems; Chair. KOO YUE-YIE.

National Chinese Seamen's Union: 115 Hang-Chow South Rd, 2nd Floor, Sec. 1, Taipei; tel. (02) 3941321; f. 1913; 27,845 mems; Pres. KING TI-HSIEN.

Regional Federations

Taiwan Federation of Textile and Dyeing Industry Workers' Unions (TFTDWU): 2 Lane 64, Chung Hsiao East Rd, Sec. 2, Taipei; tel. (02) 3415627; f. 1957; 33,031 mems; Chair. LI HSIN-NAN.

Taiwan Provincial Federation of Labour: 44 Roosevelt Rd, 11th Floor, Sec. 2, Taipei; tel. (02) 3916241; f. 1948; 69 mem. unions and 1.38m. mems; Pres. LEE CHEN-CHON; Sec.-Gen. HUANG YAO-TUNG.

Transport

RAILWAYS

Taiwan Railway Administration (TRA): 2 Yen Ping North Rd, Sec. 1, Taipei; tel. (02) 5511131; telex 21837; f. 1891; a public utility under the provincial govt of Taiwan; operates both the west line and east line systems, with a route length of 1,071.5 km, of which 498 km are electrified; the west line is the main trunk line from Keelung, in the north, to Kaohsiung, in the south, with several branches; electrification of the main trunk line was completed in 1979; the east line runs along the east coast, linking Hualien with Taitung; the north link line, with a length of 79.2 km from New Suao to Hualien, connecting Suao and Hualien, was opened in 1980; Man. Dir CHANG SHOU-TSEN.

There are also 1,454.3 km of private narrow-gauge track, operated by the Taiwan Sugar Corpn in conjunction with the Taiwan Forestry Bureau and other organizations. These railroads are mostly used for freight but they also offer a limited public passenger service.

ROADS

There were 20,040 km of highways in 1989, most of them asphalt-paved. The Sun Yat-sen (North–South) Freeway was completed in 1974. Construction of a 431-km Second Freeway, which is to extend to Pingtung, in southern Taiwan, began in July 1987 and was scheduled to be completed by the end of 1996.

Taiwan Area National Freeway Bureau: POB 75, Sinchwang, Taipei; tel. (02) 9093201; f. 1970; Dir-Gen. C. GENIH.

Taiwan Highway Bureau: 70 Chung Hsiao West Rd, Sec. 1, Taipei; tel. (02) 3110929; fax (02) 3810394; f. 1946; responsible for planning, design, construction and maintenance of provincial highways and some rural roads; Dir-Gen. CHI-CHANG YEN.

Taiwan Motor Transport Co Ltd: 17 Hsu Chang St, 5th Floor, Taipei; tel. (02) 3715364; f. 1980; operates national bus service; Chair. HSU JING-YUAN; Gen. Man. SHU LUNG-TAN.

SHIPPING

Taiwan has four international ports: Kaohsiung, Keelung, Taichung and Hualien. In 1989 the merchant fleet had a total displacement of 391,917.2 metric tons.

Evergreen Marine Corpn: 330 Minsheng East Rd, Taipei; tel. (02) 5057766; telex 11476; fax (02) 5055856; f. 1968; 33 container vessels, 1 training ship; world-wide container liner services from the Far East to the USA, the Caribbean, the Mediterranean, Europe and South-East Asia; Indian subcontinent feeder service; Chair. CHANG YUNG-FA; Pres. CHANG KUO-HUA.

Far Eastern Navigation Corpn Ltd: 348 Ming-Sheng East Rd, 5th Floor, Taipei; tel. (02) 5055561; 1 bulk carrier; Chair. C. C. HSU.

First Steamship Co Ltd: 10 Lin Sen South Rd, 8th Floor, Taipei; tel. (02) 3949412; telex 11288; 6 cargo vessels; world-wide services; Chair. J. Y. LIN.

Great Pacific Navigation Co Ltd: 79 Chung Shan North Rd, 2nd Floor, Sec. 2, Taipei; tel. (02) 5713211; telex 21983; 1 reefer vessel; fruit and refrigeration cargo services world-wide; Chair. CHEN CHA-MOU.

Taiwan Navigation Co Ltd: 17 Hsuchang St, 7th Floor, Taipei; tel. (02) 3113882; telex 11233; 4 bulk carriers, 2 general cargo, 1 passenger vessel; Chair. L. S. CHEN; Pres. C. W. ZEN.

Uniglory Marine Corpn: 340 Minsheng East Rd, 6th Floor, Taipei; tel. (02) 5019001; telex 24720; fax (02) 5017592; 9 container vessels; Chair. LOH YAO-FON; Pres. LEE MAN-CHI.

Waywiser Navigation Corpn Ltd: 200 Sunkiang Rd, 7th Floor, Taipei; tel. (02) 5221311; telex 23948; 2 bulk carriers, 1 ore carrier; Chair. C. C. HSU.

Yangming Marine Transport Corpn: Hwai Ning Bldg, 4th Floor, 53 Hwai Ning St, Taipei 10037; tel. (02) 3812911; telex 11572; fax (02) 3148058; 20 container vessels, 4 multi-purpose vessels, 2 ore carriers, 5 tankers, 3 bulk carriers; Chair. W. OUYANG; Pres. T. H. CHEN.

CIVIL AVIATION

There are two international airports, Chiang Kai-shek at Taoyuan, near Taipei, which opened in 1979, and Hsiaokang, in Kaohsiung. There are also 12 domestic airports.

China Air Lines Ltd (CAL): 131 Nanking East Rd, Sec. 3, Taipei; tel. (02) 7152626; telex 11346; fax (02) 7174641; f 1959; domestic services and international services to Hong Kong, Indonesia, Japan, Malaysia, the Philippines, Saudi Arabia, Singapore, Thailand, the Republic of Korea, the Netherlands, UAE and the USA; Chair. Gen. YEUH WU; Pres. BIEN SHIH-NIEN; fleet of 3 Boeing 737, 13 747, 6 Airbus-300, 3 A300-600R.

Eva Airways: Evergreen Bldg, 330 Minsheng East Rd, Taipei; f. 1989; plans to commence services to USA, Europe, South Pacific and Asia in 1991/92; Pres. FRANK HSU; fleet of 4 Boeing 747-400, 6 MD-11 and 2 767-300 ER on order.

Far Eastern Air Transport Corpn (FAT): 5, Alley 123, Lane 405, Tunhwa North Rd, 10592 Taipei; tel. (02) 7121555; telex 11639; fax (02) 7122428; f. 1957; domestic services and chartered flights; Chair. K. H. SIAO; Pres. T. C. HWOO; fleet of 8 Boeing 737, 2 Bell 212.

Formosa Airlines: 87 Sung Kiang Rd, 11th–15th Floors, Taipei; tel. (02) 5074188; telex 28979; fax (02) 5061542; f. 1966; domestic services; Chair. HSIN OH HSIU; fleet of 2 Saab 340, 5 Dornier 228-200, 3 B-N Islanders and 1 Short 360.

CHINA (TAIWAN)

Foshing Airlines: 150 Fu Hsing Rd, 2nd Floor, 10440 Taipei; tel. (02) 7152766; fax (02) 7129801; f. 1989; fleet of 2 ATR-42, 2 on order.

Great China Airlines: 171 Nanking East Rd, 12th Floor, Sec. 4, Taipei; tel. (02) 7150911; telex 115; f. 1989; Gen. Man. PETER SZU; fleet of 1 Dash 8-100, 5 on order.

Makung Airlines: 305 Ho-Tung Rd, Kaohsiung; tel. (07) 2211168; fax (07) 2211186; f. 1989; domestic services; Chair. CHEN WEN WU; fleet of 2 BAe 748; 2 BAe 146-300 on order.

Tourism

The principal tourist attractions are the festivals, the ancient art treasures and the island scenery. In 1989 there were 2,004,126 foreign visitors (including overseas Chinese) to Taiwan.

Tourism Bureau, Ministry of Communications: 280 Chunghsiao East Rd, 9th Floor, Sec. 4, Taipei; tel. (02) 7218541; telex 26408; fax (02) 7735487; f. 1966; Dir-Gen. CHI-KUO MAO.

Taiwan Visitors' Association: 111 Minchuan East Rd, 5th Floor, Taipei; tel. (02) 5943261; telex 20335; fax (02) 5943265; f. 1956; promotes domestic and international tourism; Chair. RICHARD C. C. CHAO.

Atomic Energy

The first nuclear power plant was integrated into the power supply system in 1977, and three nuclear power plants were operational by the late 1980s. Nuclear power generation provided about 13.0% of Taiwan's total energy supply in 1989.

Atomic Energy Council (AEC): 67 Lane 144, Keelung Rd, Sec. 4, 10772 Taipei; tel. (02) 3634180; telex 26554; fax (02) 3635377; f. 1955; promotes the advancement of nuclear science and technology, enforces safety requirements; Chair. HSU YIH-YUN; Sec.-Gen. LIU KUANG-CHI.

Institute of Nuclear Energy Research (INER): POB 3, Lung Tan 32500; tel. 3145384; telex 34154; f. 1968; national nuclear research centre; Dir JEN-CHANG CHOU.

COLOMBIA

Introductory Survey

Location, Climate, Language, Religion, Flag, Capital

The Republic of Colombia lies in the north-west of South America, with the Caribbean Sea to the north and the Pacific Ocean to the west. Its continental neighbours are Venezuela and Brazil to the east, and Peru and Ecuador to the south, while Panama connects it with Central America. The coastal areas have a tropical rain forest climate, the plateaux are temperate, and in the Andes mountains there are areas of permanent snow. The language is Spanish. Almost all of the inhabitants profess Christianity, and about 95% are Roman Catholics. There are small Protestant and Jewish minorities. The national flag (proportions 3 by 2) has three horizontal stripes, of yellow (one-half of the depth), dark blue and red. The capital is Bogotá.

Recent History

Colombia was under Spanish rule from the 16th century until 1819, when it achieved independence as part of Gran Colombia, which included Ecuador, Panama and Venezuela. Ecuador and Venezuela seceded in 1830, when Colombia (then including Panama) became a separate republic. In 1903 the province of Panama successfully rebelled and became an independent country. For more than a century, Colombia has been dominated by two political parties, the Conservatives (Partido Conservador) and the Liberals (Partido Liberal), whose rivalry has often led to violence. Liberal governments held power in 1860–84 and 1930–46, with Conservative governments in 1884–1930 and 1946–53. From 1922 to 1953, with one exception, every President of Colombia completed his four-year term of office. The assassination in April 1948 of Bogotá's left-wing Liberal mayor, Jorge Eliécer Gaitán, led to intense political violence, amounting to civil war, between Conservative and Liberal factions. According to official estimates, lawlessness between 1949 and 1958, known as 'La Violencia', caused the deaths of about 280,000 people.

President Laureano Gómez, who had been elected 'unopposed' in November 1949, ruled as a dictator until his overthrow by a coup in June 1953, when power was seized by Gen. Gustavo Rojas Pinilla. President Rojas established a right-wing dictatorship but, following widespread rioting, he was deposed in May 1957, when a five-man military junta took power.

In an attempt to restore peace and stability, the Conservative and Liberal Parties agreed to co-operate in a National Front. Under this arrangement, the presidency was to be held by Liberals and Conservatives in rotation, while cabinet portfolios would be divided equally between the two parties and both would have an equal number of seats in each house of the bicameral Congress. In December 1957, in Colombia's first vote on the basis of universal adult suffrage, this agreement was overwhelmingly approved by a referendum. It was subsequently incorporated in Colombia's Constitution.

In May 1958 the first presidential election under the amended Constitution was won by the National Front candidate, Dr Alberto Lleras Camargo, a Liberal who had been President in 1945–46. He took office in August 1958, when the junta relinquished power. During the rule of President Lleras Camargo, who was in power until 1962, left-wing guerrilla groups were established in Colombia. As provided by the 1957 agreement, he was succeeded by a Conservative, Dr Guillermo León Valencia, who held office until 1966, when another Liberal, Dr Carlos Lleras Restrepo, was elected. Despite continuing political violence, President Lleras Restrepo was able to bring about some recovery in Colombia's economy.

At the presidential election of 19 April 1970, the National Front candidate, Dr Misael Pastrana Borrero of the Conservative Party, narrowly defeated Gen. Rojas, the former dictator, who campaigned as leader of the Alianza Nacional Popular (ANAPO), with policies that had considerable appeal for the poorer sections of the population. At elections to Congress held simultaneously, the National Front lost its majority in each of the two houses, while ANAPO became the main opposition group in each. The result of the presidential election was challenged by supporters of ANAPO, who demonstrated against alleged electoral fraud. However, the result was officially upheld, after four recounts, and in August 1970 Dr Pastrana took office as President. In June 1971 ANAPO was officially constituted as a political party, advocating a populist programme of 'Colombian socialism'. However, some ANAPO supporters, in reaction to the disputed 1970 election results, formed an armed wing, the Movimiento 19 de Abril (M-19), which began guerrilla activity against the Government. They were joined by dissident members of a pro-Soviet guerrilla group, the Fuerzas Armadas Revolucionarias de Colombia (FARC), which had been established in 1966.

The bipartisan form of government ended formally with the presidential and legislative elections of April 1974, although the 1974–78 Cabinet remained subject to the parity agreement. The Conservative and Liberal Parties together won an overwhelming majority of seats in Congress, and the vote for ANAPO was greatly reduced. The presidential election was won by the Liberal Party candidate, Dr Alfonso López Michelsen, who received 56% of the total votes. President López took office in August 1974, promising wide-ranging reforms and a more equitable distribution of income. His failure to achieve these aims led to strikes, rioting and increased guerrilla violence. Meanwhile, Gen. Rojas died in January 1975 and was succeeded as leader of ANAPO by his daughter, María Eugenia Rojas de Moreno Díaz, who had been the party's presidential candidate in the 1974 election.

At elections to Congress in February 1978, the Liberal Party won a clear majority in both houses, and in June the Liberal Party candidate, Dr Julio César Turbay Ayala, won the presidential election. President Turbay kept to the National Front agreement, and attempted to tackle the problems of urban terrorism and drug trafficking, but had little success. In October 1981 a Peace Commission was set up under ex-President Lleras Restrepo. In early 1982 the guerrillas suffered heavy losses after successful counter-insurgency operations, combined with the activities of a new anti-guerrilla group which was associated with drug-smuggling enterprises, the Muerte a Secuestradores (MAS, Death to Kidnappers), whose targets later became trade union leaders, academics and human rights activists.

At congressional elections in March 1982, the Liberal Party maintained its majority in both the House of Representatives and the Senate. In the presidential election in May, the Conservative candidate, Dr Belisario Betancur Cuartas, received the most votes, benefiting from a division within the Liberal Party. President Betancur, who took office in August 1982, declared a broad amnesty for guerrillas in November, reconvened the Peace Commission and ordered an investigation into the MAS. Several hundred political prisoners were released. He embarked on a programme of radical reforms. However, the internal pacification campaign, which was begun in November 1982, met with only moderate success. An estimated 2,000 guerrillas accepted the Government's offer of amnesty.

In February 1984 President Betancur announced the resumption of talks between the Peace Commission and the principal guerrilla organizations. In late March the Peace Commission and the FARC agreed conditions for a cease-fire, which was to take effect for one year from May. Under the terms of the accord, the Government agreed to the demilitarization of rural areas. The FARC was to be allowed to assume an active political role. In July, following protracted negotiations, the M-19 group (now operating as a left-wing guerrilla movement) and the Ejército Popular de Liberación (EPL) agreed to a cease-fire but refused to relinquish their weapons. In spite of the murder of the M-19's founder, Carlos Toledo Plata, and subsequent reprisals by those guerrillas still active, the peace accord was signed in August. Factions of the FARC, EPL and the M-19 group which were opposed to the truce continued to conduct guerrilla warfare against the Government.

A major set-back to the Government's campaign for internal peace occurred in May 1984, when the Minister of Justice, Rodrigo Lara Bonilla, was assassinated. His murder was regarded as a consequence of his energetic attempts to eradicate the flourishing drugs industry, and Colombia's leading drugs dealers were implicated in the killing. The Government immediately declared a nation-wide state of siege and announced its intention to enforce its hitherto unobserved extradition treaty with the USA. The state of siege was partially lifted in October 1984.

Although members of the M-19 had begun to conduct a lawful political campaign in Colombia's main cities, reports of skirmishes between the guerrillas and the armed forces increased in early 1985. Relations between the M-19 and the armed forces continued to deteriorate, and in June the M-19 formally withdrew from the cease-fire agreement, accusing the armed forces of attempting to sabotage the truce. In November a dramatic siege by the M-19 at the Palace of Justice in Bogotá, during which more than 90 people (including 41 guerrillas and 11 judges) were killed, resulted in severe public criticism of the Government and the armed forces for their handling of events. Negotiations with the M-19 were suspended indefinitely. After three years, therefore, the only successful aspects of the Government's internal pacification programme had been the FARC's adherence to the cease-fire agreement and its foundation of a political party, the Unión Patriótica (UP), in May 1985. In response to the siege and the subsequent natural disaster caused by the eruption of the Nevado del Ruiz volcano (also in November 1985), the Government declared a state of economic and social emergency.

At congressional elections in March 1986, the traditional wing of the Partido Liberal (PL) secured a clear victory over the Partido Conservador and obtained 49% of the votes cast. The Nuevo Liberalismo wing of the PL received only 7% of the votes and subsequently withdrew from the forthcoming presidential election. The UP won seats in both houses of Congress. At the presidential election in May, Dr Virgilio Barco Vargas, candidate of the PL, was elected president with 58% of the votes cast. The large majority that the PL secured at both elections obliged the Partido Conservador to form the first formal opposition to a government for 30 years. The PL's dominant position was consolidated by the Conservatives' refusal to participate as the minority party in a coalition government with the Liberals.

On taking office in August 1986, President Barco Vargas affirmed that his Government's principal task was to solve the problem of political violence and that the new administration was committed to the peace process that had been established by former President Betancur. It was hoped that the administration's plans would benefit from the FARC's decision, in March 1986, to sign an indefinite cease-fire agreement. Further priorities for the Government were to be a campaign against poverty and the maintenance of Colombia's programme to combat the cultivation and trafficking of illicit drugs.

Despite initial optimism that the truce between the Government and the FARC would prevail and that the UP would be able to participate fully in the political process, it became apparent during 1987 that such optimism was unfounded. The deterioration in relations between the Government and the guerrillas had been largely precipitated by the Government's decision to disband the independent commissions responsible for monitoring and mediating in disputes between the authorities and guerrillas. Moreover, there was considerable hostility towards the Government because of its apparent reluctance to act against the campaign of paramilitary 'death squads' to assassinate members of the UP: between 1985 and October 1987 it was estimated that more than 450 members of the UP had been killed by such groups. In October the murder of Dr Jaime Pardo Leal, the President of the UP, heightened social tensions and led to widespread protests—many, specifically, against the Government's inadequate response to the mounting political violence. The crisis was compounded, later in the month, by the decision of six guerrilla groups, including the FARC, the Ejército de Liberación Nacional (ELN) and the M-19, to form a joint front, the Coordinadora Guerrillera Simón Bolívar (CGSB). Despite the resumption of talks between representatives of the Government and the guerrillas in late October, political violence and unrest continued.

Although the Barco Government had affirmed its commitment to eradicate Colombia's role in international drugs smuggling, it was unable to make any significant progress in 1987. In December 1986 leading drugs dealers were held responsible for the murder of a prominent newspaper director in Bogotá, and in January 1987 drugs traffickers were implicated in an attempt to assassinate the Colombian ambassador to Hungary (a former Minister of Justice). Although the Government authorized an extension of police powers against drugs dealers, its campaign was severely hampered by the Colombian Supreme Court's rulings, in December 1986 and June 1987, that Colombia's extradition treaty with the USA was unconstitutional. The inadequacy of the Government's efforts was underlined, in December, when Colombian authorities first declined to extradite, and subsequently released from custody, Jorge Luis Ochoa, a leading international cocaine trafficker. In January 1988 the internal crisis worsened, following the assassination of the Attorney-General, apparently on the orders of leading drugs dealers.

The Government responded to the assassination by issuing a new anti-terrorism decree, under which the armed forces were to be increased and rewards were to be offered to informants. In addition, the Government proposed to hold a plebiscite on the question of changes to the Constitution to counter guerrilla warfare. (The plebiscite was initially scheduled to be held concurrently with mayoral elections in March 1988, but was subsequently postponed to October. However, the Government eventually withdrew its proposal, after it was deemed to be unconstitutional by the Council of State.) The first direct elections for 1,009 mayoralties were held on 13 March. Poor results for the PL, which won in 427 municipalities, were attributed to divisions within the party. The Partido Social Conservador won in 415 municipalities, including Bogotá and Medellín. The electoral campaigns of all parties were disrupted by violence, and more than 30 candidates were killed.

In late May 1988 Colombia's internal crisis worsened, following the abduction by the M-19 group of Dr Alvaro Gómez Hurtado, a former presidential candidate of the Partido Social Conservador. Widespread protests were held in support of his release, and in June the Cabinet resigned, under public pressure. Gómez Hurtado was eventually freed by the M-19 in July, and his release appeared to give renewed impetus to the peace process; a Day of National Dialogue was held in late July, attended by representatives of political parties, trade unions and the Roman Catholic Church, although not by the Government or guerrilla groups. A Comisión de Convivencia Democrática (Commission of Democratic Cohabitation) was subsequently established, with the aim of holding further meetings between all sides in the conflict.

Moreover, at the beginning of September 1988 President Barco announced a new peace initiative, composed of three phases: pacification; transition; and definitive reintegration into the democratic system. Under the plan, the Government was committed to entering into a dialogue with those guerrilla groups that renounced violence and intended to resume civilian life. In October, despite reports of the guerrillas' willingness to resume the peace process, a major new offensive was launched by the leading guerrilla groups. Moreover, in November the President's effort to secure a cease-fire was placed in jeopardy by an appeal by the Minister of Defence for an 'all-out offensive' against the guerrillas. President Barco responded by dismissing the Minister and making new appointments to the military high command. However, within a few weeks of assuming his post, an unsuccessful attempt was made to assassinate the new Minister, Gen. Manuel Guerrero Paz. This development, coupled with the massacre of 43 people by a right-wing 'death squad' in the town of Segovia in November, prompted the Government to enact new measures to combat terrorism. In December it was estimated that some 18,000 murders had occurred in Colombia in 1988, of which at least 3,600 were attributed to political motives or related to drugs trafficking.

In January 1989 it was reported that the Government and the M-19 had concluded an agreement whereby a direct dialogue was to be initiated between the Government, all political parties in Congress and the CGSB, in an attempt to seek a political solution to the unrest. In mid-March the M-19 was reported to have signed a seven-point agreement with the Colombian Government, which provided for the reintegration of the guerrillas within Colombian society. The Government regarded the accord as an important step towards national reconciliation. In the same month, the ELN, EPL and FARC publicly confirmed their willingness to hold peace talks with the Government; in July the leading guerrilla groups (including the M-19) held a 'summit' meeting, at which they agreed to the formation of a Comisión de Notables, which was to draft proposals for a peace dialogue with the Government. The

Commission was to include two former Presidents and the Roman Catholic Archbishop of Bogotá. In September the M-19 announced that it had reached agreement with the Government on a peace treaty, under which its members were to demobilize and disarm in exchange for a full pardon. In addition, the movement was to be permitted to become a political party; in October the M-19 was formally constituted as a political party, and its leader, Carlos Pizarro León Gómez, was named presidential candidate for the movement. By 9 March 1990 (some three weeks later than scheduled) all M-19 guerrilla forces had surrendered their weapons, thereby satisfying the terms of the latest peace accord agreed with the Government. In exchange for firm commitments from the Barco administration that a referendum would be held to decide the question of constitutional reform and that proposals for comprehensive changes to the electoral law would be introduced in Congress, members of the M-19 were guaranteed a general amnesty, reintegration into civilian life and full political participation in forthcoming elections. In February Carlos Pizarro had announced the intention of the M-19 to contest congressional and municipal elections in Bogotá and the Department of Cundinamarca, scheduled for 11 March, as part of an electoral alliance (Acción Nacionalista por la Paz—with a diversity of support including the Christian Democrats and José Joaquín Matallana, a former army general who had headed state internal security (DAS) in the 1970s), although it was to present its own list of candidates elsewhere.

The election results revealed significant gains for the governing PL, which won 72 of the 114 seats in the Senate and an estimated 60% of the 199 contested seats in the House of Representatives, as well as regaining the important mayorships of Bogotá and Medellín. Ballot papers had also presented the opportunity to vote for the convening of a National Constituent Assembly (a measure which was heavily endorsed) and the selection procedure for the PL's presidential candidate, from which César Gaviria Trujillo (a former Minister of Finance and of the Interior under President Barco) emerged as a clear winner, with 60% of the votes cast.

The M-19 were thought to have secured at least two seats in the House of Representatives and the control of a small number of municipal councils, while in the contest for the mayorship of Bogotá Pizarro had received some 9% (around 80,000) of the total votes.

Bernardo Jaramillo, the presidential candidate of the UP (who had secured the only left-wing seat in the Senate), was assassinated by a hired gunman at Bogotá airport later in March 1990. It was estimated that more than 1,000 members of the UP had been murdered since its formation in 1985. While responsibility for Jaramillo's murder remained a source of speculation, public and political outrage at his assassination was directed largely at the Minister of the Interior, Carlos Lemos Simmons, who was accused of sharing responsibility for such acts of violence, owing to alleged government encouragement of anti-guerrilla death-squads and to recent comments made by Lemos, which suggested that the UP continued to maintain strong links with the revolutionary FARC. Lemos later resigned, reportedly indignant that President Barco had failed to support him in the matter.

The escalation of political violence continued in April 1990, when Carlos Pizarro became the third presidential candidate to be killed by hired assassins since August 1989; he was shot dead aboard an aircraft on a domestic flight from Bogotá to Barranquilla. Pizzaro was replaced by Antonio Navarro Wolff as presidential candidate for the M-19, in conjunction with the recently established Convergencia Democrática (later Alianza Democrática), an alliance of 13 (mainly left-wing) groups and factions. Although responsibility for the murder of Pizarro was officially ascribed to the Medellín drug cartels (as in the case of Jaramillo), spokesmen representing the cartels strenuously denied the allegations, leading to further speculation that both men had been the victims of political extremists.

A presidential election was held on 27 May 1990. A considerable escalation in the number of incidents of drug-related and politically-motivated violence in the weeks preceding the election was thought to be at least partly responsible for the poor turn-out of voters (estimated at some 46% of the electorate). César Gaviria Trujillo of the PL, who had been the most vociferous opponent of the drug cartels among the surviving candidates, was proclaimed the winner, with 47% of the votes cast, ahead of Álvaro Gómez Hurtado of the conservative Movimiento de Salvación (MSN), with 24%. Other candidates were Antonio Navarro Wolff of the Alianza Democrática—M-19 (AD—M-19), with 13%, and Rodrigo Lloreda Caicedo of the Partido Social Conservador Colombiano (PSC), with 12% of the votes cast.

Voters were also required to indicate support for, or opposition to, more detailed proposals for the creation of a National Constituent Assembly in a *de facto* referendum held simultaneously with the presidential ballot. Some 90% of voters indicated their approval of the proposal.

Gaviria's Cabinet, which was announced shortly before his inauguration on 7 August 1990, was described as a cabinet of 'national unity' and comprised seven members of the PL, four of the PSC and, most surprisingly, Antonio Navarro Wolff, who was appointed Minister of Public Health. President Gaviria emphasized, however, that the diversity in composition of the Cabinet did not represent the installation of a coalition government. Gen. Oscar Botero Restrepo was retained as Minister of Defence.

In October 1990 the creation of the National Constituent Assembly was declared constitutionally acceptable by the Supreme Court, and later in the same month Navarro Wolff resigned the health portfolio in order to head the list of candidates representing the AD—M-19 in elections to the Assembly scheduled for early December. Widespread concern was again expressed at the low level of participation in the election (turn-out was estimated at some 25%). Candidates for the AD—M-19 were particularly successful, securing around 27% of the votes cast and 19 of the 70 contested Assembly seats, forcing the ruling Liberals (with a total of 24 seats) and the Conservatives (with a combined total of 20 seats) to seek support from the AD—M-19 members and seven elected independents (including two members of the Evangelical Church and two representatives of indigenous Indian groups) for the successful enactment of reform proposals. It was suggested by the Government that the Assembly might be extended to 72 members in the future, to accommodate representatives of guerrilla groups willing to negotiate peace accords similar to that agreed with the M-19 earlier in the year.

In February 1990 the Government established the National Council for Normalization, in an attempt to repeat the success of recent peace initiatives with the M-19 in negotiations with other revolutionary groups. The EPL announced the end of its armed struggle in August and planned to join the political mainstream, along with the Comando Quintín Lame and the Partido Revolucionario de Trabajadores, in early 1991. Attempts to negotiate with the FARC and the ELN, however, proved ultimately fruitless, and violent clashes between the guerrilla groups and security forces continued throughout 1990, culminating in an intensification of guerrilla attacks against government targets in Antioquia by both the FARC and the ELN and significant escalation in counter-insurgency activities by the security forces (including the aerial bombardment in December of FARC headquarters). In January 1991 it was estimated that the total number of violent deaths in Colombia in 1990 had been more than 22,000.

During 1988 no significant progress was made by the Government in its attempt to eradicate the illegal drugs trade. Despite the decision of a US court to sentence Carlos Lehder Rivas, a leading member of the Medellín cartel of drugs smugglers, to life imprisonment in July, other leading drugs traffickers remained at liberty within Colombia, benefiting from the continuing dispute over the country's extradition policy.

In 1989 Colombia's internal situation, already regarded as highly unstable, was thrown into turmoil by the assassinations of several leading politicians and prominent figures in Colombian society, all of which were attributed to political motives or to the drugs-trafficking cartels. However, these events were overshadowed in mid-August, when Dr Luis Galán Sarmiento, leader of the Nuevo Liberalismo faction within the PL and a politician who commanded considerable popular support, was assassinated. As he had been an outspoken critic of the drugs traffickers, Galán's murder was ascribed to the drugs cartels of Medellín and Cali. President Barco responded to the assassination by introducing a series of emergency measures, including the reactivation of Colombia's extradition treaty with the USA; the immediate seizure of the extensive properties and financial assets of the principal drugs traffickers; and an extention of the security forces' powers of detention. Implementation of the measures led to a wave of arrests throughout Colombia (estimated to exceed 10,000) and the confiscation of laboratories, properties, farms, aircraft and weapons controlled by the cartels. The US administration requested the arrest by the Colombian authorities of 12 leading drugs traffickers, popularly known as the 'Extraditables', who responded to the USA's request by issuing a declaration of 'total war' against the Government and all journalists, judges and trade unionists opposed to their activities. In addition, in late August the US Government allocated emergency aid amounting to US $65m. to Colombia, and in September President George Bush announced details of the US administration's National Drug Control Strategy, under which an Andean aid programme was established to combat the production and trafficking of drugs in the region. Under the programme, Colombia's initial allocation of aid was $9.4m. Moreover, some 100 US military advisers were sent to Colombia to train security forces in the use of US military equipment. However, Colombia was strongly opposed to any direct military intervention by the USA.

Despite the Government's emergency measures, bomb attacks and assassinations continued to occur throughout Colombia. Several leading figures who were associated with the drugs cartels were detained and subsequently extradited to the USA, but the Government suffered a reverse in late September, when, following considerable speculation, the Minister of Justice resigned, after only a brief period in office, prompting a further cabinet reshuffle in October. In the same month, the Supreme Court ratified the Government's emergency measures, including the traditionally controversial extradition treaty with the USA. Following a public proposal by the 'Extraditables' for the formation of a peace commission to inaugurate further dialogue, the Government affirmed that it would not hold any negotiations with drugs traffickers. As the internal situation continued to deteriorate, the Government appeared to be losing the initiative in its campaign against the drugs cartels. However, in mid-December the Government achieved a major success in its campaign, when Gonzalo Rodríguez Gacha, a leading drugs trafficker, was killed in a confrontation with the security forces.

In early 1990, despite reports that leaders of the country's main drug cartels were prepared to adopt a more conciliatory stance towards the Government in return for constitutional and legal guarantees, President Barco reiterated his intention to exert all necessary force to combat drug-related violence and crime, refuting allegations that the Government had entered into direct negotiations with suspected drugs traffickers. The Government was sceptical of unilaterally declared truces by the cartels and continued to invoke the controversial extradition treaty with the USA for Colombian nationals suspected of drug-related crimes in the USA. This prompted accusations from leading members of the Medellín cartel that the Government had reneged on recent peace initiatives, and a new wave of violence against police forces, judges and journalists was launched.

In his inaugural address in August 1990, President Gaviria confirmed the commitment of the new Government to continuing the strenuous efforts to combat the trafficking of illicit drugs (initiated by Barco), having previously made comprehensive changes to police and military personnel in a move widely interpreted as an attempt to strengthen the Government's resistance to infiltration by the cartels. In June and August 1990 the Medellín cartel suffered serious reversals when prominent members of drug-trafficking organizations were shot dead during violent exchanges with security forces. In October the Government issued a statement proposing a new initiative by which some articles of law would be relaxed and others not invoked (including the extradition treaty) for suspected drugs traffickers who were prepared to surrender to the authorities. In November the Government was informed by spokesmen for drug-trafficking organizations that around 200-300 members of drug cartels might be willing to accept this latest initiative on the condition that further concessions were guaranteed. The release of two kidnapped journalists in late 1990 was widely regarded as a gesture of goodwill from the cartels, and by January 1991 it had been reported that Fabio and Jorge Luis Ochoa (the latter had narrowly avoided extradition in 1987), members of one of Medellín's most notorious cartels and both sought by US courts for drug-related offences in the USA, had surrendered.

Colombia has a long-standing border dispute with Venezuela. In May 1987 Venezuela rejected Colombia's proposal for a negotiated settlement of the dispute. In August the disagreement flared again, when Venezuela claimed that a Colombian naval vessel and Colombian aircraft had violated its territorial waters and airspace. In late October 1988, 14 Colombian fishermen were shot dead by Venezuelan soldiers at El Amparo, on the river border. The incident revived the controversy over military activities along the border, and it was suggested that the massacre may have been related to the large-scale smuggling of subsidized Venezuelan goods or to drugs trafficking. However, relations between the countries were expected to improve following the signing, in October 1989, of a border integration agreement, which included a provision on joint cooperation in the campaign to eradicate drugs trafficking. (Prior to this agreement, a permanent reconciliation commission to investigate the border dispute had been established in March 1989.) In March 1990 the San Pedro Alejandrino agreement, signed by the two countries, sought to initiate the implementation of recommendations made by existing bilateral border commissions and to establish a number of new commissions, including one to examine the territorial claims of both sides. In 1980 Nicaragua laid claim to the Colombian-controlled islands of Providencia and San Andrés. Colombia has a territorial dispute with Honduras over cays in the San Andrés and Providencia archipelago. In October 1986 the Colombian Senate approved a delimitation treaty of marine and submarine waters in the Caribbean Sea, which had been signed by the Governments of Colombia and Honduras in August. Former President Betancur's efforts to reverse Colombian foreign policy led to improved relations with Nicaragua and Cuba, and an attempt to revive the Andean Pact. As a member of the Contadora group, Colombia sought a new peace initiative for Central America and supported the withdrawal of US forces from El Salvador and Honduras.

Government

Executive power is exercised by the President (assisted by a Cabinet), who is elected for a four-year term by universal adult suffrage. Legislative power is vested in the bicameral Congress, consisting of the Senate (114 members elected for four years) and the House of Representatives (199 members elected for four years). The country is divided into 23 Departments, four Intendencies, five Commissaries and one Special District.

Defence

At 18 years of age, every male (with the exception of students) must present himself as a candidate for military service of between one and two years. In June 1990 the strength of the army was 115,000 (including 38,000 conscripts), the navy 14,000 (including 6,000 marines) and the air force 7,000. The paramilitary police force numbers about 80,000 men. Under the 1989 budget, defence expenditure was estimated at 206,518m. pesos.

Economic Affairs

In 1988, according to estimates by the World Bank, Colombia's gross national product (GNP), measured at average 1986-88 prices, was US $37,210m., equivalent to $1,240 per head. During 1980-88, it was estimated, GNP increased, in real terms, at an average annual rate of 3.0%, while GNP per head increased by 1.2% per year. Over the same period, the population increased by an annual average of 1.9%. Colombia's gross domestic product (GDP) increased, in real terms, by an average of 3.4% per year in 1980-88 and by 3.0% in 1989.

Agriculture (including forestry and fishing) contributed an estimated 16.7% of GDP in 1989, and employed some 29% of the labour force in 1988. The principal cash crops are coffee (which accounted for 31.1% of official export earnings in 1989), cocoa, sugar cane, bananas, tobacco, cotton and cut flowers. Rice, cassava, plantains and potatoes are the principal food crops. Timber and beef production are also important. During 1980-88 agricultural production increased by an annual average of 2.4%.

Industry (including mining, manufacturing, construction and power) employed 17% of the labour force in 1980, and contributed an estimated 36.9% of GDP in 1989. During 1980-88 industrial production increased by an annual average of 5.1%.

Mining contributed an estimated 7.4% of GDP in 1989, and employed 0.6% of the labour force in 1980. Petroleum, natural gas, coal, nickel, emeralds and gold are the principal minerals exploited. Silver, platinum, iron, lead, zinc, copper, mercury, limestone and phosphates are also mined.

In 1987 hydroelectricity provided about 75% of Colombia's electricity requirements. The country is self-sufficient in petroleum and coal, which together earned 26% of export revenues in 1988.

Manufacturing contributed an estimated 20.5% of GDP in 1989; it employed 13% of the labour force in 1980. The most important sectors are petroleum-refining, textiles, metals and food-processing.

In 1989 Colombia recorded a visible trade surplus of US $1,481m. and there was a surplus of $42m. on the current account of the balance of payments. The country's principal trading partner in that year was the USA, which provided 36% of imports and took 43.2% of exports. Other Latin American countries (especially Argentina, Brazil, Chile, Mexico and Venezuela), Japan and the European Community are important trading partners. The principal exports in 1989 were coffee, other agricultural products (chiefly bananas, cut flowers and cotton), petroleum and its derivatives, coal, chemicals, textiles and paper. The principal imports were machinery and transport equipment, chemicals, minerals, metals and food. A significant amount of foreign exchange is believed to be obtained from illegal trade in gold, emeralds and, particularly, the drug cocaine: in 1988 income from drug-trafficking was estimated at between $800m. and $1,500m.

In 1988 there was an estimated budgetary deficit of 160,800m. pesos in central government spending, equivalent to 1.4% of GDP. Colombia's total external public debt amounted to US $13,853m. in that year, and the cost of debt-servicing exceeded 39% of revenue from exports of goods and services. The average annual rate of inflation was 25.8% in 1989, and some 9% of the labour force were unemployed in that year.

Colombia is a member of ALADI (see p. 172) and of the Andean Group (see p. 93). Both organizations attempt to increase trade and economic co-operation within the region.

Colombia's economy was adversely affected by a decline in international prices for coffee in 1986–87, and by the suspension of export quotas by the International Coffee Organization in 1989, which led to a further fall in prices. However, the country's dependence on this commodity was reduced during the 1980s by an increase in exports of other agricultural products and minerals. During 1989 recurring violence, caused by guerrilla groups and rival drug-traffickers, made necessary an increase in government spending on security, and contributed to the budget deficit. Sabotage of petroleum installations by guerrillas was expected to reduce earnings from petroleum exports by 20% in that year. Unlike most Latin American countries, Colombia avoided the need to reschedule its foreign debt during the 1980s. In 1989 the Government announced plans to liberalize trade policy, to increase access for foreign investors, and to restructure the industrial and financial sectors.

Social Welfare

There is compulsory social security, paid for by the Government, employers and employees, and administered by the Institute of Social Security. It provides benefits for disability, old age, death, sickness, maternity, industrial accidents and unemployment. Large enterprises are required to provide life insurance schemes for their employees, and there is a comprehensive system of pensions. In 1977 there were 12,720 physicians working in Colombia, and in 1980 the country had 849 hospital establishments, with a total of 44,495 beds. Of total expenditure by the central Government in 1989, 126,934m. pesos (7.1%) was for health. In 1984 central government expenditure on social security and welfare amounted to 114,810m. pesos. The benefits of the health service do not reach all inhabitants, and in 1981 a report by the Family Welfare Institute estimated the level of infant mortality at 64 per 1,000 live births, one of the highest rates in the world.

Education

Primary education is free and compulsory for five years, to be undertaken by children between six and 12 years of age. No child may be admitted to secondary school unless these five years have been successfully completed. Secondary education, beginning at the age of 11, lasts for up to six years. Following completion of a first cycle of four years, pupils may pursue a further two years of vocational study, leading to the Bachiller examination. In 1986 the total enrolment at primary and secondary schools was equivalent to 83% of the school-age population. Primary enrolment included 73% of children in the relevant age-group. In 1988 there were an estimated 238 institutions of higher education. There are plans to construct an Open University to satisfy the increasing demand for higher education. Expenditure on education by the central Government in 1989 was 367,663m. pesos, representing 20.4% of total spending. In 1988 the World Bank allocated a loan of US $100m. to finance the expansion and improvement of primary education, particularly in rural areas. The rate of adult illiteracy averaged 19.2% in 1973, but, according to estimates by UNESCO, declined to 11.9% (males 10.9%; females 12.9%) in 1985.

Public Holidays

1991: 1 January (New Year's Day), 6 January (Epiphany), 19 March (St Joseph's Day), 28 March (Maundy Thursday), 29 March (Good Friday), 1 May (Labour Day), 9 May (Ascension Day), 30 May (Corpus Christi), 9 June (Thanksgiving), 29 June (SS Peter and Paul), 20 July (Independence), 7 August (Battle of Boyacá), 15 August (Assumption), 12 October (Discovery of America), 1 November (All Saints' Day), 11 November (Independence of Cartagena), 8 December (Immaculate Conception), 25 December (Christmas Day).

1992: 1 January (New Year's Day), 6 January (Epiphany), 19 March (St Joseph's Day), 16 April (Maundy Thursday), 17 April (Good Friday), 1 May (Labour Day), 28 May (Ascension Day), 9 June (Thanksgiving), 18 June (Corpus Christi), 29 June (SS Peter and Paul), 20 July (Independence), 7 August (Battle of Boyacá), 15 August (Assumption), 12 October (Discovery of America), 1 November (All Saints' Day), 11 November (Independence of Cartagena), 8 December (Immaculate Conception), 25 December (Christmas Day).

Weights and Measures

The metric system is in force.

Statistical Survey

Sources (unless otherwise stated): Departamento Administrativo Nacional de Estadística (DANE), Centro Administrativo Nacional (CAN), Avda Eldorado, Apdo Aéreo 80043, Bogotá; tel. (1) 222-1100; telex 44573; fax (1) 222-2107; Banco de la República, Carrera 7, No 14-78, Apdo Aéreo 3531, Bogotá; tel. (1) 283-1111; telex 044560.

Area and Population

AREA, POPULATION AND DENSITY

Area (sq km) Total	1,141,748*
Population (census results)	
24 October 1973	22,915,229
15 October 1985†	
Males	14,935,790
Females	15,126,410
Total	30,062,200
Population (official estimates at mid-year)	
1987	31,058,145
1988	31,677,178
1989	32,316,933
Density (per sq km) at mid-1989	28.3

* 440,831 sq miles.
† Including adjustment for underenumeration. The enumerated total was 27,875,676 (males 13,798,460; females 14,077,216).

DEPARTMENTS (population at 15 October 1985)

Department	Population*	Capital
Antioquia	4,067,207	Medellín
Atlántico	1,478,213	Barranquilla
Bolívar	1,288,985	Cartagena
Boyacá	1,209,739	Tunja
Caldas	883,024	Manizales
Caquetá	264,507	Florencia
Cauca	857,751	Popayán
César	699,428	Valledupar
Chocó	313,567	Quibdó
Córdoba	1,013,247	Montería
Cundinamarca	1,512,928	Bogotá†
La Guajira	299,995	Riohacha
Huila	693,712	Neiva
Magdalena	890,934	Santa Marta
Meta	474,046	Villaricencio
Nariño	1,085,173	Pasto
Norte de Santander	913,491	Cúcuta
Quindío	392,208	Armenia
Risaralda	652,872	Pereira
Santander del Sur	1,511,392	Bucaramanga
Sucre	561,649	Sincelejo
Tolima	1,142,220	Ibagué
Valle del Cauca	3,027,247	Cali
Intendencies		
Arauca	89,972	Arauca
Casanare	147,472	Yopal
Putumayo	174,219	Mocoa
San Andrés y Providencia Islands	35,818	San Andrés
Commissaries		
Amazonas	39,937	Leticia
Guainía	12,345	Obando
Guaviare	47,073	San José de Guaviare
Vaupés	26,178	Mitú
Vichada	18,702	Puerto Carreño
Special District		
Bogotá, DE	4,236,490	Bogotá†
Total	30,062,200	

* Including adjustment for underenumeration.
† The capital city, Bogotá, exists as the capital of a department as well as a special district. The city's population is included only in Bogotá, DE.

PRINCIPAL TOWNS
(population at 15 October 1985)*

Bogotá, DE (capital)	4,236,490	Cúcuta	388,397
Medellín	2,121,174	Bucaramanga	357,585
Cali	1,429,026	Manizales	308,784
Barranquilla	927,233	Ibagué	314,954
Cartagena	563,949	Pereira	300,224

* Including adjustment for underenumeration.

BIRTHS, MARRIAGES AND DEATHS*

	Registered live births	Registered deaths
1983	829,348	140,292
1984	825,842	137,189
1985	835,922	153,947
1986	811,600	146,346
1987	1,116,894	151,957

1988: Registered deaths 153,069.
Registered marriages: 102,448 in 1980; 95,845 in 1981.

* Data are tabulated by year of registration rather than by year of occurrence, although registration is incomplete. According to UN estimates, the average annual rates in 1980–85 were: births 31.0 per 1,000; deaths 7.7 per 1,000.

ECONOMICALLY ACTIVE POPULATION
(household survey, 1980)

Agriculture, hunting, forestry and fishing	2,412,413
Mining and quarrying	49,740
Manufacturing	1,136,735
Electricity, gas and water	44,233
Construction	242,191
Trade, restaurants and hotels	1,261,633
Transport, storage and communications	352,623
Financing, insurance, real estate and business services	278,210
Community, social and personal services	1,998,460
Activities not adequately described	690,762
Total labour force	8,467,000*

* Males 6,247,000; females 2,220,000.

1985 census (persons aged 12 years and over): Total labour force 9,557,868 (males 6,419,608; females 3,138,260).

COLOMBIA   Statistical Survey

Agriculture

PRINCIPAL CROPS ('000 metric tons)

	1987	1988	1989
Wheat	74.2	62.5	79.7
Rice (paddy)	1,864.6	1,775.4	2,101.8
Barley	91.6	97.2	84.6
Maize	859.6	907.8	1,043.8
Sorghum	703.8	706.6	695.2
Potatoes	2,242.6	2,519.8	2,696.7
Cassava (Manioc)	1,260.4	1,222.2	1,509.4
Soybeans	128.2	115.4	177.4
Seed cotton	320.5	376.4	294.5
Cane sugar (raw)	1,390.2	1,415.3	1,492.8
Bananas	1,090.9	1,140.0	1,156.9
Plantains	2,449.2	2,271.1	2,200.2
Coffee (green)	778.4	708.6	664.0
Cocoa beans	53.7	54.7	55.4
Tobacco (blond and black)	34.9	33.6	33.7

Fruit ('000 metric tons): 786.2 in 1987; 952.1 in 1988; 980.6* in 1989.
Vegetables ('000 metric tons): 1,419.9 in 1987; 1,485.0 in 1988; 1,602.8* in 1989.
* Preliminary.
Source: Ministerio de Agricultura, *Boletín Estadísticas Agropecuarias*.

LIVESTOCK ('000 head, year ending September)

	1987	1988	1989
Horses†	1,950	1,950	1,950
Mules†	600	600	600
Asses†	650	650	650
Cattle	23,971	24,307	24,671
Pigs	2,511	2,586	2,600
Sheep	2,652	2,652*	2,697*
Goats	932	932*	947*
Chickens†	36,000	39,000	40,000

* Unofficial figures.   † FAO estimates.
Source: FAO, *Production Yearbook*.

LIVESTOCK PRODUCTS ('000 metric tons)

	1987	1988	1989
Beef and veal	584	594	602
Pig meat	122†	131†	137†
Cows' milk	3,142	3,155†	3,170†
Cheese*	51	51	51
Butter and ghee*	14.4	14.4	14.5
Hen eggs	226	248†	247†
Cattle hides*	77.4	78.7	80

* FAO estimates.   † Unofficial figures.
Source: FAO, *Production Yearbook*.

Forestry

ROUNDWOOD REMOVALS (FAO estimates, '000 cu metres)

	1986	1987	1988
Sawlogs, veneer logs and logs for sleepers*	1,960	1,960	1,960
Pulpwood*	305	305	305
Other industrial wood*	408	408	408
Fuel wood	14,861	15,174	15,490
Total	17,534	17,847	18,163

* Assumed to be unchanged from 1982 official estimates.
Source: FAO, *Yearbook of Forest Products*.

SAWNWOOD PRODUCTION ('000 cu metres)

	1980	1981	1982
Coniferous sawnwood	30*	30*	1
Broadleaved sawnwood	900	936	680
Railway sleepers	40	40	40*
Total	970	1,006	721

* FAO estimates.
1983–88: Annual production as in 1982 (FAO estimates).
Source: FAO, *Yearbook of Forest Products*.

Fishing

('000 metric tons, live weight)

	1986	1987	1988
Inland waters	56.0	62.1	50.7
Atlantic Ocean	10.4	9.7	10.6
Pacific Ocean	17.0	13.6	23.5
Total catch	83.4	85.5	84.8

Source: FAO, *Yearbook of Fishery Statistics*.

Mining and Industry

SELECTED PRODUCTS
('000 metric tons, unless otherwise indicated)

	1987	1988	1989
Gold ('000 troy oz)	853.5	933.0	948.6
Silver ('000 troy oz)*	167.3	210.9	220.1
Salt (refined)	652.2	662.7	661.5
Iron ore	606.8	614.7	567.4
Crude petroleum ('000 barrels)	140,594	137,146	147,596
Diesel oil ('000 barrels)	14,054	14,117	14,818
Fuel oil ('000 barrels)	23,638	23,382	24,050
Motor fuel ('000 barrels)	28,606	27,355	27,378
Sugar	1,293.5	1,364.0	1,523.3
Cement	5,898.1	6,316.3	6,643.5
Carbonates	116.9	114.1	113.5
Caustic soda	19.5	21.3	27.6
Steel ingots	335.9	337.9	324.2

* Figures refer to purchases by the Banco de la República.
Sources: Banco de la República, Laboratorios de Fundición y Ensaye, Concesión Salinas and Empresa Colombiana de Petróleos.
Coal: 14,594,000 metric tons in 1987.

Finance

CURRENCY AND EXCHANGE RATES
Monetary Units
    100 centavos = 1 Colombian peso.

Denominations
    Coins: 1, 2, 5, 10, 20 and 50 pesos.
    Notes: 100, 200, 500, 1,000, 2,000 and 5,000 pesos.

Sterling and Dollar Equivalents (30 September 1990)
    £1 sterling = 1,002.1 pesos;
    US $1 = 534.9 pesos;
    10,000 Colombian pesos = £9.979 = $18.695.

Average Exchange Rate (pesos per US $)
    1987   242.61
    1988   299.17
    1989   382.57

COLOMBIA

BUDGET (million pesos)

Revenue	1987	1988	1989
Direct taxation	281,089	461,625	584,597
Indirect taxation	591,214	826,569	1,044,021
Rates and fines	19,351	18,083	27,801
Revenue under contracts	63,215	53,515	48,936
Credit resources	247,307	398,189	565,161
Special funds	9,308	12,035	18,264
Total	1,211,484	1,770,016	2,288,780

Expenditure*	1987	1988	1989
Congress and comptrollership	20,026	25,864	35,761
General administration	40,707	51,449	67,867
Government and foreign affairs	13,370	22,877	24,578
Finance and public credit	137,377	168,026	277,177
Public works and transportation	85,330	97,402	138,545
Defence	100,452	155,134	206,518
Police	74,735	96,217	124,400
Agriculture†	52,448	77,705	110,388
Health	68,765	86,669	126,934
Education	217,853	274,077	367,663
Development, labour, mines and communications	93,129	179,549	217,692
Justice and legal affairs	51,295	77,304	101,486
Total	961,487	1,312,323	1,799,009

*Excluding public debt. † Investment only.
Source: *Informe Anual de la Contraloría General de la República*.

INTERNATIONAL RESERVES
(US $ million at 31 December)

	1987	1988	1989
Gold*	290	468	249
IMF special drawing rights	162	154	150
Foreign exchange	2,924	3,094	3,466
Total	3,376	3,716	3,865

* Valued at market-related prices.
Source: IMF, *International Financial Statistics*.

MONEY SUPPLY (million pesos at 31 December)

	1985	1987	1988
Currency outside banks	186,730	418,820	530,660
Demand deposits at commercial banks	341,180	577,360	722,980

Note: Figures for 1986 are not available.
Source: IMF, *International Financial Statistics*.

COST OF LIVING (Consumer price index for low-income families in Bogotá; base: 1980 = 100)

	1986	1987	1988
Food	343.1	430.9	579.1
Clothing	278.1	331.3	405.3
Rent	245.4	270.4	309.1
All items (incl. others)	329.6	403.7	525.6

Source: ILO, *Year Book of Labour Statistics*.
1989 (base: 1988 = 100): Food 114.4; All items 115.8.
Source: UN, *Monthly Bulletin of Statistics*.

NATIONAL ACCOUNTS (million pesos at current prices)
Composition of the Gross National Product

	1986	1987	1888*
Compensation of employees	2,575,310	3,351,499	4,414,109
Operating surplus	} 3,414,059	4,439,895	5,939,314
Consumption of fixed capital			
Gross domestic product (GDP) at factor cost	5,989,369	7,791,394	10,353,423
Indirect taxes	837,793	1,076,166	1,334,180
Less Subsidies	39,206	43,152	55,735
GDP in purchasers' values	6,787,956	8,824,408	11,631,868
Net factor income from abroad	−149,892	−186,641	−196,944
Gross national product (GNP)	6,638,064	8,637,767	11,434,924

* Provisional.

Expenditure on the Gross Domestic Product

	1986	1987	1988
Government final consumption expenditure	665,814	868,383	1,182,370
Private final consumption expenditure	4,479,169	5,835,407	7,684,268
Increase in stocks	17,797	227,425	292,008
Gross fixed capital formation	1,204,114	1,537,235	2,287,685
Total domestic expenditure	6,366,894	8,468,450	11,446,331
Exports of goods and services	1,365,264	1,495,708	1,910,587
Less Imports of goods and services	944,202	1,139,750	1,625,570
GDP in purchasers' values	6,787,956	8,824,408	11,731,348
GDP at constant 1975 prices	621,781	655,164	681,791

Gross Domestic Product by Economic Activity

	1987	1988	1989*
Agriculture, hunting, forestry and fishing	1,594,018	1,964,916	2,538,671
Mining and quarrying	577,797	722,193	1,124,454
Manufacturing	1,792,906	2,482,111	3,112,567
Electricity, gas and water	200,970	270,592	373,958
Construction	494,644	775,750	1,005,372
Wholesale and retail trade	933,751	1,272,959	1,638,298
Transport, storage and communications	712,573	969,475	1,233,172
Other services	2,517,749	3,273,352	4,189,066
Total	8,824,408	11,731,348	15,215,558

* Estimates.

COLOMBIA

Statistical Survey

BALANCE OF PAYMENTS (US $ million)

	1987	1988	1989
Merchandise exports f.o.b.	5,661	5,343	6,029
Merchandise imports f.o.b.	−3,793	−4,516	−4,548
Trade balance	1,868	827	1,481
Exports of services	1,368	1,653	1,619
Imports of services	−3,901	−3,644	−4,086
Balance on goods and services	−665	−1,164	−986
Private unrequited transfers (net)	1,009	975	1,028
Government unrequited transfers (net)	−8	−11	—
Current balance	336	−200	42
Direct capital investment (net)	293	165	546
Other long-term capital (net)	−102	675	116
Short-term capital (net)	−203	106	−266
Net errors and omissions	67	−552	−44
Total (net monetary movements)	391	194	394
Monetization of gold	−514	175	−119
Valuation changes (net)	6	−20	−17
Official financing (net)	11	−1	—
Changes in reserves	−106	348	258

Source: IMF, *International Financial Statistics*.

External Trade

PRINCIPAL COMMODITIES (US $ million)*

Imports	1987	1988	1989
Vegetables and vegetable products	260.2	304.4	308.4
Food and drink	141.7	100.1	95.9
Mineral products	171.4	217.9	271.7
Chemical products	1,016.8	1,174.9	1,227.9
Plastic and rubber products	334.8	359.1	409.8
Paper and paper products	206.6	204.4	200.1
Textiles and textile products	137.4	128.7	184.3
Metals	562.5	672.6	887.9
Mechanical and electrical equipment	1,543.4	1,601.0	1,744.8
Transport equipment	729.4	685.7	758.7
Total (incl. others)	5,466.2	5,866.5	6,716.1

Exports†	1987	1988	1989
Agricultural, forestry and fisheries products	2,170.9	2,211.3	2,249.8
Coffee	1,674.6	1,604.1	1,530.8
Bananas	222.5	299.7	329.7
Flowers	174.1	200.8	219.8
Minerals	434.0	491.6	738.5
Coal	332.4	403.4	649.9
Foodstuffs, beverages and tobacco	153.1	220.9	259.4
Textiles, clothing, leather and footwear	319.5	474.1	617.7
Paper and publishing	143.6	126.3	129.4
Chemicals	119.8	122.7	145.9
Basic metals	116.3	219.4	241.9
Total (incl. others)‡	3,877.7	4,369.8	4,925.6

* Registrations and licences approved by the Instituto Colombiano de Comercio Exterior (INCOMEX).
† Customs data: does not include non-monetary gold.
‡ Excluding petroleum and derivatives (US $ million): 1,351.8 in 1987 and 985.7 in 1988.

PRINCIPAL TRADING PARTNERS (US $ million)

Imports c.i.f.	1987	1988	1989
Argentina	58.2	97.1	187.8
Belgium and Luxembourg	35.6	56.9	53.6
Brazil	150.5	230.3	212.8
Canada	174.5	179.4	178.9
Chile	55.7	69.4	91.3
Ecuador	37.8	58.3	50.4
France	166.0	183.8	157.5
Germany, Federal Republic	334.5	340.8	347.5
Italy	72.8	85.4	87.7
Japan	386.2	540.0	469.9
Mexico	148.6	205.4	122.8
Netherlands	75.5	77.7	54.8
Peru	66.1	91.4	120.8
Spain	114.6	121.5	109.4
United Kingdom	127.6	121.9	139.8
USA*	1,514.7	1,812.8	1,805.6
Venezuela	120.5	173.7	205.8
Total (incl. others)	4,228.0	5,005.3	5,010.2

* Including Puerto Rico.

Exports f.o.b.	1987	1988	1989
Argentina	41.9	51.4	33.7
Belgium and Luxembourg	72.4	73.4	78.7
Canada	67.5	62.4	86.7
Chile	99.6	119.0	131.7
Denmark	94.3	87.9	110.7
Ecuador	65.2	47.7	60.1
France	112.6	132.4	145.0
Germany, Federal Republic	592.3	524.8	496.3
Italy	68.3	75.5	80.7
Japan	203.7	262.0	250.2
Netherlands	212.1	252.0	328.8
Peru	118.1	87.3	60.5
Spain	80.8	86.7	96.0
United Kingdom	100.1	88.1	101.6
USA*	1,997.3	1,974.2	2,476.8
Venezuela	220.2	220.7	185.3
Total (incl. others)	5,024.4	5,026.2	5,739.3

* Including Puerto Rico.

Transport

RAILWAYS (traffic)

	1987	1988	1989
Passengers carried ('000)	1,429	1,245	1,147
Passenger-kilometres ('000)	171,121	147,962	151,994
Freight ('000 metric tons)	1,055	934	854
Freight ton-km ('000)	562,548	464,333	360,595

ROAD TRAFFIC (motor vehicles in use)

	1986	1987	1988
Passenger cars	611,978	655,201	706,922
Buses	52,136	53,354	55,111
Goods vehicles	282,386	291,070	300,254
Heavy-duty vehicles	230,034	233,555	239,524
Total (incl. others)	1,242,650	1,301,802	1,375,405

1989 (census results, Feb. 1989): Total 1,305,986.

DOMESTIC SEA-BORNE SHIPPING
(freight traffic, '000 metric tons)

	1987	1988	1989
Goods loaded and unloaded	772.1	944.8	464.6

COLOMBIA

INTERNATIONAL SEA-BORNE SHIPPING
(freight traffic, '000 metric tons)

	1987	1988	1989
Goods loaded	17,543	16,413	17,893
Goods unloaded	6,101	6,042	5,581

CIVIL AVIATION (traffic)

	1986	1987	1988
Domestic			
Passengers carried	5,448,366	5,523,842	5,517,194
Freight carried ('000 metric tons)	84,338	95,226	93,614
International			
Passengers:			
arrivals	516,554	525,987	544,282
departures	556,919	541,530	569,559
Freight ('000 metric tons):			
loaded	55,586	54,412	53,249
unloaded	69,594	60,698	62,466

Tourism
(visitors)

Country of Origin	1987	1988	1989
Argentina	6,624	7,925	8,881
Canada	21,684	33,491	27,234
Costa Rica	8,538	11,561	10,372
Ecuador	94,826	182,509	102,916
France	7,694	6,806	6,636
Germany, Federal Republic	11,146	6,913	5,094
Italy	7,603	7,527	6,308
Netherlands	7,300	2,006	1,513
Panama	8,549	10,862	9,576
Peru	9,611	9,468	16,529
Spain	8,457	9,797	11,198
United Kingdom	7,590	6,788	8,243
USA	70,000	116,244	132,810
Venezuela	220,677	366,995	340,814
Total (incl. others)	541,268	828,913	732,982

Source: Corporación Nacional de Turismo.

Communications Media

	1985	1986	1987
Telephones ('000 in use)	2,097	2,289	n.a.
Radio receivers ('000 in use)	4,000	4,500	5,000
Television receivers ('000 in use)	2,750	3,000	3,250
Daily newspapers: number	n.a.	46	n.a.

Book production (1984): 15,041 titles (incl. 8,541 pamphlets); 118,754,000 copies (incl. 70,749,000 pamphlets).

Sources: UN, *Statistical Yearbook*, and UNESCO, *Statistical Yearbook*.

Education
(1988—provisional)

	Institutions	Teachers	Pupils
Nursery	7,759	14,918	320,244
Primary	37,948	136,549	4,044,220
Secondary (general)	6,134	99,392	2,076,455
Higher (incl. universities)	238	47,990	457,834

Directory

The Constitution

The Constitution which is now in force was promulgated in 1886 and has been amended from time to time. In 1957 it was amended to provide for the alternation of the presidency between the two major parties. All citizens over 18 years of age are eligible to vote. Civil rights and social guarantees include freedom of education, the right to strike (except in the public sector), public aid to those unable to support themselves, freedom of assembly, of the press, and the right to petition. All male citizens are required to present themselves for possible military service at the age of 18.

In December 1990 a National Constituent Assembly was established to revise the Constitution.

THE PRESIDENT

Executive power is vested in the President of the Republic, who is elected by popular suffrage for a four-year term of office. The President cannot hold office for two consecutive terms but may be re-elected at a later date.

The President appoints a Cabinet, which assists in the government of the country. A substitute (primer designado) is elected by Congress, subject to biannual reappointment, to act in the event of a Presidential vacancy. The President appoints the governors of the 23 Departments, the four Intendencies and the five Commissaries.

CONGRESS

Legislative power is exercised by Congress, which is composed of the Senate and the House of Representatives. Members of both chambers are elected by direct suffrage for a period of four years. The President in each House is elected for six months.

JUDICIARY

The administration of justice is in the hands of the Supreme Court, superior district tribunals, and lower courts. The magistrates of the Supreme Court of Justice are elected by serving members of the Court. The term of office is five years and the magistrates may be re-elected indefinitely.

NATIONAL ECONOMIC COUNCIL

Direction of the nation's finances is in the hands of the Consejo Nacional de Política Económica—CONPES (National Council for Economic Policy). CONPES is composed of five ministers and also representatives of banking, industrial and agricultural interests and has functioned since 1935.

COLOMBIA   *Directory*

LOCAL GOVERNMENT

For administrative purposes the country is divided into 23 Departments, four Intendencies and five Commissaries. The Departments are further divided into Municipalities. Governors for the Departments are appointed by the President, but regional legislatures are elected by the local inhabitants and enjoy considerable autonomy, including the management of local finances. Popular elections for mayors were held for the first time in all municipalities in 1988.

AMENDMENTS

Various constitutional reforms were promulgated in December 1968, including the following amendments: to increase the membership of the Senate from 106 to 112 (later expanded to 114), and the maximum membership of the House of Representatives from 204 to 214; to increase from two to four years the term of office of representatives; to eliminate the two-thirds majority required for matters of importance; to enable the Government to legislate by decree for a maximum period of 90 days in any one year in the event of an economic crisis, though such decrees must relate only to the matters which caused the crisis; from 1970, proportional representation to be allowed in departmental and municipal elections; the same principle to apply to congressional elections after 1974. An amendment was also promulgated whereby the 'minority' party must have 'adequate' representation in government positions.

Note: A state of siege has been in force intermittently since 1948.

The Government

HEAD OF STATE

President: CÉSAR GAVIRIA TRUJILLO (took office 7 August 1990).
Primer Designado: (vacant).

CABINET
(January 1991)

Minister of Government (Interior): HUMBERTO DE LA CALLE.
Minister of Foreign Affairs: LUIS FERNANDO JARAMILLO.
Minister of Justice: JAIME GIRALDO ANGEL.
Minister of Finance and Public Credit: RUDOLF HOMMES.
Minister of National Defence: Gen. OSCAR BOTERO RESTREPO.
Minister of Agriculture: MARÍA ROSARIO SINTES DE RESTREPO.
Minister of Labour and Social Security: FRANCISCO POSADA DE LA PEÑA.
Minister of Public Health: CAMILO GONZÁLEZ POZO.
Minister of Economic Development: ERNESTO SAMPER PIZANO.
Minister of Mines and Energy: LUIS FERNANDO VERGARA.
Minister of Education: ALFONSO VALDIVIESO.
Minister of Communications: ALBERTO CASAS SANTAMARÍA.
Minister of Public Works and Transportation: JUAN FELIPE GAVARIA.

MINISTRIES

Office of the President: Casa de Nariño, Carrera 8A, No 7-26, Bogotá, DE; tel. (1) 284-3300; telex 44281.
Ministry of Agriculture: Carrera 10A, No 20–30, Bogotá, DE; tel. (1) 241-9005; telex 44470.
Ministry of Communications: Edif. Murillo Toro, Carreras 7A y 8A, Calle 12A y 13, Apdo Aéreo 14515, Bogotá, DE; tel. (1) 284-9090; telex 41249; fax (1) 286-1185.
Ministry of Economic Development: Calle 26, 13–19, 25°, 34°, 35°, Bogotá, DE; tel. (1) 241-9030; telex 44508; fax (1) 281-1103.
Ministry of Education: Centro Administrativo Nacional (CAN), Of. 501, Avda Eldorado, Bogotá, DE; tel. (1) 222-0029; telex 42456; fax (1) 222-0324.
Ministry of Finance and Public Credit: Carrera 7A, No 6-45, Of. 308, Bogotá, DE; tel. (1) 286-3676; telex 44473; fax (1) 84-5396.
Ministry of Foreign Affairs: Palacio de San Carlos, Calle 10A, No 5-51, Bogotá, DE; tel. (1) 282-7811; telex 45209.
Ministry of Government (Interior): Palacio Echeverry, Carrera 8A, No 8-09, Bogotá, DE; tel. (1) 286-2324; telex 45406.
Ministry of Justice: Calle 26, No 27-48, 2°, Bogotá, DE; tel. (1) 283-9493.
Ministry of Labour and Social Security: Avda 19, No 6-68, Bogotá, DE; tel. (1) 242-2007; telex 45445.
Ministry of Mines and Energy: Centro Administrativo Nacional (CAN), Avda Eldorado, Bogotá, DE; tel. (1) 222-2069; telex 45898.

Ministry of National Defence: Centro Administrativo Nacional (CAN), 2°, Avda Eldorado, Bogotá, DE; tel. (1) 288-4184.
Ministry of Public Health: Calle 16, No 7-39, Of. 701, Bogotá, DE; tel. (1) 282-0002.
Ministry of Public Works and Transportation: Centro Administrativo Nacional (CAN), Of. 409, Avda Eldorado, Bogotá, DE; tel. (1) 222-3782; telex 45656.

President and Legislature

PRESIDENT

Election, 27 May 1990

Candidate	Votes Cast*
CÉSAR GAVIRIA TRUJILLO (Partido Liberal)	2,783,466
Dr ALVARO GÓMEZ HURTADO (Movimiento de Salvación Nacional)	1,392,379
ANTONIO NAVARRO WOLFF (Alianza Democrática—M-19)	736,476
RODRIGO LLOREDA CAICEDO (Partido Social Conservador Colombiano)	715,146

* Figures with 95% of the vote counted.

CONGRESO

General Election, 11 March 1990

	Seats	
Party	Senate	House of Representatives*
Partido Liberal	72	n.a.
Partido Conservador	41	n.a.
Movimiento de Salvación Nacional	—	n.a.
Unión Patriótica	1	n.a.
Others	—	n.a.
Total	**114**	**199**

* In the 1990 congressional elections the Partido Liberal won approximately 60% of the seats in the House of Representatives.

President of the Senate: AURELIO IRAGORRI.
President of the House of Representatives: NORBERTO MORALES BALLESTEROS.

Note: In early December 1990 a 70-seat National Constituent Assembly, which was to revise the Constitution, was established.

Political Organizations

Alianza Democrática (AD): Bogotá, DE; f. 1990; alliance of centre-left groups (including factions of Unión Patriótica, Colombia Unida, Frente Popular and Socialismo Democrático) which supported the M-19 campaign for elections to the National Constituent Assembly in December 1990; Leader DIEGO MONTAÑA CUÉLLAR.

Alianza Nacional Popular (ANAPO): Bogotá, DE; f. 1971 by supporters of Gen. Gustavo Rojas Pinilla; populist party; Leader MARÍA EUGENIA ROJAS DE MORENO DÍAZ.

Democracia Cristiana: Avda 42, 18-08, Apdo 25867, Bogotá, DE; tel. (1) 285-6639; telex 45572; f. 1964; Christian Democrat party; 10,000 mems; Pres. JUAN A. POLO FIGUEROA; Sec.-Gen. DIEGO ARANGO OSORIO.

Frente por la Unidad del Pueblo (FUP): Bogotá, DE; extreme left-wing front comprising socialists and Maoists.

Movimiento Colombia Unida (CU): Bogotá, DE; left-wing group allied to the UP; leader ADALBERTO CARVAJAL.

Movimiento Obrero Independiente Revolucionario (MOIR): Bogotá, DE; left-wing workers' movement; Maoist; Leader MARCELO TORRES.

Movimiento de Salvación Nacional (MSN): Bogotá, DE; f. 1990; split from the Partido Social Conservador Colombiano; Leader Dr ALVARO GÓMEZ HURTADO.

Movimiento Unitario Metapolítico: Bogotá, DE; f. 1985; populist-occultist party; Leader REGINA BETANCOURT DE LISKA.

Movimiento 19 de Abril (M-19): f. 1970 by followers of Gen. Gustavo Rojas Pinilla and dissident factions from the FARC; left-wing urban guerrilla group, until formally constituted as a political

COLOMBIA

party in Oct. 1989; Leaders ANTONIO NAVARRO WOLFF, OTTY PATIÑO.

Partido Liberal (PL): Avda Jiménez 8–56, Bogotá, DE; f. 1815; divided into two factions, the official group (HERNANDO DURÁN LUSSÁN, MIGUEL PINEDO) and the independent group: Nuevo Liberalismo (New Liberalism, led by Dr ALBERTO SANTOFIMIO BOTERO, ERNESTO SAMPER, EDUARDO MESTRE.

Partido Social Conservador Colombiano (PSC): Avda 22, No 37-09, Bogotá, DE; tel. (1) 268-0006; fax (1) 269-5354; f. 1849; fmrly Partido Conservador; 2.9m. mems; Leader (vacant); Sec.-Gen. Dr HERNANDO BARJUCH MARTÍNEZ.

Unidad Democrática de la Izquierda (Democratic Unity of the Left): Bogotá, DE; f. 1982; Leader Dr GERARDO MOLINA; left-wing coalition incorporating the following parties:

Firmes: Bogotá, DE; democratic party.

Partido Comunista de Colombia (PCC): Bogotá, DE; f. 1930; Marxist-Leninist party; Leader Dr GILBERTO VIEIRA; Sec. FRANCISCO CARABALLO.

Partido Socialista de los Trabajadores (PST): Bogotá, DE; workers' socialist party; Leader MARÍA SOCORRO RAMÍREZ.

Unión Patriótica (UP): f. 1985; Marxist party formed by FARC (see below); obtained legal status in 1986; Pres. DIEGO MONTAÑA CUELLAR; Exec. Sec. OVIDIO SALINAS.

The following guerrilla groups and illegal organizations were active in the late 1980s:

Comando Ricardo Franco-Frente Sur: f. 1984; common front formed by dissident factions from the FARC and M-19 (see below); Leader JAVIER DELGADO.

Ejército de Liberación Nacional (ELN–Unión Camilista): Castroite guerrilla movement; f. 1965; 930 mems; Leaders FABIO VÁSQUEZ CASTAÑO, MANUEL PÉREZ; factions include:

Frente Simón Bolívar: (ceased hostilities in December 1985).

Frente Antonio Nariño: (ceased hostilities in December 1985).

Ejército Popular de Liberación (EPL): Maoist guerrilla movement; splinter group from Communist Party; announced end of its armed struggle in August 1990; planned to join the political mainstream; Leader FRANCISCO CARABALLO.

Fuerzas Armadas Revolucionarias de Colombia (FARC): fmrly military wing of the pro-Soviet Communist Party; composed of 39 armed fronts; 4,400 armed supporters in 1987; Leader MANUEL MARULANDA VELEZ (alias TIROFIJO); Gen. Sec. (vacant).

Movimiento de Autodefensa Obrera (MAO): workers' self-defence movement; Trotskyite; Leader ADELAIDA ABADIA REY; (reported to have joined the Unión Patriótica, July 1985).

Movimiento de Restauración Nacional (MORENA): right-wing; Leader ARMANDO VALENZUELA RUIZ.

Muerte a Secuestradores (MAS) (Death to Kidnappers): rightwing paramilitary organization; funded by drug-dealers.

Nuevo Frente Revolucionario del Pueblo: f. 1986; faction of M-19; active in Cundinamarca region.

Partido Revolucionario de Trabajadores (PRT): left-wing; began peace talks with the Government in August 1990.

Patria Libre: f. 1985; left-wing guerrilla movement.

In 1984 the Government reached agreement on a cease-fire with the M-19, the FARC and the EPL. In June 1985, however, the M-19 formally withdrew from the agreement and resumed hostilities against the armed forces. In November 1985 the EPL withdrew from the agreement. The FARC maintained their commitment to the cease-fire. In late 1985 the M-19, the Comando Ricardo Franco-Frente Sur and the Comando Quintín Lame (an indigenous organization active in the department of Cauca) announced the formation of a united front, the Coordinadora Guerrillera Nacional (CGN). In 1986 the CGN participated in joint campaigns with the Movimiento Revolucionario Tupac Amarú (Peru) and the Alfaro Vive ¡Carajo! (Ecuador). The alliance operated under the name of **Batallón América.** In October 1987 six guerrilla groups, including the ELN, the FARC and the M-19, formed a joint front, to be known as the **Coordinadora Guerrillera Simón Bolívar (CGSB).** In early 1989 the ELN, FARC, EPL and M-19 all confirmed their willingness to hold peace talks with the Government. At a 'summit' meeting held with the Government in July these groups agreed to the formation of a Comisión de Notables, which was to draft proposals for a peace dialogue. In September the M-19 announced that it had reached agreement with the Government on a peace treaty, allowing M-19 a full pardon and recognition as a political party in exchange for total demobilization and disarmament. Having received recognition as a political party, the M-19 joined the legitimate political system in early 1990, while the EPL began peace negotiations with the Government at the same time. The EPL announced the end of its armed struggle in August 1990 and stated its intention to join the political mainstream.

Diplomatic Representation

EMBASSIES IN COLOMBIA

Argentina: Avda 40A, 13-09, 16°, Bogotá, DE; tel. (1) 288-0900; telex 44576; Ambassador: DANIEL OLMOS.

Austria: Carrera 11, No 75-29, Bogotá, DE; tel. (1) 235-6628; telex 41489; Ambassador: ARTHUR SCHUSCHNIGG.

Belgium: Calle 26, No 4A-45, 7°, Bogotá, DE; tel. (1) 282-8881; telex 41203; Ambassador: WILLY J. STEVENS.

Bolivia: Calle 78, No 9-57, Of. 1103, Bogotá, DE; tel. (1) 211-8962; telex 45583; Ambassador: GUILLERMO RIVEROS TEJADA.

Brazil: Calle 93, No 14-20, 8°, Bogotá, DE; Ambassador: ALVARO DA COSTA FRANCO.

Bulgaria: Calle 81, No 7-71, Apdo Aéreo 89751, Bogotá, DE; tel. (1) 212-8028; telex 41217; Ambassador: DIMITAR PETKOV POPOV.

Canada: Calle 76, No 11-52, Apdo Aéreo 53531, Bogotá, DE; tel. (1) 217-5555; telex 44568; Ambassador: GAÉTAN LAVERTU.

Chile: Calle 100, No 11B-44, Bogotá, DE; tel. (1) 214-7926; telex 44404; Ambassador: CARLOS NEGRI CHIORRINI.

China, People's Republic: Calle 71, No 2A-41, Bogotá, DE; tel. (1) 255-8548; telex 45387; Ambassador: YUSHENG WANG.

Costa Rica: Carrera 15, No 80-87, Of. 401, Apdo Aéreo 11354, Bogotá, DE; tel. (1) 236-1098; Ambassador: RAFAEL A. CHINCHILLA FALLAS.

Czechoslovakia: Avda 13, No 104A-30, Bogotá, DE; tel. (1) 214-2240; telex 44590; Ambassador: RENÉ HANOUSEK.

Dominican Republic: Calle 87, No 16-27, 3°, Bogotá, DE; tel. (1) 218-8673; Ambassador: RODOLFO LEYBA POLANCO.

Ecuador: Calle 89, No 13-07, Bogotá, DE; tel. (1) 257-0066; telex 45776; fax (1) 257-9799; Ambassador: Dr FERNANDO CÓRDOVA.

Egypt: Carrera 19A, 98-17, Bogotá, DE; tel. (1) 236-4832; Ambassador: AHMED FATHI ABULKHEIR.

El Salvador: Carrera 9A, No 80-15, Of. 503, Apdo 089394, Bogotá, DE; tel. (1) 212-5932; telex 42072; Ambassador: JOSÉ ROBERTO ANDINO SALZAR.

Finland: Calle 72, No 8-56, Bogotá, DE; tel. (1) 212-6111; telex 44304; fax (1) 212-6106; Ambassador: RISTO REKOLA.

France: Avda 39, No 7-84, Bogotá, DE; tel. (1) 285-4311; telex 44558; Ambassador: PAUL DIJOUD.

Germany: Carrera 4, No 72-35, 6°, Apdo Aéreo 91808, Bogotá, DE8; tel. (1) 212-0511; telex 44765; Ambassador: GEORG JOACHIM SCHLAICH.

Guatemala: Transversal 29, Apdo 139A-41, Bogotá, DE; tel. (1) 259-1496; fax (1) 274-5365; Ambassador: HUGO CEREZO ARÉVALO.

Haiti: Calle 67, No 10-18, 4°, Bogotá, DE; tel. (1) 217-6209; Chargé d'Affaires: CARLO TOUSSAINT.

Holy See: Carrera 15, No 36-33, Apdo Aéreo 3740, Bogotá, DE (Apostolic Nunciature); tel. (1) 245-4260; fax (1) 285-1815; Apostolic Nuncio: Most Rev. PAOLO ROMEO, Titular Archbishop of Vulturia.

Honduras: Carrera 13, No 63-51, Bogotá, DE; tel. (1) 235-3158; telex 45540; Ambassador: RICARDO ARTURO PINEDA MILLA.

Hungary: Carrera 6A, No 77-46, Bogotá, DE; tel. (1) 217-8578; telex 43244; Ambassador: Dr VINCE KOCZIAN.

India: Calle 93B, No 13-44, Bogotá, DE; tel. (1) 236-9821; telex 41380; fax (1) 218-5393; Ambassador: G. D. Atuk.

Iran: Transversal 20, No 114-20A, Bogotá, DE; tel. (1) 215-8262; telex 42252; Ambassador: ALI ASGHAR ALMOUSAVI.

Israel: Calle 35, No 7-25, 14°, Bogotá, DE; tel. (1) 287-7782; telex 44755; Ambassador: GIDEON TADMOR.

Italy: Calle 70, No 10-25, Bogotá, DE; tel. (1) 235-4300; telex 45588; Ambassador: FILIPPO ANFUSO.

Japan: Carrera 7, No 74-21, 8° y 9°, Apdo Aéreo 7407, Bogotá, DE; tel. (1) 255-0300; telex 43327; Ambassador: RIKIWO SHIKAMA.

Korea, Republic: Calle 94, No 9-39, Bogotá, DE; tel. (1) 236-1616; telex 41468; Ambassador: YONG CHOL AHN.

Lebanon: Calle 74, No 12-44, Bogotá, DE; tel. (1) 212-8360; telex 44333; Ambassador: ROBERT ARAB.

Mexico: Calle 99, No 12-08, Bogotá, DE; tel. (1) 256-6121; telex 41264; Ambassador: RODULFO FIGUEROA.

Morocco: Carrera 13A, No 98-33, Bogotá, DE; tel. (1) 218-7147; telex 43468; Ambassador: YOUSSEF FASSI FIHRI.

Netherlands: Carrera 9, No 74-08, Bogotá, DE; tel. (1) 211-9600; telex 44629; fax (1) 211-9855; Ambassador: REIJNIER FLAES.

Nicaragua: Calle 105, No 22A-45, Bogotá, DE; tel. (1) 214-2040; telex 45388; Ambassador: OSCAR CORTÉS CORDERO.

Panama: Calle 87, No 11A-64, Bogotá, DE; tel. (1) 256-8280; Ambassador: JUSTO ARROYO SIMANCA.

COLOMBIA — *Directory*

Paraguay: Calle 57, No 7-11, Of. 702, Apdo Aéreo 20085, Bogotá, DE; tel. (1) 255-4160; Ambassador: RUBÉN RUIZ GÓMEZ.
Peru: Calle 94A, No 7A-26, Bogotá, DE; tel. (1) 257-3753; telex 44453; fax (1) 18-0133; Ambassador: (vacant).
Poland: Calle 104A, No 23-48, Bogotá, DE; tel. (1) 214-0854; telex 44591; Ambassador: MIECZYSŁAW BIERNACKI.
Portugal: Calle 71, No 11-10, Of. 703, Bogotá, DE; tel. (1) 212-4223; Ambassador: ANTÓNIO SYDER SANTIAGO.
Romania: Carrera 7, No 92-58, Bogotá, DE; tel. (1) 256-6438; telex 41238; Ambassador GEORGHE FULEA.
Spain: Calle 92, No 12-68, Bogotá, DE; tel. (1) 236-2154; telex 44779; Ambassador: SALVADOR BERMÚDEZ DE CASTRO Y BERNALES.
Sweden: Calle 72, 5-83, 9°, Bogotá, DE; tel. (1) 255-3777; telex 44626; fax (1) 210-3401; Ambassador: FREDRIK BERGENSTRÅHLE.
Switzerland: Carrera 9, No 74-08/1101, Bogotá, DE; tel. (1) 255-3945; telex 41230; Ambassador: PETER NIEDERBERGER.
USSR: Carrera 4, No 75-00, Apdo Aéreo 90600, Bogotá, DE; tel. (1) 235-7960; telex 44503; Ambassador: IGOR DMITRIEVICH BUBNOV.
United Kingdom: Torre Propaganda Sancho, Calle 98, No 9-03, 4°, Apdo 4508, Bogotá, DE; tel. (1) 218-5111; telex 44503; fax (1) 218-2460; Ambassador: KEITH MORRIS.
USA: Calle 38, No 8-61, Bogotá, DE; tel. (1) 285-1300; telex 44843; Ambassador: THOMAS E. MCNAMARA.
Uruguay: Carrera 9A, No 80-15, 11°, Apdo Aéreo 01466, Bogotá, DE; tel. (1) 235-2968; telex 43377; Ambassador: (vacant).
Venezuela: Calle 33, No 6-94, 10°, Bogotá, DE; tel. (1) 285-2286; telex 44504; Ambassador: ILDEGAR PÉREZ-SEGNINI.
Yugoslavia: Calle 93A, No 9A-22, Apdo 91074, Bogotá, DE; tel. (1) 257-0290; telex 45155; Ambassador: RADOMIR ZECEVIĆ.

Judicial System

The Supreme Court of Justice is divided into four subsidiary divisions of Civil Cassation, Criminal Cassation, Labour Cassation and Constitutional Procedure. The 24 judges of the Supreme Court hold office until the age of 65 years, although they may be removed from office if considered to be unfit by reason of conduct or age. Vacancies are filled from within the Court by election by the members. For matters of great importance and government business, the three courts of the Supreme Court sit together as a Plenary Court.

The country is divided into judicial districts, each of which has a superior court of three or more judges. There are also other Courts of Justice for each judicial district, and judges for each province and municipality.

Attorney-General: GUSTAVO ARRIETA.

SUPREME COURT OF JUSTICE

Carrera 7a, No 27-18, Edif. Banco de Crédito, 15°-24°, Bogotá, DE.

President: (vacant).
Vice-President: Dr RODOLFO MANTILLA JÁCOME.

Division of Civil Cassation: Carrera 7a, No 27-18, 22°, Bogotá, DE.
President: Dr ALBERTO OSPINA BOTERO.

Division of Criminal Cassation: Carrera 7a, No 27-18, 21°, Bogotá, DE.
President: Dr GUILLERMO DUQUE RUIZ.

Division of Labour Cassation: Carrera 7a, No 27-18, 20°, Bogotá, DE.
President: Dr JACOBO PÉREZ ESCOBAR.

Division of Constitutional Procedure: Carrera 7a, No 27-18, 23°, Bogotá, DE.
President: Dr JAIRO DUQUE PÉREZ.

Religion

Roman Catholicism is the religion of 95% of the population.

CHRISTIANITY
The Roman Catholic Church

Colombia comprises 12 archdioceses, 38 dioceses, two territorial prelatures, 10 Apostolic Vicariates and five Apostolic Prefectures.

Bishops' Conference: Conferencia Episcopal de Colombia, Apdo 7448, Carrera 8A, 84-87, Bogotá, DE; tel. (1) 218-2600; telex 44740; fax (1) 218-9650; f. 1978; Pres. Cardinal ALFONSO LÓPEZ TRUJILLO, Archbishop of Medellín.

Archbishop of Barranquilla: FÉLIX MARÍA TORRES PARRA, Carrera 42 F, No 75B-220, Apdo Aéreo 1160, Barranquilla 4; tel. (58) 35-4108.
Archbishop of Bogotá, DE: Cardinal MARIO REVOLLO BRAVO, Carrera 7a, No 10-20, Bogotá, DE; tel. (1) 243-7700.
Archbishop of Bucaramanga: HÉCTOR RUEDA HERNÁNDEZ, Calle 33, No 21-18, Bucaramanga, Santander; tel. (7) 25132.
Archbishop of Cali: PEDRO RUBIANO SÁENZ, Carrera 5A, No 11-42, 2°, Cali; tel. (23) 81-2068.
Archbishop of Cartagena: CARLOS JOSÉ RUISECO VIEIRA, Apdo Aéreo 400, Cartagena; tel. (53) 64-5308.
Archbishop of Ibagué: JOSÉ JOAQUÍN FLÓREZ HERNÁNDEZ, Calle 10, No 2-58, Ibagué, Tolima; tel. (82) 63-2680.
Archbishop of Manizales: JOSÉ DE JESÚS PIMIENTO RODRÍGUEZ, Carrera 23, No 19-22, Manizales; tel. (68) 83-1179.
Archbishop of Medellín: Cardinal ALFONSO LÓPEZ TRUJILLO, Calle 57, No 49-44, Medellín; tel. (4) 251-7700.
Archbishop of Nueva Pamplona: RAFAEL SARMIENTO PERALTA, Carrera 5, No 4-109, Nueva Pamplona; tel. (786) 82816.
Archbishop of Popayán: SAMUEL SILVERIO BUITRAGO TRUJILLO, Apdo Aéreo 593, Calle 5, No 6-71, Popayán; tel. (39) 31710.
Archbishop of Santa Fe de Antioquia: ELADIO ACOSTA ARTEAGA, Plazuela Martínez Pardo 12-11, Santa Fe; tel. (41) 26-1308.
Archbishop of Tunja: AUGUSTO TRUJILLO ARANGO, Calle 17, No 9-85, Tunja, Boyacá; tel. (92) 42-2095.

The Episcopal Church

Bishop of Colombia: Rt Rev. BERNARDO MERINO BOTERO, Carrera 6, No 49-85, Apdo Aéreo 52964, Bogotá, DE; tel. (1) 288-3167; there are 2,780 baptized mems, 1,320 communicant mems, 29 parishes, missions and preaching stations; 5 schools and 1 orphanage; 16 clergy.

Other Christian Churches

The Baptist Convention: Apdo Aéreo 51988, Medellín; tel. (4) 38-9623; Pres. RAMÓN MEDINA IBÁÑEZ; Exec. Sec. Rev. RAMIRO PÉREZ HOYOS.
Iglesia Evangélica Luterana de Colombia: Calle 75, No 20-54, Apdo Aéreo 51538, Bogotá, DE2; tel. (1) 212-5735; 2,000 mems; Pres. VIESTURS PAVASARS.

BAHÁ'Í FAITH

National Spiritual Assembly: Apdo 51387, Bogotá, DE12; tel. (1) 268-1658; adherents in 1,013 localities.

JUDAISM

There is a community of about 25,000 with 66 synagogues.

The Press

DAILIES
Bogotá

El Espacio: Avda El Dorado, No 45-35, Bogotá, DE; tel. (1) 263-6666; telex 44501; f. 1965; evening; Dir JAIME ARDILA CASAMITJANA; circ. 92,000.
El Espectador: Avda 68, No 22-71, Apdo Aéreo 3441, Bogotá, DE; tel. (1) 260-6044; telex 44718; f. 1887; morning; Dir JUAN GUILLERMO CANO; Publr LUIS GABRIEL CANO; Editor FERNANDO CANO; circ. 215,000.
La Prensa: Carretera 16, No 36-89, Bogotá, DE; tel. (1) 232-2660; Dir JUAN CARLOS PASTRANA.
La República: Calle 16, No 4-96, Apdo Aéreo 6806, Bogotá, DE; tel. (1) 282-1055; f. 1953; morning; economics; Dir RODRIGO OSPINA HERNÁNDEZ; circ. 20,000.
El Siglo: Avda El Dorado No 96-50, Apdo Aéreo 5452, Bogotá, DE; tel. (1) 298-7328; telex 44458; f. 1925; Conservative; Dir ALVARO GÓMEZ HURTADO; circ. 65,000.
El Tiempo: Avda El Dorado No 59-70, Apdo Aéreo 3633, Bogotá, DE; tel. (1) 295-9555; telex 44812; f. 1911; morning; Liberal; Dir HERNANDO SANTOS CASTILLO; Editor ENRIQUE SANTOS CALDERÓN; circ. 200,000 (weekdays), 350,000 (Sundays).

Barranquilla, Atlántico

Diario del Caribe: Calle 42, No 50B-32, Barranquilla, Atlántico; tel. (58) 41-5200; telex 00470; f. 1950; daily; Liberal; Dir EDUARDO POSADA CARBÓ; circ. 30,000.

COLOMBIA

El Heraldo: Calle 53B, No 46-25, Barranquilla, Atlántico; tel. (58) 41-6066; telex 33348; f. 1933; morning; Liberal; Dir Juan B. Fernández; circ. 65,000.

La Libertad: Carrera 53, No 55-166, Barranquilla, Atlántico; tel. (58) 31-1517; Liberal; Dir Roberto Esper Rebaje; circ. 25,000.

Bucaramanga, Santander del Sur

Diario del Oriente: Calle 35, No 12-62, 2°, Bucaramanga, Santander del Sur; tel. (7) 24759; Dir José M. Jaimes; circ. 10,000.

El Frente: Calle 35, No 12-40, Apdo Aéreo 665, Bucaramanga, Santander del Sur; tel. (7) 24949; telex 77777; f. 1942; morning; Conservative; Dir Dr Rafael Ortiz González; circ. 13,000.

Vanguardia Liberal: Calle 34, No 13-42, Bucaramanga, Santander del Sur; tel. (7) 21494; telex 77762; f. 1919; morning; Liberal; Sunday illustrated literary supplement and women's supplement; Dir and Man. Alejandro Galvis Ramírez; circ. 42,000.

Cali, Valle del Cauca

Occidente: Calle 12, No 5-22, Cali, Valle del Cauca; tel. (23) 85-1110; telex 55509; f. 1961; morning; Conservative; Dir Alvaro H. Caicedo González; circ. 50,000.

El País: Carrera 2A, No 24-46, Apdo Aéreo 1608, Cali, Valle del Cauca; tel. (23) 89-3011; telex 55527; fax (23) 83-5014; f. 1950; Conservative; Dir Alvaro José Lloreda C.; circ. 65,071 (weekdays), 72,938 (Saturdays), 108,304 (Sundays).

El Pueblo: Avda 3A, Norte 35-N-10, Cali, Valle del Cauca; tel. (23) 68-8110; telex 55669; morning; Liberal; Dir Luis Fernando Londoño Capurro; circ. 50,000.

Cartagena, Bolívar

El Universal: Calle 31, No 3-81, Cartagena, Bolívar; tel. (53) 40484; telex 37788; daily; Liberal; Dir Gonzalo Zúñiga; Man. Gerardo Araújo; circ. 28,000.

Cúcuta, Santander del Norte

Diario de la Frontera: Calle 14, No 3-44, Cúcuta, Santander del Norte; tel. (70) 28494; f. 1950; morning; Conservative; Dir Teodosio Cabeza Quiñones; circ. 10,000.

La Opinión: Avda 4, No 16-12, Cúcuta, Santander del Norte; tel. (70) 72-9994; telex 76697; fax (70) 72-7869; f. 1960; morning; Liberal; Dir Dr Eustorgio Colmenares; circ. 18,000 (Mondays), 14,500 (Mondays–Saturdays).

Manizales, Caldas

La Patria: Carrera 20, No 21-51, Apdo Aéreo 70, Manizales, Caldas; tel. (68) 23060; telex 42583; f. 1921; morning; Conservative; Dir Dr Luis José Restrepo Restrepo; circ. 25,000.

Medellín, Antioquia

El Colombiano: Calle 54, No 41-22, Apdo Aéreo 5236, Medellín, Antioquia; tel. (4) 51-0444; telex 44727; f. 1912; morning; Conservative; Dir Juan Gómez Martínez; circ. 123,707.

El Mundo: Calle 53, No 73-146, Apdo Aéreo 53874, Medellín, Antioquia; tel. (4) 34-8697; telex 65058; f. 1979; Dir Darío Arizmendi Posada; circ. 60,000.

Neiva

Diario del Huila: Calle 8A, No 6-30, Neiva; tel. (88) 22619; Dir María M. Rengifo de D.; circ. 10,000.

Pasto, Nariño

El Derecho: Calle 20, No 26-20, Pasto, Nariño; tel. (277) 2170; telex 53740; f. 1928; Conservative; Pres. Dr José Elías del Hierro; Dir Eduardo F. Mazuera; circ. 12,000.

Pereira, Risaralda

Diario del Otún: Carrera 8A, No 22-69, Apdo Aéreo 2533, Pereira, Risaralda; tel. (61) 53012; telex 8754; f. 1982; Financial Dir Javier Ignacio Ramírez Múnera; circ. 30,000.

El Imparcial: Apdo Aéreo 57, Pereira, Risaralda; tel. (61) 34-5651; fax (61) 34-6194; f. 1948; morning; Editor Zahur Klemath; circ. 20,000.

La Tarde: Carrera 9A, No 20-54, Pereira, Risaralda; tel. (61) 35-7976; telex 08832; fax (61) 35-5187; f. 1975; Dir Luis Fernando Baena Mejía; circ. 15,000.

Popayán, Cauca

El Liberal: Carrera 3, No 2-60, Apdo Aéreo 538, Popayán; tel. (39) 33555; f. 1938; Dir Aura Isabel Ocano de Muñoz; circ. 10,000.

Santa Marta, Magdalena

El Informador: Santa Marta, Magdalena; f. 1921; Liberal; Dir José B. Vives; circ. 9,000.

Tunja, Boyacá

Diario de Boyacá: Tunja, Boyacá; Dir-Gen. Dr Carlos H. Mojica; circ. 3,000.

El Oriente: Tunja, Boyacá; Dir-Gen. Luis López Rodríguez.

Villavicencio, Meta

Clarín del Llano: Villavicencio, Meta; tel. (866) 23207; Conservative; Dir Elías Matus Torres; circ. 5,000.

PERIODICALS

Bogotá, DE

Antena: Bogotá, DE; television, cinema and show business; circ. 10,000.

Arco: Carrera 6, No 35-39, Apdo Aéreo 8624, Bogotá, DE; tel. (1) 285-1500; telex 45153; f. 1959; monthly; history, philosophy, literature and humanities; Dir Alvaro Valencia Tovar; circ. 10,000.

Arte en Colombia: Apdo Aéreo 90193, Bogotá, DE; tel. (1) 262-5178; telex 44611; fax (1) 260-6339; f. 1976; quarterly; art, architecture, films and photography; English version; Dir Celia Sredni de Birbragher; circ. 13,000.

El Campesino: Carrera 39A, No 15-11, Bogotá, DE; f. 1958; weekly; cultural; Dir Joaquín Gutiérrez Macías; circ. 70,000.

Consigna: Diagonal 34, No 5-11, Bogotá, DE; tel. (1) 287-1157; fortnightly; Turbayista; Dir (vacant); circ. 10,000.

Costa Libre: Bogotá, DE; monthly; Dir Marco Antonio Contreras.

Coyuntura Económica: Calle 78, No 9-91, Apdo Aéreo 75074, Bogotá, DE; tel. (1) 211-6714; fax (1) 212-6073; f. 1970; quarterly; economics; published by Fundación para Educación Superior y el Desarrollo (FEDESARROLLO); Editor Patricia Correa; circ. 1500.

Cromos Magazine: Calle 70A, No 7-81, Apdo Aéreo 59317, Bogotá, DE; f. 1916; weekly; illustrated; general news; Dir Julio Andrés Camacho; circ. 68,000.

As Deportes: Calle 20, No 4-55, Bogotá, DE; f. 1978; sports; circ. 25,000.

Documentos Políticos: Bogotá, DE; monthly; organ of the pro-Moscow Communist Party.

Economía Colombiana: Edif. de los Ministerios, Of. 126A, No 6-40, Bogotá, DE; f. 1984; published by Contraloría General de la República; monthly; economics.

Escala: Calle 30, No 17-70, Bogotá, DE; tel. (1) 287-8200; fax (1) 232-5158; f. 1962; monthly; architecture; Dir David Serna Cárdenas; circ. 16,000.

Estrategia: Carrera 4A, 25A-12B, Bogotá, DE; monthly; economics; Dir Rodrigo Otero.

Guión: Carrera 16, No 36-89, Apdo Aéreo 19857; Bogotá, DE; tel. (1) 232-2660; f. 1977; weekly; general; Conservative; Dir Juan Carlos Pastrana; circ. 35,000.

Hit: Calle 20, No 4-55, Bogotá, DE; cinema and show business; circ. 20,000.

Hoy Por Hoy: Bogotá, DE; weekly; Dir Diana Turbay de Uribe.

El Informador Andino: Bogotá, DE; economic affairs.

MD en Español: Calle 77A, No 13A-20, Bogotá, DE; medicine.

Menorah: Apdo Aéreo 9081, Bogotá, DE; tel. (1) 263-2783; f. 1950; independent monthly review for the Jewish community; Dir Eliécer Celnik; circ. 10,000.

Nueva Frontera: Carrera 7A, No 17-01, 5°, Bogotá, DE; tel. (1) 334-3763; f. 1974; weekly; politics, society, arts and culture; Liberal; Dir Carlos Lleras Restrepo; circ. 23,000.

Pluma: Apdo Aéreo 12190, Bogotá, DE; monthly; art and literature; Dir (vacant); circ. 70,000.

Que Hubo: Bogotá, DE; weekly; general; Editor Consuelo Montejo; circ. 15,000.

Revista Diners: Carrera 10, No 64-65, 3°, Bogotá, DE; tel. (1) 217-7495; telex 45304; fax (1) 212-8931; f. 1963; monthly; Dir Consuelo Mendoza de Riaño; circ. 130,000.

Semana: Calle 93A/13A, 6-10, Bogotá, DE; tel. (1) 257-5400; fax (1) 257-9471; general; Dir Felipe López Caballero.

Síntesis Económica: Calle 70A, 10-52, Bogotá, DE; tel. (1) 212-7360; weekly; economics; Dir Daniel Mazuera Gómez.

Sucesos: Bogotá, DE; weekly; Dir Néstor Espinoza; circ. 15,000.

Teorema: Bogotá, DE; art and literature; Dir Alberto Rodríguez; circ. 5,000.

Tribuna Médica: Calle 8B, No 68A-41 and Calle 123, 8-20, Bogotá, DE; tel. (1) 261-5047; telex 43195; fax (1) 262-4459; f. 1961; monthly; medical and scientific; Editor Diego Jaramillo G.; circ. 50,000.

COLOMBIA — Directory

Tribuna Roja: Apdo Aéreo 19042, Bogotá, DE; tel. (1) 243-0371; f. 1971; quarterly; organ of the MOIR (pro-Maoist Communist party); Dir CARLOS NARANJO; circ. 300,000.

Vea: Calle 20, No 4-55, Bogotá, DE; weekly; popular; circ. 90,000.

Voz Proletaria: Carrera 34, No 9-28, Bogotá, DE; tel. (1) 247-2346; telex 45152; f. 1957; weekly; left-wing; Dir MANUEL CEPEDA VARGAS; circ. 45,000.

NEWS AGENCIES

Ciep—El País: Carrera 16, No 36-55, Bogotá, DE; tel. (1) 232-6816; Dir JORGE TÉLLEZ.

Colprensa: Diagonal 34, No 5-63, Apdo Aéreo 20333, Bogotá, DE; tel. (1) 287-2200; telex 45153; f. 1980; Dir ALBERTO SALDARRIAGA.

Foreign Bureaux

Agence France-Presse (AFP): Carrera 5, No 16-14, Of. 807, Apdo Aéreo 4654, Bogotá, DE1; tel. (1) 281-8613; telex 44726; Dir MARIE SANZ.

Agencia EFE (Spain): Carrera 16, No 39A-69, Apdo 16038, Bogotá, DE; tel. (1) 285-1576; telex 44577; Bureau Chief MANUEL RODRÍGUEZ MORA.

Agenzia Nazionale Stampa Associata (ANSA) (Italy): Carrera 4, No 67-30, Apdo Aéreo 16077, Bogotá, DE; tel. (1) 212-5409; telex 42266; Bureau Chief ALBERTO ROJAS MORALES.

Associated Press (AP) (USA): Calle 80, No 8-14, Of. 102, Apdo 093643, Bogotá, DE; tel. (1) 212-2040; telex 44641; Bureau Chief THOMAS G. WELLS.

Central News Agency Inc. (Taiwan): Carrera 13A, No 98-34, Bogotá, DE; tel. (1) 25-6342; Correspondent CHRISTINA CHOW.

Deutsche Presse-Agentur (dpa) (Germany): Carrera 7A, No 17-01, Of. 914, Apdo Aéreo 044245, Bogotá, DE; tel. (1) 281-8065; Correspondent CARLOS ALBERTO RUEDA.

Inter Press Service (IPS) (Italy): Calle 20, No 7-17, Of. 608, Apdo 7739, Bogotá, DE; tel. (1) 241-8841; fax (1) 334-2249; Correspondent MARÍA ISABEL GARCÍA NAVARRETE.

Prensa Latina: Carrera 7, 1701, Of. 914, Apdo Aéreo 30372, Bogotá, DE; tel. (1) 281-9306; telex 41467; Correspondent ROLANDO SARRAF ELÍAS.

Reuters (UK): Carrera 6A, No 14-98, Of. 1402, Apdo Aéreo 29848, Bogotá, DE; tel. (1) 243-8819; telex 44537; fax (1) 286-2506; Correspondent SIMON WALKER.

Telegrafnoye Agentstvo Sovetskovo Soyuza (TASS) (USSR): Calle 20, No 7-17, Of. 901, Bogotá, DE; tel. (1) 243-6720; telex 43329; Correspondent GENNADY KOCHUK.

United Press International (UPI) (USA): Carrera 4A, 67-30, 4°, Apdo Aéreo 57570, Bogotá, DE; tel. (1) 211-9106; telex 44892; Correspondent FEDERICO FULLEDA.

Xinhua (New China) News Agency (People's Republic of China): Calle 74, No 4-26, Apdo 501, Bogotá, DE; tel (1) 211-5347; telex 45620; Dir HOU YAOQI.

PRESS ASSOCIATIONS

Asociación Colombiana de Periodistas: Avda Jiménez, No 8-74, Of. 510, Bogotá, DE.

Asociación de Diarios Colombianos (ANDIARIOS): Calle 61, No 5-20, Apdo Aéreo 13663, Bogotá, DE; tel. (1) 211-4181; telex 41261; fax (1) 212-7894; f. 1962; 30 affiliated newspapers; Pres. CARLOS PINILLA BARRIOS; Vice-Pres. GERARDO ARAÚJO PERDOMO.

Círculo de Periodistas de Bogotá, DE: Calle 26, No 13A-23, P-23, Bogotá, DE; tel. (1) 282-4217; Pres. MARÍA TERESA HERRÁN.

Publishers

Bogotá

Comunicadores Técnicos Ltda: Carrera 18 No 46-58, Apdo Aéreo 28797, Bogotá, DE; technical; Dir PEDRO P. MORCILLO.

Ediciones Cultural Colombiana Ltd: Calle 72, No 16-15 y 16-21, Apdo Aéreo 6307, Bogotá, DE; tel. (1) 235-5494; f. 1951; textbooks; Dir JOSÉ PORTO VÁSQUEZ.

Ediciones Lerner Ltda: Calle 8A, No 68A-41, Apdo Aéreo 8304, Bogotá, DE; tel. (1) 262-4284; telex 43195; fax (1) 262-4459; f. 1959; general; Man. Dir JACK A. GRIMBERG.

Ediciones Paulinas (SSP): Carrera 9A, No 15-01, Apdo 100383, Bogotá, DE; tel. (1) 234-5036; f. 1956; religion, culture; Dir P. DAMATO TRAMAON.

Tercer Mundo Editores SA: Calle 69, No 6-46, Apdo Aéreo 4817, Bogotá, DE; tel. (1) 211-8174; telex 42192; fax (1) 257-5387; f. 1961; social sciences, fiction; Man. Dir SANTIAGO POMBO.

Editora Cinco, SA: Calle 61, No 13-23, 7°, Apdo Aéreo 15188, Bogotá, DE; tel. (1) 285-6200; telex 15188; recreation, culture, textbooks, general; Man. PEDRO VARGAS G.

Editorial El Globo, SA: Calle 16, No 4-96, Apdo Aéreo 6806, Bogotá.

Editorial Interamericana, SA: Carrera 17, No 33-71, Apdo Aéreo 6131, Bogotá, DE; tel. (1) 245-4786; university textbooks; Gen. Man. VÍCTOR CORTES.

Editorial Pluma Ltda: Carrera 20, No 39B-50, Bogotá, DE; tel. (1) 245-7606; telex 45422; politics, psychology, philosophy; Man. Dir ERNESTO GAMBOA.

Editorial Presencia, Ltda: Calle 23, No 24-20, Apdo Aéreo 006642, Bogotá, DE; tel. (1) 268-1817; textbooks, tradebooks; Gen. Man. MARÍA UMAÑA DE TANCO.

Editorial Temis SA: Calle 13, No 6-45, Apdo Aéreo 5941, Bogotá, DE; tel. (1) 269-0713; f. 1951; law, sociology, politics; Man. Dir JORGE GUERRERO.

Editorial Voluntad, SA: Carrera 7, No 24-89, 24°, Apdo Aéreo 29834, Bogotá, DE; tel. (1) 286-0666; telex 42481; fax (1) 286-5540; f. 1930; school books; Pres. GASTÓN DE BEDOUT.

Fundación Centro de Investigación y Educación Popular (CINEP): Carrera 5A, No 33A-08, Apdo Aéreo 25916, Bogotá, DE; tel. (1) 285-8977; fax (1) 211-2642; f. 1977; education and social sciences; Pres. Dr JULIO ANDRÉS CAMACHO CASTAÑO; Man. MAURICIO GAITÁN GAITÁN.

Instituto Caro y Cuervo: Carrera 11, No 64-37, Apdo Aéreo 51502, Bogotá, DE; tel. (1) 255-8289; f. 1942; philology, general linguistics and reference; Man. Dir IGNACIO CHAVES CUEVAS; Gen. Sec. GUILLERMO RUIZ LARA.

Inversiones Cromos SA: Calle 70A, No 7-81, Apdo Aéreo 59317, Bogotá, DE; tel. (1) 217-1754; telex 41384; f. 1977; Pres Dr RAFAEL SANABRIA VÁSQUEZ, JULIO ANDRÉS CAMACHO C.

Legis Editores, SA: Avda Eldorado No 81-10, Apdo Aéreo 98888, Bogotá, DE; tel. (1) 263-4100; telex 43300; f. 1952; economics, law, general; Man. VERGARA WIESNER.

Publicar SA: Avda 68 No 75A-50, 4°, Centro Comercial Metrópolis, Apdo Aéreo 8010, Bogotá, DE; tel. (1) 225-5555; telex 44588; fax (1) 225-4015; f. 1954; directories; Man. Dr FABIO CABAL P.

Siglo XXI Editores de Colombia Ltda: Carrera 14 No 80-44, Apdo Aéreo 92758, Bogotá, DE; tel. (1) 611-0787; f. 1976; arts, politics, anthropology, history, fiction, etc.; Man. Dir LINA MARÍA PÉREZ GAVIRIA.

Cali

Editorial Norma SA: 29N, No 6A-40, Apdo Aéreo 55555, Cali; tel. (23) 67-5011; f. 1964; children's, textbooks, education; Gen. Man. FERNANDO GÓMEZ C.

Medellín

Aguirre Editor: Calle 53, No 49-123, Apdo Aéreo 1395, Medellín; tel. (4) 239-4801; fiction; Dir ALBERTO AGUIRRE.

Editorial Bedout, SA: Calle 61, No 51-04, Apdo Aéreo 760, Medellín; tel. (4) 31-6900; f. 1889; social science, literature and textbooks; Man. HÉCTOR QUINTERO ARREDONDO.

ASSOCIATION

Cámara Colombiana del Libro: Carrera 17A, No 37-27, Apdo Aéreo 8998, Bogotá, DE; tel. (1) 288-6188; fax (1) 287-3320; f. 1951; Pres. JORGE VALENCIA JARAMILLO; Exec. Dir MIGUEL LAVERDE ESPEJO; 120 mems.

Radio and Television

In 1987 there were an estimated 5m. radio receivers and 3,250,000 television receivers in use.

Ministerio de Comunicaciones, División de Telecomunicaciones: Edif. Murillo Toro, Apdo Aéreo 14515, Bogotá, DE; broadcasting authority; Dir Minister of Communications.

Instituto Nacional de Radio y Televisión—INRAVISION: Centro Administrativo Nacional (CAN), Avda El Dorado, Bogotá, DE; tel. (1) 241-4068; telex 43311; f. 1954; government-run TV and radio broadcasting network; educational and commercial broadcasting; Dir FELIPE ZULETA.

RADIO

In 1988 there were 516 radio stations officially registered with the Ministry of Communications. Most radio stations belong to ASOMEDIOS. The principal radio networks are as follows:

Cadena Líder de Colombia: Calle 61, No 3B-03, Bogotá, DE; tel. (1) 217-0720; fax (1) 248-8772; Pres. ELVIRA DE PÁEZ.

COLOMBIA
Directory

CARACOL (Primera Cadena Radial Colombiana, SA): Calle 19, No 8-48, Apdo Aéreo 9291, Bogotá, DE; tel. (1) 282-2088; telex 44880; f. 1948; 126 stations; Gen. Man. RICARDO ALARCÓN GAVIRÍA.

Circuito Todelar de Colombia: Calle 48, No 18-77, Apdo Aéreo 27344, Bogotá, DE; tel. (1) 232-7327; telex 45732; f. 1953; 74 stations; Pres. JAVIER ACEVEDO.

Colmundo Radio: Diagonal 58, 26A-29, Bogotá, DE; tel. (1) 217-8911; Dir CARLOS ALVAREZ.

RCN (Radio Cadena Nacional, SA): Calle 13, No 37-32, Bogotá, DE; tel. (1) 285-0126; 64 stations; official network; Gen. Man. RICARDO LONDOÑO LONDOÑO.

Radiodifusora Nacional: CAN, Vía Eldorado, Bogotá, DE; tel. (1) 269-0350; Dir JUAN CARLOS JARAMILLO.

Super Radio: Calle 39, No 18-12, Apdo Aéreo 23316, Bogotá, DE; tel. (1) 243-3879; 27 stations; Man. ALVARO PAVA CAMELO.

TELEVISION

Television services began in 1954 and are operated by the state monopoly, INRAVISIÓN, which controls two national commercial stations and one national educational station. There are also three regional stations. Broadcasting time is distributed among competing programmers through a public tender and most of the commercial broadcast time is dominated by 35 programmers. Both channels broadcast around 77 hours per week. The educational station broadcasts some 39 hours per week. The NTSC colour television system was adopted in 1979.

ASSOCIATIONS

Asociación Nacional de Medios de Comunicación (ASOMEDIOS): Carrera 22, No 85-72, Bogotá, DE; tel. (1) 611-1300; fax (1) 236-0896; f. 1978 and merged with ANRADIO (Asociación Nacional de Radio, Televisión y Cine de Colombia) in 1980; Pres. Dr JORGE VALENCIA JARAMILLO.

Federación Nacional de Radio (FEDERADIO): Bogotá, DE; Dir LIBARDO TABORDA BOLÍVAR.

Finance

(cap. = capital; p.u. = paid up; res = reserves; dep. = deposits; m. = million; amounts in pesos, unless otherwise indicated)

Contraloría General de la República: Calle 17, No 9-82, P4, Bogotá, DE; tel. (1) 282-3549; Controller-General Dr MANUEL FRANCISCO BECERRA.

BANKING

In August 1989 the Government authorized plans to return to private ownership 65% of the assets of all financial institutions nationalized after the financial crisis of 1982.

Superintendencia Bancaria: Carrera 7A, No 4-49, 11°, Apdo Aéreo 3460, Bogotá, DE; tel. (1) 280-0187; telex 41443; fax (1) 80-0864; Banking Superintendent NÉSTOR HUMBERTO MARTÍNEZ NEIRA.

Junta Monetaria (Monetary Board): Carrera 7A, 14-78, Bogotá, DE; regulates banking operations and monetary policy; Pres. Minister of Finance and Public Credit.

Central Bank

Banco de la República: Carrera 7A, No 14-78, Apdo Aéreo 3531, Bogotá, DE; tel. (1) 831-1111; telex 44560; fax (1) 286-6008; f. 1923; sole bank of issue; cap. 153.9m., res 25,902.8m., dep. 502,922.6m. (Dec. 1989); Gov. Dr FRANCISCO J. ORTEGA ACOSTA; 28 brs.

The Banco de la República also administers the following financial funds that channel resources to priority sectors:

Fondo Agropecuario de Garantías: guarantee fund for agriculture.

Fondo de Capitalización Empresarial: company capitalization fund.

Fondo de Desarrollo Eléctrico: electric development finance fund.

Fondo Financiero Agrario: agriculture and livestock finance fund.

Fondo Financiero Forestal: forest finance fund.

Fondo Financiero Industrial: industrial finance fund.

Fondo de Inversiones Privadas: f. 1963; private investment fund for industrial development.

Commercial Banks
Bogotá

Banco Anglo-Colombiano (fmrly Bank of London and South America Ltd): Carrera 8A, No 15-46, Apdo Aéreo 3532, Bogotá, DE; tel. (1) 286-3155; telex 44884; fax (1) 283-9142; f. 1976; cap. 652.9m., res 3,213.2m., dep. 44,900.6m. (Dec. 1989); Pres. JOSÉ JOAQUÍN CASAS FAJARDO; Regional Man. M. P. MULHOLLAND; 44 brs.

Banco de Bogotá: Calle 36, No 7-47, 15°, Apdo Aéreo 3436, Bogotá, DE; tel. (1) 288-1188; telex 45621; f. 1870; cap. and res 12,238m., dep. 207,165m. (Dec. 1989); Pres. Dr ALEJANDRO FIGUEROA JARAMILLO; 238 brs.

Banco Cafetero: Calle 28, No 13A-15, POB 240332, Bogotá, DE; tel. (1) 284-6800; telex 43422; f. 1953; cap. US $58.5m., res $5.4m., dep. $710.4m. (Dec. 1988); government-owned; acts both as a commercial lending institution and development bank for rural coffee regions; Pres. LUIS PRIETO OCAMPO; 303 brs.

Banco Central Hipotecario: Carrera 6A, No 15-32, Bogotá, DE; tel. (1) 281-3840; telex 45720; fax (1) 283-2802; f. 1932; cap. 31,526m., dep. 234,939.6m. (Dec. 1988); provides urban housing development credit; Gen. Man. ARTURO FERRER CARRASCO; 137 brs.

Banco de Colombia: Calle 30A, No 6-38, Apdo Aéreo 6836, Bogotá, DE; tel. (1) 285-0300; telex 44744; f. 1874; cap. 78,787m., res 70m., dep. 143,046m. (Dec. 1988); nationalized in January 1986; sale of 65% of assets to private sector authorized in 1989; Pres. Dr GUILLERMO VILLAVECES MEDINA; 270 brs.

Banco Colombo-Americano (fmrly Bank of America): Carrera 7A, No 16-36, 46°, Apdo Aéreo 12327, Bogotá, DE; tel. (1) 281-6700; telex 44511; cap. 2,050m. dep. 7,051m. (Dec. 1988); Pres. RODOLFO ALBORELI; 12 brs.

Banco Colpatria: Carrera 7A, No 24-89, 10°, Apdo Aéreo 7762, Bogotá, DE; tel. (1) 234-0600; telex 44637; f. 1955; cap. and res 1,399m., dep. 28,054m. (Dec. 1988); Pres. ENRIQUE BRANDO PRADILLA; 26 brs.

Banco del Comercio: Calle 13, No 8-52, Apdo Aéreo 4749, Bogotá, DE; tel. (1) 282-6400; telex 44450; f. 1949; cap. 16,238m., res 36m., dep. 64,624m. (Dec. 1988); taken over by Government in August 1987; sale of 65% of assets to private sector authorized in 1989; Pres. HUGO GUILLERMO DÍAZ BÁEZ; 123 brs.

Banco de Crédito: Calle 27, No 6-48, 4°, Apdo Aéreo 6800, Bogotá, DE; tel. (1) 286-8400; telex 44789; fax (1) 286-7236; f. 1963; cap. and res 3,997m., dep. 25,789m. (Dec. 1989); Pres. LUIS FERNANDO MESA PRIETO; 17 brs.

Banco de Crédito y Comercio (fmrly Banco Mercantil): Carrera 7A, No 14-23, Apdo Aéreo 6826, Bogotá, DE; tel. (1) 284-8800; telex 44709; fax (1) 286-7919; f. 1954; cap. 2,062m., res 2,289m., dep. 48,626m. (Dec. 1988); Exec. Pres. EDUARDO GAITÁN DURÁN; 25 brs.

Banco del Estado: Carrera 10, No 18-15, 9°, POB 11392, Bogotá, DE; tel. (1) 233-8100; telex 44719; f. 1884; cap. 13,174m., res 742m., dep. 74,497m. (Dec. 1988); nationalized in 1986; sale of 65% of assets to private sector authorized in 1989; Pres. Dr HERNÁN RINCÓN GÓMEZ; 61 brs.

Banco Exterior de Los Andes y de España de Colombia—EXTEBANDES de Colombia: Calle 74, No 6-65, Apdo Aéreo 241247, Bogotá, DE; tel. (1) 212-7200; telex 45374; f. 1982; cap. and res 1,293m., dep. 10,224m. (Dec. 1988); Gen. Man. LUIS ANTONIO EFRAÍN ACEVEDO PÉREZ.

Banco Ganadero: Carrera 9A, No 72-11, 11°, Apdo Aéreo 53851, Bogotá, DE; tel. (1) 217-0100; telex 45121; fax (1) 255-2457; f. 1956; government-owned; sale of 65% of assets to private sector authorized in 1989; provides financing for development sector and international trade; cap. US $8.65m., dep. $572.3m. (May 1990); Pres. JESÚS ENRIQUE VILLAMIZAR ANGULO; 141 brs.

Banco Internacional de Colombia: Avda Jiménez, No 8-89, Bogotá, DE; tel. (1) 283-5888; telex 44721; cap. and res 2,826m., dep. 33,205m. (Dec. 1988); Pres. AVINASH CHOPRA; 23 brs.

Banco Popular: Calle 17, No 7-43, 7°, Apdo Aéreo 6796, Bogotá, DE; tel. (1) 281-5130; telex 45840; fax (1) 281-9448; f. 1951; government-owned; cap. 10,315m., res 31,284m., dep. 267,875m. (Dec. 1989); Pres. EDUARDO ROBAYO SALOM; 188 brs.

Banco Real de Colombia (fmrly Banco Real SA): Carrera 7A, No 33-80, Apdo Aéreo 034262, Bogotá, DE; tel. (1) 287-9300; telex 44688; fax (1) 287-9507; f. 1976; cap. 940m., res 124m., dep. 5,592m. (Dec. 1988); Pres. Dr JOSÉ EURÍPIDES GARCÍA; 9 brs.

Banco Santander: Carrera 10, No 28-49, 8°-13°, Edif. Bavaria Torre A, Apdo Aéreo 4740, Bogotá, DE; tel. (1) 284-3100; telex 45417; f. 1961; cap. and res 1,522m., dep. 30,866m. (Dec. 1988); Pres. JORGE J. TRUJILLO AGUDELO; 42 brs.

Banco Sudameris Colombia (fmrly Banco Francés e Italiano): Carrera 8, No 15-42, Apdo Aéreo 3440, Bogotá, DE; tel. (1) 283-8700; telex 44725; cap. 1500m., res 1400m., dep. 20,469m. (Dec. 1989); Pres. LUCIANO DALLA BONA; 6 brs.

Banco Tequendama: Diagonal 27, No 6-70, Bogotá, DE; tel. (1) 285-9900; telex 45496; f. 1976; government-owned; sale of 65% of assets to private sector authorized in 1989; cap. 5,401m., dep.

COLOMBIA

9,153m. (Dec. 1989); Pres. Héctor Manuel Muñoz Orjuela; 11 brs.

Banco de los Trabajadores: Calle 13, No 7-60, Apdo Aéreo 17645, Bogotá, DE; tel. (1) 233-8200; telex 41430; f. 1974; government-owned; sale of 65% of assets to private sector authorized in 1989; cap. and res 2,005m., dep. 12,747m. (Dec. 1988); Pres. Dr Carlos Enrique Pineda Durán; 19 brs.

Banco Unión Colombiano (fmrly Banco Royal Colombiano): Calle 72, No 10-07, Apdo Aéreo 3438, Bogotá, DE; tel. (1) 282-0077; telex 44609; f. 1925; cap. and res 1,147m., dep. 16,706m. (Dec. 1988); Pres. Phillip Bruce Arthur Williams; 17 brs.

Caja Agraria: Carrera 8A, No 15-43, 13°, Apdo Aéreo 3534, Bogotá, DE; tel. (1) 284-4600; telex 44738; f. 1931; cap. and res 17,519m., dep. 121,783m. (June 1986); government-owned development bank; Pres. José J. de Pombo Holguín; 878 brs.

Caja Social de Ahorros: Carrera 5A, No 12-42, Bogotá, DE; tel. (1) 211-2903; telex 45685; fax (1) 211-6036; f. 1911; savings bank; cap. and res US $8m., dep. $135.2m. (June 1989); Gen. Man. Augusto José Acosta Torres; 109 brs.

Cali

Banco de Occidente: Carrera 5A, No 12-42, Apdo Aéreo 4400, Cali; tel. (23) 82-3042; telex 55655; cap. and res 8,014m., dep. 118,883m. (Dec. 1988); Pres. Gabriel Mauricio Cabrera Galvis; 97 brs.

Manizales

Banco de Caldas: Carrera 22, Calle 21 esq., Apdo Aéreo 617, Manizales; tel. (68) 84-1900; telex 83512; fax (68) 840-086; f. 1965; cap. 1,804.3 m., dep. 29,132m. (1989); Pres. Luis Gonzalo Giraldo Marín; 33 brs.

Medellín

Banco Comercial Antioqueño: Edif. Vicente Uribe Rendón, 14°, Carrera 46, No 52-36, Medellín; tel. (4) 511-5200; telex 65339; f. 1912; cap. and res 7,563.7m., dep. 110,045m., (Dec. 1989); Pres. Alvaro Jaramillo Vengoechea; 142 brs.

Banco Industrial Colombiano: Calle 50, No 51-66, Apdo Aéreo 768, Medellín; tel. (4) 251-5516; telex 06743; f. 1945; cap. 1,102m., res 5,651.7m., dep. 71,383.2m. (Dec. 1988); Pres. Francisco Javier Gómez Restrepo; 98 brs.

Banking Association

Asociación Bancaria de Colombia: Carrera 7A, No 17-01, 3°, Apdo Aéreo 13994, Bogotá, DE; tel. (1) 282-1066; f. 1936; 56 mem. banks; Pres. Carlos Caballero Argáez; Vice-Pres. Santiago Gutiérrez.

STOCK EXCHANGES

Comisión Nacional de Valores: Carrera 7A, No 31-10, 4°, Apdo Aéreo 39600, Bogotá, DE; tel. (1) 287-3300; telex 44326; f. 1979 to regulate the securities market; Pres. Dr Luis Fernando Uribe Restrepo.

Bolsa de Bogotá: Carrera 8A, No 13-82, 8°, Apdo Aéreo 3584, Bogotá, DE; tel. (1) 243-6501; telex 44807; fax (1) 281-3170; f. 1928; Pres. Hernán Beltz Peralta; Vice-Pres Andres Uribe Arango; Sec.-Gen. Pedro José Bautista Moller.

Bolsa de Medellín SA: Carrera 50, No 50-48, 2°, Apdo Aéreo 3535, Medellín; tel. (4) 260-3000; telex 66788; fax (4) 251-1981; f. 1961; Pres. Francisco Piedrahita Echeverri; Vice-Pres. Libia Barreneche Gómez.

Bolsa de Occidente SA: Calle 8A, No 3-14, 17°, Cali; tel. (23) 81-7022; telex 51217; Pres. William Aguirre Peláez; Vice-Pres Jorge Ernesto Holguín B. and José Luís Munera.

INSURANCE
Principal National Companies
(selected on the basis of premium income)

Aseguradora Colseguros, SA: Calle 10, No 17-18, Apdo Aéreo 3537, Bogotá DE; tel. (1) 283-9100; telex 44710; fax (1) 284-9205; f. 1874; Pres. Dr Bernardo Botero Morales.

Aseguradora Grancolombiana, SA: Calle 31, No 6-41, 4°, Apdo Aéreo 10454, Bogotá, DE; tel. (1) 285-6520; telex 41328; Pres. Dr Julián Efrén Ossa Gómez.

Cía Agrícola de Seguros, SA: Calle 67, No 7-94, 14°-22°, Apdo Aéreo 7212, Bogotá, DE; tel. (1) 212-1100; telex 45501; fax (1) 212-3951; f. 1952; Pres. Dr Ariel Jaramillo Abad.

Cía Central de Seguros: Carrera 13, No 27-47, 12°, Apdo Aéreo 5764, Bogotá, DE; tel. (1) 288-6207; telex 45664; f. 1957; Man. Dir Julián Efrén Ossa Gómez.

Cía de Seguros Bolívar, SA: Carrera 10A, No 16-39, Apdo Aéreo 4421, Bogotá, DE; tel. (1) 283-0100; telex 44873; f. 1939; Pres. Dr José Alejandro Cortés O.

Directory

Cía Suramericana de Seguros, SA: Centro Suramericana, Carrera 64B, No 49A-30, Apdo Aéreo 780, Medellín; tel. (4) 260-2100; telex 66639; fax (4) 260-2653; f. 1944; Pres. Dr Nicanor Restrepo Santamaría.

La Interamericana Cía de Seguros Generales, SA: Calle 78, No 9-57, 5°, Bogotá, DE; tel. (1) 255-9700; telex 44631; Pres. Glenn A. Lawson.

La Nacional Cía de Seguros Generales, SA: Calle 42, No 56-01, Apdo 81077, Bogotá, DE; tel. (1) 221-5800; telex 44567; f. 1952; Pres. Dr Jaime Botero Cadavid.

Seguros Caribe, SA: Carrera 7A, No 74-36, 5°-6°, Apdo 28525, Bogotá, DE; tel. (1) 211-4183; telex 42122; Pres. Dr Fernando Escallón Morales; Vice-Pres. Stella Aparicio Hernández.

Seguros del Comercio, SA: Calle 71A, No 6-30, 2°, Apdo 57227, Bogotá, DE; tel. (1) 212-0510; telex 44582; f. 1954; Pres. Dr Maristella Sanín de Aldana.

Seguros Médicos Voluntarios, SA: Calle 72, No 6-44, 9°, Apdo 11777, Bogotá, DE; tel. (1) 212-7611; telex 43354; Gen. Man. Dr Francisco di Domenico Asti.

Skandia Seguros de Colombia, SA: Avda 19, No 113-30, Apdo 100327, Bogotá, DE; tel. (1) 214-1200; telex 43398; Pres. Terje Olsen.

Numerous foreign companies are also represented.

Insurance Association

Unión de Aseguradores Colombianos—FASECOLDA: Carrera 7a, No 26-20, 11° y 12°, Apdo Aéreo 5233, Bogotá, DE; tel. (1) 287-6611; telex 41426; f. 1976; 64 mems; Pres. Dr William R. Fadul.

Trade and Industry

CHAMBERS OF COMMERCE

Confederación Colombiana de Cámaras de Comercio—CONFECAMARAS: Carrera 13, No 27-47, Of. 502, Apdo Aéreo 29750, Bogotá, DE; tel. (1) 288-1200; telex 44416; fax (1) 288-4228; f. 1969; 53 mem. organizations; Exec.-Pres. Nicolás del Castillo Mathieu.

Cámara de Comercio de Bogotá: Carrera 9A, No 16-21, Apdo Aéreo 29824, Bogotá, DE; tel. (1) 281-9900; telex 45574; fax (1) 284-7735; f. 1878; 2,500 mem. organizations; Dir Dr Mario Suárez Melo; Pres. Alvaro Hernán Mejía Pabón.

There are also local Chambers of Commerce in the capital towns of all the Departments and in many of the other trading centres.

STATE INDUSTRIAL AND TRADE ORGANIZATIONS

Carbones de Colombia—CARBOCOL: Carrera 7A, No 31-10, 5°, Apdo Aéreo 29740, Bogotá, DE; tel. (1) 287-3100; telex 45779; fax (1) 287-3278; f. 1976; initial cap. 350m. pesos; state enterprise for the exploration, mining, processing and marketing of coal; Pres. Sergio Sokoloff Moreno; Vice-Pres. (Commerce) Dr Antonio Pretelt Emiliana.

Colombiana de Minería—COLMINAS: Bogotá, DE; state mining concern; Man. Alfonso Rodríguez Kilber.

Corporación de la Industria Aeronáutica Colombiana, SA (CIAC SA): Aeropuerto Internacional Eldorado, Entrada 1 y 2, Apdo Aéreo 14446, Bogotá, DE; tel. (1) 413-8673; telex 45254; fax (1) 268-5326; Man. Gen. Horacio García Rodríguez.

Departamento Nacional de Planeación: Calle 26, No 13-19, Mezanini 17, Bogotá, DE; tel. (1) 282-2586; telex 45634; fax (1) 281-3348; f. 1958; supervises and administers development projects; approves foreign investments; Dir Armando Montenegro.

Empresa Colombiana de Minas—ECOMINAS: Calle 32, No 13-07, Apdo Aéreo 17878, Bogotá, DE; tel. (1) 287-7136; fax (1) 87-4606; administers state resources of emerald, copper, gold, sulphur, gypsum, phosphate rock and other minerals except coal, petroleum and uranium; Gen. Man. Jorge Osorio Maya.

Empresa Colombia de Niquel—ECONIQUEL: Carrera 7, No 26-20, Bogotá, DE; tel. (1) 232-3839; telex 43262; administers state nickel resources; Dir Javier Restrepo Toro.

Empresa Colombiana de Petróleos—ECOPETROL: Carrera 13, No 36-24, Apdo Aéreo 5938, Bogotá, DE; tel. (1) 285-6400; f. 1951; responsible for exploration, production, refining and transportation of petroleum; Pres. Andrés Restrepo Londoño.

ECOPETROL Internacional: Bogotá, DE; f. 1988; conducts exploration activities in Peru and other countries in the region.

Instituto Colombiano de Petróleo; f. 1985; research into all aspects of the hydrocarbon industry; Dir Dr Medardo Gamboa Maldonado.

COLOMBIA *Directory*

Empresa Colombiana de Uranio—COLURANIO: Centro Administrativo Nacional (CAN), 4°, Ministerio de Minas y Energía, Bogotá, DE; tel. (1) 244-5440; telex 45898; f. 1977 to further the exploration, processing and marketing of radio-active minerals; initial cap. US $750,000; Dir JAIME GARCÍA.

Empresa de Comercialización de Productos Perecederos—EMCOPER: Calle 62, No 11-49, Bogotá, DE; tel. (1) 235-5507; attached to Ministry of Agriculture; Dir LUIS FERNANDO LONDOÑO RUIZ.

Empresa Nacional de Telecomunicaciones—TELECOM: Calle 23, No 13-49, Bogotá, DE; tel. (1) 269-4077; telex 44280; fax (1) 284-2171; f. 1947; national telecommunications enterprise; Pres. EMILIO SARAVIA BRAVO.

Fondo de Promoción de Exportaciones—PROEXPO: Calle 28, No 13A-15, 35°-42°, Apdo Aéreo 240092, Bogotá, DE; tel. (1) 269-0777; telex 44452; fax (1) 282-5071; f. 1967; aims to diversify exports, strengthen the balance of payments and augment the volume of trade, by granting financial aid for export operations and acting as consultant to export firms, also undertaking market studies; Dir Dr CARLOS CABALLERO ARGAÍZ.

Fondo Nacional de Proyectos de Desarrollo—FONADE: Calle 26, No 13-19, 18°-21°, Apdo Aéreo 24110, Bogotá, DE; tel. (1) 282-9400; telex 45634; fax (1) 282-6018; f. 1968; responsible for channelling loans towards economic development projects; administered by a committee under the head of the Departamento Nacional de Planeación; FONADE works in close association with other official planning organizations; Dir Dr ALBERTO VILLATE PARÍS.

Fundación para el Desarrollo Integral del Valle del Cauca—FDI: Calle 8, No 3-14, 17°, Apdo Aéreo 7482, Cali; tel. (23) 80-6660; telex 7482; fax (23) 82-4627; f. 1969; industrial development organization; Pres. GUNNAR LINDAHL HELLBERG; Exec. Pres. FABIO RODRÍGUEZ GONZÁLEZ.

Industria Militar—INDUMIL: Diagonal 40, No 47-75, Apdo Aéreo 7272, Bogotá, DE; tel. (1) 222-3001; telex 45816; fax (1) 222-4889; attached to Ministry of Defence; Man. Adm. (retd) MANUEL F. AVENDAÑO.

Instituto Colombiano Agropecuario (ICA): Calle 37, No 8-43, 4° y 5°, Apdo Aéreo 7984, Bogotá, DE; tel. (1) 285-5520; telex 44586; f. 1962; institute for promotion, co-ordination and implementation of research into and teaching and development of agriculture and animal husbandry; Dir GABRIEL MONTES LLAMAS.

Instituto Colombiano de Comercio Exterior—INCOMEX: Calle 28, No 13A-15, Apdo Aéreo 240193, Bogotá, DE; tel. (1) 283-3284; telex 44860; government agency; sets and executes foreign trade policy; Dir MARTA RAMÍREZ DE RINCÓN.

Instituto Colombiano de Energía Eléctrica—ICEL: Carrera 13, No 27-00, 3°, Apdo Aéreo 16243, Bogotá, DE; tel. (1) 242-0181; telex 43319; fax (1) 281-2890; f. 1947; formulates policy for the development of electrical energy; constructs systems for the generation, transmission and distribution of electrical energy; Man. DIEGO OTERO PRADA; Sec.-Gen. GERMÁN RUEDA ESCOBAR.

Instituto Colombiano de Hidrología, Meteorología y Adecuación de Tierras—HIMAT: Carrera 5A, No 15-80, 16°-23°, Apdo Aéreo 20032, Bogotá, DE; tel. (1) 283-6927; telex 44345; fax (1) 284-2402; f. 1976; responsible for irrigation, flood control, drainage, hydrology and meteorology; Dir CARLOS PESILLA CEPEDA.

Instituto Colombiano de la Reforma Agraria—INCORA: Avda El Dorado, (CAN), Apdo Aéreo 151046, Bogotá, DE; tel. (1) 222-0963; f. 1962; a public institution which, on behalf of the Government, administers public lands and those it acquires; reclaims land by irrigation and drainage facilities, roads, etc. to increase productivity in agriculture and stock-breeding; provides technical assistance and loans; supervises the redistribution of land throughout the country; Dir GERMÁN BULA E.

Instituto de Crédito Territorial (ICT): Carrera 13, No 18-51, Apdo Aéreo 4037, Bogotá, DE; tel. (1) 234-3560; telex 44826; Gen. Man. GABRIEL GIRALDO.

Instituto de Fomento Industrial (IFI): Calle 16, No 6-66, 7°-15°, Apdo Aéreo 4222, Bogotá, DE; tel. (1) 282-2055; telex 44642; fax (1) 283-8553; f. 1940; state finance corporation for the promotion of manufacturing activities; cap. 29,341m. pesos (Dec. 1988), res 441.4m. pesos (1986); Gen. Man. RODRIGO VILLAMIZAS.

Instituto de Mercadeo Agropecuario—IDEMA: Carrera 10, No 16-82, Apdo Aéreo 4534, Bogotá, DE; tel. (1) 282-9911; telex 43315; fax (1) 283-1838; state enterprise for the marketing of agricultural products; Man. DARÍO BUSTAMANTE.

Instituto Nacional de Fomento Municipal—INSFOPAL: Centro Administrativo Nacional (CAN), Apdo Aéreo 8638, Bogotá, DE; tel. (1) 222-3177; telex 45328; Gen. Man. JAIME MARIO SALAZAR VELÁSQUEZ.

Instituto Nacional de Investigaciones Geológico-Mineras—INGEOMINAS: Diagonal 53, No 34-53, Apdo Aéreo 4865, Bogotá, DE; tel. (1) 222-1811; telex 44909; fax (1) 222-3597; f. 1968; responsible for mineral research, geological mapping and research including hydrogeology, remote sensing, geochemistry and geophysics; Dir Dr LUIS EDUARDO JARAMILLO.

Instituto Nacional de los Recursos Naturales Renovables y del Ambiente—INDERENA: Diagonal 34, No 5-18, 3°, Apdo Aéreo 13458, Bogotá, DE; tel. (1) 285-4417; telex 44428; f. 1968; agency regulating the development of natural resources; Dir Dr GERMÁN GARCÍA DURÁN.

Sociedad de Gas Natural: Bogotá, DE; f. 1988; state gas corporation; Pres. (vacant).

Sociedad Minera del Guainía (SMG): Bogotá, DE; f. 1987; state enterprise for exploration, mining and marketing of gold; Pres. Dr JORGE BENDECK OLIVELLA.

Superintendencia de Industria y Comercio—SUPERINDUSTRIA: Carrera 13, No 27-00, 5°, Bogotá, DE; tel. (1) 234-2035; supervises chambers of commerce; controls standards and prices; Man. Dr DIEGO NARANJO MEZA; Supt FIDELIA VILLAMIZAR DE PÉREZ.

Superintendencia de Sociedades—SUPERSOCIEDADES: Avda El Dorado No 46-80, Apdo Aéreo 4188, Bogotá, DE; tel. (1) 242-2050; fax (1) 284-7659; oversees activities of local and foreign corporations; Supt LUIS FERNANDO ALVARADO ORTIZ.

There are several other agricultural and regional development organizations.

TRADE FAIR

Corporación de Ferias y Exposiciones, SA: Carrera 40, No 22C-67, Apdo Aéreo 6843, Bogotá, DE; tel. (1) 244-0100; telex 44553; fax (1) 268-8469; f. 1954; holds the biannual Bogotá International Fair and the biannual International Agricultural Fair (AGROEXPO); Man. HERNANDO RESTREPO LONOÑO.

EMPLOYERS' AND PRODUCERS' ORGANIZATIONS

Asociación Colombiana Popular de Industriales (ACOPI): Carrera 23, No 41-94, Apdo Aéreo 16451, Bogotá, DE; tel. (1) 244-2741; fax (1) 268-8965; f. 1951; association of small industrialists; Pres. JUAN A. PINTO SAAVEDRA; Man. MIGUEL CARRILLO M.

Asociación de Cultivadores de Caña de Azúcar de Colombia (ASOCAÑA): Calle 58N, No 3N-15, Apdo Aéreo 4448, Cali; tel. (23) 64-7902; telex 51136; fax (23) 64-5888; f. 1959; sugar planters' association; Pres. Dr RICARDO VILLAVECES PARDO.

Asociación Nacional de Exportadores (ANALDEX): Carrera 10, No 27, 27°, Int. 137, Of. 1009, Apdo Aéreo 29812, Bogotá, DE; tel. (1) 284-3237; telex 43326; fax (1) 284-6911; exporters' association; Pres. RICARDO SALA GAITÁN.

Asociación Nacional de Exportadores de Café de Colombia: Carrera 7, No 32-33, Of. 25-01, Bogotá, DE; tel. (1) 283-0669; telex 44802; fax (1) 283-4953; f. 1938; private association of coffee exporters; Pres. ROBERTO JUNGUITO BONET.

Asociación Nacional de Industriales (ANDI) (National Association of Manufacturers): Calle 52, No 47-48, Apdo 997, Medellín; tel. (4) 251-4444; telex 6631; fax (4) 251-8830; f. 1944; Pres. FABIO ECHEVERRI CORREA; 9 brs; 756 mems.

Expocafé: Carrera 7A, No 74-36, Of. 302, Edif. Seguros Caribe, Apdo Aéreo 41244, Bogotá, DE; tel. (1) 217-8900; telex 42379; fax (1) 217-3554; f. 1985; coffee exporting organization; comprises 53 coffee co-operatives; Pres. JOSÉ A. LÓPEZ.

Federación Colombiana de Ganaderos (FEDEGAN): Carrera 14, No 36-65, Apdo Aéreo 9709, Bogotá, DE; tel. (1) 245-3041; f. 1975; cattle raisers' association; about 350,000 affiliates; Pres. JOSÉ RAIMUNDO SOJO ZAMBRANO.

Federación Nacional de Algodoneros: Carrera 8A, No 15-73, 5°, Apdo Aéreo 8632, Bogotá, DE; tel. (1) 234-3221; telex 44864; f. 1953; federation of cotton growers; Gen. Man. ANTONIO ABELLO ROCA; 14,000 mems.

Federación Nacional de Cacaoteros: Carrera 17, No 30-39, Apdo Aéreo 17736, Bogotá, DE; tel. (1) 232-0806; fax (1) 288-4424; federation of cocoa growers; Gen. Man. Dr MIGUEL URIBE.

Federación Nacional de Cafeteros de Colombia (National Federation of Coffee Growers): Calle 73, No 8-13, Apdo Aéreo 57534, Bogotá, DE; tel. (1) 217-0600; telex 44723; f. 1927; totally responsible for fostering and regulating the coffee economy; Gen. Man. JORGE CÁRDENAS GUTIÉRREZ; 203,000 mems.

Federación Nacional de Cultivadores de Cereales (FENALCE): Carrera 14, No 97-62, Apdo Aéreo 8694, Bogotá, DE; tel. (1) 218-9366; fax (1) 218-9463; f. 1960; federation of grain growers; Gen. Man. ADRIANO QUINTANA SILVA; 12,000 mems.

Federación Nacional de Comerciantes (FENALCO): Carrera 4, No 19-85, 7°, Bogotá, DE; tel. (1) 286-0600; telex 44706; fax (1)

COLOMBIA

Directory

282-7573; federation of businessmen; Pres. Sabas Pretelt de la Vega.

Sociedad de Agricultores de Colombia (SAC) (Colombian Farmers' Society): Carrera 7A, No 24-89, 44°, Apdo Aéreo 3638, Bogotá, DE; tel. (1) 282-1989; f. 1871; Pres. Carlos Gustavo Cano.

There are several other organizations, including those for rice growers, engineers and financiers.

TRADE UNIONS

According to official figures, an estimated 900 of Colombia's 2,000 trade unions are independent.

Central Unitaria de Trabajadores (CUT): Calle 35, No 7-25, 9°, Apdo Aéreo 221, Bogotá, DE; tel. (1) 288-0557; fax (1) 287-5867; f. 1986; comprises 50 federations and 80% of all trade union members; Pres. Jorge Carillo Rojas; Sec.-Gen. Angelino Garzón.

Frente Sindical Democrática (FSD): f. 1984; centre-right trade union alliance; comprises:

Confederación de Trabajadores de Colombia (CTC) (Colombian Confederation of Workers): Calle 39, No 26A-23, 5°, Apdo Aéreo 4780, Bogotá, DE; tel. (1) 269-7119; f. 1934; mainly Liberal; 600 affiliates, including 6 national organizations and 20 regional federations; admitted to ICFTU; Pres. Alvis Fernández; 400,000 mems.

Confederación de Trabajadores Democráticos de Colombia (CTDC): Carrera 13, No 59-52, Of. 303, Bogotá, DE; tel. (1) 255-3146; fax (1) 484-581; f. 1988; comprises 23 industrial federations and 22 national unions; Pres. Mario de J. Valderrama.

Confederación General del Trabajo (CGT): Calle 19, No 13A-12, 6° y 7°, Apdo Aéreo 5415, Bogotá, DE; tel. (1) 283-5817; fax (1) 283-5895; Christian Democrat; Pres. Julio Roberto Gómez Esguerra.

Transport

Land transport in Colombia is rendered difficult by high mountains, so the principal means of long-distance transport is by air. As a result of the development of the El Cerrejón coal field, Colombia's first deep-water port has been constructed at Bahia de Portete, and a 150-km rail link between El Cerrejón and the port became operational in 1986.

Instituto Nacional del Transporte (INTRA): Edif. Minobras (CAN), 6°, Apdo Aéreo 24990, Bogotá, DE; tel. (1) 222-4100; government body; Dir Dr Guillermo Anzola Lizarazo.

RAILWAYS

Ferrocarriles Nacionales de Colombia (FNC) (National Railways of Colombia): Estación de La Sabana, Apdo Aéreo 29823, Bogotá, DE; tel. (1) 277-5577; telex 45468; f. 1954; in liquidation; will relinquish responsibility for rail services in July 1992 (see below); Pres. Dr Luis Fernando Jaramillo Correa; Man. Dr Sergio Hugo Amaya Córdoba.

The Administrative Council for the National Railways operated 2,620 km of track in 1988. The system is divided into five divisions, each with its own management: Central, Pacific, Antioquia, Santander and Magdalena.

In 1989, following the entry into liquidation of the FNC, the Government created three new companies to assume responsibility for the rail network by July 1992:

Empresa Colombiana de Vías Férreas: Calle 13, No 18-24, Bogotá, DE; tel. (1) 281-4097; responsible for the maintenance and development of the national rail network.

Sociedad Colombiana de Transporte Ferroviario, SA (STF): operates public rail services.

Fondo de Pasivo Social de Ferrocarriles Nacionales de Colombia: administers welfare services for existing and former employees of the FNC.

The Medellín urban transport project, which will provide a 29-km underground system with 24 stations, was scheduled to be operational by 1989. A similar transit project has been proposed for Bogotá, and in 1988 it was announced that Italy had been selected by the Colombian Government to construct the 44-km underground system, which was due to come into operation in 1992.

ROADS

Fondo Vial Nacional: Bogotá, DE; f. 1966; administered by the Ministerio de Obras Públicas; to execute development programmes in road transport.

In 1986 there were 106,218 km of roads, of which 25,599 km were highways and main roads and 52,826 km were secondary roads.

The country's main highways are the Caribbean Trunk Highway, the Eastern and Western Trunk Highways, the Central Trunk Highway and there are also roads into the interior. There are plans to construct a Jungle Edge highway to give access to the interior, a link road between Turbo, Bahía Solano and Medellín, a highway between Bogotá and Villavicencio and to complete the short section of the Pan-American highway between Panama and Colombia. In 1987 the World Bank granted a loan of US $180.3m. to Colombia for the rehabilitation and improvement of some 7,200 km of roads.

There are a number of national bus companies and road haulage companies.

INLAND WATERWAYS

Dirección de Navegación y Puertos: Edif. Minobras (CAN), Of. 562, Bogotá, DE; tel. (1) 222-1248; telex 45656; responsible for river works and transport; the waterways system is divided into four sectors: Magdalena, Atrato, Orinoquia, and Amazonia; Dir Alberto Rodríguez Rojas.

The Magdalena–Cauca river system is the centre of river traffic and is navigable for 1,500 km, while the Atrato is navigable for 687 km. The Orinoco system has more than five navigable rivers, which total more than 4,000 km of potential navigation (mainly through Venezuela); the Amazonas system has four main rivers, which total 3,000 navigable km (mainly through Brazil). There are plans to connect the Arauca with the Meta, and the Putamayo with the Amazon, and also to construct an Atrato–Truandó interoceanic canal.

SHIPPING

The four most important ocean terminals are Buenaventura on the Pacific coast and Santa Marta, Barranquilla and Cartagena on the Atlantic coast. The port of Tumaco on the Pacific coast is gaining in importance and there are plans for construction of a deep-water port at Bahía Solano. In 1986 the World Bank allocated a loan of US $43m. to Colombia for the rehabilitation of port facilities at Buenaventura, Cartagena and Santa Marta.

Empresa Puertos de Colombia—COLPUERTOS (Colombian Port Authority): Carrera 10A, No 15-22, 8°-10°, Apdo Aéreo 13017, Bogotá, DE; tel. (1) 234-3701; telex 44770; fax (1) 281-1501; f. 1959; Man. Enrique Javier Pacheco Sánchez.

Flota Mercante Grancolombiana, SA: Carrera 13, No 27-75, Apdo Aéreo 4482, Bogotá, DE; tel. (1) 286-0200; telex 44853; fax (1) 286-9028; owned by the Colombian Coffee Growers' Federation (80%) and Ecuador Development Bank (20%); f. 1946; one of Latin America's leading cargo carriers serving 45 countries worldwide; Pres. Dr Enrique Vargas R.; Sec.-Gen. Dr Humberto Velásquez; 21 vessels.

Colombiana Internacional de Vapores, Ltda (Colvapores): Avda Caracas, No 35-02, Apdo 17227, Bogotá, DE; cargo services mainly to the USA.

Líneas Agromar, Ltda: Calle 73, Vía 40-350, Apdo Aéreo 3259, Barranquilla; tel. (58) 45-1968; telex 31405; fax (58) 45-9634; Pres. M. del Dago F.

Several foreign shipping lines call at Colombian ports.

CIVIL AVIATION

Colombia has more than 100 airports, including 11 international airports: Bogotá (El Dorado Airport), Medellín, Cali, Barranquilla, Bucaramanga, Cartagena, Cúcuta, Leticia, Pereira, San Andrés and Santa Marta.

Airports Authority

Departamento Administrativo de Aeronáutica Civil (Aerocivil): Aeropuerto Internacional El Dorado, Bogotá, DE; tel. (1) 413-9500; telex 44844; fax (1) 413-8091; Dir Yezid Castaño González.

National Airlines

AVIANCA (Aerovías Nacionales de Colombia): Avda El Dorado 93-30, 4°, Bloque 1, Bogotá, DE; tel. (1) 263-9511; telex 44427; fax (1) 69-9131; f. 1919; operates domestic services to all cities in Colombia and international services to Argentina, Brazil, Chile, Ecuador, Mexico, Panama, Peru, Uruguay, Venezuela, the Dominican Republic, Haiti, the Netherlands Antilles, Puerto Rico, the USA, France, Germany and Spain; Pres. Edgar Lewis Garrido; fleet: 1 Boeing 747, 10 Boeing 727-100, 7 Boeing 727-200, 4 Boeing 707-320B.

Sociedad Aeronáutica de Medellín Consolidada, SA (SAM): Edif. SAM, Calle 53, No 45-112, 2°, 9° y 21°-24°, Apdo Aéreo 1085, Medellín; Avda Jiménez, No 5-14, Bogotá, DE; tel. (4) 251-5544; telex 6774; fax (4) 251-0711; f. 1945; subsidiary of Avianca; internal services; and international cargo services to Costa Rica, El Salvador, Guatemala, Nicaragua, Panama and the USA; Gen.

Man. Javier Zapata; fleet: 6 Boeing 727-100, 1 Boeing 727-100C.

Servicio Aéreo a Territorios Nacionales (Satena): Aeropuerto El Dorado, Entrada No 1, Interior No 11, Carrera 10, Bogotá, DE; tel. (1) 281-7071; telex 42332; fax (1) 413-8178; f. 1962; commercial enterprise attached to the Ministry of National Defence; internal services; Man. Luis Ángel Díaz Díaz; fleet: 1 Fokker F-28, 2 BAe-748, 3 Pilatus Porter PC 6, 11 Casa 212-200.

Transportes Aéreos Mercantiles Panamericanos (Tampa): Casilla 95542, Medellín; tel. (4) 250-2939; telex 66601; fax (4) 250-2939; f. 1974; operates international cargo services to Miami and Ostend; Pres. Jorge Coulson Rodríguez; fleet: 3 Boeing 707-320C.

In addition the following airlines operate scheduled domestic passenger and cargo services: Aerolíneas Centrales de Colombia, SA (ACES), Aerosucre Colombia, Aerovías de Pesca y Colonización del Suroeste Colombiano (Aeropesca) and Aerovías Colombianas (ARCA).

Tourism

The principal tourist attractions are the Caribbean coast (including the island of San Andrés), the 16th-century walled city of Cartagena, the Amazonian town of Leticia, the Andes mountains rising to 5,700 m above sea-level, the extensive forests and jungles, pre-Columbian relics and monuments of colonial art. Most of the 732,982 visitors in 1989 came from Venezuela, Ecuador, Canada, Europe and the USA.

Corporación Nacional de Turismo: Calle 28, No 13A-15, 16°-18°, Apdo Aéreo 8400, Bogotá, DE; tel. (1) 283-9466; telex 41350; fax (1) 284-3818; f. 1968; Gen. Man. Fernando Anchique Vaca; 9 brs throughout Colombia and brs in Europe, the USA and Venezuela.

Asociación Colombiana de Agencias de Viajes y Turismo—ANATO: Carrera 21, No 83-63/71, Apdo Aéreo 7088, Bogotá, DE; tel. (1) 256-2290; telex 45675; fax (1) 218-7103; f. 1949; Pres. Dr Oscar Rueda García.

Atomic Energy

Instituto de Asuntos Nucleares—IAN: Avda Eldorado, Carrera 50, Apdo Aéreo 8595, Bogotá 1, DE; tel. (1) 222-0600; telex 42416; fax (1) 222-0173; f. 1959; experimental facilities; Dir Dr Jaime J. Ahumada.

THE COMOROS*

Introductory Survey

Location, Climate, Language, Religion, Flag, Capital

The Federal Islamic Republic of the Comoros is an archipelago in the Mozambique Channel, between the island of Madagascar and the east coast of the African mainland. The group comprises four main islands (Njazidja, Nzwani and Mwali, formerly Grande-Comore, Anjouan and Mohéli respectively, and Mayotte) and numerous islets and coral reefs. The climate is tropical, with considerable variations in rainfall and temperature from island to island. The official languages are Arabic and French but the majority of the population speak Comoran, a blend of Swahili and Arabic. Islam is the state religion. The flag is green, with a white crescent moon and four five-pointed white stars in the centre. The capital is Moroni, on Njazidja.

Recent History

Formerly attached to Madagascar, the Comoros became a separate French Overseas Territory in 1947. The islands achieved internal self-government in December 1961, with a Chamber of Deputies and a Government Council to control local administration.

Elections in December 1972 produced a large majority for parties advocating independence, and Ahmed Abdallah became President of the Government Council. In June 1973 he was restyled President of the Government. A referendum in December 1974 resulted in a 96% vote in favour of independence, despite the opposition of the Mayotte Party, which sought the status of a French Department for the island of Mayotte.

On 6 July 1975, despite French insistence that any constitutional settlement should be ratified by all the islands voting separately, the Chamber of Deputies voted for immediate independence. The Chamber elected Abdallah to be first President of the Comoros and constituted itself as the National Assembly. Although France made no attempt to intervene, it maintained control of Mayotte. President Abdallah was deposed in August, and the Assembly was abolished. A National Executive Council was established, with Prince Saïd Mohammed Jaffar, leader of the opposition Front National Uni, as its head, and Ali Soilih, leader of the coup, among its members. In November the Comoros was admitted to the UN, as a unified state comprising the whole archipelago, but France continued to support Mayotte, although recognizing the independence of the three remaining islands in December. In February 1976 Mayotte voted overwhelmingly to retain its links with France.

As relations with France deteriorated, all development aid and technical assistance were withdrawn. Ali Soilih was elected Head of State in January 1976, and a new constitution gave him extended powers. In May 1978 Soilih was shot dead, following a coup by a group of about 50 European mercenaries, led by a Frenchman, Bob Denard, on behalf of the exiled former President, Ahmed Abdallah, and the Comoros was proclaimed a Federal Islamic Republic. In July the Comoros was expelled from the Organization of African Unity (OAU) because of the continued presence of the mercenaries.

In October 1978 a new constitution was approved in a referendum, on the three islands excluding Mayotte, by 99.31% of the votes cast. Abdallah was elected President in the same month, and in December elections were held to form a Federal Assembly. In January 1979 the Assembly approved the formation of a one-party state. Unofficial opposition groups, however, continued to exist, and 150 people were arrested in February 1981, following reports (officially denied) of an attempted coup. Ali Mroudjae, former Minister of Foreign Affairs and Co-operation, was appointed Prime Minister in February 1982, and legislative elections were held in March. Constitutional amendments, adopted in October, increased the President's power by reducing that of each island's Governor. In May 1983 President Abdallah announced an amnesty for all political prisoners who were serving sentences of less than 10 years. In December an attempted coup, planned by a group of British mercenaries on behalf of Prince Saïd Ali Kemal (a former Comoran diplomat), was prevented by the arrest of the mercenary leaders in Australia. Abdallah was the sole candidate at a presidential election in September 1984. Despite appeals by the opposition for voters to boycott the election, 98% of the electorate participated. Abdallah was re-elected President by 99.44% of the votes cast, and was therefore returned to office for a further six years. In January 1985 the Constitution was amended to abolish the position of Prime Minister, and President Abdallah assumed the office of Head of Government.

In March 1985 an attempt by presidential guardsmen to overthrow Abdallah, while he was absent on a private visit to France, failed. In November 17 people, including Mustapha Saïd Cheikh, Secretary-General of the banned opposition movement, Front démocratique (FD), were sentenced to forced labour for life, while 50 others were also imprisoned for their part in the coup attempt. In December, however, President Abdallah granted an amnesty to about 30 political prisoners, many of whom were FD members, and in May 1986 a further 15 detainees, convicted after the attempted coup, were also released. In January 1987 President Abdallah announced a further amnesty for political prisoners. In February Abdallah announced that elections for the Federal Assembly would be held on 22 March, and indicated that the elections would be open to individual candidates who opposed the Government. However, candidates other than those selected by the Government were only allowed to contest 20 seats on Njazidja, where they received 35% of the total votes, and pro-Government candidates retained full control of the 42-seat Federal Assembly. About 65% of the electorate participated. There were allegations of widespread fraud and intimidation of opposition candidates, and, according to Comoran dissidents in Réunion, about 400 people were arrested, 200–300 of whom were later imprisoned. In June three French-based opposition movements agreed to merge, during a rally in Marseille, attended by nearly 1,000 Comorans.

In July 1987, to mark the 12th anniversary of independence, Abdallah reinstated all civil servants who had been dismissed or suspended following the coup attempt in March 1985. In mid-1987 it was reported that President Abdallah was seeking to secure a third term of office, upon the expiry of his mandate in 1990, and that the Constitution, which limited the President's tenure to two six-year terms, was to be revised accordingly. In August the Government nationalized SOCOVIA, a food-retailing company, in an apparent attempt to limit the power of the European mercenaries, with whom the director of the company was associated. In November 1987, shortly after President Abdallah's departure for a conference in France, another coup attempt by a left-wing group of 14 former members of the presidential guard and members of the Comoran armed forces was foiled by the authorities with, it was believed, assistance from French mercenaries and South African military advisers. Three rebels were killed during the attack on the main barracks, and a number of civilians also died. In March 1988 anti-Government leaflets were distributed on Mwali by the Echo Mohélien, a dissident group based on Mayotte and founded by islanders who had fled from Mwali. The group aimed to attract the attention of human rights organizations to the situation on Mwali, alleging that several people had been arrested, that public funds had been diverted and that civil servants had not been paid for nine months. In April President Abdallah's son, Nassuf Abdallah, founded the Union Régionale pour la Défense de la Politique du Président Ahmed Abdallah, a pro-Government party based on the island of Nzwani.

In early November 1989 a constitutional amendment, permitting President Abdallah to remain in office for a third six-year term, was approved by 92.5% of votes cast in a popular

---

* Some of the information contained in this chapter refers to the whole Comoros archipelago, which the independent Comoran state claims as its national territory. However, the island of Mayotte (Mahore) is, in fact, administered by France. Separate information on Mayotte may be found in the chapter on French Overseas Possessions.

THE COMOROS

referendum. The restoration of the post of Prime Minister was also envisaged. The result of the referendum was disputed by the President's opponents. Violent demonstrations followed, and opposition leaders were detained. The Comoran ambassador to France claimed that the reports of violence were exaggerated.

On the night of 26–27 November 1989, however, President Abdallah was shot dead during a violent incident at the presidential palace. Although early reports suggested that the President had been attacked by a group of rebels led by the former Chief of Staff of the Armed Forces, it was subsequently revealed that the Head of State had been assassinated by members of his own 650-strong presidential guard (which included a number of European advisers), under the command of the veteran French mercenary, Bob Denard. The Constitution provided for the appointment of the president of the Supreme Court as interim Head of State, pending a presidential election. Denard, however, seized power but strongly denied responsibility for President Abdallah's death. Saïd Mohamed Djohar was appointed interim Head of State. During the coup 27 policemen were reportedly killed. The regular army was disarmed by Denard and his supporters. The European mercenaries' action provoked international condemnation. France and South Africa temporarily suspended aid to the islands. In early December hundreds of students participated in a demonstration to demand the removal of Denard and his followers. The protest was dispersed by the presidential guard.

A French naval force was sent to the area, ostensibly to prepare for the evacuation of French citizens from the Comoros. Having initially refused to surrender control of the islands, in mid-December 1989 Denard agreed to relinquish power in a peaceful manner. The withdrawal of the mercenaries commenced and, upon the arrival of French paratroops in Moroni, Denard and a further 25 mercenaries flew out of the Comoros on a South African military aircraft. Following the mercenaries' departure, Djohar announced that the French Government's troops were to remain in the Comoros for up to two years in order to train local security forces.

At the end of December 1989 the main political groups agreed to form a provisional government of national unity. An amnesty for all political prisoners was proclaimed, and an inquiry into the death of President Abdallah was instigated. A multi-candidate presidential election was to be held in January 1990, thus ending the system of single-party rule. Djohar, however, subsequently postponed the presidential election until 18 February. The election was duly held, but, following allegations of widespread electoral irregularities during the voting, was declared invalid. It was announced on 19 February that the presidential election was rescheduled for 4 March, and that a second round of voting would be held on 11 March between the two leading contenders, if none of the eight candidates contesting the election obtained 50% of the total votes cast. After an inconclusive first round, Djohar, the official candidate for the Union Comorienne pour le Progrès (Udzima), was elected President, winning 55.3% of the total votes cast, compared with 44.7% for Mohamed Taki Abdulkarim, the leader of the Union Nationale pour la Démocratie aux Comores (UNDC).

In late March 1990 Djohar appointed a new Government, which included two candidates from the presidential election: Saïd Ali Kemal, the leader of the Islands' Fraternity and Unity Party (CHUMA), and Ali Mroudjae, a former Prime Minister and the leader of the Parti Comorien pour la Démocratie et le Progrès (PCDP). In April Djohar accused Mohamed Taki Abdulkarim, who disputed the result of the election, of attempting to undermine the Government. A demonstration by supporters of Mohamed Taki resulted in clashes with the security forces, and several casualties were reported. In April Djohar also announced plans for the formal constitutional restoration of a multi-party political system and indicated that extensive economic reforms were to be undertaken.

On 18–19 August 1990 an attempted coup was staged by armed rebels, who attacked various French installations on the island of Grande-Comore. Two Comorans who were implicated in the plot, and were subsequently arrested, were reportedly supporters of Mohamed Taki. The revolt was allegedly organized by a small group of European mercenaries, who intended to provoke Djohar's resignation through the enforced removal of French forces from the islands. In September the Minister of the Interior and Administrative Reforms, Ibrahim Halidi, was dismissed for his alleged involvement in the

Introductory Survey

attempted coup. By mid-September more than 20 arrests had been made in connection with the plot. In the same month a member of the former presidential guard was imprisoned by a French court for his part in the assassination of President Ahmed Abdallah in 1989. In mid-October 1990 it was reported that the leader of the conspirators, Max Veillard, had been killed by Comoran security forces. In October Djohar implemented an extensive ministerial reshuffle.

Diplomatic relations with France had been resumed in July 1978, and in November the two countries signed agreements on military and economic co-operation, apparently deferring any decision on the future of Mayotte. In February 1979 the OAU readmitted the Comoros. At the UN General Assembly in November 1987, 128 countries voted in favour of a motion asserting the Comoran claim to Mayotte, with 22 countries abstaining and France casting the only vote against the motion.

In January 1985 the Comoros was admitted as the fourth member state of the Indian Ocean Commission (IOC), an organization founded by Madagascar, Mauritius and Seychelles to promote regional co-operation and economic development. The fourth ministerial meeting of the IOC was held in Moroni in February 1988. In June the Comoros agreed to establish diplomatic relations, and to exchange ambassadors, with Seychelles. In November Abdallah and a ministerial delegation made an official week-long visit to the People's Republic of China. In September 1990 the Comoros and South Africa signed a bilateral agreement providing for a series of South African loans towards the development of infrastructure in the Comoros.

Government

According to the Constitution of October 1978 (q.v.), the Comoros is ruled by a President, elected for six years by universal adult suffrage. He is assisted by an appointed Council of Ministers. Legislative power lies with the Federal Assembly, with 42 members directly elected for five years, while each island has a degree of autonomy under a Governor and Council. Constitutional amendments in October 1982 gave the President the power to appoint each Governor, while the Federal Government became responsible for each island's resources. Following the removal of restrictions on multi-party activity in 1989, a multi-candidate presidential election was held in March 1990. Further constitutional amendments, to permit the establishment of a multi-party system, were envisaged in 1990.

Defence

The national army, the Forces Armées Comoriennes, has 700–800 men. Following France's intervention in December 1989, French troops were to remain in the Comoros for up to two years in order to train local security forces. Government expenditure on defence in 1987 was 910.8m. Comoros francs.

Economic Affairs

In 1988, according to estimates from the World Bank, the gross national product (GNP) of the Comoros (excluding Mayotte), measured at average 1986–88 prices, was US $200m., equivalent to $440 per head. During 1980–87, it was estimated, GNP increased, in real terms, at an average annual rate of 3.6%, although GNP per head increased by only 0.1% per year. Over the same period, the population increased by an annual average of 3.5%. The Comoros' gross domestic product (GDP) increased, in real terms, by 4.2% per year between 1980 and 1985, and by an annual average of 1.8% between 1985 and 1988.

Agriculture (including hunting, forestry and fishing) contributed an estimated 34% of GDP and employed about 80% of the labour force in 1989. In the same year the agricultural sector accounted for more than 98% of total export earnings. The principal cash crops are cloves, vanilla and ylang-ylang. Food crops include cassava, sweet potatoes, rice and bananas. During the 1980s the Comoros' fishing industry received substantial aid from Japan.

Industry (including manufacturing, construction and power) contributed an estimated 25% of GDP in 1989, and employed about 6% of the labour force at mid-1980. Industry in the Comoros consists mainly of the distillation of essences, vanilla-processing, soft drinks and woodwork. Manufacturing provided an estimated 3.9% of GDP in 1987.

The Comoros suffers from a shortage of natural energy resources. Imports of petroleum products accounted for 5.7% of the total value of imports in 1989.

In 1989 the Comoros recorded a visible trade deficit of US $17.6m., but there was a surplus of $2.9m. on the current

THE COMOROS

account of the balance of payments. The main source of imports in 1977 was France, followed by Madagascar, Kenya and Tanzania, Pakistan, and the People's Republic of China. France was also the principal market for exports (65%); other sources were the USA, Madagascar, and the Federal Republic of Germany. By the late 1980s South Africa was also a major trading partner. The leading exports in 1989 were vanilla (63%), ylang-ylang (22%) and cloves (11%). The principal imports in 1989 were rice (20.4%), petroleum products (5.8%) and transport equipment (5.6%).

In 1989 there was an estimated budgetary deficit of 2,779m. Comoros francs. France continued to provide budgetary aid in 1989, the sum of 30m. French francs being allocated in that year. Comoros' total external debt was $118m. in 1987. The annual rate of inflation averaged 5.8% in 1980–88.

In 1985 the Comoros joined the Indian Ocean Commission (IOC, see p. 223). The Comoros has a relatively undeveloped economy, with high unemployment, a limited transport system, and a severe shortage of natural resources. The economy is supported by foreign aid, from France in particular (which provided 130m. French francs annually in the late 1980s), while Japan, Saudi Arabia, Kuwait, the United Arab Emirates and the EEC have also provided financial assistance. Export earnings are insufficient to cover the cost of imports, and are dependent on fluctuating prices for the principal commodities of vanilla and cloves. In 1989 a poor vanilla harvest led to a reduction in the level of export earnings. During the 1980s the Government aimed to increase the production of foodstuffs and energy, to expand communication systems, and to improve housing and regional development.

Social Welfare
In 1978 the Government administered six hospital establishments, with a total of 698 beds, and there were 20 physicians working in the country. In 1983 the Government was granted a loan of $2.8m. by the International Development Association (IDA), an affiliate of the World Bank, for a programme to curb population growth and to improve health facilities on the islands. Two new maternity clinics were planned, and existing health centres were to be renovated. Expenditure on health services by the central Government in 1987 was 1,527.2m. Comoros francs (7.3% of total spending).

Education
Education is officially compulsory for eight years between seven and 15 years of age. Primary education begins at the age of six and lasts for six years. Secondary education, beginning at 12 years of age, lasts for seven years, comprising a first cycle of four years and a second of three years. Total enrolment at primary and secondary schools, as a proportion of all school-age children, increased from 19% in 1970 to 60% (boys 72%; girls 48%) in 1980, but the ratio declined to 56% (boys 64%; girls 48%) in 1986. Enrolment at primary schools in 1986 included an estimated 59% of children in the relevant age-group (boys 66%; girls 52%). Secondary education ceased after the withdrawal of all French teaching staff in late 1975, but some schools were reopened in 1976, with the aid of teachers from other French-speaking countries. Children may also receive a basic education through traditional Koranic schools, which are staffed by Comoran teachers. In 1986 there were 62,404 pupils attending primary schools and 21,168 enrolled at secondary schools. In 1987 the Government initiated a project to improve the education system and to make it more relevant to the country's development needs. The project was partly funded by an IDA loan of US $7.9m. About 2,000 primary-school teachers and 350 lower-secondary teachers were to receive training, while a National Centre for Technical Education and Vocational Training and a business school were to be established to provide industrial and office training. Expenditure by the central Government on education in 1987 was 5,287.6m. Comoros francs, representing 25.1% of total spending. In 1988 the sector was allocated 28% of total planned current expenditure.

Public Holidays
1991: 12 February* (Leilat al-Meiraj, Ascension of the Prophet), 17 March* (Ramadan begins), 16 April* (Id al-Fitr, end of Ramadan), 23 June* (Id al-Adha, Feast of the Sacrifice), 6 July (Independence Day), 13 July* (Muharram, Islamic New Year), 22 July* (Ashoura), 21 September* (Mouloud, Birth of the Prophet), 27 November (Anniversary of President Abdallah's assassination).

1992: 1 February* (Leilat al-Meiraj, Ascension of the Prophet), 5 March* (Ramadan begins), 4 April* (Id al-Fitr, end of Ramadan), 11 June* (Id al-Adha, Feast of the Sacrifice), 2 July* (Muharram, Islamic New Year), 6 July (Independence Day), 11 July* (Ashoura), 10 September* (Mouloud, Birth of the Prophet), 27 November (Anniversary of President Abdallah's assassination).

* Religious holidays, which are dependent on the Islamic lunar calendar, may differ by one or two days from the dates given.

Weights and Measures
The metric system is in force.

Statistical Survey

Source (unless otherwise stated): Ministère de l'Economie et des Finances, BP 324, Moroni; tel. 2767; telex 219.
Note: Unless otherwise indicated, figures in this Statistical Survey exclude data for Mayotte.

AREA AND POPULATION

Area: 1,862 sq km (719 sq miles) *By island:* Njazidja (Grande-Comore) 1,146 sq km, Nzwani (Anjouan) 424 sq km, Mwali (Mohéli) 290 sq km.

Population: 335,150 (males 167,089; females 168,061), excluding Mayotte (estimated population 50,740), at census of 15 September 1980; 484,000 (official estimate), including Mayotte, at 31 December 1986.

Principal Towns (population at 1980 census): Moroni (capital) 17,267; Mutsamudu 13,000; Fomboni 5,400.

Births and Deaths (including figures for Mayotte): 24,000 registered live births (birth rate 50.4 per 1,000) in 1986; 7,500 registered deaths (death rate 15.8 per 1,000) in 1986. Average annual birth rate 46.6 per 1,000 in 1975–80, 46.4 per 1,000 in 1980–85, 45.6 per 1,000 in 1985–90; average annual death rate 17.2 per 1,000 in 1975–80, 15.9 per 1,000 in 1980–85, 14.5 per 1,000 in 1985–90 (UN estimates).

Economically Active Population (ILO estimates, '000 persons at mid-1980, including figures for Mayotte). Agriculture, forestry and fishing 150, Industry 10, Services 30, Total 191 (males 104, females 77). Source: ILO, *Economically Active Population Estimates and Projections, 1950–2025*.

AGRICULTURE, ETC.

Principal Crops (FAO estimates, '000 metric tons, 1989): Rice (paddy) 18, Maize 4, Cassava (Manioc) 55, Sweet potatoes 15, Pulses 7, Coconuts 54, Bananas 47. Source: FAO, *Production Yearbook*.

Livestock (FAO estimates '000 head, year ending September 1989): Asses 4, Cattle 86, Sheep 10, Goats 96. Source: FAO, *Production Yearbook*.

Livestock Products (FAO estimates, '000 metric tons, 1989): Meat 3 (beef and veal 2); Cows' milk 4. Source: FAO, *Production Yearbook*.

Fishing (FAO estimates, '000 metric tons, live weight): Total catch 5.3 in 1986; 5.3 in 1987; 5.5 in 1988. Source: FAO, *Yearbook of Fishery Statistics*.

INDUSTRY

Electric energy (production by public utilities): 14 million kWh in 1987. Source: UN, *Industrial Statistics Yearbook*.

FINANCE

Currency and Exchange Rates: 100 centimes = 1 Comoros franc. *Coins:* 1, 2, 5, 10 and 20 francs. *Notes:* 50, 100, 500, 1,000 and

THE COMOROS

5,000 francs. *Sterling and Dollar Equivalents* (30 September 1990): £1 sterling = 491.1 Comoros francs; US $1 = 262.1 Comoros francs; 1,000 Comoros francs = £2.036 = $3.815. *Average Exchange Rate* (Comoros francs per US $): 300.54 in 1987; 297.85 in 1988; 319.01 in 1989. Note: The Comoros franc has a fixed link to French currency, with an exchange rate of 1 French franc = 50 Comoros francs.

Budget (provisional, million Comoros francs, 1987): *Revenue:* Taxation 5,302.3 (Import duties 3,069.4); Other current revenue 1,517.7; Total 6,820.0, excluding grants received from abroad (6,889.1). *Expenditure:* General public services 2,599.7; Defence 910.8; Education 5,287.6; Health 1,527.2; Recreational, cultural and religious affairs and services 1,035.9; Economic affairs and services 9,179.6 (Fuel and energy 1,002.0; Agriculture, forestry, fishing and hunting 3,794.2; Transportation and communication 2,438.6); Total (incl. others) 21,036.7, excluding net lending (67.2). Figures refer to the consolidated operations of the central Government, including extrabudgetary accounts. Source: IMF, *Government Finance Statistics Yearbook*.

International Reserves (US $ million at 31 December 1989): Gold 0.24; IMF special drawing rights 0.08; Foreign exchange 30.69; Total 31.01 (Source: IMF, *International Financial Statistics*).

Money Supply (million Comoros francs at 31 December 1989): Currency outside deposit money banks 3,618; Demand deposits at deposit money banks 4,065 (Source: IMF, *International Financial Statistics*).

Gross Domestic Product by Kind of Economic Activity (estimates, million Comoros francs at current factor cost, 1987): Agriculture, hunting, forestry and fishing 23,703; Manufacturing 2,200; Electricity, gas and water 620; Construction 4,672; Trade, restaurants and hotels 10,307; Transport, storage and communications 2,466; Finance, insurance, real estate and business services 1,198; Public administration and defence 11,039; Other services 307; GDP at factor cost 56,512; Indirect taxes (net of subsidies) 5,030; GDP in purchasers' values 61,542. Source: UN Economic Commission for Africa, *African Statistical Yearbook*.

Balance of Payments (US $ million, 1989): Merchandise exports f.o.b. 18.05; Merchandise imports f.o.b. −35.65; *Trade balance* −17.60; Exports of services 21.59; Imports of services −42.29; *Balance on goods and services* −38.30; Private unrequited transfers 2.66; Government unrequited transfers 38.51; *Current balance* 2.86; Long-term capital (net) 5.50; Short-term capital (net) 0.96; Net errors and omissions −3.97; *Total* (net monetary movements) 5.35; Valuation changes (net) 1.87; *Changes in reserves* 7.22 (Source: IMF, *International Financial Statistics*).

EXTERNAL TRADE

Principal Commodities (million French francs, 1989): *Imports:* Rice 55.2, Petroleum products 15.6, Transport equipment 15.2, Iron and steel 6.8, Cement 6.2; Total (incl. others) 271.5. *Exports:* Vanilla 72.5, Ylang-ylang 25.5, Cloves 12.6; Total (incl. others) 115.2. Source: Banque Centrale des Comores, quoted by La Zone Franc, *Rapport 1989*.

Principal Trading Partners (million French francs, 1977): *Imports:* People's Republic of China 4.0, France 33.6, Kenya and Tanzania 7.6, Madagascar 16.1, Pakistan 6.8; Total (incl. others) 81.1. *Exports:* France 28.8, Federal Republic of Germany 1.5, Madagascar 2.2, USA 9.4; Total (incl. others) 44.0.

TRANSPORT

Road Traffic (1977): 3,600 motor vehicles in use.

International Shipping (estimated sea-borne freight traffic, '000 metric tons, 1987): Goods loaded 11; Goods unloaded 100. Source: UN Economic Commission for Africa, *African Statistical Yearbook*.

Civil Aviation (1973): 15,227 passenger arrivals, 15,674 passenger departures, 909 tons of freight handled.

COMMUNICATIONS MEDIA

Telephones (1987): 3,000 in use.

Radio receivers (1987): 62,000 in use.

Source: UN Economic Commission for Africa, *African Statistical Yearbook*.

EDUCATION

Pre-Primary (1980): 600 teachers; 17,778 pupils.

Primary (1986): 1,808 teachers; 62,404 pupils.

Secondary (1986): 449 (1980) teachers (general education 432 (1980); teacher training 10; vocational 31); 21,168 pupils (general education 20,834; teacher training 32; vocational 302).

Directory

The Constitution

The Constitution of the Federal Islamic Republic of the Comoros was approved by popular referendum on 1 October 1978. Several amendments were made in October 1982 and in January 1985. In November 1989 the electorate approved an amendment permitting the President to remain in office for a third six-year term. The Constitution is not in effect on the island of Mayotte (q.v.), which the Government envisages as eventually 'rejoining the Comoran community'. A commission to revise the Constitution for each of the three main islands of the Comoros was appointed in 1988. In 1990 plans were announced for a constitutional amendment to provide for the establishment of a multi-party political system.

GENERAL PRINCIPLES

The preamble affirms the will of the Comoran people to derive from the state religion, Islam, inspiration for the regulation of government, to adhere to the principles laid down by the Charters of the UN and the OAU, and to guarantee the rights of citizens in accordance with the UN Declaration of Human Rights. Sovereignty resides in the people, through their elected representatives. All citizens are equal before the law.

ISLAND AND FEDERAL INSTITUTIONS

The Comoros archipelago constitutes a Federal Islamic Republic. Each island has autonomy in matters not assigned by the Constitution to the federal institutions, which comprise the Presidency and Council of Government, the Federal Assembly, and the Supreme Court. There is universal secret suffrage for all citizens over 18 in full possession of their civil and political rights. The number of political parties may be regulated by federal law.

The President of the Republic is Head of State and Head of Government and is elected for six years by direct suffrage, and may not serve for more than three terms. He nominates ministers to form the Council of Government. The Governor of each island is nominated by the President of the Republic for five years, and appoints not more than four Commissioners to whom administration is delegated. Should the Presidency fall vacant, the President of the Supreme Court temporarily assumes the office until a presidential election takes place.

The Federal Assembly is directly elected for five years. Each electoral ward elects one deputy. The Assembly meets for not more than 45 days at a time, in April and October and if necessary in extraordinary sessions. Matters covered by federal legislation include defence, posts and telecommunications, external and interisland transport, civil, penal and industrial law, external trade, federal taxation, long-term economic planning, education and health.

The Council of each island is directly elected for four years. Each electoral ward elects one councillor. Each Council meets for not more than 15 days at a time, in March and December and if necessary in extraordinary sessions. The Councils are responsible for non-federal legislation.

THE JUDICIARY

The judiciary is independent of the legislative and executive powers. The Supreme Court acts as a Constitutional Council in resolving constitutional questions and supervising presidential elections, and as High Court of Justice it arbitrates in any case where the government is accused of malpractice.

The Government

HEAD OF STATE

President and Head of Government: SAÏD MOHAMED DJOHAR (took office as Acting President 26–27 November 1989, following

THE COMOROS — Directory

the assassination of President Abdallah; elected President by popular vote 11 March 1990; took office 20 March 1990).

COUNCIL OF MINISTERS
(December 1990)

Minister of Foreign Affairs and Co-operation: MTARA MAECHA.
Minister of Finance, Economy, Budget and Planning: AHMAD ABDALLAH SOURET.
Minister of the Interior, Immigration, Administrative Reform and Local Government: MOHAMED TAKI MBOREHA.
Minister of Public Health and Population: HOUMADI KAAMBI.
Minister of Justice, Civil Service and Employment: SAÏD ATTOUMANE.
Minister of National Education, Vocational and Technical Training: ABDEREMANE MOHAMED.
Minister of Information, Culture, Youth and Sports: ADAMOU MOHAMED.
Minister of State, in charge of Equipment, Posts and Telecommunications: SAÏD HASSANE SAÏD HACHIM.
Minister of State, in charge of Tourism, Transport and Urban Development: SAÏD ALI YOUSSOUF.
Minister of State, in charge of Production, Industry, Rural Development and Environment: ALI MROUDJAE.
Secretary of State for Islamic and Arab Affairs and Koranic Teaching: DAOUD ATTOUMANI.
Secretary of State for Commerce and Crafts: MOUHTARE RACHID.

MINISTRIES

Office of the Head of Government: BP 421, Moroni; tel. 2413; telex 233.
Ministry of Commerce and Crafts: Moroni.
Ministry of Defence: BP 246, Moroni; tel. 2646; telex 233.
Ministry of Equipment, Posts and Telecommunications: Moroni.
Ministry of Finance, Economy, Budget and Planning: BP 324, Moroni; tel. 2767; telex 219.
Ministry of Foreign Affairs and Co-operation: BP 428, Moroni; tel. 2306; telex 219.
Ministry of Information, Culture, Youth and Sports: BP 421, Moroni; telex 219.
Ministry of Interior, Immigration, Administrative Reform and Local Government: Moroni.
Ministry of Islamic and Arab Affairs and Koranic Teaching: Moroni.
Ministry of Justice, Civil Service and Employment: BP 520, Moroni; tel. 2411; telex 219.
Ministry of National Education, Vocational and Technical Training: BP 446, Moroni; tel. 2420; telex 229.
Ministry of Production, Industry, Rural Development and Environment: BP 41, Moroni; tel. 2292; telex 240.
Ministry of Public Health and Population: BP 42, Moroni; tel. 2277; telex 219.
Ministry of Transport, Tourism and Urban Development: Moroni; tel. 2098; telex 244.

President and Legislature

PRESIDENT

Election, 4 and 11 March 1990

In the first round of voting, on 4 March, none of the eight candidates received 50% of the total votes cast. Accordingly, a second round of voting took place on 11 March, when voters chose between the two leading candidates. SAÏD MOHAMED DJOHAR received 55.3% of the votes, while MOHAMED TAKI ABDULKARIM obtained 44.7%.

ASSEMBLÉE FÉDÉRALE

Elections for a Federal Assembly of 42 members were held on 22 March 1987. These elections were the first in which opposition candidates were officially permitted to stand since 1978. The Union comorienne pour le progrès (Udzima) retained control of all constituencies, although the opposition parties obtained 35.5% of the votes cast in 20 contested constituencies. In one district, a second run-off poll between government and opposition candidates was held on 29 March.

President: (vacant).

Political Organizations

The 1978 Constitution provided for the free activity of political parties, but in January 1979 the Federal Assembly voted for the establishment of a one-party system for the following 12 years. Between 1982 and 1989 the **Union comorienne pour le progrès (Udzima)** was the sole legal party. Following the assassination of President Abdallah in November 1989, formal restrictions on multi-party activity ceased to be applied, and various unofficial opposition groups were able to return from exile.

CHUMA (Islands' Fraternity and Unity Party): Moroni; Leader SAÏD ALI KEMAL.
Front Démocratique (FD): Moroni; Leader MOUSTAPHA SAÏD CHEIKH.
Mouvement Démocratique Populaire (MDP): Moroni; Leader ABBAS DJOUSSOUF.
Mouvement pour la Rénovation et l'Action Démocratique (MOURAD): Moroni; f. 1990; aims to promote economic and financial rehabilitation; Sec.-Gen. Dr KASSIM SAÏD.
Parti Comorien pour la Démocratie et le Progrès (PCDP): Moroni; Leader ALI MROUDJAE.
Parti Socialiste des Comores (PASOCO): Moroni; Leader MOHAMED ALI MBALYA.
Union Comorienne pour le Progrès (Udzima): Moroni; sole legal party until 1989; Leader SAÏD MOHAMED DJOHAR.
Union Nationale pour la Démocratie aux Comores (UNDC): Moroni; Leader MOHAMED TAKI ABDULKARIM; Sec.-Gen. MOUNI MADI.
Union pour une République Démocratique aux Comores (URDC): Moroni; Leader ABDULLAH MOUAZOIR.

Diplomatic Representation

EMBASSIES IN THE COMOROS

China, People's Republic: Moroni; tel. 2721; Ambassador: WEI DONG.
France: blvd de Strasbourg, BP 465, Moroni; tel. 73-07-53; telex 220; Ambassador: ROBERT SCHERRER.
Mauritius: Moroni.
USA: Moroni; Ambassador: KENNETH PELTIER.

Judicial System

The Supreme Court consists of two members chosen by the President of the Republic, two elected by the Federal Assembly, one by the Council of each island, and former Presidents of the Republic; Pres. HARIBOU CHEBANI.

Religion

The majority of the population are Muslims. In 1988 there were an estimated 2,600 adherents of the Roman Catholic Church.

CHRISTIANITY
The Roman Catholic Church

Office of Apostolic Administrator of the Comoros: Mission Catholique, BP 46, Moroni; tel. 73-05-70; Apostolic Pro-Administrator Fr JEAN PÉAULT.

The Press

Al Watwany: M'tsangani, BP 984, Moroni; tel. 73-08-61; f. 1985; weekly; state-owned; general; Dir ALLAOUI SAÏD OMAR; circ. 1,500.
L'Archipel: Moroni; f. 1988; weekly; independent; Publrs ABOUBACAR MCHANGAMA, SAINDOU KAMAL.

NEWS AGENCIES

Agence Comores Presse (ACP): Moroni.

Foreign Bureau

Agence France-Presse (AFP): c/o Radio-Comoros, BP 250, Moroni; tel. 2260; telex 241; Rep. ALI SOILIH.

Radio and Television

In 1987 there were an estimated 60,000 radio receivers in use. In 1986 the French Government announced that it would be funding

THE COMOROS

the establishment of a television station. In 1989 France announced aid of 5m. French francs towards the construction of television studios.

Radio-Comoros: BP 250, Moroni; tel. 73-05-31; telex 241; govt-controlled since 1975; home service in Comoran and French; international services in Swahili, Arabic and French; Tech. Dir KOMBO SOULAIMANA.

Finance

BANKING

(cap. = capital; dep. = deposits; res = reserves; m. = million; brs = branches; amounts in Comoros francs)

Central Bank

Banque centrale des Comores: BP 405, Moroni; tel. 73-10-02; telex 213; f. 1981; bank of issue; cap. and res 2,202.8m. (Dec. 1989); Pres. AHMED DAHALANI; Dir-Gen. MOHAMED HALIFA.

Other Banks

Banque de développement des Comores: place de France, BP 298, Moroni; tel. 73-08-18; telex 246; f. 1982; provides loans, guarantees and equity participation for small and medium-scale projects; Banque centrale des Comores and Comoran govt hold two-thirds of shares, European Investment Bank and Caisse centrale de coopération économique (France) each own one-sixth; cap. 300m. (Dec. 1988); Pres. DAROUECHE ABDALLAH; Dir-Gen. CAABI ELY-ACHROUTU.

Banque internationale des Comores (BIC): place de France, BP 175, Moroni; tel. 73-02-43; telex 242; f. 1982; subsidiary of Banque internationale pour l'Afrique occidentale; cap. 300m., res 232.6m., dep. 9,316m. (1988); Pres. MOHAMED MOUMINI; Dir-Gen. G. PIERRE BACCI; 6 brs.

BIC Afribank: Moroni; telex 274.

Trade and Industry

CEFADER: a rural design, co-ordination and support centre, with brs on each island.

Chambre de commerce, d'industrie et d'agriculture: BP 763, Moroni.

Mission permanente de coopération: Moroni; centre for administering bilateral aid from France; Dir GABRIEL COURCELLE.

Office national du commerce: Moroni, Njazidja; state-operated agency for the promotion and development of domestic and external trade; Chair. (vacant).

Société de développement de la pêche artisanale des Comores (SODEPAC): state-operated agency overseeing fisheries development programme.

Other state-owned enterprises include **BAMBAO** and the **Société comorienne des viandes (SOCOVIA)**, a company specializing in the sale of meat and other food products, which was nationalized in 1987.

TRADE UNION

Union des travailleurs des Comores: BP 405, Moroni.

Transport

ROADS

In 1987 there were about 900 km of roads in the Comoros. A major road-improvement scheme was launched in 1979, with foreign assistance, and by 1990 about 170 km of roads on Njazidja and Nzwani had been resurfaced.

SHIPPING

Large vessels anchor off Moroni, Mutsamudu and Fomboni, and the port of Mutsamudu can accommodate vessels of up to 11 m draught. In 1988 the EEC provided financial aid to develop Moroni port. Goods from Europe come via Madagascar, and coasters serve the Comoros from the east coast of Africa.

Société Comorienne de Navigation: Moroni; services to Madagascar.

CIVIL AVIATION

The international airport is at Moroni-Hahaya on Njazidja and each of the three other islands has a small airfield. In 1986 the Comoros received French aid to upgrade the Moroni-Hahaya Airport.

Air Comores (Société Nationale des Transports Aériens): BP 544, Moroni; tel. 2245; telex 218; f. 1975; state-owned; scheduled and cargo services linking Moroni to Nzwani, Mwali and Dzaoudzi; Gen. Man. DJAMALEDDINE AHMED; fleet of 1 Fokker F27, 3 DC-4.

Tourism

The principal tourist attractions are the beaches, underwater fishing and mountain scenery. In 1987 the number of visitors totalled an estimated 8,000. In 1990 the Government introduced a hotel development plan, which was financed by a loan from the South African Government.

Société Comorienne de Tourisme et d'Hôtellerie (COMOTEL): Itsandra Hotel, Njazidja; tel. 2365; national tourist agency.

THE CONGO

Introductory Survey

Location, Climate, Language, Religion, Flag, Capital

The People's Republic of the Congo is an equatorial country on the west coast of Africa. It has a coastline of about 170 km on the Atlantic Ocean, from which the country extends northward to Cameroon and the Central African Republic. It is bordered by Gabon in the west, with Zaire to the east, while in the south there is a short frontier with the Cabinda exclave of Angola. The climate is tropical, with temperatures averaging 21°–27°C (70°–80°F) throughout the year. The average annual rainfall is about 1,200 mm (47 in). The official language is French, and many African languages are also used. More than 50% of the population follow traditional beliefs, although nearly 40% are Roman Catholics. There are small Protestant and Muslim minorities. The national flag is red, with the state emblem (two green palms enclosing a crossed hammer and hoe, surmounted by a gold star) in the upper hoist. The capital is Brazzaville.

Recent History

Formerly part of French Equatorial Africa, Middle Congo became the autonomous Republic of the Congo, within the French Community, in November 1958, with the Abbé Fulbert Youlou as the first Prime Minister. In November 1959 Youlou was elected President of the Republic by the National Assembly. The Congo became fully independent on 15 August 1960. Under the provisions of a new constitution, approved by the National Assembly in March 1961, Youlou was re-elected President (unopposed) by popular vote in that month. Proposals to establish a one-party state were announced by President Youlou in August 1962 and overwhelmingly approved by the National Assembly in April 1963.

However, on 15 August 1963 (the third anniversary of independence and the date scheduled for the introduction of one-party rule) Youlou was forced to resign, following anti-Government demonstrations and strikes by trade unionists. On the following day, a provisional government was formed, with the support of military and trade union leaders. Alphonse Massamba-Débat, a former Minister of Planning, became Prime Minister. In December a national referendum approved a new constitution, and a general election was held for a new National Assembly. Later in that month, Massamba-Débat was elected President for a five-year term. The new regime adopted a policy of 'scientific socialism', and in July 1964 the Mouvement national de la révolution (MNR) was established as the sole political party. In June 1965 ex-President Youlou was sentenced to death *in absentia*.

Tension between the armed forces and the MNR culminated in a military coup in August 1968. The leader of the coup was Capt. (later Maj.) Marien Ngouabi, a paratroop officer, who became Chief of the General Staff. The National Assembly was replaced by the National Council of the Revolution, led by Ngouabi. The President was briefly restored to office, with reduced powers, but was dismissed again in September, when Capt. (later Maj.) Alfred Raoul, the new Prime Minister, also became Head of State, a position that he relinquished in January 1969 to Maj. Ngouabi, while remaining Prime Minister until the end of that year.

Ngouabi established a regime which proclaimed itself Marxist but maintained close economic ties with France. The People's Republic of the Congo, as it became in January 1970, was governed by a single political party, the Parti congolais du travail (PCT). In 1973 Ngouabi introduced a new constitution and a National Assembly with delegates elected from a single party list. However, the Ngouabi regime was threatened by attempted coups, and in 1976 he dismissed the Political Bureau of the PCT, replacing it by a Special Revolutionary General Staff.

In March 1977 Ngouabi was assassinated, reportedly by supporters of ex-President Massamba-Débat; Massamba-Débat was subsequently charged with organizing the attempted coup and executed. The Government was taken over by an 11-member Military Committee of the PCT, and in April 1977 Col (later Brig.-Gen.) Joachim Yhombi-Opango, the Chief of Staff and, like Ngouabi, a member of the Kouyou tribe, was named as the new Head of State.

The worsening economic crisis and the inherited regional and ethnic imbalances, however, made Yhombi-Opango's regime vulnerable to pressure from both left and right. In April 1977 he abrogated the Constitution and suspended the National Assembly. In August 1978 a plot to overthrow the Government was reported. In February 1979 Yhombi-Opango and the Military Committee transferred their powers to the Central Committee of the PCT. Following an election in March, Col (later Gen.) Denis Sassou-Nguesso (a member of the Mboshi ethnic group) became President of the Republic, having assumed power in the interim month as head of a Provisional Committee. In July a National People's Assembly and regional councils were also elected, and the new socialist Constitution was overwhelmingly approved in a referendum. At the third PCT Congress, in July 1984, Sassou-Nguesso was unanimously re-elected Chairman of the PCT Central Committee and President of the Republic for a second five-year term. Under the provisions of a constitutional amendment, he also became Head of Government. As a result of an extensive government reshuffle in August, Ange-Edouard Poungui, a former Vice-President, became Prime Minister in succession to Col (later Gen.) Louis Sylvain Goma, who had held the post since December 1975. Sassou-Nguesso assumed control of the Ministry of Defence and Security. Legislative elections were held in September 1984, and ex-President Yhombi-Opango, who had been detained since March 1979, was placed under house arrest in November.

In December 1985, following a reorganization of the secretariat of the PCT Central Committee, the Government was reshuffled and its membership reduced. In November 1986 the membership of the Politburo was decreased from 13 to 10, and in the following month the number of ministerial portfolios was again reduced by means of a government reshuffle.

Persistent ethnic rivalries, together with disillusionment with the Government's response to the country's worsening economic situation, resulted in an increase in opposition to the Sassou-Nguesso regime during the late 1980s. In July 1987 some 20 army officers, most of whom were members of the Kouyou tribe, were arrested for alleged complicity in a coup plot. Shortly afterwards fighting broke out in the northern Cuvette region between government forces and troops led by Pierre Anga, a supporter of ex-President Yhombi-Opango. In early September government troops suppressed the rebellion with French military assistance. Yhombi-Opango, previously under house arrest, was transferred to prison. Anga evaded arrest; however, in July 1988 it was reported that he had been killed by the Congolese security forces.

Changes in the PCT hierarchy in July 1987 were followed by a government reshuffle in August. A further reallocation of portfolios took place in July 1988. In August 1988 an amnesty was announced for all political prisoners sentenced before July 1987, to commemorate the 25th anniversary of the overthrow of the Youlou regime. During August 1988 a faction of the PCT published a document accusing the Government of having lost its revolutionary momentum, and criticizing its recourse to the IMF and its alleged links with the South African Government.

At the PCT Congress in July 1989, Sassou-Nguesso, the sole candidate, was re-elected Chairman of the PCT and President of the Republic for a third five-year term. A new Politburo was elected, comprising 13 members, six of whom were new to office. The Central Committee was reorganized to include 23 new members, who apparently held moderate views, while 21 of the existing members, considered to be conservative, were dismissed. Among those dismissed was Pierre Nze, a Marxist who had served under the regime of President Marien Ngouabi. In August Alphonse Mouissou Poaty-Souchalaty, formerly the Minister of Trade and Small and Medium-sized Enterprises, was appointed Prime Minister, and a new government was announced.

Legislative elections were held in September 1989. The single list of 133 candidates, presented by the PCT, was approved

784

by 99.2% of the voters. The list included, for the first time, candidates who were not members of the PCT: 66 were members of a front comprising youth, women's, welfare, religious and professional organizations, and eight seats were reserved for unaffiliated individuals.

In November 1989 President Sassou-Nguesso announced plans for economic reforms, heralding a departure from socialist policies. Public-sector monopolies were to be transferred to the private sector, and private enterprise was to be promoted in order to attract both foreign and domestic investment. In December a new political movement opposed to the regime, the Union pour la démocratie congolaise (UDC), was founded by Sylvain Bamba, formerly a senior government official. In the same month, 40 prisoners, who had been detained without trial since July 1987 (following an alleged plot against the State), were released.

Progress towards political reform dominated the latter half of 1990. In early July the Government announced that an extraordinary Congress of the PCT would be convened during 1991 to formulate legislation enabling the introduction of a multi-party system. Measures were also approved that would limit the role of the ruling party in the country's mass and social organizations. It was stated that, while the attainment of a socialist state remained the regime's ultimate objective, strict adherence to Marxist-Leninist dogma would be abandoned. The Congress also effected a restructuring of the PCT's secretariat, whose membership was reduced, by one-half, to four. Among those who were not re-elected to that body was Jean-Michel Boukamba-Yangouma, who, in February 1990, had stated that the introduction of a multi-party system would provoke disorder and ethnic rivalries. In mid-August, on the occasion of the 30th anniversary of the country's independence, several political prisoners were released, including the former Head of State, Yhombi-Opango, and two military officers who had been arrested in the previous month in connection with an alleged plot to overthrow the Government. At the beginning of September a reorganization of some minor government posts was announced. In mid-September a congress of the Confederation of Congolese Trade Unions (CSC) was annulled by the Government, following demands by that organization for independence from the ruling PCT, the immediate transition to a multi-party political system and increased salaries for workers in the public sector. In response to a two-day general strike, called in protest by the CSC, President Sassou-Nguesso agreed to accelerate the process of political reform and to permit free elections to the leadership of the trade union organization. In late September the Central Committee of the PCT agreed to permit the immediate registration of new political parties, and announced that constitutional amendments to legalize a multi-party system would be implemented by January 1991. A transitional government was to assume power in early 1991, in preparation for a general election. During late 1990 more than 50 new political parties were registered, including the Mouvement pour la démocratie et le développement, founded by ex-President Yhombi-Opango. In early December the Prime Minister, Alphonse Poaty-Souchalaty, resigned. On the following day, the extraordinary Congress of the PCT, which had previously been scheduled for 1991, commenced. The Central Committee of the PCT was expanded from 77 to 249 members, and Marxist-Leninism was abandoned as the party's official ideology. In late December the National Assembly approved constitutional amendments legalizing a multi-party system, with effect from January 1991. Shortly afterwards, President Sassou-Nguesso announced that a national conference to determine a date for multi-party elections would be held in February 1991. In early January 1991 Gen. Louis Sylvain Goma was appointed Prime Minister (a position he had previously held between December 1975 and August 1984).

Since the mid-1970s, the Congo has moved away from the Soviet sphere of influence, and has fostered links with neighbouring francophone countries, and also with France, the USA and the People's Republic of China. There was an improvement in relations with France following the victory of the French left in the 1981 elections. Western nations, particularly France, remain the chief source of development aid (France is the source of more than one-half of total assistance to the Congo), but some Eastern bloc aid is received in the form of military and security assistance. The Congo is committed to the survival of the OAU (see p. 190), and is a member of the Customs and Economic Union of Central Africa (UDEAC, see p. 157). In 1986/87, during his tenure of the OAU chairmanship, President Sassou-Nguesso toured a number of Western European countries. In 1988 the Congo mediated in negotiations between Angola, Cuba, South Africa and the USA, which resulted in the signing, in December, of the Brazzaville accord, regarding the withdrawal of Cuban troops from Angola and progress towards Namibian independence. In April 1989 relations between the Congo and Zaire became strained, following reciprocal expulsions from those countries of Congolese and Zairean nationals, who were alleged to be illegal residents. The situation was resolved following a visit by Sassou-Nguesso to Zaire.

In February 1990 President Sassou-Nguesso visited the USA; it was hoped that the Congolese Government's plans for economic reform, announced in November 1989, would promote co-operation between the two countries. Diplomatic relations with the Republic of Korea (severed in 1964) were restored in June 1990.

Government

Until September 1990 there was only one authorized political party, the Parti congolais du travail (PCT). The Chairman of the Central Committee of the PCT is the President of the Republic, Head of State and Head of Government, elected for a five-year term by the Congress of the PCT, which also elects the Central Committee (249 members in December 1990). To direct its policy, the Central Committee elects a Politburo, which comprised 13 members when reorganized in July 1989. The senior executive body of the PCT is the Secretariat of the Central Committee, with four members (reduced from eight members in July 1990). Supreme executive power rests with the Council of Ministers, under the chairmanship of the President of the Republic. The main legislative body is the National People's Assembly, which was re-established in 1979. The 133 members are elected by universal adult suffrage from a list proposed by the PCT. The Assembly is responsible to the Prime Minister, who is, in turn, responsible to the PCT.

In late September 1990 the Central Committee of the PCT agreed to permit the immediate registration of new political parties. By late 1990 more than 50 political parties had been registered. In late December 1990 the National Assembly approved constitutional amendments legalizing a multi-party system, with effect from January 1991. A national conference to determine a date for multi-party elections was to be held in February 1991.

Responsibility for local administration is vested in nine People's Regional Councils, each with an Executive Committee elected by universal franchise. They act under the direction of 10 Commissars designated by the PCT Central Committee.

Defence

In June 1990 the army numbered 8,000, the navy 300 and the air force 500. There were 6,100 men in paramilitary forces, and 500 Cuban troops were stationed in the country. National service is voluntary for men and women, and lasts for two years. The defence budget for 1985 was 25,000m. francs CFA.

Economic Affairs

In 1988, according to estimates by the World Bank, the Congo's gross national product (GNP), measured at average 1986–88 prices, was US $1,950m., equivalent to $930 per head. During 1980–88, it was estimated, overall GNP increased, in real terms, at an average annual rate of 4.6%. GNP per head, however, grew by only 1.1% annually. Over the same period, the population increased by an annual average of 3.4%. The Congo's gross domestic product (GDP) increased, in real terms, by an annual average of 4.0% in 1980–88.

Agriculture (including forestry and fishing) contributed 15% of GDP in 1988. About 60% of the labour force were employed in the sector at mid-1989. The staple crops are cassava and plantains, while the major cash crops are sugar cane, palm oil, cocoa and coffee. Forests cover 60% of the country's total area, and forestry is a major economic activity. During 1980–88 agricultural production increased by an annual average of 2.0%.

Industry (including mining, manufacturing, construction and power) contributed 30% of GDP in 1988, and employed an estimated 11.9% of the labour force at mid-1980. During 1980–88 industrial production increased by an annual average of 5.1%.

Mining contributed 41.8% of GDP in 1985, but, owing to the decline in petroleum prices, the proportion declined to 15.8%

in 1986. It recovered to 22.9% in 1987. The hydrocarbons sector is the only significant mining activity. The Congo's proven recoverable reserves of crude petroleum were estimated at 100m. metric tons at the beginning of 1989, and there are also deposits of natural gas. In 1984 mineral sales provided 90% of export earnings. Lead, zinc, gold and copper are produced in small quantities, and deposits of phosphate, iron ore and potash were undergoing development in 1989. In addition, the Congo has bauxite reserves.

Manufacturing contributed an estimated 8% of GDP in 1988. The most important industries are the processing of agricultural and forest products. The textile, chemical and construction materials industries are also important.

Energy is derived principally from hydroelectric power. Imports of mineral fuels comprised 7% of the value of total imports in 1987.

In 1989 the Congo recorded a visible trade surplus of US $604.0m., but there was a deficit of $80.9m. on the current account of the balance of payments. In 1985 the principal source of imports (38.8%) was France, while the USA was the principal market for exports (60.0%). Other major trading partners are Spain, the Netherlands and Italy. The principal exports in 1985 were petroleum and petroleum products. The principal imports were machinery and transport equipment, food, beverages and tobacco, and iron and steel.

The budget deficit for 1989 was forecast at 77,500m. francs CFA. The Congo's total external debt was estimated at 990,000m. francs CFA in 1989. According to World Bank estimates, debt-servicing payments were equivalent to 28.7% of total earnings from exports of goods and services in 1988. The annual rate of inflation averaged 0.8% in 1980-88, rising to 4.1% in 1989.

The Congo is a member of the Central African organs of the Franc Zone (see p. 156) and of the Communauté économique des Etats de l'Afrique centrale (CEEAC, see p. 223).

From 1985 the decline in international petroleum prices significantly reduced government revenue, leading to a decline in the construction industry and a lack of industrial growth. The agricultural sector, however, remained strong. The greatest impediment to development is the country's large external debt, which in 1989 was among the highest per caput in Africa. In 1990 the IMF approved a programme of support for the Congo. The 1990–94 Economic and Social Action Plan (PAES) was to include a programme to increase the role of the private sector in development and to rationalize the state sector. The plan was to be financed mainly by foreign loans.

Social Welfare

There is a state pension scheme and a system of family allowances and other welfare services. Expenditure on social security and welfare by the central Government was about 13,620m. francs CFA (4.4% of total spending) in 1983. In 1987 there were 43 hospitals, providing a total of 7,917 hospital beds. There were about 460 physicians working in the Congo in that year. According to a national study, the number of AIDS cases almost trebled to 3,750 between 1987 and 1988, and in 1989 more than 50% of hospital beds were occupied by AIDS patients.

Education

Education is officially compulsory for 10 years between six and 16 years of age. Primary education begins at the age of six and lasts for six years. Secondary education, from 12 years of age, lasts for seven years, comprising a first cycle of four years and a second of three years. In 1986 there were 498,588 pupils enrolled at primary schools, while 201,228 pupils were undergoing general secondary education. In addition, there were 1,591 secondary students at teacher-training colleges, and 32,231 at vocational institutions. The Marien Ngouabi University, at Brazzaville, was founded in 1971. In 1986 there were 11,008 students at university level. Some Congolese students go to France for technical instruction. In 1985, according to estimates by UNESCO, the average rate of adult illiteracy was 37.1% (males 28.6%, females 44.6%), one of the lowest in Africa. In 1965 the Government assumed control of all private schools. In November 1989 it was announced that the People's Republic of China was to provide 20m. francs CFA to assist the Congo in developing a professional primary teacher-training programme. Expenditure on education by the central Government was about 34,930m. francs CFA (11.3% of total spending) in 1983.

Public Holidays

1991: 1 January (New Year's Day), 29 March (Good Friday), 1 April (Easter Monday), 1 May (Labour Day), 15 August (Independence Day), 25 December (Christmas).

1992: 1 January (New Year's Day), 17 April (Good Friday), 20 April (Easter Monday), 1 May (Labour Day), 15 August (Independence Day), 25 December (Christmas).

Weights and Measures

The metric system is in force.

Statistical Survey

Source (unless otherwise stated): Centre National de la Statistique et des Etudes Economiques, Ministère du Plan et de l'Economie, BP 2031, Brazzaville; tel. 83-43-24; telex 5210.

Area and Population

AREA, POPULATION AND DENSITY

Area (sq km)	342,000*
Population (census results)	
7 February 1974	1,319,790
22 December 1984	1,843,421
Density (per sq km) at December 1984	5.4

* 132,047 sq miles.

REGIONS (estimated population at 1 January 1983)*

Brazzaville	456,383	Kouilou	78,738
Pool	219,329	Lékoumou	67,568
Pointe-Noire	214,466	Sangha	42,106
Bouenza	135,999	Nkayi	40,419
Cuvette	127,558	Likouala	34,302
Niari	114,229	Loubomo	33,591
Plateaux	110,379	**Total**	**1,675,067**

* Figures have not been revised to take account of the 1984 census results.

PRINCIPAL TOWNS (population at 1984 census)

Brazzaville (capital)	596,200
Pointe-Noire	298,014

THE CONGO

BIRTHS AND DEATHS (UN estimates, annual averages)

	1975-80	1980-85	1985-90
Birth rate (per 1,000)	44.7	44.5	44.4
Death rate (per 1,000)	16.9	15.4	17.2

Source: UN, *World Population Prospects: 1988.*

EMPLOYMENT
('000 persons at 1984 census)

	Males	Females	Total
Agriculture, etc.	105	186	291
Industry	61	8	69
Services	123	60	183
Total	289	254	543

Mid-1989 (FAO estimates, '000 persons): Agriculture, etc. 457; Total labour force 765 (Source: FAO, *Production Yearbook*).

Agriculture

PRINCIPAL CROPS ('000 metric tons)

	1987	1988	1989*
Maize*	9	9	9
Sugar cane*	390	400	400
Sweet potatoes*	10	12	13
Cassava (Manioc)	746	761	760
Yams*	15	15	16
Other roots and tubers	25	27	27
Dry beans*	5	5	5
Tomatoes*	9	9	9
Other vegetables*	30	31	32
Avocados*	21	22	22
Pineapples*	112	114	115
Bananas	31	32*	33
Plantains	64	65*	65
Palm kernels*	0.5	0.5	0.5
Groundnuts (in shell)	24	25	25
Coffee (green)	1	2	2
Cocoa beans	1	2	2
Natural rubber*	2	2	2

* FAO estimate(s).
Source: FAO, *Production Yearbook.*

LIVESTOCK
('000 head, year ending September)

	1987	1988	1989*
Cattle	70	69	70
Pigs	47	50	50
Sheep	97	101	102
Goats	238	240*	245

* FAO estimate(s).
Poultry (FAO estimates, million): 1 in 1987; 1 in 1988; 2 in 1989.
Source: FAO, *Production Yearbook.*

LIVESTOCK PRODUCTS (FAO estimates, '000 metric tons)

	1987	1988	1989
Beef and veal	3	3	3
Pig meat	2	2	2
Poultry meat	5	5	5
Other meat	6	6	6
Cows' milk	3	3	3
Hen eggs	1.1	1.1	1.2

Source: FAO, *Production Yearbook.*

Forestry

ROUNDWOOD REMOVALS ('000 cubic metres, excluding bark)

	1986	1987	1988
Sawlogs, veneer logs and logs for sleepers	715	694	751
Pulpwood	n.a.	254	593
Other industrial wood*	230	237	243
Fuel wood	1,636	1,682	1,728
Total	2,581	2,867	3,315

* FAO estimates.

SAWNWOOD PRODUCTION ('000 cubic metres)

	1986	1987	1988
Total (incl. boxboards)	77	60	57

Source: FAO, *Yearbook of Forest Products.*

Fishing

('000 metric tons, live weight)

	1986	1987	1988
Freshwater fishes	12.0	13.5	19.4
Common sole	0.5	0.4	0.7
Sea catfishes	0.5	0.5	0.6
Boe drum	0.7	0.7	0.8
West African croakers	0.9	1.1	1.9
Sardinellas	11.6	11.3	14.3
Bonga shad	1.0	0.5	0.0
Sharks, rays, skates, etc.	0.6	0.7	0.5
Other marine fishes (incl. unspecified)	2.1	7.1	3.6
Crustaceans	0.1	0.1	0.0
Total catch	30.0	36.0	41.8

Source: FAO, *Yearbook of Fishery Statistics.*

Mining

('000 metric tons, unless otherwise indicated)

	1985	1986	1987
Crude petroleum	5,825	5,950	6,316
Copper ore*	0.1	0.1	1.3
Gold (kg)*	16	16†	16†
Lead ore*	1.1	1.1	0.0
Zinc ore*	2.1	2.3†	2.3†

* Figures refer to the metal content of ores.
† Provisional or estimated figures.
Source: UN, *Industrial Statistics Yearbook.*
Crude petroleum ('000 metric tons): 6,600 in 1988; 7,396 in 1989 (Source: UN, *Monthly Bulletin of Statistics*).

THE CONGO

Industry

SELECTED PRODUCTS
('000 metric tons, unless otherwise indicated)

	1985	1986	1987
Palm oil (refined)	1	1	0
Wheat flour	0	10	16
Raw sugar	46	35	26
Beer ('000 hectolitres)	882	897	762
Soft drinks ('000 hectolitres)	317	257	185
Cigarettes (metric tons)	1,027	888	787
Veneer sheets ('000 cu metres)	67	51*	47*
Soap (metric tons)	1,900	1,816	1,589
Jet fuels*	0	10	12
Motor spirit (petrol)*	3	55	61
Distillate fuel oils*	5	110	90
Residual fuel oils*	40	330	340
Cement	62	2	38
Electric energy (million kWh)	293	270	281
Footwear ('000 pairs)	1,128	535	180

* Source: UN, *Industrial Statistics Yearbook*.

1988: Beer ('000 hectolitres) 744; Cigarettes (metric tons) 770; Soap (metric tons) 1,490; Electric energy (million kWh) 292; Footwear ('000 pairs) 296.

Finance

CURRENCY AND EXCHANGE RATES
Monetary Units
100 centimes = 1 franc de la Coopération financière en Afrique centrale (CFA).

Denominations
Coins: 1, 2, 5, 10, 25, 50 and 100 francs CFA.
Notes: 100, 500, 1,000, 5,000 and 10,000 francs CFA.

French Franc, Sterling and Dollar Equivalents
(30 September 1990)
1 French franc = 50 francs CFA;
£1 sterling = 491.1 francs CFA;
US $1 = 262.1 francs CFA;
1,000 francs CFA = £2.036 = $3.815.

Average Exchange Rate (francs CFA per US $)
1987 300.54
1988 297.85
1989 319.01

BUDGET ('000 million francs CFA)

Revenue	1987	1988*	1989†
Petroleum receipts	47.1	40.4	84.1
Non-petroleum receipts	88.0	84.5	82.5
Aid	0.4	0.5	0.5
Total	**135.5**	**125.4**	**167.1**

Expenditure	1987	1988*	1989†
Current expenditure	190.1	193.8	199.7
Salaries	83.7	81.2	78.5
Transfers, subsidies, goods and services	54.4	49.9	59.5
Interest	45.8	54.1	56.0
Deficits of autonomous bodies and communes	6.2	8.6	5.7
Capital expenditure	30.4	30.3	20.9
Net lending	—	6.6	10.5
Restructuring expenditure	4.0	13.9	13.5
Total	**224.5**	**244.6**	**244.6**

* Provisional figures.   † Estimates.

Source: *La Zone Franc—Rapport 1989*.

CENTRAL BANK RESERVES (US $ million at 31 December)

	1987	1988	1989
Gold*	5.37	4.52	n.a.
IMF special drawing rights	2.71	1.13	1.59
Reserve position in IMF	0.68	0.65	0.63
Foreign exchange	0.01	2.06	13.96
Total	**8.77**	**8.36**	**n.a.**

* Valued at market-related prices.
Source: IMF, *International Financial Statistics*.

MONEY SUPPLY ('000 million francs CFA at 31 December)

	1987	1988	1989
Currency outside banks	55.26	50.60	49.91
Demand deposits at commercial and development banks	41.82	41.74	46.35
Checking deposits at post office	5.26	2.56	n.a.
Total money	**102.34**	**94.90**	**n.a.**

Source: IMF, *International Financial Statistics*.

NATIONAL ACCOUNTS (million francs CFA at current prices)
National Income and Product

	1985	1986	1987
Compensation of employees	264,454	264,296	253,198
Operating surplus	390,577	133,347	183,843
Domestic factor incomes	**655,031**	**397,643**	**437,041**
Consumption of fixed capital	167,228	156,074	164,360
Gross domestic product (GDP) at factor cost	**822,259**	**553,717**	**601,401**
Indirect taxes	154,437	91,444	90,790
Less Subsidies	5,846	4,754	1,668
GDP in purchasers' values	**970,850**	**640,407**	**690,523**
Factor income from abroad	4,103	2,781	9,183
Less Factor income paid abroad	106,547	44,717	85,980
Gross national product	**868,406**	**598,471**	**613,726**
Less Consumption of fixed capital	167,228	156,074	164,360
National income in market prices	**701,178**	**442,397**	**449,366**
Other current transfers from abroad	19,085	17,470	25,403
Less Other current transfers paid abroad	32,167	25,512	35,776
National disposable income	**688,096**	**434,355**	**438,993**

Expenditure on the Gross Domestic Product

	1985	1986	1987
Government final consumption expenditure	159,693	159,804	142,115
Private final consumption expenditure	403,583	380,534	390,669
Increase in stocks	17,080	5,742	−7,811
Gross fixed capital formation	276,902	182,856	144,016
Total domestic expenditure	**857,258**	**728,936**	**668,989**
Exports of goods and services	551,863	255,152	288,254
Less Imports of goods and services	438,271	343,681	266,720
GDP in purchasers' values	**970,850**	**640,407**	**690,523**

THE CONGO

Gross Domestic Product by Economic Activity

	1985	1986	1987
Agriculture, hunting, forestry and fishing	72,331	77,424	82,434
Mining and quarrying	398,041	99,444	155,188
Manufacturing	57,587	61,277	59,757
Electricity, gas and water	11,906	9,054	10,614
Construction	55,895	38,806	21,580
Trade, restaurants and hotels	110,463	104,377	102,153
Transport, storage and communication	70,799	71,067	71,294
Finance, insurance, real estate, business, community, social and personal services	76,240	64,402	70,975
Government services	97,680	101,495	102,716
Other services	1,750	1,550	1,395
Sub-total	952,692	628,896	678,106
Import duties	34,212	27,977	25,533
Less Imputed bank service charge	16,054	16,466	13,116
GDP in purchasers' values	970,850	640,407	690,523

BALANCE OF PAYMENTS (US $ million)

	1987	1988	1989
Merchandise exports f.o.b.	876.7	843.2	1,138.0
Merchandise imports f.o.b.	−419.9	−552.7	−534.0
Trade balance	456.8	320.5	604.0
Exports of services	127.7	99.7	90.0
Imports of services	−818.3	−873.5	−796.9
Balance on goods and services	−233.8	−453.3	−102.9
Private unrequited transfers (net)	−56.8	−56.6	−29.8
Government unrequited transfers (net)	67.9	64.4	51.7
Current balance	−222.7	−445.5	−80.9
Direct capital investment (net)	43.4	9.1	−281.2
Other long-term capital (net)	−195.1	−137.4	
Short-term capital (net)	−141.8	66.4	−93.2
Net errors and omissions	27.6	40.6	100.3
Total (net monetary movements)	−488.5	−466.8	−355.0
Valuation changes (net)	−1.5	−0.3	12.8
Exceptional financing (net)	486.6	471.8	359.8
Official financing (net)	0.3	−0.4	−1.4
Changes in reserves	−3.0	4.3	16.2

Source: IMF, *International Financial Statistics*.

External Trade

Note: Figures exclude trade with other states of the Customs and Economic Union of Central Africa (UDEAC).

PRINCIPAL COMMODITIES (million francs CFA)

Imports c.i.f.	1986	1987	1988
Machinery	50,027	32,264	36,252
Transport equipment	20,090	16,791	17,532
Petroleum products	3,438	4,985	3,978
Chemicals and related products	17,437	15,445	20,290
Textile materials and manufactures	6,540	5,174	5,564
Iron and steel	19,332	13,271	12,377
Food, beverages and tobacco	37,270	28,954	34,466
Plastic and rubber goods	14,701	15,459	5,394
Precision instruments, watches, etc.	5,724	3,276	4,591
Total (incl. others)	199,394	151,738	161,958

Exports f.o.b.	1986	1987	1988
Petroleum and petroleum products	239,395	123,034	178,289
Wood	18,240	23,077	34,935
Diamonds	3,678	5,900	4,768
Coffee	642	198	202
Iron and steel	897	415	251
Total (incl. others)	268,757	155,303	223,744

PRINCIPAL TRADING PARTNERS (million francs CFA)

Imports c.i.f.	1983	1984	1985
Belgium/Luxembourg	5,133	4,782	6,214
China, People's Republic	3,063	5,505	4,279
France	143,637	136,793	118,797
Germany, Fed. Republic	10,853	15,412	12,176
Italy	9,353	7,778	21,567
Japan	8,001	9,480	8,917
Netherlands	6,186	5,827	7,010
Spain	4,456	8,639	11,495
USA	19,106	14,819	17,267
Total (incl. others)	239,970	259,820	306,198

Exports f.o.b.	1983	1984	1985
Belgium/Luxembourg	12,195	12,265	5,140
France	2,808	5,919	53,262
Germany, Fed. Republic	1,659	2,523	1,322
Italy	31,197	8,409	8,955
Netherlands	2,848	11,011	29,562
Spain	8,084	9,526	67,762
USA	176,032	400,780	293,112
Total (incl. others)	243,720	516,700	488,366

Transport

RAILWAYS (traffic)

	1985	1986	1987
Passenger-km (million)	437	456	400
Freight ton-km (million)	518	536	449

THE CONGO

ROAD TRAFFIC ('000 motor vehicles in use)

	1980	1981	1982
Passenger cars	45.4	49.0	30.5
Commercial vehicles	38.6	60.0	78.6

Source: Régie Nationale des Transports et des Travaux Publics.

INLAND WATERWAYS (freight traffic, '000 metric tons)

Port of Brazzaville	1985	1986	1987
Goods loaded	77	77	62
Goods unloaded	407	309	331

INTERNATIONAL SEA-BORNE SHIPPING
(freight traffic, '000 metric tons)

	1985	1986	1987
Goods loaded	8,525	8,893	9,113
Goods unloaded	668	621	518

CIVIL AVIATION (traffic on scheduled services)*

	1983	1984	1985
Kilometres flown (million)	3.4	3.3	3.6
Passengers carried ('000)	217	228	248
Passenger-km (million)	268	274	302
Freight ton-km (million)	20.2	19.0	20

* Including an apportionment of the traffic of Air Afrique.
Source: UN, *Statistical Yearbook*.

Tourism

	1985	1986	1987
Foreign tourist arrivals	37,000	39,000	39,000

Source: UN Economic Commission for Africa, *African Statistical Yearbook*.

Communications Media

	1985	1986	1987
Radio receivers ('000 in use)	114	116	119
Television receivers ('000 in use)	5	5	6
Telephones ('000 in use)	22	23	23

1984: Daily newspapers 1 (average circulation 8,000 copies); Non-daily newspapers 2 (average circulation 15,000 copies).
Sources: UNESCO, *Statistical Yearbook*; UN Economic Commission for Africa, *African Statistical Yearbook*.

Education

(1986)

	Institutions	Teachers	Pupils Males	Females	Total
Pre-primary	54	578	2,954	2,959	5,913
Primary	1,589	7,818	262,673	235,915	498,588
Secondary					
General	n.a.	4,849	115,181	86,047	201,228
Teacher training	n.a.	200	1,021	570	1,591
Vocational	n.a.	1,778	14,703	17,528	32,231
University level	n.a.	682	n.a.	n.a.	11,008

Source: UNESCO, *Statistical Yearbook*.

Directory

The Constitution

A new constitution was approved by national referendum on 8 July 1979. The Constitution was amended in July 1984 and in December 1990*. The following is a summary of its provisions:

FUNDAMENTAL PRINCIPLES

The People's Republic of the Congo is a sovereign independent state, in which all power springs from the people and belongs to the people. Treason against the people is the greatest crime. All nationals are guaranteed freedom of conscience and religion, and religious communities are free to practise their faith, but political organizations based on religion are banned. The land is the property of the people, and as necessary the State shall regulate its use. The State directs the economic life and development of the country according to the general plan. The right to own and inherit private property is guaranteed, and expropriation is governed by law.

HEAD OF STATE

The Chairman of the Central Committee of the Parti congolais du travail (PCT) is the President of the Republic, Head of State and Head of Government. He is elected for a five-year term by the Congress of the PCT.

THE EXECUTIVE

Executive power is vested in the Council of Ministers, under the Chairmanship of the President of the Republic. It directs and orientates the action of the Government; Ministers are appointed by the Prime Minister, who is responsible to the party.

THE LEGISLATURE

Most legislative powers are vested in the National People's Assembly. It has 133 members, elected for a five-year term by all adults over 18 years of age, with representatives from the PCT, mass organizations (including women and students), and workers, peasants and craftsmen. It is responsible to the Prime Minister and undertakes tasks entrusted to him by the party. The President

THE CONGO	Directory

of the National Assembly is second in rank only to the President of the Republic.

THE PARTY

The sole political party is the Parti congolais du travail (PCT). Its Political Bureau (of 13 members) takes part in government. Its Central Committee (of 77 members†) includes the Political Bureau, most of the Ministers and the Chief of Staff of the army, and is chaired by the President of the Republic and Head of State. The Central Committee's powers include the initiation of revisions to the Constitution, which become final when approved by the National Assembly, and the appointment of judges to the Revolutionary Court of Justice.

Note: In August 1984 a Constitutional Council was established by Presidential statute, assuming powers hitherto exercised by the Constitutional Chamber of the Supreme Court.

* In December 1990 the Constitution was amended to permit, with effect from January 1991, the existence of more than one political party. A transitional government was to be appointed in early 1991, pending multi-party elections.

† Increased to 249 members in December 1990.

The Government

HEAD OF STATE

President: Gen. DENIS SASSOU-NGUESSO (appointed President of the Provisional Committee of the PCT 8 February 1979; elected President of the Republic 31 March 1979; re-elected July 1984 and July 1989).

COUNCIL OF MINISTERS
(January 1991)

Prime Minister: Gen. LOUIS SYLVAIN GOMA.
Minister of State for Planning and Economy: PIERRE MOUSSA.
Minister of State for Youth and Rural Development: GABRIEL OBA-APOUNOU.
Minister of State for Forestry: PAUL NGATSE.
Minister of State for Foreign Affairs and Co-operation: ANTOINE NDINGA OBA.
Minister of Defence and Security: RAYMOND DAMAS NGOLLO.
Minister of the Interior, Information, Physical Education and Sport: CELESTIN NGOMA-FOUTOU.
Minister of Culture and Arts: JEAN-BAPTISTE TATI-LOUTARD.
Minister of Territorial Administration and Local Government: (vacant).
Minister of Trade and Small and Medium-sized Enterprises: ALPHONSE BOUDENESA.
Minister of Industry, Fisheries and Crafts: HILAIRE BABASSANA.
Minister of Mines, Energy and State Control: AIMÉ-EMMANUEL YOKA.
Minister of Equipment, with Responsibility for the Environment: FLORENT TSIBA.
Minister of Basic Education and Literacy: PIERRE-DAMIEN BASSOUKOU-MBOUMBA.
Minister of Labour and Social Security: JEANNE DAMBENZET.
Minister of Secondary and Higher Education, with Responsibility for Scientific Research: RODOLPHE ADADA.
Minister of Health and Social Affairs: Dr OSSEBI DOUANIAM.
Minister of Finance and Budget: EDOUARD NGAKOSSO.
Minister of Justice and Keeper of the Seals, with Responsibility for Administrative Reforms: ALPHONSE NZOUNGOU.
Minister of Tourism, Post and Telecommunications: JEAN-CLAUDE GANGA.

MINISTRIES

All Ministries are in Brazzaville.
Office of the President: Palais du Peuple, Brazzaville; telex 5210.
Ministry of Education: BP 169, Brazzaville; tel. 83-24-60; telex 5210.
Ministry of Finance and Budget: Centre Administratif, quartier Plateau, BP 2093, Brazzaville; tel. 83-06-20; telex 5210.
Ministry of Foreign Affairs and Co-operation: BP 2070, Brazzaville; tel. 83-20-28; telex 5210.
Ministry of Health and Social Affairs: Palais du Peuple, Brazzaville; tel. 83-29-35; telex 5210.
Ministry of Industry, Fisheries and Crafts: Palais du Peuple, Brazzaville; tel. 83-51-30; telex 5210.
Ministry of the Interior, Information, Physical Education and Sport: BP 2241, Brazzaville; tel. 81-03-83; telex 5291.
Ministry of Planning and Economy: BP 2031, Brazzaville; tel. 83-43-24; telex 5210.
Ministry of Trade and Small and Medium-sized Enterprises: Brazzaville; tel. 83-18-27; telex 5210.

Legislature

ASSEMBLÉE NATIONALE POPULAIRE

The National People's Assembly is elected for a five-year term and comprises 133 members. Following the most recent elections, held on 24 September 1989, 59 seats were filled by PCT members, 66 by members of a front comprising youth, women's, welfare, religious and professional organizations, and eight by unaffiliated individuals. All candidates were approved by the PCT.

President: BERNARD COMBO-MATSIONA.

In December 1990 it was announced that a national conference to determine a date for multi-party elections was to be held in February 1991.

Political Organizations

In January 1991 legislation came into effect whereby the Parti congolais du travail ceased to be the Congo's sole political party.

Assemblée pour la démocratie et le progrès social: f. 1990; Leader JEAN-PIERRE THYSTÈRE-TCHICAYA.

Mouvement congolais pour la démocratie et le developpement intégral: f. 1990; Leader BERNARD KOLELA.

Mouvement pour la démocratie et le développement: f. 1990; aims to promote a mixed economy; Leader Brig.-Gen. JOACHIM YHOMBI-OPANGO.

Mouvement patriotique du Congo (MPC): Paris, France; advocates the withdrawal of Cuban troops from the Congo.

Parti congolais du travail (PCT): Brazzaville; telex 5335; f. 1969 to replace the Mouvement national de la révolution; abandoned Marxist-Leninist ideology in 1990; the national party congress, the highest authority of the PCT, meets every five years*; a 249-mem. cen. cttee directs party policy; a 13-mem. politburo exercises the powers of the cen. cttee between its sessions; a four-mem. secr. is the sr exec. body; Pres. of Cen. Cttee Gen. DENIS SASSOU-NGUESSO; Gen. Sec. ANDRÉ OBAMI ITOU; Secr. ITH OSSE TOUMBA-LEKOUNZOU, PAUL NGATSE, DANIEL ABIBI.

* An extraordinary Congress of the PCT was held in December 1990, regarding the implementation of political reforms (see Recent History).

Parti écologiste: f. 1990.
Parti libéral congolais: f. 1990; Gen. Sec. MARCEL MAKON.
Parti social-démocrate congolais: f. 1990; Pres. CLÉMENT MIERASSA.
Union nationale pour la démocratie et le progrès: f.1990.
Union pour la démocratie congolaise (UDC): f. 1989; advocates a liberal economy; Chair. SYLVAIN BAMBA.

Diplomatic Representation

EMBASSIES IN THE CONGO

Algeria: BP 2100, Brazzaville; tel. 83-39-15; telex 5303; Ambassador: MOHAMED NACER ADJALI.
Angola: BP 388, Brazzaville; tel. 81-14-71; telex 5321; Ambassador: JOSÉ AGOSTINHO NETO.
Belgium: BP 225, Brazzaville; tel. 83-29-63; telex 5216; Ambassador: LOTHAR VERSYCK.
Cameroon: BP 2136, Brazzaville; tel. 83-34-04; telex 5242; Ambassador: JEAN-HILAIRE MBEA MBEA.
Central African Republic: BP 10, Brazzaville; tel. 83-40-14; Ambassador: CHARLES GUEREBANGBI.
Chad: BP 386, Brazzaville; tel. 81-22-22; Chargé d'affaires: NEATO-BEI BIDI.
China, People's Republic: BP 213, Brazzaville; tel. 83-11-20; Ambassador: (vacant).
Cuba: BP 80, Brazzaville; tel. 81-20-91; telex 5308; Ambassador: DIEGO ERNESTO GONZÁLEZ PÉREZ.
Czechoslovakia: BP 292, Brazzaville; tel. 82-08-37; Ambassador: LUBOMÍR HALUSKA.

THE CONGO   *Directory*

Egypt: BP 917, Brazzaville; tel. 83-44-28; telex 5248; Ambassador: MOHAMED ABDEL RAHMAN DIAB.

France: rue Alfassa, BP 2089, Brazzaville; tel. 83-14-23; telex 5239; Ambassador: ROBERT DELOS SANTOS.

Gabon: ave Fourneau, BP 2033, Brazzaville; tel. 81-05-90; telex 5225; Ambassador: CONSTANT TSOUMOU.

Germany: BP 2022, Brazzaville; tel. 83-29-90; telex 5235; Ambassador: BERNHARD KALSCHEUER.

Guinea: BP 2477, Brazzaville; tel. 81-24-66; Ambassador: BONATA DIENG.

Holy See: rue Colonel Brisset, BP 1168, Brazzaville; tel. 83-15-46; Apostolic Pro-Nuncio: Most Rev. BENIAMINO STELLA, Titular Archbishop of Midila.

Italy: 2-3 blvd Lyautey, BP 2484, Brazzaville; tel. 83-40-47; telex 5251; Ambassador: TIBOR HOOR TEMPIS LIVI.

Korea, Democratic People's Republic: BP 2032, Brazzaville; tel. 83-41-98; Ambassador: YU KWAN-CHIN.

Libya: BP 920, Brazzaville; Secretary of People's Bureau: SAAD ABDESSALEM BAAIU.

Nigeria: BP 790, Brazzaville; tel. 83-13-16; telex 5263; Ambassador: LAWRENCE OLUFOLAHAN OLADEJO OYELAKIN.

Romania: BP 2413, Brazzaville; tel. 81-32-79; telex 5259; Chargé d'affaires a.i.: DIACONESCO MILCEA.

United Kingdom: ave du Général de Gaulle, Plateau, BP 1038, Brazzaville; tel. 83-49-44; telex 5385; fax 83-49-45; Ambassador: PETER WARREN CHANDLEY.

USSR: BP 2132, Brazzaville; tel. 83-44-39; telex 5455; fax 83-69-17; Ambassador: ANATOLY SAFRONOVICH ZAITSEV.

USA: ave Amílcar Cabral, BP 1015, Brazzaville; tel. 83-20-70; telex 5367; Ambassador: LEONARD G. SHURTLEFF.

Viet-Nam: BP 988, Brazzaville; tel. 83-26-21; Ambassador: BUI VAN THANH.

Yugoslavia: BP 2062, Brazzaville; tel. 83-42-46; telex 5316; Chargé d'affaires a.i.: IBRAHIM DJIKIĆ; temporarily closed Feb. 1988.

Zaire: 130 ave de l'Indépendance, BP 2450, Brazzaville; tel. 83-29-38; Ambassador: (vacant).

Judicial System

A state security court was established in 1978 to try 'crimes against the Congolese revolution'. There is a court of appeal, labour courts, and tribunaux coutumiers (courts of common law), the latter to be replaced by tribunaux d'instance.

Supreme Court: Brazzaville; telex 5298; acts as a cour de cassation; Pres. CHARLES ASSEMEKANG.

Revolutionary Court of Justice: Brazzaville; f. 1969; has jurisdiction in cases involving the security of the State; comprises nine judges appointed by cen. cttee of PCT; Pres. (vacant).

Religion

About one-half of the population follow traditional animist beliefs. The remainder are mostly Christians. In 1978 the Government banned all religions and sects, except the Roman Catholic Church, the Congo Evangelical Church, the Salvation Army, Islam and the followers of Simon Kimbangu Prophète, Lassy Zephirin Prophète and Terynkyo.

CHRISTIANITY
The Roman Catholic Church

The Congo comprises one archdiocese and five dioceses. At 31 December 1988 there were an estimated 806,600 adherents (about 38% of the total population).

Bishops' Conference: Conférence Episcopale du Congo, BP 2301, Brazzaville; tel. 83-06-29; f. 1966; Pres. Most Rev. BARTHÉLÉMY BATANTU, Archbishop of Brazzaville.

Archbishop of Brazzaville: Most Rev. BARTHÉLÉMY BATANTU, Archevêché, BP 2301, Brazzaville; tel. 83-17-93.

Other Christian Churches

Protestant Churches: In all four equatorial states (the Congo, the CAR, Chad and Gabon) there are nearly 1,000 mission centres with a total personnel of about 2,000.

Eglise Evangélique du Congo: BP 3205, Bacongo, Brazzaville; tel. 83-43-64; f. 1909; autonomous since 1961; 110,461 mems (1985); Pres. Rev. JEAN MBOUNGOU.

ISLAM

There are an estimated 25,000 Muslims in the Congo.

Conseil Islamique: Brazzaville; Head of Islamic Community ABOU-BAKAR GOLOUOLI.

The Press

Censorship has been in force since 1972.

DAILIES

ACI: BP 2144, Brazzaville; tel. 83-05-91; telex 5285; daily news bulletin publ. by Agence Congolaise d'Information; circ. 1,000.

L'Eveil de Pointe-Noire: BP 66, Pointe-Noire.

Mweti: BP 991, Brazzaville; tel. 81-10-87; national news; Dir EMMANUEL KIALA-MATOUBA; Chief Editor HUBERT MADOUABA; circ. 8,000.

PERIODICALS

Bakento Ya Congo: BP 309, Brazzaville; tel. 83-27-44; quarterly; Dir MARIE LOUISE MAGANGA; Chief Editor CHARLOTTE BOUSSE; circ. 3,000.

Bulletin de Statistique: Centre Nationale de la Statistique et des Etudes Economiques, BP 2031, Brazzaville; tel. 83-36-94; f. 1977; quarterly; Dir-Gen. MARCEL MOUELLE.

Bulletin Mensuel de la Chambre de Commerce de Brazzaville: BP 92, Brazzaville; monthly.

Combattant Rouge: Brazzaville; tel. 83-02-53; monthly; Dir SYLVIO GEORGES ONKA; Chief Editor GILLES OMER BOUSSI.

Congo-Magazine: BP 114, Brazzaville; tel. 83-43-81; monthly; Dir GASPARD MPAN; Chief Editor THEODORE KIAMOSSI; circ. 3,000.

Effort: BP 64, Brazzaville; monthly.

Jeunesse et Révolution: BP 885, Brazzaville; tel. 83-44-13; weekly; Dir JEAN-ENOCH GOMA-KENGUE; Chief Editor PIERRE MAKITA.

La Semaine Africaine: BP 2080, Brazzaville; tel. 83-03-28; f. 1952; weekly; Roman Catholic; circulates in the Congo, Gabon, Chad and the CAR; Dir Fr FRANÇOIS DE PAUL MOUNDANGA; Chief Editor BERNARD MACKIZA; circ. 8,000.

Le Stade: BP 114, Brazzaville; tel. 81-47-18; telex 5285; f. 1985; weekly; sports; Dir ROCIL PIERRE BEMBA; Chief Editor LOUIS NGAMI; circ. 12,000.

Voix de la Classe Ouvrière (Voco): BP 2311, Brazzaville; tel. 83-36-66; six a year; Dir MICHEL JOSEPH MAYOUNGOU; Chief Editor MARIE-JOSEPH TSENGOU; circ. 4,500.

NEWS AGENCIES

Agence Congolaise d'Information (ACI): BP 2144, Brazzaville; tel. 83-05-91; telex 5285; f. 1961; Chief Editor JOSEPH GOUALA.

Foreign Bureaux

Agence France-Presse (AFP): c/o Agence Congolaise d'Information, BP 2144, Brazzaville; telex 5477; Correspondent JOSEPH GOUALA.

Associated Press (AP) (USA): BP 2144, Brazzaville; telex 5477; Correspondent ARMAND BERNARD MASSAMBA.

Informatsionnoye Agentstvo Novosti (IAN) (USSR): BP 170, Brazzaville; tel. 83-43-44; telex 5227; Bureau Chief DMITRI AMVROSIEV.

Inter Press Service (IPS) (Italy): BP 4174, Brazzaville; tel. 810565; telex 5285.

Reuters (UK): BP 2144, Brazzaville; telex 5477; Correspondent ANTOINE MOUYAMBALA.

Telegrafnoye Agentstvo Sovetskovo Soyuza (TASS) (USSR): BP 379, Brazzaville; tel. 83-44-33; telex 5203; Correspondent BORIS PHILIPOV.

Xinhua (New China) News Agency (People's Republic of China): 40 ave Maréchal Lyauté, BP 373, Brazzaville; tel. 83-44-01; telex 5230; Chief Correspondent XU ZHENQIANG.

Publishers

Imprimerie Centrale d'Afrique (ICA): BP 162, Pointe-Noire; f. 1949; Man. Dir M. SCHNEIDER.

Société Congolaise Hachette: BP 919, Brazzaville; telex 5291; general fiction, literature, education, juvenile, textbooks.

Government Publishing House

Imprimerie Nationale: BP 58, Brazzaville.

THE CONGO   *Directory*

Radio and Television

In 1987 there were an estimated 119,000 radio sets and 6,000 television receivers in use. In August 1989 the Congo and France signed an agreement whereby France was to finance the installation of a satellite ground station and equipment for the Canal France International Television Service.

Radiodiffusion-Télévision Congolaise: BP 2241, Brazzaville; tel. 83-16-76; telex 5299; Dir FIRMIN AYESSA.

Télévision Nationale Congolaise: BP 2241, Brazzaville; tel. 81-51-52; began transmission in 1963; operates for 46 hours per week, with most programmes in French but some in Lingala and Kikongo; colour transmissions began in 1983; Dir VALENTIN MAFOUTA.

La Voix de la Révolution Congolaise: BP 2241, Brazzaville; tel. 83-03-83; radio programmes in French, Lingala, Kikongo, Subia, English and Portuguese; transmitters at Brazzaville and Pointe-Noire; also broadcasts to Namibia in English and vernacular languages; Dir JEAN-PASCAL MONGO-SLYM.

Finance

(cap. = capital; res = reserves; dep. = deposits; br. = branch; m. = million; amounts in francs CFA)

BANKING

Central Bank

Banque des Etats de l'Afrique Centrale (BEAC): BP 126, Brazzaville; tel. 83-28-14; telex 5200; headquarters in Yaoundé, Cameroon; f. 1973 as the central bank of issue for mem. states of the Customs and Economic Union of Central Africa (UDEAC), comprising Cameroon, the Central African Republic, Chad, the Congo, Equatorial Guinea and Gabon; cap. 36,000m., res 162,037m. (June 1989); Gov. JEAN-FÉLIX MAMALEPOT; Dir in the Congo GABRIEL BOKILO; br. at Pointe-Noire.

Commercial Banks

Banque Commerciale Congolaise (BCC): ave Patrice Lumumba, BP 79, Brazzaville; tel. 83-08-79; telex 5237; fax 83-41-84; f. 1962; 60.4% state-owned, 25% by Crédit Lyonnais (France); cap. 5,000m. (Dec. 1988); Chair. AMBROISE NOUMAZALAYE; Gen. Man. CLÉMENT MOUAMBA; 12 brs.

Banque Internationale du Congo (BIDC): ave Amílcar Cabral, BP 645, Brazzaville; tel. 83-14-11; telex 5339; fax 83-53-82; f. 1983; 57% state-owned; undergoing reorganization in 1990; cap. 1,000m. (Dec. 1988); Gen. Man. MATHIAS DZON.

Union Congolaise de Banques SA (UCB): ave Amílcar Cabral, BP 147, Brazzaville; tel. 83-30-00; telex 5206; fax 83-65-48; f. 1974 by the merger of Société Générale de Banques au Congo and Banque Internationale pour le Commerce et l'Industrie; 89.7% state-owned; cap. 3,000m. (Dec. 1988); Chair. OSSEBI DOUANIAM; Man. Dir MATHIEU AKONGO; 12 brs.

Development Banks

Banque de développement des états de l'Afrique centrale: (see Franc Zone, p. 157).

Banque Nationale de Développement du Congo (BNDC): ave Foch, BP 2085, Brazzaville; tel. 83-30-13; telex 5312; f. 1961; 79% state-owned; cap. 1,087m. (Dec. 1986); provides financial and technical help for development projects; Pres. Minister of Finance and Budget; Man. Dir ANDRÉ BATANGA; br. at Pointe-Noire.

Financial Institution

Caisse Congolaise d'Amortissement: 410 allée du Chaillu, BP 2090, Brazzaville; tel. 83-32-41; telex 5294; f. 1971; management of state funds; Man. Dir EMILE MABONZO.

INSURANCE

Assurances et Réassurances du Congo (ARC): ave Amílcar Cabral, BP 977, Brazzaville; tel. 83-01-71; telex 5236; f. 1973 to acquire the businesses of all insurance companies operating in the Congo; 50% state-owned; cap. 500m.; Dir-Gen. RAYMOND IBATA; brs at Pointe-Noire, Loubomo and Ouesso.

Trade and Industry

DEVELOPMENT AGENCIES

Caisse Centrale de Coopération Economique (CCCE): BP 96, Brazzaville; tel. 83-15-95; telex 5202; French fund for economic co-operation; Dir JACQUES BENIER.

Mission Française de Coopération: BP 2175, Brazzaville; tel. 83-15-03; f. 1959; administers bilateral aid from France; Dir GÉRARD LA COGNATA.

Office des Cultures Vivrières (OCV): BP 894, Brazzaville; tel. 82-11-03; f. 1979; state-owned; food-crop development; Dir-Gen. GILBERT PANA.

STATE MARKETING BOARDS

Office Congolais des Bois (OCB): 2 ave Moe Vangoula, BP 1229, Pointe-Noire; tel. 94-22-38; telex 8248; f. 1974; cap. 1,486m. francs CFA; monopoly of purchase and marketing of all timber products; Man. Dir ALEXANDRE DENGUET-ATTIKI.

Office du Café et du Cacao (OCC): BP 2488, Brazzaville; tel. 83-19-03; telex 5273; f. 1978; cap. 1,500m. francs CFA; marketing and export of coffee and cocoa; Man. Dir PAUL YORA.

Office National de Commercialisation des Produits Agricoles (ONCPA): BP 144, Brazzaville; tel. 83-24-01; telex 5273; f. 1964; marketing of all agricultural products except sugar; promotion of rural co-operatives; Dir JEAN-PAUL BOCKONDAS.

Office National du Commerce (OFNACOM): BP 2305, Brazzaville; tel. 83-43-99; telex 5309; f. 1964; proposals for transfer to private ownership announced in 1987; cap. 2,158m. francs CFA; importer and distributor of general merchandise; monopoly importer of salted and dried fish, cooking salt, rice, tomato purée, buckets, enamelled goods and blankets; Dir-Gen. VALENTIN ENOUSSA NCONGO.

Office National d'Importation et de Vente de Viande en Gros (ONIVEG): BP 2130, Brazzaville; tel. 82-30-33; telex 5240; f. 1975; cap. 177m. francs CFA; monopoly importer and distributor of wholesale meats; Man. Dir ROBERT PAUL MANGOUTA.

CHAMBERS OF COMMERCE

Chambre de Commerce, d'Agriculture et d'Industrie de Brazzaville: BP 92, Brazzaville; tel. 83-21-15; Pres. MAURICE OGNAOY; Sec.-Gen. FRANÇOIS DILOU-YOULOU.

Chambre de Commerce, d'Agriculture et d'Industrie de Loubomo: BP 78, Loubomo.

Chambre de Commerce, d'Industrie et d'Agriculture du Kouilou: 3 ave Charles de Gaulle, BP 665, Pointe-Noire; tel. 94-12-80; f. 1948; Chair. FRANÇOIS-LUC MACOSSO; Sec.-Gen. GEORGES MBOMA.

PROFESSIONAL ORGANIZATION

Union Patronale et Interprofessionnelle du Congo (UNICONGO): BP 42, Brazzaville; tel. 83-05-51; fax 83-68-16; f. 1960; employers' union; Pres. BERNARD FRAUD; Sec.-Gen. MICHEL GIRARD.

NATIONALIZED INDUSTRIES

Minoterie, Aliments de Bétail, Boulangerie (MAB): BP 789, Pointe-Noire; tel. 94-19-09; telex 8283; f. 1978; cap. 2,650m. francs CFA; monopoly importer of cereals; production of flour and animal feed; Man. Dir DENIS TEMPERE.

Régie Nationale des Palmeraies du Congo (RNPC): BP 8, Brazzaville; tel. 83-08-25; f. 1966; cap. 908m. francs CFA; production of palm oil; Man. Dir RENE MACOSSO.

Société Nationale de Construction (SONACO): BP 1126, Brazzaville; tel. 83-06-54; f. 1979; cap. 479m. francs CFA; building works; Man. Dir DENIS M'BOMO.

Société Nationale de Distribution d'Eau (SNDE): ave Sergent Malamine, BP 229 and 365, Brazzaville; tel. 83-41-69; telex 5272; f. 1967; water supply and sewerage; holds monopoly over wells and import of mineral water; Chair. and Man. Dir F. S. SITA.

Société Nationale d'Elevage (SONEL): BP 81, Loutété, Massangui; f. 1964; cap. 80m. francs CFA; development of semi-intensive stock-rearing; exploitation of by-products in co-operation with SIA-CONGO; Man. Dir THÉOPHILE BIKAWA.

Société Nationale d'Exploitation des Bois (SNEB): BP 1198, Pointe-Noire; tel. 94-02-09; f. 1970; cap. 1,779m. francs CFA; production of timber; merged with wood-processing firm SONATRAB 1983; Pres. RIGOBERT NGOULOU; Man. Dir ROBERT ZINGA KANZA.

Société Nationale de Recherches et d'Exploitation Pétrolière (HYDRO-CONGO): ave Amílcar Cabral, BP 2008, Brazzaville; tel. 83-40-22; telex 5300; f. 1973; cap. 710m. francs CFA; research into and production of petroleum resources; had monopoly of distribution of petroleum products in the Congo until 1990; refinery at Pointe-Noire; manufacture of lubricants; Pres. and Man. Dir SATURNIN OKABE.

Société des Verreries du Congo (SOVERCO): BP 1241, Pointe-Noire; tel. 94-19-19; telex 8288; f. 1977; cap. 500m. francs CFA;

THE CONGO

mfrs of glassware; Chair. A. E. NOUMAZALAYE; Man. Dir NGOYOT IBARRA.

Sucrerie du Congo (SUCO): BP 71, Nkayi; tel. 92-11-00; telex 8246; f. 1978; cap. 500m. francs CFA; sugar production; Dir HENRI DJOMBO; 1,800 employees.

Unité d'Afforestation Industrielle du Congo (UAIC): BP 1120, Pointe-Noire; tel. 94-04-17; telex 8308; f. 1978; eucalyptus plantations to provide wood-pulp for export; Dir YVES LAPLACE.

TRADE UNION

Confédération Syndicale Congolaise (CSC): BP 2311, Brazzaville; tel. 83-19-23; telex 5304; f. 1964; Sec.-Gen. JEAN-MICHEL BOUKAMBA-YANGOUMA.

Transport

Agence Transcongolaise des Communications (ATC): BP 711, Pointe-Noire; tel. 94-15-32; telex 8345; f. 1969; the largest state enterprise; cap. 23,888m. francs CFA; three sections: Congo-Océan Railway, inland waterways and general transport facilities, and the port of Pointe-Noire; Man. Dir FRANÇOIS BITA.

RAILWAYS

There are 510 km of track from Brazzaville to Pointe-Noire. A 286-km section of privately-owned line links the manganese mines at Moanda (in Gabon), via a cableway to the Congo border at M'Binda, with the main line to Pointe-Noire.

ATC—Chemin de Fer Congo-Océan (CFCO): BP 651, Pointe-Noire; tel. 94-11-84; telex 8231; fax 94-12-30; Dir NOËL BOUANGA.

INLAND WATERWAYS

The Congo and Oubangui rivers form two axes of a highly developed inland waterway system. The Congo river and seven tributaries in the Congo basin provide 2,300 km of navigable river and the Oubangui river, developed in co-operation with the Central African Republic, 2,085 km.

ATC—Direction des Voies Navigables, Ports et Transports Fluviaux: BP 2048, Brazzaville; tel. 83-06-27; waterways authority; Dir MÉDARD OKOUMOU.

Compagnie Congolaise de Transports: BP 37, Loubomo; f. 1960; cap. 36m. francs CFA; Pres. and Dir-Gen. ROBERT BARBIER.

Société Congolaise de Transports (SOCOTRANS): BP 617, Pointe-Noire; tel. 94-23-31; f. 1977; cap. 17m. francs CFA; Man YVES CRIQUET.

Transcap-Congo: BP 1154, Pointe-Noire; tel. 94-01-46; telex 8218; f. 1962; cap. 100m. francs CFA; Chair. J. DROUAULT.

SHIPPING

Pointe-Noire is the major port of the Congo. Brazzaville, on the Congo river, is an inland port. A major expansion programme for Brazzaville port was scheduled for completion in the late 1980s. The project, which was to cost an estimated 1,900m. francs CFA, was part-financed by the European Investment Bank and aimed at establishing the port as a container traffic centre for several central African countries, including Chad, the CAR and the western part of Cameroon. In 1987 Congolese seaports handled 9,631,000 metric tons of goods for international transport.

ATC—Direction du Port de Brazzaville: BP 2048, Brazzaville; tel. 83-00-42; nationalized in 1977; port authority; Dir JEAN-PAUL BOCKONDAS.

ATC—Direction du Port de Pointe-Noire: BP 711, Pointe-Noire; tel. 94-00-52; telex 8318; nationalized in 1977; port authority; Dir ALPHONSE M'BAMA.

La Congolaise de Transport Maritime (COTRAM): f. 1984; national shipping co.; state-owned.

ROADS

In 1980 there were 8,246 km of roads usable throughout the year, of which 849 km were bituminized. The network consists of 4,519 km of main roads and 3,727 km of secondary roads, with the principal routes linking Brazzaville to Pointe-Noire, in the south, and to Ouesso, in the north.

Régie Nationale des Transports et des Travaux Publics: BP 2073, Brazzaville; tel. 83-35-58; f. 1965; civil engineering, upkeep of roads and public works; Man. Dir HECTOR BIENVENU OUAMBA.

CIVIL AVIATION

There are international airports at Brazzaville (Maya-Maya) and Pointe-Noire. There are also 37 smaller airfields. An aeronautical development programme covering 1982–86 included the construction of airports at six regional capitals.

Afri-Congo: Brazzaville; f. 1986; private airline operating flights to Rwanda and Burundi; fleet of 1 Hercules C-130.

Agence Nationale de l'Aviation Civile (ANAC): BP 128, Brazzaville; tel. 81-09-94; telex 5388; f. 1970; Gen. Man. GILBERT M'FOUO-OTSIALLY.

Air Afrique: BP 1126, Pointe-Noire; tel. 94-17-00; telex 8342; see under Côte d'Ivoire; Dir at Pointe-Noire JEAN-CLAUDE NDIAYE; Dir at Brazzaville I. CISSÉ DEMBA.

Lina Congo (Lignes Nationales Aériennes Congolaises): ave Amílcar Cabral, BP 2203, Brazzaville; tel. 83-30-66; telex 5243; f. 1965; state-owned; operates an extensive internal network; also services to CAR and Gabon; Man. Dir JEAN-JACQUES ONTSA-ONTSA; fleet of 1 Boeing 737-200QC, 1 Fokker F.28-1000, 1 F.27-600, 2 Twin Otter 300.

Tourism

Brazzaville has three international hotels, but there is a shortage of accommodation in Pointe-Noire, where the petroleum and business sectors have increased demand. A regional hotel chain is to be established to cater for travellers in the provinces. There are plans to convert Mbamou Island into a tourist attraction. An estimated 39,000 tourists visited the Congo in 1987.

Direction Générale du Tourisme et des Loisirs: BP 456, Brazzaville; tel. 83-09-53; telex 5210; f. 1963; Dir-Gen. JEAN FÉLIX TABA-GOMA.

COSTA RICA

Introductory Survey

Location, Climate, Language, Religion, Flag, Capital

The Republic of Costa Rica lies in the Central American isthmus, with Nicaragua to the north, Panama to the south, the Caribbean Sea to the east and the Pacific Ocean to the west. The climate is warm and damp in the lowlands (average temperature 27°C (81°F)) and cooler on the Central Plateau (average temperature 22°C (72°F)), where two-thirds of the population live. The language spoken is Spanish. Almost all of the inhabitants profess Christianity, and the overwhelming majority adhere to the Roman Catholic Church, the state religion. The national flag (proportions 3 by 2) has five horizontal stripes, of blue, white, red, white and blue, the red stripe being twice the width of the others. The state flag, in addition, has on the red stripe (to the left of centre) a white oval enclosing the national coat of arms, showing three volcanic peaks between the Caribbean and the Pacific. The capital is San José.

Recent History

Costa Rica was ruled by Spain from the 16th century until 1821, when independence was declared. The only significant interruption in the country's constitutional government since 1920 occurred in February 1948, when the result of the presidential election was disputed. The legislature annulled the election in March but a civil war ensued. The anti-Government forces, led by José Figueres Ferrer, were successful, and a revolutionary junta took power in April. Costa Rica's army was abolished in December 1948. After the preparation of a new constitution, the victorious candidate of the 1948 election took office in January 1949.

Figueres, who founded the socialist Partido de Liberación Nacional (PLN), dominated national politics for decades, holding presidential office in 1953–58 and 1970–74. Under his leadership, Costa Rica became one of the most democratic countries in Latin America. Since the 1948 revolution, there have been frequent changes of power, all achieved by constitutional means. Figueres' first Government nationalized the banks and instituted a comprehensive social security system. The presidential election of 1958, however, was won by a conservative, Mario Echandi Jiménez, who reversed many PLN policies. His successor, Francisco Orlich Bolmarich (President from 1962 to 1966), was supported by the PLN but continued the encouragement of private enterprise. Another conservative, José Joaquín Trejos Fernández, held power in 1966–70. In 1974 the PLN candidate, Daniel Oduber Quirós, was elected President. He continued the policies of extending the welfare state and of establishing friendly relations with communist states. Communist and other left-wing parties were legalized in 1975. In 1978 Rodrigo Carazo Odio of the conservative Partido Unidad Opositora (PUO) coalition (subsequently the Coalición Unidad) was elected President. During Carazo's term of office the worsening instability in Central America led to diplomatic tension, and in 1981 the President was criticized for his alleged involvement in illegal arms trafficking between Cuba and El Salvador.

At presidential and legislative elections in February 1982, Luis Alberto Monge Alvarez of the PLN gained a comfortable majority when his party won 33 of the 57 seats in the Legislative Assembly. Following his inauguration in May, President Monge announced a series of emergency economic measures, in an attempt to rescue the country from near-bankruptcy. A policy of neutrality towards the left-wing Sandinista Government of Nicaragua was continued. However, after a number of cross-border raids, a national alert was declared in May. The rebel Nicaraguan leader, Edén Pastora Gómez, was expelled so as to reduce Costa Rican involvement in the Nicaraguan conflict. Relations with Nicaragua worsened as guerrilla activity spread to San José.

Throughout 1983, President Monge came under increasing pressure, from liberal members of the Cabinet and PLN supporters, to adopt a more neutral stance in foreign policy. Three leading members of the anti-Sandinista (Contra) movement were expelled from Costa Rica in May, and 80 of Pastora's supporters were arrested in September. In addition, some 82 guerrilla camps were dismantled by the Civil Guard. In November 1983 President Monge declared Costa Rica's neutrality in an attempt to elicit foreign support for his country. This declaration was opposed by the USA and led to the resignation of the Costa Rican Minister of Foreign Affairs.

In May 1984 there were reports of an air raid by the Nicaraguan Air Force on a border village in Costa Rica and of an increasing number of incursions by the Sandinista forces. Public opposition to any renunciation of neutrality was emphasized by a demonstration in support of peace and neutrality, held in San José and attended by over 20,000 people. An attempt was made to defuse the tense situation with the establishment of a commission, supported by the Contadora group (Colombia, Mexico, Panama and Venezuela), to monitor events in the border area. In late May, however, the attempt to assassinate Edén Pastora Gómez near the Costa Rican border exacerbated the rift within the Cabinet concerning government policy towards Nicaragua.

Relations with Nicaragua deteriorated further in December 1984, following an incident involving a Nicaraguan refugee at the Costa Rican embassy in Managua. Subsequently, diplomatic relations were reduced to a minimal level. Reports of clashes between Costa Rican Civil Guardsmen and Sandinista forces along the joint border became increasingly frequent. In 1985 the Government's commitment to neutrality was disputed when it decided to establish an anti-guerrilla battalion, trained by US military advisers.

During 1983 there were signs of increasing urban unrest in response to the Government's austerity measures and to the agrarian crisis, which had produced high levels of unemployment, principally among workers on banana plantations. By August 1984 the Government's position was regarded as unstable. The division within the Cabinet over policy towards Nicaragua, coupled with the effects of the unpopular austerity programme and a protracted strike by banana plantation workers, which had resulted in two deaths, led to fears of a coup. At President Monge's request, the Cabinet resigned, and in the subsequent reshuffle four Ministers were replaced.

At presidential and legislative elections in February 1986, Oscar Arias Sánchez, the candidate of the PLN, was elected President, with 52% of the votes cast. The PLN also obtained a clear majority in the Legislative Assembly. The new Government was committed to the development of a 'welfare state', whereby 25,000 new jobs and 20,000 new dwellings were to be created each year. In addition, the Government planned to renegotiate the country's external debt and to reach agreement on a social pact with the trade unions. Furthermore, President Arias Sánchez was resolved to maintain and reinforce Costa Rica's policy of neutrality, a decision which was expected to antagonize relations with the US administration.

In February 1986 diplomatic relations with Nicaragua were fully restored, and it was decided to establish a permanent inspection and vigilance commission at the common border. In accordance with the Government's pledge to protect neutrality, Costa Rica objected to the allocation of US $100m. in US aid to the Contra forces in mid-1986. In addition, the Government embarked on a series of arrests and expulsions of Contras resident in Costa Rica. In October, however, an aeroplane crash in Nicaraguan territory, involving four US citizens, caused considerable embarrassment to the Costa Rican Government and encouraged scepticism about Costa Rica's participation in the anti-Sandinista campaign.

Throughout 1986 and 1987 President Arias became increasingly involved in the quest for peace in Central America. In February 1987 President Arias' first peace proposal was discussed at a meeting of Central American Presidents, but was not endorsed. In May President Arias began a tour of Western Europe, in an attempt to secure international support and in the hope of overcoming US reservations concerning certain aspects of the peace plan. In August, at a summit meeting in Esquipulas, Guatemala, President Arias presented a modified plan which was accepted and signed by the Presidents of El Salvador, Nicaragua, Guatemala, Honduras and Costa Rica. The plan incorporated a 90-day timetable for the implementation of various measures aimed at promoting the establishment of peace in the region. The crucial provisions of the proposals were simultaneous cease-fires in Nicaragua and El Salvador, a halt to foreign assistance to rebel groups, democratic reform in Nicaragua, and a ban on the use of foreign territory as a base for attack. National reconciliation commissions were also to be formed in each of the Central American nations, including Costa Rica, to monitor the progress of the plan. This peace proposal was regarded as the most promising yet to be formulated and as a personal triumph for President Arias, who was awarded the Nobel Peace Prize in October 1987. In September the Central American Vice-Presidents had agreed on the future creation of a unified parliament, in which each country was to hold 20 seats.

Despite the efforts of President Arias, the 90-day timetable for implementation of the proposals made at Esquipulas had to be extended until January 1988 before the second phase of verification and monitoring of progress could begin. In January President Arias brought Nicaraguan government officials and Contra leaders together in San José for their first discussions concerning the implementation of a cease-fire. Prior to this meeting, President Arias ordered three Contra leaders to leave Costa Rica or cease their military activities; subsequently, Alfredo César and Pedro Joaquín Chamorro agreed to leave, while Alfonso Robelo remained and agreed to modify his campaign. President Arias maintained his independent position by supporting discussions between the Contras and Sandinistas, held in Nicaragua in March, and by condemning any continuation of aid to the Contras. In November a border agreement was signed with Nicaragua.

In 1988 there were renewed indications of internal unrest as a result of the Government's economic policies. In March there were two one-day stoppages by public employees, to protest against concessions made to the IMF and the World Bank. In June UNSA, the co-ordinating organization for agricultural unions, proposed a week-long protest against the Government's agricultural policies. In August there were strikes by farmers who were aggrieved at the Government's 'Agriculture for Change' policy of promoting the cultivation of cash crops, and thereby sacrificing the interests of many smallholders, to appease the IMF. The Government established a commission to consider the farmers' complaints.

During 1989, however, there was increased labour unrest throughout the country. In August a coalition movement of regional trade unions, professional bodies and civic groups in the province of Limón called a strike that paralysed shipping on the Caribbean coast for four days. Trade union, farmers' and other mass organizations along the Atlantic coast continued to protest against the Government's policies of structural adjustment. In September teachers demanding higher pay and professional status held a one-day strike. Workers in the Ministry of Transport also went on strike, demanding salaries comparable to those of staff in other ministries. The dispute ended in mid-September, after the Government had agreed to revise their salary scale. Private-sector workers negotiated a 6.4% increase in wages in 1989. Moreover, President Arias promised that proportional wage increases would be awarded whenever the annual rate of inflation exceeded 7%. In September the Minister of Finance resigned, as his efforts to impose stringent austerity measures were being undermined by the increase in the budgetary deficit. He also opposed the Government's plan to reduce a tax on coffee production, claiming that, without the tax, the government deficit would exceed US $145m., which might jeopardize agreements with the IMF.

In September 1989 the Legislative Assembly's commission of enquiry into the extent of drug-trafficking and related activities published its findings. As a result, a number of public figures were asked to resign. Among these were the former President (then a senior PLN official), Daniel Oduber Quirós, a PLN deputy, Leonel Villalobos, the general manager of a leading bank and the head of the Civil Aviation Authority. A former Minister of Public Security, Benjamín Piza, was to be tried on corruption charges, and a Supreme Court Justice, Jesús Ramírez, was accused of perjury.

At presidential and legislative elections in February 1990, Rafael Angel Calderón Fournier, the candidate presented by the Partido Unidad Social Cristiana (PUSC), was elected President, with 51.3% of the votes cast. The PUSC obtained a clear majority in the Legislative Assembly, with 29 seats. It was widely believed that the decline in public support for the PLN was partly a result of the party's involvement in the drug scandal in the previous year. On assuming office in May, President Calderón was faced with the problem of a fiscal deficit of US $150m. and was therefore forced to renege on his pre-election promise of improvements in welfare and income distribution. The deficit, equivalent to 3.3% of GDP, was almost double the limit of 1.7% stipulated by the IMF in order to ensure financial support from the Fund. Principal factors contributing to the increasing deficit were rising imports, a fall in the price of coffee on the world market, and court-imposed wage increases for a steadily expanding public sector (70% of public expenditure in 1989 was spent on salaries). In an attempt to reduce the deficit, the Government introduced an adjustment programme of austerity measures, which included a rise in the price of fuel by 30% and of many goods and services by as much as 20%, and proposed tax increases. However, initially, the IMF refused to release funds for Costa Rica, insisting that approval of a stand-by loan would depend on the Legislative Assembly's approval of the tax measures. In early October 70,000–100,000 public- and private-sector employees participated in a one-day national strike to protest against the Government's economic policies. In the same month the Central Bank imposed credit restrictions on all private and state banks, in an attempt to curb rising inflation. In late October the Government reached an agreement with the IMF for a stand-by loan of $55m. On 30 October the Minister of Labour, Erick Thompson Piñeres, resigned, stating that his decision to do so reflected the rift between 'economic and social groups' within the Cabinet.

In February 1989 the Presidents of Costa Rica, El Salvador, Guatemala, Honduras and Nicaragua met and agreed to draft a plan to remove the Contra forces from base camps in Honduras, in exchange for the introduction of political reforms and the holding of free elections in Nicaragua. The plan was ratified at a second 'summit' meeting, held in August in Honduras, with the signing of the Tela Agreement. Peace proposals for El Salvador and Guatemala were also elaborated, as was an agreement on co-operation in the campaign against the trafficking and use of illicit drugs. In November, however, the conflicts in Nicaragua and El Salvador intensified. In December the deadline for the disbanding of Contra forces, agreed at Tela, passed unfulfilled, and the Presidents of the five Central American countries, meeting in Costa Rica, agreed on measures to revive the regional peace process. In February 1990, after being defeated in elections, Nicaragua's Sandinista Government decreed an immediate cease-fire. The Contras accepted this, and a cease-fire agreement was concluded in April.

The first inter-American 'summit' meeting for 22 years was held in San José in October 1989, to celebrate a centenary of democracy in Costa Rica. The 17 participating Heads of State discussed issues of democracy, development and drug-trafficking, but no final document was produced, owing to the unwillingness of President Bush of the USA to align with the Nicaraguan President, Daniel Ortega. In addition, the coffee-producing nations agreed on proposals for the reintroduction of export quotas, suspended by the International Coffee Organization in July. It was estimated that the decline in prices resulting from the suspension would cost Costa Rica US $100m. in lost export earnings in 1989. The successful renegotiation of Costa Rica's debt to foreign banks, which would reduce annual interest payments from US $150m. to $50m., was also announced.

In October 1989 Costa Rica announced that it would initiate new diplomatic efforts against Panama (where the Government had declared the results of elections in May to be invalid, following an apparent victory by its opponents), outside the OAS. Costa Rica criticized the OAS for not condemning the Panamanian Government directly in its most recent resolution. In December, however, a US military offensive overthrew Gen. Manuel Noriega's regime in Panama.

In April 1990 an extradition treaty between Costa Rica and the USA was approved by the Legislative Assembly. The treaty, which does not apply to Costa Rican citizens, was aimed at combating crime, particularly international drug-trafficking. Negotiations regarding a bilateral free-trade accord between Costa Rica and the USA were expected to commence in early 1991.

COSTA RICA

Introductory Survey

Government
Under the Constitution of 1949, executive power is vested in the President, assisted by two Vice-Presidents (or, in exceptional circumstances, one Vice-President) and an appointed Cabinet. The President is elected for a four-year term by compulsory adult suffrage, and a successful candidate must receive at least 40% of the votes. The legislative organ is the unicameral Legislative Assembly, with 57 members who are similarly elected for four years.

Defence
There have been no armed forces since 1948. In June 1989, Rural and Civil Guards totalled 7,800 men. In 1985 an anti-terrorist battalion was formed, composed of 750 Civil Guards. Expenditure on the security forces was estimated at 5,740m. colones for 1990.

Economic Affairs
In 1988, according to estimates by the World Bank, Costa Rica's gross national product (GNP), measured at average 1986–88 prices, was US $4,690m., equivalent to $1,760 per head. During 1980–88, it was estimated, GNP increased, in real terms, at an average annual rate of 2.6%, while GNP per head grew by only 0.2% per year. Over the same period, the population increased by an annual average of 2.3%. Costa Rica's gross domestic product (GDP), at purchasers' values, increased, in real terms, by an annual average of 2.4% in 1980–88 and by 5.0% in 1989.

Agriculture (including forestry and fishing) contributed 17.9% of GDP, and employed 25.9% of the labour force, in 1989. The principal cash crops are coffee (which accounted for about 20% of export earnings in 1989), bananas (about 19% of export earnings), sugar cane and cocoa. Cattle and meat exports were also significant. Maize, rice, beans and potatoes are also cultivated. During 1980–88 agricultural production increased by an annual average of 2.5%.

Industry (including mining, manufacturing, construction and power) employed 26.1% of the labour force, and provided 26.7% of GDP, in 1989. During 1980–88 industrial production increased by an annual average rate of 2.3%. Mining and manufacturing employed 18.7% of the labour force, and contributed 20.7% of GDP, in 1989. The mining sector employed only 0.1% of the labour force in 1989. In terms of the value of output, the principal branches of manufacturing in 1984 were food products (42.4%), chemical products (9.3%) and petroleum refineries (7.8%).

Energy is derived principally from petroleum and hydroelectric power. By the late 1980s hydroelectric power provided 20% of commercial energy consumption. The Arenal hydroelectricity project was inaugurated in 1979, and, at its full generating capacity of 1,974MW, was expected to fulfil Costa Rica's entire electricity requirements. Imports of petroleum and other fuels accounted for 9.3% of the value of total imports in 1988.

The services sector employed 46.1% of the labour force, and provided 55.3% of GDP, in 1989. The output of this sector increased at an average annual rate of 2.5% during 1980–88.

In 1989 Costa Rica recorded a visible trade deficit of US $254.5m. and there was a deficit of $446.9m. on the current account of the balance of payments. In 1989 the principal sources of imports were the USA (40.1%), followed by Venezuela (8.3%) and Central America (8.0%). The USA was the principal recipient of Costa Rica's exports (38.0%), followed by the Federal Republic of Germany (13.1%) and Central America (10.4%). The principal exports in 1989 were coffee and bananas. The principal imports were primary commodities, consumer non-durables, machinery and equipment.

In 1989 there was an estimated budgetary deficit of 7,405m. colones (equivalent to some 1.7% of GDP). Costa Rica's total external debt was US $3,531m. at the end of 1988. In that year the cost of debt-servicing was an estimated $715m., equivalent to 58.9% of total revenue from exports of goods and services. The annual rate of inflation averaged 26.9% in 1980–88 and 16.5% in 1989. The rate increased to 17.7% in the year to September 1990. An estimated 3.8% of the labour force were unemployed in 1989.

In October 1990 Costa Rica became a full contracting party to GATT (see p. 57). It is also a member of the Central American Common Market (CACM, see p. 110).

In May 1989 the IMF granted Costa Rica a stand-by credit of SDR 42m. In February 1990, however, disbursements were suspended because Costa Rica's fiscal deficit had exceeded the limit of 1.7% of GDP as stipulated by the IMF. In late October, following the implementation of a number of austerity measures by the Government, the IMF agreed to extend a stand-by loan of $55m. to Costa Rica. President Calderón stated that the agreement committed his administration to a reduction in the public-sector deficit from a projected 5% of GNP in 1990 to 1.4% in 1991. In June 1989 Costa Rica's debt to the 'Paris Club' of Western creditor governments was rescheduled over 10 years. In October 1989 the Legislative Assembly approved two credits, to the value of US $200m., from the World Bank and the Japanese Government, which were to fund the second phase of Costa Rica's structural adjustment plan, SAL II. By late 1990, however, $120m. of that total were still being withheld. In March 1990 Costa Rica secured an agreement to repurchase $1,150m. of its $1,800m. debt to commercial banks at 16% of its nominal value. In early October the US Agency for International Development released $27m. in aid to Costa Rica to help to support the balance of payments, thus averting a foreign-exchange crisis at the Central Bank.

Social Welfare
Costa Rica possesses one of the world's most advanced social welfare systems, which provides a complete programme of care and assistance for all wage-earners and their dependants.

All social services are co-ordinated by the National Development Plan, administered by the Ministry of National Planning and Economic Policy, and are organized by state institutions. The Social Security Fund provides health services and general social insurance, the National Insurance Institute provides professional insurance, and the Ministry of Health operates a preventive health programme through a network of health units throughout the country. Benefits include disability and retirement pensions, workers' compensation and family assistance. In 1979 there were 1,506 registered physicians, not all resident and working in Costa Rica. In 1982 there were 28 hospitals and 76 health centres, with a total of 7,706 beds. Of total expenditure by the central Government in 1986, 12,595.5m. colones (19.1%) was for health services, and a further 12,525.6m. colones (19.0%) for social security.

Education
Education at all levels is available free of charge, and elementary education is officially compulsory for children between six and 13 years of age. Official secondary education consists of a three-year basic course, followed by a more highly specialized course of two years. Attendance figures are very high: in 1987 an estimated 95% of children aged six to 11 years were enrolled at primary schools, while 70% of those aged 12 to 16 received secondary education. There are six universities, one of which is an 'open' university. In 1985, according to estimates by UNESCO, the average rate of adult illiteracy was only 6.4% (males 6.0%; females 6.8%). Costa Rica has the highest adult literacy rate in Central America. Expenditure on education by the central Government in 1987 was 11,860.5m. colones (21.6% of total spending).

Public Holidays
1991: 1 January (New Year's Day), 19 March (Feast of St Joseph), 28 March (Maundy Thursday), 29 March (Good Friday), 11 April (Anniversary of the Battle of Rivas), 1 May (Labour Day), 30 May (Corpus Christi), 29 June (St Peter and St Paul), 25 July (Anniversary of the Annexation of Guanacaste Province), 2 August (Our Lady of the Angels), 15 August (Assumption), 15 September (Independence Day), 12 October (Columbus Day), 1 December (Abolition of the Armed Forces Day), 8 December (Immaculate Conception), 25 December (Christmas Day), 28–31 December (San José only).

1992: 1 January (New Year's Day), 19 March (Feast of St Joseph), 16 April (Maundy Thursday), 17 April (Good Friday), 1 May (Labour Day), 18 June (Corpus Christi), 29 June (St Peter and St Paul), 25 July (Anniversary of the Annexation of Guanacaste Province), 2 August (Our Lady of the Angels), 15 August (Assumption), 15 September (Independence Day), 12 October (Columbus Day), 1 December (Abolition of the Armed Forces Day), 8 December (Immaculate Conception), 25 December (Christmas Day), 28–31 December (San José only).

Weights and Measures
The metric system is in force.

COSTA RICA   Statistical Survey

Statistical Survey

Source (unless otherwise stated): Dirección General de Estadística y Censos, Ministerio de Economía y Comercio,
Avda 2 y Central, Calle 10, Apdo 10.216, San José; tel. 22-1016; telex 2414.

Area and Population

AREA, POPULATION AND DENSITY

Area (sq km)	
Land	51,060
Inland water	40
Total	51,100*
Population (census results)†	
14 May 1973	1,871,780
11 June 1984	
Males	1,208,216
Females	1,208,593
Total	2,416,809
Population (official estimates at mid-year)	
1987	2,781,418
1988	2,851,085
1989	2,922,000
Density (per sq km) at mid-1989	57.2

* 19,730 sq miles.
† Excluding adjustment for underenumeration.

PROVINCES (1 January 1989)

	Area (sq km)	Population (estimates)	Capital (with population)
Alajuela	9,753	512,886	Alajuela (150,968)
Cartago	3,125	324,299	Cartago (103,898)
Guanacaste	10,141	232,414	Liberia (34,333)
Heredia	2,656	233,185	Heredia (64,356)
Limón	9,189	206,675	Limón (64,406)
Puntarenas	11,277	321,920	Puntarenas (88,342)
San José	4,960	1,055,611	San José (284,550)
Total	51,100	2,886,990	—

BIRTHS, MARRIAGES AND DEATHS (rates per 1,000)

Births 30.7 in 1986, 28.9 in 1987, 28.5 in 1988, 28.2 in 1989; Marriages 7.8 in 1986, 7.8 in 1987, 8.0 in 1988, 7.4 in 1989; Deaths 3.8 in 1986, 3.8 in 1987, 3.8 in 1988, 3.9 in 1989.

ECONOMICALLY ACTIVE POPULATION
(persons aged 12 years and over, household survey, July 1989)

	Males	Females	Total
Agriculture, hunting, forestry and fishing	248,649	17,308	265,957
Mining and quarrying	1,460	38	1,498
Manufacturing	117,138	73,650	190,788
Electricity, gas and water	10,177	1,779	11,956
Construction	63,700	649	64,349
Trade, restaurants and hotels	103,956	56,604	160,560
Transport, storage and communications	34,315	2,423	36,738
Financing, insurance, real estate and business services	24,981	8,957	33,938
Community, social and personal services	117,304	124,015	241,319
Activities not adequately defined	8,984	1,992	10,976
Unemployed persons not previously employed	2,947	4,522	7,469
Total	733,611	291,937	1,025,548

Agriculture

PRINCIPAL CROPS ('000 metric tons)

	1987	1988	1989
Rice (paddy)	163	196	229
Maize	127	98	103
Beans (dry)	23	28	28
Palm kernels†	10.0	13.0	10.0
Palm oil	47.8†	59.2†	50.0
Sugar cane	3,000	2,730†	2,600*
Bananas*	1,100	1,150	1,250
Coffee (green)	138	145	147
Cocoa beans	4	4	5†

* FAO estimate(s). † Unofficial figure(s).
Source: FAO, *Production Yearbook*.

LIVESTOCK ('000 head, year ending September)

	1987	1988	1989
Horses*	114	114	114
Cattle†	1,836	1,753	1,735
Pigs†	238	223	223

Poultry (million): 5* in 1987; 5* in 1988; 5* in 1989.
* FAO estimate(s). † Unofficial figures.
Source: FAO, *Production Yearbook*.

LIVESTOCK PRODUCTS ('000 metric tons)

	1987	1988	1989
Beef and veal	97	86†	86
Pig meat	10	10	10*
Poultry meat	5†	5†	5*
Cows' milk	410	415*	420*
Cheese*	5.9	5.9	5.9
Butter and ghee*	3.5	3.5	3.5
Hen eggs	13.9†	14.0*	14.5*
Cattle hides (fresh)*	12.2	10.4	10.3

* FAO estimate(s). † Unofficial figures.
Source: FAO, *Production Yearbook*.

Forestry

ROUNDWOOD REMOVALS
('000 cubic metres, excluding bark)

	1986	1987	1988
Sawlogs, veneer logs and logs for sleepers	720	920	941
Pulpwood	8*	4	6
Other industrial wood*	188	193	199
Fuel wood*	2,667	2,744	2,815
Total	3,583	3,861	3,961

* FAO estimate(s).
Source: FAO, *Yearbook of Forest Products*.

COSTA RICA

SAWNWOOD PRODUCTION ('000 cubic metres)

	1986	1987	1988
Coniferous (soft wood)*	12	12	12
Broadleaved (hard wood)	400*	491	503
Total	412*	503	515

* FAO estimate(s).
Source: FAO, *Yearbook of Forest Products*.

Fishing

('000 metric tons, live weight)

	1986	1987*	1988*
Inland waters	0.4	0.5	0.5
Atlantic Ocean	0.3	0.3	0.3
Pacific Ocean	20.3	19.5	19.6
Total catch	21.0	20.3	20.4

* FAO estimates.
Source: FAO, *Yearbook of Fishery Statistics*.

Industry

SELECTED PRODUCTS
('000 metric tons, unless otherwise indicated)

	1985	1986	1987
Cement	475	520*	520
Salt (unrefined)*	30	30	30
Fish (tinned)	2.2	2.1*	2.0*
Palm oil*	40	45	50
Raw sugar*	230	220	230
Cocoa powder (metric tons)	691*	n.a.	n.a.
Cocoa butter (metric tons)	985*	n.a.	n.a.
Cigarettes (million)	2,200	n.a.	n.a.
Nitrogenous fertilizers†	27	32	30
Motor spirit (petrol)	67	114	106
Kerosene	16	10	16
Distillate fuel oils	88	173	158
Residual fuel oils	188	270	237
Bitumen	22	11	14
Electric energy (million kWh)	2,826	2,949	3,133

* Estimates.
† Production in terms of nitrogen.
Source: mainly UN, *Industrial Statistics Yearbook*.

Finance

CURRENCY AND EXCHANGE RATES
Monetary Units
100 céntimos = 1 Costa Rican colón.

Denominations:
Coins: 5, 10, 25 and 50 céntimos; 1, 2, 5, 10 and 20 colones.
Notes: 5, 10, 20, 50, 100, 500 and 1,000 colones.

Sterling and Dollar Equivalents (30 September 1990)
£1 sterling = 179.54 colones;
US $1 = 95.83 colones;
1,000 Costa Rican colones = £5.570 = $10.435.

Average Exchange Rate (colones per US $)
1987   62.776
1988   75.805
1989   81.504

BUDGET (million colones)

Revenue	1987	1988	1989
Taxation	41,383	50,427	61,267
Income tax	6,513	8,036	9,607
Taxes on internal transactions	20,511	27,460	32,539
Export taxes and duties		5,164	6,312
Import taxes and duties	13,414	9,714	12,625
Other taxes on external transactions		53	184
Other revenues	1,503	2,584	1,580
Transfers	1,614	1,190	2,253
Total	44,500	54,201	65,100

Expenditure	1987	1988	1989
Current expenditure	43,630	54,570.6	69,626.6
Consumption expenditure	18,018	23,438.5	28,951.8
Current transfers	17,911	21,572.3	28,134.3
Internal debt servicing	4,391	5,859.8	8,200.5
External debt servicing	3,310	3,700.0	4,340.0
Capital expenditure	6,715	8,464.3	12,803.4
Real investment	2,386	2,764.1	3,193.7
Capital transfers	4,246	5,700.2	9,609.7
Total	50,345	63,034.9	82,430.0

Source: Ministerio de Hacienda.

CENTRAL BANK RESERVES (US $ million at 31 December)

	1987	1988	1989
IMF special drawing rights	0.01	0.01	0.05
Foreign exchange	488.85	667.97	742.52

Source: IMF, *International Financial Statistics*.

MONEY SUPPLY (million colones at 31 December)

	1987	1988	1989
Currency outside banks	14,777	24,734	21,922
Demand deposits at commercial banks	27,624	40,186	41,903

Source: IMF, *International Financial Statistics*.

COST OF LIVING (Consumer Price Index for San José metropolitan area; base: 1975 = 100)

	1987	1988	1989
Food	958.2	1,151.9	1,358.1
Clothing	398.7	466.2	542.7
Rent	615.4	760.3	871.4
Miscellaneous	1,176.5	1,419.1	1,641.5
All items	857.4	1,036.0	1,207.0

COSTA RICA

NATIONAL ACCOUNTS (million colones at current prices)
Expenditure on the Gross Domestic Product

	1987	1988	1989*
Government final consumption expenditure	42,651.8	54,629.6	68,778.7
Private final consumption expenditure	172,824.1	216,375.7	264,843.9
Increase in stocks	25,001.0	23,979.1	25,987.9
Gross fixed capital formation	56,081.7	66,320.0	82,043.1
Total domestic expenditure	296,558.6	361,304.4	441,653.6
Exports of goods and services	90,055.2	122,540.6	147,938.8
Less Imports of goods and services	101,761.2	125,625.8	160,733.7
GDP in purchasers' values	284,852.6	358,219.2	428,858.7
GDP at constant 1966 prices	10,833.4	11,242.9	11,805.0

* Preliminary.

Gross Domestic Product by Economic Activity

	1987	1988	1989*
Agriculture, hunting, forestry and fishing	51,941.7	67,160.7	76,831.8
Mining and quarrying	} 59,985.7	75,222.1	88,837.3
Manufacturing			
Electricity, gas and water	8,591.4	10,223.8	12,513.9
Construction	9,085.6	10.702.9	13,367.9
Trade, restaurants and hotels	58,829.6	72,360.4	86,036.5
Transport, storage and communications	13,990.1	17,445.6	21,213.8
Finance, insurance and business services	19,951.5	26,056.7	31,684.9
Real estate†	11,081.5	14,074.3	17,001.7
Government services	36,254.3	45,970.4	58,796.2
Other services	15,141.2	19,002.3	22,574.7
GDP in purchasers' values	284,852.6	358,219.2	428,858.7

* Preliminary.
† Including imputed rents of owner-occupied dwellings.
Source: Central American Monetary Council, *Boletín Estadístico*.

BALANCE OF PAYMENTS (US $ million)

	1987	1988	1989
Merchandise exports f.o.b.	1,106.7	1,180.7	1,322.7
Merchandise imports f.o.b.	−1,245.2	−1,278.6	−1,577.2
Trade balance	−138.5	−97.9	−254.5
Exports of services	385.6	478.1	568.9
Imports of services	−729.5	−814.1	−857.1
Balance on goods and services	−482.4	−433.9	−542.7
Private unrequited transfers (net)	38.7	40.0	40.1
Government unrequited transfers (net)	67.3	90.4	55.7
Current balance	−376.4	−303.5	−446.9
Direct capital investment (net)	75.8	121.4	114.9
Other long-term capital (net)	−486.9	−348.7	−329.3
Short-term capital (net)	−30.1	−44.6	12.3
Net errors and omissions	131.2	224.6	221.9
Total (net monetary movements)	−686.4	−350.8	−427.1
Monetization of gold (net)	−3.8	−23.1	1.4
Valuation changes (net)	−22.1	6.8	2.6
Exceptional financing (net)	729.2	585.0	576.7
Official financing (net)	−5.5	8.0	−4.2
Changes in reserves	11.4	225.9	149.4

Source: IMF, *International Financial Statistics*.

External Trade

PRINCIPAL COMMODITIES (US $ million)

Imports c.i.f.	1987	1988	1989*
Raw materials for industry	585.5	617.3	764.4
Raw materials for agriculture	63.9	70.5	76.7
Consumer non-durables	189.6	220.0	281.5
Consumer durables	89.5	88.4	112.6
Machinery and equipment	341.3	287.2	358.9
Building materials	35.5	43.2	53.3
Fuels and lubricants	55.2	64.8	75.9
Others	19.7	13.3	19.7
Total	1,380.2	1,404.7	1,743.0

* Preliminary.
Source: Banco Central de Costa Rica.

Exports f.o.b.	1987	1988*	1989*†
Coffee	334.5	316.2	286.2
Bananas	228.6	248.7	270.6
Sugar	15.1	12.4	15.4
Cattle and meat	62.5	53.8	48.7
Shellfish	15.7	n.a.	n.a.
Total (incl. others)	1,106.7	1,215.1	1,403.8

* Preliminary.
† Source: Banco Central de Costa Rica.

PRINCIPAL TRADING PARTNERS (US $ million)

Imports c.i.f.	1987	1988*	1989*
Canada	28.1	23.2	23.1
Colombia	16.6	24.2	17.7
El Salvador	34.0	36.0	44.3
Germany, Federal Republic	73.8	60.3	71.1
Guatemala	64.6	65.0	74.4
Italy	26.7	25.3	37.6
Japan	117.0	94.4	116.2
Mexico	69.3	84.5	97.6
Netherlands	22.1	17.5	15.8
Panama	24.5	26.5	34.3
United Kingdom	22.1	24.0	26.1
USA	511.1	547.1	699.4
Venezuela	96.2	102.1	144.6
Total (incl. others)	1,380.2	1,409.8	1,743.0

* Preliminary.
Source: Banco Central de Costa Rica.

Exports f.o.b.	1987	1988*	1989*
Belgium/Luxembourg	10.8	10.7	28.5
Canada	18.8	28.0	53.9
El Salvador	36.5	43.5	46.6
Finland	24.0	16.6	15.2
Germany, Federal Republic	168.2	173.3	183.3
Guatemala	43.6	55.3	60.1
Honduras	17.5	14.3	15.2
Italy	33.2	52.4	65.3
Netherlands	30.4	35.5	33.3
Nicaragua	12.1	16.7	23.4
Panama	48.5	35.1	40.9
United Kingdom	24.9	26.8	31.8
USA	512.7	502.9	533.9
Total (incl. others)	1,158.3	1,270.2	1,403.8

* Preliminary.
Source: Banco Central de Costa Rica.

COSTA RICA

Transport

RAILWAYS

	1982	1983	1984
Passenger journeys	2,397,147	2,508,959	2,000,933

Source: Ministry of Public Works and Transport.

ROAD TRAFFIC (motor vehicles in use at 31 December)

	1982	1983	1984
Cars and jeeps	91,350	101,251	106,233
Lorries	62,309	62,363	63,350
Buses	3,640	3,310	3,315
Industrial vehicles	10,322	10,812	11,109
Motor cycles	33,979	32,308	33,317
Total	201,600	210,044	217,324

1985: Cars and jeeps 109,802; Lorries 65,974; Buses 3,573.
Source: Ministry of Public Works and Transport.

INTERNATIONAL SEA-BORNE SHIPPING
(freight traffic, '000 metric tons)

	1983	1984	1985
Goods loaded	1,406	1,600	1,532
Goods unloaded	1,542	1,500	1,653

Source: UN, *Statistical Yearbook*.

CIVIL AVIATION

	1987	1988	1989
Passengers:			
Domestic	50,236	69,574	86,633
International	707,910	730,090	825,623
Freight (metric tons):			
Domestic	74,539	57,034	155,401
International	36,960	44,827	59,874

Source: Ministry of Public Works and Transport.

Tourism

	1987	1988	1989
Visitors	227,861	329,386	375,951
Revenue (US $ '000)	136,300	164,700	206,600

Source: Instituto Costarricense de Turismo.

Education

(1988)

	Institutions	Teachers	Pupils
Primary	3,196	12,834	409,322
Secondary	216	6,658	118,331

1989: Primary: 3,234 institutions, 422,102 pupils; Secondary: 218 institutions, 123,052 pupils.

Source: Ministry of Public Education.

Directory

The Constitution

The present Constitution of Costa Rica was promulgated in November 1949. Its main provisions are summarized below:

GOVERNMENT

The government is unitary: provincial and local bodies derive their authority from the national Government. The country is divided into seven Provinces, each administered by a Governor who is appointed by the President. The Provinces are divided into Cantons, and each Canton into Districts. There is an elected Municipal Council in the chief city of each Canton, the number of its members being related to the population of the Canton. The Municipal Council supervises the affairs of the Canton. Municipal government is closely regulated by national law, particularly in matters of finance.

LEGISLATURE

The government consists of three branches: legislative, executive and judicial. Legislative power is vested in a single chamber, the Legislative Assembly, which meets in regular session twice a year—from 1 May to 31 July, and from 1 September to 30 November. Special sessions may be convoked by the President to consider specified business. The Assembly is composed of 57 deputies elected for four years. The chief powers of the Assembly are to enact laws, levy taxes, authorize declarations of war and, by a two-thirds vote, suspend, in cases of civil disorder, certain civil liberties guaranteed in the Constitution.

Bills may be initiated by the Assembly or by the Executive and must have three readings, in at least two different legislative periods, before they become law. The Assembly may override the presidential vote by a two-thirds vote.

EXECUTIVE

The executive branch is headed by the President, who is assisted by the Cabinet. If the President should resign or be incapacitated, the executive power is entrusted to the First Vice-President; next in line to succeed to executive power are the Second Vice-President and the President of the Legislative Assembly.

The President sees that the laws and the provisions of the Constitution are carried out, and maintains order; has power to appoint and remove Cabinet ministers and diplomatic representatives, and to negotiate treaties with foreign nations (which are, however, subject to ratification by the Legislative Assembly). The President is assisted in these duties by a Cabinet, each member of which is head of an executive department.

ELECTORATE

Suffrage is universal, compulsory and secret for persons over the age of 18 years.

DEFENCE

A novel feature of the Costa Rican Constitution is the clause outlawing a national army. Only by a continental convention or for the purpose of national defence may a military force be organized.

The Government

HEAD OF STATE

President: Rafael Angel Calderón Fournier (took office 8 May 1990).

First Vice-President (responsible for social issues): Germán Serrano.

COSTA RICA

Second Vice-President (responsible for economic issues): ARNOLDO LÓPEZ ECHANDI.

THE CABINET
(December 1990)

Minister of the Presidency: RODOLFO MÉNDEZ MATA.
Minister of Foreign Affairs: BERND NIEHAUS QUESADA.
Minister of the Interior and Police: LUIS FISHMAN.
Minister of Finance: Prof. THELMÓ VARGAS.
Minister of Labour: CARLOS MONGE RODRÍGUEZ.
Minister of Social Welfare: Dr ELIAS JIMÉNEZ FONSECA.
Minister of Science and Technology: ORLANDO MORALES.
Minister of Health: CARLOS CASTRO CHARPANTIER.
Minister of Public Works and Transport: GUILLERMO MADRIZ DE MEZERVILLE.
Minister of Public Security: VÍCTOR EMILIO HERRERA ALFARO.
Minister of Agriculture and Livestock: JUAN RAFAEL LIZANO SÁENZ.
Minister of Public Education: MARVIN HERRERA ARAYA.
Minister of Economy, Industry and Trade: GONZALES FAJARDO SALAS.
Minister of Natural Resources, Energy and Mines: HERNÁN BRAVO TREJOS.
Minister of Culture, Youth and Sport: AIDA FISHMAN.
Minister of National Planning and Economic Policy: Dr HELIO FALLAS.
Minister of Housing and Urban Development: CRISTÓBAL ZAWADZSKI.
Minister of Foreign Trade: ROBERTO ROJAS LÓPEZ.
Minister of State Restructuring: JOHNNY MEOÑO.
Minister of Justice: ELIZABETH ODIO BENITO.
Minister of Information: (vacant).
Minister of Tourism: LUIS MANUEL CHACÓN JIMÉNEZ.
President of the Central Bank: JORGE GUARDIA.

MINISTRIES

Ministry of Agriculture and Livestock: Apdo 10.094, 1000 San José; tel. 32-4496; telex 3558.
Ministry of Culture, Youth and Sport: Apdo 10.227, 1000 San José; tel. 23-1658; fax 33-7066.
Ministry of Economy, Industry and Trade: Apdo 10.216, 1000 San José; tel. 22-1016; telex 2414; fax 22-2305.
Ministry of Finance: Apdo 5.016, San José; tel. 22-2481; telex 2277; fax 33-8267.
Ministry of Foreign Affairs: Apdo 10.027, 1000 San José; tel. 23-7555; telex 2107; fax 23-9328.
Ministry of Foreign Trade: La Llacuna 12°, Avda Central, Calle 5, San José; tel. 22-5910; telex 2936; fax 33-5090.
Ministry of Health: Apdo 10.123, 1000 San José; tel. 33-0683; fax 55-4997.
Ministry of Housing and Urban Development: Paseo Estudiantes, Apdo 222, 1002 San José; tel. 33-3665.
Ministry of the Interior and Police: Apdo 10.006, 1000 San José; tel. 23-8354; telex 3434; fax 22-7726.
Ministry of Justice: Apdo 5.685, 1000 San José; tel. 23-9739.
Ministry of Labour and Social Welfare: Apdo 10.133, 1000 San José; tel. 21-0238.
Ministry of National Planning and Economic Policy: Avda 3 y 5, Calle 4, San José; tel. 21-9524; telex 2962; fax 53-6243.
Ministry of Natural Resources, Energy and Mines: Avda 8–10, Calle 25, Apdo 10.104, 1000 San José; tel. 57-1417; telex 2363; fax 57-0697.
Ministry of the Presidency: Apdo 520, 2010 Zapote, San José; tel. 24-4092; telex 2106; fax 53-2064.
Ministry of Public Education: Apdo 10.087, 1000 San José; tel. 22-0229; fax 55-2868.
Ministry of Public Security: Apdo 4.768, 1000 San José; tel. 26-0093; telex 3308.
Ministry of Public Works and Transport: Apdo 10.176, San José; tel. 26-7311; telex 2478; fax 27-1434.
Ministry of Science and Technology: Apdo 10.318, 1000 San José; tel. 50-7110; telex 2229; fax 24-8295.
Ministry of State Restructuring: San José; fax 23-7858.
Ministry of Tourism: Edif. Genaro Valverde, Calles 5 y 7, Avda 4a, Apdo 777-1000, San José; tel. 33-9605; telex 2281; fax 55-4997.

President and Legislature

PRESIDENT

Presidential Election, 4 February 1990

Candidates	Percentage of votes cast
RAFAEL ANGEL CALDERÓN FOURNIER (PUSC)	51.3
CARLOS MANUEL CASTILLO (PLN)	47.2
VÍCTOR CAMACHO (PU)	
FERNANDO RAMÍREZ (ANC)	
ISAAC FELIPE AZOFEIFA (PP)	1.5
EDWIN BADILLA (PRT)	
RODRIGO CORDERO (PI)	

ASAMBLEA LEGISLATIVA

President: Lic. JUAN JOSÉ TREJOS FONSECA.

General Election, 4 February 1990

Party	Seats
Partido Unidad Social Cristiana (PUSC)	29
Partido de Liberación Nacional (PLN)	25
Partido Unión Generaleña	1
Vanguardia Popular (Communist)	1
Acción Agrícola Cartaginesa	1
Total	**57**

Political Organizations

Acción del Pueblo (AP): San José; Pres. ANGEL RUÍZ ZÚÑIGA; Sec. HENRY MORA JIMÉNEZ.

Acción Agrícola Cartaginesa: Cartago; provincial party; Pres. JUAN BRENES CASTILLO; Sec. RODRIGO FALLAS BONILLA.

Acción Democrática Alajuelense: Alajuela; provincial party; Pres. FRANCISCO ALFARO FERNÁNDEZ; Sec. JUAN BAUTISTA CHACÓN SOTO.

Alianza Nacional Cristiana (ANC): Pres. VÍCTOR HUGO GONZÁLEZ MONTERO; Sec. JUAN RODRÍGUEZ VENEGAS.

Coalición Pueblo Unido (PU): Calle 4, Avda 7 y 9, San José; tel. 23-0032; Sec. ALBERTO SALOM ECHEVERRÍA; left-wing coalition comprising:

    Partido del Pueblo Costarricense: Apdo 6.613, 1000 San José; tel. 22-5517; f. 1931; communist; Sec.-Gen. LENIN CHACÓN VARGAS.

    Partido Socialista Costarricense: San José; socialist; Pres. ALVARO MONTERO MEJÍA; Sec. ALBERTO SALOM ECHEVERRÍA.

    Partido de los Trabajadores: San José; Maoist; Pres. JOHNNY FRANCISCO ARAYA MONGE; Sec. ILSE ACOSTA POLONIO.

Movimiento Nacional (MN): San José; Pres. MARIO ECHANDI JIMÉNEZ; Sec. RODRIGO SANCHO ROBLES.

Partido Alajuelita Nueva: Alajuelita Centro, 100W Escuela Abraham Lincoln, San José; tel. 27-9527; telex 3076; f. 1981; Pres. CARLOS RETANA RETANA; Sec. WILLIAM CASTRO BADILLA.

Partido Auténtico Limonense: Limón; provincial party; Pres. MARVIN WRIGHT LINDO; Sec. GUILLERMO JOSEPH WIGNALL.

Partido Concordia Costarricense: Calle 2 y 4, Avda 10, San José; tel. 23-2497; Pres. EMILIO PIEDRA JIMÉNEZ; Sec. ROBERTO FRANCISCO SALAZAR MADRIZ.

Partido Independiente (PI): San José; Pres. EUGENIO JIMÉNEZ SANCHO; Sec. GONZALO JIMÉNEZ CHAVES.

Partido de Liberación Nacional (PLN): Sabana Oeste, San José; tel. 31-4022; f. 1948; social democratic party; affiliated to the Socialist International; 400,000 mems; Pres. (vacant); Sec.-Gen. WALTER COTO MOLINA.

Partido Nacional Democrático: San José; Pres. RODOLFO CERDAS CRUZ; Sec. ELADIO JARA JIMÉNEZ.

Partido Revolucionario de los Trabajadores (PRT): San José; worker's revolutionary party.

Partido Radical Demócrata: San José; Pres. JUAN JOSÉ ECHEVERRÍA BREALEY; Sec. RODRIGO ESQUIVEL RODRÍGUEZ.

Partido Republicano Nacional: San José; Pres. DELFINO RODRÍGUEZ VARELA; Sec. FERNANDO PEÑA HERRERA.

COSTA RICA
Directory

Partido Unidad Social Cristiana (PUSC): San José; Pres. Mario Quintana; Sec. Danilo Chaverri.

Partido Unión Generaleña: Pérez Zeledón, Apdo 440-8.000, San José; tel. 71-0524; f. 1981; Pres. Dr Carlos A. Fernández Vega; Sec. Hugo Sáenz Marín.

Partido Unión Nacional: San José; Pres. Olga Marta Ulate Rojas; Sec. Rodrigo González Saborío.

The following party is in suspension:

Acción Socialista: San José; Pres. Marcial Aguiluz Orellana; Sec. Arnoldo Ferreto Segura.

The following guerrilla groups are active:

Ejército del Pueblo Costarricense (EPC): f. 1984; right-wing.

Patria y Libertad: f. 1985.

Diplomatic Representation

EMBASSIES IN COSTA RICA

Argentina: Calle 27, Avda Central, Apdo 1.963, San José; tel. 21-3438; telex 2117; Ambassador: Rubén Antonio Vela.

Belgium: 4a, entrada de Los Yoses, Apdo 3.725, 1000 San José; tel. 25-6255; telex 2909; Ambassador: Baron Pangaert d'Opdorp.

Brazil: Edif. Plaza de la Artillería 7°, Calle 4, Avda Central y 1, Apdo 10.132, San José; tel. 23-4325; telex 2270; Ambassador: R. B. Denys.

Bulgaria: Edif. Delcoré 3°, 100 metros Sur Hotel Balmoral, Apdo 4.752, San José; Ambassador: Kiril Zlatkov Nikolov.

Canada: Edif. Cronos 6°, Avda Central, Calle 3, Apdo 10.303, San José; tel. 23-0446; telex 2179; Ambassador: Stanley E. Gooch.

Chile: De la Pulpería La Luz 125 metros Norte, Casa 116, Apdo 10.102, San José; tel. 24-4243; telex 2207; Ambassador: Pedro Palacios Camerón.

China (Taiwan): Edif. Mendiola 3°, Avda Central 917, Apdo 907, San José; tel. 21-3752; telex 2174; Ambassador: Shao Hsioh-Kwen.

Colombia: Apdo 3.154, 1000 San José; tel. 21-0725; telex 2918; fax 55-1705; Ambassador: María Cristina Zuleta de Patiño.

Czechoslovakia: 200 metros sur del Rótulo de la Plaza del Sol, Residencial El Prado, Carretera a Curridabat, Apdo 3.910, 1000 San José; telex 2323; Chargé d'affaires a.i.: Ing. Václav Malý.

Dominican Republic: Frente costado al norte de la Nunciatura Apostólica, Barrio Rohrmoser, Apdo 4.746, San José; telex 3210; Ambassador: José Marcos Iglesias Iñigo.

Ecuador: Edif. de la esquina sureste del Museo Nacional, 125 metros al este, Avda 2°, entre calles 19 y 21, Apdo 1.374, 1000 San José; tel. 23-6281; telex 2601; Ambassador: Lic. Andrés Córdova Galarza.

El Salvador: Edif. Trianón 3°, Avda Central y Calle 5a, Apdo 1.378, San José; tel. 22-5536; telex 2641; Ambassador: Carlos Matamoros Guirola.

France: Carretera a Curridabat Del Indoor Club, 200 al Sur y 25 al Oeste, Apdo 10.177, San José; tel. 25-0733; telex 2191; Ambassador: Daniel Guilhou.

Germany: de la Residencia de España 200 metros al norte, 50 metros al oeste, Apdo 4.017, 1000 San José; tel. 32-5533; telex 2183; fax 31-6403; Ambassador Dr Dieter Zeisler.

Guatemala: Avda Primera detrás Más y Menos del Paseo Colón, Avda 2, Apdo 328-1000, San José; tel. 31-6654; fax 31-6645; Ambassador: Lic. Ramiro Leal E.

Holy See: Urbanización Rohrmoser, Sabana Oeste, Apdo 992, Centro Colón, San José (Apostolic Nunciature); tel. 32-2128; Apostolic Nuncio: Most Rev. Pier Giacomo De Nicolò, Titular Archbishop of Martana.

Honduras: Edif. Jiménez de la Guardia 2°, Calle 1, Avda 5, Apdo 2.239, San José; tel. 22-2145; telex 2784; Ambassador: Edgardo Sevilla Idiaquez.

Israel: Calle 2, Avdas 2 y 4, Apdo 5.147, San José; tel. 21-6444; telex 2258; Ambassador: Shimon Moratt.

Italy: 5° entrada del Barrio Los Yoses, Apdo 1.729, San José; tel. 24-6574; telex 2769; Ambassador: Dr Rosario Guido Nicosia.

Japan: De la 1a entrada del Barrio Rohrmoser (Sabana Oeste) 500 metros y 100 Norte, Apdos 501 y 10.145, San José; tel. 32-1255; telex 2205; Ambassador: Hiroyuki Kimoto.

Korea, Republic: Calle 28, Avda 2, Barrio San Bosco, Apdo 3.150, San José; tel. 21-2398; telex 2512; Ambassador: Jae Hoon Kim.

Mexico: Avda 7, No 1371, Apdo 10.107, San José; tel. 22-5485; telex 2218; fax 22-6080; Ambassador: Jesús Cabrera Muñoz Ledo.

Netherlands: 2a entrada de Los Yoses, 100 metros al sur, Avda 8, Calle 37, Apdo 10.285, San José; tel. 25-3516; telex 2187; Ambassador: Jan-Willem Bertens.

Nicaragua: Edif. Trianón, Calle 25 y 27, Avda Central, San José; tel. 22-4749; telex 2316; Ambassador: Claudia Chamorro Barrios.

Panama: 200 metros al sur, 25 metros al este de Higueron, La Granja, San Pedro de Montes de Oco, San José; tel. 25-3401; Ambassador: Walter Myers.

Peru: Del Automercado de Los Yoses, 300 Sur y 75 oeste, Apdo 4.248, 1000 San José; tel. 25-9145; telex 3515; fax 53-0457; Ambassador: Enrique Rivero Vélez.

Romania: Urbanización Rohrmoser, frente al costado este del Parque La Favorita, Apdo 10.321, San José; tel. 31-0813; telex 2337; Ambassador: Nicolae Turturea.

Spain: c/32, Paseo Colón, Avda 2, Apdo 10.150, 1000 San José; tel. 221-1933; telex 2438; Ambassador: J. A. Ortiz Ramos.

Switzerland: Paseo Colón, Centro Colón, Apdo 895, San José; tel. 21-4829; telex 2512; Ambassador: Dr Johann Bucher.

USSR: Apdo 6.340, San José; tel. 25-5780; telex 2299; Ambassador: Yuri Pavlov.

United Kingdom: Edif. Centro Colón 11°, Apdo 815, 1007 San José; tel. 21-5566; telex 2169; fax 33-9938; Ambassador: William Marsden.

USA: Pavas Frente Centro Comercial, Apdo 920-1200 Pavas, San José; tel. 20-3939; fax 20-2305; Ambassador: Deane R. Hinton.

Uruguay: Calle 2, Avda 1, San José; tel. 23-2512; Ambassador: Jorge Justo Boero-Brian.

Venezuela: Avda Central 5a entrada Los Yoses, Apdo 10.230, San José; tel. 25-5813; telex 2413; Ambassador: Dr Francisco Salazar Martínez.

Yugoslavia: Calles 30 y 32, Paseo Colón, San José; tel. 22-0619; Ambassador: (vacant).

Judicial System

Ultimate judicial power is vested in the Supreme Court, the 17 justices of which are elected by the Assembly for a term of eight years, and are automatically re-elected for an equal period, unless the Assembly decides to the contrary by a two-thirds vote. Judges of the lower courts are appointed by the Supreme Court in plenary session.

The Supreme Court may also meet as the Corte Plena, with power to declare laws and decrees unconstitutional. There are also four appellate courts, criminal courts, civil courts and special courts. The jury system is not used.

La Corte Suprema: Apdo 01, 1000 San José; tel. 23-0666; telex 1548.

President of the Supreme Court: Miguel Blanco Quirós.

Religion

Under the Constitution, all forms of worship are tolerated. Roman Catholicism is the official religion of the country. Various Protestant Churches are represented. There are an estimated 7,000 members of the Methodist Church.

CHRISTIANITY
The Roman Catholic Church

Costa Rica comprises one archdiocese, three dioceses and one Apostolic Vicariate. At 31 December 1988 there were an estimated 2,620,000 adherents in the country, representing about 85% of the total population.

Bishops' Conference: Conferencia Episcopal de Costa Rica, Arzobispado, Apdo 497, San José; tel. 21-0947; f. 1977; Pres. Román Arrieta Villalobos, Archbishop of San José de Costa Rica.

Archbishop of San José de Costa Rica: Román Arrieta Villalobos, Arzobispado, Apdo 497, 1000 San José; tel. 21-7692.

The Episcopal Church

Bishop of Costa Rica: Rt Rev. Cornelius Joshua Wilson, Apdo 2773, 1000 San José; tel. 25-0209.

Other Churches

Baptist Convention of Costa Rica: Apdo 1631-2100, Guadalupe; tel. 53-4723; fax 27-0211; f. 1946; Pres. Rev. Carlos Alfaro H.; Sec. Julieta Chinchilla de Badilla.

Iglesia Evangélica Metodista de Costa Rica (Evangelical Methodist Church of Costa Rica): Apdo 5.481, 1000 San José; tel. 36-2171;

COSTA RICA
Directory

autonomous since 1973; 6,000 mems; Pres. Bishop ROBERTO DÍAZ C.

BAHÁ'Í FAITH
Bahá'í Information Centre: Apdo 3.751, 1000 San José; tel. 22-5335; telex 1050; adherents resident in 242 localities.

The Press

General Directorate of Information and the Press: Presidential House, Apdo 520, Zapote, San José; tel. 25-6205; telex 2376; Dir Lic. LIDIETTE BRENES DE CHARPENTIER.

DAILIES

Boletín Judicial: La Uruca, Apdo 5.024, San José; tel. 31-5222; f. 1878; journal of the judiciary; Dir ISAÍAS CASTRO VARGAS; circ. 2,500.

Diario Extra: Calle 4, Avda 4, Apdo 177, 1.009 San José; tel. 23-9505; fax 23-6101; f. 1978; morning; independent; Dir WILLIAM GÓMEZ; circ. 100,000.

La Gaceta: La Uruca, Apdo 5.024, San José; tel. 31-5222; f. 1878; official gazette; Dir ISAÍAS CASTRO VARGAS; circ. 5,300.

La Nación: Llorente de Tibás, Apdo 10.138, San José; tel. 40-4848; telex 2358; fax 40-6480; f. 1946; morning; independent; Dir EDUARDO ULIBARRI; circ. 90,000.

La Prensa Libre: Calle 4, Avda 4, Apdo 10.121, San José; tel. 23-6666; f. 1889; evening; independent; Dir ANDRÉS BORRASÉ SANOU; circ. 50,000.

La República: Barrio Tournón, Goicoechea, Apdo 2.130, San José; tel. 23-0266; fax 55-3950; f. 1950, reorganized 1967; morning; independent; Dir Lic. JOAQUÍN VARGAS GENE; circ. 60,000.

PERIODICALS

Abanico: Calle 4, esq. Avda 4, Apdo 10.121, San José; tel. 23-6666; weekly supplement of *La Prensa Libre*; women's interests; Editor GUISELLE BORRASÉ; circ. 50,000.

Acta Médica: Sabana Sur, Apdo 548, San José; tel. 32-3433; f. 1954; organ of the Colegio de Médicos; 3 issues per year; Editor Dr BAUDILIO MORA MORA; circ. 2,000.

Contrapunto: La Uruca, Apdo 7-1.980, San José; tel. 31-3333; f. 1978; fortnightly; publication of Sistema Nacional de Radio y Televisión; Dir FABIO MUÑOZ CAMPOS; circ. 10,000.

Eco Católico: Avda 10, Calles 5 y 7, Apdo 1.064, San José; tel. 22-5903; f. 1931; Catholic weekly; Dir ARMANDO ALFARO; circ. 20,000.

Mujer y Hogar: Avda 15, Casa 1916, Apdo 89, Barrio Aránjuez, San José; tel. 36-3128; f. 1943; weekly; women's journal; Editor and Gen. Man. CARMEN CORNEJO MÉNDEZ; circ. 15,000.

Noticiero del Café: Calle 1, Avdas 18 y 20, Apdo 37, San José; tel. 22-6411; telex 2279; f. 1964; monthly; coffee journal; owned by the Instituto del Café; Dir ROCÍO BOGANTES MADRIGAL; circ. 5,500.

Perfil: Llorente de Tibás, Apdo 10.138, San José, 1000; tel. 35-1211; telex 2358; fax 36-6485; fortnightly; women's interest; Dir PATRICIA DE LIBERMAN; circ. 24,500.

Polémica: Icadis, Paseo de los Estudiantes, Apdo 1.006, San José; tel. 33-3964; f. 1981; every 4 months; left-wing; Dir GABRIEL AGUILERA PERALTA.

Primera Plana: Sabana Este, San José; tel. 55-1590.

Rumbo: Llorente de Tibás, Apdo 10.138, 1000 San José; tel. 40-4848; telex 2358; fax 40-6480; f. 1984; weekly; general; Dir ROXANA ZÚÑIGA; circ. 15,000.

San José News: Apdo 7-2.730, San José; 2 a week; Dir CHRISTIAN RODRÍGUEZ.

Semanario Libertad: Apdo 6.613, Calle 4, Avda 8 y 10, 1000 San José; tel. 23-7651; f. 1962; weekly; organ of the Partido del Pueblo Costarricense; Dir RODOLFO ULLOA B.; Editor JOSÉ A. ZÚÑIGA; circ. 10,000.

Semanario Universidad: Ciudad Universitaria Rodrigo Facio, San Pedro Montes de Oca, Apdo 24-6661; telex 2544; fax 34-2723; f. 1970; weekly; general; Dir Lic. CARLOS MORALES CASTRO; circ. 15,000.

The Tico Times: Calle 15, Avda 8, Apdo 4.632, San José; tel. 22-0040; weekly; in English; Dir RICHARD DYER; circ. 12,000.

PRESS ASSOCIATIONS

Colegio de Periodistas de Costa Rica: Sabana Este, Calle 42, Avda 4, Apdo 5.416, San José; tel. 33-5850; fax 23-8669; f. 1969; 550 mems; Exec. Dir Licda ADRIANA NÚÑEZ.

Sindicato Nacional de Periodistas: Sabana Este, Calle 42, Avda 4, Apdo 5.416, San José; tel. 22-7589; f. 1970; 105 mems; Sec.-Gen. BERNI QUIRÓS HERRERA.

FOREIGN NEWS BUREAUX

ACAN-EFE (Central America): Costado Sur, Casa Matute Gómez, Casa 1912, Apdo 84.930, San José; tel. 22-6785; telex 3197; Correspondent WILFREDO CHACÓN SERRANO.

Agence France-Presse (France): Calle 13, entre Avdas 9 y 11 bis, Apdo 5.276, San José; tel. 33-0757; telex 2403; Correspondent DOMINIQUE PETTIT.

Agencia EFE (Spain): Avda 10, Calles 19 y 21, No 1912, Apdo 84.930, San José; tel. 22-6785; telex 3197.

Agenzia Nazionale Stampa Associata (ANSA) (Italy): c/o Diario la República, Barrio Tournón, Guadalupe, Apdo 2.130, San José; tel. 23-0840; telex 2538; Correspondent YEHUDI MONESTEL ARCE.

Associated Press (AP) (USA): San José; tel. 21-6146; Correspondent REID MILLER.

Deutsche Presse-Agentur (dpa) (Germany): Edif. Trifami, Of. 606, Calle 2, Avda 1, Apdo 7.156, San José; tel. 33-0604; Correspondent ERNESTO RAMÍREZ.

Informatsionnoye Agentstvo Novosti (IAN) (USSR): De la Casa Italiana 100 Este, 50 Norte, Apdo 1.011, San José; tel. 24-1560; telex 2711.

Inter Press Service (IPS) (Italy): Calle 11 entre Avda 1 y 3, No 152, Paseo de los Estudiantes, Apdo 70, 1002 San José; tel. 33-6952; telex 3239; fax 33-8583; Correspondent MARCO ANTONIO SIBAJA.

Prensa Latina: Avda 11, No 3185, e/31 y 33, Barrio Escalante (de la parrillada 25 al oeste), San José; tel. 53-1457; Correspondent FRANCISCO A. URIZARRI TAMAYO.

Telegrafnoye Agentstvo Sovetskovo Soyuza (TASS) (USSR): De la Casa Italia 1000 Este, 50 Norte, Casa 675, Apdo 1.011, San José; tel. 24-1560; telex 2711; Correspondent ENRIQUE MORA.

United Press International (UPI) (USA): Calle 15, Avda 2, Radioperiódicos Reloj, Apdo 4.334, San José; tel. 22-2644; Correspondent WILLIAM CESPEDES CHAVARRÍA.

Xinhua (New China) News Agency (People's Republic of China): Apdo 4.774, San José; tel. 31-3497; telex 3066; Correspondent XU BIHUA.

Publishers

Alfalit Internacional: Apdo 292, 4050 Alajuela; f. 1961; educational; Dirs GILBERTO BERNAL, OSMUNDO PONCE.

Antonio Lehmann Librería, Imprenta y Litografía, Ltda: Calles 1 y 3, Avda Central, Apdo 10.011, San José; tel. 23-1212; telex 2540; f. 1896; general fiction, educational, textbooks; Man. Dir ANTONIO LEHMANN STRUVE.

Editorial Caribe: Apdo 1.307, San José; tel. 22-7244; f. 1949; religious textbooks; Dir JOHN STROWEL.

Editorial Costa Rica: Calle 1A, Avda 18, Apdo 10.010, San José; tel. 23-4875; f. 1959; government-owned; cultural; Gen. Man. HABIB SUCCAR GUZMÁN.

Editorial Fernández Arce: Apdo 6.523, 1000 San José; tel. 21-6321; f. 1967; textbooks for primary, secondary and university education; Dir Dr MARIO FERNÁNDEZ LOBO.

Editorial Texto Ltda: Calle 26, Avdas 3, Apdo 2.988, 1000 San José; tel. 55-3106; f. 1963; Dir FRANK THOMAS GALLARDO; Asst Man. FRANK THOMAS ECHEVERRÍA.

Editorial de la Universidad Autónoma de Centroamérica (UACA): Apdo 7.637, 1000 San José; tel. 23-5822; fax 24-0391; f. 1981; Dir RODOLFO PIZA R.

Editorial de la Universidad Estatal a Distancia (EUNED): Plaza González Víquez, Apdo 474, 2050 San José; tel. 23-5430; telex 3003; f. 1979; Dir CARLOS ALBERTO ARCE.

Editorial Universitaria Centroamericana (EDUCA): Apdo 64, Ciudad Universitaria Rodrigo Facio, 2060 San José; tel. 25-8740; telex 3011; f. 1969; organ of the CSUCA; science, art, philosophy; Editorial Dir CARMEN NARANJO.

Mesen Editores: Apdo 146-2.400, Desamparados, San José; tel. 59-2455; f. 1978; general; Dir DENNIS MESÉN SEGURA.

Trejos Hermanos Sucs, SA: Curridabat, Apdo 10.096, San José; tel. 24-2411; telex 2875; f. 1912; general and reference; Man. ALVARO TREJOS.

ASSOCIATION

Cámara Costarricense del Libro: San José; Pres. Luis FERNANDO CALVO FALLAS.

COSTA RICA
Directory

Radio and Television

In 1987 there were an estimated 720,000 radio receivers and 220,000 television receivers in use.

Control Nacional de Radio: Dirección Nacional de Comunicaciones, Ministerio de Gobernación y Policia, Apdo 8.000, 1000 San José; tel. 25-7364; f. 1954; governmental supervisory department; Dir WARREN MURILLO MARTÍNEZ.

Cámara Nacional de Medios de Comunicación Colectiva (CANAMECC): Apdo 6574, 1000 San José; tel. 22-4820; f. 1954; Pres. RICARDO GONZÁLEZ VARGAS.

Cámara Nacional de Radio (CANARA): Apdo 1583, 1002 San José; tel. 33-1845; f. 1947; Pres. RIGOBERTO URBINA PINTO.

Asociación Costarricense para Información y Cultura (ACIC): San José; f. 1983; independent body; controls private radio stations; Pres. EUGENIO PIGNATARO PACHECO.

RADIO
Non-commercial

Faro del Caribe: Apdo 2.710, 1000 San José; tel. 26-2618; f. 1948; call letters TIFC; religious and cultural programmes in Spanish and English; Man. JUAN JACINTO OCHOA F.

Radio Costa Rica: Apdo 365, 1009 San José; tel. 27-4693; f. 1985; broadcasts Voice of America news bulletins (in Spanish) and locally-produced educational and entertainment programmes; Pres. ALVARO RAMOS.

Radio Fides: Avda 4, Curia Metropolitana, Apdo 5.079, 1000 San José; tel. 22-1252; f. 1952; Roman Catholic station; Dir Fr JORGE LUIS CAMPOS.

Radio Santa Clara: Santa Clara, San Carlos, Ciudad Quesada, Alajuela; tel. 47-1264; f. 1986; Roman Catholic station; Dir Fr MARCO A. SOLÍS V.

Radio Universidad de Costa Rica: Ciudad Universitaria Rodrigo Facio, San José; tel. 25-3936; f. 1949; classical music; Dir JOSÉ TASIES SOLÍS.

Commercial

There are about 40 commercial radio stations, including:

Cadena de Emisoras Columbia: Apdo 708-1000, San José; tel. 34-0355; fax 25-9275; operates Radio Columbia, Radio Uno, Radio Sabrosa, Radio Puntarenas; Dir RAÚL QUESADA M.

Cadena Musical: POB 13, Moravia 2150, San José; tel. 35-9733; fax 36-1954; f. 1954; operates Radio Musical, Radio Emperador; Gen. Man. JORGE JAVIER CASTRO.

Circuito Radial Titania: Apdo 10.279, San José; tel. 22-6033; operates Radio Titania and Radio Sensación; Dir MARIO SOTELA.

Grupo Centro: Apdo 6.133, San José; tel. 35-4509; operates Radio Centro, Radio Turrialba, Radio W Liberia, Radio W San Isidro, Canal 28 de Televisión; Dir ROBERTO HERNÁNDEZ RAMÍREZ.

Radio Chorotega: Santa Cruz de Guanacaste, Apdo 92; tel. 68-0447; f. 1983; Roman Catholic station; Dir Fr HÉCTOR ARAYA MADRIGAL.

Radio Emaus: San Vito de Coto Brus; tel. 77-3101; f. 1962; Roman Catholic station; Dir Mgr ALVARO COTO OROZCO.

Radio Fundación: Apdo 4.057, 1000 San José; tel. 59-1213; operated by the Fundación 'Ciudadelas de Libertad' to promote educational and cultural development; Man. VÍCTOR BERMÚDEZ MORA.

Radio Monumental/Radio Linda: Apdo 800, San José; tel. 22-0000; f. 1929; all news station; Dir NORA RUÍZ DE ANGULO.

Radio Sinai: Apdo 262-8000, San Isidro de El General; tel. 71-0367; f. 1957; Roman Catholic station; Dir Mgr ALVARO COTO OROZCO.

Sistema Radiofónico: Apdo 341, San José; tel. 22-4344; operates Radio Reloj and Radio Sonido 1120; Dir RÓGER BARAHONA GÓMEZ.

TELEVISION
Government-owned

Sistema Nacional de Radio y Televisión Cultural (SINART): Apdo 7-1.980, San José; tel. 31-0839; telex 2374; cultural; Dir-Gen. NELSON BRENES LÓPEZ.

Commercial

Canal 2: Apdo 2.860, San José; tel. 31-2222; Pres. RAMÓN COLL MONTERO.

Corporación Costarricense de Televisión (Canal 6): Apdo 1.860, San José; tel. 32-9255; telex 2443; Gen. Man. MARIO SOTELA BLEN.

Multivisión de Costa Rica (Canal 4): Apdo 4.666, San José; tel. 33-4444; telex 3043; operates Radio Sistema Universal A.M. (f. 1956), Channel 9 (f. 1962) and Channel 4 (f. 1964) and FM (f. 1980); Gen. Man. ARNOLD VARGAS V.

Televisora de Costa Rica (Canal 7), SA (Teletica): Apdo 3.876, San José; tel. 32-2222; telex 2220; fax 31-7545; f. 1960; operates Channel 7; Pres. OLGA DE PICADO; Gen. Man. RENÉ PICADO COZZA.

Televisora Sur y Norte (Canal 11): Apdo 5.542, San José; tel. 23-7130; Pres. FRANZ ULRICH.

Finance

(cap. = capital; p.u. = paid up; res = reserves; dep. = deposits; m. = million; brs = branches; amounts in colones)

BANKING

Banco Central de Costa Rica: Avdas Central y Primera, Calles 2-4, Apdo 10.058, San José; tel. 33-4233; telex 2163; f. 1950; cap. and res 7,996.7m., dep. 154,973.3m. (Dec. 1986); Exec. Pres. Dr JORGE GUARDIA; Gen. Man. CARLOS HERNÁNDEZ R.

State-owned Banks

Banco Anglo-Costarricense: Avda 2, Calles 1 y 3, Apdo 10.038, San José; tel. 22-3322; telex 2132; fax 57-1845; f. 1863; responsible for servicing commerce; cap. 745.1m., res 435.0m., dep. 19,549.6m. (Dec. 1987); Pres. JORGE ARAYA WESTOVER; Gen. Man. JOSÉ MANUEL PERAZA; 10 brs.

Banco de Costa Rica: Avdas Central y Segunda, Calles 4 y 6, Apdo 10.035, 1000 San José; tel. 55-1100; telex 2103; fax 55-3316; f. 1877; responsible for industry; cap. and res 930.7m., dep. 42,610.5m. (Dec. 1988); Pres. MARIO ESQUIVAL V.; Gen. Man. (vacant); 55 brs.

Banco Crédito Agrícola de Cartago: Calle 5 a 2, Apdo 297, Cartago; tel. 51-3011; telex 8006; f. 1918; responsible for housing; cap. 377,049m., dep. 3,341m. (March 1987); Pres. RAÚL MORALES VARGAS; Gen. Man. ROBERTO COSSANI RIVERA; 5 brs.

Banco Nacional de Costa Rica: Calles 2 y 4, Avda 1A, Apdo 10.015, San José; tel. 23-2166; telex 2120; fax 55-2436; f. 1914; responsible for the agricultural sector; cap. 1,696.4m., dep. 67,559.6m. (Dec. 1989); Gen. Man. LUIS ALBERTO CARRANZAS BONILLA; 125 brs.

Banco Popular y de Desarrollo Comunal: Calle 1, Avda 2 y 4, Apdo 10.190, San José; tel. 22-8122; telex 2844; fax 33-2350; f. 1969; cap. 260m., res 6m., dep. 940m. (June 1981); Pres. Ing. RODOLFO NAVAS ALVARADO; Gen. Man. ALVARO UREÑA ALVAREZ.

Private Banks

Banco de la Construcción, SA: Calle 38, Paseo Colón, Apdo 5.099, 1000 San José; tel. 21-5811; telex 2473; fax 22-6567; f. 1974; cap. p.u. 47m. (July 1988); Pres. CARLOS A. URCUYO BARRIOS; Mans CARLOS A. URCUYO P., GONZALO G. COTO F.

Banco Latinoamericano (Costa Rica), SA: San José; f. 1974; cap. 5m.; Pres. FERNANDO BERROCAL S.; Man. FRED O'NEILL G.

Banco Lyon, SA: Calle 2, Avs 6 y 8, Apdo 10.184, 1000 San José; tel. 21-2611; telex 2577; fax 21-6795; f. 1871; Pres. PETER A. LYON POWE; Gen. Man. CARLO PAGANI.

Banco de San José, SA: Calle Central, Avdas 3 y 5, Apdo 5.445, 1000 San José; tel. 21-9911; telex 2242; fax 22-8208; f. 1968; fmrly Bank of America, SA; total assets US $26.7m. (Dec. 1989); Pres. ALVARO SANCHO CASTRO; Man. MARIO MONTEALEGRE SABORÍO.

Banco de Santander (Costa Rica), SA: Avda 2, Calle Central, Apdo 6.714, San José; tel. 22-8066; telex 2666; fax 22-8840; f. 1977; cap. 60m. (1986); Pres. ABRAHAM WAIESLEDER; Gen. Man. LUIS MIER ABANS.

Credit Co-operatives

Federación Nacional de Cooperativas de Ahorro y Crédito y de Servicios Múltiples RL (Fedecrédito): Calle 20, Avdas 8 y 10, Apdo 4.748, San José; tel. 33-5666; fax 33-4596; f. 1963; 55 co-operatives, with 150,000 mems; combined cap. US $82m.; Pres. RAFAEL MURILLO; Gen. Man. Lic. MANUEL A. ARAYA BARBOZA.

STOCK EXCHANGE

Bolsa Nacional de Valores, SA: Edif. Cartagena 7°, Calle Central, Avda 1, Apdo 1.736, 1000 San José; tel. 22-8011; telex 2863; fax 55-0131; f. 1976; Exec. Pres. Ing. HUMBERTO PÉREZ BONILLA; Gen. Man. Dr RODRIGO BOLAÑOS ZAMORA.

INSURANCE

Instituto Nacional de Seguros: Calles 9 y 9B, Avda 7, Apdo 10.061, 1000 San José; tel. 23-5800; telex 2290; fax 55-3381; f. 1924; administers the state monopoly of insurance; services of foreign

COSTA RICA

insurance companies may be used only by authorization of the Ministry of Economy, Industry and Trade and only after the Instituto has certified that it will not accept the risk; cap. and res 3,389m. colones (Dec. 1983); Pres. FERNANDO ZUMBADO BERRY; Gen. Man. GERARDO ARAÚZ MONTERO.

Trade and Industry

STATE AGENCIES AND DEVELOPMENT ORGANIZATIONS

Cámara Nacional de Artesanía y Pequeña Industria de Costa Rica: Calle 11, Avda 1, Apdo 8–6.540, San José; tel. 23-2763; fax 55-4873; f. 1963; development, marketing and export of small-scale industries and handicrafts; Pres. MIREYA GUEVARA; Exec. Dir RAFAEL SÁENZ SANDÍ.

Centro de Promoción de Exportaciones e Inversiones (CENPRO): Calle 7, Avdas 1 y 3, Apdo 5.418, San José; tel. 21-7166; telex 2385; fax 23-5722; f. 1968 to encourage increased investment in export oriented activities and greater exports of non-traditional products; Exec. Dir CARLOS J. TORRES AMES.

CINDE (Costa Rican Investment and Development Co.): Apdo 7.170, 1000 San José; tel. 33-1711; telex 3514; fax 55-2281; coalition for development of initiatives to attract foreign investment for production and export of new products; Pres. MARIO ROJAS VEGA; CEO CARLOS EDUARDO ROBERT GÓNGORA.

CODESA: Apdo 10.254, 1000 San José; tel. 22-4422; telex 2405; fax 33-1355; f. 1972; development corporation; Pres. Lic. JOSÉ MANUEL SALAZAR XIRINACHS.

Consejo Nacional de Producción: Calle 36 a 12, Apdo 2.205, San José; tel. 23-6033; telex 2273; fax 33-9660; f. 1948 to encourage agricultural and fish production and to regulate production and distribution of basic commodities; Pres. Ing. JAVIER FLORES GALAGARCÍA; Man. HORACIO ZÚÑIGA CHAVARRÍA.

Instituto del Café: Calle 1, Avdas 18 y 20, Apdo 37, San José; tel. 33-2888; telex 2279; fax 22-2838; f. 1948 to develop the coffee industry, to control production and to regulate marketing; Pres. Ing. GUILLERMO CANET BRENES; Exec. Dir Lic. MARIO FERNÁNDEZ URPI.

Instituto Costarricense de Acueductos y Alcantarillados: Avda Central, Calle 5, Apdo 5120, 1000 San José; tel. 33-2155; telex 2724; fax 22-2259; water and sewerage; Exec. Pres. Ing. MARIO FERNÁNDEZ ORTIZ.

Instituto Costarricense de Electricidad (ICE): Apdo 10.032, 1000 San José; tel. 20-7720; telex 2140; fax 20-1555; state power and telecommunications agency; Exec. Pres. Ing. HERNÁN FOURNIER ORIGGI; Gen. Man. Ing. MARIO HIDALGO PACHECO.

Instituto de Desarrollo Agrícola (IDA): Apdo 5.054, 1000 San José; tel. 24-6066; Exec. Pres. Ing. SERGIO QUIRÓS MAROTO.

Instituto de Fomento y Asesoría Municipal: Apdo 10.187, San José; tel. 23-3714; f. 1970; municipal development institute; Exec. Pres. JUSTO AGUILAR FONG; Exec. Dir HARRY JAGER CONTRERAS.

Instituto Mixto de Ayuda Social (IMAS): Calle 29, entre Avdas 2 y 4, Apdo 2.613, San José; tel. 25-2555; telex 1559; fax 24-8783; Pres. CARLOS CORRALES VILLALOBOS.

Instituto Nacional de Fomento Cooperativo: Apdo 10.103, San José; tel. 23-4355; fax 55-3835; f. 1973; to encourage the establishment of co-operatives and to provide technical assistance and credit facilities; cap. 11m. (May 1986); Pres. Lic. ALVARO CHÁVEZ GÓMEZ; Exec. Dir Lic. RAFAEL A. ROJAS JIMÉNEZ.

Instituto Nacional de Vivienda y Urbanismo: Apdo 2.534, San José; tel. 21-5266; telex 2908; housing and town planning institute; Exec. Pres. Ing. FERNANDO CAÑAS ROWSON; Representative JOSÉ MANUEL AGÜERO.

Ministerio de Planificación Nacional y Política Económica: Apdo 10.127, 1000 San José; tel. 23-2322; telex 2962; fax 53-6243; f. 1963; formulates and supervises execution of the National Development Plan; main aims: to increase national productivity; to improve distribution of income and social services; to increase citizen participation in solution of socio-economic problems; Pres. Dr HELIO FALLAS, Dir Minister of National Planning and Economic Policy.

Refinadora Costarricense de Petróleo (Recope): Apdo 4.351, San José; tel. 23-9611; telex 2215; fax 55-2049; f. 1961; state petroleum organization; Dir ROBERTO DOBLES.

CHAMBERS OF COMMERCE AND INDUSTRY

Cámara de Comercio de Costa Rica: Urbanización Tournón, Apdo 1114, 1000 San José; tel. 21-0005; telex 2646; fax 33-7091; f. 1915; 1,050 mems; Pres. ANGEL NIETO CASTRO; Exec. Dir ALVARO TREJOS.

Cámara de Industrias de Costa Rica: Calles 13–15, Avda 6, Apdo 10.003, 1000 San José; tel. 23-2411; telex 2474; fax 22-1007; f. 1943; Pres. Ing. SAMUEL YANKELEWITZ BERGER; Exec. Dir GEOVANNY CASTILLO ANTONIA.

Unión de Cámaras: Apdo 539-1.002, Paseo de Estudiantes, San José; tel. 33-3555; telex 3644; fax 33-0909; f. 1974; business federation; Pres. VÍCTOR E. HERRERA ALFARO.

AGRICULTURAL ORGANIZATIONS

Cámara de Azucareros: Calle 3, Avda Fernández Güell, Apdo 1.577, 1000 San José; tel. 22-1358; f. 1949; sugar growers; Pres. RODOLFO JIMÉNEZ BORBÓN.

Cámara Nacional de Agricultura: Avda 10-10bis, Cv. 23, Apdo 1671, 1000 San José; tel. 21-6864; telex 3489; fax 33-8658; f. 1947; Pres. JUAN R. LIZANO; Exec. Dir Lic. GERARDINA GONZÁLEZ M.

Cámara Nacional de Bananeros: Calle 11, Avda 6a, Edif. Urcha, Apdo 10.273, 1000 San José; tel. 22-7891; f. 1967; banana growers; Pres. EDMUNDO TAYLOR ENRÍQUEZ.

Cámara Nacional de Cafetaleros: Calle 3, Avdas 6 y 8, Apdo 1.310, San José; tel. 21-8207; telex 2525; fax 38-0858; f. 1948; 300 mems; coffee growers; Pres. RODOLFO MONTEALEGRE ECHEVERRÍA.

Cámara Nacional de Ganaderos: Edif. Ilifílán 4°, Calles 2 y 4, Avda Central Apdo 4.564, San José; tel. 22-1652; cattle farmers; Pres. VÍCTOR WOLF FOURNIER.

TRADE UNIONS

By the end of 1987 there were only 19 unions, with a total of 4,313 members nationwide. Membership of 'solidarista' associations had risen to 16,229. A new labour code, adopted in 1988, has encouraged the further growth of these associations (in which employers' interests tend to predominate) at the expense of the trade unions.

Central de Trabajadores Costarricenses (Costa Rican Workers' Union): Calle 20 a 3 y 5, Apdo 4.137, 1000 San José; tel. 21-7701; telex 3091; Sec.-Gen. ALSIMIRO HERRERA TORRES.

Confederación Auténtica de Trabajadores Democráticos (Democratic Workers' Union): Calle 13 a 10 y 12, Solera; tel. 53-2971; Pres. LUIS ARMANDO GUTIÉRREZ; Sec.-Gen. Prof. CARLOS VARGAS.

Confederación Costarricense de Trabajadores Democráticos (Costa Rican Confederation of Democratic Workers): Calles 3–5, Avda 12, Apdo 2.167, San José; tel. 22-1981; telex 2167; f. 1966; mem. ICFTU and ORIT; Sec.-Gen. LUIS ARMANDO GUTIÉRREZ R.; 50,000 mems.

Confederación Unitaria de Trabajadores (CUT): Calles 1 y 3, Avda 12, Casa No 142, Apdo 186, 1009 San José; tel. 21-4709; f. 1980 from a merger of the Federación Nacional de Trabajadores Públicos and the Confederación General de Trabajadores; linked to Coalición Pueblo Unido; 53 affiliated unions; Pres. MARIO DEVANDAS; Sec.-Gen. ORLANDO SOLANO MEJÍAS; c. 55,000 mems.

Federación Sindical Agraria Nacional (FESIAN) (National Agrarian Confederation): Apdo 2.167, 1000 San José; tel. 33-5897; 20,000 member families; Sec.-Gen. JUAN MEJÍA VILLALOBOS.

The **Consejo Permanente de los Trabajadores**, formed in 1986, comprises six union organizations and two teachers' unions.

Transport

Ministerio de Obras Públicas y Transportes: Apdo 10.176, 1000 San José; tel. 26-7311; telex 2493; fax 27-1434; the ministry is responsible for setting tariffs, allocating funds, maintaining existing systems and constructing new ones.

Cámara Nacional de Transportes: Calle 20, Avda 7, San José; tel. 22-5394; national chamber of transport.

RAILWAYS

Instituto Costarricense de Ferrocarriles (INCOFER): Apdo No 1, 1009 FE al P Estación, Zona 3, San José; tel. 26-0011; telex 2393; government-owned; 647.4 km, of which 280.8 km are electrified; Exec. Pres. Ing. JOSÉ F. NICOLÁS ALVARADO.

INCOFER comprises:

División I: San José to Limón; Río Frío to Limón; several branch lines; f. 1986; 63.9 km of track are electrified.

División II: Alajuela to San José; San José to Puntarenas and Caldera branch; 216.9 km of track are electrified.

Other railways in Costa Rica include 48 km of track, formerly belonging to the United Fruit Company of Boston (USA), which are not presently in use.

ROADS

In 1985 there were 35,594 km of roads, of which 4,536 km were paved, excluding 663 km of the Pan-American Highway.

COSTA RICA
Directory

SHIPPING

Local services operate between the Costa Rican ports of Puntarenas and Limón and those of Colón and Cristóbal in Panama and other Central American ports. The multi-million dollar project at Caldera on the Gulf of Nicoya is now in operation as the main Pacific port; Puntarenas is being used as the second port. The Caribbean coast is served by the port complex of Limón/Moín. International services are operated by various foreign shipping lines.

Junta de Administración Portuaria y de Desarrollo Económico de la Vertiente Atlántica (JAPDEVA): Calle 17, Avda 7, Apdo 8–5.330, 1000 San José; tel. 33-5301; telex 2435; state agency for the development of Atlantic ports; Exec. Pres. Ing. JORGE ARTURO CASTRO HERRERA.

Instituto Costarricense de Puertos del Pacífico (INCOP): Calle 36, Avda 3, San José; tel. 23-7111; telex 2793; state agency for the development of Pacific ports; Exec. Pres. EDGAR GUARDIOLA MENDOZA.

CIVIL AVIATION

Costa Rica's main international airport is the Juan Santamaría Airport, 16 km from San José at El Coco and there are regional airports at Liberia, Limón and Pavas (Tobías Bolaños Airport).

Líneas Aéreas Costarricenses, SA—LACSA (Costa Rican Airlines): Edif. Lacsa, Apdo 1.531, La Uruca, San José; tel. 32-3555; telex 2188; fax 32-4178; f. 1946; operates international services to Colombia, El Salvador, Guatemala, Honduras, Mexico, Panama, Puerto Rico, Venezuela and the USA; Chair. and Chief Exec. Capt. OTTO ESCALANTE W.; fleet: 4 Airbus 320, 2 Airbus 310, 1 DC-8-55F (cargo).

Servicios Aéreos Nacionales, SA (SANSA): Paseo Colón, Apdo 999, 1.007 Centro Colón, San José; tel. 23-4179; telex 2914; subsidiary of LACSA; internal services; Gen. Man. Lic. CARLOS MANUEL DELGADO AGUILAR; fleet: 2 Aviocar C-212, 1 DC-3.

Tourism

Costa Rica boasts a system of nature reserves and national parks unique in the world. The main tourist features are the Irazú and Poás volcanoes, the Orosí valley, the ruins of the colonial church at Ujarras and the jungle train to Limón. Tourists also visit San José, the capital, the Pacific beaches of Guanacaste and Puntarenas, and the Caribbean beaches of Limón. A total of 375,951 tourists visited Costa Rica in 1989.

Instituto Costarricense de Turismo: Edif. Genaro Valverde, Calles 5 y 7, Avda 4a, Apdo 777, 1000 San José; tel. 23-1733; telex 2281; fax 55-4997; f. 1955; Exec. Pres. LUIS MANUEL CHACÓN.

Atomic Energy

Comisión de Energía Atómica de Costa Rica: Edif. Galerias del Este, 3°, Curridabat, Apdo Postal 6.681, San José; tel. 24-1591; f. 1967; Pres. Dr ENRIQUE GÓNGORA TREJOS; Dir SOLÓN CONTRERAS GARBANZO.

CÔTE D'IVOIRE

(THE IVORY COAST)

Introductory Survey

Location, Climate, Language, Religion, Flag, Capital

The Republic of Côte d'Ivoire lies on the west coast of Africa, between Ghana to the east and Liberia to the west, with Guinea, Mali and Burkina Faso to the north. The climate is hot and wet, with temperatures varying from 14°C to 39°C (57°F to 103°F). The official language is French, and a large number of African languages are also spoken. Most of the inhabitants follow traditional beliefs, while about 12% are Christians, mainly Roman Catholics, and 23% Muslims. The national flag (proportions 3 by 2) has three equal vertical stripes, of orange, white and green. The process of transferring the capital from Abidjan to Yamoussoukro (the President's birthplace), about 220 km (135 miles) north-west of Abidjan, was begun in March 1983; however, it was envisaged that Abidjan would remain the major centre for economic activity.

Recent History

Formerly a province of French West Africa, Côte d'Ivoire achieved self-government, within the French Community, in December 1958. Dr Félix Houphouët-Boigny, leader of the Parti démocratique de la Côte d'Ivoire (PDCI), became Prime Minister in 1959. The country became fully independent on 7 August 1960.

A new constitution was adopted in October 1960, and Houphouët-Boigny became President in November. Until 1990 the PDCI, founded in 1946, was Côte d'Ivoire's only legal political party: although Article 7 of the Constitution made provision for the existence of a plurality of political organizations, no opposition grouping was granted official recognition. A high rate of economic growth, particularly during the 1970s, together with strong support from France contributed, until the late 1980s, to the stability of the regime. Political unrest occurred sporadically, though without strong leadership. Two plots were uncovered in 1963, apparently representing a youthful radical element and northerners who resented southern domination in the Government. The army was reduced in size to reduce the risk of military intervention. The Government responded to criticism by implementing a policy of regional development and increased Ivorian management of commercial enterprises.

In 1977 Houphouët-Boigny replaced the Ministers of Finance, Economic Planning and Foreign Affairs, and legislation was enacted against corrupt trading and speculation in commodities. In May 1978 it was announced that, with the exception of Abidjan and Bouaké, the capitals of all the country's Departments would be administered by elected mayors, rather than by party appointees. Elections to the National Assembly were held in November 1980 and, for the first time, more than one candidate was permitted to contest each seat.

A series of strikes and demonstrations took place between late 1980 and mid-1983, mainly involving students and professional groups. The longest strike, in April and May 1983, was staged by teachers protesting against the withdrawal of free housing rights, and was supported by members of the medical profession. The strike was terminated by a presidential decree ordering a return to work, and two education ministers were subsequently dismissed from the Government. In 1984 the Government implemented anti-corruption measures, including the imprisonment of several former government officials in the state housing sector, accused of malpractice. In 1985 a much-publicized court case, concerning debts of US $58m., was brought by the Banque Nationale pour le Développement Agricole (BNDA) against COGEXIM, a private cocoa- and coffee-exporting company whose chairman was the mayor of Abidjan, Emmanuel Dioulo. The ensuing scandal prompted Dioulo to flee to Belgium; he was, however, subsequently granted amnesty, and later returned to Côte d'Ivoire.

In November 1983 the number of government ministers was reduced from 35 to 28, in an attempt to cut administrative costs. The eighth ordinary congress of the PDCI, held in Abidjan in October 1985, approved the adoption of a constitutional amendment suppressing the post of Vice-President, and allowing for the President of the National Assembly to succeed the President of the Republic, on an interim basis, in the event of a vacancy. Later that month, Houphouët-Boigny was re-elected President for a sixth five-year term. Municipal and legislative elections were held in November, and in January 1986 Henri Konan-Bédié was re-elected to the presidency of the National Assembly. In July the Council of Ministers was reorganized, and its membership increased to 40, in response to the apparent easing of the country's economic crisis.

In September 1987 three members of the secondary-school teachers' union, SYNESCI, were arrested, following divisions within the union and a disputed transference of leadership. They were subsequently imprisoned after having been convicted of embezzlement, while 11 other members were sent to a military camp for a period of 're-education'. All those detained were released in July 1988. The unexpected dismissal, in December 1987, of the Minister of Maritime Affairs, Lamine Fadika, together with the removal from office of the Chief of Staff of the Armed Forces and of four officials of the PDCI, was rumoured to be linked to the discovery of a coup plot. In September 1988 Laurent Gbagbo, the leader of the Front populaire ivoirien (FPI) opposition movement, returned to Côte d'Ivoire after a six-year period of exile in Paris. However, it was subsequently reported that prominent members of the FPI, including Gbagbo, were held in detention for a short time.

In September 1988 it was announced that the membership of the Council of Ministers was to be reduced to 39, as part of government changes that included the creation of a Ministry of Drug Control.

In September 1989 Houphouët-Boigny hosted a series of meetings, at which Côte d'Ivoire's political, economic and social problems were discussed. The meetings, which were designated 'days of national dialogue', were attended by members of the Government and of the PDCI, prominent state officials, senior officers of the armed forces and representatives of the country's trade unions and professional organizations. In the following month a national commission was established to examine the grievances expressed at the meetings. Despite this atmosphere of apparent openness, Houphouët-Boigny continued to assert that progress towards national unity would be impeded by the introduction of a multi-party system. In September the President announced the imposition of stricter security measures: armed forces were to be deployed along the country's borders, in an attempt to inhibit smuggling and illegal immigration, and also in principal towns, to assist the police force in combating crime. In the following month a security fund was established, to which all residents of Côte d'Ivoire were exhorted to contribute, in order to modernize and re-equip the country's security forces.

A reallocation of ministerial portfolios occurred in October 1989. Several ministries were abolished, and others merged, as a result of which the membership of the Council of Ministers was reduced to 29. Moïse Koumoué Koffi, who, as Minister of the Budget (a portfolio that was abolished as a result of the reorganization), had gained the respect of Côte d'Ivoire's external creditors, was appointed to the Ministry of the Economy and Finance. The reshuffle and accompanying structural changes were believed to reflect Houphouët-Boigny's desire to secure funding from external donors, notably the IMF and the World Bank, for his country's economic adjustment efforts.

In early 1990 the proposed adoption of austerity measures, in compliance with an economic revival programme that had been adopted in mid-1989, precipitated an unprecedented level of civil unrest that was ultimately to lead to the initiation of radical political changes. In February a boycott of classes by students at the University of Abidjan was followed by the occupation of the city's cathedral, as a result of which more than 100 protesters were detained. Later in the same month, it was announced that the salaries of all state employees (including government ministers) were to be reduced by as much as 40%, while a 'solidarity tax' was to be levied on income in the private sector. It was hoped that these measures would generate sufficient funds to repay the country's burgeoning external debt. A new Minister of National Education (with responsibility for secondary and higher education) was appointed; however, student unrest persisted. In early March school pupils and civil servants in Abidjan joined a students' demonstration, in protest at alleged corruption among state officials. Security forces dispersed the demonstrators, and educational establishments in the city were closed. Armed forces were deployed in the capital, as leaflets appealing for further disruption continued to circulate. Proposals for reductions in the prices of essential goods and services, to compensate for the levies on income (which were due to be imposed in late March), also failed to ease tension, and about 126 university lecturers and researchers defied a newly-imposed ban on public gatherings to protest at the impending introduction of austerity measures. Physicians and other health-sector employees withdrew their labour, but were ordered to resume their duties by the Government. Teaching staff refused to supervise classes. In early April all educational establishments were closed, and the 1989/90 academic year was declared invalid, following the death of a student when security forces intervened at an anti-Government demonstration. Armed forces also intervened when students attempted to disrupt a rally that had been organized in support of the austerity measures.

By mid-1990 it had become clear that the unpopular economic measures would fail to generate the revenue necessary to fulfil the Government's objectives. Houphouët-Boigny thus appointed Alassane Ouattara, the Governor of the Banque Centrale des Etats de l'Afrique de l'Ouest, to chair a special commission whose function would be formulate new measures that would be more economically effective and, at the same time, more politically acceptable.

In late April 1990 the Political Bureau of the ruling party advised that Article 7 of the Constitution be implemented, a recommendation that was endorsed by Houphouët-Boigny in early May. Accordingly, hitherto unofficial political organizations were granted official status, and several new parties were formed. In June representatives of four political organizations met in Korhogo and issued a joint declaration, urging the resignation of Houphouët-Boigny from the leadership of the PDCI, the dissolution of the Council of Ministers and the formation of a transitional administration.

Despite the recent political and economic changes, industrial unrest continued during May 1990. However, the Government demonstrated a relatively conciliatory attitude towards protesting army conscripts, who occupied the offices of the state broadcasting service and the airport at Abidjan, and towards police officers: both groups were subsequently given assurances regarding improved terms of service. In late May a revised programme of austerity measures was announced, in accordance with the recommendations of the Ouattara Commission.

In June 1990 Col Robert Guei was appointed Chief of the General Staff of the Armed Forces. The departure of his predecessor, Gen. Félix Ory (who was assigned to a diplomatic post), was believed to be connected with the conscripts' mutiny in the previous month. In July Daniel Kablan Duncan succeeded Moïse Koumoué Koffi as Minister of the Economy and Finance, as part of a minor reallocation of portfolios; Koffi, meanwhile, was appointed Minister-delegate at the Presidency.

Presidential and legislative elections were scheduled, respectively, for late October and late November 1990. Although these elections were to be held in the context of the country's new multi-party system, opposition leaders repeatedly accused the Government of impeding the implementation of political reform. During the second half of 1990 security forces intervened at several rallies and demonstrations that had been organized by opponents of the PDCI. In late September Houphouët-Boigny accused his opponents of complicity in an alleged plot to assassinate Pope John Paul II at the time of his visit to Côte d'Ivoire (see below).

The reopening of educational establishments was scheduled for early September 1990. However, many university students refused to resume classes, in protest at proposals to conclude the 1989/90 academic programme during the first weeks of the new term. Following several disturbances, security forces were deployed at the University of Abidjan in late September, in an attempt to restore order.

In September 1990 Laurent Gbagbo was chosen to represent the FPI in the forthcoming presidential election. Houphouët-Boigny was similarly adopted as the candidate of the PDCI, at the ninth congress of the ruling party, which was held in Yamoussoukro in early October. Delegates to that congress also approved a restructuring of the PDCI.

Côte d'Ivoire's first contested presidential election was held on 28 October 1990, when Houphouët-Boigny was re-elected for a seventh term, having reportedly received the support of 81.67% of those who voted. The FPI and its allies alleged electoral malpractice, and appealed to the Supreme Court to declare the election invalid (a petition that was rejected). The Ligue ivoirienne des droits de l'homme (LIDHO) alleged that about 120 opposition supporters had been arrested at the time of the election. In early November the National Assembly approved two constitutional amendments. The first concerned the procedure to be adopted if the presidency should become vacant: the President of the National Assembly would, henceforth, assume the functions of the President of the Republic until the expiry of the mandate of the previous incumbent. Secondly, provision was made for the appointment of a prime minister, who would be accountable to the President. Accordingly, Alassane Ouattara was subsequently designated Prime Minister.

By the time of the November 1990 legislative elections, about 26 political organizations had been officially recognized; however, it was widely believed that some of these groups had been created by the Government, in an attempt to cause confusion among the electorate and thus to consolidate support for the PDCI. Some 500 candidates, representing about 17 political parties, contested the Assembly's 175 seats. Malpractice and the harassment of opposition supporters by the authorities was again alleged. According to official results, the PDCI returned 163 deputies to the legislature, while the FPI secured nine seats (among the FPI delegates was Gbagbo). The leader of the Parti ivoirien des travailleurs (PIT), Frances Wodié, was also elected, as were two independent candidates.

The composition of the new Council of Ministers, which was announced in late November 1990, indicated that priority would be given to the country's economic recovery. Prime Minister Ouattara also assumed the Economy and Finance portfolio, while the number of ministers was reduced to 20. Several ministers who had served Houphouët-Boigny for many years, including Mathieu Ekra, Siméon Aka and Jean Konan Banny, were removed from office as a result of the changes.

The presence in Côte d'Ivoire of large numbers of Europeans, Levantines and nationals of neighbouring countries has led to sporadic clashes between Ivorians and immigrant groups: in 1981 more than 1m. foreigners were resident in the country. However, increasing unemployment among university leavers, a concern for 'Ivorianization' and the need for reductions in public spending prompted the Government to reduce the level of foreign assistance in the country; in 1989 there were about 1,600 French 'coopérants' working in Côte d'Ivoire, compared with 4,000 such workers in 1980.

In February 1986 Côte d'Ivoire resumed formal diplomatic relations with Israel, following a 13-year suspension as a result of the Arab–Israeli war in 1973. Diplomatic links with the Soviet Union and several Eastern bloc states were also renewed in 1986–87. Houphouët-Boigny is committed to a policy of dialogue between Black Africa and white-ruled South Africa, for which he has been strongly criticized by other African leaders. In October 1988 President Botha of South Africa visited Côte d'Ivoire, and in December 1989 his successor, President de Klerk, was accorded an official state reception when he met Houphouët-Boigny in Yamoussoukro. It was widely expected that Côte d'Ivoire would establish diplomatic relations with South Africa during the early 1990s.

In late 1989 the Liberian Government alleged that rebel forces, who were involved in an attempt to overthrow the incumbent regime, had entered the country through Côte d'Ivoire. In January 1990 President Doe of Liberia sought assurances from the Ivorian authorities that the safety of thousands of refugees who had fled from his country to Côte d'Ivoire, in an attempt to escape the conflict between the Liberian armed forces and the rebels, would be guaranteed.

Despite evidence to the contrary, Houphouët-Boigny denied suggestions that his Government was supporting Charles Taylor's rebel National Patriotic Forces of Liberia.

Pope John Paul II visited Côte d'Ivoire in September 1990, in order to consecrate a basilica in Yamoussoukro (Houphouët-Boigny's birthplace), which had been constructed, officially at the Ivorian President's own expense, at a cost of some 40,000m. francs CFA. As a precondition for the papal visit, the Ivorian Government undertook a number of welfare projects in Yamoussoukro, and agreed to fund the maintenance of the basilica.

In mid-1990 at least seven Ivorian embassies abroad were closed, in accordance with the provisions of the Outtara Commission's austerity measures.

In April 1986 it was announced that the country wished to be known internationally by its French name of Côte d'Ivoire, rather than by translations of it. The request was subsequently endorsed by the UN.

Government

Executive power is vested in the President, who is elected for a five-year term by direct universal suffrage. In November 1990 a constitutional amendment was adopted to provide for the President of the National Assembly to carry out the functions of the Head of State, in case of the latter's death or incapacitation, until the expiry of the previous incumbent's mandate. At the same time provision was made for the appointment of a prime minister, who is responsible to the President of the Republic. Legislative power is vested in the unicameral National Assembly, which is directly elected (using two ballots if necessary) for five years. The Assembly was expanded from 147 to 175 members following the 1985 elections. Article 7 of the Constitution provides for the existence of multiple political parties; however, this clause was not implemented until mid-1990. The first presidential and legislative elections to be held in the context of a multi-party system took place in October and November 1990. The country is divided into 49 Departments, each with its own elected Council.

Defence

Defence matters are the concern of the Regional Defence Council of the Conseil de l'Entente, through which agreements with France have been negotiated. France supplies equipment and training, and maintains a force of several hundred men. In June 1990 Côte d'Ivoire had 5,500 men in the army, 900 in the air force and 700 in the navy. In addition, there are paramilitary forces of approximately 7,800 men. The estimated defence budget for 1989 was 43,508m. francs CFA (6.7% of total budget spending).

Economic Affairs

In 1988, according to estimates by the World Bank, Côte d'Ivoire's gross national product (GNP), measured at average 1986–88 prices, was US $8,590m., equivalent to $740 per head. During 1980–88, it was estimated, GNP increased at an average annual rate of only 0.4%, while GNP per head declined by 3.7% per year. Over the same period, the population increased by an annual average of 4.2%. Côte d'Ivoire's gross domestic product (GDP) increased, in real terms, by an annual average of 2.2% in 1980–87.

Agriculture (including forestry and fishing) contributed 47.3% of GDP in 1987. About 56.7% of the labour force were employed in agriculture in 1989. Côte d'Ivoire is the world's foremost producer of cocoa (exports of cocoa and related products contributed 39.5% of total export earnings in 1987). In 1988 Côte d'Ivoire was the world's third largest producer of coffee (exports of coffee and related products accounted for 14.7% of export earnings in 1987). Other major cash crops are palm kernels, cotton, rubber, pineapples and other fruit. The principal subsistence crops are yams, cassava and plantains. The attainment of self-sufficiency in basic foodstuffs remains a priority: some 494,000 metric tons of cereals were imported in 1988. Excessive exploitation of the country's forest resources has led to a decline in the importance of this sector. Abidjan is among sub-Saharan Africa's principal fishing ports; however, the participation of Ivorian fishing fleets is minimal. During 1980–87 agricultural production increased by an annual average of 1.6%.

Industry (including mining, manufacturing, construction and power) contributed 16.3% of GDP in 1987. About 0.0% of the labour force were employed in the sector in 1980. Industrial production increased by an annual average of 10.4% in 1965–80, but declined by an average of 2.4% per year in 1980–87.

Mining contributed only 1.2% of GDP in 1987. The exploitation of the country's petroleum resources (which were discovered in 1977) has been hampered by technical difficulties, and revenue from the extraction of petroleum has, consequently, failed to meet initial expectations. Diamonds are extracted by private companies. However, much of the production is smuggled out of the country. The development of gold deposits at Ity was expected to begin during the early 1990s. The exploitation of offshore reserves of natural gas is also envisaged. Significant deposits of iron ore and copper remain unexploited. The existence of traces of nickel, phosphates, bauxite and cobalt has also been confirmed.

The manufacturing sector, which contributed 10.3% of GDP in 1987, is dominated by agro-industrial activities (such as the processing of cocoa, coffee, cotton, palm kernels, pineapples and fish). The tobacco industry, which uses imported tobacco, is also important. Crude petroleum (much of which is imported) is refined at Abidjan.

Electrical energy is derived from both thermal and hydroelectric installations. A programme to reduce the country's dependence on imported energy (which accounted for about one-fifth of the value of total imports in the late 1980s), by developing indigenous resources of natural gas, was announced in late 1989. Imports of fuel products accounted for about 15% of the value of merchandise imports in 1988.

In 1989 Côte d'Ivoire recorded a visible trade surplus of US $1,141.4m., although there was a deficit of $858.2m. on the current account of the balance of payments. In 1987 the principal source of imports (31.7%) was France, while the principal market for exports (16.9%) was the Netherlands. Other major trading partners are Italy, the Federal Republic of Germany, the USA, the United Kingdom, Nigeria and Japan. The principal exports in 1987 were cocoa, coffee (and their related products), fuels and wood. The principal imports were machinery and transport equipment, fuels, chemicals and cereals.

Budget estimates for 1989 projected a deficit of 102,997m. francs CFA. Côte d'Ivoire's total external public debt was US $8,088m. at the end of 1988. In that year the cost of debt-servicing was equivalent to 13.0% of the value of exports of goods and services. The annual rate of inflation averaged 3.8% in 1980–88; consumer prices increased by an annual average of 7.0% in 1988 and by 1.0% in 1989.

Côte d'Ivoire is a member of numerous regional and international organizations, including the Communauté Économique de l'Afrique de l'Ouest (CEAO, see p. 120), the Conseil de l'Entente (see p. 122), the Economic Community of West African States (ECOWAS, see p. 133), the West African organs of the Franc Zone (see p. 156), the International Cocoa Organization (ICCO, see p. 228) and the International Coffee Organization (ICO, see p. 228).

Following its independence, Côte d'Ivoire's strong economic growth was based upon revenue from sales of cocoa, coffee and timber. The decline, during the 1980s, in international prices for the country's major export commodities, together with the near-exhaustion of its forest resources and the inviability of the petroleum programme, precipitated a decline in economic development and Côte d'Ivoire's incapacity to service its internal and external deficits. In 1989, following the failure of an attempt by the Ivorian Government to bring about an increase in international prices for cocoa by imposing an embargo on sales of its crop, the official prices payable to producers of cocoa and coffee were reduced. External creditors subsequently agreed to fund the first phase of a four-year economic revival programme. However, the programme entailed a series of austerity measures, the proposed implementation of which precipitated a severe political and social crisis (see Recent History). A six-month programme of less stringent adjustment measures was adopted in mid-1990, and negotiations for a longer-term economic programme were initiated, in co-operation with the country's external creditors, who also agreed to provide interim financial support. A considerable reduction in state participation in the economy was expected to be a major priority of the new Ouattara Government.

Social Welfare

Medical services are organized by the State. In 1980 the country had 8,799 hospital beds and 518 physicians. There is a minimum wage for workers in industry and commerce. Projects

CÔTE D'IVOIRE

to increase the social and health services to regional centres and villages are being carried out. Of total budgetary expenditure in 1989, 4,815m. francs CFA (0.7%) was allocated to social security and welfare, and 42,730m. francs CFA (6.6%) to health. A major vaccination programme, introduced in April 1987, aimed to immunize between 75% and 80% of Ivorian children against the six major infant diseases.

Education

In 1985, according to UNESCO estimates, adult illiteracy averaged 57.3% (males 46.9%; females 68.9%). Education at all levels is available free of charge. Primary education, which is officially compulsory, usually begins at seven years of age and lasts for six years. Enrolment at primary schools in 1985 was equivalent to 70% of all children between seven and 12 years of age (82% of boys; 58% of girls). In the towns, however, average attendance is more than 90%. Secondary education, beginning at the age of 13, lasts for up to seven years, normally comprising a first cycle of four years and a second cycle of three years. In 1987 the total enrolment at secondary schools was equivalent to 19% of children aged between 13 and 19 (26% of boys; 12% of girls). The National University at Abidjan has five faculties, and in 1984/85 had 11,300 students. In addition, many students attend French universities. In 1981–85 five technical training institutes were to be built, and the University was to be decentralized. University facilities have been constructed at Yamoussoukro. About 1,600 teachers and researchers of French nationality were estimated to be working in Côte d'Ivoire in 1987. Expenditure on education in 1989 was projected at 192,488m. francs CFA (29.8% of total budget spending), the highest allocation to any sector.

Public Holidays

1991: 1 January (New Year's Day), 29 March (Good Friday), 1 April (Easter Monday), 16 April* (Id al-Fitr, end of Ramadan), 1 May (Labour Day), 9 May (Ascension Day), 20 May (Whit Monday), 23 June* (Id al-Adha, Feast of the Sacrifice), 15 August (Assumption), 1 November (All Saints' Day), 7 December (Independence Day), 25 December (Christmas).

1992: 1 January (New Year's Day), 4 April* (Id al-Fitr, end of Ramadan), 17 April (Good Friday), 20 April (Easter Monday), 1 May (Labour Day), 28 May (Ascension Day), 8 June (Whit Monday), 11 June* (Id al-Adha, Feast of the Sacrifice), 15 August (Assumption), 1 November (All Saints' Day), 7 December (Independence Day), 25 December (Christmas).

* These holidays are dependent on the Islamic lunar calendar and may vary by one or two days from the dates given.

Weights and Measures

The metric system is in force.

Statistical Survey

Source (unless otherwise stated): Direction de la Statistique, Ministère de l'Economie et des Finances, 01 BP V55, Abidjan 01; tel. 21-15-38.

Area and Population

AREA, POPULATION AND DENSITY

Area (sq km)	322,462*
Population (census of 30 April 1975)†	
Males	3,474,750
Females	3,234,850
Total	6,709,600
Population (official estimates at mid-year)	
1980	8,262,300
1983	9,334,800‡
1984	9,742,900‡
Density (per sq km) at mid-1984	30.2

* 124,503 sq miles.
† Provisional result. Revised total is 6,702,866.
‡ Provisional. Figures for 1981–82 are not available.

PROVINCES

	Area (sq km)	Population (1975 census)
Abengourou	6,900	177,692
Abidjan*	14,200	1,389,141
Aboisso	6,250	148,823
Adzopé	5,230	162,837
Agboville	3,850	141,970
Biankouma	4,950	75,711
Bondoukou	16,530	296,551
Bouaflé	8,500	263,609
Bouaké*	23,670	808,048
Bouna	21,470	84,290
Boundiali	10,095	132,278
Dabakala	9,670	56,230
Daloa	15,200	369,610
Danané	4,600	170,249
Dimbokro	14,100	475,023
Divo	10,650	278,526
Ferkessedougou	17,728	90,423
Gagnoa	6,900	259,504
—continued	Area (sq km)	Population (1975 census)
Guiglo	14,150	137,672
Katiola	9,420	77,875
Korhogo	12,500	276,816
Man	7,050	278,659
Odienné	20,600	124,010
Sassandra	25,800	191,994
Séguéla	21,900	157,539
Touba	8,720	77,786
Total	320,633†	6,702,866

* Including commune.
† Other sources give the total area as 322,462 sq km.

Source: *La Côte d'Ivoire en Chiffres*, 1979.

(Note: Following a reorganization of local government in 1985, Côte d'Ivoire comprised a total of 49 provinces.)

PRINCIPAL TOWNS (population at 15 June 1979)

Abidjan 1,423,323; Bouaké 272,640.

BIRTHS AND DEATHS (UN estimates, annual averages)

	1975–80	1980–85	1985–90
Birth rate (per 1,000)	51.1	51.0	50.9
Death rate (per 1,000)	17.3	15.6	14.2

Source: UN, *World Population Prospects: 1988*.

CÔTE D'IVOIRE

ECONOMICALLY ACTIVE POPULATION
(ILO estimates, '000 persons at mid-1980)

	Males	Females	Total
Agriculture, etc.	1,385	928	2,314
Industry	231	62	293
Services	693	248	940
Total	2,309	1,238	3,547

Source: ILO, *Economically Active Population Estimates and Projections, 1950–2025*.

Mid-1989 (estimates, '000 persons): Agriculture, etc. 2,576; Total 4,543 (Source: FAO, *Production Yearbook*).

Agriculture

PRINCIPAL CROPS ('000 metric tons)

	1987	1988	1989
Maize	435	448	450
Millet	41	42	41†
Sorghum	23	24	23†
Rice (paddy)	580	597	590
Potatoes*	24	24	24
Sweet potatoes*	12	12	18
Cassava (Manioc)	1,294	1,333	1,300
Yams	2,381	2,452	2,370
Taro (Coco yam)	272	280	250*
Pulses*	8	8	8
Tree nuts*	11	11	11
Sugar cane*	1,600	1,500	1,750
Palm kernels	40.3	33.0*	40.0*
Groundnuts (in shell)	116	119	137†
Cottonseed	115	135	160*
Coconuts*	450	470	470
Copra*	70	75	75
Tomatoes	19*	20†	21*
Aubergines (Eggplants)	22*	25†	27*
Chillies, peppers*	23	23	23
Other vegetables*	323	329	368
Oranges*	28	28	28
Other citrus fruit*	30	30	30
Bananas	136†	134†	130*
Plantains	1,045	1,076	1,030
Mangoes*	14	14	14
Pineapples†	274	265	213
Other fruit*	12	12	12
Coffee (green)	270	187	265†
Cocoa beans	664	820†	750†
Tobacco (leaves)*	2	2	2
Cotton (lint)	93	114	128
Natural rubber (dry weight)	55†	63†	65*

* FAO estimate(s). † Unofficial figure(s).

Source: FAO, *Production Yearbook*.

LIVESTOCK ('000 head, year ending September)

	1987	1988	1989
Cattle	925	960	991
Pigs*	450	450	450
Sheep*	1,500	1,500	1,500
Goats*	1,500	1,500	1,500

Poultry (million)*: 16 in 1987; 16 in 1988; 17 in 1989.

* FAO estimates.

Source: FAO, *Production Yearbook*.

LIVESTOCK PRODUCTS (FAO estimates, '000 metric tons)

	1987	1988	1989
Total meat production	124	125	135
Beef and veal	36	37	45
Mutton and lamb	6	7	7
Goats' meat	6	6	7
Pig meat	18	18	18
Poultry meat	30	30	31
Cows' milk	18	19	19
Hen eggs	11.5	11.5	12.0
Cattle hides	4.8	4.9	5.9
Sheepskins	1.5	1.6	1.6
Goatskins	1.5	1.5	1.6

Source: FAO, *Production Yearbook*.

Forestry

ROUNDWOOD REMOVALS ('000 cubic metres)

	1986	1987	1988
Sawlogs, veneer logs and logs for sleepers	3,020	2,588	2,650
Other industrial wood	674	702	732
Fuel wood*	8,683	9,051	9,431
Total	12,377	12,341	12,813

* FAO estimates.

Source: FAO, *Yearbook of Forest Products*.

SAWNWOOD PRODUCTION ('000 cubic metres)

	1986	1987	1988
Total (incl. boxboards)	765	775	775

Source: FAO, *Yearbook of Forest Products*.

Fishing

('000 metric tons, live weight)

	1986	1987	1988
Freshwater fishes	26.0	26.0	24.2
Bigeye grunt	2.3	2.5	3.6
West African croakers	1.5	1.5	0.7
Porgies, seabreams, etc.	1.2	0.6	0.7
Threadfins and tasselfishes	1.1	0.9	0.5
Sardinellas	36.6	32.0	18.7
Bonga shad	12.0	12.0	12.0
Other clupeoids	1.6	0.2	0.9
Atlantic black skipjack	0.0	5.3	0.0
Other marine fishes (incl. unspecified)	19.6	18.9	25.0
Total fish	101.8	99.9	86.2
Crustaceans	3.4	2.6	2.6
Total catch	105.2	102.5	88.8
Inland waters	29.0	28.2	28.0
Atlantic Ocean	75.4	74.3	60.8
Indian Ocean	0.7	—	—

Source: FAO, *Yearbook of Fishery Statistics*.

CÔTE D'IVOIRE   Statistical Survey

Mining

	1985	1986	1987
Crude petroleum ('000 metric tons)	1,010	1,007*	880*
Diamonds ('000 carats)†	5‡	14	20*

* UN estimates.
† Source: US Bureau of Mines.
‡ Industrial diamonds only.

Source: UN, *Industrial Statistics Yearbook*.

Industry

SELECTED PRODUCTS
('000 metric tons, unless otherwise indicated)

	1984	1985	1986
Palm oil and palm-kernel oil	244	200	223
Wheat flour	163	n.a.	n.a.
Biscuits	4.5	n.a.	n.a.
Pineapple juice (unconcentrated)	8.8	10.0†	n.a.
Salted, dried or smoked fish*	12.0	15.0	15.0
Tinned fish	35.2	22.2*	23.8*
Cocoa butter (exports)	18.6	21.7	n.a.
Raw sugar	130	112‡	120‡
Beer ('000 hectolitres)	1,245	n.a.	n.a.
Soft drinks ('000 hectolitres)	400	n.a.	n.a.
Cigarettes (million)	3,210	4,000	4,200‡
Cotton woven fabrics (million metres)	100.8	n.a.	n.a.
Synthetic textile materials ('000 metres)	1,710	1,700‡	n.a.
Footwear—excl. rubber ('000 pairs)	5,900	n.a.	n.a.
Plywood ('000 cubic metres)	26	44	44
Motor spirit (Petrol)	245	250	270
Jet fuel	96	98	97
Kerosene	318	320	321
Distillate fuel oils	650	575	478
Cement	552	535	775
Electric energy (million kWh)	1,643	2,021	2,086

1987 ('000 metric tons, unless otherwise indicated): Cigarettes (million) 3,400‡; Plywood ('000 cubic metres) 45; Motor spirit (Petrol) 295; Jet fuel 95; Kerosene 317; Distillate fuel oils 485; Electric energy (million kWh) 2,200.

* Source: FAO.   † FAO estimates.   ‡ UN estimates.

Source: UN, *Industrial Statistics Yearbook*.

Finance

CURRENCY AND EXCHANGE RATES

Monetary Units
  100 centimes = 1 franc de la Communauté financière africaine (CFA).

Denominations
  Coins: 1, 5, 10, 25, 50 and 100 francs CFA.
  Notes: 500, 1,000, 5,000 and 10,000 francs CFA.

French Franc, Sterling and Dollar Equivalents
(30 September 1990)
  1 French franc = 50 francs CFA;
  £1 sterling = 491.1 francs CFA;
  US $1 = 262.1 francs CFA;
  1,000 francs CFA = £2.036 = $3.815.

Average Exchange Rate (francs CFA per US $)
  1987   300.54
  1988   297.85
  1989   319.01

BUDGET (million francs CFA)

Revenue	1987	1988	1989*
Fiscal receipts	496,839	517,750	513,402
Taxes on income and profits	85,778	90,360	96,440
Individual taxes	51,276	52,700	51,800
Corporate and business taxes	26,552	30,460	37,580
Employers' contributions	37,899	42,030	33,785
Taxes on goods and services	116,661	120,880	116,800
Turnover taxes	67,933	61,460	55,291
Consumption taxes	35,018	44,100	41,930
Taxes on international trade and transactions	254,997	263,100	265,182
Import duties	169,569	183,420	180,340
Export duties	85,428	79,680	84,842
Other current receipts	7,451	15,936	9,837
Aid, grants and subsidies	—	2,965	19,068
Borrowing	122,569	106,297	102,997
Domestic borrowing	15,500	20,500	25,500
External borrowing	107,069	85,797	77,497
Total	**626,859**	**642,948**	**645,304**

Expenditure	1987	1988	1989*
General public services	132,788	137,029	137,468
Defence	36,900	38,155	43,508
Public order and security	31,302	32,267	33,207
Education	177,060	191,040	192,488
Health	47,928	44,971	42,730
Social security and welfare	5,044	4,822	4,815
Housing and community amenities	42,103	37,898	33,260
Other community and social services	10,183	11,911	11,687
Economic services	141,133	142,738	144,338
Agriculture, forestry and fishing	55,778	64,925	74,397
Mining, manufacturing and construction	4,470	3,833	2,368
Transport and communications	74,997	66,590	63,599
Other economic services	5,888	7,390	3,974
Other purposes	2,418	2,117	1,803
Debt repayment	2,000	1,700	1,000
Total	**626,859**	**642,948**	**645,304**

* Estimates.

Source: Banque Centrale des Etats de l'Afrique de l'Ouest.

1990 (draft budget, million francs (CFA): Current expenditure 489,800; Investment expenditure 129,578.

CENTRAL BANK RESERVES (US $ million at 31 December)

	1987	1988	1989
Gold*	21.0	18.5	17.4
IMF special drawing rights	0.2	0.7	5.1
Foreign exchange	8.7	9.7	9.8
Total	**29.9**	**28.9**	**32.4**

* Valued at market-related prices.

Source: IMF, *International Financial Statistics*.

MONEY SUPPLY ('000 million francs CFA at 31 December)

	1987	1988	1989
Currency outside banks	304.7	298.5	254.1
Demand deposits at deposit money banks*	292.3	278.3	255.6
Checking deposits at post office	1.5	1.1	1.5
Total money	**598.6**	**578.0**	**511.2**

* Excluding the deposits of public establishments of an administrative or social nature.

Source: IMF, *International Financial Statistics*.

CÔTE D'IVOIRE *Statistical Survey*

COST OF LIVING
(Consumer Price Index for Africans in Abidjan. Base: 1980 = 100)

	1984	1985	1986
Food	120.1	122.0	133.7
Fuel, light, water and soap	121.8	125.9	130.9
Clothing	203.0	207.3	214.2
Rent	150.9	152.6	152.9
All items (incl. others)	128.8	131.1	139.8

1987: Food 156.1; All items 154.1.
1988: All items 164.8.
Source: ILO, mainly *Year Book of Labour Statistics*.

NATIONAL ACCOUNTS
('000 million francs CFA at current prices)
National Income and Product

	1980	1981	1982
Compensation of employees	748.2	796.2	873.7
Operating surplus	788.2	910.3	954.1
Domestic factor incomes	1,536.5	1,706.5	1,827.9
Consumption of fixed capital	184.0	211.3	208.5
Gross domestic product (GDP) at factor cost	1,720.5	1,917.8	2,036.4
Indirect taxes, *less* subsidies*	429.4	373.6	450.2
GDP in purchasers' values	2,149.9	2,291.4	2,486.5
Factor income received from abroad	7.3	8.1	10.1
Less Factor income paid abroad	117.5	179.7	225.3
Gross national product	2,039.7	2,119.6	2,271.3
Less Consumption of fixed capital	184.0	211.3	208.5
National income in market prices	1,855.7	1,908.3	2,062.8
Other current transfers from abroad	45.0	55.4	55.8
Less Other current transfers paid abroad	138.8	135.7	160.5
National disposable income	1,761.9	1,828.0	1,958.1

* Includes the profit or loss of the Caisse de stabilisation et de soutien des prix des productions agricoles (CSSPPA).

GDP in purchasers' values ('000 million francs CFA at current prices): 2,605.9 in 1983; 2,883.4 in 1984.

Source: UN, *National Accounts Statistics*.

Expenditure on the Gross Domestic Product

	1984*	1985†	1986†
Government final consumption expenditure	427	437.1	491.7
Private final consumption expenditure	1,750	1,891.7	2,004.8
Increase in stocks	108	35.2	−25.7
Gross fixed capital formation	362	359.3	386.2
Total domestic expenditure	2,647	2,723.2	2,857.0
Exports of goods and services	1,320	1,437.9	1,262.2
Less Imports of goods and services	1,083	1,023.6	874.8
GDP in purchasers' values	2,883	3,137.6	3,244.4

* Estimates (Source: UN Economic Commission for Africa, *African Statistical Yearbook*).
† Source: UN, *National Accounts Statistics*.

Gross Domestic Product by Economic Activity

	1985*	1986	1987
Agriculture, hunting, forestry and fishing	1,077	1,228	1,382
Mining and quarrying	40	37	35
Manufacturing	286	316	302
Electricity, gas and water	33	37	36
Construction	123	114	104
Trade, restaurants and hotels	337	373	366
Transport, storage and communications	191	212	207
Finance, insurance, real estate and business services	92	102	102
Public administration and defence	311	333	348
Other services	38	42	39
GDP at factor cost	2,527	2,794	2,922
Indirect taxes, *less* subsidies	610	694	685
GDP in purchasers' values	3,138	3,489	3,606

* Estimates.
Source: UN Economic Commission for Africa, *African Statistical Yearbook*.

BALANCE OF PAYMENTS (US $ million)

	1987	1988	1989
Merchandise exports f.o.b.	2,938.4	2,774.2	2,520.6
Merchandise imports f.o.b.	−1,846.7	−1,696.2	−1,379.3
Trade balance	1,091.7	1,078.1	1,141.4
Exports of services	614.9	641.6	625.7
Imports of services	−2,297.6	−2,396.9	−2,239.1
Balance on goods and services	−591.0	−677.3	−472.1
Private unrequited transfers (net)	−501.1	−491.5	−458.9
Government unrequited transfers (net)	141.4	66.6	72.8
Current balance	−950.7	−1,102.1	−858.2
Direct capital investment (net)	87.5	22.2	25.4
Other long-term capital (net)	−126.1	−391.8	−440.7
Short-term capital (net)	67.2	231.7	11.6
Net errors and omissions	−11.1	−193.2	1,395.3
Total (net monetary movements)	−933.1	−1,433.3	133.3
Valuation changes (net)	−83.9	28.4	15.1
Exceptional financing (net)	1,087.1	1,514.7	−19.8
Official financing (net)	9.0	−18.1	−0.9
Changes in reserves	79.1	91.7	127.7

Source: IMF, *International Financial Statistics*.

CÔTE D'IVOIRE   *Statistical Survey*

External Trade

Source: Banque Centrale des Etats de l'Afrique de l'Ouest.

PRINCIPAL COMMODITIES (million francs CFA)

Imports c.i.f.	1985	1986	1987
Dairy products	23,629	23,790	24,445
Cereals	32,962	41,589	45,091
Beverages and tobacco	15,154	16,856	16,003
Fuels	170,142	111,525	100,900
Crude petroleum	156,695	104,058	93,438
Machinery and transport equipment	170,483	160,907	143,649
Electrical machinery	25,294	28,813	25,560
Non-electric machinery	54,147	69,750	60,956
Road vehicles	51,525	59,318	53,946
Air transport equipment	29,466	2,246	1,970
Chemicals	102,167	100,420	93,152
Cotton yarn and fabrics	17,240	18,569	15,066
Total (incl. others)	772,987	709,044	673,899

Exports f.o.b.	1985	1986	1987
Pineapples	25,516	25,350	21,040
Green coffee	277,657	233,131	118,053
Cocoa beans	398,409	392,877	312,615
Cocoa paste and cocoa butter	88,617	64,667	54,456
Coffee extracts and essences	20,744	20,371	18,230
Canned fish	18,643	18,783	22,457
Fuels	118,204	94,005	101,175
Latex	13,693	13,644	16,201
Wood	90,857	76,445	63,043
Cotton (ginned)	33,360	27,665	25,678
Fats and oils	30,774	15,975	18,042
Machinery and transport equipment	21,398	23,311	14,069
Chemicals	30,297	29,761	21,606
Cotton yarn and fabrics	14,311	15,115	16,869
Total (incl. others)	1,318,060	1,160,441	929,143

PRINCIPAL TRADING PARTNERS (million francs CFA)

Imports	1985	1986	1987
Belgium/Luxembourg	17,846	20,848	17,481
Brazil	5,555	7,944	4,823
Cameroon	21,040	1,737	3,348
Canada	7,890	4,042	3,383
China, People's Republic	13,219	11,838	17,120
France	247,873	219,707	213,313
Gabon	13,655	6,556	1,432
Germany, Fed. Republic	37,466	40,429	35,340
Italy	29,121	30,717	36,396
Japan	38,438	44,170	37,275
Netherlands	36,852	39,567	34,356
Nigeria	86,155	69,864	73,128
Pakistan	6,949	16,048	13,541
Senegal	15,377	11,764	9,862
Spain	27,426	26,275	23,321
Switzerland	8,026	9,845	11,298
United Kingdom	16,533	18,003	15,546
USA	52,984	29,219	29,719
Venezuela	2,835	17,173	4,113
Total (incl. others)	772,987	709,044	673,899

Exports	1985	1986	1987
Belgium/Luxembourg	51,055	52,603	41,372
Burkina Faso	38,121	30,716	22,295
France	218,371	165,256	141,567
Gabon	5,577	11,042	2,489
Germany, Fed. Republic	70,692	64,269	56,882
Ghana	11,038	12,261	15,429
Italy	120,911	90,001	67,465
Japan	13,590	15,931	5,732
Liberia	5,453	5,802	10,951
Mali	37,975	32,083	24,036
Netherlands	225,633	216,758	156,585
Niger	10,518	8,614	8,714
Nigeria	7,718	25,015	20,490
Senegal	20,629	12,010	15,519
Spain	33,901	33,915	25,196
Togo	10,706	9,400	13,656
USSR	57,522	59,027	47,660
United Kingdom	57,312	49,324	82,889
USA	154,055	121,980	97,746
Total (incl. others)	1,318,060	1,160,441	929,143

Transport

RAILWAYS (including Burkina Faso traffic)

	1982	1983	1984
Passengers ('000)	3,171.8	2,941.0	2,574.9
Passenger-km (million)	892.6	971.8	857.8
Freight ('000 metric tons)	731	601	702
Freight (million net ton-km)	610.6	468.7	530.2

ROAD TRAFFIC (motor vehicles in use at 31 December)

	1981	1982	1984†
Passenger cars	157,076	166,920	182,956
Buses and coaches	10,608	11,417	12,944
Goods vehicles*	66,795	69,467	30,057

* Including vans. † Figures for 1983 are not available.
Source: International Road Federation, *World Road Statistics*.

INTERNATIONAL SEA-BORNE SHIPPING
(freight traffic, '000 metric tons)

	1987	1988	1989
Goods loaded	4,319	4,195	4,667
Goods unloaded	6,137	6,134	6,454

Source: Banque Centrale des Etats de l'Afrique de l'Ouest.

CIVIL AVIATION (traffic on scheduled services)*

	1983	1984	1985
Kilometres flown ('000)	4,700	4,700	3,200
Passengers carried	389,000	398,000	183,000
Passenger-km ('000)	316,000	325,000	289,000
Freight ton-km ('000)	19,100	17,800	18,400
Mail ton-km ('000)	900	800	700

* Including an apportionment of the traffic of Air Afrique.
Source: UN, *Statistical Yearbook*.

CÔTE D'IVOIRE

Tourism

	1985	1986	1987
Tourist arrivals ('000)	202	184	184

Source: UN Economic Commission for Africa, *African Statistical Yearbook*.

Communications Media

	1985	1986	1987
Radio receivers ('000 in use)	1,300	1,350	1,450
Television receivers ('000 in use)	500	550	600
Daily newspapers:			
Number	n.a.	1	n.a.
Average circulation ('000 copies)	n.a.	90	n.a.

Book production (1983, excluding pamphlets): 46 titles; 3,766,000 copies.

Source: UNESCO, *Statistical Yearbook*.

Telephones (1987): 110,000 in use (Source: UN Economic Commission for Africa, *African Statistical Yearbook*).

Education

PUPILS ENROLLED

	1982/83	1983/84	1984/85
Pre-primary	7,200	7,493	8,539
Primary	1,134,915	1,159,824	1,179,456
Public	1,001,647	1,029,628	1,046,790
Private	133,268	130,196	132,666
Secondary	242,126	251,417	266,801
General	217,824	229,872	245,043
Teacher training	1,525	1,081	2,765
Vocational	22,777	20,464	18,993
Higher education	n.a.	18,872	19,660
National University	12,363	12,859	11,300

Pupils enrolled: Pre-primary 8,570 in 1985/86; Primary 1,214,511 in 1985/86; Secondary (General) 272,911 in 1987/88; Secondary (Vocational) 25,328 in 1986/87.

Teachers: Pre-primary 230 in 1983/84; Primary 33,500 in 1985/86; Secondary (General) 5,192 in 1980/81; Secondary (Vocational) 1,947 in 1981/82; Higher education 1,204 (incl. 666 at the National University) in 1981/82.

Source: UNESCO, *Statistical Yearbook*.

Directory

The Constitution

The Constitution was promulgated on 31 October 1960. It was amended in June 1971, October 1975, August 1980, November 1980, October 1985, January 1986 and November 1990.

PREAMBLE

The Republic of Côte d'Ivoire is one and indivisible. It is secular, democratic and social. Sovereignty belongs to the people who exercise it through their representatives or through referenda. There is universal, equal and secret suffrage. French is the official language.

HEAD OF STATE

The President is elected for a five-year term by direct universal suffrage and is eligible for re-election. He is Head of the Administration and the Armed Forces and has power to ask the National Assembly to reconsider a Bill, which must then be passed by two-thirds of the members of the Assembly; he may also have a Bill submitted to a referendum. In case of the death or incapacitation of the President of the Republic, the functions of the Head of State are assumed by the President of the National Assembly, until the expiry of the previous incumbent's mandate.

EXECUTIVE POWER

Executive power is vested in the President. He appoints a Prime Minister, who, in turn, appoints a Council of Ministers. Any member of the National Assembly appointed minister must renounce his seat in the Assembly, but may regain it on leaving the Government.

LEGISLATIVE POWER

Legislative power is vested in a National Assembly of 175 members, elected for a five-year term of office. Legislation may be introduced either by the President or by a member of the National Assembly.

JUDICIAL POWER

The independence of the judiciary is guaranteed by the President, assisted by a High Council of Judiciary.

ECONOMIC AND SOCIAL COUNCIL

This is an advisory commission of 120 members, appointed by the President because of their specialist knowledge or experience.

POLITICAL ORGANIZATIONS

Article 7 of the Constitution stipulates that political organizations can be formed and can exercise their activities freely, provided that they respect the principles of national sovereignty and democracy and the laws of the Republic.

The Government

HEAD OF STATE

President: Dr FÉLIX HOUPHOUËT-BOIGNY (took office November 1960, re-elected for seventh term of office 28 October 1990).

COUNCIL OF MINISTERS
(January 1991)

Prime Minister and Minister of the Economy and Finance: ALASSANE OUATTARA.

Minister-delegate to the Prime Minister, with responsibility for the Economy, Finance, Trade and Planning: DANIEL KABLAN DUNCAN.

Minister-delegate to the Prime Minister, with responsibility for Raw Materials: GUY-ALAIN EMMANUEL GAUZE.

Minister of Defence: LÉON KONAN KOFFI.

Minister of Foreign Affairs: AMARA ESSY.

Minister of the Interior and Security: EMILE CONSTANT BOMBET.

Minister of Justice and Keeper of the Seals: JACQUELINE LOHOUES OBLÉ.

Minister of National Education: VAMOUSSA BAMBA.

Minister of Scientific Research, Professional Training and Technical Education: ALHASSANE SALIF N'DIAYE.

Minister of Agriculture and Animal Husbandry: LAMBERT KOUASSI KONAN.

Minister of Industry, Mines and Energy: YED ESAÏE ANGORAN.

Minister of Public Health and Social Protection: ALAIN EKRA.

Minister of Communications and Spokesperson for the Government: AUGUSTE SÉVÉRIN MIREMONT.

Minister of Equipment, Transport and Tourism: ADAMA COULIBALY.

Minister of the Environment, Construction and Town Planning: EZAN AKÈLE.

CÔTE D'IVOIRE   *Directory*

Minister of Planning, Employment and the Civil Service: Patrice Kouamé.

Minister of Culture: Henriette Dagri Diabate.

Minister of Women's Promotion: Claire-Thérèse Elisabeth Grah.

Minister of Posts and Telecommunications: Yao Nicolas Kouassi Akon.

Minister of Youth and Sports: René Djedjemel Diby.

MINISTRIES

Ministry of Agriculture and Animal Husbandry: BP V82, Abidjan; telex 23612.

Ministry of Communications: BP V138, Abidjan; telex 23501.

Ministry of Culture: Abidjan.

Ministry of Defence: BP V11, Abidjan; telex 22855.

Ministry of the Economy and Finance: Immeuble SCIAM, ave Marchand, BP V163, Abidjan; tel. 21-05-66; telex 23747.

Ministry of the Environment, Construction and Town Planning, Posts and Telecommunications: ave Jean Paul II, BP V6, Abidjan 01; tel. 29-13-67; telex 22108.

Ministry of Equipment, Transport and Tourism: BP V184, Abidjan; tel. 21-29-92; telex 23438.

Ministry of Foreign Affairs: BP V109, Abidjan; telex 23752.

Ministry of Industry, Mines and Energy: BP V65, Abidjan; tel. 29-14-68; telex 22638.

Ministry of the Interior and Security: BP V241, Abidjan; telex 22296.

Ministry of Justice: BP V107, Abidjan.

Ministry of National Education: BP V120, Abidjan; tel. 21-12-31.

Ministry of Planning, Employment and the Civil Service: BP V93, Abidjan 01; tel. 21-04-00.

Ministry of Public Health and Social Protection: BP V4, Abidjan; telex 42213.

Ministry of Women's Promotion: Abidjan.

Ministry of Youth and Sports: BP V124, Abidjan; telex 23480.

Legislature

ASSEMBLÉE NATIONALE

Legislative elections were held on 25 November 1990, at which, for the first time, representatives of more than one party were permitted to contest the Assembly's 175 seats. According to official results, representation in the legislature is as follows:

Parti démocratique de la Côte d'Ivoire 163 seats; Front populaire ivorien 9; Parti ivoirien des travailleurs 1; Independent candidates 2.

President: Henri Konan-Bédié.

Vice-Presidents: Elhaji Lanciné Cissé (Dean of the Députés), Marthe Achi-Brou, Paul Akoto Yao, Edmond Boazo Zegbehi, Joseph Folquet, Goly Kouassi, Bamba Mamadou, Kalé Socoudé.

Political Organizations

Parti démocratique de la Côte d'Ivoire (PDCI): Maison du Parti, Abidjan; f. 1946 as the local section of the Rassemblement démocratique africain; principal organs are a Cen. Cttee of 80 mems, a 400-mem. Political Bureau and a Political Council; Chair. Dr Félix Houphouët-Boigny.

On 30 April 1990 the political bureau of the PDCI recommended that the Government implement Article 7 of the Constitution, which provides for the establishment of political organizations. President Houphouët-Boigny subsequently complied with this recommendation; by late 1990 the statutes of 26 political organizations had been approved. Among the first parties to be granted legal status were:

Front populaire ivoirien (FPI)*: Abidjan; f. 1982 in France; Leader Laurent Gbagbo.

Parti ivoirien des travailleurs (PIT)*: Abidjan; f. 1990; Leader Francis Wodié.

Parti républicain de la Côte d'Ivoire (PRCI): Abidjan; f. 1975 in France; Pres. Robert Gbai Tagro.

Parti socialiste ivoirien (PSI)*: Abidjan; f. 1990; Leader Bamba Morifère.

Union social-démocrate (USD)*: Abidjan; f. 1990; Leader Bernard Zadi-Zaourou.

* Denotes signatories to the June 1990 'Korhogo Declaration'.

Diplomatic Representation

EMBASSIES IN CÔTE D'IVOIRE

Algeria: 53 blvd Clozel, 01 BP 1015, Abidjan 01; tel. 21-23-40; telex 23243; Ambassador: (vacant).

Argentina: 08 BP 860, Abidjan 08; tel. 44-41-78; telex 26100; Ambassador: Federico Mirre.

Austria: Immeuble N'Zarama, blvd Lagunaire-Charles de Gaulle, Plateau, 01 BP 1837, Abidjan 01; tel. 33-22-00; telex 22664; Ambassador: Dr Georg Znidaric.

Belgium: Immeuble Alliance, ave Terrasson de Fougères, 01 BP 1800, Abidjan 01; tel. 21-00-88; telex 23633; Ambassador: Jacques de Montjoye.

Benin: rue des Jardins, 09 BP 238, Abidjan 09; tel. 41-44-14; telex 23922; Ambassador: Jonas Gbogbohoundada.

Brazil: Immeuble Alpha 2000, rue Gourgas, 01 BP 3820, Abidjan 01; tel. 22-23-41; telex 23443; Ambassador: Italo M. A. Mastrogiovanni.

Burkina Faso: 2 ave Terrasson de Fougères, 01 BP 908, Abidjan 01; tel. 21-13-13; telex 23453; Ambassador: Bernard Nabare.

Cameroon: 01 BP 2886, Abidjan 01; Ambassador: Paul Kamga Njike.

Canada: Immeuble Trade Centre, 01 BP 4104, Abidjan 01; tel. 21-20-09; telex 23593; Ambassador: Jean-Guy Saint-Martin.

Central African Republic: rue des Combattants, 01 BP 3387, Abidjan 01; tel. 21-36-46; telex 22102; Ambassador: Antoine Kezza.

Chile: 06 BP 380, Abidjan 06; tel. 21-92-37; telex 22173; Ambassador: Félix Cabezas.

China, People's Republic: 01 BP 3691, Abidjan 01; tel. 41-32-48; telex 22104; Ambassador: Cai Zaidu.

Colombia: 01 BP 3874, Abidjan 01; tel. 33-12-44; telex 22576; fax 32-47-31; Ambassador: Octavio Gallón Restrepo.

Czechoslovakia: Immeuble Tropique III, 01 BP 1349, Abidjan 01; tel. 21-20-30; telex 22110; Chargé d'affaires a.i.: Petr Postulka.

Denmark: Immeuble Le Mans, blvd Botreau Roussel, angle ave Noguès, Plateau, 01 BP 4569, Abidjan 01; tel. 33-17-65; telex 23871; fax 32-41-89; Chargé d'affaires: Johan Otto Stephensen.

Egypt: Immeuble El Nasr, ave du Général de Gaulle, 01 BP 2104, Abidjan 01; tel. 32-79-25; telex 23537; Ambassador: Nosrat Ali Fahmi Naim.

Ethiopia: Immeuble Nour Al-Hayat, 01 BP 3712, Abidjan 01; tel. 21-33-65; telex 23848; Ambassador: (vacant).

France: rue Lecoeur, quartier du Plateau, 17 BP 175, Abidjan 17; tel. 21-67-49; telex 23699; Ambassador: Michel Dupuch.

Gabon: Cocody Danga Nord, derrière la Direction de la Géologie, 01 BP 3765, Abidjan 01; tel. 41-51-54; telex 27188; Ambassador: Aboubakar Bokoko.

Germany: Immeuble Le Mans, blvd Boitreau Roussel, 01 BP 1900, Abidjan 01; tel. 32-47-27; telex 23642; fax 32-47-29; Ambassador: Dr Michael Schmidt.

Ghana: Résidence de la Corniche, blvd du Général de Gaulle, 01 BP 1871, Abidjan 01; tel. 21-11-24; Ambassador: J. E. A. Kotei.

Guinea: Immeuble Crosson Duplessis, 08 BP 2280, Abidjan 08; tel. 21-86-00; telex 22865; Ambassador: Richard Haba.

Holy See: 08 BP 1347, Abidjan 08 (Apostolic Nunciature); tel. 44-38-35; telex 26182; Apostolic Nuncio: Most Rev. Janusz Bolonek, Titular Archbishop of Madaurus.

India: Lot 36, Impasse, Ablaha Pokou, Cocody Danga Nord, 06 BP 318, Abidjan 06; tel. 44-52-31; telex 28103; fax 44-01-11; Ambassador: Beni Prasad Agarwal.

Israel: Immeuble Nour Al-Hayat, 01 BP 1877, Abidjan 01; tel. 21-49-53; Ambassador: Menahem Carmon.

Italy: 16 rue de la Canebière, Cocody, 01 BP 1905, Abidjan 01; tel. 44-61-70; telex 26123; Ambassador: (vacant).

Japan: Immeuble Alpha 2000, rue Gourgas, 01 BP 1329, Abidjan 01; tel. 21-28-63; telex 23400; Ambassador: Masaki Yagi.

Korea, Democratic People's Republic: BP V48, Abidjan; tel. 44-22-75; Ambassador: Yi Chae-Rim.

Korea, Republic: Immeuble Le Général, 01 BP 3950, Abidjan 01; tel. 21-22-90; telex 23638; Ambassador: Joung-Soo Lee.

Lebanon: 01 BP 2227, Abidjan 01; tel. 21-28-24; telex 22245; Ambassador: Nizar Chamas.

CÔTE D'IVOIRE

Liberia: Immeuble La Symphonie, 30 ave du Général de Gaulle, Abidjan; tel. 22-23-59; telex 23535; Ambassador: HAROLD TARR.
Mali: Maison du Mali, rue du Commerce, 01 BP 2746, Abidjan 01; tel. 21-31-47; telex 23429; Ambassador: MODIBO DIARRA.
Mauritania: 01 BP 2275, Abidjan 01; tel. 44-16-43; telex 27181; Ambassador: Col AHMEDOU OUM ABDALLAH.
Morocco: 24 rue de la Canebière, Cocody, 01 BP 146, Abidjan 01; tel. 44-58-78; telex 26147; Ambassador: MOHAMED BENNIS.
Netherlands: Immeuble Les Harmonies, blvd Carde, 01 BP 1086, Abidjan 01; tel. 22-77-12; telex 23694; Ambassador: (vacant).
Niger: 01 BP 2743, Abidjan 01; tel. 35-50-98; telex 43185; Ambassador: MADOU MAHAMADOU.
Nigeria: 35 blvd de la République, 01 BP 1906, Abidjan 01; tel. 21-38-17; telex 23532; Ambassador: Dr LAWRENCE B. EKPEBU.
Norway: Immeuble N'Zarama, blvd du Général de Gaulle, 01 BP 607, Abidjan 01; tel. 22-25-34; telex 23355; fax 32-91-99; Ambassador: KJELL ØSTREM.
Poland: 04 BP 308, Abidjan 04; tel. 44-12-25; telex 26114; Chargé d'affaires: ANDRZEJ KULESZA.
Rwanda: 01 BP 3905, Abidjan 01; tel. 41-38-31; telex 27152; fax 41-05-37; Ambassador: ISMAÏL AMRI SUED.
Senegal: Résidence Nabil, blvd du Général de Gaulle, 08 BP 2165, Abidjan 08; tel. 21-28-76; telex 23897; Ambassador: ABDOURAHMANE TOURÉ.
Spain: 01 BP 2589, Abidjan 01; tel. 44-48-50; telex 28120; fax 33-28-48; Ambassador: FERNANDO CASTILLO.
Sweden: Immeuble Alpha 2000, rue Gourgas, 04 BP 992, Abidjan 04; tel. 21-24-10; telex 23293; fax 21-21-07; Ambassador: ARNE EKFELDT.
Switzerland: Immeuble Alpha 2000, rue Gourgas, 01 BP 1914, Abidjan 01; tel. 21-17-21; telex 23492; Ambassador: JACQUES REVERDIN.
Tunisia: Immeuble Shell, 48 ave Lamblin, 01 BP 3906, Abidjan 01; tel. 21-23-04; telex 23709; Ambassador: ABDEL AZIZ AL-AYADHI.
USSR: Riviera SQ-1 Sud, 01 BP 7646, Abidjan 01; tel. 43-09-59; Ambassador: BORIS MINAKOV.
United Kingdom: Immeuble Les Harmonies, angle blvd Carde et ave Dr Jamot, Plateau, 01 BP 2581, Abidjan 01; tel. 22-68-50; telex 23706; fax 22-32-21; Ambassador: MARGARET ROTHWELL.
USA: 5 rue Jesse Owens, 01 BP 1712, Abidjan 01; tel. 21-09-79; telex 23660; Ambassador: KENNETH BROWN.
Zaire: 29 blvd Clozel, 01 BP 3961, Abidjan 01; tel. 22-20-80; telex 23795; Ambassador: LOUYA LONDOALE.

Judicial System

Since 1964 all civil, criminal, commercial and administrative cases have come under the jurisdiction of the Tribunaux de première instance (Magistrates' courts), the assize courts and the Court of Appeal, with the Supreme Court as supreme court of appeal.

The Supreme Court: rue Gourgas, BP V30, Abidjan; has four chambers: constitutional, judicial, administrative and auditing; Pres. (vacant).
Courts of Appeal: Abidjan and Bouaké; hear appeals from courts of first instance; Abidjan: First Pres. CAMILLE HOGUIE, Attorney-Gen. LOUIS FOLQUET; Bouaké: First Pres. AHIOUA MOULARE, Attorney-Gen. ANOMAN OGUIE.
The High Court of Justice: composed of Deputies elected from and by the National Assembly; has jurisdiction to impeach the President or other member of the government; Pres. HENRI KONAN-BÉDIÉ.
State Security Court: composed of a president and six regular judges, all appointed for five years; deals with all offences against the security of the State; Pres. ALPHONSE BONI.
Courts of First Instance: Abidjan, Pres. ROBERT COULOUD NATCHA; Bouaké: Pres. KABLAN AKA EDOUKOU; Daloa: Pres. WOUNE BLEKA; there are a further 25 courts in the principal centres.

Religion

It is estimated that 65% of the population follow traditional animist beliefs, while 23% are Muslims and 12% are Christians, mainly Roman Catholics.

CHRISTIANITY
The Roman Catholic Church

Côte d'Ivoire comprises one archdiocese and 11 dioceses. At 01 December 1988 there were an estimated 1,138,644 adherents (about 11.5% of the total population).

Bishops' Conference: Conférence Episcopale de la Côte d'Ivoire, 01 BP 1287, Abidjan 01; tel. 21-22-56; f. 1973; Pres. Cardinal BERNARD YAGO, Archbishop of Abidjan.
Archbishop of Abidjan: Cardinal BERNARD YAGO, Archevêché, ave Jean Paul II, 01 BP 1287, Abidjan 01; tel. 21-12-46.

Protestant Churches

Assemblée de Dieu: 04 BP 266, Abidjan 04; Pres. ADAMO OUEDRAOGO.
Christian and Missionary Alliance: BP 585, Bouaké 01; tel. 63-23-12; fax 63-54-12; f. 1929; 13 mission stations; Dir Rev. J. CLYDE RITCHEY.
Conservative Baptist Foreign Mission Society: BP 109, Korhogo; tel. 86-00-33; f. 1947; active in Abidjan and in the northern area in evangelism, teaching and medical work.
Eglise Baptiste Oeuvres et Mission: 03 BP 1032, Abidjan 03; Pres. ROBERT DION.
Eglise Nazaréenne: CEDEX 03C34, Riviera, Abidjan: Dir JOHN SEAMAN.
Eglise Protestante Méthodiste: 41 blvd de la République, 01 BP 1282, Abidjan 01; c. 120,000 mems; Pres. Pastor EMMANUEL YANDO.
Mission Baptiste du Sud: 01 BP 3722, Abidjan 01.
Mission Evangélique de l'Afrique Occidentale: 08 BP 653, Abidjan 08; tel. 44-02-68; f. 1934; 11 mission centres, 48 missionaries; Field Dir SHOERD VAN DONGE; affiliated church: Alliance des Eglises Evangéliques de Côte d'Ivoire; 85 churches, 35 full-time pastors; Pres. BOAN BI ZRÉ EMMANUEL.
Mission Norvégienne Luthérienne: BP 196, Ouaninou; Dir JOHANNES REDSE.
Union des Eglises Evangéliques du Sud-Ouest de la Côte d'Ivoire and **Mission Biblique:** 08 BP 20, Abidjan 08; f. 1927; c. 250 places of worship.

The Press

Abidjan 7 Jours: 01 BP 1965, Abidjan 01; tel. 35-39-39; telex 43171; f. 1964; weekly; local information; circ. 10,000.
Afrique-Sports: Abidjan; weekly.
L'Alternative: Abidjan; f. 1990; organ of the Front populaire ivoirien.
Bulletin mensuel de Statistiques: Direction de la Statistique, 01 BP V55, Abidjan 01; tel. 21-15-38.
Djeliba—le journal des jeunes Chrétiens: 01 BP 1287, Abidjan 01; tel. 21-69-79; f. 1974; 5 a year; Editor PIERRE TRICHET; circ. 5,500.
Eburnea: Ministry of Information, BP V138, Abidjan; telex 23781; monthly.
Entente Africaine: 01 BP 3901, Abidjan 01; publ. by Société Inter Afrique Presse; quarterly; illustrated; Editor JUSTIN VIEYRA.
Fraternité-Hebdo: 01 BP 1212, Abidjan 01; tel. 21-29-15; organ of the PDCI; weekly; Editor GUY PIERRE NOUAMA.
Fraternité-Matin: blvd du Général de Gaulle, 01 BP 1807, Abidjan 01; tel. 21-27-27; telex 23718; f. 1964; organ of the PDCI; official journal of record for govt activities; daily; Editor-in-Chief AUGUSTE MIREMONT; circ. 80,000.
Gazette du Centre: Bouaké; weekly.
Le Griot: 01 BP 495, Abidjan 01; tel. 35-72-23; telex 42258; f. 1981; weekly; classified advertisements; circ. 20,000.
Le Guido (Abidjan Jour et Nuit): 01 BP 1807, Abidjan 01; tel. 37-06-66; telex 372545; f. 1987; weekly; local information; Dir LAURENT DONA-FOLOGO.
Ivoire-Dimanche (ID): 01 BP 1807, Abidjan 01; f. 1971; weekly; circ. 75,000.
Ivoir 'Soir: blvd du Général de Gaulle, 01 BP 1807, Abidjan 01; f. 1987; organ of the PDCI; social, cultural and sporting activities; daily; Dir AUGUSTE MIREMONT; circ. 50,000.
Journal des Amis du Progrès de l'Afrique Noire: Abidjan; 5 a week.
Journal Officiel de la Côte d'Ivoire: Service Autonome des Journaux Officiels, BP V70, Abidjan; tel. 22-67-76; weekly; circ. 1,000.
Le Messager: BP 1776, Abidjan; 6 a year; Editor ANDRÉ LEROUX.
La Nouvelle: 01 BP 1287, Abidjan 01; tel. 21-69-79; f. 1989; 6 a year; Editor PIERRE TRICHET; circ. 6,500.
Le Nouvel Horizon: f. 1990; publ. by Front populaire ivoirien; weekly; circ. 15,000.

CÔTE D'IVOIRE
Directory

Revue Ivoirienne de Droit: BP 3811, Abidjan; f. 1969; publ. by the Centre ivoirien de recherches et d'études juridiques; legal affairs; circ. 1,500.

Télé-Miroir: Abidjan; monthly.

La Voix d'Afrique: Abidjan; publ. by Société Inter Afrique Presse; monthly; Editor-in-Chief GAOUSSOU KAMISSOKO.

NEWS AGENCIES

Agence Ivoirienne de Presse (AIP): 04 BP 312, Abidjan 04; telex 23781; f. 1961; Dir KONÉ SEMGUÉ SAMBA.

Foreign Bureaux

Agence France-Presse (AFP): 18 ave du Docteur Crozet, 01 BP 726, Abidjan 01; tel. 21-90-17; telex 22481; Dir BERNARD NICOLAS.

Agenzia Nazionale Stampa Associata (ANSA) (Italy): 01 BP 3570, Abidjan 01; tel. 35-60-82; telex 26118; Dir MAURIZIO LOCATELLI.

Associated Press (AP) (USA): 01 BP 5843, Abidjan 01; tel. 41-37-49; telex 28129; Correspondent ROBERT WELLER.

Reuters (UK): Résidence Les Acacias, 20 blvd Clozel, 01 BP 2338, Abidjan 01; tel. 21-27-01; telex 23921; Chief Correspondent R. M. MALONEY.

Xinhua (New China) News Agency (People's Republic of China): Cocody Danga Nord Lot 46, 08 BP 1212, Abidjan 08; tel. 44-01-24; Chief Correspondent XIONG SHANWU.

Central News Agency (Taiwan) also has an office in Abidjan.

Publishers

Le Bureau Ivoirien des Nouvelles Editions Africaines (BINEA): 01 BP 3525, Abidjan 01; tel. 21-12-51; telex 22564; f. 1972, as Nouvelles Editions Africaines, name changed 1988; bibliography, fiction, poetry, theatre, religion, art, juveniles, history, textbooks; Dir KROAH-BILÉ N'DABIAN.

Centre d'Edition et de Diffusion Africaines (CEDA): 04 BP 541, Abidjan 04; tel. 22-20-55; telex 22451; fax 21-72-62; f. 1961; general non-fiction; Chair. and Man. Dir VENANCE KACOU.

Centre de Publications Evangéliques: 08 BP 900, Abidjan 08; tel. 44-48-05; f. 1970; religious; Dir ROBERT BRYAN.

Institut africain pour le Développement Economique et Social-Edition (INADES-Edition): 08 BP 8, Abidjan 08; tel. 44-15-94; f. 1975; African studies, philosophy, religion, economics, agriculture, sociology, essays; Man. Dir RAYMOND DENIEL.

Société Inter Afrique Presse: blvd du Général de Gaulle, 01 BP 3901, Abidjan 01; tel. 37-14-75; telex 3861; Man. JUSTIN VIEYRA.

Université Nationale de Côte d'Ivoire: 01 BP V34, Abidjan 01; tel. 44-08-59; telex 26138; f. 1964; general non-fiction and periodicals; Publications Dir GILLES VILASCO.

Government Publishing House

Imprimerie Nationale: BP V87, Abidjan; telex 23868.

Radio and Television

In 1987 there were an estimated 1.5m. radio receivers and 600,000 television receivers in use.

Radiodiffusion Ivoirienne: BP V191, Abidjan 01; tel. 21-48-00; telex 22635; f. 1962; govt radio station broadcasting in French, English and local languages; MW station at Abidjan, relay at Bouaké; VHF transmitters at Abidjan, Bouaflé, Man and Koun-Abbrosso; Dir MAMADOU BERTÉ.

Télévision Ivoirienne: 08 BP 883, Abidjan 08; tel. 43-90-39; telex 22293; f. 1963; broadcasts in French; two channels; colour transmissions since 1973; stations at Abidjan, Bouaflé, Bouaké, Binao, Digo, Dimbokro, Koun, Man, Niangbo, Niangué, Séguéla, Tiémé and Touba; Man. DANIÈLE BONNI-CLAVERIE.

Finance

(br. = branch; cap. = capital; res = reserves; dep. = deposits; m. = million; amounts in francs CFA)

BANKING

Central Bank

Banque Centrale des Etats de l'Afrique de l'Ouest (BCEAO): ave Terrasson de Fougères, 01 BP 1769, Abidjan 01; tel. 21-04-66; telex 23474; fax 22-28-52; headquarters in Dakar, Senegal; bank of issue and central bank for the seven states of the Union monétaire ouest africaine (UMOA), comprising Benin, Burkina Faso, Côte d'Ivoire, Mali, Niger, Senegal and Togo; f. 1955; cap. and res 217,441m. (Sept. 1989); Gov. (vacant); Dir in Côte d'Ivoire CHARLES KONAN BANNY; 5 brs.

Other Banks

Banque Atlantique-Côte d'Ivoire: Immeuble El Nasr, ave du Général de Gaulle, 04 BP 1036, Abidjan 04; tel. 21-82-18; telex 23834; fax 21-68-52; f. 1978; cap. 1,000m. (Sept. 1988); Chair. SERGE GETTA; Man. Dir JEAN-PIERRE DUTERTRE.

Banque Internationale pour le Commerce et l'Industrie de la Côte d'Ivoire SA (BICICI): ave Franchet d'Espérey, 01 BP 1298, Abidjan 01; tel. 21-03-79; telex 23651; fax 21-22-82; f. 1962; 24% state-owned, 21% by Banque Nationale de Paris (BNP), 28% by Société Financière pour les Pays d'Outre-Mer (comprises BNP, Banque Bruxelles Lambert and Dresdner Bank); cap. 7,500m. (Sept. 1988); Chair. JOACHIM RICHMOND; Man. Dir GÉRARD LOHIER; 46 brs.

Banque Paribas Côte d'Ivoire: Immeuble Alliance, ave Terrasson de Fougères, 17 BP 09, Abidjan 17; tel. 21-86-86; telex 22870; f. 1984; 83% owned by Paribas International; cap. 1,000m. (Sept. 1988); Chair. DANIEL BÉDIN; Man. Dir GILLES BOREUX.

Banque Real de Côte d'Ivoire SA: Immeuble Botreau Roussel, 5e étage, angle ave Delafosse et blvd Botreau Roussel, 04 BP 411, Abidjan 04; tel. 21-84-52; telex 22430; fax 21-85-99; f. 1976; 99.98% owned by Banco Real SA (Brazil); cap. 1,000m. (Sept. 1988); Chair. RICARDO A. GRIBEL; Man. Dir DOMINGO SAVIO GONÇALVES.

BIAO-Côte d'Ivoire: 8/10 ave Joseph Anoma, 01 BP 1274, Abidjan 01; tel. 21-07-22; telex 23641; f. 1980; undergoing reorg. in 1990; cap. 5,000m. (Sept. 1988); Chair. and Man. Dir NIAMIEN N'GORAN; 37 brs in Côte d'Ivoire.

Compagnie Financière de la Côte d'Ivoire (COFINCI): rue Gourgas, 01 BP 1566, Abidjan 01; tel. 21-27-32; telex 22228; f. 1974; 14.6% state-owned, 55.5% by BICICI; cap. 1,400m. (Sept. 1988); Chair. JOACHIM RICHMOND; Man. Dir JOSEPH ADJOUSSOU.

Ecobank–Côte d'Ivoire: Immeuble Alliance, ave Terrasson de Fougères, 01 BP 4107, Abidjan 01; tel. 21-10-42; telex 23266; fax 21-88-16; f. 1989; 93% owned by Ecobank Transnational Inc (see ECOWAS, p. 133); cap. 1,012m. (Sept. 1989); Chair. AKA AOUÉLÉ; Man. Dir MICHAEL D. ASHMORE.

Société Générale de Banques en Côte d'Ivoire SA (SGBCI): 5–7 ave Joseph Anoma, 01 BP 1355, Abidjan 01; tel. 21-03-33; telex 23741; fax 21-80-65; f. 1962; 10.5% state-owned, 37.2% by Société Générale (France); cap. 8,000m. (Sept. 1989); Chair. and Man. Dir TIÉMOKO YADÉ COULIBALY; 48 brs.

Société Générale de Financement et de Participations en Côte d'Ivoire (SOGEFINANCE): 26 ave Jean Delafosse, 01 BP 3904, Abidjan 01; tel. 21-03-33; telex 23502; f. 1978; 15% state-owned, 58% by SGBCI, 12% by Société Générale (France); cap. 1,000m. (Sept. 1988); Chair. and Man. Dir TIÉMOKO YADÉ COULIBALY; Man. ANTOINE YÉO.

Société Ivoirienne de Banque (SIB): 34 blvd de la République, 01 BP 1300, Abidjan 01; tel. 21-00-00; telex 23751; f. 1962; 41% state-owned, 41% by Crédit Lyonnais (France); cap. 6,000m. (Sept. 1988); Man. Dir JEAN LEFEVRE; 37 brs.

Union de Banques en Côte d'Ivoire (BANAFRIQUE): Résidence Nabil, ave du Général de Gaulle, 01 BP 4132, Abidjan 01; tel. 21-15-36; telex 22513; f. 1980; 36% owned by Banque du Liban et d'Outre-mer (Lebanon); cap. 1,000m. (Sept. 1986); Chair. Dr NAAMAN AZHARI; Dir and Gen. Man. JEAN-PIERRE PARODI; 2 brs.

Financial Institution

Caisse Autonome d'Amortissement: Immeuble SCIAM, ave Marchand, 01 BP 670, Abidjan 01; tel. 21-06-11; telex 23798; f. 1959; management of state funds; Man. Dir LÉON NAKA; Sec.-Gen. MATHIEU N'GORAN.

Bankers' Association

Association Professionnelle des Banques et Etablissements Financiers de Côte d'Ivoire (APBEFCI): 01 BP 3810, Abidjan 01; tel. 21-20-08; Pres. JEAN PIERRE MEYER.

INSURANCE

Assurances Générales de Côte d'Ivoire (AGCI): Immeuble AGCI, ave Noguès, 01 BP 4092, Abidjan 01; tel. 21-99-32; telex 22502; f. 1979; cap. 1,290m.; Chair. JOACHIM RICHMOND; Man. Dir ANTOINE LE MESLE.

Assurmafer SA: 11 ave Joseph Anoma, 01 BP 62, Abidjan 01; tel. 21-10-52; telex 23231; f. 1941; cap. 160m.; Chair. ANTOINE LE MESLE; Dir GILBERT HIS.

Compagnie des Assurances Colina SA: 01 BP 3832, Abidjan 01; tel. 21-37-17; telex 20983; f. 1980; cap. 300m.; Chair. MICHEL POUPARD; Dir E. MALARTRE.

CÔTE D'IVOIRE

Mutuelle Universelle de Garantie (UNIWARRANT): 01 BP 301, Abidjan 01; tel. 32-76-32; telex 22120; fax 32-55-36; f. 1970; cap. 400m.; Chair. and Man. Dir FATIMA SYLLA.

La Nationale d'Assurances (CNA): 30 ave du Général de Gaulle, 01 BP 1333, Abidjan 01; tel. 32-08-00; telex 22176; fax 32-49-06; f. 1972; cap. 400m.; insurance and reinsurance; Chair. LÉON AMON; Man. Dir RICHARD COULIBALY.

La Sécurité Ivoirienne: Immeuble La Sécurité Ivoirienne, blvd Roume, 01 BP 569, Abidjan 01; tel. 21-50-63; telex 23817; fax 21-05-67; f. 1971; cap. 300m.; general; Chair. DIA HOUPHOUËT-BOIGNY; Dir-Gen. JACQUES BARDOUX.

Société Africaine d'Assurances et de Réassurances en République de Côte d'Ivoire (SAFFARRIV): Résidence Longchamp, blvd Roume, 01 BP 1741, Abidjan 01; tel. 21-91-57; telex 22159; f. 1975; cap. 500m.; Pres. TIÉMOKO YADÉ COULIBALY; Man. Dir JEAN-MARIE MANTOUX.

Société Ivoirienne d'Assurances Mutuelles—Mutuelle d'Assurances Transports (SIDAM—MAT): ave Houdaille, 01 BP 1217, Abidjan 01; tel. 21-97-82; telex 22670; f. 1970, restructured 1985; cap. 150m.; Chair. ABOU DOUMBIA; Dir-Gen. VAKABA KONÉ.

Société Nouvelle d'Assurances de Côte d'Ivoire (SNACI): 9 ave Houdaille, 01 BP 1014, Abidjan 01; tel. 21-10-11; telex 22225; cap. 1,008m.; subsidiary of Axa International; Chair. L. BROSSIER.

Société Tropicale d'Assurances Mutuelles Vie (STAMVIE): 15 ave Joseph Anoma, 01 BP 1337, Abidjan 01; tel. 21-20-24; telex 23774; f. 1969; cap. 150m.; life; Chair. JEAN-BAPTISTE AMETHIER; Dir ALBERT AFFOUE-FAUSTE.

L'Union Africaine Société d'Assurances et de Réassurances (UA): ave de la Fosse Prolongée, 01 BP 378, Abidjan 01; tel. 21-73-81; telex 23568; f. 1980; cap. 1,000m.; insurance and reinsurance; Chair. ERNEST AMOS DJORO; Dir JEAN-KACOU DIAGOU.

Union Africaine Vie: ave de la Fosse Prolongée, 01 BP 2016, Abidjan 01; tel. 21-77-46; telex 22200; f. 1985; cap. 550m.; life assurance; Chair. ERNEST AMOS DJORO; Dir JEAN-KACOU DIAGOU.

Trade and Industry

DEVELOPMENT ORGANIZATION

Conseil Economique et Social: 04 BP 301, Abidjan; tel. 21-20-60; reconstituted 1982; govt body overseeing economic development; Pres. PHILIPPE GRÉGOIRE YACÉ; Vice-Pres F. KONIAN KODJO, B. BEDA YAO, Mme J. CHAPMAN; 120 mems.

DEVELOPMENT AGENCIES

Caisse Centrale de Coopération Economique (France): 01 BP 1814, Abidjan 01; tel. 44-53-05; telex 28113; Dir in Côte d'Ivoire ANTOINE BAUX.

Mission Française de Coopération: 01 BP 1839, Abidjan 01; tel. 21-60-45; administers bilateral aid from France; Dir ROGER BOURDIL.

STATE COMPANIES

Caisse de Stabilisation et de Soutien des Prix des Productions Agricoles (CSSPPA): BP V132, Abidjan; tel. 21-08-33; telex 23712; f. 1964; cap. 4,000m. francs CFA; controls price, quality and export of agricultural products; offices in Paris, London and New York; Man. Dir RENÉ AMANI.

Compagnie Ivoirienne pour le Développement des Cultures Vivrières (CIDV): 01 BP 2049, Abidjan 01; tel. 21-00-79; telex 23347; f. 1988 to succeed Société pour le Développement de l'Exploitation du Palmier à Huile (SODEPALM); production of palm oil; Man. Dir BENOÎT N'DRI BROU.

Direction et Controle des Grands Travaux (DCGTX): 04 BP 945, Abidjan 04; tel. 44-28-05; telex 26193; f. 1977; commissioning, implementation and supervision of public works contracts.

Palmindustrie: 01 BP V239, Abidjan 01; tel. 36-93-88; telex 43100; f. 1969; cap. 3,365m. francs CFA; transfer to private ownership pending in 1990; development of palm, coconut and copra products; Man. Dir BERNARD DOSSONGUI KONÉ.

Société de Développement des Plantations Forestières (SODEFOR): blvd François Mitterrand, 01 BP 3770, Abidjan 01; tel. 44-29-60; telex 26156; f. 1966; cap. 50m. francs CFA; establishment and management of plantations, reafforestation, marketing of timber products; Pres. Minister of Agriculture, Water and Forestry Resources; Man. Dir KONAN SOUNDELE.

Société pour le Développement Minier de la Côte d'Ivoire (SODEMI): 31 blvd André Latrille, 01 BP 2816, Abidjan 01; tel. 44-00-04, telex 26102, fax 44-08-21; f. 1962; cap. 600m. francs CFA; geological and mineral research; Pres. N'GOLO COULIBALY; Man. Dir JOSEPH N'ZI.

Société pour le Développement de la Motorisation de l'Agriculture (MOTORAGRI): Km 5, route d'Abobo, 01 BP 3745, Abidjan 01; tel. 37-16-17; telex 23178; f. 1966; cap. 230m. francs CFA; state organization for rationalizing machinery use for agricultural development; Chair. Minister of Agriculture, Water and Forestry Resources; Man. Dir AMADOU OUATTARA.

Société pour le Développement des Plantations de Canne à Sucre, l'Industrialisation et la Commercialisation du Sucre (SODESUCRE): 16 ave du Docteur Crozet, 01 BP 2164, Abidjan 01; tel. 21-04-79; telex 23451; f. 1971; cap. 30,500m. francs CFA; transfer to private ownership pending in 1990; sugar plantations and refinery; Chair. and Man. Dir JOSEPH KOUAMÉ KRA.

Société pour le Développement des Productions Animales (SODEPRA): c/o Ministry of Animal Husbandry, 01 BP 1249, Abidjan 01; tel. 21-13-10; telex 22123; f. 1970; cap. 404m. francs CFA; rearing of livestock; Chair. CHARLES DONWAHI; Man. Dir PAUL LAMIZANA.

Société pour le Développement de la Production des Fruits et Légumes (SODEFEL): 11 ave Barthe, 01 BP 3032, Abidjan 01; tel. 21-63-40; telex 22100; f. 1968; cap. 120m. francs CFA; production and marketing of fruit and vegetables; Chair. FÉLICIEN KONAN KODJO; Man. Dir BOA BOADOU.

Société Nationale d'Opérations Pétrolières de la Côte d'Ivoire (PETROCI): Immeuble Les Hévéas, BP V194, Abidjan 12; tel. 21-85-58; telex 22135; f. 1975; transfer to private ownership pending in 1990; cap. 20,000m. francs CFA; all aspects of petroleum development; Pres. Minister of Mining; Man. Dir PAUL AHUI.

CHAMBERS OF COMMERCE

Chambre d'Agriculture de la Côte d'Ivoire: 11 ave Lamblin, 01 BP 1291, Abidjan 01; tel. 21-16-11; Pres. OKA NIANGOIN; Sec.-Gen. GBAOU DIOMANDÉ.

Chambre de Commerce de la Côte d'Ivoire: ave Joseph Anoma, 01 BP 1399, Abidjan 01; tel. 21-46-79; telex 23224; Pres. LAMINE FADIGA; Sec.-Gen. MAURICE DELAFOSSE.

Chambre d'Industrie de la Côte d'Ivoire: 11 ave Lamblin, 01 BP 1758, Abidjan 01; tel. 32-65-34; telex 22291; Pres. LAMBERT KONAN; Sec.-Gen. MAXIME EKRA.

EMPLOYERS' ASSOCIATIONS

Fédération Maritime de la Côte d'Ivoire (FEDERMAR): 04 BP 723, Abidjan 04; tel. 21-25-85; Sec.-Gen. VACABA TOURÉ.

Groupement Interprofessionnel de l'Automobile (GIPA): Immeuble Jean Lefèbvre, 14 blvd de Marseille, 01 BP 1340, Abidjan 01; tel. 35-71-42; telex 42380; f. 1953; 30 mems; Pres. DANIEL DUBOIS; Sec.-Gen. PHILIPPE MEYER.

Syndicat des Commerçants Importateurs, Exportateurs et Distributeurs de la Côte d'Ivoire (SCIMPEX): 01 BP 3792, Abidjan 01; tel. 21-54-27; Pres. JACQUES ROSSIGNOL; Sec.-Gen. PIERRE DE LA MOTTE.

Syndicat des Employeurs Agricoles (SYNDAGRI): Immeuble MGFA, 4e étage, 28 blvd Angoulvant, Plateau, 01 BP 2300, Abidjan 01; tel. 21-26-42; Pres. JEAN-BAPTISTE AMETHIER.

Syndicat des Entrepreneurs et des Industriels de la Côte d'Ivoire (SEICI): Immeuble Jean Lefèbvre, 14 blvd de Marseille, 01 BP 464, Abidjan 01; tel. 21-83-85; f. 1934; Pres. ABDEL AZIZ THIAM.

Syndicat des Entrepreneurs de Manutention du Port d'Abidjan (SEMPA): 01 BP 172, Abidjan 01; tel. 21-18-82; Vice-Pres. P. SOMICOA.

Syndicat des Exportateurs et Négociants en Bois de Côte d'Ivoire: Immeuble MGFA, 4e étage, 28 blvd Angoulvant, Plateau, 01 BP 1979, Abidjan 01; tel. 21-12-39; Pres. CLAUDE PAINPARAY.

Syndicat des Industriels de la Côte d'Ivoire: 01 BP 1340, Abidjan 01; tel. 35-71-42; Pres. ALAIN BAMBARA; Sec.-Gen. PHILIPPE MEYER.

Syndicat des Producteurs Industriels du Bois: Immeuble MGFA, 4e étage, 28 blvd Angoulvant, Plateau, 01 BP 318, Abidjan 01; tel. 21-12-39; f. 1973; Pres. ISIDORO BIANCHI.

Union des Employeurs Agricoles et Forestiers: Immeuble MGFA, 4e étage, 28 blvd Angoulvant, Plateau, 01 BP 2300, Abidjan 01; tel. 21-26-42; f. 1952; Pres. JEAN-BAPTISTE AMETHIER.

Union Patronale de Côte d'Ivoire (UPACI): 01 BP 1340, Abidjan 01; tel. 35-71-42; telex 43280; Pres. JOSEPH AKA-ANGHUI; Sec.-Gen. PHILIPPE MEYER.

TRADE UNIONS

Union Générale des Travailleurs de Côte d'Ivoire (UGTCI): 05 BP 1203, Abidjan 05; tel. 21-26-65; f. 1962; Sec.-Gen. HYACINTHE ADIKO NIAMKEY; 100,000 individual mems; 190 affiliated unions.

There are also several independent trade unions.

Transport

RAILWAYS

Société Ivoirienne des Chemins de Fer (SICF): 01 BP 1394, Abidjan 01; tel. 21-02-45; telex 23564; fax 21-39-62; f. 1989, following dissolution of Régie des Chemins de Fer Abidjan-Niger (RAN), a jt venture with Govt of Burkina Faso; 660 km of track; Pres. P. Y. KOUAKOU; Dir-Gen. K.-J. BUDIN.

ROADS

There are some 55,000 km of roads, of which 155 km are motorways. A major expansion and rehabilitation programme, which involved the resurfacing of 5,000 km of existing roads and the construction of some 1,300 km of new roads, with funding from the World Bank, the African Development Bank (ADB) and commercial banks, was completed in 1988. Financial constraints have resulted in the postponement of several projects. In 1988, however, it was confirmed that a 56-km road between Bouaké and Béoumi was to be constructed, and in 1989 the construction or upgrading of 600 km of roads, with funding from the ADB, was initiated.

Société Ivoirienne de Transports Publics: 01 BP 2949, Abidjan 01; tel. 35-33-68; telex 23685; f. 1964; road transport; Chair. JOSEPH ALLOU BRIGHT; Dir BASILE ABRE.

Société des Transports Abidjanais (SOTRA): 01 BP 2009, Abidjan 01; tel. 36-90-11; telex 43101; f. 1960; 60% state-owned; urban transport; Chair. MAURICE BAHI ZAHIRI; Dir-Gen. JEAN-BAPTISTE COFFI.

SHIPPING

Côte d'Ivoire has two major ports, Abidjan and San Pedro, both of which are industrial and commercial establishments with financial autonomy. Abidjan, which handled 10,130,703 metric tons of goods in 1989 (of which some 1,400,000 tons were containerized), is the largest container and trading port in west Africa. Access to the port is via the 2.7 km-long Vridi Canal. Rehabilitation works undertaken in the late 1980s were expected to contribute to a continued increase in Abidjan's traffic. The port at San Pedro, which handled 990,507 metric tons of goods in 1989, remains the main gateway to the south-western region of Côte d'Ivoire.

Port Autonome d'Abidjan (PAA): BP V85, Abidjan; tel. 21-01-66; telex 22778; f. 1950; public undertaking supervised by the Ministry of Defence; Man. Dir JEAN-MICHEL MOULOD.

Port Autonome de San Pedro (PASP): BP 339/340, San Pedro; tel. 71-14-79; telex 99102; f. 1971; Man. Dir OGOU ATTEMENE.

Compagnie Maritime Africaine-Côte d'Ivoire (COMAF-CI): 08 BP 867, Abidjan 08; tel. 21-56-43; telex 23357; f. 1973; naval defence and navigational equipment and management of ships; Dir STEFANO SOMMARIVA.

Société Agence Maritime de l'Ouest Africain-Côte d'Ivoire (SAMOA-CI): rue des Gallions, 01 BP 1611, Abidjan 01; tel. 21-29-65; telex 23765; f. 1955; agents for Gold Star Line, Lloyd Triestino, Seven Star Line; Man. Dir CLAUDE PERDRIAUD.

Société Ivoirienne de Navigation Maritime (SIVOMAR): 5 rue Charpentier, zone 2b, Treichville, 01 BP 1395, Abidjan 01; tel. 21-73-23; telex 22226; fax 32-38-53; f. 1977; shipments to west Africa, Mediterranean and Far East; Dir SIMPLISSE DE MESSE ZINSOU.

Société Ivoirienne de Transports Maritimes (SITRAM): ave Lamblin, 01 BP 1546, Abidjan 01; tel. 36-92-00; telex 22132; f. 1967, nationalized 1976; return to private ownership pending in 1990; services between Europe and west Africa and the USA; owns 9 cargo, passenger/cargo and reefer ships; Chair. BONIFACE PEGAWAGNABA; Dir Commdt FAKO KONE.

Société Ouest-Africaine d'Entreprises Maritimes en Côte d'Ivoire (SOAEM-CI): 01 BP 1727, Abidjan 01; tel. 21-59-69; telex 23654; f. 1978; merchandise handling, transit and storage; Chair. JACQUES PELTIER; Dir JACQUES COLOMBANI.

SOCOPAO-Côte d'Ivoire: 01 BP 1297, Abidjan 01; tel. 21-02-11; telex 23745; agents for Splošna Plovba, K Line, EAL, EAC, Morflot, DSR, POL, Nautilus Line, Gestarma, Westwind, PNSC, CNAN; air and sea freight transport; Chair. and Man. Dir SIMPLISSE DE MESSE ZINSOU.

Transcap-CI-Shipping: 01 BP 1908, Abidjan 01; tel. 21-19-37; telex 23770; f. 1960; agents for Elder Dempster Lines, Barber Line, Guinea Gulf Line, Mitsui-OSK Line, Palm Line, Nautilus Line, Nigerian National Lines, Black Star Lines, Naviera García Minaur (Madrid), Krag Shipping (Denmark), Nigerian Green Lines; Chair. CHARLES DONWAHI; Dir GÉRARD DAGOREAU.

CIVIL AVIATION

There is an international airport at Abidjan–Port-Bouët. There are regional airports at Berebi, Bouaké, Daloa, Korhogo, Man, Odienne, San Pedro, Sassandra, Tabou and Yamoussoukro. The modernization of technical facilities at Abidjan was completed in 1989.

Air Afrique (Société Aérienne Africaine Multinationale): 3 ave Joseph Anoma, 01 BP 3927, Abidjan 01; tel. 21-09-00; telex 23785; f. 1961; services between 22 African countries and to Canada, Canary Islands, France, Italy, Saudi Arabia, Switzerland and the USA; Dir-Gen. YVES ROLAND-BILLECART; Commercial Dir THÉOPHILE KOMACLO; fleet of 1 DC-8-63F, 1 DC-8-50F, 2 DC-10-30, 3 Airbus A-300 Super B-4, 1 727-200.

Air Afrique was established by an agreement between SODETRAF (Société pour le Développement du Transport Aérien en Afrique, a subsidiary of French airline UTA) and 11 states, members of the Organisation Commune Africaine et Mauricienne (OCAM), each of which had a 6% share; Togo joined later, Cameroon withdrew in 1971 and Gabon in 1976. SODETRAF has a 28% share and the following states each have a 7.2% holding: Benin, Burkina Faso, the Central African Republic, Chad, the Congo, Côte d'Ivoire, Mauritania, Niger, Senegal, Togo. A restructuring programme was introduced in 1989.

Air Ivoire: 13 ave Barthe, 01 BP 1027, Abidjan 01; tel. 21-34-29; telex 23727; fax 27-88-03; f. 1960, Govt-owned since 1976; restructuring programme pending in 1990; internal flights and services to Bamako (Mali), Conakry (Guinea) and Ouagadougou (Burkina Faso); Man. Dir Col ABDOULAYE COULIBALY; fleet of 2 Fokker F28-4000, 1 F27-600, 1 F27-400, 1 Beech Super King Air 200.

Tourism

The game reserves, forests, lagoons, rich tribal folklore and the lively city of Abidjan are all of interest to tourists. There were some 200,000 visitors in 1988. The 10-km coastal strip along the Lagune Ebrié, to the west of Abidjan, is being developed as a tourist riviera.

Direction de la Promotion Touristique et de l'Artisanat d'Art: BP V184, Abidjan; tel. 21-07-33; telex 23438; Dir DOGO YAO.

CUBA

Introductory Survey

Location, Climate, Language, Religion, Flag, Capital

The Republic of Cuba is an archipelago of two main islands, Cuba and the Isle of Youth (formerly the Isle of Pines), and about 1,600 keys and islets. It lies in the Caribbean Sea, 145 km (90 miles) south of Florida, USA. Other nearby countries are the Bahamas, Mexico, Jamaica and Haiti. The climate is tropical, with the annual rainy season from May to October. The average annual temperature is 25°C (77°F) and hurricanes are frequent. The language spoken is Spanish. Most of the inhabitants are Christians, of whom the great majority are Roman Catholics. The national flag (proportions 2 by 1) has five equal horizontal stripes, of blue, white, blue, white and blue, with a red triangle, enclosing a five-pointed white star, at the hoist. The capital is Havana (La Habana).

Recent History

Cuba was ruled by Spain from the 16th century until 1898, when the island was ceded to the USA following Spain's defeat in the Spanish–American War. Cuba became an independent republic on 20 May 1902, but the USA retained its naval bases on the island and, until 1934, reserved the right to intervene in Cuba's internal affairs. In 1933 an army sergeant, Fulgencio Batista Zaldivar, came to power at the head of a military revolt. Batista ruled the country, directly or indirectly, until 1944, when he retired after serving a four-year term as elected President.

In March 1952, however, Gen. Batista (as he had become) seized power again, deposing President Carlos Prío Socarrás in a bloodless coup. Batista's new regime soon proved to be unpopular and became harshly repressive. In July 1953 a radical opposition group, led by Dr Fidel Castro Ruz, attacked the Moncada army barracks in Santiago de Cuba. Castro was captured, with many of his supporters, but later released. He went into exile and formed a revolutionary movement which was committed to Batista's overthrow. In December 1956 Castro landed in Cuba with a small group of followers, most of whom were captured or killed. However, 12 survivors, including Castro and the Argentine-born Dr Ernesto ('Che') Guevara, escaped into the hills of the Sierra Maestra, where they formed the nucleus of the guerrilla forces which, after a prolonged struggle, forced Batista to flee from Cuba on 1 January 1959. The Batista regime collapsed, and Castro's forces occupied Havana.

The assumption of power by the victorious rebels was initially met with great popular acclaim. The 1940 Constitution was suspended in January 1959, being replaced by a new 'Fundamental Law'. Executive and legislative power was vested in the Council of Ministers, with Fidel Castro as Prime Minister and his brother Raúl as his deputy. Guevara reportedly ranked third in importance. The new regime ruled by decree but promised to hold elections within 18 months. When it was firmly established, the Castro Government adopted a radical economic programme, including agrarian reform and the nationalization of industrial and commercial enterprises. These drastic reforms, combined with the regime's authoritarian nature, provoked opposition from some sectors of the population, including former supporters of Castro, and many Cubans went into exile.

All US business interests in Cuba were expropriated, without compensation, in October 1960, and the USA severed diplomatic relations in January 1961. A US-sponsored force of anti-Castro Cuban émigrés landed in April 1961 at the Bahía de Cochinos (Bay of Pigs), in southern Cuba, but the invasion was thwarted by Castro's troops. Later in the year, all pro-Government groups were merged to form the Organizaciones Revolucionarias Integradas (ORI). In December 1961 Fidel Castro publicly announced that Cuba had become a communist state, and he proclaimed a 'Marxist-Leninist' programme for the country's future development. In January 1962 Cuba was excluded from active participation in the Organization of American States (OAS). The USA instituted a full economic and political blockade of Cuba. Hostility to the USA was accompanied by increasingly close relations between Cuba and the USSR. In October 1962 the USA revealed the presence of Soviet missiles in Cuba but, after the imposition of a US naval blockade, the weapons were withdrawn. The missile bases, capable of launching nuclear weapons against the USA, were dismantled, so resolving one of the most serious international crises since the Second World War. In 1964 the OAS imposed diplomatic and commercial sanctions against Cuba.

The ORI was replaced in 1962 by a new Partido Unido de la Revolución Socialista Cubana (PURSC), which was established, under Fidel Castro's leadership, as the country's sole legal party. Guevara resigned his military and government posts in April 1965, subsequently leaving Cuba to pursue revolutionary activities abroad. In October 1965 the PURSC was renamed the Partido Comunista de Cuba (PCC). Although ostracized by most other Latin American countries, the PCC Government maintained and consolidated its internal authority, with little effective opposition. Supported by considerable aid from the USSR, the regime made significant progress in social and economic development, including improvements in education and public health. At the same time, Cuba continued to give active support to left-wing revolutionary movements in Latin America and in many other parts of the world. Guevara was killed in Bolivia, following an unsuccessful guerrilla uprising under his leadership, in October 1967.

In July 1972 Cuba's links with the Eastern bloc were strengthened when the country became a full member of the Council for Mutual Economic Assistance (CMEA, see p. 125), a Moscow-based organization linking the USSR and other communist states. As a result of its admission to the CMEA, Cuba received preferential trade terms and more technical advisers from the USSR and East European countries.

In June 1974 the country's first elections since the revolution were held for municipal offices in Matanzas province. Cuba's first 'socialist' constitution was submitted to the first Congress of the PCC, held in December 1975, and came into force in February 1976, after being approved by popular referendum. The PCC Congress also elected a new Central Committee and an enlarged Politburo. In addition, the existing six provinces were reorganized to form 14. As envisaged by the new Constitution, elections for municipal assemblies were held in October 1976. These assemblies later elected delegates to provincial assemblies and deputies to the National Assembly of People's Power, inaugurated in December 1976 as 'the supreme organ of state'. The National Assembly chose the members of a new Council of State, with Fidel Castro as President. The second Congress of the PCC was held in December 1980, when Fidel and Raúl Castro were re-elected First and Second Secretaries respectively. At the same time, the Politburo and the Central Committee were enlarged, and details of the 1981–85 Plan were announced. Election of candidates to the 169 municipal assemblies took place in October 1981. The National Assembly was inaugurated for a second five-year term in December. Fidel Castro was re-elected by the Assembly as President of the Council of State, and Raúl Castro re-elected as First Vice-President.

Cuba continued to be excluded from the activities of the OAS, although the Organization voted in favour of allowing members to normalize their relations with Cuba in 1975. Relations with the USA deteriorated because of Cuban involvement in Angola in 1976 and in Ethiopia in 1977. The relaxation of restrictions on emigration in April 1980 resulted in the departure of more than 125,000 Cubans for Florida. Antagonism continued as Cuba's military and political presence abroad increased, threatening US spheres of influence.

In 1981 Cuba expressed interest in discussing foreign policy with the USA, and declared that the shipment of arms to guerrilla groups in Central America had ceased. High-level talks between the two countries took place in November 1981 but US hostility increased. Economic sanctions were tightened, the major air link was closed, and tourism and investment by US nationals was prohibited in April 1982. Cuba's support of Argentina during the 1982 crisis concerning the Falkland Islands improved relations with the rest of Latin America, and the country's legitimacy was finally acknowledged when it was elected to the chair of the UN General Assembly Committee on Decolonization in September 1982, while continuing to play a leading role in the Non-Aligned Movement despite its firm alliance with the Soviet bloc.

In July 1983 President Castro announced his support for the peace initiative of the Contadora group (Colombia, Mexico, Panama and Venezuela), which called for a negotiated settlement to the problems in Central America. In addition, President Castro proposed a reciprocal arrangement between Cuba and the USA to allow for a reduction in the number of military personnel in Central America and for a halt to the supply of armaments to the region. However, an increase in US military activity in Honduras and the Caribbean region led President Castro to declare a 'state of national alert' in August. The US invasion of Grenada in October, and the ensuing short-lived confrontation between US forces and Cuban personnel on the island, severely damaged hopes that the two countries might reach an agreement over Central America, and left Cuba isolated in the Caribbean, following the weakening of its diplomatic and military ties with Suriname in November.

In July 1984 official negotiations were begun with the USA on the issues of immigration and repatriation. In December agreement was reached on the resumption of Cuban immigration to the USA and the repatriation of 2,746 Cuban 'undesirables', who had accompanied other Cuban refugees to the USA in 1980. The repatriation of Cuban 'undesirables' began in February 1985, but, following the inauguration of Radio Martí (a radio station sponsored by the 'Voice of America' radio network, which began to broadcast Western-style news and other programmes to Cuba from Florida, USA), the Cuban Government suspended its immigration accord with the USA. Subsequently, all visits to Cuba by US residents of Cuban origin were banned. The US Government responded by restricting visits to the USA by PCC members and Cuban government officials. In September 1986, as a result of mediation by the Roman Catholic Church, more than 100 political prisoners and their families were permitted to leave Cuba for the USA.

In 1987 relations with the USA continued to deteriorate when, in February, the US Government launched a campaign to direct public attention to violations of human rights in Cuba. A resolution to condemn Cuba's record on human rights was narrowly defeated at a meeting of the UN Commission on Human Rights in March. In July the Cuban Government retaliated by broadcasting television programmes detailing the alleged espionage activities of officials from the US mission in Havana, who were accused of acting as intelligence agents. Nevertheless, the Cuban Government did allow 348 current and former political prisoners to return to the USA. The restoration of the 1984 immigration accord, in October 1987, led to protests by Cuban exiles detained in US prisons. Rioting in gaols at Oakdale, Louisiana, and Atlanta, Georgia, lasted several days until the US Government assured the exiles that their return to Cuba would be suspended indefinitely and that their cases would be studied individually. The accord allowed for the repatriation of 2,500 Cuban 'undesirables' in exchange for a US agreement to allow 23,000 Cubans to enter the USA annually. The USA continued its attempts to have Cuba condemned by the UN Commission on Human Rights in March 1988, but the proposal was again vetoed. A resolution was adopted, however, for a human rights' commission to visit Cuba in September. The commission published its findings in March 1989. Although it did not produce any firm conclusions or recommendations, it did document many cases in which fundamental rights had been infringed. Regarding prisoners of conscience, there had been some improvements. In 1988 the Government had released some 250 political prisoners, and in the following January President Castro pledged to release the remaining 225 political prisoners acknowledged by the regime. In 1989 human rights activists formed a co-ordinating body and increased their operations. The Government responded in August by imprisoning leading activists for up to two years for having published allegedly false information. In April 1990 the UN Commission on Human Rights, at a meeting in Geneva, voted in favour of a resolution to keep Cuba under continued UN scrutiny.

In May–June 1985 a series of ministerial changes was rumoured to have caused friction within the Government, which resulted in the postponement of a planned PCC Congress from December 1985 to February 1986. The Third Congress of the PCC duly opened in February 1986, and drastic changes were made within the Central Committee. Almost one-third of the 146 full members were replaced. Nine of the 24 members of the new Politburo were elected for the first time, with several senior members, veterans of the 1959 revolution, being replaced by younger persons. A new Council of State was elected in December. However, in 1987, despite the major reorganization of the Politburo, there was little sign that the reforms being advocated in the USSR would be pursued in Cuba; indeed, in a speech made in July 1988, President Castro indicated that changes in policy would not take place in Cuba. There was a limited degree of cultural liberalization, but, as regards the economy, there was further centralization of decision-making and restriction of free enterprise.

In June 1989 President Castro was confronted by Cuba's most serious political crisis since the 1959 Revolution. It was discovered that a number of senior military personnel were not only involved in smuggling operations in Angola but were also aiding drug-traffickers from the infamous Medellín cartel by enabling them to use Cuban airstrips as refuelling points (en route from Colombia to the USA) in return for bribes. Following court-martial proceedings, Gen. Arnaldo Ochoa Sánchez, who had led the military campaign in Angola, was found guilty of high treason and executed. Three other officers suffered the same fate. A further purge led to the imposition of harsh sentences on 14 senior officials, including the head of civil aviation and the Ministers of the Interior and of Transport, who had been found guilty of corruption. President Castro insisted that the bureaucracy in Cuba needed to undergo a process of 'purification' but not reform. However, the scandal had clearly undermined the regime's credibility at the international, as well as the domestic, level.

In the course of 1984 the number of Cuban personnel in Ethiopia was reduced, from 10,000 to 5,000 men. In Angola, where Cuban troops numbered an estimated 50,000, the peace process gathered momentum in 1988. Cuban representatives were involved for the first time at a meeting in Luanda in February. In May a large Cuban offensive almost succeeded in expelling South African forces from Angola and gave new impetus to the peace negotiations. A cease-fire was implemented, and at discussions held in New York, in October, an agreement was reached for a phased withdrawal of Cuban troops over a period of 24–30 months. By December a timetable for the withdrawal of Cuban troops had been agreed. The first troops were withdrawn on 1 April 1989, and all troops were to have left Angola by mid-1991. By October 1990 a total of 38,000 Cuban soldiers had left Angola.

In April 1989 President Gorbachev of the USSR visited Cuba. It was the first visit by a Soviet leader since 1974. The two Heads of State discussed bilateral relations, in particular ways in which Cuba's dependence on Soviet aid might be reduced, and Central American issues. The discussions culminated in the signing of a treaty of friendship and economic co-operation. Ostensibly, relations remained good. However, tensions were present, owing to Castro's resistance to Soviet-style reforms. Gorbachev made it clear that, in future, general financial aid would be replaced by assistance for specific projects, thus giving the USSR greater power to influence policy decisions in Cuba. In July President Castro strongly attacked the ideas of *perestroika* and *glasnost*, which he blamed for the 'crisis in socialism'. He pledged to eradicate all market forms of economic activity, despite the fact that Cuba's failure to integrate into the new supply-and-demand system of many Eastern European factories had led to delays in imports and acute shortages. In August a ban was imposed on two Soviet magazines. In 1990 Cuba's increasing economic isolation from the Eastern European countries in the CMEA began to become very apparent, and the Government found that it could no longer rely on the favourable terms of trade sustained for so long by large subsidies from the USSR. In the latter half of the year the number of goods on the basic rationing list (including fuel and newspapers) was increased as part of a programme of austerity measures.

In early October 1990 President Castro announced plans to reduce the PCC's bureaucracy by as much as 50%, including the reassignment of thousands of employees to more productive sectors. The number of advisory departments to the Central Committee was to be reduced from 19 to nine, the military department was to be completely disbanded and replaced by a military commission, and the Secretariat was to be reduced from seven to five members. The changes were intended to improve the efficiency of the PCC in preparation for its Congress in early 1991 and to help the party to confront the prevailing economic crisis more effectively.

In November 1990 rationing was extended to all products. Cubans were told to prepare for the possibility of a 'special wartime period' by the Minister of the Revolutionary Armed Forces, Gen. Raúl Castro, who warned of a possible US military attack if the currently intensified US economic blockade should fail. In spite of the gravity of Cuba's political and economic situation, President Castro was defiant in his rejection of recommendations that, as a condition for the removal of the blockade, Cuba should adopt a market economy and political pluralism.

In March 1990 a new Spanish-speaking television station, TV Martí (based in Florida, USA), began broadcasting to Cuba. The station, which intended to propagate anti-communist feeling in Cuba, was successfully jammed by electronic equipment in Cuban aircraft and naval vessels within an hour of beginning transmission. In mid-April Cuban officials commenced the systematic jamming of Radio Martí, which had been operating since 1985.

In early July 1990 a serious political and diplomatic crisis began when five members of the dissident Asociacíon por Arte Libre took refuge in the Czechoslovak embassy in Havana. This action prompted a succession of events involving the entry of Cuban dissidents into European embassies and diplomatic residences in Havana. At the height of the crisis, more than 50 Cubans were taking refuge, 18 of them in the Spanish embassy. One refuge-seeker had been pursued by the Cuban police and captured within the grounds of the Spanish embassy. The Spanish Government issued a strong protest against this violation of diplomatic immunity and called into question Cuba's record on human rights. As the diplomatic row escalated, the Spanish Government recalled its ambassador and suspended official aid of US $2.5m. to Cuba. Of those seeking asylum, it was widely believed in the diplomatic community that as many as one-half of them were agents provocateurs sent in with the full knowledge of the Cuban Ministery of the Interior to intimidate diplomats and to frustrate the endeavours of genuine asylum-seekers. In early September the 58-day crisis finally came to an end when the last of the refugees voluntarily surrendered.

Since 1985 Cuba has succeeded in establishing stronger ties with other Latin American countries, notably Argentina, Brazil, Peru and Uruguay. Relations with the United Kingdom were severely affected in September 1988 by the expulsion of the Cuban ambassador and an envoy at the embassy after a shooting incident in the centre of London. In the same month, however, diplomatic relations were established with the EEC. In February 1989 President Castro visited Venezuela, for the first time since 1959, to attend the inauguration of President Carlos Andrés Pérez. In May 1989 the Pope accepted an invitation to visit Cuba in December 1990; however, in mid-1990 the visit was suspended indefinitely. In October 1989 Cuba was elected to the UN Security Council (for a two-year term from January 1990) for the first time in the 30 years of President Castro's rule. Following the electoral defeat of the Sandinista Government in February 1990, Cuba announced that it would be severing its links with Nicaragua. Relations with Panama were severed completely following the ousting of Gen. Manuel Noriega by the US armed forces in December 1989 and the subsequent installation of President Guillermo Endara. Relations with Spain reached a low point between July and September 1990, during the embassy crisis (see above); however, by October they were reported to be improving, with representatives from both countries holding talks to decide on a date for a meeting of the Spanish-Cuban commission. Relations with the USA deteriorated in 1990, with the introduction of TV Martí and Cuba's defence preparations against the possibility of a US military attack.

Government

Under the 1976 Constitution (the first since the 1959 revolution), the supreme organ of state, and the sole legislative authority, is the National Assembly of People's Power, with 499 deputies elected for five years by municipal assemblies. The National Assembly elects 31 of its members to form the Council of State, the Assembly's permanent organ. The Council of State is the highest representative of the State, and its President is both Head of State and Head of Government. Executive and administrative authority is vested in the Council of Ministers, appointed by the National Assembly on the proposal of the Head of State. Municipal, regional and provincial assemblies have also been established. The Partido Comunista de Cuba (PCC), the only authorized political party, is 'the leading force of society and the state'. The PCC's highest authority is the Party Congress, which elects a Central Committee (225 members in February 1986) to supervise the Party's work. To direct its policy, the Central Committee elects a Politburo (18 members in 1990).

Defence

Conscription for military service is for a three-year period from 17 years of age, and conscripts also work on the land. In June 1990, according to Western estimates, the army numbered 145,000, the navy 13,500 and the air force 22,000. Army reserves were estimated to be 130,000. Paramilitary forces include 15,000 State Security troops, 4,000 border guards and a Youth Labour Army of about 100,000. A local militia organization (Milicias de Tropas Territoriales—MTT), comprising 1.3m. men and women, was formed in 1980. Estimated expenditure on defence and internal security for 1989 was 1,400m. pesos. Considerable aid is received from communist countries, notably the USSR. Despite Cuban hostility, the USA maintains a base at Guantánamo Bay, with 2,000 naval and 400 marine personnel in 1990.

Economic Affairs

In 1989, according to official estimates, Cuba's net material product (NMP), measured at current prices, was 12,790.9m. pesos, equivalent to 1,217 pesos per head. During 1980–85, it was estimated, NMP increased, in real terms, at an average annual rate of 8.4%. However, real NMP declined by 2.2% in 1986, and by 4.8% in 1987. It expanded by 2.5% in 1988. During 1980–89 the population increased by an annual average of 0.9%.

Agriculture (including forestry and fishing) contributed 12.2% of NMP in 1989. About 22% of the labour force were employed in this sector in 1981. The principal cash crop is sugar cane, with sugar and its derivatives accounting for 73.2% of export earnings in 1989. Other important crops are tobacco, rice, citrus fruits, plantains and bananas.

Industry (including manufacturing, mining, construction and power) contributed 45.6% of NMP in 1989. Mining, manufacturing and power employed 18.9% of the labour force in 1981. Construction contributed 9.2% of NMP in 1989, and employed 8.9% of the labour force in 1981. The most important industrial sectors, measured by gross value of output, are textiles, leather footwear, cigarettes, electricity and grey cement. Nickel is the principal mineral export. There are also deposits of copper, chromite, gold, manganese and iron ore.

Energy is derived principally from petroleum and natural gas. Imports of mineral fuels comprised 32.4% of the value of total imports in 1989.

In 1989 Cuba recorded a visible trade deficit of US $2,732m. The principal source of imports (68.0%) was the USSR, which was also the principal market for exports (59.9%). Other major trading partners were the German Democratic Republic, Czechoslovakia, Bulgaria, Romania, the People's Republic of China and Spain. The principal imports in 1989 were mineral fuels, machinery and transport equipment. The principal exports in the same year were sugar, minerals and concentrates, and agricultural produce. The re-export of mineral fuels was a major source of convertible currency, earning Cuba an estimated US $500m. in 1989. In 1990, however, imports of subsidized petroleum from the USSR, which had, hitherto, provided 95% of Cuba's total petroleum requirements, were dramatically reduced, falling short of the agreed quota by 2m. metric tons.

In the budget proposals for 1989 there was a projected deficit of 1,624m. pesos. Cuba's external debt to Western creditor nations was estimated to be US $6,800m. at mid-1989. Cuba's debt to the USSR was estimated to be $24,780m. at mid-1990. Officially, there was no unemployment in Cuba in 1988. No index of consumer prices is published. Cuba is a member of the CMEA (see p. 125), with which it conducts 87% of its foreign trade.

In 1990 Cuba suffered severe economic decline. A considerable depletion in the supply of petroleum, grain and basic raw materials from the USSR, in addition to the tightening US economic blockade and the rising price of petroleum (owing to the Gulf crisis), were the main contributing factors. With the inevitable rationing of fuel consumption, many factories closed, and state investment in construction projects was reduced to a minimum. In September the Government decided to close, indefinitely, the Ernesto Guevara nickel plant in Moa, as part of the emergency energy-saving programme. With Cuba's five-year trade agreement with the USSR coming to an end in early 1991, the Government is faced with the probability of a considerable deterioration in the terms of trade that had previously ensured a high price for Cuba's main export, sugar.

Social Welfare

Through the State Social Security System, employees receive benefits for sickness, accidents, maternity, disability, retirement and unemployment. Health services are available free of charge. In 1986 there were 5.5 hospital beds for every 1,000 inhabitants, and in 1987 there was one physician per 530 inhabitants. In 1989 the infant mortality rate was 11.1 per 1,000 live births. The 1989 budget allocation for health and education was 2,906.2m. pesos.

Education

Education is universal and free at all levels. Education is based on Marxist-Leninist principles and combines study with manual work. Day nurseries are available for all children after their 45th day, and national schools at the pre-primary level are operated by the State for children of five years of age. Primary education, from six to 12 years of age, is compulsory, and secondary education lasts from 13 to 16 (to be extended to 18) years of age. In 1987 an estimated 95% of children in the primary school age-group attended primary schools, while 70% of children in the secondary school age-group were enrolled at secondary schools. In 1987/88 there were 262,200 students in higher education. Workers attending university courses receive a state subsidy to provide for their dependants. Courses at intermediate and higher levels have an emphasis on technology, agriculture and teacher training. In 1981 the estimated illiteracy rate among persons aged 10 years and over was 3.8%. The rate for those aged 15 to 49 was only 2.2%. Adult education centres provided basic education for 292,067 people in 1984/85.

Public Holidays

1991: 1 January (Liberation Day), 1 May (Labour Day), 25–27 July (Anniversary of the 1953 Revolution), 10 October (Wars of Independence Day).

1992: 1 January (Liberation Day), 1 May (Labour Day), 25–27 July (Anniversary of the 1953 Revolution), 10 October (Wars of Independence Day).

Weights and Measures

The metric system is in force.

Statistical Survey

Source (unless otherwise stated): Cámara de Comercio de Cuba, Calle 21, No 661, Apdo 4237, Vedado, Havana; tel. 30-3356; telex 51-1752; Comité Estatal de Estadísticas, Havana, Cuba; tel. 31-5171.

Area and Population

AREA, POPULATION AND DENSITY

Area (sq km)	110,860*
Population (census results)	
6 September 1970	8,569,121
11 September 1981	
Males	4,914,873
Females	4,808,732
Total	9,723,605
Population (official estimates at mid-year)	
1987	10,288,000
1988	10,402,000
1989	10,514,000
Density (per sq km) at mid-1989	94.8

* 42,803 sq miles.

Population (estimate): 10,576,921 at 31 December 1989.

PRINCIPAL TOWNS
(estimated population at 31 December 1989)

La Habana (Havana, the capital)	2,096,054		Bayamo	125,021
Santiago de Cuba	405,354		Cienfuegos	123,600
Camagüey	283,008		Pinar del Río	121,774
Holguín	228,053		Las Tunas	119,400
Guantánamo	200,381		Matanzas	113,724
Santa Clara	194,354		Ciego de Ávila	88,102
			Sancti Spíritus	85,499

BIRTHS, MARRIAGES AND DEATHS*

	Registered live births†		Registered marriages‡		Registered deaths	
	Number	Rate (per 1,000)	Number	Rate (per 1,000)	Number	Rate (per 1,000)
1982	159,759	16.3	80,295	8.2	56,485	5.8
1983	165,284	16.7	75,920	7.7	58,334	5.9
1984	166,281	16.6	75,524	7.6	59,895	6.0
1985	182,067	18.0	80,407	8.0	64,430	6.4
1986	166,049	16.3	84,014	8.2	63,145	6.2
1987	179,477	17.4	78,146	7.6	65,079	6.3
1988	187,911	18.0	82,431	7.9	67,944	6.5
1989	184,891	17.6	85,350	8.1	67,352	6.4

* Data are tabulated by year of registration rather than by year of occurrence.
† Births registered in the National Consumers Register, established on 31 December 1964.
‡ Including consensual unions formalized in response to special legislation.

CUBA *Statistical Survey*

ECONOMICALLY ACTIVE POPULATION (1981 census)

	Males	Females	Total
Agriculture, hunting, forestry and fishing	677,565	113,304	790,869
Mining and quarrying			
Manufacturing	472,399	195,941	668,340
Electricity, gas and water			
Construction	279,327	33,913	313,240
Trade, restaurants and hotels	170,192	135,438	305,630
Transport, storage and communications	205,421	43,223	248,644
Financing, insurance, real estate and business services			
Community, social and personal services	541,387	544,665	1,086,052
Activities not adequately defined	87,778	40,139	127,917
Total labour force	2,434,069	1,106,623	3,540,692

1988 (sample survey, persons aged 15 years and over): Total employed labour force 4,570,236 (males 2,920,698; females 1,649,538).

Source: ILO, *Year Book of Labour Statistics*.

CIVILIAN EMPLOYMENT IN THE STATE SECTOR
(annual averages, '000 persons)

	1987	1988	1989
Industry*	726.9	742.8	767.5
Construction	314.1	339.4	344.3
Agriculture	602.7	653.2	690.3
Forestry	30.1	28.9	30.8
Transport	196.9	199.9	204.4
Communications	28.4	30.1	31.5
Trade	376.2	387.3	395.3
Social services	116.5	121.5	124.5
Science and technology	28.7	27.5	27.4
Education	383.0	388.2	396.4
Arts and culture	42.2	42.1	43.9
Public health	222.4	232.5	243.5
Finance and insurance	20.6	20.9	21.7
Administration	161.4	155.1	151.7
Total (incl. others)	3,299.2	3,408.4	3,526.6

* Fishing, mining, manufacturing, electricity, gas and water.

Agriculture

PRINCIPAL CROPS ('000 metric tons)

	1987	1988	1989
Sugar cane	75,536	83,138	76,443
Maize	42	36	47
Cassava (Manioc)*†	305	305	305
Potatoes	250†	277†	282
Sweet potatoes	188	164	195
Plantains	118	142	109
Rice (paddy)	466†	489	536
Tobacco (leaves)	39†	39	42
Tomatoes	211†	335	260
Oranges	496†	503†	
Lemons	75†	57†	826
Grapefruit	285†	385†	
Bananas	166†	203	183
Mangoes	81†	121	81
Coffee (green)	26†	29†	29

* FAO estimate.
† Source: FAO, *Production Yearbook*.

LIVESTOCK ('000 head)

	1987	1988	1989
Cattle	4,984	4,927	4,920
Horses	739	665	665
Pigs	1,093	1,169	1,292
Sheep	740	804	839
Goats	37	33	34

Poultry (million): 26 in 1987; 27 in 1988; 28 in 1989.

LIVESTOCK PRODUCTS ('000 metric tons)

	1987	1988	1989*
Beef and veal	140	141	141
Pig meat	99	97	97
Poultry meat	91	95	95
Cows' milk	1,128	1,122	1,180
Butter	9.1	9.4	10.0
Cheese	15.5	16.1	16.7
Hen eggs	108.0	104.9	105.0

* FAO estimates.
Source: FAO, *Production Yearbook*.

Forestry

ROUNDWOOD REMOVALS ('000 cubic metres, excluding bark)

	1986	1987	1988
Sawlogs, veneer logs and logs for sleepers	149	156	159
Other industrial wood	475	438	417
Fuel wood	2,730	2,632	2,707
Total	3,354	3,226	3,283

Source: FAO, *Yearbook of Forest Products*.

SAWNWOOD PRODUCTION ('000 cubic metres)

	1987	1988	1989
Total (incl. railway sleepers)	112	112	125

Fishing

('000 metric tons, live weight)

	1986	1987	1988
Inland waters	17.6	16.7	15.6
Atlantic Ocean	137.7	158.0	128.7
Pacific Ocean	89.4	40.4	87.0
Total catch	244.7	215.1	231.3

Source: FAO, *Yearbook of Fishery Statistics*.
1989 ('000 metric tons): Total catch 192.0.

CUBA

Mining

('000 metric tons, unless otherwise indicated)

	1987	1988	1989
Crude petroleum	894.5	716.8	718.4
Natural gas (million cu metres)	23.9	21.9	33.6
Copper concentrates*	3.5	3.0	2.8
Nickel and cobalt*	36.8	43.9	46.6
Refractory chromium	52.4	52.2	50.6
Salt (unrefined)	230.5	200.3	206.1
Silica and sand ('000 cu metres)	5,826.3	6,467.7	6,396.7
Crushed stone ('000 cu metres)	11,102.3	12,676.6	12,510.1

* Figures refer to the metal content of ores and concentrates.

Industry

SELECTED PRODUCTS
('000 metric tons, unless otherwise indicated)

	1987	1988	1989
Crude steel	401.5	320.5	314.2
Corrugated steel bars	312.9	359.7	367.1
Grey cement	3,535.3	3,565.8	3,758.8
Mosaics ('000 sq metres)	3,443.8	3,987.9	4,478.1
Motor spirit (Gasoline)	960.3	1,011.8	1,025.7
Kerosene	546.5	558.5	640.1
Sulphuric acid (98%)	372.0	392.7	381.4
Fertilizers	996.3	840.4	898.6
Tyres ('000)	324.7	428.1	315.0
Woven textile fabrics ('000 sq metres)	258,400	260,400	220,300
Cigarettes (million)	15,397.6	16,885.2	16,500
Cigars (million)	278.6	270.2	308.5
Raw sugar*	6,961.5	7,815.6	7,328.8
Leather footwear ('000 pairs)	14,200	13,300	11,000
Electric energy (million kWh)	13,593.5	14,542.3	15,239.8

* Corresponding to calendar year.

Finance

CURRENCY AND EXCHANGE RATES
Monetary Units:
100 centavos = 1 Cuban peso.

Denominations:
Coins: 1, 2, 5, 20 and 40 centavos; 1 peso.
Notes: 1, 3, 5, 10, 20 and 50 pesos.

Sterling and Dollar Equivalents (31 July 1990)
£1 sterling = 1.399 pesos;
US $1 = 75.2 centavos;
100 Cuban pesos = £71.49 = $132.98.

Note: The foregoing information relates to non-commercial exchange rates, applicable to tourism. For the purposes of foreign trade, the peso was at par with the US dollar during 1987 and 1988.

STATE BUDGET (million pesos)

	1987	1988*	1989*
Total revenue	11,272	11,386	11,903.5
Total expenditure	11,881	12,532	13,527.5
Productive sector	4,575	4,713	4,975.1
Housing and community services	680	787	859.8
Education and public health	2,725	2,857	2,906.2
Other social, cultural and scientific activities	1,850	2,060	2,300.8
Government administration and judicial bodies	565	561	524.5
Defence and public order	1,242	1,274	1,377.4
Other	244	280	583.7

* Preliminary.
Source: State Committee for Finance, Havana.

INTERNATIONAL RESERVES (million pesos at 31 December)

	1987	1988
Gold and other precious metals	17.5	19.5
Cash and deposits in foreign banks (convertible currency)	36.5	78.0
Sub-total	54.0	97.5
Deposits in foreign banks (in transferable roubles)	142.5	137.0
Total	196.5	234.5

NATIONAL ACCOUNTS
Net Material Product (NMP) by Economic Activity*
(million pesos at current prices)

	1987	1988	1989
Agriculture, forestry and fishing	1,440.8	1,532.9	1,554.6
Industry†	4,498.5	4,782.2	4,656.2
Construction	997.6	1,082.5	1,171.8
Trade, restaurants, etc.	4,205.1	4,209.5	4,294.5
Transport and communications	986.3	1,073.4	1,037.8
Other activities of the material sphere	88.4	83.4	76.0
Total	12,284.3	12,763.9	12,790.9
NMP at constant 1981 prices	13,273.2	n.a.	n.a.

* NMP is defined as the total net value of goods and 'productive' services, including turnover taxes, produced by the economy. This excludes economic activities not contributing directly to material production, such as public administration, defence and personal and professional services.
† Principally manufacturing, mining, electricity, gas and water.

CUBA

External Trade

PRINCIPAL COMMODITIES (million pesos)

Imports	1987	1988	1989
Food and live animals	716.2	730.4	925.3
Beverages and tobacco	10.9	8.1	8.1
Animal and vegetable fats and oils	67.3	77.8	78.3
Crude materials (inedible) except fuels	301.5	281.1	307.2
Mineral fuels, lubricants, etc.	2,621.0	2,589.0	2,629.9
Chemicals and related products	447.2	433.8	530.2
Basic manufactures	821.1	816.3	838.0
Machinery and transport equipment	2,353.7	2,409.5	2,530.7
Miscellaneous manufactured articles	244.7	233.8	276.5
Total	7,583.6	7,579.8	8,124.2

Exports	1987	1988	1989
Sugar and sugar products	4,012.6	4,116.5	3,948.5
Minerals and concentrates	332.2	455.0	497.7
Tobacco and tobacco products	90.5	98.4	83.6
Fish and fish preparations	144.3	149.0	128.8
Other agricultural products	250.9	248.2	211.3
Total (incl. others)	5,402.1	5,518.3	5,392.0

PRINCIPAL TRADING PARTNERS ('000 pesos)

Imports c.i.f.	1987	1988	1989
Argentina	124,339	127,506	179,198
Bulgaria	183,980	171,797	177,501
Canada	32,992	28,553	37,134
China, People's Republic	100,750	175,886	255,483
Czechoslovakia	200,134	219,453	216,283
France	48,082	27,201	34,650
German Democratic Republic	338,836	340,950	358,688
Germany, Federal Republic	52,465	57,440	76,612
Hungary	72,436	69,501	80,543
Italy	45,825	75,850	62,577
Japan	106,503	88,563	49,456
Mexico	72,064	108,022	79,954
Netherlands	18,393	13,999	22,875
Poland	81,481	64,027	57,795
Romania	182,112	179,918	155,970
Spain	165,405	146,139	184,865
Sweden	13,547	11,985	13,970
Switzerland	36,731	31,884	50,087
USSR	5,445,979	5,364,418	5,522,391
United Kingdom	70,195	59,746	81,769
Viet-Nam	17,118	8,747	20,568
Total (incl. others)	7,583,600	7,579,800	8,124,200

Exports f.o.b.	1987	1988	1989
Algeria	7,405	28,607	37,032
Bulgaria	169,073	164,339	176,940
Canada	36,848	38,490	54,835
China, People's Republic	85,468	226,253	216,071
Czechoslovakia	143,998	183,542	136,026
Eygpt	11,906	5,120	10,467
France	57,585	66,854	54,429
German Democratic Republic	281,597	311,430	285,913
Germany, Federal Republic	28,360	73,015	71,395
Hungary	66,710	35,533	55,437
Italy	36,106	49,386	36,163
Japan	77,171	109,206	104,074
Poland	43,849	37,569	54,122
Spain	84,903	81,521	86,031
Sweden	7,759	18,870	31,308
Switzerland	48,746	12,163	72,615
USSR	3,868,736	3,683,073	3,231,222
United Kingdom	13,365	42,491	113,782
Total (incl. others)	5,402,100	5,518,300	5,392,000

Transport

RAILWAYS

	1987	1988	1989
Passengers ('000)	23,600	25,200	26,400
Passenger-kilometres (million)	2,189.0	2,626.7	2,891.0
Freight carried ('000 metric tons)	15,738.5	15,531.0	15,732.4
Freight ton-kilometres (million)	2,407.6	2,429.1	2,416.2

ROAD TRAFFIC ('000 motor vehicles in use)

	1983	1984	1985
Passenger cars	190.4	200.1	206.3
Commercial vehicles	158.9	164.5	172.8

Source: UN, *Statistical Yearbook*.

INTERNATIONAL SEA-BORNE SHIPPING
(freight traffic, '000 metric tons)

	1986	1987	1988
Goods loaded	8,377.0	7,199.1	8,554.1
Goods unloaded	18,444.6	15,880.2	15,484.0

CIVIL AVIATION

	1987	1988	1989
Passengers carried ('000)	1,100	1,100	1,100
Passenger-kilometres (million)	2,997.5	3,221.0	3,177.7
Freight ton-kilometres (million)	42.9	51.4	36.5

Tourism

	1986	1987	1988
Foreign visitors	194,531	207,000	225,018

Source: Instituto Nacional de Turismo—INTUR.

Education

(1989/90)

	Schools	Teachers	Pupils
Pre-primary	n.a.	7,393	144,700
Primary	9,417	71,887	885,500
Secondary: general	2,175	108,560	1,073,100
Technical and professional	618	30,252	312,000
Higher	35	24,499	242,400

Directory

The Constitution

Following the assumption of power by the Castro regime on 1 January 1959, the Constitution was suspended and a Fundamental Law of the Republic was instituted with effect from 7 February 1959. In February 1976 Cuba's first socialist Constitution came into force after being submitted to the first Congress of the Communist Party of Cuba in December 1975 and to popular referendum in February 1976.

POLITICAL, SOCIAL AND ECONOMIC PRINCIPLES

The Republic of Cuba is a socialist state in which all power belongs to the working people. The Communist Party of Cuba is the leading force of society and the state. The socialist state carries out the will of the working people and guarantees work, medical care, education, food, clothing and housing. The Republic of Cuba is part of the world socialist community. It bases its relations with the Union of Soviet Socialist Republics and with other socialist countries on socialist internationalism, friendship, co-operation and mutual assistance. It hopes to establish one large community of nations within Latin America and the Caribbean.

The State organizes and directs the economic life of the nation in accordance with a central social and economic development plan. Foreign trade is the exclusive function of the State. The State recognizes the right of small farmers to own their lands and other means of production and to sell that land. The State guarantees the right of citizens to ownership of personal property in the form of earnings, savings, place of residence and other possessions and objects which serve to satisfy their material and cultural needs. The State also guarantees the right of inheritance.

Cuban citizenship is acquired by birth or through naturalization.

The State protects the family, motherhood and matrimony.

The State directs and encourages all aspects of education, culture and science.

All citizens have equal rights and are subject to equal duties.

The State guarantees the right to medical care, education, freedom of speech and press, assembly, demonstration, association and privacy. In the socialist society work is the right and duty, and a source of pride for every citizen.

GOVERNMENT

National Assembly of People's Power

The National Assembly of People's Power is the supreme organ of the State and is the only organ with constituent and legislative authority. It is composed of deputies over the age of 18 elected by the Municipal Assemblies of People's Power, for a period of five years. All Cuban citizens over the age of 16, except those who are mentally incapacitated or who have committed a crime, are eligible to vote. The National Assembly of People's Power holds two ordinary sessions a year and a special session when requested by one-third of the deputies or by the Council of State. More than half the total number of deputies must be present for a session to be held.

All decisions made by the Assembly, except those relating to constitutional reforms, are adopted by a simple majority of votes. The deputies may be recalled by their electors at any time.

The National Assembly of People's Power has the following functions:

to reform the Constitution;

to approve, modify and annul laws;

to supervise all organs of the State and government;

to decide on the constitutionality of laws and decrees;

to revoke decree-laws issued by the Council of State and the Council of Ministers;

to discuss and approve economic and social development plans, the state budget, monetary and credit systems;

to approve the general outlines of foreign and domestic policy, to ratify and annul international treaties, to declare war and approve peace treaties;

to approve the administrative division of the country;

to elect the President, First Vice-President, the Vice-Presidents and other members of the Council of State;

to elect the President, Vice-President and Secretary of the National Assembly;

to appoint the members of the Council of Ministers on the proposal of the President of the Council of State;

to elect the President, Vice-President and other judges of the People's Supreme Court;

to elect the Attorney-General and the Deputy Attorney-Generals;

to grant amnesty;

to call referendums.

The President of the National Assembly presides over sessions of the Assembly, calls ordinary sessions, proposes the draft agenda, signs the Official Gazette, organizes the work of the commissions appointed by the Assembly and attends the meetings of the Council of State.

Council of State

The Council of State is elected from the members of the National Assembly and represents that Assembly in the period between sessions. It comprises a President, one First Vice-President, five Vice-Presidents, one Secretary and 23 other members. Its mandate ends when a new Assembly meets. All decisions are adopted by a simple majority of votes. It is accountable for its actions to the National Assembly.

The Council of State has the following functions:

to call special sessions of the National Assembly;

to set the date for the election of a new Assembly;

to issue decree-laws in the period between the sessions of the National Assembly;

to decree mobilization in the event of war and to approve peace treaties when the Assembly is in recess;

to issue instructions to the courts and the Office of the Attorney General of the Republic;

to appoint and remove ambassadors of Cuba abroad on the proposal of its President, to grant or refuse recognition to diplomatic representatives of other countries to Cuba;

to suspend those provisions of the Council of Ministers that are not in accordance with the Constitution;

to revoke the resolutions of the Executive Committee of the local organs of People's Power which are contrary to the Constitution or laws and decrees formulated by other higher organs.

The President of the Council of State is Head of State and Head of Government and for all purposes the Council of State is the highest representative of the Cuban state.

Head of State

The President of the Council of State is the Head of State and the Head of Government and has the following powers:

to represent the State and Government and conduct general policy;

to call and preside over the sessions of the Council of State and the Council of Ministers;

to supervise the ministries and other administrative bodies;

to propose the members of the Council of Ministers to the National Assembly of People's Power;

to receive the credentials of the heads of foreign diplomatic missions;

to sign the decree-laws and other resolutions of the Council of State;

to assume command of the Revolutionary Armed Forces.

In the case of absence, illness or death of the President of the Council of State, the First Vice-President assumes the President's duties.

The Council of Ministers

The Council of Ministers is the highest-ranking executive and administrative organ. It is composed of the Head of State and Government, as its President, the First Vice-President, the Vice-Presidents, the Ministers and the President of the Central Planning Board. Its Executive Committee is composed of the President, the First Vice-President and the Vice-Presidents of the Council of Ministers.

The Council of Ministers has the following powers:

to conduct political, economic, cultural, scientific, social and defence policy as outlined by the National Assembly;

to approve international treaties;

to propose projects for the general development plan and, if they are approved by the National Assembly, to supervise their implementation;

CUBA

to conduct foreign policy and trade;

to draw up bills and submit them to the National Assembly;

to draw up the draft state budget;

to conduct general administration, implement laws, issue decrees and supervise defence and national security.

The Council of Ministers is accountable to the National Assembly of People's Power.

LOCAL GOVERNMENT

The country is divided into 14 provinces and 169 municipalities. The provinces are: Pinar del Río, Habana, Ciudad de la Habana, Matanzas, Villa Clara, Cienfuegos, Sancti Spíritus, Ciego de Avila, Camagüey, Las Tunas, Holguín, Granma, Santiago de Cuba and Guantánamo.

Voting for delegates to the municipal assemblies is direct, secret and voluntary. All citizens over 16 years of age are eligible to vote. The number of delegates to each assembly is proportionate to the number of people living in that area. A delegate must obtain more than half the number of votes cast in the constituency in order to be elected. The Municipal Assemblies of People's Power are directly elected by the local population and, in turn, elect delegates to the Provincial Assemblies. Nominations for Municipal and Provincial Executive Committees of People's Power are submitted to the relevant assembly by a commission presided over by a representative of the Communist Party's leading organ and consisting of representatives of youth, workers', farmers', revolutionary and women's organizations. The President and Secretary of each of the regional and the provincial assemblies are the only full-time members, the other delegates carrying out their functions in addition to their normal employment.

The regular and extraordinary sessions of the local Assemblies of People's Power are public. More than half the total number of members must be present in order for agreements made to be valid. Agreements are adopted by simple majority.

JUDICIARY

Judicial power is exercised by the People's Supreme Court and all other competent tribunals and courts. The People's Supreme Court is the supreme judicial authority and is accountable only to the National Assembly of People's Power. It can propose laws and issue regulations through its Council of Government. Judges are independent but the courts must inform the electorate of their activities at least once a year. Every accused person has the right to a defence and can be tried only by a tribunal.

The Office of the Attorney-General is subordinate only to the National Assembly and the Council of State and is responsible for ensuring that the law is properly obeyed.

The Constitution may be totally or partially modified only by a two-thirds majority vote in the National Assembly of People's Power. If the modification is total, or if it concerns the composition and powers of the National Assembly of People's Power or the Council of State, or the rights and duties contained in the Constitution, it also requires a positive vote by referendum.

The Government
(December 1990)

Head of State: Dr FIDEL CASTRO RUZ (took office 2 December 1976; re-elected December 1981 and December 1986).

COUNCIL OF STATE

President: Dr FIDEL CASTRO RUZ.

First Vice-President: Gen. RAÚL CASTRO RUZ.

Vice-Presidents:
JUAN ALMEIDA BOSQUE.
OSMANY CIENFUEGOS GORRIARÁN.
JOSÉ RAMÓN MACHADO VENTURA.
PEDRO MIRET PRIETO.
Dr CARLOS RAFAEL RODRÍGUEZ RODRÍGUEZ.

Secretary: Dr JOSÉ M. MIYAR BARRUECO.

Members:
JOSÉ RAMÓN BALAGUER CABRERA.
Dr ARMANDO HART DÁVALOS.
PEDRO CHÁVEZ GONZÁLEZ.
MERCEDES DÍAZ HERRERA.
RAMIRO VALDÉS MENÉNDEZ.
FÉLIX VILLAR BENCOMO.
GUILLERMO GARCÍA FRÍAS.
CARLOS LAGE DÁVILA.
ROBERTO VEIGA MENÉNDEZ.
VILMA ESPÍN GUILLOLS DE CASTRO.
JOSÉ RAMÍREZ CRUZ.
ARMANDO ACOSTA CORDERO.
SEVERO AGUIRRE DEL CRISTO.
ORLANDO LUGO FONTE.
ROBERTO ROBAINA GONZÁLEZ.
JOSÉ RAMÓN FERNÁNDEZ ALVAREZ.
PEDRO CANISIO SÁEZ JOVA.
ZEIDA SUÁREZ PREMIER.
Gen. SENÉN CASAS REGUEIRO.
Gen. ABELARDO COLOMÉ IBARRA.
LIDIA TABLADA ROMERO.

COUNCIL OF MINISTERS

President: Dr FIDEL CASTRO RUZ.

First Vice-President: Gen. RAÚL CASTRO RUZ.

Vice-Presidents:
Dr CARLOS RAFAEL RODRÍGUEZ RODRÍGUEZ.
RAMIRO VALDÉS MENÉNDEZ.
JOEL DOMENECH BENÍTEZ.
JOSÉ RAMÓN FERNÁNDEZ ALVAREZ.
JOSÉ A. LÓPEZ MORENO.
OSMANY CIENFUEGOS GORRIARÁN.
PEDRO MIRET PRIETO.
ANTONIO RODRÍGUEZ MAURELL.
ADOLFO DÍAZ SUÁREZ.
LIONEL SOTO PRIETO.
JAIME CROMBET HERNÁNDEZ-BAQUERO.

Secretary: OSMANY CIENFUEGOS GORRIARÁN.

Minister of Agriculture: CARLOS PÉREZ LEÓN.

Minister of Foreign Trade: RICARDO CABRISAS RUIZ.

Minister of Internal Trade: MANUEL VILA SOSA.

Minister of Communications: MANUEL CASTILLO RABASA.

Minister of Construction: HOMERO CRABB VALDÉS.

Minister of Culture: Dr ARMANDO HART DÁVALOS.

Minister of Education: JOSÉ IGNACIO GÓMEZ GUTIÉRREZ.

Minister of Higher Education: FERNANDO VECINO ALEGRET.

Minister of the Revolutionary Armed Forces: Gen. RAÚL CASTRO RUZ.

Minister of the Food Industry: ALEJANDRO ROCA IGLESIAS.

Minister of Sugar: JUAN HERRERA MACHADO.

Minister of the Construction Materials Industry: JOSÉ CAÑETE ALVAREZ.

Minister of Light Industry: EDDY FERNÁNDEZ BOADA.

Minister of the Fishing Industry: Capt. JORGE A. FERNÁNDEZ-CUERVO VINENT.

Minister of the Iron and Steel and Metallurgical Industries: Ing. MARCOS LAGE COELLO.

Minister of Basic Industries: MARCOS PORTAL LEÓN.

Minister of the Interior: Gen. ABELARDO COLOMÉ IBARRA.

Minister of Justice: Dr CARLOS AMAT.

Minister of Foreign Affairs: ISIDORO MALMIERCA PEOLI.

Minister of Public Health: JULIO TEJAS PÉREZ.

Minister of Transport: Gen. SENÉN CASAS REGUEIRO.

Minister, President Central Planning Board: JOSÉ LÓPEZ MORENO.

Minister, State Committee for Technical and Material Supplies: SONIA RODRÍGUEZ CARDONA.

Minister, State Committee for Economic Co-operation: ERNESTO MELÉNDEZ BACH.

Minister, State Committee for Statistics: FIDEL VASCOS GONZÁLEZ.

Minister, State Committee for Finance: RODRIGO GARCÍA LEÓN.

Minister, State Committee for Standardization: RAMÓN DARIAS RODÉS.

Minister, State Committee for Prices: ARTURO GUZMÁN PASCUAL.

Minister, State Committee for Labour and Social Security: FRANCISCO LINARES CALVO.

Minister, President of the Banco Nacional de Cuba: HÉCTOR RODRÍGUEZ LLOMPART.

Minister, President of the Academy of Sciences of Cuba: ROSA ELENA SIMEÓN.

Minister of Government: JOSÉ A. NARANJO MORALES.

Minister of Government and President of the Commission for the Economic Management System: JOAQUÍN BENAVIDES.

CUBA   *Directory*

MINISTRIES

Ministry of Agriculture: Avda Independencia, entre Conill y Sta Ana, Havana; tel. (7) 70-1434; telex 511966.

Ministry of Basic Industries: Avda Salvador Allende, No 666, Havana; tel. (7) 70-7711; telex 511183.

Ministry of Communications: Plaza de la Revolución 'José Martí', Havana; tel. (7) 70-5581; telex 511657.

Ministry of Construction: Avda Carlos M. de Céspedes y Calle 35, Havana; tel. (7) 70-9411; telex 511275.

Ministry of the Construction Materials Industry: Calle O esq. 17, Vedado, Havana; tel. (7) 32-2541; telex 51-1517.

Ministry of Culture: Calle 2 No 258, entre 11 y 13, Vedado, Havana; tel. (7) 3-9945; telex 511400.

Ministry of Education: Obispo No 160, Havana; tel. (7) 61-4888; telex 511188.

Ministry of the Fishing Industry: Barlovento, Santa Fe, Havana; tel. (7) 22-7474; telex 51-1444.

Ministry of the Food Industry: Calle 41, No 4455, Playa, Havana; tel. (7) 2-6801; telex 511163.

Ministry of Foreign Affairs: Calzada No 360, Vedado, Havana; tel. (7) 32-3279; telex 511122.

Ministry of Foreign Trade: Infanta No 16, Vedado, Havana; tel. (7) 70-9341; telex 511174; fax (7) 7-6234.

Ministry of Higher Education: Calle 23, No 565 esq. a F, Vedado, Havana; tel. (7) 3-6655; telex 511253.

Ministry of the Interior: Plaza de la Revolución, Havana.

Ministry of Internal Trade: Calle Habana, No 258, Havana; tel. (7) 62-5790; telex 511171.

Ministry of the Iron and Steel and Metallurgical Industries: Avda Rancho Boyeros y Calle 100, Havana; tel. (7) 20-4861; telex 511179.

Ministry of Justice: Calle 0, No 216e/23 y Humboldt, Vedado, Havana 4 CP 10400; tel. (7) 32-6319; telex 511331.

Ministry of Light Industry: Empedrado No 302, Havana; tel. (7) 62-4041; telex 511141.

Ministry of Public Health: Calle 23, No 301, Vedado, Havana; tel. (7) 32-2561; telex 511149.

Ministry of the Revolutionary Armed Forces: Plaza de la Revolución, Havana.

Ministry of Sugar: Calle 23, No 171, Vedado, Havana; tel. (7) 30-5061; telex 511664.

Ministry of Transport: Avda Independencia y Lombillo, Havana; tel. (7) 70-7751; telex 511181.

Central Planning Board: 20 de Mayo y Ayestarán, Plaza de la Revolución, Havana; tel. (7) 79-6115; telex 511158.

State Committee for Economic Co-operation: Calle 1a, No 201, Vedado, Havana; tel. (7) 3-6661; telex 511297.

State Committee for Finance: Obispo No 211 esq. Cuba, Havana; tel. (7) 60-4111; telex 511101.

State Committee for Labour and Social Security: Calle 23, esq. Calle P, Vedado, Havana; tel. (7) 70-4571; telex 511225.

State Committee for Prices: Amistad No 552, Havana; tel. (7) 62-0888.

State Committee for Standardization: Egido No 611 entre Gloria y Apodaca, Havana; tel. (7) 62-1367; telex 511422.

State Committee for Statistics: Calle 5ta y Paseo, Vedado, Havana; tel. (7) 31-5171; telex 511257.

State Committee for Technical and Material Supplies: Monserrate No 261, Havana; tel. (7) 62-9390; telex 511757.

Commission for the Economic Management System: Avda 23 No 21425 entre 214 y 222, La Coronela, Havana; tel. (7) 22-0256.

Legislature

ASAMBLEA NACIONAL DEL PODER POPULAR

The National Assembly of People's Power was constituted on 2 December 1976. The Assembly's third five-year term began in December 1986. It consists of 510 deputies.

President: Dr Juan Escalona Reguera.
Vice-President: Zoila Benítez de Mendoza.
Secretary: Dr Ernesto Suárez Méndez.

Political Organizations

Partido Comunista de Cuba (PCC) (Communist Party of Cuba): Havana; f. 1961 as the Organizaciones Revolucionarias Integradas (ORI) from a fusion of the Partido Socialista Popular (Communist), Fidel Castro's Movimiento 26 de Julio and the Directorio Revolucionario 13 de Marzo); became the Partido Unido de la Revolución Socialista Cubana (PURSC) in 1962; renamed as the Partido Comunista de Cuba in 1965; 225-member Central Committee (146 full mems and 79 candidate mems were elected in February 1986), Political Bureau (18 mems in 1990), Secretariat and five Commissions; 561,104 mems (1987).

Political Bureau: Full mems Dr Fidel Castro Ruz, Gen. Raúl Castro Ruz, Juan Almeida Bosque, Dr Armando Hart Dávalos, José Ramón Machado Ventura, Carlos Rafael Rodríguez Rodríguez, Pedro Miret Prieto, Jorge Risquet Valdés-Saldaña, Julio Camacho Aguilera, Osmany Cienfuegos Gorriarán, Vilma Espín Guillois de Castro, Esteban Lazo Hernández, Gen. Abelardo Colomé Ibarra, Pedro Ross Leal, Carlos Lage Dávila, Roberto Robaina González, Maj.-Gen. Sixto Batista Santana.

Secretariat: Dr Fidel Castro Ruz (First Sec.), Gen. Raúl Castro Ruz (Second Sec.), José Ramón Machado Ventura, Julián Rizo Alvarez, Carlos Aldana Escalante.

Partido pro-Derechos Humanos: f. 1988 to defend human rights in Cuba; Pres. Hiram Abi Cobas; Sec.-Gen. Tania Díaz.

Diplomatic Representation

EMBASSIES IN CUBA

Afghanistan: Calle 24, No 106, entre 1 y 3, Miramar, Havana; tel. (7) 22-1145; Ambassador: Nur Ahmad Nur.

Albania: Calle 13, No 851, Vedado, Havana; tel. (7) 30-2788; Ambassador: Clirim Cepani.

Algeria: 5a Avda, No 2802 esq. 28, Miramar, Havana; tel. (7) 2-6538; Ambassador: Abdelhamid Latreche.

Angola: Avda 5, No 1012, entre 10 y 12, Miramar, Havana; tel. (7) 29-2205; Ambassador: Luís Dokuy Paulo de Castro.

Argentina: Calle 36, No 511, entre 5a y 7a, Miramar, Havana; tel. (7) 22-5540; telex 511138; Ambassador: Juan Carlos Olima.

Austria: Calle 4, No 101 entre 1 y 3, Miramar, Havana; tel. (7) 22-4394; telex 511415; Ambassador: Dr Christoph Parisini.

Belgium: Avda 5a, No 7408, Miramar-Playa, Havana; tel. (7) 29-6440; telex 511482; Ambassador: Count Louis Cornet d'Elzius du Chenoy.

Benin: Avda 7a, No 3205, Miramar, Havana; tel. (7) 29-6142; Ambassador: Cosme Ahannon Duguenon.

Bolivia: Calle 24, No 108 entre 1 y 3, Miramar, Havana; tel. (7) 2-4426; Ambassador: Oscar Peña Franco.

Brazil: Calle 16, No 503, Miramar, Havana; tel. (7) 22-7476; Ambassador: Italo Zappa.

Bulgaria: Calle B, No 252, Vedado, Havana; tel. (7) 30-0256; Ambassador: Kiril Zlatkov.

Burkina Faso: Calle 7a, No 8401 entre 84 y 84a, Miramar, Havana; tel. (7) 22-8295; Ambassador: Timothée Some.

Cambodia: Avda 5a, No 7001, Miramar, Havana; tel. (7) 29-6779; Ambassador: Ros Kong.

Canada: Calle 30, No 518, esq. a 7a, Miramar, Havana; tel. (7) 2-6516; telex 511586; Ambassador: Robert Middleton.

Cape Verde: Calle 98, No 508, entre 5 y 5b, Miramar, Havana; tel. (7) 21-8912; Chargé d'affaires a.i.: Mário Ferreira Lopes Camões.

China, People's Republic: Calle 13, No 551, Vedado, Havana; tel. (7) 32-5205; Ambassador: Chen Jiuchang.

Congo: Avda 5, No 1003, Miramar, Havana; tel. (7) 2-6513; Ambassador: Marcel Touanga.

Czechoslovakia: Avda Kohly, No 259, Nuevo Vedado, Havana; tel. (7) 30-0024; Ambassador: (vacant).

Denmark: Paseo de Martí No 20, Apto 4-C, Havana; tel. (7) 62-1528; telex 511100; fax (7) 62-1527; Consul: Mario Arredondo.

Ecuador: Avda 5a-A, No 4407, Miramar, Havana; tel. (7) 29-6839; telex 511770; Ambassador: Gustavo Jarrín Ampudia.

Egypt: Avda 5, No 1801, Miramar, Havana; tel. (7) 22-2541; telex 511551; Ambassador: Esmat Abdel Halim Mohammad.

Ethiopia: Calle 6, No 318, Miramar, Havana; tel. (7) 22-1260; Ambassador: Abebe Belayneh.

Finland: Avda 5a, No 9202, Miramar, Playa, Apdo. 3304, Havana; tel. (7) 22-4098; telex 511485; Ambassador: Heikki Puurunen.

France: Calle 14, No 312, entre 3a y 5a Avdas, Miramar, Havana; tel. (7) 29-6048; telex 511195; Ambassador: Philippe Peltier.

Germany: Calle 13, No 652, entre A y B, Vedado, Havana; tel. (7) 3-6626; telex 511127; Ambassador: Roland Zimmermann.

CUBA

Ghana: Avda 5a, No 1808, esq. Calle 20, Miramar, Havana; tel. (7) 29-3513; Ambassador: KOFI NYIDEVU AWOONOR.

Greece: Avda 5a, No 7802, esq. 78, Miramar, Havana; tel. (7) 22-6854; Ambassador: MARINOS RAFTOPOULOS.

Guinea: Calle 20, No 504, Miramar, Havana; tel. (7) 2-6428; Ambassador: LAMINE SOUGOULÉ.

Guinea-Bissau: Calle 14, No 313 entre 3 y 5, Miramar, Havana; tel. (7) 29-6689; Ambassador: CONSTANTINO LOPES DA COSTA.

Guyana: Calle 18, No 506, Miramar, Havana; tel. (7) 22-1249; telex 511498; Ambassador: HAROLD SAHADEO.

Holy See: Calle 12, No 514, Miramar, Havana (Apostolic Nunciature); tel. (7) 2-5296; telex (28) 512267; Apostolic Pro-Nuncio: Most Rev. FAUSTINO SÁINZ MUÑOZ, Titular Archibishop of Novaliciana.

Hungary: Calle 19, No 407, Vedado, Havana; tel. (7) 32-6526; telex 511368; Ambassador: BÉLA BARDÓCZ.

India: Calle 21, No 202, Vedado, Havana; tel. (7) 32-5777; telex 511414; Ambassador: MUKUR KANTI KHISHA.

Iran: Avda 5a, No 3002, esq. a 30, Miramar, Havana; tel. (7) 29-4575; telex 512186; Ambassador: SEYED MAHMOUD SADRI TABALE ZAVAREH.

Iraq: Avda 5a, No 8201, Miramar, Havana; tel. (7) 2-6461; telex 511413; Ambassador: WALEED A. ABBASS.

Italy: Paseo No 606 (altos), Vedado, Havana; tel. (7) 30-0378; telex 511352; Ambassador: CARLOS CIVILETTI.

Jamaica: Havana; relations restored in July 1990.

Japan: Calle 62, esq. 15, Vedado, Havana; tel. (7) 32-5554; telex 511260; Ambassador: RYO KAWADE.

Korea, Democratic People's Republic: Calle 17, No 752, Vedado, Havana; tel. (7) 30-5132; telex 511553; Ambassador: PAK CHUNG-KUK.

Laos: Avda 5a, No 2808, esq. 30, Miramar, Havana; tel. (7) 2-6198; Ambassador: PONMEK DELALOY.

Lebanon: Calle 174, No 1707, entre 17 y 17a, Sihoney, Havana; tel. (7) 21-8974; Chargé d'affaires a.i.: ZOUHAIR KAZZAZ.

Libya: Calle 8, No 309, Miramar, Havana; tel. (7) 2-4892; telex 511570; Ambassador: ALI MUHAMMAD AL-EJILI.

Mexico: Calle 12, No 518, Miramar, Havana; tel. (7) 2-8634; telex 511298; Ambassador: RAÚL CASTELLANO JIMÉNEZ.

Mongolia: Calle 66, No 505, Miramar, Havana; tel. (7) 2-5080; Ambassador: OSORYN ERDENE.

Mozambique: 7a Avda, No 2203 entre 22 y 24, Miramar, Havana; tel. (7) 26445; Ambassador: ESPERANÇA MACHAVELA.

Netherlands: Calle 8, No 307, Miramar, Havana; tel. (7) 2-6511; telex 511279; Ambassador: GERHARD JOHAN VAN HATTUM.

Nicaragua: Avda 7a, No 1402, Miramar, Havana; tel. (7) 2-6810; Ambassador: (vacant).

Nigeria: Avda 5a, No 1401, Apdo 6232, Miramar, Havana; tel. (7) 29-1091; telex 1589; Ambassador: SOLOMON KIKIOWO OMOJOKUN.

Panama: Calle 26, No 109, Miramar, Havana; tel. (7) 22-4096; Ambassador: (vacant).

Peru: Calle 36, No 109 entre 3 y 5, Miramar, Havana; tel. (7) 29-4477; telex 511289; Ambassador: CARLOS ALBERTO HIGUERAS RAMOS.

Philippines: Calle 28, No 705 entre 7 y 9, Miramar, Havana; tel. (7) 2-6870; Ambassador: OPHELIA GONZALES Y SAN AGUSTIN.

Poland: Avda 5, No 4405, Miramar, Havana; tel. (7) 29-1015; Ambassador: WOJCIECH BARANSKI.

Portugal: Avda 5a, No 6604, Miramar, Havana; tel. (7) 2-6871; telex 511411; Ambassador: F. M. H. DE GOUVEIA FAVILA V.

Romania: Calle 21, No 307, Vedado, Havana; tel. (7) 32-4303; Ambassador: ION SIMINICEANU.

Spain: Cárcel No 51, esq. Zulueta, Havana; tel. (7) 62-6061; telex 511367; Ambassador: ANTONIO SERRANO DE HARO MEDIALDEA.

Sri Lanka: Calle 32, No 307 entre 5 y 7, Miramar, Havana; tel. (7) 22-7992; Ambassador: N. KANAGARATNAM RAJALINGAN.

Sweden: Avda 31, No 14A, Miramar, Havana; tel. (7) 29-8871; telex 511208; Ambassador: KRISTER GÖRANSON.

Switzerland: Calzada, Calle L y M, Vedado, Havana; tel. (7) 2-4611; telex 511194; Ambassador: MARCUS KAISER.

Syria: Avda 5, No 7402, Miramar, Havana; tel. (7) 22-5266; telex 511394; Ambassador: (vacant).

Turkey: Avda 1a A, No 4215, entre 42 y 44, Miramar, Havana; tel. (7) 22-3933; telex 511724; Ambassador: MEHMET GÜNEY.

USSR: 5ta Avenida No 6402 entre 62 y 66, Miramar, Havana; tel. (7) 22-6444; Ambassador: YURIY VLADIMIROVICH PETROV.

United Kingdom: Edif. Bolívar, Carcel No 101-103, e Morro y Prado, Apdo 1069, Havana; tel. (7) 62-3071; telex 511656; Ambassador: DAVID BRIGHTY.

USA: (Relations broken off in 1961); Interests Section: Calzada entre L y M, Vedado, Havana; tel. (7) 32-0551; Counsellor: JOHN TAYLOR.

Uruguay: Calle 14, No 506 entre 5 y 7, Miramar, Havana; tel. (7) 22-7942; Ambassador: (vacant).

Venezuela: Calle 36-A No 704 entre 7 y 42, Miramar, Havana; tel. (7) 29-4631; telex 511384; Ambassador: M. C. LÓPEZ.

Viet-Nam: Avda 5a, No 1802, Miramar, Havana; tel. (7) 2-5214; Ambassador: DO VAN TAI.

Yemen: Avda 7a, No 2207 esq. 24, Miramar, Havana; tel. (7) 22-2594; telex 511488; Ambassador: MUHAMMAD ABDULRAHMAN HUSSEIN.

Yugoslavia: Calle 42, No 115, Miramar, Havana; tel. (7) 2-4982; Ambassador: MIHAJLO POPOVIĆ.

Zaire: Calle 36, No 716 entre 7 y 9, Miramar, Havana; tel. (7) 29-1580; Ambassador: SIMBA NDOMBE.

Zimbabwe: 3ra, No 1001 esq. a 10, Miramar, Havana; tel. (7) 22-7837; Ambassador: AMOS BERNARD MUVENGWA MIDZI.

Judicial System

The judicial system comprises the People's Supreme Court, the People's Provincial Courts and the People's Municipal Courts. The People's Supreme Court exercises the highest judicial authority.

PEOPLE'S SUPREME COURT

The People's Supreme Court comprises the Plenum, the five Courts of Justice in joint session and the Council of Government. When the Courts of Justice are in joint session they comprise all the professional and lay judges, the Attorney-General and the Minister of Justice. The Council of Government comprises the President and Vice-President of the People's Supreme Court, the Presidents of each Court of Justice and the Attorney-General of the Republic. The Minister of Justice may participate in its meetings.

President: Dr JOSÉ RAÚL AMARO SALUP.

Vice-President: Dr ZENAIDA OSORIO VIZCAINO.

Criminal Court:
President: Dr GRACIELA PRIETO MARTÍN.
Eight professional judges and 64 lay judges.

Civil and Administrative Court:
President: ANDRÉS BOLAÑOS GASSO.
Two professional judges and 32 lay judges.

Labour Court:
President: Dr ANTONIO R. MARTÍN SÁNCHEZ.
Three professional judges and 32 lay judges.

Court for State Security:
President: Dr EVERILDO DOMÍNGUEZ DOMÍNGUEZ.
Three professional judges and 32 lay judges.

Military Court:
President: Col JUAN MARINO FUENTES CALZADO.
Three professional judges and 32 lay judges.

Attorney-General: Dr RAMÓN DE LA CRUZ OCHOA.

Religion

There is no established Church, and all religions are permitted, though Roman Catholicism predominates.

CHRISTIANITY

Consejo Ecuménico de Cuba (Ecumenical Council of Cuba): Calle 6, No 273, entre 12 y 13, Vedado, Havana 4; tel. (7) 3-7404; f. 1941; 13 mem. churches; Pres. Dr ADOLFO HAM REYES; Gen. Sec. RAÚL SUÁREZ RAMOS.

The Roman Catholic Church

Cuba comprises two archdioceses and five dioceses. In 1989, according to diocesan estimates, there were 1,220,000 adherents in the country, representing about 12% of the total population. The number of practising Roman Catholics was estimated at only 100,000 in 1986.

CUBA   Directory

Bishops' Conference: Conferencia Episcopal de Cuba, Calle 26 No 314, entre 3ra y 5ta Avenida, Miramar, Apdo 623, Havana 13; tel. (7) 22-3868; telex (51) 2381; fax (7) 29-3168; f. 1983; Dir Mgr Carlos Manuel de Cespedes.

Archbishop of San Cristóbal de la Habana: Jaime Lucas Ortega y Alamino, Calle Habana 152, Apdo 594, Havana; tel. (7) 6-8463.

Archbishop of Santiago de Cuba: Pedro Meurice Estiu, Sánchez Hechevarría 607, Apdo 26, Santiago de Cuba; tel. 5-4801.

The Anglican Communion

Anglicans are adherents of the Iglesia Episcopal de Cuba (Episcopal Church of Cuba).

Bishop of Cuba: Rt Rev. Emilio J. Hernández Albalate, Calle 13, No 874, entre 4 y 6, Vedado, Havana 4; tel. (7) 32-1120.

Protestant Churches

Convención Bautista de Cuba Oriental (Baptist Convention of Eastern Cuba): Apdo 581, Calle 1, No 101, Rpto Fomento, Santiago; tel. 2-0173; f. 1905; Pres. Rev. Andrés Olivares Regalado; Sec. Rev. Félix Santos Perrand.

Iglesia Metodista en Cuba (Methodist Church in Cuba): Calle 58, No 4305, Havana; tel. (7) 32-0770; autonomous since 1968; 10,000 mems; Bishop Armando Rodríguez Borges.

Iglesia Presbiteriana-Reformada en Cuba (Presbyterian-Reformed Church in Cuba): Apdo 154, Matanzas; autonomous since 1967; 8,000 mems; Gen. Sec. Rev. Dr Sergio Arce.

Other denominations active in Cuba include the Apostolic Church of Jesus Christ, the Bethel Evangelical Church, the Christian Pentecostal Church, the Church of God, the Church of the Nazarene, the Free Baptist Convention, the Holy Pentecost Church, the Pentecostal Congregational Church and the Salvation Army.

The Press

DAILIES

National

In October 1990 President Castro announced that, in accordance with other wide-ranging economic austerity measures, only one newspaper, *Granma*, would henceforth be published as a nation-wide daily. The other national dailies were to become weeklies or were to cease publication.

Bastión: Territorial esq. a General Suárez, Plaza de la Revolución, Havana; tel. (7) 79-3361; telex 51-2373; organ of the Revolutionary Armed Forces; evening; Dir Frank Agüero Gómez; circ. 65,000.

Granma: Avda General Suárez y Calle Territorial, Plaza de la Revolución José Martí, Apdo 6260, Havana; tel. (7) 70-3521; f. 1965 to replace *Hoy* and *Revolución*; official Communist Party organ; morning and weekly editions; also weekly editions in Spanish, English, French and Portuguese; Editor Jacinto Granda de Laserna; circ. 700,000.

Juventud Rebelde: Territorial esq. Gen. Suárez, Plaza de la Revolución, Apdo 6344, Havana; tel. (7) 79-0744; telex 511168; f. 1965; organ of the Young Communist Union; evening; Dir José R. Vidal Valdés; circ. 300,000.

Trabajadores: Territorial esq. Gen. Suárez, Plaza de la Revolución, Havana; tel. (7) 79-0819; telex 511402; f. 1970; organ of the trade-union movement; daily; Dir Jorge Luis Canela Ciurana; circ. 150,000.

Provincial

Adelante: Avda A, Rpto Jayamá, Camagüey; f. 1959; morning; Dir Evaristo Sardiñas Vera; circ. 42,000.

Ahora: Salida a San Germán y Circunvalación, Holguín; f. 1962; Dir Alfredo Carralero Hernández; circ. 50,000.

Cinco de Septiembre: Calle 35, No 5609, entre 56 y 58, Cienfuegos; f. 1980; Dir Francisco Valdés Petitón; circ. 18,000.

La Demajagua: Amado Estévez esq. Calle 10, Rpto R. Reyes, Bayamo; f. 1977; Dir Bartolomé Martí Pons; circ. 30,000.

Escambray: Adolfo del Castillo 10, Sancti Spíritus; f. 1979; Dir Aramis Arteaga Pérez; circ. 14,000.

Girón: Avda Camilo Cienfuegos No 10505, P. Nuero, Matanzas; f. 1960; Dir Othoniel González Quevedo; circ. 25,000.

Guerrillero: Colón esq. Delicias y Adela Azcuy, Pinar del Río; f. 1969; Dir Ronald Suárez; circ. 33,000.

El Habanero: General Suárez y Territorial, Plaza de la Revolución, Apdo 6269, Havana; tel. (7) 6160; telex 1839; f. 1987; Dir Tubal Páez Hernández; circ. 21,000.

Invasor: Marcial Gómez 401 esq. Estrada Palma, Ciego de Avila; f. 1979; Dir Migdalia Utrera Peña; circ. 10,500.

Sierra Maestra: Santa Lucía 356, Santiago de Cuba; f. 1957; Dir Orlando Guevara Núñez; circ. 35,000.

Tribuna de la Habana: Territorial esq. Gen. Suárez, Plaza de la Revolución, Havana; tel. (7) 79-0050; f. 1980; Dir Marta Esplugas Arean; circ. 60,000.

Vanguardia: Céspedes 5 (altos), Santa Clara, Matanzas; f. 1962; Dir Pedro Hernández Soto; circ. 24,000.

Venceremos: Carretera Jamaica, Km 1½, Guantánamo; f. 1962; Dir Martha Cabrales Arias; circ. 12,000.

Ventiseis: Avda Carlos J. Finley, Las Tunas; f. 1977; Dir José Infantes Reyes; circ. 21,000.

Victoria: Carretera de la Fe, Km 1½, Plaza de la Revolución, Nueva Gerona, Isla de la Juventud; f. 1967; Dir Nieve Varona Puente; circ. 9,200.

PERIODICALS

ANAP: Línea 351, Vedado, Havana; f. 1961; monthly; information for small farmers; Dir Ricardo Machado; circ. 90,000.

Bohemia: Avda Independencia y San Pedro, Apdo 6000, Havana; tel. (7) 7-2833; telex 511256; f. 1908; weekly; politics; Dir Caridad Miranda Martínez; circ. 312,000.

El Caimán Barbudo: Paseo 613, Vedado, Havana; f. 1966; monthly; cultural; Dir Alex Pausides; circ. 47,000.

Cómicos: Calle 28, No 112, e/1ra y 3ra, Miramar, Havana; tel. (7) 22-5892; monthly; humorous; circ. 70,000.

Con la Guardia en Alto: Avda Salvador Allende 601, Havana; tel. (7) 79-4443; f. 1961; monthly; for mems of the Committees for the Defence of the Revolution; Dir Omelia Guerra Pérez; circ. 60,000.

Cuba Internacional: Calle 21 No 406, Vedado, Havana 4, Apdo 3603 Havana 3; tel. (7) 32-9353; f. 1959; monthly; political; in Spanish and Russian; Dir Jesús Hernández; circ. 30,000.

Cubatabaco: Amargura 103, 10100 Havana; tel. (7) 61-8453; telex 511123; f. 1972; quarterly; tobacco industry; Dir Zoila Couceyro; circ. 8,000.

Cubatabaco International: Amargura 103, 10100 Havana; tel. (7) 61-8453; telex 511123; f. 1979; 2 a year; tobacco industry; Dir Zoila Couceyro; circ. 3,000 (in English).

Dedeté: Territorial esq. a Gen. Suárez, Plaza de la Revolución, Havana; tel. (7) 79-0952; f. 1969; 2 a month; Dir Carlos Villar; circ. 150,000.

El Deporte, Derecho del Pueblo: Vía Blanca y Boyeros, Havana; tel. (7) 40-6838; telex 511583; f. 1968; monthly; sport; Dir Manuel Vaillant Carpente; circ. 15,000.

Heraldo Episcopal: Calle 13, No 874, entre 4 y 6, Vedado, Havana; tel. (7) 32-1120; journal of the Episcopal Church of Cuba; quarterly.

Industria Alimenticia: Amargura 103, 10100 Havana; tel. (7) 61-8453; telex 511123; f. 1977; quarterly; food industry; Dir Zoila Couceyro; circ. 10,000.

Juventud Técnica: Prado y Teniente Rey 553, Havana; tel. (7) 31-1825; f. 1965; monthly; scientific-technical; Dir Germán Fernández Burguet; circ. 100,000.

Mar y Pesca: San Ignacio 303, Havana; tel. (7) 60-4569; f. 1965; monthly; fishing; Dir Arnaldo Núñez; circ. 42,000.

El Militante Comunista: Calle 11, No 160, Vedado, Havana; tel. (7) 32-7581; f. 1967; monthly; Communist Party publication; Dir Manuel Menéndez; circ. 200,000.

Moncada: Belascoaín esq. Zanja, Havana; tel. (7) 79-7109; f. 1966; monthly; Dir Ricardo Martínez; circ. 70,000.

Muchacha: Galiano 264 esq. Neptuno, Havana; tel. (7) 61-5919; f. 1980; monthly; young women's magazine; Dir Silvia Martínez; circ. 120,000.

Mujeres: Galiano 264 esq. Neptuno, Havana; tel. (7) 61-5919; f. 1961; monthly; women's magazine; Dir Regla Zulueta; circ. 270,000.

El Muñe: Calle 28, No 112, e/1ra y 3ra, Mirimar, Havana; tel. (7) 22-5892; weekly; circ. 50,000.

Opina: Edif. Focsa, M entre 17 y 19, Havana; f. 1979; 2 a month; consumer-orientated; published by Institute of Internal Demand; Dir Eugenio Rodríguez Balari; circ. 250,000.

Pablo: Calle 28, no 112, e/1ra y 3ra, Mirimar, Havana; tel. (7) 22-5892; 16 a year; circ. 53,000.

Palante: Calle 21, No 954, entre 8 y 10, Vedado, Havana; tel. (7) 3-5098; f. 1961; weekly; humorous; Dir Rosendo Gutiérrez Román; circ. 235,000.

Pionero: Calle 17, No 354, Havana 4; tel. (7) 32-4571; f. 1961; weekly; children's magazine; Dir Pedro González (Péglez); circ. 210,000.

CUBA
Directory

Prisma Latinoamericano: Calle 21 y Avda G, Vedado, Havana; tel. (7) 6-5323; f. 1979; monthly; international news; Man. Dir JESÚS HERNÁNDEZ PÉREZ; circ. 25,000 (Spanish), 20,000 (English), 15,000 (Portuguese).

Revolución y Cultura: Calle 4, No 205, entre Línea y 11 Vedado, Havana; tel. (7) 30-9766; f. 1972; monthly; cultural; Dir ROMUALDO SANTOS; circ. 20,000.

RIL: O'Reilly 358, Havana; tel. (7) 62-0777; telex 511592; f. 1972; bi-monthly; technical; Dir Exec. Council of Publicity Dept, Ministry of Light Industry; Chief Officer MIREYA CRESPO; circ. 8,000.

Sol de Cuba: Calle 19, No 60 entre M y N, Vedado, Havana 4; tel. (7) 32-9881; telex 511955; f. 1983; every 3 months; Spanish, English and French editions; Gen. Dir ALCIDES GIRO MITJANS; Editorial Dir DORIS VÉLEZ; circ. 200,000.

Somos Jóvenes: Calle 17, No 354, esq. H, Vedado, Havana; tel. (7) 32-4571; f. 1977; monthly; Dir GUILLERMO CABRERA; circ. 200,000.

Verde Olivo: Avda de Rancho Boyeros y San Pedro, Havana; tel. (7) 79-8373; f. 1959; monthly; organ of the Revolutionary Armed Forces; Dir EUGENIO SUÁREZ PÉREZ; circ. 100,000.

PRESS ASSOCIATIONS

Unión de Periodistas de Cuba: Calle 23, No 452, Vedado, Apdo 6646, Havana; tel. (7) 32-5561; telex 512297; f. 1963; Sec.-Gen. LUIS JULIO GARCÍA.

Unión de Escritores y Artistas de Cuba (Union of Writers and Artists): Calle 17, No 351, Vedado, Havana; tel. (7) 32-4571; Pres. ABEL E. PRIETO JIMÉNEZ; Exec. Vice-Pres. LISANDRO OTERO.

NEWS AGENCIES

Agencia de Información Nacional (AIN): Calle 23, No 358 esq. a J, Vedado, Havana; tel. (7) 32-1269; national news agency; Dir ROBERTO PAVÓN TAMAYO.

Prensa Latina (Agencia Informativa Latinoamericana, SA): Calle 23, No 201 esq. a N, Vedado, Havana; tel. (7) 32-5561; telex 511132; f. 1959; Dir PEDRO MARGOLLES VILLANUEVA.

Foreign Bureaux

Agence France-Presse (AFP): No 4, Calle 17, 13°, Vedado, entre N y 0, Ciudad Habana; tel. (7) 32-0949; telex 511191; Bureau Chief BERTRAND ROSENTHAL.

Agencia EFE (Spain): Calle 36, No 110, entre 1a y 3a, Apdo 5, Miramar, Havana; tel. (7) 22-4958; telex 511395; Bureau Chief JUAN J. AZNARES MOZAS.

Agenzia Nazionale Stampa Associata (ANSA) (Italy): Calle Paseo 158, Apto 403, Vedado, Havana; tel. (7) 3-7447; telex 511903; Correspondent GIANNINA BERTARELLI.

Bulgarska Telegrafna Agentsia (BTA) (Bulgaria): Edif. Focsa, Calle 17 esq. M, Apdo 22-E, Vedado, Havana; tel. (7) 32-4779; Bureau Chief VASIL MIKOULACH.

Československá tisková kancelář (ČTK) (Czechoslovakia): Edif. Fajardo, Calle 17 y M, Apto 3-A, Vedado, Havana; tel. (7) 32-6101; telex 511397; Bureau Chief PAVEL ZOVADIL.

Informatsionnoye Agentstvo Novosti (IAN) (USSR): Calle 28, No 510, entre 5a y 7a, Miramar, Havana; tel. (7) 22-4129; Bureau Chief YURI GOLOVIATENKO.

Inter Press Service (IPS) (Italy): Calle 36 A No 121, Apto 1 esq. 3ra, Miramar, Havana; tel. (7) 22-1981; telex 512247; Bureau Chief CLAUDE JOSEPH HACKIN; Correspondent FIDEL PRIETO CRUZ.

Korean Central News Agency (Democratic People's Republic of Korea): Calle 10, No 613 esq. 25, Apto 6, Vedado, Havana; tel. (7) 31-4201; Bureau Chief CHANG YON CHOL.

Magyar Távirati Iroda (MTI) (Hungary): Calle 21, 5°, esq. 21 y 4, Vedado, Havana; tel. (7) 32-8353; telex 51-1324; Bureau Chief: ZOLTÁN TAKACS; Correspondent TAMÁS SIMÁRDI.

Novinska Agencija Tanjug (Yugoslavia): Calle 5a F, No 9801 esq. 98, Miramar, Havana; tel. (7) 22-7671; Bureau Chief DUSAN DAKOVIĆ.

Polska Agencja Prasowa (PAP) (Poland): Calle 6 No 702, Apto 5, entre 7ma y 9a, Miramar; Havana; tel. (7) 20-7067; telex 51-1254; Bureau Chief PIOTR SOMMERFED.

Reuters (UK): Edif. Altamira, Apto 116, Calle O, No 58, Vedado, Havana 4; tel. (7) 32-4345; telex 511584; Bureau Chief (vacant).

Telegrafnoye Agentstvo Sovetskovo Soyuza (TASS) (USSR): Calle 96, No 317, entre 3a y 5a, Miramar, Havana 4; tel. (7) 29-2528; telex 51-1382; Bureau Chief ALEKSANDR KANICHEV.

Viet-Nam Agency (VNA): Calle 16, No 514, 1°, entre 5a y 7a, Miramar, Havana; tel. (7) 2-4455; telex 51-1794; Bureau Chief PHAM DINH LOI.

Xinhua (New China) News Agency (People's Republic of China): Calle G, No 259, esq. 13, Vedado, Havana; tel. (7) 32-4616; telex 511692; Bureau Chief GAO YONGHUA.

Publishers

Casa de las Américas: Calle 3a y Avda G, Vedado, Havana; tel. (7) 32-3587; telex 511019; f. 1960; Latin American literature and social sciences; Dir ARTURO ARANGO.

Ediciones Unión: Calle 17, No 351, Vedado, Havana; tel. (7) 32-4571; telex 511563; publishing arm of the Unión de Escritores y Artistas de Cuba; Cuban literature, art; Dir RICARDO VIÑALET.

Editora Política: Belascoaín No 864, esq. a Desagüe y Peñalver, Havana; tel. (7) 79-8553; f. 1963; publishing institution of the Partido Comunista Cubano; Dir HUGO CHINEA.

Editorial Arte y Literatura: Calle O'Reilly, No 4, esq. Tacón, Habana Vieja, Patrimonio de la Humanidad, Havana; tel. (7) 62-3708; telex 512417; f. 1967; attached to the Ministry of Culture; world literature and art; Dir ELIZABETH DÍAZ.

Editorial Abril: Virtudes 257, entre Aguila y Galiano, Centro Habana, Havana; tel. (7) 61-7038; attached to the Union of Young Communists; children's literature; Dir ERNESTO PADRÓN.

Editorial Academia: Industria No 452, esq. a San José, Habana Vieja, Havana; tel. (7) 62-9501; telex 51949; attached to the Cuban Academy of Sciences; scientific and technical; Dir MIRIAM RAYA.

Editorial Ciencias Médicas: Calle E No 452 entre 19 y 21, Apartado No 6520, Vedado, Havana 10400; tel. (7) 32-4519; telex 511202; attached to the Ministry of Public Health; books and magazines specializing in the medical sciences; Dir Dr JEREMÍAS HERNÁNDEZ OJITO.

Editorial Ciencias Sociales: Calle 14, No 4104, entre 41 y 43, Miramar, Playa, Havana; tel. (7) 2-4801; f. 1967; attached to the Ministry of Culture; social and political literature, history, philosophy, juridical sciences and economics; Dir RICARDO GARCÍA PAMPÍN.

Editorial Científico-Técnica: Calle 2, No 58, entre 3a y 5a, Vedado, Havana; tel. (7) 3-9417; attached to the Ministry of Culture; technical and scientific literature; Dir ISIDRO FERNÁNDEZ.

Editorial Gente Nueva: Palacio del Segundo Cabo, Calle O'Reilly No 4, esq. a Tacón, Havana; tel. (7) 6-8341; books for children; Dir ELENIA RODRÍGUEZ.

Editorial José Martí: Apdo 4208, Havana; tel. (7) 32-9838; f. 1983; attached to the Ministry of Culture; foreign language publishing; Dir FÉLIX SAUTIÉ MEDEROS.

Editorial Oriente: José A. Saco, No 356 entre Harman y Río Rosado, Santiago de Cuba; tel. 8096; telex 61170; publishes works from the Eastern provinces; general; Dir REINALDO CUESTA.

Editorial Pablo de la Torriente: Calle 28, No 112 e/1ra y 3ra, Miramar, Havana; tel. (7) 22-5692; f. 1985; attached to the Cuban Union of Journalists; specialized texts and the works of Cuban journalists; Dir IRMA ARMAS FONSECA.

Editorial Pueblo y Educación: Calle 3a A, No 4605, entre 46 y 60, Playa, Havana; tel. (7) 22-1490; textbooks; Dir CATALINA LAJUD HERRERO.

Letras Cubanas: Calle O'Reilly, No 4, Habana Vieja, Havana; attached to the Ministry of Culture; general, particularly classic and contemporary Cuban literature and arts; Dir ALBERTO BATISTA REYES.

Government Publishing Houses

Instituto Cubano del Libro: Palacio del Segundo Cabo, Calle O'Reilly, No 4, esq. a Tacón, Havana; tel. (7) 62-8091; state printing and publishing organization attached to the Ministry of Culture which combines several publishing houses and has direct links with others; presides over the National Editorial Council (CEN); Pres. PABLO PACHECO LÓPEZ.

Oficina de Publicaciones: Calle 17 No 552, esq. a D, Vedado, Havana; tel. (7) 32-1883; attached to the Council of State; speeches and other texts of state and party leaders; Dir PEDRO ÁLVAREZ TABÍO.

Radio and Television

In 1987 there were an estimated 3,378,000 radio receivers. In the same year there were an estimated 1,957,000 television receivers in use.

Ministerio de Comunicaciones: Plaza de la Revolución José Martí, Havana; tel. (7) 70-0911; Tech. Dir CARLOS MARTÍNEZ ALBUERNE.

CUBA

Empresa Cubana de Radio y Televisión (INTERTV): Calle K, No 352, esq a 19, Vedado, Havana 10400; tel. (7) 32-7571; telex 511600; fax (7) 32-1746; Dir ENRIQUE SOTO RODRÍGUEZ.

Instituto Cubano de Radio y Televisión: Televisión Nacional, Calle 23, No 258 entre L y M, Vedado, Havana 4; tel. (7) 32-7511; telex 511613; f. 1962; Pres. ENRIQUE ROMÁN HERNÁNDEZ; Vice-Pres. GARY GONZÁLEZ BENÍTEZ.

RADIO

In 1986 there were 5 national networks and 1 international network; 17 provincial radio stations and 32 municipal radio stations, with a total of 188 transmitters.

Radio Enciclopedia: Calle N, entre 21 y 23, Vedado, Havana; tel. (7) 32-1180; instrumental music programmes; 24 hours daily; Dir DANIEL MARÍN DELGADO.

Radio Habana Cuba: Avda Menocal, No 105, Apdo 7026, Havana; tel. (7) 7-4954; f. 1961; shortwave station; broadcasts in Spanish, English, French, Portuguese, Arabic, Esperanto, Quechua, Guaraní and Creole; Dir MILAGROS HERNÁNDEZ CUBA.

CMBF—Radio Musical Nacional: Avda Menocal No 105, Havana; tel. (7) 70-4561; telex 1766; f. 1948; national network; classical music programmes; 17 hours daily; Dir PEDRO PABLO RODRÍGUEZ.

Radio Progreso: Avda Menocal, No 105, Havana; tel. (7) 70-4561; national network; mainly entertainment and music; 24 hours daily; Dir JULIO PÉREZ MUÑOZ.

Radio Rebelde: Calle M entre 23 y 21, Vedado, Havana; Apdo 6277, Havana; tel. (7) 32-7511; telex 511777; f. 1984 (after merger of former Radio Rebelde and Radio Liberación); national network; 24-hour news programmes, music and sports; Dir-Gen. PEDRO ROJAS LORENZO.

Radio Reloj: Edif. Radiocentro, Calle 23 No 258 entre L y M, Vedado, Havana; tel. (7) 32-9689; telex 511349; f. 1947; national network; 24-hour news service; Dir MIRTHA INÉS CERVANTES.

TELEVISION

In 1986 there were two national networks with 94 transmitters.

Televisión Cubana (Cubavisión and Tele-Rebelde): Calle M, No 213 entre 21 y 23, Vedado, Havana; tel. (7) 32-5000; broadcasts in colour on channel 2 and channel 6; Dirs GARY GONZÁLEZ BENÍTEZ, RODOBALDO DÍAZ OLIVER.

CHTV: Habana Libre Hotel, Havana; f. 1990; subsidiary station of Tele-Rebelde.

Finance

Comité Estatal de Finanzas: Obispo esq. a Cuba, Havana; tel. (7) 62-5971; f. 1976; charged with the direction and control of the State's financial policy, including preparation of the budget.

BANKING

All banks were nationalized in October 1960. Legislation establishing the national banking system was approved by the Council of State in October 1984.

Central Bank

Banco Nacional de Cuba (National Bank of Cuba): Cuba 402, esq. a Lamparilla, Apdo 736, Havana 1; tel. (7) 62-5361; telex 511822; f. 1950, reorganized 1984; total assets 12,176.8m. pesos (Dec. 1986); sole bank of issue; arranges short- and long-term credits, finances investments and operations with other countries, and acts as the clearing and payments centre; 162 brs throughout the country; Pres. HÉCTOR RODRÍGUEZ LLOMPART; First Vice-Pres OSVALDO FUENTES TORRES (Domestic), LUIS GUTIÉRREZ (International).

Commercial Bank

Banco Financiero Internacional, SA: Calle Línea, No 1, Vedado, Havana; tel. (7) 32-5972; telex 512405; fax (7) 32-5981; f. 1984; autonomous; capital 10m. pesos (1985); promotes Cuban exports and banking relations; Chair. EDUARDO BENCOMO ZURDOS; Gen. Man. ARNALDO ALAYÓN.

Savings Bank

Banco Popular del Ahorro: Calle 16, No 306, entre 5a y 3a Avda, Playa, Havana; tel. (7) 22-8240; telex 511608; f. 1983; savings bank; cap. US $30m., dep. $1,678m.; Pres. MARISELA FERREYRA DE LA GÁNDARA; 474 brs.

INSURANCE

State Organizations

Agencia Internacional de Inspección y Ajuste de Averías y Servicios Conexos—INTERMAR S.A.: Obispo No 361 entre Habana y Compostela, Havana; f. 1988; controls the inspection of goods, ship and aircraft breakage; Dir-Sec. HORACIO LUNÁN WILLIAMS.

Empresa del Seguro Estatal Nacional (ESEN): Obispo No 211, 3°, Apdo 109, 10100 Havana; tel. (7) 60-4111; f. 1978; motor and agricultural insurance; Man. Dir PEDRO MANUEL ROCHE ALVAREZ.

Seguros Internacionales de Cuba—Esicuba: Cuba No 314, Apdo 79, Havana; tel. (7) 62-7119; telex 511616; fax (7) 62-0252; all classes of insurance except life; f. 1963, reorganized 1986; Chair. and Chief Exec. SALVADOR OROZCO JHONES.

Trade and Industry

IMPORT-EXPORT BOARDS

Alimport (Empresa Cubana Importadora de Alimentos): Infanta 16, 3°, Apdo 7006, Havana; tel. (7) 70-2437; telex 511454; controls import of foodstuffs and liquors; Man. Dir ARMANDO PERDOMO.

Autoimport (Empresa Central de Abastecimiento y Venta de Equipos de Transporte Ligero): Galiano 213, entre Concordia y Virtudes, Havana; tel. (7) 62-8180; telex 511417; imports cars, light vehicles, motor cycles and spare parts; Man. Dir EDELIO VERA RODRÍGUEZ.

Aviaimport (Empresa Cubana Importadora y Exportadora de Aviación): Calle 182, No 126 entre 1ra y 5ta, Reparto Flores, Havana; tel. (7) 22-6515; telex 511135; import of aircraft and components; Man. Dir MARCOS LAGO.

Caribex (Empresa Exportadora del Caribe): Edif. No 7, Barlovento, Santa Fe, Playa La Habana, Havana; tel. (7) 22-7889; telex 511471; fax (7) 22-8452; import and export of seafood and marine products; Man. Dir PEDRO SUÁREZ GAMBE.

Construimport (Empresa Central de Abastecimiento y Venta de Equipos de Construcción y sus Piezas): Carretera de Varona, Km. 1½, Capdevila, Havana; tel. (7) 44-7284; telex 511213; controls the import and export of construction machinery and equipment; Man. Dir JESÚS SERRANO.

Consumimport (Empresa Cubana Importadora de Artículos de Consumo General): Calle 23, No 55, Apdo 6427, Vedado, Havana; tel. (7) 70-0302; telex 512355; imports and exports general consumer goods; Dir EVELIO LASTRA.

Contex: Avda 1ra No 3402 esq. 34, Miramar, Havana; tel. (7) 29-2221; telex 51-2162; f. 1980; import and export of textiles, jewellery, footwear, handicrafts, etc.; Man. Dir CÉSAR CARBALLO.

Copextel (Corporación Productora y Exportadora de Tecnología Electrónica): Calle 194 y 7a, Siboney, Havana; tel. (7) 20-1735; telex 512459; exports LTEL personal computers and micro-computer software; Man. Dir LUIS J. CARRASCO.

Coprefil (Empresa Comercial y de Producciones Filatélicas): Calle Infanta No 58 esq. P, Apdo 1000, Vedado, Havana 1; tel. (7) 7-8812; telex 512479; imports and exports postage stamps, postcards, calendars, handicrafts, communications equipment, electronics, watches, etc.; Man. Dir ANTONIO GUERRA.

Corporación UNECA (Unión de Empresas Constructoras Caribe): Avda 9a, No 614, entre 6 y 10, Miramar, Havana; tel. (7) 29-4576; telex 511678; undertakes construction work abroad; Man. Dir OSCAR RODRÍGUEZ CROISSIERD.

Cubaelectrónica (Empresa Importadora y Exportadora de Productos de la Electrónica): Calle 22, No 510 entre 5 y 7, Miramar, Havana; tel. (7) 22-7316; telex 512484; fax (7) 21-8267; f. 1986; imports and exports electronic equipment and devices; Man. Dir LUIS BLANCA.

Cubaequipos (Empresa Cubana Importadora de Productos Mecánicos y Equipos Varios): Calle 23, No 55, Vedado, Havana; tel. (7) 79-2212; telex 512443; imports of mechanical goods and equipment; Man. Dir PORFIRIO MEDEROS PAIVA.

Cubaexport (Empresa Cubana Exportadora de Alimentos y Productos Varios): Calle 23, No 55, Vedado, Apdo 6647, Havana; tel. (7) 79-1669; telex 511178; export of foodstuffs; Man. Dir VIDAL M. PRIETO.

Cubafrutas (Empresa Cubana Exportadora de Frutas Tropicales): Calle 23, No 55, Apdo 6683, Vedado 4, Havana; tel. (7) 79-5653; telex 511849; fax (7) 79-5653; f. 1979; controls export of fruits, vegetables and canned foodstuffs; Man. Dir JORGE AMARO.

Cubaindustria (Empresa Cubana Exportadora de Productos Industriales): Calle 15, No 410, entre F y G, Vedado, Havana; tel. (7) 32-5522; telex 511677; fax (7) 32-2390; controls export of industrial products; Man. Dir MILDA PICOS RIVERS.

Cubalse (Empresa para Prestación de Servicios al Cuerpo Diplomático): Calle 68 No 503 entre 5ta y 5ta A, Miramar, Havana (also at Apdo 634, Marianao 13); tel. 22-5541/48; telex 51-1235; f. 1974; imports consumer goods for the diplomatic corps and foreign

CUBA

technicians residing in Cuba; exports beverages and tobacco, leather goods and foodstuffs; Man. Dir ROLANDO DE ARMAS.

Cubametales (Empresa Cubana Importadora de Metales, Combustibles y Lubricantes): Infanta 16, 4°, Apdo 6917, Vedado, Havana; tel. (7) 70-4225; telex 511452; controls import of metals (ferrous and non-ferrous), crude petroleum and petroleum products; also engaged in the export of petroleum products and ferrous and non-ferrous scrap; Dir RAFAEL PRIEDE.

Cubanacán (Corporación de Turismo y Comercio Internacional): Avda 146 No 1107 esq. 11, Cubanacán, Apdo 16036, Havana; tel. (7) 22-5511/19; telex 51-1316; f. 1987; imports and exports inputs, materials and services regarding tourist industry development; Man. Dir ABRAHAM MACIQUES MACIQUES.

Cubaniquel (Empresa Cubana Exportadora de Minerales y Metales): Calle 23, No 55, Apdo 6128, Havana; tel. (7) 7-8460; telex 511178; sole exporter of minerals and metals; Man. Dir WALTER S. LEO. TAMAJÓN.

Cubatabaco (Empresa Cubana del Tabaco): O'Reilly No 104, Apdo 6557, Havana; tel. (7) 32-5463; telex 511760; fax (7) 9-2653; f. 1962; controls export of leaf tobacco, cigars and cigarettes; Man. Dir FRANCISCO PADRÓN.

Cubatécnica (Empresa de Contratación de Asistencia Técnica): Avda 1a, No 4, entre 0 y 2, Hotel Sierra Maestra, Miramar, Havana; tel. (7) 22-2574; telex 511360; controls export and import of technical assistance; Man. Dir RAMÓN SOTO RECIO.

Cubatex (Empresa Cubana Importadora de Fibras, Tejidos, Cueros y sus Productos): Calle 23, No 55, Apdo 7115, Vedado, Havana; tel. (7) 70-3269; telex 512361; controls import of fibres, textiles, hides and by-products and export of fabric and clothing; Man. Dir REINER MARTÍN GONZÁLEZ.

Cubazucar (Empresa Cubana Exportadora de Azúcar y sus Derivados): Calle 23, No 55, Vedado, Apdo 6647, Havana; tel. (7) 70-3526; telex 511147; fax (7) 379-4303; f. 1962; controls export of sugar, molasses and alcohol; Man. Dir ALBERO BETANCOURT R.

Ecimact (Empresa Comercial de Industrias de Materiales, Construcción y Turismo): Calle 1aC entre 152 y 154, Miramar, Havana; tel. (7) 21-9783; telex 511926; controls import and export of engineering services and plant for industrial construction and tourist complexes; Man. Dir OCTAVIO CASTILLA.

Ecimetal (Empresa Comercial para la Industria Metalúrgica y Metal mecánica): Calle 1ra 201 entre A y B, Vedado, Havana 4; tel. 30-9456; telex 511555; f. 1977; controls import of plant for shaping and milling metals; Dir Ing. RAÚL RODRÍGUEZ RODRÍGUEZ.

Ediciones Cubanas (Empresa de Comercio Exterior de Publicaciones): Obispo 527, Apdo 605, Havana; tel. (7) 62-6150; telex 512337; controls import and export of books and periodicals; Man. Dir JOSÉ MANUEL CASTRO RODRÍGUEZ.

Egrem (Empresa de Grabaciones y Ediciones Musicales): Campanario No 315, entre San Miguel y Neptuno, Apdo 2217, Havana; tel. (7) 62-9762; telex 512171; controls the import and export of records, tapes, printed music and musical instruments; Man. Dir MIGUEL COMAS.

Emexcon (Empresa Exportadora de la Construcción): Calle 25, No 2606, Miramar, Havana; tel. (7) 2-4093; telex 511693; f. 1978; consulting engineer services, contracting, import and export of building materials and equipment; Pres. Lic. ELIODORO PÉREZ.

Emiat (Empresa Importadora y Exportadora de Suministros Técnicos): Calle 20, No 519, entre 5a y 7a, Miramar, Havana; tel. (7) 22-1163; telex 51-1339; f. 1983; imports technical materials, equipment and special products; exports furniture, kitchen utensils and accessories; Man. Dir MARTA ALONSO SÁNCHEZ.

Emidict (Empresa Especializada Importadora, Exportadora y Distribuidora para la Ciencia y la Técnica): Calle 16, No 102, Miramar, Havana 13; tel. 2-5782; telex 512233; controls import and export of scientific and technical products and equipment, live animals and ornamental fishes; Man. Dir MIGUEL JULIO PÉREZ.

Empoft (Empresa Operadora de Fuerza de Trabajo—UNECA): Calle 9a, No 614, entre 6 y 10, Miramar, Havana; tel. (7) 29-4576; telex 511678; manages specialized personnel for building projects; Man. Dir ALEJANDRO GAUBECA.

Empresa Cubana de Acuñaciones: Calle 18 No 306, entre 3 y 5 Avda, Miramar, Havana; tel. (7) 29-6693; telex 511939; fax (7) 22-7771; f. 1977; controls export of coins, base and precious metals; Man. Dir GUILLERMO TRIANA AGUIAR.

Energoimport (Empresa Importadora de Objetivos Electro-energéticos): Calle 7a No 2602, esq. a 26, Miramar, Havana; tel. (7) 2-8156; telex 511812; f. 1977; controls import of equipment for electricity generation; Dir LÁZARO HERNÁNDEZ GONZÁLEZ.

Eprob (Empresa de Proyectos para las Industrias de la Básica): Calle 184 No 129, entre Avda 1 y 5, Avda Rpto Flores, Playa,

Directory

Apdo 12100, Havana; tel. (7) 21-8074; telex 511404; fax (7) 30-1394; f. 1967; exports consulting services and processing of engineering construction projects, consulting services and supplies of complete industrial plants and turn-key projects; Man. Dir ANTONIO RONDA.

Eproyiv (Empresa de Proyectos para Industrias Varias): Calle 184 entre 5ta y 1ra, Rpto Flores, Miramar, Havana; tel. (7) 7-7092; telex 515004; exports consulting services to third-world countries for plant acquisition, tender analysis and tender application; industrial design; Man. Dir GONZALO RÍOS.

Esi (Empresa de Suministros Industriales): Calle Aguiar No 556 entre Teniente Rey y Muralla, Havana; tel. (7) 62-0696; telex 51-1495; f. 1985; imports machinery, equipment and components for industrial plants; Man. Dir RODOLFO PÉREZ ROJAS.

Fecuimport (Empresa Cubana Importadora y Exportadora de Ferrocarriles): Avda 7a, No 6209, entre 62 y 66, Miramar, Havana; tel. (7) 2-3764; telex 512419; imports and exports railway equipment; Man. Dir ANTONIO CONEJO MESA.

Ferrimport (Empresa Cubana Importadora de Artículos de Ferretería): Calle 23, No 55, 2°, Apdo 6258, Vedado, Havana; tel. (7) 70-2531; telex 511144; import of ironware; Man. Dir MIGUEL SOSA.

Fondo Cubano de Bienes Culturales: Muralla No 107, esq. S. Ignacio, Havana; tel. (7) 61-2859; telex 512278; controls export of fine handicraft and works of art; Man. Dir RAFAEL GUTIÉRREZ.

ICAIC (Instituto Cubano del Arte e Industria Cinematográficos): Calle 23, No 1155, Vedado, Havana 4; tel. (7) 3-4400; telex 511419; f. 1959; production, import and export of films and newsreel; Pres. JULIO GARCÍA ESPINOSA.

Imexin (Empresa Importadora y Exportadora de Infraestructura): Avda 5a, No 1007, esq. a 12, Miramar, Havana; tel. (7) 29-2700; telex 511454; f. 1977; controls import and export of infrastructure; Man. Dir RAÚL BENCE.

Imexpal (Empresa Importadora y Exportadora de Plantas Alimentarias, sus Completamientos y Derivados): Calle 22, No 313, entre 3a y 5a, Miramar, Havana; tel. (7) 29-1671; telex 511216; controls import and export of food-processing plants and related items; Man. Dir Ing. CONCEPCIÓN BUENO.

Maprinter (Empresa Cubana Importadora y Exportadora de Materias Primas y Productos Intermedios): Infanta 16, Apdo 2110, Havana; tel. (7) 7-4981; telex 511453; controls import and export of raw materials and intermediate products; Man. Dir FRANCISCO GARCÍA CARRANZA.

Maquimport (Empresa Cubana Importadora de Maquinarias y Equipos): Calle 23, No 55, Apdo 6052, Vedado, Havana; tel. (7) 70-2546; telex 511371; controls import of machinery and equipment; Man. Dir ARMANDO VERA GIL.

Marpesca (Empresa Cubana Importadora y Exportadora de Buques Mercantes y de Pesca): Conill No 580, esq. Avda 26, Nuevo Vedado, Havana; tel. (7) 30-1971; telex 511658; imports and exports ships and port and fishing equipment; Man. Dir REYNALDO LUIS CABRERA.

Medicuba (Empresa Cubana Importadora y Exportadora de Productos Médicos): Máximo Gómez 1, esq. a Egido, Havana; tel. (7) 62-3923; telex 511658; enterprise for the export and import of medical and pharmaceutical products; Man. Dir ORLANDO ROMERO.

Produimport (Empresa Central de Abastecimiento y Venta de Productos Químicos y de la Goma): Calle Consulado No 626 entre Animas y Virtudes, Havana; tel. (7) 62-9576; telex 51-2390; f. 1977; imports and exports spare parts for motor vehicles; Man. Dir RODOLFO ALONSO NAVARRO.

Quimimport (Empresa Cubana Importadora de Productos Químicos): Calle 23, No 55, Apdo 6088, Vedado, Havana; tel. (7) 70-8066; telex 511283; controls import of chemical products; Man. Dir LESLIE E. PATTERSON.

Suchel (Empresa de Jabonería): Calzada de Buenos Aires 353 esq. a Durege, Cerro Apdo 6359; tel. 40-6396; telex 51-2159; fax 40-7323; f. 1985; imports materials for the detergent, perfumery and cosmetics industry, exports cosmetics, perfumes and household products; Man. Dir JOSÉ GARCÍA DÍAZ.

Tecnoazúcar (Empresa de Servicios Técnicos e Ingeniería para la Industria Azucarera): Calle 12 No 310 entre 3ra y 5ta, Miramar, Playa, Apdo 631, Havana; tel. (7) 29-5441; telex 51-1022; imports machinery and equipment for the sugar industry, conducts feasibility studies; Man. Dir LUIS DE CÁRDENAS CABRERA.

Tecnoimport (Empresa Cubana Importadora y Exportadora de Productos Técnicos): Calle 47, No 3419, entre 34 y 36, Playa, Havana; tel. (7) 22-5069; telex 511572; imports technical products; Man. Dir Lt Col ABEL IZQUIERDO.

Tecnotex (Empresa Cubana Exportadora e Importadora de Servicios, Artículos y Productos Técnicos Especializados): Calle 39A

No 4215 entre 42 y 44, Playa, Havana; tel. (7) 2-7421; telex 51-1039; f. 1983; imports specialized technical and radiocommunications equipment, exports outdoor equipment and geodetic networks; Man. Dir RIGOBERTO ARIAS CURBELO.

Tractoimport (Empresa Central de Abastecimiento y Venta de Maquinaria Agrícola y sus Piezas): Avda Rancho Boyeros y Calle 100, Apdo 6301, Havana; tel. (7) 20-5154; telex 511162; f. 1960 for the import of tractors and agricultural equipment; also exports pumps and agricultural implements; Man. Dir MANUEL CASTRO DEL AGUILA.

Transimport (Empresa Central de Abastecimiento y Venta de Equipos de Transporte Pesados y sus Piezas): Calle 102 y Avda 63, Marianao, Apdo 6665, 11500 Havana; tel. (7) 20-0325; telex 511150; f. 1962; controls import and export of vehicles and transportation equipment; Man. Dir JESÚS DENNES RIVERO.

Unecamoto (Unión de Empresas de Camiones y Motores): Planta de Amistad Cubano-Soviética, Avda Vía Blanca y Línea del Ferrocarril, Havana; tel. (7) 99-4571/75; f. 1987; imports components and accessories for motor vehicles; Man. Dir CECILIO GONZÁLEZ.

CHAMBER OF COMMERCE

Cámara de Comercio de la República de Cuba: Calle 21, No 661/701, esq. Calle A, Apdo 4237, Vedado, Havana; tel. (7) 30-3356; telex 511752; f. 1963; mems include all Cuban foreign trade enterprises and the most important agricultural and industrial enterprises; Pres. JULIO GARCÍA OLIVERAS; Vice-Pres. SEGUNDO ABELEDO GONZÁLEZ-LARRINAGA.

AGRICULTURAL ORGANIZATION

Asociación Nacional de Agricultores Pequeños—ANAP (National Association of Small Farmers): Calle I, No 206, Vedado, Havana; tel. (7) 32-4541; telex 511294; f. 1961; 167,461 mems (Dec. 1988); Pres. ORLANDO LUGO FONTE; Vice-Pres. LUIS GONZÁLEZ ACOSTA.

TRADE UNIONS

All workers have the right to become members of a national trade union according to their industry and economic branch.

The following industries and labour branches have their own unions: Agriculture, Chemistry and Energetics, Civil Workers of the Revolutionary Armed Forces, Commerce and Gastronomy, Communications, Construction, Culture, Education and Science, Food, Forestry, Health, Light Industry, Merchant Marine, Mining and Metallurgy, Ports and Fishing, Public Administration, Sugar, Tobacco and Transport.

Central de Tradajadores de Cuba—CTC (Confederation of Cuban Workers): Palacio de los Trabajadores, San Carlos y Peñalver, Havana; tel. (7) 7-4901; telex 511403; f. 1939; affiliated to WFTU and CPUSTAL; 17 national trade unions affiliated; Gen. Sec. PEDRO ROSS LEAL; 3,060,838 mems (Dec. 1989).

Transport

The Ministry of Transport controls all public transport.

RAILWAYS

The total length of railways in 1989 was 12,605 km, of which 7,762 km were used by the sugar industry. The remaining 4,843 km are public service railways operated by Ferrocarriles de Cuba. All railways were nationalized in 1960.

Ferrocarriles de Cuba: Ministerio del Transporte, Avda Independencia y Tulipán, Havana; tel. (7) 70-7751; f. 1960; operates public services; under direct management of the Minister of Transport; divided as follows:

División Occidente: serves Pinar del Río, Ciudad de la Habana, Havana Province and Matanzas.

División Centro: serves Villa Clara, Cienfuegos and Sancti Spíritus.

División Centro-Este: serves Camagüey, Ciego de Avila and Tunas.

División Oriente: serves Santiago de Cuba, Granma, Guantánamo and Holguín.

División Camilo Cienfuegos: serves part of Havana Province and Matanzas.

ROADS

The total length of paved roads in 1987 was 13,112 km, of which 575 km were motorway. The Central Highway runs from Pinar del Río in the west to Santiago, for a length of 1,144 km. In addition to this paved highway, there are a number of secondary and 'farm-to-market' roads. A small proportion of these secondary roads is paved, but in 1985 a total of 33,443 km of roads were unpaved, and many can be used by motor vehicles only during the dry season.

SHIPPING

Cuba's principal ports are Havana (which handles 60% of all cargo), Santiago de Cuba, Cienfuegos, Nuevitas, Matanzas, Antilla, Guayabal and Mariel. Maritime transport has developed rapidly since 1959, and in 1989 there was a merchant fleet of 117 ships (with a total capacity of 1,400,900 dwt). In 1988 there was a coastal trading and deep-sea fleet of 82 ships. A supertanker port is under construction at Matanzas, with co-operation from Soviet and French enterprises. A major development of the port of Nuevitas has been planned.

Empresa Consignataria Mambisa: Lamparilla No 2, 2°, Apdo 1785, Havana; tel. (7) 62-2597; telex 511890; fax (7) 61-0445; shipping agent, ship-chandlers, bunker suppliers; Man. Dir JULIO AIRA PRADO.

Empresa Cubana de Fletes (Cuflet): Calle Oficios No 170, entre Teniente Rey y Amargura, Apdo 6755, Havana; tel. (7) 6-4731; telex 512181; freight agents for Cuban cargo; Man. Dir RAÚL I. CAMACHO AGUILERA.

Empresa de Navegación Caribe (Navecaribe): Lamparilla 2, 4°, Apdo 1784, Havana; tel. (7) 62-5736; telex 511262; f. 1965; operates Cuban coastal fleet; Dir Lic. OTTO ROCA MORALOBOS.

Empresa de Navegación Mambisa: San Ignacio No 104, Apdo 543, Havana; tel. (7) 61-9830; telex 5111268; operates dry cargo, reefer and bulk carrier vessels; Gen. Man. GUMERSINDO GONZÁLEZ FELIÚ.

Flota Cubana de Pesca: Apdo 14, Havana 1; tel. (7) 61-9223; telex 51189; fishing fleet; Dir Ing. FÉLIX SALVADOR GONZÁLEZ SORÍS.

There are regular passenger and cargo services by Cuban vessels between Cuba and northern Europe, the Baltic, the Mediterranean, the Black Sea and Japan and by Soviet, Bulgarian and Czechoslovak vessels between Cuba and the Baltic and the Black Sea. A regular Caribbean service is maintained by Empresa Multinacional del Caribe (Namucar). The Cuban fleet also runs regular container services to northern Europe, the Mediterranean and the Black Sea.

CIVIL AVIATION

There are international airports at Havana, Santiago de Cuba, Camagüey and Varadero. Improvements to Havana and Santiago de Cuba airports were scheduled for completion in 1990.

Empresa Consolidada Cubana de Aviación (Cubana): Calle 23 y P, No 64, Apdo 4299, La Rampa, Vedado, Havana; tel. (7) 7-4961; telex 512273; fax (7) 70-3690; f. 1929; international services to Angola, Argentina, Barbados, Belgium, Canada, Czechoslovakia, Dominican Republic, France, Grenada, Guinea-Bissau, Guyana, Jamaica, Mexico, Mozambique, Nicaragua, Panama, Peru, Spain, Switzerland and USSR; internal services from Havana to 12 other cities; Gen. Man. ROBERTO TEUTELÓ; fleet: 12 Ilyushin 62, 4 Ilyushin 18, 5 Tupolev B-2, 4 Tupolev 154M, 2 Ilyushin 76, 8 Antonov 24, 18 Antonov An-26, 2 Yakovlev 42 and 7 YAK 40.

Aerocarribbean SA: Calle 23, No 113, esq. 0, Havana; tel. (7) 79-7524; telex 512191; international and domestic charter services; fleet: 2 BB-253, 3 DC-3 and 1 Ilyushin 14; Gen. Man. JORGE FALCON.

Instituto de Aeronáutica Civil de Cuba (IACC): Calle 23 No 64, Havana; tel. (7) 79-6016; telex 51-1333; f. 1985; Pres. ROGELIO ACEVEDO GONZÁLEZ.

Tourism

Tourism began to develop after 1977, with the repeal of travel restrictions by the USA, and Cuba subsequently attracted European tourists. An estimated 225,000 tourists visited Cuba in 1988,

CUBA

compared with only 4,000 in 1973. Under the 1986–90 Development Plan, some 500m. pesos were to be invested in the sector.

Empresa de Turismo Internacional (Cubatur): Calle 23, No 156, entre N y O, Apdo 6560, Vedado, Havana; tel. (7) 32-4521; telex 511212; Dir Guillermo Benítez Barbosa.

Empresa de Turismo Nacional (Viajes Cuba): Calle 20, No 352, entre 21 y 23, Vedado, Havana; tel. (7) 30-0587; telex 51-1768; f. 1981; Dir Ana Elis de la Cruz García.

Instituto Nacional de Turismo (INTUR): Avda de Malecón y G, Apdo 4339, Vedado, Havana 4; tel. (7) 32-0571; telex 511238; f. 1976; Pres. Rafael Sed Pérez; Vice-Pres Enrique Rodríguez Manzano, Orosmán Quintero Herrera.

Atomic Energy

Cuba's first nuclear power station is under construction, with help from the USSR, at Juraguá, Cienfuegos, and will, when completed, have a capacity of 1,668 MW. The first 417-MW reactor was due to begin operations in 1990/91.

Comisión de Energía Atómica Cuba (CEAC): Apdo 6795, Havana 6; f. 1980; concerned with the peaceful uses of atomic energy; Pres. José R. Fernández; Exec. Sec. Fidel Castro Díaz-Balart.

Instituto de Investigaciones Nucleares: Managua, Havana; Dir Ing. Raimundo Franco Parellada.

CYPRUS

Introductory Survey

Location, Climate, Language, Religion, Flag, Capital

The Republic of Cyprus is an island in the eastern Mediterranean Sea, about 100 km south of Turkey. The climate is mild, although snow falls in the mountainous south-west between December and March. Temperatures in Nicosia are generally between 5°C (41°F) and 36°C (97°F). About 75% of the population speak Greek and almost all of the remainder speak Turkish. The Greek-speaking community is overwhelmingly Christian, and almost all Greek Cypriots adhere to the Orthodox Church of Cyprus, while most of the Turks are Muslims. The national flag (proportions 3 by 2) is white, with a gold map of Cyprus, garlanded by olive leaves, in the centre. The capital is Nicosia.

Recent History

A guerrilla war against British rule in Cyprus was begun in 1955 by Greek Cypriots seeking unification (*Enosis*) with Greece. Their movement, the National Organization of Cypriot Combatants (EOKA), was led politically by Archbishop Makarios III, head of the Greek Orthodox Church in Cyprus, and militarily by Gen. George Grivas. Archbishop Makarios was suspected by the British authorities of being involved in EOKA's campaign of violence, and in March 1956 he and three other leaders of the *Enosis* movement were deported. They were released in 1957 but not allowed to return to Cyprus. After a compromise agreement between the Greek and Turkish communities, a constitution for an independent Cyprus was finalized in 1959. Following his return from exile, Makarios was elected the country's first President in December 1959. Cyprus became independent on 16 August 1960, although the United Kingdom retained sovereignty over two military base areas.

Following a constitutional dispute, the Turks withdrew from the central government in December 1963 and serious intercommunal fighting occurred. In March 1964 the UN Peacekeeping Force in Cyprus (UNFICYP, see p. 46) was established to prevent a recurrence of fighting between the Greek and Turkish Cypriot communities. The effective exclusion of the Turks from political power led to the creation of separate administrative, judicial and legislative organs for the Turkish community. Discussions concerning the establishment of a more equitable constitutional arrangement began in 1968, and continued sporadically for six years, never producing an agreement, as the Turks favoured some form of federation, while the Greeks advocated a unitary state. Each community received military aid from its mother country, and the Greek Cypriot National Guard was controlled by officers of the Greek Army.

In 1971 Gen. Grivas returned to Cyprus, revived EOKA, and began a terrorist campaign for *Enosis*, directed against the Makarios Government and apparently supported by the military regime in Greece. Grivas died in January 1974, and in June Makarios ordered a purge of EOKA sympathizers from the police, National Guard and civil service, accusing the Greek regime of subversion. On 15 July President Makarios was deposed by a military coup, led by Greek officers of the National Guard, who appointed Nicos Sampson, an extremist Greek Cypriot politician and former EOKA terrorist, to be President. Makarios escaped from the island on the following day and travelled to the UK. At the invitation of Rauf Denktaş, the Turkish Cypriot leader, the Turkish army intervened to protect the Turkish community and to prevent Greece from using its control of the National Guard to take over Cyprus. Turkish troops landed on 20 July and rapidly occupied the northern third of Cyprus, dividing the island along what became the Attila Line, which runs from Morphou through Nicosia to Famagusta. President Sampson resigned on 23 July, and Glavkos Klerides, the President of the House of Representatives, became acting Head of State. The military regime in Greece collapsed on the same day. In December Makarios returned to Cyprus and resumed the presidency. However, the Turkish Cypriots' effective control of northern Cyprus enabled them to establish a *de facto* government, and in February 1975 to declare the establishment of the 'Turkish Federated State of Cyprus' ('TFSC'), with Denktaş as President.

President Makarios died in August 1977. He was succeeded by Spyros Kyprianou, a former Minister of Foreign Affairs, who had been President of the House of Representatives since 1976. In September 1980 a ministerial reshuffle by President Kyprianou caused the powerful communist party, AKEL, to withdraw its support from the ruling Democratic Party. Kyprianou therefore lost his overall majority in the House of Representatives. At the next general election, held in May 1981, AKEL and the Democratic Rally each won 12 seats in the House. The Democratic Party, however, won only eight seats, so the President still depended on the support of AKEL.

In the 'TFSC' a new cabinet was formed in December 1978 under Mustafa Çağatay of the National Unity Party (NUP), a former minister. In the elections held in June 1981, President Rauf Denktaş was returned to office, but his party, the NUP, lost its previous majority, and the government that was subsequently formed by Çağatay was defeated in December. In March 1982 a coalition government, comprising the NUP, the Democratic People's Party and the Turkish Unity Party, was formed by Çağatay.

In September 1980 the intermittent UN-sponsored intercommunal peace talks were resumed. In August 1981 the Turkish Cypriots offered to hand back 3%-4% of the 35% of the area of Cyprus which they controlled, and also to resettle 40,000 of the 200,000 refugees who fled from northern Cyprus in 1974. The constitutional issue remained the main problem: the Turkish Cypriots demanded equal status for the two communities, with equal representation in government and strong links with the mother country, while the Greeks, although accepting the principle of an alternating presidency, favoured a strong central government, and objected to any disproportionate representation for the Turkish community, who formed less than 20% of the population. In November 1981 a UN plan (involving a federal council, an alternating presidency and the allocation of 70% of the island to the Greek community) was presented, but discussions faltered in February 1982, when the Greek Prime Minister, Andreas Papandreou, proposed the withdrawal of all Greek and Turkish troops and the convening of an international conference, rather than the continuation of intercommunal talks.

In February 1983 Kyprianou was re-elected President, with the support of AKEL, gaining 56.5% of the votes. In May the UN General Assembly voted in favour of the withdrawal of Turkish troops from Cyprus, whereupon President Denktaş of the 'TFSC' threatened to boycott any further intercommunal talks and to seek recognition for the 'TFSC' as a sovereign state; simultaneously it was announced that the Turkish lira was to replace the Cyprus pound as legal tender in the 'TFSC'. UN proposals for a summit meeting between Denktaş and Kyprianou in late 1983 were unsuccessful.

On 15 November 1983 the 'TFSC' made a unilateral declaration of independence as the 'Turkish Republic of Northern Cyprus' ('TRNC'), with Denktaş continuing as President. An interim government was formed in December, led by Nejat Konuk (Prime Minister of the 'TFSC' from 1976 to 1978 and President of the Legislative Assembly from 1981), pending elections in 1984. Like the 'TFSC', the 'TRNC' was recognized only by Turkey, and the declaration of independence was condemned by the UN Security Council. Conciliatory proposals by the 'TRNC', including the resettlement of 40,000 Greek Cypriot refugees in Famagusta, under UN administration, were rejected by the Cyprus Government in January 1984, while the 'TRNC', in turn, refused to accept Kyprianou's proposal that the Turkish Cypriots should be allowed to administer 25% of the island, on condition that the declaration of independence be withdrawn. The establishment of diplomatic links between the 'TRNC' and Turkey in April 1984 was followed by a formal rejection by the 'TRNC' of UN proposals for a suspension of its declaration of independence prior to further talks. In August and September the Greek and Turkish Cypriots conferred (separately) with the UN Secretary-General, whose aim was to bring the two sides together for direct negotiations. The Turkish Cypriots reiterated that they would accept the proposed creation of a two-zone federation only if power were to be shared equally between the north and the south. In January 1985 the leaders of the two communities, Spyros Kyprianou and Rauf Denktaş, held a meeting, but no agreement was reached.

In July 1985 the UN Secretary-General presented further proposals, which the Greek Cypriots accepted. The proposals envisaged a bi-zonal federal Cyprus (in which the Turkish Cypriots would occupy 29% of the land), with a Greek Cypriot president and a Turkish Cypriot vice-president, both having limited power of veto over federal legislation. Ministers would be appointed in a ratio of seven Greek Cypriots to three Turkish Cypriots, and one important ministry would always be held by a Turkish Cypriot. There would be two assemblies: an upper house, with a 50:50 community representation, and a lower house, weighted 70:30 in favour of the Greek Cypriots. A tripartite body, including one non-Cypriot voting member, would have the final decision in constitutional disagreements. However, serious problems remained over the crucial questions of a timetable for the withdrawal of Turkey's troops and of the nature of international guarantees for a newly-united Republic of Cyprus. This plan was given the guaranteed support of foreign governments (in effect the USA), which were to provide financial help. The Turkish Cypriots rejected these proposals, as they wanted Turkish troops to remain on the island indefinitely, in order to protect their interests, and they felt that any peace settlement should include Turkey as a guarantor.

In November 1985, following a debate on President Kyprianou's leadership, the House of Representatives was dissolved. A general election for an enlarged House was held in December. The Democratic Rally won 19 seats, President Kyprianou's Democratic Party won 16 seats and AKEL won 15 seats. AKEL and the Democratic Rally therefore failed to secure the two-thirds majority required to amend the Constitution and thus challenge the President's tenure of power. The election result was seen as a vindication of President Kyprianou's policies.

During 1984 a 'TRNC' constituent assembly, comprising the members of the Legislative Assembly and 30 nominated members, drew up a new constitution, which was approved by a referendum in May 1985. At the 'TRNC' presidential election on 9 June, Rauf Denktaş was returned to office with over 70% of the vote. A general election followed on 23 June, with the NUP, led by Dr Derviş Eroğlu, winning 24 of the 50 seats in the Legislative Assembly. In July Dr Eroğlu became Prime Minister of the 'TRNC', leading a coalition Government formed by the NUP and the Communal Liberation Party.

In April 1986 the Turkish Cypriots accepted a plan proposed by the UN Secretary-General (which was, as before, based on the idea of establishing a bi-zonal federal republic, with participation in the federal government according to a specified ratio for the Greek and Turkish Cypriots), while the Greek Cypriots did not. Their principal objections were that the plan failed to envisage: the withdrawal of the Turkish troops in Cyprus prior to implementation of the plan; the removal from Cyprus of settlers from the Turkish mainland; the provision of suitable international guarantors for the settlement, with the exclusion of Turkey; and the assurance of the 'three basic freedoms', namely the right to reside, move and own property anywhere in Cyprus. The Greek Cypriot leaders, as well as the Government of Greece, still favoured a 'summit' meeting between Kyprianou and Denktaş, or an international conference. President Denktaş, however, stated that he would not accept an international conference that treated the Greek Cypriots as the official government of Cyprus and the Turkish Cypriots as a minority population. In July 1987 it was reported that the Cyprus Government had proposed to the UN Secretary-General that the Cypriot National Guard be dissolved, and orders for military equipment cancelled, in exchange for the withdrawal of Turkish forces from the island. In an address to the UN General Assembly in October, President Kyprianou proposed the creation of an international peace-keeping force to replace the armed forces of both the Greek and Turkish Cypriots. President Denktaş of the 'TRNC', however, maintained that negotiations on the establishment of a federal bi-zonal republic should precede any demilitarization.

A presidential election, held in the Greek Cypriot zone in February 1988, was won by Georghios Vassiliou, an economist, who presented himself as an independent, but who was unofficially supported by the communist party, AKEL. He took office later in February and promised to re-establish the National Council (originally convened by President Makarios), which was to include representatives from all the main Greek Cypriot political parties, to discuss plans for the settlement of the Cyprus problem. The only member of Kyprianou's Council of Ministers to retain his post in Vassiliou's new administration, which was sworn in at the end of February, was Georghios Iakovou, the Minister of Foreign Affairs.

In April 1988 the Prime Minister of the 'TRNC', Dr Derviş Eroğlu, and the other members of the Council of Ministers resigned from their posts, following a disagreement between the NUP and its coalition partner (since September 1986), the New Dawn Party, which was demanding greater representation in the Government. At the request of President Denktaş, however, Eroğlu resumed his post and formed a new Council of Ministers in May, comprising mainly NUP members but also including independents.

In March 1988 President Vassiliou rejected various proposals that had been submitted, via the UN, by President Denktaş of the 'TRNC', and which included a plan to form committees to study the possibilities of intercommunal co-operation. Following a meeting with the newly-revived National Council in June, however, President Vassiliou agreed to a proposal by the UN Secretary-General to resume intercommunal talks, without pre-conditions, with President Denktaş of the 'TRNC', in their capacity as the leaders of two communities. After consulting the Turkish Government in July, Denktaş also approved the proposal. Accordingly, a 'summit' meeting, under UN auspices, took place in Geneva in August, the first such meeting between Greek and Turkish Cypriot leaders since January 1985. As a result of this meeting, President Vassiliou and President Denktaş began direct negotiations, under UN auspices, in September 1988. A target date of 1 June 1989 was agreed for the conclusion of a comprehensive political settlement. By the end of 1989, however, it was apparent that no real progress had been achieved. A 'deconfrontation' agreement, implemented in mid-May 1989 under the supervision of UNFICYP, aimed to reduce tension along the Attila Line, but in July more than 100 Greek Cypriot women crossed into the UN-controlled buffer zone, in protest at the continuing partition of the island, and were detained for some days by the Turkish Cypriot authorities. In late August the Turkish Cypriot Legislative Assembly rejected proposals for a settlement, drafted by the UN Secretary-General, and declared that it would discuss only those proposals that resulted from direct negotiations between the two communities. In February 1990 Vassiliou and Denktaş resumed negotiations at the UN, but these were abandoned in March, chiefly because Denktaş demanded recognition of the right to self-determination for Turkish Cypriots. In the same month the UN Security Council adopted a resolution reiterating its support for the formation of a federal republic in Cyprus, without partition.

In April 1990 Denktaş was the successful candidate in an early presidential election in the 'TRNC', receiving nearly 67% of the votes cast. In May, at the elections to the 'TRNC' Legislative Assembly, the NUP won 34 of the 50 seats, and its leader, Dr Eroğlu, subsequently retained the office of Prime Minister.

In July 1990 the Government of Cyprus formally applied to join the European Community. Denktaş condemned the application, on the grounds that the Turkish Cypriots had not been consulted, and stated that the action would prevent the resumption of intercommunal talks. In the same month Denktaş and the Prime Minister of Turkey signed an agreement, confirming Turkey's support for the 'TRNC' economy, and expressing the intention to review and remove passport requirements for travel between the 'TRNC' and Turkey, and to consider the formation of a customs union. In October the two men also signed a joint declaration, affirming that Turkey would continue to guarantee Turkish Cypriot security, and repeating that studies were to be undertaken on the abolition of passport formalities and of customs barriers. United Nations officials continued to hold meetings with the Cypriot leaders in late 1990, but there appeared to be no immediate prospect of a resumption of discussions between Vassiliou and Denktaş, despite a reiteration by the UN Security Council in November of its support for the UN Secretary-General's 'mission of good offices' in Cyprus.

CYPRUS

Government

The 1960 Constitution provided for a system of government in which power would be shared by the Greek and Turkish communities in proportion to their numbers. This Constitution remains in force officially but since the ending of Turkish participation in the Government in 1963, and particularly since the creation of a separate Turkish area in northern Cyprus in 1974, each community has administered its own affairs, refusing to recognize the authority of the other's Government. The Greek Cypriot administration claims to be the Government of all Cyprus, and is generally recognized as such, although it has no Turkish participation. The northern area is under the *de facto* control of the 'Turkish Republic of Northern Cyprus' (for which a new constitution was drawn up in 1984 by a constituent assembly, and approved by a referendum in May 1985). Each community has its own President, Council of Ministers, legislature and judicial system.

Defence

The formation of the National Guard was authorized by the House of Representatives in 1964, after the withdrawal of the Turkish members. Men between 18 and 50 years of age are liable to 26 months' conscription. In June 1990 the National Guard comprised an army of 10,400 regulars, mainly composed of Cypriot conscripts but with an additional 1,300 seconded Greek Army officers and NCOs, and 108,000 reserves. A further 950 Greek army personnel were stationed in Cyprus in June 1990. There is also a Greek Cypriot paramilitary police force of 3,700. In 1989 government expenditure on defence in the Greek Cypriot area was C£76.6m. In June 1990 the 'TRNC' had an army of about 4,000 regulars and 26,000 reserves. Men between 18 and 50 years of age are liable to 24 months' conscription. In 1990 it was estimated that the 'TRNC' forces were being supported by about 30,000 Turkish troops. The 1990 defence budget in the 'TRNC' was 20,000m. Turkish liras. The UN Peace-keeping Force in Cyprus (UNFICYP) consisted of 2,108 military personnel in July 1990 (see p. 46). There are British military bases (with personnel numbering 4,200 in June 1990) at Akrotiri, Episkopi and Dhekelia.

Economic Affairs

In 1988, according to estimates by the World Bank, Cyprus's gross national product (GNP), measured at average 1986–88 prices, was US $4,320m., equivalent to $6,260 per head. During 1986–88, it was estimated, GNP per head increased at an average rate of 4.8% per year. Between 1980 and 1988 the population increased by an annual average of 1.1%. Cyprus's gross domestic product (GDP), according to Cyprus government figures, increased by 6.9% in 1988 and by 6% in 1989. In the 'TRNC', there was an increase of 8.1% in GDP in 1989.

Agriculture (including forestry and fishing) contributed 8% of GDP in 1988. In the government-controlled area of the country about 15% of the working population were employed in this sector in 1989. The principal crops of the government-controlled area are wheat, barley, potatoes (which accounted for about 8% of export earnings in 1989), grapes and citrus fruit. The area's agricultural output increased by 8.1% in 1988. In the 'TRNC' 32% of the working population were employed in agriculture, forestry and fishing in 1986. The principal crops of the 'TRNC' are wheat, barley, potatoes, carobs and citrus fruit.

Manufacturing and construction together employed about 29% of the working population in the government-controlled area in 1989, and accounted for 26% of GDP there in 1987. In the 'TRNC' this sector contributed about 18% of GDP in 1988.

Minerals accounted for less than 2% of domestic exports from the government-controlled sector in 1988. The principal products were asbestos, gypsum, iron pyrites and bentonite.

Measured by the value of output, the principal industrial products in the government-controlled area in 1986 were food products, clothing and metal products. Clothing exports represented 28% (by value) of total exports in 1989.

Energy is derived principally from imported petroleum, which comprised 4% of total imports in 1989.

The government-controlled area supported 18 offshore banking units at the end of 1990, and attempts are being made to promote a financial services industry.

Tourism is the largest source of income for the government-controlled area, and visitors in 1989 exceeded 1.37m. In 1985, with only 813,607 visitors, tourist receipts of C£240m. accounted for 12% of GDP. In 1988 229,401 tourists visited the 'TRNC'.

In 1989 the government-controlled area recorded a visible trade deficit of C£669m., and, despite receipts from tourism and other services, there was a current account deficit of C£73m. The trade deficit in the 'TRNC' in 1988 was US$166m., while the current account deficit was US $9m. In 1989 the principal sources of imports to the government-controlled area were France (11.8%) and the United Kingdom (11.4%); the latter was also the principal market for exports (44.2%). Other major trading partners are Arab countries, Japan, Italy and Germany. The principal exports in 1989 were clothing, footwear, potatoes and citrus fruit. The principal imports were textiles, vehicles, minerals, metals, chemicals and foodstuffs. The principal imports of the 'TRNC' in 1988 were basic manufactures, machinery and transport equipment, and mineral fuels; the principal export was foodstuffs. In 1987 the main source of imports was Turkey (42.7%). The principal destination for exports was the United Kingdom (66.6%).

In 1989 there was an estimated budgetary deficit in the government-controlled area of C£91.2m. (equivalent to some 4% of GDP). Total public debt at 31 December 1988 was C£625.5m., equivalent to 31.5% of annual GDP, and foreign liabilities were C£602.5m. The annual rate of inflation averaged 6.4% in 1980–88, and stood at 3.8% in 1988 and 4% in 1989. An estimated 1.8% of the labour force were unemployed in the first three months of 1990, and some sectors were affected by labour shortages.

The 1990 draft budget of the 'TRNC' was balanced at TL511,172m., with aid from Turkey contributing TL110,000m. to revenue. The average rate of inflation in the 'TRNC' was estimated to exceed 50% during 1989.

In 1972 Cyprus concluded an association agreement with the European Community, improving access for Cypriot exports and ensuring financial assistance for Cyprus. In 1987 an agreement was signed on the progressive establishment of a customs union with the Community, over 15 years, and in 1990 Cyprus made a formal application to become a member of the Community.

During the late 1980s the failure of efforts to reach a political settlement did not prevent a high rate of economic growth in the Greek Cypriot part of the island, particularly in the tourism sector. The principal problems there were a shortage of skilled labour and an increase in consumer demand, leading to a growth in imports, which was exacerbated by the increase in petroleum prices that followed the Iraqi invasion of Kuwait in August 1990. The economy of the 'TRNC', although less prosperous and affected by diplomatic isolation, also expanded during the late 1980s, with considerable assistance from Turkey. In 1990, however, the 'TRNC' economy was expected to be seriously affected by a financial crisis in a multinational enterprise, Polly Peck International, which owned a large proportion of agricultural and industrial undertakings and services in northern Cyprus.

Social Welfare

A comprehensive social insurance scheme, covering every working male and female and their dependants, is in operation. It includes provisions for protection against arbitrary and unjustified dismissal, for industrial welfare and for tripartite co-operation in the formulation and implementation of labour policies and objectives. Benefits and pensions from the social insurance scheme cover unemployment, sickness, maternity, widows, orphans, injury at work, old age and death. An improved scheme, involving income-related contributions and benefits, was introduced in October 1980. The provision of health services to Greek Cypriots in 1981 included 134 hospital establishments, with a total of 3,535 beds, and 601 physicians. Of total expenditure by the central Government in the Greek Cypriot area in 1987, C£34.8m. (7.0%) was for health services, and a further C£106.8m. (21.6%) for social security and welfare. In 1988 the state health service in the Turkish Cypriot zone included 21 hospital establishments, with a total of 833 beds, and there were 43 private establishments, with 193 beds. In that year there were 256 physicians, of whom 127 worked in the state health service.

Education

In the Greek Cypriot sector elementary education, which is compulsory and available free of charge, is provided in six grades for children between five-and-a-half and 12 years of age. In some towns and certain large villages there are separate junior schools consisting of the first three grades. Secondary education is free for all years of study and lasts six years, with three years at the Gymnasiun being followed by three years at a technical school or a Lyceum. There are five options of specialization at the Lyceums: classical, science, economics, commercial/secretarial and foreign languages. There are three-year technical schools. Higher education for teachers, technicians, engineers, hoteliers and caterers, foresters, nurses and health inspectors is provided by technical and vocational colleges. Adult education is conducted through youth centres in rural areas, foreign language institutes in the towns and private institutions offering courses in business administration and secretarial work. A university was due to be inaugurated in September 1991. In 1988/89 a total of 9,410 students from the Greek Cypriot area were studying in universities abroad. Expenditure on education by the central Government in the Greek Cypriot area was C£65.4m. (10.8% of total spending) in 1989.

Education in the Turkish Cypriot zone is controlled by the 'TRNC'. Primary education is free and compulsory: it comprises elementary schools for the 7–12 age group, and secondary-junior schools for the 13–15 age group. Secondary education, for the 16–18 age group, is provided by high schools (Lycées) and vocational schools, including colleges of agriculture, nursing and hotel management. A university, the Eastern Mediterranean University, was opened in 1986 near Famagusta. It has three faculties: engineering, arts and sciences, and business and economics. There is also a Teachers' Training College. A total of 3,100 students (1,700 from Turkey) were enrolled at the university in 1990.

Public Holidays

1991: 1 January (New Year's Day), 6 January (Epiphany)*, 19 January (Name Day)*, 18 February (Green Monday)*, 25 March (Greek Independence Day)*, 5–8 April (Easter)*, 16 April (Ramazam Bayram—end of Ramadan)†, 23 April (National Sovereignty and Children's Day)†, 1 May (Workers' Day and Spring Day)†, 19 May (Youth and Sports Day)†, 23 June (Kurban Bayram—Feast of the Sacrifice)†, 20 July (Peace and Freedom Day, anniversary of the Turkish invasion in 1974)†, 1 August (Communal Resistance Day)†, 30 August (Victory Day)†, 21 September (Birth of the Prophet)†, 1 October (Independence Day)*, 28 October (Greek National Day)*, 29 October (Turkish Republic Day)†, 15 November (TRNC Day)†, 25–26 December (Christmas)*.

1992: 1 January (New Year's Day), 6 January (Epiphany)*, 19 January (Name Day)*, 9 March (Green Monday)*, 25 March (Greek Independence Day)*, 4 April (Ramazam Bayram—end of Ramadan)†, 23 April (National Sovereignty and Children's Day)†, 24–27 April (Easter)*, 1 May (Workers' Day and Spring Day)†, 19 May (Youth and Sports Day)†, 11 June (Kurban Bayram—Feast of the Sacrifice)†, 20 July (Peace and Freedom Day, anniversary of the Turkish invasion in 1974)†, 1 August (Communal Resistance Day)†, 30 August (Victory Day)†, 10 September (Birth of the Prophet)†, 1 October (Independence Day)*, 28 October (Greek National Day)*, 29 October (Turkish Republic Day)†, 15 November (TRNC Day)†, 25–26 December (Christmas)*.

* Greek and Greek Orthodox.
† Turkish and Turkish Muslim.

Weights and Measures

Although the imperial and the metric systems are understood, Cyprus has a special internal system:

Weights: 400 drams = 1 oke = 2.8 lb (1.27 kg.).
44 okes = 1 Cyprus kantar.
180 okes = 1 Aleppo kantar.

Capacity: 1 liquid oke = 2.25 pints (1.28 litres).
1 Cyprus litre = 5.6 pints (3.18 litres).

Length and Area: 1 pic = 2 feet (61 cm).
Area: 1 donum = 14,400 sq ft (1,338 sq m).

Statistical Survey

Source: Department of Statistics and Research, Ministry of Finance, Nicosia; tel. (02) 303286; telex 3399; fax (02) 366080.

Note: Since July 1974 the northern part of Cyprus has been under Turkish occupation. As a result, some of the statistics relating to subsequent periods do not cover the whole island. Some separate figures for the 'TRNC' are given on p. 843.

AREA AND POPULATION

Area: 9,251 sq km (3,572 sq miles), incl. Turkish-occupied region.

Population: 612,851 (males 306,144; females 306,707), incl. estimate for Turkish-occupied region, at census of 30 September 1976; 642,731 (males 319,562; females 323,169), incl. estimate for Turkish-occupied region, at census of 1 October 1982; 695,000 (estimate for mid-1989).

Ethnic Groups (estimates for mid-1989): Greeks 556,400, Turks 129,600, others 9,000; Total 695,000.

Principal Towns (population at 1 October 1982): Nicosia (capital) 149,100 (excl. Turkish-occupied portion); Limassol 107,200; Larnaca 48,300; Famagusta (Gazi Mağusa) 39,500 (mid-1974); Paphos 20,800.

Births and Deaths (provisional estimates, 1989): Live births 12,750 (birth rate 18.3 per 1,000); Deaths 5,943 (death rate 8.6 per 1,000).

Employment (government-controlled area, provisional figures for 1989): Agriculture, hunting, forestry and fishing 35,900; Manufacturing 48,100; Construction 22,400; Trade, restaurants and hotels 58,100; Transport, storage and communications 14,100; Financing, insurance, real estate and business services 14,300; Community, social and personal services 50,000; Total (incl. others) 244,900.

AGRICULTURE, ETC.

Principal Crops (government-controlled area, '000 metric tons, 1989): Wheat 8, Barley 130, Potatoes 193, Carobs 8, Olives 9, Grapes 212, Oranges 50, Grapefruit 68, Lemons 34.

Livestock (government-controlled area, '000 head, December 1989): Cattle 45, Sheep 025, Goats 200, Pigs 281, Chickens 2,500.

Fishing (government-controlled area, metric tons, live weight, 1989): Total catch 2,600.

MINING

Exports (government-controlled area, metric tons, 1989): Asbestos 15,776*, Iron pyrites 6,610*, Gypsum 2,901, Terra umbra 4,658, Bentonite (activated) 36,763; Copper ores and concentrates 1,940; Cement Copper 955.

* Figures are for 1988.

INDUSTRY

Selected Products (government-controlled area, 1989): Cement 1,041,681 metric tons, Bricks 52.5 million, Mosaic tiles 1,830,000 sq metres, Cigarettes 3,935 million, Footwear (excluding plastic and semi-finished shoes) 7,433,000 pairs, Beer 31.8 million litres, Wines 34.1 million litres, Intoxicating liquors 4.1 million litres.

FINANCE

Currency and Exchange Rates: 100 cents = 1 Cyprus pound (Cyprus £). *Coins:* ½, 1, 2, 5, 10, 20, 50 cents; 1 pound. *Notes:* 50 cents; 1, 5 and 10 pounds. *Sterling and US Dollar Equivalents* (30 September 1990): £1 sterling = 83.174 Cyprus cents; US $1 = 44.395 Cyprus cents; Cyprus £100 = £120.23 sterling = $225.25. *Average exchange rate* (US $ per Cyprus £): 2.0802 in 1987; 2.1447 in 1988; 2.0272 in 1989.

Budget (estimates, Cyprus £ million, government-controlled area, 1989): *Revenue:* Direct taxes 150.3, Indirect taxes 204.9, Sale of goods and services 30.4, Interest, dividends, rents and royalties 26.0, Transfers 25.9, Greek government grants 3.5, Loan proceeds 66.6, Other 6.1, Total 513.7; *Expenditure:* Agriculture and forests 6.1, Water development 5.4, Public works 6.7, Customs and excise 15.0, Public debt charges 162.9, Pensions and grants 18.6, Medical 38.9, Police 33.6, Subsidies, subventions and contributions 95.4, Education grants 65.4, Other 156.1, Total 604.9.

CYPRUS

Statistical Survey

Development Budget (Cyprus £'000, government-controlled area, 1989): Water development 11,842, Road network 27,315, Harbours 19, Agriculture 3,895, Commerce and industry 1,314, Airports 1,999; Total expenditure 73,976.

International Reserves (US $ million at 31 December 1989): Gold 15.1; Reserve position in IMF 23.7, Foreign exchange 1,100.2; IMF special drawing rights 0.1; Total 1,139.1.

Money Supply (government-controlled area, Cyprus £ million at 31 December 1989): Currency outside banks 169.1, Demand deposits at deposit money banks 215.8; Total money 384.9.

Cost of Living (Retail Price Index, government-controlled area; base: 1986 = 100): 102.79 in 1987; 106.31 in 1988; 110.32 in 1989.

Gross Domestic Product in Purchasers' Values (government-controlled area, Cyprus £ million at current prices): 1,779.1 in 1987; 1,992.1 in 1988; 2,218.7 in 1989.

Balance of Payments (Cyprus £ million, government-controlled area, 1989): Merchandise exports f.o.b. 354.0, Merchandise imports f.o.b. 1,022.6, *Trade balance* 668.6; Receipts from services and transfers 940.8, Payments for services and transfers 345.0, *Current balance* −72.8; Long-term loans (net) 120.6, Other long-term capital (net) 34.5, Short-term capital (net) 61.8, Net errors and omissions 28.0. *Total* (net monetary movements) 116.1.

EXTERNAL TRADE

Principal Commodities (Cyprus £ '000, government-controlled area only, 1989): *Imports c.i.f.*: Textile and textile articles 108,198 (Clothing and clothing accessories 10,841); Aircraft and parts 84,727; Road vehicles, parts and accessories 124,058; Mineral products 108,668 (Crude oil 45,683); Base metals and articles of base metal 89,386; Chemicals and related products 68,836 (Pharmaceutical products 15,242); Prepared foodstuffs, beverages, spirits and vinegar, tobacco and manufactured tobacco substitutes 66,622 (Beverages, spirits and vinegar 7,836; tobacco and manufactured tobacco substitutes 17,081); Plastics and plastic products 32,768; Paper, paperboard and derivatives 30,832; Live animals and animal products 25,979 (Meat and edible offal 11,438); Total (incl. others) 1,130,298. *Exports f.o.b.*: Clothing 69,515; Footwear 15,502; Potatoes 20,692; Citrus fruit 17,009; Cigarettes 6,971; Cement 6,569; Pharmaceutical products 6,701; Fruit and vegetable juices 7,004; Alcoholic beverages 5,597; Fresh grapes 5,209; Total (incl. others) 246,854.

Principal Trading Partners (Cyprus £'000, government-controlled area, 1989): *Imports c.i.f.*: France 133,340; Federal Republic of Germany 103,246; Greece 69,439; Iraq 36,652; Italy 107,266; Japan 122,441; Netherlands 24,931; Spain 21,321; Taiwan 21,879; USSR 28,167; United Kingdom 128,960; USA 63,528; Total (incl. others) 1,130,298. *Exports f.o.b.*: Egypt 11,822; Federal Republic of Germany 16,365; Greece 40,232; Italy 8,898; Lebanon 33,683; Libya 9,075; Saudi Arabia 16,856; Syria 6,878; USSR 15,397; United Arab Emirates 8,568; United Kingdom 91,801; Total (incl. others) 207,464. Figures for exports exclude (Cyprus £'000): Stores for ships and aircraft plus unspecified items sent by parcel post 39,390.

TRANSPORT

Road Traffic (licensed motor vehicles, government-controlled area, 1989): Private cars 158,852, Taxis and self-drive cars 5,891, Lorries and buses 68,494, Motor cycles 47,188, Tractors, etc. 11,123, Total 291,548.

Shipping (government-controlled area, 1988): *Freight traffic* ('000 metric tons, excluding goods loaded and unloaded at Larnaca and Paphos airports): Goods loaded 2,612, Goods unloaded 4,153; *Vessels* (steam or motor vessels and sailing vessels entered, '000 net regd tons): 14,793. In 1989 a total of 1,952 ships (displacement 17,890,061 grt) were registered in Cyprus.

Civil Aviation (Cyprus Airways, 1989): Kilometres flown 13,384,040, Passenger arrivals 410,475, Passenger departures 414,599, Freight landed (metric tons) 3,336, Freight cleared (metric tons) 8,092.

TOURISM

Foreign Visitors by Country of Origin (excluding one-day visitors and visitors to the Turkish-occupied zone, 1989): Federal Republic of Germany 108,705, Greece 59,025, Israel 5,376, Lebanon 87,459, Scandinavian countries 248,088, United Kingdom 549,552, USA 13,836; Total (incl. others) 1,377,636.

EDUCATION

1989/90 (government-controlled area): Kindergarten: 540 institutions, 917 teachers, 22,008 pupils; Primary schools: 378 institutions, 2,824 teachers, 60,841 pupils; Secondary schools (Gymnasia and Lyceums): 93 institutions, 3,064 teachers, 40,102 pupils; Technical: 11 institutions, 462 teachers, 3,117 pupils; Teacher-training: 1 institution, 61 teachers, 662 students; Other post-secondary: 25 institutions, 420 teachers, 5,190 students.

'Turkish Republic of Northern Cyprus'*

Sources: Office of the London Representative of the 'Turkish Republic of Northern Cyprus', 28 Cockspur St, London SW1 (tel. (071) 839-4577; telex 8955363); K. Rüstem and Brother, North Cyprus Almanack, 1987; *Kıbrıs* (Northern Cyprus Weekly); Prime Ministry, State Planning Organization, Statistics and Research Department.

AREA AND POPULATION

Area: 3,355 sq km (1,295 sq miles).

Population (official estimate): 167,256 (1988).

Ethnic Groups (estimates, 1985): Turks 158,225, Greeks 733, Maronites 368, Others 961; Total 160,287.

Principal Towns (estimated population within the municipal boundary, 1987): Lefkoşa (Nicosia) 38,507 (Turkish-occupied area only); Gazi Mağusa (Famagusta) 20,003; Güzelyurt (Morphou) 10,179 (1985); Girne (Kyrenia) 7,107.

Births and Deaths (registered, 1988): Birth rate 16.0 per 1,000; Death rate 3.0 per 1,000. Note: Birth registration is estimated to be 95% complete, but death registration only 25% complete.

Employment (1986): Agriculture, forestry and fishing 20,320; Industry 6,497; Construction 4,581; Trade and tourism 5,923; Transport and communications 4,554; Financial institutions 1,564; Business and personal services 4,932; Public Services 14,881; Total 63,252. **Total unemployed:** 1,556.

AGRICULTURE, ETC.

Principal Crops ('000 metric tons, 1988): Wheat 27.8, Barley 127.1, Chick-peas 0.2, Potatoes 16.2, Tomatoes 2.0, Artichokes 1.2, Water melons 6.6, Sweet melons 1.6, Carobs 5.4, Olives 6.9, Lemons 18.4, Grapefruit 39.4, Oranges 103.4, Tangerines 1.2.

Livestock ('000 head, 1988): Cattle 11.8, Sheep 179.0, Goats 55.7, Chickens 1,659.4.

Livestock Products ('000 metric tons, unless otherwise indicated, 1988): Sheep's and goats' milk 11.2, Cows' milk 15.8, Mutton and lamb 2.7, Goats' meat 0.8, Beef 1.0, Poultry meat 3.3, Wool 0.3, Eggs (million) 15.2.

Fishing (metric tons, 1985); Total catch 300.

FINANCE

Currency and Exchange Rates: Turkish currency: 100 kuruş = 1 Turkish lira (TL) or pound. *Coins:* 10, 25, 50 and 100 liras. *Notes:* 100, 500, 1,000, 5,000, 10,000 and 20,000 liras. *Sterling and Dollar Equivalents* (30 September 1990): £1 sterling = 5,126.5 liras; US $1 = 2,736.3 liras; 10,000 Turkish liras = £1.951 = $3.655. *Average Exchange Rate* (liras per US dollar): 857.2 in 1987; 1,422.3 in 1988; 2,121.7 in 1989.

Draft Budget (estimates, million Turkish liras, 1990): *Revenue:* Internal revenue 310,500, Aid from Turkey 111,000, Loans 90,700, Total 511,200; *Expenditure:* Personnel 184,400, Other current expenditure 34,250, Investment projects 117,400, Transfers 115,100, Defence 20,000, Total 511,200.

Development Budget (estimate, million Turkish liras, 1986): Total expenditure 11,196.

Cost of Living (Retail Price Index; base: December 1984 = 100): 143.04 in 1985.

Gross Domestic Product (GDP) by Economic Activity (million Turkish liras, 1988): Agriculture, forestry and fishing 54,531.4; Mining and quarrying 3,693.4; Manufacturing 42,082.5; Electricity and water 7,703.7; Construction 32,709.6; Wholesale and retail trade 84.780.4; Restaurants and hotels 27,638.5; Transport and communications 37,050.9; Finance 30,009.1; Ownership of dwellings 13,290.9; Business and personal services 25,157.2; Government services 77,626.1; *Sub-total* 436,273.7; Import duties 42,791.6; *GDP in purchasers' values* 479,065.3.

Balance of Payments (US $ million, 1988): Merchandise exports f.o.b. 52.4; Merchandise imports c.i.f. −218.1; *Trade balance* −165.7; Services and unrequited transfers (net) 156.9; *Current balance* −8.8; Capital movements (net) 38.2; Net errors and omissions 3.6; *Total* (net monetary movements) 33.0.

EXTERNAL TRADE

Principal Commodities (US $ million, 1988): *Imports c.i.f.:* Food and live animals 19.8, Beverages and tobacco 10.8, Crude materials (inedible) except fuels 5.4, Mineral fuels, lubricants, etc. 20.1, Animal and vegetable oils and fats 1.8, Chemicals 15.8, Basic manufactures 66.3, Machinery and transport equipment 57.0, Miscellaneous manufactured articles 20.9; Total 218.1. *Exports f.o.b.:* Food and live animals 31.8, Beverages and tobacco 1.3, Crude materials (inedible) except fuels 1.6, Chemicals 0.6, Basic manufactures 0.6, Miscellaneous manufactured articles 16.4; Total 52.4.

Principal Trading Partners (US $ million, 1987): *Imports:* Turkey 94.3, United Kingdom 31.4, other EEC countries 40.3, Total (incl. others) 221.1; *Exports:* Turkey 7.9, United Kingdom 36.7, other EEC countries 4.7, Total (incl. others) 55.1.

TRANSPORT

Road Traffic (licensed motor vehicles, 1988): Cars (incl. taxis and self-drive cars) 30,800, Lorries, vans and buses 9,186, Motor cycles 10,277, Tractors 4,692; Total (incl. others) 55,634.

Shipping (1988): Freight traffic ('000 metric tons): Goods loaded 270.0, Goods unloaded 508.1; Vessels entered 1,832.

Civil Aviation (Turkish Cypriot Airlines Co, Ltd, 1985): Kilometres flown 1,126,848, Passenger arrivals 67,693, Passenger departures 68,392 (1987), Freight landed (metric tons) 909, Freight cleared (metric tons) 1,030.

TOURISM

Visitors (1988): 229,401; **Accommodation** (1987): Hotels 26, Hotel beds 2,761; **Receipts** (US $ million, 1987) 56.1.

EDUCATION

1990/91: *Pre-primary education:* 5 kindergartens, 26 teachers, 610 pupils; *Elementary schools:* 141 institutions, 830 teachers, 28,000 pupils; *Secondary schools:* 22 institutions, 510 teachers, 12,000 pupils; *High schools:* 14 institutions, 292 teachers, 4,482 pupils; *Vocational, technical and commercial high schools:* 10 institutions, 232 teachers, 1,950 pupils; *Teacher-training:* 1 institution, 7 teachers, 303 students; *Other higher education:* 1 open university, 35 teachers, 928 students; 3 university-level institutions, 172 teachers, 4,100 students.

* Note: Following a unilateral declaration of independence in November 1983, the 'Turkish Federated State of Cyprus' became known as the 'Turkish Republic of Northern Cyprus'.

Directory

The Constitution

The Constitution, summarized below, entered into force on 16 August 1960, when Cyprus became an independent republic.

THE STATE OF CYPRUS

The State of Cyprus is an independent and sovereign Republic with a presidential regime.

The Greek Community comprises all citizens of the Republic who are of Greek origin and whose mother tongue is Greek or who share the Greek cultural traditions or who are members of the Greek Orthodox Church.

The Turkish Community comprises all citizens of the Republic who are of Turkish origin and whose mother tongue is Turkish or who share the Turkish cultural traditions or who are Muslims.

The official languages of the Republic are Greek and Turkish.

The Republic shall have its own flag of neutral design and colour, chosen jointly by the President and the Vice-President of the Republic.

The Greek and the Turkish Communities shall have the right to celebrate respectively the Greek and the Turkish national holidays.

THE PRESIDENT AND VICE-PRESIDENT

Executive power is vested in the President and the Vice-President, who are members of the Greek and Turkish Communities respectively, and are elected by their respective communities to hold office for five years.

The President of the Republic as Head of the State represents the Republic in all its official functions; signs the credentials of diplomatic envoys and receives the credentials of foreign diplomatic envoys; signs the credentials of delegates for the negotiation of international treaties, conventions or other agreements; signs the letter relating to the transmission of the instruments of ratification of any international treaties, conventions or agreements; confers the honours of the Republic.

The Vice-President of the Republic, as Vice-Head of the State, has the right to be present at all official functions; at the presentation of the credentials of foreign diplomatic envoys; to recommend to the President the conferment of honours on members of the Turkish Community, which recommendation the President shall accept unless there are grave reasons to the contrary.

The election of the President and the Vice-President of the Republic shall be direct, by universal suffrage and secret ballot, and shall, except in the case of a by-election, take place on the same day but separately.

The office of the President and of the Vice-President shall be incompatible with that of a Minister or of a Representative or of a member of a Communal Chamber or of a member of any municipal council including a Mayor or of a member of the armed or security forces of the Republic or with a public or municipal office.

The President and Vice-President of the Republic are invested by the House of Representatives.

The President and the Vice-President of the Republic in order to ensure the executive power shall have a Council of Ministers composed of seven Greek Ministers and three Turkish Ministers. The Ministers shall be designated respectively by the President and the Vice-President of the Republic who shall appoint them by an instrument signed by them both. The President convenes and presides over the meetings of the Council of Ministers, while the Vice-President may ask the President to convene the Council and may take part in the discussions.

The decisions of the Council of Ministers shall be taken by an absolute majority and shall, unless the right of final veto or return is exercised by the President or the Vice-President of the Republic or both, be promulgated immediately by them.

The executive power exercised by the President and the Vice-President of the Republic conjointly consists of:

Determining the design and colour of the flag.

Creation or establishment of honours.

Appointment of the members of the Council of Ministers.

Promulgation by publication of the decisions of the Council of Ministers.

Promulgation by publication of any law or decision passed by the House of Representatives.

Appointments and termination of appointments as in Articles provided.

Institution of compulsory military service.

Reduction or increase of the security forces.

Exercise of the prerogative of mercy in capital cases.

Remission, suspension and commutation of sentences.

Right of references to the Supreme Constitutional Court and publication of Court decisions.

Address of messages to the House of Representatives.

The executive powers which may be exercised separately by the President and Vice-President include: designation and termination of appointment of Greek and Turkish Ministers respectively; the right of final veto on Council decisions and on laws concerning foreign affairs, defence or security; the publication of the communal laws and decisions of the Greek and Turkish Communal Chambers respectively; the right of recourse to the Supreme Constitutional Court; the prerogative of mercy in capital cases; and addressing messages to the House of Representatives.

CYPRUS

THE COUNCIL OF MINISTERS

The Council of Ministers shall exercise executive power in all matters, other than those which are within the competence of a Communal Chamber, including the following:

General direction and control of the government of the Republic and the direction of general policy.

Foreign affairs, defence and security.

Co-ordination and supervision of all public services.

Supervision and disposition of property belonging to the Republic.

Consideration of Bills to be introduced to the House of Representatives by a Minister.

Making of any order or regulation for the carrying into effect of any law as provided by such law.

Consideration of the Budget of the Republic to be introduced to the House of Representatives.

THE HOUSE OF REPRESENTATIVES

The legislative power of the Republic shall be exercised by the House of Representatives in all matters except those expressly reserved to the Communal Chambers.

The number of Representatives shall be 50, subject to alteration by a resolution of the House of Representatives carried by a majority comprising two-thirds of the Representatives elected by the Greek Community and two-thirds of the Representatives elected by the Turkish Community.

Out of the number of Representatives 70% shall be elected by the Greek Community and 30% by the Turkish Community separately from amongst their members respectively, and, in the case of a contested election, by universal suffrage and by direct and secret ballot held on the same day.

The term of office of the House of Representatives shall be for a period of five years.

The President of the House of Representatives shall be a Greek, and shall be elected by the Representatives elected by the Greek Community, and the Vice-President shall be a Turk and shall be elected by the Representatives elected by the Turkish Community.

THE COMMUNAL CHAMBERS

The Greek and the Turkish Communities respectively shall elect from amongst their own members a Communal Chamber.

The Communal Chambers shall, in relation to their respective Community, have competence to exercise legislative power solely with regard to the following:

All religious, educational, cultural and teaching matters.

Personal status; composition and instances of courts dealing with civil disputes relating to personal status and to religious matters.

Imposition of personal taxes and fees on members of their respective Community in order to provide for their respective needs.

THE PUBLIC SERVICE AND THE ARMED FORCES

The public service shall be composed as to 70% of Greeks and as to 30% of Turks.

The Republic shall have an army of 2,000 men, of whom 60% shall be Greeks and 40% shall be Turks.

The security forces of the Republic shall consist of the police and gendarmerie and shall have a contingent of 2,000 men. The forces shall be composed as to 70% of Greeks and as to 30% of Turks.

OTHER PROVISIONS

The following measures have been passed by the House of Representatives since January 1964, when the Turkish members withdrew:

The amalgamation of the High Court and the Supreme Constitutional Court (see Judicial System section).

The abolition of the Greek Communal Chamber and the creation of a Ministry of Education.

The unification of the Municipalities.

The unification of the Police and the Gendarmerie.

The creation of a military force by providing that persons between the ages of 18 and 50 years can be called upon to serve in the National Guard.

The extension of the term of office of the President and the House of Representatives by one year intervals from July 1965 until elections in February 1968 and July 1970 respectively.

New electoral provisions; abolition of separate Greek and Turkish rolls; abolition of post of Vice-President, which was re-established in 1973.

Directory

The Government*

HEAD OF STATE

President: GEORGHIOS VASSILIOU (took office 28 February 1988).

COUNCIL OF MINISTERS
(January 1991)

Minister of Foreign Affairs: GEORGHIOS IAKOVOU.
Minister of Finance: GEORGHIOS SYRIMIS.
Minister of the Interior: CHRISTODOULOS VENIAMIN.
Minister of Defence: ANDREAS ALONEFTIS.
Minister of Agriculture and Natural Resources: ANDREAS GAVRIELIDES.
Minister of Health: PANIKOS PAPAGEORGHIOU.
Minister of Education: CHRISTOFOROS CHRISTOFIDES.
Minister of Commerce and Industry: TAKIS NEMITSAS.
Minister of Communications and Works: PAVLOS SAVVIDES.
Minister of Labour and Social Insurance: Dr IACOVOS ARISTIDOU.
Minister of Justice: NICOS PAPAIOANNOU.

* Under the Constitution of 1960, the vice-presidency and three posts in the Council of Ministers are reserved for Turkish Cypriots. However, there has been no Turkish participation in the Government since December 1963. In 1968 President Makarios announced that he considered the office of Vice-President in abeyance until Turkish participation in the Government is resumed, but the Turkish community elected Rauf Denktaş Vice-President in February 1973.

MINISTRIES

All Ministries are in Nicosia.

Ministry of Agriculture and Natural Resources: Loukis Akritas Ave, Nicosia; tel. (02) 302245; telex 4660; fax (02) 445156.
Ministry of Commerce and Industry: 6 Andreas Araouzos St, Nicosia; tel. (02) 303441; telex 2283; fax (02) 366120.
Ministry of Communications and Works: Dem. Severis Ave, Nicosia; tel. (02) 302199; telex 3678; fax (02) 465462.
Ministry of Defence: 4 Emmanuel Roides St, Nicosia; tel. (02) 303532; telex 3553; fax (02) 366225.
Ministry of Education: Greg. Afxentiou St, Nicosia; tel. (02) 303331; telex 5760; fax (02) 445021.
Ministry of Finance: Dem. Severis Ave, Nicosia; tel. (02) 303291; telex 3399; fax (02) 366080.
Ministry of Foreign Affairs: 18–19 Dem. Severis Ave, Nicosia; tel. (02) 302387; telex 3001; fax (02) 451881.
Ministry of Health: tel. (02) 303157; fax (02) 303498.
Ministry of the Interior: Dem. Severis Ave, Nicosia; tel. (02) 302100; fax (02) 453465.
Ministry of Justice: 1 Dioghenous St, Engomi, Nicosia; tel. (02) 302355; fax (02) 461427.
Ministry of Labour and Social Insurance: Byron Ave, Nicosia; tel. (02) 403481; telex 6011; fax (02) 450993.

PRESIDENT

Election, 14 February 1988* and 21 February 1988

Candidates	Votes	%
GEORGHIOS VASSILIOU (Independent)	167,834 (100,748)	51.6 (30.1)
GLAVKOS KLERIDES (Democratic Rally)	157,228 (111,504)	48.4 (33.3)
SPYROS KYPRIANOU (Democratic Party)	— (91,335)	— (27.3)
Dr VASSOS LYSSARIDES (EDEK-Socialist Party)	— (30,865)	— (9.2)
THRASSOS GEORGHIADES (Independent)	— (189)	— (0.1)
Total	325,062 (334,641)	100.0 (100.0)

*Figures from the first round of voting appear in brackets.

House of Representatives

The House of Representatives originally consisted of 50 members, 35 from the Greek community and 15 from the Turkish community, elected for a term of five years. In January 1964 the Turkish

CYPRUS   *Directory*

members withdrew and set up the 'Turkish Legislative Assembly of the Turkish Cypriot Administration' (see p. 847). The Greek membership of the House was expanded from 35 to 56 members at the 1985 elections.

President: Dr VASSOS LYSSARIDES.

Elections for the Greek Representatives, 8 December 1985

Party	Votes	% of Votes	Seats
Democratic Rally	107,223	33.56	19
Democratic Party	88,322	27.65	16
AKEL (Communist Party)	87,628	27.43	15
EDEK (Socialist Party)	35,371	11.07	6
Independents	923	0.29	—
Total	319,467	100.00	56

Political Organizations

Ananeotiko Demokratiko Socialistiko Kinema (ADISOK) (Democratic Socialist Reform Movement): 19 Nikitara St, Ayii Omologites, Nicosia; tel. (02) 367345; fax (02) 367611; f. 1990; supports settlement of the Cyprus problem based on UN resolutions; Pres. PAVLOS DINGLIS; Vice-Pres. MICHAEL PAPAPETROU.

Anorthotiko Komma Ergazomenou Laou (AKEL) (Progressive Party of the Working People): POB 1827, 8 Akamas St, Nicosia; tel. (02) 441121; f. 1941; successor to the Communist Party of Cyprus (f. 1926); Marxist-Leninist; supports demilitarized, non-aligned and independent Cyprus; over 14,000 mems; Sec.-Gen. DEMETRIS CHRISTOFIAS.

Demokratiko Komma (DIKO) (Democratic Party): 50 Grivas Dhigenis Ave, Nicosia; tel. (02) 472002; fax (02) 366488; f. 1976; absorbed Enosi Kentrou (Centre Union, f. 1981) in 1989; supports settlement of the Cyprus problem based on UN resolutions; Pres. SPYROS KYPRIANOU; Vice-Pres. ALEXIS GALANOS; Sec.-Gen. N. MOUSHIOUTAS.

Demokratikos Synagemos (DISY) (Democratic Rally): POB 5305, 23 Pindarou St, Nicosia; tel. (02) 449791; fax (02) 449894; f. 1976; opposition party; absorbed Democratic National Party (DEK) in 1977 and New Democratic Front (NEDIPA) in 1988; advocates greater active involvement by the West in the settlement of the Cyprus problem; 10,000 mems; Pres. GLAVKOS KLERIDES; Gen. Sec. ALEKOS MARKIDIS.

Ethniki Demokratiki Enosi Kyprou (EDEK)—Socialistiko Komma (Cyprus National Democratic Union): POB 1064, 2 Bouboulinas St, Nicosia; tel. (02) 458617; telex 3182; fax (02) 458894; f. 1969; the Socialist Party of Cyprus; supports independent, non-aligned, unitary, demilitarized Cyprus; advocates the establishment of a socialist structure; Pres. Dr VASSOS LYSSARIDES; Sec.-Gen. TAKIS HADJIDEMETRIOU.

Komma Phileleftheron (Liberal Party): POB 7289, 1 Demetsana St, Nicosia; tel. (02) 452117; telex 2483; fax (02) 368900; f. 1986; supports settlement of the Cyprus problem based on UN resolutions; Pres. NIKOS A. ROLANDIS.

Diplomatic Representation

EMBASSIES AND HIGH COMMISSIONS IN CYPRUS

Australia: 4 Annis Komninis St, 2nd Floor, Nicosia; tel. (02) 473001; telex 2097; fax (02) 366486; High Commissioner: E. J. STEVENS.

Bulgaria: 15 St Paul St, Nicosia; tel. (02) 472486; telex 2188; Ambassador: MILEN MARINOV.

China, People's Republic: 28 Archimedes St, Engomi, Nicosia; tel. (02) 358182; Ambassador: LIN AILI.

Cuba: 39 Regas Phereos St, Acropolis, Nicosia; tel. (02) 427211; telex 2306; fax (02) 429390; Ambassador: GUILLERMO ZURBATU GÓMEZ.

Czechoslovakia: POB 1165, 7 Kastorias St, Nicosia; tel. (02) 311683; telex 2490; Ambassador: EMIL KEBLUŠEK.

Egypt: POB 1752, 3 Egypt Ave, Nicosia; tel. (02) 465144; telex 2102; Ambassador: N. M. MAHDY.

France: POB 1671, 6 Ploutarchou St, Engomi, Nicosia; tel. (02) 465258; telex 2389; Ambassador: DANIEL HUSSON.

Germany: POB 1795, 10 Nikitaras St, Nicosia; tel. (02) 444362; telex 2400; fax (02) 365601; Ambassador: Dr THILO RÖTGER.

Greece: POB 1799, 8/10 Byron Ave, Nicosia; tel. (02) 441880; telex 2394; fax (02) 473990; Ambassador: YANNIS FOTOPOULOS.

Holy See: POB 3751, Paphos Gate, Paphos St, Nicosia (Apostolic Nunciature); tel. (02) 462132; Apostolic Pro-Nuncio: Most Rev. CARLO CURIS, Titular Archbishop of Medeli.

India: POB 5544, 3 Indira Gandhi St, Engomi, Nicosia; tel. (02) 351741; telex 4146; fax (02) 350402; High Commissioner: RAJENDRA G. PARTHASARATHY.

Israel: POB 1049, 4 I. Gryparis St, Nicosia; tel. (02) 445195; telex 5978; Ambassador: AHARON LOPEZ.

Italy: POB 1452, Margarita House, 15 Themistokli Dervis St, Nicosia; tel. (02) 473183; telex 3847; Ambassador: GUIDO RIZZO VENCI.

Lebanon: POB 1924, 1 Vasilissis Olgas St, Nicosia; tel. (02) 442216; telex 3056; Ambassador: ZAIDAN ZAIDAN.

Libya: POB 3669, 14 Estias St, Nicosia; tel. (02) 496511; Secretary of People's Bureau: ALI ABDULHAMED AS-SAGHAIER.

Romania: 37 Tombazis St, Nicosia; tel. (02) 445845; telex 2431; Chargé d'affaires: ION BISTREANU.

Syria: POB 1891, Corner Androcleous and Thoukidides Sts, Nicosia; tel. (02) 474481; telex 2030; Chargé d'affaires a.i.: ABD AL-FATAH AMMOURAH.

USSR: POB 1845, 4 Gladstone St, Nicosia; tel. (02) 472141; telex 5808; fax (02) 472230; Ambassador: (vacant).

United Kingdom: POB 1978, Alexander Pallis St, Nicosia; tel. (02) 473131; telex 2208; fax (02) 367198; High Commissioner: D. J. M. DAIN.

USA: Dositheos St, and Therissos St, Lykavitos, Nicosia; tel. (02) 465151; telex 4160; fax (02) 459571; Ambassador: ROBERT LAMB.

Yemen: Nicosia; Ambassador: AHMAD MOHAMMAD AL-MOUTAWAKIL.

Yugoslavia: 2 Vasilissis Olgas St, Nicosia; tel. (02) 445511; fax (02) 445910; Ambassador: PETAR BOSKOVIĆ.

Judicial System

Supreme Council of Judicature: Nicosia. The Supreme Council of Judicature is composed of the President and Judges of the Supreme Court. It is responsible for the appointment, promotion, transfer, etc., of the judges exercising civil and criminal jurisdiction in the District Courts and the Assize Courts.

SUPREME COURT

Supreme Court: Char. Mouskos St, Nicosia; tel. (02) 402398. The Constitution of 1960 provided for a separate Supreme Constitutional Court and High Court but in 1964, in view of the resignation of their neutral presidents, these were amalgamated to form a single Supreme Court.

The Supreme Court is the final appellate court in the Republic and the final adjudicator in matters of constitutional and administrative law, including recourses on conflict of competence between state organs on questions of the constitutionality of laws, etc. It deals with appeals from Assize Courts and District Courts as well as from the decisions of its own judges when exercising original jurisdiction in certain matters such as prerogative orders of *habeas corpus*, *mandamus*, *certiorari*, etc., and in admiralty cases.

President: A. N. LOIZOU.

Judges: Y. CH. MALACHTOS, D. GR. DEMETRIADES, L. G. SAVVIDES, D. STYLIANIDES, G. M. PIKIS, A. G. KOURRIS, I. Z. PAPADOPOULLOS, CHR. C. HADJITSANGARIS, I. CH. BOYADJIS, Y. CHR. CHRYSOSTOMIS, S. NIKITAS, CHR. C. ARTEMIDES.

OTHER COURTS

Assize Courts and District Courts: As required by the Constitution a law was passed in 1960 providing for the establishment, jurisdiction and powers of courts of civil and criminal jurisdiction, i.e. of six District Courts and six Assize Courts.

Ecclesiastical Courts: There are seven Orthodox Church tribunals having exclusive jurisdiction in matrimonial causes between members of the Greek Orthodox Church. Appeals go from these tribunals to the appellate tribunal of the Church.

'Turkish Republic of Northern Cyprus'

The Turkish intervention in Cyprus in July 1974 resulted in the establishment of a separate area in northern Cyprus under the control of the Autonomous Turkish Cypriot Administration, with a Council of Ministers and separate judicial, financial, police,

CYPRUS

military and educational machinery serving the Turkish community.

On 13 February 1975 the Turkish-occupied zone of Cyprus was declared the 'Turkish Federated State of Cyprus', and Rauf Denktaş declared President. At the second joint meeting held by the Executive Council and Legislative Assembly of the Autonomous Turkish Cypriot Administration, it was decided to set up a Constituent Assembly which would prepare a constitution for the 'Turkish Federated State of Cyprus' within 45 days. This Constitution, which was approved by the Turkish Cypriot population in a referendum held on 8 June 1975, was regarded by the Turkish Cypriots as a first step towards a federal republic of Cyprus. The main provisions of the Constitution are summarized below:

The 'Turkish Federated State of Cyprus' is a democratic, secular republic based on the principles of social justice and the rule of law. It shall exercise only those functions which fall outside the powers and functions expressly given to the (proposed) Federal Republic of Cyprus. Necessary amendments shall be made to the Constitution of the 'Turkish Federated State of Cyprus' when the Constitution of the Federal Republic comes into force. The official language is Turkish.

Legislative power is vested in a Legislative Assembly, composed of 40 deputies, elected by universal suffrage for a period of five years. The President is Head of State and is elected by universal suffrage for a period of five years. No person may be elected President for more than two consecutive terms. The Council of Ministers shall be composed of a prime minister and 10 ministers. Judicial power is exercised through independent courts.

Other provisions cover such matters as the rehabilitation of refugees, property rights outside the 'Turkish Federated State', protection of coasts, social insurance, the rights and duties of citizens, etc.

On 15 November 1983 a unilateral declaration of independence brought into being the 'Turkish Republic of Northern Cyprus', which, like the 'Turkish Federated State of Cyprus', was not granted international recognition.

The Constituent Assembly, established after the declaration of independence, prepared a new constitution, which was approved by the Turkish Cypriot electorate on 5 May 1985. The new Constitution is very similar to the old one, but the number of deputies in the Legislative Assembly was increased to 50.

HEAD OF STATE

President of the 'Turkish Republic of Northern Cyprus': RAUF R. DENKTAŞ (assumed office as President of the 'Turkish Federated State of Cyprus' 13 February 1975; became President of the 'TRNC' 15 November 1983; re-elected for a five-year term 9 June 1985 and again on 22 April 1990).

COUNCIL OF MINISTERS
(January 1991)

Prime Minister: Dr DERVIŞ EROĞLU.

Minister of Foreign Affairs and Defence: Dr KENAN ATAKOL.

Minister of the Economy and Finance: NAZIF BORMAN.

Minister of Communications, Public Works and Tourism: MEHMET BAYRAM.

Minister of Trade and Industry: ATAY AHMET RAŞIT.

Minister of the Interior, Rural Affairs and Environment: SERDAR DENKTAŞ.

Minister of Health and Social Welfare: Dr ERTUĞRUL HASIPOĞLU.

Minister of Labour, Youth and Sport: ERKAN EMEKÇI.

Minister of Housing: HASAN YUMUK.

Minister of Agriculture and Forestry: İLKAY KAMIL.

Minister of National Education and Culture: EŞBER SERAKINCI.

MINISTRIES

All Ministries are in Nicosia (Lefkoşa). Address: Nicosia, Mersin 10, Turkey.

Prime Minister's Office: tel. (520) 83141; telex 57444; fax (520) 77518.

Ministry of Agriculture and Forestry: tel. (520) 83735; telex 57419; fax (520) 75299.

Ministry of Communications, Public Works and Tourism: tel. (520) 81057; telex 57169; fax (520) 81891.

Ministry of the Economy and Finance: tel. (520) 73626; telex 57268; fax (520) 78230.

Ministry of Foreign Affairs and Defence: tel. (520) 83241; telex 57178; fax (520) 76439; Şehit İdris Doğan St, Nicosia, Mersin 10, Turkey.

Ministry of Health and Social Welfare: tel. (520) 75229; fax (520) 03893.

Ministry of Housing: tel. (520) 73213.

Ministry of the Interior, Rural Affairs and Environment: tel. (520) 73645.

Ministry of Labour, Youth and Sport: tel. (520) 73611; telex 57178.

Ministry of National Education and Culture: tel. (520) 83136; fax (520) 82234.

Ministry of Tourism: tel. (520) 78269; fax (520) 81891.

Ministry of Trade and Industry: tel. (520) 71341; telex 57174.

PRESIDENT

Election, 22 April 1990

Candidates	Votes	%
RAUF R. DENKTAŞ (Independent)	61,404	66.65
İSMAIL BOZKURT (Independent)	29,568	32.09
ALPAY DURDURAN (New Cyprus Party)	1,157	1.26
Total	92,129	100.00

LEGISLATIVE ASSEMBLY

Speaker: HAKKI ATUN.
Deputy Speaker: VEHBI Z. SERTER.

General Election, 6 May 1990

Party	Seats
National Unity Party	34
Democratic Struggle Party*	14
(Republican Turkish Party)	(7)
(Communal Liberation Party)	(6)
(New Dawn Party)	(1)
Independents	2
Total	50

* See below.

POLITICAL ORGANIZATIONS

Cumhuriyetçi Türk Partisi (CTP) (Republican Turkish Party): 99A Şehit Salahi, Şevket St, Nicosia; tel. (520) 73300; f. 1970 by members of the Turkish community in Cyprus; socialist principles with anti-imperialist stand; district organizations at Famagusta, Kyrenia, Morphou and Nicosia; Leader ÖSKER ÖZGÜR; Gen. Sec. NACI TALAT USAR.

Demokratik Mucadele Partisi (DMP) (Democratic Struggle Party): Nicosia; f. 1990; opposition alliance of Republican Turkish Party, Communal Liberation Party and New Dawn Party to contest the May 1990 general election.

Toplumcu Kurtuluş Partisi (TKP) (Communal Liberation Party): 13 Mahmut Paşa St, Nicosia; tel. (520) 72555; f. 1976; merged with the Atılımcı Halk Partisi (Progressive People's Party, f. 1979) in 1989; left of centre; social democratic principles, social justice; believes in the leading role of organized labour; wants a solution of Cyprus problem as an independent, non-aligned, bi-zonal and bi-communal federal state; Leader MUSTAFA AKINCI; Gen. Sec. ERDAL SÜREÇ.

Ulusal Birlik Partisi (UBP) (National Unity Party): 9 Atatürk Meydanı, Nicosia; tel. (520) 73972; f. 1975; right of centre; based on Atatürk's reforms, social justice, political equality and peaceful co-existence in an independent, bi-zonal, bi-communal, federal state of Cyprus; Leader Dr DERVIŞ EROĞLU.

Yeni Doğuş Partisi (YDP) (New Dawn Party): 1 Cengiz Han St, Nicosia; tel. (520) 72558; f. 1984; right of centre; supports a mixed economy; Leader ORHAN UÇOK.

Yeni Kıbrıs Partisi (YKP) (New Cyprus Party): Nicosia; f. 1989; Leader ALPAY DURDURAN.

DIPLOMATIC REPRESENTATION
Embassy in the TRNC

Turkey: Bedreddin Demirel Ave, Nicosia, Mersin 10, Turkey; tel. (520) 72314; Ambassador: ERTUĞRUL KUMCUOĞLU.

Turkey is the only country to have recognized the 'Turkish Republic of Northern Cyprus'.

JUDICIAL SYSTEM

Supreme Council of Judicature: The Supreme Council of Judicature, composed of the President and judges of the Supreme Court,

CYPRUS

a member appointed by the President of the 'Turkish Republic of Northern Cyprus', a member appointed by the Legislative Assembly, the Attorney-General of the 'Turkish Republic of Northern Cyprus' and a member elected by the Bar Association, is responsible for the appointment, promotion, transfer, leave and discipline of all judges. The appointment of the President and judges of the Supreme Court must be approved by the President of the 'Turkish Republic of Northern Cyprus'.

Attorney-General: AKIN SAIT.

Supreme Court: The Supreme Court functions as the Constitutional Court, the Court of Appeal and the High Administrative Court.

President: ŞAKIR SIDKI İLKAY.

Judges: SALIH SAMI DAYIOĞLU, NAZIM ERGIN SALÂHI, NIYAZI FAZIL KORKUT, AZIZ ALTAY, CELÂL KARABACAK, TANER ERGINEL, METIN A. HAKKI.

Subordinate Courts: Judicial power other than that exercised by the Supreme Court is exercised by the Assize, District and Family Courts.

Religion

Greeks form 77% of the population and most of them belong to the Orthodox Church. Most Turks (about 18% of the population) are Muslims. At the 1960 census, religious adherence was:

Greek Orthodox	441,656
Muslims	104,942
Armenian Apostolic	3,378
Maronite	2,752
Anglican	
Roman Catholic	} 18,836
Other	

CHRISTIANITY

The Orthodox Church of Cyprus

The Autocephalous Orthodox Church of Cyprus, founded in AD 45, is part of the Eastern Orthodox Church; the Church is independent, and the Archbishop, who is also the Ethnarch (national leader of the Greek community), is elected by representatives of the towns and villages of Cyprus. The Church comprises six dioceses, and in 1985 had an estimated 442,000 members.

Archbishop of Nova Justiniana and all Cyprus: Archbishop CHRYSOSTOMOS, POB 1130, Arch. Kyprianos St, Nicosia; tel. (02) 474411; fax (02) 474180.

Metropolitan of Paphos: Bishop CHRYSOSTOMOS.

Metropolitan of Kitium: Bishop CHRYSOSTOMOS, Dem. Lipertis St, Larnaca; fax (041) 55588.

Metropolitan of Kyrenia: Bishop GREGORIOS.

Metropolitan of Limassol: Bishop CHRYSANTHOS.

Metropolitan of Morphou: Bishop CHRYSANTHOS.

The Roman Catholic Church

Latin Rite

The Patriarchate of Jerusalem covers Israel, Jordan and Cyprus. The Patriarch is resident in Jerusalem (see the chapter on Israel).

Vicar Patriarchal for Cyprus: Father XAVIER GEISER.

Maronite Rite

Most of the Roman Catholics in Cyprus are adherents of the Maronite rite. Prior to June 1988 the Archdiocese of Cyprus included part of Lebanon. At 26 October 1990 the archdiocese contained an estimated 9,000 Maronite Catholics.

Archbishop of Cyprus: Most Rev. BOUTROS GEMAYEL, POB 2249, Maronite Archbishop's House, 8 Favierou St, Nicosia; tel. (02) 458877; telex 2933; fax (02) 493987.

The Anglican Communion

Anglicans in Cyprus are adherents of the Episcopal Church in Jerusalem and the Middle East, officially inaugurated in January 1976. The Church has four dioceses, and the President is the Bishop in Jerusalem (see Israel). The diocese of Cyprus and the Gulf includes Cyprus, Iraq and the countries of the Arabian peninsula.

Bishop in Cyprus and The Gulf: Right Rev. JOHN EDWARD BROWN, POB 2075, Diocesan Office, 2 Grigoris Afxentiou St, Nicosia; tel. (02) 451220; fax (02) 466553.

Archdeacon of Cyprus: Very Rev. BRYAN G. HENRY, POB 2075, 2 Grigoris Afxentiou St, Nicosia; tel. (02) 442241.

Other Christian Churches

Among other denominations active in Cyprus are the Armenian Apostolic Church and the Greek Evangelical Church.

ISLAM

Most of the adherents in Cyprus are Sunnis of the Hanafi Sect. The religious head of the Muslim community is the Mufti.

Mufti of Cyprus: AHMET CEMAL İLKTAÇ (acting), POB 142, Nicosia, Mersin 10, Turkey.

The Press

GREEK CYPRIOT DAILIES

Agon (Struggle): POB 1417, Makarios Ave and Agapinoros St, Nicosia; tel. (02) 477181; f. 1964; morning; Greek; independent, right of centre; Owner and Dir N. KOSHIS; Chief Editor GEORGE A. LEONIDAS; circ. 9,000.

Alithia (Truth): POB 1695, 5 Pindaros and Androklis St, Nicosia; tel. (02) 463040; fax (02) 463945; f. 1952 as a weekly, 1982 as a daily; morning; Greek; right-wing; supports Democratic Rally; Dir FR. N. KOULERMOS; Chief Editor ALEKOS KONSTANTINIDES; circ. 9,000.

Apogevmatini (Afternoon): POB 1094, 5 Aegaleo St, Strovolos, Nicosia; tel. (02) 443858; f. 1972; afternoon; Greek; independent, moderate; Owner and Chief Editor ANTHOS LYKAVGHIS; circ. 10,000.

Apogevmatinos Typos (Afternoon Press): POB 1695, 5 Pindaros and Androklis St, Nicosia; tel. (02) 463505; f. 1988; afternoon; Greek; independent; publication suspended in 1990; Owner F. N. KOYLERMOS; Chief Editor ARISTOS MICHAELIDES.

Cyprus Mail: POB 1144, 24 Vassilios Voulgaroktonos St, Nicosia; tel. (02) 462074; telex 2616; f. 1945; morning; English; independent, conservative; Dir. KYRIACOS IAKOVIDES; Chief Editor ANDREAS MICHAEL; circ. 4,000.

Eleftheria Tis Gnomis (Freedom of Opinion): 9 Zinonos Kitieos St, Engomi, Nicosia; tel. (02) 450910; f. 1987; afternoon; Greek; centre-right; Dir VASSOS ANDONIADES; Chief Editor NANCIA PALALA-CHARIDES; circ. 2,000.

Eleftherotypia (Free Press): POB 3821, 50 Grivas Dhigenis Ave, Nicosia; tel. (02) 454400; f. 1981; morning; Greek; right of centre; organ of DIKO party; Dir and Chief Editor GEORGE ELIADES; circ. 6,550.

Haravghi (Dawn): POB 1556, ETAK Bldg, 6 Akamas St, Nicosia; tel. (02) 476356; fax (02) 365154; f. 1956; morning; Greek; organ of AKEL (Communist Party); Dir and Chief Editor ANDONIS CHRISTODOULOU; circ. 13,169.

Messimvrini (Midday): POB 1543, 40 Sofouli St, Nicosia; tel. (02) 366230; f. 1970; afternoon; Greek; independent, right-wing; Publr, Dir and Chief Editor ELLI HADJINICOLAOU; circ. 2,000.

Phileleftheros (Liberal): POB 1094, 36 Vyronos Ave, 3rd Floor, 'Nicosia Tower Centre', Nicosia; tel. (02) 463922; telex 4999; fax (02) 366121; f. 1955; morning; Greek; independent, moderate; Dir CHR. PATTICHIS; Chief Editor CHR. KATSAMBAS; circ. 20,000.

Proina Nea (Morning News): POB 4349, 40 Vyronos Ave, Nicosia; tel. (02) 451000; f. 1989; morning; organ of EDEK (Socialist Party); Dir R. PRENZAS; Chief Editor A. ASSOS.

Simerini (Today): POB 1836, Solea Court, 4 Annis Komnenis St, Nicosia; tel. (02) 448708; telex 3826; f. 1976; morning; Greek; right-wing; supports Democratic Rally; Dir COSTAS HADJICOSTIS; Chief Editor SAVVAS IAKOVIDES; circ. 13,000.

TURKISH CYPRIOT DAILIES

Birlik (Unity): POB 841, 43 Yediler St, Nicosia, Mersin 10, Turkey; tel. (520) 72959; f. 1980; Turkish; organ of National Unity Party; Editor Dr M. ERBILEN; circ. 4,500.

Günaydın Kıbrıs (Good Morning, Cyprus): 23/12 Posta St, Nicosia, Mersin 10, Turkey; tel. (520) 71472; telex 57240; f. 1980; Turkish; Editor REŞAT AKAR; circ. 1,900.

Halkın Sesi (Voice of the People): 172 Kyrenia St, Nicosia, Mersin 10, Turkey; tel. (520) 73141; telex 57173; f. 1942; morning; Turkish; independent Turkish nationalist; Dir Gen. and Man. Editor MEHMET KÜÇÜK; circ. 6,000.

Kıbrıs: Şht. İdris Doğan St, Nicosia, Mersin 10, Turkey; tel. (520) 73133; telex 57177; fax 78847; Editor M. A. AKPINAR; circ. 4,000.

Kıbrıs Postası (Cyprus Post): M. İrfan Bey Sok. 30, Nicosia; tel. (520) 75242; telex 57244; f. 1982; Turkish; independent; Owner and Chief Editor İSMET KOTAK; circ. 4,500.

Ortam (Conditions): 158A Girne St, Nicosia, Mersin 10, Turkey; tel. (520) 74872; Turkish; organ of the Toplumcu Kurtuluş Partisi (Communal Liberation Party); Editor KEMAL AKTUNÇ; circ. 1,250.

CYPRUS

Yenidüzen (New System): Yeni Sanayi St, Nicosia, Mersin 10, Turkey; tel. (520) 74906; Turkish; organ of the Cumhuriyetçi Türk Partisi (Republican Turkish Party); circ. 1,000.

GREEK CYPRIOT WEEKLIES

Ammochostos: 44 Egnatias, Plati, Eylenja; tel. 352918; Greek; right-wing; reflects views of Famagusta refugees; Dir and Chief Editor NIKOS FALAS; circ. 2,800.

Anexartitos (Independent): POB 1064, A. Karyos St, Engomi, Nicosia; tel. (02) 449766; f. 1973; Greek; organ of EDEK party; Chief Editor ANTONIS MAKRIDES; circ. 2,780.

Cyprus Weekly: POB 1992, 216 Mitsis 3 Bldg, Archbishop Makarios Ave, Nicosia; tel. (02) 441433; telex 2260; f. 1979; English; independent; Dirs and Editors GEORGE DER PARTHOCH, ALEX EFTHYVOULOS, ANDREAS HADJIPAPAS; circ. 15,000.

Economiki Kypros: 51 Dhigenis Akritas Ave, Nicosia; tel. (02) 472510; f. 1987; Greek; Dir and Chief Editor TASSOS ANASTASSIADES; circ. 3,000.

Eleftherotypia Tis Defteras (Monday's Free Press): POB 3821, Hadjisavvas Bldg, Eleftheria Sq, Nicosia; tel. (02) 454400; f. 1980; Greek; right of centre; organ of DIKO party.

Embros (Forward): POB 3739, 19 Nikitara St, Ay. Omoloyitae, Nicosia; tel. (02) 451280; f. 1987; Greek; left-wing, supports ADISOK; Chief Editor P. POLYDORIDES; circ. 2,500.

Enimerossi (Briefing): POB 1417, Makarios Ave and Agapinoros St, Nicosia; tel. (02) 477181; f. 1982; Greek; Dir NIKOS KOSHIS; Chief Editor PANAYIOTIS PAPADEMETRIS; circ. 10,000.

Epikeri (Current Affairs): POB 3786, 19 Bouboulinas St, Nicosia; tel. (02) 455788; f. 1987; Greek; independent; Dir and Chief Editor LAZAROS MAVROS; circ. 2,500.

Ergatiki Phoni (Workers' Voice): POB 5018, SEK Bldg, 23 Alkeou St, Engomi, Nicosia; tel. (02) 441142; telex 6180; fax (02) 476360; f. 1946; Greek; organ of Cyprus Workers' Confederation (SEK); Chief Editor GREGORIS GREGORIADES; circ. 8,850.

Ergatiko Vima (Workers' Tribune): POB 1885, 31-35 Archemos St, Nicosia; tel. (02) 473192; f. 1956; Greek; organ of the Pancyprian Federation of Labour (PEO); Editor-in-Chief PANTELIS VARNAVAS; circ. 15,850.

Exormisi (Starting Line): POB 1697, 87b Ayias Phylaxeos, Limassol; tel. (05) 332814; f. 1989; Greek; independent; Dir and Chief Editor G. EROTOKRITOU; circ. 2,500.

Flash: POB 4626, 11 Kolokotronis St, Kaimakli, Nicosia; tel. (02) 437887; f. 1978; Greek; Chief Editor LOUCAS BARBAS; circ. 12,000.

Kirykas (Herald): 12 Diagorou St, Nicosia; tel. (02) 461961; f. 1981; Greek; right of centre; organ of Centre Union party; Dir and Chief Editor GEORGE ELIADES; circ. 3,000.

Kyriakatikes Ores (Sunday Hours): POB 1450, 7 Androkleous St, Nicosia; tel. (02) 448548; Dir and Chief Editor PHIVOS MORIDES.

Official Gazette: Printing Office of the Republic of Cyprus, Nicosia; tel. (02) 462202; f. 1960; Greek; published by the Government of the Republic of Cyprus.

Paraskinio (Behind the Scenes): 39 Kennedy Ave, Nicosia; tel. (02) 313334; f. 1987; Greek; Dir and Chief Editor D. MICHAEL; cir. 4,500.

To Periodiko: Dias Bldg, 31 Archangelos Ave, Nicosia; tel. (02) 353646; telex 3826; fax (02) 352298; f. 1986; Greek; Dir PHILIPPOS STYLIANOU; circ. 23,500.

Touristica Chronika (Tourism Chronicle): POB 7083, Nicosia; tel. (02) 443240; f. 1986; every 2 months; Dir and Publr A. KAROUZIS; circ. 2,000.

TURKISH CYPRIOT WEEKLIES

Cyprus Times: A. N. Graphics Ltd, 12 A/B Hasene Ilgaz Sokak, Köşklüçiftlik, Nicosia, Mersin 10, Turkey; f. 1989; English; political, social, cultural and economic.

Ekonomi (The Economy): POB 718, Bedreddin Demirel Ave, Nicosia, Mersin 10, Turkey; tel. (520) 83760; telex 57511; fax (520) 83089; f. 1958; Turkish; published by the Turkish Cypriot Chamber of Commerce; Editor-in-Chief SAMİ TAŞARKAN; circ. 3,000.

Ekspres: Nicosia, Mersin 10, Turkey; f. 1987; Editor-in-Chief ÖNDER ASLITÜRK.

Haber: Nicosia, Mersin 10, Turkey; tel. (520) 78188; Turkish; Chief Editor MEHMET AKAR.

Special News Bulletin-Digest: Nicosia, Mersin 10, Turkey; tel. (520) 75773; telex 57169; English; publ. by the 'TRNC' Public Relations Office.

Sportmence: Nicosia, Mersin 10, Turkey; tel. (520) 72212; Turkish; Chief Editor ERTAN BİRİNCİ.

Süper Spor: Nicosia, Mersin 10, Turkey; tel. (520) 74471; Turkish; Chief Editor İBRAHIM ÖZSOY.

Türkün Sesi (Turkish Voice): Nicosia; pro-Government; Editor N. S. UĞURSAL; circ. 3,500.

OTHER WEEKLIES

Lion: British Forces Post Office 53; tel. (05) 263926; fax (05) 263181; British Sovereign Base Areas weekly with Services Sound and Vision Corpn programme guide; Editor Maj. M. P. BEAUMONT; circ. 3,600.

Middle East Economic Survey: Middle East Petroleum and Economic Publications (Cyprus), POB 4940, Nicosia; tel. (02) 445431; telex 2198; fax (02) 474988; f. 1957 (in Beirut); weekly review and analysis of petroleum, economic and political news; Publr BASIM W. ITAYIM; Editor IAN SEYMOUR.

GREEK CYPRIOT PERIODICALS

Avgherinos (Morning Star): 2nd Floor, 18 C' Makarios Ave, Nicosia; tel. (02) 454466; f. 1983; children's magazine; Publr A. CHRISTODOULIDES; circ. 4,800.

Countryman: Nicosia; tel. (02) 454733; telex 2526; f. 1943; quarterly; Greek; published by the Cyprus Press and Information Office; circ. 6,000.

Cypria (Cypriot Woman): POB 8506, Nicosia; tel. (02) 494907; f. 1984; every 2 months; Greek; Owner MARO KARAYIANNI; circ. 6,000.

Cyprus Bulletin: Nicosia; tel. (02) 451001; telex 2526; f. 1964; fortnightly; Arabic, English, French, German, Greek, Russian, Spanish; published by the Cyprus Press and Information Office; Principal Officers A. SOPHOCLEOUS, G. HADJISAVVAS; circ. 28,000.

Cyprus Diplomatist: 16-18 Halkokondyli St, POB 660, Nicosia; tel. (02) 366866; f. 1989; every 2 months; Dir and Chief Editor GEORGE LANITIS; circ. 2,000.

Cyprus Life: Flat 21, 24 Evagorou St, Nicosia; f. 1987; monthly; English; Chief Editor GARY LAKES; circ. 4,000.

Cyprus Time Out: POB 3697, 4 Pygmalion St, Nicosia; tel. (02) 452079; f. 1978; monthly; English; Chief Editor ELLADA SOPHOCLEOUS; circ. 4,000.

Cyprus Today: c/o Ministry of Education, Nicosia; tel. (02) 302442; telex 5760; fax (02) 445021; f. 1963; quarterly; English; cultural and informative review of the Ministry of Education; published and distributed by Press and Information Office; free of charge; Chair. Editorial Board YIANNIS KATSOURIS; circ. 15,000.

Dimosios Ypallilos (Civil Servant): 3 Dem. Severis Ave, Nicosia; tel. (02) 442393; fortnightly; published by the Cyprus Civil Servants' Association (PASYDY); circ. 11,000.

Economiki Kypros (Economic Cyprus): 51 Dhigenis Akritas Ave, Nicosia; tel. (02) 472510; f. 1987; monthly; Dir and Chief Editor TASSOS ANASTASIADES; circ. 3,000.

Ekloyi (The Choice): 1st Floor, 16 Stassicratous, Nicosia; tel. (02) 474168; f. 1989; monthly; Publr A. KAISSIS; circ. 2,000.

Endoskopisi: 6th Floor, 4 Annis Komninis St, Nicosia; tel. (02) 458541; fax (02) 450370; f. 1984; every 2 months; Greek; Chief Editor NICOS HADJICOSTIS; circ. 3,000.

Eso-Etimos (Ever Ready): POB 4544, Nicosia; tel. (02) 443587; f. 1913; quarterly; Greek; publ. by Cyprus Scouts' Asscn; Editor TAKIS NEOPHYTOU; circ. 2,500.

Katanalotis (Consumer): POB 4874, 20 Gladstone St, Nicosia 162; tel. (02) 451092; f. 1977; every 2 months; Greek; circ. 3,000.

Nea Epochi (New Epoch): POB 1581, Nicosia; tel. (02) 444605; f. 1959; every 2 months; Greek; literary; Editor ACHILLEAS PYLIOTIS; circ. 1,500.

Nicosia This Month: POB 1015, Nicosia; tel. (02) 473124; telex 5374; fax (02) 463363; f. 1984; monthly; English; Chief Editor ELLADA SOPHOCLEOUS; circ. 3,000.

Oikogeneia Kai Scholeio (Family and School): 18 Archbishop Makarios III Ave, 5th Floor, Flat 8, Nicosia; tel. (02) 454466; f. 1970; every 2 months; Greek; for parents and teachers; publ. by the Pancyprian School for Parents; Editor A. D. CHRISTODOULIDES; circ. 7,000.

Paediki Hara (Children's Joy): 18 Archbishop Makarios III Ave, Nicosia; tel. (02) 442638; monthly; for pupils; publ. by the Pancyprian Union of Greek Teachers; Editor COSTAS PROTOPAPAS; circ. 15,000.

Pnevmatiki Kypros (Cultural Cyprus): Nicosia; tel. (02) 659001; f. 1960; monthly; Greek; literary; Owner Dr KYPROS CHRYSANTHIS.

To Prossopo (The Face): 105 Boumboulinas St, Nicosia; tel. (02) 454222; f. 1989; monthly; cultural; Dir CHRISTOS STYLIANIDES.

Radio Programme: POB 4824, Cyprus Broadcasting Corpn, Broadcasting House, Nicosia; tel. (02) 422231; telex 2333; fax (02) 314050; fortnightly; Greek and English; published by the CyBC; radio and TV programme news; circ. 21,000.

CYPRUS

Success: POB 4706, Nicosia; tel. (02) 472510; f. 1985; monthly; English; Chief Editor Titos Kolotas; circ. 4,000.

Synergatiko Vima (The Co-operative Rostrum): Shanteclair Bldg, 4th Floor, No. 401, 2 Sofoulis St, Nicosia; tel. (02) 458757; f. 1982; fortnightly; Greek; official organ of the Pancyprian Co-operative Confederation Ltd; circ. 7,000.

Synthesis (Composition): POB 3539, 3A Roussos Point Center, 3rd Floor, Limassol; tel. (05) 377243; f. 1988; every 2 months; interior design, fashion; Dir Yiannos Kouzarides; circ. 5,500.

Touristika Chronica (Tourism Chronicle): POB 7083, Nicosia; tel. (02) 443240; f. 1986; every 2 months; Dir and Publr A. Karouzis; circ. 2,000.

Trapezikos (Bank Employee): POB 1235, Nicosia; tel. (02) 449900; f. 1960; bank employees' magazine; Greek; monthly; Editor L. Hadzicostis; circ. 4,500.

TURKISH CYPRIOT PERIODICALS

Çengel: Nicosia, Mersin 10, Turkey; tel. (520) 75225; Turkish; Owner and Publr Erdal Andiz.

Eğitim Bülteni (Education Bulletin): Ministry of National Education and Culture, Nicosia, Mersin 10, Turkey; tel. (520) 72136; fax (520) 82334; f. 1972; monthly; Turkish; circ. 3,000.

Kıbrıs—Northern Cyprus Monthly: Directorate of Press and Information, Şehit İdris Doğan Sok., Nicosia, Mersin 10, Turkey; tel. (520) 73133; telex 57177; fax (520) 78847; f. 1963; Chief Editor Eser Birey (English).

Kooperatif (Co-operative): Dept of Co-operative Development, Nicosia, Mersin 10, Turkey; tel. (520) 71207; f. 1970; monthly; Turkish; circ. 2,000.

New Cyprus: POB 327, Nicosia, Mersin 10, Turkey; tel. (520) 78194; telex 2585; fax (520) 72592; English; publ. by the North Cyprus Research and Publishing Centre; also Turkish edition *Yeni Kıbrıs*; Editor Ahmet C. Gazioğlu.

Öğretmen (Teacher): Nicosia, Mersin 10, Turkey; tel. (520) 472802; f. 1972; monthly; Turkish; organ of Cyprus Turkish Secondary Schools' Teachers' Assen; circ. 1,200.

Özgürlük: POB 327, Nicosia, Mersin 10, Turkey; Turkish; Owner and Publr Hürrem Tolga.

Uluslararası Kuzey Kıbrıs Magazin (International Northern Cyprus Magazine): Cengiz Han St, Yuva Apt, Köşlüçiftlik, Nicosia, Mersin 10, Turkey; f. 1987; quarterly; Turkish and English; publ. by YORUM Publishing House; Editor Tansu Konuralp.

OTHER PERIODICALS

The Blue Beret: POB 1642, HQ UNFICYP, Nicosia; tel. (02) 359000; monthly; English; circ. 1,100.

International Crude Oil and Product Prices: Middle East Petroleum and Economic Publications (Cyprus), POB 4940, Nicosia; tel. (02) 445431; telex 2198; fax (02) 474988; f. 1971 (in Beirut); 2 a year; review and analysis of oil price trends in world markets; Publisher Basim W. Itayim.

NEWS AGENCIES

Cyprus News Agency: POB 3947, 97 Ay. Omoloyitae Ave, Nicosia 150; tel. (02) 458413; telex 4787; fax (02) 442613; f. 1976; English and Greek; Dir Ioannis Solomou.

Kuzey Kıbrıs Haber Ajansı (Northern Cyprus News Agency): 18 Server Somuncuoğlu St, Nicosia, Mersin 10, Turkey; tel. (020) 73892; telex 57254; fax (020) 72033; f. 1977; Dir-Gen. M. Ali Akpinar.

Pan Basin Yayin Ajansi (Pan Press Agency): ATO Apt 4, Sht. İbrahim Yusuf Sok., Nicosia, Mersin 10, Turkey; tel. (020) 77813; f. 1980; Dir Arman Ratip.

Türk Ajansı Kıbrıs (TAK) (Turkish News Agency of Cyprus): 9 Server Somuncuoğlu St, Nicosia, Mersin 10, Turkey; tel. (020) 71818; telex 57448; fax (020) 71213; f. 1973; Dir Emir Hüseyin Ersoy.

Foreign Bureaux

Agence France-Presse (AFP) (France): POB 7242, Helenium Estates Bldg, 7th Floor, 36 Kypranoros St, Nicosia; tel. (02) 365050; telex 2824; fax (02) 365125; Bureau Chief Xavier Baron; Correspondent Dimitri Andreou.

Agencia EFE (Spain): 10 Katsonis St, Nicosia; tel. (02) 461311; telex 6126; Correspondent Maria Saavedra.

Agentstvo Pechati Novosti (APN) (USSR): POB 4051, Flat 16, 5A Dinokratous St, Nicosia; tel. (02) 462287; telex 2379; Bureau Chief Dinu Linovoi.

Associated Press (AP) Middle East Ltd (USA): POB 4853, Neoelen Marina, 10 Katsonis St, Nicosia; tel. (02) 367103; telex 2459; fax (02) 367103; Rep. Nicholas Ludington; Correspondent Alex Efty.

Athinaikon Praktorion Eidiseon (Greece): 10 Andreas Patsalides St, Engomi, Nicosia; tel. (02) 441110; Rep. George Leonidas.

Iraqi News Agency: POB 1098, Flat 201, 11 Ippocratous St, Nicosia; tel. (02) 472095; telex 2197; Correspondent Ahmed Suleiman.

Jamahiriya News Agency (JANA) (Libya): 93 Kennedy Ave, Nicosia; tel. (02) 453933; Rep. Muhammad Ash-Shweihdi.

Kyodo Tsushin (Japan): 10 Katsonis St, Nicosia; tel. (02) 365267; telex 5769; fax (02) 459796; Bureau Chief Toru Maruyama.

Novinska Agencija Tanjug (Yugoslavia): 26 Methonis St, Nicosia; tel. (02) 450212; telex 3087; Rep. Nada Dugonjić.

Polska Agencja Prasowa (PAP) (Poland): POB 2373, Prodromos St 24, Nicosia; Rep. Michalakis Pantelides.

Prensa Latina (Cuba): 12 Demophon St, 5th Floor, Apt 501, Nicosia; tel. (02) 464131; telex 4505; Rep. Leonel Nodal.

Reuters (UK): POB 5725, 5th and 6th Floors, George and Thelma Paraskevaides Foundation Bldg, 36 Grivas Dhigenis Ave, Nicosia; tel. (02) 365087; telex 4922; fax (02) 475487; Rep. Diana Abdallah.

Schweizerische Despechenagentur, AG (SDA) (Switzerland): Flat 402, 35 Kappadokias St, Strovolos, Nicosia; tel. (02) 314798; Rep. Birgit Cerha.

Sofia-Press Agency (Bulgaria): 3 Fokidos St, Dasoupolis, Nicosia; tel. (02) 494484; Rep. Ionka Veresie.

Syrian Arab News Agency (SANA): POB 1891, Nicosia; tel. (02) 474481; Correspondent Sayed el-Yiaroub.

Tanjug (Yugoslavia): 26 Methonis St, Lycavitos, Nicosia; tel. (02) 450212; Correspondent Nada Dugonjić.

Telegrafnoye Agentstvo Sovetskovo Soyuza (TASS) (USSR): POB 2235, 3 Philellinon St, Nicosia; tel. (02) 475375; telex 2368; Rep. Mikhail Mashkov.

United Press International (UPI) (USA): 24A Heroes Ave, Nicosia 171; tel. (02) 449809; telex 2260; Rep. Georges der Parthogh.

Xinhua (New China) News Agency (People's Republic of China): POB 7024, Flat 32, 6 Nafpaktos St, Nicosia; tel. (02) 456703; telex 5265; Rep. Zhang Shenping.

Publishers

GREEK CYPRIOT PUBLISHERS

Action Publications: POB 4676, Nicosia; tel. (02) 444104; telex 4455; fax (02) 450048; f. 1971.

Andreou Publications: POB 2298, Nicosia; tel. (02) 466813; f. 1979.

MAM (The House of Cyprus Publications): POB 1722, Nicosia; tel. (02) 472744; f. 1965.

Nicoclis Publishing House: POB 3697, Nicosia; tel. (02) 456544.

TURKISH CYPRIOT PUBLISHERS

Devlet Basımevi (Turkish Cypriot Government Printing House): Şerif Arzik St, Nicosia, Mersin 10, Turkey; tel. (520) 72010; Dir S. Kürşad.

Sebil International Press: POB 7, Nicosia, Mersin 10, Turkey; tel. (520) 72627; telex 57565; fax (520) 83474; Principal Officer E. Başaran.

Radio and Television

In December 1989, in the government-controlled areas, it was estimated that there were 175,000 radio receivers and 89,750 television receivers (including about 78,000 colour receivers) in use; while, in December 1985, in the Turkish sector of Cyprus there were an estimated 42,170 radio receivers and 75,000 television receivers in use.

Cyprus Broadcasting Corporation (CyBC): POB 4824, Broadcasting House, Nicosia; tel. (02) 422231; telex 2333; Chair. Marios Eliades; Dir-Gen. D. Kyprianou.

 Radio: f. 1952; Programme I in Greek, Programme II in Greek, Turkish, English, Arabic and Armenian; two medium wave transmitters of 20 kW in Nicosia with relay stations at Paphos and Limassol; two 30 kW ERP VHF FM stereo transmitters on Mount Olympus; international service in English and Arabic.

 Television: f. 1957; one Band III 200/20 kW transmitter on Mount Olympus with 35 transposer stations.

Bayrak Radio and TV Corpn (BRTK): Dr Fazıl Küçük Ave, Nicosia, Mersin 10, Turkey; tel. (520) 76159; telex 57264; fax (520)

CYPRUS   Directory

81991; in July 1983 it became an independent Turkish Cypriot Corpn partly financed by the Govt; Dir-Gen. ERDAL ONURHAN.

Radio Bayrak: f. 1963; home service in Turkish, overseas services in Turkish, Greek, English, Arabic, Swedish and German; broadcasts 31 hours a day; Dir of Broadcasting HÜSEYIN ÇOBANOĞLU.

Bayrak TV: f. 1976; transmits programmes in Turkish, Greek, English and Arabic on six channels; Dir of Programmes HÜSEYIN ÇOBANOĞLU.

Services Sound and Vision Corpn, Cyprus: Dhekelia, British Forces Post Office 58; tel. (04) 723326; fax (04) 723565; f. 1948; incorporates the British Forces Broadcasting Service, Cyprus; broadcasts a 24-hour radio service in English VHF and medium wave and a six-and-a-half-hour daily TV service; Gen. Man. ALAN GRACE; Engineering Man. MIKE TOWNLEY; Sr Prog. Dir CHRIS RUSSELL.

Türkiye Radyo Televizyon (TRT): 2 channels of television programmes in Turkish, transmitted to the Turkish sector of Cyprus.

Finance

(brs = branches; cap. = capital; p.u. = paid up; auth. = authorized; dep. = deposits; res = reserves; m. = million; amounts in Cyprus pounds)

BANKING
Central Bank

Central Bank of Cyprus: POB 5529, 36 Metochiou Ave, Nicosia; tel. (02) 445281; telex 2424; fax (02) 472012; f. 1963; became the Bank of Issue in 1963; cap. p.u. 100,000, res 985,000, dep. 447m. (Dec. 1989); Gov. A. C. AFXENTIOU.

Greek Cypriot Banks

Bank of Cyprus Ltd: POB 1472, 86–90 Phaneromeni St, Nicosia; tel. (02) 464064; telex 5120; fax (02) 453881; f. 1899, reconstituted 1943 by the amalgamation of Bank of Cyprus, Larnaca Bank Ltd and Famagusta Bank Ltd; cap. p.u. 23m., res 19m. (Dec. 1989); Chair. SOLON A. TRIANTAFYLLIDES; Gov. ANDREAS C. PATSALIDES; 154 brs throughout Cyprus.

Co-operative Central Bank Ltd: POB 4537, Gregoris Afxentiou St, Nicosia; tel. (02) 442921; telex 2313; fax (02) 443088; f. 1937 under the Co-operative Societies Law; banking and credit facilities to member societies, importer and distributor of agricultural requisites, insurance agent; dep. 179m. (June 1990); Chair B. BALTAYIAN; Gen. Man. D. PITSILLIDES; 5 brs.

The Cyprus Popular Bank Ltd: POB 2032, Popular Bank Bldg, 39 Archbishop Makarios III Ave, Nicosia; tel. (02) 450000; telex 2494; fax (02) 450631; f. 1901; cap. p.u. 19.5m., res 32.9m., dep. 612.1m. (Dec. 1989); Chair. EVAGORAS C. LANITIS; Group Chief Exec. KIKIS N. LAZARIDES; 120 brs.

Hellenic Bank Ltd: POB 4747, 92 Dhigenis Akritas Ave, Nicosia; tel. (02) 447000; telex 3311; fax (02) 454074; f. 1974; cap. p.u. 6.1m., res 3.9m., dep. 167.4m. (Dec. 1989); Chair. PASCHALIS L. PASCHALIDES; Gen. Man. PANOS CHR. GHALANOS; 53 brs.

Housing Finance Corpn: POB 3898, 41 Themistoklis Dervis St, Hawaii Tower, Nicosia; tel. (02) 452777; telex 4134; f. 1980; provides long-term loans for home-buying; cap. p.u. 500,000, dep. 20m., total assets 25m. (Nov. 1988); Chair. A. MOUSKOS; Gen. Man. A. PAPAGEORGIOU; 7 brs.

Lombard NatWest Bank Ltd: POB 1661, Corner of Chilon and Gladstone St, Stylianos Lenas Square, Nicosia; tel. (02) 474333; telex 2262; f. 1960; locally incorporated although foreign-controlled; cap. p.u. 2m., res 42,000 (Sept. 1989); Chair. M. G. COLOCASSIDES; Man. Dir E. IOANNOU; 5 brs.

Mortgage Bank of Cyprus Ltd: POB 1472, 86–90 Phaneromeni St, Nicosia; tel. (02) 464064; telex 5120; fax (02) 453881; f. 1944; wholly-owned subsidiary of Bank of Cyprus Ltd; cap. p.u. 1m., res 8.2m., dep. 60.3m. (Dec. 1988); Chair. SOLON A. TRIANTAFYLLIDES; Gov. ANDREAS C. PATSALIDES; 151 brs.

Turkish Cypriot Banking Association

Northern Cyprus Bank Association: Nicosia, Mersin 10, Turkey; f. 1987; 9 mems.

Turkish Cypriot Banks
(amounts in Turkish liras)

AS Bank Ltd: POB 448, 23B Sarayönü Sok., Nicosia, Mersin 10, Turkey; tel. (520) 77023; telex 57305; fax (520) 21244; f. 1986; auth. cap. 10,000m., cap. and res 2,675m., dep. 12,119m. (Sept. 1989); Chair. Dr C. A. ADADEMIR; Exec. Dir MUSTAFA ALTUNER; 4 brs.

Inter Overseas Bank Ltd: Nicosia, Mersin 10, Turkey; 3 brs.

Kıbrıs Endüstri Bankası (Cyprus Industrial Bank): 3 Memduh Asaf Sok., Nicosia, Mersin 10, Turkey; tel. (520) 71830; telex 57257; fax (520) 71830.

Kıbrıs Kredi Bankası Ltd (Cyprus Credit Bank Ltd): POB 347, İplik Pazarı St, Nicosia, Mersin 10, Turkey; tel. (520) 75026; telex 57336; fax (520) 76999; f. 1978; cap. p.u. 5,440m., res 6,167.9m., dep. 203,764.1m. (Dec. 1989); Chair. SALIH BOYACI; Gen. Man. YÜKSEL YAZGIN; 15 brs.

Kıbrıs Ticaret Bankası Ltd (Cyprus Commercial Bank Ltd): 153 Kyrenia Ave, Nicosia, Mersin 10, Turkey; tel. (520) 83180; telex 57197; fax (520) 82278; f. 1982; cap. p.u. 2,000m., res 933m. dep. 43,839m. (Dec. 1989); Chair. YÜKSEL AHMET RAŞIT; Gen. Man. Dr ERDAL ONURHAN; 9 brs.

Kıbrıs Türk Kooperatif Merkez Bankası Ltd (Turkish Cypriot Co-operative Central Bank): POB 823, 49–55 Mahmut Paşa St, Nicosia, Mersin 10, Turkey; tel. (520) 83207; telex 57216; fax (520) 76787; cap. and res 4,589m., dep. 19,493m. (Dec. 1987); banking and credit facilities to member societies and individuals; Gen. Man. Dr TUNCER ARIFOĞLU.

Kıbrıs Vakıflar Bankası Ltd: POB 212, Evkaf Dairesi Binaları, Nicosia, Mersin 10, Turkey; tel. (520) 75109; telex 57122; fax (520) 75109; f. 1982; cap. and res 987.5m., dep. 16,500m. (Dec. 1988); Chair. TANSEL LISANI İNANÇ; Gen. Man. NEJAT MANER; 6 brs.

Türk Bankası Ltd: POB 242, 92 Kyrenia St, Nicosia, Mersin 10, Turkey; tel. (520) 83313; telex 2585; fax (520) 82432; f. 1901; cap. p.u. and res 29,692m., dep. 413,103m. (1989); Chair. and Gen. Man. M. TANJU ÖZYOL; 15 brs.

Investment Organization

Cyprus Investment and Securities Corpn: POB 597, Ghinis Bldg, 4th Floor, 58–60 Dhigenis Akritas Ave, Nicosia; tel. (02) 151535; telex 4449; fax (02) 445481; f. 1982 to promote development of capital market; issued cap. 1m. (1990); Chair. J. CL. CHRISTOPHIDES; Gen. Man. SOCRATES R. SOLOMIDES.

Development Bank

The Cyprus Development Bank Ltd: POB 1415, 50 Archbishop Makarios III Ave, Alpha House, Nicosia; tel. (02) 457575; telex 2797; fax (02) 464322; f. 1963; share cap. 2m.; res 833,000 (Dec. 1989); aims to accelerate the economic development of Cyprus by providing medium- and long-term loans for productive projects, developing the capital market, encouraging joint ventures and providing technical and managerial advice; Chair. RENOS SOLOMIDES; Gen. Man. JOHN G. JOANNIDES; 1 br.

Savings Bank

Yialousa Savings Bank Ltd: POB 8510, Santarosa St, Nicosia; tel. (02) 472972; f. 1908 (closed 1974, reopened 1990); provides loan facilities and other banking services; cap. p.u. 1.1m.; Exec. Chair. R. SOLOMIDES; Gen. Man. D. MESSIOS.

Foreign Banks

Arab Bank Ltd: POB 5700, 28 Santarosa St, Nicosia; tel. (02) 457111; telex 5717; f. 1983; commercial; Area Exec. C. C. STEPHANI; 14 brs.

Barclays Bank PLC: POB 2081, Nicosia; tel. (02) 461861; telex 3400; fax (02) 461734; f. 1937; Local Dir M. J. SHADRACH; Chief Man. D. VASSILIOU; 41 brs.

National Bank of Greece SA: POB 1191, 36 Archbishop Makarios III Ave, Nicosia; tel. (02) 441412; telex 2445; f. 1907; Regional Man. N. TRIVOUREAS; 20 brs.

Türkiye Cumhuriyeti Halk Bankası AŞ: Osman Paşa Cad., Ümit Office, Nicosia, Mersin 10, Turkey; tel. (020) 72145; telex 57241.

Türkiye Cumhuriyeti Ziraat Bankası: İplik Pazarı, Dr Şemsi Kazim Pasajı, Bitişiği, Nicosia, Mersin 10, Turkey; tel. (020) 72050; telex 57110.

Türkiye İş Bankası AŞ: 9 Girne Cad., Nicosia, Mersin 10, Turkey; tel. (020) 71133; telex 57123; f. 1924; Man. BÜLENT NIŞANCIOĞLU.

Offshore Banking Units

Cyprus-based Offshore Banking Units (OBUs) are fully-staffed units which conduct all forms of banking business from within Cyprus with other offshore or foreign entities and non-resident persons. (OBUs are not permitted to accept deposits from persons of Cypriot origin who have emigrated to the United Kingdom and taken up permanent residence there.) Although exempt from most of the restrictions and regulatory measures applicable to onshore banks, OBUs are subject to supervision and inspection by the Central Bank of Cyprus. OBUs may conduct business with onshore and domestic banks in all banking matters which the latter are allowed to undertake with banks abroad. OBUs are permitted to grant loans or guarantees in foreign currencies to residents of Cyprus (conditional on obtaining an exchange control permit from the Central Bank of Cyprus). Interest and other income earned from transactions with residents is subject to the full rate of income tax (42.5%), but the Minister of Finance is empowered by law to exempt an OBU from the above tax liability if satisfied that a specific transaction substantially contributes towards the economic development of the Republic. In December 1990 there were 18 OBUs operating in Cyprus.

Allied Business Bank SAL: POB 4232, 3rd Floor, Flat 31, Lara Court, 276 Archbishop Makarios III Ave, Limassol; tel. (051) 363759; telex 6040; fax (051) 372711; Sr Man. SAMIR BADR.

Arab Jordan Investment Bank SA: POB 4384, Libra Tower, 23 Olympion St, Limassol; tel. (05) 351351; telex 4029; fax (05) 360151; f. 1989; dep. US $60m. (Dec. 1989); Man. F. ABULKHAIR.

Bank of Beirut and the Arab Countries SAL: POB 6201, Emelle Bldg, 1st Floor, 135 Archbishop Makarios III Ave, Limassol; tel. (03) 381290; telex 5444; Man. O. S. SAAB.

Bank of Credit and Commerce International SA: POB 1963, 256 Leontios I St, Limassol; tel. (05) 338336; telex 3702; fax (05) 335586; Local Man. A. Q. SIDDIQI.

Bank of Foreign Economic Affairs of the USSR (Vneshekonombank): POB 6868, Limassol; tel. (05) 342190; telex 4561; fax (05) 342192; Local Man. O. I. LAPUSHKIN.

Banque du Crédit Populaire SAL: POB 3493, P. Lordos Centre, Block C, Roundabout, Byron St, Limassol; tel. (05) 376433; telex 4424; fax (05) 376292; Local Man. A. GELLAD.

Banque Européenne pour le Moyen-Orient SA: POB 6232, Doma Court, 1st-2nd Floors, 227 Archbishop Makarios III Ave, Limassol; tel. (05) 368628; telex 5575; fax (05) 368611; Local Man. N. A. HCHAIME.

Banque Nationale de Paris 'Intercontinentale' SA: POB 4286, Steffel Court, 3 John F. Kennedy St, Limassol; tel. (05) 359533; telex 5519; fax (05) 376519; Local Man. G. RAFFAUD.

Banque SBA SA: POB 4405, Bacchus House, 241E Kanika Enaerios Complex, corner of 28th October St and Archbishop Makarios III Ave, Limassol; tel. (05) 368650; telex 3569; fax (05) 351643; Local Man. N. DAGISTANI.

Barclays Bank PLC: POB 2383, Barclays House, 2nd Floor, Dhigenis Akritas Ave, Nicosia; tel. (02) 464777; telex 5200; fax (02) 464233; Local Man. N. LANDON.

Beogradska Banka: POB 530, Ambrosia Bldg, 1st Floor, 92 Archbishop Makarios III Ave, Nicosia; tel. (02) 453493; telex 6413; fax (02) 453207; Man. B. VUCIC.

Byblos Bank SAL: POB 218, Loucaides Bldg, 1 Archbishop Kyprianou St/St Andrew St, Limassol; tel. (05) 341433; telex 5203; fax (05) 367139; Local Man. R. T. CHEMALY.

Crédit Libanais SAL (COBU): POB 3492, Chrysalia Court, 1st Floor, 206 Archbishop Makarios III Ave, Limassol; tel. (05) 376444; telex 4702; fax (05) 376807; Local Man. R. F. AWAD.

Federal Bank of the Middle East Ltd: POB 5566, Megaron Lavinia, Santa Rosa Ave and Mykinon St, Nicosia; tel. (02) 461619; telex 4677; fax (02) 461751; f. 1983; cap. US $25m. (1988); Deputy Chair. and Chief Exec. A. F. M. SAAB.

Générale de Crédit (Cyprus) Ltd: POB 8560, 7-9 Grivas Dhigenis Ave, Nicosia; tel. (02) 464885; telex 5342; fax (02) 464471; Gen. Man. ROY M. HUTTON.

Jordan National Bank SA: POB 3587, Limassol; tel. (05) 356669; telex 5471; fax (05) 356673; Local Man. G. AIN-MELK.

Lebanon and Gulf Bank SAL: POB 337, Akamia Court, 3rd Floor, corner of G. Afxentiou and Archbishop Makarios III Ave, Larnaca; tel. (04) 620500; telex 5779; fax (04) 620708; Man. MOUNIB M. HAMMOUD.

Wardley Cyprus Ltd: POB 5718, Laiki Tower, 3rd Floor, 11-13 Archbishop Makarios III Ave, Nicosia; tel. (02) 477515; telex 4980; fax (02) 464314; Man. Dir R. I. SHIPLEY.

INSURANCE

Office of the Superintendent of Insurance: Treasury Department, Ministry of Finance, Nicosia; tel. (02) 403256; telex 2366; f. 1969 to control insurance companies, insurance agents, brokers and agents for brokers in Cyprus.

Greek Cypriot Insurance Companies

Albedo Insurance Co Ltd: 4th Floor, Block 'B', Fortuna Bldg, 284 Archbishop Makarios III Ave, Limassol 225; tel. (05) 362818; telex 2948; f. 1986; Chair. and Gen. Man. COSTAS KOUTSOKOUMNIS.

Allied Assurance & Reinsurance Co Ltd: POB 5509, 12 Themistoklis Dervis St, Ivory Tower, Nicosia 136; tel. (02) 457311; telex 4265; f. 1982; offshore company operating outside Cyprus; Chair. RONALD J. CLELAND; Man. Dir EDOUARD PAPASIAN.

Apac Ltd: POB 5403, Apt 1, 5 Mourouzi St, Nicosia 133; tel. (02) 455186; telex 2766; f. 1983; captive offshore company operating outside Cyprus; Chair. KYPROS CHRYSOSTOMIDES; Principal Officer GEORGHIOS POYATZIS.

Asfalistiki Eteria I 'Kentriki' Ltd: POB 5131, Flat 201, 2nd Floor, Margarita House, 15 Themistoklis Dervis St, Nicosia 136; tel. (02) 473931; telex 4987; f. 1985; Chair. NESTOR KAKOYIANNIS; Principal Officer GEORGE GEORGALLIDES.

Atlantic Insurance Co Ltd: POB 4579, 34 Theophanis Theodotou St, Nicosia 136; tel. (02) 444052; telex 2535; f. 1983; Chair. and Man. Dir ZENIOS PYRISHIS; Gen. Man. N. MARATHOVOUNIOTIS.

Commercial Union Assurance (Cyprus) Ltd: POB 1312, Commercial Union House, 101 Archbishop Makarios Ave, Nicosia; tel. (02) 445045; telex 2547; fax (02) 459011; f. 1974; Chair. J. CHRISTOPHIDES; Gen. Man. CONSTANTINOS P. DEKATRIS.

Compass Insurance Co Ltd: POB 7501, 48 Kyriacos Matsis St, Engomi, Nicosia 161; tel. (02) 462492; telex 2270; fax (02) 461871; f. 1981; Chair. P. LOUCAIDES; Gen. Man. PHAEDON MAKRIS.

Cosmos (Cyprus) Insurance Co Ltd: POB 1770, 1st Floor, Flat 12, 6 Ayia Eleni St, Nicosia 135; tel. (02) 441235; telex 3433; fax (02) 457925; f. 1982; Chair. and Gen. Man. KYRIACOS M. TYLLIS.

Fli-Cy Life Insurance Ltd: POB 1612, Julia House, 3 Themistoklis Dervis St, Nicosia 136; tel. (02) 448278; telex 2863; f. 1986; captive offshore company operating outside Cyprus; Chair. and Gen. Man. KYPROS CHRYSOSTOMIDES.

General Insurance Co of Cyprus Ltd: POB 1668, 2-4 Themistoklis Dervis St, Nicosia; tel. (02) 450444; telex 2311; fax (02) 446682; f. 1951; Chair. A. PATSALIDES; Gen. Man. S. SOPHOCLEOUS.

Granite Insurance Co Ltd: POB 613, 2nd Floor, Block 'A', Fortuna Bldg, 284 Archbishop Makarios III Ave, Limassol 255; tel. (05) 362818; telex 2948; captive offshore company operating outside Cyprus; Chair. and Gen. Man. COSTAS KOUTSOKOUMNIS.

Greene Insurances Ltd: POB 132, 284 Archbishop Makarios III Ave, Fortuna Bldg, Block B, 2nd Floor, Limassol 255; tel. (05) 362424; telex 2566; f. 1987; Chair. GEORGHIOS CHRISTODOULOU; Principal Officer JOSIF CHRISTOU.

Hermes Insurance Co Ltd: POB 4828, 1st Floor, Office 101-103, Anemomylos Bldg, 8 Michalakis Karaolis St, Nicosia; tel. (02) 448130; telex 3466; fax (02) 461888; f. 1980; Chair. and Man. Dir P. VOGAZIANOS.

Iris Insurance Co Ltd: POB 4841, Flat H1, 8th Floor, 'Aspelia' Bldg, 20 Costis Palamas St, Nicosia 136; tel. (02) 448302; telex 3675; Chair. and Gen. Man. PAVLOS CL. GEORGHIOU.

Juniper Insurance Ltd: POB 1121, 'Stasinos' Bldg, 2 Ayias Elenis St, Nicosia 135; tel. (02) 448700; telex 2973; captive offshore company operating outside Cyprus; Chair. YUEN HONG WONG; Gen. Man. STALO ANDREOU.

Laiki Insurance Co Ltd: POB 2069, Laiki Tower, 11-39 Archbishop Makarios III Ave, Nicosia 136; tel. (02) 449900; telex 5916; f. 1981; Chair. E. K. LANITIS; Man. Y. E. SOLOMONIDES.

L.U. Lifestyle Underwriters Ltd: POB 1612, 3 Themistoklis Dervis St, Julia House, Nicosia 136; tel. (02) 453053; telex 2046; f. 1984; Chair. LELLOS DEMETRIADES; Principal Officer NIKOS AVRAAMIDES.

Merehurst (Europe) Ltd: POB 3585, Julia House, 3 Themistoklis Dervis St, Nicosia 136; tel. (02) 453053; telex 2046; f. 1985; captive offshore company operating outside Cyprus; Chair. L. DEMETRIADES; Principal Officer N. AVRAAMIDES.

Minerva Insurance Co Ltd: POB 3554, 8 Epaminondas St, Nicosia 137; tel. (02) 445134; telex 2608; fax (02) 455528; f. 1970; Chair. and Gen. Man. K. KOUTSOKOUMNIS.

North Global Insurance and Reinsurance Co Ltd: POB 1553, Apt 21, 2nd Floor, Block 'B', Fortuna Bldg, 284 Archbishop Makarios III Ave, Limassol 255; tel. (05) 362424; telex 2566; f. 1984; offshore company operating outside Cyprus; Chair. JAMIL BIN NASSER; Principal Officer CHRIS GEORGHIADES.

Pacmag Insurance Ltd: POB 1121, Stasinos Bldg, 2 Ayias Elenis St, Nicosia 135; tel. (02) 448700; telex 2973; f. 1986; captive offshore company operating outside Cyprus; Chair. YUEN HONG WONG; Gen. Man. STALO ANDREOU.

Paneuropean Insurance Co Ltd: POB 553, 3rd, 4th and 5th Floor, 88 Archbishop Makarios III Ave, Nicosia 137; tel. (02) 449960; telex 3419; fax (02) 473396; f. 1980; Chair. N. K. SHACOLAS; Gen. Man. ZENIOS DEMETRIOU.

Philiki Insurance Co Ltd: POB 2274, 1st Floor, 2 Demokritos Bldg, Corner Archbishop Makarios III Ave and J. Clerides St, Nicosia; tel. (02) 444433; telex 2353; f. 1982; Chair. LOUKIS PETRIDES; Gen. Man. DOROS ORPHANIDES.

Sage Insurance Ltd: POB 1121, Stasinos Bldg, 2 Ayias Elenis St, Nicosia 135; tel. (02) 448700; telex 2973; captive offshore company operating outside Cyprus; Chair. YUEN HONG WONG; Principal Officer STALO PAPAIOANNOU.

CYPRUS   *Directory*

Saudi Stars Insurance Co Ltd: POB 1493, No. 2, Corner Archbishop Makarios III Ave and Methonis St, Nicosia; tel. (02) 445874; telex 3156; f. 1979; offshore company operating outside Cyprus; Chair. M. F. AL-HAJRI; Principal Officer PAN. MEGALEMOS.

Saviour Insurance Co Ltd: POB 3957, 8 Michalakis Karaolis St, Anemomylos Bldg, Suite 104, Nicosia 162; tel. (02) 365085; telex 4351; fax (02) 445577; f. 1987; Chair. ROBERT SINCLAIR; Principal Officer KONSTANTINOS KITTIS.

Seven Stars Insurance Co Ltd: 11A Rega Fereou St, Limassol 251; tel. (05) 3445045; telex 2547; f. 1983; offshore company operating outside Cyprus; Chair. KYPROS CHRYSOSTOMIDES.

Universal Life Insurance Company Ltd: POB 1270, Universal Tower, 85 Dhigenis Akritas Ave, Nicosia 135; tel. (02) 461222; telex 3116; fax (02) 461343; f. 1970; Chair. J. CHRISTOPHIDES; Gen. Man. ANDREAS GEORGHIOU.

Warwick Insurance Co Ltd: POB 1612, 3 Themistoklis Dervis St, Julia House, Nicosia 136; tel. (02) 453053; telex 2046; fax (02) 475446; f. 1987; Chair. CHARLES ZAVALLIS.

WOB Insurances Ltd: 2nd Floor, Block 'A', Fortuna Bldg, 284 Archbishop Makarios III Ave, Limassol 255; tel. (05) 362818; telex 2948; captive offshore company operating outside Cyprus; Chair. and Gen. Man. KOSTAS KOUTSOKOUMNIS.

Turkish Cypriot Insurance Companies

Ak Sigorta: Türk Bankası Ltd, 92 Girne Cad., Nicosia.

As-Can Ltd: Hasan Nihat, Apt Kat 1, Daire 5, Nicosia, Mersin 10, Turkey; tel. (520) 76444.

Atlantic Sigorta: Abdi Çaruş Sok., Bahire Küçük Apt, Nicosia, Mersin 10, Turkey; tel. (520) 71667.

Genel Sigorta: 11 Cumhuriyet Sok., Nicosia, Mersin 10, Turkey; tel. (520) 72658.

Güneş Sigorta: 42–46 Girne Cad., Nicosia, Mersin 10, Turkey; tel. (520) 71132; telex 57139.

Halk Sigorta: Memduh Asaf Sok., Nicosia, Mersin 10, Turkey.

Sark Sigorta: 13A Türk Bankası Sok., Nicosia; tel. (520) 73150.

Şeker Sigorta: POB 823, K.T. Kooperatif Merkez Bankası, 49-55 Mahmut Paşa Sok., Nicosia, Mersin 10, Turkey; tel. (520) 71207; telex 57216.

Tam Sigorta: Vakıflar Bankası Ltd, Nicosia, Mersin 10, Turkey.

There were 33 foreign insurance companies operating in Cyprus in 1987.

Trade and Industry

GREEK CYPRIOT CHAMBERS OF COMMERCE AND INDUSTRY

Cyprus Chamber of Commerce and Industry: POB 1455, 38 Grivas Dhigenis Ave, Nicosia; tel. (02) 449500; telex 2077; fax (02) 449048; Pres. PHANOS EPIPHANIOU; Sec.-Gen. PANAYIOTIS LOIZIDES; 5,000 mems, 64 affiliated trade assocns.

Famagusta Chamber of Commerce and Industry: POB 3124, 339 St Andrews St, Andrea Chambers, 2nd Floor, Office No 201–202, Limassol; tel. (05) 370165; telex 4519; fax (05) 370291; f. 1952; Pres. T. KYRIAKIDES; Vice-Pres. P. PAPATHOMAS, A. MATSIS; 330 mems.

Larnaca Chamber of Commerce and Industry: POB 287, 12 Gregoris Afxentiou St, Apt 43, 4th Floor, Skouros Bldg, Larnaca; tel. (04) 655051; telex 3187; fax (04) 628281; Pres. ANDREAS MOUSKOS; Vice-Pres. K. LEFKARITIS; 400 mems.

Limassol Chamber of Commerce and Industry: POB 347, 25 Spyrou Araouzou St, Veregaria Bldg, 3rd Floor, Limassol; tel. (05) 362556; telex 2890; fax (05) 371655; Pres. CHRISTAKIS GEORGIADES; Vice-Pres. NICOS ROSSOS; 550 mems.

Nicosia Chamber of Commerce and Industry: POB 1455, 38 Grivas Dhigenis Ave, Nicosia; tel. (02) 456859; telex 2077; fax (02) 367483; Pres. COSTAS CONSTANTINIDES; 1,200 mems.

Paphos Chamber of Commerce and Industry: POB 62, Grivas Dhigenis Ave, Demetra Court, Paphos; tel. (06) 235115; telex 2888; fax (06) 244602; Pres. ANDREAS DEMETRIADES; 400 mems.

TURKISH CYPRIOT CHAMBERS OF COMMERCE AND INDUSTRY

Turkish Chamber of Industry: Müftü Raci St, Ontaş İş Hanı B24, Nicosia, Mersin 10, Turkey; tel. (020) 74607; Pres. VEDAT ÇELIK.

Turkish Cypriot Chamber of Commerce: POB 718, Bedreddin Demirel Cad., Nicosia, Mersin 10, Turkey; tel. (020) 83645; telex 57511; f. 1958; more than 5,000 regd mems; Chair. HAMZA ARMAN; Sec.-Gen. JANEL BURCAN.

EMPLOYERS' ORGANIZATIONS

Greek Cypriot Employers' Organizations

At 31 December 1980 there were 28 employers' associations, including 14 independent associations, with a total membership of 4,115.

Cyprus Employers' & Industrialists' Federation: POB 1657, 30 Grivas Dhigenis Ave, Nicosia; tel. (02) 445102; telex 4834; fax (02) 459459; f. 1960; 26 member trade associations, 400 direct and 1,600 indirect members; Dir-Gen. ANT. PIERIDES; Chair. PHAEDROS ECONOMIDES. The largest of the trade association members are: Cyprus Building Contractors' Association; Cyprus Hotel Keepers' Association; Clothing Manufacturers' Association; Cyprus Shipping Association; Shoe Makers' Association; Cyprus Metal Industries Association; Cyprus Bankers Employers' Association; Motor Cars, Tractors & Agricultural Machinery Importers' Association.

Turkish Cypriot Employers' Organizations

Kıbrıs Türk İşverenler Sendikası (Turkish Cypriot Employers Association): POB 674, Nicosia, Mersin 10, Turkey; tel. (020) 76173; Chair. ALPAY ALI RIZA GÖRGÜNER.

TRADE UNIONS

At 31 December 1980 there were 97 trade unions with 240 branches, six union federations and five confederations.

Greek Cypriot Trade Unions

Demokratiki Ergatiki Omospondia Kyprou (Democratic Labour Federation of Cyprus): POB 1625, 40 Byron Ave, Nicosia; tel. (02) 456506; fax (02) 449494; f. 1962; 4 unions with a total membership of 4,407; Gen. Sec. RENOS PRENTZAS.

Pankypria Ergatiki Omospondia—PEO (Pancyprian Federation of Labour): POB 1885, 31-35 Archermos St, Nicosia; tel. (02) 473192; fax (02) 443382; f. 1946, registered 1947; previously the Pancyprian Trade Union Committee f. 1941, dissolved 1946; 10 unions and 176 brs with a total membership of 75,000; affiliated to the World Federation of Trade Unions; Gen. Sec. AVRAAM ANTONIOU.

Pankyprios Omospondia Anexartiton Syntechnion (Pancyprian Federation of Independent Trade Unions): 1 Menadrou St, Nicosia; tel. (02) 442233; f. 1956, registered 1957; has no political orientations; 8 unions with a total membership of 798; Pres. KOSTAS ANTONIADES; Gen. Sec. KYRIACOS NATHANAEL.

Synomospondia Ergaton Kyprou (Cyprus Workers' Confederation): POB 5018, 23 Alkaiou St, Engomi, Nicosia; tel. (02) 441142; telex 6180; fax (02) 476360; f. 1944, registered 1950; 7 Federations, 5 Labour Centres, 47 unions, 12 brs with a total membership of 51,581; affiliated to the ICFTU and the ETUC; Gen. Sec. MICHAEL IOANNOU; Deputy Gen. Sec. DEMETRIS KITTENIS.

Cyprus Civil Servants' Trade Union: 2 Andreas Demetriou St, Nicosia; tel. (02) 442278; f. 1949, registered 1966; restricted to persons in the civil employment of the government and public authorities; 6 brs with a total membership of 13,030; Pres. A. PAPANASTASSIOU; Gen. Sec. G. IAKOVOU.

Union of Cyprus Journalists: c/o Andreas Kannaouros, Embros newspaper, POB 3739, 19 Nikitara St, Nicosia; tel. (02) 428844; Chair. ANDREAS KANNAOUROS.

Turkish Cypriot Trade Unions

In 1986 trade union membership totalled 20,627.

Devrimci İşçi Sendikaları Federasyonu (Dev-İş) (Revolutionary Trade Unions' Federation): 30 Beliğ Paşa Sok., Nicosia, Mersin 10, Turkey; tel. (020) 72640; f. 1976; two unions with a total membership of 4,586 (1986); affiliated to WFTU; Pres. HASAN SARICA; Gen.-Sec. BAYRAM ÇELIK.

Kıbrıs Türk İşçi Sendikaları Federasyonu (TÜRK-SEN) (Turkish Cypriot Trade Union Federation): POB 829, 7-7A Şehit Mehmet R. Hüseyin Sok., Nicosia, Mersin 10, Turkey; tel. (020) 72444; f. 1954, regd 1955; 15 unions with a total membership of 9,307 (1986); affiliated to ICFTU, ETUC, CTUC and the Confederation of Trade Unions of Turkey (Türk-İş); Pres. HÜSEYIN CURCIOĞLU; Gen. Sec. (vacant).

TRADE FAIRS

Cyprus International (State) Fair: POB 3551, Nicosia; tel. (02) 352918; telex 3344; fax (02) 352316; 16th Fair scheduled for 23 May–2 June 1991.

Transport

There are no railways in Cyprus.

ROADS

In December 1989 there were 9,830 km of roads in the government-controlled areas, of which 5,240 km were paved and 4,590 km were earth or gravel roads. The Nicosia–Limassol four-lane dual carriageway, which was completed in 1985, was subsequently extended further west with the completion of a new Limassol bypass, and a section of the link from the Nicosia–Limassol highway to Larnaca was opened in mid-1989. The north and south are now served by separate transport systems, and there are no services linking the two sectors. In 1984 the road network in the Turkish Cypriot area consisted of about 5,278 km of paved and 838 km of unpaved roads. Between 1988 and 1990 some 250 km of new highways were constructed in the area.

SHIPPING

Until 1974 Famagusta was the island's most important harbour, handling about 83% of the country's cargo. Famagusta is a natural port capable of receiving ships of a maximum draught of 9.2 m. Since its capture by the Turkish army in August 1974 the port has been officially declared closed to international traffic. However, it continues to serve the Turkish-occupied region.

The main ports which serve the island's maritime trade at present are Larnaca and Limassol, which were constructed in 1973 and 1974 respectively. Both ports have been expanded: the quay of Limassol port is 1,280 m long and 11 m deep, while the port of Larnaca has a quay length of 866 m and a depth of 10 m. There is also an industrial port at Vassiliko, with a quay 555 m long and 9 m deep, and there are three specialized petroleum terminals, at Larnaca, Dhekelia and Moni. There are plans to upgrade the facilities of Larnaca and Limassol by 1993.

In 1989 5,674 vessels, with a total net registered tonnage of 14,732,000, visited Cyprus, carrying 7,348,000 metric tons of cargo to and from Cyprus. In addition to serving local traffic, Limassol and Larnaca ports act as cargo distribution and consolidation centres for the Mediterranean area and as regional warehouse and assembly bases for the Middle East and the Persian (Arabian) Gulf. Containerized cargo in transit amounted to 2,772,000 tons in 1989.

Both Kyrenia and Karavostassi are under Turkish occupation and have been declared closed to international traffic. Karavostassi used to be the country's major mineral port, dealing with 76% of the total mineral exports. However, since the war minerals have been passed through Vassiliko and Limni, which are open road-steads. A hydrofoil service operates between Kyrenia and Mersin on the Turkish mainland. Car ferries sail from Kyrenia to Taşucu and Mersin, in Turkey.

The total number of merchant vessels registered in Cyprus on 31 March 1990 was 1,954 (with a total displacement of 18,314,699 grt).

Cyprus Ports Authority: POB 2007, Nicosia; tel. (02) 450100; telex 2833; fax (02) 365420; f. 1973; Chair. ANDREAS POUYIOUROS; Gen. Man. JOSEPH BAYADA.

Greek Cypriot Shipping Companies

Brasal Offshore Marine Services Ltd: POB 5595, Limassol; tel. (05) 373086; fax (05) 343915; salvage craft, survey launch, suction dredger, offshore supply vessel/tug; Man. Dir E. G. BRANCO.

Columbia Shipmanagement Ltd: POB 1624, Columbia House, Dodekanison St, Limassol; tel. (05) 320900; telex 3206; fax (05) 320009; f. 1978; 149 ships; (full and part management); Chair H. SCHOELLEP, Man. Dir D. FRY.

A. Elias (Overseas) Co Ltd: POB 1165, 3rd Floor, Fairway Court, 104 Archbishop Makarios III Ave, Limassol; tel. (05) 338025; telex 2108; fax (05) 367025; two cargo ships; Chair. A. ELIAS; Man. Dir Capt. JOACHIM MEYER.

Hanseatic Shipping Co Ltd: 111 Spyrou Araouzou Ave, Limassol; fax (05) 142926; f. 1972; 95 ships; Chair. Capt. JOACHIM MEYER; Dep. Man. Dir Capt. B. BEHRENS.

Interorient Navigation Co Ltd: POB 1309, 5th Floor, Meliza Court, 229 Archbishop Makarios III Ave, Limassol; tel. (05) 352047; telex 3142; fax (05) 352914; Man. Dir Capt. LISSOW.

Lefkaritis Bros Marine Ltd: POB 162, Lefkaritis Bldg, 1 Kilkis St, Larnaca; tel. (041) 52142; telex 2224; f. 1974; three tankers; Chair. and Man. Dir TAKIS C. LEFKARITIS.

Marlow Navigation Co Ltd: POB 4077, Fortuna Court, Block B, 224 Archbishop Makarios III Ave, Limassol; tel. (05) 367029; telex 2019; fax (05) 369623; Man. Dir H. EDEN.

Navigo Management Co: POB 3087, 111 Spyrou Araouzou Ave, Limassol; tel. (05) 342922; telex 5415; fax (05) 342289; Gen. Man. Capt. L. NEUDAUER.

Oldendorff Ltd, Reederei Nord Klaus E: POB 6345, Libra Tower, Olympion St, Limassol; tel. (05) 370262; telex 5938; fax (05) 370263; Chair. and Man. Dir KLAUS E. OLDENDORFF; 16 vessels.

Seatankers Management Co Ltd: POB 3562, Flat 411, Deana Beach Apartments, Promahon Eleftherias St, Limassol; tel. (05) 326111; telex 5606; fax (05) 323770; 13 vessels.

T. Solomonides and Son Ltd: POB 259, 1 Irinis St, Limassol; tel. (05) 357000; telex 2213; fax (05) 357005; f. 1945; Man. Dir TAKIS SOLOMONIDES.

Transmed Shipping Ltd: 20 Ifgenias St, Limassol; Man. Dir S. PAPANTONIOU; 5 vessels.

Uniteam Marine Ltd: POB 4086, Fortuna Court, 284–286 Archbishop Makarios III Ave, Limassol; tel. (05) 353832; telex 2848; fax (05) 341706; Man. Dir G. RUETHER.

Turkish Cypriot Shipping Companies

Fama Shipping Ltd: Onar İş Hanı, Mahkemeler Önü, Nicosia, Mersin 10, Turkey; tel. (520) 72323; telex 57249.

Fergun Maritime Co: Kyrenia (Girne), Mersin 10, Turkey; ferries to Turkish ports; Owner FEHIM KUÇUK.

Kıbrıs Türk Denizcilik Ltd, Şti (Turkish Cypriot Maritime Co Ltd): Girne Cad., Adem Kaner İş Hanı, Nicosia, Mersin 10, Turkey.

Orion Navigation Ltd: Seagate Court, Famagusta, Mersin 10, Turkey; tel. (536) 62006; telex 57228; fax (036) 67093; f. 1976; shipping agents; Dir O. LAMA; Shipping Man. L. LAMA.

Savarona Maritime Ltd: 8 Bekiroğlu İş Hanı, Müftü Ziya Efendi Sok., Nicosia, Mersin 10, Turkey; tel. (520) 75179; telex 57246.

CIVIL AVIATION

There is an international airport at Nicosia, which can accommodate all types of aircraft, including jets. It has been closed since July 1974 following the Turkish invasion. A new international airport was constructed at Larnaca, from which flights operate to Europe, the Middle East and the Gulf. Another international airport at Paphos began operations in November 1983.

In 1975 the Turkish authorities opened Ercan (formerly Tymbou) airport, and a second airport was opened at Geçitkale (Lefkoniko) in 1986.

Cyprus Airways: POB 1903, 21 Alkeou St, Engomi, Nicosia; tel. (02) 443054; telex 2225; fax (02) 443167; f. 1947; jointly owned by Cyprus Government and local interests; wholly-owned charter subsidiary Cyprair Tours Ltd; Chair. and Man. Dir K. LAZARIDES; services to Amman (suspended), Amsterdam, Athens, Bahrain, Birmingham, Cairo, Damascus, Dubai, Frankfurt, Geneva, Jeddah, Kuwait, London, Manchester, Munich, Paris, Riyadh, Salonica, Tel-Aviv, Toulouse, Vienna and Zürich from Larnaca and Paphos Airports; fleet of 4 Airbus A310-200, 8 Airbus A320, 1 BAC 1-11-500 and 1 Boeing 707-120B.

Kıbrıs Türk Hava Yolları (Turkish Cypriot Airlines): Bedreddin Demirel Ave, Yenişehir-Lelkose, Nicosia, Mersin 10, Turkey; tel. (520) 71901; telex 57133; f. 1974; jointly owned by the Turkish Cypriot Community Assembly Consolidated Improvement Fund and Turkish Airlines Ltd.; Gen. Man. (vacant); routes from Ercan Airport, Nicosia, to Ankara, Adana, Antalya, İstanbul, İzmir, Munich and London; fleet of 1 Boeing 727-200, 1 DC9-30, 1 DC10 and 1 A310.

Noble Air: Muzaffer Paşa Cad., M. Hacı Ali Apt 50–56, Nicosia, Mersin 10, Turkey; tel. (520) 83719; fax (520) 83719; charter services to and from Turkey; Dir TURAN GÜÇLÜ.

Tourism

In 1988 there were 1,111,818 foreign visitors to the Greek Cypriot area, and in 1989 there were 1,377,636 visitors. Receipts from tourism totalled C£386m. in 1988, increasing to C£485m. in 1989. The number of visitors to the Turkish Cypriot area reached 184,337 in 1987, when revenue totalled US $56.1m., 230,000 in 1988 and 342,656 in 1989 (when revenue amounted to $130m.).

Cyprus Tourism Organization: POB 4535, Zena Bldg, 18 Th. Theodotou St, Nicosia; tel. (02) 443374; telex 2165; fax (02) 366744; Chair. ANDREAS GEORGIOU; Dir-Gen. FRYNI MICHAEL.

Cyprus Turkish Tourist Enterprises, Ltd (CTTE): Kyrenia, Mersin 10, Turkey; tel. (581) 52165; telex 57128; fax (581) 52073; f. 1974; Chair. HUSREV CAGIN.

CZECHOSLOVAKIA

Introductory Survey

Location, Climate, Language, Religion, Flag, Capital

The Czech and Slovak Federative Republic (formerly the Czechoslovak Socialist Republic) lies in central Europe. Its neighbours are Poland to the north, Germany to the northwest and west, Austria to the south-west, Hungary to the south-east and the USSR to the extreme east. The state is composed of two main population groups, the Czechs (62.7% of the total population in 1989) and the Slovaks (32.0%). The climate is continental, with warm summers and cold winters. The average mean temperature is 9°C (49°F). The official languages, which are mutually understandable, are Czech and Slovak, members of the west Slavonic group. There is a Hungarian-speaking minority, resident mainly in Slovakia, numbering about 600,000 people, and also a Romany community of an estimated 400,000 people. Most of the country's inhabitants profess Christianity: about 70% are Roman Catholics, and 15% Protestants. The national flag (proportions 3 by 2) has two equal horizontal stripes, of white and red, on which is superimposed a blue triangle (half the length) at the hoist. The capital is Prague (Praha).

Recent History

At the end of the First World War, in 1918, the Austro-Hungarian Empire was dissolved, and its former western Slavonic provinces became Czechoslovakia. The boundaries of the new republic, fixed by treaty in 1919, included the Sudetenland, an area in northern Bohemia that was inhabited by about 3m. German-speaking people. After the Nazis, led by Adolf Hitler, came to power in Germany in 1933, there was increased agitation in the Sudetenland for autonomy within, and later secession from, Czechoslovakia. In 1938, to appease German demands, the British, French and Italian Prime Ministers concluded an agreement with Hitler, whereby the Sudetenland was ceded to Germany, while other parts of Czechoslovakia were transferred to Hungary and Poland. The remainder of Czechoslovakia was invaded and occupied by Nazi Germany in March 1939.

After Germany's defeat in the Second World War (1939–45), the pre-1938 frontiers of Czechoslovakia were restored, although a small area in the east was ceded to the USSR in June 1945. Almost all of the German-speaking inhabitants of Czechoslovakia were expelled, and the Sudetenland was settled by Czechs from other parts of Bohemia. At elections in 1946 the Communists emerged as the leading party, winning 38% of the votes. The Communist Party's leader, Klement Gottwald, became Prime Minister in a coalition government. After Ministers of other parties resigned, Communist control became complete on 25 February 1948. A People's Republic was established on 9 June 1948. Gottwald replaced Edvard Beneš as President, a position that he held until his death in 1953. The country aligned itself with the Soviet-led East European bloc, joining the Council for Mutual Economic Assistance (CMEA) and the Warsaw Pact (see pp. 125 and 211 respectively).

Under Gottwald, government followed a rigid Stalinist pattern, and in the early 1950s there were many political trials. Although these ended under Gottwald's successors, Antonín Zápotocký and, from 1956, Antonín Novotný, 'de-Stalinization' was late in coming to Czechoslovakia, and there was no relaxation until 1963, when a new government, with Jozef Lenárt (hitherto President of the Slovak National Council) as Prime Minister, was formed. Meanwhile, the country was renamed the Czechoslovak Socialist Republic, under a new constitution, proclaimed in July 1960.

In January 1968 Alexander Dubček succeeded Novotný as Party Secretary, and in March Gen. Ludvík Svoboda succeeded him as President. Oldřich Černík became Prime Minister in April 1968. The policies of the new Government were more independent and liberal, and envisaged widespread reforms. These were seen by other members of the East European bloc as endangering their unity, and in August 1968 Warsaw Pact forces (numbering an estimated 600,000 men) invaded Czechoslovakia, occupying Prague and other major cities. Mass demonstrations in protest at the invasion were held throughout the country, and many people were killed in clashes with occupation troops. The Soviet Government exerted heavy pressure on Czechoslovak leaders to suppress their reformist policies, and in April 1969 Dubček was replaced by Dr Gustáv Husák as First (subsequently General) Secretary of the Central Committee of the Communist Party. Although Dr Husák resisted some pressure for stricter control and political trials, there was a severe purge of Communist Party membership, and most of Dubček's supporters were removed from the Government. The first legislative elections since 1964 were held in November 1971 and showed a 99.81% vote in favour of candidates of the National Front (the communist-dominated organization embracing all the legal political parties in Czechoslovakia).

In May 1975 Dr Husák was appointed President of the Republic while still holding the positions of Chairman of the National Front and General Secretary of the Communist Party. Dr Husák was re-elected to the latter post in April 1976, in April 1981 and again in March 1986. He was re-elected President in May 1980 and May 1985. In April 1987 Mikhail Gorbachev, General Secretary of the Soviet Communist Party, paid a three-day visit, which was interpreted by some observers as an attempt to persuade the Czechoslovak Government to pursue Soviet-style political and economic reform. Disappointing results in industry fuelled speculation that a restructuring of the system of economic management was imminent, and Dr Husák duly announced a limited plan for economic reform, which he likened to that initiated by the Dubček Government in 1968.

In December 1987 Dr Husák resigned as General Secretary of the Communist Party and was replaced by Miloš Jakeš, an economist and member of the Presidium of the Party's Central Committee. However, it was announced that Dr Husák would retain the largely ceremonial post of President of the Republic. Jakeš affirmed his commitment to the moderate programme of reform, initiated by his predecessor, but in his first year of office there was little indication of a policy more liberal than that of Dr Husák, as repressive measures towards the Roman Catholic Church and dissidents continued. A new programme of economic restructuring (přestavba) was, however, instigated by Jakeš.

A major government reshuffle was implemented in April 1988 (the first in two decades), and further government changes followed in October. Lubomír Štrougal, widely regarded as an advocate of reform, resigned as Federal Prime Minister and was replaced by Ladislav Adamec, hitherto Prime Minister of the Czech State Government. During 1988 numerous changes were also made in the Communist Party leadership. An extensive reorganization of the Presidium of the Central Committee was carried out. In February Jakeš replaced Dr Husák as Chairman of the National Front.

Meanwhile, in January 1977 a manifesto known as Charter 77, protesting against the absence of civil rights in Czechoslovakia, was published in the West. Many of the hundreds of Czechoslovak intellectuals and former politicians who signed the Charter were arrested, tried on various charges and imprisoned, but, despite attempts by the Government to suppress the activists, the civil rights campaign continued. By 1985 the movement's field of comment had broadened, and in that year spokesmen for the signatories issued appeals for the dissolution of NATO and the Warsaw Pact alliance and for the withdrawal of Soviet troops and nuclear weapons from Czechoslovakia. In August 1987 representatives of Charter 77 met members of Solidarity, the Polish trade union. On the 20th anniversary of the Warsaw Pact intervention in Czechoslovakia, in August 1988, about 10,000 people demonstrated in Prague against the Government. On 28 October (the 70th anniversary of the republic's independence) several thousand Czechoslovaks held demonstrations in Prague, Brno and Bratislava, in support of demands for political reform. Large numbers were arrested, including leading human rights activists and Charter 77 members. In December the first officially-authorized human rights

CZECHOSLOVAKIA

Introductory Survey

demonstration for 20 years was held in Prague. In January 1989 demonstrations in Prague to commemorate the 20th anniversary of the suicide of a student, Jan Palach, in protest at the invasion of Czechoslovakia by Warsaw Pact forces, were violently suppressed by riot police. In the following month the playwright Václav Havel, a leading figure in the opposition movement, was sentenced to nine months in prison for his part in the demonstrations. (He was released in May, following international condemnation of his imprisonment and of Czechoslovakia's poor human rights record.) Anti-Government demonstrations followed in May, August and October 1989.

In November 1989 a process of dramatic political change began in Czechoslovakia, largely precipitated by the decline of Communist power and the trend towards greater democracy in other Eastern European countries in the late 1980s. On 17 November some 50,000 people, mainly students, participated in a peaceful anti-Government demonstration in Prague, the largest public protest for 20 years. The demonstration was violently dispersed by the police, and more than 500 people were injured. Following rumours (which later proved to be unfounded) that a student had been killed, a series of demonstrations of escalating size, involving tens of thousands of people, took place. Students in Prague established a strike committee to publicize the recent events and to attract the support of broader strata of Czechoslovak society, in particular industrial workers. The continuing daily demonstrations, which were not opposed by the police, culminated in gatherings of as many as 500,000 people in Prague, while large-scale demonstrations took place in other towns throughout the country.

A new opposition group, Civic Forum, advocating a return to democracy in Czechoslovakia, was established in November 1989 as an informal grouping embracing several existing opposition and human rights organizations, including Charter 77, the Czechoslovak Helsinki Committee and the Independent Students' Organization. Civic Forum rapidly gained widespread popular support. It was also supported by the Czechoslovak Socialist Party (CSP) and the Czechoslovak People's Party (CPP), minor parties in the communist-dominated National Front, which were openly critical of the Government for its use of violence against peaceful demonstrators. Meanwhile, Alexander Dubček, the former Secretary of the Communist Party (who had been deposed after the Warsaw Pact intervention in 1968), addressed mass rallies in Bratislava and Prague, expressing his support for the opposition's demands for reform. On 24 November 1989 it was announced that Jakeš and the entire membership of the Presidium of the Central Committee had resigned. Karel Urbánek, a member of the Presidium and formerly Chairman of the Communist Party in the Czech Republic, replaced Jakeš as General Secretary of the Party, and a new Presidium was elected. The Presidium was denounced, however, by Civic Forum, as it included no apparent reformist figures, and comprised largely members of the previous Presidium.

Discussions were initiated between representatives of Civic Forum and the Prime Minister, Ladislav Adamec. Among the demands made by the opposition were the establishment of an inquiry into the police brutality against demonstrators on 17 November 1989, the ending of censorship, and the release of all political prisoners. It was later announced that the laws on censorship had been revoked, and that all political prisoners had been released. In late November millions of Czechoslovaks took part in a two-hour general strike, organized by Civic Forum as an 'informal referendum' on one-party rule. Shortly afterwards, Civic Forum was accorded official recognition by the Government. In a further development, the Federal Assembly voted unanimously to delete from the Constitution the articles guaranteeing the Communist Party's leading role in society as well as in the National Front. The Assembly also voted to delete the clause stating that education in Czechoslovakia should be based on Marxist-Leninist principles. In early December it was announced that Czechoslovakia would dismantle sections of the 'iron curtain' along its borders with Austria and the Federal Republic of Germany, and that Czechoslovaks would no longer require exit visas for foreign travel. A parliamentary commission was established to investigate the police brutality in November (in mid-1990 six police officers were found guilty and sentenced to varying terms of imprisonment). Also, in early December, the Communist Party condemned the invasion of Czechoslovakia by Warsaw Pact forces in 1968 as 'unjustified and mistaken', and a special commission was established to re-evaluate the reforms that had been implemented under Dubček's leadership and to investigate the circumstances under which the invasion took place. Shortly afterwards, the Governments of the five countries that had invaded Czechoslovakia (the USSR, Bulgaria, Hungary, the German Democratic Republic and Poland) issued a joint statement condemning their action.

In early December 1989 a reshuffle of the Federal Government took place. Civic Forum and its Slovak counterpart, Public Against Violence (PAV), denounced the new Government, as the majority of its ministers had been members of the previous administration, and it included only five non-Communists. An estimated 200,000 people demonstrated in Prague to demand greater representation in the Government by opposition figures. Adamec subsequently resigned as Prime Minister, and was replaced by Marián Čalfa, the newly-appointed First Deputy Prime Minister. In the following week a new, interim Federal Government was formed, with a majority of non-Communist members, including seven non-party supporters of Civic Forum. The Czech and Slovak State Governments were also reorganized to include a substantial representation by non-Communist ministers. Gustáv Husák resigned as President of the Republic and, at the end of December, was replaced by Václav Havel, whose candidacy had been endorsed by Čalfa and the members of the Federal Assembly. At an emergency congress of the Communist Party, held in December, Urbánek was dismissed from the post of General Secretary of the Central Committee and this position was abolished. Ladislav Adamec was appointed to the new post of Chairman of the Party. It was later decided to reduce the party's apparatus by more than 80%.

At round-table discussions between representatives of the major political parties and groups, which were resumed in late January 1990, agreement was reached on the holding and procedure of elections to the Federal Assembly, which were to take place in June. It was also agreed to reduce forthwith the number of seats held in the legislature by the Communist Party, in order to reflect more accurately popular support for the party nationwide. Accordingly, 120 new deputies (only nine of whom were members of the Communist Party) were elected to the Federal Assembly, in place of those deputies who had resigned or had been recalled. As a result, the Communist Party lost its majority in the legislature (its number of seats in the 350-seat Assembly falling to 138). Following the structural and ideological changes which had been effected within the Communist Party, the National Front was disbanded in its entirety.

In early February 1990 Richard Sacher, the newly-appointed Federal Minister of the Interior, announced the immediate dismantling of the state security service (*Státní Bezpečnost* or StB), which, under communist rule, had been widely feared for its ruthless methods. However, in the months prior to the legislative elections, it was reported that many former officers of the StB were actively employed in the new security apparatus which had been established by the Ministry of the Interior. Moreover, it was alleged that Sacher had misused files belonging to the Ministry in order to protect members of his own party, the CPP, who were under suspicion of having collaborated with the StB in the past. In early May the Federal Assembly approved legislation aimed at purging the new security service of former employees of the StB. Despite repeated demands by the opposition that he resign, Sacher remained in his post as Minister of the Interior.

In April 1990, following heated controversy between Czech and Slovak deputies, the Federal Assembly voted to rename the country the Czech and Slovak Federative Republic. (Hitherto the official title had been the Czechoslovak Socialist Republic.)

On 8–9 June 1990 the first free legislative elections since 1946 were held in Czechoslovakia. About 97% of the electorate voted for a total of 27 parties and movements in the Czech Lands and Slovakia. Prior to the elections, the number of seats in the bicameral Federal Assembly had been reduced from 350 to 300: 150 each in the House of the People and the House of Nations. Within the House of the People, 101 seats were reserved for deputies from the Czech Republic and 49 for deputies from the Slovak Republic, while in the House of Nations each republic was to hold 75 seats. Elections to the Czech and Slovak National Councils (the legislatures of the two republics) were held simultaneously. In the elections at federal level, the largest share of the vote (about 46%) was

CZECHOSLOVAKIA

won by Civic Forum, in the Czech Lands, and by its counterpart, PAV, in Slovakia. Together, they gained 87 seats in the House of the People and 83 seats in the House of Nations. The Communist Party won a larger proportion of the total vote than had been expected: with 23 and 24 seats, respectively, in the House of the People and the House of Nations, it obtained the second largest representation in the Federal Assembly. The Christian Democratic Union (a coalition of the CPP, the Christian Democratic Party and the Slovak-based Christian Democratic Movement, CDM) won 20 seats in each of the two Houses. The recently-established Green Party failed to secure the 5% of the vote required for representation in the legislature, despite predictions of its success in a public opinion poll, held in March. The newly-elected Federal Assembly was to serve a transitional two-year term until the holding of fresh legislative elections in 1992, before which time it was to have drafted a new federal constitution and elected a new President. In late June Alexander Dubček was re-elected Chairman of the Federal Assembly.

Following the elections, Civic Forum and PAV initiated negotiations with other parties on the formation of a coalition federal government. This was announced in late June, and comprised 16 members: four from Civic Forum, three from PAV, one from the CDM and eight independents. Nine of the members (including the Prime Minister, Marián Čalfa, the Minister of Foreign Affairs, Jiří Dienstbier, and the Minister of Finance, Václav Klaus) had served in the outgoing Government. Richard Sacher was replaced as Minister of the Interior by Ján Langoš of PAV. The new Czech and Slovak Governments were announced shortly afterwards. In early July Václav Havel was re-elected to the post of President.

In the latter half of 1990 there was increasing unrest in Slovakia, as several newly-established parties and groups, most prominently the Slovak National Party (SNP, which had won 15 seats in the elections to the Federal Assembly in June), organized demonstrations and rallies as part of a campaign for Slovak autonomy. In late October an estimated 20,000 people, mainly supporters of the SNP, participated in a rally in Bratislava to protest against the adoption by the Slovak National Council of a law on languages (while Slovak was declared the official language in the Slovak Republic, the law also permitted ethnic minorities the right to use their own languages in official contacts in regions where they constituted at least 10% of the population). In an attempt to defuse the increasing ethnic tension in the country, representatives of the Federal, Czech and Slovak Governments met, in mid-November, to discuss the possible transference of powers from the Federal Government to the governments of the two republics. It was agreed that a draft constitutional law concerning the division of powers was to be submitted to all three governments for examination. In mid-December, as calls for Slovak secession increased, Havel requested that the Federal Assembly extend temporarily his presidential powers, to permit his greater involvement in decision-making on the future status of the two republics. His request was criticized by several senior Slovak politicians as unwarranted. On 12 December a compromise was achieved when the Federal Assembly voted, by 237 votes to 24, in favour of transferring broader fiscal powers to the Czech and Slovak Governments (involving the annual rotation of the presidency of the Central Bank), while the Federal Government retained jurisdiction over defence, foreign policy, economic strategy, petroleum and natural gas supplies and decisions regarding minorities.

Relations with many Western nations were enhanced considerably following Czechoslovakia's 'velvet revolution' of late 1989 and the political changes effected during 1990. In that year diplomatic relations were restored with Israel, Chile and the Holy See, and relations were also established with the Republic of Korea, Bahrain and Qatar. Czechoslovakia has traditionally enjoyed close links with other Eastern European nations through its membership of the Warsaw Pact (see p. 211) and of the CMEA (see p. 125). However, in late 1990 it was announced that the Warsaw Pact was to be dismantled in its entirety by the beginning of 1992, while the CMEA was to be replaced by a co-operative organization based on market economy principles. In February 1990 the Soviet Government pledged to withdraw its 73,500 troops from Czechoslovak territory by July 1991. By mid-1990 almost one-half of the Soviet troops had been withdrawn.

Government

Czechoslovakia is a federal state of two nations of equal rights, the Czechs and the Slovaks, and composed of two republics, each having its own government. The supreme organ of state power is the Federal Assembly, elected for a five-year term (the Assembly elected in June 1990 was to serve a transitional two year term) by all citizens over the age of 18 years, and having two chambers, the House of the People and the House of Nations. Membership of the former is proportional to the population of the country. In June 1990, 101 deputies were elected from the Czech Republic and 49 from the Slovak Republic. The House of Nations has 150 members: 75 from each of the republics. The Federal Assembly elects the President for a five-year term of office. (In July 1990 President Havel was re-elected to serve a transitional two-year term of office.) The President, in turn, appoints the Federal Government, led by the Prime Minister, to hold executive authority. Ministers are responsible to the Assembly.

Each of the two constituent republics has its own government (responsible for all matters except external relations, defence, overseas trade, transport and communications) and its own elected National Council or parliament.

Until November 1989, political power was effectively held by the Communist Party of Czechoslovakia, which dominated the National Front (including four other parties). All candidates for representative bodies were sponsored by the National Front. Following the political upheaval in Czechoslovakia in late 1989, the Federal Assembly voted to delete from the Constitution the articles guaranteeing the Communist Party's leading role in society and in the National Front. In February 1990 the National Front was disbanded.

Defence

Czechoslovakia is a member of the Warsaw Pact (to be dismantled by early 1992). Military service is compulsory and lasts for 18 months. Service with the reserve lasts until 60 years of age. In June 1990, according to Western estimates, the army numbered 125,700 (100,000 conscripts) and the air force 44,800 (18,000 conscripts); border troops numbered 13,000. The People's Militia, comprising 120,000 part-time personnel, was disbanded in December 1989. The Czechoslovak army was to be substantially reduced (by about 60,000 men) by 1993. The defence budget for 1990 was 31,180m. korunas. In February 1990 the Czechoslovak and Soviet Governments concluded an agreement, whereby the 73,500 Soviet troops stationed in Czechoslovakia were to be withdrawn by July 1991.

Economic Affairs

In 1988 Czechoslovakia's projected gross national product (GNP) was 662,000m. korunas. In the following year, net material product (NMP) was estimated to be 618,100m. korunas, an increase of almost 2% compared with 1988. Between 1980 and 1987, NMP had increased, in real terms, at an average rate of 3.0% per year. During 1980–88 the population increased by an average annual rate of 0.3%.

Agriculture (including forestry and fishing) contributed an estimated 9.1% of NMP in 1989, when 11.6% of the working population were employed in the sector. The principal crops are wheat, barley, potatoes, sugar beet and hops. (In 1988 Czechoslovakia was the third-largest producer of hops in the world.) Timber production is also significant. In 1988 agricultural production increased by 2.2%, compared with 1987.

Industry (including mining, manufacturing, power and construction) contributed 68.8% of NMP in 1989. In that year 47.9% of the working population were employed in industry. Industrial production increased by 2% in 1988.

Mining employed 2.5% of the working population in 1986. There is large-scale mining of coal and lignite. Other important minerals are copper and zinc. Large deposits of gold have also been detected, and it was expected that gold mining would be resumed in Czechoslovakia from 1995.

Manufacturing and water employed 34% of the working population in 1986. The main components of the manufacturing sector are motor vehicles, glass, beer (exported to 70 countries), ceramics, footwear and textiles. The most important source of foreign export earnings is machinery and transport equipment, which contributed 44% of total receipts in 1989.

Energy is derived principally from coal and from hydroelectric and nuclear power. In 1989 nuclear power stations generated 28% of the total output of electricity, and in 1988 natural gas contributed 14% of total energy production.

CZECHOSLOVAKIA

In 1989 Czechoslovakia recorded a visible trade surplus of US $974m. In that year 61.7% of total foreign trade was conducted with member countries of the CMEA (see p. 125), and 30.1% was with the USSR. There is considerable trade with Western European countries, notably Germany, Austria and the United Kingdom. Trade with Western nations accounted for 31% of total foreign trade in 1989, and was expected to increase substantially in the 1990s.

In 1989 there was a budgetary surplus of 486m. korunas. Czechoslovakia's total external debt was about US $7,000m. in convertible currencies and 11,900m. korunas in other currencies at the end of June 1990. The average annual rate of inflation was about 3.4% in 1989. In November 1990 an estimated 0.6% of the working population were unemployed.

Czechoslovakia is a member of the CMEA. (In November 1990 it was announced that the CMEA was to be replaced by a new co-operative organization operating on market economy principles.) In March 1990 Czechoslovakia and the EEC signed an agreement whereby mutual trade was to increase over a 10-year period. Later in 1990 Czechoslovakia was re-admitted into the IMF, which it had left in 1954.

The new Government, appointed in December 1989, pledged its commitment to extensive economic reforms which would create the foundations for a market-based economy. Accordingly, the Federal Assembly adopted, during 1990, the necessary legislation, including a law regulating private enterprise (which permitted the establishment of companies without restrictions on the numbers of employees), and a law regarding share-holding (whereby foreign individuals or companies were permitted to own as much as 100% of companies based in Czechoslovakia). The Government stressed, however, that about one-third of economic activity would remain under state control in the immediate future. A comprehensive programme of privatization was to be initiated in January 1991. In the latter half of 1990 the economy was adversely affected by a sharp decline in deliveries of petroleum from the USSR, compounded by the rise in petroleum prices following Iraq's invasion and annexation of Kuwait in August 1990. As a result, petrol rationing was introduced in Czechoslovakia.

Social Welfare

A single and universal system of social security was established in Czechoslovakia after the Second World War. All workers and employees benefit equally from the insurance scheme. Protection of health is stipulated by law, with particular emphasis on the prevention of illness rather than treatment and cure. Medical care, treatment, medicines, etc. are, in most cases, available free of charge to the entire Czechoslovak population, and 38,268m. korunas were spent on the health service in 1989. There were 57,940 physicians in 1989, when the number of inhabitants per physician was 270. In 1988 there were 123,000 hospital beds. The National Health Insurance Scheme is administered by the Federal Ministry of Labour and Social Affairs.

Education

Education at all levels is provided free of charge. Almost all children between the ages of three and six years attend kindergarten (mateřská škola). Education is compulsory between the ages of six and 16 years, when children attend basic school (základní škola). A general curriculum is followed by more specialized subjects. Most Czechoslovak children continue their education after basic school. Secondary grammar schools provide four years of general education, and prepare students for university. Education of the same level is provided by working people's secondary schools. Four-year secondary vocational schools train young people as specialists in the fields of economics, administration and culture, or prepare them for studies at institutes of higher learning. Courses at the specialized apprentice training centres last from two to four years, and prepare young people for workers' professions. In 1990 the establishment of private and religious schools was legalized. In the 1989/90 school year 636,622 children attended kindergarten, 1,961,742 attended elementary schools, 892,940 the different types of secondary school and 173,547 students were in higher education.

Public Holidays

1991: 1 January (New Year's Day), 1 April (Easter Monday), 1 May (Labour Day), 9 May (National Day, Anniversary of Liberation), 5 July (National Day, Day of the Apostles St Cyril and St Methodius), 28 October (National Day, Anniversary of Independence), 24–26 December (Christmas).

1992: 1 January (New Year's Day), 20 April (Easter Monday), 1 May (Labour Day), 9 May (National Day, Anniversary of Liberation), 5 July (National Day, Day of the Apostles St Cyril and St Methodius), 28 October (National Day, Anniversary of Independence), 24–26 December (Christmas).

Weights and Measures

The metric system is in force.

Statistical Survey

Source: mainly Federal Statistical Office, Sokolovská 142, 180 00 Prague 8; tel. (2) 814; telex 121197.

Area and Population

AREA, POPULATION AND DENSITY

Area (sq km)	127,899*
Population (census results)	
1 November 1980	15,283,095
December 1985	
Males	7,558,152
Females	7,961,150
Total	15,519,302
Population (official estimates at 31 December)	
1987	15,587,489
1988	15,624,254
1989	15,649,765
Density (per sq km) at 31 December 1989	122.4

* 49,382 sq miles.

POPULATION BY NATIONALITY
(at 31 December 1989)

	Czech Republic		Slovak Republic		Total	
	'000	%	'000	%	'000	%
Czech	9,742	94.0	64	1.2	9,806	62.7
Slovak	425	4.1	4,585	86.6	5,010	32.0
Magyar (Hungarian)	23	0.2	578	10.9	601	3.8
German	49	0.5	3	0.1	52	0.3
Polish	70	0.7	3	0.1	73	0.5
Ukrainian and Russian	15	0.1	41	0.8	56	0.4
Others and unspecified	38	0.4	14	0.3	52	0.3
Total	**10,362**	**100.0**	**5,288**	**100.0**	**15,650**	**100.0**

CZECHOSLOVAKIA

REGIONS

	Area (sq km)	Population (31 Dec. 1989)	Density (per sq km)
Czech Republic:			
Central Bohemia	10,994	1,118,214	102
Southern Bohemia	11,345	699,479	62
Western Bohemia	10,875	869,244	80
Northern Bohemia	7,819	1,190,410	152
Eastern Bohemia	11,240	1,239,757	110
Southern Moravia	15,028	2,058,002	137
Northern Moravia	11,067	1,972,111	178
Prague (city)	496	1,214,885	2,449
Total	78,864	10,362,102	131
Slovak Republic:			
Western Slovakia	14,492	1,727,845	119
Central Slovakia	17,982	1,615,391	90
Eastern Slovakia	16,193	1,503,798	93
Bratislava (city)	368	440,629	1,197
Total	49,035	5,287,663	108
Grand total	127,899	15,649,765	122

PRINCIPAL TOWNS
(estimated population at 31 December 1989)

Praha (Prague, capital)	1,214,885
Bratislava	440,629
Brno	390,986
Ostrava	331,219
Košice	235,729
Plzeň (Pilsen)	174,666
Olomouc	106,684
Ústí nad Labem	106,463
Liberec	104,142
Hradec Králové	101,082
České Budějovice	98,812
Žilina	97,167
Pardubice	96,036
Havířov	92,187
Nitra	90,689
Zlín (formerly Gottwaldov)	87,140

BIRTHS, MARRIAGES AND DEATHS

	Registered live births		Registered marriages		Registered deaths	
	Number	Rate (per 1,000)	Number	Rate (per 1,000)	Number	Rate (per 1,000)
1982	234,356	15.2	117,376	7.6	181,158	11.8
1983	229,484	14.9	120,547	7.8	186,907	12.1
1984	227,784	14.7	121,340	7.8	183,927	11.9
1985	226,036	14.6	119,583	7.7	184,105	11.9
1986	220,494	14.2	119,979	7.7	185,718	12.0
1987	214,927	13.8	122,168	7.8	179,224	11.5
1988	215,909	13.8	118,951	7.6	178,169	11.4
1989	208,472	13.3	117,787	7.5	181,649	11.6

CIVILIAN LABOUR FORCE EMPLOYED
('000 persons, excluding apprentices)

	1987	1988	1989
Agriculture	852	839	811
Forestry	94	94	95
Mining, manufacturing, gas and electricity	2,939	2,951	2,954
Construction	792	797	799
Trade, restaurants, etc.	708	712	717
Other commerce	169	170	169
Transport	400	399	403
Communications	106	106	110
Services	293	302	323
Education and culture	587	600	604
Science and research	179	181	182
Health and social services	387	397	406
Civil service, jurisdiction	118	120	115
Others	130	135	137
Total in employment	7,754	7,803	7,830
Women on maternity leave	352	358	376
Total labour force	8,106	8,161	8,206

Agriculture

PRINCIPAL CROPS ('000 metric tons)

	1987	1988	1989
Wheat and spelt	6,154	6,547	6,356
Rye	496	534	708
Barley	3,551	3,411	3,550
Oats*	406	366	330
Maize	1,160	996	1,000
Sugar beet†	6,698	5,482	6,390
Potatoes	3,072	3,659	3,167
Dry peas	175	212	178
Dry broad beans	30	22	27
Grapes	102	229	166
Linseed	10	12	16
Rapeseed	337	380	387
Sunflower seed	62	63	70
Hops	12	15	12
Tobacco	6	5	5
Carrots	170	138	160
Onions	146	129	156
Garlic	13	13	16
Tomatoes	123	124	122
Cabbages	296	281	306
Cauliflowers	73	69	77
Lettuce	20	18	19
Cucumbers and gherkins	92	103	63
Apples	308	468	552
Pears	32	49	48
Plums	21	55	49
Sweet cherries	20	23	29
Sour cherries	8	10	14
Peaches	7	15	27
Apricots	8	7	42
Strawberries	28	25	33
Currants	33	35	38
Walnuts	6	8	11
Flax fibre	19	19	25

* Including mixed crops of oats and barley.
† Including sugar beet seed.

LIVESTOCK ('000 head at end of year)

	1987	1988	1989
Cattle	5,044	5,075	5,129
Pigs	7,235	7,384	7,498
Sheep	1,075	1,047	1,051
Goats	50	50	50
Horses	45	44	42

Chickens (million): 47 in 1987; 46 in 1988; 47 in 1989.

LIVESTOCK PRODUCTS ('000 metric tons)

	1987	1988	1989
Beef and veal	412	405	407
Pig meat	858	915	934
Poultry meat	194	226	233
Edible offals	93	94	94
Cows' milk	6,921.4	6,963.4	7,101.1
Sheep's milk	42	41	42
Goats' milk	19	19	19
Butter	149.2	148.3	156.2
Cheese	215	227	233
Hen eggs	277.2	279.8	281.4
Wool:			
greasy	5.7	5.2	5.9
clean	3.4	3.1	3.5
Cattle hides	59.3	58.3	57.6

Forestry

ROUNDWOOD REMOVALS
('000 cubic metres, excluding bark)

	1987	1988	1989
Production	18,527	18,125	17,882
Deliveries	18,565	18,271	18,026
of which:			
Industrial	16,946	16,739	16,650
Fuel wood	1,619	1,532	1,376

SAWNWOOD PRODUCTION
('000 cubic metres, including boxboards)

	1987	1988	1989
Coniferous	4,270	4,212	4,112
Broadleaved	798	802	769
Total	5,068	5,014	4,881

Fishing*

(metric tons)

	1987	1988	1989
Carp	16,652	17,240	17,873
Others	4,084	4,007	3,701
Total catch	20,736	21,247	21,574

* Figures refer only to fish caught by the State Fisheries and members of the Czech and Slovak fishing unions.

Mining

('000 metric tons, unless otherwise indicated)

	1987	1988	1989
Hard coal	25,737	25,503	26,071
Brown coal	98,347	96,361	90,915
Lignite	3,639	3,558	3,348
Kaolin	697	686	698
Iron ore:			
gross weight	1,798	1,773	1,780
metal content	483	474	476
Crude petroleum	147	143	144
Salt (refined)	233	243	238
Magnesite	671	631	642
Antimony ore (metric tons)*	931	947	839
Copper concentrates (metric tons)*	24,782	23,303	20,895
Lead concentrates (metric tons)*	5,612	5,429	5,351
Mercury (metric tons)	164	168	131
Tin concentrates (metric tons)*	545	515	562
Zinc concentrates (metric tons)*	13,662	13,870	14,137

* Figures refer to the metal content of ores and concentrates.

Industry

SELECTED PRODUCTS
('000 metric tons, unless otherwise indicated)

	1987	1988	1989
Wheat flour	1,384	1,425	1,405
Refined sugar	895	708	878
Margarine (metric tons)	37,419	38,937	38,767
Wine ('000 hectolitres)	1,403	1,422	1,391
Beer ('000 hectolitres)	22,228	22,670	22,770
Cigarettes (million)	25,365	25,502	25,428
Cotton yarn—pure and mixed (metric tons)	145,157	147,220	147,079
Woven cotton fabrics ('000 metres)*	599,900	591,243	581,906
Wool yarn—pure and mixed (metric tons)	55,397	55,617	56,106
Woven woollen fabrics ('000 metres)*	58,178	58,669	59,109
Chemical fibres	196.5	204.2	208.1
Chemical wood pulp	850.9	884.9	889.9
Newsprint	64.7	73.9	74.2
Other paper	917.9	900.1	953.3
Leather footwear ('000 pairs)	53,815	55,320	55,841
Rubber footwear ('000 pairs)	5,163	4,809	4,672
Other footwear ('000 pairs)	60,449	58,959	59,776
Synthetic rubber (metric tons)	76,488	77,078	75,932
Rubber tyres ('000)	5,316	5,519	5,743
Sulphuric acid	1,264	1,249	1,142
Hydrochloric acid	246.4	247.4	237.8
Caustic soda	344.1	337.1	337.1
Soda ash	102.7	112.2	111.9
Nitrogenous fertilizers(a)†	596.4	596.4	603.8
Phosphate fertilizers(b)†	277.0	313.0	295.6
Plastics and synthetic resins	1,150	1,192	1,186
Liquefied petroleum gas	142	126	129
Motor spirit (petrol)	1,664	1,678	1,647
Kerosene and jet fuel	418	416	422
Distillate fuel oils	4,076	4,469	4,495
Residual fuel oils	6,925	6,014	5,745
Petroleum bitumen (asphalt)	1,057	1,146	1,103
Coke-oven coke	10,586	10,586	10,147
Cement	10,369	10,974	10,888
Pig iron‡	9,788	9,706	9,911
Crude steel	15,416	15,379	15,465
Rolled steel products	11,364	11,420	11,395
Aluminium—unwrought (metric tons)	32,366	31,435	32,576
Refined copper—unwrought (metric tons)	27,202	27,076	26,920
Lead—unwrought (metric tons)	26,008	26,045	26,009
Radio receivers (number)§	199,807	183,570	146,545
Television receivers (number)	506,743	481,897	524,190
Passenger cars (number)	172,355	163,834	188,611
Goods vehicles (number)	51,194	50,498	50,570
Motor cycles (number)‖	134,573	136,160	118,905
Electric locomotives (number)	99	132	107
Diesel locomotives (number)	524	507	500
Trams (number)	950	685	937
Tractors (number)	35,274	33,558	34,317
Electric energy (million kWh)	85,825	87,374	89,255
Manufactured gas (million cu metres)	7,270	6,782	6,335
Construction:			
New dwellings completed (number)	79,626	82,910	88,510

* After undergoing finishing processes.
† Production of fertilizers is measured in terms of (a) nitrogen or (b) phosphoric acid. The figures for phosphate fertilizers include ground rock phosphate.
‡ Including blast furnace ferro-alloys.   § Excluding radiograms.
‖ Engine capacity of 100 cubic centimetres and over.

CZECHOSLOVAKIA

Statistical Survey

Finance

CURRENCY AND EXCHANGE RATES

Monetary Units
100 haléřů (singular: halér—heller) = 1 koruna (Czechoslovak crown or Kčs.).

Denominations
Coins: 5, 10, 20 and 50 haléřů; 1, 2, 5 and 10 Kčs.
Notes: 10, 20, 50, 100, 500 and 1,000 Kčs.

Sterling and Dollar Equivalents (31 July 1990)
£1 sterling = 31.620 Kčs.;
US $1 = 17.000 Kčs. (non-commercial rates);
1,000 Kčs. = £31.63 = $58.82.

Note: The rates quoted above are applicable to tourism. Foreign trade transactions are valued according to the commercial exchange rate. On this basis, the average value of the koruna was: 18.29 US cents in 1987; 18.78 US cents in 1988; 6.65 US cents in 1989. However, in December 1990 this two-tier system was replaced by a unified exchange rate, initially fixed at US $1 = 28 korunas.

BUDGET (million Kčs.)

Revenue	1987	1988	1989
State budget	245,191	258,400	259,607
From socialist economy	276,747	291,387	308,252
Taxes and rates	35,121	36,423	2,159
Other receipts	2,762	3,000	4,412
Less grants and subsidies to local administrative organs	69,439	72,410	55,216
Budgets of local administrative organs	138,541	145,645	155,825
Total	383,732	404,045	415,432

Expenditure	1987	1988	1989
State budget	245,191	258,400	263,107
National economy	94,891	103,638	86,801
Science and technology	9,731	9,754	9,636
Money-order and technical services	6,393	6,740	6,715
Culture and social welfare	101,320	104,447	111,765
Defence	28,496	29,236	43,784
Administration	4,360	4,585	4,406
Budgets of local administrative organs	136,960	142,799	151,839
Total	382,151	401,199	414,946

COST OF LIVING
(Consumer Price Index; base: 1 January 1984 = 100)

	1987	1988	1989
Food	104.2	103.9	104.0
Industrial goods	101.6	101.9	104.5
Public catering	112.8	113.5	114.6
Services	99.7	100.6	101.4
All items	103.3	103.5	104.9

NATIONAL ACCOUNTS

Net Material Product*
('000 million Kčs. at current market prices)

Activities of the material sphere	1987	1988	1989
Agriculture, hunting and fishing	38.7	38.7	56.3
Forestry and logging	4.5	4.2	5.9
Industry†	350.0	362.2	360.0
Construction	62.4	65.0	65.4
Trade, restaurants, etc.	96.2	104.2	100.1
Transport and storage	23.6	23.9	21.9
Communications	5.4	5.6	5.7
Others	2.5	2.6	2.8
Total	583.3	606.4	618.1

* Defined as the total net value of goods and 'productive' services, including turnover taxes, produced by the economy. This excludes economic activities not contributing directly to material production, such as public administration, defence and personal and professional services.
† Principally manufacturing, mining, electricity, gas and water supply.

External Trade

Note: The value of external trade has been recalculated on the basis of the exchange rates for the koruna that took effect on 1 January 1989.

PRINCIPAL COMMODITIES
(distribution by SITC, million Kčs.)

Imports f.o.b.	1987	1988	1989
Food and live animals	12,993	14,843	14,906
Vegetables and fruit	3,834	4,628	4,507
Crude materials (inedible) except fuels	17,090	17,598	18,814
Cotton fibres and waste	2,140	2,543	2,798
Metalliferous ores and metal scrap	5,315	4,374	4,784
Mineral fuels, lubricants, etc. (incl. electric current)	45,539	39,898	37,164
Coal, coke and briquettes	2,818	2,487	2,197
Petroleum, petroleum products, etc.	29,679	24,830	22,385
Gas (natural and manufactured)	15,986	11,108	10,766
Chemicals and related products	n.a.	n.a.	n.a.
Organic chemicals	2,237	3,170	3,565
Manufactured fertilizers	1,690	1,640	1,790
Basic manufactures	19,680	19,446	22,369
Iron and steel	4,161	3,030	3,357
Non-ferrous metals	5,187	6,653	7,508
Machinery and transport equipment	71,863	75,835	79,324
Power generating machinery and equipment	5,303	3,776	5,747
Machinery specialized for particular industries	17,117	21,654	20,942
Agricultural machinery (excl. tractors) and parts	3,698	3,254	2,972
Civil engineering and contractors' plant, equipment and parts	5,039	8,123	7,752
Metalworking machinery	5,120	5,865	6,184
Machine-tools for working metal	3,573	4,294	1,697
General industrial machinery, equipment and parts	22,662	21,236	19,790

CZECHOSLOVAKIA

Statistical Survey

Imports f.o.b.—continued	1987	1988	1989
Office machines and automatic data processing equipment	6,056	5,699	6,382
Automatic data processing machines and units	4,868	4,419	4,702
Road vehicles and parts*	6,209	6,048	7,088
Parts and accessories for cars, buses, lorries, etc.*	4,385	4,190	4,220
Miscellaneous manufactured articles	11,321	12,930	13,208
Total (incl. others)	203,750	209,554	214,702

* Excluding tyres, engines and electrical parts.

Exports f.o.b.	1987	1988	1989
Food and live animals	6,278	7,114	10,076
Crude materials (inedible) except fuels	7,146	6,108	8,000
Mineral fuels, lubricants, etc. (incl. electric current)	9,327	8,854	11,292
Coal, coke and briquettes	3,262	3,552	3,880
Coal, lignite and peat	1,759	2,040	2,225
Petroleum, petroleum products, etc.	4,566	3,862	5,612
Chemicals and related products	14,543	17,641	16,434
Organic chemicals	3,376	5,738	5,271
Artificial resins, plastic materials, etc.	2,663	4,754	3,776
Basic manufactures	38,921	40,335	48,814
Textile yarn, fabrics, etc.	6,436	7,994	8,132
Non-metallic mineral manufactures	5,852	6,017	10,095
Iron and steel	12,921	16,038	18,726
Bars, rods, angles, shapes, etc.	3,724	4,795	3,865
Universals, plates and sheets	2,847	4,436	5,121
Tubes, pipes and fittings	3,170	2,315	3,127
Machinery and transport equipment	99,574	101,016	96,563
Power generating machinery and equipment	7,799	9,344	8,761
Steam power units, steam engines and parts	2,534	4,356	3,656
Machinery specialized for particular industries	26,829	24,216	24,876
Agricultural machinery (excl. tractors) and parts	3,227	2,852	2,688
Civil engineering and contractors' plant, equipment and parts	5,765	5,166	6,751
Textile and leather machinery and parts	8,504	7,396	6,970
Metalworking machinery	7,523	7,032	6,788
Machine-tools for working metal	5,616	5,279	2,197
General industrial machinery, equipment and parts	29,358	26,472	22,273
Office machines and automatic data processing equipment	3,146	2,465	2,055
Telecommunications and sound equipment	2,975	2,410	2,969
Other electrical machinery, apparatus, etc.	6,417	6,045	6,766
Road vehicles and parts*	18,827	16,331	15,854
Motor vehicles for goods transport and special purposes	7,740	6,041	5,222
Parts and accessories for cars, buses, lorries, etc.*	7,540	6,828	6,365
Railway vehicles and associated equipment	7,419	5,880	5,442
Miscellaneous manufactured articles	22,687	22,829	21,028
Furniture and parts	2,786	2,740	2,537
Footwear	4,047	4,427	4,100
Total (incl. others)	201,558	213,887	217,530

* Excluding tyres, engines and electrical parts.

PRINCIPAL TRADING PARTNERS
(million Kčs., country of consignment)

Imports f.o.b.	1987	1988	1989
Austria	10,268	11,102	11,830
Belgium	1,485	1,644	1,593
Brazil	915	1,072	1,639
Bulgaria	5,081	5,210	4,808
China, People's Republic	3,996	5,441	5,902
Cuba	1,469	1,550	1,645
France	3,332	3,407	3,350
German Democratic Republic	16,153	17,190	16,797
Germany, Federal Republic*	18,935	19,580	19,931
Hungary	8,224	9,282	10,294
Iran	1,142	638	1,090
Italy	4,050	3,804	3,695
Japan	1,399	1,183	1,113
Netherlands	2,406	2,529	2,184
Poland	15,665	17,280	18,485
Romania	3,215	3,762	3,561
Switzerland	6,070	7,240	7,407
USSR	69,401	65,465	63,792
United Kingdom	3,861	4,553	4,731
Yugoslavia	7,086	6,968	7,170
Total (incl. others)	203,750	209,554	214,702

* Excluding imports from West Berlin.

Exports f.o.b.	1987	1988	1989
Austria	7,625	8,896	9,938
Bulgaria	5,654	5,919	5,073
China, People's Republic	4,377	6,225	5,546
Cuba	1,833	1,938	1,699
France	2,965	3,325	3,936
German Democratic Republic	14,553	14,916	14,257
Germany, Federal Republic†	15,304	16,573	17,964
Hungary	8,775	9,082	8,641
Iraq	3,119	841	1,296
Italy	3,364	3,751	4,623
Libya	1,542	474	1,043
Netherlands	2,606	2,854	3,316
Poland	15,008	17,238	18,438
Romania	3,288	3,307	3,938
Switzerland	2,689	3,283	3,805
Syria	662	691	1,368
Turkey	554	1,183	1,748
USSR	68,191	71,924	66,439
United Kingdom	4,007	4,413	4,396
Yugoslavia	8,011	6,826	7,095
Total (incl. others)	201,558	213,887	217,530

† Excluding exports to West Berlin.

Transport

	1987	1988	1989
Railway transport:			
Freight ('000 tons)	291,093	294,844	283,674
Passengers (million)	416	415	411
Public road transport:			
Freight ('000 tons)	337,575	339,458	328,984
Passengers (million)	2,333	2,342	2,320
Waterway transport:			
Freight ('000 tons)	14,265	15,206	13,524
Air transport:			
Freight (tons)	26,579	28,066	29,123
Passengers ('000)	1,368	1,449	1,493

CZECHOSLOVAKIA

ROAD TRAFFIC (vehicles in use at 30 June)

	1987	1988	1989
Passenger cars	2,903,947	2,999,987	3,122,307
Buses and coaches	36,595	37,720	39,382
Goods vehicles	412,969	422,971	446,725
Motorcycles and scooters	555,252	546,576	551,497

Tourism

	1986	1987	1988
Foreign tourist arrivals*	19,030,469	21,756,306	24,486,814

* Including excursionists and visitors in transit. Visitors spending at least one night in the country totalled 5,330,252 in 1986; 6,263,914 in 1987; 7,054,035 in 1988.

1989: 29.7m. foreign tourist arrivals.

Communications Media

	1987	1988	1989
Telephones in use	3,838,437	3,979,819	4,131,679
Radio receivers (licensed)	3,965,689	4,228,991	4,216,838
Television receivers (licensed)	4,424,529	4,661,775	4,660,543
Book production: titles*	7,067	6,977	6,863
Newspapers (dailies)	30	30	30
Periodicals	1,080	1,087	1,086

* Figures include pamphlets, and refer to titles produced by centrally managed publishing houses only. The total number of titles produced in 1989 was 9,294.

Education

(1989/90)

	Institutions	Teachers*	Students
Nursery	11,380	50,519	636,622
Primary (classes 1–8)	6,206	98,038	1,961,742
Secondary (classes 9–12)			
Universal	351	10,769	153,179
Special (technical, etc.)	563	18,630	274,298
Continuation schools	957	17,233	465,463
Higher	36	20,317	173,547

* Teachers in full-time employment.

Directory

The Constitution

A new constitution was proclaimed on 11 July 1960. It was amended in October 1968, July 1971 and May 1975. A summary of the main provisions of the Constitution follows:

The Czechoslovak Socialist Republic* is a Federal State of two fraternal nations possessing equal rights, the Czechs and the Slovaks.

According to the Constitution, work in the interests of the community is a primary duty and the right to work a primary right of every citizen. All citizens have equal rights and equal duties without regard to nationality and race. Remuneration for work done is based on its quantity, quality and social importance. Men and women have equal status. All citizens have the right to health protection, education and leisure after work including paid holidays. Other rights include: freedom of expression, assembly, inviolability of the person, the home, mail, etc. Everyone has the right to profess any religious faith or to be without religious conviction.

The economic foundation of the State is the Socialist economic system which excludes every form of exploitation of man by man. The means of production are socially owned and the entire national economy is directed by plan. Socialist ownership includes both national property such as mineral wealth, the means of industrial production, banks, etc., and co-operative property. The land of members of agricultural co-operatives remains the personal property of the individual members, but is jointly farmed by the co-operative. Small private enterprises based on the labour of the owner himself and excluding exploitation of another's labour power are permitted. Personal ownership of consumer goods, family houses and savings derived from labour is inviolable. Inheritance of such personal property is guaranteed.

The Czechoslovak Constitution does not restrict itself to laying down a system of state organs but also sets forth the principles by which the life of society is to be guided. It is not just a Constitution of the State but a constitution for the whole of society. In economic, political and cultural life, in questions of social security and many other spheres it emphasizes the participation of citizens in the administration of public affairs and even transfers a number of functions that have hitherto pertained to state organs to the working people and their voluntary organizations.

The guiding force in society and in the State is the Communist Party of Czechoslovakia, a voluntary militant alliance of the most active and politically conscious citizens. It is associated with the other political parties, the Trade Union Movement and other people's organizations in the National Front of Czechs and Slovaks.†

FEDERAL ASSEMBLY

The supreme organ of state power in the Czechoslovak Socialist Republic is the Federal Assembly (Parliament) which is elected for a five-year term and elects the President of the Republic. The President may be relieved of his or her duties by the Assembly in the event of having been unable to fulfil them for over a year. The Federal Assembly consists of two chambers of equal rights: the House of the People and the House of Nations. The composition of the House of the People, which has 200 deputies, corresponds to the composition of the population of the Czechoslovak Socialist Republic§. The House of Nations has 150 deputies on parity basis: 75 are elected in the Czech Socialist Republic and 75 in the Slovak Socialist Republic.

PRESIDENT AND FEDERAL GOVERNMENT

The President, elected by the Federal Assembly, appoints the Federal Government. The Government is the supreme executive organ of state power in Czechoslovakia; it consists of a Prime Minister, four Deputy Prime Ministers and 12 Ministers. The Ministries of Foreign Affairs, of Defence, of Foreign Trade, of Transport and of Telecommunications, are within the exclusive competence of the Federation, i.e. there are no corresponding portfolios in the governments of the republics. The second group of Federal Government organs share authority with organs of the two republics, i.e. there are corresponding portfolios in the national governments.

ELECTORAL SYSTEM‡

All representative bodies are elected, and the right to elect is universal, equal and by secret ballot. Every citizen has the right to vote on reaching the age of 18, and is eligible for election on reaching the age of 21. Deputies must maintain constant contacts with their constituents, heed their suggestions and be accountable to them for their activity. A member of any representative body may be recalled by his or her constituents at any time.

CZECHOSLOVAKIA

For election purposes, the country is divided into electoral districts; there are 200 electoral districts in the Czechoslovak Socialist Republic, each represented by one deputy in the House of the People§, and 75 electoral districts each in the Czech and Slovak Socialist Republics, which send one deputy each to the House of Nations.

All candidates are National Front candidates, presented by the Communist Party of Czechoslovakia and by the other political parties and social organizations associated in the National Front. One or more candidates can be nominated for one electoral district. Appropriate National Front organs select the candidates from the list of nominees, and submit their names for registration.‖

The principle of simple majority obtains in the elections: the candidate is elected when he obtains more than 50% of the votes cast, provided that the majority of all voters in his electoral district exercise their right to vote. When either of the two conditions is not met, new elections are held in the electoral district concerned within two weeks. When a seat becomes vacant, the Presidium of the Federal Assembly calls a by-election in the constituency; this is not mandatory in the last year of the deputies' term of office.

NATIONAL COUNCILS

Each of the republics has its own legislature: the Czech National Council and the Slovak National Council. The members are elected for a five-year term of office. The Czech National Council has 200 deputies, the Slovak National Council 150 deputies. There are also separate Czech and Slovak Governments.

NATIONAL COMMITTEES

National committees are the organs of popular self-government in the regions, districts and localities. The members are elected for a five-year term of office. They rely on the active participation of the working people of their area and co-operate with other organizations of the people. They direct local economic and cultural development, ensure the protection of socialist ownership and the maintenance of socialist order in society, see to the implementation and observance of laws, etc. They take part in drafting and carrying out the state plan for the development of the national economy and draw up their own budgets which form a part of the state budget. Commissions elected by the national committees are charged with various aspects of public work and carry out their tasks with the aid of a large number of citizens who need not be elected members of the national committees.

JUDICIAL SYSTEM

The execution of justice is vested in elected and independent courts. Benches are composed of professional judges and of judges who carry out their function in addition to their regular employment. Both categories are equal in making decisions. Judges are independent in the discharge of their office and bound solely by the legal order of the socialist State. The supervision of the observance of the laws and other legal regulations by public bodies and by individual citizens rests with the Office of the Procurator. The Procurator-General is appointed and recalled by the President of the Republic and is accountable to the Federal Assembly.

* Renamed the Czech and Slovak Federative Republic in April 1990.
† The provisions in this paragraph were deleted in late November 1989.
‡ Reformed in 1990.
§ The number of seats in the House of the People was reduced to 150 in 1990.
‖ The provisions in this paragraph were amended in late November 1989.

A new draft constitution, approved by Civic Forum, was submitted to the Federal Assembly in December 1989. The new Assembly, elected in June 1990, was to have drafted a new constitution by mid-1992.

The Government
(January 1991)

HEAD OF STATE

President of the Republic: Václav Havel (took office 29 December 1989; re-elected 5 July 1990).

FEDERAL GOVERNMENT

A coalition of Civic Forum/Public Against Violence (PAV), the Christian Democratic Movement (CDM) and Independents.

Prime Minister: Marián Čalfa (PAV).

Deputy Prime Ministers: Václav Valeš (Independent), Pavel Rychetský (Independent), Jozef Mikloško (CDM).
Deputy Prime Minister and Minister of Foreign Affairs: Jiří Dienstbier (Civic Forum).
Minister of Defence: Luboš Dobrovský (Independent).
Minister of the Interior: Ján Langoš (PAV).
Minister of Finance: Dr Václav Klaus (Civic Forum).
Minister of Foreign Trade: (vacant).
Minister of Labour and Social Affairs: Petr Miller (Civic Forum).
Minister of Transport: Jiří Nezval (Independent).
Minister of Telecommunications: Theodor Petrík (Independent).
Minister of the Economy: Vladimír Dlouhý (Civic Forum).
Minister of Economic Planning: Pavel Hoffmann (Independent).
Minister of the Environment: Josef Vavroušek (Independent).
Minister in charge of the Control Commission: Květoslava Kořínková (Independent).

FEDERAL MINISTRIES

Office of the Presidium of the Federal Government: Nábř. kpt. Jaroše 4, 125 09 Prague 1; tel. (2) 2102.
Federal Committee for the Environment: Slezská 9, 120 29 Prague 2; tel. (2) 2151111.
Federal Ministry of Control: Jankovcova 63, 170 04 Prague 7; tel. (2) 8734.
Federal Ministry of Defence: Nám. Svobody 471, 161 00 Prague 6; tel. (2) 330802.
Federal Ministry of Economic Planning: Nábř. kpt. Jaroše 1000, 170 32 Prague 7; tel. (2) 3891111.
Federal Ministry of the Economy: Nábř. kpt. Jaroše 1000, 170 32 Prague 7; tel. (2) 3891111.
Federal Ministry of Finance: Letenská 15, 118 10 Prague 1; tel. (2) 5141111.
Federal Ministry of Foreign Affairs: Loretánské nám. 5, 125 10 Prague 1; tel. (2) 21931111.
Federal Ministry of Foreign Trade: Politických vězňů 20, 112 49 Prague 1; tel. (2) 21261111.
Federal Ministry of the Interior: Dr. M. Horákové 85, 170 34 Prague 7; tel. (2) 33511111.
Federal Ministry of Labour and Social Affairs: Palackého nám. 4, 128 01 Prague 2; tel. (2) 2118.
Federal Ministry of Telecommunications: Klimentská 27, 125 02 Prague 1; tel. (2) 2323924.
Federal Ministry of Transport: Nábř. L. Svobody 12, 125 11 Prague 1; tel. (2) 28911111.

STATE GOVERNMENTS
Czech Government

Prime Minister: Petr Pithart.
Deputy Prime Ministers: František Vlasák, Antonín Baudyš, Milan Lukeš.
Minister of Housing: Ludvík Motyčka.
Minister of Trade and Tourism: Vlasta Štěpová.
Minister of the Environment: (vacant).
Minister of Finance: Karel Špaček.
Minister of Education: Petr Vopěnka.
Minister of Culture: Milan Uhde.
Minister of Health: Martin Bojar.
Minister of Justice: Leon Richter.
Minister of the Interior: Tomáš Sokol.
Minister of Industry: Jan Vrba.
Minister of Food and Agriculture: Bohumil Kubát.
Minister of Economic Planning and Development: Karel Dyba.
Minister of Engineering: Miroslav Grégr.
Minister of International Relations and Contacts with the Federal and Slovak Governments: Jaroslav Šabata.
Minister of Administration and Privatization of National Wealth: Tomáš Ježek.
Minister of Labour and Social Affairs: Milan Horálek.
Minister, Chairman of the People's Control Committee: Bohumil Tichý.

CZECHOSLOVAKIA   Directory

Slovak Government

Prime Minister: VLADIMÍR MEČIAR.
First Deputy Prime Minister: JÁN ČARNOGURSKÝ.
Deputy Prime Ministers: JOZEF KUČERÁK, VLADIMÍR ONDRUŠ, GÁBOR ZÁSZLÓS.
Minister of the Interior: LADISLAV PITTNER.
Minister of the Economy: JOZEF BELCÁK.
Minister of Housing: JOZEF DUBNÍČEK.
Minister of Food and Agriculture: MICHAL DŽATKO.
Minister of Planning: RUDOLF FILKUS.
Minister of Industry: JÁN HOLČÍK.
Minister of Administration and Privatization of National Wealth: AUGUSTÍN MARIÁN HÚSKA.
Minister of Trade and Tourism: JOZEF CHREN.
Minister of International Relations: MILAN KŇAŽKO.
Minister of Justice: LADISLAV KOŠŤA.
Minister of Education, Science, Youth and Sports: JÁN PIŠÚT.
Minister of Finance: MICHAL KOVÁČ.
Minister of Labour and Social Affairs: STANISLAV NOVÁK.
Minister of Forestry and Water Resources: VILIAM OBERHAUSER.
Minister of Health: ALOJZ RAKÚS.
Minister of Culture: LADISLAV SNOPKO.
Minister of the Environment: IVAN TIRPÁK.
Minister, Chairman of the People's Control Committee: MARTIN HVOZDÍK.

Legislature

FEDERÁLNÍ SHROMÁŽDĚNÍ
(Federal Assembly)

The Federal Assembly consists of 300 deputies elected for a five-year term. The Assembly is bicameral, comprising the House of the People and the House of Nations, each containing 150 members. General elections to both chambers were held on 8–9 June 1990. Deputies were to serve a transitional two-year term of office until the holding of fresh legislative elections in mid-1992.
Chairman: ALEXANDER DUBČEK.

Sněmovna lidu
(House of the People)

This House has 150 members. At the June 1990 elections, 101 were from the Czech Republic, and 49 from the Slovak Republic.
Chairman: RUDOLF BATTEK.

Sněmovna národů
(House of Nations)

This House has 150 members: 75 each from the Czech and Slovak Republics.
Chairman: MILAN SUTOVEC.

General election, 8–9 June 1990

Parties and Groups	House of the People % of votes	Seats	House of Nations % of votes	Seats	Total seats in the Federal Assembly
Civic Forum/Public Against Violence (PAV)	46.6	87	45.9	83	170
Communist Party of Czechoslovakia (CPCZ)	13.6	23	13.7	24	47
Christian Democratic Union (CDU)*	12.0	20	11.3	20	40
Movement for Autonomous Democracy-Society for Moravia and Silesia (MAD-SMS)	5.4	9	3.6	7	16
Slovak National Party (SNP)	3.5	6	6.2	9	15
Coexistence (Soužití)	2.8	5	2.7	7	12
Others	16.1	0	16.6	0	0
Total	100.0	150	100.0	150	300

* A coalition of the Czechoslovak People's Party (CPP), the Christian Democratic Party (CDP) and the Christian Democratic Movement (CDM).

NATIONAL COUNCILS

Czech National Council: Prague; 200 deputies were elected in June 1990 (127 from Civic Forum, 32 from the Communist Party of Czechoslovakia, 22 from the Movement for Autonomous Democracy-Society for Moravia and Silesia and 19 from the Christian Democratic Union); Chair. DAGMAR BUREŠOVÁ.

Slovak National Council: Bratislava; 150 deputies were elected in June 1990 (48 from Public Against Violence, 31 from the Christian Democratic Movement, 22 from the Communist Party of Czechoslovakia, 22 from the Slovak National Party, 14 from Coexistence, 7 from the Democratic Party and 6 from the Green Party); Chair. FRANTIŠEK MIKLOŠKO.

Political Organizations

Agrarian Party (Zemědělská strana): f. 1990; seeks compensation for farmers whose property was confiscated during collectivization; Chair. Dr FRANTIŠEK TRNKA.

Christian Democratic Movement (CDM): Bratislava; f. 1990; Chair. JÁN ČARNOGURSKÝ.

Christian Democratic Party (CDP): Prague; f. 1989; Leader VÁCLAV BENDA.

Civic Forum (Občanské fórum): Ústřední úřad, Václavské nám., Prague; f. 1989 as an informal coalition of independent opposition groups; re-formed as a political party in 1991; Chair. VÁCLAV KLAUS.

Communist Party of Czechoslovakia—CPCZ (Komunistická strana Československa—KSČS): nábř. Ludvíka Svobody 12, 125 11 Prague 1; tel. (2) 2199; f. 1921; incorporating the former Czechoslovak Social Democratic Party and the Slovak Labour Party; 760,000 mems; Chair. of Federal Council PAVOL KANIS.

Communist Party of Slovakia—CPSL (Komunistická strana Slovenska—KSS): Mierová 21, 827 05 Bratislava; tel. (7) 231276; telex 92722; fax (7) 235323; Chair. of Exec. Cttee of Central Cttee PETER WEISS.

Czechoslovak National Congress: Prague; f. 1990; unites right-wing political parties and movements throughout Czechoslovakia; 10,000 mems; Chair. VILEM NEDOROST.

Czechoslovak People's Party (CPP): Revoluční 5, 110 15 Prague 1; f. 1919; Christian party; 90,000 mems; Chair. JOSEF LUX; Gen. Sec. JIŘÍ ČERNÝ.

Czechoslovak Social Democratic Party: Prague; re-established 1989; Chair. Prof. JIŘÍ HORÁK.

Czechoslovak Socialist Party (CSP): nám. Republiky 7, 111 49 Prague 1; tel. (2) 313051; telex 121432; f. 1948; Chair. LADISLAV DVOŘÁK.

Democratic Party (Demokratická strana): Malinovského 70, 812 78 Bratislava; tel. (7) 498020; fax (7) 492273; f. 1944; prohibited 1948; restored 1989; approx. 12,000 mems; Chair. JÁN HOLČÍK.

Green Party: f. 1990; Chair. JAN JECMÍNEK.

National Social Party: f. 1990; considers itself successor to the Czechoslovak National Socialist Party (f. 1897); Dep. Chair. JOSEF LESÁK.

Party of Tradesmen and Entrepreneurs (Strana živnostníků a podnikatelů): Prague; f. 1990; promotes private enterprise; Chair. JAROSLAV SAMEK.

Public Against Violence (PAV) (Verejnosť proti násiliu): Bratislava; f. 1989; Slovak-based counterpart of Civic Forum; Chair. of Co-ordination Centre FEDOR GÁL.

Republican Union: Prague; f. 1990; 2,000 mems; Chair. ZDENĚK ZÁHORSKÝ.

Slovak Democratic Party: Malinovského 70, 812 78 Bratislava; f. 1989 from the Slovak Revival Party; Chair. Ing. JÁN HOLČÍK; Sec.-Gen. ALOJZ ČMELO.

Slovak Freedom Party (Strana slobody): Obrancov mieru 8, 816 18 Bratislava; f. 1946 as a splinter party from the Slovak Democratic Party; Chair. (vacant).

Slovak National Party—SNP (Slovenská národná strana): Bratislava; advocates independence for Slovakia; Chair. (vacant).

Slovak Social Democratic Party (Sociálno-demokratická strana na Slovensku): Bratislava; re-established 1990; Chair. BORIS ZÁLA.

Other independent organizations and parties that were established or revived in late 1989 and 1990 included the following: Coexistence (Soužití, also known, in Hungarian, as Együtteles—a coalition of Hungarian, Polish and other ethnic minority groups, Leader MIKLÓS DURAY), the Movement for Autonomous Democracy-Society for Moravia and Silesia (MAD-SMS, Chair. BOLESLAV BARTA), the Obroda (Renewal) Club for Socialist Restructuring, the Liberal European Party and the Party of Independent Democrats.

CZECHOSLOVAKIA

Diplomatic Representation

EMBASSIES IN CZECHOSLOVAKIA

Afghanistan: U Vorlíku 17, 125 01 Prague 6; tel. (2) 381532; Ambassador: MOHAMMAD ARAF SAKHRA.
Albania: Pod Kaštany 22, 160 00 Prague; Ambassador: IDRIZ DHRAMI.
Algeria: Korejská 16, 125 21 Prague; tel. (2) 322021; Ambassador: ABDELHAMID LATRECHE.
Argentina: Washingtonova 25, 125 22 Prague 1; Ambassador: JULIO BARBOZA.
Austria: Viktora Huga 10, 125 43 Prague 5; tel. (2) 546550; telex 121849; Ambassador: KARL PETERLIK.
Belgium: Valdštejnská 6, 125 24 Prague 1; tel. (2) 534051; telex 122362; Ambassador: Baron HENRY BEYENS.
Bolivia: Ve Smečkách 25, 125 59 Prague 1; tel. (2) 263209; Ambassador: JUAN CARLOS QUIROGA.
Brazil: Bolzanova 5, 125 01 Prague 1; tel. (2) 229254; telex 122292; Ambassador: CARLOS EDUARDO DE AFFONSECA ALVES DE SOUZA.
Bulgaria: Krakovská 6, 125 00 Prague 1; tel. (2) 264310; telex 121381; Ambassador: TONCHO CHAKAROV.
Cambodia: Na Hubálce 1, 169 00 Prague 6; tel. (2) 352603; Ambassador: UNG SEAN.
Canada: Mickiewiczova 6, 125 33 Prague 6; tel. (2) 326941; telex 121061; Ambassador: BARRY M. MAWHINNEY.
China, People's Republic: Majakovského 22, 160 00 Prague 6; Ambassador: WANG XINGDA.
Colombia: Příčná 1, 110 00 Prague 1; tel. (2) 291330; Ambassador: ENRIQUE PAREJO GONZÁLEZ.
Costa Rica: Dlouhá 36, 110 00 Prague 1; tel. (2) 2619073; telex 121776; fax (2) 2320878; Ambassador: CARLOS E. FERNÁNDEZ GARCÍA.
Cuba: Sibiřské nám. 1, 125 35 Prague 6; tel. (2) 341341; telex 93184; Ambassador: MARIO RODRÍGUEZ MARTÍNEZ.
Denmark: U Havličkových sadů 1, 120 21 Prague 2; tel. (2) 254715; telex 122209; Ambassador: VIGAND LOSE.
Ecuador: Opletalova 43, 125 01 Prague 1; tel. (2) 261258; telex 123286; Ambassador: OSWALDO RAMÍREZ LANDAZURI.
Egypt: Majakovského 14, 125 46 Prague 6; tel. (2) 341051; telex 123552; Ambassador: NABIL HELMY.
Ethiopia: V Průhledu 9, 125 01 Prague 6; tel. (2) 352268; Ambassador: WONDWOSSEN HAILU.
Finland: Dřevná 2, 125 01 Prague 2; tel. (2) 205541; telex 121060; Ambassador: EERO YRJÖLÄ.
France: Velkopřevorské nám. 2, 110 00 Prague 1; tel. (2) 533042; fax (2) 539926; Ambassador: JEAN GUÉGUINOU.
Germany: Vlašska 19, 125 60 Prague 1; tel. (2) 532351; telex 122814; Ambassador: HERMANN HUBER.
Ghana: V Tisine 4, 160 00 Prague 6; tel. (2) 373058; telex 122263; Ambassador: MOSES KWASI AHMAD AGYEMAN.
Greece: Na Ořechovce 19, 125 45 Prague 6; tel. (2) 354279; Ambassador: CONSTANTIN POLITIS.
Hungary: Mičurinova I, 125 37 Prague 6; tel. (2) 365041; telex 123535; Ambassador: MIKLÓS BARITY.
India: Valdštejnská 6, 125 28 Prague 1; tel. (2) 532642; telex 121901; Ambassador: BHUPATRAY OZA.
Indonesia: Nad Buďánkami II/7, 125 29 Prague 5; tel. (2) 526041; telex 121443; Ambassador: H. R. ENAP SURATMAN.
Iran: Nám. Družby 9, Prague 6; tel. (2) 322745; telex 122732; Ambassador: HAMID REZA HOSSEINI.
Iraq: Na Zátorce 10, 125 01 Prague 6; Ambassador: MUNTHER AHMED AL-MUTLAK.
Italy: Nerudova 20, 125 31 Prague 1; tel. (2) 530666; telex 122704; Ambassador: GIOVANNI CASTELLANI PASTORIS.
Japan: Maltézské nám. 6, 125 32 Prague 1; tel. (2) 535751; telex 121199; fax (2) 539997; Ambassador: TISATI CATO.
Korea, Democratic People's Republic: R. Rollanda 10, 160 00 Prague 6; tel. (2) 373953; Ambassador: KIM KWANG SOP.
Korea, Republic: Prague; Ambassador SON CHUN-YONG.
Lebanon: Gottwaldovo nábřeží 14, 110 00 Prague 1; tel. (2) 293633; telex 123583; Ambassador: SLEIMAN YOUNES.
Libya: Na baště sv. Jiří 7, 160 00 Prague 6; Secretary of People's Cttee: MUHAMMAD MUSBAH KHALIFA.
Mexico: Nad Kazankou 8, 171 00 Prague 7; tel. (2) 8555554; telex 121947; fax (2) 8550477; Ambassador: ALFONSO HERRERA SALCEDO.
Mongolia: Korejská 5, 160 00 Prague 6; tel. (2) 328992; telex 121921; Ambassador: DJAMSRAGIYN DULMA.
Morocco: Petrska 24, 124 47 Prague 1; tel. (2) 310935; Ambassador: TAJEDDINE BADDOU.
Myanmar: Romaina Rollanda 3, 125 23 Prague 6; Ambassador: U THAN TUN.
Netherlands: Maltézské nám. 1, 110 00 Prague 1; tel. (2) 531378; telex 122643; fax (2) 531368; Ambassador: Count LAMBERT D'ANSEMBOURG.
Nicaragua: Na Baště sv. Jiří 3, 125 46 Prague 6; tel. (2) 324410; telex 123336; Ambassador: MAYRA PASOS MARCIAQ.
Nigeria: Před Bateriemi 18, 160 00 Prague 6; tel. (2) 354294; telex 123575; Ambassador: Dr MUSA OTIGBA.
Norway: Na Ořechovce 69, 162 00 Prague 6; tel. (2) 354526; telex 122200; Ambassador: KNUT TARALDSET.
Peru: Hradecká 18, 125 01 Prague 3; tel. (2) 742024; telex 123345; Ambassador: IGOR VELÁZQUEZ RODRÍGUEZ.
Poland: Valdštejnská 8, 125 42 Prague 1; tel. (2) 536951; telex 121841; fax (2) 536427; Ambassador: JACEK BALUCH.
Portugal: Bubenská 3, 170 00 Prague 7; tel. (2) 878472; telex 121354; Ambassador: LUÍS QUARTIN.
Romania: Nerudova 5, 125 44 Prague; tel. (2) 533059; Ambassador: GHEORGHE HOMOSTEAN.
Spain: Pevnostní 9, 162 00 Prague 6; tel. (2) 327124; telex 121974; fax (2) 323573; Ambassador: JOSÉ LUIS DICENTA BALLESTER.
Sudan: Malostranské nábřeží 1, 125 01 Prague; tel. (2) 536547; Ambassador: SAYYID ABD AL-MUTASIM.
Sweden: Úvoz 13, 125 52 Prague 1; tel. (2) 533344; telex 121840; Ambassador: L. A. NILSSON.
Switzerland: Pevnostní 7, 162 00 Prague 6; tel. (2) 320406; Ambassador: SERGE F. SALVI.
Syria: Pod Kaštany 16, 125 01 Prague 6; tel. (2) 326231; telex 121532; Ambassador: SUBHI HADDAD.
Tunisia: Nad Kostelem 8, 142 00 Prague 4; tel. (2) 460652; telex 122512; Ambassador: NOUREDDINE BOUJELLABIA.
Turkey: Pevnostní 3, 160 00 Prague 6; tel. (2) 320597; Ambassador: CENAP KESKIN.
USSR: Pod Kaštany 1, 160 00 Prague 6; tel. (2) 381943; Ambassador: BORIS PANKIN.
United Kingdom: Thunovská 14, 125 50 Prague 1; tel. (2) 533347; telex 121011; fax (2) 539927; Ambassador: P. LAURENCE O'KEEFFE.
USA: Tržiště 15, 125 48 Prague; tel. (2) 536641; telex 121196; fax (2) 532457; Ambassador SHIRLEY TEMPLE BLACK.
Uruguay: Václavské nám. 64, 111 21 Prague 1; tel. (2) 351989; telex 121291; Ambassador: ANTONIO CAMPS VALGOI.
Venezuela: Janáčkovo nábřeží 49, 150 00 Prague; tel. (2) 536051; telex 122146; Ambassador: JOSÉ DE JESÚS OSÍO.
Viet-Nam: Holečkova 6, 125 55 Prague; tel. (2) 536127; telex 121824; Ambassador: NGUYEN PHU SOAI.
Yemen: Washingtonova 17, 125 22 Prague 1; tel. (2) 222411; telex 123300; Ambassador: ABD AL-LATIF MUHAMMAD DHAIF ALLAH.
Yugoslavia: Mostecká 15, 118 00 Prague; tel. (2) 531443; telex 123284; Ambassador: DUSAN RODIĆ.

Judicial System

Justice is executed through elected courts which consist of three ranks of law courts: the Supreme Court of the Czech and Slovak Federative Republic (together with Supreme Courts of the Czech and Slovak Republics), Regional and District Courts. There are also Military Courts which are subject to special regulations. Judges of the Czechoslovak Supreme Court are elected by the Federal Assembly; judges of the Czech and Slovak Supreme Courts and of the Regional and District Courts are elected by the National Councils of the respective republics. Judges are of two kinds, professional and lay judges, the latter having other occupations, but both types have equal authority. Lay judges are elected by District National Committees. Supervision of the observance of laws and legal regulations rests with the Procurator-General who is appointed by the President of the Republic and accountable to the Federal Assembly.

Chairman of the Supreme Court: Dr OTAKAR MOTEJL.
Procurator-General: Dr IVAN GASPAROVIČ.

Religion

CHRISTIANITY

Ekumenická rada církví v České a Slovenské federativní republice (Czechoslovak Ecumenical Council of Churches): Vítkova 13,

CZECHOSLOVAKIA

186 00 Prague 8; tel. (2) 227581; f. 1955, present name since 1990; 11 mem. churches; Chair. Rev. Dr JOSEF HROMÁDKA; Vice-Chair. RUDOLF BORSKI; Gen. Sec. Rev. PAVEL VYCHOPEŇ.

The Roman Catholic Church
Czechoslovakia comprises three archdioceses and 10 dioceses, including one (directly responsible to the Holy See) for Catholics of the Slovak (Byzantine) rite.

Latin Rite
Archbishop of Prague: Cardinal FRANTIŠEK TOMÁŠEK, Hradčanské nám. 16, 119 02 Prague 1; tel. (2) 539548.

Archbishop of Olomouc: Mgr Dr FRANTIŠEK VAŇÁK, Wurmova 9, 771 01 Olomouc; tel. (68) 25726.

Archbishop of Trnava: Mgr JÁN SOKOL, Svätoplukovo 3, 917 66 Trnava; tel. (805) 26235.

Slovak Rite
Bishop of Prešov: Mgr JÁN HIRKA, Greckokatolický biskupský úrad, Hlavná ulica 8, Prešov; tel. (91) 34622; 361,060 adherents (December 1988); 201 parishes.

The Orthodox Church
Pravoslavaná Církev v ČSFR (Orthodox Church of Czechoslovakia): V Jámě, 6, 111 21 Prague 1; divided into four eparchies: Prague, Olomouc, Prešov, Michalovce; Head of the Autocephalous Church. Metropolitan of Prague and of all Czechoslovakia JAN MÍRKO; 200,000 mems; 127 parishes; Theological Faculty in Prešov.

Protestant Churches
Brethren Church: Soukenická 15,110 00 Prague 1; 10,000 mems, 35 congregations, 190 preaching stations; Pres. JAROSLAV KUBOVÝ; Sec. K. TASCHNER.

Christian Corps: Brno; 3,200 mems; 123 brs; Rep. Ing. PETR ZEMAN.

Czechoslovak Baptists: Na Topolce 14, 140 00 Prague 4; tel. (2) 430974; f. 1919; 4,000 mems; Pres. Rev. PAVEL VYCHOPEŇ.

Evangelical Church of Czech Brethren (Presbyterian): Jungmannova 9, 111 21 Prague 1; tel. (2) 2360924; telex 123363; fax (2) 2350251; united since 1918; activities extend over Bohemia, Moravia, and Silesia; 180,000 adherents and 268 parishes; Pres. Rev. Dr JOSEF HROMÁDKA; Gen. Sec. MIROSLAV BROŽ.

Reformed Christian Church of Slovakia: Jókaiho 36, 945 01 Komárno; tel. (819) 2788; 150,000 mems and 310 parishes; Bishop EUGEN MIKÓ; Gen. Sec. BARTOLOMEJ GÖÖZ.

Silesian Evangelical Church of the Augsburg Confession in the Czech Republic (Silesian Lutheran Church): Na Nivách 7, 737 01 Český Těšín; tel. (659) 56656; founded in the 16th century during the Lutheran Reformation, reorganized in 1948; 46,800 mems; Bishop VILÉM STONAWSKI.

Slovak Lutheran Church (Evangelical Church of the Augsburg Confession in Czechoslovakia); 326 parishes in 14 seniorates; 369,000 baptized mems; 327 parishes; Bishop-Gen. PAVEL UHORSKAI, Palisády 46, 811 06 Bratislava; tel. (7) 330827; Eastern District Bishop Dr JÚLIUS FILLO, Jesenského 1, 040 01 Košice; Bishop of the Western District RUDOLF KOŠTIAL, Námestie SNP 17, 960 01 ZVOLEN.

Unitarians: Karlova 8, 110 00 Prague 1; tel. (2) 266730; f. 1923; 5,000 mems; 4 parishes; Presiding Officer Dr D. J. KAFKA.

United Methodist Church: Ječná 19, 120 00 Prague 2; tel. (2) 290623; 3,688 mems; 21 parishes; Supt JOSEF ČERVEŇÁK.

Unity of Brethren (Jednota bratrská) (Moravian Church): Hálkova 5, 120 00 Prague 2; tel. (2) 2361340; f. 1457; 5,000 mems; 17 parishes; Pres. Rev. RUDOLF BORSKI.

Other Christian Churches
Apostolic Church: f. 1989; 2,000 mems; Chair. of Central Council of Elders RUDOLF BUBÍK.

Church of the Seventh-day Adventists: Zálesí 50, 142 00 Prague 4; tel. (2) 4723745; 12,000 mems; 106 preaching stations; Pres. KAREL NOWAK.

Czechoslovak Hussite Church: Kujbyševa 5, 166 26 Prague 6; tel. (2) 320041; f. 1920; 400,000 mems; five dioceses divided into 327 parishes; Bishop-Patriarch Dr VLASTIMIL ZÍTEK.

Old Catholic Church (Synodní rada církve starokatolické): Hládkov 3, 160 00 Prague 6; tel. (2) 357051; f. 1871; 1,800 mems, 6 parishes; Bishop Dr AUGUSTIN PODOLÁK.

JUDAISM
The present community is estimated at approximately 6,000 people, and is divided under two central organizations:

Council of Jewish Communities in the Czech Republic (Rada židovských náboženských obcí v České republice): Maislova 18, 101 01 Prague 1; tel. (2) 2318559; 6,000 mems; Chair. (vacant); Sec.-Gen. (vacant); Chief Rabbi of Prague DANIEL MAYER.

Union of the Jewish Religious Communities in the Slovak Republic (Ústredný zväz židovských náboženských obcí ve Slovenskej republike): Šmeralova ul. 29, 800 00 Bratislava; 3,300 mems; Chair. JURAJ RAIF; Chief Rabbi SAMUEL GROSSMANN (Košice).

The Press

The Czechoslovak people far exceed other East European nations in their consumption per head of newspapers and magazines. There are about 30 daily newspapers (with a combined circulation of 5.1m. copies per issue in 1988), including nine in Prague and nine (one in Hungarian and the remainder in Slovak) in Bratislava. In 1989 there were 1,086 magazines and newspapers published in Czechoslovakia, as well as numerous less frequent periodicals.

In November 1989, during Czechoslovakia's 'velvet revolution', the laws on censorship were revoked, and many publications and literary works, hitherto banned, became freely available. Among the most influential and widely read of the new independent publications, established in 1990, were *Fórum* (a weekly magazine with a circulation of 200,000) and the daily *Občanský deník*, both published by Civic Forum. Also important was the daily *Lidové noviny* (formerly an underground publication). *Rudé právo*, the chief organ of the Czechoslovak Communist Party, retained a wide daily circulation (520,000 in 1990).

PRINCIPAL DAILIES
Prague
Československý sport (Czechoslovak Sport): Na poříčí 30, 115 23 Prague 1; tel. (2) 2322528; telex 121514; central organ of the Czech Union of Physical Education; Editor JAROMÍR TOMÁNEK; circ. 195,000.

Hospodářské noviny (Economic News): Na Florenci 3, 115 43 Prague 1; tel. (2) 225740; telex 121435; fax (2) 2356467; published by the Economia joint-stock company; Editor-in-Chief Dr JIŘÍ SEKERA; circ. 140,000.

Lidová demokracie (People's Democracy): Karlovo nám. 5, 120 78 Prague 2; tel. (2) 291505; telex 121403; f. 1945; morning; official organ of the Czechoslovak People's Party; Editor Dr JIŘÍ NAVRÁTIL; circ. 228,502.

Lidové noviny (People's News): Václavské nám. 47, 111 21 Prague 1; tel. (2) 2351045; telex 123147; fax (2) 266611; re-established 1990; Editor-in-Chief RUDOLF ZEMAN.

Mladá fronta dnes (Youth Front Today): Panská 8, 112 22 Prague 1; tel. (2) 224141; telex 122468; fax (2) 2368453; f. 1945; morning; Editor-in-Chief LÍBOR ŠEVČÍK; circ. 330,048.

Občanský deník (Civic Daily): Na Florenci 19, 113 29 Prague 1; tel. (2) 2327324; telex 121856; fax (2) 2320925; f. 1990; published by Civic Forum; Editor-in-Chief KAREL STANĚK.

Práce (Labour): Václavské nám. 15, 112 58 Prague 1; tel. (2) 266039; telex 121134; f. 1945; morning; published by the Czech and Slovak Confederation of Trade Unions; Editor-in-Chief FRANTIŠEK COŇK; circ. 353,414.

Rudé právo (Red Right): Na Florenci 19, 112 86 Prague 1; tel. (2) 2367487; telex 121184; fax (2) 2321979; f. 1920; morning; central organ of the Czechoslovak Communist Party; Editor-in-Chief ZDENĚK PORYBNÝ; circ. 520,000.

Svoboda (Freedom): Na Florenci 3, 113 29 Prague 1; tel. (2) 2321634; telex 121856; organ of the Central Bohemian Regional Cttee of the Communist Party of Czechoslovakia; Editor-in-Chief JIŘÍ NOVOTNÝ; circ. 61,683.

Svobodné slovo (Free Word): Václavské nám. 36, 112 12 Prague 1; tel. (2) 260341; telex 121432; f. 1907; organ of the Czechoslovak Socialist Party; Editor-in-Chief LUBOMÍR PETRÍK; circ. 220,000.

Večerní Praha (Evening Prague): Na Florenci 19, 112 86 Prague 1; tel. (2) 2327324; telex 121883; f. 1955; evening; edited by the Prague Municipal Cttee of the Communist Party; Editor-in-Chief Dr JAROSLAV LEMÁK; circ. 170,000.

Zemědělské noviny (Farmer's News): Václavské nám. 47, 113 78 Prague 1; tel. (2) 265951-9; telex 121435; f. 1945; Editor-in-Chief VLADIMÍR KULHÁNEK; circ. 381,275.

Banská Bystrica
Smer (Course): Čs. armády 10, 975 43 Banská Bystrica; tel. 25466; telex 70261; fax 25506; f. 1948; independent; Editor-in-Chief IVAN BAČA; circ. 45,000.

Bratislava
Hlas l'udu (Voice of the People): Martanovičova 25, 819 06 Bratislava; tel. (7) 55521; telex 93398; f. 1949; morning; West Slovakia region; Editor-in-Chief PAVOL DINKA; circ. 49,337.

CZECHOSLOVAKIA

Ľud (People): Gorkého 5/1, 812 78 Bratislava; tel. (7) 58854; telex 93254; f. 1948; organ of the Slovak Reconstruction Party; Editor-in-Chief ENGELBERT MERKL; circ. 13,589.

Narodna obroda (National Renewal): Bratislava; f. 1990; independent; published by the Slovak State Government; Editor-in-Chief JURAJ VERES; circ. 100,000.

Práca (Labour): Odborárská nám. 3, 812 71 Bratislava; tel. (7) 64547; telex 93283; fax (7) 212985; f. 1946; published by the Czech and Slovak Confederation of Trade Unions; Editor-in-Chief MILOS NEMEČEK; circ. 260,300.

Pravda (Truth): Martanovičova 25, 819 08 Bratislava; tel. (7) 52503; telex 93386; fax (7) 58305; f. 1920; independent; published by the Perex joint-stock co; Editor-in-Chief PETER SITÁNYI; circ. 260,000.

Roľnícke noviny (Farmer's News): Martanovičova 25, 819 11 Bratislava; tel. (7) 54449; telex 93211; fax (7) 51282; f. 1946; organ of the Slovak Ministry of Agriculture and Food; Editor-in-Chief JURAJ ŠESTÁK; circ. 80,000.

Smena (Shift): Dostojevského rad 1, 812 84 Bratislava; tel. (7) 54255; telex 93341; f. 1947; Editor-in-Chief LUBOMÍR CHORVATOVIČ; circ. 141,867.

Šport (Sport): Martanovičova 25, 819 23 Bratislava; tel. (7) 54727; fax (7) 211380; Editor-in-Chief Dr JÚLIUS KOZMA; circ. 70,000.

Új Szó (New World): Gorkého 10, 815 81 Bratislava; tel. (7) 53220; telex 92308; f. 1948; midday; Hungarian-language paper of the Communist Party of Slovakia; Editor-in-Chief JOZEF KISS; circ. 98,330.

Večerník (Evening Paper): Martanovičova 25, 819 16 Bratislava; tel. (7) 55085; telex 92296; f. 1956; evening; publ. by GEMIAL; Editor-in-Chief Dr RUDOLF MACHALA; circ. 80,400.

Verejnosť (Public): Martanovičova 25, 819 02 Bratislava; tel. (7) 58807; f. 1990; published by Public Against Violence; Editor-in-Chief PETER DUHAN.

Brno

Brněnský večerník (Brno Evening News): Jakubské nám. 7, 658 44 Brno; tel. (5) 228446; f. 1968; organ of the Brno City Cttee of the Communist Party; Editor-in-Chief Dr DANUŠE ŠKLÍBOVÁ; circ. 33,000.

Rovnost (Equality): Moravské nám. 13, 658 22 Brno; tel. (5) 749000; telex 62342; fax (5) 743832; f. 1885; morning; Editor-in-Chief LUBOMÍR SELINGER; circ. 100,000.

České Budějovice

Jihočeská Pravda (South Bohemia Truth): Vrbenská 23, 370 45 České Budějovice; tel. (38) 22081; published by the South Bohemian Regional Cttee of the Communist Party; Editor-in-Chief VLADIMÍR DOLEŽAL; circ. 67,515.

Hradec Králové

Pochodeň (Torch): Škroupova 695, 501 72 Hradec Králové; tel. (49) 613511; published by the East Bohemian Regional Cttee of the Communist Party; Editor-in-Chief OLDŘICH ENGE; circ. 74,188.

Košice

Východ (East): Šmeralova 18, 042 66 Košice; tel. (95) 33261; East Slovakia region; Editor-in-Chief ŠTEFAN KOČUTA; circ. 58,000.

Ostrava

Nezávislá Nová Svoboda (Independent New Freedom): Novinářská 3, 709 07 Ostrava; tel. (69) 261682; telex 66427; f. 1945; morning; published by the Delta Publishing House; Editor-in-Chief OLDŘICH VLK; circ. 150,000.

Ostravský večerník (Ostrava Evening News): Zeyerova 11, 728 85 Ostrava; tel. (69) 232023; published by the City Cttee of the Communist Party and the Municipal National Cttee; Editor-in-Chief JOSEF ZLOMEK; circ. 28,607.

Plzeň

Pravda (Truth): Leninova 15, 304 83 Plzeň; tel. (19) 222000; telex 154302; f. 1919; published by the West Bohemian Regional Cttee of the Communist Party; Editor-in-Chief JAROSLAV PÁV; circ. 85,385.

Ústí nad Labem

Severočeský deník (North Bohemian Daily): Velká hradební, 400 90 Ústí nad Labem; tel. (47) 22244-6; telex 184221; fax (47) 23676; f. 1920; published by the Delta Publishing House, Prague; Editor-in-Chief JAROSLAV HAIDLER; circ. 100,000.

PRINCIPAL PERIODICALS
Czech language

100+1ZZ: Zirovnická 2389, 106 00 Prague 10; tel. (2) 7192248; monthly foreign press digest of the Czechoslovak News Agency (ČTK); Editor-in-Chief JAN BLAŽÍK; circ. 155,000.

Ahoj na sobotu (Hallo Saturday): Václavské nám. 36, 112 12 Prague 1; tel. (2) 264663; illustrated family weekly published by the Czechoslovak Socialist Party; Editor-in-Chief MARIE ŠOLLEOVÁ; circ. 178,000.

Československý architekt (Czechoslovak Architect): Letenská 5, 118 45 Prague 1; tel. (2) 539768; telex 122064; f. 1955; fortnightly; Editor Dr JAN NOVOTNÝ; circ. 7,500.

Československý život (Czechoslovak Life): Vinohradská 46, 120 41 Prague 2; tel. (2) 257741; telex 122948; f. 1946; illustrated monthly magazine; political, economic, social, cultural and sports; published by Orbis Press Agency in English, French, German, Italian and Spanish; Editor (vacant); circ. 90,000.

Chatař (Weekend House Owner): Václavské náměstí 47, 113 11 Prague 1; tel. (2) 264592; monthly; published by State Agricultural Publishing House; Editor-in-Chief Ing. JIŘÍ TRNAVSKÝ; circ. 100,000.

Chovatel (Breeder): Václavské náměstí 47, 113 11 Prague 1; tel. (2) 2352045; monthly; published by the Czech Union of Breeders; Editor-in-Chief Ing. OLGA MAKARIUSOVÁ; circ. 100,000.

Čtení (Reading): Národní tř. 25, 110 000 Prague 1; tel. (2) 268011; monthly; about life in the USSR; published by the Union of Czechoslovak-Soviet Friendship; Editor-in-Chief EMILIE HORÁKOVÁ; circ. 275,000.

Dikobraz (Porcupine): Na Florenci 3, 112 86 Prague 1; tel. (2) 2356760; telex 121184; f. 1945; satirical weekly; Editor-in-Chief ZDENĚK DVOŘÁK; circ. 531,000.

Film a doba (Film and Time): Slavíčkova 5, 160 00 Prague 6; tel. (2) 375062; monthly; Editor EVA ZAORALOVÁ; circ. 7,000.

Fórum: Sněmovní 3, 118 00 Prague 1; tel. (2) 518586; fax (2) 539828; f. 1990; weekly; current affairs, economy, culture, ecology; publ. by Civic Forum; Editor-in-Chief JAN VÁVRA; circ. 200,000.

Fotografie (Photography): Mrštíkova 23, 101 00 Prague 10; tel. (2) 781553; f. 1946; monthly; photographic; Editor (vacant); circ. 57,000.

Hudební rozhledy (Musical Review): Maltézské nám. 1, 118 00 Prague 1; tel. (2) 532931; f. 1948; monthly review; published by the Assen of Musicians and Musicologists; Editor JAN SMOLÍK; circ. 4,200.

Katolický týdeník (Catholic Weekly): Sněmovní 9, 118 01 Prague 1; tel. (2) 533017; fax (2) 533017; weekly; published by Czech Catholic Charity; Editor-in-Chief JOSEF GABRIEL; circ. 128,000.

Kino (Cinema): Slavíčkova 5, 160 00 Prague 6; tel. (2) 375063; an illustrated film magazine published by the Panorama Publishing House; fortnightly; Editor-in-Chief JANA BÍLKOVÁ; circ. 160,000.

Květy (Flowers): Na Florenci 3, 112 86 Prague 1; tel. (2) 2323451; telex 12184; f. 1834; illustrated weekly; published by Czechoslovak Communist Party; Editor-in-Chief Dr MILAN CODR; circ. 401,000.

Magazín Co vás zajímá (What Interests You ?): Na Florenci 3, 112 86 Prague 1; tel. (2) 2323451; monthly; published by Rudé právo Publishing House; Editor-in-Chief Dr MIROSLAVA PAPEŽOVÁ; circ. 165,000.

Mladý svět (Young World): Panská 8, 112 22 Prague 1; tel. (2) 223726; telex 121510; fax (2) 220039; independent; illustrated weekly for young people; Editor-in-Chief LUBOŠ BENIAK; circ. 450,000.

Motor (Motoring): Jungmannova 24, 113 66 Prague 1; tel. (2) 2362439; f. 1969; monthly; published by State Cttee for Road Traffic Security; Editor-in-Chief PETR DUFEK; circ. 116,000.

Naše rodina (Our Family): Karlovo nám. 5, 120 00 Prague 2; tel. (2) 294196; f. 1968; Christian and cultural weekly published by Czechoslovak People's Party; Editor-in-Chief Dr LIBUŠE DAŇKOVÁ; circ. 179,700.

Obrana lidu (People's Defence): Jungmannova 24, 113 66 Prague 1; tel. (2) 246886; weekly; published by the Political Administration of the People's Army; Editor-in-Chief MIROSLAV PROCHÁZKA; circ. 87,786.

Odborář (Trade Unionist): Senovážné nám. 23, 112 82 Prague 1; tel. (2) 2363418; fortnightly; published by the Central Trade Unions Council; Editor-in-Chief Ing. HELENA MANDOVÁ; circ. 121,000.

Ohníček (Little Flame): Radlická 61, 150 00 Prague 5; tel. (2) 536523; fortnightly magazine for Czechoslovak children; published by the Mladá fronta dnes Publishing House; Editor-in-Chief Dr EVA VONDRÁŠKOVÁ; circ. 250,000.

Prager Volkszeitung (Prague People's Newspaper): Helénská 4, 120 00 Prague 2; tel. (2) 2355565; weekly; general politics and culture; published by Rudé právo Publishing House and the Cultural Union of the German citizens in Czechoslovakia; Editor HERIBERT PANSTER; circ. 17,000.

Praktická žena (Practical Woman): Na rybníčku 1, 120 00 Prague 2; tel. (2) 224642; f. 1950; monthly; published by the Czechoslovak Union of Women; Editor-in-Chief MIRKA LÁNSKÁ; circ. 272,000.

CZECHOSLOVAKIA

Právník (The Lawyer): Národní třída 18, 116 91 Prague 1; tel. (2) 201620; f. 1861; monthly; law; published by Czechoslovak Academy of Sciences (Institute of State and Law); Editor JOSEF BLAHOŽ; circ. 4,700.

Rozhlas (Radio): Na Florenci 3, 112 86 Prague 1; fax (2) 2356467; f. 1923; weekly; cultural and sound radio journal; published by the Delta Publishing House; Editor STANISLAV PSCHEIDT; circ. 270,000.

Sedmička (Seven): Radlická 61, 150 00 Prague 5; tel. (2) 540013; telex 123302; weekly; published by the Mladá fronta dnes Publishing House; Editor-in-Chief SVATAVA HIRSCHOVÁ; circ. 250,000.

Signál (Signal): Hybernská 7, 110 00 Prague 1; tel. (2) 2357323; telex 121572; f. 1965; weekly; illustrated family magazine; published by Federal Ministry of the Interior; Editor-in-Chief Ing. PAVEL MINAŘÍK; circ. 295,000.

Stadion (Stadium): Klimentská 1, 115 88 Prague 1; tel. (2) 2312898; illustrated sport weekly published by the Czech Central Cttee for Physical Education; Editor-in-Chief MILAN MACHO; circ. 166,000.

Svět motorů (World of Motors): Jungmannova 24, 113 66 Prague 1; tel. (2) 240280; f. 1947; weekly; published by the Union for Co-operation with the army of the ČSSR; motoring; Editor-in-Chief MIROSLAV EBR; circ. 359,000.

Svět práce (The World of Labour): Václavské nám. 15, 112 58 Prague 1; telex 121134; f. 1946, reorganized 1968; political, economic and cultural weekly; published by Czech and Slovak Confederation of Trade Unions; Editor FRANTIŠEK ŘÍHA; circ. 85,000.

Svět (The World): Smetanovo nábř. 18, 110 00 Prague 1; tel. (2) 241216; illustrated weekly; published by the Union of Czechoslovak-Soviet Friendship; Editor-in-Chief MIROSLAV TULEJA; circ. 115,000.

Svět v obrazech (World in Pictures): Pařížská 9, 110 00 Prague 1; tel. (2) 2324771; f. 1945; illustrated weekly published by the Odeon Publishing House; Editor-in-Chief Dr ZDENĚK HRABICA; circ. 150,000.

Světová literatura (World Literature): Na Florenci 3, 115 86 Prague 1; tel. (2) 2256774; f. 1956; published by Odeon, bi-monthly; contemporary foreign literature; Editor VÁCLAV FALADA; circ. 12,000.

Tvorba (Production): Na poříčí 30, 112 86 Prague 1; tel. (2) 2321146; f. 1925; weekly; political, scientific and cultural; published by the Rudé právo Publishing House; Editor-in-Chief IVAN MATĚJKA; circ. 80,000.

Týdeník Československé televize (Czechoslovak Television Weekly): nám. Lidových milicí 5, 190 00 Prague 9; tel. (2) 839856; telex 121184; f. 1965; weekly cultural and television journal; published by Rudé právo; Editor-in-Chief JANA KOLÁROVÁ; circ. 510,000.

Věda a život (Science and Life): POB 395, 659 95 Brno; tel. (5) 22778; f. 1936; monthly; published by the Kolorit Publishing House; Editor JIŘÍ CICVÁREK; circ. 15,000.

Vesmír (Universe): Jungmannova 12, 110 00 Prague 1; fax (2) 266022; f. 1871; a monthly popular science magazine of the Czechoslovak Academy of Science; Editor IVAN M. HAVEL; circ. 31,000.

Vlasta: Jindřišská 5, 116 08 Prague 1; tel. (2) 2357883; f. 1946; illustrated weekly for women; Editor-in-Chief MARIE FORMÁČKOVÁ; circ. 700,000.

Zahrádkář (Gardener): Čkalova 22, 160 41 Prague 6; tel. (2) 323105; monthly; published by Czech Union of Gardeners; Editor-in-Chief Dr STANISLAV PELEŠKA; circ. 320,000.

Zápisník (Notebook): Vlastina 23, 160 65 Prague 6; tel. (2) 368866; monthly; army-related topics; published by the Political Administration of the People's Army; Editor-in-Chief Col. Ing. MIROSLAV LINKA; circ. 225,000.

Zdraví (Health): Thunovská 18, 118 04 Prague 1; tel. (2) 532342; monthly; published by the Czechoslovak Red Cross; Editor-in-Chief KAREL PRŮŠA; circ. 125,000.

Žena a móda (Women and Fashion): Na příkopě 27, 113 49 Prague 1; tel. (2) 261187; monthly; published by the Mona Publishing House; Editor-in-Chief Dr VLADIMÍRA KVĚCHOVÁ; circ. 257,000.

Zlatý máj (Golden May): Na Perštýně 1, 110 01 Prague 1; telex 121605; magazine on literature for children; 10 a year; published by Albatros Publishing House; Editor Dr ZDENĚK SLABÝ; circ. 3,500.

Zora: Krakovská 21, 115 17 Prague 1; tel. (2) 262783; for the visually handicapped; Editor-in-Chief JIŘÍ REICHEL.

Slovak language

Dievča (Girl): Leninovo náměstí 12, 815 05 Bratislava; tel. (7) 334171; every 2 months; published by the Slovak Union of Women; Editor-in-Chief Dr ELENA GIRETHOVÁ; circ. 175,000.

Družba (Friendship): Sasinkova 5, 815 60 Bratislava; tel. (7) 60303; 10 a year; activities of the Union of Czechoslovak-Soviet Friendship; published by the Slovak Ministry of Education; Editor-in-Chief VIERA LABUZOVÁ; circ. 240,000.

Eva: Gorkého 13, 815 85 Bratislava; tel. (7) 52271; every 2 months; magazine for women; Editor-in-Chief Dr GITA PECHOVÁ; circ. 150,000.

Expres: Martanovičova 25, 815 80 Bratislava; tel. (7) 334209; f. 1969; weekly digest of the foreign press; published by the Pravda Publishing House; Editor-in-Chief KAROL HULMAN; circ. 80,000.

Horizont: Banskobystrická 18, 815 85 Bratislava; tel. (7) 331117; f. 1965; monthly; magazine of the Union of Czechoslovak-Soviet Friendship; Editor VOJTECH KONDEL; circ. 30,000.

Kamarát (Friend): Pražská 11, 812 84 Bratislava; tel. (7) 48541-5; Editor-in-Chief ANNA HOLOŠKOVÁ; circ. 130,000.

Katolícke noviny (Catholic News): Kapitulská 20, 815 21 Bratislava; tel. (7) 331717; f. 1849; weekly; published by the St Adalbert Association; Editor-in-Chief LADISLAV BELÁS; circ. 130,000.

Krásy Slovenska (Beauty of Slovakia): Vajnorská 100, 832 58 Bratislava; illustrated monthly; published by Sport, publishing house of the Slovak Physical Culture Organization; Editor Dr MILAN KUBIŠ; circ. 19,000.

Móda (Fashion): Leninova náměstí 12, 815 05 Bratislava; tel. (7) 334172; monthly; published by the Slovak Union of Women; Editor-in-Chief EMILIA SÁNDOROVÁ; circ. 145,000.

Nové slovo (New Word): Martanovičova 25, 819 07 Bratislava; tel. (7) 50334; f. 1944; weekly; politics, culture, economy; independent; published by the Perex joint-stock co; Editor-in-Chief EMIL POLÁK; circ. 65,000.

Ohník (Little Flame): Dostojevského rad 1, 812 84 Bratislava; tel. (7) 56168; fortnightly; youth; published by the Smena Publishing House; Editor-in-Chief MAGDALÉNA GOCNÍKOVÁ; circ. 130,000.

Roháč (Stag-Beetle): Obráncov mieru 47, 816 06 Bratislava; tel. (7) 40517; f. 1948; humorous, satirical weekly; published by Pravda, publishing house of the Communist Party of Slovakia; Editor-in-Chief PETER BÁN; circ. 120,000.

Slovenka (Slovak Woman): Štúrova 12, 814 92 Bratislava; tel. (7) 55061; f. 1949; weekly pictorial published by the Slovak Women's Union; Editor in Chief LÝDIA BRADCOVÁ; circ. 235,000.

Svet (World): Bezručova 9, 815 87 Bratislava; tel. (7) 52959; f. 1951; illustrated weekly; Editor-in-Chief VLADO KALINA; circ. 140,000.

Štart (Start): Vajnorská 100/A, 832 58 Bratislava; tel. (7) 69666; f. 1956; illustrated weekly; organ of the Slovak Central Cttee of the Czechoslovak Union of Physical Education; Editor-in-Chief MATEJ SZÉHER; circ. 81,000.

Technické noviny (Technology News): Martanovičova 25, 819 25 Bratislava; tel. (7) 213483; f. 1953; weekly of the Slovak Council of Trade Unions; Editor-in-Chief Ing. EDUARD DROBNÝ; circ. 80,000.

Televízia (Television): Martanovičova 25, 819 14 Bratislava; tel. (7) 2104194; telex 92661; fax (7) 50995; weekly; published by Euroscop Inc.; Editor-in-Chief TAŇA LUCKÁ; circ. 210,000.

Tip: Vajnorská 32, 832 58 Bratislava; tel. (7) 212100; telex 92650; fax (7) 213778; f. 1969; weekly; football and ice-hockey; published by the Slovak Physical Training Organization; Editor FERDINAND KRÁLOVIČ; circ. 60,000.

Výber (Digest): Októbrové nám. 7, 814 76 Bratislava; tel. (7) 316640; f. 1968; weekly; digest of home and foreign press; in Czech and Slovak; published by the Slovak Syndicate of Journalists; Editor-in-Chief VERONIKA TÖKÖLYOVÁ; circ. 50,000.

Život (Life): Martanovičova 25, 819 17 Bratislava; tel. (7) 53046; f. 1951; illustrated weekly; political, economic, social and cultural matters; published by the Pravda Publishing House; Editor-in-Chief PETER ZEMAN; circ. 220,000.

Foreign languages

Czechoslovak Foreign Trade: ul. 28 října 13, 112 79 Prague 1; tel. (2) 2139381; telex 121142; fax (2) 2327520; f. 1960; monthly; journal of the Czechoslovak Chamber of Commerce and Industry; published in English, German, Spanish, Russian and French by Rapid, Czechoslovak Advertising Agency; Editor-in-Chief Dr PAVLA PODSKALSKÁ; circ. 15,000.

Czechoslovak Trade Unions: Václavské nám. 17, 112 58 Prague 1; tel. (2) 356107; telex 122607; f. 1975; review of the Central Council of Trade Unions; 6 a year; English, French, German, Russian, Italian, Swedish, Portuguese and Spanish; Editor-in-Chief VLASTIMIL SVOBODA; circ. 33,000.

The Democratic Journalist: Rooseveltova 18, 160 00 Prague 6; tel. (2) 326806; telex 122631; fax (2) 2320426; f. 1953; monthly; press organ of the International Organization of Journalists; English, French, Russian, Spanish and quarterly digest in Arabic; Editor-in-Chief RUDOLF PŘEVRÁTIL; circ. 16,000.

For You from Czechoslovakia: ul. 28 října 13, 112 79 Prague 1; tel. (2) 139393; telex 121142; quarterly; published by Rapid in

CZECHOSLOVAKIA

English, German, Russian, Spanish and French; Editor-in-Chief MARIE ŠUVOVÁ; circ. 15,900.

Lacho Lav (Good Word): f. 1990; monthly; published, in Romany, for Czechoslovakia's Romany community; Editor-in-Chief VINCENT DANIHEL.

Neue Prager Presse: Vinohradská 46, 120 41 Prague 1; tel. (2) 256165; telex 123078; fax (2) 254385; weekly; politics, culture, economy, tourism; published by Orbis in German; Editor-in-Chief JAROSLAV FRIDRICH; circ. 10,000.

World Student News: ul. 17 listopadu 58, 110 00 Prague 1; tel. (2) 2312812; published by the International Union of Students in English, French, German and Spanish; Editors MARTA HUBIČKOVÁ, IRENE COXOVÁ; circ. 20,000.

NEWS AGENCY

Československá tisková kancelář (ČTK) (Czechoslovak News Agency): Opletalova 5–7, 111 44 Prague 1; tel. (2) 2147; telex 122841; f. 1918; news and photo exchange service with all international and many national news agencies; maintains wide network of foreign correspondents; English, Russian, French and Spanish news service for foreign countries; publishes weekly bulletin in Russian, English, Spanish, French and German; publs specialized economic bulletins and documentation surveys in Czech; Gen. Dir Ing. PETR UHL.

Foreign Bureaux

Agence France-Presse (AFP): Žitná 10, 120 00 Prague 2; tel. (2) 296927; telex 121124; Bureau Chief BERNARD MEIXNER.

Agenzia Nazionale Stampa Associata (ANSA) (Italy): Ve Smečkách 2, 110 00 Prague 1; tel. (2) 2361826; telex 122734; fax (2) 376133; Bureau Chief LUCIO ATTILIO LEANTE.

Allgemeiner Deutscher Nachrichtendienst (ADN) (Germany): Milevska 835, 140 00 Prague 4; tel. (2) 6921911; Bureau Chief WOLFGANG JASINSKI.

Associated Press (AP) (USA): Růžová 7, 110 00 Prague 1; tel. (2) 364838; telex 121987; Correspondent ONDŘEJ HEJMA.

Bulgarska Telegrafna Agentsia (BTA) (Bulgaria): Ždanova 46, 160 00 Prague 6; telex 121066; Bureau Chief LYUBCHO KHRISTOV.

Dan News Agency (Argentina): Dejvická 52, 160 00 Prague 6; tel. (2) 3278594; Correspondent ETIL CHROMOY.

Deutsche Presse-Agentur (dpa) (Germany): Želivského 11/4/13, 130 31 Prague 3; tel. (2) 276595; telex 122706; Bureau Chief THOMAS WOLF.

Informatsionnoye Agentstvo Novosti (IAN) (USSR): Italská 26, 120 00 Prague 3; tel. (2) 2354459; telex 122235; Bureau Chief VLADIMIR FEDOROV; also br. in Bratislava.

Magyar Távirati Iroda (MTI) (Hungary): U Smaltovny 17, 6th Floor, 170 00 Prague 7; tel. 801649; telex 121827; Bureau Chief JÁNOS KÁRPÁTI.

Novinska Agencija Tanjug (Yugoslavia): U Smaltovny 19, 170 00 Prague 7; tel. (2) 806987; Correspondent BRANKO STOŠIĆ.

Polska Agencja Prasowa (PAP) (Poland): Petrské nám. 1, 110 00 Prague 1; tel. (2) 2325223; Correspondent STANISŁAW MAZAN.

Prensa Latina (Cuba): Petrské nám. 1, 110 00 Prague 1; telex 121083; Bureau Chief EDEL SUÁREZ VENEGAS.

Telegrafnoye Agentstvo Sovetskovo Soyuza (TASS) (USSR): Pevnostní 5, 162 00 Prague 6; tel. (2) 327527; Bureau Chief A. P. SHAPOVALOV.

Xinhua (New China) News Agency (People's Republic of China): Majakovského 22, Prague 6; tel. (2) 326144; telex 121561; Correspondent LIU TIENPAI.

PRESS ASSOCIATIONS

Slovak Syndicate of Journalists: Októbrové nám. 7, 815 68 Bratislava; tel. (7) 335071; fax (7) 335434; f. 1968; reorganized in 1990; 2,630 mems; Chair. PETER ZEMAN.

Syndicate of Journalists of the Czech Republic: Pařížská 9, 116 30 Prague 1; tel. (2) 2325109; fax (2) 2326337; f. 1877; reorganized in 1990; 5,720 mems; Chair. RUDOLF ZEMAN.

Publishers

CZECH PUBLISHING HOUSES

Academia: Vodičkova 40, 112 29 Prague 1; tel. (2) 2363065; fax (2) 266022; f. 1953; publishing house of the Czechoslovak Academy of Sciences; scientific books, periodicals; Dir Ing. VÁCLAV ZVĚŘINA.

Albatros: Na Perštýně 1, 110 01 Prague 1; telex 121605; f. 1949; literature for children and young people; Dir PETR HOŘEJŠ.

Artia: Ve Smečkách 30, 111 27 Prague 1; tel. (2) 2137111; telex 121065; fax (2) 2315206; f. 1953; part of the Artia Foreign Trade Corporation; children's books, art books and encyclopaedias; Dir RICHARD DAVID.

Avicenum: Malostranské nám. 28, 118 02 Prague 1; tel. (2) 530640; f. 1953; medical books and periodicals; Dir VÁCLAV CIPRA.

Blok: Rooseveltova 4, 657 00 Brno; tel. (5) 27244; f. 1957; regional literature, fiction, general; Dir JAROSLAV NOVÁK.

Československý spisovatel (Czechoslovak Writer): Národní 9, 111 47 Prague 1; tel. (2) 2320924; telex 122645; fax (2) 2328719; publishing house of the Czech Literary Fund; poetry, fiction, literary theory and criticism; Dir Dr MILOŠ POHORSKÝ.

Horizont: Nekázanka 7, 111 21 Prague 1; tel. (2) 268617; f. 1968; publishing house of the Komenský Academy; general; Dir Dr ZDENĚK PERGNER.

Kartografie: Kostelní 42, 170 30 Prague 7; tel. (2) 378851; telex 121471; f. 1954; state map publishing house; Dir Ing. MIROSLAV MIKŠOVSKÝ.

Kruh: Dlouhá 108, 500 21 Hradec Králové; tel. (49) 22076; f. 1966; regional literature, fiction and general; Dir Dr JAN DVOŘÁK.

Lidové nakladatelství: Václavské nám. 36, 110 00 Prague 1; tel. (2) 226383; f. 1968; classical and contemporary fiction, general, magazines; Dir Dr KORNEL VAVRINČÍK.

Melantrich: Václavské nám. 36, 112 12 Prague 1; tel. (2) 261372; telex 121432; fax (2) 225012; f. 1919; publishing house of the Czechoslovak Socialist Party; general, fiction, humanities, newspapers and magazines; Dir MILAN NEVOLE.

Merkur: Senovážné nám. 11, 115 69 Prague 1; tel. (2) 2362891; telex 121648; commerce, tourism, catering; Dir JIŘÍ LINHART.

Mladá fronta dnes: Panská 8, 112 22 Prague 1; tel. (2) 224121; telex 121510; f. 1945; literature for young people, fiction and non-fiction, newspapers and magazines; Dir MARIE KOŠKOVÁ.

Nakladatelství dopravy a spojů: Hybernská 5, 115 78 Prague 1; state publishing house for transport and communications; Dir Dr OLDŘICH BREJCHA.

Nakladatelství Svoboda: Revoluční 15, 113 03 Prague 1; tel. (2) 2317051; f. 1945; publishing house of the Central Committee of the Communist Party of Czechoslovakia; politics, history, philosophy, fiction, general; Dir STEFAN SZERYŃSKI.

Naše vojsko: Na Děkance 3, 128 12 Prague 1; tel. (2) 299451; f. 1945; publishing house of the Czechoslovak Army; fiction, general; Dir Dr STANISLAV MISTR.

Odeon: Národní třída 36, 115 87 Prague 1; tel. (2) 260179; telex 123055; f. 1953; literature, poetry, fiction (classical and modern), literary theory, art books, reproductions; Dir Ing. JAN ŠRANK.

Olympia: Klimentská 1, 115 88 Prague 1; tel. (2) 2314861; telex 121717; f. 1954; sports, tourism, illustrated books; Dir Ing. KAREL ZELNÍČEK.

Panorama: Hálkova 1, 120 72 Prague 2; tel. (2) 2361391; Dir Ing. VLADIMÍR NEKOLA.

Panton: Radlická 99, 150 00 Prague 5; tel. (2) 548627; fax (2) 548627; f. 1958; publishing house of the Czech Musical Fund; books on music, sheet music, records; Dir. KAREL ČERNÝ.

Práce: Václavské nám. 17, 112 58 Prague 1; tel. (2) 266151; telex 121134; f. 1945; trade union movement, fiction, general, periodicals; Dir PAVEL LANDA.

Profil: Ciklářská 51, 702 00 Ostrava 1; regional literature, fiction and general; Dir IVAN ŠEINER.

Rapid: ul. 28 října 13, 112 79 Prague 1; tel. (2) 2139111; telex 121142; fax (2) 2327520; advertising; Dir Dr Ing. MIROSLAV HEDBÁVNÝ.

Růže: Žižkovo nám. 5, 370 96 České Budějovice; tel. (38) 38676; f. 1960; regional literature, fiction and general; Dir MIROSLAV HULE.

Severočeské nakladatelství: Velká Hradební 33, 400 21 Ústí nad Labem; regional literature, fiction and general; Dir JIŘÍ ŠVEJDA.

SNTL—Nakladatelství technické literatury: Spálená 51, 113 02 Prague 1; tel. (2) 297670; technology, applied sciences, dictionaries, periodicals; Dir Dr ALEXANDER SCHÜTZ.

Státní pedagogické nakladatelství: Ostrovní 30, 113 01 Prague 1; tel. (2) 203787; f. 1775; state publishing house; school and university textbooks, dictionaries, literature; Dir Ing. JINDŘICH KLŮNA.

Středočeské nakladatelství a knihkupectví: U Prašné brány 3, 116 29 Prague 1; regional literature, fiction, general; Dir Dr VLADIMÍR PÍSA.

Supraphon: Palackého 1, 122 99 Prague 1; tel. (2) 268141; telex 121218; fax (2) 262562; f. 1946; publishing house for gramophone records, compact discs, musicassettes and music; Gen. Dir ZDENĚK ČEJKA.

CZECHOSLOVAKIA *Directory*

Ústřední církevní nakladatelství: Ječná 2, 120 00 Prague 2; f. 1952; religion; Dir Dr Jiří Kafka.

Vyšehrad: Karlovo nám. 5, 120 78 Prague 2; tel. (2) 297726; publishing house of the Czechoslovak People's Party; general fiction, newspapers and magazines; Dir Josef Daněk.

Západočeské nakladatelství: B. Smetany 1, 301 35 Plzeň; tel. (19) 34783; f. 1955; regional literature, fiction, general; Dir Dipl. Ing. Jaroslav Hák.

Zemědělské nakladatelství–Brázda: Václavské nám. 47, 113 11 Prague 1; agricultural publishing house; periodicals; Man. Dir Ing. Jan Dienstbier.

SLOVAK PUBLISHING HOUSES

Alfa: Hurbanovo nám. 3, 815 89 Bratislava; tel. (7) 331441; fax (7) 59443; previously the Slovak Publishing House of Technical Literature; technical and economic literature, dictionaries; Dir Martin Parajka.

Církevné vydavatel'stvo: Palisády 64, 801 00 Bratislava; religious literature; Stefánia Hrebíková.

Matica Slovenská: Hostihora 2, 036 52 Martin; f. 1863; literary science, bibliography, biography and librarianship; literary archives and museums; life of the Slovaks living abroad; Dir Ondrej Kučera.

Mladé Léta (Young Years); nám. SNP 12, 815 19 Bratislava; tel. (7) 50475; telex 92721; state publishing house; f. 1950; literature for children and young people; Dir Anton Hykisch.

Obzor (Horizon): ul. Čs. armády 35, 815 85 Bratislava; tel. (7) 53021; state publishing house; educational, encyclopedias, popular scientific, fiction, textbooks, law; Dir Ing. Richard Damé.

Osveta (Education): Osloboditelov 55, 036 54 Martin; tel. 32921; f. 1953; medical, educational, photographic and regional literature; Editor-in-Chief Bohuslav Kortman.

Práca: Obráncov mieru 19, 897 17 Bratislava; f. 1946; publishing house of the Confederation of Slovak Trade Unions; economics, labour, work safety, etc.; Dir Ján Duži.

Pravda: Gundulíčova 12, 882 05 Bratislava; f. 1969; publishing house of the Central Committee of the Communist Party of Slovakia; politics, philosophy, history, economics, fiction, children's literature; Dir Ján Hanzlík.

Príroda: Križkova 7, 894 17 Bratislava; agricultural literature, gardening books; Dir Ing. Vincent Sugár.

Slovenské pedagogické nakladatel'stvo: Sasinková 5, 891 12 Bratislava; pedagogical literature, educational, school texts, dictionaries; Dir Dr Sergej Troščák.

Slovenský spisovatel: Leningradská 2, 897 28 Bratislava; publishing house of the Union of Slovak Writers; fiction, poetry; Dir Vladimír Dudáš.

Smena: Pražská 11, 812 84 Bratislava; fiction, literature for young people; Dir Jaroslav Šišolák.

Šport: Vajnorská 100/A, 832 58 Bratislava; tel. (7) 69195; telex 93330; publishing house of the Central Committee of the Slovak Physical Culture Organization; sport, physical culture, guide books, periodicals; Dir Dr Bohumil Golian.

Tatran: Michalská 9, 815 82 Bratislava; tel. (7) 335849; fax (7) 335777; f. 1949; fiction, art books, children's books, literary theory; Dir Dr Karol Wlachovský.

Veda (Science): Klemensova 19, 814 30 Bratislava; tel. (7) 56321; f. 1953; publishing house of the Slovak Academy of Science; scientific and popular scientific books and periodicals; Dir Ján Jankovič.

Východoslovenské vydavatel'stvo: Alejová 3, 040 11 Košice; tel. (95) 65710; f. 1960; regional literature, fiction, general; Dir Dr Imrich Gofus.

WRITERS' UNIONS

Svaz československých spisovatelů (Union of Czechoslovak Writers): Národní třída 11, 110 47 Prague 1; Chair. Miroslav Válek.

Svaz českých spisovatelů (Union of Czech Writers): Národní třída 11, 111 47 Prague 1; f. 1972; 165 mems; reorganizing 1990.

Zväz slovenských spisovatel'ov (Union of Slovak Writers): Obrancov mieru 14, 815 08 Bratislava; tel. (7) 43615; f. 1949; reorganizing 1990.

Radio and Television

In 1989 there were 4,216,838 radio receivers and 4,660,543 television receivers licensed.

RADIO

There are seven national networks in Czechoslovakia: Radios Prague and Bratislava (medium wave and VHF), Radio Czechoslovakia (long, medium and VHF—popular and news programmes), Radios Vltava and Děvín (VHF from Prague and Bratislava respectively—programmes on Czech, Slovak and world culture), Radio EM (long, medium and VHF—youth programmes), and Interprogramme Radio Prague (short, medium and VHF—for foreign visitors to Czechoslovakia, in English, German and French).

Local stations broadcast from Prague (Central Bohemian Studio), Banská Bystrica, Bratislava, Brno, České Budějovice, Hradec Králové, Košice, Ostrava, Plzeň, Prešov, Ústí nad Labem and other towns.

Foreign broadcasts are made in English, French, German, Hungarian, Spanish, Ukrainian, and Czech and Slovak.

Československý rozhlas (Czechoslovak Radio): Vinohradská 12, 120 99 Prague 2; tel. (2) 2115; telex 121100; fax (2) 2321020; f. 1923; Dir-Gen. Dr František Pavlíček.

Český rozhlas (Czech Radio): Vinohradská 12, 120 99 Prague 2; tel. (2) 2115; telex 121100; Dir Jaroslav Fridrich.

Československé zahraniční vysílání (Czechoslovak Foreign Broadcasts): Vinohradská 12, 120 99 Prague 2; tel. (2) 2360823; telex 121189; fax (2) 2321020; Dir Ing. Karel Lánský.

Slovenský rozhlas Bratislava (Slovak Radio Bratislava): Mýtna 1, 812 90 Bratislava; tel. (7) 44462; telex 93353; fax (7) 48923; f. 1926; Dir Dr Vladimír Štefko.

TELEVISION

There are television studios in Prague, Brno, Ostrava, Bratislava and Košice.

Československá televize (Czechoslovak Television): Jindřišská 16, 111 50 Prague 1; tel. (2) 221247; telex 121800; f. 1953; Dir-Gen. Jiří Kanturek.

Slovenská televízia (Slovak Television): Asmolovova 28, 845 45 Bratislava; telex 92277; fax (7) 328101; Dir Petr Zeman.

Finance

(cap. = capital; dep. = deposits; res = reserves; m. = million; Kčs. = korunas)

BANKS

The Czechoslovak banking system has been extensively reorganized. In January 1990 the functions of issue and credit of the State Bank were separated. An independent central bank as well as independent credit banks and savings banks were established.

Agrobanka a.s.: Ve Smečkách 33, 110 00 Prague 1; tel. (2) 269209; f. 1990; cap. 650m. Kčs., res 104m. Kčs., dep. 1,300m. Kčs.; Dir Ing. Jan Král.

Bankovní dům SKALA: Frágnerova 2384, 160 00 Prague 6; tel. (2) 3115391; fax (2) 3115391; f. 1990; cap. 50m. Kčs.; Dir Ing. Miroslav Roskot.

Československá obchodní banka a.s. (Commercial Bank of Czechoslovakia): Na Příkopě 14, 115 20 Prague 1; tel. (2) 2132; telex 122201; fax (2) 229034; f. 1965; commercial and foreign exchange transactions; cap. 7,600m. Kčs., res 1,256m. Kčs., dep. 15,700m. Kčs. (1989); Man. Dir Ing. Rostislav Petráš.

Investiční banka: Na Příkopě 28, 110 00 Prague 1; tel. (2) 2353547; telex 122459; fax (2) 2356189; f. 1990; cap. 800m. Kčs., res 2,849m. Kčs., dep. 35,600m. Kčs.; Gen. Dir Prof. Ing. Miroslav Tuček.

Komerční banka Praha: Na Příkopě 33, 110 05 Prague 1; tel. (2) 21221111; telex 121093; f. 1990; cap. 3,900m. Kčs., res 6,499m. Kčs., dep. 81,200m. Kčs.; Gen. Dir Ing. Jan Velek.

Polnohospodárska banka: Steinerova 50, 820 00 Bratislava; fax (7) 57834; f. 1991; cap. 290m. Kčs.; Gen. Dir Ing. Ludovít Pósa.

Poštovní banka a.s.: Plzeňská 139, 150 00 Prague 5; tel. (2) 549251/333; f. 1990; cap. 250m. Kčs.; Chair. Ing. Jaroslav Vopálecký.

Pragobanka a.s.: Jungmannova 32, 110 00 Prague 1; tel. (2) 220128; fax (2) 220128; f. 1990; cap. 60m. Kčs.; Dir Ing. Jiří Bek.

Slovenská Tatra banka: Vajanského nábr. 5, 811 02 Bratislava; tel. (7) 331351-7; fax (7) 224656; f. 1990; Dir Ing. Jozef Rakús.

Státní banka československá (State Bank of Czechoslovakia): Na Příkopě 28, 110 03 Prague 1; tel. (2) 2112; telex 2444; fax (2) 2354141; f. 1950; the State Monetary Agency; bank of issue, the central authority of Czechoslovakia in the monetary sphere, legislation and permission, central bank for directing and securing monetary policy, regulation of activities of other banks and savings banks. Statutory fund 1,400m. Kčs.; reserve fund 1,400m. Kčs. (Jan. 1990); Chair. Ing. Josef Tosovský.

CZECHOSLOVAKIA

Tatra Banka a.s.: Vajanského nábr. 5, 811 02 Bratislava; tel. (7) 55055; fax (7) 334656; cap. 400m. Kčs.; Gen. Dir MILAN VRŠKOVÝ.

Všeobecná úverová banka Bratislava: nám. SNP 19, 818 56 Bratislava; tel. (7) 58921; telex 93346-7; fax (7) 56867; f. 1990; cap. 1,850m. Kčs., res 2,890m. Kčs., dep. 36,100m. Kčs.; Gen. Dir Ing. JOZEF MUDRÍK.

Živnostenská banka: Na Příkopě 20, 113 80 Prague 1; tel. (2) 224346; telex 122313; fax (2) 263381; f. 1868; cap. 250m. Kčs., res 374m. Kčs., dep. 12,488m. Kčs. (Dec. 1989); Gen. Man. Ing JIŘÍ KUNERT.

SAVINGS BANKS

Česká státní spořitelna (Czech State Savings Bank): Václavské nám. 42, 113 98 Prague 1; tel. (2) 225237; telex 121010; fax (2) 267023; accepts deposits and issues loans; 15,239,363 depositors (June 1990); Gen. Dir Dipl. Ing. MILOSLAV KOHOUTEK.

Slovenská štátna sporiteľňa (Slovak State Savings Bank): nám. SNP 18, 816 07 Bratislava; tel. (7) 52300; telex 93300; fax (7) 52087; Pres. ALOJZ ONDRA.

INSURANCE

Česká státní pojišťovna (Czech State Insurance and Reinsurance Corporation): Spálená 16, 114 00 Prague 1; tel. (2) 2148111; telex 121112; fax (2) 299146; f. 1827; many home branches and some agencies abroad; controls all insurance; issues life, accident, fire, aviation and marine policies, all classes of reinsurance; Lloyd's agency; Gen. Man. Dr VLASTIMIL UZEL.

Slovenská štátna poisťovňa (Slovak State Insurance Corporation): Strakova 1, 815 74 Bratislava; telex 93375; fax (7) 827948; Gen. Dir RASTISLAV HAVERLIK.

Trade and Industry

CHAMBER OF COMMERCE

Československá obchodní a průmyslová komora (Czechoslovak Chamber of Commerce and Industry): Argentinská 38, 170 05 Prague 7; tel. (2) 8724111; telex 121862; fax (2) 879134; f. 1850; has 1,304 members (foreign trade corporations, industrial enterprises, banks, research institutes and private enterprises; Pres. Ing. JAROSLAV JAKUBEC.

FOREIGN TRADE CORPORATIONS

Artia Ltd: Ve Smečkách 30, 111 27 Prague 1; tel. (2) 2137111; telex 121065; fax (2) 2315206; imports and exports cultural commodities; Gen. Dir EMANUEL PAVLÍČEK.

Centrotex: nám. Hrdinů 3/1634, 140 61 Prague 4; tel. (2) 415; fax (2) 438771; imports and exports textiles; Gen. Dir Ing. JIŘÍ KOUTNÍK.

Čechofracht: Na Příkopě 8, 111 83 Prague 1; tel. (2) 2129111; telex 122221; fax (2) 2327137; f. 1949; shipping and international forwarding corporation; Gen. Dir Ing. STANISLAV MACH.

Chemapol: Kodaňská 46, 100 10 Prague 10; tel. (2) 715; telex 122021; fax (2) 737007; f. 1948; imports and exports chemical and pharmaceutical products and raw materials; Gen. Dir Ing. VÁCLAV VOLF.

Czechoslovak Ceramics: V Jámě 1, 111 91 Prague 1; tel. (2) 214121; telex 121118; fax (2) 267673; exports and imports ceramics; Gen. Dir Ing. MIROSLAV DOBEŠ.

Czechoslovak Filmexport: Václavské nám. 28, 111 45 Prague 1; tel. (2) 2365385; telex 122259; fax (2) 2358432; f. 1957; import and export of films; Gen. Dir JIŘÍ JANOUŠEK.

Drevounia: Dr V. Clementisa 10, 826 10 Bratislava; tel. (7) 229962; telex 93291; fax (7) 236164; imports and exports wood and furniture; Gen. Dir Ing. JIŘÍ JIRAVA.

Exico: Panská 9, 111 77 Prague 1; tel. (2) 246941; telex 122211; fax (2) 2321030; f. 1966; exports and imports leather, shoes, skins; Gen. Dir Ing. FRANTIŠEK FREMUND.

Ferromet: Opletalova 27, 111 81 Prague 1; tel. (2) 2141; telex 121411; fax (2) 2360801; imports and exports metallurgical products; Gen. Dir Ing. BŘETISLAV SEDLÁK.

Imex: Revoluční 25, 110 15 Prague 1; tel. (2) 2311000; telex 121977; fax (2) 2317191; imports and exports goods and equipment for sales and sales equipment; Gen. Man. Dipl. Ing. L. KRÁSA.

Inspekta: Na Strži 63, 140 62 Prague 4; tel. (2) 4141111; telex 121938; fax (2) 434390; control of goods in foreign trade; Gen. Dir Ing. JAN ŠVIHEL.

Intercoop: ul. Dr Vl. Clementisa 10, 826 08 Bratislava; tel. (7) 229162; telex 93365; fax (7) 224393; imports and exports toys, fruits, vegetables, honey and wine.

Jablonex Ltd: Palackého 41, 466 37 Jablonec nad Nisou; tel. (428) 510; telex 186238; fax (428) 27362; f. 1949; imports and exports fashion jewellery and decorations; Gen. Dir JAN BERNARD.

Koospol: Leninova 178, 160 67 Prague 6; tel. (2) 3361111; telex 121121; fax (2) 345572; imports and exports foodstuffs; Gen. Dir JAROSLAV ŘÍHA.

Kovo: Jankovcova 2, 170 88 Prague 7; tel. (2) 8741111; telex 121481; fax (2) 800162; imports and exports precision engineering products; Gen. Dir JOSEF KUDRHALT.

Ligna: Vodičkova 41, 112 09 Prague 1; tel. (2) 2134; telex 122066; fax (2) 263525; imports and exports timber, wood products, musical instruments and paper; Gen. Dir Ing. MILOŠ SVACH.

Martimex Ltd: Červenej armády 1, 036 65 Martin; tel. (842) 33311; telex 75488; fax (842) 39118; imports and exports shipbuilding equipment, industrial locomotives, forestry machinery and equipment, industrial robots and manipulators; Pres. MILAN LAUKO.

Merkuria: Argentinská 38, 170 05 Prague 7; tel. (2) 8724111; telex 121022; fax (2) 802950; exports and imports tools and consumer goods; Gen. Dir Ing. JOSEF CHUCHVALEC.

Metalimex: Štěpánská 34, 112 17 Prague 1; tel. (2) 2359580; telex 121405; fax (2) 2320630; imports and exports non-ferrous metals, natural gas and solid fuels; Gen. Dir Ing. MIROSLAV HLAVIČKA.

Motokov: Na Strži 63, 140 62 Prague 4; imports and exports vehicles and light engineering products; Gen. Dir Ing. DALIBOR MOŠOVSKÝ.

Omnipol: Nekázanka 11, 112 21 Prague 1; telex 121299; fax (2) 226792; import and export of sports and civil aircraft; Gen. Dir Ing. FRANTIŠEK HÁVA.

Petrimex: ul. Dr Vl. Clementisa 10, 826 08 Bratislava; tel. (7) 229962; telex 935259; fax (7) 235622; imports and exports chemicals, raw materials.

Pragoexport: Jungmannova 34, 112 59 Prague 1; tel. (2) 2366065; telex 121085; fax (2) 2358964; f. 1948; imports and exports consumer goods; Gen. Dir PAVEL MAJOR.

Pragoinvest: Českomoravská 23, 180 56 Prague 9; tel. (2) 822741; telex 122379; fax (2) 823472; import and export of machinery and complete plant equipment; Gen. Dir Ing. MILOSLAV KOČÁREK.

Skloexport: tř. 1. máje 52, 461 74 Liberec; tel. 315; telex 186267; fax 421027; exports glass; Gen. Dir Ing. JAROSLAV KŘIVÁNEK.

Škodaexport: Václavské nám. 56, 113 32 Prague 1; tel. (2) 2131; telex 122413; exports and imports power engineering and metallurgical plants, engineering works, electrical locomotives and trolleybuses, tobacco machines; Gen. Dir Ing. MILOSLAV MIKEŠ.

Strojexport: POB 662, Václavské nám. 56, 113 26 Prague 1; tel. (2) 2131; telex 121753; fax (2) 2323084; f. 1953; imports and exports machines and machinery equipment, civil engineering works; Gen. Dir Ing. JOSEF REGNER.

Strojimport Co Ltd: Vinohradská 184, 130 52 Prague 3; tel. (2) 713; telex 122241; fax (2) 777554; f. 1953; imports and exports machine tools, tools and gauges, and industrial plants; Gen. Dir Ing. IVAN ČAPEK.

Technoexport: Václavské nám. 1, 113 34 Prague 1; tel. (2) 2364325; telex 121268; fax (2) 229024; imports and exports chemical and foodstuff engineering plant; Gen. Dir Ing. OLDŘICH KUCHTA.

Tuzex: Rytířská 13, 113 43 Prague 1; tel. (2) 220292; telex 121012; fax (2) 221808; retail goods for foreign currency; Gen. Dir Ing. ANTONÍN RAČANSKÝ.

TRADE UNIONS

Česká a Slovenská konfederace odborových svazů–ČSKOS (Czech and Slovak Confederation of Trade Unions): nám. W. Churchilla 2, 113 59 Prague 3; tel. (2) 2350357; telex 121517; fax (2) 2350784; f. 1945 as the Central Council of Trade Unions; reformed as above 1990; embraces 61 trade unions with 7.5m. mems; Pres. ROMAN KOVÁČ.

Českomoravská komora ČSKOS (Czech-Moravian Chamber of the ČSKOS): nám. W. Churchilla 2, 113 59 Prague 3; tel. (2) 2368426; Pres. VLADIMÍR PETRUS.

Konfederácia odborových zväzov Slovenskej republiky (Confederation of Trade Unions of the Slovak Republic):Vajnorská 1, 815 70 Bratislava; tel. (7) 62265; fax (7) 213303; Pres. SVETOZÁR KORBEL.

Konfederace umění a kultury (Confederation of Arts and Culture): Senovážné nám. 23, 112 82 Prague 1; tel. (2) 2114919; f. 1990; independent trade union centre, not affiliated to ČSKOS; Pres. JAN KŘTITEL SÝKORA.

CZECHOSLOVAKIA

Directory

Českomoravský odborový svaz pracovníků služeb (Czech-Moravian Trade Union of Workers in Services): Senovážné nám. 23, 112 82 Prague 1; tel. (2) 21142726; Pres. RICHARD FALBR; 281,058 mems.

Českomoravský odborový svaz školství (Czech-Moravian Trade Union of Workers in Education): Senovážné nám. 23, 112 82 Prague 1; tel. (2) 2311335; Pres. JAROSLAV RÖSSLER; 280,698 mems.

Československý odborový svaz pracovníků kovoprůmyslu (Czechoslovak Trade Union of Metalworkers): nám. W. Churchilla 2, 113 59 Prague 3; tel. (2) 2368974; telex 121517; fax (2) 2350784; Pres. IGOR PLESKOT; 1,466,886 mems.

Federální odborový svaz energetiků (Federal Trade Union of Power Industry Workers): nám. W. Churchilla 2, 113 59 Prague 3; tel. (2) 270081; Pres. PAVEL HÁJEK; 102,050 mems.

Federální odborový svaz pracovníků chemického průmyslu (Federal Trade Union of Workers in the Chemical Industry): nám. W. Churchilla 2, 113 59 Prague 3; tel. (2) 2355489; telex 121517; Pres. VLADIMÍR ŽIŽKA; 180,152 mems.

Federální odborový svaz pracovníků hornictví, geologie, naftařského průmyslu (Federal Trade Union of Miners, Geologists and Oilmen): nám. W. Churchilla 2, 113 59 Prague 3; tel. (2) 2366260; fax (2) 2369349; Pres. STANISLAV HOŠEK; 365,106 mems.

Federální odborový svaz pracovníků sklářského, keramického, bižuterního průmyslu a porcelánu (Federal Trade Union of Workers in the Glass, Ceramics, Costume Jewellery and Porcelain Industries): nám. W. Churchilla 2, 113 59 Prague 3; tel. (2) 2353561; Pres. JAROSLAV KUCH; 103,294 mems.

Federální odborový svaz pracovníků spojů (Federal Trade Union of Telecommunication Workers): nám W. Churchilla 2, 113 59 Prague 3; tel. (2) 278529; Pres. ZDENĚK KUBĚNA; 146,285 mems.

Federální odborový svaz pracovníků ve stavebnictví a výrobě stavebních hmot, inženýrsko-investorských, projektových a výzkumných organizací (Federal Trade Union of Construction Workers, of Workers in Production of Construction Materials, Civil Engineering and Investments, Design and Research Organizations): Senovážné nám. 23, 112 82 Prague 1; tel. (2) 21142723; Pres. JIŘÍ KOTEN; 637,864 mems.

Odborové sdružení železničářů (federální) (Trade Union Association of Railwaymen (Federal)): nám. W. Churchilla 2, 113 59 Prague 3; tel. (2) 2353561; telex 124484; Pres. VÁCLAV VANĚK; 324,360 mems.

Odborový svaz pracovníků dřevozpracujícího odvětví, lesního a vodního hospodářství v České republice (Trade Union of Workers in Woodworking Industry, Forestry and Management of Water Supplies in the Czech Republic): nám. W. Churchilla 2, 113 59 Prague 3; tel. (2) 279159; telex 121484; fax (2) 2350784; Pres. ROBERT ZEDNÍK; 212,870 mems.

Odborový svaz pracovníků textilního, oděvního a kožedělného průmyslu Čech a Moravy (Trade Union of Workers in Textile, Clothing and Leather Industry of Bohemia and Moravia): nám. W. Churchilla 2, 113 59 Prague 3; tel. (2) 2360782; telex 121517; Pres. MARCEL MÖSTL; 323,548 mems.

Odborový svaz pracovníků zdravotnictví, sociálních a technicko-zdravotnických služeb CR (Trade Union of Workers in Health Service, of Health Technician Workers and Social Care in the Czech Republic): nám. W. Churchilla 2, 113 59 Prague 3; tel. (2) 2368267; Pres. JIŘÍ SCHLANGER; 343,379 mems.

Odborový svaz pracovníků zemědělství a výživy Čech a Moravy (Trade Union of Workers in Agriculture and Food Industry of Bohemia and Moravia): nám. W. Churchilla 2, 113 59 Prague 3; tel. (2) 2355783; telex 121484; Pres. VÁCLAV GUTTENBERG; 324,440 mems.

Odborový zväz pracovníkov drevárského, nábytkárského, papierenského priemyslu, lesného a vodného hodpodárstva (Slovak Trade Union of Workers in Woodworking, Furniture and Paper Industries, in Forests and Management of Water Supplies): Vajnorská 1, 815 70 Bratislava; tel. (7) 213660; Pres. BORISLAV MAJTÁN; 133,626 mems.

Odborový zväz pracovníkov pol'nohospodárstva na Slovensku (Trade Union of Workers in Agriculture in Slovakia): Vajnorská 1, 815 70 Bratislava; tel. (7) 213942; Pres. EMIL KUČERA; 170,490 mems.

Slovenský odborový zväz pracovníkov textilného, odevného a kožiarského priemyslu (Slovak Trade Union of Workers in Textile, Clothing and Leather Industry): Vajnorská 1, 815 70 Bratislava; tel. (7) 213389; telex 92382; Pres. PAVOL JAKUBIK; 131,679 mems.

TRADE FAIR

BVV Trade Fairs and Exhibitions: Výstaviště 1, 602 00 Brno; tel. (5) 3141111; telex 62239; fax (5) 333998; f. 1959; international engineering fair yearly in September; international consumer goods fair yearly in April; Gen. Dir Ing. ANTONÍN SURKA.

Transport

RAILWAYS

At 31 December 1989 the total length of the Czechoslovak railways was 13,106 km; of this total, 3,816 km were electrified, including the connection Prague–Warsaw via Bohumín. The densest section of the network links the north with the south, and there is a direct rail link between the west and east of the country.

Československé státní dráhy (Czechoslovak State Railways): nábř. L. Svobody 12, 110 15 Prague 1; tel. (2) 2891; telex 121096; Dir Ing. IVO MALINA.

Prague Metropolitan Railway: Dopravní podnik hlavního města Prahy, Bubenská 1, 170 26 Prague 7; tel. (2) 878278; telex 122443; fax (2) 878786; the Prague underground railway opened in 1974, and by Nov. 1990, 38.5 km were operational; there are 41 stations; Gen. Dir Ing. VAVŘINEC BODENLOS.

ROADS

In January 1989 there were 73,444 km of roads in Czechoslovakia, including 518 km of motorways. More than 90% of the total road network is hard-surfaced. The Prague–Brno–Bratislava motorway was opened in 1980.

Československá státní automobilová doprava—ČSAD (Czechoslovak State Road Transport): Hybernská 32, 111 21 Prague 1; f. 1949; the organization has 11 regional head offices.

Sdružení československých mezinárodních automobilových dopravců (ČESMAD) (Czechoslovak International Road Transport Enterprises Association): Perucká 5, 120 67 Prague 2; tel. (2) 6911920; telex 122303; fax (2) 256273; f. 1966; Chair. Ing. JOZEF MRÁŽIK; Gen. Sec. Dipl. Ing. JIŘÍ KLADIVA.

INLAND WATERWAYS

The total length of navigable waterways in Czechoslovakia is 480 km. The Elbe and its tributary the Vltava connect the country with the North Sea via the port of Hamburg. The Oder provides a connection with the Baltic Sea and the port of Szczecin. The Danube provides a link with Germany, Austria, Hungary, Yugoslavia, Bulgaria, Romania and the USSR. Czechoslovakia's river ports are Prague Holešovice, Prague Radotín, Kolín, Mělník, Ústí nad Labem and Děčín on the Vltava and Elbe, and Bratislava and Komárno on the Danube.

Československá plavba dunajská (Czechoslovak Danube River Shipping): Červenej armády 35, 815 24 Bratislava; telex 92338; three ships totalling 6,080 grt; Man. Dir Ing. JURAJ PAVELEK.

Československá plavba labsko-oderská (ČSPLO) (Czechoslovak Elbe-Oder River Shipping): K. Čapka 1, 405 91 Děčín; telex 184241; fax 23470; carries out transport of goods on the Vltava, Elbe and Oder rivers as well as other waterways; transfer and storage of goods in Czechoslovak ports; operates the river ports of Prague, Mělník, Kolín, Ústí nad Labem and Děčín; Man. Dir JIŘÍ ASTR.

SHIPPING

Československá námořní plavba, mezinárodní akciová společnost (Czechoslovak Ocean Shipping, International Joint-Stock Company): Počernická 168, 100 99 Prague 10; tel. (2) 778941; telex 122137; fax (2) 773962; f. 1959; shipping company operating the Czechoslovak sea-going fleet; 18 ships totalling 442,096 dwt; Man. Dir Capt. VLADIMÍR PODLENA.

CIVIL AVIATION

There are civil airports at Prague (Ruzyně), Brno, Bratislava, Karlovy Vary, Košice, Mariánské Lázně, Ostrava, Pieštany, Poprad-Tatry, Sliač (Banská Bystrica) and Zlín, served by ČSA's internal flights. International flights serve Prague, Bratislava, Poprad-Tatry, Ostrava, Brno, Košice and Karlovy Vary.

ČSA (Československé aerolinie) (Czechoslovak Airlines): Head Office: Ruzyně Airport, 160 08 Prague; telex 120338; f. 1923; external services to most European capitals, the Near, Middle and Far East, North and Central America and North Africa; Gen. Dir Ing. JIŘÍ NULÍČEK; fleet of 9 Ilyushin Il-62M, 10 Tupolev TU-134A, 7 Tupolev TU-154-M and 6 Yakovlev Yak-40.

CZECHOSLOVAKIA

Slov-Air: Ivanka Airport, 823 12 Bratislava; tel. (7) 226172; telex 93270; f. 1969; domestic scheduled and charter services; Dir Dipl. Ing. LUBOMÍR KOVÁČIK; fleet of small turboprop aircraft including four Let L-410 and two An-2.

Tourism

Czechoslovakia has magnificent scenery, with winter sports facilities. Prague is the best known of the historic cities, and there are famous castles and cathedrals, numerous resorts and 57 spas with natural mineral springs. In 1989 foreign visitor arrivals totalled 29.7m., including excursionists. Receipts from tourism totalled US $698m. in 1989.

Čedok (Travel and Hotels Corporation): Na Příkopě 18, 111 35 Prague 1; tel. (2) 2127111; telex 121109; fax (2) 2321656; the official Czechoslovak Travel Agency; 163 travel offices; 19 branches throughout Europe and in Japan and the USA; Pres. MILOSLAV HOLUB.

Atomic Energy

Nuclear power accounted for 28% of total electricity production in 1989.

Československá komise pro atomovou energii (ČSKAE) (Czechoslovak Atomic Energy Commission): Slezská 9, 120 29 Prague 2; tel. (2) 2151111; responsible for the peaceful utilization of atomic energy and for co-ordinating the atomic energy programme; Chair. Ing. STANISLAV HAVEL.

Federální ministerstvo paliv a energeticky (Federal Ministry of Fuel and Energy): Vinohradská 8, 120 70 Prague 2; tel. (2) 262698; telex 122083; responsible for development and functioning of Czechoslovakia's fuel and energy complex; nuclear power station construction plants at Jaslovské Bohunice (1,760 MW in operation), Dukovany (1,760 MW in operation), Mochovce (1,760 MW under construction), Temelín (4,000 MW under construction).

Ústav jaderného výzkumu (Institute of Nuclear Research): 250 68 Řež; tel. (2) 896231; telex 122626; f. 1955; Dir JAN MRKOS.

DENMARK

Introductory Survey

Location, Climate, Language, Religion, Flag, Capital

The Kingdom of Denmark is situated in northern Europe. It consists of the peninsula of Jutland, the islands of Zealand, Funen, Lolland, Falster and Bornholm, and 401 smaller islands. The country lies between the North Sea, to the west, and the Baltic Sea, to the east. Denmark's only land frontier is with Germany, to the south. Norway lies to the north of Denmark, across the Skagerrak, while Sweden, whose most southerly region is separated from Zealand by a narrow strait, lies to the north-east. Outlying territories of Denmark are Greenland and the Faeroe Islands in the North Atlantic Ocean. Denmark is low-lying and the climate is temperate, with mild summers and cold, rainy winters. The language is Danish. Almost all of the inhabitants profess Christianity: the Evangelical Lutheran Church, to which 91% of the population belong, is the established Church, and there are also small communities of other Protestant groups and of Roman Catholics. The national flag (proportions 37 by 28) displays a white cross on a red background, the upright of the cross being to the left of centre. The capital is Copenhagen (København).

Recent History

In 1945, following the end of German wartime occupation, Denmark recognized the independence of Iceland, which had been declared in the previous year. Home rule was granted to the Faeroe Islands in 1948 and to Greenland in 1979. Denmark was a founder member of NATO in 1949 and of the Nordic Council in 1952. Following a referendum, Denmark entered the EEC in January 1973.

In 1947 King Frederik IX succeeded to the throne on the death of his father, Christian X. Denmark's Constitution was radically revised in 1953: new provisions allowed for female succession to the throne, abolished the upper house of parliament and amended the franchise. King Frederik died in January 1972, and his eldest daughter, Margrethe, became the first queen to rule Denmark for nearly 600 years.

The system of proportional representation which is embodied in the 1953 Constitution makes it difficult for a single party to gain a majority in the Folketing (Parliament), and the tendency of Danish parties to fragment has, in recent years, produced a series of coalition and minority governments, all of which have had to face economic problems and popular discontent with Denmark's EEC membership. The Liberal Party's minority Government, led by Poul Hartling and formed in 1973, was followed in 1975 by a minority Social Democratic Government under the leadership of Anker Jørgensen. Jørgensen led various coalitions and minority governments until 1982. There were general elections in 1977, 1979 and 1981, held against a background of growing unemployment and attempts to tighten control of the economy. By September 1982, Jørgensen's economic policy, including attempts to reduce the budget deficit by introducing new taxes, had once more led to disagreements within the Cabinet, and the Government resigned.

The Conservatives, who had been absent from Danish coalitions since 1971, formed a centre-right four-party government (with the Liberals, the Centre Democrats and the Christian People's Party), led by Poul Schlüter, who became Denmark's first Conservative Prime Minister since 1894. Holding only 66 of the Folketing's 179 seats, the coalition narrowly avoided defeat in October 1982, when it introduced stringent economic measures (including a six-month 'freeze' on wages), and again in September 1983, when larger reductions in public spending were proposed. In December the anti-tax Progress Party withdrew its support for further cuts in expenditure, and the Government was defeated. A general election to the Folketing was held in January 1984, and Schlüter's Government remained in office, with its component parties holding a total of 77 seats, and relying on the support of the Radical Liberal members.

A general election took place in September 1987 and was contested by 16 political parties, nine of which won seats in the Folketing. Schlüter's coalition retained only 70 seats, and the Radical Liberals gained one seat, while the opposition Social Democratic Party lost two of its 56 seats. Jørgensen later resigned as leader of the latter party. Several of the smaller and extremist parties made considerable gains, with the result that the outgoing coalition was weakened, while the main opposition parties were unable to command a working majority. Schlüter eventually formed a new cabinet which comprised representatives of the former four-party governing coalition. However, the Radical Liberals had earlier declared that they would not support any administration that depended on the support of the Progress Party. This therefore left a precarious balance of power within the Folketing.

In the Folketing a government is expected to resign only if its defeated proposals have been presented as a 'vital element' of policy. This practice enabled the coalition to survive a series of defeats on foreign policy during the early 1980s, including several attempts by the Folketing to dissociate itself from particular aspects of NATO defence strategy. In November 1984 the Government ignored a Folketing decision in favour of a ban on any first use of nuclear weapons by the Western alliance. In March 1985 the Folketing voted against any inclusion of nuclear power stations in public energy plans, and in May a majority approved a motion opposing Danish involvement in research connected with the US Government's 'Strategic Defense Initiative' (a plan, first announced by President Ronald Reagan in March 1983, to test the feasibility of creating a space-based defensive 'shield' against attack by ballistic missiles). This vote constituted a further defeat for Schlüter's Government. The left-wing parties also committed the Government to work actively towards the creation of a nuclear-free zone in the Nordic region.

In April 1988, however, the Folketing adopted an opposition-sponsored resolution requiring the Government to inform visiting warships of the country's ban on nuclear weapons. The British and US Governments were highly critical of the resolution. Schlüter therefore announced an early general election for May 1988, on the issue of Denmark's membership of NATO and defence policy. Twelve political parties contested the elections in metropolitan Denmark, and eight won seats in the Folketing. The Common Course party lost parliamentary representation, and the right-wing Progress Party increased its number of seats from nine to 16. For the main parties, however, the election result was inconclusive, and three weeks of negotiations took place before Schlüter was appointed to seek a basis for viable government. At the beginning of June a new minority coalition formed a cabinet under Schlüter. The Conservatives retained nine cabinet positions, but the Liberals secured only seven (compared with their former eight) posts, although they gained the defence portfolio. Their new partners, the Radical Liberals, provided five cabinet members. One of the first acts of the new Government was to restore good relations with its NATO allies. This was done with a formula that requested all visiting warships to respect Danish law in its territorial waters, while making no specific reference to nuclear weapons. The Schlüter Government did receive some criticism from NATO, however, for its refusal to increase defence expenditure.

The Government also proposed large reductions in social welfare provision for 1989, and attacked Progress Party demands for less taxation as unrealistic. The Progress Party, however, continued to increase in popularity, and in November 1989 its share of the vote rose significantly in municipal elections, while the Conservatives lost support. The Government therefore determined to implement its proposals for reductions in the rates of taxation in 1990, despite Social Democratic opposition to decreases in welfare expenditure. The budget proposals for 1990 were enacted in December 1989, only with the support of the six right-wing parties in the Folketing. This included the Progress Party, which voted for the Finance Act for the first time since entering the Folketing. In September 1990 the Government held talks with the Social Democratic Party, in an attempt to obtain its support for the Government's programme of economic reform, which included proposals to reduce the highest rate of taxation from 68% to

DENMARK

62%. Divisions within the Progress Party became apparent in November, when its founder, Mogens Glistrup, was expelled from the 16-member Folketing group. Shortly after the emergence of the split in the Progress Party, the talks between the Government and the Social Democratic Party collapsed. The Government consequently lacked the requisite support to guarantee the adoption of its economic reforms by the Folketing, and Schlüter called an early general election for 12 December. Although the Social Democratic Party retained the largest share of the vote (winning an additional 14 seats to bring its total to 69), Schlüter indicated that he would form a minority coalition government, comprising the Conservative party, which had lost five seats in the election, and the Liberal Party, which had gained an additional seven seats. It was expected that the Radical Liberals, while no longer part of the Government, would continue to support the majority of the new coalition Government's policies.

In January 1986 tension arose between Denmark and the other members of the EEC when the left-wing parties in the Folketing combined to defeat proposals for a programme of EEC reforms. These reforms had been designed to accelerate decision-making by the EEC's Council of Ministers, by removing the need for unanimity, and to lift internal trade barriers within the Community. The Social Democrats, who led the opposition, argued that the adoption of the reforms would lead to a diminution of Denmark's powers to protect its own environmental standards, forcing the country to alter its stringent import controls. The reform proposals were rejected in the Folketing by a narrow majority, making any amendment to the EEC's Treaty of Rome impossible, since a positive vote by the legislatures of all member states was required. Schlüter announced that a national referendum on the issue would take place in February, arguing that Danish rejection of the proposals would be the first stage towards Denmark's withdrawal from the EEC, and all parties agreed to respect the referendum result: 56.2% of the votes cast were in favour of the reforms, which were formally approved by the Folketing in May.

De-oxygenization of the Kattegat, the strait between Denmark and Sweden, resulted in the destruction of lobster colonies in the latter half of 1986. This caused widespread concern about ecological matters, and the Folketing responded by enacting legislation that set the world's most rigorous standards of environmental protection. Many of the requirements were expensive for farmers and industrialists, and some measures conflicted with EEC regulations. Environmental concerns, however, were heightened in 1988 by two ecological disasters, both attributed to pollutants. A massive increase in the concentration of algae devastated marine life around Denmark and southern Scandinavia, and this was followed by a virulent outbreak of a canine distemper virus that reduced the seal population of the North and Baltic Seas by two-thirds.

In August 1988 the Danish Government decided to submit a dispute with Norway, concerning maritime economic zones between Greenland and Jan Mayen island, to the International Court of Justice at The Hague.

The legality of tender terms (which referred to the use of Danish materials and labour) and the award of the contract for the building of a bridge across the Great Belt, between the islands of Zealand and Funen, were challenged by the Commission of the EEC in mid-1989. The Commission accused the Danish Government of serious transgressions of EEC law and of violating the principle of non-discrimination that is embodied in the Treaty of Rome. The Commission ceased its proceedings in the European Court in Luxembourg in September 1989, when the Danish Government acknowledged the validity of the allegations made against it (an injunction suspending work on the bridge would have added greatly to the costs). The Government also committed itself to never repeating the offence and to allowing the unsuccessful tenderers to seek compensation in the Danish courts.

Government

Denmark is a constitutional monarchy. Under the 1953 constitutional charter, legislative power is held jointly by the hereditary monarch (who has no personal political power) and the unicameral Folketing (Parliament), with 179 members, including 175 from metropolitan Denmark and two each from the Faeroe Islands and Greenland. Members are elected for four years (subject to dissolution) on the basis of proportional representation. A referendum in September 1978 reduced the age of suffrage from 20 to 18. Executive power is exercised by the monarch through a Cabinet, led by the Prime Minister, which is responsible to the Folketing. Denmark comprises 14 counties (amtskommuner), one city and one borough, all with elected councils.

Defence

In June 1990 Denmark maintained an army of some 19,400 (including 9,900 conscripts), a navy of 5,400 (900 conscripts) and an air force of 6,900 (700 conscripts). There were, in total, about 72,700 reservists, and a volunteer Home Guard numbering 70,500. Military service is for nine–12 months. Denmark abandoned its neutrality after the Second World War and has been a member of NATO since 1949. In 1988 it became the first NATO country to include women in front-line units (there were 900 women on active service in June 1990). The defence budget for 1990/91 was 14,290m. kroner.

Economic Affairs

In 1988, according to estimates by the World Bank, Denmark's gross national product (GNP), measured at average 1986–88 prices, was US $94,792m., equivalent to $18,470 per head. Denmark's level of GNP per head is one of the highest among industrialized countries. It was estimated that both overall GNP and GNP per head increased at an average rate of 2.3% per year, in real terms, between 1980 and 1988, although between 1986 and 1988 GNP per head decreased by 0.5% per year. Denmark's population in 1988 was only 0.1% higher than in 1980. Denmark's gross domestic product (GDP) increased, in real terms, by an annual average of 2.2% in 1980–88, and by 1.1% in 1989.

Agriculture (including forestry and fishing) employed about 5.8% of the civilian labour force and contributed 4.6% of GDP in 1989. In 1988, 65% of Denmark's land area was used for agriculture. The principal activities are pig farming (Denmark is the world's principal exporter of pork products) and dairy farming. Most of Denmark's agricultural production is exported, and the sector accounted for 25.8% of total exports in 1989. During 1980–87 agricultural production increased by an annual average of 4.3%. The fishing industry alone accounted for 5.7% of total export earnings in 1989.

Industry (including mining, manufacturing, construction, power and water) employed 27.5% of the working population and provided 27.7% of GDP in 1989. During 1980–87 industrial production increased by an annual average of 3.1%.

In 1989 mining accounted for only 0.1% of employment and 1.0% of GDP. Denmark has few natural resources, but exploration for hydrocarbon reserves in the Danish sector of the North Sea in the 1970s proved successful. Natural gas has also been extensively exploited. In 1989, in north-western Jutland, it was established that there was a significant reserve of sand which could be exploited for rich yields of titanium, zircon and yttrium.

Manufacturing employed about 19.9% of the civilian labour force and contributed 18.7% of GDP in 1989. The most important manufacturing industries, measured by the value of output, are food-processing, steel and metals, chemicals and pharmaceuticals, printing and publishing, machinery and electronic goods. Manufacturing exports constituted some 65% of the value of total commodity exports in 1987.

Energy is derived principally from petroleum and natural gas. Denmark supplied some 40% of its own energy requirements, according to an estimate in 1988, and, the following year, mineral fuels comprised only 7.2% of the total cost of imports. The use of renewable sources of energy (including wind power) has been encouraged.

Service industries are a major contributor to the economy, notably government, business and financial services. Changes in legislation and policy, and the approach of the EEC's implementation of a single internal market, brought about an increasing number of closures and mergers of banks in the late 1980s and in 1990. Danish banking, like most other sectors of the economy, traditionally consists of small- and medium-sized, locally-based businesses.

In 1989 Denmark recorded a visible trade surplus of US $2,433m., but there was a deficit of US $1,414m. on the current account of the balance of payments. Most Danish trade is with the EEC (49.9% of imports and 50.4% of exports in 1989). The principal source of imports in 1989 was the Federal Republic of Germany (22.2%), which was also the principal market for exports (17.5%). Other major trading partners

DENMARK

include Sweden and the United Kingdom. The principal exports are food and food products, chemicals and manufactures such as industrial machinery. The principal imports are chemicals, machinery and basic manufactures such as iron, steel and paper.

In the financial year ending 31 December 1989 there was a budgetary deficit of 1,223m. kroner, and for 1990 it was estimated that this would increase to 2,784m. kroner. Denmark has one of the highest levels of debt per head of population among industrialized nations. By the end of 1988 the foreign debt stood at 296,000m. kroner, and it was initially estimated that interest payments would account for 18.4% of budgetary expenditure in 1989. The average annual rate of inflation was 4.8% in 1989. In the year to July 1990, however, inflation fell to 0.4%. Some 9.4% of the labour force were unemployed in 1989.

Denmark is a member of the EEC (see p. 135), the Nordic Council (p. 179) and the Nordic Council of Ministers (p. 180).

The main factor in the development of Denmark's economy is the movement towards a wider European market from 1992, and the resulting need for bigger economic units that are able to compete effectively. In 1989 legislation permitted the formation of larger farms, signifying a change in the policy that had protected the traditional family farms, many of which have become seriously indebted. The problems of the agricultural sector were compounded by the expense of environmental-protection legislation (see Recent History) and changes in EEC agricultural policies. Mergers in the industry and banking sectors have led to the creation of larger companies. The Danish Government is under considerable pressure to reform the rates of taxation in preparation for 1992 and the single European market (see the EEC, p. 135). Serious obstacles to such reform, however, are the comprehensive nature of welfare provision and the size of the national debt.

Social Welfare

Denmark was one of the first countries to introduce state social welfare schemes. The principal benefits cover unemployment, sickness, old age and disability, and are financed largely by state subventions. The Government introduced a new system in 1984, whereby social benefits are regulated according to the individual's means. In 1985 Denmark had 120 hospital establishments, with 36,000 beds, and in 1986 there were 13,144 physicians working in the country. In 1990, 34% of proposed budget expenditure was allocated to social services.

Education

Education is compulsory for nine years between seven and 16 years of age, though exemption may be granted after seven years. The State is obliged to offer a pre-school class and a tenth voluntary year. State-subsidized private schools are available, but about 90% of pupils attend municipal schools. The 1975 Education Act, with effect from August 1976, increased parental influence, introduced a comprehensive curriculum for the first 10 years and offered options on final tests or a leaving certificate thereafter.

Primary and lower secondary education begins at six or seven years of age and lasts for nine (optionally 10) years. At the age of 16 or 17, pupils may transfer to an upper secondary school (Gymnasium), leading to the Upper Secondary School Leaving Examination (Studentereksamen) after three years, or they may take a two-year course, leading to the Higher Preparatory Examination; both courses give admission to university studies. Students may transfer to vocational courses or apprenticeship training at this point. Enrolment at primary and secondary schools is equivalent to virtually 100% of school-age children.

There are three universities, two university centres, and several other institutions of further and higher education. The traditional folk high schools offer a wide range of further education opportunities, which do not confer any professional qualification. In 1990 proposed government expenditure on education represented 8.2% of total budget spending.

Public Holidays

1991: 1 January (New Year's Day), 29 March–1 April (Easter), 26 April (General Prayer Day), 9 May (Ascension Day), 20 May (Whit Monday), 5 June (Constitution Day), 25–26 December (Christmas).

1992: 1 January (New Year's Day), 17–20 April (Easter), 15 May (General Prayer Day), 28 May (Ascension Day), 5 June (Constitution Day), 8 June (Whit Monday), 25–26 December (Christmas).

Weights and Measures

The metric system is in force.

Statistical Survey

Note: The figures in this survey relate only to metropolitan Denmark, excluding the Faeroe Islands and Greenland, which are dealt with in separate chapters (see pp. 898 and 901 respectively).
Source (unless otherwise stated): Danmarks Statistik, Sejrøgade 11, POB 2550, 2100 Copenhagen Ø; tel. 31-29-82-22; telex 16236; fax 31-18-48-01.

Area and Population

AREA, POPULATION AND DENSITY

Area (sq km)	43,093*
Population (census results)	
9 November 1970	4,937,579
1 January 1981	
Males	2,528,225
Females	2,595,764
Total	5,123,989
Population (official estimates at 1 January)	
1988	5,129,254
1989	5,129,778
1990	5,135,409
Density (per sq km) at 1 January 1990	119.2

* 16,638 sq miles.

PRINCIPAL TOWNS (population at 1 January 1990)

Ålborg (Aalborg)	155,019		Kolding	57,285
Odense	176,133		Helsingør	
København			(Elsinore)	56,701
(Copenhagen,			Horsens	55,210
the capital)	1,337,114		Vejle	51,263
Århus (Aarhus)	261,437		Roskilde	49,081
Esbjerg	81,504		Næstved	45,175
Randers	61,020			

* Copenhagen metropolitan area, including Frederiksberg and 25 suburb municipalities. The estimated population of the Copenhagen municipality was 466,723 at 1 January 1990.

DENMARK

BIRTHS, MARRIAGES AND DEATHS

	Registered live births Number	Rate (per 1,000)	Registered marriages Number	Rate (per 1,000)	Registered deaths Number	Rate (per 1,000)
1982	52,658	10.3	24,330	4.8	55,368	10.8
1983	50,822	9.9	27,096	5.3	57,156	11.2
1984	51,800	10.1	28,624	5.6	57,109	11.2
1985	53,749	10.5	29,322	5.7	58,378	11.4
1986	55,370	10.8	30,778	6.0	58,139	11.7
1987	56,221	11.0	31,132	6.1	58,136	11.3
1988	58,844	11.5	32,080	6.3	58,984	11.5
1989	61,467	12.0	30,780	6.0	59,420	11.6

Expectation of life at birth: Males 71.8 years; females 77.7 years (1987–88).

CIVILIAN LABOUR FORCE EMPLOYED
(ISIC Major Divisions, '000 persons)

	1987	1988	1989
Agriculture, forestry and fishing	162.4	156.9	151.0
Mining and quarrying	2.6	2.3	2.4
Manufacturing	529.2	513.8	514.0
Electricity, gas and water	16.8	17.0	17.4
Construction	187.7	183.5	176.7
Trade, restaurants and hotels	347.6	344.7	337.0
Transport, storage and communications	181.9	182.2	179.9
Financing, insurance, real estate and business services	250.3	250.5	253.4
Community, social and personal services	931.6	944.2	949.6
Total	2,610.1	2,595.2	2,581.5

Agriculture

PRINCIPAL CROPS ('000 metric tons)

	1987	1988	1989
Wheat	2,285	2,080	3,224
Barley	4,292	5,419	4,959
Rye	512	366	487
Oats	94	202	125
Potatoes	957	1,246	1,238
Pulses	519	508	475
Rapeseed	556	504	655
Sugar beet	2,632	3,379	3,309

LIVESTOCK ('000 head at June-July)

	1987	1988	1989
Horses	32.8	34.3	35.4
Cattle	2,350.8	2,262.1	2,221.5
Pigs	9,266.4	9,217.5	9,190.0
Sheep	100.8	124.3	144.2
Chickens	14,619.1	14,767.9	16,266.3
Turkeys	345.3	245.9	312.0
Ducks	525.6	443.9	569.7
Geese	50.2	66.1	46.2

LIVESTOCK PRODUCTS ('000 metric tons)

	1987	1988	1989
Beef and veal	254.9	235.9	222.2
Pig meat	1,198.5	1,217.6	1,214.2
Poultry meat	113.0	116.8	128.0
Cows' milk	4,859.6	4,739.0	4,747.3
Butter	96.2	93.8	92.3
Cheese	272.3	259.6	276.7
Eggs	76.5	79.4	82.0

Forestry

ROUNDWOOD REMOVALS ('000 cu m, excl. bark)

	1986	1987	1988
Sawlogs, veneer logs and logs for sleepers	941*	806	806*
Pulpwood	612	506	510
Other industrial wood	356*	285	285*
Fuel wood	406	481	481*
Total	2,315	2,078	2,082

* FAO estimate.
Source: FAO, *Yearbook of Forest Products*.

SAWNWOOD PRODUCTION ('000 cu m, incl. boxboards)

	1983	1984*	1985
Coniferous (softwood)	400	400	450
Broadleaved (hardwood)	400	400	400*
Total	800	800	850

1986, 1987 and 1988: Annual production as in 1985 (FAO estimates).
Railway sleepers ('000 cu m): 29* in 1986; 11 in 1987; 11* in 1988.
* FAO estimates.
Source: FAO, *Yearbook of Forest Products*.

Fishing*

('000 metric tons, live weight)

	1986	1987	1988
Trouts	24.4	25.8	28.5
European plaice	41.1	37.0	32.4
Atlantic cod	154.1	150.0	128.1
Haddock	20.3	11.4	11.7
Norway pout	194.5	219.2	181.2
Blue whiting (Poutassou)	69.8	72.7	134.6
Sandeels (Sandlances)	847.5	617.1	799.3
Grey gurnard	0.3	46.6	38.2
Atlantic horse mackerel	52.6	53.9	117.4
Atlantic herring	150.5	156.6	184.2
European sprat (brisling)	105.0	134.5	149.9
Atlantic mackerel	25.0	31.5	26.0
Other fishes (incl. unspecified)	60.6	44.2	54.4
Total fish	1,746.1	1,600.5	1,885.9
Crustaceans	15.1	20.2	12.2
Blue mussel	87.5	85.7	72.5
Total catch (incl. other aquatic animals)	1,848.7	1,706.4	1,971.8
Inland waters	21.1	23.3	23.9
Atlantic Ocean	1,827.5	1,683.1	1,947.9

* Data include quantities landed by Danish fishing craft in foreign ports and exclude quantities landed by foreign fishing craft in Danish ports.

Source: FAO, *Yearbook of Fishery Statistics*.

DENMARK
Statistical Survey

Mining

('000 metric tons)

	1987	1988	1989
Crude petroleum	4,552	4,700	5,416
Salt (unrefined)	537	548	552
Sulphur*	11	14	19
Limestone flux and calcareous stone	1,362	1,968	2,383

* Sulphur of all kinds, other than sublimed sulphur, precipitated sulphur and colloidal sulphur.

Industry

SELECTED PRODUCTS
('000 metric tons, unless otherwise indicated)

	1987	1988	1989
Pig meat:			
Fresh, chilled or frozen	n.a.	727	644
Salted, dried or smoked	152	132	100
Poultry meat and offals	107	102	116
Fish fillets: fresh, chilled, frozen	108	93	94
Salami, sausages, etc	70	76	80
Meat in airtight containers:			
Hams	58	72	66
Other meat	26	25	29
Meat preparations, pâtés, etc	89	n.a.	n.a.
Beet and cane sugar (solid)	522	468	503
Beer ('000 hectolitres)	8,755	9,160	9,217
Flours, meals and pastes of fish	450	363	341
Oil cake and meal	129	154	208
Cigarettes (million)	11,162	11,145	11,209
Cement	1,886	1,620	1,999
Motor spirit (Petrol)	1,360	1,560	1,688
Motor and fuel oils	5,002	5,600	5,318
Powder asphalt	3,117	2,950	2,378
Washing powders, etc	194	n.a.	171
Refrigerators for household use ('000)	229	146	147
New dwellings completed (number)	27,250	25,435	26,272
Electric energy (million kWh)	27,227	25,789	20,929
Manufactured gas ('000 gigajoules)	2,337	1,950	1,666

Finance

CURRENCY AND EXCHANGE RATES

Monetary Units
100 øre = 1 Danish krone (plural: kroner).

Denominations
Coins: 25 and 50 øre; 1, 5, 10 and 20 kroner.
Notes: 50, 100, 500 and 1,000 kroner.

Sterling and Dollar Equivalents (30 September 1990)
£1 sterling = 11.195 kroner;
US $1 = 5.975 kroner;
1,000 Danish kroner = £89.33 = $167.36.

Average Exchange Rate (kroner per US $)
1987 6.840
1988 6.732
1989 7.310

Budget

BUDGET (million kroner)

Revenue	1989*	1990†
Income and property taxes	119,680	123,465
Customs and excise duties	122,110	123,673
Other revenue	−20,271	−21,259
Interest (net)		
Total	221,519	225,879

Expenditure	1989*	1990†
Ministry of Social Affairs	74,330	77,778
Ministry of Education	18,473	18,784
Ministry of Defence	13,993	14,300
Public corporations	2,694	849
Ministry of Agriculture	2,403	2,532
Ministry of Justice	4,004	4,717
Ministry of Finance	3,211	4,164
Other expenditure	103,639	105,539
Total	222,742	228,663

* Approved.   † Estimates.

NATIONAL BANK RESERVES (million kroner)

	1987	1988	1989
Gold	4,858	4,595	4,340
IMF special drawing rights	1,301	1,542	1,850
European currency units	3,777	10,454	4,625
Gross foreign assets	54,078	59,063	33,180
Reserve position in IMF	6,148	6,565	6,173
Total official reserves	70,162	82,219	50,168

MONEY SUPPLY ('000 million kroner at 31 December)

	1987	1988	1989
Currency outside banks	31.43	27.91	32.83
Demand deposits with commercial banks and savings banks	209.88	246.20	245.31
Savings deposits with commercial banks and savings banks	102.53	82.43	82.30
Short-term government bills outside banks	20.61	17.77	38.05
Total money	364.45	374.31	398.49

COST OF LIVING
(Consumer Price Index. Base: 1980 = 100)

	1987	1988	1989
Food	152	158	164
Fuel and power	166	167	179
Clothing and footwear	150	160	169
Rent	161	171	182
All items	157.8	165.0	172.9

DENMARK

NATIONAL ACCOUNTS (million kroner at current prices)

National Income and Product

	1987	1988	1989
Compensation of employees	389,309	403,759	416,226
Operating surplus	130,658	138,462	163,502
Domestic factor incomes	519,966	542,221	579,728
Consumption of fixed capital	61,900	66,200	71,158
Gross domestic product at factor cost	581,866	608,421	650,886
Indirect taxes	135,982	140,081	139,289
Less Subsidies	22,011	24,455	24,806
GDP in purchasers' values	695,837	724,047	765,369
Factor income from abroad	20,829	27,149	35,704
Less Factor income paid abroad	48,784	55,799	68,003
Gross national product	667,883	695,397	733,071
Less Consumption of fixed capital	61,900	66,200	71,158
National income in market prices	605,983	629,197	661,912
Other current transfers from abroad	8,913	10,101	9,104
Less Other current transfers paid abroad	14,807	16,351	15,587
National disposable income	600,088	622,947	655,429

Expenditure on the Gross Domestic Product

	1987	1988	1989
Government final consumption expenditure	176,214	186,983	194,015
Private final consumption expenditure	377,686	386,156	403,817
Increase in stocks	−4,000	−4,000	3,223
Gross fixed capital formation	133,078	133,103	139,141
Total domestic expenditure	682,978	702,242	740,196
Exports of goods and services	220,085	237,071	266,930
Less Imports of goods and services	207,226	215,266	241,755
GDP in purchasers' values	695,837	724,047	765,369

Gross Domestic Product by Economic Activity (at factor cost)

	1987	1988	1989
Agriculture and hunting	24,162	23,401	27,237
Forestry and logging	1,011	1,039	1,107
Fishing	2,152	2,097	2,458
Mining and quarrying	5,360	4,681	6,515
Manufacturing	118,176	121,758	125,953
Electricity, gas and water	8,212	9,537	11,138
Construction	40,133	40,984	42,729
Wholesale and retail trade	79,338	81,457	87,055
Restaurants and hotels	8,581	8,884	9,148
Transport, storage and communication	45,958	49,232	52,965
Finance and insurance	21,609	20,312	21,170
Owner-occupied dwellings	51,674	52,782	59,026
Business services	32,310	34,962	39,136
Market services of education and health	7,044	7,474	7,740
Recreational and cultural services	5,413	5,760	6,958
Household services (incl. vehicle repairs)	16,866	18,303	20,050
Government services	131,770	142,112	147,380
Other producers	4,145	4,446	4,790
Sub-total	603,914	629,221	672,555
Less Imputed bank service charges	22,048	20,800	21,660
Total	581,866	608,421	650,886

BALANCE OF PAYMENTS (US $ million)

	1987	1988	1989
Merchandise exports f.o.b.	25,695	27,537	28,718
Merchandise imports f.o.b.	−24,900	−25,664	−26,285
Trade balance	795	1,873	2,433
Exports of services	10,475	12,883	14,050
Imports of services	−14,051	−16,316	−17,754
Balance on goods and services	−2,781	−1,560	−1,271
Private unrequited transfers (net)	−56	−88	80
Government unrequited transfers (net)	−164	−131	−223
Current balance	−3,002	−1,779	−1,414
Long-term capital (net)	8,153	2,909	−3,268
Short-term capital (net)	−793	805	1,207
Net errors and omissions	85	−619	−347
Total (net monetary movements)	4,443	1,316	−3,821
Valuation changes (net)	1,370	−731	−516
Official financing (net)	−712	120	−16
Changes in reserves	5,102	705	−4,354

Source: IMF, *International Financial Statistics*.

External Trade

PRINCIPAL COMMODITIES
(distribution by SITC, million kroner)

Imports c.i.f.	1987*	1988	1989
Food and live animals	18,313.1	18,916	20,513
Fish, crustaceans and molluscs	5,681.7	5,594	6,218
Animal feeding-stuff (excl. cereals)	3,633.1	3,998	4,404
Crude materials (inedible) except fuels	7,411.5	8,253	8,778
Mineral fuels, lubricants, etc.	13,779.5	11,346	14,151
Coal, coke and briquettes	3,026.1	2,758	3,500
Petroleum, petroleum products, etc.	10,308.2	8,006	9,545
Crude petroleum oils, etc.	3,826.6	n.a.	n.a.
Refined petroleum products	5,903.4	n.a.	n.a.
Chemicals and related products	19,249.9	21,043	22,665
Artificial resins and plastic materials, etc.	6,396.4	7,419	7,634
Products of polymerization, etc.	4,480.4	n.a.	n.a.
Basic manufactures	35,097.0	35,655	39,311
Paper, paperboard and manufactures	6,804.5	6,989	7,618
Textile yarn, fabrics, etc.	6,235.4	5,683	5,814
Iron and steel	6,922.2	7,998	9,426
Machinery and transport equipment	51,860.2	50,278	58,949
Machinery specialized for particular industries	7,124.3	6,216	6,534
General industrial machinery, equipment and parts	7,467.5	7,318	8,172

DENMARK

Imports c.i.f.—continued	1987*	1988	1989
Office machines and automatic data processing equipment	7,358.3	7,451	8,267
Automatic data processing machines, etc.	3,908.2	n.a.	n.a.
Telecommunications and sound equipment	4,424.7	4,315	4,817
Other electrical machinery, apparatus, etc.	7,398.5	7,756	8,499
Road vehicles and parts (excl. tyres, engines and electrical parts)	12,437.8	8,891	9,947
Passenger motor cars (excl. buses)	5,246.2	n.a.	n.a.
Motor vehicles for the transport of goods, etc.	3,458.6	n.a.	n.a.
Miscellaneous manufactured articles	22,307.7	21,886	23,851
Clothing and accessories (excl. footwear)	6,321.8	5,931	6,400
Total (incl. others)	173,917.9	174,429	195,328

* Provisional figures. Beginning in 1988, revised SITC classifications have been used. The values of certain transactions are not, therefore, strictly comparable with those in earlier years.
† Revised total (million kroner) 174,066.1.

Exports f.o.b.	1987*	1988	1989
Food and live animals	46,232.2	47,068	52,930
Meat and meat preparations	18,346.2	18,668	21,081
Fresh, chilled or frozen meat	11,663.5	n.a.	n.a.
Dairy products and birds' eggs	6,567.0	6,609	7,778
Cheese and curd	3,603.5	n.a.	n.a.
Fish, crustaceans and molluscs	11,245.7	10,765	11,659
Fresh, chilled or frozen fish	5,838.9	n.a.	n.a.
Cereals and cereal preparations	4,144.4	4,465	4,696
Crude materials (inedible) except fuels	11,744.4	11,868	12,082
Hides, skins and furskins	4,552.5	3,838	3,356
Mineral fuels, lubricants, etc.	5,106.3	4,713	6,827
Petroleum, petroleum products, etc.	4,245.3	3,798	5,801
Refined petroleum products	2,362.7	n.a.	n.a.
Chemicals and related products	16,226.8	18,077	20,436
Medicinal and pharmaceutical products	5,741.4	6,223	7,179
Basic manufactures	20,154.2	20,712	23,327
Textile yarn, fabrics, etc.	4,045.1	3,918	4,216
Machinery and transport equipment	42,493.2	46,739	52,991
Power generating machinery and equipment	2,905.4	2,918	3,628
Machinery specialized for particular industries	6,734.5	7,449	8,854
General industrial machinery, equipment and parts	12,934.4	13,857	15,692
Telecommunications and sound equipment	4,057.5	4,069	4,928
Other electrical machinery, apparatus, etc.	5,810.1	5,787	6,559
Transport equipment	6,843.1	9,201	9,604
Ships, boats and floating structures	3,354.6	n.a.	n.a.
Miscellaneous manufactured articles	28,480.8	28,632	32,337
Furniture and parts	6,515.2	6,258	7,518
Clothing and accessories (excl. footwear)	5,100.2	4,438	4,705
Professional, scientific and controlling instruments, etc.	3,972.3	4,250	4,703
Total (incl. others)	175,096.5	182,415	205,508

* Provisional figures. Beginning in 1988, revised SITC classifications have been used. The values of certain transactions are not, therefore, strictly comparable with those in earlier years.
† Revised total (million kroner) 175,302.4.

PRINCIPAL TRADING PARTNERS* (million kroner)

Imports c.i.f.	1987	1988	1989
Austria	2,168.9	2,148.7	2,366.6
Belgium/Luxembourg	5,996.9	5,933.8	6,331.8
China, People's Republic	1,653.4	2,148.5	2,349.2
Finland	5,433.3	5,435.4	5,675.4
France (incl. Monaco)	9,273.1	8,642.4	9,720.3
Germany, Fed. Rep.	41,006.4	39,907.5	43,389.5
Greenland	2,056.3	2,024.3	2,162.6
Italy	7,063.9	6,835.7	7,702.8
Japan	7,712.5	7,265.6	7,598.3
Kuwait	1,787.9	2,253.7	3,160.2
Netherlands	9,296.3	10,434.2	11,033.0
Norway	7,377.1	7,798.5	8,577.0
Sweden	21,267.1	21,377.6	23,604.8
Switzerland	3,730.7	3,802.8	3,931.3
United Kingdom	13,272.7	12,320.0	13,585.0
USA	9,305.7	10,472.0	13,468.3
Total (incl. others)	174,066.1	174,428.8	195,327.9

Exports f.o.b.	1987	1988	1989
Belgium/Luxembourg	3,573.6	3,671.2	4,111.5
Finland	4,006.2	4,545.8	5,620.7
France (incl. Monaco)	9,713.9	10,426.1	12,387.2
Germany, Fed. Rep.	29,718.7	31,934.3	35,945.7
Greenland	2,772.9	2,179.4	1,865.2
Italy	8,484.1	8,589.0	9,835.4
Japan	6,661.1	7,788.8	8,871.0
Netherlands	7,546.5	7,491.7	8,591.6
Norway	12,971.5	12,412.7	11,898.6
Spain (excl. Canary Is.)	2,308.6	2,883.1	3,639.6
Sweden	20,114.8	20,958.3	25,061.3
Switzerland	4,094.6	4,170.4	4,465.4
United Kingdom	20,195.0	21,746.3	24,812.3
USA	12,385.1	10,671.0	11,481.8
Total (incl. others)	175,302.4	182,414.8	205,508.0

* Imports by country of production; exports by country of consumption.

Transport

RAILWAYS (traffic)

	Private railways 1988	State railways 1987	State railways 1988
Number of journeys ('000)	10,911	145,767	143,106
Passenger-kilometres ('000)	191,168	4,782,000	4,797,000
Ton-kilometres ('000)	13,663	1,680,000	1,639,000

ROAD TRAFFIC (motor vehicles in use at 31 December)

	1986	1987	1988
Private cars	1,544,284	1,574,251	1,582,297
Taxis, hire cars, etc.	13,596	13,168	13,137
Buses, coaches	8,105	8,110	8,093
Vans, lorries	274,991	286,415	293,543
Tractors	142,649	141,022	139,381
Trailers	248,372	269,378	287,248
Motor cycles	41,868	42,456	87,861

DENMARK

SHIPPING

Danish Merchant Marine
(vessels exceeding 100 gross registered tons, at 1 July)

	1989		1990	
	Number	Gross tonnage	Number	Gross tonnage
Dry cargo	452	2,290,600	440	2,518,100
Tankers	73	2,494,900	83	2,181,700
Total	525	4,785,500	523	4,699,800

Source: Danmarks Rederiforening, Copenhagen.

Sea-borne Freight Traffic at Danish Ports*
('000 metric tons loaded and unloaded)

	1987	1988	1989
Ålborg	3,268	2,998	2,819
Århus	5,890	6,684	6,377
Copenhagen	6,163	5,629	5,618
Fredericia	6,676	7,119	7,290
Kalundborg	4,072	3,818	3,843
Skaelskør	5,046	6,365	6,302
Others	33,353	31,213	34,451
Total	64,468	63,826	66,700

* Including domestic traffic, excluding international ferry traffic.

International Sea-borne Shipping*
(freight traffic, '000 metric tons)

	1987	1988	1989
Goods loaded	12,020	13,480	14,719
Goods unloaded	32,317	30,501	30,695

* Excluding international ferry traffic.
Source: Danmarks Rederiforening, Copenhagen.

CIVIL AVIATION (Scandinavian Airlines System)

	1987	1988	1989
Kilometres flown ('000)	138,900	152,900	169,400
Passengers carried ('000)	12,662	13,341	14,005
Passenger-kilometres (million)	13,207	14,024	15,229
Cargo and mail ton-kilometres (million)	429	451	481

Tourism
(income from visitors, million kroner)

	1987	1988	1989
Scandinavian visitors	5,731	6,373	6,264
German visitors	3,345	3,429	3,719
All other visitors	6,110	6,506	6,915
Total	15,185	16,308	16,898

OVERNIGHT STAYS (foreign visitors)

	1987	1988	1989
In hotels	4,480,300	4,377,700	5,131,900
At camping sites	3,289,600	3,213,800	3,506,200
Total	7,769,900	7,591,500	8,638,100

Communications Media

	1987	1988	1989
Radio licences	2,313,000	2,022,000	2,620,000
Television licences (black and white)	243,000	243,000	187,000
Television licences (colour)	1,698,000	1,699,000	1,760,000
Telephones in use	4,434,000	4,509,000	4,397,776
Number of newspapers	47	46	46
Total circulation (weekdays)	1,848,000	1,842,000	1,853,000
Books published	11,129	10,584	10,762

Education
(1988/89)

	Institutions	Teachers	Students
Pre-primary			
Primary	3,049	62,700	669,822
Secondary: first stage			
Secondary: second stage			
General	162	7,500	71,723
Vocational			
Teacher-training	325	n.a.	201,717
Technical education			
Universities	5	n.a.	51,355
Other university-level	59	n.a.	42,540

Directory

The Constitution

The constitutional charter (*Grundlov*), summarized below, was adopted on 5 June 1953.

GOVERNMENT

The form of government is a limited (constitutional) monarchy. The legislative authority rests jointly with the Crown and Parliament. Executive power is vested in the Crown, and the administration of justice is exercised by the courts. The Monarch can constitutionally 'do no wrong'. She exercises her authority through the Ministers appointed by her. The Ministers are responsible for the government of the country. The Constitution establishes the principle of Parliamentarism under which individual Ministers or the whole Cabinet must retire when defeated in Parliament by a vote of no confidence.

MONARCH

The Monarch acts on behalf of the State in international affairs. Except with the consent of the Parliament, she cannot, however, take any action which increases or reduces the area of the Realm or undertake any obligation, the fulfilment of which requires the co-operation of the Parliament or which is of major importance. Nor can the Monarch, without the consent of the Parliament, terminate any international agreement which has been concluded with the consent of the Parliament.

Apart from defence against armed attack on the Realm or on Danish forces, the Monarch cannot, without the consent of the Parliament, employ military force against any foreign power.

PARLIAMENT

The Parliament is an assembly consisting of not more than 179 members, two of whom are elected in the Faeroe Islands and two in Greenland. It is called the Folketing. Danish nationals, having attained 18 years of age, with permanent residence in Denmark, have the franchise and are eligible for election. The members of the Folketing are elected for four years. Election is by a system of proportional representation, with direct and secret ballot on lists in large constituencies. A bill adopted by the Folketing may be submitted to referendum, when such referendum is claimed by not less than one-third of the members of the Folketing and not later than three days after the adoption. The bill is void if rejected by a majority of the votes cast, representing not less than 30% of all electors.

The Government

HEAD OF STATE

Queen of Denmark: HM QUEEN MARGRETHE II (succeeded to the throne 14 January 1972).

THE CABINET
(January 1991)

A coalition of the Conservative People's Party (KF) and the Liberal Party (V).

Prime Minister: POUL SCHLÜTER (KF).
Minister of Foreign Affairs: UFFE ELLEMANN-JENSEN (V).
Minister of Finance: HENNING DYREMOSE (KF).
Minister of Justice: HANS ENGELL (KF).
Minister of Economic and Fiscal Affairs: ANDERS FOGH RASMUSSEN (V).
Minister of Defence: KNUD ENGÅRD (V).
Minister of Education and Research: BERTEL HÅRDER (V).
Minister of Fisheries: KENT KIRK (KF).
Minister of Labour: KNUD E. KIRKEGÅRD (KF).
Minister of the Interior and for Nordic Affairs: THOR PEDERSEN (V).
Minister of Transport: KAJ IKAST (KF).
Minister of Industry and Energy: ANNE BIRGITTE LUNDHOLT (KF).
Minister of Housing and Building: SVEND ERIK HOVMAND (V).
Minister of Agriculture: LAURITS TØRNÆS (V).
Minister of Cultural Affairs: GRETHE ROSTBØLL (KF).
Minister of the Environment: PER STIG MÖLLER (KF).
Minister of Social Affairs: ELSE WINTHER ANDERSEN (V).
Minister of Ecclesiastical Affairs and Communications: TORBEN RECHENDORFF (KF).
Minister of Health: ESTER LARSEN (V).

MINISTRIES

Office of the Prime Minister: Christiansborg, Prins Jørgens Gård 11, 1218 Copenhagen K; tel. 33-92-33-00; telex 27027; fax 33-11-16-65.
Ministry of Agriculture: Slotsholmsgade 10, 1216 Copenhagen K; tel. 33-92-33-01; fax 33-14-50-42.
Ministry of Cultural Affairs: Nybrogade 2, 1203 Copenhagen K; tel. 33-92-33-70; telex 27385; fax 33-91-33-88.
Ministry of Defence: Slotsholmsgade 10, 1216 Copenhagen K; tel. 33-92-33-20.
Ministry of Ecclesiastical Affairs: Frederiksholms Kanal 21, 1220 Copenhagen K; tel. 33-14-62-63; fax 33-92-39-13.
Ministry of Economic and Fiscal Affairs: Slotsholmsgade 12, 1216 Copenhagen K; tel. 33-92-32-22; telex 16833; fax 33-93-60-20.
Ministry of Education and Research: Frederiksholms Kanal 21–25, 1220 Copenhagen K; tel. 33-92-50-00; telex 16243; fax 33-92-55-47.
Ministry of the Environment: Slotsholmsgade 12, 1216 Copenhagen K; tel. 33-92-33-88; fax 33-32-22-27.
Ministry of Finance: Christiansborg Slotsplads 1, 1218 Copenhagen K; tel. 33-92-33-33; telex 16140; fax 33-32-80-30.
Ministry of Fisheries: Stormgade 2, 1470 Copenhagen K; tel. 33-92-65-00; telex 16144; fax 33-92-65-79.
Ministry of Foreign Affairs: Asiatisk Plads 2, 1448 Copenhagen K; tel. 33-92-00-00; telex 31292; fax 31-54-05-33.
Ministry of Health: Herluf Trolles Gade 11, 1052 Copenhagen K; tel. 33-92-33-60; fax 33-93-15-63.
Ministry of Housing and Building: Slotsholmsgade 12, 1216 Copenhagen K; tel. 33-92-61-00; telex 31401; fax 33-92-61-04.
Ministry of Industry and Energy: Slotsholmsgade 12, 1216 Copenhagen K; tel. 33-92-33-50; telex 22373.
Ministry of the Interior: Christiansborg Slotsplads 1, 1218 Copenhagen K; tel. 33-92-33-80; fax 33-11-12-39.
Ministry of Justice: Slotsholmsgade 10, 1216 Copenhagen K; tel. 33-92-33-40; telex 15530.
Ministry of Labour: Laksegade 19, 1063 Copenhagen K; tel. 33-92-59-00; telex 19320.
Ministry of Social Affairs: Slotsholmsgade 6, 1216 Copenhagen K; tel. 33-12-25-17; telex 27343.
Ministry of Transport: Frederiksholms Kanal 25–27, 1220 Copenhagen K; tel. 33-92-33-55; telex 22275; fax 33-12-38-93.

Legislature

FOLKETING

President of the Folketing: HANS PETER CLAUSEN.
Secretary-General: HELGE HJORTDAL.
Clerk of the Folketing: L. E. HANSEN-SALBY.

General Election, 12 December 1990
(metropolitan Denmark only)

	% of votes	Seats
Social-Democratic Party	37.4	69
Conservative People's Party	16.0	30
Socialist People's Party	8.3	15
Liberals	15.8	29
Radical Liberals	3.5	7
Centre Democrats	5.1	9
Progress Party	6.4	12
Christian People's Party	2.3	4
Others	5.2	—
Total	**100.0**	**175**

The Folketing also contains two members from Greenland and two from the Faeroe Islands.

DENMARK

Political Organizations

Centrum-Demokraterne (Centre Democrats): Folketinget, Christiansborg, 1240 Copenhagen K; tel. 33-37-48-77; f. 1973; opposes extreme ideologies, supports EEC and NATO; Leader MIMI JACOBSEN, Sec.-Gen. ERHARD JACOBSEN.

Danmarks Kommunistiske Parti (Danish Communist Party): Dr Tværgade 3, 1302 Copenhagen K; f. 1919; Chair. OLE SOHN.

Danmarks Retsforbund (Justice Party): Landssekretariatet, Lyngbyvej 42, 2100 Copenhagen Ø; tel. 31-20-44-88; fax 31-20-44-50; f. 1919; programme is closely allied to Henry George's teachings (single tax, free trade); Chair. POUL GERHARD C. KRISTIANSEN.

Europæiske Centrum-Demokrater (European Centre Democrats): Christiansborg, 1240 Copenhagen K; tel. 33-11-66-00; f. 1974; supports co-operation within EEC and provides information about the workings of the EEC; Chair. MIMI JACOBSEN.

Fælles Kurs (Common Course): Copenhagen.

Fremskridtspartiet (Progress Party): Folketinget, Christiansborg, 1218 Copenhagen K; tel. 33-11-66-00; telex 19461; f. 1972; movement whose policies include gradual abolition of income tax, disbandment of most of the civil service, and abolition of diplomatic service and about 90% of legislation; Chair. ANNETTE JUST.

De Grønne (Green Environmentalists' Party): Landssekretariatet, Sterrebyvej 6, 5762 Vester Skerning, Fyn; International Secretariat, Slugten 10, 3300 Frederiksvaerk; tel. 42-34-89-19; f. 1983.

Det Humanistiske Parti (Humanistic Party): Ryesgade 111, 2100 Copenhagen Ø; tel. 31-42-76-80.

Internationalen-Socialistiisk Arbejderparti (Socialist Workers' Party): Blegdamsvej 28c, 2200 Copenhagen N.

Kommunistisk Arbejderparti (Communist Workers' Party): Studiestræde 24, 1455 Copenhagen K; tel. 33-15-21-33; f. 1968.

Konservative Folkeparti (Conservative People's Party): Tordenskjoldsgade 21, POB 1515, 1020 Copenhagen K; tel. 33-13-41-40; fax 33-93-37-73; f. 1916; advocates free initiative and the maintenance of private property, but recognizes the right of the State to take action to keep the economic and social balance; Chair. POUL SCHLÜTER; Sec.-Gen. JOHN WAGNER.

Kristeligt Folkeparti (Christian People's Party): Bernhard Bangs Allé 23, 2000 Frederiksberg; tel. 38-88-51-52; fax 38-88-31-15; f. 1970; interdenominational grouping opposed to pornography and abortion; favours social-liberal economic policy, and emphasizes significance of cultural and family policy; Chair. JANN SJURSEN; Sec.-Gen. NIELS CHRESTEN ANDERSEN.

Marxistisk-Leninistisk Parti (Marxist-Leninist Party): Griffenfeldsgade 26, 2200 Copenhagen N; tel. 31-35-60-69; Sec.-Gen. CLAUS RIIS.

Det Radikale Venstre (Radical Liberal Party): Det Radikale Venstres sekretariat, Christiansborg, 1240 Copenhagen K; tel. 33-12-72-51; f. 1905; supports international détente and co-operation within regional and world organizations, social reforms without socialism, incomes policy, workers' participation in industry, state intervention in industrial disputes, state control of trusts and monopolies, strengthening private enterprise; Chair. THORKILD MØLLER; Leader MARIANNE JELVED; Gen. Sec. KURT BUCH JENSEN.

Schleswigsche Partei (Schleswig Party): Vestergade 30, 6200 Åbenrå; tel. 74-62-38-33; fax 74-62-79-39; represents the German minority in North Schleswig.

Socialdemokratiet (Social Democratic Party): Thorvaldsensvej 2, 1998 Frederiksberg C; tel. 31-39-15-22; telex 22309; fax 31-39-40-30; f. 1871; finds its chief adherents among workers, employees and public servants; 100,000 members; Leader SVEND AUKEN; Gen. Sec. STEEN CHRISTENSEN.

Socialistisk Folkeparti (Socialist People's Party): Folketinget, Christiansborg, 1240 Copenhagen K; tel. 33-12-70-11; telex 21509; fax 33-14-70-10; f. 1959 by Aksel Larsen; socialist; Chair. GERT PETERSEN; Sec. CHRISTIAN FISCHER.

Venstre (Liberal Party): Søllerødvej 30, 2840 Holte; tel. 42-80-22-33; fax 42-80-38-30; f. 1870; supports free trade, a minimum of state interference, and the adoption, in matters of social expenditure, of a modern general social security system; Chair. UFFE ELLEMANN-JENSEN; Sec.-Gen. CLAUS HJORT FREDERIKSEN.

Venstresocialisterne (Left Socialist Party): Rosenørns Allé 44, 1970 Frederiksberg C; tel. 31-35-60-99; fax 31-35-62-98; f. 1967 as a result of a split from the Socialist People's Party; non-dogmatic Marxist party of the post-1968 'New Left'; collective leadership.

Diplomatic Representation

EMBASSIES IN DENMARK

Argentina: Store Kongensgade 45, 1264 Copenhagen K; tel. 33-15-80-82; telex 27182; Ambassador: JORGE H. MAUHOURAT.

Australia: Kristianiagade 21, 2100 Copenhagen Ø; tel. 31-26-22-44; telex 22308; fax 35-43-22-18; Ambassador: JEFFREY A. BENSON.

Austria: Grønningen 5, 1270 Copenhagen K; tel. 33-12-46-23; telex 27023; fax 33-32-15-42; Ambassador: Dr FRANZ WUNDER-BALDINGER.

Belgium: Øster Allé 7, 2100 Copenhagen Ø; tel. 31-26-03-88; telex 22624; Ambassador: ERIK BAL.

Brazil: Ryvangs Allé 24, 2100 Copenhagen Ø; tel. 31-20-64-78; telex 19322; Ambassador: SERGIO PAULO ROUANET.

Bulgaria: Gamlehave Allé 7, 2920 Charlottenlund; tel. 31-64-24-84; telex 27020; Ambassador: (vacant).

Burkina Faso: Svanemøllevej 20, 2100 Copenhagen Ø; tel. 31-18-40-22; telex 19375; Ambassador: ANNE KONATE.

Canada: Kr. Bernikowsgade 1, 1105 Copenhagen K; tel. 33-12-22-99; telex 27036; fax 33-14-05-85; Ambassador: DOROTHY J. ARMSTRONG.

Chile: Kastelsvej 15, 2100 Copenhagen Ø; tel. 31-38-58-34; telex 15099; Ambassador: MARIO VALENZUELA.

China, People's Republic: Øregårds Allé 25, 2900 Hellerup; tel. 31-62-58-06; Ambassador: ZHANG LONGHAI.

Colombia: Kastelsvej 15, 2100 Copenhagen Ø; tel. 33-26-22-97; telex 27072; fax 31-26-22-97; Chargé d'affaires a.i.: NORELLA MESA DE MUTIS.

Côte d'Ivoire: Gersonsvej 8, 2900 Hellerup; tel. 31-62-88-22; telex 22351; Ambassador: (vacant).

Czechoslovakia: Ryvangs Allé 14, 2100 Copenhagen Ø; tel. 31-29-18-88; telex 19188; fax 31-29-15-98; Ambassador: (vacant).

Egypt: Nyropsgade 47, 1602 Copenhagen V; tel. 31-12-76-41; telex 19892; Ambassador: ADEL MOHAMED ABBAS ZAKI.

Finland: Skt. Annae Plads 24, 1250 Copenhagen K; tel. 33-13-42-14; telex 27084; fax 33-13-43-41; Ambassador: JOHANNES BÄCKSTRÖM.

France: Kongens Nytorv 4, 1050 Copenhagen K; tel. 33-15-51-22; telex 27029; fax 33-93-97-52; Ambassador: MICHEL DRUMETZ.

Germany: Stockholmsgade 57, 2100 Copenhagen Ø; tel. 31-26-16-22; telex 27166; fax 31-26-71-05; Ambassador: RÜDIGER VON PACHELBEL.

Ghana: Egebjerg Allé 13, 2900 Hellerup; tel. 31-62-82-22; telex 19471; fax 31-62-16-52; Ambassador: CHRISTINE ODURO.

Greece: Borgergade 16, 1300 Copenhagen K; tel. 33-11-45-33; telex 27279; Ambassador: EVANGELOS GEORGIOU.

Holy See: Immortellevej 11, 2950 Vedbæk (Apostolic Nunciature); tel. 42-89-35-36; Apostolic Pro-Nuncio: Most Rev. HENRI LEMAÎTRE, Titular Archbishop of Tongeren.

Hungary: Strandvejen 170, 2920 Charlottenlund; tel. 31-63-00-52; telex 27186; Ambassador: Dr LÁSZLÓ DEMUS.

Iceland: Dantes Plads 3, 1556 Copenhagen V; tel. 33-15-96-04; telex 15954; fax 33-93-05-06; Ambassador: HÖRDUR HELGASON.

India: Vangehusvej 15, 2100 Copenhagen Ø; tel. 31-18-28-88; telex 15964; fax 39-27-02-18; Ambassador: ROMA MAZUMDAR.

Indonesia: Ørehøj Allé 1, 2900 Hellerup; tel. 31-62-44-22; telex 16274; Ambassador: HARINGUN HARDJOTANOJO.

Iran: Grønningen 5, 1270 Copenhagen K; tel. 33-14-12-38; Ambassador: MANSOUR GHARAVI.

Ireland: Østbanegade 21, 2100 Copenhagen Ø; tel. 31-42-32-33; telex 22995; fax 35-43-18-58; Ambassador: SEAN O'HUIGINN.

Israel: Lundevangsvej 4, 2900 Hellerup; tel. 31-62-62-88; telex 27136; Ambassador: AMOS GANOR.

Italy: Gammel Vartov Vej 7, 2900 Hellerup; tel. 31-62-68-77; telex 27078; fax 31-62-25-99; Ambassador: MARIO MANCA.

Japan: Pilestræde 61, 1112 Copenhagen K; tel. 31-11-33-44; telex 27082; Ambassador: YOSHIFUMI MATSUDA.

Korea, Democratic People's Republic: Skelvej 2, 2900 Hellerup; tel. 31-62-50-70; Ambassador: O UNG GWON.

Korea, Republic: Svanemøllevej 104, 2900 Hellerup; Ambassador: SUN-SUP CHANG.

Lesotho: Østerkildevej 14, 2820 Gentofte; tel. 31-65-14-42; telex 16687; fax 31-65-33-64; Ambassador: BISHOP AUSTIN TLELASE.

Libya: Rosenvængets Hovedvej 4, 2100 Copenhagen Ø; tel. 31-26-36-11; telex 22652; Head of People's Bureau; (vacant).

Mexico: Gammel Vartov Vej 18, 2900 Hellerup; tel. 31-20-86-00; telex 27503; fax 31-20-82-48; Ambassador: MARIO RUÍZ MASSIEU.

Morocco: Øregårds Allé 19, 2900 Hellerup; tel. 31-62-45-11; telex 22913; fax 31-62-24-49; Ambassador: OMAR BELKORA.

Netherlands: Toldbodgade 95, 1253 Copenhagen K; tel. 33 15 62 93; telex 27093; fax 33 14 03 50; Ambassador: WILLEM DAMSTÉ.

Norway: Trondhjems Plads 4, 2100 Copenhagen Ø; tel. 31-38-89-85; telex 27114; fax 31-38-09-15; Ambassador: ARNE ARNESEN.

DENMARK

Pakistan: Valeursvej 17, 2900 Hellerup; tel. 31-62-11-88; Chargé d'affaires a.i.: QAZI HUMAYUN.
Poland: Richelieus Allé 12, 2900 Hellerup; tel. 31-62-72-44; telex 19264; fax 31-62-71-20; Ambassador: JANUSZ ROSZKOWSKI.
Portugal: Hovedvagtsgade 6, 1103 Copenhagen K; tel. 33-13-13-01; telex 16586; fax 33-13-24-87; Ambassador: ANTÓNIO CASCAIS.
Romania: Strandagervej 27, 2900 Hellerup; tel. 31-62-42-04; telex 27017; Ambassador: MARIN UNGUREANU.
Saudi Arabia: Lille Strandvej 27, 2900 Hellerup; tel. 31-62-12-00; telex 15931; fax 31-62-60-09; Chargé d'affaires a.i.: ABDUL RAHMAN A. OWAIDAH.
South Africa: Gammel Vartov Vej 8, Box 128, 2900 Hellerup; tel. 31-18-01-55; Ambassador: EDUARD ANTONIE LOUBSER.
Spain: Upsalagade 26, 2100 Copenhagen Ø; tel. 31-42-47-00; telex 27145; fax 31-26-30-99; Ambassador: CARLOS FERNÁNDEZ-LONGORIA.
Swaziland: Kastelsvej 19, 2100 Copenhagen Ø; tel. 31-42-61-11; Ambassador: MPHUMELELO JOSEPH NDUMISO HLOPHE.
Sweden: Skt Annæ Plads 15A, 1250 Copenhagen K; tel. 33-14-22-42; telex 22960; fax 33-32-90-35; Ambassador: CARL-JOHAN GORTH.
Switzerland: Amaliegade 14, 1256 Copenhagen K; tel. 33-14-17-96; telex 16239; Ambassador: DANIEL P. DAYER.
Thailand: Norgesmindevej 18, 2900 Hellerup; tel. 31-62-50-10; telex 16216; fax 31-62-50-59; Ambassador: TONGCHAN JOTIKASTHIRA.
Turkey: Vestagervej 16, 2100 Copenhagen Ø; tel. 31-20-55-00; telex 27476; fax 31-22-90-68; Ambassador: BAKI ILKIN.
Uganda: Sofievej 15, 2900 Hellerup; tel. 31-62-09-66; telex 15689; Ambassador: EDITH GRACE SSEMPALA.
USSR: Kristianiagade 5, 2100 Copenhagen Ø; tel. 31-42-55-85; fax 31-42-37-41; Ambassador: GENNADI GEORGIYEVICH VEDERNIKOV.
United Kingdom: Kastelsvej 36–40, 2100 Copenhagen Ø; tel. 31-26-46-00; telex 27106; fax 31-38-10-12; Ambassador: NIGEL C. R. WILLIAMS.
USA: Dag Hammarskjølds Allé 24, 2100 Copenhagen Ø; tel. 31-42-31-44; telex 22216; fax 35-43-02-23; Ambassador: KEITH LAPHAM BROWN.
Venezuela: Hammerensgade 3 (2nd Floor), 1267 Copenhagen K; tel. 33-93-63-11; telex 15309; fax 33-15-69-11; Ambassador: RAMÓN DELGADO-VALDERRAMA.
Yemen: Strandvejen 153, 1st Floor, 2900 Hellerup; tel. 31-62-30-40; Ambassador: SALEM ABDUL SHEIKH FARES.
Yugoslavia: Svanevænget 36, 2100 Copenhagen Ø; tel. 31-29-71-61; Ambassador: NADA FILIPOVIĆ.

Judicial System

In Denmark the judiciary is independent of the Government. Judges are appointed by the Crown on the recommendation of the Minister of Justice and cannot be dismissed except by judicial sentence.

The ordinary courts are divided into three instances, the Lower Courts, the High Courts and the Supreme Court. There is one Lower Court for each of the 82 judicial districts in the country. These courts must have at least one judge trained in law and they hear the majority of minor cases. The two High Courts serve Jutland and the islands respectively. They serve as appeal courts for cases from the lower courts, but are also used to give first hearing to the more important cases. Each case must be heard by at least three judges. The Supreme Court, at which at least five judges must sit, is the court of appeal for cases from the Higher Courts. Usually only one appeal is allowed from either court, but in special instances the Minister of Justice may give leave for a second appeal, to the Supreme Court, from a case which started in a lower court.

There is a special Maritime and Commercial Court in Copenhagen, consisting of a President and two Vice-Presidents with legal training and a number of commercial and nautical assessors; and also a Labour Court, which deals with labour disputes.

An Ombudsman is appointed by Parliament, after each general election, and is concerned with defects in the laws or administrative provisions. He must present an annual report to Parliament.

President of the Supreme Court: P. M. CHRISTENSEN.
President of the East High Court: K. HAULRIG.
President of the West High Court: O. AGERSNAP.
President of the Maritime and Commercial Court: EMIL FRANK POULSEN.
President of the Labour Court: JOHANNES BANGERT.
Ombudsman: HANS GAMMELTOFT-HANSEN.

Religion

CHRISTIANITY

Det Økumeniske Fællesraad i Danmark (Ecumenical Council of Denmark): Nørregade 11, 1165 Copenhagen K; tel. 33-15-59-27; f. 1939; associate council of the World Council of Churches; seven mem. churches, one observer; Chair. INGE MARIE NIELSEN; Gen. Sec. JØRGEN THOMSEN.

The National Church

Den evangelisk-lutherske Folkekirke i Danmark (Evangelical Lutheran Church of Denmark): Nørregade 11, 1165 Copenhagen K; tel. 33-13-35-08; telex 16217; fax 33-15-38-60; the established Church of Denmark, supported by the State; no bishop exercises a presiding role, but the Bishop of Copenhagen is responsible for ecumenical relations, together with the Ecumenical Council of Denmark; membership in 1988 was 4,602,210 (90% of the population).

Bishop of Copenhagen: OLE BERTELSEN.
Bishop of Helsingør: JOHS JOHANSEN.
Bishop of Roskilde: B. WIBERG.
Bishop of Nykøbing: TH. GRÆSHOLT.
Bishop of Odense: V. LIND.
Bishop of Ålborg: HENRIK CHRISTIANSEN.
Bishop of Viborg: GEORG S. GEIL.
Bishop of Århus: H. ERIKSEN.
Bishop of Ribe: H. SKOV.
Bishop of Haderslev: O. LINDEGÅRD.

Other Protestant Churches

Apostolic Church in Denmark: Lykkegaards vej 100, 6000 Kolding; tel. 75-52-47-95.
Danish Mission Covenant Church: Rosenlanden 17, 5000 Odense C; tel. 66-14-83-00; Rev. LEIF LUNDTOFT.
Det Danske Baptistsamfund (Baptist Union of Denmark): Købnerhus, Lærdalsgade 5.1, 2300 Copenhagen S; tel. 31-59-07-08; f. 1839; 6,000 mems; Pres. LEIF DAMKIER; Gen. Sec. Rev. OLE JÖRGENSEN.
German Lutheran Church: Sankt Petri Church Office, Larslejsstræde 11[1], 1451 Copenhagen K; tel. 33-13-38-34.
Methodist Church: Metodistkirkens Hjaelpearbejde, Rigensgade 21A, 1316 Copenhagen K; f. 1910; tel. 33-93-25-96; Gen. Sec. EGON HJULER.
Moravian Brethren: The Brethren Community, 6070 Christiansfeld; f. in Denmark 1773; Pastor HELGE RØNNOW, Lindegade 26, 6070 Christiansfeld; tel. 74-56-14-20.
Norwegian Lutheran Church: Kong Håkons Kirke, Ved Mønten 9, 2300 Copenhagen S; tel. 31-57-11-03.
Reformed Church: Reformed Synod of Denmark, Gothersgade 109[3], 1123 Copenhagen K; tel. 33-13-87-53; Rev. ULRICH DUSSE.
Seventh-day Adventists: Adventistsamfundet, Concordiavej 16, 2850 Nærum; tel. 42-80-56-00; fax 42-80-70-75.
Society of Friends: Danish Quaker Centre, Vendersgade 29, 1363 Copenhagen K; tel. 33-11-82-48.
Swedish Lutheran Church: Svenska Gustafskyrkan, Folke Bernadottes Allé, 2100 Copenhagen Ø; tel. 33-15-54-58; also V. Strandvej 24, 9990 Skagen; tel. 98-44-23-11.
Unitarians: Unitarernes Hus, Dag Hammarskjølds Allé 30, 2100 Copenhagen Ø; Chair. P. BOVIN; mems: 100 families.

The Salvation Army is also active in the country.

The Roman Catholic Church

Denmark comprises a single diocese, directly responsible to the Holy See. At 31 December 1988 there were an estimated 28,386 adherents in the country. The Bishop participates in the Scandinavian Episcopal Conference (based in Norway).

Bishop of Copenhagen: HANS LUDVIG MARTENSEN, Katolsk Bispekontor, Bredgade 69A, 1260 Copenhagen K; tel. 33-11-60-80; fax 33-14-60-86.

Other Christian Churches

Church of England: St Alban's House, Stigårdsvej 6, 2900 Hellerup; tel. 31-62-77-36; f. 1728; Chaplain Rev. DENNIS R. CAPES.
Church of Jesus Christ of Latter-day Saints (Mormons): Informationstjenesten, Annexgårdsvej 37, 2610 Rødovre; tel. 31-70-90-43; f. (in Denmark) 1850; 4,500 mems.
First Church of Christ, Scientist: Nyvej 7, 1851 Frederiksberg C; also in Århus.

DENMARK

Russian Orthodox Church: Alexander Nevski Church, Bredgade 53, 1260 Copenhagen K.; tel. 33-13-60-46.

BAHÁ'Í FAITH

Bahá'í: Det Nationale Åndelige Råd, Sofievej 28, 2900 Hellerup; tel. 31-62-35-18; National Centre for the Bahá'í faith in Denmark.

ISLAM

The Muslim Community: Nusrat Djahan Mosque (and Ahmadiyya Mission), Eriksmunde Allé 2, 2650 Hvidovre, Copenhagen; tel. 31-75-35-02; telex 16600; fax 31-75-00-07.

JUDAISM

Jewish Community: The Synagogue, Krystalgade 12, Copenhagen; Mosaisk Trossamfund, Ny Kongensgade 6, 1472 Copenhagen K; tel. 33-12-88-68; 8,000 mems; Chief Rabbi BENT MELCHIOR.

The Press

Denmark's long press history dates from the first newspaper published in 1666, but it was not until press freedom was introduced by law in 1849 that newspapers began to assume their present importance. The per caput circulation of Danish newspapers is one of the highest in the world. There are more than 220 separate newspapers, including more than 40 principal dailies. The average total circulation of newspapers in the first half of 1989 was 1,855,719 on weekdays and 1,519,883 on Sundays.

The freedom of the press is embodied in the 1953 Constitution and all censorship laws have been abolished. The legal limits to press comment are wide, legislation on defamation being chiefly concerned to protect the reputation of the individual. The Law of 1938 included provision for a Board of Denials and Corrections to be established to guard the individual's right to require a newspaper to correct factual errors. This Press Law makes editors legally responsible for the contents of a paper with the exception of signed articles for which the author is responsible.

Most newspapers and magazines are privately owned and published by joint concerns, co-operatives or limited liability companies. The main concentration of papers is held by the Berlingske Tidende Group which owns *Berlingske Tidende*, *Weekendavisen*, *B.T.*, the provincial *Jydske Tidende* and *Amtsavisen*, and three weekly magazines. Another company, Politiken A/S, owns several dailies, including *Politiken* and *Ekstra Bladet*, one weekly and a large publishing house. De Bergske Blade owns a group of six Liberal papers, including *Folkebladet Sydjylland*, *Frederiksborg Amts Avis* and *Ringkøting Amts Dagblad*.

There is no truly national press. Copenhagen accounts for 16% of the national dailies and about half the total circulation. The provincial press has declined since the last war, but still tends to be more politically orientated than the majority of Copenhagen dailies. The Communist Party's *Land og Folk* is the only paper to be directly owned by a political party, although all papers show a fairly pronounced political leaning. The three Social Democrat papers, headed by Copenhagen's *Aktuelt*, are owned and subsidized by the trade unions.

The major Copenhagen dailies are *Berlingske Tidende*, *Ekstra Bladet*, *B.T.*, *Politiken* and *Aktuelt*. The evening paper *Information* and the weekly *Weekendavisen* are also influential. The *Aalborg Stiftstidende*, published at Ålborg, the *Århuus Stiftstidende* (Århus), the *Jyllands-Posten*, *Morgenavisen* (Viby), and the *Fyens Stiftstidende* (Odense), are the most important provincial papers.

PRINCIPAL DAILIES

Åbenrå

Jydske Tidende: Storetorv 10, 6200 Åbenrå; tel. 74-62-62-11; telex 51340; fax 74-62-63-91; morning; independent; to merge in 1991 with *Vestkysten* to form new daily called *Jydske Vestkysten*; Chief Editor ERIK RANDEL; Man. FLEMMING CHRISTENSEN; circ. weekdays 75,111, Sundays 98,273.

Ålborg

Aalborg Stiftstidende: Langagervej 1, 9220 Ålborg Ø; tel. 98-15-15-15; telex 69747; fax 98-15-89-11; f. 1767; weekday evenings; Saturday and Sunday mornings; Liberal independent; Publisher and Chief Editor ERLING BRÖNDUM; approx. circ. weekdays 74,635, Sundays 97,255.

Århus

Århuus Stiftstidende: Olof Palmes Allé 39, 8200 Århus N; tel. 86-78-40-00; fax 86-78-44-00; f. 1794; evening; Liberal independent; Editors ÅGE HOLM-PEDERSEN, ÅGE LUNDGÅRD; circ. weekdays 69,283, Sundays 88,389.

Copenhagen

Berlingske Tidende: Pilestræde 34, 1147 Copenhagen K; tel. 33-15-75-75; telex 27143; fax 33-13-10-12; f. 1749; morning; Conservative independent; Chief Editor HANS DAM; circ. weekdays 130,424, Sundays 174,901.

Børsen: Møntergade 19, 1140 Copenhagen K; tel. 33-32-01-02; telex 22903; fax 33-12-24-45; f. 1896; morning; independent; business news; Chief Editor JAN CORTZEN; circ. 42,933.

B.T.: Kr. Bernikowsgade 6, 1147 Copenhagen K; tel. 33-14-12-34; fax 33-91-14-75; f. 1916; morning; independent; Chief Editor PETER DALL; circ. weekdays 211,748, Sundays 221,122.

Ekstra Bladet: Rådhuspladsen 37, 1585 Copenhagen V; tel. 33-11-85-11; telex 16885; fax 33-14-10-00; f. 1904; evening; Liberal; Editor-in-Chief SV. O. GADE; Man. Dir E. SANDAL; circ. weekdays 211,748, Sundays 231,655.

Erhvervs-Bladet: Vesterbrogade 12, 1620 Copenhagen V; tel. 31-21-36-36; telex 19890; fax 31-21-80-36; circ. 108,682.

Det Fri Aktuelt: Rådhuspladsen 45–47, 1595 Copenhagen V; tel. 33-32-40-01; telex 19785; fax 33-13-45-80; f. 1871; morning; Social Democratic; Editor JØRGEN FLINDT PEDERSEN; Dir LISBETH KNUDSEN; circ. weekdays, 49,915.

Information: Store Kongensgade 40, POB 188, 1006 Copenhagen K; tel. 33-14-14-26; telex 22658; fax 33-93-80-83; f. 1943 (underground during occupation), legally 1945; morning; independent; Chief Editor LASSE ELLEGAARD; circ. 25,901.

Kristeligt Dagblad: Fanøgade 15, 2100 Copenhagen Ø; tel. 39-27-12-35; fax 39-27-08-00; f. 1896; morning; independent; Editors GUNNAR RYTGÅRD, JENS RAVN OLESEN; Dir IB NORDLAND; circ. 15,060.

Politiken: Politikens Hus, Rådhuspladsen 37, 1585 Copenhagen V; tel. 33-11-85-11; telex 16885; fax 33-15-41-17; f. 1884; morning; Liberal; Editors HERBERT PUNDIK, AGNER AHM, JØRGEN GRUNNET; Man. Dir E. SANDAL; circ. weekdays 152,435, Sundays 200,342.

Esbjerg

Vestkysten: Banegårdspladsen, 6700 Esbjerg; tel. 75-12-45-00; telex 54123; fax 75-13-62-62; f. 1917; evening; to merge in 1991 with **Jydske Tidende** to form new daily called **Jydske Vestkysten**; Liberal; Editors THYGE MADSEN, EGON HANSEN; circ. 54,177.

Fredericia

Fredericia Dagblad: 6 Jolivej 1, 7000 Fredericia; tel. 75-92-26-00; fax 75-92-33-55; f. 1890; evening; independent; Editor MOGENS SØRENSEN; Man. VAGN NYGÅRD; circ. 8,000.

Herning

Herning Folkeblad: Østergade 25, 7400 Herning; tel. 97-12-37-00; fax 97-22-36-00; f. 1869; evening; Liberal; Chief Editor GORM ALBRECHTSEN; circ. 16,714.

Hillerød

Frederiksborg Amts Avis: Milnersvej 44–46, 3400 Hillerød; tel. 42-26-31-00; fax 42-25-48-40; f. 1874; morning; Liberal; Editor SEJR CLAUSEN; circ. weekdays 30,201, Sundays 40,683.

Hjørring

Vendsyssel Tidende: Frederikshavnsvej 79–81, 9800 Hjørring; tel. 98-92-17-00; fax 98-92-16-70; f. 1872; evening; Liberal; Editor CLAUS DINDLER; Man. Dir L. JUHL ANDERSEN; circ. weekdays 25,735, Sundays 78,340.

Holbæk

Holbæk Amts Venstreblad: Ahlgade 1, 4300 Holbæk; tel. 53-43-20-48; telex 44148; fax 53-44-28-10; f. 1905; evening; Radical Liberal; Editor ALFRED HANSEN; circ. 22,443.

Holstebro

Dagbladet Holstebro-Struer: Lægårdvej 86, 7500 Holstebro; tel. 97-42-17-22; fax 97-41-03-20; evening; Liberal independent; Editor ERIK MØLLER; circ. 13,849.

Horsens

Horsens Folkeblad: Søndergade 47, 8700 Horsens; tel. 75-62-45-00; telex 61626; fax 75-61-07-97; f. 1866; evening; Liberal; Editor MOGENS AHRENKIEL; circ. 24,485.

Kalundborg

Kalundborg Folkeblad: Skibbrogade 40–42, 4400 Kalundborg; tel. 53-51-24-60; telex 44351; fax 53-51-02-80; f. 1917; evening; Liberal Democrat; Editor JØRGEN JENSEN; circ. 10,003.

Kolding

Folkebladet Sydjylland: Jernbanegade 33–35, 6000 Kolding; tel. 75-52-20-00; fax 75-53-21-44; f. 1871; evening; Liberal; Editor TAGE RASMUSSEN; circ. 18,229.

DENMARK

Nakskov

Ny Dag: Højevej 15, 4900 Nakskov; tel. 53-92-14-00; fax 53-92-11-09; evening; Social Democrat; Editor KLAUS SIVEBÆK; circ. 10,200.

Næstved

Næstved Tidende: Ringstedgade 13, 4700 Næstved; tel. 53-72-45-11; fax 55-77-01-57; f. 1866; Liberal; Editor POUL KRISTENSEN; circ. 21,839.

Nykøbing

Lolland-Falsters Folketidende: Tværgade 14, 4800 Nykøbing F; tel. 54-85-20-66; fax 54-85-38-52; f. 1873; evening; Liberal; Editor PER WESTERGAARD-ANDERSEN; circ. 24,257.

Odense

Fyens Stiftstidende: Blangstedgårdsvej 2–6, 5220 Odense SØ; tel. 66-11-11-11; telex 59858; fax 65-93-25-74; f. 1772; evening; independent; Editors BENT A. KOCH, EGON TØTTRUP; circ. weekdays 74,335, Sundays 100,901.

Randers

Amtsavisen: Nørregade 7, 8900 Randers; tel. 86-42-75-11; telex 65173; fax 86-41-81-50; f. 1810; evening; independent; Chief Editor OLE C. JØRGENSEN; circ. 30,224.

Ringkøbing

Ringkøbing Amts Dagblad: Sct Blichersvej 5, 6950 Ringkøbing; tel. 97-32-07-22; fax 97-32-05-46; evening; Editor KRISTIAN SAND; circ. 15,746.

Ringsted

Dagbladet: Søgade 4–12, 4100 Ringsted; tel. 53-61-25-00; fax 53-61-07-17; evening; Liberal; Editor TORBEN DALBY LARSEN; circ. 32,419.

Rønne

Bornholms Tidende: Nørregade 11–13, 3700 Rønne; tel. 53-95-14-00; fax 53-95-31-19; evening; Liberal; Chief Editor THOMAS E. JENSEN; circ. 11,115.

Silkeborg

Midtjyllands Avis: Vestergade 30, 8600 Silkeborg; tel. 86-82-13-00; fax 86-81-35-77; f. 1857; daily except Sundays; Chief Editor VIGGO SØRENSEN; circ. 22,655.

Skive

Skive Folkeblad: Gemsevej 7, 7800 Skive; tel. 97-51-34-11; fax 97-51-28-35; f. 1880; Social-Liberal; Editor HANS LARSEN; circ. 14,186.

Slagelse

Sjællands Tidende: Korsgade 4, 4200 Slagelse; tel. 53-52-37-00; telex 45372; fax 53-52-64-78; f. 1815; evening; Liberal; for western part of Zealand; Editor POUL KRISTENSEN; circ. 19,602.

Svendborg

Fyns Amts Avis: Sct Nicolaigade 3, 5700 Svendborg; tel. 62-21-46-21; telex 58118; fax 62-22-06-10; f. 1863; Liberal; Editor ARNE MARIAGER; circ. 24,276.

Thisted

Thisted Dagblad: Jernbanegade 15–17, 7700 Thisted; tel. 97-92-33-22; fax 97-91-07-20; Liberal independent; Editor HANS PETER KRAGH; circ. 11,372.

Vejle

Vejle Amts Folkeblad: Bugattivej 8, 7100 Vejle; tel. 75-85-77-88; fax 75-85-72-47; f. 1865; evening; Liberal; Editor VAGN NYGÅRD; circ. 27,364.

Viborg

Viborg Stifts Folkeblad: Sct Mathiasgade 7, 8800 Viborg; tel. 86-62-68-00; fax 86-62-22-20; f. 1877; Liberal Democrat; evening; also published: *Viborg Nyt*, *Skive Bladet* (weekly); *Aktuel Jordbrug* (monthly); Editor PER SUNESEN; circ. 13,505.

Viby

Jyllands-Posten Morgenavisen: Grøndalsvej 3, 8260 Viby J; tel. 86-14-66-77; telex 68747; fax 86-14-82-92; independent; Editors-in-Chief N. THOSTRUP, T. TOLSTRUP; circ. weekdays 140,000, Sundays 230,285.

OTHER NEWSPAPERS

Den Blå Avis (East edition): Strandboulevarden 122, 2100 Copenhagen Ø; tel. 39-27-39-39; fax 39-27-34-24; 2 a week; circ. 73,000.

Den Blå Avis (West edition): Frederiksgade 45, POB 180, 8000 Århus C; tel. 86-19-14-11; fax 86-20-20-02; Thursday; circ. 46,160.

Weekendavisen Berlingske: Gammel Mønt 1, 1147 Copenhagen K; tel. 33-15-75-75; telex 27143; fax 33-11-48-61; f. 1749; independent Conservative; Friday; Chief Editor TØGER SEIDENFADEN; circ. 42,682.

POPULAR PERIODICALS

ALT for Damerne: Vognmagergade 11, 1148 Copenhagen K; tel. 33-15-19-25; telex 16705; fax 33-91-05-85; f. 1946; weekly; women's magazine; Editor-in-Chief HANNE HØIBERG; circ. 90,000.

Anders And & Co: Vognmagergade 11, 1148 Copenhagen K; tel. 33-15-19-25; telex 21143; fax 33-15-99-95; weekly; children's magazine; Editor STEFEN VEDSTED; circ. 144,420.

Arte-Nyt: Hvidkildevej 64, 2400 Copenhagen NV; tel. 31-10-16-22; fax 38-33-20-83; 3 a year; arts; Editor MOGENS HJORT; circ. 41,814.

Bådnyt (Boats): Strandboulevarden 130, 2100 Copenhagen Ø; tel. 31-29-55-00; telex 15712; fax 31-29-01-99; monthly; Editor LARS BANG JENSBY; circ. 24,572.

Basserne: Krogshøjvej 32, 2880 Bagsværd; tel. 44-44-32-33; telex 22426; fax 44-44-36-33; 26 a year; children and youth; circ. 64,000.

Det Bedste fra Reader's Digest A/S: Jagtvej 169B, 2100 Copenhagen Ø; tel. 31-18-12-13; telex 27357; fax 31-18-12-36; monthly; Danish *Reader's Digest*; Editor OLE KNUDSEN; circ. 130,763.

Bilen Motor og Sport: Strandboulevarden 130, 2100 Copenhagen Ø; tel. 31-29-55-00; telex 15712; fax 31-29-01-99; monthly; cars, motor sport; Editor FLEMMING HASLUND; circ. 60,102.

Billed-Bladet: Vesterbrogade 16, 1506 Copenhagen V; tel. 31-23-16-11; fax 31-24-10-08; f. 1938; weekly; family picture magazine; Editor ANDERS THISTED; circ. 227,000.

Bo Bedre: Strandboulevarden 130, 2100 Copenhagen K; tel. 31-29-55-00; telex 15712; fax 31-29-01-99; monthly; homes and gardens; Editor-in-Chief KAREN LYAGER HORVE; circ. 104,260.

Bo & Fritid: Munkehatten 17, 5220 Odense SØ; tel. 65-93-00-80; 4 a year; leisure; circ. 203,021.

Camping: Gammel Kongevej 74, 1850 Copenhagen; tel. 31-21-06-04; telex 22611; fax 31-21-01-08; monthly; circ. 44,107.

Familie Journalen: Vigerslev Allé 18, 2500 Valby, Copenhagen; tel. 31-30-33-33; telex 22390; fax 31-30-24-40; f. 1877; weekly; Editor ANKER SVENDSEN-TUNE; circ. 328,909.

Femina: Vigerslev Allé 18, 2500 Valby, Copenhagen; tel. 36-30-33-33; fax 36-44-19-79; f. 1873; weekly; Editor JUTTA LARSEN; circ. 99,513.

Gør det selv: Strandboulevarden 130, 2100 Copenhagen Ø; tel. 31-29-55-00; telex 15712; fax 31-29-01-99; monthly; do-it-yourself; circ. 60,613.

Helse—Familiens Lægemagasin: Classensgade 36, 2100 Copenhagen Ø; tel. 31-26-79-00; fax 31-26-87-60; 10 a year; family health; circ. 340,000.

Hendes Verden: Bygmesteivej 2, 2400 Copenhagen NV; tel. 31-81-70-70; fax 35-82-12-41; f. 1937; weekly; for women; Editor EVA RAVN; circ. 78,046.

Hi-Fi & Elektronik: Strandboulevarden 130, 2100 Copenhagen Ø; tel. 31-29-55-00; telex 15712; fax 31-29-01-99; monthly; electronics; Editor TORRY LINDSTROM; circ. 25,285.

Hjemmet (The Home): Vognmagergade 11, 1148 Copenhagen K; tel. 33-15-19-25; telex 16705; fax 33-91-15-62; weekly; Chief Editor KAJ DORPH-PETERSEN; circ. 275,000.

Idé-nyt: Gl. Klausdalsbrovej 482, 2730 Herlev; tel. 44-53-40-00; telex 35148; fax 44-92-11-21; quarterly; free magazine; homes and gardens; circ. 2,400,000.

Iform: Strandboulevarden 130, 2100 Copenhagen Ø; tel. 31-29-55-00; telex 15712; fax 31-29-01-99; monthly; sport, health; Editor ANKER TIEDEMANN; circ. 57,927.

Illustreret Videnskab: Strandboulevarden 130, 2100 Copenhagen Ø; tel. 31-29-55-00; telex 15712; fax 31-29-01-99; monthly; popular science; Editor BIRGITTE ENGEN; circ. 108,465.

IN: Vesterbrogade 16, 1506 Copenhagen V; women's magazine; tel. 31-23-16-11; Editor CAMILLA LINDEMANN; circ. 59,843.

Landbrugsmagasinet: Vester Farimagsgade 6, 1606 Copenhagen V; tel. 33-12-99-50; fax 33-12-63-62; weekly; farming; circ. 24,376.

Landsbladet: Vester Farimagsgade 6, 1606 Copenhagen V; tel. 33-11-22-22; fax 33-11-31-48; farmer's weekly; Man. Dir TOVE MALZER; circ. 82,197.

Mit Livs Novelle: Krogshøjvej 32, 2880 Bagsværd; tel. 44-44-32-33; fax 44-44-36-33; young women's magazine; fortnightly; circ. 22,954.

Motor: Firskovvej 32, POB 500, 2800 Lyngby; tel. 45-93-08-00; telex 15857; fax 45-93-32-42; fortnightly; cars and motor-tourism; circ. 205,687.

DENMARK

Directory

Penny: Vognmagergade 11, 1148 Copenhagen K; tel. 33-15-19-25; fax 33-91-05-85; monthly; children's magazine; circ. 43,000.

Praxis: Gl. Bjert 22, 6092 Varmark; tel. 75-57-27-00; 10 a year; health; circ. 70,000.

Samvirke: Roskildevej 65, 2620 Albertslund; tel. 42-64-88-11; telex 33311; f. 1928; consumer monthly; Publr and Chief Editor POUL DINES; circ. 700,000.

Satellitserien: Vognmagergade 11, 1148 Copenhagen K; tel. 33-15-19-25; fax 33-91-05-85; monthly; children's magazine; circ. 40,000.

Se og Hør: Vigerslev Allé 18, 2500 Valby; tel. 31-30-33-33; telex 22390; fax 31-30-24-40; f. 1940; news and TV; Editor MOGENS E. PEDERSEN; circ. 314,623.

Sofus' Lillebror: Krogshøjvej 32, 2880 Bagsværd; tel. 44-44-32-33; fax 44-44-36-33; monthly; children and youth; circ. 44,000.

TIPS-bladet: Alsgarde Centret 2, 3140 Alsgarde; tel. 42-10-93-00; fax 42-10-88-30; weekly; sport; circ. 39,467.

TV Bladet: Gl. Mønt 1, 1147 Copenhagen K; tel. 33-15-20-55; telex 27094; weekly; television and radio programmes; circ. 287,730.

Ude og Hjemme: Vigerslev Allé 18, 2500 Valby, Copenhagen; tel. 36-30-33-33; fax 36-30-74-44; f. 1926; family weekly; Editor JØRN BAUENMAND; circ. 232,000.

Ugemagasinet Søndag: Vesterbrogade 16, POB 424, 1505 Copenhagen V; tel. 31-23-16-11; fax 31-24-10-08; f. 1921; weekly; family magazine; Editor JØRGEN BJERRE; circ. 116,863.

Ugens Rapport: Skt Annæ Plads 8, 1250 Copenhagen K; tel. 33-13-60-60; fax 33-15-64-46; f. 1971; men's weekly; Editor-in-chief JAN SCHIWE NIELSEN; circ. 50,733.

Vi på Landet: Købmagergade 58, 1150 Copenhagen K; tel. 33-91-12-24; 4 a year; farming life; circ. 278,000.

Vi Unge: Finsensvej 80, 2000 Frederiksberg; tel. 38-88-32-22; fax 38-88-30-38; f. 1958; teenagers' monthly; Editor CARL W. BAERENTZEN; circ. 20,163.

SPECIALIST PERIODICALS

Aktuel Elektronik: Skelbækgade 4, 1780 Copenhagen V; tel. 31-21-68-01; fax 31-21-23-96; 39 a year; computing and information technology; circ. 21,357.

Alt om Data: St. Kongensgade 72, 1264 Copenhagen K; tel. 33-91-28-33; f. 1983; monthly; Chief Editor KLAUS NORDFELD; circ. 23,000.

Amt- og Kommunebladet: Tordenskjoldsgade 27, 1055 Copenhagen K; tel. 33-14-00-10; fax 33-14-00-10; monthly; public works and administration; circ. 19,723.

Andelsboligbladet ABF-Nyt: Istedgade 1, 1650 Copenhagen V; tel. 31-24-75-02; fax 31-24-75-27; 6 a year; Editor JAN HANSEN; circ. 26,837.

Annonce Avisen Erhvery: Farum Gydevej 59, 3520 Farum; tel. 42-95-72-10; fax 42-95-57-25; 6–8 a year; management; circ. 96,000.

Arbejde og Daginstitution: Pædagogisk Medhjælper Forbund, Sct Kongensgade 79, 1264 Copenhagen K; tel. 33-11-03-43; fax 33-13-27-01; 36 a year; teaching; circ. 26,627.

Arbejdsgiveren: Vester Voldgade 113, 1790 Copenhagen V; tel. 33-93-40-00; telex 16464; fax 33-12-29-76; 20 a year; management; Editor SVEND BIE; circ. 44,660.

Arbejdslederen: Vermlandsgade 65–67, 2300 Copenhagen S; tel. 31-57-56-22; fax 31-57-90-22; 15 a year; circ. 73,585.

Automatik: Algade 10, POB 80, 4500 Nykøbing sj; tel. 73-41-23-10; engineering; monthly; circ. 39,250.

Bankstanden: Esplanaden 8, 1014 Copenhagen K; tel. 33-15-83-11; monthly; bank employees; circ. 40,000.

Beboerbladet: Studiestræde 50, 1554 Copenhagen V; tel. 33-11-11-22; 4 a year; home-renting; circ. 433,380.

Bil Snak: Park Allé 355, 2605 Brøndby; tel. 42-63-11-22; fax 42-63-27-22; quarterly; cars; circ. 113,538.

Boligen: Studiestraede 50, 1554 Copenhagen V; tel. 33-11-11-22; 11 a year; housing associations, architects; Editor HELGE MØLLER; circ. 23,000.

Byg-tek: Hovedvejen 182, 2600 Glostrup; tel. 42-45-10-63; fax 43-43-13-28; 11 a year; building and construction; circ. 30,000.

Chef Nyt: Sydvestvej 49, 2600 Glostrup; tel. 42-63-02-22; fax 42-63-01-21; 25 a year; managers; circ. 72,682.

Civilforsvar: Nørrebrogade 66D, 2200 Copenhagen N; tel. 35-37-75-00; fax 35-37-73-95; 6 a year; civil defence; circ. 18,014.

Communalbladet: H. C. Andersens Boulevard 50, 1501 Copenhagen V; tel. 33-12-43-43; 23 a year; municipal administration, civil servants; Editor KIM HUNDEVADT; circ. 65,835.

Computerworld: Krumtappen 4, 2500 Valby; tel. 36-44-28-00; f. 1981; weekly; computing; Chief Officers JENS MICHAEL DAMM, LARS OLSEN; circ. 19,751.

Cyklister: Dansk Cyklist Forbund, Kjeld Langes Gade 14, 1367 Copenhagen K; tel. 33-32-31-21; fax 33-32-76-83; f. 1905; 6 a year; organ of Danish Cyclists' Asscn; Editor POUL JENSEN; circ. 24,500.

Dansk Jagt: Einer-Jensens Vænge 1, 2000 Frederiksberg; tel. 38-33-29-11; fax 31-19-02-41; monthly; hunting; circ. 48,500.

Effektivt Landbrug: Skelbækgade 4, 1717 Copenhagen V; tel. 31-21-68-01; fax 31-21-53-50; 23 a year; farming; circ. 34,759.

Elev-bladet: Ryesgade 105 st., 2100 Copenhagen Ø; tel. 31-42-92-10; 7 a year; organ of secondary school students' union; circ. 60,000.

Folkeskolen: Vandkunsten 12, 1467 Copenhagen K; tel. 33-11-82-55; fax 33-93-89-90; 43 a year; teaching; Editor THORKILD THEJSEN; circ. 78,400.

Forbrugsforeningsbladet: Knabrostræde 12, 1210 Copenhagen K; tel. 33-15-88-26; monthly; for civil servants and doctors; circ. 60,000.

Havebladet: Hvidehusv 24, POB 173, 3450 Allerød; tel. 42-27-14-09; fax 42-27-72-88; 6 a year; gardening; circ. 47,000.

Haven: Åby Bækgardsvej 6, 8230 Åbyhøj; tel. 86-15-56-88; fax 86-15-33-23; 11 a year; horticulture and gardening; circ. 79,998.

High Fidelity: St. Kongensgade 72, 1264 Copenhagen K; tel. 33-11-25-47; f. 1968; 11 a year; Chief Editor MICHAEL MADSEN; circ. 22,000.

Hjemmeværnsbladet: Kastellet 82, 2100 Copenhagen Ø; tel. 33-93-32-10; 10 a year; organ of the Home Guard; circ. 80,000.

Hunden: Parkvej 1, 2680 Solrød Strand; tel. 53-14-15-66; fax 53-14-30-03; 10 a year; organ of the kennel club; circ. 31,000.

Ingeniøren: Skelbækgade 4, 1717 Copenhagen V; tel. 31-21-68-01; fax 31-21-67-01; weekly engineers' magazine; circ. 69,478.

Jagt og Fiskeri: Frydendalsvej 20, 1809 Frederiksberg; tel. 31-31-51-52; fax 31-31-51-60; 11 a year; hunting, fishing, sport; Editor VILLY ANDERSEN; circ. 60,000.

Jern- og Maskinindustrien: Falkoner Allé 90, 2000 Frederiksberg; tel. 35-36-37-00; telex 21317; fax 35-36-37-90; 22 a year; iron and metallic industries; circ. 25,295.

Jyllands Ringens program: Vilvordevej 102, 2920 Charlottenlund; tel. 31-64-46-92; 5 a year; cars and motor cycles; circ. 280,000.

Kamera: Finsensvej 80, 2000 Frederiksberg; tel. 38-88-32-22; fax 38-88-30-38; f. 1960; 2 a year; photography; Editor FINN NESGAARD; circ. 55,484.

Kontor/Bladet: Sydvestvej 49, 2600 Glostrup; tel. 42-63-02-22; fax 42-63-01-21; monthly; management in trade and industry; circ. 97,165.

Kvinde i Danmark: Virringvej 11, Virring, 8900 Randers; tel. 86-48-02-17; 6 a year; home management; Editor KIRSTEN WULFF; circ. 25,000.

Metal: Nyropsgade 38, 1602 Copenhagen V; tel. 33-12-82-12; telex 16526; fax 33-12-82-28; 22 a year; iron and metal industries; circ. 147,658.

New COMputer Magasin: St. Kongensgade 72, 1264 Copenhagen K; tel. 33-91-28-33; fax 33-91-01-21; f. 1985; 11 a year; Commodore computers; Editor-in-Chief CHRISTIAN MARTENSEN; circ. 35,000.

ny elektronik: St. Kongensgade 72, 1264 Copenhagen K; tel. 33-11-25-47; f. 1977; 11 a year; electronics; Chief Editor JANN KALF LARSEN; circ. 21,500.

Produktion: Vester Farimagsgade 3, 1606 Copenhagen V; tel. 33-12-14-19; fax 33-12-61-48; 8 a year; farming; circ. 120,000.

Rotary Norden: Lundtoftevej 1, 2800 Lyngby; tel. 42-88-12-00; fax 42-93-12-44; members of the Scandinavian rotary associations; circ. 65,000.

Samtid: Nordkysvej, 8961 Allingåbro; tel. 86-49-51-53; 17 a year; for school pupils aged 14–18; circ. 25,000.

Spejd: Lundsgade 6, 2100 Copenhagen Ø; tel. 31-26-12-11; 8 a year; organ of the Scout Movement; circ. 35,000.

Sundhedsbladet: Børstenbindervej 4, 5230 Odense M; tel. 66-15-88-43; every 2 months; health; circ. 35,000.

Sygeplejersken: Vimmelskaftet 38, POB 1084, 1008 Copenhagen K; tel. 33-15-15-55; 50 a year; nursing; circ. 62,232.

Tidernes Tegn: Børstenbindervej 4, 5230 Odense M; tel. 66-15-88-43; telex 155743; every 2 months; religion; Editor AAGE ANDERSEN; circ. 11,000.

Tidsskrift for Sukkersyge—Diabetes: Filosofgangen 24, 5000 Odense C; tel. 66-12-90-06; fax 65-91-49-08; f. 1940; 5 a year; diabetes; Dir FLEMMING KJERSGÅRD JOHANSEN; circ. 28,000.

Ugeskrift for Læger: Trondhjemsgade 9, 2100 Copenhagen Ø; tel. 31-38-55-00; weekly; medical; circ. 21,000.

NEWS AGENCY

Ritzaus Bureau I/S: Mikkel Bryggersgade 3, 1460 Copenhagen K; tel. 33-12-33-44; telex 22362; fax 33-93-53-27; f. 1866; general, financial and commercial news; works in conjuction with Reuters,

DENMARK

Agence France-Presse, Deutsche Presse-Agentur and European national agencies; owned by all Danish newspapers; Chair. of Board of Dirs HANS DAM; Gen. Man. and Editor-in-Chief PER WINTHER.

Foreign Bureaux

Agence France-Presse (AFP): Mikkel Bryggersgade 5, 1460 Copenhagen K; tel. 33-13-23-31; telex 19584; Bureau Chief SLIM ALLAGUI.

Agencia EFE (Spain): c/o Int. Press Centre, Snaregade 14, 1205 Copenhagen K; Correspondent MARÍA CAMINO SÁNCHEZ.

Agenzia Nazionale Stampa Associata (ANSA) (Italy): Hvalsøvej 6, 2700 Brønshøj; tel. 31-80-04-13; telex 19315; fax 33-91-16-13; Agent VITTORIO SPADANUDA.

Allgemeiner Deutscher Nachrichtendienst (ADN) (Germany): 2660 Brøndbystrand, Kisumparken 65 st. th., Copenhagen; Bureau Chief HERBERT HANSCH.

Associated Press (AP) (USA): Kristen Bernikowsgade 4 (2nd floor), 1105 Copenhagen K; tel. 33-11-15-04; telex 22381; fax 33-32-36-60; Bureau Chief ANDREW TORCHIA.

Deutsche Presse-Agentur (dpa) (Germany): Mikkel Bryggersgade 5, 1460 Copenhagen K; tel. 33-14-22-19; Chief Correspondent THOMAS BORCHERT.

Informatsionnoye Agentstvo Novosti (IAN) (USSR): Vestagervej 7, 2100 Copenhagen Ø; tel. 31-20-04-44; telex 15618; fax 31-20-19-42; Chief Editor SERGEI SEREBRYAKOV.

Reuters (UK): Badstuestræde 18, 1209 Copenhagen K; tel. 33-93-21-42; telex 16846; fax 33-12-32-72.

Telegrafnoye Agentstvo Sovetskovo Soyuza (TASS) (USSR): Uraniavej 9B, 1, 1878 Copenhagen; tel. 31-24-04-03; telex 19304; Correspondent ALEXANDER SIDOROV.

United Press International (UPI) (USA): Sprydet 47, 3070 Snekkersten; tel. 42-22-53-54; telex 41270; fax 42-22-53-59; Correspondent JULIAN ISHERWOOD.

PRESS ASSOCIATIONS

Danske Dagblades Forening (Danish Newspapers Association): Pressens Hus, Skindergade 7, 1159 Copenhagen K; tel. 33-12-21-15; telex 27183; fax 33-14-23-25; comprises managers and editors-in-chief of all newspapers; general spokesman for the Danish press.

Illustrated Press Publishers' Association: Copenhagen; publishers of magazines.

Københavnske Dagblades Samraad (Copenhagen Newspaper Publishers' Association): c/o Det Berlingske Hus, Pilestræde 34, 1147 Copenhagen K; Chair. CHR. W. REVES.

Publishers

Forlaget åløkke A/S: 26 Tulinpanparken, 8700 Horsens; tel. 75-65-77-84; fax 75-65-72-07; educational, audio-visual and other study aids; Dir BERTIL TOFT HANSEN.

Akademisk Forlag AmbA: Store Kannikestræde 6–8, POB 54, 1002 Copenhagen K; tel. 33-11-98-26; fax 33-32-05-70; f. 1962; history, philosophy, psychology, engineering, general science, linguistics, university textbooks, educational materials; Man. Dir PETER KRISTIANSEN; Chief Editor POUL ERIK MUNK NIELSEN.

Alrune Forlaget: Snertinge Markvej 57, 4760 Vordingborg; tel. 53-78-25-73; children's books.

Apostrof Forlaget: Berggreensgade 24, 2100 Copenhagen Ø; tel. 31-20-84-20; fax 31-20-84-53; f. 1980; Dirs MIA THESTRUP, OLE THESTRUP.

Arnkrone Publishers Ltd: Fuglebækvej 4, 2770 Kastrup; tel. 31-50-70-00; f. 1941; popular medicine, art and cultural history; children's fiction and non-fiction, psychotherapy, contemporary fiction and humour; Man. Dir J. JUUL RASMUSSEN.

Peter Asschenfeldt's Stjernbøger A/S: Gerdasgade 37, 2500 Valby; tel. 36-44-11-20; telex 19387; bestseller paperbacks; Dir BENNY FREDERIKSEN.

Bibelselskabets Forlag og Vajsenhusets Forlag: Frederiksborggade 50, 1360 Copenhagen K; tel. 33-12-78-35; fax 33-93-21-50; religious works; Gen. Sec. NIELS JØRGEN CAPPELØRN.

Bibliotekscentralens Forlag: 7–11 Tempovej, 2750 Ballerup; tel. 42-97-40-00; telex 35370; fax 42-65-53-10; f. 1939; bibliographies, indexes and library literature; Man. Dir ASGER HANSEN.

Thomas Bloms Forlag A/S: Rudolph Berghsgade 18, 2100 Copenhagen Ø; tel. 31-29-17-49; non-fiction, children's books; Owners CONNIE BLOM, THOMAS BLOM.

Bierman og Bierman A/S: Vestergade 126, 7200 Grindsted; tel. 75-32-02-88; fax 75-32-15-48; f. 1968; fiction, non-fiction, children's books, general culture, magazines; Man. Dirs B. LORENTZEN, T. SELMER-PETERSEN.

Bogans Forlag: Kastaniebakken 8, POB 39, 3540 Lynge; tel. 42-18-80-55; f. 1974; general paperbacks, popular science, humour and occult; Owner EVAN BOGAN.

Bonniers Specialmagasiner A/S: Strandboulevarden 130, 2100 Copenhagen Ø; tel. 31-29-55-00; telex 15712; fax 31-29-46-65; f. 1960 as Fogtdals Blade A/S; handbooks, part-works and magazines; Man. Dir STEEN HAU.

Borberg Forlagsbureau: Købrmagergade 11, 1150 Copenhagen K; tel. 33-91-36-56; non-fiction, computer packaging; Man. Dir HENRIK BORBERG.

Borgens Forlag A/S: Valbygårdsvej 33, 2500 Valby; tel. 31-46-21-00; fax 36-44-14-88; f. 1948; owned by Forlaget Vindrose; fiction, non-fiction, handicrafts, religion, children's, computer books, large-print books and textbooks; Man. Dir JARL BORGEN; Dirs ERIK CRILLESEN, NIELS BORGEN.

Børnegudstjeneste-Forlaget: Korskærvej 25, 7000 Fredericia; tel. 75-93-44-55; religion, children's books; Man. Dir CURT GRAVEN NIELSEN.

Børsen Forlaget A/S: Møntergade 19, 1140 Copenhagen K; tel. 33-32-01-02; telex 22903; fax 33-12-24-45; business information (daily news, magazines, newsletters and books), electronic publishing; Man. Dir PREBEN SCHACK.

Branner og Korchs Forlag A/S: H.C. Ørstedsvej 7B, 1879 Frederiksberg C; tel. 31-22-45-11; f. 1949; handbooks, fiction, juveniles; Dir TORBEN SCHUR.

Carit Andersens Forlag A/S: Skudehavnsvej 27, 2100 Copenhagen Ø; tel. 31-29-19-80; telex 16121; fax 31-29-60-90; illustrated books, non-fiction, fiction, science fiction; Dir ERIK ALBRECHTSEN.

Centrum, Jyllands-Posten Forlag: Gunnar Clausensvej 66, 8260 Viby J; tel. 86-29-69-77; fax 86-29-30-90; fiction, handbooks, children's, school books; Dir SVEN BEDSTED.

Dansk Historisk Håndbogsforlag A/S: Klintevej 25, 2800 Lyngby; tel. 45-93-48-00; fax 45-93-47-47; f. 1976; genealogy, heraldry, culture and local history, facsimile editions, microfiches produced by subsidiary co; Owners and Man. Dirs RITA JENSEN, HENNING JENSEN.

Dansklærerforeningens Forlag: Nørre Søgade 49c, 1370 Copenhagen K; tel. 33-15-04-99; fax 33-15-07-20; f. 1885; school books, Danish literature, educational slides and videos; Man. Dir ASGER UHD JEPSEN.

Christian Ejlers' Forlag A/S: Brolæggerstræde 4, POB 2228, 1018 Copenhagen K; tel. 33-12-21-14; f. 1967; general, art, social and political science; Dir CHRISTIAN EJLERS.

Chr. Erichsens Forlag A/S: Nørrebrogade 53B, 2200 Copenhagen N; tel. 31-39-51-25; fax 31-39-40-54; f. 1902; fiction, non-fiction, general trade books.

Forlaget Europa: Nyhavn 40, 1051 Copenhagen K; tel. 33-15-62-73; telex 19280; school and university texts, tourist and restaurant guides; Dir LARS KVISTSKOV LARSEN.

FADL's Forlag A/S (Foreningen af danske Lægestuderendes Forlag): Prinsesse Charlottegade 29, 2200 Copenhagen N; tel. 31-35-62-87; f. 1962; medicine, biology; Man. Dir HANS JESPERSEN.

Fiskers Forlag; Mariendalsvej 33, 2000 Frederiksberg; tel. 38-34-80-76; illustrated books, travel, fiction books about Greenland; Owners JÖRGEN FISKER, LIZ SCHOU.

Forlaget for Faglitteratur A/S: Vandkunsten 6, 1467 Copenhagen K; tel. 33-13-79-00; medicine, technology.

Forlaget Forum A/S: Snaregade 4, 1205 Copenhagen K; tel. 33-14-77-91; f. 1940; history, fiction, quality paperbacks and children's books; Dir CLAUS BRØNDSTED.

Forlaget Fremad af 1979 A/S: Rentemestervej 45–47, 2400 Copenhagen NV; tel. 38-33-40-40; f. 1912; fiction, non-fiction, popular science, textbooks, juveniles, reissues; Man. Dir PETER JOHANSEN.

J. Frimodts Forlag: Korskærvej 25, 7000 Fredericia; tel. 75-93-44-55; religion, fiction, devotional; Man. Dir CURT GRAVEN NIELSEN.

FSR's Forlag: Kronprinsessegade 8, 1306 Copenhagen K; tel. 33-93-91-91; telex 22491; fax 33-11-09-13; textbooks, legal, economic, financial, business; Publications Man. VIBEKE CHRISTIANSEN.

G.E.C. Gad Publishers: Vimmelskaftet 32, 1161 Copenhagen K; tel. 33-15-05-58; fax 33-12-38-35; university and school books, legal, reference, science, natural history; Man. AXEL KIELLAND.

Gjellerup og Gad Forlagsaktieselskab: Vimmelskaftet 32, 1161 Copenhagen K; tel. 33-15-05-58; fax 33-12-38-35; textbooks, school books, audio-visual aids; Man. GRETHE BRYNER.

Forlaget GMT: Meilgård, 8585 Glæsborg; tel. 86-31-75-11; f. 1971; history, philosophy, politics, social sciences, general fiction, textbooks; Publrs HANS JØRN CHRISTENSEN, ERIK BJØRN OLSEN.

Grafisk Forlag A/S: Klosterrisvej 7, 2100 Copenhagen Ø; tel. 31-29-44-22; telex 16987; fax 39-27-10-10; f. 1914; school and textbooks.

DENMARK

Grevas Forlag: Auningvej 33, Sdr. Kastrup, 8544 Mørke; tel. 86-16-83-87; fax 86-99-70-65; f. 1966; novels, debate; Dir LUISE HEMMER PIHL.

Gyldendals Forlag A/S: Klareboderne 3, 1115 Copenhagen K; tel. 33-11-07-75; telex 15887; fax 33-11-03-23; f. 1770; fiction, non-fiction, reference books, paperbacks, children's books, textbooks; Dirs PER HEDEMAN, KURT FROMBERG, KLAUS RIFBJERG, EGON SCHMIDT.

P. Hâse & Søns Forlag A/S: Løvstræde 8, 1152 Copenhagen K; tel. 33-11-59-99; fax 33-11-59-59; f. 1877; Man. Dir N. J. HÂSE; educational books, audio-visual aids, children's books, fiction, non-fiction.

Forlaget Hamlet A/S: 25 Linnésgade, 1361 Copenhagen K; tel. 33-13-16-50; handbooks, art books.

Hekla Forlag: Store Kongensgade 61A–B, POB 9011, 1022 Copenhagen K; tel. 33-91-19-33; fax 33-91-19-49; f. 1979; general trade fiction and non-fiction; Owner HELGA W. LINDHARDT.

Hernovs' Forlag: Bredgade 14–16, 1260 Copenhagen K; tel. 33-15-62-84; fax 33-15-62-09; f. 1941; fiction, memoirs, children's; Owner JOHS. G. HERNOV; Dir PER LESLIE HOLST.

Forlag Hønsetryk: Rosenørns Allé 18, 1970 Copenhagen V; tel. 31-54-81-51; Owner Gjellerup Forlags-Aktieselskab.

Høst & Søns Forlag: Nørre Søgade 35, 1016 Copenhagen K; tel. 33-15-30-31; fax 33-15-51-55; f. 1836; crafts and hobbies, languages, books on Denmark, children's books; Skarv imprint (travel, ecology, etc.); Dir ERIK C. LINDGREN.

Forlaget Hovedland: Stenvej 19, 8270 Højberg; tel. 86-27-65-00; fax 86-27-29-28; Owner STEEN PIPER.

Finn Jacobsens Forlag: Gothersgade 56, 1123 Copenhagen K; tel. 33-14-36-32; non-fiction, science, cultural history; Owner FINN JACOBSEN.

Forlaget Kaleidoscope A/S: Njalsgade 19, 2300 Copenhagen S; tel. 31-95-83-33; fax 31-95-93-38; educational, audio-visual, modern languages, fiction for youth; Publr JENS BENDTSEN.

Forlaget Per Kofod A/S: Krystalgade 7, 1172 Copenhagen K; tel. 33-15-03-47.

Komma og Clausen: Emdrupvej 28C, 2100 Copenhagen Ø; tel. 31-18-34-77; fax 31-20-20-75; f. 1977; reference, sport, maritime, cookery, instructional; Man. Dir LISBETH ANDERSEN SKOV.

Morten A. Korch's Forlag: Aurehøjvej 2, 2900 Hellerup; tel. 31-62-08-59; children's books; Owner MORTEN KORCH.

Krak: Virumgardsvej 21, 2830 Virum; tel. 45-83-45-83; fax 45-83-10-11; f. 1770; reference works, maps and yearbooks; Dir IB LE ROY TOPHOLM.

Lademann Ltd, Publishers: Linnésgade 25, 1361 Copenhagen K; tel. 33-13-16-50; telex 19149; fax 33-93-18-50; f. 1954; novels, history, text books, reference books, encyclopaedias, paperbacks; Man. Dir JØRGEN LADEMANN.

Lindhardt og Ringhof, Forlag A/S, og Jespersen og Pio's Forlag: Studiestræde 14, 1455 Copenhagen K; tel. 33-11-19-55; fax 33-14-45-70; f. 1971; general fiction and non-fiction, paperbacks; Man. Dirs OTTO B. LINDHARDT, GERT RINGHOF.

Lohses Forlag: Korskærvej 25, 7000 Fredericia; tel. 75-93-44-55; f. 1868; religion, memoirs, fiction; Man. Dir CURT GRAVEN NIELSEN.

Mallings Forlag A/S: Strandvejen 638, 2930 Klampenborg; tel. 31-64-35-55; fax 31-64-35-98; f. 1975; Dir HANNAH MALLING.

Martins Forlag: Thorsbjerggård L1, Fjellenstrupvej 25, 3250 Gilleleje; tel. 48-30-11-00; telex 19203; fiction, non-fiction, juveniles; Man. Dir JENS ERIK HALKIER.

Medicinsk Forlag A/S: Tranevej 2, 3650 Ølstykke; tel. 42-17-65-92; medical and scientific books; Man. Dir ANNI LINDELØV.

Forlaget Melgård A/S: Storegade 5, 4171 Glumsø; tel. 53-64-63-30; travel, general fiction, non-fiction; Owner SØREN MELGÅRD.

Modtryk-Socialistisk forlag AmbA: Anholtsgade 4, 8000 Århus C; tel. 86-12-79-12; fax 86-13-27-78; f. 1972; politics, children's and school books, fiction, thrillers and poetry; Man. Dir PREBEN BACH.

Münksgård International Publishers Ltd: Nørre Søgade 35, POB 2148, 1016 Copenhagen K; tel. 33-12-70-30; telex 19431; fax 33-12-93-87; f. 1917; agents to Royal Danish Academy, and various learned societies; specializing in medical and natural science, international scientific journals, humanities, school books and computer software; also own Forlaget Rosinante; Man. Dir JOACHIM MALLING.

Forlaget Natur og Harmoni: Løvstræde 8, 1152 Copenhagen K; tel. 33-11-59-99; fax 33-11-59-59; alternative health books; Owner P. Haase & Søns Forlag A/S.

Nyt Nordisk Forlag-Arnold Busck A/S: Købmagergade 49, 1150 Copenhagen K; tel. 33-11-11-03; fax 33-93-44-90; f. 1896; textbooks, school books, non-fiction; Man. Dir OLE ARNOLD BUSCK.

Det Schønbergske Forlag A/S: Landemærket 5, 1119 Copenhagen K; tel. 33-11-30-66; f. 1857; fiction, travel, history, biography, paperbacks, textbooks; Mans OLE STENDER, OLE THESTRUP.

Forlaget Optima A/S: Møllevænget 16, 7800 Skive; tel. 97-53-55-80; education; Dir INGRID SCHIØLER.

Jørgen Paludans Forlag A/S: Fiolstræde 16, 1171 Copenhagen K; tel. 33-15-06-75, ext. 38; language teaching, natural sciences, psychology, history, sociology, politics, economics, reference; Man. Dir JØRGEN PALUDAN.

Politikens Forlag A/S: Vestergade 26, 1456 Copenhagen K; tel. 33-11-21-22; fax 33-93-21-52; f. 1947; dictionaries, reference books, handbooks, yearbooks, collected works and maps; Man. Dir JOHANNES RAVN.

Rasmus Navers Forlag: Løvstræde 8, 1152 Copenhagen K; tel. 33-11-59-99; fax 33-11-59-59; humour, fiction; Owner P. Haase & Søns Forlag A/S.

Hans Reitzel Publishers Ltd: POB 1073, Nørre Søgade 35, 1008 Copenhagen K; tel. 33-14-04-51; fax 33-15-51-55; f. 1949; reference and textbooks, psychology, sociology, Hans Christian Andersen; Man. Dir ERIK C. LINDGREN; Editors PETER THIELST, OLE GAMMELTOFT.

C.A. Reitzels Booksellers and Publishers Ltd: Nørregade 20, 1165 Copenhagen K; tel. 33-12-24-00; fax 33-14-02-70; f. 1819; Owner and Man. Dir SVEND OLUFSEN.

Rhodos, International Science and Art Publishers: Niels Brocks Gård, Strandgade 36, 1401 Copenhagen K; tel. 31-54-30-20; telex 31502; fax 31-95-47-42; f. 1959; science, art, literature, politics, professional, criticism; Man. Dir NIELS BLAEDEL.

Rosenkilde og Baggers Forlag: POB 2184, 1017 Copenhagen K; tel. 33-93-70-07; f. 1941; manuals, cultural history, facsimiles; Owner HANS R. BAGGER.

Samlerens Forlag A/S: Snaregade 4, 1205 Copenhagen K; tel. 33-13-10-23; telex 15887; fax 33-14-43-14; general fiction, contemporary history and politics, psychology, biographies; Man. Dir JOHANNES RIIS.

A/S J. H. Schultz Forlag: Møntergade 21[1], 1116 Copenhagen K; tel. 33-12-11-95; f. 1661; printers, publishers, booksellers; printers to the Danish Government and the Copenhagen University; division of Schultz Information; Publishing Man. JOHN M. MADSEN.

Semic Forlagene A/S: Krogshøjvej 32, 2880 Bagsværd; tel. 44-44-32-33; fax 44-44-36-33.

Forlaget Sesam A/S: Frederiksborggade 26A, 1360 Copenhagen K; tel. 33-15-37-00; telex 19149; history, educational, children's; Dir GEORG VEJEN.

A/S Skattekartoteket: Informationskontor, Palægade 4, 1261 Copenhagen K; tel. 33-11-78-74; fax 33-93-80-09; books and computer software on taxation; Man. Dir P. TAARNHØJ.

Sommer & Sørensen Forlag A/S: Mynstersvej 19, 1827 Frederiksberg C; tel. 31-23-25-55; Dirs AAGE BØRGLUM SØRENSEN, ERIK SOMMER.

Spektrum Publishers Ltd: Skindergade 14, 1159 Copenhagen K; tel. 33-32-63-22; fax 33-32-64-54; non-fiction, biography, art, science; Man. Dir WERNER SVENDSEN.

Strandbergs Forlag A/S: Vedbæk Strandvej 475, 2950 Vedbæk; tel. 42-89-47-60; fax 42-89-47-01; cultural history, computer science, travel, humour; Owner HANS JØRGEN STRANDBERG.

Strubes Forlag A/S: POB 827, 2100 Copenhagen Ø; tel. 31-42-07-16; psychic, occult, philosophy, art, naval; Man. Dir POUL STRUBE.

Teaterforlaget Drama: Ladegårdsskov 14, 6300 Gråsten; tel. 74-65-11-41; theatrical literature, drama; Man. Dir STIG JARL.

Teknisk Forlag A/S: Skelbækgade 4, 1717 Copenhagen V; tel. 31-21-68-01; telex 16368; fax 31-21-23-96; f. 1948; technical books and periodicals; Man. Dir PETER MÜLLER.

Teknologisk Institus Forlag: Gregersensvej, 2630 Tåstrup; tel. 42-99-66-11; fax 42-99-54-36; technical, crafts, industries.

Tellerup Forlagsaktieselskab: Vesterbrogade 40, 1620 Copenhagen V; tel. 31-31-01-11; fax 31-31-81-71; f. 1972; children's, young adults fiction, science fiction, fiction; Dir K. TELLERUP.

Thaning & Appels Forlag A/S: H.C. Ørstedsvej 7B, 1879 Frederiksberg C; tel. 31-22-45-11; f. 1866; fiction, art, popular sciences; Dir AKSEL PEDERSEN.

Forlaget Tiderne Skifter A/S: Skt Peder Stræde 28B, 1453 Copenhagen K; tel. 33-13-65-03; fax 33-14-42-05; fiction, sexual and cultural politics, psychology, criticism, arts, children's books; Man. Dir CLAUS CLAUSEN.

Forlaget Tommeliden: Odensevej 92, Harrested, 5853 Ørbæk; tel. 65-98-23-74; fiction, school books, handbooks, juveniles; Man. Dir JES TRØST JØRGENSEN.

Unitas Forlag: Valby Langgade 19, 2500 Valby; tel. 31-16-60-33; fax 31-16-08-18; religion, fiction, education; Man. Dir INGE MADSEN.

DENMARK

Vandrer mod Lysets Forlag A/S: Ellevadsvej 3, 2920 Charlottenlund; tel. 31-63-22-26; religion, science, philosophy, ethics; Dir BØRGE BRØNNUM.

Forlaget Vindrose A/S: Nybrogade 24, 1203 Copenhagen K; tel. 33-13-50-00; f. 1980; general trade, fiction and non-fiction; Dir ERIK VAGN JENSEN.

Vitafakta A/S: Kohavevej 28, 2950 Vedbæk; tel. 42-89-21-03; health books, school books; Dir INGER MARIE HAUT.

Wangels Forlag A/S: Gerdasgade 37, 2500 Valby; tel. 36-44-11-20; telex 19387; f. 1946; fiction, book club; Gen. Man. BENNY FREDERIKSEN.

Edition Wilhelm Hansen A/S: Bornholmsgade 1, 1266 Copenhagen K; tel. 33-11-78-88; telex 19912; fax 33-14-81-78; f. 1855; music publishers; Owner G. SCHIRMER.

Winthers Forlag A/S: Gerdasgade 35, 2500 Valby; tel. 36-44-11-20; telex 19387; fax 36-44-11-36; f. 1945; general fiction, paperbacks; Man. Dir JESPER HOLM.

Forlaget Wøldike K/S: Stægers Allé 13, 2000 Frederiksberg; tel. 31-86-39-54; fax 38-33-70-80; fiction and non-fiction; Publr OVE MØLBECK.

Government Publishing House

Statens Informationstjeneste (State Information Service): Bredgade 20, POB 1103, 1009 Copenhagen K; tel. 33-92-92-00; fax 33-92-92-81; acts as press, public relations and information body for the Government in all media; publishes Official Gazette, etc.; Dir NICK DALUM.

PUBLISHERS' ASSOCIATION

Den danske Forlæggerforening: Købmagergade 11, 1150 Copenhagen K; tel. 33-15-65-88; f. 1837; 78 mems; Chair. OLE A. BUSCK; Dir ERIK V. KRUSTRUP.

Radio and Television

There were 2.6m. licences for radio receivers and 1.9m. licences for television receivers in 1989.

General Directorate of Posts and Telegraphs: Tietgensgade 37, 1530 Copenhagen V; Dir-Gen. HELGE ISRAELSON.

RADIO

Danmarks Radio (Radio Denmark): Radio Hus, Rosenørns Allé 22, 1999 Frederiksberg C; tel. 31-35-06-47; telex 22695; fax 39-66-12-33; govt-owned statutory corpn; Dir-Gen. HANS JØRGEN JENSEN; Dir of Radio Programmes HANS JØRGEN SKOV; operates a foreign service, 10 regional stations and three national channels:

Channel 1 broadcasts for 115 hours per week on FM, in Danish (Greenlandic programmes weekly); Head METTE WINGE.

Channel 2, a serious music channel, broadcasts on FM, for 35 hours per week nationally, in Danish, as well as regional and special (for foreign workers) programmes; Head STEEN FREDERIKSEN.

Channel 3 broadcasts on FM for 24 hours per day, in Danish; primarily a popular music channel, there is news in Greenlandic, in Faeroese and, weekly, in English, German and French; Head PALLE ÅRSLEV.

There are also some 300 operators licensed for low-power FM transmissions of local and community radio, etc.

TELEVISION

Danmarks Radio—TV: TV-Byen, 2860 Søborg; tel. 31-67-12-33; telex 22695; fax 39-66-10-36; Dir-Gen. HANS JØRGEN JENSEN; Dir of Television Programmes HENRIK ANTONSEN.

TV 2: Rugårdsvej 25, 5100 Odense C; tel. 65-91-12-44; telex 59660; fax 65-91-33-22; began broadcasts in October 1988; Denmark's first national commercial TV station; only a third of its finances come from licence fees, the rest from advertising; Dir-Gen. JØRGEN SCHLEIMANN.

There were 19 local television stations, and another 52 planned, in Denmark in 1988.

Finance

The first Danish commercial bank was founded in 1846. In January 1975 restrictions on savings banks were lifted, giving commercial and savings banks equal rights and status. Several foreign banks have representative offices in Copenhagen, and in January 1975 restrictions on the establishment of full branches of foreign banks were removed. In October 1988 all remaining restrictions on capital movements were ended. In 1988 there were about 225 banks, considerably fewer than 20 years earlier, and in 1989 there was a succession of important mergers between leading banks. All banks are under government supervision, and public representation is obligatory on all bank supervisory boards.

BANKING

(cap. = capital; p.u. = paid up; res = reserves; dep. = deposits; m. = million; brs = branches; amounts in kroner)

Supervisory Authority

Tilsynet med Banker og Sparekasser (Government Supervision of Banks and Savings Banks): Gammel Kongevej 74A, 1850 Frederiksberg C; fax 31-23-88-13; agency of the Ministry of Industry and Energy ; Dir EIGIL MOELGÅRD.

Central Bank

Danmarks Nationalbank: Havnegade 5, 1093 Copenhagen K; tel. 33-14-14-11; telex 27051; fax 33-14-59-02; f. 1818; self-governing; sole right of issue; conducts monetary policy; administers reserves of foreign exchange; capital fund 50m.; cap. and res 29,110m.; gold in coin and bullion 4,340m.; notes in circ. 23,290m. (1989); Govs E. HOFFMEYER, O. THOMASEN, BODIL N. ANDERSEN.

Commercial Banks

Åbenrå Kreditbank A/S: Ramsherred 27, 6200 Åbenrå; tel. 74-62-46-00; telex 52124; f. 1926; cap. 17.8m., res 36m., dep. 289.2m. (Dec. 1988); Chair. ULRICH JANSEN.

Aktivbanken A/S: POB 2350, Ladegårdsvej 3, 7100 Vejle; tel. 75-85-71-00; telex 61113; fax 75-85-81-55; f. 1971; absorbed Århus Discontobank A/S in Jan. 1988; cap. 228.5m., res 777.2m., dep. 6,173.8m. (1988); Man. Dirs GERT KRISTIANSEN, ERIK SØFELOE; 58 brs.

Amagerbanken A/S: Amagerbrogade 25, 2300 Copenhagen S; tel. 31-95-60-90; telex 31262; fax 31-54-45-34; f. 1903; cap. 152m., res 548m., dep. 8,641m. (Dec. 1989); Chief Gen. Man. KNUD CHRISTENSEN; 31 brs.

Amtssparekassen for Fyns Amt: Vestre Stationsvej 7, POB 189, 5100 Odense C; tel. 66-14-04-74; telex 5559778; fax 65-91-01-10; f. 1974; cap. 101.3m., res 366.6m., dep. 5,735.4m. (Dec. 1988); Chair. JOHN KOERNER; 46 brs.

Andelsbanken Danebank: 1–3 Staunings Plads, 1643 Copenhagen V; tel. 33-14-51-14; telex 27086; fax 33-91-21-10; cap. 890.7m., res 2,690m., dep. 57,869.4m. (Dec. 1989); Chair. A. C. JACOBSEN.

Arbejdernes Landsbank A/S: Vesterbrogade 5, 1502 Copenhagen V; tel. 33-14-88-77; telex 15633; fax 33-32-18-73; f. 1919; cap. 300m., res 699m., dep. 11,216.8m. (Dec. 1989); Man. Dirs E. MIDTGÅRD, P. E. LETH, E. CASTELLA; 57 brs.

Baltica Bank A/S: Bredgade 40, 1296 Copenhagen K; tel. 33-33-99-99; telex 27212; fax 33-33-97-97; f. 1987; cap. 250m., res 390.7m., dep. 7,609.1m. (Dec. 1989); Chair. H. C. HANSEN; Pres. PETER VEJE JENSEN.

Bank of Copenhagen: Ostergade 4-6, 1100 Copenhagen K; tel. 33-11-15-15; telex 15977; fax 33-32-60-04; f. 1979; 90% owned by ICAF (Luxembourg); cap. 62.5m., res 43.7m., dep. 873m. (Dec. 1989); Chair. and Jt Man. Dir JOERGEN MOELVANG; CEO and Jt Man. Dir NIELS DAHL-SØRENSEN.

Bankaktieselskabet Alm. Brand Bank: Jarmers Plads 7, 1551 Copenhagen V; tel. 33-13-11-88; telex 16858; fax 33-14-11-88; f. 1983 as SJL-Banken A/S, changed name to above in Oct. 1988; cap. 75m., res 41.3m., dep. 859.8m. (Dec. 1988); Chair. SVEN KJEMS; Gen. Mans JESPER STOKHOLM, HENRIK NORDAM.

Bonusbanken A/S: Dalgasgade 30, POB 239, 7400 Herning; tel. 97-12-11-14; telex 62314; fax 97-21-44-54; f. 1958; cap. 10m., res 33.5m., dep. 367m. (Dec. 1989); Gen. Man. I. ØSTERBY HANSEN; 1 br.

Bornholmerbanken A/S: St. Torv 15, 3700 Rønne, Bornholm; tel. 53-95-00-61; telex 48117; fax 53-95-05-70; f. 1966; cap. 22.5m., res 77.2m., dep. 663.2m. (Dec. 1989); Man. SØREN ANDERSEN; 7 brs.

Danske Andelskassers Bank A/S: Baneskellet 1, Hammershoj; 8830 Tjele; tel. 86-45-14-11; telex 65211; fax 86-45-00-14; f. 1970; cap. 40m., res 7.7m., dep. 450.9m. (Dec. 1989); Chair. KNUD LARSEN.

Den Danske Bank A/S: Holmens Kanal 2–12, 1092 Copenhagen K; tel. 33-15-65-00; telex 27000; f. 1871 as Danske Landmandsbank; merged with Copenhagen Handelsbank and Provinsbanken in April 1990 to form Den Danske Bank A/S; cap. 5,292.5m., res 17,432.2m., dep. 313,226.9m. (Jan. 1990); Chair. POUL J. SVANHOLM; Dep. Chair. A. BJØRN RÜHNE.

Djurslands Bank: 5 Torvet, 8500 Grenå; tel. 86-32-15-55; telex 63488; fax 86-32-75-77; f. 1965; cap. and res 171m., dep. 1,262m. (1989); Gen. Man. V. STENAGER; 32 brs.

Egnsbank Fyn A/S: Vestergade 33, POB 60, 5100 Odense C; tel. 66-11-46-11; telex 59876; fax 66-11-66-10; f. 1902; cap. 18m., res

DENMARK

74.7m., dep. 521.1m. (Dec. 1989); Chair LEIF LADBYE-HANSEN; 12 brs.

Egnsbank Nord A/S: Jernbanegade 4–6, POB 701, 9900 Frederikshavn; tel. 98-42-04-33; telex 67102; fax 98-42-47-92; f. 1970; cap. 285m., dep. 1,993m. (Dec. 1989); Gen. Mans B. WAMMEN, JENS OLE JENSEN, OLE KRISTENSEN; 21 brs.

Erhvervs-og Investeringsbanken: Nikolaj Plads 34, 1018 Copenhagen K; tel. 33-14-41-66; telex 16789; fax 33-14-95-65; f. 1973; cap. 40m., res 11.3m., dep. 459.6m. (Dec. 1989); Chair. JOHN MADSEN; Man. Dir MOGENS PIHL.

Esbjerg Bank A/S: Kongensgade 70, 6700 Esbjerg; tel. 75-12-82-00; telex 54161; fax 75-12-27-21; f. 1917; cap. 25m., res 76.5m., dep. 791.2m. (Dec. 1989); Man. B. HÄBER CHRISTIANSEN; 6 brs.

Fjerritslev Bank A/S: Vestergade 16, POB 19, 9690 Fjerritslev; tel. 98-21-41-11; fax 98-21-34-94; f. 1898; cap. 12m., res 62.3m., dep. 485.3m. (Dec. 1986); Chair. A. NORSKOV PEDERSEN.

Forstædernes Bank A/S: Malervangen 1, 2600 Glostrup; tel. 42-96-17-20; telex 33261; fax 42-63-11-20; f. 1902; total assets 3,600m. (Sept. 1988); Chair. V. B. CHRISTENSEN; Gen. Man. F. MARCUSSEN; 16 brs.

Haandværker-, Handels- og Landbrugsbanken A/S: Jernbanegade 9, 4700 Næstved; tel. 53-72-45-55; telex 46255; fax 53-72-75-55; f. 1901; cap. 18m., res 63m., dep. 531m. (1988); Man. OLE MEYER; 8 brs.

Hafnia Merchant Bank Ltd: Borgergade 24, POB 1064, 1347 Copenhagen K; tel. 33-11-27-33; telex 22396; fax 33-15-96-48; f. 1940 as Fællesbanken for Danmarks Sparekasser; a subsidiary of Hafnia Invest since Dec. 1987; cap. 250m., res 263m., dep. 5,291.7m. (Dec. 1989); Man. Dir H. BAROUDY; 9 brs.

Himmerlandsbanken A/S: Adelgade 31, 9500 Hobro; tel. 98-52-10-00; telex 65864; fax 98-52-18-94; f. 1892; cap. 37m., res 83.1m., dep. 1,108m. (Dec. 1989); Man. BENT HANSEN; 13 brs.

Holstebro Bank A/S: Storetorv 1, 7500 Holstebro; tel. 97-41-21-44; telex 66433; fax 97-41-61-82; f. 1871; cap. 190.8m., dep. 1,207.6m. (1987); Man. N. K. NIELSEN; 9 brs.

Horsens Landbobank A/S: Jessensgade 6–8, 8700 Horsens; tel. 75-62-42-22; telex 61680; fax 75-62-42-42; f. 1925; cap. 25m., res 52.4m., dep. 730.5m. (Dec. 1989); Gen. Mans SØREN PETER HANSEN, OLE POULSEN; 16 brs.

Hvidbjerg Bank A/S: Ostergade 2, 7790 Hvidbjerg; tel. 97-87-13-00; fax 97-87-16-83; f. 1912; cap. 10m., res 18.7m., dep. 159.5m. (Dec. 1989); Chair. VIGGO PEDERSEN; Gen. Man. H. LAUSTEN.

Jyske Bank A/S: Vestergade 8–16, 8600 Silkeborg; tel. 86-82-11-22; telex 63231; fax 86-82-41-66; f. 1855, amalgamated in 1967; cap. 600m., res 2,881.6m., dep. 48,849.2m. (Dec. 1989); Chief Exec. KAJ STEENKJÆR; 158 brs.

Lån & Spar Bank: Reventlowsgade 12, 1651 Copenhagen V; tel. 33-22-10-80; telex 15908; fax 33-23-34-52; f. 1880 as Laane-Og Sparekassen For offentligt Ansatte, name changed to above in Jan. 1990; cap. 6.1m., res 91m., dep. 1,365.2m. (Dec. 1988); Chair. MARTIN RØMER; Chief Gen. Man. PETER SCHOU.

Langelands Bank A/S: Ørstedsgade 6, 5900 Rudkøbing; tel. 62-51-10-22; telex 50594; fax 62-51-10-23; f. 1872; cap. 9m., res 57m., dep. 429.7m. (Dec. 1989); Man. TORBEN RASMUSSEN; 17 brs.

Lokalbanken i Hjørring A/S: Østergade 4A, POB 39, 9800 Hjørring; tel. 98-92-12-33; telex 67881; fax 98-90-12-33; f. 1929; cap. 12.5m., res 33.8m., dep. 497.1m. (Dec. 1987); Pres. JØRGEN SKOVEN; Chair. JØRN HOLM; 2 brs.

Lollands Bank A/S: Nybrogade 3, 4900 Nakskov, Lolland; tel. 53-92-11-33; telex 47542; fax 53-92-87-67; f. 1907; cap. 18.3m., res 54.8m., dep. 377.5m. (1989); Man. MOGENS NIELSEN; 4 brs.

Midtbank A/S: Østergade 2, 7400 Herning; tel. 97-12-48-00; telex 62142; fax 97-22-43-38; f. 1965; cap. and res 395m., dep. 3,838m. (July 1990); Gen. Mans KJELD FREDERIKSEN, JØRN ASTRUP HANSEN; 30 brs.

Møns Bank: Storegade Nr 29, POB 92, 4780 Stege; tel. 55-81-51-11; fax 55-81-17-07; f. 1967; cap. 24m., res 52.4m., dep. 432.8m. (Dec. 1989); Chair. HANS CARSTENSEN; Man. Dirs SØREN JUHLER, HANS K. OLSEN; 6 brs.

Morsø Bank A/S: Algade, 7900 Nykøbing M.; tel. 97-72-14-00; telex 60714; fax 97-72-58-37; f. 1876; cap. 32m., res 63m., dep. 668m. (July 1990); Man. Dir H. J. CHRISTENSEN; 11 brs.

Næstved Diskontobank A/S (Diskonto Banken): Axeltorv 4, 4700 Næstved; tel. 53-72-15-00; telex 46227; fax 53-17-03-41; f. 1871; cap. 40m., res 188.5m., dep. 1,406.4m. (Dec. 1989); Gen. Man. A. HOVE ANDREASEN; 9 brs.

Nordfyns Bank A/S: Adelgade 49, 5400 Bogense; tel. 64-81-17-37; telex 50338; fax 64-81-30-44; f. 1897; cap. 16m., res 38.2m., dep. 380.3m. (Dec. 1989); Chair. HANS HVIID NICOLAISEN; Man. Dir PREBEN SANDBERG.

Nordvestbank A/S: Torvet 4–5, 7620 Lemvig; tel. 97-82-07-77; telex 66536; fax 97-81-01-77; f. 1874; cap. and res 200m., dep. 846m. (1989); Chair. P. GRANKÆR; Gen. Man. J. HOLT; 8 brs.

Nørresundby Bank A/S: Torvet 4, 9400 Nørresundby; tel. 98-17-33-33; telex 69776; fax 98-19-18-78; f. 1898; cap. 40m., res 105.5m., dep. 2,180.9m. (Dec. 1989); Chair. HUGO PEDERSEN; Gen. Man. HAKON WORMSLEV; 14 brs.

Østjydsk Bank AS: Østergade 6–8, 9550 Mariager; tel. 98-54-14-44; telex 65872; fax 98-54-17-19; f. 1897; cap. 18m., res. 22.7m., dep. 406m. (Dec. 1989); Chair. THORVALD CHRISTENSEN; Gen. Man. POUL BERTELSEN.

Ringkjøbing Bank: Torvet 2, POB 19, 6950 Ringkøbing; tel. 97-32-03-22; telex 62442; fax 97-32-15-41; f. 1872; cap. 32m., res 189.7m., dep. 1,903.1m. (Dec. 1989); Chair. NIELS SKYTTE; Man. Dir MOGENS SVENSSON; 7 brs.

Ringkjøbing Landbobank A/S: Torvet 1, 6950 Ringkøbing; tel. 97-32-11-66; telex 60385; fax 97-32-18-18; f. 1886; cap. 27m., res 237m., dep. 1,366m. (1989); Chair. OLE KRISTENSEN; Gen. Man. BENT NAUR KRISTENSEN; 11 brs.

Roskilde Bank A/S: Algade 14, POB 39, 4000 Roskilde; f. 1884; tel. 42-35-17-00; telex 43122; fax 42-36-32-30; cap. and res 320m., dep. 2,060m. (1989); Man. N. VALENTIN HANSEN; 18 brs.

Salling Bank A/S: Frederiksgade 6, 7800 Skive; tel. 97-52-33-66; telex 66726; fax 97-51-06-96; f. 1926; cap. 27m., dep. 930m. (1988); Chair. LARS E. ANDERSEN; Man. P. E. BASTRUP; 12 brs.

Skælskør Bank A/S: Algade 18, 4230 Skælskør; tel. 53-59-60-70; telex 40139; fax 53-59-62-25; f. 1876; cap. 24m., res 53.6m., dep. 588.2m. (Dec. 1989); Man. P. W. OLSEN; 6 brs.

Skjern Bank A/S: Jernbanegade 1, 6900 Skjern; tel. 97-35-13-33; telex 60324; fax 97-35-35-01; f. 1906; cap. 18.8m., res 87.2m., dep. 965.7m. (Dec. 1989); Chair. HANS ABILDGÅRD; Man. Dir JENS LUNDØE POULSEN; 9 brs.

Sydbank Sønderjylland A/S: Kirkeplads 2, POB 169, 6200 Åbenrå; tel. 74-62-12-22; telex 52114; fax 74-62-01-42; f. 1970; cap. and res 1,597m., dep. 10,642m., total assets 27,097m. (1989); Gen. Mans C. ANDERSEN, S. OLSEN, J. ANDERSEN; 68 brs.

Sydfyns Discontobank A/S: Torvet 1, POB 71, 5600 Faborg; tel. 62-61-17-17; telex 50389; fax 62-61-18-53; f. 1924; cap. 45.5m., res 37.5m., dep. 896.6m. (Dec. 1989); Chair. M. JOERGENSEN; Vice-Pres. H. BASTRUP; 6 brs.

Tarm Bank A/S: Storegade 6–10, 6880 Tarm; tel. 97-37-14-11; telex 60326; fax 97-37-13-72; f. 1911; cap. 18m., res 22.5m., dep. 346.8m. (Dec. 1989); Chair. GUNNAR ASMUSSEN; Vice-Chair. KNUD MOGENSEN; 10 brs.

Totalbanken A/S: Bredgade 5, 5560 Årup; tel. 64-43-12-34; telex 59675; fax 64-43-31-16; f. 1911, present name 1989; cap. 28m., res. 62.9m., dep. 332.2m. (Dec. 1989); Chair. H. PEDERSEN; Gen. Man. P. E. JENSEN; 4 brs.

Trier (Brødr.) Bank A/S: Nyropsgade 17, 1505 Copenhagen V; tel. 33-11-22-10; telex 16894; fax 33-11-61-06; f. 1877 as Brødr Trier Bankiers & Fondsborsvekseler, became a bank in May 1988; cap. 25m., res 3.7m., dep. 190.2m. (Dec. 1989); Chair. TORBEN ROSSBERG; Gen. Man. ANDERS CHRISTENSEN.

UNIbankDanmark A/S: Torvegade 2, POB 1000, 2300 Copenhagen S; tel. 33-11-11-11; telex 27196; fax 31-95-14-38; f. 1990 by merger of Andelsbanken (f. 1925), Privatbanken (f. 1857) and SDS (f. 1973); Man. Dir STEEN RASBORG; 750 brs.

Varde Bank A/S: Kongensgade 62–64, 6701 Esbjerg; tel. 75-12-68-11; fax 75-13-15-44; f. 1872; cap. 200m., res 1,403m., dep. 6,231m. (1989); Chair. JENS M. KRISTENSEN; Man. Dir J. O. OCKHOLM; 48 brs.

Vestfyns Bank A/S: Østergade 42, 5610 Assens; tel. 64-71-50-50; fax 64-71-24-74; f. 1896; cap. 15m., res 55.8m., dep. 561.8m. (1988); Chair. GEORG GUNDERSEN; Gen. Man. and Man. Dir N. J. FORD; 3 brs.

Vestjysk Bank (Hostelbro Landmandsbank) A/S: Vestergade 1, 7500 Holstebro; tel. 97-42-26-11; telex 66412; fax 97-41-21-85; f. 1887; cap. 73.1m., res 173.5m., dep. 1,828.3m. (Dec. 1989); Mans FRANK HOMÅ, GUNNAR V. MOLLER; 3 brs.

Vordingborg Bank A/S: Algade 52, POB 119, Vordingborg; tel. 53-77-01-19; fax 55-34-00-19; f. 1890; cap. 9m., res 24.9m., dep. 212.7m. (Dec. 1989); Chair. ELVAR THOMSEN.

Savings Banks

Sparbank Vest Skive Sparekasse: Adelgade 8, 7800 Skive; tel. 97-52-33-11; telex 66724; fax 97-52-73-11; f. 1857; cap. 46m., res 281.5m., dep. 1,455.8m. (Dec. 1988); Gen. Man. PREBEN RASMUSSEN.

Sparekassen Bikuben A/S: Silkegade 8, 1113 Copenhagen K; tel. 33-12-01-33; telex 19832; fax 33-12-09-33; f. 1877; merged in Jan. 1989 with Sparekassen DK; cap. 215m., res 1,882m., dep. 50,854m.

DENMARK

Directory

(Jan. 1989); Gen. Mans HANS ERIK BALLE, KNUD BRANDENBORG, BØRGE MUNK EBBESEN, PEDER ELKJÆR, GERT KRISTENSEN, TOMMY PEDERSEN; 311 brs.

Sparekassen Lolland: Nygade 4, POB 129, 4900 Nakskov; tel. 53-92-33-44; telex 47547; fax 53-92-87-69; cap. 23.9m., res 143.8m., dep. 1,522.5m. (Dec. 1988); Chair. ERIK HOEJGÅRD; 13 brs.

Sparekassen Nordjylland A/S: Karlskogavej 4, POB 162, 9100 Alborg; tel. 98-18-73-11; telex 69662; fax 98-18-56-77; f. 1967; cap. 433.6m., res 1,174.1m., dep. 21,093.5m. (Dec. 1989); Chair. HENRY JENSEN; Man. Dirs J. GIVERSEN, T. OLSSON; 87 brs.

Sparekassen Sydjylland: Soldalen 8, 7100 Vejle; tel. 75-84-04-00; telex 61122; fax 75-83-25-01; f. 1819; cap. 873.6m., res 447.3m., dep. 18,199m. (Dec. 1989); Chair. SIGFRED BUHL; 89 brs.

Sparekassen Thy: Store Torv 1, 7700 Thisted; tel. 97-92-23-00; telex 66631; fax 97-92-09-08; cap. 55.1m., res 70.8m., dep. 1,046.3m. (Dec. 1988); Man. Dirs JORGEN PEDERSEN, POUL JENSEN.

Bankers' Organizations

Danmarks Sparekasseforening (Danish Savings Banks Association): Købmagergade 62, POB 2189, 1017 Copenhagen K; tel. 33-15-18-11; telex 15965; fax 33-11-23-48; Gen. Man. SVEND JAKOBSEN.

Finansrådet—Danske Pengeinstitutters Forening (Danish Bankers' Association): Finansrådets Hus, Amaliegade 7, 1256 Copenhagen K; tel. 33-12-02-00; telex 16102; fax 33-93-02-60; f. 1990; 193 mems; Man. Dir SVEN JAKOBSEN.

STOCK EXCHANGE

Københavns Fondsbørs (Copenhagen Stock Exchange): Nikolaj Plads 6, POB 1040, 1007 Copenhagen K; tel. 33-93-33-66; telex 16496; fax 33-12-86-13; f. 1861; Pres. BENT MEBUS; Chair. SVEN CASPERSEN.

INSURANCE
Principal Companies

Alm. Brand af 1792: Lyngby Hovedgade 4, POB 1792, 2800 Lyngby; tel. 45-93-17-92; telex 37512; fax 45-87-17-92; f. 1792; subsidiaries: finance, life, non-life and reinsurance; Chief Gen. Man. BENT KNIE-ANDERSEN.

Baltica Holding A/S: Klausdalsbrovej 601, 2750 Ballerup; tel. 44-68-68-44; fax 44-87-49-79; f. 1985; in 1990 acquired 80% of Statsanstalten for Livsforsikring (see below); Chief Gen. Mans PETER CHRISTOFFERSEN, JØRGEN HAGEN HANSEN, CLAUS GORDON NIELSEN.

Baltica Forsikring A/S: Klausdalsbrovej 601, 2750 Ballerup; tel. 44-68-68-44; telex 16322; f. 1915 by merger; all classes; subsidiaries: pensions, workers' liabilities, life; Gen. Mans STEEN HEMMINGSEN, JENS ERIK CHRISTENSEN, HOLGER FOGED, MICHAEL PRAM RASMUSSEN.

Forsikringsaktieselskabet KOMPAS A/S: Bredgade 40, 1260 Copenhagen K; tel. 33-32-00-32; telex 16375; fax 33-93-35-34; travel, health; Chief Gen. Man. NIELS HORST LAURSEN.

Max Levig & Co Eft. A/S: Bredgade 40, 1260 Copenhagen K; tel. 33-14-67-00; telex 27519; fax 33-93-67-01; f. 1890; Gen. Man. ERNST KÅS WILHJELM.

Statsanstalten for Livsforsikring: Kampmannsgade 4, 1645 Copenhagen V; tel. 33-15-15-15; telex 15283; fax 33-32-37-32; f. 1842 as state insurance co; privatized in 1990; 80%-owned by Baltica Holding A/S.

Forsikringsselskabet Codan A/S: Codanhus, Gl. Kongevej 60, Frederiksberg C; tel. 31-21-21-21; telex 15469; fax 31-21-21-22; f. 1915; all classes except life; subsidiaries: workers' liability, life; Gen. Man. PETER ZOBEL.

Hafnia Holdings A/S: Holbergsgade 3, 1010 Copenhagen K; tel. 33-32-45-11; telex 16193; f. 1984; subsidiaries: all classes of insurance and reinsurance; merchant bank; Chair. E. J. B. CHRISTENSEN; Chief Gen. Man. PER VILLUM HANSEN.

A/S Det Kjøbenhavnske Reassurance-Compagni: Amaliegade 39, POB 2093, 1256 Copenhagen K; tel. 33-14-30-63; telex 19617; fax 33-32-52-70; f. 1915; reinsurance; Gen. Mans BENT KNIE ANDERSEN, CLAUS POULSEN, LEIF CORINTH-HANSEN, HENNING KANSTRUP LUNDE, PETER JERVING.

Købstædernes almindelige Brandforsikring: Grønningen 1, 1270 Copenhagen K; tel. 33-14-37-48; fax 33-32-06-66; f. 1761; fire; Chair. INGVARDT PEDERSEN; Gen. Man. ALF TORP-PEDERSEN.

Det kongelige octroierede almindelige Brandassurance-Co. A/S (The Royal Chartered General Fire Insurance Co. Ltd): Hojbro Plads 10, 1248 Copenhagen K; tel. 33-14-15-16; telex 16016; f. 1798; all branches; subsidiaries: workers' liability, life; Gen. Man. SVEN A. BLOMBERG.

Nordisk Reinsurance Company A/S: Grønningen 25, 1270 Copenhagen K; tel. 33-14-13-67; telex 15367; fax 33-14-36-41; f. 1894; reinsurance, life and non-life, international; Gen. Man. KAJ AHLMAN.

PFA Pension: Marina Park, Sundkrogsgade 4, 2100 Copenhagen Ø; tel. 31-20-77-11; telex 16183; fax 31-18-64-60; f. 1917; life; non-life, property; Gen. Mans ANDRÉ LUBLIN, A. KÜHLE, JAN IHLEMANN, HANS TJELLESON.

Topdanmark A/S: Borupvang 4, 2750 Ballerup; tel. 44-68-33-11; telex 35107; fax 44-68-28-05; f. 1985; all classes, with subsidiaries; Man. Dir HENNING BIRCH.

Tryg Forsikring gs: Forsikringshuset, Parallelvej, POB 300, 2800 Lyngby; tel. 42-87-88-11; telex 37449; fax 45-93-24-42; f. 1973 by merger; all classes, with subsidiaries; Chief Gen. Man. STEEN RODE.

Insurance Association

Assurandør-Societetet: Amaliegade 10, 1256 Copenhagen K; tel. 33-13-75-55; telex 12208; fax 33-11-23-53; Chair. STEEN HEMMINGSEN; Dir STEEN LETH JEPPESEN; 139 mems.

Trade and Industry

ADVISORY BODIES

Det Økonomiske Råd (Economic Council): Kampmannsgade 1 IV, 1604 Copenhagen V; tel. 33-13-51-28; f. 1962, under the Economic Co-ordination Act, to watch national economic development and help to co-ordinate the actions of economic interest groups; 27 members representing both sides of industry, the Government and independent economic experts; Co-Chair. Prof. ARNE LARSEN, Prof. PEDER J. PEDERSEN, Prof. C. VASTRUP; Sec.-Gen. J. SØNDERGÅRD.

Industrirådets Industriregister (Federation of Danish Industries' Register of Industries): H. C. Andersens Blvd 18, 1790 Copenhagen V; tel. 33-15-22-33; telex 112217; fax 33-32-32-81; register of exporters and products.

Landsforeningen Dansk Arbejde (National Association for Danish Enterprise): Gravene 2, 8800 Viborg; tel. 86-62-42-22; fax 86-62-45-88.

CHAMBERS OF COMMERCE

Det Danske Handelskammer (Danish Chamber of Commerce): Børsen, 1217 Copenhagen K; tel. 33-91-23-23; telex 19520; fax 33-32-52-16; f. 1742; approx. 12,000 mems.; Man. Dir H. SEJER-PETERSEN; Pres. KLAVS OLSEN.

ICC Denmark, International Chamber of Commerce: Børsen, 1217 Copenhagen K; Chair. ERIK B. RASMUSSEN; Sec.-Gen. H. SEJER-PETERSEN.

EMPLOYERS' ORGANIZATIONS

Bryggeriforeningen (Danish Brewers' Association): Frederiksberggade 11, 1459 Copenhagen K; tel. 33-12-62-41; fax 33-14-25-13; f. 1899; Chair. POUL J. SVANHOLM; Dir POUL ANTONSEN; 12 mems.

Danmarks Textiltekniske Forening (Textile Technical Society): Fredericiavej 99, 7100 Vejle; f. 1942; Pres. AAGE JESPERSEN; Vice-Pres. MOGENS NISSEN; 500 mems.

Dansk Arbejdsgiverforening (Danish Employers' Confederation): Vester Voldgade 113, 1790 Copenhagen V; tel. 33-93-40-00; telex 16464; fax 33-12-29-76; f. 1896; Chair. POUL HEDEGÅRD; Dir-Gen. HANS SKOV CHRISTENSEN; 30,283 mems.

Dansk Pelsdyravlerforening (DPF) (Danish Fur Breeders' Association): Langagervej 60, 2600 Glostrup; tel. 43-43-44-00; telex 33171; fax 42-45-25-46; co-operative of 5,000 mems.

Danske Husmandsforeninger (Danish Family Farmers' Association): Landbrugsmagasinet, Vester Farimagsgade 6, 1606 Copenhagen V; tel. 33-12-99-50; fax 33-93-63-62; f. 1906; Chair. CHR. SØRENSEN; Sec.-Gen. OLAV POVLSGÅRD; 30,000 mems.

Danske Mejeriers Fællesorganisation (Danish Dairy Board): Frederiks Allé 22, 8000 Århus; tel. 86-13-26-11; telex 64307; fax 86-13-26-93; f. 1912; Chair. KNUD ERIK JENSEN; Sec. K. THAYSEN; 63 mems.

Fællesforeningen for Danmarks Brugsforeninger (Co-operative of Denmark): Roskildevej 65, 2620 Albertslund; f. 1896; Chair. BJARNE MØGELHØJ; 975,000 mems.

Foreningen af danske Cementfabrikker (Association of Cement Manufacturers): N. Voldgade 34, Copenhagen; f. 1898; Chair. POUL SKOVGÅRD; Sec. PER LAURENTS; 4 mems.

Foreningen af Fabrikanter i Jernindustrien i Provinserne (Manufacturers' Federation of the Provincial Iron Industry): N. Voldgade 34, Copenhagen; tel. 33-14-34-14; telex 16068; fax 33-14-12-33; f. 1895; Chair. VAGN-ÅGE JENSEN; Sec. GLENN SØGÅRD; 550 mems.

DENMARK

Directory

Håndværksrådet (Federation of Crafts and Smaller Industries): Amaliegade 15, 1256 Copenhagen K; tel. 33-93-20-00; telex 16600; fax 33-32-01-74; f. 1879; comprises about 450 asscns with 57,000 mems; Chair. KLAUS BONDE LARSEN; Man. LARS JØRGEN NIELSEN.

Industrirådet (Federation of Danish Industries): H. C. Andersens Blvd 18, 1790 Copenhagen V; tel. 33-15-22-33; telex 112217; fax 33-32-32-81; f. 1910; Pres. BENT J. LE FÈVRE; Dir OVE MUNCH; 2,500 mems.

Jernindustrielle Arbejdsgivere i København (Copenhagen Metal Industry Employers' Federation): Nørre Voldgade 34, 1358 Copenhagen K; tel. 33-14-34-14; telex 16068; fax 33-14-12-33; Chair. FRANK BOTTRUP; Sec. H. ENGELHARDT; 475 mems.

Det kongelige danske Landhusholdningsselskab (The Royal Agricultural Society of Denmark): Rolighedsvej 26, 1958 Frederiksberg C; tel. 31-35-02-27; fax 31-35-09-49; f. 1769 to promote agricultural progress; Pres A. NEIMANN-SØRENSEN, JON KRABBE, PETER SKAK OLUFSEN; Dir JENS WULFF; 3,100 mems.

De danske Landboforeninger (Farmers' Unions): Axelborg, Vesterbrogade 4A, 1620 Copenhagen V; tel. 33-12-75-61; telex 327662; fax 33-32-76-62; f. 1893; Pres. H. O. A. KJELDSEN; Chief Sec. JØRGEN SKOVBAK; 85,000 mems.

Landbrugsrådet (Agricultural Council): Axelborg, Axeltorv 3, 1609 Copenhagen V; tel. 33-14-56-72; telex 16772; fax 33-14-95-74; f. 1919; Pres. HANS O. A. KJELDSEN; Dir KJELD EJLER; 32 mems.

Sammenslutningen af Arbejdsgivere indenfor den keramiske Industri (Federation of Employers of the Ceramic Industry): N. Voldgade 34, Copenhagen; tel. 33-14-34-34; fax 33-12-12-33; f. 1918; Chair. L. LAUTRUP LARSEN; Sec. K. MAXEN; 22 mems.

Sammenslutningen af Landbrugets Arbejdsgiverforeninger (SALA) (Federation of Agricultural Employers' Associations): Magstræde 6, 1204 Copenhagen K; tel. 33-13-46-55; fax 33-11-89-53.

Skibsværftsforeningen (Association of Danish Shipbuilders): St. Kongensgade 128, 1264 Copenhagen K; tel. 33-13-24-16; telex 19582; fax 33-11-10-96.

Textilindustrien (Federation of Textile Industries): Bredgade 41, POB 300, 7400 Herning; tel. 97-12-13-66; telex 62199; fax 97-12-23-50; f. 1895; Pres. C. WICHMANN MADSEN; Man. Dirs J. BOLLERUP JENSEN, S. HOLM PEDERSEN; 310 mems.

TRADE UNIONS

Landsorganisationen i Danmark (LO) (Danish Federation of Trade Unions): Rosenørns Allé 12, 1634 Copenhagen V; tel. 31-35-35-41; telex 16170; fax 31-37-37-41; Pres. FINN THORGRIMSON; Vice-Pres. HANS JENSEN; 1,412,767 mems (on 1 January 1989); 1,371 brs.

Principal Affiliated Unions

Blik- og Rørarbejderforbundet i Danmark (Metal and Steel Workers): Ålholmvej 55, 2500 Valby; tel. 31-71-30-22; fax 31-71-29-97; Pres. JORN-OLUF OLSEN; 8,988 mems.

Dansk Beklædnings- og Tekstilarbejderforbund (Textile and Garment Workers); Nyropsgade 14, 1602 Copenhagen V; tel. 33-11-67-65; fax 33-32-99-94; f. 1978 by merger of Garment Workers' Union and Textile Workers' Union; Gen. Sec. ANNE M. PEDERSEN; 25,000 mems.

Dansk Bogbinder- og Kartonnagearbejder Forbund (Bookbinders and Cardboard Box Workers): Grafisk Forbundshus, Lygten 16, 2400 Copenhagen NV; tel. 31-81-42-22; fax 31-81-24-25; Pres. SVEND MÅBJERG; 8,782 mems.

Dansk El-Forbund (Electricians' Union): Vodroffsvej 26, 1900 Frederiksberg C; tel. 31-21-14-00; fax 31-21-84-00; Pres. FREDDY ANDERSEN; 25,175 mems.

Dansk Funktionærforbund (Service Trade Employees); Upsalagade 20, 2100 Copenhagen Ø; tel. 31-38-65-95; fax 31-38-71-59; Pres. HANS JØRGEN JENSEN; 23,000 mems.

Dansk Jernbaneforbund (Railway Workers); Bredgade 21, 1260 Copenhagen K; tel. 33-14-33-00; fax 33-91-14-33; f. 1899; Pres. E. NYGÅRD JESPERSEN; 11,095 mems.

Dansk Kommunal Arbejderforbund (Municipal Workers); Nitivej 6, 2000 Frederiksberg; tel. 31-19-90-22; telex 27481; fax 31-19-51-09; Pres. POUL WINCKLER; 124,000 mems.

Dansk Metalarbejderforbund (Metalworkers); Nyropsgade 38, 1602 Copenhagen V; tel. 33-12-82-12; telex 16526; fax 33-12-82-28; f. 1888; Pres. GEORG POULSEN; 137,532 mems.

Dansk Postforbund (Postmen): Vodroffsvej 13A, 1900 Frederiksberg C; tel. 31-21-41-24; fax 31-21-06-42; f. 1908; Pres. JOHAN OVERGÅRD; 15,267 mems.

Dansk Tele Forbund (Telecommunications): Rolfsvej 37, 2000 Frederiksberg; tel. 38-88-00-55; fax 38-88-15-11; Pres. BJARNI POULSEN; 9,787 mems.

Dansk Typograf-Forbund (Printers): Grafisk Forbundshus, Lygten 16, 2400 Copenhagen NV; tel. 31-81-42-22; fax 35-82-24-22; Pres. KAJ PEDERSEN; 9,735 mems.

Handels- og Kontorfunktionærernes Forbund i Danmark (Commercial and Clerical Employees): H. C. Andersens Blvd 50, POB 268, 1553 Copenhagen V; tel. 33-12-43-43; fax 33-11-40-68; f. 1900; Pres. JØRGEN EIBERG; 317,469 mems.

Husligt Arbejder Forbund (Domestic Workers): Rådhuspladsen 77, 1550 Copenhagen V; tel. 33-13-40-00; fax 33-93-76-15; Pres. MARGIT VOGNSEN; 72,000 mems.

Kvindeligt Arbejderforbund (Women Workers); Ewaldsgade 3–9, 2200 Copenhagen N; tel. 31-39-31-15; fax 31-39-05-40; f. 1901; Pres. LILLIAN KNUDSEN; 96,532 mems.

Malerforbundet i Danmark (Housepainters): Tomsgårdsvej 23C, 2400 Copenhagen NV; tel. 31-34-75-22; f. 1890; Pres. FINN ANDERSEN; 13,829 mems.

Murerforbundet i Danmark (Bricklayers): Mimersgade 47, 2200 Copenhagen N; tel. 31-81-99-00; fax 35-82-07-44; Pres. BENDT JENSEN; 12,337 mems.

Nærings- og Nydelsesmiddelarbejder Forbundet (Food, Sugar Confectionery, Chocolate, Dairy Produce and Tobacco Workers): C.F. Richs Vej 103, 2000 Frederiksberg; tel. 31-87-15-22; fax 31-87-11-97; Pres. E. ANTON JOHANNSEN; 43,025 mems.

Pædagogisk Medhjælper Forbund (Teachers' Assistants): St. Kongensgade 79, 1264 Copenhagen K; tel. 33-11-03-43; f. 1974; Pres. JAKOB SØLVHØJ; 24,482 mems.

Restaurations-og Bryggeriarbejder Forbundet og Arbejdløshedskasse (Restaurant and Brewery Workers): Thoravej 29-33, 2400 Copenhagen NV; tel. 38-33-89-89; fax 38-33-67-91; Chair. BENT MOOS; 22,000 mems.

Snedker- og Tømrerforbundet i Danmark (Joiners, Cabinetmakers and Carpenters): Mimersgade 47, 2200 Copenhagen N; tel. 31-81-99-00; fax 35-82-07-44; Pres. BENT LARSEN; 48,275 mems.

Socialpædagogernes Landsforbund (Social Workers): Brolæggerstræde 9, 1211 Copenhagen K; tel. 33-14-00-58; fax 33-93-06-04; Pres. JENS ASGER HANSEN; 17,800 mems.

Specialarbejderforbundet i Danmark (General Workers' Union in Denmark): Nyropsgade 30, 1602 Copenhagen V; tel. 33-14-21-40; telex 19596; fax 33-32-14-50; Pres. HARDY HANSEN; 310,133 mems.

Træindustriforbundet i Danmark (Woodworkers); Mimersgade 47, 2200 Copenhagen N; tel. 31-81-99-00; fax 35-82-07-44; Pres. ERIK NIELSEN; 21,575 mems.

Other Unions

Akademikernes Centralorganisation (Academic employees): Nørre Voldgade 29, 1358 Copenhagen K; tel. 33-12-85-40; fax 33-93-85-40.

Den Almindelige Danske Lægeforening (Danish Medical Association): Trondhjemsgade 9, 2100 Copenhagen Ø; tel. 31-38-55-00; fax 31-42-66-78.

Dansk Journalistforbund (Journalists): Gammel Strand 46, 1202 Copenhagen K; tel. 33-14-23-88; fax 33-14-23-01; f. 1961; Pres. LARS POULSEN; 6,200 mems.

Funktionærernes og Tjenestemændenes Fællesråd (Federation of Civil Servants' and Salaried Employees' Organizations): Niels Hemmingsensgade 12, 1010 Copenhagen K; tel. 33-15-30-22; fax 33-91-30-22; f. 1952; Chair. ANKER CHRISTOFFERSEN; 360,000 mems.

Transport

In June 1986 government plans were announced for a 20-km combined tunnel-and-bridge link across the Great Belt, linking the islands of Zealand and Funen. Work began in 1987; the bridge was due to be completed in 1993, the tunnel in 1996. A meeting between the Governments of Denmark and Sweden was held in October 1986 to discuss plans for a bridge link between the two countries. However, in 1987 the Swedish Government decided to delay its decision and to conduct an inquiry into plans for a tunnel link.

RAILWAYS

DSB (Danish State Railways): Sølvgade 40C, 1349 Copenhagen K; tel. 33-14-04-00; telex 22225; fax 33-14-04-00; controls 2,476 km of line, of which 225 km are electrified; the Director-General is directly responsible to the Minister of Transport; Dir-Gen. PETER LANGAGER.

A total of 523 km, mostly branch lines, is run by 15 private companies.

DENMARK

ROADS

At 31 December 1988 Denmark had 70,666 km of paved roads, including 599 km of motorways and 3,958 km of other national roads.

FERRIES

DSB (Danish State Railways): Sølvgade 40, 1349 Copenhagen K; tel. 33-14-04-00; telex 22225; fax 33-14-04-00; operates passenger train and motor car ferries between the mainland and principal islands. Train and motor car ferries are also operated between Denmark, Sweden and Germany in co-operation with German Federal Railways, and German and Swedish State Railways; Gen. Man. N. RIECHERS.

Other services are operated by private companies.

SHIPPING

The Port of Copenhagen is the largest port in Denmark and the only one including a Free Port Zone. The other major ports are Århus, Ålborg, Fredericia and Esbjerg, which provides daily services to the United Kingdom. There are oil terminals at Kalundborg, Fredericia and Skælskør.

Farvandsvæsenet (Royal Danish Administration of Navigation and Hydrography): Overgaden oven Vandet 62B, POB 1919, 1023 Copenhagen K; tel. 31-57-40-50; telex 31319; fax 31-57-43-41.

Principal Shipping Companies

(Figures for the number of ships and their displacement refer only to Danish flag vessels at 1 July 1990, unless otherwise indicated.)

Rederiet Otto Danielsen: Kongevejen 40, 2840 Holte; tel. 42-42-32-55; telex 15704; fax 42-42-32-05; 11 dry cargo vessels, totalling 13,500 grt under foreign flags; general tramp trade, chartering, ship sales; Man. Dirs ULLA DANIELSEN, OTTO DANIELSEN, Jr.

Dannebrog Rederi A/S: Rungsted Strandvej 113, 2960 Rungsted Kyst; tel. 42-86-65-00; telex 37204; fax 42-57-14-46; f. 1883; owners of tankers and roll-on, roll-off vessels; 7 vessels of 34,014 grt (1990); liner service US–Europe, US Gulf–Caribbean, Mediterranean–Caribbean; Man. Owner Baron E. WEDELL-WEDELLSBORG.

DFDS A/S—DFDS Seaways: Skt Annæ Plads 30, 1295 Copenhagen; tel. 33-15-63-00; telex 19435; fax 33-15-49-93; f. 1866; 6 car/passenger ships of 94,600 grt and 4 roll-on, roll-off vessels of 18,600 grt; passenger and car ferry services between Denmark, Sweden, the UK, Germany and Norway, liner trade to Spain, Portugal and South America; Lauritzen owns majority share; Man. Dir NIELS BACH.

The East Asiatic Co Ltd A/S: Holbergsgade 2, 1099 Copenhagen K; tel. 35-27-27-27; telex 12100; fax 33-12-37-00; f. 1897; trading, industry, plantations, shipping; totally owned and managed tonnage: 6 container vessels of 189,300 grt, 3 bulk carriers of 80,100 grt and 5 product chemical tankers of 124,400 grt; consists of 130 companies, and with interests in 37 associate companies; worldwide services; Chair. T. W. SCHMITH; Board of Management HENNING H. SPARSØ, JOHN ARTHUR HANSEN, FLEMMING HASLE.

Elite Shipping I/S: Vestagervej 17, 2900 Hellerup; tel. 31-18-24-33; telex 15301; fax 31-18-20-17; 19 dry cargo vessels of 26,100 grt; tramp; Man. Dir RINO LANGE.

Knud I. Larsen: Vedbæk Strandvej 341, POB 40, 2950 Vedbæk; tel. 45-66-00-90; telex 19251; fax 45-66-09-90; f. 1942; 24 vessels of 54,000 grt; general cargo, container ships, chemical tankers; Man. Owners KNUD I. LARSEN, FINN SAKSØ LARSEN.

J. Lauritzen A/S: Skt Annæ Plads 28, 1291 Copenhagen K; tel. 33-11-12-22; telex 15522; fax 33-11-85-13; f. 1884; world-wide service with refrigerated vessels, product/gas tankers and bulk carriers; drilling rigs; 17 chartered reefers of 131,800 grt, 11 poolships of 117,300 grt, 2 drilling rigs of 13,100 grt, 1 container vessel and 5 dry cargo vessels of 58,700 grt; Man. Dir PETER WEITEMEYER.

Lauritzen Kosan Tankers: Toldbodgade 18, 1291 Copenhagen K; tel. 33-14-34-00; telex 22214; fax 33-91-00-39; f. 1951; 18 gas carriers of 31,000 grt; Gen. Man. LIEF SVANBERG.

Mercandia Rederierne: Amaliegade 27, 1256 Copenhagen K; tel. 33-12-01-55; telex 19762; fax 33-32-55-47; f. 1964; 27 roll-on, roll-off vessels and car ferries totalling 246,000 grt; tramp and liner services; Man. Dir H. DRACHMANN.

A. P. Møller: Esplanaden 50, 1098 Copenhagen K; tel. 33-14-15-14; telex 19632; fax 33-93-15-14; f. 1904; fleet of 77 vessels of 2,927,000 grt and 5 drilling rigs of 60,000 grt; subsidiary shipping companies in the United Kingdom, Spain, Singapore and Canada; wide variety of services, world-wide liner service under the name of **Mærsk Line:** services between Europe, USA, West Africa, Middle East, Far East; Chair. MÆRSK MCKINNEY MØLLER.

Mortensen & Lange: Strandvejen 32D, POB 2703, 2100 Copenhagen Ø; tel. 31-29-55-33; telex 15100; fax 31-29-50-60; f. 1961; 19 dry cargo vessels of 15,600 grt; worldwide tramping; Dirs STEEN OLSEN, FINN OLLENDORFF.

Dampskibsselskabet Norden A/S: Amaliegade 49, 1256 Copenhagen K; tel. 33-15-04-51; telex 22374; fax 33-15-61-99; f. 1871; 8 bulk carriers and product tankers of 283,100 grt; tramp; Man. Dir STEEN KRABBE.

Sønderborg Rederiaktieselskab: Havnevej 18, POB 20, 6320 Egernsund; tel. 74-44-14-35; telex 52815; fax 74-44-14-75; 9 livestock carriers of 8,483 grt; shipowners, managers, chartering agents; worldwide; Chair. B. CLAUSEN.

A/S Em. Z. Svitzer Bjergnings-Enterprise: Park Allé 350B, 2605 Brøndby; tel. 43-43-43-71; telex 15983; fax 43-43-60-22; f. 1833; 20 tugs and salvage vessels; worldwide salvage, towage and offshore services; Gen. Man. JØRN HANSEN.

A/S D/S Torm: Marina Park, Sundkrogsgade 10, 2100 Copenhagen Ø; tel. 31-18-01-33; telex 22315; fax 31-20-07-33; f. 1889; fleet of bulk carriers and product tankers totalling 262,000 grt; liner services USA–West Africa; Man. Dir ERIK BEHN.

Association

Danmarks Rederiforening (Danish Shipowners' Assen): Amaliegade 33, 1256 Copenhagen K; tel. 33-11-40-88; telex 16492; fax 33-11-62-10; f. 1884; representing 4,156,000 grt (July 1990); Chair. of the Board IB KRUSE; Man. Dir KNUD PONTOPPIDAN.

CIVIL AVIATION

The International Airport is about 10 km from the centre of Copenhagen. Domestic airports include Roskilde in Zealand, Tirstrup at Århus, Ålborg, Billund, Esbjerg, Karup, Skrydstrup, Stauning, Sønderborg and Thisted in Jutland, Rønne in Bornholm and Odense in Funen.

Statens Luftfartsvæsen (Civil Aviation Administration): Luftfartshuset, POB 744, 2450 Copenhagen SV; tel. 36-44-48-48; telex 27096; fax 36-44-03-03; Dir-Gen. V. K. H. EGGERS.

Det Danske Luftfartselskab A/S—DDL (Danish Airlines): Industriens Hus, H. C. Andersens Blvd 18, 1553 Copenhagen V; tel. 33-14-13-33; fax 33-14-28-28; f. 1918; 50% govt-owned; Danish parent company of the designated national carrier, Scandinavian Airline Systems—SAS (see under Sweden), SAS Commuter and SCAN-AIR; Chair. TAGE ANDERSEN; Man. Dir FREDE AHLGREEN ERIKSEN.

National Airlines

Cimber Air Denmark: Sønderborg Airport, 6400 Sønderborg; tel. 74-42-22-77; telex 52315; fax 74-42-65-11; f. 1950; operates own service between Copenhagen, Sønderborg, Esbjerg, Montpellier (France) and Humberside (United Kingdom); operates services between Copenhagen and Sønderborg for Danair; operates charter flights and total route systems for other companies; Chair. I. L. NIELSEN; Man. Dir H. I. NIELSEN; fleet of 2 Aérospatiale 262, 4 ATR-42-300, 2 Fokker F28-3000, 1 Beech King Air 200.

Conair A/S (Consolidated Aircraft Corporation): Hangar 276, Copenhagen Airport, 2791 Dragør; tel. 31-53-17-00; telex 31423; fax 31-53-12-20; f. 1964; operates charter and inclusive-tour flights to Europe and North and West Africa for Spies Travel Organization, which owns the airline; Chair. JANNI SPIES; Man. Dir VERNER MØLLER; fleet of 3 Airbus A300 B4-120.

Danair A/S: Kastruplundgade 13, 2770 Kastrup; tel. 31-51-50-55; fax 31-51-55-70; f. 1971; owned by SAS (see under Sweden—57%), Mærsk Air (38%) and Cimber Air (5%); f. 1971; operates domestic services between Copenhagen and Ålborg, Billund, Esbjerg, Karup, Odense, Rønne, Skrydstrup, Sønderborg, Thisted, Århus and the Faeroe Islands; Chair. KURT THYREGOD; Man. Dir GUNNAR TIETZ; leased fleet of MD 80, DC-9, Fokker F27 (SAS), Shorts 360 (Mærsk), ATR-42 (Cimber).

Mærsk Air: Copenhagen Airport South, 2791 Dragør; tel. 31-53-44-44; telex 31125; fax 31-53-35-50; f. 1969; provides charter flights for Scandinavian tour operators, operates domestic services between Copenhagen and Billund, Esbjerg, Odense, Rønne, Skrydstrup, Vagar and the Faeroe Islands, and international flights to Brussels (Belgium), Stockholm (Sweden), Amsterdam (The Netherlands), Cologne and Bonn (Germany), Gatwick (United Kingdom) and Stavanger (Norway); owned by Møller Group (see under Shipping); subsidiaries: Mærsk Helicopters, Mærsk Air Cargo; interests in several British cos; Pres. BJARNE HANSEN; Exec. Vice-Pres. OLE DIETZ; fleet of 5 Boeing 737-200, 10 737-300, 2 Bell 212, 2 Aérospatiale Super Puma, 8 Fokker 50, 1 Hawker Siddeley 125-700B, 1 Shorts SD3-60.

Muk Air: Anekæret 39, 3520 Farum; tel. 42-95-23-33; telex 37697; fax 42-95-26-06; f. 1979; operates scheduled services between Odense and Ålborg, and Oslo (Norway); fmrly air taxi operator; Man. Capt. KNUT LINDAU; fleet of 3 Bandeirante, 2 Beech 99, 1 Fairchild F-27J, 1 Cessna 402C, 1 Navajo.

DENMARK

Star Air: Røbenhavns Lufthavn Syd, 2791 Dragør; fax 31-53-25-88; f. 1987; operates cargo services in Europe; fleet of 4 Fokker F27-600.

Sterling Airways: Hangar 144, Copenhagen Airport, 2791 Dragør; tel. 31-53-53-53; telex 31231; fax 31-53-13-91; f. 1962; owned by Tjæreborg International Holdings A/S, operates inclusive-tour flights to Europe, North Africa, North America and the Indian Ocean; subsidiaries in Norway and Sweden; Chair. NIELS HEERING; Pres. EINAR LUNDT; fleet of 10 Boeing 727-200, 1 DC-8-63, 6 Caravelle 10B.

Tourism

Tourists visit Denmark for the peaceful charm of its countryside and old towns, or the sophistication of Copenhagen. There were an estimated 8,638,100 overnight stays by foreign visitors (in hotels and at camping sites) in 1989. Revenue from tourism totalled 16,898m. kroner in that year.

Danmarks Turistråd (Tourist Board): Vesterbrogade 6D, 1620 Copenhagen V; tel. 33-11-14-15; telex 27586; fax 33-91-14-16; Information Bureau, H. C. Andersens Blvd 22, 1553 Copenhagen V; tel. 33-11-13-25; telex 27586; f. 1967; Dir JØRGEN BERTELSEN.

Atomic Energy

Danish Energy Agency: Landemærket 11, 1119 Copenhagen K; tel. 33-92-67-00; telex 22450; f. 1976; under Ministry of Industry and Energy; Dir HANS VON BÜLOW.

Risø National Laboratory: Forskningscenter Risø, POB 49, 4000 Roskilde; tel. 42-37-12-12; telex 43116; fax 42-36-06-09; f. 1958; environmental and energy research centre; Man. Dir H. BJERRUM MØLLER; Technical Dir K. SINGER.

DANISH EXTERNAL TERRITORIES

THE FAEROE ISLANDS

Introductory Survey

Location, Climate, Language, Religion, Flag, Capital

The Faeroe (Faroe) Islands are a group of 18 islands (of which 17 are inhabited) in the Atlantic Ocean, between Scotland and Iceland. The main island is Streymoy, where more than one-third of the population resides. The climate is mild in winter and cool in summer, with a mean temperature of 7°C (45°F). Most of the inhabitants profess Christianity: the majority of Faeroese belong to the Evangelical Lutheran Church of Denmark. The principal language is Faeroese, but Danish is a compulsory subject in all schools. The flag (proportions 22 by 16) displays a red cross, bordered with blue, on a white background, the upright of the cross being to the left of centre. The capital is Tórshavn, which is situated on Streymoy.

History and Government

The Faeroe Islands have been under Danish administration since Queen Margrethe I of Denmark inherited Norway in 1380. The islands were occupied by the United Kingdom while Denmark was under German occupation during the Second World War, but they were restored to Danish control immediately after the war. The Home Rule Act of 1948 gave the Faeroese control over all their internal affairs. There is a local parliament (the Løgting), but the Danish Folketing, to which the Faeroese send two members, is responsible for defence and foreign policy, constitutional matters and the judicial and monetary systems. The Faeroes control fishing resources within their territorial waters, but jurisdiction over resources beneath the bed of the sea in the area adjacent to the islands has yet to be settled with Copenhagen. Until the dispute is resolved, and until Faeroese fears of being overwhelmed by an 'oil culture' can be allayed, exploration for petroleum cannot begin. Any further independence from Denmark is unlikely before the size of the Danish subsidy is reduced. The Faeroe Islands did not join the EEC with Denmark in 1973.

The centre-left coalition Government of the Social Democratic Party (SDP), Republicans and the People's Party, formed in 1978, collapsed in 1980 over a plan, opposed by the conservative People's Party, to extend through the winter months a government-owned ferry service linking the islands with Denmark, Norway and Scotland. At a general election, held in November, conservative political groups slightly increased their share of the popular vote. Although there was no material change in the balance of party representation in the Løgting, the Union Party formed a centre-right coalition with the People's Party and the Home Rule Party in January 1981. A general election was held in November 1984, and in December a four-party, centre-left coalition government was formed under the premiership of Atli Dam, comprising his SDP, the Home Rule Party, the Republican Party and the Christian People's Party combined with the Progressive and Fishing Industry Party (CPP-PFIP).

Elections in 1988 demonstrated a shift to the right in the Faeroes, to the benefit of the People's Party. Its one member in the Danish Folketing increased his support in the national elections of September 1987 and May 1988. At a Faeroese general election in November 1988 the incumbent Government lost its majority, and the People's Party became the largest party in the Løgting. In January 1989, after 10 weeks of various negotiations, a centre-right coalition comprising the People's Party, the Republican Party, the Home Rule Party and the CPP-PFIP, and led by Jógvan Sundstein (Chairman of the People's Party), was formed. The coalition was committed to economic austerity and support for the fishing industry. In June 1989, however, the CPP-PFIP and the Home Rule Party withdrew their support for the Government. After three weeks of political paralysis, a new coalition was formed. Sundstein remained Løgmadur (Prime Minister), and his People's Party was supported by the Republican and Union Parties. In October 1990, however, the Republican Party and the Union Party withdrew their support for the coalition Government. As a result, an early general election was held on 17 November. The SDP obtained the largest share of the vote, winning 10 seats (an increase of three), while the People's Party, which led the outgoing coalition, won seven seats (a loss of one seat).

In international affairs, the Faeroe Islanders earned opprobium for their traditional slaughter of pilot whales for food. After foreign journalists first publicized the whaling in 1986, the manner in which it is practised has been even more strictly regulated. Whale meat, however, accounted for one-half of the meat produced, and one-quarter of the meat eaten, in 1986. Responsibility for foreign policy lies in Copenhagen, but in 1983 the Løgting unanimously declared the Faeroe Islands a 'nuclear-free zone', and in 1987, as a consequence of this policy, requested the Danish Government to curtail a US naval visit. There have also been several declarations of 'non-aligned' status, notwithstanding NATO membership as part of the Kingdom of Denmark. When the People's Party changed its policy, however, to advocate closer co-operation with the NATO alliance, the party ended political unanimity on the issue and made gains in the elections of 1987 and 1988.

Economic Affairs

In 1987, according to estimates by the World Bank, gross national product (GNP), measured at average 1985–87 prices, was US $686m., equivalent to $14,600 per head. Between 1973 and 1986, it was estimated, GNP increased, in real terms, at an average rate of 4.3% per year, with real GNP per head rising by 3.2% annually. The average annual rate of population growth between 1980 and 1989 was 1.1%.

Agriculture and fishing contributed 16.8% of gross domestic product (GDP) in 1988. Agriculture was formerly the main activity of the islanders, particularly sheep farming (Faeroe Islands means Sheep Islands). In 1989 there were an estimated 73,000 sheep on the islands, but local agriculture supplies only about one-third of the total consumption of lamb and mutton. Potatoes (about 1,000 metric tons a year being grown) and other vegetables are the main crops. Only about 6% of the land surface is cultivated.

Fishing is the dominant industry. Fishing and fish-processing accounted for 27% of GDP, employed 26% of the labour force and provided over 80% of exports in 1987. Most fishing has taken place within the 200-nautical-mile (370-km) exclusive economic zone imposed around the Faeroes in 1977, and there has been massive investment in developing the fishing fleet and the processing plants on the islands. In the 1980s fish farming began to be encouraged and, by October 1987, 52 licences had been granted. In 1989 farmed fish amounted to 8,132 metric tons, an increase of 49% on the previous year, when the sector had earned 269m. kroner. The traditional hunting of whales (see Recent History) is an important source of meat.

Industry (including mining, manufacturing, construction and power) contributed 33.3% of GDP in 1988. The dominant industry is dependent on fishing, but there are other activities. Coal is mined on Suderoy, and a small textile industry exports traditional Faeroese woollens. Manufacturing alone accounted for 21.4% of GDP in 1988. The export of machinery and transport equipment accounted for some 6.6% of total exports in 1989, and consists mainly of sea-going vessels (there are three shipyards) and some specialized machinery. About 25% of the islands' energy requirements are provided by a hydroelectric power plant. There are hopes of discovering petroleum reserves on or around the islands.

In 1989 the Faeroe Islands recorded a visible trade deficit of 8.3m. kroner, and a deficit of 819m. kroner on the current account of the balance of payments. Denmark remains the Faeroes' principal trading partner, supplying 44.4% of imports and receiving 16.2% of exports in 1989. Other important markets for Faeroese exports were the United Kingdom (13.6%), the Federal Republic of Germany (13.4%) and the USA (9.8%). The principal imports are machinery and transport equipment. In 1940 the Faeroese krona was introduced. It must, however, always be freely interchangeable with the Danish krone at the rate of 1:1 (for exchange rate, see under Denmark).

Danish subsidies are an important source of income to the islands, and accounted for about 16% of GDP in 1986. In 1989 including the central government grant of 730.3m. kroner as revenue, the Faeroese Government recorded a budget surplus of 603.5m. kroner. In 1986 the net external debt was equivalent to some 67% of GDP but, since it was owed primarily in Denmark, it was not a foreign currency debt. In 1989 it was suggested that certain Japanese institutions might take over as creditors of the Faeroese debt. The average annual rate of inflation was 4.5% in 1986. There is an acute labour shortage in the Faeroes and, in 1987, immigrant workers formed 5% of the labour force.

The Faeroe Islands, as part of the Kingdom of Denmark, is a member of the UN and NATO. Membership of more specifically economic organizations is not dictated by Denmark. The Faeroe Islands did not join the EEC with Denmark in 1973, but did secure

DANISH EXTERNAL TERRITORIES

The Faeroe Islands

favourable terms of trade with Community members and special concessions in Denmark and the United Kingdom. Other nations maintained the Faeroes' EFTA trading concessions. (Denmark had joined EFTA in 1959, but the Faeroes were not included until 1967, and membership lapsed in 1973.) In international fisheries organizations, where Denmark is represented by the EEC, the Kingdom maintains separate membership in respect of the Faeroe Islands (and Greenland). The Faeroe Islands is also a member of the Nordic Council (see p. 179).

The Faeroese economy is vulnerable to factors beyond its control, particularly changes in international prices. Fluctuations in the fishing catch can have a serious effect, but mainly on income rather than on employment. The authorities attempt to minimize this vulnerability by strict control of the fisheries, the encouragement of fish farming and the diversification of trade and industry. Some tourism is being developed. The large Danish subsidies also protect the economy, and have contributed to a high standard of living in the islands.

Education and Social Welfare

The education system is similar to that of Denmark, except that Faeroese is the language of instruction. Danish is, however, a compulsory subject in all schools. The Faeroese Academy was upgraded to the University of the Faeroe Islands in May 1990.

In 1989 government medical services included three hospitals, with a total of 349 beds.

In 1989 government expenditure on social welfare represented 25.3% of total budget spending, while education received a further 11.4% of the total.

Statistical Survey

Sources: Føroya Landsstýri (Faeroese Government), Tinganes, 3800 Tórshavn, Faeroe Islands; *Statistisk årbog*, Danmarks Statistik, Sejrøgade 11, 2100 Copenhagen Ø.

AREA AND POPULATION

Area: 1,398.9 sq km (540.1 sq miles).

Population: 47,840 (males 24,961, females 22,879) at census of 31 December 1989.

Density (1989): 34.20 per sq km.

Principal Town: Tórshavn (capital), estimated population 16,256 in 1989.

Births and Deaths (1989): Registered live births 911 (birth rate 19.0 per 1,000); Deaths 369 (death rate 7.7 per 1,000) (Source: UN, *Population and Vital Statistics Report*).

Labour Force (census of 22 September 1977): Males 12,808; Females 4,777; Total 17,585.

AGRICULTURE, ETC.

Livestock (FAO estimates, '000 head, year ending September 1989): Cattle 2; Sheep 73 (Source: FAO, *Production Yearbook*).

Fishing ('000 metric tons, live weight, 1988): Salmon and trout 5.5, Atlantic cod 49.7, Haddock 12.6, Saithe (Pollock) 45.9, Norway pout 28.6, Blue whiting (Poutassou) 77.6, Golden redfish 14.0, Sandeels (Sandlances) 15.5, Capelin 48.5, Other fishes 35.7, Northern prawn 14.3, Other crustaceans and molluscs 8.9; total catch 356.8. Figures include quantities landed by Faeroes fishing craft in foreign ports but exclude quantities landed by foreign fishing craft in Faeroes ports. Number of cetaceans caught (1988): 1,600 (Source: FAO, *Yearbook of Fishery Statistics*).

FINANCE

Government Accounts ('000 kroner, 1989): Revenue 3,099,300; Danish state subsidy 730,300; Expenditure 3,226,100.

Cost of Living (Consumer Price Index; base: 1987 = 100): *1988:* Food 106; Fuel and power 99.8; Clothing 106.6; Rent 107.5; All items 105.2; *1989:* Food 114.4; Fuel and power 115.9; Clothing 109.7; Rent 112.3; All items 112.8.

Gross Domestic Product by Economic Activity (million kroner at current factor cost, 1988): Agriculture, fishing, etc. 986; Mining and quarrying 8; Manufacturing 1,254; Electricity, gas and water 161; Construction 530; Trade, restaurants and hotels 936; Transport, storage and communications 523; Community, social and personal services 217; Business services, etc. 238; Non-market services 1,142; *Less* imputed bank service charges 522; Gross domestic product at factor cost 5,865.

EXTERNAL TRADE

Principal Commodities (million kroner, 1989): *Imports c.i.f.:* Food and live animals 368.1; Mineral fuels, lubricants, etc. 251.2 (Petroleum products 250.8); Chemicals and related products 152.8; Basic manufactures 405.1; Machinery and transport equipment 741.7 (Machinery for special industries 70.3, General industrial machinery 83.9, Electric machinery, apparatus, etc. 90.1, Road vehicles and parts 126.8); Miscellaneous manufactured articles 339.2; Total (incl. others) 2,514.1. *Exports f.o.b.:* Food and live animals 2,264.2; Animal feeding-stuff (excl. cereals) 98.1; Crude materials 59.9; Machinery and transport equipment 165.0; Total (incl. others) 2,505.8.

Principal Trading Partners (million kroner, 1989): *Imports c.i.f.:* Denmark 1,115.7; Fed. Repub. of Germany 147.4; Japan 78.2; Norway 409.4; Sweden 146.4; United Kingdom 94.0; Total (incl. others) 2,514.1. *Exports f.o.b.:* Denmark 406.7; France (incl. Monaco) 230.8; Fed. Repub. of Germany 335.3; Greenland 43.5; Italy 176.1; Norway 86.7; Spain 182.7; Sweden 79.6; United Kingdom 341.9; USA 244.9; Total (incl. others) 2,505.8.

TRANSPORT

Road Traffic (registered vehicles, 1989): Private motor cars 13,986; Goods vehicles 3,551; Buses 118; Coaches 233; Trailers 773; Motor cycles 113.

Shipping (1989): Merchant fleet (displacement) 99,415 gross registered tons (fishing vessels 67,537 grt); International sea-borne freight traffic ('000 metric tons): Goods loaded 255.1, Goods unloaded 553.6 (excluding landings of raw fish).

Directory

The Government

The legislative body is the Løgting (Lagting in Danish) which consists of 32 members, elected on a basis of proportional representation in seven constituencies, with up to five supplementary seats dependent upon the numbers of people voting. All Faeroese over the age of 18 years have the right to vote. Based on the strength of the parties in the Løgting, a Government of six members, the Landsstýri, is formed. This is the administrative body in certain spheres, chiefly relating to Faeroese economic affairs. The Løgmaður (Prime Minister) has to ratify all Løgting laws. Power is decentralized and there are about 50 local authorities. The Ríkisumboðsmaður, or High Commissioner, represents the Danish Government, and has the right to address the Løgting and to advise on joint affairs. All Danish legislation must be submitted to the Landsstýri before becoming law in the Faeroe Islands.

Ríkisumboðsmaður: BENT KLINTE.

LANDSSTÝRI
(February 1991)

Prime Minister (Løgmaður): ATLI P. DAM (Social Democratic Party).

Deputy Prime Minister and Minister of Finance: JÓGVAN SUNDSTEIN (People's Party).

Minister of Fisheries: JOHN PETERSEN (People's Party).

Minister of Industry and Commerce: THOMAS ARABO (Social Democratic Party).

Minister of Education and Justice: MARITA PETERSEN (Social Democratic Party).

Minister of Transport and Energy: SVEND AAGE ELLEFSEN (People's Party).

Minister of Health and Social Services: JÓANNES EIDESGAARD (Social Democratic Party).

Government Offices

Rigsombudsmanden (High Commission): Amtmansbrekkan 4, 110 Tórshavn; tel. 11040; fax 10864.

Føroya Landsstýri (Faeroese Government): POB 64, 110 Tórshavn; tel. 11080; telex 81310; fax 14942.

Føroya Tollstova (Faeroese Customs Authority): Vágsbotnur 11, POB 3, 110 Tórshavn; tel. 10260; telex 81310; fax 10588.

Fiskivinnuumsitingin (Fisheries Administration): POB 87, 110 Tórshavn; tel. 11080; telex 81310; fax 14942.

LØGTING

The Løgting has 32 members, elected by universal adult suffrage.

Speaker: JØRGEN THOMSEN (Social Democratic Party).

DANISH EXTERNAL TERRITORIES

Election, 17 November 1990

	Votes	Seats
Javnaðarflokkurin (Social Democratic Party)	7,805	10
Fólkaflokkurin (People's Party)	6,234	7
Sambandsflokkurin (Union Party)	5,367	6
Tjóveldisflokkurin (Republican Party)	4,178	4
Sjálvstýrisflokkurin (Home Rule Party)	2,489	3
Kristiligi fólkaflokkurin, Føroya framburds-og Fiskivinnuflokkurin (Christian People's Party, Progressive and Fishing Industry Party)	1,681	2
Socialistiski Loysingarflokkurin (Socialist Independence Party)	666	—

Political Organizations

The address of each of the following organizations is Løgtingið, Áarvegut, 110 Tórshavn; tel. 10850.

Fólkaflokkurin (People's Party): f. 1940; conservative-liberal party, favours free enterprise and wider political and economic autonomy for the Faeroes within the Kingdom of Denmark; Chair. ANFINN KALLSBERG.

Javnaðarflokkurin (Social Democratic Party—SDP): f. 1928; Chair. ATLI P. DAM.

Kristiligi fólkaflokkurin, Føroya framburds- og Fiskivinnuflokkurin (The Christian People's Party, Progressive and Fishing Industry Party—CPP-PFIP): f. 1984; non-socialist, social, anti-communist centre party; Chair. TORDUR NICLASEN.

Sambandsflokkurin (Union Party): f. 1906; favours the maintenance of close relations between the Faeroes and the Kingdom of Denmark; conservative in internal affairs; Chair. EDMUND JOENSEN.

Sjálvstýrisflokkurin (Home Rule Party): f. 1906; social-liberal party advocating eventual political independence for the Faeroes within the Kingdom of Denmark; Chair. LASSI KLEIN.

Socialistiski Loysingarflokkurin (Socialist Independence Party).

Tjóveldisflokkurin (Republican Party): f. 1948; left-wing party, advocates the secession of the Faeroes from Denmark; Chair. FINNBOGI ISAKSON.

Religion

CHRISTIANITY

The Faeroes Church comes under the jurisdiction of the Bishop of Copenhagen (Evangelical Lutheran Church of Denmark), who exercises control through a suffragan bishop. The largest independent group is the 'Plymouth Brethren'. There is also a small Roman Catholic community.

Evangelical Lutheran Church

Biskupur Føroya (Bishop for the Faeroes): HANS J. JOENSEN, Paturssonargøta, 100 Tórshavn.

The Press

There are no daily papers in the Faeroe Islands.

Dagblaðið: POB 23, 110 Tórshavn; tel. 17600; fax 17708; 3 a week; People's Party; circ. 5,000.

Dimmalætting: Smyrilsvegur, 110 Tórshavn; tel. 11212; telex 81222; fax 10941; 3 a week; Union Party; circ. 13,000.

Eysturoyggin: 110 Tórshavn; circ. 800.

Fríu Føroyar: Argjavegur 26, POB 2055, 165 Argir; tel. 16444; fax 18813; f. 1983; weekly; independent; socialist; circ. 1,300.

Nordlýsið: á Hædd, 700 Klaksvík; tel. 56285; fax 56498; weekly; circ. 1,200.

Oyggjatíðindi: R. C. Effersøesgøta 7, 110 Tórshavn; tel. 14411; fax 16410; 2 a week; circ. 5,000.

Tíðindablaðið Sosialurin: POB 76, 110 Tórshavn; tel. 11820; fax 14720; f. 1927; 5 a week; Editor TORFINN SMITH; Social Democratic Party; circ. 6,400.

Tingakrossur: Dr Jacobsengøta 16, POB 193, 110 Tórshavn; tel. 15474; fax 14786; f. 1901; 2 a week; Home Rule Party; circ. 2,500.

14 September: POB 2079, 165 Argir; tel. 14412; fax 14469; 2 a week; Republican Party; circ. 3,800.

The Faeroe Islands

NEWS AGENCY

Faeroe Press Agency: P/f Salvará, Tjarnardeild 12, Tórshavn; f. 1980; covers Ritzaus Bureau of Copenhagen, Danmarks Radio and Morgunblaðið of Reykjavík, Iceland; Man. JÓGVAN ARGE.

Publisher

Útvarp Føroya: Norðari Ringvegur, POB 328, 110 Tórshavn; tel. 16568; telex 81226; fax 10471; f. 1957; fiction and periodicals; Man. NIELS JUEL ARGE.

Radio and Television

In 1987 there were an estimated 11,000 television receivers, and 18,000 radio receivers in use.

Sjónvarp Føroya (Faeroese Television): M. A. Winthersgøta, POB 21, 110 Tórshavn; tel. 17780; telex 81391; fax 11345; f. 1982; Gen. Man. J. A. SKAALE.

Útvarp Føroya (Faeroese Broadcasting Corporation): Norðari Ringevur, POB 328, 110 Tórshavn; tel. 16566; telex 81226; fax 10471; f. 1957; Man. JÓGVAN JESPERSEN.

Finance

BANKS

(cap. = capital; res = reserves; dep. = deposits; m. = million; amounts in kroner; brs = branches)

Føroya Banki P/f: Niels Finsensgøta 15, POB 14, 110 Tórshavn; tel. 11350; telex 81227; fax 15850; f. 1906; cap. 137.5m., res 367.9m., dep. 4,147.3m., total assets 6,253m. (Dec. 1989); Chair. POUL JOHS. JOHANSEN; Gen. Mans HANS-JÓRGEN LAURSEN, JOHAN SIMONSEN, NIELS JOEL NATTESTAD; 32 brs.

Føroya Sparikassi (Faeroese Savings Bank): Sverrisgøta 3, POB 34, 110 Tórshavn; tel. 14800; telex 81318; fax 19948; f. 1832.

Fossbankin: Niels Finsensgøta 37, POB 1120, 110 Tórshavn; tel. 12400; telex 81306; fax 17440; f. 1986; cap. 30m., res. 10m., dep. 238m. (Dec. 1987); Man. HJARNAR DJURHUUS; Gen. Man. HELGI FOSSADAL.

Landsbanki Føroya: Yviri við Strond 29, 100 Tórshavn; tel. 18305; fax 18537.

Norðoya Sparikassi: Biskopsstøðgøta, 700 Klaksvik; tel. 56366; fax 56761.

Sjóvinnubankin P/F (Fisheries Bank): J. Húsag. 3, POB 48, 110 Tórshavn; tel. 14900; telex 81229; fax 16950; f. 1932; cap. 98m., res 310m., dep. 3,494.7m. (Dec. 1989); Chair. BIRGIR DANIELSEN; Mans STEINGRIM NIELSEN, REGIN OLSEN; 32 brs.

INSURANCE

Tryggingarsambandið Føroyar: Kongabrúgvin, POB 329, 110 Tórshavn; tel. 14590; telex 81253; fax 15590; marine, fire, accident and life; only insurance co. in islands.

Trade and Industry

ASSOCIATIONS

L/F Føroya Fiskasøla (Faeroe Seafood): POB 68, 110 Tórshavn; tel. 14960; telex 81224; fax 12520; f. 1948; union of co-operative fish producers; markets approx. 75% of fish product exports; Chair. BJARTI MOHR.

Føroya Reiðarafelag (Faeroe Fishing Vessel-Owners' Association): R.C. Effersøesgøta, POB 179, 110 Tórshavn; tel. 11864; telex 81388; fax 17278.

TRADE UNION

Føroya Arbeiðarafelag (Faeroese Labour Organization): Tjarndeild 5, POB 56, 110 Tórshavn; tel. 12101; telex 82416; fax 15374.

Transport

There are about 433 km of roads in the Faeroe Islands. The main harbour is at Tórshavn; the other ports are at Fuglafjordur,

DANISH EXTERNAL TERRITORIES   *The Faeroe Islands, Greenland*

Klaksvík, Skálafjorður, Tvøroyri, Vágur and Vestmanna. Between mid-May and mid-September, a summer roll-on, roll-off ferry service links the Faeroe Islands with Iceland, Shetland (United Kingdom), Denmark and Norway.

There is an airport on Vágar. Icelandair operates services to Bergen and Copenhagen, Danair to Copenhagen, and Icelandair operates a service between Reykjavík (Iceland) and Glasgow (United Kingdom) via the Faeroes. The Danish and Faeroese authorities administer aviation jointly.

Atlantic Airways: Vága Floghavn, 380 Sørvágur; tel. 33344; telex 82440; fax 33380; f. 1987; scheduled passenger services to Copenhagen; fleet of 1 BAe 146-200.

Tourism

Ferðaráð Føroya—Turistráð Færøernes (Faeroese Tourist Board): Reyngøta 17, 110 Tórshavn; tel. 16055; fax 10858; f. 1985; Man. JAKUP VEYHE.

GREENLAND

Introductory Survey

Location, Climate, Language, Religion, Flag, Capital

Greenland (Kalaallit Nunaat) is the world's largest island, with a total area of 2,175,600 sq km, and lies in the North Atlantic Ocean, east of Canada. Most of it is permanently covered by ice, but 341,700 sq km of coastland are habitable. Greenlandic, an Inuit (Eskimo) language, and Danish are the official languages. The majority of the population profess Christianity and belong mainly to the Evangelical Lutheran Church of Denmark. There are also small communities of other Protestant groups and of Roman Catholics. The flag (proportions 3 by 2) consists of two equal horizontal stripes (white above red) on which is superimposed a representation of the rising sun (a disc divided horizontally, red above white) to the left of centre. Nuuk (Godthåb) is the capital.

Recent History

Greenland first came under Danish rule in 1380. In the revision of the Danish Constitution in 1953, Greenland became part of the Kingdom and acquired the representation of two members in the Danish Folketing. In October 1972 the Greenlanders voted by 9,658 to 3,990 against joining the European Community but, as part of Denmark, were bound by the Danish decision to join. Resentment of Danish domination of the economy, education and the professions continued, taking expression in 1977 when the nationalist Siumut movement formed a left-wing party. In 1975 the Minister for Greenland appointed a commission to devise terms for Greenland home rule, and its proposals were approved by 73.1% to 26.9% in a referendum among the Greenland electorate in January 1979. The Siumut, led by a Lutheran pastor, Jonathan Motzfeldt, secured 13 seats in the 21-member Landsting (the local legislature) at a general election in April, and a five-member Landsstyre, with Motzfeldt as Prime Minister, took office in May. Since 1979 the island has been gradually assuming full administration of its internal affairs.

In February 1982 a referendum was held to decide Greenland's continued membership of the European Community. This resulted in a 53% majority in favour of withdrawal. Negotiations were begun in May 1982, with the Danish Government acting on Greenland's behalf, and were concluded in March 1984 (with effect from 1 February 1985): Greenland was accorded the status of an overseas territory in association with the Community, with preferential access to EEC markets.

At the April 1983 general election to the Landsting (enlarged, by measures adopted in 1982, to between 23 and 26 seats, depending on the proportion of votes cast), the Siumut and Atassut parties won 12 seats each, while the Inuit Ataqatigiit (IA) won two seats. The Siumut party once again formed a government, led by Motzfeldt, dependent on the support of the IA members in the Landsting: this support was withdrawn in March 1984, when the IA members voted against the terms of withdrawal from the European Community, and Motzfeldt resigned. In the ensuing general election, held in June, the Siumut and Atassut parties won 11 seats each while the IA won three. Motzfeldt once again formed a coalition government, comprising the Siumut party and the IA.

In March 1987 the coalition Government collapsed, following a dispute between the Siumut party and the IA over policy towards the modernization of the US radar facility at Thule, which was claimed by the IA to be in breach of the 1972 US-Soviet Anti-Ballistic Missile Treaty. A general election was held in May. The Siumut party lost its status as the largest party, obtaining 39.8% of the total votes, but the proportion of votes won by the Atassut party also declined, to 40.1%. Each party retained 11 seats in the Landsting; the IA won three seats, and the remaining seat was won by the newly-formed Issittup-partii-a, which was demanding the privatization of the trawler fleet. Motzfeldt eventually formed a new coalition government with the IA, although his candidature for head of government was challenged by left-wing members of the Siumut, after he had attempted to negotiate a coalition with the Atassut party. In May 1988, in elections to the Danish Folketing, Siumut once more became the party winning the most votes. In June the coalition between Siumut and the IA collapsed, and Motzfeldt formed a new Siumut government, with support from the Atassut party. In the municipal elections of April 1989, Siumut's share of the votes cast increased to 41.8%, while support for Atassut fell to only 31.3%. In December 1990, when the Atassut party withdrew its support for the Siumut administration (following allegations that government ministers had misused public funds), Motzfeldt called an early general election for 6 March 1991.

In February 1988 a massive vaccination programme attempted to control a virulent outbreak of canine distemper among the island's estimated 30,000 husky sledge-dogs. Despite this, most of the dogs in the northern area of Thule perished. The husky sledge-dogs are important to the economy of Greenland, with one-fifth of the local Inuit (Eskimo) population dependent on them for hunting. This activity, however, probably accounts for the spread of the canine distemper virus to the seal population of the North Sea, with the devastating results apparent later in 1988 (see chapter on Denmark).

Denmark remains responsible for Greenland's foreign relations. Greenland does have separate representation on the Nordic Council (see p. 179), and is a member of the Inuit Circumpolar Conference (see p. 237). Denmark, a member of NATO, retains its responsibility for defence, and Danish-American military co-operation in Greenland began in 1951. Under a 1981 agreement on the defence of Greenland, two US radar bases were established on Greenland, at Thule and at Kangerlussuaq (Søndre Strømfjord). An agreement between the USA and Denmark for the reduction of the bases from 325,000 ha to 160,000 ha took effect from 1 October 1986, and the land, thus becoming available, was returned to the Inuit.

In June 1980 the Danish Government declared an economic zone extending 200 nautical miles (370 km) off the east coast of Greenland. This, however, caused a dispute with Norway over territorial waters, owing to the existence of the small Norwegian island of Jan Mayen, 460 km off the east coast of Greenland. In 1988 Denmark requested the International Court of Justice to arbitrate on the issue of conflicting economic zones.

Government

Greenland is part of the Kingdom of Denmark, and the Danish Government, which remains responsible for foreign affairs, defence and justice, is represented by the Rigsombudsmand, or High Commissioner, in Nuuk (Godthåb). Most functions of government are administered by the 'Home Rule Government', the Landsstyre. The formation of this executive is dependent upon support in the local legislature, the Landsting. The Landsting has 27 members elected for a maximum term of four years, on a basis of proportional representation. Greenland also elects two members to the Danish Folketing.

Defence

The Danish Government, which is responsible for Greenland's defence, co-ordinates military activities through its Greenland Command. The Greenland Command, which also undertakes fisheries control and sea rescues, is based at the Grønnedal naval base, in south-west Greenland. Greenlanders are not liable for military service. As part of the Kingdom of Denmark, Greenland belongs to NATO. The USA operates two air bases, at Pituffik in Thule and at Kangerlussuaq (Søndre Strømfjord). The Danish Government spent 397m. kroner (14.8% of total central government expenditure on Greenland) on defence in 1989, of which 172m. kroner was spent on the Fisheries Inspectorate.

DANISH EXTERNAL TERRITORIES

Greenland

Economic Affairs

In 1986, according to estimates by the World Bank, Greenland's gross national product (GNP), measured at average 1984–86 prices, was US $465m., equivalent to US $8,780 per head. Between 1973 and 1986, it was estimated, GNP increased, in real terms, at an average annual rate of only 0.5%, with real GNP per head declining by 0.2% per year. In 1986, however, GNP per head rose by about 8% in real terms. The population increased at an average annual rate of 1.0% between 1980 and 1988.

Fishing, hunting and agriculture constitute the main sector of the economy. Fishing dominates the commercial economy, as well as being important to the traditional way of life. In 1989 the fishing industry accounted for 77.9% of Greenland's total export revenue, earning some 2,375.6m. kroner. It was estimated that the industry, including the processing of the catch, employed about one-sixth of the paid labour force in the late 1980s. The traditional occupation of the Greenlanders, however, is seal-hunting, which remains important in the north. Seal-skins, and also fox-skins, are sold both commercially and to augment the income of rural families. The only feasible agricultural activity in the harsh climate is livestock-rearing, and only sheep-farming has proved to be of any commercial significance. Climatic difficulties caused a reduction in the number of sheep-farms from 153 in 1970 to 69 in 1985. There are also herds of domesticated reindeer.

Industry (including mining, manufacturing, construction and public works) employed some 25% of those in paid employment in March 1987. Mining, which is controlled jointly by the central and Home Rule Governments, employed less than 1% of the labour force, but nevertheless earned 565.1m. kroner, or 18.5% of total export revenue, in 1989. A Swedish company extracted lead, zinc and some silver at the important mine at Marmorilik in the northwest. The mine was closed, however, in 1990. Greenland does have other mineral deposits which, it is hoped, can be exploited, including significant reserves of gold found in east Greenland in 1986.

Manufacturing is mainly dependent upon the fishing industry, but there is also a printing press, a brewery and some small shipyards. Construction work is an important activity. Tanneries and work-shops have been established to process seal-skins, and to manufacture finished goods. It is hoped that Greenland will have ample resources of electricity for such activities by exploiting water power (meltwater from the ice-cap and glaciers). All mineral fuels are imported, as exploration for petroleum has not, hitherto, met with success. Nevertheless, mineral fuels accounted for less than 10% of total imports in 1989.

In 1989 Greenland recorded a visible trade surplus of 169.6m. kroner. The principal trading partner remains Denmark, although its monopoly on trade ceased in 1950. Denmark supplied 69.2% of imports and received 25.9% of exports in 1989. Trade is still dominated by KNJ, the Royal Greenland Trade Department company, and, internally, by KNI, Greenland Trade, both of which are owned by the Home Rule Government. The principal exports are fish and fish products, and the principal imports are machinery and transport equipment.

Greenland is dependent upon large grants from the central Danish Government. In 1989 central government expenditure on Greenland amounted to 2,723m. kroner, of which 1,529m. was in the form of a direct grant to the Home Rule Government. In that year this grant constituted 42.7% of the Home Rule Government's revenue. There was a budgetary surplus of 265m. kroner. Greenland has few debts, and also receives valuable revenue from the EEC (see below) for fishing licences. The average annual rate of inflation was 5.8% in 1989. As of May 1987 there were 1,668 people seeking paid employment (compared with some 23,000 employed).

Greenland, although a part of the Kingdom of Denmark, withdrew from the EEC in 1985 (see Recent History). It remains a territory in association with the EEC, however, and has preferential access to European markets. The loss of EEC development aid has been offset by the annual payment of 26.5m. ECUs for Community member countries to retain fishing rights in Greenlandic waters. In 1988 this agreement was extended until 1995.

Greenland's economy is dominated by the fishing industry, but remains a subsistence, barter economy for a large part of the population. Migration to the towns and the rejection of a traditional life-style by many young people have eroded this latter feature, but have created new social and economic problems. Any development or progress is possible only with Danish aid, which is already fundamental to Greenlandic finances. Furthermore, even small climate changes can have dramatic effects on the precarious, but vital, primary sector of the economy. Owing to climate change in the 1960s, for example, shrimps replaced cod as the main catch on the south-west coast. Greenland therefore views environmental problems with particular concern.

Education and Social Welfare

The educational system is based on that of Denmark, except that the main language of instruction is Greenlandic. Danish is, however, quite widely used. There is a school in every settlement. In 1988/89 there were about 90 primary and lower secondary schools, with 8,943 pupils and 1,110 teachers. There is a teacher-training college in Nuuk, and a university centre opened in 1987. In 1987 expenditure on education by the Home Rule Government (including allocations to the municipalities) represented 17% of total budget spending.

There is a free health service for all residents, administered by the Danish Government, with a total of 16 hospitals and 444 beds in 1989. In 1988 there were 78 physicians working in Greenland. In 1989 the central Government spent 502m. kroner, or 18.4% of its total expenditure on Greenland, on health. In 1989 the Home Rule Government spent 516m. kroner, or 23.2% of current expenditure, on social welfare.

Statistical Survey

Sources: Ministry for Greenland, *Annual Report*; Greenland Home Rule Government—Denmark Bureau, Sjælebøderne 2, 1122 Copenhagen K; tel. 33-13-42-24; telex 15804; fax 33-32-20-24; Greenland Bureau of Statistics, Box 1025, 3900 Nuuk; tel. 23000; fax 22954.

AREA, POPULATION AND DENSITY

Area: Total 2,175,600 sq km (840,000 sq miles); Ice-free portion 341,700 sq km (131,930 sq miles).

Population: 55,558 (males 30,057; females 25,501) at census of 1 January 1990 (incl. 46,142 born in Greenland).

Density (1990): 0.026 per sq km.

Capital: Nuuk (Godthåb), population 12,217 (1990).

Births and deaths (1988): Registered live births 1,213 (birth rate 22.2 per 1,000); Deaths 434 (death rate 8.0 per 1,000).

Marriages (1988): Registered marriages 407 (marriage rate 7.5 per 1,000).

Labour Force (census of 26 October 1976): Males 14,234; Females 7,144; Total 21,378. 1987 (paid employment in May): 23,062.

AGRICULTURE, ETC.

Livestock (1989): Sheep 17,363, Reindeer 6,000 (1988).

Hunting (1989): Fox skins 358, Polar bears 42, Seals 45,038 (Ringed seal 34,640), Minke whales 90 (1987).

Fishing ('000 metric tons, live weight, 1988): Greenland halibut 8.3, Atlantic cod 54.0, Greenland cod 1.4, Other fishes 4.7, Northern prawn 65.1; Total catch 133.5 (Source: FAO, *Yearbook of Fishery Statistics*). The total excludes seals and whales, which are recorded by number rather than by weight (see Hunting, above).

MINING

Production (concentrates, '000 metric tons, 1989): Lead 36; Zinc 131.

FINANCE

Danish currency is in use

Central Government Expenditure (by Ministry, million kroner, 1989): *Current:* Prime Minister's Office 18, Traffic 71, Justice 103, Defence 233 (Fisheries Inspectorate 172), Finance 1,545 (Grant to Home Rule Govt 1,529), Energy 57, Health 463, Other 22, Total 2,512. *Capital:* Total 211 (Defence 164, Health 39). *Total:* 2,723.

Home Rule Government Accounts (million kroner, 1989): *Revenue:* Current 3,118 (Income tax 539, Import and production duties 694, Fishing licences 224, Danish central govt grant 1,529, Other 132), Capital 462, Total 3,580. *Expenditure:* Current 2,221 (Grants to municipalities 570, Education, church and culture 442, Trade and industry 374), Capital 1,094 (Industry 604, Housing 176), Total 3,315.

Cost of Living (consumer price index at 1 January; base: January 1981 = 100): 177.4 in 1988; 185.2 in 1989; 195.9 in 1990.

Gross Domestic Product (million kroner at current factor cost): 4,594 in 1986; 5,542 in 1987; 5,643 in 1988.

EXTERNAL TRADE

Principal Commodities (million kroner, 1989): *Imports c.i.f.:* Food and live animals 381.6 (Meat and meat preparations 110.0); Beverages and tobacco 148.2 (Beverages 119.8); Mineral fuels, lubricants etc. 276.7 (Petroleum products 273.1); Chemicals 132.5; Basic manufactures 489.7; Machinery and transport equipment 745.6 (Machinery 552.1, Transport equipment 193.5); Miscellaneous manufactured articles 290.1; Total (incl. others) 2,878.5. *Exports f.o.b.:* Shrimps and mussels 1,819.6; Cod 449.6; Other fish products 106.4; Crude materials (inedible) except fuels 565.1 (Lead ores and concentrates 83.9, Zinc ores and concentrates 481.2); Total (incl. others) 3,048.1.

Principal Trading Partners (million kroner, 1989): *Imports c.i.f.:* Denmark 1,991.6, Federal Republic of Germany 127.9, Japan 100.4, Norway 109.2, Sweden 86.5, USA 106.7; Total (incl. others) 2,878.5. *Exports f.o.b.:* Denmark 770.5, France and Monaco 208.8, Federal Republic of Germany 413.4, Japan 585.4, Sweden 266.1, United Kingdom 404.5; Total (incl. others) 3,048.1.

TRANSPORT

Road Traffic (registered vehicles, excl. those on radio, weather or military stations, 1989): Passenger cars 1,743, Lorries and trucks 1,429, Total (incl. others) 3,547 (of which 2,667 privately owned).

Shipping (number of fishing vessels, 1989): 453 (15 govt-owned).

International Transport (passengers conveyed between Greenland and Denmark): Ship (1983) 94; Aircraft (1989) 82,753.

Directory

The Government

The legislative body is the Landsting, with 27 members elected for four years, on a basis of proportional representation. Greenlanders and Danes resident in Greenland over the age of 18 years have the right to vote. Based on the strength of the parties in the Landsting, an executive, the Landsstyre, is formed. During a transitional period the Landsstyre will gradually assume control of the administration of Greenland's internal affairs. Jurisdiction in constitutional matters, foreign affairs and defence remains with the Danish Government, the highest representative of which, in Greenland, is the Rigsombudsmand or High Commissioner.

Rigsombudsmand: TORBEN HEDE PEDERSEN.

LANDSSTYRE
(January 1991)

Prime Minister and Secretary for Administration and the Environment: JONATHAN MOTZFELDT.

Secretary for the Economy, Trade and Traffic: EMIL ABELSEN.

Secretary for Fisheries, Industry and Outlying Districts: KAJ EGEDE.

Secretary for Schools, Education and Labour: JENS LYBERTH.

Secretary for Social Affairs and Housing: MOSES OLSEN.

Government Offices

Rigsombudsmanden i Grønland (High Commissioner for Greenland): POB 1030, 3900 Nuuk; tel. 21001; telex 90604; fax 24171.

Grønlands Hjemmestyre (Greenland Home Rule Government): POB 1015, 3900 Nuuk; tel. 23000; telex 90613; fax 25002; Denmark Bureau, Sjæleboderne 2, 1122 Copenhagen K; tel. 33-13-42-24; telex 15804; fax 33-32-20-24.

Statsministeriet, Grønlandsafdelingen (Prime Minister's Office, Greenland Section): Hausergade 3, 1128 Copenhagen K; tel. 33-92-33-00; telex 27125; fax 33-93-68-15.

LANDSTING
Election, 27 May 1987

	Votes cast Number	%	Seats
Atassut (Solidarity)	10,004	40.1	11
Siumut (Forward)	9,987	39.8	11
Inuit Ataqatigiit (Inuit Brotherhood)	3,823	15.3	4
Issittup-partii-a (Polar Party)	1,119	4.5	1
Others	95	0.4	—
Total	25,068	100.0	27

Political Organizations

Atassut (Solidarity): POB 399, 3900 Nuuk; f. 1978 and became political party in 1981; supports the close links with Denmark; part of Liberal group in the Nordic Council; conservative party; Leader KONRAD STEENHOLDT.

Inuit Ataqatigiit (Inuit Brotherhood): POB 321, 3900 Nuuk, f. 1978; Socialist organization, demanding that Greenland citizenship be restricted to those of Inuit parentage; advocates Greenland's eventual independence from Denmark; Chair. ARQALUK LYNGE.

Issittup-partii-a (Polar Party): 3900 Nuuk; f. 1987; aims to reduce govt involvement in the economy and to improve the status of private tradesmen, private fishermen and other private organizations; Leader KRISTIAN NIELSEN.

Siumut (Forward): POB 357, 3900 Nuuk; tel. 22077; fax 22319; f. 1971 and became political party in 1977; aims to promote collective ownership and co-operation, and to develop greater reliance on Greenland's own resources; favours greatest possible autonomy within the Kingdom of Denmark; social democratic party; Chair. LARS EMIL JOHANSEN.

Judicial System

The island is divided into 18 court districts and these courts all use lay assessors. For most cases these lower courts are for the first instance and appeal is to the Landsret, the higher court in Nuuk, which is the only one with a professional judge. This court hears the more serious cases in the first instance and appeal in these cases is to the High Court (Østre Landsret) in Copenhagen.

Religion

CHRISTIANITY

The Greenlandic Church, of which most of the population are adherents, comes under the jurisdiction of the Landsstyre and of the Bishop of Copenhagen (Evangelical Lutheran Church of Denmark), who exercises control through a suffragan bishop.

Vicebiskoppen for Grønland (Suffragan Bishop of Greenland): KRISTIAN MØRCH, Evangelical Lutheran Church, 3900 Nuuk.

There are also small groups of other Protestant churches and of Roman Catholics.

The Press

There are no daily newspapers in Greenland.

Atuagagdliutit/Grønlandsposten: POB 39, 3900 Nuuk; fax 25483; 3 a week; Editor PHILIP LAURITZEN.

Niviarsiaq: POB 357, 3900 Nuuk; fax 22319; organ of Siumut; monthly.

Sermitsiaq: POB 150, 3900 Nuuk; weekly; Editor POUL KARUP.

Publisher

Atuakkiorfik/Det Grønlandske Forlag: Hans Egedesvej 3, POB 840, 3900 Nuuk; tel. 22122; fax 22500; f. 1956; general, children's and textbooks; public relations; Man. P. P. PÉRONARD; Chief Editor SVEND MØLLER.

Radio and Television

In 1988 there were an estimated 18,000 radio receivers and 12,000 television receivers in use.

Kalaallit Nunaata Radioa (KNR)—Grønlands Radio: POB 1007, 3900 Nuuk; tel. 21172; telex 90606; fax 24703; 5 AM stations, 38 FM stations; bilingual programmes in Greenlandic and Danish, 17 hours a day; Man. Dir HANS A. HANSEN; Admin. Dir JØRGEN MUNK.

Kujataata Radioa: POB 158, 3920 Qaqortoq; regional station in south Greenland.

Aavannaata Radioa: POB 223, 3952 Ilulissat; regional station in north Greenland.

KNR TV: POB 1007, 3900 Nuuk; tel. 25333; broadcasts from Nuuk by microwave link; distributed by cable and transmitter to most inhabited parts of Greenland; commercial; most programmes in Danish; Dir. of Television H. P. MØLLER ANDERSEN.

American Forces Radio and Television Service (AFRTS)—Air Force Arctic Broadcasting Squadron (AFABS): Station Manager, OL-A Det 1 AFABS, APO New York, NY 09121, USA; station at Søndre Strømfjord; 2 FM radio stations broadcast 24 hours a day, television transmissions 16 hours daily.

Thule Air Base Radio—50Z20: DAC POB 1117, 3970 Dundas; FM, non-commercial station; broadcasts 24 hours a day; news, music, etc.; Station Man. KURT CHRISTENSEN.

Finance

BANKS

(cap. = capital; dep. = deposits; m. = million; amounts in kroner; br. = branch)

Grønlandsbanken A/S—The Bank of Greenland: POB 1033, 3900 Nuuk; tel. 21380; telex 90611; fax 23918; f. 1967; cap. 229m., dep. 1,096m. (1989); Man. S. E. Danielsen; 6 brs.

Nuna Bank A/S: Skibshavnsvej 33, POB 1031, 3900 Nuuk; tel. 21360; telex 90610; fax 23665; f. 1985; cap. 166.8m., dep. 895.9m. (Dec. 1989), commercial bank; Gen. Man. René Nielsen; 6 brs.

Trade and Industry

Grønlandske Handel (KNJ)—Royal Greenland Trade Department: Grønlandshavnen, POB 8100, 9220 Ålborg Ø, Denmark; tel. 98-15-76-77; telex 69688; fax 98-15-99-89; f. 1774; trade monopoly ended 1950; Home Rule Govt assumed control 1985; exporter and importer; Admin. Head Niels Duysen.

Kalaallit Nieuerfiat (KNI)—Greenland Trade: POB 1008, 3900 Nuuk; fax 24431; f. 1985; statutory wholesale and retail trading co; owned by Home Rule Govt.

Transport

Domestic traffic is mainly by aircraft (fixed-wing and helicopter), boat and dog-sled. There are airports or heliports in all towns for domestic flights. Flights to Copenhagen are operated by Scandinavian Airline Systems (SAS) from Kangerlussuaq (Søndre Strømfjord), and by Greenlandair from Narsarsuaq via Iceland. There are international flights from Nuuk (Godthåb) to Frobisher Bay in Canada, and to Reykjavík, Iceland, which also receives flights from Constable Pynt, on the east coast. In summer, two Icelandic air companies operate passenger services between Iceland and Kulusuk (Ammassalik; on the east coast).

The main port is at Nuuk; there are also all-year ports at Paamiut (Frederikshåb), Maniitsoq (Sukkertoppen) and Sisimiut (Holsteinsborg). Coastal motor vessels operate passenger services along the west coast from Upernavik to Nanortalik.

Grønlandsfly A/S (Greenlandair Inc.): POB 1012, 3900 Nuuk; tel. 28888; telex 90602; fax 27288; f. 1960; air services to the 16 principal centres in Greenland, and to Copenhagen (Denmark), Reykjavík and Keflavík (Iceland) and Frobisher Bay (Northwest Territories, Canada); supply, survey, ice-reconnaissance services; subsidiaries incl. Greenlandair Charter (light helicopters) and Greenair (int. heavy helicopter charters); owned by Danish and Home Rule Govts and SAS; Chair. Lars Emil Johansen; Pres. Jan K. Rasmussen; fleet of 3 Dash 7, 3 Twin Otter, 4 Sikorsky S-61N, 5 Jet Ranger, 6 Bell-212, 3 Aérospatiale AS350B1, 1 Beechcraft King Air E-90, 1 Piper Super Cub, 1 Cessna 172 Skyhawk.

DJIBOUTI

Introductory Survey

Location, Climate, Language, Religion, Flag, Capital

The Republic of Djibouti is in the Horn of Africa, at the southern entrance to the Red Sea. It is bounded on the north, west and south-west by Ethiopia, and on the south-east by Somalia. The land is volcanic desert and the climate hot and arid. There are two main ethnic groups, the Issa, who are of Somali origin and comprise 50% of the population, and the Afar, who comprise 40% of the population and are of Ethiopian origin. Both groups are Muslims, and they speak related Cushitic languages. The official languages are Arabic and French. The flag has two equal horizontal stripes, of blue and green, with a white triangle, enclosing a five-pointed red star, at the hoist. The capital is Djibouti.

Recent History

French involvement in the territory began in 1859 and centred on the port of Djibouti, whose position at the entrance to the Red Sea invests the country with its strategic importance and economic potential. In 1945 the area (then known as French Somaliland) was proclaimed an overseas territory, and in 1967 was renamed the French Territory of the Afars and the Issas. The Afars and the Issas have strong connections with Ethiopia and Somalia respectively.

In the late 1950s divisions between the two communities were not marked, the Issas dominating local politics through their greater numbers in the port, but in the 1960s conflicting interests in the Horn of Africa and the French policy of favouring the minority Afar community combined to reveal tensions in the Territory. Demands for independence were growing, and the violence which had been sporadic since 1967 brought matters to a head in 1975, when Ali Aref Bourhan, Vice-President of the Council of Ministers, lost the support of 13 of his deputies. International assurances to respect the rights of a free Djibouti ushered in negotiations for its independence.

Ali Aref resigned in July 1976, and it was finally agreed that a referendum on independence and elections to a new Chamber of Deputies would be held simultaneously in May 1977, and that independence would follow in June; all parties united to form the Rassemblement populaire pour l'indépendance, which became the Rassemblement populaire pour le progrès (RPP) in 1979.

The Territory voted overwhelmingly for independence in the referendum, while in the parallel elections to the Chamber of Deputies 77% of votes cast were in support of a single list of candidates. Hassan Gouled Aptidon was elected President and on 27 June 1977 Djibouti became independent.

The most important task facing the new State was that of resolving tensions between Afar and Issa. The first administration attempted to balance all ethnic and political interests, but the Afars soon complained of discrimination and attacked the Government's pro-Somali policies; following the arrest of 600 Afars in December 1977, Ahmed Dini, the Prime Minister, and four other Afar ministers resigned. A special Commission of Afars was created, and the President agreed to its demands for more Afar representation in the Government, the civil service and the armed forces, and the release of most Afar detainees. In February 1978 a new Council of Ministers, with a careful tribal balance, was announced, and in September Barkad Gourad Hamadou, a former Minister of Health, became Prime Minister and declared a policy of 'rapid detribalization'.

In February 1981 a law providing for the election of the President by universal suffrage was passed; President Gouled, the sole candidate, was subsequently re-elected in June. Other laws, passed in October, led to the establishment of a one-party state. Legislative elections were held in May 1982, when candidates were chosen from a single list approved by the RPP, with 91% of the electorate voting. The new Government, formed in June, differed little from its predecessor. In October 1986 President Gouled announced a ministerial reshuffle, in which three newcomers joined the Government. Tension was renewed within Djibouti during the weeks preceding the presidential and legislative elections of April 1987. In March a bomb exploded at a Djibouti café used by French soldiers, killing 11 people, including eight Europeans. The attack, however, was discovered to have been carried out by a member of an extremist group opposed to the French military presence in Djibouti, and not by Djiboutian dissidents. At the presidential election, President Gouled, the sole candidate, was re-elected with the endorsement of about 90% of the registered electorate. At the same time, 65 candidates for the Chamber of Deputies, presented on a single list approved by the RPP, were elected unopposed by 87% of the electorate. In November President Gouled announced the dissolution of the Government. The new Council of Ministers was enlarged to comprise 16 members. The success of a presidential tour of remote areas of Djibouti in February 1988 was claimed to have demonstrated national unity. In the same month, however, an attack on the border town of Balho was attributed to the Mouvement populaire pour la libération de Djibouti (MPLD) and regarded as a sign of increasing clan tensions. In November the President reorganized the RPP Politburo to include three new appointees among its 15 members.

Separate treaties of friendship and co-operation were signed in 1981 with Ethiopia, Somalia, Kenya and Sudan in an effort to begin the peace process in East Africa. In August 1984 the Minister of Foreign Affairs reaffirmed Djibouti's policy of maintaining a neutral stance in the conflict between its neighbours in the Horn of Africa, and expressed his Government's willingness to act as a mediator. A joint ministerial committee has been formed between Djibouti and Ethiopia, to strengthen existing relations and co-operation between the two countries, and at the first session, held in July 1985, it was agreed to improve technical and scientific co-operation in the agricultural sector. Relations deteriorated in 1986, however, after Aden Robleh Awalleh (a former Minister of Commerce, Transport and Tourism), charged with conducting 'massive propaganda campaigns' against the RPP, fled to Ethiopia, where he was granted asylum and subsequently formed a new opposition group, the Mouvement national djiboutien pour l'instauration de la démocratie (MNDID).

Djibouti's role in promoting regional co-operation was illustrated by the creation, in February 1985, of the six-nation Inter-Governmental Authority on Drought and Development (IGADD, see p. 223); Djibouti was chosen as the site of the new organization's permanent secretariat, and President Gouled became the first chairman. At IGADD's inaugural session, in January 1986, the Heads of State of Ethiopia and Somalia met for the first time in 10 years. In April 1988, following a further meeting in Djibouti between the two leaders, Ethiopia and Somalia agreed to re-establish diplomatic relations, to withdraw troops from their common border and to exchange prisoners of war. In March 1988 President Gouled was elected chairman of IGADD for a second term of office.

Djibouti suspended air and sea links with the People's Democratic Republic of Yemen in August 1986, following an incident in which an Air Djibouti aircraft was intercepted by Yemeni fighter aircraft and forced to land at Aden. Djibouti had played a prominent part in the evacuation of foreign nationals from Aden during the fighting there in January 1986. Communications were restored in November.

In April 1984 a new scheme for repatriating Ethiopian refugees (estimated to number 35,000), under the aegis of the UNHCR, was begun. By December 1984 it was estimated that around 16,000 had returned to Ethiopia. However, the recurrence of drought and the political situation in Ethiopia caused some refugees to return, and by June 1987 the number of 'official' refugees in Djibouti was 17,200. In August 1986 a new repatriation programme was announced by the Djibouti Government, in consultation with the Ethiopian Government and the UNHCR. According to Djiboutian sources, the number of voluntary repatriations under this programme had reached 2,000 by the end of March 1987. The burden that 'official' refugees have imposed on the economy has been exacerbated by an influx of illegal immigrants from Somalia and Ethiopia, and in June 1987 the Government announced tighter controls on border crossings and identity papers. Following discussions in February 1988, Djibouti and Ethiopia agreed to control movements across their common border and to curb the influx of refugees into Djibouti. In January 1989 illegal immigrants were alleged to have taken part in a violent confrontation between the security forces and inhabitants of Balbala, a densely populated shanty-town close to Djibouti city, in which four people died and 100 were injured. In April inter-tribal hostilities erupted in Djibouti city and the Afar town of Tadjourah, reportedly leading to the deaths of more than 10 people. Tension increased in Afar-inhabited areas in May, and in a speech to mark the end of the Muslim period of Ramadan President Gouled instructed the army to deal firmly with tribal hostilities. At the same time he announced that measures were to be taken against illegal refugees, who were not only an economic burden on the country, but also a source of instability. In May 1990 fighting between members of the Issa and the Gadabursi communities in Djibouti city led to two deaths and to increased conern over internal security. In June the Djibouti armed forces carried out a raid on the town of Tadjourah and arrested Afars who were suspected of involvement in the MPLD. In September there was speculation that a grenade attack on a Djibouti café frequented by French military personnel might have been made in response to the involvement of French troops in the multinational force deployed to defend Saudi Arabia following Iraq's invasion of Kuwait in August 1990.

In December 1987 President Mitterrand visited Djibouti, the first visit by a French President since 1977. President Gouled made an official visit to France in June 1989, during which he described relations with France as of an 'exceptional quality' and praised the stabilizing influence of the French military presence in Djibouti. However, the French military presence became more controversial following Iraq's invasion of Kuwait in August 1990 and the onset of the 'Gulf crisis'. French troops in Djibouti were reinforced and Djibouti became the base of operations connected with France's participation in the multinational force deployed in Saudi Arabia. By supporting the UN resolutions which have been formulated against Iraq, Djibouti has jeopardized its future relations with Iraq, which was emerging as an important supplier of economic and military aid. Iraq is believed to have sought to conclude a security pact with Djibouti in 1989, and in May 1990, following an abrupt deterioration in Djibouti's relations with Somalia, Iraq reportedly supplied Djibouti with military equipment. In the same month the C-in-C of the Iraqi armed forces made a visit to Djibouti to discuss future military aid.

Government

Executive power is vested in the President, who is directly elected by universal adult suffrage for a six-year term. Legislative power is held by the Chamber of Deputies, consisting of 65 members elected for five years. The Council of Ministers, presided over by a Prime Minister, is responsible to the President. The Republic forms a single electoral district. Djibouti became a one-party state in October 1981. The Political Bureau of the ruling party, the Rassemblement populaire pour le progrès, is appointed by the President.

Defence

Since French withdrawal, a large portion of the annual budget has been allocated to military expenditure, and defence costs were budgeted at US $26m. in 1989. In June 1990 there were about 4,000 French troops stationed in Djibouti. The French military presence was reinforced following Iraq's invasion of Kuwait in August 1990. The total armed forces of Djibouti itself, in which all services form part of the army, numbered 2,890 (including 90 naval and 100 air force personnel), and there was a paramilitary force of 1,200 gendarmes.

Economic Affairs

In 1985, according to UN estimates, Djibouti's gross domestic product (GDP), measured at current prices, was US $407m., equivalent to $1,118 per head. In 1987, however, the country's gross national product (GNP) per head was estimated at $600. Djibouti's overall GDP expanded, in real terms, at an average rate of 2.2% annually in 1980-85, reversing an average annual decline of 2.7% in 1977-79. However, as a result of rapid population increase, GDP per head declined, in real terms, during 1980-85. Over that period, population rose by about 4% annually, owing partly to the influx of refugees from neighbouring Ethiopia and Somalia. GDP grew by 13.6% in 1982, but by only 0.9% in 1983, 0.5% in 1984 and 0.6% in 1985.

The agricultural sector (including hunting, forestry and fishing) accounted for 4.9% of GDP in 1983. There is little arable farming, owing to Djibouti's unproductive terrain, and the country is able to produce only about 3% of its total food requirements. More than one-half of the population are pastoral nomads, herding goats, sheep and camels.

Industry (comprising mining, manufacturing, construction and utilities) provided 21.5% of GDP in 1983, but industrial activity is mainly limited to a few small-scale enterprises. Manufacturing accounted for 9.3% of GDP in 1983, and almost all consumer goods have to be imported. The construction of an oil refinery, funded by Saudi Arabia, commenced in mid-1990. The refinery is due to become operative in 1994, with a planned daily production capacity of 100,000 barrels of petrol, kerosene and liquefied gas.

In 1986 work commenced on a major geothermal exploration project, funded by the World Bank and foreign aid. In June 1986 Saudi Arabia gave Djibouti a grant of US $21.4m. for the purchase and installation of three electricity generators, with a combined capacity of 15 MW. Total electricity generation capacity rose from 40 MW to 80 MW in 1988, when the second part of the Boulaos power station became operative. Imported fuels satisfy 90% of Djibouti's energy requirements.

Djibouti's economic viability is based on trade through the international port of Djibouti, and on the developing service sector, which accounted for 73.7% of GDP in 1983. Almost 1.6m. metric tons of goods were handled by the port of Djibouti in 1986. In 1988, however, only 563,170 tons of goods were handled by the port. Almost all consumer goods are imported, mainly from France. The cost of Djibouti's imports totalled 33,475m. Djibouti francs in 1986, while the revenue from exports, in the same year, amounted to 3,628m. Djibouti francs. Somalia is Djibouti's principal export market.

The 1990 budget was projected to balance at 23,987m. Djibouti francs. In 1989 new tax laws were adopted, which sought to improve the collection of government revenues, and thus to assist in the reduction of the budgetary deficit (estimated at US $560,000 in 1986). Djibouti's external debt was estimated to have reached US $300m. by the end of 1988, equivalent to 73% of annual GNP. In that year the cost of debt-servicing amounted to 1,000m. Djibouti francs, equivalent to 5% of total budgeted expenditure.

Djibouti is heavily dependent on foreign assistance, the principal donors being France and Saudi Arabia. Since 1986, however, there has been a reduction in foreign aid, resulting in financial problems. Co-operation agreements have been signed with Pakistan, the People's Republic of China, the Republic of Korea and Uganda. Budgetary aid for 1990, totalling 37.5m. French francs, was promised by the French Government. Djibouti is a member of the African Development Bank, the IMF, the Islamic Development Bank, the World Bank and the International Finance Corporation.

Djibouti suffers from periodic drought, although flooding destroyed part of the capital and damaged infrastructure in April 1989. The Ogaden War of 1977-78 between Ethiopia and Somalia led to the temporary closure of the Djibouti-Addis Ababa railway, exemplifying the Djibouti economy's vulnerability to events in neighbouring countries. The vulnerability has become all the more apparent since the onset of the 'Gulf crisis' in August 1990. In September the Government estimated that total losses resulting from the 'Gulf crisis' would amount to $218m. This estimate took into account increases in the price of imports and in transport expenses, and the postponement of investments pledged by Kuwait, Saudi Arabia and Iraq. In recent years Djibouti port has experienced increasing competition from nearby developing Arab ports. It is also feared that the development by Ethiopia of container facilities may reduce trade through Djibouti port. The main hope for the future is to develop Djibouti as a major entrepôt for trade between East Africa and the Arab countries. Recent development plans have, therefore, tended to concentrate on the improvement of Djibouti's infrastructure. The 1984-89 Development Plan envisaged total expenditure of US $570m.

Social Welfare

The social insurance scheme in Djibouti is divided into three categories, according to whether the worker is employed in

DJIBOUTI

the private sector, the civil service or the army. Employees receive benefits in case of accidents at work, and are allocated retirement pensions after the age of 55 years. Budgetary expenditure on health in 1986 was 1,631m. Djibouti francs. In 1987 there were 18 hospital establishments, with a total of 1,285 beds, and more than 700 medical personnel, including 89 physicians.

Education

Since independence, the Government has assumed overall responsibility for education. Primary education generally begins at seven years of age and lasts for six years. Secondary education, usually starting at the age of 13, lasts for seven years. Budgetary expenditure on education in 1986 was 1,651m. Djibouti francs. In 1986/87 there were 27,136 primary school pupils and 7,895 pupils at secondary and technical schools.

Public Holidays

1991: 1 January (New Year's Day), 16 April* (Id al-Fitr, end of Ramadan), 1 May (Workers' Day), 23 June* (Id al-Adha, Feast of the Sacrifice), 27 June (Independence Day), 13 July* (Muharram, Islamic New Year), 21 September* (Mouloud, Birth of the Prophet), 25 December (Christmas Day).

1992: 1 January (New Year's Day), 4 April* (Id al-Fitr, end of Ramadan), 1 May (Workers' Day), 11 June* (Id al-Adha, Feast of the Sacrifice), 27 June (Independence Day), 2 July* (Muharram, Islamic New Year), 10 September* (Mouloud, Birth of the Prophet), 25 December (Christmas Day).

* These holidays are dependent on the Islamic lunar calendar and may vary by one or two days from the dates given.

Weights and Measures

The metric system is in force.

Statistical Survey

Source (unless otherwise stated): Ministère du Commerce, de l'Industrie, des Transports et du Tourisme, BP 1846, Djibouti; tel. 35331.

AREA AND POPULATION

Area: 23,200 sq km (8,958 sq miles).

Population: 220,000 (1976 estimate), including Afars 70,000, Issas and other Somalis 80,000, Arabs 12,000, Europeans 15,000, other foreigners 40,000; 483,000 (including refugees and resident foreigners) at mid-1987 (official estimate).

Principal Towns: Djibouti (capital), population 200,000 (1981); Dikhil; Ali-Sabieh; Tadjourah; Obock.

AGRICULTURE, ETC.

Principal Crops (FAO estimate, '000 metric tons, 1989): Vegetables 16.

Livestock (FAO estimates, '000 head, year ending September 1989): Cattle 72, Sheep 415, Goats 501, Asses 8, Camels 58.

Livestock Products: (FAO estimates, metric tons, 1989): Meat 7,000, Goatskins 440.

Fishing (metric tons, live weight): Total catch 410 in 1986; 427 in 1987; 454 in 1988. (Source: FAO, *Yearbook of Fishery Statistics*).

INDUSTRY

Electric energy (million kWh): 164 in 1985; 171 in 1986; 172 in 1987.

FINANCE

Currency and Exchange Rates: 100 centimes = 1 Djibouti franc. *Coins:* 1, 2, 5, 10, 20, 50 and 100 Djibouti francs. *Notes:* 500, 1,000 and 5,000 Djibouti francs. *Sterling and Dollar Equivalents* (30 September 1990): £1 sterling = 332.96 Djibouti francs; US $1 = 177.72 Djibouti francs; 1,000 Djibouti francs = £3.003 = $5.627. *Exchange Rate:* Fixed at US $1 = 177.721 Djibouti francs since February 1973.

Budget (million Djibouti francs, 1986): *Revenue:* Taxation 17,041, Non-tax current revenue 1,727, Grants 1,662, Repayment of loans 254, Transfers from reserve fund 3,639, Advances from the Treasury 170, Total 24,494; *Expenditure:* General administration 9,908, Defence 4,632, Education 1,651, Health 1,631, Economic services 1,341, Debt servicing 968, Other current expenditure 1,694, Total 23,133. 1988 (provisional, million Djibouti francs): *Revenue* 25,498 (excl. grants received 1,400); *Expenditure* 22,234 (Source: IMF, *International Financial Statistics*); 1989 (provisional, million Djibouti francs): Expenditure 23,919.2; 1990 (estimate, million Djibouti francs): Expenditure 23,987.

International Reserves (US $ million at 31 December 1989): IMF special drawing rights 0.27; Reserve position in IMF 1.24; Foreign exchange 57.17; Total 58.68. Source: IMF, *International Financial Statistics*.

Money Supply (million Djibouti francs at 31 December 1989): Currency outside banks 8,197; Demand deposits at commercial banks 16,444. Source: IMF, *International Financial Statistics*.

Gross Domestic Product by Economic Activity (million Djibouti francs at current prices, 1987): Agriculture, hunting, forestry and fishing 3,143; Manufacturing 5,265; Electricity, gas and water 2,186; Construction 4,601; Trade, restaurants and hotels 8,811; Transport, storage and communications 6,342*; Finance, insurance, real estate and business services 6,780; Government services 17,463*; Other community, social and personal services 1,027*; GDP at factor cost 51,879; Indirect taxes less subsidies 13,741; GDP in purchasers' values 65,620.

* Estimate.

Source: UN Economic Commission for Africa, *African Statistical Yearbook*.

Balance of Payments (million Djibouti francs, 1982): Exports f.o.b. (incl. re-exports) 20,830, Imports c.i.f. −38,523, *Trade Balance* −17,693; Services, port 847, Unrequited transfers (net) 8,909, *Current Balance* −4,366; Capital movements 1,942, Changes in reserves −2,424.

EXTERNAL TRADE

Principal Commodities (million Djibouti francs, 1983): *Imports:* Machinery and electrical equipment 4,301, Textiles 4,713, Food 7,488, Qat 3,550, Petroleum and derivatives 3,708, Road vehicles 4,749; Total (incl. others) 39,307. *Exports:* Live animals 592, Food 356; Total (incl. others) 1,919.

Total imports (million Djibouti francs): 35,670 in 1985; 33,475 in 1986; 36,133 in 1987.

Total exports (million Djibouti francs): 2,488 in 1985; 3,628 in 1986; 1,193 in 1987.

Principal Trading Partners (million Djibouti francs, 1984): *Imports:* Benelux 2,214, Ethiopia 4,926, France and Monaco 22,044, Italy 2,915, United Kingdom 1,592; Total (incl. others) 47,832. *Exports:* France and Monaco 1,704, Italy 89, Somalia 179, Spain and Portugal 2, United Kingdom 23; Total (incl. others) 3,306.

TRANSPORT

Railways (Djibouti-Ethiopian Railway, 1987): Freight traffic ('000 metric tons): 291.7; Passengers 1.3m.

Road Traffic ('000 motor vehicles, 1984): Passenger cars 18.4; Commercial vehicles 6.7 (Source: UN, *Statistical Yearbook*).

Shipping (Djibouti port, 1986): Vessels entered 1,723; Goods loaded 155,000 metric tons; Goods unloaded 466,000 metric tons.

Civil Aviation (Djibouti airport, 1987): Freight loaded 1,612 metric tons; Freight unloaded 6,036 metric tons; Passenger arrivals 67,856; Passenger departures 61,518.

COMMUNICATIONS MEDIA

Radio Receivers (1990): 60,000 in use.

Television Receivers (1990): 40,000 in use.

Telephones (1987): 4,452 in use.

DJIBOUTI

EDUCATION

Primary (1986/87): 59 schools (52 state schools, 7 private schools); 27,136 pupils (24,606 at state schools, 2,530 at private schools); 559 teachers (state schools only).

Secondary and Technical (1986/87): 21 schools (8 state schools, 13 private schools); 7,895 pupils (6,203 at state schools, 1,692 at private schools); 302 teachers (state schools only).

Teacher Training (1987/88): 117 pupils; 13 teachers.

Directory

The Constitution

In February 1981 the National Assembly approved the first constitutional laws controlling the election and terms of office of the President, who is elected by universal suffrage for six years and may serve for no more than two terms. Candidates for the presidency must be presented by a regularly constituted political party and represented by at least 25 members of the Chamber of Deputies.

Deputies are elected for five years from a single list of candidates proposed by the Rassemblement populaire pour le progrès.

In October 1984 a new constitutional law was proposed, specifying that, when the office of President falls vacant, the President of the Supreme Court will assume the power of Head of State for a minimum of 20 days and a maximum of 35 days, during which period a new President shall be elected.

Laws approving the establishment of a single-party system were adopted in October 1981.

The Government

HEAD OF STATE

President and Commander-in-Chief of the Armed Forces: Hassan Gouled Aptidon (took office 27 June 1977; re-elected June 1981 and April 1987).

COUNCIL OF MINISTERS
(January 1991)

Prime Minister and Minister of Planning and Land Development: Barkad Gourad Hamadou.
Minister of the Interior, Posts and of Telecommunications: Khaireh Allaleh Hared.
Minister of Justice and Islamic Affairs: Ougoure Hassan Ibrahim.
Minister of Foreign Affairs and Co-operation: Moumin Bahdon Farah.
Minister of Defence: Ismail Ali Youssouf.
Minister of Commerce, Transport and Tourism: Ahmed Ibrahim Abdi.
Minister of Finance and National Economy: Moussa Bourale Roble.
Minister of the Civil Service and Administrative Reform: Suleiman Farah Lodon.
Minister of Industry and Industrial Development: Salem Abdou Yahyam.
Minister of Labour and Social Welfare: Elaf Orbiss Ali.
Minister of Education: Omar Chirdon Abass.
Minister of Public Works and Housing: Ibrahim Idris Muhammad.
Minister of Agriculture and Rural Development: Muhammad Moussa Chehem.
Minister of Health and Social Affairs: Muhammad Djama Elabe.
Minister of Ports and Maritime Affairs: Ahmed Aden Youssouf.
Minister of Youth, Sports and Cultural Affairs: Hussein Barkat Siraj.

MINISTRIES

Office of the Prime Minister: BP 2086, Djibouti; tel. 351494; telex 5871; fax 355049.
Ministry of Agriculture and Rural Development: BP 453, Djibouti; tel. 351297; telex 5871.
Ministry of the Civil Service: BP 155, Djibouti; tel. 351464; telex 5871.
Ministry of Commerce, Transport and Tourism: BP 121, Djibouti; tel. 352540; telex 5871.
Ministry of Defence: BP 42, Djibouti; tel. 352034; telex 5871.
Ministry of Education, Youth and Sports: BP 2102, Djibouti; tel. 351689; telex 5871.
Ministry of Finance and National Economy: BP 13, Djibouti; tel. 350297; telex 5871; 35601.
Ministry of Foreign Affairs and Co-operation: BP 1863, Djibouti; tel. 352471; telex 5871.
Ministry of Health and Social Affairs: BP 296, Djibouti; tel. 353331; telex 5871.
Ministry of Industry and Industrial Development: BP 175, Djibouti; tel. 350137; telex 5871.
Ministry of the Interior: BP 33, Djibouti; tel. 350791; telex 5871.
Ministry of Justice and Islamic Affairs: BP 12, Djibouti; tel. 351506; telex 5871.
Ministry of Labour and Social Welfare: BP 170, Djibouti; tel. 350497; telex 5871.
Ministry of Ports and Maritime Affairs: BP 2107, Djibouti; tel. 350105; telex 5871.
Ministry of Public Works and Housing: BP 11, Djibouti; tel. 350006; telex 5871.
Ministry of Telecommunications: Djibouti; tel. 350971; telex 5871.

Legislature

CHAMBRE DES DÉPUTÉS

Elections for the 65-seat Chamber of Deputies were held on 24 April 1987. A single list of candidates, which was claimed to reflect the traditional balance between different ethnic groups and clans, was presented by the Rassemblement populaire pour le progrès. All candidates were elected unopposed.

President of the Chamber: Abdoulkader Waberi Askar.

Political Organizations

Rassemblement populaire pour le progrès (RPP): Djibouti; f. 1979 to succeed the Ligue populaire africaine pour l'indépendance; sole legal party since 1981; 15-mem. Political Bureau; Pres. Hassan Gouled Aptidon; Sec.-Gen. Moumin Bahdon Farah.

The following organizations are banned:

Front de libération de la Côte des Somalis (FLCS): f. 1963; Issa-supported; based in Mogadishu, Somalia; Chair. Abdulla Waberi Khalif; Vice-Chair. Omar Osman Rabeh.

Mouvement populaire pour la libération de Djibouti (MPLD): f. 1964; Afar-supported; based in Dire Dawa, Ethiopia; Leader Shehem Daoud.

Parti populaire djiboutien: f. 1981; mainly Afar-supported; Leader Moussa Ahmad Idris.

Union de mouvements démocratiques (UMD): f. 1990 by merger of the fmr Front démocratique pour la libération de Djibouti and the Mouvement national djiboutien pour l'instauration de la démocratie; Leader Aden Robleh Awalleh.

Diplomatic Representation

EMBASSIES IN DJIBOUTI

China, People's Republic: Djibouti; tel. 352246; telex 5926; Ambassador: Xu Chenghua.
Egypt: BP 1989, Djibouti; tel. 351231; telex 5880; Ambassador: Mohsen T. Azmi.

DJIBOUTI

Ethiopia: BP 230, Djibouti; tel. 350718; Ambassador: BERHANU DINKA.
France: 45 blvd du Maréchal Foch, BP 2039, Djibouti; tel. 350963; telex 5861; Ambassador: CLAUDE SOUBESTE.
Iraq: BP 1983, Djibouti; tel. 353469; telex 5877; Ambassador: ABDEL AZIZ AL-GAILANI.
Libya: BP 2073, Djibouti; tel. 353339; telex 5874; Ambassador: JALAL MUHAMMAD AL-DAGHELY.
Oman: BP 1996, Djibouti; tel. 350852; telex 5876; Ambassador: SAOUD SALEM HASSAN AL-ANSI.
Saudi Arabia: BP 1921, Djibouti; tel. 351645; telex 5865; fax 352284; Chargé d'affaires: MOWAFFAK AL-DOLIGANE.
Somalia: BP 549, Djibouti; tel. 353521; telex 5815; Ambassador: MUHAMMAD SHEK MUHAMMAD MALINGUR.
Sudan: Djibouti; tel. 351483; Ambassador: TAG EL-SIR MUHAMMAD ABASS.
USSR: BP 1913, Djibouti; tel. 352051; telex 5906; Ambassador: VIKTOR ZHURAVLEV.
USA: Villa Plateau du Serpent, blvd Maréchal Joffré, BP 185, Djibouti; tel. 353995; Ambassador: ROBERT S. BARRETT.
*Yemen Arab Republic: BP 194, Djibouti; tel. 352975; Ambassador: MUHAMMAD ABDOUL WASSI HAMID.
*Yemen, People's Democratic Republic: BP 1932, Djibouti; tel. 353704; Chargé d'affaires: AWAD SALEM BAABAD.

* Merged to form the Republic of Yemen in May 1990.

Judicial System

The Supreme Court was established in October 1979. There is a High Court of Appeal and a 'tribunal de première instance' in Djibouti; each of the five administrative districts has a 'tribunal coutumier'.

Religion

ISLAM
Almost the entire population are Muslims.
Qadi of Djibouti: MOGUE HASSAN DIRIR, BP 168, Djibouti; tel. 352669.

CHRISTIANITY
The Roman Catholic Church
Djibouti comprises a single diocese, directly responsible to the Holy See. There were an estimated 8,500 adherents in the country at 31 December 1988.
Bishop of Djibouti (vacant): Apostolic Administrator: Fr GEORGES PERRON, Evêché, blvd de la République, BP 94, Djibouti; tel. 350140.

The Anglican Communion
Within the Episcopal Church in Jerusalem and the Middle East, Djibouti lies within the jurisdiction of the Bishop in Egypt.

Other Christian Churches
Eglise Protestante: blvd de la République, BP 416, Djibouti; tel. 351820; f. 1957; Pastor PASCAL VERNIER.
Greek Orthodox Church: blvd de la République, Djibouti; tel. 351325; c. 350 adherents; Archimandrite STAVROS GEORGANAS.
The Ethiopian Orthodox Church is also represented in Djibouti.

The Press

Carrefour Africain: BP 393, Djibouti; fax 354916; fortnightly; publ. by the Roman Catholic mission; circ. 500.
Djibouti Aujourd'hui: Djibouti; f. 1977; monthly; Editor ISMAEL OMAR GUELLEH.
La Nation de Djibouti: place du 27 juin, BP 32, Djibouti; tel. 352201; weekly; Dir ISMAEL H. TANI; circ. 4,000.

NEWS AGENCIES
Agence Djiboutienne de Presse (ADP): BP 32, Djibouti; tel. 350201; telex 5871

Foreign Bureau
Agence France-Presse (AFP): BP 97, Djibouti; tel. 352294; telex 5863; Correspondent HAIDAR KHALID ABDALLAH.

Radio and Television

There were an estimated 60,000 radio receivers and 40,000 television receivers in use in 1990. In 1980 Djibouti became a member of the Arab Satellite Communication Organization, and opened an earth station for radio, television and telecommunications; a second earth station was inaugurated in June 1985.

Radiodiffusion-Télévision de Djibouti (RTD): BP 97, Djibouti; tel. 352294; telex 5863; f. 1956; state-controlled; programmes in French, Afar, Somali and Arabic; 24 hours radio and 7 hours television daily; Dir-Gen. MUHAMMAD FARAH MOUSSA.

Finance

(cap. = capital; p.u. = paid up; dep. = deposits; m. = million; res = reserves; br. = branch; amounts in Djibouti francs)

BANKING
Central Bank
Banque Nationale de Djibouti: BP 2118, Djibouti; tel. 352751; telex 5838; f. 1977; bank of issue; Gov. LUC A. ADEN.

Commercial Banks
Bank of Credit and Commerce International: 10 ave Pierre Pascal, BP 2105, Djibouti; tel. 351741; telex 5810; fax 352030; Man. Dir CHRISTIAN HOLLANDER.
Banque de Djibouti et du Moyen Orient SA: 6 rue de Marseille, BP 2471, Djibouti; tel. 351133; telex 5943; fax 355828; f. 1983; 55% owned by Middle East Bank; cap. 300m. (Dec. 1987); Man. Dir IAN J. MITCHELL.
Banque Indosuez (Mer Rouge) (France): 10 place Lagarde, BP 88, Djibouti; tel. 353016; telex 5829; fax 351638; f. 1908; cap. and res 1,650m., dep. 17,873m. (Dec. 1989); Chair. and Man. Dir FRANÇOIS GRIFFE; 5 brs.
Banque pour le Commerce et l'Industrie (Mer Rouge): place Lagarde, BP 2122, Djibouti; tel. 380857; telex 5821; fax 354260; f. 1977; 51% owned by Banque Nationale de Paris Intercontinentale; cap. and res. 3,220m., dep. 27,523m. (Dec. 1989); Pres. JEAN-CLAUDE CLARAC; 7 brs.
British Bank of the Middle East (Hong Kong): place Lagarde, BP 2112, Djibouti; tel. 353291; telex 5826; Man. CHRISTOPHER REDDINGTON.
Commercial and Savings Bank of Somalia: BP 2004, Djibouti; tel. 351282; telex 5879; Dir ABDULKADIR HASSAN EGAL.
Commercial Bank of Ethiopia: rue de Marseilles, BP 187, Djibouti; tel. 352101; telex 5835; f. 1980; Man. ASSEBEWORK ZEGEYE.

Development Bank
Caisse de Développement de Djibouti: rue de l'Ethiopie, BP 520, Djibouti; tel. 353391; f. 1983; 51% govt-owned; cap. 500m. (Dec. 1988); Pres LUC ADEN; Dir NOUH OMAR MIGUIL.

Banking Association
Association Professionnelle des Banques: c/o Banque pour le Commerce et l'Industrie (Mer Rouge), place Lagarde, BP 2122, Djibouti; tel. 350857; Pres. MUHAMMAD ADEN.

INSURANCE
Assurances Générales de France (AGF): 3 rue Marchand, Djibouti; tel. 352339.
State Insurance Co of Somalia (SICOS): BP 50, Djibouti; tel. 352707; telex 5819; all classes of insurance.
About 10 European insurance companies maintain agencies in Djibouti.

Trade and Industry

Chambre Internationale de Commerce et d'Industrie: place Lagarde, BP 84, Djibouti; tel. 351070; telex 5957; f. 1906; 24 mems; 12 assoc. mems; Pres. SAID ALI COUBECHE; First Vice-Pres. MUHAMMAD ADEN.

Djibouti Labour Federation: Pres. IDRIS OMAR.

Transport

RAILWAYS
Compagnie du Chemin de Fer Djibouti-Ethiopien: BP 2116, Djibouti; tel. 350353; telex 5953; POB 1051, Addis Ababa; tel.

447250; telex 21414; f. 1908, adopted present name in 1981; jtly-owned by govts of Djibouti and Ethiopia; plans to grant autonomous status were announced by the two govts in July 1985; 781 km of track (100 km in Djibouti) linking Djibouti with Addis Ababa; Pres. Y. AHMED; Vice-Pres. MOUSSA BOURALE ROBLE.

ROADS

In 1987 there were 3,037 km of roads, of which over 400 km were bitumen-surfaced, including the 185-km road along the Ethiopian frontier. Of the remainder, 1,000 km are serviceable throughout the year, the rest only during the dry season. Half the roads are usable only by lorries. In 1981 the 40-km Grand Bara road was opened, linking the capital with the south.

SHIPPING

Djibouti was established as a free port in 1981.

Port Autonome International de Djibouti: Djibouti; Dir ADEN AHMED DOUALE.

Principal Shipping Agents

Compagnie Générale Maritime: Immeuble Plein Ciel, BP 182, Djibouti; tel. 353825; telex 5817; agents for Mitsui OSK, CGM/Svedel, CGM, SNC, Hapaglloyd and Seal Lines.

Compagnie Maritime Auxiliaire d'Outre-Mer: ave des Messageries Maritimes, BP 89, Djibouti; tel. 352022; telex 5825; agents for Adriatic Red Sea Line, British Petroleum, Compagnie Générale Maritime, Comp. Navale des Pétroles, Deutsche Ost Afrika Line, Djakarta Lloyd, Hapaglloyd, Hungarian Shipping Line, Jadranska Line, Nedlloyd Line, Scandinavian East Africa Line, Shell International, Sovinflot; Gen. Man. L. J. HUGHES.

Gellatly Hankey et Cie (Djibouti) SA: rue de Genève, BP 81, Djibouti; tel. 352012; telex 5843; fax 353294; f. 1942; Lloyd's agents, and shipping agents for Nippon Yusen Kaisha, Waterman Line, P & O, Cosco, Sinochart and others; Man. Dir ERIK VANDENDRIESSCHE.

J. J. Kothari & Co Ltd: BP 171, rue de Soleillet, Djibouti; tel. 350219; telex 5860; fax 351778; agents for American President Lines, Bangladesh Shipping Corpn, Pacific International Line, Ratnakar Shipping Co, Shipping Corpn of Saudi Arabia, United Thai Shipping Co, Shipping Corpn of India, Mogul Line, United Arab Maritime, Sudan Shipping Line, Finland Steamship Co; also ship managers, stevedores, freight forwarders; Dirs S. J. KOTHARI, N. KOTHARI.

Mitchell Cotts Djibouti SARL: blvd de la République, BP 85, Djibouti; tel. 351204; telex 5812; fax 355851; agents for Adriatic Tankers, Beacon, Central Gulf, Cunard Ellerman, Dan Bunkering Denmark, Dry Tank/Piraeus, Harrison, Khan Shipping, Marship Operators, Mobil/Fairfax/London, Naftomar, Pand OCL, Scan-Shipping/Denmark and other shipping and forwarding cos; Dir FAHMY SAID CASSIM.

Société d'Armement et de Manutention de la Mer Rouge (SAMER): BP 10, Djibouti; agents for Pacific International Line, Cunard Brocklebank, Wilhelm Wilhelmsen Co, Pakistan Shipping Lines, Aktiebolaget Svenska Östasiatiska Kompaniet, Texaco, Chevron Shipping Co, Kie Hock Shipping Co, Barber Lines, Supreme Shipping Co, Scandutch; Chair. JOHN COLLINS; Man. Dir VINCENT DELL'AQUILLA.

Société Maritime L. Savon et Ries: ave Saint-Laurent du Var, BP 2125, Djibouti; fax 351103; agents for Chargeurs Réunis, NCHP, Sudcargos, Svedel Line, Lloyd Triestino, Hellenic Lines, Messina, Polish Ocean Lines; Dir M. AARSTAD.

CIVIL AVIATION

The international airport is at Ambouli, 6 km from Djibouti, and there are six internal airports.

Air Djibouti (Red Sea Airlines): BP 505, rue Marchand, Djibouti; tel. 352651; telex 5820; fax 354363; f. 1971, when Air Somalie took over the fmr Air Djibouti (f. 1963); the Djibouti govt holds 62.5% of shares, and Air France 32.3%; internal flights connecting the six major centres and international services to Yemen, Somalia, the United Arab Emirates, France, Italy, Egypt, Kenya, Ethiopia, Saudi Arabia and Uganda; Gen. Man. PAUL BOTBOL; fleet of 2 Twin Otter and 2 DC-9-30.

Tourism

Djibouti's principal attractions are the desert scenery of the interior and, on the coast, its watersport facilities. In 1989 a total of 40,762 tourists stayed in hotels in Djibouti.

Office National du Tourisme et de l'Artisanat: place du 27 juin, BP 1938, Djibouti; tel. 352800; telex 5938; fax (253) 356322.

DOMINICA

Introductory Survey

Location, Climate, Language, Religion, Flag, Capital

The Commonwealth of Dominica is situated in the Windward Islands group of the West Indies, lying between Guadeloupe, to the north, and Martinique, to the south. The climate is tropical, though tempered by sea winds which sometimes reach hurricane force, especially from July to September. The average temperature is about 27°C (80°F), with little seasonal variation. Rainfall is heavy, especially in the mountainous areas, where the annual average is 6,350 mm (250 inches), compared with 1,800 mm (70 inches) along the coast. English is the official language but a local French patois, or Creole, is widely spoken. In parts of the north-east an English dialect, known as Cocoy, is spoken by the descendents of Antiguan settlers. There is a small community of Carib Indians on the east coast. Almost all of the inhabitants profess Christianity, and about 80% are Roman Catholics. The national flag has a green field, with equal stripes of yellow, white and black forming an upright cross, on the centre of which is superimposed a red disc containing a parrot surrounded by ten five-pointed green stars (one for each of the island's parishes). The capital is Roseau.

Recent History

Dominica was first settled by Arawaks and then Caribs. Control of the island was fiercely contested by the Caribs, British and French during the 17th and 18th centuries. The British eventually prevailed and Dominica formed part of the Leeward Islands federation until 1939. In 1940 it was transferred to the Windward Islands and remained attached to that group until the federal arrangement was ended in December 1959. Under a new constitution, effective from January 1960, Dominica (like each other member of the group) achieved a separate status, with its own Administrator and an enlarged Legislative Council. Dominica was a member of the West Indies Federation between 1958 and its dissolution in 1962.

At the January 1961 elections to the Legislative Council, the ruling Dominica United People's Party was defeated by the Dominica Labour Party (DLP), formed from the People's National Movement and other groups. Edward LeBlanc, leader of the DLP, became Chief Minister. In March 1967 Dominica became one of the West Indies Associated States, gaining full autonomy in internal affairs, with the United Kingdom retaining responsibility for defence and foreign relations only. The Legislative Council was replaced by a House of Assembly, the Administrator became Governor and the Chief Minister was restyled Premier. At elections to the House in October 1970, the Premier was returned to power.

In July 1974 LeBlanc retired, being replaced as DLP leader and Premier by Patrick John, formerly Deputy Premier and Minister of Finance. Elections to an enlarged House of Assembly were held in March 1975, when the DLP was returned again, winning 16 of the 21 elective seats. Following a decision in 1975 by the Associated States to seek independence separately, Dominica became an independent republic within the Commonwealth on 3 November 1978. Patrick John became Prime Minister, and Frederick Degazon, formerly Speaker of the House of Assembly, was eventually elected President.

In May 1979 two people were killed by the Defence Force at a demonstration against the Government's attempts to introduce legislation which would restrict the freedom of the trade unions and the press. The killings fuelled increasing popular opposition to the Government, and a Committee for National Salvation (CNS) was formed to press for John's resignation. On his refusal to do so, opponents of the Government organized a general strike which lasted 25 days, with John relinquishing power only after all his cabinet ministers had resigned and President Degazon had gone into hiding abroad (there was a succession of Acting Presidents; Degazon finally resigned in February 1980). Oliver Seraphin, the candidate proposed by the CNS, was elected Prime Minister, and an interim government was then formed to prepare for elections after six months.

Elections were eventually held in July 1980, when the Dominica Freedom Party (DFP) gained a convincing victory, winning 17 of the 21 elective seats in the House of Assembly. Eugenia Charles, the party's leader, became the Caribbean's first woman Prime Minister. Both Patrick John, who contested the elections as leader of the DLP, and Oliver Seraphin, who stood as leader of the newly formed Democratic Labour Party (DEMLAB), lost their seats. The DFP's victory was attributed to its continued integrity, while the DLP and DEMLAB had suffered from major political scandals.

Fears for the island's security dominated 1981. In January the Government disarmed the Defence Force, following reports that weapons were being traded for marijuana. Against a background of increasing violence and the declaration of a state of emergency, however, there were two coup attempts involving former Defence Force members. Patrick John, the former Prime Minister, was also implicated and imprisoned. In June 1982 John and his fellow prisoners were tried and acquitted but the Government secured a retrial in October 1985. John and the former deputy commander of the Defence Force each received a prison sentence of 12 years (they were released in May 1990). In 1986 the former commander of the Defence Force was hanged for the murder of a policeman during the second coup attempt. The death sentences on five other soldiers were commuted to life imprisonment.

After his release in June 1982, John attempted to form a new left-wing coalition party, and in 1983 a new DLP was formed upon its reunification with DEMLAB. In January 1985 agreement was reached between the DLP, the United Dominica Labour Party and the Dominica Liberation Movement, to form a united left-wing grouping, known as the Labour Party of Dominica (LPD), to contest the next general election, with Michael Douglas, a former Minister of Finance, as leader. During the election campaign, Eugenia Charles stressed the economic achievements of her administration, and, at the general election, held on 1 July 1985, the DFP was returned to power, winning 15 of the 21 elective seats in the House of Assembly. The opposition LPD won five seats, with the remaining seat being won by Rosie Douglas, the brother of the LPD leader, whose candidature was not officially endorsed by the LPD. Following the election, the LPD began an 18-month boycott of the House, in protest at the Government's decision to curtail live broadcasts of parliamentary proceedings. By July 1987, the DFP's strength in the House had increased to 17 seats, with four seats still being held by the LPD.

Dissatisfaction at continued government austerity measures was offset by the success of the land reform programme. Since independence, the Government had acquired nearly all the large estates, often in an attempt to forestall violence. In 1986 the first of the estates was divided, and tenure granted to the former workers. This process was continued and, with the accompanying development programme, received widespread support. The opposition DLP and the Dominica United Workers' Party (UWP—formed in 1988) bitterly denounced many other government policies and criticized Prime Minister Charles' style of leadership. The two opposition parties failed to agree on the formation of an electoral alliance, however, and the DFP was returned for a third term in government at the general election in May 1990. There was a relatively low level of participation in the election, in which the DFP won a total of 11 seats, the UWP became the official opposition (with six seats) and the LPD won four seats. The results were reported to indicate the electorate's disenchantment with the traditional parties, and participation and voting preferences were determined by personality rather than policy.

In foreign policy, Dominica has close links with France and the USA. France helped in suppressing the coup attempts against the DFP Government, and Dominica was the first Commonwealth country to benefit from the French aid agency, FAC. In October 1983 Dominica, as a member of OECS (see p. 109), contributed forces to the US-backed invasion of Grenada. Since the mid-1980s, the OECS has discussed the possible formation of a political union, although some islands displayed considerable reluctance. Nevertheless, in 1988 four countries of the Windward group, Dominica, Grenada, Saint Lucia and Saint Vincent and the Grenadines, decided to proceed with further plans. In 1990 the four countries decided to convene a constituent assembly, with referendums to be held in the following year. In November, however, the opposition parties of the region (grouped in the Standing Committee of Popular Democratic Parties—Scope) threatened to boycott the assembly's first session, scheduled for the end of the month. Scope expressed fears that any resulting political union might institutionalize the dominance of the ruling party in each country. Dominica is also a member of CARICOM (see p. 108), and secured limited protection for some of its industries when the organization removed its internal trade barriers in October 1988.

Government

Legislative power is vested in the unicameral House of Assembly, containing 30 members (nine nominated and 21 elected for five years by universal adult suffrage). Executive authority is vested in the President, elected by the House, but in most matters the President is guided by the advice of the Cabinet and acts as a constitutional Head of State. He appoints the Prime Minister, who must be able to command a majority in the House, and (on the Prime Minister's recommendation) other Ministers. The Cabinet is responsible to the House. The island is divided into ten administrative divisions, known as parishes, and there is limited local government in Roseau and in the Carib Territory.

Defence

The Dominican Defence Force was officially disbanded in April 1981. There is a police force of about 300, which includes a coastguard service. A patrol boat was received from the USA in 1983. The country participates in the US-sponsored Regional Security System.

Economic Affairs

In 1988, according to estimates by the World Bank, Dominica's gross national product (GNP), measured at average 1986–88 prices, was US $130m., equivalent to $1,650 per head. Between 1980 and 1988, it was estimated, GNP increased, in real terms, at an average rate of 4.4% per year, and GNP per head by 3.1%. Over the same period, the population increased by an annual average of 1.3%. Gross domestic product (GDP), in real terms, increased significantly during the 1980s, growing by 7.9% in 1988, before declining by 1.6% in 1989.

Agriculture is the principal economic activity, accounting for 31% of GDP in 1988 (including forestry and fishing). According to the census of 1981, 31.0% of the labour force were employed in agriculture. The principal cash crop is bananas, of which 72,800 metric tons were produced in 1988, with exports earning EC $103.3m., or some 70% of total export revenue (in 1989, following hurricane damage, banana production fell to 46,000 tons, which earned EC $67m. in export revenue). There were almost 6,000 active banana farmers at the end of 1987. Other important crops include coconuts (which provide copra for export as well as edible oil and soap), citrus fruits and, mainly for domestic consumption, vegetables. Livestock-rearing and fishing are also practised for local purposes, although in the 1980s there were efforts to develop the fishing industry. Dominica has extensive timber reserves (more than 40% of the island's total land area is forest and woodland), and international aid agencies are encouraging the development of a balanced timber industry.

Industry (comprising mining, manufacturing, construction and utilities) provided 14.8% of GDP in 1987, and engaged 19.3% of the employed labour force in 1981. Industrial activity is mainly small-scale and dependent upon agriculture. The mining sector contributed only 0.7% of GDP in 1987. There is some quarrying of pumice, and there are extensive reserves of limestone and clay. Pumice is useful to the construction industry, which accounted for 5.1% of GDP in 1987 and employed 9.1% of the labour force in 1981. Extensive infrastructure development by the Government maintained the high levels of activity in the construction sector during the 1980s. The Government has also encouraged the manufacturing sector in an attempt to diversify the economy. In 1987 manufacturing contributed 6.4% of GDP (the sector employed some 5.6% of the labour force in 1981). There is a banana-packaging plant and factories for the manufacturing and refining of crude and edible vegetable oils and for the production of soap, canned juices and cigarettes. Soap accounted for some 16% of total domestic exports in 1987 (98% of production is exported).

By 1992 it is hoped that all Dominica's energy requirements will be satisfied by hydroelectric power. Investment in a hydroelectric development scheme and in the water supply system has been partially financed by the export of water, from Dominica's extensive reserves, to drier Caribbean islands such as Aruba. By 1988 Dominica had reduced imports of mineral fuels to 5.6% of the value of total imports.

The tourist industry is small and exploits Dominica's natural history and scenery. Hotels and restaurants contributed only 1.2% to GDP in 1987. In 1990 it was decided to proceed with the construction of an international airport.

In 1988 Dominica recorded a visible trade deficit of US $23.95m., and a deficit of US $9.39m. on the current account of the balance of payments. The principal source of imports in 1988 was the USA (21.8%), but CARICOM as a whole provided 26.5% (Saint Lucia 8.1%, the rest of the OECS 3.6%, Trinidad and Tobago 8.4%) and the EEC 27.8% (the United Kingdom alone accounted for 18.4% of imports). The principal market for exports is the United Kingdom, which receives virtually all Dominica's banana production. In 1988 the United Kingdom received 60.9% of total exports (the rest of the EEC taking a further 11.2%). CARICOM bought 21.0% of exports in 1988, with Jamaica the main market (10.4%). The principal imports are food and live animals, basic manufactures such as paper, and machinery and transport equipment. The principal exports are bananas and other agricultural produce.

For the financial year ending 30 June 1991 there was a projected recurrent budget surplus of EC $12.3m. In September 1988 the total foreign debt was only US $18.1m. The average annual rate of inflation rose to 6.3% in 1989, but unemployment had fallen to under 10% by May 1989. Labour shortages have occurred in the agricultural and construction sectors.

Dominica is a member of the OAS (see p. 194), CARICOM (see p. 108) and the OECS (see p. 109). The Charles Government has received considerable aid from the United Kingdom, France, the USA and various international aid agencies. Dominica concluded a fishing agreement with the EEC in 1987 and is a signatory of the Lomé Convention (see p. 151).

The Dominican economy is heavily dependent upon the banana industry, which is, however, very vulnerable to adverse weather conditions. In 1979 Dominica was devastated by Hurricane David, and in 1989 suffered further severe damage from Hurricane Hugo. There is also a perceived threat to the protected banana market in the United Kingdom upon the implementation of the EEC's single internal market during 1992. In 1990 the Charles Government caused some anxiety in the region by expressing more willingness to reach a compromise solution than other Eastern Caribbean administrations. The Charles Government has encouraged efficiency and quality in the banana industry, and has developed agriculture generally through land reform (see Recent History) and investment in road building and other infrastructure. In recent years Dominica has become favoured as a recipient of international aid. Unlike other countries of the region, Dominica is unlikely to become a major tourist destination, on account of its black, volcanic sand. It does, however, possess considerable natural beauty and resources.

Social Welfare

There are main hospitals at Roseau and Portsmouth, with 242 and 50 beds respectively, and two cottage hospitals, at Marigot and Grand Bay. There is a polyclinic at the Princess Margaret Hospital, Roseau. There are 44 health centres, located throughout the island. In 1986 there were 27 physicians working in Dominica.

Education

Education is free and is provided by both government and denominational schools. There are also a number of schools for the mentally and physically handicapped. Education is compulsory for 10 years between five and 15 years of age. Primary education begins at the age of five and lasts for seven years. Secondary education, beginning at 12 years of age, also lasts for seven years, comprising a first cycle of five years and a second of two years. A teacher-training college provides

DOMINICA

further education, and there is also a branch of the University of the West Indies on the island. The rate of adult illiteracy was only 5.6% in 1986.

Public Holidays

1991: 1 January (New Year's Day), 11-12 February (Masquerade, Carnival), 29 March (Good Friday), 1 April (Easter Monday), 6 May (May or Labour Day), 20 May (Whit Monday), 5 August (Emancipation, August Monday), 4 November (for Independence Day), 5 November (Community Service Day), 25-26 December (Christmas).

1992: 1 January (New Year's Day), 2-3 March (Masquerade, Carnival), 17 April (Good Friday), 20 April (Easter Monday), 4 May (May or Labour Day), 8 June (Whit Monday), 3 August (Emancipation, August Monday), 3 November (Independence Day), 4 November (Community Service Day), 25-26 December (Christmas).

Weights and Measures

The imperial system is in use, although the metric system is to be introduced.

Statistical Survey

Sources (unless otherwise stated): Ministry of Finance, Roseau; OECS Economic Affairs Secretariat, *Annual Digest of Statistics*.

AREA AND POPULATION

Area: 749.8 sq km (289.5 sq miles).

Population: 70,513 at census of 7 April 1970; 74,625 at census of 7 April 1981; 81,200 (estimate, 1988).

Density (1988): 108.3 per sq km.

Population by Ethnic Group (*de jure* population, excl. those resident in institutions, 1981): Negro 67,272; Mixed race 4,433; Amerindian (Carib) 1,111; White 341; Total (incl. others) 73,795 (males 36,754, females 37,041). Source: UN, *Demographic Yearbook*.

Principal Towns (population at 1981 census): Roseau (capital) 8,279; Portsmouth 2,200.

Births and Deaths (1987): Birth rate 21.4 per 1,000; Death rate 4.6 per 1,000.

Economically Active Population (1981 census): Agriculture, hunting, forestry and fishing 7,843; Mining and quarrying 8; Manufacturing 1,417; Electricity, gas and water 245; Construction 2,306; Trade, restaurants and hotels 1,613; Transport, storage and communications 914; Financing, insurance, real estate and business services 257; Community, social and personal services 4,980; Activities not adequately defined 1,004; Total employed 20,587 (males 14,057; females 6,530); Unemployed 4,746 (males 2,641; females 2,105); Total labour force 25,333 (males 16,698, females 8,635) (Source: ILO, *Year Book of Labour Statistics*).

AGRICULTURE, ETC.

Principal Crops (FAO estimates, '000 metric tons, 1989): Bananas 46*, Roots and tubers 28 (Taro—Dasheen—11), Vegetables 6, Coconuts 16, Sugar cane 6, Citrus fruits 28 (Grapefruit 17, Limes 6), Mangoes 4. Source: FAO, *Production Yearbook*.

* Official figure.

Livestock (FAO estimates, '000 head, year ending September 1989): Cattle 9, Pigs 5, Sheep 10, Goats 10. Source: FAO, *Production Yearbook*.

Livestock Products (FAO estimates, metric tons, 1989): Meat 1,000; Cows' milk 5,000; Hen eggs 149. Source: FAO, *Production Yearbook*.

Fishing (metric tons, live weight): Total catch 640 in 1985; 644 in 1986; 650 per year (FAO estimates) in 1987 and 1988. Source: FAO, *Yearbook of Fishery Statistics*.

MINING

Pumice ('000 metric tons, 1987): Estimated production 108.9 (Source: US Bureau of Mines).

INDUSTRY

Production (1987): Soap 6,571 metric tons; Electricity 26.6 million kWh.

FINANCE

Currency and Exchange Rates: 100 cents = 1 East Caribbean dollar (EC $). *Coins:* 1, 2, 5, 10, 25 and 50 cents. *Notes:* 1, 5, 20 and 100 dollars. *Sterling and US Dollar Equivalents* (30 September 1990): £1 sterling = EC $5.058; US $1 = EC $2.700; EC $100 = £19.77 = US $37.04. *Exchange Rate:* Fixed at US $1 = EC $2.70 since July 1976.

Budget (government estimates, EC $ million, year ending 30 June 1991): Recurrent revenue 130.8; Recurrent expenditure 118.5; Capital expenditure 110.2.

International reserves (US $ million at 31 December 1989): Reserve position in IMF 0.01; Foreign exchange 11.25; IMF special drawing rights 0.42; Total 11.68. Source: IMF, *International Financial Statistics*.

Money Supply (EC $ million at 31 December 1988): Currency outside banks 22.83; Demand deposits 38.41; Total money 61.24. Source: IMF, *International Financial Statistics*.

Cost of Living (Retail Price Index, base: 1985 = 100): All items 108.4 in 1987; 110.4 in 1988; 117.3 in 1989. Source: IMF, *International Financial Statistics*.

National Accounts (EC $ million at current factor cost): Gross domestic product 281.8 in 1987; 324.3 in 1988; 339.5 in 1989.

Balance of Payments (US $ million, 1988): Merchandise exports f.o.b. 55.60, Merchandise imports f.o.b. -79.55; *Trade balance* -23.95; Exports of services 13.50, Imports of services -16.15; *Balance on goods and services* -26.60; Private unrequited transfers (net) 8.40; Government unrequited transfers (net) 8.81; *Current balance* -9.39; Direct investment 6.90; Other long-term capital (net) 3.50, Short-term capital (net) -10.06; Net errors and omissions 9.31; *Total* (net monetary movements) 0.27; Valuation changes (net) -1.56; Exceptional financing (net) 0.07; *Changes in reserves* -1.23. Source: IMF, *International Financial Statistics*.

EXTERNAL TRADE

Principal Commodities (EC $ '000, 1988): *Imports c.i.f.:* Food and live animals 42,899; Beverages and tobacco 9,716; Mineral fuels, lubricants, etc. 13,197; Chemicals and related products 32,920; Basic manufactures 60,303; Machinery and transport equipment 40,892; Miscellaneous manufactured articles 16,135; Total (incl. others) 236,334. *Exports f.o.b.:* Food and live animals 110,188 (Bananas 103,300); Animal and vegetable oils, fats and waxes 1,571; Chemicals and related products 28,149; Basic manufactures 1,755; Machinery and transport equipment 2,038; Miscellaneous manufactured articles 4,824; Total (incl. others) 149,866.

Principal Trading Partners (EC $ '000, 1988): *Imports c.i.f.:* Barbados 8,479; Canada 7,508; France and the French West Indies 9,652 (France 3,182); Saint Lucia 19,072; Trinidad and Tobago 19,924; United Kingdom 43,531; USA 51,581; Total (incl. others) 236,334. *Exports f.o.b.:* Antigua and Barbuda 2,034; Barbados 3,154; France and the French West Indies 3,099 (Guadeloupe 2,651); Guyana 2,031; Italy 13,246; Jamaica 15,555; Saint Lucia 2,622; Trinidad and Tobago 2,169; United Kingdom 91,341; USA 6,621; Total (incl. others) 149,866.

TRANSPORT

Road Traffic (registered motor vehicles): 4,573 in 1985; 5,254 in 1986; 6,072 in 1987.

Shipping (international sea-borne freight traffic, '000 metric tons, estimates, 1985): Goods loaded 33; Goods unloaded 51. Source: UN, *Monthly Bulletin of Statistics*.

Civil Aviation (1987): Aircraft arrivals 12,964.

EDUCATION

Institutions (1987): 63 pre-primary, 66 primary, 9 secondary, 1 sixth-form college, 1 teacher-training college, 1 nursing school, 1 technical college.

Teachers (1987): 99 pre-primary, 835 primary and general secondary, 27 vocational, 15 teacher-training (1982), 17 tertiary (1984).

DOMINICA

Pupils (1987): 2,598 pre-primary, 12,600* primary, 6,150 general secondary, 60 teacher-training (1982), 259 vocational (1985).

* Estimates.

Source: mainly UNESCO, *Statistical Yearbook*.

TOURISM

Tourist arrivals (arrivals by air and cruise-ship passengers): 36,639 in 1987*; 36,739 in 1988; 27,254 (23,554 arrivals by air, 3,700 cruise-ship passengers) in 1989.

* There were also 2,034 stop-over arrivals by sea in 1987.

Directory

The Constitution

The Constitution came into effect at the independence of Dominica on 3 November 1978. Its main provisions are summarized below:

FUNDAMENTAL RIGHTS AND FREEDOMS

The Constitution guarantees the rights of life, liberty, security of the person, the protection of the law and respect for private property. The individual is entitled to freedom of conscience, of expression and assembly and has the right to an existence free from slavery, forced labour and torture. Protection against discrimination on the grounds of sex, race, place of origin, political opinion, colour or creed is assured.

THE PRESIDENT

The President is elected by the House of Assembly for a term of five years. A presidential candidate is nominated jointly by the Prime Minister and the Leader of the Opposition and on their concurrence is declared elected without any vote being taken; in the case of disagreement the choice will be made by secret ballot in the House of Assembly. Candidates must be citizens of Dominica aged at least 40 who have been resident in Dominica for five years prior to their nomination. A President may not hold office for more than two terms.

PARLIAMENT

Parliament consists of the President and the House of Assembly, composed of 21 elected Representatives and nine Senators. According to the wishes of Parliament, the latter may be appointed by the President—five on the advice of the Prime Minister and four on the advice of the Leader of the Opposition—or elected. The life of Parliament is five years.

Parliament has the power to amend the Constitution. Each constituency returns one Representative to the House who is directly elected in accordance with the Constitution. Every citizen over the age of 18 is eligible to vote.

THE EXECUTIVE

Executive authority is vested in the President. The President appoints as Prime Minister the elected member of the House who commands the support of a majority of its elected members, and other Ministers on the advice of the Prime Minister. Not more than three Ministers may be from among the appointed Senators. The President has the power to remove the Prime Minister from office if a resolution of 'no confidence' in the Government is passed by the House and the Prime Minister does not resign within three days or advise the President to dissolve Parliament.

The Cabinet consists of the Prime Minister, other Ministers and the Attorney-General in an ex officio capacity.

The Leader of the Opposition is appointed by the President as that elected member of the House who, in the President's judgement, is best able to command the support of a majority of the elected members who do not support the Government.

The Government

HEAD OF STATE

President: Sir CLARENCE AUGUSTUS SEIGNORET (assumed office 19 December 1983; second term began 20 December 1988).

CABINET
(January 1991)

Prime Minister and Minister of Finance and Defence: MARY EUGENIA CHARLES.
Minister of External Affairs: BRIAN G. K. ALLEYNE.
Minister of Trade, Industry and Tourism: CHARLES MAYNARD.
Minister of Housing, Communications, Public Works and Road Construction: ALLEYNE CARBON.
Minister of Community Development and Social Affairs: HENRY GEORGE.
Minister of Labour and Immigration: HESKEITH ALEXANDER.
Minister of Education: Senator RUPERT SORHAINDO.
Minister of Health: ALLAN GUYE.
Minister of Agriculture: MAYNARD JOSEPH.
Minister without Portfolio: Senator DERMOT SOUTHWELL.
Attorney-General: JENNER ARMOUR.

MINISTRIES

Office of the President: Morne Bruce, Roseau; tel. 82054.
Office of the Prime Minister: Government Headquarters, Kennedy Ave, Roseau; tel. 82406.

All other Ministries are at Government Headquarters, Kennedy Ave, Roseau; tel. 82401.

CARIB TERRITORY

This reserve of the remaining Amerindian population is located on the central east coast of the island. The Caribs enjoy a measure of local government and elect their chief.

Chief: IRVINCE AUGUISTE.

Waitukubuli Karifuna Development Committee: Salybia, Carib Territory.

Legislature

HOUSE OF ASSEMBLY

Speaker: CRISPIN SORHAIDOO.
Clerk: ALBERTHA JNO BAPTISTE.
Senators: 9.
Elected Members: 21.

Election, 28 May 1990

Party	Votes cast	%	Seats
Dominica Freedom Party	16,529	49.4	11
Dominica United Workers' Party	8,979	26.8	6
Labour Party of Dominica	7,860	23.5	4
Dominica Progressive Party	74	0.2	—
Total	33,442	100.0	21

Political Organizations

Dominica Freedom Party (DFP): Cross St, Roseau; tel. 82104; Leader MARY EUGENIA CHARLES.

Dominica Progressive Party: Roseau; f. 1990; Leader LEONARD (PAPPY) BAPTISTE.

Dominica United Workers' Party (UWP): Roseau; f. 1988; Chair. EDISON JAMES.

Labour Party of Dominica (LPD): Roseau; f. 1985; merger and reunification of left-wing groups, incl. the Dominica Labour Party (f. 1961); Leader MICHAEL A. DOUGLAS; Gen. Sec. JEROME BARZEY.

Diplomatic Representation

EMBASSIES IN DOMINICA

China (Taiwan): Morne Daniel, POB 56, Roseau; tel. 91385; telex 8661; fax 92085; Chargé d'affaires: GEORGE CHAN.

DOMINICA

Venezuela: 3rd Floor, 37 Cork St, Roseau; tel. 83348; telex 8643; fax 86198; Ambassador: HÉCTOR GRIFFIN.

Judicial System

Justice is administered by the Eastern Caribbean Supreme Court (based in Saint Lucia), consisting of a Court of Appeal and a High Court. One of the six puisne judges of the High Court is resident in Dominica and presides over the Court of Summary Jurisdiction. The District Magistrate Courts deal with summary offences and civil offences involving limited sums of money (specified by law).

Religion

Most of the population profess Christianity, but there are some Muslims, Hindus, Jews and Bahá'ís. The largest denomination is the Roman Catholic Church (76.9% of the inhabitants, according to the 1981 census).

CHRISTIANITY

The Roman Catholic Church

Dominica comprises the single diocese of Roseau, suffragan to the archdiocese of Castries (Saint Lucia). At 31 December 1988 there were an estimated 57,500 adherents in the country, representing a large majority of the inhabitants. The Bishop participates in the Antilles Episcopal Conference (currently based in Kingston, Jamaica).

Bishop of Roseau: Rt Rev. ARNOLD BOGHAERT; Bishop's House, 20 Virgin Lane, POB 339, Roseau; tel. 82837.

The Anglican Communion

Anglicans in Dominica are adherents of the Church in the Province of the West Indies. The country forms part of the diocese of the North Eastern Caribbean and Aruba. The Bishop, who is also Archbishop of the Province, is resident in Antigua.

Other Christian Churches

There are churches of various denominations, including Methodist, Pentecostal, Baptist, Church of God, Presbyterian, the Assemblies of Brethren, Moravian and Seventh-day Adventist groups, and the Jehovah's Witnesses.

BAHÁ'Í FAITH

National Spiritual Assembly: 21 Margaret's Gap, POB 367, Roseau; tel. 84269.

The Press

New Chronicle: 7 Queen Mary St, POB 124, Roseau; tel. 82121; telex 8625; fax 85984; f. 1909; Friday; progressive independent; Gen. Man. J. A. WHITE; Editor MORRIS CYRILLE; circ. 4,500.

Official Gazette: Government Printery, Roseau; tel. 82401, ext. 330; telex 8613; weekly; circ. 550.

Radio and Television

There were an estimated 40,000 radio receivers and 4,000 television receivers in use in 1987. There is no national television service, although there is a cable television network serving one-third of the island.

RADIO

Dominica Broadcasting Corporation: Victoria St, POB 1, Roseau; tel. 83283; government station; daily broadcasts in English; 2 hrs daily in French patois; 10 kW transmitter on the medium wave band; programmes received throughout Caribbean excluding Jamaica and Guyana; Gen. Man. GEORGE JOHN; Programme Dir SHERMAINE GREEN.

Voice of Life Radio—ZGBC: Gospel Broadcasting Corpn, Loubiere, POB 205, Roseau; tel. 84391; linked to the US Christian Reformed Church; 126 hrs weekly; Man. Dir WAYNE K. DEBOER.

Voice of the Islands Radio—VOI: Pte Michel, POB 402, Roseau; tel. 84042; religious; managed by Racom Int.; 126 hrs weekly; Exec. Dir Rev. RAYMOND CONARD.

TELEVISION

Marpin-TV: POB 382, Roseau; tel. 84107; fax 82965; commercial; cable service; Prog. Man. RON ABRAHAM.

Finance

The Eastern Caribbean Central Bank (see p. 109), based in Saint Christopher, is the central issuing and monetary authority for Dominica.

BANKS

Agricultural, Industrial and Development (AID) Bank: 64 Hillsborough St, POB 215, Roseau; tel. 82853; telex 8620; fax 84903; f. 1971; state-owned; cap. EC $5m. (1988); Man. PATRICIA CHARLES.

Bank of Nova Scotia (Canada): 12 Hillsborough St, POB 520, Roseau; tel. 85800; telex 8671.

Banque Française Commerciale (France): Corner of Queen Mary St and Gt Marlborough St, POB 166, Roseau; tel. 84040; telex 8629; fax 85335; Man. P. INGLISS.

Barclays Bank (United Kingdom): Old St, POB 4, Roseau; tel. 82571; telex 8618; fax 83471; Man. C. MCINTYRE; sub-branch in Portsmouth.

Dominica Co-operative Bank: 9 Gt Marlborough St, Roseau; tel. 82580.

International Bank of Roseau: 14 Cork St, Roseau; tel. 88106.

National Commercial Bank of Dominica: 64 Hillsborough St, POB 271, Roseau; tel. 84401; telex 8620; fax 83982; govt-owned; Chair. FRANK A. BARON; Gen. Man. LAMBERT V. LEWIS.

Royal Bank of Canada: Bay St, POB 144, Roseau; tel. 82771; telex 8637; fax 85398; Man. H. PINARD.

INSURANCE

Several British, regional and US companies have agents in Roseau. Local companies include the following:

J. B. Charles and Co Ltd: Old St, POB 121, Roseau; tel. 82876.

Tonge Inc—Insurance Specialist and Consultant: 19–21 King George V St, POB 20, Roseau; tel. 84027; telex 8631; fax 85778.

Windward Islands Crop Insurance Co (Wincrop): Gt Marlborough St, Roseau; tel. 83955; f. 1987; regional; coverage for weather destruction of, mainly, banana crops; total assets (1988) EC $6.2m.; Man. KERWIN FERREIRA; brs in Grenada and Saint Lucia.

Trade and Industry

Dominica Association of Industry and Commerce (DAIC): 15 King George V St, POB 85, Roseau; tel. 82874; f. 1972 by a merger of the Manufacturers' Association and the Chamber of Commerce; represents the business sector, liaises with the Government, and stimulates commerce and industry; 91 mems; Pres. SHERIDAN GREGOIRE; Exec. Sec. FERDINAND A. AZILLE.

Dominica Employers' Federation: 14 Church St, POB 85, Roseau; tel. 82314; Pres. FRANCIS A. EMMANUEL; Exec. Dir SHIRLEY GUYE.

Eastern Caribbean States Export Development Agency (ECSEDA): c/o Govt Headquarters, Kennedy Ave, Roseau; f. 1990; OECS regional development org.; Exec. Dir JUSTIN VINCENT.

STATE ENTERPRISES AND STATUTORY CORPORATIONS

Co-operative Citrus Growers' Association: 21 Hanover St, Roseau; tel. 82062; telex 8615; f. 1954; processing and marketing of citrus fruits; Pres. P. NORMAN ROLLE.

DOMLEC: Castle St, POB 13, Roseau; tel. 82681; telex 8655; state-owned national electricity service.

Dominica Banana Marketing Corporation (DBMC): Corner of Queen Mary St and Turkey Lane, Roseau; tel. 82671; telex 8648; f. 1934 as Dominica Banana Growers' Association; restructured 1982; state-supported; Chair. VANOULST JNO CHARLES; Gen. Man. AMBROSE V. GEORGE.

Dominica Export-Import Agency (Dexia): POB 173, Roseau; tel. 82780; telex 8626; fax 86308; f. 1986; replaced the Dominica Agricultural Marketing Board and the External Trade Bureau; export development and importer of basic foodstuffs.

National Development Corporation (NDC): Bath Estate, POB 293, Roseau; tel. 82045; telex 8642; fax 85840; f. 1988 by merger of Industrial Development Corpn (f. 1974) and Tourist Board; promotes local and foreign investment to increase employment, production and exports; promotes and co-ordinates tourism; Chair. Senator DERMOT SOUTHWELL; Gen. Man. KENNETH ALLEYNE.

MARKETING AND CO-OPERATIVE ORGANIZATIONS

At the end of 1986 there were 22 registered credit unions, with 39,218 members and share capital of EC $29.5m. There were also 36 other registered co-operatives, of which 19 were agricultural (citrus, fisheries, craft, poultry, vegetables, bay oil, bananas and sugar cane), with 1,861 members and share capital of approximately EC $72,000.

TRADE UNIONS

Civil Service Association: Valley Rd/Windsor Lane, Roseau; tel. 82102; f. 1940 and registered as a trade union in 1960; representing all grades of civil servants, including firemen, prison officers, nurses, teachers and postal workers; Pres. ARTHUR R. SMITH; Sec. ALVIN THOMAS; 1,700 mems.

Dominica Amalgamated Workers' Union (DAWU): 40 Kennedy Ave, POB 137, Roseau; tel. 83048; f. 1960; Gen. Sec. DARRYL D. GAGE; 500 mems.

Dominica Farmers' Union: 17 Church St, Roseau; tel. 84244.

Dominica Trade Union: 70–71 Queen Mary St, Roseau; tel. 82903; f. 1945; Pres. KENNEDY PASCAL; Gen. Sec. LEO J. BERNARD NICHOLAS; 850 mems.

National Workers Union: Corner of Church St and Old St, Roseau; tel. 84465; f. 1977; Pres. RAWLINS JERMOTT; Gen. Sec. DAVIDSON BERTRAND; 800 mems.

Waterfront and Allied Workers' Union: 43 Hillsborough St, Roseau; tel. 82343; f. 1965; Pres. LOUIS BENOIT; Gen. Sec. CURTIS AUGUSTUS; 1,500 mems.

Transport

ROADS

At the end of 1984 there were 327 km (231 miles) of first-class, 262 km (163 miles) of second-class and 117 km (73 miles) of third-class motorable roads, as well as 282 miles (454 km) of tracks. Extensive road development was completed in 1986 and further improvements continued, despite the problem of damage caused by heavy rains.

SHIPPING

A deep-water harbour at Woodbridge Bay serves Roseau, which is the principal port. Several foreign shipping lines call at Roseau, and there is a high-speed ferry service between Antigua and Guadeloupe which goes via Montserrat and Dominica. Ships of the Geest Line call at Portsmouth, to collect bananas, and cruise-ship facilities were constructed there during 1990. There are other specialized berthing facilities on the west coast.

Dominica Ports Authority: POB 243, Roseau; tel. 84431; fax 86131.

CIVIL AVIATION

Melville Hall Airport, 64 km (40 miles) from Roseau, and Canefield Airport, 5 km (3 miles) from Roseau, are the two airports on the island. In 1990 it was decided to proceed with the construction of an international airport. The regional airline, LIAT (based in Antigua and Barbuda, and in which Dominica is a shareholder), provides daily services and, with Air Guadeloupe, Air Martinique, Air BVI and Winlink (Saint Lucia), connects Dominica with all the islands of the Eastern Caribbean, including the international airports of Puerto Rico, Antigua, Guadeloupe and Martinique.

Tourism

The Government has designated areas of the island as nature reserves, to preserve the beautiful, lush scenery and the rich natural heritage that is Dominica's main tourist attraction. Birdlife is particularly prolific, and includes several rare and endangered species, such as the Imperial parrot. There are also two marine reserves. Tourism is not as developed as it is among Dominica's neighbours. There were 27,254 visitors in 1989.

National Development Corporation (NDC)—Division of Tourism: Valley Rd, POB 73, Roseau; tel. 82351; telex 8642; fax 85840; f. 1988, when Tourist Board merged with Industrial Development Corpn; Dir of Tourism MARIE-JOSE EDWARDS.

Dominica Hotel Association: POB 270, Roseau; tel. 84436; telex 8607.

THE DOMINICAN REPUBLIC

Introductory Survey

Location, Climate, Language, Religion, Flag, Capital

The Dominican Republic occupies the eastern part of the island of Hispaniola, which lies between Cuba and Puerto Rico in the Caribbean Sea. The country's only international frontier is with Haiti, to the west. The climate is sub-tropical, with an average annual temperature of 27°C (80°F). In Santo Domingo, temperatures are generally between 19°C (66°F) and 31°C (88°F). The west and south-west of the country are arid. Hispaniola lies in the path of tropical cyclones. The official language is Spanish. Almost all of the inhabitants profess Christianity, and more than 90% are Roman Catholics. There are small Protestant and Jewish communities. The national flag (proportions 23 by 15) is blue (upper hoist and lower fly) and red (lower hoist and upper fly), quartered by a white cross. The state flag has, in addition, the national coat of arms, showing a quartered shield in the colours of the flag (on which are superimposed national banners, a cross and an open Bible) between scrolls above and below, at the centre of the cross. The capital is Santo Domingo.

Recent History

The Dominican Republic became independent in 1844, although it was occupied by US military forces between 1916 and 1924. General Rafael Leonidas Trujillo Molina overthrew the elected President, Horacio Vázquez, in 1930 and dominated the country until his assassination in May 1961. The dictator ruled personally from 1930 to 1947 and indirectly thereafter. His brother, Héctor Trujillo, was President from 1947 until August 1960, when he was replaced by Dr Joaquín Balaguer, hitherto Vice-President. After Rafael Trujillo's death, President Balaguer remained in office, but in December 1961 he permitted moderate opposition groups to participate in a Council of State, which exercised legislative and executive powers. Balaguer resigned in January 1962, when the Council of State became the Provisional Government. A presidential election in December 1962, the country's first free election for 38 years, was won by Dr Juan Bosch Gaviño, the founder and leader of the Partido Revolucionario Dominicano (PRD), who had been in exile since 1930. President Bosch, a left-of-centre democrat, took office in February 1963 but was overthrown in the following September by a military coup. The leaders of the armed forces transferred power to a civilian triumvirate, led by Emilio de los Santos. In April 1965 a revolt by supporters of ex-President Bosch overthrew the triumvirate. Civil war broke out between pro-Bosch forces and military units headed by Gen. Elías Wessin y Wessin, who had played a leading role in the 1963 coup. The violence was eventually suppressed by the intervention of some 23,000 US troops, who were formally incorporated into an Inter-American peace force by the Organization of American States (OAS) after they had landed. The peace force withdrew in September 1965.

Following a period of provisional government under Héctor García Godoy, a presidential election in June 1966 was won by ex-President Balaguer, the candidate of the Partido Reformista Social Cristiano (PRSC), who won 57% of the votes cast, while ex-President Bosch won 39%. The PRSC, founded in 1964, also won a majority of seats in both houses of the National Congress. President Balaguer took office in July. A new constitution was promulgated in November 1966. Despite his association with the Trujillo dictatorship, Balaguer initially proved to be a popular leader, and in May 1970 he was re-elected for a further four years. In February 1973 a state of emergency was declared when guerrilla forces landed on the coast. Captain Francisco Caamaño Deño, the leader of the 1965 revolt, and his followers were killed. Bosch and other opposition figures went into hiding. Bosch later resigned as leader of the PRD (founding the Partido de la Liberación Dominicana—PLD), undermining hopes of a united opposition in the May 1974 elections, when President Balaguer was re-elected with a large majority. In June 1975 guerrilla forces of Dominican *émigrés* from Cuba landed on the island in an unsuccessful attempt to overthrow Balaguer.

In the May 1978 presidential election, Dr Balaguer was defeated by the PRD candidate, Silvestre Antonio Guzmán Fernández. This was the first occasion in the country's history when an elected President yielded power to an elected successor. An attempted military coup in favour of Dr Balaguer was prevented by pressure from the US Government. On assuming office in August, President Guzmán undertook to professionalize the armed forces by removing politically ambitious high-ranking officers. In June 1981 he declared his support for Jacobo Majluta Azar, his Vice-President, as his successor but in November the PRD rejected Majluta's candidacy in favour of Dr Salvador Jorge Blanco, a left-wing senator, who was elected President in May 1982. In the congressional elections, held at the same time, the PRD gained a majority in both the Senate and the Chamber of Deputies. President Guzmán committed suicide in July after allegations of fraud were made against his Government and members of his family. Vice-President Majluta was immediately sworn in as interim President until Dr Blanco assumed office in August. Although a member of the Socialist International, Blanco maintained good relations with the USA (on which the country is economically dependent) and declared that he would not resume relations with Cuba. In December 1982 the Government revealed that it would not nationalize foreign property, including extensive holdings owned by petroleum companies, in the Dominican Republic.

In 1983 popular discontent with the Government's austerity programme led to the occupation of the Ministry of Agriculture by peasants, and calls for agrarian reform. In August 1983 a two-week purge of subversives took place on the orders of President Blanco. Two visiting Cuban academics were deported, and Socialist and Communist Party sympathizers were arrested. The Government's move came in response to a report which implicated Cuban and Nicaraguan involvement in the increased left-wing activity in the country.

In April 1984 a series of public protests against substantial increases in the cost of essential items erupted into violent confrontations between government forces and demonstrators in Santo Domingo and four other cities, which lasted for three days. In the course of the protests, more than 50 people were killed, some 200 injured and over 4,000 arrested. The Government held opposition groups of the extreme right and left responsible for the unrest. In May the Government responded to the prospect of further demonstrations by ordering the arrest of more than 100 trade union and left-wing leaders. In August, in anticipation of civil unrest at the announcement of new price increases, more arrests were made among trade union and opposition leaders. Rumours of a plot against the Government by left-wing sympathizers caused serious disquiet throughout the country. Further demonstrations, including one attended by 40,000 people in Santo Domingo, were held in protest at the continuing economic decline.

In February 1985 a further series of substantial price increases led to violent clashes between demonstrators and police, during which four people died and more than 50 were injured. Public unrest was exacerbated by the Government's decision, in April, to accept the IMF's terms for further financial aid. In June a 24-hour general strike was organized by trade unions, in protest at the Government's economic policy and its refusal to increase the minimum wage. In July, however, the threat of a 48-hour general strike prompted the Government to order an immediate increase in the minimum wage.

Further violence preceded the presidential and legislative elections of May 1986. Several people were killed, and many more injured, in clashes between rival political supporters. The three principal candidates in the presidential election were all former Presidents: Dr Joaquín Balaguer of the PRSC; Jacobo Majluta, who, having registered La Estructura, his right-wing faction of the PRD, as a separate political party in July 1985, nevertheless secured the candidacy of the ruling PRD; and Dr Juan Bosch of the PLD. The counting of votes was suspended twice, following allegations by Majluta of fraud by the PRSC and by the Central Electoral Board, two of the three members of which then resigned. Dr Balaguer was finally declared the winner by a narrow margin of votes over Majluta, his closest rival. In the simultaneous legislative elections, the PRSC won 21 of the 30 seats in the Senate and 56 of the 120 seats in the Chamber of Deputies.

Upon taking office as President (for the fifth time) in August 1986, Dr Balaguer initiated an investigation into alleged corrupt practices by members of the outgoing administration. The former President was charged with embezzlement and the illegal purchase of military vehicles. The financial accounts of the armed forces were examined, and the former Secretary of State for the Armed Forces was subsequently imprisoned. In July 1987 a general strike was organized by the trade unions, in support of a demand for an increase of 62% in the minimum wage. In September the Cabinet resigned, at the request of the President, to enable him to restructure the Government. Some 35,000 government posts were abolished in an attempt to reduce public spending, and the money thus becoming available was to be used to finance a programme of public works projects which were expected to create almost 100,000 new jobs. Nevertheless, strike action continued. The situation worsened in February 1988, when demonstrations took place throughout the country, to protest against the high cost of living, after the price of staple foods was increased. Six people were killed as the police intervened to quell the protests. Subsequently, the Roman Catholic Church mediated between the opposing sides, and President Balaguer agreed to stabilize prices of staple foods and to increase the minimum wage by 33%. However, prices continued to rise, provoking a new wave of strikes in June.

In 1989 opposition to the Government's economic policies intensified. The elimination of preferential exchange rates, which took effect in January, resulted in further price increases for basic commodities. In an unpopular measure to stabilize the peso, the Government had earlier curbed the activities of unlicensed money-traders, so restricting the flow of dollars from remittances from *émigrés* in the USA. Thus, a major source of foreign exchange was eliminated, thereby preventing a large section of the population from receiving financial support from relatives in the USA. Popular discontent was aggravated by the deterioration of public utilities, particularly water and electricity. In March a strike by teachers demanding higher wages led to violent clashes in the Duarte province between demonstrators and police. In June the Conferencia Nacional de Organizaciones Populares called a 48-hour general strike. More than 300 organizations supported the action, which reportedly paralysed the country for two days. The major demands were the doubling of the minimum wage, the implementation of the 1988 tripartite agreement on workers' conditions and benefits, a reduction in the prices of staple commodities and medicines, and the ending of interruptions in the supplies of water and electricity. Four people were killed, and an estimated 3,000 arrested, during the protests. Despite mediation efforts by the Roman Catholic Church, the Government made no concessions to union demands. In October, following a 66% rise in fuel prices, there were further violent demonstrations.

In September 1989 President Balaguer implemented a number of ministerial changes, in an attempt to enhance the popular appeal of his Government. In the same month, the governor of the Central Bank was dismissed after publicly criticizing the Government.

With presidential and legislative elections due to take place in May 1990, President Balaguer's prospects for re-election were hampered considerably by the continuing deterioration of the economy (particularly rapid inflation), the worsening energy crisis, and criticism of government spending on expansive public works programmes which had resulted in a severe depletion of the country's reserves of foreign exchange. The principal contender for the presidency was the PLD candidate, Dr Juan Bosch, who concentrated his election campaign on seeking support from the private sector, promising privatization of state-owned companies. In opinion polls conducted in the period preceding the presidential election, Bosch appeared to have a clear advantage. When the initial results indicated a narrow victory for Balaguer, Bosch accused the ruling PRSC and the Junta Central Electoral of a 'colossal fraud', necessitating a re-count, supervised by monitors from the OAS. Almost two months after the election, Balaguer was declared the official winner.

In August 1990, in an attempt to reduce inflation by cutting government subsidies, the Government announced a programme of austerity measures, including substantial increases in the cost of fuel and food. Petrol and essential foodstuffs were almost doubled in price. In an attempt to stimulate exports and to divert foreign currency from the 'black market' and into the Central Bank, the currency was devalued. The trade unions reacted angrily to the austerity measures, calling a 48-hour general strike. This action was violently suppressed by units of the army, and the ensuing conflict resulted in as many as 14 deaths. The price increases were partially offset by an increase of 30% in the salaries of army personnel and civilian employees in the public sector. The trade unions, however, rejected an identical offer by the private sector and threatened further strike action if their demands for basic food subsidies and considerable wage increases were not satisfied. In September a three-day general strike, organized by the Organizaciones Colectivas Populares (OCP), led to further arrests, injuries and at least one death. In the following month a further general strike was called by the OCP and the Central General de Trabajadores (CGT), with the stated aim of ousting Balaguer from power. Violent clashes with the army in Santo Domingo resulted in a further four deaths.

Relations with Haiti remained tense in 1988. Dominican soldiers were accused of arresting immigrant Haitians in order to use them as cutters during the sugar harvest. The problem was eased somewhat when the deposed Haitian leader, Gen. Henri Namphy, was refused permission to remain in the Dominican Republic. Subsequently, however, Gen. Namphy was unable to find a country willing to accept him as a political exile, and the Dominican Government was obliged to allow him to stay. In January 1989 a traffic accident, in which 47 Haitian sugar workers were killed, focused attention on the continuing illegal import of plantation labour into the Dominican Republic from Haiti.

In November 1988 the former President, Dr Salvador Jorge Blanco, was convicted, in his absence, of corruption during his presidency. He returned to the country from the USA in December, and was sentenced to 20 years' imprisonment. In April 1989, however, he obtained a further consideration of his case. In March 1990 a warrant for his arrest was issued, after he failed to obey a summons to appear in court.

Government

The Dominican Republic comprises 26 provinces, each administered by an appointed governor, and a Distrito Nacional (DN) containing the capital. Under the 1966 Constitution, legislative power is exercised by the bicameral National Congress, with a Senate of 30 members and a Chamber of Deputies (120 members). Members of both houses are elected for four years by universal adult suffrage. Executive power lies with the President, who is also elected by direct popular vote for four years. He is assisted by a Vice-President and a Cabinet containing Secretaries of State.

Defence

Military service is voluntary and lasts for four years. In June 1990 the armed forces totalled 22,800 men: army 15,000, air force 3,800 and navy 4,000. Paramilitary forces number 1,000. Defence expenditure for 1987 was estimated at RD $294.5m.

Economic Affairs

In 1988, according to estimates by the World Bank, the Dominican Republic's gross national product (GNP), measured at average 1986–88 prices, was US $4,690m., equivalent to $680 per head. During 1980–88, it was estimated, GNP increased, in real terms, at an average rate of 0.8% per year. GNP per head, however, declined by 1.6% annually. Over the same period, the population increased by an annual average of 2.4%. The Dominican Republic's gross domestic product (GDP) increased, in real terms, by an annual average of 2.2% in 1980–88.

Agriculture, including forestry and fishing, contributed 15.1% of GDP in 1989. In that year an estimated 37% of the labour force were employed in the agricultural sector. The principal cash crops are sugar cane (raw sugar and molasses accounted for 18.1% of total export earnings in 1989), coffee and cocoa beans. During 1980–88 agricultural production increased by an annual average of 0.8%.

THE DOMINICAN REPUBLIC

Introductory Survey

Industry (including mining, manufacturing, construction and power) employed 18.2% of the labour force in 1981, and contributed 32.3% of GDP in 1989. During 1980–88 industrial production increased by an annual average of 2.5%.

Mining contributed 4.0% of GDP in 1989, but employed only 0.3% of the labour force in 1981. The major mineral exports are ferro-nickel (providing 40.2% of total export earnings in 1989) and doré, a gold-silver alloy (7.5%).

Manufacturing contributed 16.4% of GDP in 1989, and employed 12.6% of the labour force in 1981. Based on the value of sales, the most important branches of manufacturing in 1984 were food products (accounting for 38.9% of the total), petroleum refineries (11.3%), beverages (11.3%) and chemicals (8.4%).

Energy is derived principally from petroleum. Imports of mineral fuels comprised 18.8% of the value of total imports in 1986.

The services sector contributed 52.6% of GDP in 1989. Around 23.9% of the labour force were employed in this sector in 1981, which expanded at an average annual rate of 2.5% during 1980–88. Receipts from tourism were expected to reach US $650m. in 1989.

In 1989 the Dominican Republic recorded a visible trade deficit of US $1,039.4m., and there was a deficit of $127.2m. on the current account of the balance of payments. In 1986 the principal source of imports (37.9%) was the USA. In 1989 the USA was the principal market for exports (50.5%). Other major trading partners are Venezuela and Mexico. The principal exports in 1989 were ferro-nickel and raw sugar. The principal imports in 1986 were petroleum and petroleum products, and machinery.

In 1989 there was an estimated budgetary surplus of 122.1m. pesos. The Dominican Republic's total external public debt at the end of 1988 was US $3,216m. In that year the cost of debt-servicing was equivalent to 13.4% of revenue from exports of goods and services. By the end of 1990 the total foreign debt was expected to reach $4,500m. The average annual rate of inflation was estimated at 100% in 1990. An estimated 30% of the labour force were unemployed in 1989.

In July 1984 the Dominican Republic was granted observer status in CARICOM (see p. 108). In December 1989 the country was accepted as a member of the ACP nations covered by the Lomé Convention (see p. 151). In 1990 the Dominican Republic's application for membership of CARICOM was threatened when ACP nations accused the Dominican Republic of breaking an agreement made under the Lomé Convention concerning the export of bananas to EEC countries.

In 1988 there was a sharp decline in economic growth, as a result of a fall in domestic consumption and private investment. Real wages were severely depressed by a high rate of inflation and fluctuating exchange rates. Exports of coffee and minerals declined, as external demand decelerated. Consequently, in 1988 real GDP grew by less than 1%, despite high public capital expenditure, and remained at a similar level in 1989, the difficulties being exacerbated by a poor sugar harvest. The elimination of the preferential exchange rate for the peso in early 1989 led to a sharp reduction in the supply of foreign exchange. In 1990 the worsening energy crisis (insufficient and outmoded electricity network and fuel shortages) and lack of foreign exchange severely affected the country's economy. Industry suffered, in particular, with interruptions, lasting up to 20 hours per day, in the supply of electric power.

Social Welfare

A voluntary national contributory scheme, introduced in 1947, provides insurance cover for sickness, unemployment, accidental injury, maternity, old age and death. Only 42% of the population are thought to benefit from the system. In 1980 there were 571 hospitals and clinics, 2,142 physicians and 8,953 hospital beds under the auspices of the public health and welfare department and the Institute of Social Security. The 1989 budget allocated 338.7m. pesos (5.7% of total expenditure) to the health sector.

Education

Education is, where possible, compulsory for children between the ages of seven and 14 years. Primary education begins at the age of seven and lasts for six years. Secondary education, starting at 13 years of age, also lasts for six years, comprising a first cycle of two years and a second of four years. In 1986 the total enrolment at primary and secondary schools was equivalent to 91% of the school-age population, while primary enrolment included 79% of children in the relevant age-group. In 1983/84 there were an estimated 5,864 primary schools and 1,664 secondary schools. There are eight universities. Budgetary expenditure on education by the central Government in 1989 was 393.1m. pesos, representing about 6.6% of total spending. In 1985, according to UNESCO estimates, the average rate of adult illiteracy was 22.7%.

Public Holidays

1991: 1 January (New Year's Day), 6 January (Epiphany), 21 January (Our Lady of Altagracia), 26 January (Duarte), 27 February (Independence), 29 March (Good Friday), 14 April (Pan-American Day), 1 May (Labour Day), 16 July (Foundation of Sociedad la Trinitaria), 16 August (Restoration Day), 24 September (Our Lady of Mercedes), 12 October (Columbus Day), 24 October (United Nations Day), 1 November (All Saints' Day), 25 December (Christmas Day).

1992: 1 January (New Year's Day), 6 January (Epiphany), 21 January (Our Lady of Altagracia), 26 January (Duarte), 27 February (Independence), 14 April (Pan-American Day), 17 April (Good Friday), 1 May (Labour Day), 16 July (Foundation of Sociedad la Trinitaria), 16 August Restoration Day), 24 September (Our Lady of Mercedes), 12 October (Columbus Day), 24 October (United Nations Day), 1 November (All Saints' Day), 25 December (Christmas Day).

Weights and Measures

The metric system is officially in force but the imperial system is often used.

Statistical Survey

Source (unless otherwise stated): Oficina Nacional de Estadísticas, Edif. de Oficinas Públicas, Avda México esq. Leopoldo Navarro, Santo Domingo; Banco Central de la República Dominicana, Santo Domingo; tel. 689-8141; telex 346-0052.

Area and Population

AREA, POPULATION AND DENSITY

Area (sq km)	
Land	48,072
Inland water	350
Total	48,422*
Population (census results)†	
9 January 1970	4,009,458
12 December 1981	
Males	2,832,454
Females	2,815,523
Total	5,647,977
Population (official estimates at mid-year)	
1987	6,716,000
1988	6,867,000
1989	7,012,367
Density (per sq km) at mid-1989	144.8

* 18,696 sq miles.
† Excluding adjustment for underenumeration.

Births and Deaths: Registered live births 175,935 (birth rate 28.1 per 1,000) in 1984; Registered deaths 27,844 (death rate 4.3 per 1,000) in 1985.

PRINCIPAL TOWNS (population at 1981 census)

Santo Domingo, DN (capital)	1,313,172
Santiago de los Caballeros	278,638
La Romana	91,571
San Pedro de Macorís	78,562
San Francisco de Macorís	64,906
Concepción de la Vega	52,432
San Juan	49,764
Barahona	49,334
San Felipe de Puerto Plata	45,348

ECONOMICALLY ACTIVE POPULATION (1981 census)*

	Males	Females	Total
Agriculture, hunting, forestry and fishing	378,274	42,189	420,463
Mining and quarrying	4,304	439	4,743
Manufacturing	166,748	57,689	224,437
Electricity, gas and water	12,090	1,801	13,891
Construction	77,880	2,970	80,850
Trade, restaurants and hotels	131,634	60,547	192,181
Transport, storage and communications	36,577	3,893	40,470
Financing, insurance, real estate and business services	14,944	7,425	22,369
Community, social and personal services	157,398	205,727	363,125
Activities not adequately defined	284,822	136,806	421,628
Total	**1,264,671**	**519,486**	**1,784,157**

* Figures exclude persons seeking work for the first time, totalling 131,231 (males 96,438; females 34,793), but include other unemployed persons, totalling 220,163 (males 144,823; females 75,340).

Source: ILO, *Year Book of Labour Statistics*.

Agriculture

PRINCIPAL CROPS ('000 metric tons)

	1987	1988	1989
Rice (paddy)	515	499	467†
Maize	47	56	84
Sorghum	39	39	50
Potatoes	27	27	30
Sweet potatoes	38	45	86
Cassava (Manioc)	98	126	156
Yams	4	9	10
Other roots and tubers	33	40	49
Dry beans	52	54	75
Groundnuts (in shell)	39†	34*	36*
Coconuts	71	129	118
Copra	14	26	23
Tomatoes	173	163	170*
Sugar cane	8,772	8,375	8,718†
Oranges*	64	65	65
Lemons and limes*	9	9	9
Avocados*	133	133	133
Mangoes*	192	192	190
Pineapples	72	44	44*
Bananas	373†	391†	384
Plantains†	672	651	809
Coffee (green)	67	68	42
Cocoa beans	39	41	49†
Tobacco (leaves)	29	30	29

* FAO estimate(s).   † Unofficial figure(s).
Source: FAO, *Production Yearbook*.

LIVESTOCK ('000 head, year ending September)

	1987	1988	1989
Horses*	300	310	310
Mules*	130	132	132
Asses*	140	142	142
Cattle	2,092	2,129	2,245
Pigs	389	409	429
Sheep†	95	100	110
Goats†	521	534	543

* FAO estimates.   † Unofficial figures.

Chickens (FAO estimates, million): 19 in 1987; 22 in 1988; 25 in 1989.

Source: FAO, *Production Yearbook*.

LIVESTOCK PRODUCTS ('000 metric tons)

	1987	1988	1989
Beef and veal	67	69	71*
Poultry meat	89	99	112
Cows' milk	289†	290*	290*
Butter*	1.5	1.5	1.5
Cheese*	2.5	2.5	2.5
Hen eggs	17.9	19.1	28.8†
Cattle hides (fresh)*	7.9	8.1	8.4

*FAO estimates.   † Unofficial figures.
Source: FAO, *Production Yearbook*.

THE DOMINICAN REPUBLIC

Fishing

('000 metric tons, live weight)

	1986	1987	1988*
Inland waters	0.8	1.9	2.0
Atlantic Ocean	16.3	18.5	16.8
Total catch	17.2	20.3	18.8

* FAO estimates.
Source: FAO, *Yearbook of Fishery Statistics*.

Mining*

	1987	1988	1989
Ferro-nickel (metric tons)	85,567	77,209	82,260
Gold (troy oz)	250,714	203,655	172,154
Silver (troy oz)	1,092,933	1,419,532	700,417

* Figures are provisional.

Industry*

SELECTED PRODUCTS

	1987	1988	1989
Wheat flour and derivatives ('000 quintals†)	5,644.8	4,902.1	4,951.0
Refined sugar ('000 metric tons)	85.6	98.9	108.3
Molasses ('000 US gallons)	52,052.2	54,951.0	47,502.4
Cement ('000 sacks)	27,918.3	28,756.6	29,866.9
Beer ('000 litres)	120,818.3	143,509.4	146,636.9
Spirits ('000 litres)	34,417.9	31,629.8	32,895.0
Cigarettes (million)	4,329.5	4,942.1	4,823.5

* Figures are provisional.
† Figures are in terms of the old Spanish quintal, equivalent to 46 kg (101.4lb).
Electric energy: 5,296 million kWh in 1987.

Finance

CURRENCY AND EXCHANGE RATES
Monetary Units
  100 centavos = 1 Dominican Republic peso (RD $ or peso oro)
Denominations
  Coins: 1, 5, 10, 25 and 50 centavos; 1 peso.
  Notes: 1, 5, 10, 20, 50, 100, 500 and 1,000 pesos.
Sterling and Dollar Equivalents (30 September 1990)
  £1 sterling = 19.39 pesos;
  US $1 = 10.35 pesos;
  1,000 Dominican Republic pesos = £51.57 = US $96.62.
Average Exchange Rate (RD $ per US $)
  1987 3.8448
  1988 6.1125
  1989 6.3400

CENTRAL BANK RESERVES (US $ million at 31 December)

	1987	1988	1989
Gold*	8.9	7.7	7.5
Foreign exchange	180.6	253.5	167.7
Total	189.5	261.2	175.2

* Valued at market-related prices.

MONEY SUPPLY (RD $ million at 31 December)

	1987	1988	1989
Currency outside banks	1,317.7	1,855.9	2,665.5
Demand deposits at commercial banks	1,249.3	2,047.7	2,521.3

BUDGET (RD $ million)

Revenue	1987	1988	1989
Tax revenue	2,553.5	3,889.4	5,306.4
Non-tax revenue	297.2	503.0	405.6
Other receipts*	234.7	388.3	347.2
Total	3,085.4	4,780.7	6,059.2

* Including loans from domestic banks and from abroad.

Expenditure	1987	1988	1989
Presidency	1,765.2	2,543.0	3,166.1
Interior and police	180.0	263.1	313.3
Armed forces	218.9	280.3	332.6
Education	257.0	337.1	393.1
Health	182.6	259.6	338.7
Others	684.2	1,151.1	1,393.3
Total	3,287.9	4,834.2	5,937.1

COST OF LIVING
(Consumer Price Index. Base: Year ending April 1977 = 100)

	1987	1988	1989
Food, beverages and tobacco	381.0	584.2	865.7
Housing	336.2	452.2	622.1
Clothing, shoes and accessories	542.6	782.5	1,257.4
Others	317.4	403.2	548.8
All items	367.8	531.2	772.5

NATIONAL ACCOUNTS
National Income and Product
(RD $ million at current prices)

	1987	1988	1989
GDP in purchasers' values	19,536.1	28,352.7	42,421.3
Net factor income from abroad	−1,068.3	−1,542.4	−1,470.7
Gross national product (GNP)	18,467.8	26,810.3	40,950.6
Less Consumption of fixed capital	1,162.4	1,687.0	2,524.1
National income in market prices	17,305.4	25,123.3	38,426.5

THE DOMINICAN REPUBLIC

Expenditure on the Gross Domestic Product
(RD $ million at current prices)

	1987	1988	1989‡
Government final consumption expenditure	1,205.2	1,783.1	2,956.8
Private final consumption expenditure*	15,361.3	21,807.8	33,073.0
Increase in stocks†	117.5	87.5	9,173.9
Gross fixed capital formation	4,801.7	6,367.8	
Total domestic expenditure	21,485.7	30,046.2	45,203.7
Exports of goods and services	5,432.2	10,067.0	13,548.1
Less Imports of goods and services	7,381.8	11,760.5	16,358.8
GDP in purchasers' values	19,536.1	28,352.7	42,393.0
GDP at constant 1970 prices	3,467.4	3,505.9	3,640.7

* Obtained as a residual.
† Including only mining, manufacturing, groundnuts, raw tobacco and beans.
‡ Provisional.

Gross Domestic Product by Economic Activity*
(RD $ million at constant 1970 prices)

	1987	1988	1989
Agriculture	323.2	315.1	317.4
Livestock	196.7	196.9	205.8
Forestry and fishing	23.9	24.5	24.9
Mining	150.7	140.2	145.1
Manufacturing	610.0	588.2	598.6
Construction	297.4	325.1	370.9
Wholesale and retail trade	517.9	505.0	515.1
Transport	221.5	215.1	219.4
Communications	50.7	58.7	68.7
Electricity	69.4	67.1	61.5
Finance	150.7	174.2	194.6
Owner-occupied dwellings	219.4	223.9	224.3
Government services	314.6	339.5	349.7
Other services	321.3	332.4	344.9
Total	3,467.4	3,505.9	3,640.9

* Provisional.

BALANCE OF PAYMENTS (US $ million)

	1987	1988	1989
Merchandise exports f.o.b.	711.3	889.7	924.4
Merchandise imports f.o.b.	−1,591.5	−1,608.0	−1,963.8
Trade balance	−880.2	−718.3	−1,039.4
Exports of services	859.9	1,014.8	1,228.9
Imports of services	−678.1	−676.1	−706.4
Balance of goods and services	−698.4	−379.6	−516.9
Private unrequited transfers (net)	277.4	292.9	305.8
Government unrequited transfers (net)	57.5	64.8	83.9
Current balance	−363.5	−21.9	−127.2
Direct capital investment (net)	89.0	106.1	110.0
Other long-term capital (net)	−29.5	23.9	119.2
Short-term capital (net)	132.8	−110.2	−35.6
Net errors and omissions	28.4	11.8	−101.6
Total (net monetary movements)	−142.8	9.7	−35.2
Valuation changes (net)	−39.6	15.3	3.1
Exceptional financing (net)	9.1	112.7	37.2
Changes in reserves	−173.3	137.7	5.1

Source: IMF, *International Financial Statistics*.

External Trade

PRINCIPAL COMMODITIES (US $ '000)

Imports	1984*	1985*	1986*
Cars and other vehicles (incl. spares)	65,300	84,633	161,619
Chemical and pharmaceutical products	59,649	64,436	106,229
Cotton and manufactures	9,660	15,212	7,045
Foodstuffs	112,295	171,793	115,248
Petroleum and petroleum products	504,842	426,782	253,849
Iron and steel manufactures (excl. building materials)	56,874	43,500	56,357
Machinery (incl. spares)	83,360	119,311	218,185
Total (incl. others)	1,257,134	1,285,910	1,351,732

* Figures are provisional.

Total imports (US $ million): 1,591.5 in 1987; 1,608.0 in 1988; 1,963.8 in 1989.

Exports f.o.b.	1987*	1988*	1989*
Raw sugar	127,089	123,198	157,090
Molasses	12,924	11,788	9,878
Cocoa beans	66,336	64,036	42,962
Coffee (green)	63,326	66,494	63,776
Tobacco (unmanufactured)	14,176	18,330	10,563
Ferro-nickel	115,244	308,836	371,946
Alloy of gold and silver	120,042	98,066	69,776
Furfural	19,999	17,865	19,208
Total (incl. others)	711,253	889,696	924,388

* Figures are provisional.

PRINCIPAL TRADING PARTNERS (US $ '000)

Imports	1984	1985*	1986*
Belgium and Luxembourg	7,540	9,334	12,304
Brazil	21,537	22,514	23,491
Canada	19,222	17,507	24,351
France	9,351	8,598	15,096
Germany, Federal Republic	33,396	48,611	45,164
Italy	9,745	13,073	28,499
Japan	58,621	78,357	105,630
Mexico	147,660	101,795	112,981
Netherlands	14,752	11,789	12,693
Netherlands Antilles (incl. Aruba)	23,159	6,715	2,932
Puerto Rico	21,869	19,378	23,901
Spain	27,942	21,712	26,028
United Kingdom	11,661	13,462	14,266
USA	407,646	452,786	511,700
Venezuela	332,726	332,250	134,307
Total (incl. others)	1,257,134	1,285,910	1,351,732

* Figures are provisional.

Exports	1987	1988	1989*
Belgium and Luxembourg	30,002	36,803	10,827
Canada	25,097	19,826	9,909
Haiti	5,200	7,938	27,539
Italy	2,416	2,380	4,875
Japan	9,783	42,350	54,216
Morocco	10,920	5,957	8,278
Netherlands	29,833	105,076	166,729
Puerto Rico	64,118	75,603	65,705
Spain	7,440	16,931	9,979
USA	468,028	488,634	467,265
Total (incl. others)	711,252	889,696	924,388

* Figures are provisional.

THE DOMINICAN REPUBLIC

Transport

ROAD TRAFFIC ('000 motor vehicles in use)

	1983	1984	1985
Passenger cars	92.4	108.7	101.5
Commercial vehicles	58.0	60.4	52.0

Source: UN, *Statistical Yearbook*.

INTERNATIONAL SEA-BORNE SHIPPING
(freight traffic, '000 metric tons)*

	1985	1986	1987
Goods loaded	1,500	1,214	1,806
Goods unloaded	3,844	3,988	5,048

1988 ('000 metric tons): Goods unloaded: 5,681.
* Figures are provisional.

CIVIL AVIATION (traffic on scheduled services)

	1983	1984	1985
Kilometres flown (million)	4.8	4.4	4.9
Passengers carried ('000)	447	605	734
Passengers-km (million)	429	479	606
Freight ton-km (million)	7.1	9.7	8.5

Source: UN, *Statistical Yearbook*.

Tourism

(provisional figures)

	1986	1987	1988
Total visitors	886,282	1,037,481	1,221,735

Education

(1986)

	Institutions	Teachers	Students
Pre-primary	n.a.	n.a.	125,780
Primary	4,853	31,275	1,296,366
Secondary:			
general	n.a.	9,963	426,962
teacher training	n.a.	108	3,602
vocational	n.a.	n.a.	21,156*
Higher	n.a.	6,539*	123,748*

* 1985.
Source: UNESCO, *Statistical Yearbook*.

Directory

The Constitution

The present Constitution of the Dominican Republic was promulgated on 28 November 1966. Its main provisions are summarized below:

The Dominican Republic is a sovereign, free, independent state; no organizations set up by the State can bring about any act which might cause direct or indirect intervention in the internal or foreign affairs of the State or which might threaten the integrity of the State. The Dominican Republic recognizes and applies the norms of general and American international law and is in favour of and will support any initiative towards economic integration for the countries of America. The civil, republican, democratic, representative Government is divided into three independent powers: legislative, executive and judicial.

The territory of the Dominican Republic is as laid down in the Frontier Treaty of 1929 and its Protocol of Revision of 1936.

The life and property of the individual citizen are inviolable; there can be no sentence of death, torture nor any sentence which might cause physical harm to the individual. There is freedom of thought, of conscience, of religion, freedom to publish, freedom of unarmed association, provided that there is no subversion against public order, national security or decency. There is freedom of labour and trade unions; freedom to strike, except in the case of public services, according to the dispositions of the law.

The State will set about agrarian reform, dedicating the land to useful interests and gradually eliminating the latifundios (large estates). The State will do all in its power to support all aspects of family life. Primary education is compulsory and all education is free. Social security services will be developed. Every Dominican has the duty to give what civil and military service the State may require. Every legally entitled citizen must exercise the right to vote, i.e. all persons over 18 years of age and all who are or have been married even if they are not yet 18.

GOVERNMENT

Legislative power is exercised by Congress which is made up of the Senate and Chamber of Deputies, elected by direct vote. Senators, one for each of the 26 Provinces and one for the Distrito Nacional, are elected for four years; they must be Dominicans in full exercise of their citizen's rights, and at least 25 years of age. Their duties are to elect judges, the President and other members of the Electoral and Accounts Councils, and to approve the nomination of diplomats. Deputies, one for every 50,000 inhabitants or fraction over 25,000 in each Province and the Distrito Nacional, are elected for four years and must fulfil the same conditions for election as Senators.

Decisions of Congress are taken by absolute majority of at least half the members of each house; urgent matters require a two-thirds majority. Both houses normally meet on 27 February and 16 August each year for sessions of 90 days, which can be extended for a further 60 days.

Executive power is exercised by the President of the Republic, who is elected by direct vote for a four-year term. The President must be a Dominican citizen by birth or origin, over 30 years of age and in full exercise of citizen's rights. The President must not have engaged in any active military or police service for at least a year prior to election. The President takes office on 16 August following the election. The President of the Republic is Head of the Public Administration and Supreme Chief of the armed forces and police forces. The President's duties include nominating Secretaries and Assistant Secretaries of State and other public officials, promulgating and publishing laws and resolutions of Congress and seeing to their faithful execution, watching over the collection and just investment of national income, nominating, with the approval of the Senate, members of the Diplomatic Corps, receiving foreign Heads of State, presiding at national functions, decreeing a State of Siege or Emergency or any other measures necessary during a public crisis. The President may not leave the country for more than 15 days without authorization from Congress. In the absence of the President, the Vice-President will assume power, or failing him, the President of the Supreme Court of Justice.

LOCAL GOVERNMENT

Government in the Distrito Nacional and the Municipalities is in the hands of local councils, with members elected proportionally to the number of inhabitants, but numbering at least five. Each Province has a civil Governor, designated by the Executive.

THE DOMINICAN REPUBLIC

JUDICIARY

Judicial power is exercised by the Supreme Court of Justice and the other Tribunals; no judicial official may hold another public office or employment, other than honorary or teaching. The Supreme Court is made up of at least nine judges, who must be Dominican citizens by birth or origin, at least 35 years old, in full exercise of their citizen's rights, graduates in law and have practised professionally for at least 12 years. There are also five Courts of Appeal, a Lands Tribunal and a Court of the First Instance in each judicial district; in each Municipality and in the Distrito Nacional there are also Justices of the Peace.

Elections are directed by the Central Electoral Board. The armed forces are essentially obedient and apolitical, created for the defence of national independence and the maintenance of public order and the Constitution and Laws.

The artistic and historical riches of the country, whoever owns them, are part of the cultural heritage of the country and are under the safe-keeping of the State. Mineral deposits belong to the State. There is freedom to form political parties, provided they conform to the principles laid down in the Constitution. Justice is administered without charge throughout the Republic.

This Constitution can be reformed if the proposal for reform is supported in Congress by one-third of the members of either house or by the Executive. A special session of Congress must be called and any resolutions must have a two-thirds majority. There can be no reform of the method of government, which must always be civil, republican, democratic and representative.

The Government

HEAD OF STATE

President: Dr Joaquín Balaguer Ricardo (took office 16 August 1986; re-elected 16 May 1990).

Vice-President: Carlos Morales Troncoso.

CABINET
(January 1991)

Secretary of State to the Presidency: Dr Rafael Bello Andino.
Secretary of State for External Relations: Joaquín Ricardo García.
Secretary of State for Defence, the Interior and Police: Atilio Guzmán Fernández.
Secretary of State for Finance: Licelot Marte de Barrios.
Secretary of State for Energy: Celestino Armas.
Secretary of State for Education and Culture: Nicolás Almanzar.
Secretary of State for Agriculture: Manuel de Jesús Pina Cacarels.
Secretary of State for Public Works and Communications: Ing. Marcos Subero Sajuín.
Secretary of State for Health and Social Welfare: Rafael Bello.
Secretary of State for Industry and Commerce: Ramón Martínez Moya.
Secretary of State for Labour: Washington de Peña.
Secretary of State for Tourism: Lic. Fernando Rainieri Marranzini.
Secretary of State for Sport, Physical Education and Recreation: Temistocles Metz.
Secretaries of State without Portfolio: Ing. Manuel Guaroa Liranzo, Simón Tomás Fernández, Dr Donald Reid Cabral, Juan Rafael Peralta.
Administrative Secretary to the Presidency: Luis Toral.
Technical Secretary to the Presidency: Roberto Martínez Villanueua.
Governor of the Central Bank: Luis Julián Pérez.

SECRETARIATS OF STATE

Secretariat of State for Agriculture: Centro de los Héroes de Constanza, Santo Domingo, DN; tel. 533-7171; telex 346-0393.
Secretariat of State for Defence: Plaza de la Independencia, Avda 27 de Febrero, Santo Domingo, DN; tel. 533-5131; telex 346-0652.
Secretariat of State for Education and Culture: Avda Máximo Gómez, Santo Domingo, DN; tel. 689-9161.
Secretariat of State for External Relations: Avda Independencia, Santo Domingo, DN; tel. 533-4121; telex 326-4192.
Secretariat of State for Finance: Avda México, Santo Domingo, DN; telex 346-0437.

Directory

Secretariat of State for Health and Social Welfare: Santo Domingo, DN.
Secretariat of State for Industry and Commerce: Edif. de Oficinas Gubernamentales 7°, Avda México, Santo Domingo, DN; tel. 685-5171.
Secretariat of State for the Interior and Police: Edif. de Oficinas Gubernamentales, 3°, Avda Leopoldo Navarro a esq. México, Santo Domingo, DN; tel. 689-1979.
Secretariat of State for Labour: Santo Domingo, DN.
Secretariat of State for the Presidency: Santo Domingo, DN.
Secretariat of State for Public Works and Communications: Ensanche La Fé, Santo Domingo, DN; tel. 567-4929.
Secretariat of State for Sport, Physical Education and Recreation: Calle Pedro Henríquez Ureña, Santo Domingo, DN; tel. 688-0126; telex 346-0471.
Secretariat of State for Tourism: Avda George Washington, Apdo 497, Santo Domingo, DN; tel. 682-8181; telex 346-0303.

President and Legislature

PRESIDENT

Election, 16 May 1990

Candidates	% of votes
Dr Joaquín Balaguer Ricardo (PRSC)	36.0
Dr Juan Bosch Gaviño (PLD)	33.9
José Francisco Peña Gómez (PRD)	23.2
Lic. Jacobo Majluta Azar (PRI)	6.9
Total	**100.0**

CONGRESO NACIONAL

President: Luis José González Sánchez.
Vice-President: Máximo Antonio Nova Zapata.

The National Congress comprises a Senate and a Chamber of Deputies.

General Election, 16 May 1990

	Senate	Chamber
Partido Reformista Social Cristiano (PRSC)	16	42
Partido de la Liberación Dominicana (PLD)	12	44
Partido Revolucionario Dominicano (PRD)	2	32
Partido Revolucionario Independiente (PRI)	—	2
Total	**30**	**120**

Political Organizations

Movimiento de Conciliación Nacional (MCN): Calle Pina 207, Santo Domingo, DN; f. 1969; centre party; 659,277 mems; Pres. Dr Jaime M. Fernández; Sec. Víctor Mena.

Movimiento de Integración Democrática (MIDA): Las Mercedes 607, Santo Domingo, DN; tel. 687-8895; centre-right; Leader Dr Francisco Augusto Lora.

Movimiento Popular Dominicano: Santo Domingo, DN; left-wing; Leader Julio de Peña Valdés.

Partido Comunista Dominicano: Avda Independencia 89, Santo Domingo, DN; tel. 685-3540; f. 1944; outlawed 1962-77; Leader José Israel Cuello; Sec.-Gen. Narciso Isa Conde.

Partido Demócrata Popular: Arz. Meriño 259, Santo Domingo, DN; tel. 685-2920; opposition party; Leader Luis Homero Lájara Burgos.

Partido de la Liberación Dominicana (PLD): Avda Independencia 401, Santo Domingo, DN; tel. 685-3540; f. 1973 by breakaway group of PRD; left-wing; Leader Dr Juan Bosch Gaviño; Sec.-Gen. Lidio Cadet.

Partido Quisqueyano Demócrata (PQD): 27 de Febrero 206, altos, Santo Domingo, DN; tel. 565-0244; f. 1968; right-wing; 600,000 mems; Pres. Lic. Pedro Bergés; Sec.-Gen. Lic. Elias Wessin Chávez.

Partido Reformista Social Cristiano (PRSC): Avda San Cristóbal, Ensanche La Fe, Apdo 1332, Santo Domingo, DN; tel. 566-

7089; f. 1964; centre-right party; Leader Dr JOAQUÍN BALAGUER RICARDO.

Partido Revolucionario Dominicano (PRD): Espaillat 118, Santo Domingo, DN; tel. 687-2193; f. 1939; democratic socialist; mem. of Socialist International; 400,000 mems; Pres. JOSÉ FRANCISCO PEÑA GÓMEZ; Sec.-Gen. HATUEY DECAMPS.

Partido Revolucionario Independiente (PRI): Santo Domingo; f. 1985 after split by the PRD's right-wing faction; Pres. JACOBO MAJLUTA AZAR.

Partido Revolucionario Social Cristiano (PRSC): Las Mercedes 141, Santo Domingo, DN; tel. 688-3511; f. 1961; left-wing; Pres. Dr CLAUDIO ISIDORO ACOSTA; Sec.-Gen. Dr ALFONSO LOCKWARD.

Partido de los Trabajadores Dominicanos: Avda Duarte No 69, altos, Santo Domingo, DN; tel. 685-7705; f. 1979; workers' party; Sec.-Gen. JOSÉ GONZÁLEZ ESPINOZA.

Other parties include Unión Cívica Nacional (UCN), Partido Alianza Social Demócrata (ASD—Leader Dr JOSÉ RAFAEL ABINADER), Movimiento Nacional de Salvación (MNS—Leader LUIS JULIÁN PÉREZ), Partido Comunista del Trabajo de la República Dominicana (Sec.-Gen. RAFAEL CHALJUB MEJÍA), Partido de Veteranos Civiles (PVC), Partido Acción Constitucional (PAC), Partido Unión Patriótica (PUP—Leader ROBERTO SANTANA), Partido de Acción Nacional (right-wing) and Movimiento de Acción Social Cristiana (ASC).

An opposition front, the Frente Izquierda Dominicana, has been formed by 53 political organizations and trade unions.

Diplomatic Representation

EMBASSIES IN THE DOMINICAN REPUBLIC

Argentina: Avda Máximo Gómez 10, Santo Domingo, DN; tel. 682-2977; telex 346-0154; Ambassador: JORGE VÁSQUEZ.

Brazil: Avda Winston Churchill 32, Edif. Franco-Acra y Asociados, 2°, Apdo 1655, Santo Domingo, DN; tel. 532-0868; telex 346-0155; Ambassador: P. G. VILAS-BÔAS CASTRO.

Chile: Avda Anacaona 11, Mirador del Sur, Santo Domingo, DN; tel. 532-7800; telex 346-0395; fax 532-7979; Ambassador: RICARDO LIRA GÓMEZ.

China (Taiwan): Edif. Palic, 1°, Avda Abraham Lincoln, esq. José Amado Soler, Santo Domingo, DN; tel. 562-5555; fax 541-5207; Ambassador: MENG-HSIEN WANG.

Colombia: Avda Abraham Lincoln 502, 2°, Santo Domingo, DN; tel. 567-6836; telex 346-0448; Ambassador: Dr ERNESTO TORRES DÍAZ.

Costa Rica: Andrés Julio Aybar 15, Santo Domingo, DN; tel. 565-7294; Chargé d'affaires: ODALISCA AUED RODRÍGUEZ.

Ecuador: Gustavo M. Ricart 90, Santo Domingo, DN; tel. 565-0822; telex 326-4556; Ambassador: ADAIBERTO ORTIZ Q.

El Salvador: Calle José A. Brea Peña 12, Ensanche Evaristo Morales, Santo Domingo, DN; tel. 565-4311; fax 541-7503; Ambassador: Dr BYRON F. LARIOS L.

France: Avda Jorge Washington 353, Santo Domingo, DN; tel. 689-2161; telex 346-0392; Ambassador: CLAUDE FOUQUET.

Germany: Mejía y Cotes 37, Santo Domingo, DN; tel. 565-8811; telex 326-4125; Ambassador: ULRICH SCHOENING.

Guatemala: Z No 8, Naco, Santo Domingo, DN; tel. 566-8881; Ambassador: (vacant).

Haiti: Cub Scouts 11, Naco, Santo Domingo, DN; tel. 567-2511; telex 346-0851; Ambassador: ALBERT CHASSAGNE.

Holy See: Máximo Gómez No 27, Apdo 312, Santo Domingo, DN (Apostolic Nunciature); tel. 682-3773; Apostolic Nuncio: Most Rev. BLASCO FRANCISCO COLLAÇO, Titular Archbishop of Octava.

Honduras: Calle Porfirio Herrera No 9 esq. Respaldo Federico Geraldino Ensanche Piantini, Santo Domingo, DN; tel. 566-5707; telex 346-4104; Ambassador: IVÁN ROMERO MARTÍNEZ.

Israel: Pedro Henríquez Ureña 80, Santo Domingo, DN; tel. 686-7359; fax 687-7888; Ambassador: GAVRIEL LEVY.

Italy: Rodríguez Objío 4, Santo Domingo, DN; tel. 689-3684; telex 346-0543; Ambassador: ROBERTO ROSELLINI.

Japan: Torre BHD, 8°, Avda Winston Churchill esq. Luis F. Thomén, Santo Domingo, DN; tel. 567-3365; telex 4154; fax 566-8013; Ambassador: TSUNODA KATSUHIKO.

Korea, Republic: Avda Sarasota 98, Santo Domingo, DN; tel. 532-4314; telex 326-4368; Ambassador: KIM SUNG-SHIK.

Mexico: Rafael Hernández 11, Ensanche Naco, Santo Domingo, DN; tel. 565-2744; telex 326-4187; Ambassador: HUMBERTO LIRA MORA.

Nicaragua: El Recodo, Santo Domingo, DN; tel. 532-8846; telex 326-4542; Ambassador: Dr DANILO VALLE MARTÍNEZ.

Panama: E de Marchena 36, Santo Domingo, DN; tel. 685-6950; Chargé d'affaires a.i.: Lic. CRISTÓBAL SARMIENTO.

Peru: Cancillería, Avda Winston Churchill, Santo Domingo, DN; tel. 565-5851; Ambassador: RAÚL GUTIÉRREZ.

Romania: Santo Domingo, DN; Ambassador: (vacant).

Spain: Independencia 1205, Santo Domingo, DN; tel. 533-1424; telex 346-0158; fax 535-7001; Ambassador: FERNANDO GONZÁLEZ-CAMINO.

USA: César Nicolás Pensón, esq. Leopoldo Navarro, Santo Domingo, DN; tel. 541-2171; telex 346-0013; Ambassador: PAUL D. TAYLOR.

Uruguay: Avda México 169, Santo Domingo, DN; tel. 565-2669; telex 346-0442; Ambassador: JAIME WOLFSON KOT.

Venezuela: Cancillería, Avda Bolívar 832, Santo Domingo, DN; tel. 687-5066; telex 326-4279; Ambassador: Lic. ABEL CLAVIJO OSTOS.

Judicial System

The Judicial Power resides in the Supreme Court of Justice, the Courts of Appeal, the Tribunals of the First Instance, the municipal courts and the other judicial authorities provided by law. The Supreme Court is composed of nine judges and the Attorney-General and exercises disciplinary authority over all the members of the judiciary. The Attorney-General of the Republic is the Chief of Judicial Police and of the Public Ministry which he represents before the Supreme Court of Justice. All judges are elected by the Senate.

Corte Suprema: Centro de los Héroes de Constanza, Santo Domingo, DN; tel. 533-3522.

President: NÉSTOR COYTÍN AYBAR.

Attorney-General: SEMÍRAMIS OLIVO DE PICHARDO.

Religion

More than 90% of the inhabitants belong to the Roman Catholic Church, but freedom of worship exists for all denominations. The Baptist, Evangelist, Seventh-day Adventist and Jewish churches are also represented.

CHRISTIANITY

The Roman Catholic Church

The Dominican Republic comprises one archdiocese and eight dioceses.

Bishops' Conference: Conferencia del Episcopado Dominicano, Apdo 186, Santo Domingo, DN; tel. 685-3141; f. 1985; Pres. Mgr. NICOLÁS DE JESÚS LÓPEZ RODRÍGUEZ, Archbishop of Santo Domingo.

Archbishop of Santo Domingo: NICOLÁS DE JESÚS LÓPEZ RODRÍGUEZ, Arzobispado, Apdo 186, Isabel la Católica No 55, Santo Domingo, DN; tel. 685-3141.

Episcopal Church

Bishop of the Dominican Republic: Rt Rev. TELÉSFORO A. ISAAC, Apdo 764, Santo Domingo, DN; tel. 685-1635; fax 685-3293.

BAHÁ'Í FAITH

National Spiritual Assembly of the Bahá'ís of the Dominican Republic: Cambronal 152 esq. Beller, Santo Domingo, DN; f. 1961; tel. 687-1726; 392 localities.

The Press

DAILIES

Santo Domingo, DN

El Caribe: Autopista Duarte, Km 7½, Apdo 416, Santo Domingo, DN; tel. 566-8161; f. 1948; morning; Dir GERMÁN E. ORNES; circ. 28,000.

Diario Las Américas: Avda Tiradentes, Santo Domingo, DN; tel. 566-4577.

Hoy: Santo Domingo, DN.

Listín Diario: Calle 19 de Marzo 59, Apdo 1455, Santo Domingo, DN; tel. 689-7171; f. 1889; morning; Dir RAFAEL HERRERA; circ. 55,000.

THE DOMINICAN REPUBLIC

El Nacional: Avda San Martín 236, Santo Domingo, DN; tel. 565-5581; f. 1966; evening and Sunday; Dir MARIO ALVAREZ DUGAN; circ. 45,000.

La Noticia: Julio Verne 14, Santo Domingo, DN; tel. 687-3131; f. 1973; evening; Pres. JOSÉ A. BREA PEÑA; Dir SILVIO HERASME PEÑA.

El Sol: Carrera Sánchez, Km 6½, Santo Domingo, DN; tel. 532-9511; morning; Pres. QUITERIO CEDEÑO; Dir-Gen. MIGUEL ANGEL CEDEÑO.

Ultima Hora: Paseo de los Periodistas 52, Ensanche Miraflores, Santo Domingo, DN; tel. 688-3361; telex 346-0206; fax 686-6594; f. 1970; evening; Dir ANÍBAL DE CASTRO; circ. 50,000.

Puerto Plata

El Porvenir: Calle Imbert No 5, Apdo 614, Puerto Plata; f. 1872; Dir CARLOS ACEVEDO.

Santiago de los Caballeros, SD

La Información: Carretera Licey Km 3, Santiago de los Caballeros, SD; tel. 581-1915; fax 581-7770; f. 1915; morning; Editor ADRIANO MIGUEL TEYADA; circ. 15,000.

PERIODICALS AND REVIEWS
Santo Domingo, DN

Agricultura: Santo Domingo, DN; organ of the State Secretariat of Agriculture; f. 1905; monthly; Dir MIGUEL RODRÍGUEZ, Jr.

Agroconocimiento: Apdo 345-2, Santo Domingo, DN; monthly; agricultural news and technical information; Dir DOMINGO MARTE; circ. 10,000.

¡Ahora!: Avda San Martín 236, Apdo 1402, Santo Domingo, DN; tel. 565-5581; telex 346-0423; f. 1962; weekly; Dir MARIO ALVAREZ DUGAN.

La Campiña: San Martín 236, Apdo 1402, Santo Domingo, DN; f. 1967; Dir Ing. JUAN ULISES GARCÍA B.

Carta Dominicana: Avda Tiradentes 56, Santo Domingo, DN; tel. 566-0119; f. 1974; monthly; economics; Dir JUAN RAMÓN QUIÑONES M.

Deportes: San Martín 236, Apdo 1402, Santo Domingo, DN; f. 1967; sports; fortnightly; Dir L. R. CORDERO; circ. 5,000.

Eva: San Martín 236, Apdo 1402, Santo Domingo, DN; f. 1967; fortnightly; Dir MAGDA FLORENCIO.

Horizontes de América: Alexander Fleming 2, Santo Domingo, DN; tel. 565-9717; f. 1967; monthly; Dir ARMANDO LEMUS CASTILLO.

Letra Grande, Arte y Literatura: Leonardo da Vinci 13, Mirador del Sur, Santo Domingo, DN; tel. 533-4522; f. 1980; monthly; art and literature; Dir JUAN RAMÓN QUIÑONES M.

Renovación: Calle José Reyes esq. El Conde, Santo Domingo, DN; fortnightly; Dir OLGA QUISQUEYA Viuda MARTÍNEZ.

FOREIGN PRESS BUREAUX

Agencia EFE (Spain): Avda 27 de Febrero, Galerías Comerciales, 5°, Of. 507, Santo Domingo, DN; tel. 567-7617; telex 202-4176; Bureau Chief ANTONIO CASTILLO URBERUAGA.

Agenzia Nazionale Stampa Associata (ANSA) (Italy): Calle Leopoldo Navarro 79, 3°, Sala 17, Apdo 20324, Huanca, Santo Domingo, DN; tel. 685-8765; telex 201-4537; Bureau Chief HUMBER ANDRÉS SUAZO.

Inter Press Service (IPS) (Italy): Edif. Palamara, El Conde 407, Apto 202, Santo Domingo, DN; tel. 689-6449; Correspondent ANGELA HERNÁNDEZ.

United Press International (UPI) (USA): Carrera A. Manoguaybo 16, Manoguaybo, DN; tel. 689-7171; telex 346-0206; Chief Correspondent SANTIAGO ESTRELLA VELOZ.

Publishers

Santo Domingo, DN

Arte y Cine, C por A: Isabel la Católica 42, Santo Domingo, DN.

Editora Alfa y Omega: José Contreras 69, Santo Domingo, DN; tel. 532-5577.

Editora de las Antillas: Calle Pedro Henríquez Ureña, Santo Domingo, DN; tel. 685-2197.

Editora Colonial, C por A: Calle Moca 27-B, Apdo 2569, Santo Domingo, DN; tel. 688-2394; Pres. DANILO ASENCIO.

Editora Dominicana, SA: 23 Oeste, No 3 Lup., Santo Domingo, DN; tel. 688-0846.

Editora El Caribe, C por A: Autopista Duarte, Km 7½, Apdo 416, Santo Domingo, DN; tel. 566-8161; f. 1948; Dir Dr GERMÁN E. ORNES.

Editora El País: Carretera Sánchez, Km 6½, Santo Domingo, DN; tel. 532-9511.

Editora Hoy, C por A: Avda San Martín, 236, Santo Domingo, DN; tel. 566-1147; telex 346-0423.

Editora Listín Diario, C por A: Paseo de los Periodistas 52, Apartado 1455, Ensanche Miraflores, Santo Domingo, DN; tel. 689-7171; telex 346-0206; fax 686-6594; f. 1889; Pres. Dr ROGELIO A. PELLERANO.

Editorama, SA: Avda Tiradentes 56, Apdo 2074, Santo Domingo, DN; tel. 566-0119.

Editorial Padilla: San F. de Macorís 14, Santo Domingo, DN; tel. 682-3101.

Editorial Santo Domingo: Santo Domingo, DN; tel. 532-9431.

Editorial Stella: 19 de Marzo, Santo Domingo, DN; tel. 682-2281.

Julio D. Postigo e Hijos: Mercedes 49, Santo Domingo, DN; f. 1949; fiction; Man. J. D. POSTIGO.

Publicaciones América: Arz. Meriño, Santo Domingo, DN; Dir PEDRO BISONÓ.

Santiago de los Caballeros, SD

Editora el País, SA: Carrera Sánchez, Km 6½, Santiago de los Caballeros, SD; tel. 532-9511.

Radio and Television

In 1989 there were about 1m. radio receivers and 675,000 television receivers in use.

Dirección General de Telecomunicaciones: Isabel la Católica 203, Santo Domingo, DN; tel. 689-4161; government supervisory body; Dir-Gen. LEOPOLDO NÚÑEZ SANTOS.

RADIO

There were more than 140 commercial stations in 1989. The government-owned broadcasting network Radio Televisión Dominicana operates 10 radio stations.

TELEVISION

Radio Televisión Dominicana: Dr Tejada Florentino 8, Apdo 969, Santo Domingo, DN; tel. 689-2121; government station; three channels, two relay stations; Dir-Gen. ADRIANO RODRÍGUEZ; Gen. Man. AGUSTÍN MERCADO.

Rahintel Televisión: Centro de los Héroes de Constanza, Apdo 1220, Santo Domingo, DN; tel. 532-2531; telex 346-0213; fax 535-4575; commercial station; two channels; Pres. LEONEL ALMONTE V.

Color-Visión (Corporación Dominicana de Radio y Televisión): Calle Emilio A. Morel esq. Luis E. Pérez, Ensanche La Fé, Apdo 30043, Santo Domingo, DN; tel. 566-5875; telex 326-4327; commercial station; two channels: Channel 2 (Santiago) and Channel 9 (Santo Domingo, Puerto Plata, La Romana, San Juan); Dir-Gen. M. QUIROZ.

Teleantillas: Autopista Duarte, Km 7½, Apdo 30404, Santo Domingo, DN; tel. 567-7751; telex 346-0863; Gen. Man. MARITZA DE LOS SANTOS.

Telecentro, SA: Avda Pasteur 204, Santo Domingo, DN; tel. 687-9161; telex 346-0091; channel 13 for Santo Domingo and east region; Pres. JASINTO PEYNADO.

Tele-Inde Canal 13: 30 de Marzo, No 80, Santo Domingo, DN; commercial station; Proprietor JOSÉ A. SEMORILE.

Telesistema Dominicana: El Vergel 88, Ensanche El Vergel, Santo Domingo; tel. 567-5151; Pres. JOSÉ L. CORREPIO.

Finance

(cap. = capital; dep. = deposits; m = million; p.u. = paid up; res = reserves; amounts in pesos)

BANKING
Supervisory Body

Superintendencia de Bancos: Avda México esq. Leopoldo Navarro, Apdo 1326, Santo Domingo, DN; tel. 685-8141; telex 346-0653; f. 1947; Superintendent Dr JORGE MARTÍNEZ LAVANDIER.

Central Bank

Banco Central de la República Dominicana: Calle Pedro Henríquez Ureña esq. Leopoldo Navarro, Apdo 1347, Santo

THE DOMINICAN REPUBLIC
Directory

Domingo, DN; tel. 689-7121; telex 346-0052; fax 687-7488; f. 1947; cap. 0.7m., res 61.9m., dep. 1,098.6m. (Dec. 1989); Gov. Dr GUILLERMO CARÁM; Man. Dr JORGE MATOS FELIZ.

Commercial Banks

Banco del Comercio Dominicano: Avda 27 de Febrero, esq. Winston Churchill, Apdo 1440, Santo Domingo, DN; tel. 567-8871; telex 326-4533; fax 565-7541; f. 1980; cap. 214.3m., res. 38.4m., dep. 1,866.2m. (Dec. 1989); Pres. JOSÉ UREÑA ALMONTE; 28 brs.

Banco Dominicano del Progreso, SA: Avda John F. Kennedy 3, Apdo 1329, Santo Domingo, DN; tel. 566-7171; telex 346-0181; fax 566-8645; f. 1974; cap. and res 6.1m., dep. 62.6m. (June 1985); Exec. Vice-Pres. MICHAEL A. KELLY; 13 brs.

Banco Español: Avda John F. Kennedy, Santo Domingo, DN; tel. 565-8555; telex 346-0260; fax 565-2829; f. 1949 as Banco de Crédito y Ahorros, later renamed Banco de Santander Dominicano; cap. and res 8.9m., dep. 94.6m. (June 1985); Pres. EMILIO BOTÍN; 12 brs.

Banco Gerencial y Fiduciario Dominicano, SA: Avda San Martín 122, Apdo 1101, Santo Domingo, DN; tel. 565-9971; f. 1983; cap. and res 5.1m., dep. 17.8m. (June 1985); Exec. Vice-Pres. GEORGE MANUEL HAZOURY PEÑA.

Banco Metropolitano: Avda Lope de Vega esq. Gustavo Mejía Ricart, Apdo 1872, Santo Domingo, DN; tel. 562-2442; telex 346-0419; f. 1974; cap. and res 17.1m., dep. 196.4m. (Dec 1986); Gen. Dir ADALBERTO PÉREZ PERDOMO; 7 brs.

Banco Nacional de Crédito: Avda Lope de Vega 95, Apdo 1502, Santo Domingo, DN; tel. 542-7556; telex 346-0633; fax 567-4954; f. 1981; cap. 39.5m., res 10.5m., dep. 334.7m. (Dec. 1988); Dir MARINA DE GARRIGÓ; 11 brs.

Banco Popular Dominicano: Isabel la Católica 251, Apdo 1441, Santo Domingo, DN; tel. 544-5600; telex 346-0105; fax 544-5899; f. 1963; cap. and res 139.6m., dep. 1,750.5m. (Dec. 1989); Pres. MANUEL A. GRULLÓN ; 39 brs.

Banco de Reservas de la República Dominicana: Isabel la Católica 201, Apdo 1353, Santo Domingo, DN; tel. 688-8223; telex 346-0012; fax 685-0602; f. 1941; cap. and res 257.8m., dep. 3,421.1m. (Dec. 1988); Gen. Man. Lic. EMILIO DE LUNA PEGUERO; 18 brs.

Banco de los Trabajadores de la República Dominicana: El Conde esq. Arz. Meriño, Apdo 1446, Santo Domingo, DN; tel. 688-0181; telex 346-4500; f. 1972; state-controlled; cap. and res 9.4m., dep. 16.7m. (June 1987); Pres. Lic. JOSÉ A. RODRÍGUEZ ESPAILLAT; 4 brs.

Banco Universal, SA: El Conde 105, Apdo 2065, Santo Domingo, DN; tel. 688-6666; f. 1982; cap. and res 5.0m., dep. 13.1m. (June 1985); Pres. LEONEL ALMONTE.

A further eight commercial banks were operating in 1989.

Development Banks

Banco Agrícola de la República Dominicana: Avda G. Washington 601, Apdo 1057, Santo Domingo, DN; tel. 533-1171; telex 346-0026; f. 1945; government agricultural development bank; cap. and res 230.9m., dep. 115.5m. (Dec 1985); Gen. Administrator PEDRO BRETUN; 31 brs.

Banco de Crédito Hipotecario, SA: Avda Bolívar esq. Socorro Sánchez, Apdo 497-2, Santo Domingo, DN; tel. 682-3191; telex 346-0820; f. 1983; cap. and res 6.4m., dep. 9.0m. (Oct. 1988); Pres. Lic. ENRIQUE DALET LOZANO.

Banco Hipotecario Mercantil, SA: Juan I. Jiménez 1, Santo Domingo, DN; tel. 689-8005; f. 1983; cap. and res 10.6m., dep. 11.7m. (Aug 1988); Exec. Vice-Pres. Lic. JOSÉ MANUEL LÓPEZ VÁLDEZ.

Banco Hipotecario de la Construcción, SA (BANHICO): Avda Tiradentes (Altos Plaza Naco), Santo Domingo, DN; tel. 562-1281; f. 1977; cap. and res 8.4m., dep. 0.4m. (June 1985); Man. Dr JAIME ALVAREZ DUGAN.

Banco Hipotecario Dominicano, SA: Avda 27 de Febrero esq. Winston Churchill, Apdo 266-2, Santo Domingo, DN; tel. 567-7281; telex 4546; fax 541-4949; f. 1972; housing development bank; cap. and res 66.2m.; Pres. DAISY PERELLO; 5 brs.

Banco Hipotecario Financiero, SA: Avda 27 de Febrero esq. Avda Tiradentes, Apdo 385-2, Santo Domingo, DN; tel. 566-5151; f. 1978; cap. and res 2.6m., dep. 12.9m. (June 1985); Pres. Lic. JOSÉ DE POOL D.

Banco Hipotecario Horizontes, SA: Avda Rómulo Betancourt 1410, Santo Domingo, DN; tel. 532-2527; telex 346-0782; f. 1984; cap. and res 3.5m., dep. 4.5m. (Aug. 1987); Pres. HÉCTOR MARTÍNEZ CASTRO.

Banco Hipotecario Miramar, SA: Avda John F. Kennedy 10, Apdo 2424, Santo Domingo, DN; tel. 566-5681; telex 326-4202; fax 567-0926; f. 1976; cap. 30.7m., dep. 34.1m. (June 1989); Pres. Ing. GUILLERMO ARMENTEROS; 5 brs.

Banco Hipotecario Popular, SA: Avda 27 de Febrero 261, Santo Domingo, DN; tel. 544-6700; f. 1978; cap. 43.5m., dep. 232.2m. (August 1989); Pres. MANUEL E. JIMÉNEZ F.

Banco Hipotecario Unido, SA: Calle Del Sol 42, Apdo 290, Santiago; tel. 583-0401; f. 1983; cap. and res 1.8m., dep. 0.7m. (June 1985); Exec. Pres. LUIS MARTÍNEZ VILCHEZ.

Banco Hipotecario Universal, SA: Avda Santa Rosa esq. Gregorio Luperón, Apdo 259, La Romana; tel. 556-2183; f. 1979; cap. and res 3.9m., dep. 0.1m. (June 1985); Pres. LEONEL ALMONTE; 2 brs.

Banco Inmobiliario Dominicano, SA: Calle Del Sol 10, Santiago; tel. 583-4331; telex 346-1111; f. 1979; cap. and res 13.6m., dep. 0.5m. (June 1985); Dir Dr J. MANUEL PITTALUGA NIVAR; 3 brs.

Banco Nacional de la Construcción: Avda Alma Mater esq. Pedro Henríquez Ureña, Santo Domingo, DN; tel. 685-9776; f. 1977; cap. and res 3.7m., dep. 0.9m. (June 1985); Gen. Man. LUIS MANUEL PELLERANO.

There were 36 other development banks operating in 1989.

Foreign Banks

Bank of Nova Scotia (Canada): Avda John F. Kennedy esq. Lope de Vega, Santo Domingo, DN; tel. 566-5671; telex 346-0067; f. 1920; cap. and res 9.5m., dep. 101.1m. (June 1985); Gen. Man. IVAN L. LESSARD; 12 brs.

Chase Manhattan Bank (USA): Avda John F. Kennedy, Apdo 1408, Santo Domingo, DN; tel. 565-4441; telex 346-0096; f. 1962; cap. and res 8.6m., dep. 554.1m. (Sept. 1989); Man. VÍCTOR M. CAÑAS; 6 brs.

Citibank NA (USA): Avda John F. Kennedy 1, Apdo 1492, Santo Domingo, DN; tel. 566-5611; telex 346-0083; f. 1962; cap. and res 14.1m., dep. 421.4m. (Dec. 1985); Vice-Pres. MICHAEL CONTRERAS; 5 brs.

INSURANCE
Supervisory Body

Superintendencia de Seguros: Secretaría de Estado de Finanzas, Leopoldo Navarro esq. Avda México, Santo Domingo, DN; tel. 688-1245; f. 1969; Superintendent Dr JUAN ESTEBAN OLIVERO FELIZ.

National Companies

American Life and General Insurance Co, C por A: Edif. Alico, 4°, Avda Abraham Lincoln, Santo Domingo, DN; tel. 562-7131; telex 346-0366; general; Gen. Man. FRANK CABREJA.

La Americana, SA: Edif. La Cumbre, Avda Tiradentes, Apdo 25241, Santo Domingo, DN; tel. 567-0181; telex 346-0185; f. 1975; life; Pres. MARINO GINEBRA H.

Aseguradora Dominicana Agropecuaria C por A (ADACA): Isabel la Católica, 212, Santo Domingo, DN; tel. 685-6191; agriculture; Pres. Ing. PEDRO BRETÓN.

Centro de Seguros La Popular, C por A: Gustavo Mejía Ricart 61, Apdo 1123, Santo Domingo, DN; tel. 566-1988; fax 567-9389; f. 1965; general except life; Pres. Lic. FABIO A. FIALLO.

Centroamericana de Seguros, SA: Edif B H D, Avda 27 de Febrero esq. Tiradentes, Santo Domingo, DN; tel. 566-5151; general; Pres. Lic. JOSÉ E. DE POOL.

Citizens Dominicana, SA: Avda Winston Churchill esq. Paseo de los Locutores, 4°, Santo Domingo, DN; tel. 562-2705; f. 1978; Pres. MIGUEL E. SAVIÑON TORRES.

Cía Dominicana de Seguros, C por A: Edif. Buenaventura, Avda Independencia 201, Dr Delgado esq., Apdo 176, Santo Domingo, DN; tel. 689-6127; general except life; Pres. Lic. HUGO VILLANUEVA.

Cía Nacional de Seguros, C por A: Avda Máximo Gómez 31, Apdo 916, Santo Domingo, DN; tel. 685-2121; telex 346-0117; general; Pres. Dr MÁXIMO A. PELLERANO.

Cía de Seguros Quisqueyana, SA: Edif. Banco Antillano, Avda Abraham Lincoln, 953, Santo Domingo, DN; tel. 541-3550; telex 346-0637; general; Pres. POLIBIO DÍAZ.

La Colonial, SA: Edif. Haché, 2°, Avda John F. Kennedy, Santo Domingo, DN; tel. 565-9926; f. 1971; general; Pres. Dr MIGUEL FERIS IGLESIAS.

El Condor Seguros, SA: Avda 27 de Febrero No 12, Apdo 20077, Santo Domingo, DN; tel. 689-4146; telex 346-0210; f. 1977; general; Pres. JUAN PABLO REYES.

General de Seguros, SA: Avda Sarasota No 55, Bella Vista, Santo Domingo, DN; tel. 685-9102; fax 532-4451; f. 1981; general; Pres. Dr FERNANDO A. BALLISTA DÍAZ.

Inter-Oceania de Seguros, SA: Calle el Conde, 105, Santo Domingo, DN; tel. 689-2088; general; Pres. LEONEL ALMONTE.

La Intercontinental de Seguros, SA: Plaza Naco, 2°, Avda Tiradentes, Apdo 825, Santo Domingo, DN; tel. 562-1211; telex 346-0034; general; Pres. Lic. RAMÓN BÁEZ ROMANO.

THE DOMINICAN REPUBLIC

Directory

Latinoamericana de Seguros, SA: Edif. Salco, Avda W. Churchill esq. Max Henríquez Ureña, Santo Domingo, DN; tel. 541-5400; life; Pres. RAFAEL CASTRO MARTÍNEZ.

Magna Compañía de Seguros, SA: Edif. Magna Motors, Avda Abraham Lincoln esq. John F. Kennedy, Santo Domingo, DN; tel. 562-6591; telex 346-0812; fax 562-5723; f. 1974; general and life; Man. DARÍO LAMA.

La Metropolitana de Seguros, C por A: Edif. Alico, 4a, Avda Abraham Lincoln, Apdo 131, Santo Domingo, DN; tel. 532-0541; telex 346-0366; managed by American International Underwriters (AIU); Gen. Man. RAFAEL ARMANDO PICHARDO.

La Mundial de Seguros, SA: Edif. Torre BHD, Avda W. Churchill, esq. 27 de Febrero, Santo Domingo, DN; tel. 541-1451; telex 346-0466; general except life and financial; Gen. Man. FREDERICK RONALD AXELSON.

Patria, SA: Avda 27 de Febrero 10, Santo Domingo, DN; tel. 687-3151; general except life; Pres. Dr MIGUEL ANGEL LUNA MORALES.

La Peninsular de Seguros, SA: Edif. Corp. Corominas Pepín, 7°, Avda 27 de Febrero 234, Santo Domingo, DN; tel. 567-9095; general; Pres. Lic. ERNESTO RÓMERO LANDRÓN.

La Principal de Seguros, SA: Max Henríquez Ureña, esq. Virgilio Díaz Ordoñez, Santo Domingo, DN; tel. 566-8141; telex 4112; fax 541-4868; f. 1986; general; Pres. VIRTUDES GONZÁLEZ DE CÉSPEDES.

La Real de Seguros, SA: Avda 27 de Febrero 80, Santo Domingo, DN; tel. 566-5195; general; Pres. Lic. HÉCTOR MARTÍNEZ.

Reaseguradora Internacional, SA: Avda Pasteur 17, Santo Domingo, DN; tel. 685-3909; general; Pres. Lic. FABIO A. FIALLO.

Reaseguradora Nacional, SA: Avda Máximo Gómez 31, Apdo 916, Santo Domingo, DN; tel. 685-2121; f. 1971; general; Pres. MÁXIMO A. PELLERANO.

Reaseguradora Profesional, SA: Edif. La Universal de Seguros, 4°, Avda Winston Churchill 1100, Santo Domingo, DN; tel. 544-7400; telex 326-4545; fax 544-7099; f. 1981; Gen. Man. Lic. MANUEL DE JS. COLÓN.

Reaseguradora Santo Domingo, SA: Centro Comercial Jardines del Embajador, 2a Planta, Avda Sarasota, Apdo 25005, Santo Domingo, DN; tel. 532-2586; telex 346-0566; general; Man. DOUGLAS HARMAND.

Seguros San Rafael, C por A: Leopoldo Navarro 61, esq. San Francisco de Macorís, Santo Domingo, DN; tel. 688-2231; telex 346-0169; general; Admin. HECTOR COCCO.

Seguros La Alianza: Padre Fantino Falcó, Plaza Naco, Avda Tiradentes, Santo Domingo, DN; tel. 562-6361; general; Pres. Ing. LORENZO GARCÍA TRONCOSO.

Seguros América, C por A: Edif. La Cumbre, 4°, Avda Tiradentes, Santo Domingo, DN; tel. 567-0181; telex 346-0185; f. 1966; general except life; Pres. Dr LUIS GINEBRA HERNÁNDEZ.

Seguros La Antillana, SA: Avda Abraham Lincoln No 708, Apdo 146 y 27, Santo Domingo, DN; tel. 567-4481; telex 346-0411; general; Pres. ANDRÉS A. FREITES V.

Seguros Bancomercio, SA: Edif. E. León Jiménez, 2°, Avda John F. Kennedy 16, Santo Domingo, DN; tel. 565-3070; general; Pres. DIOMEDES DE LOS SANTOS.

Seguros del Caribe, SA: José Andrés Aybar Castellano No 105, Ensanche El Vergel, Santo Domingo, DN; tel. 567-0242; general; Pres. CARLOS P. PORTES.

Seguros Pepín, SA: Edif. Corp. Corominas Pepín, Avda 27 de Febrero, 233, Santo Domingo, DN; tel. 562-1006; general; Pres. Dr BIENVENIDO COROMINAS.

El Sol de Seguros, SA: Torre Hipotecaria 2A Planta, Avda Tiradentes 25, Santo Domingo, DN; tel. 562-2547; general; Pres. GUILLERMO ARMENTEROS.

Unión de Seguros, C por A: Avda 27 de Febrero 263, Santo Domingo, DN; tel. 566-2191; f. 1964; general; Pres. BELARMINIO CORTINA.

La Universal de Seguros, C por A: Torre La Universal de Seguros, Avda Winston Churchill 1100, Apdo 1052, Santo Domingo, DN; tel. 562-3011; fax 544-7099; general; Pres. ERNESTO IZQUIERDO.

There are also 11 foreign-owned insurance companies in the Dominican Republic.

Insurance Association

Cámara Dominicana de Aseguradores y Reaseguradores, Inc.: Edif. Central, 1°, Avda Winston Churchill esq. Max Henríquez Ureña, Santo Domingo, DN; Pres. MARINO GINEBRA HURTADO.

Trade and Industry

TRADE AND DEVELOPMENT ORGANIZATIONS

Asociación Dominicana de Hacendados y Agricultores Inc.: Avda Sarasota No 20, Santo Domingo, DN; tel. 565-0542; farming and agricultural organization; Pres. Lic. SILVESTRE ALBA DE MOYA.

Asociación de Industrias de la República Dominicana Inc.: Avda Sarasota 20, Apdo 850, Santo Domingo, DN; tel. 532-5523; f. 1962; industrial organization; Pres. JORGE ABOUT.

Centro Dominicano de Promoción de Exportaciones (CEDOPEX): Plaza de la Independencia, Apdo 199-2, Santo Domingo, DN; tel. 530-5505; telex 346-0351; fax 530-8208; organization for the promotion of exports; Dir Lic. RAMÓN HERNÁNDEZ BUENO.

Consejo Estatal del Azúcar (CEA) (State Sugar Council): Centro de los Héroes, PO Box 1256/1258, Santo Domingo, DN; tel. 533-1161; telex 346-0043; f. 1966; autonomous administration for each of the 12 state sugar mills; Dir Ing. JUAN ARTURO BIACHE.

Consejo Promotor de Inversiones (Investment Promotion Council): Avda Abraham Lincoln, 2°, Santo Domingo; tel. 532-3281; fax 533-7029; Exec. Dir and CEO FREDERIC EMAM ZADÉ.

Corporación Dominicana de Electricidad: Avda Independencia, Santo Domingo, DN; tel. 533-1131; state electricity company; Dir Ing. RAMÓN PÉREZ MARTÍNEZ.

Corporación Dominicana de Empresas Estatales (CORDE) (Dominican State Corporation): Avda General Antonio Duvergé, Apdo 1378, Santo Domingo, DN; tel. 533-5171; telex 346-0311; f. 1966 to administer, direct and develop 26 state enterprises; auth. cap. RD $25m.; Exec. Dir Lic. LUIS TAVERAS ANDÚJAR.

Corporación de Fomento Industrial (CFI): Avda 27 de Febrero, Apdo 1472, Santo Domingo, DN; tel. 547-3328; telex 346-0049; f. 1962 to promote agro-industrial development; auth. cap. RD $25m.; Dir Lic. JULIO CÉSAR PINEDA.

Dirección General de Minería e Hidrocarburos: Edif. de Oficinas Gubernamentales, 10°, Avda México esq. Leopoldo Navarro, Santo Domingo, DN; tel. 685-8191; f. 1947; government mining and hydrocarbon organization; Dir-Gen. Ing. GERARD MARTEN ELLIS.

Fondo de Inversión para el Desarrollo Económico—FIDE (Economic Development Investment Fund): c/o Banco Central de la República Dominicana, Avda Pedro Henríquez Ureña esq. Leopoldo Navarro, Santo Domingo, DN; tel. 682-6336; fax 686-0885; f. 1965; associated with AID, IDB; resources US $300m.; encourages economic development in productive sectors of economy, excluding sugar; authorizes complementary financing to private sector for establishing and developing industrial and agricultural enterprises and free-zone industrial parks; Dir Lic. VIRGILIO MALAGÓN ALVAREZ.

Fundación Dominicana de Desarrollo (Dominican Development Foundation): Calle Mercedes No 4, Apdo 857, Santo Domingo, DN; f. 1962 to mobilize private resources for collaboration in financing small-scale development programmes; 384 mems; assets US $10.7m.; Dir EDUARDO LA TORRE.

Instituto Agrario Dominicano (IAD): Avda 27 de Febrero, Santo Domingo, DN; tel. 530-8272; Dir Ing. GUSTAVO ADOLFO TAVARES.

Instituto Azucarero Dominicano (INAZUCAR): Avda Jiménez Moya, Apdo 667, Santo Domingo, DN; tel. 532-5571; sugar institute; f. 1965; Exec. Dir JIMMY GARCÍA SAVIÑÓN.

Instituto de Desarrollo y Crédito Cooperativo (IDECOOP): Centro de los Héroes, Santo Domingo, DN; tel. 532-4960; f. 1963 to encourage the development of co-operatives; cap. 100,000 pesos; Dir Ing. GILBERTO VÁLDEZ VIDAURRE.

Instituto de Estabilización de Precios (INESPRE): Avda Luperón, Santo Domingo, DN; tel. 530-0020; price commission; Dir RAFAEL AUGUSTO COLLADO.

Instituto Nacional de la Vivienda: Antiguo Edif. del Banco Central, Avda Pedro Henríquez Ureña esq. Leopoldo Navarro, Apdo 1506, Santo Domingo, DN; tel. 685-4181; f. 1962; low-cost housing institute; Dir Ing. MANUEL DE LA CRUZ.

CHAMBERS OF COMMERCE

Cámara de Comercio y Producción del Distrito Nacional: Arz. Nouel 206, Apdo Postal 815, Santo Domingo, DN; tel. 682-7206; telex 346-0877; f. 1910; 1,500 active mems; Pres. JOSÉ MANUEL ARMENTEROS; Exec. Dir Lic. VILMA ARBAJE.

Cámara Americana de Comercio de la República Dominicana: Torre BHD, 4°, Avda Winston Churchill, Santo Domingo, DN; tel. 544-2222; telex 346-0958; fax 544-0502; Pres. JOSÉ VITIENES.

There are official Chambers of Commerce in the larger towns.

THE DOMINICAN REPUBLIC

EMPLOYERS' ASSOCIATIONS

Confederación Patronal de la República Dominicana: Edif. Mella, Cambronal/G. Washington, Santo Domingo, DN; tel. 688-3017; Pres. Ing. HERIBERTO DE CASTRO.

Consejo Nacional de Hombres de Empresa Inc.: Edif. Motorámbar, 7°, Avda Abraham Lincoln 1056, Santo Domingo, DN; tel. 562-1666; Pres. Ing. LUIS AUGUSTO GINEBRA HERNÁNDEZ.

Federación Dominicana de Comerciantes: Carretera Sánchez Km 10, Santo Domingo, DN; tel. 533-2666; Pres. PEDRO MERCEDES.

TRADE UNIONS

It is estimated that 13% of the total work-force belong to trade unions.

Central General de Trabajadores (CGT): Calle 26 esq. Duarte, Santo Domingo, DN; tel. 688-3932; f. 1972; 13 sections; Sec.-Gen. FRANCISCO ANTONIO SANTOS; 65,000 mems.

Central de Trabajadores Independientes (CTI): Calle Juan Erazo 133, Santo Domingo, DN; tel. 688-3932; f. 1978; left-wing; Sec.-Gen. RAFAEL SANTOS.

Central de Trabajadores Mayoritarias (CTM): Tunti Cáceres 222, Santo Domingo, DN; tel. 562-3392; Sec.-Gen. NÉLSIDA MARMOLEJOS.

Confederación Autónoma de Sindicatos Clasistas (CASC) (Autonomous Confederation of Trade Unions): J. Erazo 39, Santo Domingo, DN; tel. 687-8533; f. 1962; supports PRSC; Sec.-Gen. GABRIEL DEL RÍO.

Confederación Nacional de Trabajadores Dominicanos (CNTD) (National Confederation of Dominican Workers): Santo Domingo, DN; f. 1988 by merger of Confederación de Trabajadores Dominicanos (f. 1920) and the Unión General de Trabajadores Dominicanos (f. 1978); 11 provincial federations totalling 150 unions are affiliated; Sec.-Gen. JULIO DE PEÑA VÁLDEZ; 188,000 mems (est.).

Transport

RAILWAYS

Dirección General de Tránsito Terrestre: Avda San Cristóbal, Santo Domingo, DN; tel. 567-4610; f. 1966; run by Secretary of State for Public Works and Communications; Dir-Gen. Ing. ARIF ABUD ABREU.

Ferrocarril Unidos Dominicanos: Santo Domingo; government-owned; 142 km of track from La Vega to Sánchez principally used for the transport of exports.

There are also a number of semi-autonomous and private railway companies for the transport of sugar cane, including:

Ferrocarril de Central Romana: La Romana; 375 km open; Pres. C. MORALES.

Ferrocarril Central Río Haina: Apdo 1258, Haina; 113 km open.

ROADS

In 1985 there were 17,120 km of roads. There is a direct route from Santo Domingo to Port-au-Prince in Haiti. In 1980 a project to improve the main road between Santo Domingo and Santiago de los Caballeros, at a cost of US $61m., was launched. In 1989 the Government allocated 888.4m. pesos for expenditure on the construction and improvement of 1,240 km of roads.

SHIPPING

The Dominican Republic has 14 ports, of which Santo Domingo is by far the largest, handling about 80% of imports. In 1983 the country's merchant fleet had a total displacement of 11,963 grt.

A number of foreign shipping companies operate services to the island.

Armadora Naval Dominicana, SA: Calle Isabel la Católica 165, Apdo 2677, Santo Domingo, DN; tel. 689-6191; telex 346-0465; Man. Dir Capt. EINAR WETTRE.

Líneas Marítimas de Santo Domingo, SA: José Gabriel García 8, Apdo 1148, Santo Domingo, DN; tel. 689-9146; telex 326-4274; fax 685-4654; Pres. C. LLUBERES; Vice-Pres. JUAN T. TAVARES.

CIVIL AVIATION

There are international airports at Santo Domingo (Aeropuerto Internacional de las Américas) and Puerto Plata. The airport at La Romana is authorized for international flights, providing that three days' notice is given. Most main cities have domestic airports.

Aerolíneas Argo: Avda 27 de Febrero 409, Santo Domingo, DN; tel. 566-1844; telex 346-0531; f. 1971; cargo and mail services to USA, Puerto Rico and US Virgin Islands; fleet: 1 L-749 Constellation, 1 Curtiss C-46.

Aerolíneas Litoral: Aeropuerto Las Américas, Santo Domingo; tel. 549-0547; f. 1987; services from Veracruz to Nuevo Laredo, Tampico, Minatitlán and Villahermosa; Pres. FILIPO D'PLANA; fleet: 1 Curtiss C-46, 2 Lockheed Super Constellations.

Aerotours Dominicano: Aeropuerto Las Américas, Santo Domingo; tel. 687-7111; charter carrier; fleet: 1 Caravelle 3.

Agro Air International Dominicana: POB 520941, Miami, Florida 33152, USA; tel. 942-4910; telex 803135; operates cargo charter services from Santo Domingo base; fleet: 1 Boeing 720, 2 C-97G, 2 McDonnell Douglas DC-50F.

Compañía Dominicana de Aviación C por A: Avda Jiménez de Moya esq. José Contreras, Apdo 1415, Santo Domingo, DN; tel. 532-8511; telex. 346-0390; f. 1944; operates on international routes connecting Santo Domingo with the Netherlands Antilles, Aruba, the USA, Haiti, Panama and Venezuela; charter flights in USA, Canada and Europe; Chair. Dr EUDORO SÁNCHEZ Y SÁNCHEZ; fleet: 1 Boeing 727-100, 1 727-100C, 2 727-200, 1 707-320C, 2 DC-6B.

Alas del Caribe, C por A: Avda Luperón, Aeropuerto de Herrera, Santo Domingo, DN; tel. 566-2141; f. 1968; internal routes; Pres. JACINTO B. PEYNADO; Dir MANUEL PÉREZ NEGRÓN.

Tourism

In 1989 tourist receipts were expected to total US $650m., with tourist arrivals by air reaching 1m. In 1989 there were 16,500 hotel rooms in the Dominican Republic, with a further 6,500 under construction. Strenuous efforts to improve the tourist infrastructure are being made, with 200m. pesos to be spent on increasing the number of hotel rooms by 50%, road improvements, and a new development, costing 160m. pesos, planned at Bahía de Manzanillo.

Secretaría de Estado de Turismo: Avda George Washington, Santo Domingo, DN; tel. 682-8181; telex 346-0303; Sec. of State for Tourism Lic. FERNANDO RAINIERI MARRANZINI.

Asociación Dominicana de Agencias de Viajes: Carrera Sánchez 201, Santo Domingo, DN; tel. 687-8984; Pres. RAMÓN PRIETO.

Atomic Energy

Comisión Nacional de Asuntos Nucleares: Edif. de la Defensa Civil, Dr Delgado 58, Santo Domingo, DN; tel. 565-5090; telex 346-0461; Pres. Dr ABEL GONZÁLEZ MASSENET.

ECUADOR

Introductory Survey

Location, Climate, Language, Religion, Flag, Capital

The Republic of Ecuador lies on the west coast of South America. It is bordered by Colombia to the north, by Peru to the east and south, and by the Pacific Ocean to the west. The Galapagos Islands, about 1,000 km (600 miles) off shore, form part of Ecuador. The climate is affected by the Andes mountains, and the topography ranges from the tropical rain forest on the coast and in the eastern region to the tropical grasslands of the central valley and the permanent snowfields of the highlands. The official language is Spanish, but Quechua and other indigenous languages are very common. Almost all of the inhabitants profess Christianity, and about 90% are Roman Catholics. The national flag (proportions 2 by 1) has three horizontal stripes, of yellow (one-half of the depth), blue and red. The state flag has, in addition, the national emblem (an oval cartouche, showing Mt Chimborazo and a steamer on a lake, surmounted by a condor) in the centre. The capital is Quito.

Recent History

Ecuador was ruled by Spain from the 16th century until 1822, when it achieved independence as part of Gran Colombia. In 1830 Ecuador seceded and became a separate republic. A long-standing division between Conservatives (Partido Conservador), whose support is generally strongest in the highlands, and Liberals (Partido Liberal, subsequently Partido Liberal Radical), based in the coastal region, began in the 19th century. Until 1948 Ecuador's political life was characterized by a rapid succession of presidents, dictators and juntas. Between 1830 and 1925 the country was governed by 40 different regimes. From 1925 to 1948 there was even greater instability, with a total of 22 heads of state.

Dr Galo Plaza Lasso, who was elected in 1948 and remained in power until 1952, was the first President since 1924 to complete his term of office. He created a climate of stability and economic progress. Dr José María Velasco Ibarra, who had previously been President in 1934–35 and 1944–47, was elected again in 1952 and held office until 1956. A 61-year-old tradition of Liberal Presidents was broken in 1956, when a Conservative candidate, Dr Camilo Ponce Enríquez, was elected in June (though with only 29% of the votes cast) and took office in September. He was succeeded in September 1960 by ex-President Velasco, who campaigned as a non-party Liberal. In November 1961, however, President Velasco was deposed by a coup, and was succeeded by his Vice-President, Dr Carlos Julio Arosemena Monroy. The latter was himself deposed in July 1963 by a military junta, led by Capt. (later Rear-Adm.) Ramón Castro Jijón, the Commander-in-Chief of the Navy, who assumed the office of President. In March 1966 the High Command of the Armed Forces dismissed the junta and installed Clemente Yerovi Indaburu, a wealthy businessman and a former Minister of Economics, as acting President. Yerovi was forced to resign when the Constituent Assembly, elected in October 1966, proposed a new constitution which prohibited the intervention of the armed forces in politics. In November he was replaced as provisional President by Dr Otto Arosemena Gómez, who held office until the elections of June 1968, when Dr Velasco returned from exile to win the Presidency for the fifth time. He took office in September.

In June 1970 President Velasco, with the support of the army, suspended the Constitution, dissolved the National Congress and assumed dictatorial powers to confront a financial emergency. In February 1972 he was overthrown for the fourth time by a military coup, led by Brig.-Gen. Guillermo Rodríguez Lara, the Commander-in-Chief of the Army, who proclaimed himself Head of State. In January 1976 President Rodríguez resigned, and power was assumed by a three-man military junta, led by Vice-Adm. Alfredo Poveda Burbano, the Chief of Staff of the Navy. The new junta announced its intention to lead the country to a truly representative democracy. A national referendum approved a newly-drafted constitution in January 1978 and presidential elections took place in July. No candidate achieved an overall majority, and a second round of voting was held in April 1979, when a new Congress was also elected. Jaime Roldós Aguilera of the Concentración de Fuerzas Populares (CFP) was elected President and he took office in August, when the Congress was inaugurated and the new Constitution came into force. President Roldós promised social justice and economic development, and guaranteed freedom for the press, but he met antagonism from both the conservative sections of the Congress and the trade unions. In May 1981 the President died in an air crash and was replaced by the Vice-President, Dr Osvaldo Hurtado Larrea, who was confronted by opposition from left-wing politicians and unions for his efforts to reduce government spending. He was also opposed by right-wing and commercial interests, which feared encroaching state intervention in the private economic sector.

A dispute between Hurtado and Vice-President León Roldós Aguilera in January 1982 led to the resignation of two ministers belonging to Roldós' party, Pueblo, Cambio y Democracia (PCD), which then went into opposition. Hurtado replaced the ministers with members of the CFP, creating a new pro-Government majority with a coalition of members of Democracia Popular-Unión Demócrata Cristiana (DP-UDC), CFP, Izquierda Democrática (ID) and seven independents. The heads of the armed forces resigned and the Minister of Defence was dismissed in January 1982, when they opposed Hurtado's attempts to settle amicably the border dispute with Peru (see below). In August Hurtado lost his majority again when two CFP Ministers resigned over energy policy. A state of emergency was declared in October, after a general strike and violent demonstrations against price rises, but it was lifted in November.

In March 1983 the Government introduced a series of austerity measures, which encountered immediate opposition from the trade unions and workers in the private sector. Three ministers resigned in July, and a new cabinet was appointed in August. Discontent with the Government's performance was reflected in the results of the concurrent presidential and general elections of January 1984, when the ruling party, DP-UDC, lost support. Seventeen political parties contested the elections. Of the nine presidential candidates competing for votes, the two leading contenders were León Febres Cordero, leader of the Partido Social Cristiano (PSC) and candidate of the conservative Frente de Reconstrucción Nacional (FRN), and Dr Rodrigo Borja Cevallos, representing the left-wing ID. As neither candidate won an absolute majority, a second round of voting was held in May 1984. After an often acrimonious campaign, Febres Cordero unexpectedly won the second round, securing 52.2% of the votes cast. He took office in August.

In September 1984 a serious constitutional dispute developed between the Government and Congress over the appointments procedure for the Supreme Court. The dispute was finally settled in December, after violent confrontations in Congress and fears of a coup, when Congress agreed to allow the Government to appoint the new Supreme Court justices.

In March 1984 a state of emergency was declared for 11 days in two northern provinces, following unrest and acts of sabotage by workers in the petroleum industry. In October a 24-hour general strike was called by the Frente Unitario de Trabajadores (FUT) and opposition groups, to protest against the restrictions on press freedom and the austerity measures that had been imposed by the new Government. In January 1985 a 48-hour general strike was called by the opposition after the Government announced increases in the cost of petroleum products and public transport fares. In the course of public demonstrations, seven people were killed and more than 100 were arrested. The trade unions staged another 24-hour general strike in September 1986, aimed at doubling the minimum wage. In October 1987 a general strike was called in protest at the Government's decision to reject a resolution, approved by Congress, accusing the Minister of the Interior, Luis Robles Plaza, of violations of human rights, and demanding his resignation. The Government imposed a state of emergency for two days. Further unrest in May 1988 led to the implementation of a state of emergency, prior to a one-day general strike, organized by the FUT. In early June President Febres Cordero appeared before the Court of Constitutional Guarantees, accused of contravening Article 78 of the Constitution by imposing the state of emergency in anticipation of the forthcoming strike.

The dismissal of the Chief of Staff of the Armed Forces, Lt-Gen. Frank Vargas Pazzos, brought about a military crisis in March 1986. Lt-Gen. Vargas and his supporters barricaded themselves inside the Mantas military base until they had forced the resignation of both the Minister of Defence, Gen. Luis Piñeiros, and the army commander, Gen. Manuel Albuja, who had been accused by Lt-Gen. Vargas of embezzlement. Lt-Gen. Vargas then staged a second rebellion at the military base where he had been detained. Troops loyal to the President made an assault on the base, captured Lt-Gen. Vargas and arrested his supporters. In January 1987 President Febres Cordero was abducted and, after he had been held for 11 hours, was released in exchange for Lt-Gen. Vargas, who was granted an amnesty. In July 58 members of the air force were sentenced to up to 16 years' imprisonment for involvement in the abduction of the President.

In June 1986, after unfavourable results in mid-term elections in 59 provincial seats, President Febres Cordero lost the majority that his coaliton of parties had held in the Congress. The President retained enough support, however, to survive a vote in the Congress on a resolution demanding his resignation. A total of 10 candidates (including Lt-Gen. Vargas) contested the presidential election of January 1988. The most successful candidates, Dr Rodrigo Borja Cevallos (of the ID) and Abdalá Bucaram Ortiz of the Partido Roldosista Ecuatoriano (PRE), received 20% and 15% respectively of the total votes cast, and advanced to the second round of voting. Sixto Durán Ballén, the PSC candidate, finished third, with 13% of the votes, and was eliminated from the presidential contest. In the second round of voting, held in May, Rodrigo Borja secured 46% of the votes cast, thus defeating Abdalá Bucaram, who won 41%. The President-elect promised to act promptly to address Ecuador's increasing economic problems and to change the country's isolationist foreign policy. Meanwhile, Abdalá Bucaram had fled to Panama, following accusations of corruption when in office as mayor of Guayaquil. During his inauguration in August, President Borja re-established Ecuador's diplomatic relations with Nicaragua, which had been severed in October 1985. He also pledged to join the Contadora group of countries (Colombia, Mexico, Panama and Venezuela). In September 1988 there were large demonstrations in protest against the rise in the price of fuel and against other economic measures which had been implemented to combat inflation. In October the guerrilla organization, Montoneros Patria Libre (MPL), proposed the establishment of dialogue between the Government and the rebels. In the same month the President of the Supreme Court of Justice, Ivan Martínez Vela, was murdered in Quito by unknown assassins.

In February 1989 the Government conducted a campaign to confiscate weapons belonging to paramilitary organizations. This measure followed an incident in which gunmen prevented security police from arresting Miguel Orellana, the former private secretary to ex-President Febres Cordero, who was accused of misusing public funds. In March Alfaro Vive ¡Carajo! (AVC), a leading opposition (hitherto guerrilla) group, urged paramilitary groups across the political spectrum to surrender their weapons. The Government agreed to guarantee the civil rights of AVC members and promised to initiate a national dialogue in return for the group's demobilization. In the same month the MPL dissociated itself from the agreement between the Government and the AVC and pledged to continue violent opposition. Terrorist activities continued, including a bomb attack on the Congress building in June, which caused only minor damage.

In July 1989 the DP-UDC alliance announced that it would withdraw from the Government in order to present independent candidates for the presidential election that was due to take place in 1992. Consequently, the sole DP member in the Government, Juan José Pons Arízaga, resigned from his post of Minister of Industry, Trade, Integration and Fisheries. In early August 1989, however, the alliance and the ID signed an agreement to maintain the coalition, thus in effect guaranteeing a working majority in Congress for the ID. In November, following the Government's decision to increase the price of vegetable oils, the ruling majority was again placed in jeopardy as the alliance between the ID and the DP-UDC was suspended.

In October 1989 a plot to organize a coup to overthrow the President and replace him with Vice-President Luis Parodí Valverde was revealed in a Federal German newspaper. The alleged conspirators were based in the Guayaquil municipality, where the local business community resented the perceived growing centralization of power in Quito. Radical right-wing groups, headed by former President Febres Cordero, led the movement. In January 1990 Febres Cordero was detained and charged with embezzlement of public funds.

In June 1989 the border with Colombia was temporarily closed, following a number of serious incidents involving Ecuadorean lorry drivers and police. The lorry drivers were engaged in prolonged industrial action, in protest against the Government's policies of economic adjustment.

The Government's plans to restructure the petroleum industry engendered further industrial disputes. In July 1989 the President requested military intervention to ensure that production continued at the state petroleum corporation, where there had been a number of work stoppages. In September workers at the Texaco concession went on strike to demand severance pay prior to the nationalization of the company's pipeline in October. The action resulted in a six-day suspension of petroleum exports in October, despite the fact that the Government had decreed a state of emergency in September in an effort to avoid any disruption to the normal supply and export of petroleum.

In September 1989 the Andean Parliament held a two-day session in Quito and established the Seventh Commission against Drugs in the region. The Ecuadorean Government decided to adopt measures to halt intensive 'money-laundering' operations in the country, and requested US aid to combat the drug-traffickers. In October a leading figure of the Medellín drug-trafficking ring was arrested and extradited to Colombia. In January 1990 the Government opposed the operation of US warships in Ecuador's territorial waters, but affirmed its support for President Bush's intention to confront the drug-trafficking problem in the region. In the same month legislation aimed at curbing the influence of drug-traffickers was drafted, including a proposed amendment to the Constitution with regard to the extradition of nationals. In September the US Government provided Ecuador with US $1.7m. in aid towards a programme to combat drug-trafficking.

With mid-term legislative elections due to take place in June 1990 and President Borja's popularity apparently waning (owing to sustained fiscal and monetary controls, the high rate of unemployment and shortages of basic commodities), the Government was faced with the possibility of losing its majority in Congress. In May 1990 President Borja introduced a tariff-reduction scheme in an attempt to stimulate export growth and to aid economic recovery. Despite these measures, there was no apparent revival of popular support for the President. At the legislative elections, which were held, as scheduled, in the following month, the ID lost 16 seats and conceded control of Congress to an informal alliance of the PSC and the PRE.

In October 1990 a serious conflict arose between the Government and Congress when the newly-elected president of Congress, Dr Averroes Bucaram, attempted to stage a legislative coup against President Borja. Bucaram's first move was the impeachment of several ministers, who were subsequently dismissed by Congress. Congress then dismissed the 16 Supreme Court justices and other high-ranking members of the judiciary, and appointed new courts with shortened mandates. Both the Government and the judiciary refused to recognize these actions, on the grounds that Congress had exceeded its constitutional powers. Bucaram then announced that Congress would initiate impeachment proceedings against President Borja himself. However, this move was averted when three opposition deputies transferred their allegiance, so restoring Borja's congressional majority. Bucaram was subsequently dismissed as President of Congress.

In May 1990 about 1,000 indigenous Indians, representing 70 socio-political Indian organizations, marched into Quito to present President Borja with a 16-point petition demanding official recognition of land rights for the indigenous population. In the following month the Confederación Nacional de Indígenas del Ecuador (Coniae, the National Confederation of the Indigenous Population of Ecuador) organized an uprising covering seven Andean provinces. Roads were blockaded, *haciendas* occupied, and supplies to the cities interrupted. Following the arrest of 30 Indians by the army, the rebels took military hostages. The Government offered to hold conciliatory negotiations with Coniae, in return for the release of the hostages. Among the demands made by the Indians were the return of traditional community-held lands, recognition of Quechua as an official language and compensation from petroleum companies for environmental damage. Discussions between Coniae and President Borja collapsed in August. In January 1991 the FUT announced a joint campaign with Coniae. The FUT, which organized a strike in July 1990 that had limited success, was protesting against the Government's decision to increase the minimum monthly wage by only 38%, to 44,000 sucres, and insisted that the minimum should be raised to 150,000 sucres.

The long-standing border dispute with Peru over the Cordillera del Cóndor erupted into war in January 1981. A cease-fire was declared a few days later under the auspices of the guarantors of the Rio Protocol of 1942 (Argentina, Brazil, Chile and the USA). The Protocol was not recognized by Ecuador as it awarded the area, which affords access to the Amazon river system, to Peru. Further clashes occurred along the border with Peru in December 1982 and January 1983. In addition, skirmishes between Ecuadorean and Colombian forces were reported to have taken place in the border zone in December 1982. Following his inauguration in August 1988, President Borja stated that he wished to negotiate a settlement with Peru over the disputed border areas.

Government

Ecuador comprises 20 provinces, including the Galapagos Islands. Each province has a Governor, who is appointed by the President. Executive power is vested in the President, who is directly elected by universal adult suffrage for a four-year term. The President is not eligible for re-election. Legislative power is held by the 71-member unicameral Congress, which is also directly elected: 12 members are elected on a national basis and serve a four-year term, while 59 members are elected on a provincial basis and are replaced every two years, being ineligible for re-election. In April 1980 the future formation of an upper chamber was agreed.

Defence

Military service, which lasts two years, is selective for men at the age of 20. In June 1990 there were 57,800 men in the armed forces: army 50,000, navy 4,800 (including 1,600 marines) and air force 3,000. Defence expenditure for 1989 was estimated to be 70,000m. sucres.

Economic Affairs

In 1988, according to estimates by the World Bank, Ecuador's gross national product (GNP), measured at average 1986-88 prices, was US $10,920m., equivalent to $1,080 per head. During 1980-88, it was estimated, GNP increased, in real terms, at an average annual rate of 1.7%, although GNP per head decreased by 1.1% per year. Over the same period, the population increased by an annual average of 2.8%. Ecuador's gross domestic product (GDP) increased, in real terms, by an annual average of 2.0% in 1980-88, but growth of only 0.5% was estimated for 1989.

Agriculture (including forestry and fishing) contributed 17.2% of GDP in 1989. An estimated 31.1% of the labour force were employed in the agricultural sector in that year. The principal cash crops are bananas, coffee and cocoa. The seafood sector, particularly the shrimp industry, expanded rapidly in the 1980s. Ecuador's extensive forests yield valuable hardwoods, and the country is a leading producer of balsawood. During 1980-88 agricultural production increased by an annual average of 4.3%.

Industry (including mining, manufacturing, construction and power) employed 20.6% of the labour force in 1982, and provided 34.3% of GDP in 1989. During 1980-88 industrial production increased by an annual average of 2.2%.

Mining and petroleum-refining contributed 13.2% of GDP in 1989, although the mining sector employed only 0.3% of the labour force in 1982. Petroleum and its derivatives remained the major exports in 1989. Natural gas is extracted, but only a small proportion is retained. Gold, silver, copper, antimony and zinc are also mined.

Manufacturing contributed 15.9% of GDP in 1989, and employed 12.7% of the labour force in 1982. Measured by the value of output, the most important branches of manufacturing in 1986 were food products, chemicals, textiles and petroleum refineries.

Energy is derived principally from thermoelectric and hydroelectric plants. Imports of mineral fuels and lubricants comprised only 3.8% of the value of total imports in 1989.

The services sector contributed 48.4% of GDP in 1989. Around 43% of the active population were employed in this sector in 1982. The sector's output increased at an average annual rate of 1.1% during 1980-88.

In 1989 Ecuador recorded a visible trade surplus of US $661m., while there was a deficit of $532m. on the current account of the balance of payments. In 1989 the principal source of imports (33.7%) was the USA, which was also the principal market for exports (58.1%). Other major trading partners were Japan, the Federal Republic of Germany and Brazil. The principal exports in 1989 were petroleum and petroleum derivatives (48.7%), seafood and seafood products (18.4%) and bananas (15.7%). The principal imports were raw materials for industry (45.2%), capital goods for industry (21.0%) and transport equipment (11.1%).

In 1989 there was a budgetary surplus of 89,813m. sucres. Ecuador's total external public debt was US $9,353m. at the end of 1988. In that year the cost of debt-servicing was equivalent to 21.1% of revenue from exports of goods and services. The average annual rate of inflation was 75.6% in 1989. An estimated 14.3% of the labour force were unemployed in 1990.

Ecuador is a member of the Andean Group (see p. 93), of ALADI (p. 172) and of OPEC (p. 200).

In June 1989, after assessing the results of the economic emergency measures implemented since President Borja's inauguration, Ecuador resumed payment of interest on its external debt to commercial debtors, thus ending a two-year moratorium. In September and October Ecuador concluded two important credit agreements with the Spanish and French Governments, worth US $350m. and 310m. French francs respectively. In December the Ecuadorean Government announced a new range of economic liberalization measures, aimed at promoting the private sector and at improving exports. This programme received approval from the IMF, which, in turn, granted a stand-by credit facility of US $143m. to Ecuador. Of this credit, two disbursements of $40.8m. each were approved in March 1990. In November the IDB approved a loan of $104m. for Ecuador, aimed at fostering economic autonomy at local-government level and supporting municipal investment projects. Throughout 1990 Ecuador limited its debt-service payments to 30% of the amounts due. Revenue from exports of petroleum increased considerably towards the end of the year, as a result of the increase in the price of petroleum on the international market, following the annexation of Kuwait by Iraq in August. As a consequence of this increase in revenue, Ecuador's reserves of foreign exchange stood at $609.3m. at the end of 1990, and the Government was able to resume a credit programme, providing credit at low rates of interest for industrial enterprises in the private sector.

Social Welfare

Social insurance is compulsory for all employees. Benefits are available for sickness, industrial accidents, disability, maternity, old age, widowhood and orphanhood. In 1980 about 125,000 peasants were integrated into social security schemes; the 1980-84 Development Plan aimed to increase the number to 335,000. Hospitals and welfare institutions are administered by Central Public Assistance Boards. In 1973 Ecuador had 221 hospital establishments, with a total of 13,594 beds, and in 1977 there were 4,660 physicians working in the country. Budgetary expenditure on health and community development by the central Government was estimated at 60,710m. sucres (6.5% of total spending) in 1989.

Education

Education is compulsory for six years, to be undertaken between six and 14 years of age, and all public schools are free. Private schools continue to play a vital role in the educational system. Primary education begins at six years of age and lasts for six years. Secondary education, in general and specialized technical or humanities schools, begins at the age of 12 and lasts for up to six years, comprising two equal cycles of three years each. In 1987 the total enrolment at primary and secondary schools was equivalent to 89% of the school-age population (117% in primary schools and 56% in

ECUADOR

secondary schools). In 1983/84 there were 11,480 primary schools and 1,099 secondary schools. University courses extend for up to six years, and include programmes for teacher training. A number of adult schools and literacy centres have been built, aimed at reducing the rate of adult illiteracy, which averaged 25.8% in 1974 and 19.8% (males 15.8%; females 23.8%) in 1982. There are 16 universities. Budgetary expenditure on education and culture by the central Government was estimated at 156,260m. sucres (16.8% of total spending) in 1989. In many rural areas, Quechua and other indigenous Indian languages are used in education.

Public Holidays

1991: 1 January (New Year's Day), 6 January (Epiphany), 11–12 February (Carnival), 28 March (Holy Thursday), 29 March (Good Friday), 30 March (Easter Saturday), 1 May (Labour Day), 24 May (Battle of Pichincha), 24 July (Birth of Simón Bolívar), 10 August (Independence of Quito), 9 October (Independence of Guayaquil), 12 October (Discovery of America), 1 November (All Saints' Day), 2 November (All Souls' Day), 3 November (Independence of Cuenca), 6 December (Foundation of Quito), 25 December (Christmas Day).

1992: 1 January (New Year's Day), 6 January (Epiphany), 2–3 March (Carnival), 16 April (Holy Thursday), 17 April (Good Friday), 18 April (Easter Saturday), 1 May (Labour Day), 24 May (Battle of Pichincha), 24 July (Birth of Simón Bolívar), 10 August (Independence of Quito), 9 October (Independence of Guayaquil), 12 October (Discovery of America), 1 November (All Saints' Day), 2 November (All Souls' Day), 3 November (Independence of Cuenca), 6 December (Foundation of Quito), 25 December (Christmas Day).

Weights and Measures

The metric system is in force.

Statistical Survey

Sources (unless otherwise stated): Banco Central de Ecuador, Quito; Ministerio de Industrias, Comercio e Integración, Quito; Instituto Nacional de Estadística y Censos, 10 de Agosto 229, Quito; tel. (2) 519-320.

Area and Population

AREA, POPULATION AND DENSITY

Area (sq km)	
Land	263,950
Inland water	6,720
Total	270,670*
Population (census results)†	
8 June 1974	6,521,710
28 November 1982	
Males	4,021,034
Females	4,039,678
Total	8,060,712
Population (official estimates at mid-year)†	
1988	10,203,722
1989	10,490,249
1990	10,781,613
Density (per sq km) at mid-1990	39.8

* 104,506 sq miles.

† Figures exclude nomadic tribes of indigenous Indians. Census results also exclude any adjustment for underenumeration, estimated to have been 5.6% in 1982.

PROVINCES (estimated population at mid-1990)*

	Population	Capital
Azuay	562,725	Cuenca
Bolívar	168,034	Guaranda
Cañar	213,364	Azogues
Carchi	150,778	Tulcán
Cotopaxi	332,962	Latacunga
Chimborazo	383,544	Riobamba
El Oro	464,709	Machala
Esmeraldas	335,229	Esmeraldas
Guayas	2,841,945	Guayaquil
Imbabura	300,298	Ibarra
Loja	426,844	Loja
Los Ríos	591,550	Babahoyo
Manabí	1,126,310	Portoviejo
Morona Santiago	99,365	Macas
Napo	192,109	Tena
Pastaza	44,476	Puyo
Pichincha	1,984,743	Quito
Tungurahua	403,484	Ambato
Zamora Chinchipe	71,480	Zamora
Archipiélago de Colón (Galápagos)	9,710	Puerto Baquerizo (Isla San Cristóbal)
Total	**10,703,659**	

* Figures exclude persons in unspecified areas, totalling 77,954.

Note: An additional province, Sucumbios (capital Nueva Loja), has been created.

PRINCIPAL TOWNS (estimated population at mid-1990)

Guayaquil	1,764,170	Portoviejo	163,898
Quito (capital)	1,281,849	Manta	155,757
Cuenca	227,212	Ambato	137,418
Machala	166,270	Esmeraldas	136,370

ECUADOR

BIRTHS, MARRIAGES AND DEATHS*
(excluding nomadic Indian tribes)

	Registered live births		Registered marriages		Registered deaths	
	Number	Rate (per 1,000)	Number	Rate (per 1,000)	Number	Rate (per 1,000)
1981	264,963	31.7	49,936	6.0	54,910	6.6
1982	262,102	30.5	49,341	5.7	53,009	6.2
1983	253,990	28.7	49,571	5.6	55,202	6.2
1984	257,044	28.2	54,038	5.9	53,118	5.8
1985	262,260	28.0	56,560	6.0	51,134	5.5
1986	257,234	26.7	60,205	6.2	50,957	5.3
1987	261,312	26.3	61,301	6.2	51,567	5.2
1988	211,392	20.7	66,468	6.5	52,732	5.2

* Registration is incomplete. According to UN estimates, the average annual rates were: births 36.8 per 1,000 in 1980–85, 35.4 per 1,000 in 1985–90; deaths 8.1 per 1,000 in 1980–85, 7.6 per 1,000 in 1985–90.

ECONOMICALLY ACTIVE POPULATION*
(ISIC Major Divisions, 1982 census)

	Males	Females	Total
Agriculture, hunting, forestry and fishing	727,880	59,092	786,972
Mining and quarrying	6,912	494	7,406
Manufacturing	214,063	72,467	286,530
Electricity, gas and water	11,946	1,237	13,183
Construction	154,683	3,326	158,009
Trade, restaurants and hotels	185,127	86,787	271,914
Transport, storage and communications	96,345	4,976	101,321
Financing, insurance, real estate and business services	29,865	14,251	44,116
Community, social and personal services	343,627	211,288	554,915
Activities not adequately defined	28,567	10,027	38,594
Total labour force	**1,799,015**	**463,945**	**2,262,960**

* Figures refer to persons aged 12 years and over, excluding those seeking work for the first time, totalling 83,103 (males 62,637; females 20,466).

Mid-1989 (official estimate, persons aged 12 years and over): Total labour force 3,551,017 (males 2,484,959; females 1,066,058).

Agriculture

PRINCIPAL CROPS ('000 metric tons)

	1987	1988	1989
Wheat	31.4	34.2	25.6
Rice (paddy)	780.8	954.5	867.4
Barley	43.5	50.8	55.9
Maize	385	397.6	532.5
Potatoes	353.9	338.2	362.2
Cassava (Manioc)	131.2	123‡	113.6
Dry beans	21.8	25.6	31.9
Soybeans (Soya beans)	146.1	131.3	153.9
Seed cotton	20.1	23.9	32.8
Coconuts	34.6	103.9	42*
Pumpkins, squash and gourds	100*	100*	98*
Sugar cane‡	5,612	5,411	5,700*
Oranges	77.6	86.6	71.4
Pineapples	54	56‡	55*
Bananas	2,386.5	2,576.1	2,576.2
Plantains	848.4	959.1	1,053.4
Coffee (green)	112†	144‡	129.3
Cocoa beans	57.5	85.1	82.9

* FAO estimate.   † Unofficial estimate.
‡ Source: FAO, *Production Yearbook*.
Source: mainly Sistema Estadístico Agropecuario Nacional.

LIVESTOCK ('000 head)

	1987	1988*	1989
Cattle	3,884.3	4,007	4,176
Sheep	1,619.8	1,707†	1,329
Pigs*	4,160‡	4,160†	2,092

* Source: FAO, *Production Yearbook*.
† FAO estimate.   ‡ Unofficial estimate.
Source: Sistema Estadístico Agropecuario Nacional.

Poultry (million, year ending September): 49 in 1987; 48 in 1988; 48 in 1989 (FAO estimate).
Source: FAO, *Production Yearbook*.

LIVESTOCK PRODUCTS ('000 metric tons)

	1987	1988	1989
Beef and veal	92	95	116†
Mutton and lamb*	7	7	7
Pig meat*	67	67	67
Poultry meat*	46	46	62
Cows' milk	1,270†	1,406	1,400
Butter*	4.5	4.5	4.5
Cheese*	13.2	13.2	13.2
Hen eggs	45.3	44.2	42*
Wool:			
greasy*	2.4	2.4	2.4
clean*	1.2	1.2	1.2
Cattle hides (fresh)*	14.1	14.5	16.6

* FAO estimate(s).   † Unofficial figure.
Source: FAO, *Production Yearbook*.

Forestry

ROUNDWOOD REMOVALS ('000 cubic metres, excluding bark)

	1986	1987	1988
Sawlogs, veneer logs and logs for sleepers	2,285	2,580	2,610
Pulpwood	260*	261	264
Other industrial wood	86	86*	86*
Fuel wood	6,238	6,304*	6,376*
Total	**8,869**	**9,231**	**9,336**

* FAO estimate.
Source: FAO, *Yearbook of Forest Products*.

SAWNWOOD PRODUCTION ('000 cubic metres)

	1986	1987	1988
Total (incl. boxboards)	1,256	1,263	1,278

Source: FAO, *Yearbook of Forest Products*.

Fishing

('000 metric tons, live weight)

	1986	1987	1988
Freshwater fishes	0.9	1.1	0.9
Herrings, sardines, anchovies, etc.	688.6	363.1	369.5
Chub mackerel	107.7	116.6	146.9
Other marine fishes	146.5	117.6	168.1
Shrimps	52.8	78.7	80.8
Other sea creatures	6.9	2.9	2.9
Total catch	**1,003.4**	**680.1**	**769.1**

Source: FAO, *Yearbook of Fishery Statistics*.

ECUADOR

Mining

	1986	1987	1988
Crude petroleum ('000 barrels)	106,995	63,687	112,553
Natural gas (million cu metres)*	734.6	460.8	n.a.
Natural gasoline ('000 barrels)	298.9	156.0	231.6
Gold (kilograms)†	9,870	9,553	n.a.

* Including wasted gas and shrinkage.
† Estimates by the US Bureau of Mines.

1989 (provisional, '000 barrels): Crude petroleum 102,592; Natural gasoline 181.1.

Industry

SELECTED PRODUCTS
('000 metric tons, unless otherwise indicated)

	1985	1986	1987
Jet fuels	145	135	161
Kerosene	274	287	204
Gasoline	913	1,030	816
Distillate fuel oils	748	842	854
Residual fuel oils	1,865	2,087	1,839
Liquefied natural gas	42*	66	22
Crude steel	18	17	25*
Cement	2,008	2,087*	2,875*
Electric energy (million kWh)	4,750	5,301	5,668

* Estimate.

Source: UN, *Industrial Statistics Yearbook*.

1988 ('000 metric tons): Kerosene and jet fuels 425; Gasoline 1,338; Distillate fuel oils 1,233; Residual fuel oils 2,522; Cement 2,927.
1989 ('000 metric tons): Cement 2,942.

Finance

CURRENCY AND EXCHANGE RATES

Monetary Units
100 centavos = 1 sucre.

Denominations
Coins: 50 centavos; 1, 5, 10, 20 and 50 sucres.
Notes: 5, 10, 20, 50, 100, 500, 1,000 and 5,000 sucres.

Sterling and Dollar Equivalents (30 September 1990)
£1 sterling = 1,552.6 sucres;
US $1 = 828.7 sucres;
10,000 sucres = £6.441 = $12.067.

Average Exchange Rate (sucres per US dollar)
1987   170.46
1988   301.61
1989   526.35

BUDGET (million sucres)

Revenue	1987	1988	1989‡
Petroleum revenue	89,632.9	164,798.0	391,872.8
Tax revenue	7,539.7	5,056.9	5,276.9
Non-tax revenue	82,093.2	159,741.1	386,595.9
Price increases on petroleum by-products for internal consumption	19,438.5	43,618.3	81,131.2
Release of resources	90.1	1,739.0	22,678.7
Surplus on exports of crude petroleum by CEPE*	35,286.4	42,910.2	211,967.5
Surplus quota on TEXACO and CITY exports	12,806.3	57,614.3	38,702.9
Non-petroleum revenue	150,240.1	250,267.8	435,282.5
Tax revenue	142,063.5	225,337.3	410,390.0

Revenue—continued	1987	1988	1989‡
External trade	41,858.5	67,024.1	108,638.0
Exports	145.0	28.4	25.7
Imports	41,713.5	66,995.7	108,612.3
Domestic taxes	100,205.0	158,313.2	301,752.0
Income tax	26,536.5	36,505.8	79,600.9
Taxes on financial transactions	5,660.0	13,607.3	23,050.5
Taxes on production and consumption	62,644.4	99,129.8	156,840.0
Non-tax revenue	8,176.6	24,930.5	24,892.5
Transfers	1,496.9	408.5	964.2
Sub-total	241,369.9	415,474.3	828,119.5
Less CATs†	4,608.3	18.5	125.4
Total	236,761.6	415,455.8	827,994.1

* Corporación Estatal Petrolera Ecuatoriana, renamed Petróleos del Ecuador in 1989.
† Certificados de Abono Tributario y Bonos IERAC.
‡ Provisional.

Expenditure	1987	1988	1989*
General services	67,000.1	115,739.5	197,870.1
Education and culture	70,411.7	98,235.4	156,260.0
Social welfare and labour	3,761.5	4,796.3	14,938.9
Health and community development	25,668.6	40,340.3	60,710.0
Farming and livestock development	9,155.7	13,674.7	25,205.1
Natural and energy resources	3,543.2	5,481.7	5,260.5
Industry and trade	7,046.9	21,046.3	32,392.7
Transport and communications	29,857.1	32,511.9	50,761.9
Public debt interest	37,242.3	75,898.2	163,654.6
General appropriations	10,092.7	8,970.5	—
Other purposes	16,688.9	132.9	31,127.7
Sub-total	280,468.7	416,827.7	738,181.5
Less Withdrawals	1,880.6	—	—
Total	278,588.1	416,827.7	738,181.5

* Provisional.

CENTRAL BANK RESERVES (US $ million at 31 December)

	1987	1988	1989
Gold*	165.7	165.7	165.7
IMF special drawing rights	0.9	1.3	0.9
Foreign exchange	490.2	396.3	539.5
Total	655.8	563.3	706.1

* Valued at $400 per troy ounce.

Source: IMF, *International Financial Statistics*.

MONEY SUPPLY (million sucres at 31 December)

	1987	1988	1989
Currency outside banks	73,494	122,470	174,307
Private-sector deposits at central bank	2,071	5,017	2,542
Demand deposits at private banks	144,010	210,180	289,458
Total money	219,575	337,667	466,307

COST OF LIVING (Consumer Price Index; annual averages for middle- and low-income families in urban area; base: May 1978–April 1979 = 100)

	1987	1988	1989
Food and drink	818.4	1,344.9	2,527.9
Housing	378.5	525.5	782.3
Clothing	552.7	850.5	1,425.3
Miscellaneous	609.6	967.2	1,607.6
All items	627.7	993.2	1,744.4

ECUADOR

NATIONAL ACCOUNTS

Expenditure on the Gross Domestic Product
(million sucres at current prices)

	1987	1988	1989
Government final consumption expenditure	230,417	337,003	499,620
Private final consumption expenditure	1,269,416	2,140,102	3,896,928
Increase in stocks	234	15,824	52,223
Gross fixed capital formation	406,598	666,857	1,125,703
Total domestic expenditure	1,906,665	3,159,786	5,574,474
Exports of goods and services	431,538	865,318	1,482,600
Less Imports of goods and services	543,702	920,765	1,592,461
Gross domestic product in purchasers' values	1,794,501	3,104,339	5,464,613

Gross Domestic Product by Economic Activity
(million sucres at constant 1975 prices)

	1987	1988	1989
Agriculture, hunting, forestry and fishing	27,323	29,678	30,581
Petroleum and other mining*	11,107	25,319	23,501
Manufacturing*	28,729	29,381	28,272
Electricity, gas and water	2,616	2,789	2,871
Construction	7,011	6,359	6,282
Trade, restaurants and hotels	25,397	26,256	26,392
Transport, storage and communications	12,829	13,486	14,175
Finance, insurance, real estate and business services	21,095	22,978	19,629
Community, social and personal services	10,067	10,190	10,478
Sub-total	146,174	166,436	162,181
Less Imputed bank service charge	7,122	8,683	5,114
Domestic product of industries	139,052	157,753	157,067
Government services	15,002	14,231	14,501
Domestic services of households	756	778	800
Sub-total	154,810	172,762	172,368
Customs duties (net of import subsidies)	4,206	4,104	4,776
GDP in purchasers' values	159,016	176,866	177,144

* Petroleum-refining is included in mining and excluded from manufacturing.

BALANCE OF PAYMENTS (US $ million)

	1987	1988	1989
Merchandise exports f.o.b.	2,021.0	2,202.0	2,354.0
Merchandise imports f.o.b.	−2,054.0	−1,614.0	−1,693.0
Trade balance	−33.0	588.0	661.0
Exports of services	444.0	455.0	529.0
Imports of services	−1,674.0	−1,676.0	−1,819.0
Balance on goods and services	−1,263.0	−633.0	−629.0
Private unrequited transfers (net)	132.0	97.0	97.0
Government unrequited transfers (net)			
Current balance	−1,131.0	−536.0	−532.0
Direct capital investment (net)	75.0	80.0	80.0
Other long-term capital (net)	96.0	−760.0	−291.0
Short-term capital (net)	56.0	280.0	−212.0
Net errors and omissions	−718.6	−248.2	−9.4
Total (net monetary movements)	−1,622.6	−1,184.2	−964.4
Valuation changes (net)	−61.6	−23.2	26.0
Exceptional financing (net)	1,560.0	1,248.0	1,171.0
Official financing (net)	−36.0	−51.0	−14.0
Changes in reserves	−160.3	−10.4	218.5

Source: IMF, *International Financial Statistics*.

External Trade

PRINCIPAL COMMODITIES (US $ million)

Imports c.i.f.	1987	1988	1989
Durable consumer goods	83.6	63.4	47.6
Non-durable consumer goods	124.8	101.2	136.8
Fuels and lubricants	294.5	58.7	71.1
Raw material for agriculture	52.7	62.1	90.6
Raw material for industry	791.7	707.5	839.0
Construction materials	73.5	51.3	52.1
Capital goods for agriculture	28.8	12.3	13.4
Capital goods for industry	500.8	404.1	389.3
Transport equipment	202.4	249.3	205.7
Total (incl. others)	2,158.1	1,713.5	1,854.8

Exports f.o.b.	1987	1988	1989
Bananas	266.9	297.8	369.5
Coffee	192.3	152.4	142.0
Cocoa	82.8	77.6	55.6
Seafood	421.1	423.3	377.2
Petroleum	645.8	875.2	1,032.7
Cocoa products	57.1	47.7	52.8
Seafood products	58.6	86.6	56.7
Petroleum derivatives	78.2	100.9	114.7
Total (incl. others)	1,927.7	2,192.6	2,353.9

ECUADOR

PRINCIPAL TRADING PARTNERS (US $ million)

Imports c.i.f.	1987	1988	1989
Argentina	13.8	17.5	34.3
Belgium and Luxembourg	13.6	13.5	22.5
Brazil	117.3	109.8	173.7
Chile	38.1	33.4	30.3
Colombia	43.3	34.8	45.0
France	41.3	37.8	39.0
Germany, Federal Republic	172.3	106.6	125.2
Italy	80.6	64.2	83.8
Japan	282.4	238.4	152.7
Mexico	92.0	56.8	55.7
Netherlands	26.0	18.6	17.9
Peru	24.1	21.8	30.5
Spain	65.3	67.8	54.3
Switzerland	51.3	35.3	46.3
Taiwan	36.7	32.4	34.8
United Kingdom	48.8	35.3	45.6
USA	558.8	567.6	625.9
Venezuela	173.5	21.5	17.2
Total (incl. others)	2,158.1	1,713.5	1,854.8

Exports f.o.b.	1987	1988	1989
Belgium and Luxembourg	10.0	15.7	26.0
Chile	33.7	58.7	81.9
Colombia	35.6	43.5	41.4
Germany, Federal Republic	66.8	90.8	78.7
Italy	15.1	29.2	26.3
Japan	47.1	54.1	59.2
Mexico	76.5	19.3	26.0
Netherlands	20.0	21.0	12.3
Panama	53.2	34.8	61.7
Peru	51.3	129.0	135.1
Spain	15.2	23.1	38.9
Taiwan	44.2	47.6	47.9
USA	1,056.4	1,006.2	1,367.6
Venezuela	37.9	4.5	6.2
Total (incl. others)	1,927.7	2,192.9	2,353.9

Transport

RAILWAYS (traffic)

	1983	1984	1985
Passenger-kilometres (million)	43	49	52
Net ton-kilometres (million)	8	6	9

Source: UN, *Statistical Yearbook*.

ROAD TRAFFIC (motor vehicles in use at 31 December)

	1985	1986	1987
Passenger cars	250,805	273,352	272,282
Buses and coaches	12,771	14,005	13,364
Goods vehicles	24,247	27,965	27,867

Source: International Road Federation, *World Road Statistics*.

INTERNATIONAL SEA-BORNE SHIPPING
(freight traffic, '000 metric tons)

	1986	1987	1988
Goods loaded	16,901	9,198	8,402
Goods unloaded	2,443	2,544	2,518

Source: UN, *Monthly Bulletin of Statistics*.

CIVIL AVIATION (traffic on scheduled services)

	1983	1984	1985
Passengers carried ('000)	618	634	665
Passenger-km (million)	762	893	969
Freight ton-km (million)	33.0	42.5	50.7

Source: UN, *Statistical Yearbook*.

Tourism

	1983	1984	1985
Foreign visitors	192,900	219,200	238,100

Source: UN, *Statistical Yearbook*.

Education

(1987)

	Teachers	Pupils/Students
Pre-primary	4,756	108,348
Primary	58,326	1,822,252
Secondary:		
General	36,730	504,481
Teacher-training		6,597
Vocational	16,838	260,850
Higher:		
Universities, etc.	12,278	264,941
Distance-learning	172	7,015
Other institutions	n.a.	2,795*

* 1984 figure.

Source: UNESCO, *Statistical Yearbook*.

Directory

The Constitution

The 1945 Constitution was suspended in June 1970. In January 1978 a referendum was held to choose between two draft Constitutions, prepared by various special constitutional committees. In a 90% poll, 43% voted for a proposed new Constitution and 32.1% voted for a revised version of the 1945 Constitution. The new Constitution came into force on 10 August 1979. Its main provisions are summarized below:

CHAMBER OF REPRESENTATIVES

The Constitution of 1979 states that legislative power is exercised by the Chamber of Representatives which sits for a period of 60 days from 10 August. The Chamber is required to set up four full-time Legislative Commissions to consider draft laws when the House is in recess. Special sessions of the Chamber of Representatives may be called.

Representatives are elected for four years from lists of candidates drawn up by legally-recognized parties. Twelve are elected nationally; two from each Province with over 100,000 inhabitants, one from each Province with fewer than 100,000; and one for every 300,000 citizens or fractions of over 200,000. Representatives are eligible for re-election.

In addition to its law-making duties, the Chamber ratifies treaties, elects members of the Supreme and Superior Courts, and (from panels presented by the President) the Comptroller-General, the Attorney-General and the Superintendent of Banks. It is also able to overrule the President's amendment of a bill which it has submitted for Presidential approval. It may reconsider a rejected bill after a year or request a referendum, and may revoke the President's declaration of a state of emergency. The budget is considered in the first instance by the appropriate Legislative Commission and disagreements are resolved in the Chamber.

PRESIDENT

The presidential term is four years, and there is no re-election. The President appoints the Cabinet, the Governors of Provinces, diplomatic representatives and certain administrative employees, and is responsible for the direction of international relations. In the event of foreign invasion or internal disturbance, the President may declare a state of emergency and must notify the Chamber, or the Tribunal for Constitutional Guarantees if the Chamber is not in session.

As in other post-war Latin-American Constitutions, particular emphasis is laid on the functions and duties of the State, which is given wide responsibilities with regard to the protection of labour; assisting in the expansion of production; protecting the Indian and peasant communities; and organizing the distribution and development of uncultivated lands, by expropriation where necessary.

Voting is compulsory for every Ecuadorean citizen who is literate and over 18 years of age. An optional vote has been extended to illiterates (under 15% of the population by 1981). The Constitution guarantees liberty of conscience in all its manifestations, and states that the law shall not make any discrimination for religious reasons.

The Government

HEAD OF STATE

President: Dr RODRIGO BORJA CEVALLOS (took office 10 August 1988).
Vice-President: Ing. LUIS PARODÍ VALVERDE.

THE CABINET
(January 1991)

Minister of Government and Justice (Interior): Econ. CÉSAR VERDUGA VÉLEZ.
Minister of Foreign Affairs: Dr DIEGO CORDÓVEZ ZÉGERS.
Minister of Finance and Public Credit: JUAN FALCONI.
Minister of Industry, Trade, Integration and Fisheries: PABLO BETTER.
Minister of Agriculture and Livestock: ALFREDO SALTOS.
Minister of Energy and Mines: Ing. DIEGO TAMARIZ SERRANO.
Minister of Labour and Human Resources: ROBERTO GÓMEZ.
Minister of Education, Culture and Sport: ALFREDO VERA ARRATA.
Minister of Defence: Gen. (retd) JORGE FÉLIX MENA.
Minister of Public Health: Dr PLUTARCO NARANJO VARGAS.
Minister of Social Welfare: Ing. RÁUL BACA CARBO.
Minister of Public Works and Communications: RAÚL CARRASCO ZAMORA.
Secretary-General for Public Administration: Econ. WASHINGTON HERRERA.
Secretary-General for Public Information: Dr GONZALO ORTIZ CRESPO.
President of the National Monetary Board: GERMÁNICO SALGADO.
General Manager of the Central Bank: EDUARDO VALENCIA.

MINISTRIES

Office of the President: Palacio Nacional, García Moreno 1043, Quito; tel. (2) 216-300; telex 23751.
Office of the Vice-President: Manuel Larrea y Arenas, Edif. Consejo Provincial de Pichincha, 21°, Quito; tel. (2) 504-953; telex 22058; fax (2) 503-379.
Ministry of Agriculture and Livestock: Avda Eloy Alfaro y Amazonas, Quito; tel. (2) 548-708; telex 2291.
Ministry of Defence: Exposición 208, Quito; tel. (2) 216-150; telex 3986.
Ministry of Education, Culture and Sport: Mejía 322, Quito; tel. (2) 216-224; telex 1267.
Ministry of Energy and Mines: Santa Prisca 223 y Manuel Larrea, Quito; tel. (2) 572-011; telex 2271.
Ministry of Finance and Public Credit: Avda 10 de Agosto 1661 y Jorge Washington, Quito; tel. (2) 544-500; telex 2358.
Ministry of Foreign Affairs: Avda 10 de Agosto y Carrión, Quito; tel. (2) 230-100; telex 22705.
Ministry of Industry, Trade, Integration and Fisheries: Roca 582 y Juan León Mera, Quito; tel. (2) 527-988; telex 2166.
Ministry of the Interior: Espejo y Benalcázar, Quito; tel. (2) 580-970; telex 2354.
Ministry of Labour and Human Resources: Ponce y Luis Felipe Borja, Quito; tel. (2) 524-666; telex 2898.
Ministry of Public Health: Juan Larrea 444, Quito; tel. (2) 521-114.
Ministry of Public Works and Communications: Avda 6 de Diciembre 1184, Quito; tel. (2) 561-180; telex 2663.
Ministry of Social Welfare: Robles 850 y Amazonas, Quito; tel. (2) 540-750; telex 2497.

President and Legislature

PRESIDENTIAL ELECTION

In the first round of voting, held on 31 January 1988, there were 10 candidates, among whom RODRIGO BORJA CEVALLOS (ID) polled an estimated 20% of the votes cast and ABDALÁ BUCARAM ORTIZ (PRE) polled 15%. In the second round of voting, held on 8 May, RODRIGO BORJA CEVALLOS received 46% of the votes cast and ABDALÁ BUCARAM ORTIZ polled 41%. RODRIGO BORJA CEVALLOS was thus elected President.

CONGRESO NACIONAL

Cámara Nacional de Representantes

President of Congress: EDELBERTO BONILLA OLEAS.
Vice-President of Congress: FLAVIO TORRES.

ECUADOR
Directory

Party	Seats after elections*	
	31 January 1988	17 June 1990
Partido Social Cristiano (PSC)	6	16
Izquierda Democrática (ID)	27	14
Partido Roldosista Ecuatoriano (PRE)	4	13
Partido Socialista Ecuatoriano (PSE)	3	8
Democracia Popular-Unión Demócrata Cristiana (DP-UDC)	7	7
Concentración de Fuerzas Populares (CFP)	6	3
Partido Liberal Radical (PLR)	2	3
Partido Conservador (PC)	1	3
Frente Radical Alfarista (PRA)	1	2
Frente Amplio de la Izquierda (FADI)	2	2
Movimiento Popular Democrático (MPD)	4	1
Total	71	72

* The 60 seats allocated on a provincial basis are renewable after two years.

Political Organizations

Concentración de Fuerzas Populares (CFP): Quito; f. 1946; Leader GALO VAYAS; Dir Dr AVERROES BUCARAM SAXIDA.

Democracia Popular-Unión Demócrata Cristiana (DP-UDC): Calle Luis Saá No 153 y Hnos Pazmiño, Casilla 2300, Quito; tel. (2) 547-388; f. 1978; Christian democrat; Pres. JAMIL MAHUAD.

Frente Progresista Democrático: f. 1984 to succeed Convergencia Democrática; regrouped June 1986; also known as Bloque Progresista; left-wing coalition comprising the following parties:

Frente Amplio de la Izquierda (FADI): Quito; f. 1977; left-wing alliance comprising the following parties: Partido Comunista Ecuatoriano, Partido Socialista Revolucionario, Movimiento para la Unidad de la Izquierda, Movimiento Revolucionario de la Izquierda Cristiana; Dir Dr RENÉ MAUGÉ M.

Izquierda Democrática (ID): Juan León Mera 268 y Jorge Washington, Quito; f. 1977; Leader RODRIGO BORJA CEVALLOS; Dir XAVIER LEDESMA.

Movimiento Popular Democrático (MPD): Maoist; Leader Dr JAIME HURTADO GONZÁLEZ.

Partido Demócrata (PD): Quito; Leader Dr FRANCISCO HUERTA MONTALVO.

Partido Socialista Ecuatoriano (PSE): San Luis 340, Of. 105, entre Santa Prisca y Ante, Quito; tel. (2) 570-065; f. 1926; Sec.-Gen. Dr VÍCTOR GRANDA AGUILAR.

Pueblo, Cambio y Democracia (PCD) Popular Roldosista: Quito; f. 1980; centre-left; committed to policies of fmr Pres. Jaime Roldós; Dir LEÓN ROLDÓS AGUILERA; Sec.-Gen. ERNESTO BUENANO CABRERA.

Unión Democrática Popular (UDP): Leader JORGE CHIRIBOGA.

Frente Radical Alfarista (FRA): Quito; f. 1972; Leader IVÁN CASTRO PATIÑO.

Frente de Reconstrucción Nacional (FRN): centre-right coalition comprising the following parties:

Alianza Popular Revolucionaria Ecuatoriana (APRE): centrist.

Coalición Nacional Republicana (CNR): Quito; f. 1986; fmrly Coalición Institucionalista Demócrata (CID).

Partido Conservador (PC): Quito; f. 1855, traditional rightist party; Dir JOSÉ TERÁN VAREA.

Partido Liberal Radical (PLR): Quito; f. 1895; held office from 1895 to 1944 as the Liberal Party, which subsequently divided into various factions; perpuates the traditions of the old party; Dir CARLOS JULIO PLAZA A.

Partido Nacionalista Revolucionario (PNR): Calle Pazmiño 245, Of. 500, Quito; f. 1969; supporters of fmr President Dr Carlos Julio Arosemena Monroy; Dir Dr MAURICIO GÁNDARA.

Partido Nacional Velasquista (PNV): f. 1952; centre-right; Leader ALFONSO ARROYO ROBELLY.

Partido Social Cristiano (PSC): Quito; f. 1951; centre-right party; Pres. ECON. NICOLÁS LAPENTTI CARRIÓN; Leaders SIXTO DURÁN BALLÉN, LEÓN FEBRES CORDERO RIVADENEIRA.

Fuerzas Armadas Populares Eloy Alfaro—Alfaro Vive ¡Carajo! (AVC) (Eloy Alfaro Popular Armed Forces—Alfaro Lives, Damn it!): f. 1982; left-wing; supports Izquierda Democrática; guerrilla group until Feb. 1989; joined legitimate political system in August 1990; Leader ROSA MIREYA CÁRDENAS; 3,000 mems.

Partido Comunista Marxista-Leninista de Ecuador: Sec.-Gen. CAMILO ALMEYDA.

Partido Republicano (PR): Quito; 1988 Presidential Candidate GUILLERMO SOTOMAYOR.

Partido Roldosista Ecuatoriano (PRE): Quito; f. 1982; Dir ABDALÁ BUCARAM ORTIZ.

Unión del Pueblo Patriótico (UPP): Quito; 1988 Presidential Candidate Lt-Gen. FRANK VARGAS PAZZOS.

The following guerrilla group is active:

Montoneros Patria Libre (MPL): f. 1986; advocates an end to authoritarianism.

Diplomatic Representation

EMBASSIES IN ECUADOR

Argentina: Avda Amazonas 477, Apdo 2937, Quito; tel. (2) 562-292; telex 2136; Ambassador: RICARDO H. ILLIA.

Austria: Avda Patria y Amazonas, Edif. Cofiec 11°; tel. (2) 545-336.

Belgium: Austria 219 e Irlanda, Quito; telex 2767; Ambassador: F. FRANZ.

Bolivia: Quito; Ambassador: EUSEBIO MOREIRA.

Brazil: Calle Amazonas 1429 y Colón, Apdo 231, Quito; tel. (2) 563-846; telex 22218; Ambassador: ADOLPHO BENEVIDES.

Bulgaria: Calle Colina 331 y Orellana, Quito; tel. (2) 552-553; telex 22047; Chargé d'affaires: LUBOMIR IVANOV.

Canada: Edif. Belmonte 6°, Avda Corea 126 y Amazonas; tel. (2) 458-102.

Chile: Edif. Rocafuerte 4° y 5°, Avda Amazonas 325 y Washington, Quito; telex 2167; Ambassador: GABRIEL VAN SCHOUWEN FIGUEROA.

China, People's Republic: Quito; Ambassador: PANG GANGHUA.

Colombia: Calle San Javier 169, Casilla 2923, Quito; telex 2156; Ambassador: LAUREANO ALBERTO ARELLANO.

Costa Rica: Quito; Ambassador: FÉLIX CÓRTEZ.

Cuba: Quito; Ambassador: CARLOS ZAMORA.

Czechoslovakia: Calle General Salazar 459 y Coruña, Quito; telex 2478; Ambassador: JULIUS STANG.

Dominican Republic: Avda 6 de Diciembre 4629, Quito; Ambassador: MARIO PENA.

Egypt: Edif. Araucaria 9°, Baquedano 222 y Reina Victoria, Apdo 9355, Sucursal 7, Quito; tel. (2) 235-046; telex 2154; Ambassador: KHAIRAT ISSA.

El Salvador: Avda de los Shyris 1240 y Portugal, Edif. Albatros, Apdo 8386, Quito; tel. (2) 433-823; telex 22931; Ambassador: BYRON FERNANDO LARIOS L.

France: Plaza 107 y Avda Patria, Apdo 536, Quito; tel. (2) 560-789; telex 2146; Ambassador: JEAN-MICHEL GAUSSOT.

Germany: Avda Patria y 9 de Octubre, Edif. Eteco 6°, Quito; tel. (2) 232-660; telex 2222; Ambassador: Dr JOACHIM Graf SCHIRNDING.

Guatemala: Avda 6 de Diciembre 2636, Quito; Ambassador: JUAN RENDÓN M.

Holy See: (Apostolic Nunciature), Avda Orellana 692, Apdo 4543-A, Quito; tel. (2) 564-938; telex 2053; Apostolic Nuncio: Most Rev. LUIGI CONTI, Titular Archbishop of Gratiana.

Honduras: Cordero 279 y Plaza, Quito; telex 2805; Ambassador: ANTONIO MOLINA O.

Hungary: Avda República de El Salvador 733 y Avda Portugal, Quito; tel. (2) 459-700; telex 2255; Chargé d'affaires: PÁL LANDESZ.

Israel: Avda Eloy Alfaro 969 y Avda Amazonas, Quito; tel. (2) 565-509; telex 2174; Ambassador: ABRAHAM SETTON.

Italy: Calle La Isla 111, POB 072-A, Quito; tel. (2) 561-077; telex 22715; Ambassador: GIOVANNI BATTISTA CROSETTI.

Japan: Avda Amazonas 239 y 18 de Septiembre, Quito; telex 2185; Ambassador: H. NISHAMIYA.

Korea, Republic: Calle Reina Victoria 1539 y Avda Colón, Edif. Banco de Guayaquil 11°, Quito; tel. (2) 560-573; telex 2868; Ambassador: HAE YUNG CHUNG.

Mexico: Avda 6 de Diciembre 4843 y Naciones Unidas, Casilla 6371, Quito; tel. (2) 457-820; telex 2395; Ambassador: IGNACIO VILLASEÑOR.

Netherlands: Edif. Club de Leones Central 5°, Avda de las Naciones Unidas entre Avdas 10 de Agosto y Amazonas, Apdo 2840, Quito; telex 2576; Ambassador: Dr J. WEIDEMA.

ECUADOR

Panama: Calle Pazmiño 245 y Avda 6 de Diciembre, Quito; Ambassador: ROBERTO SAMUEL FÁBREGA GOYTIA.
Paraguay: Avda Gaspar de Villarroel 2013 y Avda Amazonas, Casilla 139-A, Quito; tel. (2) 245-871; telex 2260; Ambassador: Dr GILBERTO CANIZA SÁNCHIZ.
Peru: Edif. España Pent-House, Avda Colón y Amazonas, Quito; tel. (2) 554-161; telex 2864; fax (2) 562-349; Ambassador: EDUARDO PONCE VIVANCO.
Poland: Quito; Chargé d'affaires: CZESŁAW BUGAJSKI.
Romania: Avda República del Salvador 482 e Irlanda, Quito; telex 2230; Ambassador: GHEORGHE DOBRA.
Spain: La Pinta 455 y Amazonas, Casilla 9322, Quito; tel. (2) 564-373; telex 22816; Ambassador: JUAN MANUEL EGEA IBÁÑEZ.
Sweden: Edif. Las Cámaras 2°, Avda República y Amazonas, Apdo 420-A, Quito; tel. (2) 454-872; telex 2396; Ambassador: CHRISTIAN BAUSCH.
Switzerland: Edif. Xerox, Avda Amazonas 3617 y Juan Pablo Sanz, 2°, Casilla 4815, Quito; tel. (2) 434-948; telex 2592; fax (2) 449-314; Chargé d'affaires a.i.: G. F. PEDOTTI.
USSR: Reina Victoria 462 y Roca, Quito; Ambassador: GERMAN E. SHLIAPNIKOV.
United Kingdom: Avda González Suárez 111, Casilla 314, Quito; tel. (2) 560-670; telex 2138; fax (2) 560-730; Ambassador: FRANK B. WHEELER.
USA: Avda 12 de Octubre y Patria 120, Quito; tel. (2) 562-890; telex 2329; Ambassador: PAUL LAMBERT.
Uruguay: Edif. Sonelsa 2°, Calle Mariscal Foch s/n y Avda 6 de Diciembre, Quito; tel. (2) 237-151; telex 2657; Ambassador: Dr JORGE PÉREZ OTERMIN.
Venezuela: Coruña 1733 y Belo Horizonte, Apdo 688, Quito; tel. (2) 564-626; telex 22160; Ambassador: LUIS RODRÍGUEZ MALASPINA.
Yugoslavia: Gen. Francisco Salazar 958 y 12 de Octubre, Quito; tel. (2) 526-218; telex 2633; Ambassador: SAMUILO PROTIĆ.

Judicial System

Note: In August 1984 an amendment to the Constitution was passed to reduce the term of Supreme Court justices from six to four years. Following the appointment of the 16 Supreme Court justices by Congress, a dispute broke out between Congress and the Government, which opposed the appointments on the grounds that they were 'unconstitutional'. In December 1984 the dispute was resolved when Congress agreed to waive its prerogative to select the 16 Supreme Court justices and allowed the Government to make the new appointments.

Attorney-General: Dr JORGE MAZÓN JARAMILLO.
Supreme Court of Justice: Palacio de Justicia, Avda 6 de Diciembre y Piedrahita, Quito; tel. (2) 236-550; telex 22976; fax (2) 551-516; Pres. RAMIRO LARREA SANTOS; 15 Judges and two Fiscals.
Higher or Divisional Courts: Ambato, Azogues, Babahoyo, Cuenca, Esmeraldas, Guaranda, Guayaquil, Ibarra, Latacunga, Loja, Machala, Portoviejo, Quito, Riobamba and Tulcán; 90 judges.
Provincial Courts: there are 40 Provincial Courts in 15 districts; other courts include 94 Criminal; 219 Civil; 29 dealing with labour disputes; 17 Rent Tribunals.
Special Courts: National Court for Juveniles.

Religion

There is no state religion but about 90% of the population are Roman Catholics. There are representatives of various Protestant Churches and of the Jewish faith in Quito and Guayaquil.

CHRISTIANITY
The Roman Catholic Church

Ecuador comprises three archdioceses, 10 dioceses, two territorial prelatures, seven Apostolic Vicariates and one Apostolic Prefecture.

Bishops' Conference: Conferencia Episcopal Ecuatoriana, Apdo 1081, Avenida América 1866 y La Gasca, Quito; tel. (2) 524-568; telex 2427; f. 1939; Pres. ANTONIO J. GONZÁLEZ ZUMÁRRAGA, Archbishop of Quito.
Archbishop of Cuenca: LUIS ALBERTO LUNA TOBAR, Apdo 46, Calle Bolívar 7-64, Cuenca; tel. (7) 827-792.
Archbishop of Guayaquil: JUAN IGNACIO LARREA HOLGUÍN, Arzobispado, Apdo 254, Calle Clemente Ballén 501 y Chimborazo, Guayaquil; tel. (4) 528-872.
Archbishop of Quito: ANTONIO J. GONZÁLEZ ZUMÁRRAGA, Arzobispado, Apdo 106, Calle Chile 1140, Quito; tel. (2) 210-703.

The Baptist Church
The Baptist Convention of Ecuador: POB 3236, Guayaquil; tel. (4) 384-865; Pres. Rev. HAROLT SANTE MATA; Sec. JORGE MORENO CHAVARRÍA.

The Episcopal Church
Bishop of Ecuador: Rt Rev. Dr ADRIÁN D. CÁCERES, Apdo 353-A, Quito.

The Methodist Church
The Methodist Church: Evangelical United Church, Rumipamba 915, Apdo 236-A, Quito; 800 mems, 2,000 adherents.

BAHÁ'Í FAITH
The National Spiritual Assembly of the Bahá'ís: Apdo 869-A, Quito; tel. (2) 563-484; mems resident in 1,121 localities.

The Press

PRINCIPAL DAILIES
Quito

El Comercio: Kilómetro 6 Sur, Apdo 57, Quito; tel. (2) 260-020; telex 2246; fax (2) 614-466; f. 1906; morning; independent; Proprs Compañía Anónima El Comercio; Dir SANTIAGO JERVIS; circ. 130,000.
Hoy: Avda Colón 936, Apdo 9069, Quito; tel. (2) 539-888; telex 22718; f. 1982; liberal; Editor BENJAMÍN ORTIZ; circ. 55,000.
El Tiempo: Avda América y Villalengua, Apdo 3117, Quito; f. 1965; morning; independent; Proprs Editorial La Unión, CA; Pres. ANTONIO GRANDA CENTENO; Editor EDUARDO GRANDA GARCES; circ. 35,000.
Ultimas Noticias: Chile 1345, Apdo 57, Quito; tel. (2) 260-020; telex 2246; f. 1938; evening; independent; commercial; Proprs Compañía Anónima El Comercio; Dir DAVID MANTILLA CASHMORE; circ. 90,000.

Guayaquil
Expreso: Avda 9 de Octubre 427 y Chimborazo, Guayaquil; morning; independent; Dir GALO MARTÍNEZ; circ. 30,000.
La Razón: Frente al Terminal Aéreo, Junto a Canal 10, Casilla 5832, Guayaquil; tel. (4) 280-100; evening; independent; f. 1965; Dir JIMMY JAIRALA VALLAZZA; circ. 28,000.
El Telégrafo: Avda 10 de Agosto 601 y Boyacá, Apdo 415, Guayaquil; tel. (4) 323-265; telex 3473; f. 1884; morning; independent; commercial; Proprs El Telégrafo CA; Dir-Gen. Gen. EDUARDO AROSEMENA GÓMEZ; Man. ROBERTO YCAZA VEGA; circ. 35,000 (weekdays), 52,000 (Sundays).
El Universo: Escobedo y 9 de Octubre, Apdo 531, Guayaquil; tel. (4) 324-630; telex 435566; f. 1921; morning; independent; Dir CARLOS PÉREZ PERAZO; circ. 174,000 (weekdays), 255,000 (Sundays).

There are local daily newspapers of very low circulation in other towns.

PERIODICALS
Quito

La Calle: Casilla 2010, Quito; f. 1956; weekly; politics; Dir CARLOS ENRIQUE CARRIÓN; circ. 20,000.
Carta Económica del Ecuador: Toledo 1448 y Coruña, Apdo 3358, Quito; f. 1969; weekly; economic, financial and business information; Pres. Dr LINCOLN LARREA B.; circ. 8,000.
El Colegial: Calle Carlos Ibarra No 206, Quito; tel. (2) 216-541; f. 1974; publ. of Student Press Association; Dir WILSON ALMEIDA MUÑOZ; circ. 20,000.
Comercio Ecuatoriano: Avdas Amazona y República, Casilla 202, Quito; tel. (2) 453-011; telex 2638; f. 1906; monthly; commerce.
Ecuador Guía Turística: Meja 438, Oficina 43, Quito; f. 1969; tourist information in Spanish and English; Propr Prensa Informativa Turística; Dir JORGE VACA O.; circ. 30,000.
Integración: Solano 836, Quito; quarterly; economics of the Andean countries.
Letras del Ecuador: Casa de la Cultura Ecuatoriana, Avda 6 de Diciembre, Casilla 67, Quito; f. 1944; monthly; literature and art; non-political; Dir Dr TEODORO VANEGAS ANDRADE.
El Libertador: Olmedo 931 y García Moreno, Quito; f. 1926; Pres. Dr BENJAMÍN TERÁN VAREA.
Mensajero: Benalcázar 562, Apdo 4100, Quito; f. 1884; monthly; religion, culture, economics and politics; Dir JOSÉ GONZÁLEZ POYATOS, S.J.; circ. 5,000.

ECUADOR

Nueva: Apdo 3224, Quito; monthly; left-wing; Dir MAGDALENA JARAMILLO DE ADOUM.

Solidaridad: Calle Oriente 725, Quito; tel. (2) 216-541; f. 1982; monthly; publ. of Confederation of Catholic Office Staff and Students of Ecuador; Dir WILSON ALMEIDA MUÑOZ; Man. JOHNY MERIZALDE; circ. 15,000.

This is Ecuador: La Niña 555 y Avda Amazonas, Quito; f. 1968; monthly; English; tourism; Dir GUSTAVO VALLEJO.

Guayaquil

Análasis Semanal: Apdo 4925, Elizalde 119 7°, Guayaquil; fax (4) 326-842; weekly; economic and political affairs; Editor WALTER SPURRIER BAQUERIZO.

Boletín del Sindicato Médico: Guayaquil; f. 1911; monthly; scientific, literary; independent.

Ecuador Ilustrado: Guayaquil; f. 1924; monthly; literary; illustrated.

Revista Estadio: Aguirre 730 y Boyacá, Apdo 1239, Guayaquil; tel. (4) 327-200; telex 3423; fax (4) 320-499; f. 1962; fortnightly; sport; Editor JOSÉ CALDERÓN; circ. 70,000.

Hogar: Aguirre 724 y Boyacá, Apdo 1239, Guayaquil; tel. (4) 327-200; telex 3423; f. 1964; monthly; Man. Editor ROSA AMELIA ALVARADO; circ. 35,000.

Vistazo: Aguirre 724 y Boyacá, Apdo 1239, Guayaquil; tel. (4) 327-200; telex 3423; f. 1957; fortnightly; general; Pres. XAVIER ALVARADO ROCA; circ. 85,000.

NEWS AGENCIES
Foreign Bureaux

Agencia EFE (Spain): Palacio Arzobispal, Chile 1178, Apdo 4043, Quito; tel. (2) 512-427; telex 2602; Bureau Chief EMILIO CRESPO.

Agenzia Nazionale Stampa Associata (ANSA) (Italy): Calle Venezuela 1013 y esq. Mejía, Of. 26, Quito; tel. (2) 580-794; telex 1362; fax (2) 580-782; Correspondent FERNANDO LARENAS.

Associated Press (AP) (USA): Edif. Sudamérica, 4°, Of. 44, Calle Venezuela 1018 y Mejía, Apdo 3056, Quito; tel. (2) 570-235; telex 2296; Correspondent CARLOS CISTERNAS.

Deutsche Presse-Agentur (dpa) (Germany): González Suárez 894 y Gonnessiat, Edif. Atrium, Of. 5-7, Quito; tel. (2) 568-986; Correspondent JORGE ORTIZ.

Inter Press Service (IPS) (Italy): Edif. Sudamérica 1°, Of. 14, Calle Venezuela 1018 y Mejía, Quito; tel. (2) 215-616; Correspondent VIRGINIA AGUIRRE.

Prensa Latina (Cuba): Edif. Sudamérica 2°, Of. 24, Calle Venezuela 1018 y Mejía, Quito; tel. (2) 519-333; telex 2625; Bureau Chief ENRIQUE GARCÍA MEDINA.

Reuters (UK): Chile 1345, 4°, Casilla 4112, Quito; tel. (2) 510-972; telex 22620; Correspondent JORGE AGUIRRE.

Telegrafnoye Agentstvo Sovetskovo Soyuza (TASS) (USSR): Calle Roca 328 y 6 de Diciembre, 2°, Dep. 6, Quito; tel. (2) 511-631; telex 3566; Correspondent VLADIMIR GOSTEV.

United Press International (UPI) (USA): Quito; Correspondent RICARDO POLIT.

Xinhua (New China) News Agency (People's Republic of China): Edif. Portugal, Avda Portugal y Avda de la República del Salvador No 730, 10°, Quito; telex 2268; Bureau Chief LIN MINZHONG.

Publishers

Artes Gráficas Ltda: Avda 12 de Octubre 1637, Apdo 533, Casilla 456-A, Quito; Man. MANUEL DEL CASTILLO.

Cromograf, SA: Coronel 2207, Casilla 4285, Guayaquil; tel. (4) 346-400; telex 3387; children's books, paperbacks, art productions.

Editorial Ariel: Avda 10 de Agosto No 504, Guayaquil; tel. (4) 519-282; literature, sociology and history.

Editorial de la Casa de la Cultura Ecuatoriana 'Benjamín Carrión': Avda 6 de Diciembre 794, Apdo 67, Quito; tel. (2) 566-070; f. 1944; general fiction and non-fiction, general science; Pres. MILTON BARRAGÁN DUMET.

Editorial Claridad: Quito; tel. (2) 517-442; economics, history, sociology and politics.

Editorial y Librería Selecciones: Avda 9 de Octubre No 724 y Boyacá, Guayaquil; tel. (4) 305-807; history, geography and sociology.

Libros Técnicos Litesa Cía Ltda: Avda América 542, Apdo 456A, Quito; tel. (2) 528-537; Man. MANUEL DEL CASTILLO.

Pontificia Universidad Católica del Ecuador: 12 de Octubre 1076 y Carrión, Apdo 2184, Quito; tel. (2) 529-240; fax (2) 567-117; literature, natural science, law, anthropology, sociology, politics,

economics, theology, philosophy, history, archaeology, linguistics, languages and business.

Universidad Central del Ecuador: Departamento de Publicaciones, Servicio de Almacén Universitario, Ciudad Universitaria, Quito.

Universidad de Guayaquil: Departamento de Publicaciones, Biblioteca General, Apdo 3834, Guayaquil; tel. (4) 392-430; f. 1930; general literature, history, philosophy, fiction; Man. Dir LEONOR VILLAO DE SANTANDER.

Radio and Television

In 1987 there were about 2,900,000 radio receivers and 800,000 television receivers in use.

Asociación Ecuatoriana de Radiodifusión: 911–915 Edif. Gran Pasaje, Guayaquil; independent association; Pres. JORGE AGUILAR V.

Instituto Ecuatoriano de Telecomunicaciones—IETEL: Casilla 3066, Quito; telex 2202; Gen. Man. Ing. GONZALO GUERRERO JORDÁN.

RADIO

There are nearly 300 commercial stations, 10 cultural stations and 10 religious stations. The following are some of the most important commercial stations:

CRE (Cadena Radial Ecuatoriana): Edif. El Torreón 9, Avda Boyacá 642, Apdo 4144, Guayaquil; tel. (4) 304290; telex 43825; fax (4) 327031; Dir RAFAEL GUERRERO.

Emisoras Gran Colombia: Galápagos 112 y Guayaquil, Casilla 2246, Quito; tel. (2) 211-670; fax (2) 580-170; f. 1943; Dir EDUARDO CEVALLOS CASTEÑEDA.

Radio Colón: Diguja 327, Quito; tel. (2) 453-288; Dir ATAHUALPA RUIZ RIVA.

Radio Cristal: Luque 1407, Guayaquil; Dir ARMANDO ROMERO RODAS.

Radio Nacional del Ecuador: Chile 1267, Quito.

Radio Quito-La Voz de la Capital: POB 57, Calle Chile 1347, Quito; tel. (2) 514-398; telex 22043; fax (2) 514-676; f. 1940; Dir G. ACQUAVIVA.

Radio Tropicana: Edif. El Torreón 8°, Avda Boyacá 642, Apdo 4144, Guayaquil; tel. (4) 307-900; telex 3825; Dir ANTONIO GUERRERO G.

La Voz de los Andes: Villalengua 278, Quito; tel. (2) 241-550; telex 22734; fax (2) 447-263; f. 1931; operated by World Radio Missionary Fellowship; programmes in 17 languages including Spanish, English and Quechua; private, non-commercial, cultural, religious; Pres. Dr RONALD A. CLINE; Dir of Broadcasting GLEN VOLKHARDT.

TELEVISION

Corporación Ecuatoriana de Televisión: C. del Carmen, Casilla 1239, Guayaquil; tel. (4) 300-150; telex 3409; fax (4) 303-677; f. 1967; Pres. XAVIER ALVARADO ROCA; Gen. Man. FRANCISCO AROSEMENA ROBLES.

Cadena Ecuatoriana de Televisión: Avda de las Américas, frente al Aeropuerto, Casilla 673, Guayaquil; tel. (4) 393-248; telex 3530; fax (4) 287-544; f. 1969; commercial; Gen. Man. JORGE E. PÉREZ P.

Canal Universitario Católica: Avda Humbolt 3170, Cuenca; tel. (7) 827-862; telex 48775; fax (7) 831-040; Dir Dr CÉSAR CORDERO-MOSCOSO.

Diario Ediasa: Apdo 50, Portoviejo; Dir PEDRO EDUARDO IZAGUIRRE.

Teleamazonas: Casilla 4844, Quito; tel. (2) 430-313; telex 2244; commercial; Pres. ANTONIO GRANDA CENTENO.

Tele Cuatro Guayaquil, SA: Edif. Casa de Cultura, 5°, 9 de Octubre 1200, Guayaquil; tel. (4) 308-194; telex 3198; fax (4) 313-436; Pres. Dr CARLOS MUÑOZ INSUA.

Televisión Esmeraldeña Compañía de Economía Mixta—TESEM: Edif. Mutual V. Torres, Casilla 108, Esmeraldas; tel. (2) 710-090; Dir HÉCTOR ENDARA E.

Televisión del Pacífico, SA (Telenacional): Murgeón 732, Casilla 130-B, Quito; tel. (2) 540-877; telex 2435; commercial; Man. MODESTO LUQUE BENÍTEZ.

Televisora Ecuatoriana: Rumipamba 1039, Quito; commercial; Dir GERARDO BABORICH.

Televisora Nacional Cía Ltda—Canal 8: Bellavista, Casilla 3888, Quito; tel. (2) 244-888; telex 2888; commercial; Exec. Pres. CRISTINA MANTILLA DE LARA.

Ultravision: 9 de Octubre y Córdova, Guayaquil; Dir BOLIVAR MALTA A.

ECUADOR

Finance

(cap. = capital, p.u. = paid up; res = reserves; dep. = deposits; .n. = million; amounts in sucres)

Junta Monetaria Nacional (National Monetary Board): Quito; tel. (2) 514-833; telex 2182; f. 1927; Pres. Lic. ANDRÉS VALLEJO ARCO.

Supervisory Authority

Superintendencia de Bancos y Seguros: Avda 12 de Octubre 1561, Apdo 424, Quito; tel. (2) 569-526; telex 22148; fax (2) 563-652; f. 1927; supervises national banking system, including state and private banks and other financial institutions; Superintendent Dr FERNANDO GUERRERO GUERRERO.

BANKING

State Banks

Banco Central del Ecuador: Avda 10 de Agosto, Plaza Bolívar, Casilla 339, Quito; tel. (2) 519-384; telex 2165; fax (2) 570-701; f. 1927; cap. 1,482m., res 2,533m., dep. 666,608m. (Dec. 1987); Chair. Dr RODRIGO ESPINOZA B.; Gen. Man. FERNANDO SEVILLA H..

Banco de Desarrollo del Ecuador, SA (BEDE): Páez 655 y Ramírez Dávalos, Casilla 373, Quito; tel. (2) 546-404; telex 2655; f. 1979; cap. 39,992m., res 2,001m. (Dec. 1986); Pres. Ing. GUSTAVO ESPINOSA CHIMBO; Gen. Man. Econ. EDUARDO VALENCIA.

Banco Ecuatoriano de la Vivienda: Avda l0 de Agosto 2270 y Cordero, Casilla 3244, Quito; tel. (2) 521-311; telex 2399; f. 1962; cap. 5,006m., res 952m., dep. 7,389m. (Dec. 1986); Pres. Abog. JUAN PABLO MONCAGATTA.; Gen. Man. Dr FAUSTO VÁSQUEZ MORALES.

Banco Nacional de Fomento: Ante 107 y 10 de Agosto, Casilla 685, Quito; tel. (2) 230-010; telex 22256; f. 1928; cap. 3,000m., res 14,914m., dep. 117,067m. (Dec. 1987); Pres. Dr IGNACIO HIDALGO VILLAVICENCIO; Gen. Man. MARCELO PEÑA DURINI; 70 brs.

Corporación Financiera Nacional (CFN): Juan León Mera 130 y Avda Patria, Casilla 163, Quito; tel. (2) 564-900; telex 2193; f. 1964; cap. 2,000m., res 8,417m. (July 1987); Pres. Econ. JORGE NÚÑEZ DAHIK; Gen. Man. Lic. RODRIGO MALO GONZÁLEZ.

Commercial Banks

Quito

Banco Amazonas, SA: Avda Amazonas y Santa María, Casilla 1211, Quito; tel. (2) 545-123; telex 2393; fax (2) 560-310; f. 1976; affiliated to Banque Paribas; cap. 800m., res 702.1m., dep. 1,811m. (Dec. 1986); Pres. Dr FRANCISCO PARRA GIL; Gen. Man. CARLOS MOSQUERA.

Banco de los Andes: Avda Amazonas 477, Casilla 3761, Quito; tel. (2) 554-215; telex 2214; f. 1973; affiliated to Banco de Bogotá; cap. 247m., res 57m., dep. 1,298m. (June 1984); Pres. Dr AUGUSTO DEL POZO; Gen. Man. GUILLERMO DUEÑAS ITURRALDE.

Banco Caja de Crédito Agrícola Ganadero, SA: Avda 6 de Diciembre 225 y Piedrahita, Quito; tel. (2) 528-521; telex 2559; f. 1949; cap 132m., res 41m., dep. 592m. (Aug. 1984); Man. HUGO GRIJALVA GARZÓN; Pres. NICOLÁS GUILLÉN.

Banco Consolidado del Ecuador: Avda Patria 740 y 9 de Octubre, Apdo 9150, Suc. 7, Quito; tel. (2) 560-369; telex 2634; fax (2) 560-719; f. 1981; cap. 575m., res 33.4m., dep. 3,861.0m. (June 1989); Pres. Dr MARCO TULIO GONZÁLEZ; Gen. Man. RAÚL DAZA M.

Banco de Co-operativas del Ecuador: Avda 10 de Agosto 937, Casilla 2244, Quito; tel. (2) 551-933; telex 2651; f. 1965; cap. 113m., res 8m., dep. 1,100m. (Sept. 1988); Pres. Dr JACINTO MONTERO; Gen. Man. LUIS G. CORNEJO C.

Banco Internacional: Avda Patria 660 y Avda Amazonas, Casilla 2114, Quito; tel. (2) 565-547; telex 2195; f. 1973; cap. 2,000m., res 598m., dep. 21,619m. (Dec. 1989); Pres. FRANCISCO URIBE LASSO; Gen. Man. MARCO ANTONIO SUÁREZ CUERVO; 6 brs.

Banco del Pichincha, SA: Avda 10 de Agosto y Bogotá, Casilla 717-A, Quito; tel. (2) 235-861; telex 2618; fax (2) 551-893; f. 1906; cap. 1,650m., res 394m., dep. 28,585m. (July 1987); Pres. Dr GONZALO MANTILLA MATA; Gen. Man. JAIME ACOSTA VELASCO; 31 brs.

Banco Popular del Ecuador: Amazonas 3535 y Juan Pablo Sanz, Casilla 696, Quito; tel. (2) 444-700; telex 2234; f. 1953; cap. 8,000m., res 496m., dep. 75,000m. (April 1990); Pres. and Gen. Man. NICOLÁS LANDES; 21 brs.

Banco de Préstamos, SA: Calle Venezuela 659 y Sucre, Casilla 279, Quito; tel. (2) 216-360; telex 2854; fax (2) 570-239 f. 1909; cap. 1,215m., res 356m., dep. 20,440m. (June 1989); Pres. ALFREDO ALBÓRNOZ ANDRADE; Gen. Man. MAURO INTRIAGO DUNN; 2 brs.

Banco de la Producción, SA: Avda Amazonas y Japón, Apdo 38-A, Quito; tel. (2) 454-100; telex 2376; f. 1978; cap. 260m., res 91m., dep. 1,099m. (June 1984); Pres. RODRIGO PAZ DELGADO; Exec. Pres. Econ. ABELARDO PACHANO BERTERO.

Directory

Ambato

Banco de Tungurahua: Montalvo 630, Casilla 173, Ambato; tel. (2) 821-122; telex 7186; f. 1979; cap. 50m., res 2m., dep. 329m. (June 1984); Pres. GEORG SONNENHOLZNER; Gen. Man. PEDRO CALVACHE MOYA.

Cuenca

Banco del Austro: Sucre y Borrero (esq.), Casilla 167, Cuenca; tel. (7) 831-646; telex 8560; fax (7) 832-633; f. 1977; cap. 1,400m., dep. 21,254m. (May 1990); Pres. JUAN ELJURI ANTÓN; Gen. Man. PATRICIO ROBAYO IDROVO.

Banco del Azuay, SA: Bolívar 797, Casilla 33, Cuenca; tel. (7) 831-811; telex 8579; f. 1913; cap. 267m., res 33m., dep. 1,860m. (June 1984); Pres. LUIS ARCENTALES GONZÁLEZ; Gen. Man. DENNIS R. SHEETS.

Guayaquil

Banco Bolivariano: Pichincha 412, Casilla 10184, Guayaquil; tel. (4) 321-420; telex 3659; fax (4) 325-654; f. 1980; cap. 1,275m., res 1,097m., dep. 23,322m. (Dec. 1987); Pres. Abog. JOSÉ SALAZAR BARRAGÁN; Gen. Man. ALBERTO AVILÉS CEPEDA ; 10 brs.

Banco Continental: General Cordova 811 y Víctor Manuel Rendón, Casilla 9348, Guayaquil; tel. (4) 303-300; telex 3418; fax (4) 312-669; f. 1974; cap. 3,000m., res 1,847m., dep. 34,965m. (Dec. 1988); Pres. and Gen. Man. Dr LEÓNIDAS ORTEGA TRUJILLO.

Banco de Crédito e Hipotecario: P. Icaza 302, Casilla 4173, Guayaquil; tel. (4) 310-055; telex 3336; f. 1871; cap. 639m., res 15m., dep. 2,468m. (June 1988); Pres. LUIS NOBOA NARANJO; Exec. Vice-Pres. FERNANDO LEÓN BARBA.

FILANBANCO: Avda 9 de Octubre y Pichincha, Apdo 149, Guayaquil; tel. (4) 511-780; telex 3173; f. 1908; cap. 920m., res 189m., dep. 7,020m. (June 1984); Chair. Dr LUIS PERE CABANAS; Gen. Man. MIGUEL BADUY AHUAD.

Banco de Guayaquil: Pichincha 105 y P. Ycaza, Casilla 1300, Guayaquil; tel. (4) 309-300; telex 3671; fax (4) 327-373; f. 1923; cap. 3,300m., res 138.6m., dep. 20,535m. (1988); Pres. Dr JOSÉ SANTIAGO CASTILLO; Gen. Man. DANILO CARRERA DROUET.

Banco Industrial y Comercial—Baninco: Pichincha 335 e Illingworth, Casilla 5817, Guayaquil; tel. (4) 323-488; telex 3199; f. 1965; cap. and res 2m., dep. 10m. (June 1988); Pres. Ing. CARLOS MANZUR PERES; Gen. Man. GABRIEL MARTÍNEZ INTRIAGO; 2 brs.

Banco del Pacífico: P. Ycaza 200 y Pichincha, Casilla 988, Guayaquil; tel. (4) 311-010; telex 3240; f. 1972; cap. 5,000m., res 806m., dep. 84,847m. (June 1989); Chair. VÍCTOR MASPONS Y BIGAS; Exec. Pres. MARCEL J. LANIADO; 5 brs.

Banco del Progreso, SA: Primero de Mayo y P. Moncayo, Casilla 11100, Guayaquil; tel. (4) 312-100; telex 3662; f. 1981; cap. and res 2,506m., dep. 29,697m. (May 1990); Pres. ARCADIO AROSEMENA GALLARDO; Gen. Man. FERNANDO ASPIAZU S.

Banco La Previsora: Avda 9 de Octubre 110 y Pichincha, POB 1324, Guayaquil; tel. (4) 306-100; telex 3219; fax (4) 313-832; f. 1919; cap. 3,546m., res 153m., dep. 33,609m. (June 1989); Pres. FRANCISCO SOLA MEDINA; Gen. Man. ALVARO GUERRERO FERBER.

Banco Sociedad General de Crédito: 9 de Octubre 1404 y Machala, Casilla 5501, Guayaquil; tel. (4) 286-490; telex 3138; fax (4) 283-952; f. 1972; cap. 300m., res 199.6m., dep. 4,638m. (Dec. 1986); Pres. SANTIAGO MASPONS GUZMÁN; Gen. Man. EDUARDO SIMÓN PEREIRA CABRAL; 3 brs.

Banco Territorial: Panamá 814 y V. M. Rendón, Casilla 227, Guayaquil; tel. (4) 305-210; f. 1886; cap. 225.0m., res 112.5m., dep. 484.5m. (Oct. 1989); Pres. FEDERICO GOLDBAUM; Gen. Man. HUGO SUÁREZ BAQUERIZO.

Loja

Banco de Loja: esq. Bolívar y Rocafuerte, Casilla 300, Loja; tel. (4) 960-381; telex 4132; f. 1968; cap. 40m., res 47m., dep. 731m. (June 1984); Pres. Dr VÍCTOR EMILIO VALDIVIESO C.; Gen. Man. OSWALDO BURNEO VALDIVIEZO.

Machala

Banco de Machala: Avda 9 de Mayo y Rocafuerte, Casilla 711, Machala; tel. (4) 920-022; telex 4479; f. 1972; cap. 330m., res 121.4m., dep. 2,698m. (June 1986); Pres. Dr JOSÉ UGARTE VEGA; Gen. Man. ESTEBAN QUIROLA FIGUEROLA; 6 brs.

Portoviejo

Banco Comercial de Manabí, SA: 10 de Agosto 600 y 18 Octubre, Portoviejo; tel. (4) 653-888; telex 6180; f. 1980; cap. 117m., res 21m., dep. 720m. (June 1985); Pres. Dr RUBÉN DARÍO MORALES; Gen. Man. ARISTO ANDRADE DÍAZ.

Foreign Banks

Banco Holandés Unido, SA (Netherlands): Avda 10 de Agosto 911, Casilla 42, Quito; tel. (2) 239-765; telex 2153; f. 1959; cap.

ECUADOR

358m., res 138m., dep. 1,335m. (Dec. 1986); Gen. Man. KEES DOEFF; br. at Guayaquil.

Bank of America (USA): Calle Guayaquil 1938, Casilla 344, Quito; tel. (2) 550-510; telex 3143; f. 1966; cap. 250m., res 180m., dep. 1,500m. (Dec. 1986); Vice-Pres. JOHN TURNER; br. at Guayaquil.

Citibank, NA (USA): Juan León Mera 130 y Patria, Casilla 1393, Quito; tel. (2) 563-300; telex 2134; f. 1959; cap. 253m., res 563m., dep. 7,333m. (March 1987); Gen. Man. JAMES V. DEANE; 4 brs.

Lloyds Bank (BLSA) Ltd (UK): Avda Amazonas 580 esq. Jerónimo Carrión, Casilla 556-A, Quito; tel. (2) 564-177; telex 2215; fax (2) 568 997; f. 1988 (in succession to the Bank of London and South America, f. 1936); cap. 301m., res 283m., dep. 3,238m. (June 1987); Man. J. E. FRANKE.

Finance Corporations

COFIEC—Compañía Financiera Ecuatoriana de Desarrollo: Avdas Patria y Amazonas, Edif. COFIEC, 14°, Casilla 411, Quito; tel. (2) 546-177; telex 2131; fax (2) 564-224; f. 1966; cap. 678m., res 85m. (July 1984); Pres. JOSÉ LOUIS ALVAREZ; Exec. Pres. CÉSAR ROBALINO.

Financiera Guayaquil, SA: Carchi 702 y 9 de Octubre, 6°, Casilla 2167, Guayaquil; telex 43431; f. 1976; cap. 900m., res 142m. (June 1987); Gen. Man. Dr MIGUEL BABRA LYON.

FINANSA—Financiera Nacional, SA: Avda 6 de Diciembre 2417, entre Orellana y la Niña, Casilla 6420-CCI, Quito; tel. (2) 546-200; telex 2884; f. 1976; cap. 694m., res 103.6m. (June 1986); Gen. Man. RICHARD A. PEARSE.

FINANSUR—Financiera del Sur, SA: 9 de Mayo y 9 de Octubre, Casilla 7436, Machala; f. 1979; cap. 600m., res 30m. (July 1984); Pres. Econ. DANILO CARRERA DROUET.

Associations

Asociación de Bancos Privados del Ecuador: Edif. Banco de Préstamos, Avdas 10 de Agosto y Patria, Casilla 768A, Quito; f. 1965; 28 mems; Pres. Ing. MARCEL J. LANIADO.

Asociación de Compañías Financieras del Ecuador—AFIN: Robles 653 y Amazonas, 13°, Of. 1310-1311, Casilla 9156, Quito; tel. (2) 550-623; telex 2809; Pres. Dr JOSÉ ANTONIO CORREA.

STOCK EXCHANGE

Bolsa de Valores de Quito CA: Avda Río Amazonas 540 y J. Carrión, Quito; tel. (2) 526-805; telex 2565; f. 1969; volume of operations in 1989, 30,400m. sucres; Pres Dr JOSÉ MARÍA RUMAZO ARCOS; Gen. Man. Dr BOLÍVAR CHIRIBOGA VALDIVIESO.

INSURANCE

Instituto Ecuatoriano de Seguridad Social: Avda 10 de Agosto y Bogotá, Apdo 2640, Quito; tel. (2) 547-400; telex 221459; fax (2) 504-572; f. 1928; various forms of state insurance provided; the Institute directs the Ecuadorean social insurance system; it provides social benefits and medical service; Dir-Gen. MARCO MORALES TOBAR.

National Companies

In 1981 there were 27 insurance companies operating in Ecuador. The following is a list of the eight principal companies, selected by virtue of capital.

Amazonas Cía Anónima de Seguros: V. M. Rendón y Córdova, Apdo 3285, Guayaquil; tel. (4) 306-300; telex 3176; f. 1966; cap. 175m. sucres (1988); Exec. Pres. ANTONIO AROSEMENA G.-L.

Cía Reaseguradora del Ecuador, SA: Junín No 105 y Malecón Simón Bolívar, Casilla 6776, Guayaquil; f. 1977; tel. (4) 304-458; telex 42960; cap. 45m. sucres (1989); Man. Dir Dr EDUARDO PEÑA TRIVIÑO.

Cía de Seguros Condor, SA: P. Ycaza 302, Apdo 5007, Guayaquil; tel. (4) 312-300; telex 43755; fax (4) 320-144; f. 1966; cap. 151m. sucres; Gen. Man. JAIME GUZMÁN ITURRALDE.

Cía de Seguros Ecuatoriano-Suiza, SA: Avda 9 de Octubre 2101 y Tulcán, Apdo 397, Guayaquil; tel. (4) 372-222; telex 3386; f. 1954; cap. 65m. sucres (1986); Gen. Man. Econ. ENRIQUE SALAS CASTILLO.

La Nacional Cía de Seguros Generales, SA: Panamá 809, Apdo 1085, Guayaquil; tel. (4) 307-700; telex 3420; f. 1941; cap. 100m. sucres (1984); Gen. Man. LUCIANO CAGNATO CALIGO.

Panamericana del Ecuador, SA: Avda Amazonas 477 entre Roca y Robles, Edif. Banco de los Andes, 4°, Apdo 3902, Quito; tel. (2) 235-358; telex 22352; fax (2) 563-875; f. 1973; cap. 100m. sucres (1989); Gen. Man. HANS G. GRIEBACH.

Seguros Rocafuerte, SA: P. Carbo 505 y 9 de Octubre, Apdo 3401, Guayaquil; f. 1967; cap. 40m. sucres; Gen. Man. Ing. DANIEL CAÑIZARES AGUILAR.

La Unión Cía Nacional de Seguros: Km. 5½ Vía a la Costa, Apdo 1294, Guayaquil; tel. (4) 354-800; telex 3421; f. 1943; cap. 106.5m. sucres; Man. DAVID ALBERTO GOLDBAUM MORALES.

Trade and Industry

CHAMBERS OF COMMERCE AND INDUSTRY

Federación Nacional de Cámaras de Comercio del Ecuador: Avda Olmedo 414, Casilla y Boyaca, Guayaquil; tel. (4) 323130; telex 3466; fax (4) 323478; federation of chambers of commerce; Pres. ANDRÉS BARREIRO VIVAS.

Cámara de Comercio de Cuenca: Avda Federico Malo 1-90, Casilla 4929, Cuenca; tel. (7) 827531; telex 8630; f. 1919; 5,329 mems; Pres. EDUARDO MALO ABAD.

Cámara de Comercio de Quito: Avdas República y Amazonas, Edif. Las Cámaras 6° piso, Casilla 202, Quito; tel. (2) 435810; telex 2638; f. 1906; 6,000 mems; Pres. MARCELO PALLARES SEVILLA.

Cámara de Comercio de Guayaquil: Avda Olmedo 414 y Boyaca, Guayaquil; tel. (4) 323130; telex 3466; fax (4) 323478; f. 1889; 3,700 mems; Pres. ANDRÉS BARREIRO VIVAS.

Federación Nacional de Cámaras de Industrias: Avdas República y Amazonas, Casilla 2438, Quito; tel. (2) 452994; telex 2770; f. 1974; Pres. Ing. PEDRO KOHN.

Cámara de Industrias de Cuenca: Edif. Las Cámaras, Avda Federico Malo 1-90, Casilla 326, Cuenca; tel. (7) 830845; telex 8631; fax (7) 830945; f. 1936; Pres. Arq. GASTÓN RAMÍREZ SALCEDO.

Cámara de Industrias de Guayaquil: Avda 9 de Octubre 910, Casilla 4007, Guayaquil; tel. (4) 302705; telex 3686; fax (4) 320924; f. 1936; Pres. RODOLFO KRONFLE AKEL.

STATE ENTERPRISES AND DEVELOPMENT ORGANIZATIONS

Centro de Desarrollo Industrial del Ecuador—CENDES: Avda Orellana 1715 y 9 de Octubre, Casilla 2321, Quito; tel. (2) 527-100; f. 1962; carries out industrial feasibility studies, supplies technical and administrative assistance to industry, promotes new industries, supervises investment programmes; Gen. Man. CLAUDIO CREAMER GUILLÉN.

Centro Nacional de Promoción de la Pequeña Industria y Artesanía—CENAPIA: Quito; agency to develop small-scale industry and handicrafts; Dir Econ. EDGAR GUEVARA (acting).

Centro de Reconversión Económica del Austro (CREA): Bolívar y Cueva, Cuenca; tel. (7) 830-799; telex 8610; f. 1959; development organization; Dir Dr JUAN TAMA.

Consejo Nacional de Desarrollo—CONADE: Juan Larrea y Arenas, Quito; formerly Junta Nacional de Planificación y Coordinación Económica; aims to formulate a general plan of economic and social development and supervise its execution; also to integrate local plans into the national; Chair. Ing. LUIS PARODÍ VALVERDE.

Empresa de Comercio Exterior (ECE): Quito; f. 1980 to promote non-traditional exports; State owns 33% share in company; share capital 25m. sucres.

Empresa Pesquera Nacional: Velex 131 y Chile, 5°, Guayaquil; tel. (4) 524-913; state fishing enterprise.

Fondo de Desarrollo del Sector Rural Marginal—FODERUMA: f. 1978 to allot funds to rural development programmes in poor areas.

Fondo Nacional de Desarrollo—FONADE: f. 1973; national development fund to finance projects as laid down in the five-year plan.

Fondo Nacional de Preinversión—FONAPRE: Jorge Washington 624 y Avda Amazonas, Casilla 3302, Quito; tel. (2) 563-261; telex 2772; f. 1973 to undertake feasibility projects before investment is made by FONADE; Pres. LUIS PARODI; Gen. Man. Ing. EDUARDO MOLINA GRAZZIANI.

Fondo de Promoción de Exportaciones—FOPEX: Juan León Mera 130 y Avda Patria, Casilla 163, Quito; tel. (2) 564-900; telex 2193; fax (2) 562-519; f. 1972; export promotion; Dir Econ. DANIEL OCAMPO C.

Instituto de Colonización de la Región Amazónica—INCREA: f. 1978 to encourage settlement in and economic development of the Amazon region; Dir Dr DIMAS GUZMÁN.

Instituto Ecuatoriano de Electrificación—INECEL: 6 de Diciembre y Orellana, Casilla 565-A y 9076, Suc. 7, Quito; tel. (2) 237-422; telex 2243; f. 1961; state enterprise for the generation, transmission and distribution of electric energy; under the control of the Ministry of Energy and Mines; Gen. Man. Ing. MARCELO JARAMILLO AGUILAR.

Instituto Ecuatoriano de Recursos Hidráulicos—INERHI: undertakes irrigation and hydroelectric projects; Man. Ing. EDUARDO GARCÍA GARCÍA.

ECUADOR

Directory

Instituto Ecuatoriano de Reforma Agraria y Colonización (IERAC): f. 1973 to supervise the Agrarian Reform Law under the auspices and co-ordination of the Ministry of Agriculture and Livestock; Dir LUIS LUNA GAYBOR.

Organización Comercial Ecuatoriana de Productos Artesanales (OCEPA): Avda República 1527 e Inglaterra, Casilla 2948, Quito; tel. (2) 542-045; telex 22062; fax (2) 430839; f. 1964; to develop and promote national arts and crafts; Gen. Man. Ing. GUADALUPE HURTADO.

Petróleos del Ecuador—PETROECUADOR: Avda Colón No 1021, 8° piso, Edif. Banco Continental, Casillas 5007/8, Quito; tel. (2) 544-939; telex 2861; f. 1972; fmrly the Corporación Estatal Petrolera Ecuatoriana (CEPE); reorg. 1989; state petroleum corpn; promotes exploration for, and exploitation of, petroleum and natural gas deposits by initiating joint ventures with foreign and national companies; acts as the agency controlling the concession of onshore and offshore exploration rights; began international marketing of crude petroleum in 1974 and assumed responsibility for the domestic marketing and distribution of petroleum products in 1976; Exec. Pres. LUIS ROMÁN.

Programa Nacional del Banano y Frutas Tropicales: Pichincha 103, Guayaquil; to promote the development of banana and tropical fruit cultivation; Dir Ing. JORGE GIL CHANG.

Programa Regional de Desarrollo del Sur del Ecuador—PREDESUR: 9 de Octubre 275 y Jorge Washington, Quito; tel. (2) 230-531; f. 1972 to promote the development of the southern area of the country; Dir Econ. JORGE PIEDRA.

Superintendencia de Compañías del Ecuador: Roca 660 y Avda Amazonas, Casilla 687, Quito; tel. (2) 525-022; telex 22595; fax (2) 565-685; f. 1964; responsible for the legal and accounting control of commercial enterprises; Supt Dr LUIS SALAZAR BECKER.

EMPLOYERS' ASSOCIATIONS

Asociación de Cafecultores del Cantón Piñas: García Moreno y Abdón Calderón; coffee growers' association.

Asociación de Comerciantes e Industriales: Boyacá 1416, Guayaquil; traders' and industrialists' association.

Asociación de Industriales Textiles del Ecuador (AITE): Avdas República y Amazonas, Edif. Las Cámaras 8°, Casilla 2893, Quito; telex 2770; f. 1938; textile manufacturers' association; 33 mems; Pres. RICHARD C. HANDAL; Sec.-Gen. JOSÉ LUIS ALARCÓN.

Asociación de Productores Bananeros del Ecuador—APROBANA: Malecón 2002, Guayaquil; banana growers' association.

Asociación Nacional de Empresarios—ANDE: Edif. España 6°, Of. 67, Avda Colón y Amazonas, Casilla 3489, Quito; tel. (2) 238-507; telex 22298; fax (2) 503-271; national employers' association.

Asociación Nacional de Exportadores de Cacao y Café: Casilla 4774, Manta; cocoa and coffee exporters' association.

Cámara de Agricultura: Casilla 21-322, Quito; tel. (2) 230-195; Pres. Ing. IGNACIO PÉREZ ARTETA .

Consorcio Ecuatoriano de Exportadores de Cacao y Café: cocoa and coffee exporters' consortium.

Corporación Nacional de Exportadores de Cacao y Café: Sucre 106 y Malecón, Guayaquil; cocoa and coffee exporters' corporation.

Federación Nacional de Cooperativas Cafetaleras: Guayaquil 1242, Of. 304, Quito; coffee co-operatives federation.

There are several other coffee and cocoa organizations.

TRADE UNIONS

Frente Unitario de Trabajadores (FUT): f. 1971; left-wing; 300,000 mems; Pres. FAUSTO DUTÁN; comprises:

Confederación Ecuatoriana de Organizaciones Clasistas—CEDOC: POB 3207, Calle Río de Janeiro 407 y Juan Larrea, Quito; tel. (2) 548-086; f. 1938; affiliated to CMT and CLAT; humanist; Pres. RAMIRO ROSALES NARVÁEZ; Sec.-Gen. JORGE MUÑOZ; 150,000 mems (est.) organized in 20 provinces.

Confederación Ecuatoriana de Organizaciones Sindicales Libres (CEOSL): Casilla 1373, Quito; tel. (2) 522-511; f. 1962; affiliated to ICFTU and ORIT; Pres. JOSÉ CHÁVEZ CHÁVEZ; Sec.-Gen. JULIO CHANG CRESPO.

Confederación de Trabajadores del Ecuador (CTE) (Confederation of Ecuadorean Workers): Olmedo y Benalcázar, 3°, Casilla 4166, Quito; telex 22582; fax (2) 580-747; f. 1944; admitted to WFTU and CPUSTAL; Leaders EDGAR PONCE; 1,200 affiliated unions, 70 national federations.

Central Católica de Obreros: Avda 24 de Mayo 344, Quito; tel. (2) 213-704; f. 1906; craft and manual workers and intellectuals; Pres. CARLOS E. DÁVILA ZURITA.

A number of trade unions are not affiliated to the above groups. These include the Federación Nacional de Trabajadores Marítimos y Portuarios del Ecuador (FNTMPE) (National Federation of Maritime and Port Workers of Ecuador) and both railway trade unions.

Transport

Ministerio de Obras Públicas y Comunicaciones: Avda 6 de Diciembre y Wilson 1184, Quito; tel. (2) 242-660; telex 2353.

RAILWAYS

All railways are government-controlled. Extensive construction work is being undertaken.

Empresa Nacional de Ferrocarriles del Estado: POB 159, Calle Bolívar 443, Quito; tel. (2) 216-180; Gen. Man. Ing. L. TOSCANO.

Total length 965 km (1987).

There are divisional state railway managements for the following lines: Guayaquil–Quito, Sibambe–Cuenca and Quito–San Lorenzo.

ROADS

There were 37,636 km of roads in 1988, of which 6,325 km were paved. The Pan-American Highway runs north from Ambato to Quito and to the Colombian border at Tulcán and south to Cuenca and Loja. The severe weather of 1982/83 damaged 1,120 km of roads, which were subsequently repaired. The earthquake of March 1987 resulted in further damage to roads and bridges, but by 1988 these were passable again.

SHIPPING

Some US $160m. is to be invested in the modernization of Ecuador's principal ports: Guayaquil, Esmeraldas, Manta and Puerto Bolívar.

Flota Bananera Ecuatoriana, SA: Edif. Gran Pasaje 9°, P. Icaza 437, Casilla 6883, Guayaquil; tel. (4) 309-333; telex 43218; f. 1967; owned by Government of Ecuador and private stockholders; Pres. DIEGO SÁNCHEZ; Gen. Man. JORGE BARRIGA; 5 vessels.

Flota Mercante Grancolombiana, SA: Calle 2 Aguirre 104 y Malecón Simón Bolívar, Casilla 3714, Guayaquil; tel. (4) 512-791; telex 3210; f. 1946 with Colombia and Venezuela; on Venezuela's withdrawal in 1953, Ecuador's 10% interest was increased to 20%; operates services from Colombia and Ecuador to European ports, US Gulf ports and New York, Mexican Atlantic ports and East Canada; offices in Quito, Cuenca, Bahía, Manta and Esmeraldas; Man. Naval Capt. J. ALBERTO SÁNCHEZ; fleet of 29 vessels (21 owned by it and 8 chartered).

Flota Petrolera Ecuatoriana—FLOPEC: Edif. CONTEMPO, Avda Amazonas 1188 y Cordero, Casilla 535-A, Quito; tel. (2) 552-100; telex 2211; f. 1973; 5 vessels; Pres. H. UNDA A.; Gen. Man. E. GALLEGOS.

Naviera del Pacífico, CA: El Oro 101, Apdo 529, Guayaquil; tel. (4) 342-055; telex 3144; 10 vessels.

Transportes Navieros Ecuatorianos—Transnave: Edif. Citibank 6°, Avda 9 de Octubre 416 y Chile, Apdo 4706, Guayaquil; tel. (4) 308-400; telex 43249; 9 vessels; transports general cargo within the European South Pacific Magellan Conference, Japan West Coast South America Conference and Atlantic and Gulf West Coast South America Conference; Pres. Vice-Adm. FERNANDO ALFARO ECHEVERRÍA; Gen. Man. Rear-Adm. RUBÉN LANDÁZURI ZAMBRANO.

Various foreign lines operate between Ecuador and European ports.

CIVIL AVIATION

There are two international airports: Mariscal Sucre, near Quito, and Simón Bolívar, near Guayaquil.

Aerolíneas Nacionales del Ecuador, SA—ANDES: Apdo 4113, Aeropuerto Simón Bolívar, Guayaquil; tel. (4) 394490; telex 3228; f. 1961; headquarters in Miami, USA; regular cargo services Miami–Panamá–Quito–Guayaquil, Cuenca; Gen. Man. Dr ROBERTO PÓLIT; fleet: 1 DC-8-50F, 1 DC-8-30F.

Empresa Ecuatoriana de Aviación (EEA): Condominios Almagro, Avda Reina Victoria y Colón Esp., Apdo 505, Quito; tel. (2) 563003; telex 21143; nationalized 1974; international scheduled passenger services and cargo and mail services to Argentina, Brazil, Chile, Colombia, Costa Rica, Mexico, Panama, Peru, USA and Venezuela; Pres. and Chair. EDUARDO EMMANUEL; fleet: 1 DC-10-30, 3 Boeing 707-320-B, 1 707-320-C.

Transportes Aéreos Militares Ecuatorianos (TAME): Avda 10 de Agosto 239, Casilla 8736, Suc. Almagro, Quito; tel. (2) 510-211; telex 22567; brs in Guayaquil and 10 other cities; f. 1962; domestic scheduled services for passengers and freight; charter services

ECUADOR

abroad; Gen. Man. Lt-Gen. (retd.) ARMANDO DURÁN NÚÑEZ.; fleet: 1 L-188 Electra, 1 Fokker F.28-4000, 1 Boeing 727-200, 3 727-100.

The following airlines also offer national and regional services: Aerotaxis Ecuatorianos, SA—ATESA; Cía Ecuatoriana de Transportes Aéreos (CEDTA); Ecuastol Servicios Aéreos, SA; Ecuavia Cía Ltda; Sociedad Ecuatoriana de Transportes Aéreos—SAETA; Servicios Aéreos Nacionales (SAN); Aeroturismo Cía Ltda—SAVAC.

Tourism

The number of tourists visiting Ecuador in 1985 totalled 238,100.

Asociación Ecuatoriana de Agencias de Viajes y Turismo—ASECUT: POB 9377 Suc. 7, Avda Amazonas 2468, Quito; tel. (2) 552617; telex 2749; fax (2) 552916; f. 1953; Pres. GONZALO RUEDA U.

Corporación Ecuatoriana de Turismo: Reina Victoria 514 y Roca, Quito; f. 1964; tel. (2) 527-002; telex 21158; fax (2) 568-198; Exec. Dir BRUNA STORNAIOLO DE AVILIA.

Atomic Energy

Comisión Ecuatoriana de Energía Atómica: San Javier 295 y Avda Orellana, Casilla 2517, Quito; tel. (4) 528-405; telex 21461; fax (2) 566-343; f. 1968; research in nuclear physics, radio-isotopes, radio-biology, chemistry, medicine and radioactive minerals; in 1975 it took over the production and sale of radioactive minerals; nuclear information centre; Exec. Dir. PATRICIO PEÑAHERRERA S.

EGYPT

Introductory Survey

Location, Climate, Language, Religion, Flag, Capital

The Arab Republic of Egypt occupies the north-eastern corner of Africa, with an extension across the Gulf of Suez into the Sinai Peninsula, sometimes regarded as lying within Asia. Egypt is bounded to the north by the Mediterranean Sea, to the north-east by Israel, to the east by the Red Sea, to the south by Sudan, and to the west by Libya. The climate is arid, with a maximum annual rainfall of only 200 mm (8 in) around Alexandria. More than 90% of the country is desert, and some 99% of the population live in the valley and delta of the River Nile. Summer temperatures reach a maximum of 43°C (110°F) and winters are mild, with an average day temperature of about 18°C (65°F). Arabic is the official language. Many educated Egyptians also speak English or French. More than 80% of the population are Muslims, mainly of the Sunni sect. The remainder are mostly Christians, principally Copts, who number some 6m. The national flag (proportions 3 by 2) has three equal horizontal stripes, of red, white, and black; the white stripe has, in the centre, the national emblem (a shield superimposed on a hawk, with a scroll beneath) in gold. The capital is Cairo.

Recent History

Egypt, a province of Turkey's Ottoman Empire from the 16th century, was occupied by British forces in 1882. The administration was controlled by British officials, although Egypt remained nominally an Ottoman province until 1914, when a British protectorate was declared. The United Kingdom (UK) granted nominal independence to Egypt on 28 February 1922. Fuad I, the reigning Sultan since 1917, became King of Egypt. He was succeeded in 1936 by his son, King Faruq (Farouk). The Anglo-Egyptian Treaty of 1936 recognized full Egyptian sovereignty and provided for the gradual withdrawal of British troops, while giving the UK the right to maintain a garrison on the Suez Canal, which links the Mediterranean and Red Seas, and to use Alexandria and Port Said as naval bases. The Italian invasion of Egypt in 1940 and the subsequent Libyan campaign postponed the departure of British forces. After the Second World War, British forces withdrew from Egypt, except for a military presence in the Suez Canal Zone. When the British mandate in Palestine was ended in 1948, Arab armies intervened to oppose the newly-proclaimed State of Israel. A cease-fire was agreed in 1949, leaving Egyptian forces occupying the Gaza Strip, a coastal strip, around the town of Gaza, in southern Palestine.

On 23 July 1952 King Farouk's unpopular regime, widely recognized as corrupt, was overthrown by a bloodless military coup. Power was seized by a group of young army officers, the 'Free Officers', led by Lt-Col Gamal Abd an-Nasir (Nasser). Three days later, Farouk abdicated in favour of his infant son, Ahmad Fuad II, and went into exile. After the coup, Gen. Muhammad Nagib (Neguib) was appointed Commander-in-Chief of the Army and Chairman of the Revolution Command Council (RCC), a nine-member military junta. In September 1952 Gen. Neguib was appointed Prime Minister and Military Governor of Egypt, with Col Nasser as Deputy Prime Minister. In December 1952 the 1923 Constitution was abolished, and in January 1953 all political parties were dissolved. On 18 June 1953 the monarchy was abolished and Egypt was proclaimed a republic, with Gen. Neguib as President and Prime Minister. In April 1954 President Neguib was succeeded as Prime Minister by Col Nasser. In October Egypt and the UK signed an agreement concerning the Suez Canal, providing for the withdrawal of all British forces by June 1956. In November 1954, following a dispute within the military regime, President Neguib was relieved of all his remaining posts, and Col Nasser became acting Head of State.

The establishment of military rule was accompanied by wide-ranging reforms, including the redistribution of land, the promotion of industrial development and the expansion of social welfare services. In foreign affairs, the new regime was strongly committed to Arab unity, and Egypt played a prominent part in the Non-Aligned Movement. In 1955, having failed to secure Western armaments on satisfactory terms, Egypt accepted military assistance from the USSR.

In January 1956 Col Nasser proclaimed a new Egyptian constitution, providing for a strong presidency. On 23 June the Constitution was approved by a national referendum, and Nasser was elected President (unopposed). The RCC was dissolved on the next day. In July 1956, following the departure of British forces, the US and British Governments withdrew their offers of financial assistance for Egypt's construction of the Aswan High Dam on the River Nile. In response, President Nasser announced the nationalization of the Suez Canal Company, so that revenue from Canal tolls could be used to finance the High Dam's construction. The take-over of the Canal was a cause of great concern to Israel, Britain and France, and Israel invaded the Sinai Peninsula on 29 October. Britain and France began military operations against Egypt two days later. Strong pressure from the UN and the US Government resulted in a cease-fire on 6 November, and supervision by the UN of the invaders' withdrawal.

Egypt and Syria, although geographically separate, merged in February 1958 to form the United Arab Republic (UAR), with Nasser as President. The new nation strengthened earlier ties with the USSR and other countries of the East European bloc. In September 1961 Syria seceded from the UAR, and resumed its separate independence, after the army had seized power there. However, Egypt retained the title of UAR until September 1971. Further attempts at federating Egypt, Syria and Iraq during the early 1960s proved unsuccessful. Earlier, in 1958, the UAR and Yemen formed a federation called the United Arab States, but this was dissolved at the end of 1961. Following the death in September 1962 of the Imam Ahmad of Yemen, a military coup deposed his successor, and the rebels proclaimed the Yemen Arab Republic (YAR). Civil war broke out between royalist forces, supported by Saudi Arabia, and republicans, aided by Egyptian troops. The republicans eventually gained control, and Egyptian forces withdrew from the YAR in 1967.

President Nasser enjoyed immense prestige throughout the Arab world and beyond. Internally, he was regarded as the founder of modern Egypt. In December 1962 he established the Arab Socialist Union (ASU) as the country's only recognized political organization. In May 1967 he secured the withdrawal of the UN Emergency Force from Egyptian territory. Egypt subsequently reoccupied Sharm esh-Sheikh, near the southern tip of the Sinai Peninsula, and closed the Straits of Tiran to Israeli shipping. These actions provoked the 'Six-Day War' of June 1967, when Israel quickly defeated neighbouring Arab states, including Egypt. The war left Israel in control of the Gaza Strip and a large area of Egyptian territory, including the whole of the Sinai Peninsula. The Suez Canal was blocked, and remained closed until June 1975.

In December 1969 the office of Vice-President was re-established when Col Anwar Sadat, who had held the post in 1964–66, was reappointed. President Nasser died suddenly in September 1970, and was succeeded by Col Sadat. In September 1971 the UAR was renamed the Arab Republic of Egypt, and a new constitution took effect. In the early years of his rule, Sadat attempted to follow Nasser's aim of unity with other Arab states. The Federation of Arab Republics (Egypt, Libya and Syria) came into being in 1972, but proved ineffective. In March 1976 Egypt terminated its Treaty of Friendship with the USSR. Relations with the USA, on the other hand, became closer as President Sadat came to rely increasingly on US aid.

An uneasy cease-fire with Israel lasted until October 1973, when Egyptian troops crossed the Suez Canal to recover territory which had been lost in 1967. After 18 days of fighting, a cease-fire was arranged. Dr Henry Kissinger, the US Secretary of State, negotiated disengagement agreements in 1974 and September 1975, by which Israel evacuated territory in Sinai, and Israeli and Egyptian forces were separated by a buffer zone under the control of UN forces.

A dramatic peace-making initiative was made by President Sadat in November 1977, when he visited Israel and addressed the Knesset. Many Arab countries opposed the visit on the grounds that it undermined Arab unity. The leaders of Syria, Libya, Algeria, Iraq, the People's Democratic Republic of Yemen (PDRY) and the Palestine Liberation Organization (PLO) condemned Egypt and met in Tripoli in December to discuss what action they should take, but Egypt pre-empted their decision and broke off diplomatic relations with the five.

In September 1978, after talks at Camp David in the USA (under the guidance of President Carter), President Sadat and Menachem Begin, Prime Minister of Israel, signed two agreements. The first was a 'framework of peace in the Middle East' and the second was a 'framework for the conclusion of a peace treaty between Egypt and Israel'. The first agreement provided for a five-year transitional period during which the inhabitants of the Israeli-occupied West Bank of the Jordan and the Gaza Strip would obtain full autonomy and self-government, and the second agreement provided for the signing of a peace treaty between Egypt and Israel by 17 December 1978. The peace treaty was signed in March 1979, and Israel subsequently made phased withdrawals from the Sinai Peninsula, the last of which took place in April 1982. Syria, Algeria, Libya and the PLO had condemned the Camp David agreements, and in March 1979 the Council of the Arab League expelled Egypt from the League and introduced political and economic sanctions. Oman, Sudan and Somalia were the only Arab countries that did not sever their ties with Egypt. Egypt, however, continued to strengthen relations with Israel, and in February 1980 the two countries exchanged ambassadors for the first time.

In 1974 Sadat began to introduce a more liberal political and economic regime. Political parties (banned since 1953) were allowed to participate in the 1976 elections for the People's Assembly (Majlis ash-Sha'ab). They were legalized in June 1977 but overshadowed in July 1978, when Sadat formed a new political party, the National Democratic Party (NDP), with himself as leader. In April 1979 the special constitutional status of the ASU was terminated. In October 1981 Sadat was assassinated by members of Islamic Jihad, a group of fundamentalists (belonging to the community of Islamic extremists called gamaat, or 'the (Islamic) groups'), led by Lt Khalid Islambouly, who was later executed. Sadat was succeeded by Lt-Gen. Hosni Mubarak, who had been Vice-President since April 1975 and was previously Commander-in-Chief of the Air Force. The state of emergency was extended for another year in October 1982 and October 1983.

An electoral law, adopted in July 1983, required parties to receive a minimum of 8% of the total vote to be represented in the People's Assembly. This prompted opposition parties to boycott elections to local councils and to the Shura (Advisory) Council. In January 1984 the legality of the re-formed New Wafd Party, perhaps the only opposition party with any prospect of wide popular support, was upheld by the courts after the Government had refused to recognize it on its re-emergence in August 1983. At elections to the People's Assembly on 27 May 1984, the ruling NDP received 72.9% of the total vote, winning 389 of the 448 elective seats in the Assembly. Of the four other participating parties, only the New Wafd, with 15.1% of the vote, crossed the 8% threshold, and won the remaining 59 seats. Dr Ahmad Fuad Mohi ed-Din, who had been Prime Minister since January 1982 and was also Secretary-General of the NDP, died on 5 June 1984. As a result, President Mubarak reorganized the Council of Ministers, appointing Gen. Kamal Hassan Ali, hitherto a Deputy Prime Minister and the Minister of Foreign Affairs, as Prime Minister.

In foreign affairs, a division in the Arab world between a 'moderate' grouping (including Jordan, Iraq and, less vocally, the Gulf States), which viewed the participation of Egypt as indispensable to any diplomatic initiatives for solving the problems of the region, and a 'radical' grouping, led by Syria (which devoted itself to taking Egypt's place as the leader of the Arab community), became increasingly evident. The PLO leader, Yasser Arafat, visited President Mubarak for discussions in Cairo in December 1983, signifying the end of a six-year period of estrangement between Egypt and the PLO. In September 1984 Jordan decided to resume diplomatic relations with Egypt. In 1984 Egypt proposed two formulas for a peaceful settlement of the Gulf War, but neither was adopted by Iran or Iraq. President Mubarak, accompanied by King Hussein of Jordan, made a surprise visit to Baghdad in March 1985, to demonstrate his support for the Iraqi President, Saddam Hussain, despite the fact that there had been no formal diplomatic relations between Egypt and Iraq since 1979. Owing to alleged Libyan terrorist and espionage activities, and the continuing problem of Muslim fundamentalists pursuing Islamic revolution, the Egyptian Government extended the national state of emergency for 18 months from October 1984 and for a further two years from April 1986. Relations with Libya, however, continued to deteriorate. In July 1985 the Libyan leader, Col Qaddafi, barred Egyptian workers (of whom there were some 100,000 in the country at the time) from Libya, in retaliation against a similar Egyptian measure preventing Libyans from working in Egypt. However, in 1988, after the improvement in Egypt's relations with other Arab states following its recognition of the independent Palestinian State (declared in November), Egypt announced that Libyan commercial aircraft would be permitted to operate in Egyptian airspace and to land in Cairo.

The resumption of full diplomatic relations with the USSR was announced in April 1984, and ambassadors were exchanged later in the year. Relations had ceased in 1981, when President Sadat expelled the Soviet ambassador and 1,000 Soviet experts from Egypt.

President Mubarak, King Hussein of Jordan and Yasser Arafat of the PLO continued their discussions in pursuit of a negotiated settlement of the Palestinian question during 1984 and 1985. Mubarak endorsed the agreement of February 1985, concluded by Arafat and King Hussein, establishing the principle of a joint Jordanian-Palestinian delegation to participate in a proposed Middle East peace conference, to include the permanent members of the UN Security Council.

The credibility of the PLO as a participant in peace negotiations, and of the Jordanian-Palestinian agreement, was further compromised in October 1985, when an Italian cruise liner, the *Achille Lauro*, was hijacked in the eastern Mediterranean by four Palestinians, belonging to one faction of the divided Palestine Liberation Front (PLF). The terrorists murdered an American passenger before surrendering to the Egyptian authorities in Port Said. In November an EgyptAir airliner was hijacked to Malta by Palestinians, whom Egypt immediately linked with the renegade PLO leader, Abu Nidal, and his Libyan supporters. Egyptian special forces were sent to Malta to release the 98 passengers, but their assault on the aircraft resulted in the deaths of 58 hostages and strong criticism of Egypt's conduct of the affair.

The campaign by Muslim fundamentalists in Egypt for the legal system fully to adopt the principles of the Shari'a (Islamic holy law) intensified in 1985. An amendment to the Constitution, approved by the People's Assembly in 1980, made Islamic law the basis of Egyptian law, and this provision was largely, although not fully, implemented. In May 1985 the People's Assembly rejected proposals for immediate changes in the legal system, and advocated a thorough study of the small proportion of Egyptian law that does not conform to Islamic precepts before proceeding further. Numerous Muslim fundamentalists, including militant leader Sheikh Hafez Salama, were detained in July for crimes of agitation. Dr Ali Lutfi, a former Minister of Finance under President Sadat, was appointed Prime Minister in September, following the resignation of Gen. Kamal Hassan Ali and his Council of Ministers. The new Council of Ministers contained three members with the rank of Deputy Prime Minister, a post already held by the Minister of Defence, Field Marshal Muhammad Abd al-Halim Abu Ghazalah.

Relations between Egypt and Israel, meanwhile, were strained by the latter's invasion of Lebanon in June 1982, and Israel repeatedly accused Egypt of contraventions of the military provisions of the 1979 peace treaty. In January 1985 Israel and Egypt began a series of negotiations, the first for two years, to determine the sovereignty of the small coastal strip of Taba, on the Red Sea, which Israel did not vacate when it completed its withdrawal from the Sinai Peninsula in 1982. In January 1986 Israel agreed to submit the dispute to international arbitration, on condition that this was preceded by a period of conciliation, during which a compromise solution would be sought before the chosen arbitrators delivered a binding decision. After the appointment of arbitrators (three independent and one each from Egypt and Israel) and the demarcation of the Taba enclave had been agreed, the arbitration document was finally approved by both countries in

September. The process of arbitration began in December. In September 1988 the arbitration panel awarded sovereignty to Egypt, but left an important border undefined. Discussions on the final arrangements for the Taba enclave were held in January 1989, and Egypt assumed control over the area in March.

In September 1986 President Mubarak of Egypt and Prime Minister Peres of Israel met in Alexandria, Egypt, to discuss ways of reviving the Middle East peace process. After the 'summit' meeting (the first between Egypt and Israel since August 1981), and following the signing of the Taba arbitration agreement, President Mubarak appointed Muhammad Bassiouni, Egypt's former chargé d'affaires in Tel-Aviv, as ambassador to Israel. The previous Egyptian ambassador had been recalled from Israel in 1982, after the Israeli invasion of Lebanon.

In November 1986 President Mubarak accepted the resignation of the Prime Minister, Ali Lutfi, and a new Council of Ministers, containing, among 11 changes, a new Minister of Finance and three other new ministers in positions related to the management of the economy, was appointed under a new Prime Minister, Dr Atif Sidqi, hitherto the head of the Central Auditing Agency. President Mubarak was believed to be critical of Ali Lutfi for his indecisive approach to the country's economic problems.

A referendum was held on 12 February 1987 to decide whether the People's Assembly should be dissolved, prior to the holding of a general election on the basis of a new electoral law, whereby 48 of the Assembly's 458 seats would be contested by candidates on an individual, rather than a party-list, basis. An overwhelming vote in the referendum in favour of the dissolution of the People's Assembly enabled the holding of a general election on 6 April. The Socialist Labour Party (SLP), the Liberal Socialist Party (LSP) and the Muslim Brotherhood (which was legally barred from operating as a political party in its own right) formed an electoral alliance, principally in order to overcome the requirement for individual parties to win at least 8% of the total votes to qualify for seats in the People's Assembly. The election campaign was marred by sectarian clashes between Muslims and Christians in several towns in February and March, and the opposition parties accused the Government of electoral corruption. The election resulted in a large, although reduced, majority for the ruling NDP in the People's Assembly. Of the 448 elective seats, the NDP won 346 (compared with 389 at the 1984 election), the opposition parties together won 95, and independents seven. The SLP/LSP/Muslim Brotherhood alliance won a combined total of 60 seats, of which the Brotherhood took 37, thus becoming the largest single opposition group in the new Assembly.

In July 1987 Hosni Mubarak was nominated by the necessary two-thirds majority of the members of the People's Assembly, as the sole presidential candidate, to seek a second six-year term of office, and he was confirmed as President by national referendum on 5 October. Prime Minister Atif Sidqi submitted the resignation of the Government and formed a new Council of Ministers, with only minor changes in personnel. In March 1988 the state of emergency was renewed for a further three years. In August, following disturbances in Cairo, 92 Muslim fundamentalists were remanded in custody, charged with various offences, including attempted murder and illegal possession of weapons. Further anti-Government demonstrations, not only by Muslim fundamentalists but also by striking workers, followed later in the year. In December it was reported that more than 500 militant Muslim students in Cairo and Asyut had been arrested on suspicion of involvement in 'anti-state activities'; and in May 1989, faced with increasing popular discontent over price increases and food shortages, the Government acted to pre-empt disturbances during the month of Ramadan by detaining more than 2,000 Muslim fundamentalists. In June elections to the 210-member Shura Council were contested by opposition parties (the 'Islamic Alliance', consisting of the Muslim Brotherhood, the LSP and the SLP) for the first time since the establishment of the Council in 1980. Other political parties, however, continued to boycott the elections in protest at the prevailing state of emergency. None of the candidates from the 'Islamic Alliance' was elected, and it was subsequently alleged that the NDP had achieved its victory by fraudulent means.

In July and August 1989, in a further attempt by the Government to suppress political opposition, large numbers of alleged 'leftists' and Shi'ite Muslims, including prominent members of the Muslim Brotherhood, were arrested by the Egyptian security forces. By early September, following international protests, it was reported that most of the detainees had been released. In December 1989 there was speculation that Muslim fundamentalists had been responsible for the attempted assassination of the Minister of the Interior, Maj.-Gen. Zaki Badr.

In January 1990 Badr was dismissed from his post and replaced by Muhammad Abd al-Halim Moussa. In April three new political parties, the Green Party, the Democratic Unionist Party (DUP) and the Young Egypt Party (YEP), were legalized, bringing the total number of officially recognized political parties in Egypt to nine.

In May 1990 a constitutional crisis arose after Egypt's Supreme Constitutional Court ruled that elections to the People's Assembly in 1987 had been unconstitutional because the electoral law, promulgated in 1986, unfairly discriminated against independent candidates. Legislation which had subsequently been adopted by the Assembly was deemed to be valid, but the Court declared that any new laws approved after 2 June 1990 could not enter into force. In September President Mubarak announced that a popular referendum would be held on 11 October in order to decide whether the People's Assembly should be dissolved; and that the electoral law would be amended with regard to the limited number of independent candidates previously permitted to participate in elections. (The People's Assembly, in recess since 4 June, had granted the President permission to legislate by decree in its absence.) Some 58.6% of the electorate subsequently participated in the referendum, and, of these, 94.34% voted for the dissolution of the Assembly. The People's Assembly was duly dissolved on 12 October.

The legislative elections, held on 29 November and on 6 December 1990, were boycotted by the principal opposition parties (the SLP, the LSP and the Muslim Brotherhood, which had together contested the previous general election as a coalition, and the New Wafd Party), even though they were conducted under new electoral laws. The former requirement for political parties to win a minimum of 8% of the total vote in order to gain representation in the Assembly was abolished, and restrictions on independent candidates were removed, but the Government refused to concede the opposition parties' demands that the elections be removed from the supervision of the Ministry of the Interior, and that the state of emergency (in force since 1981) be repealed. The credibility of any mandate which the Government might receive in the elections was thus undermined in advance. Moreover, in the event, the electoral turnout was estimated to have been no greater than 20%–30%. Of the 444 elective seats in the new Assembly (see Directory, Legislature), the NDP won 348 (compared with 346 at the 1987 general election), the National Progressive Unionist Party won six, and independent candidates (including members of the main opposition parties which officially boycotted the elections) 83. Voting in the remaining seven seats was suspended.

On 12 October 1990 the Speaker of the People's Assembly, Dr Rifa'at el-Mahgoub, was assassinated in Cairo. The Ministry of the Interior claimed that eight members of an Islamic fundamentalist group, Al-Jihad (arrested at the end of October), had been responsible for the assassination. During the elections held on 29 November and 6 December five people were reported to have been killed, and 92 injured, in gun battles and riots which occurred in some constituencies.

A rift between Egypt and the PLO was precipitated by the reunification of the Palestinian liberation movement that took place at a session of the Palestine National Council (PNC) in Algiers in April 1987. The influence of dissident factions that were returning to the mainstream of the movement, under Yasser Arafat's leadership, resulted in the adoption by the PNC of a resolution urging the reappraisal of PLO links with Egypt, and making future contacts dependent on Egypt's abrogation of the Camp David accords and the 1979 peace treaty with Israel. President Mubarak responded by closing the PLO's offices in Egypt. However, President Mubarak and Yasser Arafat conferred in July in Addis Ababa, Ethiopia, and the PLO's Egyptian offices were subsequently reopened. Both leaders endorsed proposals for the convening of an international peace conference on the Middle East, under UN auspices, involving the five permanent members of the UN Security Council and all parties to the conflict, including the PLO.

In November 1987, at a 'summit' conference in Amman, Jordan, which was attended by the majority of Arab leaders, the Syrian President, Hafiz Assad, obstructed proposals to readmit Egypt to membership of the League of Arab States. However, recognizing Egypt's support for Iraq in the Gulf War and acknowledging the influence that Egypt (as the most populous and, militarily, the most powerful Arab nation) could bring to bear on the problems of the region, the conference approved a resolution putting the establishment of diplomatic links with Egypt at the discretion of member governments. Such links had previously been prohibited. One week after the end of the conference, nine Arab states (the United Arab Emirates, Iraq, Kuwait, Morocco, the Yemen Arab Republic, Bahrain, Saudi Arabia, Mauritania and Qatar) had re-established full diplomatic relations with Egypt. Of the remaining 12 members of the League, three (Sudan, Somalia and Oman) had maintained diplomatic links with Egypt throughout the period of the boycott, Jordan and Djibouti had re-established them in 1985 and 1986, respectively, and the PLO (to which the League accords nation status) had recently begun to settle its differences with Egypt. In February 1988 the PDRY re-established full diplomatic relations with Egypt, leaving Algeria, Lebanon, Libya and Syria as the only Arab League members not to have done so. Libya was the most outspoken critic of the change in the League's policy towards Egypt, complaining that the 1979 peace treaty with Israel, the original reason for Egypt's ostracism, remained in force. In November 1988 Algeria announced that it would re-establish diplomatic relations with Egypt, and in June 1989 full diplomatic relations with Lebanon were restored.

Following Jordan's decision, in July 1988, to sever its legal and administrative links with the West Bank region (annexed by Jordan in 1950 but, like the Gaza Strip, under Israeli occupation since 1967), President Mubarak urged the PLO to exercise caution in its plans to declare an independent Palestinian state and to form a government-in-exile. In September, during a tour of Western Europe, he expressed reservations regarding the PLO's commitment to renounce terrorism and recognize Israel. At the same time, he sought support for proposals to convene an international conference on the Middle East. In November Egypt granted full recognition to the newly-declared independent Palestinian State, and President Mubarak was believed to have persuaded the USA to initiate contact with the PLO in December, after Arafat had explicitly renounced terrorism and recognized Israel's right to exist.

The visit of King Fahd of Saudi Arabia to Cairo in March 1989 was a further indication of Egypt's improved status in the Arab world. In May President Mubarak represented Egypt at an emergency 'summit' conference of the League of Arab States in Casablanca, Morocco. The meeting, which was convened to rally support for the diplomatic initiatives of Yasser Arafat following the Palestinian declaration of independence, was preceded by a meeting of the Ministers of Foreign Affairs of the majority of Arab League member states, at which Egypt's formal readmission to the Arab League, after an absence of 10 years, was endorsed. Despite Libya's opposition to Egypt's readmission, Col Qaddafi attended the 'summit' meeting and held separate discussions with President Mubarak. In June it was announced that Egypt was preparing to reopen its border with Libya, and in October Col Qaddafi visited Egypt, the first such visit for 16 years, for further discussions with President Mubarak. In July President Mubarak was elected chairman of the Organization of African Unity for 1989/90.

In August 1989 the Egyptian Minister of State for Foreign Affairs, Dr Boutros Boutros-Ghali, visited Israel to confer with the Israeli Prime Minister, Itzhak Shamir. However, his offer to mediate between Israel and the PLO was rejected. Egypt denounced the abduction by Israeli agents, in July 1989, of Sheikh Abdul Karim Obeid, a leading Shi'a Muslim, from southern Lebanon as a terrorist act likely to endanger the already fragile Middle East peace process.

In April 1989, in response to increasing international diplomatic pressure, Israel announced details of a four-point peace initiative for a resolution of the Middle East conflict. The most important component of the plan was a proposal to hold elections in the West Bank and the Gaza Strip. However, the initiative was ambiguous with regard to several crucial aspects of the Middle East conflict.

In September 1989 President Mubarak sought to persuade the Israeli Government to accept 10 points clarifying its peace initiative, so that direct Palestinian-Israeli negotiations concerning the election plans could begin. The 10 points in question were: a commitment by Israel to accept the results of the proposed elections; the supervision of the elections by international observers; the granting of immunity to elected representatives; the withdrawal of the Israeli Defence Force from the balloting area; a commitment by Israel to begin negotiations, within three to five years after the proposed elections, on the final status of the Occupied Territories; the ending of Israeli settlement of the West Bank; complete freedom as regards election propaganda; a ban on entry of all Israelis to the Occupied Territories on the day of the proposed elections; the participation of residents of East Jerusalem in the elections; a commitment by Israel to the principle of exchanging land for peace. In early December, following two months of US diplomatic support for (and development of) the 'Cairo initiative', Egypt accepted, with conditions, a five-point US framework for the holding of Palestinian elections in the Occupied Territories.

On 27 December 1989, in a move presaged by the restoration, earlier in the month, of air links between Cairo and Damascus, and by the announcement that Presidents Mubarak and Assad would hold a 'summit' meeting (subsequently scheduled for January 1990), Egypt and Syria restored full diplomatic relations after a break lasting 12 years, leaving Libya as the only Arab State not to have re-established relations with Egypt. However, the reconciliation between Egypt and Libya also appeared to be gathering pace, as President Mubarak and Col Qaddafi met in December for the fourth occasion in 1989.

By early 1990 there had been no appreciable progress in the Middle East peace process, which had been further complicated by Israel's apparent intention to settle in the Occupied Territories some of the Soviet Jewish immigrants who had arrived in the country in large numbers in 1989 and continued to do so in 1990. Egypt's increasing frustration at the lack of progress in the peace process and its concern about the escalation of the Palestinian *intifada* (especially after the murder of seven Palestinians by an Israeli civilian at Rishon LeZiyyon in May 1990) led it to assume a more critical stance towards the Israeli Government in the first half of 1990. Following the suspension by the US Government of its dialogue with the PLO in June 1990, Egypt attributed the disintegration of the peace process to 'Israeli intransigence' and urged the resumption of the US-PLO dialogue. In July Egyptian diplomats were reportedly attempting to mediate betweeen the USA and the PLO, in order to bring about a resumption of their dialogue.

In November 1989 reports of widespread acts of violent discrimination against Egyptian expatriate workers in Iraq threatened the special relationship which had developed between Egypt and Iraq during the Gulf War, when Egypt provided Iraq with military equipment and advisers. Prior to the crisis in the Gulf (precipitated by Iraq's invasion and annexation of Kuwait in August 1990), Egypt sought to mediate in the dispute between Iraq and Kuwait, appealing for dialogue between the two sides in the interests of Arab solidarity. Following the invasion of Kuwait, Egypt sought initially to maintain its role as a mediator, immediately convening an emergency 'summit' meeting of Arab leaders. At the 'summit' meeting, held on 10 August in Cairo, Egypt firmly demanded the withdrawal of Iraqi forces from Kuwait, and 12 of the 20 Arab League member states participating in the meeting voted to send an Arab force to the Gulf in response to the Saudi Arabian Government's request for multinational assistance to deter aggression by Iraq.

In response to Egypt's support for the economic sanctions imposed on Iraq by the UN, Iraq urged the Egyptian people to overthrow the Egyptian Government. However, there was no evidence of widespread popular support in Egypt for President Saddam Hussain of Iraq, and the Government's action was judged to have bolstered its domestic popularity. While it condemned Iraq's invasion of Kuwait, however, the Muslim Brotherhood, the largest opposition group in the People's Assembly (prior to its dissolution in October 1990, see above), demanded the immediate withdrawal of US forces from the Gulf and opposed the sending of Egyptian troops to Saudi Arabia as part of an Arab deterrent force. It was feared, too, that the influx of Egyptian expatriate workers (totalling some 1m. in Iraq and some 150,000 in Kuwait before the Iraqi invasion), returning in large numbers from Iraq and Kuwait to almost certain unemployment in Egypt, might have a destabilizing effect.

EGYPT

On 28 August 1990 President Mubarak and President Assad of Syria met in Alexandria to discuss Arab efforts to avert the outbreak of war in the Gulf. An extraordinary meeting of Ministers of Foreign Affairs of Arab League member states took place in Cairo on 30 August, but it was attended by representatives of only 12 member states (those which had supported the sending of an Arab deterrent force to Saudi Arabia), reflecting the divisions which had arisen in the Arab world as a result of Iraq's invasion of Kuwait. In late October President Mubarak visited Saudi Arabia, the UAE and other Gulf states. Qatar, the UAE, Saudi Arabia and Kuwait's government-in-exile were reported to have cancelled some US $7,700m. of Egyptian debt, in support of Egypt's commitment to the defence of the Saudi Arabia.

In late October 1990 the USA also agreed to waive the US $7,000m. military debt owed to it by Egypt. Egypt's prompt support for the UN economic sanctions against Iraq, and its participation in the multinational defence force in Saudi Arabia, appeared to reinforce the USA's perception of Egypt as an important force for stability in the Middle East. Similarly, the renewed vigour with which Egypt pursued a Middle East peace agreement in 1989 was partly motivated by Egypt's wish to reinforce its positive image in the USA.

In mid-November 1990, amid growing confusion regarding the precise nature of the command structure of the multinational force in Saudi Arabia, President Mubarak indicated that Egyptian armed forces would not enter Iraqi territory in the event of offensive action against Iraq. He stated, however, that Egyptian forces would be allowed to enter Kuwait as part of a peace-keeping force. Following talks in Damascus (also in mid-November), Presidents Mubarak and Assad accused Iraq of thwarting attempts to convene a further emergency 'summit' meeting of Arab leaders, by insisting that the resolutions which had been agreed at the emergency 'summit' meeting held in Cairo on 10 August be annulled before it would attend such a meeting.

In early December 1990 the Ministers of Foreign Affairs of Egypt, Syria and Saudi Arabia met in Cairo and renewed their demand for Iraq to withdraw from Kuwait. Saudi Arabia was reported to have promised Egypt a further US $1,500m. to offset the financial losses that Egypt had incurred as a result of sending troops to Saudi Arabia. The Egyptian forces in Saudi Arabia were reported to number 27,000 (under Saudi Arabian command) in January 1991.

In early 1991, in an attempt to develop a new initiative to resolve the crisis in the Gulf, Presidents Mubarak and Assad conferred with Col Qaddafi of Libya and Lt-Gen. Bashir of Sudan in Misurata, Libya.

Following the outbreak of military conflict in the Gulf in January 1991, and Iraqi missile attacks on Israel, President Mubarak warned Israel not to become involved in the fighting. It was feared that Israeli involvement in the conflict might cause Egypt, and other Arab states participating in the multinational force ranged against Iraq, to reconsider their positions. However, it subsequently appeared that Egypt would be prepared to sanction limited retaliatory attacks by Israeli forces against Iraq.

In late January 1991 the USA, Japan, Germany, France, the UK, Italy and Canada agreed to waive more than one-third (some US $14,000m.) of the total debt owed to them by Egypt. This decision was taken in the light of Egypt's unwavering support for the multinational forces fighting to liberate Kuwait, in accordance with the UN Security Council's Resolution 678.

Government

Legislative power is held by the unicameral Majlis ash-Sha'ab (People's Assembly), which has 454 members: 10 nominated by the President and 444 directly elected for five years from 222 constituencies. The Assembly nominates the President, who is elected by popular referendum for six years (renewable). The President has executive powers and appoints one or more Vice-Presidents, a Prime Minister and a Council of Ministers. There is also a 210-member advisory assembly, the Shura Council. The country is divided into 26 governorates.

Defence

In June 1990 Egypt had total armed forces of 450,000 (army 320,000, air defence command 80,000, navy 20,000, air force 30,000), with 623,000 reserves. There is a selective three-year period of national service. Defence expenditure for 1990/91 was budgeted at £E4,400m.

Economic Affairs

In 1988, according to estimates by the World Bank, Egypt's gross national product (GNP), measured at average 1986–88 prices, was US $33,250m., equivalent to $650 per head. During 1980–88, it was estimated, GNP increased, in real terms, at an average rate of 5.6% per year, while GNP per head increased by an annual average of 2.8%. Over the same period, the population increased by an annual average of 2.7%. The average annual growth of overall gross domestic product (GDP), measured in constant prices, was 5.7% in 1980–88.

Agriculture (including forestry and fishing) contributed 21% of GDP in 1988, and employed an estimated 41% of the labour force in 1989. The principal crops include cotton, rice, wheat, sugar cane and maize. Exports of food and live animals accounted for about 11% of total exports in 1987. During 1980–88 agricultural production increased by an annual average of 2.6%.

Industry (including mining, manufacturing, construction and power) employed 20% of the working population in 1984, and provided 25% of GDP in 1988. During 1980–88 industrial production increased by an annual average of 5.1%.

Mineral resources include petroleum, natural gas, phosphates, manganese, uranium, coal, iron ore and gold. The petroleum industry contributed 16.1% of GDP in 1985/86, and petroleum and petroleum products accounted for 35.4% of total export earnings in 1987. However, the mining sector employed only 0.3% of the working population in 1984, although it provided 13.8% of GDP (at 1981/82 prices) in 1986/87.

Manufacturing contributed 14% of GDP in 1988, and employed 13.9% of the working population in 1984. Food-processing, petroleum-refining and textiles are the most important industries.

Energy is derived principally from hydroelectric power and coal. Petroleum production averaged 890,000 barrels per day in 1989, and by the beginning of 1990 Egypt's proven published petroleum reserves totalled 4,500m. barrels. Egypt has proven natural gas reserves of 325,000m. cu m.

In 1989 Egypt recorded a visible trade deficit of US $7,664m. and there was a deficit of $1,691m. on the current account of the balance of payments. In 1987 the principal source of imports (13.7%) was the USA, while Italy was the principal market for exports (13.7%). Other major trading partners were the Federal Republic of Germany, Japan and the USSR. Egypt's principal exports in 1987 were petroleum and petroleum products, textiles, and food and live animals. The principal imports were cereals, chemicals, machinery and transport equipment, and basic manufactures.

In the financial year ending 30 June 1988 there was an estimated budgetary deficit of £E680m. Egypt's total external debt was estimated at US $42,100m. at the end of 1988. In the same year the cost of servicing the foreign debt was equivalent to 13.9% of the value of exports of goods and services. The annual rate of inflation averaged 10.6% in 1980–88, rising to more than 21% in 1989. The rate in the year to August 1990 was 20%. In mid-1989 government officials estimated that the number of unemployed persons was between 20% and 22% of the total labour force.

Egypt is a member of the Arab League (see p. 174), the Organization of Arab Petroleum Exporting Countries (see p. 197), the Arab Co-operation Council (see p. 222), the Organization of the Islamic Conference (see p. 198) and the Gulf Organization for Development in Egypt.

The fundamental difficulty confronting the Egyptian economy is the pressure on resources, owing to one of the world's highest ratios of population to habitable and cultivable land. Egypt imports as much as 60% of its food requirements, and the Government's granting of subsidies to imports of food and petroleum has contributed to a large trade deficit and an unmanageable foreign debt. The crisis which has developed in the Gulf since August 1990 has damaged the prospects for the tourist sector, one of the most dynamic in the Egyptian economy, and has caused the return of many expatriate workers from Iraq and Kuwait and the consequent loss of their remittances. The 1987–92 Five-Year Plan required total projected investment of £E46,500m. This Plan aimed to achieve an average annual economic growth rate of 5.8%, and to increase agricultural output and petroleum production.

Social Welfare

Great progress has been made in social welfare services in recent years. There are comprehensive state schemes for sick-

EGYPT

Introductory Survey, Statistical Survey

ness benefits, pensions, health insurance and training. In 1982 Egypt had 1,521 hospital establishments, with a total of 87,685 beds, and there were 58,761 physicians working in the country. Of total expenditure by the central Government in the financial year 1986/87, £E447m. (2.5%) was for health services, and a further £E2,004m. (11.1%) for social security and welfare.

Education

Primary education is officially compulsory for six years between six and 12 years of age. In 1987, however, enrolment at primary schools was equivalent to 90% of children in the relevant age-group (boys 100%; girls 79%). Secondary education, beginning at 12 years of age, lasts for a further six years, comprising two equal cycles of three years each. Enrolment at secondary schools in 1987 was equivalent to 69% of children in this age-group (boys 79%; girls 58%). About 11m. people were receiving state education in the 1985/86 school year. There are 13 universities. Education at all levels is available free of charge. Expenditure on education by the central Government in the financial year 1986/87 was £E2,177m. (12.0% of total spending). In 1976 adult illiteracy averaged 61.8% (males 46.4%; females 77.6%), but by 1986, according to government estimates, the rate had declined to 49.3%.

Public Holidays

1991: 1 January (New Year), 12 February (Leilat al-Meiraj, Ascension of Muhammad), 8 April (Sham an-Nessim, Coptic Easter Monday), 16 April (Id al-Fitr, end of Ramadan), 18 June (Evacuation Day, proclamation of the republic), 23 June (Id al-Adha, Feast of the Sacrifice), 13 July (Islamic New Year), 23 July (Revolution Day), 21 September (Mouloud, Birth of Muhammad), 6 October (Armed Forces Day), 24 October (Popular Resistance Day), 23 December (Victory Day).

1992: 1 January (New Year), 1 February (Leilat al-Meiraj, Ascension of Muhammad), 4 April (Id al-Fitr, end of Ramadan), 27 April (Sham an-Nessim, Coptic Easter Monday), 11 June (Id al-Adha, Feast of the Sacrifice), 18 June (Evacuation Day, proclamation of the republic), 2 July (Islamic New Year), 23 July (Revolution Day), 10 September (Mouloud, Birth of Muhammad), 6 October (Armed Forces Day), 24 October (Popular Resistance Day), 23 December (Victory Day).

Coptic Christian holidays include: Christmas (7 January), Palm Sunday and Easter Sunday.

Weights and Measures

The metric system is in force, but some Egyptian measurements are still in use.

Statistical Survey

Sources (unless otherwise stated): Central Agency for Public Mobilization and Statistics, POB 2086, Nasr City, Cairo; tel. (02) 604632; telex 92395; Research Department, National Bank of Egypt, Cairo.

Area and Population

AREA, POPULATION AND DENSITY

Area (sq km)	997,738.5*
Population (census results)	
22–23 November 1976	36,626,204†
17–18 November 1986 (provisional)‡	
Males	24,655,297
Females	23,549,752
Total	48,205,049
Population (official estimates at mid-year)§	
1987	50,740,000
1988	51,897,000
1989	53,080,000
Density (per sq km) at mid-1989	53.2

* 385,229 sq miles. Inhabited and cultivated territory accounts for 35,189 sq km (13,587 sq miles).
† Excluding Egyptian nationals abroad, totalling 1,572,000.
‡ Including Egyptian nationals abroad, totalling an estimated 2,250,000.
§ Including Egyptian nationals abroad. Data have not been adjusted to take account of the 1986 census results.

GOVERNORATES (population at 1986 census*)

Governorate	Area (sq km)	Population ('000)	Capital
Cairo	214.2	6,052.8	Cairo
Alexandria	2,679.4	2,917.3	Alexandria
Port Said	72.1	399.8	Port Said
Ismailia	1,441.6	544.4	Ismailia
Suez	17,840.4	326.8	Suez
Damietta	589.2	741.3	Damietta
Dakahlia	3,470.9	3,500.5	Mansoura
Sharkia	4,179.5	3,420.1	Zagazig
Kalyubia	1,001.1	2,514.2	Benha
Kafr esh-Sheikh	3,437.1	1,800.1	Kafr esh-Sheikh
Gharbia	1,942.2	2,871.0	Tanta
Menufia	1,532.1	2,227.1	Shibin el-Kom
Behera	10,129.5	1,770.6	Damanhur
Giza	85,153.2	3,700.1	Giza
Beni Suef	1,321.7	1,443.0	Beni Suef
Fayum	1,827.2	1,544.0	Fayum
Menia	2,261.7	2,648.0	Menia
Asyut	1,553.0	2,223.0	Asyut
Suhag	1,547.2	2,455.1	Suhag
Qena	1,850.7	2,252.3	Qena
Aswan	678.5	801.4	Aswan
Al-Bahr al-Ahmar	203,685.0	90.5	Al-Ghaurdaqah
Al-Wadi al-Jadid	376,505.0	113.8	Al-Kharijah
Matruh	212,112.0	160.6	Matruh
North Sinai*	60,714.0	171.5	El-Arish
South Sinai*		29.0	Et-Toor

* Preliminary results.

EGYPT

PRINCIPAL TOWNS (estimated population at 1 July 1986)

El-Qahira (Cairo, the capital)	6,052,836*	Asyut	291,000
		Zagazig	274,000
El-Iskandariyah (Alexandria)	2,893,000	Es-Suweis (Suez)	265,000
		Ismailia	236,000
El-Giza	1,857,508*	El-Fayoum	227,000
Shoubra el-Kheima	710,794*	Damanhur	226,000
El-Mahalla el-Koubra	385,000	El-Minya (Menia)	203,000
Bur Sa'id (Port Said)	382,000	Aswan	196,000
Tanta	374,000	Kafr ed-Dawar	194,000
El-Mansoura	358,000	Beni Suef	163,000

* Census of 17–18 November 1986.

BIRTHS AND DEATHS

	Registered live births		Registered deaths	
	Number	Rate (per 1,000)	Number	Rate (per 1,000)
1980	1,569,247	37.3	421,227	10.0
1981	1,593,698	36.8	432,264	9.9
1982	1,601,265	36.0	441,621	9.9
1983*	1,710,000	37.2	412,700	9.0
1984*	1,820,000	38.6	400,600	8.5
1985	1,817,297	37.5	442,258	9.1
1986*	1,878,000	37.9	468,000	9.4
1987	2,087,302	40.7	466,161	9.1

* Figures are provisional.

Marriages (registrations): 442,280 (marriage rate 9.1 per 1,000) in 1985 (provisional).

EMPLOYMENT (Egyptians only, '000 persons)

	1982/83	1983/84	1984/85
Agriculture, forestry and fishing	4,296.4	4,384.9	4,464.2
Manufacturing and mining	1,514.2	1,603.2	1,722.0
Petroleum and petroleum products	25.2	26.5	27.0
Housing and construction	867.3	917.4	982.2
Electricity, gas and water	138.3	139.4	147.0
Transport and communications	446.3	463.8	492.2
Suez Canal	18.9	19.2	19.7
Trade	1,161.2	1,187.8	1,214.2
Finance and insurance	88.4	92.5	96.4
Tourism, hotels and restaurants	144.2	149.7	157.2
Social and private services	942.2	939.9	956.9
Social insurance	31.5	33.0	34.9
Government services	2,436.6	2,511.7	2,576.7
Total	**12,110.7**	**12,469.0**	**12,890.6**

OTHER PRINCIPAL CROPS ('000 metric tons)

	1987	1988	1989
Wheat†	2,721	2,839	3,148
Rice (paddy)†	2,406	2,132	2,680
Barley†	136	109	126
Maize	3,019	4,087†	3,748†
Sorghum	551	587†	585†
Potatoes	1,678	1,862†	1,005†
Sweet potatoes	63	40*	27†
Taro (Coco yam)	107	112*	115*
Dry broad beans	337	358	370*
Soybeans (Soya beans)	134	130†	136†
Cottonseed	584	510†	530†
Cabbages	431	452†	450†
Tomatoes	4,921	4,212†	4,800†
Cauliflowers	113	115*	120*
Pumpkins, squash and gourds	436	450*	480*
Cucumbers and gherkins	275	290*	300*
Aubergines	431	435*	450*
Chillies and peppers	261	280*	285*
Onions (dry)	613	650*	700*
Garlic	148	180*	200*
Green beans	157	160*	165*
Carrots	116	120*	125*
Watermelons	1,370	1,390*	1,400*
Melons	452	479*	485*
Grapes	510	540†	555†
Dates†	491	542	560
Sugar cane†	10,162	10,832	10,795
Sugar beets	835	908	950†
Oranges	1,387	1,400†	1,370†
Tangerines, mandarins, clementines and satsumas	134	151†	155†
Lemons and limes	209	220*	225*
Mangoes	106	100*	100*
Bananas	278	280*	300*

* FAO estimate.   † Unofficial estimates.

Source: FAO, *Production Yearbook*.

LIVESTOCK ('000 head, year ending September)

	1987*	1988	1989*
Cattle	1,870	1,900†	1,950
Buffaloes	2,550	2,600†	2,650
Sheep*	1,200	1,300	1,320
Goats	1,595	1,600†	1,650
Pigs*	15	15	15
Horses*	9	10	10
Asses*	1,900	1,950	1,960
Camels	70	75†	77

Chickens (million): 30* in 1987, 1988 and 1989.
Ducks (million): 4* in 1987, 1988 and 1989.

* FAO estimates.   † Unofficial estimate.

Source: FAO, *Production Yearbook*.

Agriculture

PRODUCTION OF LINT COTTON
(by type of staple; '000 kantars*, year ending 30 June)

	1984	1985	1986
Long†	1,947	1,814	1,914
Medium long‡	4,710	6,782	4,988
Medium§	2	3	—
Total	**6,659**	**8,599**	**6,902**

* 1 metric kantar = 50 kg.   † 1.375 in (3.4925 cm) and longer.
‡ 1.25 in–1.375 in (3.175 cm–3.4925 cm.).
§ 1.125 in–1.25 in (2.8575 cm–3.175 cm).

EGYPT

LIVESTOCK PRODUCTS ('000 metric tons)

	1987	1988	1989
Beef and veal*	200	185	188
Buffalo meat*	168	165	170
Mutton and lamb*	29	32	35
Goats' meat*	23	24	24
Pig meat*	3	3	3
Poultry meat*	136	112	107
Other meat*	48	49	54
Edible offals*	78	77	82
Cows' milk*	970	980	1,000
Buffaloes' milk*	1,400	1,420	1,440
Sheep's milk*	24	24	25
Goats' milk*	9	9	9
Butter and ghee*	80.0	80.8	81.7
Cheese*	306.3	313.3	315.5
Hen eggs†	153.8	142.0	143.0
Honey	12.4	12.5*	13.0*
Wool: greasy*	1.8	1.9	1.9
Cattle and buffalo hides*	51.0	50.4	53.0
Sheep skins*	3.8	3.9	4.1
Goat skins*	3.4	3.4	3.5

* FAO estimate(s). † Unofficial figures.

Source: FAO, mainly *Production Yearbook*.

Forestry

ROUNDWOOD REMOVALS
(FAO estimates, '000 cubic metres, excluding bark)

	1986	1987	1988
Industrial wood	97	100	103
Fuel wood	1,999	2,054	2,108
Total	2,096	2,154	2,211

Source: FAO, *Yearbook of Forest Products*.

Fishing

('000 metric tons, live weight)

	1985	1986	1987*
Marine	37.8	39.0	48.3
Freshwater	178.1	190.0	201.7
Total catch	215.9	229.1	250.0

1988: Catch as in 1987 (FAO estimates).
* FAO estimates.

Source: FAO, *Yearbook of Fishery Statistics*.

Mining

('000 metric tons, year ending 30 June)

	1984/85	1985/86	1986/87
Crude petroleum	43,241	41,970	43,178
Iron ore*	1,950	2,135	2,048
Salt (unrefined)	1,061	1,040	1,233
Phosphate rock†	599	639	580
Natural gas	3,179	4,247	4,491

Small quantities of lead and zinc are also mined.
* Figures refer to the metal content of ores.
† Source: US Bureau of Mines.

Industry

SELECTED PRODUCTS ('000 metric tons, unless otherwise indicated; year ending 30 June)

	1984/85	1985/86	1986/87
Wheat flour*	3,579	3,737	3,706
Refined sugar	764	791	841
White sugar crystal	473	479	n.a.
Cottonseed oil	260	274	277
Beer ('000 hectolitres)	423	461	470
Cigarettes ('000 million)	48	44	48
Cotton yarn (pure)	243	225	251
Jute yarn	27	24	26
Jute fabrics	23	24	n.a.
Woollen yarn	18	18	19
Paper	161	172	187
Rubber tyres and tubes ('000)†	3,256	3,526	3,411
Ethyl alcohol ('000 hectolitres)	300	270	—
Sulphuric acid (100%)	46	55	60
Caustic soda (Sodium hydroxide)	48	55	54
Nitrogenous fertilizers‡	626	576	602
Phosphate fertilizers§	112	149	188
Motor spirit (petrol)	1,940	1,993	2,090
Kerosene	2,123	2,257	2,325
Distillate fuel oils	3,408	3,300	3,604
Residual fuel oil (Mazout)	9,787	9,501	10,353
Petroleum bitumen (asphalt)	581	539	597
Cement	5,275	7,612	8,762
Pig-iron	241	294	296
Gypsum and plaster of Paris	1,009	556	n.a.
Radio receivers ('000)	221	180	18
Television receivers ('000)	895	443	333
Passenger motor cars—assembly (number)	20,790	19,243	17,939
Electric energy (million kWh)	30,300	32,150	32,500

* Figures refer to the calendar years 1985–87.
† Tyres and inner tubes for road motor vehicles (including motor-cycles) and bicycles.
‡ Production in terms of nitrogen.
§ Production in terms of phosphoric acid.

Finance

CURRENCY AND EXCHANGE RATES

Monetary Units
1,000 millièmes = 100 piastres = 5 tallaris = 1 Egyptian pound (£E).

Denominations
Coins: 1, 2, 5 and 10 piastres.
Notes: 5, 10, 25 and 50 piastres; 1, 5, 10, 20 and 100 pounds.

Sterling and Dollar Equivalents (30 September 1990)
£1 sterling = £E3.747;
US $1 = £E2.000;
£E100 = £26.69 sterling = $50.00.

Note: The information on exchange rates refers to the official rate of the Central Bank. This rate was fixed at US $1 = 700 millièmes (£E1 = $1.4286) between January 1979 and August 1989. It was adjusted to $1 = £E1.100 in August 1989, and to $1 = £E2.000 in July 1990. However, a system of multiple exchange rates is in operation, and the official rate is applicable only to a limited range of transactions, including payments for selected imports and exports. At 30 September 1990 the banks' free market rate, applicable to most other transactions, was $1 = £E2.753 (£E1 = 36.32 US cents). The average of this secondary rate (£E per US $) was: 1.518 in 1987; 2.223 in 1988; 2.517 in 1989.

EGYPT

BUDGET ESTIMATES (£E million, year ending 30 June)*

	1985/86	1986/87	1987/88
Expenditure	19,910	20,246	23,058.9
Current spending	12,480	11,146	13,745.3
Investment	5,430	7,400	5,800.0
Capital transfer	n.a.	n.a.	3,513.6
Subsidies	2,000	1,700	1,700.0
Revenue	15,010	14,386	18,113.2
Gross deficit	4,900	5,860	4,947.7
Financing	4,000	5,080	4,267.7
Net deficit	900	780	680.0

Source: *Al-Ahram*, Cairo.

* The Government does not provide up-to-date figures on actual spending and income. A number of observers, including the IMF, believe that the actual gross and net deficits since 1982/83 have been higher than budgeted. A major reason for the discrepancy is that the expenditure on subsidies tends to exceed its allocation. Estimates by the IMF assess actual spending on subsidies in 1984/85 at about £E2,600m.

CENTRAL BANK RESERVES (US $ million at 31 December)

	1987	1988	1989
Gold*	814	794	679
Foreign exchange	1,378	1,263	1,520
Total	2,192	2,057	2,199

* Valued at market-related prices.
Source: IMF, *International Financial Statistics*.

MONEY SUPPLY (£E million at 31 December)

	1987	1988	1989
Currency outside banks	9,537	10,406	10,934
Demand deposits at deposit money banks	7,460	8,308	9,742

Source: IMF, *International Financial Statistics*.

COST OF LIVING (Consumer Price Index; base: 1980 = 100)

	1987	1988	1989
Food	304.0	373.8	473.1
Fuel and light	123.8	133.5	137.2
Clothing	237.4	274.5	315.5
Rent	100.0	100.7	106.8
All items (incl. others)	281.4	335.5	408.6

Source: ILO, *Year Book of Labour Statistics*.

NATIONAL ACCOUNTS
(£E million, year ending 30 June)
Expenditure on the Gross Domestic Product (at current prices)

	1986/87	1987/88	1988/89
Government final consumption expenditure	6,330	7,373	8,189
Private final consumption expenditure	35,947	42,729	52,066
Increase in stocks	100	150	240
Gross fixed capital formation	8,050	13,037	15,029
Total domestic expenditure	50,427	63,289	75,524
Exports of goods and services	8,006	12,944	14,010
Less Imports of goods and services	13,184	21,680	24,847
GDP in purchasers' values	45,249	54,553	64,688

Source: IMF, *International Financial Statistics*.

Gross Domestic Product by Economic Activity
(at constant 1981/82 factor cost)

	1984/85	1985/86	1986/87
Agriculture, hunting, forestry and fishing	4,394.0	4,540.0	4,670.0
Mining and quarrying	3,910.6	3,949.3	3,866.5
Manufacturing	3,584.1	3,849.1	4,128.7
Electricity, gas and water	178.5	219.3	240.8
Construction	1,224.0	1,272.9	1,241.7
Trade, restaurants and hotels	5,251.0	5,395.3	5,694.2
Transport, storage and communications	2,541.3	2,704.8	2,839.5
Finance, insurance, real estate and business services	497.7	536.9	579.8
Other services	4,029.0	4,361.6	4,695.8
Total	25,610.2	26,829.2	27,957.0

Source: UN, *National Accounts Statistics*.

BALANCE OF PAYMENTS (US $ million)

	1987	1988	1989
Merchandise exports f.o.b.	3,115	2,619	3,755
Merchandise imports f.o.b.	−8,095	−9,370	−11,419
Trade balance	−4,980	−6,751	−7,664
Exports of services	4,130	4,982	6,617
Imports of services	−3,725	−3,858	−6,035
Balance on goods and services	−4,575	−5,627	−7,082
Private unrequited transfers (net)	3,604	3,770	4,253
Government unrequited transfers (net)	725	666	1,137
Current balance	−245	−1,190	−1,691
Direct capital investment (net)	929	1,178	1,586
Other long-term capital (net)	173	266	672
Short-term capital (net)	−1,434	−178	−1,791
Net errors and omissions	893	−177	529
Total (net monetary movements)	315	−101	−696
Valuation changes (net)	−149	52	824
Exceptional financing (net)	266	6	158
Changes in reserves	431	−42	286

Source: IMF, *International Financial Statistics*.

External Trade

Note: Figures exclude trade in military goods.

PRINCIPAL COMMODITIES
(distribution by SITC, US $ million)

Imports c.i.f.	1985	1986	1987
Food and live animals	2,278.7	2,617.2	3,778.4
Meat and meat preparations	280.2	358.6	542.2
Fresh, chilled and frozen meat	254.9	314.6	499.0
Meat of bovine animals	170.8	233.0	366.5
Dairy products and birds' eggs	243.5	226.6	429.7
Cereals and cereal preparations	1,007.6	1,130.8	1,503.2
Wheat and meslin (unmilled)	489.3	662.4	817.1
Maize, unmilled	207.4	194.1	331.2
Wheat, etc., meal or flour	304.7	265.7	337.6
Flour of wheat or meslin	304.7	259.0	327.7

EGYPT

Statistical Survey

Imports c.i.f.—continued	1985	1986	1987
Crude materials (inedible) except fuels	759.6	644.6	1,074.4
Cork and wood	512.4	453.9	687.9
Simply worked wood and railway sleepers	454.6	420.7	603.2
Simply worked coniferous wood	451.3	419.9	579.3
Sawn coniferous wood	449.7	418.3	574.3
Mineral fuels, lubricants, etc. (incl. electric current)	377.4	394.7	450.0
Animal and vegetable oils, fats and waxes	191.4	609.8	358.5
Fixed vegetable oils and fats	144.1	375.4	291.8
Soft fixed vegetable oils	123.6	344.5	266.4
Chemicals and related products	908.9	1,078.4	1,971.4
Medicinal and pharmaceutical products	161.6	206.7	343.0
Artificial resins, plastic materials, etc.	211.8	267.4	554.2
Products of polymerization, etc.	158.6	206.6	461.4
Basic manufactures	2,409.6	2,618.0	3,203.5
Paper, paperboard and manufactures	244.4	199.1	385.5
Paper and paperboard (not cut to size or shape)	224.3	179.8	359.5
Non-metallic mineral manufactures	574.5	628.2	635.4
Lime, cement and building products	475.4	489.6	406.7
Cement	469.5	486.1	404.9
Iron and steel	882.6	989.2	976.0
Bars, rods, angles, shapes, etc.	536.4	597.1	426.7
Machinery and transport equipment	2,526.5	2,952.1	4,618.6
Machinery specialized for particular industries	614.5	854.9	989.1
General industrial machinery, equipment and parts	448.7	572.8	923.9
Telecommunications and sound equipment	167.6	215.8	387.3
Other electrical machinery, apparatus, etc.	378.6	458.4	826.0
Road vehicles and parts*	582.2	492.4	896.1
Parts and accessories for cars, buses, lorries, etc.*	221.5	248.4	389.9
Miscellaneous manufactured articles	298.0	394.8	549.2
Total (incl. others)	9,961.5	11,502.3	16,225.8

* Excluding tyres, engines and electrical parts.

Exports f.o.b.	1985	1986	1987
Food and live animals	191.3	196.4	489.0
Vegetables and fruit	154.4	124.1	375.2
Fresh or simply preserved vegetables	49.5	52.6	113.8
Fresh and dried fruit and nuts (excl. oil nuts)	96.7	62.8	242.7
Oranges, mandarins, etc.	86.5	44.2	226.1
Oranges	86.5	44.1	149.5
Crude materials (inedible) except fuels	455.4	479.3	463.6
Textile fibres and waste	434.1	451.5	409.4
Cotton	429.6	442.7	393.6
Raw cotton (excl. linters)	427.1	440.6	388.8
Mineral fuels, lubricants, etc.	2,531.3	1,504.0	1,555.6
Petroleum, petroleum products, etc.	2,526.7	1,492.9	1,540.7
Crude petroleum	2,002.9	1,140.0	1,123.2
Refined petroleum products	517.8	348.5	410.6
Kerosene and other medium oils	186.5	56.9	138.2
Residual fuel oils	288.1	247.2	226.4
Chemicals and related products	28.8	41.9	90.3
Basic manufactures	450.0	639.4	1,609.6
Textile yarn, fabrics, etc.	291.0	432.2	1,170.7
Textile yarn	221.5	325.3	934.3
Cotton yarn	220.9	319.5	930.6
Woven cotton fabrics (excl. narrow or special fabrics)	60.3	93.8	202.2
Non-ferrous metals	147.8	166.6	345.2
Aluminium and aluminium alloys	147.2	164.8	341.8
Aluminium bars, wire, etc.	147.2	163.2	338.0
Miscellaneous manufactured articles	40.6	69.1	133.7
Clothing and accessories (excl. footwear)	21.2	34.5	85.1
Total (incl. others)	3,714.2	2,934.3	4,351.5

Source: UN, *International Trade Statistics Yearbook*.

PRINCIPAL TRADING PARTNERS
(countries of consignment, £E million)

Imports c.i.f.	1986	1987	1988
Australia	287.2	272.9	415.1
Austria	86.5	163.5	n.a.
Belgium/Luxembourg	159.2	210.2	306.8
Czechoslovakia	80.7	146.9	156.2
Finland	79.6	166.7	174.8
France	538.7	885.7	1,375.6
Germany, Fed. Repub.	777.5	1,227.1	1,788.0
Greece	159.7	214.7	180.3
India	54.4	106.0	143.3
Italy	559.2	784.1	1,143.9
Japan	436.5	726.1	822.9
Netherlands	229.7	405.3	606.8
Romania	396.9	322.7	576.8
Saudi Arabia	86.3	111.5	128.5
Spain	157.1	186.1	178.1
Sweden	132.7	221.9	372.6
Switzerland	170.4	322.3	510.2
Turkey	124.5	149.9	259.5
USSR	281.3	307.5	509.5
United Kingdom	311.1	475.9	691.9
USA	1,230.7	1,561.4	1,944.8
Yugoslavia	166.0	230.0	412.5
Total (incl. others)	8,051.4	11,357.8	16,308.6

Exports f.o.b.	1986	1987	1988
Belgium/Luxembourg	31.3	79.9	n.a.
Czechoslovakia	43.7	60.1	79.5
France	77.8	149.6	233.6
German, Dem. Repub.	40.4	41.2	54.1
Germany, Fed. Repub.	61.9	128.0	169.7
Greece	50.3	29.7	92.1
Israel	213.5	209.6	n.a.
Italy	289.6	418.1	443.6
Japan	55.7	66.3	187.4
Netherlands	99.8	178.7	275.2
Poland	16.6	35.5	5.9
Romania	241.2	101.9	51.0
Saudi Arabia	56.1	86.3	129.7
Sudan	35.9	85.6	89.5
Switzerland	10.3	33.2	38.1
USSR	120.4	404.5	486.6
United Kingdom	42.4	88.8	109.5
USA	60.3	235.4	251.2
Yugoslavia	43.2	33.5	12.4
Total (incl. others)	2,054.0	3,046.0	3,994.4

EGYPT

Transport

RAILWAYS (year ending 30 June)

	1983/84	1984/85	1985/86
Total freight (million ton-km)	2,631	2,792	2,927
Total passengers (million passenger-km)	24,104	26,232	28,350
Track length (km)	5,327	5,367	5,355

ROAD TRAFFIC (motor vehicle licences at 31 December)

	1987	1988	1989
Passenger cars	783,306	791,245	826,915
Buses and coaches	29,534	31,590	29,508
Goods vehicles	302,379	318,478	330,854
Vans	175,733	184,358	190,287
Motor cycles	282,682	298,929	n.a.

SHIPPING (Suez Canal traffic)

	1987	1988	1989
Transits (number)	17,541	18,190	17,628
Displacement ('000 net tons)	347,038	356,913	373,429
Northbound goods traffic ('000 metric tons)	152,951	140,401	150,348
Southbound goods traffic ('000 metric tons)	103,984	119,093	115,471
Net tonnage of tankers ('000)	126,275	126,658	134,924

Source: Suez Canal Authority.

CIVIL AVIATION (traffic on scheduled services)

	1983	1984	1985
Kilometres flown (million)	36.5	35.3	37.8
Passengers carried ('000)	2,618	2,786	2,786
Passenger-km (million)	4,118	4,386	4,427
Freight ton-km (million)	69.7	88.2	98.5

Source: UN, *Statistical Yearbook*.

Tourism

TOURIST ARRIVALS BY REGION ('000)

	1985	1986	1987
Arabs	564	528	616
OECD nationals	818	613	932
Nationals of socialist countries	28	40	43
Others	109	130	204
Total	1,518	1,311	1,795

Education

	Teachers		Pupils/Students	
	1986	1987	1986	1987
Pre-primary	3,414	4,067	135,820	152,371
Primary	211,092*	235,586*	6,613,503	7,034,617
Secondary:				
General	142,293*	155,941*	3,018,401	3,123,233
Teacher training	7,754*	8,509*	98,390	106,308
Vocational	58,200	65,639	924,811	901,271
Higher:				
Universities, etc.	31,173*	n.a.	775,530	685,587†
Others	2,014‡	n.a.	102,793	104,812

* Excluding teachers in Al-Azhar education.
† Excluding post-graduate students.
‡ Figure refers to 1985.

Source: UNESCO, *Statistical Yearbook*.

Directory

The Constitution

A new constitution for the Arab Republic of Egypt was approved by referendum on 11 September 1971.

THE STATE

Egypt is an Arab Republic with a democratic, socialist system based on the alliance of the working people and derived from the country's historical heritage and the spirit of Islam.

The Egyptian people are part of the Arab nation, who work towards total Arab unity.

Islam is the religion of the State; Arabic is its official language and the Islamic code is a principal source of legislation. The State safeguards the freedom of worship and of performing rites for all religions.

Sovereignty is of the people alone which is the source of all powers.

The protection, consolidation and preservation of the socialist gains is a national duty: the sovereignty of law is the basis of the country's rule, and the independence of immunity of the judiciary are basic guarantees for the protection of rights and liberties.

THE FUNDAMENTAL ELEMENTS OF SOCIETY

Social solidarity is the basis of Egyptian society, and the family is its nucleus.

The State ensures the equality of men and women in both political and social rights in line with the provisions of Muslim legislation.

Work is a right, an honour and a duty which the State guarantees together with the services of social and health insurance, pensions for incapacity and unemployment.

The economic basis of the Republic is a socialist democratic system based on sufficiency and justice in a manner preventing exploitation.

Ownership is of three kinds, public, co-operative and private. The public sector assumes the main responsibility for the regulation and growth of the national economy under the development plan.

Property is subject to the people's control.

Private ownership is safeguarded and may not be sequestrated except in cases specified in law nor expropriated except for the general good against fair legal compensation. The right of inheritance is guaranteed in it.

Nationalization shall only be allowed for considerations of public interest in accordance with the law and against compensation.

Agricultural holding may be limited by law.

The State follows a comprehensive central planning and compulsory planning approach based on quinquennial socio-economic and cultural development plans whereby the society's resources are mobilized and put to the best use.

The public sector assumes the leading role in the development of the national economy. The State provides absolute protection

EGYPT

of this sector as well as the property of co-operative societies and trade unions against all attempts to tamper with them.

PUBLIC LIBERTIES, RIGHTS AND DUTIES

All citizens are equal before the law. Personal liberty is a natural right and no one may be arrested, searched, imprisoned or restricted in any way without a court order.

Houses have sanctity, and shall not be placed under surveillance or searched without a court order with reasons given for such action.

The law safeguards the sanctities of the private lives of all citizens; so have all postal, telegraphic, telephonic and other means of communication which may not therefore be confiscated, or perused except by a court order giving the reasons, and only for a specified period.

Public rights and freedoms are also inviolate and all calls for atheism and anything that reflects adversely on divine religions are prohibited.

The freedom of opinion, the Press, printing and publications and all information media are safeguarded.

Press censorship is forbidden, so are warnings, suspensions or cancellations through administrative channels. Under exceptional circumstances, as in cases of emergency or in war time, censorship may be imposed on information media for a definite period.

Egyptians have the right to permanent or provisional emigration and no Egyptian may be deported or prevented from returning to the country.

Citizens have the right to private meetings in peace provided they bear no arms. Egyptians also have the right to form societies which have no secret activities. Public meetings are also allowed within the limits of the law.

SOVEREIGNTY OF THE LAW

All acts of crime should be specified together with the penalties for the acts.

Recourse to justice, it says, is a right of all citizens, and those who are financially unable, will be assured of means to defend their rights.

Except in cases of *flagrante delicto*, no person may be arrested or their freedom restricted unless an order authorizing arrest has been given by the competent judge or the public prosecution in accordance with the provisions of law.

SYSTEM OF GOVERNMENT

The President, who must be of Egyptian parentage and at least 40 years old, is nominated by at least one-third of the members of the People's Assembly, approved by at least two-thirds, and elected by popular referendum. His term is for six years and he 'may be re-elected for another subsequent term'. He may take emergency measures in the interests of the State but these measures must be approved by referendum within 60 days.

The People's Assembly, elected for five years, is the legislative body and approves general policy, the budget and the development plan. It shall have 'not less than 350' elected members, at least half of whom shall be workers or farmers, and the President may appoint up to 10 additional members. In exceptional circumstances the Assembly, by a two-thirds vote, may authorize the President to rule by decree for a specified period but these decrees must be approved by the Assembly at its next meeting. The law governing the composition of the People's Assembly was amended in May 1979 (see People's Assembly, below).

The Assembly may pass a vote of no confidence in a Deputy Prime Minister, a Minister or a Deputy Minister, provided three days' notice of the vote is given, and the Minister must then resign. In the case of the Prime Minister, the Assembly may 'prescribe' his responsibility and submit a report to the President: if the President disagrees with the report but the Assembly persists, then the matter is put to a referendum: if the people support the President the Assembly is dissolved; if they support the Assembly the President must accept the resignation of the Government. The President may dissolve the Assembly prematurely, but his action must be approved by a referendum and elections must be held within 60 days.

Executive Authority is vested in the President, who may appoint one or more Vice-Presidents and appoints all Ministers. He may also dismiss the Vice-Presidents and Ministers. The President has 'the right to refer to the people in connection with important matters related to the country's higher interests.' The Government is described as 'the supreme executive and administrative organ of the state'. Its members, whether full Ministers or Deputy Ministers, must be at least 35 years old. Further sections define the roles of Local Government, Specialized National Councils, the Judiciary, the Higher Constitutional Court, the Socialist Prosecutor General, the Armed Forces and National Defence Council and the Police.

POLITICAL PARTIES

In June 1977 the People's Assembly adopted a new law on political parties, which, subject to certain conditions, permitted the formation of political parties for the first time since 1953. The law was passed in accordance with Article Five of the Constitution which describes the political system as 'a multi-party one' with four main parties: 'the ruling National Democratic Party, the Socialist Workers (the official opposition), the Liberal Socialists and the Unionist Progressive'. (The legality of the re-formed New Wafd Party was established by the courts in January 1984.)

1980 AMENDMENTS

On 30 April 1980 the People's Assembly passed a number of amendments, which were subsequently massively approved at a referendum the following month. A summary of the amendments follows:

(i) the regime in Egypt is socialist-democratic, based on the alliance of working people's forces.

(ii) the political system depends on multiple political parties; the Arab Socialist Union is therefore abolished.

(iii) the President is elected for a six-year term and can be elected for 'other terms'.

(iv) the President shall appoint a Consultative Council to preserve the principles of the revolutions of 23 July 1952 and 15 May 1971.

(v) a Supreme Press Council shall safeguard the freedom of the press, check government censorship and look after the interests of journalists.

(vi) Egypt's adherence to Islamic jurisprudence is affirmed. Christians and Jews are subject to their own jurisdiction in personal status affairs.

(vii) there will be no distinction of race or religion.

The Government

THE PRESIDENCY

President: Muhammad Hosni Mubarak (confirmed as President by referendum, 13 October 1981, after assassination of President Sadat; re-elected and confirmed by referendum 5 October 1987).

Vice-President: (vacant).

Presidential Assistant: Field-Marshal Muhammad Abd al-Halim Abu Ghazalah.

COUNCIL OF MINISTERS
(January 1991)

Prime Minister and Minister of International Co-operation: Dr Atif Sidqi.

Deputy Prime Minister and Minister of Foreign Affairs: Dr Ahmad Esmat Abd al-Meguid.

Deputy Prime Minister and Minister of Planning: Dr Kamal Ahmad al-Ganzouri.

Deputy Prime Minister and Minister of Agriculture and Land Reclamation: Dr Yousuf Amin Wali.

Minister of Defence and Military Production: Gen. Yusef Sabri Abu Taleb.

Minister of Finance: Dr Muhammad Ahmad ar-Razzaz.

Minister of Social Insurance and Social Affairs: Dr Amal Abd ar-Rahim Osman.

Minister of Manpower and Vocational Training: Asim Abd al-Haq Salih.

Minister of Justice: Farouk Sayf an-Nasr.

Minister of Transport, Communications and Naval Transport: Eng. Sulayman Mutawalli Sulayman.

Minister of Electricity and Energy: Eng. Muhammad Mahir Abazah.

Minister of Culture: Farouk Hosni.

Minister of Information: Muhammad Safwat Muhammad Yousuf ash-Sharif.

Minister of Health: Dr Muhammad Ragib Duwaydar.

Minister of Tourism and Civil Aviation: Dr Fouad Sultan.

Minister of Economy and Foreign Trade: Dr Yusri Ali Mustafa.

Minister of Supply and Internal Trade: Dr Muhammad Jalal ad-Din Abu hdi Dhahab.

Minister of the Interior: Muhammad Abd al-Halim Moussa.

Minister of Industry: Eng. Muhammad Farag Abd al-Wahhab.

EGYPT

Minister of Petroleum and Mineral Resources: ABD AL-HADI MUHAMMAD KANDIL.

Minister of Works and Water Resources: Eng. ISAM RADI ABD AL-HAMID RADI.

Minister of Cabinet Affairs and Minister of State for Administrative Development: Dr ATIF MUHAMMAD OBEID.

Minister of National Education: (vacant).

Minister of Development, New Communities, Housing and Public Utilities: Eng. HASABALLAH MUHAMMAD AL-KAFRAWI.

Minister of Awqaf (Islamic Endowments): Dr MUHAMMAD ALI MAHGOUB.

Minister for People's Assembly and Shura (Advisory) Council Affairs: Dr AHMAD SALAMAH MUHAMMAD.

Minister of State for Foreign Affairs: Dr BOUTROS BOUTROS GHALI; **Minister of State for Military Production:** Dr GAMAL AS-SAYED IBRAHIM; **Minister of State for Immigration and Egyptian Expatriates:** Dr FOUAD ISKANDAR; **Minister of State for Scientific Research:** Dr ADEL ABD AL-HAMID IZZ; **Minister of State for International Co-operation:** Dr MAURICE MAKRAMALLAH; **Minister of State for People's Assembly and Shura (Advisory) Council Affairs:** (vacant).

MINISTRIES

Ministry of Agriculture: Sharia Wizaret az-Ziraa, Dokki, Giza; tel. (02) 702677; telex 93006.

Ministry of Awqaf (Islamic Endowments): Sharia Sabri Abu Alam, Ean el-Luk, Cairo; tel. (02) 746305.

Ministry of Civil Aviation: Sharia Matar, Cairo (Heliopolis); tel. (02) 969555.

Ministry of Communications: 26 Sharia Ramses, Cairo; tel. (02) 909090.

Ministry of Culture: 110 Sharia al-Galaa, Cairo; tel. (02) 971995.

Ministry of Development, New Communities, Housing and Public Utilities: 1 Ismail Abaza, Qasr el-Eini, Cairo; tel.: Development (02) 3540419; New Communities (02) 3540590; Public Utilities (02) 3540110; telex: Development and New Communities 20807; Public Utilities 92188.

Ministry of Economic Co-operation: 9 Sharia Adly, Cairo; telex 348.

Ministry of Economy: 8 Sharia Adly, Cairo; tel. (02) 907344.

Ministry of Scientific Research: 4 Sharia Ibrahim Nagiv, Cairo (Garden City).

Ministry of Electricity and Energy: Cairo (Nasr City); tel. (02) 829565.

Ministry of Finance: Sharia Maglis esh-Sha'ab, Lazoughli Sq., Cairo; tel. (02) 24857; telex 92169.

Ministry of Foreign Affairs: Tahrir Sq., Cairo; telex 92220.

Ministry of Foreign Trade: Lazoghli Sq., Cairo; tel. (02) 25424.

Ministry of Health: Sharia Magles esh-Sha'ab, Cairo; tel. (02) 903939; telex 94107.

Ministry of Industry: 2 Sharia Latin America, Cairo (Garden City); tel. (02) 3550641; telex 93112.

Ministry of Information: Radio and TV Bldg, Corniche en-Nil, Cairo (Maspiro); tel. (02) 974216.

Ministry of International Co-operation: 8 Sharia Adly, Cairo; tel. (02) 3909707; fax (02) 3915167.

Ministry of Irrigation: Sharia Qasr el-Eini, Cairo; tel. (02) 3552120.

Ministry of Justice: Justice Bldg, Cairo (Lazoughli); tel. (02) 31176.

Ministry of Land Reclamation: Land Reclamation Bldg, Dokki, Giza; tel. 703011.

Ministry of Manpower and Vocational Training: Sharia Yousuf Abbas, Nasr City, Abbasia, Cairo.

Ministry of Military Production: 5 Sharia Ismail Abaza, Kasr el-Eini, Cairo; tel. (02) 3553063; telex 92167.

Ministry of National Education: Sharia el-Falaky, Cairo; tel. (02) 8544805.

Ministry of Naval Transport: 4 Sharia el-Bataisa, Alexandria; tel. 35763; telex 54147.

Ministry of Petroleum and Mineral Resources: 2 Sharia Latin America, Cairo (Garden City); tel. (02) 3545022; telex 92197.

Ministry of Planning: Sharia Salah Salem, Cairo (Nasr City); tel. (02) 600096.

Ministry of Social Affairs: Sharia Sheikh Rihan, Cairo; telex 94105.

Ministry of Social Insurance: 3 Sharia el-Alfi, Cairo; tel. (02) 922717.

Ministry of Supply and Internal Trade: 99 Sharia Qasr el-Eini, Cairo; tel. (02) 3552600; telex 93497.

Ministry of Tourism: Misr Travel Tower, Abbassia Sq., Cairo; tel. (02) 2828450; telex 94040.

Ministry of Transport: Sharia Qasr el-Eini, Cairo; tel. (02) 3557402; telex 92802.

Legislature

MAJLIS ASH-SHA'AB
(People's Assembly)

The law governing election to, and the composition of, the People's Assembly was amended in October 1990. In May 1990 the Supreme Constitutional Court had ruled that the previous elections to the People's Assembly, held in 1987, had been unconstitutional because amendments to the 1972 electoral law discriminated against independent candidates. There are now 222 constituencies, which each elect two deputies to the Assembly. Ten deputies are appointed by the President, giving a total of 454 seats. Parties are no longer required to gain a minimum of 8% of the total vote in order to be represented in the Assembly.

On 12 October 1990, following a popular referendum, the People's Assembly was dissolved. A new Assembly was elected, in accordance with the provisions of the new electoral law, on 29 November.

Speaker: Dr AHMAD FATHI SURUR.

Deputy Speakers: Dr ABD AL-AHAD GAMAL AD-DIN, AHMAD ABU ZEID.

Elections, 29 November and 6 December 1990

Party	% of votes received	Seats
National Democratic Party	79.6	348
National Progressive Unionist Party	1.4	6
Independents*	19.0	83
Total	100.0	437†

* The elections were boycotted by the principal opposition parties (the Socialist Labour Party, the Muslim Brotherhood and the New Wafd Party), which refused to offer candidates unless legislation providing for the declaration of states of emergency was repealed, and the elections were supervised by magistrates.

† Voting was suspended in three constituencies, and for one of the seats of a fourth. There are, in addition, 10 deputies appointed by the President.

MAJLIS ASH-SHURA
(Advisory Council)

In September 1980 elections were held for a 210-member **Shura (Advisory) Council**, which replaced the former Central Committee of the Arab Socialist Union. Of the total number of members, 140 are elected and the remaining 70 are appointed by the President. The National Democratic Party holds all the elected seats. The opposition parties boycotted elections to the Council in October 1983, and again in October 1986, in protest against the 8% electoral threshold. In June 1989 elections to 153 of the Council's 210 seats were contested by opposition parties (the 'Islamic Alliance', consisting of the Muslim Brotherhood, the LSP and the SLP). However, all of the seats in which voting produced a result (143) were won by the National Democratic Party. A supplementary poll was to be held at a later date to elect a further 10 members.

Speaker: Dr ALI LUTFI.

Deputy Speakers: THARWAT ABAZAH, AHMAD AL-IMADI.

Political Organizations

Democratic Unionist Party: f. 1990.

Green Party: f. 1990.

Ikhwan (Brotherhood): f. 1928; officially illegal, the (Muslim) Brotherhood advocates the adoption of the Shari'a, or Islamic law, as the sole basis of the Egyptian legal system; Sec.-Gen. MAAMOUN AL-HODAIBY.

Liberal Socialist Party: Cairo; f. 1976; advocates expansion of 'open door' economic policy and greater freedom for private enterprise; Leader MUSTAFA KAMEL MURAD.

National Democratic Party: Cairo; f. July 1978; government party established by Anwar Sadat; has absorbed Arab Socialist Party; Leader MUHAMMAD HOSNI MUBARAK; Sec.-Gen. Dr YOUSUF AMIN

EGYPT

WALI; Political Bureau: Chair. MUHAMMAD HOSNI MUBARAK; mems: KAMAL HASSAN ALI, Dr MUSTAFA KHALIL, Dr RIFA'AT EL-MAHGOUB, Dr SUBHI ABD AL-HAKIM, Dr MUSTAFA KAMAL HILMI, FIKRI MAKRAM OBEID, Dr ISMAT ABD AL-MEGUID, Dr AMAL OSMAN, SAFWAT ASH-SHARIF, Dr YOUSUF AMIN WALI, HASSAN ABU BASHA, KAMAL HENRY BADIR, Dr AHMAD HEIKAL.

National Progressive Unionist Party (Tagammu): 1 Sharia Karim ed-Dawlah, Cairo; f. 1976; left wing; Leader KHALED MOHI ED-DIN; Sec. Dr RIFA'AT ES-SAID; 160,000 mems.

New Wafd Party: Cairo; original Wafd Party f. 1919; banned 1952; re-formed as New Wafd Party February 1978; disbanded June 1978; re-formed August 1983; Leader FOUAD SERAG ED-DIN; Sec.-Gen. IBRAHIM FARAG.

Socialist Labour Party: 12 Sharia Awali el-Ahd, Cairo; f. September 1978; official opposition party; Leader IBRAHIM SHUKRI.

Umma (National) Party: Islamic religious party, based in Khartoum, Sudan; Leader SADIQ AL-MAHDI (fmr Prime Minister of Sudan).

Young Egypt Party: f. 1990.

Diplomatic Representation

EMBASSIES IN EGYPT

Afghanistan: Interests served by India.

Albania: 29 Sharia Ismail Muhammad, Cairo (Zamalek); tel. (02) 3415651; Ambassador: ALKYZ CERGA.

Algeria: Interests served by India.

Angola: 12 Midan en-Nasr, Cairo (Dokki); tel. (02) 707602; Ambassador: KAMU D'ALMEIDA.

Argentina: 8 Sharia as-Saleh Ayoub, Cairo (Zamalek); tel. (02) 3401501; Ambassador: JORGE H. DE BELAUSBEGUI.

Australia: 5th Floor, South Bldg, Cairo Plaza Annexe, Corniche en-Nil, Cairo; tel. (02) 777900; telex 92257; fax (02) 768220; Ambassador: JOHN H. CRIGHTON.

Austria: Sharia en-Nil, Cnr of Sharia Wissa Wassef, Cairo (Giza); tel. (02) 737640; telex 92258; Ambassador: FRANZ BOGEN.

Bahrain: Interests served by Pakistan.

Bangladesh: 47 Sharia Ahmed Heshmat, Cairo (Zamalek); tel. (02) 3412642; Ambassador: M. NURUN NABI CHOWDHURY.

Belgium: 20 Sharia Kamel esh-Shennawi, Cairo (Garden City); tel. (02) 3547494; telex 92264; Ambassador: ALAIN RENS.

Bolivia: Cairo; tel. (02) 3550917; Chargé d'affaires (a.i.): ENRIQUE SORIA NAU.

Brazil: 1125 Corniche en-Nil, 11561 Cairo (Maspiro); tel. (02) 756938; telex 92044; Ambassador: IVAN VELLOSO DA SILVEIRA BATALHA.

Brunei: Room 401, Nile Hilton, Tahrir Sq., Cairo; tel. (02) 750666.

Bulgaria: 141 Sharia Tahrir, Cairo (Dokki); tel. (02) 982691.

Burkina Faso: Ramses Centre, 3 Sharia Abd al-Khawi Ahmad, POB 306, Cairo; tel. (02) 3440301; telex 93871; Ambassador: YAYA GNESSIEN.

Burundi: 13 Sharia el-Israa, Madinet el-Mohandessin, Cairo (Dokki); tel. (02) 3419940; telex 20091; Ambassador: ZACHARIE BANYIYEZAKO.

Cambodia: 2 Sharia Tahawia, Cairo (Giza); tel. (02) 3489966; Ambassador: IN SOPHEAP.

Cameroon: POB 2061, 15 Sharia Israa, Madinet el-Mohandessin, Cairo (Dokki); tel. (02) 341101; telex 92088; Ambassador: MOUCHILI NJI MFOUAYO.

Canada: 6 Sharia Muhammad Fahmy es-Sayed, Cairo (Garden City); tel. (02) 3543110; telex 92677; fax (02) 3557276; Ambassador: JACQUES T. SIMARD.

Central African Republic: 13 Sharia Chehab, Madinet el-Mohandessin, Cairo (Dokki); tel. (02) 713291; Ambassador: PIERRE FIDÈLE BAKRI.

Chad: 12 Midan ar-Refaï, Cairo (Dokki); tel. (02) 703232; telex 92285; Ambassador: KOCHE ABDEL KADER ADOUN.

Chile: 5 Sharia Chagaret ed-Dorr, Cairo (Zamalek); tel. (02)

China, People's Republic: 14 Sharia Bahgat Aly, Cairo (Zamalek); tel. (02) 3417691; Ambassador: ZHAN SHILIANG.

Colombia: 20/A Gamal ed-Din Aboul Mahassen, Cairo (Garden City); tel. (02) 3546152; telex 3036; fax (02) 3557087; Chargé d'affaires a.i.: Dr JAIRO MONTES MORENO.

Côte d'Ivoire: 39 Sharia el-Kods esh-Sherif, Madinet el-Mohandessin, Cairo (Dokki); tel. (02) 699009; telex 2334; Ambassador: Gen. FÉLIX ORY.

Cuba: 6 Fawakeh St, Madinet el-Mohandessin, Cairo (Dokki); tel. (02) 710525; telex 93966; Ambassador: JORGE CUBILES HERNÁNDEZ.

Cyprus: 23A Sharia Ismail Muhammad, Cairo (Zamalek); tel. (02) 3411288; telex 92059; Ambassador: ALECOS H. SHAMBOS.

Czechoslovakia: 4 Sharia Dokki, Cairo (Giza); tel. (02) 3485531; Ambassador: IVAN VOLEŠ.

Denmark: 12 Sharia Hassan Sabri, Cairo (Zamalek); tel. (02) 3407411; telex 92254; Ambassador: JØRGEN BØJER.

Djibouti: 157 Sharia Sudan, Madinet el-Mohandessin, Cairo (Dokki); tel. (02) 709787; telex 93143.

Ecuador: 8 Sharia Abd ar-Rahman Fahmy, Cairo (Garden City); tel. (02) 3546372; Ambassador: LUCINDO ALMEIDA.

Ethiopia: 12 Midan Bahlawi, Cairo (Dokki); tel. (02) 705372; Ambassador: Ato BETROU KIDANE MARIAM.

Finland: 3 Abu el-Feda St, Cairo (Zamalek); tel. (02) 3411487; Ambassador: ELISABETH TIGERSTEDT-TÄHTELÄ.

France: 29 ave en-Nil, Cairo (Giza); tel. (02) 728346; telex 92032; Ambassador: PIERRE HUNT.

Gabon: 15 Sharia Mossadek, Cairo (Dokki); tel. (02) 702963; telex 92323; Ambassador: ALAIN MAURICE MAYOMBO.

Germany: 8 Sharia Hassan Sabri, Cairo (Zamalek); tel. (02) 3410015; telex 92023; Ambassador: Dr MARTIN ELSÄSSER.

Ghana: 24 Sharia el-Batal Ahmad Abd al-Aziz, Cairo (Dokki); tel. (02) 704275; Ambassador: Dr W. C. YAW ANOFF.

Greece: 18 Sharia Aicha et-Taimouria, Cairo (Garden City); tel. (02) 3550443; telex 92036; Ambassador: PANDEUS MENGLIDIS.

Guatemala: POB 8062, 3rd Floor, Apt 13, 4 Sharia Dr al-Batrawi, Cairo; tel. (02) 2611813; telex 93242; fax (02) 2611814; Ambassador: RODOLFO ROSALES MURALLES.

Guinea: 46 Sharia Muhammad Mazhar, Cairo (Zamalek); tel. (02) 3411088; Ambassador: AMIROU DIALLO.

Guinea-Bissau: 37 Sharia Lebanon, Madinet el-Mohandessin, Cairo (Dokki).

Holy See: Apostolic Nunciature, Safarat al-Vatican, 5 Sharia Muhammad Mazhar, Cairo (Zamalek); tel. (02) 3402250; fax (02) 3406152; Pro-Nuncio: Most Rev. ANTONIO MAGNONI, Titular Archbishop of Boseta.

Hungary: 55 Sharia Muhammad Mazhar, Cairo (Zamalek); tel. (02) 3405091; Ambassador: Dr ERNÖ SIMONYI.

India: 5 Sharia Aziz Abaza, Cairo (Zamalek); tel. (02) 3413051; telex 92081; Ambassador: PASCAL ALAN NAZARETH; also looks after Afghanistan interests at 39 Sharia Orouba (Heliopolis) (tel. (02) 666653), Algerian interests at 14 Sharia Brasil (Zamalek) (tel. (02) 3402466).

Indonesia: POB 1661, 13 Sharia Aicha at-Taimouria, Cairo (Garden City); tel. (02) 3547200; Ambassador: R. ACHMAD DJUMIRIL.

Iraq: Interests served by Yugoslavia.

Ireland: POB 2681, 3 Sharia Abu el-Feda, Cairo (Zamalek); tel. (02) 3408264; telex 92778; Ambassador: EAMONN O'TUATHAIL.

Israel: 6 Sharia ibn el-Malek, Cairo (Giza); tel. (02) 729329; telex 93363; Ambassador: EPHRAIM DUBEK.

Italy: 15 Sharia Abd ar-Rahman Fahmi, Cairo (Garden City); tel. (02) 3543974; telex 94229; Ambassador: PATRIZIO SCHMIDLIN.

Japan: Immeuble Cairo Centre, 3rd Floor, 2 Sharia Abd al-Kader Hamza, 106 Kasr el-Eini; tel. (02) 3551477; telex 92226; Ambassador: HIROSHI HASHIMOTO.

Jordan: 6 Sharia Juhaini, Cairo (Zamalek); tel. (02) 3487543; Ambassador: NABIH AN-NIMR.

Kenya: POB 362, Cairo (Dokki), 8 Sharia Medina Mounawara; tel. (02) 704546; telex 92021; Ambassador: OCHIENG ADALA.

Korea, Democratic People's Republic: 6 Sharia es-Saleh Ayoub, Cairo (Zamalek); tel. (02) 650970; Ambassador: O CHANG RIM.

Korea, Republic: 6 Sharia el-Hesn, Cairo (Giza); tel. (02) 729162.

Kuwait: 12 Sharia Nabil el-Wakkad, Cairo (Dokki); tel. (02) 701611.

Lebanon: 5 Sharia Ahmad Nessim, Cairo (Giza); tel. (02) 728454; telex 92227; Ambassador: ABDEL RACHMAN.

Liberia: 11 Sharia Brasil, Cairo (Zamalek); tel. (02) 3419864; telex 92293; Ambassador: GABRIEL FARNGALO.

Malaysia: 7 Sharia Wadi en-Nil, Mohandessin, Cairo (Agouza); tel. (02) 699162; Ambassador: ABDULLAH ZAWAWI BIN HAJI MUHAMMAD.

Mali: 3 Sharia al-Kawsar, Cairo (Dokki); tel. (02) 701641; Ambassador: MUPHTAH AG-HAIRY.

Mauritania: 31 Sharia Syria, Cairo (Dokki); tel. (02) 707229; telex 93074.

Mauritius: 72 Sharia Abd el-Monehm Riad, Cairo (Agouza); tel. (02) 3470929; telex 93631; fax (02) 3452425; Ambassador: MAHMOOD EDAH TALLY.

EGYPT

Mexico: 5 Sharia Dar es-Shifa, Cairo; tel. (02) 3543422; telex 92277; fax (02) 3557953; Ambassador: Prof. GRACIELA DE LA LAMA.
Mongolia: 3 Midan en-Nasr, Cairo (Dokki); tel. (02) 650060; Ambassador: SONOMDORJIN DAMBADARJAA.
Morocco: *Interests served by Senegal.*
Myanmar: 24 Sharia Muhammad Mazhar, Cairo (Zamalek); tel. (02) 3404176; Ambassador: U AYE THEIN.
Nepal: 9 Sharia Tiba, Cairo (Dokki); tel. (02) 704447; Ambassador: KRISHNA BAHADUR MONANDHAR.
Netherlands: 18 Sharia Hassan Sabri, Cairo (Zamalek); tel. (02) 3406434; telex 92028; fax (02) 3415249; Ambassador: L. J. HANRATH.
Niger: 28 Sharia Pahlaw, Cairo (Dokki); tel. (02) 987740; telex 2880; Ambassador: SORY MAMADOU DIALLO.
Nigeria: 13 Sharia Gabalaya, Cairo (Zamalek); tel. (02) 3406042; telex 92038; Ambassador: MUSTAFA SAM.
Norway: 8 Sharia el-Gezireh, Cairo (Zamalek); tel. (02) 3403340; telex 92259; fax (02) 3420709; Ambassador: KNUT MORKVED.
Oman: 30 Sharia el-Montazah, Cairo (Zamalek); tel. (02) 3407811; telex 92272; Ambassador: GHALEB ABDULLAH JOUBRAN.
Pakistan: 8 Sharia es-Salouli, Cairo (Dokki); tel. (02) 3487677; fax (02) 3480310; Ambassador: GUL HANEEF; also looks after Bahrain interests at 8 Sharia Jamaiat an-Nisr, Cairo (Dokki); tel. (02) 705052; telex 2084.
Panama: 5 Shagaret ed-Dorr St, 11211 Cairo (Zamalek); tel. (02) 3411093; telex 92776; fax 3411092; Chargé d'affaires a.i.: Dr E. MONTERREY.
Peru: 8 Kamel esh-Shenawi St, Cairo (Garden City); tel. (02) 3562973; telex 93663; Ambassador: CLAUDIO ENRIQUE SOSA V.
Philippines: 5 Sharia ibn el-Walid, Cairo (Dokki); tel. (02) 3480396; telex 92446; Ambassador: KASAN A. MAROHOMBSAR.
Poland: 5 Sharia el-Aziz Osman, Cairo (Zamalek); tel. (02) 3417456; Ambassador: ROMAN CZYZYCKI.
Portugal: 15A Sharia Mansour Muhammad, Cairo (Zamalek); tel. (02) 3405583; telex 20325; Ambassador: JOSÉ DE MATTOS-PARREIRA.
Qatar: 10 Sharia ath-Thamar, Midan an-Nasr, Madinet al-Mohandessin, Cairo; tel. (02) 704537; telex 92287.
Romania: 6 Sharia Kamel Muhammad, Cairo (Zamalek); tel. (02) 3409546; telex 93807; Ambassador: ION COZMA.
Rwanda: 9 Sharia Ibrahim Osman, Mohandessin, Cairo, POB 485; tel. (02) 3461126; telex 92552; fax (02) 3461079; Ambassador: CÉLESTIN KABANDA.
Saudi Arabia: 12 Sharia al-Kamel Muhammad, Cairo (Zamalek); tel. (02) 819111; Ambassador: M. JALLOH.
Senegal: 46 Sharia Abd al-Moneim Riad, Mohandessin, Cairo (Dokki); tel. (02) 3458479; telex 92047; Ambassador: SHAMS ED-DINE NDOYE; also looks after Moroccan interests at 10 Sharia Salah ed-Din Ayoub, Cairo (Zamalek).
Sierra Leone: *Interests served by Saudi Arabia.*
Singapore: POB 356, 40 Sharia Babel, Cairo (Dokki); tel. (02) 704744; telex 21353; Ambassador: TAN KENG JIN.
Somalia: 38 Sharia esh-Shahid Abd el-Moneim Riad, Cairo (Dokki); tel. (02) 704038; Ambassador: HUSSEIN HASSAN FAREH.
Spain: 9 Hod el-Laban, Cairo (Garden City); tel. (02) 3547069; telex 92255; Ambassador: CARLOS FERNÁNDEZ-LONGORIA.
Sri Lanka: POB 1157, 8 Sharia Sri Lanka, Cairo (Zamalek); tel. (02) 3417138; telex 23375; Ambassador: T. D. S. A. DISSANAYAKE.
Sudan: 4 Sharia el-Ibrahimi, Cairo (Garden City); tel. (02) 3549661; Ambassador: AL-AMIN ABD AL-LATIF.
Sweden: POB 131, 13 Sharia Muhammad Mazhar, Cairo (Zamalek); tel. (02) 3414132; telex 92256; Ambassador: LARS-OLOF BRILIOTH.
Switzerland: 10 Sharia Abd al-Khalek Saroit, POB 633, Cairo; tel. (02) 758133; telex 92267; Ambassador: CLAUDIO CARATSCH.
Syria: 14 Ahmad Hechmar St, Cairo (Zamalek); Ambassador: (vacant).
Tanzania: 9 Sharia Abd al-Hamid Lotfi, Cairo (Dokki); tel. (02) 704155; telex 23537; Ambassador: MUHAMMAD A. FOUM.
Thailand: 2 Sharia al-Malek el-Afdal, Cairo (Zamalek); tel. (02) 3408356; telex 94231; Ambassador: CHAMRAS CHOMBHUBOL.
Tunisia: 26 Sharia el-Jazirah, Cairo (Zamalek); tel. (02) 3404940; Ambassador: MAHMOUD MESTIRI.
Turkey: ave en-Nil, Cairo (Giza); tel. (02) 726115; Ambassador: BERDUK OLGAÇAY; also looks after United Arab Emirates interests at 4 Sharia ibn Sina, al-Gezira, Cairo; tel. (02) 729955.
Uganda: 9 Midan el-Messaha, Cairo (Dokki); tel. (02) 3485544; telex 92087; Ambassador: DAUDI M. TALIWAKU.
USSR: 95 Sharia Giza, Cairo (Giza); tel. (02) 731416; Ambassador: VLADIMIR POLYAKOV.
United Arab Emirates: *Interests served by Turkey.*
United Kingdom: Sharia Ahmad Raghab, Cairo (Garden City); tel. (02) 3540852; telex 94188; fax (02) 3540859; Ambassador: Sir JAMES ADAMS.
USA: 5 Sharia Latin America, Cairo (Garden City); tel. (02) 3557371; telex 93773; Ambassador: ROBERT PELLETREAU.
Uruguay: 6 Sharia Lotfallah, Cairo (Zamalek); tel. (02) 3415137; telex 92435; Ambassador: RAMIRO PIRIZ BALLÓN.
Venezuela: 15A Sharia Mansour Muhammad, Cairo (Zamalek); tel. (02) 3413517; telex 93638; Ambassador: Dr JOSÉ A. MARTÍNEZ-RAMÍREZ.
Viet-Nam: 47 Sharia Ahmad Hishmat, Cairo (Zamalek); tel. (02) 3402401; Ambassador: VU BACH MAI.
Yemen: Cairo.
Yugoslavia: 33 Sharia Mansour Muhammad, Cairo (Zamalek); tel. (02) 3404061; telex 21046; Ambassador: Dr IVAN IVEKOVIĆ.
Zaire: 5 Sharia Mansour Muhammad, Cairo (Zamalek); tel. (02) 3403662; telex 92294; Ambassador: NGANDU MWALBA.
Zambia: POB 253, 10 Midan al-Gomhouriya Muttahada, Mohandessin-e-Giza, 12311 Cairo; tel. (02) 3610282; telex 92262; fax (02) 3610833; Ambassador: KALENGA KANGWA.

Judicial System

The Courts of Law in Egypt are principally divided into two juridical court systems: Courts of General Jurisdiction and Administrative Courts. Since 1969 the Supreme Constitutional Court has been at the top of the Egyptian judicial structure.

THE SUPREME CONSTITUTIONAL COURT

The Supreme Constitutional Court is the highest court in Egypt. It has specific jurisdiction over: (i) judicial review of the constitutionality of laws and regulations; (ii) resolution of positive and negative jurisdictional conflicts and determination of the competent court between the different juridical court systems, e.g. Courts of General Jurisdiction and Administrative Courts, as well as other bodies exercising judicial competence; (iii) determination of disputes over the enforcement of two final but contradictory judgments rendered by two courts each belonging to a different juridical court system; (iv) rendering binding interpretation of laws or decree laws in the event of a dispute in the application of said laws or decree laws, always provided that such a dispute is of a gravity requiring conformity of interpretation under the Constitution.

COURTS OF GENERAL JURISDICTION

The Courts of General Jurisdiction in Egypt are basically divided into four categories, as follows: (i) The Court of Cassation (ii) The Courts of Appeal; (iii) The Tribunals of First Instance; (iv) The District Tribunals; each of the above courts is divided into Civil and Criminal Chambers.

(i) Court of Cassation: Is the highest court of general jurisdiction in Egypt. Its sessions are held in Cairo. Final judgments rendered by Courts of Appeal in criminal and civil litigation may be petitioned to the Court of Cassation by the Defendant or the Public Prosecutor in criminal litigation and by any of the parties in interest in civil litigation on grounds of defective application or interpretation of the law as stated in the challenged judgment, on grounds of irregularity of form or procedure, or violation of due process, and on grounds of defective reasoning of judgment rendered. The Court of Cassation is composed of the President, 41 Vice-Presidents and 92 Justices.

President: Hon. ABD AL-BORHAN NOOR.

(ii) The Courts of Appeal: Each has geographical jurisdiction over one or more of the governorates of Egypt. Each Court of Appeal is divided into Criminal and Civil Chambers. The Criminal Chambers try felonies, and the Civil Chambers hear appeals filed against such judgment rendered by the Tribunals of First Instance where the law so stipulates. Each Chamber is composed of three Superior Judges. Each Court of Appeal is composed of President, and sufficient numbers of Vice-Presidents and Superior Judges.

(iii) The Tribunals of First Instance: In each governorate there are one or more Tribunals of First Instance, each of which is divided into several Chambers for criminal and civil litigations. Each Chamber is composed of: (a) a presiding judge, and (b) two sitting judges. A Tribunal of First Instance hears, as an Appellate Court, certain litigations as provided under the law.

(iv) District Tribunals: Each is a one-judge ancillary Chamber of a Tribunal of First Instance, having jurisdiction over minor civil and criminal litigations in smaller districts within the jurisdiction of such Tribunal of First Instance.

EGYPT

PUBLIC PROSECUTION

Public prosecution is headed by the Attorney General, assisted by a number of Senior Deputy and Deputy Attorneys General, and a sufficient number of chief prosecutors, prosecutors and assistant prosecutors. Public prosecution is represented at all levels of the Courts of General Jurisdiction in all criminal litigations and also in certain civil litigations as required by the law. Public prosecution controls and supervises enforcement of criminal law judgments.

Attorney General: GAMAL SHOMAN.
Prosecutor-General: MUHAMMAD ABD AL-AZIZ EL-GINDI.

ADMINISTRATIVE COURTS SYSTEM (CONSEIL D'ETAT)

The Administrative Courts have jurisdiction over litigations involving the State or any of its governmental agencies. The Administrative Courts system is divided into two courts: the Administrative Courts and the Judicial Administrative Courts, at the top of which is the High Administrative Court. The Administrative Prosecutor investigates administrative crimes committed by government officials and civil servants.

President of Conseil d'Etat: Hon. MUHAMMAD HILAL QASIM.
Administrative Prosecutor: Hon. RIFA'AT KHAFAGI.

THE STATE COUNCIL

The State Council is an independent judicial body which has the authority to make decisions in administrative disputes and disciplinary cases within the judicial system.

THE SUPREME JUDICIAL COUNCIL

The Supreme Judicial Council was reinstituted in 1984, having been abolished in 1969. It exists to guarantee the independence of the judicial system from outside interference and is consulted with regard to draft laws organizing the affairs of the judicial bodies.

Religion

About 90% of Egyptians are Muslims, and almost all of these follow Sunni tenets. According to government figures from 1986, there are about 2m. Copts (a figure contested by Coptic sources, whose estimates range between 6m. and 7m.), forming the largest religious minority, and about 1m. members of other Christian groups. There is also a small Jewish minority.

ISLAM

Grand Sheikh of al-Azhar: Sheikh JAD AL-HAQ ALI JAD AL-HAQ.
Grand Mufti of Egypt: Dr MUHAMMAD SAYED ATTIYAH TANTAWI.

CHRISTIANITY

Orthodox Churches

Coptic Orthodox Church: St Mark Cathedral, Anba Ruess, 222 Ramses St, Abbasiya, POB 9035, Cairo; telex 23281; fax (02) 2825983; f. AD 61; Leader Pope SHENOUDA III; c. 10m. followers in Egypt, Sudan, other African countries, the USA, Canada, Australia, Europe and the Middle East. In September 1981 Pope Shenouda was banished to a monastery by President Sadat, and a committee of five bishops was appointed to administer the Church. This decree was rescinded in April 1982, and the Church's synod was summoned to elect a new pope. However, Pope Shenouda was released from internal exile by President Mubarak and permitted to resume his duties in January 1985.

Greek Orthodox Patriarchate: POB 2006, Alexandria; tel. (03) 36839; f. AD 64; Pope and Patriarch of Alexandria and All Africa His Beatitude PARTHENIOS III; 350,000 mems.

The Roman Catholic Church

Armenian Rite

The Armenian Catholic diocese of Alexandria, with an estimated 1,500 adherents at 31 December 1988, is suffragan to the Patriarchate of Cilicia. The Patriarch is resident in Beirut, Lebanon.

Bishop of Alexandria: RAPHAËL BAYAN, Patriarcat Arménien Catholique, 36 Sharia Muhammad Sabri Abou Alam, Cairo; tel. (02) 3938429.

Chaldean Rite

The Chaldean Catholic diocese of Cairo had an estimated 500 adherents at 31 December 1988.

Bishop of Cairo: YOUSSEF IBRAHIM SARRAF, Evêché Chaldéen Sanctuaire Notre Dame de Fatima, 141 Sharia Nouzha, 11361 Heliopolis, Cairo; tel. (02) 2455718.

Coptic Rite

Egypt comprises the Coptic Catholic Patriarchate of Alexandria and five dioceses. At 31 December 1988 there were an estimated 152,584 adherents in the country.

Patriarch of Alexandria: His Beatitude STEPHANOS II (ANDREAS GHATTAS), Patriarcat Copte Catholique, POB 69, 34 Sharia Ibn Sandar, Koubbeh Bridge, Cairo; tel. (02) 2571740.

Latin Rite

Egypt comprises the Apostolic Vicariate of Alexandria (incorporating Heliopolis and Port Said), containing an estimated 8,126 adherents at 31 December 1988.

Vicar Apostolic: Fr EGIDIO SAMPIERI (Titular Bishop of Ida in Mauretania), 10 Sharia Sidi Metwalli, Alexandria; tel. (03) 4836065; also at 2 Sharia Banque Misr, Cairo, and at 30 Sharia Ibrahim, Port Said.

Maronite Rite

The Maronite diocese of Cairo had an estimated 4,350 adherents at 31 December 1988.

Bishop of Cairo: JOSEPH DARGHAM, Evêché Maronite, 15 Sharia Hamdi, Daher, Cairo; tel. (02) 923327.

Melkite Rite

His Beatitude MAXIMOS V HAKIM (resident in Damascus, Syria) is the Greek-Melkite Patriarch of Antioch, of Alexandria and of Jerusalem.

Patriarchal Vicariate of Egypt and Sudan: Patriarcat Grec-Melkite Catholique, 16 Sharia Daher, Cairo; tel. (02) 905790; 8,000 adherents (31 December 1988); Vicar Patriarchal Mgr PAUL ANTAKI, Titular Archbishop of Nubia.

Syrian Rite

The Syrian Catholic diocese of Cairo had an estimated 2,000 adherents at 31 December 1988.

Bishop of Cairo: BASILE MOUSSA DAOUD, Evêché Syrien Catholique, 46 Sharia Daher, Cairo; tel. (02) 901234.

The Anglican Communion

The Anglican diocese of Egypt, suspended in 1958, was revived in 1974 and became part of the Episcopal Church in Jerusalem and the Middle East, formally inaugurated in January 1976. The Church has four dioceses, and its President is the Bishop in Jerusalem (see the chapter on Israel). The Bishop in Egypt has jurisdiction also over the Anglican chaplaincies in Algeria, Djibouti, Ethiopia, Libya, Somalia and Tunisia.

Bishop in Egypt: Rt Rev. GHAIS ABD AL-MALIK, Diocesan Office, POB 87, Zamalek, Cairo.

Other Christian Churches

Armenian Apostolic Church: 179 ave Ramses, Cairo, POB 48-Faggalah; tel. 901385; Archbishop ZAVEN CHINCHINIAN; 10,000 mems.

Protestant Churches of Egypt: POB 1304, Cairo; tel. (02) 904995; f. 1854, independent since 1926; 200,000 mems (1985); Gen. Sec. Rev. Dr SAMUEL HABIB.

Other denominations active in Egypt include the Coptic Evangelical Church (Synod of the Nile) and the Union of the Armenian Evangelical Churches in the Near East.

JUDAISM

The 1976 census recorded 1,631 Jews in Egypt.

Jewish Community: Office of the Chief Rabbi, Rabbi HAIM DOUEK, 13 Sharia Sebil el-Khazindar, Abbassia, Cairo.

The Press

Despite a fairly high illiteracy rate in Egypt, the country's press is well developed. Cairo is the biggest publishing centre in the Middle East and Africa.

Legally all newspapers and magazines come under the guidance of the Supreme Press Council. The four major publishing houses of al-Ahram, Dar al-Hilal, Dar Akhbar al-Yawm and Dar al-Tahrir, operate as separate entities and compete with each other commercially. Dar al-Hilal is concerned only with magazines and publishes *Al-Musawar*, *Hawa'a* and *Al-Kawakeb*. Dar Akhbar al-Yawm publishes the daily newspaper *Al-Akhbar*, the weekly newspaper *Akhbar al-Yawm* and the weekly magazine *Akher Saa*.

Dar at-Tahrir publishes the daily *Al-Gomhouriya*, the daily English language paper *Egyptian Gazette*, the daily French newspaper *Le Progrès Egyptien* and the afternoon paper *Al-Misaa'*.

The most authoritative daily newspaper is the very long-established *Al-Ahram*. Other popular large circulation magazines are *Rose al-Yousuf*, *Sabah al-Kheir* and *Al-Iza'a wat-Television*.

EGYPT

In May 1975 President Sadat established the Supreme Press Council, under the chairmanship of the First Secretary of the Arab Socialist Union, to supervise the press.

In November 1978 President Sadat abolished the Ministry of Culture and Information, but major papers remained under government ownership. A Press Law of July 1980 liberalized the organization of the major papers and, while continuing to provide for 49% ownership by the employees, arranged for the transfer of the remaining 51% from the defunct Arab Socialist Union to the new Shura (Advisory) Council. The editorial board of a national newspaper should consist of at least five members, headed by an editor-in-chief who is selected by the Shura Council. In June 1984 the Shura Council approved a proposal made by the Supreme Press Council that the posts of chairman of the board and editor-in-chief be held separately and not by one individual.

DAILIES

Alexandria

Bareed ach-Charikat (Companies' Post): POB 813, Alexandria; f. 1952; Arabic; evening; commerce, finance, insurance and marine affairs, etc.; Editor S. BENEDUCCI; circ. 15,000.

Al-Ittihad al-Misri (Egyptian Unity): 13 Sharia Sidi Abd ar-Razzak, Alexandria; f. 1871; Arabic; evening; Propr ANWAR MAHER FARAG; Dir HASSAN MAHER FARAG.

Le Journal d'Alexandrie: 1 Sharia Rolo, Alexandria; French; evening; Editor CHARLES ARCACHE.

La Réforme: 8 passage Sherif, Alexandria; f. 1895; French; noon; Propr Comte AZIZ DE SAAB; circ. 7,000.

As-Safeer (The Ambassador): 4 Sharia as-Sahafa, Alexandria; f. 1924; Arabic; evening; Editor MUSTAFA SHARAF.

Tachydromos-Egyptos: 4 Sharia Zangarol, Alexandria; tel. 35650; f. 1879; Greek; morning; liberal; Publr PENY COUTSOUMIS; Editor DINOS COUTSOUMIS; circ. 2,000.

Cairo

Al-Ahram (The Pyramids): Sharia al-Galaa, Cairo; tel. (02) 745666; telex 92002; f. 1875; Arabic; morning, incl. Sundays (international edition published in London, England; North American edition published in New York, USA); Editor and Chair. IBRAHIM NAFEH; circ. 900,000 (weekdays), 1.1m. (Friday).

Al-Akhbar (The News): Dar Akhbar al-Yawm, Sharia as-Sahafa, Cairo; tel. (02) 758888; telex 92215; f. 1952; Arabic; Chair. and Chief Editor SAID SONBUL; circ. 789,268.

Arev: 3 Sharia Soliman Halaby, Cairo; tel. 754703; f. 1915; Armenian; evening; official organ of the Armenian Liberal Democratic Party; Editor AVEDIS YAPOUDJIAN.

Egyptian Gazette: 24–26 Sharia Zakaria Ahmad, Cairo; tel. (02) 751511; telex 92475; f. 1880; English; morning; Editor-in-Chief MOHAMED EL-EZABI; circ. 35,000.

Al-Gomhouriya (The Republic): 24 Sharia Zakaria Ahmad, Cairo; tel. (02) 751511; telex 92475; f. 1953; Arabic; morning; Chair. SAMIR RAGAB; Editor MAHFOUZ AL-ANSARI; circ. 650,000.

Journal d'Egypte, Le: 1 Sharia Borsa Guédida, Cairo; f. 1936; French; morning; Gen. Man. LITA GALLAD; Editor-in-Chief MUHAMMAD RACHAD; circ. 72,000.

Mayo (May): Sharia al-Galaa, Cairo; organ of National Democratic Party; Supervisor MUHAMMAD SAFWAT ASH-SHARIF; Chair. ABDULLAH ABD AL-BARY; Chief Editor ANIS MANSOUR; circ. 500,000.

Al-Misaa' (The Evening): 24 Sharia Zakaria Ahmad, Cairo; telex 92475; f. 1956; Arabic; evening; Editor-in-Chief SAMIR RAGAB; circ. 105,000.

Misr (Egypt): Cairo; f. 1977; organ of the Arab Socialist Party.

Phos: 14 Sharia Zakaria Ahmad, Cairo; f. 1896; Greek; morning; Editor S. PATERAS; Man. BASILE A. PATERAS; circ. 20,000.

Le Progrès Egyptien: 24 Sharia Zakaria Ahmad, Cairo; tel. (02) 741611; telex 92475; f. 1890; French; morning including Sundays; Editor-in-Chief KHALED ANWAR BAKIR; circ. 21,000.

PERIODICALS

Alexandria

Al-Ahad al-Gedid (New Sunday): 88 Sharia Said M. Koraim, Alexandria; tel. 807874; f. 1936; Editor-in-Chief and Publr GALAL M. KORAITEM; circ. 60,000.

Alexandria Medical Journal: 4 G. Carducci, Alexandria; f. 1922; English, French and Arabic; quarterly; publ. by Alexandria Medical Asscn; Editor AMIN RIDA; circ. 1,500.

Amitié Internationale: 59 avenue Hourriya, Alexandria; tel. 23639; f. 1957; publ. by Asscn Egyptienne d'Amitié Internationale; Arabic and French; quarterly; Editor Dr ZAKI BADAOUI.

L'Annuaire des Sociétés Egyptiennes par Actions: 23 Midan Tahrir, Alexandria; f. 1930; annually in December; French; Propr ELIE I. POLITI; Editor OMAR ES-SAYED MOURSI.

L'Echo Sportif: 7 Sharia de l'Archevêché, Alexandria; French; weekly; Propr MICHEL BITTAR.

L'Economiste Egyptien: 11 Sharia de la Poste, Alexandria, POB 847; f. 1901; weekly; Proprs MARGUERITE and JOFFRE HOSNI.

Egypte-Sports-Cinéma: 7 avenue Hourriya, Alexandria; French; weekly; Editor EMILE ASSAAD.

Egyptian Cotton Gazette: POB 433, Alexandria; organ of the Cotton Exporters Association; English; 2 a year; Chief Editor AHMAD H. YOUSSEF.

Egyptian Cotton Statistics: Alexandria; English; weekly.

Egyptian Customs Magazine: 2 Sharia Sinan, Alexandria; deals with invoicing, receipts, etc.; Man. MUHAMMAD ALI EL-BADAWI.

La Gazette d'Orient: 5 Sharia Borsa Guédida, Alexandria; Propr MAURICE BETITO.

Guide des Industries: 2 Sharia Adib, Alexandria; French; annual; Editor SIMON A. BARANIS.

Informateur des Assurances: 1 Sharia Sinan, Alexandria; f. 1936; French; monthly; Propr ELIE I. POLITI; Editor SIMON A. BARANIS.

Répertoire Permanent de Législation Egyptienne: 27 Tariq el-Gaish, Chatby-les-Bains, Alexandria; f. 1932; French and Arabic; Editor V. SISTO.

Sina 'at en-Nassig (L'Industrie Textile): 5 rue de l'Archevêché, Alexandria; Arabic and French; monthly; Editor PHILIPPE COLAS.

Voce d'Italia: 90 Sharia Farahde, Alexandria; Italian; fortnightly; Editor R. AVELLINO.

Cairo

Al-Ahali (The People): 23 Sharia Abd al-Khalek, Tharwat, Cairo; tel. (02) 759114; weekly; published by the National Progressive Unionist Party; Chair. LOTFI WAKID; Editor-in-Chief MAHMOUD AL-MARAGI.

Al-Ahram al-Iqtisadi (The Economic Al-Ahram): Sharia al-Galaa, Cairo; telex 20185; fax (02) 745888; Arabic; weekly; economic and political affairs; owned by Al-Ahram publrs; Chief Editor ISSAM RIFA'AT; circ. 67,000.

Al-Ahrar (The Liberals): Cairo; f. 1977; weekly; published by Liberal Socialist Party; Editor WAHID GHAZI.

Akhbar al-Yaum (Daily News): 6 Sharia as-Sahafa, Cairo; f. 1944; Arabic; weekly (Saturday); Chair. SAID SONBUL; Editor-in-Chief IBRAHIM ABU SADAH; circ. 1,087,177.

Akher Sa'a (Last Hour): Dar Akhbar al-Yawm, Sharia as-Sahafa, Cairo; telex 92215; f. 1934; Arabic; weekly (Wednesday); independent; Editor-in-Chief MUHAMMAD WAJDI KANDIL; circ. 97,832.

Al-Azhar: Idarat al-Azhar, Sharia al-Azhar, Cairo; f. 1931; Arabic; Islamic monthly; supervised by the Egyptian Council for Islamic Research of Al-Azhar University; Dir MUHAMMAD FARID WAGDI.

Al-Bitrul (Petroleum): Cairo; monthly; published by the Egyptian General Petroleum Corporation.

Contemporary Thought: University of Cairo, Cairo; quarterly; Editor Dr Z. N. MAHMOUD.

Ad-Da'wa (The Call): Cairo; Arabic; monthly; organ of the Muslim Brotherhood.

Ad-Doctor: 8 Sharia Hoda Shaarawy, Cairo; f. 1947; Arabic; monthly; Editor Dr AHMAD M. KAMAL; circ. 30,000.

Echos: 1–5 Sharia Mahmoud Bassiouni, Cairo; f. 1947; French; weekly; Dir and Propr GEORGES QRFALI.

The Egyptian Mail: 24–26 Sharia Zakaria Ahmad; telex 92475; weekly; Saturday edition of The Egyptian Gazette; English; circ. 35,000.

Al-Fusoul (The Seasons): 17 Sharia Sherif Pasha, Cairo; Arabic; monthly; Propr and Chief Editor MUHAMMAD ZAKI ABD AL-KADER.

Al-Garidat at-Tigariyat al-Misriya (The Egyptian Business Paper): 25 Sharia Nubar Pasha, Cairo; f. 1921; Arabic; weekly; circ. 7,000.

Hawa'a (Eve): Dar al-Hilal, 16 Sharia Muhammad Ezz el-Arab, Cairo; telex 92703; women's magazine; Arabic; weekly; Chief Editor SUAD AHMAD HILMI; circ. 160,837.

Al-Hilal Magazine: Dar al-Hilal, 16 Sharia Muhammad Ezz el-Arab, Cairo; telex 92703; f. 1895; Arabic; literary monthly; Editor Dr HUSSAIN MONES.

Industrial Egypt: POB 251, 26A Sharia Sherif Pasha, Cairo; tel. (02) 3928317; telex 92624; fax (02) 3928075; f. 1924; quarterly bulletin and year book of the Federation of Egyptian Industries in English and Arabic; Editor DARWISH M. DARWISH.

Informateur Financier et Commercial: 24 Sharia Soliman Pasha, Cairo; f. 1929; weekly; Dir HENRI POLITI; circ. 15,000.

EGYPT — Directory

Al-Iza'a wat-Television (Radio and Television): 13 Sharia Muhammad Ezz el-Arab, Cairo; f. 1935; Arabic; weekly; Editor and Chair. SAKEENA FOUAD; circ. 80,000.

Al-Kerazeh (The Sermon): Cairo; Arabic; weekly newspaper of the Coptic Orthodox Church.

Al-Kawakeb (The Stars): Dar al-Hilal, 16 Sharia Muhammad Ezz el-Arab, Cairo; tel. (02) 27954; f. 1952; Arabic; weekly; film magazine; Editor HOSN SHAH; circ. 86,381.

Kitab al-Hilal: Dar al-Hilal, 16 Sharia Muhammad Ezz el-Arab, Cairo; monthly; Founders EMILE and SHOUKRI ZEIDAN; Editor MOUSTAFA NABIL.

Al-Liwa' al-Islami (Islamic Standard): 11 Sharia Sherif Pasha, Cairo; f. 1982; Arabic; weekly; government paper to promote official view of Islamic revivalism; Propr AHMAD HAMZA; Editor MUHAMMAD ALI SHETA; circ. 30,000.

Lotus Magazine (Afro-Asian Writings): 104 Sharia Qasr el-Eini, Cairo; f. 1968; quarterly; English, French and Arabic.

Magallat al-Mohandeseen (The Engineer's Magazine): 28 avenue Ramses, Cairo; f. 1945; published by The Engineers' Syndicate; Arabic and English; 10 a year; Editor and Sec. MAHMOUD SAMI ABD AL-KAWI.

Al-Magallat az-Zira'ia (The Agricultural Magazine): Cairo; monthly; agriculture; circ. 30,000.

Medical Journal of Cairo University: Manyal University Hospital, Sharia Qasr el-Eini, Cairo; f. 1933; Kasr el-Eini Clinical Society; English; quarterly.

The Middle East Observer: 8 Sharia Chawarby, Cairo; f. 1954; English; weekly; specializing in economics of Middle East and African markets; also publishes supplements on law, foreign trade and tenders; Man. Owner AHMAD FODA; Chief Editor AHMAD SABRI; circ. 30,000.

Al-Musawar: Dar al-Hilal, 16 Sharia Muhammad Ezz el-Arab, Cairo; tel. (02) 27954; telex 92703; f. 1924; Arabic; weekly; Editor-in-Chief MAKRAM MUHAMMAD AHMAD; circ. 130,423.

October: 1119 Sharia Corniche en-Nil, Cairo; tel. (02) 746834; telex 847031; monthly; Chair. and Editor-in-Chief SALAH MONTASSIR; circ. 140,500.

Al-Omal (The Workers): 90 Sharia Galal, Cairo; telex 93255; published by the Egyptian Trade Union Federation: Arabic; weekly; Chief Editor AHMAD HARA.

Progrès Dimanche: 24 Sharia Galal, Cairo; tel. 741611; telex 92475; French; weekly; Sunday edition of Le Progrès Egyptien; Editor-in-Chief KHALED ANWAR BAKIR.

Riwayat al-Hilal: Dar al-Hilal, 16 Sharia Muhammad Ezz el-Arab, Cairo; Arabic; monthly; Editor Dr HUSSAIN MONES.

Rose al-Yousuf: 89A Sharia Qasr el-Eini, Cairo; f. 1925; Arabic; weekly; political; circulates throughout all Arab countries; Chair. of Board and Editor MUHAMMAD TUHAMI; circ. 35,000.

As-Sabah (The Morning): 4 Sharia Muhammad Said Pasha, Cairo; f. 1922; Arabic; weekly; Editor MUSTAFA EL-KACHACHI.

Sabah al-Kheir (Good Morning): 18 Sharia Muhammad Said Pasha, Cairo; Arabic; weekly; light entertainment; Chief Editor MOFEED FAWZI; circ. 70,000.

Ash-Shaab (The People): Sharia Corniche en-Nil, Cairo; organ of Socialist Labour Party; weekly; Editor-in-Chief ADEL HUSSEIN; circ. 50,000.

At-Tahrir (Liberation): 5 Sharia Naguib, Rihani, Cairo; Arabic; weekly; Editor ABD AL-AZIZ SADEK.

At-Taqaddum (Progress): c/o 1 Sharia Jarim ed-Dawlah, Cairo; f. 1978; organ of National Progressive Unionist Party.

Tchehreh Nema: 14 Sharia Hassan el-Akbar (Abdine), Cairo; f. 1904; Iranian; monthly; political, literary and general; Editor MANUCHEHR TCHEHREH NEMA MOADEB ZADEH.

Up-to-Date International Industry: 10 Sharia Galal, Cairo; Arabic and English; monthly; foreign trade journal.

Al-Wafd: Cairo; f. 1984; weekly; organ of the New Wafd Party; Editor-in-Chief GAMAL BADAWI; circ. 360,000.

Watani (My Country): Cairo; French; weekly newspaper of the Coptic Orthodox Church; Editor MEGUID ATTAIA.

Yulio (July): July Press and Publishing House, Cairo; f. 1986; weekly; Nasserist; Editor ABDULLAH IMAM; and a monthly cultural magazine, Editor MAHMOUD AL-MARAGHI.

NEWS AGENCIES

Middle East News Agency: 4 Sharia Hoda Sharawi, Cairo; tel. (02) 3935000; telex 92252; fax (02) 3935055; f. 1955; regular service in Arabic, English and French; Chair. and Editor-in-Chief MUSTAFA NAGUIB.

Foreign Bureaux

Agence France-Presse (AFP): 33 Sharia Qasr en-Nil, Apt 12-06, Cairo; tel. (02) 3921044; telex 92225; fax (02) 3925673; Correspondent MICHEL TRICHET.

Agencia EFE (Spain): 35a Sharia Abul Feda, 4th Floor, Apt 14, Cairo (Zamalek); Correspondent JOSÉ LUIS VIDAL COY.

Agenzia Nazionale Stampa Associata (ANSA) (Italy): 19 Sharia Abd al-Khalek Sarwat, Cairo; tel. (02) 3929821; telex 93365; Chief VITTORIO FRENQUELLUCCI.

Allgemeiner Deutscher Nachrichtendienst (ADN) (Germany): 17 Sharia el-Brazil, Apt 59, Cairo (Zamalek); tel. (02) 3404006; telex 92339; Correspondent RALF SCHULTZE.

Associated Press (AP) (USA): 33 Sharia Qasr en-Nil, POB 1077, Cairo; tel. (02) 3936096; telex 92211; Chief WILLIAM C. MANN.

Bulgarska Telegrafna Agentsia (BTA) (Bulgaria): 13 Sharia Muhammad Kamel Morsi, Aguza, Cairo; Chief DIMITER MASLAROV.

Československá Tisková Kancelář (CTK) (Czechoslovakia): 28 Abu el-Fittah Bldgs, Pyramids St, Cairo; telex 20987.

Deutsche Presse-Agentur (dpa) (Germany): 33 Sharia Qasr en-Nil, Apt 13/4, Cairo; tel. (02) 3928019; telex 92054; Chief Dr JUNG FISCHER.

Jiji Tsushin-Sha (Japan): Room 12, 5th Floor, 3 Gezira el-Wosta, Cairo (Zamalek); tel. (02) 3401443; telex 20940; fax (02) 3405244; Correspondent TOSHIYA HATANO.

Kyodo News Service (Japan): Flat 2, 9 Sharia el-Kamel Muhammad, Zamalek, Cairo; tel. (02) 3411571; telex 20435; fax (02) 3406105; Correspondent KENICHIRO HAYASHI.

Magyar Távirati Iroda (MTI) (Hungary): 11 Sharia Ahmad Heshmat, Flat 15, Cairo (Zamalek); Chief KÁROLY PATAK.

Reuters (United Kingdom): 21st Floor, Bank Misr Tower, 153 Sharia Muhammad Farid, Cairo, POB 2040; tel. (02) 3925667; telex 92210; Chief Correspondent J. ROGERS.

Telegrafnoye Agentstvo Sovetskovo Soyuza (TASS) (USSR): 30 Sharia Muhammad Mazhar, Cairo (Zamalek); tel. 3419784; telex 93008; fax (02) 3417268; Dir MIKHAIL I. KROUTIKHIN.

United Press International (UPI) (USA): 4 Sharia Eloui, POB 872, Cairo.

Xinhua (New China) News Agency (People's Republic of China): 2 Moussa Galal Sq., Mohandessin, Cairo; tel. (02) 3448950; telex 93812.

The Iraqi News Agency (INA) reopened its office in Cairo in October 1985.

Publishers

General Egyptian Book Organization: 117 Sharia Corniche en-Nil, Cairo; tel. (02) 775000; telex 93932; f. 1961; affil. to Min. of Culture; Chair. Dr SAMIR SARHAN.

Alexandria

Alexandria University Press: Shatby, Alexandria.

Artec: 10 Sharia Stamboul, Alexandria.

Dar Nashr ath-Thaqata: Alexandria.

Egyptian Book Centre: A. D. Christodoulou and Co, 5 Sharia Adib, Alexandria; f. 1950.

Egyptian Printing and Publishing House: Ahmad es-Sayed Marouf, 59 Safia Zaghoul, Alexandria; f. 1947.

Maison Egyptienne d'Editions: Ahmad es-Sayed Marouf, Sharia Adib, Alexandria; f. 1950.

Maktab al-Misri al-Hadith li-t-Tiba wan-Nashr: 7 Sharia Noubar, Alexandria; also at 2 Sharia Sherif, Cairo; Man. AHMAD YEHIA.

Cairo

Al-Ahram Establishment: Sharia al-Galaa, Cairo; tel. (02) 758333; telex 92001; fax 745888; f. 1875; publishes newspapers, magazines and books, incl. Al-Ahram; Chair. IBRAHIM NAFEA.

Akhbar al-Yawm Publishing House: 6 Sharia as-Sahafa, Cairo; f. 1944; publishes Al-Akhbar (daily), Akhbar al-Yawm (weekly), and colour magazine Akher Sa'a; Pres. MOUSA SABRI; Dir-Gen. AMIN ADLY.

Al-Arab Publishing House: 28 Sharia Faggalah, 11271 Cairo; tel. (02) 908025; fax 771140; f. 1900; fiction, poetry, history, biography, philosophy, Arabic language, literature, politics, etc.; Man. Dir Dr SALADIN BOUSTANY.

Argus Press: 10 Sharia Zakaria Ahmad, Cairo; Owners KARNIG HAGOPIAN and ABD AL-MEGUID MUHAMMAD.

Dar al-Gomhouriya: 24 Sharia Zakaria Ahmad, Cairo; affiliate of At-Tahrir Printing and Publishing House; publications include

EGYPT

the dailies, *Al-Gomhouriya, Al-Misaa', Egyptian Gazette* and *Le Progrès Egyptien*; Pres. MOHSEN MUHAMMAD.

Dar al-Hilal Publishing Institution: 16 Sharia Muhammad Ezz el-Arab, Cairo; tel. (02) 20610; f. 1892; publishes *Al-Hilal, Riwayat al-Hilal, Kitab al-Hilal, Tabibak al-Khass* (monthlies); *Al-Mussawar, Al-Kawakeb, Hawaa, Samir, Mickey* (weeklies); Chair. MAKRAN MUHAMMAD AHMAD.

Dar al-Kitab al-Arabi: Misr Printing House, Sharia Noubar, Bab al-Louk, Cairo; f. 1968; Man. Dir Dr SAHAIR AL-KALAMAWI.

Dar al-Kitab al-Masri: 33 Sharia Kasr en-Nil, POB 156, Cairo; tel. (02) 3922168; telex 22481; fax (02) 3924657; f. 1929; religion, history, geography, poetry, philosophy, science, etc.; Man. Dir HASSAN EL-ZEIN.

Dar al-Maaref: 1119 Sharia Corniche en-Nil, Cairo; tel. (02) 777077; telex 92199; fax (02) 744999; f. 1890; publishing, printing and distribution of all kinds of books in Arabic and other languages; publishers of *October* magazine; Chair. and Man. Dir SALAH MUNTASSAR.

Dar an-Nashr (formerly Les Editions Universitaires d'Egypte): 41 Sharia Sherif Pasha, Cairo; tel. (02) 393451º, university textbooks, academic works, encyclopaedia.

Dar ash-Shorouk: 16 Sharia Gawad Hosni, Cairo; tel. (02) 774814; telex 93091; f. 1968; publishing, printing and distribution; publishers of books on modern Islamic politics, philosophy and art, and books for children; Chair. M. I. EL-MOALLIM.

Documentation and Research Centre for Education (Ministry of Education): 33 Sharia Falaky, Cairo; f. 1956; bibliographies, directories, information and education bulletins; Dir Mrs ZEINAB M. MEHREZ.

Editions Horus: 1 Midan Soliman Pasha, Cairo.

Editions le Progrès: 6 Sharia Sherif Pasha, Cairo; Propr WADI SHOUKRI.

Egyptian Co for Printing and Publishing: 40 Sharia Noubar, Cairo; tel. (02) 21310; Chair. MUHAMMAD MAHMOUD HAMED.

Higher University Council for Arts, Letters and Sciences: University of Cairo, Cairo.

Lagnat at-Taalif wat-Targama wan-Nashr (Committee for Writing, Translating and Publishing Books): 9 Sharia el-Kerdassi (Abdine), Cairo.

Librairie La Renaissance d'Egypte (Hassan Muhammad & Sons): 9 Sharia Adly, POB 2172, Cairo; f. 1930; religion, history, geography, medicine, architecture, economics, politics, law, philosophy, psychology, children's books, atlases, dictionaries; Man HASSAN MUHAMMAD.

Maktabet Misr: POB 16, 3 Sharia Kamal Sidki, Cairo; tel. (02) 908920; f. 1932; publs wide variety of fiction, biographies and textbooks for schools and universities; Man. AMIR SAID GOUDA ES-SAHHAR.

Muhammad Abbas Sid Ahmad: 55 Sharia Noubar, Cairo.

National Library Press (Dar al-Kutub): Midan Ahmad Maher, Cairo; bibliographic works.

New Publications: J. Meshaka and Co, 5 Sharia Maspiro, Cairo.

The Public Organization for Books and Scientific Appliances: Cairo University, Orman, Ghiza, Cairo; f. 1965; state organization publishing academic books for universities, higher institutes, etc.; also imports books, periodicals and scientific appliances; Chair. KAMIL SEDDIK; Vice-Chair. FATHY LABIB.

Senouhy Publishers: 54 Sharia Abd al-Khalek Sarwat, Cairo; f. 1956; Dirs LEILA A. FADEL, OMAR RASHAD.

At-Tahrir Printing and Publishing House: 24 Sharia Zakaria Ahmad, Cairo; tel. (02) 751511; telex 92475; f. 1953; affil. to Shura (Advisory) Council; Chair. MOHSEN MUHAMMAD; Man. Dir ABD AL-HAMID HAMROUSH.

Radio and Television

In 1987 there were an estimated 15.5m. radio receivers and 4.15m. television receivers in use.

RADIO

Egyptian Radio and Television Corporation (ERTV): Radio and TV Building, Sharia Maspiro, Corniche en-Nil, POB 1186, Cairo; tel. (02) 757155; telex 92152; f. 1928; 300 hours daily. Home Service radio programmes in Arabic, English, French, Armenian, German, Greek, Italian and Hebrew; foreign services in Arabic, English, French, Swahili, Hausa, Bengali, Urdu, German, Spanish, Indonesian, Malay, Thai, Hindi, Pushtu, Persian, Turkish, Somali, Portuguese, Fulani, Italian, Zulu, Shona, Sindebele, Lingala, Afar, Amharic, Yoruba, Wolof, Bambara; Pres. HUSSEIN ENAN.

Directory

Middle East Radio: Société Egyptienne de Publicité, 24-26 Sharia Zakaria Ahmad, Cairo; f. 1964; commercial service with 500-kW transmitter; UK Agents: Radio and Television Services (Middle East) Ltd, 21 Hertford St, London, W1.

TELEVISION

Egyptian Television Organization: Radio and TV Bldg, Sharia Maspiro, Corniche en-Nil, POB 1186, Cairo; tel. (02) 757155; telex 92152; f. 1960; 22.5 hours daily (three channels); Pres. Mrs SAMIA SADIQ.

Finance

(cap. = capital; auth. = authorized; p.u. = paid up; dep. = deposits; res = reserves; m. = million; brs = branches; amounts in £ Egyptian unless otherwise stated)

BANKING

The whole banking system was nationalized in 1961. Since 1974 foreign and private sector banks have been allowed to play a role in the economy, and about 72 joint-venture banks, branches of foreign banks and private banks have been established. More than 200 financial institutions are now operating in Egypt.

Central Bank

Central Bank of Egypt: 31 Sharia Qasr en-Nil, Cairo; tel. (02) 3931688; telex 92237; f. 1961; state-owned; cap. 5.0m., dep. 21,506.8m., res 708.7m., total assets 22,707.1m. (June 1989); Gov. and Chair. Dr MAHMOUD SALAH ED-DIN HAMID; 3 brs.

Commercial and Specialized Banks

Agricultural Bank: there are 17 Agricultural Banks in governorates throughout Egypt.

Alexandria Commercial and Maritime Bank: POB 2376, 85 avenue el-Hourriya, Alexandria 21519; tel. (03) 4921556; telex 54553; f. 1981; cap. 32,078.3m., dep. 286.5m., total assets 467.2m. (Dec. 1989); Chair. ADEL GHALEB MAHMOUD; Man. Dir MUHAMMAD MAHMOUD FAHMY.

Bank of Alexandria, SAE: 6 Sharia Salah Salem, Alexandria; and 49 Sharia Kasr en-Nil, Cairo; tel. (03) 4836073 (Alexandria), (02) 3913822 (Cairo); telex 54107 (Alexandria), 92069 (Cairo); f. 1957; state-owned; cap. p.u. 85m., total assets 6,700.7m. (Dec. 1989); Chair. ABD AL-GHANI GAMEH; 91 brs.

Bank of Commerce and Development: POB 1373, 13 Midan 26 July Sq., Sphinx, Mohandessin, Cairo; tel. (02) 3479461; telex 21607; fax (02) 3450581; f. 1980; cap. 100m., dep. 318.7m., total assets 426.7m. (Dec. 1988); Chair. and Man. Dir SAMIR MUHAMMAD FOUAD EL-QASRI; 6 brs.

Banque du Caire, SAE: 30 Roushdy St, POB 1495, Cairo; tel. (02) 3904554; telex 92022; f. 1952; state-owned; cap. p.u. 782m., dep. 6,548m., total assets 7,763m. (Dec. 1989); Chair. MAHMOUD HASSAN ALI ABDALLA; 143 brs.

Banque Misr: 151 Sharia Muhammad Farid, Cairo; tel. (02) 3912711; telex 92242; fax 3919779; f. 1920; state-owned since 1960; cap. 100m., dep. 12,809.4m. (June 1989); Chair. MAHMOUD MUHAMMAD MAHMOUD; 300 brs.

Crédit Foncier Egyptien: 11 Sharia el-Mashadi, POB 141, Cairo; tel. (02) 910197; telex 93863; f. 1880; state-owned; cap. p.u. 25m.; Chair. ADEL MAHMOUD ABD AL-BAKI; Gen Man. IBRAHIM ABD AL-HALIM KHOR ED-DIN; 7 brs.

Development Industrial Bank: 110 Sharia el-Galaa, Cairo; tel. (02) 779087; telex 92643; f. 1975; cap. p.u. 34m., dep. 30m., total assets 402m. (Dec 1985); Chair. HUSSAIN MAHMOUD ES-SENNARI; 4 brs.

Egyptian Export Development Bank: Evergreen Bldg, 10 Sharia Talaat Harb, Cairo; f. 1983 to replace National Import-Export Bank; tel. (02) 777033; telex 20850; cap. p.u. 35.6m., total assets 89.2m. (Dec. 1986); Chair. Dr HAZEM EL-BEBLAWY.

Egyptian Workers Bank: 90 Sharia el-Galaa, Cairo; telex 23520; f. 1983; Workers Union has a 50% interest, Banque Misr and other Egyptians interests 50%.

Hong Kong Egyptian Bank: Abu el-Feda Bldg, 3 Sharia Abu el-Feda, POB 126 D, Zamalek, Cairo; tel. (02) 3404849; telex 22505; f. 1982; the Hongkong and Shanghai Banking Corporation has a 40% shareholding, Egyptian interests 43%, Egyptian Reinsurance Co 8%, other Arab interests 9%; cap. 16.8m., dep. 280m. res 5m., total assets 360.7m. (Dec. 1989); Chair. Dr HAMED ES-SAYEH; 2 brs.

National Bank for Development: 5 Sharia el-Borsa el-Gedida, POB 647, Cairo; tel. (02) 3923528; telex 20878; f. 1980; cap. p.u. 37.5m., dep. 948m., res 20.4m., total assets 1,203m. (Dec. 1989);

EGYPT

Chair. MUHAMMAD ALI Z. EL-ORABI; 11 brs; there are affiliated National Banks for Development in 16 governorates.

National Bank of Egypt: 24 Sharia Sherif, Cairo; tel. (02) 3924143; telex 92238; f. 1898; nationalized 1960; handles all commercial banking operations; cap. 100m., dep. 15,030m., total assets 36,190m. (June 1989); Chair. MUHAMMAD NABIL IBRAHIM; 182 brs.

Commercial International Bank (Egypt), SAE: Nile Tower Bldg, 21-23 Sharia Giza, POB 2430, Giza; tel. (02) 726132; telex 20201; fax (02) 728419; f. 1975; National Bank of Egypt has 99.997% interest; name changed 1987; cap. 50m., dep. 1,542.9m., res 213m., total assets 2,288.5m. (Dec. 1989); Exec. Chair. MAHMOUD ABD AL-AZIZ MUHAMMAD; 13 brs.

Principal Bank for Development and Agricultural Credit: 110 Sharia Qasr el-Eini, POB 11612, Cairo; tel. (02) 3551204; telex 93045; f. 1976 to succeed former Credit organizations; state-owned; cap. p.u. 55.7m., dep. 706.9m., res 77.8m, total assets 2,490.9m. (June 1986); Chair. ADEL HUSSEIN EZZI; Gen. Man. ABED AR-RAOUF DEKHEL.

Société Arabe Internationale de Banque: 56 Sharia Gamet ed-Dowal al-Arabia, POB 124, Mohandessin, Giza; tel. (02) 3499460; telex 22087; f. 1976; cap. p.u. US $16m., dep. US $145.4m., res 8.3m., total assets 207.9m. (Dec. 1988); Chair. Dr HASSAN ABBAS ZAKI; Gen. Man. HISHAM ESH-SHIATI; 4 brs.

Social Bank

Nasser Social Bank: 35 Sharia Qasr en-Nil, POB 2552, Cairo; tel. (02) 744377; telex 92754; f. 1971; state-owned; interest-free savings and investment bank for social and economic activities, participating in social insurance, specializing in financing co-operatives, craftsmen and social institutions; cap. p.u. 20m.; Chair. NASSIF TAHOON.

Multinational Banks

Arab African International Bank: 5 Midan es-Saray al-Koubra, POB 60, Garden City, Maglis esh-Shaab, 11516 Cairo; tel. (02) 3545094; telex 93531; f. 1964; auth. cap. US $500m.; cap. p.u. US $400m. (Dec. 1987); commercial investment bank; shareholders are Governments of Kuwait, Egypt, Algeria, Jordan and Qatar, Bank Al-Jazira (Saudi Arabia), Rafidain Bank (Iraq), individuals and Arab institutions; Chair. ALI R. AL-BADR; Deputy Chair. and Man. Dir MUHAMMAD ABD AL-MONEIM ROUSHDY; brs in Cairo, Alexandria, Heliopolis, Beirut, Dubai, Abu Dhabi, London (2), Nassau, and New York.

Arab International Bank: 35 Sharia Abd al-Khalek Sarwat, POB 1563, Cairo; tel. (02) 3916120; telex 92098; f. 1971 as Egyptian International Bank, renamed 1974; cap. p.u. US $165m., res US $84.5m., dep. US $1,754.6m., total assets US $2,467.3m. (June 1989); offshore bank; aims to promote trade and investment in shareholders' countries and other Arab countries; owned by Egypt, Libya, UAE, Oman, Qatar and private Arab shareholders; Chair. Dr MUSTAFA KHALIL; 3 brs in Egypt, 1 in Bahrain.

Commercial Foreign Venture Banks

Alexandria-Kuwait International Bank: 10 Sharia Talaat Harb, 4th Floor, POB 92, Maglis esh-Shaab, Cairo; tel. (02) 779766; telex 20398; f. 1978; cap. 17.9m., dep. 456.2m., res 11.5m., total assets 632.6m. (Dec. 1988); Egyptian/Kuwaiti businessmen have 48.4% interest, Bank of Alexandria 25%, Principal Bank for Development and Agric. Credit 4.5%, Egyptian cos 8.8%, UAE cos 13.3%; Chair. and Man. Dir ES-SAYED FOUAD MUHAMMAD EL-HABASHY; Gen. Man. MAMDOUH SHABRI ABOU ALAM; 5 brs.

Alwatany Bank of Egypt: 1113 Sharia Corniche en-Nil, POB 750, Cairo; tel. (02) 740705; telex 93268; f. 1980; cap. p.u. 17.5m., dep. 389.9m., res 9.6m., total assets 583.1m. (Dec. 1988); Chair. FAT'HALLAH RIFA'AT MUHAMMAD; Man. Dir TAWFIQ GAMIL YASSIN; 5 brs.

Arab Land Bank: Amir Muhammad St, POB 6729, Cairo; tel. (02) 628357; telex 21208; f. 1958; Egyptian/Jordanian joint venture; cap. p.u. 5m. (Dec. 1988); Chair. HASSOUMA HASSAN HASIB; 10 brs.

Bank of Credit and Commerce (Misr), SAE: 56-A Gameat ed-Dowal al-Arabia St, POB 788, Mohandessen Yiza; tel. (02) 3607361; telex 02679; fax (02) 3609054; f. 1981; member of BCC Group; cap. p.u. 20m., dep. 1,326m., total assets 1,800.0m. (Dec. 1989); Chair. Dr ALY ABD AL-MEGUID ABDOU; Man. Dir ARIF MAQSOOD HAMIDI; 19 brs.

Banque du Caire Barclays International, SAE: 12 Midan esh-Sheikh Yousuf, POB 10, Garden City, Cairo; tel. (02) 3549422; telex 93734; f. 1975 as Cairo Barclays Int. Bank; name changed 1983; Banque du Caire has 51%, Barclays Bank 49%; cap. 10m., dep. 471.3m., total assets 833m. (Dec. 1989); Chair. MAHMOUD HASSAN ABDALLAH; Joint Man. Dirs MUHAMMAD ABD AL-FATH ABD AL-AZIZ and DENNIS OUTRAM; 8 brs.

Banque du Caire et de Paris: 3 Sharia Latin America, Garden City, POB 2441, Cairo; tel. (02) 3548323; telex 93722; f. 1977;

Directory

Banque du Caire has 51% interest and Banque Nationale de Paris 49%; cap. p.u. 10.3m., dep. 142.5m. (Dec. 1989); Chair. MUHAMMAD ES-SABBAGH; Gen. Man. MUHAMMAD ADEL EL-FAZZARI; 3 brs.

Cairo Far East Bank: 104 Corniche en-Nil, POB 757, Cairo (Dokki); tel. (02) 710280; telex 93977; f. 1978; cap. p.u. 7m., dep. 246.3m., total assets 344.2m. (Dec. 1989); Chair. Dr AHMAD ABU ISMAIL; 2 brs.

Crédit International d'Egypte: 2 Sharia Talaat Harb, POB 831, Cairo; tel. (02) 759950; telex 93680; f. 1977; National Bank of Egypt has 51% interest, Crédit Commercial de France 39% and Berliner Handels und Frankfurter Bank 10%; cap. 7m., dep. 83.8m., res 4m., total assets 191.9m. (Dec. 1985); Chair. ABD AL-GHANI HAMID GAMEH; Gen. Man. ANIS RIZKALLAH ABD AL-MALIK.

Delta International Bank: 1113 Corniche en-Nil, POB 1159, Cairo; tel. (02) 753484; telex 93833; fax (02) 750954; f. 1978; cap. p.u. 20m., dep. 721.9m. (Dec. 1989); Chair. MAHMOUD SEDQI MOURAD; Gen. Man. IBRAHIM SHEHATA MUSTAFA; 14 brs.

Egyptian American Bank: 4 Sharia Hassan Sabri, Zamalek, POB 1825, Cairo; tel. (02) 3416150; telex 92683; f. 1976; Bank of Alexandria has 51% interest and American Express Int. Banking Corpn 49%; dep. 1,229.4m., total assets 1,760.3m. (Dec. 1988); Chair. ABD AL-GHANI GAMEH; Man. Dir ELIE S. BAROUDI; 13 brs.

Egyptian Gulf Bank: 8–10 Sharia Ahmad Nessim, POB 56, el-Orman, Giza; tel. (02) 736181; telex 20214; f. 1981; cap. p.u. 17.8m., dep. 545.9m., total assets 734.9m. (Dec. 1988); Chair. KAMAL HASSAN ALI; Gen. Man. GAMIL HUSSAM ED-DIN ABUS-SU'UD; 5 brs.

Egyptian-Saudi Finance Bank: 12 Sharia Itehad el-Mohameen el-Arab, Garden City, Cairo; tel. (02) 3547112; telex 20623; fax (02) 3555914; f. 1980 as Pyramids Bank; cap. p.u. 60.2m. (Dec. 1989); Chair. Sheikh SALEH ABDULLAH KAMEL.

Faisal Islamic Bank of Egypt: 1113 Corniche en-Nil, POB 2446, Cairo; tel. (02) 753109; telex 93877; fax (02) 777301; f. 1979; all banking operations conducted according to Islamic principles; auth. cap. US $500m., cap. p.u. US $70m., dep. US $1,389.7m. (Aug. 1989); Chair. Prince MUHAMMAD AL-FAISAL AS-SAOUD; Gov. AHMED ZANDO; 12 brs.

Misr Exterior Bank, SAE: Cairo Plaza Bldg, Corniche en-Nil, POB 272, Ataba, Cairo; tel. (02) 778380; telex 94061; f. 1981; Banco Exterior de España has 40% interest, Banque Misr 40%, Egyptian/Saudi Arabian businessmen 20%; cap. p.u. 16.1m., dep. 677.2m., res 34.2m., total assets 784.4m. (Dec. 1989); Chair. MUHAMMAD NABIL IBRAHIM; Gen. Mans and Man. Dirs ABDULLAH ABD AL-FATAH TAYEL, AURELIO OLAVARRIETA; 5 brs.

Misr International Bank, SAE: 54 Sharia al-Batal Ahmed Abd al-Aziz, Mohandessen, Cairo 12411; tel. (02) 3497091; telex 22840; fax (02) 3498072; f. 1975; cap. p.u. 27.3m., dep. 3,367m., total assets 3,892m. (Dec. 1989); Chair. MAHMOUD MUHAMMAD MAHMOUD; Vice-Chair. and Man. Dir MUHAMMAD ALI HAFEZ; 9 brs.

Misr-America International Bank: 5 Midan es-Saraya el-Kobra, POB 1003, Garden City, Cairo; tel. (02) 3554359; telex 23505; f. 1977; Banque du Caire has 33% interest, Misr Insurance Co 33%, Development Industrial Bank 17%, Red Sea Enterprises 17%; cap. p.u. 45m., total assets 330.6m. (Dec. 1985); Chair. and Man. Dir ISMAIL HASSAN MUHAMMAD; 5 brs.

Misr-Romanian Bank, SAE: POB 35, 15 Sharia Abu al-Feda, Zamalek, Cairo; tel. (02) 3419275; telex 93653; fax (02) 3420481; f. 1977; Banque Misr has 51% interest, Romanian Bank for Foreign Trade (Bucharest) 19%, Bank for Agriculture and Food Industries (Bucharest) 15%, and Investments Bank (Bucharest) 15%; cap. p.u. 7.6m., dep. 242.7m., res 87.6m. (Dec. 1989); Chair. ESSAM AD-DIN MUHAMMAD AL-AHMADY; 3 brs in Egypt, 1 in Romania.

Mohandes Bank: 30 Sharia Ramses, POB 2778, Cairo; tel. (02) 751973; telex 93950; f. 1979; cap. p.u. 12.5m., dep. 319.9m., res 4.3m., total assets 604.6m. (Dec. 1988); Chair. Eng. AHMAD ALI KAMAL; Man. Dir MUHAMMAD ABD AS-SALAM BADR AD-DIN.

Nile Bank, SAE: 35 Sharia Ramses, POB 2741, Cairo; tel. (02) 741417; telex 22344; f. 1978; cap. p.u. 32.2m., dep. 743.4m., total assets 848.8m. (Dec. 1989); Chair. and Man. Dir ISSA EL-AYOUTY; 16 brs.

Suez Canal Bank: 11 Sharia Muhammad Sabry Abu Alam, POB 2620, Cairo; tel. (02) 3931033; telex 93852; f. 1978; cap. p.u. 15m., dep. 1,531.1m., res 106.2m., total assets 2,212.8m. (Dec. 1989); Chair. and Man. Dir AHMAD FOUAD; 9 brs.

Non-Commercial Banks

Arab Investment Bank (Federal Arab Bank for Development and Investment): 1113 Corniche en-Nil, POB 1147, Cairo; tel. (02) 753301; telex 93025; f. 1978; cap. p.u. 18.5m., dep. 473m., total assets 659.1m. (Dec. 1988); Chair. Prof. FOUAD HASHEM AWAD; 6 brs.

Banque Nationale Société Générale, SAE: 4 Sharia Talaat Harb, Evergreen Office Bldg, 3rd Floor, Cairo; tel. (02) 770291; telex

EGYPT

93894; National Bank of Egypt has 51% interest, Société Générale, Paris has 49%; f. 1978; cap. 10m.; Chair. Mahmoud Abd al-Aziz; Gen. Man. Jean Dubois.

Egypt Arab African Bank: POB 61, Magli esh-Shaab, 5 Midan es-Saray, el-Koubra, Garden City, Cairo; tel. (02) 3550948; telex 20965; f. 1982; Arab African International Bank has 49% interest, Egyptian businessmen have 16%, Arab African International Bank Pension Fund, Bank of Alexandria, Banque du Caire, Egyptian Reinsurance Co, and Development Industrial Bank each have 7%; cap. p.u. 20m., dep. 500.1m., res 83.1m., total assets 688.2m. (Dec. 1989); merchant and investment bank services; Chair. and Man. Dir Muhammad Ibrahim Farid; Gen. Man. Bahi ed-Din M. es-Sadiq; 5 brs.

Egyptian Investment Finance Corporation: Cairo; f. 1985; cap. 17m.; merchant bank services.

Housing and Development Bank: 26 Batal Ahmad Abd al-Aziz, POB 234, Cairo (Dokki); tel. (02) 717170; telex 94075; fax (02) 3600728; f. 1979; cap. p.u. 18m., dep. 121.6m., res. 40m. (Dec. 1989); Chair. and Man. Dir Mahmoud Nabih el-Minshawi; 3 brs.

Islamic International Bank for Investment and Development: 4 Sharia Addy, Mesaha Sq., Dokki, POB 180, Cairo; tel. (02) 3489973; f. 1980; auth. cap. US $100, cap. p.u. US $12m. (Dec. 1987); Chair. Hassan Ahmad Nagi; Gen. Man. Adel Khalifa Tantawi; 5 brs.

Misr Iran Development Bank: The Nile Tower, 21 Sharia Giza, POB 219, El-Orman; tel. (02) 727311; telex 22407; f. 1975; cap. p.u. US $40m., res 11.5m.; dep. US $347.7m. (Dec. 1987); Chair. Fathi Muhammad Ibrahim; Gen. Man. Dr Ibrahim Moukhtar; 5 brs.

National Investment Bank: 18 Sharia Abd el-Meguid ar-Remaly, Bab el-Louk, Cairo; tel. (02) 3541336; telex 23414; fax (02) 3557399; f. 1980; state-owned; responsible for government projects; Chair. Gamal al-Ganzouri; Sec.-Gen. Abd al-Kaher al-Sayed Ali.

National Société Générale Bank, SAE: 4 Sharia Talaat Harb, POB 2664, Cairo; tel. (02) 747396; telex 93895; f. 1978; investment and merchant bank; Chair. Yousuf Ahmad Allouba.

Offshore Bank

Manufacturers Hanover Trust Co: 3 Sharia Ahmad Nessim, Giza, POB 1962, Giza, Cairo; tel. (02) 726703; telex 92297; Vice-Pres. and Man. R. Dolan.

STOCK EXCHANGES

Capital Market Authority: 20 Sharia Emad ed-Din, Cairo; tel. (02) 779696; telex 94282; fax (02) 755339; f. 1979; Chair. Dr Muhammad Hassan Fag an-Nour.

Cairo Stock Exchange: 4 Sharia esh-Sherifein, Cairo; tel. (02) 3921447; f. 1904; Chair. Fouad Shahen.

Alexandria Stock Exchange: 11 Sharia Talaat Harb, Alexandria; tel. (03) 4824015; fax (03) 4823039; f. 1861; Chair. Edward Anis Gebrayil.

INSURANCE

Arab International Insurance Co: POB 2704, 28 Sharia Talaat Harb, Cairo; tel. (02) 746322; telex 92599; f. 1976; a joint-stock free zone company established by Egyptian and foreign insurance companies; Chair. Gamal el-Borollossi; Gen. Man. Hassan M. Hafez.

Ach-Chark Insurance Co, SAE: 15 Sharia Kasr en-Nil, Cairo; tel. (02) 740455; telex 92276; f. 1931; Chair. Ezzat M. Abd al-Bary; general and life.

Egyptian Reinsurance Co, SAE: 7 Sharia Dar esh-Shifa, Garden City, POB 950, Cairo; tel. (02) 3543354; telex 92245; fax (02) 3557483; f. 1957; Chair. Essam ed-Din Omar.

L'Epargne, SAE: Immeuble Chemla, Sharia 26 July, POB 548, Cairo; all types of insurance.

Al-Iktisad esh-Shabee, SAE: 11 Sharia Emad ed-Din, POB 1635, Cairo; f. 1948; Man. Dir and Gen. Man. W. Khayat.

Misr Insurance Co: 44A Sharia Dokki, Giza; tel. 700158; telex 93320; f. 1934; all classes of insurance and reinsurance; cap. p.u. 12m., res 414.5 m. (June 1987); Chair. Fathi Muhammad Ibrahim.

Mohandes Insurance Co: 36 Sharia Batal Ahmad Abd al-Aziz, Mohandesin, POB 363, Giza; tel. 701074; telex 93392.

Al-Mottahida: 9 Sharia Soliman Pasha, POB 804, Cairo; f. 1957.

National Insurance Co of Egypt, SAE: 33 Sharia en-Nabi Danial, POB 446, Alexandria; tel. (03) 4923034; telex 54212; f. 1900; Chair. Ahmad Fouad el-Ansari.

Provident Association of Egypt, SAE: 9 Sharia Sherif Pasha, POB 390, Alexandria; f. 1936; Man. Dir G. C. Vorloou.

Trade and Industry

CHAMBERS OF COMMERCE

Federation of Chambers of Commerce: 4 el-Falaki Sq., Cairo; tel. (02) 3551164; telex 92645.

Alexandria

Egyptian Chamber of Commerce, Alexandria: Sharia el-Ghorfa Altogariya, Alexandria; tel. (03) 808993; Pres. Abd al-Hamid Serri; Gen. Dir Muhammad Fathi Mahmoud.

Cairo

Cairo Chamber of Commerce: 4 Sharia Midan el-Falaki, Cairo; tel. (02) 3558261; telex 92453; fax (02) 3563603; f. 1913; Pres. Mahmoud al-Araby; Sec.-Gen. Mostafa Zaki Taha.

INVESTMENT ORGANIZATION

General Authority for Investment and Free Zones: 8 Sharia Adly, POB 1007, Cairo; tel. (02) 3906804; telex 92235; Deputy Chair. Mohi ed-Din el-Ghareb.

NATIONALIZED ORGANIZATIONS

In November 1975 a Presidential Decree ratified the establishment of Higher Councils for the various sectors of industry. During 1978, however, various government ministries took increasing control of industries. In 1980 it was estimated that the Government controlled about 350 companies. The majority of the larger, more important industrial and commercial companies are now either state-owned or operate under government supervision.

MINERALS

Egyptian Geological Survey and Mining Authority (EGSMA): 3 Sharia Salah Salem, Abbassiya, Cairo; tel. (02) 831242; telex 22695; fax (02) 820128; f. 1896; state supervisory authority concerned with planning of policies relating to mining activities in Egypt; Chair. Ahmad Abd al-Halim Hassan.

PETROLEUM

Egyptian General Petroleum Corporation (EGPC): 4th Sector, Sharia Palestine, POB 2130, New Maadi, Cairo; tel. (02) 3531340; telex 92049; state supervisory authority generally concerned with the planning of policies relating to petroleum activities in Egypt with the object of securing the development of the oil industry and ensuring its effective administration; Chair. Dr Eng. Hamdy al-Banbi.

Belayim Petroleum Co (PETROBEL): Sharia Gharb el-Istad, Nasr City, Cairo; tel. (02) 608456; telex 92449; f. 1978; capital equally shared between EGPC and International Egyptian Oil Co, which is a subsidiary of ENI of Italy; oil and gas exploration, drilling and production.

General Petroleum Co (GPC): 8 Sharia Dr Moustafa Abou Zahra, Nasr City, Cairo; f. 1957; wholly owned subsidiary of EGPC; operates mainly in Eastern Desert.

Gulf of Suez Petroleum Co (GUPCO): POB 2400, Cairo; f. 1965; partnership between EGPC and Amoco-Egypt Co, USA; developed the el-Morgan oilfield in the Gulf of Suez, also holds other exploration concessions in the Gulf of Suez and the Western Desert; Chair. Dr Eng. Hamdi el-Banbi.

Western Desert Petroleum Co (WEPCO): POB 412, Alexandria; tel. (03) 4928710; telex 54075; f. 1967 as partnership between EGPC (50% interest) and Phillips Petroleum (35%) and later Hispanoil (15%); developed Alamein, Yidma and Umbarka fields in the Western Desert and later Abu Qir offshore gas field in 1978 followed by NAF gas field in 1987; Chair. Eng. Muhammad Mohi ed-Din Bahgat.

Arab Petroleum Pipelines Co (SUMED): 431 el-Geish Ave, Loran, Alexandria; tel. (03) 5863139; telex 54295; f. 1974; Suez-Mediterranean crude oil transportation pipeline (capacity: 80m. tons per year) and oil terminal operators; Chair. and Man. Dir Eng. Hafez Muhammad el-Sherbini.

Numerous foreign oil companies are prospecting for oil in Egypt under agreements with EGPC.

EMPLOYERS' ORGANIZATION

Federation of Egyptian Industries: POB 251, 26A Sharia Sherif Pasha, Cairo, and 65 Gamal Abdel Nasser Ave, Alexandria; tel. (02) 3557642 (Cairo), (03) 28622 (Alexandria); f. 1922; Pres. Dr Adel Gazarein; represents the industrial community in Egypt.

TRADE UNIONS

Egyptian Trade Union Federation (ETUF): 90 Sharia Galaa, Cairo; tel. (02) 740362; telex 93255; f. 1957; 23 affiliated unions;

5m. mems; affiliated to the International Confederation of Arab Trade Unions and to the Organization of African Trade Union Unity; Pres. Ahmed Ahmed el-Ammawi; Gen. Sec. Abd al-Rahman Kedr.

General Trade Union of Agriculture: 31 Sharia Mansour, Bab el-Louq, Cairo; 150,000 mems; Pres. Mukhtar Abd al-Hamid; Gen. Sec. Muhammad Abd al-Khalek Gouda.

General Trade Union of Air Transport: 5 Sharia Ahmad Sannan, St Fatima, Heliopolis; 11,000 mems; Pres. Abd al-Monem Farag Eisa; Gen. Sec. Shekata Abd al-Hamid.

General Trade Union of Banks and Insurance: 2 Sharia el-Kady el-Fadel, Cairo; 56,000 mems; Pres. Mahmoud Muhammad Dabbour; Gen. Sec. Abdou Hassan Muhammad Ali.

General Trade Union of Building Workers: 9 Sharia Emad ed-Din, Cairo; 150,000 mems; Pres. Hamid Hassan Barakat; Gen. Sec. Salem Abd ar-Razek.

General Trade Union of Chemical Workers: 90 Galaa St, Cairo; telex 93255; 120,000 mems; Pres. Ahmed Ahmed el-Ammawi; Gen.-Sec. Gaafer Abd el-Monem.

General Trade Union of Commerce: 70 Sharia el-Gomhouriya, Cairo; tel. (02) 914124; f. 1903; more than 100,000 mems; Pres. Abd ar-Razek esh-Sherbeeni; Gen. Sec. Kamel Hussein A. Awad.

General Trade Union of Food Industries: 3 Sharia Housni, Hadaek el-Koba, Cairo; 111,000 mems; Pres. Saad M. Ahmad; Gen. Sec. Adly Tanous Ibrahim.

General Trade Union of Health Services: 22 Sharia esh-Sheikh Qamar, es-Sakakiny, Cairo; 56,000 mems; Pres. Ibrahim Abou el-Muti Ibrahim; Gen. Sec. Ahmad Abd al-Latif Salem.

General Trade Union of Maritime Transport: 36 Sharia Sharif, Cairo; 46,000 mems; Pres. Thabet Muhammad es-Sefari; Gen. Sec. Muhammad Ramadan Abou Tor.

General Trade Union of Military Production: 90 Sharia el-Galaa, Cairo; telex 93255; 64,000 mems; Pres. Moustafa Muhammad Moungi; Gen. Sec. Fekry Imam.

General Trade Union of Mine Workers: 5 Sharia Ali Sharawi, Hadaek el-Koba, Cairo; 14,000 mems; Pres. Abbas Mahmoud Ibrahim; Gen. Sec. Amin Hassan Amer.

General Trade Union of Petroleum Workers: 5 Sharia Ali Sharawi, Koba Hadek, Cairo; telex 93255; 55,000 mems; Pres. Anwar Ashmawi; Gen. Sec. Abd al-Kader Hassan Abd al-Kader.

General Trade Union of Postal Workers: 90 Sharia el-Galaa, Cairo; telex 93255; 80,000 mems; Pres. Hassan Muhammad Eid; Gen. Sec. Salem Mahmoud Salem.

General Trade Union of Press, Printing and Information: 90 Sharia el-Galaa, Cairo; tel. (02) 740324; telex 93255; 55,000 mems; Pres. Muhammad Ali el-Fikki; Gen. Sec. Ahmed ed-Dessouki.

General Trade Union of Public and Administrative Workers: 2 Sharia Muhammad Haggag, Midan et-Tahrir, Cairo; tel. (02) 742134; telex 93255; 210,000 mems; Pres. Abd ar-Rahman Khedr; Gen. Sec. Mahmoud Muhammad Abd el-Khalek.

General Trade Union of Public Utilities: 22 Sharia Sharif, Cairo; 64,000 mems; Pres. Mansour Abd al-Monem Mansour; Gen. Sec. Muhammad Talaat Hassan.

General Trade Union of Railway Workers: 15 Sharia Emad ed-Din, POB 84 (el-Fagalah), Cairo; tel. (02) 930305; 89,000 mems; Pres. Muhammad Sharawi Muhammad; Gen. Sec. Sabr Ahmad Hussein.

General Trade Union of Road Transport: 90 Sharia el-Galaa, Cairo; tel. (02) 7403254; telex 93255; 245,000 mems; Pres. Muhammad Kamal Labib; Gen. Sec. Mounir Badr Sheta.

General Trade Union of Textile Workers: 327 Sharia Shoubra, Cairo; 244,000 mems; Pres. Ali Muhammad Doufdaa; Gen. Sec. Hassan Toulba Marzouk.

General Trade Union of Hotels and Tourism Workers: 90 Sharia el-Galaa, Cairo; 50,000 mems; Pres. Mustafa Ibrahim; Gen. Sec. Muhammad hell ech-Charkawi.

General Trade Union of Workers in Engineering, Metal and Electrical Industries: 90 Sharia el-Galaa, Cairo; tel. (02) 742519; telex 93255; 160,000 mems; Pres. Said Gomaa; Gen. Sec. Muhammad Fares.

General Trade Union of Telecommunications Workers: POB 651, Cairo; telex 93255; 60,000 mems; Pres. Khairi Hachem; Sec.-Gen. Ibrahim Saleh.

Transport

RAILWAYS

The area of the Nile Delta is well served by railways. Lines also run from Cairo southward along the Nile to Aswan, and westward along the coast to Sollum.

Egyptian Railways: Station Bldg, Midan Ramses, Cairo; tel. (02) 347600; telex 922616; f. 1852; length 4,548 km; 42 km electrified; a 430-km line to carry phosphate and iron ore from the Bahariya mines, in the Western Desert, to the Helwan iron and steel works in south Cairo, was opened in August 1973; Chair. H. Gado.

Alexandria Passenger Transport Authority: 2 Sharia Aflatone, POB 466, Alexandria; tel. (03) 5975223; telex 54637; f. 1863; controls City Tramways (28 km), Ramleh Electric Railway (16 km), suburban buses (544.5 km); 159 tram cars, 42 light railway three-car sets; Chair. Eng. Muhammad Saleh ed-Din Abd al-Moneim; Tech. Dir Eng. Fikry Amin Abd al-Malek.

Cairo Metro: National Authority for Tunnels, Ministry of Transport, Sharia Qasr el-Eini, Cairo; construction of the first underground transport system in Africa and the Middle East began in Cairo in 1982; planned to connect existing electrified Helwan line of Egyptian railways with Koubri el-Lamoun to el-Marg line, via a 4.2-km tunnel with five stations beneath central Cairo, making a 42.5-km regional line with a total of 33 stations; gauge 1,435 mm, electrified; work on the first stage of the system was completed in July 1987, and it was opened in September; the second and final stage was completed in April 1989; Gen. Dir H. Abd es-Salam.

Cairo Transport Authority: POB 254, Madinet Nasr, Cairo; tel. (02) 830533; length 78 km (electrified); gauge 1,000 mm; operates 16 tram routes and 24 km of light railway; 441 cars.

Heliopolis Co for Housing and Inhabiting: 28 Sharia Ibrahim el-Lakkany, Heliopolis, Cairo; 50 km, 148 railcars; Gen. Man. Abd al-Moneim Seif.

Lower Egypt Railway: Mansura; f. 1898; length 160 km; gauge 1,000 mm; 20 diesel railcars.

ROADS

There are good metalled main roads as follows: Cairo–Alexandria (desert road); Cairo–Benna–Tanta–Damanhur–Alexandria; Cairo–Suez (desert road); Cairo–Ismailia–Port Said or Suez; Cairo–Fayum (desert road); in 1989 there were 45,500 km of roads, including 18,300 km of highways. The Ahmad Hamdi road tunnel (1.64 km) beneath the Suez Canal was opened in October 1980. A 320-km macadamized road linking Mersa Matruh, on the Mediterranean coast, with the oasis town of Siwa was completed in 1986.

Egyptian General Organization of Inland Transport for Provinces Passengers: Sharia Qasr el-Eini, Cairo; Pres. Hassan Mourad Kotb.

SHIPPING

Egypt's principal ports are Alexandria, Port Said and Suez. A port constructed at a cost of £E315m. and designed to handle up to 16m. tons of grain, fruit and other merchandise per year (22% of the country's projected imports by the year 2000) in its first stage of development, was opened at Damietta in July 1986. The second stage will increase handling capacity to 25m. tons per year. A ferry link between Nuweibeh and the Jordanian port of Aqaba was opened in April 1985.

Alexandria Port Authority: 66 ave Gamal Abd an-Nasser, Alexandria; Head Office: 106 Sharia el-Hourriya, Alexandria; tel. (03) 34321; telex 54147; Chair. Adm. Anwar Hegazi.

Major Shipping Companies

Alexandria Shipping and Navigation Co: 557 ave el-Hourriya, POB 812, Alexandria; tel. (03) 62923; telex 54029; services between Egypt, N. and W. Europe, USA, Red Sea and Mediterranean; 9 vessels; Chair. and Man. Dir Eng. Mahmoud Ismail; Man. Dir Abd al-Aziz Qadri.

Arab Bridge Maritime Co: Aqaba, Jordan; tel. (03) 316317; telex 62354; fax (03) 316313; f. 1987; joint venture by Egypt, Iraq and Jordan to improve economic co-operation; an expansion of the company that established a ferry link between the ports of Aqaba, Jordan, and Nuweibeh, Egypt, in 1985; Chair. Nabeeh al-Abwah.

Egyptian Navigation Co: 2 Sharia en-Nasr, POB 82, Alexandria; tel. (03) 800050; telex 4131; f. 1930; owners and operators of Egypt's mercantile marine; services Alexandria/Europe, USA, Black Sea, Adriatic Sea, Mediterranean Sea, Indian Ocean and Red Sea; 47 vessels; Chair. Adly Abd al-Mouti.

Pan-Arab Shipping Co: 404 El Horreya Ave, Rouchdy, POB 39, Alexandria; tel. (03) 5468835; telex 54123; fax (03) 5469533; f. 1974; Arab League Co; 8 vessels; Gen. Man. Capt. Hassan Said Mahmoud.

THE SUEZ CANAL

In 1989 a total of 17,628 vessels, with a net displacement of 373.4m. tons, used the Suez Canal, linking the Mediterranean and Red Seas.

Length of Canal 195 km, maximum permissible draught. 16.15 m (53 ft); breadth of canal at water level and breadth between buoys

EGYPT

defining the navigable channel 365 m and 180 m respectively in the northern section and 305 m and 175 m in the southern section.

Suez Canal Authority (Hay'at Canal as-Suess): Irshad Bldg, Ismailia; tel. (064) 220000; telex 63238; fax (064) 64220784; Cairo Office: 6 Sharia Lazoghli, Garden City, Cairo; f. 1956; Chair. MUHAMMAD EZZAT ADEL.

CIVIL AVIATION

The main international airports are at Heliopolis (23 km from the centre of Cairo) and Alexandria (7 km from the city centre). A second terminal was opened at Cairo International Airport in July 1986. An international airport was opened at Nuzhah in December 1983.

EgyptAir: Cairo International Airport, Heliopolis, Cairo; tel. (02) 455099; telex 22221; f. 1932 as Misr Airwork; known as United Arab Airlines 1960–1971; operates internal services in Egypt and external services throughout the Middle East, Far East, Africa, Europe and the USA; Chair. Gen. MUHAMMAD FAHIM RAYAN; fleet of one Boeing 747-100, one Boeing 747-200, two 747-300 Combi, 3 Boeing 767-200 ER, 6 Boeing 707-320C, 7 Boeing 737-200, 7 Airbus A300B4, one DC10, 2 Fokker F-27.

Egyptian Civil Aviation Authority: 31 Sharia 26 July, Cairo; tel. (02) 742853; telex 24430; fax (02) 2475473; Chair. ALI OSMAN ZIKO.

Zarkani Air Services (ZAS): Cairo; operates internal services and external services to Amsterdam, Belgrade, Kampala, Lisbon, Mogadishu and Valletta, *inter alia*.

In September 1990 Kuwait Airways announced that it was relocating its office to Cairo. In October the airline recommenced flights between Cairo, Jeddah, Dubai and Bahrain; and announced plans to recommence flights between London and New York, one of which would operate via Cairo.

Tourism

Ministry of Tourism: Misr Travel Tower, Abbassia Sq., Cairo; tel. (02) 2828450; telex 94040; f. 1965; brs at Alexandria, Port Said, Suez, Luxor and Aswan; Minister of Tourism and Civil Aviation Dr FOUAD SULTAN.

Egyptian General Authority for the Promotion of Tourism: Misr Travel Tower, Abbassia Sq., Cairo; tel. (02) 823570; telex 20799; Chair. SAYED MOUSSA.

Egyptian General Co for Tourism and Hotels: 4 Latin America St, Garden City, Cairo; tel. (02) 32158; telex 92363; f. 1961; affiliated to the Ministry of Tourism.

Authorized foreign exchange dealers for tourists include the principal banks and the following:

American Express of Egypt Ltd: 15 Sharia Qasr en-Nil, POB 2160, Cairo; tel. (02) 750444; telex 92715; f. 1919; 7 brs.

Thomas Cook Overseas Ltd: 12 Midan El Sheikh Youssef, POB 165, Garden City, 11511 Cairo; tel. (02) 3564650; telex 21031; fax (02) 3545886.

Atomic Energy

A 32-member Higher Nuclear Council was formed in August 1975. Work has begun on two of the eight 1,000-MW nuclear power stations to be built by the year 2000, which, it is hoped, will provide 40% of Egypt's total energy requirements.

Atomic Energy Organization: 101 Sharia Qasr el-Eini, Cairo; f. 1955; Chair. Dr IBRAHIM HAMOUDA; Dir of Nuclear Research Centre Dr E. ABD AL-AZIZ; Dir of Nat. Centre for Radiation Research and Technology Dr H. R. EL-KADI.

Nuclear Power Plants Authority: POB 8191, Masaken, Nasr City, 108 Abbassia; tel. 608291; telex 20761; fax 2616476; f. 1976; Chair. Dr A. F. AS-SAIDI.

EL SALVADOR

Introductory Survey

Location, Climate, Language, Religion, Flag, Capital

The Republic of El Salvador lies on the Pacific coast of Central America. It is bounded by Guatemala to the west and by Honduras to the north and east. The climate varies from tropical on the coastal plain to temperate in the uplands. The language is Spanish. About 87% of the population are Roman Catholics, and other Christian churches are represented. The national flag (proportions 3 by 2) consists of three equal horizontal stripes, of blue, white and blue, with the national coat of arms in the centre of the white stripe. The capital is San Salvador.

Recent History

El Salvador was ruled by Spain until 1821, and became independent in 1839. Since then the country's history has been one of frequent coups and outbursts of political violence. General Maximiliano Hernández Martínez became President in 1931, and ruthlessly suppressed a peasant uprising, with an alleged 30,000 killings (including that of Farabundo Martí, the leader of the rebel peasants), in 1932. President Hernández was deposed in 1944, and the next elected President, Gen. Salvador Castañeda Castro, was overthrown in 1948. His successor as President, Lt-Col Oscar Osorio (1950–56), relinquished power to Lt-Col José María Lemus, who was deposed by a bloodless coup in 1960. He was replaced by a military junta, which was itself supplanted by another junta in January 1961. Under this Junta, the conservative Partido de Conciliación Nacional (PCN) was established and won all 54 seats in the elections to the Legislative Assembly in December 1961. A member of the Junta, Lt-Col Julio Adalberto Rivera, was elected unopposed to the presidency in 1962. He was succeeded by a former Minister of the Interior, Gen. Fidel Sánchez Hernández, the candidate of the ruling PCN, in 1967.

In the 1972 presidential election Col Arturo Armando Molina Barraza, candidate of the ruling PCN, was elected. His rival, José Napoleón Duarte, the leader of the left-wing coalition party Unión Nacional de Oposición, launched an abortive coup in March, and Col Molina took office in July, despite allegations of massive electoral fraud. These allegations were repeated in the 1977 presidential election, after which the PCN candidate, Gen. Carlos Humberto Romero Mena, took office.

Reports of violations of human rights by the Government were widespread in 1979. The polarization of left and right after 1972 was characterized by an increase in guerrilla activity. In October 1979 President Romero was overthrown and replaced by a junta of civilians and army officers. The Junta, which promised to install a democratic system and to organize elections, declared a political amnesty and invited participation from the guerrilla groups, but violence continued between government troops and guerrilla forces, and elections were postponed. In January 1980 an ultimatum from progressive members of the Government resulted in the formation of a new government, a coalition of military officers and the Partido Demócrata Cristiano (PDC). In March the country moved closer to full-scale civil war with the assassination of the Roman Catholic Archbishop of San Salvador, Oscar Romero y Galdames, an outspoken supporter of human rights.

In December 1980 José Napoleón Duarte, the 1972 presidential candidate and a member of the Junta, was sworn in as President. In January 1981 the guerrillas launched their 'final offensive' and, after initial gains, the opposition front, Frente Democrático Revolucionario—FDR (allied with the guerrilla front, the Frente Farabundo Martí de Liberación Nacional—FMLN), proposed negotiations with the USA. The US authorities referred them to the Salvadorean Government, which refused to recognize the FDR while it was linked with the guerrillas. The USA affirmed its support for the Duarte Government and provided civilian and military aid. During 1981 the guerrilla forces unified and strengthened their control over the north and east of the country. They continued their attacks on important economic targets, while the army retaliated by acting indiscriminately against the local population in guerrilla-controlled areas. By December 1981 there were an estimated 300,000 Salvadorean refugees, many of whom had fled to neighbouring countries. Large areas of Morazán, Chalatenango and Cabañas provinces were almost completely depopulated.

At elections to a National Constituent Assembly in March 1982 the PDC failed to win an absolute majority against the five right-wing parties, which, together having obtained 60% of the total votes, formed a Government of National Unity. Major Roberto D'Aubuisson Arrieta, leader of the extreme right-wing Alianza Republicana Nacionalista (ARENA), emerged as the most powerful figure and became President of the National Constituent Assembly. In April a politically independent banker, Dr Alvaro Magaña Borja, was elected interim President of El Salvador, after pressure from the armed forces. However, the Assembly voted itself wide powers over the President. Military leaders then demanded that five ministerial posts be given to members of the PDC, fearing that, otherwise, US military aid would be withdrawn. A presidential election was scheduled for 1983, and a new constitution was to be drafted.

During 1982 about 1,600 Salvadorean troops were trained in the USA, and US military advisers were reported to be actively participating in the conflict. Agrarian reform was suspended in May by the Government, which ruled out negotiation with guerrillas. It was estimated that 4,000 civilians were killed in the first nine months of 1982, making a total of about 35,000 deaths in three years. In November a military coup was forestalled by Gen. José Guillermo García, the Minister of Defence, who removed several right-wingers from key military posts. President Magaña's position was strengthened in December, when a split within the PCN gave the moderates a majority in the Assembly.

The presidential election, originally planned for 1983, was postponed until March 1984, as a result of disagreement in the National Constituent Assembly over the new Constitution, which finally became effective in December 1983. The agrarian reform programme caused a serious dispute between Maj. D'Aubuisson's ARENA party and the PDC, and led to a campaign by right-wing 'death squads' against trade unionists and peasant leaders. In October 1983 the Assembly voted to allow a maximum permissible holding of 262 ha per landowner. This result represented a victory for the ARENA party, which had been isolated in the Assembly following the collapse of its alliance with the PCN in February.

The issue of human rights abuse continued to be a serious problem for the Government throughout 1983. Following a period of intense activity by the death squads in September and October, when the weekly total of murders exceeded 200, the US Government called for the removal of several high-level officials, military officers and political figures who were linked with death squads. The failure of the US-trained 'rapid reaction' battalions and frequent reports of army atrocities (including the murder of the President of the Human Rights Commission, Marianela García Villas, in March 1983) undermined both public confidence in the Government and President Ronald Reagan's efforts to secure further US aid for El Salvador. Following their capture of the strategically important towns of Berlín and San Miguel, the guerrillas struck a crucial blow against the Government with the attack on the garrison at El Paraíso and the destruction of the Cuscatlán bridge in January 1984. In February the FDR-FMLN proposed the formation of a broad-based provisional government, as part of a peace plan without preconditions. The plan was rejected by the Government. The guerrillas refused to participate in the presidential election, due to be held in March 1984, and threatened to prevent voting in various provinces. The election was marked by a low turn-out of voters, resulting partly from chaotic voting conditions and poor organization and partly from disruptions by the guerrillas. As no candidate emerged with a clear majority, a second round of voting was held in May, when the contest was between José Napoleón Duarte, candidate of the PDC, and Maj. D'Aubuisson, candidate of ARENA. Duarte secured a clear majority over D'Aubuisson, obtaining 54% of the votes cast.

Following his inauguration in June 1984, President Duarte instituted a purge of the armed forces and the reorganization of the police force, including the disbanding of the notorious Treasury Police. Both the FDR-FMLN and the President expressed their willingness to commence peace negotiations. Following pressure from the Roman Catholic Church and trade unions, the Government opened discussions with guerrilla leaders in Chalatenango in October. A second round of negotiations was held in November but the talks ended amid accusations of intransigence from both sides.

In August 1984 President Duarte appointed a five-member commission to investigate various crimes against human rights, including the murder of Archbishop Romero y Galdames. The Government had been prompted to act following reports of the massacre of more than 150 peasants by the armed forces in Cabañas and Chalatenango.

Contrary to public predictions, the PDC won a convincing victory over the ARENA-PCN electoral alliance at the legislative and municipal elections in March 1985, thereby securing a clear majority in the new National Assembly. The PDC's victory, coupled with internal divisions within the right-wing grouping, precipitated a decline in the popularity and influence of the alliance, which culminated in the resignation of ARENA's leader, Roberto D'Aubuisson, in September. Following its electoral success, the Government announced plans to introduce extensive social reforms in the spheres of health, education and local government services. Although President Duarte reaffirmed his intention to resume talks with the FDR-FMLN, both parties failed to agree on preconditions for renewing their dialogue.

Public discontent with President Duarte, prompted by his conduct in response to the abduction by guerrillas of his eldest daughter in September 1985, was compounded by the introduction of a series of controversial austerity measures in January 1986. The new policy was intended to revive El Salvador's economy, but it succeeded only in antagonizing the trade unions and the private sector. The trade unions demonstrated their opposition by holding strikes and protests throughout the year. A further problem for the Government was the deterioration in its relations with the Roman Catholic Church, following allegations that the Church was offering assistance to members of the rebel forces.

In October 1986 a severe earthquake caused extensive damage to the capital, San Salvador; some 1,500 people were reported to have died and more than 10,000 people were injured. An estimated 300,000 people were made destitute by the earthquake, which caused damage estimated to be in excess of US $1,500m.

Throughout 1985 and 1986 there was reported to be a noticeable decline in the number of politically-motivated murders and violations of human rights. In April 1986 private discussions were held in Lima, Peru, between representatives of the Salvadorean Government and the guerrillas, and in June President Duarte made a firm offer to the guerrillas to resume negotiations in September, with mediation by the Roman Catholic Church. Although the FDR-FMLN agreed to attend, the negotiations failed to take place, after a dispute between the Government and the guerrillas over the agenda for the meeting and security arrangements. Although these developments enabled President Duarte to affirm his commitment to securing a negotiated settlement with the FDR-FMLN, there was increasing speculation that a military solution would be sought to end the civil war. Such speculation was supported by reports of the armed forces' growing domination of the conflict and by the success of the army's 'Unidos para reconstruir' campaign, a social and economic programme, launched in July 1986, to recover areas that had been devastated by the protracted fighting. Although the guerrillas mounted a successful attack against the army garrison at San Miguel in June, they failed to make any significant gains in 1986.

During the early months of 1987 President Duarte's Government came under severe pressure from all sections of the opposition. As a result of the ARENA-PCN alliance's decision to boycott the legislature, the Government was unable to obtain approval for the reimposition of the state of siege, which subsequently lapsed in January. In February the Government suffered a humiliating defeat when its attempt to introduce a 'War Tax' was ruled unconstitutional by the Supreme Court. Furthermore, in March guerrillas carried out a successful attack on the army garrison at El Paraíso, Chalatenango, which enabled them to take the military initiative in the civil war. Other problems for the Government were posed by the opposition of both trade unions and the business community to its economic policies. When, in June, the Government endeavoured to regain public confidence by submitting some 41 legislative proposals and seven executive decrees to the legislature (including proposals for an amnesty and for reform of the penal code), its opponents remained unconvinced, and the Government's credibility was regarded as very low.

Later in 1987, however, the Salvadorean Government's participation in the peace plan for Central America (see p. 795), which was signed on 7 August in Guatemala City, encouraged hopes that a peaceful solution could be found to the civil war. President Duarte urged the FDR-FMLN to enter into the peace process, and, in spite of an initial reluctance, the guerrillas subsequently agreed to open a dialogue with the Government, but insisted that there should be no preconditions attached to the talks. Discussions between the Government and the FDR-FMLN were eventually held in October; agreement was reached on the formation of two committees to study the possibility of a cease-fire and an amnesty, but no consensus was reached on the crucial issue of a cease-fire. Following further talks in late October, new discussions were scheduled for November. However, the murder, in October, of the President of the Human Rights Commission, Herbert Anaya Sanabria, prompted the guerrillas to withdraw from the talks.

Despite the Government's proclamation, in November 1987, of a unilateral cease-fire, the armed forces launched a new campaign, Operation Concordia, against the guerrillas. Moreover, the guerrillas refused to adhere to the Government's cease-fire and authorized a continuation of guerrilla activities; by December an estimated 1,300–1,500 people had been killed in the conflict during 1987, and, despite the return from exile, in November, of the opposition leaders Guillermo Ungo and Rubén Zamora, it was clear that attempts to implement the peace plan would continue to encounter serious obstacles. In late 1987 the political situation deteriorated further, following President Duarte's public denunciation of Roberto D'Aubuisson's complicity in the murder of Archbishop Romero y Galdames in March 1980.

In early 1988 there were increasing reports of the resurgence of 'death squads', and it was suggested that abuses of human rights were rapidly returning to the level reached at the beginning of the internal conflict. In February the FMLN launched a campaign of bombings and bans on traffic movements, in order to disrupt preparations for the forthcoming legislative and municipal elections, due to be held in March. The elections took place in an atmosphere of public apathy. ARENA secured control of more than 200 municipalities, including San Salvador, hitherto held for more than 20 years by the PDC. However, a dispute developed over the distribution of seats in the legislature, with both ARENA and the PDC claiming the same seat in one region. Following protracted arguments, ARENA was able to resume an overall majority in the Assembly, when a deputy of the PCN transferred allegiance to ARENA, thereby giving the party 31 seats, compared with the PDC's 23 seats.

The PDC's poor performance at the elections had been widely anticipated, and was largely attributed to public disenchantment with the party, fuelled by a series of corruption scandals concerning the misappropriation of US funds by high-ranking PDC officials. (By contrast, ARENA had made a concerted attempt to present a more moderate image to the electorate.) Moreover, the PDC was deeply divided over the question of the party's candidate for the next presidential election, scheduled for March 1989. Two former ministers, Julio Rey Prendes and Dr Fidel Chávez Mena, both sought the candidacy. Rey Prendes commanded considerable support within the PDC but was closely linked with the corruption scandal; Dr Chávez Mena enjoyed the support of the US administration. In April 1988, in an attempt to resolve the dispute, President Duarte proposed an alternative PDC candidate for the presidency, but his suggestion was rejected by Rey Prendes, who was subsequently nominated as presidential candidate at the PDC convention. However, his nomination was disallowed by the election commission, and Dr Chávez Mena was named as candidate in August. Rey Prendes responded by establishing his own political movement in October, in order to contest the presidential election. Earlier in the year, in May, the PDC suffered another reverse when it was revealed that President

Duarte was suffering from a terminal illness (he died in February 1990).

In mid-1988 the Convergencia Democrática, a left-wing alliance comprising two of the leading groups within the FDR-FMLN and the Partido Social Demócrata, announced that Dr Guillermo Ungo would be its candidate at the forthcoming presidential election. In September, however, the guerrillas launched a major new offensive, with particular emphasis on targets in residential areas. In November the guerrillas, taking advantage of a transition period following the installation of a new military high command, undertook an audacious attack against the headquarters of the National Guard in San Salvador.

Despite the Government's willingness to participate in negotiations to revive the Central American peace plan, no progress was made in 1988 in resolving the internal conflict. Indeed, an estimated 11,000 Salvadoreans were killed or injured during the year, including 1,750 civilian deaths. By the end of 1988, it was estimated that between 65,000 and 70,000 Salvadoreans had died in the course of the civil war, while the US administration had provided some US $3,000m. in aid to the Government. Moreover, by early 1989 many areas appeared to be without government, following the resignations of some 75 mayors and nine judges, purportedly because of death threats by the FMLN. The resurgence of the 'death squads' and the new guerrilla offensive appeared to confirm that El Salvador's internal crisis had worsened. In late January, however, radical new peace proposals were announced by the FMLN, which, for the first time, expressed its willingness to participate in the electoral process. The FMLN proposed that the presidential election be postponed from March to September, and offered a 60-day cease-fire (30 days on each side of a September election date). However, negotiations about this proposal failed to produce agreement. When Duarte announced that the election would proceed on the scheduled date of 19 March, the FMLN advocated a boycott of the election and intensified its campaign of violence, more than 40 people being killed on election day alone.

The election result was, as expected, a victory for the ARENA candidate, Alfredo Cristiani Burkard, who obtained 53.81% of the votes cast, thus obviating the need for a second round of voting. Dr Fidel Chávez Mena of the ruling PDC received 36.59% of the votes. The level of abstention was estimated at almost 50%. Cristiani took office on 1 June 1989. In spite of the assassinations of the Attorney-General, Roberto García Alvarado, on 19 April and of the new Minister for the Presidency, José Antonio Rodríguez Porth, on 9 June, prospects for progress on peace negotiations were initially favourable.

In August 1989 the Heads of State of five Central American countries signed an agreement in Tela, Honduras. The accord included an appeal to the FMLN to abandon its military campaign and to 'initiate dialogue' with the Salvadorean Government. In the spirit engendered by the Tela agreement, representatives of the Government and the FMLN began negotiations in Mexico City on 13 September. The FMLN offered an eventual halt to all hostilities in return for its future integration into the country's political life. It also demanded the cessation of US military aid to the Salvadorean Government. The September talks in Mexico City were planned as the first of a monthly series to discuss these proposals. A second round of discussions took place in San José, Costa Rica, in mid-October, and a third round was planned for Caracas, Venezuela, in November. The talks in Caracas, however, were never held, because on 31 October a bomb attack was made, allegedly by the Salvadorean army, on the headquarters of the Salvadorean Workers' National Union Federation (FENASTRAS), in which 10 people were killed and 29 wounded. On 2 November the FMLN suspended participation in the Caracas talks, although President Cristiani was prepared to continue with them. On 7 November, in accordance with the Tela agreement, the UN Security Council authorized the creation of the UN Observer Group for Central America (ONUCA), a multinational military force, to monitor developments in the region.

On 11 November 1989 the FMLN launched a military offensive, and throughout the month the fiercest fighting for nine years took place. The Government declared a state of siege, and tension rose when, on 16 November, gunmen murdered the head of a San Salvador Jesuit university and five other Jesuit priests. Two women servants were also killed. Both the UN and the Organization of American States appealed for a cease-fire. Although the fighting moderated in December and in January 1990, no cease-fire was observed. On 12 January 1990, however, the FMLN announced that it would accept a Salvadorean government offer whereby the UN Secretary-General, Javier Pérez de Cuéllar, was to arrange the reopening of peace talks. The renewal of peace negotiations, however, was jeopardized by the assassination, in Guatemala, of Héctor Oquelí Colindres, the deputy leader of the Movimiento Nacional Revolucionario, one of the parties comprising the FDR-FMLN.

In March 1990 President Cristiani announced that he was willing to offer a comprehensive amnesty, territorial concessions and the opportunity to participate fully in political processes to members of the FMLN, as part of a broad-based peace proposal. Later in 1990, however, hopes for the successful negotiation of a peaceful settlement (including the implementation of a cease-fire in mid-September) were frustrated by the failure of the two sides to reach a consensus, at a series of UN-sponsored discussions, on the crucial issue of the future role, structure and accountability of the armed forces. Demands by guerrilla leaders that the army be at least partially dismantled, that its leaders be replaced and that soldiers who were suspected of participation in abuses of human rights be brought to trial were rejected by the Government, which, in turn, offered to disband rural civil defence forces, to transfer control of two of the three existing police units from military to civilian authority and to reduce the number of troops by an unspecified number. Although agreement was reached in July on proposals to establish a UN commission to monitor abuses of human rights after the proposed September cease-fire, this was later rejected by the FMLN, which demanded that more immediate measures be taken to protect human rights.

In May 1990 guerrilla forces had launched their first major offensive since November 1989, coinciding with demonstrations in San Salvador by some 40,000 trade unionists and opposition supporters in protest at economic austerity measures and the breakdown of peace negotiations. By the end of September all hopes for a cease-fire had been abandoned, and the FMLN had publicly advocated a 'democratic revolution' to abolish the armed forces, to create a civilian-controlled public security force, to effect judicial, electoral and political reform, to expand existing proposals for agrarian reform and to introduce specific economic measures to benefit the poor. A renewed FMLN offensive, undertaken by the newly-proclaimed National Army for Democracy (the establishment of which marked the reorganization of the FMLN's previous divisions into a more conventional army structure) in several departments in November, was named 'Punishment for the Anti-Democratic Armed Forces'. The conflict was considered to have entered into a new phase when, in the same month, a government aircraft was shot down by guerrilla forces armed with surface-to-air missiles (allegedly supplied by Nicaraguan military personnel). In January 1991 a US military helicopter, en route to operations in Honduras, was shot down by rebel forces in El Salvador. Public and political outrage in the USA increased when it became known that two of the three US servicemen who died in the incident had been executed, following the crash, by members of the FMLN. This incident, together with the escalating violence of the latest FMLN offensive and an apparent advance in the sophistication of the guerrilla forces' weaponry, prompted the US Government to initiate the restoration of full military aid to the Salvadorean Government. In October 1990 the disbursement of one-half of El Salvador's military allocation of around US $85m. for 1991 had been conditionally suspended by the US Congress in order to penalize Cristiani's Government for its failure to secure a peaceful settlement with the FMLN and to bring to justice those responsible for the perpetration of recent atrocities against foreign nationals in El Salvador (see below).

In January 1991, following the FMLN's declaration of a unilateral cease-fire, it was reported that the guerrilla forces had entered into clandestine negotiations with the Government, in an attempt to reach agreement on the creation of a UN observer group to oversee crucial municipal and legislative elections, due to be held in March 1991.

In January 1990 President Cristiani admitted that members of the Salvadorean army had been involved in the murder of the six Jesuits in the previous November. Nine soldiers, including a colonel, were charged in connection with the massacre. The successful prosecution of those implicated in the affair was, however, severely impeded by the disappearance of important

EL SALVADOR

evidence in May 1990. In January 1991 two leading state prosecutors resigned from the case, complaining of military obstruction and interference by the Attorney-General.

In November 1989, meanwhile, Cristiani had suspended relations with Nicaragua, after an aircraft, en route from Nicaragua, made a crash landing in El Salvador and was found to contain 24 Soviet-made surface-to-air missiles. This confirmed the suspicions of the Salvadorean Government that Nicaragua had been supplying weapons to the FMLN. In January 1991 four officers of the Nicaraguan armed forces were placed under arrest by the Nicaraguan Government and charged with supplying anti-aircraft missiles to the FMLN guerrilla forces.

El Salvador has a territorial dispute with Honduras over three islands in the Gulf of Fonseca and a small area of land on the joint border. In an attempt to resolve the issue, President Duarte and President Azcona of Honduras submitted the dispute to the International Court of Justice for arbitration in December 1986. The case remained under consideration in 1990.

Government

Executive power is held by the President, assisted by the Vice-President and the Council of Ministers. The President is elected for a five-year term by universal adult suffrage. Legislative power is vested in the National Assembly (which replaced the National Constituent Assembly in March 1985), with 60 members elected by universal adult suffrage for a three-year term.

Defence

Military service is by compulsory selective conscription of men between 18 and 30 years of age for two years. In June 1990 the army totalled 40,000 men, the navy 2,200 and the air force 2,400. Paramilitary forces number 13,400 men, and the territorial civil defence force also 12,500. Defence expenditure in 1988 was 777.3m. colones. The US Government granted US $85m. in military aid to El Salvador for 1990.

Economic Affairs

In 1988, according to estimates by the World Bank, El Salvador's gross national product (GNP), measured at average 1986-88 prices, was US $4,780m., equivalent to $950 per head. During 1980-88, it was estimated, GNP declined, in real terms, at an average annual rate of 0.4%, while real GNP per head declined by 1.8% per year. Over the same period, the population increased by an annual average of 1.4%. El Salvador's gross domestic product (GDP) in 1988 was no higher, in real terms, than in 1980.

Agriculture (including forestry and fishing) contributed 13.7% of GDP, and employed 38% of the labour force, in 1988. The principal cash crops are coffee (which accounted for about 59% of export earnings in 1988), sugar cane and cotton. Maize, rice and beans form the principal food crops. Shrimps are a significant export commodity. During 1980-88 agricultural production was estimated to have declined by an annual average of 1.4%.

Industry (including mining, manufacturing, construction and power), contributed 22.7% of GDP in 1988, and employed 21.8% of the labour force in 1980. During 1980-88 industrial production grew by an annual average of only 0.4%.

El Salvador has no significant mineral resources, and the mining sector employed only 0.3% of the labour force in 1980.

Manufacturing contributed 17.6% of GDP in 1988, and employed 15.8% of the labour force in 1980. Measured by the gross value of output, the most important branches of manufacturing in 1988 were food products (about 45% of the total), petroleum products, beverages, chemical products and textiles.

Energy is derived principally from imported petroleum, which accounted for 8% of the cost of imports in 1988. Hydroelectric power is also important.

In 1988 El Salvador recorded a visible trade deficit of US $355.9m., and there was a deficit of $129.2m. on the current account of the balance of payments. The country's principal trading partner is the USA, which took 39.2% of exports and provided 37.4% of imports in 1988. Other Central American countries, the EEC and Japan are also important trading partners. In 1988 the main exports were coffee, sugar, cotton and other agricultural products, shrimps, pharmaceuticals and textiles. The principal imports were petroleum, other minerals, cereals, chemicals, iron and steel, machinery and transport equipment.

Introductory Survey

In 1988 there was an estimated budgetary deficit of 616.8m. colones, equivalent to about 23% of GDP. The total external public debt at the end of 1988 was US $1,630m. In that year the cost of debt-servicing exceeded 16% of revenue from exports of goods and services. In 1989 the average annual rate of inflation was 17.6% (compared with an annual average of 16.8% in 1980-88). An estimated 30% of the labour force were unemployed in 1985.

El Salvador is a member of the Central American Common Market (CACM, see p. 110), which aims to increase trade within the region and to encourage monetary and industrial co-operation.

During the 1980s El Salvador's economy was devastated by the civil war and by guerrilla attacks on agricultural areas and sabotage of power installations and roads; natural disasters, including a major earthquake in October 1986, a hurricane in October 1988 and recurrent drought, also had a severe effect. The Government depended on US aid to counteract deficits on the balance of payments and on budgetary spending, and to finance military activity against its opponents. In July 1989 the newly-elected administration of President Cristiani introduced austerity measures to reduce public spending, to end most controls on prices, and to increase the cost of public utilities. Measures were also taken to simplify the taxation system, to liberalize the country's import policy and to reduce currency speculation. In August 1990 a stand-by agreement was approved by the IMF for some US $50m. to be made available to the Government, over a 12-month period, in support of economic and financial programmes.

Social Welfare

In 1952 the Instituto Salvadoreño del Seguro Social (ISSS) was established. This institute provides hospital facilities, medicines and benefits for industrial injury, sickness, accident, disability, maternity, old age and death. Health and welfare insurance is financed by contributions from workers, employers and the State. In 1981 El Salvador had 46 government-controlled hospital establishments, with a total of 7,375 beds, and there were 1,793 physicians working in the country. The Ministry of Public Health and Social Welfare administers 250 medical units, including 14 hospitals. In 1988 budgetary expenditure by the central Government (excluding the ISSS) included 216.0m. colones on health and a further 88.5m. colones on social security and welfare.

Education

In 1985 there were 4,034 public and private schools. There is one national university and 33 private universities. Education is provided free of charge in state schools, and there are also numerous private schools. Primary education, beginning at seven years of age and lasting for nine years, is officially compulsory. In 1987, however, only about 71% of children in the relevant age-group were enrolled at primary schools. Secondary education begins at the age of 16 and lasts for three years. In 1984 only 15% of children in this age-group attended secondary schools. In 1985, according to estimates by UNESCO, the illiteracy rate among people aged 15 years and over was 27.9% (males 25.0%, females 30.7%). Budgetary expenditure on education by the central Government in 1988 was 516.0m. colones.

Public Holidays

1991: 1 January (New Year's Day), 29 March-1 April (Easter), 1 May (Labour Day), 30 May (Corpus Christi), 4-6 August* (San Salvador Festival), 15 September (Independence Day), 12 October (Discovery of America), 2 November (All Souls' Day), 5 November (First Call of Independence), 24-25 December (Christmas).

1992: 1 January (New Year's Day), 17-20 April (Easter), 1 May (Labour Day), 18 June (Corpus Christi), 4-6 August* (San Salvador Festival), 15 September (Independence Day), 12 October (Discovery of America), 2 November (All Souls' Day), 5 November (First Call of Independence), 24-25 December (Christmas).

* 5-6 August in other cities.

Weights and Measures

The metric system is officially in force. Some old Spanish measures are also used, including:
   25 libras = 1 arroba;
   4 arrobas = 1 quintal (46 kg).

EL SALVADOR

Statistical Survey

Sources (unless otherwise stated): Banco Central de Reserva de El Salvador, 1a Calle Poniente y 7a Avda Norte, San Salvador; tel. 22-1144; telex 20088; Dirección General de Estadística y Censos, 1a Calle Poniente y 43a Avda Norte, Apdo 2670, San Salvador; tel. 71-5011.

Area and Population

AREA, POPULATION AND DENSITY

Area (sq km)	
Land	21,073
Inland water	320
Total	21,393*
Population (census results)†	
2 May 1961	2,510,984
28 June 1971	
Males	1,763,190
Females	1,791,458
Total	3,554,648
Population (official estimates at mid-year)	
1987	5,009,000
1988	5,107,000
1989	5,207,000
Density (per sq km) at mid-1989	243.4

* 8,260 sq miles.
† Excluding adjustments for underenumeration.

PRINCIPAL TOWNS
(estimated population at mid-1985)

San Salvador (capital)	462,652	San Miguel	175,553
Santa Ana	224,302	Mejicanos	107,278

BIRTHS AND DEATHS (registered data, per 1,000)

	1984	1985	1986
Birth rate	29.8	29.0	29.5
Death rate	6.0	5.6	5.2

Note: Registration is incomplete. According to UN estimates, the average annual rates in 1985–90 were: births 36.3 per 1,000; deaths 8.5 per 1,000.

ECONOMICALLY ACTIVE POPULATION*
(household survey, January–June 1980)

	Males	Females	Total
Agriculture, hunting, forestry and fishing	520,699	115,918	636,617
Mining and quarrying	4,103	291	4,394
Manufacturing	144,115	103,506	247,621
Electricity, gas and water	8,828	853	9,681
Construction	79,737	352	80,089
Trade, restaurants and hotels	78,785	177,301	256,086
Transport, storage and communication	62,994	2,599	65,593
Financing, insurance, real estate and business services	10,430	5,433	15,863
Community, social and personal services	121,145	129,013	250,158
Activities not adequately defined	112	112	224
Total labour force	1,030,948	535,378	1,566,326

* Excluding persons seeking work for the first time, totalling 27,027 (males 8,498; females 18,529).

Agriculture

PRINCIPAL CROPS (production in '000 quintals*)

	1986	1987	1988†
Coffee (green)	3,004	3,215	2,615
Cotton (lint)	283	258	215
Maize	9,500	12,578	12,956
Beans	1,080	534	1,240
Rice (milled)	751	594	810
Millet	2,924	565	3,333
Sugar cane‡	3,647	3,405	2,736

* Figures are in terms of the old Spanish quintal, equivalent to 46 kg (101.4 lb).
† Provisional.
‡ Figures are in terms of '000 metric tons.

LIVESTOCK ('000 head, year ending September)

	1987	1988	1989
Horses*	93	93	93
Mules*	23	23	23
Cattle	1,088	1,144	1,162
Pigs	418	442	450†
Sheep*	5	5	5
Goats*	15	15	15

* FAO estimates.   † Unofficial figure.

Chickens (million): 5 in 1987; 5 in 1988; 5 in 1989 (FAO estimate).
Source: FAO, *Production Yearbook*.

LIVESTOCK PRODUCTS ('000 metric tons)

	1987	1988	1989
Beef and veal	19	22	23†
Pigmeat*	14	14	14
Poultry meat	29	28	28†
Cows' milk	240	295	283
Cheese*	15.4	15.4	15.4
Hen eggs	42.0	42.5	24.5

* FAO estimates.   † Unofficial figure.
Source: FAO, *Production Yearbook*.

Forestry

ROUNDWOOD REMOVALS
(FAO estimates, '000 cubic metres, excluding bark)

	1986	1987	1988
Sawlogs, veneer logs and logs for sleepers	56	56	56
Other industrial wood	25	25	25
Fuel wood	4,076	4,149	4,234
Total	4,157	4,230	4,315

Source: FAO, *Yearbook of Forest Products*.

EL SALVADOR

SAWNWOOD PRODUCTION (FAO estimates, '000 cubic metres)

	1985	1986	1987
Coniferous	28	29	29
Broadleaved	9	9	9
Total	37	38	38

1988: Production as in 1986 and 1987.
Source: FAO, *Yearbook of Forest Products*.

Fishing

('000 metric tons, live weight)

	1986	1987	1988
Freshwater fishes	1.9	1.7	0.7
Skipjack tuna	0.9	1.9	1.9
Other marine fishes	5.7	2.9	2.9
Squat lobsters	7.6	11.5	2.9
Pacific seabobs	1.7	1.0	1.4
Other crustaceans	1.9	1.9	2.4
Molluscs	0.1	0.1	0.8
Total catch	19.8	21.0	12.9

Source: FAO, *Yearbook of Fishery Statistics*.

Industry

SELECTED PRODUCTS
('000 metric tons, unless otherwise indicated)

	1985	1986	1987
Raw sugar	279	292	262
Cigarettes (million)	2,300*	2,100*	2,100*
Motor spirit (petrol)†	130	125	120
Distillate fuel oils	180	175	170
Residual fuel oils	190	180	185
Cement	450	443	606
Electric energy (million kWh)	1,785	1,757	1,971

* Estimated production.
† Including aviation gasoline.
Source: UN, *Industrial Statistics Yearbook*.

Finance

CURRENCY AND EXCHANGE RATES
Monetary Units
100 centavos = 1 Salvadorean colón.

Denominations
Coins: 1, 2, 3, 5, 10, 25 and 50 centavos; 1 colón.
Notes: 1, 2, 5, 10, 25, 50 and 100 colones.

Sterling and Dollar Equivalents (30 September 1990)
£1 sterling = 9.37 colones;
US $1 = 5.00 colones;
100 Salvadorean colones = £10.675 = $20.000.

Exchange Rate
Prior to January 1986, the official exchange rate was fixed at US $1 = 2.50 colones. In January 1986 a new rate of $1 = 5.00 colones was introduced.

BUDGET (million colones)

Revenue	1989	1990*
Taxes	2,457.4	3,486.6
Other current revenue	202.9	270.3
Capital revenue	522.7	766.0
Total	3,183.0	4,522.9

Expenditure	1989	1990*
Remunerations	2,059.0	2,361.6
Purchase of goods and services	500.3	508.0
Interest on public debt	287.6	409.0
Private sector transfers	157.3	124.7
Public sector transfers	385.3	525.7
Foreign transfers	8.9	20.5
Capital investment	745.9	1,246.9
Amortization of public debt	325.6	310.7
Total	4,469.9	5,507.1

* Provisional.

CENTRAL BANK RESERVES (US $ million at 31 December)

	1987	1988	1989
Gold*	19.8	19.8	19.8
Foreign exchange	186.1	161.6	265.9
Total	205.9	181.4	285.7

* Valued at US $42.22 per troy ounce.
Source: IMF, *International Financial Statistics*.

MONEY SUPPLY (million colones at 31 December)

	1987	1988	1989
Currency outside banks	1,298	1,326	1,727
Deposits of non-financial public enterprises at central bank	17	18	14
Demand deposits at deposit money banks	1,370	1,567	1,568
Total money (incl. others)	2,762	2,996	3,370

Source: IMF, *International Financial Statistics*.

COST OF LIVING (Consumer Price Index for Urban Areas. Base: December 1978 = 100)

	1987	1988	1989
Food	431.5	558.1	708.4
Clothing	427.3	458.6	489.9
Rent	422.0	453.1	463.7
Miscellaneous	363.6	412.9	454.9
All items	416.6	498.9	586.9

EL SALVADOR

Statistical Survey

NATIONAL ACCOUNTS (million colones at current prices)

National Income and Product

	1986	1987	1988*
Domestic factor incomes†	16,933.9	20,422.5	24,559.2
Consumption of fixed capital	815.3	954.6	1,128.9
Gross domestic product at factor cost	17,749.2	21,377.1	25,688.1
Indirect taxes, *less* subsidies	2,013.7	1,763.5	1,677.7
GDP in purchasers' values	19,762.9	23,140.6	27,365.8
Net factor income from abroad	−472.0	−524.5	−509.0
Gross national product	19,290.9	22,616.1	26,856.8
Less Consumption of fixed capital	815.3	954.6	1,128.9
National income in market prices	18,475.6	21,661.5	25,727.9

* Provisional.
† Compensation of employees and the operating surplus of enterprises. The amount is obtained as a residual.

Expenditure on the Gross Domestic Product

	1986	1987	1988*
Government final consumption expenditure	2,802.6	3,181.3	3,484.2
Private final consumption expenditure	15,206.2	18,744.3	22,150.8
Increase in stocks	25.7	−297.4	85.3
Gross fixed capital formation	2,593.5	3,157.9	3,417.3
Total domestic expenditure	20,628.0	24,786.1	29,137.6
Exports of goods and services	4,875.2	4,394.6	4,326.7
Less Imports of goods and services	5,740.3	6,040.1	6,098.5
GDP in purchasers' values	19,762.9	23,140.6	27,365.8
GDP at constant 1962 prices	3,012.5	3,093.5	3,143.8

* Provisional.

Gross Domestic Product by Economic Activity

	1986	1987	1988*
Agriculture, hunting, forestry and fishing	3,968.9	3,198.4	3,736.0
Mining and quarrying	26.7	38.1	47.0
Manufacturing	3,085.7	4,044.8	4,808.5
Construction	547.1	710.4	814.5
Electricity, gas and water	418.1	497.2	535.3
Transport, storage and communications	815.8	1,060.8	1,205.5
Wholesale and retail trade	5,626.5	7,275.3	8,793.3
Finance, insurance, etc.	564.0	640.0	779.2
Owner-occupied dwellings	939.3	1,182.1	1,520.3
Public administration	1,976.5	2,207.1	2,377.6
Private services	1,794.3	2,286.4	2,748.6
Total	19,762.9	23,140.6	27,365.8

* Provisional.

BALANCE OF PAYMENTS (US $ million)

	1986	1987	1988
Merchandise exports f.o.b.	777.9	589.6	610.6
Merchandise imports f.o.b.	−902.3	−938.7	−966.5
Trade balance	−124.4	−349.1	−355.9
Exports of services	277.9	361.1	352.2
Imports of services	−420.0	−415.0	−471.0
Balance on goods and services	−266.5	−403.0	−474.7
Private unrequited transfers (net)	149.6	180.5	202.1
Government unrequited transfers (net)	99.7	154.4	143.5
Current balance	−17.1	−68.2	−129.2
Direct capital investment (net)	24.1	18.3	17.0
Other long-term capital (net)	−5.5	−55.0	12.2
Short-term capital (net)	27.0	−22.4	23.2
Net errors and omissions	−141.8	7.0	−107.2
Total (net monetary movements)	−113.2	−120.3	−184.1
Valuation changes (net)	−9.1	−5.1	1.1
Exceptional financing (net)	176.1	203.5	164.5
Official financing (net)	−19.0	−1.3	—
Changes in reserves	34.8	76.7	−18.5

Source: IMF, *International Financial Statistics*.

External Trade

PRINCIPAL COMMODITIES (million colones)

Imports c.i.f.	1986	1987	1988
Live animals, animal and vegetable products	255.3	377.5	354.9
Wheat	82.3	68.7	80.0
Animal and vegetable oils and fats	136.8	100.9	137.3
Food industry products, beverages and tobacco	201.4	248.0	305.0
Mineral products	488.1	628.9	545.8
Crude petroleum	410.0	521.7	405.2
Chemicals and related products	846.2	800.9	810.3
Plastics, artificial resins, natural and synthetic rubber	297.4	353.6	393.2
Paper and paper products	185.9	238.1	283.5
Textiles and textile products	184.3	172.5	154.5
Ceramics and glass	85.2	79.5	90.6
Metals and metal products	314.1	456.9	444.8
Machines, mechanical and electrical apparatus	573.3	757.0	747.0
Transport equipment	537.2	523.2	542.3
Total (incl. others)	4,674.4	4,970.3	5,034.9

EL SALVADOR

Exports f.o.b.	1986	1987	1988
Live animals and animal products	105.8	132.8	106.0
Shrimps	85.9	102.6	80.2
Vegetable products	2,827.6	1,843.2	1,873.2
Coffee	2,761.9	1,769.1	1,804.0
Food industry products, beverages and tobacco	171.8	106.6	165.1
Sugar (unrefined)	126.6	60.4	95.8
Mineral products	47.0	57.3	21.2
Chemicals	156.3	178.3	186.4
Paper and paper products	73.4	110.8	131.8
Textiles and textile manufactures	173.1	255.6	262.5
Footwear	40.5	65.4	63.9
Metals and metal products	67.2	96.7	112.0
Machinery and electrical equipment	29.4	44.7	47.4
Total (incl. others)	3,774.6	2,954.7	3,043.8

PRINCIPAL TRADING PARTNERS ('000 colones)

Imports c.i.f.	1986*	1987*	1988
Belgium-Luxembourg	43,585	38,021	44,410
Canada	31,262	75,289	52,012
Colombia	46,508	21,643	25,270
Costa Rica	188,832	194,262	239,100
France	25,838	22,095	n.a.
Germany, Federal Republic	212,224	249,415	216,940
Guatemala	543,321	640,447	666,310
Honduras	46,142	51,260	70,740
Italy	38,687	39,969	47,520
Japan	166,474	311,576	250,120
Mexico	306,350	450,727	401,840
Netherlands	64,097	69,294	93,130
Panama	68,561	44,802	32,054
Spain	45,009	40,533	44,910
Sweden	21,678	16,222	24,054
Switzerland	28,723	30,242	31,370
Taiwan	32,472	64,378	48,610
USA	1,761,107	1,810,875	1,884,911
Venezuela	286,415	338,675	319,920
Total (incl. others)	4,674,440	4,970,335	5,034,850

Exports f.o.b.	1986*	1987*	1988
Belgium-Luxembourg	62,618	73,963	7,990
Canada	98,523	43,218	91,300
Costa Rica	130,357	160,976	160,620
Germany, Federal Republic	860,339	509,482	703,210
Guatemala	239,163	364,268	459,470
Honduras	37,903	46,516	63,820
Japan	134,306	127,675	137,910
Netherlands	8,082	72,884	81,056
Nicaragua	26,093	26,232	15,470
Panama	53,177	54,241	33,930
Puerto Rico	6,509	11,316	11,550
Spain	61,869	77,199	13,920
Taiwan	528	3,399	n.a.
USA	1,752,222	1,320,034	1,193,045
Total (incl. others)	3,774,562	2,954,705	3,043,790

* Provisional.

Transport

RAILWAYS (traffic)

	1985	1986	1987
Passengers ('000)	307.7	322.2	364.0
Freight ('000 metric tons)	324.4	322.3	353.3

Source: Comisión Ejecutiva Portuaria Autónoma.

ROAD TRAFFIC (motor vehicles in use at 31 December)

	1985	1986	1987
Passenger cars	136,163	136,927	138,276
Buses and coaches	6,073	6,463	6,774
Goods vehicles	13,388	16,463	16,607

Source: IRF, *World Road Statistics*.

SHIPPING

	1985	1986	1987
Vessels entered ('000 tons)	4,015	4,049	3,820
Freight ('000 metric tons)			
Loaded	345.9	255.1	175.0
Unloaded	993	1,038.1	971.6

Source: Comisión Ejecutiva Portuaria Autónoma.

CIVIL AVIATION (traffic on scheduled services)

	1985	1986	1987
Passengers arriving	161,368	167,186	180,469
Passengers leaving	171,666	168,457	165,828
Freight loaded (tons)	4,428	3,160	4,747
Freight unloaded (tons)	6,174	5,677	6,784

Source: Comisión Ejecutiva Portuaria Autónoma.

Tourism

	1987	1988	1989
Tourist arrivals ('000)	125	134	131

Communications Media

	1985	1986	1987
Radio receivers ('000 in use)	1,900	2,000	2,000
Television receivers ('000 in use)	350	400	410
Telephones ('000 in use)	133	129	n.a.
Daily newspapers	6	7	n.a.

Source: mainly UNESCO, *Statistical Yearbook*.

Education

(1985)

	Institutions	Teachers	Students
Pre-primary	916	1,561	62,500
Primary	2,799	24,295	923,597
Secondary	285	3,880	90,288
Higher	34	3,404	60,994

EL SALVADOR

Directory

The Constitution

The Constitution of the Republic of El Salvador came into effect on 20 December 1983.

The Constitution provides for a republican, democratic and representative form of government, composed of three Powers—Legislative, Executive, and Judicial—which are to operate independently. Voting is a right and duty of all citizens over 18 years of age. Presidential and congressional elections may not be held simultaneously.

The Constitution binds the country, as part of the Central American Nation, to favour the total or partial reconstruction of the Republic of Central America. Integration in a unitary, federal or confederal form, provided that democratic and republican principles are respected and that basic rights of individuals are fully guaranteed, is subject to popular approval.

LEGISLATIVE ASSEMBLY

The Legislative Power is vested in a single Chamber, the Legislative Assembly, whose members are elected every three years and are eligible for re-election. The Assembly's term of office begins on 1 May. The Assembly's duties include the choosing of the President and Vice-President of the Republic from the two citizens who shall have gained the largest number of votes for each of these offices, if no candidate obtains an absolute majority in the election. It also selects the members of the Supreme and subsidiary courts; of the Elections Council; and the Accounts Court of the Republic. It fixes taxes; ratifies treaties concluded by the Executive with other States and international organizations; sanctions the Budget; regulates the monetary system of the country; determines the conditions under which foreign currencies may circulate; and suspends and reimposes constitutional guarantees. The right to initiate legislation may be exercised by the Assembly (as well as by the President, through the Council of Ministers, and by the Supreme Court). The Assembly may override, with a two-thirds majority, the President's objections to a Bill which it has sent for presidential approval.

PRESIDENT

The President is elected for five years, the term beginning and expiring on 1 June. The principle of alternation in the presidential office is established in the Constitution, which states the action to be taken should this principle be violated. The Executive is responsible for the preparation of the Budget and its presentation to the Assembly; the direction of foreign affairs; the organization of the armed and security forces; and the convening of extraordinary sessions of the Assembly. In the event of the President's death, resignation, removal or other cause, the Vice-President takes office for the rest of the presidential term; and, in case of necessity, the Vice-President may be replaced by one of the two Designates elected by the Legislative Assembly.

JUDICIARY

Judicial Power is exercised by the Supreme Court and by other competent tribunals. The Magistrates of the Supreme Court are elected by the Legislature, their number to be determined by law. The Supreme Court alone is competent to decide whether laws, decrees and regulations are constitutional or not.

The Government

HEAD OF STATE

President: Lic. ALFREDO FÉLIX CRISTIANI BURKARD (sworn in 1 June 1989).
Vice-President: JOSÉ FRANCISCO MERINO LÓPEZ.

COUNCIL OF MINISTERS
(January 1991)

Minister for the Presidency: Dr OSCAR ALFREDO SANTAMARÍA.
Minister of Foreign Affairs: Dr JOSÉ MANUEL PACAS CASTRO.
Minister of Planning and Co-ordination of Economic and Social Development: Lic. MIRNA LIÉVANO DE MÁRQUEZ.
Minister of the Interior: Col JUAN ANTONIO MARTÍNEZ VARELA
Minister of Justice: (vacant).
Minister of Finance: Lic. RAFAEL ALVARADO CANO.
Minister of Economy: Ing. ARTURO ZABLAH.
Minister of Education: Dr RENÉ HERNÁNDEZ VALIENTE.
Minister of Defence and Public Security: Col. RENÉ EMILIO PONCE.
Minister of Labour and Social Security: Lic. MAURICIO GONZÁLEZ DUBÓN.
Minister of Public Health and Social Welfare: Dr LISANDRO VÁSQUEZ SOSA.
Minister of Agriculture and Livestock: Ing. ANTONIO CABRALES.
Minister of Public Works: Ing. MAURICIO STUBIG.
Secretary of Information: Lic. MAURICIO SANDÓVAL.

MINISTRIES

Ministry for the Presidency: Avda Cuba, Calle Darió González 806, Barro San Jacinto, San Salvador; tel. 21-8483; telex 20552.
Ministry of Agriculture and Livestock: OSPA 31 Avda Sur 627, San Salvador; tel. 23-2598; telex 20228.
Ministry of Culture and Communications: 17 Avda Sur 430, San Salvador; tel. 22-9152.
Ministry of Defence and Public Security: Km 5, Carretera a Santa Tecla, San Salvador; tel. 23-0233; telex 30345.
Ministry of Economy: Paseo General Escalón 4122, Apdo 0119, San Salvador; tel. 24-3000; telex 20269; fax 98-1965.
Ministry of Education: 17 Avda Sur 430, San Salvador; tel. 22-9152.
Ministry of Finance: 13 Calle Poniente y 7a Avda Norte, San Salvador; tel. 71-4466; telex 20647.
Ministry of Foreign Affairs: Blvd Dr Manuel Enrique Araújo, Km 6, San Salvador; tel. 23-7145; telex 20179.
Ministry of the Interior: Centro de Gobierno, San Salvador; tel. 21-5438.
Ministry of Justice: Avda Masferrer 612B, Colonia Escalón, San Salvador; tel. 24-0326.
Ministry of Labour and Social Security: Edif. 2A, Avda Norte 428, San Salvador; tel. 77-1250; telex 20016.
Ministry of Planning and Co-ordination of Economic and Social Development: Km 1, Carretera a Planes de Renderos, atrás de ALFA, San Salvador; tel. 71-3266; telex 20809.
Ministry of Public Health and Social Welfare: Calle Arce 827, San Salvador; tel. 21-0966; telex 20704.
Ministry of Public Works: 1A Avda Sur 630, 5°, San Salvador; tel. 22-2466.

President

In the first and only round of voting in the presidential election, held on 19 March 1989, Lic. ALFREDO FÉLIX CRISTIANI BURKARD, candidate of the Alianza Republicana Nacionalista (ARENA), received 53.81% of the 576,339 votes cast. Dr FIDEL CHÁVEZ MENA, candidate of the Partido Demócrata Cristiano (PDC), received 36.59%. RAFAEL MORÓN (Partido de Conciliación Nacional (PCN) received 4.21%, while GUILLERMO UNGO (Convergencia Democrática) received 3.20%. Other candidates received 1% or less than 1% of the total votes cast.

Legislature

ASAMBLEA NACIONAL

President: Lic. RICARDO ALVARENGA VALDIVIESO (ARENA).

General Election, 20 March 1988

Party	Seats
Alianza Republicana Nacionalista (ARENA)	31
Partido Demócrata Cristiano (PDC)	23
Partido de Conciliación Nacional (PCN)	6
Total	**60**

Note: Legislative and municipal elections were due to be held in March 1991.

EL SALVADOR
Directory

Political Organizations

Alianza Republicana Nacionalista (ARENA): San Salvador; f. 1981; right-wing; Leader ALFREDO CRISTIANI BURKARD; Chair. ARMANDO CALDERÓN SOL; Pres. for Life ROBERTO D'AUBUISSON ARRIETA; Sec.-Gen. MARIO REDAELLI.

Movimiento Estable Republicano Centrista (MERECEN): San Salvador; f. 1982; centre party; Sec.-Gen. JUAN RAMÓN ROSALES Y ROSALES.

Partido Acción Democrática (AD): Apdo 01124, San Salvador; f. 1981; centre-right; observer mem. of Liberal International; Leader RICARDO GONZÁLEZ CAMACHO.

Partido Acción Renovadora (PAR): San Salvador; f. 1944; advocates a more just society; Leader ERNESTO OYARBIDE.

Partido Auténtico Institucional Salvadoreño (PAISA): San Salvador; f. 1982; formerly right-wing majority of the PCN; Sec.-Gen. Dr ROBERTO ESCOBAR GARCÍA.

Partido de Conciliación Nacional (PCN): Calle Arce 1128, San Salvador; f. 1961; right-wing; Pres. CIRO ZEPEDA; Leader FRANCISCO JOSÉ GUERRERO; Sec.-Gen. RAFAEL MORÁN CASTANEDA.

Partido Demócrata Cristiano (PDC): 3a Calle Poniente 836, San Salvador; f. 1960; 150,000 mems; anti-imperialist, advocates self-determination and Latin American integration; Leader Dr PABLO MAURICIO ALVERGUE; Sec.-Gen. Dr FIDEL CHÁVEZ MENA; factions include:

Movimiento Auténtico Cristiano (MAC): f. 1988; Leader JULIO ADOLFO REY PRENDES.

Partido de Orientación Popular (POP): San Salvador; f. 1981; extreme right-wing.

Partido Popular Salvadoreño (PPS): POB (01) 425, San Salvador; tel. 24-5546; fax 24-5523; f. 1966; right-wing; represents business interests; Sec.-Gen. FRANCISCO QUIÑÓNEZ ÁVILA.

Partido Unionista Centroamericana (PUCA): San Salvador; advocates reunification of Central America; Pres. Dr GABRIEL PILOÑA ARAÚJO.

Other parties include Partido Centrista Salvadoreño (f. 1985; Leader TOMÁS CHAFOYA MARTÍNEZ); Partido de Empresarios, Campesinos y Obreros (ECO, Leader Dr LUIS ROLANDO LÓPEZ) and Partido Independiente Democrático (PID, f. 1985; Leader EDUARDO GARCÍA TOBAR); Partido de la Revolución Salvadoreña (Sec.-Gen. JOAQUÍN VILLALOBOS); Patria Libre (f. 1985; right-wing; Leader HUGO BARRERA) and Partido Social Demócrata (PSD, f. 1987; left-wing; Sec.-Gen. MARIO RENI ROLDÁN).

OPPOSITION GROUPING

Frente Democrático Revolucionario-Frente Farabundo Martí de Liberación Nacional (FDR-FMLN): San Salvador; f. 1980 as a left-wing opposition front to the PDC-military coalition Government; the FDR is the political wing and the FMLN is the guerrilla front; military operations are co-ordinated by the Dirección Revolucionaria Unida (DRU); Pres. (FDR) Dr GUILLERMO MANUEL UNGO; Vice-Pres (FDR) Ing. EDUARDO CALLES, RUBÉN ZAMORA RIVAS; General Command (FMLN) FERMÁN CIENFUEGOS, ROBERTO ROCA, JOAQUÍN VILLALOBOS, LEONEL GONZÁLEZ, SHAFIK JORGE HANDEL; the front comprises c. 20 groups, of which the principal are:

Bloque Popular Revolucionario (BPR): guerrilla arm: Fuerzas Populares de Liberación (FPL; Leader 'Commander GERÓNIMO'); based in Chalatenango; First Sec. LEONEL GONZÁLEZ; Second Sec. DIMAS RODRÍGUEZ.

Frente de Acción Popular Unificado (FAPU): guerrilla arm: Fuerzas Armadas de la Resistencia Nacional (FARN); Leaders FERMÁN CIENFUEGOS, SAÚL VILLALTA.

Frente Pedro Pablo Castillo: f. 1985.

Ligas Populares del 28 de Febrero (LP-28): guerrilla arm: Ejército Revolucionario Popular (ERP); Leaders JOAQUÍN VILLALOBOS, ANA GUADALUPE MARTÍNEZ.

Movimiento Nacional Revolucionario (MNR): San Salvador; Sec.-Gen. Dr GUILLERMO MANUEL UNGO.

Movimiento Obrero Revolucionario Salvado Cayetano Carpio (MOR).

Movimiento Popular Social Cristiano (MPSC): formed by dissident members of PDC; Leader RUBÉN ZAMORA RIVAS.

Partido Comunista Salvadoreño (PCS): guerrilla arm: Fuerzas Armadas de Liberación (FAL); Leader JORGE SCHAFIK HANDAL; Deputy Leader AMÉRICO ARAÚJO RAMÍREZ.

Partido Revolucionario de los Trabajadores Centroamericanos (PRTC): Leaders ROBERTO ROCA, MARÍA CONCEPCIÓN DE VALLADARES (alias Commdr NIDIA DÍAZ).

Unión Democrática Nacionalista (UDN): f. 1969; left-wing; Sec.-Gen. MARIO AGUINADA CARRANZA.

In November 1987 the PSD, MNR and MPSC united to form a left-wing alliance, the **Convergencia Democrática** Leader Dr GUILLERMO MANUEL UNGO; Gen. Co-ordinator RUBÉN ZAMORA RIVAS. The MNR and MPSC were, however, to remain as members of the FDR-FMLN.

OTHER GROUPS

Partido de Liberación Nacional (PLN): political-military organization of the extreme right; the military wing is the Ejército Secreto Anti-comunista (ESA); Sec.-Gen. and C-in-C AQUILES BAIRES.

The following guerrilla groups are dissident factions of the Fuerzas Populares de Liberación (FPL):

Frente Clara Elizabeth Ramírez: f. 1983; Marxist-Leninist group.

Movimiento Laborista Cayetano Carpio: f. 1983.

There are also several right-wing guerrilla groups and 'death squads' not officially linked to any of the right-wing parties.

Diplomatic Representation

EMBASSIES IN EL SALVADOR

Argentina: 79 Avda Norte 704, Colonia Escalón, Apdo 01-384, San Salvador; tel. 24-4238; telex 20221; Ambassador: JUAN CARLOS IBÁÑEZ.

Brazil: Edif. la Centroamericana, 5°, Alameda Roosevelt 3107, San Salvador; tel. 23-1214; telex 20096; Ambassador: MARIO LOUREIRO DIAS COSTA.

Chile: Pasaje Belle Vista No 121, Entre 9a C.P. y 9a C.P. bis, Colonia Escalón, San Salvador; tel. 23-7132; telex 20377; Ambassador: RENÉ PÉREZ NEGRETE.

China (Taiwan): 89a Avda Norte 335, Colonia Escalón, San Salvador; tel. 23-6920; telex 20152; Ambassador: Gen. LO YU-LUM.

Colombia: Edif. Inter-Capital, 2°, Paseo General Escalón y Calle La Ceiba, Colonia Escalón, San Salvador; tel. 23-0126; telex 20247; Ambassador: Dr LUIS GUILLERMO VÉLEZ TRUJILLO.

Costa Rica: Edif. la Centroamericana, 3°, Alameda Roosevelt 3107, San Salvador; tel. 23-8283; telex 20171; Ambassador: Lic. JESÚS M. FERNÁNDEZ.

Dominican Republic: San Salvador; tel. 23-6636; Ambassador: ALBERTO EMILIO DESPRADEL CABRAL.

Ecuador: Blvd Hipódromo 803, Colonia San Benito, San Salvador; tel. 24-5921; telex 20445; Ambassador: JAIME SÁNCHEZ LEMOS.

France: Pasaje A 41-46, Colonia La Mascota, Casilla 474, San Salvador; tel. 23-0728; telex 20243; Ambassador: GASTON LE PAUDERT.

Germany: 3a Calle Poniente 3831, Colonia Escalón, Apdo 693, San Salvador; tel. 23-6140; telex 20149; fax 23-6173; Ambassador: GUIDO HEYMER.

Guatemala: 15 Avda Norte 135, San Salvador; tel. 21-6097; Ambassador: Brig.-Gen. LUIS FEDERICO FUENTES CORADO.

Holy See: 87a Avda Norte y 7a Calle Poniente, Colonia Escalón, Apdo 01-95, San Salvador (Apostolic Nunciature); tel. 23-2454; fax 23-7607; Apostolic Nuncio: Most Rev. FRANCESCO DE NITTIS, Titular Archbishop of Tunis.

Honduras: 9a Calle Poniente 4612 y 89a Avda Norte, Colonia Escalón, San Salvador; tel. 24-6662; telex 20524; Ambassador: MARIO MALDONADO MUÑOZ.

Israel: 85 Avda Norte, No 619, Colonia Escalón, Apdo 1776, San Salvador; tel. 23-8770; telex 20777; Ambassador: ARYEH AMIR.

Italy: Boulevard del Hipódromo 330 y Avda La Capilla 1, Colonia San Benito, San Salvador; tel. 23-7325; telex 20418; Ambassador: Dr ARRIGO LÓPEZ CELLY (also represents the interests of Somalia).

Japan: Avda La Capilla 615, Colonia San Benito, San Salvador; tel. 24-4597; Chargé d'affaires: HIROYUKI KIMOTO.

Mexico: Paseo General Escalón 3832, San Salvador; tel. 98-1084; telex 20070; fax 98-1178; Ambassador: Lic. HERMILIO LÓPEZ-BASSOLS.

Nicaragua: 27a Avda Norte 1134, Colonia Layco, San Salvador; tel. 25-7281; telex 20546; Chargé d'affaires: FRANCISCO TENORIO MORA.

Panama: Edif. Balam Quitzé 68-1, Calle Circunvalación y 89a Avda Sur, Colonia Escalón, San Salvador; tel. 23-7893; Ambassador: (vacant).

Paraguay: Avda La Capilla 414, Colonia San Benito, San Salvador; tel. 23-5951; Ambassador: JUAN ALBERTO LLÁNEZ.

Peru: Edif. La Centroamericana, 2°, Alameda Roosevelt 3107, POB 1620, San Salvador; tel. 23-0008; telex 20791; fax 23-5672; Ambassador: MAX DE LA FUENTE PREM.

EL SALVADOR

Spain: 51 Avda Norte 138, San Salvador; tel. 23-7961; telex 20372; Ambassador: FRANCISCO CÁDIZ.
United Kingdom: Edif. Inter Inversión, Paseo General Escalón 4828, Apdo 1591, San Salvador; tel. 24-0473; telex 20033; fax 23-5817; Ambassador: PETER STREAMS (resident in Honduras).
USA: 25 Avda Norte 1230, San Salvador; tel. 26-7100; telex 20648; Ambassador: WILLIAM WALKER.
Uruguay: Edif. Intercapital, 1°, Calle La Ceiba y Paseo General Escalón, San Salvador; tel. 24-6661; telex 20391; Ambassador: ALFREDO LAFONE.
Venezuela: 93 Avda Norte 619, Colonia Escalón, San Salvador; tel. 23-5809; telex 20388; Ambassador: Dr PEDRO E. COLL.

Judicial System

Supreme Court of Justice: Centro de Gobierno José Simeón Cañas, San Salvador; tel. 71-3511; fax 71-3379; f. 1824; composed of 14 Magistrates, one of whom is its President. The Court is divided into four chambers: Constitutional Law, Civil Law, Penal Law and Litigation.
President: Dr GABRIEL MAURICIO GUTIÉRREZ CASTRO.
Chambers of 2nd Instance: 14 chambers composed of two Magistrates.
Courts of 1st Instance: 87 courts in all chief towns and districts.
Courts of Peace: 193 courts throughout the country.
Attorney-General: ROBERTO MENDOZA JEREZ.

Religion

Roman Catholicism is the dominant religion, but other denominations are also permitted. In 1982 there were about 200,000 Protestants. Seventh-day Adventists, Jehovah's Witnesses, the Baptist Church and the Church of Jesus Christ of Latter-day Saints (Mormons) are represented.

CHRISTIANITY
The Roman Catholic Church

El Salvador comprises one archdiocese and eight dioceses. About 87% of the country's inhabitants are adherents.
Bishops' Conference: Conferencia Episcopal de El Salvador, 15 Avda Norte 1420, Colonia Layco, Apdo 1310, San Salvador; tel. 25-8997; f. 1974; Pres. Mgr ROMEO TOVAR ASTORGA, Bishop of Zacatecoluca.
Archbishop of San Salvador: Most Rev. ARTURO RIVERA Y DAMAS, Arzobispado, Urbanización Isidro Menéndez, Calle San José y Avenida las Americas, San Salvador; tel. 26-6066.

The Baptist Church
Baptist Association of El Salvador: Apdo 347, San Salvador; tel. 26-6287; f. 1933; Exec. Sec. Rev. CARLOS ISIDRO SÁNCHEZ.

The Press

DAILY NEWSPAPERS
San Salvador

El Diario de Hoy: 11a Calle Oriente y Avda Cuscatancingo 271, Apdo 495, San Salvador; tel. 22-2344; fax 22-5482; f. 1936; independent; Dir ENRIQUE ALTAMIRANO MADRIZ; circ. 86,458 (weekdays), 82,052 (Sundays).
Diario Latino: 23a Avda Sur 225, Apdo 96, San Salvador; tel. 21-3240; f. 1890; evening; Editor MIGUEL ÁNGEL PINTO; circ. 20,000.
Diario Oficial: 4a Calle Poniente 829, San Salvador; tel. 21-9101; f. 1875; Dir ALONSO MIRA; circ. 2,100.
El Mundo: 2a Avda Norte 211, Apdo 368, San Salvador; tel. 71-4400; f. 1967; evening; Dir CRISTÓBAL IGLESIAS; circ. 58,032 (weekdays), 61,822 (Sundays).
La Noticia: 1a Avda. Norte 316, San Salvador; tel. 22-7906; f. 1986; evening; general information; independent; Dir CARLOS SAMAYOA MARTÍNEZ; circ. 25,000 (weekdays).
La Prensa Gráfica: 3a Calle Poniente 130, San Salvador; tel. 71-3333; f. 1915; general information; conservative, independent; Editor RODOLFO DUTRIZ; circ. 97,312 (weekdays), 115,564 (Sundays).

Santa Ana
Diario de Occidente: 1a Avda Sur 3, Santa Ana; tel. 41-2931; f. 1910; Editor ALEX E. MONTENEGRO; circ. 6,000.

PERIODICALS

Anaqueles: 8a Avda Norte y Calle Delgado, San Salvador; review of the National Library.
Cultura: Ministerio de Educación, 17 Avda Sur 430, San Salvador; tel. 22-9152; annually; educational; Dir Dr DAVID ESCOBAR GALINDO.
El Salvador Filatélico: Avda España 207, Altos Vidrí Panades, San Salvador; f. 1940; publ. quarterly by the Philatelic Society of El Salvador.
Orientación: 1a Calle Poniente 3412, San Salvador; tel. 24-5166; fax 26-4979; f. 1953; Catholic weekly; Dir P. JESÚS DELGADO; circ. 8,000.
Proceso: Apdo 01-575, San Salvador; tel. 24-0011; f. 1980; weekly newsletter, published by the Documentation and Information Centre of the Universidad Centroamericana José Simeón Cañas.
Revista del Ateneo de El Salvador: 13a Calle Poniente, Centro de Gobierno, San Salvador; tel. 22-9686; f. 1912; 3 a year; official organ of Salvadorean Athenaeum; Pres. Dr MANUEL LUIS ESCAMILLA; Sec.-Gen. Dr CARLOS RIVAS TEJADA.
Revista Judicial: Centro de Gobierno, San Salvador; tel. 22-4522; organ of the Supreme Court; Dir Dr MANUEL ARRIETA GALLEGOS.

PRESS ASSOCIATION

Asociación de Periodistas de El Salvador (Press Association of El Salvador): Edif. Casa del Periodista, Paseo General Escalón 4130, San Salvador; tel. 23-8943; Pres. CARLOS SAMAYOA MARTÍNEZ.

FOREIGN NEWS AGENCIES

Agencia EFE (Spain): Edif. OMSA, 2°, Of. 1, 21 Calle Poniente, San Salvador; tel. 26-0110; telex 20455; Bureau Chief RICARDO CHACÓN.
Agenzia Nazionale Stampa Associata (ANSA) (Italy): Edif. 'Comercial 29', 29 Calle Poniente y 11 Arda Norte, San Salvador; tel. 26-6427; telex 20083; Bureau Chief RENÉ ALBERTO CONTRERAS.
Associated Press (AP) (USA): Hotel Camino Real, Suite 201, Blvd de Los Héroes, San Salvador; tel. 24-4885; telex 20463; Correspondent BRYNA BRENNAN.
Deutsche Presse-Agentur (dpa) (Germany): Avda España 225, 2°, Of. 1, San Salvador; tel. 22-2640; Correspondent JORGE ARMANDO CONTRERAS.
Inter Press Service (IPS) (Italy): Apdo 05152, San Salvador; tel. 98-0760; telex 20523; Correspondent PABLO IACUB.
Reuters (UK): 7 Calle Poniente 3921, Colonia Escalón, San Salvador; tel. 23-4736; telex 20634; Bureau Chief ADRIAN R. ALDANA.
United Press International (UPI) (USA): Calle y Pasaje Palneral, Col. Toluca, Apdo 05-185, San Salvador; tel. 25-4033; telex 30131; Correspondent EDA CHÁVEZ.

Publishers

Editorial Universitaria: Ciudad Universitaria, Universidad de El Salvador, Apdo 1703, San Salvador; tel. 25-6604; f. 1923; Dir ALFREDO MONTTI.
Dirección de Publicaciones e Impresos: Ministerio de Cultura y Comunicaciones, 17 Avda Sur 430, San Salvador; tel. 22-9152; f. 1953; educational and general; Dir Ing. ARMANDO ALVAREZ MATALSOL.
UCA Editores: Apdo 01-575, San Salvador; tel. 24-0011; f. 1975; social science, religion, economy, literature and textbooks; Dir RODOLFO CARDENAL.

PUBLISHERS' ASSOCIATIONS

Asociación Salvadoreña de Agencias de Publicidad: San Salvador; f. 1962.
Cámara Salvadoreña del Libro: Calle Arce No 423, Apdo 2296, San Salvador; tel. 21-7206; f. 1974; Pres. OTTO KURT WAIIN CABRALES.

Radio and Television

In 1987 there were an estimated 2m. radio receivers and 410,000 television receivers in use.
Administración Nacional de Telecomunicaciones—ANTEL: Edif. Administrativo ANTEL, Centro de Gobierno, San Salvador; tel. 71-7171; telex 20252; f. 1963; Pres. Ing. JULIO CÉSAR GÓMEZ; Man. Dr MAURICO DANIEL VIDES CASANOVA.

EL SALVADOR   *Directory*

RADIO

Asociación Salvadoreña de Radiodifusores—ASDER: Edif. Azucena 457, 2°, No 22, 85 Avda y Sur y Calle Juan José Cañas, Paseo General Escalón, San Salvador; tel. 24-4692; f. 1965; Pres. Manuel Antonio Flores Barrera.

YSS Radio El Salvador: Dirección General de Medios, 3a Avda Norte y 11 Calle Poniente, San Salvador; tel. 21-4376; telex 20145; non-commercial cultural station; Dir-Gen. (vacant).

There are 64 commercial radio stations. The guerrilla group, ERP, operates its own station, Radio Venceremos, and the FPL operate Radio Farabundo Martí. Radio Verdad broadcasts right-wing material hostile to the FMLN.

TELEVISION

Canal 2, SA: Alameda Dr Manuel Enrique Araujo, Planta; Boquerón del Volcán de San Salvador; telex 20443; commercial; Pres. B. Eserski; Gen. Man. Eduardo Anaya.

Canal 4, SA: Edificio YSU, Col. Escalón, Planta; Boquerón del Volcán de San Salvador; commercial; Pres. Boris Eserski; Man. Ronald Calvo.

Canal 6, SA: Km. 6 Carretera a Santa Tecla, Planta; Boquerón del Volcán de San Salvador; commercial; Pres. José A. González L.; Man. Dr Pedro Leonel Moreno Monge.

Canal 8 and 10: Final 13 Avda Sur, Santa Tecla, Planta; Picacho del Volcán de San Salvador; telex 21046; f. 1965; government station; Dir Carlos Díaz Chapetón.

Canal 12: 5a Avda las Acacias 130, Colonia San Benito, San Salvador; tel. 24-6171.

Canal 19: 37, C.O. 413, Col. La Rádida, San Salvador; commercial.

Canal 25 (Canal Evangélico): Pje. Rosedal 8, Reparto El Rosal, San Salvador; commercial.

Finance

(cap. = capital; p.u. = paid up; res = reserves; dep. = deposits; m. = million; brs = branches; amounts in colones unless otherwise stated).

BANKING

The banking system was nationalized in March 1980. In October 1990 the Government announced plans to return the banking system to private ownership.

Supervisory Body

Superintendencia del Sistema Financiero: 4a Calle Poniente No. 2223, Colonia Flor Blanca, Apdo 2942, San Salvador; tel. 98-0733; fax 79-1819; Superintendent Lic. José Luis Avalos.

Central Bank

Banco Central de Reserva de El Salvador: Calle Rubén Darío y 17 Avda Norte, San Salvador; tel. 22-5022; telex 20088; fax 71-0381; f. 1934; nationalized Dec. 1961; sole right of note issue; cap. p.u. 2.5m., res 243.5m., dep. 5,725.6m. (June 1989); Pres. José Roberto Orellana Milla; Gen. Man. Armando Barrios; 3 brs.

Commercial and Mortgage Banks

Banco Agrícola Comercial de El Salvador: Paseo General Escalón No. 3635, San Salvador; tel. 71-2666; fax 23-6516; f. 1955; cap. 30m., res 13.1m., dep. 1,113.8m. (June 1987); Pres. Ing. Ramón Ernesto González Giner; 17 brs.

Banco Capitalizador, SA: Alameda Roosevelt y 43 Avda Sur, San Salvador; tel. 24-1039; fax 24-5516; f. 1955; cap. 24m., res 30.8m., dep. 575.6m. (Dec. 1988); Pres. Oscar A. Hinds V.; 17 brs.

Banco de Comercio de El Salvador: Calle y Casa Loma Linda No 104, Colonia San Benito, San Salvador; tel. 24-4659; fax 24-0890; f. 1949; cap. 35m., res 5.7m., dep. 839.7m. (June 1987); Pres. Lic. Ramón Avila Quehl; Gen. Man. Lic. Marco Tulio Mejía; 21 brs.

Banco de Crédito Popular: Calle Nueva No. 2, Casa 21, Colonia Escalón, San Salvador; tel. 23-9283; f. 1957; cap. 35m., res 1.8m., dep. 483.6m. (Dec. 1989); Pres. Juan Samuel Quinteros; 12 brs.

Banco Cuscatlán: Alameda Roosevelt y 41 Avda Sur, Edificio Bustamante, San Salvador; tel. 24-6333; telex 20220; fax 23-2952; f. 1972; cap. p.u. 75m., res 68.2m., dep. 1,561.4m. (Dec. 1989); Pres. Lic. Eduardo Vilanova M.; Man. José Antonio Manzano; 15 brs.

Banco de Desarrollo e Inversión, SA: 67a Avda Norte y Blvd San Antonio Abad, Plaza las Américas, San Salvador; tel. 23-7888; fax 24-4316; f. 1978; cap. 17m., res 7.5m., dep. 265.1m. (June 1988); Pres. Lic. Gerardo Balzaretti Kriete; 7 brs.

Banco Financiero: Edificio Torre Roble, Boulevard Los Héroes 1°, San Salvador; tel. 23-6066; telex 20319; f. 1977; cap. 5m., res 0.3m., dep. 86.9m. (June 1987); Pres. Lic. José Luis Zablah Touché; 3 brs.

Banco Hipotecario de El Salvador: 4a Calle Oriente No. 124, San Salvador; tel. 71-5852; fax 71-1120; f. 1934; mortgage bank; cap. p.u. 0.9m., res 21.6m., dep. 954.6m. (June 1987); Pres. Lic. Augusto Ramón Avila; Man. Lic. Arturo Francisco Guzmán Trigueros; 16 brs.

Banco Mercantil, SA: Avda Olímpica y 59 Avda Sur, Edificio La Tapachulteca, San Salvador; tel. 23-3022; fax 79-1159; f. 1978; cap. 10m., res 4.6m., dep. 187.8m. (June 1987); Pres. Maximino Belloso; 4 brs.

Banco Salvadoreño, SA: Calle Rubén Darío 1236, Apdo 01-101, San Salvador; tel. 71-6069; fax 71-3606; f. 1885; cap. 38m., res 6.6m., dep. 731m. (Dec. 1988); Pres. Lic. Félix José Simán; 17 brs.

Public Institutions

Banco de Fomento Agropecuario: Km 10, Carretera a la Libertad, San Salvador; tel. 28-0060; telex 20089; fax 28-2666; f. 1973; cap. 82m., res 8.7m., dep. 59.2m. (July 1987); Pres. Carlos Antonio Borja Letona; Gen. Man. Gustavo Adolfo Escobar Tobías; 27 brs.

Banco Nacional de Fomento Industrial—BANAFI: 1a Calle Poniente 2310, San Salvador; tel. 24-6677; fax 24-4956; f. 1982; Pres. Lic. René Orlando Santamaría; Man. Lic. Juan José Manzanares.

Financiera Nacional de la Vivienda (FNV): 49 Avda Sur No. 820, San Salvador; tel. 23-8822; fax 23-9985; national housing finance agency; f. 1963 to improve housing facilities through loan and savings associations; cap. 5.2m., res 20.8m. (June 1990); Pres. Lic. Ricardo F. J. Montenegro Palomo; Man. Lic. Adalberto Elías Campos.

Financiera Nacional de Tierras Agrícolas—FINATA: Blvd del Hipódromo 643, Col. San Benito, San Salvador; tel. 71-2444; fax 79-1237; Pres. Lic. Raúl García Prieto; Gen. Man. Lic. José Angel Villeda Castillo.

Savings and Loan Associations

Asociación de Ahorro y Préstamo, SA (ATLACATL): 55 Avda Sur No. 221, San Salvador; tel. 79-0033; fax 24-4278; f. 1964; savings and loan association; cap. 19.2m., dep. 305.4m. (June 1987); Pres. Ing. Gastón de Clairmont Dueñas; 17 brs.

Ahorro, Préstamos e Inversiones, SA—APRISA: Edificio Metroplaza, Oficina Central, San Salvador; tel. 98-0411; fax 24-1288; f. 1977; cap. 3.1m., res 0.7m., dep. 105.8m. (June 1987); Pres. Lic. Gino Rolando Bettaglio; 9 brs.

Ahorros Metropolitanos, SA—AHORROMET: Paseo General Escalón, Contiguo a CURACAO, Salvador del Mundo, Edificio Ahorromet, San Salvador; tel. 71-0888; fax 24-2884; f. 1972; cap. 4.5m., res 0.5m., dep. 187.9m. (June 1987); Pres. Lic. Juan Federico Salaverria; 12 brs.

La Central de Ahorros, SA: 43 Avda Sur, Alameda Roosevelt, San Salvador; tel. 24-4840; fax 23-3783; f. 1979; cap. 5m., dep. 60m. (June 1989); Pres. Lic. Guillermo Alfaro Castillo; 7 brs.

Construcción y Ahorro SA—CASA: 75 Avda Sur 209, Colonia Escalón, Apdo 2215, San Salvador; tel. 71-4617; fax 71-5533; f. 1964; saving and building finance; cap. 13m. (Nov. 1989), dep. 397m. (April 1990); Pres. Harold Hill Arguello; 18 brs.

CRECE, SA: 59 Avda Norte, Alameda Roosevelt, Apdo 05-25, San Salvador; tel. 23-8299; fax 23-5072; f. 1973; cap. 5.5m., res 0.7m., dep. 122.3m. (June 1987); Pres. Lic. José Benedicto Morataya; 8 brs.

Crédito Inmobiliario, SA—CREDISA: Edif. CREDISA, Alameda Juan Pablo II, San Salvador; tel. 23-4111; fax 24-4378; f. 1964; cap. 9m., res 2.8m., dep. 240.2m. (June 1987); Pres. Ing. José Alberto Gómez; 14 brs.

Foreign Banks

Banco de Santander y Panamá, SA: Calle La Reforma No. 183, San Salvador; tel. 24-1099; fax 23-9554; Pres. María Laura Baires (acting).

Bank of America NT and SA (USA): Edif. San José, Planta Alta, 29 Avda Norte 1223, Apdo 01163, San Salvador; tel. 26-7391; telex 20072; Pres. Dr Armando Peña Quezada.

Banking Associations

Federación de Asociaciones Cooperativas de Ahorro y Crédito de El Salvador de Responsabilidad Limitada—FEDECACES: 23 Avda Norte y 25 Calle Poniente, No. 1301, Colonia San Jorge, Apdo 156, San Salvador; tel. 26-8925; fax 26-8925; f. 1966; Pres. Carlos Alberto Baires; Gen. Man. Héctor David Córdova.

Federación de Cajas de Crédito—FEDECREDITO: 25a Avda Norte y 23 Calle Poniente, San Salvador; tel. 25-5922; telex 20392; f. 1943; Pres. Lic. OSCAR RAYMUNDO MELGAR; Man. VÍCTOR NOSTHAS MENA.

STOCK EXCHANGE

Bolsa de El Salvador: San Salvador; tel. 23-8342; f. 1964.

INSURANCE

American Life Insurance Co.: Edif. Omnimotores, 2°, Km 4½, Carretera a Santa Tecla, Apdo (06) 169, San Salvador; tel. 23-4925; telex 20627; f. 1963; cap. 1m.; Man. CARLOS F. PEREIRA.

Aseguradora Agrícola Comercial, SA: Alameda Roosevelt 3104, Apdo 1855, San Salvador; tel. 23-8200; fax 23-9897; f. 1973; cap. 1.5m.; Pres. JUAN PABLO BOLENS.

Aseguradora Popular, SA: Paseo General Escalón No. 5338, Colonia Escalón, San Salvador; tel. 24-2693; fax 24-6977; f. 1975; cap. 2m.; Exec. Pres. Dr CARLOS ARMANDO LAHUD.

Aseguradora Suiza Salvadoreña, SA: Calle la Reforma, Colonia San Benito, San Salvador; tel. 23-2111; telex 20581; fax 23-1688; f. 1969; cap. 6m.; Pres. MAURICIO M. COHEN.

La Auxiliadora, SA: Avda Olímpica y 63 Avda Sur, Colonia Escalón, Apdo 665, San Salvador; tel. 23-7736; telex 20753; fax 71-4961; f. 1958; cap. 1.5m., dep. 11m.; Pres. MARÍA EUGENIA BRIZUELA DE ÁVILA.

La Centro Americana, SA, Cía Salvadoreña de Seguros: Alameda Roosevelt 3107, Apdo 527, San Salvador; tel. 23-6666; fax 23-7203; f. 1915; cap. 5m.; Pres. Dr ALEJANDRO GÓMEZ VIDES.

Compañía Anglo Salvadoreña de Seguros, SA: Paseo General Escalón 3848, San Salvador; tel. 24-2399; telex 20466; fax 24-4394; f. 1976; cap. 3m.; Pres. Lic. RICARDO BARRIENTOS; Vice-Pres. JULIO E. PAYES.

Compañía General de Seguros, SA: 7a Calle Poniente No. 4623 entre 89a y 91a Avda Norte, Colonia Escalón, San Salvador; tel. 98-0922; fax 23-2376; f. 1955; cap. 6m.; Pres. Dr RAFAEL CÁCERES VIALE.

La Seguridad Salvadoreña: Carretera a Santa Tecla y Calle Nueva No. 2, Edificio Omnimotores, San Salvador; tel. 24-3816; fax 24-5990; f. 1974; cap. 2m.; Pres. JOSÉ MAURICIO LOUCEL.

Seguros Desarrollo, SA: Calle Loma Linda No. 265, Colonia San Benito, Apdo 05-92, San Salvador; tel. 24-3800; telex 20773; fax 24-3388; f. 1975; cap. 2m.; Exec. Pres. ISMAEL WARLETA FERNÁNDEZ.

Seguros e Inversiones, SA (SISA): Alameda Dr Manuel Enrique Araújo 3530, Apdo 1350, San Salvador; tel. 23-1200; telex 20772; fax 23-2460; f. 1962; cap. 6m.; Pres. JACOBO ESTEBAN NASSER.

Seguros Universales, SA: Avda sur Mo. 164, 69A, Colonia Escalón, San Salvador; tel. 23-3177; fax 24-3999; Pres. Dr ENRIQUE GARCÍA PRIETO.

Unión de Seguros, SA: Blvd Constitución No. 339, Colonia Escalón, San Salvador; tel. 23-4825; telex 20533; fax 23-4817; f. 1974; cap. 2m.; Pres. FRANCISCO R. R. DE SOLA.

Trade and Industry

CHAMBER OF COMMERCE

Cámara de Comercio e Industria de El Salvador: 9a Avda Norte y 5a Calle Poniente, Apdo (06) 1640, San Salvador; tel. 71-2055; telex 20753; fax 71-4461; f. 1915; 1,355 mems; Pres. RICARDO F. SÍMAN; Gen. Man. Ing. FRANCISCO CASTRO FUNES. Branch offices in San Miguel, Santa Ana and Sonsonate.

TRADE ORGANIZATIONS

Asociación Cafetalera de El Salvador (ACES): Condominio Colonial, Esquina Opuesta Cine Colonial, Colonia Jardines de Guadaloupe, Apdo 112, San Salvador; tel. 79-1607; fax 73-2135; f. 1930; coffee growers' asscn; Pres. Ing. EDUARDO E. BARRIENTOS.

Asociación de Ganaderos de El Salvador: 1a Avda Norte 1332, San Salvador; tel. 25-7208; telex 20213; f. 1932; livestock breeders' asscn; Pres. Lic. CARLOS ARTURO MUYSHONDT.

Asociación Salvadoreña de Beneficiadores y Exportadores de Café—ABECAFE: 87a Avda Norte 720, Colonia Escalón, Apdo A, San Salvador; tel. 23-3292; telex 20231; fax 23-3292; coffee producers' and exporters' asscn; Pres. VICTORIA DALTÓN DE DÍAZ.

Asociación Salvadoreña de Industriales: Calles Roma y Liverpool, Colonia Roma, Apdo Postal 06-40, San Salvador, tel. 23-1788; telex 20235; fax 23-8004; f. 1958; 100 mems; manufacturers' asscn; Pres. Ing. ROBERTO VILANOVA M.; Exec. Dir Lic. ROBERTO ORTIZ AVALOS.

Co-operativa Algodonera Salvadoreña Ltda: 7a Avda Norte 418, Apdo 06-616, San Salvador; tel. 22-0399; telex 20112; f. 1940; 414 mems; cotton growers' asscn; Pres. ULISES FERNANDO GONZÁLEZ; Gen. Man. Lic. ARMANDO JIMÉNEZ GONZÁLEZ.

Instituto Nacional del Azúcar: Paseo General Escalón y 87a Avda Norte, San Salvador; tel. 24-6044; telex 20430; national sugar institute; Pres. Lic. WOLF H. VON HUNDELSHAUSEN.

Instituto Nacional del Café—INCAFE: 6a Avda Sur 133, San Salvador; tel. 71-3311; telex 20138; f. 1942; national coffee institute; Pres. ROBERT SUÁREZ SUAY; Gen. Man. MIGUEL ÁNGEL AGUILAR.

UCAFES: San Salvador; union of coffee-growing co-operatives; Pres. FRANCISCO ALFARO CASTILLO.

STATE AND DEVELOPMENT ORGANIZATIONS

Comisión Ejecutiva Hidroeléctrica del Río Lempa (CEL): 9a Calle Poniente 950, San Salvador; tel. 71-0855; telex 20303; fax 28-1911; state energy agency dealing with electricity generation, transmission, distribution and non-conventional energy sources; Pres. Col SIGIFREDO OCHOA PÉREZ.

Corporación de Exportadores de El Salvador—COEXPORT: Condomínios del Mediterráneo, Edif. A No 23, Colonia Jardines de Guadalupe, San Salvador; tel. 23-1888; telex 20235; fax 98-0951; f. 1973 to promote Salvadorean exports; Exec. Dir Lic. SILVIA M. CUÉLLAR.

Corporación Salvadoreña de Inversiones—CORSAIN: 1a Calle Poniente entre 43 y 45 Avda Norte, San Salvador; tel. 24-4242; telex 20257; fax 24-6877; Pres. Lic. MARIO EMILIO REDAELLI.

Fondo de Financiamiento y Garantía para la Pequeña Empresa—FIGAPE: Diagonal Principal y 1a Diagonal, Urbanización La Esperanza, Apdo 1990, San Salvador; tel. 25-9466; f. 1973; government body to assist small-sized industries; Pres. Lic. GUILLERMO FUNES ARAÚJO.

Fondo de Garantía para el Crédito Educativo—EDUCREDITO: Avda España 726, San Salvador; tel. 22-2181; f. 1973.

Fondo Social para la Vivienda (FSV): Edif. Magaña, C. Aree y 13a Avda Sur, San Salvador; tel. 74-4011; f. 1973; Pres. Lic. EDWÍN SAGRERA.

Instituto Salvadoreño de Transformación Agraria (ISTA): Km 5, Carretera a Santa Tecla, San Salvador; tel. 24-6000; f. 1976 to promote rural development; empowered to buy inefficiently cultivated land; Pres. RAMÓN APARACIO.

Instituto de Vivienda Urbana (IVU): Avda Don Bosco, Cento Urbano Libertad, San Salvador; tel. 25-3011; f. 1950; government housing agency; Pres. Lic. PEDRO ALBERTO HERNÁNDEZ P.

EMPLOYERS' ORGANIZATIONS

There are several business associations, the most important of which is the Asociación Nacional de Empresa Privada (National Private Enterprise Association).

TRADE UNIONS

Asociación de Sindicatos Independientes—ASIES (Association of Independent Trade Unions).

Central de Trabajadores Democráticos (CTD) (Democratic Workers' Confederation): 6 Avda sur y 8 Calle Oriente No. 438, San Salvador; tel. 21-5405; Pres. SALVADOR CARAZO.

Central de Trabajadores Salvadoreños (CTS) (Salvadorean Workers' Confederation): Calle Darío, González No. 616, Barrio San Jacinto, San Salvador; f. 1966; Christian Democratic; 35,000 mems; Sec.-Gen. MIGUEL ÁNGEL VÁSQUEZ.

Confederación General de Sindicatos (CGS) (General Confederation of Unions): 3a Calle Oriente 226, San Salvador; f. 1958; admitted to ICFTU/ORIT; 27,000 mems.

Confederación General del Trabajo (CGT) (General Confederation of Workers): 2 Avda Norte 619, San Salvador; tel. 24-3824; f. 1983; 26 affiliated unions; Sec.-Gen. JOSÉ LUIS GRANDE PREZA; 80,000 mems.

Coordinadora de Solidaridad de los Trabajadores (CST): f. 1985; conglomerate of independent left-wing trade unions.

Federación Campesina Cristiana de El Salvador-Unión de Trabajadores del Campo—FECCAS-UTC: Universidad Nacional, Apdo 4000, San Salvador; allied illegal Christian peasants' organizations.

Federación Nacional de Sindicatos de Trabajadores de El Salvador—FENASTRAS (Salvadorean Workers' National Union Federation): San Salvador; f. 1975; left-wing; 35,000 mems in 16 affiliates.

Federación Revolucionaria de Sindicatos (Revolutionary Federation of Unions): Sec. Gen. SALVADOR CHÁVEZ ESCALANTE.

Federación Unitaria Sindical Salvadoreña (FUSS) (United Salvadorean Union Federation): Apdo 2226, Centro de Gobierno, San

EL SALVADOR

Salvador; tel. 21-5911; f. 1965; left-wing; Sec.-Gen. Juan Edito Genovez.

MUSYGES (United Union and Guild Movement): labour federation previously linked to FDR; 50,000 mems (est.).

Unión Comunal Salvadoreña (UCS) (Salvadorean Communal Union): 4a Calle Oriente 6-4, Santa Tecla, La Libertad; tel. 284-836; peasants' association; 100,000 mems; Gen. Sec. Guillermo Blanco.

Unidad Nacional de Trabajadores Salvadoreños (UNTS): San Salvador; f. 1986; largest trade union conglomerate; Leader Marco Tulio Lima; affiliated unions include:

Unidad Popular Democrática (UPD): San Salvador; f. 1980; led by a committee of 10; 500,000 mems.

Unión Nacional Obrera-Campesina (UNOC): San Salvador; f. 1986; centre-left labour organization; 500,000 mems.

Some unions, such as those of the taxi drivers and bus owners, are affiliated to the Federación Nacional de Empresas Pequeñas Salvadoreñas—Fenapes, the association of small-scale business.

Transport

Comisión Ejecutiva Portuaria Autónoma (CEPA): Edif. Torre Roble, Blvd de Los Héroes, Apdo 2667, San Salvador; tel. 24-1133; telex 20194; fax 24-1355; f. 1952; operates and administers the ports of Acajutla (on Pacific coast) and Cutuco (on Gulf of Fonseca) and the El Salvador International Airport, as well as Ferrocarriles Nacionales de El Salvador; Chair. Col. Carlos Humberto Figueroa; Gen. Man. Lic. Arturo Germán Martínez.

RAILWAYS

There are about 600 km of railway track in the country. The main track links San Salvador with the ports of Acajutla and Cutuco and with San Jerónimo on the border with Guatemala. The International Railways of Central America run from Anguiatú on the El Salvador–Guatemala border to the Pacific ports of Acajutla and Cutuco and connect San Salvador with Guatemala City and the Guatemalan Atlantic ports of Puerto Barrios and Santo Tomás del Castillo.

Ferrocarriles Nacionales de El Salvador—FENADESAL: Avda Peralta 903, Apdo 2292, San Salvador; tel. 22-9000; telex 20194; 600 km open; in 1975 Ferrocarril de El Salvador and the Salvadorean section of International Railways of Central America (429 km open) were merged and are administered by the Railroad Division of CEPA (see above); Man. Ing. José Guillermo Merlos.

ROADS

The country's highway system is well integrated with its railway services. There are some 12,164 km of roads, including: the Pan-American Highway: 306 km; paved highways: 1,700 km; improved roads: 2,827 km; dry-weather roads: 3,872 km. A coastal highway, with interconnecting roads, was under construction in the late 1980s.

SHIPPING

The ports of Acajutla and Cutuco are administered by CEPA (see above). Services are also provided by foreign lines.

CIVIL AVIATION

AESA Aerolíneas de El Salvador, SA de CV: Avda. Las Palmas 129 Col. San Benito, Apdo 06-1830, San Salvador; tel. 24-6588; cargo and mail service between San Salvador and Miami; Pres. E. Cornejo López; Gen. Man. José Roberto Santana.

TACA International Airlines: Edif. Caribe, 2°, San Salvador; tel. 23-2244; telex 20456; fax 23-3757; f. 1939; passenger and cargo services to Belize, Guatemala, Honduras, Mexico, Panama and the USA; Pres. Dr Enrique Borgo Bustamante; Exec. Pres. Federico Bloch; fleet: 2 Boeing 737-300, 3 Boeing 737-200, 1 Boeing 767-200.

Tourism

El Salvador was one of the centres of the ancient Mayan civilization, and the ruined temples and cities are of great interest. The volcanoes and lakes of the uplands provide magnificent scenery, while there are fine beaches along the Pacific coast. The civil war, in progress since 1979, has severely affected the tourist industry. The number of tourist arrivals declined from 293,000 in 1978 to 82,000 in 1981, although the total rose to 134,024 in 1988.

Buró de Convenciones y Visitantes de la Ciudad de San Salvador: Suites 274–276, Hotel Presidente, Avda La Revolución, Colonia San Benito, Apdo 2124, San Salvador; tel. 24-0819; telex 20037; fax 23-4912; f. 1973; assists in organization of national and international events; Pres. Lucio Bustillo Fuentes; Exec. Dir Carolina Dalton de Magaña.

Cámara Salvadoreña de Turismo: Hotel Sheraton, 89 Avda Norte y 11 Calle Poniente, Colonia Escalón, San Salvador; tel. 24-9992; Pres. Carlos Olivo.

Comité Nacional de Turismo—CONATUR: San Salvador; tel. 23-4566; comprises hotels, restaurants, tour operators, airlines and Instituto Salvadoreño de Turismo; Sec. Mercedes Meléndez.

Instituto Salvadoreño de Turismo—ISTU (National Tourism Institute): Calle Rubén Darío 619, San Salvador; tel. 22-8000; telex 20775; f. 1950; Pres. Carlos Hirlemann; Man. Dir Lic. Ricardo Escoto.

Atomic Energy

Comisión Salvadoreña de Energía Nuclear—COSEN: c/o Ministerio de Economía, 4a Avda Norte 233, San Salvador; f. 1961; atomic energy research institute.

EQUATORIAL GUINEA

Introductory Survey

Location, Climate, Language, Religion, Flag, Capital

The Republic of Equatorial Guinea consists of the islands of Bioko (formerly Fernando Póo and subsequently renamed Macías Nguema Biyogo under the regime of President Macías), Corisco, Great Elobey, Small Elobey and Annobón (previously known also as Pagalu), and the mainland territory of Río Muni (Mbini) on the west coast of Africa. Cameroon lies to the north and Gabon to the east and south of Río Muni, while Bioko lies off shore from Cameroon and Nigeria. The small island of Annobón lies far to the south, beyond the islands of São Tomé and Príncipe. The climate is hot and humid, with average temperatures higher than 26°C (80°F). The official language is Spanish. In Río Muni the Fang language is spoken, as well as those of coastal tribes such as the Combe, Balemke and Bujeba, while in Bioko the principal local language is Bubi, although pidgin English and Ibo are also widely understood. An estimated 94% of the population are adherents of the Roman Catholic Church. The national flag (proportions 3 by 2) has three equal horizontal stripes, of green, white and red, with a light blue triangle at the hoist. The state flag has, in addition, the national coat of arms (a white shield, containing a tree, with six yellow stars above and a scroll beneath) on the white stripe. The capital is Malabo (formerly Santa Isabel).

Recent History

Portugal ceded the territory to Spain in 1778. The mainland region and the islands were periodically united for administrative purposes. In July 1959 Spanish Guinea, as the combined territory was known, was divided into two provinces: Río Muni, on the African mainland, and Fernando Póo (with other nearby islands). From 1960 the two provinces were represented in the Spanish legislature. In December 1963 they were merged again, to form Equatorial Guinea, with a limited measure of self-government.

After 190 years of Spanish rule, independence was declared on 12 October 1968. Francisco Macías Nguema, Equatorial Guinea's first President, formed a coalition government from all the parties represented in the new National Assembly. Relations with Spain became strained in early 1969, following a series of anti-European incidents. In March 1969 the Minister for Foreign Affairs, Atanasio Ndongo Miyone, was killed by security forces during a failed coup attempt.

In February 1970 the President outlawed all existing political parties and formed the Partido Unico Nacional (PUN), which later became the Partido Unico Nacional de los Trabajadores (PUNT). Macías appointed himself Life President in July 1972. A new constitution, giving absolute powers to President Macías and abolishing the provincial autonomy previously enjoyed by the island of Fernando Póo (then renamed Macías Nguema Biyogo), was adopted in July 1973. President Macías controlled both radio and press and all citizens were forbidden to leave the country, although many fled during his rule. During 1975–77 there were many arrests and executions. Nigerian workers were repatriated in 1976, following reports of maltreatment and forced labour. The Macías regime maintained close relations with the Soviet bloc.

In August 1979 President Macías was overthrown in a coup, led by his nephew, Lt-Col (later Brig.-Gen.) Teodoro Obiang Nguema Mbasogo, hitherto the Deputy Minister of Defence. (Obiang Nguema subsequently ceased to use his forename.) Macías was later captured, tried on charges of treason, genocide, embezzlement and violation of human rights, and was executed by a military firing squad. The Spanish Government, which admitted prior knowledge of the coup, was the first to recognize the new regime, and remained a major supplier of financial and technical aid. Obiang Nguema appointed civilians to the Government for the first time in December 1981. In August 1982 he was reappointed President for a further seven years, and later that month a new constitution, which provided for an eventual return to civilian government, was approved by 95% of voters in a referendum. Equatorial Guinea held its first legislative elections in more than 19 years in August 1983, when an estimated 50,000 voters elected 41 candidates (unopposed) to a new House of Representatives. Further legislative elections were held in July 1988, when it was reported that 99.2% of voters endorsed a single list of candidates who had been nominated by Obiang Nguema.

During the 1980s Obiang Nguema's rule was threatened on a number of occasions. Attempted coups were reported in April 1981, May 1983 and November 1983. In January 1986, following rumours of discontent among the Río Muni armed forces, the President reorganized the Government and reinforced his control by assuming the post of Minister of Defence. In July 1986 an attempt to occupy the presidential palace in Malabo was quelled by loyalist forces, and in August a military tribunal imposed sentences on 13 senior civilian and military officials who had been convicted of complicity in the coup attempt. The alleged leader, Eugenio Abeso Mondu (a former diplomat and a member of the House of Representatives), was sentenced to death and executed by firing squad, while prison sentences were imposed on 12 others, including two government ministers and the national director of the Banque des Etats de l'Afrique Centrale (BEAC).

The persistence of economic depression during the early 1980s and the existence, between 1979 and 1987, of a ban on organized political activity within Equatorial Guinea contributed towards continued opposition to Obiang Nguema's regime from Equato-Guineans living in exile (estimated to number around 130,000 in 1983). In April 1983 representatives of five opposition groups met at Zaragoza, in Spain, and formed a Junta Coordinadora de las Fuerzas de Oposición Democrática (Co-ordinating Board of Democratic Opposition Forces), and in the following year the Convergencia Social Democrática was formed in Paris by two further groups. In August 1987, on the eighth anniversary of his accession to power, Obiang Nguema ended the ban on political formations by announcing the establishment of a 'governmental party', the Partido Democrático de Guinea Ecuatorial (PDGE), and suggesting that other political parties could be created at a later date. In June 1988 representatives of the Junta Coordinadora de las Fuerzas de Oposición Democrática visited Equatorial Guinea, in order to establish local opposition groups in preparation for the presidential election that was to be held in 1989. However, Obiang Nguema rejected their demands for the legalization of opposition parties. In September 1988, following the discovery of a plot to overthrow Obiang Nguema, seven civilians, including the Secretary-General of the Partido del Progreso de Guinea Ecuatorial, José Luis Jones, were given severe prison sentences. Two army officers were sentenced to death for their part in the plot, but these sentences were subsequently commuted to life imprisonment. Jones (who had received a 17-year prison sentence), was released in January 1989, prior to an official visit, by Obiang Nguema, to Spain.

In June 1989 Obiang Nguema was elected, unopposed, to the office of President, in the first presidential election to be held since independence. Voting was compulsory, and Obiang Nguema reportedly received the support of more than 99% of the electorate. Members of opposition groupings criticized the conduct of the election, and declared the result invalid. Following his success, the President appealed to dissidents to return to Equatorial Guinea, and declared an amnesty for political prisoners. However, Obiang Nguema reiterated his opposition to the establishment of a multi-party system. In August a government reshuffle was implemented.

In September 1990 the human rights organization, Amnesty International, accused the Equato-Guinean authorities of torturing political prisoners. A reorganization of the Council of Ministers was effected in October. In December it was reported that about 30 people had been imprisoned after having advocated the introduction of a multi-party political system.

While Spain remains a major trading partner and aid donor, Equatorial Guinea's entry into the Customs and Economic Union of Central Africa (UDEAC, see p. 156) in December 1983 represented a significant move towards a greater integration with neighbouring francophone countries. In January 1985 the country joined the Franc Zone (see p. 156), with financial assistance from France, which also applied pressure on the 'Paris Club' of creditor nations to achieve a rescheduling of Equatorial Guinea's debts in July of that year. French was expected to become a compulsory subject in Equato-Guinean schools during the early 1990s. In September 1988 Obiang Nguema made an official visit to France, during which Equatorial Guinea's formal entry into the francophone bloc was discussed. Obiang Nguema cancelled a visit to Spain which had been scheduled to take place in October 1988, following allegations, in the Spanish legislature, of the misappropriation of Spanish development aid to the former colony (similar allegations were made by exiled Equato-Guinean opposition groupings). In January 1989, however, Obiang Nguema visited Spain, where the continuation of bilateral links between the two countries was confirmed, and the Spanish Government agreed to cancel one-third of Equatorial Guinea's public debt to Spain, and to reschedule the remainder of the bilateral debt. In March relations between the two countries again deteriorated, when Equato-Guinean dissident groupings and Spanish opposition parties signed an agreement, known as the 'Pacto de Madrid para la Democratización y el Autodesarrollo en Guinea Ecuatorial'. The pact, in which proposals for the future democratization and self-development of Equatorial Guinea were outlined, was widely interpreted as a condemnation of existing co-operation agreements between Spain and Equatorial Guinea. In May a prominent Spanish development-aid administrator was expelled from Equatorial Guinea. None the less, representatives of the Spanish Government attended Obiang Nguema's installation as President in August.

Despite Equatorial Guinea's close military links with Nigeria, relations between the two countries underwent some strain in 1988, when it became clear that Equatorial Guinea, anxious to attract foreign investment, had formed links with South Africa. The Nigerian Government claimed that contracts between the Governments of Equatorial Guinea and South Africa, for the construction of a satellite-tracking station on Bioko and for the extension and modernization of the airport at Malabo, constituted a threat to Nigerian security, and demanded that all South African nationals be expelled from Equatorial Guinea. Following a visit to Malabo by the Nigerian Minister of External Affairs, it was announced that all South African personnel had been expelled from Equatorial Guinea. However, the Nigerian Government subsequently provided evidence that a number of South African workers (whom the Obiang Nguema Government claimed to be agricultural advisers) had returned to Equatorial Guinea.

Government

After the coup of August 1979, the Supreme Military Council ruled by decree. In August 1982 a new constitution was approved in a referendum, making provision for presidential and legislative elections by universal suffrage, a State Council of 11 members and a House of Representatives of the People (elected for a five-year term).

Defence

In June 1990 there were 1,300 men in the army, 100 in the navy and 100 in the air force. There were also paramilitary forces of 2,000. Military service is voluntary. The estimated defence expenditure for 1982 was US $6m. Spain has provided military advisers and training since October 1979, and the presidential guard is staffed by Morocco, which maintains about 360 troops in the country. Foreign military aid totalled $150,000 in 1988.

Economic Affairs

In 1988, according to estimates by the World Bank, Equatorial Guinea's gross national product (GNP), measured at average 1986–88 prices, was US $140m., equivalent to $350 per head. Between 1986 and 1988, it was estimated, GNP per head increased, in real terms, at an average annual rate of 3.6%. In 1980–88 the population increased by an annual average of 1.9%. According to estimates by the UN Statistical Office, Equatorial Guinea's gross domestic product (GDP) increased, in real terms, by an annual average of 2.5% in 1980–86, while GDP per head declined by an average of 0.5% per year over the same period.

Agriculture (including forestry and fishing) contributed 58% of GDP in 1988. An estimated 58% of the labour force were employed in the agricultural sector in 1989. The principal cash crops are cocoa, which contributed 42.1% of export earnings in 1987, and coffee. The principal subsistence crops are cassava and sweet potatoes. Some 8,000 tons of cereals were imported in 1986. Exploitation of the country's forest resources (principally of okoumé timber) provides a significant proportion of export revenue. All industrial fishing activity is practised by foreign fleets, notably by those of countries of the EEC.

Industry (including mining, manufacturing, construction and power) contributed 11.2% of GDP in 1987. About 11.3% of the population were employed in the sector in 1980.

Despite the existence of significant mineral resources, extractive activities are minimal. However, the development of onshore and offshore reserves of petroleum and of offshore deposits of natural gas (which remained unexploited during the 1980s, owing to the weakness of international prices for both commodities) was expected to commence in the early 1990s. The existence of deposits of other minerals, including iron ore, tantalum and manganese, has also been confirmed.

The manufacturing sector contributed only 1.9% of GDP in 1987, with the processing of cocoa and coffee constituting the only commercial manufacturing activities.

A total of 17m. kWh of electric energy was generated in 1987. A 3.6-MW hydroelectric installation, constructed on the Riaba river, on Bioko, became operational in mid-1989. A further installation is planned for the mainland. Imports of fuel products comprised 22.4% of the value of total imports in 1981.

In 1988 there was an estimated trade deficit of 3,166m. francs CFA, while the deficit on the current account of the balance of payments was estimated at 902m. francs CFA. In the 1980s Spain and France were the principal sources of imports; the two countries also constituted the main markets for exports. In the late 1980s sales of cocoa, wood and coffee remained the principal sources of export revenue. In 1981 the principal imports were food, beverages and tobacco, petroleum and related products, motor vehicles and machinery, iron and steel products, and clothing.

Budget estimates for 1989 envisaged a deficit of 2,479m. francs CFA. Equatorial Guinea's total external public debt was US $175m. at the end of 1987. In that year the cost of debt-servicing was equivalent to 23.1% of the value of exports of goods and services. Consumer prices declined significantly in 1986 and 1987; in 1988, however, the average annual rate of inflation was 2.3%, increasing to 5.9% in 1989.

Equatorial Guinea is a member of the central African organs of the Franc Zone (see p. 156) and of the Communauté Economiqe des Etats de l'Afrique centrale (CEEAC, see p. 223).

Equatorial Guinea suffered a severe economic decline under the Macías regime. The Obiang Nguema administration has achieved some success in rehabilitating and diversifying the primary sector. However, extractive and industrial activities remain minimal, and the transport infrastructure and power-generating facilities are inadequate. A medium-term (1989–91) economic development programme, which envisaged the reform of fiscal and budgetary procedures, and of the ailing banking sector, while encouraging private investment, has received financial support from bilateral and multilateral creditors, including the IMF. Spain and France are important bilateral donors.

Social Welfare

Health services are extremely limited, and diseases such as malaria, infectious hepatitis, whooping cough and dysentery are endemic. In 1975 Equatorial Guinea had only five physicians, compared with 25 in 1971. There were 65 hospital establishments, with a total of 3,577 beds, in 1977.

Education

The 1982 Constitution made education the State's first priority, and free and compulsory basic education was to be provided. Education is officially compulsory for eight years between the ages of six and 14 years. Primary education starts at six years of age and normally lasts for six years. Secondary education, beginning at the age of 12, also spans a six-year period, comprising a first cycle of four years and a second cycle of two years. In 1982 the total enrolment at primary and secondary schools was equivalent to 55% of the school-age population. In 1986 primary education in nine grades was provided for 65,000 pupils in 550 schools. More advanced education for 3,013 pupils was provided in 14 centres, with 288 teachers, in 1980/81. A major programme of restructuring was planned for the

EQUATORIAL GUINEA

primary-education sector in 1987, with the International Development Association (IDA) providing funds of US $5.1m.

Since 1979, assistance in the development of the educational system has been provided by Spain, which had 100 teaching staff working in Equatorial Guinea in 1986. Two higher education centres, at Bata and Malabo, are administered by the Spanish Universidad Nacional de Educación a Distancia (UNED), and had 500 students in 1986. The French Government also provides considerable financial assistance, and French was expected to become a compulsory subject in Equato-Guinean schools during the early 1990s. In 1980, according to official estimates, the average rate of adult illiteracy was 63%.

Public Holidays

1991: 1 January (New Year's Day), 5 March (Independence Day), 29 March–1 April (Easter), 1 May (Labour Day), 25 May (OAU Day), 10 December (Human Rights Day), 25 December (Christmas).

1992: 1 January (New Year's Day), 5 March (Independence Day), 17–20 April (Easter), 1 May (Labour Day), 25 May (OAU Day), 10 December (Human Rights Day), 25 December (Christmas).

Weights and Measures

The metric system is in force.

Statistical Survey

Source (unless otherwise stated): Dirección Técnica de Estadística, Secretaría de Estado para el Plan de Desarrollo Económico y Cooperación, Malabo.

AREA AND POPULATION

Area: 28,051 sq km (Río Muni (Mbini) 26,017 sq km, Bioko 2,017 sq km, Annobón 17 sq km).

Population: 246,941 (Río Muni 200,106, Bioko 44,820, Annobón 2,015) at December 1965 census; 300,000 (Río Muni 240,804, Bioko 57,190, Annobón 2,006), comprising 144,268 males and 155,732 females, at census of 4–17 July 1983 (Source: Ministerio de Asuntos Exteriores, Madrid); 341,000 (official estimate) at mid-1989.

Provinces (population, census of July 1983): Kié-Ntem 70,202, Litoral 66,370, Centro-Sur 52,393, Wele-Nzas 51,839, Bioko Norte 46,221, Bioko Sur 10,969, Annobón 2,006.

Principal towns (population at 1983 census): Malabo (capital) 15,253, Bata 24,100.

Births and Deaths (UN estimates, annual averages): Birth rate 42.5 per 1,000 in 1980–85, 42.4 per 1,000 in 1985–90; Death rate 21.0 per 1,000 in 1980–85, 19.0 per 1,000 in 1985–90. (Source: UN, *World Population Prospects: 1988*).

Economically Active Population (estimates, '000 at mid-1980): Agriculture, etc. 104 (males 48, females 56); Industry 18 (males 16, females 2); Services 36 (males 28, females 8); Total 159 (males 93, females 65). Source: ILO, *Economically Active Population Estimates and Projections, 1950–2025*. Mid-1989 (estimates, '000): Agriculture, etc. 101; Total 179 (Source: FAO, *Production Yearbook*).

AGRICULTURE, ETC.

Principal Crops (FAO estimates, metric tons, 1989): Sweet potatoes 37,000, Cassava 57,000, Coconuts 8,000, Palm kernels 3,000, Bananas 21,000, Cocoa beans (unofficial estimate) 8,000, Green coffee 7,000 (Source: FAO, *Production Yearbook*).

Livestock (FAO estimates, year ending September 1989): Cattle 5,000, Pigs 5,000, Sheep 35,000, Goats 8,000 (Source: FAO, *Production Yearbook*).

Forestry (1988): Roundwood removals (FAO estimates, '000 cu m): Fuel wood 447, Industrial wood 160, Total 607 (Source: FAO, *Yearbook of Forest Products*).

Fishing (metric tons, live weight): Total catch 4,400 in 1986; 4,000 (FAO estimate) in 1987; 4,000 (FAO estimate) in 1988 (Source: FAO, *Yearbook of Fishery Statistics*).

INDUSTRY

Palm oil (FAO estimates, '000 metric tons): 5.0 in 1987; 5.0 in 1988; 5 in 1989 (Source: FAO, *Production Yearbook*).

Veneer sheets ('000 cubic metres): 2 (FAO estimate) in 1983; 3 in 1984; 10 in 1985 (Source: FAO, *Yearbook of Forest Products*).

Electric energy (million kWh): 22 in 1985; 16 in 1986; 17 in 1987 (Source: UN, *Industrial Statistics Yearbook*).

FINANCE

Currency and Exchange Rates: 100 centimes = 1 franc de la Coopération financière en Afrique centrale (CFA). *Coins:* 1, 2, 5, 10, 25, 50, 100 and 500 francs CFA. *Notes:* 100, 500, 1,000, 5,000 and 10,000 francs CFA. *French Franc, Sterling and Dollar Equivalents* (30 September 1990): 1 French franc = 50 francs CFA; £1 sterling = 491.1 francs CFA; US $1 = 262.1 francs CFA; 1,000 francs CFA = £2.036 = $3.815. *Average Exchange Rate* (francs CFA per US dollar): 300.54 in 1987; 297.85 in 1988; 319.01 in 1989. *Note:* In January 1985 Equatorial Guinea adopted the franc CFA in place of the epkwele (plural: bipkwele), which had been linked to the Spanish peseta at the rate of 1 peseta = 2 bipkwele since June 1980. Some of the figures in this Survey are still in terms of bipkwele.

Budget (estimates, million francs CFA, 1989): *Revenue* Fiscal receipts 4,858, Other receipts 1,420; Sub-total 6,278; Taxes on sales of petroleum by Total-Guinée Equatoriale not yet remitted to the Government, Cheques issued to banks in liquidation –422; Total 5,856. *Expenditure:* Compensation of employees 2,062; Interest payments 2,300; Other goods and services 1,832; Transfers and subsidies 707; Capital expenditure 1,434; Total 8,335 (Source: *La Zone Franc–Rapport 1989*).

International Reserves (US $ million at 31 December 1989): IMF special drawing rights 0.12; Foreign exchange 0.71; Total 0.83 (Source: IMF, *International Financial Statistics*).

Money Supply ('000 million francs CFA at 31 December 1988): Currency outside deposit money banks 2.48; Demand deposits at deposit money banks 3.15; Total money 5.63 (Source: IMF, *International Financial Statistics*).

Cost of Living (Consumer price index for Africans in Malabo; base: January 1985 = 100): 132.5 in 1987; 135.6 in 1988; 143.7 in 1989 (Source: BEAC, *Etudes et Statistiques*).

Gross Domestic Product by Economic Activity (million bipkwele at current prices, 1987): Agriculture, hunting, forestry and fishing 24,453; Manufacturing 776; Electricity, gas and water 669; Construction 3,024; Trade, restaurants and hotels 3,627; Transport and communications 744; Finance, insurance, real estate and business services 803; Government services 5,445; Other services 495; Sub-total 40,036; Import duties 1,878; GDP in purchasers' values 41,914. (Source: UN, *National Accounts Statistics*).

Balance of Payments (estimates, million francs CFA, 1988): Merchandise exports f.o.b. 11,929, Merchandise imports c.i.f. –15,095, *Trade balance* –3,166; Current transactions (net) 2,264, *Current balance* –902; Capital balance 430; Total –472.

EXTERNAL TRADE

Principal Commodities (million bipkwele, 1981): *Imports:* Food, beverages and tobacco 1,990, Petroleum and petroleum products 1,787, Clothing 478, Iron and steel products 993, Motor vehicles and machinery 1,389; Total (incl. others) 7,982. *Exports:* Cocoa 1,788, Coffee 70, Timber 611; Total (incl. others) 2,502. **1982** (million bipkwele): Total imports 10,857; Total exports 3,837. **1986** (exports, million francs CFA): Cocoa beans 4,110; Wood 3,817; Coffee 434. **1987** (exports, million francs CFA): Cocoa beans 3,542; Coffee 1,681. **1988** (exports, million francs CFA): Cocoa beans 3,426 (Source for 1986–88: IMF, *International Financial Statistics*).

Principal Trading Partners (million bipkwele, 1981): *Imports:* Cameroon 574, Spain 6,375; Total (incl. others) 7,982. *Exports:* Federal Republic of Germany 87, Netherlands 81, Spain 2,170; Total (incl. others) 2,502.

TRANSPORT

Shipping (international sea-borne freight traffic, '000 metric tons, 1987): Goods loaded 97, Goods unloaded 57 (Source: UN Economic Commission for Africa, *African Statistical Yearbook*).

EQUATORIAL GUINEA

COMMUNICATIONS MEDIA
Radio receivers 103,000 in use in 1987; Television receivers 2,000 in use in 1987; Daily newspapers 1 in 1986, estimated circulation 1,000 (Source: UNESCO, *Statistical Yearbook*).

EDUCATION
Primary (1980/81): Schools 511; Teachers 647; Pupils 40,110.
Secondary and Further (1980/81): Schools 14; Teachers 288; Pupils 3,013. There were 175 pupils studying abroad.

Directory

The Constitution

A new constitution was approved by referendum on 15 August 1982.

FUNDAMENTAL PRINCIPLES

Education is the first priority of the State. Civil liberties and basic human rights are guaranteed. The State has sole control of minerals and coal mines, electricity and water supply, posts and telecommunications, and radio and television.

PRESIDENT OF THE REPUBLIC

The President, who is Head of State, leader of the Government and Supreme Commander of the Armed Forces, has the power to appoint and dismiss ministers and to determine and direct national policy. At the expiry of the presidential term of seven years, an election by universal suffrage was to be held. (President Obiang Nguema was appointed for a term of seven years immediately before the publication of the Constitution and was, accordingly, elected President in June 1989.)

STATE COUNCIL

The State Council has 11 members (including the Chairman of the House of Representatives, the President of the Supreme Tribunal and the Minister of Defence), and is responsible for defending national sovereignty, unity between the territorial units of Equatorial Guinea, peace and justice, and the proper conduct of democracy. The Council acts as an electoral college to approve or reject a presidential candidature, may refuse to accept the resignation of the President of the Republic, and may declare the President physically or mentally unfit to continue in office.

HOUSE OF REPRESENTATIVES

The House of Representatives is elected for a term of five years, and its members should be between 45 and 60 years of age. It sits twice a year, in March and September, for two-month periods, unless an extraordinary session is requested by the President, or by petition of three-quarters of the members of the House.

The Government

HEAD OF STATE

President: Brig.-Gen. (TEODORO) OBIANG NGUEMA MBASOGO (assumed office 25 August 1979; elected President 25 June 1989).

COUNCIL OF MINISTERS
(January 1991)

President and Head of Government: Brig.-Gen. (TEODORO) OBIANG NGUEMA MBASOGO.
Prime Minister in charge of Political and Administrative Co-ordination: Lt-Col CRISTINO SERICHE BIOKO MALABO.
Deputy Prime Minister, Minister of Education, Youth and Sport: ISIDORO EYI MOSUY ANDEME.
Minister of State, Minister Secretary-General at the Presidency: CASTRO NVONO AKELE.
Minister of State, Minister of the Economy, Commerce and Planning: MARCELINO NGUEMA ONGUENE.
Minister of State at the Presidency, in charge of Missions: ALEJANDRO EVUNA OWONO ASANGONO.
Deputy Minister Secretary-General at the Presidency: MARTÍN NKA ESONO NSING.
Minister of Justice and Religion: SILVESTRE SIALE BILEKA.
Minister of Public Works, Housing and Transport: ALEJANDRO ENVORO OVONO.
Minister of Agriculture, Livestock, Fisheries and Forestry: ANATOLIO NDONG MBA.
Minister of Industry and Energy: SEVERINO OBIANG BENGONO.
Minister of Labour and Social Promotion: JUAN BALBOA BONEKE.
Minister-delegate at the Presidency, in charge of Mines and Hydrocarbons: JUAN OLO MBA NSENG.
Minister-delegate at the Presidency, in charge of Culture, Tourism and Artisanal Promotion: LEANDRO MBOMIO NSUE.
Minister-delegate at the Ministry of Foreign Affairs and Co-operation: SANTIAGO ENEME OVONO.
Minister-delegate at the Ministry of National Defence: Maj. MELANIO EBENDENG NSOMO.
Minister-delegate at the Ministry of Territorial Administration and Communications: SEGUNDO MUÑOZ ILATA.
Minister-delegate at the Ministry of Health: ALEJANDRO MASOKO BENGONO.
Minister-delegate at the Ministry of Women's Promotion: PURIFICACIÓN ANGUE ONDO.

MINISTRIES

All Ministries are in Malabo.

Ministry of the Economy, Commerce and Planning: Malabo; tel. 20-43.
Ministry of Foreign Affairs and Co-operation: Malabo; tel. 32-20.

Legislature

CÁMARA DE REPRESENTANTES DEL PUEBLO

The 41-member House of Representatives of the People was elected for a five-year term on 28 August 1983. All candidates were nominated by President Obiang Nguema and were elected unopposed. Further legislative elections were held in July 1988.

Political Organizations

Partido Democrático de Guinea Ecuatorial (PDGE): Malabo; f. 1987 as a 'governmental party'.

Movements (in exile in 1991) seeking the restoration of democracy include the following:

Convergencia Social Democrática (CSD): Paris, France; f. 1984; comprises:

Partido Socialista de Guinea Ecuatorial (PSAGE): Oviedo, Spain.

Reunión Democrática para la Liberación de Guinea Ecuatorial (RDLGE): Paris, France: f. 1981; formed 12-mem. provisional Govt-in-exile 1983; Pres. MANUEL RUBÉN NDONGO.

Junta Coordinadora de las Fuerzas de Oposición Democrática (Co-ordinating Board of Opposition Forces): Zaragoza, Spain; f. 1983; Pres. TEODORO MACKUANDJI BONDJALE OKO; Sec.-Gen. SEVERO MOTO NSA; comprises:

Alianza Nacional de Restauración Democrática de Guinea Ecuatorial (ANRDGE)*: BP 335, 1211 Geneva 4, Switzerland; f. 1974; Sec.-Gen. MARTÍN NSOMO OKOMO.

Frente de Liberación de Guinea Ecuatorial (FRELIGE)*.

Movimiento de Liberación y Futuro de Guinea Ecuatorial (MOLIFUGE)*.

Partido del Progreso de Guinea Ecuatorial (PPGE)*: Madrid, Spain; Pres. SEVERO MOTO NSA; Sec.-Gen. JOSÉ LUIS JONES.

Reforma Democrática.

Partido Socialdemócrata de Guinea Ecuatorial (PSGE)*: Madrid, Spain; f. 1990; Pres. MARCELINO MANGUE MBA.

Movimiento para la Unificación Nacional de Guinea Ecuatorial (MUNGE): Kinshasa, Zaire; f. 1990.

EQUATORIAL GUINEA *Directory*

Revolutionary Command Council of Socialist Guinean Patriots and Cadres: f. 1981; Leader DANIEL OYONO.

Unión Eriana*.

Unión para la Democracia y el Desarrollo Social (UDDS): Libreville, Gabon; f. 1990; Sec.-Gen. ANTONIO SIBACHA.

* Signatories to the March 1989 'Pacto de Madrid para la Democratización y el Autodesarrollo en Guinea Ecuatorial.

Diplomatic Representation

EMBASSIES IN EQUATORIAL GUINEA

Cameroon: BP 292, Malabo; tel. 22-63; telex 1111; Ambassador: JOHN NCHOTU AKUM.

China, People's Republic: Malabo; Ambassador: DAI SHIQI.

Cuba: Malabo; Ambassador: (vacant).

France: Carreterra del Aeropuerto, Malabo; tel. 20-05; Ambassador: JACQUES GAZON.

Gabon: Apdo 648, Douala, Malabo; tel. 420; telex 1125; Ambassador: JEAN BAPTISTE MBATCHI.

Korea, Democratic People's Republic: Malabo; Ambassador: CHI YONG-HO.

Nigeria: 4 Paseo de los Cocoteros, Apdo 78, Malabo; tel. 23-86; Ambassador: JOHN SHINKAME.

Spain: Malabo; Ambassador: MANUEL ALABART FERNÁNDEZ CABADA.

USSR: Malabo; Ambassador: LEV ALEKSANDROVICH VAKHRAMEYEV.

USA: Casilla 597, Malabo; tel. 25-07; Ambassador: CHESTER NORRIS.

Judicial System

The structure of judicial administration was established in February 1981. The Supreme Tribunal in Malabo, consisting of a President of the Supreme Tribunal, the Presidents of the three chambers (civil, criminal and administrative), and two magistrates from each chamber, is the highest court of appeal. There are Territorial High Courts in Malabo and Bata, which are also courts of appeal. Courts of the First Instance exist in Malabo and Bata, and may be convened in the other provincial capitals, and Local Courts may be convened when necessary.

President of the Supreme Tribunal: JULIO ELA NDONG.

Religion

An estimated 94% of the population are adherents of the Roman Catholic Church. Traditional forms of worship are also followed.

CHRISTIANITY

The Roman Catholic Church

Equatorial Guinea comprises one archdiocese and two dioceses. There were an estimated 323,000 adherents in the country at 31 December 1988.

Bishops' Conference: Arzobispado, Apdo 106, Malabo; f. 1984; Pres. Mgr RAFAEL MARÍA NZE ABUY, Archbishop of Malabo.

Archbishop of Malabo: Mgr RAFAEL MARÍA NZE ABUY, Arzobispado, Apdo 106, Malabo; tel. 21-76.

Protestant Church

Iglesia Evangélica de Guinea Ecuatorial (Evangelical Church of Equatorial Guinea): Apdo 195, Malabo; f. 1960; c. 8,000 mems; Sec.-Gen. Rev. SAMUEL OKE ESONO ATUGU.

The Press

Africa 2000: Apdo 180, Malabo; tel. 27-20; Spanish; cultural review; quarterly; publ. by Centro Cultural Hispano-Guineano; Editor DONATO NDONGO-BIDYOGO.

Ebano: Malabo; Spanish; irregular; circ. 1,000.

Hoja Parroquial: Malabo; weekly.

Potopoto: Apdo 230, Bata, Fang and Spanish; irregular; Dir FRANCISCO DE ABHA FRANGO.

Unidad de la Guinea Ecuatorial: Malabo; irregular.

FOREIGN NEWS BUREAU

Agencia EFE (Spain): 50 Calle del Presidente Nasser, Malabo; tel. 31-65; Bureau Chief DONATO NDONGO BIDYOGO.

Publisher

Centro Cultural Hispano-Guineano: Apdo 180, Malabo; tel. 27-20.

Radio and Television

There were an estimated 103,000 radio receivers and 2,000 television receivers in use in 1987.

RADIO

There are three radio stations, all of which are operated by the Government.

Africa 2000: Camino de Basilé, Malabo; tel. 2490; f. 1988; cultural and educational programmes; broadcasts in Spanish; Dir MATÍAS NAVARRO.

Radio Ecuatorial Bata: Apdo 749, Bata; tel. 182; commercial station; programmes in Spanish, French and vernacular languages; Dir JESÚS OBIANG NGUEMA NDONG.

Radio Santa Isabel: Apdo 195, Malabo; tel. 382; programmes in Spanish, French, Fang, Bubi, Annobonés and Combe; Dir JUAN EYENE OPKUA NGUEMA.

TELEVISION

Director of Television: MAXIMILIANO MBA.

Finance

(cap. = capital; res = reserves; m. = million; br. = branch; amounts in francs CFA)

BANKING

Central Bank

Banque des Etats de l'Afrique Centrale (BEAC): Apdo 1917, Malabo; tel. 22-25-05; telex 8343; headquarters in Yaoundé, Cameroon; f. 1973 as the central bank of issue for mem. states of the Customs and Economic Union of Central Africa (UDEAC), comprising Cameroon, the Central African Republic, Chad, the Congo, Equatorial Guinea and Gabon; cap. 36,000m., res 162,037m. (June 1989); Gov. JEAN-FÉLIX MAMALEPOT; Dir in Equatorial Guinea MARTÍN-CRISANTO EBE MBA; br. in Bata.

Commercial Bank

BIAO-Guinea Ecuatorial: 6 Calle de Argelia, Apdo 686, Malabo; tel. 28-87; telex 913103; f. 1986; cap. 300m. (Dec. 1988); undergoing reorganization in 1991; Pres. CASTRO NVONO AKELE; Gen. Man. PAUL A. AUDUC; 2 brs.

Financial Institution

Caja Autónoma de Amortización de la Deuda Pública: Ministry of the Economy, Commerce and Planning, Malabo; management of state funds; Dir PATRICIO EKA NGUEMA.

Trade and Industry

Cámara de Comercio, Agrícola y Forestal de Malabo: Apdo 51, Malabo; tel. 151.

Cámaras Oficiales Agrícolas de Guinea: Bioko and Bata; buys cocoa and coffee from indigenous planters, who are partially grouped in co-operatives.

Empresa General de Industria y Comercio (EGISCA): Malabo; f. 1986; parastatal body jtly operated with the French Société pour l'Organisation, l'Aménagement et le Développement des Industries Alimentaires et Agricoles (SOMDIA); import-export agency.

INPROCAO: Malabo; production, marketing and distribution of cocoa.

Oficina para la Cooperación con Guinea Ecuatorial (OCGE): Malabo; f. 1981; administers bilateral aid from Spain.

Sociedad Anónima de Desarrollo del Comercio (SOADECO-Guinée): Malabo; f. 1986; parastatal body jtly operated with the French Société pour l'Organisation, l'Aménagement et le Développement des Industries Alimentaires et Agricoles (SOMDIA); development of commerce.

EQUATORIAL GUINEA

Total-Guinée Equatoriale: Malabo; f. 1984; cap. 150m. francs CFA; 50% state-owned, 50% by CFP-Total (France); petroleum marketing and distribution; Chair. of Board of Dirs Minister of Public Works, Housing and Transport.

TRADE UNIONS

There is no officially active trade unionism in Equatorial Guinea.

Transport

RAILWAYS

There are no railways in Equatorial Guinea.

ROADS

Bioko: a semi-circular tarred road serves the northern part of the island from Malabo down to Batete in the west and from Malabo to Bacake Grande in the east, with a feeder road from Luba to Moka and Bahía de la Concepción; total length of roads: about 160 km.

Río Muni: a tarred road links Bata with Mbini (Río Benito) in the west; another road, partly tarred, links Bata with the frontier post of Ebebiyin in the east and then continues into Gabon; other earth roads join Acurenam, Mongomo de Guadelupe and Nsork; total length of roads: 1,015 km.

SHIPPING

The main ports are Malabo (general cargo), Luba (bananas, timber), Bata (general), Mbini and Kogo (timber). A regular monthly service is operated by the Spanish Compañia Transmediterránea from Barcelona, calling at Malabo and Bata, and by other carriers.

CIVIL AVIATION

There is an international airport at Malabo, and a smaller airport at Bata. South Africa is to participate in the modernization of facilities at Malabo, and plans to upgrade facilities at Bata, at a cost of some 3,500m. francs CFA (with assistance from the African Development Bank, the Banque Arabe pour le Développement économique en Afrique and the Kuwait Fund for Arab Economic Development) were announced in 1988.

The national carrier, Compañia Ecuato-Guineana de Aviación, went into liquidation in early 1990. The regional airline, Air Afrique, agreed to maintain the country's national and regional flights, pending the establishment of a new carrier.

Tourism

Prior to the overthrow of President Macías Nguema in 1979, few foreigners visited Equatorial Guinea. Tourism remains undeveloped.

ETHIOPIA

Introductory Survey

Location, Climate, Language, Religion, Flag, Capital

The People's Democratic Republic of Ethiopia extends inland from the Red Sea coast of eastern Africa. The country has a long frontier with Somalia near the Horn of Africa. Sudan lies to the west, Djibouti to the east and Kenya to the south. The climate is mainly temperate because of the high plateau terrain, with an average annual temperature of 13°C (55°F), abundant rainfall in some years and low humidity. The lower country and valley gorges are very hot and subject to recurrent drought. The official language is Amharic, but many other local languages are also spoken. English is widely used in official and commercial circles, and Arabic is spoken in the province of Eritrea. The Ethiopian Orthodox (Tewahido) Church, an ancient Christian sect, has a wide following in the north and on the southern plateau. In much of the south and east there are Muslims and followers of animist beliefs. The national flag (proportions 3 by 2) has three horizontal stripes, of green, yellow and red. The capital is Addis Ababa.

Recent History

Ethiopia was dominated for more than 50 years by Haile Selassie, who became Regent in 1916, King in 1928 and Emperor in 1930. He ruled the country, except during the Italian occupation of 1936–41, until his deposition by the armed forces in September 1974 in the wake of serious regional famine, inflation and unemployment, and growing demands for democratic reform. The Emperor's rule was highly personal and autocratic, but he consolidated the expansion of Ethiopian territory and the gradual process of national modernization which had been begun by the Emperor Menelik (1865–1913). The former Italian colony of Eritrea was merged with Ethiopia, in a federal arrangement, in September 1952, and annexed to Ethiopia as a province in November 1962. Haile Selassie died, a captive of the military regime, in August 1975.

The revolution of September 1974 was engineered by an Armed Forces Co-ordinating Committee, known popularly as the Dergue ('Shadow'), which controlled ultimate power. The Dergue established a Provisional Military Government (PMG), headed by Lt-Gen. Aman Andom. In November, after a dispute in the military leadership, Gen. Andom was deposed and shot. The PMG was replaced by a Provisional Military Administrative Council (PMAC), led by Brig.-Gen. Teferi Benti; the monarchy was abolished in March 1975. Ethiopia was declared a socialist state in December 1974, and a national programme, called Ethiopia Tikdem (Ethiopia First), was implemented in the following year. Insurance companies, banks, financial institutions, large industrial enterprises, rural and urban land and schools were nationalized, while peasant co-operatives and industrial workers' councils were established.

Widespread unrest continued throughout 1975 and 1976, despite moves by the Dergue to ease tension by releasing some detainees and promising a return to civilian rule, at an unspecified date. Strains within the Dergue were reflected by its reorganization in December 1976. However, in February 1977 Lt-Col Mengistu Haile Mariam executed Brig.-Gen. Teferi Benti and his closest associates, and replaced him as Chairman of the PMAC and Head of State.

The Government continued to meet political and armed opposition from various groups, both Marxist and anti-Marxist. During 1977 and 1978 thousands of opponents of the Government were killed or imprisoned in a programme of 'rehabilitation' or 'liquidation'. Until July 1977 the Dergue was assisted by Mei'son (the Marxist All-Ethiopia Socialist Movement) but later formed its own party, Abyot Seded (Revolutionary Flame), which sought to enlist civilian support. However, all political groupings were theoretically swept away in late 1979 when a Commission for Organizing the Party of the Working People of Ethiopia (COPWE) was established.

The Central Committee of COPWE, which was dominated by military personnel, held its first congress in June 1980. The third congress and the formal establishment of the Workers' Party of Ethiopia (WPE), which replaced COPWE, took place in September 1984, to coincide with the 10th anniversary of the revolution. Lt-Col Mengistu was unanimously elected Secretary-General of the party, which was modelled on the Communist Party of the Soviet Union. The congress also elected an 11-member Politburo and a 136-member Central Committee.

In June 1986, in preparation for the eventual transfer of power from the PMAC to a civilian government, a draft constitution was published. Following extensive consultative procedures, the draft constitution was endorsed by 81% of the votes cast in a referendum held in February 1987. In June 85% of Ethiopia's registered voters (more than 15.7m.) participated in elections for an 835-seat legislature, the National Shengo (Assembly), to which Lt-Col Mengistu and all members of the Politburo of the WPE were returned as deputies. At the inaugural meeting of the National Shengo in September, the PMAC was abolished and the People's Democratic Republic of Ethiopia (PDRE) was declared. The National Shengo unanimously elected Lt-Col Mengistu as President of the PDRE, and a 24-member Council of State was also elected, to be the Shengo's permanent organ.

Numerous insurgent movements, encouraged by the confusion resulting from the revolution, are engaged in armed struggle with the Ethiopian Government. These movements are strongest in the Ogaden, Eritrea and Tigre. Somalia lays claim to the Ogaden, which is inhabited mainly by ethnic Somalis, and regular Somali troops have supported incursions by forces of the Western Somali Liberation Front (WSLF). In 1977 the Somalis made major advances in the Ogaden, but in 1978 were forced to retreat. By the end of 1980 Ethiopian defence forces were in control of virtually the whole of the Ogaden, but armed clashes continued in the region. In 1980 an OAU committee declared the Ogaden to be an integral part of Ethiopia.

A secessionist movement has existed in Eritrea since its annexation in 1962, and insurgent groups have pursued a military campaign in Tigre with the aim of creating a government of 'genuine democratic forces'. The Eritrean Liberation Front (ELF) was originally founded in Egypt in 1958, but the movement subsequently split into numerous factions. In January 1982 the Ethiopian Government announced 'Operation Red Star', to bring the political, social and economic development of Eritrea into conformity with programmes in operation in the rest of the country. However, the accompanying military campaign to enforce the implementation of these projects had failed by May. The Government launched an offensive against the Eritrean People's Liberation Front (EPLF) outside its stronghold of Nakfa in mid-1983, while a similar campaign was waged against the Tigre People's Liberation Front (TPLF) in western Tigre province. In early 1984 the EPLF started a major new campaign, and, during heavy fighting, government troops suffered severe losses. The EPLF captured the town of Tessenei, near the Sudanese border, and defeated the army on three fronts in the Eritrean highlands. In January 1985 three of the Eritrean factions agreed to form the Eritrean Unified National Council (EUNC), but the EPLF refused to collaborate with this group. It was revealed that, since 1977, the EPLF and the Ethiopian Government had sporadically conducted secret negotiations, which had the aim of reaching agreement on autonomy for the region, but had so far been unproductive. In March 1985 the Government launched a large-scale offensive in Tigre and Eritrea, and by September had made significant gains, including the recapture of the strategic towns of Barentu and Tessenei. In mid-1986, however, government forces again abandoned the north-east coast, and EPLF attacks on strategic installations continued. In March 1987 it was disclosed that further secret negotiations between the EPLF and the Government had recently taken place. Meanwhile, the EUNC alliance of three Eritrean groups had not proved successful, and it suffered a further set-back upon the death of its chairman in April 1987. The various factions of the Eritrean movement as a whole remained divided. In September 1987 the newly-elected National Shengo announced that five areas, including Eritrea and Tigre, were to become 'autonomous regions' under the new Constitution. Eritrea was granted the greatest degree of self-government, but both the EPLF and the TPLF have rejected the new provisions. At the end of 1990 it was still far from clear when the new structures would become operative, although elections were held for the shengos (regional assemblies) of 11 Administrative Regions and the Autonomous Regions of Dire Dawa, Assab and Ogaden in May 1989.

In December 1987 the EPLF announced the start of an offensive aiming to expel Ethiopian government troops from Eritrea. In March 1988 the EPLF captured the town of Afabet and claimed to have killed one-third of all Ethiopian troops in Eritrea. Following the capture of Afabet, the TPLF took advantage of the movement of government forces from Tigre to Eritrea and overran all the garrisons in north-western and north-eastern Tigre. In April the EPLF and the TPLF were reported to have restored contact and to be aiming to co-ordinate their military operations. Ideologically, however, the two groups remained far apart. The expulsion of foreign relief officials from Eritrea and Tigre in April, and the Government's declaration of a state of emergency there in May, emphasized the extent of the rebel forces' military successes. In late June government troops regained control of some of the captured garrison towns, suffering heavy losses in the process. However, in early 1989, after major defeats in north-west Tigre (including one inflicted by a joint TPLF-EPLF force), the government forces abandoned virtually the whole region to the TPLF.

Attempts by government forces to launch counter-offensives in Eritrea and Tigre have been handicapped by heavy losses and poor morale. In May 1989 the Government acted to pre-empt a coup which had been prepared by numerous senior army officers, including the chief-of-staff, the commander of the air force and the commander of the army in Eritrea. The entire military command structure was subsequently reshaped, casting further doubt upon the army's efficiency and its ability to conduct an effective campaign in the northern regions.

In mid-September 1989 it was reported that the TPLF, now allied with the Ethiopian People's Democratic Movement (EPDM) in the Ethiopian People's Revolutionary Democratic Front (EPRDF), had captured the one town, Maychew, which had remained under the control of government forces in the Tigre region, and all of the north-western part of the neighbouring Wollo region. Further southward, advances by the TPLF in October threatened the government-held garrison town of Dese, 370 km north of Addis Ababa, and in late October the TPLF reportedly captured the town of Mekane Selam, 200 km north of the capital.

While the EPLF and the TPLF pursued their military campaigns throughout 1989, both groups engaged in dialogue with the Government in an attempt to facilitate diplomatic solutions to the conflicts in Eritrea and Tigre. The diplomatic process began in January 1989 with the endorsement by the National Shengo of a proposal by some elements of the Eritrean Liberation Front (ELF) to divide Eritrea into two autonomous regions (one for the predominantly Muslim-populated lowlands and one for the mainly Christian highlands). However, the proposal was condemned by the EPLF. In June, at an emergency session, the National Shengo voted unanimously in favour of a proposal to commence peace negotiations with secessionist groups. The discussions were to be held without any preconditions in the presence of international observers, but the proposal made no mention of the TPLF (which seeks the creation of a government of 'genuine democratic forces', not secession from Ethiopia), and President Mengistu subsequently indicated that the Government was unwilling to compromise with regard to Eritrean independence. The EPLF was accordingly critical of the Government's initiative, but by the end of June both the EPLF and the TPLF had agreed to negotiate with the Government in the presence of international observers.

Negotiations between delegations representing the Ethiopian Government and the EPLF commenced in Atlanta, USA, under the chairmanship of the former US President, Jimmy Carter, in early September 1989, and were followed by a further round of talks in Nairobi, Kenya, in November. It was agreed to hold substantive discussions in April 1990, but it was clear from the outset that neither side was prepared to compromise on the issue of Eritrean independence; and that neither side was strongly motivated to negotiate. Following the capture of the port of Massawa by the EPLF in February 1990, the talks were postponed indefinitely. In January 1991 the USA announced that it would act as an intermediary between the Ethiopian Government and the EPLF, which had reportedly agreed to recommence negotiations in February.

Negotiations between delegations representing the Government and the ELF began in San'a, Yemen, in April 1990. Procedural matters were reportedly resolved, and the talks concluded with both sides agreeing to proceed to substantive negotiations within five months (by mid-January 1991, however, no further discussions had been held).

In November 1989 representatives of the TPLF met an Ethiopian government delegation in Rome, in the presence of Italian observers, for preliminary discussions aiming to establish an agenda for peace negotiations. Unlike the talks between the Government and the EPLF (during which a *de facto* ceasefire was maintained), the opening of negotiations between the Government and the TPLF coincided with an increase in the latter's military activities. The preliminary discussions concluded with a commitment by each side to recommence talks in mid-December. These were duly held, but ended inconclusively. A third round of talks was held in Rome in March 1990, but collapsed over the TPLF's insistence that substantive negotiations should involve a joint delegation of the TPLF and the EPDM.

Following the capture of the port of Massawa by the EPLF in February 1990 (presenting a direct threat to the continued survival of the Ethiopian army in Eritrea), President Mengistu was obliged to make further concessions to his critics. In March 1990 Ethiopian socialism was virtually abandoned. The WPE was renamed the Ethiopian Democratic Unity Party (EDUP), and membership was opened to non-Marxists. Mengistu also indicated that opposition groups would be allowed to participate in the political process, under an 'umbrella of unity'. With regard to the economy, Mengistu commenced dismantling many of the structures created after the revolution and establishing a mixed economy. Free-market principles were again to take precedence over planning, although a state sector was to remain.

Mengistu's reforms provoked a mixed reaction. The traditionalist element of the renamed WPE was outraged, although the announcement that large-scale, privately-owned farms were to be established on uncultivated land, and that peasants would be able to bequeath land to their children, was widely welcomed. Peasant organizations were nevertheless quick to remove party representatives, and the Government began, unexpectedly, to lose authority in rural areas.

Between April and June 1990 further defeats of government forces by both the EPLF and the TPLF (sometimes within 120 km of Addis Ababa) led President Mengistu to admit that Ethiopia was on the brink of collapse. In June Mengistu visited Kenya, where he was believed to have discussed a peace initiative for Ethiopia with President Moi of Kenya, and in the same month both the USA's President Bush and the USSR's President Gorbachev advocated the convening of an international peace conference on Ethiopia.

The continued fighting in the north during 1984–85 compounded difficulties being experienced in areas of Ethiopia already severely affected by famine. In 1984 the rains failed for the third consecutive crop season, and in May the Relief and Rehabilitation Commission estimated that 7m. people could suffer starvation. Ethiopia received emergency food aid from many Western nations, but distribution of the aid posed a major problem, as ports rapidly became congested. Some famine relief was airlifted to affected areas, while Western food agencies sent food and medical supplies into Eritrea through Sudan. Some rainfall in 1985 eased the drought in the northern provinces, but Ethiopia remained dependent on foreign aid.

In September 1987, following severe drought and the virtual total failure of all crops in the northern regions of Eritrea, Tigre, Wollo and Northern Shoa, the Ethiopian Government requested about 1m. tons of food aid from Western donors for the estimated 5m. people at risk of starvation (later revised to 1.4m. tons for 5.2m. people). As in 1984–85, the relief campaign that the international community subsequently mounted was hindered by Ethiopia's inadequate infrastructure, which exacerbated the problems of distributing food to the country's inaccessible northern regions. In late 1987 the EPLF's attacks on UN convoys, carrying vital food aid to the drought-stricken areas, were universally condemned. The EPLF, however, claimed that the vehicles were transporting military equipment on behalf of the Ethiopian Government. The UN refused to negotiate with the rebels (both the EPLF and the TPLF), but nevertheless resumed relief operations. In April 1988 the Government ordered the expulsion of all foreign relief workers from Eritrea and Tigre, claiming that it was about to launch a counter-offensive against the EPLF and the TPLF. This action prompted international condemnation. It was feared that the Government's Relief and Rehabilitation Commission, and the other national agencies which were left in charge of relief operations, would be unable to distribute food on the scale necessary to avert widespread famine. By May, however, it was clear that the relief operations being undertaken by the EPLF and the TPLF were capable of reaching large numbers of people. In June 1988 the League of Red Cross and Red Crescent Societies was granted permission to initiate a major famine relief operation in the northern Administrative Regions. The need for another major relief campaign, so soon after the famine of 1984-85, prompted renewed criticism of the Ethiopian Government's commitment to collectivist agricultural policies and its 'villagization' programme which, in late 1989, was reported to have affected some 40% of the total population.

In November 1989, following severe drought and the almost total failure of all crops in Eritrea and Tigre, the UN estimated that as many as 4m. people in those regions would require food aid in 1990. As in previous years of famine, it was clear that those who needed the food most would be inaccessible from the principal distribution centres, and would depend on air-drops and cross-border operations from Sudan. While local relief organizations, such as the Relief Society of Tigre and the Eritrean Relief Association, were believed to be capable of surmounting the logistical problems of food distribution, their participation in the relief operation was politically controversial, owing to their association with the TPLF and the EPLF.

In February 1990 the EPLF captured the port of Massawa, which had been the main staging-post for relief supplies to Eritrea and northern Tigre, and bombing by the Ethiopian air force subsequently destroyed grain stocks which had already arrived there. Following these developments (which left most of the famine-affected areas of northern Ethiopia under the control of the insurgent movements), international activity concentrated on securing an 'open roads' policy in order to guarantee the supply of food to these areas. The Ethiopian Government agreed to this policy in March 1990, and the first food convoy was despatched in the middle of that month. However, relief workers warned that convoys, even if permitted to continue, would be able to reach only one-quarter of the total number of people at risk of starvation. Non-governmental organizations continued to convey food-relief supplies across the Ethiopia-Sudan border, but these operations were hampered by air attacks, poor roads, shortage of transport and the dual use of lorries to transport both military equipment and food relief.

In May 1990 the Government warned food-aid donors not to attempt to deliver supplies to Massawa, while donors themselves appealed for an immediate cessation of all hostilities to enable food-aid to be supplied through neutral organizations. In July, however, the UN World Food Programme announced that both the Government and the EPLF had signalled their willingness to allow supplies of food-aid to the northern provinces to pass through Massawa.

In November 1990 the Ethiopian Relief and Rehabilitation Committee warned that 4.28m. people in northern Ethiopia would require some 850,000 tons of food-aid in 1991. In December the Government and the EPLF agreed to allow emergency food-aid to pass through the port of Massawa. The first shipment of relief supplies was reported to have left Djibouti for Massawa in early January 1991.

After Lt-Col Mengistu's coup in February 1977, the USSR supplanted the USA as the principal supplier of armaments to Ethiopia. In 1978 a treaty of friendship and co-operation between Ethiopia and the USSR was signed. However, this relationship has weakened as a result of the USSR's disengagement from Afghanistan and Angola, and of the Soviet Government's support for political, rather than military, solutions to Ethiopia's regional conflicts.

Relations with the USA improved slightly in December 1985, when Ethiopia agreed to pay compensation to US companies, on claims dating back to the 1975 nationalizations. In April 1989 Ethiopia sought to upgrade its diplomatic relations with the USA, receiving a cautious initial response. In September the USA provided a venue for direct talks between the Ethiopian Government and the EPLF, following diplomatic efforts by the former US President, Jimmy Carter. In November 1990 the US Assistant Secretary of State for African Affairs, Herman Cohen, held talks with the Ethiopian Minister of Foreign Affairs in Addis Ababa. It was noted that Ethiopia's relations with the USA had improved considerably as a result of the former's firm support for the sanctions implemented by the UN against Iraq, following its invasion of Kuwait in August 1990.

Ethiopia has developed closer diplomatic links with its neighbours, Kenya and Djibouti, which have attempted to bring about a reconciliation with Somalia. In January 1986, under the mediation of the President of Djibouti, Mengistu met the Somali President, Mohamed Siad Barre, for the first time since 1977. Talks between the two Ministers of Foreign Affairs took place later in 1986, when the issue of the Ogaden was discussed. Relations between Ethiopia and Somalia deteriorated in 1987, however, following a border clash in February, in which both sides reportedly sustained heavy casualties. In April 1988, after a further meeting between Lt-Col Mengistu and President Siad Barre had taken place in Djibouti, Ethiopia and Somalia agreed to re-establish diplomatic relations, to withdraw troops from their common border and to exchange prisoners of war. Ethiopia had previously insisted that the question of border demarcation be settled before the discussion of other issues. However, it was prompted to seek an improvement in relations with Somalia, owing to its urgent need to redeploy some of its estimated 50,000-70,000 troops in the Ogaden region to reinforce the military presence in the northern Administrative Regions of Eritrea and Tigre. On 25 April the first withdrawal of troops from the common border took place, followed, in August, by an exchange of prisoners who had been in captivity since the Ogaden war of 1978. In November 1990 President Mengistu was reported to have offered assistance to the Somali National Movement, the United Somali Congress and the Somali Patriotic Front if they united to overthrow President Siad Barre of Somalia. Other reports, however, indicated that Mengistu was seeking the normalization of relations between Ethiopia and Somalia.

Following the military coup in Sudan in April 1985, which displaced President Nimeri, full diplomatic relations were restored between Ethiopia and Sudan. In April 1987 Lt-Col Mengistu paid a four-day visit to Egypt for talks with President Mubarak. In December Sudan's Prime Minister, Sadiq al-Mahdi, met President Mengistu in Uganda. Since this meeting, Sudan has actively encouraged the Eritrean insurgent movements to negotiate with the Ethiopian Government, while Ethiopia has supported meetings between the Sudanese People's Liberation Army (SPLA) and Sudanese politicians. Relations between Ethiopia and Sudan were strained by the influx into Ethiopia, in late 1987 and early 1988, of thousands of Sudanese refugees, fleeing from famine and civil war in Southern Sudan. By May 1988 their numbers were estimated to have reached more than 300,000. It was also estimated that, since May 1988, about 400,000 Somalis had fled fighting in northern Somalia and had entered Ethiopia. Both groups were reported to be in need of substantial amounts of food aid in early 1990. In January 1991, following fighting between Somali government forces and rebels, 84,000 refugees were reported to have fled Somalia for Ethiopia. According to the UN, however, some 50% of the refugees were Ethiopians who had fled to Somalia after the 1977-78 Ogaden war.

In November 1989 Ethiopia re-established formal diplomatic relations with Israel. Ethiopia's previously close ties with Israel had been severed in 1973, in support of OAU policy. However, Israel provided anti-guerrilla training in 1976, and supplied weapons and spare parts for US military equipment until 1978. In 1984 about 13,000 Falashas, a Jewish group in Ethiopia, reached Sudan, from where they were flown to Israel in a secret airlift. Following the renewal of relations between Ethiopia and Israel in November 1989, the Ethiopian Government removed restrictions on Falashas leaving the country, and Israel began to provide more anti-guerrilla training and armaments. Israel was also believed to have obtained from Ethiopia the use of some naval and monitoring facilities on the Dahlak Islands in the Red Sea.

The re-establishment of relations with Israel had an immediate effect on Ethiopia's relations with Arab states. Relations with Libya were close in 1981, when a tripartite treaty between Ethiopia, Libya and the People's Democratic Republic of Yemen was signed, but by the mid-1980s the treaty had become moribund. Efforts to improve relations with other Arab states,

ETHIOPIA

Introductory Survey

many of which provided spasmodic support for the Eritrean secessionist cause, were also made, but with little success. These overtures ceased abruptly in 1989, when the renewal of relations with Israel precipitated immediate and considerable outside support for the EPLF and the TPLF.

Israel is interested both in keeping some part of the Red Sea free from Arab control and in aiding the cause of the SPLA in southern Sudan, which also receives support from Ethiopia. In November 1990 the Ethiopian Government announced that all Falashas remaining in the country, numbering an estimated 15,000, would be permitted to leave for Israel.

Government

Between 1974 and 1987 Ethiopia was ruled by a Provisional Military Administrative Council (PMAC), chaired by the Head of State. Under the new Constitution, adopted in 1987, legislative power is held by the National Shengo, with 835 members elected by universal suffrage for a five-year period. The Constitution provides for the election, by the National Shengo, of a President, who is Head of State and Head of Government. From its members, the National Shengo also elects the Council of State (its permanent organ) and the Council of Ministers, which is headed by a Prime Minister. The President and Vice-President of the country are also, respectively, President and Vice-President of the Council of State. Until March 1990 the Marxist-Leninist Workers' Party of Ethiopia (WPE) was the only legal political party. In that month the WPE was renamed the Ethiopian Democratic Unity Party (EDUP), and President Mengistu indicated that opposition groups would be permitted to participate in the political process. However, as the civil war escalated in 1990, political reform appeared increasingly irrelevant to the Government's prospects of remaining in power. Ethiopia is divided into 24 administrative regions and five autonomous regions, the 1987 Constitution providing for the formation of regional assemblies (shengos).

Defence

In June 1990, according to Western estimates, the army (including the People's Militia) numbered 430,800, the air force 4,500 and the navy 3,500. Military service is compulsory, and lasts for 30 months. In addition, all men and women between 18 and 50 years of age undergo six months' reserve training. Ethiopia receives armaments and technical assistance from Warsaw Pact countries, Cuba, Libya, Yemen and Israel. Defence expenditure in 1988/89 was estimated at 1,500m. birr.

Economic Affairs

In 1988, according to estimates by the World Bank, Ethiopia's gross national product (GNP), measured at average 1986–88 prices, was US $5,760m., equivalent to $120 per head: the second lowest recorded level of GNP per caput for any country in the world. During 1980–88, it was estimated, GNP increased, in real terms, at an average annual rate of 1.1%, although GNP per head declined by 1.4% per year. Over the same period the population increased by an annual average of 2.5%. Ethiopia's gross domestic product (GDP) increased, in real terms, by an annual average of 1.4% in 1980–88.

Agriculture (including forestry and fishing) contributed 42% of GDP in 1988. About 75% of the labour force were employed in agriculture in 1989. The principal cash crop is coffee (which accounted for about 58% of export earnings in 1988). The principal subsistence crops are cereals (barley, maize, sorghum and teff) and sugar cane. During 1980–88 agricultural production declined by an annual average of 1.1%.

Industry (including mining, manufacturing, construction and power) employed about 8% of the labour force in 1980, and contributed 17% of GDP in 1988. During 1980–88 industrial production increased by an annual average of 3.5%.

Mining contributed only about 0.1% of GDP in 1985/86. Ethiopia has reserves of petroleum, although these have not been exploited, and there are also small deposits of gold, platinum, copper and potash.

Manufacturing contributed 12% of GDP in 1988. Measured by the value of output, the principal branches of manufacturing in 1985/86 were food products (accounting for 20.2% of the total), petroleum refineries (19.1%), beverages (14.5%) and textiles (13.2%).

In years of normal rainfall, energy is derived principally from Ethiopia's massive hydroelectric power resources. Imports of mineral fuels comprised less than 15% of the value of total imports in 1985.

In 1988 Ethiopia recorded a visible trade deficit of US $556.0m. and there was a deficit of $227.9m. on the current account of the balance of payments. In 1985 the principal source of imports (17.4%) was the USSR, while the principal market for exports (18.5%) was the Federal Republic of Germany. Other major trading partners are Italy, Japan and the USA. The principal exports in 1985 were coffee, hides and skins and petroleum products. The principal imports were cereals and cereal preparations, mineral fuels, basic manufactures and machinery and transport equipment.

Services, which consisted mainly of wholesale and retail trade, public administration and defence, and transport and communications, contributed 40% of GDP in 1988.

In the fiscal year 1988/89 it was estimated that Ethiopia's budgetary deficit would total 1,600m. birr. It was estimated that this, together with military spending, would account for around 20% of GDP. Ethiopia is the principal African recipient of concessionary funding, and the largest recipient of EEC aid (ECU 230m. under the Third Lomé Convention). At the end of 1988 Ethiopia's total external public debt was US $2,790m. The cost of debt-servicing in 1988 was equivalent to an estimated 37.4% of total earnings from the export of goods and sevices. The annual rate of inflation averaged 2.1% in 1980–88. It was 7.1% in 1988 and 7.8% in 1989.

Ethiopia is a member of the African Development Bank (see p. 91), the Organization of African Unity (see p. 190), and adheres to the Third Lomé Convention of the EEC (see p. 151).

During the 1980s Ethiopia's agricultural development was severely disrupted by recurrent, catastrophic drought. The development of all sectors of the economy has suffered from the Government's diversion of as much as 50% of the regular budget to finance its war effort against insurgent forces in Eritrea and Tigre. The economy is dependent on foreign aid and is heavily, although not uncontrollably, indebted. The Government's 'ideological inflexibility' in addressing the problems resulting from the drought has been criticized by Western donors and development agencies. In 1989 the Government approved a five-year Development Plan which aimed to provide more incentives for private investors to participate in industry, agriculture and tourism. In late 1990 and early 1991 it was reported that large areas of the country were again threatened with severe shortages of food, with millions of people at risk of starvation.

Social Welfare

The scope of modern health services has been greatly extended since 1960, but they still reach only a small section of the population. In 1977 free medical care for the needy was introduced. In 1980 Ethiopia had 86 hospital establishments. Between 1974 and 1987, 26 new hospitals were built. By 1987 there were a total of 11,400 beds, while 1,204 physicians and 3,105 nurses were working in the health service. Relative to the size of the population, the provision of hospital beds and physicians was the lowest among African countries. By 1987 there were also 2,095 clinics and 159 health centres. With foreign assistance, health centres and clinics are steadily expanding into the rural areas. In times of famine, however, Ethiopian health services are totally inadequate. The 1986/87 budget allocated 8.7% (341.1m. birr) of total expenditure to health, social security and welfare.

Education

Education in Ethiopia is free and, after a rapid growth in numbers of schools, it is hoped to introduce compulsory primary education shortly. Since September 1976 most primary and secondary schools have been controlled by local peasant associations and urban dwellers' associations. Primary education begins at seven years of age and lasts for six years. Secondary education, beginning at 13 years of age, lasts for a further six years, comprising a first cycle of two years and a second of four years. As a proportion of male children in the relevant age-group, enrolment at primary, junior and senior schools was 35%, 21% and 11%, respectively, in 1988. The corresponding ratios for female children were 27%, 18% and 9%. There are three universities. The 1986/87 budget allocated 10.6% (413.7m. birr) of total expenditure to education. A major literacy campaign was launched in 1979. By 1987 more than 20m. people had been enrolled for tuition programmes, and the rate of adult illiteracy had reportedly been reduced from 93% to 29%.

ETHIOPIA

Public Holidays

1991: 7 January* (Christmas), 19 January* (Epiphany), 2 March (Battle of Adowa), 1 April* (Palm Monday), 6 April (Victory Day), 8 April* (Easter Monday), 16 April† (Id al-Fitr, end of Ramadan), 1 May (May Day), 23 June† (Id al-Adha/Arafat), 11 September (New Year's Day), 12 September (Popular Revolution Commemoration Day), 21 September† (Mouloud, Birth of the Prophet), 27 September* (Feast of the True Cross).

1992: 7 January* (Christmas), 19 January* (Epiphany), 2 March (Battle of Adowa), 4 April† (Id al-Fitr, end of Ramadan), 6 April (Victory Day), 20 April* (Palm Monday), 27 April* (Easter Monday), 1 May (May Day), 11 June† (Id al-Adha/Arafat), 10 September† (Mouloud, Birth of the Prophet), 11 September (New Year's Day), 12 September (Popular Revolution Commemoration Day), 27 September* (Feast of the True Cross).

* Coptic holidays.
† These holidays are dependent on the Islamic lunar calendar and may vary by one or two days from the dates given.

Note: Ethiopia uses its own solar calendar; the Ethiopian year 1983 began on 11 September 1990.

Weights and Measures

The metric system is officially in use. There are many local weights and measures.

Statistical Survey

Source (unless otherwise stated): Central Statistical Office, POB 1143, Addis Ababa; tel. 113010.

Area and Population

AREA, POPULATION AND DENSITY

Area (sq km)	1,251,282*
Population (census of 9 May 1984)†	
Males	21,080,209
Females	21,104,743
Total	42,184,952
Population (official estimates at mid-year)	
1987	46,184,000
1988	47,882,000
1989	49,513,000
Density (per sq km) at mid-1989	39.6

* 483,123 sq miles.
† Including an estimate for areas not covered by the census.

ADMINISTRATIVE REGIONS (census of 9 May 1984)*

	Area (sq km)	Population	Density (per sq km)
Arussi	23,674.7	1,662,232	70.2
Bale	127,052.8	1,006,490	7.9
Eritrea	93,679.1	2,614,699	27.9
Gemu Goffa	40,374.8	1,248,033	30.9
Gojam	61,224.3	3,224,881	52.7
Gondar	79,579.4	2,921,124	36.7
Hararge	272,636.9	4,181,167	15.3
Illubabor	46,367.1	963,554	20.8
Kefa (Kaffa)	56,633.6	2,450,468	43.3
Shoa†	85,315.6	9,503,140	111.4
Sidamo	119,760.4	3,790,577	31.7
Tigre	64,921.3	2,409,599	37.1
Wollega	70,481.0	2,477,276	35.1
Wollo	82,143.6	3,642,013	44.3
Assab Administration	27,464.5	89,299	3.3
Total	**1,251,281.9**	**42,184,952**	**33.7**

* Following the adoption of a new constitution in 1987, the 15 existing regions were replaced by 24 Administrative Regions and five Autonomous Regions.
† Data include the capital, Addis Ababa, which is also a separate Administrative Region (area 222.0 sq km; population 1,412,577).

PRINCIPAL TOWNS (population at 1984 census)

Addis Ababa (capital)	1,412,577	Dessie	68,848
Asmara	275,385	Harar	62,160
Dire Dawa	98,104	Mekele	61,583
Gondar (incl. Azeso)	80,886	Jimma	60,992
		Bahir Dar	54,800
		Akaki	54,146
Nazret	76,284	Debre Zeit	51,143

BIRTHS AND DEATHS (official estimates)

Average annual birth rate 46.0 per 1,000 in 1970–81; death rate 18.1 per 1,000 in 1970–81.

ECONOMICALLY ACTIVE POPULATION
(ILO estimates, '000 persons at mid-1980)

	Males	Females	Total
Agriculture, etc.	8,164	5,877	14,040
Industry	960	422	1,383
Services	1,547	623	2,170
Total	**10,671**	**6,922**	**17,593**

Source: ILO, *Economically Active Population Estimates and Projections, 1950–2025*.

1984 census: Total labour force 18,492,300 (males 11,243,065; females 7,249,235).

Agriculture

PRINCIPAL CROPS ('000 metric tons)

	1987	1988	1989
Wheat	834†	850†	850*
Barley†	1,024	1,098	1,100
Maize	1,560†	1,600†	1,600*
Oats	41*	30†	30*
Millet (Dagusa)	188†	180†	180*
Sorghum	950†	964†	964*
Other cereals	1,130	1,201	1,201
Potatoes*	370	370	370
Sweet potatoes*	136	143	144
Yams*	230	240	250
Other roots and tubers*	870	900	920
Dry beans	30*	60†	60*
Dry peas	77†	78†	80*
Dry broad beans	259†	259†	260*
Chick-peas	130†	115†	115*
Lentils	28†	27†	28*
Other pulses*	92	102	104
Sugar cane*	1,600	1,700	1,750
Soybeans†	6	6	6
Groundnuts (in shell)*	50	50	53
Castor beans*	12	12	13
Rapeseed	23†	26†	26*
Sesame seed*	37	37	38
Linseed	26†	36†	37*
Safflower seed*	33	34	34
Cottonseed†	44	38	36
Cotton (lint)†	20	19	18
Vegetables and melons*	577	586	591
Bananas*	75	76	77
Other fruit (excl. melons)	143*	147	149*
Tree nuts*	61	62	63
Coffee (green)	186	170	200
Tobacco (leaves)*	3	3	4
Fibre crops (excl. cotton)*	17	17	17

* FAO estimate(s). † Unofficial estimate(s).

Source: FAO, *Production Yearbook*.

ETHIOPIA

LIVESTOCK ('000 head, year ending September)

	1987	1988	1989
Cattle*	27,000	27,000	28,900
Sheep*	24,000	24,000	24,000
Goats*	18,000	18,000	18,000
Asses*	4,700	4,800	4,900
Horses†	2,500	2,550	2,600
Mules†	530	550	570
Camels†	1,050	1,060	1,070
Pigs†	19	19	20

* Unofficial estimates.   † FAO estimates.
Poultry (FAO estimates, million): 57 in 1987, 1988 and 1989.
Source: FAO, *Production Yearbook*.

LIVESTOCK PRODUCTS
(FAO estimates, unless otherwise indicated; '000 metric tons)

	1987	1988	1989
Beef and veal*	206	206	237
Mutton and lamb*	79	79	82
Goats' meat	66	66	66
Pig meat	1	1	1
Poultry meat	136	112	107
Other meat	60	87	95
Edible offals	89	89	96
Cows' milk	602	602	624
Goats' milk	95	95	95
Sheep's milk	65	65	65
Butter	9.1	9.2	9.2
Hen eggs	78.0	78.7	78.7
Honey	22.2	22.5	22.6
Wool:			
greasy	12.6	12.6	12.6
clean	6.6	6.6	6.6
Cattle hides	39.5	39.5	45.5
Sheep skins	14.3	14.3	14.7
Goat skins	14.0	14.0	14.1

* Unofficial estimates.
Source: FAO, *Production Yearbook* and *Quarterly Bulletin of Statistics*.

Forestry

ROUNDWOOD REMOVALS
(FAO estimates, '000 cubic metres, excluding bark)

	1986	1987	1988
Sawlogs, etc.*	120	120	120
Other industrial wood*	1,693	1,693	1,693
Fuel wood	35,647	36,333	37,083
Total	37,460	38,146	38,896

* Assumed to be unchanged since 1983.
Source: FAO, *Yearbook of Forest Products*.

SAWNWOOD PRODUCTION ('000 cubic metres)

	1981	1982	1983
Total (including boxboards)	65*	45	45

* FAO estimate.
1984–88: Annual production as in 1983 (FAO estimates).
Source: FAO, *Yearbook of Forest Products*.

Fishing
('000 metric tons, live weight)

	1986*	1987*	1988†
Inland waters	3.5	3.5	3.3
Indian Ocean	0.6	0.5	0.7
Total catch	4.1	4.0	4.1

* FAO estimates.   † Official estimates.
Source: FAO, *Yearbook of Fishery Statistics*.

Mining
(year ending 10 September)

	1983/84	1984/85	1985/86
Gold (kilograms)	661.6	918.1	923.0
Platinum (kilograms)	0.2	0.1	2.4

Industry

SELECTED PRODUCTS ('000 metric tons, unless otherwise indicated; year ending 10 September)

	1984/85	1985/86	1986/87
Wheat flour	181	195	n.a.
Macaroni	18	19	n.a.
Raw sugar	180	181	n.a.
Wine ('000 hectolitres)	100	104	n.a.
Beer ('000 hectolitres)	818	797	n.a.
Soft drinks ('000 hectolitres)	755	796	n.a.
Mineral waters ('000 hectolitres)	237	245	n.a.
Cigarettes (million)	2,229	2,629	n.a.
Cotton yarn	9.4	10.6	n.a.
Woven cotton fabrics (million sq metres)	78	84	n.a.
Blankets (number)	1,274	1,215	n.a.
Woollen carpets ('000 sq metres)	28	33	n.a.
Nylon fabrics (million sq metres)	5.9	5.7	n.a.
Footwear ('000 pairs)	7,682	8,868	n.a.
Soap	12.9	15.5	n.a.
Ethyl alcohol ('000 hectolitres)	10	13	n.a.
Liquefied petroleum gas	5*	6	7
Motor gasoline	101	107	122
Distillate fuel oils	195	199	215
Residual fuel oils	310	311	338
Clay building bricks (million)	21	13	n.a.
Quicklime	6	8	n.a.
Cement	228	270	n.a.
Electric energy (million kWh)	750	759	764

* Provisional.
Source: UN, *Industrial Statistics Yearbook*.

ETHIOPIA

Finance

CURRENCY AND EXCHANGE RATES

Monetary Units
100 cents = 1 birr.

Denominations
Coins: 1, 5, 10, 25 and 50 cents.
Notes: 1, 5, 10, 50 and 100 birr.

Sterling and Dollar Equivalents (30 September 1990)
£1 sterling = 3.878 birr;
US $1 = 2.070 birr;
100 birr = £25.79 = $48.31.

Exchange Rate
Fixed at US $1 = 2.070 birr since February 1973.

GENERAL BUDGET (estimates, million birr, year ending 7 July)

Revenue*	1984/85	1985/86	1986/87
Taxation	1,685.0	1,883.0	2,098.2
Taxes on income, profits, etc.	646.6	722.0	860.5
Taxes on property	42.0	44.4	46.2
Sales taxes	173.4	190.2	219.5
Excises	353.5	373.7	409.3
Import duties	275.9	268.8	387.1
Export duties	172.8	263.0	153.7
Stamp taxes	13.9	14.5	16.4
Entrepreneurial and property income	395.9	538.4	491.9
Administrative fees and charges, etc.	79.2	46.6	50.8
Other current revenue	94.4	249.8	191.7
Capital revenue	11.5	12.6	15.2
Total revenue	**2,266.0**	**2,730.4**	**2,847.8**

Expenditure†	1984/85	1985/86	1986/87
General public services and defence	1,056.6	993.0	1,166.7
Public order and safety	165.7	166.9	173.4
Education	364.4	381.0	413.7
Health	114.7	122.1	139.3
Social security and welfare	200.2	209.6	201.8
Housing and community amenities	118.0	134.0	160.8
Recreational, cultural and religious affairs and services	38.8	118.4	49.4
Economic affairs and services	823.0	1,125.2	1,178.7
Fuel and energy	112.1	221.0	213.5
Agriculture, forestry and fishing	310.5	486.2	422.4
Mining, manufacturing and construction	155.0	167.3	230.0
Transport and communication	203.9	211.7	252.6
Other purposes	827.8	690.3	428.3
Total expenditure	**3,709.2**	**3,940.5**	**3,912.1**
Current‡	3,078.6	3,109.0	3,063.3
Capital	630.6	831.5	848.8

* Excluding grants received from abroad (million birr): 631.3 (current 538.8, capital 92.5) in 1984/85; 443.1 (current 369.9, capital 73.2) in 1985/86; 322.0 (current 247.7, capital 74.3) in 1986/87. Figures include estimates of the value of grants in kind and technical assistance received by Ethiopia.
† Excluding net lending (million birr): 56.9 in 1984/85; 46.1 in 1985/86; 12.6 in 1986/87.
‡ Including interest payments (million birr): 225.4 in 1984/85; 192.7 in 1985/86; 235.2 in 1986/87.
Source: IMF, *Governmental Finance Statistics Yearbook*.

1987/88 (estimates, million birr): Revenue 3,377.7, excluding grants received (274.4); Expenditure 4,482.0. Source: IMF, *International Financial Statistics*.

NATIONAL BANK RESERVES (US $ million at 31 December)

	1987	1988	1989
Gold*	21.3	21.3	17.3
IMF special drawing rights	1.7	—	0.1
Foreign exchange	121.0	64.2	46.0
Total	**144.0**	**85.5**	**63.4**

* National valuation.
Source: IMF, *International Financial Statistics*.

MONEY SUPPLY (million birr at 31 December)

	1987	1988	1989
Currency outside banks	1,744	1,962	2,341
Demand deposits at commercial banks	1,597	1,759	1,981
Total money	**3,341**	**3,722**	**4,322**

Source: IMF, *International Financial Statistics*.

COST OF LIVING (General Index of Retail Prices for Addis Ababa, excluding rent; base: 1980 = 100)

	1985	1986	1987
Food	155.3	131.6	123.6
Fuel, light and soap*	128.2	137.6	151.0
Clothing	97.2	99.0	134.7
All items (incl. others)	**144.1**	**130.0**	**126.8**

* Including certain kitchen utensils.
1988: Food 133.4; All items 135.8.
1989: Food 142.1; All items 146.4.
Source: ILO, mainly *Year Book of Labour Statistics*.

NATIONAL ACCOUNTS
(million birr at current prices, year ending 7 July)
Expenditure on the Gross Domestic Product

	1986/87	1987/88	1988/89
Government final consumption expenditure	2,164	2,775	3,026
Private final consumption expenditure*	8,650	8,204	8,930
Gross fixed capital formation	1,633	1,805	1,783
Total domestic expenditure	**12,447**	**12,784**	**13,739**
Exports of goods and services	1,289	1,353	1,438
Less Imports of goods and services	2,541	2,598	2,822
GDP in purchasers' values	**11,196**	**11,539**	**12,355**

* Including increase in stocks. The figures are obtained as a residual.
Source: IMF, *International Financial Statistics*.

ETHIOPIA

Gross Domestic Product by Economic Activity

	1983/84	1984/85	1985/86‡
Agriculture, hunting, forestry and fishing	4,070.2	3,915.8	4,354.5
Mining and quarrying	12.3	15.1	15.3
Manufacturing	1,009.2	1,023.0	1,072.9
Electricity, gas and water	67.6	73.6	109.9
Construction	387.3	374.5	387.6
Wholesale and retail trade	997.5	962.1	1,036.3
Transport, storage and communications	564.9	614.0	718.1
Finance, insurance and real estate*	510.4	542.9	577.4
Public administration and defence	750.9	770.0	781.6
Other community, social and personal services†	503.1	539.9	582.4
Other services	70.1	70.8	71.6
GDP at factor cost	8,943.5	8,901.7	9,707.6
Indirect taxes, *less* subsidies	1,057.5	979.1	1,096.0
GDP in purchasers' values	10,000.1	9,880.8	10,803.6

* Including imputed rents of owner-occupied dwellings.
† Including, restaurants, hotels and business services.
‡ Figures are provisional. The revised total is 10,823 million birr.

Source: UN, *National Accounts Statistics*.

BALANCE OF PAYMENTS (US $ million)

	1986	1987	1988
Merchandise exports f.o.b.	477.1	355.2	400.0
Merchandise imports f.o.b.	−932.6	−932.7	−956.0
Trade balance	−455.4	−577.4	−556.0
Exports of services	277.9	318.7	288.9
Imports of services	−332.9	−366.4	−402.9
Balance on goods and services	−510.4	−625.1	−670.0
Private unrequited transfers (net)	69.4	129.6	180.5
Government unrequited transfers (net)	113.7	278.0	261.6
Current balance	−327.3	−217.5	−227.9
Long-term capital (net)	240.6	292.8	292.9
Short-term capital (net)	−1.0	—	6.8
Net errors and omissions	201.6	−182.7	−94.0
Total (net monetary movements)	113.9	−107.4	−22.3
Valuation changes (net)	−9.4	−32.7	3.9
Exceptional financing	—	0.4	—
Changes in reserves	104.5	−139.7	−18.4

Source: IMF, *International Financial Statistics*.

External Trade

PRINCIPAL COMMODITIES
(distribution by SITC, US $ '000)

Imports c.i.f.	1983	1984	1985
Food and live animals	103,814	82,909	241,820
Dairy products and birds' eggs	n.a.	11,028	33,066
Milk and cream	n.a.	9,926	28,769
Preserved milk and cream	n.a.	9,926	28,765
Dried milk with up to 1.5% fat content	n.a.	8,911	24,421
Cereals and cereal preparations	n.a.	59,104	186,778
Wheat and meslin (unmilled)	n.a.	38,575	77,427
Wheat, etc., meal or flour	n.a.	6,561	65,541
Flour of wheat or meslin	n.a.	5,461	33,363
Wheat meal and groats	n.a.	1,099	32,178
Crude materials (inedible) except fuels	n.a.	20,901	32,651
Textile fibres and waste	n.a.	9,547	24,120
Mineral fuels, lubricants, etc.	n.a.	174,150	146,292
Petroleum, petroleum products, etc.	n.a.	174,107	146,288
Crude petroleum oils, etc.	160,521	146,453	133,488
Refined petroleum products	16,192	26,413	11,681
Animal and vegetable oils, fats and waxes	n.a.	11,773	47,867
Fixed vegetable oils and fats	n.a.	6,363	44,208
Soft fixed vegetable oils	n.a.	4,111	22,133
Soya bean oil	n.a.	3,484	20,615
Other fixed vegetable oils	n.a.	2,252	22,075
Chemicals and related products	75,368	99,503	72,673
Medicinal and pharmaceutical products	22,413	24,266	22,847
Medicaments	n.a.	22,108	21,988
Basic manufactures	123,321	140,198	133,232
Paper, paperboard and manufactures	10,600	12,443	20,968
Textile yarn, fabrics, etc.	22,237	17,971	25,878
Iron and steel	n.a.	41,284	29,964
Metal structures and parts	n.a.	20,089	13,445
Machinery and transport equipment	300,159	373,947	284,147
Machinery specialized for particular industries	n.a.	91,927	64,311
General industrial machinery, equipment and parts	n.a.	21,290	21,715
Electrical machinery, apparatus, etc.	n.a.	41,937	34,764
Road vehicles and parts*	92,117	92,540	116,618
Motor vehicles for goods transport, etc.	n.a.	35,988	53,753
Goods vehicles (lorries and trucks)	n.a.	31,060	49,474
Parts and accessories for cars, buses, lorries, etc.*	n.a.	32,686	29,913
Other transport equipment*	n.a.	110,025	23,279
Aircraft, etc., and parts*	n.a.	107,201	21,697
Miscellaneous manufactured articles	n.a.	29,735	25,851
Total (incl. others)	876,003	942,563	988,620

* Excluding tyres, engines and electrical parts.
Source: UN, *International Trade Statistics Yearbook*.

ETHIOPIA

Statistical Survey

Exports f.o.b.	1983	1984	1985
Food and live animals	n.a.	299,377	235,022
Live animals for food	8,448	5,831	9,170
Vegetables and fruit	n.a.	11,483	8,692
Fresh or simply preserved vegetables	13,185	10,552	7,054
Dried leguminous vegetables	11,676	8,008	4,769
Coffee, tea, cocoa and spices	n.a.	265,651	209,783
Coffee and coffee substitutes	251,176	263,627	209,045
Crude materials (inedible) except fuels	n.a.	79,187	64,675
Hides and skins	n.a.	46,752	53,720
Raw hides and skins (excl. furs)	40,637	46,751	53,718
Raw bovine and equine hides	n.a.	8,819	9,376
Goatskins	n.a.	8,981	12,172
Sheepskins with wool	n.a.	28,951	32,094
Oil seeds and oleaginous fruit	n.a.	8,067	4,484
Seeds for soft fixed oils	11,400	7,696	4,401
Vegetable materials used in pharmacy	13,638	15,466	2,003
Mineral fuels, lubricants, etc.	n.a.	30,846	33,146
Petroleum, petroleum products, etc.	n.a.	30,846	33,146
Refined petroleum products	n.a.	30,846	33,146
Residual fuel oils	n.a.	30,846	33,146
Total (incl. others)*	402,682	417,188	337,783

* Excluding platinum.

Source: UN, *International Trade Statistics Yearbook*.

1986 (million birr): *Imports:* Total 2,280.4; *Exports:* Coffee 725.6; Hides and skins 109.9; Total (incl. others) 941.6.
1987 (million birr): *Imports:* Total 2,205.9; *Exports:* Coffee 414.0; Hides and skins 123.7; Total (incl. others) 735.2.
1988 (million birr): *Imports:* Total 2,336.2; *Exports:* Coffee 513.4; Hides and skins 129.3; Total (incl. others) 888.6.

(Source: IMF, *International Financial Statistics*).

PRINCIPAL TRADING PARTNERS ('000 birr)

Imports	1983	1984	1985
China, People's Rep.	8,775	8,213	8,118
France	51,494	64,231	66,524
German Dem. Rep.	39,086	31,724	29,080
Germany, Fed. Rep.	179,419	201,346	203,791
India	8,098	9,587	9,224
Italy	243,045	190,418	164,184
Japan	168,147	126,042	123,638
Kenya	9,757	9,394	8,098
Korea, Rep.	46,257	20,172	51,378
Netherlands	51,879	37,571	58,201
Saudi Arabia	18,002	9,994	18,142
Sweden	36,108	25,976	63,163
Switzerland	38,798	42,401	40,698
USSR	379,063	452,996	356,339
United Kingdom	137,638	124,589	178,300
USA	83,192	298,219	330,469
Total (incl. others)	1,813,325	1,951,104	2,046,443

Source: Ethiopian Chamber of Commerce.

Exports	1983	1984	1985
Djibouti	65,363	59,856	25,274
Egypt	6	1	2,908
France	63,320	43,720	26,335
Germany, Fed. Rep.	137,809	155,688	129,099
Italy	62,184	63,696	53,809
Japan	62,805	64,510	71,720
Netherlands	16,476	17,471	92,266
Saudi Arabia	47,931	36,440	25,609
Sudan	1,525	10,337	12,690
USSR	3,684	39,074	36,872
United Kingdom	13,435	20,055	22,185
USA	169,665	167,802	73,317
Yemen, People's Dem. Rep.	54,893	49,679	56,819
Yugoslavia	2,204	2,012	3,452
Total (incl. others)	832,973	863,579	698,712

Transport

RAILWAYS (traffic)*

	1981/82	1982/83	1983/84
Addis Ababa–Djibouti:			
Passenger-km ('000)	307,000	360,000	268,000
Freight ('000 net ton-km)	108,000	122,000	117,000

* Excluding Eritrea but including traffic on the portion of the Djibouti–Addis Ababa line which runs through the Republic of Djibouti.

ROAD TRAFFIC (motor vehicles in use at 31 December)

	1987	1988	1989
Cars	30,212	41,512	39,942
Buses and coaches	4,542	4,465	4,515
Goods vehicles	6,368	12,619	12,615
Motorcycles and scooters	1,516	1,697	1,708
Total	42,638	60,293	58,780

Source: IRF, *World Road Statistics*.

SHIPPING (Ports of Assab and Massawa, year ending 7 July)

	1981/82*	1982/83	1983/84
Vessels entered ('000 net reg. tons)	2,681	2,961	3,024
Goods loaded ('000 metric tons)	625	650	711
Goods unloaded ('000 metric tons)	1,753	1,856	1,955

* Provisional figures.

CIVIL AVIATION (traffic on scheduled services)

	1983	1984*	1985*
Kilometres flown (million)	14.9	14.6	16.7
Passengers carried ('000)	346	399	471
Passenger-km (million)	767	858	1,016
Freight ton-km (million)	24.5	43.8	66.4

* Source: UN, *Statistical Yearbook*.

Tourism

	1984	1985	1986
Tourist arrivals ('000)	60	61	59

Source: UN, *Statistical Yearbook*.

ETHIOPIA

Communications Media

	1982	1983	1984
Telephones ('000 in use)	101	110	116
Radio receivers ('000 in use)	3,000	3,000	3,000
Television receivers ('000 in use)	45	45	50
Book production: titles*	n.a.	457	349
Daily newspapers: Number	3	3	3
Average circulation ('000 copies)	40	n.a.	40
Non-daily newspapers: Number	4	n.a.	4
Average circulation ('000 copies)	39	n.a.	40
Other periodicals: Number	n.a.	n.a.	3
Average circulation ('000 copies)	n.a.	n.a.	178

* Including pamphlets (214 in 1983; 157 in 1984).

1987: Book production 335 titles; Radio receivers 8.5m.; Television receivers 70,000.

Source: mainly UNESCO, *Statistical Yearbook*.

Education

	Teachers		Pupils/Students	
	1986	1987	1986	1987
Pre-primary	1,622	1,900	74,107	87,000
Primary	56,684	58,400	2,736,517	2,884,000
Secondary: general	16,987	18,580	742,351	842,700
Vocational	n.a.	n.a.	5,859	n.a.
Universities	1,022	1,098	23,633	22,701
Other higher	337	297	6,577	6,552

Source: UNESCO, *Statistical Yearbook*.

Directory

The Constitution

The 1931 Constitution was abolished by military decree in September 1974. In June 1986 a draft constitution, prepared by the Workers' Party of Ethiopia (WPE, subsequently renamed the Ethiopian Democratic Unity Party), was published, providing for a unitary state comprising administrative and autonomous regions. The new Constitution was approved by referendum in February 1987. Based on Marxist-Leninist principles, it provides for the election of an 835-seat National Shengo (Assembly), which is the highest organ of government. Candidates for election must either be members of the WPE, or be nominated by representative organizations, such as trade unions, or the armed forces. The term of office of the National Shengo is five years, and its deputies are responsible for the election of the President of the People's Democratic Republic of Ethiopia (PDRE) (established at the inaugural session of the National Shengo in September 1987), and of the Council of State, which oversees state affairs when the National Shengo is not in session. The National Shengo also appoints a Council of Ministers (Cabinet). Under the terms of the Constitution, the President and Vice-President of the PDRE are also President and Vice-President, respectively, of the Council of State.

The Government

HEAD OF STATE

President: Lt-Col Mengistu Haile Mariam (elected 11 September 1987).
Vice-President: Fisseha Desta.

COUNCIL OF STATE
(January 1991)

President: Lt-Col Mengistu Haile Mariam.
Vice-Presidents: Fisseha Desta, Emanuel Amdemikhail, Yusuf Ahmed, Lt-Col Berhanu Bayih, Lema Gutema.
Secretary: Embibe Ayele.
Members:
Capt. Fikre Selassie Wogderes
Lt-Gen. Tesfaye Gebre-Kidan
Addis Tedla
Hailu Yimenu
Alemu Agebe
Fasika Sidelil
Tesfaye Dinka
Shewandagn Belete
Endalle Tessema
Ashagre Yigletu
Tefera Wondie
Kasaye Aragaw
Tadese Tamirat
Abdela Sonesa
Haile Gabriel Dagne
Asegedech Bizuneh
Getachew Robele.

COUNCIL OF MINISTERS
(January 1991)

Prime Minister: Hailu Yimenu (acting).
Deputy Prime Ministers: Alemu Agebe, Ashagre Yigletu, Wole Chekol.
Minister of Foreign Affairs: Tesfaye Dinka.
Minister of Internal Affairs: Col Tesfaye Wolde-Selassie.
Minister of Construction: Kassa Gebre.
Minister of Labour and Social Affairs: Shimeles Adugna.
Minister of Information: Abdul Hafez Yusuf.
Minister of Culture, Sports and Youth Affairs: Maj. Giram Yilma.
Minister of Defence: (vacant).
Minister of Industry: Tadeos Hagere Work.
Minister of Coffee and Tea Development: Hambissa Wakoya.
Minister of Agriculture: Geremew Debele.
Minister of Finance: Tekola Dejene.
Minister of Housing and Urban Development: Tadese Kidane Mariam.
Minister of Health: Brig.-Gen. Dr Gizaw Tsehay.
Minister of Mines and Energy: Eng. Tekize-Shoa Ayitenfisu.
Minister of State Farms: Yoseph Muleta.
Minister of Foreign Trade: Getachew Habte Selassie.
Minister of Law and Justice: Wondayen Mehretu.
Minister of Education: Dr Yayehrad Kitaw.
Minister of Domestic Trade: Mersha Wodajo.
Minister of Transport and Communications: Assegid Wolde-Ammanuel.
Minister for the Co-ordination of Regional Affairs: Tsegaw Ayele.
Minister for the Co-ordination of Religious Affairs: Dibekulu Zewde.
Director of the Institute of Nationalities (with rank of Minister): Hailu Wolde Amanuel.
Ministers in the President's Office: Feleke Gedle-Ghiorghis, Maj.-Gen. Kefelegn Yibza, Neguse Wolde Mikael, Maj.-Gen. Seyoum Mekonen.
Commissioner for Relief and Rehabilitation: Yilma Kasaye.
Commissioner for Hotels and Tourism: Dawit Getachew.
Commissioner for National Water Resources: Argaw Tirunch.

ETHIOPIA — *Directory*

MINISTRIES AND COMMISSIONS

Office of the Prime Minister: POB 1013, Addis Ababa; tel. 123400.

Ministry of Agriculture: POB 1223, Addis Ababa; tel. 448040; fax 513042.

Ministry of Coffee and Tea Development: POB 3222, Addis Ababa; tel. 518088; telex 21130.

Ministry of Construction: Addis Ababa; tel. 155406.

Ministry of Culture, Sports and Youth Affairs: POB 1902, Addis Ababa; tel. 446338.

Ministry of Defence: POB 125, Addis Ababa; tel. 445555; telex 21261.

Ministry of Domestic Trade: POB 1769, Addis Ababa; tel. 448200.

Ministry of Education: POB 1362, Addis Ababa; tel. 112039.

Ministry of Finance: POB 1905, Addis Ababa; tel. 113400; telex 21147.

Ministry of Foreign Affairs: POB 393, Addis Ababa; tel. 447345; telex 21050.

Ministry of Foreign Trade: POB 2559, Addis Ababa; tel. 151066; telex 21320.

Ministry of Health: POB 1234, Addis Ababa; tel. 157011.

Ministry of Housing and Urban Development: POB 3386, Addis Ababa; tel. 150000.

Ministry of Industry: POB 704, Addis Ababa; tel. 448025.

Ministry of Information: POB 1020, Addis Ababa; tel. 111124.

Ministry of Internal Affairs: POB 2556, Addis Ababa; tel. 113334.

Ministry of Labour and Social Affairs: POB 2056, Addis Ababa; tel. 447080.

Ministry of Law and Justice: POB 1370, Addis Ababa; tel. 447390.

Ministry of Mines and Energy: POB 486, Addis Ababa; tel. 448250; telex 21448; fax 517874.

Ministry of State Farms: POB 1223, Addis Ababa; tel. 154600.

Ministry of Transport and Communications: POB 1629, Addis Ababa; tel. 155011; fax 515665.

Commission for Hotels and Tourism: POB 2183, Addis Ababa; tel. 447470; telex 21067.

Commission for National Water Resources: POB 486, Addis Ababa; tel. 447597; telex 21219.

Commission for Relief and Rehabilitation: POB 5686, Addis Ababa; tel. 153011; telex 21281.

Legislature

NATIONAL SHENGO

Parliament was suspended by military decree in September 1974. Provision for an elected national assembly was contained in the new Constitution, approved by referendum in February 1987. At elections held on 14 June 1987, 835 members were elected by universal adult suffrage from a list of candidates approved by the Workers' Party of Ethiopia (since renamed the Ethiopian Democratic Unity Party). The National Shengo subsequently elected a 24-member Council of State, which oversees state affairs when the National Shengo is not in session.

Political Organizations

Ethiopian Democratic Unity Party (EDUP): Addis Ababa; f. 1984 as Workers' Party of Ethiopia; adopted present name in March 1990, when its adherence to Marxist-Leninist ideology was relaxed and membership opened to non-Marxist and opposition groups; sole legal political party; c. 50,000 mems (1989); Sec.-Gen. Lt-Col MENGISTU HAILE MARIAM.

Political Bureau

Members:

Lt-Col MENGISTU HAILE MARIAM
Capt. FIKRE SELASSIE WOGDERES
FISSEHA DESTA
Lt-Gen. TESFAYE GEBRE-KIDAN
Lt-Col BERHANU BAYIH
ADDIS TEDLA
LEGESSE ASFAW
HAILU YIMENU
AMANUEL AMDE-MIKHAIL
ALEMU AGEBE
SHIMELIS MAZENGIA

Alternate members:

FASIKA SIDELU
SHEWANDAGN BELETE
TESFAYE DINKA
TESFAYE WOLDE SELASSIE
KASSA GEBRE

The following groups are in conflict with the Ethiopian Government:

Afar Liberation Front (ALF): operates in Hararge and Wollo Administrative Regions; Leader ALI MIRAH.

Eritrean Liberation Front (ELF): f. 1958 (in Cairo, Egypt) with aim of achieving autonomy for Eritrea; commenced armed struggle in 1961; subsequently split into numerous factions; mainly Muslim support; Chair. ABDULLAH MUHAMMAD.

Eritrean People's Liberation Front (EPLF): f. 1970 by secession from the Eritrean Liberation Front; Marxist-Leninist; Christian and Muslim support; seeks total independence for Eritrea; maintains Eritrean People's Liberation Army (EPLA) of 40,000–50,000 men; Sec.-Gen. ISSAIAS AFEWERKI.

Ethiopian People's Democratic Movement (EPDM): operates in Tigre Administrative Region; since August 1989 has fought in alliance with the TPLF as the **Ethiopian People's Revolutionary Democratic Front (EPRDF)**.

Oromo Liberation Front (OLF): operates among the Oromo (or Galla) people in Shoa Administrative Region; has received Somali military assistance.

Somali Abo Liberation Front (SALF): operates in Bale Administrative Region; has received Somali military assistance; Sec.-Gen. MASURAD SHU'ABI IBRAHIM.

Tigre People's Liberation Front (TPLF): f. 1975; Marxist; operates in Tigre Administrative Region; seeks autonomy within Ethiopia; 20,000 mems; Chair. MELES ZENAWI.

Western Somali Liberation Front (WSLF): POB 978, Mogadishu, Somalia; f. 1975; aims to unite the Ogaden region with Somalia; maintains guerrilla forces of c. 3,000 men; has received support from regular Somali forces; Sec.-Gen. ISSA SHAYKH ABDI NASIR ADAN.

Diplomatic Representation

EMBASSIES IN ETHIOPIA

Algeria: POB 5740, Addis Ababa; tel. 441334; telex 21302; Ambassador: HOCINE MESLOUB.

Argentina: Addis Ababa; telex 21172; Ambassador: Dr H. R. M. MOGUES.

Australia: POB 5798; Addis Ababa; tel. 114500; telex 21488; Ambassador: J. P. C. SHEPPARD.

Austria: POB 1219, Addis Ababa; tel. 712144; telex 21060; Ambassador: Dr HORST-DIETER RENNAU.

Belgium: Fikre Mariam St, Higher 16, Kebelo, POB 1239, Addis Ababa; tel. 181813; telex 21157; Ambassador: Baron d' ANETHAN.

Bulgaria: POB 987, Addis Ababa; tel. 153822; telex 21450; Ambassador: G. P. KASSOV.

Burundi: POB 3641, Addis Ababa; tel. 651300; telex 21069; Ambassador: THARCISSE MIDONZI.

Cameroon: Bole Rd, POB 1026, Addis Ababa; telex 21121; Ambassador: DOMINIQUE YONG.

Canada: African Solidarity Insurance Bldg, 6th Floor, Churchill Ave, POB 1130, Addis Ababa; tel. 151343; telex 21053; fax 512818; Ambassador: F. M. FILLEUL.

Chad: Addis Ababa; telex 21419; fax 612050; Ambassador: J. B. LAOKOLE.

China, People's Republic: POB 5643, Addis Ababa; telex 21145; Ambassador: GU JIAJI.

Congo: POB 5571, Addis Ababa; tel. 154331; telex 21406; Ambassador: C. STANISLAS BATHEAS-MOLLOMB.

Côte d'Ivoire: POB 3668, Addis Ababa; tel. 711213; telex 21061; Ambassador: ANTOINE KOUADIO-KIRINE.

Cuba: Jimma Road Ave, POB 5623, Addis Ababa; tel. 202010; telex 21306; Ambassador: ANTONIO PÉREZ HERRERO.

Czechoslovakia: POB 3108, Addis Ababa; tel. 516382; telex 21021; Ambassador: DUŠAN ROVENSKY.

Djibouti: POB 1022, Addis Ababa; tel. 183200; telex 21317; Chargé d'affaires: DJIBRIL DJAMA ELABE.

Egypt: POB 1611, Addis Ababa; tel. 113077; telex 21254; Ambassador: SAMIR AHMED.

Equatorial Guinea: POB 246, Addis Ababa; Ambassador: SALVADOR ELA NSENG ABEGUE.

Finland: Tedla Desta Bldg, Bole Rd, POB 1017, Addis Ababa; tel. 513900; telex 21259; Chargé d'affaires a.i.: ERIK BREHMER.

France: Kabana, POB 1464, Addis Ababa; tel. 110681; telex 21040; Ambassador: FRANÇOIS MICHEL.

Gabon: POB 1256, Addis Ababa; tel. 181075; telex 21208; Ambassador: DENIS DANGUE REWAKA.

ETHIOPIA

Germany: Kabana, POB 660, Addis Ababa; tel. 550433; telex 21015; fax 551311; Ambassador: Dr KURT STÖCKL.

Ghana: POB 3173, Addis Ababa; tel. 711402; telex 21249; Ambassador: BONIFACE KWAME ATEPOR.

Greece: Africa Ave, POB 1168, Addis Ababa; tel. 110612; telex 21092; Chargé d'affaires: M. DIAMANTOPOULOS.

Guinea: POB 1190, Addis Ababa; tel. 449712; Ambassador: PIERRE BASSAMBA CAMARA.

Holy See: POB 588, Addis Ababa (Apostolic Nunciature); tel. 712100; telex 21815; Apostolic Pro-Nuncio: Most Rev. PATRICK COVENEY, Titular Archbishop of Satriano.

Hungary: Abattoirs Rd, POB 1213, Addis Ababa; tel. 651850; telex 21176; Ambassador: Dr SÁNDOR ROBEL.

India: Kabana, POB 528, Addis Ababa; tel. 552100; telex 21148; fax 552521; Ambassador: K. P. BALAKRISHNAN.

Indonesia: Mekanisa Rd, POB 1004, Addis Ababa; tel. 202104; telex 21264; Ambassador: T.M. MOCHTAR MOHAMAD THAJEB.

Iran: 317/02 Jimma Rd, Old Airport Area, POB 1144, Addis Ababa; tel. 200369; telex 21118; Chargé d'affaires: HASSEN DABIR.

Israel: New Tafari Makonnen School, POB 1075, Addis Ababa; Chargé d'affaires: MEIR YAFE.

Italy: Villa Italia, POB 1105, Addis Ababa; tel. 551565; telex 21342; fax 550218; Ambassador: SERGIO ANGELETTI.

Jamaica: Off Bole Rd, POB 5633, Addis Ababa; tel. 613656; telex 21137; Ambassador: OWEN A. SINGH.

Japan: Finfinne Bldg, Revolution Sq., POB 5650, Addis Ababa; tel. 448215; telex 21108; Ambassador: SUKETORO ENOMOTO.

Kenya: Fikre Mariam Rd, POB 3301, Addis Ababa; tel. 610303; telex 21103; Ambassador: MUDE DAE MUDE.

Korea, Democratic People's Republic: POB 2378, Addis Ababa; Ambassador: SOK TAE UK.

Korea, Republic: Jimma Rd, Old Airport Area, POB 2047, Addis Ababa; tel. 444490; telex 21140; Ambassador: DEUK PO KIM.

Liberia: POB 3116, Addis Ababa; tel. 513655; telex 21083; Ambassador: THOMAS C. T. BESTMAN.

Libya: POB 5728, Addis Ababa; telex 21214; Secretary of People's Bureau: K. BAZELYA.

Malawi: POB 2316, Addis Ababa; tel. 44829536; telex 21087; Ambassador: D. P. W. KACHIKUWO.

Mexico: Tsige Mariam Bldg 292/21, 4 Piso, Churchill Rd, POB 2962, Addis Ababa; tel. 443456; telex 21141; Ambassador: CARLOS FERRER.

Mozambique: Addis Ababa; telex 21008; Ambassador: ALBERTO SITHOLE.

Netherlands: Old Airport Area, POB 1241, Addis Ababa; tel. 711100; telex 21049; Ambassador: A. HELDRING.

Niger: POB 5791, Addis Ababa; tel. 161175; telex 21284; Ambassador: ABDOURAHAMANE HAMA.

Nigeria: POB 1019, Addis Ababa; tel. 120644; telex 21028; Ambassador: HALIDU HANNANNIYA.

Poland: Bole Rd, POB 1123, Addis Ababa; tel. 610197; telex 21185; Ambassador: TADEUSZ WUJEK.

Romania: Africa Ave, POB 2478, Addis Ababa; tel. 181191; telex 21168; Ambassador: BARBU POPESCU.

Rwanda: Africa House, Higher 17 Kelele 20, POB 5618, Addis Ababa; tel. 610300; telex 21199; fax 610411; Ambassador: JEAN-MARIE VIANNEY NDAGIJIMANA.

Saudi Arabia: Old Airport Area, POB 1104, Addis Ababa; tel. 448010; telex 21194; Chargé d'affaires: HASSAN M. ATTAR.

Senegal: Africa Ave, POB 2581, Addis Ababa; tel. 611376; telex 21027; Ambassador: PAPA LOUIS FALL.

Sierra Leone: POB 5619, Addis Ababa; tel. 710033; telex 21144; Ambassador: ABDUL G. KOROMA.

Somalia: Addis Ababa; Ambassador: ABRAHIM HAJI NUR.

Spain: Entoto St, POB 2312, Addis Ababa; tel. 550222; telex 21107; Ambassador: A. MARTÍNEZ-MORCILLO.

Sudan: Kirkos, Kabele, POB 1110, Addis Ababa; telex 21293; Ambassador: UTHMAN ADAM.

Sweden: Ras Tesemma Sefer, POB 1029, Addis Ababa; tel. 516699; telex 21039; Ambassador: BIRGITTA KARLSTROM DORPH.

Switzerland: Jimma Rd, Old Airport Area, POB 1106, Addis Ababa; tel. 711107; telex 21123; Ambassador: GAUDENZ B. RUF.

Tanzania: POB 1077, Addis Ababa; tel. 441064; telex 21268; Ambassador: FATUMA TATU NURU.

Tunisia: Kesetegna 20, Kebele 39, POB 10069, Addis Ababa; Ambassador: MOHAMED BACHROUCH.

Turkey: POB 1506, Addis Ababa; tel. 152321; telex 21257; Ambassador: SUPHI MERIÇ.

Uganda: POB 5644, Addis Ababa; tel. 513088; telex 21143; fax 514355; Ambassador: SWAIB MATUMBWE MUSOKE.

USSR: POB 1500, Addis Ababa; telex 21404; Ambassador: A. DIMITRIEV.

United Kingdom: Fikre Mariam Abatechan St, POB 858, Addis Ababa; tel. 612354; telex 21299; fax 610588; Ambassador: M. J. C. GLAZE.

USA: Entoto St, POB 1014, Addis Ababa; tel. 110666; telex 21282; Chargé d'affaires: JAMES R. CHEEK.

Venezuela: Dedre Zeit Rd, POB 5584, Addis Ababa; tel. 654790; telex 21102; Chargé d'affaires: ALFREDO HERNÁNDEZ-ROVATI.

Viet-Nam: POB 1288, Addis Ababa; Ambassador: NGUYEN DUY KINH.

*****Yemen Arab Republic:** POB 664, Addis Ababa; telex 21346; Ambassador: Lt-Col HUSSEIN MOHASIN AL-GHAFFARI.

*****Yemen, People's Democratic Republic:** POB 664, Addis Ababa; telex 21357; Ambassador: SALIH ABU BAKR BIN HUSAYNUN.

Yugoslavia: POB 1341; Addis Ababa; tel. 517804; Ambassador: IVAN SENIČAR.

Zaire: Makanisa Rd, POB 2723, Addis Ababa; tel. 204385; telex 21043; Ambassador: WAKU YIZILA.

Zambia: POB 1909; Addis Ababa; tel. 711302; telex 21065; Ambassador: BASIL R. KABWE.

Zimbabwe: POB 5624, Addis Ababa; tel. 183872; telex 21351; Ambassador: TICHAONA J. B. JOKONYA.

* Merged to form the Republic of Yemen since May 1990.

Judicial System

Special People's Courts were established in 1981 to replace the former military tribunals. Judicial tribunals are elected by members of the urban dwellers' and peasant associations. In 1987 the Supreme Court ceased to be administered by the Ministry of Law and Justice and became an independent body.

Procurator-General: BILILIGNE MANDEFRO.

The Supreme Court: Addis Ababa; comprises civil, criminal and military sections; in 1987 its jurisdiction (previously confined to hearing appeals from the High Court) was extended to include supervision of all judicial proceedings throughout the country; the Supreme Court is also empowered, when ordered to do so by the Procurator-General or at the request of the President of the Supreme Court, to review and decide cases upon which final rulings have been made by the courts, including the Supreme Court, but where basic judicial errors have occurred; judges are elected by the National Shengo; Pres. ASEFA LIBEN.

The High Court: Addis Ababa; hears appeals from the Provincial and sub-Provincial Courts; has original jurisdiction.

Awraja Courts: Regional courts composed of three judges, criminal and civil.

Warada Courts: Sub-regional; one judge sits alone with very limited jurisdiction, criminal only.

Religion

About 45% of the population are Muslims and about 40% belong to the Ethiopian Orthodox (Tewahido) Church. There are also significant Evangelical Protestant and Roman Catholic communities. The Pentecostal Church and the Society of International Missionaries carry out mission work in Ethiopia. There are also Hindu and Sikh religious institutions and a small Jewish population.

CHRISTIANITY
Ethiopian Orthodox (Tewahido) Church

The Ethiopian Orthodox (Tewahido) Church is one of the five oriental orthodox churches. It was founded in AD 328, and in 1989 had more than 22m. members, 20,000 parishes and 290,000 clergy. The Supreme Body is the Holy Synod and the National Council, under the chairmanship of the Patriarch. The Church comprises 25 archdioceses and dioceses (including those in Jerusalem, Sudan, Djibouti and the Western Hemisphere). There are 32 Archbishops and Bishops. The Church administers 1,139 schools and 12 relief and rehabilitation centres throughout Ethiopia.

Patriarchate Head Office: POB 1283, Addis Ababa; tel. 116507; telex 21489; Patriarch Archbishop ABUNE MERKOREWOS; Gen. Sec. L. M. DEMTSE GEBRE MEDHIN.

ETHIOPIA — Directory

Other Christian Churches

Armenian Orthodox Church: Deacon VARTKES NALBANDIAN, St George's Armenian Church, POB 116, Addis Ababa; f. 1923.

Ethiopian Evangelical Church (Mekane Yesus): Pres. Ato FRANCIS STEPHANOS, POB 2087, Addis Ababa; tel. 111200; telex 21528; f. 1958; affiliated to Lutheran World Fed., All Africa Conference of Churches and World Council of Churches; 870,388 mems (1989).

Greek Orthodox Church: Metropolitan of Axum Most Rev. PETROS GIAKOUMELOS, POB 571, Addis Ababa.

The Roman Catholic Church: At 31 December 1988 there were an estimated 118,550 adherents of the Alexandrian-Ethiopian rite and 165,022 adherents of the Latin rite.

Alexandrian-Ethiopian Rite: There is one archdiocese (Addis Ababa) and two dioceses (Adigrat and Asmara); Archbishop of Addis Ababa HE Cardinal PAULOS TZADUA, POB 210903, Addis Ababa; tel. 111667.

Latin Rite: There are five Apostolic Vicariates (Asmara, Awasa, Harar, Nekemte and Soddo-Hosanna) and one Apostolic Prefecture (Meki); Apostolic Administrator of Asmara Fr LUCA MILESI, 107 National Ave, POB 224, Asmara; tel. 110631.

Seventh-day Adventist Church: Pres. Pastor BEKELE BIRI, POB 145, Addis Ababa; tel. 158300; telex 21549; f. 1907; 46,000 mems.

ISLAM

Leader: Haji MOHAMMED HABIB SANI.

JUDAISM

Following the secret airlifts to Israel in 1984–85 of about 13,000 Falashas (Ethiopian Jews), and further emigrations during 1989 and 1990, there are estimated to be some 15,000 Falashas still in the country, living mainly in Gondar and Tigre Administrative Regions.

TRADITIONAL BELIEFS

It is estimated that between 5% and 15% of the population follow animist rites and ceremonies.

The Press

DAILIES

The following three newspapers are published by the Ministry of Information:

Addis Zemen: POB 30145, Addis Ababa; f. 1941; Amharic; Editor-in-Chief TSEHAJU DEBALKEW (acting); circ. 37,000.

Ethiopian Herald: POB 30701, Addis Ababa; tel. 119050; f. 1943; English; Editor-in-Chief KIFLOM HADGOI; circ. 6,000.

Hibret: POB 247, Asmara; Tigrinya; Editor-in-Chief GURJA TESFA SELASSIE; circ. 4,000.

PERIODICALS

Al-Alem: POB 30232, Addis Ababa; weekly; Arabic; publ. by the Ministry of Information; Editor-in-Chief TELSOM AHMED; circ. 2,500.

Berisa: POB 30232, Addis Ababa; f. 1976; weekly; Oromogna; publ. by the Ministry of Information; circ. 2,000.

Ethiopia: POB 247, Asmara; weekly; Amharic; publ. by Ministry of Information; Editor-in-Chief ABRAHA GEBRE HIWOT; circ. 2,000.

Ethiopian Trade Journal: POB 517, Addis Ababa; tel. 448240; telex 21213; quarterly; English; publ. by the Ethiopian Chamber of Commerce; Editor-in-Chief GETACHEW ZICKE.

Maedot (Passover): POB 1283, Addis Ababa; tel. 116507; telex 21489; Amharic and English; publ. by the Ethiopian Orthodox Church.

Meskerem: POB 80001, Addis Ababa; quarterly; theoretical politics; circ. 100,000.

Negarit Gazzetta: POB 1031, Addis Ababa; fortnightly; Amharic and English; official gazette of laws, orders and notices.

Nigdina Limat: POB 2458, Addis Ababa; tel. 158039; telex 21213; monthly; Amharic; publ. by the Ethiopian Chamber of Commerce.

Revolutionary Police: POB 40046, Addis Ababa; fortnightly; Amharic; police journal.

Serto Ader (Worker): POB 80123, Addis Ababa; f. 1980; weekly; organ of the EDUP; Editor TESFAYE TADESE; Dep. Editor GEZA HEGN GEBRE; circ. 100,000.

Tatek (Get Armed): POB 1901, Addis Ababa; fortnightly; Amharic; army journal.

Tinsae (Resurrection): POB 1283, Addis Ababa; tel. 116507; telex 21489; Amharic and English; publ. by the Ethiopian Orthodox Church.

Trade and Development Bulletin: POB 856, Asmara; tel. 110814; telex 42079; monthly; Amharic and English; publ. by the Ethiopian Chamber of Commerce; Editor TAAME FOTO.

Yezareitu Ethiopia (Ethiopia Today): POB 30232, Addis Ababa; weekly; Amharic; publ. by the Ministry of Information; Editor-in-Chief ABIYE MEIZURIA (acting); circ. 30,000.

NEWS AGENCIES

Ethiopia News Agency (ENA): Patriots' St, POB 530, Addis Ababa; tel. 120014; telex 21068.

Foreign Bureaux

Agence France-Presse (AFP): POB 3537, Addis Ababa; tel. 511006; telex 21031; Chief SEYOUM AYELE.

Agentstvo Pechati Novosti (APN) (USSR): POB 239, Addis Ababa; telex 21237; Chief VITALI POLIKARPOV.

Agenzia Nazionale Stampa Associata (ANSA) (Italy): POB 1001, Addis Ababa; telex 115704; Chief BRAHAME GHEBREZGHI-ABIHER.

Novinska Agencija Tanjug (Yugoslavia): POB 5743, Addis Ababa; telex 21150; Chief RADOSLAV JOVIĆ.

Prensa Latina (Cuba): Gen. Makonnen Bldg, 5th Floor, nr Ghion Hotel, opposite National Stadium, POB 5690, Addis Ababa; tel. 519229; telex 21151; Chief HUGO RIUS BLEIN.

Telegrafnoye Agentstvo Sovetskovo Soyuza (TASS) (USSR): POB 998, Addis Ababa; tel. 181255; telex 21091; Chief GENNADI G. GABRIELYAN.

Xinhua (New China) News Agency (People's Republic of China): POB 2497, Addis Ababa; tel. 151064; telex 21504; Correspondent TENG WENQI.

PRESS ASSOCIATION

Ethiopian Journalists' Association: Addis Ababa; Chair. IMERU WORKU (acting).

Publishers

Addis Ababa University Press: POB 1176, Addis Ababa; tel. 119148; telex 21205; f. 1968; educational and reference works in English; Editor INNES MARSHALL.

Ethiopia Book Centre: POB 1024, Addis Ababa; tel. 116844; f. 1977; privately-owned; publisher, importer, wholesaler and retailer of educational books.

Kuraz Publishing Agency: POB 30933, Addis Ababa; state-owned.

Government Publishing House

Government Printing Press: POB 1241, Addis Ababa.

Radio and Television

In 1990 there were an estimated 9m. radio receivers and an estimated 200,000 television receivers in use.

Board of Telecommunications of Ethiopia: POB 1047, Addis Ababa; Gen. Man. G. ENGDAYEHU.

RADIO

Voice of Ethiopia: POB 1020, Addis Ababa; tel. 121011; f. 1941; Amharic, English, French, Arabic, Afar, Oromigna, Tigrinya and Somali; Gen. Man. MOGUS TAFFESSE.

TELEVISION

Ethiopian Television: POB 5544, Addis Ababa; tel. 116701; telex 21429; f. 1964; state-controlled; commercial advertising is accepted; programmes are transmitted from Addis Ababa to 18 regional stations; broadcasts cover all of Ethiopia except two Administrative Regions; Dir-Gen. WOLE GURMU.

Finance

(cap. = capital; p.u. = paid up; dep. = deposits;
m. = million; res = reserves; amounts in birr)

BANKING

All privately-owned banks and other financial institutions were nationalized in 1975.

ETHIOPIA

Central Bank
National Bank of Ethiopia: POB 5550, Addis Ababa; tel. 447430; telex 21020; f. 1964; bank of issue; cap. and res 147.1m. (June 1986); Gov. BEKELE TAMIRAT.

Other Banks
Agricultural and Industrial Development Bank: Joseph Broz Tito St, POB 1900, Addis Ababa; tel. 511188; telex 21173; fax 511606; provides development finance for industry and agriculture, technical advice and assistance in project evaluation; cap. p.u. 100m. (June 1988); Gen. Man. TSEGAYE ASFAW; 21 brs.

Commercial Bank of Ethiopia: Unity Square, POB 255, Addis Ababa; tel. 515000; telex 21037; f. 1964, reorg. 1980; state-owned; cap. 65m. (June 1990); Gen. Man. ALEMU ABERRA; 158 brs.

Housing and Savings Bank: Higher 21 Kebele 04, POB 3480, Addis Ababa; tel. 512300; telex 21869; f. 1975; provides credit for construction of houses and commercial bldgs; cap. p.u. 15.3m. (June 1990); Gen. Man. TASSEW DEMISSIE; 13 brs.

INSURANCE
Ethiopian Insurance Corporation: POB 2545, Addis Ababa; tel. 156348; telex 21120; f. 1976 to undertake all insurance business; Gen. Man. AYALEW BEZABEH.

Trade and Industry

CHAMBER OF COMMERCE
Ethiopian Chamber of Commerce: Mexico Sq., POB 517, Addis Ababa; tel. 518240; telex 21213; f. 1947; city chambers in Addis Ababa, Asmara, Awassa, Bahir Dar, Dire Dawa, Nazret, Jimma, Gondar and Dessie; Pres. DAMTE BEREDED; Sec.-Gen. WORKENEH MENGESHA.

AGRICULTURAL ORGANIZATION
Ethiopia Peasants' Association (EPA): f. 1978 to promote improved agricultural techniques, cottage industries, education, public health and self-reliance; comprises 30,000 peasant asscns with c. 7m. mems; Chair. ABDELA SONESA.

TRADE AND INDUSTRIAL ORGANIZATIONS
Ethiopian Beverages Corporation: POB 1285, Addis Ababa; tel. 186185; telex 21373.

Ethiopian Cement Corporation: POB 5782, Addis Ababa; tel. 552222; telex 21308; fax 551572.

Ethiopian Chemical Corporation: POB 5747, Addis Ababa; tel. 184305; telex 21011.

Ethiopian Coffee Marketing Corporation: POB 2591, Addis Ababa; tel. 155330; telex 21174; fax 510762.

Ethiopian Food Corporation: Higher 21, Kebele 04, Mortgage Bldg, Addis Ababa; tel 158522; telex 21292; fax 513173; f. 1975; produces and distributes food items including edible oil, ghee substitute, pasta, bread, maize, wheat flour etc.

Ethiopian Fruit and Vegetable Marketing Enterprise: POB 2374, Addis Ababa; tel. 449192; telex 21106; f. 1980; sole wholesale domestic distributor and exporter of fruit and vegetables, spices and floricultural products; Gen. Man. HAILU BALCHA.

Ethiopian Handicrafts and Small-Scale Industries Development Agency: POB 5758, Addis Ababa; tel. 157366.

Ethiopian Import and Export Corporation (ETIMEX): POB 2313, Addis Ababa; tel. 512400; telex 21235; fax 514396; f. 1975; state trading corpn under the supervision of the Ministry of Foreign Trade; import of building materials, foodstuffs, stationery and office equipment, textiles, clothing, chemicals, general merchandise, capital goods.

Ethiopian Livestock and Meat Corporation: POB 5579, Addis Ababa; tel. 159341; telex 21095; f. 1984; state trading organization responsible for the development and export of livestock and livestock products.

Ethiopian National Metal Works Corporation: Addis Ababa; fax 510714.

Ethiopian Oil Seeds and Pulses Export Corporation: POB 5719, Addis Ababa; tel. 159536; telex 21133; Gen. Man. EPHRAIM AMBAYE.

Ethiopian Petroleum Corporation: POB 3375, Addis Ababa; telex 21054; fax 512938; f. 1976; operates Assab petroleum refinery; Gen. Man. MAMO GEBRE MESKEL.

Ethiopian Pharmaceuticals and Medical Supplies Corporation: POB 21904, Addis Ababa; tel. 134577; telex 21248; f. 1976; manufacture, import, export and distribution of pharmaceuticals, chemicals, dressings, surgical and dental instruments, hospital and laboratory supplies; Gen. Man. BERHANU ZELEKE.

Ethiopian Sugar Corporation: POB 133, Addis Ababa; tel. 519700; telex 21038; fax 513488.

National Leather and Shoe Corporation: POB 2516, Addis Ababa; tel. 514075; telex 21096; fax 513525; f. 1975; produces and sells semi-processed hides and skins, finished leather, leather goods and footwear.

National Textiles Corporation: POB 2446, Addis Ababa; tel. 157316; telex 21129; fax 511955; f. 1975; production of yarn, fabrics, knitwear, blankets, bags, etc.; Gen. Man. BEKELE HAILE.

Natural Gums Processing and Marketing Enterprise: POB 62322, Addis Ababa; tel. 159930; telex 21336.

TRADE UNIONS
All trade unions must register with the Ministry of Labour and Social Affairs, and 'subordinate' unions must comply with directives issued by 'higher' unions.

Ethiopian Trade Union (ETU): POB 3653, Addis Ababa; tel. 514366; telex 21618; f. 1975 to replace the Confed. of Ethiopian Labour Unions; comprises nine industrial unions and 22 regional unions with a total membership of 320,000 (1987); Chair. TADESSE TAMRAT.

Transport

RAILWAYS
Ethio-Djibouti Railway Co: POB 1051, Addis Ababa; tel. 517250; telex 21414; f. 1908, adopted present name in 1981; jtly-owned by Govts of Ethiopia and Djibouti; plans to grant autonomous status were announced by the two Govts in July 1985; 781 km of track, of which 681 km in Ethiopia, linking Addis Ababa with Djibouti; Pres. MOUSSA BOURALE ROBLE; Man. Dir ASRAT MENDERIL.

ROADS
In 1988 the total road network comprised 39,482 km of primary, secondary and feeder roads and trails, of which 18,482 km were main roads. A highway links Addis Ababa with Nairobi in Kenya, forming part of the Trans-East Africa Highway.

Ethiopian Transport Construction Authority: POB 1770, Addis Ababa; tel. 447170; telex 21180; f. 1951; constructs roads, bridges, airfields, ports and railways, and maintains roads and bridges throughout Ethiopia; Gen. Man. KELLETTA TESFA MICHAEL.

National Freight Transport Corporation: POB 2538, Addis Ababa; tel. 151841; telex 21238; f. 1974; truck and tanker operations throughout the country.

Public Transport Corporation: POB 5780, Addis Ababa; tel. 153117; telex 21371; fax 510720; f. 1977; urban bus services in Addis Ababa, Asmara, Jimma, Massawa, and services between towns; Gen. Man. TESFAYE SHENKUTE.

Road Transport Authority: POB 2504, Addis Ababa; fax 510715; enforcement of road transport regulations, registering of vehicles and issuing of driving licences.

SHIPPING
Port and maritime services were nationalized in September 1979. The Ethiopian merchant shipping fleet totalled 28,409 grt in July 1983. There are irregular services by foreign vessels to Massawa and Assab (the port for Addis Ababa), which can handle over 1m. metric tons of merchandise annually. It has an oil refinery with an annual capacity of 500,000 metric tons. Much trade passes through Djibouti (in the Republic of Djibouti) to Addis Ababa, and Ethiopia has permission to use the Kenyan port of Mombasa.

Ethiopian Shipping Lines Corporation: POB 2572, Addis Ababa; tel. 514204; telex 21045; fax 519525; f. 1964; state-owned; serves Red Sea, Europe and Far East with its own and chartered vessels; Chair. Minister of Transport and Communications; Gen. Man. TESEMA GEZAW; 12 vessels.

Marine Transport Authority: POB 1861, Addis Ababa; tel. 446448; telex 21280; fax 516015; f. 1978; administers and operates the ports of Assab and Massawa, manages inland waterways, handles cargo.

Maritime and Transit Services Corporation: POB 1186, Addis Ababa; tel. 510666; telex 21057; fax 514097; f. 1979; handles cargoes for import and export; operates shipping agency service.

CIVIL AVIATION
Ethiopia has four international airports and around 40 airfields.

Civil Aviation Authority: POB 978, Addis Ababa; tel. 180266; telex 21162; constructs and maintains airports; provides air navigational facilities.

ETHIOPIA

Ethiopian Airlines: Bole International Airport, POB 1755, Addis Ababa; tel. 182222; telex 21012; fax 611474; f. 1945; operates regular domestic services and flights to 31 international destinations in Africa, Europe, Middle East, India and the People's Republic of China; Chair. Minister of Transport and Communications; Gen. Man. Capt. MUHAMMAD AHMAD; fleet of 3 Boeing 767-200ER, 2 Boeing 707-320C, 3 Boeing 727-200, 2 Boeing 737-200, 7 DC-3, 2 DHC-5A Transporter, 6 Twin Otter, 2 ART 42.

Tourism

The principal tourist attractions are the early Christian monuments and churches, and the ancient capitals of Gondar and Axum. Tourist arrivals in 1986 were about 59,000. Tourism provided an estimated 47m. birr in foreign exchange in that year.

Ethiopian Commission for Hotels and Tourism: POB 2183, Addis Ababa; tel. 517470; telex 21067; f. 1961; Commr DAWIT GETACHEW.

FIJI

Introductory Survey

Location, Climate, Language, Religion, Flag, Capital

The Republic of Fiji comprises more than 300 islands, of which 100 are inhabited, situated about 1,930 km (1,200 miles) south of the equator in the Pacific Ocean. The four main islands are Viti Levu (on which almost 70% of the country's population lives), Vanua Levu, Tavenui and Kadavu. The climate is tropical, with temperatures ranging from 16° to 32°C (60°–90°F). Rainfall is heavy on the windward side. Fijian and Hindi are the principal languages but English is also widely spoken. In 1986 about 53% of the population were Christians (mainly Methodists), 38% Hindus and 8% Muslims. The national flag (proportions 2 by 1) is light blue, with the United Kingdom flag as a canton in the upper hoist. In the fly is the main part of Fiji's national coat of arms: a white field quartered by a red upright cross, the quarters containing sugar canes, a coconut palm, a bunch of bananas and a dove bearing an olive branch; in chief is a red panel with a yellow lion holding a coconut. The capital is Suva, on Viti Levu.

Recent History

The first Europeans to settle on the islands were sandalwood traders, missionaries and shipwrecked sailors, and in October 1874 Fiji was proclaimed a British possession. In September 1966 the British Government introduced a new constitution for Fiji. It provided for a ministerial form of government, an almost wholly elected Legislative Council and the introduction of universal adult suffrage. Rather than using a common roll of voters, however, the Constitution introduced an electoral system that combined communal (Fijian and Indian) rolls with cross-voting. In September 1967 the Executive Council became the Council of Ministers, with Ratu Kamisese Mara, leader of the multiracial (but predominantly Fijian) Alliance Party (AP), as Fiji's first Chief Minister. Following a constitutional conference in April–May 1970, Fiji achieved independence, within the Commonwealth, on 10 October 1970. The Legislative Council was renamed the House of Representatives, and a second parliamentary chamber, a nominated Senate, was established. The British-appointed Governor became Fiji's first Governor-General, while Ratu Sir Kamisese Mara (as he had become in 1969) took office as Prime Minister.

Fiji was troubled by racial tensions, however. Although the descendants of indentured Indian workers who were brought to Fiji in the late 19th century had grown to outnumber the native inhabitants, they were discriminated against in political representation and land ownership rights. A new electoral system was adopted in 1970 to ensure a racial balance in the legislature.

At the general election held in March and April 1977 the National Federation Party (NFP), traditionally supported by the Indian population, won 26 of the 52 seats in the House of Representatives but was unable to form a government and subsequently split into two factions. The AP governed in a caretaker capacity until the holding of a further general election in September, when it was returned with its largest-ever majority. While these two main parties professed multiracial ideas, the Fijian Nationalist Party campaigned in support of its 'Fiji for the Fijians' programme in order to foster nationalist feeling.

In 1980 Ratu Sir Kamisese Mara's suggestion that a government of national unity be formed was overshadowed by renewed political disagreement between the AP and the NFP (whose two factions had drawn closer together again) over land ownership. Fijians owned 83% of the land and were strongly defending their traditional rights, while the Indian population was pressing for greater security of land tenure. The general election held in July 1982 was also dominated by racial issues. The AP retained power after winning 28 seats, but their majority had been cut from 20 to four. The NFP won 22 seats and the Western United Front (WUF), which professed a multiracial outlook, took the remaining two seats. Allegations by the two major political parties that foreign political and business interests had been involved in each other's election campaign prompted the appointment of a Royal Commission of Inquiry which, however, failed to uncover any conclusive proof of the allegations during its investigations in 1983. The opposition parties in the House of Representatives supported their leader, Jai Ram Reddy, in his boycott of Parliament, which had begun in December 1983 over a point of protocol. The boycott ended in June 1984, after Reddy had resigned his seat in May and had been replaced as parliamentary leader of the NFP, and of the opposition coalition, by Siddiq Koya, whom he had defeated for the leadership in 1977.

In February 1985 the Government held its first economic 'summit conference'; the meeting was boycotted, however, by both the parliamentary opposition and the Fiji Trades Union Congress (FTUC), in protest against a government-imposed 'freeze' on wages, which had been in force since November 1984. A meeting of union leaders in May 1985 marked the beginning of discussions which culminated in the founding of the Fiji Labour Party (FLP), officially inaugurated in Suva in July 1985. Sponsored by the FTUC, and under the presidency of Dr Timoci Bavadra, the new party was formed with the aim of presenting a more effective parliamentary opposition, and declared the provision of free education and a national medical scheme to be among its priorities. The FLP hoped to work through farmers' organizations to win votes among rural electorates, which traditionally supported the NFP.

During 1985 and 1986 disagreements between the Government and the FTUC over economic policies became increasingly acrimonious, and in February 1986, having failed to reach agreement with the unions on an acceptable increase in wages for 1986, the Government arbitrarily fixed the increase at 2.25%. This provoked an outbreak of labour unrest, leading to the withdrawal, in June 1986, of government recognition of the FTUC as the unions' representative organization. The FTUC responded by holding public protest rallies and by seeking an international suspension of air and sea links with Fiji. The dispute was finally settled in January 1987, when the FTUC, the Fiji Employers' Consultative Association and the Government signed an agreement whereby a guideline of 5.5% was fixed for pay increases in that year.

At the general election held in April 1987 a coalition of the FLP and NFP won 28 seats (19 of which were secured by ethnic Indian candidates) in the House of Representatives, thus defeating the ruling AP, which won only 24 seats. The new Government, led by Dr Timoci Bavadra of the FLP, was therefore the first in Fijian history to contain a majority of ministers of Indian, rather than Melanesian, origin. Dr Bavadra, himself, was of Melanesian descent. On 14 May, however, the Government was overthrown by a military coup, led by Lt-Col (later Maj.-Gen.) Sitiveni Rabuka. The Governor-General, Ratu Sir Penaia Ganilau, responded by declaring a state of emergency and appointed a 19-member advisory council, including Bavadra and Rabuka. However, Bavadra refused to participate in the council, denouncing it as unconstitutional and biased in its composition.

Widespread racial violence followed the coup, and there were several public demands for Bavadra's reinstatement as Prime Minister. In July 1987 the Great Council of Fijian Chiefs, comprising the country's 80 hereditary Melanesian leaders, approved plans for constitutional reform. In September negotiations began, on the initiative of Ganilau, between delegations led by the two former Prime Ministers, Bavadra and Mara, to resolve the political crisis. On 22 September it was announced that the two factions had agreed to form an interim bipartisan government.

However, on 25 September 1987, before the new plan could be implemented, Rabuka staged a second coup and announced his intention to declare Fiji a republic. Despite Ganilau's refusal to recognize the seizure of power, Rabuka revoked the Constitution on 1 October and proclaimed himself Head of State, thus deposing the Queen. Ganilau conceded defeat and resigned as Governor-General. At a meeting in Canada, Commonwealth Heads of Government formally declared that Fiji's membership of the Commonwealth had lapsed. An interim cabinet, comprising mainly Melanesians, was installed by

Rabuka. Senior judges who had opposed the coup were removed from office. Australia and New Zealand refused to recognize the Rabuka regime, although France, Indonesia and the People's Republic of China indicated that they were prepared to expand trade links with Fiji. In late October Rabuka announced that he would resign as Head of State as soon as he had appointed a new President of the Republic. Several cases of violations of human rights by the Fijian army were reported as the regime assumed powers of detention without trial and suspended all political activity.

On 6 December 1987 Rabuka resigned as Head of State. Although he had previously refused to accept the post, Ratu Sir Penaia Ganilau, the former Governor-General, became the first President of the Fijian Republic. Ratu Sir Kamisese Mara was reappointed Prime Minister, and Rabuka became Minister of Home Affairs. A new cabinet was announced on 9 December, containing 11 members of Rabuka's administration, but no member of Bavadra's deposed Government.

In February 1988 Rotuma, an island to the north-west of Suva, declared itself politically independent of Fiji, whose newly-acquired republican status it refused to recognize. Rotuma appealed to the Governments of Australia, New Zealand and the United Kingdom for assistance. However, Fijian troops were dispatched to the island and soon quelled the dissent.

A new draft constitution was approved by the interim Government in September 1988. The proposed Constitution was rejected, however, by a multiracial constitutional committee, which considered unnecessary the specific reservation of the principal offices of state for ethnic Fijians. In September 1989 the committee published a revised draft, which was still, however, condemned by Bavadra and the FLP-NFP coalition. In November Bavadra died and was replaced as leader of the FLP-NFP coalition by his widow, Adi Kuini Bavadra.

In September 1989 the Australian media published a copy of the Fijian military leadership's verbal submission to the constitutional committee. It was reported that, in the event of Mara's retirement, the plans envisaged the necessity of military intervention and the establishment of a military executive to administer the country for the following 15 years. Ganilau described the document as a statement of concern by certain members of the armed forces and not a set of government policies. In January 1990 Rabuka resigned from the Cabinet and returned to his military duties. Mara agreed to remain as Prime Minister until the restoration of constitutional government. In March the Great Council of Chiefs met to debate the constitutional proposals, and at a further meeting in June the draft Constitution was approved. At the same time, the Great Council of Chiefs stated its intention to form a new party, the Fijian Political Party, to advocate the cause of ethnic Fijians. The new Constitution was finally promulgated on 25 July by President Ganilau: a development which was reported to have been prompted by fears of another coup. The Constitution was immediately condemned by the FLP-NFP coalition, which announced that it would boycott any elections held in accordance with the Constitution's provisions. Angered by the fact that a legislative majority was guaranteed to ethnic Fijians (who were reserved 37 of the 70 elective seats, compared with 27 Indian seats), and that the Great Council of Chiefs was to nominate ethnic Fijians to 24 of the 34 seats in the Senate and to appoint the President of the Republic, the opposition organized anti-Constitution demonstrations, at which it burned copies of the new document. The new Constitution was similarly condemned for its racial bias by India, New Zealand and Australia at the UN General Assembly, meeting in New York in October.

In November 1989 the Fijian Government expelled the Indian ambassador to Fiji for allegedly interfering in Fiji's internal affairs, and the status of the Indian embassy was downgraded to that of a consulate. Relations between Fiji and India have deteriorated since the coup of May 1987, and many ethnic Indians (including many members of the professions) have emigrated. In January 1989 statistical information, released by the interim Government, indicated that the islands' ethnic Fijians were in a majority for the first time since 1946.

In July 1990 the visit of New Zealand's Minister for Disarmament and Arms Control and for Tourism, Fran Wilde, to Fiji constituted the first direct contact between the two countries since the 1987 coups, and was followed in November by requests from the Fijian interim Government for the resumption of military aid from New Zealand. In 1990 Fiji received an increased amount of military aid from France, although relations between the two countries remained overshadowed by France's consistent use of the area for nuclear-weapons testing. The organization Nuclear-Free and Independent Pacific (NFIP), which was founded in Fiji in 1975, has continued to campaign for the establishment of a nuclear-free zone in the Pacific and for a restriction in foreign military control in the area.

Government

Until October 1987 the Head of State was the British sovereign, represented locally by an appointed Governor-General, who was required to act in accordance with the advice of the Cabinet except in certain constitutional functions. Following two military coups, however, the 1970 Constitution was revoked, and on 15 October 1987 Fiji became a Republic.

An interim constitution replaced that of 1970. A new constitution, drafted in 1988, was approved by the interim Government, but was revised during 1989. The new Constitution was finally promulgated on 25 July 1990 by President Ganilau, following its approval, in the previous month, by the Great Council of Chiefs. The Constitution of a 'sovereign, democratic republic', it provided for a parliamentary form of government with a bicameral legislature comprising an elected 70-seat House of Representatives and an appointed Senate of Chiefs with 34 members. The Constitution established a permanent majority of 37 seats in the House to be elected by indigenous Fijians, with 27 seats to be elected by those of Indian descent, four by other races (General Electors) and one by voters on the island of Rotuma. Only five Fijian seats were reserved for the urban centres, where approximately one-third of the ethnic Fijian population reside. The Senate of Chiefs was to be appointed by the President of the Republic, 24 members on the advice of the Great Council of Chiefs (an 80-member traditional body comprising every hereditary chief (Ratu) of a Fijian clan) from among their own number, one member on the advice of the Rotuma Island Council, and the remaining nine selected from 'prominent citizens' among the other racial communities, on the President's 'own deliberate judgement'.

Defence

The Fiji Military Forces consist of men in the regular army, the Naval Squadron, the conservation corps and the territorials. The conservation corps was created in 1975 to make use of unemployed labour in construction work. In June 1990 the total armed forces numbered 5,000 men: 4,700 in the army and 300 in the navy. The defence budget for 1990 was $F 29.8m. In October 1990 the creation of a security service was announced.

Economic Affairs

In 1988, according to estimates by the World Bank, Fiji's gross national product (GNP), measured at average 1986–88 prices, was US $1,130m., equivalent to $1,540 per head. During 1980–88, it was estimated, GNP declined, in real terms, at an average annual rate of 0.4%, while GNP per head decreased by 2.2% per year. Over the same period, the population increased by an annual average of 1.9%. Fiji's gross domestic product (GDP) declined, in real terms, by 7.8% in 1987, but expanded by 2% in 1988, and by a further 12.6% in 1989. Between 1980 and 1989 GDP increased by an annual average of 2.0%.

Agriculture (including forestry and fishing) contributed 21% of GDP in 1988. Some 44% of the labour force were employed in the sector in 1986. The principal cash crop is sugar cane, which normally accounts for about 80% of total agricultural production. Sugar and its derivatives provided some 37% of export earnings in 1989. Other important export crops are coconuts and ginger, while the most important subsistence crop is paddy rice (of which Fiji provided about 72% of its domestic requirements in 1989). Agricultural output declined by 5.8% in 1987, but increased by 5% in 1988.

Industry (including mining, manufacturing, construction and power) employed 13.8% of the labour force in 1986, and provided 19.3% of GDP in 1988. Industrial production increased by about 6% in 1988 and by 8.9% in 1989. Mining contributed 2.7% of GDP in 1988, and employed 1.7% of the labour force in 1990. Gold and silver are the major mineral exports.

Manufacturing contributed 9.3% of GDP in 1988, and employed 7.5% of the labour force in 1986. Manufacturing output expanded by 19% in 1989. The most important sector is food-processing, in particular sugar, molasses and copra. The ready-made garment industry is also important and has particularly benefited from the tax-exemption scheme implemented by the Government in 1987. At the end of 1989 about 10.2% of the labour force were employed in tax-exempt factories, 77% of which were in the ready-made garment industry.

Energy is derived principally from hydroelectric power. Electricity, gas and water contributed 3.9% of GDP in 1988. Imports of mineral fuels represented 16.9% of the total cost of imports in 1989.

Tourism is Fiji's second largest source of foreign exchange, earning some $F 281m. in 1989, when visitor arrivals totalled 250,565. Revenue from tourism was expected to total about $F 310m. in 1990, when arrivals were provisionally estimated at 273,668.

In 1989 Fiji recorded a visible trade deficit of US $160.9m., and there was a deficit of $21.7m. on the current account of the balance of payments. In 1989 the principal sources of imports were Australia (30.9%), New Zealand (17.3%) and Japan (13.9%). The principal markets for exports were the United Kingdom (25.1%), Australia (20.1%) and New Zealand (11.6%). The principal imports in 1989 were machinery and transport equipment, basic manufactured goods and petroleum products. The principal exports were sugar, gold, re-exported petroleum products and ready-made garments.

In 1990 there was a projected budgetary deficit of $F 61.3m. Fiji's total external debt was $F 470.7m. at the end of 1989. The annual rate of inflation averaged 5.7% in 1980–88. The rate declined from 11.8% in 1988 to 6.2% in 1989, but rose to 8.1% in the year ending June 1990. An estimated 6.4% of the labour force were unemployed in 1990.

Fiji is a member of the UN Economic and Social Commission for Asia and the Pacific (see p. 25), the Colombo Plan for Co-operative Economic and Social Development in Asia and the Pacific (see p. 112), the South Pacific Forum (see p. 207), the South Pacific Commission (see p. 205) and the International Sugar Organization (see p. 229). Fiji is also a signatory of the South Pacific Regional Trade and Economic Cooperation Agreement—SPARTECA (see p. 207) and the Lomé Convention with the EEC (see p. 151).

Fiji's economic performance in the 1980s was adversely affected by the world recession and by political instability resulting from the two *coups d'état* of 1987. The tourist and sugar industries, in particular, were disrupted by the political unrest, and the country's reserves of foreign exchange declined substantially in 1987. The economy expanded slightly in 1988, with the introduction of tax incentives for exporters and free trade zones, and grew significantly in 1989. Since 1987 Fiji's economy has suffered considerably from large-scale emigration. It was estimated that, of the average 5,000 emigrants per year in 1987–89, 30% were professional or semi-professional workers. During 1990 Fiji's economy benefited from strong sugar prices on the international market, an increase in tourist arrivals, the introduction of tax-free zones, and growth in foreign investment (notably from Japan). The Fijian Government stated that it planned to broaden the country's industrial base in 1991, in an attempt to attract a wider range of manufacturing industries to its tax-free zones. Another important economic change, announced in the 1991 budget speech, was the adoption of a 10% value-added tax (VAT), which was to come into effect from 1 July 1992. In addition, farmers, who have enjoyed a 10-year exemption, became liable to pay income tax as of 1 January 1991.

Social Welfare

The Fiji National Provident Fund, established in 1966, contains provision for retirement pensions, widows' pensions, an insurance scheme and housing loans. Employers and employees contribute equally. In June 1987 there were 146,812 members. Medical and dental treatment is provided for all at a nominal charge. In 1987 Fiji had 25 hospitals (with a total of 1,747 beds), 56 health centres, 94 nursing centres and 358 physicians. Of total budgetary expenditure by the central Government in 1988, $F 29.1m. (7.3%) was for health services, and a further $F 23.2m. (5.8%) for social security and welfare.

Education

Education in Fiji is not compulsory, but in 1986 about 94% of school-age children were enrolled at the country's schools, and the Government provided free education for the first eight years of schooling. Primary education begins at six years of age and lasts for six years. Secondary education, beginning at the age of 12, lasts for a further six years. State subsidies are available for secondary and tertiary education in cases of hardship. In 1989 there were 678 state primary schools (with a total enrolment of 141,408 pupils), 141 state secondary schools (with an enrolment of 47,848 pupils) and 41 vocational and technical institutions (with 3,603 students in 1986). In 1988 there were three teacher-training colleges (with 530 students) and, in 1989, two schools of medicine (with 493 students). There were 876 holders of Fiji government scholarships at the University of the South Pacific in Fiji in 1981. In 1989 university students on campus totalled 2,386, and extension students totalled 6,648. Budgetary expenditure on education by the central Government in 1989 was $F 78.5m., representing 14.5% of total spending. The adult illiteracy rate in 1976 averaged 21% (males 16%; females 26%), but in 1986 the rate was only 13% (males 10%; females 16%).

Public Holidays

1991: 1 January (New Year's Day), 29 March–1 April (Easter), 10 June (Queen's Official Birthday), 29 July (Bank Holiday), 21 September* (Birth of the Prophet Muhammad), 14 October (for Independence Day), October/November (Diwali), 11 November (for Birthday of the Prince of Wales), 25–27 December (Christmas).

1992: 1 January (New Year's Day), 17–20 April (Easter), 11 June† (for Queen's Official Birthday), 30 July (Bank Holiday), 10 September* (Birth of the Prophet Muhammad), 8 October (for Independence Day), October/November (Diwali), 12 November† (for Birthday of the Prince of Wales), 25–27 December (Christmas).

* This Islamic holiday is dependent on the lunar calendar and may vary by one or two days from the dates given.
† These holidays may vary by one or two days from the dates given.

Weights and Measures

The metric system is in force.

Statistical Survey

Source (unless otherwise stated): Bureau of Statistics, POB 2221, Government Bldgs, Suva; tel. 315144; telex 2167; Reserve Bank of Fiji, POB 1220, Suva; tel. 313611; telex 2164.

AREA AND POPULATION

Area (incl. the Rotuma group): 18,376 sq km (7,095 sq miles). Land area of 18,333 sq km (7,078 sq miles) consists mainly of the islands of Viti Levu (10,429 sq km—4,027 sq miles) and Vanua Levu (5,556 sq km—2,145 sq miles).

Population: 588,068 (296,950 males, 291,118 females) at census of 13 September 1976; 715,375 (362,568 males, 352,807 females) at census of 31 August 1986; 727,104 (official estimate) at 31 December 1989.

Density (1989): 39.6 per sq km.

Principal Towns: Suva (capital), population 69,665 at 1986 census; Lautoka (estimate, 1986) 29,000.

Ethnic Groups (at census of 31 August 1986): Indians 348,704, Fijians 329,305, Others 37,366, Total 715,375.

Births, Marriages and Deaths (registrations, 1986): Live births 19,045 (birth rate 26.7 per 1,000); Marriages 6,289 (marriage rate 8.8 per 1,000); Deaths 3,917 (death rate 5.5 per 1,000).

Economically Active Population (persons aged 15 years and over, census of 31 August 1986): Agriculture, hunting, forestry and fishing 106,305; Mining and quarrying 1,345; Manufacturing 18,106; Electricity, gas and water 2,154; Construction 11,786; Trade, restaurants and hotels 26,010; Transport, storage and communications 13,151; Financing, insurance, real estate and business services 6,016; Community, social and personal services 36,619; Activities not adequately defined (incl. persons seeking work for the first time) 19,668; Total labour force 241,160 (males 189,929, females 51,231). *1989* (total labour force at 31 December): 252,100.

AGRICULTURE, ETC.

Principal Crops (FAO estimates, metric tons, 1989): Sugar cane 3,200,000, Coconuts 152,000, Cassava 26,000, Rice (paddy) 37,000, Sweet potatoes 2,000, Bananas 6,000, Yams 4,000, Taro 10,000. Source: FAO, *Production Yearbook*.

Livestock (FAO estimates, '000 head, year ending September 1989): Cattle 160, Pigs 16, Goats 75, Horses 42. Source: FAO, *Production Yearbook*.

Livestock Products (metric tons, 1989): Poultry meat 4,674; Beef 4,000; Goat meat 786; Pig meat 600.

Forestry (FAO estimates, 1988): *Roundwood removals* ('000 cu m): Sawlogs and veneer logs 205, Fuel wood and charcoal 37, Other industrial wood 7; Total 249. Source: FAO, *Yearbook of Forest Products*.

Fishing (metric tons, live weight): Total catch 27,002 in 1986; 35,266 in 1987; 38,347 in 1988. Source: FAO, *Yearbook of Fishery Statistics*.

MINING

Production: Gold 4,222 kg (1989), Silver 988 kg (1988), Crushed metal 133,891 cu m (1984).

INDUSTRY

Production (metric tons unless otherwise stated, 1988): Beef 3,565, Sugar 363,000, Copra 10,713, Coconut oil 6,576, Soap 7,915, Cement 44,201, Paint 1,778 ('000 litres), Beer 15,650 ('000 litres), Soft drinks 4,428 ('000 litres), Cigarettes 466,098,650 (number), Timber 204 ('000 cu m), Matches 145 ('000 gross boxes).

FINANCE

Currency and Exchange Rates: 100 cents = 1 Fiji dollar ($F). *Coins:* 1, 2, 5, 10, 20 and 50 cents. *Notes:* 1, 2, 5, 10 and 20 dollars. *Sterling and US Dollar Equivalents* (30 September 1990): £1 sterling = $F2.683; US $1 = $F1.432; $F100 = £37.27 = US $69.82. *Average Exchange Rate* ($F per US $): 1.2439 in 1987; 1.4303 in 1988; 1.4833 in 1989.

Budget ($F '000, 1989): *Revenue:* Customs and Excise 188,563, Inland Revenue 184,458, Non-tax revenue 93,353, Grants 10,346, Total 476,448. *Expenditure:* Administration 106,947, Social services 148,526, Economic services 52,006, Infrastructure 64,257, Public debt charges 127,170, Total (incl. others) 565,038.

International Reserves (US $ million at 31 December 1989): Gold (valued at market-related prices) 0.30, IMF special drawing rights 20.29, Reserve position in IMF 10.37, Foreign exchange 180.33, Total 211.89. Source: IMF, *International Financial Statistics*.

Money Supply ($F million at 31 December 1989): Currency outside banks 78.0; Demand deposits at commercial banks 196.6; Total money 275.7. Source: IMF, *International Financial Statistics*.

Cost of Living (Consumer Price Index; base: 1985 = 100): 107.6 in 1987, 120.2 in 1988, 127.7 in 1989. Source: IMF, *International Financial Statistics*.

Gross Domestic Product by Economic Activity ($F million at current factor cost, 1988): Agriculture, forestry and fishing 279.6; Mining and quarrying 39.1; Manufacturing 137.2; Electricity, gas and water 56.9; Building and construction 50.4; Trade, hotels and restaurants 273.4; Transport and communications 151.6; Finance, real estate etc. 197.0; Government and other services 273.4; Sub-total (incl. others) 1,470.3; *Less* Imputed bank service charges 85.2; Total 1,385.1.

Balance of Payments (US $ million, 1989): Merchandise exports f.o.b. 383.1; Merchandise imports f.o.b. −544.0; *Trade balance* −160.9; Exports of services 384.4; Imports of services −265.0; *Balance on goods and services* −41.5; Private unrequited transfers (net) −14.6; Government unrequited transfers (net) 34.5; *Current balance* −21.7; Direct capital investment (net) 32.4; Other long-term capital (net) −31.1; Short-term capital (net) −7.8; Net errors and omissions 14.5; *Total* (net monetary movements) −13.9; Valuation changes (net) −6.9; *Change in reserves* −20.7. Source: IMF, *International Financial Statistics*.

EXTERNAL TRADE

Principal Commodities (provisional, $F '000, 1989): *Imports c.i.f.* (distribution by SITC): Food 128,373, Beverages and tobacco 8,980, Crude materials 8,175, Mineral fuels 162,225, Oils and fats 10,461, Chemicals 80,624, Manufactured goods 215,625, Machinery and transport equipment 243,385, Miscellaneous manufactured items 90,971, Total (incl. others) 961,870. *Exports f.o.b.:* Sugar 208,152, Gold 76,197, Coconut oil 5,277, Molasses 8,078, Green ginger 3,808, Veneer sheets 2,461, Bakery products 2,174, Prepared fish 39,443, Other fish 5,100, Cement 2,091, Lumber 24,996, Re-exports 104,192, Total (incl. others) 589,200.

Principal Trading Partners (provisional, $F '000, 1989): *Imports c.i.f.:* Australia 290,577, China, People's Republic 30,459, Germany, Federal Republic 12,794, Hong Kong 29,133, India 7,928, Japan 130,592, New Zealand 162,553, Other Pacific countries 2,168, Singapore 57,370, Taiwan 36,292, United Kingdom 27,150, USA 48,265. *Exports:* Australia 116,745, China, People's Republic 829, Germany, Federal Republic 4,832, Hong Kong 2,696, Japan 38,910, New Zealand 67,115, Other Pacific countries 61,936, Singapore 879, Taiwan 4,684, United Kingdom 145,336, USA 29,542.

TRANSPORT

Road Traffic (motor vehicles registered at 31 December 1988): Passenger cars 34,895, All other vehicles 36,513.

Shipping (international freight traffic, '000 metric tons, 1988): Goods loaded 585; Goods unloaded 595. Source: UN, *Monthly Bulletin of Statistics*.

Civil Aviation (1987): Passengers arriving 221,057, Passengers departing 246,778, Transit passengers 158,726.

TOURISM

Foreign Tourist Arrivals: 208,155 in 1988; 250,565 in 1989; 273,668 (provisional estimate) in 1990.

COMMUNICATIONS MEDIA

Radio receivers (1987): 410,000 in use.

Television receivers (1988): 55,000 in use.

Telephones (1988): 62,373 in use.

Book production (1980): 110 titles (84 books, 26 pamphlets); 273,000 copies (229,000 books, 44,000 pamphlets).

Daily newspapers (1988): 2 (combined circulation 40,000 copies per issue).

Non-daily newspapers (1982): 4 (combined circulation 74,300).

EDUCATION

Pre-primary (1986): 214 schools, 325 teachers, 5,400 pupils.

Primary (1989)*: 678 schools, 4,713 teachers, 141,408 pupils.

FIJI
Statistical Survey, Directory

General Secondary (1989)*: 141 schools, 2,815 teachers, 47,848 pupils.

Vocational and Technical: 36 institutions (1984), 41 institutions (1989), 2,941 students (1985), 3,603 students (1986).

Teacher Training (1988): 3 institutions, 530 students.
Medical (1989): 2 institutions, 493 students.
University (1989): 1 institution, 9,034 students (2,386 on campus).
* State sector only.

Directory

The Constitution

The Constitution which came into force on 10 October 1970, when Fiji achieved independence, was formally revoked on 1 October 1987, following the military coup of 25 September 1987. Ratu Sir Penaia Ganilau resigned as Governor-General on 15 October 1987, and Fiji became a Republic. An interim constitution recognized Ratu Ganilau as President of the Republic and vested executive authority in him.

On 25 July 1990 President Ganilau promulgated a new Constitution, after the Bose Levu Vakaturaga (Great Council of Chiefs—a traditional body, with some 70 members, consisting of every hereditary chief or Ratu of each Fijian clan) had approved the draft. The following is a summary of the main provisions:

The Constitution, which declares Fiji to be a sovereign, democratic republic, guarantees fundamental human rights, a universal, secret and equal suffrage and equality before the law for all Fijian citizens. Citizenship may be acquired by birth, descent, registration or naturalization and is assured for all those who were Fijian citizens before 6 October 1987. Parliament may make provision for the deprivation or renunciation of a person's citizenship. Ethnic Fijians, and the Polynesian inhabitants of Rotuma, receive special constitutional consideration, including positive discrimination for employment in the judiciary and by the government (no less than 50% of those employed—although provision is made for exceptions). A Judicial and Legal Services Commission, a Public Service Commission and a Police Service Commission are established as supervisory bodies. The Constitution also declares that those involved in the two military coups of 1987 and the members of the military government, which held office until 5 December 1987, will be immune from any consequent civil or criminal prosecution.

THE GREAT COUNCIL OF CHIEFS

The Great Council of Chiefs (Bose Levu Vakaturaga) derives its authority from the status of its members and their chiefly lineage. The Great Council appoints the President of the Republic and selects the 24 Fijian nominees for appointment to the Senate, the upper chamber of the Parliament.

THE EXECUTIVE

Executive authority is vested in the President of the Republic, who is appointed by the Great Council of Chiefs, for a five-year term, to be a constitutional Head of State and Commander-in-Chief of the armed forces. A Presidential Council advises the President on matters of national importance. The President, and Parliament, can be empowered to introduce any necessary measures in an emergency or in response to acts of subversion which threaten Fiji.

In most cases the President is guided by the Cabinet, which conducts the government of the Republic. The Cabinet is led by a Prime Minister, who must be an ethnic Fijian and is appointed by the President from among the members of Parliament, on the basis of support in the legislature. The Prime Minister selects the other members of the Cabinet (the Attorney-General, the minister responsible for defence and security and any other ministers) from either the House of Representatives or the Senate. The Cabinet is responsible to Parliament.

THE LEGISLATURE

Legislative power is vested in the Parliament, which comprises the President, the appointed upper house or Senate and an elected House of Representatives. The maximum duration of a parliament is five years.

The Senate has 34 members, appointed by the President of the Republic for the term of the Parliament. Twenty-four senators are ethnic Fijians, nominated by the Great Council of Chiefs; one Rotuman is appointed on the advice of the Rotuma Island Council; the remaining nine senators are appointed at the President's discretion from among other groups, with particular regard to minority communities. The Senate is a house of review, with some powers to initiate legislation, but with limited influence on financial measures. The Senate is important in the protection of ethnic Fijian interests, and its consent is essential to any attempt to amend, alter or repeal any provisions affecting ethnic Fijians, their customs, land or tradition.

The House of Representatives has 70 elected members, who themselves elect their presiding officials, the Speaker and Deputy Speaker, from outside the membership of the House. Voting is communal, with universal suffrage for all citizens of the Republic aged over 21 years. For general elections to the House, ethnic Fijians vote in five single-member urban constituencies and 14 rural constituencies, to elect 37 representatives in all. There are 27 seats for those on the Indian electoral roll, one seat for Rotumans and five seats for other races (General Electors). Elections must be held at least every five years and are to be administered by an independent Supervisor of Elections. An independent Boundaries Commission determines constituency boundaries.

THE JUDICIARY

The judiciary is independent and comprises the High Court, the Fiji Court of Appeal and the Supreme Court. The High Court and the Supreme Court are the final arbiters of the Constitution. The establishment of Fijian courts is provided for, and decisions of the Native Lands Commission (relating to ethnic Fijian customs, traditions and usage, and on disputes over the headship of any part of the Fijian people, with the customary right to occupy and use any native lands) are declared to be final and without appeal.

The Government

HEAD OF STATE

President: Ratu Sir PENAIA GANILAU (took office 6 December 1987).

THE CABINET
(January 1991)

Prime Minister, Minister of Foreign Affairs and Minister of Home Affairs: Ratu Sir KAMISESE MARA.

Minister for Fijian Affairs and Rural Development: Col VATILIAI NAVUNISARAVI.

Minister of Finance and Economic Planning: JOSEFATA KAMIKAMICA.

Minister of Education, Youth and Sport: FILIPE BOLE.

Minister for Primary Industries and Cooperatives: VILIAME GONELEVU.

Minister of Trade and Commerce: BERENADO VUNIBOBO.

Minister of Health: APENISA KURISAQILA.

Minister for Infrastructure and Public Utilities: APISAI TORA.

Attorney-General and Minister of Justice: SAILOSI KEPA.

Minister of Tourism, Civil Aviation and Energy: DAVID PICKERING.

Minister of Indian Affairs: IRENE JAI NARAYAN.

Minister of Forests: OVINI BOKINI.

Minister of Employment and Industrial Relations: TANIELA VEITATA.

Minister of Women's Affairs and Social Welfare: FINAU TABAKAUCORO.

Minister of Housing and Urban Development: TOMASI VAKATORA.

Minister of Lands and Mineral Resources: Ratu WILLIAM TOGANIVALU.

Minister of Information, Broadcasting, Television and Telecommunications: Ratu INOKE KUBUABOLA.

FIJI *Directory*

MINISTRIES

All Ministries are based at the Government Buildings, Suva.

Legislature

PARLIAMENT

During the coup of 14 May 1987 a group of soldiers forcibly entered the House of Representatives and arrested all 28 members of the ruling coalition. Parliament has not convened since that time.

The chamber of the House of Representatives was demolished in 1988, but a new Parliament building was under construction at Veiuto, Suva, and was due to be completed by 1991.

The Constitution of July 1990 provided for a bicameral legislature, with elections to the House of Representatives to be held on a communal basis. A general election was expected in late 1991.

The Senate

There were 22 appointed members.
President: W. J. CLARK.

House of Representatives

Speaker: MILITONI LEWANIQILA.

General Election, 5–11 April 1987

	Seats
FLP-NFP coalition	28
AP	24
Total	**52**

Political Organizations

All political activity was suspended on 24 October 1987, but by early 1990 some limited political activity had been permitted to resume.

Alliance Party (AP): 41 Gladstone Rd, POB 688, Suva; f. 1965; mainly indigenous Fijian support, but comprised of the Fijian Association, the Indian Alliance and the General Electors' Association (now the General Voters' Party: see below); ruling party 1970–87; considered defunct since coups of 1987; Pres. Ratu Sir KAMISESE K. T. MARA.

Fijian Conservative Party: Suva; f. 1989 by former mems of the FNP and AP; Leader ISIRELI VUIBAU.

Fiji Labour Party (FLP): Suva; f. 1985; affiliated to Fiji Trades Union Congress; formed coalition govt with NFP following April 1987 election; began moves towards merger with NFP in 1989; Pres. Adi KUINI BAVADRA; Sec.-Gen. KRISHNA DATT.

Fijian Nationalist Party (FNP): POB 1336, Suva; tel. 314700; f. 1974; seeks additional parliamentary representation for persons of Fijian ethnic origin and the introduction of other pro-Fijian reforms; Leader SAKIASI BUTADROKA.

Fijian Political Party: Suva; f. 1990 by Great Council of Chiefs; supports constitutional dominance of ethnic Fijians but accepts multi-racialism.

General Voters' Party: Suva; f. 1990; formerly the General Electors' Association (one of the three wings of the AP); represents the interests of the minority Chinese and European communities and people from other Pacific Islands resident in Fiji, all of whom are classed as General Electors under the new Constitution; Leader LEO SMITH.

National Federation Party (NFP): POB 228, Suva; f. 1960 by merger of the Federation Party, which was multiracial but mainly Indian and the National Democratic Party; joined FLP in coalition govt following April 1987 election; began moves towards merger with FLP in 1989; Leader HARISH CHANDRA SHARMA; Pres. Dr BALWANT SINGH RAKKA.

Taukei Solidarity Movement: f. 1988, following merger of Taukei Liberation Front and Domo Ni Taukei; extreme right-wing indigenous Fijian nationalist group; Vice-Pres. MELI VESIKULA.

Western United Front (WUF): POB 263, Sigatoka; f. 1981; mainly Fijian; advocates co-existence and co-operation among all communities; 10,000 mems; Pres. Ratu OSEA GAVIDI; Sec. ISIKELI NADALO. There are supporters of secession in Rotuma and in the western districts of Fiji.

Diplomatic Representation

EMBASSIES IN FIJI

Australia: Dominion House, POB 214, Suva; tel. 312844; telex 2126; fax 300900; Ambassador: ROBERT COTTON.

China, People's Republic: 147 Queen Elizabeth Drive, Suva; tel. 322425; telex 2136; Ambassador: XU MINGYUAN.

France: 1st Floor, Dominion House, Thomson St, Suva; tel. 312925; telex 2326; Ambassador: HENRI JACOLIN.

Japan: 2nd Floor, Dominion House, Suva; tel. 302122; telex 2253; Chargé d'affaires a.i.: YASUO TAKAHASHI.

Korea, Republic: 8th Floor, Vanua House, PMB, Suva; tel. 311977; telex 2175; Ambassador: HYON CHIN KIM.

Malaysia: Air Pacific House, POB 356, Suva; tel. 312166; telex 2295; fax 303350; Ambassador: SYED ARIFF FADZILLAH.

New Zealand: 10th Floor, Reserve Bank of Fiji Bldg, POB 1378, Suva; tel. 311422; telex 2161; Ambassador: BRIAN ABSOLUM.

Papua New Guinea: 6th Floor, Ratu Sukuna House, POB 2447, Suva; tel. 325420; telex 2113; Ambassador: MAIMU RAKA-NOU.

Tuvalu: POB 14449, Suva; tel. 301023; telex 2297; Ambassador: AMASONE KILEI.

United Kingdom: Victoria House, 47 Gladstone Rd, POB 1355, Suva; tel. 311033; telex 2129; fax 301406; Ambassador: A. B. PETER SMART.

USA: 31 Loftus St, POB 218, Suva; tel. 314466; telex 2255; fax 300081; Ambassador: EVELYN I. H. TEEGEN.

Fiji, and several other countries, recognize as embassies the Suva representation of the US associated states: the Republic of the Marshall Islands (Ambassador: vacant) and the Federated States of Micronesia (Ambassador: ALIK L. ALIK).

Judicial System

Justice is administered by the Supreme Court, the Fiji Court of Appeal, the High Court and the Magistrates' Courts. The Supreme Court of Fiji is the superior court of record presided over by the Chief Justice, who is also the President of the Fiji Court of Appeal. The Chief Justice and six senior judges were removed from office on 15 October 1987, following the military coup of 25 September. In January 1988 the former Chief Justice, Sir Timoci Tuivaga, resumed his post in a newly-constituted judicial system and a further three High Court judges were appointed. Many judicial appointees come from overseas. Since the 1987 coups about two-thirds of Fiji's lawyers have left the country. The judicial arrangements were regularized by the Constitution promulgated on 25 July 1990. This also provided for the establishment of Fijian customary courts and declared as final decisions of the Native Lands Commission in cases involving Fijian custom, etc.

Chief Justice: Sir TIMOCI TUIVAGA.

Religion

CHRISTIANITY

Most ethnic Fijians are Christians. Methodists are the largest Christian group, followed by Roman Catholics. In the census of 1986 about 53% of the population were Christian (mainly Methodists).

Fiji Council of Churches: POB 2300, Government Buildings, Suva; tel. (1) 313798; f. 1964; seven mem. churches; Pres. HENRY MANUELI; Gen. Sec. Rev. GERALD MCNICHOLAS (acting).

The Anglican Communion

Anglicans in Fiji are adherents of the Church of the Province of New Zealand. The Primate and Archbishop of New Zealand is the Bishop of Wellington (New Zealand). The missionary diocese of Polynesia is based in Fiji but also includes Wallis and Futuna, Tuvalu, Kiribati, French Polynesia, Cook Islands, Tonga, Samoa and Tokelau.

Bishop in Polynesia: Rt Rev. JABEZ LESLIE BRYCE, Bishop's House, 7 Disraeli Rd, POB 35, Suva; tel. 302553; fax 302152.

The Roman Catholic Church

Fiji comprises a single archdiocese. At 31 December 1988 there were an estimated 65,311 adherents in the country.

Bishops' Conference: Episcopal Conference of the Pacific Secretariat, POB 289, Suva; tel. 300340; fax 303143; f. 1968; 17 mems; Pres. Most Rev. ANTHONY APURON, Archbishop of Agaña, Guam.

Archbishop of Suva: Most Rev. PETERO MATACA, Archdiocesan Office, Nicolas House, Pratt St, POB 109, Suva; tel. 301955; fax 300909.

Other Christian Churches

Methodist Church in Fiji (Lotu Wesele e Viti): Epworth Arcade, Nina St, POB 357, Suva; tel. 324097; f. 1835; autonomous since

FIJI

1964; 170,820 mems (1985); Pres. Rev. ISIRELI CAUCAU; Gen. Sec. Rev. MANASA LASARO.

Other denominations active in the country include the Assembly of God (with c. 7,000 mems), the Baptist Mission, the Congregational Christian Church and the Presbyterian Church.

HINDUISM

Most of the Indian community are Hindus. According to the census of 1986, 38% of the population were Hindus.

ISLAM

In 1986 some 8% of the population were Muslim. There are several Islamic organizations:

Fiji Muslim League: Suva; Pres. ABDUL RAUF.

BAHÁ'Í FAITH

National Spiritual Assembly: Pacific Regional Office, POB 639, Suva; tel. 381747; mems resident in 486 localities; local church has regional office for consultancy and co-ordination.

The Press

Sunday newspapers have not been published since the military coup of September 1987.

NEWSPAPERS AND PERIODICALS

Coconut Telegraph: POB 249, Savusavu, Vanua Levu; f. 1975; monthly; serves widely-scattered rural communities; Editor Mrs LEMA LOW.

Daily Post: 422 Fletcher Rd, POB 2071, Govt Bldgs, Suva; f. 1987 as *Fiji Post*, daily from 1989; English; Publr TANIELA BOLEA.

Fiji Beach Press: POB 2193, Govt Bldgs, Suva; tel. 313755; telex 2631; fortnightly in English (circ. 8,000), twice a year in English for overseas (circ. 40,000); free tourist information; Editor MERE MOMOIVALU.

Fiji Magic: George Rubine Ltd, POB 12511, Suva; tel. 313944; monthly; English; Editor-in-Chief GABRIEL SINGH; circ. 10,000.

Fiji Republic Gazette: Printing Dept, POB 99, Suva; f. 1874; weekly; English.

Fiji Times: 20 Gordon St, POB 1167, Suva; tel. 304111; telex 2124; fax 301521; f. 1869; publ. by Fiji Times Ltd; daily; English; Man. Dir GEOFFREY HUSSEY; circ. 27,000.

Fiji Trade Review: George Rubine Ltd, POB 12511, Suva; tel. 313944; monthly; English; Editor-in-Chief GEORGE MATAI.

Fiji Women: George Rubine Ltd, POB 12511, Suva; tel. 313944; monthly women's magazine; Editor-in-Chief GEORGE MATAI.

Islands Business: 46 Gordon St, POB 12718, Suva; tel. 303108; fax 301423; f. 1980, present name since 1985; monthly; English; Publr ROBERT KEITH-REID; Editor PETER LOMAS; circ. 8,500.

Na Tui: 422 Fletcher Rd, POB 2071, Govt Bldgs, Suva; f. 1988; weekly; Fijian; Publr TANIELA BOLEA; Editor Ratu NET NAWALOWALO; circ. 7,000.

Nai Lalakai: 20 Gordon St, POB 1167, Suva; tel. 314111; telex 2124; f. 1962; publ. by Fiji Times Ltd; weekly; Fijian; Editor DALE TONAWAI; circ. 18,000.

Nav Jyoti (New Light): c/o Ministry of Information, Govt Bldgs, Suva; f. 1989; govt-owned; free monthly; Hindi.

Sartaj: John Beater Enterprises Ltd, Raiwaqa, POB 5141, Suva; f. 1988; weekly; Hindi; Editor S. DASO; circ. 15,000.

Shanti Dut: 20 Gordon St, POB 1167, Suva; f. 1935; publ. by Fiji Times Ltd; weekly; Hindi; Editor M. C. VINOD; circ. 8,000.

Siga Rarama: Newspapers of Fiji Ltd, POB 354, Suva; tel. 311944; telex 2333; f. 1974; weekly; Fijian; Editor MIKA TURAGA; circ. 10,000.

PRESS ASSOCIATION

Pacific Islands News Association: Suva; regional press asscn; Exec. Dir TAVAKE FUSIMALOHI.

Publishers

Fiji Times Ltd: POB 1167, Suva; tel. 304111; telex 2124; fax 302011; f. 1869; largest newspaper publr; also publrs of books and magazines; Man. Dir GEOFFREY HUSSEY.

Government Publishing House
Printing Department: POB 98, Suva.

Radio and Television

There were an estimated 410,000 radio receivers in use in 1987, and some 55,000 television receivers (for programmes on videotape) in use in 1988.

The coups of 1987 ended earlier plans to establish a television broadcasting service in Fiji. In 1989 the interim Government resumed negotiations with several companies, including Television New Zealand, for such a service.

The content of all broadcasts has been subject to government control since the military coup of 25 September 1987.

Fiji Broadcasting—FBC (Radio Fiji): Broadcasting House, POB 334, Suva; tel. 314333; telex 2142; fax 301643; f. 1954; statutory body; jointly funded by govt grant and advertising revenue; Chair. Ratu JOSUA TOGANIVALU; Gen. Man. EPELI KACIMAIWAI.

Radio Fiji 1 broadcasts nationally on AM in English and Fijian.

Radio Fiji 2 broadcasts nationally on AM in English and Hindi.

Radio Fiji 3-FM broadcasts English programmes, but is not received throughout the islands.

FM 98, mainly with musical programmes, broadcasts for 24 hours per day in Hindi, but cannot be received everywhere.

FBC Radio West (based in Lautoka) is the leading FBC local service, serving the western district of the Republic.

Communications Fiji Ltd: 23 Stewart St, PMB, Suva; tel. 314766; telex 2496; f. 1985; operates two commercial stations; Man. Dir WILLIAM PARKINSON.

FM 96, f. 1985, broadcasts 24 hours per day, on FM, in English and Fijian.

Navtarang, f. 1989, broadcasts 24 hours per day, on FM, in Hindi.

Fiji National Video Centre (FNVC): c/o Ministry of Information, Govt Bldgs, Suva; video library; production unit established by Govt and Hanns Seidel Foundation (Germany); educational programmes.

Finance

The central bank is the Reserve Bank of Fiji. Other locally-based banks are a merchant bank, a development bank and a commercial bank. There were four other, foreign-owned commercial banks in Fiji in 1989. There were one reinsurance and 13 insurance companies operating in Fiji in 1989 (and five inoperative companies). The other major financial institutions are the Fiji National Provident Fund, the Unit Trust of Fiji Ltd, the Housing Authority and the Home Finance Co Ltd.

BANKING

(cap. = capital; res = reserves; dep. = deposits; m. = million; brs = branches; amounts in Fiji dollars)

Central Bank

Reserve Bank of Fiji: POB 1220, Suva; tel. 313611; telex 2164; fax 301688; f. 1984 to replace Central Monetary Authority of Fiji; bank of issue; administers Office of Commissioner of Insurance; cap. and res 58.5m., dep. 103.3m. (1989); Chair. and Gov. JONE YAVALA KUBUABOLA.

Commercial Bank

National Bank of Fiji: 107 Victoria Parade, POB 1166, Suva; tel. 311999; telex 2135; f. 1974; cap. and res 3.3m. (June 1988), dep. 106m. (June 1989); Chair. PAUL MANUELI; Chief Man. VISANTI MAKRAVA; 11 brs; 128 agencies.

Development Bank

Fiji Development Bank: 360 Victoria Parade, POB 104, Suva; tel. 314886; telex 2578; f. 1967; finances the development of natural resources, agriculture, transportation and other industries and enterprises; statutory body; cap. and res 49.6m. (June 1989), dep. 89.2m. (June 1988); Chair. LYLE N. CUPIT; Man. Dir LAISENIA QARASE; 8 brs.

Merchant Bank

Merchant Bank of Fiji Ltd: Burns Philp Bldg, Usher St, Suva; tel. 314955; fax 300026; f. 1986; jointly owned by the Fiji Development Bank (50%), Westpac and the World Bank; Man. RASIK MASTER.

FIJI
Directory

Foreign Banks

Australia and New Zealand (ANZ) Banking Group Ltd: 4th Floor, Civic House, Town Hall Rd, POB 179, Suva; tel. 314000; telex 2194; bought Bank of New Zealand in Fiji (8 brs) in 1990; Gen. Man. (Pacific Islands) L. W. COOKE.

Bank of Baroda (India): POB 57, Suva; telex 2120; fax 302510; Chief Man. D. J. M. PEREIRA.

Habib Bank (Pakistan): Suva; licensed to operate in Fiji 1990; 3 brs.

Westpac Banking Corporation (Australia): Town Hall Rd, POB 238, Suva; tel. 311666; telex 2133; Man. B. H. MUDGE; 11 brs.

INSURANCE

Blue Shield (Pacific) Ltd: Suva; Fijian co; life insurance.

Colonial Mutual Life Assurance Society Ltd: Private Bag, Suva; tel. 314400; telex 2254; f. 1876; inc in Australia; life; Man. T. VUETILOVONI.

Dominion Insurance Ltd: partly owned by Flour Mills of Fiji Ltd; general insurance.

Fiji Reinsurance Corpn Ltd: Suva; 20% govt-owned; reinsurance; Chair. Commissioner of Insurance.

National Insurance Co of Fiji Ltd: Suva; owned by New Zealand interests.

Queensland Insurance (Fiji) Ltd: Queensland Insurance Center, Victoria Parade, POB 101, Suva; tel. 315455; telex 2414; owned by Australian interests; Gen. Man. J. WENNERBOM.

There are also two Indian companies operating in Fiji.

Trade and Industry

DEVELOPMENT AGENCIES

Commonwealth Development Corporation: Office of the Representative for Pacific Islands, Velop House, 371 Victoria Parade, POB 161, Suva; tel. 302577; telex 2412; fax 302303; Rep. D. H. BISHOP.

Fiji Development Company Ltd: POB 161, Suva; tel. 304661; telex 2412; fax 302303; f. 1960; subsidiary of the Commonwealth Development Corpn; Man. V. W. YEE.

Fiji Trade and Investment Board: 3rd Floor, Civic House, Town Hall Rd, POB 2303, Govt Bldgs, Suva; tel. 315988; telex 2355; fax 301783; f. 1980, restyled 1988, to promote and stimulate foreign and local economic development investment; Chair. Prof. ASESELA RAVUVU; Dir SURENDRA SHARMA.

Fijian Development Fund Board: POB 122, Suva; tel. 312601; fax 302585; f. 1951; funds derived from payments of $F20 a metric ton from the sales of copra by indigenous Fijians; deposits receive interest at 2.5%; funds used only for Fijian development schemes; dep. $F1m. (1990); Chair. Minister of Fijian Affairs; CEO N. MORRIS.

Land Development Authority: c/o Ministry for Primary Industries, POB 358, Suva; tel. 311233; f. 1961 to co-ordinate development plans for land and marine resources; Chair. Ratu Sir JOSAIA TAVAIQIA.

CHAMBERS OF COMMERCE

Nadi Chamber of Commerce: Nadi.

Suva Chamber of Commerce: 7th Floor, Honson Bldg, Thomson St, POB 337, Suva; fax 300475; f. 1902; Pres. J. SINGH; Sec. R. DUNSTAN; 94 mems.

Viti Chamber of Chamber: Pres. Ms KOTO VAKAREWAKOBAU.

MARKETING ORGANIZATIONS

Fiji Sugar Cane Growers' Council: 4th Floor, Dominion House, Thomson St, Suva; tel. 314855; telex 2271; f. 1985; aims to develop the sugar industry and protect the interests of registered growers; CEO KALU KARAN SINGH; Chair. Ratu JOSUA CAVALEVU; Sec. (vacant).

Fiji Sugar Corporation Ltd: 5th Floor, Dominion House, Thomson St, POB 283, Suva; tel. 313455; telex 2119; nationalized 1974; buyer of sugar cane and raw sugar mfrs; Chair. LYLE N. CUPIT; Man. Dir RASHEED A. ALI.

Fiji Sugar Marketing Co Ltd: 5th Floor, Dominion House, Thomson St, POB 1402, Suva; tel. 311588; telex 2271; fax 300607; Man. Dir JOHN MAY.

National Marketing Authority: POB 5085, Raiwaqa, Suva; tel. 395989; telex 2412; f. 1971; a statutory body set up to develop markets for agricultural and marine produce locally and overseas; exporters of fresh fruit and vegetables, coconut, chilli and ginger products, doruka and palusami; Chair. V. PRASAD; CEO SOLOMONE MAKASIALE.

Native Land Trust Board: Suva; manages holdings of ethnic Fijian landowners.

Sugar Commission of Fiji: 4th Floor, Dominion House, Thomson St, Suva; tel. 315488; fax 301488; Chair. GERALD BARRACK.

CO-OPERATIVES

In 1986 there were 1,203 registered co-operatives.

EMPLOYERS' ORGANIZATIONS

Fiji Employers' Consultative Association: 7th Floor, Honson Bldg, Thomson St, POB 575, Suva; tel. 313188; fax 302183; represents 160 major employers; Pres. R. A. STORCK; Dir KENNETH A. J. ROBERTS.

Fiji Inter-Island Ship Owners' Association: Suva; Pres. LEO SMITH.

Fiji Manufacturers' Association: 7th Floor, Honson Bldg, Thomson St, POB 1308, Suva; f. 1902; Pres. CHANDU RANIGA; Sec. P. B. SLOAN; 108 mems.

Garment Manufacturers' Association: c/o POB 337, Suva; Chair. PADAM LALA.

TRADE UNIONS

Fiji Trades Union Congress (FTUC): 32 Des Voeux Rd, POB 1418, Suva; tel. 315377; fax 300306; f. 1951; affiliated to ICFTU and ICFTU—APRO; 39 affiliated unions; more than 42,000 mems; Pres. MICHAEL COLOMBUS; Nat. Sec. MAHENDRA P. CHAUDHRY. Principal affiliated unions:

Air Pacific Employees Association: c/o Air Pacific Centre, 263-269 Grantham Rd, Raiwaqa; f. 1951.

Association of USP Staff: POE 1168, Suva; tel. 313900; telex 2276; fax 301305; Pres. SATENDRA PRASAD; Sec. CLAIRE SLATTER.

Federated Airline Staff Association: c/o FTUC, POB 1418, Suva.

Fiji Association of Garment Workers: c/o FTUC, POB 1418, Suva; Sec. EMA DRUAVESI.

Fiji Public Service Association: 298 Waimanu Rd, POB 1405, Suva; tel. 311922; fax 301099; 4,640 mems; Pres. RAJESHWAR SINGH; Gen. Sec. M. P. CHAUDHRY.

Fiji Registered Ports Workers' Union: f. 1947; Gen. Sec. (vacant).

Fiji Sugar and General Workers' Union: POB 330, Lautoka; tel. 360746; 2,500 mems; Pres. SHIU LINGAM; Gen. Sec. FELIX ANTHONY.

Fiji Teachers' Union: 211 Edinburgh Drive, POB 3582, Samabula; tel. 381585; fax 385021; f. 1930; 3,000 mems; Pres. ANIL KUMAR SUDHAKAR; Gen. Sec. PRATAP CHAND.

Mineworkers' Union of Fiji: Vatukoula; f. 1986.

National Farmers' Union: 298 Waimanu Rd, POB 1405, Suva; tel. 311662; fax 301099; 10,000 mems (sugar cane farmers); Pres. GIRJA PRASAD; Gen. Sec. M. CHAUDHRY.

National Union of Factory and Commercial Workers: POB 989, Suva; 3,800 mems; Pres. CAMA TUILEVUKA; Gen. Sec. JAMES R. RAMAN.

Public Employees' Union: POB 781, Suva; tel. 313744; 6,752 mems; Pres. JAMES SAMUJH; Gen. Sec. (vacant).

Transport and Oil Workers' Union: f. 1988; following merger of Oil and Allied Workers' Union and Transport Workers' Union; Gen. Sec. MICHAEL COLUMBUS.

There are several independent trade unions.

Transport

RAILWAYS

Fiji Sugar Corporation Railway: Rarawai Mill, POB 155, Ba; tel. 74044; telex 6248; fax 74822; for use in cane-harvesting season, May–Dec.; 595 km of permanent track and 225 km of temporary track (gauge of 600 mm), serving cane-growing areas at Ba, Lautoka and Penang on Viti Levu and Labasa on Vanua Levu; Gen. Man. R. BOKINI.

In 1985 the Asian Development Bank sponsored a feasibility study of the potential for the creation of a major passenger railway system.

ROADS

At the end of 1989 there were 1,206 km of roads in Fiji, of which 1,250 km were main or national roads and 563 km secondary roads.

FIJI

A 500-km highway circles the main island of Viti Levu. Of the total road network, 13% is paved.

SHIPPING

There are ports of call at Suva, Lautoka and Levuka. The main port, Suva, handles more than 800 ships a year, including large passenger liners. Lautoka handles more than 300 vessels and liners and Levuka, the former capital of Fiji, mainly handles commercial fishing vessels. A fourth port, at Savusavu on the island of Vanua Levu, was expected to open in the early 1990s.

Fuji Maritime Services Ltd: c/o Ports Authority of Fiji (PAF), Suva; f. 1989 by PAF and the Ports Workers' Union; services between Lautoka and Vanua Levu ports.

Inter-Ports Shipping Corpn Ltd: 25 Eliza St, Walu Bay; POB 152, Suva; tel. 313638; telex 2703; f. 1984; Man. Dir Leo B. Smith.

Transcargo Express Fiji Ltd: POB 936, Suva; f. 1974; Man. Dir Leo B. Smith.

Williams Taoniu Shipping Co Ltd: POB 1270, Suva; inter-island shipping.

The main foreign companies serving Fiji are: Karlander (Aust.) Pty Ltd, Sofrana-Unilines (Fiji Express Line), Pacific Forum Line, and Pacific Navigation of Tonga operating cargo services between Australia and Fiji; Blue Star Line Ltd and Crusader Shipping Co Ltd calling at Fiji between North America and New Zealand, and P & O between the USA and Australia; Nedlloyd operates to Fiji from New Zealand, the UK and Northern Europe; Bank Line Ltd from the UK and the Netherlands; NYK Line and Daiwa Lines from Japan; Marshall Islands Maritime Co from Honolulu and Tonga; Kyowa Shipping Co Ltd from Hong Kong, Taiwan, the Republic of Korea and Japan; and Jebsen Line from various Asian ports.

CIVIL AVIATION

There is an international airport at Nadi (about 210 km from Suva), a domestic airport at Nausori (Suva) and 15 other airfields. Nadi is an important transit airport in the Pacific and, in 1990, direct flights to Japan also began.

Air Coral Coast: Korolevu; telex 3241; domestic airline; Man. Dir Gordon Oliver; fleet of 1 Britten Norman Islander, 1 Cessna 206.

Air Pacific Ltd: Air Pacific Centre, 263-269 Grantham Rd, Raiwaqa, Suva, pending relocation to Nadi International Airport; tel. 386444; telex 2131; fax 300976; f. 1951 as Fiji Airways, name changed in 1971; domestic services from Nausori Airport (serving Suva) to Nadi and international services to Tonga, Solomon Islands, Vanuatu, Western Samoa, Japan, Australia and New Zealand; in December 1984 management was taken over by the Australian airline Qantas; in 1990 the Govt owned about 80% and Qantas 10% of shares in the airline; Chair. Gerald Barrack; Man. Dir and CEO Andrew Drysdale; fleet of 1 Boeing 747-200, 1 Boeing 737-200, 1 Boeing 767-200, 2 ATR 42-300.

Fiji Air Ltd: 219 Victoria Parade, POB 1259, Suva; tel. 314666; telex 2258; fax 300771; domestic airline operating 46 scheduled services a week to 13 destinations; international service to Tuvalu; charter operations, aerial photography and surveillance also conducted; partly owned by the Fijian Govt; CEO Martin C. D. Tyler; fleet of 2 DHC6 Twin Otters, 3 Britten Norman Islander, 1 Beech Baron C55, 2 Riley Heron DH114; 2 Casa on order.

Sunflower Airlines Ltd: POB 9452, Nadi International Airport, Nadi; tel. 73555; telex 5183; fax 790085; f. 1980; domestic airline; Man. Dir Don Ian Collingwood; fleet of 5 Britten Norman Islander, 2 De Havilland Twin Otter, 2 Cessna, 1 Riley Heron, 1 Piper Chieftain, 1 Queenair Excalibur.

Tourism

Scenery, climate and fishing attract visitors to Fiji, where tourism is an important industry. The number of foreign visitors increased from 250,565 in 1989 to an estimated 273,668 in 1990. Further expansion of the tourist industry is constrained, however, by limited airline capacity and a shortage of skilled personnel.

Fiji Hotel Association (FHA): Suva; represents about 70 hotels; Chief Exec. Kevin Mutton.

Fiji Visitors Bureau: POB 92, Suva; tel. 302433; telex 2180; fax 300970; f. 1923; Chair. Sakeasi Waqanivavalagi; Gen. Man. Isimeli Bainimara.

Regional Organization

Tourism Council of the South Pacific: POB 13119, Suva; tel. 315277; telex 2306; fax 301995; regional tourism development organization.

FINLAND

Introductory Survey

Location, Climate, Language, Religion, Flag, Capital

The Republic of Finland lies in northern Europe, bordered to the far north by Norway and to the north-west by Sweden. The USSR adjoins the whole of the eastern frontier. Finland's western and southern shores are washed by the Baltic Sea. The climate varies sharply, with warm summers and cold winters. The mean annual temperature is 5°C (41°F) in Helsinki and −0.4°C (31°F) in the far north. There are two official languages: 93.6% of the population speak Finnish and 6.0% speak Swedish. Finnish is a member of the small Finno-Ugrian group of languages, which includes Hungarian. There is a small Lapp population in the north. Almost all of the inhabitants profess Christianity, and nearly 90% belong to the Evangelical Lutheran Church. The Orthodox Church has the status of a second national church, while there are small groups of Roman Catholics, Methodists, Jews and other religious sects. The national flag (proportions 18 by 11) displays an azure blue cross (the upright to the left of centre) on a white background. The state flag has, at the centre of the cross, the national coat of arms (a yellow-edged red shield containing a golden lion and nine white roses). The capital is Helsinki.

Recent History

Finland was formerly an autonomous part of the Russian Empire. During the Russian revolution of 1917 the territory proclaimed its independence. Following a brief civil war, a democratic constitution was adopted in 1919. The Soviet regime which came to power in Russia attempted to regain control of Finland but acknowledged the country's independence in 1920.

Demands by the USSR for military bases in Finland and for the cession of part of the Karelian isthmus, in south-eastern Finland, were rejected by the Finnish Government in November 1939. As a result, the USSR attacked Finland, and the two countries fought the 'Winter War', a fiercely contested conflict lasting 15 weeks, before Finnish forces were defeated. Following its surrender, Finland ceded an area of 41,880 sq km (16,170 sq miles) to the USSR in March 1940. In the hope of recovering the lost territory, Finland joined Nazi Germany in attacking the USSR in 1941. However, a separate armistice between Finland and the USSR was concluded in 1944.

In accordance with a peace treaty signed in February 1947, Finland agreed to the transfer of about 12% of its pre-war territory (including the Karelian isthmus and the Petsamo area on the Arctic coast) to the USSR, and to the payment of reparations which totalled about US $570m. when completed in 1952. Meanwhile, in April 1948, Finland and the USSR signed the Finno-Soviet Pact of Friendship, Co-operation and Mutual Assistance (the YYA treaty), which was extended for periods of 20 years in 1955, 1970 and again in 1983. A major requirement of the treaty is that Finland repel any attack made on the USSR by Germany, or its allies, through Finnish territory. Finnish policy, however, is one of neutrality in foreign affairs.

Since becoming independent in 1917, the politics of Finland have been characterized by premature elections, a rapid succession of coalition governments (including numerous minority coalitions) and the development of consensus. The Social Democratic Party (SDP) and the Centre Party (KP) have been the dominant participants in government. The conservative opposition gained significant support at a general election in March 1979, following several years of economic crises. A new centre-left coalition government was formed in May, however, by Dr Mauno Koivisto, a Social Democratic economist and former Prime Minister. This four-party Government, comprising the KP, the SDP, the Swedish People's Party (SFP) and the Finnish People's Democratic League (SKDL—an electoral alliance which includes the Communists), continued to pursue deflationary economic policies although crises arose within the Council of State (Cabinet) in 1981, owing to disagreements over social welfare policy and budgetary matters.

Dr Urho Kekkonen, President since 1956, resigned in October 1981. Dr Koivisto was elected President in January 1982. He was succeeded as head of the coalition by a former Prime Minister, Kalevi Sorsa, a Social Democrat. Towards the end of 1982 the SKDL refused to support austerity measures or an increase in defence spending. This led to the re-formation of the coalition in December, without the SKDL, until the general election of March 1983.

At this election the SDP won 57 (compared with 52 in the 1979 election) of the 200 seats in the Eduskunta (Parliament), while the conservative opposition National Coalition Party (Kok) lost three seats. In May Sorsa formed another centre-left coalition, comprising the SDP, the SFP, the KP and the Rural Party (SMP): the coalition parties had a total of 122 parliamentary seats. The aims of the new Government, which retained office throughout 1984 and 1985 without any major disruption, were to reduce inflation and unemployment, to curb the rise in gross taxation, to limit state borrowing, and to expand trade with Western countries. In May 1985 the coalition was threatened when the Government announced that it would resign if an anti-nuclear parliamentary motion, introduced by the SMP and the SFP, was not withdrawn. The motion, which demanded the dismantling of Finland's four nuclear reactors, was subsequently withdrawn by both parties. The Government also survived a motion of 'no confidence', proposed by the conservative opposition, for its alleged failure to provide accurate information following the accident in April 1986 at the Chernobyl nuclear power station in the USSR, which resulted in radioactive fall-out over Finland.

In 1985 relations between Finland and the USSR were threatened when the Communist Party of Finland (SKP) expelled several groups of pro-Soviet dissidents. This 'Stalinist' minority formed a separate electoral organization, and eventually registered as a distinct political party, known as the Democratic Alternative (later, the SKP–Y).

At a general election held in March 1987, the combined non-socialist parties gained a majority in the Eduskunta for the first time since the election of 1945. Although the SDP remained the largest single party, losing one seat and retaining 56, the system of modified proportional representation enabled the Kok to gain an additional nine seats, winning a total of 53, while increasing its share of the votes cast by only 1%. The Communist parties suffered a decline in popularity: although the SKDL retained all of its 16 seats, the number of seats held by the Democratic Alternative was reduced from 10 to four. President Koivisto eventually invited Harri Holkeri, a former chairman of the Kok, to form a coalition government comprising the Kok, the SDP, the SFP and the SMP, thus avoiding a polarization of the political parties within the Eduskunta. The four parties controlled 131 of the 200 seats. Holkeri became the first conservative Prime Minister since 1946, and the Centre Party joined the opposition for the first appreciable length of time since independence. Sorsa resigned as SDP chairman, but retained office as Deputy Prime Minister and Minister for Foreign Affairs.

The arrival of the Kok in government represented a major change in Finnish politics, but did not destroy the long-established consensus. The success of the basic Kok-SDP alliance was tested in two elections in 1988. In February Koivisto retained office after the first presidential election by direct popular vote. He campaigned for a reduction in presidential power. He did not win the required absolute majority, however, and the electoral college was convened. Koivisto was re-elected after an endorsement by Prime Minister Holkeri, who was third in terms of direct votes (behind Paavo Väyrynen, leader of the KP).

Local elections in October 1988 confirmed the continuing strength of the ruling coalition, with very little change in the balance of support for the parties. The coalition parties were successful despite a dispute between some unions and Holkeri, who was accused of condoning the regime of President Pinochet of Chile by guaranteeing a state-owned company's mining

FINLAND

operations in that country. The SDP was affected by internal disputes, with none of the Social Democratic ministers willing to resign in order to allow the party chairman, Pertti Paasio, to join the Council of State. In January 1989, however, Sorsa resigned in an attempt to solve the problem. This threatened the Kok's agreement to the coalition, and SDP support for planned austerity measures. In August 1990 the SMP withdrew from the governing coalition, following a disagreement over proposals concerning pensions in the 1991 budget. The extreme left also continued to experience internal problems. In 1988 the communists suffered financial losses and scandals within the SKP, and further fragmentation following a split in the SKP—Y. In April 1990 the SKP, the SKP—Y and the SKDL merged to form the Left-Wing Alliance.

In foreign affairs, Finland is neutral, but President Koivisto continued the Passiviki-Kekkonen policy (named after the two post-war Presidents) of pursuing friendly relations with the USSR. In October 1989 Mikhail Gorbachev became the first Soviet Head of State to visit Finland since 1975, and recognized Finland's neutral status. This was regarded by Finland as a significant diplomatic success. Finland joined the United Nations and the Nordic Council (see p. 179) in 1955 but decided to become a full member of EFTA (see p. 154) only in 1985. In 1989 Finland joined the Council of Europe (see p. 129). However, Koivisto excluded the possibility of Finnish membership of the European Communities (a trade agreement between Finland and the EEC has been in effect since 1974). In September 1989 Finland and the USSR concluded an accord whereby the USSR agreed to halve sulphur emissions from the Kola Peninsula by the end of 1995, and Finland agreed to finance the modernization of the nickel factories in the region (the pollution was seriously affecting Finland's forests and waterways).

Government

Finland has a republican constitution which combines a parliamentary system with a strong presidency. The unicameral Parliament (Eduskunta) has 200 members, elected by universal adult suffrage for four years (subject to dissolution by the President) on the basis of proportional representation. The President, entrusted with supreme executive power, is elected for six years by direct popular vote. If no candidate wins an absolute majority, a 301-member electoral college is convened. Legislative power is exercised by Parliament in conjunction with the President. For general administration, the President appoints a Council of State (Cabinet), which is headed by a Prime Minister and is responsible to Parliament. Finland has 12 provinces, each administered by an appointed Governor. The province of Ahvenanmaa (the Åland Islands) has, in addition, a local parliament (landsting), elected by the predominantly Swedish-speaking residents of the islands, which has independent rights of legislation in internal affairs.

Defence

The armed forces of Finland are restricted by treaty to 41,900, and in June 1990 numbered 31,000 (of whom 23,700 were conscripts serving up to 11 months), comprising an army of 27,800 (22,300 conscripts), an air force of 1,800 (800 conscripts) and a navy of 1,400 (600 conscripts). There were also 1,073 serving abroad with UN forces, some 700,000 reserves and 4,400 frontier guards. The estimated defence budget for 1990 was 7,200m. markkaa.

Economic Affairs

In 1988, according to estimates by the World Bank, Finland's gross national product (GNP), measured at average 1986–88 prices, was US $92,015m., equivalent to $18,610 per head. During 1980–88, it was estimated, GNP increased, in real terms, at an average annual rate of 3.2%, and GNP per head increased by 2.7% per year. Over the same period, the population increased by an annual average of 0.4%. The country's gross domestic product (GDP) increased, in real terms, by an annual average of 2.8% in 1980–88.

Agriculture (including hunting, forestry and fishing) contributed 6.2% of GDP and employed 8.8% of the working population in 1989. Forestry is the most important branch of the sector. According to the Bank of Finland, the wood industry provided 42% of export earnings in 1988. Animal husbandry is the predominant form of farming. The major crops are oats, sugar beet and potatoes. During 1980–87 agricultural production declined by an annual average of 1.1%.

Introductory Survey

Industry (including mining, manufacturing, construction and power) contributed 34.6% of GDP and employed 30.8% of the working population in 1989. During 1980–87 industrial production increased by an annual average of 2.7%.

Mining and quarrying contributed 0.4% of GDP and employed 0.2% of the working population in 1989. Gold is the major mineral export. Zinc ore, silver, copper ore and lead ore are mined in small quantities.

Manufacturing provided 22.4% of GDP in 1989, and in the same year employed 21.4% of the working population. In 1987 the most important branches of manufacturing, measured by gross value of output, were paper and paper products (accounting for 17.2% of the total), food products (16.7%), machinery (13.4%), metals and metal products (10%) and wood products (including furniture). During 1980–88 the output of the manufacturing sector increased at an average rate of 3.1% per year.

Energy is derived principally from petroleum, coal and nuclear power. Imports of mineral fuels comprised 9.8% of the total value of imports in 1989.

Services contributed 59.3% of GDP and employed 60.3% of the working population in 1989. During 1980–87 the output of the services sector grew by an annual average of 3.9%.

In 1989 Finland recorded a visible trade deficit of US $219m., and there was a deficit of $5,128m. on the current account of the balance of payments. In 1989 the principal source of imports (17.3%) was the Federal Republic of Germany, and the principal market for exports (14.3%) was Sweden. Other major trading partners are the USSR and the United Kingdom. The principal exports in 1989 were paper and paper products, machinery and transport equipment, and crude materials (mainly wood and pulp). The principal imports were machinery and transport equipment, basic manufactures, and mineral fuels.

The budget surplus for 1991 was forecast at 2m. markkaa. Finland's total external debt was estimated at 69,600m. markkaa in 1989. The average annual rate of inflation was 6.6% in 1989. In November 1990, 4.3% of the labour force were unemployed.

Finland is a member of the Nordic Council (see p. 179), the European Free Trade Association (p. 154) and the Organization for Economic Co-operation and Development (p. 186).

Finland experienced a high rate of economic growth during the 1980s, but this was expected to decline in the 1990s. In the late 1980s Finland and other members of EFTA were engaged in negotiations with the EEC to ensure access to the EEC's internal market after the completion of the 'single European market' in 1992, and there were plans to deregulate Finland's financial markets to facilitate free trade with European countries. Finland has maintained strong economic ties with the USSR, and in 1989 the two countries renewed a bilateral trade agreement (for 1991–95). In December 1990, however, the Soviet Union announced that the clearing-house trade system in operation between Finland and the USSR would end, without a transition period, at the end of that month and would be replaced by a system of trade based on convertible currency.

Social Welfare

Social policy covers social security (national pensions, disability insurance, sickness insurance), social assistance (maternity, child, housing, education and other allowances and accident compensation) and social welfare (care of children, the aged, disabled and maladjusted, including residential services). Sickness insurance covers a considerable part of the costs of medical care outside hospital, while the general hospitals charge moderate fees. The National Health Act of 1972 provided for the establishment of health centres in every municipality, and the abolition of doctors' fees. In 1985 Finland had 61,082 hospital beds. In the same year there were 10,193 physicians working in the country. Of total general budget expenditure in 1989, 11,515m. markkaa (8.9%) was for health, and a further 23,155m. markkaa (17.9%) for social security. In addition, significant expenditure on these services is provided from social security funds under the control of the central Government. In 1987 such funds spent 3,378m. markkaa on health and 20,733m. markkaa on social security and welfare.

Education

Compulsory education, introduced in 1921, lasts for nine years between seven and 16 years of age. By the 1977/78 school year, the whole country had transferred to a new comprehensive education system. Tuition is free and instruc-

FINLAND

tion is the same for all students. The compulsory course comprises six years at primary school, beginning at the age of seven, followed by three years at secondary school, beginning at the age of 13. After completing compulsory education, the pupil may transfer to an upper secondary school or other vocational school or institute for a further three years. In 1987 the total enrolment at all primary and secondary schools was equivalent to 103% of the school-age population. After three years in upper secondary school, a student takes a matriculation examination. Students who pass this examination are entitled to seek admission at one of the 23 universities and colleges of further education. General budget expenditure on education by the central Government in 1989 was 23,050m. markkaa (17.8% of total spending).

Public Holidays

1991: 1 January (New Year's Day), 6 January (Epiphany), 29 March (Good Friday), 1 April (Easter Monday), 1 May (May Day, Labour Day), 4 May (for Ascension Day), 18–19 May (Whitsun), 24 June (Midsummer Day, Flag Day), 2 November (for All Saints' Day), 6 December (Independence Day), 25–26 December (Christmas).

1992: 1 January (New Year's Day), 6 January (Epiphany), 17 April (Good Friday), 20 April (Easter Monday), 1 May (May Day, Labour Day), 28 May (for Ascension Day), 6–7 June (Whitsun), 24 June (Midsummer Day, Flag Day), 3 November (for All Saints' Day), 6 December (Independence Day), 25–26 December (Christmas).

Weights and Measures

The metric system is in force.

Statistical Survey

Sources (unless otherwise specified): Central Statistical Office of Finland, POB 504, Annankatu 44, 00101 Helsinki; tel. (90) 17341; telex 1002111; fax (90) 17342279; *Maataloustilastollinen Kuukausikatsaus* (Monthly Review of Agricultural Statistics), Board of Agriculture Statistical Office, Mariankatu 23, 00170 Helsinki; and *Bank of Finland Monthly Bulletin*.

Note: Figures in this Survey include data for the autonomous Åland Islands, treated separately on pp. 1031–1032.

Area and Population

AREA, POPULATION AND DENSITY

Area (sq km)
Land	304,623
Inland water	33,522
Total	338,145*

Population (census results)
1 November 1980	4,784,710
17 November 1985	
Males	2,377,978
Females	2,532,641
Total	4,910,619

Population (official estimates at 31 December)
1987	4,938,602
1988	4,954,359
1989	4,974,383
Density (per sq km) at 31 December 1989	14.7

* 130,559 sq miles.

31 December 1990 (provisional estimate): Population 4,994,000.

PROVINCES (estimated population at 31 December 1989)

	Land Area (sq km)*	Population
Uudenmaan (Nylands)	9,898	1,235,460
Turun-Porin (Åbo-Björneborgs)	22,170	716,639
Ahvenanmaan (Åland)	1,527	24,231
Hämeen (Tavastehus)	17,010	688,267
Kymen (Kymmene)	10,783	335,466
Mikkelin (St Michels)	16,342	208,156
Kuopion (Kuopio)	16,510	256,381
Pohjois-Karjalan (Norra Karelens)	17,782	176,566
Vaasan (Vasa)	20,447	444,624
Keski-Suomen (Mellersta Finlands)	16,230	251,206
Oulun (Uleåborgs)	56,868	437,414
Lapin (Lapplands)	93,056	199,973
Total	**304,623**	**4,974,383**

* Excluding inland waters, totalling 33,522 sq km.

PRINCIPAL TOWNS
(estimated population at 31 December 1989)

Helsinki (Helsingfors) (capital)	490,629
Tampere (Tammerfors)	171,561
Espoo (Esbo)	169,851
Turku (Åbo)	159,469
Vantaa (Vanda)	152,262
Oulu (Uleåborg)	100,281
Lahti	93,132
Kuopio	80,002
Pori (Björneborg)	76,456
Jyväskylä	66,387
Kotka	56,933
Lappeenranta (Villmanstrand)	54,804
Vaasa (Vasa)	53,364
Joensuu	47,204
Hämeenlinna (Tavastehus)	43,098

BIRTHS, MARRIAGES AND DEATHS

	Registered live births*		Registered marriages†		Registered deaths*	
	Number	Rate (per 1,000)	Number	Rate (per 1,000)	Number	Rate (per 1,000)
1982	66,106	13.7	30,459	6.3	43,408	9.0
1983	66,892	13.8	29,474	6.1	45,388	9.3
1984	65,076	13.3	28,550	5.8	45,098	9.2
1985	62,796	12.8	25,794	5.3	48,198	9.8
1986	60,799	12.4	25,866	5.3	47,117	9.6
1987	59,825	12.2	26,376	5.3	47,949	9.7
1988	63,313	12.8	26,453	5.3	10,026	0.0
1989	63,388	12.8	25,043	5.0	49,072	9.9

* Including Finnish nationals temporarily outside the country.
† Data relate only to marriages in which the bride was domiciled in Finland.

FINLAND

ECONOMICALLY ACTIVE POPULATION*
('000 persons aged 15 to 74 years)

	1987	1988	1989
Agriculture, forestry and fishing	251	238	218
Mining and quarrying	7	6	6
Manufacturing	534	519	528
Electricity, gas and water	28	28	28
Construction	184	188	199
Trade, restaurants and hotels	348	354	368
Transport, storage and communications	182	182	179
Finance, insurance, real estate and business services	177	190	194
Community, social and personal services	710	724	749
Activities not adequately described	3	3	2
Total employed	**2,423**	**2,432**	**2,470**
Unemployed	130	116	89
Total labour force	**2,554**	**2,548**	**2,559**

* Excluding persons on compulsory military service (29,000 in 1987; 28,000 in 1988; 24,000 in 1989).

Agriculture

PRINCIPAL CROPS
('000 metric tons; farms with arable land of 1 hectare or more)

	1987	1988	1989
Wheat	281.1	284.6	507.2
Barley	1,089.2	1,611.8	1,629.9
Rye	74.2	48.9	195.9
Oats	723.2	857.3	1,443.8
Mixed grain	14.8	23.1	31.9
Potatoes	490.5	854.5	981.3
Rapeseed	89.7	121.1	125.4
Sugar beet	466.2	943.7	989.8

LIVESTOCK ('000 head at 1 June; farms with arable land of 1 hectare or more)

	1987	1988	1989
Horses	19.9	15.1	15.6
Cattle	1,497.9	1,443.4	1,357.4
Sheep	126.2	119.0	107.3
Reindeer	366.0	364.0	407.0
Pigs*	1,341.9	1,305.1	1,298.0
Chickens / Other poultry	6,790.7	6,678.2	6,138.9
Beehives†	42.0	47.0	50.0

* Including piggeries of dairies.   † '000 hives.

LIVESTOCK PRODUCTS ('000 metric tons)

	1987	1988	1989
Beef	122.0	110.0	109.8
Veal	0.7	0.4	0.3
Pig meat	174.8	168.2	178.7
Poultry meat	26.6	27.7	30.2
Cows' milk*	2,692.0	2,531.0	2,546.8
Butter	60.7	60.9	63.9
Cheese	85.2	86.6	90.5
Hen eggs	78.0	74.4	75.7
Cattle hides	15.2	12.6	12.6

* Million litres.

Forestry

ROUNDWOOD REMOVALS ('000 cu m, excl. bark)

	1986	1987	1988
Sawlogs, veneer logs and logs for sleepers	17,026	17,488	19,740
Pulpwood	19,428	21,117	24,500
Other industrial wood	1,206	1,269	1,269*
Fuel wood	3,009	2,956	3,111
Total	**40,669**	**42,830**	**48,620**

* FAO estimate.
Source: FAO, *Yearbook of Forest Products*.

SAWNWOOD PRODUCTION ('000 cu m, incl. boxboards)

	1986	1987	1988
Coniferous (softwood)	7,035	7,460	7,720
Broadleaved (hardwood)	75	70	70*
Total	**7,110**	**7,530**	**7,790**

Railway sleepers ('000 cu m): 33 per year (1986–88).
* FAO estimate.
Source: FAO, *Yearbook of Forest Products*.

Fishing

('000 metric tons, live weight)

	1986*	1987	1988
Freshwater fishes	26.7	2.2	2.6
Diadromous fishes	23.8	18.9	22.2
Atlantic herring	94.8	82.5	92.8
Other marine fishes	9.4	2.7	3.5
Total catch	**154.7**	**106.3**	**121.1**
Inland waters	32.9	8.6	8.3
Atlantic Ocean	121.8	97.7	112.7

* Figures include recreational fishing, estimated to account for 5% of the total catch.
Source: FAO, *Yearbook of Fishery Statistics*.

Mining

('000 metric tons, unless otherwise indicated)

	1987	1988	1989
Copper ore*	21.4†	18.4†	23.8
Lead ore*	2.4	1.9	2.6
Zinc ore*	55.1	63.9	58.2
Silver (metric tons)	33.2†	29.9†	34.6
Gold (kilograms)	708†	594†	696

* Figures refer to metal content.
† Provisional.

FINLAND

Statistical Survey

Industry

SELECTED PRODUCTS
(provisional figures, '000 metric tons, unless otherwise indicated)

	1987	1988	1989
Cellulose	5,118	5,322	5,531
Machine pulp (for sale)	2,790	1,244	884
Newsprint	1,374	1,273	1,184
Other paper, boards and cardboards	6,845	7,559	7,865
Plywoods and veneers ('000 cubic metres)	636	586	602
Cement	1,579	1,504	1,596
Pig iron and ferro-alloys	2,064	2,173	2,312
Electricity (million kWh)	52,564	51,156	50,765
Cotton yarn (metric tons)	6,214	3,174	2,120
Cotton fabrics (metric tons)	7,815	5,269	4,122
Sugar (metric tons)	204,142	185,411	137,872
Rolled steel products (metric tons)	2,024	2,191	2,539
Copper cathodes (metric tons)	59,538	53,939	55,751
Cigarettes (million)	9,061	9,474	8,932

Finance

CURRENCY AND EXCHANGE RATES

Monetary Units
100 penniä (singular: penni) = 1 markka (Finnmark).

Denominations
Coins: 5, 10, 20 and 50 penniä; 1, 5 and 10 markkaa.
Notes: 5, 10, 50, 100, 500 and 1,000 markkaa.

Sterling and Dollar Equivalents (30 September 1990)
£1 sterling = 6.963 markkaa;
US $1 = 3.7215 markkaa;
100 markkaa = £14.36 = $26.87.

Average Exchange Rate (markkaa per US $)
1987   4.3956
1988   4.1828
1989   4.2912

BUDGET* (million markkaa)

Revenue	1987	1988	1989
Direct taxes	29,454	34,498	38,513
Indirect taxes	57,538	67,389	77,536
Social security	—	—	71
Other	21,658	16,782	18,708
Total	108,650	118,669	134,828

Expenditure	1987	1988	1989
Education	18,363	20,459	23,050
Social security	20,191	21,765	23,155
Health	9,420	10,368	11,515
Agriculture and forestry	9,501	10,001	9,854
Transport and communications	9,578	10,350	10,916
Defence	5,772	6,414	6,748
Public debt	4,987	5,391	9,416
Other	29,176	32,533	34,805
Total	106,988	117,281	129,459

Budget Estimates (million markkaa): 1990: Revenue 141,611, Expenditure 141,609; 1991: Revenue 157,655, Expenditure 157,653.

* Figures refer to the General Budget only, excluding the operations of the Social Insurance Institution and of other social security funds with their own budgets.

INTERNATIONAL RESERVES (US $ million at 31 December)

	1987	1988	1989
Gold*	539.3	510.4	537.1
IMF special drawing rights	227.7	268.9	239.2
Reserve position in IMF	200.8	225.6	235.0
Foreign exchange	5,989.0	5,874.7	4,636.9
Total	6,956.8	6,879.6	5,648.2

* Valued at market-related prices.
Source: IMF, *International Financial Statistics*.

MONEY SUPPLY (million markkaa at 31 December)

	1987	1988	1989
Currency outside banks	7,259	8,418	8,772
Demand deposits at deposit money banks	23,047	27,472	32,634
Total money*	30,342	35,921	41,444

* Including private-sector deposits at the Bank of Finland.
Source: IMF, *International Financial Statistics*.

COST OF LIVING (Consumer Price Index; base: 1981 = 100)

	1987	1988	1989
Food	147	151	156
Beverages and tobacco	155	171	179
Clothing and footwear	135	137	141
Rent, heating and lighting	135	142	162
Furniture, household equipment	140	146	152
All items	145	152	162

NATIONAL ACCOUNTS (million markkaa at current prices)
National Income and Product

	1987	1988	1989
Compensation of employees	214,672	237,260	265,183
Operating surplus	72,875	83,669	94,208
Domestic factor incomes	287,547	320,929	359,391
Consumption of fixed capital	58,143	64,956	73,473
Gross domestic product at factor cost	345,690	385,885	432,864
Indirect taxes	57,593	66,925	76,180
Less Subsidies	11,686	11,271	13,604
GDP in purchasers' values	391,597	441,539	495,440
Factor income received from abroad	5,586	8,422	11,021
Less Factor income paid abroad	13,599	16,789	21,718
Gross national product	383,584	433,172	484,743
Less Consumption of fixed capital	58,143	64,956	73,473
National income in market prices	325,441	368,216	411,270

FINLAND

Expenditure on the Gross Domestic Product

	1987	1988	1989*
Government final consumption expenditure	81,339	88,731	97,998
Private final consumption expenditure	213,984	234,946	256,019
Increase in stocks	−889	3,006	6,424
Gross fixed capital formation	93,270	111,048	135,923
Statistical discrepancy	1,638	4,924	7,552
Total domestic expenditure	389,342	442,655	503,916
Exports of goods and services	100,030	108,750	117,061
Less Imports of goods and services	97,775	109,866	125,537
GDP in purchasers' values	391,597	441,539	495,440

* Provisional figures.

Gross Domestic Product by Economic Activity

	1987	1988	1989*
Agriculture, hunting, forestry and fishing	22,444	24,476	27,514
Mining and quarrying	1,026	1,350	1,715
Manufacturing	85,710	93,801	100,193
Electricity, gas and water	10,002	9,937	10,728
Construction	27,691	33,401	42,102
Trade, restaurants and hotels	40,709	45,168	50,487
Transport, storage and communication	28,934	31,927	35,347
Finance, insurance and business services	39,224	47,015	55,358
Owner-occupied dwellings	21,369	22,958	25,495
Public administration and defence	16,461	18,318	20,023
Other community, social and personal services	62,815	69,362	78,408
Sub-total	356,385	397,713	447,370
Less Imputed bank service charge	11,458	13,251	16,373
GDP in basic values	344,927	384,462	430,997
Commodity taxes	54,523	63,667	72,103
Less Commodity subsidies	7,853	6,590	7,660
GDP in purchasers' values	391,597	441,539	495,440

* Provisional figures.

BALANCE OF PAYMENTS (US $ million)

	1987	1988	1989
Merchandise exports f.o.b.	19,079	21,826	22,882
Merchandise imports f.o.b.	−17,700	−20,686	−23,100
Trade balance	1,379	1,140	−219
Exports of services	4,805	5,994	6,848
Imports of services	−7,506	−9,383	−11,097
Balance on goods and services	−1,322	−2,249	−4,468
Private unrequited transfers (net)	−162	−87	−195
Government unrequited transfers (net)	−328	−425	−465
Current balance	−1,812	−2,762	−5,128
Direct capital investment (net)	−807	−1,700	−2,598
Other long-term capital (net)	875	3,172	4,910
Short-term capital (net)	7,099	485	1,243
Net errors and omissions	−1,332	1,059	514
Total (net monetary movements)	4,022	255	−1,058
Valuation changes (net)	609	−306	−179
Official financing (net)	11	3	−10
Changes in reserves	4,642	−48	−1,246

Source: IMF, *International Financial Statistics*.

External Trade

PRINCIPAL COMMODITIES
(distribution by SITC, million markkaa)

Imports c.i.f.	1987	1988	1989
Food and live animals	4,442.4	4,361.7	4,699.7
Coffee, tea, cocoa and spices	1,277.0	1,056.7	1,112.1
Crude materials (inedible) except fuels	4,827.0	5,549.4	5,899.9
Mineral fuels, lubricants, etc.	11,617.2	8,447.0	10,364.6
Coal, coke and briquettes	1,341.1	1,175.5	1,527.9
Petroleum, petroleum products, etc.	9,002.4	5,922.0	7,133.6
Crude petroleum oils, etc.	6,368.6	4,064.4	5,059.2
Refined petroleum products	2,592.1	1,770.6	1,965.0
Gas oils (distillate fuels)	1,141.6	887.5	811.2
Chemicals and related products	9,053.5	9,530.2	11,038.9
Chemical elements and compounds	2,419.7	2,555.0	2,865.5
Plastic materials, etc.	2,781.2	2,985.2	3,451.0
Basic manufactures	14,012.3	13,997.7	17,313.0
Textile yarn, fabrics, etc.	3,260.6	2,914.8	3,102.2
Woven textile fabrics (excl. narrow or special fabrics)	2,203.9	1,137.5	1,142.0
Iron and steel	2,995.5	2,958.1	4,029.2
Non-ferrous metals	1,361.4	1,762.4	2,343.0
Other metal manufactures	2,344.1	2,299.5	2,791.2
Machinery and transport equipment	31,799.9	34,627.0	42,290.4
Non-electric machinery	14,932.3	15,538.1	19,127.2
Electrical machinery, apparatus, etc.	7,241.8	7,603.7	9,055.3
Transport equipment	9,582.2	11,485.7	11,469.3
Road vehicles and parts*	8,250.8	9,032.4	8,915.0
Passenger motor cars (excl. buses)	4,026.1	4,450.6	5,514.7
Miscellaneous manufactured articles	10,462.1	11,218.7	13,283.6
Scientific instruments, watches, etc.	2,628.7	2,636.8	3,044.3
Total (incl. others)	86,696.4	88,228.6	105,518.8

* Excluding tyres, engines and electrical parts.

Exports f.o.b.	1987	1988	1989
Food and live animals	1,714.9	1,503.1	1,779.4
Crude materials (inedible) except fuels	11,165.7	11,212.5	11,986.6
Wood, lumber and cork	4,696.5	4,761.3	4,614.1
Shaped or simply worked wood	4,130.2	4,445.1	4,310.3
Shaped coniferous lumber	4,110.1	4,416.1	4,274.0
Sawn coniferous lumber	3,737.0	4,278.6	3,918.2
Pulp and waste paper	3,993.6	4,636.9	5,268.2
Chemical wood pulp	3,836.9	n.a.	n.a.
Mineral fuels, lubricants, etc.	1,939.5	1,549.1	935.6
Petroleum, petroleum products, etc.	1,879.2	1,490.3	877.5
Refined petroleum products	1,831.7	1,451.3	839.8
Chemicals and related products	4,738.0	5,174.3	6,321.8
Basic manufactures	35,159.9	38,677.0	42,114.1
Wood and cork manufactures (excl. furniture)	2,310.0	2,264.7	2,338.1
Veneers, plywood boards, etc.	1,851.4	1,968.3	2,073.1
Paper, paperboard and manufactures	22,415.8	25,130.9	26,604.3
Paper and paperboard	20,699.7	23,074.5	24,573.6
Newsprint paper	3,270.3	3,031.3	2,666.3
Other printing and writing paper in bulk	10,111.7	12,615.3	13,701.6
Kraft paper and paperboard	1,766.9	2,310.4	2,461.8
Articles of paper pulp, paper or paperboard	1,833.9	2,056.4	2,030.7
Iron and steel	n.a.	4,560.1	5,330.2
Non-ferrous metals	2,139.3	3,004.8	3,768.2
Other metal manufactures	1,735.7	1,445.9	1,675.9

FINLAND

Statistical Survey

Imports c.i.f.—*continued*	1987	1988	1989
Machinery and transport equipment	23,523.7	24,930.6	28,820.1
Non-electric machinery	11,478.4	11,192.2	13,940.4
Electrical machinery, apparatus, etc.	5,385.8	5,400.5	6,852.6
Transport equipment	6,659.4	8,338.0	8,027.1
Ships and boats	2,446.4	4,427.3	3,951.6
Miscellaneous manufactured articles	8,922.4	7,443.3	7,444.8
Clothing (excl. footwear)	2,956.2	2,525.7	8,087.7
Clothing not of fur	2,714.1	2,310.8	1,895.5
Non-knitted textile clothing (excl. accessories and headgear)	1,985.4	1,659.3	1,310.5
Total (incl. others)	87,564.1	90,853.7	99,781.8

PRINCIPAL TRADING PARTNERS (million markkaa)*

Imports c.i.f.	1987	1988	1989
Austria	1,116.5	1,089.4	1,294.6
Belgium/Luxembourg	2,234.5	2,231.7	2,931.9
Denmark	2,453.5	2,588.6	3,289.7
France	3,719.5	3,589.7	4,417.5
Germany, Federal Republic	15,130.4	14,859.7	18,233.7
Iran	17.5	8.8	10.6
Italy	3,789.5	3,924.3	4,900.2
Japan	6,136.8	6,522.5	7,695.3
Netherlands	2,675.8	2,867.6	3,416.1
Norway	1,904.8	2,096.4	2,456.6
Poland	847.5	852.3	1,065.2
Saudi Arabia	703.7	394.7	378.0
Sweden	11,205.4	11,765.3	14,314.2
Switzerland	1,743.1	1,639.2	1,829.1
USSR	12,461.9	10,592.2	12,152.7
United Kingdom	6,192.4	5,941.9	6,897.9
USA	4,539.4	5,616.0	6,669.1
Total (incl. others)	86,696.4	88,228.6	105,518.8

Exports f.o.b.	1987	1988	1989
Belgium/Luxembourg	1,566.4	1,789.3	1,946.6
Denmark	3,407.7	3,204.1	3,257.1
France	4,615.3	4,835.2	5,453.3
Germany, Federal Republic	9,580.9	9,842.4	10,784.6
Iraq	30.4	42.2	90.9
Italy	2,239.7	2,462.8	2,989.1
Netherlands	3,141.0	3,312.8	3,961.2
Norway	4,132.0	3,137.3	2,920.0
Sweden	12,424.7	12,835.2	14,314.0
Switzerland	1,564.7	1,553.7	1,680.4
USSR	13,522.5	13,562.9	11,495.9
United Kingdom	10,109.2	11,863.8	11,958.0
USA	5,070.0	5,245.1	6,387.7
Total (incl. others)	87,564.1	90,853.7	99,781.8

* Imports by country of production; exports by country of consumption.

Transport

RAILWAYS (traffic)

	1987	1988	1989
Passenger-km (million)	3,106	3,147	3,208
Freight ton-km (million)	7,402	7,815	7,958

ROAD TRAFFIC (registered motor vehicles at 31 December)

	1987	1988	1989
Passenger cars	1,698,671	1,795,908	1,896,895
Buses and coaches	9,233	9,229	9,268
Goods vehicles	51,956	52,736	53,818
Vans	146,219	160,901	187,827
Special purpose vehicles	13,640	15,392	n.a.

SHIPPING
Merchant Fleet (1989)

	Ships	Displacement ('000 gross reg. tons)
Passenger vessels	181	365
Tankers	25	230
Others	235	458
Total	441	1,053

International Sea-borne Freight Traffic

	1987	1988	1989
Vessels ('000 net reg. tons):			
Entered	68,203	70,420	85,265
Cleared	68,807	n.a.	n.a.
Goods ('000 metric tons):			
Loaded	22,437	23,353	22,425
Unloaded	31,285	31,874	22,632

CANAL TRAFFIC

	1987	1988	1989
Vessels in transit	64,194	77,788	85,291
Timber rafts in transit	7,287	7,301	7,065
Goods carried ('000 metric tons)	6,106	5,809	6,616
Passengers carried ('000)	267	303	297

CIVIL AVIATION (scheduled services, '000)

	1987	1988	1989
Kilometres flown	43,362	48,602	55,415
Passenger-kilometres	3,588,000	4,034,400	4,625,000
Cargo ton-kilometres	97,938	107,924	137,479

Tourism

NUMBER OF NIGHTS AT ACCOMMODATION FACILITIES (excl. camping sites)

Country of Domicile	1987	1988	1989
Denmark	62,202	69,569	72,147
France	61,888	66,433	71,269
Germany, Federal Republic	280,953	321,592	353,506
Netherlands	41,743	46,266	52,189
Norway	142,211	122,201	115,463
Sweden	523,418	557,463	584,866
Switzerland	70,306	73,365	76,152
USSR	262,115	214,487	313,549
United Kingdom	116,553	131,711	141,205
USA	199,655	202,202	209,150
Total (incl. others)	2,207,484	2,298,300	2,517,300

FINLAND

Communications Media

	1987	1988	1989
Telephone lines	2,365,486	2,470,000	2,582,000
Television receivers*	1,843,000	1,862,479	1,887,369
Book production: titles†	9,106	10,386	10,097
Newspapers and periodicals	5,228	5,053‡	n.a.

* Number of licensed sets.
† Including pamphlets (2,098 in 1987; 2,366 in 1988).
‡ Comprising 66 daily newspapers, 327 non-daily newspapers and 4,660 other periodicals.

Education

(1987/88)

	Institutions	Staff*	Students
First level	5,340	47,045	390,469
Secondary, general			287,490
Secondary vocational	536	16,842	111,577
Universities and other education at the third level	20	7,538	139,375

* Excluding part-time teachers paid by the hour.

Directory

The Constitution

The Constitution (summarized below) was adopted on 17 July 1919. The first report of the Constitutional Committee on possible reforms of the fundamental laws was presented in April 1974. Generally, the right-wing parties are suspicious of reform, but the left has won some support from the centre.

Three main topics have been discussed by the Committee: the respective powers of the President, the Council of State (Cabinet) and Parliament (Eduskunta); legislative procedure, particularly the strength of the protection to be given to parliamentary minorities; the basic economic, social and cultural rights of the individual and security of ownership. The Committee has also recommended the implementation of employee participation in decision-making. The most basic reform under discussion is the left's proposal that Parliament should be the supreme state organ, and that much of the President's power should be transferred to the Council of State. Proposals that citizens vote directly for a presidential candidate were implemented in February 1988. If no candidate wins an absolute majority, the 301-member electoral college is convened.

GOVERNMENT

For the general administration of the country, there is a Council of State, appointed by the President, and composed of the Prime Minister and the Ministers of the various Ministries. The members of the Council, who must enjoy the confidence of the Parliament, are collectively responsible to it for their conduct of affairs, and for the general policy of the administration, while each member is responsible for the administration of his own Ministry.

To this Council the President can appoint supernumerary Ministers, who serve either as assistant Ministers or as Ministers without portfolio. The President also appoints a Chancellor of Justice, who must see that the Council and its members act within the law. If, in the opinion of the Chancellor of Justice, the Council of State or an individual Minister has acted in a manner contrary to the law, the Chancellor must report the matter to the President of the Republic or, in certain cases, to the Parliament. In this way Ministers are rendered legally as well as politically responsible for their official acts.

Finland is divided into 461 self-governing municipalities. Members of the municipal councils are elected by universal suffrage for a period of four years.

THE PRESIDENT

The President is elected for a term of six years by direct popular vote. The 301 members of the electoral college, which convenes if no presidential candidate wins an absolute majority, are chosen by public vote in the same manner as members of Parliament.

The President of the Republic is entrusted with supreme executive power. The President's decisions are made known in meetings of the Council of State on the basis of the recommendation of the minister responsible for the matter. The President has the right to depart even from a unanimous opinion reached by the Council of State. Legislative power is exercised by the Parliament in conjunction with the President. Both the President and the Parliament have the right of initiative in legislation. Laws passed by the Parliament are submitted to the President, who has the right of veto. If the President has not within three months assented to a law, this is tantamount to a refusal of assent. A law to which the President has not given assent will nevertheless come into force, if the Parliament elected at the next general election adopts it without alteration.

The President has also the right to issue decrees in certain events, to order new elections to the Parliament, to grant pardons and dispensations, and to grant Finnish citizenship to foreigners.

The President's approval is necessary in all matters concerning the relations of Finland with foreign countries. The President is Supreme Commander of the Defence Forces of the Republic.

Such decisions as are arrived at by the President are made in the Council of State, except in matters pertaining to military functions and appointments.

THE PARLIAMENT

The Parliament is an assembly of one chamber with 200 members elected for four years by universal suffrage on a system of proportional representation, every man and woman aged 18 years or over being entitled to vote and everyone over 20 being eligible. It assembles annually at the beginning of February. The ordinary duration of a session is 120 days but the Parliament can, at its pleasure, extend or shorten its session. The opposition of one-third of the members can cause ordinary legislative proposals to be deferred until after the next elections. Discussion of questions relating to the constitutional laws belongs also to Parliament, but for the settlement of such questions certain delaying conditions (fixed majorities) are prescribed. The Parliament, besides taking part in legislation, has the right to determine the estimates, which, though not technically a law, are published as a law.

Furthermore, the Parliament has the right, in a large measure, to supervise the administration of the Government. For this purpose it receives special reports (the Government also submitting an account of its administration every year) and a special account of the administration of national finances. The Chancellor of Justice submits a yearly report on the administration of the Council of State. The Parliament elects five auditors, who submit to it annual reports of their work, to see that the estimates have been adhered to. The Parliament also appoints every four years a Parliamentary Ombudsman (Judicial Delegate of Parliament) who submits to it a report, to supervise the observance of the laws.

The Parliament has the right to interrogate the Government. It can impeach a member of the Council of State or the Chancellor of Justice for not having conformed to the law in the discharge of his duties. Trials are conducted at a special court, known as the Court of the Realm, of 13 members, six of whom are elected by Parliament for a term of four years.

The Government

(January 1991)

HEAD OF STATE

President: Dr MAUNO KOIVISTO (assumed duties 10 September 1981; elected 26 January 1982; re-elected 15 February 1988).

COUNCIL OF STATE
(Valtioneuvosto)

In April 1987 a coalition of the National Coalition Party (Kok), Social Democratic Party (SDP), Swedish People's Party (SFP) and Finnish Rural Party (SMP) was formed. The SMP withdrew from the coalition in August 1990.

Prime Minister: HARRI HOLKERI (Kok).

Deputy Prime Minister and Minister for Foreign Affairs: PERTTI PAASIO (SDP).

FINLAND

Minister of Foreign Trade: Pertti Salolainen (Kok).
Minister of Justice: Tarja Halonen (SDP).
Minister of the Interior: Jarmo Rantanen (SDP).
Minister of Education: Ole Norrback (SFP).
Second Minister of Education: Anna-Liisa Kasurinen (SDP).
Minister of Finance: Matti Louekoski (SDP).
Second Minister of Finance: Ulla Puolanne (Kok).
Minister of Defence: Elisabeth Rehn (SFP).
Minister of Agriculture and Forestry: Toivo T. Pohjola (Kok).
Minister of Transport and Communications: Ilkka Kanerva (Kok).
Minister of Trade and Industry: Ilkka Suominen (Kok).
Minister of Social Affairs and Health: Mauri Miettinen (Kok).
Second Minister of Social Affairs and Health: Tuulikki Hämäläinen (SDP).
Minister of Labour: Matti Puhakka (SDP).
Minister of the Environment: Kaj Bärlund (SDP).

MINISTRIES

Prime Minister's Office: Aleksanterinkatu 3D, 00170 Helsinki; tel. (90) 1601; fax (90) 1602099.

Ministry of Agriculture and Forestry: Hallituskatu 3A, 00170 Helsinki; tel. (90) 1601; telex 125621.

Ministry of Defence: Et. Makasiinikatu 8A, 00130 Helsinki; tel. (90) 625801; telex 124667.

Ministry of Education: Meritullinkatu 10, POB 293, 00171 Helsinki; tel. (90) 134171; telex 122079; fax (90) 6121335.

Ministry of the Environment: POB 399, 00121 Helsinki; tel. (90) 19911; telex 123717; fax (90) 1991499.

Ministry of Finance: Snellmaninkatu 1A, 00170 Helsinki; tel. (90) 1601; telex 123241; fax (90) 1603090.

Ministry of Foreign Affairs: Merikasarmi, POB 176, 00161 Helsinki; tel. (90) 134151; telex 124636.

Ministry of the Interior: Kirkkokatu 12, 00170 Helsinki; tel. (90) 1601; telex 123644.

Ministry of Justice: Eteläesplanadi 10, 00130 Helsinki; tel. (90) 18251; fax (90) 1825430.

Ministry of Labour: Eteläesplanadi 4, 00130 Helsinki; tel. (90) 18561; telex 121441.

Ministry of Social Affairs and Health: Snellmaninkatu 4-6, 00170 Helsinki; tel. (90) 1601; telex 125073; fax (90) 1605763.

Ministry of Trade and Industry: Aleksanterinkatu 10, POB 230, 00170 Helsinki; tel. (90) 1601; telex 124645; fax (90) 1603666.

Ministry of Transport and Communications: Eteläesplanadi 16, 00130 Helsinki; tel. (90) 17361; telex 125472; fax (90) 1736270.

President and Legislature

PRESIDENT
Elections of 31 January–1 February and 15 February 1988

	Popular vote (%)	Electoral College First Ballot	Electoral College Second Ballot
Mauno Koivisto	47.92	144	189
Paavo Väyrynen	20.15	68	68
Harri Holkeri	18.06	63	18
Kalevi Kivistö	10.45	26	26
Jouko Kajanoja	1.41	—	—

EDUSKUNTA
(Parliament)

Speaker: Kalevi Sorsa (SDP).
First Deputy Speaker: Elsi Hetemäki-Olander (Kok).
Second Deputy Speaker: Veijo Pesala (KP).
Secretary-General: Erkki Ketola.

General Election, 15–16 March 1987

	Votes	%	Seats
Social Democratic Party	694,666	24.14	56
National Coalition Party	665,477	23.13	53
Centre Party	507,384	17.63	40
Finnish People's Democratic League	269,678	9.37	16
Swedish People's Party	153,141	5.32	12
Finnish Rural Party	181,557	6.31	9
Finnish Christian Union	74,011	2.57	5
Democratic Alternative*	122,115	4.24	4
Green Party	115,830	4.03	4
Others	93,661	3.25	1†
Total	**2,877,520**	**100.00**	**200**

* The party subsequently adopted the title of Communist Party of Finland–Unity (SKP–Y).
† Åland delegate.

Political Organizations

Kansallinen Kokoomus (Kok) (National Coalition Party): Kansakoulukuja 3, 00100 Helsinki; tel. (90) 69381; fax (90) 6943702; f. 1918; moderate conservative political ideology; 80,000 mems; Chair. Ilkka Suominen; Sec.-Gen. Pekka Kivela; Chair. Parliamentary Group Iiro Viinanen.

Keskustapuolue (KP) (Centre Party): Pursimiehenkatu 15, Helsinki; tel. (90) 170311; fax (90) 653589; f. 1906; a radical centre party founded to promote the interests of the rural population, especially that of the numerous small farmers, on the lines of individual enterprise; also favours decentralization; 304,000 mems; Chair. Paavo Väyrynen; Sec. Seppo Kääriänen; Chair. Parliamentary Group Kauko Juhantalo.

Liberaalinen Kansanpuolue (LKP) (Liberal People's Party): Fredrikinkatu 58A 6, Helsinki; tel. (90) 440227; f. 1965 as a coalition of the Finnish People's Party and the Liberal Union; in 1982 became mem. organization of the Centre Party; 8,000 mems; Chair. Kyösti Lallukka; Sec.-Gen. Jari P. Havia.

Kommunistinen Pyovaenpuolue (KTP) (Communist Workers' Party): POB 93, 01301 Vantaa; tel. (90) 8571022; f. 1989; Marxist-Leninist; Chair. T. Lahdenmäki.

Perustuslaillinen Oikeistopuolue-Konstitutionella högerpartiet r.p. (Constitutional Party of the Right): Mannerheimintie 146A, 00270 Helsinki; tel. (90) 419063; f. 1973; conservative; seeks to protect constitutional rights and parliamentary democracy; Chair. Georg C. Ehrnrooth; Sec. Panu Toivonen.

Suomen Eläkeläisten Puolue (Finnish Pensioners' Party): Helsinki; f.1986; represents the interests of pensioners; Chair. Yrjoe Virtanen.

Suomen Kristillinen Liitto (SKL) (Finnish Christian Union): Töölönkatu 50 D, 00250 Helsinki 25; fax (90) 440450; f. 1958; 17,000 mems; Chair. Toimi Kankaanniemi; Sec. Jouko Jääskeläinen; Chair. Parliamentary Group C. P. Eeva-Liisa Moilanen.

Suomen Maaseudun Puolue (SMP) (Finnish Rural Party): Hämeentie 157, 00560 Helsinki; tel. (90) 790299; fax (90) 790299; f. 1959; non-socialist programme; represents lower-middle-class elements, small farmers, small enterprises etc.; Chair. Heikki Riihijärvi; Sec. Tina Maekelae (acting); Chair. Parliamentary Group Sulo Aittoniemi.

Suomen Sosialidemokraattinen Puolue (SDP) (Finnish Social Democratic Party): Saariniemenkatu 6, 00530 Helsinki; tel. (90) 77511; telex 121560; fax (90) 712752; f. 1899; constitutional socialist programme; mainly supported by the working and middle classes and small farmers; approx. 97,000 mems; Chair. Pertti Paasio; Gen.-Sec. Ulpu Iivari; Chair. Parliamentary Group Pertti Hietala.

Svenska Folkpartiet (SFP) (Swedish People's Party): Gräsviksgatan 14, POB 282, 00181 Helsinki; tel. (90) 6942322; fax (90) 6931968; f. 1906; a liberal party representing the interests of the Swedish-speaking minority; 50,000 mems; Chair. Ole Norrback; Sec. Peter Stenlund; Chair. Parliamentary Group Jörn Donner.

Vasemmistoliitto (Left-Wing Alliance): Pasilanraitio 5, 00240 Helsinki; tel. (90) 1485100; fax (90) 1483425; f. 1990 as a merger of the Finnish People's Democratic League (f. 1944), the Communist Party of Finland (f. 1918) and the Communist Party of Finland–Unity (f. 1980); Chair. Claes Andersson.

Vihrea Eduskuntaryhma (Green Union of Finland): Tallberginkatu 1C, 00180 Helsinki; tel. (90) 6933366; fax (90) 6933799; Chair. Erkki Pulliainen.

FINLAND

Directory

Vihreä Liitto (Green Association): Helsinki; f. 1988; Leader HEIDI HAUTALA.

Diplomatic Representation

EMBASSIES IN FINLAND

Argentina: Bulevardi 10A 14, 00120 Helsinki; tel. (90) 607630; telex 122794; Ambassador: NEREO IGNACIO MELO FERRER.

Austria: Eteläesplanadi 18, 00130 Helsinki; tel. (90) 171322; fax (90) 665084; Ambassador: HANS GEORG RUDOFSKY.

Belgium: Kalliolinnantie 5, 00140 Helsinki; tel. (90) 170412; telex 121390; fax (90) 628842; Ambassador: JACQUES IVAN D'HONDT.

Brazil: Mariankatu 7A 3, 00170 Helsinki; tel. (90) 177922; Ambassador: CARLOS LUZILDE HILDEBRANDT.

Bulgaria: Itäinen puistotie 10, 00140 Helsinki; tel. (90) 661707; fax (90) 663723; Ambassador: VALERI PCHELINTSHEV.

Canada: Pohjoisesplanadi 25B, 00100 Helsinki; tel. (90) 171141; telex 121363; fax (90) 601060; Ambassador: MARY VANDENHOFF.

Chile: Etelaranta 4, 00130 Helsinki; tel. (90) 134511; Ambassador: LUCIO PARADA DAGNINO.

China, People's Republic: Vanha Kelkkamäki 9-11, 00570 Helsinki; tel. (90) 6848371; fax (90) 6849551; Ambassador: YU LIXUAN.

Colombia: Fredrikinkatu 61, 00100 Helsinki; tel. (90) 6931255; telex 126210; Ambassador: NICOLÁS SALOM-FRANCO.

Cuba: Paasivuorenkatu 3, 00530 Helsinki; tel. (90) 766199; telex 121017; Ambassador: OSCAR FERNÁNDEZ MELL.

Czechoslovakia: Armfeltintie 14, 00150 Helsinki; tel. (90) 171169; telex 121804; fax (90) 630655; Ambassador: PAVEL ŠTULRAJTER.

Denmark: Yrjönkatu 9, POB 178, 00121 Helsinki; tel. (90) 641948; telex 124782; fax (90) 608169; Ambassador: SKJOLD G. MELLBIN.

Egypt: Stenbäckinkatu 22A, 00250 Helsinki; tel. (90) 413288; telex 124216; Ambassador: HOSNY SAAD EL-DIN EL-AGIZY.

France: Itäinen puistotie 13, 00140 Helsinki; tel. (90) 171521; fax (90) 6933514; Ambassador: MARCEL MAÎTRE.

Germany: Fredrikinkatu 61, 00100 Helsinki; tel. (90) 6943355; telex 124568; fax (90) 6932564; Ambassador: HANS PETER BAZING.

Greece: Lönnrotinkatu 15C 26, 00120 Helsinki; tel. (90) 645202; fax (90) 6801038; Ambassador: ANASTÁSSIOS SIDERIS.

Holy See: Bulevardi 5 as. 12, 00120 Helsinki (Apostolic Nunciature); tel. (90) 644664; Apostolic Pro-Nuncio: Most Rev. HENRI LEMAÎTRE, Titular Archbishop of Tongeren (resident in Denmark).

Hungary: Kuusisaarenkuja 6, 00340 Helsinki; tel. (90) 484144; fax (90) 480497; Ambassador: BÉLA JAVORSZKY.

India: Satamakatu 2A 8, 00160 Helsinki; tel. (90) 608927; telex 125202; fax (90) 6221208; Ambassador: THANGKIMA CHERPOOT.

Indonesia: Eerikinkatu 37, 00180 Helsinki; tel. (90) 6947744; fax (90) 6949394; Ambassador: ROCHSID SETYOKO.

Iran: Bertel Jungin tie 4, 00570 Helsinki; tel. (90) 6847133; fax (90) 6849412; Ambassador: M. MOHAMMAD REZA DOKHANCHI.

Iraq: Lars Sonckin tie 2, 00570 Helsinki; tel. (90) 6849177; Ambassador: ANWAR ABDUL KADIR MOHAMMED AL-HADITHI.

Israel: Vironkatu 5A, 00170 Helsinki; tel. (90) 1356177; fax (90) 1356959; Ambassador: YOSEF HASEEN.

Italy: Fabianinkatu 29C 4, 00100 Helsinki; tel. (90) 175144; telex 121753; fax (90) 175976; Ambassador: GIANCARLO CARRARA CAGNI.

Japan: Yrjönkatu 13, 00120 Helsinki; tel. (90) 644206; fax (90) 611344; Ambassador: HISAMI KUROKOCHI.

Korea, Democratic People's Republic: Kulosaaren puistotie 32, 00570 Helsinki; tel. (90) 6848195; fax (90) 6848995; Ambassador: SUNG CHOL RYO.

Korea, Republic: Mannerheimintie 76A 7, 00250 Helsinki; tel. (90) 498955; telex 122589; Ambassador: SANG JIN CHOI.

Mexico: Fredrikinkatu 51-53A, 00100 Helsinki; tel. (90) 640637; telex 122021; fax (90) 6801227; Ambassador: RICARDO VILLANUEVA HALLAL.

Netherlands: Raatimiehenkatu 2A 7, 00140 Helsinki; tel. (90) 661737; telex 121779; fax (90) 654734; Ambassador: HUGO C. G. CARSTEN.

Norway: Rehbinderintie 17, 00150 Helsinki; tel. (90) 171234; fax (90) 657807; Ambassador: KJELL RASMUSSEN.

Peru: Fredrikinkatu 16A 22, 00120 Helsinki; tel. (90) 631354; telex 123650; Ambassador: ALBERTO MONTAGNE.

Poland: Armas Lindgrenintie 21, 00570 Helsinki; tel. (90) 6848077; fax (90) 6848907; Ambassador: (vacant).

Portugal: Itäinen puistotie 11B, 00140 Helsinki; tel. (90) 171717; telex 121877; Ambassador: FERNANDO DA COSTA FIGUEIRINHAS.

Romania: Stenbäckinkatu 24, 00250 Helsinki; tel. (90) 413624; Ambassador: VASILE FLOREA.

South Africa: Rahapajankatu 1A 5, 00160 Helsinki; tel. (90) 658288; fax (90) 655884; Ambassador: J. C. LÖTTER.

Spain: Bulevardi 10A 8, 00120 Helsinki; tel. (90) 647351; telex 122193; fax (90) 601742; Ambassador: LUIS JORDANA DE POZAS FUENTES.

Sweden: P. Esplanadi 7B, 00170 Helsinki; tel. (90) 651255; fax (90) 655285; Ambassador: KNUT THYBERG.

Switzerland: Uudenmaankatu 16A, 00120 Helsinki; tel. (90) 649422; fax (90) 6801343; Ambassador: OTHMAR UHL.

Turkey: Topeliuksenkatu 3B A 1-2, 00260 Helsinki; tel. (90) 406058; Ambassador: TUNCER TOPUR.

USSR: Tehtaankatu 1B, 00140 Helsinki; tel. (90) 661876; Ambassador: BORIS IVANOVICH ARISTOV.

United Kingdom: Itäinen puistotie 17, 00140 Helsinki; tel. (90) 661293; telex 121122; fax (90) 661342; Ambassador: NEIL SMITH.

USA: Itäinen puistotie 14A, 00140 Helsinki; tel. (90) 171931; telex 121644; Ambassador: JOHN GIFFEN WEINMANN.

Venezuela: Mannerheimintie 14B, 00100 Helsinki; tel. (90) 641522; fax (90) 640791; Ambassador: GERMÁN DE PÉREZ CASTILLO.

Yugoslavia: Kulosaarentie 36, 00570 Helsinki; tel. (90) 6848522; telex 122099; Ambassador: MITO PEJOVSKI.

Judicial System

The administration of justice is independent of the Government and judges can be removed only by judicial sentence.

SUPREME COURT

Korkein oikeus: Consists of a President and 21 Justices appointed by the President of the Republic. Final court appeal in civil and criminal cases, supervises judges and executive authorities, appoints judges.

President: OLAVI HEINONEN.

SUPREME ADMINISTRATIVE COURT

Korkein hallinto oikeus: Consists of a President and 21 Justices appointed by the President of the Republic. Highest tribunal for appeals in administrative cases.

President: ANTTI SUVIRANTA.

COURTS OF APPEAL

There are Courts of Appeal at Turku, Vaasa, Kuopio, Helsinki, Kouvola, and Rovaniemi, consisting of a President and an appropriate number of members.

DISTRICT AND MUNICIPAL COURTS

Courts of first instance for almost all suits. Appeals lie to the Court of Appeal, and then to the Supreme Court. District Courts consist of a judge and from five to seven jurors. The decision rests with the judge, but the jurors may overrule him if they are unanimous. Municipal Courts are the municipal equivalent of District Courts, consisting of three judges of whom one or two may be lay judges, and presided over by the burgomaster.

CHANCELLOR OF JUSTICE

The Oikeuskansleri is responsible for seeing that authorities and officials comply with the law. He is the chief public prosecutor, and acts as counsel for the Government.

Chancellor of Justice: JORMA S. AALTO.

PARLIAMENTARY SOLICITOR-GENERAL

The Eduskunnan Oikeusasiamies is the Finnish Ombudsman appointed by Parliament to supervise the observance of the law.

Parliamentary Solicitor-General: OLAVI E. HEINONEN.

Religion

CHRISTIANITY

Suomen ekumeeninen neuvosto/Ekumeniska Rådet i Finland (Ecumenical Council of Finland): Luotsikatu 1A, POB 185, 00161 Helsinki; tel. (90) 18021; telex 122357; fax (90) 1802337; f. 1919; 10 mem. churches; Pres. Dr JOHN VIKSTRÖM (Archbishop, Evangelical Lutheran Church of Finland); Gen. Sec. Rev. Dr JAAKKO RUSAMA.

FINLAND

National Churches

Suomen Evankelisluterilainen Kirkko (Evangelical Lutheran Church of Finland): Office of Foreign Affairs, Satamakatu 11, POB 185, 00161 Helsinki; tel. (90) 18021; telex 122357; fax (90) 1802428; about 88% of the population are adherents; Archbishop Dr JOHN VIKSTRÖM.

Suomen Ortodoksinen Kirkko (Orthodox Church of Finland): Karjalankatu 1, 70110 Kuopio; tel. (Admin.) (971) 122611; fax (971) 118017; 56,762 mems; Leader JOHANNES, Archbishop of Karelia and All Finland.

Protestant Churches

Finlands Svenska Baptistmission (Baptists, Swedish-speaking): Rådhusgatan 44A, 65100 Vaasa; tel. (961) 118559; f. 1856; 1,761 mems (Dec. 1988).

Jehovan Todistajat (Jehovah's Witnesses): Kuismatie 58, 01300 Vantaa; tel. (90) 826488; 17,300 mems.

Myöhempien Aikojen Pyhien Jeesuksen Kristuksen Kirkko (Church of Jesus Christ of Latter-day Saints—Mormon): Neitsytpolku 3A, 00140 Helsinki; tel. (90) 177311; 4,550 mems.

Suomen Adventtikirkko (Adventist Church of Finland): Uudenmaantie 50, 20720 Turku; tel. (921) 365100; f. 1894; 6,217 mems; Pres. OLAVI ROUHE; Sec. JOEL NIININEN.

Suomen Baptistiyhdyskunta (Baptists, Finnish-speaking): Kissanmaankatu 19, 33530 Tampere; tel. (931) 530901; 1,834 mems; Pres. Rev. JOUKO NEULANEN.

Suomen Metodistikirkko (Methodist Church of Finland): Punavuorenkatu 2, 00120 Helsinki; 1,940 mems; Moderators Rev. TAPANI RAJAAMA (Finnish-speaking), FREDRIK WEGELIUS, KAIJA-RIIKA WÄXBY (Swedish-speaking).

Suomen Vapaakirkko (Evangelical Free Church of Finland): Sibeliuksenkatu 17, 13100 Hämeenlinna; tel. (917) 122150; f. 1923; 13,192 mems; Moderator ERKKI VERKKONEN.

Svenska Kyrkan i Finland (Church of Sweden in Finland): Minervagatan 6, 00100 Helsinki; f. 1919; 1,779 mems; Rector Dr JARL JERGMAR.

Other Christian Churches

Anglican Church in Finland: Putouskuja 5B 7, 01600 Vantaa; tel. (90) 5634829; telex 121122; chaplaincy founded 1921; part of diocese of Gibraltar in Europe; Chaplain Rev. TYLER A. STRAND.

Katolinen kirkko Suomessa (Roman Catholic Church in Finland): Rehbinderintie 21, 00150 Helsinki; tel. (90) 637907; fax (90) 639820; Finland comprises the single diocese of Helsinki, directly responsible to the Holy See; 4,429 mems; Bishop of Helsinki PAUL M. VERSCHUREN; Vicar-Gen. Rev. JOHANNES AARTS.

JUDAISM

Helsingin Juutalainen Seurakunta (Jewish Community of Helsinki): Synagogue and Community Centre, Malminkatu 26, 00100 Helsinki; tel. (90) 6941302; fax (90) 6941302; 900 mems; Pres. GIDEON BOLOTOWSKY.

ISLAM

Suomen Islam-Seurakunta (Islamic Community of Finland): Fredrikinkatu 33A, 00120 Helsinki; tel. (90) 643579; 926 mems.

The Press

The 1919 Constitution provided safeguards for press freedom in Finland, and in the same year the Freedom of the Press Act developed and qualified this principle by defining the rights and responsibilities of editors and the circumstances in which the Supreme Court may confiscate or suppress a publication. In practice there are few restrictions. The most notable offences for newspapermen concern libel and copyright. Two notable features of the press are the public's legal right of access to all official documents (with important exceptions), and since 1966 the right of the journalist to conceal his source of news.

Almost all daily newspapers are independent companies, most of which are owned by large numbers of shareholders. Newspaper chains are virtually unknown, but the Finnish press is a party press. The small number of papers that are generally considered left-orientated are usually owned by the political parties concerned, by trade unions, or by other workers' associations (the Social Democratic Party's chief organ is *Demari* and the Left-Wing Alliance publishes *Kansan Uutiset*). Most of the right-wing newspapers are owned by private shareholders, and some belong to private endowments. The leading organ of the National Coalition Party is *Aamulehti* in Tampere. The left-wing papers are subject to considerably closer influence from the parties to which they are affiliated than their right-wing counterparts. Privately owned newspapers—including some of the largest such as *Helsingin Sanomat* and *Turun Sanomat*—are usually independent of political parties.

Helsinki is the only large press centre, with a large number of daily papers. Several large dailies are produced in provincial towns, as are a number of weekly and twice-weekly papers. In 1989 there were 66 daily newspapers in Finland, with a total circulation of about 3,253,000. Twelve of these dailies are printed in Swedish. A further 175 local non-daily papers, with a total circulation of 1,311,786, were also registered.

The most popular daily papers are *Helsingin Sanomat*, *Aamulehti*, *Turun Sanomat*, *Ilta-Sanomat*, *Uusi Suomi* and *Savon Sanomat*. Those most respected for their standard of news coverage and commentary are *Helsingin Sanomat*, an independent paper, and the smaller *Uusi Suomi*.

The total circulation of periodicals amounts to about 23m. copies per issue, of which the business and trade press contribute 11.5m. The largest publishers are Kustannusosakeyhtiö Apulehti, Yhtyneet Kuvalehdet Oy, Lehtimiehet Oy and Sanoma Osakeyhtiö. Consumer co-operatives use their periodicals as information media for both their members and their customers. *Pirkka*, *YV*, *Me* and *Yhteishyvä* are among the most important.

There are about 1,100 periodicals, of which some 200 are in the nation's second language, Swedish. Among the leading weekly periodicals are the general interest *Seura*, *Apu* and the illustrated news magazine *Suomen Kuvalehti*. The publications of the consumer co-operatives enjoy large circulations, as do the chief women's magazines *Anna*, *Me naiset* and *Kotiliesi*. The more popular serious magazines include the fortnightly *Pellervo* specializing in agricultural affairs, and *Valitut Palat*, the Finnish *Reader's Digest*.

PRINCIPAL DAILIES

Helsinki

Demari: Paasivuorenkatu 3, 00530 Helsinki; tel. (90) 701041; telex 124433; fax (90) 7534688; f. 1918; chief organ of the Social Democratic Party; Editor-in-Chief JUKKA HALONEN; circ. 36,013.

Helsingin Sanomat: Ludviginkatu 6-8, POB 975, 00101 Helsinki; tel. (90) 1221; telex 124897; f. 1889; independent; Publr SEPPO KIEVARI; Editor-in-Chief JANNE VIRKKUNEN; circ. 477,215 weekdays, 565,048 Sunday.

Hufvudstadsbladet: Mannerheimvägen 18, 00101 Helsinki; tel. (90) 12531; telex 124402; fax (90) 642930; f. 1864; Swedish language; independent; Editor HÅKAN HELLBERG; circ. 67,230 weekdays, 70,202 Sunday.

Iltalehti: POB 139, 00101 Helsinki; tel. (90) 507721; telex 124898; fax (90) 538549; f. 1981; independent; Editor-in-Chief VELI-ANTTI SAVOLAINEN; circ. 103,818 afternoon, 151,013 Saturday.

Ilta-Sanomat: Korkeavuorenkatu 34, POB 375, 00101 Helsinki; tel. (90) 1221; telex 124897; fax (90) 1223419; f. 1932; afternoon; independent; Editor-in-Chief VESA-PEKKA KOLJONEN; circ. 213,660 weekdays, 243,200 weekend.

Insinööriuutiset—Tekniikka ja Talous: Ratavartijankatu 2, 00520 Helsinki; tel. (90) 15901; daily; technology and economy; Editor-in-Chief RISTO TUOMAINEN.

Kansan Uutiset: Niitaajankatu 8, 00810 Helsinki; tel. (90) 75881; telex 12663; f. 1957; organ of the Left-Wing Alliance; Editor ERKKI KAUPPILA; circ. 45,731 weekdays, 57,262 Sunday.

Kauppalehti (The Commercial Daily): POB 189, 00101 Helsinki; tel. (90) 50781; telex 125827; f. 1898; morning; Editor-in-Chief LAURI HELVE; circ. 81,798.

Suomenmaa: Mannerheimint 30, Eduskunta, 00270 Helsinki; tel. (90) 4322858; f. 1908; Centre; Editor SEPPO SARLUND; circ. 12,270.

Uusi Suomi: POB 139, 00101 Helsinki; tel. (90) 50771; telex 124898; fax (90) 531646; f. 1847; morning; independent; Editors ARI VALJAKKA, MAUNO SAARI, JYRKI VESIKANSA; circ. 84,500 morning, 87,880 Sunday.

Hämeenlinna

Hämeen Sanomat: Vanajantie 7, POB 530, 13111 Hämeenlinna; tel. 23011; f. 1879; independent; Man. JUSSI ALA-NIKKOLA; Editor-in-Chief ESKO OJALA; circ. 33,119.

Hyrylä

Keski-Uusimaa: Klaavolantie 5, 04300 Hyrylä; tel. (90) 255255; independent; Editor-in-Chief AUVO KANTOLA; circ. 24,590.

Joensuu

Karjalainen: Torikatu 33, POB 99, 80101 Joensuu; tel. (973) 1551; telex 46126; f. 1874; National Coalition; Editor SEPPO VENTO; circ. 56,151.

FINLAND

Jyväskylä

Keskisuomalainen: Aholaidantie 3, POB 159, 40101 Jyväskylä; tel. (0941) 201211; telex 28211; f. 1871; Centre; Editor ERKKI LAATIKAINEN; circ. 81,456 weekdays.

Kajaani

Kainuun Sanomat: Viestitie 2, POB 150, 87700 Kajaani; tel. (986) 1661; telex 33172; fax (986) 23013; f. 1918; Centre; Editor KEIJO KORHONEN; circ. 30,357.

Kemi

Pohjolan Sanomat: POB 17, 94101 Kemi; tel. (80) 2911; telex 3643; f. 1915; Centre; Editors MATTI LAMMI, REIJO ALATÖRMÄNEN; circ. 42,203.

Kokkola

Keskipohjanmaa: Kosila, POB 45, 67101 Kokkola; tel. (968) 28511; fax (968) 25039; f. 1917; Centre; Editor LASSI JAAKKOLA; circ. 35,004.

Kotka

Kotkan Sanomat: POB 27, 48101 Kotka; tel. (952) 16300; fax (952) 16377; f. 1902; independent; Editor JUKKA VENKASALO; circ. 24,457.

Kouvola

Kouvolan Sanomat: Lehtikaari 1, POB 40, 45101 Kouvola; tel. (951) 28911; telex 52210; fax (951) 15335; f. 1909; Editor MARTTI TURTOLA; circ. 34,783.

Kuopio

Savon Sanomat: Vuorikatu 21, POB 68, 70101 Kuopio; tel. (71) 303111; telex 42111; f. 1907; Centre; Dir RISTO SUHONEN; Editor REINO MYÖHÄNEN; circ. 90,488.

Lahti

Etelä-Suomen Sanomat: Ilmarisentie 7, POB 80, 15101 Lahti; tel. (918) 57511; telex 16132; fax (918) 575467; f. 1900; independent; Dir JAAKKO UKKONEN; Editors-in-Chief KAUKO MÄENPÄÄ, PENTTI VUORIO; circ. 71,018.

Lappeenranta

Etelä-Saimaa: POB 3, 53101 Lappeenranta; tel. (953) 15600; telex 58217; fax (953) 53292; f. 1885; Centre; Man. Dir ESA LAVENDER; Editor LAURI SARHIMAA; circ. 36,183.

Mikkeli

Länsi-Savo: POB 6, 50101 Mikkeli; tel. (955) 10555; telex 55154; circ. 29,182.

Oulu

Kaleva: POB 70, 90101 Oulu; tel. (981) 277111; telex 32112; f. 1899; Liberal independent; Editor TEUVO MÄLLINEN; circ. 95,461.

Kansan Tahto: POB 61, 90101 Oulu; tel. (981) 221722; fax (981) 16457; f. 1906; organ of the Left-Wing Alliance; circ. 16,936.

Liitto: Lekatie 4, 90150 Oulu; tel. (981) 336333; morning; Centre; circ. 18,135.

Pori

Satakunnan Kansa: POB 58, 28101 Pori; tel. (939) 328111; telex 66102; fax (939) 328392; f. 1873; independent; Editor ERKKI TEIKARI; circ. 62,630.

Rauma

Länsi-Suomi: Kaivopuistontie 1, 26100 Rauma; tel. (38) 3361; telex 65160; fax (38) 240959; f. 1905; daily; National Coalition Party; circ. 20,000.

Rovaniemi

Lapin Kansa: Veitikantie 6–8, 96100 Rovaniemi; tel. (960) 2911; telex 37213; fax (960) 291305; f. 1928; independent; Editor HEIKKI TUOMI-NIKULA; circ. 43,121.

Salo

Salon Seudun Sanomat: Örninkatu 14, POB 117, 24101 Salo; tel. (924) 30021; circ. 21,539.

Savonlinna

Itä-Savo: POB 35, 57101 Savonlinna; tel. (957) 29171; telex 5611; Centre; circ. 23,617 weekdays, 20,122 Sunday.

Seinäjoki

Ilkka: POB 60, Kouluk, 60101 Seinäjoki; tel. (964) 141100; telex 72130; f. 1906; organ of Centre Party; Editor KARI HOKKANEN; circ. 56,645.

Tampere

Aamulehti: Patamäenkatu 7, Tampere; tel. (931) 666111; telex 22111; fax (931) 666259; f. 1881; National Coalition; Editors SAKARI KUMPULAINEN, RAIMO SEPPÄLÄ; circ. 145,162 weekdays, 152,220 Sunday.

Turku

Turun Sanomat: Kauppiaskatu 5, 20100 Turku; tel. (921) 693311; telex 62213; fax (921) 693274; f. 1904; independent; Man. Dir KEIJO KETONEN; Editor JARMO VIRMAVIRTA; circ. 136,517 weekdays, 146,372 Sunday.

Vaasa

Pohjalainen: Pitkäkatu 37, POB 37, 65101 Vaasa; tel. (961) 111411; telex 74212; f. 1903; National Coalition; Editor ERKKI MALMIVAARA; circ. 64,534.

Vasabladet: Sandögatan 6, POB 52, 65101 Vaasa; tel. (961) 121866; telex 74269; fax (961) 129003; f. 1856; Swedish language; Liberal independent; Editor BIRGER THÖLIX; circ. 27,385.

PRINCIPAL PERIODICALS

Akava: Rautatielaisenkatu 6, 00520 Helsinki; tel. (90) 141822; fax (90) 142595; economy and administration; Editor PERTTI RONKKO; circ. 200,078.

Aku Ankka (Donald Duck): POB 113, 00381 Helsinki; tel. (90) 1201; telex 125848; fax (90) 1205599; f. 1951; weekly; children's; Editor KIRSTI TOPPARI; circ. 304,671.

Anna: Maistraatinportti 1, 00240 Helsinki; tel. (90) 15661; telex 1482025; f. 1963; weekly; women's; Editor-in-Chief RIITTA TULONEN; circ. 163,222.

Apu: Hitsaajankatu 7, 00810 Helsinki; tel. (90) 75961; telex 124732; fax (90) 781911; f. 1933; weekly; family journal; Editor-in-Chief MATTI SAARI; circ. 279,215.

Asu Hyvin: Rauhankatu 15, 00170 Helsinki; tel. (90) 175566; fax (90) 175426; 10 a year; housebuilding; Editor LAURI LEHTINEN; circ. 177,121.

Avotakka: Hitsaajankatu 7, 00811 Helsinki; tel. (90) 75961; telex (90) 124732; fax (90) 781911; interior decorating; Editor LEENA NOKELA; circ. 51,961.

Eeva: Hitsaajankatu 10, 00810 Helsinki; tel. (90) 782311; telex 124732; f. 1933; monthly; women's; Editor-in-Chief ULLA LESKINEN; circ. 126,694.

et-lehti: POB 113, 00381 Helsinki; tel. (90) 1201; telex 125848; fax (90) 1205428; pensioners' magazine; Editor KAISA LARMELA; circ. 166,267.

Hymy: Maistraatinportti 1, 00241 Helsinki; tel. (90) 15661; fax (90) 144595; monthly; family journal; Editor-in-Chief ISMO VALKKI; circ. 137,646.

Kaks' Plus: Maistraatinportti 1, 00241 Helsinki; tel. (90) 15661; fax (90) 145650; general; Editor ANTTI NURMINEN; circ. 58,783.

Kalamies: Svinhufvudintie 11, 00570 Helsinki; tel. (90) 6849022; fax (90) 6849904; 10 a year; fishing; Editor-in-Chief TIMO SEPPÄLÄ; circ 69,705.

Kameralehti: Sibeliuksenkatu 11B, 00250 Helsinki; tel. (90) 441323; fax (90) 407029; f. 1950; 11 a year; photographic; Editor PEKKA PUNKARI; circ. 14,026.

Katso: Hitsaajankatu 7, 00810 Helsinki; weekly; tel. (90) 782311; telex 124732; fax (90) 781911; TV, radio and video; Editor-in-Chief ANJA TUOMI; circ. 69,857.

Kauppa ja Koti: Työpajakatu 13, 00580 Helsinki; tel. (90) 6191; fax (90) 6197882; free to customers of retail stores; Editor-in-Chief TAPANI LEHMUSVAARA; circ. 420,188.

Käytännön Maamies: Maistraatinpoorti 1, 00241 Helsinki; tel. (90) 15661; fax (90) 145650; monthly; agriculture; Editor JORMA MUURINEN; circ. 36,277.

Kodin Kuvalehti: POB 113, 00381 Helsinki; tel. (90) 1201; telex 125848; fortnightly; family magazine; Editor MAIJA ALFTAN; circ. 171,841.

Koiramme–Våra Hundar: Kamreerintie 8, 02770 Espoo; tel. (90) 8057722; monthly; dogs; circ. 79,856.

Koneviesti: Simonkatu 6, 00100 Helsinki; tel. (90) 131151; fax (90) 13115209; bi-monthly; farming and forestry; Editor RISTO KNAAPI; circ. 51,479.

Kotilääkäri: Maistraatinportti 1, 00240 Helsinki; tel. (90) 15661; telex 122772; fax (90) 145650; f. 1889; monthly; health and beauty; Editor-in-Chief IRMA HEYDEMANN; circ. 52,554.

Kotiliesi: Maistraatinportti 1, 00240 Helsinki; tel. (90) 15661; telex 121364; f. 1922; fortnightly; home journal; Editor-in-Chief ELINA SIMONEN; circ. 195,742.

Kotimaa: Norrsväng 15, 00200 Helsinki; tel. (90) 6922591; 3 a week; circ. 77,898.

FINLAND

Kotivinkki: Kalevankatu 1C, 00100 Helsinki; tel. (90) 642911; fax (90) 604500; 11 a year; family; circ. 199,651.

Koululainen: Maistraatinportti 1, 00241 Helsinki; tel. (90) 15661; telex 121364; fax (90) 145650; 17 a year; for pupils of comprehensive schools; Editor IRMA HOYDEMANN; circ. 66,322.

Look at Finland: POB 625, 00101 Helsinki; tel. (90) 403011; quarterly; tourist information, travel and general articles; publ. by Finnish Tourist Board and Ministry for Foreign Affairs; Editor-in-Chief BENGT PIHLSTRÖM; circ. 32,000.

Maito ja Me: POB 440, 00101 Helsinki; tel. (90) 131151; telex 122474; fax (90) 6944766; f. 1989; 10 a year; dairy farming; Editor-in-Chief REIJO VATANEN; circ. 70,000.

Me naiset: POB 113, 00381 Helsinki; tel. (90) 1205599; telex 125848; fax (90) 1205599; f. 1952; weekly; women's; Editor ULLA-MAIJA PAAVILAINEN; circ. 108,482.

Metsälehti: Maistraatinportti 4A, 00240 Helsinki; tel. (90) 1562333; fax (90) 1562335; f. 1933; fortnightly; forestry; Editor PAAVO SEPPÄNEN; circ. 70,269.

Nykyposti: Maistraatinportti 1, 00240 Helsinki; tel. (90) 15661; fax (90) 144595; f. 1977; monthly; family journal; Editor-in-Chief LASSE ASKOLIN; Man. Editor IRMA KARAMA; circ. 160,124.

Opettaja: Rautatieläisenkatu 6, 00520 Helsinki; tel. (90) 15021; weekly; teachers; Editor-in-Chief HANNU LAAKSOLA; Man. Editor SIRPPA KAHRI; circ. 57,000.

Seura: Maistraatinportti 1, 00240 Helsinki; tel. (90) 15661; telex 121364; fax (90) 145650; f. 1934; weekly; family journal; Editors-in-Chief HANNU PARPOLA, HEIKKI PARKKONEN; circ. 296,463.

Silver News: Runeberginkatu 5, 00101 Helsinki; tel. (90) 4041; fax (90) 4042957; Editor TUULA EROLA; circ. 208,349.

Sosiaalinen Aikakauskirja: Snellmaninkatu 4-6, 00170 Helsinki; tel. (90) 1605411; telex 125073; 6 a year; social policy; summaries in English; Editor KARI PURO.

STTK—FTFK: Pohjoisranta 4A, 00171 Helsinki; tel. (90) 625871; fax (90) 652367; economy; Editor ERKII HUSU; circ. 153,250.

Suomen Kuvalehti: Maistraatinportti 1, 00240 Helsinki; tel. (90) 15661; telex 121364; fax (90) 144076; f. 1916; weekly; illustrated news; Editor-in-Chief PEKKA HYVÄRINEN; circ. 107,819.

Suosikki: Eerikinkatu 3B, 00100 Helsinki; tel. (90) 6943311; telex 122730; fax (90) 6826206; 16 a year; youth, music; Editor-in-Chief JYRKI HÄMÄLÄINEN; circ. 110,439.

Suuri Käsityökerho: POB 107, 00381 Helsinki; tel. (90) 1201; telex 125848; fax (90) 1205428; f. 1974; monthly; needlework and clothing magazine; Editor KRISTINA TÖTTERMAN; circ. 108,500.

Sydän: Hjärtsjukdomsförbundet i Finland, POB 196, 00121 Helsinki; tel. (90) 650288; fax (90) 175085; 7 a year; information on cardiovascular treatment; circ. 110,000.

Tekniikan Maailma: Melkonkatu 10C, 00210 Helsinki; tel. (90) 68261; telex 122730; fax (90) 6826313; 20 a year; technical review; Editor-in-Chief MAURI J. SALO; circ. 124,613.

Tekniset: POB 146, 00131 Helsinki; tel. (90) 658611; telex 122728; fax (90) 653620; 14 a year; industrial technology; Editor LAURI TUOMINEN; circ. 79,353.

Tuulilasi: Hitsaajankatu 7, 00810 Helsinki; tel. (90) 75961; fax (90) 787311; monthly; motoring; Editor-in-Chief ERKKI RAUKKO; circ. 101,721.

Työ Terveys Turvallisuus: Topeliuksenkatu 41A, 00250 Helsinki; tel. (90) 47471; 15 a year; occupational health; Editor-in-Chief MATTI TAPIAINEN; circ. 93,677.

Valitut Palat: Halsuantie 4, 00420 Helsinki; tel. (90) 5632011; telex 122489; monthly; Finnish Reader's Digest; Editor-in-Chief RAIMO MÖYSÄ; circ. 338,377.

Vene: Melkonkatu 10C, POB 116, 00101 Helsinki; tel. (90) 68261; telex 122730; fax (90) 6826206; monthly; sailing; Editor-in-Chief MATTI MURTO; circ. 33,936.

CO-OPERATIVE JOURNALS

Elanto, Elanto-Tidningen: Hämeentie 11, 00530 Helsinki; tel. (90) 7342360; monthly magazine of Elanto Co-operative Society; circ. 137,000.

Kymppi: Korkeavuorenkatu 45, POB 42, 00131 Helsinki; tel. (90) 13341; fax (90) 1334870; f. 1954; 8 a year; publ. by Skopbank of Finland Banks Assen, free to customers; Editor-in-Chief VELI-MATTI HEPOLUHTA; circ. 180,000.

Me: Hameentie 19A, 00500 Helsinki; tel. (90) 7331; telex 124454; fax (90) 7333264; f. 1916; 10 per year; family magazine for mems. of Co-op Eka Corpn; Editor-in-Chief HILKKA KEMPPINEN; circ. 310,000.

Moidän Liiket: POB 73, 00501 Helsinki; tel. (90) 7331; fax (90) 7333264; 6 a year; management and elected officials of co-operative societies; Editor KALEVI SUOMELA; circ. 7,818.

Pellervo: POB 77, 00101 Helsinki; tel. (90) 6955203; fax (90) 6948845; f. 1899; monthly; agricultural and co-operative journal; organ of the Central Union of Agricultural Co-operative Societies; Editor-in-Chief MARTTI SEPPÄNEN; circ. 82,594.

Pirkka: Rauhankatu 15, 00170 Helsinki; tel. (90) 175566; monthly; Swedish; free to customers of retail stores; Editor-in-Chief OSMO LAMPINEN; circ. 1,717,803.

Samarbete: Vilhelmsgatan 7, 00100 Helsinki; tel. (90) 1881; telex 121341; fax (90) 1882332; f. 1909; monthly; free to members of co-operative shops; circ. 36,328.

Yhteishyvä: Vilhonkatu 7, 00100 Helsinki; tel. (90) 1881; telex 121341; fax (90) 1882332; f. 1905; monthly; free to members of co-operative shops; Editor-in-Chief JOUKO TYYRI; circ. 455,792.

YV: Arkadiankatu 23, POB 480, 00101 Helsinki; tel. (90) 4041; monthly; free to customers of co-operative banks; Editor-in-Chief MATTI PAAVONSALO; circ. 559,700.

NEWS AGENCIES

Oy Suomen Tietotoimisto-Finska Notisbyrån Ab (STT-FNB): Yrjönkatu 22C, 00100 Helsinki; tel. (90) 646224; telex 124534; fax (90) 602936; f. 1887; eight provincial branches; independent national agency distributing domestic and international news in Finnish and Swedish; Chair. KEIJO KETONEN; Gen. Man. and Editor-in-Chief PER-ERIK LÖNNFORS.

Foreign Bureaux

Agence France-Presse (AFP) (France): c/o STT-FNB, Yrjönkatu 22, 00100 Helsinki; tel. (90) 646800.

Agencia EFE (Spain): Helsinki; Correspondent HANNU VUORI.

Agenzia Nazionale Stampa Associata (ANSA) (Italy): Helsinki; tel. (90) 639799; Agent MATTI BROTHERUS.

Allgemeiner Deutscher Nachrichtendienst (ADN) (Germany): Aarholmankuja 4C 27, 00840 Helsinki; Correspondent RALF JARKOWSKI.

Associated Press (AP) (USA): 2nd floor, Yrjönkatu 27A, 00100 Helsinki; tel. (90) 646883; fax (90) 602979; Correspondent MATTI HUUHTANEN.

Informatsionnoye Agentstvo Novosti (IAN) (USSR): Lönnrotinkatu 25A, 5 Kerros, 00180 Helsinki; tel. (90) 6942022; telex 124662; Correspondent L. LAASKO.

Inter Press Service (IPS) (Italy): Suomen IPS, 5th floor, Mannerheimintie 5C, 01000 Helsinki; tel. 6121447; Editor MILLA SUNDSTRØM.

Reuters (UK): c/o STT-FNB, POB 550, 00101 Helsinki.

Telegrafnoye Agentstvo Sovetskogo Soyuza (TASS) (USSR): Ratakatu 1A 10, 00120 Helsinki; Correspondent ALEXANDER SOURIKOV.

United Press International (UPI) (USA): Ludviginkatu 3-5, 00130 Helsinki; tel. (90) 605701; telex 124403; Bureau Man. SIRKA LIISA KANKURI.

Xinhua (New China) News Agency (People's Republic of China): Hopeasalmentie 14, 00570 Helsinki; tel. (90) 687587; telex 122552; Correspondent ZHENG HUANGING.

PRESS ASSOCIATIONS

Aikakauslehtien Liitto (Periodical Publishers' Association): Lönnrotinkatu 33A 1, 00180 Helsinki; tel. (90) 641516; fax (90) 603478; f. 1946; protects the interests of periodical publishers and liaises with the authorities, postal services and advertisers; organizes training courses to improve the quality of periodicals; Man. Dir MATTI ÄHTOMIES.

Suomen Sanomalehtimiesten Liitto (Union of Journalists): Hietalandenkatu 2B, 00180 Helsinki; tel. (90) 647326; telex 121394; fax (90) 640361; f. 1921; 8,400 mems; Pres. ANTERO LAINE; Sec.-Gen. EILA HYPPÖNEN.

Sanomalehtien Liitto—Tidningarnas Förbund (Newspaper Publishers' Association): Kalevankatu 4, 00100 Helsinki; tel. (90) 607786; telex 123990; fax (90) 607989; f. 1908; negotiates newsprint prices, postal rates; represents the press in relations with Government and advertisers; undertakes technical research; 107 mems; Man. Dir VEIKKO LÖYTTYNIEMI.

Publishers

Gummerus Publishers: Erottajankatu 5C, POB 2, 00131 Helsinki; tel. (90) 644301; telex 123727; fax (90) 604998; f. 1872; fiction, non-fiction, encyclopaedias and reference books; Man. Dir RISTO LEHMUSOKSA.

Holger Schildts Förlagsaktiebolag: Nylandsgatan 17, 00120 Helsinki; tel. (90) 604892; fax (90) 611979; f. 1913; subjects mainly in Swedish; Man. Dir STIG-BJÖRN NYBERG.

FINLAND

Karisto Oy: Paroistentie 2, POB 102, 13101 Hämeenlinna; tel. (917) 161551; telex 2348; fax (917) 161555; f. 1900; non-fiction and fiction; Man. Dir SIMO MOISIO.

Kirjayhtymä Oy: Eerikinkatu 28, 00180 Helsinki; tel. (90) 6944522; fax (90) 6947265; f. 1958; fiction, non-fiction, textbooks; Man. Dir HEIKKI RÖNNQVIST; Publishing Dirs PERTTI LASSILA, JUHANI KARVINEN.

Kustannusosakeyhtiö Kansanvalta: Paasivuorenkatu 3, 00530 Helsinki; tel. (90) 701041; telex 124433; f. 1918; Social Democratic publishing company; publishes newspaper *Demari*; Dir RISTO UOSUKAINEN.

Kustannusosakeyhtiö Otava: Uudenmaankatu 10, 00120 Helsinki; tel. (90) 19961; telex 124560; fax (90) 643136; f. 1890; non-fiction, fiction, science, juvenile, textbooks and encyclopaedias; Chair. HEIKKI A. REENPÄÄ; Man. Dir OLLI REENPÄÄ.

Kustannusosakeyhtiö Tammi: Eerikinkatu 28, 00180 Helsinki; tel. (90) 6942700; telex 125482; fax (90) 6942711; f. 1943; fiction, non-fiction, juvenile; Man. Dir OLLI ARRAKOSKI.

Sanoma Corporation: POB 240, 00101 Helsinki; tel. (90) 1221; telex 122772; fax (90) 1223229; f. 1889; publishes daily newspapers *Helsingin Sanomat* and *Ilta-Sanomat*; also magazines and books, cable television and electronic publishing; Chair. AATOS ERKKO; Man. Dir JAAKKO RAURAMO.

Söderström & Co. Förlags Ab: Wavulinsvägen 4, 00210 Helsinki; tel. (90) 6923681; fax (90) 6926346; f. 1891; all subjects in Swedish only; Man. Dir CARL APPELBERG.

Weilin ja Göös: Ahertajantie 5, 02100 Espoo; tel. 43771; telex 122597; f. 1872; fiction, reference books, juvenile, textbooks, software; Dir OLLE KOSKINEN.

Werner Söderström Osakeyhtiö: Bulevardi 12, 00120 Helsinki; tel. (90) 61681; telex 122644; fax (90) 6168405; f. 1878; fiction and non-fiction, science, juvenile, textbooks, graphic industry; Man. Dir ANTERO SILJOLA.

Government Printing Centre

Valtion Painatuskeskus: Hakuninmaantie 2, POB 516, 00101 Helsinki; tel. (90) 56601; telex 123458; fax (90) 5660374; f. 1859; Man. Dir OLAVI PERILÄ.

PUBLISHERS' ASSOCIATION

Suomen Kustannusyhdistys: Merimiehenkatu 12A 6, 00150 Helsinki; tel. (90) 179185; fax (90) 6221143; f. 1858; Chair. ANTERO SILJOLA; Sec. VEIKKO SONNINEN; 68 mems.

Radio and Television

In 1988 there were an estimated 4.9m. radio receivers in use, and 1,862,479 television licences. Some 130,000 homes are linked to cable television in Finland.

Office of the Director-General of Posts and Telecommunications: POB 1001, 00101 Helsinki; tel. (90) 1954004; telex 124557; fax (90) 1954015; Dir-Gen. PEKKA VENNAMO.

Oy Yleisradio Ab (YLE) (Finnish Broadcasting Company): Kesäkatu 2, 00260 Helsinki; tel. (90) 441141; telex 124735; fax (90) 4013421; f. 1926, state controlled since 1934, with management appointed according to the political character of Parliament; Dir-Gen. REINO PAASILINNA; Dir of Admin. and Deputy Dir-Gen. JOUNI MYKKÄNEN; Dir of Radio OLLI ALHO; Dir of TV Programme 1 ARNO KAILA; Dir of TV Programme 2 ARNE WESSBERG; Dir of Swedish Radio and TV BENGT BERGMAN; Dir of News and Regional Programming TAPIO SIIKALA; Dir of Engineering ERKKI LARKKA.

RADIO

Oy Yleisradio Ab (YLE) (Finnish Broadcasting Company): POB 10, 00241 Helsinki; tel. (90) 418811; telex 124735; Finnish main programme: both light and serious programmes; Finnish second programme: mainly musical and educational; Swedish programme: Swedish language and music; also regional stations, belonging to a local radio union; Foreign Service: broadcasts to Europe, Africa, the Middle and Far East and America in Finnish, Swedish, German and English.

Experimental Finnish local radio began operations in 1984, and by October 1987, 38 such licences had been granted.

TELEVISION

The State operates three television channels, and broadcasting time is leased from them by commercial companies. A teletext news service is operated in co-operation with Sweden and Denmark.

Oy Yleisradio Ab (YLE) (Finnish Broadcasting Company): Radio Programme 1: POB 10, 00241 Helsinki; tel. (90) 418811; telex 121270; Radio Programme 2: Tohlopinranta 12, 33270 Tampere; tel. (31) 445445; telex 22176. Also operates television service:

TV Programme 1: about 45 hours per week (commercial programmes included).
TV Programme 2: about 40 hours per week (commercial programmes included).
TV Programme 3: about 50 hours per week (commercial).

MTV Oy: Ilmalantori 2, 00240 Helsinki; tel. (90) 15001; telex 125144; fax (90) 1500721; f. 1957; independent commercial television company producing programmes on all channels; about 21 hours per week; Pres. EERO PILKAMA.

Oy Kolmostelevisio Ab (Channel 3): Ilmalankatu 2C, 00240 Helsinki; tel. (90) 15001; telex 126068; fax (90) 1500677.

Finance

The Bank of Finland is the country's central bank and the centre of Finland's monetary and banking system. It functions 'under guarantee and supervision of Parliament and the Bank supervisors delegated by Parliament'.

There are three deposit bank groups in Finland: commercial banks, savings banks and co-operative banks, and Postipankki Ltd. The total number of branches in 1989 was 3,500.

The commercial banks constitute the most important group of deposit banks. At the end of 1989 there were 14 commercial banks, with a total of 976 offices. Two of these banks are national, and four are foreign-owned.

The savings banks and co-operative banks are regional, providing mainly local banking services. At 31 December 1989 there were 178 savings banks and 360 co-operative banks. Postipankki had 67 branch offices. At December 1989 2,902 post offices handled certain Postipankki operations.

There are seven mortgage banks operating in Finland, and several special credit institutions. The insurance institutions, of which 56 are private companies, granted credits in 1985. Finance companies, development companies and other special institutions have also joined the money-market.

BANKING

(cap. = capital; p.u. = paid up; dep. = deposits; m. = million; res = reserves; brs = branches; amounts in markkaa)

Central Bank

Suomen Pankki/Finlands Bank (The Bank of Finland): Snellmaninaukio, POB 160, 00101 Helsinki; tel. (90) 1831; telex 121224; fax (90) 174872; f. 1811; Bank of Issue under the guarantee and supervision of Parliament; cap. and res 5,436m. (Dec. 1989); Gov. ROLF KULLBERG; 12 brs.

Commercial and Mortgage Banks

Kansallisluottopankki Oy (Kansallis Mortgage Bank Ltd): Erottajankatu 19B, 00130 Helsinki; tel. (90) 1631; f. 1985; cap. and res 143m. (1989); Chair. JAAKKO LASSILA; Man. Dir EERO HERTTOLA.

Kansallis-Osake-Pankki: Aleksanterinkatu 42, POB 10, 00101 Helsinki; tel. (90) 1631; telex 124412; fax (90) 1633595; f. 1889; cap. and res 9,986m., dep. 63,371m. (Dec. 1989); Chair. MARKUS MANNERKOSKI; CEO JAAKKO LASSILA; 487 brs.

MB Corporate Bank Ltd: Fabianinkatu 23, 00130 Helsinki; tel. (90) 131011; telex 121840; fax (90) 1310; f. 1956; subsidiary of Postipankki Ltd; cap. 336m. (Dec. 1989); Chair. MATTI JAATINEN; Man. Dir ILPO NIITTI.

Midland Montagu Osakepankki: Eteläesplanadi 22A, POB 212, 00131 Helsinki; tel. (90) 601766; telex 124210; fax (90) 603479; f. 1986; owned by Midland Bank PLC; cap. p.u. 70m.; Chair. KURT GEIGER; Man. Dir KAI LUOTONEN.

OKO—Investointipankki Oy (OKO—Mortgage Bank Ltd): Malminkatu 30, POB 930, 00101 Helsinki; tel. (90) 4041; telex 124714; fax (90) 4044209; f. 1916; cap. and res 295m. (Dec. 1989); Chair. PAULI KOMI; Man. Dir. OSSIAN ANTSON.

Okobank (Osuuspankkien Keskuspankki Oy) (Central Bank of the Co-operative Banks of Finland Ltd): POB 308, Arkadiankatu 23, 00101 Helsinki; tel. (90) 4041; telex 124714; fax (90) 4042652; f. 1902; cap. and res 2,502m., dep. 1,537m. (Dec. 1989); Chair. of Board of Admin. ESA TIMONEN; Chair. of Board of Management PAULI KOMI; 1,224 brs.

Postipankki Ltd: Unioninkatu 22, 00007 Helsinki; tel. (90) 1641; telex 121698; fax (90) 1642608; f. 1886, a limited company 1988; operates through its head office, 89 branches and 1,000 local post offices; assets 72,738m., dep. 27,923m. (Dec. 1989); Chair. of Supervisory Board MATTI JAATINEN; Chair. and Chief Exec. SEPPO LINDBLOM.

PSP—Kuntapankki Oy (PSP Municipality Bank Ltd): Fabianinkatu 23, 00007 Helsinki; tel. (90) 1641; telex 121428; cap. and res

81.1m. (Dec. 1989); Chair. SEPPO LINDBLOM; Man. Dir PERTTI MATTILA.

Skopbank (Säästöpankkien Keskus-Osake-Pankki) (Central Bank of the Finnish Savings Banks): Mikonkatu 4, POB 400,00101 Helsinki; tel. (90) 13341; telex 122284; fax (90) 1334896; f. 1908; mem. of Norden Banking Group; cap. and res 4,500m., dep. 1,452m. (Dec. 1989); Chair. and Chief Gen. Man. CHRISTOPHER WEGELIUS.

Suomen Hypoteekkiyhdistys (Mortgage Society of Finland): Yrjönkatu 9, POB 509, 00101 Helsinki; tel. (90) 647401; fax (90) 647443; f. 1860; cap. and res 102m. (Dec. 1989); Pres. RISTO PIEPPONEN.

Suomen Kiinteistöpankki Oy (Finnish Real Estate Bank Ltd): Erottajankatu 7A, POB 428, 00101 Helsinki; tel. (90) 13341; telex 122284; fax (90) 1335129; f. 1907; cap. and res 320m. (June 1990); Pres. HEIKKI PERHO; Man. Dir TOIVO IHO.

Suomen Teollisuuspankki Oy (Industrial Bank of Finland Ltd): Fabianinkatu 8, 00130 Helsinki; tel. (90) 177521; telex 121839; fax (90) 608951; f. 1924; cap. and res 386m. (Dec. 1988); Chair. KURT STENVALL; Man. Dir JARMO KARPPI.

STS-Bank Ltd: POB 53, 00531 Helsinki; tel. (90) 73181; telex 126196; fax (90) 73182540; f. 1909; cap. 814.3m., dep. 6,817.6m. (Dec. 1989); Chief Gen. Man. ULF SUNDQVIST; 102 brs.

Union Bank of Finland Ltd: Aleksanterinkatu 30, POB 868, 00101 Helsinki; tel. (90) 1651; telex 124407; fax (90) 1652648; f. 1862; mem. of Scandinavian Banking Partners; cap. and res 10,729m., dep. 39,023m. (Dec. 1989); Chair. AHTI HIRVONEN; 366 brs.

Banking Associations

Osuuspankkien Keskusliitto r.y. (Central Association of the Finnish Co-operative Banks): Arkadiankatu 23, POB 308, 00100 Helsinki; tel. (90) 4041; f. 1928; in 1989 there were 360 co-operative banks (1,206 brs) with a membership of 650,000; Man. Dir TAISTO JOENSUU.

Säästöpankkiliitto (Finnish Savings Bank Association): Pohjoisesplanadi 35A, 00100 Helsinki; tel. (90) 13341; fax (90) 1334870; f. 1906; 230 mems; 1,315 offices; Chair. PAAVO PREPULA; Man. Dir KALEVI KAUNISKANGAS.

Suomen Pankkiyhdistys r.y. (Finnish Bankers' Association): Kansakoulukatu 1A, POB 1009, 00101 Helsinki; tel. (90) 6948422; fax (90) 6947844; f. 1914; Chair. JAAKKO LASSILA; Man. Dir MATTI SIPILÄ.

STOCK EXCHANGE

Helsinki Stock Exchange: Fabianinkatu 14, POB 361, 00101 Helsinki; tel. (90) 1733301; telex 123460; fax (90) 17330399; f. 1912; Chair. of Supervisory Bd JAAKKO LASSILA; Chair of Bd of Dirs VESA VAINIO; Pres. JUHANI ERMA.

INSURANCE

EFFOA-yhtymän Keskinäinen Vakuutusyhtiö (Effoa Gp Mutual Insurance Co): c/o Neptun Maritime (Finland) Co Ltd, Sinikalliontie 18A, 02630 Espoo; tel. (90) 5021211; telex 121897; fax (90) 5021250; f. 1942; insurance for Effoa-Finland Steamship Co; marine; Chair. N. G. PALMGREN.

Finnish Marine Insurance Co Ltd/Suomen Merivakuutus Osakeyhtiö: Melkonkatu 22A, 00210 Helsinki; tel. (90) 6927166; telex 121013; f. 1898; Man. Dir CARL-HENRIK LUNDELL.

Kansa Corporation Ltd: Hämeentie 33, POB 78, 00501 Helsinki; tel. (90) 73161; telex 122209; fax (90) 711915; f. 1919; insurance, reinsurance, pensions, finance; Pres. and Chief Exec. MATTI PACKALÉN.

Keskeytysvakuutusosakeyhtiö Otso (Otso Loss of Profits Insurance Co Ltd): Bulevardi 10, POB 00121 Helsinki; tel. (90) 68071; telex 121061; f. 1939; non-life; Gen. Man. MAGNUS NORDLING.

Keskinäinen Vakuutusyhtiö Palonvara (Palonvara Mutual Insurance Co): Rautatienkatu 19, 15110 Lahti; tel. (918) 52261; f. 1912; non-life; Man. Dir JUHANI SORRI.

Keskinäinen Vakuutusyhtiö Tulenvara (Tulenvara Mutual Insurance Co): Porkkalankatu 9, 00180 Helsinki; tel. (90) 13211; telex 124633; f. 1947; non-life; Man. Dir YRJÖ PESSI.

Keskinäinen yhtiö Yrittäjäinvakuutus-Fennia (Enterprise-Fennia Mutual Insurance Co): Asemamiehenkatu 3, 00520 Helsinki; tel. (90) 450351; telex 121280; f. 1928; non-life; Man. Dir KARI ELO.

Lähivakuutus Keskinäinen Yhtiö (Local Mutual Insurance Co): Annankatu 25, 00100 Helsinki; tel. (90) 12941; fax (90) 642173; f. 1917; Gen. Man. SIMO CASTRÉN.

Meijerien Keskinäinen Vakuutusyhtio (Dairies' Mutual Insurance Co): Meijerite 6, POB 68, 00371 Helsinki; tel. (90) 5681; f. 1920; Gen. Man. KEIJO RAUTIO.

Osuuspankkien Keskinäinen Vakuutusyhtiö (Mutual Insurance Co of the Co-operative Banks): Temppelikatu 6B, POB 308, 00101 Helsinki; tel. (90) 4041; f. 1964; non-life; Gen. Man. ASKO KUTVONEN.

Patria Group: Vattuniemenkuja 8A, POB 12, 00211 Helsinki; tel. (90) 69611; telex 124832; f. 1881; non-life, reinsurance; Man. Dir CARL-OLAF HOMÉN.

Pohjola Group: Lapinmäentie 1, 00300 Helsinki; tel. (90) 5591; telex 124556; marine, life and non-life insurance, reinsurance; Chair. and Man. Dir YRJO NISKANEN.

Säästöpankkien Keskinäinen Vakuutusyhtiö (Savings Banks' Mutual Insurance Co): Iso Roobertinkatu 4-6, POB 154, 00121 Helsinki; tel. (90) 13341; fax (90) 1335180; f. 1971; Gen. Man. JUHANI LAINE.

Sampo Group: Yliopistonkatu 27, POB 216, 20101 Turku; tel. (921) 663311; telex 62242; life, non-life, pensions, reinsurance; Man. Dir KAUKO PIHLAVA.

Svensk-Finland Ömsesidiga Försäkringsbolaget (Svensk-Finland Mutual Insurance Co): Malminkatu 20, POB 549, 00101 Helsinki; tel. (90) 69351; telex 125093; fax (90) 6935300; f. 1925; non-life; Man. Dir STIG TAMMELIN.

Tapiola Insurance Group: Revontulentie 7, POB 30, 02101 Espoo; tel. (90) 4531; telex 121073; fax (90) 4532146; life, non-life, livestock, pensions, reinsurance; Chair. and Man. Dir ASMO KALPALA.

Vakuutusosakeyhtiö Pankavara (Pankavara Insurance Co Ltd): Kanavaranta 1, POB 309, 00101 Helsinki; tel. (90) 16291; telex 121438; fax (90) 1629471; f. 1943; non-life; Man. Dir ESKO MÄKELÄINEN.

Varma Group: Annankatu 18A, POB 175, 00121 Helsinki; tel. (90) 61651; telex 125415; f. 1919; pensions, life, non-life, reinsurance; Man. Dir JUHANI KOLEHMAINEN.

Verdandi Group: Olavintie 2, POB 133, 20101 Turku; tel. (921) 690011; telex 62601; fax (921) 690690; life, pensions, reinsurance; Man. Dir KURT LJUNGMAN.

Wärtsilän Keskinäinen Vakuutusyhtiö (Wärtsilä Mutual Insurance Co): John Stenbergin ranta 2, 00530 Helsinki; tel. (90) 70951; telex 124623; fax (90) 736674; f. 1943; non-life; Gen. Man. HENRIK DIESEN.

Insurance Associations

Federation of Accident Insurance Institutions: Bulevardi 28, 00120 Helsinki; tel. (90) 19251; telex 123511; fax (90) 1925389; f. 1920; Man. Dir TAPANI MIETTINEN.

Federation of Employment Pension Institutions: Lastenkodinkuja 1, 00180 Helsinki; tel. (90) 6940122; f. 1964; Man. Dir PENTTI KOSTAMO.

Federation of Finnish Insurance Companies: Bulevardi 28, 00120 Helsinki; tel. (90) 19251; telex 123511; fax (90) 1925216; f. 1942; Chair. YRJÖ NISKANEN; Man. Dir MATTI L. AHO; 50 mems.

Finnish Atomic Insurance Pool, Finnish Pool of Aviation Insurers, Finnish General Reinsurance Pool: Bulevardi 10, 00120 Helsinki; tel. (90) 61691; telex 121061; Man. Dir K.-M. STRÖMMER.

Finnish Marine Underwriters' Association: Bulevardi 28, 00120 Helsinki; tel. (90) 19251; telex 123511; fax (90) 611096; f. 1956; Man. Dir LARS BECKMAN.

Finnish Motor Insurers' Bureau: Bulevardi 28, 00120 Helsinki; tel. (90) 19251; telex 123511; fax (90) 1925368; f. 1938; Man. Dir PENTTI AJO.

Insurance Rehabilitation Agency: Asemamiehenkatu 3, 00520 Helsinki; tel. (90) 15041; fax (90) 1504230; f. 1964; joint bureau of the Finnish carriers of employment accident insurance, motor insurance and pension insurance, to carry out vocational rehabilitation as part of the insurance compensation; Man. Dir RISTO SEPPÄLÄINEN.

Trade and Industry

CHAMBERS OF COMMERCE

Central Chamber of Commerce (Keskuskauppakamari): Fabianinkatu 14, POB 1000, 00101 Helsinki; tel. (90) 650133; telex 123814; fax (90) 650303; f. 1918; Pres. JAAKKO LASSILA; Gen. Man. MATTI AURA; 23 local chambers of commerce represented by 8 mems each on Board.

Finnish Foreign Trade Association: Arkadiankatu 4-6B, POB 908, 00101 Helsinki; tel. (90) 69591; telex 121696; fax (90) 6940028; f. 1919; Chair. MATTI KANKAANPÄÄ; Chair. of Board TIMO RELANDER; Man. Dir PERTTI HUITU.

Helsinki Chamber of Commerce: Kalevankatu 12, 00100 Helsinki; tel. (90) 644601; f. 1917; Pres. PENTTI KIVINEN; Man. Dir HEIKKI HELIÖ; 4,100 mems.

FINLAND

TRADE AND INDUSTRIAL ORGANIZATIONS

Eka Corporation: Hämeentie 19, 00500 Helsinki; tel. (90) 7331; telex 124454; fax (90) 7332921; f. 1983 as a merger of 40 co-operatives; Pres. EERO KANTALA.

Enigheten Centrallaget (Butter and Cheese Export): Päiväläisentie 2, 00390 Helsinki; tel. (90) 5624188; telex 122835; fax (90) 5622630; Chair. and Man. Dir E. ÖRNDAHL; 8 mems.

Finnish Cabinet Makers' and Wood Turners' Association: Helsinki; f. 1944; Man. Dir JUHO SAVIO.

Finnish Joinery Association: Helsinki; Man. Dir JUHO SAVIO.

Hankkija Group: POB 80, 00101 Helsinki; tel. (90) 7291; telex 124660; f. 1905; agricultural produce and supplies, farm machinery, engineering, food technology, construction, automobiles; Chair. and Chief Exec. PERTTI TUOMALA.

Kalatalouden Keskusliitto (Federation of Fisheries Associations): Köydenpunojankatu 7B 23, 00180 Helsinki; tel. (90) 640126; fax (90) 608309; f. 1891; Sec. M. MYLLYLÄ; 398,000 mems.

Kaukomarkkinat Oy: Kutojantie 4, 02631 Espoo; tel. (90) 5211; telex 124469; f. 1947; international trade; Pres. JUHANI RIUTTA.

Kesko Oy (Retailers' Wholesale Co): Satamakatu 3, 00160 Helsinki; tel. (90) 1981; telex 124748; fax (90) 655473; f. 1941; retailer-owned wholesale corporation, trading in foodstuffs, textiles, shoes, consumer goods, agricultural and builders' supplies, and machinery; Pres. EERO UTTER.

Kotimaisen Työn Liitto (Association for Domestic Work): Bulevardi 5A, POB 177, 00121 Helsinki; tel. (90) 645733; f. 1978; public relations for Finnish products and for Finnish work; Chair. of Council ILKKA SUOMINEN; Chair. of Board of Dirs TIMO PELTOLA; Man. Dir RAUNO BISTER; about 1,500 mems.

Kulutusosuustoiminnan Keskusliitto (KK) r.y. (Central Union of Consumer Co-operation): Hämeentie 19, POB 72, 00501 Helsinki; tel. (90) 7331; telex 124454; fax (90) 733-2921; f. 1916; Chair. VÄINÖ HAKALA; Sec.-Gen. KALEVI SUOMELA; 2 mem. societies with 560,000 individuals.

Oy Labor Ab (Agricultural Machinery): Mikkolantie 1, 00640 Helsinki; tel. (90) 7291; telex 124660; f. 1898; Gen. Man. KIMMO VARJOVAARA.

Maataloustuottajain Keskusliitto (Central Union of Agricultural Producers): Simonkatu 6, 00100 Helsinki; tel. (90) 131151; telex 122474; f. 1917; Chair. of Board of Dirs HEIKKI HAAVISTO; Sec.-Gen. MARKKU NEVALA; 278,273 mems.

Munakunta (Co-operative Egg Producers' Association): POB 43, 00721 Helsinki; tel. (90) 372755; telex 1001079; f. 1921; Chair. and Man. Dir TUOMO YLI-KETOLA; 4,920 mems.

Pellervo-Seura (Pellervo Society): Simonkatu 6, 00100 Helsinki; tel. (90) 69551; fax (90) 6948845; f. 1899; central organization of farmers' co-operatives; Man. Dir SAMULI SKURNIK; 600 mem. societies (incl. 8 central co-operative societies).

Suomen Betoniteollisuuden Keskusjärjestö r.y. (Association of the Concrete Industry of Finland): Iso Roobertinkatu 30, 00120 Helsinki; tel. (90) 648212; telex 121394; fax (90) 642597; f. 1929; Chair. ERKKI INKINEN; Man. Dir ERKKI TIKKANEN; 78 mems.

Suomen Metsäteollisuuden Keskusliitto r.y. (Central Association of Finnish Forest Industries): Eteläesplanadi 2, 00130 Helsinki; tel. (90) 13261; telex 121823; fax (90) 174479; f. 1918; Chair. CARL G. BJÖRNBERG; Man. Dir JARL KÖHLER; mems: 70 companies in the forestry industry and the following sales or trade associations:

Converta (Finnish Paper and Board Converters' Association): Fabianinkatu 9, POB 35, 00131 Helsinki; tel. (90) 131711; telex 124622; fax (90) 650152; f. 1944; Man. Dir LEO MAMONTOFF; 8 mems.

Finnboard (Finnish Board Mills Association): Eteläesplanadi 2, POB 36, 00131 Helsinki; tel. (90) 13251; telex 121460; fax (90) 652934; f. 1943; Man. Dir MATTI LINDAHL; 12 mems.

Finncell (Finnish Pulp Exporters' Association): Eteläesplanadi 2, POB 60, 00101 Helsinki; tel. (90) 18051; telex 124459; fax (90) 1805372; f. 1918; Man. Dir T. NYKOPP; 8 mems.

Finnpap (Finnish Paper Mills' Association): Eteläesplanadi 2, POB 380, 00101 Helsinki; tel. (90) 13241; telex 124429; fax (90) 658949; f. 1918; marketing organization for 7 paper companies; Man. Dir and CEO THOMAS NYSTÉN; 7 mems.

Suomen Kuitulevy-yhdistys (Finnish Wood Fibre Panel Association—FFA): Opastinsilta 8B B, 00520 Helsinki; tel. (90) 141122; telex 124858; f. 1953, reorganized 1960; Man. Dir A. PENTINSAARI; 4 mems.

Suomen Lastulevy-yhdistys (Finnish Particle Board Association): Opastinsilta 8B B, 00520 Helsinki; tel. (90) 141122; telex 124858; fax (90) 1496590; Man. Dir PENTTI SAARRO; 3 mems.

Suomen Sahanomistajayhdistys (Finnish Sawmill Owners' Association): Fabianinkatu 29c, 00100 Helsinki; tel. (90) 661801; telex 121851; fax (90) 657053; f. 1895; Man. Dir PEKKA SNÄLL; 24 mems.

Suomen Vaneriyhdistys (Association of Finnish Plywood Industry): Opastinsilta 8B B, 00520 Helsinki; tel. (90) 141122; telex 124858; fax (90) 1496590; f. 1939; Man. Dir PENTTI SAARRO; 6 mems.

Suomen Osuuskauppojen Keskusliitto (SOKL) (Finnish Co-operative Union): Vilhonkatu 7, 00100 Helsinki; tel. (90) 1881; telex 124456; fax (90) 1882332; f. 1908; Chair. SEPPO TÖRMÄLÄ; 77 mems.

Suomen Teknillinen Kauppaliitto (Finnish Technical Traders Association): Helsinki; f. 1918; organization of the main importers dealing in iron, steel, and non-ferrous metals, machines and equipment, heavy chemicals and raw materials; Chair. K. KUOSMANEN; Man. Dir KLAUS VARTIOVAARA; 67 mems.

Svenska Lantbruksproducenternas Centralförbund (Union of Swedish Agricultural Producers): Fredriksgatan 61, 00100 Helsinki; fax (90) 6941358; f. 1945; Swedish-speaking producers; Chair. O. ROSENDAHL; 20,518 mems.

Teknisen Tukkukaupan Keskusliitto (TTK) (Central Federation of Technical Wholesale Traders): Mannerheimint 76B, Helsinki; fax (90) 407643; 10 branch asscns with 250 mems.

Tukkukaupan Keskusliitto (Federation of Finnish Wholesalers and Importers): Mannerheimint 76A, 00250 Helsinki; tel. (90) 441651; fax (90) 496142; f. 1988 to replace previous Association (f. 1920); Man. Dir GUY WIRES; 24 mem. asscns with over 800 firms.

Tuottajain Lihakeskuskunta (Farmers' Central Meat Administration): Vanha talvitie 5, 00500 Helsinki; tel. (90) 717911; telex 124813; f. 1936; Pres. VOITTO KOSKENMÄKI; 7 mem. co-operatives.

Valio Finnish Co-operative Dairies' Association: POB 390, 00101 Helsinki; tel. (90) 5681; telex 123-427; f. 1905; Man. Dir IIKKA HAKA; 134 mems (dairies).

EMPLOYERS' ORGANIZATIONS

Liiketyönantajain Keskusliitto (LTK) r.y. (Confederation of Service Industries): Eteläranta 10, 00130 Helsinki; tel. (90) 172831; fax (90) 655588; f. 1945; six mem. asscns consisting of about 7,100 enterprises with about 300,000 employees; Chair. EERO UTTER; Man. Dir JARMO PELLIKKA.

Suomen Työnantajain Keskusliitto (STK) (Finnish Employers' Confederation): Eteläranta 10, POB 30, 00131 Helsinki; tel. (90) 17281; telex 124635; f. 1907 to safeguard the interests of its member enterprises by negotiating and signing collective agreements and by influencing general decisions which affect business life; comprises 28 branch asscns consisting of about 6,300 enterprises employing about 625,000 employees. Chair. KRISTER AHLSTRÖM; Dir-Gen. TAPANI KAHRI.

Autoalan Työnantajaliitto r.y. (Federation of Motor Vehicle Trade Employers): Liisankatu 21B 11, 00170 Helsinki; tel. (90) 171410; Chair. ROLF EHRNROOTH; Man. Dir LEO GYLDÉN; 407 mems.

Autoliikenteen Työnantajaliitto r.y. (Employers' Federation of Road Transport): Nuijamiestentie 7A, 00400 Helsinki; tel. (90) 5885022; Chair. JUHANI HEIKKILÄ; Man. Dir HANNU PARVELA; 580 mems.

Autonrengasliitto r.y. (Tyre Federation): Nordenskiöldinkatu 6A 1, 00250 Helsinki; tel. (90) 492054; f. 1944; Chair. HEIKKI HELENIUS; Man. Dir AIMO WASENIUS; 50 mems, 16 assoc. mems.

Elintarviketeollisuuden Työnantajiliitto r.y. (Food Industry Employers' Association): Eteläranta 10, 00130 Helsinki; tel. (90) 172841; Chair. PETER FAZER; Man. Dir PEKKA HÄMÄLÄINEN; 462 mems.

Graafisen Teollisuuden Työnantajaliitto (Employers' Association of the Graphic Arts Industries): Lönnrotinkatu 11A, 00120 Helsinki; tel. (90) 602911; fax (90) 603527; Chair. JAAKKO RAURAMO; Man. Dir MATTI SUTINEN; 490 mems.

Kemianteollisuuden Työnantajalitto r.y. (Chemical Industry Employers' Association): Eteläranta 10, 00130 Helsinki; tel. (90) 172841; Chair. YRJÖ PESSI; Man. Dir MARTTI NISKANEN; 200 mems.

Kenkäteollisuuden Työnantajaliitto r.y. (Employers' Association of the Footwear Industry): Eteläranta 10, 00130 Helsinki; tel. (90) 172841; Chair. ESKO HEINO; Man. Dir JUHANI SALONIUS; 34 mems.

Konttorikoneliikkeiden Yhdistys r.y. (Association of Office Machine Traders): Mariankatu 26B 5, 00170 Helsinki; tel. (90) 656667; Chair. TOM HYNNINEN; Man. Dir KALLE-VEIKKO HAVAS; 133 mems.

Kultaseppien Työnantajaliitto r.y. (Employers' Association of Goldsmiths): Eteläranta 10, 00130 Helsinki; tel. (90) 172841; Chair. and Man. Dir ILKKA KUNNAS; 25 mems.

FINLAND

Directory

Metalliteollisuuden Työnantajaliitto (Metal Industries Employers' Association): Eteläranta 10, 00130 Helsinki; tel. (90) 19231; telex 124997; fax (90) 624462; f. 1903; Chair. REIJO KAUKONON; Man. Dir HARRI MALMBERG; 850 mems.

Metsäteollisuuden Työnantajaliitto (Employers' Association of Forest Industries): Fabianinkatu 9A, POB 5, 00131 Helsinki; tel. (90) 174877; telex 122986; fax (90) 657923; Chair. OLLI PAROLA; Man. Dir MAURI MOREN; 116 mems.

Nahkateollisuuden Työnantajaliitto r.y. (Employers' Association of the Leather Industry): Eteläranta 10, 00130 Helsinki; tel. (90) 172841; Chair. PERTTI HELLEMAA; Man. Dir JUHANI SALONIUS; 32 mems.

Puhelinlaitosten Työnantajaliitto (Employers' Association of Telephone Companies): Yrjönkatu 13A V, 00120 Helsinki; tel. (90) 642811; telex 124845; Chair. ERKKI RIPATTI; 51 mems.

Puusepänteollisuuden Liitto r.y. (Employers' Association of the Furniture and Joinery Industries): Fabianinkatu 9A, 00130 Helsinki; tel. (90) 174877; fax (90) 657923; f. 1917; Chair. HANNU ROINE; Man. Dir MARTTI UOTI; 125 mems.

Rannikko- ja Sisävesiliikenteen Työnantajaliitto (RASILA) r.y. (Employers' Federation of Coastal and Inland Waterways Transportation): see under Shipping.

Sähkö-ja telealan työnantajaliitto (Finnish Association of Electrical and Telecommunication Employers): Yrjönkatu 13A, 00120 Helsinki; tel. (90) 642811; telex 124845; fax (90) 644383; Chair. KALEVA NUMMINEN; Man. Dir MATTI HÖYSTI; 370 mems.

Suomen Kiinteistöliitto r.y. (Finnish Real-Estate Federation): Annankatu 24, 00100 Helsinki; tel. (90) 641331; f. 1907; Chair. KARI RAHKAMO; Man. Dir UKKO LAURILA; 17,000 mems.

Suomen Konsulttitoimistojen Liitto (SKOL) r.y. (Finnish Association of Consulting Firms—SKOL): Pohjantie 12A, 02100 Espoo; tel. (90) 460122; Chair. KALLE VARTOLA; Man. Dir TIMO MYLLYS; 200 mems.

Suomen Lasitus- ja Hiomoliitto r.y. (Finnish Glass Dealers' and Glaziers' Association): Eteläranta 10, 00130 Helsinki; tel. (90) 172841; telex 124665; fax (90) 179588; Chair. PEKKA RAITANIEMI; Dir RAIMO KILPIÄINEN; 153 mems.

Suomen Lastauttajain Liitto (SLL) r.y. (Federation of Finnish Master Stevedores): Köydenpunojankatu 8, 00180 Helsinki; tel. (90) 6949800; fax (90) 6944585; f. 1906; Chair. JUHANI FORSS; Man. Dir HARRI TUULENSU; 36 mems.

Suomen Rakennusteollisuusliitto r.y. (Federation of the Finnish Building Industry): Unioninkatu 14 VI, 00130 Helsinki; tel. (90) 12991; telex 125321; f. 1946; Chair. HANNO ISOTALO; Man. Dir MATTI LOUKOLA; 1,974 mems.

Suomen Tiiliteollisuusliitto r.y. (Finnish Brick Industry Association): Laturinkuja 2, 02600 Espoo; tel. (90) 519133; fax (90) 514017; Chair. LEO SEPPÄLÄ; Man. Dir JUKKA SUONIO; 13 mems.

Suomen Varustamoyhdistys r.y. (Finnish Shipowners' Association): see under Shipping.

Tekstiiliteollisuusliitto (Association of Textile Industries): Aleksis Kiven katu 10, 33211 Tampere; tel. (931) 32277; fax (931) 37457; f. 1905; Chair. AXEL CEDERCREUTZ; Man. Dir MATTI JÄRVENTIE; 155 mems.

Työnantajain Yleinen Ryhmä (Employers' General Group): Eteläranta 10, 00130 Helsinki; tel. (90) 172841; telex 124665; fax (90) 179588; Chair. GEORG EHRNROOTH; Gen. Dir JUHANI SALONIUS; 933 mems.

Vaatetusteollisuuden Työnantajaliitto r.y. (Clothing Industry Employers' Federation): Eteläranta 10, 00130 Helsinki; tel. (90) 172841; Chair. SIMO HIILAMO; Man. Dir JUHANI SALONIUS; 129 mems.

Voimalaitosrakentajain Liitto (Association of Power Plant Builders): Yrjönkatu 13A V, 00120 Helsinki; tel. (90) 642811; telex 124845; Chair. ERKKI LAASKO; Man. Dir MATTI HÖYSTI; 18 mems.

Voimalaitosten Työnantajaliitto r.y. (Employers' Association of Electrical Contractors): Yrjönkatu 13A V, 00120 Helsinki; tel. (90) 642811; telex 124845; f. 1945; Chair. KALEVI NUMMINEN; Man. Dir MATTI HÖYSTI; 93 mems.

TRADE UNIONS

Suomen Ammattiliittojen Keskusjärjestö (SAK) r.y. (Central Organization of Finnish Trade Unions): Siltasaarenkatu 3A, 00530 Helsinki; tel. (90) 77211; telex 122346; fax (90) 7721447; f. 1907; 24 affiliated unions; 1,092,405 mems (1988); Pres. LAURI IHALAINEN; Vice-Pres AARNO AITAMURTO, RAIMO KANTOLA

Principal affiliated unions (membership of over 5,000):

Auto- ja Kuljetusalan Työntekijäliitto (AKT) r.y. (Transport Workers): Haapaniemenkatu 7-9B, 00530 Helsinki; tel. (90) 70911; fax (90) 739287; f. 1948; Pres. RISTO KUISMA; Secs KAUKO LEHIKOINEN, LEO ROPPOLA; 45,225 mems.

Hotelli- ja Ravintolahenkilökunnan Liitto (HRHL) r.y. (Hotel and Restaurant Workers): Toinen Linja 3, 00530 Helsinki; tel. (90) 77561; fax (90) 7756223; f. 1933; Pres. MATTI HAAPAKOSKI; Sec. JORMA KALLIO; 50,882 mems.

Kemian Työntekijäin Liitto r.y. (Chemical Workers): Haapaniemenkatu 7-9B, POB 324, 00530 Helsinki; tel. (90) 70911; fax (90) 7538040; f. 1970; Pres. HEIKKI POHJA; Sec. RALF SUND; 22,651 mems.

Kiinteistötyöntekijäin Liitto r.y. (Caretakers): Viherniemenkatu 5A, 00530 Helsinki; tel. (90) 750075; fax (90) 761427; f. 1948; Pres. MATTI SIKANEN; Sec. TAUNO ROSTEN; 10,763 mems.

Kumi- ja Nahkatyöväen Liitto (KNL) r.y. (Rubber and Leather Workers): Siltasaarenkatu 4, 00530 Helsinki; tel. (90) 750044; fax (90) 714989; f. 1897; Pres. HILKKA HÄKKILÄ; Sec. KALEVI URPELAINEN; 11,000 mems.

Kunnallisten työntekijäin ja viranhaltijain liitto (KTV) r.y. (Municipal Workers and Employees): Kolmas linja 4, 00530 Helsinki; tel. (90) 77031; fax (90) 7703397; f. 1931; Pres. JOUNI RISKILÖ; 200,278 mems.

Lasi- ja Posliinityöväen Liitto r.y. (Glass and Porcelain Workers): Haapaniemenkatu 7-9B, POB 319, 00531 Helsinki; tel. (90) 70911; fax (90) 7091215; f. 1906; Pres. RISTO SAINIO; Sec. TOIVO PARTANEN; 5,130 mems.

Liikealan ammattiliitto r.y. (Commercial Employees): Paasivuorenkatu 4-6, 00530 Helsinki; tel. (90) 77571; fax (90) 7011119; f. 1987; Pres. MAJ-LEN REMAHL; Secs NILS KOMI, JARMO KOSKI; 117,213 mems.

Liikelaitosunioni (Employees in State-owned Business Enterprises): Ratamestarinkatu 11B, 00520 Helsinki; tel. (90) 1551; f. 1990; Chair. HEIKKI MÄKINEN; 14,000 mems.

Maaseututyöväen Liitto r.y. (Forest and Agricultural Workers): Haapaniemenkatu 7-9B, 00531 Helsinki; tel. (90) 70911; fax (90) 7532506; f. 1945; Pres. RAIMO LINDLÖF; Secs HANNU HEDEMÄKI, KALEVI HÄNNINEN; 22,000 mems.

Metallityöväen Liitto r.y. (Metalworkers): Siltasaarenkatu 3A, 00530 Helsinki; tel. (90) 77071; telex 122571; fax (90) 7532506; f. 1899; Pres. PER-ERIK LUNDH; Secs OSMO ISOVIITA, VEIKKO LEHTONEN; 151,382 mems.

Paperiliitto r.y. (Paperworkers): Pl.326, 00531 Helsinki; tel. (90) 70891; fax (90) 701-2279; f. 1906; Pres. ANTERO MÄKI; Gen. Sec. ARTTURI PENNANEN; 49,611 mems.

Puutyöväen Liitto r.y. (Woodworkers): Haapaniemenkatu 7-9B, 00530 Helsinki; tel. (90) 70911; fax (90) 761160; f. 1973; Pres. HEIKKI PELTONEN; Sec. KALEVI HÖLTTÄ; 40,000 mems.

Rakennustyöläisten Liitto r.y. (Construction Workers): Siltasaarenkatu 4, 00530 Helsinki; tel. (90) 77021; telex 121394; fax (90) 7702241; f. 1930; Pres. PEKKA HYNÖNEN; Sec. HANNU ALANOJA; 98,285 mems.

Suomen Elintarviketyöläisten Liitto r.y. (Food Workers): Siltasaarenkatu 6, POB 213, 00531 Helsinki; tel. (90) 393881; fax (90) 712059; f. 1905; Pres. JARL SUND; Sec. ARTO TALASMÄKI; 39,404 mems.

Suomen Kirjatyöntekijäin Liitto r.y. (Bookworkers): Ratakatu 9, 00120 Helsinki; tel. (90) 649717; fax (90) 604461; f. 1894; Pres. PENTTI LEVO; Sec. PEKKA LAHTINEN; 28,916 mems.

Suomen Merimies-Unioni r.y. (Seamen): Siltasaarenkatu 6, 00530 Helsinki; tel. (90) 716177; telex 124795; fax (90) 7016253; f. 1916; Pres. REIJO ANTTILA; Sec. PER-ERIK NELIN; 9,721 mems.

Suomen Sähköalantyöntekijäin Liitto r.y. (Electricity Workers): Aleksanterinkatu 15, 33101 Tampere; tel. (931) 520111; fax (931) 520210; f. 1955; Pres. SEPPO SALISMA; Sec REIJO TIHINEN; 30,738 mems.

Tekstiili- ja Vaatetustyöväen Liitto r.y. (Textile and Garment Workers): POB 87, 33101 Tampere; tel. (931) 593111; fax (931) 593343; f. 1970; Pres. TUULIKKI KANNISTO; Secs PIRKKO OKSA, TOIVO KERÄNEN; 31,282 mems.

Virkamiesten ja Työntekijäin Yhteisjärjestö (VTY) r.y. (Joint Organization of Civil Servants and Workers): Haapaniemenkatu 7-9B, 00530 Helsinki; tel. (90) 70911; fax (90) 739513; f. 1946; Pres. RAIMO RANNISTO; Sec.-Gen. PERTTI AHONEN; 101,832 mems.

Toimihenkilö- ja Virkamiesjärjestöjen Keskusliitto (TVK) r.y. (Confederation of Salaried Employees): Asemamiehenkatu 4, 00520 Helsinki; tel. (90) 1551; telex 122505; fax (90) 143058; f. 1922; 15 affiliates; Chair MATTI KINNUNEN, RIITTA PRUSTI; approx. 390,000 mems.

FINLAND

Directory

Principal affiliated unions (membership of over 5,000):

Auto- ja Konekaupan Toimihenkilöliitto (Car and Machine Commerce Employees): Hämeentie 10A, 00530 Helsinki; tel. (90) 716433; f. 1985; Chair. ERKKI MÄKELÄ; 5,500 mems.

Erityisalojen Toimihenkilöliitto (ERTO) (Special Service and Clerical Employees): Asemamiehenkatu 2, 00520 Helsinki; tel. (90) 1551; f. 1968; Chair. MATTI HELLSTEN; 11,500 mems.

Kunnallisvirkamiesliitto r.y. (KVL) (Municipal Officers): Asemamiehenkatu 4, 00520 Helsinki; tel. (90) 1551; f. 1918; Chair. TAISTO MURSULA; 65,000 mems.

Pankkitoimihenkilöliitto (Bank Employees): Ratamestarinkatu 12, 00520 Helsinki; tel. (90) 141066; fax (90) 141460; f. 1931; Pres. CHRISTINA HOLMLUND; Sec.-Gen. RAIMO POHJAVÄRE; 40,500 mems.

Poliisijärjestöjen Liitto (Police): Haapaniemenkatu 7-9B, 00520 Helsinki; tel. (90) 1551; f. 1990; Chair. TIMO MIKKOLA; 11,000 mems.

Suomen Perushoitajaliitto (Enrolled Nurses): Asemamiehenkatu 2, 00520 Helsinki; tel. (90) 141833; f. 1948; Chair. SALME PIHL; 31,000 mems.

Suomen Teollisuustoimihenkilöiden Liitto (Salaried Employees in Industry): Asemamiehenkatu 4, 00520 Helsinki; tel. (90) 1551; f. 1917; Pres. TUULIKKI VÄLINIEMI; Gen. Sec. TARMO HYVÄRINEN; 45,500 mems.

Terveydenhuoltoalan ammattijärjestö Tehy (Health Professionals): Asemamiehenkatu 4, 00520 Helsinki; tel. (90) 1551; telex 122505; fax (90) 1483038; f. 1982; Chair. RAIJA HUKKAMÄKI; 83,000 mems.

Vakuutusväen Liitto (Insurance Employees): Asemamiehenkatu 2, 00520 Helsinki; tel. (90) 1551; telex 122505; f. 1945; Chair. JORMA VIRPIÖ; Exec. Dir PEKKA PORTTILA; 10,000 mems.

Valtion Laitosten ja Yhtiöiden Toimihenkilöliitto (Employees in State-owned Institutions and Companies): Topparikuja 7, 00520 Helsinki; f. 1945; Chair. JARMO RANTANEN; 14,000 mems.

Virkamiesliitto (Civil Servants): Ratamestarinkatu 11, 00520 Helsinki; tel. (90) 1551; f. 1917; Chair. KEIJO RANTALA; 42,000 mems.

STATE-OWNED INDUSTRIES

It has never been government policy in Finland to nationalize industries. Occasionally, however, it has been found necessary for various reasons to give substantial state aid in setting up a company and the State has retained a majority of shares in these companies. All are administered as limited companies, the State being represented on the Board of Management and at the General Meeting of Shareholders by either the relevant Minister or an official of the relevant Ministry.

Alko Ltd: Salmisaarenranta 7, POB 350, 00101 Helsinki; tel. (90) 13311; telex 121045; f. 1932; production, import, export and sale of alcoholic beverages and spirits; has monopoly of retail sale of all alcoholic beverages except medium beer; 99.9% state-owned; Chair. of Board of Dirs HEIKKI KOSKI; 2,900 employees.

Enso-Gutzeit Oy: Kanavaranta 1, 00160 Helsinki; tel. (90) 16291; telex 124438; fax (90) 1629471; f. 1872; wood processing, paper, forestry, acquiring and installing hydro-electric power; 50.3% state-owned; Chair. of Board of Dirs PENTTI SALMI; Pres. and Chief Exec. JUKKA HÄRMÄLÄ; 17,915 employees.

Finnair Oy: see Civil Aviation.

Imatran Voima Oy: POB 138, 00101 Helsinki; tel. (90) 5081; telex 124608; fax (90) 6946654; f. 1932; electric power, including nuclear energy, district heating; 95.6% state-owned; Pres. KALEVI NUMMINEN; Chair. of Admin. Council TAPANI MÖRTTINEN; 4,700 employees.

Kemijoki Oy: POB 457, 00101 Helsinki; tel. (90) 6944811; telex 124608; f. 1954; electric power; 77.08% state-owned; Chair. of Supervisory Board PAAVO VÄYRYNEN; Chair. of Board of Management PERTTI KIVINEN; 468 employees.

Kemira Group: Porkkalankatu 3, POB 330, 00101 Helsinki; tel. (90) 13211; telex 121191; fax (90) 6946167; f. 1920; 15 plants in Finland, 18 overseas; fertilizers, agricultural and industrial chemicals, organic fine chemicals, biotechnical products, explosives, safety equipment, man-made fibres, paints, filters and autocatalysts; Chair. of Supervisory Board HEIKKI PERHO; Chair. of Board of Management YRJÖ PESSI; 16,000 employees.

Neste Oy: Keilaniemi, 02150 Espoo; tel. (90) 4501; telex 124641; f. 1948; oil refining, petrochemicals, plastics, industrial chemicals and lubricants, shipping, natural gas, batteries; 97.96% state-owned; (see also under Shipping); Chair. of Supervisory Board ULF SUNDQVIST; Chair. of Board of Management JAAKKO IHAMUOTILA; 5,370 employees.

Outokumpu Oy: POB 280, 00101 Helsinki; tel. (90) 4211; telex 124441; fax (90) 4213888; f. 1932; exploration, mining, mineral processing, metal refining and processing, equipment manufacture, engineering contracting; 57% state-owned; Chair. of Supervisory Board PAAVO LIPPONEN; Chair. of Board of Dirs and Pres. PERTTI VOUTILAINEN; 18,000 employees.

Rautaruukki Oy: Kiilakiventie 1, POB 217, 90101 Oulu; tel. (81) 327711; telex 32109; fax (81) 327506; f. 1960; steel processing; 87% state-owned; Chair. of Supervisory Board EINO SIURUAINEN; Chair. of Board of Management, Pres. MIKKO KIVIMÄKI; 9,000 employees.

Oy Sisu-Auto Ab: Ristipellontie 19, 00390 Helsinki; tel. (90) 547841; telex 121245; fax (90) 541488; f. as private company in 1931; in 1975 the State bought 70% of the shares; 99.8% state-owned (1989); manufacture, marketing and maintenance of trucks, terminal tractors and defence vehicles; Chair. of Supervisory Board MATTI LUTTINEN; Chair. of Board of Management and Chief Exec. JORMA S. JERKKU; 1,500 employees.

Valmet Corporation: Punanotkonkatu 2, POB 155, 00131 Helsinki; tel. (90) 13291; telex 124427; fax (90) 179677; f. 1946; engineering, automation; 79.8% state-owned; Chair. of Admin. Council HARRI HOLKERI; Chair. of Board of Dirs MATTI KANKAANPÄÄ; 19,200 employees.

Valvilla Oy: POB 108, 20101 Turku; telex 62156; f. 1978; wool and cotton spinning, weaving and sales; 99.4% state-owned; Chair. of Supervisory Board BROR WAHLROOS; Chair. of Board of Management MATTI VAINIO; 630 employees.

Veitsiluoto Oy: 94830 Kemi; tel. (980) 6988141; fax (980) 698 814890; f. 1932; pulp and paper industry, chemical industry; 88.8% state-owned; Chair. of Supervisory Board JAAKKO PAJULA; Chair. of Board of Management NIILO PELLONMAA; 4,970 employees.

TRADE FAIRS

Osuuskunta Suomen Messut (Finnish Fair Corporation): Helsinki Fair Centre, POB 21, 00521 Helsinki; tel. (90) 15091; telex 121119; fax (90) 142358; f. 1919; principal annual events: Helsinki International Boat Show, Medicine, Caravan, Skiexpo (skiing and winter tourism), Matka (Finnish International Travel Fair), Finnish Chemical Congress; biennial events: Business Machines and Equipment, Elkom (professional electronics), FinnConsum (Helsinki International Trade Fair), Habitare (furniture and interior decoration), FinnBuild (Helsinki International Building Fair); triennial: FinnTec (Helsinki International Technical Fair), PacTec (packaging), FinnTexMa (textile industry machines and accessories), Transportation; every 4 years: Hepac (heating, plumbing and air-conditioning), Eltek (electrical technology, household technology); Chair. of Supervisory Board RAIMO ILASKIVI; Chair. of Admin. Board KARI O. SOHLBERG; Man. Dir MATTI HURME.

Transport

RAILWAYS

There are 5,869 km of railways, providing internal services and connections with Sweden and the USSR, and 1,636 km of track are electrified. An underground railway service has been provided by Helsinki City Transport since 1982.

Karhula Railway: Ratakatu 8, 48600 Karhula; tel. (952) 298221; telex 53170; fax (952) 298225; f. 1937; goods transport; Man. PERTTI HONKALA; Man. of Traffic OLLI KOKKOMÄKI.

Valtionrautatiet (VR) (State Railways): Finnish State Railways' Headquarters, Vilhonkatu 13, POB 488, 00101 Helsinki; tel. (90) 7071; telex 301151; fax (90) 7073700; began operating 1862; operates 5,863 km of railways; wide gauge (1,524 mm); privately-owned total 6 km; 1,636 km of route are electrified; Dir-Gen. EINO SAARINEN; Dep. Dir-Gen. PANU HAAPALA.

ROADS

At 31 December 1989 there were 76,717 km of public roads, of which 215 km were motorways, 11,494 km other main roads (I and II class), 29,373 km other highways and 35,378 km local roads (excluding urban streets). In addition, there are about 56,779 km of private roads, the maintenance of which is subsidized.

Tiehallitus (National Road Administration): POB 33, 00521 Helsinki; tel. (90) 1541; telex 124589; fax (90) 1542698; f. 1799; central office and 13 road and waterways districts; in charge of developing road traffic, including planning, constructing and maintaining roads, bridges and ferries; Dir-Gen. JOUKO LOIKKANEN.

INLAND WATERWAYS

Lakes cover 31,500 sq km. The inland waterway system comprises 6,100 km of buoyed-out channels, 40 open canals and 25 lock canals. The total length of canals is 76 km. In 1989 the canals carried about 6.6m. metric tons of goods and 297,000 passengers.

FINLAND

Directory

In 1968 the southern part of the Saimaa Canal, which was leased to Finland by the USSR, was opened for vessels. In 1986 a total of 1,464,000 tons of goods were transported along the canal.

Suomen Uittajainyhdistys r.y. (Association of Finnish Floaters): POB 33, 70501 Kuopio; tel. (971) 116701; 332 mems; Chair. KAARLO PALMROTH; Sec. ILKKA PURHONEN.

SHIPPING

The chief port of export is Kotka, where construction of a new deep harbour was due to start in the late 1980s; the main port of import is Helsinki, which has five specialized harbours. The West Harbour handles most of the transatlantic traffic, the East Harbour coastal and North Sea freight, and the South Harbour passenger traffic. North Harbour deals only in local launch traffic. Sörnäinen is the timber and coal harbour; Herttoniemi specializes in petroleum. Other important international ports are Turku (Åbo), Rauma and Hamina. The ports handled 45.1m. metric tons of cargo in 1989.

Associations

Rannikko- ja Sisävesiliikenteen Työnantajaliitto (RASILA) r.y. (Employers' Federation of Coastal and Inland Waterways Transportation): Satamakatu 4A, 00160 Helsinki; tel. (90) 170485; telex 122751; fax (90) 669251; branch of STK (see Trade and Industry); Chair. TIMO SAARINEN; Man. Dir HENRIK LÖNNQVIST; 11 mems.

Suomen Varustamoyhdistys (Finnish Shipowners' Association): Satamakatu 4, POB 155, 00161 Helsinki; tel. (90) 170401; telex 122751; fax (90) 669251; f. 1932; Chair. RAIMO ROOS; Man. Dir PER FORSSKÅHL; 12 mems.

Principal Companies

Oy Bore Line Ab: Pohjoisranta 2D, Norra kajen, POB 151, 00171 Helsinki; tel. (90) 135311; telex 126023; f. 1897; routes: Baltic and North Sea cargo services; Man. Dir JARMO SALONEN.

Effoa—Finland Steamship Co Ltd: POB 290, 00130 Helsinki; tel. (90) 179933; telex 121410; fax (90) 176623; f. 1883; to merge operations with Johnsson Line (Sweden) in 1989; liner and contract services: see Finncarriers; passenger services operated by Elf John International; Man. Dir ROBERT G. EHRNROOTH; fully-owned: 2 cargo vessels, 3 cruise ferries and holdings in six cruise ferries.

Etelä-Suomen Laiva Oy: Suolakivenkatu 10, 00810 Helsinki; tel. (90) 7595777; telex 124453; fax (90) 787315; world-wide tramp services; Man. Dir H. HÖCKERT; 4 cargo vessels.

Oy Finnlines Ltd: Lönnrotinkatu 21, POB 406, 00121 Helsinki; tel. (90) 16221; telex 12441; f. 1947; cargo traffic, chartering; ship management, marine consulting; member of freight pools; Pres. RAIMO ROOS; 34 cargo vessels (10 general cargo carriers, 9 barges, 9 roll-on roll-off ships, 2 pushers, 2 bulk carriers, 1 ore carrier, 1 car/passenger ferry).

Oy Finncarriers Ab: Eteläranta 8, POB 185, 00130 Helsinki; tel. (90) 1781; telex 122822; f. 1975; liner and contract services between Finland and other European countries, the Mediterranean, North Africa, the Middle East and South and Central America; Man. Dir BO ÅBERG.

Neste Oy: Keilaniemi, 02150 Espoo 15; tel. (90) 4501; telex 124641; f. 1948; (see also under State-owned Industries); Pres. JAAKKO IHAMUOTILA; Corporate Vice-Pres. Shipping RAIMO ROOS; 17 tankers, 3 LPG carriers, 4 tugs; 942,241 dwt.

The Nielsen Group: Lönnrotinkatu 18, 00120 Helsinki; tel. (90) 17291; telex 121377; fax (90) 1729256; f. 1923; managing owners for about 119,815 dwt tanker and dry cargo; shipbrokers, liner- and forwarding-agents; Man. BERNDT NIELSEN.

CIVIL AVIATION

An international airport is situated at Helsinki-Vantaa, 19 km from Helsinki. Internal flights connect Helsinki to Enontekiö, Ivalo, Joensuu, Jyväskylä, Kajaani, Kemi, Kittilä, Kokkola/Pietarsaari, Kuopio, Kuusamo, Lappeenranta, Mariehamn, Mikkeli, Oulu, Pori, Rovaniemi, Savonlinna, Tampere, Turku, Vaasa and Varkaus.

In 1989, 10.2m. passengers passed through Finnish airports.

Finnair Oy: Head Office: Dagmarinkatu 4, 00100 Helsinki; tel. (90) 81881; telex 124946; f. 1923; 70% state-owned; 22 domestic services and services to 38 cities in Europe, the Middle East, South-East Asia and North America; Pres. ANTTI POTILA; fleet of 5 ATR 72, 17 DC-9, 5 DC-10, 3 MD-87, 9 MD-82/83, 2 Airbus A300B4-203, 6 Saab 340, 1 B737.

Finnaviation Oy (FA): POB 39, 01531 Vantaa; tel. (90) 870941; telex 122635; fax (90) 8709588; f. 1979; 90% owned by Finnair Oy; scheduled domestic services, also to Göteborg, Malmö and Stockholm in Sweden and Copenhagen in Denmark; Man. Dir PAAVO TURTIAINEN; fleet of 6 SF-340.

Karair Oy: 01530 Vantaa; tel. (90) 81851; telex 124769; fax (90) 8701906; f. 1957; scheduled domestic routes; Man. Dir PEKKA VÄLIMÄKI; fleet of 1 DHC-6-300 Twin Otter, 5 ATR 72.

Tourism

Europe's largest inland water system, vast forests, magnificent scenery and the possibility of holiday seclusion are Finland's main attractions. Most visitors come from other Nordic countries, Germany and the USSR. There were 2,517,300 tourist arrivals (including excursionists) in 1989, and tourist receipts totalled 3,729m. markkaa in 1987.

Matkailun edistämiskeskus (Tourist Board): Asemapäällikönkatu 12B, 00520 Helsinki; tel. (90) 144511; telex 122690; f. 1973; Chair. KALERVO HENTILÄ; Dir BENGT PIHLSTRÖM.

Atomic Energy

At December 1989 there were 4 nuclear power reactors in operation, with a total capacity of 2,310 MW.

Atomic Energy Commission: Ministry of Trade and Industry, Aleksanterinkatu 10, 00170 Helsinki; tel. (90) 1605226; telex 125452; fax (90) 14884333; advises the Government; the Ministry of Trade and Industry is the administrative and licensing authority; Chair. Prof. JORMA ROUTTI; Sec.-Gen. S. IMMONEN; Admin. Sec. M. HOVI.

Finnish Centre for Radiation and Nuclear Safety: POB 268, 00101 Helsinki; tel. (90) 70821; telex 122691; fax (90) 7082210; f. 1958; responsible for the supervision of radiation protection and nuclear safety.

Finnish Nuclear Society: c/o Technical Research Centre of Finland, Nuclear Engineering Laboratory, Lönnrotinkatu 37, 00180 Helsinki; tel. (90) 648931; telex 122972.

Lappeenranta University of Technology: Dept of Energy Technology, POB 20, 53851 Lappeenranta; tel. (953) 5711; telex 58290; fax (953) 5712799; f. 1969.

Technical Research Centre of Finland: Vuorimiehentie 5, 02150 Espoo; tel. (90) 4561; telex 122972; fax (90) 460419; six divisions.

Teknillinen korkeakoulu (Helsinki University of Technology): Department of Technical Physics, 02150 Espoo; tel. (90) 4511; telex 125161; fax (90) 4513195; the Department provides engineering education in experimental and theoretical solid-state and atomic physics, semiconductor physics and technology, optoelectronics, materials science, nuclear engineering and energy technology, biophysics and medical engineering, optics and laser technology; Dir Dr R. SALOMAA, Dep. Dir Dr P. HAUTOJÄRVI.

Imatran Voima Oy: see State-Owned Industries.

Teollisuuden Voima Oy (Industrial Power Co Ltd): Fredrikinkatu 51–53, 00100 Helsinki; tel. (90) 605022; telex 122065; fax (90) 605135.

FINNISH EXTERNAL TERRITORY

THE ÅLAND ISLANDS

Introductory Survey

Location, Language, Religion, Flag, Capital

The Åland Islands (Ahvenanmaa) are a group of 6,554 islands (of which some 50 are inhabited) in the Gulf of Bothnia, between Finland and Sweden. About 95% of the inhabitants are Swedish-speaking; the majority profess Christianity and belong to the Evangelical Lutheran Church of Finland. The flag displays a red cross, bordered with yellow, on a blue background, the upright of the cross being to the left of centre. The capital is Mariehamn (Maarianhamina), which is situated on Åland, the largest island in the group.

History and Government

For geographical and economic reasons, the Åland Islands were traditionally associated closely with Sweden. In 1809, when Sweden was forced to cede Finland to Russia, the islands were incorporated into the Finnish Grand Duchy. However, following Finland's declaration of independence from the Russian Empire, in 1917, the Ålanders demanded the right to self-determination and sought to be reunited with Sweden. Their demands were supported by the Swedish Government and people. In 1920 Finland granted the islands autonomy but refused to acknowledge their secession, and in 1921 the Åland question was referred to the League of Nations. In June the League granted Finland sovereignty over the islands, while directing that certain conditions pertaining to national identity be included in the autonomy legislation offered by Finland and that the islands should be a neutral and non-fortified region. Elections were held in accordance with the new legislation, and the new provincial parliament (Landsting) held its first plenary session on 9 June 1922.

The revised Autonomy Act of 1951 provides for independent rights of legislation in internal affairs and for autonomous control over the islands' economy. This Act cannot be amended or repealed by the Finnish Eduskunta without the consent of the Åland Landsting. At a general election to the Landsting, held on 18–19 October 1987, the Centre Party secured nine of the 30 seats, and the Liberal Party won eight. The Moderates and the Social Democrats won five and four seats respectively, while the Green Party and the Independents each won two.

In 1988 constitutional reform introduced the principle of a majority parliamentary government. Previously the executive council (Landskapsstyrelse) of the province consisted of the six members of the Landsting who had received the most votes from the 30-member parliament. Thus, any party with at least five members in the Landsting could secure a representative on the Landskapsstyrelse. From April 1988, however, this system was to function only if a majority government could not be formed by the Lantrådskandidat, the member of the Landsting nominated to conduct negotiations. This nominee must first try to form a government consisting of representatives from all the larger parties, before proceeding to an attempt to form a majority coalition.

Following these reforms, the first formal parliamentary government and opposition were established. The governing coalition consisted of the three largest parties in the Landsting (the Centre Party, the Liberals and the Moderates), which together held 22 seats in the legislature.

Economic Affairs

In 1985 the gross domestic product (GDP) of the Åland Islands, measured at current prices, was 1,890.4m. marks.

Agriculture, fishing and shipping employed about 60% of the labour force in 1960. Forests cover most of the islands, and only 7% of the total land area is arable. The principal crops are cereals, onions, cucumbers and fruit. Dairy-farming and sheep-rearing are also important.

The budget surplus for 1988 was 369,000 marks.

Since 1960 the economy of the islands has expanded and diversified. Fishing has declined as a source of income, and shipping, trade and tourism have become the dominant economic sectors. The political autonomy of the islands and their strategic location between Sweden and Finland have contributed to an expanding banking and finance sector.

Education and Social Welfare

The education system is similar to that of Finland, except that Swedish is the language of instruction. In 1985 government medical services included two hospitals, with a total of 240 beds, and 34 physicians.

Statistical Survey

Source: Ålands Landsting, POB 69, 22101 Mariehamn; tel. (928) 25000; fax (928) 13302.

AREA, POPULATION AND DENSITY

Area: 1,552 sq km (599 sq miles), of which 25 sq km (9.7 sq miles) is inland waters.

Population (estimate, 25 December 1989): 24,167.

Density (1989): 15.6 per sq km.

Births and Deaths (1988): Registered live births 348 (birth rate 14.5 per 1,000); Deaths 218 (death rate 9.1 per 1,000).

Labour Force (census of 17 November 1985): Males 6,299; Females 5,345; Total 11,644.

FINANCE

Currency: Finnish currency: 100 penni (penniä) = 1 mark (markka).

Government Accounts ('000 marks, 1988): Revenue 517,508; Expenditure 517,139.

Cost of Living (consumer price index; base: 1985 = 100): 102.2 in 1986; 106.1 in 1987; 111.8 in 1988.

Gross Domestic Product (million marks at current prices): 1,519.9 in 1983; 1,621.8 in 1984; 1,890.4 in 1985.

EXTERNAL TRADE

1984 (million marks): Imports 1,433.9; Exports 967.9.

TRANSPORT

Shipping (1987): Merchant fleet 40 vessels; total displacement 159,000 grt (Source: *Yearbook of Nordic Statistics*).

TOURISM

Tourist Arrivals (1988): 1,281,961.

Directory

Government and Legislature

The legislative body is the Landsting, comprising 30 members, elected every four years on a basis of proportional representation. All Ålanders over the age of 18 years resident in the islands have the right to vote. An executive council (Landskapsstyrelse) is either formed by parties with the support of a majority in the Landsting, or it is directly elected by the Landsting. The Provincial Governor (Lantråd), is Chairman of the Landskapsstyrelse and is appointed by the President of Finland after consultation with the Speaker (Talman) of the Åland Landsting. The President has the right to veto Landsting decisions only when the Landsting exceeds its legislative competence, or when there is a threat to the security of the country.

LANDSKAPSSTYRELSE
(January 1991)

Governor (Lantråd): John Sune Eriksson.
Deputy Governor: May Valborg Flodin.
Members: Göran Bengtz, Holger Eriksson, Karl-Göran Eriksson, Ragnar Erlandsson, Magnus Lundberg.

The governing coalition comprises members of the Centre Party, the Liberal Party and the Moderate Party.

LANDSTING

Speaker (Talman): Sven Olof Jansson.
First Deputy Speaker: Karl-Gunnar Fagerholm.

FINNISH EXTERNAL TERRITORY

The Åland Islands

Second Deputy Speaker: JAN-ERIK H. T. LINDFORS.

Election, 18–19 October 1987

	Seats
Åländsk Center (Centre Party)	9
Liberalerna på Åland (Liberal Party)	8*
Frisinnad samverkan (Moderate Party)	5*
Ålands socialdemokrater (Social Democratic Party)	4†
Gröna på Åland (Green Party)	2†
Independents	2
Total	**30**

* A Liberal member subsequently joined the Moderate Party.
† A Green member subsequently joined the Social Democratic Party.

Political Organizations

Åländsk Center (Centre Party): Ålands Landsting, POB 69, 22101 Mariehamn; Chair. RAGNAR ERLANDSSON; Leader ANDERS ERIKSSON; Sec.-Gen. MARIANNE GRÖNHOLM.

Ålands socialdemokrater (Social Democratic Party): Ålands Landsting, POB 69, 22101 Mariehamn; Chair. LASSE WIKLÖF; Leader BARBO SUNDBACK; Sec.-Gen. OLA ANDERSSON.

Frisinnad samverkan (Moderate Party): Ålands Landsting, POB 69, 22101 Mariehamn; tel. (928) 25000; fax (928) 11155; Chair. NORAH LINDHOLM; Leader ROGER JANSSON; Sec.-Gen. JENS BOMAN.

Gröna på Åland (Green Party): 13 Mariegatan, 22100 Mariehamn; tel. (928) 11528; f. 1987; Chair. and Leader CHRISTINA HEDMAN-JAAKKOLA.

The Independents: Cityjuristen Ab, Torggatan 9B, 22100 Mariehamn; tel. (928) 17200; Chair. and Leader BERT HAGGBLOM.

Liberalerna på Åland (Liberal Party): Ålands Landsting, POB 69, 22101 Mariehamn; Chair. GUNNEVI NORDMAN; Leader KARL-GUNNAR FAGERHOLM; Sec.-Gen. LISBETH ERIKSSON.

The Press

Läsarägda Nya Åland: POB 21, 22101 Mariehamn; tel. (928) 23444; 3 a week; circ. 7,874.

Tidningen Åland: POB 50, 22101 Mariehamn; tel. (928) 26026; 5 a week; circ. 11,326.

Radio and Television

Radio Åland: POB 46, 22101 Mariehamn; tel. (928) 26060; broadcasts 10 hours a week.

Finance

BANKS

(cap. = capital; res = reserves; dep. = deposits; m. = million; amounts in marks; brs = branches)

Ålandsbanken Ab (Bank of Åland Ltd): Nygatan 2, 22100 Mariehamn; tel. (928) 29011; telex 63157; fax (928) 29228; f. 1919; cap. and res 309.4m., dep. 2,271.2m. (Dec. 1989); Chair. FOLKE WOIVALIN; Chief Gen. Man. FOLKE HUSELL; 21 brs.

Ålands Hypoteksbank Ab: Nygatan 2, 22100 Mariehamn; tel. (928) 29011; telex 63119; f. 1986; cap. and res 5m. (Dec. 1987); Chair. GÖRAN FAGERLUND; Chief Man. Dir LARS DONNER.

Ålands Sparbank: POB 7, 22101 Mariehamn; tel. (928) 16200; telex 63154; Dirs ERLING GUSTAVSSON, ERIK SUNDBERG, JAN-ERIK RASK.

Andelsbanken för Åland: POB 34, 22101 Mariehamn; tel. (928) 26000; Dirs HÅKAN CLEMES, ROLAND KARLSSON.

Lappo Andelsbank: 22840 Lappo; tel. (928) 56621; Dir TORSTEN NORDBERG.

INSURANCE

Alandia Group: Ålandsvägen 31, 22100 Mariehamn; tel. (928) 29000; telex 63117; fax (928) 12290; f. 1938; life, non-life and marine; comprises three subsidiaries; Gen. Man. JOHAN DAHLMAN.

Ålands Ömsesidiga Försäkringsbolag: Köpmansgatan 6, POB 64, 22101 Mariehamn; tel. (928) 15100; telex 63191; f. 1866; property; subsidiary: Hamnia Reinsurance; Man. Dir BJARNE OLOFSSON.

Trade and Industry

CHAMBER OF COMMERCE

Ålands Handelskammare: Nygatan 9, 22100 Mariehamn; tel. (928) 29029; f. 1945; brs in Helsinki and Stockholm; Chair. SVEN-HARRY BOMAN; Man. Dir HARRY JANSSON.

EMPLOYERS' ORGANIZATIONS

Ålands arbetsgivareförening (Åland Employers' Asscn): Nygatan 9, 22100 Mariehamn; tel. (928) 29474; fax (928) 29438; f. 1969; Chair. INGMAR JANSSON; Sec. ASKO ANNALA.

Ålands företagareförening (Åland Business Asscn): Nygatan 9, 22100 Mariehamn; tel. (928) 29033; fax (928) 29438; f. 1957; Chair. SIGVARD PERSSON; Sec. AGNETA ERLANDSSON.

Ålands köpmannaförening (Åland Businessmen's Asscn): Nygatan 9, 22100 Mariehamn; f. 1927; Chair. ROLF NORDLUND; Sec. VIKING GRANSKOG.

Ålands producentförbund (Åland Agricultural Producers' Asscn): Styrmansgatan 1B, 22100 Mariehamn; fax (928) 11410; f. 1946; Chair. GÖRAN HELLING; Vice-Chair. HENRIK BECKMAN.

TRADE UNIONS

AKAVA-Åland (Professional Asscn): Styrmansgatan 1B, 22100 Mariehamn; tel. (928) 16348; Chair. KARL-JOHAN EDLUND; Gen. Sec. Maj. BRITT LIND.

FFC/SAK: s Lokalorganisation på Åland (SAK's Regional Trade Union in Åland): POB 108, 22101 Mariehamn; tel. (928) 16207; fax (928) 17207; Chair. FREJVID GRANQVIST; Gen. Sec. KURT GUSTAFSSON.

Fackorgan för offentliga arbetsomraden på Åland (FOA-Å) (Joint Organization of Civil Servants and Workers (VTY) in Åland): Styrmansgatan 1B, 22100 Mariehamn; tel. (928) 16976; Chair. ÅKE WIRTANEN; Gen. Sec. BRITT-MARIE LUND.

TOC/TVK: s Tjänstemannaorganisationer på Åland (TOC-TÅ) (TVK's Union of Salaried Employees in Åland): Styrmansgatan 6, 22100 Mariehamn; tel. (928) 16210; Chair. BENGT DAHLEN; Gen. Sec. TUULA MATTSSON.

Transport

The islands are linked to the Swedish and Finnish mainlands by ferry services and by air services from Mariehamn airport.

SHIPPING

Ålands Redarförening r.f. (Åland Shipowners' Association): Ålandsvägen 31, 22100 Mariehamn; tel. (928) 13430; telex 63117; f. 1934; Chair. JARL DANIELSSON; Man. Dir HANS AHLSTRÖM.

Principal Companies

Birka Line Ab: Östra Esplanadg. 7, 22100 Mariehamn; tel. (928) 27027; telex 63163; fax (928) 15118; f. 1971; passenger service; Chair. TRYGVE ERIKSSON; Man. Dir OLOF BERGROTH.

Lundqvist Rederierna: N. Esplanadgt. 9, 22100 Mariehamn; tel. (928) 26050; telex 63113; f. 1927; liner services; Pres. STIG LUNDQVIST; total tonnage 1m. dwt.

Rederiaktiebolaget Gustaf Erikson: POB 49, 22101 Mariehamn; tel. (928) 27070; telex 63112; fax (928) 12670; f. 1913; Man. Dir BO LIMNELL; 14 dry cargo and refrigerated vessels.

Rederiaktiebolaget Sally: Hamngatan 8, 22100 Mariehamn; tel. (928) 16711; telex 63115; ferry services to Sweden, England, France; Caribbean cruises; Man. Dir INGMAR INGVESGÅRD; 6 ferries and 2 cruisers; total tonnage 71,571 grt.

SF Line Ab: Norragatan 4, 22100 Mariehamn; tel. (928) 27000; telex 63151; fax (928) 12099; f. 1963; 5 car/passenger vessels; Chair. STIG LUNDQVIST; Man. Dir NILS-ERIK EKLUND; total tonnage 161,324 grt.

Tourism

Ålands turistförbund (Åland Tourist Union): Storagatan 11, 22100 Mariehamn; tel. (928) 27310; fax (928) 27315; f. 1989; Chair. KARL-GÖRAN ERIKSSON; Man. Dir ANDERS INGVES.

FRANCE

Introductory Survey

Location, Climate, Language, Religion, Flag, Capital

The French Republic is situated in Western Europe. It is bounded to the north by the English Channel, to the east by Belgium, Luxembourg, Germany, Switzerland and Italy, to the south by the Mediterranean Sea and Spain, and to the west by the Atlantic Ocean. The island of Corsica is part of metropolitan France, while four overseas departments, two overseas 'collectivités territoriales' and four overseas territories also form an integral part of the Republic. The climate is temperate throughout most of the country, but in the south it is of the Mediterranean type, with warm summers and mild winters. Temperatures in Paris are generally between 0°C (32°F) and 24°C (75°F). The principal language is French, which has numerous regional dialects, and small minorities speak Breton and Basque. Almost all French citizens profess Christianity, and about 80% are adherents of the Roman Catholic Church. Other Christian denominations are represented, and there are also Muslim and Jewish communities. The national flag (proportions three by two) has three equal vertical stripes, of blue, white and red. The capital is Paris.

Recent History

In September 1939, following Nazi Germany's invasion of Poland, France and the United Kingdom declared war on Germany, thus entering the Second World War. In June 1940, however, France was forced to sign an armistice, following a swift invasion and occupation of French territory by German forces. After the liberation of France from German occupation in 1944, a provisional government took office under Gen. Charles de Gaulle, leader of the 'Free French' forces during the wartime resistance. The war in Europe ended in May 1945, when German forces surrendered at Reims. In 1946, following a referendum, the Fourth Republic was established and Gen. de Gaulle retired from public life.

France had 26 different governments from 1946 until the Fourth Republic came to an end in 1958 with an insurrection in Algeria (then an overseas department) and the threat of civil war. In May Gen. de Gaulle was invited by the President, René Coty, to form a government. In June he was invested as Prime Minister by the National Assembly, with the power to rule by decree for six months. A new constitution was approved by referendum in September 1958 and promulgated in October; thus the Fifth Republic came into being, with Gen. de Gaulle taking office as its first President in January 1959. The new system provided a strong, stable executive. Real power rested in the hands of the President, who strengthened his authority through direct appeals to the people in national referendums.

The early years of the Fifth Republic were overshadowed by the Algerian crisis. De Gaulle suppressed a revolt of French army officers and granted Algeria independence in 1962, withdrawing troops and repatriating French settlers. A period of relative tranquillity was ended in 1968, when dissatisfaction with the Government's authoritarian policies on education and information, coupled with discontent at low wage rates and lack of social reform, fused into a serious revolt of students and workers. For a month the republic was threatened, but the student movement collapsed and the general strike was settled by large wage rises. In April 1969 President de Gaulle resigned after defeat in a referendum on regional reform.

Georges Pompidou, who had been Prime Minister between April 1962 and July 1968, was elected President in June 1969. He attempted to continue Gaullism, while also responding to the desire for change. The Gaullist hold on power was threatened, however, by the Union of the Left, formed in 1972 by the Parti Socialiste (PS) and the Parti Communiste Français (PCF). Leaders of the PS and the PCF agreed a common programme for contesting legislative elections. At a general election for the National Assembly in March 1973, the Government coalition was returned with a reduced majority.

President Pompidou died in April 1974. Valéry Giscard d'Estaing, formerly leader of the Républicains Indépendants (RI), supported by the Gaullist Union des Démocrates pour la République (UDR) and the centre parties, was elected President in May, narrowly defeating François Mitterrand, the First Secretary of the PS and the candidate of the Union of the Left (which was abandoned in 1977). A government was formed from members of the RI, the UDR and the centre parties. In August 1976 Jacques Chirac resigned as Prime Minister and was replaced by Raymond Barre, hitherto Minister of External Trade. Chirac undertook the transformation of the UDR into a new Gaullist party, the Rassemblement pour la République (RPR). In February 1978 the non-Gaullist parties in the Government formed the Union pour la Démocratie Française (UDF), to compete with RPR candidates in the National Assembly elections held in March, when the governing coalition retained a working majority.

In the April/May 1981 presidential elections, Mitterrand, the candidate of the PS, defeated Giscard d'Estaing, with the support of Communist voters. Pierre Mauroy was appointed Prime Minister and formed France's first left-wing Council of Ministers for 23 years. At elections for a new Assembly, held in June, the PS and associated groups, mainly the Mouvement des Radicaux de Gauche (MRG), won an overall majority of the seats. The Government was reshuffled to include four members of the PCF in the Council of Ministers. The new Government introduced a programme of reforms: social benefits and working conditions were substantially improved; several major industrial enterprises and financial institutions were brought under state control; and administrative and financial power was transferred from government-appointed Préfets to locally-elected departmental assemblies.

By 1983 the effects of economic recession had led to the adoption of deflationary policies, including reductions in public expenditure. Following a decline in support for the PS and other left-wing parties at nationwide municipal elections held in March 1983, Mauroy resigned, but was immediately requested to form a new administration by President Mitterrand. Elections for one-third of the seats in the newly-enlarged Senate in September 1983 resulted in an overall majority for the opposition right-wing and centre parties. In the June 1984 elections to the European Parliament, the PS suffered a serious set-back, taking only 20 of the 81 seats allocated to France, while the RPR-UDF opposition alliance won 41 seats. The extreme right-wing Front National (FN) and the PCF each took 10 seats.

Dissension between the PCF and the PS over the Government's continued programme of economic austerity became increasingly bitter as plans for further 'industrial restructuring' were revealed. After forceful protest by opposition politicians and Roman Catholic pressure-groups, a government proposal to introduce a unified, state-run secular education system was abandoned in July 1984, and the Minister of Education, Alain Savary, resigned. President Mitterrand accepted Mauroy's subsequent resignation, and appointed Laurent Fabius, the former Minister for Industry, as Prime Minister. Following Fabius's declared intention to continue policies of economic rigour, the PCF refused to participate in the new Council of Ministers.

A general election for an enlarged National Assembly (increased from 491 to 577 seats) was held in March 1986. In accordance with legislation introduced in 1985, the voting, except in three small overseas possessions, was based on a system of proportional representation (with voters choosing from party lists in each department or territory), rather than under the previous system of single-member constituencies. As in the 1981 general election, the PS and the MRG formed a left-wing alliance, while the RPR and the UDF formed a centre-right alliance. Although the PS remained the largest single party in the new Assembly, the RPR-UDF was able to control a majority of seats, with the support of 14 deputies from minor right-wing parties. The PCF suffered a severe decline in support, whereas the FN won seats in the Assembly for the first time. President Mitterrand invited Jacques Chirac, the leader of the RPR (the dominant party in the centre-right alliance), to become Prime Minister (Chirac, the Mayor of Paris since 1977, had previously been Prime Minister in 1974–76). A new Council of Ministers, comprising RPR-UDF politicians and a few non-party members, was formed. This resulted in an unprecedented situation in France: a right-wing government 'cohabiting' with a Socialist President, as Mitterrand's presidential term of office did not expire until 1988. On the same day as the election for the National Assembly, voting took place throughout France for regional councils, using direct suffrage in all areas for the first time (the councils in metropolitan France had previously been chosen by indirect election, except in Corsica—see below). The regional elections also resulted in a swing to the right, although in nine regional councils right-wing parties had to form coalitions with the FN in order to maintain their control.

In April 1986 Chirac introduced highly controversial enabling legislation to allow his Government to legislate by decree on economic and social issues, and on the proposed reversion to the single-seat majority voting system for elections to the National Assembly. However, President Mitterrand insisted on his presidential right to refuse to sign decrees that undermined the previous Government's achievements on social reform. Chirac was therefore forced to use the 'guillotine' procedure (setting a time-limit for parliamentary consideration of legislative proposals) to gain parliamentary approval for contentious legislation, which the President would be constitutionally obliged to sign within 15 days, following its approval by the Senate (with a large right-wing majority) and the Constitutional Council. In July 1986 the 'guillotine' procedure was used to enact legislation which provided for the 'privatization' of 65 state-owned companies (by November 1987 shares in 11 major companies and their subsidiaries had been offered for sale to private investors). From 1986 the Government implemented its programme of deregulation of the French broadcasting system and established a new broadcasting authority, the Commission Nationale de la Communication et des Libertés (CNCL), to oversee the reforms. Stringent legislation to control immigration was adopted by the National Assembly in July 1986, and in September tough anti-terrorism measures were implemented, following a series of bombings in Paris, which were carried out by the Committee of Solidarity with Arab and Middle Eastern Political Prisoners (CSPPA). In elections for one-third of the seats in the enlarged Senate in late September, the right-wing parties consolidated their majority.

By the end of 1986 the Government's popularity had slumped, owing to two consecutive crises. In December 1986 the Minister Delegate attached to the Minister of National Education resigned, and the Government was forced to withdraw proposed legislation on education, which aimed to introduce selection procedures for university places, to increase registration fees, and to reform the degree and baccalauréat systems, after large student demonstrations took place throughout France. Following widespread strikes by the transport unions, the Government abandoned plans to introduce merit-linked salaries in January 1987, but remained determined that increases in wages should not exceed the limit of 2%–3% per year, set by the austerity policy.

By 1987 the RPR-UDF coalition had become increasingly divided, as the UDF resented the RPR's domination of major ministries. In April 1987 Chirac attempted to unify the RPR-UDF coalition by seeking a vote of confidence in the Government's past and future policies. In June François Léotard, the Minister for Culture and Communication and Secretary-General of the Parti Républicain (PR), affiliated to the UDF, announced that he would not support Chirac's presidential candidacy in 1988. In the following month Raymond Barre, a prominent member of the UDF and a former Prime Minister (1976–81), announced that he would be a candidate for the presidency and would base his campaign on criticism of Chirac's economic and foreign policies. Further splits developed in the right-wing coalition, as Chirac reintroduced proposals, previously introduced in 1986, to remove the right of automatic French citizenship from children of foreign parents, with the aim of attracting FN support for his candidacy in the second round of the presidential election. However, UDF and moderate RPR members of the coalition rejected any accommodation with the FN, and the RPR hastily distanced itself from the FN, after Le Pen described the Nazi gas chambers as 'un point de détail' in the history of the Second World War, during a television interview in mid-September.

Towards the end of 1987, scandals relating to the PS term of government were revealed. In October the National Assembly withdrew parliamentary immunity from Christian Nucci, the former PS Minister of Co-operation, thus enabling him to be examined by five special magistrates over his alleged role in the embezzlement of about 5m. francs of development aid during his tenure of office. In November a secret report was disclosed on illegal shipments of French-made weapons to Iran, with the alleged complicity of senior defence officers, under the Socialist Government. Following further allegations that the PS had received commissions from the illegal sales of armaments, President Mitterrand declared his support for a series of proposals which would oblige politicians to declare their incomes, and presidential candidates to declare their sources of funding.

During the last session of the National Assembly in December 1987, Chirac sought a vote of confidence in his Government's policies, in an attempt to deflect widespread criticism over the alleged means by which relations had been normalized with Iran (see below). The National Assembly also adopted 16 legislative proposals, including the reduction of the powers of examining magistrates, the reform of the Bourse and the introduction of a new statute for the French overseas territory of New Caledonia. During an extraordinary session in February 1988, the Assembly adopted legislation requiring elected office-holders to be financially accountable, and regulating the financing of political parties and electoral campaigns.

In early 1988, in the months leading up to the presidential election, President Mitterrand gained a tactical advantage over the other presidential candidates by delaying the announcement of his intention to seek a second five-year term of office until just five weeks before the first round of voting was due to take place, whereas Jacques Chirac of the RPR and Raymond Barre of the UDF had declared their candidacies many weeks in advance. In the first round of the election on 24 April, Mitterrand established a lead, with 34.1% of the votes, while right-wing support was split between Chirac and Barre, who gained 19.9% and 16.5% of the votes respectively. There was an unexpected resurgence in support for the extreme right-wing candidate, Jean-Marie Le Pen, who won 14.4% of the votes, while the PCF official candidate, André Lajoinie, received only 6.8% of the votes. The rate of absention was 18.6%. Mitterrand and Chirac proceeded to the second round of the election. The PCF recommended its supporters to vote for Mitterrand, while the UDF urged its supporters to vote for Chirac. Le Pen, however, refused to endorse Chirac's candidacy. On 8 May Mitterrand was re-elected President, with 54% of the votes, while Chirac received 46%. Of the total electorate, 15.9% failed to participate. Chirac subsequently resigned as Prime Minister, and Mitterrand appointed Michel Rocard, who had been the Minister of Agriculture in the previous Socialist Government, as his successor. However, Rocard's Government failed to command a reliable majority in the National Assembly, which was promptly dissolved by Mitterrand.

A general election for a new National Assembly was held on 5 and 12 June 1988. The voting was based on the single-seat majority system, which had been reintroduced by Chirac after the 1986 elections. The PS formed a left-wing alliance with the MRG, while the RPR and the UDF decided to contest the elections jointly as the Union du Rassemblement et du Centre (URC). The first round of the election, on 5 June, was characterized by an unusually high abstention rate of 34.3%. The PS-MRG alliance received 37.6% of the votes cast, while the URC received 37.7%. The PCF recovered support, winning 11.3% of the votes, while the FN's share of the votes was 9.7%, as in the 1986 general election. The second round of voting, on 12 June 1988, was restricted to constituencies where no candidate had won an absolute majority. The election was contested by candidates who had received at least 12.5% of the votes in the first round. The PCF agreed not to contest the same constituencies as the PS, and a similar, but controversial, pact was reached between URC and FN candidates in Marseille and the surrounding Bouches-du-Rhône department. Although the PS won the most seats, it failed to win an overall majority: the PS-MRG alliance received 48.7% of the second-round votes and won a total of 276 seats, and the URC secured 46.8% and won 272 seats (the RPR received 20.1% and took 127 seats, the UDF won 21.8% and took 129 seats, while the other right-wing candidates, who campaigned as URC candidates in the second round, won 2.6% of the votes and secured 16 seats).

FRANCE

The PCF, with 3.4%, won 27 seats, while the FN received 1.1% and won only 1 seat. The abstention rate remained high, at 30.1%. After the election, Mitterrand announced that he would form a minority government and seek parliamentary majorities on a case-by-case basis. Meanwhile, Pierre Méhaignerie, the leader of the Centre des Démocrates Sociaux (CDS, a party affiliated to the UDF), announced the formation of a new independent centrist group comprising 40 deputies, the Union du Centre (UDC), with the aim of establishing effective opposition to the Government. Barre subsequently announced that he was allying himself with the UDC.

In late June Rocard was reappointed Prime Minister, and he formed a new Council of Ministers. Although members of the previous Government held the main portfolios, six members of the new Council of Ministers were drawn from the UDF and 13 were independent 'technocrats', thus demonstrating the new Government's wish to attract centrist support in the National Assembly. However, the Government's attempt to gain reliable PCF support, in preparation for the introduction of a potentially controversial series of measures later in the year, received a set-back in July, when a clause of the Amnesty Law (traditionally introduced after the presidential election) that had been proposed by the PCF, seeking to reinstate dismissed trade union officials, was rejected by the Constitutional Council, following an appeal by the RPR. In the cantonal elections on 25 September and 2 October, the PS made a gain of 89 additional seats, but the abstention rate reached its highest post-war levels (50.9% in the first round and 53.0% in the second round).

In October 1988 the Government introduced a series of legislative proposals which aimed to encourage an 'everyday democracy' by protecting the underprivileged. A major proposal, to introduce a minimum guaranteed income, was approved almost unanimously (the FN subsequently expelled its one deputy from the party for supporting the measure), although, to ensure right-wing support, the Government had to introduce a clause whereby those benefiting from the measure would have their allowances suspended if they failed to accept job-training or social employment. A proposal to introduce a 'wealth and solidarity' tax, along with a series of other tax reforms was also approved, owing to abstentions by the PCF and the UDC. However, legislation to replace the broadcasting authority, the CNCL (which had been criticized for alleged right-wing bias), with a 'more impartial' Conseil Supérieur de l'Audiovisuel provoked much opposition, and Rocard subsequently invoked a procedure whereby a measure was automatically accepted if opposition parties failed to achieve the adoption of a motion of censure.

However, the Government's success in implementing its programme was overshadowed by a series of strikes in protest against its attempts to restrict public-sector wages and thus reduce the budgetary deficit. In September 1988 nurses went on strike, and in the following month the unrest spread to most other public sectors, including schools, urban transport, railways and the civil service. Eventually the Government was forced to concede to the strikers' demands, and by early December most trade unions had reached a settlement. Although the PCF had been criticized by the Government during the unrest for encouraging union discontent, it refused to vote for a motion of censure against the Government which was presented by the RPR in mid-December, in response to the unrest. In January 1989 the PCF agreed not to combine with right-wing deputies to defeat the Government, and formed an electoral alliance with the PS in preparation for the municipal elections in March.

In early 1989, however, details emerged of two 'insider trading' scandals which involved individuals close to President Mitterrand and the Ministry of the Economy, Finance and the Budget. The first scandal focused on the purchase of American Can from the US company, Triangle Holding, by the French state-owned aluminium and packaging company, Péchiney, in November 1988. A few individuals, including a close friend of President Mitterrand, Roger-Patrice Pelat, and a left-wing financier, bought large amounts of Triangle shares before the Péchiney bid and subsequently made substantial profits. It was suspected that these investors might have received insider information, and it was noted that, as Péchiney was a state-owned company, senior officials in the Ministries of the Economy, Finance and the Budget, and of Industry and Regional Planning, as well as in the Prime Minister's and the President's Offices would have known about the bid beforehand. The second scandal focused on attempts by Pierre Bérégovoy, the Minister of the Economy, Finance and the Budget, to oust the controlling groups of right-wing shareholders created by the Chirac Government during its privatization programme. In October 1988 hostile bidders, financed by a state savings bank (with the alleged implicit support of the Ministry of the Economy, Finance and the Budget), unsuccessfully attempted to acquire a controlling interest in a major privatized bank, the Société Générale. During the attempted takeover, several individuals, including one person who was later implicated in the Péchiney scandal, made substantial profits. In January 1989, in an attempt to limit the impact of these scandals, Rocard announced new proposals to increase the powers of the Commission des Opérations de Bourse (COB), the supervisory body of the stock exchange. The head of Bérégovoy's private office resigned, in order to 'defend his honour' against accusations of irregular conduct in the Péchiney takeover. At the end of the month, the COB, which had been investigating the Péchiney takeover, presented a dossier on the affair to the Public Prosecutor. In February the COB opened investigations into the Société Générale affair. In the same month, five people were charged with insider trading offences in the Péchiney affair, including Pelat, who later died of a heart attack.

Despite the embarrassment caused to the Government by this scandal, the results of the local elections in March 1989 constituted a triumph for the PS, while Les Verts, an environmentalist group, emerged as a serious force in French politics. In April the established leadership of the right-wing opposition was challenged by a group of 12 deputies, known as the Rénovateurs, who threatened to form their own list for elections to the European Parliament in June, and made a public appeal for Giscard d'Estaing, the leader of the UDF, to relinquish his leadership of the right-wing list. Although support for the Rénovateurs increased, a meeting of the UDF National Council voted in favour of the party's official electoral strategy by a majority of 87%. This division was considered to have strengthened the position of the PS. In June, however, Giscard d'Estaing succeeded in forming an alliance between the UDF and the RPR, which defeated the PS in the European elections by 28.9% to 23.6% of the votes cast in France. At partial elections to the Senate in September, the RPR was able to consolidate its position. In October an 'intergroupe' was created by the RPR, UDF and UDC, although differences between the party leaders remained unresolved.

The extreme right-wing FN achieved an unexpected rise in popularity in October 1989, following a dispute concerning the large Muslim community in France. The immediate cause of the controversy was the demand by three Muslim schoolgirls to wear their headscarves at school, despite the strong tradition of secularity (forbidding the wearing of religious emblems in schools). The matter was referred to the Conseil d'Etat, which ruled that the wearing of scarves, providing that it did not constitute propaganda, did not compromise the separation of church and state. However, the issue released general anti-immigration sentiments, which contributed to the victory of the FN, in two local elections in late October. In early December Prime Minister Rocard acknowledged that the success of the FN, which had provoked tension within the PS, would force the Government to alter its policy on immigration. In the first part of 1990 immigration and race relations continued to be important issues. Following an increase in racist attacks, the desecration of Jewish cemeteries and a government survey revealing that 75% of French people believed that there were too many North Africans resident in France, the National Assembly passed legislation, in early May, strengthening the 1972 anti-racism laws. The legislation, which was proposed by the PCF, was approved by 307 votes to 265, despite the use of blocking tactics by Marie-France Stirbois, the sole FN deputy. Only the PS and the PCF voted for the bill, although it had been hoped that it would have won cross-party support. The bill stated that those found guilty of all racist, anti-semitic or xenophobic acts would be subject to heavier fines or imprisonment, and could be barred from seeking public office or from state employment. In addition, it became an offence to contest the existence of Nazi gas chambers during the Second World War. At the same time, however, the Government prepared plans for more stringent action as regards illegal immigrants, who were estimated to number between 300,000 and 1m. The annual budgets of the Office français de protection des réfugiés et apatrides (OFPRA) and of the appeals commission were increased three-fold in order to expedite applications for asylum.

Following the overthrow of the Romanian regime in late December 1989, the Secretary-General of the PCF, Georges Marchais, was accused of having had close connections with the former Romanian leader, Nicolae Ceaușescu. A group known as the Réconstructeurs demanded that the entire Government resign, owing to its support of the previous regime. In December ministers also pressed for the resignation of Socialist leader Pierre Mauroy, whose traditional left-wing policies were blamed for election defeats and dissension within the party. In January 1990 the PS divided into factions over the question of the succession to President Mitterrand in 1995. The three main contenders were considered to be Prime Minister Rocard, Lionel Jospin (the Minister of State for National Education) and Laurent Fabius, the President of the National Assembly and a former Prime Minister. Meanwhile, the RPR leader, Jacques Chirac, was criticized by two former ministers, Charles Pasqua and Philippe Séguin, over his defeat in the 1988 presidential election. Nevertheless Chirac was unanimously re-elected as RPR President in February 1990.

In June 1990 Chirac and Giscard d'Estaing announced the formation of a confederation of their parties, which was to be known as the Union pour la France (UPF), with the intention of introducing US-style primary elections to choose a single candidate from among right-wing groups for the 1995 presidential election. This agreement was intended to counter support for the FN, but it was immediately criticized by François Léotard, the President of the Parti Républicain (the largest group within the UDF), who claimed that the FN's political standing would not be adversely affected, since the new union lacked credibility. The Government's own moral position had been severely damaged by the introduction, in December 1989, of new amnesty legislation which appeared to discriminate in favour of elected politicians by protecting them as regards politically-related crimes. The political amnesty was appended to a law which exonerated all persons guilty of offences relating to party finances that had been committed before June 1989 and instituted rigorous rules governing such finances henceforth. However, in June 1990 the public prosecutor committed for trial several businessmen and construction company officials, who had allegedly been involved in channelling money into local party funds, but amnestied the party officials involved. The judiciary was outspoken in its condemnation of the implications of the amnesty, notably regarding the case of the exoneration of Christian Nucci, a former PS minister, who was alleged to have personally benefited from the diversion of 10m. francs into his election campaign fund. In protest at insufficient funding and increasing political interference, the judges staged their first strike for nine years.

On 5 November 1990, the day on which the National Assembly was debating its financial provisions for education in the 1991 budget, secondary-school students held demonstrations to demand heightened security in schools (following several serious attacks on students and teachers), improved conditions and more teachers. The demonstrations ended in clashes between students and the police. The Government stated that it had already agreed to create an additional 1,100 administrative posts and 3,000 jobs for student teachers, and that the annual education budget was to rise by 20,000m. francs, to 248,000m. francs (which was higher than the sum to be allocated to defence). The students dismissed these actions as derisory, and marched again on 12 November. Following this second demonstration, representatives of the students held discussions with President Mitterrand and Lionel Jospin, the Minister of National Education, Youth and Sports, and the Government promised to provide an additional 4,500m. francs to the education sector in the 1991 budget.

As a result of the decentralization legislation of 1982, Corsica was elevated from regional status to that of a 'collectivité territoriale', with its own directly-elected 61-seat Assembly, and an administration with greater executive powers in economic, social and other spheres. This measure failed to pacify the pro-independence Front de Libération Nationale de la Corse (FLNC) and the Consulte des Comités Nationalistes (CCN), which were banned in 1983, following a terrorist campaign. A new independence movement, the Mouvement Corse pour l'Autodétermination (MCA), was immediately formed by members of the banned CCN, and terrorist activities continued from 1984. In January 1987 the MCA, which had six members in the Corsican Assembly in alliance with the Union du Peuple Corse (UPC), was banned after police investigations revealed alleged links with the FLNC, and the UPC later suspended the alliance. In October the police seized an FLNC article, published in a Corsican nationalist newspaper, which advocated the 'physical elimination' of French mainlanders on Corsica and new terrorist operations to be directed against the police. One gendarme was killed, and five were injured, in a series of terrorist attacks in March and April 1988. At the end of May, the FLNC announced a suspension of violent operations, with the aim of achieving a dialogue with the newly-elected Socialist Government. In November the Government proposed that discussions be held with MCA councillors and announced proposals to redress some of the nationalists' grievances. The proposals included measures to introduce the teaching of the Corsican language in all Corsican schools and to encourage economic development on the island. In January 1989, however, the MCA councillors rejected an invitation to meet the Minister of the Interior, Pierre Joxe, although they stressed that this did not imply an end to the dialogue or to the FLNC truce.

In March 1989 a strike by public-service officials in Corsica, in support of a claim for an insularity bonus, blockaded air- and seaports, and effectively isolated the island. The Regional Assembly demanded the recognition of the island as a 'zone zéro', a region with a high cost of living. The failure of negotiations in April was followed by riots and violent incidents. In mid-April, however, the unions accepted Prime Minister Rocard's suggestion to hold discussions on the structural problems of the Corsican economy, and the strike finally came to an end at the beginning of May. In mid-1989 the FLNC ended its suspension of violence, and declared hostilities against the tourist trade on the island. In subsequent months several holiday flats were destroyed in major terrorist attacks. In January 1990 a unit of 60 armed men blew up part of a complex of holiday homes. It was feared that these incidents signified the beginning of a campaign to destroy foreign tourist investment on Corsica.

In November 1990 the French Government proposed legislation granting greater autonomy to Corsica. The bill included proposals to strengthen the powers of Corsica's fragmented regional government, to recognize formally the existence of the Corsican people for the first time, to reform the electoral rules to encourage political stability, and to prepare new voting lists to curb electoral irregularities. The bill, which was known as the Joxe Plan (after its instigator, Pierre Joxe, the Minister of the Interior), envisaged that Corsica would be governed by an executive council consisting of seven members from a 51-member Corsican assembly to be elected in 1992. The Plan also stated that it would seek to ensure a strong political leadership by giving six additional seats to the group holding the majority in the new assembly. Despite opposition from right-wing parties in the National Assembly and from Corsicans who thought that the measures were insufficient, the bill passed its first reading. A bombing campaign and a series of assassinations that took place in Corsica in December 1990 and January 1991 served only to make the Government more determined to ensure that the bill would be approved in a special session of the National Assembly to be held in early 1991.

From 1984 the French Government was confronted by increasing terrorist activity in the Pacific overseas territory of New Caledonia, where Kanak (indigenous Melanesian) separatists were campaigning for independence from metropolitan France. In September 1987 the French Government held a referendum in New Caledonia, with voters choosing between total independence and adoption of a statute to incorporate the territory firmly as part of the French Republic. The FLNKS advocated a boycott of the referendum, as it had not been consulted by the Government over the issue, and instigated a campaign of civil disobedience in the period preceding the referendum. In a low turn-out of 58.9% of the electorate (owing mainly to the FLNKS boycott), 98.3% of voters chose to remain part of France. In December a new statute, granting greater autonomy to the territory by establishing four elected regional councils, was adopted. However, the FLNKS urged a boycott of the elections for the new regional councils, which were to be held concurrently with the first round of the French presidential elections on 24 April 1988. Several days before the elections were held, 30 Kanak separatists killed four gendarmes and took 27 gendarmes hostage. (See p. 1100 for further details.) In May the new French Prime Minister, Michel Rocard, dispatched a six-member mission to New Caledonia to re-establish a dialogue with the Kanaks and to formulate proposals for the territory's future. Meanwhile, controversy arose over the release of the hostages, when the unauthorized disclosure of a report by the commander of the French paratroopers who had been sent to the hostages' rescue seemed to imply that the Chirac Government had favoured a military solution, rather than a negotiated settlement, to the crisis. After a series of discussions between Rocard and the leaders of the FLNKS and the anti-independence party, the Rassemblement pour la Calédonie dans la République, agreement was reached in August to transfer the administration of New Caledonia to the central Government in Paris for 12 months, and then to appoint a High Commissioner to administer the territory, along with three elected regional councils, for 10 years, prior to a referendum on self-determination, to be held in 1998. The programme was presented to the French electorate in a referendum on 6 November 1988. Of the 36.9% of the electorate who voted, 80% approved the Government's plan. In May 1989, however, the assassination of Jean-Marie Tjibaou and Yeiwéné Yeiwéné, two leaders of the FLNKS, threatened to jeopardize previous agreements and to provoke further outbreaks of violence. Nevertheless, Prime Minister Rocard decided that local elections would take place, as planned, in June. The elections established three regional councils (with the FLNKS winning an absolute majority in two), thus ending administrative control by the central Government.

Terrorist attacks in the Basque region of south-western France escalated in 1983 and 1984, as violence between Spanish right-wing extremists and members of the Basque separatist movement, ETA, spread across the border from Spain. In 1984 the French Government agreed to stop granting refugee status to ETA members seeking asylum in France, and in July 1986 the Government agreed to increase collaboration with the Spanish authorities to curb ETA. Many ETA members were subsequently deported, detained, or expelled to other countries. In July 1987 the French Government banned another Basque separatist group, (IK) Iparretarrak, which had been responsible for terrorist operations since 1973 and had renewed a bombing campaign in 1986, in protest against the expulsions of ETA members. In September and October French and Spanish police conducted the largest ever series of arrests of suspected members of ETA and IK, and in January 1989 French police arrested the leader of the military wing of ETA and other suspected ETA members.

France is a founder-member of the European Communities. In 1966 it withdrew from the integrated military structure of NATO, but remained a member of the alliance. In 1986 France agreed with the Federal Republic of Germany to intensify military links and to play a more active joint role in international affairs. In January 1988 France and the Federal Republic of Germany signed new agreements on defence and economic co-operation, to commemorate the 25th anniversary of the Franco-German Treaty, the original aims of which had never been realized. In October a joint Franco-German military brigade was formed, which was intended to strengthen the European element within NATO and the French commitment to use conventional forces to defend the Federal Republic of Germany. However, French relations with NATO in 1988 were uneasy. In February other NATO states expressed a wish for closer French co-operation with the Alliance. In March Mitterrand became the first French President to attend a NATO 'summit' meeting since 1966, owing to French concern over the implications of the Intermediate-Range Nuclear Forces Treaty, signed by the USA and the USSR in December 1987. In the same month Mitterrand criticized NATO's plans to modernize its short-range nuclear weapons, arguing that European security would be better served by disarmament. In July Mitterrand welcomed Soviet proposals for the convening of a Soviet-European 'summit' meeting on conventional disarmament, in contrast with NATO's response. In November France incurred NATO's disapproval for its insistence on linking the issue of disarmament with that of human rights in Eastern bloc countries, and for proposing that neutral and non-aligned European countries be given a decisive role in negotiations on conventional forces, thus repudiating NATO's decision that only NATO and Warsaw Pact states should be directly involved in such negotiations. In 1989 it was decided that France would participate with other NATO members in a plan to redistribute equipment among allies to prevent the destruction of new weapons in accordance with the terms of a treaty to limit armaments.

Meanwhile, President Mitterrand placed a new emphasis on improving France's relations with the USSR and Eastern European countries. In January 1988 Mitterrand met Erich Honecker, thus becoming the first leader of a Western signatory to the Berlin Agreement of 1945 to meet the leader of the German Democratic Republic. In early November the French Government withdrew charges against three people who had been arrested in 1987 for allegedly spying for the USSR. Franco-Soviet relations had deteriorated following the arrests, with the two countries engaging in retaliatory expulsions of diplomatic personnel. Later in November 1988, Mitterrand visited the USSR and attended the launch of the second joint Franco-Soviet space mission. During his visit, Mitterrand signed an agreement allowing for the creation of a line of credit from a French banking consortium to the USSR and for the establishment of a joint venture to construct an aluminium plant in Armenia. He also agreed in principle to the holding of a human rights conference in Moscow in 1991. Mitterrand visited Czechoslovakia in December 1988.

In 1989 and 1990 France's foreign policy was affected by events in Eastern Europe. Following the rapid political developments between the German Democratic Republic and the Federal Republic of Germany, the threat to stability in Europe became a matter of concern to France. President Mitterrand, who held the Presidency of the EEC Council of Ministers in the second half of 1989, responded by urging faster progress towards economic and monetary integration within the EEC and the adoption of measures leading to closer political union. Shortly before the meeting of EEC heads of government at Strasbourg in December, the Federal Republic of Germany unexpectedly rejected its common policy with France over monetary union. At the Strasbourg meeting, however, the leaders agreed to support the reunification of Germany in principle, while the Federal German Chancellor, Dr Helmut Kohl, withdrew his objections to monetary union. In January 1990 Dr Kohl agreed to Mitterrand's concept of a future European Confederation between the EEC and the countries of Eastern Europe. At the Franco-German 'summit' meeting held in September 1990 in Munich, France announced plans to withdraw all of its 50,000 troops from Germany over the next few years. In addition, the two countries set a target date for European economic and monetary union of January 1993 and pledged to work towards political union within the European Community (EC).

Meanwhile, France continued its efforts to establish economic links with the USSR and other Eastern European countries. During an official two-day visit to France in July 1989, the Soviet leader, Mikhail Gorbachev, signed more than 20 agreements on economic, scientific and cultural co-operation. Mitterrand's three-day visit to the German Democratic Republic in December was the first by a foreign head of state since the changes there, and reflected his concern for future developments. Six agreements on economic, industrial and technical co-operation were signed during his visit. In January 1990 President Mitterrand paid an official visit to Hungary. In October Gorbachev visited France, and the first treaty of friendship with the Soviet Union by a Western country was signed.

Agricultural policy adversely affected relations between France and the United Kingdom on two separate occasions in 1990. In May France announced a ban on the import of British beef, including live cattle, owing to fears that bovine spongiform encephalopathy (BSE), a disease affecting cattle, might be passed on to humans who ate meat from infected animals. The ban was revoked in June (following the exertion of pressure by the EC), when the British Government agreed to provide certain guarantees about the meat's origin. Later in June, French farmers, claiming to be nearing bankruptcy because of declines in meat prices, resorted to violent measures to try to prevent the import of beef and lamb from the United Kingdom, Belgium, the Netherlands and the Federal Republic of Germany. They attacked lorries from these countries, sometimes slaughtering the cargo, and blockaded roads and ports. In August the French Government announced an aid programme of 1,200m. francs for livestock farmers affected by reduced prices and drought; but the attacks continued. In September the British Government threatened to institute judicial proceedings against France at the European Court of Justice if the attacks continued. The French Government announced a further aid programme, worth 350m. francs, and a debt-relief fund, worth 1,400m. francs, financed by Crédit

Agricole. Organizations representing British and French farmers agreed to conduct a joint campaign to seek additional aid from the EC and to secure more stringent controls on cheap imports of beef and cattle from Eastern Europe.

France has been conducting tests of nuclear weapons on the South Pacific atoll of Mururoa, in French Polynesia, since 1966, despite protests from countries in the region, particularly Australia and New Zealand. In mid-1985 France's relations with these countries were further damaged by the discovery that French secret service agents had been responsible for the sinking of the trawler *Rainbow Warrior* (flagship of the international environmental protection group, Greenpeace) in the New Zealand port of Auckland. In September 1985 the head of the secret service, Adm. Pierre Lacoste, was dismissed, and the Minister of Defence, Charles Hernu, was forced to resign. In December the French Government agreed to compensate Greenpeace, and in July 1986 the new right-wing French Government issued a formal apology and paid US $7m. compensation to New Zealand, and approved New Zealand butter quotas, while New Zealand returned the secret service agents, whom the New Zealand authorities had imprisoned on charges of manslaughter, on the condition that they were confined to Hao Atoll, a French military base in the Pacific, for three years. There was renewed tension between France and New Zealand, after the two secret service agents were flown back to France on humanitarian grounds in December 1987 and in May 1988, without New Zealand's consent, thus breaking the terms of the 1986 agreement. In May 1990 an international tribunal ruled that France's repatriation of the agents constituted a substantial violation of the agreement, but it said the agents would not be required to return to Hao Atoll. The tribunal recommended that France pay an initial US $2m. into a joint fund intended to foster close and friendly relations between the two countries. France accepted the tribunal's recommendations.

France granted independence to most of its former colonies after the Second World War. In Indo-China, after prolonged fighting, Laos, Cambodia and Viet-Nam became fully independent in 1954. In Africa most of the French colonies in the West and Equatorial regions attained independence in 1960, but have retained their close economic and political ties with France. In 1983, under the terms of a co-operation agreement, a large contingent of French troops was sent to Chad as a result of continuing hostilities between government forces and Libyan-backed rebels. France became increasingly involved in the conflict between Chad and Libya (see chapter on Chad for further details), and in 1987 increased its military presence by 1,000 men. In February 1990, however, the French troops in Chad were reduced from 1,300 to 1,000 men. None the less, the French Government consistently expressed its support for Chad's efforts to maintain its territorial integrity.

In 1986 the Chirac Government changed the direction of French foreign policy in the Middle East. From 1978 France had the largest contingent of soldiers in the UN Interim Force in Lebanon (UNIFIL), but in November 1986 the Government announced the withdrawal of more than one-half of the French contingent from Lebanon, owing to increasing numbers of casualties among French soldiers. In 1986 the French Government reached a settlement with Iran over the repayment of a US $1,000m. loan from the Iranian Government of the late Shah in 1974, expelled leaders of the Mujaheddin resistance (opposed to the Iranian regime of Ayatollah Khomeini) from France and closed the Mujaheddin headquarters in Paris. Improved relations between France and Iran resulted in the release of five French hostages being detained by a pro-Iranian group in Lebanon. In 1987, however, French relations with Iran deteriorated after a series of arrests of suspected members of a pro-Iranian terrorist network in Paris, and an incident involving an interpreter at the Iranian embassy in Paris, who was implicated in the bombing campaign carried out by the CSPPA in 1986 (see above). In July France severed diplomatic relations with Iran. France subsequently reinforced its naval fleet in the Persian (Arabian) Gulf and announced a ban on imports of Iranian crude petroleum. By late November relations between France and Iran had improved, after secret negotiations resulted in the release of two out of five French hostages being detained by a pro-Iranian group in Lebanon. The French Government was widely criticized in France and in Europe, after allegations that it had paid a ransom of US $5m. for the return of the hostages. In early December 17 members of the Mujaheddin resistance (14 Iranians and three Kurdish nationalists from Turkey) were expelled from France to Gabon, in a move which intensified suspicions of a secret French deal with Iran. Following protests in France and abroad, seven of the Iranians were allowed to return to France in January 1988. In May, before the second round of the French presidential election, the three remaining French hostages being held by a pro-Iranian group in Lebanon were released, prompting speculation that a further secret agreement between France and Iran had been made. Later that month, diplomatic relations between France and Iran were restored, and in December the French Government revoked its ban on imports of Iranian crude petroleum.

In June 1989 Chirac revived the controversy over the hostages by suggesting the release of a pro-Iranian terrorist, Anis Naccache, imprisoned in France. It was speculated this was in part-exchange for the release of the French hostages. However, reversing an earlier decision to refuse to grant an amnesty to Naccache, Mitterrand decided to pardon him, together with his four accomplices, in July 1990, and they were released at the end of the month. This action provoked a series of prison revolts in August, as inmates protested against the length of their sentences. However, Naccache's release removed the last obstacle to an increase in economic co-operation between France and Iran.

Following Iraq's invasion and occupation of Kuwait in August 1990, France attempted to find a diplomatic resolution to the crisis, right up to the UN Security Council's deadline of 15 January 1991 for the complete withdrawal of Iraqi forces. When these attempts failed, France committed land, sea and air contingents (10,000 personnel, 12 ships and 54 aircraft) to the multinational forces deployed in the region of the Persian (Arabian) Gulf. On 17 January, the day following the outbreak of hostilities between Iraq and the allied forces, the Minister of Defence, Jean-Pierre Chevènement, announced that French troops would fight in Kuwait but not in Iraq. In the event, however, this position proved to be untenable. At the end of the month, Chevènement resigned from his post and was replaced by Pierre Joxe, the former Minister of the Interior. French participation in the anti-Iraq coalition forces was a sensitive domestic issue, owing to the presence in France of about 3m. Arabs (mainly from North Africa) and other Muslims, many of whom sympathized with the Iraqi Government's anti-Western stance. Following the outbreak of hostilities, there were a few violent incidents, including bomb explosions, believed to be related to the war, and official security measures were intensified. In February, however, the French military presence in the Gulf region was reinforced, bringing its total strength to about 14,000.

Government

Under the 1958 Constitution, legislative power is held by the bicameral Parliament, comprising a Senate and a National Assembly. The Senate has 321 members (296 for metropolitan France, 13 for the overseas departments, 'collectivités territoriales' and territories, and 12 for French nationals abroad). Senators are elected for a nine-year term by an electoral college composed of the members of the National Assembly, delegates from the Councils of the Departments and delegates from the Municipal Councils. One-third of the Senate is renewable every three years. The National Assembly has 577 members, with 555 for metropolitan France and 22 for overseas departments, 'collectivités territoriales' and territories. In the June 1988 general election, members of the Assembly were elected by universal adult suffrage, under the reintroduced single-member constituency system of direct election, using a second ballot if the first ballot failed to produce an absolute majority for any one candidate. The Assembly's term is five years, subject to dissolution. Executive power is held by the President. Since 1962 the President has been directly elected by popular vote (using two ballots if necessary) for seven years. The President appoints a Council of Ministers, headed by the Prime Minister, which administers the country and is responsible to Parliament.

Metropolitan France comprises 21 administrative regions containing 96 departments. Under the decentralization law of March 1982, administrative and financial power in metropolitan France was transferred from the Préfets, who became Commissaires de la République, to locally-elected departmental assemblies (Conseils généraux) and regional assemblies (Conseils regionaux). The special status of a 'collectivité territoriale' was granted to Corsica, which has its own directly-elected

FRANCE

legislative Assembly. There are four overseas departments (French Guiana, Guadeloupe, Martinique and Réunion), two overseas 'collectivités territoriales' (Mayotte and St Pierre and Miquelon) and four overseas territories (French Polynesia, the French Southern and Antarctic Territories, New Caledonia and the Wallis and Futuna Islands), all of which are integral parts of the French Republic (see p. 1078). Each overseas department is administered by an elected Conseil général and Conseil régional, each 'collectivité territoriale' by an appointed government commissioner, and each overseas territory by an appointed high commissioner.

Defence

French military policy is decided by the Supreme Defence Council. Military service is compulsory and lasts for 12–18 months (this period was to be reduced to 10 months from 1992). In June 1990 the total armed forces numbered 461,250 (including 235,250 conscripts), comprising an army of 288,550, a navy of 65,300, an air force of 93,100, inter-service central staffs of 3,600, a Service de Santé of 8,700 and a Service des Essences of 2,000. In addition, there was a paramilitary gendarmerie of 91,800 (including 10,700 conscripts). Total reserves stood at 419,000 (army 325,000; navy 24,000; air force 70,000). The defence budget for 1990 was 189,440m. francs. France is a member of NATO, but withdrew from its integrated military organization in 1966, and possesses its own nuclear weapons.

Economic Affairs

In 1989, according to estimates by the World Bank, France's gross national product (GNP), measured at average 1987–89 prices, was $1,000,866m., equivalent to $17,830 per head. During 1980–89, it was estimated, GNP expanded, in real terms, at an average annual rate of 2.0%, while GNP per head increased by 1.6% per year. Over the same period, the population increased by an annual average of 0.4%. France's gross domestic product (GDP) increased, in real terms, by an annual average of 1.8% in 1980–88.

Agriculture (including forestry and fishing) contributed about 3.5% of GDP in 1988. An estimated 5.5% of the labour force were employed in the sector in 1989. The principal crops in 1989 were wheat, sugar beet, maize and barley. Livestock, dairy products and wine are also important. During 1980–88 agricultural production increased by an annual average of 2.3%.

Industry (including mining, manufacturing, construction and power) provided 30.6% of GDP in 1988, and employed 30.5% of the working population in 1987. During 1980–88 industrial production increased by an annual average of 0.1%.

Mining contributed 0.7% of GDP and employed 0.5% of the working population in 1987. Coal is the principal mineral produced, while petroleum and natural gas are also extracted. In addition, metallic minerals, including iron ore and zinc, are mined.

Manufacturing provided about 22% of GDP in 1988, and employed 21.7% of the working population in 1987. Measured by the value of output, the most important branches of manufacturing in 1987 were food products, beverages and tobacco (accounting for 15.3% of the total), transport equipment (12.8%), metals and metal products (12.1%), chemicals (9.6%), non-electric machinery (8.9%) and electrical machinery (7.6%).

Energy is derived principally from coal and petroleum products. Imports of mineral fuels comprised 8.2% of the value of total imports in 1988.

In 1989 France recorded a trade deficit of US $10,703m., and there was a deficit of $3,892m. on the current account of the balance of payments. In 1989 the principal source of imports (19.3%) was the Federal Republic of Germany, which was also the principal market for exports (16.0%). Other major trading partners were Italy, Belgium and Luxembourg, and the Netherlands. The principal exports in 1989 were machinery and transport equipment, basic manufactures, road vehicles, armaments, and chemicals. The principal imports were machinery and transport equipment, basic manufactures and miscellaneous manufactured articles.

In 1990 the projected budgetary deficit was 90,000m. francs (equivalent to some 1.4% of GDP). The annual rate of inflation averaged 3.6% in 1989 and decreased to 3.4% in the year ending November 1990. An estimated 9.0% of the labour force were unemployed in November 1990.

France is a member of the European Community (see p. 135) and of the Organization for Economic Co-operation and Development (see p. 186), which annually examines the economic situation of member countries.

France is one of the world's leading industrial countries, although it suffers from a higher level of debt than other European countries. The heavy trade deficit is due, in part, to the decline of France's share of world trade in manufactured goods. A 10th National Plan (1989–92) is designed to prepare France for the EC's proposed single European market in 1992 (see p. 140). The Government aims to restrict the rise in unemployment, and to increase investments and exports, with the object of achieving a trade surplus by 1992. In addition, in January 1990 France removed its remaining exchange controls in a gesture of the country's commitment to European monetary integration.

Social Welfare

France has evolved a comprehensive system of social security, which is compulsory for all wage-earners and self-employed people. State insurance of wage-earners requires contributions from both employers and employees, and provides for sickness, unemployment, maternity, disability through industrial accident, and substantial allowances for large families. The self-employed must make these contributions in full. War veterans receive pensions and certain privileges, and widows the equivalent of three months' salary and pension. About 95% of all medical practitioners adhere to the state scheme. The patient pays directly for medical treatment and prescribed medicines, and then obtains reimbursement for all or part of the cost. Sickness benefits and pensions are related to the insured person's income, age and the length of time for which he or she has been insured. In 1985 expenditure by the central Government included about 437,500m. francs for health, and a further 787,000m. francs for social security and welfare. In 1987 France had 3,560 hospital establishments, with a total of 499,326 beds in 1985, equivalent to one for every 92 inhabitants. In 1986 there were 128,000 physicians registered in France. A national minimum hourly wage is in force, and is periodically adjusted in accordance with fluctuations in the cost of living.

Education

France is divided into 27 educational districts, called Académies, each responsible for the administration of education, from primary to higher levels, in its area. Education is compulsory and free for children aged six to 16 years. Primary education begins at six years of age and lasts for five years. At the age of 11 all pupils enter the first cycle of the Enseignement secondaire, with a four-year general course. At the age of 15 they may then proceed to the second cycle, choosing a course leading to the baccalauréat examination after three years or a course leading to the brevet d'études professionnelles after two years, with commercial, administrative or industrial options. In 1963 junior classes in the Lycées were gradually abolished in favour of new junior comprehensives, called Collèges. Alongside the collèges and lycées, technical education is provided in the Lycées professionnels and the Lycées techniques. About 17% of children attend France's 10,000 private schools, most of which are administered by the Roman Catholic Church. The Socialist Government's plans to merge private schools into the state system were abandoned in 1984, following strong public protest; compromise measures were introduced, however, involving continued government financial assistance and greater involvement in the appointment of teachers at private schools.

Educational reforms, introduced in 1980, aimed to decentralize the state school system: the school calendar now varies according to three zones, and the previously rigid and formal syllabus has been replaced by more flexibility and choice of curricula. Further decentralization measures have included, from 1986, the transfer of financial responsibility for education to the local authorities. In January 1989 the Socialist Government initiated a series of reforms aiming to 'develop, diversify and renovate' the education system. The legislation identified four targets for the system: no one should leave school without a recognized form of qualification; 80% of all schoolchildren should achieve the baccalauréat, or its equivalent; everyone who passes the baccalauréat examination should have the right to continue to higher education; and teaching methods should be reformed.

The minimum qualification for entry to university faculties is the baccalauréat. There are three cycles of university edu-

FRANCE

cation. The first level, the Diplôme d'études universitaires générales (DEUG), is reached after two years of study, and the first degree, the Licence, is obtained after three years. The master's degree (Maîtrise) is obtained after four years of study, while the doctorate requires six or seven years' study and the submission of a thesis. The prestigious Grandes Ecoles complement the universities; entry to them is by competitive examination, and they have traditionally supplied France's administrative élite. The 1968 reforms in higher education aimed to increase university autonomy and to render teaching methods less formal. Several new diploma courses were instituted in 1982 and 1984, and more directly vocational and professional qualifications are planned. However, Government plans to revise the baccalauréat, to introduce further selection procedures for entry to the universities, to restrict places on courses and to award separate degrees in each university were abandoned in December 1986, following student protests. In 1989 there was a huge increase in student enrolment, which universities were unable to accommodate. In 1990 the Government increased the financial provisions for education, following student demonstrations (see above).

Expenditure on education by central and local government in 1990 was projected at 227,400m. francs. Different forms of financial aid are available to university students, but in 1985/86 only 16% of French students obtained a grant.

Primary teachers are trained in Ecoles Normales. Secondary teachers must hold either the Certificat d'Aptitude au Professorat d'Enseignement Général des Collèges (CAPEGC), the Certificat d'Aptitude au Professorat de l'Enseignement du Second Degré (CAPES) or the Agrégation.

Public Holidays

1991: 1 January (New Year's Day), 1 April (Easter Monday), 1 May (Labour Day), 8 May (Liberation Day), 9 May (Ascension Day), 20 May (Whit Monday), 14 July (National Day, Fall of the Bastille), 15 August (Assumption), 1 November (All Saints' Day), 11 November (Armistice Day), 25 December (Christmas Day).

1992: 1 January (New Year's Day), 20 April (Easter Monday), 1 May (Labour Day), 8 May (Liberation Day), 28 May (Ascension Day), 8 June (Whit Monday), 14 July (National Day, Fall of the Bastille), 15 August (Assumption), 1 November (All Saints' Day), 11 November (Armistice Day), 25 December (Christmas Day).

Weights and Measures

The metric system is in force.

Statistical Survey

Unless otherwise indicated, figures in this survey refer to metropolitan France, excluding Overseas Departments and Territories.
Source (unless otherwise stated): Institut national de la statistique et des études économiques, 18 boulevard Adolphe-Pinard, 75675 Paris Cedex 14; tel. (1) 45-40-12-12.

Area and Population

AREA, POPULATION AND DENSITY

Area (sq km)	543,965*
Population (census results, *de jure*)†	
20 February 1975	52,655,802
4 March 1982	54,334,871
Population (official estimates at mid-year)	
1987	55,630,000
1988	55,884,000
1989	56,160,000
Density (per sq km) at mid-1989	103.2

* 210,026 sq miles.
† Excluding professional soldiers and military personnel outside the country with no personal residence in France. These were estimated at 44,000 in 1975.

NATIONALITY OF THE POPULATION (1982 census*)

Country of citizenship	Population	%
France	50,593,100	93.22
Algeria	795,920	1.47
Belgium	50,200	0.09
Germany	43,840	0.08
Italy	333,740	0.61
Morocco	431,120	0.79
Poland	64,820	0.12
Portugal	764,860	1.41
Spain	321,440	0.59
Tunisia	189,400	0.35
Turkey	123,540	0.23
Yugoslavia	64,420	0.11
Others	496,800	0.93
Total	**54,273,200**	**100.00**

* Figures based on a 5% sample of census returns.

REGIONS (1 January 1988)

	Area (sq km)	Population (estimated)	Density (per sq km)
Ile-de-France	12,012.3	10,319,700	859.1
Champagne-Ardenne	25,605.8	1,360,000	53.1
Picardie (Picardy)	19,399.5	1,783,400	91.9
Haute-Normandie	12,317.4	1,710,500	138.9
Centre	39,150.9	2,347,500	60.0
Basse-Normandie	17,589.3	1,385,300	78.8
Bourgogne (Burgundy)	31,582.0	1,613,900	51.1
Nord-Pas-de-Calais	12,414.1	3,925,000	316.2
Lorraine	23,547.4	2,320,700	98.6
Alsace	8,280.3	1,613,900	194.9
Franche-Comté	16,202.3	1,088,200	67.2
Pays de la Loire	32,081.8	3,054,500	95.2
Bretagne (Brittany)	27,207.9	2,772,900	101.9
Poitou-Charentes	25,809.5	1,599,600	62.0
Aquitaine	41,308.4	2,737,200	66.3
Midi-Pyrénées	45,347.9	2,377,300	52.4
Limousin	16,942.3	732,000	43.2
Rhône-Alpes	43,698.2	5,205,000	119.1
Auvergne	26,012.9	1,328,300	51.1
Languedoc-Roussillon	27,375.8	2,079,900	76.0
Provence-Alpes-Côte d'Azur	31,399.6	4,148,200	132.1
Corse (Corsica)	8,679.8	247,300	28.5
Total	**543,965.4**	**55,750,300**	**102.5**

1040

FRANCE   Statistical Survey

PRINCIPAL TOWNS
(population at 1982 census)

Paris (capital)	2,188,918	Le Mans	.	150,331
Marseille (Marseilles)	878,689	Dijon	.	145,569
Lyon (Lyons)	418,476	Limoges	.	144,082
Toulouse	354,289	Angers	.	141,143
Nice	338,486	Tours	.	136,483
Strasbourg	252,264	Amiens	.	136,358
Nantes	247,227	Nîmes	.	129,924
Bordeaux	211,197	Aix-en-Provence	.	124,550
Saint-Etienne	206,688	Besançon	.	119,687
Montpellier	201,067	Metz	.	118,502
Le Havre	200,411	Villeurbanne	.	118,330
Rennes	200,390	Caen	.	117,119
Reims (Rheims)	181,985	Mulhouse	.	113,794
Toulon	181,405	Perpignan	.	113,646
Lille	174,039	Orléans	.	105,589
Brest	160,355	Rouen	.	105,083
Grenoble	159,503	Boulogne-Billancourt	.	102,595
Clermont-Ferrand	151,092	Roubaix	.	101,886

BIRTHS, MARRIAGES AND DEATHS*

	Registered live births		Registered marriages		Registered deaths	
	Number	Rate (per 1,000)	Number	Rate (per 1,000)	Number	Rate (per 1,000)
1982	797,223	14.6	312,405	5.7	543,104	10.0
1983	748,525	13.7	300,513	5.5	559,655	10.2
1984	759,939	13.8	281,402	5.1	542,490	9.9
1985	768,431	13.9	269,419	4.9	552,496	10.0
1986	778,468	14.1	265,678	4.8	546,926	9.9
1987	767,828	13.8	265,177	4.8	527,466	9.5
1988†	770,690	13.8	271,100	4.9	524,290	9.4
1989†	765,000	13.6	281,000	5.0	528,000	9.4

* Including data for national armed forces outside the country.
† Provisional figures.

Expectation of Life at Birth (1987): Males 72.03 years; Females 80.27 years.

IMMIGRATION AND EMIGRATION

	1986	1987	1988
Algerian workers and their families:			
Arriving from Algeria in France	1,261,955	1,151,492	1,272,013
Returning from France to Algeria	1,308,440	1,094,163	1,069,131
Other immigrants:			
Permanent	38,370	39,000	43,939
Seasonal	81,670	76,647	70,547

ECONOMICALLY ACTIVE POPULATION
(sample survey, March 1987)*

	Males	Females	Total
Agriculture, hunting, forestry and fishing	1,034,752	559,937	1,594,689
Mining and quarrying	96,005	10,985	106,990
Manufacturing	3,249,847	1,397,568	4,647,415
Electricity, gas and water	152,341	40,565	192,906
Construction	1,441,284	135,296	1,576,580
Trade, restaurants and hotels	1,833,434	1,615,236	3,448,670
Transport, storage and communications	951,969	345,200	1,297,169
Finance, insurance, real estate and business services	906,398	852,141	1,758,539
Community, social and personal services	2,695,776	3,990,118	6,685,894
Activities not adequately defined	61,466	34,685	96,151
Total employed	12,423,272	8,981,731	21,405,003
Unemployed	1,172,384	1,394,915	2,567,299
Total labour force	13,595,656	10,376,646	23,972,302

* Figures include regular members of the armed forces, officially estimated at 304,200 (males 286,000; females 18,200) in 1986, but exclude persons on compulsory military service, totalling about 251,000.

Source: ILO, *Year Book of Labour Statistics*.

Agriculture

PRINCIPAL CROPS ('000 metric tons)

	1987	1988	1989
Wheat	27,415	29,677	31,817
Rye	299	276	262
Barley	10,489	10,086	9,810
Oats	1,122	1,074	1,025
Maize*	12,470	14,120	12,926
Sorghum	209	234	300
Rice (paddy)	54	65	97
Sugar beet	26,471	28,606	23,220
Potatoes	7,500‡	6,900‡	5,750
Pulses	2,072	2,831	2,854
Soybeans	210	255	311
Sunflower seed	2,659	2,350	2,054
Rapeseed	2,655	2,469	1,830
Tobacco (leaves)	38	33	29
Artichokes	36	91	97
Cabbages	298†	274	233
Carrots	529	540	485
Cauliflowers	541	568	585
Cucumbers and gherkins	101	104	105
Melons	280	281	285
Onions (dry)	219	184	202
Peas (green)	158	190	188
Tomatoes	709	743	756
Apples	2,389	2,473	2,339
Apricots	97	95	130
Grapes	9,186‡	7,419‡	7,555‡
Peaches and nectarines	488	457	551
Pears	440	345	344
Plums	203	229	146

* Figures refer to main, associated and catch crops.
† FAO estimate.
‡ Unofficial estimate.
Source: FAO, *Production Yearbook*.

FRANCE

LIVESTOCK ('000 head at 31 December)

	1986	1987	1988
Cattle	22,803	22,189	21,780
Pigs	12,419	12,643	12,480
Sheep*	10,580*	11,397	12,001
Goats	1,090	1,091	1,103
Horses	300	292	269
Asses†	24	25	25
Mules†	12	12	12
Chickens (million)†	188	189	190
Ducks (million)†	11	11	12
Turkeys (million)†	19	20	20

* Unofficial figure. † FAO estimates.
Source: FAO, *Production Yearbook*.

LIVESTOCK PRODUCTS ('000 metric tons)

	1987	1988	1989
Beef and veal	1,955	1,826	1,716†
Mutton and lamb*	158	156	150
Goats' meat	8†	8†	8†
Pig meat	1,729	1,852	1,840†
Horse meat	22	17	17†
Poultry meat	1,384	1,377	1,426
Other meat	295	292	292
Edible offals†	415	401	395
Cows' milk	27,146	26,606	27,250†
Sheep's milk	1,065	1,068	1,075
Goats' milk	456	434	468
Butter	571	516	539
Cheese	1,327	1,360	1,388
Hen eggs	884	931	891*
Wool:			
greasy*	24	23	23
clean*	13	13	13
Cattle hides†	158	159	160
Sheep skins†	16	17	17

* Unofficial figure. † FAO estimate.
Source: FAO, *Production Yearbook*.

Forestry

ROUNDWOOD REMOVALS
('000 cubic metres, excluding bark)

	1986	1987	1988
Sawlogs, veneer logs and logs for sleepers	19,260	20,410	21,914
Pulpwood	9,599	9,722	9,722
Other industrial wood	580	571	571
Fuel wood*	10,430	10,430	10,436
Total	39,869	41,124	42,643

* FAO estimate.
Source: FAO, *Yearbook of Forest Products*.

SAWNWOOD PRODUCTION
('000 cubic metres, including boxboards)

	1986	1987	1988
Coniferous (softwood)	5,740	5,956	6,450
Broadleaved (hardwood)	3,390	3,447	3,675
Total	9,130	9,403	10,125

Railway sleepers ('000 cubic metres): 188 in 1986; 209 in 1987.
Source: FAO, *Yearbook of Forest Products*.

Fishing*
('000 metric tons, live weight)

	1986	1987	1989
Rainbow trout	29.1	30.6	30.7
Atlantic cod	64.2	64.1	61.8
Blue ling	14.7	13.3	10.3
Haddock	14.2	14.0	9.3
Saithe (Pollock)	81.2	72.7	63.0
Whiting	28.3	33.0	33.1
European hake	21.7	18.2	21.9
Angler (Monk)	18.2	18.2	18.2
Atlantic herring	9.5	9.2	20.9
European pilchard (sardine)	28.7	26.0	27.7†
Skipjack tuna	50.8	55.5	53.7
Yellowfin tuna	48.4	54.4	80.6
Sharks, rays, skates, etc.	25.2	23.5	24.7
Other fishes (incl. unspecified)	162.4	163.8	170.1†
Total fish	596.7	596.5	626.1
Crustaceans	24.9	28.1	25.1†
Oysters	146.3	138.4	137.8†
Blue mussel	63.9	56.4	50.8
Other molluscs	38.6	41.3	57.6
Other marine animals	0.3	0.2	0.3†
Total catch	870.7	861.0	897.6†
Inland waters	39.3	39.9	41.6
Mediterranean and Black Sea	46.3	44.8	45.6†
Atlantic Ocean	704.7	693.0	708.4
Indian Ocean	80.4	83.4	102.1

* Figures exclude aquatic plants ('000 metric tons): 68.8 in 1986; 61.7 in 1987; 106.1 in 1988. Also excluded are corals and sponges.
† FAO estimates.
Source: FAO, *Yearbook of Fishery Statistics*.

Mining
('000 metric tons, unless otherwise indicated)

	1986	1987	1988
Hard coal	16,315	13,490	12,140
Brown coal (incl. lignite)	2,136	2,090	1,660
Iron ore:			
gross weight	12,436	11,235	9,983
metal content	3,861	3,514	3,225
Bauxite	1,238	1,271	878
Crude petroleum	2,942	3,236	3,355
Potash salts*	1,617	1,665	1,612
Native sulphur	1,170	1,092	1,022
Salt (unrefined)	7,083	7,013	6,752
Lead concentrates (metric tons)†	1,800	1,600	1,400
Zinc concentrates (metric tons)†	39,200	30,100	32,000
Natural gas (million cu m)	4,388	5,495	4,644

* Figures refer to recovered quantities of K_2O.
† Figures refer to the metal content of concentrates.
Source: Ministère de l'Industrie et de l'Aménagement du Territoire; and Institut national de la statistique et des études économiques.

FRANCE

Statistical Survey

Industry

SELECTED PRODUCTS
('000 metric tons, unless otherwise indicated)

	1986	1987	1988
Wheat flour*	4,969	5,113	n.a.
Raw sugar	3,734†	3,973†	4,424†
Margarine	153.6	161.6	n.a.
Wine ('000 hectolitres)	74,221	70,360	63,790
Beer ('000 hectolitres)	18,850	18,024	n.a.
Cigarettes (million)	59,122	54,160	53,307
Cotton yarn—pure and mixed (metric tons)[1]	193,074	196,476	191,527
Woven cotton fabrics—pure and mixed (metric tons)	116,988	113,627	111,376
Wool yarn—pure and mixed (metric tons)	97,547	87,570	76,034
Woven woollen fabrics—pure and mixed (metric tons)	48,372	42,901	43,471
Rayon and acetate continuous filaments (metric tons) / Rayon and acetate discontinuous fibres (metric tons)[2]	20,500	22,900	n.a.
Non-cellulosic continuous filaments (metric tons)	61,800	55,500	n.a.
Non-cellulosic discontinuous fibres (metric tons)	122,838	125,328	n.a.
Woven fabrics of non-cellulosic (synthetic) fibres (metric tons)[3]	70,308	66,972	n.a.
Mechanical wood pulp	430	463	526
Chemical wood pulp	1,584	1,628	1,665
Newsprint	304	299	373
Other printing and writing paper	2,196	2,309	2,486
Other paper and paperboard	3,080	3,224	3,454
Synthetic rubber	542	539	569
Rubber tyres ('000)[4]	51,138	55,570	59,930
Sulphuric acid	3,956	3,960	4,081
Caustic soda (Sodium hydroxide)	1,517	1,430	1,494
Nitrogenous fertilizers (a)[5]	1,690	1,530	1,435
Phosphate fertilizers (b)[5]	1,023	1,000	955
Potash fertilizers (b)[5]	1,719	1,549	1,564
Liquefied petroleum gas[6]	2,411	2,260	n.a.
Motor spirit (petrol)	16,207	16,638	18,513
Kerosene and jet fuels	4,286	4,149	4,539
Distillate fuel oils	28,077	25,923	27,456
Residual fuel oil	14,155	12,914	11,194
Petroleum bitumen (asphalt)	2,572	2,790	n.a.
Coke-oven coke	8,258	7,464	7,428
Cement	22,596	23,557	30,863
Pig-iron	13,982	13,449	14,786
Crude steel	17,865	17,693	19,122
Rolled steel products	15,849	16,252	17,428
Aluminium (unwrought): primary	386	381.8	388
secondary (incl. alloys)	170	186.3	213
Refined copper—unwrought (metric tons)	41,294	39,323	43,239
Lead (unwrought): primary	131.9	138.7	147
secondary	92.9	39.3	47
Zinc (unwrought)[7]	257.4	249.3	264.2

—continued	1986	1987	1988
Radio receivers ('000)	2,161	2,182	1,983
Television receivers ('000)	1,869	2,015	2,081
Merchant ships launched ('000 gross reg. tons)	185	204	12
Passenger motor cars ('000)	2,773.1	3,051.8	3,224.0
Lorries and vans ('000)	409.3	429.1	456.7
Mopeds and motorcycles ('000)	291.2	280.0	311.6
Construction: dwellings completed ('000)[8]	236.6	251.0	286.7
Electric energy (million kWh)	346,298	360,744	n.a.

* Deliveries.
† Estimate.

[1] Including tyre-cord yarn. [2] Including cigarette filtration tow.
[3] Including fabrics of natural silk.
[4] Tyres for road motor vehicles other than bicycles and motor cycles.
[5] Figures refer to estimated output during the 12 months ending (a) 30 June or (b) 30 April of year stated. Production is in terms of plant nutrients: nitrogen, phosphoric acid and K_2O.
[6] Excluding production in natural gas processing plants ('000 metric tons): 203 in 1986; 163 in 1987.
[7] Primary production only.
[8] Including restorations and conversions but excluding single rooms without kitchens.

Source: Ministère de l'Industrie et de l'Aménagement du Territoire; and Institut national de la statistique et des études économiques.

Finance

CURRENCY AND EXCHANGE RATES

Monetary Units:
100 centimes = 1 French franc.

Denominations:
Coins: 1, 5, 10, 20 and 50 centimes; 1, 2, 5, 10 and 100 francs.
Notes: 10, 50, 100, 200 and 500 francs.

Sterling and Dollar Equivalents (30 September 1990)
£1 sterling = 9.8225 francs;
US $1 = 5.2425 francs;
1,000 French francs = £101.81 = $190.75.

Average Exchange Rate (francs per US $)
1987   6.011
1988   5.957
1989   6.380

BUDGET (million francs)

Revenue	1987	1988	1989
Tax revenue	1,139,894	1,233,770	1,321,170
Income tax	222,600	233,000	243,830
Corporation tax	117,000	134,900	154,500
Value-added tax	500,260	545,500	586,965
Stamp duty, etc.*	63,900	70,570	73,075
Petroleum revenue	95,300	107,400	113,600
Other taxes	140,834	179,750	202,500
Non-tax revenue	65,195	79,755	99,408
Sub-total	1,205,089	1,313,525	1,420,578
Tax relief and reimbursements	−109,410	−130,900	−153,100
Other deductions, e.g. EEC	−153,190	−177,004	−185,351
Total	942,489	1,005,621	1,082,127

* Including registration duties and tax on stock exchange transactions.

FRANCE
Statistical Survey

Expenditure	1987	1988	1989
Public authorities, general administration	133,888	142,038	147,944
Education and culture	250,377	260,820	277,613
Social services, health and employment	202,672	205,383	223,175
Agriculture and rural areas	24,465	24,291	24,331
Housing and town planning	47,954	52,387	54,541
Transport and communications	47,569	47,148	47,524
Industry and services	49,939	51,049	34,782
Foreign affairs	42,953	44,117	53,459
Defence	177,856	182,877	190,812
Other purposes	124,770	142,897	123,009
Total	**1,102,443**	**1,153,007**	**1,177,190**

Source: Ministère de l'Economie, des Finances et du Budget.

BANK OF FRANCE AND EXCHANGE FUND RESERVES*
(US $ million at 31 December)

	1987	1988	1989
Gold†	41,496	33,686	33,982
IMF special drawing rights	1,502	1,390	1,329
Reserve position in IMF	1,914	1,615	1,414
Foreign exchange	29,634	22,359	21,868
Total	**74,546**	**59,050**	**58,593**

* Excluding deposits made with the European Monetary Co-operation Fund.
† Valued at market-related prices.
Source: IMF, *International Financial Statistics*.

CURRENCY IN CIRCULATION
('000 million francs at 31 December)

	1987	1988	1989
Currency outside banks	221.8	235.7	246.4

Source: Banque de France, Paris.

COST OF LIVING
(Consumer Price Index for Urban Households, average of monthly figures; base: 1980 = 100)

	1987	1988	1989
Food	167.3	169.9	177.2
Fuel and light	149.1	147.6	154.7
Clothing and household linen	175.9	181.6	186.8
Rent	173.8	185.1	195.3
All items (incl. others)	**167.3**	**171.8**	**178.0**

Source: ILO, *Year Book of Labour Statistics*.

NATIONAL ACCOUNTS
National Income and Product (million francs at current prices)*

	1985	1986	1987
Compensation of employees	2,581,077	2,696,068	2,801,578
Operating surplus	928,068	1,086,456	1,159,010
Domestic factor incomes	**3,509,145**	**3,782,524**	**3,960,588**
Consumption of fixed capital	590,445	628,830	664,406
Gross domestic product at factor cost	**4,099,590**	**4,411,354**	**4,624,994**
Indirect taxes	737,565	780,366	831,471
Less Subsidies	142,198	156,790	167,766
GDP in purchasers' values	**4,694,957**	**5,034,930**	**5,288,699**

—continued	1985	1986	1987
Factor income received from abroad	201,021	173,530	168,788
Less Factor income paid abroad	226,740	190,779	188,088
Gross national product (GNP)	**4,669,238**	**5,017,681**	**5,269,399**
Less Consumption of fixed capital	590,445	628,830	664,406
National income in market prices	**4,078,793**	**4,388,851**	**4,604,993**

* Figures are provisional. Revised totals of GDP in purchasers' values (in '000 million francs) are: 4,700.1 in 1985; 5,069.3 in 1986; 5,320.8 in 1987.
Source: Ministère de l'Economie, des Finances et du Budget.

Expenditure on the Gross Domestic Product
('000 million francs at current prices)

	1987	1988	1989
Government final consumption expenditure	1,015.9	1,071.1	1,132.5
Private final consumption expenditure	3,231.1	3,422.4	3,649.6
Increase in stocks*	19.4	31.0	29.2
Gross fixed capital formation*	1,046.2	1,164.4	1,268.7
Total domestic expenditure	**5,312.6**	**5,688.9**	**6,080.0**
Exports of goods and services	1,103.2	1,221.9	1,428.7
Less Imports of goods and services	1,095.0	1,218.0	1,406.5
GDP in purchasers' values	**5,320.8**	**5,692.7**	**6,102.2**
GDP at constant 1985 prices	**4,924.8**	**5,113.6**	**5,299.5**

* Construction of non-residential buildings is included in 'Increase in stocks'.
Source: IMF, *International Financial Statistics*.

Gross Domestic Product by Economic Activity
(provisional, million francs at current prices)

	1985	1986	1987
Agriculture and hunting	165,731	170,649	166,944
Forestry and logging	11,304	12,622	13,747
Fishing	3,509	4,407	4,316
Mining and quarrying	39,021	34,039	33,306
Manufacturing	1,039,206	1,116,889	1,152,208
Electricity, gas and water	115,669	119,538	123,337
Construction	250,242	265,601	287,096
Wholesale and retail trade	570,166	624,182	657,881
Restaurants and hotels	112,046	122,453	133,798
Transport, storage and communications	283,701	304,812	315,948
Finance, insurance, real estate and business services*	850,521	942,878	1,020,435
Government services	795,718	845,158	873,588
Other community, social and personal services	230,843	255,140	274,654
Sub-total	**4,467,677**	**4,818,368**	**5,057,258**
Value-added tax and import duties†	414,088	429,719	459,246
Less Imputed bank service charges	186,808	213,157	227,805
Total	**4,694,957**	**5,034,930**	**5,288,699**

* Including imputed rents of owner-occupied dwellings.
† Including other adjustments (million francs): −163 in 1985; −173 in 1986; −447 in 1987.
Source: mainly UN, *National Accounts Statistics*.

FRANCE

Statistical Survey

BALANCE OF PAYMENTS (US $ million)*

	1987	1988	1989
Merchandise exports f.o.b.	141,658	160,184	170,752
Merchandise imports f.o.b.	−150,325	−168,727	−181,455
Trade balance	−8,667	−8,544	−10,703
Exports of services	79,344	87,788	100,421
Imports of services	−69,713	−76,018	−85,234
Balance on goods and services	964	3,226	4,484
Private unrequited transfers (net)	−2,297	−2,437	−2,661
Government unrequited transfers (net)	−3,114	−4,294	−5,714
Current balance	−4,446	−3,504	−3,892
Direct capital investment (net)	−4,071	−6,006	−9,116
Other long-term capital (net)	6,282	6,183	17,566
Short-term capital (net)	−6,945	2,305	−4,540
Net errors and omissions	850	927	3,509
Total (net monetary movements)	−8,329	−95	−2,473
Valuation changes (net)	4,228	−2,517	119
Official financing (net)	5,727	−5,067	1,613
Changes in reserves	1,627	−7,679	−742

* Figures refer to transactions of metropolitan France, Monaco and the French overseas departments and territories with the rest of the world.

Source: IMF, *International Financial Statistics*.

External Trade

Note: Figures refer to the trade of metropolitan France and Monaco with the rest of the world, excluding trade in war materials, goods exported under the off-shore procurement programme, war reparations and restitutions and the export of sea products direct from the high seas. The figures include trade in second-hand ships and aircraft, and the supply of stores and bunkers for foreign ships and aircraft.

PRINCIPAL COMMODITIES
(distribution by SITC, million francs)

Imports c.i.f.	1987	1988‡	1989‡
Food and live animals	90,857.7	97,864.3	106,389.4
Meat and meat preparations	17,019.1	18,471.8	25,057.6
Fresh, chilled or frozen meat	15,182.2	16,540.1	19,529.5
Vegetables and fruit	23,968.0	23,305.1	27,183.9
Beverages and tobacco	9,134.0	10,589.6	11,908.7
Crude materials (inedible) except fuels	41,637.6	48,209.1	55,786.1
Mineral fuels, lubricants, etc. (incl. electric current)	102,021.3	86,654.1	107,704.4
Petroleum, petroleum products, etc.	79,135.5	64,676.7	82,825.7
Crude petroleum oils, etc.	50,389.1	42,614.7	55,204.1
Refined petroleum products	26,797.2	20,218.8	25,547.5
Gas (natural and manufactured)	15,712.6	14,579.6	15,800.1
Animal and vegetable oils, fats and waxes	3,127.1	3,663.9	4,252.1
Chemicals and related products	101,083.8	116,724.2	132,067.6
Organic chemicals	23,894.5	27,699.1	30,988.3
Artificial resins, plastic materials, etc.	25,286.4	29,379.9	33,551.4
Products of polymerization, etc.	16,445.8	n.a.	n.a.

Imports c.i.f.—*continued*	1987	1988‡	1989‡
Basic manufactures	164,745.8	190,459.5	221,495.3
Paper, paperboard and manufactures	23,128.1	26,723.9	30,139.6
Paper and paperboard	17,476.7	20,259.0	22,595.8
Textile yarn, fabrics, etc.	33,344.7	34,758.6	39,216.4
Non-metallic mineral manufactures	17,437.0	19,714.0	22,787.7
Iron and steel	30,429.6	36,240.0	43,361.6
Non-ferrous metals	20,541.9	29,402.2	37,273.3
Other metal manufactures	22,849.5	26,070.8	29,800.0
Machinery and transport equipment	298,366.0	350,399.1	406,608.1
Power generating machinery and equipment	24,348.7	22,144.2	29,289.4
Machinery specialized for particular industries	30,695.1	36,974.6	43,394.7
General industrial machinery, equipment and parts	35,743.8	41,800.8	48,632.6
Office machines and automatic data processing equipment	42,007.2	48,842.7	54,539.8
Automatic data processing machines and units	24,832.3	29,114.0	33,225.4
Parts and accessories for office machines, etc.	12,898.2	15,027.8	16,085.6
Telecommunications and sound equipment	18,801.9	22,932.0	25,400.9
Other electrical machinery, apparatus, etc.	47,182.0	55,703.3	61,503.7
Road vehicles and parts*	83,333.1	93,463.3	113,804.9
Passenger motor cars (excl. buses)	45,008.9	50,270.3	63,687.3
Motor vehicles for goods transport, etc.	11,185.7	12,762.7	15,106.7
Parts and accessories for cars, buses, lorries, etc.*	18,016.1	19,980.1	22,241.8
Other transport equipment and parts*	9,071.2	18,683.9	19,028.2
Aircraft, associated equipment and parts*	7,170.6	15,937.0	16,897.2
Miscellaneous manufactured articles	130,870.0	145,918.8	165,763.4
Furniture and parts	13,527.3	15,215.6	16,991.4
Clothing and accessories (excl. footwear)	33,570.6	35,909.9	40,848.5
Professional, scientific and controlling instruments, etc.	16,518.5	18,470.1	20,672.2
Photographic apparatus, optical goods, watches and clocks	12,215.0	13,588.2	15,071.5
Other commodities and transactions†	3,201.2	3,316.1	4,674.6
Total	945,044.5	1,053,798.6	1,216,649.7

* Excluding tyres, engines and electrical parts.
† Including items not classified according to kind (million francs): 421.5 in 1987; 686.6 in 1988; 973.3 in 1989.
‡ Data are based on a revised classification. Some figures are not strictly comparable with those for 1987.

Exports f.o.b.	1987	1988‡	1989‡
Food and live animals	98,336.3	114,487.6	129,922.6
Meat and meat preparations	11,876.8	13,768.2	16,385.1
Dairy products and birds' eggs	14,875.9	17,543.6	19,037.5
Cereals and cereal preparations	31,331.5	35,629.2	39,864.6
Wheat and meslin (unmilled)	13,202.8	16,212.2	17,781.3
Beverages and tobacco	30,356.2	33,000.1	37,788.2
Beverages	29,615.1	32,246.1	36,912.3
Alcoholic beverages	27,823.4	30,144.0	34,273.5
Crude materials (inedible) except fuels	33,666.5	41,440.3	44,594.7
Mineral fuels, lubricants, etc. (incl. electric current)	19,541.4	19,617.9	23,960.8
Animal and vegetable oils, fats and waxes	1,802.4	2,368.5	2,962.8

FRANCE

Statistical Survey

Exports f.o.b.—continued	1987	1988‡	1989‡
Chemicals and related products	122,280.6	140,524.9	152,579.1
Organic chemicals	28,247.8	32,378.4	35,792.9
Hydrocarbons and their derivatives	17,714.7	19,494.7	20,602.9
Inorganic chemicals	18,583.3	19,305.9	16,765.9
Medicinal and pharmaceutical products	14,206.4	15,441.4	18,583.4
Essential oils, perfume materials and cleansing preparations	17,100.2	19,517.1	22,918.9
Perfumery, cosmetics and toilet preparations (excl. soaps)	12,267.5	14,220.9	16,865.5
Artificial resins, plastic materials, etc.	23,884.0	28,961.7	30,426.6
Products of polymerization, etc.	16,089.2	n.a.	n.a.
Basic manufactures	154,274.7	172,224.8	200,604.7
Rubber manufactures	14,142.1	15,373.6	16,497.2
Paper, paperboard and manufactures	16,168.2	18,040.6	21,174.6
Textile yarn, fabrics, etc.	27,195.3	27,483.5	31,647.6
Non-metallic mineral manufactures	16,990.0	18,949.2	21,309.0
Iron and steel	39,710.9	46,377.2	54,234.5
Non-ferrous metals	14,120.5	18,358.2	23,210.0
Other metal manufactures	19,826.2	21,440.0	25,402.4
Machinery and transport equipment	303,642.5	338,326.2	392,544.0
Power generating machinery and equipment	25,005.0	29,019.4	32,141.8
Internal combustion piston engines and parts	9,633.5	14,590.8	17,005.9
Machinery specialized for particular industries	25,220.6	28,848.2	33,420.6
General industrial machinery, equipment and parts	33,513.0	37,662.5	44,397.2
Office machines and automatic data processing equipment	28,902.2	29,122.2	33,058.7
Automatic data processing machines and units	14,377.1	14,318.3	16,118.4
Telecommunications and sound equipment	14,919.7	15,205.4	18,472.5
Other electrical machinery, apparatus, etc.	44,814.4	50,427.1	55,089.3
Switchgear, etc.	12,055.5	13,575.9	15,525.2
Road vehicles and parts*	100,872.2	107,903.5	123,604.8
Passenger motor cars (excl. buses)	50,847.3	58,146.6	68,015.4
Parts and accessories for cars, buses, lorries, etc.*	37,944.6	35,236.5	37,931.0
Other transport equipment and parts*	26,213.7	34,358.6	46,666.1
Aircraft, associated equipment and parts*	18,590.8	27,282.3	40,162.5
Miscellaneous manufactured articles	87,936.6	98,490.8	111,660.1
Clothing and accessories (excl. footwear)	18,260.7	19,627.9	23,112.8
Professional, scientific and controlling instruments, etc.	14,590.1	15,884.8	16,846.0
Other commodities and transactions†	5,943.7	3,266.9	5,793.8
Total	857,781.1	963,747.9	1,102,410.8

* Excluding tyres, engines and electrical parts.
† Including items not classified according to kind (million francs): 3,143.0 in 1987; 965.3 in 1988; 2,893.8 in 1989.
‡ Data are based on a revised classification. Some figures are not strictly comparable with those for 1987.

PRINCIPAL TRADING PARTNERS (million francs)*

Imports c.i.f.	1987	1988	1989
Algeria	8,535.1	8,298.2	9,460.6
Australia	5,695.4	6,241.7	6,343.5
Austria	7,709.3	9,060.7	10,246.3
Belgium and Luxembourg	88,679.9	96,313.4	111,766.4
Brazil	7,502.2	9,535.7	10,892.1
Canada	6,539.2	7,740.5	8,836.2
China, People's Republic	6,589.8	8,578.3	11,020.4
Denmark	8,400.9	8,880.0	10,102.3
Finland	6,978.1	8,060.1	8,872.0
Germany, Federal Republic	186,648.1	208,012.1	235,169.6
Iran	3,833.3	761.5	6,635.9
Iraq	5,954.9	4,479.8	5,437.1
Ireland	7,374.3	8,512.9	10,546.4
Italy	110,810.2	122,779.1	140,341.7
Japan	36,056.5	44,051.0	50,253.1
Korea, Republic	6,650.6	8,559.7	7,915.4
Morocco	6,380.4	7,293.8	8,555.7
Netherlands	53,271.0	55,835.9	62,969.9
Norway	10,807.8	11,748.9	17,278.4
Portugal	9,282.9	10,275.1	12,623.0
Saudi Arabia	7,448.4	9,045.0	12,172.3
Spain (excl. Canary Is.)	41,238.9	44,388.3	54,245.8
Sweden	15,684.4	17,670.0	20,168.9
Switzerland and Liechtenstein	23,625.4	26,496.3	29,948.9
Taiwan	7,405.7	9,193.4	10,720.8
USSR	15,348.3	16,746.2	16,742.7
United Kingdom	67,179.0	76,899.2	86,874.8
USA and Puerto Rico	67,586.9	81,507.9	93,671.4
Total (incl. others)	945,044.5	1,053,798.6	1,216,649.7

Exports f.o.b.	1987	1988	1989
Algeria	11,755.3	9,443.5	12,775.4
Australia	3,261.5	4,461.8	6,131.8
Austria	7,146.1	8,407.0	9,843.9
Belgium and Luxembourg	79,864.9	86,722.8	97,735.7
Brazil	5,249.2	4,431.6	4,469.6
Canada	8,741.3	12,080.8	10,903.8
China, People's Republic	5,086.3	5,504.0	9,888.5
Denmark	7,734.0	7,888.6	8,488.3
Egypt	5,360.9	5,428.7	5,590.4
Finland	4,255.1	4,832.9	5,954.1
Germany, Federal Republic	142,699.3	157,741.3	176,526.7
Greece	6,714.4	7,451.5	8,196.3
Guadeloupe	4,544.3	5,156.2	5,955.7
Hong Kong	4,748.0	6,140.1	6,864.6
India	5,148.7	3,923.6	7,214.8
Italy	103,597.8	117,706.2	133,410.4
Japan	13,210.3	16,533.6	21,019.4
Korea, Republic	4,700.7	5,513.4	5,919.3
Martinique	4,464.4	5,176.2	5,469.2
Morocco	6,475.9	7,656.5	10,291.2
Netherlands	43,600.7	54,006.9	62,370.9
Norway	5,378.3	4,127.0	4,154.5
Portugal	9,328.6	11,853.9	14,906.2
Réunion	5,367.7	6,202.3	6,905.2
Saudi Arabia	6,663.8	6,575.8	6,932.2
Singapore	3,504.2	4,091.2	6,203.6
Spain (excl. Canary Is.)	45,491.3	51,773.9	63,017.0
Sweden	11,830.5	12,593.2	14,850.0
Switzerland and Liechtenstein	36,786.1	40,066.1	46,289.5
Taiwan	2,744.2	3,853.4	5,854.3
Tunisia	5,040.8	5,475.0	7,147.3
USSR	10,482.9	11,580.1	10,957.0
United Kingdom	75,512.5	94,290.9	105,302.5
USA and Puerto Rico	62,525.0	70,658.5	72,428.7
Total (incl. others)	857,781.1	963,747.9	1,102,410.8

* Imports by country of production; exports by country of last consignment.

Source: Direction Générale des Douanes et Droits Indirects.

FRANCE   *Statistical Survey*

Transport

RAILWAYS (traffic)

	1986	1987	1988
Paying passengers ('000 journeys)	794,330	799,400	810,000
Freight carried ('000 metric tons)	145,860	142,290	144,900
Passenger-km (million)	59,860	59,970	63,290
Freight ton-km (million)*	51,690	51,300	52,290

* Including passengers' baggage.
Source: Société Nationale des Chemins de Fer Français, Paris.

ROAD TRAFFIC ('000 motor vehicles in use at 31 December)

	1987	1988	1989
Passenger cars	21,970	22,520	23,010
Goods vehicles	4,160	4,355	4,790
Buses and coaches	65	65	68
Motor cycles and mopeds	3,370	n.a.	n.a.

Source: International Road Federation, *World Road Statistics*.

INLAND WATERWAYS

	1986	1987	1988
Freight carried ('000 metric tons)	63,118	60,720	64,587
Freight ton-km (million)	7,767	7,370	7,334

SHIPPING
Merchant Fleet (vessels registered at 30 June)

	Displacement ('000 gross reg. tons)		
	1983	1984	1985
Oil tankers	5,443	4,785	4,346
Total (incl. others)	9,868	8,945	8,237

Source: UN, *Statistical Yearbook*.
Total Fleet ('000 grt at 30 June): 4,506 in 1988; 4,413 in 1989 (Source: *Lloyd's Register of Shipping*).

Sea-borne Freight Traffic ('000 metric tons)

	1986	1987	1988
Goods loaded (excl. stores)	75,271	77,782	77,364
International	64,732	66,680	67,839
Coastwise	10,539	11,182	9,525
Goods unloaded (excl. fish)	206,071	203,253	109,446
International	194,022	190,014	96,872
Coastwise	12,049	13,239	12,574

Source: Direction des Ports et de la Navigation Maritimes, Ministère délégué chargé de la Mer.

CIVIL AVIATION (revenue traffic on scheduled services)

	1983	1984	1985
Kilometres flown (million)	275.2	270.8	275.8
Passengers carried ('000)	23,278	23,694	24,492
Passenger-km (million)	38,599	38,712	39,559
Freight ton-km (million)	2,483.7	2,797.7	2,873.3
Mail ton-km (million)	112.9	112.8	119.1
Total ton-km (million)	6,027	6,350	6,506

Source: UN, *Statistical Yearbook*.

Tourism

FOREIGN TOURIST ARRIVALS BY COUNTRY ('000)

	1986	1987	1988
Belgium and Luxembourg	3,099	3,111	3,146
Canada	386	349	344
Germany, Federal Republic	8,417	8,915	9,113
Italy	2,798	3,157	9,441
Latin America	696	780	751
Netherlands	4,012	3,936	4,047
Spain	1,043	1,223	1,310
Switzerland	3,524	3,372	3,378
United Kingdom and Ireland	6,299	6,368	6,645
USA	1,668	1,802	1,950
Total (incl. others)	36,080	36,974	38,288

Net earnings from tourism (million francs): 23,245 (receipts 82,097, expenditure 57,852) in 1988; 39,649 (receipts 103,646, expenditure 63,997) in 1989.
Source: Ministère du Tourisme, Direction des Industries Touristiques.

Communications Media

	1985	1986	1987
Radio receivers ('000 in use)	48,000	49,000	49,500
Television receivers ('000 in use)	21,500	22,000	n.a.
Book production (titles)*	37,860	38,701	43,505

* Including pamphlets (about 32% of all titles produced in 1984).
Daily newspapers (1986): 92 titles (combined circulation 10,670,000 copies per issue).
Non-daily newspapers (1981): 526 titles (circulation 16,282,000 copies).
Source: UNESCO, *Statistical Yearbook*.
Telephones (1985): 34,347,000 in use.

Education

(1988/89)

	Institutions	Staff	Students
Pre-primary	18,186	73,795*	2,504,125
Primary	45,686	198,922*	4,085,508
Secondary	11,268	333,740*	5,380,072
Universities, etc.	n.a.	47,570	1,040,949

* Figures are for 1987/88 and refer to teachers in public education only.
Source: Institut national de la statistique et des études économiques.

Directory

The Constitution

The Constitution of the Fifth Republic was adopted by referendum on 28 September 1958 and promulgated on 6 October 1958.

PREAMBLE

The French people hereby solemnly proclaims its attachment to the Rights of Man and to the principles of national sovereignty as defined by the Declaration of 1789, confirmed and complemented by the Preamble of the Constitution of 1946.

By virtue of these principles and that of the free determination of peoples, the Republic hereby offers to the Overseas Territories that express the desire to adhere to them, new institutions based on the common ideal of liberty, equality and fraternity and conceived with a view to their democratic evolution.

Article 1. The Republic and the peoples of the Overseas Territories who, by an act of free determination, adopt the present Constitution thereby institute a Community.

The Community shall be based on the equality and the solidarity of the peoples composing it.

I. ON SOVEREIGNTY

Article 2. France shall be a Republic, indivisible, secular, democratic and social. It shall ensure the equality of all citizens before the law, without distinction of origin, race or religion. It shall respect all beliefs.

The national emblem shall be the tricolour flag, blue, white and red.

The national anthem shall be the 'Marseillaise'.

The motto of the Republic shall be 'Liberty, Equality, Fraternity'.

Its principle shall be government of the people, by the people, and for the people.

Article 3. National sovereignty belongs to the people, which shall exercise this sovereignty through its representatives and through the referendum.

No section of the people, nor any individual, may attribute to themselves or himself the exercise thereof.

Suffrage may be direct or indirect under the conditions stipulated by the Constitution. It shall always be universal, equal and secret.

All French citizens of both sexes who have reached their majority and who enjoy civil and political rights may vote under the conditions to be determined by law.

Article 4. Political parties and groups may compete for votes. They may form and carry on their activities freely. They must respect the principles of national sovereignty and of democracy.

II. THE PRESIDENT OF THE REPUBLIC

Article 5. The President of the Republic shall see that the Constitution is respected. He shall ensure, by his arbitration, the regular functioning of the public powers, as well as the continuity of the State.

He shall be the guarantor of national independence, of the integrity of the territory, and of respect for Community agreements and for treaties.

Article 6. The President of the Republic shall be elected for seven years by direct universal suffrage. The method of implementation of the present article shall be determined by an organic law.

Article 7. The President of the Republic shall be elected by an absolute majority of the votes cast. If such a majority is not obtained at the first ballot, a second ballot shall take place on the second following Sunday. Those who may stand for the second ballot shall be only the two candidates who, after the possible withdrawal of candidates with more votes, have gained the largest number of votes on the first ballot.

Voting shall begin at the summons of the Government. The election of the new President of the Republic shall take place not less than 20 days and not more than 35 days before the expiration of the powers of the President in office. In the event that the Presidency of the Republic has been vacated for any reason whatsoever, or impeded in its functioning as officially declared by the Constitutional Council, after the matter has been referred to it by the Government and which shall give its ruling by an absolute majority of its members, the functions of the President of the Republic, with the exception of those covered by Articles 11 and 12 hereunder, shall be temporarily exercised by the President of the Senate and, if the latter is in his turn unable to exercise his functions, by the Government.

In the case of vacancy or when the impediment is declared to be final by the Constitutional Council, the voting for the election of the new President shall take place, except in case of force majeure officially noted by the Constitutional Council, not less than 20 days and not more than 35 days after the beginning of the vacancy or of the declaration of the final nature of the impediment.

If, in the seven days preceding the latest date for the lodging of candidatures, one of the persons who, at least 30 days prior to that date, publicly announced his decision to be a candidate dies or is impeded, the Constitutional Council can decide to postpone the election.

If, before the first ballot, one of the candidates dies or is impeded, the Constitutional Council orders the postponement of the election.

In the event of the death or impediment, before any candidates have withdrawn, of one of the two candidates who received the greatest number of votes in the first ballot, the Constitutional Council shall declare that the electoral procedure must be repeated in full; the same shall apply in the event of the death or impediment of one of the two candidates standing for the second ballot.

All cases shall be referred to the Constitutional Council under the conditions laid down in paragraph 2 of article 61 below, or under those determined for the presentation of candidates by the organic law provided for in Article 6 above.

The Constitutional Council can extend the periods stipulated in paragraphs 3 and 5 above provided that polling shall not take place more than 35 days after the date of the decision of the Constitutional Council. If the implementation of the provisions of this paragraph results in the postponement of the election beyond the expiry of the powers of the President in office, the latter shall remain in office until his successor is proclaimed.

Articles 49 and 50 and Article 89 of the Constitution may not be put into application during the vacancy of the Presidency of the Republic or during the period between the declaration of the final nature of the impediment of the President of the Republic and the election of his successor.

Article 8. The President of the Republic shall appoint the Premier. He shall terminate the functions of the Premier when the latter presents the resignation of the Government.

At the suggestion of the Premier, he shall appoint the other members of the Government and shall terminate their functions.

Article 9. The President of the Republic shall preside over the Council of Ministers.

Article 10. The President of the Republic shall promulgate the laws within 15 days following the transmission to the Government of the finally adopted law.

He may, before the expiration of this time limit, ask Parliament for a reconsideration of the law or of certain of its articles. This reconsideration may not be refused.

Article 11. The President of the Republic, on the proposal of the government during [Parliamentary] sessions, or on joint motion of the two Assemblies published in the *Journal Officiel*, may submit to a referendum any bill dealing with the organization of the public powers, entailing approval of a Community agreement, or providing for authorization to ratify a treaty that, without being contrary to the Constitution, might affect the functioning of the institutions.

When the referendum decides in favour of the bill, the President of the Republic shall promulgate it within the time limit stipulated in the preceding article.

Article 12. The President of the Republic may, after consultation with the Premier and the Presidents of the Assemblies, declare the dissolution of the National Assembly.

General elections shall take place 20 days at the least and 40 days at the most after the dissolution.

The National Assembly shall convene by right on the second Thursday following its election. If this meeting takes place between the periods provided for ordinary sessions, a session shall, by right, be opened for a 15 day period.

There may be no further dissolution within a year following these elections.

Article 13. The President of the Republic shall sign the ordinances and decrees decided upon in the Council of Ministers.

He shall make appointments to the civil and military posts of the State.

Councillors of State, the Grand Chancellor of the Legion of Honour, Ambassadors and Envoys Extraordinary, Master Councillors of the Audit Office, prefects, representatives of the Government in the Overseas Territories, general officers, rectors of academies [regional divisions of the public educational system] and directors of central administrations shall be appointed in meetings of the Council of Ministers.

An organic law shall determine the other posts to be filled in meetings of the Council of Ministers, as well as the conditions under which the power of the President of the Republic to make appointments to office may be delegated by him to be exercised in his name.

Article 14. The President of the Republic shall accredit Ambassadors and Envoys Extraordinary to foreign powers; foreign Ambassadors and Envoys Extraordinary shall be accredited to him.

Article 15. The President of the Republic shall be commander of the armed forces. He shall preside over the higher councils and committees of national defence.

Article 16. When the institutions of the Republic, the independence of the nation, the integrity of its territory or the fulfilment of its international commitments are threatened in a grave and immediate manner and the regular functioning of the constitutional public powers is interrupted, the President of the Republic shall take the measures required by these circumstances, after official consultation with the Premier and the Presidents of the Assemblies, as well as with the Constitutional Council.

He shall inform the nation of these measures in a message.

These measures must be prompted by the desire to ensure to the constitutional public powers, in the shortest possible time, the means of accomplishing their mission. The Constitutional Council shall be consulted with regard to such measures.

Parliament shall meet by right.

The National Assembly may not be dissolved during the exercise of exceptional powers.

Article 17. The President of the Republic shall have the right of pardon.

Article 18. The President of the Republic shall communicate with the two Assemblies of Parliament by means of messages, which he shall cause to be read, and which shall not be the occasion for any debate.

Between sessions, the Parliament shall be convened especially to this end.

Article 19. The acts of the President of the Republic, other than those provided for under Articles 8 (first paragraph), 11, 12, 16, 18, 54, 56 and 61, shall be counter-signed by the Premier and, should circumstances so require, by the appropriate ministers.

III. THE GOVERNMENT

Article 20. The Government shall determine and conduct the policy of the nation.

It shall have at its disposal the administration and the armed forces.

It shall be responsible to the Parliament under the conditions and according to the procedures stipulated in Articles 49 and 50.

Article 21. The Premier shall direct the operation of the Government. He shall be responsible for national defence. He shall ensure the execution of the laws. Subject to the provisions of Article 13, he shall have regulatory powers and shall make appointments to civil and military posts.

He may delegate certain of his powers to the ministers.

He shall replace, should the occasion arise, the President of the Republic as the Chairman of the councils and committees provided for under Article 15.

He may, in exceptional instances, replace him as the chairman of a meeting of the Council of Ministers by virtue of an explicit delegation and for a specific agenda.

Article 22. The acts of the Premier shall be counter-signed, when circumstances so require, by the ministers responsible for their execution.

Article 23. The functions of Members of the Government shall be incompatible with the exercise of any parliamentary mandate, with the holding of any office, at the national level, in business, professional or labour organizations, and with any public employment or professional activity.

An organic law shall determine the conditions under which the holders of such mandates, functions or employments shall be replaced.

The replacement of the members of Parliament shall take place in accordance with the provisions of Article 25.

IV. THE PARLIAMENT

Article 24. The Parliament shall comprise the National Assembly and the Senate.

The deputies to the National Assembly shall be elected by direct suffrage.

The Senate shall be elected by indirect suffrage. It shall ensure the representation of the territorial units of the Republic. Frenchmen living outside France shall be represented in the Senate.

Article 25. An organic law shall determine the term for which each Assembly is elected, the number of its members, their emoluments, the conditions of eligibility, and the system of ineligibilities and incompatibilities.

It shall likewise determine the conditions under which, in the case of a vacancy in either Assembly, persons shall be elected to replace the deputy or senator whose seat has been vacated until the holding of new complete or partial elections to the Assembly concerned.

Article 26. No Member of Parliament may be prosecuted, searched for, arrested, detained or tried as a result of the opinions or votes expressed by him in the exercise of his functions.

No Member of Parliament may, during parliamentary session, be prosecuted or arrested for criminal or minor offences without the authorization of the Assembly of which he is a member except in the case of *flagrante delicto.*

When Parliament is not in session, no Member of Parliament may be arrested without the authorization of the Secretariat of the Assembly of which he is a member, except in the case of *flagrante delicto*, of authorized prosecution or of final conviction.

The detention or prosecution of a Member of Parliament shall be suspended if the assembly of which he is a member so demands.

Article 27. Any compulsory vote shall be null and void.

The right to vote of the members of Parliament shall be personal.

The organic law may, under exceptional circumstances, authorize the delegation of a vote. In this case, no member may be delegated more than one vote.

Article 28. Parliament shall convene by right in two ordinary sessions a year.

The first session shall begin on the first Tuesday of October and shall end on the third Friday of December.

The second session shall open on the last Tuesday of April; it may not last longer than three months.

Article 29. Parliament shall convene in extraordinary session at the request of the Premier or of the majority of the members comprising the National Assembly, to consider a specific agenda.

When an extraordinary session is held at the request of the members of the National Assembly, the closure decree shall take effect as soon as the Parliament has exhausted the agenda for which it was called, and at the latest 12 days from the date of its meeting.

Only the Premier may ask for a new session before the end of the month following the closure decree.

Article 30. Apart from cases in which Parliament meets by right, extraordinary sessions shall be opened and closed by decree of the President of the Republic.

Article 31. The members of the Government shall have access to the two Assemblies. They shall be heard when they so request.

They may call for the assistance of Commissioners of the Government.

Article 32. The President of the National Assembly shall be elected for the duration of the legislature. The President of the Senate shall be elected after each partial re-election [of the Senate].

Article 33. The meetings of the two Assemblies shall be public. An *in extenso* report of the debates shall be published in the *Journal Officiel.*

Each Assembly may sit in secret committee at the request of the Premier or of one-tenth of its members.

V. ON RELATIONS BETWEEN PARLIAMENT AND THE GOVERNMENT

Article 34. Laws shall be voted by Parliament.

They shall establish the regulations concerning:

Civil rights and the fundamental guarantees granted to the citizens for the exercise of their public liberties; the obligations imposed by the national defence upon the person and property of citizens;

Nationality, status and legal capacity of persons; marriage contracts, inheritance and gifts;

Determination of crimes and misdemeanours as well as the penalties imposed therefor; criminal procedure; amnesty; the creation of new juridical systems and the status of magistrates;

The basis, the rate and the methods of collecting taxes of all types; the issue of currency;

They likewise shall determine the regulations concerning:

The electoral system of the Parliamentary Assemblies and the local assemblies;

The establishment of categories of public institutions;

The fundamental guarantees granted to civil and military personnel employed by the State;

The nationalization of enterprises and the transfers of the property of enterprises from the public to the private sector.

Laws shall determine the fundamental principles of:
The general organization of national defence;
The free administration of local communities, of their competencies and their resources;
Education;
Property rights, civil and commercial obligations;
Legislation pertaining to employment unions and social security.

The financial laws shall determine the financial resources and obligations of the State under the conditions and with the reservations to be provided for by an organic law.

Laws pertaining to national planning shall determine the objectives of the economic and social action of the State.

The provisions of the present article may be detailed and supplemented by an organic law.

Article 35. Parliament shall authorize the declaration of war.

Article 36. Martial law shall be decreed in a meeting of the Council of Ministers.

Its prorogation beyond 12 days may be authorized only by Parliament.

Article 37. Matters other than those that fall within the domain of law shall be of a regulatory character.

Legislative texts concerning these matters may be modified by decrees issued after consultation with the Council of State. Those legislative texts which shall be passed after the entry into force of the present Constitution shall be modified by decree only if the Constitutional Council has stated that they have a regulatory character as defined in the preceding paragraph.

Article 38. The Government may, in order to carry out its programme, ask Parliament for authorization to take through ordinances, during a limited period, measures that are normally within the domain of law.

The ordinances shall be enacted in meetings of Ministers after consultation with the Council of State. They shall come into force upon their publication but shall become null and void if the bill for their ratification is not submitted to Parliament before the date set by the enabling act.

At the expiration of the time limit referred to in the first paragraph of the present article, the ordinances may be modified only by the law in those matters which are within the legislative domain.

Article 39. The Premier and the Members of Parliament alike shall have the right to initiate legislation.

Government bills shall be discussed in the Council of Ministers after consultation with the Council of State and shall be filed with the secretariat of one of the two Assemblies. Finance bills shall be submitted first to the National Assembly.

Article 40. The bills and amendments introduced by the Members of Parliament shall be inadmissible when their adoption would have as a consequence either a diminution of public financial resources or an increase in public expenditure.

Article 41. If it shall appear in the course of the legislative procedure that a Parliamentary bill or an amendment is not within the domain of law or is contrary to a delegation granted by virtue of Article 38, the Government may declare its inadmissibility.

In case of disagreement between the Government and the President of the Assembly concerned, the Constitutional Council, upon the request of one or the other, shall rule within a time limit of eight days.

Article 42. The discussion of bills shall pertain, in the first Assembly to which they have been referred, to the text presented by the Government.

An Assembly given a text passed by the other Assembly shall deliberate on the text that is transmitted to it.

Article 43. Government and Parliamentary bills shall, at the request of the Government or of the Assembly concerned, be sent for study to committees especially designated for this purpose.

Government and Parliamentary bills for which such a request has not been made shall be sent to one of the permanent committees, the number of which is limited to six in each Assembly.

Article 44. Members of Parliament and of the Government have the right of amendment.

After the opening of the debate, the Government may oppose the examination of any amendment which has not previously been submitted to committee.

If the Government so requests, the Assembly concerned shall decide, by a single vote, on all or part of the text under discussion, retaining only the amendments proposed or accepted by the Government.

Article 45. Every Government or Parliamentary bill shall be examined successively in the two Assemblies of Parliament with a view to the adoption of an identical text.

When, as a result of disagreement between the two Assemblies, it has been impossible to adopt a Government or Parliamentary bill after two readings by each Assembly, or, if the Government has declared the matter urgent, after a single reading by each of them, the Premier shall have the right to bring about a meeting of a joint committee composed of an equal number from both Assemblies charged with the task of proposing a text on the matters still under discussion.

The text elaborated by the joint committee may be submitted by the Government for approval of the two Assemblies. No amendment shall be admissible except by agreement with the Government.

If the joint committee does not succeed in adopting a common text, or if this text is not adopted under the conditions set forth in the preceding paragraph, the Government may, after a new reading by the National Assembly and by the Senate, ask the National Assembly to rule definitively. In this case, the National Assembly may reconsider either the text elaborated by the joint committee, or the last text voted by it, modified when circumstances so require by one or several of the amendments adopted by the Senate.

Article 46. The laws that the Constitution characterizes as organic shall be passed and amended under the following conditions:

A Government or Parliamentary bill shall be submitted to the deliberation and to the vote of the first Assembly notified only at the expiration of a period of 15 days following its introduction;

The procedure of Article 45 shall be applicable. Nevertheless, lacking an agreement between the two Assemblies, the text may be adopted by the National Assembly on final reading only by an absolute majority of its members;

The organic laws relative to the Senate must be passed in the same manner by the two Assemblies;

The organic laws may be promulgated only after a declaration by the Constitutional Council on their constitutionality.

Article 47. The Parliament shall pass finance bills under the conditions to be stipulated by an organic law.

Should the National Assembly fail to reach a decision on first reading within a time limit of 40 days after a bill has been filed, the Government shall refer it to the Senate, which must rule within a time limit of 15 days. The procedure set forth in Article 45 shall then be followed.

Should Parliament fail to reach a decision within a time limit of 70 days, the provisions of the bill may be enforced by ordinance.

Should the finance bill establishing the resources and expenditures of a fiscal year not be filed in time for it to be promulgated before the beginning of that fiscal year, the Government shall urgently request Parliament for the authorization to collect the taxes and shall make available by decree the funds needed to meet the Government commitments already voted.

The time limits stipulated in the present article shall be suspended when the Parliament is not in session.

The Audit Office shall assist Parliament and the Government in supervising the implementation of the finance laws.

Article 48. The discussion of the bills filed or agreed upon by the Government shall have priority on the agenda of the Assemblies in the order determined by the Government.

One meeting a week shall be reserved, by priority, for questions asked by Members of Parliament and for answers by the Government.

Article 49. The Premier, after deliberation by the Council of Ministers, shall make the Government responsible, before the National Assembly, for its programme or, should the occasion arise, for a declaration of general policy.

When the National Assembly adopts a motion of censure, the responsibility of the Government shall thereby be questioned. Such a motion is admissible only if it is signed by at least one-tenth of the members of the National Assembly. The vote may not take place before 48 hours after the motion has been filed. Only the votes that are favourable to a motion of censure shall be counted; the motion of censure may be adopted only by a majority of the members comprising the Assembly. Should the motion of censure be rejected, its signatories may not introduce another motion of censure during the same session, except in the case provided for in the paragraph below.

The Premier may, after deliberation by the Council of Ministers, make the Government responsible before the National Assembly for the adoption of a vote of confidence. In this case, this vote of confidence shall be considered as adopted unless a motion of censure, filed during the twenty-four hours that follow, is carried under the conditions provided for in the preceding paragraph.

The Premier shall have the right to request the Senate for approval of a declaration of general policy.

Article 50. When the National Assembly adopts a motion of censure, or when it disapproves the programme or a declaration of general policy of the Government, the Premier must hand the resignation of the Government to the President of the Republic.

Article 51. The closure of ordinary or extraordinary sessions shall by right be delayed, should the occasion arise, in order to permit the application of the provisions of Article 49.

VI. ON TREATIES AND INTERNATIONAL AGREEMENTS

Article 52. The President of the Republic shall negotiate and ratify treaties.

He shall be informed of all negotiations leading to the conclusion of an international agreement not subject to ratification.

Article 53. Peace treaties, commercial treaties, treaties or agreements relative to international organization, those that commit the finances of the State, those that modify provisions of a legislative nature, those relative to the status of persons, those that call for the cession, exchange or addition of territory may be ratified or approved only by a law.

They shall go into effect only after having been ratified or approved.

No cession, no exchange, no addition of territory shall be valid without the consent of the populations concerned.

Article 54. If the Constitutional Council, the matter having been referred to it by the President of the Republic, by the Premier, or by the President of one or the other Assembly, shall declare that an international commitment contains a clause contrary to the Constitution, the authorisation to ratify or approve this commitment may be given only after amendment of the Constitution.

Article 55. Treaties or agreements duly ratified or approved shall, upon their publication, have an authority superior to that of laws, subject, for each agreement or treaty, to its application by the other party.

VII. THE CONSTITUTIONAL COUNCIL

Article 56. The Constitutional Council shall consist of nine members, whose mandates shall last nine years and shall not be renewable. One-third of the membership of the Constitutional Council shall be renewed every three years. Three of its members shall be appointed by the President of the Republic, three by the President of the National Assembly, three by the President of the Senate.

In addition to the nine members provided for above, former Presidents of the Republic shall be members *ex officio* for life of the Constitutional Council.

The President shall be appointed by the President of the Republic. He shall have the deciding vote in case of a tie.

Article 57. The office of member of the Constitutional Council shall be incompatible with that of minister or Member of Parliament. Other incompatibilities shall be determined by an organic law.

Article 58. The Constitutional Council shall ensure the regularity of the election of the President of the Republic.

It shall examine complaints and shall announce the results of the vote.

Article 59. The Constitutional Council shall rule, in the case of disagreement, on the regularity of the election of deputies and senators.

Article 60. The Constitutional Council shall ensure the regularity of the referendum procedure and shall announce the results thereof.

Article 61. Organic laws, before their promulgation, and regulations of the parliamentary Assemblies, before they come into application, must be submitted to the Constitutional Council, which shall rule on their constitutionality.

To the same end, laws may be submitted to the Constitutional Council, before their promulgation, by the President of the Republic, the Premier, the President of the National Assembly, the President of the Senate, or any 60 deputies or 60 senators.

In the cases provided for by the two preceding paragraphs, the Constitutional Council must make its ruling within a time limit of one month. Nevertheless, at the request of the Government, in case of urgency, this period shall be reduced to eight days.

In these same cases, referral to the Constitutional Council shall suspend the time limit for promulgation.

Article 62. A provision declared unconstitutional may not be promulgated or implemented.

The decisions of the Constitutional council may not be appealed to any jurisdiction whatsoever. They must be recognised by the public powers and by all administrative and juridical authorities.

Article 63. An organic law shall determine the rules of organization and functioning of the Constitutional Council, the procedure to be followed before it, and in particular of the periods of time allowed for laying disputes before it.

VIII. ON JUDICIAL AUTHORITY

Article 64. The President of the Republic shall be the guarantor of the independence of the judicial authority.

He shall be assisted by the High Council of the Judiciary.

An organic law shall determine the status of magistrats. Magistrates may not be removed from office.

Article 65. The High Council of the Judiciary shall be presided over by the President of the Republic. The Minister of Justice shall be its Vice-President *ex officio*. He may preside in place of the President of the Republic.

The High Council shall, in addition, include nine members appointed by the President of the Republic in conformity with the conditions to be determined by an organic law.

The High Council of the Judiciary shall present nominations for judges of the Court of Cassation [Supreme Court of Appeal] and for First Presidents of courts of appeal. It shall give its opinion under the conditions to be determined by an organic law on proposals of the Minister of Justice relative to the nominations of the other judges. It shall be consulted on questions of pardon under conditions to be determined by an organic law.

The High Council of the Judiciary shall act as a disciplinary council for judges. In such cases, it shall be presided over by the First President of the Court of Cassation.

Article 66. No one may be arbitrarily detained.

The judicial authority, guardian of individual liberty, shall ensure the respect of this principle under the conditions stipulated by law.

IX. THE HIGH COURT OF JUSTICE

Article 67. A High Court of Justice shall be instituted.

It shall be composed, in equal number, of members elected, from among their membership, by the National Assembly and by the Senate after each general or partial election to these Assemblies. It shall elect its President from among its members.

An organic law shall determine the composition of the High Court, it rules, as well as the procedure to be applied before it.

Article 68. The President of the Republic shall not be held accountable for actions performed in the exercise of his office except in the case of high treason. He may be indicted only by the two Assemblies ruling by identical vote in open balloting and by an absolute majority of the members of said Assemblies. He shall be tried by the High Court of Justice.

The members of the Government shall be criminally liable for actions performed in the exercise of their office and rated as crimes or misdemeanours at the time they were committed. The procedure defined above shall be applied to them, as well as to their accomplices, in case of a conspiracy against the security of the State. In the cases provided for by the present paragraph, the High Court shall be bound by the definition of crimes and misdemeanours, as well as by the determination of penalties, as they are established by the criminal laws in force when the acts are committed.

X. THE ECONOMIC AND SOCIAL COUNCIL

Article 69. The Economic and Social Council, at the referral of the Government, shall give its opinion on the Government bills, ordinances and decrees, as well as on the Parliamentary bills submitted to it.

A member of the Economic and Social Council may be designated by the latter to present, before the Parliamentary Assemblies, the opinion of the Council on the Government or Parliamentary bills that have been submitted to it.

Article 70. The Economic and social council may likewise be consulted by the Government on any problem of an economic or social character of interest to the Republic or to the Community. Any plan, or any bill dealing with a plan, of an economic or social character shall be submitted to it for advice.

Article 71. The composition of the Economic and Social Council and its rules of procedure shall be determined by an organic law.

XI. ON TERRITORIAL UNITS

Article 72. The territorial units of the Republic shall be the communes, the Departments, and the Overseas Territories. Any other territorial unit shall be created by law.

These units shall be free to govern themselves through elected councils and under the conditions stipulated by law.

In the Departments and the Territories, the Delegate of the Government shall be responsible for the national interests, for administrative supervision, and for seeing that the laws are respected.

Article 73. Measures of adjustment required by the particular situation of the Overseas Departments may be taken with regard to the legislative system and administrative organization of those Departments.

Article 74. The Overseas Territories of the Republic shall have a particular organization, taking account of their own interests within the general interests of the Republic. This organization shall be defined and modified by law after consultation with the Territorial Assembly concerned.

Article 75. Citizens of the Republic who do not have ordinary civil status, the only status referred to in Article 34, may keep their personal status as long as they have not renounced it.

Article 76. The Overseas Territories may retain their status within the Republic.

If they express the desire to do so by decision of their Territorial Assemblies taken within the time limit set in the first paragraph of Article 91, they shall become either Overseas Departments of the Republic or, organized into groups among themselves or singly, member States of the Community.

XII. ON THE COMMUNITY

Article 77. In the Community instituted by the present Constitution, the States shall enjoy autonomy; they shall administer themselves and, democratically and freely, manage their own affairs.

There shall be only one citizenship in the Community.

All citizens shall be equal before the law, whatever their origin, their race and their religion. They shall have the same duties.

Article 78. The Community shall have jurisdiction over foreign policy, defence, the monetary system, common economic and financial policy, as well as the policy on strategic raw materials.

In addition, except by special agreement, control of justice, higher education, the general organization of external and common transport, and telecommunications shall be within its jurisdiction.

Special agreements may establish other common jurisdictions or regulate the transfer of jurisdiction from the Community to one of its members.

Article 79. The member States shall benefit from the provisions of Article 77 as soon as they have exercised the choice provided for in Article 76.

Until the measures required for implementation of the present title go into force, matters within the common jurisdiction shall be regulated by the Republic.

Article 80. The President of the Republic shall preside over and represent the Community.

The Community shall have, as organs, an Executive Council, a Senate and a Court of Arbitration.

Article 81. The member States of the Community shall participate in the election of the President according to the conditions stipulated in Article 6.

The President of the Republic, in his capacity as President of the Community, shall be represented in each State of the Community.

Article 82. The Executive Council of the Community shall be presided over by the President of the Community. It shall consist of the Premier of the Republic, the heads of Government of each of the member States of the Community, and of the ministers responsible for the common affairs of the Community.

The Executive Council shall organize the co-operation of members of the Community at Government and administrative levels.

The organization and procedure of the Executive Council shall be determined by an organic law.

Article 83. The Senate of the Community shall be composed of delegates whom the Parliament of the Republic and the legislative assemblies of the other members of the Community shall choose from among their own membership. The number of delegates of each State shall be determined, taking into account its population and the responsibilities it assumes in the Community.

The Senate of the Community shall hold two sessions a year, which shall be opened and closed by the President of the Community and may not last more than one month each.

The Senate of the Community, upon referral by the President of the Community, shall deliberate on the common economic and financial policy, before laws in these matters are voted upon by the Parliament of the Republic, and, should circumstances so require, by the legislative assemblies of the other members of the Community.

The Senate of the Community shall examine the acts and treaties or international agreements, which are specified in Articles 35 and 53, and which commit the Community.

The Senate of the Community shall take enforceable decisions in the domains in which it has received delegation of power from the legislative assemblies of the members of the Community. These decisions shall be promulgated in the same form as the law in the territory of each of the States concerned.

An organic law shall determine the composition of the Senate and its rules of procedure.

Article 84. A Court of Arbitration of the Community shall rule on litigations occurring among members of the Community.

Its composition and its competence shall be determined by an organic law.

Article 85. By derogation from the procedure provided for in Article 89, the provisions of the present title that concern the functioning of the common institutions shall be amendable by identical laws passed by the Parliament of the Republic and by the Senate of the Community.

The provisions of the present title may also be revised by agreements concluded between all states of the Community: the new provisions are enforced in the conditions laid down by the Constitution of each state.

Article 86. A change of status of a member State of the Community may be requested, either by the Republic, or by a resolution of the legislative assembly of the State concerned confirmed by a local referendum, the organization and supervision of which shall be ensured by the institutions of the Community. The procedures governing this change shall be determined by an agreement approved by the Parliament of the Republic and the legislative assembly concerned.

Under the same conditions, a Member State of the Community may become independent. It shall thereby cease to belong to the Community.

A Member State of the Community may also, by means of agreement, become independent without thereby ceasing to belong to the Community.

An independent State which is not a member of the Community may, by means of agreements, adhere to the Community without ceasing to be independent.

The position of these States within the Community is determined by the agreements concluded for that purpose, in particular the agreements mentioned in the preceding paragraphs as well as, where applicable, the agreements provided for in the second paragraph of Article 85.

Article 87. The particular agreements made for the implementation of the present title shall be approved by the Parliament of the Republic and the legislative assembly concerned.

XIII. ON AGREEMENTS OF ASSOCIATION

Article 88. The Republic or the Community may make agreements with States that wish to associate themselves with the Community in order to develop their own civilisations.

XIV. ON AMENDMENT

Article 89. The initiative for amending the Constitution shall belong both to the President of the Republic on the proposal of the Premier and to the Members of Parliament.

The Government or Parliamentary bill for amendment must be passed by the two Assemblies in identical terms. The amendment shall become definitive after approval by a referendum.

Nevertheless, the proposed amendment shall not be submitted to a referendum when the President of the Republic decides to submit it to Parliament convened in Congress; in this case, the proposed amendment shall be approved only if it is accepted by a three-fifths majority of the votes cast. The Secretariat of the Congress shall be that of the National Assembly.

No amendment procedure may be undertaken or followed if it is prejudicial to the integrity of the territory.

The republican form of government shall not be the object of an amendment.

XV. TEMPORARY PROVISIONS

Article 90. The ordinary session of Parliament is suspended. The mandate of the members of the present National Assembly shall expire on the day that the Assembly elected under the present Constitution convenes.

Until this meeting, the Government alone shall have the authority to convene Parliament.

The mandate of the members of the Assembly of the French Union shall expire at the same time as the mandate of the members of the present National Assembly.

Article 91. The institutions of the Republic, provided for by the present Constitution, shall be established within four months counting from the time of its promulgation.

This period shall be extended to six months for the institutions of the Community.

The powers of the President of the Republic now in office shall expire only when the results of the election provided for in Articles 6 and 7 of the present Constitution are proclaimed.

FRANCE

The Member States of the Community shall participate in this first election under the conditions derived from their status at the date of the promulgation of the Constitution.

The established authorities shall continue in the exercise of their functions in these States according to the laws and regulations applicable when the Constitution goes into force, until the establishment of the authorities provided for by their new regimes.

Until its definitive constitution, the Senate shall consist of the present members of the Council of the Republic. The organic laws that shall determine the definitive constitution of the Senate must be passed before 31 July 1959.

The powers conferred on the Constitutional Council by Articles 58 and 59 of the Constitution shall be exercised, until the establishment of this Council, by a committee composed of the Vice-President of the Council of State, as Chairman, the First President of the Court of Cassation, and the First President of the Audit Office.

The peoples of the member States of the Community shall continue to be represented in Parliament until the entry into force of the measures necessary to the implementation of Chapter XII.

Article 92. The legislative measures necessary to the establishment of the institutions and, until they are established, to the functioning of the public powers, shall be taken in meetings of the Council of Ministers, after consultation with the Council of State, in the form of ordinances having the force of law.

During the time limit set in the first paragraph of Article 91, the Government shall be authorized to determine, by ordinances having the force of law and passed in the same way, the system of elections to the Assemblies provided for by the Constitution.

During the same period and under the same conditions, the Government may also adopt measures, in all domains, which it may deem necessary to the life of the nation, the protection of citizens or the safeguarding of liberties.

ELECTORAL LAW, 1985

At the elections of March 1986, the 577 Deputies of the National Assembly for Metropolitan France and for the Overseas Possessions (except Mayotte, St Pierre and Miquelon and the Wallis and Futuna Islands) were elected under a system of proportional representation, the increase from 491 to 577 giving a ratio of approximately one deputy per 108,000 inhabitants. Within each department, seats were allocated to candidates in the order in which they appeared on party lists, and the votes for any party receiving less than 5% of the total vote were reapportioned among the remaining lists.

ELECTORAL LAW, JULY 1986

The 577 Deputies of the National Assembly are to be directly elected under the former single-member constituency system. Participating parties can nominate only one candidate and designate a reserve candidate, who can serve as a replacement if the elected Deputy is appointed a Minister or a member of the Constitutional Council, or is sent on a government assignment scheduled to last more than six months, or dies. A candidate must receive an absolute majority and at least one-quarter of registered votes in order to be elected to the National Assembly. If these conditions are not fulfilled, a second ballot will be held a week later, for voters to choose between all candidates receiving 12.5% of the total votes on the first ballot. The candidate who receives a simple majority of votes on the second ballot will then be elected. Candidates polling less than 5% of the votes will lose their deposit.

The Government

HEAD OF STATE

President: François Mitterrand (took office 21 May 1981, re-elected May 1988).

COUNCIL OF MINISTERS
(January 1991)

A coalition of the Parti Socialiste (PS), Mouvement des Radicaux de Gauche (MRG), members of the Union pour la Démocratie Française (UDF) and its affiliated parties—the Parti Républicain (PR), the Parti Républicain Radical et Radical-Socialiste (Rad.) and the Centre des Démocrates Sociaux (CDS)—and non-party representatives.

Prime Minister: Michel Rocard (PS).

Minister of State for the Economy, Finance and the Budget: Pierre Bérégovoy (PS).

Minister of State for National Education, Youth and Sport: Lionel Jospin (PS).

Minister of State for Foreign Affairs: Roland Dumas (PS).

Minister of State for the Civil Service and Administrative Reform: Michel Durafour (UDF/Rad.).

Minister of Justice and Keeper of the Seals: Henri Nallet (PS).

Minister of Defence: Pierre Joxe (PS).

Minister of the Interior: Philippe Marchand (PS).

Minister of Industry and Regional Planning: Roger Fauroux.

Minister of Equipment, Housing, Transport and the Sea: Louis Besson (PS).

Minister of Labour, Employment and Professional Training: Jean-Pierre Soisson (UDF/PR).

Minister of Co-operation and Development: Jacques Pelletier (UDF).

Minister of Culture, Communications and Major Works: Jack Lang (PS).

Minister of Overseas Departments and Territories and Government Spokesman: Louis Le Pensec (PS).

Minister of Agriculture and Forestry: Louis Mermaz (PS).

Minister of Postal Services, Telecommunications and Space: Paul Quilès (PS).

Minister for Relations with Parliament: Jean Poperen (PS).

Minister of Social Affairs and Solidarity: Claude Evin (PS).

Minister of Research and Technology: Hubert Curien (PS).

Minister of Foreign Trade: Jean-Marie Rausch (UDF/CDS).

Minister of Urban Affairs: Michel Delebarre PS).

Minister Delegate attached to the Prime Minister:
  Environment and the Prevention of Technological and Natural Disasters: Brice Lalonde.

Minister Delegate attached to the Minister for the Economy, Finance and the Budget:
  Budget: Michel Charasse (PS).

Ministers Delegate attached to the Minister for Foreign Affairs:
  European Affairs: Elisabeth Guigou.
  Francophone Countries: Alain Decaux.
  Foreign Affairs: Edwige Avice (PS).

Minister Delegate attached to the Minister of Justice and Keeper of the Seals:
  Without Portfolio: Georges Kiejman.

Ministers Delegate attached to the Minister of Industry and Regional Planning:
  Regional Planning and Redeployment: Jacques Chérèque.
  Trade and Artisan Industries: François Doubin (MRG).
  Tourism: Jean-Michel Baylet (CDS).

Minister Delegate attached to the Minister of Culture and Communications:
  Communications: Catherine Tasca.

Minister Delegate attached to the Minister of Social Affairs and Solidarity:
  Health: Bruno Durieux (UDF-CDS).

Ministers Delegate attached to the Minister of Equipment, Housing, Transport and the Sea:
  The Sea: Jacques Mellick (PS).
  Housing: (vacant).

SECRETARIES OF STATE

Attached to the Prime Minister:
  Planning: Lionel Stoléru (UDF).
  Without Portfolio: Tony Dreyfus (PS).
  Humanitarian Policy: Bernard Kouchner.

Attached to the Minister of National Education, Youth and Sport:
  Technical Education: Robert Chapuis (PS).
  Youth and Sport: Roger Bambuck.

FRANCE
Directory

Attached to the Minister for the Economy, Finance and the Budget:
  Consumer Affairs: VÉRONIQUE NEIERTZ (PS).

Attached to the Minister of Foreign Affairs:
  International Cultural Relations: THIERRY DE BEAUCÉ.

Attached to the Minister of Equipment, Housing, Transport and the Sea:
  Road Transport and Waterways: GEORGE SARRE (PS).

Attached to the Minister of Labour, Employment and Professional Training:
  Professional Training: ANDRÉ LAIGNEL (PS).

Attached to the Minister of Culture, Communications and Major Works:
  Major Works: EMILE BIASINI.

Attached to the Minister of Social Affairs and Solidarity:
  The Family and the Elderly: HÉLÈNE DORLHAC DE BORNE (UDF).
  The Disabled and Casualties of Life: MICHEL GILLIBERT.

Secretary of State for Defence: GÉRARD RENON.
Secretary of State for Women's Rights: MICHÈLE ANDRÉ (PS).
Secretary of State for War Veterans and War Victims: ANDRÉ MÉRIC (PS).

MINISTRIES

Office of the President: Palais de l'Elysée, 55–57 rue du Faubourg Saint Honoré, 75008 Paris; tel. (1) 42-92-81-00; telex 650127.

Office of the Prime Minister: 57 rue de Varenne, 75700 Paris; tel. (1) 42-75-80-00; telex 200724.

Ministry of Agriculture and Forestry: 78 rue de Varenne, 75700 Paris; tel. (1) 49-55-49-55; telex 205202; fax (1) 45-55-95-50.

Ministry of the Civil Service and Administrative Reform: 69 rue de Varenne, 75700 Paris; tel. (1) 42-75-80-00.

Ministry of Co-operation and Development: 20 rue Monsieur, 75700 Paris; tel. (1) 47-83-10-10; telex 202363; fax (1) 43-06-74-82.

Ministry of Culture, Communications and Major Works: 3 rue de Valois, 75042 Paris Cedex 01; tel. (1) 40-15-80-00; telex 210293.

Ministry of Defence: 14 rue Saint Dominique, 75700 Paris; tel. (1) 40-65-30-11; telex 201375; fax (1) 45-52-58-55.

Ministry of the Economy, Finance and the Budget: 139 rue de Bercy, 75572 Paris Cedex 12; tel. (1) 40-04-04-04; telex 217068.

Ministry of Equipment, Housing, Transport and the Sea: Grande Arche-La Défense, 92055 Paris-La Défense Cedex 04; tel. (1) 40-81-21-22.

Ministry of European Affairs: 32 ave Raymond Poincaré, 75016 Paris; tel. (1) 47-55-54-00.

Ministry of Foreign Affairs: 37 quai d'Orsay, 75700 Paris; tel. (1) 47-53-53-53; telex 202329.

Ministry of Foreign Trade: 139 rue de Bercy, 75572 Paris, Cedex 12; fax (1) 40-04-04-04.

Ministry of Industry and Regional Planning: 101 rue de Grenelle, 75700 Paris; tel. (1) 45-56-36-36; fax (1) 45-56-36-36.

Ministry of the Interior: place Beauvau, 75800 Paris; tel. (1) 49-27-49-27; telex 290922.

Ministry of Justice: 13 place Vendôme, 75042 Paris Cedex 01; tel. (1) 44-77-60-60; telex 211320; fax (1) 42-61-98-34.

Ministry of Labour, Employment and Professional Training: 127 rue de Grenelle, 75700 Paris; tel. (1) 40-56-60-00; fax (1) 40-56-67-60.

Ministry of National Education, Youth and Sport: 110 rue de Grenelle, 75700 Paris; tel. (1) 49-55-10-10; telex 201244.

Ministry of Overseas Departments and Territories: 27 rue Oudinot, 75700 Paris; tel. (1) 47-83-01-23.

Ministry of Postal Services, Telecommunications and Space: 20 ave de Ségur, 75700 Paris; tel. (1) 45-64-22-22; telex 270496; fax (1) 45-38-98-96.

Ministry for Relations with Parliament: 72 rue de Varenne, 75700 Paris; tel. (1) 42-75-80-00.

Ministry of Research and Technology: 1 rue Descartes, 75005 Paris; tel. (1) 46 34 35 35; fax (1) 46 34 38 35.

Ministry of Social Affairs and Solidarity: 8 ave de Ségur, 75700 Paris; tel. (1) 40-56-60-00.

President and Legislature

PRESIDENT
Elections of 24 April and 8 May 1988

	First ballot	Second ballot
RAYMOND BARRE (Union pour la Démocratie Française)	5,031,849	—
PIERRE BOUSSEL IMBERT (Mouvement pour un Parti des Travailleurs)	116,823	—
JACQUES CHIRAC (Rassemblement pour la République)	6,063,514	14,218,970
PIERRE JUQUIN (Independent Communist)	639,084	—
ARLETTE LAGUILLER (Lutte Ouvrière)	606,017	—
ANDRÉ LAJOINIE (Parti Communiste Français)	2,055,995	—
JEAN-MARIE LE PEN (Front National)	4,375,894	—
FRANÇOIS MITTERRAND (Parti Socialiste)	10,367,220	16,704,279
ANTOINE WAECHTER (Les Verts)	1,149,642	—

Figures published by Ministry of the Interior, after corrections by the Conseil Constitutionnel (see p. 1051).

PARLEMENT
(Parliament)

Assemblée Nationale
(National Assembly)

President: LAURENT FABIUS.

General election, 5 and 12 June 1988

Parties and Groups	% of votes cast in first ballot	% of votes cast in second ballot*	Seats
Parti Socialiste (PS)	34.76	45.31	
Mouvement des Radicaux de Gauche (MRG)	1.14	1.28	276†
Affiliated to PS	1.65	2.08	
Union pour la Démocratie Française (UDF)‡	18.50	21.18	129
Rassemblement pour la République (RPR)‡	19.18	23.09	127
Parti Communiste Français (PCF)	11.32	3.43	27
Various right-wing parties‡	2.85	2.58	16
Front National (FN)	9.66	1.07	1§
Others	0.93	—	1‖
Total	100.00	100.00	577¶

* Held where no candidate had won the requisite overall majority in the first round of voting, between candidates who had received at least 12.5% of the votes in that round.
† Of which: PS 260, MRG 9, various left-wing affiliates 7.
‡ The UDF and the RPR contested the elections jointly as the Union du Rassemblement et du Centre (URC). The various right-wing parties joined the URC prior to the second ballot.
§ Subsequently expelled from the FN.
‖ Seat held by centre-left candidate.
¶ Including two representatives from French Polynesia, where elections took place on 12 and 26 June 1988.

Note: On 15 June 1988 the formation of a new centrist group, the Union du Centre (UDC), was announced. This separate grouping was led by the president of the CDS, hitherto part of the UDF. In September 1988 the composition of the National Assembly was as follows: PS and associates 275, RPR and associates 132, UDF and associates 90, UDC and associates 40, PCF and associates 25, unattached 15 (including one FN).

Sénat
(Senate)

President: ALAIN POHER.

Members of the Senate are indirectly elected for a term of nine years, with one-third of the seats renewable every three years.

After the most recent election, held on 24 September 1989, the Sénat had 321 seats: 296 for metropolitan France; 13 for the overseas departments and territories; and 12 for French nationals abroad. The strength of the parties was as follows:

FRANCE

	Seats
Groupe du Rassemblement pour la République	91
Groupe de l'Union centriste des Démocrates de Progrès	68
Groupe socialiste	66
Groupe de l'Union des Républicains et des Indépendants	52
Groupe de la Gauche démocratique	23
Groupe communiste	16
Non-attached	5
Total	**321**

Note: Until the September 1989 election, the Senate had 319 seats. The two additional members represent French nationals abroad.

Political Organizations

Centre National des Indépendants et Paysans (CNIP): 170 rue de l'Université, 75007 Paris; tel. (1) 47-05-49-64; fax (1) 45-56-02-63; f. 1949; right-wing; Pres. YVON BRIANT; Sec.-Gen. JEAN-ANTOINE GIANSILY.

Fédération des Socialistes Démocrates (FSD): 8 rue Saint Marc, 75002 Paris; Pres. CHRISTIAN CHAUVEL; Sec.-Gen. GILBERT PÉROT.

Front National (FN): 8 rue du Général Clergerie, 75116 Paris; tel. (1) 47-27-56-66; fax (1) 47-55-96-67; f. 1972; extreme right-wing nationalist; Pres. JEAN-MARIE LE PEN; Sec.-Gen. CARL LANG.

Ligue Communiste Révolutionnaire (LCR): c/o Rouge, 2 rue Richard Lenoir, 93108 Montreuil; tel. (1) 48-59-23-00; fax (1) 48-59-23-28; f. 1974; Trotskyist; French section of the Fourth International; Leader ALAIN KRIVINE.

Lutte Ouvrière (LO): BP 233, 75865 Paris Cedex 18; Trotskyist; Leaders ARLETTE LAGUILLER, F. DUBURG, J. MORAND.

Mouvement des Démocrates: 71 rue Ampère, 75017 Paris; tel. (1) 47-63-81-43; f. 1974; Leader MICHEL JOBERT.

Mouvement gaulliste populaire (MGP): 11 rue de la Cerisaie, 75004 Paris; f. 1982 by merger of Union démocratique du travail and Fédération des républicains de progrès; Gaulliste party; Leaders JACQUES DUBÛ-BRIDEL, PIERRE DABEZIES.

Mouvement des Radicaux de Gauche (MRG): 3 rue la Boétie, 75008 Paris; tel. (1) 47-42-22-41; fax (1) 47-42-82-93; f. 1973; formed by splinter group from Parti Radical; left-wing; Pres. EMILE ZUCCARELLI.

Mouvement des Rénovateurs Communistes (MRC): Paris; f. 1988; Leader CLAUDE LLABRÈS.

Nouvelle Gauche: 2 allée des Helvètes, 91300 Massy; f. 1988 by 'renovators' expelled from the PCF; Leader PIERRE JUQUIN.

Parti Communiste Français (PCF): 2 place du Colonel Fabien, 75940 Paris Cedex 19; tel. (1) 40-40-12-12; subscribed to the common programme of the United Left (with the Parti Socialiste) until 1977 when the United Left split over nationalization issues; aims to follow the democratic path to socialism and advocates an independent foreign policy; mems 702,800 (1979); Sec.-Gen. GEORGES MARCHAIS.

Parti Socialiste (PS): 10 rue de Solférino, 75007 Paris; tel. (1) 45-56-77-00; telex 200174; fax (1) 47-05-15-78; f. 1971; subscribed to the common programme of the United Left (with the Parti Communiste) until 1977, when the United Left split over nationalization issues; advocates a planned economy, full employment and the eventual attainment of socialism through the nationalization of key industries; 200,000 mems; First Sec. PIERRE MAUROY.

Parti Socialiste Unifié (PSU): 40 rue de Malte, 75011 Paris; tel. (1) 43-57-44-80; f. 1960; left-wing party; 3,000 mems; National Sec. SERGE DEPAQUIT.

Rassemblement pour la République (RPR): 123 rue de Lille, 75007 Paris; tel. (1) 49-55-63-00; telex 260820; fax (1) 45-51-44-79; f. 1976 from the Gaullist party Union des Démocrates pour la République (UDR) after the resignation of Jacques Chirac as Prime Minister in Giscard d'Estaing's Government; joined UDF to campaign as Union du Rassemblement et du Centre (URC) at 1988 legislative elections; Pres. JACQUES CHIRAC; Sec.-Gen. ALAIN JUPPÉ.

Union Centriste et Radicale (UCR): f. 1984 after dissolution of Mouvement des Sociaux Libéraux; Pres. OLIVIER STIRN; Sec.-Gen. FRANÇOIS GARCIA.

Union des Démocrates Gaullistes et Républicains de Progrès (UDGRP): f. 1988; Pres. JEAN-PIERRE CÉVAER.

Union pour la Démocratie Française (UDF): 12 rue François I, 75008 Paris; tel. (1) 43-59-79-59; fax (1) 42-25-03-81; formed in 1978 to unite for electoral purposes non-Gaullist 'majority' candidates; joined RPR to campaign as Union du Rassemblement et du Centre (URC) at 1988 legislative elections; Chair. VALÉRY GISCARD D'ESTAING; Sec.-Gen. MICHEL PINTON; Leader CHARLES MILLON. Affiliated parties:

Centre des Démocrates Sociaux (CDS): 133 bis rue de l'Université, 75007 Paris; tel. (1) 45-55-75-75; fax (1) 45-55-94-62; f. 1976 by merger of Centre Démocrate and Centre Démocratie et Progrès; formed independent group in National Assembly known as Union du Centre after 1988 election; Pres. PIERRE MÉHAIGNERIE; Sec.-Gen. JACQUES BARROT.

Parti Républicain (PR): 105 rue de l'Université, 75007 Paris; tel. (1) 47-53-99-99; fax (1) 47-53-97-97; formed May 1977 as a grouping of the Fédération Nationale des Républicains Indépendants (FNRI) and three smaller 'Giscardian' parties; Pres. (vacant); Sec.-Gen. ALAIN MADELIN.

Parti Radical Socialiste (Parti Républicain Radical et Radical-Socialiste): 1 place de Valois, 75001 Paris; tel. (1) 42-61-56-32; fax (1) 42-61-49-65; f. 1901; Pres. YVES GALLAND; Sec.-Gen. AYMERI DE MONTESQUIOU.

Parti social-démocrate (PSD): 191 rue de l'Université, 75007 Paris; tel. (1) 47-53-84-28; fax (1) 47-53-84-41; f. 1973 as Mouvement des démocrates socialistes de France, name changed 1982; Pres. MAX LEJEUNE; Sec.-Gen. ANDRÉ SANTINI.

Les Verts: 19 rue Titon, 75011 Paris; tel. (1) 43-79-38-38; fax (1) 43-79-30-44; f. 1984; ecologist party; National Sec. GUY CAMBOT.

Small left-wing parties include Organisation Communiste Internationale, Communistes Démocrates et Unitaires, Révolution, Parti communiste révolutionnaire (marxiste-léniniste), and Union des communistes de France (marxiste-léniniste). Small right-wing parties include Nouvelle Action Française (f. 1971), Oeuvre Française (f. 1968), Parti Démocrate Française (f. 1982), Parti des Forces Nouvelles (f. 1974), Restauration Nationale (f. 1947), Travail et Patrie (f. 1987) and Rassembler, Agir pour la France (f. 1988). There are also regional movements in Brittany, the Basque country, Corsica and Occitania (Provence-Languedoc).

Diplomatic Representation

EMBASSIES IN FRANCE

Afghanistan: 32 ave Raphaël, 75016 Paris; tel. (1) 45-27-66-09; Chargé d'affaires a.i.: M. WAHIDULLAH.

Albania: 131 rue de la Pompe, 75116 Paris; tel. (1) 45-53-51-32; telex 611534; Ambassador: KSENOFON NUSHI.

Algeria: 50 rue de Lisbonne, 75008 Paris; tel. (1) 42-25-70-70; Ambassador: SMAIL HAMDANI.

Angola: 19 ave Foch, 75116 Paris; tel. (1) 45-01-58-20; telex 649847; Ambassador: ELISIO DE FIGUEIREDO.

Argentina: 6 rue Cimarosa, 75116 Paris; tel. (1) 45-53-14-69; telex 613819; Ambassador: FERNANDO GELBARD.

Australia: 4 rue Jean Rey, 75724 Paris Cedex 15; tel. (1) 45-75-62-00; telex 202313; Ambassador: EDWARD ROBERT POCOCK.

Austria: 6 rue Fabert, 75007 Paris; tel. (1) 40-59-33-00; telex 200708; fax (1) 45-55-63-65; Ambassador: WOLFGANG SCHALLENBERG.

Bahrain: 15 ave Raymond Poincaré, 75116 Paris; tel. (1) 45-53-01-19; telex 620924; Ambassador: ABD AL-AZIZ BUALI.

Bangladesh: 5 sq. Pétrarque, 75016 Paris; tel. (1) 45-53-41-20; telex 630868; Ambassador: Dr A. TOZAMMEL HUQ.

Belgium: 9 rue de Tilsit, 75840 Paris Cedex 17; tel. (1) 43-80-61-00; telex 650484; Ambassador: ALFRED CAHEN.

Benin: 87 ave Victor Hugo, 75116 Paris; tel. (1) 45-00-98-82; telex 610110; Ambassador: SOULER ISSIFOU IDRISSOU.

Bolivia: 12 ave Président Kennedy, 75016 Paris; tel. (1) 42-24-93-44; telex 611879; fax (1) 45-25-86-23; Chargé d'affaires a.i.: FERNANDO LAREDO.

Brazil: 34 cours Albert 1er, 75008 Paris; tel. (1) 42-25-92-50; telex 650063; fax (1) 42-89-03-45; Ambassador: JOÃO HERMES PEREIRA DE ARAÚJO.

Bulgaria: 1 ave Rapp, 75007 Paris; tel. (1) 45-51-85-90; Ambassador: MILAN MILANOV.

Burkina Faso: 159 blvd Haussmann, 75008 Paris; tel. (1) 43-59-90-63; telex 641870; Ambassador: SERGE THÉOPHILE BALIMA.

Burundi: 3 rue Octave Feuillet, 75116 Paris; tel. (1) 45-20-60-61; telex 611463; Chargé d'affaires a.i.: Pasteur NZINAHORA.

Cameroon: 73 rue d'Auteuil, 75016 Paris; tel. (1) 47-43-98-33; telex 620312; Ambassador: SIMON NKO'O ETOUNGOU.

Canada: 35 ave Montaigne, 75008 Paris; tel. (1) 47-23-01-01; telex 280806; Ambassador: CLAUDE T. CHARLAND.

Central African Republic: 29 blvd de Montmorency, 75116 Paris; tel. (1) 42-24-42-56; telex 611908; Ambassador: JOSEPH HETMAN-EL-ROOSALEM.

FRANCE

Chad: 65 rue des Belles Feuilles, 75116 Paris; tel. (1) 45-53-36-75; telex 610629; Ambassador: AHMED ALLAM-MI.

Chile: 2 ave de la Motte-Piquet, 75007 Paris; tel. (1) 45-51-46-68; telex 260075; Ambassador: JOSÉ-MIGUEL BARROS.

China, People's Republic: 11 ave George V, 75008 Paris; tel. (1) 47-23-34-45; telex 270114; Ambassador: ZHOU JUE.

Colombia: 22 rue de l'Elysée, 75008 Paris; tel. (1) 42-65-46-08; telex 640935; Ambassador: FERNANDO REY.

Comoros: 13-15 rue de la Néva, 75008 Paris; tel. (1) 47-63-81-78; telex 642390; Ambassador: ALI MLAHAILI.

Congo: 37 bis rue Paul Valéry, 75016 Paris; tel. (1) 45-00-60-57; telex 611954; Ambassador: JEAN-MARIE EWENGUÉ.

Costa Rica: 135 ave de Versailles, 75116 Paris; tel. (1) 45-25-52-23; telex 648046; Ambassador: ENRIQUE CASTILLO.

Côte d'Ivoire: 102 ave Raymond Poincaré, 75116 Paris; tel. (1) 45-01-53-10; telex 611915; Ambassador: EUGÈNE AIDARA.

Cuba: 16 rue de Presles, 75015 Paris; tel. (1) 45-67-55-35; telex 200815; Ambassador: FERNANDO FLÓREZ IBARRA.

Cyprus: 23 rue Galilée, 75116 Paris; tel. (1) 47-20-86-28; telex 610664; fax (1) 40-70-13-44; Ambassador: GEORGES LYCOURGOS.

Czechoslovakia: 15 ave Charles Floquet, 75007 Paris; tel. (1) 47-34-29-10; telex 611032; fax (1) 47-83-50-78; Ambassador: JAROSLAV ŠEDIVÝ.

Denmark: 77 ave Marceau, 75116 Paris; tel. (1) 47-23-54-20; telex 620172; fax (1) 47-20-03-90; Ambassador: GUNNAR RIBERHOLDT.

Djibouti: 26 rue Emile Ménier, 75116 Paris; tel. (1) 47-27-49-22; telex 614970; Chargé d'affaires a.i.: AHMED OMAR FARAH.

Dominican Republic: 2 rue Georges-Ville, 75116 Paris; tel. (1) 45-01-88-81; telex 615333; Chargé d'affaires a.i.: CAONABO FERNÁNDEZ NARANJO.

Ecuador: 34 ave de Messine, 75008 Paris; tel. (1) 45-61-10-21; telex 641333; fax (1) 42-56-06-64; Ambassador: JUAN CUEVA.

Egypt: 56 ave d'Iéna, 75116 Paris; tel. (1) 47-20-97-70; telex 611691; fax (1) 47-23-06-43; Ambassador: AHMED SIDKY.

El Salvador: 12 rue Galilée, 75116 Paris; tel. (1) 47-20-42-02; fax (1) 40-70-01-95; Ambassador: ANA CRISTINA SOL.

Equatorial Guinea: 6 rue Alfred de Vigny, 75008 Paris; tel. (1) 47-66-44-33; Ambassador: FAUSTINO NGUEMA ESONO.

Ethiopia: 35 ave Charles Floquet, 75007 Paris; tel. (1) 47-83-83-95; telex 260008; Chargé d'affaires: HABTEMARIAM SEYOUM.

Finland: 2 rue Fabert, 75007 Paris; tel. (1) 47-05-35-45; telex 200054; fax (1) 45-51-63-23; Ambassador: MATTI HÄKKÄNEN.

Gabon: 26 bis ave Raphaël, 75016 Paris; tel. (1) 42-24-79-60; telex 610146; Ambassador: FRANÇOIS BANGA EBOUMI.

Germany: 13–15 ave Franklin D. Roosevelt, 75008 Paris; tel. (1) 42-99-78-00; telex 280136; fax (1) 43-59-74-18; Ambassador: Dr FRANZ PFEFFER.

Ghana: 8 Villa Said, 75116 Paris; tel. (1) 45-00-09-50; telex 611020; Ambassador: THERESE STRIGGNER SCOTT.

Greece: 17 rue Auguste Vacquerie, 75116 Paris; tel. (1) 47-23-72-28; telex 612747; Ambassador: ALEXANDRE RAPHAEL.

Guatemala: 73 rue de Courcelles, 75008 Paris; tel. (1) 42-27-78-63; telex 650850; fax (1) 47-54-02-06; Ambassador: GUILLERMO PUTZEIS-ALVAREZ.

Guinea: 51 rue de la Faisanderie, 75016 Paris; tel. (1) 47-04-81-48; telex 648497; Ambassador: MARCEL MARTIN.

Haiti: 10 rue Théodule Ribot, 75017 Paris; tel. (1) 47-63-47-78; Chargé d'affaires a.i.: SERGE VIEUX.

Holy See: 10 ave du Président Wilson, 75116 Paris (Apostolic Nunciature); tel. (1) 47-23-58-34; Apostolic Nuncio: Most Rev. LORENZO ANTONETTI, Titular Archbishop of Roselle.

Honduras: 6 place Vendôme, 75001 Paris; tel. (1) 42-61-34-75; fax (1) 42-61-12-99; Chargé d'affaires a.i.: SONIA MENDIETA DE BADAROUX.

Hungary: 5 bis sq. de l'Avenue Foch, 75116 Paris; tel. (1) 45-00-41-59; telex 610822; Ambassador: GÁBOR NAGY.

Iceland: 124 blvd Haussmann, 75008 Paris; tel. (1) 45-22-81-54; telex 290314; Ambassador: ALBERT GUDMUNDSSON.

India: 15 rue Alfred Dehodencq, 75016 Paris; tel. (1) 45-20-39-30; telex 610621; Ambassador: SOONU KOCHAR.

Indonesia: 49 rue Cortambert, 75116 Paris; tel. (1) 45-03-07-60; telex 648031; fax (1) 45-04-50-32; Ambassador: DODDY A. TISNA AMIDJAJA.

Iran: 4 ave d'Iéna, 75116 Paris; tel. (1) 47-23-61-22; telex 610600; Ambassador: Dr ALI AHANI.

Iraq: 53 rue de la Faisanderie, 75116 Paris; tel. (1) 45-01-51-00; telex 613706; Ambassador: ABD AR-RAZZAK AL-HACHEMI.

Ireland: 4 rue Rude, 75116 Paris; tel. (1) 45-00-20-87; telex 620557; Ambassador: TADHG O'SULLIVAN.

Israel: 3 rue Rabelais, 75008 Paris; tel. (1) 42-56-47-47; telex 650831; fax (1) 42-25-64-15; Ambassador: OVADIA SOFER.

Italy: 51 rue de Varenne, 75007 Paris; tel. (1) 45-44-38-90; telex 270827; Ambassador: GIACOMO ATTOLICO.

Japan: 7 ave Hoche, 75008 Paris; tel. (1) 47-66-02-22; telex 660493; Ambassador: MASATOSHI INAMI.

Jordan: 80 blvd Maurice Barrès, 92200 Neuilly-sur-Seine; tel. (1) 46-24-23-78; telex 630084; Chargé d'affaires a.i.: AWAD AL-KHALIDI.

Kenya: 3 rue Cimarosa, 75116 Paris; tel. (1) 45-53-35-00; telex 620825; Ambassador: SIMEON B. ARAP BULLUT.

Korea, Republic: 125 rue de Grenelle, 75007 Paris; tel. (1) 47-53-01-01; Ambassador: YOUNG CHAN LO.

Kuwait: 2 rue de Lubeck, 75016 Paris; tel. (1) 47-23-54-25; telex 620513; Ambassador: TAREK RAZZOUQI.

Laos: 74 ave Raymond Poincaré, 75116 Paris; tel. (1) 45-53-02-98; telex 610711; Ambassador: PHOUNE KHAMMOUNHEUAG.

Lebanon: 3 villa Copernic, 75116 Paris; tel. (1) 45-00-22-25; telex 611087; Ambassador: JOHNNY ABDOU.

Liberia: 8 rue Jacques Bingen, 75017 Paris; tel. (1) 47-63-58-55; telex 290288; Ambassador: GEORGE AARON.

Libya (People's Bureau): 2 rue Charles Lamoureux, 75116 Paris; tel. (1) 47-04-71-60; telex 620643; Sec. of People's Bureau: SAAD MUJBER.

Luxembourg: 33 ave Rapp, 75007 Paris; tel. (1) 45-55-13-37; telex 204711; Ambassador: PIERRE WURTH.

Madagascar: 4 ave Raphaël, 75116 Paris; tel. (1) 45-04-62-11; telex 610394; Ambassador: FRANÇOIS DE PAUL RABOTOSON.

Malawi: 20 rue Euler, 75008 Paris; tel. (1) 47-20-20-27; telex 642804; fax (1) 47-23-62-48; Ambassador: WILLIE S. KHOZA.

Malaysia: 2 bis rue Bénouville, 75116 Paris; tel. (1) 45-53-11-85; Ambassador: Datuk ISMAIL AMBIA.

Mali: 89 rue du Cherche-Midi, 75006 Paris; tel. (1) 45-48-58-43; telex 260002; Ambassador: H'FAGNANAMA KONE.

Malta: 92 ave des Champs Elysées, 75008 Paris; tel. (1) 45-62-53-01; telex 641023; fax (1) 45-62-00-36; Ambassador: ALBERT BORG OLIVIER DE PUGET.

Mauritania: 5 rue de Montévidéo, 75116 Paris; tel. (1) 45-04-88-54; telex 620506; Ambassador: MUHAMMAD EL HAUCHI OULD MUHAMMAD SALEH.

Mauritius: 68 blvd de Courcelles, 75017 Paris; tel. (1) 42-27-30-19; telex 644233; fax (1) 40-53-02-91; Ambassador: EDDY JOSEPH CHANGKYE.

Mexico: 9 rue de Longchamp, 75116 Paris; tel. (1) 45-53-76-43; telex 610332; Ambassador: MANUEL TELLO.

Monaco: 22 blvd Suchet, 75116 Paris; tel. (1) 45-04-74-54; telex 611088; Ambassador: CHRISTIAN ORSETTI.

Mongolia: 5 ave Robert Schuman, 92100 Boulogne-Billancourt; tel. (1) 46-05-28-12; telex 200656; Ambassador: LUVSANDORJIIN MUNDAGBAATAR.

Morocco: 3–5 rue Le Tasse, 75016 Paris; tel. (1) 45-20-69-35; telex 611025; Ambassador: ABBES EL-FASSI.

Mozambique: 82 rue Laugier, 75017 Paris; tel. (1) 47-64-91-32; telex 641527; Ambassador: MURADE MURARGY.

Myanmar: 60 rue de Courcelles, 75008 Paris; tel. (1) 42-25-56-95; telex 642190; Ambassador: U SAW TUN.

Nepal: 45 bis rue des Acacias, 75017 Paris; tel. (1) 46-22-48-67; Ambassador: DILLY RAJ UPRETY.

Netherlands: 7-9 rue Eblé, 75007 Paris; tel. (1) 43-06-61-88; telex 200070; fax (1) 40-56-01-32; Ambassador: HENRY WIJNAENDTS.

New Zealand: 7 ter rue Léonard de Vinci, 75116 Paris; tel. (1) 45-00-24-11; fax (1) 45-01-26-39; Ambassador: Mrs JUDITH C. TROTTER.

Nicaragua: 11 rue de Sontay, 75116 Paris; tel. (1) 45-00-35-42; telex 612017; Ambassador: ROBERTO ARGÜELLO HURTADO.

Niger: 154 rue de Longchamp, 75116 Paris; tel. (1) 45-04-80-60; telex 611080; Ambassador: YACOUBA SANDI.

Nigeria: 173 ave Victor Hugo, 75116 Paris; tel. (1) 47-04-68-65; telex 620106; Ambassador: OLUYEMI ADENIJI.

Norway: 28 rue Bayard, 75008 Paris; tel. (1) 47-23-72-78; telex 280947; fax (1) 47-23-97-40; Ambassador: ARNE LANGELAND.

Oman: 50 ave d'Iéna, 75116 Paris; tel. (1) 47-23-01-63; telex 613765; Ambassador: MUNIR A. MAKKI.

Pakistan: 18 rue Lord Byron, 75008 Paris; tel. (1) 45-62-23-32; telex 644000; Ambassador: SHAHID AMIN.

Panama: 145 ave de Suffren, 75015 Paris; tel. (1) 47-83-23-32; telex 205970; fax (1) 45-67-99-43; Ambassador: ANTONIA DE ROUX AROSEMENA.

FRANCE
Directory

Paraguay: 8 ave Charles Floquet, 75007 Paris; tel. (1) 47-83-54-77; Ambassador: ANÍBAL FILARTIGA CARRILLO.

Peru: 50 ave Kléber, 75116 Paris; tel. (1) 47-04-34-53; telex 611081; Chargé d'affaires a.i.: NORAH NALVARTE.

Philippines: 39 ave Georges Mandel, 75116 Paris; tel. (1) 47-04-65-50; telex 611572; fax (1) 47-04-49-92; Ambassador: FELICIDAD BENGZON-GONZALES.

Poland: 1–3 rue Talleyrand, 75007 Paris; tel. (1) 45-51-60-80; telex 611029; Ambassador: RYSZARD FIJALKOWSKI.

Portugal: 3 rue de Noisiel, 75116 Paris; tel. (1) 47-27-35-29; telex 620905; Ambassador: LUÍS GASPAR DA SILVA.

Qatar: 57 quai d'Orsay, 75007 Paris; tel. (1) 45-51-90-71; telex 270074; Ambassador: ABD AR-RAHMAN AL-ATTIYAH.

Romania: 5 rue de l'Exposition, 75007 Paris; tel. (1) 47-05-57-64; Chargé d'affaires a.i.: SABIN POP.

Rwanda: 12 rue Jadin, 75017 Paris; tel. (1) 42-27-36-31; telex 650930; Ambassador: DENIS MAGIRA-BIGIRIMANA.

San Marino: 6 ave Franklin Roosevelt, 75008 Paris; tel. (1) 43-59-22-28; telex 643445; Minister: CAMILLO DE BENEDETTI.

Saudi Arabia: 5 ave Hoche, 75008 Paris; tel. (1) 47-66-02-06 and 42-27-81-12; telex 641508; Ambassador: JAMIL AL-HEJAILAN.

Senegal: 14 ave Robert Schuman, 75007 Paris; tel. (1) 47-05-39-45; telex 611563; Ambassador: MASSAMBA SARRE.

Seychelles: 53 bis rue François 1er, 75008 Paris; tel. (1) 47-23-98-11; telex 649634; Ambassador: CALLIXTE D'OFFAY.

Singapore: 12 sq. de l'Avenue Foch, 75116 Paris; tel. (1) 45-00-33-61; telex 630994; fax (1) 45-00-61-79; Ambassador: DAVID SAUL MARSHALL.

Somalia: 26 rue Dumont d'Urville, 75116 Paris; tel. (1) 45-00-76-51; telex 611828; Ambassador: Said Hagi MUHAMMAD FARAH.

South Africa: 59 quai d'Orsay, 75007 Paris; tel. (1) 45-55-92-37; telex 200280; Ambassador: HENDRIK GELDENHUYS.

Spain: 13 ave Georges V, 75008 Paris; tel. (1) 47-23-61-83; telex 280689; Ambassador: JUAN DURÁN-LÓRIGA RODRIGÁÑEZ.

Sri Lanka: 15 rue d'Astorg, 75008 Paris; tel. (1) 42-66-35-01; telex 642337; Chargé d'affaires a.i.: Dr ANANDA W. P. GURUGÉ.

Sudan: 56 ave Montaigne, 75008 Paris; tel. (1) 47-20-07-34; telex 660268; Ambassador: AWAD EL-KARIM FADULALLA.

Sweden: 17 rue Barbet de Jouy, 75007 Paris; tel. (1) 45-55-92-15; telex 204675; fax (1) 45-50-26-43; Ambassador: CARL LIDBOM.

Switzerland: 142 rue de Grenelle, 75007 Paris; tel. (1) 45-50-34-46; telex 270969; fax (1) 45-51-34-77; Ambassador: CARLO JAGMETTI.

Syria: 20 rue Vaneau, 75007 Paris; tel. (1) 45-50-24-90; Ambassador: HONEIN HATEM.

Tanzania: 70 blvd Péreire, 75017 Paris; tel. (1) 47-66-21-77; telex 643968; Ambassador: TATU NURU.

Thailand: 8 rue Greuze, 75116 Paris; tel. (1) 47-04-32-22; telex 611626; Ambassador: WICHIAN WATANAKUN.

Togo: 8 rue Alfred Roll, 75017 Paris; tel. (1) 43-80-12-13; telex 290497; Ambassador: BOUMBÉRA ALASSOUNOUMA.

Tunisia: 25 rue Barbet de Jouy, 75007 Paris; tel. (1) 45-55-95-98; telex 200639; fax (1) 45-56-02-64; Ambassador: IBRAHIM TURKI.

Turkey: 16 ave de Lamballe, 75016 Paris; tel. (1) 45-24-52-24; telex 611784; fax (1) 45-20-41-91; Ambassador: ILTER TÜRKMEN.

Uganda: 13 ave Raymond Poincaré, 75116 Paris; tel. (1) 47-27-46-80; telex 630028; Ambassador: FRANCIS X. S. HATEGA.

USSR: 40–50 blvd Lannes, 75116 Paris; tel. (1) 45-04-05-50; telex 611761; Ambassador: YURI DUBININ.

United Arab Emirates: 3 rue de Lota, 75116 Paris; tel. (1) 45-53-94-04; telex 620003; Chargé d'affaires a.i.: ALI MOUBARAK AL-MANSOURI.

United Kingdom: 35 rue du Faubourg Saint Honoré, 75383 Paris Cedex 08; tel. (1) 42-66-91-42; telex 650264; fax (1) 42-66-95-90; Ambassador: Sir EWEN FERGUSSON.

USA: 2 ave Gabriel, 75008 Paris; tel. (1) 42-61-80-75; telex 650221; Ambassador: WALTER J. P. CURLEY, Jr.

Uruguay: 15 rue Le Sueur, 75116 Paris; tel. (1) 45-00-81-37; telex 610564; Ambassador: HORACIO TERRA GALLINAL.

Venezuela: 11 rue Copernic, 75116 Paris; tel. (1) 45-53-29-98; telex 610683; fax (1) 47-55-64-56; Ambassador: ISIDRO MORALES-PAUL.

Viet-Nam: 62 rue Boileau, 75016 Paris; tel. (1) 45-24-50-63; telex 613240; Ambassador: PHAM BINH.

Yemen: 25 rue Georges Bizet, 75116 Paris; tel. (1) 47-23-61-76; telex 610231; fax (1) 47-23-69-41; Ambassador: ALI MUTHANA HASSON.

Yugoslavia: 54 rue de la Faisanderie, 75116 Paris; tel. (1) 45-04-05-05; telex 610846; Ambassador: BOZIDAR GAGRO.

Zaire: 32 cours Albert 1er, 75008 Paris; tel. (1) 42-25-57-50; telex 280661; Ambassador: RAMAZANI BAYA.

Zambia: 76 ave d'Iéna, 75116 Paris; tel. (1) 47-23-43-52; telex 610483; Ambassador: MATHIAS MAINZA CHONA.

Zimbabwe: 5 rue de Tilsit, 75008 Paris; tel. (1) 47-63-48-31; telex 643505; Ambassador: BEN KUFAKUNESU JAMBGA.

Judicial System

The Judiciary is independent of the Government. Judges of the Court of Cassation and the First President of the Court of Appeal are appointed by the executive from nominations of the High Council of the Judiciary.

Subordinate cases are heard by Tribunaux d'instance, of which there are 471, and more serious cases by Tribunaux de grande instance, of which there are 181. Parallel to these Tribunals are the Tribunaux de commerce, for commercial cases, composed of judges elected by traders and manufacturers among themselves. These do not exist in every district. Where there is no Tribunal de commerce, commercial disputes are judged by Tribunaux de grande instance.

The Conseils de Prud'hommes (Boards of Arbitration) consist of an equal number of workers or employees and employers ruling on the differences which arise over Contracts of Work.

The Tribunaux correctionnnels (Correctional Courts) for criminal cases correspond to the Tribunaux de grande instance for civil cases. They pronounce on all graver offences (délits), including those involving imprisonment. Offences committed by juveniles of under 18 years go before specialized tribunals for children.

From all these Tribunals appeal lies to the Cours d'appel (Courts of Appeal).

The Cours d'assises (Courts of Assize) have no regular sittings, but are called when necessary to try every important case, for example, murder. They are presided over by judges who are members of the Cours d'appel, and are composed of elected judges (jury). Their decision is final, except where shown to be wrong in law, and then recourse is had to the Cour de cassation (Court of Cassation). The Cour de cassation is not a supreme court of appeal but a higher authority for the proper application of the law. Its duty is to see that judgments are not contrary either to the letter or the spirit of the law; any judgment annulled by the Court involves the trying of the case anew by a court of the same category as that which made the original decision.

COUR DE CASSATION

Palais de Justice, 5 quai de l'Horloge, 75001 Paris; tel. (1) 43-29-12-55.

First President: PIERRE DRAI.

Presidents of Chambers: BERNARD DUTHEILLET-LAMONTHÉZIE (2ème Chambre Civile), ROLAND DEFONTAINE (Chambre Commerciale), CHRISTIAN LE GUNEHEC (Chambre Criminelle), JEAN SENSELME (3ème Chambre Civile), YVES JOUHAUD (1ère Chambre Civile), JEAN COCHARD (Chambre Sociale).

Solicitor-General: PIERRE BEZIO.

There are 84 Counsellors, one First Attorney-General and 19 Attorneys-General.

Chief Clerk of the Court: DANIEL AUTIÉ.

Council of Advocates at Court of Cassation: Pres. CHARLES CHOUCROY.

COUR D'APPEL DE PARIS

Palais de Justice, blvd de Palais, 75001 Paris.

First President: MYRIAM EZRATTY.

There are also 57 Presidents of Chambers.

Solicitor-General: PIERRE TRUCHE.

There are also 128 Counsellors, 21 Attorneys-General and 37 Deputies.

TRIBUNAL DE GRANDE INSTANCE DE PARIS

Palais de Justice, blvd de Palais, 75001 Paris; fax (1) 43-29-12-55.

President: ROBERT DIET.

Solicitor of Republic: BRUNO COTTE.

TRIBUNAL DE COMMERCE DE PARIS

1 quai de Corse, 75181 Paris Cedex 04.

President: PHILIPPE GRANDJEAN.

TRIBUNAUX ADMINISTRATIFS

Certain cases arising between civil servants (when on duty) and the government, or between any citizen and the government are judged by special administrative courts.

FRANCE

The Tribunaux administratifs, of which there are 22, are situated in the capital of each area; the Conseil d'Etat (see below) has its seat in Paris.

TRIBUNAL DES CONFLITS

Decides whether cases shall be submitted to the ordinary or administrative courts.

President: The Minister of Justice.
Vice-President: PIERRE NICOLAI.

There are also four Counsellors of the Cour de cassation and three Counsellors of State.

COUR DES COMPTES

13 rue Cambon, 75100 Paris; tel. (1) 42-98-95-00.

An administrative tribunal competent to judge the correctness of public accounts. It is the arbiter of common law of all public accounts laid before it. The judgments of the Court may be annulled by the Conseil d'Etat.

First President: ANDRÉ CHANDERNAGOR.
Presidents: JUSTIN ROHMER, RENÉ VACQUIER, CHARLES DE VILLAINES, MAURICE BERNARD, FRANCIS RAISON, FRANÇOIS MOSES, GÉRARD DUCHER, JEAN PRADA, PAUL THERRE.
Attorney-General: JEAN RAYNAUD.
Deputy Attorneys-General: JEAN-PIERRE GASTINEL, JEAN-LOUIS BEAUD DE BRIVE.
Secretary-General: ALAIN PICHON.
Deputy Secretaries-General: ALAIN LEFOULON, ALAIN HESPEL.

CHAMBRES RÉGIONALES DES COMPTES

In 1983 jurisdiction over the accounts of local administrations (Régions, Départements and Communes) and public institutions (hospitals, council housing, etc.) was transferred from the Cour des comptes to local Chambres régionales. The courts are autonomous but under the jurisdiction of the State. Appeals may be brought before the Cour des comptes.

CONSEIL D'ETAT

Palais-Royal, 75100 Paris; tel. (1) 42-61-52-29.

A council of the central power and an administrative tribunal. As the consultative organ of the government, it gives opinions in the legislative and administrative domain (interior, finance, public works and social sections). In administrative jurisdiction it has three functions: to judge in the first and last resort such cases as appeals against excess of power laid against official decrees or individuals; to judge appeals against judgments made by Tribunaux administratifs and resolutions of courts of litigation; and to annul decisions made by various specialized administrative authorities which adjudicate without appeal, such as the Cour des comptes.

President: The Prime Minister.
Vice-President: MARCEAU LONG.
Presidents of Sections: Jacques Boutet, Fernand Grevisse, Suzanne Grevisse, Guy Braibant, Michel Combarnous, Michel Bernard.
General Secretary: JEAN-PIERRE AUBERT.

In 1987 the Government introduced proposals to create five Cours administratives d'appel (at Paris, Lyon, Bordeaux, Nancy and Nantes) in 1989. These courts would judge appeals against judgments made by Tribunaux administratifs on any case with the given facts already supplied. The new courts were to be headed by a Conseiller d'Etat and to be composed of members of the Tribunaux administratifs, which would be renamed Corps des Tribunaux administratifs et des Cours administratives d'appel. However, the Conseil d'Etat would retain its power to judge appeals against excess of power and the application of the law, and to pronounce on electoral disputes. The Conseil d'Etat would also be empowered to quash judgments made by the Cours administratives d'appel.

Religion

CHRISTIANITY

Conseil d'Eglises Chrétiennes en France: 31 rue de la Marne, 94230 Cachan; tel. (1) 46-63-49-02; fax (1) 46-63-77-18; f. 1987; ecumenical organization comprising representatives from all Christian denominations to express opinions on social issues; 21 mems; Secs Pastor FREYCHET, Fr DAMIEN SICARD, Fr MICHEL EVDOKIMOV.

The Roman Catholic Church

For ecclesiastical purposes, France comprises nine Apostolic Regions, together forming 19 archdioceses (of which two, Marseille and Strasbourg, are directly responsible to the Holy See), 93 dioceses (including one, Metz, directly responsible to the Holy See) and one Territorial Prelature. The Archbishop of Paris is also the Ordinary for Catholics of Oriental Rites. An estimated 80% of the population of France are adherents of the Roman Catholic Church.

Bishops' Conference: Conférence Episcopale Française, 106 rue de Bac, 75341 Paris Cedex 07; tel. (1) 42-22-57-08; telex 260757; fax (1) 45-48-13-39; f. 1975; Pres. Cardinal ALBERT DECOURTRAY, Archbishop of Lyon and Primate of Gaul.

Latin Rite

Archbishop of Lyon and Primate of Gaul: Cardinal ALBERT DECOURTRAY, Archevêché, 1 place de Fourvière, 69321 Lyon Cedex 05; tel. 78-25-12-27; telex 380835; fax 78-36-06-00.
Archbishop of Aix: Most Rev. BERNARD PANAFIEU.
Archbishop of Albi: Most Rev. ROGER MEINDRE.
Archbishop of Auch: Most Rev. GABRIEL VANEL.
Archbishop of Avignon: Most Rev. RAYMOND BOUCHEX.
Archbishop of Besançon: Most Rev. LUCIEN DALOZ.
Archbishop of Bordeaux: Most Rev. PIERRE EYT.
Archbishop of Bourges: Most Rev. PIERRE PLATEAU.
Archbishop of Cambrai: Most Rev. JACQUES DELAPORTE.
Archbishop of Chambéry: Most Rev. CLAUDE FEIDT.
Archbishop of Marseille: Most Rev. ROBERT COFFY.
Archbishop of Paris: Cardinal JEAN-MARIE LUSTIGER.
Archbishop of Reims: Most Rev. JEAN BALLAND.
Archbishop of Rennes: Most Rev. JACQUES JULLIEN.
Archbishop of Rouen: Most Rev. JOSEPH DUVAL.
Archbishop of Sens: Most Rev. EUGÈNE ERNOULT.
Archbishop of Strasbourg: Most Rev. CHARLES-AMARIN BRAND.
Archbishop of Toulouse: Most Rev. ANDRÉ COLLINI.
Archbishop of Tours: Most Rev. JEAN HONORÉ.

Armenian Rite

Bishop of Sainte-Croix-de-Paris: KRIKOR GHABROYAN, 10 bis rue Thouin, 75005 Paris; tel. (1) 43-26-50-43; 30,000 adherents (1988).

Ukrainian Rite

Apostolic Exarch of France: MICHEL HRYNCHYSHYN (Titular Bishop of Zygris), 186 boulevard Saint-Germain, 75006 Paris; tel. (1) 45-48-48-65; 16,000 adherents (1988).

Protestant Churches

There are some 850,000 Protestants in France.

Fédération Protestante de France: 47 rue de Clichy, 75009 Paris; tel. (1) 48-74-15-08; telex 206959; fax (1) 42-81-40-01; f. 1906; Pres. JACQUES STEWART; Vice-Pres MICHEL HOEFFEL, JEAN-PIERRE MONSARRAT, NELLY SELORON, ANDRÉ THOBOIS; Gen. Sec. LOUIS SCHWEITZER.

The Federation comprises the following Churches:

Alliance Nationale des Eglises Luthériennes de France: 1A quai Saint Thomas, Strasbourg; tel. 88-25-90-05; fax 88-25-90-99; f. 1945; 250,000 mems; groups the two Lutheran churches below; Pres. Mme PIERRETTE RICHARD.

Eglise de la Confession d'Augsbourg d'Alsace et de Lorraine: 1A quai Saint Thomas, 67081 Strasbourg Cedex; tel. 88-25-90-05; Pres. MICHEL HOEFFEL; Gen. Secs Pastor W. JURGENSEN, D. BIRMELE.

Eglise Evangélique Luthérienne de France: 13 rue Godefroy, 75013 Paris; tel. (1) 45-82-19-99; 65 parishes grouped in 2 directorates: Paris and Montbéliard; Pres. JEAN-MICHEL STURM; Sec. Pastor MICHEL DAUTRY.

Eglise Méthodiste: 3 rue Paul Verlaine, 30100 Alès; the total Methodist community was estimated at 2,900 mems in 1982.

Eglise Réformée d'Alsace et de Lorraine: 1 quai St Thomas, 67081 Strasbourg; fax 88-25-90-99; 45,000 mems; Pres. Pastor ANTOINE PFEIFFER.

Eglise Réformée de France: 47 rue de Clichy, 75009 Paris; tel. (1) 48-74-90-92; Pres. National Council Pastor JEAN-PIERRE MONSARRAT.

Fédération des Eglises Evangéliques Baptistes de France: 48 rue de Lille, 75007 Paris; tel. (1) 42-61-13-96; Pres. Pastor ROBERT SOMERVILLE; Sec. JEAN-PIERRE DASSONVILLE.

Union Nationale des Eglises Réformées Evangéliques Indépendantes: 7 rue Goum, 30900 Nîmes, tel. 67 50 00 01; Pres. Pastor MAURICE LONGEIRET; Gen. Sec. A. LEWIN.

FRANCE   *Directory*

The Orthodox Churches

Administration of Russian Orthodox Churches in Europe (Jurisdiction of the Oecumenical Patriarchate): 12 rue Daru, 75008 Paris; presided over by His Eminence the Most Reverend GEORGES, Archbishop of Russian Orthodox Churches in Europe.

Greek Orthodox Cathedral of St Etienne: 7 rue Georges Bizet, 75116 Paris; tel. (1) 47-20-82-35; Superior The Most Rev. MELETIOS CARABINIS, Greek Archbishop of France, Spain and Portugal.

The Anglican Communion

Within the Church of England, France forms part of the diocese of Gibraltar in Europe. The Bishop is resident in London.

Anglican Chaplain in Nice and Vence and Archdeacon of the Riviera: Ven. J. M. LIVINGSTONE, 11 rue de la Buffa, 06000 Nice; tel. 93-87-19-83.

Archdeacon of Northern France: Ven. M. B. LEA, 5 rue d'Aguesseau, 75008 Paris; tel. (1) 47-42-70-88.

Other Christian Churches

Société Religieuse des Amis (Quakers) et Centre Quaker International: 114 rue de Vaugirard, 75006 Paris; tel. (1) 45-48-74-23.

ISLAM

Islam is the second most important religion in France; in 1985 there were about 2.5m. adherents, of whom more than 750,000 resided in the Marseille area.

Fédération Nationale des Musulmans de France (FNMF): Paris; f. 1985; 20 asscns; Pres. DANIEL YOUSSOF LECLERQ.

Muslim Institute of the Paris Mosque: place du Puits de l'Ermite, 75005 Paris; tel. (1) 45-35-97-33; f. 1923; cultural, diplomatic, social, judicial and religious sections; research and information and commercial annexes; Dir Cheikh TEDJINI HADDAM.

JUDAISM

Consistoire Central—Union des Communautés Juives de France: 17 rue Saint Georges, 75009 Paris; tel. (1) 45-26-02-56; fax (1) 40-16-06-11; f. 1808; 120 asscns; Chief Rabbi of France JOSEPH SITRUK; Pres. JEAN PAUL ELKANN; Exec. Dir LÉON MASLIAH.

Consistoire Israélite de Paris (Jewish Consistorial Association of Paris): 17 rue Saint Georges, 75009 Paris; tel. (1) 40-82-76-76; Pres. BENNY COHEN; Chief Rabbi ALAIN GOLDMANN; Sec.-Gen. SERGE GUEDJ.

BUDDHISM

World Federation of Buddhists, French Regional Centre: 98 chemin de la Calade, 06250 Mougins; Sec. Mme TEISAN PERUSAT STORK.

Association Zen Internationale: 17 rue des Cinq Diamants, 75013 Paris; tel. (1) 45-80-10-00; Sec. JANINE MANNOT.

The Press

The legislation under which the French press operates mostly dates back to an Act of 1881, which established very liberal conditions for journalism, asserting the right of individuals to produce newspapers without any prior authorization. At the same time the law defined certain offences which the press might commit, such as incitement to crime, disturbance of the peace by the publication of false information, libel and defamation, the publication of material offensive to the President and revealing official secrets. Further legislation in the 1940s extended these restrictions, particularly with regard to children's literature. A law to prevent the concentration of newspaper and magazine ownership in the hands of a small number of press conglomerates was adopted in 1984. However, by June 1986 the new right-wing Government had abrogated the 1984 law and a 1944 ordinance, thus increasing the proportion of the total circulation of daily newspapers that an individual was permitted to control. The Constitutional Council added amendments which attempted to prevent the use of 'front' companies and intermediaries to increase an individual company's holdings in the French press.

In 1984 504 newspapers and 2,378 periodicals were published in France. In 1983 there were 11 daily newspapers published in Paris with a national circulation and 80 provincial dailies covering all the French regions. The circulations of the two groups in 1983 were 2.7m. for the Parisian press and 7.5m. for the provincial press. These figures showed a remarkable decline from the situation in 1946, when 28 Parisian dailies had a circulation of 5m. and 175 provincial dailies shared 9m. circulation. In recent years sharply rising costs and falling advertising revenue have increased the difficulties caused by declining circulation. The prestigious daily, *Le Monde*, issued shares to avoid a financial crisis in late 1985. In January 1988 the left-wing daily, *Le Matin de Paris*, was declared bankrupt and published its last edition.

The provincial press, already strong under the Third Republic, achieved a leading role during the German occupation (1940–44), when Paris was cut off from the rest of France. Since the war, it has proved more adept than the national press at dealing with the fall in revenue and rising costs. The best-selling provincial dailies can now almost match the most popular Paris dailies for circulation and they have initiated various rationalization schemes. Groups of provincial papers have been formed to pool advertising and, in some cases, copy and printing facilities. In an attempt to prevent the domination of the press in Lyon by the Hersant Group (following its take-over of *Le Progrès* in January 1986), two national dailies, *Le Monde* and *Libération*, started to produce regional editions in Lyon. By late 1986 the Hersant Group had launched a regional edition of *Le Figaro* in Lyon, which was merged with *Le Journal Rhône-Alpe*, another publication owned by the Hersant Group, to become *Journal Rhône-Alpes-Lyon-Figaro* in 1987.

The weekly news magazines have expanded in recent years; the two best examples of this are *L'Express* and *Le Nouvel Observateur*. Radio and TV magazines have greatly increased in popularity, and were estimated to reach 40% of French homes in 1987. Both national and regional newspapers have started to launch weekly TV supplements and, in response to increased competition in 1987, the Hachette Group, the owner of *Télé-7-Jours*, proposed the creation of another weekly, *Télé Couleur*, to sell as a supplement to regional publications.

The only major daily which acts as the organ of a political party is the Communist paper, *L'Humanité*. All others are owned by individual publishers or by the powerful groups which have developed round either a company or a single personality. The major groups are as follows:

Amaury Group: 25 ave Michelet, 93408 Saint-Ouen Cedex; tel. (1) 40-10-30-30; telex 234341; fax (1) 40-11-27-10; owns *Le Parisien*, the provincial dailies *Le Courrier de l'Ouest*, *Le Maine Libre* and *Liberté Dimanche*, the sports daily *L'Equipe*, the weeklies *L'Equipe Magazine* and *France-Football*, and the monthly, *Tennis de France*; Man. Dir PHILIPPE AMAURY.

Bayard Presse: 3 rue Bayard, 75008 Paris; tel. (1) 45-62-51-51; telex 641868; fax (1) 42-56-08-64; important Catholic press group; owns 37 publs, incl. the national *La Croix-L'Evénement*, *Pèlerin Magazine*, *Panorama Aujourd'hui*, *Notre Temps*, important magazines for young people and several specialized religious publications; Pres. BERNARD PORTE.

Editions Mondiales: 9-13 rue du Colonel Pierre Avia, 75754 Paris Cedex 15; tel. (1) 46-62-20-00; formerly Del Duca Group; owns several popular weekly magazines, incl. *Nous Deux*, *Le Nouvel Intimité*, *Les Veillées des Chaumières*, *Télé-Poche*, *Auto Plus*, *Le Sport* and also specialized magazines, incl. *Grands Reportages*, *Diapason*, *Cameravidéo*, *Photo Reporter* and *Montagnes Magazine*; Man. Dir FRANCIS MOREL.

Expansion Group: 67 ave de Wagram, 75017 Paris; tel. (1) 47-63-12-11; telex 650242; f. 1967; owns a number of magazines, incl. *L'Expansion*, *L'Entreprise*, *Architecture d'Aujourd'hui*, *Harvard L'Expansion*, *Voyages*, *Agefi*, *La Vie Française*, *La Tribune*; Chair. and Man. Dir JEAN-LOUIS SERVAN-SCHREIBER.

Filipacchi Group: 63 ave des Champs Elysées, 75008 Paris; tel. (1) 42-56-72-72; telex 290294; controls a number of large-circulation magazines incl. *Paris-Match*, *Salut*, *7 à Paris*, *OK!*, *Podium*, *Top 50*, *Newlook*, *Penthouse*, *Union*, *Echo des Savanes*, *Les Grands Ecrivains*, *Femme*, *Pariscope*, *Jazz Magazine*, *Lui*, *Les Grands Peintres*, *Les Grands Personnages*, *Jeune et Jolie*, *Fortune* and *Photo*; Pres. DANIEL FILIPACCHI.

Hachette Groupe Presse: 6 rue Ancelle, 92525 Neuilly-sur-Seine Cedex; tel. (1) 40-88-60-00; telex 611462; fax (1) 45-63-93-61; f. 1826; publs incl. *Le Journal du Dimanche*, *France-Dimanche*, *Elle*, *Télé-7-Jours*, *Parents*, *Le Provençal*, *Le Méridional*, *Var Matin*, *Les Dernières*, *Nouvelles d'Alsace*; has 32.6% holding in *Le Parisen Libéré* and *l'Equipe*; Chair. JEAN-LUC LAGARDÈRE; Man. Dir DANIEL FILIPACCHI.

Hersant Group: one of the largest of the provincial daily press groups; owns 20 dailies, numerous weeklies, fortnightlies and periodicals; dailies incl. *Le Progrès*, *L'Eclair*, *Le Dauphiné Libéré*, *Nord-Matin* and *Nord-Eclair*; has a majority holding in *Le Figaro*, *France-Soir*, *l'Aurore* and *Paris-Turf*; Chair. and Man. Dir ROBERT HERSANT.

Among the metropolitan dailies, the outstanding papers are *Le Monde* (circulation 362,443) and *Le Figaro* (433,496). Also popular are *France-Soir* and *Le Parisien Libéré*. The English language *International Herald Tribune* (174,200) is also important. The major provincial dailies are *Ouest-France* (Rennes), *Sud-Ouest* (Bordeaux), *Le Dauphiné Libéré* (Grenoble), *La Voix du Nord* (Lille), *Le Progrès* (Lyon), and *L'Est Républicain* (Nancy). Many provincial dailies cater for rural readership by producing local subsidiary editions.

FRANCE

Metropolitan weekly papers range from the popular press, such as *France-Dimanche* (721,000) and *L'Humanité-Dimanche* (360,000), through to the more serious current affairs magazines like *L'Express*, *Le Nouvel Observateur* and the satirical *Le Canard Enchaîné*. Among the popular periodicals must be mentioned the weekly illustrated *Paris-Match* (690,000) and the women's journals *Marie-Claire* (599,362), *Elle* (395,007) and *Marie-France* (522,284).

DAILY PAPERS (PARIS)

L'Aurore: 133 Champs-Elysées, 75008 Paris; telex 220310; f. 1944; Dir ROGER ALEXANDRE; circ. 35,000 (1983).

La Croix l'Evénement: 3-5 rue Bayard, 75008 Paris; tel. (1) 45-62-51-51; telex 280626; fax (1) 42-56-08-64; f. 1883; Catholic; Dirs BERNARD PORTE, CHARLES-JEAN PRADELLE; Editors-in-Chief BRUNO CHENU, CHRISTIAN LATU, NOËL COPIN; circ. 113,028.

Les Echos: 67 ave des Champs Elysées, 75381 Paris Cedex 08; tel. (1) 45-62-19-68; telex 290275; f. 1908; economic and financial; Chair. FRANK BARLOW (acting); circ. 72,992.

L'Equipe: 4 rue Rouget-de-Lisle, 92137 Issy-les-Moulineaux Cedex; tel. 40-93-20-20; telex 203004; f. 1946; sport; Man. Dir JEAN-PIERRE COURCOL; circ. 268,320.

Le Figaro: 25 ave Matignon, 75398 Paris Cedex 08; tel. (1) 42-56-80-80; telex 211112; fax (1) 42-21-64-05; f. 1828; morning; news and literary; magazine on Saturdays; Chair. ROBERT HERSANT; Editor-in-Chief FRANZ-OLIVIER GIESBERT; circ. 433,496.

France-Soir: rue de Bercy, 75112 Paris; tel. (1) 45-08-28-00; f. 1941 as *Défense de la France*, present title 1944; merged with *Paris-Presse L'Intransigeant* 1965; magazine on Saturdays, merged with *TV-France-Soir*, 1987; Chair. and Man. Dir PHILIPPE VILLIN; Editor-in-Chief MICHEL SCHIFRES; circ. 301,716 (1988).

L'Humanité: 5 rue du Faubourg Poissonière, 75440 Paris Cedex 09; tel. (1) 42-46-82-69; f. 1904 by Jean Jaurès; organ of the French Communist Party; morning; Dir ROLAND LEROY; Editor-in-Chief CLAUDE CABANES; circ. 117,005.

International Herald Tribune: 181 ave Charles de Gaulle, 92521 Neuilly-sur-Seine Cedex; tel. (1) 46-37-93-00; telex 612718; fax (1) 46-37-93-70; f. 1887; English language; Co-Chairs W. S. PALEY, K. GRAHAM, A. O. SULZBERGER; circ. 178,000.

Le Journal Officiel de la République Française: 26 rue Desaix, 75727 Paris Cedex 15; tel. (1) 40-58-75-00; telex 201176; fax (1) 40-58-77-80; f. 1870; official journal of the Government; publishes laws, decrees, parliamentary proceedings, and economic bulletins; Dir BERNARD SARAZIN.

Libération: 11 rue Béranger, 75154 Paris Cedex 03; tel. (1) 42-76-17-89; telex 217656; fax (1) 42-72-94-93; f. 1973; non-conformist; Publ. Dir SERGE JULY; Dir-Gen. JEAN-LOUIS PÉNINOU; circ. 195,098 (1988).

Le Monde: 7 rue des Italiens, 75427 Paris Cedex 09; tel. (1) 42-47-97-27; telex 650572; fax (1) 45-23-06-81; f. 1944; liberal; independent; week-end supplements; Man. Editor JACQUES LESOURNE; Editor-in-Chief DANIEL VERNET; circ. 362,443.

Paris-Turf/Sport Complet: Paris; racing, sport; Dir PIERRE JANROT; circ. 150,000.

Le Parisien: 25 ave Michelet, 93400 Saint Ouen; tel. (1) 40-10-30-30; telex 660041; f. 1944; morning; Chair. and Man. Dir PHILLIPE AMAURY; Man. Dir JEAN-PIERRE COURCOL; Dir-Gen. ANDRÉ FERRAS; circ. 402,085.

Le Quotidien du Médecin: Le France, 2 rue Ancelle, 92200 Neuilly-sur-Seine; medical journal; Dir Dr MARIE CLAUDE TESSON MILLET; Editor RICHARD LISCIA; circ. 62,000.

Le Quotidien de Paris: Neuilly-sur-Seine; tel. (1) 47-47-12-32; telex 610806; f. 1974, relaunched 1979; Man. Dir JEAN-MICHEL SAINT-OUEN; Editor PHILIPPE TESSON; circ. 75,000 (1987).

La Tribune de l'Economie: 12 rue Béranger, 75003 Paris; tel. (1) 48-04-99-99; telex 230735; f. 1986; economic and financial; Dir JACQUES JUBLIN; circ. 59,000.

SUNDAY PAPERS (PARIS)

France-Dimanche: 6 rue Ancelle, 92525 Neuilly-sur-Seine Cedex; tel. (1) 40-88-64-52; telex 611462; Dir ANNE-MARIE CORRE; circ. 706,388.

L'Humanité-Dimanche: rue Jean Jaurès, Saint Denis, Cedex 93528; tel. (1) 49-22-72-72; telex 234915; fax (1) 49-22-73-00; f. 1946; weekly magazine of the French Communist Party; Dir ROLAND LEROY; Editor Mme BULARD; circ. 360,000.

PRINCIPAL PROVINCIAL DAILY PAPERS

Amiens

Le Courrier Picard: 11 rue Alphonse Paillant, 80010 Amiens Cedex; f. 1944; Chair. FRANCIS LACHAT; Man. Dir DANIEL HUTIER; circ. 89,000.

Angers

Courrier de l'Ouest: blvd Albert Blanchoin, BP 728, 49005 Angers Cedex; tel. 41-66-21-31; telex 720997; f. 1944; Chair. and Man. Dir J. M. DESGREES DU LOU; circ. 108,423 (1988).

Angoulême

La Charente Libre: Zone Industrielle no. 3, BP 106, 16001 Angoulême Cedex; tel. 45-69-33-33; telex 791950; Dir LOUIS-GUY GAYAN; circ. 39,600.

Auxerre

L'Yonne Républicaine: 8-12 ave Jean Moulin, BP 399, 89006 Auxerre Cedex; f. 1944; Gen. Man. J. F. COMPÉRAT; circ. 41,606.

Besançon

Le Comtois: 60 rue Grande, 25000 Besançon; f. 1914; Dir. PIERRE BRANTUS; circ. 15,532.

Bordeaux

La France—Nouvelle République: 3 Zone industrielle, BP 3, 16004 Angoulême Cedex; tel. 45-69-30-69; f. 1944; Dir JEAN-MICHEL BLANCHY; circ. 10,270.

Sud-Ouest: 8 rue de Cheverus, BP 521, 33000 Bordeaux; tel. 56-90-92-72; telex 570670; f. 1944; independent; Man. Dir HENRI DE GRANDMAISON; Chief Editor PIERRE VEILLETET; circ. 366,387 (1988).

Calais

Nord Littoral: 39 blvd Jacquard, 62100 Calais; tel. 21-34-41-00; f. 1944; Editor JEAN-JACQUES BARATTE; circ. 9,819.

Chalon-sur-Saône

Courrier de Saône-et-Loire: 9 rue des Tonneliers, 71104 Chalon-sur-Saône; f. 1826; Dir RENÉ PRÉTET; circ. 46,021.

Charleville-Mézières

L'Ardennais: 36 cours Aristide Briand, 08102 Charleville-Mézières; tel. 24-32-91-51; f. 1944; Man. Dir PIERRE DIDRY; circ. 29,872.

Chartres

L'Echo Républicain: 39 rue de Châteaudun, 28004 Chartres; f. 1929; Chair. and Man. Dir ALAIN GASCON; Editor-in-Chief ALAIN BOUZY; circ. 31,817.

Chaumont

La Haute-Marne Libérée: 14 rue du Patronage Laïque, 52003 Chaumont Cedex; tel. 25-32-19-88; telex 840934; fax 25-32-67-87; f. 1944; Editor JEAN BLETNER; circ. 10,100.

Cherbourg

La Presse de la Manche: 14 rue Gambetta, 50104 Cherbourg; tel. 33-94-16-16; telex 171623; f. 1944; Chair. and Man. Dir (vacant); circ. 29,660.

Clermont-Ferrand

La Montagne (Centre-France): 28 rue Morel Ladeuil, 63003 Clermont-Ferrand; tel. 73-93-22-91; telex 990588; f. 1919; independent; Dir RENÉ BONJEAN; circ. 252,691 (1988).

Dijon

Le Bien Public: 7 blvd Chanoine Kir, 21015 Dijon Cedex; f. 1850; Pres. and Dir-Gen. A. THÉNARD; Dir-Gen. L. DE BROISSIA; circ. 53,383.

Les Dépêches: 5 rue Pierre Palliot, BP 570, 21015 Dijon; tel. 80-42-16-16; f. 1936; Chair. XAVIER ELLIE; Man. Dir PIERRE VILLEZ; circ. 42,000.

Epinal

Liberté de l'Est: 40 quai des Bons Enfants, 88001 Epinal Cedex; tel. 29-82-98-00; f. 1945; Man. SERGE CLÉMENT; Editor-in-Chief JACQUES DALLÉ; circ. 31,319.

Grenoble

Le Dauphiné Libéré: Les Iles Cordées, 38113 Veurey-Voroize; tel. 76-88-71-00; telex 320822; f. 1944; Chair. DENIS HUERTAS; circ. 294,200 (1988).

Le Havre

Havre Libre: BP 1384, 76066 Le Havre; tel. 35-21-37-70; fax 35-21-37-81; f. 1944; Editor-in-Chief RENÉ LENHOF; circ. 26,000.

Lille

Nord-Matin: 15 rue du Caire, Lille Cedex; f. 1944; Gen. Man. ROGER GRUSS; circ. 73,798.

FRANCE

La Voix du Nord: 8 place du Général de Gaulle, 78167 Lille; f. 1944; Chair. and Man. Dir RENÉ DECOCK; circ. 374,050 (1988).

Limoges

L'Echo du Centre: 46 rue Turgot, 87000 Limoges; tel. 55-34-46-35; f. 1943; five editions; Communist; Dir CHRISTIAN AUDOUIN; Chief Editor JEAN SAVARY; circ. 65,000.

Le Populaire du Centre: 9 place Fontaine-des-Barres, Limoges Cedex; f. 1905; four editions; Chair and Man. Dir RENÉ BONJEAN; Editor-in-Chief ROGER QUEYROI; circ. 56,493.

Lyon

Le Progrès: 93 chemin de Saint-Priest, 69680 Chassieu; tel. 72-22-23-23; f. 1859; Chair. XAVIER ELLIE; circ. Mon.–Sat. 411,000, Sun. 540,000.

Marseille

La Marseillaise: 17 cours Honoré d'Estienne d'Orves, BP 1862, 13222 Marseille Cedex 1; tel. 91-54-92-13; f. 1944; Communist; Dir PAUL BIAGGINI; Editor-in-Chief ALAIN FABRE; circ. 159,039.

Le Méridional-La France: 4 rue Cougit, 13316 Marseille Cedex 15; f. 1944; independent; 12 regional editions; Chair. RENÉ MERLE; circ. 72,750.

Le Provençal: 248 ave Roger Salengro, BP 100, 13316 Marseille Cedex 15; tel. 91-84-45-45; telex 440805; fax 91-84-49-95; f. 1944; the biggest daily paper in the south-east (evening edition **Le Soir**); Chair. and Man. Dir LAURENT PERPERE; circ. 162,389 (1988).

Metz

Le Républicain Lorrain: 3 rue de St Eloy, BP 89, 57104 Metz-Woippy; tel. 87-33-22-00; telex 860346; f. 1919; independent; Pres. Mme MARGUERITE PUHL-DEMANGE; Dir-Gen. CLAUDE PUHL; circ. 194,178 (1988).

Montpellier

Midi-Libre: Le Mans de Grille, route de Sète, Saint-Jean de Vedas, 34063 Montpellier Cedex; tel. 67-42-00-44; f. 1944; Dir CLAUDE BUJON; circ. 185,817 (1988).

Morlaix

Le Télégramme de Brest et de l'Ouest: rue Anatole Le Braz, BP 243, 29205 Morlaix Cedex; tel. 98-62-11-33; telex 940652; fax 98-63-45-45; f. 1944; Dir JEAN-PIERRE COUDURIER; circ. 206,648.

Mulhouse

L'Alsace: 25 ave du Président Kennedy, 68053 Mulhouse; tel. 89-43-99-44; telex 881818; f. 1944; Editor GILBERT KLEIN; circ. 125,244 (1989).

Nancy

L'Est Républicain: rue Theophraste Renaudot Houdemont, 54185 Heillecourt Cedex; tel. 83-56-80-54; telex 850019; f. 1889; Dir GÉRARD LIGNAC; circ. 267,588.

Nantes

L'Eclair: 5 rue Santeuil, BP 1116, 44010 Nantes Cedex 01; tel. 40-73-44-45; fax 40-73-05-88; f. 1945; Gen. Man. ROLANDE HERSANT; Dir-Gen. JEAN LUCAS; circ. 20,230.

Presse Océan: 7–8 allée Duguay Trouin, BP 1142, 44024 Nantes Cedex 01; tel. 40-44-24-00; telex 700439; f. 1944; independent; Chair. and Man. Dir PHILIPPE MESTRE; Editor-in-Chief JEAN-MARIE GAUTIER; circ. 93,180.

Nevers

Journal du Centre: 3 rue du Chemin de Fer, BP 14, 58000 Nevers; f. 1943; Editor PAUL BERTHELOT; circ. 37,834.

Nice

Nice-Matin: 214 route de Grenoble, BP 4, 06200 Nice Cedex; tel. 93-21-71-71; telex 460788; f. 1944; Chair. and Man. Dir MICHEL BAVASTRO; circ. 265,104 (1988).

Orléans

La République du Centre: 45 rue de la Halte, Saran, BP 35, 45403 Fleury les Aubrais Cedex; tel. 38-86-37-68; telex 780702; f. 1944; Chair. and Man. Dir MARC CARRÉ; Editor JACQUES RAMEAU; circ. 67,144.

Pau

Eclair-Pyrénées: 40 rue Emile Guichenné, 64006 Pau; f. 1944; Dir HENRI LOUSTALAN; circ. 9,801.

Perpignan

L'Indépendant: 4 rue Emmanuel Brousse, 66004 Perpignan; tel. 68-35-51-51; telex 500982; f. 1846; also **Indépendant-Dimanche** (Sunday); Dir DOMINIQUE PRETET; circ. 84,621.

Poitiers

Centre Presse: 5 rue Victor Hugo, BP 299, 86007 Poitiers; f. 1958; Man. Dir CYRILLE DUVAL; Editor-in-Chief ROLAND BARKAT; circ. 20,000.

Reims

L'Union: 87–91 place Drouet d'Erlon, 51083 Reims Cedex; f. 1944; telex 830751; fax 26-47-83-95; Dir PHILIPPE HERSANT; Dir-Gen. and Editor-in-Chief PIERRE-JEAN BOZO; circ. 117,812.

Rennes

Ouest-France: Zone Industrielle Rennes-Chantepie, 35051 Rennes Cedex; tel. 99-32-60-00; telex 730965; f. 1944; Chair. FRANÇOIS-RÉGIS HUTIN; circ. 786,463 (1989).

Roubaix

Nord-Eclair: 21 rue du Caire, 59052 Roubaix Cedex 1; tel. 20-75-92-56; telex 160740; f. 1944; Chair. A. DILIGENT; Man. Dir A. FARINE; circ. 102,773.

Rouen

Paris-Normandie: 19 place du Général de Gaulle, BP 563, 76004 Rouen; f. 1944; tel. 35-14-56-56; telex 771507; Publr Société Normande de Presse Républicaine; Chair. and Man. Dir JEAN ALLARD; circ. 119,925 (1988).

Saint-Etienne

La Tribune: 33 ave Général de Gaulle, 26201 Montelimar Cedex; tel. 75-01-69-66; Editor LOUIS AYZAC; circ. 23,352.

La Tribune—Le Progrès: 16 place Jean Jaurès, 42007 Saint-Etienne Cedex; tel. 77-32-45-45; Editor XAVIER ELLIE; circ. 130,000.

Strasbourg

Dernières Nouvelles d'Alsace: 17-19-21 rue de la Nuée Bleue, BP 406/R1, 67000 Strasbourg; tel. 88-23-31-23; telex 880445; f. 1877; non-party; Dir JACQUES PUYMARTIN; circ. 220,082.

Le Nouvel Alsacien: Strasbourg; tel. 88-32-37-14; f. 1885; Man. BERNARD DECK; circ. 15,245.

Tarbes

La Nouvelle République des Pyrénées: 48 ave Bertrand Barère, 65001 Tarbes; tel. (Tarbes) 93-90-90; f. 1944; Man. JEAN GAITS; circ. 17,765.

Toulon

Var Matin: route de la Seyne à Ollioules, 83190 Toulon; tel. 94-06-91-91; telex 440691; fax 94-63-34-49; f. 1946; Man. Dir LAURENT PERPERE; circ. 81,858.

Toulouse

Dépêche du Midi: ave Jean-Baylet, 31095 Toulouse; f. 1870; radical; Gen. Man. Mme EVELYNE-JEAN BAYLET; circ. 241,514 (1988).

Tours

La Nouvelle République du Centre-Ouest: 232 ave de Grammont, 37048 Tours Cedex; tel. 47-31-70-00; telex 750693; f. 1944; non-party; Chair JACQUES SAINT-CRICQ; circ. 268,777 (1989).

Troyes

L'Est-Eclair: 55 rue Urbain IV, 10000 Troyes; tel. 25-79-90-10; f. 1945; Dir ANDRÉ BRULEY; circ. 33,000.

Libération-Champagne: 126 rue Général de Gaulle, BP 713, 10003 Troyes Cedex; tel. 25-73-11-55; Dir GILBERT BOUTSOQUE; circ. 21,074.

SELECTED PERIODICALS

The following is a selection from the total of 2,378 periodicals (1984) published in France.

General, Political and Literary

Annales—Economies, sociétés, civilisations: 54 blvd Raspail, 75006 Paris; tel. (1) 49-54-23-75; f. 1929; every 2 months; eight Dirs.

Aspects de la France: 10 rue Croix des Petits Champs, 75001 Paris; tel. (1) 40-39-92-06; f. 1947; weekly; monarchist; organ of L'Action Française; Dir PIERRE PUJO.

Autre Journal: 7 rue d'Argout, 75002 Paris; tel. (1) 42-36-33-86; f. 1984, fmrly *Nouvelles Littéraires*; monthly; literature, medicine, science, technology, news; Dir MICHEL BUTEL; circ. 220,000.

Le Canard Enchaîné: 173 rue Saint Honoré, Paris 75001; tel. (1) 42-60-31-36; f. 1915; weekly; political satire; Chair. and Man. Dir ANDRÉ RIBAUD; circ. 450,000.

FRANCE
Directory

Carrefour: Paris; f. 1944; weekly; moderate; Dir JEAN DANNENMULLER; circ. 100,000.

Le Crapouillot: 49 ave Marceau, 75016 Paris; f. 1915; satire and humorous; Man. Dir J.-C. GOUDEAU; Editor PATRICE BOIZEAU.

Critique: Editions de Minuit, 7 rue Bernard Palissy, 75006 Paris; tel. (1) 45-44-23-16; f. 1946; monthly; general review of French and foreign literature; Editor JEAN PIEL.

Croissance: Le monde en développement: 163 blvd Malesherbes, 75017 Paris; tel. (1) 48-88-46-00; telex 649333; fax (1) 47-64-04-53; f. 1961 as *Croissance des Jeunes Nations*; monthly on developing nations; circ. 25,000.

Diogène: Unesco House, 1 rue Miollis, 75732 Paris Cedex 15; tel. (1) 45-68-27-34; telex 204461; fax (1) 40-65-94-80; f. 1951; quarterly; international review of human sciences; four editions, in Arabic, English, French and Spanish; anthologies in Chinese, Hindi, Japanese and Portuguese; Editor JEAN D'ORMESSON.

Les Ecrits de Paris: 9 passage des Marais, 75010 Paris; tel. (1) 42-01-40-51; f. 1944; monthly; current affairs; circ. 15,000.

Esprit: 212 rue St-Martin, 75003 Paris; tel. (1) 48-04-92-90; f. 1932; monthly; Dir OLIVIER MONGIN; circ. 10,000.

Europe: 146 rue du Faubourg Poissonnière, 75010 Paris; tel. (1) 42-81-91-03; fax (1) 48-74-19-99; f. 1923; monthly; literary review; Chair. PIERRE GAMARRA; Editors CHARLES DOBZYNSKI, JEAN-BAPTISTE PARA; circ. 16,000.

L'Evénement du Jeudi: 2 rue Christine, 75006 Paris; tel. (1) 43-54-84-80; telex 205802; fax 46-34-69-36; f. 1984; weekly; current affairs; Editorial Dir JEAN-MARCEL BOUGUEREAU; circ. 260,000.

L'Express: 61 ave Hoche, 75008 Paris; tel. (1) 40-54-30-00; telex 280805; fax (1) 40-54-99-72; f. 1953; weekly; Head of Publication WILLY STRICKER; Editor-in-Chief YANN DE L'ECOTAIS; circ. 669,600.

Le Hérisson: 2-12 rue de Bellevue, 75019 Paris; f. 1936; weekly; humorous; Dir J. P. VENTILLARD; Editor-in-Chief PHILIPPE CARPENTIER; circ. 270,000.

Ici-Paris: 29 rue Galilée, 75116 Paris; tel. (1) 47-23-78-77; f. 1941; weekly; Editor LOUIS BALAYÉ; circ. 372,386.

Jours de France: 49 ave Marceau, 75116 Paris; tel. (1) 40-70-15-15; f. 1954; weekly; news and fashion magazine; Chief Editor MARCEL DASSAULT; circ. 673,000.

Lire: 38 ave Hoche, 75008 Paris; tel. (1) 42-89-05-98; fax (1) 45-63-48-14; monthly; literary review; Editor-in-Chief JEAN-MAURICE DE MONTREMY; Editor DAVID GUIRAUD; circ. 125,070.

Lutte Ouvrière: BP 233, 75865 Paris Cedex 18; f. 1968; weekly; Editor MICHEL RODINSON.

Minute: 31 rue Saint-Lazare, 75009 Paris; tel. (1) 42-85-54-54; fax (1) 48-74-23-64; f. 1962; right-wing weekly; Pres. and Dir-Gen. J. C. GOUDEAU; Editor-in-Chief J. ROBERTO; circ. 220,000.

Le Monde Diplomatique: 5 rue Antoine Bourdelle, 75015 Paris; tel. (1) 40-65-25-25; telex 650572; fax (1) 45-48-23-96; f. 1954; monthly; political and cultural; Dir IGNACIO RAMONET; Editor MICHELINE PAUNET; circ. 165,000.

Le Nouvel Observateur: 14 rue Dussoubs, 75081 Paris; telex 680729; f. 1964; weekly; left-wing political and literary; Dir CLAUDE PERDRIEL; Editorial Dir LAURENT JOFFRIN; circ. 324,200.

La Nouvelle Revue Française (NRF): 5 rue Sébastien Bottin, 75007 Paris; tel. (1) 45-44-39-19; telex 204121; f. 1909; monthly; literary; Editor JACQUES REDA.

Parents: 6 rue Ancelle, 92521 Neuilly-sur-Seine; tel. (1) 47-38-43-21; magazine for parents; circ. 367,571.

Paris-Match: 63 ave des Champs Elysées, 75008 Paris; telex 290294; f. 1949; weekly; magazine of French and world affairs; Dir ROGER THÉROND; circ. 690,000.

Passages: 17 rue Simone Weil, 75013 Paris; tel. (1) 45-86-30-02; f. 1987; monthly; Jewish current affairs, humour and literary review; Dir EMILE MALET; Editor BERNARD ULMANN; circ. 75,000.

Le Peuple: 263 rue de Paris, Case 432, 93516 Montreuil Cedex; tel. 48-51-83-06; telex 235091; f. 1921; fortnightly; official organ of the Confédération Générale du Travail (trade union confederation); Dir JEAN-CLAUDE LAROZE; Editor-in-Chief LUCIEN POSTEL.

Poétique: Editions du Seuil, 27 rue Jacob, 75261 Paris Cedex 06; tel. (1) 40-46-50-50; telex 270024; fax (1) 40-46-51-43; f. 1970; quarterly; literary review.

Le Point: 140 rue de Rennes, 75006 Paris; tel. (1) 45-44-39-00; telex 202784; fax (1) 45-49-30-20; f. 1972; politics and current affairs; Man. Dir BERNARD WOUTS; Editor CLAUDE IMBERT; circ. 329,658.

Point de Vue-Images du Monde: Paris; weekly; Dir C. GIRON; circ. 370,311.

Politique Hebdo: 14–16 rue des Petits Hotels, 75010 Paris; weekly; review of world socialist studies and practice.

Politique Internationale: 11 rue du Bois de Boulogne, 75116 Paris; 4 a year.

Quinzaine Littéraire: 43 rue du Temple, 75004 Paris; tel. (1) 48-87-48-58; fax (1) 48-87-13-01; f. 1966; fortnightly; Dir MAURICE NADEAU; circ. 40,000.

Révolution: 15 rue Montmartre, 75001 Paris; tel. (1) 42-33-61-26; f. 1980; weekly; political and cultural; Dir GUY HERMIER; Chief Editors JEAN-PAUL JOUARY, GÉRARD STREIFF.

Revue des Deux Mondes: 170 rue de Grenelle, 75007 Paris; tel. (1) 47-53-71-10; fax (1) 47-05-66-74; f. 1829; monthly; current affairs; Dir JEAN-MICHEL PLACE.

Revue d'Histoire Littéraire de la France: 112 rue Monge, 75005 Paris; f. 1894; 6 a year; Editor RENÉ POMEAU.

Rivarol: 9 passage des Marais, 75010 Paris; tel. (1) 42-06-40-51; fax (1) 42-38-03-08; f. 1951; weekly; political, literary and satirical; circ. 45,000.

Rouge: 2 rue Richard Lenoir, 93100 Montreuil; tel. 48-59-00-80; f. 1969; weekly; extreme left; circ. 10,000.

Sélection du Reader's Digest: 212 blvd Saint Germain, 75007 Paris; tel. (1) 46-64-16-16; telex 200882; monthly; Chair. HENRI CAPDEVILLE; circ. 1,130,000.

Les Temps Modernes: 26 rue de Condé, 75006 Paris; tel. (1) 43-29-08-47; f. 1945 by J.-P. Sartre; monthly; literary review; publ. by Les Presses d'Aujourd'hui.

Art

L'Architecture d'Aujourd'hui: 67 ave de Wagram, 75017 Paris; tel. (1) 47-63-12-11; telex 650242; f. 1930; publ. by Groupe Expansion; Editor-in-Chief FRANÇOIS CHASLIN; circ. 25,791.

Art et Décoration: 16–18 rue de l'Amiral Mouchez, 75014 Paris; tel. (1) 45-65-48-48; f. 1897; 8 a year; Dir JEAN MASSIN; circ. 451,443.

Gazette des Beaux-Arts: 140 Faubourg Saint Honoré, 75008 Paris; tel. (1) 42-89-08-04; f. 1859; monthly; the oldest review of the history of art; Dir DANIEL WILDENSTEIN.

L'Oeil: 10 rue Guichard, 75116 Paris; tel. (1) 45-25-85-60; fax (1) 42-88-65-87; f. 1955; monthly; Vice-Chair. FRANÇOIS DAULTE; Gen. Sec. and Editor SOLANGE THIERRY.

Bibliography

Bulletin des Bibliothèques de France: 61/65 rue Dutot, 75732 Paris Cedex 15; tel. (1) 40-65-63-78; fax (1) 40-65-60-93; f. 1956; 6 a year; circ. 2,200.

Livres-Hebdo: 30 rue Dauphine, 75006 Paris; tel. (1) 43-29-73-50; fax (1) 43-29-77-85; f. 1979; 46 a year; Dir JEAN-MARIE DOUBLET.

Livres de France: 30 rue Dauphine, 75006 Paris; tel. (1) 43-29-73-50; fax (1) 43-29-77-85; f. 1979; 11 a year; Dir JEAN-MARIE DOUBLET.

Economic and Financial

L'Expansion: 25 rue Leblanc, 75015 Paris; tel. (1) 47-63-12-11; telex 650242; f. 1967; every 2 weeks; economics and business; Pres. JEAN-LOUIS SERVAN-SCHREIBER; Dir JEAN BOISSONNAT; Editor-in-Chief ALBERT DU ROY; circ. 200,565.

Le Nouvel Economiste: 65 ave des Champs-Elysées, 75008 Paris; tel. (1) 40-74-70-00; telex 648991; fax (1) 42-25-94-73; f. 1975 by merger of *l'Entreprise* and *Les Informations*; weekly; Chair. FRANK TENOT; circ. 117,090.

La Revue du Courtage: 31 rue d'Amsterdam, 75008 Paris; tel. (1) 42-82-91-10; f. 1923; monthly; review produced by Syndicat National des Courtiers d'Assurances; Editor-in-Chief ALAIN FARSHIAN; circ. 2,000.

Revue Economique: 54 blvd Raspail, 75006 Paris; tel. (1) 49-54-25-65; f. 1950; every 2 months; Chair. J. M. PARLY.

Science et Vie Economie: 1 rue du Colonel Pierre Avia, 75015 Paris; tel. (1) 46-48-48-48; fax (1) 46-48-48-09; f. 1984; monthly; economics; Dir PAUL DUPUY; Editor-in-Chief DIDIER POURQUERY; circ. 124,600.

L'Usine Nouvelle: 59 rue du Rocher, 75008 Paris; tel. (1) 43-87-37-88; telex 640485; f. 1945; weekly with monthly supplements; technical and industrial journal; Chair. and Man. Dir JACQUES MONNIER; circ. 60,000.

Valeurs Actuelles: 14 rue d'Uzès, 75081 Paris Cedex 02; tel. (1) 42-33-21-84; fax (1) 40-26-01-33; f. 1967; weekly; politics, economics, international affairs; Editor R. BOURGINE; circ. 150,000.

La Vie Française: 2 rue Béranger, 75003 Paris; tel. (1) 48-04-99-99; telex 670092; f. 1945; weekly; economics and finance; Dir and Editor-in-Chief BRUNO BERTEZ; Editorial Dir FRANÇOIS DE WITT; circ. 125,000.

History and Geography

Acta geographica: 184 blvd Saint Germain, 75006 Paris; tel. (1) 40-48-54-62; f. 1821; quarterly; Chair. JACQUELINE BEAUJEU-GARNIER.

FRANCE

Annales de géographie: 103 blvd Saint Michel, 75240 Paris Cedex 05; tel. (1) 46-34-12-19; telex 201269; fax (1) 43-26-96-38; f. 1891; every 2 months; seven Dirs.

Cahiers de civilisation médiévale: 24 rue de la Chaine, 86022 Poitiers; tel. 49-41-03-86; f. 1958; quarterly; Dirs PIERRE BEC, ROBERT FAVREAU.

XVIIe siècle: c/o Collège de France, 11 place Marcelin Berthelot, 75231 Paris Cedex 05; tel. (1) 45-48-85-24; f. 1948; quarterly; Dir R. ZUBER; Pres. J. TRUCHET; circ. 1,500.

Historia: 61 rue de la Tombe-Issoire, 75104 Paris; f. 1946; monthly; Dirs JACQUES JOURQUIN, CHRISTIAN MELCHIOR-BONNET; circ. 104,097.

Revue d'histoire diplomatique: 13 rue Soufflot, 75005 Paris; fax (1) 46-34-07-60; f. 1887; quarterly; Dir GEORGES DETHAN.

Revue Historique: Archives Nationales, 60 rue des Francs-Bourgeois, 75003 Paris; f. 1876; quarterly; Dirs JEAN FAVIER, RENÉ RÉMOND.

Revue de synthèse: Centre International de Synthèse, 12 rue Colbert, 75002 Paris; tel. (1) 42-97-50-68; f. 1900; quarterly; Dir JEAN-CLAUDE PERROT.

Law

Propriété Immobilière: 17 rue d'Uzès, 75002 Paris; f. 1945; monthly; Chair. MARC N. VIGIER; Man. Dir JEAN-MARC PILPOUL; circ. 5,846.

Revue Critique de Droit International Privé: 22 rue Soufflot, 75005 Paris; f. 1905; quarterly; publ. by Editions Sirey; Dirs Prof P. LAGARDE, Prof. PH. FRANCESCAKIS; Editor-in-Chief Prof. Y. LEQUETTE.

Leisure

Cahiers du Cinéma: 9 passage de la Boule Blanche, 75012 Paris; tel. (1) 43-43-92-20; telex 215092; f. 1951; monthly; film reviews; Dir and Editor SERGE TOUBIANA; circ. 80,000.

France-Football: 4 rue Rouget-de-Lisle, 92137 Issy-les-Moulineaux Cedex; tel. (1) 40-93-20-20; telex 203004; fax (1) 40-93-20-08; weekly; owned by Amaury Group; circ. 158,553.

Le Miroir du Cyclisme: Paris; tel. (1) 42-60-31-06; telex 640067; monthly; cycling; circ. 87,536.

Photo: 65 ave des Champs-Elysées, 75360 Paris; tel. (1) 42-56-75-72; telex 29294; f. 1960; monthly; specialist photography magazine; circ. 191,908.

Télé-Magazine: Asnières; f. 1955; weekly; circ. 273,958.

Télé-Poche: 2 rue des Italiens, 75009 Paris; tel. (1) 48-24-46-21; telex 660712; fax (1) 47-70-51-56; f. 1966; weekly; television magazine; Pres. and Dir-Gen. FRANCIS MOREL; circ. 1,800,000.

Télérama: 129 blvd Malesherbes, 75017 Paris; tel. (1) 48-88-48-88; fax (1) 40-54-06-45; f. 1972; weekly; radio, TV, film, literature and music; circ. 526,000.

Télé 7 Jours: 2 rue Ancelle, 92525 Neuilly-sur-Seine Cedex; tel. (1) 47-38-43-21; telex 611462; f. 1960; weekly; television; Dir PAUL GIANOLLI; Chief Editor ALAIN LAVILLE; circ. 3,335,000.

Military

Armées d'Aujourd'hui: 14 rue St Dominique, 75997 Paris; 10 a year; military and technical; produced by the Service d'information et de relations publiques des armées (SIRPA); circ. 130,000.

Revue 'Défense Nationale': Ecole Militaire, 1 place Joffre, 75700 Paris; tel. (1) 45-55-31-90; fax (1) 45-55-31-89; f. 1939; monthly; publ. by Committee for Study of National Defence; military, economic, political and scientific problems; Chair. PAUL-MARIE DE LA GORCE; Editor Adm. JACQUES HUGON.

Music

Diapason-Harmonie: 9–13 rue du Colonel Pierre Avia, 75754 Paris Cedex 15; tel. (1) 46-62-20-00; fax (1) 46-62-25-33; f. 1956; monthly; Pres. and Dir-Gen. JEAN-PIERRE ROGER; Chief Editor YVES PETIT DE VOIZE; circ. 70,000.

Revue de Musicologie: 2 rue Louvois, 75002 Paris; f. 1917; 2 a year; publ. by Société française de musicologie; Editors CHRISTIAN MEYER, GEORGIE DUROSOIR; circ. 1,000.

Overseas and Maritime

Le Droit Maritime Français: 190 blvd Haussmann, 75008 Paris; tel. (1) 45-63-11-55; telex 290131; f. 1949; monthly; maritime law; Pres. SERGE MARPAUD.

Europe Outremer: 178 Quai Louis Blériot, 75016 Paris; tel. (1) 46-47-78-44; f. 1923; monthly; Dir R. TATON; circ. 17,800.

Industries et Développement International: 190 blvd Haussmann, 75008 Paris; tel. (1) 45-63-11-55; f. 1953; monthly; analysis and information on developing economies; Pres. SERGE MARPAUD.

Directory

Le Journal de la Marine Marchande et du Transport Multimodal: 190 blvd Haussmann, 75008 Paris; tel. (1) 45-63-11-55, telex 290131; fax (1) 42-89-08-72; f. 1919; weekly shipping publication; Pres. SERGE MARPAUD.

Marchés Tropicaux et Méditerranéens: 190 blvd Haussmann, 75008 Paris; tel. (1) 45-63-11-55; telex 290131; f. 1945; weekly; African trade review; Pres. SERGE MARPAUD.

Navires, Ports et Chantiers: 190 blvd Haussmann, 75008 Paris; tel. (1) 45-63-11-55; telex 290131; f. 1950; monthly; international shipbuilding and harbours; Pres. SERGE MARPAUD.

La Pêche Maritime: 190 blvd Haussmann, 75008 Paris; tel. (1) 45-63-11-55; telex 290131; f. 1919; monthly; fishing industry; Pres. SERGE MARPAUD.

Philosophy, Psychology

Bibliographie de la Philosophie: Librairie J. Vrin, 6 place de la Sorbonne, 75005 Paris; tel. (1) 43-54-03-47; fax (1) 43-54-48-18; f. 1937; quarterly.

Psychologie française: 28 rue Serpente, 75006 Paris; tel. (1) 42-34-99-37; f. 1956; quarterly; revue of the Société Française de Psychologie; Editor C. BONNET.

Revue d'Esthétique: 162 rue Saint Charles, 75740 Paris Cedex 15; tel. (1) 61-23-09-26; telex 521001; f. 1948; 2 a year; Dirs OLIVIER REVAULT D'ALLONNES, MIKEL DUFRENNE; circ. 2,500.

Revue des sciences philosophiques et théologiques: Librairie J. Vrin, 6 place de la Sorbonne, 75005 Paris; tel. (1) 43-54-03-47; fax (1) 43-54-48-18; f. 1907; quarterly.

Revue philosophique de la France et de l'étranger: 12 rue Jean de Beauvais, 75005 Paris; tel. (1) 43-26-22-16; f. 1876; quarterly; Dir YVON BRÉS; circ. 1,200.

Religion

L'Actualité Religieuse dans le Monde: 163 blvd Malesherbes, 75017 Paris; tel. (1) 48-88-46-00; telex 649333; f. 1983; Editor JEAN-PAUL GUETNY; circ. 30,000.

Etudes: 14 rue d'Assas, 75006 Paris; tel. (1) 45-48-52-51; f. 1856; monthly; general interest; Editor JEAN-YVES CALVEZ.

France Catholique: 12 rue Edmond Valentin, 75007 Paris; tel. (1) 47-05-43-31; fax (1) 45-51-11-87; weekly; Dir A. CHABADEL; circ. 20,000.

Pèlerin Magazine: 3 rue Bayard, 75008 Paris; tel. (1) 45-62-51-51; f. 1873; weekly; Dir GUY BAUDRILLART; Editors-in-Chief HENRY CARO, GUY MAURATILLE; circ. 386,000.

Prier: 163 blvd Malesherbes, 75017 Paris; tel. (1) 48-88-46-00; telex 649333; fax (1) 42-27-29-03; f. 1978; monthly; review of modern prayer and contemplation; circ. 85,000.

Témoignage Chrétien: 49 rue du Faubourg Poissonnière, 75009 Paris; tel. (1) 42-46-37-50; telex 290562; f. 1941; weekly; cultural; Dir GEORGES MONTARON; circ. 52,000.

La Vie Catholique: 163 blvd Malesherbes, 75017 Paris; tel. (1) 47-66-01-86; telex 649333; f. 1945; weekly; Chair. and Man. Dir ANDRÉ SCHAFTER; Dir JOSÉ DE BROUCKER; circ. 400,000.

Science and Mathematics

Annales de Chimie—Science des Matériaux: 120 blvd Saint Germain, 75280 Paris Cedex 06; tel. (1) 46-34-21-60; f. 1789; 8 a year; chemistry and material science.

Astérisque: Ecole Normale Supérieure, Tour L, 1 rue Maurice Arnoux, 92120 Montrouge; tel. (1) 40-84-80-55; fax (1) 40-84-80-52; f. 1973; monthly; mathematics; Dir M. HERMAN; Sec. D. BOLLOT.

L'Astronomie: 3 rue Beethoven, 75016 Paris; tel. (1) 42-24-13-74; f. 1887; monthly; publ. by Société Astronomique de France; Chair. P. DE LA COTARDIÈRE.

Biochimie: Collège de France, 11 place Marcellin-Berthelot, 75231 Paris Cedex 05; tel. (1) 43-29-12-11; f. 1914; monthly; bio-chemistry; Chief Editor Mme M. GRUNBERG-MANAGO.

Bulletin de la Société mathématique de France: Ecole Normale Supérieure, Tour L, 1 rue Maurice Arnoux, 92120 Montrouge; tel. (1) 40-84-80-55; fax (1) 40-84-80-52; f. 1872; quarterly; mathematics; Dir P. SCHAPIRA; Sec. D. BOLLOT.

Bulletin des sciences mathématiques: Centrale des Revues, 11 rue Gossin, 92543 Montrouge Cedex; telex 260776; f. 1870; quarterly; circ. 800.

Science et vie: 5 rue de la Baume, 75382 Paris; telex 641866; fax (1) 45-63-70-24; f. 1913; monthly; Pres. PAUL DUPUY.

Technical and Miscellaneous

L'Argus de l'Automobile: 1 place Boieldieu, 75002 Paris; tel. (1) 42-61-83-03; telex 214633; f. 1927; motoring weekly.

Aviation Magazine International: 15–17 quai de l'Oise, 75019 Paris; tel. (1) 42-02-40-41; telex 211678; f. 1950; fortnightly; circ. 30,000.

FRANCE *Directory*

Bureaux d'Études Automatismes: 60–62 rue d'Hauteville, 75010 Paris; tel. (1) 48-24-82-82; telex 280274; fax (1) 48-24-02-02; 9 issues a year; industrial design and CAD; publ. by CEP Information Technologie; Editor-in-Chief JEAN-FRANÇOIS DESCLAUX; circ. 7,500.

L'Echo de la Presse: 19 rue des Prêtres Saint-Germain l'Auxerrois, 75039 Paris Cedex 01; f. 1945; weekly; journalism, advertising; Editor NOEL JACQUEMART; circ. 8,100.

Ingénieurs de l'Automobile: 3 ave Président-Wilson, 75116 Paris; tel. (1) 47-20-93-23; f. 1927; monthly; formerly *Journal de la S.I.A.*; technical automobile review; Dir PAUL BARDEZ.

Matériaux et Techniques: 76 rue de Rivoli, 75004 Paris; tel. (1) 42-78-52-20; fax (1) 42-74-40-48; f. 1913; monthly; review of engineering research and progress on industrial materials; Chief Editor R. DROUHIN.

Le Monde de l'Education: 5 rue des Italiens, 75427 Paris; tel. (1) 42-47-97-10; telex 650572; f. 1974; monthly; circ. 115,000.

Le Moniteur des Travaux Publics et du Bâtiment: 17 rue d'Uzès, 75002 Paris; tel. (1) 42-96-15-50; telex 680876; f. 1903; weekly; Editor-in-Chief JEAN MARCHAND; Gen. Man. JACQUES GUY; circ. 75,952.

La Revue Générale des Chemins de Fer: C.D.R., 11 rue Gossin, 92543 Montrouge Cedex; telex 260776; f. 1878; monthly; Chief Editor J. P. BERNARD; circ. 4,000.

Revue Pratique du Froid et du Conditionnement de l'Air: 5 ave de Verdun, BP 105, 94208 Ivry-sur-Seine Cedex; tel. (1) 49-60-86-36; telex 263424; fax (1) 46-72-41-85; f. 1945; fortnightly; industrial and technical review on cold storage, heat pumps and heat recovery and air-conditioning; Dir P. BENICHOU; Editor-in-Chief MICHÈLE LERY; circ. 4,948.

Techniques et Equipements de Production: 59 rue du Rocher, 75008 Paris; tel. (1) 42-94-01-04; fax (1) 43-87-05-15; f. 1906 as *Machine Moderne*; monthly; technical magazine; Dir JACQUES-YVES DUQUENNOY; circ. 13,000.

Technologies et Formations: 5 ave de Verdun, BP 105, 94208 Ivry-sur-Seine Cedex; tel. (1) 49-60-86-36; telex 263424; fax (1) 46-72-41-85; f. 1945; every 2 months; review intended for vocational schools and training managers; Dir P. BENICHOU; circ. 2,833.

Traitement Thermique: 5 ave de Verdun, BP 105, 94208 Ivry-sur-Seine Cedex; tel. (1) 49-60-86-36; telex 263424; fax (1) 46-72-41-85; f. 1963; 9 a year; technical review for engineers and technicians of heat treatment; Dir PIERRE BENICHOU; circ. 3,022.

La Vie des Métiers: 28 rue du Montmartre, 75009 Paris; tel. (1) 47-70-84-85; fax (1) 47-70-61-55; monthly; Man. Editor MICHÈLE ANSOLA.

Women's and Fashion

Bonne Soirée Télé: 26 rue de la Trémoille, 75008 Paris; tel. (1) 40-70-98-93; f. 1922; weekly; Chief Editor M. H. ADLER; circ. 234,637.

Echo de la Mode: 9 rue d'Alexandrie, 75002 Paris; f. 1890; weekly; publ. by Editions de Montsouris; Chair. and Man. Dir ALBERT DE SMAELE; circ. 405,000.

Elle: 6 rue Ancelle, 92521 Neuilly-sur-Seine Cedex; tel. (1) 40-88-60-00; telex 611462; fax (1) 47-45-38-12; f. 1945; weekly; Dir JEAN DEMACHY; circ. 395,007.

Femme d'Aujourd'hui: 73 rue Pascal, 75013 Paris; tel. (1) 43-36-11-11; telex 649964; f. 1933; weekly; circ. 850,000.

Femme Pratique: 34 rue Eugène-Flachat, 75017 Paris; tel. (1) 42-27-49-49; telex 649964; f. 1958; monthly; French and Belgian; circ. 380,000.

Intimité: 2 rue des Italiens, 75009 Paris; f. 1949; weekly; illustrated stories; Dir ANTOINE DE CLERMONT-TONNERRE; circ. 509,622.

Jardin des Modes: 80 ave du Maine, 75014 Paris; tel. (1) 43-20-13-11; telex 615142; fax (1) 47-23-94-81; f. 1922; monthly; Publr and Editor ALICE MORGAINE; circ. 15,000.

Maison et Jardin: 10 blvd du Montparnasse, 75724 Paris Cedex 15; tel. (1) 45-67-35-05; telex 204191; fax (1) 45-67-99-60; f. 1950; 10 a year, 3 special issues; associated with *House and Garden*, New York and London, *Casa Vogue*, Italy; Publr PATRICK DELCROIX; circ. 89,477.

Marie-Claire: 11 bis rue Boissy d'Anglas, 75008 Paris; tel. (1) 42-66-93-64; telex 240387; f. 1954; monthly; Dir EVELYNE PROUVOST; circ. 599,362.

Marie-Claire Maison: 11 bis rue Boissy d'Anglas, 75008 Paris; tel. (1) 42-66-88-88; telex 240387; f. 1967; home interest; Dir EVELYNE PROUVOST; circ. 200,801.

Marie-France: 13 rue Bleue, 75009 Paris; tel. (1) 40-22-19-32, telex 281100; fax 48-24-00-03, f. 1944, monthly, Man. Dir LUDWIG M. TRÄNKNER; Chief Editor MICHÈLE FAURE; circ. 315,058.

Modes et travaux: 10 rue de la Pépinière, 75380 Paris Cedex 08; tel. (1) 45-22-78-05; telex 280286; f. 1919; monthly; Dir PHILIPPE CHOPIN; circ. 1,500,000.

Nous Deux: 2 rue des Italiens, 75009 Paris; f. 1947; illustrated stories; Dir ANTOINE DE CLERMONT-TONNERRE; circ. 823,397.

Vogue: Paris; tel. (1) 45-50-32-32; telex 260752; f. 1921; 10 a year, plus 10 a year of *Vogue Hommes* and 2 a year of *Vogue Enfants*; Dirs JEAN PONIATOWSKI (*Vogue*), BERNARD CHAPUIS (*Vogue Hommes*).

NEWS AGENCIES

Agence France-Presse: 11–15 place de la Bourse, 75002 Paris; tel. (1) 40-41-46-46; telex 210064; fax (1) 42-33-44-66; f. 1944; 24-hour service of world political, financial, sporting news, and photographs; 150 agencies and 2,000 correspondents all over the world; Chair. and Man. Dir CLAUDE MOISY; Gen. Man. PIERRE JEANTET.

Agence Parisienne de Presse: 18 rue Saint Fiacre, 75002 Paris; f. 1949; Man. Dir MICHEL RAVELET.

Agence Républicaine d'Information: 22 rue de Châteaudun, 75009 Paris; French domestic and foreign politics; Dir ALBERT LEBACQZ.

Presse Services: 111 ave Victor Hugo, 75116 Paris; f. 1929; Chair. and Man. Dir C. CAZENAVE DE LA ROCHE.

Science-Service–Agence Barnier: 10 rue Notre Dame de Lorette, 75009 Paris; medical, scientific, technical, recreation news; Man. Dir DENISE BARNIER.

Foreign Bureaux

Agencia EFE (Spain): 60 rue de la Chaussée d'Antin, 75009 Paris; tel. (1) 40-16-90-72; telex 660829; fax (1) 40-16-82-99; Delegate FERNANDO CASARES.

Agenzia Nazionale Stampa Associata (ANSA) (Italy): 29 rue Tronchet, 75008 Paris; tel. (1) 42-65-55-16; telex 290120; Bureau Chief ADA PRINCIGALLI.

Associated Press (AP) (USA): 162 rue du Faubourg Saint-Honoré, 75008 Paris; tel. (1) 43-59-86-76; telex 280770; fax (1) 40-74-00-45; Bureau Chief HARRY DUNPHY.

Československá tisková kancelář (ČTK) (Czechoslovakia): 6 rue du Dr Finlay, 75015 Paris; tel. (1) 45-79-00-24; telex 201735; Bureau Man. KAREL BARTAK.

Deutsche Presse-Agentur (dpa) (Germany): 30 rue Saint Augustin, 75002 Paris; tel. (1) 47-42-95-02; fax (1) 47-42-51-75; Bureau Chief PEER MEINERT.

Informatsionnoye Agentstvo Novosti (IAN) (USSR): 14 place du Général Catroux, 75017 Paris; tel. (1) 42-27-79-21; telex 650673; Bureau Chief V. NEDBAEV.

Inter Press Service (Italy): 6 rue Jean Lantier, 2 ème étage, 75001 Paris; tel. (1) 42-21-14-19; telex 217511; Correspondent DANIEL GATTI.

Jiji Tsushin-sha (Japan): 27 blvd des Italiens, 75002 Paris; tel. (1) 42-66-96-57; telex 660616; Bureau Chief JOJI HARANO.

Kyodo Tsushin (Japan): 19 rue Paul Lelong, 75002 Paris; tel. (1) 42-60-13-16; telex 680516; fax (1) 40-20-08-87; Bureau Chief KAZUO KATO.

Magyar Távirati Iroda (MTI) (Hungary): 8 rue Octave Feuillet, 75116 Paris; Correspondent LÁSZLÓ BALÁZS.

Middle East News Agency (Egypt): 6 rue de la Michodière, 75002 Paris; tel. (1) 47-42-16-03; telex 230011; f. 1956; Dir ESSAM SALEH.

Prensa Latina (Cuba): 22 ave de l'Opéra, 75001 Paris; tel. (1) 42-60-22-18; telex 213688; Bureau Chief RAMÓN MARTÍNEZ CRUZ.

Reuters (UK): 101 rue Réaumur, 75080 Paris Cedex 02; tel. (1) 42-21-50-00; telex 210003; fax (1) 40-26-69-70; Chief Editor F. DURIAUD.

Telegrafnoye Agentstvo Sovetskovo Soyuza (TASS) (USSR): 27 ave Bosquet, 75007 Paris; telex 201807; Correspondent YURI LOPATIN.

United Press International (UPI) (USA): 2 rue des Italiens, 75009 Paris; tel. (1) 47-70-91-70; telex 650547; Correspondents JOHN PHILLIPS, BRENDAN MURPHY.

Wikalat al-Maghreb al-Arabi/Agence Maghreb Arabe Presse (Morocco): 4 place de la Concorde, 75008 Paris; tel. (1) 42-65-40-45; fax (1) 42-66-26-43; f. 1959; Correspondent CHAKIB LAROUSSI.

Xinhua (New China) News Agency (People's Republic of China): 148 rue Petit Leroy, Chevilly-Larue, 94150 Rungis; tel. (1) 46-87-12-08; telex 204398; Correspondent WANG WEN.

The following Agencies are also represented: Jamahiriya News Agency (Libya) and Central News Agency (Taiwan).

PRESS ASSOCIATIONS

Comité de Liaison Professionnel de la Presse: liaison organization for press, media and cinema; mems Chambre Syndicale de la Presse Filmée, Confédération de la Presse Française, Fédér-

FRANCE

ation Française des Agences de Presse, Fédération Nationale de la Presse Française; Gen. Sec. CHRISTIAN LOYAUTÉ.

Confédération de la Presse Française: 17 place des Etats Unis, 75116 Paris; tel. (1) 47-23-36-36; Chair. PIERRE ARCHAMBAULT; Dir JEAN-CLAUDE GATINEAU.

Fédération Française des Agences de Presse et d'Informations Audiovisuelles (FFAPA): 32 rue de Laborde, 75008 Paris; tel. (1) 42-93-42-57; fax (1) 42-93-15-32; Pres. ELIE DAVIDSON.

Fédération Nationale de la Presse Française: 6 bis rue Gabriel Laumain, 75010 Paris; tel. (1) 48-24-98-30; f. 1944; mems. Syndicat de la Presse Parisienne, Syndicat de la Presse Hebdomadaire Parisienne, Syndicat des Quotidiens Régionaux, Syndicat des Quotidiens Départementaux, Fédération de la Presse Hebdomadaire et Périodique, Union Nationale de la Presse Périodique d'Information, Fédération Nationale de la Presse d'Information Spécialisée; Chair. CLAUDE PUHL; Dir MICHEL CABART; Gen. Sec. PHILIPPE NONIN.

Fédération Nationale de la Presse d'Information Spécialisée: 6 bis rue Gabriel Laumain, 75484 Paris Cedex 10; tel. (1) 47-70-93-86; telex 642473; fax (1) 42-46-14-03; Chair. SOPHIE ROBERT; Dir MAURICE VIAU.

Fédération Nationale des Syndicats et Associations Professionnelles de Journalistes Français: Paris; tel. (1) 48-24-65-71; f. 1888, under present title since 1937; 7,000 mems; Chair. ARMAND MACÉ.

Union Nationale de la Presse Périodique d'Information: 6 bis rue Gabriel Laumain, 75010 Paris; tel. (1) 48-24-98-30; f. 1978; mems Syndicat National de la Presse Hebdomadaire Régionale d'Information, Syndicat National des Publications Régionales, Syndicat de la Presse Judiciaire de Province; Chair. ALBERT GARRIGUES.

PRESS INSTITUTE

Institut Français de Presse et des Sciences de l'Information: 92 rue d'Assas, 75006 Paris; tel. (1) 43-20-12-24; fax (1) 43-25-33-20; f. 1953; studies and teaches all aspects of communication and the media; maintains research and documentation centre; open to research workers, students, journalists; Dir PIERRE ALBERT.

Publishers

Editions Albin Michel: 22 rue Huyghens, 75014 Paris Cedex 14; tel. (1) 42-79-10-00; telex 203379; fax (1) 43-27-21-58; f. 1901; general, fiction, history, classics; Chair. and Man. Dir FRANCIS ESMÉNARD.

Editions Arthaud: 20 rue Monsieur-le-Prince, 75006 Paris; tel. (1) 40-51-31-00; telex 205641; fax (1) 43-29-21-48; f. 1870; literature, arts, history, travel books, reference, sports; Chair. and Man. Dir CHARLES-HENRI FLAMMARION; Dir ROSELYNE DE AYALA.

Assimil: 13 rue Gay Lussac, BP 25, Z.I. 94430 Chennevières-sur-Marne; tel. (1) 45-76-87-37; telex 264337; fax (1) 45-94-06-55; f. 1929; self-study language methods; Man. Dir JEAN-LOUP CHEREL.

Editions Aubier: 13 quai de Conti, 75006 Paris; tel. (1) 43-26-55-59; telex 205641; f. 1924; literature, philosophy, history and sociology; Chair and Man. Dir CHARLES-HENRI FLAMMARION; Dir PATRICE MENTHA.

J. B. Baillière: 37 ave des Champs Elysées, 75008 Paris; tel. (1) 49-53-69-00; telex 650378; f. 1814; science, medicine, agriculture and technical books; Dir-Gen. CHRISTOPHE POUTHIER.

Editions Balland: 33 rue Saint André des Arts, 75006 Paris; tel. (1) 43-25-74-40; telex 270840; fax (1) 46-33-56-21; f. 1967; fine art, literature, history, humanities; Pres. GERARD NOËL; Dir-Gen. MAURICE PARTOUCHE.

Bayard-Presse: 3–5 rue Bayard, 75008 Paris; tel. (1) 45-62-51-51; telex 280626; f. 1873; children's books, religion, literature; owns *La Croix, Le Pèlerin, Notre Temps, Panorama d'Aujourd'hui, Grain de Soleil,* etc.; Chair. BERNARD PORTE; Dir NICHOLAS BARDINET.

Beauchesne Editeur: 72 rue des Saints Pères, 75007 Paris; tel. (1) 45-48-80-28; fax (1) 42-22-59-79; f. 1900; scripture, religion and theology, philosophy, religious history, politics, encyclopaedias, periodicals; Dir MONIQUE CADIC.

Editions Belfond: 216 blvd Saint Germain, 75007 Paris; tel. (1) 45-44-38-23; telex 260717; fax (1) 45-44-98-04; f. 1963; fiction, poetry, documents, history, arts; Chair. PIERRE BELFOND; Dir-Gen. FRANCA BELFOND.

Berger-Levrault SA: 229 blvd Saint Germain, 75006 Paris; tel. (1) 47-05-56-14; f. 1976; architecture, social and economic sciences, law; Pres. MARC FRIEDEL; Man. Dir BERNARD AJAC.

De Boccard, Edition-Diffusion: 11 rue de Médicis, 75006 Paris; tel. (1) 43-26-00-37; fax (1) 43-54-85-83; f. 1866; history, archaeology, religion, orientalism, medievalism; Dir DOMINIQUE CHAULET.

Bordas: 17 rue Rémy Dumoncel, BP 50, 75661 Paris Cedex 14; tel. (1) 42-79-62-00; telex 260776; fax (1) 43-22-85-18; f. 1946; encyclopaedic, scientific, technical, dictionaries, history, geography, arts, children's and educational; Chair. and Man. Dir JEAN MANUEL BOURGOIS.

Editions Bornemann: 15 rue de Tournon, 75006 Paris; tel. (1) 43-26-05-88; f. 1829; art, fiction, sports, nature, easy readers; Chair. and Man. Dir JACQUES HERSANT.

Bottin SA: 31 Cours de Juilliottes, 94706 Maisons-Alfort Cedex; tel. (1) 49-81-56-56; telex 262407; fax (1) 49-77-85-28; data bases, videotex, business directories; Chair. JEAN-PAUL DEVAI.

Buchet-Chastel: 18 rue de Condé, 75006 Paris; tel. (1) 43-26-06-20; f. 1929; dietetics, religion, sociology, history, music, literature, biographies, documents; Dir GUY BUCHET.

Calmann-Lévy, SA: 3 rue Auber, 75009 Paris; tel. (1) 47-42-38-33; telex 290993; fax (1) 47-42-77-81; f. 1836; fiction, history, social sciences, economics, sport, religion; Chair. and Man. Dir JEAN-ETIENNE COHEN-SÉAT.

Casterman: 66 rue Bonaparte, 75006 Paris; tel. (1) 43-25-20-05; telex 200001; f. 1780; juvenile, comics, fiction, education, leisure interests; Chair. and Man. Dir ROBERT VANGÉNEBERG.

Les Editions du Cerf: 29 blvd de Latour Maubourg, 75340 Paris Cedex 07; tel. (1) 45-50-34-07; telex 200684; fax (1) 45-56-04-27; f. 1929; juvenile, religion, social science; Pres. and Dir-Gen. PASCAL MOITY.

Chiron (Editions): 40 rue de Seine, 75006 Paris; tel. (1) 46-33-18-93; telex 200233; fax (1) 43-25-61-56; f. 1907; technical, sport, education, leisure; Chair. and Man. Dir DENYS FERRANDO-DURFORT.

Armand Colin: 103 blvd Saint Michel, 75240 Paris Cedex 05; tel. (1) 46-34-12-19; telex 201269; f. 1870; philosophy, history, law, geography and science, pedagogy, music, poetry, maps and textbooks; Chair. and Man. Dir JÉRÔME TALAMON.

Editions du CNRS (Centre National de la Recherche Scientifique): 15 quai Anatole-France, 75700 Paris Cedex; tel. (1) 45-55-92-25; telex 260034; f. 1946; public institution under the Ministry of Research and Technology; science and social science; Dir GÉRARD LILAMAND.

Dalloz: 11 rue Soufflot, 75240 Paris Cedex 05; tel. (1) 43-29-50-80; telex 206446; f. 1824; law, philosophy, political science, business and economics; Chair. and Man. Dir PATRICE VERGÉ.

Dargaud: 12 rue Blaise Pascal, BP 155, 92200 Neuilly-sur-Seine; tel. (1) 47-47-11-33; telex 620631; f. 1943; juvenile, cartoons, music, science-fiction; Chair. and Man. Dir GEORGES DARGAUD.

La Découverte: 1 place Paul Painlevé, 75005 Paris; tel. (1) 46-33-41-16; fax (1) 46-33-46-77; f. 1959; economic, social and political science, literature, history; Man. Dir FRANÇOIS GÈZE.

Librairie Delagrave (SARL): 15 rue Soufflot, 75240 Paris Cedex 05; tel. (1) 43-25-88-66; telex 204252; fax (1) 46-34-11-33; f. 1865; textbooks; Man. FABRICE DELAGRAVE.

Editions Denoël: 30 rue de l'Université, 75007 Paris; tel. (1) 42-61-50-87; fax (1) 42-61-14-90; f. 1930; general literature, sport, politics, economics; Dir HENRY MARCELLIN.

Editions Des Femmes: 6 rue de Mézières, 75006 Paris; tel. (1) 42-22-60-74; fax (1) 42-22-62-73; f. 1973; mainly women authors; fiction, essays, art, history, politics, psychoanalysis, talking books; Dirs ANTOINETTE FOUQUE, MARIE-CLAUDE GRUMBACH.

Desclée De Brouwer: 76 bis rue des Saints Pères, 75007 Paris; tel. (1) 45-44-07-63; telex 202098; f. 1875; religion, reference, textbooks, arts, psychiatry; Chair. and Man. Dir MICHEL HOUSSIN.

Deux Coqs d'Or: 28 rue la Boétie, 75008 Paris; tel. (1) 45-62-10-52; telex 650780; f. 1949; children's books, encyclopaedias; Chair. and Man. Dir JEAN-MICHEL AZZI; Dir FRANÇOIS MARTINEAU.

La Documentation Française: 29–31 quai Voltaire, 75340 Paris Cedex 07; tel. (1) 40-15-70-00; telex 204826; fax (1) 40-15-72-30; f. 1945; government publs; political, economical, topographical, historical, sociological documents and audio-visual material; Dir JEAN JENGER.

ESF Editeur: 17 rue Viète, 75854 Paris Cedex 17; tel. (1) 47-63-68-76; fax (1) 46-22-67-45; f. 1947; business, humanities, social sciences; Chair. GÉRARD DIDIER; Man. Dir FRANÇOISE DAUZAT.

Eyrolles: 61 blvd Saint Germain, 75240 Paris Cedex 05; tel. (1) 46-34-21-99; telex 203385; f. 1918; scientific, technical; Chair. and Man. Dir SERGE EYROLLES.

Fayard: 75 rue des Saints Pères, 75278 Paris Cedex 06; tel. (1) 45-44-38-45; telex 240918; f. 1850; general fiction, literature, biography, history, religion, essays, philosophy, geography, music, science; Chair. and Man. Dir CLAUDE DURAND.

Librairie Ernest Flammarion: 26 rue Racine, 75278 Paris Cedex 06; tel. (1) 40-51-31-00; telex 205641; fax (1) 43-29-21-48; f. 1875;

general literature, art, human sciences, history, children's books, medicine; Chair. CHARLES-HENRI FLAMMARION.

Fleuve Noir: 6 rue Garancière, 75278 Paris Cedex 06; tel. (1) 46-34-12-80; telex 204870; f. 1949 (Presses de la Cité); crime and science fiction, paperbacks; Dir Gen. CHRISTIAN CHALMIN.

Foucher: 128 rue de Rivoli, 75038 Paris Cedex 01; tel. (1) 42-36-38-90; telex 240231; f. 1935; science, economics, law, medicine; Chair. and Man. Dir BERNARD FOULON.

Editions Gallimard: 5 rue Sébastien-Bottin, 75007 Paris; tel. (1) 45-44-39-19; telex 204121; f. 1911; general fiction, literature, history, poetry, philosophy; Chair. and Man. Dir ANTOINE GALLIMARD.

Librairie Générale de Droit et de Jurisprudence: 26 rue Vercingétorix, 75014 Paris; tel. (1) 43-35-01-67; telex 203918; fax (1) 43-20-07-42; f. 1836; law and economy; Pres. and Man. Dir L. GUERIN; Dir N. JOUVEN.

Librairie Générale Française—Le Livre de Poche: 79 blvd Saint Germain, 75006 Paris; tel. (1) 46-34-86-34; telex 204434; *Livres de Poche* paperback series, general literature, dictionaries, encyclopaedias; f. 1953; Pres. DOMINIQUE GOUST.

Librairie Orientaliste Paul Geuthner SA: 12 rue Vavin, 75006 Paris; tel. (1) 46-34-71-30; fax (1) 43-29-75-64; f. 1901; philology, travel books, studies and learned periodicals concerned with the Orient; Dir MARC F. SEIDL-GEUTHNER.

Editions Grasset et Fasquelle: 61 rue des Saints Pères, 75006 Paris; tel. (1) 45-44-38-14; f. 1907; contemporary literature, criticism, general fiction and children's books; Chair. and Man. Dir JEAN CLAUDE FASQUELLE.

Groupe de la Cité: 8 rue Garancière, 75285 Paris Cedex 06; tel. (1) 46-34-12-80; telex 204807; f. 1942 as Presses de la Cité; renamed 1988; general fiction, history, paperbacks; group comprises Bordas, Garancière, Garnier, Plon, G.P. Rouge et Or, Solar, Librairie Académique Perrin, Julliard, Presses Pocket, Editions Fleuve Noir, Messageries Centrales du Livre, Editions Christian Bourgeois, le Rocher, UGE 10/18, Olivier Orban, M. A.-Edition, OCI; Pres. and Dir-Gen. CHRISTIAN BREGOU.

Librairie Gründ: 60 rue Mazarine, 75006 Paris; tel. (1) 43-29-87-40; telex 204926; fax (1) 43-29-49-86; f. 1880; art, natural history, children's, books, guides; Chair. ALAIN GRÜND.

Hachette Groupe Livre: 24 blvd Saint Michel, 75006 Paris; tel. (1) 46-34-86-34; telex 204434; f. 1826; general; all types of book, especially text-books; Editorial Dir JEAN-CLAUDE LATTÈS.

Librairie A. Hatier, SA: 8 rue d'Assas, 75006 Paris; tel. (1) 49-54-49-54; telex 202732; f. 1880; text books, art, audio-visual materials, dictionaries, general literature, geographical maps, books for young people, computer software; Pres. MICHEL FOULON.

Hermann: 293 rue Lecourbe, 75015 Paris; tel. (1) 45-57-45-40; telex 200595; fax (1) 40-60-12-93; f. 1870; sciences and art, humanities; Chair. and Man. Dir PIERRE BERÈS.

I.D. Music SA: 34 rue Kleber, 92400 Courbevoie; tel. (1) 47-88-25-92; telex 613711; fax (1) 47-68-74-28; f. 1972; music; Dir PHILIPPE AGEON.

J'ai Lu: 27 rue Cassette, 75006 Paris; tel. (1) 45-44-38-76; telex 202765; fax (1) 45-44-65-52; f. 1958; fiction, paperbacks; subsidiary of Flammarion; Chair. CHARLES-HENRI FLAMMARION; Gen. Dir JACQUES GOUPIL; Literary Dir JACQUES SADOUL.

Editions René Julliard: 8 rue Garancière, 75285 Paris Cedex 06; tel. (1) 46-34-12-80; telex 204807; f. 1931; general literature, history, political science, biographies and documents; Chair. and Man. Dir JEAN-MANUEL BOURGOIS; Man. Dir CATHERINE BLANCHARD.

Editions Klincksieck: 11 rue de Lille, 75007 Paris; tel. (1) 42-60-38-25; f. 1842; human sciences, architecture, literature, history, fine art, philosophy, music; Chair. and Man. Dir Mme ANDRÉE LAURENT-KLINCKSIECK; Dir MICHEL PIERRE.

Jeanne Laffitte: 25 Cours d'Estienne-d'Orves, BP 1903, 13225 Marseille Cedex 02; tel. 91-54-14-44; fax 91-54-76-33; f. 1972; art, geography, culture, medicine, history; Chair. and Man. Dir JEANNE LAFFITTE.

Editions Robert Laffont: 6 place Saint Sulpice, 75279 Paris Cedex 06; tel. (1) 43-29-12-33; telex 270607; f. 1941; literature, history, art, translations; Chair. and Man. Dir ROBERT LAFFONT.

Librairie Larousse SA: 17 rue du Montparnasse, 75298 Paris Cedex 06; tel. (1) 45-44-38-17; telex 250828; f. 1852; general, specializing in dictionaries, illustrated books on scientific subjects, encyclopaedias, classics, textbooks and periodicals; Pres. and Dir-Gen. CHRISTIAN BRÉGOU.

Editions Jean-Claude Lattès: 17 rue Jacob, 75006 Paris; tel. (1) 46-34-03-10; telex 205652; f. 1968; general fiction and non-fiction, biography, music; Man. Dir PIERRE-ANTOINE ULLMO.

Letouzey et Ané: 87 blvd Raspail, 75006 Paris; tel. (1) 45-48-80-14; f. 1885; biblical exegesis; history and archaeology of Catholic Church; history of religions; ecclesiastical encyclopaedias and dictionaries, biography; Dirs JEAN LETOUZEY, FLORENCE LETOUZEY-DUMONT.

Editions Magnard: 122 blvd Saint Germain, 75264 Paris Cedex 06; tel. (1) 43-26-39-52; telex 202294; f. 1933; children's and educational books; Man. Dir LOUIS MAGNARD.

Maloine, SA: 27 rue de l'Ecole-de-Médecine, 75006 Paris; tel. (1) 43-25-60-45; telex 203215; f. 1881; medical textbooks, sciences and humanities; Chair. and Man. Dir DANIEL VIGOT.

Editions Maritimes et d'Outre-mer: 17 rue Jacob, 75006 Paris; tel. (1) 46-34-03-10; telex 205652; f. 1839; yachting, marine, maritime history, navigation; Chair. and Man. Dir PIERRE GUTELLE.

Masson: 120 blvd Saint Germain, 75280 Paris Cedex 06; tel. (1) 46-34-21-60; telex 260946; fax (1) 43-37-12-30; f. 1804; medicine and science, books and periodicals; publrs for various academies and societies; Chair. and Man. Dir JÉROME TALAMON.

Mercure de France, SA: 26 rue de Condé, 75006 Paris; tel. (1) 43-29-21-13; f. 1890; general fiction, history, psychology, sociology; Chair. and Man. Dir SIMONE GALLIMARD.

Les Editions de Minuit: 7 rue Bernard Palissy, 75006 Paris; tel. (1) 42-22-37-94; f. 1945; general literature; Chair. and Man. Dir JÉRÔME LINDON.

Fernand Nathan Editeur: 9 rue Méchain, 75676 Paris Cedex 14; tel. (1) 45-87-50-00; telex 204525; f. 1881; affiliated to Librairie Larousse; school, and children's books, encyclopaedias, educational journals and games, fine arts, literature; Chair. and Man. Dir BERTRAND EVENO.

Les Editions d'Organisation (Editions Hommes et Techniques): 26 ave Emile-Zola, 75015 Paris; tel. (1) 45-78-61-81; f. 1952; management and business economy; Chair. SERGE EYROLLES; Man. DOMINIQUE BIDART.

Editions Ouvrières: 12 ave Soeur-Rosalie, 75621 Paris Cedex 13; tel. (1) 43-37-93-85; f. 1929; religious, educational, political and social, including labour movement; Dir ANDRÉ JONDEAU.

Payot-Paris: 106 blvd Saint Germain, 75006 Paris; tel. (1) 43-29-74-10; telex 203246; f. 1912; general science, biography, philosophy, religion, education, history; Chair. and Man. Dir JEAN-FRANÇOIS LAMUNIÈRE.

Editions Perrin: 8 rue Garancière, 75285 Paris Cedex 06; tel. (1) 46-34-12-80; telex 204807; f. 1884; historical and literary biographies, fine arts, humanities, trade books; Dir FRANÇOIS-XAVIER DE VIVIE.

A. et J. Picard: 82 rue Bonaparte, 75006 Paris; tel. (1) 43-26-97-78; telex 305551; fax (1) 43-26-42-64; f. 1869; archaeology, architecture, history of art, history, pre-history, auxiliary sciences, linguistics, musicological works, antiquarian books, *Catalogue Varia* (old and rare books, documentary books, quarterly); Chair. and Man. Dir CHANTAL PASINI-PICARD.

Plon: 8 rue Garancière, 75285 Paris, Cedex 06; tel. (1) 46-34-12-80; telex 204807; f. 1844; fiction, travel, history, anthropology, science, trade books; Dir-Gen. JEAN-LUC PIDOUX-PAYOT.

Présence Africaine: 25 bis rue des Ecoles, 75005 Paris; tel. (1) 43-54-13-74; telex 200891; f. 1949; general books; Dir-Gen. YANDÉ CHRISTIANE DIOP.

Presses de la Fondation Nationale des Sciences Politiques: 27 rue Saint Guillaume, 75341 Paris Cedex 07; tel. (1) 45-49-50-50; f. 1975; history, politics, linguistics, economics, sociology; Chair. and Man. Dir LOUIS BODIN.

Presses Universitaires de France: 108 blvd Saint Germain, 75279 Paris Cedex 06; tel. (1) 46-34-12-01; telex 600474; fax (1) 46-33-61-21; f. 1921; philosophy, psychology, psychoanalysis, psychiatry, education, sociology, theology, history, geography, economics, law, linguistics, literature, science, the 'Que Sais-Je?' series, and official publs of universities; Chair. PIERRE ANGOULVENT.

Presses Universitaires de Grenoble: Domaine Universitaire, BP 47 X, 38400 Saint Martin d'Hères, 38040 Grenoble Cedex; tel. 76-82-56-51; telex 980910; fax 76-82-56-54; f. 1972; architecture, anthropology, law, economics, management, history, statistics, literature, medicine, science, politics; Dir CHRISTIAN AUGUSTE.

Privat, SA: 14 rue des Arts, 31068 Toulouse Cedex; tel. 61-23-09-26; telex 521001; f. 1839; regional publs, history, medicine, philosophy, religion, tourism, education; Pres. JEAN LISSARRAGUE.

Quillet: 6 rue Ancelle, 92200 Neuilly-sur-Seine; tel. (1) 40-88-63-10; telex 611462; fax (1) 47-45-33-75; f. 1898; general; specializes in dictionaries and encyclopaedias; Chair. G. DE ROQUEMAUREL.

Editions Seghers, SA: 6 place Saint Sulpice, 75279 Paris Cedex 06; tel. (1) 43-29-12-33; telex 270607; f. 1939; poetry, novels, politics, philosophy, biographies; Dir DANIEL RADFORD.

Editions du Seuil: 27 rue Jacob, 75261 Paris Cedex 06; tel. (1) 40-46-50-50; telex 650505; f. 1560; modern literature, fiction, illustrated books, non-fiction; Chair. and Man. Dir CLAUDE CHERKI.

FRANCE

Slatkine-France: 7 quai Malaquais, 75006 Paris; tel. (1) 46-34-07-29; fax (1) 46-34-64-06; f. 1973; medieval literature, music, law, history, psychology, comics, ethnology, linguistics; Dir MICHEL SLATKINE.

Editions Stock: 103 blvd St Michel, 75005 Paris; tel. (1) 46-34-89-34; telex 206023; f. 1708; subsidiary of Librairie Hachette; foreign literature, novels, general literature, law, science, philosophy, sport; Dir ALAIN CARRÌERE.

Editions de la Table Ronde: 9 rue Huysmans, 75006 Paris; tel. (1) 42-22-28-91; fax (1) 42-22-03-42; f. 1944; history, leisure, medicine, children's books; Pres. ALAIN LEFEBVRE.

Editions Tallandier: 61 rue de la Tombe Issoire, 75677 Paris Cedex 14; tel. (1) 43-20-14-33; telex 210311; f. 1865; literature, history, magazines, popular editions, book club edition; Chair. and Man. Dir JACQUES JOURQUIN.

Editions Vigot: 23 rue de l'Ecole de Médecine, 75006 Paris; tel. (1) 43-29-54-50; telex 201708; f. 1890; medicine, pharmacology, languages, tourism, veterinary science, sport, architecture; Chair. and Man. Dir CHRISTIAN VIGOT; Dir DANIEL VIGOT.

Vilo: 25 rue Ginoux, 75015 Paris; tel. (1) 45-77-08-05; telex 200305; fax (1) 45-79-97-15; f. 1950; non-fiction, art, history, geography, tourism, sport, architecture; Chair. ROGER SABATER; Man. Dir MAURICE DESSEMOND.

Librairie Philosophique J. Vrin: 6 place de la Sorbonne, 75005 Paris; tel. (1) 43-54-03-47; fax (1) 43-54-48-18; f. 1911; university textbooks, philosophy, education, science, law, religion; Chair. and Man. Dir A. PAULHAC-VRIN.

Librairie Vuibert: 63 blvd Saint Germain, 75006 Paris; tel. (1) 43-25-61-00; telex 201005; fax (1) 43-25-75-86; f. 1877; economics, business, mathematics, physics, science; Chair. JEAN ADAM.

CARTOGRAPHERS

Blondel La Rougery: 7 rue Saint Lazare, 75009 Paris; tel. (1) 48-78-95-54; f. 1902; maps; specialized prints of maps and charts; Chair. J. BARBOTTE.

Girard et Barrère: 2 place du Puits de l'Ermite, 75005 Paris; f. 1780; maps and globes; Mans MM BARRY, GOURIER, VUILLERET.

Institut Géographique National: 136 bis rue de Grenelle, 75700 Paris; tel. (1) 43-98-80-00; telex 204989; fax (1) 45-55-07-85; f. 1940; surveying and mapping of France and many other countries; Dir JEAN-FRANÇOIS CARREZ.

Cartes Taride: 2 bis place du Puits de l'Ermite, 75005 Paris; f. 1852; tourists' maps, guides and maps of the world, globes; Mans MM BARRY, GOURIER, VUILLERET.

PUBLISHERS' ASSOCIATIONS

Cercle de la Librairie (Syndicat des Industries et Commerces du Livre): 35 rue Grégoire de Tours, 75006 Paris Cedex; tel. (1) 43-29-10-00; telex 270838; fax (1) 43-29-77-85; f. 1847; a syndicate of the book trade, grouping the principal asscns of publishers, booksellers and printers; Chair. MARC FRIEDEL; Man. Dir JEAN-MARIE DOUBLET.

Chambre Syndicale des Editeurs de Musique de France: 215 rue du Faubourg Saint-Honoré, 75008 Paris; tel. (1) 42-89-17-13; telex 649693; fax (1) 45-63-62-91; f. 1873; music publishers' asscn; Chair. JEAN-MANUEL MOBILLION DE SCARANO; Sec. ISABELLE BERTHOU.

Chambre Syndicale de l'Edition Musicale (CSDEM): 62 rue Blanche, 75009 Paris; tel. (1) 48-74-09-29; fax (1) 42-81-19-87; f. 1978; music publishers; Chair. RENÉ BOYER.

Fédération Française des Syndicats de Libraires: 43 rue de Châteaudun, 75009 Paris; tel. (1) 42-82-00-03; fax (1) 42-82-10-51; f. 1892; booksellers' asscn; 2,000 mems; Chair. PATRICE VAN MOE; Gen. Man. MICHÈLE BOURGUIGNON.

Syndicat Général des Imprimeries de Paris et de l'Ile-de-France: 46 rue de Bassano, 75008 Paris; tel. (1) 47-20-45-90; fax (1) 47-23-06-79; f. 1970; printers' asscn; 600 mems; Chair. GEORGES AIMÉ.

Syndicat National de l'Edition: 35 rue Grégoire de Tours, 75006 Paris; tel. (1) 43-29-75-75; fax (1) 43-25-35-01; f. 1892; c. 350 mems; publishers' asscn; Chair. ALAIN GRUND; Man. Dir ALAIN ROLAND KIRSCH.

Syndicat National de la Librairie: 40 rue Grégoire-de-Tours, 75006 Paris; tel. (1) 46-34-74-20; Pres. ALAIN DIART.

Syndicat Professionnel Annuaires, Télématique, Communication (ATC): 35 rue Grégoire de Tours, 75279 Paris Cedex 06; tel. (1) 43-29-55-03; f. 1984; Pres. HUBERT MOULET.

Union Parisienne des Syndicats Patronaux de l'Imprimerie: 46 rue de Bassano, 75008 Paris; tel. (1) 47-20-45-90; f. 1923; Chair. JACQUES NOULET.

Directory

Radio and Television

From 1964 to 1974 broadcasting was administered by the Office de Radiodiffusion-Télévision Française (ORTF), under the tutelage of the Ministry of Information. The ORTF was replaced by seven independent state-financed companies and, in 1982, their functions were taken over by a nine-member committee. In 1986 the right-wing Government replaced the committee with a 13-member Commission Nationale de la Communication et des Libertés (CNCL), and in December the CNCL announced a series of new three-year appointments to the chairs of television and radio networks. The creation of the CNCL provoked criticism from the opposition parties, which alleged that the commission was an instrument for the Government to extend its influence over broadcasting. In 1989 the new Socialist Government replaced the CNCL with a nine-member Conseil Supérieur de l'Audiovisuel.

In 1987 there were an estimated 49.5m. radio receivers in use, and in 1986 there were an estimated 22m. television receivers in use.

Conseil Supérieur de l'Audiovisuel (CSA): Tour Mirabeau, 39–43 quai André Citroën, 75739 Paris Cedex 15; tel. (1) 40-58-38-00; telex 200365; fax (1) 45-79-00-06; f. 1989; supervises all French broadcasting, allocates concessions for privatized channels, distributes cable networks and frequencies, appoints heads of state-owned radio and television companies, oversees telecommunications sectors, monitors programme standards; consists of nine members, of whom three are appointed for eight years, three for six years and three for four years: three nominated by the Pres. of the Republic; three by the Pres. of the National Assembly; and three by the Pres. of the Senate; Pres. JACQUES BOUTET.

Institut National de l'Audiovisuel: 4 ave de l'Europe, 94366 Bry Sur Marne Cedex; tel. (1) 49-83-20-00; telex 262493; fax (1) 43-47-64-00; f. 1975; research and professional training in the field of broadcasting; radio and TV archives; Pres. GEORGES FILLIOUD; Dir of Communications YANN COTTEN.

Radio Télévision Française d'Outre-Mer (RFO): 5 ave du Recteur Poincaré, 75016 Paris; tel. (1) 45-24-71-00; controls broadcasting in the French overseas territories; Chair. JEAN-CLAUDE MICHAUD; Dir of DOM-TOM CLAUDE LEFÈVRE; Dir of Foreign Affairs ANDRÉ BRIÈRE.

Société Française de Production et de Création Audiovisuelles (SFP): 36 rue des Alouettes, 75935 Paris; tel. (1) 40-03-50-00; telex 240888; fax (1) 42-03-18-35; f. 1975; production of major programmes for cinema and TV; Chair. JEAN-PIERRE HOSS; Gen. Man. ALAIN AUCLÈRE.

Société France Media International (FMI): 78 ave Raymond Poincare, 75116 Paris; tel. (1) 45-01-55-90; telex 614186; fax (1) 45-01-28-39; f. 1983 and privatized in 1987; distribution and merchandising in France and abroad for all TV programmes except news and sport, co-productions with foreign TV companies: Chair. JEAN-MARC JANCOVICHI; Man. Dir ANDRÉ HARRIS.

Télédiffusion de France (TDF), SA: 21–27 rue Barbès, 92542 Montrouge Cedex; tel. (1) 46-57-11-15; telex 25738; fax (1) 45-55-35-35; f. 1975, partly privatized in 1987; responsible for broadcasting programmes produced by the production companies (Radio France, A2, FR3), for the organization and maintenance of the networks, for study and research into radio and television equipment; administrative council comprising 16 members, of which six are representatives of the State; Pres. XAVIER GOUYOU-BEAUCHAMPS; Man. Dir PHILIPPE LEVRIER.

RADIO

Société Nationale de Radiodiffusion (Radio France): 116 ave Président Kennedy, 75786 Paris Cedex 16; tel. (1) 42-30-22-22; telex 200002; fax (1) 42-30-14-88; f. 1975; production of radio programmes; Chair. and Man. Dir JEAN MAHEU; Dir JEAN IZARD; Dir France Inter (programmes) PIERRE BOUTEILLER; Information Dir IVAN LEVAÏ; Dir France Culture JEAN-MARIE BORZEIX; Dir of programmes and musical services CLAUDE SAMUEL; Radio France Internationale Dir-Gen. ANDRÉ LARQUIÉ.

Radio France Home Services

France-Inter: Entertains and informs. Broadcasts transmitted for 24 hours a day; they can be received by 98% of the population and by listeners outside France. France-Inter is broadcast on long wave, medium wave and frequency modulation (FM) transmitters.

FIP: Music and news broadcast 24 hours daily; FM transmission available only in Paris.

France-Info: Information broadcast 24 hours daily on FM transmitters.

France Culture: Stereophonic transmission on FM transmitters; art, culture and thought; broadcasts can be received by 95% of the population.

France Musique: Stereophonic transmission on FM transmitters. Nearly 95% of the programme is devoted to music.

Radio Bleue: Medium-wave transmission for the elderly.

Radio-Sorbonne: Low-power transmission of educational programmes. Only available in the Paris region.

There are 47 local radio stations, which relay Parisian programmes as well as transmitting their own broadcasts.

Radio France International

Home Service: Broadcasts in France for foreign workers in African-French, Arabic, Cambodian, Lao, Portuguese, Serbo-Croat, Spanish, Turkish and Vietnamese.

Foreign Service: Broadcasts 24 hours daily to Europe (in French, German, Portuguese, Polish, Romanian and Spanish), Eastern Europe (in French and Russian), Africa/Indian Ocean (in French, English and Portuguese), North America (in French), Latin America (in French, Portuguese and Spanish) and Asia (in French).

Private Radio

A number of radio stations based in countries on France's perimeter have very large French audiences. These include notably RTL (Luxembourg), Europe No. 1 (Saarbrücken), Radio Monte Carlo (Monaco). The state monopoly of broadcasting was ended in 1982, and in 1986 the French Government sold its controlling stake in Europe No. 1 to Hachette, the largest publishing group in France, and planned to sell its 83% shareholding in Radio Monte Carlo after the presidential election in 1988.

By August 1986 1,527 private radio stations ('radios libres') had been authorized. Advertising on private radio was legalized in 1984. In 1987 the CNCL introduced new regulations for local private radio stations, which stipulated that stations had to provide at least 84 hours of programmes per week, of which a minimum of 20% had to be produced by the owners of the stations. In July the CNCL authorized 96 radio stations to broadcast on the FM airwaves in Paris, which had previously been open to any station. In February 1989 there were an estimated 1,740 private radio stations.

TELEVISION

In 1989 there were two state-run channels. A2 is on a 625-line system in colour, which can be received by 96.5 per cent of the population. FR3, introduced in 1973, is on a 625-line system in colour and can be received by 70% of the population. Government approval was granted in 1984 for the transmission of France's first early-morning television, and by 1986 free videotex data screens had been installed in millions of homes. In August 1989 one chairman was appointed to both public networks. The post was created under a controversial law that was intended to help state-controlled television to overcome competition from private channels.

Télé-Luxembourg, Télé-Belge and Télé-Monte-Carlo have large regional audiences in France. German-speaking inhabitants of Alsace watch programmes transmitted from Germany.

Société Nationale de Télévision en Couleur—Antenne 2 (A2): 22 ave Montaigne, 75387 Paris Cedex 08; tel. (1) 42-99-42-42; telex 204068; f. 1975; production of programmes on the second TV channel; Chair. PHILIPPE GUILHAUME; Pres. Mme CHRISTIANE DORÉ; Sec.-Gen. LOUIS BÉRIOT; Dir JEAN-MICHEL GAILLARD.

Société Nationale de Programmes—France Régions 3 (FR3): 116 ave du Président-Kennedy, 75790 Paris Cedex 16; tel. (1) 42-30-22-22; telex 630720; f. 1975; production of programmes on the third TV channel; responsible for regional and overseas TV; Pres. PHILIPPE GUILHAUME; Dir-Gen. Mme DOMINIQUE ALDUY.

Private Television

There were four national private television channels in 1990. Canal Plus, the first private channel (introduced in 1984), transmits on a 625-line system in colour, and provides 20 hours of daily broadcasts, mainly films and sport, to 1.5m. subscribers. The channel is financed mainly by subscription, and carries a limited amount of advertising. In 1987 Canal + attempted to raise further revenue by offering shares to the public. In 1985 the Socialist Government approved the formation of two new commercial networks, La 5 and TV6, and both channels started broadcasting in February 1986. In late 1986 the new right-wing Government introduced restrictions on the ownership of media outlets, with the aim of preventing a single communications company from owning more than 25% of a national television channel, and subsequently cancelled the contracts of La 5 and TV6. In 1987 the CNCL reallocated the contract for La 5 to the Hersant consortium, chaired by Robert Hersant, a right-wing National Assembly deputy and newspaper owner. La 5 broadcasts mainly foreign light entertainment programmes and films. In late 1987 the channel suffered a financial crisis, owing to low audience figures and a subsequent decline in revenue from advertising. In September 1989 Robert Hersant's position as Chairman was threatened by rival factions, headed by Jérôme Seydoux and Silvio Berlusconi, after the channel was fined 60m. Frs for failing to fulfil commitments to transmit 50% French programmes. The contract for TV6, the music and video channel, was allocated to the Métropole TV consortium, which renamed the channel M6 and started to broadcast general interest programmes. In 1987 the state-run first channel, TF1, was transferred to private ownership: the CNCL awarded 50% ownership and a 10-year initial contract to the Bouygues consortium, and the remaining 50% of shares were sold to small investors and TF1 employees. TF1 transmits on a 819-line system, and is accessible to 98.5% of the population. In 1987 the CNCL approved the formation of Télé-Toulouse, a private local television channel, and offered to other potential private local channels the right to broadcast on the La 5 and M6 systems.

Canal +: 78 rue Olivier de Serres, 75015 Paris; tel. (1) 45-33-74-74; telex 201141; f. 1984; 24.7% owned by Havas, 21.3% by Compagnie Générale des Eaux, 6.9% by L'Oréal, 6% by Groupe Caisse des Dépôts and 5.9% by Geneval; coded programmes financed by audience subscription; uncoded programmes financed by advertising sold by Canal +; Pres. ANDRÉ ROUSSELET.

La 5: 241 blvd Péreire, 75017 Paris; tel. (1) 40-55-55-55; telex 640635; fax (1) 46-47-80-48; f. 1987; 25% owned by Groupe Hersant, 25% by Groupe Berlusconi, 22% by Groupe Hachette and 22% by Groupe Vernes; financed by advertising sold by La 5; Pres. ROBERT HERSANT.

M6: 16 cours Albert 1er, 75008 Paris; tel. (1) 44-21-66-66; telex 649781; fax (1) 45-63-78-52; f. 1986 as TV6, re-formed as M6 in 1987; owned by Métropole TV consortium, of which 25% is owned by Compagnie Luxembourgeoise de Télédiffusion, 25% by Lyonnaise des Eaux, 10% by Crédit Agricole, 2.5% by Marin Karmitz and 37.5% by financial institutions; Pres. and Dir-Gen. JEAN DRUCKER.

Télévision Française 1 (TF1): 17 rue de l'Arrivée, 75015 Paris; tel. (1) 42-75-12-34; telex 250878; f. 1975 as a state-owned channel, privatized 1987; 25% owned by Bouygues SA, 12% by Maxwell Group, 24% by various French companies, 35% by individual shareholders and 4% by TF1 employees; Pres. PATRICK LE LAY; Dir-Gen. ETIENNE MOUGEOTTE.

Satellite Television

In 1984 TV5 began broadcasting programmes relayed from French, Belgian and Swiss television stations by satellite. In the same year, the French Government reached an agreement with Luxembourg to finance jointly a communal direct-broadcasting satellite television system (TDF-1). TDF-1 was to operate four television channels and 16 sound channels, thus enabling each television channel to broadcast in four different languages. In late 1986 the Government cancelled concessions which had been granted to a European consortium to operate two of the channels, and offered them to the general market on new financial terms. One channel was allocated to La SEPT, a projected French state cultural channel, and in 1987 the CNCL examined applications for the remaining three channels. In April 1989 the CSA determined that TDF-1 was to operate five channels, which were allocated respectively to Canal + (including Canal + Allemagne), Sept, Sport 2/3, Canal Enfants and Euromusique. TDF-1 was inaugurated in October 1988, after a series of technical problems, and another satellite television system, TDF-2 (to be financed by private investors), was planned to be launched in September 1989.

Société d'Edition de Programmes de Télévision (La SEPT): 35 quai André Citroën, 75015 Paris; tel. (1) 40-59-39-77; fax (1) 45-78-09-27; f. 1986; Franco-German cultural channel launched in May 1990; Pres. JÉRÔME CLÉMENT; Chair. GEORGES DUBY.

TV5: Centre Alfred Lelluch 15, rue Cognacq-Jay, 75330 Paris Cedex 07; telex 201090; fax (1) 45-56-00-04; communal channel for francophone European countries, transmitted by EUTEL satellite; Chair. PATRICK IMHAUS.

Cable Television

After two years of controversy, government approval was given in 1984 to plans to develop a national cable television network. In 1986 the responsibility for the construction of the network was opened to private communications companies, rather than to the state-owned postal and telecommunications service. In 1987 the Government announced that the cable network would be developed initially in 52 towns, and in October new regulations were introduced, which extended contracts for the networks from five to 20 years and applied the conditions governing national television channels to services transmitted by cable television. Foreign transmissions being broadcast by cable were allocated a maximum of 50% of the channels on a cable network, and were obliged to conform to the French regulations, if broadcasting in the French language. Private cable operators have announced their interest in providing local services and specialist cable television channels,

FRANCE   *Directory*

such as Canal J, a channel specializing in children's programmes, which was launched in 1985. However, by October 1987 cable television was received by only 13,170 subscribers in France, and in December a campaign was launched to publicize the medium. In June 1989 an estimated 78,000 subscribers received cable television.

Finance

(cap. = capital; p.u. = paid up; dep. = deposits;
res = reserves; m. = million; Frs = Francs)

BANKING

In 1982 the Socialist Government nationalized 36 banks, bringing 95% of all deposits under state control. These banks are marked * in the following list. Those marked † had previously been nationalized and became wholly nationalized in 1982. The banking law of July 1984 strengthened government control of local banks. Most banks, including foreign-controlled banks, became unified 'credit establishments', supervised by the Association française des établissements de crédit. A 'credit establishment' is defined as a company whose main business is conducting banking operations, which comprise accepting funds from the public, lending, and managing the payments system. The 'credit establishments' consist of banks that are authorized to accept demand deposits and time deposits with maturities of less than two years. These include banks authorized to conduct all banking operations and banks that conduct only the banking operations permitted by their statutes, such as mutual and co-operative banks (Crédit Agricole, Crédit Mutuel, Crédit Co-opératif and the Banques Populaires), savings banks (caisses d'épargne et de prévoyance) and caisses de crédit municipal. Other 'credit establishments' may accept demand deposits or time deposits with maturities of less than two years with authorization by an additional order. These comprise finance companies (hire purchase, mortgage or leasing companies) and specialized financial institutions (Crédit National and Crédit Foncier de France) which conduct only those banking operations that are necessary for fulfilling their particular functions. The 1984 law did not apply to the public accounts system, to the postal and telecommunications (PTT) financial services, nor to the Caisse des Dépôts et Consignations. In 1985 the banks were deprived of their monopoly of issuing short-term loans, after a market for 'commercial paper' (negotiable instruments) was inaugurated (see below). In 1986 the right-wing Government adopted a Privatization Law, and produced a plan to denationalize 65 state-owned companies including banks, in the following three years. Banks that have been denationalized are marked ‡ in the following list. The Government also introduced proposals to reduce state control over banking operations. In late 1986 quantitative controls on bank lending were ended, although banks were required to maintain a minimum level of reserves to cover at least 60% of long-term borrowing. Banks were allowed to open, close, or transfer their branches without government authorization, and could establish their own interest rates on deposits lasting over three months. Non-banking activities were limited to 10% of a bank's operations. From 1988 banks were to be allowed to hold capital in, and eventually gain control of, official stockbroking firms operating on the Bourse, during the gradual deregulation of the French financial markets (see below).

Central Bank

Banque de France: 39 rue Croix des Petits Champs, BP 140, 75001 Paris; tel. (1) 42-92-42-92; telex 220932; fax (1) 42-96-04-23; f. 1800; cap. and res 229,434.4m. Frs (Dec. 1989); nationalized from 1946; acts as banker to the Treasury, issues bank notes, controls credit and money supply and administers France's gold and currency assets; the Governor and two Deputy Governors are nominated by decree of the President of the Republic; the bank has 211 offices or brs throughout France; Gov. JACQUES DE LAROSIÈRE; Dep. Govs PHILIPPE LAGAYETTE, DENIS FERMAN.

Commercial Banks

American Express Bank (France) SA: 12–14 Rond Point des Champs Elysées, 75008 Paris; tel. (1) 42-25-15-16; telex 643177; f. 1957; cap. 150m. Frs, dep. 2,600.3m. Frs, res 41.3m. Frs (1986); Chair. DAVID C. WINN; 4 brs.

Bank of Credit and Commerce International (Overseas) Ltd: 125 ave des Champs Elysées, 75008 Paris; tel. (1) 47-23-90-19; telex 611710; Dir NAZIZ CHINOY.

Banque Arabe et Internationale d'Investissement (BAII): 12 place Vendôme, 75001 Paris; tel. (1) 47-03-23-45; telex 680330; fax (1) 47-03-28-00; f. 1973; investment bank; cap. 1,015m. Frs (Dec. 1989); subsidiary of Baii Holdings, Luxembourg; Chair. and CEO FRANÇOIS HECKER.

Banque Centrale des Coopératives et des Mutuelles: 12 place de la Bourse, 75002 Paris; tel. (1) 42-21-88-88; telex 211038; fax (1) 40-26-14-44; f. 1922; cap. 72.3m. Frs, dep. 15,801.2m. Frs, res 17.9m. Frs (Dec. 1987); two-thirds of shares are held by 136 co-operative socs; Chair. JEAN LOUIS PETRIAT; 95 brs.

Banque CGER France: 21 blvd Malesherbes, 75008 Paris; tel. (1) 42-68-62-00; telex 283040; fax 42-66-35-30; f. 1933; fmrly Banque Française de l'Agriculture et du Crédit Mutuel; cap. 150m. Frs, dep. 10,259m. Frs, res 34m. Frs (Dec. 1989); Chair. PAUL HENRION; 14 brs.

Banque CGER France: 21 blvd Malesherbes, 75008 Paris; tel. (1) 42-68-62-00; telex 283040; fax (1) 42-66-35-30; f. 1933; fmrly Banque Française de l'Agriculture et du Crédit Mutuel; cap. 150m. Frs, dep. 10,259m. Frs, res 34m. Frs (Dec. 1989); Chair. PAUL HENRION; 14 brs.

Banque Courtois: 33 rue de Rémusat, 31000 Toulouse; tel. 61-29-61-29; telex 531580; f. 1760; cap. 55.6m. Frs, dep. 2,651.5m. Frs, res 41.1m. Frs (Dec. 1989); Chair. and Gen. Man. GILBERT COURTOIS DE VIÇOSE.

***Banque de Bretagne:** 283 ave du Général Patton, 35000 Rennes Cedex; tel. 99-28-36-44; telex 730094; fax (1) 99-28-38-02; f. 1909; cap. 65.9m. Frs, dep. 8,498m. Frs, res 91.6m. Frs (Dec. 1988); Chair. XAVIER HENRY DE VILLENEUVE; 81 brs.

Banque de la Méditerranée-France, SA: 49 ave Hoche, 75008 Paris; tel. (1) 40-54-55-56; telex 648528; fax 47-66-89-36; f. 1976; cap. 300m. Frs, dep. 4,357m. Frs, res 34.5m. Frs (Dec. 1989); Chair. and Man. Dir JOSEPH GHOLAM.

Banque de Neuflize, Schlumberger, Mallet: 3 ave Hoche, 75008 Paris; tel. (1) 47-66-61-11; telex 640653; fax (1) 47-66-62-89; f. 1966; subsidiary of Algemene Bank Nederland NV; cap. 672m. Frs, dep. 29,023.3m. Frs, res 336.2m. Frs (Dec. 1989); Chair. Supervisory Bd JEAN FRANÇOIS; Chair. Man. Bd ANTOINE DUPONT-FAUVILLE; 18 brs.

***Banque de l'Union Européenne:** 4 rue Gaillon, BP 89, 75107 Paris Cedex 02; tel. (1) 42-66-70-00; telex 210942; fax (1) 42-66-78-90; f. 1920; merged with CIC group April 1984; cap. 500m. Frs, dep. 42,587.8m. Frs, res 560m. Frs (Dec. 1989); Chair. and CEO PAUL ALIBERT; 6 brs.

Banque Européenne de Tokyo: 4–8 rue Sainte Anne, 75001 Paris; tel. (1) 42-61-58-55; telex 210436; fax (1) 49-27-97-81; f. 1968; cap. 75m. Frs, dep. 415m. Frs, res 120m. Frs (Dec. 1989); Pres. and Gen. Man. KAORU HAGIWARA.

Banque Fédérative du Crédit Mutuel SA: 34 rue du Wacken, 67000 Strasbourg; tel. 88-35-90-35; telex 880034; fax 88-25-13-14; f. 1940; cap. 400m. Frs, dep. 54,250m. Frs, res 702.4m. Frs (Dec. 1989); Chair. Supervisory Board ETIENNE PFIMLIN; Chair. Management Board RAYMOND CROMBECQUE; 13 brs.

Banque Française Commerciale, SA: 3 rue Amélie, 75007 Paris; tel. (1) 45-55-06-25; telex 280833; fax (1) 45-55-07-09; f. 1922; cap. 92.8m. Frs, dep. 3,166.5m. Frs, res 65.4m. Frs (Dec. 1989); Pres. DOMINIQUE RAMBURE; 24 brs.

Banque Française de Crédit Coopératif: parc de la Défense, 33 rue des Trois Fontanot, BP 211, 592002 Nanterre Cedex; tel. (1) 47-24-85-00; telex 620496; fax (1) 47-24-89-25; f. 1969; cap. 120.8m. Frs, dep. 14,450.9m. Frs, res 104.3m. Frs (Dec. 1989); Chair. Supervisory Board JACQUES MOREAU; 35 brs.

Banque Française du Commerce Extérieur: 21 blvd Haussmann, 75009 Paris; tel. (1) 48-00-48-00; telex 660370; fax (1) 48-00-41-51; f. 1947; cap. 1,000m. Frs, dep. 260,718.2m. Frs, res 231m. Frs (Dec. 1989); Chair. MICHEL FREYCHE; Man. Dir PIERRE ANTONI.

Banque Française de l'Orient: 33 rue Monceau, 75008 Paris; tel. (1) 43-59-51-88; telex 640820; fax (1) 45-63-98-22; f. 1989, following merger of Banque Libano-Française (France) and Al Saudi Banque; cap. 310.3m. Frs, dep. 9,966.6m. Frs, res 248.1m. Frs (Sept. 1989); Chair. BERNARD VERNHES.

***Banque Hervet SA:** 1 Place de la Préfecture, 18004 Bourges; tel. 46-40-90-00; telex 620433; fax 46-40-92-77; f. 1830; cap. 142.4m. Frs, dep. 10,835.2m. Frs, res 284.7m. Frs (Dec. 1988); Chair. PATRICK CAREIL; 70 brs.

‡Banque Indosuez: 96 blvd Haussmann, 75008 Paris; tel. (1) 44-20-20-20; telex 650409; fax (1) 44-20-29-67; f. 1975; cap. 2,620.2m. Frs, dep. 309,526.2m. Frs, res 6,986.5m. Frs (Dec. 1989); Chair. ANTOINE JEANCOURT-GALIGNANI; 13 brs.

‡Banque Industrielle et Mobilière Privée, SA: 22 rue Pasquier, 75383 Paris Cedex 08; tel. (1) 40-06-60-00; telex 640586; fax (1) 42-66-27-88; f. 1967; cap. 31.4m. Frs, dep. 6,027.9m. Frs, res 109.8m. Frs (Dec. 1989); Chair. CHARLES FROISSART.

Banque Intercontinentale Arabe: 67 ave Franklin Roosevelt, 75008 Paris; tel. (1) 43-59-61-49; telex 644030; fax (1) 42-89-09-59; f. 1975; cap. 310m. Frs, dep. 18m. Frs, res 1,438m. Frs (1984); Chair. MOURAD KHELLAF.

Banque Internationale de Commerce, SA: 62 ave Marceau, 75008 Paris; tel. (1) 47-20-57-39; telex 630151; fax (1) 47-23-24-53; f. 1919;

cap. 70m. Frs, dep. 1,160.2m. Frs, res 7.2m. Frs (Dec. 1989); Chair. EROL AKSOY.

Banque Louis-Dreyfus, SA: 6 rue Rabelais, BP 285, 75384 Paris Cedex 08; tel. (1) 44-21-70-00; telex 290063; fax (1) 43-59-07-59; f. 1905; cap. 240m. Frs, res 161m. Frs, dep. 19,158m. Frs (Dec. 1988); Chair. JEAN-CLAUDE SEYS.

†**Banque Nationale de Paris, SA:** 16 blvd des Italiens, 75009 Paris; tel. (1) 40-14-45-46; telex 280605; f. 1966; cap. 2,963m. Frs, dep. 1,304,334.2m. Frs, res 28,757.6m. Frs (Dec. 1989); Chair. and Man. Dir RENÉ THOMAS.

Banque Nationale de Paris 'Intercontinentale', SA: 20 blvd des Italiens, BP 315-09, 75009 Paris; tel. (1) 40-14-78-04; telex 283419; fax (1) 40-14-69-34; f. 1940; cap. 159.5m. Frs, dep. 8,486.4m. Frs, res 595.1m. Frs (Dec. 1988); Chair. RENÉ THOMAS; 134 brs.

‡**Banque OBC—Odier Bungener Courvoisier, SA:** 57 ave d'Iéna, BP 195, 75783 Paris Cedex 16; tel. (1) 45-02-40-00; telex 630889; fax (1) 45-00-77-79; f. 1960; cap. 155.4m. Frs, dep. 5,659.8m. Frs, res 48.5m. Frs (Dec. 1989); Chair. and Man. Dir FRANÇOIS PROPPER.

‡**Banque Paribas:** 3 rue d'Antin, 75002 Paris; tel. (1) 42-98-12-34; telex 210041; fax (1) 42-98-13-31; f. 1872; cap. 2,223m. Frs, dep. 404,612m. Frs, res 9,720m. Frs (Dec. 1989); Chair. ANDRÉ LEVY-LANG; Dirs-Gen. GILLES COSSON, DOMINIQUE HOENN, PHILIPPE DULAC.

‡**Banque Parisienne de Crédit:** 56 rue de Châteaudun, 75009 Paris; tel. (1) 42-80-68-68; telex 280179; fax (1) 42-81-53-35; f. 1920; cap. 220.2m. Frs, dep. 16,394.1m. Frs, res 538.7m. Frs (Dec. 1989); Chair. GUY CHARTIER; 64 brs.

*****Banque Régionale de l'Ain, SA:** 2 ave Alsace-Lorraine, 01001 Bourg-en-Bresse; tel. 74-32-50-00; telex 310435; f. 1849; mem. of Crédit Industriel et Commercial Group; cap. 60m. Frs; dep. 3,623.6m. Frs, res 34.9m. Frs (1986); Pres. JEAN-NOËL RELIQUET; 50 brs.

*****Banque Régionale de l'Ouest, SA:** 7 rue Gallois, 41003 Blois Cedex; tel. 54-78-96-28; telex 750408; f. 1913; mem. of Crédit Industriel et Commercial Group; cap. 100m. Frs, dep. 9,784.5m. Frs, res 74.8m. Frs (1988); Chair. JEAN DE LA CHAUVINIÈRE.

Banque Rivaud: 13 rue Notre Dame des Victoires, 75002 Paris; tel. (1) 42-61-52-43; telex 680231; fax (1) 42-60-93-08; f. 1906; cap. 200.2m. Frs, dep. 5,888.2m. Frs, res 60.7m. Frs (Dec. 1989); Chair. Comte DE RIBES.

Banque Scalbert-Dupont: 37 rue du Molinel, BP 322, 59020 Lille Cedex; tel. 20-06-92-52; telex 820650; fax 20-06-88-40; f. 1838; cap. 150m. Frs, dep. 24,034.4m. Frs, res 257.6m. Frs (Dec. 1989); Chair. and Man. Dir CLAUDE LAMOTTE.

Banque Sudameris: 4 rue Meyerbeer, 75009 Paris; tel. (1) 45-23-72-22; telex 283669; fax (1) 42-46-32-13; f. 1910; cap. 395.6m. Frs, dep. 37,127.5m. Frs, res 1,322.2m. Frs (1989); Chair. and Pres. G. RAMBAUD; 7 brs.

Banque Transatlantique, SA: 17 blvd Haussmann, 75428 Paris Cedex 09; tel. (1) 40-22-80-00; telex 650729; fax (1) 48-24-01-75; f. 1881; cap. 102.6m. Frs, dep. 4,361m. Frs, res 111.9m. Frs (1989); Chair. FRANÇOIS DE SIÈYES.

‡**Banque Vernes et Commerciale de Paris, SA:** 52 ave Hoche, 75008 Paris; tel. (1) 47-54-40-40; telex 290322; fax (1) 47-54-46-57; f. 1971; cap. 500m. Frs, dep. 3,960m. Frs (1989); Pres. FABRIZIO GIANNI; 25 brs.

*****Banque Worms SA:** Le Voltaire, 1 place des Degrés Cedex 58, 92059 Paris La Défense; tel. (1) 49-07-50-50; telex 616023; fax (1) 49-07-59-11; f. 1928; cap. 650m. Frs, dep. 68,154.5m. Frs, res 808.9m. Frs (Dec. 1989); Chair. JEAN-MICHEL BLOCH-LAINÉ; 24 brs.

Barclays Bank SA: 33 rue du Quatre Septembre, BP 24X, 75002 Paris; tel. (1) 40-06-85-85; telex 210015; fax (1) 47-42-78-99; f. 1968; cap. 850m. Frs, dep. 30,256.8m. Frs, res 89.7m. Frs (1988); Chair. and Gen. Man. JACQUES RAMBOSSON; 34 brs.

Caisse Centrale des Banques Populaires: 115 rue Montmartre; 75002 Paris; tel. (1) 40-39-00-00; telex 210993; fax (1) 40-26-62-27; f. 1921; the central banking institution of 31 co-operative regional Banques Populaires; cap. 1,110m. Frs, dep. 127,078.3m. Frs, res. 1,236.3m. Frs (1989); Chair. JACQUES DELMAS-MARSALET; Gen. Man. PAUL LORIOT.

Caisse Nationale de Crédit Agricole (CNCA), SA: 91–93 blvd Pasteur, 75015 Paris; tel. (1) 43-23-52-02; telex 250971; fax (1) 43-23-21-12; f. 1920; central institution for 91 regional co-operative banks; the Crédit Agricole group is the densest banking network in France, with 9,746 domestic branch offices; broad range of banking services with special emphasis on agribusiness; international network includes brs in Chicago, Frankfurt, London, New York, Milan, Hong Kong and Madrid, rep. offices in Barcelona, Rio de Janeiro, San Francisco, Beijing, Cairo, Tokyo, Singapore, Bangkok, Jakarta and Caracas; total assets 1,276,031.7m. Frs, cap.

and res 51,514.4m. Frs, dep. 870,973.7m. Frs (Dec. 1988); Chair. and Man. Dir PHILIPPE JAFFRÉ.

*****Centrale de Banque, SA:** 5 blvd de la Madeleine, 75001 Paris; tel. (1) 40-15-92-47; telex 680014; fax (1) 42-60-54-32; f. 1880; cap. 168.7m. Frs, dep. 8,099.6m. Frs, res 11m. Frs (Dec. 1989); Chair. PIERRE PICHOT; 37 brs.

Compagnie Parisienne de Réescompte, SA: 4 Cité de Londres, 75009 Paris; tel. (1) 40-23-24-25; telex 282511; fax (1) 40-23-25-55; f. 1928; discount bank; cap. 327.7m. Frs, dep. 50,683.2m. Frs, res –18m. Frs (Dec. 1989); Chair. and Gen. Man. HENRI CUKIERMAN; 2 brs.

*****Crédit Chimique SA:** 20 rue Treilhard, 75008 Paris; tel. (1) 49-61-94-00; telex 650838; fax (1) 42-89-40-40; f. 1889; cap. 225m. Frs, dep. 9,411.6m. Frs, res 126.2m. Frs (1989); Chair. and Man. Dir JEAN-LUC JAVAL; 2 brs.

‡**Crédit Commercial de France (CCF) SA:** 103 ave des Champs Elysées, 75008 Paris; tel. (1) 40-70-70-40; telex 630300; fax (1) 47-23-71-04; f. 1894; cap. 1,085m. Frs, dep. 181,085m. Frs, res 2,334.7m. Frs (1987); Pres. GABRIEL PALLEZ; Chair. and CEO MICHEL PÉBEREAU; 209 brs.

‡**Crédit du Nord:** 28 place Rihour, 59000 Lille (reg. office); tel. 20-30-61-61; telex 120342; 6–8 blvd Haussmann, 75009 Paris (administrative headquarters); tel. (1) 42-47-12-34; telex 641379; fax (1) 42-47-10-72; f. 1974; cap. 871.9m. Frs, dep. 104,184.7m. Frs, res 365.7m. Frs (1989); Chair. BRUNO DE MAULDE; 501 brs.

Crédit Foncier de France, SA: 19 rue des Capucines, 75050 Paris; tel. (1) 42-44-80-00; telex 213098; fax (1) 42-44-99-96; f. 1852; cap. 2,883.1m. Frs, dep. 297,457.8m. Frs, res 7,056.6m. Frs (Dec. 1989); Gov. GEORGES BONIN.

*****Crédit Industriel d'Alsace et de Lorraine (CIAL):** 31 rue Jean Wenger-Valentin, 67000 Strasbourg; tel. 88-37-61-23; telex 890167; fax 88-35-09-70; f. 1919; cap. 143.7m. Frs, dep. 40,934m. Frs, res 1,529.7 (Dec. 1989); Chair. and Gen. Man. JEAN WEBER; 146 brs.

*****Crédit Industriel de l'Ouest, SA:** 4 rue Voltaire, 44040 Nantes Cedex 01; tel. 40-35-91-20; telex 700590; fax 40-35-92-07; f. 1957; cap. 130m. Frs, dep. 15,294m. Frs (Dec. 1989); Chair. BERNARD MADINIER; Man. Dir JEAN-LOUIS RUSTERHOLTZ.

*****Crédit Industriel de Normandie, SA:** 15 place de la Pucelle d'Orléans, 76000 Rouen; tel. 35-08-64-00; telex 180671; fax 35-98-63-72; f. 1932; cap. 84m. Frs, dep. 8,035.6m. Frs, res 36.1m. Frs (1988); Chair. and Man. Dir JEAN DURAMÉ.

*****Crédit Industriel et Commercial de Paris, SA:** 66 rue de la Victoire, 75009 Paris; tel. (1) 42-80-80-80; telex 290692; fax (1) 42-80-97-17; f. 1859; cap. 1,609.9m. Frs, dep. 84,282.5m. Frs, res 204.4m. Frs (1989); Chair. JEAN-PIERRE AUBERT; 118 brs.

†**Crédit Lyonnais, SA:** Head Office: 18 rue de la République, 69002 Lyon; Central Office: 19 blvd des Italiens, 75002 Paris; tel. (1) 42-95-70-00; telex 615310; fax (1) 42-95-11-96; f. 1863; cap. 4,451m. Frs, dep. 1,168,011m. Frs, res 20,013m. Frs (1989); Chair. JEAN-YVES HABERER; 2,500 brs.

‡**L'Européenne de Banque:** 21 rue Lafitte, 75428 Paris Cedex 09; tel. (1) 42-47-82-47; telex 280952; fax (1) 42-47-82-52; f. 1817; affiliated to Crédit Commercial de France 1984; cap. 209m. Frs, dep. 13,103.9m. Frs, res 410.2m. Frs (Dec. 1989); Chair. and Man. Dir ROGER PRAIN; 15 brs.

Midland Bank, SA: 6 rue Piccini, BP 4416, 75761 Paris Cedex 16; tel. (1) 44-28-80-80; telex 648022; fax (1) 44-28-85-99; f. 1978; cap. 452.1m. Frs, dep. 925.2m. Frs, res 526m. Frs (Dec. 1989); Chair. CLAUDE-ERIC PAQUIN; 14 brs.

National Bank of Kuwait (France), SA: 90 ave des Champs Elysées, 75008 Paris; tel. (1) 43-59-99-49; telex 642528; fax (1) 45-62-95-76; f. 1969 as Frab-Bank International; cap. 150m. Frs, res 44m. Frs (March 1990); Chair. MOHAMED ABDUL MOHSIN AL-KHARAFI; Gen. Man. DAVID M. LOWREY.

Société Bancaire de Paris: 24 rue Murillo, 75008 Paris; tel. (1) 47-66-02-00; telex 643203; fax (1) 46-22-63-95; f. 1927; cap. 75m. Frs, dep. 915.3m. Frs, res 7.3m. Frs (1989); Chair. MANUEL RICARDO ESPIRITO SANTO SILVA; 1 br.

*****Société Bordelaise de Crédit Industriel et Commercial, SA:** 42 cours du Chapeau Rouge, 33001 Bordeaux; tel. 56-56-10-00; telex (Foreign Dept) 550850; fax 56-79-08-71; f. 1880; cap. 135m. Frs, dep. 7,650.4m. Frs, res 3.3m. Frs (1987); Chair. and Man. Dir JEAN DE LA CHAUVINIÈRE.

Société de Banque Occidentale (SDBO): 8 rue de la Rochefoucauld, 75009 Paris; tel. (1) 49-95-70-00; telex 650159; fax (1) 49-95-72-00; f. 1969; wholly-owned subsidiary of Crédit Lyonnais; cap. 340m. Frs, dep. 8,909.3m. Frs, res 253m. Frs (Dec. 1989); Chair. MICHEL GALLOT; 6 brs.

‡**Société Générale, SA:** 29 blvd Haussmann, 75009 Paris; tel. (1) 40-98-20-00; telex 290842; fax (1) 40-98-20-99; f. 1864; cap. 1,000m. Frs, dep. 302,430m. Frs, res 17,656.6m. Frs (1989); Chair. MARC VIÉNOT; 2,200 brs.

FRANCE   *Directory*

‡**Société Générale Alsacienne de Banque (SOGENAL):** 8 rue du Dôme, 67000 Strasbourg; tel. 88-32-99-27; telex 870720; f. 1881; cap. 332.7m. Frs, dep. 60,478.9m. Frs, res 744.2m. Frs (1988); Chair. RENÉ GERONIMUS; 126 brs.

***Société Lyonnaise de Banque SA:** 8 rue de la République, 69001 Lyon; tel. 78-92-02-12; telex 330532; f. 1865; cap. 400m. Frs, dep. 41,810.6m. Frs, res 326.3m. Frs (Dec. 1986); Chair. and Man. Dir HENRI MOULARD; 300 brs.

***Société Marseillaise de Crédit, SA:** 75 rue Paradis, 13006 Marseille; tel. 91-54-91-12; telex 430232; fax 91-37-90-23; f. 1865; cap. 100m. Frs, dep. 13,022m. Frs, res 125m. Frs (1989); Chair. and CEO JEAN-PAUL ESCANDE; 190 brs.

***Société Nancéienne Varin-Bernier (SNVB):** 4 place André Maginot, 5400 Nancy; tel. 83-37-65-45; telex 960205; fax 83-34-52-00; f. 1881; cap. 115m. Frs, dep. 25,376.1m. Frs, res 455.8m. Frs (1989); Pres. BERNARD YONCOURT; 168 brs.

Standard Chartered Bank: 4 rue Ventadour, BP 43, 75001 Paris; tel. (1) 42-61-82-20; telex 213097; 2 brs.

‡**Union de Banques à Paris, SA:** 22 place de la Madeleine, 75008 Paris; tel. (1) 45-30-44-44; telex 206791; f. 1935; cap. 100m. Frs, dep. 11,086.6m. Frs, res. 380.7m. Frs. (Dec. 1989); Chair. ROGER PUJOL; 49 brs.

Union de Banques Arabes et Françaises (UBAF): 190 ave Charles de Gaulle, 92523 Neuilly Cedex; tel. (1) 46-40-61-01; telex 610334; fax (1) 47-38-13-88; f. 1970; cap. 925m. Frs, dep. 39,097.4m. Frs, res 383.4m. Frs (1989); Chair. ALY NEGM; Vice-Chairs ABOUBAKER A. AL-SHERIF, BERNARD THIOLON; 5 brs.

Union Française de Banques (UFB LOCABAIL): 43 quai de Grenelle, 75738 Paris Cedex 15; tel. (1) 45-71-60-60; telex 200015; f. 1950; cap. 521.7m. Frs, dep. 29,587.5m. Frs, res 328m. (Dec. 1989); Pres. J. M. BOSSUAT; 65 brs.

Supervisory Body

Association Française des Etablissements de Crédit: 36 rue Taitbout, 75009 Paris; tel. (1) 48-24-34-34; f. 1983; advises government on monetary and credit policy and supervises the banking system; Pres. ETIENNE PFLIMLIN; Gen. Man. ROBERT PELLETIER.

Banking Association

Association Française des Banques: 18 rue La Fayette, 75009 Paris; tel. (1) 48-00-52-52; telex 660282; fax (1) 42-46-76-40; f. 1941; 407 mems; Chair. DOMINIQUE CHATILLON; Delegate-Gen. JEAN-JACQUES BURGARD.

STOCK EXCHANGES

Since 1808 there have been 45 broking houses operating on the Paris Bourse, and 16 in the six provincial exchanges (at Bordeaux, Lille, Lyon, Marseille, Nancy and Nantes). In 1987 the Government introduced proposals to allow French and foreign banks to hold up to 30% of the capital of a broking house from 1988, increasing to 49% in 1989 and to 100% by 1990. By 1992 the limit of 45 broking houses operating on the Bourse was to be removed, and brokers would be able to extend their activities into investment banking operations. The Conseil des Bourses de Valeur would then examine new broking houses.

In 1985 a market for 'commercial paper' (negotiable instruments) was inaugurated. This allowed companies to borrow directly from each other and from other lenders, and in 1987 the first French market in financial 'futures', the Marché à Terme des Instruments Financiers (MATIF), and the first options exchange, the Marché des Options Négociables sur Actions (MONA), were opened. The Government later announced plans to merge the markets for commodities and financial futures under the authority of MATIF, and thus to enable brokers dealing in commodities futures to deal in the financial futures markets.

La Bourse de Paris: Palais de la Bourse, 4 place de la Bourse, 75080 Paris Cedex 02; tel. (1) 40-26-85-90; f. 1808; Dir GUY BÉRARD; run by:

  Société des Bourses Françaises: 4 place de la Bourse, 75080 Paris Cedex 02; tel. (1) 40-41-10-00; telex 215561; fax (1) 40-26-31-40; undertakes the organization and management of French stock exchanges; 61 mems; Chair. BRUNO DE MAULDE.

Stock Exchange Association

Commission des Opérations de Bourse (COB): Tour Mirabeau 39–43 quai André Citroën, 75739 Paris Cedex 15; tel. (1) 45-78-33-33; telex 205238; f. 1967; 150 mems; Chair. JEAN SAINT-GEOURS; Sec.-Gen. PATRICK MORDACQ.

INSURANCE

A list is given below of some of the more important insurance companies:

L'Alsacienne: 1 chemin du Wacken, 67000 Strasbourg; tel. 88-25-95-60; telex 870039; f. 1820; Chair. JACQUES JARDEL (Leader of L'Alsacienne Groupe d'Assurances, composed of: L'Alsacienne, La Cité, La Cité Européenne and L'Alsacienne Finances).

Assurances Mutuelles de France: 7 ave Marcel-Proust, 28032 Chartres Cedex; tel. 37-28-82-28; telex 760511; f. 1819; Chair. CHRISTIAN SASTRE.

Caisse Industrielle d'Assurance Mutuelle (CIAM): 7 rue de Madrid, 75383 Paris Cedex 08; tel. (1) 42-94-37-37; telex 290679; fax (1) 45-22-81-81; f. 1891; Chair. MICHEL LEONET; Gen. Man. HENRI DORON.

Compagnie du Midi SA: 21 rue de Châteaudun; 75447 Paris, Cedex 09; tel. (1) 42-82-82-12; telex 280638; Chair. CLAUDE BEBEAR.

La Concorde: 5 rue de Londres, 75439 Paris Cedex 09; tel. (1) 42-80-66-00; telex 650734; fax (1) 48-74-54-69; f. 1905; Pres. EUGENIO COPPOLA DI CANZANO; Gen. Man. GASTON ALEXANDRE.

La France IARD: 7–9 blvd Haussmann, 75309 Paris Cedex 09; tel. (1) 48-00-80-00; telex 660272; fax (1) 42-46-17-04; f. 1837; Pres. and Dir-Gen. ANTOINE BERNHEIM; Dir-Gen. GEORGES SOLEIL-HAVOUP.

Garantie Mutuelle des Fonctionnaires: 76 rue de Prony, 75857 Paris Cedex 17; tel. (1) 47-54-10-10; telex 640377; f. 1934; Pres. and Dir-Gen. JEAN-LOUIS PETRIAT; Dir ANDRÉ RIALS.

Groupe de Paris: 21 rue de Châteaudun, 75447 Paris Cedex 09; tel. (1) 42-82-82-12; telex 280-638; composed of La Paternelle R.D., La Paternelle Vie, Seine et Rhône, La Défense Civile, Trans Expansion-Vie, Prévoyance Mutuelle MACL, Mutuelle de Marseille; Chair. PIERRE YVES SOLEIL.

Groupe des Assurances Générales de France: 87 rue de Richelieu, 75060 Paris Cedex 02; tel. (1) 42-44-04-44; telex 210697; f. 1968 by merger of Assurances Générales and Phénix, both f. 1819; insurance and reinsurance; cap. 407m. Frs; Chair. MICHEL ALBERT; Man. Dirs JEAN DANIEL LE FRANC, YVES MANSION.

Groupe des Assurances Nationales (GAN): 2 rue Pillet Will, 75448 Paris Cedex 09; tel. (1) 42-47-50-00; telex 280006; fax (1) 42-47-57-56; f. 1820 (fire), 1830 (life), 1865 (accident), reorganized 1968; Chair. FRANÇOIS HEILBRONNER; Dir-Gen. JEAN-JACQUES BONNAUD.

Groupement Français d'Assurances (GFA): 38 rue de Châteaudun, 75439 Paris Cedex 09; tel. (1) 42-80-63-72; telex 660418; Pres. ARNO MORENZ; Dir-Gen. JEAN-MARC JACQUET.

Groupe Victoire (Abeille Assurances): 52 rue de la Victoire, 75009 Paris; tel. (1) 42-80-75-75; cap. 850.2m. Frs; Chair. JEAN ARVIS.

Mutuelle Centrale d'Assurances (MCA): 65 rue de Monceau, 75008 Paris; tel. (1) 45-63-08-00; telex 280343; fax (1) 45-61-92-05; Pres. PAUL ARNAUD; Dir-Gen. ANDRÉ JANNIN.

La Mutuelle du Mans: 37 rue Chanzy, 72035 Le Mans Cedex; tel. 43-41-72-72; telex 720664; f. 1828 (fire); Chair. and Man. Dir J. PERROUD.

Les Mutuelles du Mans, Groupe des Sociétés: 19–21 rue Chanzy, 72030 Le Mans Cedex; tel. 43-41-72-72; telex 720764; life and general insurance; f. 1883; Chair. JEAN CLAUDE JOLLAIN; Gen. Man. MICHEL COSSON.

Mutuelles Unies Assurances: 3037x, 76029 Rouen Cedex, and 14 rue de Londres, 75440 Paris Cedex 09; tel. 35-80-40-40 (Rouen), (1) 42-80-62-19 (Paris); telex 180559 (Rouen), 640584 (Paris); f. 1817; comprises Mutuelles Unies Assurances IARD, Mutuelles Unies Assurances-Vie, La Mutualité Générale Risques Divers; Chair. and Gen. Man. C. BEBEAR.

Preservatrice Foncière d'Assurances (PFA): 92076 Paris la Défense 43; tel. (1) 42-91-10-10; telex 615030; fax (1) 42-91-12-20; Chair. GUY VERDEIL; Gen. Man. GÉRARD BOUCHER.

Présence Assurances: 56 rue de la Victoire, 75308 Paris Cedex 09; tel. (1) 40-23-56-09; telex 660191; f. 1986 from merger between Présence-Vie, La Providence IARD and Le Secours; Pres. and Dir-Gen. VICTOR-CLAUDE ROSSET; Dir-Gen. CLAUDE TENDIL.

La Réunion Française: 5 rue Cadet, 75009 Paris; tel. (1) 48-24-03-04; telex 648083; fax (1) 42-46-14-93; f. 1899; insurance and reinsurance; Chair. ALAIN DU COUËDIC; Gen. Man. FRANÇOIS DROUAULT.

Rhin et Moselle-Assurances Françaises: 1 rue des Arquebusiers, BP 52, 67002 Strasbourg Cedex; tel. 88-25-31-31; telex 890332; fax 88-36-60-52; f. 1881; comprises Compagnie Générale d'Assurances et de Réassurances and Compagnie d'Assurances sur la Vie; Pres. EMMANUEL GAUTIER; Dir-Gen. PHILIPPE TOURNEUR.

Société Anonyme Française de Réassurances (SAFR): 34–36 blvd de Courcelles, 75849 Paris Cedex 17; tel. (1) 42-27-86-82; telex 650493; reinsurance; Chair. and Gen. Man. J. BOURTHOUMIEUX.

Société Commerciale de Réassurance (SCOR): Immeuble SCOR, 1 ave du Président Wilson, 92074 Paris la Défense Cedex 39; tel. (1) 42-91-04-32; telex 614151; f. 1969; reinsurance; Chair. PATRICK PEUGEOT; Gen. Man. FRANÇOIS NEGRIER.

FRANCE — Directory

Société de Réassurance des Assurances Mutuelles Agricoles (SOREMA): 20 rue Washington, 75008 Paris; tel. (1) 40-74-66-00; telex 640774; fax (1) 45-63-25-47; f. 1978; reinsurance; Chair. and CEO L. BORDEAUX-MONTRIEUX; Gen. Man. D. PLOTON.

UAP Réassurances: Tour Voltaire, Cedex 58, 92059 Paris la Défense; tel. (1) 49-07-75-75; telex 616411; fax (1) 49-07-75-01; f. 1919; reinsurance; Chair. and Man. Dir PATRICK PEUGEOT; Man. Dir GÉRARD FRANÇOIS.

L'Union des Assurances de Paris (UAP): 9 place Vendôme, 75001 Paris; tel. (1) 42-60-33-40; telex 210798; includes L'UAP-Vie, L'UAP-Incendie-Accidents and L'UAP-Capitalisation; Chair. JEAN PEYRELEVADE.

Via Assurances IARD: 20 rue Le Peletier, 75439 Paris Cedex 09; tel. (1) 45-23-60-00; telex 660918; Chair. EMMANUEL GAUTIER; Man. Dir JACQUES LEFÈVRE.

Insurance Associations

Fédération Française des Sociétés d'Assurances: 26 blvd Haussmann, 75311 Paris Cedex 09; tel. (1) 42-47-90-00; telex 640477; fax (1) 42-47-93-11; f. 1925; Chair. DENIS KESSLER.

Fédération Nationale des Syndicats d'Agents Généraux d'Assurances de France: 104 rue Jouffroy, 75847 Paris Cedex 17; tel. (1) 44-01-18-00; fax (1) 46-22-76-29; Chair. DANIEL ORLUC.

Syndicat Français des Assureurs-Conseils: 14 rue de la Grange Batelière, 75009 Paris; tel. (1) 45-23-25-26; Chair. GILBERT BAYOU.

Syndicat National des Courtiers d'Assurances et de Réassurances: 31 rue d'Amsterdam, 75008 Paris; tel. (1) 48-74-19-12; fax (1) 42-82-91-10; f. 1896; Chair. PATRICK LUCAS; c. 900 mems.

Trade and Industry

CHAMBERS OF COMMERCE

There are Chambers of Commerce in all the larger towns for all the more important commodities produced or manufactured.

Chambre de Commerce et d'Industrie de Paris: 27 ave de Friedland, 75382 Paris Cedex 08; tel. (1) 42-89-70-00; telex 650100; fax (1) 42-89-78-68; f. 1803; Chair. BERNARD CAMBOURNAC; Man. Dir FRANÇOIS ESSIG.

DEVELOPMENT ORGANIZATION

Institut de Développement Industriel (IDI): 4 rue Ancelle, 92521 Neuilly-sur-Seine; tel. (1) 47-47-71-17; telex 630006; fax (1) 47-47-72-06; f. 1970 as a state agency assisting small and medium-sized businesses by taking equity shares in enterprises and offering advisory services; Chair. CLAUDE MANDIL.

TRADE COUNCIL

Conseil National du Commerce: 53 ave Montaigne, 75008 Paris; tel. (1) 42-25-01-25; fax (1) 45-63-21-83; Chair. J. DERMAGNE.

EMPLOYERS' ORGANIZATION

Conseil National du Patronat français (CNPF): 31 ave Pierre Ier de Serbie, 75016 Paris; tel. (1) 47-23-61-58; fax (1) 47-23-61-61; f. 1946; an employers' organization grouping some 900,000 industrial, trading and banking concerns; Chair. FRANÇOIS PÉRIGOT; Vice-Pres. MICHEL MAURY-LARIBIÈRE.

INDUSTRIAL AND TRADE ASSOCIATION

Syndicat Général du Commerce et de l'Industrie—Union des Chambres Syndicales de France: 163 rue Saint Honoré, 75001 Paris; tel. (1) 42-60-66-83; Pres. MAGDELEINE THÉNAULT-MONDOLONI.

INDUSTRIAL ORGANIZATIONS

Assemblée Permanente des Chambres d'Agriculture (APCA): 9 ave George V, 75008 Paris; tel. (1) 47-23-55-40; telex 280720; fax (1) 47-23-84-97; f. 1929; Chair. PIERRE CORMORECHE; Gen. Sec. JEAN FRANÇOIS HERVIEU.

Association Nationale des Industries Agro-alimentaires (ANIA): 52 rue Faubourg Saint Honoré, 75008 Paris; tel. (1) 42-66-40-14; telex 641784; f. 1971; food and agricultural produce; Chair. FRANCIS LEPATRE; 43 affiliated federations.

Centre de Liaisons Intersyndicales des Industries et des Commerces de la Quincaillerie: 91 rue du Miromesnil, 75008 Paris; tel. (1) 45-61-99-44; telex 650680; f. 1913; hardware; Chair. MM. BLANC; Pres. OLIVIER BLONDET; Sec.-Gen. M. PASSEBOSC; mems 14 syndicates.

Centre des Jeunes Dirigeants d'Entreprise (CJD): 13 rue Dufour, 75007 Paris; tel. (1) 47-83-42-28; telex 200298; fax (1) 42-73-32-90; f. 1938; junior management; Pres. ALAIN BEUNAUD; Sec.-Gen. LUC BERNIMOLIN; 3,000 mems.

Chambre Syndicale de la Sidérurgie Française: Elysées la Défense, 19 le Parvis Cedex 35, 92072 Paris la Défense; tel. (1) 47-67-85-88; telex 65039; fax (1) 47-67-85-77; f. 1945; steel-making; Chair. FRANCIS MER; Delegate-Gen. YVES-THIBAULT DE SILGUY.

Chambre Syndicale de l'Ameublement, Négoce de Paris et de l'Ile de France: 15 rue de la Cerisaie, 75004 Paris; tel. (1) 42-72-13-79; f. 1860; furnishing; Chair. NICOLE PHILIBERT; Sec.-Gen. CHRISTINE ERRANT; 407 mems.

Chambre Syndicale de l'Amiante: 10 ave de la Pépinière, 75008 Paris; tel. (1) 45-22-12-34; telex 281133; fax (1) 42-94-98-86; f. 1898; asbestos; Chair. CYRIL X. LATTY; 17 mems.

Chambre Syndicale des Céramistes et Ateliers d'Art: 62 rue d'Hauteville, 75010 Paris; tel. (1) 47-70-95-83; telex 660005; fax (1) 47-70-10-54; f. 1937; ceramics and arts; Chair. M. BLIN; 1,200 mems.

Chambre Syndicale des Constructeurs de Navires: 47 rue de Monceau, 75008 Paris; tel. (1) 45-61-99-11; telex 280756; shipbuilding; Chair. ALAIN GRILL; Gen. Man. BERTRAND VIEILLARD-BARON.

Comité Central de la Laine et des Fibres Associées (Groupement Général de l'Industrie et du Commerce Lainiers Français): BP 249, 37–39 rue de Neuilly, 92113 Clichy; telex 212591; f. 1922; manufacture of wool and associated textiles; Chair. ROBERT SERRÈS; Vice-Chair. PHILIPPE VANDEPUTTE; 510 mems.

Comité Central des Armateurs de France: 73 blvd Haussmann, 75008 Paris; tel. (1) 42-65-36-04; telex 660532; fax (1) 42-65-71-89; f. 1903; shipping; Pres. GILLES BOUTHILLIER; Delegate-Gen. AGNÈS DE FLEURIEU; 120 mems.

Comité des Constructeurs Français d'Automobiles: 2 rue de Presbourg, 75008 Paris; tel. (1) 47-23-54-05; telex 610-446; fax (1) 47-23-54-05; f. 1909; motor manufacturing; Chair. RAYMOND RAVENEL; 9 mems.

Confédération des Commerçants-Détaillants de France: 21 rue du Château d'Eau, 75010 Paris; tel. (1) 42-08-17-15; retailers; Chair. M. FOUCAULT.

Confédération des Industries Céramiques de France: 44 rue Copernic, 75116 Paris; tel. (1) 45-00-18-56; telex 611913; fax (1) 45-00-47-56; f. 1937; ceramic industry; Chair. FRÉDÉRIC LEBOUCHARD; Man. Dir PIERRE BOISAUBERT; 300 mems, 12 affiliates.

Confédération Générale des Petites et Moyennes Entreprises: 1 ave du Général de Gaulle, Terrasse Bellini, 92806 Puteaux Cedex; tel. (1) 47-62-73-73; telex 630358; fax (1) 47-73-08-86; f. 1945; small and medium-sized enterprises; Chair. LUCIEN REBUFFEL; 3,000 affiliated assens.

Fédération des Chambres Syndicales de l'Industrie du Verre: 3 rue de la Boétie, 75008 Paris; tel. (1) 42-65-60-02; f. 1874; glass industry; Chair. PIERRE BREITENSTEIN.

Fédération des Chambres Syndicales des Minerais et Métaux non-Ferreux: 30 ave de Messine, 75008 Paris; tel. (1) 45-63-02-66; telex 650438; f. 1945; minerals and non-ferrous metals; Chair. JEAN-SEBASTIEN LETOURNEUR; Delegate-Gen. G. JOURDAN; 16 affiliated syndicates.

Fédération des Exportateurs des Vins et Spiritueux de France: 95 rue de Monceau, 75008 Paris; tel. (1) 45-22-75-73; telex 280695; fax (1) 45-22-94-16; f. 1921; exporters of wines and spirits; Pres. CLAUDE TAITTINGER; Delegate-Gen. LOUIS RÉGIS AFFRE; 450 mems.

Fédération des Industries Electriques et Electroniques (FIEE): 11 rue Hamelin, 75783 Paris Cedex 16; tel. (1) 45-05-70-70; telex 611045; fax (1) 45-53-03-93; f. 1925; electrical and electronics industries; Chair. ROGER SEGUY; Delegate-Gen. PAUL ROGER SALLEBERT; c. 1,000 mems.

Fédération des Industries Mécaniques et Transformatrices des Métaux: BP 3515, 11 ave Hoche, 75382 Paris Cedex 08; tel. (1) 45-63-02-00; telex 280900; f. 1840; mechanical and metal-working; Chair. ALAIN BANZET; Man. Dir G. IMBERT.

Fédération des Industries Nautiques: Port de la Bourdonnais, 75007 Paris; tel. (1) 45-55-10-49; telex 203963; fax (1) 47-53-94-75; f. 1965; pleasure-boating; Chair. MICHEL RICHARD; Sec.-Gen. PIERRE-EDOUARD DE BOIGNE; 700 mems.

Fédération Française de la Bijouterie, Joaillerie, Orfèvrerie du Cadeau, Diamants, Pierres et Perles et Activités qui s'y rattachent (BJOC): 58 rue du Louvre, 75002 Paris; tel. (1) 42-33-61-33; fax (1) 40-26-29-51; jewellery, gifts and tableware; Chair. MAURICE GRUSON; 1,500 mems.

Fédération Française de la Tannerie-Mégisserie: 122 rue de Provence, 75008 Paris; tel. (1) 45-22-96-45; telex 290785; fax (1) 42-93-37-44; f. 1885; leather industry; 180 mems.

Fédération Française de l'Imprimerie et des Industries graphiques (FFIIG): 115 blvd Saint Germain, 75006 Paris; tel. (1) 40-34-21-15; fax (1) 46-33-73-34; printing; Pres. DOMINIQUE HARLEY.

FRANCE

Fédération Française du Commerce du Bois: 8 rue du Colonel Moll, 75017 Paris; tel. (1) 42-67-64-75; telex 640438; timber trade; Chair. GÉRARD LEMAIGNEN; Man. Dir DENIS SPIRE.

Fédération Nationale de la Musique: 62 rue Blanche, 75009 Paris; tel. (1) 48-74-09-20; f. 1946; includes Chambre Syndicale de la Facture Instrumentale, Syndicat National de l'Édition Phonographique and other groups; musical instruments and recordings; Chair. LUCIEN ADES; Sec.-Gen. PIERRE CHESNAIS.

Fédération Nationale de l'Industrie Hôtelière (FNIH): 22 rue d'Anjou, 75008 Paris; tel. (1) 42-65-04-61; telex 640033; Chair. JACQUES THÉ.

Fédération Nationale des Entreprises à Commerces Multiples: 11 rue Saint Florentin, 75008 Paris; tel. (1) 42-60-36-02; f. 1937; Chair. JACQUES PERRILLIAT.

Fédération Nationale des Industries Électrométallurgiques, Éléctrochimiques et Connexes: 30 ave de Messine, 75008 Paris; tel. (1) 45-61-06-63; fax (1) 45-63-61-54; Chair. BRUNO ANGLÈS D'AURIAC.

Fédération Nationale du Bâtiment: 33 ave Kléber, 75784 Paris Cedex 16; tel. (1) 40-69-51-00; f. 1906; building trade; Chair. JACQUES BRUNIER; Dir-Gen. CHRISTIAN MAURETTE; 55,000 mems.

Fédération Nationale du Bois: 1 place André Malraux, 75001 Paris; tel. (1) 42-60-30-27; telex 215409; fax (1) 42-60-58-94; timber and wood products; Chair. J. NANTY; Dir PIERRE VERNERET; 4,000 mems.

Groupement des Industries Françaises Aéronautiques et Spatiales: 4 rue Galilée, 75782 Paris Cedex 16; tel. (1) 47-23-55-56; telex 630615; fax (1) 40-70-91-41; aerospace industry; Pres. HENRI MARTRE; Delegate-Gen. BERNARD NICOLAS.

Syndicat Général de l'Industrie Cotonnière Française: BP 249, 37 rue de Neuilly, 92110 Clichy; tel. (1) 47-56-30-40; telex 614529; f. 1902; cotton manufacturing; Chair. JEAN CAULLIEZ; Vice-Chair. DENIS CHAIGNE; mems 71 (spinning), 153 (weaving).

Syndicat Général des Cuirs et Peaux Bruts: Bourse de Commerce, 2 rue de Viarmes, 75040 Paris Cedex 01; tel. (1) 45-08-08-54; f. 1977; untreated leather and hides; Chair. PIERRE DUBOIS; 60 mems.

Syndicat Général des Fabricants de Papiers, Cartons et Celluloses de France: 154 blvd Haussmann, 75008 Paris; tel. (1) 45-62-87-07; telex 290544; f. 1864; paper, cardboard and cellulose; Chair. PAUL BRETON; Gen. Man. JEAN-FRANÇOIS HEMON-LAURENS; 133 firms affiliated.

Syndicat Général des Fabricants d'Huile et de Tourteaux de France: 10 rue de la Paix, 75002 Paris; tel. (1) 42-61-57-21; fax (1) 47-03-98-78; f. 1928; edible oils; Pres. RICHARD RANTAG; Sec.-Gen. J. C. BARSACQ.

Syndicat Général des Fondeurs de France et Industries Connexes: 2 rue Bassano, 75783 Paris Cedex 16; tel. (1) 47-23-55-50; telex 620617; fax (1) 47-20-44-15; f. 1897; metal smelting; Chair. ANDRÉ DOAT; Delegate-Gen. GÉRARD CORNET; 400 mems.

Syndicat National de l'Industrie Pharmaceutique (CSNIP): 88 rue de la Faisanderie, 75782 Paris Cedex 16; tel. (1) 45-03-21-01; fax (1) 45-04-47-71; telex 612828; pharmaceuticals; Chair. RENÉ SAUTIER.

Union des Armateurs à la Pêche de France: 59 rue des Mathurins, 75008 Paris; tel. (1) 42-66-32-60; telex 660143; fax (1) 47-42-91-12; f. 1945; fishing-vessels; Chair. CLAUDE SENECHAL; Delegate-Gen. A. PARRES.

Union des Chambres Syndicales de l'Industrie du Pétrole: 16 ave Kléber, 75116 Paris; tel. (1) 45-02-11-20; telex 630545; fax (1) 45-00-84-81; petroleum industry; Chair. JEAN-LOUIS BREUIL-JARRIGE.

Union des Fabricants de Porcelaine de Limoges: 7 bis rue du Général Cérez, 87000 Limoges; tel. 55-77-29-18; fax 55-77-36-81; porcelain manufacturing; Chair. ANDRÉ RAYNAUD; Sec.-Gen. MARIE-THÉRÈSE PASQUET.

Union des Industries Chimiques: 64 ave Marceau, 75008 Paris; tel. (1) 47-20-56-03; telex 630611; fax (1) 47-20-48-69; f. 1860; chemical industry; Chair. J.-C. ACHILLE; Dir-Gen. C. MARTIN; 58 affiliated unions.

Union des Industries Métallurgiques et Minières: 56 ave de Wagram, 75017 Paris; tel. (1) 40-54-20-20; fax (1) 47-66-51-15; metallurgy and mining; Chair. JEAN LEENHARDT; Vice-Pres. JEAN D'HUART.

Union des Industries Textiles (Production): BP 249, 37 rue de Neuilly, 92113 Clichy Cedex; tel. (1) 47-56-31-21; telex 615280; fax (1) 47-30-25-28; f. 1901; Chair. LOUIS-CHARLES BARY; 2,500 mems.

TRADE UNIONS

There are three major trade union organizations:

Confédération Générale du Travail (CGT): Complexe Immobilier Intersyndical CGT, 263 rue de Paris, 93516 Montreuil Cedex; tel. (1) 48-51-80-00; telex 235069; fax (1) 48-57-15-20; f. 1895; a founder member of the World Federation of Trade Unions since 1945; National Congress is held every three years; Sec.-Gen. HENRI KRASUCKI; approx. 1.6m. mems.

Affiliated unions:

Agroalimentaire et Forestière (FNAF): 263 rue de Paris, 93100 Montreuil Cedex; Sec.-Gen. FREDDY HUCK.

Bois (Woodworkers): 263 rue de Paris, 93100 Montreuil Cedex; Sec.-Gen. GEORGES LHERICEL.

Cheminots (Railway Workers): 263 rue de Paris, 93100 Montreuil Cedex; Sec.-Gen. GEORGES LANOUE.

Construction (Building): 263 rue de Paris, 93100 Montreuil Cedex; Sec.-Gen. ROBERT BRUN.

Education, Recherche et Culture: 263 rue de Paris, 93100 Montreuil Cedex; Sec.-Gen. JOËL HEDDE.

Energie: 16 rue de Candale, 93057 Pantin Cedex; tel. 48-43-93-24; telex 240194; fax 48-91-36-96; f. 1905; Sec.-Gen. DENIS COHEN.

Energie Atomique: Bâtiment 38, Centre d'Etudes Nucléaires de Saclay, 91191 Gif-sur-Yvette Cedex; Sec.-Gen. J. TRELIN.

Enseignements Techniques et Professionnels (Technical and Professional Teachers): 12 promenée Venise Gosnat, 94200 Ivry-sur-Seine; tel. (1) 46-70-01-59; Sec.-Gen. MICHÈLE BARACAT.

Equipement et l'Environnement: 263 rue de Paris, Case 543, 93515 Montreuil Cedex; tel. (1) 48-51-82-81; Sec.-Gen. JEAN-CLAUDE BOUAL.

Finances: 263 rue de Paris, 93100 Montreuil Cedex; tel. (1) 48-51-82-21; Sec.-Gen. JEAN-CHRISTOPHE LE DUIGOU.

Fonctionnaires (Civil Servants): 263 rue de Paris, 93515 Montreuil Cedex; tel. (1) 48-51-82-31; telex 218912; groups National Education, Finance, Technical and Administrative, Civil Servants, Police, etc.; mems about 70 national unions covered by six federations; Sec.-Gen. THÉRÈSE HIRSZBERG.

Industries Chimiques (Chemical Industries): 263 rue de Paris, 93100 Montreuil Cedex; tel. (1) 48-51-80-36; fax (1) 48-51-80-35; f. 1950; Sec.-Gen. JEAN VINCENT.

Industries du Livre du Papier et de la Communication (FILPAC) (Printing and Paper Products): Case 426, 263 rue de Paris, 93514 Montreuil Cedex; tel. (1) 48-51-80-45; Sec.-Gen. MICHEL MULLER.

Ingénieurs, Cadres et Techniciens (Engineers, Managerial Staff and Technicians): 263 rue de Paris, 93514 Montreuil Cedex; tel. (1) 48-51-81-25; Sec.-Gen. ALAIN OBADIA.

Journalistes: 50 rue Edouard Pailleron, 75019 Paris; tel. (1) 42-06-16-50; fax (1) 42-06-02-46; Sec.-Gen. GÉRARD GATINOT.

Marine Marchande (Merchant Marine): Fédération des Officiers CGT, Cercle Franklin, Cours de la République, 76600 Le Havre; tel. 35-25-04-81; fax 35-24-23-77; Sec.-Gen. D. LEFÈBVRE.

Métaux (Metal): 263 rue de Paris, 93514 Montreuil Cedex; Sec.-Gen. JEAN DESMAISON.

Organismes Sociaux: 263 rue de Paris, 93100 Montreuil Cedex; tel. 48-51-83-56; fax 48-59-24-75; Sec.-Gen. PHILIPPE HOURCADE.

Personnels du Commerce, de la Distribution et des Services: Case 425, 263 rue de Paris, 93514 Montreuil Cedex; tel. (1) 48-51-83-11; Sec.-Gen. MICHELLE COMMERGNAT.

Police: Case 550, 263 rue de Paris, 93514 Montreuil Cedex; tel. (1) 48-51-81-85; Sec.-Gen. PASCAL MARTINI.

Ports et Docks: 263 rue de Paris, 93100 Montreuil Cedex; Sec.-Gen. DANIEL LEFÈVRE.

Postes et Télécommunications: 263 rue de Paris, 93100 Montreuil Cedex; Sec.-Gen. MARYSE DUMAS.

Santé, Action Sociale (Health and Social Services): Case 583, 263 rue de Montreuil, 93515 Montreuil Cedex; tel. (1) 48-51-80-91; f. 1907; Sec.-Gen. BERNARD DESORMIÈRE.

Secteurs Financiers: 263 rue de Paris, 93100 Montreuil Cedex; Sec.-Gen. J. DOMINIQUE SIMONPOLI.

Services Publics (Community Services): 263 rue de Paris, 93100 Montreuil Cedex; Sec.-Gen. ALAIN POUCHOL.

Sous-sol (Miners): Case 535, 263 rue de Paris, 93515 Montreuil Cedex; Sec.-Gen. JACKY BERNARD.

Spectacle, Audio-Visuel et Action Culturelle (Theatre, Media and Culture): 14-16 rue des Lilas, 75019 Paris; tel. (1) 42-40-14-95; Sec.-Gen. JEAN VOIRIN.

Syndicats Maritimes (Seamen): Case 420, 263 rue de Paris, 93514 Montreuil Cedex; tel. (1) 48-51-84-21; fax (1) 48-51-59-21; Sec.-Gen. MARCEL HALYK.

Tabac et Allumettes (Tobacco and Matches): 263 rue de Paris, 93100 Montreuil Cedex; Sec.-Gen. BERTRAND PAGE.

THC (Textiles): 263 rue de Paris, 93100 Montreuil Cedex; Sec.-Gen. CHRISTIAN LAROSE.

FRANCE

Transports: 263 rue de Paris, 93100 Montreuil Cedex; Sec.-Gen. Sylvie Salmon.

Travailleurs de l'Etat (State Employees): 263 rue de Paris, 93100 Montreuil Cedex; Sec.-Gen. Henri Berry.

Verre et Céramique (Glassworkers and Ceramics): Case 417, 263 rue de Paris, 93514 Montreuil Cedex; tel. (1) 48-51-80-13; Sec.-Gen. Jacques Beauvoir.

Voyageurs-Représentants, Cadres et Techniciens de la Vente (Commercial Travellers): 67 rue de Turbigo, 75003 Paris; tel. (1) 42-72-96-99; Sec.-Gen. Alain Serre.

Force Ouvrière: 198 ave du Maine, 75680 Paris Cedex 14; tel. (1) 45-39-22-03; telex 203405; fax (1) 45-45-34-52; f. 1947 by breakaway from the CGT (above); Force Ouvrière is a member of ICFTU and of the European Trade Union Confederation; Sec.-Gen. Marc Blondel; approx. 1.1m. mems (1985).

Affiliated federations:

Action Sociale: 8 rue de Hanovre, 75002 Paris; tel. (1) 42-68-08-01; Sec. Michel Pinaud.

Agriculture et Alimentation (Food and Agriculture): 198 ave du Maine, 75680 Paris Cedex 14; tel. (1) 45-39-22-03; Secs-Gen. Gérard Fosse, Alain Kerbriand, Daniel Dreux.

Bâtiment, Travaux Publics, Bois, Céramiques, Papier-Carton et Matériaux de Construction (Building and Building Materials, Public Works, Wood, Ceramics and Pasteboard): 170 ave Parmentier, 75010 Paris; tel. (1) 42-01-30-00; Sec.-Gen. Emile Apain.

Cadres et Ingénieurs (UCI) (Engineers): 2 rue de la Michodière, 75002 Paris; tel. (1) 47-42-39-69; Sec.-Gen. Hubert Bouchet.

Cheminots (Railway Workers): 60 rue Vergniaud, 75640 Paris Cedex 13; tel. (1) 45-80-22-98; f. 1948; Sec.-Gen. Jean Jacques Carmentran; 16,350 mems.

Coiffeurs, Esthétique et Parfumerie (Hairdressers, Beauticians and Perfumery): 130 ave Isementier, 75011 Paris; tel. (1) 43-57-31-80; Sec.-Gen. Michel Bourlon.

Cuirs-Textiles-Habillement (Leather and Textiles): 8 rue de Hanovre, esc. B., 75002 Paris; tel. (1) 47-42-92-70; Sec. Francis Desrousseaux.

Employés et Cadres (Managerial Staff): 28 rue des Petits Hôtels, 75010 Paris; tel. (1) 42-46-46-64; Sec.-Gen. Yves Simon.

Energie Electrique et Gaz (Gas and Electricity): 60 rue Vergniaud, 75640 Paris Cedex 13; tel. (1) 45-88-91-51; f. 1947; Sec.-Gen. Gabriel Gaudy; 22,000 mems.

Enseignement, Culture et Formation Professionelle: 155 rue de Vaugirard, 75015 Paris; tel. (1) 45-67-94-49; Sec.-Gen. François Chaintron; 50,000 mems.

Equipement, Transports et Service (Transport and Public Works): 46 rue des Petites Ecuries, 75010 Paris; tel. (1) 42-46-36-63; telex 643115; f. 1932; Sec.-Gen. René Valladon; 50,000 mems.

Finances: 46 rue des Petites Ecuries, 75010 Paris; tel. (1) 42-46-75-20; Sec. Jacky Lesuer.

Fonctionnaires (Civil Servants): 46 rue des Petites Ecuries, 75010 Paris; tel. (1) 42-46-48-56; fax (1) 42-46-97-80; Sec. Roland Gaillard.

Industries Chimiques (Chemical Industries): 60 rue Vergniaud, 75640 Paris Cedex 13; tel. (1) 45-80-14-90; f. 1948; Sec.-Gen. F. Grandazzi.

Livre (Printing Trades): 198 ave du Maine, 75014 Paris Cedex 14; tel. (1) 45-40-69-44; Sec.-Gen. Roger Carpentier.

Métaux (Metals): 9 rue Baudoin, 75013 Paris; tel. (1) 45-82-01-00; fax (1) 45-83-78-87; Sec.-Gen. Michel Huc.

Mineurs, Miniers et Similaires (Mine Workers): 169 ave de Choisy, 75624 Paris Cedex 13; tel. (1) 45-87-10-98; Sec.-Gen. René Mertz.

Défense des Industries, de l'Armement et des Secteurs Assimilés (National Defence): 46 rue des Petites Ecuries, 75010 Paris; tel. (1) 42-46-00-05; Sec.-Gen. René Allais.

Personnels des Services des Départements et des Régions: 46 rue des Petites Ecuries, 75010 Paris; tel. (1) 42-46-50-52; Sec.-Gen. Michèle Simonnin.

Pharmacie (Chemists): 198 ave du Maine, 75680 Paris Cedex 14; tel. (1) 45-39-97-22; Sec.-Gen. Marguerite Adenis.

Police: 6 rue Albert Bayet, 75013 Paris; tel. (1) 45-82-28-08; f. 1948; Sec. Jean-Louis Cerceau; 11,000 mems.

PTT (Post, Telegraphs and Telephones): 60 rue Vergniaud, 75640 Paris Cedex 13; tel. (1) 40-78-31-50; telex 200644; fax (1) 40-78-30-58; Sec.-Gen. Jacques Marçot.

Services d'Administration Générale de l'Etat: 46 rue des Petites Ecuries, 75010 Paris; tel. (1) 42-46-46-19; f. 1948; Sec.-Gen. Francis Lamarque; 20,000 mems.

Services Publics et de Santé (Health and Public Services): 153–155 rue de Rome, 75017 Paris; tel. (1) 46-22-26-00; f. 1947; Sec.-Gen. René Champeau; 130,000 mems.

Spectacles, Presse et Audiovisuel (Theatre and Cinema Performers, Press and Broadcasting): 2 rue de la Michodière, 75002 Paris; tel. (1) 47-42-35-86; Sec.-Gen. Georges Donaud.

Transports: 198 ave du Maine, 75680 Paris Cedex 14; tel. (1) 45-40-68-00; Sec. Gilbert Doriat.

Voyageurs-Représentants-Placiers (Commercial Travellers): 6–8 rue Albert-Bayet, 75013 Paris; tel. (1) 45-82-28-28; f. 1930; Sec. Henry Dupille.

Confédération Française Démocratique du Travail (CFDT): 4 blvd de la Villette, 75955 Paris Cedex 19; tel. (1) 42-03-80-00; telex 240832; constituted in 1919 as Confédération Française des Travailleurs Chrétiens—CFTC, present title and constitution adopted in 1964; co-ordinates 2,500 trade unions, 102 departmental and overseas unions and 22 affiliated professional federations, all of which are autonomous. There are also 22 regional orgs; in 1990 its membership was estimated at 539,000; affiliated to European Trade Union Confederation and to CSL; Sec.-Gen. Jean Kaspar.

Principal affiliated federations:

Agroalimentaire (FGA): 47/49 ave Simon Bolivar, 75950 Paris Cedex 19; tel. (1) 42-02-50-05; fax (1) 42-02-55-79; f. 1980; Sec.-Gen. Jean Alegre.

Anciens Combattants (War Veterans): 37 rue Bellechasse, 75007 Paris Cedex 09; tel. (1) 45-56-84-67; Sec.-Gen. Nicole Delvaux.

Banques (Fédération des Syndicats CFDT de Banques et Sociétés Financières) (Banking): 47/49 ave Simon Bolivar, 75950 Paris Cedex 19; tel. (1) 42-02-50-38; fax (1) 42-02-61-20; Sec.-Gen. Jean-Luc Wabant.

Construction-Bois: 47/49 ave Simon Bolivar, 75950 Paris Cedex 19; tel. (1) 42-02-50-58; fax (1) 42-02-62-24; f. 1934; Sec.-Gen. Michel Jalmain.

EDF-GDF (Electricity and Gas of France): 47/49 ave Simon Bolivar, 75950 Paris Cedex 19; tel. (1) 42-02-44-55; fax (1) 45-02-48-78; f. 1946; Sec.-Gen. Bruno Lechevin.

Education Nationale (SGEN-CFDT) (National Education): 47/49 ave Simon Bolivar, 75950 Paris Cedex 19; tel. (1) 42-02-50-11; fax (1) 42-02-50-97; f. 1937; Sec.-Gen. Jean Michel Boullier.

Enseignement Privé (Non-State education): 47/49 ave Simon Bolivar, 75950 Paris Cedex 19; tel. (1) 42-02-44-90; Sec.-Gen. Jacques André.

Establissements et Arsenaux de l'Etat: 47/49 ave Simon Bolivar, 75950 Paris Cedex 19; tel. (1) 42-02-44-62; Sec.-Gen. Pierre-Henri Guinet.

Finances et Affaires Economiques (Finance): 47/49 ave Simon Bolivar, 75950 Paris Cedex 19; tel. (1) 42-02-45-85; f. 1936; civil servants and workers within government financial departments; Sec.-Gen. Philippe Leclezio.

Fonctionnaires et Assimilés (UFFA-CFDT) (Civil Servants): 47/49 ave Simon Bolivar, 75950 Paris Cedex 19; tel. (1) 42-02-44-70; f. 1972; Sec.-Gen. Roselyne Vieillard.

Habillement, Cuir et Textile (HACUITEX): 47/49 ave Simon Bolivar, 75950 Paris Cedex 19; tel. (1) 42-02-50-20; telex 660154; fax (1) 42-02-48-78; f. 1963; Sec.-Gen. Yvonne Delemotte.

Industries Chimiques (FUC—CFDT) (Chemicals): 47/49 ave Simon Bolivar, 75950 Paris Cedex 19; tel. (1) 42-02-42-09; telex 660154; fax (1) 42-02-48-78; Sec.-Gen. Jacques Kheliff.

Information, Livre, Audiovisuel et Culture (FILAC): 47/49 ave Simon Bolivar, 75950 Paris Cedex 19; tel. (1) 42-02-57-22; fax (1) 42-02-59-74; Sec.-Gen. Michel Mortelette.

Ingénieurs et Cadres (UCC-CFDT): 47/49 ave Simon Bolivar, 75950 Paris Cedex 19; tel. (1) 42-02-44-43; fax (1) 42-02-48-58; Sec.-Gen. Daniel Croquette.

Justice: 25 rue de la Fontaine au Roi, 75011 Paris; tel. (1) 48-05-70-56; fax (1) 48-05-60-61; Sec.-Gen. Yves Rousset.

Mines et Métallurgie (Miners and Metal Workers): 47/49 ave Simon Bolivar, 75950 Paris Cedex 19; tel. (1) 42-02-42-40; telex 660154; Sec.-Gen. Gérard Dantin.

Personnel du Ministère de l'Intérieur et des Collectivités Locales (INTERCO): 47/49 ave Simon Bolivar, 75950 Paris Cedex 19; tel. (1) 40-40-85-50; telex 660154; fax (1) 42-02-46-49; Sec.-Gen. Jacques Nodin.

Protection Sociale, Travail-Emploi (Social Security): 47/49 ave Simon Bolivar, 75950 Paris Cedex 19; tel. (1) 42-02-51-22; fax (1) 42-02-53-13; Sec.-Gen. Michel Weissberger.

PTT (Post, Telegraph and Telephone Workers): 47/49 ave Simon Bolivar, 75950 Paris Cedex 19; tel. (1) 42-02-42-00; telex 660154; fax (1) 42-02-42-10; Sec.-Gen. Jean-Claude Desrayaud.

FRANCE

Santé et Services Sociaux (Hospital Workers): 47/49 ave Simon Bolivar, 75950 Paris Cedex 19; tel. (1) 40-40-85-00; fax (1) 42-02-48-08; Sec.-Gen. MARC DUPONT.

Services: 47/49 ave Simon Bolivar, 75950 Paris Cedex 19; tel. (1) 42-02-50-48; telex 660154; fax (1) 42-02-56-55; Sec.-Gen. RÉMY JOUAN.

Transports et Equipement: 47/49 ave Simon Bolivar, 75950 Paris Cedex 19; tel. (1) 42-02-48-88; fax (1) 42-02-49-96; f. 1977; Sec.-Gen. MICHEL PERNET.

Union Confédérale des Retraités (UCR): 47/49 ave Simon Bolivar, 75950 Paris Cedex 19; tel. (1) 42-02-43-83; Sec.-Gen. MARCEL GONIN.

Confédération Française de l'Encadrement (CGC): 30 rue de Gramont, 75002 Paris; tel. (1) 42-61-81-76; telex 215116; fax (1) 42-96-45-97; f. 1944; organizes managerial staff, professional staff and technicians; co-ordinates unions in every industry and sector; Pres. PAUL MARCHELLI; Gen.-Sec. MARC VILBÈNOÎT; 300,000 mems.

Confédération Française des Travailleurs Chrétiens (CFTC): 13 rue des Ecluses Saint Martin, 75483 Paris Cedex 10; tel. (1) 42-40-02-02; telex 214046; fax (1) 42-00-44-04; f. 1919; present form in 1964 after majority CFTC became CFDT (see above); absorbed Confédération Générale des Syndicats Indépendants 1977; Chair. JEAN BORNARD; Gen. Sec. GUY DRILLEAUD; 250,000 mems in 1985.

Confédération des Syndicats Libres (CSL) (formerly Confédération française du Travail): 13 rue Péclet, 75015 Paris; tel. (1) 45-33-62-62; telex 201390; f. 1959; right-wing; Sec.-Gen. AUGUSTE BLANC; 250,000 mems.

Fédération de l'Education Nationale (FEN): 48 rue La Bruyère, 75440 Paris Cedex 09; tel. (1) 42-85-71-01; telex 648356; fax (1) 40-16-05-92; f. 1948; federation of teachers' unions; Sec.-Gen. YANNICK SIMBRON; 395,000 mems in 1988.

Fédération Nationale des Syndicats Autonomes: 19 blvd Sébastopol, 75001 Paris; f. 1952; groups unions in the private sector; Sec.-Gen. MICHEL-ANDRÉ TILLIÈRES.

Fédération Nationale des Syndicats d'Exploitants Agricoles (FNSEA) (National Federation of Farmers' Unions): 11 rue de la Baume, 75008 Paris; tel. (1) 45-63-11-77; telex 660587; fax (1) 45-63-91-25; f. 1946; divided into 92 departmental federations and 30,000 local unions; Chair. RAYMOND LACOMBE; Dir-Gen. GEORGES-PIERRE MALPEL; Sec.-Gen. LUC GUYAU; 700,000 mems.

PRINCIPAL STATE-CONTROLLED COMPANIES

Aerospatiale: 37 blvd de Montmorency, 75781 Paris Cedex 16; tel. (1) 45-24-43-21; fax (1) 45-24-43-21; manufacturer of aircraft, helicopters, strategic missiles, space and ballistic systems; 35,222 employees; Chair. and Gen. Man. HENRI MARTRE; Dir PHILIPPE COUILLARD.

Avions Marcel Dassault—Breguet Aviation: 33 rue du Professeur Victor Pauchet, 92420 Vaucresson; tel. (1) 47-41-79-21; telex 203944; f. 1967 by merger; state took 46% of shares in 1982; design and production of civil and military aircraft; 14,676 employees; turnover 15,545m. Frs (1987); Pres. SERGE DASSAULT.

Charbonnages de France (CdF): Tour Albert ler, 65 ave de Colmar, 92507 Rueil Malmaison; tel. (1) 47-52-92-52; telex 631450; fax (1) 45-63-11-20; established under the Nationalization Act of 1946; responsible for coal mining, sales and research in metropolitan France; there are also engineering and informatics divisions; 25,000 employees; Pres. and Dir-Gen. BERNARD PACHE.

Electricité de France: 32 rue de Monceau, 75008 Paris; tel. (1) 47-55-94-10; telex 280098; fax (1) 47-64-27-06; established under the Electricity and Gas Industry Nationalization Act of 1946; responsible for generating and supplying electricity for distribution to consumers in metropolitan France; 123,000 employees; Chair. PIERRE DELAPORTE; Man. Dir JEAN BERGOUGNOUX.

Société Nationale Elf Aquitaine (SNEA) (Groupe Elf, 2 place de la Coupole, Paris la Défense 6, Courbevoie; tel. (1) 47-44-45-46; telex 615400; 67% owned by ERAP—Entreprise de Recherches et d'Activités Pétrolières, a state enterprise; undertakes exploration for and production of petroleum and natural gas, chiefly in France, Africa (Cameroon, the Congo, Gabon and Nigeria), the North Sea and the USA; in 1987 it produced 17.8m. metric tons of crude petroleum and 14,400m. cu m of natural gas; has four refineries in France and a share in four others, with total capacity of 34.8m. tons per year. Elf Aquitaine also exploits uranium and non-energy minerals, and has subsidiaries in petrochemicals (ATOCHEM) and pharmaceuticals (SANOFI); 76,100 employees; Chair. and CEO LE FLOCH PRIGENT.

Gaz de France: 23 rue Philibert Delorme, 75840 Paris Cedex 17; tel. (1) 47-54-20-20; telex 650483; fax (1) 47-54-21-87; established under the Electricity and Gas Industry Nationalization Act of 1946; responsible for distribution of gas in metropolitan France; about 17.5% of gas is produced in France (Aquitaine) and the rest imported from Algeria, the Netherlands, Norway and the USSR; Chair. FRANCIS GUTMANN; Dir-Gen. PIERRE GADONNEIX.

Orkem: Tour Albert ler, 65 ave de Colmar, 92507 Rueil Malmaison; f. 1986, originally part of CdF; chemicals; 15,000 employees; turnover 20,000m. Frs (1987); Chair. SERGE TCHURUK.

Péchiney: 23 rue Balzac, 75008 Paris; tel. (1) 45-61-61-61; telex 290503; fax (1) 45-61-50-00; nationalized 1982; aluminium, fine metallurgy and advanced materials, ferroalloys and carbon products, copper fabrication; 49,160 employees; turnover 29,009m. Frs (1983); Chair. and CEO JEAN GANDOIS.

Régie Nationale des Usines Renault: 34 quai du Point du Jour, BP 103, 92109 Boulogne-Billancourt; tel. (1) 46-09-15-30; telex 205677; fax (1) 42-25-18-57; nationalized in 1945; in 1987 1.6m. passenger cars and small vans were manufactured; sales totalled 115,744m. Frs; Chair. RAYMOND LÉVY.

Rhône-Poulenc: 25 quai Paul Doumer, 92408 Courbevoie Cedex; tel. (1) 47-68-12-34; f. 1858; nationalized 1982; chemicals, pharmaceuticals, animal foodstuffs, film, textiles, communications; 80,000 employees (of whom 48,000 in France); turnover 56,000m. Frs (1984); Chair. and CEO JEAN-RENÉ FOURTOU; Man. Dir JEAN-MARC BRUEL.

Société Nationale d'Etude et de Construction de Moteurs d'Avion (SNECMA): 2 blvd Victor, 75724 Paris Cedex 15; tel. (1) 45-54-92-00; telex 202834; f. 1905; nationalized 1945; manufactures engines for civil and military aircraft, electronic and meteorological equipment; Chair. and Man. Dir Gen. LOUIS GALLOIS.

Société Nationale d'Exploitation Industrielle des Tabacs et des Allumettes (SEITA): 53 quai d'Orsay, 75340 Paris Cedex 07; tel. (1) 45-56-61-50; telex 250604; responsible for the production and marketing of tobacco and matches in France; sales totalled 10,300m. Frs in 1989; 6,200 employees; Chair. and Man. Dir B. DE GALLÉ.

Thomson, SA: Cedex 67, 92045 Paris La Défense; tel. (1) 49-07-80-00; telex 616780; fax (1) 49-07-83-00; f. 1893 as Compagnie Française Thomson-Houston; nationalized 1982; holding company for Thomson group; professional electronics; 100,000 employees; turnover 76,700m. Frs (1989); Chair. ALAIN GOMEZ.

Usinor Sacilor: Immeuble 'Ile de France', Cedex 33, 92070 Paris la Défense; tel. (1) 49-00-60-10; telex 614730; f. 1948 as two companies, Sacilor and Usinor; Usinor nationalized 1981; Sacilor nationalized 1982; two companies merged as Usinor Sacilor 1987; steel; 97,000 employees (1990); Chair. and Man. Dir FRANCIS MER.

Transport

RAILWAYS

Most of the French railways are controlled by the Société Nationale des Chemins de fer Français (SNCF) which took over the activities of the five largest railway companies in 1937. The SNCF is divided into 23 régions (areas), all under the direction of a general headquarters in Paris. In 1989 the SNCF operated 34,322 km of track, of which 12,430 km were electrified. The Parisian transport system is controlled by a separate authority, the Régie Autonome des Transports Parisiens (RATP, see below). A number of small railways in the provinces are run by independent organizations. In 1987 the French and British Governments signed a treaty to construct a rail link between the two countries, under the English Channel, which would be completed by 1993. The rail link was to be constructed and operated by the Anglo-French Eurotunnel Consortium. Construction of a high-speed railway line between Paris and the tunnel is due for completion by 1993: the line is to form the main artery of a high-speed rail network serving Belgium, the Netherlands, Germany and France.

Société Nationale des Chemins de fer Français (SNCF): 88 rue Saint Lazare, 75436 Paris Cedex 09; tel. (1) 42-85-60-00; telex 290936; f. 1937; formerly 51% state-owned, wholly nationalized Jan. 1983; Dir-Gen. JEAN COSTET; Pres. JACQUES FOURNIER.

Metropolitan Railways

Régie Autonome des Transports Parisiens (RATP): 53 ter quai des Grands Augustins, BP 70-06, 75271 Paris Cedex 06; tel. (1) 40-46-41-41; telex 200000; f. 1948; state-owned; operates the Paris underground and suburban railways, and buses; Chair. CHRISTIAN BLANC; Gen. Man. (vacant).

Three provincial cities also have underground railway systems: Marseille (first section opened 1977), Lyon and Lille.

ROADS

At 31 December 1989 there were 6,950 km of motorways (autoroutes). There are also about 28,500 km of national roads (routes nationales), 350,000 km of secondary roads, 420,000 km of other urban roads and 700,000 km of rural roads. In 1987 the Government

FRANCE

introduced a programme to construct 2,700 km of motorways by 1995, which would be partly financed by 2,000m. francs of receipts from the privatization programme.

Fédération Nationale des Transports Routiers (FNTR): 6 rue Paul Valéry, 75116 Paris; tel. (1) 45-63-16-00; road transport; Chair. MAURICE VOIRON.

INLAND WATERWAYS

In 1987 there were 8,500 km of navigable waterways, of which 1,647 km were accessible to craft of 3,000 tons. In 1987 the Government initiated a programme, with a projected cost of 2,800m. francs, to modernize navigable waterways and construct a canal linking the Rivers Rhône and Rhine.

SHIPPING

At 30 June 1989 the French merchant shipping fleet (921 vessels) had a total displacement of 4,413,464 grt. In 1965 control of the six major seaports (Marseille, Le Havre, Dunkerque, Rouen, Nantes–Saint-Nazaire and Bordeaux) was transferred from the State to autonomous authorities. The State retains supervisory powers. An independent consultative body, the Conseil National des Communautés Portuaires, was established in 1987 as a co-ordinating organization for ports and port authorities.

Conseil National des Communautés Portuaires: f. 1987; central independent consultative body for ports and port authorities; over 50 mems including 10 trade union mems; Pres. JACQUES DUPUY-DAUBY.

Principal Shipping Companies

CETRAMAR, Consortium Européen de Transports Maritimes: 87 ave de la Grande Armée, 75782 Paris Cedex 16; tel. (1) 40-66-11-11; telex 611234; fax (1) 45-00-23-97; tramping; Man. Dir ANDRÉ MAIRE; displacement 149,021 grt.

Chargeurs Delmas: Tour Franklin, Cedex 11, 92081 Paris La Défense; tel. (1) 49-02-49-02; telex 62005; fax (1) 47-76-41-31; f. 1964; services between Asia and West Africa, Europe and southern Africa, Mediterranean and West Indies (French Guiana); Chair. T. VIELJEUX; displacement 154,483 grt.

Compagnie de Navigation: 93–95 rue de Provence, 75009 Paris; tel. (1) 49-95-94-98; telex 282534; fax (1) 49-95-95-01; Chair. PIERRE DE DEMANDOLX-DEDONS.

Compagnie Générale Maritime et Financière: 22 quai Galliéni, 92158 Suresnes Cedex; tel. (1) 46-25-70-00; telex 630387; f. 1976 from merger of Compagnie Générale Transatlantique and Compagnie des Messageries Maritimes; holding co. Compagnie Générale Maritime et Financière (CGMF); 99.9% state-owned; freight services to USA, Canada, West Indies, Central and South America, Northern Europe, USSR, the Middle East, India, Australia, New Zealand, Indonesia and other Pacific and Indian Ocean areas; Chair. CLAUDE ABRAHAM; capacity of fleet 1,160,000 dwt.

Compagnie Nationale de Navigation: 50 blvd Haussmann, 75441 Paris Cedex 09; tel. (1) 42-85-19-00; telex 290673; fax (1) 42-81-20-37; f. 1930 as Compagnie Navale Worms; merged with Compagnie Nationale de Navigation and Société Française de Transports Maritimes, and changed name to Compagnie Nationale de Navigation in 1986; holding co. with subsidiaries: Société Française de Transports Pétroliers, Cie Morbihannaise de Navigation, Feronia International Shipping (FISH) and other subsidiaries abroad; Pres. and Dir-Gen. GILLES BOUTHILLIER; Dir-Gen. PIERRE DE DEMANDOLX.

Esso SAF: 6 ave André Prothin, 92093 Paris la Défense Cedex 2; tel. (1) 43-34-60-00; telex 620031; fax (1) 43-41-17-01; ocean-going tankers; Chair. M. KOPFF; Marine Man. A. CALVARIN; fleet of 4 cargo carriers (1m. grt) and 2 coasters.

Gazocéan: Tour Fiat, 1 place de la Coupole, 92084 Paris la Défense Cedex 16; tel. (1) 47-96-60-60; telex 615234; fax (1) 47-96-60-93; f. 1957; fleet with a capacity of about 115,000 cu m of liquefied gas; world-wide gas sea transportation; Chair. GÉRARD PIKETTY.

Louis-Dreyfus et Cie: 87 ave de la Grande Armée, 75782 Paris Cedex 16; tel. (1) 40-66-11-11; telex 611234; fax (1) 45-00-23-97; tramping; Chair. C. BOQUIN; Man. Dir P. D'ORSAY; displacement of fleet 630,000 grt.

Mobil Oil Française: Tour Septentrion, 92081 Paris la Défense Cedex 09; tel. (1) 47-73-42-41; telex 610412; bulk petroleum transport; refining and marketing of petroleum products; Chair. GEORGES DUPASQUIER.

Nouvelle Compagnie de Paquebots: Marseille; tel. 91-91-91-21; telex 440003; f. 1965; cap. 10,229,100 Frs; passenger cruise services; Chair. and Man. Dir BERNARD MAURIAC; displacement 27,658 grt.

Sealink Voyages: 23 rue Louis le Grand, 75002 Paris; tel. (1) 47-42-86-87; telex 281710; fax (1) 42-65-10-17; cross-Channel passenger, accompanied motorcar, freight and roll on/roll off on train-ferries and car-ferries; Pres. M. BONNET; displacement 45,000 grt.

Société Maritime des Pétroles BP et Cie: 10 quai Paul Doumer, 92412 Courbevoie Cedex; tel. (1) 47-68-40-00; telex 630546; fax (1) 47-68-37-25; oil tankers; Man. Dir PHILIPPE VALOIS; capacity of fleet 539,632 dwt.

Société Maritime Shell: 29 rue de Berri, 75397 Paris Cedex 08; tel. (1) 45-61-82-82; telex 644487; fax (1) 45-61-75-36; oil tankers; Man. Dir P. SESBOUÉ.

Société Nationale Maritime Corse-Méditerranée: 61 blvd des Dames, 13002 Marseille; tel. 91-56-32-00; telex 440068; passenger and roll on/roll off ferry services between France and Corsica, Sardinia, North Africa; Pres. J. RIBIÈRE; Man. Dir J. P. ISOARD; 13 vessels.

Société Navale Caennaise: 58 ave Pierre Berthelot, BP 6183, 14061 Caen Cedex; tel. 31-82-21-76; telex 170122; fax (1) 42-65-95-05; f. 1901; regular lines; Chair. JEAN-MICHEL BLANCHARD; Man. Dir Y. LENEGRE; displacement 43,501 grt.

Société Navale et Commerciale Delmas-Vieljeux: 16 ave Matignon, 75008 Paris; tel. (1) 42-56-44-33; telex 290354; f. 1867; cargo service from North and South European ports to West and North Africa; Chair. TRISTAN VIELJEUX; Vice-Pres. PATRICE VIELJEUX; capacity of fleet 444,114 dwt.

Soflumar Van Ommeren France: 5 ave Percier, 75008 Paris; tel. (1) 45-62-50-50; telex 650252; coastal tankers and tramping; Chair. F. VALLAT; Man. Dir P. DECAVELE; displacement 120,718 grt.

Total Compagnie Française de Navigation: Tour Mirabeau, 39–43 quai André Citroen, 75739 Paris Cedex 15; tel. (1) 45-78-33-33; telex 201604; fax (1) 45-78-30-30; f. 1931; cap. 120m. Frs; oil tankers; Chair. PHILIPPE GUERIN; capacity of fleet 117,947,000 dwt.

CIVIL AVIATION

There are international airports at Orly, Roissy and Le Bourget (Paris), Bordeaux, Lille, Lyon, Marseille, Nice, Strasbourg and Toulouse.

National Airlines

Air France: 1 sq Max Hymans, 75757 Paris Cedex 15; tel. (1) 43-23-81-81; telex 200666; fax (1) 43-23-92-79; f. 1933; international, European and inter-continental services; flights to Africa, Madagascar, Americas, Middle and Far East and West Indies; Chair. BERNARD ATTALI; Pres. JEAN-DIDIER BLANCHET; fleet (1990) 7 Concorde, 27 Boeing 747, 16 Boeing 737, 15 Airbus A300, 18 Boeing 727, 9 Airbus A310, 12 Airbus A320, 9 Boeing 747 Cargo.

Air Inter: 1 ave du Maréchal Devaux, 91550 Paray Vieille Poste; tel. (1) 46-75-12-12; telex 265952; fax (1) 46-75-12-22; f. 1954; operates internal services within metropolitan France; Air France Group (Air France and UTA) and the SNCF are the part owners; Chair and Man. Dir JEAN-CYRIL SPINETTA; fleet of 22 Airbus A300, 14 Airbus A320, 11 Mercure, 8 Super 12.

Private Airlines

Union de Transports Aériens (UTA): 3 blvd Malesherbes, 75008 Paris; tel. (1) 42-66-30-30; telex 610692; fax (1) 42-68-46-25; f. 1963; services to West and South Africa, Middle and Far East, Australia, New Caledonia, New Zealand, Japan, Tahiti, Guadeloupe, Martinique and the west coast of Africa; 54.6% stake purchased by Air France, Jan. 1990; Chair. BERNARD ATTALI; Vice-Pres. DANIEL-CHARLES RICHON; fleet of 4 Boeing 747-300, 1 Boeing 747-200F, 1 Boeing 747-400, 6 DC 10-30.

About 20 small private companies provide regional air services. Small private airlines flying services outside France include:

Euralair: 93350 Aéroport du Bourget, Paris; tel. (1) 49-34-62-00; telex 235688; fax 49-34-63-00; f. 1964; Chair. ALEXANDRE COUVELAIRE; fleet of 6 Boeing 737-200, 2 BAe 146, 2 Citation I, 2 Citation II, 1 Citation III, 2 Citation V, 2 Dassult Falcon 10, 2 Falcon 20.

Europe Aéro Service SA: Aérodrome de Perpignan-Rivesaltes, 66028 Perpignan; telex 500084; f. 1965; internal passenger and cargo services and services to Spain; Chair. GEORGES MASUREL; fleet of 11 Caravelle 10B, 2 Boeing 727-200, 3 Boeing 737-200, 1 Saab 340.

Transport Aérien Transrégional (TAT): Aérogare Civile, BP 0237, 37100 Tours Cedex; tel. 47-54-21-45; telex 750876; fax 47-54-29-50; f. 1968; took over Air Alpes 1981; took over Air Alsace routes following its demise in 1982; Chair. and Man. Dir MICHEL MARCHAIS; fleet of 7 Fokker F.28-1000, 4 F.28-2000, 5 F.28-4000, 14 Fairchild FH-227B, 2 Fairchild F.27A, 2 ATR 42-300, 5 Twin Otter, 3 Beech 99, 3 Metro, 1 Nord 262.

Airlines Association

Chambre Syndicale du Transport Aérien (CSTA): 43 blvd Malesherbes, 75008 Paris; tel. (1) 47-42-11-00; telex 281491; f. 1946 to represent French airlines at national level; Chair. ALEXANDRE COUVELAIRE; Delegate-Gen. JEAN-LOUIS GASCHET; 17 mems.

Tourism

France draws tourists from all over the world. Paris is famous for its boulevards, historic buildings, theatres, art treasures, fashion houses and restaurants, and for its many music halls and night clubs. The Mediterranean and Atlantic coasts and the French Alps are the most popular tourist resorts. Among other attractions are the many ancient towns, the châteaux of the Loire, the fishing villages of Brittany and Normandy, and spas and places of pilgrimage, such as Vichy and Lourdes. There were 38,288,000 tourist arrivals in 1988, when tourist receipts totalled 82,097m. francs. Most visitors are from the Federal Republic of Germany, Belgium, the United Kingdom, the Netherlands and Switzerland.

Ministère du Tourisme: 11 ave d'Iéna, 75007 Paris; fax (1) 45-56-36-36; Minister Delegate for Tourism JEAN-MICHEL BAYLET.

 Direction des Industries Touristiques: 2 rue Linois, 75740 Paris Cedex 15; tel. (1) 45-75-62-16; telex 870974; fax (1) 45-79-90-20; Dir JEAN-LUC MICHAUD.

 Maison de la France: 8 ave de l'Opéra, Paris; tel. (1) 42-96-10-23; Pres. JEAN MARC JANAILLAC.

There are Regional Tourism Committees in the 23 regions and 4 overseas départements. There are over 3,200 Offices de Tourisme and Syndicats d'Initiative (tourist offices run by the local authorities) throughout France.

Atomic Energy

In 1989 France had 55 nuclear reactors in operation, with a total generating capacity of 52,863 MW.

Commissariat à l'Energie Atomique (CEA) (Atomic Energy Commissariat): 31–33 rue de la Fédération, 75752 Paris Cedex 15; tel. (1) 40-56-10-00; telex 200671; fax (1) 40-56-25-38; f. 1945; Gen. Administrator PHILIPPE ROUVILLOIS; High Commissioner JEAN TEILLAC; Sec.-Gen. JEAN MARMOT.

The CEA is an establishment of scientific, industrial and technological character. Its function is to promote the uses of nuclear energy in science, industry and national defence; the fields in which it is active, either directly or through its own subsidiaries and participation in private companies, are: production of nuclear materials; reactor development; fundamental research; innovation and transfer of technologies; military applications; bio-technologies; robotics; electronics; new materials; radiological protection and nuclear safety.

Administration is the responsibility of a 15-member Comité de l'Energie Atomique (Atomic Energy Committee), presided over by the Prime Minister and consisting of government officials and representatives of sciences and industry.

Institutes and Administrative Bodies:

 Direction des Applications Militaires (Military Applications Division): Dir ROGER BALERAS.

 Direction des Sciences de la Matière: CEN de Saclay, 91191 Gif-sur-Yvette Cedex; tel. (1) 69-08-75-15; fax (1) 69-08-38-16; Dir ROBERT AYMAR.

 Groupe ORIS: BP 6, 91192 Gif-sur-Yvette Cedex; tel. 69-85-70-70; telex 692431; fax 69-85-70-71; f. 1985, fmrly Compagnie ORIS Industrie; Pres. and Dir-Gen. YVES LE GALLIC.

 Institut de Protection et de Sûreté Nucléaire (Institute for Nuclear Protection and Security): CEN/Fontenay-aux-Roses, BP 6, 92260 Fontenay-aux-Roses; Dir FRANÇOIS COGNE.

 Institut de Recherche Technologique et de Développement Industriel (Institute of Technological Research and Industrial Development): Centre d'Etudes Nucléaires de Saclay, 91191 Gif-sur-Yvette Cedex; tel. (1) 69-08-66-16; telex 604641; fax (1) 69-08-79-85; Dir JEAN CHATOUX.

 Agence Nationale pour la Gestion des Déchets Radioactifs: 31–33 rue de la Fédération, 75752 Paris Cedex 15; tel. (1) 40-56-15-15; Dir FRANÇOIS CHENEVIER.

 Institut National des Sciences et Techniques Nucléaires (National Institute of Nuclear Science and Technology): CEN Saclay-INSTN, 91191 Gif-sur-Yvette Cedex; tel. (1) 69-08-63-14; telex 604641; fax (1) 69-08-79-93; f. 1956; Dir. Y. CHELET.

Research Centres:

 Centre d'Etudes Nucléaires de Cadarache (CEN-Ca) (Cadarache Nuclear Research Centre): 13108 Saint-Paul-les-Durance Cedex, Bouches-du-Rhône; tel. 42-25-70-00; telex 440678; f. 1960; Dir GÉRARD VIAL.

 Centre d'Etudes Nucléaires de Fontenay-aux-Roses (Fontenay-aux-Roses Nuclear Research Centre): BP 6, 92265 Fontenay-aux-Roses Cedex; tel. (1) 46-54-70-80; f. 1945; Dir YVES MARTIN.

 Centre d'Etudes Nucléaires de Grenoble (CEN-G) (Grenoble Nuclear Research Centre): BP 85X, 38041 Grenoble Cedex; tel. 76-88-44-00; telex 320323; fax 76-88-51-75; f. 1955; 40 laboratories; Dir FRANCIS DECOOL.

 Centre d'Etudes Nucléaires de Saclay (CENS) (Saclay Nuclear Research Centre): 91191 Gif-sur-Yvette Cedex; tel. 69-08-60-00; telex 604641; f. 1949; Dir JEAN BAZIN.

 Centre d'Etudes Nucléaires de la Vallée du Rhône (CEN-VALRHO): BP 171, 30205 Bagnols-sur-Cèze Cedex; tel. 66-79-60-00; telex 480816; Dir ALBERT TEBOUL.

 Société des Participations du CEA: CEA-Industrie: 31–33 rue de la Fédération, 75752 Paris Cedex 15; tel. (1) 40-56-10-00; telex 200671; fax (1) 42-73-32-77; principal affiliates CISI, COGEMA, FRAMATOME, TECHNICATOME, Groupe ORIS, INTER-CONTROLE STMI, etc.; Pres. PHILIPPE ROUVILLOIS; Dir-Gen. ACHILLE FERRARI.

Centre National de la Recherche Scientifique (CNRS): 15 quai Anatole France, 75700 Paris; tel. (1) 47-53-15-15; telex 260-034; fax (1) 45-51-73-07; there are nuclear research centres attached to this institution in Strasbourg, Grenoble and Orsay.

 Groupe de Laboratoires de Strasbourg-Cronenbourg: rue du Loess, BP 20 CRO, 67037 Strasbourg Cedex; tel. 88-28-63-00; telex 890032; fax 88-28-09-90; f. 1957; Dirs P. DEJOURS, C. GAILLARD, A. MUZET, R. SELTZ, G. VINCENDON.

FRENCH OVERSEAS POSSESSIONS

Ministry of Overseas Departments and Territories: rue Oudinot 27, 75700 Paris, France; tel. 47-83-01-23.
Minister: Louis Le Pensec.

The national flag of France, proportions three by two, with three equal vertical stripes, of blue, white and red, is used in the Overseas Possessions.

French Overseas Departments

The four Overseas Departments (départements d'outre-mer) are French Guiana, Guadeloupe, Martinique and Réunion. They are integral parts of the French Republic. Each Overseas Department is administered by a Prefect, appointed by the French Government, and the administrative structure is similar to that of the Departments of metropolitan France. Overseas Departments, however, have their own Courts of Appeal. In 1974 each of the Overseas Departments was granted the additional status of a region (a unit devised for the purpose of economic and social planning, presided over by a Regional Council). Under the decentralization law of March 1982, the executive power of the Prefect in each Overseas Department was transferred to the locally-elected General Council. A proposal to replace the General Council and the indirectly-elected Regional Council by a single assembly was rejected by the French Constitutional Council in December 1982. As a compromise between autonomy and complete assimilation into France, the Regional Councils' responsibility for economic, social and cultural affairs was increased in 1983. In February the first direct elections for the Regional Councils were held. The Overseas Departments continue to send elected representatives to the French National Assembly and to the Senate in Paris, and also to the European Parliament in Strasbourg.

FRENCH GUIANA

Introductory Survey

Location, Climate, Language, Religion, Capital
French Guiana (Guyane) lies on the north coast of South America, with Suriname to the west and Brazil to the south and east. The climate is humid, with a season of heavy rains from April to July and another short rainy season in December and January. Average temperature at sea-level is 27°C (85°F), with little seasonal variation. French is the official language but a creole patois is also spoken. The majority of the population belong to the Roman Catholic Church, although other Christian churches are represented. The capital is Cayenne.

Recent History
French occupation commenced in the early 17th century. After brief periods of Dutch, English and Portuguese rule, the territory was finally confirmed as French in 1817. The colony steadily declined, after a short period of prosperity in the 1850s as a result of the discovery of gold in the basin of the Approuague river. French Guiana, including the notorious Devil's Island, was used as a penal colony, and as a place of exile for convicts and political prisoners, before the practice was stopped in 1937. The colony became a department of France in 1946.

French Guiana's reputation as an area of political and economic stagnation was dispelled by the growth of pro-independence sentiments, and the use of violence by a small minority, compounded by tensions between the Guyanais and large numbers of immigrant workers. In 1974 French Guiana was granted regional status, as part of France's governmental reorganization, thus acquiring greater economic autonomy. In that year, however, demonstrations against unemployment, the worsening economic situation, and French government policy with regard to the department, led to the detention of leading trade unionists and pro-independence politicians. In 1975 the French Government announced plans to improve the economic situation by increasing investment in French Guiana. However, these were unsuccessful, owing partly to the problems of developing French Guiana's interior. As a result of industrial and political unrest in the late 1970s, there were demands for greater autonomy for the department by the Parti Socialiste Guyanais (PSG), the strongest political party. In 1980 there were several bomb attacks against 'colonialist' targets by an extremist group known as Fo nou Libéré la Guyane (FNLG). Reforms, introduced by the French Socialist Government in 1982 and 1983, devolved some power over local affairs to a new Regional Council. The French Government, however, refused to countenance any change in French Guiana's departmental status.

In the February 1983 elections to the Regional Council, the left-wing parties gained a majority of votes, but not of seats, and the balance of power was held by the separatist Union des Travailleurs Guyanais (UTG), which was restyled the Parti National Populaire Guyanais (PNPG) in November 1985. In May 1983 French Guiana was the target for bombings by the Alliance Révolutionnaire Caraïbe (ARC), an extremist independence movement based in Guadeloupe, another French Overseas Department in the West Indies. At elections to the General Council, held in March 1985, the PSG and left-wing independents succeeded in increasing their representation to 13 seats out of a total of 19.

For the general election to the French National Assembly in March 1986, French Guiana's representation was increased from one to two deputies. The incumbent deputy, a member of the PSG, received 48.1% of the total votes (voting at this election being based on a system of proportional representation), and was re-elected. The other seat was won by the right-wing Rassemblement pour la République (RPR). On the same day as the elections to the Assembly, direct elections were held for the 31 seats on the Regional Council. The PSG, with 42.1% of the votes, increased its strength on the Council from 14 to 15 members, and Georges Othily of the PSG was re-elected President of the Council. The RPR won nine seats, and the centrist Union pour la Démocratie Française (UDF) three, while four seats were secured by Action Démocratique Guyanaise.

A French presidential election was held in April and May 1988. Of the votes cast in French Guiana, the incumbent President Mitterrand of the Parti Socialiste (PS) obtained 52% in the first round, and 60% in the second round against Jacques Chirac of the RPR. Nevertheless, in the legislative elections held in June (when the former constituency system was reintroduced), the RPR succeeded in retaining one of the two seats in the National Assembly in Paris. In September–October the left-wing parties consolidated their control of local government by winning 14 of the 19 seats at elections to the General Council.

In March 1989 municipal elections were held. The left-wing parties were victorious in 13 of the 20 municipalities, including Cayenne. At elections to the European Parliament in June, the centre-right UDF-RPR alliance was the most successful grouping. The abstention rate, however, was estimated at 88.5%.

In September 1989 Georges Othily, the President of the Regional Council, was elected to take French Guiana's one seat in the French Senate. In June Othily had been expelled from the PSG for having worked too closely with the opposition parties. However, he attracted support from those who regarded the party's domination of French Guiana as corrupt. Thus, his victory over the incumbent senator, a PSG member, was believed to reflect the level of dissatisfaction within the party.

In January 1990 a commission, appointed by the Minister of Overseas Departments and Territories, published its report on the question of social equality with metropolitan France and economic development in the four departments. The report contained 50 proposals for the rectification of social and economic shortcomings in the departments, and recommended a development programme of two three-year stages.

In 1986-87 French Guiana's relations with neighbouring Suriname deteriorated as increasing numbers of Surinamese refugees fled across the border to escape rebel uprisings in their own country. In late 1986 additional French troops were brought in to patrol the border, as a result of which the Surinamese Government accused the French Government of preparing an invasion of Suriname via French Guiana. It was also reported that Surinamese rebels were using French Guiana as a conduit for weapons and supplies. By 1989, according to official estimates, the number of Surinamese refugees in French Guiana was about 7,000. In the same year there was an escalation in violent crime, which was generally attributed to the immigrant and refugee population. In August a 24-hour strike, in protest against the high rate of crime, was called by the Chamber of Commerce. The strike was widely supported by trade unions and business proprietors alike. In response to demands for more effective policing, the French Government dispatched 100 riot police from France as reinforcements for the department's regular police.

Government

France is represented in French Guiana by an appointed Prefect. There are two Councils with local powers: the General Council, with 19 members, and the Regional Council, with 31 members. Both are elected by universal adult suffrage for a period of six years. French Guiana elects two representatives to the French National Assembly in Paris, and sends one elected representative to the French Senate. French Guiana is also represented at the European Parliament in Strasbourg.

Defence

In 1990 France maintained a military force of about 8,800 in French Guiana and the Antilles.

Economic Affairs

The economy of French Guiana is heavily dependent on France for budgetary aid and imports of food and manufactured goods. In 1986, according to estimates by the UN, the gross domestic product (GDP), measured at current prices, was US $231m., equivalent to $2,718 per head. Between 1980 and 1986, it was estimated, GDP declined, in real terms, at an average rate of 0.6% per year, and GDP per head declined by 2.8% annually. In 1980-88 the population increased by an annual average of 3.3%.

Local production is mainly in the agricultural sector, particularly forestry and fisheries. In 1989 exports of fisheries products (particularly shrimps) provided about 60% of total export earnings. Tropical forests covered 90% of the territory in the late 1980s, and in 1987 exports of cork and wood provided 7.3% of export earnings. The prinicpal crops for local consumption are cassava, vegetables and rice; production of rice and pineapples for export expanded in 1988 and 1989, but production of sugar cane (for making rum) declined by 80% in 1983-88. Cattle, pigs and poultry are the principal livestock.

Gold (which provided 7.6% of export earnings in 1987) and crushed rock for the construction industry are the only minerals extracted in significant quantities, although deposits of bauxite and kaolin are present.

There is little manufacturing activity, except for the processing of fisheries products (mainly shrimp-freezing) and the distillation of rum.

Energy is derived principally from petroleum. In 1987 petroleum and petroleum products represented 9.7% of expenditure on imports. A barrage on the River Sinnamary, for hydroelectric power production, was expected to be operational in 1994, and was to provide twice the territory's energy requirements (at 1989 levels).

The tourist sector expanded during the 1980s, but improvements are needed in transport and hotel facilities if tourism is to become more than a secondary activity.

In 1988 French Guiana recorded a trade deficit of $456m. In 1987 the principal source of imports was France (62.1%), which was also the principal market for exports (33.8%). Other major trading partners were the Federal Republic of Germany, Japan and the USA. The principal imports were food and live animals, petroleum, chemicals, machinery and transport equipment and manufactured articles. The principal exports were fish and fish preparations, gold, rice and wood.

By September 1988 French Guiana's external debt had reached $1,200m. The annual rate of inflation averaged 8.0% during 1980-88 and 4.0% in 1989. The rate was 3.3% in the year to August 1990. In 1989 the average rate of unemployment was 12.2%, but there was a shortage of skilled labour, offset partly by immigration.

As an integral part of France, French Guiana belongs to the European Community, and was to receive 73m. ECUs in Community aid during the period 1989-93, in order to adapt to the requirements of the single European market, due to become operational in 1992.

Despite its potential for forestry, fisheries and tourism, the development of French Guiana's economy has been hindered by a lack of infrastructure and of skilled labour, although the European Space Agency's satellite-launching centre at Kourou (established in 1964 and to be expanded during the 1990s) has stimulated the economy. In 1989 the French Government agreed to provide 377.5m. French francs during the period 1989-93 to fulfil a programme for economic development over five years. The aim was to improve the economic, social and cultural conditions of the department through training, research, job creation and regional planning.

Social Welfare

In 1986 there were two hospitals (with a total of 611 beds in 1984), a health centre and two private clinics. The Institut Pasteur undertakes research into malaria and other tropical diseases. There is a system of social security similar to the French model. In 1987 there were 237 physicians working in French Guiana.

Education

Education is modelled on the French system, and is compulsory for 10 years between the ages of six and 16 years. Primary education begins at six years of age and lasts for five years. Secondary education, beginning at 11 years of age, lasts for up to seven years, comprising a first cycle of four years and a second of three years. Education at state schools is provided free of charge. Between 1974 and 1986 the number of children attending primary schools increased from 6,465 to 16,916 (including 1,711 pupils at six private schools). Over the same period, the total enrolment at secondary (including technical) schools rose from 5,251 to 10,429. This expansion placed a strain on the education system: new schools were to be built in 1989-93. Higher education in law and administration is provided by a branch of the Université Antilles-Guyane in Cayenne, and one department of a technical institute opened at Kourou in 1988. There is also a teacher-training college and an agricultural college.

Public Holidays

1991: 1 January (New Year's Day), 12-13 February (Lenten Carnival), 29 March-1 April (Easter), 1 May (Labour Day), 9 May (Ascension Day), 20 May (Whit Monday), 14 July (National Day), 11 November (Armistice Day), 25 December (Christmas Day).

1992: 1 January (New Year's Day), 3-4 March (Lenten Carnival), 17-20 April (Easter), 1 May (Labour Day), 28 May (Ascension Day), 8 June (Whit Monday), 14 July (National Day), 11 November (Armistice Day), 25 December (Christmas Day).

Weights and Measures

The metric system is in use.

Statistical Survey

Sources (unless otherwise stated): Institut national de la statistique et des études économiques, 1 rue Maillard, 97306 Cayenne; tel. 31-5603; telex 910344; Service de Presse et d'Information, Ministère des départements et territoires d'outre-mer, 27 rue Oudinot, 75700 Paris; tel (1) 47-83-0123.

AREA AND POPULATION

Area: 90,000 sq km (34,750 sq miles).

Population: 73,012 (males 38,448; females 34,564) at census of 9 March 1982; 114,600 (census of 15 March 1990); *Capital:* Cayenne, population 41,637 (1990). *Other towns:* Kourou 13,963; Saint-Laurent-du-Maroni 13,893.

Births and Deaths (1989): Registered live births 3,178 (provisional birth rate 33.5 per 1,000); Registered deaths 527 (provisional death rate 5.5 per 1,000). Figures exclude live-born infants dying before registration of birth.

Economically Active Population (persons aged 16 years and over, 1982 census): Agriculture, hunting, forestry and fishing 3,706; Mining and quarrying 163; Manufacturing 1,359; Electricity, gas and water 380; Construction 2,837; Trade, restaurants and hotels 2,025; Transport, storage and communications 1,347; Financing, insurance, real estate and business services 3,662; Community, social and personal services 8,931; Activities not adequately defined 2,013; Total civilians employed 26,423 (males 17,205, females 9,218); Unemployed 4,760 (males 2,389, females 2,371); Armed Forces 1,192 (all males); Total labour force 32,375 (males 20,786, females 11,589).

FRENCH OVERSEAS DEPARTMENTS

AGRICULTURE, ETC.

Principal Crops (metric tons, 1988): Sugar cane 2,500, Cassava (Manioc) and other tubers 13,358, Rice (paddy) 14,325.

Livestock (1988): Cattle 14,450, Pigs 8,000, Goats and sheep 3,200, Poultry 117,000.

Livestock Products (metric tons, unless otherwise indicated, 1988): Beef 380, Pork 750, Poultry meat 536, Cows' milk 5,900 hl, Eggs 4,000,000 (number).

Forestry ('000 cu m, 1989): Sawlogs 80.2, Sawnwood 85.5.

Fishing (landings in metric tons, 1989): Fish 3,120, Shrimps 4,319; Total 7,439.

MINING

Production (1989): Gold 544 kg. Source: Le Secrétariat du Comité Monétaire de la Zone Franc: *La Zone Franc, Rapport 1989*.

INDUSTRY

Production (1988): Rum 756 hl, Electricity 268 million kWh.

FINANCE

Currency and Exchange Rates: 100 centimes = 1 French franc. *Coins:* 5, 10, 20 and 50 centimes; 1, 2, 5 and 10 francs. *Notes:* 20, 50, 100, 200 and 500 francs. *Sterling and Dollar Equivalents* (30 September 1990): £1 sterling = 9.8225 francs; US $1 = 5.2425 francs; 1,000 French francs = £101.81 = $190.75. *Average Exchange Rate* (French francs per US dollar): 6.011 in 1987; 5.957 in 1988; 6.380 in 1989.

Budget (estimates, 1990): Revenue and expenditure to balance at 566 million francs. Source: *La Zone Franc, Rapport 1989*.

Expenditure by Metropolitan France (1988): 1,578 million francs.

Cost of Living (Consumer Price Index for Cayenne; base: 1980 = 100): 181.2 in 1987; 185.3 in 1988; 192.7 in 1989.

Gross Domestic Product (million francs at current prices): 2,232.6 in 1984; 2,595.4 in 1985; 3,035.0 (provisional) in 1986.

EXTERNAL TRADE

Principal Commodities (US $ million, 1987): *Imports c.i.f.:* Food and live animals 65.8 (Meat and meat preparations 16.3); Beverages and tobacco 20.1 (Beverages 17.7); Petroleum and petroleum products 38.4 (Refined petroleum products 37.8); Chemicals and related products 23.3; Basic manufactures 57.7; Machinery and transport equipment 125.9 (General industrial machinery, equipment and parts 16.8; Electrical machinery, apparatus, etc. 36.6; (Road vehicles and parts 43.2); Miscellaneous manufactured articles 54.9; Total (incl. others) 394.4. *Exports f.o.b.:* Fish and fish preparations 33.4 (Fresh and frozen shellfish 31.1); Rice (milled) 3.4; Cork and wood 3.9 (Non-coniferous lumber 3.7); Machinery and transport equipment 3.0; Non-monetary gold 4.1; Total (incl. others) 53.8.

Principal Trading Partners (US $ million, 1987): *Imports c.i.f.:* France 245.1; Federal Republic of Germany 13.5; Italy 12.8; Japan 12.6; Trinidad and Tobago 36.8; USA 17.0; Total (incl. others) 394.4. *Exports f.o.b.:* France 16.8; Guadeloupe 7.7; Japan 5.8; Martinique 5.5; USA 11.8; Total (incl. others) 49.7.

Source: UN, *International Trade Statistics Yearbook*.

1988 (million francs): Imports c.i.f. 3,038; Exports f.o.b. 306. Source: UN, *Monthly Bulletin of Statistics*.

TRANSPORT

Road Traffic (vehicles in use, 31 December 1986): Passenger cars 27,010; Buses and coaches 1,120; Goods vehicles 7,208. Source: IRF, *World Road Statistics*.

International Sea-borne Shipping (freight traffic, '000 metric tons, 1988): Goods loaded 65; Goods unloaded 457.

Civil Aviation (1989): Freight carried 6,349 metric tons, Passengers carried 345,134.

EDUCATION

Primary (1988): 73 schools; 16,312 pupils.

Secondary (1988): Secondary and technical schools 20; 9,260 pupils.

Higher (1988): College of Law and Administration (Université Antilles-Guyane) 290 students; Technical institute 25 students.

Directory

The Government
(February 1991)

Prefect: Jean François de Chaunac

President of the General Council: Elie Castor (PSG).

French Guiana

Deputies to the French National Assembly: Elie Castor (PSG), Léon Bertrand (RPR).

Representative to the French Senate: Georges Othily (PSG-Dissident).

REGIONAL COUNCIL

President: Georges Othily (PSG-Dissident).

Election, 16 March 1986

	Votes	%	Seats
PSG	6,704	43.00	15
RPR	4,319	27.69	9
ADG	1,906	12.22	4
UDF	1,390	8.91	3
FN	571	3.66	—
PNPG	533	1.41	—
Others	490	3.14	—
Total	15,913	100.00	31

Political Organizations

Action Démocratique Guyanaise (ADG): Cayenne; Leader André Lecante.

Front National: BP 478, 97384 Kourou Cedex; tel. 32-1034; f. 1984; extreme right-wing; Leader Guy Malon.

Parti National Populaire Guyanais (PNPG): Cayenne; f. 1985; independence party; Leader Claude Robo.

Parti Socialiste Guyanais (PSG): Cité Césaire, Cayenne; f. 1956; Sec.-Gen. Antoine Karam.

*****Rassemblement pour la République (RPR):** 84 ave Léopold Héder, 97300 Cayenne; tel. 31-6660; f. 1946; right-wing (Gaullist); Pres. Paulin Bruné.

*****Union pour la Démocratie Française (UDF):** 111 bis rue Christophe Colomb, BP 472, 97331 Cayenne; tel. 31-1710; f. 1979; centrist; Leader Claude Ho A Chuck.

* The RPR and the UDF allied to contest the 1988 legislative elections as the Union du Rassemblement du Centre (URC).

Judicial System

See: Judicial System, Martinique.

Religion

The majority of the population belong to the Roman Catholic Church.

CHRISTIANITY

The Roman Catholic Church

French Guiana comprises the single diocese of Cayenne, suffragan to the archdiocese of Fort-de-France, Martinique. At 31 December 1989 there were an estimated 75,000 adherents in French Guiana, representing almost 75% of the total population.

Bishop of Cayenne: François-Marie Morvan, Evêché, BP 378, 24 rue Madame-Payé, 97328 Cayenne; tel. 31-0118; fax 30-2033.

The Anglican Communion

Within the Church in the Province of the West Indies, French Guiana forms part of the diocese of Guyana. The Bishop is resident in Georgetown, Guyana.

Other Churches

The Seventh-day Adventists, Evangelist Church, Assembly of God, and Jehovah's Witnesses are also represented.

The Press

France-Guyane: 28 rue Félix Eboué, Cayenne; telex 910552; 2 a week; Dir Luc Germain; circ. 4,000.

La Presse de Guyane: 26 rue Lieutenant Brassé, 97300 Cayenne; daily; Dir Fabien Roubaud; circ. 1,000.

Radio and Television

In 1987 there were an estimated 60,000 radio receivers and 14,000 television receivers in use.

FRENCH OVERSEAS DEPARTMENTS

Cayenne FM: Hôtel PLM Montabo, BP 581, 97334 Cayenne; tel. 31-3938; 120 hours weekly.
Radio-Télévision Française d'Outre-mer (RFO): rue du Dr Devèze, BP 336, 97305 Cayenne; tel. 31-1500; telex 910526; Radio-Guyane Inter: 16 hours broadcasting daily; Téléguyane: 2 channels, 32 hours weekly; Dir Maurice Grimaud.
Radio Antipa: 1 place Schoëlcher, Cayenne; tel. 31-0037; 126 hours weekly.
Radio Nou Men: broadcasts in Creole and Boni.
Radio Tout Moune: route de Montabo, BP 74, Cayenne; tel. 31-8074; 24 hours a day; Dir Hector Jean-Louis.

Finance

(cap. = capital; dep. = deposits; m. = million; frs = French francs; brs = branches)

BANKING
Central Bank
Caisse Centrale de Coopération Economique: 13 rue Louis Blanc, Cayenne; tel. 31-4133; telex 910570; Dir Hervé Maurice.

Commercial Banks
Banque Française Commerciale: 8 place Palmistes, Cayenne; tel. 30-3577; telex 910559; Dir André Gerolimatos; 2 brs.
Banque Nationale de Paris-Guyane (BNP Guyane): 2 place Victor Schoëlcher, BP 35, Cayenne; tel. 30-3866; telex 910522; f. 1855; cap. 50m. frs, res 56.7m. frs, dep. 1,462.6m. frs (Dec. 1989); Chair. of the Board Jean-Claude Clarac; Dir M. Blondel; 5 brs.
Crédit Populaire Guyanais: Caisse de Crédit Mutuel, 93 rue Lallouette, BP 818, 97338 Cayenne; tel. 30-1523; Dir Lei-San Eliane.

Development Bank
Société financière de développement de la Guyane (SOFIDEG): 25 rue F. Arago, Cayenne; tel. 30-0418; telex 910556; f. 1982; Dir Patrice Pin.

Trade and Industry

Chambre de Commerce de la Guyane: BP 49, 97321 Cayenne; tel. 30-3000; telex 910537; Pres. Jean-Pierre Prévôt.
Jeune Chambre Economique de Cayenne: 2 bis rue Docteur Saint-Rose, BP 1094, Cayenne; Pres. Madeleine Georges.

TRADE UNIONS
Centrale Démocratique des Travailleurs de la Guyane (CDTG): 113 rue Christophe Colomb, BP 383, Cayenne; tel. 31-0232; Sec.-Gen. René Sydalza.
Fédération de l'Education Nationale: 68 rue Justin Catayee, BP 807, Cayenne; Sec.-Gen. Eliane Niel.
Force Ouvrière (FO): 107 rue Barthélemy, Cayenne; Sec.-Gen. M. Xavero.
Syndicat National des Instituteurs (SNI): Ecole Maximilien Sabas, BP 265, Cayenne; Sec.-Gen. Claude Leonardi.
Union des Travailleurs Guyanais (UTG): 7 ave Ronjon, Cayenne; tel. 31-2642; Sec.-Gen. Paul Cécilien.

Transport

RAILWAYS
There are no railways in French Guiana.

ROADS
In 1989 there were 670 km of roads in French Guiana, of which 304 km were main roads.

SHIPPING
Dégrad-des-Cannes, on the estuary of the river Mahury, is the principal port, handling 80% of maritime traffic in 1989. There are other ports at Le Larivot, Saint-Laurent-du-Maroni and Kourou. Saint-Laurent is used primarily for the export of timber, and Larivot for fishing vessels. There are river ports on the Oyapock and on the Approuague. There is a ferry service across the Maroni river between Saint-Laurent and Albina, Suriname. The rivers provide the best means of access to the interior, although numerous rapids prevent navigation by large vessels.

CIVIL AVIATION
Rochambeau International Airport, situated 17.5 km (11 miles) from Cayenne, is equipped to handle the largest jet aircraft. Air Guyane operates internal air services.

Air Guyane: Aéroport de Rochambeau, 97307 Matoury.
Guyane Air Transport (GAT): Aéroport de Rochambeau, 97307 Matoury; tel. 35-6555; telex 910619; f. 1980; Dir-Gen. Guy Malidor.

Tourism

The main attractions are the natural beauty of the tropical scenery and the Amerindian villages of the interior. There were 800 hotel rooms in 1988.

Délégation Régionale au Tourisme pour la Guyane: BP 7008, 97307 Cayenne; tel. 31-8491; telex 910532; fax 30-5222.

GUADELOUPE

Introductory Survey

Location, Climate, Language, Religion, Capital

Guadeloupe is the most northerly of the Windward Islands group in the West Indies. Dominica lies to the south, and Antigua and Montserrat to the north-west. Guadeloupe is formed by two large islands, Grande-Terre and Basse-Terre, separated by a narrow sea channel, with a smaller island, Marie-Galante, to the south-east, and another, La Désirade, to the east. There are also a number of small dependencies, mainly Saint-Barthélemy and the northern half of Saint-Martin (the remainder being part of the Netherlands Antilles), among the Leeward Islands. The climate is tropical, with an average temperature of 26°C (79°F), and a more humid and wet season between June and November. French is the official language, but a creole patois is widely spoken. The majority of the population profess Christianity, and belong to the Roman Catholic Church. The capital is the town of Basse-Terre; the other main town and principal commercial centre is Pointe-à-Pitre on Grande-Terre.

Recent History

Guadeloupe was first occupied by the French in 1635, and has remained French territory, apart from a number of brief occupations by the British in the 18th and early 19th century. It gained departmental status in 1946.

The deterioration of the economy and an increase in unemployment provoked industrial and political unrest during the 1960s and 1970s, including outbreaks of serious rioting in 1967. Pro-independence parties (which had rarely won more than 5% of the total vote at elections in Guadeloupe) resorted, in some cases, to violence as a means of expressing their opposition to the economic and political dominance of white, pro-French landowners and government officials. In 1980 and 1981 there was a series of bomb attacks on hotels, government offices and other targets by a group called the Groupe Libération Armée (GLA), and in 1983 and 1984 there were further bombings by a group called the Alliance Révolutionnaire Caraïbe (ARC). The Government responded by outlawing the ARC and reinforcing the military and police presence on the islands. In 1984, however, the ARC merged with the Mouvement populaire pour une Guadeloupe indépendante (MPGI) in order to continue its campaign. Further sporadic acts of violence continued into 1985, but in October the ARC suspended its bombing campaign, prior to the holding of legislative elections. In November 1986, however, a further series of bomb attacks began. In January 1988 a series of bomb explosions occurred in various parts of the island. Responsibility was claimed by a previously unknown pro-independence group, the Organisation Révolutionnaire Armée.

In 1974 Guadeloupe was granted the status of a region, and an indirectly-elected Regional Council was formed. In direct elections to a new Regional Council in February 1983, held as a result of the decentralization reforms that were introduced by the Socialist Government of President Mitterrand, the centre-right coalition succeeded in gaining a majority of the seats and control of the administration. In January 1984 Lucette Michaux-Chevry, the President of the General Council, formed a new conservative centre party, Le Parti de la Guadeloupe (LPG), which remained in alliance with the right-wing Rassemblement pour la République (RPR). However, at the elections for the General Council, held in March 1985, the left-wing combination of the Parti Socialiste (PS) and the Parti Communiste Guadeloupéen (PCG) gained a majority of seats on the enlarged Council, and Dominique Larifla of the PS was elected its President. In July demonstrations and a general strike, organized by pro-separatist activists in order to obtain the release of a leading member of the MPGI, quickly intensified into civil disorder and rioting in the main town, Pointe-à-Pitre.

For the general election to the French National Assembly in March 1986, Guadeloupe's representation was increased from three to four deputies. The local branches of the RPR and the Union pour la Démocratie Française (UDF), which had campaigned jointly at the 1981 general election and the 1983 regional elections, presented separate candidates (voting for the 1986 election being based on a system of proportional representation). In February 1986 the President of the Regional Council, José Moustache, resigned from the RPR and joined the UDF. The incumbent PCG and PS members of the Assembly were re-elected, but the UDF deputy was not; the two remaining seats were won by RPR candidates (Lucette Michaux-Chevry and Henri Beaujean).

In the concurrent elections for the 41 seats on the Regional Council, the two left-wing parties together received 52.4% of the total votes (compared with 43.1% in 1983) and won a majority of seats, increasing their combined strength from 20 to 22 members (PS 12, PCG 10). As a result, Moustache was replaced as President of the Council by Félix Proto of the PS. The elections were boycotted by the separatist Union Populaire pour la Libération de la Guadeloupe (UPLG). In September 1986 the publication of a report (prepared at Proto's request) criticizing the management of finances by the former RPR/UDF majority on the Regional Council, led by Moustache, caused disruption within the Council and, as expected, had repercussions on the indirect elections for the two Guadeloupe members of the French Senate later in the month: there was a decline in support for centre-right candidates, and, as before, two left-wing Senators were elected (one from the PCG and one from the PS).

At the French presidential elections held in April and May 1988, the incumbent President Mitterrand of the PS received 55% of the votes cast in Guadeloupe in the first round, and 69% in the second round against Jacques Chirac of the RPR. At legislative elections in June, the constituency system was reintroduced. Dominique Larifla of the PS defeated Henri Beaujean of the RPR, while the three other deputies to the National Assembly retained their seats. In September–October the left-wing parties won 26 of the 42 seats at elections to the General Council.

At the municipal elections held in March 1989, the left-wing parties were victorious in 20 municipalities, including Basse-Terre, Pointe-à-Pitre and the principal tourist resorts of Le Gosier and Capesterre-Belle-Eau. The right-wing parties won control in 13 municipalities.

In June 1989 elections to the European Parliament were held, but the level of participation in Guadeloupe was very low, with an abstention rate of 90% being recorded. The grouping of the PS, with 39.2% of the votes cast, was slightly ahead of the UDF-RPR grouping.

In April 1989 the UPLG held protests in Port Louis to demand the release of 'political prisoners', which led to violent clashes with the police. A number of activists of the now disbanded ARC (including its leader, Luc Reinette) went on hunger strike while awaiting trial in Paris, accused in connection with politically-motivated offences in the overseas departments. In the following month the Comité Guadeloupéen de Soutien aux Prisonniers Politiques (COGUASEP) united 11 organizations in demonstrations against the Government. Demands included the release of the prisoners held in France, a rejection of the Single European Act (which aimed to create a unified market within the EEC by 1992) and the granting of a series of social demands. In June 1989 the French National Assembly approved legislation granting an amnesty for crimes that had taken place before July 1988, and that were intended to undermine the authority of the French Republic in the overseas departments. The agreement of those seeking greater independence in Guadeloupe to work within the democratic framework had gained parliamentary support for the amnesty. However, when the freed activists returned to Guadeloupe in July, they advocated increased confrontation with the authorities in order to achieve autonomous rule. In March 1990 the UPLG declared that it would henceforth participate in elections, and would seek associated status for Guadeloupe, rather than full independence.

In January 1990 a commission, appointed by the Minister of Overseas Departments and Territories, published its report on the question of social equality with metropolitan France and economic development in the four departments. The report contained 58 proposals for the rectification of social and economic shortcomings in the departments, and recommended a development programme of two three-year stages.

Government

France is represented in Guadeloupe by an appointed Prefect. There are two councils with local powers: the 42-member General Council and the 41-member Regional Council. Both are elected by universal adult suffrage for a period of up to six years. Guadeloupe elects four deputies to the French National Assembly in Paris, and sends two indirectly-elected representatives to the Senate. The department is also represented at the European Parliament in Strasbourg.

Defence

In 1990 France maintained a military force of about 8,800 in French Guiana and the Antilles.

Economic Affairs

Guadeloupe's economy is based on agriculture, tourism and light industry, but is heavily dependent on French aid and imports. In 1986 the gross domestic product (GDP), measured at current prices, was 10,569m. French francs (about 31,600 francs per head). Over the period 1980–86, according to UN estimates, GDP increased, in real terms, at an average annual rate of 1.3%, but real GDP per head declined by 1.0% per year. Between 1982 and 1990 the population increased by an annual average of 2.1%.

The primary sector (agriculture, forestry and fishing) contributed 11.1% of GDP in 1986. According to the 1982 census, this sector employed 14% of the working population. The principal cash crops are bananas (which accounted for 51.3% of export earnings in 1988), sugar cane and exotic fruits (coconuts, pineapples and melons); yams, sweet potatoes and plantains are the chief subsistence crops. Meat production from cattle, pigs, goats and poultry fulfilled less than 50% of consumer demand in the department in 1989. Fishing, mostly at artisanal level, fulfilled about three-quarters of domestic requirements in 1989; shrimp-farming was developed during the 1980s.

The secondary sector (including manufacturing, construction and power) contributed 15.9% of GDP in 1986, and, according to the 1982 census, employed 18% of the working population. The main industrial activity is food processing, particularly sugar production, rum distillation, and flour-milling. Manufacturing has been slow to develop, despite government efforts to promote this sector.

Tourism superseded sugar production in 1988 as the department's principal source of income. In 1988 there were 328,726 tourist arrivals.

Energy is derived principally from mineral fuels. In 1987 petroleum and petroleum products represented 4.3% of expenditure on imports.

In 1988 Guadeloupe recorded a trade deficit of US $1,049m. In 1987 the principal source of imports (64.5%) was France, which was also the principal market for exports (68.2%). Other major trading partners were the Federal Republic of Germany, Italy, Japan, Martinique, French Guiana and the USA. The principal exports in 1987 were bananas, machinery and transport equipment, wheat flour and distilled alcoholic beverages. The principal imports in 1987 were machinery and transport equipment, foodstuffs, basic manufactures and miscellaneous manufactured articles.

The annual rate of inflation averaged 7.1% in 1980–88 and 2.4% in 1989. The rate was 2.6% in the year to July 1990. An estimated 24% of the labour force were unemployed in 1988.

As an integral part of France, Guadeloupe belongs to the European Community, and was to receive 166m. ECUs in Community aid during the period 1989–93, in order to adapt to the requirements of the single European market, due to become operational in 1992.

The economic activity of Guadeloupe was severely disrupted in September 1989, when Hurricane Hugo struck the islands, causing widespread devastation and leaving some 12,000 people homeless. Banana cultivation and the tourist industry were particularly badly affected. The French Government undertook to provide more than 2,000m. francs for reconstruction, and additional aid for the modernization of the sugar industry.

Social Welfare

In 1986 there was one departmental hospital, eight general hospitals, six maternity hospitals, a psychiatric hospital and a sanatorium. There were also 13 private clinics. In that year there were 451 physicians and 114 dentists working in Guadeloupe. The social security legislation of metropolitan France is applicable in Guadeloupe.

FRENCH OVERSEAS DEPARTMENTS

Education
Education is free and compulsory in state schools between the ages of six and 16 years. The system is similar to that of France, with primary, junior and secondary academic and technical education. Primary education begins at six years of age and lasts for five years. Secondary education, beginning at the age of 11, lasts for up to seven years, comprising a first cycle of four years and a second of three years. Higher education is provided by a branch of the Université Antilles-Guyane, containing faculties of law, economics and science. There is also a teacher-training college. In 1982 the average rate of adult illiteracy was 10.0% (males 10.4%; females 9.6%).

Public Holidays
1991: 1 January (New Year's Day), 11–12 February (Lenten Carnival), 29 March–1 April (Easter), 1 May (Labour Day), 9 May (Ascension Day), 20 May (Whit Monday), 14 July (National Day), 21 July (Victor Schœlcher Day), 11 November (Armistice Day), 25 December (Christmas Day).

1992: 1 January (New Year's Day), 2–3 March (Lenten Carnival), 17–20 April (Easter), 1 May (Labour Day), 28 May (Ascension Day), 8 June (Whit Monday), 14 July (National Day), 21 July (Victor Schœlcher Day), 11 November (Armistice Day), 25 December (Christmas Day).

Weights and Measures
The metric system is in use.

Statistical Survey

Sources (unless otherwise stated): Institut national de la statistique et des études économiques, ave Paul Lacavé, BP 96, 97102 Basse-Terre; tel. 81-4250; Service de Presse et d'Information, Ministère des départements et territoires d'outre-mer, 27 rue Oudinot, 75700 Paris; tel. 47-83-01-23.

AREA AND POPULATION

Area: 1,780 sq km (687.3 sq miles), of which dependencies (La Désirade, Les Saintes, Marie-Galante, Saint-Barthélemy, Saint-Martin) 269 sq km.

Population: 327,002 (males 160,112; females 166,890) at census of 9 March 1982; 386,988 (census of 15 March 1990, preliminary results); *Principal Towns* (population at 1990 census): Les Abymes 62,809; Pointe-à-Pitre 26,083; Basse-Terre (capital) 14,107, Capesterre (1989) 26,500.

Births and Deaths (1988): Registered live births 7,126 (birth rate 21.0 per 1,000); Registered deaths 2,228 (death rate 6.6 per 1,000).

Economically Active Population (persons aged 16 years and over, 1982 census): Agriculture, forestry and fishing 12,997; Manufacturing, mining and quarrying 6,643; Electricity, gas and water 703; Construction 9,997; Wholesale and retail trade 10,062; Transport, storage and communications 4,819; Financing, insurance, real estate and business services 15,109; Community, social and personal services (incl. restaurants and hotels) 26,106; Activities not adequately defined 5,963; Total employed 92,399 (males 54,529, females 37,870); Unemployed 29,427 (males 14,629, females 14,798); Civilian labour force 121,826 (males 69,158, females 52,668); Armed forces 2,062 (all males); Total labour force 123,888. (*Estimate at 31 December 1986:* Total Employed 97,300.)

AGRICULTURE, ETC.

Principal Crops ('000 metric tons, 1989): Sweet potatoes 7; Yams 12; Coconuts 3 (1987); Vegetables 20; Melons 2; Pineapples 4 (1987); Bananas 159 (1988); Plantains 9; Sugar cane 871 (1988); Aubergines 1 (1987). Source: mainly Secrétariat du Comité de la Zone Franc: *La Zone Franc, Rapport 1989.*

Livestock ('000 head, 1988): Cattle 65; Pigs 29; Goats 28; Sheep 3; Chickens 320.

Forestry (1979): Roundwood removals 17,000 cubic metres.

Fishing (metric tons, live weight): Total catch 8,080 in 1986; 8,000 in 1987; 8,150 in 1988. Production of shrimps by aquaculture: 52 metric tons (1988).

INDUSTRY

Production (1988): Raw sugar 76,127 metric tons, Rum 74,552 hl, Electricity 681 million kWh.

FINANCE

Currency and Exchange Rates: French currency is used (see French Guiana).

Guadeloupe

Budget (estimates, 1990): Revenue and expenditure to balance at 1,695 million francs.

Expenditure by Metropolitan France (1988): 757 million francs.

Cost of Living (Consumer Price Index for urban areas; base: 1980 = 100): 170.3 in 1987; 173.7 in 1988; 177.8 in 1989. Source: UN, *Monthly Bulletin of Statistics.*

Gross Domestic Product (million francs at current prices): 9,049.1 in 1984; 9,650.3 in 1985; 10,568.8 in 1986. Source: *La Zone Franc, Rapport 1989.*

EXTERNAL TRADE

Principal Commodities (US $ million, 1987): *Imports c.i.f.:* Food and live animals 184.2 (Meat and meat preparations 45.2; Cereals and cereal preparations 37.1); Beverages and tobacco 43.8 (Beverages 39.0); Petroleum and petroleum products 44.8 (Refined petroleum products 42.2); Chemicals and related products 96.1; Basic manufactures 166.7; Machinery and transport equipment 308.4 (Electrical machinery, apparatus, etc. 68.6; Road vehicles and parts 113.5); Miscellaneous manufactured articles 161.4; Total (incl. others) 1,040.2. *Exports f.o.b.:* Food and live animals 62.2 (Wheat meal or flour 7.7; Bananas and plantains 47.0; Raw sugar 3.1); Beverages 9.1 (Distilled alcoholic beverages 7.6); Basic manufactures 4.6; Machinery and transport equipment 9.0 (Power generating equipment 3.6); Miscellaneous manufactured articles 3.2; Total (incl. others) 91.7; Source: UN, *International Trade Statistics Yearbook.*

Principal Trading Partners (US $ million, 1987): *Imports c.i.f.:* France 670.5; Fed. Rep. of Germany 38.4; Italy 45.4; Japan 27.8; Martinique 30.0; USA 34.4; Total (incl. others) 1,040.1. *Exports f.o.b.:* France 62.3; French Guiana 2.8; Martinique 20.4; Réunion 2.7; Total (incl. others) 91.7. Source: UN, *International Trade Statistics Yearbook.*

1988 (million francs): Imports c.i.f. 7,169; Exports f.o.b. 909. Source: UN, *Monthly Bulletin of Statistics.*

TRANSPORT

Road Traffic (vehicles in use, 1986): Passenger cars 69,200, Buses and coaches 500, Goods vehicles 500. Source: IRF, *World Road Statistics.*

Shipping (international sea-borne traffic, '000 metric tons, 1988): Freight loaded 464; Freight unloaded 1,571.

Civil Aviation (commercial traffic, 1988): Number of flights 29,251; Passengers carried 1,383,817, Freight carried 11,431 metric tons.

TOURISM

Visitors (1988): 328,726.

EDUCATION

Primary (1988): Schools 304; Students 52,780.

Secondary (1988): Schools 75; Students 46,654.

Higher (1988): 2,373 students (Université Antilles-Guyane).

Directory
The Government
(February 1991)

Prefect: JEAN-PAUL PROUST.

President of the General Council: DOMINIQUE LARIFLA (PS).

President of the Economic and Social Committee: GUY FRÉDÉRIC.

Deputies to the French National Assembly: ERNEST MOUTOUSSAMY (PCG), FRÉDÉRIC JALTON (PS), LUCETTE MICHAUX-CHEVRY (RPR), DOMINIQUE LARIFLA (PS).

Representatives to the French Senate: HENRI BANGOU (PCG), FRANÇOIS LOUISY (PS).

FRENCH OVERSEAS DEPARTMENTS　　　　　　　　　　　　　　　　　　*Guadeloupe*

REGIONAL COUNCIL

President: Félix Proto (PS).

Election, 16 March 1986

	Votes	%	Seats
RPR	25,371	33.09	15
PS	21,969	28.65	12
PCG	18,229	23.77	10
UDF	8,217	10.71	4
Others	2,876	3.78	—
Total	76,662	100.00	41

Political Organizations

Fédération Guadeloupéenne du Parti Socialiste (PS): Les Abymes; in March 1987 the PS announced plans to become autonomous party, while maintaining links with PS in France; First Sec. Dominique Larifla.

*Fédération Guadeloupéenne du Rassemblement pour la République (RPR): 1 rue Baudot, Basse-Terre; tel. 81-1069; Gaullist; Pres. Daniel Beaubrun.

*Fédération Guadeloupéenne de l'Union pour la Démocratie Française (UDF): Pointe-à-Pitre; centrist; Pres. Marcel Esdras.

Mouvement populaire pour une Guadeloupe indépendante (MPGI): Pointe-à-Pitre; f. 1982; extremist independence party; Sec.-Gen. Simone Faisans-Renac.

Alliance Révolutionnaire Caraïbe (ARC): Pointe-à-Pitre; f. 1983; illegal pro-independence alliance; left-wing; supports armed struggle; officially dissolved, but merged with MPGI in 1984 and continued activities; Leader Luc Reinette (arrested July 1987, released July 1989).

Mouvement Socialiste Départmentaliste Guadeloupéen: Mairie de Morne-à-l'Eau, 97111 Morne-à-l'Eau; Sec.-Gen. Abdon Saman.

Parti Communiste Guadeloupéen (PCG): 119 rue Vatable, 97110 Pointe-à-Pitre; telex 919419; f. 1944; Sec.-Gen. Christian Celeste.

Union Populaire pour la Libération de la Guadeloupe (UPLG): Basse-Terre; f. 1978; pro-independence movement; Pres. Dr Claude Makouké.

* The RPR and the UDF allied to contest the 1988 legislative elections as the Union du Rassemblement du Centre (URC).

In June 1987 three leaders of the separatist movement, Luc Reinette, Henri Amédien and Henri Bernard, announced the formation of the Conseil National de la Résistance Guadeloupéenne (CNRG), which was to organize a provisional government whose aim was to establish conditions for the creation of a future Republic of Guadeloupe.

Judicial System

Cour d'Appel: Palais de Justice, 97100 Basse-Terre; tel. 81-2759; telex 919890; fax 81-8591; First Pres. Jean Levanti; Procurator-Gen. Jerry Sainte-Rose; two Tribunaux de Grande Instance, four Tribunaux d'Instance.

Religion

The majority of the population belong to the Roman Catholic Church.

CHRISTIANITY
The Roman Catholic Church

Guadeloupe comprises the single diocese of Basse-Terre, suffragan to the archdiocese of Fort-de-France, Martinique. At 31 December 1988 there were an estimated 312,050 adherents, representing more than 90% of the total population. The Bishop participates in the Antilles Episcopal Conference, based in Kingston, Jamaica.

Bishop of Basse-Terre: Mgr Ernest Mesmin Lucien Cabo, Evêché, place Saint-François, BP 50, 97101 Basse-Terre; tel. 81-3669.

The Press

Combat Ouvrier: Valette, 97180 St Anne; monthly; trade union publ.

L'Etincelle: 119 rue Vatable, 97110 Pointe-à-Pitre; telex 919419; weekly; organ of the Communist Party; Dir Raymond Baron; circ. 5,000.

France-Antilles: 1 rue Hincelin, BP 658, 97159 Pointe-à-Pitre; telex 919728; daily; Dir Claude Provençal; circ. 25,000.

Guadeloupe 2000: Résidence Massabielle, 97110 Pointe-à-Pitre; fortnightly; right-wing extremist; Dir Edouard Boulogne; circ. 4,000.

Information Caraïbe (ICAR): BP 958, Pointe-à-Pitre; tel. 82-5606; f. 1973; weekly; Dir P. Fertin.

Jakata: 18 rue Condé, 97110 Pointe-à-Pitre; f. 1977; fortnightly; Dir Frantz Succab; circ. 6,000.

Magwa: Résidence Vatable, Bâtiment B, BP 1286, 97178 Pointe-à-Pitre; tel. 91-7698; monthly; independent; Editor Dannick Zandronis; circ. 4,000.

Match: 33 rue St John Perse, 97110 Pointe-à-Pitre; tel. 82-0187; fortnightly; Dir Camille Jabbour; circ. 6,000.

Moun: BP 128, 97184 Pointe-à-Pitre; quarterly; culture; circ. 3,500.

Le Progrès social: rue Toussaint L'Ouverture, 97100 Basse-Terre; tel. 81-1041; weekly; Dir Henri Rodes; circ. 5,000.

Télé Sept Jours: Agence Promovente, Immeuble Lagland Bergevin, 97110 Pointe-à-Pitre; weekly; TV.

NEWS AGENCIES

Agence Centrale Parisienne de Presse (ACP): BP 1105, 97181 Pointe-à-Pitre; tel. 82-1476; telex 919728; fax 91-7831; Rep. René Cazimir-Jeanon.

Foreign Bureaux

Agencia EFE (Spain): BP 1016, 97178 Pointe-à-Pitre; Correspondent Dannick Zandronis.

United Press International (UPI) (USA): BP 658, 97159 Pointe-à-Pitre; Rep. Stéphane Delannoy.

Radio and Television

In 1987 there were an estimated 85,000 radio receivers and 72,000 television receivers in use. The establishment of a private local television channel was approved in 1987.

Société nationale de radio-télévision française d'Outre-Mer (RFO): BP 402, 97163 Pointe-à-Pitre Cedex; tel. 90-2424; 24 hours radio and 24 hours television broadcast daily; Dir Bernard Joyeux.

Radio Antilles: 55 rue Henri IV, 97110 Pointe-à-Pitre.

Radio Caraïbes International: Tour Cecid, Blvd Legitimus, 97110 Pointe-à-Pitre; tel. 82-1746; telex 19083. Dir Olivier Garon.

Radio Actif: Pointe-à-Pitre; satellite link to Radio Monte-Carlo (France).

Finance

(cap. = capital; dep. = deposits; m. = million;
frs = French francs; brs = branches)

BANKING
Central Bank

Caisse Centrale de Coopération Economique: Faubourg Frébault, BP 160, 97154 Pointe-à-Pitre; tel. 83-3272; telex 919074.

Commercial Banks

Banque des Antilles Françaises: place de la Victoire, 97110 Pointe-à-Pitre; tel. 26-8007; telex 919866; rue de Cours Nolivos, 97100 Basse-Terre; f. 1853; cap. 32.583m. frs, res 17.1m. frs, dep. 1,973.9m. frs (Dec. 1989); Chair. Jacques Girault; Gen. Man. Georges Migliore; 4 brs.

Banque Française Commerciale: 21 rue Gambetta, 97110 Pointe-à-Pitre; tel. 82-1201; telex 919764; f. 1977; cap. 21m. frs (Dec. 1981); Dir René Mouttet; 7 brs.

Banque Nationale de Paris: place de la Rénovation, 97110 Pointe-à-Pitre; tel. 82-9696; telex 919706; Dir Henri Betbeder; 13 brs.

Banque Populaire de la Guadeloupe—Crédit Guadeloupéen: 10 rue Achille René-Boisneuf, 97110 Pointe-à-Pitre; f. 1926; tel. 91-4560; telex 919713; dep. 550m. frs (1983); Pres. Christian Rimbaud; Dir Richard Nalpas; 6 brs.

Caisse Régionale de Crédit Agricole Mutuel de la Guadeloupe: BP 134, Zone artisanale de petit perou, 97154 Pointe-à-Pitre; tel. 90-6565; telex 919708; Dir Thélème Gedeon; 5 brs.

FRENCH OVERSEAS DEPARTMENTS — Guadeloupe, Martinique

Crédit Martiniquais: Angle des rues P. Lacavé et Cités Unies, 97100 Pointe-à-Pitre; tel. 83-1859; f. 1987, in succession to Chase Manhattan Bank (USA).

Société Générale de Banque aux Antilles (SGBA): 30 rue Frébault, POB 630, 97110 Pointe-à-Pitre; tel. 82-5423; telex 919735; f. 1979; Pres. Jacques de Maleville; Dir Henri Gilles; 6 brs.

INSURANCE

Mutuelle Antillaise d'Assurances, Société d'Assurances à forme mutuelle: 12 rue Gambetta, BP 409, 97110 Pointe-à-Pitre; tel. 83-2332; telex 919945; f. 1937; Dir-Gen. Félix Cherdieu d'Alexis; Man. A. Zogg; Dir Alain Buffon.

Foreign Companies

Some 30 of the principal European insurance companies are represented in Pointe-à-Pitre, and another six companies have offices in Basse-Terre.

Trade and Industry

Agence pour la promotion industrielle de la Guadeloupe (APRIGA): BP 1229, 97184 Pointe-à-Pitre; tel. 83-4897; telex 919780; fax 90-2187; f. 1979; development agency; Pres. Roland Michel; Dir Charly Blondeau.

Centre Technique de la Canne et du Sucre: Morne l'Epingle, 97139 Les Abymes; tel. 82-9470; Pres. Antoine Andreze-Louison; Dir Philippe Douchel.

Chambre de Commerce et d'Industrie de Pointe-à-Pitre: rue F. Eboué, BP 64, 97152 Pointe-à-Pitre; tel. 90-0808; telex 919780; fax 90-2187; Pres. Georges Marianne; Dir-Gen. Jean-Claude Paris.

Chambre de Commerce et d'Industrie de Basse-Terre: 6 rue Victor Hugues, 97100 Basse-Terre; tel. 81-1656; telex 919781; fax 81-2117; f. 1832; 24 mems; Pres. Gérard Penchard; Sec.-Gen. Jean-Claude Baptistide.

Chambre d'Agriculture de la Guadeloupe: 27 rue Sadi-Carnot, 97110 Pointe-à-Pitre; tel. 82-1130; telex 919286; fax 91-8873; Pres. Christian Flereau; Dir Victorin Lurel.

Société d'Intérêt Collectif Agricole (Sica-Assobag): Desmarais, 97100 Basse-Terre; tel. 81-0552; telex 919727; f. 1967; banana producers; Pres. François Le Metayer; Dir Jean-Claude Petrelluzzi.

Syndicat des Producteurs-Exportateurs de Sucre et de Rhum de la Guadeloupe et Dépendances: Zone Industrielle de la Pointe Jarry, 97122 Baie-Mahault, BP 2015, 97191 Pointe-à-Pitre; tel. 26-6212; telex 919824; f. 1937; 4 mems; Pres. Amédée Huyghues-Despointes.

TRADE UNIONS

Confédération Générale du Travail de la Guadeloupe (CGTG): 4 cité Artisanale de Bergevin, 97173 Pointe-à-Pitre; tel. 82-3461; telex 919061; f. 1973; Sec.-Gen. Claude Morvan; 15,000 mems.

Union Départementale de la Confédération Française des Travailleurs Chrétiens: Pointe-à-Pitre; f. 1937; Sec.-Gen. E. Democrite; about 3,500 mems.

Union Départementale des Syndicats CGT-FO: 59 rue Lamartine, Pointe-à-Pitre; Gen. Sec. Clotaire Bernos; about 1,500 mems.

Union Générale des Travailleurs de la Guadeloupe: 5 Immeuble Diligenti, 97110 Pointe-à-Pitre; tel. 83-1007; confederation of pro-independence trade unions; Sec.-Gen. Rosan Mounien.

Union Interprofessionnelle de la Guadeloupe (UIG): Logement TEFT, Bergevin, 97181 Pointe-à-Pitre; tel. 83-1650; (affiliated to the Confédération Française Démocratique du Travail—CFDT—of France); Institut National de la Recherche Agronomique (INRA), Domaine de Duclos, 97170 Petit-Bourg; Sec.-Gen. A. Mephon.

Transport

RAILWAYS

There are no railways in Guadeloupe.

ROADS

In 1988 there were 2,093 km of roads in Guadeloupe, of which 330 km were Routes Nationales.

SHIPPING

The major port is at Pointe-à-Pitre, and a new port for the export of bananas has been built at Basse-Terre.

CIVIL AVIATION

Raizet International Airport is situated 3 km (2 miles) from Pointe-à-Pitre and is equipped to handle jet-engined aircraft. There are smaller airports on the islands of Marie-Galante, La Désirade and Saint-Barthélémy.

Air Guadeloupe: Raizet Airport, 97110 Abymes; tel. 82-2161; telex 919008; f. 1970; regular flights to Antigua, Dominica, Saint-Martin and Saint Thomas; connects the various dependent islands; fleet of 2 Fairchild F-27-J, 4 Twin Otters, 2 ATR 42, 1 Dornier 228.

Tourism

Guadeloupe is a popular tourist destination, especially for visitors from France and the USA. The main attractions are the beaches, the mountainous scenery and the unspoilt beauty of the island dependencies. In 1988 there were 4,722 hotel rooms. The number of visitors totalled 328,726 in 1988; of these, 67% were from France, 14% from other European countries, 14% from the USA and 6% from Canada.

Office du Tourisme: 5 square de la Banque, POB 1099, 97181 Pointe-à-Pitre; tel. 82-0930; telex 919715; Dir-Gen. Erick W. Rotin; Pres. Philippe Chaulet.

Bureau Industrie et Tourisme: Préfecture de la Guadeloupe, rue de Lardenoy, 97109 Basse-Terre; tel. 81-7681; telex 919707; Dir François Vosgien.

Syndicat d'Initiative de la Guadeloupe: 28 rue Sadi-Carnot, 97110 Pointe-à-Pitre; Pres. Dr Edouard Chartol.

MARTINIQUE

Introductory Survey

Location, Climate, Language, Religion, Capital

Martinique is one of the Windward islands in the West Indies, with Dominica to the north and Saint Lucia to the south. The island is dominated by the volcanic peak of Mont Pelée. The climate is tropical, but tempered by easterly and north-easterly breezes. The more humid and wet season runs from July to November, and the average temperature is 26°C (80°F). French is the official language, but a creole patois is widely spoken. The majority of the population profess Christianity and belong to the Roman Catholic Church. The capital is Fort-de-France.

Recent History

Martinique has been a French possession since 1635. The prosperity of the island was based on the sugar industry, which was dealt a devastating blow by the volcanic eruption of Mont Pelée in 1902. Martinique became a department of France in 1946, when the Governor was replaced by a Prefect, and an elected General Council was created.

During the 1950s there was a growth of nationalist feeling, as expressed by Aimé Césaire's Parti Progressiste Martiniquais (PPM), and the Parti Communiste Martiniquais (PCM). However, economic power remained concentrated in the hands of the *békés* (descendants of white colonial settlers), who owned most of the agricultural land, and controlled the lucrative import/export market. This allowed little incentive for innovation or self-sufficiency, and there was resentment against lingering colonial attitudes.

In 1974 Martinique, together with Guadeloupe and French Guiana, was given regional status as part of France's governmental reorganization. An indirectly-elected Regional Council was created, with some control over the local economy. In 1982 and 1983 the Socialist Government of President François Mitterrand, which had pledged itself to decentralizing power in favour of the overseas departments, made further concessions towards autonomy by giving the local councils greater control over taxation, local police and the economy. At the first direct elections to the new Regional

FRENCH OVERSEAS DEPARTMENTS

Martinique

Council, held in February 1983, left-wing parties (the PPM, the PCM and the Fédération Socialiste de la Martinique—FSM) obtained a small majority of votes and seats. This success, and the election of Aimé Césaire as the Council's President, strengthened his influence against the pro-independence elements in his own party. (Full independence for Martinique attracted support only from a small minority of the population; the majority sought reforms that would bring greater autonomy, while retaining French control.) The Mouvement Indépendantiste Martiniquais (MIM), the most vocal of the separatist parties, fared badly in the elections, obtaining less than 3% of the total vote. In late 1983, and in 1984, Martinique became a target for the activities of the outlawed Alliance Révolutionnaire Caraïbe (ARC), which claimed responsibility for a number of bombings on the island. At elections to an enlarged General Council, held in March 1985, the left-wing parties increased their representation, but the centre-right coalition of the Union pour la Démocratie Française (UDF) and the Rassemblement pour la République (RPR) maintained their control of the administration.

For the general election to the French National Assembly in March 1986, Martinique's representation was increased from three to four deputies. Martinique was the only French department in which the major left-wing parties presented a unified list of candidates (voting for the 1986 election being based on a system of proportional representation). The left-wing alliance received 51.2% of the votes, and two of its candidates were elected: Aimé Césaire (who retained his seat) and a member of the FSM. The joint list of the RPR and the UDF obtained 42.4% of the votes, and each party won one seat. For the concurrent elections to the Regional Council, the Union of the Left (including the PPM, the FSM and the PCM) similarly campaigned with a joint programme, winning 21 of the 41 seats (as the three parties had together won in 1983), although with a reduced share (41.3%) of the votes. The RPR and the UDF together obtained 49.8% of the votes and won the 20 remaining seats. Aimé Césaire retained the presidency of the Council until June 1988, when he relinquished the post to Camille Darsières.

In September 1986 indirect elections were held for the two Martinique seats in the French Senate. As in the March elections, the left-wing parties united, and, as a consequence, Martinique acquired a left-wing Senator for the first time since 1958, a PPM member, while the other successful candidate belonged to the UDF.

Following the recent trend in Martinique, the incumbent Socialist President won a decisive majority of the island's votes at the 1988 presidential election. President Mitterrand obtained 71% of the votes cast in Martinique in the second round of voting against Jacques Chirac of the RPR. Left-wing candidates secured all four seats at elections to the National Assembly in June (when the former single-member constituency system was reintroduced). Furthermore, in September–October, for the first time in 40 years the parties of the left achieved a majority at elections to the General Council, winning 23 of the 45 seats.

At the municipal elections held in March 1989, the right-wing parties won in 18 of the municipalities, losing three to the left and one to the independents. The left-wing parties won in 16 of the municipalities, including Fort-de-France. Elections to the European Parliament were held in June. At these, the centre-right UDF-RPR won the highest proportion of votes cast (43.5%), followed by the Parti Socialiste (35.6%). The level of participation in the voting was low, however, and an abstention rate of 83.9% was recorded.

In January 1990 a commission, appointed by the Minister of Overseas Departments and Territories, published its report on the question of social equality with metropolitan France and economic development in the four departments. The report contained 58 proposals for the rectification of social and economic shortcomings in the departments, and recommended a development programme of two three-year stages.

In June 1990 the results of the 1986 election to the Regional Council were annulled because of a technicality, and another election was therefore held in October 1990. Pro-independence candidates won nearly 22% of the votes, and secured nine seats (of which seven were won by the MIM). The PPM, the FSM and the PCM again formed a joint electoral list, but won 14 seats, compared with 21 in 1986, thus losing their absolute majority on the Council; the PPM's secretary-general, Camille Darsières, was, however, re-elected to the presidency of the Council. The success of the 'indépendantistes' was attributed to local apprehension concerning the completion of the European Community's single market (due to take place in 1992), which would, it was feared, expose Martinique's economy to excessive competition.

Government

France is represented in Martinique by an appointed Prefect. There are two councils with local powers: the 45-member General Council and the 41-member Regional Council. Both are elected by universal adult suffrage for a period of up to six years. Martinique elects four deputies to the French National Assembly in Paris, and sends two indirectly-elected representatives to the Senate. The department is also represented at the European Parliament in Strasbourg.

Defence

In 1990 France maintained a military force of about 8,800 in French Guiana and the Antilles.

Economic Affairs

In 1986 Martinique's gross domestic product (GDP), measured at current prices, was 13,846m. French francs, equivalent to about 41,700 francs per head. Over the period 1980–86, according to UN estimates, GDP increased, in real terms, at an average rate of 4.3% per year, and real GDP per head rose by 2.0% annually. During 1982–90 the population increased by an annual average of 1.1%.

The primary sector (including agriculture, forestry and fishing) contributed 12.0% of GDP in 1986, and employed 8.2% of the working population in 1989. The principal cash crops are bananas (which accounted for 48% of export earnings in 1988), sugar cane (primarily for the production of rum), avocados, limes, melons and pineapples. Roots and tubers and vegetables are cultivated for local consumption. Meat production fulfilled about 55% of local demand in 1989, while fisheries provided about one-third of domestic consumption of fish.

The secondary sector (including mining, manufacturing, construction and power) contributed 16.7% of GDP in 1986, and employed 14.7% of the working population. The most important industrial activities are food processing (particularly sugar) and rum production. Exports of rum provided about 11% of export earnings in 1988. Other areas of activity include metals, chemicals, plastics, wood, printing and textiles. There is also a petroleum refinery and a cement plant. About 4,000 people were employed in industry in 1988.

Tourism is a major activity on the island and one of the most important sources of foreign exchange. In 1988 the tourism sector recorded a 9% increase in total hotel reservations. The number of cruise-ship passengers increased by 26% in 1988.

Energy is derived principally from mineral fuels. Imports of crude petroleum comprised 7.2% of the value of total imports in 1987.

In 1988 Martinique recorded a trade deficit of 6,521m. French francs. In that year the principal source of imports (64%) was France, which was also the principal market for exports (64%). Other major trading partners were the Federal Republic of Germany, Italy, Japan, the United Kingdom and Venezuela. The principal exports in 1988 were bananas, rum, canned pineapple and refined petroleum products. The principal imports were machinery and transport equipment, food and live animals, miscellaneous manufactured articles, basic manufactures, chemicals and crude petroleum.

In 1988 the French Government's expenditure on Martinique totalled 4,486m. French francs. Unemployment affected an estimated 29% of the labour force in 1988. The annual rate of inflation averaged 7.9% in 1980–88 and 2.9% in 1989.

As an integral part of France, Martinique belongs to the European Community, and was to receive 164m. ECUs in Community aid during the period 1989–93, in order to adapt to the requirements of the single European market, due to become operational in 1992.

Martinique's economic development has created a society that combines a relatively high standard of living with a weak economic base in agricultural and industrial production, and a chronic trade deficit. This has contributed to problems such as high unemployment, emigration and social unrest. The linking of wage levels to those of metropolitan France, despite the island's lower level of productivity, has increased labour costs and restricted development.

Social Welfare

Martinique has a system of social welfare similar to that of metropolitan France. In 1986 there were 17 hospitals (including five maternity hospitals and a psychiatric hospital), with a total of 3,711 beds, and 519 physicians.

Education

The educational system is similar to that of metropolitan France (see chapter on Guadeloupe). There is free and compulsory education in government schools for children aged six to 16 years. Higher education in law, science and economics is provided in Martinique by a branch of the Université Antilles-Guyane. There are also two teacher-training institutes, and colleges of agriculture, fisheries, hotel management, nursing, midwifery and child care.

FRENCH OVERSEAS DEPARTMENTS — Martinique

The average rate of adult illiteracy in 1982 was only 7.2% (males 8.0%; females 6.6%).

Public Holidays

1991: 1 January (New Year's Day), 29 March–1 April (Easter), 1 May (Labour Day), 9 May (Ascension Day), 20 May (Whit Monday), 14 July (National Day), 11 November (Armistice Day), 25 December (Christmas Day).

1992: 1 January (New Year's Day), 17–20 April (Easter), 1 May (Labour Day), 28 May (Ascension Day), 8 June (Whit Monday), 14 July (National Day), 11 November (Armistice Day), 25 December (Christmas Day).

Weights and Measures
The metric system is in use.

Statistical Survey

Source: Institut national de la statistique et des études économiques, Pointe de Jaham Schœlcher, BP 605, 97261 Fort-de-France; tel. 616149.

AREA AND POPULATION

Area: 1,100 sq km (424.7 sq miles).

Population: 326,717 (males 158,415, females 168,302) at census of 9 March 1982; 359,572 (census of 15 March 1990, preliminary result); *Capital:* Fort-de-France, population 101,540 (1990). *Other towns* (population at 1990 census): Le Lamentin 30,596; Schoelcher 19,874; Sainte-Marie 19,760; Le François 17,065.

Births, Marriages and Deaths (1988): Registered live births 6,386 (birth rate 19.0 per 1,000); Registered marriages 1,556 (marriage rate 4.6 per 1,000); Registered deaths 2,092 (death rate 6.2 per 1,000). Figures exclude live-born infants dying before registration of birth.

Economically Active Population (persons aged 16 years and over, 1982 census): Agriculture, hunting, forestry and fishing 9,844; Mining and quarrying 1,853; Manufacturing 4,001; Electricity, gas and water 1,006; Construction 7,832; Trade, restaurants and hotels 9,864; Transport, storage and communications 5,197; Financing, insurance, real estate and business services 17,878; Community, social and personal services 29,382; Activities not adequately defined 7,707; Total employed 94,564 (males 54,121, females 40,443); Unemployed 35,936 (males 18,086, females 17,850); Total labour force 130,500 (males 72,207, females 58,293). **1986:** Total employed 94,800 (males 48,300, females 46,500); Unemployed 42,587 (males 19,592, females 22,995); Total labour force 137,400 (males 68,900, females 69,500).

AGRICULTURE, ETC.

Principal Crops (FAO estimates, '000 metric tons, 1989): Roots and tubers 34, Sugar cane 207, Bananas 155, Plantains 8, Pineapples 17. Source: FAO, *Production Yearbook*.

Livestock (1989): Cattle 35,000, Pigs 21,200, Sheep 36,100, Goats 16,500. Source: Secrétariat du Comité Monétaire de la Zone Franc: *La Zone Franc, Rapport 1989*.

Forestry (1987): Roundwood removals 13,000 cubic metres.

Fishing (metric tons, live weight): Total catch 4,083 (FAO estimate) in 1986; 4,576 (FAO estimate) in 1987; 3,060 in 1988. Source: FAO, *Yearbook of Fishery Statistics*.

INDUSTRY

Production (1988): Raw sugar 7,501 metric tons, Rum 85,487 hl, Cement 200,000 metric tons (1986), Refined petroleum products 569,755 metric tons, Electricity 585 million kWh.

FINANCE

Currency and Exchange Rates: French currency is used (see French Guiana).

Budget (estimates, 1990): Revenue and expenditure to balance at 1,785 million francs.

Expenditure by Metropolitan France (1988): 4,486 million francs.

Cost of Living (consumer price index for Fort-de-France; base: 1980=100): 179.1 in 1987; 183.4 in 1988; 188.8 in 1989. Source: UN, *Monthly Bulletin of Statistics*.

Gross Domestic Product (million francs at current prices): 11,019.7 in 1984; 12,576.9 in 1985; 13,845.5 in 1986. Source: *La Zone Franc, Rapport 1989*.

EXTERNAL TRADE

Principal Commodities (US $ million, 1987): *Imports c.i.f.:* Food and live animals 188.8 (Meat and meat preparations 48.2); Petroleum and petroleum products 91.2 (Crude petroleum oils 80.3); Chemicals and related products 97.6; Basic manufactures 159.0; Machinery and transport equipment 348.1 (Electrical machinery, apparatus, etc. 67.5; Road vehicles and parts 106.6; Ships, boats, etc. 72.2); Miscellaneous manufactured articles 167.1; Total (incl. others) 1,120.1. *Exports f.o.b.:* Food and live animals 105.2 (Bananas and plantains 92.6); Beverages 27.4 (Distilled alcoholic beverages 25.8); Refined petroleum products 27.0 (Gas oils 10.3; Residual fuel oils 8.6); Basic manufactures 9.9; Total (incl. others) 193.5. Source: UN, *International Trade Statistics Yearbook*.

Principal Trading Partners (US $ million, 1987): *Imports c.i.f.:* France 730.6; Fed. Repub. of Germany 33.4; Italy 41.7; Japan 28.2; United Arab Emirates 24.0; United Kingdom 69.3; USA 24.2; Total (incl. others) 1,119.9. *Exports f.o.b.:* France 125.1; Fed. Repub. of Germany 10.8; Guadeloupe 46.7; Total (incl. others) 193.5. Source: UN, *International Trade Statistics Yearbook*.

1988 (million francs): Imports c.i.f. 7,692; Exports f.o.b. 1,171.

TRANSPORT

Road Traffic (motor vehicles in use at 31 December 1984): Passenger cars 140,000; Buses and coaches 700; Goods vehicles 2,000. Source: IRF, *World Road Statistics*.

Shipping (freight traffic in '000 metric tons, 1988): Goods loaded 706.9; Goods unloaded 1,568.0.

Civil Aviation (1988): Passengers carried 1,276,131, Freight 12,303 metric tons.

TOURISM

Tourist Arrivals (1988): 230,000.

EDUCATION

Primary (1983): 224 schools, 2,004 teachers; 49,980 students (1988).
Secondary: 75 schools (1986); 3,065 teachers (1983); 42,787 students (1988).
Higher (1988): 2,743 students (Université Antilles-Guyane).

Directory

The Government
(February 1991)

Prefect: JEAN-CLAUDE ROURE.

President of the General Council: EMILE MAURICE (RPR).

Deputies to the French National Assembly: AIMÉ CÉSAIRE (PPM), LOUIS-JOSEPH DOGUÉ (FSM), GUY LORDINOT (PPM/PCM/FSM), CLAUDE LISE (PPM).

Representatives to the French Senate: ROGER LISE (UDF), RODOLPHE DÉSIRÉ (PPM).

REGIONAL COUNCIL

President: CAMILLE DARSIÈRES (PPM).

Election, 14 October 1990

	Votes	%	Seats
PPM/FSM/PCM	29,961	32.8	14
UDF-RPR	20,364	22.3	9
MIM	15,090	16.5	7
Independent left	10,658	11.7	5
Independent right	8,907	9.7	4
Ecological/pro-independence list	4,795	5.2	2
France Unie	1,658	1.8	—
Total*	91,433	100.0	41

* Total does not include 8,681 spoiled or blank votes.

Political Organizations

Fédération Socialiste de la Martinique (FSM): Cité la Meynard, 97200 Fort-de-France; tel. 503477; local branch of the Parti Socialiste; First Secretary JEAN CRUSOL.

France Unie: Fort-de-France; Leader EMMANUEL ARGO.

FRENCH OVERSEAS DEPARTMENTS / Martinique

Groupe Révolution Socialiste (GRS): 40 rue Pierre Semar, 97200 Fort-de-France; tel. 703649; f. 1973; Trotskyist; Leader GILBERT PAGO.
Mouvement Indépendantiste Martiniquais (MIM): Fort-de-France; pro-independence party; also known as La Parole au peuple; Leader ALFRED MARIE-JEANNE.
Parti Communiste Martiniquais (PCM): Fort-de-France; f. 1920; affiliated to French Communist Party until 1957; Leader ARMAND NICOLAS.
Parti Progressiste Martiniquais (PPM): Fort-de-France; f. 1957; Pres. AIMÉ CÉSAIRE; Sec.-Gen. CAMILLE DARSIÈRES.
***Rassemblement pour la République (RPR):** BP 448, 97205 Fort-de-France; Gaullist; Sec. STEPHEN BAGOE.
***Union pour la Démocratie Française (UDF):** Fort-de-France; centrist; Pres. JEAN MARAN.
  Parti Républicain (PR): Fort-de-France; Leader JEAN BALLY.
* The RPR and the UDF allied to contest the 1988 legislative elections as the Union du Rassemblement du Centre (URC).

Judicial System

Cour d'Appel de Fort-de-France: Fort-de-France; tel. 706262; telex 912525; highest court of appeal for Martinique and French Guiana; Pres. RENÉ CASES; Procurator-Gen. (vacant).

There are two Tribunaux de Grande Instance, at Fort-de-France and Cayenne (French Guiana), and three Tribunaux d'Instance (two in Fort-de-France and one in Cayenne).

Religion

The majority of the population belong to the Roman Catholic Church.

CHRISTIANITY
The Roman Catholic Church

Martinique comprises a single archdiocese, with an estimated 290,000 adherents (about 88% of the total population) at 31 December 1988. The Archbishop participates in the Antilles Episcopal Conference, currently based in Kingston, Jamaica.
Archbishop of Fort-de-France: Most Rev. MAURICE MARIE-SAINTE, Archevêché, 5–7 rue de R. Père Pinchon, BP 586, 97207 Fort-de-France; tel. 637070; fax 63-40-39.

The Press

Antilla: BP 46, Lamentin; tel. 500868; weekly; Dir ALFRED FORTUNE.
L'Arbalète: Cité Saint-Georges, Fort-de-France; weekly.
Aujourd'hui Dimanche: Presbytère de Bellevue, Fort-de-France; tel. 714897; weekly; Dir Père GAUTHIER; circ. 12,000.
Carib Hebdo: 23 rue Yves Goussard, 97200 Fort-de-France; f. 1989; Dir GISELE DE LA FARGUE.
Combat Ouvrier: BP 386, 97258 Fort-de-France; weekly; Dir M. G. BEAUJOUR.
France-Antilles: place Stalingrad, 97200 Fort-de-France; tel. 630883; telex 912677; fax 604024; f. 1964; daily; Dir CHRISTIAN COUSTAL; circ. 30,000 (Martinique edition).
Information Caraïbe (ICAR): 18 allée des Perruches, 97200 Fort-de-France; tel. 643740; weekly; Editor DANIEL COMPÈRE; circ. 1,500.
Justice: rue E. Zola, Fort-de-France; weekly; organ of the PPM; Dir G. THIMOTÉE; circ. 8,000.
Le Naif: voie no 7, route du Lamentin, Fort-de-France; weekly; Dir R. LAOUCHEZ.
Le Progressiste: rue de Tallis Clarière, Fort-de-France; weekly; organ of the PPM; Dir PAUL GABOURG; circ. 13,000.
Révolution Socialiste: BP 1031, 97200 Fort-de-France; tel. 703649; f. 1973; weekly; organ of the GRS; Dir PHILIPPE PIERRE CHARLES; circ. 2,500.
L'Union: Fort-de-France; weekly; organ of l'Union Departmentaliste Martiniquaise; Dir JEAN MARAN.

Radio and Television

In 1987 there were an estimated 59,000 radio receivers and 45,000 television receivers in use. The establishment of a private local television channel was approved in 1987.

Radio-Télévision Française d'Outre-mer (RFO): La Clairère, BP 662, Fort-de-France; tel. 711660; Dir PIERRE GIRARD.
Radio Caraïbe Internationale (RCI): BP 1111, 97248 Fort-de-France; tel. 636555; telex 912579; Dir-Gen. OLIVIER GARON.

Finance

(cap. = capital; dep. = deposits; m. = million; frs = French francs; brs = branches)

BANKING
Central Bank

Caisse Centrale de Coopération Economique: 12 blvd du Général de Gaulle, BP 804, 97200 Fort-de-France; Dir JEAN BRUTOT.

Major Commercial Banks

Banque des Antilles Françaises: 34 rue Lamartine, BP 582, 97200 Fort-de-France; tel. 739344; telex 912636; fax 635894; f. 1853; cap. 32.5m. frs (1983); Pres. Dir LUCIEN ELSENSOHN.
Banque Française Commerciale: 6–10 rue Ernest Deproge, 97200 Fort-de-France; telex 912526; cap. 50m. frs (1983); Dir HENRI DE MALEZIEUX.
Banque Nationale de Paris: 72 ave des Caraïbes, 97200 Fort-de-France; tel. 737111; telex 912619; Dir MICHEL MASSE.
Caisse Nationale d'Epargne et de Prévoyance: 82 rue Perrinon, 97200 Fort-de-France; telex 912435; Dir Mme M. E. ANDRE.
Caisse Régionale de Crédit Agricole Mutuel: 106 blvd Général de Gaulle, BP 583, 97207 Fort-de-France; tel. 717607; telex 912657; f. 1950; 9,500 mems; Pres. M. SAINTE-ROSE; Dir MAURICE LAOUCHEZ; 27 brs.
Crédit Maritime Mutuel: 45 rue Victor Hugo, 97200 Fort-de-France; tel. 730093; telex 912477.
Crédit Martiniquais: 17 rue de la Liberté, Fort-de-France; tel. 599300; telex 912612; f. 1922; associated since 1987 with Chase Manhattan Bank (USA) and, since 1990, with Mutuelles du Mans Vie (France); cap. 156.8m. frs (1990); Pres. PIERRE MICHAUX; 11 brs.
Crédit Ouvrier: 30 rue Franklin Roosevelt, Fort-de-France; Dir ALAIN LOUTOBY.
Crédit Populaire: ave Jean Jaurès, 97200 Fort-de-France; Dir M. L. ASSELIN DE BEAUVILLE.
Crédit Social des Fonctionnaires: 63 rue Perrion, 97200 Fort-de-France; Dir FRED AUGUSTIN.
Société Générale de Banque aux Antilles: 19 rue de la Liberté, BP 408, 97200 Fort-de-France; tel. 716983; telex 912545; f. 1979; cap. 15m. frs; Dir MICHEL SAMOUR.
Société Martiniquaise de Financement (SOMAFI): route de Saint Thérèse, 97200 Fort-de-France; Dir JEAN MACHET.

INSURANCE

Cie Antillaise d'Assurances: 19 rue de la Liberté, 97205 Fort-de-France; tel. 730450.
Caraïbe Assurances: 11 rue Victor Hugo, BP 210, 97202 Fort-de-France; tel. 639229; telex 912096.
Groupement Français d'Assurances: 46–48 rue Ernest Deproge, 97205 Fort-de-France; tel. 605455; telex 912403.
La Nationale (GAN): 30 blvd Général de Gaulle, BP 185, Fort-de-France; tel. 713007; Reps MARCEL and ROGER BOULLANGER.
La Protectrice: 27 rue Blénac, 97205 Fort-de-France; tel. 702545; Rep. RENÉ MAXIMIN.
Le Secours: 74 ave Duparquet, 97200 Fort-de-France; tel. 700379; Dir Y. ANGANI.
L'Union des Assurances de Paris: 28 rue de la République, Fort-de-France; tel. 700470; Rep. R. DE REYNAL.

Trade and Industry

CHAMBER OF COMMERCE

Chambre de Commerce et d'Industrie de la Martinique: 50–56 rue Ernest Deproge, Fort-de-France; tel. 552800; telex 912633; fax 606668; f. 1907; Pres. MARCEL OSENAT; Dir-Gen. GUY ORCEL; 26 mems.

DEVELOPMENT

Agence pour le Développement Economique de la Martinique: 20 rue Lamartine, BP 800, 97211 Fort-de-France; tel. 704791; telex 912946; fax 724138; f. 1979; promotion of industry.

FRENCH OVERSEAS DEPARTMENTS

Martinique, Réunion

Bureau de l'Industrie de l'Artisanat: Préfecture, 97262 Fort-de-France; tel. 713627; telex 029650; f. 1960; government agency; research, documentation and technical and administrative advice on investment in industry and tourism; Dir RAPHAËL FIRMIN.

Société de Crédit pour le Développement de la Martinique (SODEMA): 12 blvd du Général de Gaulle, BP 575, 97242 Fort-de-France; tel. 605758; telex 912402; fax 630595; f. 1970; cap. 22.8m. frs; medium- and long-term finance; Dir.-Gen. A. LE SAUSSE.

Société de Développement Régional Antilles-Guyane (SODERAG): 109 rue Ernest Deproge, 97200 Fort-de-France; tel. 635978; telex 912343; fax 633888; Dir-Gen. FERNAND LERYCHARD; Sec.-Gen. OLYMPE FRANCIL.

ASSOCIATIONS

Chambre Départementale d'Agriculture: 55 rue Isambert, BP 432, Fort-de-France; tel. 715146; Pres. MARCEL FABRE.

Chambre des Métiers de la Martinique: Morne Tartenson, 97200 Fort-de-France; tel. 713222; fax 704730; f. 1970; 7,768 mems; Pres. MAURICE TAILAME.

Groupement de Producteurs d'Ananas de la Martinique: BP 12, 97201 Fort-de-France; f. 1967; Pres. C. DE GRYSE.

Société Coopérative d'Intérêt Collectif Agricole Bananière de la Martinique (SICABAM): Domaine de Montgéralde, Dillon, 97200 Fort-de-France; telex 912617; f. 1961; 1,000 mems; Pres. ALEX ASSIER DE POMPIGNAN; Dir GÉRARD BALLY.

Syndicat des Distilleries Agricoles: Immeuble Clément, rive droite Levassor, Fort-de-France; tel. 712554.

Syndicat des Producteurs de Rhum Agricole: Dillon, 97200 Fort-de-France.

Union Départementale des Coopératives Agricoles de la Martinique: Fort-de-France; Pres. M. URSULET.

TRADE UNIONS AND PROFESSIONAL ORGANIZATIONS

Centrale Démocratique Martiniquaise des Travailleurs: BP 21, 97201 Fort-de-France; Sec.-Gen. LINE BEAUSOLEIL.

Chambre Syndicale des Hôtels de Tourisme de la Martinique: Entrée Montgéralde, Route de Chateauboeuf, BP 1011, Fort-de-France; tel. 702780.

Confédération Générale du Travail: Maison des Syndicats, Jardin Desclieux, Fort-de-France; tel. 712589; f. 1936; affiliated to WFTU; Sec.-Gen. VICTOR LAMON; about 12,000 mems.

Ordre des Médecins de la Martinique: 80 rue de la République, 97200 Fort-de-France; tel. 632701; Pres. Dr RENÉ LEGENDRI.

Ordre des Pharmaciens de la Martinique: Zone Industrielle de la Lézarde, 97232 Lamentin; tel. 511356.

Syndicat National des Instituteurs: 3 rue de la Mutualité, Fort-de-France.

Union Départementale des Syndicats—FO: BP 1114, 97209 Fort-de-France; affiliated to ICFTU; Sec.-Gen. R. FABIEN; about 2,000 mems.

Transport

RAILWAYS
There are no railways in Martinique.

ROADS
There are 267 km of autoroutes and first-class roads, and 615 km of secondary roads.

SHIPPING

Alcoa Steamship Co, Alpine Line, Agdwa Line, Delta Line, Raymond Witcomb Co, Moore MacCormack, Eastern Steamship Co: c/o Ets René Cottrell, 48 rue Ernest Deproge, Fort-de-France.

Compagnie Générale Maritime: BP 574, ave Maurice Bishop, 97206 Fort-de-France; tel. 630040; telex 912049; also represents other passenger and freight lines; Rep. GUY ADAM.

Compagnie de navigation Mixte: Immeuble Rocade, La Dillon, BP 1023, 97209 Fort-de-France; Rep. R. M. MICHAUX.

Chargeurs Delmas: c/o Plissonneau SA, 34 rue Ernest Deproge, 97200 Fort-de-France; Rep. ARNAUD DE RAYNAL.

CIVIL AVIATION

Martinique's international airport is at Le Lamentin, 6 km from Fort-de-France, and is served by the following airlines: Air Canada, American Airlines (USA), Air France, LIAT (Antigua) and Air Martinique. A new terminal is to be built at Le Lamentin, at a projected cost of 300m. francs, and is due to be completed in 1993.

Air Martinique (Compagnie Antillaise d'Affrètement Aérien-CAAA): Aéroport de Fort-de-France, 97232 Le Lamentin; tel. 510809; telex 912048; fax 515394; f. 1981; offers charter services within the Lesser Antilles; scheduled flights operate to Dominica, Saint Lucia, Saint Vincent, Union Island, Mustique, Canouan, Barbados and Antigua; new points anticipated for 1990 were Point-à-Pitre (Guadeloupe) and Paris, the latter served by a leased Boeing 747; services are also undertaken on behalf of Air France; Chair. JEAN BALLY; Chief Exec. MICHEL ZIEGLER; Gen. Man. MICHEL GOUZE; fleet of 2 Dornier 228 and 2 ATR 42.

Tourism

Martinique's tourist attractions are its beaches and coastal scenery, its mountainous interior, and the historic towns of Fort-de-France and Saint Pierre. Earnings from the tourist industry totalled US $180m. in 1987. In that year there were 3,394 hotel rooms. Tourist arrivals totalled 230,000 in 1988.

Délégation Régionale au Tourisme: 41 rue Gabriel Péri, 97200 Fort-de-France; tel. 631861; Dir GILBERT LECURIEUK.

Office du Tourisme: Pavillon du Tourisme, blvd Alfassa, BP 520, 97206 Fort-de-France; tel. 637960; telex 912678; fax 736693; Pres. RODOLPHE DÉSIRÉ; Dir JACQUES GUANNEL.

Syndicat d'Initiative: BP 299, 97203 Fort-de-France; Pres. M. R. ROSE-ROSETTE.

RÉUNION

Introductory Survey

Location, Climate, Language, Religion, Capital

Réunion is an island in the Indian Ocean, lying about 800 km (500 miles) east of Madagascar. The climate varies greatly according to altitude: at sea-level it is tropical, with average temperatures between 20°C (68°F) and 28°C (82°F), but in the uplands it is much cooler, with average temperatures between 8°C (46°F) and 19°C (66°F). Rainfall is abundant, averaging 4,714 mm annually in the uplands, and 686 mm at sea-level. The population is of mixed origin, including people of European, African, Indian and Chinese descent. The official language is French. A large majority of the population are Christians belonging to the Roman Catholic Church. The capital is Saint-Denis.

Recent History

Réunion was first occupied by France in 1642, and was ruled as a colony until 1946, when, in common with certain Caribbean territories, it received full departmental status. In 1974 it became an Overseas Department with the status of a region.

In June 1978 the liberation committee of the Organization of African Unity (OAU, see p. 190) adopted a report recommending measures to hasten the independence of the island, and condemned its occupation by a 'colonial power'. However, this view seemed to have little popular support in Réunion. Although the left-wing political parties on the island advocated increased autonomy (amounting to virtual self-government), few people were in favour of complete independence.

In 1982 the French Government proposed a decentralization scheme, envisaging the dissolution of the General and Regional Councils in the Overseas Departments and the creation in each department of a single assembly, to be elected on the basis of proportional representation. However, this plan met with considerable opposition in Réunion and the other Overseas Departments, and the Government was eventually forced to abandon the project. Revised legislation on decentralization in the Overseas Departments was approved by the French National Assembly in December 1982. Elections for the new Regional Council were held in Réunion in February 1983, when left-wing candidates won 50.77% of the votes cast.

For the general election to the French National Assembly in March 1986, Réunion's representation was increased from three to five deputies. At this election voting was based on a system of proportional representation. The Parti Communiste Réunionnais (PCR) won two seats, while the Union pour la Démocratie Française (UDF), the Rassemblement pour la République (RPR) and a newly-formed right-wing party, France-Réunion-Avenir (FRA), each secured one seat. In the concurrent elections to the Regional Council, the centre-right RPR-UDF alliance and FRA together received 54.1% of the votes cast, winning 18 and eight of the 45 seats respectively, while the PCR won 13 seats. Pierre Lagourgue of FRA was elected President of the Regional Council.

In September 1986 the French Government's plan to introduce a programme of economic reforms provoked criticism from the left-wing parties, which claimed that the proposals should grant the Overseas Departments social equality with metropolitan France through similar levels of taxation and benefits. In October Paul Vergès, the PCR Secretary-General and a deputy to the French National Assembly, accused France of instituting 'social apartheid' in the Overseas Departments, and presented his case to the European Parliament in Strasbourg. In October 1987 Vergès and the other PCR deputy, Elie Hoarau, resigned from the National Assembly, in protest against the Government's proposals, and Laurent Vergès, Paul Vergès's son, and Claude Hoarau, the PCR mayor of Saint-Louis, filled the vacated seats.

In January 1988 a French government proposal to redraw the boundaries of Réunion's administrative districts (cantons) was rejected by the General Council. The proposal was initiated by Auguste Legros, the RPR President of the General Council and mayor of Saint-Denis, and Michel Debré, the island's RPR deputy (and a former French Prime Minister). It was opposed by the Parti Socialiste (PS), the PCR, and by UDF councillors from the RPR-UDF alliance, who resented the extent of power held by Legros, and believed that the proposed boundary changes would, if implemented, be detrimental to the rural districts.

In the second round of the French presidential election on 8 May 1988, François Mitterrand, the incumbent President and PS candidate, received 60.3% of the votes cast in Réunion, whereas Jacques Chirac, the RPR Prime Minister, obtained only 39.7%. Mitterrand won an absolute majority of votes in all five electoral districts in Réunion, including the RPR stronghold of Saint-Denis, owing partly to the transfer of votes from supporters of the PCR and the centre-right parties. Following his re-election, Mitterrand called a general election for the French National Assembly in June, when the system of single-member constituencies was reintroduced. As in the previous general election, the PCR won two of the Réunion seats, while the UDF, the RPR (these two parties allying to form the Union du Rassemblement du Centre—URC) and the FRA each won one seat. The RPR and FRA deputies subsequently became independents, although they maintained strong links with the island's right-wing groups.

Following the general election in June 1988, relations between the PCR and the PS deteriorated, as the PCR accused the PS of failing to encourage its supporters to transfer their support to the PCR candidate for Saint-André in the second round of the election, thus ensuring that the rival UDF candidate won the seat. The PS counterclaimed that the PCR had advised its supporters not to vote for the PS candidate for Saint-Denis in the second round. In July the PCR criticized the Socialist Government for continuing to allocate lower levels of benefits and revenue to the Overseas Departments, despite President Mitterrand's promise, made during his visit to Réunion in February, to grant these departments social equality with metropolitan France.

In the elections for the newly-enlarged 44-member General Council in September and October 1988, the PCR and the PS won nine and four seats respectively, while other left-wing candidates won two seats. The UDF secured six seats and other right-wing candidates 19, but the RPR, which had previously held 11 seats, won only four. Later in October, Eric Boyer, a right-wing independent, was elected to succeed Legros as President of the General Council. In the same month, the PCR deputy, Laurent Vergès, was killed in a road accident. His seat was subsequently taken by Alexis Pota, another member of the PCR. However, Paul Vergès, the PCR Secretary-General, asked Pota to resign, with the apparent intention of taking the seat himself upon the expiry of his term of office as a member of the European Parliament in 1989. Pota refused, and in December he announced that he would not support a list of PCR candidates for Saint-Paul, to be compiled by Vergès in preparation for the municipal elections in March 1989, as Vergès had excluded him from the electoral campaign.

The results of the municipal elections in March 1989 represented a slight decline in support for the left-wing parties. Nevertheless, for the first time since the 1940s, a PS candidate became mayor of Saint-Denis, thus ousting Legros. The PCR endeavoured to retain support, in an attempt to uphold the powerful 'syndicat intercommunal', established in 1983 by six communist municipalities and led by Paul Vergès. At Saint-Pierre the incumbent mayor and PCR deputy to the French National Assembly, Elie Hoarau, unilaterally declared himself the winner, discounting 1,500 votes which had been secured by two minor lists. The result was therefore declared invalid by the administrative tribunal. This incident led to a rift between the PS and the PCR, and, when a fresh election in that municipality was held in September, Elie Hoarau was unable to form an alliance. Hoarau was, however, re-elected mayor, securing just over 50% of the votes cast. Municipal elections in Sainte-Suzanne, Sainte-Marie and Sainte-Rose were also declared invalid, owing to electoral irregularities, in March, May and June respectively, and were subsequently reheld. Second elections were also necessary for two cantons of Saint-Denis, where both leading candidates had failed to gain the support of the equivalent of one-quarter of the electorate in the first election.

The elections to the European Parliament in June 1989 showed a high level of abstention, with only 22.9% of the electorate participating. The UDF-RPR list won 34.05% of the total votes cast, marginally ahead of the PS list (which received 33.47% of the votes).

In August 1989 sugar-cane planters, fearing heavy losses in production after a cyclone in January, picketed sugar factories and blockaded main roads on the island. The barricading of the road linking Saint-Pierre and Saint-Denis led to violent confrontations with the police, in which eight policemen were wounded. The strike ended in early September, after the Government announced new measures compensating the producers for their losses.

In March 1990 violent protests took place in support of an unauthorized television service, Télé Free-DOM. The demonstration followed a decision by the French national broadcasting commission to award a broadcasting permit to a rival company.

In November 1990 the French Minister for Overseas Departments and Territories, Louis Le Pensec, visited Réunion and announced a series of proposed economic and social measures to the General and Regional Councils, in accordance with pledges made by Mitterrand in 1988 regarding the promotion of economic development and social equality between the Overseas Departments and metropolitan France. These measures were criticized as insufficient by right-wing groups and by the PCR.

Following the restructuring of the RPR under the new local leadership of Alain Defaud, right-wing groups began a process of union in preparation for the regional elections in 1992. In November 1990 the refusal of two of the opposition deputies to the French National Assembly, Jean-Paul Virapoullé (a member of the Centre des Démocrates Sociaux, part of the UDF) and André Thien-Ah-Koon (a right-wing independent), to support a motion of censure against the French Government compromised these efforts. Although there were many potential local leaders of a right-wing coalition (including Boyer, Legros and Defaud), they did not declare themselves, fearing that their rivals would unite against them.

In December 1990 Guy Zitte, a right-wing independent, resigned from the General Council, following a six months' suspended sentence for electoral corruption. He was supported throughout his trial by Legros and Boyer.

In January 1986 France was admitted to the Indian Ocean Commission (IOC, see p. 223), owing to its sovereignty over Réunion. Réunion was given the right to host ministerial meetings of the IOC, but would not be allowed to occupy the presidency, owing to its status as a non-sovereign state.

Government

France is represented in Réunion by an appointed Prefect. There are two councils with local powers: the 44-member General Council and the 45-member Regional Council. Both are elected for up to six years by direct universal suffrage. Réunion sends five directly-elected deputies to the National Assembly in Paris and three indirectly-elected representatives to the Senate. The department is also represented at the European Parliament in Strasbourg.

Defence

Réunion is the headquarters of French military forces in the Indian Ocean. In June 1990 there were 3,300 French troops stationed on Réunion and Mayotte.

Economic Affairs

Réunion's gross national product (GNP) per head in 1987 was estimated at 36,000 francs. During 1980–89 Réunion's population increased at an average rate of 1.6% per year. Réunion's gross domestic product (GDP) per head in 1988 was estimated at 39,500 francs. GDP increased, in real terms, by an annual average of 1.0% in 1973–86.

Agriculture (including hunting, forestry and fishing) contributed 9% of GDP in 1988. An estimated 9.3% of the working population were employed in the sector in 1987. The principal cash crops are sugar cane (sugar and molasses accounted for 76.4% of export

FRENCH OVERSEAS DEPARTMENTS — Réunion

earnings in 1988), maize, tobacco, vanilla, and geraniums and vetiver root, which are cultivated for the production of essential oils. Fishing is also important to the economy. In 1988 agricultural production increased by 6%.

Industry (including mining, manufacturing, construction and power) contributed 23% of GDP in 1985, and employed an estimated 23.1% of the working population in 1987. The principal branch of manufacturing is food-processing, particularly the production of sugar and rum, while civil and agricultural construction is becoming increasingly important. There are no mineral resources on the island. Imports of mineral fuels comprised 4.6% of the value of total imports in 1987. Energy is derived principally from thermal and hydroelectric power, which constituted 55.3% and 44.7%, respectively, of total electricity production (762.8m. kWh) in 1988.

Services (including transport, communications, trade and finance) contributed 67.8% of GDP in 1983, and employed 67.6% of the working population in 1987. The public sector accounts for about one-half of employment in the services sector. Commerce expanded by 14% in 1988. The tourist industry was also developing rapidly: tourist arrivals increased by 19% in 1989, compared with the previous year.

In 1988 Réunion recorded a trade deficit of US $1,028m. The principal source of imports (67.4%) in 1988 was France, which was also the principal market for exports (70.4%). Other major trading partners were Italy, Bahrain, the Federal Republic of Germany, Japan and South Africa. The principal exports in 1988 were sugar, rum, oil of geranium, vanilla, and oil of vetiver root. The principal imports in 1987 were food, machinery and transport equipment, chemicals, mineral fuels and clothing.

In 1989 there was an estimated budgetary deficit of 425m. francs. The annual rate of inflation averaged 6.8% in 1980-88. The rate increased from 1.3% in 1988 to 3.9% in 1989, and to 4.6% in the year to September 1990. An estimated 35% of the labour force were unemployed at the end of 1987.

Réunion is represented by France in the Indian Ocean Commission (IOC, see p. 223). As an integral part of France, Réunion belongs to the European Community, and was to receive 347m. ECUs in Community aid during the period 1989-93, in order to adapt to the requirements of the single European market, which was due to become operational in 1992.

Réunion has a relatively developed economy. Nevertheless, it is dependent on financial aid from France. The economy is dominated by agriculture, and is therefore vulnerable to adverse climatic conditions. In 1989 the agricultural sector suffered from the effects of a cyclone, including the reduction of sugar production to its lowest level for 30 years. However, industrial development was stimulated by the resultant investment in reconstruction. In January 1989 legislation establishing a guaranteed minimum income was approved. In 1990 there was widespread concern that more than 20% of the population of Réunion were dependent on this income supplement. In January 1990 a French government commission, appointed in 1989 to examine the economic condition of the Overseas Departments, published a report containing 58 proposals for the rectification of social and economic shortcomings in Réunion, and recommended a programme of improvements, to be phased over two three-year stages.

Social Welfare

In 1989 Réunion had 3,270 hospital beds, 928 physicians, 185 nurses and 250 dentists. There is a system of social welfare similar to that of metropolitan France.

Education

Education is compulsory for children aged six to 16 years, and consists of five years' primary and five years' secondary schooling. In 1987 there were 354 primary schools and 69 secondary schools, comprising 59 junior comprehensives, or collèges, and 10 lycées, on the island. There is a university, with several faculties, a teacher-training college, a technical institute and an agricultural college. In 1982 the illiteracy rate among the population over 15 years of age averaged 21.4% (males 23.5%; females 19.5%).

Public Holidays

The principal holidays of metropolitan France are observed.

Weights and Measures

The metric system is in use.

Statistical Survey

Source: Institut National de la Statistique et des Etudes Economiques, Service Régional de la Réunion, 15 rue de l'Ecole, 97490 Sainte-Clotilde; tel. 29-51-57; telex 916405.

AREA AND POPULATION

Area: 2,512 sq km (970 sq miles).

Population: 515,798 (males 252,997, females 262,801) at census of 9 March 1982; 596,600 (provisional) at census of 15 March 1990.

Principal Towns (population at census of 15 March 1990, provisional): Saint-Denis (capital) 121,999; Saint-Paul 71,669; Saint-Pierre 58,846; Le Tampon 47,593.

Births and Deaths (1988): Registered live births 13,561 (birth rate 23.6 per 1,000); Registered deaths 3,163 (death rate 5.5 per 1,000). Figures exclude live-born infants dying before registration of birth.

Economically Active Population (1982 census): Employed 118,490 (males 77,270, females 41,220); Unemployed 54,338 (males 33,548, females 20,790). Mid-1989 (FAO estimates): Agriculture 26,000; Total labour force 220,000.

AGRICULTURE, ETC.

Principal Agricultural Products (metric tons, 1988): Sugar cane 2,225,700, Raw sugar 252,400, Maize 13,019, Oil of geranium 20.6, Oil of vetiver root 7.9, Vanilla 54.4, Tobacco 192.8.

Livestock (agricultural census, year ending August 1989): Cattle 18,601; Pigs 70,921; Goats 31,318; Chickens 1,348,000.

Forestry: Roundwood removals: 33,000 cubic metres in 1976; estimated at 33,000 cubic metres annually in 1977-88. Source: FAO, *Yearbook of Forest Products*.

Fishing (metric tons, live weight): Total catch 1,694 in 1986; 1,746 in 1987; 1,931 (fishes 1,583, crustaceans 348) in 1988. Source: FAO, *Yearbook of Fishery Statistics*.

FINANCE

Currency and Exchange Rates: French currency is used (see French Guiana).

Budget Estimate (million francs, 1990): Revenue (incl. loans) 3,412; Expenditure 3,412.

Cost of Living (Consumer Price Index for urban areas, average of monthly figures; base: 1980 = 100): 166.9 in 1987; 169.1 in 1988; 175.7 in 1989. Source: UN, *Monthly Bulletin of Statistics*.

Expenditure on the Gross Domestic Product (million francs at current prices, 1987): Government final consumption expenditure 6,503; Private final consumption expenditure 16,811; Increase in stocks 125; Gross fixed capital formation 4,560; *Total domestic expenditure* 27,999; Exports of goods and services 1,115; *Less* Imports of goods and services 8,751; *GDP in purchasers' values* 20,363.

Gross Domestic Product by Economic Activity (million francs at current prices, 1982): Agriculture, hunting, forestry and fishing 828.2; Mining and manufacturing 1,125.8; Electricity, gas and water 225.1; Construction 638.5; Trade, restaurants and hotels 1,751.2; Transport, storage and communications 561.0; Finance, insurance, real estate and business services 1,340.7; Government services 3,495.7; Other community, social and personal services 1,558.6; Other services 301.5; *Sub-total* 11,826.3; Import duties 488.1; Value-added tax 510.6; *Less* Imputed bank service charge 538.7; *Total* 12,286.2.

EXTERNAL TRADE

Principal Commodities (million francs): *Imports* (1987): Agricultural, fishing and forestry products 1,250, Processed agricultural products 550, Fuels 400, Intermediate goods 1,500, Capital goods 2,900, Consumer goods 2,150; Total 8,750. *Exports* (1988): Sugar 747.7, Molasses 7.4, Rum 17.0, Oil of geranium 15.1, Vanilla 7.2, Oil of vetiver root 9.5, Spiny lobsters 27.3; Total (incl. others) 987.8.

Principal Trading Partners (million francs): *Imports* (1988): Bahrain 279.5, France 6,747.4, Federal Republic of Germany 347.6, Italy 355.2, Japan 263.7, South Africa 208.2; Total (incl. others) 10,006.5. *Exports* (1988): France 695.4, Others 292.4.

TRANSPORT

Road Traffic (1990): Motor vehicles in use 139,000.

Shipping (1988): Vessels entered 418; Freight unloaded 1,565,300 metric tons; Freight loaded 337,600 metric tons; Passenger arrivals 332; Passenger departures 79.

Civil Aviation (1988): Passenger arrivals 308,470; Passenger departures 323,720; Freight unloaded 11,332 metric tons; Freight loaded 3,434 metric tons.

TOURISM

Tourist Arrivals (by country of residence, 1989): France 132,200, Switzerland 2,800, Federal Republic of Germany 2,600, Italy 1,050; Total (incl. others) 182,000.

FRENCH OVERSEAS DEPARTMENTS
Réunion

COMMUNICATIONS MEDIA

Radio receivers (1988): 135,000 in use.
Television receivers (1989): 96,756 in use.
Telephones (1989): 136,355 in use.
Book production (1985): 73 titles (41 books; 32 pamphlets).
Daily newspapers (1986): 2 (average circulation 49,000 copies).
Non-daily newspapers (1982): 2 (average circulation 9,000 copies).

EDUCATION

Pre-primary: Teachers 1,336 (1986), Pupils 41,137 (1989/90), Schools 151 (1987).
Primary: Teachers 3,917 (1986), Pupils 74,002 (1989/90), Schools 354 (1987).
Secondary: Teachers 4,370 (1988/89), Pupils 76,498 (1989/90), Schools 69 (1987).
University: Teaching Staff 90 (1986/87), Students 3,564 (1987/88). There is also a teacher training college, a technical institute and an agricultural college.

Directory

The Government
(February 1991)

Prefect: DANIEL CONSTANTIN.
President of the General Council: ERIC BOYER (Right-wing independent).
President of the Economic and Social Committee: TONY MANGLOU.
Deputies to the French National Assembly: AUGUSTE LEGROS (Right-wing independent), ALEXIS POTA (PCR), ELIE HOARAU (PCR), JEAN-PAUL VIRAPOULLÉ (UDF/CDS), ANDRÉ THIEN-AH-KOON (Right-wing independent).
Representatives to the French Senate: JOSEPH SINIMALÉ (RPR-UDF), ALBERT RAMASSAMY (PS), LOUIS VIRAPOULLÉ (Independent).

REGIONAL COUNCIL
Palais Rontaunay, rue Rontaunay, 97488 Saint-Denis.
President: PIERRE LAGOURGUE (FRA).

Election, 16 March 1986

Party	% of Votes	Seats
RPR-UDF	36.8	18
PCR	28.2	13
FRA and other right-wing	17.3	8
PS	14.1	6
Others	3.6	—
Total	100.0	45

Political Organizations

France-Réunion-Avenir (FRA): Saint-Denis; f. 1986; centre-right.
Front National (FN): Saint-Denis; f. 1972; extreme right-wing; Leader ALIX MOREL.
Mouvement des Radicaux de Gauche (MRG): BP 991, 97479 Saint-Denis; f. 1977; advocates full independence and an economy separate from, but assisted by, France; Pres. JEAN-MARIE FINCK.
Mouvement pour l'Indépendance de la Réunion (MIR): f. 1981 from the fmr Mouvement pour la Libération de la Réunion; grouping of parties favouring autonomy.
Parti Communiste Réunionnais (PCR): Saint-Denis; f. 1959; Sec.-Gen. PAUL VERGÈS.
Parti Socialiste (PS)—Fédération de la Réunion: 85 rue d'Après, 97400 Saint-Denis; tel. 21-77-95; telex 916445; left-wing; Sec.-Gen. JEAN-CLAUDE FRUTEAU.
Rassemblement des Démocrates pour l'Avenir de la Réunion (RADAR): BP 866, 97477 Saint-Denis Cedex; f. 1981; centrist.
Rassemblement des Socialistes et des Démocrates (RSD): Saint-Denis; Sec.-Gen. DANIEL CADET.
Rassemblement pour la République (RPR): 25 rue Labourdonnais, 97400 Saint-Denis; tel. 20-21-18; telex 916080; Gaullist; Sec. for Réunion ALAIN DEFAUD.

Union pour la Démocratie Française (UDF): Saint-Denis; f. 1978; centrist; Sec.-Gen. GILBERT GÉRARD; affiliated parties:
  Centre des Démocrates Sociaux (CDS).
  Parti Républicain (PR).

Judicial System

Cour d'appel: Palais de Justice, 166 rue Juliette Dodu, 97488 Saint-Denis; tel. 40-58-58; telex 916149; fax 21-95-32; Pres. ROBERT DUFOURGBURG.
There are two **Tribunaux de grande instance**, one **Cour d'assises**, four **Tribunaux d'instance**, two **Tribunaux pour enfants** and two **Conseils de prud'hommes**.

Religion

A substantial majority of the population are adherents of the Roman Catholic Church. There is a small Muslim community.

CHRISTIANITY
The Roman Catholic Church
Réunion comprises a single diocese, directly responsible to the Holy See. At 31 December 1988 there were an estimated 520,000 adherents, representing about 90% of the population.
Bishop of Saint-Denis-de-La Réunion: Mgr GILBERT AUBRY, Evêché, 36 rue de Paris, BP 55, 97462 Saint-Denis; tel. 21-28-49; fax 41-77-15.

The Press

DAILIES

Journal de l'Ile de la Réunion: 42 rue Alexis de Villeneuve, BP 98, 97463 Saint-Denis; tel. 21-32-64; telex 916453; f. 1956; Dir PHILIPPE BALOUKJY; circ. 26,000.
Quotidien de la Réunion: BP 303, 97467 Saint-Denis Cedex; tel. 28-10-10; tel. 29-10-10; telex 916183; fax 28-25-28; f. 1976; Dir MAXIMIN CHANE KI CHUNE; circ. 28,000.
Témoignages: 21 bis rue de l'Est, BP 192, 97465 Saint-Denis; f. 1944; organ of the Parti Communiste Réunionnais; Dir ELIE HOARAU; circ. 6,000.

PERIODICALS

Al-Islam: 31 rue M. A. Leblond, BP 437, 97410 Saint-Pierre; tel. 25-19-65; publ. by the Centre Islamique de la Réunion; monthly; Dir SAÏD INGAR.
Cahiers de la Réunion et de l'Océan Indien: 24 blvd des Cocotiers, 97434 Saint-Gilles-les-Bains; monthly; Man. Dir CLAUDETTE SAINT-MARC.
Les Cahiers du Centre Universitaire de la Réunion: ave de la Victoire, 97400 Saint-Denis; Dir ANNE JACQUEMIN.
L'Economie de la Réunion: c/o INSEE, 15 rue de l'Ecole, Le Chaudron, 97490 Sainte-Clotilde; tel. 29-51-57; telex 916405; 6 a year; Dir M. JACOD; Editor-in-Chief GILLES LE COINTRE.
Gazette de l'Ile de la Réunion: Saint-Denis; weekly.
Le Memento Industriel et Commercial Réunionnais: 80 rue Pasteur, 97400 Saint-Denis; tel. 21-94-12; fax 41-10-85; Dir CATHERINE LOUAPRE POTTIER; circ. 10,000.
974 Ouest: Montgaillard, 97400 Saint-Denis; monthly; Dir DENISE ELMA.
Les Nouvelles Economiques: 5 bis rue de Paris, BP 120, 97463 Saint-Denis; tel. 21-53-66; telex 916278; fax 41-80-34; monthly; Dir JEAN-PIERRE FOURTOY.
La Réunion Agricole: Chambre d'Agriculture, 24 rue de la Source, BP 134, 97464 Saint-Denis Cedex; tel. 21-25-88; fax 41-17-84; monthly; Dir MARCEL BOLON; Chief Editor SULLY DAMOUR; circ. 8,000.
Télé 7 Jours Réunion: BP 405, 9469 Saint-Denis; weekly; Dir MICHEL MEKDOUD; circ. 25,000.
Témoignage Chrétien de la Réunion: 21 bis rue de l'Est, 97465 Saint-Denis; weekly; Dir RENÉ PAYET; circ. 2,000.
Visu: BP 3000, 97402 Saint-Denis; tel. 29-10-10; weekly; Editor-in-Chief J. J. AYAN; circ. 53,000.

Radio and Television

There were an estimated 135,000 radio receivers in use in 1988 and 96,756 television receivers (including 63,135 colour receivers)

FRENCH OVERSEAS DEPARTMENTS — Réunion

in use in 1989. Since 1985 there has been a growth in the number of private local radio stations. In March 1990 the French national broadcasting commission granted 18m. francs to the television service Antenne Réunion to broadcast on the island. A complementary service, to be provided by Canal Réunion, was approved in July.

Antenne Réunion: Saint-Denis; broadcasts five hours daily.

Canal Réunion: Saint-Denis; subscription television channel; broadcasts a minimum of 12 hours daily.

Société Nationale de Radio-Télévision Française d'Outre-Mer (RFO): 1 rue Jean Chatel, 97405 Saint-Denis Cedex; tel. 40-67-67; telex 916842; fax 21-64-84; home radio and television relay services in French; operates two television channels; Dir JEAN-PHILIPPE ROUSSY.

Télé Free-DOM: BP 666, 97474 Saint-Denis Cedex; tel. 41-30-30; telex 916174; fax 41-25-71; f. 1986; privately-owned TV service, operating without authorization from the French national broadcasting commission; Dir Dr CAMILLE SUDRE.

Other privately-owned television services include TVB, RTV, Télé-Réunion and TV-Run.

Finance

(cap. = capital; res = reserves; m. = million; dep. = deposits; brs = branches; amounts in French francs)

BANKING

Central Bank

Institut d'Emission des Départements d'Outre-Mer: 1 cité du Retiro, 75008 Paris, France; Office in Réunion: 4 rue de la Compagnie, 97487 Saint-Denis Cedex; tel. 21-18-96; telex 916176; fax 21-41-32; Dir JACQUES PIERRAT.

Commercial Banks

Banque Française Commerciale: 60 rue Alexis de Villeneuve, 97400 Saint-Denis; tel. 40-55-55; telex 916162; affiliate of Banque Indosuez; Dir JEAN-PIERRE PARSI; 8 brs.

Banque Nationale de Paris Intercontinentale: 67 rue Juliette Dodu, BP 113, 97463 Saint-Denis; tel. 40-30-30; telex 916133; fax 41-39-09; Man. Dir JEAN-CLAUDE LALLEMANT; 13 brs.

Banque de la Réunion, SA: 27 rue Jean-Chatel, 97400 Saint-Denis; tel. 40-01-23; telex 916134; fax 41-48-14; f. 1849; affiliate of Crédit Lyonnais; cap. and res. 203.2m., dep. 2,843.6m. (1988); Pres. XAVIER BESSON; Man. Dir MICHEL GENADINOS; 15 brs.

Caisse Régionale de Crédit Agricole Mutuel de la Réunion: parc Jean de Cambiaire, cité des Lauriers, BP 84, 97462 Saint-Denis Cedex; tel. 40-81-81; telex 916139; fax 40-81-40; f. 1949; affiliate of Caisse Nationale de Crédit Agricole; Chair. CHRISTIAN DE LA GIRODAY; Dir HENRI PAVIE.

Development Bank

Banque Populaire Fédérale de Développement: 33 rue Victor MacAuliffe, 97400 Saint-Denis; tel. 21-18-11; telex 916582; Dir OLIVIER DEVISME; 3 brs.

INSURANCE

More than 20 major European insurance companies are represented in Saint-Denis.

Trade and Industry

Association pour le Développement Industriel de la Réunion: 18 rue Milius, 97468 Saint-Denis Cedex; tel. 21-42-69; telex 916666; fax 20-37-57; f. 1975; 190 mems; Pres. PAUL MARTINEL.

Chambre d'Agriculture: 24 rue de la Source, BP 134, 97464 Saint-Denis Cedex; tel. 21-25-88; telex 916843; Pres. ANGÉLO LAURET.

Chambre de Commerce et d'Industrie de la Réunion: 5 bis rue de Paris, BP 120, 97463 Saint-Denis Cedex; tel. 21-53-66; telex 916278; fax 41-80-34; f. 1830; Pres. ALEX HOW-CHOONG; Man. Dir JEAN-PIERRE FOURTOY.

Direction de l'Action Economique: Secrétariat Général pour les Affaires Economiques, ave de la Victoire, 97405 Saint-Denis; tel. 21-86-10; telex 916111.

Jeune Chambre Economique de Saint-Denis de la Réunion: 25 rue de Paris, BP 1151, 97483 Saint-Denis; f. 1963; 30 mems; Chair. OLIVIER MOREAU.

Société de Développement Economique de la Réunion — SODERE: 26 rue Labourdonnais, 97469 Saint-Denis; tel. 20-01-68; telex 916471; fax 20-05-07; f. 1964; Chair. PIERRE PEYRON; Man. Dir ALBERT TRIMAILLE.

Syndicat des Exportateurs d'Huiles Essentielles, Plantes Aromatiques et Medicinales de Bourbon: 38 bis rue Labourdonnais, 97400 Saint-Denis; tel. 20-10-23; exports oil of geranium, vetiver and vanilla; Pres. RICO PLOENIÈRES.

Syndicat des Fabricants de Sucre de la Réunion: BP 57, 97462 Saint-Denis; tel. 21-67-00; telex 916138; fax 41-24-13; Chair. MAXIME RIVIÈRE.

Syndicat des Producteurs de Rhum de la Réunion: BP 57, 97462 Saint-Denis; tel. 21-67-00; telex 916138; fax 41-24-13; Chair. PIERRE GORCE.

Syndicat Patronal du Bâtiment de la Réunion: BP 108, 97463 Saint-Denis; tel. 21-03-81; telex 916393; fax 21-55-07; Pres. R. ROLAND; Sec.-Gen. C. OZOUX.

TRADE UNIONS

Confédération Générale du Travail de la Réunion (CGTR): 104 rue Maréchal Leclerc, 97400 Saint-Denis; Sec.-Gen. BRUNY PAYET.

Réunion also has its own sections of the major French trade union confederations, **Confédération Française Démocratique du Travail (CFDT)**, **Force Ouvrière (FO)**, **Confédération Française de l'Encadrement** and **Confédération Française des Travailleurs Chrétiens (CFTC)**.

Transport

ROADS

A route nationale circles the island, generally following the coast and linking all the main towns. Another route nationale crosses the island from south-west to north-east linking Saint-Pierre and Saint-Benoît. In 1982 there were 345.7 km of routes nationales, 731.5 km of departmental roads and 1,602.9 km of other roads. A cyclone in February 1987 extensively damaged the island's road network.

SHIPPING

In 1986 work was completed on the expansion of the Port de la Pointe des Galets, which was divided into the former port in the west and a new port in the east (the port Ouest and the port Est). In 1989 a total of nearly 2.1m. tons of freight were loaded and discharged at the two ports.

Compagnie Générale Maritime (CGM): 2 rue de l'Est, BP 2010, 97822 Le Port Cedex; tel. 42-00-88; telex 916106; fax 43-23-04; agents for Mitsui OSK Lines, Unicorn Lines, Marine Chartering, Compagnie Générale Maritime, Tropic Lines; Dir RENAUD SAUVAGET.

Navale et Commerciale Havraise Péninsulaire: rue de St Paul, BP 29, 97420 Le Port; freight only.

Société de Manutention et de Consignation Maritime (SOMACOM): BP 7, Le Port; agents for Scandinavian East Africa Line, Bank Line, Clan Line, Union Castle Mail Steamship Co and States Marine Lines.

CIVIL AVIATION

There is an international airport at Saint-Denis Gillot.

Air Outre-Mer: Saint-Denis; f. 1990; scheduled services to Paris; Chair. RENÉ MICAUD.

Air Réunion: BP 611, 97473 Saint-Denis; tel. 28-22-60; telex 916236; f. 1975; subsidiary of Air France; scheduled services to Madagascar and the Comoros; Gen. Man. Mme B. POPINEAU; fleet of 1 HS748, 1 Navajo Chieftain, 1 Cherokee Six, 2 SA315B Lama, 1 Alouette II, 1 Alouette III, 1 Dauphin C2, 1 Fokker F28/1000.

Tourism

Tourism is being extensively developed. A 'holiday village' has been opened in Saint-Gilles, and in 1989 the island had 29 hotels with a total of 1,256 rooms. In 1989 a total of 182,000 tourists visited the island.

Comité du Tourisme de la Réunion: BP 1119, 97482 Saint-Denis Cedex; tel. 41-84-41; fax 41-84-29; Pres. BERTHO AUDIFAX.

Délégation Régionale au Commerce, à l'Artisanat et au Tourisme: Préfecture de la Réunion, 97400 Saint-Denis; tel. 40-77-58; telex 916111; fax 41-73-74; Dir JEAN-FRANÇOIS DESROCHES.

Office du Tourisme: rue Rontaunay 97400 Saint-Denis; tel. 21-24-53; telex 916486; Chair. S. PERSONNÉ.

FRENCH OVERSEAS COLLECTIVITÉS TERRITORIALES — *Mayotte*

French Overseas Collectivités Territoriales

The two Overseas Collectivités Territoriales are Mayotte and St Pierre and Miquelon. Their status is between that of an overseas department and that of an overseas territory. They are integral parts of the French Republic and are both administered by a Prefect, appointed by the French Government. The Prefect is assisted by an elected General Council. The collectivités territoriales are represented in the French National Assembly and in the Senate in Paris, and also in the European Parliament in Strasbourg.

MAYOTTE

Introductory Survey

Location, Climate, Language, Religion, Capital

The island of Mayotte forms part of the Comoro archipelago, which lies between the island of Madagascar and the east coast of the African mainland. The climate is tropical, with temperatures averaging between 24°C and 27°C (75°F to 81°F) throughout the year. The official language is French, and Islam is the main religion. The capital is Dzaoudzi.

Recent History

Since the Comoros unilaterally declared independence in July 1975, Mayotte (Mahoré) has been administered separately by France. The independent Comoran state claims Mayotte as part of its territory and officially represents it in international organizations, including the United Nations. In December 1976 France introduced the special status of collectivité territoriale for the island. Following the coup in the Comoros in May 1978, Mayotte rejected the new Government's proposal that it should rejoin the other islands under a federal system, and reaffirmed its intention of remaining linked to France. In December 1979 the French National Assembly approved legislation to prolong Mayotte's special status for another five years, during which the islanders were to be consulted. However, in October 1984 the National Assembly further prolonged Mayotte's status, and the referendum on the island's future was postponed indefinitely. The UN General Assembly has adopted several resolutions reaffirming the sovereignty of the Comoros over the island, and urging France to come to an agreement with the Comoran Government as soon as possible. The main political party on Mayotte, the Mouvement Populaire Mahorais (MPM), demands full departmental status for the island, but France has been reluctant to grant this in view of Mayotte's lack of development. In June 1989 Tanzania and the Comoros expressed concern over the question of sovereignty over Mayotte, and issued a joint communiqué urging an early solution to the problem.

Following the general election to the French National Assembly in March 1986, the RPR-UDF alliance formed a new government in mainland France. At the election, a UDF/CDS candidate was elected as deputy for Mayotte. In October Jacques Chirac became the first French Prime Minister to visit Mayotte, and he assured the islanders that they would remain French citizens for as long as they wished. Meanwhile, the French Government prepared a five-year Development Plan which included the reform of laws relating to land, labour, town-planning, public markets and penal procedure, to be implemented by decree if necessary. In March 1987 there were clashes between islanders and illegal Comoran immigrants. Order was eventually restored, following the arrival of gendarmes from Réunion. In August the Comoros boycotted the Indian Ocean's first 'Youth Games', in protest against the participation of Mayotte. Relations between the MPM and the French Government rapidly deteriorated after the Franco-African summit in November, when Chirac expressed his reservations to the Comoran President concerning the elevation of Mayotte to the status of an overseas department despite the announcement, made by him during the RPR-UDF alliance's election campaign in early 1986, that he shared the MPM's aim to upgrade Mayotte's status.

In the first round of the 1988 French presidential election, which was held on 24 April, the islanders favoured the candidacy of Raymond Barre, from the centre-right, to that of Chirac, the RPR candidate. In the second round of the election on 8 May, which was contested by Chirac and the incumbent Socialist President, François Mitterrand, supporters of Barre on Mayotte transferred a large proportion of their votes to Mitterrand, rather than to Chirac. Mitterrand received 50.3% of the votes cast on Mayotte in the second round, compared with only 4% in the first round.

At the general election for the French National Assembly, which was held in June after Mitterrand's re-election as President, the UDF/CDS deputy for Mayotte retained his seat. (Later that month, he joined the newly-formed centrist group in the French National Assembly, the Union du Centre (UDC), which aimed to provide constructive opposition to the newly-elected Socialist Government.) In the cantonal election in September and October, the MPM retained the majority of seats in the General Council. At municipal elections in March 1989 the MPM again secured the majority of votes. In June, at elections to the European Parliament, the centre parties won the greatest number of votes.

In November 1988 the General Council had urged the French Government to introduce measures to curb immigration to Mayotte from neighbouring islands, particularly from the Comoros. Mayotte was affected by the situation in the Comoros, following the assassination of President Ahmed Abdallah in November 1989 (see p. 779). As the only island in the archipelago under French administration, Mayotte was used as a strategic military base, where additional French troops were amassed in December, in preparation for possible military intervention.

In 1989 and 1990 concern about the growing number of Comoran immigrants seeking employment on the island led to an increase in racial tension. In 1989 more than 150 Comoran refugees were prevented from landing on Mayotte by security forces. In mid-January 1990 demonstrators in the town of Mamoudzou protested against illegal immigration to the island. A paramilitary organization, 'Caiman', which demanded the expulsion of illegal immigrants, was subsequently formed, but was refused legal recognition by the authorities.

(For further details of the recent history of the island, see the chapter on the Comoros, p. 778.)

Government

The French Government is represented in Mayotte by an appointed Prefect. There is a General Council, with 17 members, elected by universal adult suffrage. Mayotte elects one deputy to the French National Assembly, and one representative to the Senate. Mayotte is also represented at the European Parliament in Strasbourg.

Defence

In June 1990 there were 3,300 French troops stationed in Mayotte and Réunion.

Economic Affairs

The economy of Mayotte is based entirely on agriculture. The principal crops are vanilla, ylang-ylang, coffee and coconuts. Rice, cassava and maize are cultivated for domestic consumption. Livestock-rearing and fishing are also important activities. However, Mayotte imports large quantities of foodstuffs, which comprised 22% of the value of total imports in 1988.

Construction is the sole industrial sector. There are no mineral resources on the island. Imports of mineral products comprised 4.4%, and metals 10.5%, of the value of total imports in 1988.

In 1989 Mayotte recorded a trade deficit of 302.6m. francs. The principal source of imports in 1988 was France (65.8%), which was also the principal market for exports. Other major trading partners are South Africa, Thailand and Réunion. The principal exports in 1989 were oil of ylang-ylang (accounting for 78% of domestic exports) and vanilla (21%). The principal imports were foodstuffs, machinery, transport equipment and metals.

In 1986 Mayotte's external assets totalled 203.8m. francs, and banking aid reached 6.3m. francs. In 1990 Mayotte's budget expenditure was an estimated 338m. francs.

Mayotte suffers from a high trade deficit, owing to its reliance on imports, and is largely dependent on French aid. A five-year

FRENCH OVERSEAS COLLECTIVITÉS TERRITORIALES — Mayotte

Development Plan (1986–91) included proposals for investment in public works. Substantial aid from France during the period 1987–92 aims to encourage the development of tourism on the island by financing the construction of a deep-water port and an airport. Mayotte's remote location, however, remains an obstacle to the development of the tourist sector.

Social Welfare

Medical services on Mayotte are available free of charge. The island is divided into six sectors, each of which is allocated a doctor or medical worker. Mayotte has two hospitals, situated at Mamoudzou and at Dzaoudzi, which provide a total of 77 beds. In 1985 there were nine physicians and 51 qualified nurses working in Mayotte.

Education

Education is compulsory for children aged six to 16 years, and comprises five years' primary and five years' secondary schooling. In 1986 there were 28 primary schools and two secondary colleges on the island. In the same year 15,632 primary school pupils and 1,392 secondary school pupils were enrolled. Further technical training is available in Réunion.

Public Holidays

The principal holidays of metropolitan France are observed.

Statistical Survey

Source: mainly Office of the Prefect, Government Commissioner, Dzaoudzi.

AREA AND POPULATION

Area: 374 sq km (144 sq miles).

Population: 67,167 (census of August 1985); 73,000 (estimate for 1 January 1988). *Principal towns* (population at 1985 census): Dzaoudzi (capital) 5,865, Mamoudzou 12,026, Pamanzi-Labattoir 4,106.

FINANCE

Currency and Exchange Rates: French currency is used (see French Guiana).

Budget (estimates, million francs): Total expenditure 301.7 in 1988; 371.6 (current 197.2, capital 174.4) in 1989; 338 (current 236, capital 102) in 1990.

EXTERNAL TRADE

Principal Commodities ('000 francs, 1988): *Imports:* Foodstuffs 65,014; Machinery and appliances 61,097; Metals and metal products 31,061; Transport equipment 50,097; Total (incl. others) 294,981. *Exports:* Oil of ylang-ylang 8,188; Vanilla 1,810; Coffee (green) 178; Total (incl. others) 10,189. Figures exclude re-exports (42.9 million francs in 1988). *1989* (million francs): Total imports 338.1; Total exports 35.5.

Principal Trading Partners ('000 francs): *Imports* (1988): France 193,984; Singapore 9,507; South Africa 26,854; Thailand 12,617; Total (incl. others) 294,981. *Exports* (1983): France 4,405.
Source: Secrétariat du Comité Monétaire de la Zone Franc: *La Zone Franc, Rapport 1988*.

TRANSPORT

Roads (1984): 93 km of main roads, of which 72 km are tarred, 137 km of local roads, of which 40 km are tarred, and 54 km of tracks unusable in the rainy season; 1,528 vehicles.

Civil Aviation (1984): *Arrivals:* 7,747 passengers, 120 metric tons of freight; *Departures:* 7,970 passengers, 41 metric tons of freight.

EDUCATION

Primary (1986): 28 schools, 366 teachers, 15,632 pupils.

Secondary (1986): 2 schools, 65 teachers, 1,392 pupils.

Directory

The Constitution

At a referendum in April 1976, the population of Mayotte voted to renounce the status of an overseas territory. They expressed their desire for departmental status, but this has been rejected by the French Government. The change in status of the island to a collectivité territoriale involved the election of a General Council with 17 members to assist the Prefect in the administration of the island. In December 1979 the French National Assembly voted to extend this status for five years. A further referendum was due to be held in 1984, but was postponed indefinitely in December of that year.

The Government

(February 1991)

Prefect: DANIEL LIMODIN.
Secretary-General: PHILIPPE SCHAEFER.
Deputy to the French National Assembly: HENRY JEAN-BAPTISTE (UDC).
Representative to the French Senate: MARCEL HENRY (MPM).

GENERAL COUNCIL

The General Council has 17 members, of whom nine represent the Mouvement Populaire Mahorais (MPM). The most recent elections were held in September and October 1988.

President of the General Council: YOUSSOUF BAMANA.

Political Organizations

Fédération de Mayotte du Rassemblement pour la République: Dzaoudzi, 97610 Mayotte; local branch of the French (Gaullist) RPR; holds six seats in the General Council; Sec.-Gen. MANSOUR KAMARDINE.

Mouvement Populaire Mahorais (MPM): Dzaoudzi, 97610 Mayotte; seeks departmental status for Mayotte; Leader YOUSSOUF BAMANA.

Parti pour le Rassemblement Démocratique des Mahorais (PRDM): Dzaoudzi, 97610 Mayotte; f. 1978; seeks unification with the Federal Islamic Republic of the Comoros; Leader DAROUÈCHE MAOULIDA.

Union pour la Démocratie Française (UDF): centrist.
 Centre des Démocrates Sociaux (CDS).

Prior to the French general election of June 1988, the two major French right-wing political parties, the **Rassemblement pour la République (RPR)** and the **Union pour la Démocratie Française (UDF)**, formed an electoral alliance, the **Union du Rassemblement du Centre (URC)**. After the election, 40 UDF deputies, including the deputy from Mayotte, formed a new centrist parliamentary group, the **Union du Centre (UDC)**.

Judicial System

Tribunal Supérieur d'Appel: 97600 Mayotte; tel. 61-12-65; fax 61-19-63; Pres. JEAN-BAPTISTE FLORI.
Procureur de la République: PATRICK BROSSIER.
Tribunal d'Instance: Pres. ARLETTE MEALLONNIER-DUGUE.

Religion

Muslims comprise about 98% of the population. Most of the remainder are Christians, mainly Roman Catholics.

CHRISTIANITY

The Roman Catholic Church

Mayotte is within the jurisdiction of the Apostolic Administrator of the Comoros.

Vicar-General for Mayotte: Fr ADRIEN TOULORGE.

The Press

Le Journal de Mayotte: BP 181, Mamoudzou, 97600 Mayotte; tel. 61-16-95; f. 1983; weekly; circ. 15,000.

Radio and Television

In 1989 there were an estimated 30,000 radio receivers in use.
Société Nationale de Radio-Télévision Française d'Outre-mer (RFO)—Mayotte: BP 103, Dzaoudzi, 97610 Mayotte; tel. 60-10-17; telex 915822; fax 60-18-52; f. 1977; govt-owned; radio broadcasts in French and Mahorian; television transmissions began in 1986; Regional Dir YVES RAMBEAU; Technical Dir J. BLASCO.

Finance

BANKS

Institut d'Emission d'Outre-mer: Dzaoudzi, 97610 Mayotte.
Banque Française Commerciale: Mamoudzou, 97600 Mayotte; br. at Dzaoudzi.

Transport

ROADS

The main road network totals approximately 93 km, of which 72 km are bituminized. There are 137 km of local roads, of which 40 km are tarred, and 54 km of minor tracks which are unusable during the rainy season.

SHIPPING

Coastal shipping is provided by locally-owned small craft. A deep-water port is under construction at Longoni.

CIVIL AVIATION

There is an airfield at Dzaoudzi, serving four-times weekly commercial flights to Réunion and twice-weekly services to Njazidja, Nzwani and Mwali.

Tourism

The main tourist attraction is the natural beauty of the tropical scenery. In 1985 the island had six hotels, providing a total of approximately 100 beds. Tourist arrivals number an annual average of 1,200 (two-thirds of whom are from France). In 1987 an investment programme, which aimed to encourage the development of tourism on the island, was implemented.

Office du Tourisme de Mayotte: 10 rue de Presbourg, 75116 Paris, France; tel. (1) 45-01-28-30.

ST PIERRE AND MIQUELON

Introductory Survey

Location, Climate, Language, Religion, Capital

The territory of St Pierre and Miquelon (Iles Saint-Pierre-et-Miquelon) consists of a number of small islands which lie about 25 km (16 miles) from the southern coast of Newfoundland, Canada, in the North Atlantic Ocean. The climate is cold and wet, with temperatures falling to −20°C (−4°F) in winter, and averaging between 10° and 20°C (50°–68°F) in summer. The islands are often shrouded in mist and fog. The language is French, and the majority of the population profess Christianity and belong to the Roman Catholic Church. The capital is Saint-Pierre, on the island of St Pierre.

Recent History

The islands of St Pierre and Miquelon are the remnants of the once extensive French possessions in North America. They were confirmed as French territory in 1816, and gained departmental status in July 1976. The departmentalization proved unpopular with many of the islanders, since it incorporated the territory's economy into that of the EEC, and failed to take into account the islands' isolation and their dependence on Canada for supplies and transport links. In March 1982 Socialist and other left-wing candidates, campaigning for a change in the islands' status, were elected unopposed to all seats in the department's General Council. St Pierre and Miquelon was excluded from the Mitterrand Government's decentralization reforms, undertaken in 1982.

In 1976 Canada imposed an economic interest zone extending to 200 nautical miles (370 km) around its shores. As a result of French fears over the loss of traditional fishing areas, and the threat to the livelihood of the fishermen of St Pierre, the Government claimed a similar zone around the islands. The possibility of discovering valuable reserves of petroleum and natural gas in the area heightened the tension between France and Canada. In December 1984 legislation was approved to help solve both the internal and external problems by giving the islands the status of a collectivité territoriale with effect from June 1985. This would, it was hoped, allow St Pierre and Miquelon to receive the investment and development aid suitable for its position, and would allay Canadian fears of EEC exploitation of its offshore waters. Local representatives, however, remained apprehensive about the outcome of negotiations between the French and Canadian Governments to settle the dispute over coastal limits. (France had been claiming a 200-mile fishing and economic zone around St Pierre and Miquelon, while Canada wanted the islands to have only a 12-mile zone.)

In January 1987 it was decided that the dispute over the maritime border around St Pierre and Miquelon should be submitted to international arbitration. Discussions began in March, and negotiations to determine quotas for France's catch of Atlantic cod over the period 1988–91 were to take place simultaneously. In the mean time, Canada and France agreed on an interim fishing accord which would allow France to increase its cod quota by about 15,000 metric tons in 1987. In October, however, the discussions collapsed, and French trawlers were prohibited from fishing in Canadian waters. In February 1988 Albert Pen and Gérard Grignon, St Pierre's elected representatives to the French legislature (see below), together with two members of the St Pierre administration and 17 sailors, were arrested for fishing in Canadian waters. This episode, and the arrest of a Canadian trawler captain in May for fishing in St Pierre's waters, led to an unsuccessful resumption of negotiations in September. In November Enrique Iglesias, the President of the Inter-American Development Bank, was appointed as mediator in the dispute.

In March 1989 Iglesias successfully negotiated an agreement on fishing rights in the area, which was signed by the French and Canadian Governments. Accordingly, France's annual quotas for Atlantic cod and other species were determined for the period until the end of 1991. For 1989, France's quota was set at 42,000 metric tons, to be divided between the fleets of St Pierre and Miquelon and that of Saint-Malo, in metropolitan France. At the same time, the Governments agreed upon the composition of an international arbitration tribunal which would delineate the disputed maritime boundaries and exclusive economic zones.

In January 1989 two factory fishing ships from Saint-Malo sailed to the area to catch the fish allowed by government quotas, but there were protests by the islanders, who feared that damage might be caused to fishing stocks by the factory ships. After discussions with the French Prime Minister, Michel Rocard, it was agreed that one of the factory ships would return to France. In October 1990 the islanders again protested to the Government, concerning illegal fishing in their waters by a company based in Saint-Malo.

A general election to the French National Assembly was held in March 1986. The islands' incumbent deputy, Albert Pen (representing the Parti Socialiste, PS), was re-elected. Pen was also the sole candidate at the indirect election to choose the islands' representative in the French Senate in September. A fresh election for a deputy to the National Assembly was held in November, when Gérard Grignon, representing the Union pour la Démocratie Française (UDF), was elected. At the 1988 French presidential election Jacques Chirac received 56% of the votes cast by the islanders in the second round, in May, against the successful incumbent, President Mitterrand. In June Gérard Grignon was re-elected to the National Assembly. In September–October, however, the parties of the left won a majority at elections to the General Council, securing 13 of the 19 seats. In March 1989 municipal elections were held. Candidates supporting the PS took control of 23 municipalities, while the centre-right opposition candidates won only six municipalities. At elections to the European Parliament in June, the PS obtained 27.96% of the votes cast, marginally more than the centre-right alliance of the UDF and the Rassemblement pour la République (RPR). An abstention rate of 74.2%, however, was recorded.

FRENCH OVERSEAS COLLECTIVITÉS TERRITORIALES *St Pierre and Miquelon*

Government

The French Government is represented in St Pierre by an appointed Prefect. There is a General Council, with 19 members (15 for St Pierre and four for Miquelon) elected by adult universal suffrage for a period of six years. St Pierre and Miquelon elects one deputy to the French National Assembly and one representative to the Senate in Paris, and is also represented at the European Parliament in Strasbourg.

Economic Affairs

The soil and climatic conditions of St Pierre and Miquelon do not favour agricultural production, which is mainly confined to smallholdings, except for market-gardening and the production of eggs and chickens. Pig-meat production was abandoned in 1988, following an epidemic.

The principal economic activity of the islands is traditionally fishing and related industries, which employed some 19% of the working population in 1989. Trawler-fishing accounts for most of the catch (96% in 1989). In 1988 the size of catches recorded by trawlers decreased overall by 43% (from 15,133 metric tons in 1987) to 8,631 tons. In 1989, however, the catch increased to 9,045 tons, following an agreement on quotas (see Recent History).

Processing of fish provides the basis for industrial activity. It is dominated by two major companies which produce frozen and salted fish, and fish meal for fodder. In 1988 the industry recorded a sharp decrease in production (to 3,710 tons), compared with preceding years; total production increased to 4,082 tons in 1989.

The replenishment of ships' supplies is an important economic activity. In 1989 1,232 ships entered the port of Saint-Pierre.

During the late 1980s efforts were made to promote tourism. In 1989 there were 14,200 tourist visitors, an increase of 3% compared with the previous year. The opening of the St Pierre–Montréal air route in 1987 led to an increase in air traffic.

In 1989 St Pierre and Miquelon recorded a trade deficit of 332m. French francs; total exports were 200m. francs. The principal sources of imports were Canada and France. The principal market for exports was France; the USA, Canada and Spain were also important. The only exports in that year were fish and fish meal. The principal imports were fuel and building materials from Canada. Items such as clothing and other consumer goods were imported from France.

In 1986 average prices decreased by 1%. In 1987 the inflation rate stood at 1%. Unemployment affected 13.3% of the labour force in 1987.

In 1988 the economy of St Pierre and Miquelon suffered the effects of the Canadian Government's decision (in 1987) to close its ports to foreign trawlers, to reduce France's quota for the quantity of fish to be caught in Canadian waters and to restrict France's access to certain fishing areas. In March 1989, however, France and Canada signed an agreement (effective until the end of 1991) which, it was hoped, would end the conflict and restore the economic stability of the islands (see Recent History, above). The development of the port of Saint-Pierre and the expansion of tourism (particularly from Canada and the USA) were regarded by the administration as the principal means of maintaining economic progress in the 1990s.

Social Welfare

In 1981 there was one general hospital, with 68 beds, and maternity and hospice establishments. In 1977 there were six physicians working in the islands. A new general hospital was completed in 1988.

Education

The education system is modelled on the French system, and education is compulsory for children between the ages of six and 16 years. There are nine primary schools (of which five are privately-controlled), three secondary schools (of which two are private) and six technical schools.

Public Holidays

1991: 1 January (New Year's Day), 29 March–1 April (Easter), 1 May (Labour Day), 9 May (Ascension Day), 20 May (Whit Monday), 14 July (National Day), 11 November (Armistice Day), 25 December (Christmas Day).

1992: 1 January (New Year's Day), 17–20 April (Easter), 1 May (Labour Day), 28 May (Ascension Day), 8 June (Whit Monday), 14 July (National Day), 11 November (Armistice Day), 25 December (Christmas Day).

Weights and Measures

The metric system is in use.

Statistical Survey

Source (unless otherwise stated): Préfecture, Place du Lieutenant-Colonel Pigeaud, BP 4200, 97500 Saint-Pierre; tel. 412801; telex 914410.

AREA AND POPULATION

Area: 242 sq km (93.4 sq miles).

Population: 6,392 (census of 15 March 1990): Saint-Pierre 5,683, Miquelon 709.

Births and Deaths (1989): Live births 77; Deaths 43.

Economically Active Population (1989): Agriculture 5, Fishing 117, Construction 170, Fish-processing 373, Transport 56, Dockers 50, Commerce 60, Restaurants and hotels 80, Business services 350, Government employees 1,081, Activities not adequately defined 288; Total employed 2,630; Unemployed 220; Total labour force 2,850.

FISHING

Total Catch (metric tons, live weight): 15,616 in 1987; 8,952 in 1988; 9,401 in 1989 (of which artisanal fishing: 483 in 1987; 321 in 1988; 356 in 1989). Source: Secrétariat du Comité Monétaire de la Zone Franc: *La Zone Franc, Rapport 1989*.

FINANCE

Currency and Exchange Rates: French currency is used (see French Guiana).

Expenditure by Metropolitan France (1988): 235 million francs.

Budget (estimates, million francs, 1990): Expenditure 127.9 (current 87.4; capital 40.5). Source: *La Zone Franc, Rapport 1989*.

EXTERNAL TRADE

Total (million francs, 1989): *Imports:* 533; *Exports:* 200 (Fish, fish meal fodder). Most trade is with Canada, France and the USA.

TRANSPORT

Road Traffic (1989): 2,634 motor vehicles in use.

Shipping (1989): Ships entered 1,232; Freight entered 119,440 metric tons, Freight cleared 6,817 metric tons.

Civil Aviation (1989): Passengers carried 27,786, Freight carried 229 metric tons.

TOURISM

Tourist Arrivals (1989): 14,200.

EDUCATION

Primary (1989): 8 schools; 50 teachers (1987); 875 students.
Secondary (1989): 3 schools; 55 teachers (1987); 500 students.
There are also 2 technical schools.

Directory

The Government

(February 1991)

Prefect: Jean-Pierre Marquié.

President of the Economic and Social Committee: Rémy Briand.

Deputy to the French National Assembly: Gérard Grignon (UDF/CDS).

Representative to the French Senate: Albert Pen (PS).

GENERAL COUNCIL

The General Council has 19 members (St Pierre 15, Miquelon four). At the most recent election, held in September–October 1988, 13 seats were won by the Parti Socialiste (PS) and other left-wing candidates, the remaining six being taken by the Union pour la Démocratie Française (UDF) and right-wing candidates.

President of the General Council: Marc Plantegenest (PS).

Political Organizations

Parti Socialiste (PS): 97500 Saint-Pierre; left-wing.

Rassemblement pour la République (RPR): 97500 Saint-Pierre; Gaullist.

FRENCH OVERSEAS COLLECTIVITÉS TERRITORIALES St Pierre and Miquelon

Union pour la Démocratie Française (UDF): 97500 Saint-Pierre; centrist.

Centre des Démocrates Sociaux (CDS): 97500 Saint-Pierre.

Judicial System

Tribunal Supérieur d'Appel at Saint-Pierre (Pres. ETIENNE DIXIMIER); Tribunal de Première Instance (Pres. GÉRARD EGRON-REVERSEAU).

Religion

Almost all of the inhabitants are adherents of the Roman Catholic Church.

CHRISTIANITY
The Roman Catholic Church

The islands form the Apostolic Vicariate of the Iles Saint-Pierre et Miquelon. At 31 December 1988 there were an estimated 6,100 adherents (about 99% of the total population).

Vicar Apostolic: FRANÇOIS JOSEPH MAURER (Titular Bishop of Chimaera), Vicariat Apostolique, BP 4245, 97500 Saint-Pierre; tel. 412035.

The Press

The Government Printer produces a number of publications, including *L'Echo des Caps, Le Vent de la Liberté* and *Receuil des Actes administratifs*.

Recueil des Actes administratifs: Saint-Pierre; published by the Government Printer; f. 1886; fortnightly.

Radio and Television

In 1989 there were an estimated 3,000 radio receivers and 2,000 television receivers in use.

Radio-Télévision Française d'Outre-mer (RFO): BP 4227, 97500 Saint-Pierre; tel. 413824; telex 914443; the government station, broadcasts 24 hours of radio programmes daily, and 105 hours of television programmes weekly on two channels; Dir ALAIN QUINTRIE-LAMOTTE.

Finance

MAJOR BANKS

Banque des Iles Saint-Pierre-et-Miquelon: rue Jacques-Cartier, Saint-Pierre; tel. 412217; telex 914435; fax 412531; f. 1889; cap. 15m. francs (1987); Pres. and Gen. Man. CHARLES-PIERRE LANDRY; Man. GUY ROULET.

Crédit Saint Pierrais: 20 place du Général de Gaulle, BP 4218, Saint-Pierre; tel. 412249; telex 914429; fax (508) 412596; cap. 20m. francs (1989); Pres. RENÉ DAGORT; Man. G. JOULOU.

PRINCIPAL INSURANCE COMPANIES

Mutuelle Générale Française: Saint-Pierre; Rep. J. ANDRIEUX.

Préservatrice Foncière Assurances: 16 rue M. Georges Lefèvre, BP 4222, 97500 Saint-Pierre; tel. 414355; telex 914420; Reps GUY PATUREL, BERNARD HARAN.

Trade and Industry

Chambre de Commerce, d'Industrie et de Métiers: 4 blvd Constant Colmay, BP 4207, 97500 Saint-Pierre; tel. 414512; telex 914437; fax 413209; Pres. LOUIS E. HARDY.

TRADE UNION

Force Ouvrière (FO): 15 rue Dr Dunan, BP 4241, 97500 Saint-Pierre; tel. 412522; fax 414655; Sec.-Gen. MAX OLAÏSOLA.

Transport

SHIPPING

Packet boats run to Halifax, Sydney and Louisbourg in Canada, and there are container services between Saint-Pierre and Halifax, Nova Scotia. The seaport at Saint-Pierre has three jetties and 1,200 metres of quays.

CIVIL AVIATION

There is an airport on St Pierre, served by airlines linking the territory with France and Canada.

Air Saint-Pierre: 18 rue Albert Briand St Pierre, POB 4225, 97500 Saint-Pierre; tel. 412720; telex 914422; f. 1961; connects the territory with Sydney (Canada) and directly with Halifax, Nova Scotia, and Montréal, Québec; Pres. RÉMY L. BRIAND; fleet of 2 HS. 748, 1 Navajo Chieftain, 1 Aztec.

Atlantic Airways: connects the archipelago with Newfoundland; fleet of 1 Navajo, 1 Merlin.

Tourism

There were 13,785 tourist arrivals in 1988, increasing to 14,200 in 1989.

Agence Régionale du Tourisme: rue du 11 Novembre, BP 4274, 97500 Saint-Pierre; tel. 412222; telex 914437; fax 413355; f. 1959; Pres. MARC PLANTEGENEST; Man. BERNARD VIGNEAU.

French Overseas Territories

The four Overseas Territories (territoires d'outre-mer) are French Polynesia, the French Southern and Antarctic Territories, New Caledonia, and the Wallis and Futuna Islands. They are integral parts of the French Republic. Each is administered by a High Commissioner or Chief Administrator, who is appointed by the French Government. Each permanently inhabited Territory also has a Territorial Assembly or Congress, elected by universal adult suffrage. Certain members of the Territorial Assembly or Congress sit in the French National Assembly and the Senate of the Republic in Paris. The Territories have varying degrees of internal autonomy.

FRENCH POLYNESIA

Introductory Survey

Location, Climate, Language, Religion, Flag, Capital

French Polynesia comprises several scattered groups of islands in the south Pacific Ocean, lying about two-thirds of the way between the Panama Canal and New Zealand. Its nearest neighbours are the Cook Islands, to the west, and the Line Islands (part of Kiribati), to the north-west. French Polynesia consists of the following island groups: the Iles du Vent (including the islands of Tahiti and Moorea) and the Iles Sous le Vent (located about 160 km north-west of Tahiti) which, together, constitute the Society Archipelago; the Tuamotu Archipelago, which comprises 78 islands scattered east of the Society Archipelago in a line stretching north-west to south-east for about 1,500 km; the Gambier Islands, located 1,600 km south-east of Tahiti; the Austral Islands, lying 640 km south of Tahiti; and the Marquesas Archipelago, which lies 1,450 km north-east of Tahiti. There are 120 islands in all. The average monthly temperature throughout the year varies between 20°C (68°F) and 29°C (84°F), and most rainfall occurs between November and April, the average annual precipitation being 1,625 mm. The official language is French, and Polynesian languages are spoken by the indigenous population. The principal religion is Christianity, 55% of the population being Protestant and 24% Roman Catholic. Provision was made in a statute of 6 September 1984 for the adoption of a French Polynesian flag, to fly alongside the French tricolour. The capital is Papeete, on the island of Tahiti.

Recent History

Tahiti, the largest of the Society Islands, was declared a French protectorate in 1842, and became a colony in 1880. The other island groups were annexed during the last 20 years of the 19th century. The islands were governed from France under a decree of 1885 until 1957, when French Polynesia became an Overseas Territory, administered by a Governor in Papeete. A Territorial Assembly and a Council of Government were elected to advise the Governor.

Between May 1975 and May 1982 a majority in the Territorial Assembly sought independence for French Polynesia. Following pressure by Francis Sanford, leader of the largest autonomist party in the Assembly, a new constitution for the Territory was negotiated with the French Government and approved by a newly-elected Assembly in 1977. Under the provisions of the new statute, France retained responsibility for foreign affairs, defence, monetary matters and justice, but the powers of the territorial Council of Government were increased, especially in the field of commerce. The French Governor was replaced by a High Commissioner, who was to preside over the Council of Government and was head of the administration, but had no vote. The Council's elected Vice-President, responsible for domestic affairs, was granted greater powers. An Economic and Social Committee, responsible for all development matters, was also created, and French Polynesia's economic zone has been extended to 200 nautical miles (370 km) from the islands' coastline.

Following elections to the Territorial Assembly in May 1982, the Tahoeraa Huiraatira Party of Gaston Flosse, with 13 of the 30 seats, formed successive ruling coalitions, first with the Ai'a Api Party and in September with John Teariki's Pupu Here Ai'a Party. Seeking greater (but not full) independence from France, especially in economic matters, elected representatives of the Assembly held discussions with the French Government in Paris in 1983. In spite of feelings expressed by the Assembly, that the French proposals for increased internal autonomy did not go far enough, a new statute was approved by the French National Assembly in September 1984. This allowed the territorial government greater powers, mainly in the sphere of commerce and development; the Council of Government was replaced by a Council of Ministers, whose President was to be elected from among the members of the Territorial Assembly. Gaston Flosse became the first President of the Council of Ministers.

In February 1985 Flosse and his New Caledonian counterpart, Dick Ukeiwé, signed an anti-independence alliance protocol, calling for closer economic, cultural and political co-operation within the French Republic; it was immediately described as 'illegal' and 'unconstitutional' by France's High Commissioner to New Caledonia, and subsequently annulled by a French administrative tribunal in that territory.

The testing of nuclear devices by the French Government began in 1966 at Mururoa Atoll, in the Tuamotu Archipelago. In 1983, in spite of strong protests by many Pacific nations, the Government indicated that tests would continue for a number of years. In October 1983 Australia, New Zealand and Papua New Guinea accepted a French invitation jointly to send scientists to inspect the test site, but the team's subsequent report was widely criticized for being inconclusive with regard to the problem of nuclear waste disposal, and, although the French test programme appeared to present no immediate health hazards, there was definite evidence of environmental damage, resulting from the underground explosions, which had caused subsidence by weakening the rock structure of the atoll. Significant levels of radioactivity were also detected.

A series of tests in May and June 1985, involving bigger explosions than hitherto, prompted a renewed display of opposition. In July the trawler *Rainbow Warrior*, the flagship of the anti-nuclear environmentalist group, Greenpeace, which was to have led a protest flotilla to Mururoa, was sunk in Auckland Harbour, New Zealand, in an explosion that killed one crew member. Two agents of the French secret service, the Direction générale de sécurité extérieure (DGSE), were subsequently convicted of manslaughter and imprisoned in New Zealand. In July 1986, however, they were transferred to Hao Atoll, in the Tuamoto Archipelago, after a ruling by the UN Secretary-General (acting as mediator), which effectively reduced the agents' sentences from 10 to three years' imprisonment, in return for a French payment of $NZ 7m. in compensation to the New Zealand Government. Relations between France and New Zealand worsened still further in 1987, when the French Prime Minister, Jacques Chirac, approved the removal of one of the prisoners to Paris, owing to illness. By the terms of the UN ruling, 'mutual consent' by both Governments was to be necessary for any such repatriation. An exchange of letters between the Prime Ministers of the two countries failed to resolve the issue, and in 1988 the other prisoner was also flown back to Paris after she became pregnant (see chapter on New Zealand for further details). In September 1985 the French President, François Mitterrand, had visited the test site to reaffirm France's nuclear policy and its strategic interests in the Pacific, and had declared that the tests at Mururoa would continue for as long as necessary. In October the Greenpeace yacht, *Vega*, was seized by French naval commandos, as it sailed into the prohibited zone around the atoll, in an unsuccessful attempt to disrupt further scheduled tests; although the protest as a whole ended in deadlock, it succeeded in attracting world-wide attention. Further tests were conducted, however, and in July 1989, under increasing pressure from anti-nuclear hunger strikers, the Territorial Government consented to request a special session of the Assembly to debate the question of French nuclear explosions. In August the French Prime Minister, Michel Rocard, visited the territory and warned that the outcome of any local meetings or referendums could not be binding on the defence policies of the entire French Republic, a statement that was reiterated by President Mitterrand when he visited the territory in May 1990. In October 1989, however, an unofficial French anti-nuclear delegation was received in Tahiti, and the President of the Council of Ministers, Alexandre Léontieff, stressed that France should compensate the territory for damage to its economy incurred as a result of the French nuclear-test programme. By November 1989 France had performed 110 underground nuclear tests in the territory since 1975. In a move aimed at ending the secrecy surrounding the area, the French Government permitted foreign television cameras to film at the nuclear-test sites, for the first time, in October 1990.

At elections held in March 1986 the Tahoeraa Huiraatira Party/Rassemblement pour la République (RPR) gained the first outright majority to be achieved in the territory, winning 24 of the 41 seats in the Territorial Assembly, after a recount in one constituency, and the decision of two successful independent candidates to join the ruling party. Leaders of opposition parties subsequently expressed dissatisfaction with the election result, claiming that the Tahoeraa Huiraatira Party's victory had been secured only as a result of the allocation of a disproportionately large number of seats in the Territorial Assembly to one of the five constituencies, whereby the influence of its constituents' votes was effectively increased. The constituency at the centre of the dispute was that comprising the Mangareva and Tuamotu islands, where the two French army bases at Hao and Mururoa constituted a powerful body of support for Flosse and the Tahoeraa Huiraatira Party, which, in spite of winning a majority of seats, had obtained a minority of individual votes in the election (30,571, compared with the opposition parties' 43,771). At the concurrent elections for French Polynesia's two seats in the National Assembly in Paris, Flosse and Alexandre Léontieff, the candidates of the RPR, were elected, Flosse subsequently ceding his seat to Edouard Fritch. Later in March the French Prime Minister, Jacques Chirac, appointed Flosse to a post in the French Council of Ministers, assigning him the portfolio of Secretary of State for Pacific Affairs. At the June 1988 elections to the National Assembly, Léontieff retained his seat, while the other was won by Emile Vernaudon, the leader of Ai'a Api.

In April 1986 Flosse was re-elected President of the Council of Ministers, supported by the votes of 25 of the 41 members of the Territorial Assembly. Meanwhile, in March, the incoming French Prime Minister, Jacques Chirac, appointed Flosse to a post in the French Council of Ministers, assigning him the portfolio of Secretary of State for South Pacific Problems. Flosse faced severe criticism from leaders of the opposition for his allegedly inefficient and extravagant use of public funds, and was accused, in particular, of corrupt electoral practice, through having distributed government-financed gifts of construction materials, food and clothing, in an attempt to influence voters during his pre-election campaign. In September 1986 a formal complaint against Flosse was made by Enrique ('Quito') Braun-Ortega, one of the leaders of the Amuitahiraa Mo Porinesia (a coalition of opposition parties), who accused Flosse of appropriating public funds for his own personal and political purposes. Flosse resigned as President of the Territory's Council of Ministers in February 1987, and was replaced by Jacques Teuira.

Unrest among dock-workers led to serious rioting in October 1987. More than 100 people were arrested, and 27 injured, as arson and looting broke out across Papeete. Paramilitary police and French Legionnaires were flown in from Paris and Mururoa Atoll, with the Government declaring a state of emergency and imposing a dusk-to-dawn curfew in Papeete and four neighbouring districts. Daniel Millaud, French Polynesia's representative to the French Senate, demanded the holding of a public inquiry into the rioting, and in November the French High Commissioner, Pierre Angéli, was recalled and replaced by Jean Montpezat.

In December 1987, amid growing discontent over his policies, Teuira resigned as President of the Council of Ministers, along with the seven remaining ministers (the three other ministers, including Alexandre Léontieff, having resigned a few days previously). Léontieff, the leader of the Te Tiarama party (a breakaway faction of the Tahoeraa Huiraatira Party), was elected President of the Council of Ministers by a new alliance of 28 of the Territorial Assembly's 41 members. Jean Juventin, the Mayor of Papeete, replaced Roger Doom as President of the Territorial Assembly. The new Council of Ministers included only two members of the previous administration. However, several members of the realigned Assembly had refused to resume their seats, in protest at the alleged illegitimacy of the new Government, as the outgoing administration, which had continued on a caretaker basis, had announced the dissolution of the Assembly, in preparation for the holding of new elections, shortly before the appointment of Léontieff.

In November 1988 Quito Braun-Ortega and two other ministers resigned from the Government and formed a new six-member group in the Assembly. To ensure the approval of the budget proposals, therefore, three ministers resigned from the Council of Ministers in order to resume their seats in the Assembly. They were reinstated following the confirmation of the budget. In March 1989, however, the Administrative Court declared the reappointment of the three to be unconstitutional, and also annulled the appointment during 1988 of two other ministers. A special session of the Territorial Assembly was required to endorse the Government of Léontieff because there was a constitutional requirement for the Council of Ministers to comprise a minimum of six members. In July 1989 it was announced in Paris that there would be an inquiry into the territory's judicial system. In the first half of 1990 the Léontieff Government survived two further challenges in the Territorial Assembly to its continuation in office.

All political parties in French Polynesia urged a boycott of elections to the European Parliament in June 1989. An abstention rate of almost 90% was recorded.

Amendments to the Polynesian Constitution, which were approved by the French Parliament and enacted by July 1990, augmented the powers of the President of the Territorial Government and increased the competence of the Territorial Assembly. In addition, five consultative Archipelago Councils were established, comprising Territorial and municipal elected representatives. The major purpose of these amendments, which were described as modifications of the 1984 internal autonomy statute, was to clarify the areas of responsibility of the State, the Territory and the judiciary. The amendments were widely regarded as a further step towards independence for French Polynesia.

In September 1989 the Prime Minister of the Cook Islands, Geoffrey Henry, visited Tahiti, and relations between the two Polynesian territories improved. Common policies concerning fisheries protection were discussed. An agreement settling the delimitation of the conflicting exclusive economic zones claimed by the Cook Islands and French Polynesia was signed in August 1990.

Government

The French Government is represented in French Polynesia by its High Commissioner to the territory, and controls various important spheres of government, including defence, foreign diplomacy and justice. A local Territorial Assembly, with 44 members, is elected for a five-year term by universal adult suffrage. The Assembly may elect a President of an executive body, the Territorial Council of Ministers, who, in turn, submits a list of between five and 12 members of the Assembly to serve as Ministers, for approval by the Assembly.

In addition, French Polynesia elects two deputies to the French National Assembly in Paris and one representative to the French Senate, all chosen on the basis of universal adult suffrage. French Polynesia is also represented at the European Parliament in Strasbourg.

Defence

France has been testing nuclear weapons at Mururoa Atoll, in the Tuamotu Archipelago, since 1966 and was maintaining a force of 5,400 military personnel in the territory in June 1990.

Economic Affairs

In 1985, according to estimates by the World Bank, French Polynesia's gross domestic product (GDP), measured at average 1983–85 prices, was US $1,370m., equivalent to $7,840 per head. According to official statistics, GDP increased from 280,000m. francs CFP in 1988 to 285,000 francs CFP in 1989, but GDP per head declined from 1,490 francs CFP to 1,481 francs CFP. Between the censuses of 1983 and 1988 the population increased by an annual average of 2.5%.

Agriculture and fishing contributed only about 4% of GDP in 1987, but provide most of French Polynesia's exports. Some 11.8% of the working population were employed in the sector in 1988. Coconuts are the principal cash crop, and in 1988 the estimated harvest was 150,000 metric tons. Vegetables, fruit (especially pineapples and citrus fruit), vanilla and coffee are also cultivated. Most commercial fishing, principally for tuna, is conducted, under licence, by Japanese and Korean fleets. The total catch by French Polynesian vessels in 1988 was 2,800 metric tons. Another important activity is the production of cultured black pearls, of which the quantity exported increased from 112 kg in 1984 to 636 kg in 1989.

Industry (comprising mining, manufacturing, construction and utilities) employed 17.7% of the working population in 1988, and provided 19% of GDP in 1984. There is a small manufacturing sector, which is heavily dependent on agriculture. Coconut oil and copra are produced, as are beer, dairy products and vanilla essence. Important deposits of phosphates and cobalt were discovered during the 1980s. The manufacturing sector (with mining and quarrying) employed 7.0% of the working population in 1983.

In 1988 some 76% of electricity was provided by the Papeete thermal power station and hydroelectric and solar energy also make a significant contribution. In 1988 it was announced that six new hydroelectric power dams were to be constructed by 1991, with the capacity to generate the electricity requirements of 45% of Tahiti's population.

FRENCH OVERSEAS TERRITORIES

French Polynesia

Tourism is the territory's major industry. In 1987 it contributed 20% of GDP, and in 1989 a total of 139,705 tourists visited French Polynesia. In 1989 it was announced that French Polynesia's hotel capacity was to be doubled to 5,000 rooms over the next five years. The services sector employed 68% of the working population in 1988, and provided 77% of GDP in 1984.

In 1989 French Polynesia recorded a trade deficit of 78,443m. francs CFP. In 1989 the principal sources of imports were France (which provided 54.1% of total imports), the USA (12.9%), Australia (6.1%) and New Zealand (5.0%). The principal markets for exports in 1987 were France (which received 53.5% of total exports) and the USA (18.6%). The principal imports in that year were petroleum products, hydraulic cement and flour. The principal exports were cultured black pearls (which provided 36.8% of export revenue in 1989) and coconut oil.

In 1989 there was an estimated territorial budgetary deficit of 1,200m. francs CFP. In 1988 expenditure by the French State in the Territory totalled 62,317m. francs CFP, 37.8% of which was on the military budget. Zero inflation was recorded in 1990. In that year an estimated 15% of the labour force were unemployed.

French Polynesia forms part of the Franc Zone (see p. 156), and is a member of the South Pacific Commission (see p. 205), which provides technical advice, training and assistance in economic, cultural and social development to countries in the region.

French Polynesia's traditional agriculture-based economy was distorted by the presence of large numbers of French military personnel (in connection with the nuclear-testing programme which began in 1966), stimulating employment in the construction industry and services at the expense of agriculture, and encouraging migration from the outer islands to Tahiti, where 75% of the population currently reside. These dramatic changes effectively transformed French Polynesia from a state of self-sufficiency to one of import dependency in less than a generation. The development of tourism had a similar effect. In 1988 some 80% of the territory's food requirements had to be imported, while exports of vanilla and coffee, formerly important cash crops, were negligible, owing to a long-term decline in investment; production of copra also declined during the late 1980s, affected by low prices on the international market.

As the Territory gradually achieves a greater degree of independence from metropolitan France, it is seeking closer ties with countries of Asia and the Pacific (particularly, Australia, New Zealand, Japan and South Korea) in the hope of improving its poor export performance.

Social Welfare

In 1980 there were 31 hospitals in French Polynesia, with a total of 982 beds, and there were 143 physicians working in the territory. From 1 January 1991, all medical services were to be provided free of charge for the inhabitants of French Polynesia. An estimated US $94m. was spent on social security services in the Territory in 1990.

Education

Education is compulsory for eight years between six and 14 years of age. It is free of charge for day pupils in government schools. Primary education, lasting six years, is financed by the territorial budget, while secondary and technical education are supported by state funds. In 1987/88 there were 254 kindergartens and primary schools, with 13,995 pupils attending kindergartens and 28,740 at primary schools. Secondary education is provided by both church and government schools. In 1987/88 there were 15,002 pupils at general secondary schools, while 4,113 secondary pupils were enrolled at vocational institutions in 1986. France announced plans to create a university on Tahiti in 1986. In the 1988/89 budget the territory envisaged expenditure of US $226m. on its 311 schools. The French Government was to contribute about 68% of the total expenditure on education.

Public Holidays

1991: 1 January (New Year's Day), 1 April (Easter Monday), 6 May (for Labour Day), 8 May (Liberation Day), 9 May (Ascension Day), 20 May (Whit Monday), 14 July (Fall of the Bastille), 11 November (Armistice Day), 25 December (Christmas Day).

1992: 1 January (New Year's Day), 20 April (Easter Monday), 4 May (for Labour Day), 8 May (Liberation Day), 28 May (Ascension Day), 8 June (Whit Monday), 14 July (Fall of the Bastille), 11 November (Armistice Day), 25 December (Christmas Day).

Weights and Measures

The metric system is in force.

Statistical Survey

Source (unless otherwise indicated): Institut Territorial de la Statistique, Immeuble Donald (2ᵉ étage), Angle rue Jeanne d'Arc et blvd Pomare, BP 395, Papeete; tel. 37196; telex 537; fax 427252.

AREA AND POPULATION

Area: Total 4,000 sq km (1,544 sq miles); Land area 3,660 sq km (1,413 sq miles).

Population: 166,753 (86,914 males, 79,839 females) at census of 15 October 1983; 188,814 (98,345 males, 90,469 females) at census of 6 September 1988; 194,600 (official estimate) at January 1990. *Towns* (population, 1983): Papeete 23,496, Faaa 21,927, Pirae 12,023, Uturoa 2,733.

Density (1990): 48.7 per sq km.

Ethnic Groups (1983 census): Polynesian 114,280; 'Demis' 23,625 (Polynesian-European 15,851, Polynesian-Chinese 6,356, Polynesian-Other races 1,418); European 19,320; Chinese 7,424; European-Chinese 494; Others 1,610; Total 166,753.

Births and Deaths (1989): Live births 5,364 (birth rate 27.9 per 1,000); Deaths 1,019 (death rate 5.3 per 1,000).

Economically Active Population (persons aged 14 years and over, 1988 census): Agriculture, hunting, forestry and fishing 7,555; Mining and manufacturing 4,938; Electricity, gas and water 478; Construction 5,548; Trade, restaurants and hotels 10,304; Transport, storage and communications 2,780; Financing, insurance, real estate and business services 1,161; Community, social and personal services 21,525; Activities not adequately defined 9,717; Total employed 64,006 (males 41,651, females 22,355); Unemployed 11,387 (males 5,783, females 5,604); Total labour force 75,393 (males 47,434, females 27,959). Figures exclude persons on compulsory military service. Source: International Labour Office, *Year Book of Labour Statistics*.

AGRICULTURE, ETC.

Principal Crops (metric tons, 1989): Roots and tubers 1,109, Vegetables (sold commercially) 5,200, Fresh fruit 8,970, Copra 10,925, Vanilla 54, Coffee 2.7 (1988).

Livestock (FAO estimates, year ending September 1989): Cattle 8,000, Horses 2,000, Pigs 58,000, Goats 4,000, Sheep 2,000. Source: FAO, *Production Yearbook*.

Livestock Products (metric tons unless otherwise indicated, 1989): Cows' milk ('000 litres) 1,864; Beef and veal 190; Pig meat 986; Poultry meat 326; Rabbit meat 9; Hen eggs ('000) 21,372; Honey (litres, 1986) 16,000.

Fishing (metric tons, live weight): Total catch 2,252 in 1986; 2,671 in 1987; 3,112 in 1988. Data refer only to quantities sold at the principal fish markets. Source: FAO, *Yearbook of Fishery Statistics*.

INDUSTRY

Production: Coconut oil 9,104 metric tons (1987), Oilcake 4,477 (1987), Beer 120,000 hectolitres (1987), Printed cloth 200,000 m (1979), Japanese sandals 600,000 pairs (1979), Electric energy (Tahiti) 271.3m. kWh (1989).

FINANCE

Currency and Exchange Rates: 100 centimes = 1 franc des Comptoirs français du Pacifique (franc CFP or Pacific franc). *Coins:* 50 centimes; 1, 2, 5, 10, 20 and 50 francs CFP. *Notes:* 100, 500, 1,000 and 5,000 francs CFP. *Sterling, Dollar and French Franc Equivalents* (30 September 1990): £1 sterling = 178.59 francs CFP; US $1 = 95.32 francs CFP; 1 French franc = 18.182 francs CFP; 1,000 francs CFP = £5.599 = $10.491 = 55 French francs.

Territorial Budget (estimates, million francs CFP, 1989): *Revenue:* Current 54,400 (Indirect taxation 37,500), Extraordinary 17,700, Total 72,100. *Expenditure:* Current 55,600, Capital 17,700, Total 73,300.

French State Expenditure (million francs CFP, 1988): Civil budget 35,646 (Current 27,736, Pensions 6,211, Capital 1,699); Military budget 23,552 (Current 20,342, Capital 3,210); Total (incl. others) 62,317.

Money Supply (million French francs at 31 December 1988): Currency in circulation 343; Demand deposits 1,929, Total money 2,266.

Cost of Living (Consumer Price Index; base: Dec. 1988 = 100): 96.4 in 1987; 98.9 in 1988; 101.3 in 1989.

Gross Domestic Product (million francs CFP at current prices): 280,000 in 1987; 280,000 in 1988; 285,000 (provisional) in 1989.

EXTERNAL TRADE

Principal Commodities (million francs CFP, 1989): *Imports c.i.f.:* Total 88,754. *Exports f.o.b.:* Fresh fruit 16; Vanilla 46; Coconut oil

317; Monoi (scented coconut oil) preparations 19; Cultured pearls 3,791; Mother-of-pearl 144; Total (incl. others) 10,311.

Principal Trading Partners (million francs CFP): *Imports* (1989): France (metropolitan) 47,985; Other EEC countries 10,055; Australia 5,402; Japan 3,648; New Zealand 4,411; USA 11,476; Total (incl. others) 88,754. *Exports* (1987): France (metropolitan) 4,863; USA 1,691; Total (incl. others) 9,095.

TRANSPORT

Road Traffic (1987): Total vehicles registered 54,979.

Shipping (1989): *International traffic:* passengers carried 51,081; freight handled 665,743 metric tons. *Domestic traffic:* passengers carried 601,305; freight handled 274,553 metric tons.

Civil Aviation (1989): *International traffic:* passengers carried (incl. those in transit) 631,564; freight handled 6,575 metric tons. *Domestic traffic:* passengers carried 400,055; freight handled 647 metric tons.

TOURISM

Visitors (excluding cruise passengers and excursionists): 142,820 in 1987; 135,387 in 1988; 139,705 (50,406 from the USA, 20,828 from France) in 1989.

EDUCATION

Institutions (unless otherwise indicated, 1987/88): Pre-primary and primary 254 (incl. 17 private—1985/86), General secondary 20, Technical and vocational 14, University 1.

Teachers (unless otherwise indicated, 1986/87): Pre-primary 462 (1984), Primary 1,337 (1984), General secondary 855, Vocational secondary 385, Higher 12 (1982).

Students (unless otherwise indicated, 1987/88): Pre-primary 13,995, Primary 28,740, General secondary 15,002, Vocational secondary 4,113 (1986), Higher 180 (1983).

Directory

The Constitution

The constitutional system in French Polynesia is established under the aegis of the Constitution of the Fifth French Republic and specific laws of 1977, 1984 and 1990. The French Polynesia Statute 1984, the so-called 'internal autonomy statute', underwent amendment in a law of July 1990.

French Polynesia is declared to be an autonomous Territory of the French Republic, of which it remains an integral part. The High Commissioner, appointed by the French Government, exercises the prerogatives of the State in matters relating to defence, foreign relations, the maintenance of law and order, communications and citizenship. The head of the local executive and the person who represents the Territory is the President of the Territorial Government, who is elected by the Territorial Assembly from among its own number. The Territorial President appoints and dismisses the Council of Ministers (which has a maximum number of 12) and has competence in international relations as they affect French Polynesia and its exclusive economic zone, in control of foreign investments and in immigration. The Territorial Assembly, which has financial autonomy in budgetary affairs and legislative authority within the Territory, is elected for a term of up to five years on the basis of universal adult suffrage. There are 41 members: 22 elected by the people of the Windward Islands (Iles du Vent—Society Islands), eight by the Leeward Islands (Iles Sous le Vent—Society Islands), five by the Tuamotu Archipelago and the Gambier Islands and three each by the Austral Islands and by the Marquesas. The Assembly elects a Permanent Commission of between seven and nine of its members, and itself meets for two ordinary sessions each year and upon the demand of the majority party, the Territorial President or the High Commissioner. Local government is conducted by the municipalities; there are five regional, consultative Archipelago Councils, comprised of all those elected to the Territorial Assembly and the municipalities by that region (the Councils represent the same areas as the five constituencies for the Territorial Assembly). There is an Economic and Social Committee (composed of representatives of professional groups, trade unions and other organizations and agencies which participate in the economic, social and cultural activities of the Territory), a Territorial Audit Office and a judicial system which includes a Court of the First Instance, a Court of Appeal and an Administrative Court. The Territory, as a part of the French Republic, also elects two deputies to the National Assembly and one member of the Senate, and has representation in the European Parliament.

The Government
(January 1991)

High Commissioner: JEAN MONTPEZAT (appointed 1988).
Secretary-General: RAYMOND VERGNE.

COUNCIL OF MINISTERS

President: ALEXANDRE LÉONTIEFF.

Vice-President and Minister for Agriculture, Traditional Crafts and Cultural Heritage: GEORGES KELLY.

Minister for Social Affairs, Housing and Unity: Mme HUGUETTE HONG KIOU.

Minister for Labour, Employment and Professional Training, Tourism and Sports: NAPOLÉON SPITZ.

Minister for the Sea, Equipment and Energy: BORIS LÉONTIEFF.

Minister for Finance and the Economy: LOUIS SAVOIE.

Minister for Archipelago Development, Demesne and Real Estate Affairs: IOANE TEMAURI.

Minister for Health, the Environment and Scientific Research: JACQUI DROLLET.

Minister for Education and Public Services: RAYMOND VAN BASTOLAER.

Minister for Regions, Archipelago Administration and Posts and Telecommunications: EMILE VERNAUDON.

Minister for Town Planning, Ground Transport and General Administration (responsible for administrative reforms): FRANÇOIS NANAI.

GOVERNMENT OFFICES

Office of the High Commissioner of the Republic: Bureau de l'Haut Commissaire, Gouvernement de Polynésie Française, BP 115, Papeete; tel. 422000.

Office of the President of the Territorial Government: BP 2551, Papeete; tel. 424413.

Territorial Government of French Polynesia: BP 2551, Papeete; all ministries; Delegation in Paris: Blvd Saint-Germain 28, 75005 Paris, France; tel. (1) 46-34-50-70.

Economic and Social Committee: BP 1657, Papeete; tel. 424300; Pres. TERAIEFA CHANG; Representative to National Economic and Social Council RAYMOND DESCLAUX.

Legislature
ASSEMBLÉE TERRITORIALE

President: JEAN JUVENTIN.
Vice-President: HENRI MARERE.
Territorial Assembly: Assemblée Territoriale, BP 28, Papeete; tel. 416100.

Election, 16 March 1986

Party	Seats
Tahoeraa Huiraatira/RPR	24*
Amuitahiraa Mo Porinesia†	6
Pupu Here Ai'a	4
Ia Mana Te Nunaa	3
Front de Libération	2
Others	2
Total	**41**

* Increased from preliminary result of 21 seats, following a recount in one constituency and the decision of two members, elected as independents, to join the ruling party. In November 1987, 15 members of Tahoeraa formed the Te Tiarama party and a new ruling coalition.

† A coalition of parties under the leadership of EMILE VERNAUDON and ENRIQUE ('QUITO') BRAUN-ORTEGA.

PARLEMENT

Deputies to the French National Assembly: ALEXANDRE LÉONTIEFF (RPR)*, EMILE VERNAUDON (Ai'a Api).

Representative to the French Senate: DANIEL MILLAUD (Union centriste des Démocrates de Progrès).

* In November 1987 Léontieff formed a new party, leaving Tahoeraa, the affiliate of RPR.

FRENCH OVERSEAS TERRITORIES   *French Polynesia*

Political Organizations

Ai'a Api (New Land): BP 11055, Mahina, Tahiti; tel. 481135; f. 1982 after split in Te E'a Api; Leader EMILE VERNAUDON.

Free Tahiti Party: Pres. CHARLIE CHING.

Front de Libération de la Polynésie (FLP)/Tavini Huiraatira: independence movement; anti-nuclear; Leader OSCAR TEMARU.

Ia Mana Te Nunaa: rue du Commandant Destrémau, BP 1223, Papeete; tel. 426699; f. 1976; advocates 'socialist independence'; Sec.-Gen. JACQUES DROLLET.

Pupu Here Ai'a Te Nunaa Ia Ora: BP 3195, Papeete; tel. 420766; f. 1965; advocates autonomy; 8,000 mems; Pres. JEAN JUVENTIN.

Pupu Taina/Rassemblement des Libéraux: rue Cook, BP 169, Papeete; tel. 429880; f. 1976; seeks to retain close links with France; associated with the French Union pour la Démocratie Française (UDF); Leader MICHEL LAW.

Taatiraa Polynesia: BP 283, Papeete; tel. 428619; f. 1976; Leader ARTHUR CHUNG.

Tahoeraa Huiraatira/Rassemblement pour la République—RPR: rue du Commandant Destrémeau, BP 471, Papeete; tel. 429898; telex 249; f. 1958; supports links with France, with internal autonomy; Pres. GASTON FLOSSE; Hon. Pres. JACQUES TEUIRA.

Te E'a No Maohi Nui: Leader MARIUS RAAPOTO.

Te Tiarama: Papeete; f. 1987 by split from Tahoeraa Huiraatira; Leader ALEXANDRE LÉONTIEFF.

Judicial System

Court of Appeal: Cour d'Appel de Papeete, BP 101, Papeete; tel. 420117; telex 308; Pres. HENRI DE LABRUSSE; Attorney-General PAUL MARCHAUD.

Court of the First Instance: Tribunal de Première Instance de Papeete, BP 101, Papeete; tel. 420116; telex 308; Pres. LUC COMPAIN; Procurator JEAN-YVES DUVAL; Clerk of the Court DANIEL SALMON.

Court of Administrative Law: Tribunal Administratif, BP 4522, Papeete; tel. 422482; Pres. JEAN LAVOIGNAT; Cllrs BERNARD LEPLAT, JEAN BRENIER, PASCAL JOB.

Religion

About 55% of the population are Protestant Christians.

CHRISTIANITY

Protestant Church

L'Eglise évangélique de Polynésie française (Ekalesia Evanelia no Polynesia Farani): BP 113, Papeete; tel. 420029; fax 419357; f. 1884; autonomous since 1963; c. 80,000 mems; Pres. of Council Rev. JACQUES TERAI IHORAI; Sec.-Gen. ROCKY MEUEL.

The Roman Catholic Church

French Polynesia comprises the archdiocese of Papeete and the suffragan diocese of Taiohae o Tefenuaenata (based in Nuku Hiva, Marquesas Is). At 31 December 1988 there were an estimated 66,640 adherents in the territory, representing about 37% of the total population. The Archbishop and the Bishop participate in the Episcopal Conference of the Pacific, based in Fiji.

Archbishop of Papeete: Most Rev. MICHEL-GASPARD COPPENRATH, Archevêché, BP 94, Papeete; tel. 420251.

Other Churches

There are small Sanito, Church of Jesus Christ of Latter-day Saints (Mormon), and Seventh-day Adventist missions.

The Press

La Dépêche de Tahiti: Société Polynésienne de Presse, BP 50, Papeete; tel. 424343; f. 1964; daily; Dir MICHEL ANGLADE; Man. PHILIPPE MAZELLIER; circ. 15,000.

Les Nouvelles de Tahiti: Place de la Cathédrale, BP 629, Papeete; tel. 434445; f. 1956; daily; French; Editor HENRY MORNY; CEO LOUIS BRESSON.

Tahiti Sun Press: BP 887, Papeete; tel. 426850; f. 1980; weekly; English; Man. Editor AL PRINCE; circ. 4,000.

Ve'a Porotetani: BP 113, Papeete; tel. 420029; fax 419357; monthly; French and Tahitian; publ. by the Evangelical Church.

Foreign Bureaux

Agence France-Presse (AFP): BP 2679, Papeete; tel. 482121; Correspondent JEAN-PAUL PERÉA.

Associated Press (AP) (USA): BP 912, Papeete; tel. 437562; telex 537; Correspondent AL PRINCE.

Reuters (UK): BP 50, Papeete; tel. 424343; fax 421820; Correspondent DANIEL PARDON.

Publishers

Haere Po No Tahiti: BP 1958, Papeete; tel. 422469; f. 1981; travel, history, botany, linguistics and local interest.

Government Printer

Imprimerie Officielle: BP 117, Papeete; tel. 425067; printers, publrs.

Radio and Television

In 1988 there were an estimated 80,000 radio receivers and 35,000 television receivers in use, of which about 30,000 were colour receivers.

Radio-Télé-Tahiti: 410 rue Dumont d'Urville, BP 125, Papeete; tel. 430551; telex 290; fax 413155; f. 1951 as Radio-Tahiti; television service began 1965; operated by Société Nationale de Radio-Télévision Française d'Outre-Mer (RFO), Paris; daily programmes in French and Tahitian; Dir GUY SARTHOULET.

Finance

(cap. = capital; res = reserves; dep. = deposits; m. = million; brs = branches; amounts in CFP francs)

BANKING

Commercial Banks

Banque Paribas de Polynésie: BP 4479, Papeete; tel. 437100; telex 392; f. 1985; 50.1% govt-owned, 19.9% owned by Banque Paribas (France).

Banque de Polynésie SA: blvd Pomare, BP 530, Papeete; tel. 428688; telex 230; fax 431418; f. 1973; 80% owned by Société Générale (France); cap. and res 810m., dep. 24,219m. (Dec. 1985); Pres. JEAN-MICHEL LE PETIT; Gen. Man. RAYMOND CLAVIER; 13 brs.

Banque de Tahiti SA: rue François Cardella, BP 1602, Papeete; tel. 417000; telex 237; fax 423376; f. 1969; owned by Bank of Hawaii (USA—38%) and Crédit Lyonnais (France—44%); cap. 600m., dep. 29,021m. (Dec. 1989); Pres. CLAUDE GRANGIS; Dirs MICHEL DUPIEUX, GÉRARD MULLER, GÉRARD E. SEIDL; 13 brs.

SOCREDO—Société pour le Crédit et le Développement en Océanie: BP 130, Papeete; tel. 436626; telex 289; fax 433661; f. 1959; public body; affiliated to Banque Nationale de Paris (France) and Crédit Agricole (France).

Westpac Banking Corporation (Australia): 2 place Notre-Dame, Papeete; tel. 427526; telex 395; fax 431333; acquired operations of Banque Indosuez in French Polynesia in 1990; Regional Man. HOWARD SPENCER.

Trade and Industry

Chambre de Commerce et d'Industrie de Polynésie Française: BP 118, Papeete; tel. 420344; telex 274; fax 435184; f. 1880; 27 mems; Pres. GÉRARD AFO.

Chambre d'Agriculture et d'Elevage (CAEP): route de l'Hippodrome, BP 5383, Pirae; tel. 425393; f. 1886; 10 mems; Pres. SYLVAIN MILLAUD.

DEVELOPMENT ORGANIZATIONS

Caisse Centrale de Coopération Economique (CCCE): BP 578, Papeete; tel. 430486; telex 231; fax 434645; public body; development finance institute.

Service du Développement de l'Industrie et des Métiers: BP 20728, Papeete; tel. 422020; industry and crafts development.

Société pour le Développement de l'Agriculture et de la Pêche: BP 1247, Papeete; tel. 436788; agriculture and marine industries.

SODEP—Société pour le Développement et l'Expansion du Pacifique: BP 4441, Papeete; tel. 429449; f. 1961 by consortium of banks and private interests; regional development and finance co.

FRENCH OVERSEAS TERRITORIES   French Polynesia, French Southern and Antarctic Territories

EMPLOYERS' ORGANIZATIONS

Chambre Syndicale des Entrepreneurs du Bâtiment et des Travaux Publics: BP 2218, Papeete; tel. 425309; Pres. Claude Gutierrez.

Conseil des Employeurs: Immeuble FARA, rue E. Ahnne, BP 972, Papeete; tel. 438898; fax 423237; f. 1983; Pres. Joseph Diebold; Sec.-Gen. Astrid Pasquier.

Fédération Polynésienne de l'Agriculture et de l'Elevage: Papara, Tahiti; Pres. Michel Lehartel.

Fédération Polynésienne de l'Hôtellerie et des Industries Touristiques: BP 118, Papeete; tel. 423596; f. 1967; Pres. Michel Agid.

Syndicat des Importateurs et des Négociants: BP 1607, Papeete; Pres. Jules Changues.

Union Interprofessionnelle du Tourisme de la Polynésie Française: BP 4560, Papeete; tel. 439114; f. 1973; 1,200 mems; Pres. Paul Maetz; Sec.-Gen. Jean Corteel.

Union Patronale: BP 317, Papeete; tel. 420257; f. 1948; 63 mems; Pres. Dominique Auroy.

TRADE UNIONS

A Tia I Mua: Ave Georges Clemenceau, BP 4523, Papeete; tel. 436038; affiliated to CFDT (France); Pres. Hiro Tefaarere.

Fédération des Syndicats de la Polynésie Française: BP 1136, Papeete; Pres. Marcel Ahini.

Syndicat des Cadres de la Fonction Publique: Papeete; Pres. Pierre Allain.

Syndicat Territorial des Instituteurs et Institutrices de Polynésie: BP 3007, Papeete; Sec.-Gen. Willy Urima.

Union des Syndicats Autonomes des Travailleurs de Polynésie: BP 1201, Papeete; tel. 426049; Pres. Coco Teraiefa Chang; Sec.-Gen. Théodore Céran Jérusalemy.

Union des Syndicats de l'Aéronautique: Papeete; Pres. Joseph Conroy.

Union des Travailleurs de Tahiti et des Iles: rue Albert Leboucher, BP 3366, Papeete; tel. 437369; Pres. John Tefatua-Vaiho.

Transport

ROADS

French Polynesia has 792.2 km of roads, of which about one-third are bitumen-surfaced and two-thirds stone-surfaced.

SHIPPING

The principal port is Papeete, on Tahiti.

Agence Maritime Internationale de Tahiti: BP 274, Papeete; tel. 428972; telex 227; fax 432184; agents for Blue Star Line, Hyundai Merchant Marine, Polynesia Line, Sofrana Unilines; services to New Zealand, USA, Australia, American Samoa, New Caledonia.

Agence Tahiti Poroi: Fare Ute, BP 83, Papeete; tel. 420070; telex 211; fax 435335; f. 1956; travel agents, tour operators.

Compagnie Générale Maritime: ave du Général de Gaulle, BP 96, Papeete; tel. 420890; telex 259; shipowners and agents; freight services between Europe and many international ports; agents in French Polynesia for Shell, Chevron, Total, Morflot, Cunard Line, Holland America Line and Sitmar Cruises, Norwegian American Cruises, Arcalia Shipping, Deilmann Reederei, Dilmun Navigation and Hapag Lloyd; Dir (vacant).

Other companies operating services to, or calling at, Papeete are: Daiwa Line, Karlander, Hamburg-Sued, China Navigation Co, Nedlloyd, Shipping Corpn of New Zealand Ltd, Bank Line and Kyowa Line.

CIVIL AVIATION

There is one international airport, Faaa airport, 6 km from Papeete, on Tahiti and there are about 40 smaller airstrips. International services are operated by Air France, Qantas (Australia), Air New Zealand, UTA (France), LAN Chile and Hawaiian Airlines (USA).

Air Moorea: BP 6019, Papeete; tel. 424834; telex 314; fax 435897; f. 1968; operates internal services between Tahiti and Moorea Island and some inter-territorial services; since 1985 the airline has been 90% govt-owned; Pres. Marcel Galenon; Dir-Gen. François Martin; Sec.-Gen. Jean Gillot; fleet of 4 Britten Norman Islander, 1 Dornier 228-212, 1 Piper Chieftain.

Air Tahiti: Blvd Pomare, BP 314, Papeete; tel. 422333; fax 420759; f. 1953, Air Polynésie 1970–87; inter-island services to 35 islands; service to Los Angeles (USA); 19% govt-owned, with 7% still retained by the French airline UTA; Chair. Christian Vernaudon; Gen. Man. Marcel Galenon; fleet of 4 ATR-42, 1n Dornier 228-212; 1 leased DC-10.

Tourism

Tourism is an important and developed industry in French Polynesia, particularly on Tahiti, and 139,705 people visited the Territory in 1989, excluding cruise passengers and excursionists.

Office de Promotion et d'Animation Touristiques de Tahiti et ses Iles (OPATTI): Fare Manihini, blvd Pomare, BP 65, Papeete; tel. 429626; telex 254; fax 436619; f. 1966; autonomous public body; tourist promotion; Pres. Napoléon Spitz; Dir Pierre Meuel.

Service du Tourisme: Fare Manihini, blvd Pomare, BP 4527, Papeete; tel. 429330; telex 254; govt dept; manages Special Fund for Tourist Development; Dir Gérard Vanizette.

Syndicat d'Initiative de la Polynésie Française: BP 326, Papeete; Pres. Mme Piu Bambridge.

FRENCH SOUTHERN AND ANTARCTIC TERRITORIES

The French Southern and Antarctic Territories (Terres australes et antarctiques françaises) form an Overseas Territory but are administered under a special statute. The territory comprises Adélie Land, a narrow segment of the mainland of Antarctica, and several islands (the Kerguelen and Crozet Archipelagos, St Paul and Amsterdam) in the southern Indian Ocean.

Under the terms of legislation approved by the French Government on 6 August 1955, the French Southern and Antarctic Territories were placed under the authority of a chief administrator, who was responsible to the Ministry of Overseas Departments and Territories. The Chief Administrator is assisted by a consultative council, which meets at least twice annually. The Consultative Council is composed of seven members who are appointed for five years by the Ministers of Defence and of Overseas Departments and Territories (from among members of the Office of Scientific Research and from those who have participated in scientific missions in the Antarctic islands and Adélie Land) and by the Minister of Research and Technology and the Minister of Transport and the Sea.

In 1987 certain categories of vessels were allowed to register under the flag of the Kerguelen Archipelago if 25% of their crew were French, including the captain and at least two officers. In January 1989 work began on the construction of a 1,100m airstrip in Adélie Land, which aimed to improve access to research facilities. However, violent clashes took place between construction workers and members of Greenpeace, the international environmental protection group, who occupied the site in protest against the project, which, they claimed, would involve the destruction of large penguin-breeding colonies. The French authorities subsequently agreed to allow Greenpeace to conduct an independent assessment of the environmental impact of the airstrip, before resuming work several days later. Greenpeace announced the end of its campaign in mid-January, following the French decision to allow the scientific study.

Statistical Survey

Area (sq km): Kerguelen Archipelago 7,215, Crozet Archipelago 515, Amsterdam Island 60, St Paul Island 7, Adélie Land (Antarctica) 432,000.

Population (the population, comprising members of scientific missions, fluctuates according to season, being higher in the summer;

the figures given are approximate): Kerguelen Archipelago, Port-aux-Français 100; Amsterdam Island at Martin de Viviès 40; Adélie Land at Base Dumont d'Urville 30; the Crozet Archipelago at Alfred-Faure 40; St Paul Island is uninhabited. Total population (January 1985): 210.

Fishing (catch in metric tons): Crayfish (spiny lobsters) in Amsterdam and St Paul: 330 (1988); fishing by French and foreign fleets in the Kerguelen Archipelago: 10,000 annually.

Currency: French currency is used (see French Guiana).

Budget: Balanced at approx. 160m. francs annually.

External Trade: Exports consist mainly of crayfish and other fish to France and Réunion.

Directory

Government: Chief Administrator CLAUDE CORBIER; there is a Central Administration in Paris (34 rue des Renaudes, 75017 Paris, France; telex 640980).

Consultative Council: Pres. CLAUDE FREJACQUES.

Transport: Shipping: A charter vessel calls five times a year in the Antarctic islands, and another calls twice a year in Adélie Land. Civil Aviation: a landing strip of 1,100 m is being built, at a projected cost of 100m. francs, to serve the research station in Adélie Land.

Research Stations: There are meteorological stations and geophysical research stations on Kerguelen, Amsterdam, Adélie Land and Crozet.

NEW CALEDONIA

Introductory Survey

Location, Climate, Language, Religion, Capital

The territory of New Caledonia comprises one large island and several smaller ones, lying in the south Pacific Ocean, about 1,500 km (930 miles) east of Queensland, Australia. The main island, New Caledonia (la Grande-Terre), is long and narrow, and has a total area of 16,750 sq km. Rugged mountains divide the west of the island from the east, and there is little flat land. The nearby Loyalty Islands, which are administratively part of the territory, are 2,353 sq km in area, and a third group of islands, the uninhabited Chesterfield Islands, lies about 400 km north-west of the main island. The climate is generally a mild one, with an average temperature of about 23°C (73°F) and a rainy season between December and March. The average rainfall in the east of the main island is about 2,000 mm (80 in) per year, and in the west about 1,000 mm (40 in). French is the official language and the mother tongue of the Caldoches (French settlers); the indigenous Kanaks also speak Melanesian languages. Other immigrants speak Polynesian and Asian languages. New Caledonians are almost all Christians; about 59% are Roman Catholics, and there is a substantial Protestant minority. The capital is Nouméa, on the main island.

Recent History

New Caledonia became a French possession in 1853, when the island was annexed as a dependency of Tahiti. In 1884 a separate administration was established, and in 1946 it became an overseas territory of the French Republic. Early European settlers on New Caledonia, supported by legislation, quickly assumed possession of Melanesian land, which provoked a number of rebellions by the indigenous Melanesian (Kanak) population.

In 1956 the first Territorial Assembly, with 30 members, was elected by universal adult suffrage, although the French Governor effectively retained control of the functions of government. New Caledonian demands for a measure of self-government were answered in December 1976 by a new statute, which gave the Council of Government, elected from the Territorial Assembly, responsibility for certain internal affairs. The post of Governor was replaced by that of French High Commissioner to the Territory. In 1978 the Melanesian-supported, pro-independence parties obtained a majority of the posts in the Council of Government. In March 1979, however, the French Government dismissed the Council, following its failure to support a proposal for a 10-year 'contract' between France and New Caledonia, because the plan did not acknowledge the possibility of New Caledonian independence. The Territory was then placed under the direct authority of the High Commissioner. A general election was held in July, but a new electoral law, which affected mainly the pro-independence parties, ensured that minor parties were not represented in the Assembly. Two parties loyal to France together won 22 of the 36 seats.

Tension increased in September 1981 after the assassination of Pierre Declercq, Secretary-General of the pro-independence party, Union Calédonienne. In December of that year the French Government made proposals for change that included fiscal reform, equal access for all New Caledonians to positions of authority, land reforms, the wider distribution of mining revenue and the fostering of Melanesian cultural institutions. To assist in effecting these reforms, the French Government simultaneously announced that it would rule by decree for a period of at least one year. In June 1982, accusing its partner in the ruling coalition of 'active resistance to evolution and change' in New Caledonia, the Fédération pour une Nouvelle Société Calédonienne (FNSC) joined with the opposition Front Indépendantiste (FI) to form a government which was more favourable to the proposed reforms.

In July 1983 the French Government held a meeting in Paris with representatives of the territory's main political groupings. A statute was drafted, providing for a five-year period of increased autonomy from July 1984 and a referendum in 1989 to determine New Caledonia's future, with independence as one of the options to be offered. The statute was opposed in New Caledonia, both by parties in favour of earlier independence and by those against, and it was rejected by the Territorial Assembly in April 1984. However, the proposals were approved by the French National Assembly in September 1984. Under the provisions of the statute, the territorial Council of Ministers was given responsibility for many internal matters of government, its President henceforth being an elected member instead of the French High Commissioner; a second legislative chamber, with the right to be consulted on development planning and budgetary issues, was created at the same time. All of the main parties seeking independence, except the Libération Kanake Socialiste (LKS) party, which left the FI, boycotted elections for a new Territorial Assembly in November 1984 and, following the dissolution of the FI, formed a new movement called the Front de Libération Nationale Kanake Socialiste (FLNKS), whose congress instituted a 'provisional government', headed by Jean-Marie Tjibaou, on 1 December. The elections to the Territorial Assembly attracted only 50.12% of electors, and the anti-independence party Rassemblement pour la Calédonie dans la République (RPCR) won 34 of the 42 seats and 70.9% of the total vote. An escalation of violence by both Kanaks and Caldoches (French settlers) began in November, and a number of deaths had resulted before political leaders successfully appealed for peace.

In January 1985 Edgard Pisani, the new High Commissioner, announced a plan by which the Territory might become independent 'in association with' France on 1 January 1986, subject to the result of a referendum in July 1985, in which all adults resident in the territory for at least three years would have the right to vote. A major obstacle to the success of such a plan was the fact that Melanesians constituted only 43% of the population of the Territory, with people of European (37%) and other, mainly Asian and Pacific, origin accounting for the balance; Melanesian groups seeking independence had hitherto insisted that the indigenous population be allowed to determine its own fate. A resurgence of violence followed the announcement of Pisani's plan, and a state of emergency was declared after Eloi Machoro, a leading member of the FLNKS, was shot dead by police.

In April 1985 the French Prime Minister, Laurent Fabius, made new proposals for the future of New Caledonia, whereby the referendum on independence was deferred until an unspecified date not later than the end of December 1987. Meanwhile, the Territory was to be divided into four regions, each to be governed by its own elected autonomous council, which would have extensive powers in the spheres of planning and development, education, health and social services, land rights, transport and housing. The elected members of all four councils together would serve as regional representatives in a Territorial Congress (to replace the Territorial Assembly).

The 'Fabius plan' was well received by the FLNKS, which, at its third Congress in May 1985, voted in favour of participating in the regional elections, although it reaffirmed the ultimate goal of independence. It was also decided to maintain the 'provisional government' under Tjibaou at least until the end of December. The RPCR, however, condemned the plan as giving a more favourable ratio of seats to voters in the pro-independence regions, and the proposals were rejected by the predominantly anti-independence Territorial Assembly at the end of May. However, the necessary legislation was approved by the French National

Assembly in July, and the Fabius plan came into force. The elections were held in September 1985, and, as expected, only in the Centre region around Nouméa, where the bulk of the population is non-Melanesian, was an anti-independence majority recorded. However, the pro-independence Melanesians, in spite of their majorities in the three non-urban regions, would be in a minority in the Territorial Congress.

The FLNKS boycotted the general election to the French National Assembly in March 1986, in which the Socialists were defeated by a centre-right alliance. Only about 50% of the eligible voters in New Caledonia participated in the election, at which the Territory's two seats in the Assembly were won by RPCR candidates.

In May 1986 the French Council of Ministers approved a draft law providing for a referendum to be held in New Caledonia within 12 months, whereby voters would choose between independence and a further extension of regional autonomy. The proposal was opposed by the Socialist President, François Mitterrand, but was approved by the French National Assembly. In December the French Government acceded to the request of the FLNKS that the electorate eligible to participate in the referendum on independence be limited to those who had been resident in New Caledonia for at least three years. In the same month, in spite of strong French diplomatic opposition, the UN General Assembly voted to reinscribe New Caledonia on the UN list of non-self-governing territories.

In May 1987 the FLNKS decided to advocate an 'active but peaceful' boycott of the referendum, which, a month later, the French Government officially fixed for 13 September. In August six Kanaks were arrested during protests against the proposed referendum, which occurred despite a French ban on demonstrations in the Territory. President Mitterrand condemned his Government's handling of the affair, criticizing, in particular, the brutality with which police units had dispersed the protesters.

At the referendum on 13 September 1987, 48,611 votes were cast in favour of New Caledonia's continuation as part of the French Republic (98.3% of the total) and only 842 (1.7%) were cast in favour of independence. Of the registered electorate, almost 59% voted, a higher level of participation than was expected, although 90% of the electorate abstained in constituencies inhabited by a majority of Melanesians.

In November 1987 the French Government submitted a plan, designed to give the Territory a limited administrative independence, to New Caledonia's Territorial Congress. The plan received 24 votes (out of 46 cast), although FLNKS members refused to participate, claiming that it would reduce New Caledonia to a position of 'economic slavery'.

In October 1987 seven pro-French loyalists were acquitted on a charge of murdering 10 Kanak separatists in 1984. Tjibaou, who reacted to the ruling by declaring that his followers would have to abandon their stance of pacifism, and his deputy, Yeiwéné Yeiwéné, were indicted for 'incitement to violence'. In December Yeiwéné was arrested and formally charged, but was soon released.

In April 1988 four gendarmes were killed, and 27 held hostage in a cave, on the island of Ouvéa by supporters of the FLNKS. Two days later, Kanak separatists prevented about one-quarter of the Territory's polling stations from opening, when local elections, scheduled to coincide with the French presidential election, were held. The FLNKS boycotted the elections. Although 12 of the gendarmes taken hostage were subsequently released, six members of a French anti-terrorist squad were captured. French security forces immediately laid siege to the cave and, in the following month, made an assault upon it, leaving 19 Kanaks and two gendarmes dead. Following the siege, allegations that three Kanaks had been executed or left to die, after being arrested, led to an announcement by the new French Socialist Government that a judicial inquiry into the incident was to be opened.

At the elections to the French National Assembly in June 1988, both New Caledonian seats were retained by the RPCR. Michel Rocard, the new French Prime Minister, chaired negotiations, at the Hôtel Matignon (his official residence) in Paris, between the President of the RPCR, Jacques Lafleur, and the President of the FLNKS, Jean-Marie Tjibaou, who agreed to transfer the administration of the Territory to Paris for 12 months. Under the provisions of the agreement (known as the Matignon Accord), the Territory was to be divided into three administrative provinces (with three elected assemblies, whose members would together form the Territorial Congress) until 1998, when a territorial plebiscite on independence was to be held. Only people resident in the Territory in 1988, and their direct descendants, would be allowed to vote in the plebiscite. The agreement also provided for a programme of economic development, training in public administration for Kanaks, and institutional reforms. The Matignon Accord was presented to the French electorate in a referendum, held on 6 November 1988, and approved by 80% of those voting (although an abstention rate of 63% of the electorate was recorded). The programme was approved by a 57% majority in New Caledonia, where the rate of abstention was 37%. In November, under the terms of the agreement, 51 separatists were released from prison, including 26 Kanaks implicated in the incident on Ouvéa.

In May 1989 the leaders of the FLNKS, Tjibaou and Yeiwéné, were murdered by separatist extremists, alleged to be associated with the Front Uni de Libération Kanake (FULK), a grouping which had until then formed part of the FLNKS, but which opposed the Matignon Accord on the grounds that it conceded too much to the European settlers. The assassination was regarded as an attempt to disrupt the implementation of the Accord. Elections to the three Provincial Assemblies were nevertheless held, as scheduled, in June: the FLNKS won a majority of seats in the North province and the Loyalty Islands, while the RPCR obtained a majority in the South province, and also emerged as the dominant party in the Territorial Congress, with 27 of the 54 seats, while the FLNKS secured 19 seats. The fact that some 69% of the electorate participated in the voting was interpreted as indicating widespread support for the Matignon Accord.

The year of direct rule by France ended, as agreed, on 14 July 1989, when the Territorial Congress and Provincial Assemblies assumed the administrative functions allocated to them in the Matignon Accord (see below under Government). Agencies for administrative training and for the development of Kanak culture were also established, as stipulated by the Accord. The Agence de Développement Rural et d'Aménagement Foncier (ADRAF), which had been established in 1986 to supervise rural development and the redistribution of land, was reorganized in September, following an official investigation into allegations that the agency (which included prominent members of the RPCR) had ignored traditional Kanak land claims in transferring land to private ownership.

In November 1989 the French National Assembly approved an amnesty (as stipulated in the Matignon Accord) for all who had been involved in politically-motivated violence in New Caledonia before August 1988: the amnesty, whose beneficiaries included those who had been accused of killing the four gendarmes in April 1988, was strongly opposed by the right-wing French parties.

Relations between the FLNKS and the RPCR generally improved during 1990, owing partly to Lafleur's announcement, in April, that he was to sell his substantial private nickel-mining interests to the Provincial Government, thereby assisting the integration of the Kanaks into the Territory's principal economic activity. However, Lafleur repeatedly advocated the need to encourage the immigration of skilled workers from France and other European countries (as part of attempts to foster economic growth in the Territory), a stance which provoked strong opposition among Kanak leaders.

In November 1990 two secondary school students in Nouméa staged a brief hunger strike, to draw attention to their allegations of discrimination against Kanak children in schools.

Government

The French Government is represented in New Caledonia by its High Commissioner to the Territory, and controls a number of important spheres of government, including external relations, defence, justice, finance, external trade and secondary education. In July 1989 administrative reforms were introduced, as stipulated in the Matignon Accord (which had been approved by national referendum in November 1988). The Territory was divided into three Provinces (North, South and Loyalty Islands), each governed by an Assembly, which is elected by direct universal suffrage. The members of the three Provincial Assemblies together form the Territorial Congress. Members are subject to re-election every six years. The responsibilities of the Territorial Congress include the Territory's budget and fiscal affairs, infrastructure and primary education, while the responsibilities of the Provincial Assemblies include local economic development, land reform and cultural affairs. These institutions were to remain in place until the holding, in 1998, of a territorial referendum on the question of self-determination for New Caledonia.

In addition, New Caledonia elects two deputies to the French National Assembly in Paris, one representative to the French Senate and one Economic and Social Councillor, all of whom are chosen on the basis of universal adult suffrage. The territory is also represented at the European Parliament in Strasbourg.

Defence

In June 1990 France was maintaining a force of 4,900 personnel in New Caledonia, including a gendarmerie of 1,100.

Economic Affairs

In 1986, according to estimates by the UN, New Caledonia's gross domestic product (GDP) totalled US $1,027m., equivalent to $6,541 per head. During 1980–86 it was estimated, New Caledonia's GDP declined, in real terms, at an average annual rate of 1.2%, while

FRENCH OVERSEAS TERRITORIES

New Caledonia

GDP per head declined by 2.6% per year. The Territory's population increased by an annual average of 1.7% in 1980–89.

Agriculture and fishing contributed only 1.8% of GDP in 1988, although 14% of the employed labour force were engaged in the sector in 1989. Some 95% of agriculturally productive land was used for pasture or fodder in 1988, mainly for cattle and pigs. Maize, yams, sweet potatoes and coconuts are the principal crops. The main fisheries products are tuna (most of which is exported to Japan) and shrimps.

Industry (comprising mining, manufacturing, construction and utilities) provided 26% of GDP in 1985, and employed 19% of the working population in 1989. Mining employed only 1.6% of the working population in 1989, but it constitutes the most important industrial sector of New Caledonia's economy: in 1985 mining contributed 15.6% of GDP. The Territory possesses the world's largest known nickel deposits, accounting for about 30% of the world's known reserves. Sales of nickel accounted for 92.8% of export revenues in 1989. Chromium is also extracted, but the principal mine was expected to close at the end of 1989. There are also deposits of cobalt, iron, manganese, lead and zinc.

The manufacturing sector, which provided 4.7% of GDP in 1985 and employed 8.4% of the working population in 1989, consists mainly of small and medium-sized enterprises, most of which are situated around the capital, Nouméa, producing building materials, furniture, salted fish and perishable foods.

Electrical energy is provided by thermal power stations (55% in 1988) and by hydroelectric plants. Mineral fuels accounted for 9% of total imports in 1987. Construction of a new thermal power station, at Nepoui in North Province (at an estimated cost of US $59m.), was due for completion by late 1992.

During the late 1980s there was considerable investment in the tourism industry, and several new hotels were built. There were 82,161 visitors in 1989 (compared with 60,502 in 1988). In 1989 there was a trade deficit of 571m. French francs, compared with a surplus of 27m. in 1988 (which had been due to an increase in international prices for nickel). The principal imports in 1989 were mineral fuels, foodstuffs and machinery and transport equipment. France is the chief trading partner, providing 44.1% of imports and taking 36.4% of exports in 1989; other major trading partners in that year were Australia, the Federal Republic of Germany, Japan and the USA.

Almost one-third of New Caledonia's budget for 1987 was financed by a subsidy from France. The budget for 1989 envisaged revenue and expenditure of 2,848m. francs CFP; fiscal receipts were expected to contribute 1,592m. francs CFP, or 56% of budgetary revenue. The annual rate of inflation averaged 7.4% in 1980–88. The rate increased from 2.5% in 1988 to 4.0% in 1989, but declined to 2.9% in the year ending July 1990. Almost 16% of the labour force were unemployed at the time of the 1989 census.

New Caledonia forms part of the Franc Zone (see p. 156) and is a member, in its own right, of the South Pacific Commission (see p. 205).

During the 1980s New Caledonia's two principal sources of income, nickel production and tourism, were both affected by political unrest. Fluctuations in international prices for nickel also illustrated the disadvantages of relying on one commodity. In 1985 the French Government began a programme of investment in hotel-building and the promotion of tourism. Plans for rural development during the decade emphasized the cultivation of cash crops (especially coffee and fruit) and the production of shrimps for export. The Matignon Accord, approved by referendum in 1988 (see Recent History), stipulated that a programme of economic development should be undertaken, with the aim of improving the economic conditions of the Kanak population and increasing their participation in the market economy and in public administration. Investment in local projects was to be increased, in order to prevent the drift of the poor and unemployed from rural areas to Nouméa.

Social Welfare
In 1981 there were 38 hospitals in New Caledonia, with a total of 1,536 beds, and there were 168 physicians working in the territory.

Education
Education is compulsory for 10 years between six and 16 years of age. Schools are operated by both the State and churches, under the supervision of the Department of Education. The French Government finances the state secondary system. Primary education begins at six years of age, and lasts for five years; secondary education, beginning at 11 years of age, comprises a first cycle of four years and a second, three-year cycle. In 1989 there were 278 pre-primary and primary schools, 44 secondary schools, 29 vocational institutions and five institutions of higher education. Some students attend universities in France. Part of a regional university, the Université française du Pacifique, is based in New Caledonia. In 1976 the rate of adult illiteracy averaged 8.7% (males 7.8%, females 9.7%).

Public Holidays
1991: 1 January (New Year's Day), 1 April (Easter Monday), 6 May (for Labour Day), 8 May (Liberation Day), 9 May (Ascension Day), 20 May (Whit Monday), 14 July (Fall of the Bastille), 11 November (Armistice Day), 25 December (Christmas Day).

1992: 1 January (New Year's Day), 20 April (Easter Monday), 4 May (for Labour Day), 8 May (Liberation Day), 28 May (Ascension Day), 8 June (Whit Monday), 14 July (Fall of the Bastille), 11 November (Armistice Day), 25 December (Christmas Day).

Weights and Measures
The metric system is in force.

Statistical Survey

Source (unless otherwise stated): Institut Territorial de la Statistique et des Etudes Economiques, BP 823, Nouméa; tel. 275481; fax 288148.

AREA AND POPULATION

Area (sq km): New Caledonia island (Grande-Terre) 16,750; Loyalty Is 1,981 (Lifou 1,150, Maré 650, Ouvéa 130); Total 19,103 (7,376 sq miles).

Population: 145,368 (males 74,285, females 71,083) at census of 15 April 1983; 164,173 (males 83,862, females 80,311) at census of 4 April 1989.

Density (1989): 8.6 per sq km.

Principal Town (1989): Nouméa (capital), population 65,110.

Ethnic Groups (census of 1989): Melanesians 73,598, French and other Europeans 55,085, Wallisians and Futunans (Polynesian) 14,186, Indonesians 5,191, Tahitians (Polynesian) 4,750, Others 11,363.

Births and Deaths (1989): Live births 3,945; deaths 990.

Economically Active Population (persons aged 14 years and over, 1989 census): Agriculture, hunting, forestry and fishing 7,763; Mining and quarrying 910; Manufacturing 4,668; Electricity, gas and water 576; Construction 4,476; Trade, restaurants and hotels 9,454; Transport, storage and communications 3,087; Financing, insurance, real estate and business services 2,475; Community, social and personal services 22,016 (incl. 2,500 members of the armed forces); Total employed 55,425 (males 34,905, females 20,520); Unemployed 10,520 (males 6,306, females 4,214); Total labour force 65,945 (males 41,211, females 24,734). Source: ILO, *Year Book of Labour Statistics*.

AGRICULTURE, ETC.

Principal Crops (FAO estimates, metric tons, 1989): Maize 2,000, Taro 3,000, Potatoes 3,000, Sweet potatoes 4,000, Yams 12,000, Coconuts 14,000, Cassava 3,000, Vegetables and melons 4,000, Fruit 7,000. Source: FAO, *Production Yearbook*.

Livestock (FAO estimates, '000 head, year ending September 1989): Horses 10, Cattle 139, Pigs 41, Sheep 3, Goats 23 (Source: FAO, *Production Yearbook*); Rabbits (1984) 5.3.

Forestry: Roundwood removals: 12,000 cubic metres in 1979; estimated at 12,000 cubic metres annually in 1980–88. Source: FAO, *Yearbook of Forest Products*.

Fishing (metric tons, live weight): Total catch 4,006 in 1986; 4,797 in 1987; 3,683 in 1988; (FAO, *Yearbook of Fishery Statistics*).

MINING

Production ('000 metric tons): Nickel ore (gross weight) 2,790 in 1987; 3,385 in 1988; 4,855 in 1989.

INDUSTRY

Production (1989): Ferro-nickel and nickel matte 46,900 metric tons; Electric energy 1,192m. kWh.

FINANCE

Currency and Exchange Rates: see French Polynesia.

Budget (million French francs, 1989): Expenditure: Ordinary expenditure 2,404.64, Extraordinary expenditure 443.62, Total 2,848.26; Revenue: Ordinary receipts 2,404.64, Extraordinary receipts 443.62, Total 2,848.26. Source: Secrétariat du Comité Monétaire de la Zone Franc.

Aid from France (francs CFP, FIDES 1982): Local section 153m.; General section 1,018m.

Money Supply (million French francs at 31 December 1988): Currency in circulation 341; Demand deposits 1,907; Total money 2,248.

FRENCH OVERSEAS TERRITORIES

Cost of Living (Consumer Price Index for Nouméa; base: 1980 = 100): 173.2 in 1987; 177.6 in 1988; 184.7 in 1989.

Gross Domestic Product (million francs CFP at current prices): 139,650 in 1985; 151,281 in 1986; 162,627 in 1987.

EXTERNAL TRADE

Principal Commodities (million francs CFP, 1989): *Imports:* Petroleum products 8,138; Solid mineral fuels 932; Cement and clinker 417; Rice 397; Sugar 346; Wine 955; Total (incl. others) 88,608. *Exports:* Ferro-nickel 49,050; Nickel ore 12,691; Nickel matte 10,580; Total (incl. others) 77,900.

Principal Trading Partners (million francs CFP, 1989): *Imports:* Australia 8,082; France (metropolitan) 39,044; Federal Republic of Germany 5,252; Japan 4,716; USA 9,187; Total (incl. others) 88,608. *Exports:* France (metropolitan) 28,356; Federal Republic of Germany 6,658; India 2,333; Japan 22,104; USA 4,851; Total (incl. others) 77,900.

TRANSPORT

Road Traffic (1986): Motor vehicles (incl. tractors) 44,551.

Shipping (1989): Vessels entered 543; Freight unloaded 977,000 metric tons, Freight loaded 2,220,000 metric tons.

Civil Aviation (La Tontouta airport, Nouméa, 1989): Passengers arriving 139,951, Passengers departing 139,483; Freight unloaded 4,782 metric tons, Freight loaded 1,496 metric tons.

TOURISM

Visitors: 60,502 in 1988; 82,161 in 1989.

EDUCATION

Pre-primary and Primary (1989): 278 schools; 1,660 teachers; 33,872 (Pre-primary 10,330, Primary 23,542) pupils.

Secondary (1989): 73 schools (44 general, 29 vocational); 1,509 teachers; 20,152 pupils (13,675 general, 6,477 vocational).

Higher (1989): 5 institutions; 57 teachers; 927 students.

Directory

The Constitution

The constitutional system in New Caledonia and its dependencies is established under the Constitution of the Fifth French Republic and specific laws, the most recent of which were enacted in July 1989 in accordance with the terms agreed by the Matignon Accord. A referendum on the future of New Caledonia is to be conducted in 1998. The islands are declared to be an Overseas Territory of the French Republic, of which they remain an integral part. The High Commissioner is the representative of the State in the Territory and is appointed by the French Government. The High Commissioner is responsible for external relations, defence, law and order, finance and secondary education. The Territory is divided into three Provinces, of the South, the North and the Loyalty Islands. Each is governed by a Provincial Assembly, which is elected by direct universal suffrage and is responsible for local economic development, land reform and cultural affairs. Members of the Assemblies (32 for the South, 15 for the North and seven for the Loyalty Islands) are subject to re-election every six years. The members of the three Provincial Assemblies together form the Territorial Congress, which is responsible for the territorial budget and fiscal affairs, infrastructure and primary education. The Assemblies and the Congress each elect a President to lead them; the Presidents join the High Commissioner as part of the territorial executive. Provision is also made for the maintenance of Kanak tradition: there are eight custom regions, each with a Regional Consultative Custom Council. These eight Councils, with other appropriate authorities, are represented on the Territorial Custom Council, which is consulted by the Congress and the Government. Local government is conducted by 32 communes. The Territory also elects two deputies to the National Assembly in Paris, one Senator and one Economic and Social Councillor, all on the basis of universal adult suffrage. The Territory is represented in the European Parliament.

The Government
(January 1991)

High Commissioner: ALAIN CHRISTNACHT (appointed 1991).
Secretary-General: JACQUES IÉKAWÉ.

Legislature

ASSEMBLÉES PROVINCIALES

The three provinces each elect an autonomous Provincial Assembly, which, in turn, elects the President of the respective Provincial Government. The Assembly of the Province of the North has 15 members, that of the Province of the South 32 members and that of the Province of the Loyalty Islands seven members.

Election, 11 June 1989 (results by province)

Party	North	South	Loyalty Islands
RPCR	4	21	2
FLNKS	11	4	4
Front National	—	3	—
Calédonie Demain	—	2	—
Union Océanienne	—	2	—
Front Anti-Néocolonialiste	—	—	1

Province of the North: President LÉOPOLD JORÉDIÉ (FLNKS).
Province of the South: President JACQUES LAFLEUR (RPCR).
Province of the Loyalty Islands: President RICHARD KALOÏ (FLNKS).

CONGRÈS TERRITORIAL

The members of the three Provincial Assemblies sit together, in Nouméa, as the Territorial Congress. There are, therefore, 54 members in total.

President: SIMON LOUECKHOTE (RPCR).

Election, 11 June 1989* (results for the Territory as a whole)

Party	Votes	%	Seats
RPCR	27,777	44.46	27
FLNKS	17,898	28.65	19
Front National	4,204	6.73	3
Calédonie Demain	3,219	5.15	2
Union Océanienne	2,429	3.89	2
Others	6,943	11.11	1
Total	**62,470**	**100.00**	**54**

* The election was boycotted by the Front Uni de Libération Kanak (FULK). The abstention rate was 30.7%.

PARLEMENT

Deputies to the French National Assembly: JACQUES LAFLEUR (RPCR), MAURICE NÉNOU-PWATAHO (RPCR).

Representative to the French Senate: DICK UKEIWÉ (RPCR).

GOVERNMENT OFFICES

Office of the High Commissioner: Haut-commissariat de la République en Nouvelle-Calédonie et dépendances, Nouméa.

Territorial Government: Gouvernement de la Nouvelle-Calédonie, Nouméa; fax 272828.

Government of the Province of the Loyalty Islands: Gouvernement Provincial des Iles Loyauté, Wé, Lifou, Loyalty Is.

Government of the Province of the North: Gouvernement Provincial du Nord, Koné, Grande-Terre.

Government of the Province of the South: Gouvernement Provincial du Sud, Nouméa.

Political Organizations

Calédonie Demain: Nouméa; right-wing; comprises former adherents of the RPCR and the Front national; Leader BERNARD MARANT.

Fédération pour une Nouvelle Société Calédonienne (FNSC): 8 rue Gagarine, Nouméa; tel. 252395; f. 1979; Leader JEAN-PIERRE AÏFA; favours a degree of internal autonomy for New Caledonia; a coalition of the following parties:

Mouvement Wallisien et Futunien: f. 1979; Pres. FINAU MELITO.

Parti Républicain Calédonien (PRC): f. 1979; Leader LIONEL CHERRIER.

Union Démocratique (UD): f. 1968; Leader GASTON MORLET.

Union Nouvelle Calédonienne (UNC): f. 1977; Leader JEAN PIERRE AÏFA.

FRENCH OVERSEAS TERRITORIES
New Caledonia

Front Calédonien (FC): extreme right-wing; Leader M. SARRAN.

Front de Libération Nationale Kanake Socialiste (FLNKS): BP 3553, Nouméa; tel. 274033; f. 1984 (following dissolution of Front indépendantiste); pro-independence; Pres. PAUL NÉAOUTYINE; Vice-Pres. ROCK WAMYTAN; a grouping of the following parties:

Parti de Libération Kanak (PALIKA): f. 1975; 5,000 mems; Leaders PAUL NÉAOUTYINE, ELIE POIGOUNE.

Parti Socialiste Calédonien (PSC): f. 1975; Leader M. VIOLETTE.

Union Calédonienne (UC): f. 1952; 5,000 mems; Pres. FRANÇOIS BURCK; Vice-Pres. ROCK WAMYTAN; Sec.-Gen. FRANÇOIS VOUTY.

Union Progressiste Mélanésienne (UPM): f. 1974 as the Union progressiste multiraciale; 2,300 mems; Pres. EDMOND NEKIRIAI; Sec.-Gen. VICTOR TUTUGORO.

Front National (FN): Nouméa; extreme right-wing; Leader GUY GEORGE.

Front Uni de Libération Kanak (FULK): Nouméa; f. 1974; pro-independence, but opposes the Matignon Accord; expulsion from FLNKS confirmed in January 1990; Leader YANN CÉLÉNÉ UREGEÏ.

Libération Kanake Socialiste (LKS): Maré, Loyalty Is; pro-independence; Leader NIDOÏSH NAISSELINE.

Rassemblement pour la Calédonie dans la République (RPCR): 8 avenue Foch, BP 306, Nouméa; tel. 282620; f. 1977; affiliated to the metropolitan Rassemblement pour la République (RPR); in favour of retaining the status quo in New Caledonia; Leader JACQUES LAFLEUR; a coalition of the following parties:

Centre des Démocrates Sociaux (CDS): f. 1971; Leader JEAN LÈQUES.

Parti Républicain (PR): Leader PIERRE MARESCA.

Un Pays pour Tous: Nouméa; left-wing, comprising mainly people of European origin; Leader JEAN-PIERRE AIFA.

Union Océanienne: Nouméa; f. 1989 by split from RPCR; represents people whose origin is in the French Overseas Territory of Wallis and Futuna; conservative; Leader MICHEL HEMA; Gen. Sec. ALOISIO SAKO.

Union pour Construire (UPC): f. 1988, by mems of the LKS who opposed their party's decision to boycott regional elections; pro-independence; Leaders M. LETHEZER, FRANCIS POADOUY.

Other political organizations participating in the elections of June 1989 included: **Front Anti-Néocolonialiste** (formed in the Loyalty Islands by the LKS and pro-independence moderates); **Front Uni pour Construire Ensemble** (Left-wing group in the Loyalty Islands; Leader M. LALIÉ); **Regroupement des Centristes et Modérés** (Leader M. BAILLY); **Vérité, Dialogue, Fraternité** (multiracial; Leader M. CHRÉTIEN).

Judicial System

Court of Appeal: Palais de Justice, BP F4, Nouméa; First Pres. JEAN-PAUL COLLOMP; Procurator-Gen. (vacant).

Court of the First Instance: Nouméa; Pres. DIDIER MARSHALL; Procurator of the Republic YVES LEBOURDON. From January 1990 two subsidiary courts, with resident magistrates, were established at Koné (Province du Nord, Grande-Terre) and Wé (Lifou).

Custom Consultative Council: Conseil Coutumier Territorial, c/o Gouvernement Territorial de la Nouvelle Calédonie, Nouméa; f. 1990; consulted by Govt on all matters affecting land and Kanak tradition; mems: 40 authorities from eight custom areas; Pres. CHARLES ATTITTI; Vice-Pres. PAUL SIHAZE.

Religion

The majority of the population is Christian, with Roman Catholics comprising about 59% of the total in 1989. About 3% of the inhabitants are Muslims.

CHRISTIANITY

The Roman Catholic Church

The Territory comprises a single archdiocese, with an estimated 97,200 adherents in 1989. The Archbishop participates in the Catholic Bishops' Conference of the Pacific, based in Fiji.

Archbishop of Nouméa: Most Rev. MICHEL-MARIE-BERNARD CALVET, Archevêché, BP 3, 4 rue Mgr-Fraysse, Nouméa; tel. 273149; fax 272374.

The Anglican Communion

Within the Church of the Province of Melanesia, New Caledonia forms part of the diocese of Vanuatu (q.v.). The Archbishop of the Province is the Bishop of Central Melanesia (resident in Honiara, Solomon Islands).

Protestant Churches

Eglise évangélique en Nouvelle-Calédonie et aux Iles Loyauté: BP 277, Nouméa; f. 1960; Pres. Rev. SAILALI PASSA; Gen. Sec. Rev. TELL KASARHEROU.

Other churches active in the Territory include the Assembly of God, the Free Evangelical Church, the Presbyterian Church and the Tahitian Evangelical Church.

The Press

L'Avenir Calédonien: 10 rue Gambetta, Nouméa; organ of the Union Calédonienne; Dir PAÏTA GABRIEL.

Dixit: BP 370, Nouméa; tel. 286631; telex 3078; f. 1984; annual; French (circ. 12,000) and English (circ. 8,000); Dir HUBERT CHAVELET.

Eglise de Nouvelle-Calédonie: BP 170, Nouméa; f. 1976; fortnightly; official publ. of the Roman Catholic Church; circ. 450.

La France Australe: 5 rue de la Somme, BP 25, Nouméa; tel. 274444; daily.

Le Journal Calédonien: BP 3002, Nouméa; weekly.

Les Nouvelles Calédoniennes: 41–43 rue de Sébastopol, BP 179, Nouméa; tel. 272584; telex 3812; f. 1971; daily; Publr HENRI MORNY; Dir MAXIME BRIANÇON; Editor HENRI PERRON; circ. 18,000.

NEWS AGENCY

Agence France-Presse (AFP): 2 rue Arthur Pelletier, Quartier Trianon, Nouméa; tel. 263033; telex 3826; Correspondent BERNARD DEGIOANNI.

Publishers

Editions d'Art Calédoniennes: 40 rue de Paris, BP 1626, Nouméa; tel. 261184; telex 3048; art, reprints, travel.

Les Editions du Devenir: 7 rue Mascart, Rivière Salée, BP 4481, Nouméa; tel. 285752; telex 3045; magazines, politics, tourism.

Radio and Television

In 1989 there were an estimated 90,000 radio receivers and 35,500 television receivers in use, of which about 25,000 were colour receivers.

RADIO

Radiodiffusion Française d'Outre-mer (RFO): BP G3, Nouméa Cedex; tel. 274327; telex 3052; fax 281252; f. 1942; 20 hours of daily programmes in French; Dir ALAIN LE GARREC.

Radio Djiido: 29 rue du Maréchal Juin, BP 1671, Nouméa; tel. 253433; Dir OCTAVE TOGNA.

Radio Latitude Sud: Nouméa; f. 1990; broadcasts in French and several other languges; multi-ethnic.

Radio Rythme Bleu: BP 1390, Nouméa; tel. 283357.

TELEVISION

Télé Nouméa: Société Nationale de Radiodiffusion Française d'Outre-mer, BP G3, Nouméa; tel. 274327; telex 3052; fax 281252; f. 1965; transmits 10 hours daily; Dir ALAIN LE GARREC.

Finance

(cap. = capital; res = reserves; m. = million; brs = branches; amounts in CFP francs unless otherwise stated)

BANKING

Banque Nationale de Paris Nouvelle Calédonie (France): 37 ave Henri Lafleur, BP K3, Nouméa; tel. 275555; telex 3022; fax 277969; f. 1969 as Banque Nationale de Paris; present name adopted in 1978; cap. 30m. French francs, res 64m. French francs, dep. 1,367.6m. French francs (Dec. 1989); Pres. JEAN-LOUIS HAUTCOEUR; Gen. Man. CHRISTIAN FAUCILHON; 8 brs.

Banque de Nouvelle-Calédonie (BNC) (Crédit Lyonnais): 23–25 ave de la Victoire ave Henri Lafleur, BP L3, Nouméa Cedex; tel. 285069; telex 3091; fax 274147; f. 1974; cap. 285m. (Oct. 1989); Pres., Dir-Gen. BERNARD THIOLON; Dir GUY JAVELAUD.

FRENCH OVERSEAS TERRITORIES

New Caledonia, Wallis and Futuna Islands

Banque Paribas Pacifique (Nouvelle-Calédonie): 33 rue de l'Alma, BP J3, Nouméa; tel. 275181; telex 3086; fax 275619; f. 1971; cap. 600m., res 292.4m., dep. 22,254.8m. (Dec. 1989); Chair. PIERRE MARTINAUD; Gen. Man. CHRISTIAN DE BERNEDE.

Société Générale Calédonienne de Banque: 56 ave de la Victoire, BP G2, Nouméa Cedex; tel. 272264; telex 3067; f. 1981; cap. 275m., res 596.5m., dep. 15,638.3m. (Dec. 1987); Gen. Man. RAYMOND CLAVIER; 6 brs.

Westpac Banking Corporation (Australia): BP G5, Nouméa; acquired operations of Banque Indosuez in New Caledonia in 1990; Man. LYALL MACKINTOSH.

Trade and Industry

Chambre d'Agriculture: BP 111, Nouméa; tel. 272056; f. 1909; 46 mems; Pres. ROGER PENE.

Chambre de Commerce et d'Industrie: BP M3, Nouméa Cedex; tel. 272551; telex 3045; fax 278114; f. 1879; 20 mems; Pres. ARNOLD DALY; Gen. Man. GEORGES GIOVANNELLI.

DEVELOPMENT ORGANIZATIONS

Agence de développement rural et d'aménagement foncier (ADRAF): 12 rue de Verdun, BP 4228, Nouméa; tel. 284242; fax 284322; f. 1986, reorganized 1989; rural development projects, acquisition and redistribution of land; Chair. ALAIN CHRISTNACHT; Dir-Gen. BRUNO ARBOUET.

Institut Calédonien de Participation: Nouméa; f. 1989 to finance development projects and encourage the Kanak population to participate in the market economy.

STATE-OWNED INDUSTRIES

Société Minière du Sud-Pacifique (SMSP): Nouméa; 85% owned by Province of the North since 1990; nickel-mining co; subsidiaries: Compagnie Maritime Calédonienne (stevedoring), and tourism cos Compagnie d'Investissement Touristiques, Nord Tourisme.

Société Le Nickel (SLN): Doniambo, Grande-Terre; nickel mining, processing and sales co.

EMPLOYERS' ORGANIZATION

Fédération Patronale de Nouvelle-Calédonie et Dépendances: Immeuble Carcopino 3000, 21 ave des Frères Carcopino, BP 466, Nouméa; tel. 273525; telex 3045; f. 1936; represents the leading companies of New Caledonia in the defence of professional interests, co-ordination, documentation and research in socio-economic fields; Pres. DIDIER LEROUX; Sec.-Gen. ANNIE BEUSTES.

TRADE UNIONS

Confédération des Travailleurs Calédoniens: Nouméa; Sec.-Gen. R. JOYEUX; grouped with:

Fédération des Fonctionnaires: Nouméa; Sec.-Gen. GILBERT NOUVEAU.

Syndicat Général des Collaborateurs des Industries de Nouvelle Calédonie: Sec.-Gen. H. CHAMPIN.

Union syndicale des Travailleurs kanaks exploités (USTKE): Nouméa, BP 4372; Leader LOUIS KOTRA UREGEÏ.

Union des Syndicats Ouvriers et Employés de Nouvelle-Calédonie (USOENC): Nouméa; Sec.-Gen. GUY MENNESSON.

Union Territoriale Force Ouvrière: 13 rue Jules Ferry, BP 4773, Nouméa; tel. 274950; f. 1982; Sec.-Gen. BERNARD CHENAIE.

Transport

ROADS

In 1983 there was a total of 5,980 km of roads in New Caledonia; 766 km were bitumen-surfaced, 589 km unsealed, 1,618 km stone-surfaced and 2,523 km tracks in 1980. The outer islands had a total of 470 km of roads and tracks in 1980.

SHIPPING

Most traffic is through the port of Nouméa. Passenger and cargo services, linking Nouméa to other towns and islands, are regular and frequent. There are plans to develop Nepoui, in the Province of the North, as a deep-water port and industrial centre.

Shipping companies operating cargo services include Hamburg-Sued, Nedlloyd and Bank Line (which connect Nouméa with European ports), Kyowa Line (with Hong Kong, Taiwan, the Republic of Korea and Japan), Somacal (with Sydney, Australia), Sofrana-Unilines (with various Pacific islands and ports on the west coast of Australia), Daiwa Line (with Sydney, Australia, Japan, and various Pacific Islands), Compagnie des Chargeurs Calédoniens (with Sydney, Australia, and European and Mediterranean ports) and the China Navigation Co (with New Zealand, Fiji and Japan).

CIVIL AVIATION

There is an international airport, Tontouta, 47 km from Nouméa, and an internal network, centred on Magenta airport, which provides air services linking Nouméa to other towns and islands.

Air Calédonie: BP 212, Nouméa; tel. 252339; telex 3249; fax 254869; f. 1955; services throughout New Caledonia and to the Loyalty Islands, and to Vanuatu for ACI; Chair. FRANCK WAHUZUE; Man. Dir PIERRE SEGUI; fleet of 3 ATR 42, 2 DO 228.

Air Calédonie International: POB 3736, Nouméa; tel. 283333; telex 3177; fax 272772; f. 1983; 62% owned by Territorial Govt; services to Sydney, Brisbane and Melbourne (Australia), Auckland (New Zealand), Fiji, Papeete (French Polynesia), Wallis Island and Vanuatu; Pres. JEAN-PIERRE VARNIER; CEO ALAIN BALLEREAU; fleet of 1 Boeing 737,300, 1 Twin Otter.

Tourism

The number of visitors to New Caledonia declined from 92,982 in 1984, to 51,190 in 1985, owing to the political unrest. An investment programme was begun in 1985 with the aim of developing and promoting tourism. In 1989 there were 82,161 visitors.

Destination Nouvelle-Calédonie: Immeuble Manathan 39, 41 rue de Verdun, BP 688, Nouméa; tel. 272632; telex 3063; fax 274623; f. 1960; Dir JEAN-MICHEL FOUTREIN.

WALLIS AND FUTUNA ISLANDS

Introductory Survey

Location, Climate, Language, Religion, Capital

The territory of Wallis and Futuna comprises two groups of islands: the Wallis Islands, including Wallis Island (also known as Uvea) and 22 islets on the surrounding reef, and, to the south-east, Futuna (or Hooru), comprising the two small islands of Futuna and Alofi. The islands are located north-east of Fiji and west of Western Samoa. Temperatures are generally between about 23°C (73°F) and 30°C (86°F), and there is a cyclone season between October and March. French and Wallisian, the indigenous Polynesian language, are spoken in the territory, and the entire population is nominally Roman Catholic. The capital is Mata-Utu, on Wallis Island.

Recent History

The Wallis and Futuna Islands were settled first by Polynesian peoples, Wallis from Tonga and Futuna from Samoa. Three kingdoms had emerged by 1842, when a French protectorate was proclaimed, coinciding with a similar proclamation in Tahiti (now French Polynesia). Protectorate status was formalized in 1887 for Wallis and in 1888 for the two kingdoms of Futuna, but domestic law remained in force. The islands were never formally annexed, and nor were French law or representative institutions introduced, although Wallis and Futuna were treated as a dependency of New Caledonia. In 1959 the traditional kings and chiefs requested the Commissioner for integration into the French Republic. The islands formally became on Overseas Territory in July 1961, following a referendum in December 1959, in which 94.4% of the electorate requested this status (almost all the opposition was in Futuna, which itself recorded dissent from only 22.2% of the voters; Wallis was unanimous in its acceptance; workers overseas also were entitled to vote).

Although there is no movement in Wallis and Futuna seeking secession of the territory from France (in contrast with the situation in the other French Pacific territories, French Polynesia and New Caledonia), the two kings whose kingdoms share the island of Futuna requested in November 1983, through the Territorial Assembly, that the island groups of Wallis and Futuna become separate overseas territories of France, arguing that the administration and affairs of the territory had become excessively concentrated on Wallis Island.

At elections to the 20-member Territorial Assembly in March 1982, the Rassemblement pour la République (RPR) and its allies won 11 seats, while the remaining nine went to candidates belonging to, or associated with, the Union pour la Démocratie Française (UDF). Later in 1982 one member of the Lua kae tahi, a group affiliated to the metropolitan UDF, defected to the RPR group, thereby strengthening the RPR's majority. In November 1983, however, three of the 12 RPR members joined the Lua kae tahi, forming a new majority. In the subsequent election for President of the Territorial Assembly, this 11-strong block of UDF-associated members supported the ultimately successful candidate, Falakiko Gata, even though he had been elected to the Territorial Assembly in 1982 as a member of the RPR.

In April 1985 Gata formed a new political party, the Union populaire locale (UPL), which was committed to giving priority to local, rather than metropolitan, issues. At a meeting with the French Prime Minister in Paris in June, Gata reaffirmed that it was in the territory's interests to remain French and not to seek independence.

In March 1986 Benjamin Brial, the candidate of the RPR, was re-elected as the territory's deputy to the French National Assembly, obtaining 2,798 votes (44.4%) of the total 6,302 votes cast in the second ballot. In October the islands' Chief Administrator, Jacques Le Hénaff, declared a state of emergency in the territory for one day, following a stone-throwing incident during a display of unrest among some local chiefs. The latter had expressed dissatisfaction with the French Secretary-General of the territory, Georges Jaymes, and requested his removal and repatriation, owing to his transfer of a number of highly-respected French civil servants from their posts in the territory. As a precautionary measure, 30 gendarmes were dispatched to the islands from New Caledonia to restore order, but the disturbance was not renewed.

In 1987 a dispute broke out between two families both laying claim to the throne of Sigavé, one of the two kingdoms on the island of Futuna. The conflict arose following the deposition of the former King, Sagato Keletaona, and his succession by Sosepho Vanaï. The intervention of the island's administrative authorities, who attempted to ratify Vanaï's accession to the throne, was condemned by the Keletaona family as an interference in the normal course of local custom, according to which such disputes are traditionally settled by a fight between the protagonists.

At elections to the Territorial Assembly held in March 1987, the UDF (together with affiliated parties) and the RPR each won seven seats. However, by forming an alliance with the UPL, the RPR maintained its majority, and Gata was subsequently re-elected President, receiving 13 of the 20 votes cast in the Territorial Assembly, the remaining seven being in favour of Basil Tui, an affiliate of the UDF. In October 1987 Gérard Lambotte replaced Jacques Le Hénaff as the islands' Chief Administrator, and in July 1988 was himself replaced by Roger Dumec. At elections for the French National Assembly in June 1988, Benjamin Brial was re-elected deputy. However, when the result was contested by an unsuccessful candidate, Kamilo Gata, the election was investigated by the French Constitutional Council and the result declared invalid, owing to electoral irregularities. When the election was held again in January 1989, Gata was elected deputy, obtaining 3,390 votes, or 57.4% of the total.

In August 1989 members of the RPR/UPL majority grouping in the Territorial Assembly, led by Clovis Logologofolau (who had replaced Falakiko Gata as President of the Assembly), accused the Chief Administrator, Dumec, of abusing his powers by excluding the traditional chiefs and the Assembly majority from decision-making. Dissatisfaction continued to be expressed in 1990, and in August the French Government announced that 'round-table' discussions regarding the Territory's social, economic and political development would take place in 1991. In September 1990 a new Chief Administrator-designate, Robert Pommies, was appointed. At the same time, Philippe Deblonde was appointed acting Chief Administrator.

Government

The territory of Wallis and Futuna is administered by a representative of the French Government, the Chief Administrator, who is assisted by a Territorial Assembly. The Assembly has 20 members and is elected for a five-year term. The three traditional kingdoms, from which the territory was formed, one on Wallis and two sharing Futuna, have equal rights, although the kings' powers are limited. In addition, the territory elects one deputy to the French National Assembly in Paris and one representative to the French Senate. The islands are also represented at the European Parliament in Strasbourg.

Economic Affairs

Most monetary income in Wallis and Futuna is derived from government employment and remittances sent home by islanders employed in New Caledonia. Coconut products (chiefly copra) and handicrafts are the only significant export commodities, which together earned 0.2m. francs CFP in export revenue in 1985. Yams, taro, bananas, cassava and other food crops are also cultivated. Imports, which are provided mainly by metropolitan France and New Caledonia, cost 1,350m. francs CFP in 1985 and consisted principally of raw materials, manufactured goods and petroleum products. Mineral fuels are the main source of electrical energy, although it is hoped that hydroelectric power can be developed, especially on Futuna.

In 1985 the President of the Territorial Assembly informed the French Government that, in his opinion, the policies relating to agricultural and fisheries development since 1960 had been a complete failure. It was hoped that these areas of the economy could be improved through new administrative arrangements, whereby development funding would be channelled through traditional chiefs.

In December 1986 almost all the cultivated vegetation on the island of Futuna, notably the banana plantations, was destroyed by a cyclone. In response to the cyclone damage, the French Government announced, in February 1987, that it was to provide exceptional aid of 55m. French francs to alleviate the situation. No copra was exported in 1987, but it was hoped that export levels would recover to about 100 metric tons per year by 1990. In August 1989 the French Prime Minister visited the islands, inaugurated a new earth station for satellite communications, and announced that additional funds were to be made available for the development of agriculture and fisheries.

Social Welfare

In 1981 there were three state hospitals in Wallis and Futuna, with a total of 93 beds, and there were four physicians working in the islands.

Education

In 1987 there were 13 state-financed primary and lower-secondary schools in Wallis and Futuna, with a total of 4,622 pupils.

Public Holidays

1991: 1 January (New Year's Day), 1 April (Easter Monday), 6 May (for Labour Day), 8 May (Liberation Day), 9 May (Ascension Day), 20 May (Whit Monday), 14 July (Fall of the Bastille), 11 November (Armistice Day), 25 December (Christmas Day).

1992: 1 January (New Year's Day), 20 April (Easter Monday), 4 May (for Labour Day), 8 May (Liberation Day), 28 May (Ascension Day), 8 June (Whit Monday), 14 July (Fall of the Bastille), 11 November (Armistice Day), 25 December (Christmas Day).

Weights and Measures

The metric system is in force.

Statistical Survey

AREA AND POPULATION

Area (sq km): 274. *By island:* Uvea (Wallis Island) 60, Other Wallis Islands 99; Futuna Island 64, Alofi Island 51.

Population (1983 census): 12,408: Wallis Islands 8,084, Futuna Island 4,324; Alofi Island uninhabited; about 12,000 Wallisians and Futunans live in New Caledonia and in Vanuatu.

Density (1983): 45.3 per sq km.

Principal Town: Mata-Utu (capital), population 815 at 1983 census.

AGRICULTURE, ETC.

Principal Crops (FAO estimates, '000 metric tons, 1989): Cassava 2, Yams 1, Taro (Coco yam) 2, Coconuts 3, Bananas 4, Other fruit 5, Vegetables and melons 1. Source: FAO, *Production Yearbook*.

Livestock (FAO estimates, year ending September 1989): Pigs 32,000, Goats 8,000. Source: FAO, *Production Yearbook*.

Fishing (FAO estimates, metric tons, live weight): 900 in 1984; 1,000 per year in 1985–88. Source: FAO, *Yearbook of Fishery Statistics*.

FINANCE

Currency and Exchange Rates: see French Polynesia.

Budget (1983): 20,350,000 French francs.

Aid from France (1982): 55,000,000 French francs.

FRENCH OVERSEAS TERRITORIES — *Wallis and Futuna Islands*

EXTERNAL TRADE
1985 (francs CFP): *Imports:* 1,350m. *Exports:* 0.21m.

TRANSPORT
Civil Aviation: Uvea (Wallis Island—1980): aircraft arrivals and departures 581; freight handled 171 metric tons; passenger arrivals 4,555, passenger departures 4,300; mail loaded and unloaded 72 metric tons.

TOURISM
Visitors: 400 in 1985.
Hotels (1985): Number 3; Rooms 25.

EDUCATION
Primary and Lower Secondary (1987): 13 state-financed schools, 4,622 pupils.

Directory

The Constitution

The Territory of the Wallis and Futuna Islands is administered according to a statute of 1961, and subsidiary legislation, under the Constitution of the Fifth Republic. The Statute declares the Wallis and Futuna Islands to be an Overseas Territory of the French Republic, of which it remains an integral part. The Statute established an administration, a Council of the Territory, a Territorial Assembly and national representation. The administrative, political and social evolution envisaged by, and enacted under, the Statute is intended to effect a smooth integration of the three customary Kingdoms with the new institutions of the Territory. The Kings are assisted by Ministers and the traditional chiefs. The Chief Administrator, appointed by the French Government, is the representative of the State in the Territory and is responsible for external affairs, defence, law and order, financial and educational affairs. The Chief Administrator is required to consult with the Council of the Territory, which has six members: three by right (the Kings of Wallis, Sigave and Alo) and three appointed by the Chief Administrator upon the advice of the Territorial Assembly. This Assembly assists in the administration of the Territory; there are 20 members elected on a common roll, on the basis of universal adult suffrage, for a term of up to five years. The Territorial Assembly elects, from among its own membership, a President to lead it. The Territory elects national representatives (one deputy to the National Assembly, one Senator and one Economic and Social Councillor) and votes for representatives to the European Parliament in Strasbourg.

The Government
(February 1991)

Chief Administrator (Administrateur Supérieur): ROBERT POMMIES (designate, appointed September 1990).
Acting Chief Administrator: PHILIPPE DEBLONDE.

CONSEIL DU TERRITOIRE
Chair: Chief Administrator.
Members by Right: King of Wallis, King of Sigave, King of Alo.
Appointed Members: PAINO TUUGAHALA (Kalae Kivalu), ATOLO UHILA (Kulitea), ESTELLE LAKALAKA.

GOVERNMENT OFFICE
Government Headquarters: Bureau de l'Administrateur Supérieur, Mata-Utu, Uvea, Wallis Islands, Wallis and Futuna (via Nouméa, New Caledonia); telex 5074; all departments.

Legislature

ASSEMBLÉE TERRITORIALE
President: CLOVIS LOGOLOGOFOLAU (RPR).

Election, 15 March 1987

	Seats
Rassemblement pour la République (RPR)	7
Union Populaire Locale (UPL)	6
Union pour la Démocratie Française (UDF)	7
Lua kae tahi	
Total	**20**

PARLEMENT
Deputy to the French National Assembly: KAMILO GATA (MRG).
Representative to the French Senate: SOSEFO MAKAPE PAPILIO (RPR).

The Kingdoms

WALLIS
(Capital: Mata-Utu on Uvea)

Lavelua, King of Wallis: TOMASI KULIMOETOKE.
Council of Ministers: Prime Minister (Kivalu) and five other Ministers.

The Kingdom of Wallis is divided into three districts (Hihifo, Hihake, Mua), and its traditional hierarchy includes three district chiefs (Faipule) and 19 village chiefs (Pule).

SIGAVE
(Capital: Sigave on Futuna)

Tuisigave, King of Sigave: LAFAELE MALAU.
Council of Ministers: five Ministers, chaired by the King.

The Kingdom of Sigave is located in the north of the island of Futuna; there are five village chiefs.

ALO
(Capital: Alo on Futuna)

Tuigaifo, King of Alo: LOMANO MUSULAMU.
Council of Ministers: five Ministers, chaired by the King.

The Kingdom of Alo comprises the southern part of the island of Futuna and the entire island of Alofi. There are seven village chiefs.

Political Organizations

Lua kae tahi: c/o Assemblée Territoriale, Mata-Utu, Uvea, Wallis Islands, Wallis and Futuna (via Nouméa, New Caledonia); affiliated to UDF.
Mouvement des Radicaux de Gauche (MRG): c/o Assemblée Territoriale, Mata-Utu, Uvea, Wallis Islands, Wallis and Futuna (via Nouméa, New Caledonia); left-wing.
Rassemblement pour la République (RPR): c/o Assemblée Territoriale, Mata-Utu, Uvea, Wallis Islands, Wallis and Futuna (via Nouméa, New Caledonia); Gaullist; Territorial Leader CLOVIS LOGOLOGOFOLAU.
Union Populaire Locale (UPL): c/o Assemblée Territoriale, Mata-Utu, Uvea, Wallis Islands, Wallis and Futuna (via Nouméa, New Caledonia); f. 1985; emphasizes importance of local issues; strongest in Futuna; Leader FALAKIKO GATA.
Union pour la Démocratie Française (UDF): c/o Assemblée Territoriale, Mata-Utu, Uvea, Wallis Islands, Wallis and Futuna (via Nouméa, New Caledonia); centrist; based on Uvean (Wallis) support.

Religion

Almost all of the inhabitants profess Christianity and are adherents of the Roman Catholic Church.

CHRISTIANITY
The Roman Catholic Church

The Territory comprises a single diocese, suffragan to the archdiocese of Nouméa (New Caledonia). The diocese estimated that the entire population were adherents, and that this totalled some 16,000 in number on 31 December 1988. The Bishop participates in the Catholic Bishops' Conference of the Pacific, based in Fiji.
Bishop of Wallis and Futuna: Mgr LOLESIO FUAHEA, Evêché, Lano, BP 15, Mata-Utu, Uvea, Wallis Islands, Wallis and Futuna (via Nouméa, New Caledonia); tel. 722783.

Radio and Television

Radiodiffusion Française d'Outre-mer (RFO): RFO Wallis et Futuna, BP 102, Mata-Utu, Uvea, Wallis Islands, Wallis and Futuna (via Nouméa, New Caledonia); tel. 722020; telex 250500; transmitters at Mata-Utu (Uvea) and Alo (Futuna); programmes in Uvean (Wallisian), Futunan and French; a television service, transmitting for five to six hours daily, began operation in 1986; Man. RENÉ DENIS.

Transport

ROADS
Uvea has a few kilometres of road, one route circling the island, and there is also a road circling the island of Futuna; the only surfaced roads are in Mata-Utu.

SHIPPING
Mata-Utu serves as the seaport of Uvea and the Wallis Islands, while Sigave is the only port on Futuna.

Compagnie de Navigation Wallisienne: Mata-Utu, Uvea, Wallis Islands, Wallis and Futuna (via Nouméa, New Caledonia); inter-island services and to Nouméa (New Caledonia), Suva (Fiji), Port Vila and Santo (Vanuatu); 2 vessels.

CIVIL AVIATION
There is an international airport in Hihifo district on Uvea (Wallis), about 5 km from Mata-Utu. Air Calédonie (New Caledonia) operates three flights a week from Wallis to Futuna, and one flight a week from Wallis to Nouméa (New Caledonia); Air Calédonie International also serves Wallis and Futuna. The airport on Futuna is in the south-east, in the Kingdom of Alo.

Tourism

Tourism remains undeveloped. There are three small hotels in Mata-Utu, on Uvea, Wallis Islands. In 1985 there were some 400 tourist visitors, in total, to the islands. There is no commercial accommodation for visitors on Futuna.

GABON

Introductory Survey

Location, Climate, Language, Religion, Flag, Capital

The Gabonese Republic is an equatorial country on the west coast of Africa, with Equatorial Guinea and Cameroon to the north and the Congo to the south and east. The climate is tropical, with an average annual temperature of 26°C (79°F) and an average annual rainfall of 2,490 mm (98 in). The official language is French, but Fang (in the north) and Bantu dialects (in the south) are also widely spoken. About 60% of the population are Christians, mainly Roman Catholics. Most of the remainder follow animist beliefs. The national flag (proportions 4 by 3) has three equal horizontal stripes, of green, yellow and blue. The capital is Libreville.

Recent History

Formerly a province of French Equatorial Africa, Gabon gained internal autonomy in 1957. It achieved self-government, within the French Community, in November 1958 and attained full independence on 17 August 1960.

At the time of independence, there were two main political parties: the Bloc démocratique gabonaise (BDG), led by Léon M'Ba, and the Union démocratique et sociale gabonaise (UDSG), led by Jean-Hilaire Aubame. The two parties were almost evenly matched in support and neither had a majority in the National Assembly. However, with the backing of independent deputies, M'Ba became Prime Minister in 1958 and Head of State at independence. He favoured close relations with France, and his rule was generally conservative. Members of the UDSG joined the Council of Ministers after independence, and the two parties agreed on a joint list of candidates for elections in February 1961, when a new constitution came into effect. In that month M'Ba was elected Gabon's first President, with 99.6% of the votes cast, and Aubame, his long-standing rival, was appointed Minister for Foreign Affairs. The BDG wanted the two parties to merge but the UDSG resisted this proposal. As a result, all the UDSG ministers were forced to resign in February 1963. President M'Ba dissolved the National Assembly in January 1964, in preparation for new elections.

In February 1964, five days before the date set for the elections, President M'Ba was deposed by a military coup, staged by army supporters of Aubame. However, French forces immediately intervened, and the M'Ba Government was restored. Aubame was found guilty of treason, and sentenced to 10 years' imprisonment. At the elections, held in April, the BDG won 31 of the 47 seats in the National Assembly. The UDSG was formally outlawed and, over the next two years, almost all of the opposition members in the Assembly joined the BDG.

In February 1967, with President M'Ba in poor health, the Constitution was revised to provide for the succession of a Vice-President if the President died or resigned. At the next elections, in March, there were no opposition candidates and the BDG was returned to power. President M'Ba was re-elected for a seven-year term, with Albert-Bernard Bongo, previously Deputy Prime Minister, as Vice-President. M'Ba died in November 1967 and was succeeded by Bongo, then aged 31. On 12 March 1968 Bongo announced the formal institution of one-party government in Gabon and the creation of a single new party, the Parti démocratique gabonais (PDG).

In February 1973 Bongo was re-elected President. In September he announced his conversion to Islam, adopting the forename Omar. In April 1975 President Bongo abolished the Vice-Presidency, appointing Léon Mébiame, who had been Vice-President since 1968, to the new post of Prime Minister. At the same time, local administration was reorganized to confer considerable autonomous powers on the provinces.

In 1977 President Kerekou of Benin accused Gabon of having aided an airborne mercenary attack on Cotonou. President Bongo strongly denied these accusations, and ordered the expulsion of all nationals of Benin from Gabon. In May 1981 several thousand Cameroonians resident in Gabon were airlifted back to Cameroon following violence against the Cameroonian communities in Libreville and Port-Gentil.

At a meeting of the PDG Congress in January 1979, elections were held to the party's Central Committee, thus introducing the first element of democracy into Gabon's political system. Following his nomination by the PDG, President Bongo stood as the sole candidate in the presidential election held in December 1979, and was re-elected for another seven-year term, receiving 99.96% of the votes cast. In early 1980 legislative and municipal elections were held, in which, for the first time since 1960, independents were free to stand against party candidates. All seats in the National Assembly were, none the less, won by members of the PDG. In a government reshuffle in August 1981, Bongo relinquished the title of Head of Government (thereafter conferred upon the Prime Minister, Léon Mébiame) and his ministerial portfolios. PDG candidates received 99.5% of the total votes at a general election in March 1985 for an enlarged National Assembly, and at the party's third ordinary congress, held in September 1986, the memberships of the Central Committee and Political Bureau were also increased. At the next presidential election, held in November, Bongo (the sole candidate) received an estimated 99.97% of the votes. In January 1987, in response to a steadily worsening economic situation, a reallocation and reduction in the number of ministerial portfolios was announced. Elections to assemblies in the country's nine provinces, 37 prefectures and 12 municipal districts were held in June. Further reorganizations of the Council of Ministers occurred in August and October 1988.

In accordance with the Bongo Government's attempts to secure the support of international creditors for its economic adjustment efforts, a policy of retrenchment in the state sector was initiated. In late 1988 public-sector employees withdrew their labour, in protest at the imposition of compulsory reductions in salaries. Following intervention by the Confédération syndicale gabonaise (COSYGA), President Bongo announced that austerity measures would, henceforth, be pursued only to the extent that they did not undermine the country's social and political cohesion. In July 1989 the Government withdrew proposals for modifications to its labour code, which had been advocated by the World Bank. In the following month, none the less, it was announced that the salaries of employees of the Office du chemin de fer transgabonais (OCTRA) were to be reduced, and that some railway workers were to be made redundant. In December employees at the Société d'energie et d'eau du Gabon (SEEG) took industrial action, following the announcement of reductions in benefits.

President Bongo has sought to repress political dissent. An illegal opposition group, the Mouvement de redressement national (MORENA), emerged in November 1981, advocating the establishment of a multi-party system in Gabon. In November 1982 a total of 29 MORENA sympathizers, including a former government minister, were found guilty of endangering state security, and received prison sentences, some with hard labour. Although they were all subsequently released, with the last group being granted clemency in May 1986, Bongo refused to sanction MORENA's existence as an official political grouping. When MORENA announced the formation of a government-in-exile in Paris during August 1985, Bongo sought assurances from the French Government that it would deny any form of recognition to that organization. An air-force captain was executed in the same month, following his conviction on charges of plotting a coup. Although a MORENA candidate stood against Bongo in the November 1986 presidential election, he was prevented from organizing a campaign.

In May 1989 the chairman of MORENA, Fr Paul M'Ba Abessolo, visited Gabon. Following a meeting with President Bongo, the opposition leader announced that he and many of his supporters would return to Gabon in the near future. M'Ba Abessolo and Bongo held further discussions in December. Although President Bongo repeated his opposition to the establishment of a multi-party system, M'Ba Abessolo announced his support for the Bongo Government. In January 1990 representatives of MORENA announced that M'Ba Abessolo had been dismissed from the leadership of the movement. M'Ba

Abessolo subsequently formed a breakaway faction, which was known as MORENA des bûcherons.

In October 1989 it was announced that a number of arrests had been made, following the discovery of a plot to overthrow the Bongo Government. Among those detained were prominent members of the security forces. It was alleged that the plot had been instigated by the leader of the Union du peuple gabonais (UPG, an opposition movement based in Paris), Pierre Mamboundou. Copies of a periodical, Le Patriote, which had reiterated Mamboundou's suggestion that two government ministers had been involved in the attempt, were seized by the Gabonese authorities. Two of the alleged conspirators later died in custody, officially of natural causes. Five others were released in January 1990; a further 21 detainees awaited trial by the Court of State Security. Further arrests were made in November 1989, in connection with the alleged discovery of a second plot to overthrow the incumbent regime. In December 1990 the two alleged instigators of the plot were sentenced to six and eight years in prison.

In January 1990 students at the Université Omar Bongo boycotted classes and staged demonstrations in protest against the shortage of academic staff and the inadequacy of facilities. The protests were joined by secondary school pupils. Shops (most of which were owned by Lebanese immigrants) were looted as the protests escalated. About 250 demonstrators were stated to have been arrested, and many injuries were reported, following intervention by the security forces. Following a meeting between President Bongo and students' representatives, it was announced that a commission was to be established to examine the grievances that had been expressed, and that a new university rector would be appointed. In February Bongo announced a programme of major social and political reforms. Unrest continued during that month, however, leading to strikes by workers protesting about economic austerity measures.

On 22 February 1990 a 'special commission for democracy', established by the PDG in the previous month, announced its conclusions, which condemned Gabon's single-party political system. On the following day, Bongo announced that immediate and fundamental political reforms would be introduced and proposed that the ruling party be replaced by a Rassemblement social-démocrate gabonais (RSDG), which was to cover a diverse ideological spectrum. However, continuing action by staff at the national airline, government departments and financial institutions led to severe disruption. In addition, all educational establishments were closed, following further student unrest. Changes in the Council of Ministers were implemented in late February and early March.

In early March 1990 a joint session of the Central Committee of the PDG and the National Assembly ruled that legislative elections, which had been scheduled for April, be postponed for a six-month period to allow time for constitutional amendments. On 9 March the Political Bureau of the PDG anounced that a multi-party system was to be introduced, under the supervision of the RSDG, at the end of a five-year transitional period.

A national conference was convened in late March 1990 to determine the programme for the transfer to multi-party democracy. A curfew was imposed, and strikes were prohibited for the duration of the gathering. The conference, which was attended by some 2,000 delegates (representing more than 70 political organizations, as well as professional bodies and other special interest groups), rejected Bongo's proposals for a transitional period of political reform under the aegis of the RSDG, and approved instead the immediate establishment of a multi-party system and the formation of a new government, which would hold office only until the October legislative elections. President Bongo acceded to the decisions of the conference, and in late April Casimir Oye Mba, the Governor of the Banque des états de l'Afrique centrale, was appointed Prime Minister in a 29-member transitional administration. Several members of opposition movements received ministerial posts.

On 22 May 1990 the Central Committee of the PDG and the National Assembly approved constitutional amendments that would facilitate the transition to a multi-party political system. The existing presidential mandate (effective until 1994) was to be retained; thereafter, elections to the presidency would be contested by more than one candidate, and the tenure of office would be reduced to five years, renewable only once. At the same time, President Bongo resigned as Secretary-General of the PDG (claiming that this role was now incompatible with his position as Head of State), and the party post was assumed by Jean Adiahenot. In the same month, however, the death, in suspicious circumstances, of Joseph Rendjambe, the Secretary-General of the opposition Parti gabonais du progrès (PGP), led to violent protests by demonstrators, who alleged Bongo's complicity in the death. A country-wide curfew was imposed as unrest spread. Protests were particularly violent in Port-Gentil (the centre for the petroleum industry), Rendjambe's birthplace. French troops were dispatched to Gabon, to protect the interests of the 20,000 resident French nationals and several hundred Europeans were evacuated. A state of emergency was imposed in Port-Gentil and its environs, and at least two deaths were reported after Gabonese security forces intervened to restore order. In early June it was announced that the French military reinforcements were to be withdrawn. The national curfew was repealed in early July; however, the state of emergency remained in force in the area surrounding Port-Gentil until mid-August.

Following an interministerial conference in August, legislative elections were scheduled for 16 and 23 September. Under new regulations, only political parties which had registered during the national conference in March were allowed to present candidates. The first round of multi-party elections on 16 September was disrupted by violent protests by voters, who claimed that electoral fraud was being practised, to favour the PDG. Following allegations by opposition parties of widespread electoral malpractices, results in 32 constituencies were declared invalid, although the election of 58 candidates (of whom 36 were members of the PDG) was confirmed. The interim Government subsequently conceded that electoral irregularities had taken place, and the second round of elections was postponed until 21 and 28 October. A commission, which represented both the PDG and opposition movements, was established in late September to prevent further irregularities, although two opposition parties withdrew from it in early October. At the elections, held on 21 and 28 October, the PDG won an overall majority, with 62 seats (including three seats gained by independent candidates affiliated to the PDG), while opposition candidates secured 55 seats. The two most prominent opposition movements, MORENA des bûcherons and the PGP, received 19 and 18 seats respectively. On 4 and 11 November a further round of elections was held in three constituencies, where voting had been abandoned, owing to alleged irregularities. The PDG and MORENA des bûcherons each gained an additional seat. In February 1991, however, the Government announced the annulment of election results in five constituencies. By-elections for the resultant vacant seats were scheduled to be held on 24 and 31 March.

On 27 November 1990 the formation of a government of national unity was announced. Casimir Oye Mba, the head of the former transitional Government, was appointed Prime Minister. Sixteen portfolios were allocated to members of the PDG, while the remaining eight portfolios were distributed between members of five opposition parties. However, three other opposition movements refused President Bongo's offer of inclusion in the Government. A new draft constitution, which had been submitted to the National Assembly in September, was promulgated on 22 December. Reforms that had been initiated under a transitional constitution, which had been adopted in May to facilitate the introduction of the multi-party political system, were endorsed. Further measures included the proposed establishment of an upper house, to be known as the Senate, which was to control the balance and regulation of power. A constitutional council was to replace the administrative chamber of the Supreme Court. A national communications council was also to be formed to ensure the impartial treatment of information by the state media.

Under Gabon's liberal economic system, efforts have been made to attract foreign companies and investors to the country. However, since January 1974 all companies operating in Gabon are required to have their headquarters there, and the State must be given a 10% share in all new foreign enterprises setting up in the country. Deteriorating economic conditions led to the imposition of controls on immigrant workers in May 1986. In June 1988 about 3,500 foreign nationals, described by the Government as illegal immigrants, were arrested by the Gabonese security forces. This action was followed by the announcement of new nationality regulations.

Bongo has pursued a policy of close co-operation with France in the fields of economic and foreign affairs. Relations with France became strained in October 1983, however, as a result of the publication in Paris of a book which was critical of the Bongo regime, and a six-week ban on news pertaining to France was imposed on the Gabonese media. Tension was reduced following a visit to Libreville in April 1984 by the French Prime Minister, Pierre Mauroy, and relations between the two countries were finally restored in October 1984, when Bongo paid a three-day state visit to Paris. In early 1988, however, copies of three French newspapers were seized, following the publication of allegations concerning Bongo's misuse of French financial aid. In late 1989 President Bongo accused the Benelux countries of involvement in attempts to destabilize his Government, and thus to gain control of Gabon's mineral resources.

President Bongo maintains that Gabon does not have an exclusive relationship with any country, and in recent years he has attempted to diversify Gabon's external relations. Bongo has also acted as an intermediary in regional disputes, chairing the OAU *ad hoc* committee charged with resolving the border dispute between Chad and Libya, and encouraging dialogue between Angola and the USA. In 1989 President Bongo held negotiations with the Heads of State of Cameroon and the Congo, as a result of which the three countries issued joint appeals, to their external creditors, for the formulation of a programme of debt relief.

Government

The 1961 Constitution, as subsequently revised, vests executive power in the President, who is directly elected by universal suffrage for a period of five years. The President appoints the Prime Minister, who is Head of Government; the President also appoints, and presides over, a Council of Ministers. The legislative organ is the National Assembly. The Assembly has 120 members, who are elected by direct universal suffrage for a term of five years. The Parti démocratique gabonais (PDG) was the sole legal party from 1968 until May 1990, when constitutional amendments provided for the introduction of a multi-party system. A new constitution was promulgated in December 1990 (see Recent History), which included the proposed formation of an upper house. The country is divided into nine provinces, each under an appointed governor, and 37 prefectures.

Defence

In June 1990 the army consisted of 3,250 men, the air force of 1,000 men, and the navy of 500 men. Paramilitary forces numbered 4,800 (including a gendarmerie of 2,000). Military service is voluntary. France maintains a military detachment of 800 in Gabon. Expenditure on defence, including internal security, in 1988 was 45,800m. francs CFA (23% of total administrative spending).

Economic Affairs

In 1989, according to estimates by the World Bank, Gabon's gross national product (GNP), measured at average 1987–89 prices, was US $3,060m., equivalent to $2,770 per head. During 1980–89, it was estimated, GNP increased, in real terms, at an average annual rate of only 1.0%, while GNP per head declined by 2.6% per year (although increasing by an annual average of 4.0% in 1987–89). The population grew by an annual average of 3.7% between 1980 and 1989. Gabon's gross domestic product (GDP) declined, in real terms, by an annual average of 0.2% in 1980–88 (compared with an average increase of 9.5% per year in 1965–80).

Agriculture (including forestry and fishing) contributed 11% of GDP in 1989. About 68.6% of the working population were employed in the sector in that year. Cocoa, coffee, the oil palm and rubber are cultivated for export. Gabon has yet to achieve self-sufficiency in staple crops: imports of foods accounted for 13.2% of the value of total imports in 1989. The principal subsistence crops are cassava, plantains and maize. The exploitation of Gabon's forests (which cover about 75% of the land area) is a principal economic activity. However, the sector is dominated by foreign (mainly French) investors. In the late 1980s the cultivation and exploitation of okoumé timber accounted for about 70% of all forestry activities. Although Gabon's territorial waters contain important fishing resources, their commercial exploitation is minimal. According to estimates by the FAO, agricultural production increased by an annual average of 0.9% in 1980–89.

Industry (including mining, manufacturing, construction and power) contributed 51% of GDP in 1988. About 10.8% of the working population were employed in the sector in 1980.

Extractive activities contributed more than 50% of annual GDP in 1984 and 1985. In 1986, however, the contribution of mining declined to 26.1%, owing to the decline in international prices for petroleum (Gabon's principal source of export revenue). In 1989, however, sales of petroleum and petroleum products provided 70.8% of export revenue (compared with 62.5% in 1988), while petroleum exploitation and research accounted for 32.5% of GDP (compared with 21.0% in 1988). Gabon is among the world's foremost producers and exporters of manganese. Significant deposits of uranium are also exploited. Major reserves of iron ore remain undeveloped, owing to the lack of appropriate transport facilities. Small amounts of gold are extracted, and the existence of many mineral deposits, including niobium (columbium), talc, barytes, phosphates, rare earths, titanium and cadmium, has also been confirmed.

The manufacturing sector contributed 4.5% of GDP in 1986. The principal activities are the refining of petroleum and the processing of other minerals, the preparation of timber and other agro-industrial processes. The chemicals industry is also significant.

Electrical energy is derived principally from hydroelectric installations (which accounted for more than 75% of total production in the mid-1980s). Imports of mineral fuels comprised only 1.6% of the value of total imports in 1989.

In 1989 Gabon recorded a visible trade surplus of US $867.1m., although there was a deficit of $106.6m. on the current account of the balance of payments. In 1985 the principal source of imports was France (which supplied an estimated 45.5% of goods); other major sources were the USA and the Federal Republic of Germany. France was also the principal market for exports (taking 33.3% of exports in that year); other major purchasers were the USA and Spain. The principal exports in 1989 were petroleum and petroleum products, manganese, timber and uranium. The principal imports were machinery and apparatus, transport equipment, food products and metals and metal products.

Budget estimates for 1990 envisaged a deficit of 154,100m. francs CFA. Gabon's total external public debt was US $2,128m. at the end of 1988. In that year the cost of debt-servicing was equivalent to 6.2% of revenue from exports of goods and services. The average annual rate of inflation was 0.9% in 1980–88.

Gabon is a member of the Central African organs of the Franc Zone (see p. 156), of the Communauté économique des Etats de l'Afrique centrale (CEEAC, see p. 223) and of OPEC (see p. 200).

Gabon's potential for economic growth is based upon its considerable, and sustainable, mineral and forestry resources. In the mid-1980s, however, the country's vulnerability to fluctuations in international prices and demand for its principal commodities precipitated a decline in export and budget revenue, and thus necessitated a reduction in investment expenditure. Since 1986 the Bongo Government's economic adjustment efforts, which have received the support of international creditors, have sought to reduce the external current-account deficit, while containing the rate of inflation and promoting the development of non-petroleum activities. Private enterprise has been encouraged, and a policy of retrenchment in the public sector has been initiated. In early 1990 the disruption of petroleum production, owing to political unrest in Port-Gentil (see p. 1115), severely weakened the economy. Later that year, however, the rise in the cost of petroleum on the international market, following the crisis in the Persian Gulf (see chapter on Iraq) resulted in an increase in export revenue.

Social Welfare

There is a national Fund for State Insurance, and a guaranteed minimum wage. In January 1985 Gabon had 28 hospitals, 87 medical centres and 312 dispensaries, with a total of 5,156 hospital beds. In 1984 there were 300 physicians in the country. Maternal and infant health is a major priority. The 1988 budget allocated 18,000m. francs CFA (10% of total administrative spending) to health expenditure.

Education

Education is officially compulsory for 10 years between six and 16 years of age: in 1984 an estimated 75% of children in the relevant age-group attended primary and secondary schools (78% of boys; 72% of girls). Primary and secondary education is provided by state and mission schools. Primary education

GABON

begins at the age of six and lasts for six years. Secondary education, beginning at 12 years of age, lasts for up to seven years, comprising a first cycle of four years and a second of three years. The Université Omar Bongo, at Libreville, had 2,741 students in 1986. The Université des Sciences et des Techniques de Masuku was opened in 1987. Many students go to France for university and technical training. In 1990, according to estimates by UNESCO, adult illiteracy averaged 39.3% (males 26.5%; females 51.5%). Education is a major priority, and the 1988 budget allocated 47,000m. francs CFA (26% of total administrative spending) to expenditure on education and culture.

Public Holidays

1991: 1 January (New Year's Day), 12 March (Anniversary of Renovation, foundation of the Parti démocratique gabonais), 1 April (Easter Monday), 16 April* (Id al-Fitr, end of Ramadan), 1 May (Labour Day), 20 May (Whit Monday), 23 June* (Id al-Adha, feast of the Sacrifice), 17 August (Anniversary of Independence), 21 September* (Mouloud, birth of Muhammad), 1 November (All Saints' Day), 25 December (Christmas).

1992: 1 January (New Year's Day), 12 March (Anniversary of Renovation, foundation of the Parti démocratique gabonais), 4 April* (Id al-Fitr, end of Ramadan), 20 April (Easter Monday), 1 May (Labour Day), 8 June (Whit Monday), 11 June* (Id al-Adha, feast of the Sacrifice), 17 August (Anniversary of Independence), 10 September* (Mouloud, birth of Muhammad), 1 November (All Saints' Day), 25 December (Christmas).

* These holidays are dependent on the Islamic lunar calendar and may vary by one or two days from the dates given.

Weights and Measures

The metric system is in official use.

Statistical Survey

Source (unless otherwise stated): Direction Générale de l'Economie, Ministère de la Planification, de l'Economie et de l'Administration Territoriale, Libreville.

Area and Population

AREA, POPULATION AND DENSITY

Area (sq km)	267,667*
Population (census results)†	
8 October 1960–May 1961	
Males	211,350
Females	237,214
Total	448,564
Population (official estimate at mid-year)	
1985‡	1,206,000
Density (per sq km) at mid-1985	4.5

* 103,347 sq miles.
† The results of a census in August 1980 were officially repudiated and a decree in May 1981 declared a population of 1,232,000, including 122,000 Gabonese nationals resident abroad.
‡ Both the World Bank and the UN dispute Gabonese official population estimates. For mid-1989 the World Bank assumes a population of 1,105,000, while the UN estimates a population of 1,132,000.

REGIONS

Region	Population (1976 estimate)	Chief town
Estuaire	311,300	Libreville
Haut-Ogooué	187,500	Franceville
Moyen-Ogooué	50,500	Lambaréné
N'Gounié	122,600	Mouila
Nyanga	89,000	Tchibanga
Ogooué-Ivindo	56,500	Makokou
Ogooué-Lolo	50,500	Koula-Moutou
Ogooué-Maritime	171,900	Port-Gentil
Woleu-N'Tem	162,300	Oyem
Total	**1,202,100**	

PRINCIPAL TOWNS (population in 1988)

Libreville (capital)	352,000	Franceville	75,000
Port-Gentil	164,000		

BIRTHS AND DEATHS (UN estimates, annual averages)

	1975–80	1980–85	1985–90
Birth rate (per 1,000)	30.9	33.8	38.8
Death rate (per 1,000)	18.9	18.1	16.4

Source: UN, *World Population Prospects: 1988*.

ECONOMICALLY ACTIVE POPULATION
(ILO estimates, '000 persons at mid-1980)

	Males	Females	Total
Agriculture, etc.	205	174	379
Industry	49	5	54
Services	50	19	69
Total labour force	**305**	**198**	**502**

Source: ILO, *Economically Active Population Estimates and Projections, 1950–2025*.

Mid-1989 (estimates, '000 persons): Agriculture, etc. 342; Total 498 (Source: FAO, *Production Yearbook*).

Agriculture

PRINCIPAL CROPS (FAO estimates, '000 metric tons)

	1987	1988	1989
Maize	10	12	12
Cassava (Manioc)	255	260	260
Yams	95	100	100
Taro (Coco yam)	58	60	62
Vegetables	29	29	30
Bananas	9	9	9
Plantains	138	135	132
Cocoa beans	2*	2*	2
Coffee (green)	1	2	2
Groundnuts (in shell)	9	9	9
Sugar cane	195	205	205

* Unofficial estimate.
Source: FAO, *Production Yearbook*.

GABON

LIVESTOCK
(FAO estimates, '000 head, year ending September)

	1987	1988	1989
Cattle	9	9	10
Pigs	153	154	155
Sheep	83	84	84
Goats	63	63	64

Poultry (FAO estimates, million): 2 in 1987; 2 in 1988; 2 in 1989.
Source: FAO, *Production Yearbook*.

LIVESTOCK PRODUCTS
1989 (FAO estimates, '000 metric tons): Meat 22; Hen eggs 1.5.

Forestry

ROUNDWOOD REMOVALS ('000 cubic metres)

	1986	1987	1988
Sawlogs, veneer logs and logs for sleepers	1,295*	1,222*	1,222†
Fuel wood†	2,236	2,315	2,396
Total	3,531	3,537	3,618

* Unofficial estimate. † FAO estimate(s).
Source: FAO, *Yearbook of Forest Products*.
Production of logs (official estimates, '000 cubic metres): 1,310 in 1986.

SAWNWOOD PRODUCTION ('000 cubic metres)

	1983	1984	1985
Total	88*	97	106

* FAO estimate.
Railway sleepers ('000 cubic metres): 20 per year in 1983–85 (FAO estimates).
1986–88: Annual output as in 1985 (FAO estimates).
Source: FAO, *Yearbook of Forest Products*.

Fishing
('000 metric tons, live weight)

	1985	1986	1987*
Freshwater fishes	1.8	2.0	1.9
West African croakers	2.7	2.6*	2.6
Lesser African threadfin	1.8	1.8*	1.8
Bonga shad	9.8	9.6*	9.7
Other marine fishes (incl. unspecified)	3.3	3.2*	3.3
Total fish	19.3	19.1*	19.2
Southern pink shrimp	1.7	1.7*	1.7
Total catch	21.0	20.8	20.9

* FAO estimate(s).
1988: Catch as in 1987 (FAO estimates).
Source: FAO, *Yearbook of Fishery Statistics*.

Mining
('000 metric tons, unless otherwise indicated)

	1987	1988	1989
Crude petroleum	7,763	7,968	10,389
Natural gas (petajoules)*	7	n.a.	n.a.
Uranium ore (metric tons)†	794	929	870
Manganese ore‡	2,589	2,254	2,550
Gold (kilograms)*†§	78	n.a.	n.a.

* Source: UN, *Industrial Statistics Yearbook*.
† Figures refer to the metal content of ores.
‡ Figures refer to gross weight. In 1987 the manganese content was 1,106,800 metric tons.
§ Estimates by the US Bureau of Mines.

Industry

PETROLEUM PRODUCTS ('000 metric tons)

	1985	1986	1987
Liquefied petroleum gas*	6	6	5
Motor spirit (petrol)	65	62	59
Kerosene	87	72	70
Jet fuel	70	71	67
Distillate fuel oils	208	256	251
Residual fuel oil	390	375	381
Bitumen (asphalt)	9	2	1

* Provisional or estimated data.
Source: UN, *Industrial Statistics Yearbook*.

SELECTED OTHER PRODUCTS
(metric tons, unless otherwise indicated)

	1987	1988	1989
Palm oil (refined)	8,349	10,346	2,307
Flour	27,428	23,105	25,976
Refined sugar	19,232	18,459	20,905
Soft drinks ('000 hectolitres)	395.7	318.6	297.2
Beer ('000 hectolitres)	571.5	511.3	460.2
Cement ('000 metric tons)	139	131	117
Electric energy (million kWh)	894.9	910.0	901.0

Plywood ('000 cu metres): 131 per year (FAO estimates) in 1986–88 (Source: FAO, *Yearbook of Forest Products*).
Veneer sheets ('000 cu metres): 97 per year (FAO estimates) in 1986–88 (Source: FAO, *Yearbook of Forest Products*).

Finance

CURRENCY AND EXCHANGE RATES
Monetary Units
  100 centimes = 1 franc de la Coopération financière en Afrique centrale (CFA).

Denominations
  Coins: 1, 2, 5, 10, 25, 50 and 100 francs CFA.
  Notes: 100, 500, 1,000, 5,000 and 10,000 francs CFA.

French Franc, Sterling and Dollar Equivalents (30 September 1990)
  1 French franc = 50 francs CFA;
  £1 sterling = 491.1 francs CFA;
  US $1 = 262.1 francs CFA;
  1,000 francs CFA = £2.036 = $3.815.

Average Exchange Rate (francs CFA per US $)
  1987 300.54
  1988 297.85
  1989 319.01

GABON

Statistical Survey

BUDGET ('000 million francs CFA)

Revenue	1988	1989*	1990†
Revenue from petroleum	74.5	78.0	120.0
Non-petroleum revenue	182.6	200.5	204.5
Total	257.1	278.5	324.5

Expenditure	1988	1989*	1990†
Current expenditure	376.3	376.8	385.4
Administrative expenditure	198.9	192.0	193.0
Interest payments	177.4	184.8	192.4
Investment expenditure	77.1	68.2	78.8
Other expenditure	−10.9	11.4	14.4
Total	442.5	456.4	478.6

* Provisional figures.   † Estimated figures.

FIFTH DEVELOPMENT PLAN, 1984–88*
(proposed expenditure, million francs CFA at 1983 prices)

Productive sector	239,054
Infrastructure	595,662
Social services and education	213,972
General investments	162,520
Total	1,228,478

Source: *Annuaire National de la République Gabonaise 1983-84*.
* The Plan was later extended until 1990.

CENTRAL BANK RESERVES (US $ million at 31 December)

	1987	1988	1989
Gold*	6.19	5.21	n.a.
IMF special drawing rights	11.62	8.80	0.22
Reserve position in IMF	0.04	0.04	0.05
Foreign exchange	0.34	56.85	34.29
Total	18.19	70.90	n.a.

* Valued at market-related prices.
Source: IMF, *International Financial Statistics*.

MONEY SUPPLY ('000 million francs CFA at 31 December)

	1986	1987	1988
Currency outside banks	47.39	49.47	50.15
Demand deposits at commercial and development banks	103.91	82.91	94.63
Checking deposits at post office	1.08	0.89	1.69
Total money	152.39	133.26	146.47

1989 ('000 million francs CFA): Currency outside banks 57.5; Demand deposits 113.4
Source: IMF, *International Financial Statistics*.

COST OF LIVING (Retail Price Index for African families in Libreville; base: 1985 = 100)

	1987	1988	1989
All items	105.3	95.0	101.6

Source: IMF, *International Financial Statistics*.

NATIONAL ACCOUNTS
('000 million francs CFA at current prices)

Expenditure on the Gross Domestic Product

	1987	1988	1989
Government final consumption expenditure	247.0	229.5	220.0
Private final consumption expenditure	499.5	510.6	524.8
Increase in stocks	−7.0	−12.1	−10.0
Gross fixed capital formation	301.1	325.0	298.1
Total domestic expenditure	1,040.6	1,053.0	1,032.9
Exports of goods and services	415.1	369.1	534.1
Less Imports of goods and services	412.0	441.4	454.8
GDP in purchasers' values	1,043.7	980.7	1,112.2

Gross Domestic Product by Economic Activity

	1987	1988	1989
Agriculture, stock-breeding and fishing	88.9	91.3	90.3
Forestry	21.9	22.3	18.8
Petroleum exploitation and research	256.2	195.8	345.7
Mining and quarrying	42.7	42.6	51.6
Timber industry	11.2	10.4	10.7
Refining	24.8	25.7	23.8
Processing industries	52.5	52.5	50.5
Electricity, water, gas and steam	27.5	29.5	28.8
Construction	68.2	57.2	44.5
Trade	87.6	89.1	86.8
Hotels, cafés and restaurants	11.8	12.2	12.2
Transport	54.7	54.6	54.5
Financial institutions	33.2	30.4	31.9
Public administration and services to households	134.9	134.3	129.5
Other services	82.6	83.6	84.3
Sub-total	998.7	931.5	1,063.9
Import duties	64.4	66.2	68.2
Less Imputed bank service charge	19.4	17.0	19.9
Total	1,043.7	980.7	1,112.2

BALANCE OF PAYMENTS (US $ million)

	1987	1988	1989
Merchandise exports f.o.b.	1,286.4	1,195.6	1,621.9
Merchandise imports f.o.b.	−731.8	−791.2	−754.8
Trade balance	554.5	404.3	867.1
Exports of services	130.8	228.1	269.6
Imports of services	−1,011.1	−1,104.6	−1,128.5
Balance on goods and services	−325.8	−472.2	8.2
Private unrequited transfers (net)	−147.8	−154.6	−134.5
Government unrequited transfers (net)	24.4	11.2	19.7
Current balance	−449.1	−615.6	−106.6
Direct capital investment (net)	82.2	121.4	−39.2
Other long-term capital (net)	473.8	531.3	325.4
Short-term capital (net)	−191.1	−15.4	−174.6
Net errors and omissions	−52.3	−23.1	−96.7
Total (net monetary movements)	−136.5	−1.4	−91.7
Valuation changes (net)	57.3	0.3	4.6
Exceptional financing (net)	−63.1	—	56.3
Official financing (net)	1.3	−18.0	−3.1
Changes in reserves	−141.1	−19.1	−33.9

Source: IMF, *International Financial Statistics*.

External Trade

Note: Figures exclude trade with other countries in the Customs and Economic Union of Central Africa (UDEAC): Cameroon, the Central African Republic, Chad (since January 1984), the Congo and Equatorial Guinea (since January 1985).

PRINCIPAL COMMODITIES ('000 million francs CFA)

Imports	1987	1988	1989
Machinery and apparatus	42.3	48.8	70.6
Transport equipment	31.1	21.2	24.2
Food products	42.1	33.9	31.8
Metals and metal products	24.2	32.8	27.2
Chemical products	8.0	8.9	13.1
Vegetable and animal products (non-food)	4.2	3.3	3.5
Precision instruments	5.7	9.1	14.4
Textiles and textile products	6.2	5.3	4.3
Hygiene and cleaning products	9.5	8.9	10.5
Vehicles	3.9	5.8	6.0
Mineral products	3.5	3.6	3.8
Total (incl. others)	216.7	215.8	241.8

Exports	1987	1988	1989
Petroleum and petroleum products	266.6	222.6	361.0
Manganese	32.4	45.0	59.3
Timber	46.9	48.3	48.1
Uranium	24.0	22.1	21.1
Total (incl. others)	386.9	356.1	509.6

PRINCIPAL TRADING PARTNERS ('000 million francs CFA)

Imports	1983	1984	1985*
Belgium/Luxembourg	4.7	10.1	15.1
France	141.5	172.5	176.2
Germany, Fed. Republic	13.3	18.0	22.2
Italy	8.2	14.9	16.1
Japan	19.3	22.1	24.5
Netherlands	9.9	9.4	8.8
Spain	6.5	7.5	6.1
United Kingdom	9.4	11.7	16.0
USA	28.8	25.1	38.9
Total (incl. others)	276.5	320.4	387.0

Exports	1983	1984	1985*
Canada	24.9	54.6	34.3
France	171.0	271.8	295.3
Germany, Fed. Republic	6.3	33.2	6.0
Italy	30.8	9.9	20.8
Netherlands	26.9	20.3	30.0
Spain	37.6	60.6	62.8
United Kingdom	22.9	16.2	37.1
USA	144.1	195.5	164.8
Total (incl. others)	762.2	881.7	887.0

* Estimated figures.
Source: *La Zone Franc-Rapport 1988*.

Transport

RAILWAYS (traffic)

	1984	1985	1986*
Passengers carried	135,913	137,111	125,816
Freight carried (metric tons)	664,605	723,034	666,412

* Estimated figures.

ROAD TRAFFIC (motor vehicles in use)

	1983	1984	1985
Passenger cars	15,150	15,650	16,093
Buses and coaches	479	508	546
Goods vehicles	9,240	9,590	9,960

Source: the former Ministère des Transports Terrestres, Ferroviaires, Fluviaux et Lagunaires.

INTERNATIONAL SEA-BORNE SHIPPING (freight traffic, '000 metric tons)

	1986	1987	1988
Goods loaded	8,738	8,305	8,890
Goods unloaded	507	521	610

Source: UN, *Monthly Bulletin of Statistics*.

CIVIL AVIATION (traffic on scheduled services)

	1983	1984	1985
Kilometres flown ('000)	6,100	5,800	6,900
Passengers carried	428,000	436,000	456,000
Passenger-kilometres ('000)	435,000	468,000	516,000
Freight ton-kilometres ('000)	30,900	31,800	36,000
Mail ton-kilometres ('000)	1,000	600	500

Source: UN, *Statistical Yearbook*.

Tourism

	1985	1986	1987
Tourist arrivals	5,248	4,917	3,454

Source: the former Ministère du Tourisme, de la Communication Sociale et des Loisirs.

Communications Media

	1986	1987	1988
Radio receivers ('000 in use)	117	125	147
Television receivers ('000 in use)	23	24	25
Daily newspapers:			
Number	1	n.a.	1
Average circulation ('000 copies)	15	n.a.	15

Source: UNESCO, *Statistical Yearbook*.

Telephones (1983): 14,000 in use (Source: UN, *Statistical Yearbook*).

Education

(1987)

	Institutions	Teachers	Pupils		
			Males	Females	Total
Primary	992	4,229	98,563	96,486	195,049
Secondary:					
General	n.a.	1,512	18,173	14,749	32,922
Vocational	n.a.	475	6,712	3,255	9,967
Teacher-training	n.a.	284	2,422	2,963	5,385
University	1	364*	1,940	935	2,875
Other higher	n.a.	257†	908	267	1,175

* 1986 figure. † 1983 figure.

Source: UNESCO, *Statistical Yearbook*.

Directory

The Constitution

The Constitution of the Gabonese Republic was adopted on 21 February 1961. It was revised in February 1967, April 1975, August 1981, September 1986, May 1990 and December 1990. The main provisions are summarized below:

PREAMBLE

Upholds the Rights of Man, liberty of conscience and of the person, religious freedom and freedom of education. Sovereignty is vested in the people, who exercise it through their representatives or by means of referenda. There is direct, universal and secret suffrage.

HEAD OF STATE

The existing presidential mandate is valid for a period of seven years (until 1994). Thereafter, the President will be elected by direct universal suffrage for a five-year term, renewable only once. The President is Head of State and of the Armed Forces. The President may, after consultation with his Ministers and leaders of the National Assembly, order a referendum to be held. The President appoints the Prime Minister, who is Head of Government and who is accountable to the President. The President is the guarantor of national independence and territorial sovereignty.

EXECUTIVE POWER

Executive power is vested in the President and the Council of Ministers, who are appointed by the President and are responsible to him. The President presides over the Council.

LEGISLATIVE POWER

The National Assembly is elected by direct universal suffrage for a five-year term and normally holds two sessions a year. It may be dissolved or prorogued for up to 18 months by the President, after consultation with the Council of Ministers and President of the Assembly. The President may return a Bill to the Assembly for a second reading, when it must be passed by a majority of two-thirds of the members. If the President dissolves the Assembly, elections must take place within 40 days.

POLITICAL ORGANIZATIONS

Article 2 of the Constitution states that 'Political parties and associations contribute to the expression of universal suffrage. They are formed and exercise their activities freely, within the limits delineated by the laws and regulations. They must respect the principles of democracy, national sovereignty, public order and national unity'.

JUDICIAL POWER

The President guarantees the independence of the Judiciary and presides over the Conseil Supérieur de la Magistrature. There is a Supreme Court and a High Court of Justice. The High Court, which is composed of deputies of the National Assembly elected from among themselves, has power to try the President or members of the government.

Note: Under a new constitution, which was approved by the National Assembly in December 1990, a Senate (or upper house) was to be established to control the balance and regulation of power. In addition, a constitutional council was to replace the administrative chamber of the Supreme Court.

The Government

HEAD OF STATE

President: El Hadj Omar (Albert-Bernard) Bongo (took office 2 December 1967, elected 25 February 1973, re-elected December 1979 and November 1986).

COUNCIL OF MINISTERS
(February 1991)

A coalition of the Parti démocratique gabonais (PDG), the Mouvement de redressement national (MORENA), the Parti gabonais du progrès (PGP), the Union socialiste gabonais (USG) and the Association pour le socialisme au Gabon (APSG).

Prime Minister: Casimir Oye Mba.

Minister of Justice: Michel Anchouey.

Minister of Equipment and Construction: Zacharie Myboto.

Minister of Decentralization: Simon Oyono-Aba'a.

Minister of Foreign Affairs, Co-operation and Francophone Affairs: Ali Bongo.

Minister of National Defence, Public Security and Immigration: Martin Fidèle Magnaga.

Minister of Land Administration and Local Communities: Antoine Mboumbou Miyakou.

Minister of the Civil Service and Administrative Reform: Paulette Moussavou Missambo.

Minister of Mines, Energy and Hydraulic Resources: Jean Ping.

Minister of Finance, the Budget and State Shareholdings: Paul Toungui.

Minister of Planning, the Economy and Territorial Administration: Marcel-Doumpamby Matoka.

Minister of State Control and Parastatal Reform: Jean-Baptiste Obiang Etoughe.

Minister of Information, Posts and Telecommunications, and Spokesperson for the Government: Jean-Rémy Pendy-Bouick.

Minister of Labour, Employment, Human Resources and Professional Training: Serge Mba.

Minister of Commerce and Industry: André Dieudonné Berre.

Minister of Small and Medium-sized Enterprises and Artisans' Affairs: Victor Mapangou Moucani Muetsa.

Minister of Waterways and Forests: Eugène Capito.

Minister of National and Higher Education and Scientific Research: Marc Ropivia.

Minister of Agriculture, Livestock and Rural Development: Emmanuel Ondo Methogo.

GABON — Directory

Minister of Transport: Jérôme Ngoua Bekale.

Minister of Youth, Sport, Art and Culture: Pierre Claver Nzeng.

Minister of Public Health and Population: Eugène Kalou Mayaka.

Minister of Social Affairs and National Solidarity: Patrice Nziengui.

Minister of Human Rights and Relations with the Assemblies: André Mba Obame.

Minister of Tourism, the Environment and National Parks: Pépin Mongockodji.

Minister of Housing, Land Registry and Town Planning: Adrien Nkoghe Essingone.

There are, in addition, 10 secretaries of state.

MINISTRIES

Office of the Prime Minister: BP 546, Libreville; telex 5409.

Ministry of Agriculture, Livestock and Rural Development: BP 551, Libreville; tel. 76-29-43; telex 5587.

Ministry of the Civil Service and Administrative Reform: Libreville.

Ministry of Commerce and Industry: BP 3906, Libreville; tel. 76-30-55; telex 5347.

Ministry of Decentralization: Libreville.

Ministry of Equipment and Construction: BP 371, Libreville; tel. 76-14-87.

Ministry of Finance, the Budget and State Shareholdings: BP 165, Libreville; tel. 72-12-10; telex 5238.

Ministry of Foreign Affairs, Co-operation and Francophone Affairs: BP 2245, Libreville; tel. 76-22-70; telex 5255.

Ministry of Housing, Land Registration and Town Planning: Libreville.

Ministry of Human Rights and Relations with the Assemblies: Libreville.

Ministry of Information, Posts and Telecommunications: BP 2280, Libreville; tel. 76-16-92; telex 5361.

Ministry of Justice: Libreville; tel. 72-26-95.

Ministry of Labour, Employment, Human Resources and Professional Training: BP 4577, Libreville; tel. 74-32-18.

Ministry of Land Administration and Local Communities: BP 2110, Libreville; tel. 74-35-06; telex 5638.

Ministry of Mines, Energy and Hydraulic Resources: Libreville; tel. 72-31-96; telex 5629.

Ministry of National Defence, Public Security and Immigration: Libreville; tel. 76-25-95; telex 5453.

Ministry of National and Higher Education and Scientific Research: BP 6, Libreville; tel. 72-17-41; telex 5501.

Ministry of Planning, the Economy and Territorial Administration: Libreville.

Ministry of Public Health, Population, Social Affairs and National Solidarity: Libreville; tel. 76-35-90; telex 5385.

Ministry of Small and Medium-sized Enterprises and Artisans' Affairs: Libreville.

Ministry of State Control and Parastatal Reform: BP 178, Libreville; tel. 76-34-62; telex 5711.

Ministry of Tourism, the Environment and National Parks: BP 403, Libreville.

Ministry of Transport: BP 3974, Libreville; tel. 72-11-62; telex 5479; fax 77-33-31.

Ministry of Waterways and Forests: Libreville.

Ministry of Youth, Sports, Art and Culture: Libreville; tel. 76-35-76; telex 5642.

Legislature

ASSEMBLÉE NATIONALE

At legislative elections, held in October and November 1990, 64 of the 120 elective seats, were won by candidates selected by the Parti démocratique gabonais (the sole legal party until May 1990). The remaining 54 seats were secured by candidates belonging to six opposition movements.

President: Jules Bourdés Ogouliguende.

Secretary-General: Pierre N'Guema-Mvé.

Political Organizations

Parti démocratique gabonais (PDG): Libreville; f. 1968; sole legal party until May 1990; principal organs are a supreme congress, a perm. cttee of 13 mems, a political bureau of 44 mems and a cen. cttee of 297 mems; there are nine regional delegates, numerous local cttees and four specialized organs: Ecole des cadres du parti, Union des jeunes (UJPDG), Union des femmes du PDG (UFPDG) and Fédération des syndicats gabonais (FESYGA); Sec.-Gen. Jean Adiahenot.

On 22 May 1990 the Central Committee of the PDG and the National Assembly approved amendments to the Constitution that would facilitate the introduction of a multi-party system. On 22 December the revised Constitution, endorsing political pluralism came into effect. Among the most prominent political organizations in early 1991 were:

Association pour le socialisme au Gabon (APSG).

Cercle pour le renoveau et le progres (CRP).

Front uni des associations et partis de l'opposition (FUAPO): f. 1990, as a syndicate of 13 political movements; Leader Nan Nguema.

Mouvement de redressement national (MORENA): f. 1981 in Paris, France; formed a government-in-exile in 1985; merged with former breakaway faction, MORENA des bûcherons, in December 1990.

Parti gabonais du progrès (PGP): f. 1990; Pres. Agondjo Okawe; Sec.-Gen. Anselme Nzoghe.

Rassemblement des bûcherons: f. 1990; Leader Fr Paul M'Ba Abessole.

Union du peuple gabonais (UPG): f. 1989 in Paris, France; Leader Pierre Mamboundou.

Union pour la démocratie et le développement Mayumba.

Union socialiste gabonais (USG): Leader Serge Mba Bekale.

Diplomatic Representation

EMBASSIES IN GABON

Algeria: BP 4008, Libreville; tel. 73-23-18; telex 5313; Ambassador: Benyoucef Baba-Ali.

Angola: BP 4884, Libreville; tel. 73-04-26; telex 5565; Ambassador: Bernardo Dombele M'Bala.

Argentina: BP 4065, Libreville; tel. 74-05-49; telex 5611; Ambassador: Hugo Hurtubei.

Belgium: BP 4079, Libreville; tel. 73-29-92; telex 5273; Ambassador: Paul de Wulf.

Brazil: BP 3899, Libreville; tel. 76-05-35; telex 5492; Ambassador: Jaime Villa-Lobos.

Cameroon: BP 14001, Libreville; tel. 73-28-00; telex 5396; Chargé d'affaires a.i.: Nyemb Nguene.

Canada: BP 4037, Libreville; tel. 74-34-64; telex 5527; Ambassador: Jean Nadeau.

Central African Republic: BP 2096, Libreville; tel. 72-12-28; telex 5323; Ambassador: François Diallo.

China, People's Republic: BP 3914, Libreville; tel. 74-32-07; telex 5376; Ambassador: Yang Shanghuh.

Congo: BP 269, Libreville; tel. 73-29-06; telex 5541; Ambassador: Pierre Obou.

Côte d'Ivoire: BP 3861, Libreville; tel. 72-05-96; telex 5317; Ambassador: Jean-Obeo Coulibaly.

Egypt: BP 4240, Libreville; tel. 73-25-38; telex 5425; Ambassador: Effat Reda.

Equatorial Guinea: BP 14262, Libreville; tel. 76-30-15; Ambassador: Crisantos Ndongo Aba Messian.

France: BP 2125, Libreville; tel. 74-04-75; telex 5249; Ambassador: Louis Dominici.

Germany: BP 299, Libreville; tel. 76-01-88; telex 5248; Ambassador: Jürgen Goldschmidt.

Guinea: BP 4046, Libreville; tel. 70-11-46; Chargé d'affaires: Mamadi Koly Kourouma.

Iran: BP 2158, Libreville; tel. 73-05-33; telex 5502; Ambassador: Dr Abbasse Safarian.

Italy: Immeuble Personnaz et Gardin, rue de la Mairie, PB 2251, Libreville; tel. 74-28-92; telex 5287; Ambassador: Alfredo Matacotta.

Japan: BP 2259, Libreville; tel. 73-22-97; telex 5428; fax 73-60-60; Ambassador: Hideo Kakinuma.

Korea, Democratic People's Republic: BP 4012, Libreville; tel. 73-26-68; telex 5486; Ambassador: Yim Kun Chun.

GABON

Korea, Republic: BP 2620, Libreville; tel. 73-40-00; telex 5356; fax 73-00-79; Ambassador: PARK CHANG IL.
Lebanon: BP 3341, Libreville; tel. 73-14-77; telex 5547; Ambassador: MAMLOUK ABDELLATIF.
Mauritania: BP 3917, Libreville; tel. 74-31-65; telex 5570; Ambassador: El Hadj THIAM.
Morocco: BP 3983, Libreville; tel. 73-31-03; telex 5434; Chargé d'affaires a.i.: TAGMA MOHA OUALI.
Nigeria: BP 1191, Libreville; tel. 73-22-03; telex 5605; Ambassador: JOE-EFFIONG UDOH EKONG.
Philippines: BP 1198, Libreville; tel. 72-34-80; telex 5279; Chargé d'affaires: ARCADIO HERRERA.
São Tomé and Príncipe: BP 409, Libreville; tel. 72-15-46; telex 5557; Ambassador: JOSEPH FRET LAU CHONG.
Senegal: BP 3856, Libreville; tel. 73-26-87; telex 5332; Ambassador: OUMAR WELE.
Spain: BP 1157, Libreville; tel. 77-30-68; telex 5258; Ambassador: GERMÁN ZURITA Y SÁENZ DE NAVARRETE.
Togo: BP 14160, Libreville; tel. 73-29-04; telex 5490; Ambassador: AHLONKO KOFFI AQUEREBURU.
Tunisia: BP 3844, Libreville; tel. 73-28-41; Ambassador: EZZEDINE KERKENI.
USSR: BP 3963, Libreville; tel. 73-27-46; telex 5797; Ambassador: YURI SHMANEVSKI.
United Kingdom: Immeuble CK2, blvd de l'Indépendance, BP 476, Libreville; tel. 74-31-83; telex 5538; Ambassador: PHILIP PRIESTLEY.
USA: blvd de la Mer, BP 4000, Libreville; tel. 76-20-03; telex 5250; Ambassador: KEITH L. WAUCHOPE.
Uruguay: BP 5556, Libreville; tel. 74-30-44; telex 5646; Ambassador: Dr ALVARO ALVAREZ.
Venezuela: BP 3859, Libreville; tel. 73-31-18; telex 5264; fax 73-30-67; Ambassador: VÍCTOR CROQUER-VEGA.
Yugoslavia: BP 930, Libreville; tel. 73-30-05; telex 5329; Ambassador: ČEDOMIR STRBAC.
Zaire: BP 2257, Libreville; tel. 74-32-54; telex 5335; Ambassador: KABANGI KAUMBU BULA.
Zimbabwe: Libreville.

Judicial System

Supreme Court: BP 1043, Libreville; tel. 72-17-00; four chambers: constitutional, judicial, administrative* and accounts; Pres. Gen. GEORGES NKOMA.
High Court of Justice: Libreville; mems appointed by and from the deputies of the National Assembly; Pres. GASTON BOUCKAT-BOUZIENGUI.
Courts of Appeal: Libreville, Franceville, Port-Gentil.
Court of State Security: Libreville; 13 mems; Pres. FLORENTIN ANGO.
Conseil Supérieur de la Magistrature: Libreville; Pres. El Hadj OMAR BONGO; Vice-Pres. Minister of Justice (ex officio).

There are also Tribunaux de Première Instance (County Courts) at Libreville, Franceville, Port-Gentil, Lambaréné, Mouila, Oyem, Koula-Moutou, Makokou and Tchibanga.

* Provision for the establishment of a constitutional chamber, which was to replace the administrative chamber of the Supreme Court, was made in the new Constitution promulgated in December 1990.

Religion

About 60% of Gabon's population are Christians, mainly adherents of the Roman Catholic Church. About 40% are animists, and fewer than 1% are Muslims.

CHRISTIANITY
The Roman Catholic Church
Gabon comprises one archdiocese and three dioceses. At 31 December 1988 there were an estimated 604,900 adherents in the country (about 52% of the total population).
Bishops' Conference: Conférence Episcopale du Gabon, BP 209, Oyem; tel. 98-63-20; f. 1989; Pres. Mgr Rt Rev. BASILE ENGONE MVÉ, Bishop of Oyem.
Archbishop of Libreville: Mgr ANDRÉ-FERNAND ANGUILÉ, Archevêché, Sainte-Marie, BP 2146, Libreville; tel. 72-20-73.

Protestant Churches
Christian and Missionary Alliance: active in the south of the country; 16,000 mems.
Eglise Evangélique du Gabon: BP 10080, Libreville; tel. 72-41-92; f. 1842; independent since 1961; 120,000 mems; Pres. Pastor SAMUEL NANG ESSONO; Sec. Rev. EMILE NTETOME.
The Evangelical Church of South Gabon and the Evangelical Pentecostal Church are also active in the country.

The Press

Bulletin Evangélique d'Information et de Presse: BP 80, Libreville; monthly; religious.
Bulletin Mensuel de la Chambre de Commerce, d'Agriculture, d'Industrie et des Mines: BP 2234, Libreville; tel. 72-20-64; telex 5554; monthly.
Bulletin Mensuel de Statistique de la République Gabonaise: BP 179, Libreville; monthly; publ. by Direction Générale de l'Economie.
Dialogue: Maison du PDG, BP 213, Libreville; f. 1969; publ. by the PDG; monthly; Man. ELOIE CHAMBRIEN; circ. 3,000.
L'Economiste Gabonais: BP 3906, Libreville; quarterly; publ. by the Centre gabonais du commerce extérieur.
Gabon d'Aujourd'hui: BP 750, Libreville; weekly; publ. by the Ministry of Information, Posts and Telecommunications.
Gabon-Matin: BP 168, Libreville; daily; publ. by Agence Gabonaise de Presse; Man. HILARION VENDANY; circ. 18,000.
Journal Officiel de la République Gabonaise: BP 563, Libreville; f. 1959; fortnightly; Man. EMMANUEL OBAMÉ.
Ngondo: BP 168, Libreville; monthly; publ. by Agence Gabonaise de Presse.
Le Patriote: Libreville; irregular; satirical.
Promex: BP 3906, Libreville.
Sept Jours: BP 213, Libreville; weekly.
L'Union: BP 3849, Libreville; f. 1975; 75% state-owned; daily; official govt publication; Man. Dir ALBERT YANGARI; Dir RENÉ KOUPANGOYE; circ. 15,000.

NEWS AGENCIES
Agence Gabonaise de Presse (AGP): BP 168, Libreville; tel. 21-26; telex 5628.

Foreign Bureau
Agence France-Presse (AFP): Villa 32, Borne 2, Cité du 12 mars, BP 788, Libreville; tel. 76-14-36; telex 5239; Correspondents PATRICK VAN ROEKEGHEM, LAURENT MENNELET.

Publishers

Imprimerie Centrale d'Afrique (IMPRIGA): BP 154, Libreville; tel. 70-22-55; fax 70-05-19; f. 1973; Chair. ROBERT VIAL; Dir FRANCIS BOURQUIN.
Multipress Gabon: blvd Léon-M'Ba, BP 3875, Libreville; tel. 73-22-33; telex 5389; f. 1973; Chair. PAUL BORY.
Société Imprimerie de l'Ogooué—SIMO: BP 342, Port-Gentil; f. 1977; Man. Dir URBAIN NICOUE.
Société Nationale de Presse et d'Edition—SONAPRESSE: BP 3849, Libreville; tel. 73-21-84; telex 5391; f. 1975; Pres. and Man. Dir JOSEPH RENDJAMBE.

Radio and Television

In 1988 there were an estimated 147,000 radio receivers and 25,000 television receivers in use.

RADIO
The national network, 'La Voix de la Rénovation', and a provincial network broadcast for 24 hours each day in French and local languages. Proposals for the construction of 13 new FM radio stations were announced in 1986.
Africa No. 1: BP 1, Libreville; tel. 76-00-01; telex 5558; f. 1980; 35% state-controlled; international commercial radio station; broadcasts began in 1981; daily programmes in French and English; Pres. LOUIS BARTHÉLEMY MAPANGOU; Mans MICHEL KOUMBANGOYE, RENAUD LAFARGUE.

GABON

Radiodiffusion-Télévision Gabonaise (RTG): BP 150, Libreville; tel. 73-20-25; telex 5342; f. 1959; state-controlled; Dir-Gen. WILLIAM OYONNE; Dir of Radio PAUL MBADINGA-MATSIENDI.

TELEVISION

Television transmissions can be received as far inland as Kango and Lambaréné; in 1986 proposals were announced for the extension and modernization of the network to cover the whole of Gabon, including the construction of 13 new TV broadcasting stations. Programmes are also transmitted by satellite to other African countries. Colour broadcasts began in 1975. Negotiations began in 1988 with Canal Plus Afrique, a subsidiary of Canal Plus (France), for the establishment of a private television channel.

Radiodiffusion-Télévision Gabonaise (RTG): BP 150, Libreville; tel. 73-20-25; telex 5342; fax 73-21-53; f. 1959; state-controlled; Dir-Gen. WILLIAM OYONNE; Dir of Television CHARLES-NOËL BOURDETTE AW'VELEKAMBANY.

Télé-Africa: Libreville; tel. 76-20-33; private channel; daily broadcasts in French.

Finance

(cap. = capital; res = reserves; dep. = deposits; brs = branches; m. = million; amounts in francs CFA)

BANKING

Central Bank

Banque des Etats de l'Afrique Centrale (BEAC): BP 112, Libreville; tel. 76-13-52; telex 5215; fax 74-45-63; headquarters in Yaoundé, Cameroon; f. 1973 as central bank of issue for mem. states of the Customs and Economic Union of Central Africa (UDEAC), comprising Cameroon, the Central African Republic, Chad, the Congo, Equatorial Guinea and Gabon; cap. 36,000m., res 162,037m. (June 1989); Gov. JEAN-FELIX MAMALEPOT; Dir in Gabon JEAN-PAUL LEYIMANGOYE; 2 brs.

Commercial Banks

Banque du Gabon et du Luxembourg: blvd de l'Indépendance, BP 3879, Libreville; tel. 72-28-62; telex 5344; f. 1974; cap. 1,200m.; activities temporarily suspended by the Govt.

Banque Internationale pour le Commerce et l'Industrie du Gabon SA (BICIG): ave du Colonel Parant, BP 2241, Libreville; tel. 76-26-13; telex 5526; fax 76-41-95; f. 1973; 27.7% state-owned, 26% Société Financière pour les Pays d'Outre-Mer, 25% Banque Nationale de Paris; cap. 6,000m. (Dec. 1988); Pres. GUY-ETIENNE MOUVAGHA-TCHIOBA; Man. Dir EMILE DOUMBA; 9 brs.

Banque Internationale pour le Gabon (BIPG): Immeuble Concorde, blvd de l'Indépendance, BP 106, Libreville; tel. 76-26-27; telex 5221; fax 76-20-63; f. 1975; undergoing reorg. in 1990; cap. 1,260m. (Dec. 1988); Pres. PAUL BIYOGHE MBA; Man. Dir SAMSON NGOMO; 6 brs.

Banque Paribas Gabon: blvd de l'Indépendance, BP 2253; Libreville; tel. 76-40-35; telex 5265; fax 74-08-94; f. 1971; 33.4% state-owned, 24.6% owned by Paribas International; cap. 7,892m. (Dec. 1989); Pres. ETIENNE MOUSSIROU; Man. Dir HENRI-CLAUDE OYIMA; br. at Port-Gentil.

Banque Privée de Gestion et de Crédit: Immeuble Phoebus, ave Charles de Gaulle, BP 4013, Libreville; tel. 76-11-19; telex 5482; f. 1987; 53.8% owned by private Gabonese interests, 45% by private Swiss interests; cap. 1,000m. (Dec. 1988); Chair. GUSTAVE BONGO; Man. Dir RAYMOND LE GRAND.

Union Gabonaise de Banque SA (UGB): ave du Colonel Parant, BP 315, Libreville; tel. 76-15-14; telex 5232; fax 76-46-16; f. 1962; 25% state-owned, 56.3% owned by Crédit Lyonnais (France); cap. 2,000m. (Dec. 1988); Pres. MATHIEU NGUEMA; Vice-Pres. and Gen. Man. BERNARD FOURNIER; 6 brs.

Development Banks

Banque Gabonaise de Développement (BGD): rue Alfred Marche, BP 5, Libreville; tel. 76-24-29; telex 5430; fax 74-26-99; f. 1960; 69% state-owned; cap. 10,500m. (Dec. 1989); Pres. MICHEL ANCHOUEY; Man. Dir JEAN-FÉLIX MAMALEPOT; brs in Franceville, Port-Gentil.

Banque Nationale de Crédit Rural (BNCR): ave Bouet, BP 1120, Libreville; tel. 72-47-42; telex 5830; f. 1986; 87% state-owned; cap. 1,150m. (Dec. 1988); Pres. Minister of Planning, the Economy and Territorial Administration; Man. Dir JACQUES DIOUF.

Société Gabonaise de Participations et de Développement—SOGAPAR: blvd de l'Indépendance, BP 1624, Libreville; tel. 76-23-26; telex 5209; fax 74-08-54; f. 1971; studies and promotes projects conducive to national economic development; 25% state-owned, 64% owned by Paribas International; cap. 2,063m. (Dec. 1987); Pres. DANIEL BÉDIN; Man. Dir HENRI-CLAUDE OYIMA.

Société Nationale d'Investissements du Gabon—SONADIG: BP 479, Libreville; tel. 72-09-22; f. 1968; cap. 100m.; state-owned investment co; Pres. ANTOINE OYIEYE; Dir-Gen. SIMON EDOU-EYENNE.

Financial Institution

Caisse Autonome d'Amortissement du Gabon: BP 912, Libreville; tel. 76-41-43; telex 5537; management of state funds; Dir-Gen. MAURICE EYAMBA TSIMAT.

INSURANCE

Agence Gabonaise d'Assurance et de Réassurance (AGAR): BP 1699, Libreville; tel. 74-02-22; fax 76-59-25; f. 1987; cap. 50m.; Man. Dir LOUIS GASTON MAYILA.

Assurances Générales Gabonaises (AGG): ave du Colonel Parant, BP 2148, Libreville; tel. 76-09-73; telex 5473; f. 1974; cap. 66.5m.; Chair. JEAN DAVIN, JACQUES NOT.

Assureurs Conseils Franco-Africains du Gabon—ACFRA-GABON: BP 1116, Libreville; tel. 72-32-83; telex 5485; cap. 43.4m.; Chair. FRÉDÉRIC MARRON; Dir M. GARNIER.

Assureurs Conseils Gabonais-Faugère et Jutheau & Cie: Immeuble Shell-Gabon, rue de la Mairie, BP 2138, Libreville; tel. 72-04-36; telex 5435; fax 76-04-39; cap. 10m.; represents foreign insurance cos; Dir GÉRARD MILAN.

Mutuelle Gabonaise d'Assurances: ave du Colonel Parant, BP 2225, Libreville; tel. 72-13-91; telex 5240; Sec.-Gen. M. YENO-OLINGOT.

Omnium Gabonais d'Assurances et de Réassurances (OGAR): blvd Triomphal Omar Bongo, BP 201, Libreville; tel. 76-15-96; telex 5505; f. 1976; 10% state-owned; cap. 340m.; general; Pres. MARCEL DOUPAMBY-MATOKA; Man. Dir EDOUARD VALENTIN; brs in Oyem, Port-Gentil, Franceville.

Société Nationale Gabonaise d'Assurances et de Réassurances—SONAGAR: ave du Colonel Parant, BP 3082, Libreville; tel. 76-28-97; telex 5366; f. 1974; activities taken over in 1987 by l'Union des Assurances de Paris (France); Dir-Gen. JEAN-LOUIS MESSAN.

SOGERCO-Gabon: BP 2102, Libreville; tel. 76-09-34; telex 5224; f. 1975; cap. 10m.; general; Dir M. RABEAU.

L'Union des Assurances du Gabon (UAG): ave du Colonel Parant, BP 2141, Libreville; tel. 74-34-34; telex 5404; f. 1976; cap. 280.5m.; 65% owned by l'Union des Assurances de Paris International; Chair. ALBERT ALEVINA-CHAVIHOT; Dir FRANÇOIS SIMON.

Trade and Industry

GOVERNMENT ADVISORY BODY

Conseil Economique et Social de la République Gabonaise: BP 1075, Libreville; tel. 76-26-68; comprises representatives from salaried workers, employers and Govt; commissions on economic, financial and social affairs and forestry and agriculture; Pres. EDOUARD ALEXIS M'BOUY-BOUTZIT; Vice-Pres. M. RICHEPIN EYOGO-EDZANG.

CHAMBER OF COMMERCE

Chambre de Commerce, d'Agriculture, d'Industrie et des Mines du Gabon: BP 2234, Libreville; tel. 72-20-64; telex 5554; f. 1935; regional offices at Port-Gentil and Franceville; Pres. EDOUARD ALEXIS M'BOUY-BOUTZIT; Sec.-Gen. DOMINIQUE MANDZA.

EMPLOYERS' FEDERATIONS

Confédération Patronale Gabonaise: BP 410, Libreville; tel. 76-02-43; f. 1959; represents the principal industrial, mining, petroleum, public works, forestry, banking, insurance, commercial and shipping concerns; Pres. M. ANDRÉ DIEUDONNÉ BERRE; Sec.-Gen. ERIC MESSERSCHMITT.

Conseil National du Patronat Gabonais (CNPG): Libreville; Pres. RAHANDI CHAMBRIER; Sec.-Gen. THOMAS FRANCK EYA'A.

Syndicat des Entreprises Minières du Gabon—SYNDIMINES: BP 260, Libreville; telex 5388; Pres. ANDRÉ BERRE; Sec.-Gen. SERGE GREGOIRE.

Syndicat des Importateurs Exportateurs du Gabon—SIMPEX: BP 1743, Libreville; Pres. ALBERT JEAN; Sec.-Gen. R. TYBERGHEIN.

Syndicat des Producteurs et Industriels du Bois du Gabon: BP 84, Libreville; tel. 72-26-11; Pres. CLAUDE MOLENAT.

Syndicat Professionnel des Usines de Sciages et Placages du Gabon: BP 417, Port-Gentil; f. 1956; Pres. PIERRE BERRY.

Union des Représentations Automobiles et Industrielles (URAI): BP 1743, Libreville; Pres. M. MARTINENT; Sec. R. TYBERGHEIN.

Union Nationale du Patronat Syndical des Transports Urbains, Routiers et Fluviaux du Gabon—UNAPASYFTUROGA: BP

1025, Libreville; f. 1977 as Syndicat National des Transporteurs Urbains et Routiers du Gabon—SYNTRAGA: Pres. Laurent Bellal Bibang-Bi-Edzo; Sec.-Gen. Martin Kombila-Mombo.

PRINCIPAL DEVELOPMENT ORGANIZATIONS

Agence Nationale de Promotion de la Petite et Moyenne Entreprise (PROMO-GABON): BP 3939, Libreville; tel. 74-31-16; telex 000576; f. 1964; state-controlled; promotion of and assistance to small and medium-sized industries; Pres. Simon Boulamatari; Man. Dir Jean-Fidèle Otando.

Caisse Centrale de Coopération Economique (CCCE) (France): BP 64, Libreville; tel. 72-23-89; telex 5362; Dir Jacques Albugues.

Centre Gabonais de Commerce Extérieur (CGCE): BP 3906, Libreville; tel. 76-11-67; telex 5347; promotion of foreign trade and investment in Gabonese interests; Man. Dir Michel Leslie Teale.

Commerce et Développement—CODEV: BP 2142, Libreville; tel. 76-06-73; telex 5214; f. 1976; cap. 2,000m. francs CFA; 95% state-owned; future transfer to private ownership announced 1986; import and distribution of capital goods and food products; Chair. and Man. Dir Jérôme Ngoua-Bekale.

Mission Française de Coopération: BP 2105, Libreville; administers bilateral aid from France; Dir François Chappellet.

Office Gabonais d'Amélioration et de Production de Viande—OGAPROV: BP 245, Moanda; tel. 66-12-67; f. 1971; development of private cattle farming; manages ranch at Lekedi-Sud; Pres. Paul Kounda Kiki; Dir-Gen. Vincent Eyi-Ngui.

Palmiers et Hévéas du Gabon—PALMEVEAS: BP 75, Libreville; f. 1956; cap. 145m. francs CFA; state-owned; palm-oil development.

Société de Développement de l'Agriculture au Gabon (AGROGABON): BP 2248, Libreville; tel. 76-40-82; telex 5468; f. 1976; cap. 7,356m. francs CFA; 96% state-owned; Man. Dir André Le Roux.

Société de Développement de l'Hévéaculture (HEVEGAB): BP 316, Libreville; tel. 70-03-43; telex 5615; fax 70-19-89; f. 1981; cap. 5,500m. francs CFA; 99.9% state-owned; development of rubber plantations in the Mitzic, Bitam and Kango regions; Chair. Emmanuel Ondo-Methogo; Man. Dir Guy de Roquemaurel.

Société Gabonaise de Recherches et d'Exploitations Minières—SOGAREM: blvd de Nice, Libreville; state-owned; research and development of gold mining; Chair. Arsène Bounguenza; Man. Dir Serge Gassita.

Société Gabonaise de Recherches Pétrolières—GABOREP: BP 564, Libreville; tel. 77-23-86; telex 5829; fax 77-23-85; exploration and exploitation of hydrocarbons; Chair. Hubert Perrodo; Man. Dir P. F. Leca.

Société Nationale de Développement des Cultures Industrielles—SONADECI: BP 256, Libreville; tel. 76-33-97; telex 5362; f. 1978; cap. 600m. francs CFA; state-owned; agricultural development; Chair. Paul Kounda Kiki; Man. Dir Georges Bekalé.

TRADE UNIONS

Confédération Syndicale Gabonaise—COSYGA: BP 14017, Libreville; telex 5623; f. 1969, by the Govt, as a specialized organ of the PDG, to organize and educate workers, to contribute to social peace and economic development, and to protect the rights of trade unions; Gen. Sec. Martin Allini.

Transport

RAILWAYS

The Transgabon railway, which will eventually open up the densely-forested interior, was begun in 1974. The first phase, from Owendo (the port of Libreville) to Booué (340 km), was inaugurated in January 1983, and the second phase, from Booué to Franceville (330 km), in December 1986. By 1989, regular services were operating between Libreville and Franceville. More than 829,000 metric tons of freight (including 584,000 tons of timber) and 118,400 passengers were carried on the network in 1988. The construction of a 235-km spur from Booué to Belinga, to serve future iron-ore mines in the north-east, was planned for the 1990s, but has been postponed indefinitely, owing to reductions in public investment expenditure and to a lack of private finance. The manganese mine at Moanda is connected with Pointe-Noire (Congo) by a 76-km cableway and a 296-km railway. However, the importance of this link was expected to diminish after 1988, following the commissioning of a minerals-handling terminal at Owendo (see Shipping).

Office du Chemin de Fer Transgabonais—OCTRA: BP 2198, Libreville; tel. 70-24-78; telex 5307; fax 74-51-45; f. 1972; cap. 231,243m. francs CFA; state-owned; Chair. Charles Tsibah; Dir Gen. Richard Damas.

ROADS

In late 1987 there were 6,898 km of roads, of which 735 km were surfaced. In 1989 the World Bank approved a loan of US $30m., in support of a project for the repair and maintenance of the road network. The three-year programme, which was estimated to cost $137m., was initiated in mid-1990. The African Development Bank is providing ECU 25m. for the financing of road construction projects.

Société Africaine de Transit et d'Affrètement Gabon (SATA-GABON): blvd de l'Indépendance, BP 2258, Libreville; tel. 76-11-28; telex 5439; f. 1961; cap. 300m. francs CFA; freight; Man. Dir Yves Lerays.

INLAND WATERWAYS

The principal river is the Ogooué, navigable from Port-Gentil to Ndjolé (310 km) and serving the towns of Lambaréné, Ndjolé and Sindara.

Compagnie de Navigation Intérieure (CNI): BP 3982, Libreville; tel. 72-39-28; telex 5289; f. 1978; cap. 500m. francs CFA; state-owned; inland waterway transport; agencies at Port-Gentil, Mayumba and Lambaréné; Chair. Jean-Pierre Mengwang me Ngyema; Dir Mathurin Anotho-Onanga.

SHIPPING

The principal deep-water ports are Port-Gentil, which handles mainly petroleum exports, and Owendo, 15 km from Libreville, which services mainly barge traffic. The principal ports for timber are at Owendo, Mayumba and Nyanga, and there is a fishing port at Libreville. The construction of a deep-water port at Mayumba is planned. A new terminal for the export of minerals, at Owendo, was opened in December 1988. The terminal has an annual handling capacity of 2.5m. metric tons of manganese ore. At mid-1985 the merchant shipping fleet had a total displacement of 98,000 grt, of which 74,000 grt were oil tankers.

Compagnie de Manutention et de Chalandage d'Owendo—COMACO: BP 2131, Libreville; tel. 70-26-35; telex 5208; f. 1974; cap. 1,500m. francs CFA; Pres. Georges Rawiri; Dir in Libreville M. Raymond.

Office des Ports et Rades du Gabon—OPRAG: BP 1051, Libreville; tel. 70-17-98; telex 5319; f. 1974; state-owned; national port authority; Man. Dir Marius Foungues.

Société Nationale d'Acconage et de Transit (SNAT): BP 3897, Libreville; tel. 70-04-04; telex 5420; fax 70-13-11; f. 1976; cap. 600m. francs CFA; 51% state-owned; freight transport; Chair. Maurice Leflem; Man. Dir Claude Ayo-Iguendha.

Société Nationale de Transports Maritimes—SONATRAM: BP 3841, Libreville; tel. 74-06-32; telex 5289; fax 74-59-67; f. 1976; cap. 1,500m. francs CFA; 51% state-owned; river and ocean cargo transport; Man. Dir Raphael Moara Walla.

Société Ouest Africaine d'Entreprises Maritimes (SOAEM-GABON): BP 518, Port-Gentil; tel. 75-21-71; telex 5205; freight shipping; Chair. René Kolowski; Man. Dir T. de Pontbriand.

Société du Port Minéralier d'Owendo: f. 1987; cap. 4,000m. francs CFA; majority holding by COMILOG; management of new terminal for minerals at Owendo.

SOCOPAO-Gabon: BP 4, Libreville; tel. 70-21-40; telex 5212; fax 70-02-76; f. 1963; cap. 120m. francs CFA; freight transport and storage; Dir Henri Lecordier.

Terminal Frigorifique Transgabonais: Owendo; f. 1989; operation of refrigeration facilities at Owendo.

CIVIL AVIATION

There are international airports at Libreville, Port-Gentil and Franceville, 65 other public and 50 private airfields linked mostly with forestry and petroleum industries. The second phase of a project to modernize and extend Libreville's Léon M'Ba airport was completed in early 1988. A third phase, to expand the airport's passenger-handling capacity, was financed by France, and completed in mid-1990.

Air Affaires Gabon: BP 3962, Libreville; tel. 73-25-13; telex 5360; fax 73-49-98; f. 1975; cap. 950m. francs CFA; domestic passenger chartered and scheduled flights; Chair. Raymond Bellanger; Dir Ange Acostini; fleet of 2 King Air 90, 1 Super King 200, 1 Bandeirante E110, 1 Lear 35, 1 HS 125-600, 2 B-58.

Air Service Gabon (ASG): BP 2232, Libreville; tel. 73-24-07; telex 5522; fax 73-60-69; f. 1965; cap. 750m. francs CFA; charter flights; Chair. Jérôme Okinda; Gen. Man. Francis Lascombes.

Compagnie Nationale Air Gabon: BP 2206, Libreville; tel. 73-21-97; telex 5213; fax 73-01-11; f. 1951 as Compagnie Aérienne Gabonaise, name changed 1968 and 1974; began operating international services in 1977, following Gabon's withdrawal from Air

GABON

Afrique (see under Côte d'Ivoire); cap. 6,500m. francs CFA; 80% state-owned; internal and international cargo and passenger services; Chair. MARTIN BONGO; Dir-Gen. JEAN-CLAUDE LABOUBA; fleet of 1 Boeing 747-200C, 1 Boeing 737-200C, 2 Fokker F28-2000, 1 F-100, 1 Lockheed L 100-30.

Société de Gestion de l'Aéroport de Libreville (ADL): BP 363, Libreville; tel. 73-62-44; telex 5459; fax 76-61-28; f. 1988; cap. 340m. francs CFA; 26.5% state-owned; management of airport at Libreville; Pres. CHANTAL LIDJI BADINGA; Dir-Gen. CHRISTIAN ROGNONE.

Tourism

Tourism is being extensively developed, with new hotels and several important projects, including a 'holiday village' near Libreville (opened in 1973), reorganization of Pointe-Denis tourist resort, and the promotion of national parks. In 1987 there were 74 hotels, with a total of 3,077 rooms. Measures aimed at increasing the role of private investors in the tourism sector were expected to be implemented during the early 1990s.

Centre de Promotion Touristique du Gabon (GABONTOUR): Libreville.

Ministère du Tourisme, de L'Environnement et des Parcs Nationaux: BP 403, Libreville.

Office National Gabonais du Tourisme: BP 161, Libreville; tel. 72-21-82.

THE GAMBIA

Introductory Survey

Location, Climate, Language, Religion, Flag, Capital

The Republic of The Gambia is a narrow territory around the River Gambia on the west coast of Africa. The country has a short coastline on the Atlantic Ocean but is otherwise surrounded by Senegal. The climate is tropical and, away from the river swamps, most of the terrain is covered by savanna bush. The average annual temperature in the capital, Banjul, is 27°C (80°F). English is the official language, while the principal vernacular languages are Mandinka, Fula and Wolof. About 85% of the inhabitants are Muslims, and most of the remainder are Christians, with some adherents of animism. The national flag (proportions 3 by 2) has red, blue and green horizontal stripes, with two narrow white stripes bordering the central blue band. The capital is Banjul (formerly called Bathurst).

Recent History

The Gambia was formerly a British dependency. It became a separate colony in 1888, having previously been united with Sierra Leone. The principle of election was introduced for the first time in the 1946 Constitution. Political parties were formed in the 1950s, and another constitution was adopted in 1960. This was amended in April 1962, when the office of Premier was created. Following elections in May, the leader of the People's Progressive Party (PPP), Dr (later Sir) Dawda Kairaba Jawara, took office as Premier in June 1962. Full internal self-government followed in October 1963.

On 18 February 1965 The Gambia became an independent country within the Commonwealth, with Dr Jawara as Prime Minister. The country became a republic on 24 April 1970, with Sir Dawda Jawara (as he had become in 1966) taking office as President. He was re-elected in 1972 and again in April 1977, as a result of PPP victories in legislative elections. In September 1978 the only United Party member remaining in the House of Representatives, following a by-election defeat in May 1977, joined the PPP, leaving only the five members of the National Convention Party (NCP) as opposition.

In October 1980 the Government was obliged to ask neighbouring Senegal to dispatch troops to The Gambia to assist in maintaining internal security under the terms of a mutual defence pact. A more serious threat arose in July 1981, when a coup was staged during President Jawara's absence. Left-wing rebels formed a 12-member National Revolutionary Council, and proclaimed their leader, Kukoi Samba Sanyang, as Head of State. Senegalese troops again assisted in the suppression of the rebellion. A state of emergency was announced, and more than 1,000 people were arrested. During the resulting trials, held in subsequent months, more than 60 people were sentenced to death, but by late 1987 most of the sentences had been commuted to life imprisonment and no executions had taken place. The state of emergency was finally revoked in February 1985.

In The Gambia's first presidential election by direct popular vote, held in May 1982, President Jawara was re-elected, obtaining 72% of the votes cast, while the leader of the NCP, Sherif Mustapha Dibba (at that time in detention for his alleged involvement in the abortive coup), secured 28% of the votes. In the concurrent legislative elections, the PPP won 27 of the 35 elective seats in the House of Representatives. Following the elections, the PPP sought further to restore its public standing by bringing a number of younger, reformist ministers into the Cabinet. However, the resignation of the Minister of Justice in June 1984, amid unconfirmed reports of financial misconduct, and the dismissal of the Minister of Economic Planning in January 1985, following allegations of abuse of power, indicated that corruption remained a major problem.

Legislative and presidential elections took place in March 1987. The PPP overcame an intensified challenge from opposition groups, winning 31 of the 36 directly-elected seats in the House of Representatives. Three other parties presented candidates: the NCP (which won the remaining five elective seats) and two newly-formed groupings, the Gambia People's Party (GPP) and the People's Democratic Organization for Independence and Socialism (PDOIS). In the presidential election, Dr Jawara was re-elected with 59% of the votes cast, while Sherif Dibba (who had been acquitted and released from detention in June 1982) and the GPP leader, Assan Musa Camara (a former Vice-President), received 27% and 14% of the votes respectively.

In January 1988 the authorities detained 10 people, including six Senegalese, following the discovery of a coup plot. Musa Sanneh, Amadou Badjie, Adrien Sambou (both Badjie and Sambou being members of the Senegalese separatist movement, the Mouvement des forces démocratiques de la Casamance) and Ousman Sanneh were brought to trial in April, on charges of high treason and conspiracy to overthrow the Gambian Government. During the trial, it was alleged that false travel documents had been supplied to Gambian and Senegalese citizens, with a view to receiving military training abroad. The involvement in the plot of both Kukoi Samba Sanyang (the leader of the 1981 coup, who was resident in Libya) and the Senegalese opposition leader, Abdoulaye Wade, was suggested by witnesses. Musa Sanneh, Badjie and Ousman Sanneh subsequently received prison sentences, with hard labour, of between nine and 30 years, while Sambou was acquitted. Allegations concerning the involvement of Wade were deemed to be unfounded. In late 1989 an appeal against the sentences was rejected by the Court of Appeal.

In February 1989 the retirement, owing to ill health, of Sheriff Saidula Sisay prompted a reallocation of ministerial portfolios. Sisay was replaced as Minister of Finance and Trade by the former Minister of Agriculture, Saihou Sabally. Sabally was one of four government ministers who had been named in October 1988 in an article in a Banjul periodical, *The Torch*, which alleged widespread corruption among prominent public officials. The editor of that publication, Sana Manneh, was sued for libel and defamation by three of the ministers. Only one minor charge, which had been brought by Alhaji Landing Jallow Sonko, was upheld, and in April 1989 Manneh was cautioned and the case dismissed. The Minister of Justice and Attorney-General, Hassan B. Jallow, appealed against the verdict of the trial, and in mid-1990, in spite of allegations made by Manneh regarding irregularities in the conduct of the appeal, Jallow ordered a reversal of the earlier acquittals. In early May 1990 Dr Lamin K. Saho (one of those who had brought criminal charges against Manneh) was dismissed from the Ministry of Information and Tourism. In the following month Momodou Cadi Cham (hitherto Minister of Works and Communications), who had been implicated in the allegations of corruption but had declined to take action against the editor of *The Torch*, was similarly removed from office.

In January 1990 an amnesty was announced for four of those who had been convicted of involvement in the July 1981 coup attempt. A further amnesty was announced in February 1991.

In early December 1990 President Jawara made official visits to the United Kingdom and to the Canary Islands. Later in that month the Gambian authorities denied persistent rumours of an attempt to overthrow Jawara during his absence.

Plans were announced in August 1981 for the merger of The Gambia and Senegal, in a confederation to be called Senegambia. These proposals were approved by the Gambian House of Representatives in December, and came into effect on 1 February 1982. The first Confederal Council of Ministers, headed by President Abdou Diouf of Senegal (with President Jawara as his deputy), was announced in November 1982 and held its inaugural meeting in January 1983, as did the new, 60-member, Confederal Assembly. Subsequent meetings led to agreements on co-ordination of foreign policy, communications, defence and security. However, the Senegalese authorities were critical of President Jawara's apparent reluctance to complete the process of confederation, in the interests of minimizing the economic cost to The Gambia. In August 1989 President Diouf of Senegal announced that his country's troops were to be withdrawn from The Gambia. This decision was apparently taken in protest at a request by President Jawara that The Gambia be accorded more power within the confederal agreement. Later in that month Diouf stated that, in view of The Gambia's reluctance to proceed towards full political and economic integration with Senegal, the functions of the nominal confederation should be suspended, and the two countries should endeavour to formulate more attainable co-operation accords. The confederation was dissolved in September. Relations between The Gambia and Senegal subsequently deteriorated; it was reported that the Senegalese authorities had introduced restrictions concerning customs duties and travel that were unfavourable to Gambian interests, and that supplies of important commodities were being prevented from entering The Gambia via Senegal. Relations between The Gambia and Senegal remained strained during 1990. In January 1991, however, the Gambian Minister of External Affairs, Alhaji Omar Sey, and his Senegalese counterpart, Seydina Oumar Sy, met in Banjul, where they signed a bilateral agreement of friendship and co-operation.

In mid-1990, in his capacity as Chairman of the Conference of Heads of State and Government of the Economic Community of West African States (ECOWAS), President Jawara contributed to attempts to mediate in the civil conflict in Liberia. Gambian troops subsequently formed part of the ECOWAS Monitoring Group that was dispatched to Liberia in August.

Government

Legislative power is held by the unicameral House of Representatives, with 50 members: 36 directly elected by universal adult suffrage for five years; five Chiefs' Representatives Members, elected by the Chiefs in Assembly; eight non-voting nominated members; and the Attorney-General. The President is elected by direct universal suffrage for a five-year term. He is Head of State and appoints a Vice-President (who is leader of government business in the House) and a Cabinet consisting of elected members of the House or other nominees.

Defence

In June 1990 the Gambian armed forces comprised 900 men (including a gendarmerie of at least 600). A Presidential Guard was formed in 1989, following the withdrawal from The Gambia of Senegalese military forces (from whose ranks the Gambian Presidential Guard had hitherto been recruited). All bilateral defence protocols that had been signed by The Gambia and Senegal lapsed upon the dissolution, in September 1989, of the Senegambia Confederation. Military service is mainly voluntary. The Gambia's defence budget for 1985/86 was estimated at 7.8m. dalasi.

Economic Affairs

In 1989, according to estimates by the World Bank, The Gambia's gross national product (GNP), measured at average 1987-89 prices, was US $196m., equivalent to $230 per head. Between 1980 and 1989, it was estimated, GNP increased, in real terms, at an average annual rate of 2.2%, while GNP per head declined by 1.0% per year. Over the same period, the population increased by an annual average of 3.3%. The Gambia's gross domestic product (GDP) increased, in real terms, by an annual average of 5.0% in 1980-87.

Agriculture (including forestry and fishing) contributed 34% of GDP in 1989. About 81.3% of the labour force were employed in the sector in that year. The principal agricultural activity is the cultivation of groundnuts. Exports of groundnuts and related products accounted for 25.9% of total export earnings (and 78.6% of domestic exports) in the year ending 30 June 1986; however, a significant proportion of the crop is smuggled into Senegal. Cotton is also cultivated for export. The principal staple crops are millet, sorghum, rice and maize. None the less, some 70,000 metric tons of cereals were imported into The Gambia in 1986. In the 1980s the Government encouraged the development of the livestock-rearing and fishing sectors. During 1980-89 agricultural production increased by an annual average of 3.6%.

Industry (including mining, manufacturing, construction and power) contributed 11% of GDP in 1987. About 4.2% of the labour force were employed in the sector in 1983. During 1980-87 industrial production increased by an annual average of 5.8%.

Manufacturing contributed 6% of GDP in 1987, and employed about 2.5% of the labour force in 1983. The sector is dominated by the processing of groundnuts and by other agro industrial activities. Beverages and construction materials are also produced.

Imports of fuels accounted for 4% of the value of total imports in 1987; however, as a significant proportion of imports are destined for re-export, the actual percentage (as a proportion of imports for domestic consumption) is much greater. Efforts to reduce The Gambia's dependence on imported energy from Senegal were initiated in 1989, following the dissolution of the Senegambia confederal agreement in September of that year.

In the early 1990s the tourism sector contributed about 10% of GDP and employed some 7,000 people.

In 1989 The Gambia recorded a visible trade deficit of US $25.16m.; however, there was a surplus of $15.02m. on the current account of the balance of payments. In 1985/86 the principal source of imports (14.4%) was France; other major sources were the United Kingdom, Thailand and the People's Republic of China. The principal market for exports in that year was Switzerland (which took 22.9% of exports); other major purchasers were the Netherlands, Guinea-Bissau and the United Kingdom. The principal domestic exports in 1985/86 were groundnuts and related products, fish and fish preparations and cotton (lint). The principal imports were food and live animals, basic manufactured goods, machinery and transport equipment, fuels and fuel products and chemicals.

Budget estimates for 1990/91 envisaged a deficit of 59.4m. dalasi. The Gambia's total external public debt was US $273m. at the end of 1987. In that year the cost of debt-servicing was equivalent to 12.9% of the value of exports of goods and services. The average annual rate of inflation was 13.8% in 1980-87; consumer prices increased by an average of 8.3% in 1989, and by 13% in the year ending 30 June 1990.

The Gambia is a member of the Economic Community of West African States (ECOWAS, see p. 133) and of The Gambia River Basin Development Organization (OMVG, see p. 223).

Since 1985, when a major Economic Recovery Programme (ERP) was inaugurated, the Jawara Government has sought to reduce the dependence of the Gambian economy on revenue from sales of groundnuts, and thus its vulnerability to fluctuations in output of, and international prices for, the crop. Funding has been obtained from bilateral and international donors, in support of the Government's adjustment efforts, which envisage the diversification of the agricultural sector, a policy of retrenchment and rehabilitation in the public sector, and the fostering of private enterprise (notably in the agriculture and tourism sectors). Considerable success has been achieved in curtailing the rate of inflation, while ensuring sustained GDP growth. However, The Gambia remains heavily dependent on imported commodities (especially petroleum) and manufactured goods, and the ability of the country's resources to accommodate a relatively high rate of population growth remains in doubt. Seismic surveys have indicated the existence of significant reserves of petroleum, which, if developed, could result in the further diversification of the economy.

Social Welfare

In 1978 The Gambia had 16 hospital establishments, with a total of 699 beds. At the end of 1980 there were 43 government physicians, 23 private practitioners and five dentists. There were four hospitals and a network of 12 health centres, 17 dispensaries and 68 maternity and child welfare clinics throughout the country. Of total expenditure by the central Government in the financial year 1981/82, about 12.7m. dalasi (8.0%) was for health services, and a further 5.75m. dalasi (3.6%) for social security and welfare. A national health development project, to cost US $19.8m. over five years, was announced in 1987.

Education

Primary education, beginning at eight years of age, is free but not compulsory and lasts for six years. On completion of this period, pupils may sit a common entrance examination, leading either to five years of secondary high school or to four years of secondary technical school. High schools offer an academic-based curriculum leading to examinations at the 'Ordinary' level of the General Certificate of Education (GCE), under the auspices of the West African Examinations Council (WAEC). Two of the high schools provide two-year courses leading to GCE 'Advanced' level. In 1989/90 a total of 18,118 candidates from The Gambia were examined by the WAEC. Gambia College, at Brikama, offers post-secondary courses in teacher-

THE GAMBIA

training, agriculture and health; other post-secondary education is provided by technical training schools. Non-formal education services are being expanded to offer increased educational opportunities in rural areas, and to provide for primary-school leavers who are unable to continue their studies. University education must be obtained abroad. In 1988 enrolment at primary schools was equivalent to 61% of children in the relevant age-group (76% of boys; 47% of girls). Secondary enrolment in 1987 was equivalent to only 16% of students aged between 14 and 20 (23% of boys; 10% of girls). According to UNESCO estimates, adult illiteracy in 1985 averaged 74.9% (males 64.4%, females 84.9%). A long-term restructuring of the education system was undertaken in 1990. In 1977 The Gambia introduced Koranic studies at all stages of education; in addition, many children attend Koranic schools. Expenditure on education by the central Government in 1981/82 was 27.7m. dalasi (17.4% of total spending).

Public Holidays

1991: 1 January (New Year's Day), 18 February (Independence Day), 29 March–1 April (Easter), 16 April* (Id al-Fitr, end of Ramadan), 1 May (Labour Day), 23 June* (Id al-Adha, Feast of the Sacrifice), 15 August (Assumption), 21 September* (Mouloud, Birth of the Prophet), 25 December (Christmas).

1992: 1 January (New Year's Day), 18 February (Independence Day), 4 April* (Id al-Fitr, end of Ramadan), 17–20 April (Easter), 1 May (Labour Day), 11 June* (Id al-Adha, Feast of the Sacrifice), 15 August (Assumption), 10 September* (Mouloud, Birth of the Prophet), 25 December (Christmas).

* These holidays are dependent on the Islamic lunar calendar and may vary by one or two days from the dates given.

Weights and Measures

Imperial weights and measures are used. Importers and traders also use the metric system.

Statistical Survey

Source (unless otherwise stated): Directorate of Information and Broadcasting, 14 Hagan St, Banjul; tel. 27230.

AREA AND POPULATION

Area: 11,295 sq km (4,361 sq miles).

Population: 493,499 (census of 23–30 April 1973); 698,817 (census of 24 April 1983). *Principal ethnic groups* (April 1963 census): Mandinka (40.8%), Fula (13.5%), Wolof (12.9%), Jola (7.0%), Serahuli (6.7%).

Density: 61.9 per sq km (April 1983).

Principal Towns (1983 census): Serrekunda 68,433, Banjul (capital) 44,188, Brikama 19,584, Bakau 19,309, Farafenni 10,168, Sukuta 7,227, Gunjur 7,115.

Births and Deaths (1983 census): Birth rate 49.0 per 1,000; death rate 21.0 per 1,000.

Economically Active Population (persons aged 10 years and over, 1983 census): Agriculture, hunting, forestry and fishing 239,940; Quarrying 66; Manufacturing 8,144; Electricity, gas and water 1,233; Construction 4,373; Trade, restaurants and hotels 16,551; Transport, storage and communication 8,014; Public administration and defence 8,295; Education 4,737; Medical services 2,668; Personal and domestic services 6,553; Activities not adequately defined 25,044; Total 325,618 (males 174,856, females 150,762); Figures exclude persons seeking work for the first time. **Mid-1989** (estimates in '000): Agriculture, etc. 311; Total labour force 382 (Source: FAO, *Production Yearbook*).

AGRICULTURE, ETC.

Principal Crops ('000 metric tons, 1989): Millet and sorghum 71 (unofficial figure), Rice (paddy) 30 (unofficial figure), Maize 16 (unofficial figure), Cassava (Manioc) 6 (FAO estimate), Palm kernels 2 (FAO estimate), Groundnuts (in shell) 120 (unofficial figure), Seed (unginned) cotton 1 (FAO estimate) (Source: FAO, *Production Yearbook*).

Livestock ('000 head, year ending September 1989): Cattle 300 (FAO estimate), Goats 190, Sheep 163, Asses 41, Horses 18, Pigs 13 (FAO estimate) (Source: FAO, *Production Yearbook*).

Livestock Products (FAO estimates, '000 metric tons, 1989): Meat 8, Cows' milk 5 (Source: FAO, *Production Yearbook*).

Forestry (FAO estimates, 1988): *Roundwood removals* ('000 cu m): Sawlogs, veneer logs and logs for sleepers 14, Other industrial wood 7, Fuel wood 889; Total 910 (Source: FAO, *Yearbook of Forest Products*).

Fishing ('000 metric tons, live weight, 1987): Inland waters 2.7; Atlantic Ocean 11.7; Total catch 14.4; 1988 (FAO estimates): catch as in 1987. (Source: FAO, *Yearbook of Fishery Statistics*).

INDUSTRY

Production ('000 metric tons, unless otherwise indicated, 1987): Palm oil 3 (FAO estimate), Salted, dried or smoked fish 4 (FAO figure), Electric energy 44 million kWh (Source: UN, *Industrial Statistics Yearbook*).

FINANCE

Currency and Exchange Rates: 100 butut = 1 dalasi (D). *Coins:* 1, 5, 10, 25 and 50 butut; 1 dalasi. *Notes:* 1, 5, 10, 25 and 50 dalasi. *Sterling and Dollar Equivalents* (30 September 1990): £1 sterling = 14.000 dalasi; US $1 = 7.473 dalasi; 1,000 dalasi = £71.43 = $133.82. *Average Exchange Rate* (dalasi per US $): 7.0744 in 1987; 6.7086 in 1988; 7.5846 in 1989.

Budget ('000 dalasi, year ending 30 June): 1985/86 revised estimates: Recurrent revenue 247,250; Recurrent expenditure 182,100; Development expenditure 83,500. 1986/87 budget proposals: Recurrent revenue 296,700; Recurrent expenditure 262,530; Development expenditure 201,200. 1987/88 revised budget proposals: Recurrent revenue 386,709; Recurrent expenditure 379,954.

Second National Development Plan (proposed investment, '000 dalasi, 1981/82–1985/86): Agriculture and natural resources 131,300, Industry 29,200, Public utilities 67,300, Transport and communications 143,900, Tourism, trade and finance 7,300, Education, youth, sports and culture 37,000, Health, labour and social welfare 15,000, Housing 21,000, Total (incl. others) 475,000 (Source: *National Development Plan, 1981/82–1985/86*).

International Reserves (US $ million at 31 December 1989): IMF special drawing rights 1.35, Reserve position in IMF 0.07, Foreign exchange 19.17, Total 20.59 (Source: IMF, *International Financial Statistics*).

Money Supply (million dalasi at 31 December 1989): Currency outside banks 134.78; Demand deposits at commercial banks 120.03 (Source: IMF, *International Financial Statistics*).

Cost of Living (Consumer price index for Banjul and Kombo St Mary, year ending 30 June; base: 1985 = 100): 193.4 in 1987; 216.0 in 1988; 233.9 in 1989 (Source: IMF, *International Financial Statistics*).

Gross Domestic Product by Economic Activity ('000 dalasi at constant 1976/77 prices, year ending 30 June 1986): Agriculture, etc. 108,400; Manufacturing 18,500; Electricity, gas and water 3,300; Construction 13,800; Trade 93,600; Other services 141,500; GDP at factor cost 379,100; Indirect taxes, *less* subsidies 35,000; GDP at market prices 414,100.

Balance of Payments (US $ million, year ending 30 June 1989): Merchandise exports f.o.b. 100.2, Merchandise imports f.o.b. −125.35, *Trade Balance* −25.16; Exports of services 67.73, Imports of services −66.41, *Balance on Goods and Services* −37.65; Private unrequited transfers (net) 6.68, Government unrequited transfers (net) 32.17, *Current Balance* 15.02; Direct investment 14.79, Other long-term capital (net) −4.29, Short-term capital (net) −2.42, Net errors and omissions −21.97, *Total (net monetary movements)* 1.13; Valuation changes (net) 8.39, Exceptional financing (net) −11.08, *Change in Reserves* −1.57. (Source: IMF, *International Financial Statistics*).

THE GAMBIA

EXTERNAL TRADE

Principal Commodities ('000 dalasi, year ending 30 June 1986): *Imports:* Food and live animals 175,280, Beverages and tobacco 27,881, Inedible crude materials (except fuels) 8,167, Mineral fuels, lubricants, etc. 56,630, Animal and vegetable oils and fats 3,146, Chemicals 34,008, Basic manufactured goods 113,916, Machinery and transport equipment 97,850, Miscellaneous and manufactured articles 27,322, Total (incl. others) 567,631. *Exports* (excl. re-exports): Groundnuts (shelled) 33,570, Groundnut cake 4,142, Groundnut oil 15,132, Fish and fish preparations 2,507, Hides and skins 1,652, Cotton (lint) 3,862, Total (incl. others) 67,257. *Re-exports:* 136,938.

Principal Trading Partners ('000 dalasi, year ending 30 June 1986): *Imports:* Belgium 18,998, People's Republic of China 31,157, France 81,457, Federal Republic of Germany 28,835, Japan 22,096, Malawi 6,439, Netherlands 30,135, Thailand 32,409, United Kingdom 64,294, USA 26,633, Total (incl. others) 567,631. *Exports:* Belgium 3,334, France 8,123, Guinea 4,654, Guinea-Bissau 16,959, Mali 8,807, Netherlands 30,263, Nigeria 918, Sweden 1,579, Switzerland 46,706, United Kingdom 13,686, Total (incl. others) 204,195.

TRANSPORT

Road Traffic (motor vehicles in use, estimates, 31 December 1985): Passenger cars 5,200; Buses and coaches 100; Goods vehicles 600; Tractors and trailers 200; Motorcycles, scooters and mopeds 2,000 (Source: IRF, *World Road Statistics*).

International Shipping (estimated sea-borne freight traffic, '000 metric tons, 1988): Goods loaded 155; Goods unloaded 210 (Source: UN, *Monthly Bulletin of Statistics*).

Civil Aviation (1984/85): 1,576 aircraft landed.

TOURISM

Tourist Arrivals: 112,381 in 1988/89.

COMMUNICATIONS MEDIA

Radio receivers 115,000 in use in 1987; Newspapers 6 in 1986 (average circulation 4,000 copies); Book production 74 titles in 1987; Telephones 7,000 in use in 1987 (Sources: UNESCO, *Statistical Yearbook*; UN Economic Commission for Africa, *African Statistical Yearbook*).

EDUCATION

Primary (1988/89): 226 schools, 2,604 teachers, 73,673 pupils (28,540 females).

Secondary: General (1986/87) 658 teachers, 15,978 pupils (4,881 females); Teacher training (1984/85) 30 teachers, 353 pupils (73 females); Vocational (1984/85) 148 teachers, 1,107 pupils (423 females) Source: UNESCO, *Statistical Yearbook*.

Post-secondary (1984/85): 8 schools, 179 teachers, 1,489 pupils.

Directory

The Constitution

The Gambia's present Constitution took effect on 24 April 1970, when the country became a republic. Its major provisions are summarized below:

Executive power is vested in the President, who is Head of State and Commander-in-Chief of the armed forces. Following a constitutional amendment in March 1982, the President is elected by direct universal suffrage, and serves a five-year term. The President appoints a Vice-President, who is leader of government business in the House of Representatives, and other Cabinet Ministers from members of the House.

Legislative power is vested in the unicameral House of Representatives, with 50 members: 36 elected by universal adult suffrage, five Chiefs (elected by the Chiefs in Assembly), eight non-voting nominated members and the Attorney-General.

The Government

HEAD OF STATE

President: Alhaji Sir DAWDA KAIRABA JAWARA (took office 24 April 1970; re-elected 1972, 1977, 1982 and 1987).

CABINET
(February 1991)

President and Minister of Defence: Alhaji Sir DAWDA KAIRABA JAWARA.
Vice-President and Minister of Education, Youth, Sports and Culture: BAKARY B. DARBO.
Minister of Justice and Attorney-General: HASSAN B. JALLOW.
Minister of External Affairs: Alhaji OMAR SEY.
Minister of the Interior: Alhaji LAMIN KITTY JABANG.
Minister of Finance and Trade: Alhaji SAIHOU SABALLY.
Minister of Information and Tourism: JAMES ALKALI GAYE.
Minister of Health, Labour, Social Welfare and the Environment: LOUISE N'JIE.
Minister of Agriculture: Alhaji OMAR AMADOU JALLOW.
Minister of Economic Planning and Industrial Development: MBEMBA JATTA.
Minister of Local Government and Lands: Alhaji LANDING JALLOW-JONKO.
Minister of Works and Communications: MATTHEW YAYA BALDEH.

Minister of Water Resources, Forestry and Fisheries: SARJO TOURAY.

MINISTRIES

Office of the President: State House, Banjul; tel. 27208; telex 2204; fax 27034.
Ministry of Agriculture: The Quadrangle, Banjul; tel. 2147.
Ministry of Economic Planning and Industrial Development: Central Bank Bldg, Banjul; tel. 28229; telex 2293.
Ministry of Education, Youth, Sports and Culture: Bedford Place Bldg, Banjul; tel. 28231.
Ministry of External Affairs: The Quadrangle, Banjul; tel. 28291; telex 2351; fax 28060.
Ministry of Finance and Trade: The Quadrangle, Banjul; tel. 28291; telex 2264.
Ministry of Health, Labour, Social Welfare and the Environment: MacCarthy Square, Banjul; tel. 27223; telex 2263; fax 27122.
Ministry of Information and Tourism: The Quadrangle, Banjul; tel. 28496; telex 2204.
Ministry of the Interior: 71 Dobson St, Banjul; tel. 28611.
Ministry of Justice: Marina Parade, Banjul; tel. 28181.
Ministry of Local Government and Lands: The Quadrangle, Banjul; tel. 28291.
Ministry of Water Resources, Forestry and Fisheries: 5 Marina Parade, Banjul; tel. 27431; telex 2204.
Ministry of Works and Communications: Half-Die, Banjul; tel. 27449.

President and Legislature

PRESIDENT

Presidential Election, 11 March 1987

	Votes	% of total
Alhaji Sir DAWDA JAWARA (PPP)	123,385	58.71
SHERIF MUSTAPHA DIBBA (NCP)	57,343	27.29
ASSAN MUSA CAMARA (GPP)	29,400	14.00
Total	**210,128**	**100.00**

THE GAMBIA

HOUSE OF REPRESENTATIVES

Speaker: Alhaji Momodou B. N'Jie.

Election, 11 March 1987

	Votes	% of total	Seats
People's Progressive Party	117,599	56.61	31
National Convention Party	57,340	27.60	5
Gambia People's Party	30,606	14.73	—
PDOIS	2,069	1.00	—
Independent	105	0.05	—
Total	207,719	100.00	36

In addition to the 36 members directly elected, the House has 14 other members: the Attorney-General, five Chiefs and eight nominated (non-voting) members.

Political Organizations

Gambia People's Party (GPP): Banjul; f. 1986 by fmr mems of the PPP; socialist; Leader Assan Musa Camara.

National Convention Party (NCP): 4 Fitzgerald St, Banjul; f. 1975; advocates social reform and more equitable distribution of national wealth; 50,000 mems; Leader Sheriff Mustapha Dibba.

People's Democratic Organisation for Independence and Socialism (PDOIS): Banjul; f. 1986; radical socialist; aims to maintain economic and political independence of The Gambia; Leaders Halifa Sallah, Sam Sarr, Sidia Jatta.

People's Progressive Party (PPP): 21 Leman St, Banjul; f. 1959; merged in 1965 with Democratic Congress Alliance, and in 1968 with Gambia Congress Party; ruling party; favours continued membership of the Commonwealth; Nat. Pres. I. A. A. Kelepha Samba; Sec.-Gen. Alhaji Sir Dawda Kairaba Jawara.

The following organizations were banned in November 1980:

Gambia Socialist Revolutionary Party (GSRP).

Movement for Justice in Africa-The Gambia (MOJA-G): Leader Koro Sallah.

Diplomatic Representation

EMBASSIES AND HIGH COMMISSIONS IN THE GAMBIA

China, People's Republic: Fajara, Banjul; tel. 23835; Chargé d'affaires: An Yongyu.

Nigeria: Garba Jahumpa Ave, Banjul; tel. 95805; High Commissioner: Mark Nnabugwu Eze.

Senegal: 10 Cameron St, Banjul; tel. 27469; High Commissioner: Saliou Cissé.

Sierra Leone: 67 Hagan St, Banjul; tel. 28206; High Commissioner: H. R. S. Bultman.

United Kingdom: 48 Atlantic Rd, Fajara, POB 507, Banjul; tel. 95133; telex 2211; fax 96134; High Commissioner: Alan J. Pover.

USA: Kairaba Ave, Fajara, POB 19, Banjul; tel. 92858; fax 92475; Ambassador: Arlene Render (designate).

Judicial System

The judicial system of The Gambia is based on English Common Law and legislative enactments of the Republic's Parliament which include an Islamic Law Recognition Ordinance by which an Islamic Court exercises jurisdiction in certain cases between, or exclusively affecting, Muslims.

The Supreme Court consists of the Chief Justice and puisne judges; has unlimited jurisdiction; appeal lies to the Court of Appeal.

Chief Justice: Emmanuel Olayinka Ayoola.

The Gambia Court of Appeal is the Superior Court of Record and consists of a president, justices of appeal and other judges of the Supreme Court ex officio. Final appeal, with certain exceptions, to the Judicial Committee of the Privy Council in the United Kingdom.

President: (vacant).

The Banjul Magistrates Court, the Kanifing Magistrates Court and the **Divisional Courts** are courts of summary jurisdiction presided over by a magistrate or in his absence by two or more lay justices of the peace. There are resident magistrates in all divisions. The magistrates have limited civil and criminal jurisdiction, and appeal lies from these courts to the Supreme Court.

Islamic Courts have jurisdiction in matters between, or exclusively affecting, Muslim Gambians and relating to civil status, marriage, succession, donations, testaments and guardianship. The Courts administer Islamic Law. A cadi, or a cadi and two assessors, preside over and constitute an Islamic Court. Assessors of the Islamic Courts are Justices of the Peace of Islamic faith.

District Tribunals are appeal courts which deal with cases touching on customs and traditions. Each court consists of three district tribunal members, one of whom is selected as president, and other court members from the area over which it has jurisdiction.

Religion

About 85% of the population are Muslims. The remainder are mainly Christians, and there are a few animists, mostly of the Jola and Karoninka tribes.

ISLAM

Imam of Banjul: Alhaji Abdoulie M. Jobe, 39 Lancaster St, POB 562, Banjul; tel. 27369.

CHRISTIANITY

The Gambia Christian Council: POB 27, Banjul; tel. 92092; telex 2290; f. 1966; seven mems (churches and other Christian bodies); Pres. Rt Rev. Michael J. Cleary (Roman Catholic Bishop of Banjul); Sec.-Gen. Solomon Billy Dalliah.

The Anglican Communion

The diocese of The Gambia, which includes Senegal and Cape Verde, forms part of the Church of the Province of West Africa. There are about 1,500 adherents in The Gambia.

Bishop of The Gambia: Rt Rev. Solomon Tilewa Johnson, Bishop's Court, POB 51, Banjul; tel. 27405; telex 2203; fax 29313.

The Roman Catholic Church

The Gambia comprises a single diocese, directly responsible to the Holy See. At 31 December 1988 there were an estimated 15,300 adherents in the country. The Bishop of Banjul is a member of the Inter-territorial Catholic Bishops' Conference of The Gambia, Liberia and Sierra Leone (based in Freetown, Sierra Leone).

Bishop of Banjul: Rt Rev. Michael J. Cleary, Bishop's House, POB 165, Banjul; tel. 93437; telex 2201.

Other Christian Churches

Methodist Church: POB 288, Banjul; tel. 27425; Chair. and Gen. Supt Rev. K. John A. Stedman; Sec. Rev. Titus K. A. Pratt.

The Press

Foroyaa (Freedom): Bundunka Kunda, POB 2306, Serrekunda; organ of the PDOIS; Editors Halifa Sallah, Sam Sarr, Sidia Jatta.

The Gambia Onward: 48 Grant St, Banjul; Editor Rudolph Allen.

The Gambia Outlook: 29 Grant St, Banjul; Editor M. B. Jones.

The Gambia Weekly: 14 Hagan St, Banjul; tel. 27230; telex 2308; f. 1943 as Gambia News Bulletin, name changed 1989; govt newspaper; Editor C. A. Jallow; circ. 2,500.

The Gambian: 60 Lancaster St, Banjul; Editor Ngaing Thomas.

The Gambian Times: 21 Leman St, POB 698, Banjul; tel. 445; f. 1981; fortnightly; publ. by the People's Progressive Party; Editor Momodou Gaye.

The Nation: People's Press, 3 Boxbar Rd, POB 334, Banjul; fortnightly; Editor W. Dixon-Colley.

The Toiler: 31 Leman St, POB 698, Banjul; Editor Pa Modou Fall.

The Torch: 59 Gloucester St, Banjul; f. 1984; Editor Sana Manneh.

The Worker: 6 Albion Place, POB 508, Banjul; publ. by the Gambia Labour Congress; Editor M. M. Ceesay.

NEWS AGENCIES

Gambia News Agency (GAMNA): Information Office, 14 Hagan St, Banjul; tel. 26621; telex 2308.

THE GAMBIA

Foreign Bureau

Agence France-Presse (AFP): 6 Allen St, POB 279/280, Banjul; tel. 28133; Correspondent DEYDA HYDARA.

Associated Press (USA) is also represented in The Gambia.

Publishers

Government Printer: MacCarthy Sq., Banjul; tel. 27399; telex 2204.

Inter Africa Press Inc: Banjul; Pres. PETER ENAHORO.

Radio and Television

There were an estimated 115,000 radio receivers in use in 1987. There is no national television service, but transmissions can be received from Senegal.

Radio Gambia: Mile 7, Banjul; tel. 95101; telex 2204; f. 1962; non-commercial govt service of information, education and entertainment; one transmitting station of two 10-kW transmitters broadcasting about 17 hours daily in English, Mandinka, Wolof, Fula, Jola, Serer and Serahuli; Dir MARCEL THOMASI.

Radio Syd: POB 279/280, Banjul; tel. 26490; commercial station broadcasting 20 hours a day, mainly music; programmes in English, French, Wolof, Mandinka, Fula, Jola and Serahuli; tourist information in Swedish; Dir CONSTANCE W. ENHÖRNING.

Finance

(cap. = capital; res = reserves; dep. = deposits; br. = branch; m. = million; amounts in dalasi unless otherwise stated)

BANKING

Central Bank

Central Bank of The Gambia: 1–2 Buckle St, Banjul; tel. 28103; telex 2218; fax 26969; f. 1971; bank of issue; cap. and res 10m., dep. 384m.; Gov. ABDOU A. B. NJIE; Gen. Man. EDWARD E. FILLINGHAM.

Other Banks

The Gambia Commercial and Development Bank: 3–4 Buckle St, POB 666, Banjul; tel. 28651; telex 2221; f. 1972; 52% state-owned; transfer to private-sector ownership pending in 1990; cap. and res 3.8m., dep. 136m. (1981); Chair. M. M. DIBBA; Man. Dir (vacant); 3 brs.

Standard Chartered Bank Gambia Ltd: 8 Buckle St, POB 259, Banjul; tel. 28681; telex 2210; fax 27714; f. 1978; 15% state-owned, 75% by Standard Chartered Bank of Africa; cap. and res 12.1m., dep. 146.3m. (Dec. 1989); Chair. HARRY LLOYD-EVANS; Man. Dir EDWARD G. BELL; 4 brs.

INSURANCE

Capital Insurance Co Ltd: 23 Anglesea St, Banjul; tel. 28544; telex 2320; fax 29219; f. 1986; Man. Dir MOMODOU M. TAAL.

The Gambia National Insurance Corporation: 6 Leman St, POB 750, Banjul; tel. 28412; telex 2268; f. 1979; Man. Dir (vacant).

Greater Alliance Insurance Co: 10 Cameron St, Banjul; tel. 27839; telex 2245; fax 26687; f. 1989.

Senegambia Insurance Co Ltd: 23 Buckle St, Banjul; tel. 28866; f. 1984; Man. Dir Alhaji BABOU CEESAY.

Trade and Industry

CHAMBER OF COMMERCE

Gambia Chamber of Commerce and Industry: 78 Wellington St, POB 33, Banjul; tel. 765; f. 1961; Exec. Sec. PIERRE W. F. N'JIE.

TRADE AND MARKETING ORGANIZATIONS

Gambia Produce Marketing Board: Marina Foreshore, Banjul; tel. 27572; telex 2205; fax 28037; state-controlled; Chair. M. M. JALLOW; Man. SAIKOU DARAMMEH.

National Trading Corporation of The Gambia Ltd (NTC): 1–3 Wellington St, POB 81, Banjul; tel. 28005; telex 2259; f. 1979; transfer to private ownership pending in 1990; Chair. and Man. Dir MOMODOU CHAM; 15 brs.

EMPLOYERS' ASSOCIATION

Gambia Employers' Association: POB 333, Banjul; f. 1961; Vice-Chair. G. MADI; Sec. P. W. F. N'JIE.

TRADE UNIONS

Gambia Labour Union: 6 Albion Place, POB 508, Banjul; tel. 641; f. 1935; 25,000 mems; Pres. B. B. KEBBEH; Gen. Sec. MOHAMED CEESAY.

Gambia Workers' Confederation: Banjul; f. 1958 as The Gambia Workers' Union, adopted present name in 1985; the govt withdrew recognition from the union 1977–85; Sec.-Gen. PA MODOU FALL.

The Gambia Trades Union Congress: POB 307, Banjul; Sec.-Gen. SAM THORPE.

Transport

RAILWAYS

There are no railways in The Gambia.

ROADS

In 1985 there were 2,358 km of roads in The Gambia. Of this total, 757 km were main roads, and 452 km were secondary roads. Some roads are impassable in the rainy season, as only 21% of the road network is paved. The South Bank Trunk Road links Banjul with the Trans-Gambian Highway, which intersects it at Mansakonko. The South Bank Trunk Road is bituminized as far as Basse, about 386 km from Banjul. The North Bank Trunk Road connects Barra with Georgetown. A major highways maintenance project was announced in 1986 and aimed to rehabilitate 1,250 km of roads. A road linking Banjul and Serrekunda was completed in early 1990. The construction of a road linking Lamin Koto with Passimas is being funded by the Arab Bank for Economic Development in Africa (BADEA), the Islamic Development Bank and the OPEC Fund for International Development.

Gambia Public Transport Corporation: POB 801, Banjul; tel. 92501; telex 2243; fax 92454; f. 1979; fleet of 50 buses; Chair. Alhaji A. J. SENGHORE; Man. Dir ISMAILLA CEESAY.

SHIPPING

The River Gambia is well suited to navigation. The port of Banjul receives about 300 ships annually, and there are intermittent sailings to and from North Africa, the Mediterranean and the Far East. A weekly river service is maintained between Banjul and Basse, 390 km above Banjul, and a ferry plies between Banjul and Barra. Construction of a barrage across the river at Balingho is planned. Small ocean-going vessels can reach Kaur, 190 km above Banjul, throughout the year.

Gambia Ferry Services Co Ltd: 36 Wellington St, POB 487, Banjul; tel. 27132; telex 2235; domestic and regional services.

Gambia Ports Authority: Wellington St, POB 617, Banjul; tel. 27266; telex 2235; fax 27268; administers Banjul port, which was substantially expanded in 1974; further improvements were completed in 1984; transfer to private ownership pending in 1990; Man. Dir Alhaji O. B. CHAM.

The Gambia Shipping Agencies Ltd: Wellington St, Banjul; tel. 27432; telex 2202; fax 27929; shipping agents and forwarders; Man. STEN C. HEDEMANN; 30 employees.

The Gambia River Basin Development Organization (Organisation de mise en valeur du fleuve Gambie), a joint project with Senegal, Guinea and Guinea-Bissau to develop the river and its basin, was founded in 1978 and is based in Dakar, Senegal (see p. 223).

Regular shipping services to Banjul are maintained by **Elder Dempster Agencies**. Other British and Scandinavian lines run occasional services. The Gambia is also served by **Nigerian National** and **Black Star** (Ghana) Lines.

CIVIL AVIATION

There is an international airport at Yundum, 27 km from Banjul. Facilities at Yundum have been upgraded by the US National Aeronautics and Space Administration (NASA), to enable the airport to serve as an emergency landing site for space shuttle vehicles.

Air-Gambia: 7–9 Cameron St, POB 432, Banjul; tel. 27824; telex 2255; fax 29354; f. 1990; weekly flights to London (UK) and Freetown (Sierra Leone); fleet of 1 Boeing DC-10.

Gambia Air Shuttle: 32–33 Buckle St, Banjul; tel. 26998; telex 2303; fax 26428; f. 1987; 60% owned by private Swedish interests,

40% by private Gambian interests; daily flights to Dakar (Senegal), twice-weekly flights to Guinea-Bissau, weekly flights to Bamako, Mopti and Tombouctou (Mali), Nouakchott (Mauritania) and Las Palmas de Gran Canaria; Chair. LENNART HESSELBERG; Man. Dir C. J. GARSTEN; fleet of 2 Vickers Viscount.

Gambia Airways: City Terminal, 68–69 Wellington St, POB 535, Banjul; tel. 26733; telex 2214; f. 1964; 60% state-owned, 40% owned by British Airways; operates regional service; sole handling agent at Yundum, sales agent; Man. Dir SALIFU M. JALLOW.

Tourism

In 1988/89, 112,381 tourists visited The Gambia. Tourists come mainly from the United Kingdom (54.4% of the total in 1988/89), Sweden, France and Germany. In 1987/88 there were 4,500 hotel beds in resort areas. A major expansion of facilities for tourists was under way in the late 1980s.

Ministry of Information and Tourism: The Quadrangle, Banjul; tel. 28496; telex 2204.

GERMANY

Introductory Survey

Location, Climate, Language, Religion, Flag, Capital

The Federal Republic of Germany, which was formally established in October 1990 upon the unification of the Federal Republic of Germany (FRG, West Germany) and the German Democratic Republic (GDR, East Germany), lies in the heart of Europe. Its neighbours to the west are the Netherlands, Belgium, Luxembourg and France, to the south Switzerland and Austria, to the east Czechoslovakia and Poland, and to the north Denmark. The climate is temperate, with an average annual temperature of 9°C (48°F), although there are considerable variations between the North German lowlands and the Bavarian Alps. The language is German. There is a small Sorbian-speaking minority (numbering about 100,000 people) in the territory formerly constituting the GDR. Almost all citizens of the former FRG profess Christianity, and adherents are about equally divided between Protestants and Roman Catholics. About 35% of the inhabitants of the former GDR are Protestants (mainly belonging to the Evangelical Church) and about 7% Roman Catholics (the remainder are non-adherents). The national flag (proportions 5 by 3) consists of three equal horizontal stripes, of black, red and gold. The capital is Berlin. The provisional seat of government is Bonn.

Recent History

After the defeat of the Third Reich in 1945, Germany was divided, according to the Berlin Agreement, into US, Soviet, British and French occupation zones. Berlin was similarly divided. The former German territories east of the Oder and Neisse rivers, with the city of Danzig, became part of Poland, while the northern part of East Prussia was transferred to the USSR. After the failure of negotiations to establish a unified German administration, the three Western-occupied zones were integrated economically in 1948. A provisional constitution, the Grundgesetz (Basic Law), came into force in the three zones (excluding Saarland) in May 1949. The first federal elections were held in August 1949, when the Christlich-Demokratische Union Deutschlands/Christlich-Soziale Union (CDU/CSU, Christian Democratic Union/Christian Social Union) and the Sozialdemokratische Partei Deutschlands (SPD, Social Democratic Party) emerged as the two largest political parties. The Federal Republic of Germany (FRG) was established on 21 September 1949, although its sovereignty was limited by the continuing Allied military occupation. The first President of the Republic was Theodor Heuss. In October 1949 the Soviet-occupied zone of Germany declared itself the German Democratic Republic (GDR), with the Soviet-occupied zone of Berlin as its capital. This left the remainder of Berlin, known as West Berlin, as an exclave of the FRG in GDR territory. Wilhelm Pieck and Otto Grotewohl were elected President and Prime Minister, respectively, of the GDR. These two men were joint Chairmen of the Sozialistische Einheitspartei Deutschlands (SED, Socialist Unity Party of Germany), which had been formed in April 1946 by the merger of the Communist Party and the Social Democratic Party in the Soviet zone. The USSR granted complete sovereignty to the GDR on 27 March 1954. Following the establishment of the FRG, the military occupation there was converted into a contractual defence relationship. The Paris Agreement of 1954 gave full sovereign status to the FRG from 5 May 1955, and also gave it membership of NATO. In 1957 the Bundestag (Federal Assembly) declared Berlin the capital of Germany, and the FRG continued to aim for a united Germany. Until such time, the FRG would not recognize the GDR as an independent state and the seat of the FRG Government was to be Bonn. Saarland, under French occupation, was reunited with the FRG administratively in 1957 and became economically incorporated in 1959.

In the immediate post-war period, the USSR compensated for a small part of its wartime losses with equipment, money and livestock from the Soviet zone. More than 200 industrial concerns became Soviet joint-stock companies and were returned, after reconstruction, to the GDR in 1953. Soviet policy also involved the creation of a communist economic and political system in the GDR. As early as 1945 the large agricultural estates were dissolved and nationalized. In July 1946 all large-scale industrial concerns became state-owned. The policy of nationalization was continued by the SED regime as the USSR gradually transferred control. The increasing 'Sovietization' of administrative and economic affairs, coupled with severe food shortages, led to uprisings and strikes in June 1953. These were forcibly suppressed by Soviet troops. In 1960 it was announced that 50% of those farms which remained outside state control were to be nationalized. This measure led to a sudden rush of refugees to West Berlin, which, in turn, was the main reason for the construction by GDR 'shock troops' of a wall between East and West Berlin in August 1961.

The first (local) elections in the GDR took place in September 1946, when the SED received 57.1% of the total votes, the Christlich-Demokratische Union Deutschlands (CDU, Christian Democratic Union of Germany) and the Liberal-Demokratische Partei Deutschlands (LDPD, Liberal Democratic Party of Germany), together 39.9% and others 3.0%. The composition of the National Front, a co-ordinating body formed in January 1950 for the various political parties and mass organizations, effectively gave the SED and its partners an overall majority. The SED continued to be the dominant political force and there was no visible relaxation in its harsh policy towards political and religious dissent.

Walter Ulbricht took office as Secretary-General (later restyled First Secretary) of the SED in 1950, and was Chairman of the Council of State (Head of State) from September 1960 until his death in August 1973. He had been replaced by Erich Honecker as First Secretary of the SED in May 1971. (This post was later restyled General Secretary.) In October 1976 Honecker was also named Chairman of the Council of State, replacing Willi Stoph, who was reappointed Chairman of the Council of Ministers, the post that he had held from 1964 to 1973.

Under the chancellorship of Dr Konrad Adenauer (1949–63) and the direction of his Economics Minister, Dr Ludwig Erhard, who succeeded Adenauer as Chancellor in 1963, the FRG rebuilt itself rapidly to become one of the most affluent and economically dynamic states of Europe, allying itself with the West, to avoid the threat of 'expansionist' communism, and becoming a founder member of the European Communities. Owing to the Government's insistence on reunification, maintaining that the 1937 borders of the Reich remained legally valid until the signing of a peace treaty by the government of a united Germany, the FRG became completely isolated from Eastern Europe. The CDU/CSU, which had formed the Government from 1949, ruled in coalition with the SPD from 1966 to 1969, under the chancellorship of Dr Kurt Kiesinger. After the general election of October 1969, a new coalition of the SPD and the Freie Demokratische Partei (FDP, Free Democratic Party) formed the Government, under the chancellorship of Willy Brandt, adopting a fresh policy towards Eastern Europe (Ostpolitik) and particularly towards the GDR. Following elections in November 1972, the SPD became, for the first time, the largest party in the Bundestag. Chancellor Brandt resigned in May 1974, after the discovery that his personal assistant had been a clandestine agent of the GDR, and was succeeded by Helmut Schmidt, hitherto the Minister of Finance. In the same month, Walter Scheel, Brandt's Vice-Chancellor and Minister for Foreign Affairs, was elected Federal President in place of Gustav Heinemann. A deteriorating economic situation was accompanied by a decline in the popularity of the Government and increasing tension between the coalition partners. In the general election of October 1976 the SPD lost its position as largest party in the Bundestag, but the SPD-FDP coalition retained a slender majority. Traditional partnerships between parties became less certain: the Bavarian CSU split from, and then rejoined, the CDU in 1976. In July

1979 Dr Karl Carstens of the CDU, President of the Bundestag, succeeded Scheel as President of the FRG.

In the general election of October 1980 the SPD-FDP coalition achieved a majority of 45 seats in the Bundestag. At local elections in 1981 and 1982, however, the coalition suffered severe set-backs and became increasingly unstable, while disputes over nuclear power, defence policy and economic measures continued to divide the parties. By September 1982 the two parties were disagreeing openly and the FDP eventually withdrew from the coalition, thus ending a 13-year partnership. On 1 October, after a 'constructive vote of no confidence', Schmidt was replaced as Chancellor by the CDU leader, Dr Helmut Kohl, and the FDP agreed to form a coalition with the CDU/CSU. This partnership was confirmed by the results of the general election held in March 1983, when the CDU/CSU substantially increased its share of votes cast, obtaining 48.8% of the total, while the SPD, led by Hans-Jochen Vogel after Helmut Schmidt's retirement, received only 38.8%. The environmentalist Green Party entered the Bundestag for the first time.

The Federal Government suffered a series of domestic crises in 1983 and 1984. There was disunity between the coalition partners over several questions of policy, while in November 1983 the deployment of US missiles in the FRG provoked a large-scale confrontation with the country's anti-nuclear movement. In May–June 1984 the Government was confronted by the first major industrial conflict since 1978, as trade union demands for a shorter working week led to a seven-week strike in the engineering and metal industry, which brought the country's production of motor cars almost to a standstill. In July Dr Richard von Weizsäcker, the former Governing Mayor of West Berlin, became Federal President, succeeding Dr Karl Carstens. At the next general election, held in January 1987, the CDU/CSU/FDP coalition returned to power, although with a reduced majority. In March Dr Kohl's reappointment as Chancellor was approved by the Bundestag, but he received only four more votes than the requisite absolute majority, the poorest result for any FRG Chancellor since 1949. At a CDU party congress, held in September 1989, Kohl was re-elected Chairman of the party. However, the fact that almost 20% of the delegates voted against his re-election provided evidence of increasing loss of support for Kohl within the party.

The Grundgesetz (the FRG's provisional Constitution, which was proclaimed in 1949) stipulated German unification as one of the FRG's principal goals. During 1970 representatives of the FRG and the GDR conducted formal discussions for the first time, and there was a significant increase in diplomatic contacts between the FRG and the other Communist countries of Europe. Treaties were signed with the USSR on the Renunciation of Force, and with Poland, recognizing the Oder-Neisse Line as the border between Germany (actually the GDR) and Poland. The FRG also renounced German claims to the eastern territories of the old Reich. Further negotiations between the FRG and the GDR, following a Quadripartite Agreement on West Berlin in September 1971, clarified the details of access rights to West Berlin and also allowed West Berliners to visit the GDR. In December 1972 the two states signed a Basic Treaty, agreeing to develop normal good-neighbourly relations with each other, on the basis of equality of rights, and to be guided by the United Nations Charter. In March 1974 a further agreement was signed in Bonn, implementing Article 8 of the Basic Treaty, to install Permanent Representative Missions in Bonn and East Berlin. As a result, many Western countries were able to establish diplomatic relations with the GDR. Meanwhile, the GDR and the FRG both joined the UN in September 1973.

In October 1980 inter-German relations deteriorated when the GDR Government increased the minimum exchange requirement for foreign visitors and renewed its old demands for recognition as an independent state. In December 1981, however, the first official meeting between the two countries' leaders for 11 years took place, when Chancellor Helmut Schmidt of the FRG travelled to the GDR for discussions with Honecker. In April 1983 Honecker cancelled a proposed visit to Bonn, following the death of three West Germans at a border checkpoint. The situation was further threatened by the deployment, in late 1983, of US nuclear missiles in the FRG, and by the subsequent siting of additional Soviet missiles in the GDR. Nevertheless, relations improved steadily under Chancellor Kohl, and in 1983–84 there was a series of meetings between East and West German politicians. In 1986 relations were again strained, when a large number of refugees, mainly from developing countries, were allowed by the GDR to cross into West Berlin. The issue was resolved in September, when the GDR agreed to restrict access for the refugees. In 1987, the 750th anniversary of the founding of Berlin, Eberhard Diepgen, the Governing Mayor of West Berlin, invited Honecker to attend celebrations in the western half of the city, and received a reciprocal invitation from Honecker to attend celebrations in East Berlin. The invitations gave rise to concern that acceptance by either might undermine the four-power status of Berlin, and both were declined. In September, however, Honecker made his first, and long-awaited, visit to the FRG. The Government of the FRG described this as a 'working' visit, rather than a state visit, since it did not wish to grant *de facto* recognition to the GDR as an independent state.

Relations between the two German states were affected dramatically as a result of the political upheavals which took place in the GDR in late 1989 and 1990. In the latter half of 1989 many thousands of disaffected GDR citizens emigrated illegally to the FRG, via Czechoslovakia, Poland and Hungary. Many of them had taken refuge in the FRG's embassies in those countries, as well as in its permanent mission in East Berlin. The exodus was accelerated by the Hungarian Government's decision, in early September 1989, to allow GDR citizens to leave Hungary without exit visas. As popular dissent increased in the GDR, an independent citizens' action group, New Forum (Neues Forum), was founded. Its declared aim was to serve as a platform for discussions on democratic reforms, justice and environmental issues. By late October more than 100,000 signatures had been collected for a petition supporting the foundation of New Forum.

In early October 1989 the GDR celebrated the 40th anniversary of its foundation. Following the official celebrations (which were attended by the Soviet leader, Mikhail Gorbachev), demonstrations were held in East Berlin. These were suppressed by the police. Civil unrest spread to other major towns: in Dresden a series of daily demonstrations, involving several thousand people, began, while in Leipzig weekly protest marches were organized, with the participation of as many as 120,000 people. The demonstrations attracted an increasing number of people, and intervention by the police eventually ceased. (It was later reported that a proposal to use the armed forces to suppress the demonstrations had been narrowly rejected in a vote by the SED Politburo.) In mid-October, as the political situation became increasingly troubled, Honecker resigned as General Secretary of the SED, Chairman of the Council of State and Chairman of the National Defence Council. While it was officially declared that he had relinquished his posts for health reasons, there was speculation that pressure had been applied by Gorbachev for the appointment of a more reformist leader in the GDR, consistent with the political changes taking place in other Eastern European countries. Honecker was replaced in all his posts by Egon Krenz, a member of the SED Politburo and the Secretary of the party's Central Committee for Security, Youth Affairs and Sport. Dialogue was initiated with members of New Forum (which was legalized in early November) and with church leaders, and there was a noticeable liberalization of the media. An amnesty was announced for all persons who had been imprisoned for attempting to leave the country without authorization, as well as for those who had been detained during the recent demonstrations. However, large-scale demonstrations, in support of demands for further reforms, continued in many towns throughout the GDR. As many as 300,000 people attended the weekly demonstrations in Leipzig in late October, and more than 500,000 took part in a rally in East Berlin in early November. On 7 November the entire membership of the Council of Ministers announced its resignation. Hans Modrow, a member of the Central Committee of the SED and the First Secretary of the SED for the Dresden area, was subsequently elected Chairman, replacing Willi Stoph. Modrow was widely regarded as an advocate of reform, and enjoyed considerable popular support. A new Council of Ministers, composed largely of SED members, was formed. The SED Politburo also resigned and was reorganized. The new Government pledged to introduce comprehensive political and economic reforms and to hold free elections in 1990. In an attempt to quell the growing unrest and the continuing exodus, the Government abolished restrictions on foreign travel for GDR citizens, and opened all border crossings to the FRG. During the weekend of 10–11 November 1989 an estimated 2m. GDR citizens crossed into West Berlin, and the GDR Government promptly began to dismantle sections of the wall dividing the city. Many new crossing points were opened along the GDR's border with the FRG.

In early December 1989 the Volkskammer (People's Chamber), the GDR's legislature, voted almost unanimously to delete from the Constitution the provisions guaranteeing the SED's leading role in society. Other radical measures that were taken included the establishment of a special commission to investigate cases of abuse of office, corruption and personal enrichment by members of the former leadership. Honecker and Stoph, among other senior figures in the former leadership, were expelled from the SED and placed under house arrest, pending legal proceedings. The mass demonstrations continued, prompted by revelations of high-level corruption and abuse of power by the state security service (Staatssicherheitsdienst, known colloquially as the Stasi—subsequently disbanded). As the internal situation became increasingly unstable, the entire Politburo and the Central Committee of the SED, including Krenz, resigned, and an interim working committee was established to manage the party's affairs. Krenz retained his office as Chairman of the Council of State, but was shortly afterwards replaced, on an acting basis, by Dr Manfred Gerlach, the Chairman of the LDPD. The SED then voted to replace the Politburo with an Executive Board, and the post of General Secretary with that of Chairman. Dr Gregor Gysi, a prominent defence lawyer who was sympathetic to the opposition, was elected Chairman of the SED (subsequently restyled the Party of Democratic Socialism, PDS). A series of round-table talks was initiated between the Government and members of the opposition, as well as church representatives. In February 1990 a new electoral law was adopted, which provided for proportional representation in the Volkskammer and permitted political associations, as well as parties, to present candidates at elections.

The first free legislative elections in the GDR were held on 18 March 1990, with the participation of more than 93% of the electorate. The Christian Democratic Union (CDU), which had received considerable financial and technical assistance from its sister party in the FRG, received 40.8% of the total votes cast, substantially more than had been anticipated. The newly re-established Social Democratic Party (SPD), which was also strongly supported by its counterpart in the FRG, obtained only 21.8% of the votes, despite predictions that it would win the election by a large majority. The PDS (the reformed successor of the SED) secured 16.4% of the total votes (although in East Berlin it won 30%). In early April a 'grand coalition' Government was formed, chaired by Lothar de Maizière, the leader of the CDU. The new Government comprised five parties—the CDU, the right-wing German Social Union and the Christian-orientated Democratic Departure (which together had campaigned in the elections as the Alliance for Germany), the SPD and the League of Free Democrats. The PDS was not represented. At local elections, held in May, the CDU's position as the dominant party in the GDR was reconfirmed.

Following the abolition by the GDR Government of all travel restrictions to the FRG, contact between Germans of both countries became freely possible at all levels. Inevitably, the issue of possible unification of the two German states emerged, particularly in the GDR, where large-scale demonstrations in favour of a united Germany were held in many parts of the country in late 1989 and early 1990. In late November 1989 Chancellor Kohl presented to the Bundestag a 10-point plan envisaging an eventual unification of the FRG and the GDR. He proposed that the first stage towards this objective should be the forming of 'confederative structures' by the two countries after legislative elections in the GDR, including a joint committee for permanent consultations, joint technical committees, and a joint parliamentary body. The plan received broad approval in the Bundestag. In order to allay the fears of neighbouring countries, Kohl stressed that an eventual unification would in no way affect the stability of the borders determined as a result of the Second World War, nor would it jeopardize the FRG's commitment to the establishment of the EEC's single European market in 1992. In December 1989 Chancellor Kohl made his first official visit to the GDR. During discussions with the GDR Prime Minister, Hans Modrow, it was agreed to establish joint economic, cultural and environmental commissions and to develop relations between the two countries at all levels. Chancellor Kohl also reiterated his plan for 'confederative structures' leading to eventual unification. The GDR leadership was initially insistent that the GDR should remain a sovereign, independent state. However, in February 1990, in response to the continuing exodus of GDR citizens to the FRG and the escalating demonstrations in favour of unification, Modrow publicly advocated the creation of a united Germany, proposing a four-point plan towards achieving this goal. Following discussions between Chancellor Kohl and President Gorbachev of the USSR in Moscow in mid-February, it was reported that the Soviet leader had endorsed the principle of unification, stating that the two German states should themselves decide the timing and form of an eventual unification, although within the framework of the Final Act adopted at Helsinki, Finland, in 1975 by the 35-nation Conference on Security and Co-operation in Europe (CSCE). Shortly afterwards, Kohl and Modrow held further consultations in Bonn, at which it was agreed to establish a joint commission to elaborate steps towards full economic and monetary union. There was disagreement, however, on the issue of membership of NATO by an eventually unified Germany. In late February the GDR Minister of National Defence, Adm. Theodor Hoffmann, proposed the creation of a joint army for a united Germany, which would be reduced to less than one-third of the combined size of the FRG's and the GDR's armed forces. He also suggested that the two countries should remain in their respective military alliances, pending further negotiations following the elections in the GDR. Later in the month, at a meeting in Camp David in the USA, Chancellor Kohl and the US President, George Bush, reaffirmed their commitment to Germany's full membership of NATO, following unification. They stressed, however, that the territory formerly constituting the GDR would initially enjoy a 'special military status', to protect the security interests of the USSR.

The new coalition Government of the GDR, formed in April 1990, pledged its determination to 'achieve the unity of Germany swiftly and responsibly for the whole of the GDR ... on the basis of Article 23 of the Grundgesetz' (the FRG's provisional Constitution). In early May the first round of the so-called 'two-plus-four' talks on German unification was held in Bonn, in accordance with a plan adopted in February 1990 by the Ministers of Foreign Affairs of 23 NATO and Warsaw Pact nations, at a meeting in Ottawa, Canada. Under the plan, it was agreed that the Ministers of Foreign Affairs of the two German states and of the four powers that occupied Germany following the Second World War—the USA, the USSR, the United Kingdom and France—would meet to 'discuss external aspects of the establishment of German unity, including the issues of security of the neighbouring states'. Three further sessions of the 'two-plus-four' talks were subsequently held—in June, July and September 1990. In mid-May the legislative bodies of the FRG and the GDR signed the Treaty Between the FRG and the GDR Establishing a Monetary, Economic and Social Union (this treaty came into force on 1 July). In late June the respective German legislatures approved a resolution recognizing the inviolability of Poland's borders as determined after the Second World War and confirming the Oder-Neisse rivers as the bilateral border between Poland and a future united Germany. (In November 1990 a treaty confirming this border was signed by the united Germany and Poland. A final treaty on good-neighbourliness and co-operation was expected to be ratified by the legislatures of the two countries by the end of February 1991.) At talks between Chancellor Kohl and President Gorbachev, meeting in the USSR in mid-July 1990, it was agreed that the united Germany would exercise full sovereignty, could decide freely to which military alliance it would belong, and was to reduce the strength of its armed forces to 370,000 within four years. The USSR pledged to withdraw its forces from GDR territory within the same period. Later in July the Volkskammer approved the re-establishment on GDR territory of the five Länder (states)—Brandenburg, Mecklenburg-Vorpommern (Mecklenburg-Western Pomerania), Sachsen (Saxony), Sachsen-Anhalt (Saxony-Anhalt) and Thüringen (Thuringia)—which had been abolished by the GDR Government after the Second World War and replaced by 14 Bezirke (districts).

On 31 August 1990, following disagreement between parties in both German states regarding the date and modalities of unification, a second state treaty, the Treaty between the FRG and the GDR on the Establishment of German Unity, was signed in East Berlin by officials of the respective Governments. This treaty stipulated, among other provisions, that the five newly re-established Länder in the GDR were to accede to the FRG on 3 October 1990, and that the 23 boroughs of East and West Berlin were to form jointly the Land (state) of Berlin. The capital of the united Germany (which would continue to be known as the Federal Republic of Germany) was to be Berlin, although the seat of government—Bonn or Berlin—was to be decided after unification. At the fourth and final session of the 'two-plus-four' talks, which was held in Moscow in early September, the Treaty on the Final Settlement with Respect to Germany, covering the external aspects of unification, was signed by the Ministers of Foreign Affairs of the participating countries. On the following day, a fourth treaty, on Good-neighbourliness, Partnership and Co-operation between the FRG and the USSR, was signed by officials of the respective countries. In late September the GDR Minister of Defence and Disarmament and the Commander-in-Chief of the Armed Forces of the Warsaw Pact concluded an agreement which provided for the GDR's immediate withdrawal from the Warsaw Pact. On 1 October, in New York, representatives of the four countries which occupied Germany after the Second World War signed a document in which Germany's full sovereignty was recognized. Finally, on 3 October, the two German states were formally unified. It was officially declared that the united Germany would be a full member of NATO. The area which had comprised the GDR was automatically integrated into the EEC (although only 80% of EEC legislation was to apply initially, pending economic and other adjustments in the area). The Bundestag (which had been expanded from 519 to 663 members, to permit the representation of deputies from the former GDR Volkskammer) met on 4 October, and adopted a new electoral law, which was to be valid only for the first all-German legislative elections, scheduled for 2 December 1990, and under which voting procedures would operate separately in the areas formerly constituting the FRG and the GDR. At the same session, five prominent politicians of the former GDR were sworn in as Ministers without Portfolio in the Federal Government. These included de Maizière, who had previously been elected to the post of Deputy Chairman of the united CDU (prior to unification, the CDU, the SPD and the FDP of the GDR had merged with their respective counterparts in the FRG to form three single parties).

At state elections in the five newly-acceded Länder, held on 14 October 1990, the CDU obtained an average of 41% of the total votes and won control of four Land legislatures. The SPD, which won an average of 27% of the total votes, secured a majority only in Brandenburg, where it formed a government in coalition with the FDP and with Alliance 90 (a group of opposition parties and movements, including the Green Party in eastern Germany and New Forum, which had been formed in early 1990 and had played a significant role in the democratic movement in the GDR). In Sachsen the Land government was formed solely from members of the CDU, which had won an absolute majority of votes cast there. In each of the remaining three Länder a coalition government of the CDU-FDP was established. As a result of the elections, the SPD lost its majority (which it had held since May 1990) in the Bundesrat (Federal Council), the second chamber of the national legislature, to the CDU-CSU-FDP coalition.

Elections to the Bundestag (the first all-German elections since 1933) were held on 2 December 1990, and confirmed the recent surge of support for Chancellor Kohl and the CDU. Together with the CSU (its sister party in Bayern—Bavaria), the CDU obtained 43.8% of the total votes and secured, as a result, a joint total of 319 seats in the new Bundestag (now with a total membership of 662). The SPD achieved its poorest result in a general election since 1957, receiving 33.5% of the votes and winning 239 seats in the legislature. Its failure to challenge the CDU/CSU was attributed, in large part, to the somewhat cautious stance on the issue of unification which it had adopted before and during the election campaign. (Following the elections, the SPD Chairman, Hans-Jochen Vogel, resigned, and was replaced by Björn Engholm, the Minister-President of Schleswig-Holstein.) With 11% of the votes, and consequently 79 seats in the Bundestag, the FDP achieved its most successful result in legislative elections since 1961. Its success, it was believed, was due to the widespread popularity of Hans-Dietrich Genscher, one of the party's most prominent members, and current Federal Minister for Foreign Affairs (a post which he had held since 1974). Unexpectedly, the Green Party (which had pioneered the environmental movement in Western Europe in the early 1980s) lost the 42 seats that it had previously held in the legislature, having failed to obtain the 5% of the votes cast in the area formerly constituting the FRG necessary for representation. However, as a result of a special clause incorporated in the electoral law (adopted in October 1990), which permitted representation in the Bundestag for parties of the former GDR that received at least 5% of the total votes cast there, the Green Party's East German counterpart, in coalition with Alliance 90, secured eight seats in the legislature. Under the same ruling, the PDS won 17 seats in the Bundestag (having obtained almost 10% of the votes cast in the area formerly constituting the GDR). State elections in Berlin (the first joint elections in the city since 1946) were held simultaneously with the general election. The CDU won the largest share of the votes (40%), despite widespread predictions of success for the SPD (which secured only 30%). The extreme right-wing Republican Party, which had been founded in the FRG in 1983, lost the 11 seats that it had won at elections in West Berlin in January 1989, and consequently was no longer represented in any of the Land legislatures. Both Green Parties (West and East) won seats. A coalition Senate (government) of CDU and SPD members was formed in Berlin (the only example of such a coalition in the 16 Länder).

In mid-January 1991 Dr Kohl was formally re-elected to the post of Federal Chancellor, immediately following the formation of the new Federal Government. This contained 20 members and included only three politicians from the former GDR. The FDP's representation was increased from four to five ministers, reflecting the party's success in the recent legislative elections. Hans-Dietrich Genscher retained his posts as Vice-Chancellor and Minister for Foreign Affairs. Other members of the outgoing Government who were reappointed included Wolfgang Schäuble, Theodor Waigel and Gerhard Stoltenberg, respectively the Ministers of the Interior, Finance and Defence. The new Government did not include Lothar de Maizière, who, in mid-December 1990, had resigned as Minister without Portfolio in the outgoing Government (and also as Deputy Chairman of the CDU), in response to allegations (subsequently disproved) that he had colluded with the Stasi in the past. Similar allegations had prompted the resignation or dismissal of many other former GDR politicians and members of the PDS, as investigations into the abuse of power by the SED regime were undertaken during 1990. In January 1991 the Berlin authorities suspended efforts to arrest Erich Honecker on charges of manslaughter (for the deaths of those who had been killed while attempting to escape from the GDR), owing to the severe ill health of the former GDR leader.

At state elections in Hessen (Hesse), held in late January 1991, the SPD received 40.8% of the total votes, while the CDU obtained 40.2%. Each party secured 46 seats in the Land parliament, while the Green Party and the FDP won 10 and eight seats, respectively. It was expected that the SPD would seek to re-establish a coalition government with the Green Party (such a coalition had been defeated by the CDU-FDP at the previous election, in 1987). The success of the SPD and the Green Party in the election was largely attributable to the pacifist policies advocated by both parties (in early 1991 there was widespread popular opposition in Germany to the Gulf War currently in progress—see below).

Owing to its geopolitical location at the dividing line between East and West Europe, and to the experiences of its recent history, Germany's policies as regards foreign relations are essentially in pursuit of peace. The fundamental objectives of its foreign policy are: the continuation of the process of European integration (the FRG was a founder member of the EEC), the maintenance and strengthening of NATO (which the FRG joined in 1955), support for (and co-operation with) developing countries, and the policy of détente with the East. Relations between the FRG and the USSR improved substantially during the 1980s, culminating in the signature, in September 1990, of a Treaty on Good-neighbourliness, Partnership and Co-operation. The treaty (which was to be valid for a period of 20 years) provided, inter alia, for economic, industrial and technical co-operation as well as regular consultations at ministerial level between the united Germany and the USSR, and also regulated the status and eventual withdrawal of Soviet troops stationed on the territory of the former GDR. In early 1991 mass demonstrations were held in many parts of Germany in protest at the war being waged in the Persian (Arabian) Gulf region, following Iraq's invasion and annexation of Kuwait in

GERMANY *Introductory Survey*

August 1990 (see chapter on Iraq). According to a public opinion poll conducted in January 1991, nearly 80% of Germans were opposed to the use of force against Iraq. The German Government supported the actions of the US-led allied forces in combat against Iraq as being 'justified', and in early 1991 contributed substantial amounts of financial and technical aid (totalling US $11,000m. by mid-February) to the allied war effort. Despite criticism from certain countries participating in the alliance, Germany reiterated its decision not to send troops to fight in the Gulf region (intervention of this kind, outside the NATO area, being prohibited by a provision incorporated in the Grundgesetz). However, in early January 1991 Germany deployed 18 Alpha fighter aircraft at the Erhaç air base in southern Turkey (a fellow member of NATO), to be used in the event of an Iraqi attack on the base. Germany also intended to send anti-aircraft missiles (with 600 soldiers to operate them) to help protect the Erhaç and one other air base in Turkey, should the need arise. By mid-February Germany was expected to have sent some 3,000 servicemen to Turkey and the Mediterranean region, in a purely peace-keeping capacity.

Government

Germany is composed of 16 Länder (states), each Land having its own constitution, legislature and government.

The country has a parliamentary regime, with a bicameral legislature. The Upper House is the Bundesrat (Federal Council), with 68 seats. Each Land has between three and six seats, depending on the size of its population. The term of office of Bundesrat members varies with Land election dates. The Lower House, and the country's main legislative organ, is the Bundestag (Federal Assembly), with 662 deputies, who are elected for four years by universal adult suffrage (using a mixed system of proportional representation and direct voting).

Executive authority rests with the Federal Government, led by the Federal Chancellor, who is elected by an absolute majority of the Bundestag and appoints the other Ministers. The Federal President is elected by a Federal Convention (Bundesversammlung) which meets only for this purpose and consists of the Bundestag and an equal number of members elected by Land parliaments. The President is a constitutional Head of State with little influence on government.

Each Land has its own legislative assembly, with the right to enact laws except on matters which are the exclusive right of the Federal Government, such as defence, foreign affairs and finance. Education, police, culture and environmental protection are in the control of the Länder. Local responsibility for the execution of Federal and Land laws is undertaken by the city boroughs and counties.

Defence

Germany is a member of NATO. Conscription, which came into force in the FRG (West Germany) in 1956, lasts for 15 months. In June 1990 the armed forces of the FRG totalled 469,000, including 204,500 conscripts. The strength of the army stood at 308,000, including 161,000 conscripts. The navy numbered 32,000 (including 7,000 conscripts), and there were 106,000 in the air force (36,500 conscripts). The remaining 23,000 were inter-service staff. Defence expenditure for 1990 was estimated at DM52,520m.

At German unification, the National People's Army of the former GDR was dissolved, and 50,000 of its members were incorporated into the German Bundeswehr (armed forces). According to a Soviet-German agreement, concluded in July 1990, Germany was to reduce the strength of its armed forces to 370,000 men within four years, and the USSR was to have withdrawn its 370,000 troops from the territory of the former GDR within the same period. In late 1990 the USA, the United Kingdom and France had approximately 400,000 troops stationed in Germany. Some 150,000 foreign military personnel in the territory of the former FRG (including 32,500 troops belonging to Belgium and the Netherlands) were to be withdrawn in the early 1990s.

Economic Affairs of the Former GDR

In 1988, according to Western estimates, the GDR's gross national product (GNP) was US $207,000m., equivalent to about $12,400 per head. In 1989 net material product (NMP), measured at 1985 prices, was estimated to be 273,670m. DDR-Marks. In that year NMP increased by just over 2%, compared with the previous year. During 1980–89 the population decreased by an annual average of 0.1%.

Agriculture (including forestry) provided an estimated 10.0% of NMP in 1989. In that year about 11% of the working population were employed in the sector. The principal crops were potatoes, sugar beet, barley and wheat. The economic importance of agriculture entered a decline in the 1980s. In 1988 agricultural production decreased by about 4%.

Industry (including construction, fishing and handicrafts) contributed 72.1% of NMP in 1989, according to provisional figures. In that year the industrial sector employed about 44% of the working population. In terms of production, the GDR was one of the world's leading industrial nations in the 1980s. In 1988 industrial production increased by 3.7%. However, as the GDR's economy entered a severe decline, industrial production decreased, between August 1989 and August 1990, by an estimated 50%. The main branches of the manufacturing sector were chemical products (which in the late 1980s accounted for about 20% of national industrial output), textiles and metal products.

The GDR's only major mineral resource was lignite, a low-grade form of brown coal. In 1989 about 301m. metric tons of lignite were extracted. Copper ore, potash salts, tin ore and nickel ore were also mined.

The GDR's most important source of energy was lignite. In 1990 about 85% of the national demand for electricity was fulfilled by lignite. Nuclear power accounted for 10.9% of total electricity generation in 1989. Most of the GDR's domestic petroleum requirements were supplied by pipeline from the USSR.

In 1989 the GDR recorded a visible trade deficit of 3,614.2m. DDR-Marks (in foreign currency equivalent). In that year there was a deficit of US $2,400m. on the current account of the balance of payments. In 1989 about 66% of GDR trade was with other member states of the CMEA (see p. 125). The USSR was traditionally the GDR's major trading partner (accounting for about 23% of total trade—imports plus exports—in 1989). The FRG was the most important trading partner outside the CMEA and accounted for 21% of total trade in 1989. The principal imports in 1989 were machinery and transport equipment, basic manufactures and mineral fuels. The principal exports were machinery and transport equipment, basic manufactures and chemical products.

In the 1989 state budget, revenue was envisaged at 301,521.0m. DDR-Marks and expenditure at 301,365.6m. The GDR's net external debt in convertible currencies was estimated to be between US $7,000m. and $9,000m. in 1989. In that year, according to official sources, the average annual rate of inflation was 0%. In late August 1990 an estimated 350,000 people (equivalent to about 4% of the labour force) were unemployed.

The GDR was a member of the CMEA, the International Bank for Economic Co-operation (see p. 160) and the International Investment Bank (see p. 165). A number of agreements on economic co-operation existed between the GDR and the FRG. In its trade with the FRG, the GDR benefited from a system of 'swing' loans, which provided the country with interest-free credit from the FRG.

Economic Affairs of the Former FRG

In 1989, according to estimates by the World Bank, the FRG's gross national product (GNP), measured at average 1987–89 prices, was US $1,272,959m., equivalent to $20,750 per head. During 1980–89, it was estimated, GNP increased, in real terms, at an average annual rate of 2.0%, while GNP per head increased by 2.1% per year. During 1980–89 the population decreased by an annual average of 0.1%. The FRG's gross domestic product (GDP) increased, in real terms, by an annual average of 1.8% in 1980–88.

Agriculture (including forestry and fishing) contributed 1.7% of GDP, and employed 3.8% of the working population, in 1989. The principal cash crops were potatoes, sugar beet, wheat and barley. Wine production was also important. During 1980–88 agricultural production increased by an annual average of 1.9%.

Industry (including mining, power, manufacturing and construction) contributed 40.8% of GDP in 1989, when 41% of the working population were employed in industrial activity. During 1980–88 industrial production increased by an annual average of 0.4%.

Mining and power contributed 3.3% of GDP in 1989. In that year mining and quarrying employed just over 1% of the working population. Hard coal, lignite and salt were the most important mineral deposits. In 1989 about 1% of the working

GERMANY

population were employed in power (electricity, gas and water). The Government sought to increase the contribution of nuclear energy to total electricity output (in 1988 it provided almost 40%). In 1987 about one-third of the natural gas consumed in the FRG was supplied from local sources.

Manufacturing contributed over 32% of GDP in 1989, when 32% of the working population were employed in the sector. The most important branches of manufacturing were mechanical engineering, electrical engineering and electronics, vehicles, chemicals, and food-processing. In 1989 the FRG was the world's third largest producer of cars. During 1980–88 production in the manufacturing sector increased by an annual average of 1.0%.

In 1989 the FRG recorded a visible trade surplus of US $76,660m. and there was an estimated surplus of US $55,430m. on the current account of the balance of payments. In 1989 the FRG was among the world's largest exporters in US dollar terms. In that year the principal market for exports (13.2%) was France, which was also the principal source of imports (11.9%). The other EEC countries were important trading partners (in 1988 around 53% of the FRG's trade was conducted with the EEC). The principal exports in 1989 were machinery and transport equipment (accounting for 48.6% of total exports), basic manufactures and chemical products. The major imports were chemicals, electrical products, motor vehicles, farm and forest products, and mining products.

In 1989 there was an estimated budgetary deficit of DM 26,639m. (equivalent to around 1.2% of GDP). The average annual rate of inflation was 2.7% in 1990. In October 1990 an estimated 6.5% of the labour force were unemployed.

The FRG was a founder member of the EEC (see p. 135). It traditionally allotted substantial amounts of financial aid annually to developing countries, in particular through the specialized agencies of the UN, the World Bank and its subsidiaries, and the EEC.

Economic Affairs of Germany

After the destruction caused by the Second World War, the FRG made a remarkable economic recovery which was sustained over a number of years (the so-called 'Wirtschaftswunder', or economic miracle). By October 1990, when German unification was achieved, the FRG was among the world's largest exporters in US dollar terms, and its economy was one of the strongest in the world. By comparison, the economy of the GDR, following 40 years of communist-style command economy, was in a state of severe decline. Following economic, monetary and social union, which took effect in July 1990, all the economically relevant laws of the FRG were introduced in the GDR, and an extensive process of renewal was undertaken. It was anticipated that a long period of adjustment would need to elapse before the enormous economic differences between the eastern and western parts of Germany, in particular the disparity in levels of salaries and standards of living, might be eliminated.

In March 1990 the Treuhandanstalt (trustee agency) was created by the FRG Government to supervise the transfer to private ownership of the approximately 8,000 state-owned enterprises in the GDR. By February 1991, however, only 600 of these had been privatized (the majority having been acquired by companies operating in the former FRG), and it was expected that more than three-quarters of the total would be liquidated. One of the German Government's most pressing economic problems is the level of unemployment in the Länder formerly constituting the GDR. By January 1991 this had reached 757,200 (8.6% of the labour force in eastern Germany). At the same time, a further 1.8m. people were in short-time employment, and in early 1991 unemployment in eastern Germany increased at an average rate of 11,000 people per day. It was estimated that some 350,000 East Germans had resettled in western Germany in the latter half of 1990, while a further 200,000 commuted to work there. Conversely, in January 1991, the level of unemployment in western Germany had fallen to 6.4% (compared with 7.5% in January 1990), despite the influx during 1990 of more than 1m. immigrants and refugees, mainly from Eastern Europe and the GDR. In 1990, it was reported, gross national product (GNP) in the former FRG increased, in real terms, by 4.6%, compared with 1989, the highest rate of growth recorded since 1976. This was attributed largely to the enormous surge in domestic demand, particularly in eastern Germany, following economic and monetary union. In 1990 (including the former GDR for the second half of the year) Germany recorded a surplus of DM 75,500m. on the current account of the balance of payments.

Social Welfare

Social legislation has established comprehensive insurance cover for sickness, accidents, retirement, disability and unemployment. The insurance schemes for disability, retirement and unemployment are compulsory for all employees, and, in the former FRG, more than 80% of the population was covered. Insurance is administered by autonomous regional and local organizations. Pensions are the highest in Europe; the amount is based on contributions paid, is related to national average earnings and regularly adjusted. Sickness insurance pays for all medical attention and provides a benefit of 85% to 90% of the normal wage. The Treaty between the FRG and the GDR Establishing a Monetary, Economic and Social Union, signed in May 1990, envisaged the gradual adoption in the territory of the former GDR of the systems of social, unemployment, pension and health insurance, in operation in the FRG.

In 1991 there were approximately 3,540 hospitals in Germany (3,070 and 470, respectively, in the territory of the former FRG and GDR).

Education

The Basic Law gives the control of education entirely to the Land governments. They do, however, co-operate quite closely to ensure a large degree of conformity in the system. Education is compulsory for children aged six to 18 years. At least nine years of education must be full-time. Primary education is free, and grants are made for secondary education wherever fees are payable. Attendance at the Grundschule (elementary school) is obligatory for all children during the first four years of their school life, after which they go on to one of three other types of school. Approximately one-half of this age-group attend the Hauptschule (general school) for five or six years, after which they go into employment, but continue their education part-time for three years at a vocational school. Alternatively, pupils may attend the Realschule (intermediate school) for six years, or the Gymnasium (grammar school) for nine years. The Abitur (grammar school leaving certificate) is a necessary prerequisite for university education. In 1988 the total enrolment at primary and secondary schools in the FRG was equivalent to 100% of the school-age population, while the comparable ratio in the GDR was 87%.

Following German unification, a radical restructuring of the education system in the former GDR was undertaken, in an attempt to standardize it with the system in operation in the rest of Germany. The Unification Treaty guaranteed that school, vocational or higher education certificates or degrees obtained or officially recognized in the GDR would continue to be valid in the united Germany.

Public Holidays

1991: 1 January (New Year's Day), 6 January (Epiphany)*, 29 March (Good Friday), 1 April (Easter Monday), 1 May (Labour Day), 9 May (Ascension Day), 20 May (Whit Monday), 30 May (Corpus Christi)*, 15 August (Assumption)*, 3 October (Day of Unity), 1 November (All Saints' Day)*, 20 November (Day of Prayer and Repentance), 25–26 December (Christmas).

1992: 1 January (New Year's Day), 6 January (Epiphany)*, 17 April (Good Friday), 20 April (Easter Monday), 1 May (Labour Day), 28 May (Ascension Day), 8 June (Whit Monday), 18 June (Corpus Christi)*, 15 August (Assumption)*, 3 October (Day of Unity), 1 November (All Saints' Day)*, 18 November (Day of Prayer and Repentance), 25–26 December (Christmas).

* Religious holidays observed in certain Länder only.

Weights and Measures

The metric system is in force.

GERMANY

Statistical Survey

Source: Statistisches Bundesamt, 6200 Wiesbaden 1, Gustav-Stresemann-Ring 11, Postfach 5528; tel. (0611) 75-1; telex 4186511; fax (0611) 753425.

Area and Population

AREA, POPULATION AND DENSITY (31 December 1989)

Area (sq km)	356,945*
Population†	79,070,000
Density (per sq km)†	221.5

* 137,817 sq miles. † Provisional figures.

STATES

	Area (sq km)	Population ('000) at 31 Dec. 1989	Density (per sq km)	Capital
Baden-Württemberg	35,751	9,619	269	Stuttgart
Bayern (Bavaria)	70,554	11,221	159	München
Berlin	883	3,410	3,862	Berlin
Brandenburg	29,059	2,641	91	Potsdam
Bremen	404	674*	1,668*	Bremen
Hamburg	755	1,626	2,154	Hamburg
Hessen (Hesse)	21,114	5,661	268	Wiesbaden
Mecklenburg-Vorpommern (Mecklenburg-Western Pomerania)	23,838	1,964	82	Schwerin
Niedersachsen (Lower Saxony)	47,344	7,238†	153†	Hannover
Nordrhein-Westfalen (North Rhine-Westphalia)	34,070	17,104	502	Düsseldorf
Rheinland-Pfalz (Rhineland-Palatinate)	19,849	3,702	186	Mainz
Saarland	2,570	1,065*	414*	Saarbrücken
Sachsen (Saxony)	18,337	4,901	267	Dresden
Sachsen-Anhalt (Saxony-Anhalt)	20,445	2,965	145	Magdeburg
Schleswig-Holstein	15,729	2,595	165	Kiel
Thüringen (Thuringia)	16,251	2,684	165	Erfurt
Total	356,945	79,070*	222*	—

* Provisional figures.   † At 30 September 1989.

Statistical Survey of the Former German Democratic Republic

Source (unless otherwise stated): *Statistisches Jahrbuch 1990 der DDR*.

Area and Population

AREA, POPULATION AND DENSITY

Area (sq km)	108,333*
Population (census results)	
1 January 1971	17,068,318
31 December 1981	
Males	7,849,112
Females	8,856,523
Total	16,705,635
Population (official estimates at 31 December)	
1987	16,661,423
1988	16,674,632
1989	16,433,796
Density (per sq km) at 31 December 1989	151.7

* 41,828 sq miles.

DISTRICTS (each district is named after its capital)

	Area (sq km)	Population at 31 December 1989 ('000)			Density (per sq km)
		Male	Female	Total	
Berlin (city)	403	608.9	670.3	1,279.2	3,174
Cottbus	8,262	426.1	449.5	875.6	106
Dresden	6,738	812.0	901.1	1,713.1	254
Erfurt	7,349	586.5	636.4	1,222.9	166
Frankfurt (a.d. Oder)	7,186	344.9	361.2	706.1	98
Gera	4,004	347.9	380.1	728.1	182
Halle (a.d. Saale)	8,771	836.5	911.5	1,748.0	199
Karl-Marx-Stadt (Chemnitz)	6,009	853.5	964.0	1,817.5	302
Leipzig	4,966	631.1	702.0	1,333.1	268
Magdeburg	11,526	594.5	643.4	1,237.9	107
Neubrandenburg	10,948	301.2	314.6	615.8	56
Potsdam	12,568	537.3	573.9	1,111.2	88
Rostock	7,075	444.7	465.1	909.8	129
Schwerin	8,672	285.8	304.4	590.2	68
Suhl	3,856	262.3	283.0	545.3	141
Total	108,333	7,873.3	8,560.5	16,433.8	152

PRINCIPAL TOWNS (estimated population at 31 December 1989)

East Berlin (capital)	1,279,212	Erfurt	217,035	
Leipzig	530,010	Potsdam	141,430	
Dresden	501,417	Gera	132,257	
Karl-Marx-Stadt*	301,918	Schwerin	129,492	
Magdeburg	288,355	Cottbus	128,943	
Rostock	252,956	Zwickau	118,914	
Halle an der Saale	230,728	Jena	105,825	
		Dessau	101,262	

* The town's former name, Chemnitz, was restored in April 1990.

BIRTHS, MARRIAGES AND DEATHS

	Registered live births		Registered marriages		Registered deaths	
	Number	Rate (per 1,000)	Number	Rate (per 1,000)	Number	Rate (per 1,000)
1982	240,102	14.4	124,890	7.5	227,975	13.7
1983	233,756	14.0	125,429	7.5	222,695	13.3
1984	228,135	13.7	133,900	8.0	221,181	13.3
1985	227,648	13.7	131,514	7.9	225,353	13.5
1986	222,269	13.4	137,208	8.3	223,536	13.4
1987	225,959	13.6	141,283	8.5	213,872	12.9
1988	215,734	12.9	137,165	8.2	213,111	12.8
1989	198,922	12.0	130,989	7.9	205,711	12.4

Life expectancy (years at birth, 1987): Males 69.84; Females 75.92.

EMPLOYMENT ('000 persons at 30 September each year)*

	1987	1988	1989
Industry†	3,479.4	3,482.5	3,186.9
Agriculture and forestry	928.5	928.2	923.5
Construction	568.9	566.6	559.9
Commerce	881.0	883.2	876.8
Transport and communications	632.7	636.0	639.1
Others	2,080.2	2,097.9	2,094.6
Total	8,570.7	8,594.4	8,547.3
Males	4,370.3	4,390.5	4,369.7
Females	4,200.3	4,203.9	4,177.7

* Excluding apprentices, numbering (at 30 September each year): 383,700 in 1987; 385,300 in 1988; 338,500 in 1989.
† Including fishing and handicraft.

Agriculture

PRINCIPAL CROPS ('000 metric tons)

	1987	1988	1989
Wheat	4,040	3,699	3,477
Rye	2,283	1,785	2,103
Barley	4,198	3,798	4,683
Oats	637	507	476
Sugar beet	7,683	4,625	6,220
Potatoes	12,228	11,546	9,167
Pulses	90	86	88
Rapeseed	366	424	419
Carrots†	377	237	277
Onions (dry)‡	117	102	106
Tomatoes‡	52	70	79
Cabbages†	443	411	415
Cauliflowers†	148	148	148
Green beans†	35	34	30
Green peas†	21	20	21
Cucumbers and gherkins‡	65	72	71
Apples‡	516	697	757
Pears‡	51	77	84
Plums‡	31	161	39
Currants‡	37	32	33
Strawberries‡	37	28	31

† Production from socialist enterprises only.
‡ Source: FAO, *Production Yearbook*.

GERMANY   Statistical Survey

LIVESTOCK ('000 head recorded at December)

	1987	1988	1989
Cattle	5,721	5,710	5,724
Pigs	12,503	12,464	12,013
Sheep	2,656	2,634	2,603
Goats	19	19	19
Horses	104	102	100
Poultry	50,719	49,430	49,270
Beehives	531	506	468

LIVESTOCK PRODUCTS ('000 metric tons)

	1987	1988	1989
Beef and veal	445*	438*	420†
Mutton and lamb	18*	22*	23†
Pig meat*	1,357	1,360	1,368
Poultry meat	160*	161*	159†
Other meat	17	16	17
Edible offals	102	101	102
Cows' milk	9,235	9,204	9,300*
Goats' milk†	17	15	15
Butter	309.9	305.8	315.0*
Cheese	263.7	272.5	274.3
Condensed and evaporated milk†	133.6	134.4	136.8
Dried milk	171	173	173†
Hen eggs	335.1	335.0*	333.0†
Honey	6.5	6.2	6.3†
Wool (clean)	8.3	8.3	8.0*
Cattle hides and calf skins†	52.3	52.0	52.3
Sheep skins†	1.7	2.0	2.0

* Unofficial figure.   † FAO estimate.

Source: FAO, *Production Yearbook* and *Quarterly Bulletin of Statistics*.

Forestry

ROUNDWOOD REMOVALS
('000 cubic metres, excluding private consumption)

	1986	1987	1988
Industrial wood	10,115	10,121	10,164
Fuel wood	710	710*	710*
Total	10,825	10,831	10,874

* FAO estimate.

Source: FAO, *Yearbook of Forest Products*.

SAWNWOOD PRODUCTION ('000 cubic metres)

	1986	1987	1988
Coniferous (softwood)	1,832	1,876	1,900
Broadleaved (hardwood)	502	468	468*
Total	2,334	2,344	2,368

* FAO estimate.

Railway sleepers ('000 cubic metres): 97 in 1986; 121 in 1987; 121 in 1988.

Source: FAO, *Yearbook of Forest Products*.

Fishing
('000 metric tons, live weight)

	1986	1987	1988
Common carp	13.1	12.8	14.0
Rainbow trout	6.9	7.7	7.0
Atlantic redfishes	10.6	8.5	18.5
Jack and horse mackerels	62.5	47.4	23.6
Atlantic herring	53.1	50.0	53.5
Sardinellas	1.8	8.4	0.7
Atlantic mackerel	18.9	18.7	21.6
Other fishes	39.9	38.6	30.5
Total fish	206.9	192.2	169.3
Crustaceans	1.0	0.7	0.7
Argentine shortfin squid	3.9	3.5	9.2
Other molluscs	0.2	0.0	0.0
Total catch	211.9	196.5	179.2
Inland waters	22.7	23.0	20.8
Atlantic Ocean	188.3	172.7	157.8
Indian Ocean	1.0	0.7	0.7

Source: FAO, *Yearbook of Fishery Statistics*.

Mining
('000 metric tons, unless otherwise indicated)

	1985	1986	1987
Brown coal (incl. lignite)[1]	312,156	311,260	308,976
Copper ore (metric tons)[2,3]	12,000	13,000	13,000
Tin ore (metric tons)[2,4]	2,200	1,600	1,800
Nickel ore (metric tons)[2,3]	2,000	1,670	1,690
Salt (unrefined)	5,104	5,212	6,083
Potash salts (crude)[5]	3,465	3,485	3,510
Sulphur[6,7]	109	117	110
Silver (metric tons)[7]	41	41	37
Natural gas (million cu m.)[8]	7,650	7,350	7,550
Crude petroleum	40	39	41

[1] Gross weight.
[2] Figures refer to the metal content of ores.
[3] Estimated production (Source: Metallgesellschaft Aktiengesellschaft, Frankfurt am Main).
[4] Estimated production (Source: *World Metal Statistics*).
[5] Figures refer to the K_2O content or equivalent of potash salts mined.
[6] Figures refer to sulphur recovered as by-products in the purification of coal-gas, petroleum refineries, gas plants and from copper, lead and zinc sulphide ores.
[7] Estimated production (Source: Bureau of Mines, US Department of the Interior).
[8] Net calorific value 3,120 kilocalories per cubic metre.

Source: mainly UN, *Industrial Statistics Yearbook*.

1988 ('000 metric tons): Brown coal 310,314; Potash salts 3,510.
1989 ('000 metric tons): Brown coal 301,058; Potash salts 3,200.

Industry

SELECTED PRODUCTS
('000 metric tons, unless otherwise indicated)

	1987	1988	1989
Flour[1]	1,391.5	1,407.4	1,373.0
Refined sugar	894.8	791.3	736.6
Margarine	177.9	179.6	171.6
Spirits ('000 hectolitres)	2,712.2	2,765.7	2,717.4
Beer ('000 hectolitres)	24,128	24,521	24,843
Non-alcoholic beverages ('000 hectolitres)	15,534	16,741	17,611

GERMANY

SHIPPING
Inland Waterways (traffic)

	1987	1988	1989
Passenger journeys (million)	7	8	7
Passenger-km (million)	188	206	189
Freight ton-km (million)	2,361	2,532	2,286

Merchant Fleet (at 31 December)

	1987	1988	1989
Number of ships	170	164	163
Displacement (grt)	1,332,181	1,313,556	1,292,718

International Sea-borne Freight Traffic ('000 metric tons)

	1987	1988	1989
Goods loaded and unloaded	24,805	25,515	25,144

CIVIL AVIATION (traffic)

	1987	1988	1989
Kilometres flown ('000)	37,166	39,437	38,054
Passengers carried	1,506,000	1,582,000	1,616,000
Passenger-km ('000)	2,846,000	3,229,000	3,324,000
Freight ton-km ('000)*	78,805	92,171	87,055

* Figures refer to both cargo and mail.

Tourism

FOREIGN TOURIST ARRIVALS*

Country of Origin	1987	1988	1989
Bulgaria	13,277	20,433	20,951
Czechoslovakia	122,264	141,738	121,510
Hungary	17,977	16,168	18,805
Poland	68,440	56,972	35,052
USSR	125,908	130,839	116,387
Total (incl. others)	674,481	705,588	662,585

* Figures refer only to holidays and short visits arranged by the State Travel Bureau, excluding excursionists (447,256 in 1987; 503,839 in 1988; 468,872 in 1989).

Tourist arrivals from the Federal Republic of Germany and West Berlin: 227,158 in 1988; 271,885 in 1989.

Communications Media

	1987	1988	1989
Radio licences	6,758,000	6,781,000	6,729,000
Television licences	6,199,000	6,233,000	6,201,000
Telephones in use	3,875,000	3,977,000	4,087,000
Book production: titles	6,572	6,590	6,093
Newspapers and magazines:			
Number	542	542	543
Circulation (total, million)	285.1	288.3	289.0

Education

(1989)

	Institutions	Students
Infant schools	13,452	747,140
General polytechnic schools	5,226	1,986,314
Extended polytechnic schools and special schools	702	103,240
Vocational schools	951	314,234
Technical schools	234	152,700
Universities (incl. technical)	54	131,188

Statistical Survey of the Former Federal Republic of Germany

Source (unless otherwise stated): Statistisches Bundesamt, 6200 Wiesbaden 1, Gustav-Stresemann-Ring 11, Postfach 5528; tel. (0611) 75-1; telex 4186511; fax (0611) 753425.
(All statistical data relate to the Federal Republic of Germany, including West Berlin, except where indicated.)

Area and Population

AREA, POPULATION AND DENSITY

Area (sq km)	248,628*
Population (census results)	
27 May 1970	60,650,599
25 May 1987	
Males	29,322,923
Females	31,754,119
Total	61,077,042
Population (official estimates at 31 December)	
1987	61,238,079
1988	61,715,103
1989	62,679,035
Density (per sq km) at 31 December 1989	252.1

* 95,996 sq miles.

PRINCIPAL TOWNS (estimated population at 31 December 1989)

Town	Pop.	Town	Pop.
West Berlin	2,130,525	Wiesbaden	256,885
Hamburg	1,626,220	Braunschweig (Brunswick)	256,323
München (Munich)	1,206,683	Mönchengladbach	255,905
Köln (Cologne)	946,280	Münster	253,123
Frankfurt am Main	635,151	Augsburg	250,197
Essen	624,445	Kiel	243,579
Dortmund	594,058	Krefeld	240,208
Düsseldorf	574,022	Aachen (Aix-la-Chapelle)	236,987
Stuttgart	570,699	Oberhausen	222,419
Bremen	544,327	Lübeck	212,932
Duisburg	532,152	Hagen	212,460
Hannover (Hanover)	505,872	Kassel	191,598
Nürnberg (Nuremberg)	485,717	Saarbrücken	190,466
Bochum	393,053	Freiburg im Breisgau	187,767
Wuppertal	378,312	Hamm	179,109
Bielefeld	315,096	Mainz	177,062
Mannheim	305,974	Herne	176,472
Gelsenkirchen	289,791	Mülheim an der Ruhr	176,149
Bonn (capital)	287,117		
Karlsruhe	270,659		

STATES (31 December 1989)

	Area (sq km)	Population ('000)	Density (per sq km)	Capital	Population of capital ('000)
Schleswig-Holstein	15,730.5	2,594.6	165	Kiel	243.6
Hamburg	755.3	1,626.2	2,153	Hamburg	1,626.2
Niedersachsen (Lower Saxony)	47,348.7	7,283.8	154	Hannover (Hanover)	505.9
Bremen	404.2	673.7	1,667	Bremen	544.3
Nordrhein-Westfalen (North Rhine-Westphalia)	34,071.1	17,103.6	502	Düsseldorf	574.0
Hessen (Hesse)	21,114.2	5,660.6	268	Wiesbaden	256.9
Rheinland-Pfalz (Rhineland-Palatinate)	19,848.8	3,701.7	186	Mainz	177.1
Baden-Württemberg	35,751.4	9,618.7	269	Stuttgart	570.7
Bayern (Bavaria)	70,553.9	11,220.7	159	München (Munich)	1,206.7
Saarland	2,570.2	1,064.9	414	Saarbrücken	190.5
West Berlin	480.2	2,130.5	4,437	West Berlin	2,130.5
Total	248,628.4	62,679.0	252	Bonn	287.1

BIRTHS, MARRIAGES AND DEATHS (Federal Republic)

	Registered live births		Registered marriages		Registered deaths	
	Number	Rate (per 1,000)	Number	Rate (per 1,000)	Number	Rate (per 1,000)
1982	621,173	10.1	361,966	5.9	715,857	11.6
1983	594,177	9.7	369,963	6.0	718,337	11.7
1984	584,157	9.5	364,140	5.9	696,118	11.3
1985	586,155	9.6	364,661	6.0	704,296	11.5
1986	625,963	10.3	372,112	6.1	701,890	11.5
1987	642,010	10.5	382,564	6.3	687,419	11.2
1988	677,259	11.0	397,738	6.5	687,516	11.2
1989*	681,537	11.0	397,639	6.4	697,730	11.3

* Provisional figures.

EMPLOYMENT (civilian labour force employed, '000 persons aged 15 years and over)

	1987	1988	1989
Agriculture, hunting, forestry and fishing	1,180	1,155	1,039
Mining and quarrying	286	277	360
Manufacturing	8,574	8,662	8,754
Electricity, gas and water	269	265	270
Construction	1,739	1,843	1,849
Trade, restaurants and hotels	4,038	4,014	4,093
Transport, storage and communications	1,550	1,556	1,573
Financing, insurance, real estate and business services	2,038	2,057	2,181
Community, social and personal services	6,877	7,012	7,199
Total	26,550	26,841	27,216
Males	16,045	16,234	16,422
Females	10,505	10,607	10,794

GERMANY

Agriculture

PRINCIPAL CROPS ('000 metric tons)

	1987	1988	1989
Wheat	9,932	11,922	11,032
Rye	1,599	1,579	1,797
Barley	8,571	9,587	9,717
Oats	2,008	2,039	1,534
Maize	1,217	1,535	1,573
Mixed grain	444	449	460
Sugar beets*	19,049	18,590	20,767
Potatoes	6,836	7,434	7,451
Rapeseed	1,265	1,216	1,450
Cabbages	430	575	527
Carrots	139	167	198
Grapes†	1,280	1,450§	1,450§
Apples‡	500	767	766
Pears‡	26	33	29
Plums‡	24	29	23
Currants†	130	142	130‖

* Deliveries to sugar factories.
† Source: FAO, *Production Yearbook*.
‡ Marketed production.
§ FAO estimate.
‖ Unofficial figure.

LIVESTOCK ('000 head at December)

	1987	1988	1989
Horses	n.a.	375.0	n.a.
Cattle	14,886.9	14,659.3	14,563.4
Pigs	23,669.6	22,589.4	22,164.8
Sheep	1,413.7	1,464.3	1,532.5
Chickens	n.a.	72,034.6	n.a.
Geese	n.a.	514.9	n.a.
Ducks	n.a.	1,165.4	n.a.
Turkeys	n.a.	3,169.0	n.a.

LIVESTOCK PRODUCTS ('000 metric tons)

	1987	1988	1989
Beef and veal	1,702.6	1,613.7	1,600.3
Mutton and lamb*	26.6	25.1	26.2
Pig meat	3,285.8	3,250.4	3,093.2
Poultry meat	389.2	410.8	425.2
Edible offals	327.7	317.3	306.5
Cows' milk	24,436.2	23,974.4	24,243.4
Butter	464.3	391.8	398.4
Cheese	1,085.5	1,144.3	1,188.4
Hen eggs	729	722	713

* Including goat meat.
Source: FAO, mainly *Quarterly Bulletin of Statistics*.

Forestry

ROUNDWOOD REMOVALS
('000 cubic metres, excluding bark)

	1986	1987	1988
Sawlogs, veneer logs and logs for sleepers	16,287	16,330	17,417
Pulpwood	9,026	12,363	12,491
Other industrial wood*	1,390	1,390	1,390
Fuel wood	3,656	3,656*	3,656*
Total	30,359	33,739	34,954

* FAO estimates.
Source: FAO, *Yearbook of Forest Products*.

SAWNWOOD PRODUCTION
('000 cubic metres, including boxboards)

	1987	1988	1989
Coniferous (softwood)	8,111	8,747	9,731
Broadleaved (hardwood)	1,571	1,576	1,599
Total	9,682	10,323	11,330

Railway sleepers ('000 cu metres): 93 in 1986; 86 in 1987; 72 in 1988.

Fishing

('000 metric tons, live weight)

	1987	1988	1989
Rainbow trout	14.5	14.5	18.0
Common carp	5.4	5.4	7.0
Other freshwater fishes	4.2	5.6	4.4
Atlantic cod	45.3	46.1	53.9
Saithe (Pollock)	28.8	24.9	16.1
Atlantic redfishes	13.9	10.0	6.6
Atlantic herring	14.1	21.9	48.8
Atlantic mackerel	15.6	19.1	22.5
Other fishes	13.2	16.9	25.6
Common shrimp	17.0	14.3	13.3
Blue mussel	25.9	29.7	18.6
Other aquatic animals	3.9	1.1	2.0
Total catch	201.8	209.5	236.8
Inland waters	24.1	25.5	29.0
Marine waters	177.7	184.0	207.8

Source: mainly FAO, *Yearbook of Fishery Statistics*.

Mining

('000 metric tons)

	1987	1988	1989
Hard coal	76,300	73,304	71,428
Brown coal	108,799	108,563	110,081
Crude petroleum	3,800	3,937	3,770

* Metal content.

GERMANY

Statistical Survey

Industry

SELECTED PRODUCTS
('000 metric tons, unless otherwise indicated)

	1987	1988	1989
Electricity (million kWh)	418,262	431,171	440,893
Manufactured gas from gas works (terajoules)*	18,780	17,163	16,846
Manufactured gas from cokeries (terajoules)	166,105	154,441	156,691
Hard coal briquettes	1,001	825	723
Hard coal coke	19,674	18,274	18,384
Brown coal briquettes	3,188	2,526	2,214
Pig-iron	28,517	32,453	33,777
Steel ingots	35,919	40,669	40,700
Motor spirit (petrol)	18,832	19,719	20,360
Diesel oil	10,928	11,706	12,344
Cement	25,268	26,215	28,499
Potash (K_2O)	2,199	2,290	2,182
Sulphuric acid	3,323	3,308	3,288
Soda ash	1,448	1,404	1,443
Caustic soda	3,635	3,664	3,541
Chlorine	3,452	3,500	3,443
Nitrogenous fertilizers (N)	1,056	941	878
Phosphatic fertilizers (P_2O_5)	395	333	302
Artificial resins, plastics	8,546	9,218	9,176
Primary aluminium (unwrought)	738	744	742
Refined copper (unwrought)	400	427	475
Zinc (unwrought)	385.3	n.a.	n.a.
Refined lead (unwrought)†	260.5	n.a.	n.a.
Rubber tyres ('000)	47,083	48,645	49,467
Wool yarn	52.7	49.0	46.0
Cotton yarn	226	197	193
Machine tools	342	339	382
Agricultural machinery	298	318	334
Textile machinery	225	270	272
Passenger cars and minibuses ('000)	4,008	3,980	4,106
Motor cycles ('000)	60	49	n.a.
Bicycles ('000)	2,877	2,998	3,424
Radio receivers ('000)	5,141	4,758	4,975
Television receivers ('000)	3,537	3,737	3,236
Clocks and watches ('000)	28,946	29,822	31,856
Footwear ('000 pairs)	74,589	69,121	66,394
Cameras ('000)	664	413	67
Dwellings completed (number)	196,112	186,191	214,438

* Production from local gas works only.
† Excluding antimonial lead and production from imported bullion.

Finance

CURRENCY AND EXCHANGE RATES

Monetary Units
100 Pfennige = 1 Deutsche Mark (DM).

Denominations
Coins: 1, 2, 5, 10 and 50 Pfennige; 1, 2, 5 and 10 DM.
Notes: 5, 10, 20, 50, 100, 500 and 1,000 DM.

Sterling and Dollar Equivalents (30 September 1990)
£1 sterling = 2.935 DM;
US $1 = 1.566 DM;
100 DM = £34.07 = $63.86.

Average Exchange Rate (DM per US $)
1987 1.7974
1988 1.7562
1989 1.8800

BUDGET (million DM)*

Revenue	1987	1988	1989
Current receipts	558,341	571,142	628,578
Taxes and similar revenue	451,291	465,966	513,698
Income from economic activity	36,130	29,591	35,670
Interest	2,937	2,850	2,938
Allocations and grants for current purposes	110,380	114,911	122,615
Other receipts	58,003	61,708	64,072
Less Deductible payments on the same level	100,400	103,884	110,415
Capital receipts	21,225	22,189	20,252
Sale of property	8,162	8,411	7,256
Loans and grants for investment	26,185	26,013	27,623
Repayment of loans	9,617	10,203	9,412
Public sector borrowing	2,621	2,919	3,198
Less Deductible payments on the same level	25,360	25,357	27,237
Total	579,566	593,331	648,830

Expenditure	1987	1988	1989
Current expenditure	530,112	546,347	569,542
Personnel expenses	208,187	213,411	218,629
Goods and services	102,608	104,227	109,325
Interest	58,850	60,628	61,313
Allocations and grants for current purposes	260,867	271,965	290,690
Less Deductible payments on the same level	100,400	103,884	110,415
Capital expenditure	98,639	99,297	105,927
Construction	39,988	41,228	43,983
Purchase of property	13,917	13,770	15,251
Allocations and grants for investment	45,351	44,329	48,906
Loans	19,880	20,522	20,201
Sale of shares	3,275	3,338	3,267
Repayment expenses in the public sector	1,589	1,467	1,556
Less Deductible payments on the same level	25,360	25,357	27,237
Total	628,751	645,644	675,469

* Figures represent a consolidation of the accounts of all public authorities, including the Federal Government and state administrations.

INTERNATIONAL RESERVES* (US $ million at 31 December)

	1987	1988	1989
Gold†	8,656	7,690	8,063
IMF special drawing rights	1,964	1,857	1,804
Reserve position in IMF	3,900	3,346	3,043
Foreign exchange	72,893	53,324	55,862
Total	87,413	66,217	68,772

* Data on gold and foreign exchange holdings exclude deposits made with the European Monetary Co-operation Fund.
† National valuation.
Source: IMF, *International Financial Statistics*.

MONEY SUPPLY (million DM at 31 December)

	1987	1988	1989
Currency outside banks	124,092	142,596	146,916

GERMANY

COST OF LIVING (Consumer Price Index. Base: 1985 = 100)

	1987	1988	1989
Food	100.1	100.3	102.6
Clothes and shoes	103.2	104.5	106.0
Rent	103.4	105.6	108.8
Energy	80.3	78.1	82.0
Furniture, domestic appliances and other household expenses	102.2	103.3	104.9
Transport and communications	97.4	98.9	103.3
Health	103.2	104.7	108.6
Entertainment and culture	101.6	102.7	103.8
Personal expenses	106.0	110.0	113.1
All items	100.1	101.4	104.2

NATIONAL ACCOUNTS
(provisional, million DM at current prices)

National Income and Product

	1987	1988	1989
Compensation of employees	1,079,050	1,121,600	1,172,040
Operating surplus*	474,390	519,120	554,050
Domestic factor incomes	1,553,440	1,640,720	1,726,090
Consumption of fixed capital	249,450	260,410	276,740
Gross domestic product at factor cost	1,802,890	1,901,130	2,002,830
Indirect taxes	245,640	257,220	278,160
Less Subsidies	44,780	47,670	45,410
GDP in purchasers' values	2,003,750	2,110,680	2,235,580
Factor income from abroad	62,010	67,440	87,870
Less Factor income paid abroad	50,160	54,920	62,150
Gross national product	2,015,600	2,123,200	2,261,300
Less Consumption of fixed capital	249,450	260,410	276,740
National income in market prices	1,766,150	1,862,790	1,984,560
Other current transfers from abroad	15,190	19,170	20,650
Less Other current transfers paid abroad	46,250	52,590	59,180
National disposable income	1,735,090	1,829,370	1,946,030

* Obtained as a residual.

Expenditure on the Gross Domestic Product

	1987	1988	1989
Government final consumption expenditure	397,510	412,650	418,960
Private final consumption expenditure	1,110,300	1,154,280	1,211,300
Increase in stocks	4,390	18,130	29,180
Gross fixed capital formation	389,970	415,980	458,410
Total domestic expenditure	1,902,170	2,001,040	2,117,850
Exports of goods and services	577,320	620,420	699,240
Less Imports of goods and services	475,740	510,780	581,510
GDP in purchasers' values	2,003,750	2,110,680	2,235,580
GDP at constant 1980 prices	1,630,180	1,690,490	1,745,660

Gross Domestic Product by Economic Activity

	1987	1988	1989
Agriculture and livestock	26,280	28,770	36,110
Forestry and fishing	4,180	4,340	
Mining[1]	13,690	11,910	72,220
Electricity, gas and water	55,480	57,670	
Manufacturing[1,2,3]	626,770	655,560	695,030
Construction[2]	100,920	106,460	116,000
Wholesale and retail trade	182,740	189,250	199,710
Transport, storage and communications	115,460	122,600	129,620
Finance, insurance and dwellings[4]	235,020	245,020	260,020
Restaurants and hotels	28,440	30,450	370,210
Community, social and personal services[3,5]	284,460	317,330	
Less Imputed bank service charges	82,270	85,080	89,190
Domestic product of industries	1,591,170	1,684,280	1,789,730
Government services	226,180	232,430	239,120
Private non-profit services to households	40,620	42,550	44,600
Domestic services of households	1,540	1,510	1,500
Sub-total	1,859,510	1,960,770	2,074,950
Non-deductible sales tax	125,250	130,200	137,520
Import duties	18,990	19,710	23,110
GDP in purchasers' values	2,003,750	2,110,680	2,235,580

[1] Quarrying is included in manufacturing.
[2] Structural steel erection is included in manufacturing.
[3] Publishing is included in community, social and personal services.
[4] Including imputed rents of owner-occupied dwellings.
[5] Business services and real estate, except dwellings, are included in community, social and personal services.

BALANCE OF PAYMENTS (US $ million)

	1987	1988	1989
Merchandise exports f.o.b.	278,090	308,180	324,320
Merchandise imports f.o.b.	−208,210	−228,780	−247,660
Trade Balance	69,880	79,400	76,660
Exports of services	82,430	87,330	99,620
Imports of services	−89,980	−98,240	−102,440
Balance of goods and services	62,330	68,490	73,840
Private unrequited transfers (net)	−5,540	−6,350	−6,170
Government unrequited transfers (net)	−10,680	−11,690	−12,240
Current balance	46,100	50,450	55,430
Direct capital investment (net)	−7,260	−9,850	−7,660
Other long-term capital (net)	−6,090	−39,770	−4,670
Short-term capital (net)	−13,350	−22,730	−59,060
Net errors and omissions	950	3,480	5,350
Total (net monetary movements)	20,350	−18,430	−10,620

Source: IMF, *International Financial Statistics*.

GERMANY

DEVELOPMENT AID (public and private development aid to developing countries and multilateral agencies, million DM)

	1986	1987	1988
Public development co-operation	8,317	7,895	8,319
Bilateral	5,736	5,557	5,578
Multilateral	2,581	2,338	2,741
Other public transactions	1,994	1,622	2,276
Bilateral	2,003	1,626	2,275
Multilateral	−9	−4	1
Private development aid	1,183	1,159	1,223
Other private transactions	5,162	4,238	8,951
Bilateral	4,141	3,522	8,160
Multilateral	1,021	716	791
Total	**16,656**	**14,914**	**20,769**

External Trade

Note: Figures include trade in second-hand ships, and stores and bunkers for foreign ships and aircraft. Imports also exclude military supplies under the off-shore procurement programme and exports exclude war reparations and restitutions, except exports resulting from the Israel Reparations Agreement. Official figures exclude trade with the German Democratic Republic, which is compiled separately (see table below).

PRINCIPAL COMMODITIES (distribution by SITC, million DM)

Imports c.i.f.	1987	1988*	1989*
Food and live animals	40,147.3	41,445.6	43,764.7
Meat and meat preparations	5,533.2	5,857.1	6,723.8
Fresh, chilled or frozen meat	4,734.8	1,738.6	1,900.8
Dairy products and birds' eggs	4,268.7	4,600.0	4,901.1
Cereals and cereal preparations	3,289.7	3,180.2	3,335.6
Vegetables and fruit	14,092.3	14,224.2	14,694.2
Fresh and dried fruit and nuts (excl. oil nuts)	5,742.2	5,474.8	5,624.8
Coffee, tea, cocoa and spices	5,742.2	5,678.0	5,678.6
Coffee and coffee substitutes	3,352.0	3,445.5	3,558.8
Animal feeding stuff (excl. cereals)	2,602.7	2,961.0	3,023.3
Beverages and tobacco	4,472.4	4,381.4	4,698.0
Crude materials (inedible) except fuels	25,111.8	28,511.9	33,393.4
Oilseeds and oleaginous fruit	3,058.2	3,111.8	3,010.6
Cork and wood	2,610.0	2,713.0	3,265.5
Metalliferous ores and metal scrap	5,731.7	7,336.8	9,667.9
Mineral fuels, lubricants, etc.	39,508.4	33,516.9	38,344.7
Petroleum, petroleum products, etc.	30,399.8	25,738.9	30,315.4
Crude petroleum oils, etc.	16,016.9	14,830.3	17,046.4
Refined petroleum products	13,251.2	9,912.6	12,062.7
Motor spirit and other light oils	4,294.4	3,675.3	4,983.1
Gas oils	6,333.4	4,248.5	4,708.4
Gas (natural and manufactured)	6,869.2	5,747.5	6,041.6
Petroleum gases, etc. in the gaseous state	6,562.7	n.a.	n.a.
Animal and vegetable oils, fats and waxes	1,173.2	1,454.1	1,729.9
Chemicals and related products	38,512.2	42,620.1	47,701.0
Organic chemicals	10,018.9	11,005.1	13,167.5
Inorganic chemicals	4,275.0	4,499.9	4,308.2
Artificial resins and plastic materials, etc.	10,837.5	n.a.	n.a.

Imports c.i.f.—continued	1987	1988*	1989*
Basic manufactures	71,642.8	80,471.5	94,631.0
Paper, paperboard and manufactures	9,510.5	10,292.4	11,402.0
Paper and paperboard (not cut to size or shape)	7,856.5	8,505.8	9,288.0
Textile yarn, fabrics, etc.	14,712.2	15,175.3	16,921.1
Non-metallic mineral manufactures	6,653.2	7,270.7	8,255.5
Iron and steel	13,524.6	16,402.5	20,185.0
Non-ferrous metals	9,768.9	13,257.2	17,352.2
Other metal manufactures	8,426.9	9,170.0	10,922.1
Machinery and transport equipment	114,475.5	128,137.9	154,364.8
Power generating machinery and equipment	7,405.2	8,520.8	10,033.0
Machinery specialized for particular industries (excl. metalworking)	7,784.0	8,589.7	10,332.6
General industrial machinery, equipment and parts	11,849.8	12,946.8	15,487.9
Office machines and automatic data processing equipment	16,399.2	18,258.0	22,633.9
Telecommunications and sound equipment	10,169.8	11,494.5	12,812.7
Other electrical machinery, apparatus and appliances	19,702.7	22,726.8	26,474.3
Road vehicles (incl. air-cushion vehicles) and parts[1]	28,718.9	31,225.2	36,129.5
Passenger motor cars (excl. buses)	17,678.4	18,223.2	20,369.6
Motor vehicle parts and accessories[1]	7,347.5	8,748.4	10,424.4
Other transport equipment	9,130.7	10,847.1	16,204.3
Aircraft and associated equipment	8,399.5	10,260.5	15,519.0
Miscellaneous manufactured articles	61,537.6	65,699.1	73,320.3
Furniture and parts	4,333.6	4,885.9	5,810.5
Articles of apparel and clothing accessories (excl. footwear)	25,386.0	25,536.6	27,491.7
Footwear	5,323.2	5,698.9	6,453.1
Professional, scientific and controlling instruments, etc.	6,509.9	7,000.5	8,077.7
Photographic apparatus, optical goods, watches and clocks	5,327.1	5,814.7	6,207.7
Other commodities and transactions[2]	13,060.0	13,370.7	14,517.2
Special transactions[3]	10,813.3	10,864.2	12,197.9
Total[2]	**409,641.3**	**439,609.4**	**506,464.7**

* Data for 1988 and 1989 are based on a revised version of the SITC, so the classification is not strictly comparable with that used for 1987.

[1] Excluding tyres, engines and electrical parts.
[2] Including monetary gold.
[3] Including government imports. Also included are returns and replacements, not allocated to their appropriate headings.

GERMANY

Statistical Survey

Exports f.o.b.	1987	1988*	1989*
Food and live animals	21,103.1	23,644.3	25,995.4
Dairy products and birds' eggs	5,741.4	7,489.5	6,863.7
Beverages and tobacco	3,095.6	3,249.2	3,617.1
Crude materials (inedible) except fuels	9,240.8	10,639.1	12,368.6
Mineral fuels, lubricants, etc.	7,103.9	6,918.4	7,884.1
Coal, coke and briquettes	2,504.2	2,573.7	2,737.4
Petroleum, petroleum products, etc.	3,248.6	3,058.1	3,886.7
Animal and vegetable oils, fats and waxes	1,322.2	1,596.5	1,817.7
Chemicals and related products	68,485.2	76,908.4	83,082.6
Organic chemicals	16,048.3	18,314.9	19,510.7
Inorganic chemicals	5,360.9	5,500.3	6,266.9
Dyeing, tanning and colouring materials	7,303.5	7,960.2	8,688.7
Medicinal and pharmaceutical products	7,268.5	8,195.2	8,904.9
Artificial resins and plastic materials, etc.	18,326.1	6,798.7	7,540.7
Basic manufactures	93,344.3	102,554.7	117,154.6
Rubber manufactures	4,737.6	5,164.8	5,630.5
Paper, paperboard and manufactures	10,673.0	11,993.3	13,790.4
Textile yarn, fabrics, etc.	17,576.9	18,455.7	20,800.5
Non-metallic mineral manufactures	9,103.4	9,938.9	10,867.5
Iron and steel	21,153.0	23,835.3	27,790.6
Bars, rods, angles, shapes and sections	2,767.6	3,227.3	3,836.7
Universals, plates and sheets	6,081.0	n.a.	n.a.
Tubes, pipes and fittings	4,887.6	5,773.2	6,311.0
Non-ferrous metals	9,326.5	11,316.5	13,574.4
Other metal manufactures	16,582.1	17,870.8	20,305.5
Machinery and transport equipment	255,132.3	272,817.7	311,684.4
Power generating machinery and equipment	15,161.2	16,175.3	18,018.8
Internal combustion piston engines and parts	7,611.4	9,030.2	9,013.9
Machinery specialized for particular industries (excl. metalworking)	34,238.6	36,638.4	41,847.5
Textile and leather machinery	7,770.5	8,432.3	9,051.3
Metalworking machinery	9,045.5	9,917.4	11,209.7
Machine-tools for working metal, etc.	7,352.4	n.a.	n.a.
General industrial machinery and equipment	33,397.0	37,011.2	42,262.9
Mechanical handling equipment	4,728.1	4,838.1	5,596.2
Office machines and automatic data processing equipment	14,066.8	13,895.3	15,984.4
Telecommunications and sound equipment	10,977.6	10,659.8	11,702.6
Other electrical machinery, apparatus and appliances	32,236.6	36,809.9	42,145.9
Switchgear, etc.	8,965.2	9,876.1	11,268.2
Road vehicles (incl. air-cushion vehicles) and parts[1]	92,624.4	95,745.8	108,192.7
Passenger motor cars (excl. buses)	59,518.5	58,213.5	66,475.5
Motor vehicles for goods transport, etc.	7,501.1	8,374.5	9,751.3
Goods vehicles	6,565.3	7,203.6	8,298.7
Motor vehicle parts and accessories[1]	21,264.7	24,319.0	26,133.4
Other transport equipment	9,754.5	11,804.5	16,620.3

Exports f.o.b.—*continued*	1987	1988*	1989*
Miscellaneous manufactured articles	56,837.4	62,363.7	69,706.1
Furniture and parts	5,997.7	6,189.7	6,902.7
Articles of apparel and clothing accessories (excl. footwear)	9,051.5	9,477.1	10,587.3
Professional scientific and controlling instruments, etc.	12,973.6	14,325.5	15,318.5
Measuring, checking, analysing and controlling instruments	9,386.7	10,031.6	10,727.6
Photographic apparatus, optical goods, watches and clocks	5,924.8	6,398.2	7,023.6
Other commodities and transactions[2]	11,711.9	6,962.0	7,730.2
Special transactions[3]	10,476.0	5,441.3	6,192.6
Total[2]	527,376.7	567,654.0	641,040.7

* Data for 1988 and 1989 are based on a revised version of the SITC, so the classification is not strictly comparable with that used for 1987.
[1] Excluding tyres, engines and electrical parts.
[2] Including monetary gold.
[3] Including returns and replacements, not allocated to their appropriate headings.

PRINCIPAL TRADING PARTNERS*
(million DM, including gold)

Imports c.i.f.	1987	1988	1989*
Austria	17,292.8	18,916.9	20,994.6
Belgium/Luxembourg	29,129.3	31,160.1	34,975.2
Brazil	3,994.0	4,952.7	5,644.5
Canada	3,366.8	3,625.8	4,353.6
China, People's Republic	3,455.8	4,343.4	5,796.1
Denmark	7,669.8	8,280.6	9,242.9
Finland	4,259.7	4,642.2	5,177.5
France	47,482.1	53,052.0	60,421.5
Greece	3,369.4	3,199.8	3,412.9
Hong Kong	4,259.6	4,597.1	4,703.9
Ireland	3,520.0	3,662.2	4,365.9
Italy	39,206.4	40,216.8	45,196.6
Japan	25,245.1	28,365.7	32,185.6
Korea, Republic	4,012.5	4,528.7	4,234.5
Libya	2,079.2	2,680.0	3,146.2
Netherlands	44,934.5	45,421.0	51,972.1
Norway	5,534.8	6,154.8	7,281.2
Poland	2,477.1	2,911.0	3,584.0
Portugal	2,846.3	3,081.3	3,992.5
South Africa	2,242.6	3,024.9	3,183.5
Spain (excl. Canary Is)	8,060.2	8,845.5	10,503.0
Sweden	9,979.3	10,748.7	12,793.6
Switzerland	18,968.4	19,652.8	21,249.4
Taiwan	4,284.4	4,940.1	5,596.9
Turkey	3,706.5	3,781.1	4,670.3
USSR	7,260.6	6,876.9	8,391.9
United Kingdom	29,393.6	30,442.6	34,698.1
USA	25,612.9	29,095.2	38,265.7
Yugoslavia	4,887.2	5,330.2	6,350.9
Total (incl. others)	409,641.3	439,609.4	506,647.6

* Provisional.

GERMANY   Statistical Survey

Exports f.o.b.	1987	1988	1989
Australia	3,458.5	3,689.0	4,739.0
Austria	28,410.5	31,868.0	35,275.2
Belgium/Luxembourg	38,845.6	42,040.2	45,979.0
Brazil	2,666.8	2,709.8	3,167.7
Canada	4,759.9	4,844.5	5,116.8
China, People's Republic	4,999.6	4,918.9	4,618.7
Denmark	11,165.0	11,281.5	12,297.3
Finland	5,827.4	6,271.7	7,679.7
France	63,608.8	71,271.6	84,357.8
Greece	4,950.6	5,523.9	6,434.8
Hong Kong	2,196.6	2,857.2	3,398.6
Hungary	2,891.7	2,759.3	3,651.2
India	3,230.7	2,934.2	3,043.3
Italy	46,056.3	51,652.4	59,830.5
Japan	10,544.5	13,111.1	15,269.1
Korea, Republic	2,799.0	3,257.7	4,172.0
Netherlands	46,087.5	49,189.0	54,422.0
Norway	5,790.3	5,130.2	5,233.4
Poland	2,390.3	2,888.3	4,470.4
Portugal	3,701.2	4,574.9	5,543.3
Singapore	1,936.4	2,521.7	3,064.1
South Africa	4,554.2	5,867.1	6,129.7
Spain (excl. Canary Is)	14,559.4	17,346.1	21,755.4
Sweden	15,841.7	16,650.2	18,354.3
Switzerland	32,126.3	34,442.3	38,149.3
Taiwan	2,664.6	3,115.3	3,973.8
Turkey	4,748.7	4,498.4	4,534.4
USSR	7,845.6	9,423.8	11,528.1
United Kingdom	46,632.4	52,873.7	59,363.8
USA	49,879.0	45,678.1	46,659.4
Yugoslavia	5,783.8	6,122.7	7,266.4
Total (incl. others)	527,376.7	567,654.0	641,341.7

* Imports by country of production; exports by country of consumption. Totals exclude trade with the German Democratic Republic (see below). The distribution by countries excludes stores and bunkers for ships and aircraft (million DM): Imports 261.2 in 1987, 279.9 in 1988, 324.5 in 1989; Exports 839.2 in 1987, 823.6 in 1988, 979.7 in 1989.

TRADE WITH THE GERMAN DEMOCRATIC REPUBLIC
(million DM)

	1987	1988	1989
Purchases from the GDR	6,647	6,789	7,205
Deliveries to the GDR	7,367	7,234	8,104

Transport

FEDERAL RAILWAYS (traffic)

	1987	1988	1989*
Passengers (million)	1,088	1,121	1,127
Passenger-km (million)	39,965	41,760	44,973
Freight net ton-km (million)	60,231	61,180	63,325

* Provisional figures.

ROAD TRAFFIC ('000 licensed vehicles at July each year)

	1987	1988	1989
Passenger cars	27,908.2	28,878.2	29,755.4
Lorries	1,305.3	1,321.8	1,345.3
Buses	70.2	70.2	70.2
Motor cycles	1,391.1	1,372.1	1,378.5
Trailers	1,940.6	2,038.8	2,138.9

SHIPPING
Inland Waterways

	1987	1988	1989
Freight ton-km (million)	49,721	52,854	54,041

Sea-borne Shipping

	1987	1988	1989
Merchant fleet (gross registered tons)*	3,767,928	3,728,394	4,005,152
Vessels entered ('000 net registered tons)†			
Domestic (coastwise)	13,331	15,104	15,580
International	155,938	162,784	169,542
Vessels cleared ('000 net registered tons)†			
Domestic	13,216	14,713	15,331
International	135,987	141,305	150,792
Freight unloaded ('000 metric tons)‡			
International	89,681	93,435	92,351
Freight loaded ('000 metric tons)‡			
International	42,631	44,133	46,727
Total domestic freight ('000 metric tons)	1,994	2,886	1,876

* Vessels of more than 100 grt at 31 December.
† Loaded vessels only.
‡ Including transhipments.

CIVIL AVIATION (traffic)

	1987	1988	1989
Kilometres flown (million)	763	869	954
Passenger-km (million)	97,853	109,718	115,922
Freight ton-km (milion)	4,381	4,675	5,685
Mail ton-km (million)	321	338	344

Tourism

FOREIGN TOURIST ARRIVALS*

Country of Residence	1987	1988	1989
Austria	488,411	506,274	545,392
Belgium and Luxembourg	497,320	517,856	556,228
Canada	167,937	169,977	195,312
Denmark	648,835	657,699	680,758
France	687,899	714,545	808,102
Italy	635,888	724,486	850,151
Japan	588,615	622,770	762,554
Netherlands	1,856,538	1,878,699	1,954,574
Norway	296,718	288,737	311,482
Spain	222,197	258,323	298,568
Sweden	746,387	818,923	942,251
Switzerland	605,549	633,258	706,668
United Kingdom	1,174,602	1,186,131	1,355,507
USA	2,071,647	1,878,557	2,067,317
Total (incl. others)	12,779,904	13,113,017	14,653,201

* Figures refer to arrivals at registered accommodation establishments.

Communications Media

	1982	1983	1984
Radio receivers in use	24,158,000	24,299,855	24,856,997
Television receivers in use	21,834,000	21,959,483	22,340,623
Telephones in use	31,370,000	35,137,000	36,582,000
Book production: titles	61,332	60,598	51,733
Daily newspaper circulation	25,882,000	25,834,000	25,619,000

1985: Telephones in use 37,899,000; Book production: titles 57,623; Daily newspaper circulation 25,439,000.
1986: Book production: titles 63,679; Daily newspaper circulation 25,255,000.
1987: Book production: titles 65,680; Daily newspaper circulation 25,470,000.
1988: Radio receivers 26,340,933; Television receivers 23,010,526; Book production: titles 68,611; Daily newspaper circulation 24,525,000.

Education

(1988)

	Institutions	Teachers	Students ('000)
Pre-primary	29,089	84,764	1,646
Primary	14,002	136,155	2,388
General Secondary:			
First stage	12,565	277,798	3,381
Second stage	2,867	64,466	579
Vocational Secondary:			
Second stage (full-time)	6,360	101,467	2,259
Second stage (part-time)			27
Special	3,106	44,612	254
Higher:			
Non-university institutions	2,861	47,261	222
Universities and equivalent institutions*	243	150,980	1,465

* Universities and other institutions of similar standing, including colleges of art and music, colleges of theology, colleges of education and institutions of vocational training.

Directory

The Constitution

The Basic Law (Grundgesetz), which came into force in the British, French and US Zones of Occupation in Germany (excluding Saarland) on 23 May 1949, was and is intended as a provisional Constitution to serve until a permanent one for Germany as a whole can be adopted. The Parliamentary Council which framed the Basic Law intended to continue the tradition of the Constitution of 1848–49, and to preserve some continuity with subsequent German constitutions (with Bismarck's Constitution of 1871, and with the Weimar Constitution of 1919), while avoiding the mistakes of the past. It contains 146 articles, divided into 11 sections, and is introduced by a short preamble.

With the accession of the five newly re-established eastern Länder and East Berlin to the Federal Republic of Germany on 3 October 1990, the Basic Law became the Constitution of the united German people. Article 4 of the Unification Treaty stipulates that the Basic Law 'will lose its validity on the day that a new Constitution comes into force, that has been resolved freely by the German people'. The all-German legislature, elected in December 1990, was to have adopted any amendments to the Basic Law within a period of two years.

I. BASIC RIGHTS

The opening articles of the Constitution guarantee the dignity of man, the free development of his personality, the equality of all persons before the law, and freedom of faith and conscience. Men and women shall have equal rights, and no one may be prejudiced because of sex, descent, race, language, homeland and origin, faith or religion or political opinion.

No one may be compelled against his conscience to perform war service as a combatant (Article 4). All Germans have the right to assemble peacefully and unarmed and to form associations and societies. Everyone has the right freely to express and to disseminate his opinion through speech, writing or pictures. Freedom of the press and freedom of reporting by radio and motion pictures are guaranteed (Article 5). Censorship is not permitted.

The State shall protect marriage and the family, property and the right of inheritance. The care and upbringing of children is the natural right of parents. Illegitimate children shall be given the same conditions for their development and their position in society as legitimate children. Schools are under the supervision of the State. Religion forms part of the curriculum in the State schools, but parents have the right to decide whether the child shall receive religious instruction (Article 7).

A citizen's dwelling is inviolable; house searches may be made only by Court Order. No German may be deprived of his citizenship if he would thereby become stateless. The politically persecuted enjoy the right of asylum (Article 16).

II. THE FEDERATION AND THE LÄNDER

Article 20 describes the Federal Republic (Bundesrepublik Deutschland) as a democratic and social federal state. The colours of the Federal Republic are to be black-red-gold, the same as those of the Weimar Republic. Each Land within the Federal Republic has its own Constitution, which must, however, conform to the principles laid down in the Basic Law. All Länder, districts and parishes must have a representative assembly resulting from universal, direct, free, equal and secret elections (Article 28). The exercise of the power of state is the concern of the Länder, in so far as the Basic Law does not otherwise prescribe. Where there is incompatibility, Federal Law supersedes Land Law (Article 31). Every German has in each Land the same civil rights and duties.

Political parties may be freely formed in all the states of the Federal Republic, but their internal organization must conform to democratic principles, and they must publicly account for the sources of their funds. Parties which seek to impair or abolish the free and democratic basic order or to jeopardize the existence of the Federal Republic of Germany are unconstitutional (Article 21). So are activities tending to disturb the peaceful relations between nations, and, especially, preparations for aggressive war, but the Federation may join a system of mutual collective security in order to preserve peace (Articles 26 and 24). The rules of International Law shall form part of Federal Law and take precedence over it and create rights and duties directly for the inhabitants of the Federal territory (Article 25).

The territorial composition of the Länder may be reorganized by Federal law, subject to plebiscite and with due regard to regional unity, territorial and cultural connections, economic expediency and social structure.

III. THE BUNDESTAG

The Federal Assembly (Bundestag) is the Lower House. Its members are elected by the people in universal, free, equal, direct and secret elections, for a term of four years.* Any person who has reached the age of 18 is eligible to vote and any person who has reached the age of 18 is eligible for election (Article 38). A deputy may be arrested for a punishable offence only with the permission of the Bundestag, unless he be apprehended in the act or during the following day.

The Bundestag elects its President and draws up its Standing Orders. Most decisions of the House require a majority vote. Its

---

* The elections of 1949 were conducted on the basis of direct election, with some elements of proportional representation. In January 1953 the draft of a new electoral law was completed by the Federal Government and was approved shortly before the dissolution. The new law represents a compromise between direct election and proportional representation, and is designed to prevent the excessive proliferation of parties in the Budestag.

IV. THE BUNDESRAT

The Federal Council (Bundesrat) is the Upper House, through which the Länder participate in the legislation and the administration of the Federation. The Bundesrat consists of members of the Land governments, which appoint and recall them (Article 51). Each Land has at least three votes; Länder with more than two million inhabitants have four, and those with more than six million inhabitants have five. Länder with more than seven million inhabitants have six votes. The votes of each Land may only be given as a block vote. The Bundesrat elects its President for one year. Its decisions are taken by simple majority vote. Meetings are in public, but the public may be excluded. The members of the Federal Government have the right, and, on demand, the obligation, to participate in the debates of the Bundesrat.

V. THE FEDERAL PRESIDENT

The Federal President (Bundespräsident) is elected by the Federal Convention (Bundesversammlung), consisting of the members of the Bundestag and an equal number of members elected by the Länder Parliaments (Article 54). Every German eligible to vote in elections for the Bundestag and over 40 years of age is eligible for election. The candidate who obtains an absolute majority of votes is elected, but if such majority is not achieved by any candidate in two ballots, whoever receives most votes in a further ballot becomes President. The President's term of office is five years. Immediate re-election is admissible only once. The Federal President must not be a member of the Government or of any legislative body or hold any salaried office. Orders and instructions of the President require the counter-signature of the Federal Chancellor or competent Minister, except for the appointment or dismissal of the Chancellor or the dissolution of the Bundestag.

The President represents the Federation in International Law and accredits and receives envoys. The Bundestag or the Bundesrat may impeach the President before the Federal Constitutional Court on account of wilful violation of the Basic Law or of any other Federal Law (Article 61).

VI. THE FEDERAL GOVERNMENT

The Federal Government (Bundesregierung) consists of the Federal Chancellor (Bundeskanzler) and the Federal Ministers (Bundesminister). The Chancellor is elected by an absolute majority of the Bundestag on the proposal of the Federal President (Article 63). Ministers are appointed and dismissed by the President upon the proposal of the Chancellor. Neither he nor his Ministers may hold any other salaried office. The Chancellor determines general policy and assumes responsibility for it, but within these limits each Minister directs his department individually and on his own responsibility. The Bundestag may express its lack of confidence in the Chancellor only by electing a successor with the majority of its members; the President must then appoint the person elected (Article 67). If a motion of the Chancellor for a vote of confidence does not obtain the support of the majority of the Bundestag, the President may, upon the proposal of the Chancellor, dissolve the House within 21 days, unless it elects another Chancellor within this time (Article 68).

VII. THE LEGISLATION OF THE FEDERATION

The right of legislation lies with the Länder in so far as the Basic Law does not specifically accord legislative powers to the Federation. Distinction is made between fields of exclusive legislation of the Federation and fields of concurrent legislation of Bund and Länder. In the field of concurrent legislation the Länder may legislate so long and so far as the Federation makes no use of its legislative right. The Federation has this right only in so far as a matter cannot be effectively regulated by Land legislation, or the regulation by Land Law would prejudice other Länder, or if the preservation of legal or economic unity demands regulation by Federal Law. Exclusive legislation of the Federation is strictly limited to such matters as foreign affairs, citizenship, migration, currency, copyrights, customs, railways, post and telecommunications. In most other fields, as enumerated (Article 74), concurrent legislation exists.

The legislative organ of the Federation is the Bundestag, into which Bills are introduced by the Government, by members of the Bundestag or by the Bundesrat (Article 76). After their adoption they must be submitted to the Bundesrat, which may demand, within three weeks, that a committee of members of both houses be convened to consider the Bill (Article 77). In so far as its express approval is not needed, the Bundesrat may veto a law within two weeks. This veto can be overruled by the Bundestag, with the approval of a majority of its members.

An alteration of the Basic Law requires a majority of two-thirds in both houses, but an amendment by which the division of the Federation into Länder and the basic principles contained in Articles 1 and 20 would be affected, is inadmissible (Article 79).

The Federal Government or the Länder Governments may be authorized by law to issue ordinances. A state of legislative emergency for a Bill can be declared by the President on the request of the Government with the approval of the Bundesrat. If then the Bundestag again rejects the Bill, it may be deemed adopted nevertheless in so far as the Bundesrat approves it. An emergency may not last longer than six months and may not be declared more than once during the term of office of any one Government (Article 81).

VIII. THE EXECUTION OF FEDERAL LAWS AND THE FEDERAL ADMINISTRATION

The Länder execute the Federal Laws as their own concern in so far as the Basic Law does not otherwise determine. In doing so, they regulate the establishment of the authorities and the administrative procedure, but the Federal Government exercises supervision in order to ensure that the Länder execute the Federal Laws in an appropriate manner. For this purpose the Federal Government may send commissioners to the Land authorities (Article 84). Direct Federal administration is foreseen for the Foreign Service, Federal finance, Federal railways, postal services, Federal waterways and shipping.

In order to avert imminent danger to the existence of the democratic order, a Land may call in the police forces of other Länder; and if the Land in which the danger is imminent is itself not willing or able to fight the danger, the Federal Government may place the police in the Land, or the police forces in other Länder, under its instructions (Article 91).

IX. THE ADMINISTRATION OF JUSTICE

Judicial authority is invested in independent judges, who are subject only to the law and who may not be dismissed or transferred against their will (Article 97).

Justice is exercised by the Federal Constitutional Court, by the Supreme Federal Courts and by the Courts of the Länder. The Federal Constitutional Court decides on the interpretation of the Basic Law in cases of doubt, on the compatibility of Federal Law or Land Law with the Basic Law, and on disputes between the Federation and the Länder or between different Länder. Supreme Federal Courts are to be established for the spheres of ordinary, administrative, finance, labour and social jurisdiction. If a Supreme Federal Court intends to judge a point of law in contradiction to a previous decision of another Supreme Federal Court, it must refer the matter to a special senate of the Supreme Courts. Extraordinary courts are inadmissible.

The freedom of the individual may be restricted only on the basis of a law. No one may be prevented from appearing before his lawful judge (Article 101). Detained persons may be subjected neither to physical nor to mental ill-treatment. The police may hold no one in custody longer than the end of the day following the arrest without the decision of a court. Any person temporarily detained must be brought before a judge who shall either issue a warrant of arrest or set him free, at the latest on the following day. A person enjoying the confidence of the detainee must be notified forthwith of any continued duration of a deprivation of liberty. An act may be punished only if it was punishable by law before the act was committed, and no one may be punished more than once on account of the same criminal act. The death sentence shall be abolished.

X. FINANCE

The Federation has the right of exclusive legislation only on customs and financial monopolies; on most other taxes, especially on income, property and inheritance, it has concurrent legislation rights with the Länder (see VII above).

Customs, financial monopolies, excise taxes (with exception of the beer tax), the transportation tax, the value added tax and property dues serving non-recurrent purposes, are administered by Federal finance authorities, and the revenues thereof accrue to the Federation. The remaining taxes are administered, as a rule, by the Länder and the Gemeinden to which they accrue. The Federation and the Länder shall be self-supporting and independent of each other in their budget economy (Article 109). In order to ensure the working efficiency of the Länder with low revenues and to equalize their differing burden of expenditure, there exists a system of revenue sharing among the Länder; in addition, the Federation may make grants, out of its own funds, to the poorer Länder. (In the case of the newly acceded Länder, a special ruling was to apply for a transitional period until the end of 1994.) All

GERMANY

revenues and expenditures of the Federation must be estimated for each fiscal year and included in the budget, which must be established by law before the beginning of the fiscal year. Decisions of the Bundestag or the Bundesrat which increase the budget expenditure proposed by the Federal Government require its approval (Article 113).

XI. TRANSITIONAL AND CONCLUDING PROVISIONS

The Articles 116–146 regulate a number of disconnected matters of detail, such as the relation between the old Reich and the Federation, the Federal Government and Allied High Commission, the expenses for occupation costs which have to be borne by the Federation, and the status of former German nationals who now may regain their citizenship. Article 143 contains those divergences from the Basic Law, with regard to the newly-acceded Länder, as stipulated in the Unification Treaty.

Major Constitutional Amendments

I. SOVEREIGNTY AND RESPONSIBILITY

An amending bill of 1954:

(1) Laid down under an amendment to Article 73 of the Basic Law that the Federal Parliament had full powers to legislate in all matters relating to national defence 'including obligatory national service for men over 18 years of age';

(2) Introduced a new article (142A) which declared that 'the treaties signed in Bonn and Paris on 26 and 27 May 1952 (i.e. the Bonn Conventions and European Defence Community Treaty) were not contrary to the Federal Constitution'.

Until September 1954 the operation of the Basic Law was conditioned by two further instruments: the first, the Occupation Statute of 1949 (with subsequent amendments) defining the rights and obligations of the United States, Great Britain and France with respect to Germany; and the second, the Bonn Conventions, designed to replace the Occupation Statute and to grant almost full sovereignty to the German people.

The Bonn Conventions, 1952

(1) The Occupation Statute was abolished, and the Federal Government inherited full freedom in so far as the international situation permits.

(2) Allied forces in Germany were no longer occupation forces, but part of 'the defence of the free world, of which the Federal Republic and West Berlin form a part'.

(3) A number of problems which would normally be settled by a Peace Treaty were resolved; the Conventions were in effect a provisional treaty to end the war between the Federal Republic and the Three Powers, pending a final treaty between the whole of Germany and the Four. Under this heading the following provisions were made:

(a) The Federal Republic would have full control over its internal and foreign affairs and relations with the Three Powers would be conducted through ambassadors.

(b) Only because of the international situation would the Three Powers claim their rights regarding the stationing of armed forces on German soil, matters concerning Berlin, the reunification of Germany and the final Peace Treaty.

(c) The Federal Republic undertook to conduct its policy according to the principles of the United Nations.

(d) In their negotiations with states with which the Federal Republic has no relations, the Three Powers would consult with the Federal Government.

(e) The Federal Republic would participate in the European Defence Community.

(f) The Three Powers and the Federal Republic agreed that a freely negotiated peace settlement for the whole of Germany was their common aim, and that determination of the final boundaries of Germany must await such a treaty.

The Conventions also included supplementary contractual agreements concerning the rights and obligations of foreign troops in Germany, taxation of the armed forces, a Finance Convention, and a Convention on the settlement of matters arising out of the war and the occupation.

The London and Paris Agreements

The terms of the London Agreement of 1954 were that Germany and Italy should enter an expanded Brussels Treaty Organization; that German sovereignty should be restored and that Germany should, on agreed terms, enter NATO, and that an Agency for the control of armaments on the continent of Europe should be set up. The Paris Agreement later that year established the details of the points agreed in London.

German Sovereignty

On 5 May 1955, with the depositing of the instruments of ratification of the London and Paris Agreements, the Federal Republic of Germany attained its sovereignty. The three-power status in West Berlin ceased to exist upon the signature of the so-called 'Two-plus-Four' Treaty (in September 1990).

II. OTHER AMENDMENTS

In June 1968 legislation was finally passed providing for emergency measures to be taken during a time of crisis.

The main provisions of this, the 17th Amendment to the Constitution, were to allow the authorities to place certain restrictions on the secrecy of correspondence and telecommunications, to conscript men into the armed forces and to use the armed forces to fight armed insurgents if the free democratic status of the Federal Republic or of any Land was threatened. A new Article 53A provided for the establishment of a committee of 33 members, two-thirds members of the Bundestag and one-third members of the Bundesrat, which must be informed by the Federal Government of any plans in the event of a defence emergency. The life of parliamentary bodies and the terms of office of the Federal President and his deputy might be extended during a defence emergency.

The Government

(February 1991)

HEAD OF STATE

Federal President: Dr RICHARD VON WEIZSÄCKER (took office 1 July 1984; re-elected 23 May 1989).

THE FEDERAL GOVERNMENT

A coalition of the Christian Democratic Union (CDU)/Christian Social Union (CSU) and the Free Democratic Party (FDP).

Federal Chancellor: Dr HELMUT KOHL (CDU).

Vice-Chancellor and Minister for Foreign Affairs: HANS-DIETRICH GENSCHER (FDP).

Minister for Special Tasks and Head of the Federal Chancellery: RUDOLF SEITERS (CDU).

Minister of the Interior: Dr WOLFGANG SCHÄUBLE (CDU).

Minister of Justice: Dr KLAUS KINKEL (FDP).

Minister of Finance: Dr THEODOR WAIGEL (CSU).

Minister of Economics: JÜRGEN MÖLLEMANN (FDP).

Minister of Food, Agriculture and Forestry: IGNAZ KIECHLE (CSU).

Minister of Labour and Social Affairs: DR NORBERT BLÜM (CDU).

Minister of Defence: Dr GERHARD STOLTENBERG (CDU).

Minister for Family Affairs and Senior Citizens: HANNELORE RÖNSCH (CDU).

Minister for Women and Youth: Dr ANGELA MERKEL (CDU).

Minister for Health: GERDA HASSELFELDT (CSU).

Minister of Transport: Prof. Dr GÜNTHER KRAUSE (CDU).

Minister for the Environment, Nature Conservation and Nuclear Safety: Prof. Dr KLAUS TÖPFER (CDU).

Minister of Posts and Telecommunications: Dr CHRISTIAN SCHWARZ-SCHILLING (CDU).

Minister for Regional Planning, Housing and Urban Development: Dr IRMGARD ADAM-SCHWAETZER (FDP).

Minister of Research and Technology: Dr HEINZ RIESENHUBER (CDU).

Minister for Education and Science: Prof. Dr RAINER ORTLIEB.

Minister for Economic Co-operation: KARL-DIETER SPRANGER (CSU).

MINISTRIES

Office of the Federal President: 5300 Bonn 1, Kaiser-Friedrich-Str. 18; tel. (0228) 2001; telex 886393; fax (0228) 200200.

Office of the Federal Chancellor: 5300 Bonn 1, Adenauerallee 141; tel. (0228) 561; telex 886750; fax (0228) 2357.

Office of the Head of the Press and Information Office of the Federal Government: 5300 Bonn 1, Welckerstr. 11; tel. (0228) 2080; telex 886741; fax (0228) 208-2555.

GERMANY   Directory

Ministry of Defence: 5300 Bonn 1, Hardthöhe, Postfach 1328; tel. (0228) 121; telex 886575; fax (0228) 12-5357.

Ministry of Economic Co-operation: 5300 Bonn 1, Karl-Marx-Str. 4–6; tel. (0228) 5350; telex 8869452; fax (0228) 535202.

Ministry of Economics: 5300 Bonn 1, Villemombler Str. 76; tel. (0228) 615-1; telex 886747; fax (0228) 6154436.

Ministry of Education and Science: 5300 Bonn 2, Heinemannstr. 2; tel. (0228) 571; telex (17) 228315; fax (0228) 57-2096.

Ministry of the Environment, Nature Conservation and Nuclear Safety: 5300 Bonn 2, Kennedyallee 5; tel. (0228) 305-0; telex 885790.

Ministry of Family Affairs and Senior Citizens: 5300 Bonn 2, Kennedyallee 105–107; tel. (0228) 308-0; telex 885517; fax (0228) 308-2221.

Ministry of Finance: 5300 Bonn 1, Graurheindorfer Str. 108; tel. (0228) 682-0; telex 886645; fax (0228) 682-4420.

Ministry of Food, Agriculture and Forestry: 5300 Bonn 1, Rochusstr. 1; tel. (0228) 5291; telex 886844; fax (0228) 529.

Ministry of Foreign Affairs: 5300 Bonn 1, Adenauerallee 99–103; tel. (0228) 170; telex 886591; fax (0228) 17-3402.

Ministry of the Interior: 5300 Bonn 1, Graurheindorfer Str. 198; tel. (0228) 6811; telex 886896; fax (0228) 681-4665.

Ministry of Justice: 5300 Bonn 2, Heinemannstr. 6, Postfach 200365; tel. (0228) 581; fax (0228) 584525.

Ministry of Labour and Social Affairs: 5300 Bonn 1, Rochusstr. 1, Postfach 140280; tel. (0228) 5271; telex 886641; fax (0228) 527-2965.

Ministry of Posts and Telecommunications: 5300 Bonn 2, Heinrich-von-Stephan-Str. 1; tel. (0228) 140; telex 886707; fax (0228) 14-8872.

Ministry of Regional Planning, Housing and Urban Development: 5300 Bonn 2, Deichmannsaue; tel. (0228) 3370; telex 885462; fax (0228) 337-509.

Ministry of Research and Technology: 5300 Bonn 2, Heinemannstr. 2; tel. (0228) 591; telex 885674; fax (0228) 593601.

Ministry of Transport: 5300 Bonn 2, Robert-Schumann-Platz 1; tel. (0228) 300-0; telex 885700; fax (0228) 300-3428.

Legislature

BUNDESTAG
(Federal Assembly)

President: Prof. Dr Rita Süssmuth (CDU).

Vice-Presidents: Helmut Becker (SPD), Dieter Julius Cronenberg (FDP), Hans Klein (CSU), Renate Schmidt (SPD).

General Election, 2 December 1990*

Parties and Groups	Votes†	%	Seats
Christian Democratic Union (CDU)	17,051,128	36.71	268
Social Democratic Party (SPD)	15,539.977	33.46	239
Free Democratic Party (FDP)	5,123,936	11.03	79
Christian Social Union (CSU)	3,301,239	7.11	51
Green Party (West)	1,788,214	3.85	—
Party of Democratic Socialism (PDS)	1,129,290	2.43	17
Republican Party	985,557	2.12	—
Alliance 90/Green Party (East)	558,552	1.20	8
Others	966,165	2.08	—
Total	**46,444,058**	**100.00**	**662**

* The general election was conducted in two areas, representing the former FRG and GDR. In each area, parties required a minimum of 5% of the total votes to gain representation in the Bundestag. This ruling was adopted in favour of smaller parties in the former GDR.

† Figures refer to valid second votes (i.e. for state party lists). Details of the numbers of valid first votes (for individual candidates) are not available.

BUNDESRAT
(Federal Council)

President: Dr Henning Voscherau.

The Bundesrat has 68 members. Each Land has three, four, five or six votes, depending on the size of its population, and sends as many members to the sessions as it has votes. The head of government of each Land is automatically a member of the Bundesrat. Ministers and Members of the Federal Government attend the sessions, which are held every two to three weeks.

Länder	Seats
Nordrhein-Westfalen (North Rhine-Westphalia)	6
Bayern (Bavaria)	6
Baden-Württemberg	6
Niedersachsen (Lower Saxony)	6
Hessen (Hesse)	4
Sachsen (Saxony)	4
Rheinland-Pfalz (Rhineland-Palatinate)	4
Berlin	4
Sachsen-Anhalt (Saxony-Anhalt)	4
Thüringen (Thuringia)	4
Brandenburg	4
Schleswig-Holstein	4
Mecklenburg-Vorpommern (Mecklenburg-Western Pomerania)	3
Hamburg	3
Saarland	3
Bremen	3

The Land Governments

The 16 Länder of Germany are autonomous but not sovereign states, enjoying a high degree of self-government and wide legislative powers.

NORDRHEIN-WESTFALEN (NORTH RHINE-WESTPHALIA)

The present Constitution was adopted by the Diet on 6 June 1950, and was endorsed by the electorate in the elections held on 18 June. The Land Government is presided over by the Minister-President who appoints his Ministers. It is formed from the majority SPD.

Minister-President: Johannes Rau (SPD).

The Diet, elected on 13 May 1990, is composed as follows:

President of Diet: Ingeborg Friebe (SPD).

Party	Seats
Social Democratic Party	122
Christian Democratic Union	89
Free Democratic Party	14
Green Party (West)	12

The state is divided into five governmental districts: Düsseldorf, Münster, Arnsberg, Detmold and Köln.

BAYERN (BAVARIA)

The Constitution of Bayern allows for a two-chamber Parliament and a Constitutional Court. Provision is also made for a popular referendum. The Minister-President is elected by the Diet for four years. He appoints the Ministers and Secretaries of State with the consent of the Diet. The State Government is formed from the majority party (CSU).

Minister-President: Dr Max Streibl (CSU).

The composition of the Diet, as a result of elections held on 14 October 1990, is as follows:

President of Diet: Dr Franz Heubl (CSU).

Party	Seats
Christian Social Union	127
Social Democratic Party	58
Green Party (West)	12
Free Democratic Party	7

The Senate, or second chamber, consists of 60 members, divided into 10 groups representing professional interests, e.g. agriculture, industry, trade, free professions and religious communities. Every two years one-third of the Senate is replaced at elections.

President of the Senate: Dr Hans Weiss.

Bayern is divided into seven districts: Mittelfranken, Oberfranken, Unterfranken, Schwaben, Niederbayern, Oberpfalz and Oberbayern.

GERMANY

BADEN-WÜRTTEMBERG

The Constitution was adopted by the Land Assembly in Stuttgart on 19 November 1953. The Minister-President is elected by the Diet. He appoints and dismisses his Ministers. The Government, which is responsible to the Diet, is formed by the majority party (CDU).

Minister-President: ERWIN TEUFEL (CDU).

The composition of the Diet, as the result of elections held on 20 March 1988, is as follows:

President of Diet: ERICH SCHNEIDER (CDU).

Party	Seats
Christian Democratic Union	66
Social Democratic Party	42
Green Party (West)	10
Free Democratic Party	7

The Land is divided into four administrative districts: Stuttgart, Karlsruhe, Tübingen and Freiburg.

NIEDERSACHSEN (LOWER SAXONY)

The Provisional Constitution was adopted by the Diet on 13 April 1951, and came into force on 1 May 1951. The Land Government is formed from a coalition of the SPD and the Green Party.

Minister-President: GERHARD SCHRÖDER (SPD).

As a result of elections held on 13 May 1990, the Diet is composed as follows:

President of Diet: HORST MILDE (CDU).

Party	Seats
Social Democratic Party	71
Christian Democratic Union	67
Free Democratic Party	9
Green Party (West)	8

Niedersachsen is divided into four governmental districts: Braunschweig, Hannover, Lüneburg and Weser-Ems.

HESSEN (HESSE)

The Constitution of this Land dates from 11 December 1946. The Minister-President is elected by the Diet and he appoints and dismisses his Ministers with its consent. The Diet can force the resignation of the State Government by a vote of no-confidence. The Government is formed from a coalition of the CDU and the FDP*.

Minister-President: Dr WALTER WALLMANN (CDU)*.

The Diet, elected on 20 January 1991, is composed as follows:

President of Diet: (vacant).

Party	Seats
Social Democratic Party	46
Christian Democratic Union	46
Green Party (West)	10
Free Democratic Party	8

Hessen is divided into two governmental districts: Kassel and Darmstadt.

* Following the state elections in January 1991 (which were won by the Social Democratic Party, SPD, with 40.8% of the total votes, as against the 40.2% won by the Christian Democratic Union), it was expected that the SPD would form a government in coalition with the Green Party. The CDU-FDP Government was to retain office until 4 April 1991.

SACHSEN (SAXONY)

The Land Government is formed by the majority party (CDU).

Minister-President: Prof. Dr KURT BIEDENKOPF (CDU).

The composition of the Diet, as a result of elections held on 14 October 1990, is as follows:

President of Diet: ERICH ILLTGEN.

Party	Seats
Christian Democratic Union	92
Social Democratic Party	32
Party of Democratic Socialism	17
Alliance 90/Green Party (East)	10
Free Democratic Party	9

RHEINLAND-PFALZ (RHINELAND-PALATINATE)

The three chief agencies of the Constitution of this Land are the Diet, the Government and the Constitutional Court. The Minister-President is elected by the Diet, with whose consent he appoints and dismisses his Ministers. The Government, which is dependent on the confidence of the Diet, is made up from a coalition of the CDU and the FDP.

Minister-President: Dr CARL-LUDWIG WAGNER (CDU).

The members of the Diet are elected according to a system of proportional representation. Its composition, as the result of elections held on 17 May 1987, is as follows:

President of Diet: Dr HEINZ PETER VOLKERT (CDU).

Party	Seats
Christian Democratic Union	48
Social Democratic Party	40
Free Democratic Party	7
Green Party (West)	5

Rheinland-Pfalz is divided into three districts: Koblenz, Rheinhessen-Pfalz (Rheinhessen-Palatinate) and Trier.

BERLIN

The House of Representatives (Abgeordnetenhaus) is the legislative body, and has 240 members. The executive agency is the Senate, which is composed of the Governing Mayor (Regierender Bürgermeister), his deputy, and up to 15 Senators. The Governing Major is elected by a majority of the House of Representatives. The Senate is responsible to the House of Representatives and dependent on its confidence. The Senate is composed of a coalition of the CDU and the SPD.

Regierender Bürgermeister: EBERHARD DIEPGEN (CDU).

The state of parties in the House of Representatives, as the result of elections held on 2 December 1990, is as follows:

President of House of Representatives: (not available).

Party	Seats
Christian Democratic Union	100
Social Democratic Party	76
Party of Democratic Socialism	23
Free Democratic Party	18
Green Party (West)/Alternative List*	12
Alliance 90/Green Party (East)	11

* AL, the Green Party of western Berlin.

SACHSEN-ANHALT (SAXONY-ANHALT)

The Land Government is formed from a coalition of the CDU and the FDP.

Minister-President: Dr GERD GIES (CDU).

The composition of the Diet, as a result of elections held on 14 October 1990, is as follows:

President of Diet: (not available).

Party	Seats
Christian Democratic Union	48
Social Democratic Party	27
Free Democratic Party	14
Party of Democratic Socialism	12
Green Party (East)/New Forum	5

THÜRINGEN (THURINGIA)

The Land Government is formed from a coalition of the CDU and the FDP.

Minister-President: JOSEF DUCHAC (CDU).

The composition of the Diet, as a result of elections held on 14 October 1990, is as follows:

President of Diet: Dr GOTTFRIED MÜLLER.

Party	Seats
Christian Democratic Union	44
Social Democratic Party	21
Free Democratic Party	9
Party of Democratic Socialism	9
Green Party (East)/New Forum/Democracy Now	6

GERMANY

BRANDENBURG

The Land Government is formed from a coalition of the SPD, the FDP and Alliance 90.

Minister-President: Dr MANFRED STOLPE (SPD).

The composition of the Diet, as a result of elections held on 14 October 1990, is as follows:

President of Diet: Dr KNOBLICH.

Party	Seats
Social Democratic Party	36
Christian Democratic Union	27
Party of Democratic Socialism	13
Free Democratic Party	6
Alliance 90	6

SCHLESWIG-HOLSTEIN

The Provisional Constitution was adopted by the Diet on 13 December 1949. The Land Government consists of the Minister-President and the Ministers appointed by him. Following an inconclusive election in September 1987, a new election was held in May 1988.

Minister-President: BJÖRN ENGHOLM (SPD).

The composition of the Diet, as the result of elections held on 8 May 1988, is as follows:

President of Diet: LIANNE PAULINA-MÜRL.

Party	Seats
Social Democratic Party	46
Christian Democratic Union	27
Südschleswigscher Wählerverband	1

MECKLENBURG-VORPOMMERN (MECKLENBURG-WESTERN POMERANIA)

The Land Government is formed from a coalition of the CDU and the FDP.

Minister-President: Dr ALFRED GOMOLKA (CDU).

The composition of the Diet, as a result of elections held on 14 October 1990, is as follows:

President of Diet: RAINER PRACHTEL.

Party	Seats
Christian Democratic Union	29
Social Democratic Party	21
Party of Democratic Socialism	12
Free Democratic Party	4

HAMBURG

The Constitution of the 'Free and Hanseatic City of Hamburg' was adopted in June 1952. There is complete parity between the Town Assembly and the Land Diet on the one hand and between the Mayor and the President on the other. The members of the Senate are elected by the City Council. The Senate in turn elects the President and his deputy from its own ranks. The President remains in office for one year, but may offer himself for re-election. The Senate has a coalition Government formed by the SPD and the FDP.

President of Senate and First Bürgermeister: Dr HENNING VOSCHERAU (SPD).

The City Council was elected on 17 May 1987, and is composed as follows:

President: HELGA ELSTNER (SPD).

Party	Seats
Social Democratic Party	55
Christian Democratic Union	49
Free Democratic Party	8
Green Party (West)	8

SAARLAND

By the Constitution which came into force on 1 January 1957, Saarland became politically integrated with the FRG as a Land. It became economically integrated with the FRG in July 1959. The Minister-President is elected by the Diet. The Government is formed by the SPD.

Minister-President: OSKAR LAFONTAINE (SPD).

The composition of the Diet, as a result of elections held on 28 January 1990, is as follows:

President of the Diet: ALBRECHT HEROLD (SPD).

Party	Seats
Social Democratic Party	30
Christian Democratic Union	18
Free Democratic Party	3

BREMEN

The Constitution of the Free Hanseatic City of Bremen was sanctioned by referendum of the people on 12 October 1947. The main constitutional organs are the City Council, the Senate and the Constitutional Court. The Senate is the executive organ elected by the Council for the duration of its own tenure of office. The Senate elects from its own ranks two Bürgermeister, one of whom becomes President of the Senate. The Senators cannot be simultaneously members of parliament. A vote of no-confidence can only be given under special conditions. Decisions of the Council are subject to the delaying veto of the Senate. The Senate is formed from the majority party (SPD).

First Bürgermeister and President of the Senate: KLAUS WEDEMEIER (SPD).

The Council consists of 100 members elected for four years. The election of 13 September 1987 resulted in the following composition:

President of the Bürgerschaft: Dr DIETER KLINK (SPD).

Party	Seats
Social Democratic Party	54
Christian Democratic Union	25
Free Democratic Party	10
Green List	10
German People's Union	1

Political Organizations

Bündnis 90/Grüne (Alliance 90/Green Party-East): 1080 Berlin, Friedrichstr. 165; tel. (02) 2202091; telex 114099; fax (02) 2291645; f. 1990 as an electoral alliance in the former GDR; comprises the following: Democracy Now, the Initiative for Peace and Human Rights, New Forum, the Independent Women's Association, and the Green Party (East).

Christlich-Demokratische Union Deutschlands (in Bavaria: **Christlich-Soziale Union Deutschlands**) **(CDU/CSU)** (Christian Democratic and Christian Social Union):

CDU: 5300 Bonn 1, Konrad-Adenauer-Haus, Friedrich-Ebert-Allee 73–75; tel. (0228) 5441; telex 886804; fax (0228) 544216; f. 1945, became a federal party in 1950; stands for the united action between Catholics and Protestants for rebuilding German life on a Christian-Democratic basis, while guaranteeing private property and the freedom of the individual and for a 'free and equal Germany in a free, politically united and socially just Europe'; other objectives are to guarantee close ties with allies within NATO and the principle of self-determination; in October 1990 incorporated the CDU of the former GDR; c. 800,000 mems (Jan. 1991); Chair. Dr HELMUT KOHL; Sec.-Gen. VOLKER RÜHE.

CSU: 8000 München 2, Nymphenburger Str. 64; tel. (089) 1243-0; telex 898666; fax (089) 1243-220; f. 1946; Christian Democratic party, aiming for a free market economy 'in the service of man's economic and intellectual freedom'; also combines national consciousness with support for a united Europe; 190,000 mems; Chair. Dr THEO WAIGEL; Sec.-Gen. ERWIN HUBER.

Deutsche Kommunistische Partei (DKP) (German Communist Party): 4000 Düsseldorf, Prinz-Georg-Str. 79; telex 8584387; fax (0211) 481001; 47,500 mems (1988); Chair. HELGA ROSENBERG, ROLF PRIEMER, HEINZ STEHR, ANNA FROHNWEILER.

Freie Demokratische Partei (FDP) (Free Democratic Party): 5300 Bonn, Baunscheidtstr. 15, Thomas-Dehler-Haus; tel. (0228) 5470; telex 886580; fax (0228) 547298; f. 1948; represents democratic and social liberalism and makes the individual the focal point of the state and its laws and economy; in August 1990 incorporated the three liberal parties of the former GDR, the Association of Free Democrats, the German Forum Party and the FDP; approx. 200,000 mems (Oct. 1990); Chair. Dr OTTO GRAF LAMBSDORFF; Deputy Chair. Dr IRMGARD ADAM-SCHWAETZER, GERHART

GERMANY

Rudolf Baum, Dr Wolfgang Gerhardt; Chair. in Bundestag Wolfgang Mischnick; Sec.-Gen. Cornelia Schmalz-Jacobsen.

Die Grünen (Green Party—West): 5300 Bonn 1, Colmantstr. 36; tel. (0228) 726130; telex 886330; fax (0228) 72613-99; f. 1980; largely comprised of the membership of the Grüne Aktion Zukunft, the Grüne Liste Umweltschutz and the Aktionsgemeinschaft Unabhängiger Deutscher, also includes groups of widely varying political views; essentially left-wing party programme includes ecological issues, dissolution of NATO and Warsaw Pact military blocs, breaking down of large economic concerns into smaller units, 35-hour week and unlimited right to strike; has links with the Green Party of the former GDR (see Bündnis 90/Grüne, above); approx. 40,600 mems (1990); Jt Speakers of Exec. Renate Damus, Heide Rühle, Christian Ströbele; Gen. Sec. Eberhard Walde.

Nationaldemokratische Partei Deutschlands (NPD) (National Democratic Party of Germany): 7000 Stuttgart 10, Postfach 103528; tel. (0711) 610605; telex 244012; f. 1964; right-wing; 15,000 mems; youth organization Junge Nationaldemokraten (JN), 6,000 mems; Chair. Martin Mussgnug.

Neues Forum (New Forum): 1080 Berlin, Friedrichstr. 165; tel. (02) 202091; f. 1989 as a citizens' action group; played a prominent role in the democratic movement in the former GDR; affiliated to Bündnis 90; Leaders Rolf Henrich, Bärbel Bohley.

Partei des Demokratischen Sozialismus (PDS) (Party of Democratic Socialism): 1020 Berlin, Kleine Alexanderstr. 28; tel. (02) 2824155; telex 112511; fax (02) 2814169; the dominant political force in the former GDR until late 1989; formed in 1946 as the Socialist Unity Party (SED), as a result of a unification of the Social Democratic Party and the Communist Party in Eastern Germany; in Dec. 1989 renamed the SED-PDS; adopted present name in Feb. 1990; 345,000 mems (Nov. 1990); Chair. Dr Gregor Gysi; Hon. Chair. Hans Modrow; Deputy Chair. Wolfgang Pohl, Marlies Deneke, Andre Brie.

Die Republikaner (REP) (Republican Party): f. 1983; approx. 25,000 mems; extreme right-wing; Chair. Franz Schönhuber.

Sozialdemokratische Partei Deutschlands (SPD) (Social Democratic Party of Germany): 5300 Bonn, Ollenhauerstr. 1; tel. (0228) 5321; telex 2283620; fax (0228) 532410; f. 1863; the party maintains that a vital democracy can be built only on the basis of social justice; advocates for the economy as much competition as possible, as much planning as necessary to protect the individual from uncontrolled economic interests; a positive attitude to national defence, while favouring controlled disarmament; a policy of religious toleration; rejects any political ties with Communism; in September 1990 incorporated the SPD of the former GDR; approx. 944,000 mems (Dec. 1990); Chair. Björn Engholm; Deputy Chair. Johannes Rau, Oskar Lafontaine, Herta Däubler-Gmelin, Wolfgang Thierse; Chair. of Parliamentary Party Dr Hans-Jochen Vogel.

There are also numerous other small parties, none of them represented in the Bundestag, covering all shades of the political spectrum and various regional interests.

Diplomatic Representation

EMBASSIES IN GERMANY

Afghanistan: 5300 Bonn 1, Liebfrauenweg 1A; tel. (0228) 251927; Chargé d'affaires: Dr Makhan Shinwari.

Albania: 5300 Bonn 2, Dürenstr. 35–37; tel. (0228) 351044; telex 8869669; fax (0228) 351048; Ambassador: Andon Berxholi.

Algeria: 5300 Bonn 2, Rheinallee 32–34; tel. (0228) 82070; telex 885723; Ambassador: Kamel Hacene.

Angola: 5300 Bonn 1, Kaiser-Karl-Ring 20c; tel. (0228) 55570-8; telex 885775; fax (0228) 659282; Ambassador: Hermínio Escórcio.

Argentina: 5300 Bonn 1, Adenauerallee 50–52; tel. (0228) 222011; telex 886478; fax (0228) 229636; Ambassador: Dr Carlos Alfredo Mandry.

Australia: 5300 Bonn 2, Godesberger Allee 107; tel. (0228) 81030; telex 885466; fax (0228) 376268; Ambassador: John Stewart Bowan.

Austria: 5300 Bonn 1, Johanniterstr. 2; tel. (0228) 53006; telex 886780; fax (0228) 5300645; Ambassador: Dr Friedrich Bauer.

Bangladesh: 5300 Bonn 2, Bonner Str. 48; tel. (0228) 352525; telex 885640; fax (0228) 354142; Ambassador: Anwar Hossain.

Belgium: 5300 Bonn 1, Kaiser-Friedrich-Str. 7; tel. (0228) 212001; telex 886777; fax (0228) 220857; Ambassador: Georges Vander Espt.

Benin: 5300 Bonn 2, Rüdigerstr. 10; tel. (0228) 344031; telex 885594; fax (0228) 857192; Ambassador: Saturnin K. Soglo.

Bolivia: 5300 Bonn 2, Konstantinstr. 16; tel. (0228) 362038; telex 885785; fax (0228) 355952; Ambassador: Bernardo Bauer Kyllmann.

Brazil: 5300 Bonn 2, Kennedyallee 74; tel. (0228) 376976; telex 885471; fax (0228) 373696; Ambassador: João Carlos Pessoa Fragoso.

Bulgaria: 5300 Bonn 2, Auf der Hostert 6; tel. (0228) 363061; telex 885739; Ambassador: Georgi Evtimov.

Burkina Faso: 5300 Bonn 2, Wendelstadtallee 18; tel. (0228) 332063; telex 885508; Ambassador: Moumouni Fabré.

Burundi: 5307 Wachtberg-Niederbachem, Drosselweg 2; tel. (0228) 345032; telex 885745; Ambassador: Sébastien Ntahuga.

Cameroon: 5300 Bonn 2, Rheinallee 76; tel. (0228) 356037; telex 885480; Ambassador: Jean Melaga.

Canada: 5300 Bonn 1, Friedrich-Wilhelm-Str. 18; tel. (0228) 231061; telex 886421; fax (0228) 230857; Ambassador: William Thomas Delworth.

Cape Verde: 5300 Bonn 1, Meckenheimer Allee 113; tel. (0228) 651604; telex 885505; fax (0228) 630588; Ambassador: António Rodrigues Pires.

Central African Republic: 5300 Bonn 3, Rheinaustr. 120; tel. (0228) 469724; telex 8861166; Ambassador: Christian Lingama-Toléqué.

Chad: 5300 Bonn 2, Basteistr. 80; tel. (0228) 356025; telex 8869305; fax (0228) 355887; Ambassador: Dr Issa Hassan Khayar.

Chile: 5300 Bonn 2, Kronprinzenstr. 20; tel. (0228) 363089; telex 885403; fax (0228) 353766; Ambassador: Dr Carlos Huneeus.

China, People's Republic: 5300 Bonn 2, Kurfürstenallee 12; tel. (0228) 361095; telex 885655; Ambassador: Mei Zhaorong.

Colombia: 5300 Bonn 1, Friedrich-Wilhelm-Str. 35; tel. (0228) 234565; telex 886305; fax (0228) 236845; Ambassador: Luis Guillermo Giraldo Hurtado.

Congo: 5300 Bonn 2, Rheinallee 45; tel. (0228) 357085; telex 886690; Ambassador: Charles Ngouoto-Moukolo.

Costa Rica: 5300 Bonn 1, Borsigallee 2; tel. (0228) 252940; telex 8869661; fax (0228) 252950; Ambassador: José Joaquín Chaverri.

Côte d'Ivoire: 5300 Bonn 1, Königstr. 93; tel. (0228) 212098; telex 886524; fax (0228) 217313; Ambassador: Lambert Amon-Tanoh.

Cuba: 5300 Bonn 2, Kennedyallee 22–24; tel. (0228) 3091; telex 885733; Ambassador: Raúl Barzaga Navas.

Cyprus: 5300 Bonn 2, Kronprinzenstr. 58; tel. (0228) 363336; telex 885519; fax (0228) 353626; Ambassador: Andreas Jacovides.

Czechoslovakia: 5300 Bonn 1, Ferdinandstr. 27; tel. (0228) 284765; telex 8869322; fax (0228) 284369; Ambassador: Dr Milan Kadnár.

Denmark: 5300 Bonn 1, Pfälzer Str. 14; tel. (0228) 729910; telex 886892; fax (0228) 7299131; Ambassador: Knud-Erik Tygrsen.

Dominican Republic: 5300 Bonn 2, Burgstr. 87; tel. (0228) 364956; fax (0228) 352576; Ambassador: (vacant).

Ecuador: 5300 Bonn 2, Koblenzer Str. 37; tel. (0228) 352544; telex 8869527; Ambassador: Dr Miguel Espinosa Páez.

Egypt: 5300 Bonn 2, Kronprinzenstr. 2; tel. (0228) 364008; telex 885719; Ambassador: Ahmed Raouf Ghoneim.

El Salvador: 5300 Bonn 1, Burbacherstr. 2; tel. (0228) 221351; fax (0228) 218824; Ambassador: Dr José Saguer Saprissa.

Ethiopia: 5300 Bonn 1, Brentanostr. 1; tel. (0228) 233041; telex 8869498; Ambassador: Tibebu Bekele.

Finland: 5300 Bonn 2, Friesdorfer Str. 1; tel. (0228) 38298-0; telex 885626; fax (0228) 3829850; Ambassador: Kai Helenius.

France: 5300 Bonn 2, Kapellenweg 1A; tel. (0228) 362031; telex 885445; Ambassador: Serge Boidevaix.

Gabon: 5300 Bonn 2, Kronprinzenstr. 52; tel. (0228) 354084; telex 885520; Ambassador: Léon N'Dong.

Ghana: 5300 Bonn 2, Rheinallee 58; tel. (0228) 352011; telex 885660; fax (0228) 363498; Ambassador: Kwame Samuel Adusei-Poku.

Greece: 5300 Bonn 2, Koblenzerstr. 103; tel. (0228) 83010; telex 885636; fax (0228) 353284; Ambassador: Alexandros Zafiriou.

Guatemala: 5300 Bonn 2, Zietenstr. 16; tel. (0228) 351579; telex 8869983; fax (0228) 354940; Ambassador: Lucrecia Rivera de Ampuero.

Guinea: 5300 Bonn 1, Rochusweg 50; tel. (0228) 231097; telex 886448; Ambassador: Jean Delacroix Camara.

Haiti: 5300 Bonn 2, Schlossallee 10; tel. (0228) 340351; fax (0228) 856829; Ambassador: Jean-Robert Saget.

Holy See: 5300 Bonn 2, Turmstr. 29 (Apostolic Nunciature); tel. (0228) 376901; telex 8869794; fax (0228) 379180; Apostolic Nuncio: Mgr Giuseppe Uhač, Titular Archbishop of Tharros.

Honduras: 5300 Bonn 2, Ubierstr. 1; tel. (0228) 356394; telex 889496; fax (0228) 351981; Ambassador: Rafael Aguilar Paz C.

GERMANY

Hungary: 5300 Bonn 2, Turmstr. 30; tel. (0228) 376797; telex 886501; fax (0228) 374994; Ambassador: Dr István Horváth.

Iceland: 5300 Bonn 2, Kronprinzenstr. 6; tel. (0228) 364021; telex 885690; fax (0228) 361398; Ambassador: Hjalmar W. Hannesson.

India: 5300 Bonn 1, Adenauerallee 262–264; tel. (0228) 54050; telex 8869301; fax (0228) 5405154; Ambassador: Anantanarayan Madhavan.

Indonesia: 5300 Bonn 2, Bernkasteler Str. 2; tel. (0228) 38299-0; telex 886352; fax (0228) 311393; Ambassador: Dr Hasjim Djalal.

Iran: 5300 Bonn 2, Godesberger Allee 133–137; tel. (0228) 8100521/22; telex 885697; Ambassador: Mehdi Ahari Mostafavi.

Iraq: 5300 Bonn 2, Dürenstr. 33; tel. (0228) 82031; telex 8869471; Ambassador: Abdul Jabbar Omar Ghani.

Ireland: 5300 Bonn 2, Godesberger Allee 119; tel. (0228) 376937; telex 885588; fax (0228) 373500; Ambassador: Kester W. Heaslip.

Israel: 5300 Bonn 2, Simrockallee 2; tel. (0228) 8231; fax (0228) 356093; Ambassador: Benjamin Navon.

Italy: 5300 Bonn 2, Karl-Finkelnburg-Str. 51; tel. (0228) 822-0; fax (0228) 822-169; Ambassador: Marcello Guidi.

Jamaica: 5300 Bonn 2, Am Kreuter 1; tel. (0228) 354045; telex 885493; Ambassador: M. Patricia Durrant.

Japan: 5300 Bonn 1, Bonn-Center, H1 701, Bundeskanzlerplatz; tel. (0228) 5001; telex 886878; Ambassador: Keizo Kimura.

Jordan: 5300 Bonn 2, Beethovenallee 21; tel. (0228) 357046; telex 885401; Ambassador: Fawaz Sharaf.

Kenya: 5300 Bonn 2, Villichgasse 17; tel. (0228) 353066; telex 885570; Ambassador: Vincent John Ogutu-Obare.

Korea, Republic: 5300 Bonn 1, Adenauerallee 124; tel. (0228) 267960; telex 8869508; Ambassador: Shin Dong-Won.

Kuwait: 5300 Bonn 2, Godesberger Allee 77–81; tel. (0228) 378081; telex 886525; Ambassador: Khalid al-Babtain.

Lebanon: 5300 Bonn 2, Rheinallee 27; tel. (0228) 352075; telex 8869339; Ambassador: Souheil Chammas.

Lesotho: 5300 Bonn 2, Godesberger Allee 50; tel. (0228) 376868; telex 8869370; Ambassador: Mokheseng Reginald Tekateka.

Liberia: 5300 Bonn 2, Hohenzollernstr. 73; tel. (0228) 352394; telex 886637; Ambassador: Nathaniel Eastman.

Libya: 5300 Bonn 2, Beethovenallee 12A; tel. (0228) 820090; telex 885738; fax (0228) 364260; Secretary of the People's Committee: Ali Mahmoud el-Gheriani.

Luxembourg: 5300 Bonn 1, Adenauerallee 108; tel. (0228) 214008; telex 886557; fax (0228) 222920; Ambassador: Adrien Ferdinand Josef Meisch.

Madagascar: 5300 Bonn 2, Rolandstr. 48; tel. (0228) 331057; telex 885781; fax (0228) 334628; Chargé d'affaires: Rajaonah Rene Fidele.

Malawi: 5300 Bonn 2, Mainzer Str. 124; tel. (0228) 343016-19; telex 8869689; Ambassador: Macdonald Amon Banda.

Malaysia: 5300 Bonn 2, Mittelstr. 43; tel. (0228) 376803; telex 885683; fax (0228) 376584; Ambassador: Dato' Zainal Abidin bin Ibrahim.

Mali: 5300 Bonn 2, Basteistr. 86; tel. (0228) 357048; telex 885680; Ambassador: Modibo Keïta.

Malta: 5300 Bonn 2, Viktoriastr. 1; tel. (0228) 363017; telex 885748; fax (0228) 363019; Ambassador: Richard Lapira.

Mauritania: 5300 Bonn 2, Bonnerstr. 48; tel. (0228) 364024; telex 885550; fax (0228) 361788; Ambassador: Dr Youssouf Diagana.

Mexico: 5300 Bonn 1, Adenauerallee 100; tel. (0228) 218043; telex 886819; fax (0228) 211113; Ambassador: Juan José Bremer.

Monaco: 5300 Bonn 1, Zitelmannstr. 16; tel. (0228) 232007; Ambassador: René Bocca.

Mongolia: 5310 Troesdorf-Siegler, Siebengebirgsblick 4-6; tel. (0228) 402727; Ambassador: Agvaanborjeen Tsolnon.

Morocco: 5300 Bonn 2, Gotenstr. 7–9; tel. (0228) 355044; telex 885428; fax (0228) 357894; Ambassador: Abdel Aziz Benjelloun.

Mozambique: 5300 Bonn 1, Adenauerallee 46A; tel. (0228) 224024; Ambassador: Amadeo Paul Samuel da Conceição.

Myanmar: 5300 Bonn 1, Schumann Str. 112; tel. (0228) 210091; telex 8869560; fax (0228) 219316; Ambassador: U Win Aung.

Nepal: 5300 Bonn 2, Im Hag 15; tel. (0228) 343097; telex 8869297; fax (0228) 856747; Ambassador: (vacant).

Netherlands: 5300 Bonn 1, Strässchensweg 10; tel. (0228) 5305-0; telex 886826; fax (0228) 238621; Ambassador: Jan Gerard van der Tas.

New Zealand: 5300 Bonn 1, Bonn Center, III 902, Bundeskanzlerplatz 2-10; tel. (0228) 228070; fax (0228) 221687; Ambassador: Dr Richard Grant.

Nicaragua: 5300 Bonn 2, Konstantinstr. 41; tel. (0228) 362505; telex 885734; Chargé d'affaires a.i.: Ramón-Alfonso Estrada Centeno.

Niger: 5300 Bonn 2, Dürenstr. 9; tel. (0228) 356057; telex 885572; fax (0228) 363246; Ambassador: Youssofa Mamadou Maiga.

Nigeria: 5300 Bonn 2, Goldbergweg 13; tel. (0228) 322071; telex 885522; Ambassador: Asuquo Eta Hogan Emenyi.

Norway: 5300 Bonn 2, Mittelstr. 43; tel. (0228) 819970; telex 885491; fax (0228) 373498; Ambassador: Per Martin Ølberg.

Oman: 5300 Bonn 2, Lindenallee 11; tel. (0228) 357031; telex 885688; fax (0228) 357045; Ambassador: Saud bin Suliman al-Nabhani.

Pakistan: 5300 Bonn 2, Rheinallee 24; tel. (0228) 352004; telex 885787; Ambassador: Najmuddin A. Shaikh.

Panama: 5300 Bonn 2, Lützowstr. 1; tel. (0228) 361036; telex 885600; fax (0228) 363558; Ambassador: Maximiliano E. Jiménez.

Papua New Guinea: 5300 Bonn 2, Gotenstr. 163; tel. (0228) 376855; telex 886340; fax (0228) 375103; Ambassador: Andrew M. D. Yauieb.

Paraguay: 5300 Bonn 2, Plittersdorfer Str. 121; tel. (0228) 356727; Ambassador: Dr Nicolás Lüthold F.

Peru: 5300 Bonn 2, Godesbergerallee 127; tel. (0228) 373045; telex 886325; fax (0228) 379475; Ambassador: Gabriel García Pike.

Philippines: 5300 Bonn 1, Argelanderstr. 1; tel. (0228) 267990; telex 8869571; fax (0228) 221968; Ambassador: Bienvenido A. Tan, Jr.

Poland: 5000 Köln 51, Lindenallee 7; tel. (0221) 380261; telex 8881040; fax (0221) 343089; Ambassador: Janusz Reiter.

Portugal: 5300 Bonn 2, Ubierstr. 78; tel. (0228) 363011; telex 885577; fax (0228) 352864; Ambassador: António Pinto da França.

Qatar: 5300 Bonn 2, Brunnenallee 6; tel. (0228) 351074; telex 885476; fax (0228) 351170; Ambassador: Ahmed Abdulla al-Khal.

Romania: 5300 Bonn 1, Legionsweg 14; tel. (0228) 555860; telex 8869791-3; fax (0228) 680247; Ambassador: Radu Comşa.

Rwanda: 5300 Bonn 2, Beethovenallee 72; tel. (0228) 355058; telex 885604; Ambassador: Juvénal Renzaho.

Saudi Arabia: 5300 Bonn 2, Godesberger Allee 40–42; tel. (0228) 379013; telex 885442; fax (0228) 375593; Ambassador: Abbas Faig Ghazzawi.

Senegal: 5300 Bonn 1, Argelanderstr. 3; tel. (0228) 218008; telex 8869644; Ambassador: Faye Gassama.

Sierra Leone: 5300 Bonn 2, Rheinallee 20; tel. (0228) 352001; Ambassador: Dauda Suleiman Kamara.

Singapore: 5300 Bonn 2, Südstr. 133; tel. (0228) 312007; telex 885642; fax (0228) 310527; Ambassador: Tony K. Siddique.

Somalia: 5300 Bonn 2, Hohenzollernstr. 12; tel. (0228) 355084; telex 885724; Ambassador: Dr Hassan Abshir Farah.

South Africa: 5300 Bonn 2, Auf der Hostert 3; tel. (0228) 82010; telex 885720; fax (0228) 352579; Ambassador: Albert Erich van Niekerk.

Spain: 5300 Bonn 1, Schlossstr. 4; tel. (0228) 217094; telex 886792; fax (0228) 223405; Ambassador: Eduardo Foncillas.

Sri Lanka: 5300 Bonn 2, Rolandstr. 52; tel. (0228) 332055; telex 885612; fax (0228) 331829; Ambassador: Mrs Irangani Manel Abeysekera.

Sudan: 5300 Bonn 2, Koblenzerstr. 99; tel. (0228) 363074; telex 885478; Ambassador: Ahmed Eltayeb Yousif Elkordofani.

Sweden: 5300 Bonn 2, Allianzplatz, Haus I, Heussallee 2–10; tel. (0228) 260020; telex 886667; fax (0228) 223837; Ambassador: Torsten Örn.

Switzerland: 5300 Bonn 2, Gotenstr. 156; tel. (0228) 810080; telex 885646; fax (0228) 8100819; Ambassador: Alfred Hohl.

Syria: 5300 Bonn 1, Andreas-Hermes-Strasse 5; tel. (0228) 819920; telex 885757; Ambassador: Suleyman Haddad.

Tanzania: 5300 Bonn 2, Theaterplatz 26; tel. (0228) 358051; telex 885569; fax (0228) 358226; Ambassador: James L. Kateka.

Thailand: 5300 Bonn 2, Ubierstr. 65; tel. (0228) 355065; telex 886574; Ambassador: Sokol Vanabriksha.

Togo: 5300 Bonn 2, Beethovenallee 13; tel. (0228) 355091; telex 885595; fax (0228) 351639; Ambassador: Dr Fousseni Mamah.

Tunisia: 5300 Bonn 2, Godesberger Allee 103; tel. (0228) 376981; telex 885477; fax (0228) 374223; Ambassador: Muhammad Karboul.

Turkey: 5300 Bonn 2, Ute Str. 47; tel. (0228) 346052; telex 885521; Ambassador: Reşat Arim.

Uganda: 5300 Bonn 2, Dürenstr. 44; tel. (0228) 355027; telex 885578; fax (0228) 351692; Ambassador: Mrs Freda Blick.

GERMANY

USSR: 5300 Bonn 2, Waldstr. 42; tel. (0228) 312086; fax (0228) 364561; Ambassador: Vladislav Petrovich Terekhov.

United Arab Emirates: 5300 Bonn 1, Erste Fährgasse 6; tel. (0228) 267070; telex 885741; fax (0228) 2670714; Ambassador: Dr Saeed Mohammad al-Shamsi.

United Kingdom: 5300 Bonn 1, Friedrich-Ebert-Allee 77; tel. (0228) 234061; telex 886887; fax (0228) 234070; Ambassador: Sir Christopher Mallaby.

USA: 5300 Bonn 2, Deichmanns Aue 29; tel. (0228) 3391; telex 885452; fax (0228) 339-2663; Ambassador: Vernon A. Walters.

Uruguay: 5300 Bonn 2, Gotenstr. 1–3; tel. (0228) 356570; telex 885708; Ambassador: Dr Augustín Espinosa Lloveras.

Venezuela: 5300 Bonn 3, Im Rheingarten 7; tel. (0228) 400920; telex 885447; fax (0228) 4009228; Ambassador: Dr Rafael León Morales.

Viet-Nam: 5300 Bonn 2, Konstantinstr. 37; tel. (0228) 357022; telex 8861122; fax (0228) 351866; Ambassador: Bui Hong Phuc.

Yemen: 5300 Bonn 1, Adenauerallee 77; tel. (0228) 220273; telex 885765; fax (0228) 229364; Ambassador: Mostafa Ahmed Yacoub.

Yugoslavia: 5300 Bonn 2, Schlossallee 5; tel. (0228) 344051; telex 885530; fax (0228) 344057; Ambassador: Dr Boris Frlec.

Zaire: 5300 Bonn 2, Im Meisengarten 133; tel. (0228) 346071; telex 885573; Ambassador: Mabolia Inengo Tra Bwato.

Zambia: 5300 Bonn 2, Mittelstr. 39; tel. (0228) 376811; telex 885511; Ambassador: Windsor Kapalakonje Nkowani.

Zimbabwe: 5300 Bonn 2, Villichgasse 7; tel. (0228) 356071; telex 885580; Ambassador: Prof. Dr George Payne Kahari.

Judicial System

The Unification Treaty, signed by the FRG and the GDR in August 1990, provided for the extension of Federal Law to the territory formerly occupied by the GDR, and also stipulated certain exceptions where GDR Law was to remain valid.

Judges are not removable except by the decision of a court. Half of the judges of the Federal Constitutional Court are elected by the Bundestag and half by the Bundesrat. A committee for the selection of judges participates in the appointment of judges of the Superior Federal Courts.

FEDERAL CONSTITUTIONAL COURT

Bundesverfassungsgericht (Federal Constitutional Court): 7500 Karlsruhe, Schlossbezirk 3; tel. (0721) 1491; telex 8869679.

President: Prof. Dr Roman Herzog.

Vice-President: Dr Ernst Gottfried Mahrenholz.

Judges: Dr Karin Grasshof, Dr Everhardt Franssen, Konrad Kruis, Prof. Dr Alfred Söllner, Prof. Dr Thomas Dieterich, Prof. Dr Paul Kirchof, Helga Seibert, Klaus Winter, Dr Otto Seidl, Prof. Dr Johann Friedrich Henschel, Prof. Dr Ernst-Wolfgang Böckenförde, Prof. Dr Hans Hugo Klein, Prof. Dr Dieter Grimm, Dr Jürgen Kühling.

SUPERIOR FEDERAL COURTS

Bundesgerichtshof (Federal Court of Justice): 7500 Karlsruhe, Herrenstr. 45A; tel. (0721) 159-0; telex 07825828; fax (0721) 159-830.

President: Prof. Dr Walter Odersky.

Vice-President: Hannskarl Salger.

Presidents of the Senate: Karl-Dietrich Bundschuh, Dr Otto Friedrich Freiherr von Gamm, Heinrich Wilhelm Laufhütte, Karlheinz Boujong, Eckhard Wolf, Dr Arnold Lang, Friedrich Lohmann, Gerhard Herdegen, Dr Günter Krohn, Franz Merz, Dr Erich Steffen, Dr Horst Schauenburg, Dr Karl Bruchhausen, Dr Wolfgang Russ, Prof. Dr Horst Hagen, Herbert Schimansky.

Federal Solicitor-General: Alexander von Stahl.

Federal Prosecutors: Reiner Schulte, Gerhard Löchner, Dr Rainer Müller.

Bundesverwaltungsgericht (Federal Administrative Court): 1000 Berlin 12, Hardenbergstr. 31; tel. (030) 3197-1.

President: Prof. Dr Horst Sendler.

Vice-President: Prof. Dr Otto Schlichter.

Presidents of the Senate: Jürgen Saalmann, Prof. Dr Felix Weyreuther, Dr Günter Korbmacher, Dr Paul Schwarz, Helmut Hacker, Dr Ingeborg Franke, Dr Charlotte Eckstein, Dr Alfred Dickersbach, Erich Bermel, Werner Meyer.

Bundesfinanzhof (Federal Financial Court): 8000 München 80, Ismaningerstr. 109; tel. (089) 9231-1.

President: Prof. Dr Franz Klein.

Vice-President: Dr Claus Grimm.

Presidents of the Senate: Prof. Heinrich Beisse, Dr Max Rid, Dr Klaus Ebling, Dr Albert Beermann, Dr Lothar Woerner, Prof. Dr Ludwig Schmidt, Dr Klaus Offerhaus, Erich Hauter.

Religion

CHRISTIANITY

Arbeitsgemeinschaft christlicher Kirchen in Deutschland (Association of Christian Churches in Germany): 6000 Frankfurt/Main 1, Neue Schlesingergasse 22–24; tel. (069) 20334; fax (069) 289347; f. 1948; 15 Churches are affiliated to this Council, including the Roman Catholic Church and the Greek Orthodox Metropoly; Pres. Rev. Hans-Beat Motel.

The Roman Catholic Church

It is estimated that about 45% of the population of the former FRG and about 7% of the inhabitants of the former GDR are adherents of the Roman Catholic Church.

Bishops' Conferences: Deutsche Bischofskonferenz, 5300 Bonn, Kaiserstr. 163; tel. (0228) 1030; telex 8869438; Pres. Dr Dr Karl Lehmann, Bishop of Mainz; Sec. Prälat Wilhelm Schätzler; Berliner Bischofskonferenz, 1086 Berlin, Französische Str. 34; tel. (02) 2000946; fax (02) 2082408; Pres. Georg Sterzinsky, Bishop of Berlin.

Archbishop of Bamberg: Dr Elmar Maria Kredel, Erzbischöfliches Ordinariat, 8600 Bamberg, Domplatz 3, Postfach 4034.

Archbishop of Freiburg im Breisgau: Dr Oskar Saier, 7800 Freiburg im Breisgau, Herrenstr. 35.

Archbishop of Köln: Cardinal Joachim Meisner, Generalvikariat, 5000 Köln 1, Marzellenstr. 32; tel. (0221) 16421.

Archbishop of München and Freising: Cardinal Friedrich Wetter, 8000 München 33, Postfach 360; tel. (089) 21371.

Archbishop of Paderborn: Dr Johannes Joachim Degenhardt, Erzbischöfliches Generalvikariat, 4790 Paderborn, Domplatz 3.

Commissariat of German Bishops—Catholic Office: 5300 Bonn, Kaiser-Friedrich-Str. 9; tel. 218015; (represents the German Conference of Bishops before the Federal Government on political issues); Leader Prälat Paul Bocklet.

Central Committee of German Catholics: 5300 Bonn 2, Hochkreuzallee 246; tel. (0228) 316056; telex (17) 2283 748; f. 1868; summarizes the activities of Catholic laymen and lay-organizations in the Federal Republic; Pres. Prof. Dr Hans Maier; Gen. Sec. Dr Friedrich Kronenberg.

Protestant Churches

Until 1969 the Protestant churches in both the FRG and the GDR were united in the Evangelische Kirche in Deutschland (EKD), a federation established at the Conference of Eisenach (Thuringia) in 1948. In 1969, however, the churches in the GDR declared themselves organizationally independent and established the Bund der Evangelischen Kirchen in der DDR (BEKDDR). The Vereinigte Evangelisch-Lutherische Kirche Deutschlands (VELKD), one of the federations within the EKD, also divided in 1968 and was paralleled in the GDR by the VELKDDR. The Evangelische Kirche der Union (EKU) was partly divided and spanned both the FRG and the GDR. Following German unification, the BEKDDR was renamed the Bund der Evangelischen Kirchen (BEK). The BEK, and those Churches affiliated to it, merged with the EKD in February 1991.

About 41.6% of the population of the former FRG (25.5m.) are members of the Protestant Church, the great majority belonging to churches forming the EKD. The total membership of the Lutheran churches is almost 10m., of the United Churches about 13.5m., and of the Reformed Churches about 448,000. Approximately 35% of the inhabitants of the former GDR are Protestants (mainly belonging to the Evangelical Church).

Outside the EKD are numerous small Protestant Free Churches, such as the Baptists, Methodists, Mennonites and the Lutheran Free Church, with a membership of approximately 400,000 in all.

Evangelische Kirche in Deutschland (EKD) (Evangelical Church in Germany): 3000 Hannover 21, Herrenhäuser Str. 12, Postfach 210120; tel. (0511) 71110; telex 923445; fax (0511) 7111-707; Berlin Office: 1000 Berlin 12, Jebensstr. 3. The governing bodies of the EKD are its Synod of 120 clergy and lay members which meets at regular intervals, the Conference of member churches, and the Council, composed of 15 elected members; the EKD has an

GERMANY

ecclesiastical secretariat of its own (the Protestant Church Office), including a special office for foreign relations; Chair. of the Council Bischof Dr MARTIN KRUSE; Pres. of the Office OTTO Frhr VON CAMPENHAUSEN.

Synod of the EKD: 3000 Hannover 21, Herrenhäuserstr. 12; tel. (0511) 71110; telex 923445; Pres. Dr JÜRGEN SCHMUDE.

Deutscher Evangelischer Kirchentag (German Protestant Church Assembly): 6400 Fulda, Magdeburgerstr. 59, Postfach 480; tel. (0661) 601091; fax (0661) 607310; Pres. Dr ERIKA REIHLEN; Gen. Sec. CHRISTIAN KRAUSE.

Churches and Federations within the EKD:

Vereinigte Evangelisch-Lutherische Kirche Deutschlands (VELKD) (The United Evangelical-Lutheran Church of Germany): 3000 Hannover 1, Richard-Wagner-Str. 26; tel. (0511) 62611; telex 922673; f. 1949; mems 9.4m.; a body uniting all but two of the Lutheran territorial Churches within the Protestant Church in Germany; Presiding Bishop Landesbischof Prof. Dr GERHARD MÜLLER (Braunschweig).

Evangelische Kirche der Union (EKU) (Protestant Church of the Union): Chancellery, Western Region: 1000 Berlin 12, Jebensstr. 3; Eastern Region: 1040 Berlin, Auguststr. 80; tel. (030) 319001-0; fax (030) 3139967; composed of Lutheran and Reformed elements; includes the Protestant Churches of Berlin-Brandenburg, Westphalia and the Rhineland (Western Region), Berlin-Brandenburg, Saxony, Pomerania, Görlitz (Silesia) and Anhalt (Eastern Region); Chair. of Council Präses PETER BEIER (Western Region), Bischof Prof. Dr JOACHIM ROGGE (Eastern Region); Chair of Synod Präses MANFRED KOCK (1000 Berlin 12, Jebensstr. 3) (Western Region), Präses DIETRICH AFFELD (Eastern Region); Pres. of Administration WERNER RADATZ (Western Region), Dr FRIEDRICH WINTER (Eastern Region).

Arnoldshainer Konferenz: 1000 Berlin 12, Jebensstr. 3; tel. (030) 319001-0; fax (030) 3139967; f. 1967; a loose federation of the church governments of one Lutheran, one Reformed Territorial and all United Churches, aiming at greater co-operation between them; Chair. of Council HELMUT SPENGLER.

Reformierter Bund (Reformed League): 5600 Wuppertal 1, Vogelsangstr. 20; f. 1884; unites the Reformed Territorial Churches and Congregations of Germany. The central body of the Reformed League is the 'Moderamen', the elected representation of the various Reformed Congregations; Moderator Prof. Dr HANS-JOACHIM KRAUS (5600 Wuppertal 23, Zur Gloria 25); Gen. Sec. Pfarrer HERMANN SCHÄFER.

Affiliated to the EKD:

Bund Evangelisch-Reformierter Kirchen (Association of Protestant Reformed Churches): 2000 Hamburg 1, Ferdinandstr. 21; tel. (040) 337260; Chair. Präses P. Dr ULRICH FALKENROTH.

Evangelical-Lutheran Church in Braunschweig: 3340 Wolfenbüttel, Neuer Weg 88–90; tel. (05331) 8020; fax (05331) 802-220; Landesbischof Prof. Dr GERHARD MÜLLER DD.

Herrnhuter Brüdergemeine or **Europäisch-Festländische Brüder-Unität** (Moravian Church): f. 1457; there are 24 congregations in Germany, Switzerland, Denmark and the Netherlands, with approximately 30,000 mems; Chair. of Western District Rev. Dr HELMUT BINTZ (7325 Bad Boll, Badwasen 6; tel. (07164) 8010; fax (07164) 801-99).

†**Protestant Church in Baden:** 7500 Karlsruhe 1, Blumenstr. 1; tel. (147) 234; Landesbischof Prof. Dr KLAUS ENGELHARDT.

*Protestant-Lutheran Church in Bayern:** 8000 München 2, Meiserstr. 13; tel. (089) 55951; telex 529674; Landesbischof D. Dr phil., Mag. theol. JOHANNES HANSELMANN DD.

†**Protestant Church in Berlin-Brandenburg:** Konsistorium: 1000 Berlin 21, Bachstr. 1-2; tel. (030) 390910; fax (030) 39091431; Bischof Dr MARTIN KRUSE.

†**Bremen Evangelical Church:** 2800 Bremen 1, Franziuseck 2–4, Postfach 10 69 29; tel. (0421) 55970; Pres. HEINZ HERMANN BRAUER.

*Protestant-Lutheran Church of Hannover:** 3000 Hannover 1, Haarstr. 6; tel. (0511) 12411; Landesbischof HORST HIRSCHLER.

†**Protestant Church in Hessen and Nassau:** 6100 Darmstadt, Paulusplatz 1; tel. (06151) 4050; telex 4197176; fax (06151) 405-440; Pres. Rev. HELMUT SPENGLER.

†**Protestant Church of Kurhessen-Waldeck:** 3500 Kassel-Wilhelmshöhe, Wilhelmshöher Allee 330; tel. (0561) 30830; fax (0561) 3083400; Bischof Dr HANS-GERNOT JUNG.

Church of Lippe: 4930 Detmold 1, Leopoldstr. 27; tel. (05231) ...; fax (05231) 740345; Landessuperintendent Dr AKO ECK.

Protestant-Lutheran Church of North Elbe: Bischof HANS-CHRISTIAN KNUTH (2380 Schleswig, Plessenstr. 5A; tel. (04621) 24622); Bischof Prof. Dr ULRICH WILCKENS (2400 Lübeck, Bäckerstr. 3–5; tel. (0451) 797176); Bischof Prof. D. PETER KRUSCHE (2000 Hamburg 11, Neue Burg 1; tel. (040) 3689-216); Pres. of North Elbian Church Administration Dr KLAUS BLASCHKE (2300 Kiel, Dänische Str. 21–35; tel. (0431) 991-1).

†**Protestant-Reformed Church in North-West Germany:** 2950 Leer, Saarstr. 6; tel. (0491) 8030; fax (0491) 803-301; Moderator Rev. HINNERK SCHRÖDER; Synod Clerks Rev. WALTER HERRENBRÜCK, Dr WINFRIED STOLZ.

†**Protestant-Lutheran Church in Oldenburg:** 2900 Oldenburg, Philosophenweg 1; tel. (0441) 77010; Bischof Dr WILHELM SIEVERS.

†**Protestant Church of the Palatinate:** 6720 Speyer, Domplatz 5; tel. (06232) 1091; Pres. WERNER SCHRAMM.

†**Protestant Church in the Rhineland:** 4000 Düsseldorf 30, Hans-Böckler-Str. 7; tel. (0211) 45620; fax (0211) 4562444; Pres. PETER BEIER.

*Protestant-Lutheran Church of Schaumburg-Lippe:** 3062 Bückeburg, Herderstr. 27; tel. (05722) 25021; Landesbischof HEINRICH HERRMANNS; Pres. Dr MICHAEL WINCKLER.

†**Protestant Church of Westfalen:** 4800 Bielefeld 1, Altstädter Kirchplatz 5; tel. (0521) 5940; fax (0521) 594129; Präses D. HANS-MARTIN LINNEMANN.

†**Protestant-Lutheran Church of Württemberg:** 7000 Stuttgart 10, Gänsheidestr. 4, Postfach 101342; tel. (0711) 2149-0; telex 72559080; fax (0711) 2149236; Landesbischof D. THEO SORG.

(* Member of the VELKD; † member of the EKU)

Other Protestant Churches

Bund Evangelisch-Freikirchlicher Gemeinden (Union of Protestant Free Church Congregations; Baptists): 6380 Bad Homburg v. d. H. 1, Friedberger Str. 101; tel. (06172) 80040; fax (06172) 800436; f. 1849; Pres. WALTER ZESCHKY; Dirs Rev. GERD RUDZIO, Rev. ECKHARD SCHAEFER.

Bund Freier evangelischer Gemeinden (Covenant of Free Evangelical Churches in Germany): 5810 Witten (Ruhr), Goltenkamp 4; tel. (02302) 39901; fax (02302) 31463; f. 1854; Pres. KARL H. KNÖPPEL; Administrator JÜRGEN HEDFELD; 25,100 mems.

Evangelisch-methodistische Kirche (United Methodist Church): 6000 Frankfurt/Main 1, Wilhelm-Leuschner-Str. 8; tel. (069) 239373; fax (069) 239375; f. 1968 when the former Evangelische Gemeinschaft and Methodistenkirche united; Bishop Dr WALTER KLAIBER.

Selbständige Evangelisch-Lutherische Kirche (Independent Evangelical-Lutheran Church): Schopenhauerstr. 7, 3000 Hannover 61; tel. (0511) 557808; f. 1972; Bishop Dr JOBST SCHÖNE, D.D.; Exec. Sec. Rev. ARMIN ZIELKE.

Vereinigung der deutschen Mennonitengemeinden (Union of German Mennonite Congregations): 2970 Emden, Brückstr. 74; tel. (04921) 22966; f. 1886; Chair. Dr HEINOLD FAST.

Other Christian Churches

Alt-Katholische Kirche (Old Catholic Church): 5300 Bonn 1, Gregor-Mendelstr. 28; tel. (0228) 232285; seceded from the Roman Catholic Church as a protest against the declaration of Papal infallibility in 1870; belongs to the Utrecht Union of Old Catholic Churches; in full communion with the Anglican Communion; Pres. Bischof Dr SIGISBERT KRAFT (Bonn); 28,000 mems.

Protestant Churches in the former GDR

Bund der Evangelischen Kirchen (BEK) (Federation of Evangelical Churches): 1040 Berlin, Auguststr. 80; tel. 28860; some 4m. people, about 25% of the population of the former GDR, belong to one of the Territorial Churches united in the BEK, compared with an estimated 70% in the 1950s; Pres. of Synod Rev. ROSEMARIE CYNKIEWICZ; Exec. Sec. Oberkirchenrat MARTIN ZIEGLER.

Arbeitsgemeinschaft Christlicher Kirchen (Association of Christian Churches): 1040 Berlin, Auguststr. 80; tel. 28860; f. 1970; unites member churches of BEK with other churches; 17 full mems, four observers; Chair. Dr EBERHARD NATHO; Gen. Sec. Rev. MARTIN LANGE.

Konferenz der Evangelischen Kirchenleitungen (Conference of Evangelical Church Leaders): 1040 Berlin, Auguststr. 80; Chair. Bischof Dr CHRISTOPH DEMKE.

Affiliated to the BEK

Evangelische Kirche der Union (EKU): Kirchenkanzlei (Chancellery): 1040 Berlin, Auguststr. 80; tel. 28860; Pres. Dr FRIEDRICH WINTER.

†**Evangelical Church of Anhalt:** Kirchenpräsident: Dr EBERHARD NATHO (1500 Dessau, Otto-Grotewohl-Str. 22; tel. (047) 7247).

GERMANY

†**Evangelical Church in Berlin-Brandenburg:** 1020 Berlin, Neue Grünstr. 19–22; tel. 278020; Bischof Dr GOTTFRIED FORCK (1120 Berlin-Weissensee, Parkstr. 21).

†**Evangelical Church of the Church Region of Görlitz:** 8900 Görlitz, Berliner Str. 62; tel. 6247; formerly Church Province of Silesia; Bischof Prof. Dr JOACHIM ROGGE.

Evangelical-Lutheran Church of Mecklenburg: 2751 Schwerin, Münzstr. 8; tel. 864165; Landesbischof CHRISTOPH STIER.

†**Evangelical Church of Pomerania:** 2200 Greifswald, Bahnhofstr. 35–36; tel. 5261; formerly Evangelical Church of Greifswald; Bischof EDUARD BERGER.

†**Evangelical Church of the Church Province of Saxony:** 3010 Magdeburg, Am Dom 2; tel. (091) 31881; Bischof Dr CHRISTOPH DEMKE.

Evangelical-Lutheran Church of Saxony: 8032 Dresden, Lukasstr. 6; tel. 475841; Landesbischof Dr JOHANNES HEMPEL.

Evangelical-Lutheran Church in Thuringia: 5900 Eisenach, Dr-Moritz-Mitzenheim Str. 2A; tel. 5226; Landesbischof Dr WERNER LEICH.

(† Member of the EKU)

Other Protestant Churches in the former GDR

Bund Evangelisch-Freikirchlicher Gemeinden (Union of Evangelical Free Church Congregations): 1034 Berlin, Gubener Str. 10; tel. 5891832; Pres. Rev. MANFRED SULT; Gen. Sec. Rev. ULRICH MATERNE.

Bund Freier evangelischer Gemeinden (Federation of Free Evangelical Congregations): 1199 Berlin, Handjerystr. 29-31; tel. 6762665; Federal Chair. Rev. JOHANNES SCHMIDT.

Evangelische Brüder-Unität, Distrikt Herrnhut (Unitas Fratrum-Moravian Church in the District of Herrnhut); 8709 Herrnhut, Zittauer Str. 20; tel. 258; Pres. Rev. CHRISTIAN MÜLLER.

Evangelisch-Lutherische (altlutherische) Kirche (Evangelical Lutheran (Old Lutheran) Church): 1020 Berlin, Annenstr. 53; tel. 2793583; f. 1830; c. 8,000 mems; Sec. Kirchenrat JOHANNES ZELLMER.

Evangelisch-Methodistische Kirche (United Methodist Church): 8020 Dresden, Wiener Str. 56; tel. 477441; Bischof Dr RÜDIGER MINOR.

Kirchenbund Evangelisch-Reformierter Gemeinden (Church Federation of Evangelical Reformed Congregations): 7010 Leipzig, Tröndlinring 7; tel. 291079; Pastor HANS-JÜRGEN SIEVERS.

Mennonitengemeinde (Mennonite Congregation): 1054 Berlin, Schwedter Str. 262; Dir Pastor KNUTH HANSEN.

Other Christian Churches in the former GDR

Apostelamt Jesu Christi: 7500 Cottbus, Otto-Grotewohl-Str. 57; tel. 713297; Pres. WALDEMAR ROHDE.

Gemeindeverband der Altkatholischen Kirche (Union of the Old Catholic Church): 3720 Blankenburg, Georgstr. 7; tel. 2297; Deaconess URSULA BUSCHLÜTER.

Gemeinschaft der Siebenten-Tags-Adventisten (Seventh-day Adventist Church): 1160 Berlin, Helmholtzstr. 1; tel. 6351320; Pres. LOTHAR REICHE.

Religiöse Gesellschaft der Freunde (Quäker) (Society of Friends): 1086 Berlin, Planckstr. 20; tel. 2082284; f. 1969; 51 mems; Sec. HANS-ULRICH TSCHIRNER.

Russische Orthodoxe Kirche—Mitteleuropäisches Exarchat (Russian Orthodox Church): 1157 Berlin, Wildensteiner Str. 10; tel. 5082024; Archbishop GERMAN.

JUDAISM

The Jewish community in Germany is estimated to number about 35,000.

Zentralrat der Juden in Deutschland (Central Council of Jews in Germany): 5300 Bonn 2, Rüngsdorfer Str. 6; tel. (0228) 357023; telex 8869230; fax (0228) 361148; Pres. Board of Dirs Dr HEINZ GALINSKI; Sec.-Gen. MICHA GUTTMANN.

Jüdische Gemeinde zu Berlin (Jewish Community in Berlin): 1000 Berlin 12, Fasanenstr. 79–80; Pres. Dr HEINZ GALINSKI.

The Press

Article 5 of the 1949 Basic Law of the Republic stipulates: 'Everyone has the right freely to express or to disseminate his opinion by speech, writing and pictures and freely to inform himself from generally accessible sources. Freedom of the press and freedom of reporting by radio and motion pictures are guaranteed. There shall be no censorship. These rights are limited by the provisions of the general laws, the provisions of the law for the protection of youth, and by the right to inviolability of personal honour.' These last qualifications refer to the Federal law penalizing the sale to young people of literature judged to endanger morality, and to articles in the Penal Code relating to defamation, in particular Article 187A concerning defamation of public figures.

There is no Federal Press Law, all legal action being normally referred back to the Constitution. But the press is subject to general items of legislation, some of which may significantly limit press freedom. Article 353C of the Penal Code, for example, dating from the Nazi period, prohibits the publication of official news supposed to be secret; under it a journalist may be required to reveal his sources. The Code of Criminal Procedure also constitutes a danger in that it authorizes the Government to confiscate objects potentially important as evidence in a legal investigation, which may be construed to include papers, print, etc.

Freedom of the press is stipulated in each of the Constitutions of the individual Länder. Many Länder have enacted laws defining the democratic role of the press and some give journalists access to sources of government information; some authorize the journalist to refuse to disclose his sources; others qualify, and even withhold this right. Some permit printed matter to be confiscated on suspicion of an indictable offence only if authorized by an independent judge; others allow a district attorney or even the police to give this authorization.

The German Press Council was founded in 1956 and is composed of publishers and journalists. It lays down guidelines, investigates complaints against the press and enjoys considerable standing.

The Federal German press is quite free of government control. While some 10% of papers support a political party, the majority of newspapers, including all the major dailies, are politically independent.

The political and economic conditions prevalent in the FRG after 1949 fostered the rapid development of a few large publishing groups.

In 1968 a government commission laid down various limits on the proportions of circulation one group should be allowed to control: (1) 40% of the total circulation of newspapers or 40% of the total circulation of magazines; (2) 20% of the total circulation of newspapers and magazines together; (3) 15% of the circulation in one field if the proportion owned in the other field is 40%. At that time the Springer Group's estimated ownership was 39.2% of newspaper circulation (65–70% in Berlin) and 17.5% of magazine circulation. In June 1968 Springer reduced his share of the periodical market to around 11%.

In 1990 (prior to German unification) there were 356 daily newspapers in the FRG, with a combined circulation of 20.8m. copies. There were five Sunday papers, with a circulation of 3.9m., and 37 weekly papers, with a circulation of 1.8m. In 1988 a total of 39 daily newspapers appeared in the GDR, with a combined circulation of 9.4m. copies per issue. In 1989 there were 543 periodicals and illustrated magazines in the GDR, with a combined average circulation of 21.9m. Until early 1990 all newspapers and periodicals in the GDR were owned and managed by political or related organizations such as party committees, trade unions, cultural associations, youth organizations, etc. Almost all dailies were controlled by or affiliated to a political party. In 1990 the majority of party-owned publications were transferred to private ownership. The most important and influential national dailies in the united Germany include *Frankfurter Allgemeine Zeitung*, *Süddeutsche Zeitung* (München) and *Berliner Zeitung* (formerly published in the GDR). The newspaper with the largest circulation is *Bild-Zeitung* (circ. 5.3m.) which is printed in 15 different provincial centres. The most influential weekly newspapers include *Die Zeit* and the Sundays *Bild am Sonntag* and *Welt am Sonntag*. Periodicals with circulations of over 1m. include the illustrated news weeklies *Der Spiegel*, *Stern* and *Quick*, the TV and Radio magazines *Hörzu* and *TV Hören + Sehen*, and the women's magazines *Brigitte* and *burda moden*.

The principal newspaper publishing groups are:

Axel Springer Group: 1000 Berlin 61, Kochstr. 50; tel. (030) 25-91-0; telex 184257; and 2000 Hamburg 36, Kaiser-Wilhelm-Str. 6; tel. (040) 3-47-1; telex 403242; the largest newspaper publishing group in continental Europe; includes five major dailies *(Die Welt, Hamburger Abendblatt, Bild Zeitung, Berliner Morgenpost, BZ)*, two Sunday papers *(Welt am Sonntag, Bild am Sonntag)*, three radio, television and family magazines *(Hörzu, Funk Uhr, Bildwoche)*, two women's journals *(JOURNAL für die Frau, Bild der Frau)*, the weekly motoring magazine *Auto-Bild*, and the book publishing firm Verlag Ullstein GmbH; Propr Axel Springer Verlag AG.

Gruner und Jahr AG & Co Druck- und Verlagshaus: 2210 Itzehoe, Am Vossbarg, Posfach 1240; telex 28289; and 2000 Hamburg 11, Postfach 110011; telex 219520; fax (040) 3703600; owns

GERMANY *Directory*

Stern, Brigitte, Essen und Trinken, Geo, Capital, Eltern, Marie Claire, Häuser, Yps, Schöner Wohnen, Hamburger Morgenpost.

Süddeutscher-Verlag: 8000 München 2, Sendlingerstr. 80; tel. (089) 21830; telex 523426; fax (089) 2183787; owns *Süddeutsche Zeitung*; 5 Mans.

Jahreszeiten-Verlag GmbH: 2000 Hamburg 60, Possmoorweg 5; tel. (040) 2717-0; telex 213214; fax (040) 27172056; f. 1948; owns amongst others the periodicals *Für Sie, Petra* and *Zuhause*; Pres. THOMAS GANSKE.

Heinrich-Bauer-Verlag: 2000 Hamburg 1, Burchardstr. 11 and 8000 München 83, Charles-de-Gaulle-Str.; telex 212845; owns 29 popular illustrated magazines, including *Quick* (München), *Neue Revue* (Hamburg), *Praline, Neue Post, Das Neue Platt* and *Bravo*; Pres. HEINRICH BAUER.

Burda GmbH: 7600 Offenburg, Postfach 1230; tel. (0781) 8401; telex 528000; owns *Bunte, Bild+Funk, Freundin, Pan, Freizeit Revue, Meine Familie und ich, Mein Schöner Garten, Das Haus, Architectural Digest (Deutsch)* and *Ambiente*; 7 Mans.

PRINCIPAL DAILIES

Aachen

Aachener Nachrichten: 5100 Aachen, Dresdner Str. 3, Postfach 110; tel. (0241) 5101-1; telex 832365; f. 1872; Publrs Zeitungsverlag Aachen; Edited by Verlagsanstalt Cerfontaine GmbH & Co., 5100 Aachen, Theaterstr. 24–34; circ. 67,000.

Aachener Volkszeitung: 5100 Aachen, Dresdner Str. 3, Postfach 110; tel. (0241) 51010; telex 832851; f. 1946; Publishers Zeitungsverlag Aachen; Editor-in-Chief Dr ANTON STERZL; circ. 106,000.

Ansbach

Fränkische Landeszeitung: 8800 Ansbach, Nürnberger Str. 9–17, Postfach 1362; tel. (0981) 95000; telex 17981837; Editors-in-Chief GERHARD EGETEMAYER, PETER M. SZYMANOWSKI; circ. 50,000.

Aschaffenburg

Main-Echo: 8750 Aschaffenburg (Main), Goldbacher Str. 25–27, Postfach 548; tel. (06021) 3961; telex 4188837; fax (06021) 20641; Editors Dr GEROLD MARTIN, HELMUT WEISS, Dr HELMUT TEUFEL; circ. 86,000.

Augsburg

Augsburger Allgemeine: 8900 Augsburg 1, Curt-Frenzel-Str. 2, Postfach 100054; tel. (0821) 70071; telex 53837; fax (0821) 704471; Editor-in-Chief GERNOT RÖMER; circ. 350,000.

Baden-Baden

Badisches Tagblatt: 7570 Baden-Baden, Stefanienstr. 1–3, Postfach 120; tel (07221) 2151; telex 781158; Editor UDO F. A. ROTZOLL; circ. 41,100.

Bamberg

Fränkischer Tag: 8600 Bamberg, Gutenbergstr. 1; tel. (0951) 1880; telex 662426; Publr BERNHARD WAGNER; circ. 83,900.

Bautzen

Nowa Doba: 8600 Bautzen, Tuchmacher Str. 27; tel. (054) 511316; telex 287220; morning; Sorbian language paper; Editor SIEGHARD KOSEL; circ. 1,957.

Berlin

Bauern-Echo: 1040 Berlin, Reinhardtstr. 14; tel. (02) 28930; telex 114424; f. 1948; morning; Editor LEONHARD HELMSCHROTT; circ. 93,969.

Berliner Morgenpost: 1000 Berlin 61, Kochstr. 50, Postfach 110303; tel. (030) 25910; telex 183508; fax (030) 2510828; f. 1898; published by Ullstein Verlag GmbH & Co KG; Editor BRUNO WALTERT; circ. 182,000.

Berliner Zeitung: 1026 Berlin, Karl-Liebknecht-Str. 29; tel. (02) 2440; telex 114854; f. 1945; morning; publ. by Gruner & Jahr AG and Maxwell Communications; Editor HANS EGGERT; circ. 450,000.

Berliner Zeitung (BZ) am Abend: 1026 Berlin, Karl-Liebknecht-Str. 29; tel. (02) 2440; telex 114854; evening; Editor HORST HERTELT; circ. 203,653.

BZ (Berliner Zeitung): 1000 Berlin 61, Kochstr. 50; tel. (030) 25910; telex 183508; fax (030) 2510828; f. 1877; published by Ullstein Verlag GmbH & Co KG; Editor WILHELM PANNIER; circ. 291,500.

Deutsches Sport-Echo: 1086 Berlin, Neustädtische Kirchstr. 15; sports; Editor DIETER WALES; circ. 184,960.

Junge Welt: 1026 Berlin, Karl-Liebknecht-Str. 29; tel. (02) 2440; telex 114857; f. 1947; morning; Editor JENS KÖNIG; circ. 1,380,477.

Der Morgen: 1086 Berlin, Johannes-Dieckmann-Str. 17; tel. (02) 220218; telex 112704; f. 1945; morning; Editor GERHARD FISCHER; circ. 61,682.

National-Zeitung: 1055 Berlin, Prenzlauer Allee 36; tel. (02) 4300215; telex 112714; f. 1948; morning; Editor DIETHARD WEND; circ. 55,450.

Neue Zeit: 1086 Berlin, Mittelstr. 2–4; tel. (02) 2000942; telex 112536; fax (02) 2004757; f. 1945; morning; independent; Editor Dr MONIKA ZIMMERMANN; circ. 113,054.

Neues Deutschland: 1017 Berlin, Franz-Mehring-Platz 1; tel. (02) 58310; telex 112051; f. 1946; morning; publ. by the PDS; Editor WOLFGANG SPICKERMANN; circ. 200,000.

Der Tagesspiegel: 1000 Berlin 30, Potsdamer Str. 87; tel. (030) 26009-0; telex 183773; f. 1945; circ. 134,864.

Bielefeld

Neue Westfälische: 4800 Bielefeld 1, Niederstr. 23–27, Postfach 26; tel. (0521) 5550; telex 932799; fax (0521) 555-348; f. 1967; Editors GÜNTER BROZIO, JÜRGEN JUCHTMANN; circ. 227,850.

Westfalen-Blatt: 4800 Bielefeld, Südbrackstr. 14–18, Postfach 8740; tel. (0521) 5850; f. 1946; Editor CARL-W. BUSSE; circ. 148,400.

Bonn

Bonner Rundschau: 5300 Bonn, Thomas-Mann-Str. 51–53, Postfach 1248; tel. (0228) 7211; telex 886702; f. 1946; Dir Dr HEINRICH HEINEN; circ. 24,300.

General-Anzeiger: 5300 Bonn, Justus von Liebig-Str. 15, Postfach 1609; tel. (0228) 66880; telex 8869616; fax (0228) 6688411; f. 1725; independent; Publrs HERMANN NEUSSER, HERMANN NEUSSER, Jr; Editor FRIEDHELM KEMNA; circ. 85,200.

Die Welt: 5300 Bonn, Godesberger Allee 99; tel. (0228) 3041; telex 885715; fax (0228) 373465; f. 1946; published by Axel Springer Verlag; Editors MANFRED SCHELL, PETER GILLIES; circ. 225,200.

Braunschweig

Braunschweiger Zeitung: 3300 Braunschweig, Hamburger Str. 277 (Pressehaus), Postfach 3263; tel. (0531) 39000; telex 952722; Editor Dr ARNOLD RABBOW; circ. 169,300.

Bremen

Bremer Nachrichten: 2800 Bremen, Martinistr. 43; tel. (0421) 36710; telex 244720; f. 1743; Publr HERBERT C. ORDEMANN; Editors DIETRICH IDE, WALFRIED ROSPEK; circ. 44,000.

Weser-Kurier: 2800 Bremen 1, Martinistr. 43, Postfach 107801; tel. (0421) 36710; telex 244709; f. 1945; Publr HERBERT C. ORDEMANN; circ. 185,000.

Bremerhaven

Nordsee-Zeitung: 2850 Bremerhaven 1, Hafenstr. 140; tel. (0471) 597-0; telex 238761; Chief Editor CLAUS PETERSEN; circ. 77,500.

Chemnitz

Chemnitzer Tageblatt: 9072 Chemnitz, Dimitroffstr. 2A; tel. (071) 44526; telex 7288; f. 1946; morning; circ. 10,000.

Freie Presse: 9010 Chemnitz 1, Karl-Marx Allee 15-19; tel. (071) 656280; telex 7233; morning; Editor DIETMAR GRIESHEIMER; circ. 603,000.

Cottbus

Lausitzer Rundschau: 7500 Cottbus, Strasse der Jugend 54; tel. (059) 4810; telex 17210; fax (059) 481375; independent; morning; Editors EVELIN SOBOTTKA, BERNHARD LISKE; circ. 275,000.

Darmstadt

Darmstädter Echo: 6100 Darmstadt, Holzhofallee 25–31, Postfach 110269; tel. (06151) 3871; telex 419363; f. 1945; Publrs Dr HANS-PETER BACH, HORST BACH; Editor-in-Chief ROLAND HOF; circ. 120,000.

Dortmund

Ruhr-Nachrichten: 4600 Dortmund 1, Pressehaus, Westenhellweg 86–88, Postfach 105051; telex 822106; f. 1949; Editor FLORIAN LENSING-WOLFF; circ. 269,000.

Dresden

Dresdner Neueste Nachrichten: 8060 Dresden, Antonstr. 8; tel. (051) 52757; telex 2369; morning; Editor-in-Chief WOLFGANG SCHÜTZE; circ. 34,000.

Sächsische Zeitung: 8010 Dresden, Julian-Grimau-Allee; tel. (051) 4864240; telex 2251; f. 1946; morning; Editor JOHANNES SCHULZ; circ. 525,000.

Die Union: 8060 Dresden, Str. der Befreiung 21; tel. (051) 53357; telex 2910; fax (051) 51024; f. 1946; morning; publ. by the Dresdner Zeitungsverlag; Editors A. RICHTER, A. HOLZBERGER; circ. 60,000.

GERMANY   Directory

Düsseldorf

Handelsblatt: 4000 Düsseldorf 1, Kasernenstr. 67, Postfach 1102; tel. (0211) 8870; telex 8581815; fax (0211) 326759; 5 a week; only economics, business and finance newspaper with national circulation; Man. Dir GEORG VON HOLTZBRINCK; circ. 140,000.

Rheinische Post: 4000 Düsseldorf, Schadowstr. 11; tel. (0211) 5050; telex 8581901; f. 1946; Dirs Dr J. SCHAFFRATH; Editor Dr JOACHIM SOBOTTA; circ. 347,500.

Westdeutsche Zeitung: 4000 Düsseldorf 1, Königsallee 27, Postfach 1132; tel. (0211) 83820; Editor-in-Chief PAULHEINZ GRUPE; Publisher and Editor Dr M. GIRARDET; circ. 192,300.

Erfurt

Thüringer Allgemeine: 5010 Erfurt, Juri-Gagarin-Ring 113–117; tel. (061) 530316; telex 61212; f. 1946; morning; Editor-in-Chief SERGEJ LOCHTHOFEN; circ. 350,000.

Essen

Neue Ruhr Zeitung: 4300 Essen, Friedrichstr. 34–38, Postfach 104161; tel. (0201) 20640; telex 85750130; Editor-in-Chief JENS FEDDERSEN; circ. 215,000.

Westdeutsche Allgemeine Zeitung: 4300 Essen, Friedrichstr. 34–38, Postfach 104161; tel. (0201) 20640; telex 8579951; Editor RALF LEHMANN; circ. 1,211,900.

Westfälische Rundschau: 4300 Essen, Friedrichstr. 34–38; tel. (0201) 20640; telex 8579951; Editor GÜNTER HAMMER; circ. 250,000.

Frankfurt am Main

Frankfurter Allgemeine Zeitung: 6000 Frankfurt a.M., Hellerhofstr. 2–4, Postfach 100808; tel. (069) 75910; telex 41223; f. 1949; Editors FRITZ ULLRICH FACK, JOACHIM C. FEST, JÜRGEN JESKE, HUGO MÜLLER-VOGG, JOHANN GEORG REISSMÜLLER; circ. 380,000.

Frankfurter Neue Presse: 6000 Frankfurt a.M., Frankenallee 71–81, Postfach 100801; tel. (069) 75010; telex 411054; fax (069) 7306192; independent; Editor WERNER WIRTHLE; circ. 130,000.

Frankfurter Rundschau: 6000 Frankfurt a.M., Grosse Eschenheimer Str. 16–18, Postfach 100660; tel. (069) 21991; telex 411651; fax (069) 2199521; Editor WERNER HOLZER; circ. 204,000.

Frankfurt an der Oder

Märkische Oderzeitung: 1200 Frankfurt a.d. Oder, Karl-Marx-Str. 23; tel. (030) 311211; telex 16288; morning; Editor HERBERT THIEME; circ. 210,507.

Freiburg

Badische Zeitung: 7800 Freiburg i. Br., Basler Landstr. 3; tel. (0761) 4960; telex 772820; f. 1946; Editor Dr ANSGAR FÜRST; circ. 175,800.

Gera

Ostthüringer Nachrichten: 6500 Gera, Julius-Fucik-Str. 18; tel. (070) 612262; telex 58227; morning; Editor LOTHAR OBERÜCK; circ. 237,537.

Göttingen

Göttinger Tageblatt: 3400 Göttingen, Dransfelder Str. 1, Postfach 1953; tel. (0551) 9011; telex 96800; f. 1889; Man. Dir MANFRED DALLMANN; Editor-in-Chief HORST STEIN; circ. 49,600.

Hagen

Westfalenpost: 5800 Hagen, Mittelstr. 32; tel. (02331) 2041; telex 823861; f. 1946; Chief Editor Dr FRITZ HEIMPLÄTZER; circ. 160,000.

Halle

Hallesches Tageblatt: 4002 Halle, Gr. Brauhausstr. 16–17; tel. (046) 38396; telex 4359; fax (046) 28691; f. 1945; morning; Editor AXEL MEIER; circ. 57,000.

Mitteldeutsche Zeitung: 4020 Halle, Str. der DSF 76; tel. (046) 38461; telex 4265; f. 1946; morning; Editor Dr HANS-DIETER KRÜGER; circ. 530,000.

Der Neue Weg: 4000 Halle, Klement-Gottwald-Str. 61; telex 4417; f. 1946; morning; CDU; Editor KLAUS-PETER BIGALKE; circ. 37,100.

Hamburg

Bild–Zeitung: 2000 Hamburg 36, Axel-Springer-Platz 1; tel. (040) 3471; telex 2170010; fax (040) 345811; f. 1952; published by Axel Springer Verlag; Chief Editors PETER BARTELS, HANS-HERMANN TIEDJE; circ. 5,283,502.

Hamburger Abendblatt: 2000 Hamburg 36, Axel-Springer-Platz 1; tel. (040) 3471; telex 217001101; published by Axel Springer Verlag; Editor-in-Chief KLAUS KORN; circ. 303,000 (Saturdays 358,000).

Hamburger Morgenpost: 2000 Hamburg 50, Postfach 501060; tel. (040) 883031; telex 2161837; Editor WOLFGANG CLEMENT; circ. 162,200.

Hannover

Hannoversche Allgemeine Zeitung: 3000 Hannover 71, Bemeroder Str. 58, Postfach 209; tel. (0511) 5180; telex 923911-15; fax (0511) 513175; Editor LUISE MADSACK; circ. 263,000.

Heidelberg

Rhein-Neckar-Zeitung: 6900 Heidelberg, Hauptstr. 23, Postfach 104560; tel. (06221) 519-1; telex 461751; fax (06221) 519217; f. 1945; Publrs Dr LUDWIG KNORR, WINFRIED KNORR, Dr DIETER SCHULZE; circ. 114,000.

Heilbronn

Heilbronner Stimme: 7100 Heilbronn, Allee 2, Postfach 2040; tel. (07131) 615-1; telex 728729; f. 1946; Editor-in-Chief Dr WERNER DISTELBARTH; circ. 104,000.

Hof-Saale

Frankenpost: 8670 Hof-Saale, Poststr. 11, Postfach 1320; tel. (09281) 8160; telex 643601; Publr Frankenpost Verlag GmbH; Editor-in-Chief HEINRICH GIEGOLD; circ 110,000.

Ingolstadt

Donau Kurier: 8070 Ingolstadt, Stauffenbergstr. 2A, Postfach 340; tel. (0841) 6800; telex 55845; fax (0841) 680255; f. 1872; Publr and Dir Dr W. REISSMÜLLER; circ. 81,100.

Karlsruhe

Badische Neueste Nachrichten: 7500 Karlsruhe 1, Linkenheimer Landstr. 133, Postfach 311168; tel. (0721) 7890; telex 7826960; Publr and Editor HANS W. BAUR; circ. 174,000.

Kassel

Hessische/Niedersächsische Allgemeine: 3500 Kassel, Frankfurter Str. 168, Postfach 101009; tel. (0561) 2030; telex 99635; f. 1959; independent; Editor-in-Chief LOTHAR ORZECHOWSKI; circ. 201,400.

Kempten

Allgäuer Zeitung: 8960 Kempten, Kotternerstr. 64, Postfach 1129; tel. (0831) 2060; telex 54871; fax (0831) 27020; f. 1968; Publrs GEORG FÜRST VON WALDBURG-ZEIL, GÜNTER HOLLAND; Editor-in-Chief GERNOT RÖMER; circ. 118,000.

Kiel

Kieler Nachrichten: 2300 Kiel 1, Fleethörn 1–7, Postfach 1111; tel. (0431) 9030; telex 292768; Chief Editor WOLFGANG KRYSZOHN; circ. 114,100.

Koblenz

Rhein-Zeitung: 5400 Koblenz, August-Horch-Str. 28, Postfach 1540; tel. (0261) 89200; telex 862611; Editor HANS PETER SOMMER; circ. 244,700.

Köln

Express: 5000 Köln 1, Breite Str. 70, Postfach 100410; tel. (0221) 2240; telex 8882965; f. 1964; Publr ALFRED NEVEN DUMONT; Editor MICHAEL H. SORENG; circ. 314,700.

Kölner Stadt-Anzeiger: 5000 Köln 1, Breite Str. 70, Postfach 100410; tel. (0221) 2240; telex 8881162; f. 1876; Publr ALFRED NEVEN DUMONT; Editor HANS-JOACHIM DECKERT; circ. 288,300.

Kölnische Rundschau: 5000 Köln 1, Stolkgasse 25–45, Postfach 101910; tel. (0221) 16320; telex 8882361; fax (0221) 1632-491; f. 1946; Publr Dr HEINRICH HEINEN; Editor-in-Chief JÜRGEN C. JAGLA; circ. 162,000.

Konstanz

Südkurier: 7750 Konstanz, Südkurierhaus, Postfach 4300; tel. (07531) 2820; telex 733231; f. 1945; Publr Dr PIERRE GERCKENS; circ. 139,100.

Leipzig

Leipziger Tageblatt: 7010 Leipzig, Neumarkt 6; tel. (041) 295251; telex 512236; f. 1946; morning; part of the Axel Springer Group; circ. 40,000.

Leipziger Volkszeitung: 7010 Leipzig, Peterssteinweg 19; tel. (041) 71540; telex 51495; fax (041) 311948; f. 1894; morning; Editor BERND RADESTOCK; circ. 420,000.

Mitteldeutsche Neueste Nachrichten: 7010 Leipzig, Thomasiusstr. 2; morning; Editor RAINER DUCLAUD; circ. 20,499.

GERMANY *Directory*

Leutkirch
Schwäbische Zeitung: 7970 Leutkirch 1, Rudolf-Roth-Str. 18, Postfach 1145; tel. (07561) 800; telex 7321915; fax (07561) 80-134; f. 1945; Editor Chrysostomus Zodel; circ. 198,900.

Lübeck
Lübecker Nachrichten: 2400 Lübeck, Königstr. 53–57; tel. (0451) 1441; telex 26801; f. 1945; Chief Editor Klaus J. Groth; circ. 114,100.

Ludwigshafen
Die Rheinpfalz: 6700 Ludwigshafen/Rhein, Amtsstr. 5–11, Postfach 211147; tel. (0621) 590201; telex 464822; Dir Dr Dieter Schaub; circ. 248,300.

Magdeburg
Volksstimme: 3010 Magdeburg, Bahnhofstr. 17; tel. (091) 3880; telex 8462; fax (091) 388240; f. 1890; morning; publ. by Magdeburger Verlags- und Druckhaus GmbH & Co KG; Editor-in-Chief Karl-Heinz Schwarzkopf.

Mainz
Allgemeine Zeitung: 6500 Mainz, Grosse Bleiche 44–50, Postfach 3120; tel. (06131) 144-1; telex 4187753; part of the Rhein-Main-Presse; circ. 133,100.

Mannheim
Mannheimer Morgen: 6800 Mannheim 1, Am Marktplatz, Postfach 121231; tel. (0621) 17020; telex 462171; fax (0621) 1702-376; f. 1946; Publrs Dr K. Ackermann, R. v. Schilling; Chief Editors Sigmar Heilmann, Horst-Dieter Schiele; circ. 198,755.

München
Abendzeitung/8-Uhr-Blatt: 8000 München 2, Sendlingerstr. 79; tel. (089) 23770; telex 17897123; f. 1948; Publr Dr Johannes Friedmann; Editor-in-Chief Dr Uwe Zimmer; circ. 252,100.

Münchner Merkur: 8000 München 2, Paul-Heyse-Str. 2–4, Pressehaus; tel. (089) 53060; telex 522100; Publr Dr Dirk Ippen; Editor Werner Giers; circ. 186,500.

Süddeutsche Zeitung: 8000 München 2, Sendlingerstr. 80, Postfach 202220; tel. (089) 21830; telex 523426; f. 1945; Editor-in-Chief Dieter Schröder; circ. 383,500.

Münster
Münstersche Zeitung: 4400 Münster, Neubrückenstr. 8–11, Postfach 5560; tel. (0251) 5920; fax (0251) 592212; f. 1871; independent; Editor Dr Ralf Richard Koerner; circ. 66,308.

Westfälische Nachrichten: ZENO-Zeitungen, 4400 Münster, Soester Str. 13, Postfach 8680; tel. (0251) 6900; telex 892830; fax (0251) 690717; Chief Editor Jost Springensguth; circ. 215,000.

Neubrandenburg
Neubrandenburg Nordkurier: 2000 Neubrandenburg, Str. der Befreiung 27; tel. (090) 5850; telex 33211; f. 1990; Dir Klaus Strachardt; circ. 180,000.

Nürnberg
Nürnberger Nachrichten: 8500 Nürnberg, Marienplatz 1/5; tel. (0911) 2160; telex 622339; f. 1945; Editor Bruno Schnell; circ. 336,175.

Oberndorf-Neckar
Schwarzwälder Bote: 7238 Oberndorf-Neckar, Postfach 1380; tel. (07423) 780; telex 762814; circ. 135,576.

Oelde
Die Glocke: 4740 Oelde, Engelbert-Holterdorf-Str. 4–6; tel. (02522) 73-0; telex 89543; f. 1880; Editors Karl Friedrich Gehring, Engelbert Holterdorf; circ. 65,000.

Offenbach
Offenbach-Post: 6050 Offenbach, Grosse Marktstr. 36–44, Postfach 164; tel. (069) 80631; telex 4152864; f. 1947; Publr Udo Bintz; circ. 54,000.

Oldenburg
Nordwest-Zeitung: 2900 Oldenburg, Peterstr. 28–34, Postfach 2525; tel. (0441) 2391; telex 25878; published by the Druck- und Pressehaus GmbH; Editor B. Schulte; circ. 122,000.

Osnabrück
Neue Osnabrücker Zeitung: 4500 Osnabrück, Breiter Gang 11–14 und Grosse Str. 17/19, Postfach 1960; tel. (0541) 3250; telex 94832; fax (0541) 310334; f. 1967 from merger of *Neue Tagespost* and *Osnabrücker Tageblatt*; Chief Editor F. Schmedt; circ. 299,572.

Passau
Passauer Neue Presse: 8390 Passau, Neuburger Str. 28, Postfach 2040; tel. (0851) 5020; telex 57879; fax (0851) 502-256; f. 1946; Editor-in-Chief Ulrich Zimmermann; circ. 163,000.

Potsdam
Brandenburgische Neueste Nachrichten: 1500 Potsdam, Leninallee 185; morning; Editor Georg Jopke; circ. 22,453.

Märkische Volksstimme: 1500 Potsdam, Friedrich-Engels-Str. 24; tel. (033) 3240; telex 15333; morning; independent; Editor Hans-Ulrich Konrad; circ. 347,495.

Regensburg
Mittelbayerische Zeitung: 8400 Regensburg 1, Kumpfmühler Str. 11; tel. (0941) 2070; telex 65841; fax (0941) 27173; f. 1945; Editor Karlheinz Esser; circ. 120,000.

Rostock
Der Demokrat: 2500 Rostock, Kröpelinerstr. 44–47; tel. (081) 36111; telex 31205; f. 1945; CDU; Editor Wolfgang Voss; circ. 18,200.

Norddeutsche Neueste Nachrichten: 2500 Rostock, Kröpelinerstr. 21; tel. (081) 94161; telex 031105; f. 1953; morning; Editor Wolf-Dietrich Gehrke; circ. 38,827.

Ostsee-Zeitung: 2500 Rostock, Richard-Wagner-Str. 1A; tel. (081) 3650; telex 31241; fax (081) 365302; f. 1952; independent; Editor Gerd Spilker; circ. 260,000.

Saarbrücken
Saarbrücker Zeitung: 6600 Saarbrücken, Gutenbergstr. 11–23, Postfach 296; tel. (0681) 5020; telex 4421262; f. 1761; Editors Rudolf Bernhard, Uwe Jacobsen; circ. 205,000.

Schwerin
Norddeutsche Zeitung: 2751 Schwerin, Graf-Schack-Allee 11; tel. (084) 865091; telex 32238; f. 1946; morning; belongs to the Axel Springer Group; Editor Günter Grasmeyer; circ. 20,500.

Schweriner Volkszeitung: 2791 Schwerin, Hermann-Duncker-Str. 27; tel. (084) 3530; telex 32247; fax (084) 375140; f. 1946; Editor Christoph Hamm; circ. 185,000.

Stuttgart
Stuttgarter Nachrichten: 7000 Stuttgart 80, Plieniger Str. 150; tel. (0711) 72050; telex 7255395; f. 1946; Editor-in-Chief Jürgen Offenbach; circ. 260,000.

Stuttgarter Zeitung: 7000 Stuttgart 80, Plieniger Str. 150, Postfach 106032; tel. (0711) 72050; telex 7255384; fax (0711) 7205-300; f. 1945; Chief Editor Jürgen Dannenmann; circ. 509,710.

Suhl
Freies Wort: 6000 Suhl, Wilhelm-Pieck-Str. 6; tel. (066) 5130; telex 62205; morning; Editor Helmut Linke; circ. 177,460.

Trier
Trierischer Volksfreund: 5500 Trier, Nikolaus-Koch-Platz 1–3, Postfach 3770; tel. (0651) 7199-0; telex 472860; fax (0651) 7199990; Chief Editors Dr Hajo Goertz, Norbert Kohler; circ. 97,600.

Ulm
Südwest Presse: 7900 Ulm, Frauenstr. 77, Postfach 3333; tel. (0731) 15601; telex 7124612; circ. 361,924.

Weiden
Der Neue Tag: 8480 Weiden, Weigelstr. 16, Postfach 1340; tel. (0961) 850; telex 63880; Editor-in-Chief Horst Homberg; circ. 84,100.

Weimar
Thüringer Neueste Nachrichten: 5300 Weimar, Goetheplatz 9A; tel. (0621) 4192; telex 618924; f. 1951; Editor Klaus-Rainer Lorenz; circ. 32,055.

Thüringer Tageblatt: 5300 Weimar, Coudraystr. 6; tel. (0621) 2411; telex 618922; fax (0621) 3493; f. 1946; morning; Editor Thomas Bickelhaupt; circ. 25,000.

Thüringische Landeszeitung: 5300 Weimar, Marienstr. 14; tel. (0621) 3201; telex 618937; f. 1945; morning; Editor H.-D. Woithon; circ. 68,000.

Wetzlar
Wetzlarer Neue Zeitung: 6330 Wetzlar, Elsa-Brandström-Str. 18, Postfach 2940; tel. (06441) 7010; telex 483883; f. 1945; Editor Janos Bardi; circ. 70,000.

GERMANY

Wiesbaden

Wiesbadener Kurier: 6200 Wiesbaden 1, Langgasse 21, Postfach 6029; tel. (06221) 3550; telex 4186841; Chief Editor HILMAR BÖRSING; circ. 65,000.

Würzburg

Main-Post: 8700 Würzburg, Berner Str. 2; tel. (0931) 60010; telex 68845; fax (0931) 6001-242; f. 1883; independent; Publrs JOHANNES VON GUTTENBERG, GERHARD WIESEMANN; Editors-in-Chief REINER F. KIRST, DIETER W. ROCKENMAIER; circ. 153,000.

SUNDAY AND WEEKLY PAPERS

Bayernkurier: 8000 München 19, Nymphenburger Str. 64; tel. (089) 120041; weekly; organ of the CSU; Chief Editor W. SCHARNAGL; circ. 161,802.

Bild am Sonntag: 2000 Hamburg 36, Kaiser-Wilhelm-Str. 6, Postfach 566; tel. (040) 3471; telex 403242; f. 1956; Sunday; Published by Axel Springer Verlag; Chief Editor EWALD STRUWE; circ. 2,400,000.

Deutsches Allgemeines Sonntagsblatt: 2000 Hamburg 13, Mittelweg 111; tel. (040) 41419-0; telex 212973; fax (040) 41419111; f. 1948; Friday; Dir NORBERT MEYER; circ. 115,000.

Die Märkische: 1080 Berlin, Mittelstr. 2–4; tel. (030) 2000942; weekly; Editor-in-Chief PETER MUGAY; circ. 15,000.

Rheinischer Merkur Christ und Welt: 5300 Bonn 2, Godesberger Allee 157; tel. (0228) 8840; f. 1946; weekly; Editor THOMAS KIELINGER; circ. 133,000.

Welt am Sonntag: 2000 Hamburg 36, Axel-Springer-Platz 1; tel. (040) 3471; telex 403242; Sunday; published by Axel Springer Verlag; Editor MANFRED GEIST; circ. 360,000.

Die Zeit: 2000 Hamburg 1, Postfach 10 68 20, Speersort 1, Pressehaus; tel. (040) 3280-0; telex 886433; f. 1946; weekly; Publr HILDE VON LANG; Editor-in-Chief Dr THEO SOMMER; circ. 488,000.

SELECTED PERIODICALS

Agriculture

Agrar Praxis: 7022 Leinfelden-Echterdingen, Ernst-Mey-Str. 8; tel. (0711) 7594-423; telex 7255421; f. 1882; monthly; Editor-in-Chief KLAUS NIEHÖRSTER; circ. 60,250.

Agrarwirtschaft: 6000 Frankfurt 1, Mainzerlandstr. 251; tel. (069) 7595-01; telex 4170335; fax (069) 7595-2999; f. 1952; monthly; agricultural management, market research and agricultural policy; Publr ALFRED STROTHE; Editor Prof. Dr BUCHHOLZ; circ. 1,900.

Bayerisches Landwirtschaftliches Wochenblatt: 8000 München 2, Postfach 400320, Lothstr. 29; f. 1810; weekly; organ of the Bayerischer Bauernverband; Editor LUDWIG M. GAUL; circ. 106,621.

Eisenbahn-Landwirt: 4300 Essen 11, Am Ellenbogen 12, Postfach 110664; tel. (0201) 670525; f. 1918; monthly; Dir HANS HÜSKEN; circ. 120,000.

Land und Garten: 3000 Hannover, Bemeroder Str. 58, Postfach 3720; f. 1920; weekly; agriculture and gardening; Editor LUISE MADSACK; circ. 80,000.

Das Landvolk: 3000 Hannover, Warmbüchenstr. 3; telex 9230457; fortnightly; issued by Landbuch-Verlag GmbH; Chief Editor GÜNTHER MARTIN BEINE; circ. 104,000.

Die Landpost: 7000 Stuttgart 70, Wollgrasweg 31; tel. (0711) 451091; fax (0711) 456603; f. 1945; weekly; agriculture and gardening; Editors Dr KONRAD BINKERT, ERICH REICH.

Neue Deutsche Bauernzeitung: 1040 Berlin, Reinhardtstr. 14; tel. (030) 2893; telex 112728; f. 1960; agricultural weekly; Editor Dr UDO AUGUSTIN; circ. 145,000.

Art, Drama, Architecture and Music

AIT Architektur, Innenarchitektur, Technischer Ausbau: 7000 Stuttgart 1, Postfach 3081; tel. (0711) 75911; fax (0711) 7591-266; f. 1890; monthly; Editors E. HOEHN, R. SELLIN; circ. 10,000.

Bildende Kunst: 1040 Berlin, Oranienburger Str. 67–68; tel. (02) 2879306; telex 112302; fax (02) 2829458; f. 1947; monthly; painting, sculpture and graphics; Editor MATTHIAS FLÜGGE; circ. 20,000.

Die Kunst: 8000 München 90, Elisenstr. 3; telex 522745; f. 1885; monthly; arts and antiques; published by Karl Thiemig AG München; circ. 6,500.

Das Kunstwerk: 7000 Stuttgart 80, Hessbrühlstr. 69; tel. (0711) 7863-0; telex 7-255820; fax (0711) 7863-393; f. 1946; quarterly; modern art; circ. 2,500.

Musica: 3500 Kassel, Postfach 10 03 29; telex 992376; fax (0561) 3105-240; Editor Prof. Dr CLEMENS KÜHN; circ. 7,000.

Neue Werbung: 1055 Berlin, Am Friedrichshain 22; tel. (02) 4387232; telex 114566; fax (02) 4361249; monthly; graphic design and advertising.

Theater der Zeit: 1040 Berlin, Oranienburger Str. 67; tel. (02) 2879259; telex 112302; f. 1946; monthly; theatre, drama, opera, operetta, musical, puppet theatre, ballet; Editor MARTIN LINZER; circ. 12,000.

Theater heute: 1000 Berlin 30, Lützowplatz 7; tel. (030) 2617003; fax (030) 2617002; f. 1960; monthly; Editors Prof. Dr HENNING RISCHBIETER, Dr PETER VON BECKER, Dr MICHAEL MERSCHMEIER.

Economics, Finance and Industry

Absatzwirtschaft: 4000 Düsseldorf 1, Kasernenstr. 67, Postfach 1102; tel. (0211) 8388493/4; fax (0211) 328229; f. 1958; monthly; journal for marketing; Dir UWE HOCH; Editor FRIEDHELM PÄLIKE; circ. 17,000.

Atomwirtschaft-Atomtechnik: 4000 Düsseldorf 1, Kasernenstr. 67, Postfach 1102; tel. (0211) 8388-498; telex 17211308; fax (0211) 326759; f. 1956; monthly; technical, scientific and economic aspects of nuclear engineering and technology; Editors Dipl.-Ing. R. HOSSNER, Dipl.-Ing. W.-M. LIEBHOLZ; circ. 5,000.

Baurundschau: 2000 Hamburg 11, Gr. Burstah 49; monthly; published by Robert Mölich Verlag; Editor ROBERT MÖLICH.

Der Betrieb: 4000 Düsseldorf 1, Kasernenstr. 67, Postfach 1102; tel. (0211) 8870; telex 11308; fax (0211) 328229; weekly; business administration, revenue law, labour and social legislation; circ. 28,000.

Capital: 2000 Hamburg, Postfach 302040; telex 2195213; f. 1956; business and economics; circ. 248,876.

Creditreform: 4000 Düsseldorf, Kasernenstr. 67, Postfach 1102; tel. (0211) 887-0; telex 17211308; fax (0211) 328229; f. 1879; 11 a year; Editor KLAUS-WERNER ERNST; circ. 94,000.

Finanzwirtschaft: 1055 Berlin, Am Friedrichshain 22; tel. (02) 4387237; telex 114566; fax (02) 4361249; 12 a year; finance and economics; circ. 34,000.

Getränketechnik, Zeitschrift für das technische Management: 8500 Nürnberg 1, Breite Gasse 58–60; tel. (0911) 23830; telex 623081; fax (0911) 204956; 6 a year; trade journal for the brewing and beverage industries; circ. 8,518.

HV-Journal Der Handelsvertreter und Handelsmakler: 6000 Frankfurt a.M., Mainzer-Land-Str. 251, Postfach 101937, Siegel-Verlag Otto Müller GmbH; tel. (069) 759506; telex 411699; f. 1949; fortnightly; Editor ERNST H. HAUMANN; circ. 23,000.

Industrie-Anzeiger: 7022 Leinfelden-Echterdingen, Postfach 100252; f. 1879; 2 a week; Editor W. GIRARDET; circ. 26,000.

Management International Review: 6200 Wiesbaden, Taunusstr. 54; tel. (0611) 53435; telex 4186567; fax (0611) 53489; f. 1960; quarterly; issued by Betriebswirtschaftlicher Verlag Dr Th. Gabler; English; Editor Prof. Dr K. MACHARZINA (Stuttgart-Hohenheim).

VDI Nachrichten: 4000 Düsseldorf 1, Postfach 8228, Heinrichstr. 24; tel. (0211) 61880; telex 8587743; fax (0211) 6188306; f. 1946; weekly; circ. 135,000.

Versicherungswirtschaft: 7500 Karlsruhe 1, Klosestr. 22; tel. (0721) 3509-0; telex 7826943; fax (0721) 31833; f. 1946; fortnightly; Editor-in-Chief KARL-HEINZ REHNERT; circ. 11,000.

Wirtschaft und Statistik: 6500 Mainz 42, Postfach 421120; tel. (06131) 59094; telex 4187768; monthly; organ of the Federal Statistical Office; published by Verlag W. Kohlhammer GmbH; Editor Dr GERHARD BÜRGIN; circ. 5,000.

Wirtschaftswoche: 4000 Düsseldorf 1, Kasernenstr. 67, Postfach 3734; tel. (0211) 877-0; telex 8582048; fax (0211) 133374; weekly; business; Publrs Dr HEIK AFHELDT, Prof. Dr WOLFRAM ENGELS; Editor WOLFRAM BAENTSCH; circ. 142,184.

Education and Youth

Bravo: 8000 München 83, Postfach 201728; telex 524350; weekly; for young people; circ. 1,190,495.

Deutsche Lehrerzeitung: 1086 Berlin, Lindenstr. 54A; tel. (02) 20343294; telex 112181; fax (02) 2273453; f. 1954; weekly for teachers; Editor ELKE SCHILLING; circ. 100,000.

Erziehung und Wissenschaft: 4300 Essen, Goldammerweg 16; tel. (0201) 41757; telex 8579801; f. 1948; monthly; Editor-in-Chief DIRK-PETER ORTH; circ. 187,000.

Geographische Rundschau: 3300 Braunschweig, Georg-Westermann-Allee 66; tel. (0531) 708385; telex 952841; fax (0531) 708127; f. 1949; monthly; Man. Editor VERENA PICKART; circ. 15,581.

Jugend + Technik: 1026 Berlin, Postfach 43, Mauerstr. 39–40; tel. (02) 2233427; telex 114483; f. 1953; popular scientific/technological monthly for young people; circ. 205,000.

Junge Generation: 1026 Berlin, Postfach 43, Mauerstr. 39–40; tel. (02) 2233321; f. 1947; monthly; youth; circ. 72,000.

GERMANY

neues leben: 1080 Berlin, Mauerstr. 39-40; monthly; youth; circ. 550,111.

Pädagogik: 6940 Weinheim, Hauptbahnhof 10; tel. (040) 454595; f. 1949; monthly; Editor Dr J. BASTIAN; circ. 12,000.

Praxis Deutsch: 3016 Seelze, Postfach 100150; tel. (0511) 400040; telex 922923; 6 a year; German language and literature; circ. 28,786.

Rocky—Das Freizeit Magazine: 8000 München 19, Arnulfstr. 197; monthly; pop music magazine for young people; circ. 475,662.

Law

Deutsche Richterzeitung: 5300 Bonn-Bad Godesberg, Seufertstr. 27; fax (0228) 334723; f. 1909; monthly; circ. 11,000.

Juristenzeitung: 7400 Tübingen, Wilhelmstr. 18, Postfach 2040; tel. (07071) 26064; telex 7262872; fax (07071) 51104; fortnightly; circ. 6,000.

Juristische Rundschau: 1000 Berlin 30, Genthiner Str. 13; tel. (030) 26005-0; telex 184027; monthly; Editors Prof. Dr DIRK OLZEN, Prof. Dr HERBERT TRÖNDLE.

Neue Juristische Wochenschrift: 6000 Frankfurt a.M. 1, Palmengartenstr. 14, and 8 Munich 40, Wilhelmstr. 5-9; tel. (069) 7560910; fax (069) 748683; f. 1947; weekly; 6 Editors; circ. 55,000.

Rabels Zeitschrift für ausländisches und internationales Privatrecht: 2000 Hamburg 13, Mittelweg 187; tel. (040) 4127-263; telex 212893; fax (040) 4127-288; f. 1927; quarterly; Editors ULRICH DROBNIG, HEIN KÖTZ, ERNST-JOACHIM MESTMÄCKER.

Versicherungsrecht: 7500 Karlsruhe 1, Klosestr. 22; tel. (0721) 3509-0; telex 7826943; fax (0721) 31833; f. 1950; 3 a month; Editors Prof. Dr EGON LORENZ, KARL-HEINZ REHNERT; circ. 7,850.

Zeitschrift für die gesamte Strafrechtswissenschaft: 1000 Berlin 30, Genthiner Str. 13; tel. (030) 26005-0; telex 184027; f. 1881; quarterly; Chief Editor Prof. Dr Dr HANS JOACHIM HIRSCH.

Politics, Literature, Current Affairs

Akzente: 8000 München 86, Kolbergerstr. 22; tel. (089) 92694-0; fax (089) 915919; f. 1954; Editor MICHAEL KRÜGER.

Buch Aktuell: 4600 Dortmund 1, Westfalendamm 67, Postfach 101852/62; tel. (0231) 4344-0; telex 822214; fax (0231) 4344214; 4 a year; Editor EVA ROSENKRANZ; circ. 630,000.

Europa-Archiv, Zeitschrift für internationale Politik: 5300 Bonn, Adenauerallee 131; tel. (0228) 2675-0; telex 886822; fax (0228) 2675-173; f. 1946; 2 a month; journal of the German Society for Foreign Affairs; published by the Verlag für Internationale Politik GmbH, Bonn; Editor WOLFGANG WAGNER; Man. Editor JOCHEN THIES; circ. 4,500.

Die Fackel: 5300 Bonn 2, Wurzerstr. 2-4; tel. (0228) 82093-0; telex 885464; fax (0228) 8209343; f. 1950; monthly; Publr Verband der Kriegs- und Wehrdienstopfer, Behinderten und Sozialrentner Deutschland eV; Exec. Dir ULRICH LASCHET; circ. 1,000,000.

Gegenwartskunde: Leske Verlag + Budrich GmbH, 5090 Leverkusen 3 (Opladen), Postfach 300406; tel. (02171) 2079; quarterly; economics, politics, education; Editors W. GAGEL, H.-H. HARTWICH, B. SCHÄFERS.

Geist und Tat: 6000 Frankfurt a.M., Elbestr. 46; Bonn, Postfach 364; monthly; political, cultural; Editor W. EICHLER; circ. 3,500.

horizont international: 1026 Berlin, Karl-Liebknecht-Str. 29; tel. (02) 2442663; telex 114854; fax (02) 2123900; f. 1968; weekly; international politics and economics; Editor GERHARD ZAZWORKA; circ. 50,000.

Merian: 2000 Hamburg 13, Harvestehuder Weg 42; tel. (040) 441880; telex 214259; fax (040) 44188310; f. 1948; monthly; every issue deals with a country or a city; Chief Editor MANFRED BISSINGER; circ. 250,000.

Merkur (Deutsche Zeitschrift für europäisches Denken): 8000 München 5, Angertorstr. 1a; tel. (089) 2609644; fax (089) 2608307; f. 1947; monthly; literary, political; Editor KARL HEINZ BOHRER; circ. 6,000.

Neue Deutsche Literatur: 1086 Berlin, Friedrichstr. 169; tel. (02) 2335059; f. 1953; monthly; review of literature; Editor WERNER LIERSCH.

Neue Deutsche Presse: 1086 Berlin, Friedrichstr. 101; tel. (02) 2000106; telex 114947; f. 1946; monthly; journalist affairs, press, radio, television; Editor ERIKA GELHAAR; circ. 5,000.

Die Neue Gesellschaft—Frankfurter Hefte: 5300 Bonn 1, Godesberger Allee 143; tel. (0228) 883539; telex 885479; f. 1946; monthly; cultural, political; Editors WALTER DIRKS, EUGEN KOGON, HEINZ KÜHN, JOHANNES RAU, HEINZ O. VETTER, HANS-JOCHEN VOGEL, HERBERT WEHNER; circ. 11,000.

Neue Rundschau: 6000 Frankfurt a.M. 70, Postfach 700355, Hedderichstr. 114; tel. (069) 60620; telex 412877; fax (069) 6062319; f. 1890; quarterly; literature and essays; Editors UWE WITTSTOCK, GÜNTHER BUSCH; circ. 6,000.

Politik und Kultur: 5300 Bonn 1, Remigiusstr. 1; f. 1983; quarterly; Editor Dr W. W. SCHUTZ.

Sozialdemokrat Magazin: 5300 Bonn 2, Am Michaelshof 8; tel. (0228) 361011; telex 885603; Publisher Vorwärts Verlag GmbH; circ. 834,599.

Universitas: 7000 Stuttgart 1, Birkenwaldstr. 44, Postfach 105339; tel. (0711) 2582-0; telex 723636; fax (0711) 291450; f. 1946; monthly; scientific, literary and philosophical; Editor Dr CHRISTIAN ROTTA; circ. 7,200; quarterly editions in English and Spanish (circ. 4,800).

Die Weltbühne: 1080 Berlin, Oberwasserstr. 12; tel. (02) 2071435; weekly; politics, art, economics; Editor Dr HELMUT REINHARDT; circ. 30,000.

Welt des Buches: 5300 Bonn 2, Godesberger Allee 99; telex 885714; f. 1971; weekly; literary supplement of *Die Welt*.

Westermanns Monatshefte: 3300 Braunschweig, Georg-Westermann-Allee 66; telex 952973; f. 1856; monthly; circ. 100,000.

Wille und Weg: 8000 München 34, Schellingstr. 31, Postfach 340144; tel. (089) 2117-0; telex 5212394; fax (089) 2117-258; f. 1948; monthly; published by Verband der Kriegs- und Wehrdienstopfer, Behinderten und Sozialrentner Deutschlands eV, Landesverband Bayern eV; Editor MICHAEL PAUSDER; circ. 320,000.

Popular

Anna: 7600 Offenburg, Am Kestendamm 2; tel. (0781) 8402; telex 752804; f. 1974; knitting and needlecrafts; Editor AENNE BURDA.

Das Beste aus Readers Digest: 7000 Stuttgart 1, PO Box 106020, Augustenstr. 1; tel. (0711) 66020; telex 723539; magazines, books and recorded music programmes; Man. Dir WILFRIED RUSS; circ. 1,300,000.

Bild + Funk: 8000 München 81, Arabellastr. 23; tel. (089) 9250-0; telex 522043; radio and television weekly; Editor GÜNTER VAN WAASEN; circ. 1,040,829.

Bild und Ton: 7031 Leipzig, Karl-Heine-Str. 16; tel. (041) 49500; telex 51451; f. 1947; special photographic and cinematographic monthly; Editor Dr WALTER.

Brigitte: Gruner und Jahr AG, 2000 Hamburg 36, Postfach 302040; tel. (040) 41182550; telex 2195228; fortnightly; women's magazine; circ. 1,300,000.

Bunte Illustrierte: 7600 Offenburg, Burda-Hochhaus, Hauptstr. 130; tel. (0781) 8402; telex 528000; f. 1948; weekly family illustrated; circ. 1,140,439.

burda moden: 7600 Offenburg, Am Kestendamm 2, Postfach 1160; tel. (0781) 8402; telex 752804; fax (0781) 843319; f. 1949; monthly; fashion, beauty, cookery; Editor AENNE BURDA; circ. 2,300,000.

Deine Gesundheit: 1020 Berlin, Neue Grünstr. 18; tel. (02) 2700516; popular monthly dealing with health and welfare; circ. 242,700.

Eltern: 2000 Hamburg 1, Postfach 302040; Pressehaus Gruner und Jahr; tel. (089) 41520; telex 529324; fax (089) 4152720; f. 1966; monthly; for young parents; Editor NORBERT HINZE; circ. 599,181.

Eulenspiegel: 1017 Berlin, Franz-Mehring-Platz 1; tel. (02) 58312207; telex 112051; political satirical and humorous weekly; Editors JÜRGEN NOWAK, HARTMUT BERLIN; circ. 492,568.

FF-dabei: 1026 Berlin, Karl-Liebknecht-Str. 29; tel. (02) 2440; telex 114854; weekly; Editor ALFRED WAGNER; circ. 1,483,495.

Filmspiegel: 1040 Berlin, Oranienburger Str. 67-68; tel. (02) 2879254; telex 112302; fortnightly; films and cinematography; circ. 200,000.

Film und Fernsehen: 1040 Berlin, Oranienburger Str. 67-68; tel. (02) 2879265; telex 112302; f. 1973; monthly; organ of the Union of Film and TV Artists; Editor GÜNTER NETZEBAND; circ. 10,700.

Fotografie: 7031 Leipzig, Karl-Heine-Str. 16; tel. (041) 49500; telex 51451; f. 1946; special photographic monthly; Editor Dr WALTER.

Fotokino-Magazin: 7031 Leipzig, Karl-Heine-Str. 16; tel. (041) 49500; telex 51451; f. 1962; popular photographic monthly; Editor Dr WALTER.

Frau aktuell: 4000 Düsseldorf 1, Adlerstr. 22; tel. (0211) 36660; telex 8587669; fax (0211) 3666-231; f. 1965; Editor DIETER ULRICH; circ. 307,284.

Frau im Spiegel: 2000 Hamburg 50, Griegstr. 75; tel. (040) 88303-5; fax (040) 8802709; women's magazine; circ. 749,834.

Freie Welt: 1026 Berlin, Karl-Liebknecht-Str. 29; tel. (02) 2440; telex 114854; fax (02) 2442997; weekly; travel; Editor GÜNTHER WOLFRAM; circ. 100,000.

Freundin: 8000 München 81, Arabellastr. 23; telex 522274; f. 1948; fortnightly for young women; Chief Editor EBERHARD HENSCHEL; circ. 745,556.

Funk Uhr: 2000 Hamburg 36, Axel-Springer-Platz 1, Postfach 304630; tel. (040) 3471; telex 403242; fax (040) 343180; radio and

GERMANY

television weekly; published by Axel Springer Verlag AG; Editor IMRE KUSZTRICH; circ. 2,013,072.

Für Dich: 1026 Berlin, Karl-Liebknecht-Str. 29; tel. (02) 2440; telex 114854; fax (02) 2443327; f. 1962; women's weekly; Editors HANS EGGERT, Dr PETER PANKAU; circ. 350,000.

Für Sie: 2000 Hamburg 60, Possmoorweg 5; telex 213214; women's magazine; circ. 959,838.

FUWO—Die Neue Fussballwoche: 1086 Berlin, Neustädtische Kirchstr. 15; tel. (02) 2212420; telex 2853; weekly; football; Editor JÜRGEN NÖLDNER; circ. 284,993.

Gong: 8500 Nürnberg, Innere Cramer-Klett-Str. 6; telex 9118134; f. 1948; radio and TV weekly; Editor HELMUT MARKWORT; circ. 1,016,415.

Guter Rat: 1026 Berlin, Mollstr. 1; tel. (0161) 2123865; fax (0161) 2909511; f. 1948; monthly consumer magazine; circ. 500,000.

Heim und Welt: 3000 Hannover, Am Jungfernplan 3; tel. (0511) 855757; telex 921158; fax (0511) 854603; weekly; Editor H. G. BRÜNEMANN; circ. 300,000.

Hörzu: 2000 Hamburg 36, Axel-Springer-Platz 1, Postfach 304630; tel. (040) 3471; telex 217001210; f. 1946; radio and television; published by Axel Springer Verlag; Editor KLAUS STAMPFUSS; circ. 3,857,000.

Illustrierter Motorsport: 1086 Berlin, Neustädtische Kirch-Str. 15; monthly; cars, motorcycles and motor-boats; Editor WOLFGANG ESCHMENT.

Kicker-Sportmagazin: 8500 Nürnberg 1, Badstr. 4–6; tel. (0911) 2160; telex 622906; f. 1946; sports weekly illustrated; published by Olympia Verlag; Man. Dir HERMANN KRAEMER; circ. 226,884.

Das Magazin: 1026 Berlin, Karl-Liebknecht-Str. 29; tel. (02) 2443435; telex 114854; f. 1954; monthly; Editor MANFRED GEBHARDT; circ. 560,000.

Meine Familie & ich: 8000 München 81, Arabellastr. 23; tel. (089) 9250-0; telex 522802; fax (089) 9250-3030; circ. 756,662.

Die Mode: 7010 Leipzig, Friedrich-Ebert-Str. 76–78; 2 a year; fashion; circ. 23,300.

Modische Maschen: 7010 Leipzig, Friedrich-Ebert-Str. 76–78; tel. (041) 71790; telex 512733; f. 1963; popular women's monthly for fashion and knitting; Editor-in-Chief HEIDRUN SCHELMAT; circ. 220,000.

Neue Berliner Illustrierte: 1026 Berlin, Karl-Liebknecht-Str. 29; tel. (02) 2440; telex 114854; fax (02) 2123880; f. 1945; weekly; Editor SIEGFRIED SCHRÖDER; circ. 794,102.

Neue Post: 2000 Hamburg 1, Burchardstr. 11, Postfach 100444; telex 2163770; weekly; circ. 1,728,750.

Neue Revue: 2000 Hamburg 1, Burchardstr. 11, Postfach 100444; tel. (040) 3019-0; telex 2163770; f. 1946; illustrated weekly; Editor-in-Chief RICHARD MAHKORN; circ. 1,121,184.

Neue Welt: 4000 Düsseldorf 1, Adlerstr. 22; telex 8587669; f. 1932; weekly; Editors PETER PREISS, GÜNTHER GROTKAMP; circ. 499,885.

Pardon: 6000 Frankfurt a.M., Oberweg 157, Postfach 180426; f. 1962; satirical monthly; Editor HANS A. NIKEL; circ. 70,000.

Petra: Jahreszeiten-Verlag, 2000 Hamburg 60, Possmoorweg 1; telex 213214; monthly; circ. 496,305.

Praline: 2000 Hamburg 1, Burchardstr. 11; telex 2163770; weekly; women's magazine; circ. 760,369.

Pramo: 7010 Leipzig, Friedrich-Ebert-Str. 76–78; tel. (041) 71790; telex 51733; monthly; practical fashion for women and children; circ. 753,100.

Quick: 8000 München 83, Charles-de-Gaulle Str. 8; tel. (089) 67860; telex 2163770; f. 1948; illustrated weekly; Editor GERT BRAUN; circ. 843,908.

Saison: 7010 Leipzig, Friedrich-Ebert-Str. 76–78; quarterly; fashion; circ. 209,500.

Scala: 6000 Frankfurt a.M. 1, Frankenallee 71–81; tel. (069) 75010; telex 411655; fax (069) 7306192; 6 a year; independent; Editor WERNER WIRTHLE; circ. 330,000; editions in German, English, French, Spanish, Portuguese.

Schöner Wohnen: 2000 Hamburg 11, Am Baumwall 11, Postfach 110011; tel. (040) 3703-0; telex 2195228; monthly; homes and gardens; Editor ANGELIKA JAHR; circ. 365,000.

Sibylle: 1080 Berlin, Friedrichstr. 81–82; tel. (0161) 2202141; fax (0161) 2909477; f. 1956; 12 a year; women's fashion and lifestyle magazine; Editor-in-Chief ERIKA BÜTTNER; circ. 100,000.

7 Tage: 7570 Baden-Baden, Augustaplatz 10; telex 781410; f. 1843; weekly; Editor HELMUT EILERS; circ. 480,000.

Sonntag: 1086 Berlin, Niederwallstr. 39; cultural weekly; Editor Dr WILFRIED GEISSLER; circ. 22,598.

Der Spiegel: 2000 Hamburg 11, Brandstwiete 19/Ost-West-Str., Postfach 110420; telex 2162477; f. 1947; weekly; political, general;

Directory

Publr RUDOLF AUGSTEIN; Editors-in-Chief Dr WERNER FUNK, HANS WERNER KILZ; circ. 1,090,000.

Stern: Gruner und Jahr AG, 2000 Hamburg 36, Postfach 302040; tel. (040) 41181; telex 2195213; illustrated weekly; Publr ROLF SCHMIDT-HOLTZ; Editors-in-Chief MICHAEL JÜRGS, HERBERT RIEHL-HEYSE; circ. 1,478,926.

TV Hören+Sehen: 2000 Hamburg 1, Burchardstr. 11; tel. (040) 30194001; telex 2163770; fax (040) 326274; Chief Editor HAJO PAUS; circ. 2,343,848.

Wochenend: 2000 Hamburg 1, Burchardstr. 11, Postfach 100444; telex 2163770; f. 1948; weekly; Editor GERD ROHLOF; circ. 668,278.

Wochenpost: 1026 Berlin, Karl-Liebknecht-Str. 29; tel. (02) 2440; telex 114854; f. 1953; weekly; Editor BRIGITTE ZIMMERMANN; circ. 1,243,264.

Religion and Philosophy

Christ in der Gegenwart: 7800 Freiburg i. Br., Hermann-Herder-Str. 4; f. 1948; weekly; Editor MANFRED PLATE; circ. 36,000.

Die Christliche Familie: 4300 Essen-Werden, Ruhrtalstr. 52–60; f. 1885; weekly; Publisher Dr ALBERT E. FISCHER; Editor Dr HEINRICH HÖPKER; circ. 85,724.

Der Dom: 4790 Paderborn, Liboristr. 1–3; telex 936807; weekly; Catholic; Publr Bonifatius GmbH, Druck-Buch-Verlag; circ. 126,500.

Europa: 8000 München 5, Ickstattstr. 7, Postfach 140620; tel. (089) 2015505; telex 5215020; Publr VZV Zeitschriften-Verlags-GmbH; circ. 15,800.

Evangelischer Digest: 7000 Stuttgart 10, Landhausstr. 82, Postfach 104864; tel. (0711) 26863-0; telex 722985; fax (0711) 2686345; f. 1958; monthly; Publr Verlag Axel B. Trunkel; circ. 9,300.

Evangelische Theologie: 8000 München 40, Isabellastr. 20; 6 a year; f. 1934; Editor GERHARD SAUTER; circ. 3,400.

Katholischer Digest: 7000 Stuttgart 10, Landhausstr. 82, Postfach 104864; tel. (0711) 268630; telex 722985; fax (0711) 2686345; f. 1949; monthly; Publr Verlag Axel B. Trunkel; circ. 28,900.

Katholisches Sonntagsblatt: 7302 Ostfildern 1, Senefelderstr. 12; tel. (0711) 4406-0; telex 723556; fax (0711) 442349; f. 1848; weekly; Publr Schwabenverlag AG; circ. 120,000.

Die Kirche: 1020 Berlin, Sophienstr. 3; tel. (02) 2823097; f. 1945; Protestant weekly; Editor-in-Chief GERHARD THOMAS; circ. 40,000.

Kirche und Leben: 4400 Münster, Antoniuskirchplatz 21; tel. (0251) 525379; telex 892888; f. 1945; weekly; Catholic; Chief Editor Dr GÜNTHER MEES; circ. 215,542.

Kirchenzeitung für das Erzbistum Köln: 5000 Köln, Ursulaplatz 1; tel. (0221) 1619-131; telex 8881128; fax (0221) 1619-216; weekly; Chief Editor Mgr ERICH LÄUFER; circ. 120,000.

Philosophisches Jahrbuch: 7800 Freiburg i. Breisgau, Hermann-Herder Str. 4; f. 1893; 2 a year; Editors Prof. Dr H. KRINGS, Prof. Dr L. OEING-HANHOFF, Prof. Dr H. ROMBACH, Prof. Dr A. HALDER, Prof. Dr A. BARUZZI.

St Hedwigsblatt: 1086 Berlin, Hinter der Katholischen Kirche 3, Postfach 1343; tel. (02) 2082560; f. 1954; weekly; organ of the Catholic Church, Berlin diocese; circ. 25,000.

Der Sonntagsbrief: 7000 Stuttgart 10, Landhausstr. 82, Postfach 104864; tel. (0711) 268630; telex 722985; fax (0711) 2686345; f. 1974; monthly; Publr AXEL B. TRUNKEL; circ. 81,400.

Standpunkt: 1190 Berlin, Fennstr. 16; tel. (02) 6350915; f. 1973; Protestant monthly; circ. 3,000.

Der Weg: 4000 Düsseldorf, Postfach 6409; tel. (0211) 3610-1; telex 8582627; weekly; protestant; Editor Dr GERHARD E. STOLL; circ. 70,000.

Weltbild: 8900 Augsburg, Frauentorstr. 5; telex 533105; 2 a month; Catholic; Editor EUGEN GEORG SCHWARZ; circ. 310,000.

Science, Medicine

Angewandte Chemie: VCH Verlagsgesellschaft mbH, 6940 Weinheim, Postfach 101161; tel. (06201) 602315; fax (06201) 602328; f. 1888; monthly; circ. 4,000; monthly international edition in English, f. 1962, circ. 3,000.

Archiv der Pharmazie: 6940 Weinheim/Bergstr., Pappelallee 3; f. 1822; monthly; Editor Prof. Dr J. KNABE; circ. 1,000.

Ärztliche Jugendkunde: 7010 Leipzig, Salomonstr. 18B, Postfach 109; tel. (041) 70131; f. 1888; 5 a year; medical; Editor Prof. Dr K. JÄHRIG; circ. 750.

Ärztliche Praxis: 8032 München-Gräfelfing, Hans-Cornelius-Str. 4; tel. (089) 855021; telex 522451; 2 a week; Editor Dr EDMUND BANASCHEWSKI; circ. 52,000.

Berichte der Bunsen-Gesellschaft für physikalische Chemie: VCH Verlagsgesellschaft mbH, 6940 Weinheim/Bergstr., Pappelallee 3; tel. (06201) 6020; telex 465516; f. 1894; monthly; Editors K. G. WEIL, A. WEISS; circ. 2,300.

GERMANY

Chemie-Ingenieur-Technik: VCH Verlagsgesellschaft mbH, 6940 Weinheim, Boschstr. 12, Postfach 101161; tel. (06201) 606117; telex 465516; fax (06201) 606184; f. 1928; monthly; Editor G. WELLHAUSEN; circ. 7,807.

Chemische Industrie: 6000 Frankfurt a.M. 1, Karlstr. 21; tel. (069) 2556454; telex 411372; fax (069) 239564; f. 1949; industrial chemistry, the environment and economics; Dir UWE HOCH; Editor M. KERSTEN; circ. 5,000.

Chemische Technik: 7031 Leipzig, Karl-Heine-Str. 27; tel. (041) 4081011; monthly; chemistry, chemical engineering.

Der Chirurg: 6900 Heidelberg 1, Postfach 105280; tel. (06621) 487387; telex 461723; f. 1929; monthly; Editors Prof. Dr Ch. HERFARTH, Prof. Dr G. HEBERER, Prof. Dr E. KERN; circ. 6,750.

Deutsche Apotheker Zeitung: 7000 Stuttgart 1, Birkenwaldstr. 44, Postfach 40; tel. (0711) 25820; telex 723636; f. 1861; weekly; Editor Dr WOLFGANG WESSINGER; circ. 22,518.

Deutsche Automobil-Revue: 6000 Frankfurt a.M., Städelstr. 19; f. 1926; Editor Dr JÜRGEN CHRIST.

Deutsche Medizinische Wochenschrift: 7000 Stuttgart 30, Rüdigerstr. 14; weekly; Editors F. KÜMMERLE, P. C. SCRIBA, W. SIEGENTHALER, A. STURM, R. AUGUSTIN, W. KUHN; circ. 33,142.

Deutsche Zahnärztliche Zeitschrift: 8000 München 2, Kolbergerstr. 22, Postfach 860420; monthly; dental medicine; Editors Prof. Dr A. KRÖNCKE, Dr G. MASCHINSKI.

Deutsche Zeitschrift für Mund-, Kiefer- und Gesichtschirurgie: 4400 Münster, Waldeystr. 30; quarterly; oral and maxillofacial surgery and oral pathology; Editors Dr R. BECKER, Dr H. SCHEUNEMANN, Dr G. SEIFERT.

Elektrie: 1020 Berlin, Verlag Technik GmbH, Oranienburger Str. 13-14; tel. (02) 2870344; telex 112228; fax (02) 2870259; f. 1947; monthly for electrical engineering; circ. 5,000.

Elektro-Anzeiger: 7022 Leinfelden-Echterdingen, Postfach 100252; tel. (0711) 7594-0; telex 7255421; fax (0711) 7594-390; f. 1948; monthly; Editor Dipl.-Ing. W. OTTO; circ. 18,100.

Europa Chemie: 6000 Frankfurt a.M. 1, Karlstr. 21, tel. (069) 2556464; telex 411372; fax (069) 239564; topical news service of the review *Chemische Industrie*; Dir UWE HOCH; Editor Dipl. Chem. H. SEIDEL; circ. 5,200.

Geologische Rundschau: Geologische Vereinigung e.V., 5442 Mendig, Industriestr. 8; tel. (02652) 1508; general, geological; Pres. Dr A. KRÖNER; circ. 2,800.

Handchirurgie, Mikrochirurgie, Plastische Chirurgie: 7000 Stuttgart 30, Rüdigerstr. 14; tel. (0711) 89310; telex 7252275; fax (0711) 8931453; 6 a year; Editors Prof. Dr med. D. BUCK-GRAMCKO, Prof. Dr H. MILLESI, Prof. Dr E. BIEMER.

Historisches Jahrbuch: 78 Freiburg i. Breisgau, Hermann-Herder Str. 4; f. 1879; 2 double vols a year; Editor Prof. Dr J. SPÖRL.

Humanitas: 1020 Berlin, Neue Grünstr. 18; fortnightly for medical and social welfare; circ. 47,707.

Informatik: 1055 Berlin, Am Friedrichshain 22; tel. (02) 43870; telex 114566; 6 a year; scientific journal.

ING. Das Ingenieur-Magazin: 1080 Berlin, Kronenstr. 18; tel. (02) 2000966; telex 114841; fax (02) 2265256; f. 1990; monthly; technology; circ. 160,000.

Journal of Neurology: Springer-Verlag, 1000 Berlin 33, Heidelberger Platz 3; tel. (030) 8207-0; telex 0183319; f. 1891; continuation of *Deutsche Zeitschrift für Nervenheilkunde*; Editors-in-Chief Prof. A. COMPSTON, Prof. Dr K. POECK.

Kerntechnik: 8014 Neubiberg, Werner-Heisenberg-Weg 39; tel. (089) 6004-2017; telex 5215800; fax (089) 6004-3560; f. 1958; published by Carl Hanser GmbH; 6 a year; independent journal on nuclear engineering, energy systems and radiation; Editor Prof. Dr A. KRAUT; circ. 1,200.

Kosmos: 7000 Stuttgart 10, Neckarstr. 121, Postfach 106012; tel. (0711) 2631-0; telex 7111193; fax (0711) 2631-292; f. 1904; monthly; popular nature journal; Editor Dr RAINER KÖTHE; circ. 70,000.

Medizinische Klinik: 8000 München 2, Lindwurmstr. 95; tel. (089) 514150; telex 521701; f. 1905; fortnightly; Editor Dr HELGA SCHICHTL; circ. 11,827.

Mikrokosmos: 7000 Stuttgart 1, Pfizerstr. 5-7; tel. (0711) 2191304; telex 721669; fax (0711) 2191360; f. 1906; monthly; microscopical studies; Editor Dr D. KRAUTER; circ. 3,000.

Nachrichten aus Chemie, Technik und Laboratorium: 6940 Weinheim, Postfach 101161; tel. (06201) 602318; telex 465516; f. 1953; fortnightly; circ. 24,000.

Naturwissenschaftliche Rundschau: 7000 Stuttgart 10, Birkenwaldstr. 44, Postfach 105280; tel. (0711) 25820; telex 723636; fax (0711) 201450; f. 1948; monthly; scientific; Editors HANS ROTTA, ROSWITHA SCHMID; circ. 7,600.

Planta medica: 7000 Stuttgart 30, Rüdigerstr. 14, Postfach 104853; tel. (0711) 8931-0; telex 7252275; f. 1952; every 2 months; publ. by Society of Medicinal Plant Research; Editor E. REINHARD.

Plaste und Kautschuk: 7031 Leipzig, Karl-Heine-Str. 27; tel. (041) 4081011; fax (041) 4012571; f. 1954; monthly; chemistry, physics, processing and application; Editor-in-Chief JOHANN ARNDT.

Radio Fernsehen Elektronik: 1020 Berlin, Postfach 201, Oranienburger Str. 13-14; tel. (02) 2870333; telex 112228; fax (02) 2870259; f. 1952; monthly; practice of electronics and microelectronics; circ. 52,000.

Therapie der Gegenwart: 8000 München 15, Lindwurmstr. 95; tel. (089) 51415-0; fax (089) 536052; f. 1890; weekly; Chief Editor Dr TILL UWE KEIL; circ. 38,500.

Urania: 1080 Berlin, Otto-Nuschke-Str. 28; tel. (02) 2002403; f. 1924; popular scientific monthly; Editor-in-Chief LUTZ BUCHMANN; circ. 116,000.

Zahnärztliche Praxis: 8032 München-Gräfelfing, Hans-Cornelius-Str. 4; monthly; dentistry; Editor Dr EDMUND BANASCHEWSKI; circ. 12,000.

Zahntechnik: 1136 Berlin, Verlag Gesundheit GmbH, Strasse der Befreiung 60; tel. (02) 51612727; telex 11448; fax (02) 2754983; every 2 months; dentistry; circ. 4,700.

ZAMM: 1199 Berlin, Rudower Chaussee 5; tel. (02) 6745611; monthly; applied mathematics and mechanics; circ. 1,900.

Zeitschrift für Allgemeinmedizin: 7000 Stuttgart 30, Rüdigerstr. 14; tel. (0711) 89310; fax (0711) 8931-453; f. 1924; 3 a month; general medicine; publ. by Hippokrates Verlag GmbH; Editors Dr W. MAHRINGER, Prof. Dr P. DOENECKE, Prof. Dr M. KOCHEN, Dr G. VOLKERT, Prof. Dr W. HARDINGHAUS; circ. 40,000.

Zeitschrift für Chemie: 7031 Leipzig, Karl-Heine-Str. 27; tel. (041) 4081011; monthly; chemistry.

Zeitschrift für Kinderchirurgie: 7000 Stuttgart 10, Postfach 102263; tel. (0711) 89310; telex 7252275; fax (0711) 8931453; f. 1964; 6 a year; Editors Prof. Dr A. M. HOLSCHNEIDER, Prof. Dr M. BETTEX.

Zeitschrift für Klinische Medizin (Das deutsche Gesundheitswesen): 1020 Berlin, Neue Grünstr. 18; fortnightly for the medical profession.

Zeitschrift für Klinische Psychologie u. Psychotherapie: 78 Freiburg i. Breisgau, Hermann-Herder-Str. 4; f. 1952; quarterly; Editor Dr W. J. REVERS.

Zeitschrift für Metallkunde: 7000 Stuttgart 80, Heisenbergstr. 5; tel. (0711) 6861200; telex 7111576; f. 1911; monthly; metal research; Editors G. PETZOW, P. HAASEN, V. SCHUMACHER.

Zeitschrift für Physik: 6900 Heidelberg 1, Philosophenweg 19; 16 a year; Editors-in-Chief (Atomic Nuclei) Prof. Dr H. A. WEIDENMÜLLER, (Condensed Matter) Prof. Dr H. HORNER, Prof. Dr F. STEGLICH, (Particles and Fields) Prof Dr G. KRAMER, Prof. Dr W. SATZ, (Atoms, Molecules and Clusters) Prof. Dr. I. V. HERTEL.

Zeitschrift für Psychologie mit Zeitschrift für angewandte Psychologie: 7010 Leipzig, Salomonstr. 18B, Postfach 109; tel. (041) 70131; f. 1890; 4 a year; psychology and applied psychology; Editors Prof. Dr F. KLIX, Prof. Dr W. HACKER, Dr E. VAN DER MEER, Dr J. MEHL, Dr F. KUKLA, Dr M. ZIESSLER; circ. 1,300.

Zentralblatt für Neurochirurgie: 7010 Leipzig, Salomonstr. 18B, Postfach 109; tel. (041) 70131; f. 1936; 4 a year; neuro-surgery; Editors Prof. Dr H.-G. NIEBELING, Dr W.-E. GOLDHAHN; circ. 850.

NEWS AGENCIES

Allgemeiner Deutscher Nachrichtendienst (ADN): 1026 Berlin, Mollstr. 1; tel. (02) 230; telex 1146010; fax (02) 2354474; f. 1946; formerly the official news agency of the GDR; maintains seven branch offices in Germany; has eight offices as well as additional correspondents abroad; provides a daily news service and features in German; Man. Dir GÜNTER HUNDRO.

dpa Deutsche Presse-Agentur GmbH: 2000 Hamburg 13, Mittelweg 38; tel. (040) 41131; telex 212995; fax (040) 4113351; f. 1949; supplies all the daily newspapers, broadcasting stations and more than 1,000 further subscribers throughout Germany with its national and regional news services. English, Spanish, Arabic and German language news is also transmitted regularly to 550 press agencies, newspapers, radio and television stations and ministries of information in over 85 countries; Dir Gen. Dr WALTER RICHTBERG; Editor-in-Chief Dr WILM HERLYN.

VWD: 6236 Eschborn 1, Niederurseler Allee 8-10, Postfach 6105; tel. (06196) 405-0; telex 4072895; fax (06196) 482007; economic news.

Foreign Bureaux

Agence France-Presse (AFP): 5300 Bonn 1, Friedrich-Ebert-Allee 13; tel. (0228) 225031; telex 886898; fax (0228) 225580; Man. PIERRE LEMOINE.

GERMANY

Agencia EFE (Spain): 5300 Bonn 1, Heussallee 2-10, Pressehaus II/12-14; tel. (0228) 214058; telex 886556; fax (0228) 224147; Bureau Chief HEDWIG MUTH DE ESPINOSA.

Agenzia Nazionale Stampa Associata (ANSA) (Italy): 5300 Bonn 1, Dahlmannstr. 36; tel. (0228) 214770; telex 886857; Correspondent SANDRO DE ROSA.

Associated Press (AP) (USA): 6000 Frankfurt am Main 1, Moselstr. 27; tel. (069) 2713-0; telex 412118; fax (069) 234434; also in Hanover, Hamburg, Stuttgart, Wiesbaden, Saarbrücken, Bonn, Berlin, Munich and Düsseldorf; Man. STEPHEN H. MILLER.

Central News Agency (Taiwan): 5307 Wachtberg-Pech, Auf dem Girzen 4; tel. (0228) 324972; Correspondent FRANCIS FINE.

Československá tisková kancelář (ČTK) (Czechoslovakia): 5300 Bonn, Heussallee 2-10, Pressehaus I/207; tel. (0228) 215811; telex 886772.

Inter Press Service (IPS) (Italy): 5300 Bonn 1, Heussallee 2-10, Pressehaus II/205; tel. (0228) 219138; fax (0228) 261205; Correspondents RAMESH JAURA, JORGE GILLIES, ROBERTO AMPUERO ESPINOZA.

Jiji Tsushin-sha (Japan): 2000 Hamburg 13, Mittelweg 38; tel. (040) 445553; telex 211470; fax (040) 456849; Correspondent HIROYOSHI OHNO.

Kyodo Tsushin (Japan): 5300 Bonn 1, Bundeskanzlerplatz 2-10; tel. (0228) 225543; telex 886308; fax (0228) 222198; Chief Correspondent MASARU IMAI.

Magyar Távirati Iroda (MTI) (Hungary): 5300 Bonn 1, Heussallee 2-10, Pressehaus I/202; tel. (0228) 210820; telex 8869652; Correspondent ISTVÁN FLESCH.

Prensa Latina (Cuba): 5300 Bonn 1, Heussallee 2-10, Pressehaus II/201; tel. (0228) 211330; telex 886517; Man. FAUSTO TRIANA.

Reuters (UK): 5300 Bonn 1, Bonn-Center, Bundeskanzlerplatz 2-10, Postfach 120324; tel. (0228) 260970; telex 886677; Chief Correspondent BJÖRN EDLUND.

Telegrafnoye Agentstvo Sovetskovo Soyuza (TASS) (USSR): 5300 Bonn, Heussallee 2-10, Pressehaus I/133; telex 886472; fax (0228) 210627.

United Press International (UPI) (USA): 5300 Bonn 1, Heussallee 2-10, Pressehaus 2, Zimmer 224; tel. (0228) 215031; telex 885638; Bureau Man. PATRICK MOSER; Chief Correspondent J. B. FLEMING.

Xinhua (New China) News Agency (People's Republic of China): 5300 Bonn 2, Lyngsbergstr. 33; tel. (0228) 331845; telex 885531; Chief Correspondent HU YONGZHEN.

IAN (USSR) is also represented.

PRESS AND JOURNALISTS' ASSOCIATIONS

Bundesverband Deutscher Zeitungsverleger eV (Association of Newspaper Publishers): 5300 Bonn 2, Riemenschneiderstr. 10, Postfach 205002; tel. (0228) 810040; telex 885461; there are 10 affiliated Land Associations; Pres. ROLF TERHEYDEN; Chief Sec. Dr DIRK M. BARTON.

Deutscher Journalisten-Verband (German Journalists' Association): 5300 Bonn 1, Bennauerstr. 60; tel. (0228) 222971-8; telex 886567; fax (0228) 214917; Chair. Dr HERMANN MEYN; Sec. HUBERT ENGEROFF; 12 Land Associations.

Deutscher Presserat (German Press Council): 5300 Bonn 2, Wurzerstr. 46, Postfach 260163; tel. (0228) 361087; fax (0228) 361089; 20 mems; Man. DOROTHEE RÜFFER.

Verband Deutscher Zeitschriftenverleger eV (Association of Publishers of Periodicals): 5300 Bonn 2, Winterstr. 50; tel. (0228) 382030; telex 8869391; fax (0228) 3820340; there are six affiliated Land Associations; Pres. Dr WERNER HIPPE; Man. Dir Dr WINFRIED RESKE.

Verein der Ausländischen Presse in der BRD (VAP) (Foreign Press Association): 5300 Bonn 1, Heussallee 2-10, Pressehaus I/35; tel. (0228) 210885; f. 1951; Chair. EWALD KÖNIG.

Publishers

Prior to German unification, there were about 1,850 publishing firms in the FRG, of which nearly 80% produced fewer than 10 books per year. There is no national publishing centre.

ADAC Verlag: 8000 München 70, Am Westpark 8; tel. (089) 76760; telex 528404; fax (089) 76762500; f. 1958; travel, guidebooks, legal brochures, technical manuals, maps, magazines ADAC-Motorwelt, Deutsches Autorecht; Man. Dir MANFRED M. ANGELE.

Akademie-Verlag: 1086 Berlin, Leipziger Str. 3-4, Postfach 1233; tel. (02) 22360; telex 114420; f. 1946; books and periodicals on scientific theory and practice; Dir Dr BERNHARD TESCHE.

Akademische Verlagsgesellschaft Geest & Portig K.-G.: 7010 Leipzig, Sternwartenstr. 8, Postfach 106; tel. (041) 293158; telex 512381; f. 1906; mathematics, physics, science, engineering, history of science.

Karl Alber Verlag GmbH: 7800 Freiburg i.Br., Hermann-Herder-Str. 4; tel. (0761) 273495; telex 7721440; f. 1939; philosophy, history and theory of science, psychology, sociology, political science, communications; Man. Dir Dr MEINOLF WEWEL.

Altberliner Verlag GmbH: 1020 Berlin, Neue Schönhauser Str. 8; tel. (02) 2806634; f. 1945; books for children; Dir Dr G. DAHNE.

Arani-Verlag GmbH: 1000 Berlin 31, Kurfürstendamm 126, Postfach 31 0829; tel. (030) 8911008; f. 1947; fiction, general; Man. HORST MEYER.

Arena Verlag GmbH: 8700 Würzburg 1, Rottendorfer Str. 16; tel. (0931) 75011; telex 68833; fax (0931) 882391; f. 1949; books for children and juveniles, non-fiction; Dir HANS-GEORG NOACK.

Artemis und Winkler Verlag GmbH: 8000 München 2, Hackenstr. 5; tel. (089) 231198-0; telex 5215517; fax (089) 264499; f. 1957; literature, encyclopaedias; Dir FRANZ EBNER.

Aschendorffsche Verlagsbuchhandlung: 4400 Münster/Westfalen, Soesterstr. 13, Postfach 1124; tel. (0251) 6900; telex 892830; fax (0251) 690405; f. 1720; Catholic theology, philosophy, psychology, education, jurisprudence, general and church history, philology; Dir Dr ANTON WILHELM HÜFFER.

Aufbau-Verlag Berlin und Weimar: 1086 Berlin, Französische Str. 32; tel. (02) 2202421; telex 114739; f. 1945; literature, German and foreign, classical literature and criticism; Dir ELMAR FABER.

Aussaat- und Schriftenmissions-Verlag: 4133 Neukirchen-Vluyn, Andreas-Braemstr. 18-20, Postfach 1265; tel. (02845) 392239; f. 1981; religion, juveniles; Man. Dirs Dr RUDOLF WETH, LIESEL RENNSCHEIDT.

Badenia Verlag und Druckerei GmbH: 7500 Karlsruhe 21, Rudolf-Freytag-Str. 6, Postfach 210248; tel. (0721) 578041; telex 7826726; fax (0721) 579890; f. 1874; religion, text-books, school books, fiction; Dir Dr HELMUT WALTER.

Friedrich Bahn Verlag GmbH: 7750 Konstanz, Zasiusstr. 8, Postfach 100165; tel. (07531) 23054; f. 1891; religion, literature; Dir HERBERT DENECKE.

Bardtenschlager Verlag GmbH: 8000 München 81, Oberfoehringerstr. 105A; tel. (089) 952043; f. 1852; juvenile literature, pedagogics; Dir PETER EISMANN.

Johann Ambrosius Barth: 7010 Leipzig, Salomonstr. 18B, Postfach 109; tel. (041) 70131; f. 1780; textbooks, monographs and periodicals, medicine, stomatology, physics, chemistry, astronomy and psychology; Dir K. WIECKE.

Otto Wilhelm Barth Verlag: 8000 München 19, Stievestr. 9; tel. (089) 172237; telex 5215282; fax (089) 174030; f. 1924; a division of Scherz Verlag, Berne; Far East religions, philosophy, meditation, healing, mysticism, etc.; Dir RUDOLF STREIT-SCHERZ; Editor STEPHAN SCHUHMACHER.

Bastei-Verlag: 5060 Bergisch Gladbach 2, Scheidtbachstr. 23-31; tel. (02202) 1210; telex 887922; f. 1949; paperbacks; Man. Dir GUSTAV LÜBBE.

Verlag für Bauwesen: 1086 Berlin, Französische Str. 13-14; tel. (02) 20410; telex 112229; building; Dir R. SCHWANKE.

Bayerische Verlagsanstalt GmbH: 8600 Bamberg, Laubanger 23; tel. (0951) 7902-0; telex 9518118; f. 1949; Dir HELMUT TREML.

Bechtle-Verlag: 7300 Esslingen, Zeppelinstr. 116; tel. (0711) 3108-1; telex 256487; fax (0711) 3169488; f. 1868; biography, history, literature, humour, poetry; Man. Dir OTTO W. BECHTLE.

Verlag C. H. Beck: 8000 München 40, Wilhelmstr. 9; tel. (089) 381890; telex 5215085; fax (089) 38189-398; f. 1763; law, science, theology, archaeology, philosophy, philology, history, politics, art, literature; Dirs Dr HANS DIETER BECK, WOLFGANG BECK.

Beltz Verlag: 6940 Weinheim, Am Hauptbahnhof 10, Postfach 1120; tel. (06201) 63071; telex 465500; f. 1841; textbooks; Man. Dir Dr MANFRED BELTZ-RÜBELMANN.

Berghaus Verlag: 8347 Kirchdorf/Inn, Ramerding 18; tel. (08571) 2042; fax (08571) 6567; f. 1973; art; Man. Dir URSULA BADER.

Verlagsgruppe Bertelsmann: 8000 München 80, Neumarkterstr. 18; tel. (089) 431890; telex 523259; f. 1970; general, reference; Man. Dirs Dr H. BENZING, B. VON MINCKWITZ, O. PAESCHKE, K. CHRISTOCHOWITZ, F. WÖSSNER.

Beuroner Kunstverlag: 7792 Beuron 1; tel. (07466) 17228; fax (07466) 17209; f. 1898; fine art, religion, calendars; Dir LEO P. GABRIEL GAWLETTA.

Bibliographisches Institut und F.A. Brockhaus AG: 6800 Mannheim 1, Dudenstr. 6, Postfach 100311; tel. (0621) 390101; telex 462107; fax (0621) 3901389; f. (1805/1826) 1984; encyclopaedia, reference books, scientific books, atlases; Man. Dirs HUBERTUS BROCKHAUS, CLAUS W. GREUNER, ANDREAS LANGENSCHEIDT, Dr FLORIAN LANGENSCHEIDT, Dr MICHAEL WEGNER.

GERMANY

Bibliographisches Institut und Verlag Enzyklopädie GmbH Leipzig: 7010 Leipzig, Gerichtsweg 26; tel. (041) 7801; telex 512773; fax (041) 286307; f. 1826; encyclopaedias, German language books, reference books, bibliographies, biographies, information and documentation; Dir (vacant).

Biederstein Verlag: 8000 München 40, Wilhelmstr. 9; tel. (089) 381890; telex 05-215085; fax (089) 38189398; f. 1946; belles-lettres, non-fiction; Man. Dir WOLFGANG BECK.

Georg Bitter Verlag KG: 4350 Recklinghausen, Herner Str. 24; tel. (02361) 25888; f. 1968; children's books; Dir Dr GEORG BITTER.

Blanvalet Verlag: 8000 München 80, Neumarkter Str. 18, Postfach 800 360; tel. (089) 431890; telex 523259; fax (089) 43189431; fiction; Man. OLAF PAESCHKE, KLAUS ECK.

BLV Verlagsgesellschaft mbH: 8000 München 40, Lothstr. 29; tel. (089) 127050; telex 5215087; fax (089) 12705354; f. 1946; cookery, sports, gardening, equitation, technical books, nature, motoring, etc.; Chair. Dr D. IPPEN; Man. Dir HEINZ HARTMANN.

Hermann Böhlaus Nachf. Verlag: 5300 Weimar, Meyerstr. 50A; tel. (0621) 2071; f. 1624; literary history and criticism, history, law; Man. Dir Dr BERNHARD TESCHE.

Böhlau-Verlag GmbH: 5000 Köln 60, Niehlerstr. 272-274; tel. (0221) 769340; fax (0221) 762199; f. 1951; history, music, art; Man. Dir Dr PETER RAUCH.

Boje-Verlag GmbH: 8520 Erlangen, Am Pestalozziring 14, Postfach 2829; tel. (09131) 6060-0; telex 629766; f. 1947; children's books; Man. Dirs Dr RHEINHOLD WEIGAND, NORBERT FRANKE.

Harald Boldt Verlag GmbH: 5407 Boppard am Rhein 1, Postfach 1110; tel. (06742) 2511; f. 1951; history, reference, general and social science, demography; Man. Dirs HARALD BOLDT, PETER BOLDT.

Gebrüder Borntraeger Verlagsbuchhandlung: 7000 Stuttgart 1, Johannesstr. 3A; tel. (0711) 625001; telex 723363; fax (0711) 625005; f. 1790; geology, palaeontology, mineralogy, biology, botany, oceanography, meteorology, geophysics, geomorphology, geography, metallography, periodicals; Proprs Dr E. NÄGELE, KLAUS OBERMILLER.

Verlag G. Braun: 7500 Karlsruhe, Karl-Friedrich-Str. 14-18; tel. (0721) 1650; telex 7826904; f. 1813; physics, mathematics, flow mechanics, medicine; Dirs Dr EBERHARD KNITTEL, HELLO Graf VON RITTBERG, Dipl. Ing. FRIEDRICH WERTH.

Braun & Schneider: 8000 München 2, Maximiliansplatz 9; tel. (089) 555580; f. 1843; children's literature, fiction; Dirs Dr J. SCHNEIDER, FRIEDRICH SCHNEIDER.

Breitkopf & Härtel: 6200 Wiesbaden, Walkmühlstr. 52, Postfach 1707; tel. (0611) 4903-0; telex 4182647; fax (0611) 490359; f. 1719; music and music books; Dirs LIESELOTTE SIEVERS, GOTTFRIED MÖCKEL.

F. A. Brockhaus GmbH: 6800 Mannheim 1, Dudenstr. 6, Postfach 5305; tel. (0621) 390101; telex 462107; f. 1805; encyclopaedias, dictionaries, travel, natural sciences, memoirs, archaeology; Dirs HUBERTUS BROCKHAUS, Dr MICHAEL WEGNER.

Verlag Bruckmann München: 8000 München 20, Nymphenburgerstr. 86, Postfach 27; tel. (089) 125701; telex 523739; f.1858; books, calendars, video cassettes, magazines, fine art prints, original prints; Man. Dir Dr JORG D. STIEBNER.

Buchhändler-Vereinigung GmbH: 6000 Frankfurt a.M.1, Grosser Hirschgraben 17-21; tel. (069) 13060; telex 413573; f. 1846; publishing dept of Börsenverein des Deutschen Buchhandels eV (German Book Trade Asscn); Dir W. ROBERT MÜLLER.

Verlag Busse und Seewald GmbH: 4900 Herford, Ahmser Str. 190, Postfach 1344; tel. (05221) 7750; telex 17-5221855; fax (05221) 775-215; politics, economics, contemporary history, biography, sociology, wine, interior decoration, carpets, etc.; Man. HELMUT RUSS.

Butzon & Bercker GmbH: 4178 Kevelaer 1, Postfach 215; tel. (02832) 2906; telex 812207; f. 1870; Catholic religion and theology, meditation, prayers, liturgy, children's books; Dirs KLAUS BERCKER, Dr EDMUND BERCKER.

Verlag Georg D. W. Callwey GmbH & Co: 8000 München 80, Streitfeldstr. 35; tel. (089) 436005-0; fax (089) 436005-13; f. 1884; history, cultural history, architecture, sculpture, painting, gardens, art restoration; Man. Dirs HELMUTH BAUR-CALLWEY, Dr VERONIKA BAUR-CALLWEY.

Verlag Hans Carl GmbH & Co KG: 8500 Nürnberg 1, Breite Gasse 58-60; tel. (0911) 2383-0; telex 623081; fax (0911) 204956; f. 1861; technical, scientific and general literature; Man. Dirs RAIMUND SCHMITT, TRAUDEL SCHMITT.

Carlsen Verlag GmbH: 2000 Hamburg 50, Völckersstr. 14-20, Postfach 500380; tel. (040) 351865-0; telex 217070; fax (040) 381000 02; f. 1950; comic books; Dirs CARL JOHAN BONNIER, VIKTOR NIEMANN.

Christliche Verlagsanstalt GmbH: 7750 Konstanz, Zasiusstr. 8; tel. (07531) 23054; f. 1892; religion, children's books, literature; Dir HERBERT DENECKE.

Colloquium Verlag GmbH: 1000 Berlin 45, Unter den Eichen 93; tel. (030) 8328085; f. 1948; biography, history, political and social science, Latin-American studies; Dirs OTTO H. HESS, STEFAN HESS; Editor Dr GABRIELE PANGRATZ.

Columbus Verlag Paul Oestergaard GmbH: 7056 Weinstadt 1, Postfach 1180, Columbus Haus; tel. (07151) 68011; telex 724382; fax (07151) 66196; f. 1909; globes; Dir PETER OESTERGAARD.

Cornelsen Verlag Hirschgraben GmbH & Co: 6000 Frankfurt 1, Fürstenbergerstr. 223, Postfach 180 245; tel. (069) 550491; telex 176997604; fax (069) 5976409; f. 1946; school books; Dirs ALFRED GRÜNER, Dr F. LÖFFELHOLZ, WERNER THIELE.

Cornelsen Verlag Schwann-Girardet GmbH & Co KG: 4000 Düsseldorf 1, Postfach 7640, Am Wehrhahn 100; tel. (0211) 16479-0; fax (0211) 16479-20; f. 1987; pedagogics, languages, art, history, dictionaries, mathematics, religion; Dir Dr HANS WEYMAR.

Deutsche Verlags-Anstalt GmbH: 7000 Stuttgart 1, Neckarstr. 121, Postfach 106012; tel. (0711) 26310; fax (0711) 2631-292; f. 1831; general; Dirs ULRICH FRANK-PLANITZ, Dr HANS GLÜCKER.

Deutscher Apotheker Verlag: 7000 Stuttgart 10, Birkenwaldstr. 44, Postfach 101061; tel. (0711) 25820; telex 723636; fax (0711) 291450; f. 1861; pharmacy; Dirs Dr WOLFGANG WESSINGER, VINCENT SIEVEKING, REINHOLD HACK.

Deutscher Verlag für Grundstoffindustrie: 7031 Leipzig, Karl-Heine-Str. 27; tel. (041) 4081011; telex 51451; fax (041) 4012571; f. 1960; technical books and journals for science and industry; Dir H. BROMMA.

Deutscher Instituts-Verlag: 5000 Köln 51, Gustav-Heinemann-Ufer 84-88, Postfach 510670; tel. (0221) 370801; telex 8882768; f. 1951; economic literature; attached to Institut der deutschen Wirtschaft, Köln (German Economics Institute); Man. Dir Prof. Dr GERHARD FELS.

Deutscher Kunstverlag GmbH: 8000 München 21, Vohburgerstr. 1; tel. (089) 568145; fax (089) 564837; f. 1921; art books.

Deutscher Verlag für Kunstwissenschaft GmbH: 1000 Berlin 61, Lindenstr. 76; tel. (030) 25913864; telex 183723; f. 1964; German art; Dirs KLAUS MÜLLER-CREPON, Prof. HENNING BOCK, Prof. PETER BLOCH.

Deutscher Landwirtschaftsverlag: 1040 Berlin, Reinhardtstr. 14; tel. (02) 28930; f. 1960; agriculture, hunting; Dir G. HOLLE.

Deutscher Verlag für Musik: 7010 Leipzig, Karlstr. 10; tel. (041) 7351; f. 1954; classical and contemporary and vocal music and literature on music; Dir Dr G. HEMPEL.

Deutscher Verlag der Wissenschaften GmbH: 1080 Berlin, Johannes-Dieckmann-Str. 10; tel. (02) 203050; telex 114390; f. 1954; mathematics, physics, chemistry, philosophy, psychology, history; Dir Dr L. WALTER.

Deutscher Taschenbuch Verlag GmbH & Co KG (dtv): 8000 München 40, Friedrichstr. 1A; tel. (089) 381706-0; telex 5215396; fax (089) 346428; f. 1961; general fiction, history, music, art, reference, children, general and social science, medicine, textbooks; Man. Dir Dr WOLFRAM GÖBEL.

Eugen Diederichs Verlag: 5000 Köln 1, Merlosstr. 8; tel. (0221) 720672; f. 1896; literature, cultural sciences, psychology, sociology, philosophy; Dirs KLAUS DIEDERICHS, ULF DIEDERICHS.

Verlag Moritz Diesterweg: 6000 Frankfurt 63, Wächtersbacherstr. 89, Postfach 630180; tel. (069) 42081-0; fax (069) 42081-100; f. 1860; text books, economics, social sciences, sciences, pedagogics; Dir DIETRICH HERBST.

Dieterich'sche Verlagsbuchhandlung: 7022 Leipzig, Mottelerstr. 8; tel. (041) 58726; f. 1766; literature; Dir Dr F. BERGER.

Dietz Verlag Berlin GmbH: 1020 Berlin, Wallstr. 76-79; tel. (02) 27030; telex 114741; fax (02) 2793233; f. 1947; social science, politics, history, philosophy, memoirs, periodicals; Dir G. FIEBIG.

Domowina-Verlag GmbH: 8600 Bautzen, Tuchmacherstr. 27; tel. (054) 5770; telex 287220; f. 1958; Slavonic studies; books in Sorbian and in German on Sorbian culture, children's books, belles-lettres, newspapers and periodicals in Sorbian; Dir Dr P. VÖLKEL.

Droemersche Verlagsanstalt Th. Knaur Nachf GmbH & Co: 8000 München 80, Rauchstr. 9-11; tel. (089) 92710; telex 6105802; fax (089) 9271-168; f. 1901; general literature, non-fiction, art books, paperbacks; Man. Dirs PETER SCHAPER, Dr KARL H. BLESSING.

Droste Verlag GmbH: 4000 Düsseldorf 11, Druckzentrum Düsseldorf, Zülpicher Str. 10, Postfach 1135; tel. (0211) 5052604; telex 8582495; f. 1711; fiction, non-fiction, German and foreign literature; Publ. Dir Dr M. LOTSCH.

Duncker & Humblot GmbH: 1000 Berlin 41, Dietrich-Schäfer-Weg 9; tel. (030) 790006-0; fax (030) 790006-31; f. 1798; economics, sociology, law, science, history, philosophy, political sciences.

GERMANY

Econ Verlagsgruppe: 4000 Düsseldorf 30, Kaiserswertherstr. 282, Postfach 300321; tel. (0211) 439060; telex 8587327; fax (0211) 4390668; general fiction and non-fiction; Publr Dr HERO KIND; Man. Dir MICHAEL STAEHLER.

Edition Leipzig—Verlag für Kunst und Wissenschaft: 7030 Leipzig, Karl-Liebknecht-Str. 77; tel. (041) 312412; telex 512918; f. 1960; arts and history of civilization, scientific and bibliophilic reprints, science and technics, general; Dir Prof. Dr D. NADOLSKI.

Edition Peters: 7010 Leipzig, Talstr. 10, Postfach 746; tel. (041) 7721; telex 512381; f. 1800; classical and contemporary music, music books: *Musikwissenschaftliche Studienbibliothek Peters, Peters-Textbücher;* Dir N. MOLKENBUR.

Ehrenwirth Verlag GmbH: 8000 München 2, Schwanthalerstr. 91; tel. (089) 539193; telex 529667; fax (089) 534739; f. 1945; general literature, fiction, education, textbooks, periodicals; Dir MARTIN EHRENWIRTH.

N. G. Elwert Verlag: 3550 Marburg/Lahn, Reitgasse 7–9; tel. (06421) 25023; f. 1726; history, religion, law, social science; Man. Dir Dr W. BRAUN-ELWERT.

Ferdinand Enke Verlag: 7000 Stuttgart 10, Postfach 101254, and 7000 Stuttgart 30, Rüdigerstr. 14; tel. (0711) 89310; telex 07252275; fax (0711) 8931-419; f. 1837; medicine, veterinary medicine, sciences (geosciences), psychology, social sciences; books and periodicals; Man. Dr MARLIS KUHLMANN.

Wilhelm Ernst & Sohn: 1000 Berlin 31, Hohenzollerndamm 170; tel. (030) 860003-0; telex 184143; f. 1851; architecture, technology.

Eulenspiegel. Das Neue Berlin Verlagsgesellschaft mbH: 1080 Berlin, Kronenstr. 73–74; tel. (02) 2202126; f. 1954; humour, satire, caricature, cartoons; Dir WOLFGANG GATZKE.

Europäische Verlagsanstalt GmbH: 2000 Hamburg 13, Parkallee 2; tel. (040) 492915; fax (040) 4912010; f. 1946; social sciences, politics, culture, history, economics, education; Publr Dr SABINE GROENEWOLD.

Evangelische Haupt-Bibelgesellschaft zu Berlin: 1040 Berlin, Ziegelstr. 30; tel. (02) 2837191; f. 1814; religion; Dirs E. RUNGE, K. WEBER.

Evangelische Verlagsanstalt GmbH: 1040 Berlin, Ziegelstr. 30; tel. (02) 28370; f. 1946; religion; Dir Dr S. BRÄUER.

Fachbuchverlag GmbH Leipzig: 7031 Leipzig, Karl-Heine-Str. 16, Postfach 67; tel. (041) 49500; telex 51451; f. 1949; mathematics, physics and technical, basic sciences, textiles, commerce, printing, catering, etc, and technical periodicals; Dir Dr E. WALTER.

Fackelträger-Verlag GmbH: 3000 Hannover 1, Goseriede 10–12; tel. (0511) 14648; fax (0511) 18877; f. 1949; Man. Dirs SIEGFRIED LIEBRECHT, PETER SEIFRIED.

Fackelverlag Fackelversand G. Bowitz GmbH: 7000 Stuttgart 80, Schockenriedstr. 46; tel. (0711) 20171; telex 722875; f. 1919; popular literature; Man. DIETER BOWITZ.

Verlag für Medizin, Dr Ewald Fischer: 6900 Heidelberg 1, Fritz-Frey-Str. 21, Postfach 105767; tel. (06221) 49974; telex 461683; fax (06221) 400727; f. 1967; medicine; Man. Dir Dr E. FISCHER.

Gustav Fischer Verlag GmbH: 6900 Jena, Villengang 2; tel. (078) 27332; telex 588676; f. 1878; biological science, human and veterinary medicine; Dir JOHANNA SCHLÜTER.

S. Fischer Verlag GmbH: 6000 Frankfurt a.M. 70, Hedderichstr. 114, Postfach 700355; tel. (069) 60620; telex 412410; f. 1886; general, paperbacks; Publr MONIKA SCHOELLER; Man. Dir Dr ARNULF CONRADI.

Fleischhauer & Spohn Verlag: 7000 Stuttgart 30, Maybachstr. 18, Postfach 301160; tel. (0711) 89340; telex 723113; f. 1830; fiction, literature.

Focus-Verlag: 6300 Giessen, Lonystr. 19, Postfach 110328; tel. (0641) 71799; fax (0641) 71641; f. 1971; history, reference, literature, ecology, social science; Man. Dir HELMUT SCHMID; Publ. Man. RAYMUND NEUHOFER.

Franckh'sche Verlagshandlung, W. Keller & Co: 7000 Stuttgart 1, Pfizerstr. 5–7, Postfach 106011; tel. (0711) 21910; telex 721669; fax (0711) 2191360; f. 1822; science, natural history, railway books, field guides, children's books; Dir Dr JÜRGEN BACH.

Verlag Frauenoffensive: 8000 München 80, Knollerstr. 3; tel. (089) 339128; fax (089) 339129; f. 1976; feminist publs; Dir GERLINDE KOWITZKE.

Friedrich Frommann Verlag, Günther Holzboog: 7000 Stuttgart 50 (Bad Cannstatt), König-Karl-Str. 27, Postfach 500460; tel. (0711) 569039; fax (0711) 563892; f. 1727; philosophy, theology, sociology, politics, linguistics, mathematics, history of science; Man. GÜNTHER HOLZBOOG.

Dr Th. Gabler Betriebswirtschaftlicher Verlag GmbH: 6200 Wiesbaden 1, Taunusstr. 54, Postfach 1546; tel. (0611) 5340; telex 4186567; fax (0611) 53489; f. 1928; business, banking, insurance; Dirs Dr FRANK LUBE, Dr HANS-DIETER HAENEL.

Dr Rudolf Georgi Verlag: 5100 Aachen, Theaterstr. 77; tel. (0241) 477910; telex 832337; f. 1932; history, calendars, art, general science; Man. Dirs WERNER, MANFRED GEORGI.

Wilhelm Goldmann Verlag: 8000 München 80, Neumarkter Str. 18; tel. (089) 43189-0; telex 529965; f. 1922; fiction, non-fiction, paperbacks; Man. Dir JÜRGEN KREUZHAGE.

Gräfe und Unzer GmbH: 8000 München 40, Isabellastr. 32; tel. (089) 272720; telex 5216929; fax (089) 27272113; f. 1722; cookery, health, nature; Man. Dirs KURT PRELINGER, PETER SASSNINK, DIETER BANZHAF.

Greifenverlag: 6820 Rudolstadt, Heidecksburg, Postfach 142; tel. 22085; f. 1919; belles-lettres; Dir Dr URSULA STEINHAUSSEN.

Verlag Kurt Gross: 6000 Frankfurt a.M. 1, Zeppelinallee 43, Postfach 970148; tel. (069) 793009-0; telex 4189621; f. 1949; law; Man. Dir NICO DE GIER.

G. Grote'sche Verlagsbuchhandlung KG: 5000 Köln 40, Max-Planck-Str. 12, Postfach 400263; tel. (02234) 1060; telex 8882662; f. 1861; social and political science, history, law, economics, administration, periodicals; Dir F. PLAGGE.

Matthias-Grünewald-Verlag GmbH: 6500 Mainz-Weisenau 1, Max-Hufschmidt-Str. 4A, Postfach 3080; tel. (06131) 839055; fax (06131) 834322; f. 1918; theology, philosophy, history, psychology, children's books; Dir Dr JAKOB LAUBACH.

Walter de Gruyter & Co Verlag: 1000 Berlin 30, Genthiner Str. 13; tel. (030) 260050; telex 184027; fax (030) 26005251; f. 1919; humanities and theology, law, science, medicine, mathematics, economics, data processing, general; Man. Dirs Dr KURT LUBASCH, Dr KURT-GEORG CRAM, Dr HELWIG HASSENPFLUG.

Gütersloher Verlagshaus Gerd Mohn: 4830 Gütersloh 1, Königstr. 23–25, Postfach 1343; tel. (05241) 862-0; telex 933868; f. 1959; theology, politics, paperbacks; Man. HANS-JÜRGEN MEURER.

Verlag Anton Hain: 6000 Frankfurt a.M., Savignystr. 53, Postfach 170101; tel. (069) 740261; fax (069) 747822; f. 1946; philosophy, psychology, politics, sociology, economics, quarterly periodicals; Publr IRMELA RÜTTERS.

Carl Hanser Verlag: 8000 München 80, Kolbergerstr. 22; tel. (089) 92694-0; telex 522837; fax (089) 984809; f. 1928; modern literature, plastics, technology, chemistry, science, dentistry; Man. Dirs JOACHIM SPENCKER, F.-J. KLOCK.

Peter Hanstein Verlag GmbH: 6000 Frankfurt a.M., Savignystr. 53, Postfach 170101; tel. (069) 740261; fax (069) 747822; f. 1878; religion, economics; Publr AXEL RÜTTERS.

Verlag Otto Harrassowitz: 6200 Wiesbaden 1, Taunusstr. 14, Postfach 2929; tel. (0611) 530-0; telex 4186135; fax (0611) 530-570; f. 1872; oriental studies, linguistics, history of Eastern Europe, slavic studies, librarianship.

Harth Musik Verlag GmbH: 7010 Leipzig, Karl-Liebknecht-Str. 12; tel. (041) 312612; f. 1946; Dir RITA PREISS.

Verlag Gerd Hatje: 7000 Stuttgart 50, Wildungerstr. 83, Postfach 500468; tel. (0711) 561109; fax (0711) 569652; f. 1945; modern art, architecture and design, general; Propr GERD HATJE.

Dr Ernst Hauswedell & Co: 7000 Stuttgart 1, Rosenberg Str. 113; tel. (0711) 638264; fax (0711) 6369010; f. 1927; bibliographies, book trade, fine arts, humanities, literature, illustrated periodicals, collecting; Man. Dirs GERD HIERSEMANN, Dr REIMAR W. FUCHS.

Henschel Verlag GmbH: 1040 Berlin, Oranienburgerstr. 67-68; tel. (02) 28790; telex 112302; fax (02) 2829458; f. 1945; stage, music, literature, film, art; Dir K. MITTELSTÄDT.

Henssel Verlag: 1000 Berlin 39, Glienicker Str. 12; tel. (030) 8051493; f. 1938; poetry, literature, general fiction, travel, humour; Man. Dir KARL-HEINZ HENSSEL.

F. A. Herbig Verlagsbuchhandlung: 8000 München 22, Thomas-Wimmer-Ring 11; tel. (089) 2350080; telex 5215045; fax (089) 23500844; f. 1821; fine arts, popular sciences, fiction, hobbies; Publr Dr HERBERT FLEISSNER.

Verlag Herder GmbH & Co KG: 7800 Freiburg i. Br., Hermann-Herder-Str. 4; tel. (0761) 27171; fax (0761) 2717-520; f. 1801; religion, philosophy, history, education, art, music, encyclopaedias, children's books; Propr Dr H. HERDER.

Hermann Haack Verlagsgesellschaft mbH: 5800 Gotha, Justus-Perthes-Str. 1–9; tel. (0622) 53302; telex 615333; fax (0622) 52200; f. 1785; maps, atlases, geographical and cartographical books and periodicals; Dir D. GEUTEBRÜCK.

Carl Heymanns Verlag KG: 5000 Köln 41, Luxemburger Str. 449; tel. (0221) 460100; telex 8881888; fax (0221) 4601069; brs at Berlin, Bonn and München; f. 1815; law, political science and administration; periodicals; Man. Dir BERTRAM GALLUS.

Anton Hiersemann Verlag: 7000 Stuttgart 1, Rosenbergstr. 113, Postfach 102251; tel. (0711) 638264; fax (0711) 6369010; f. 1884; library, documentation, history, philology, literature, theatre, religion, art, bibliography; Pres. KARL G. HIERSEMANN.

GERMANY

Hinstorff Verlag GmbH Rostock: 2500 Rostock, Lagerstr. 7; tel. (081) 34441; fax (081) 34601; f. 1831; German and north European literature, regional literature, maritime literature; Dir BIRGIT HEINZE.

S. Hirzel Verlag GmbH & Co: 7000 Stuttgart 10, Birkenwaldstr. 44, Postfach 102237; tel. (0711) 25820; telex 723636; fax (0711) 291450; f. 1853; chemistry, physics, philosophy, psychology; Dirs Dr WOLFGANG WESSINGER, VINCENT SIEVEKING, REINHOLD HACK.

Julius Hoffmann Verlag: 7000 Stuttgart 1, Neckarstr. 121; tel. (0711) 26310; architecture, art, technology, handbooks.

Hoffmann & Campe Verlag: 2000 Hamburg 13, Harvestehuderweg 45; tel. (040) 214259; telex 214259; f. 1781; biography, fiction, history, economics, science, also magazine *Merian*; Man. Dir THOMAS GANSKE.

Friedrich Hofmeister Musikverlag: 7010 Leipzig, Karlstr. 10; tel. (041) 7351; f. 1807; classical, contemporary, vocal and folk music; Dir Dr G. HEMPEL.

Insel Verlag: 6000 Frankfurt 1, Lindenstr. 29, Suhrkamp Haus, Postfach 101130; tel. (069) 756010; fax (069) 75601522; f. 1899; literature, general; Dir Dr SIEGFRIED UNSELD.

Axel Juncker-Verlag: 8000 München 40, Neusser Str. 3, Postfach 401120; tel. (089) 360960; f. 1902; dictionaries, phrase-books; Man. Dir Dr FLORIAN LANGENSCHEIDT.

Verlag Junge Welt GmbH: 1026 Berlin, Postfach 43; tel. (0161) 22330; telex 114483; fax (0161) 7208440; f. 1952; books and periodicals for children and young people; Dirs D. BARTSCH, W. TITZE.

Chr. Kaiser Verlag GmbH: 8000 München 80, Lilienstr. 70; tel. (089) 483014; f. 1845; theological; Dir MANFRED WEBER.

Hermann Kessler Verlag für Sprachmethodik: 5300 Bonn 2, Plittersdorfer Str. 91; tel. (0228) 363004; f. 1953; German, English and Chinese language; Publr HANS-PETER DÜRR-AUSTER.

Gustav Kiepenheuer Verlag: 7022 Leipzig, Mottelerstr. 8; tel. (041) 58726; f. 1909; general; Gustav-Kiepenheuer library; literature, history, arts; Dir Dr FRIEDEMANN BERGER.

Verlag Kiepenheuer & Witsch & Co: 5000 Köln 51, Rondorferstr. 5; tel. (0221) 376850; telex 8881142; f. 1948; general fiction, biography, history, sociology, politics; Man. Dir Dr REINHOLD NEVEN DU MONT.

Kinderbuchverlag Berlin: 1080 Berlin, Behrenstr. 40–41; tel. (02) 20933200; f. 1949; children's books; Dir A. HEMPEL.

Kindler Verlag GmbH: 8000 München 40, Leopoldstr. 54; tel. (089) 394041; telex 5215678; f. 1951; biography, literature, psychology, fiction; Man. Dirs Dr KARL BLESSING, RÜDIGER HILDEBRANDT.

Kirchheim & Co GmbH: 6500 Mainz 1, Kaiserstr. 41; tel. (06131) 671081; telex 4187521; f. 1736; science, law, medicine, periodicals; Dir MANUEL ICKRATH.

Ernst Klett Gruppe: 7000 Stuttgart 1, Rotebühlstr. 77; tel. (0711) 66720; telex 722225; f. 1844; secondary school and university textbooks (especially German as a foreign language), dictionaries, atlases, teaching aids; Dirs MICHAEL KLETT, ROLAND KLETT, Dr THOMAS KLETT.

Klett-Cotta Verlagsgemeinschaft: 7000 Stuttgart 1, Rotebühlstr. 77; tel. (0711) 66720; telex 722225; f. 1977; literature, linguistics, education, humanities, social sciences, psychology, history, philosophy, fine arts; Dirs MICHAEL KLETT, ROLAND KLETT, Dr THOMAS KLETT.

Erika-Klopp-Verlag GmbH: 8000 München 40, Hohenzollernstr. 86; tel. (089) 3072219; fax (089) 3083068; f. 1925; children's books; Man. JULIANE HEHN-KYNAST.

Vittorio Klostermann GmbH: 6000 Frankfurt a.M. 90, Frauenlobstr. 22; tel. (069) 774011; fax (069) 708038; f. 1930; bibliography, philosophy, literature, history, law, periodicals; Man. Dirs MICHAEL and VITTORIO E. KLOSTERMANN.

Verlag Josef Knecht: 6000 Frankfurt a.M. 1, Liebfrauenberg 37; tel. (069) 281767; f. 1946; politics, religion, arts; Man. Dirs Dr HERMANN HERDER, Dr MARIANNE REGNIER.

Knorr & Hirth Verlag GmbH: 3016 Seelze 1, Hannoversche Str. 41; tel. (05137) 7037-21; fax (05137) 7037-99; f. 1894; art, travel, guide-books, postcards; Dirs ROLF SCHRÖER, WILFRIED SEIBEL.

Koehler & Amelang Verlagsgesellschaft mbH Berlin-Leipzig: 1086 Berlin, Charlottenstr. 79; tel. (030) 2202711; f. 1789; history, history of culture and art, theology; Dir Dr HANS-JOACHIM MIETHKE.

K. F. Koehler Verlag: 7000 Stuttgart 80, Schockenriedstr. 39; tel. (0711) 7860; telex 7255344; f. 1789; biography, history, sociology, political science, law, geography; Publr TILL GRUPP.

Koehlers Verlagsgesellschaft mbH: 4900 Herford, Steintorwall 17, Postfach 2352; tel. (05221) 59910; telex 934801; fax (05221) 500125; f. 1780; international shipping, marine reference books.

W. Kohlhammer GmbH: 7000 Stuttgart 80, Heßbrühlstr. 69, Postfach 800430; tel. (0711) 7863-0; telex 7255820; fax (0711) 7863263; f. 1866; periodicals, general textbooks; Man. Dirs Dr JÜRGEN GUTBROD, HANS-JOACHIM NAGEL.

Kommentator Verlag: 6000 Frankfurt a.M. 1, Zeppelinallee 43, Postfach 970148; tel. (069) 793009-0; telex 4189621; fax (069) 79300948; f. 1947; mem. of Hermann Luchterhand Verlag; law, taxation; Man. Dir NICO DE GIER.

Konradin-Fachzeitschriften-Verlag GmbH: 7022 Leinfelden-Echterdingen, Ernst-Mey-Str. 8; tel. (0711) 7594-0; telex 7255421; f. 1865; technical and trade journals; Publr KONRAD KOHLKAMMER.

Kösel-Verlag: 8000 München 19, Flüggenstr. 2; tel. (089) 179008-0; telex 5215492; fax (089) 17900811; f. 1593; philosophy, religion, psychology, esoteric, family and education; Dir Dr CHRISTOPH WILD.

Kreuz Verlag GmbH: 7000 Stuttgart 80, Breitwiesenstr. 30, Postfach 800669; tel. (0711) 788030; fax (0711) 7880310; f. 1983; theology, psychology, pedagogics; Man. Dir DIETER BREITSOHL.

Alfred Kröner Verlag: 7000 Stuttgart 1, Reinsburgstr. 56, Postfach 102862; tel. (0711) 620221; f. 1904; humanities, handbooks, reference; Man. Dirs ARNO KLEMM, WALTER KOHRS.

Verlag der Kunst: 8019 Dresden, Spenerstr. 21; tel. (051) 34486; telex 2311; f. 1952; art books and reproductions; Dir Dr K. SELBIG.

Kyrios-Verlag GmbH: 8050 Freising, Luckengasse 8/10; tel. (08161) 5527; f. 1916; religion, meditation, calendars, periodicals; Dir URSULA BLUM.

Lambertus-Verlag: 7800 Freiburg i. Br., Wölflinstr. 4, Postfach 1026; tel. (0761) 31566; f. 1898; social work, social sciences, education, theology, periodicals; Dirs FRITZ BOLL, GERHILD NEUGART.

Landbuch Verlag GmbH: 3000 Hannover 1, Kabelkamp 6, Postfach 160; tel. (0511) 67806-0; telex 921169; fax (0511) 67806-45; f.1945; agriculture, animal breeding, forestry, hunting, gardening, nature; Dir FRIEDRICH BUTENHOLZ.

Langenscheidt-Verlag: 1000 Berlin 62, Crellestr. 29–30; 8000 Munich 40, Neusser Str. 3, Postfach 401120; tel. (089) 360960; telex 183175; f. 1856; foreign languages, German for foreigners, dictionaries, textbooks, records, tapes, cassettes; Man. Dir KARL ERNST TIELEBIER-LANGENSCHEIDT.

Karl Robert Langewiesche Nachfolger Hans Köster KG: 6240 Königstein im Taunus, Am grünen Weg 6, Postfach 1327; tel. (06174) 7333; fax (06174) 25205; f. 1902; art, music, history, monographs; Owner and Man. HANS-CURT KÖSTER.

Leske Verlag & Budrich GmbH: 5090 Leverkusen 3 (Opladen), Gerhart-Hauptmann-Str. 27, Postfach 300 406; tel. (02171) 2079; f. 1820; economics, politics, psychology, sociology, educational and school books; Man. Dir EDMUND BUDRICH.

Lichtenberg Verlag GmbH: 8000 München 40, Leopoldstr. 54; tel. (089) 394041; telex 5215678; f. 1962; popular fiction, non-fiction; Dir PETER NIKEL.

Lied der Zeit GmbH, Musikverlag und Bühnenvertrieb: 1020 Berlin, Rosa-Luxemburgstr. 41; tel. (02) 2805113; f. 1954; dance, brass band and light music, sheet-music, musical comedies, books on music, children's books, almanacs, posters, autographs; Dir K. EISENBARTH.

Limes Verlag: 8000 München 22, Thomas-Wimmer-Ring 11; tel. (089) 235008-0; telex 5215045; f. 1945; poetry, essays, novels, art, contemporary history, translations; Publr Dr HERBERT FLEISSNER.

Paul List Verlag und Schroedel Schulbuchverlag GmbH: 8000 München 2, Goethestr. 43; tel. (089) 51480; telex 522405; fax (089) 5148185; school books, atlases; Man. Dirs ANTON KEMPER, Dr WOLFGANG REISTER.

Hermann Löffler: 1000 Berlin 49, Schillerstr. 115; tel. (030) 7425818; f. 1903; music; Propr H. LÖFFLER.

Hermann Luchterhand Verlag GmbH & Co: 5450 Neuwied, Heddesdorfer Str. 31, Postfach 1780; tel. (02631) 8010; telex 867853; f. 1924; insurance, law, taxation, labour; Man. N. W. A. DE GIER.

Otto Maier Verlag GmbH: 7980 Ravensburg, Marktstr. 22–26, Postfach 1860; tel. (0751) 861; telex 732926; f. 1883; games, puzzles, hobbies, children's crafts, art, design, educational; Man. Dir CLAUS RUNGE.

Gebr. Mann Verlag GmbH & Co: 1000 Berlin 61, Lindenstr. 76; tel. (030) 25913864; telex 183723; f. 1917; archaeology, art; Dir KLAUS MÜLLER-CREPON.

Maximilian-Verlag: 4900 Herford, Steintorwall 17, Postfach 2352; tel. (05221) 59910; telex 934801; fax (05221) 599125; textbooks, history, social sciences, law, administration.

Felix Meiner Verlag: 2000 Hamburg 76, Richardstr. 47; tel. (040) 294870; fax (040) 2993614; f. 1911; re-f. 1951 in Hamburg; humanities, especially philosophy; Dirs R. MEINER, M. MEINER.

J. B. Metzlersche Verlagsbuchhandlung und C. E. Poeschel Verlag GmbH: 7000 Stuttgart 10, Kernerstr. 43, Postfach 103241;

GERMANY

tel. (0711) 2290290; telex 7262891; fax (0711) 2290290; literature, pedagogics, linguistics, history, economics, commerce, textbooks; Dir Dr Günther Schweizer.

Alfred Metzner Verlag: 6000 Frankfurt a.M. 1, Postfach 970148, Zeppelinallee 43; tel. (069) 793009-0; telex 4189621; f. 1909; mem. of Hermann Luchterhand Verlag; law; Man. Dir Nico de Gier.

Gertraud Middelhauve Verlag GmbH & Co KG: 5000 Köln 80, Wiener Platz 2; tel. (0221) 612703; fax (0221) 614982; f. 1947; children's and picture books; Dirs Gertraud Middelhauve, Dr Robert Abt.

Mitteldeutscher Verlag GmbH: 4020 Halle/Saale, Grosse Brauhausstr. 17A; tel. (046) 33662; f. 1946; general fiction and non-fiction; Man. Dir Dr Eberhard Günther.

Verlag E. S. Mittler & Sohn GmbH: 4900 Herford, Steintorwall 17, Postfach 2352; tel. (05221) 59910; telex 934801; fax (05221) 599125; also 5300 Bonn 2, Austr. 19; military sciences, aviation, philosophy, history.

Verlag Moderne Industrie AG: 8910 Landsberg, Justus-von-Liebig-Str. 1; tel. (08191) 125-1; telex 527114; f. 1952; management, investment, technical; Man. Dir Dr Reinhard Möstl.

Verlag Modernes Lernen Borgmann KG: 4600 Dortmund, Hohe Str. 39; tel. (0231) 128008; telex (17) 231329; fax (0231) 125640; f. 1969; modern learning and educational books; Dir D. Borgmann.

J. C. B. Mohr (Paul Siebeck): 7400 Tübingen, Wilhelmstr. 18; tel. (07071) 26064; telex 7262872; fax (07071) 51104; f. 1801; religion, philosophy, law, economics, sociology, history, political science; Propr G. Siebeck.

Buchverlag Der Morgen: 1170 Berlin, Seelenbinderstr. 152; tel. (02) 6504151; telex 6504151; f. 1958; belles-lettres, politics; Dir Dr W. Tenzler.

C. F. Müller Juristischer Verlag: 6900 Heidelberg 1, Im Weiher 10, Postfach 102640; tel. (06221) 489250; telex 461727; fax (06221) 489410; f. 1973; periodicals, humanities, insurance, law, science, technology; Dir Dr Hans Windsheimer.

Muster-Schmidt-Verlag Christian Hansen-Schmidt: 3400 Göttingen 1, Grünberger Weg 6; tel. (0551) 71741; telex 96720; f. 1905; history, scientific works; Dirs Hans Hansen-Schmidt, Frau E. Gerhardy.

Verlag der Nation: 1040 Berlin, Friedrichstr. 113; tel. (02) 28390; f. 1948; literature, politics, biographies, paperbacks; Man. H.-O. Lecht.

Verlag Das Neue Berlin: 1080 Berlin, Kronenstr. 73-74; tel. (02) 2202126; f. 1946; crime, adventure, science fiction; Dir W. Sellin.

Verlag Neues Leben: 1080 Berlin, Behrenstr. 40-41; tel. (02) 20932765; telex 114781; f. 1946; books for young people and fiction; Dir Rudolf Chowanetz.

Verlag Neue Musik: 1086 Berlin, Leipziger Str. 26; tel. (02) 2202051; f. 1957; music and literature on music; Dir Ferdinand Hirsch.

Verlag Neue Wirtschafts-Briefe: 4690 Herne 1, Eschstr. 22; tel. (02323) 141-0; telex 8229870; fax (02323) 141123; f. 1947; accountancy, industrial management, political economics; Man. Dir E.-O. Kleyboldt.

Verlag Günther Neske: 7417 Pfullingen, Kloster, Postfach 7240; tel. (07121) 71339; telex 729790; f. 1951; poetry, psychiatry, philosophy, theology, jurisprudence, picture books; Propr Günther Neske.

Neumann Verlag Radebeul: 8122 Radebeul, Dr-Schmincke-Allee 19; tel. (051) 75749; f. 1946; books on home and garden, nature.

Max Niemeyer Verlag GmbH & Co KG: 7400 Tübingen 1, Pfrondorferstr. 6, Postfach 2140; tel. (07071) 81104; fax (07071) 87419; f. 1870; scholarly books on philology, philosophy, history, linguistics; Dir R. Harsch-Niemeyer.

Nymphenburger Verlagshandlung: 8000 München 22, Thomas-Wimmer-Ring 11; tel. (089) 235008-0; telex 5215045; fax (089) 23500844; f. 1946; belles lettres, history, adventure, sports and music; Publr Dr Herbert Fleissner; Man. Dir Ingeborg Castell.

R. Oldenbourg Verlag GmbH: 8000 München 80, Rosenheimerstr. 145; tel. (089) 41120; telex 529296; f. 1858; technology, science, history, textbooks, mathematics, economics, dictionaries, periodicals; Dirs Dr T. von Cornides, W. Dick, G. Ohmeyer, Johannes Oldenbourg.

Georg Olms Verlag AG: 3200 Hildesheim, Hagentorwall 7; tel. (05121) 37007; telex 927454; fax (05121) 32007; f. 1945; classical antiquity, study of languages and literature, philosophy, theology, musicology; Publr W. Georg Olms, Dr E. Mertens.

Paul Parey: 2000 Hamburg 1, Spitalerstr. 12; tel. (040) 339690; telex 2161391; and 1000 Berlin 61, Lindenstr. 44-47; tel. (030) 2599040; telex 184777; f. 1848; biology, botany, zoology, ethology, veterinary science, laboratory animals science, food technology and control, agriculture, starch research and technology, brewing and distilling, forestry, horticulture, phytomedicine, plant and environment protection, water management, hunting, fishing, dogs, equitation; technical and scientific journals; Dirs Dr Friedrich Georgi, Dr Rudolf Georgi.

Pattloch-Bibel Verlags GmbH: 8751 Haibach Unterfranken, Haydnstr. 8; tel. (06021) 68328; telex 4188517; f. 1827; theology; Man. Dirs Wolfgang Lowitzki, Klemens Pattloch.

Paulinus-Verlag: 5500 Trier, Fleischstr. 62/65, Postfach 3040; tel. (0651) 4604-162; telex 472735; fax (0651) 4604-153; f. 1875; religious literature and theology, periodicals; Dir Siegfried Fäth.

Physik Verlag GmbH: 6940 Weinheim/Bergstr., Pappelallee 3; tel. (06201) 602-0; telex 465516; f. 1947; physics journals; Man. Dirs Dr W. Heinicke, Dr Eva E. Wille.

R. Piper GmbH & Co KG Verlag: 8000 München 40, Georgenstr. 4, Postfach 430120; tel. (089) 381801-0; telex 5215385; f. 1904; literature, philosophy, theology, psychology, natural sciences, political and social sciences, history, biographies, music; Dirs Dr Klaus Piper, Dr Ernst R. Piper.

Polyglott-Verlag: 8000 München 40, Neusser Str. 3, Postfach 401120; tel. (089) 36096-0; telex 5215379; fax (089) 36096288; f. 1902; travel guides, menu guides, dictionaries, phrase-books; Man. Dir Dr Florian Langenscheidt.

Postreiter-Verlag: 4020 Halle/Saale, Ernst-Toller-Str. 18; tel. (046) 28097; f. 1947; children's books; Dir Ch. Kupfer.

Prestel-Verlag: 8000 München 40, Mandlstr. 26; tel. (089) 381709-0; telex 5216366; fine arts, arts and crafts, art history, travel; Dirs Georgette Capellmann, Gustav Stresow, Jürgen Tesch.

Prisma-Verlag Leipzig: 7013 Leipzig, Leibnizstr. 10; tel. (041) 281411; f. 1957; popular science, art history, novels; Dir Klaus-Jürgen Heiber.

Pro Musica Verlag GmbH: 7010 Leipzig, Karl-Liebknecht-Str. 12; tel. (041) 312612; f. 1946; Dir Rita Preiss.

Verlag Friedrich Pustet: 8400 Regensburg 11, Gutenbergstr. 8, Postfach 110441; tel. (0941) 96049; telex 65672; f. 1826; religion, art, liturgical books, folklore; also periodical *Liturgie Konkret*; Man. Dir Friedrich Pustet.

Quell Verlag: 7000 Stuttgart 1, Furtbachstr. 12A, Postfach 897; tel. (0711) 60100-0; f. 1830; Protestant literature; Dirs Dr Wolfgang Reister, Walter Waldbauer.

Quelle & Meyer Verlag: 6200 Wiesbaden, Luisenplatz 2, Postfach 4747; tel. (06121) 373071; fax (06121) 374351; f. 1906; religion, natural and social science, textbooks; Man. Dirs Günther Fertig, Gerhard Stahl.

Räthgloben-Verlag Leipzig: 7033 Leipzig, Raimundstr. 14; tel. (041) 475169; telex 512923; f. 1917; Dir H. Goeschel.

Walter Rau Verlag: 4000 Düsseldorf 12, Benderstr. 168A, Postfach 120407; tel. (0211) 283095; telex 8586682; fax (0211) 283827; literature, magazines, translations, hobbies; Dirs Gisela Rau, Beatrix Rau-Siegert.

Karl Rauch Verlag KG: 4000 Düsseldorf 1, Grafenberger Allee 100; tel. (0211) 16795-0; fax (0211) 662216; history, translations, art; Dir Harald Ebner.

Ravenstein-Verlag: 6232 Bad Soden, Auf der Krautweide 24; tel. (06196) 609630; telex 4072538; fax (06196) 27450; f. 1830; maps and atlases; Man. Dirs Rüdiger Bosse, Helga Ravenstein.

Philipp Reclam jun. Verlag GmbH: 7257 Ditzingen bei Stuttgart, Siemensstr. 32, Postfach 1349; tel. (07156) 1630; telex 7266704; f. 1828; literature, literary criticism, fiction, history of culture and literature, philosophy and religion, biography, fine arts, music; Acting Partner Dr Dietrich Bode.

Reclam-Verlag Leipzig: 7031 Leipzig, Nonnenstr. 38; tel. (041) 474501; f. 1828; *Reclam-Bibliothek*: pocket-book series (including philosophy, history and culture, language and literature, biographies) and works of world literature in attractive format; Dir Stefan Richter.

Regensbergsche Buchhandlung und Buchdruckerei GmbH & Co: 4400 Münster, Daimlerweg 58, Postfach 6748; tel. (0251) 717061; fax (0251) 717725; f. 1591; Catholic and scientific books; Dir Dr Bernhard Lucas.

Dietrich Reimer Verlag: 1000 Berlin 45, Unter den Eichen 57; tel. (030) 8314081; fax (030) 8136323; f. 1845; geography, ethnology, sociology, scientific, archaeology, history of civilization, art; Propr Dr Friedrich Kaufmann.

Verlag Ernst Reinhardt GmbH & Co: 8000 München 19, Kemnatenstr. 46; tel. (089) 1783005; fax (089) 1781827; f. 1899; psychology, education, philosophy, psychotherapy, social sciences; Man. Karl Münster.

Dr Riederer Verlag GmbH: 7000 Stuttgart 1, Gutbrodstr. 9, Postfach 104052; tel. (0711) 639797; f. 1947; technology, metallography; Dir H. Schneider.

GERMANY

Rowohlt Verlag GmbH and **Rowohlt Taschenbuch Verlag GmbH:** 2057 Reinbek bei Hamburg, Hamburgerstr. 17; tel. (040) 72721; telex 217854; f. 1908/1953; politics, science, fiction, translations of international literature; Dirs Dr MICHAEL NAUMANN, HORST VARRELMANN, Dr HELMUT DÄHNE, ERWIN STEEN.

Rütten & Loening Berlin: 1086 Berlin, Französische Str. 32; f. 1844; tel. (02) 2202421; telex 114739; belles-lettres, literary criticism magazines; Dir ELMAR FABER.

St Benno Verlag GmbH: 7033 Leipzig, Thüringerstr. 1–3; tel. (041) 474161; f. 1951; Catholic publications; Dirs F.-J. CORDIER, C. BOCKISCH.

K.G. Saur Verlag: 8000 München 71, Heilmannstr. 17, Postfach 711009; tel. (089) 791040; telex 5212067; fax (089) 7910499; f. 1949; library science, reference, dictionaries, microfiches; brs in New York, London, Oxford and Paris; subsidiary of Butterworths & Co (Publishers) Ltd, London.

Moritz Schauenburg Verlag GmbH & Co: 7630 Lahr 1, Schillerstr. 13, Postfach 2120; tel. (07821) 2783-0; telex 754943; f. 1794; fiction, literature, linguistics, philosophy, music; Dir Dipl.-Kfm. JÖRG SCHAUENBURG.

Fachverlag Schiele & Schön GmbH: 1000 Berlin 61, Markgrafenstr. 11; tel. (030) 2516029; telex 181470; fax (030) 2517248; f. 1946; technology, telecommunications, textile and clothing industry, biomedical engineering, optics, reference; Dir PETER SCHÖN.

Schlütersche Verlagsanstalt und Druckerei GmbH & Co: 3000 Hannover 1, Georgswall 4, Postfach 5440; tel. (0511) 12360; telex 923978; fax (0511) 1236-290; f. 1747; non-fiction, periodicals, Yellow Pages; Man. Dir HORST DRESSEL.

Erich Schmidt Verlag GmbH & Co: 1000 Berlin 30, Genthinerstr. 30G; tel. (030) 250085-0; telex 183671; fax (030) 25008521; law, economics, philology, technology; Man. CLAUS-MICHAEL RAST.

Wilhelm Schmitz Verlag: 6304 Lollar, Staufenbergerweg 22; tel. (06406) 2324; f. 1847; German studies, East European studies, Slavonic folklore; Dir S. SCHMITZ.

Franz Schneekluth Verlag: 8000 München 22, Widenmayerstr. 34; tel. (089) 221391; telex 529070; fax (089) 2289385; f. 1949; general literature; Publr ULRICH STAUDINGER.

Franz Schneider Verlag: 8000 München 40, Frankfurter Ring 150; tel. (089) 381910; telex 5215804; f. 1913; children's books; Publr Dr HUBERTUS SCHENKEL.

Verlag Lambert Schneider GmbH: 6900 Heidelberg, Hausackerweg 16, Postfach 105802; tel. (06221) 21354; fax (06221) 12794; f. 1925; literature, philosophy, religion, Judaism (especially the publications of Martin Buber); Dir L. STIEHM.

Verlag Schnell & Steiner GmbH: 8000 München 60, Paganinistr. 92, Postfach 112; tel. (089) 8112015; fax (089) 8115484; f. 1933; art, travel, history; Man. Dir ELISABETH ZUBER.

B. Schott's Söhne: 6500 Mainz 1, Weihergarten 5, Postfach 3640; tel. (06131) 246-0; telex 4187 821; fax (06131) 246-211; f. 1770; sheet music, music books, records, music periodicals; Man. Dirs Dr PETER HANSER-STRECKER, ROLF REISINGER.

Verlag J. F. Schreiber: 7300 Esslingen, Postfach 285; tel. (07153) 22011; telex 7266880; fax (07153) 22014; f. 1831; children's books, juveniles; Man. Dir JÜRGEN MEISSNER.

Carl Ed. Schünemann KG: 2800 Bremen 1, 2 Schlachtpforte 7, Postfach 106067; tel. (0421) 36903-0; telex 244397; fax (0421) 36903-48; f. 1810; art, periodicals; Dirs CARL SCHÜNEMANN, CARL FRITZ SCHÜNEMANN.

Schwabenverlag AG: 7302 Ostfildern 1; tel. (0711) 4406-0; telex 723556; fax (0711) 442349; f. 1848; regional history, literature, theology, picture books; Man. Dir ROBERT BIENDARRA.

J. Schweitzer Verlag: 6000 Frankfurt a.M. 1, Zeppelinallee 43, Postfach 970148; tel. (069) 793009-0; telex 4189621; f. 1949; mem. of Hermann Luchterhand Verlag; law, jurisprudence; Man. Dir NICO DE GIER.

E. Schweizerbart'sche Verlagsbuchhandlung: 7000 Stuttgart 1, Johannesstr. 3A; tel. (0711) 625001; telex 723363; fax (0711) 625005; f. 1826; geology, palaeontology, mineralogy, hydrobiology, limnology, botany, zoology, fisheries, anthropology; periodicals; Proprs KLAUS OBERMILLER, Dr E. NÄGELE.

E. A. Seemann Buch- und Kunstverlagsgesellschaft mbH: 7010 Leipzig, Jacobstr. 6; tel. (041) 7736; f. 1858; art books and reproductions; Dir R. WINKLER.

Societäts-Verlag: 6000 Frankfurt a.M. 1, Frankenallee 71–81, Postfach 100801; tel. (069) 75010; telex 411655; f. 1921; literature, art, economics; Publr W. WIRTHLE.

Sonnenweg-Verlag: 7750 Konstanz, Raitenaugasse 11, Postfach 100165; tel. (07531) 23054; f. 1922; religion, literature; Dir HERBERT DENECKE.

W. Spemann Verlag: 7000 Stuttgart 1, Pfizerstr. 5/7; tel. (0711) 21910; telex 721669; f. 1873; history, culture, art, military; Dirs G KELLER, F. KELLER, E. NEHMANN.

Adolf Sponholtz Verlag: 3250 Hameln, Osterstr. 19; tel. (05151) 200310; telex 92859; f. 1894; literature, poetry; Publ. Dir HANS FREIWALD.

Sportverlag: 1086 Berlin, Neustädtische Kirchstr. 15, Postfach 1218; tel. (0161) 22120; telex 112853; fax (0161) 2304307; f. 1947; sports, recreation, technical, sport education, reports; Dir BERND MORCHUTT.

Springer-Verlag GmbH & Co KG: 1000 Berlin 33, Heidelberger Platz 3; tel. (030) 8207-0; telex 183319; fax (030) 183319; f. 1842; medicine, biology, mathematics, physics, chemistry, psychology, engineering, geosciences, philosophy, law, economics; Proprs Dr Dres. h.c. HEINZ GÖTZE, Dr KONRAD F. SPRINGER, Dipl.-Kfm. CLAUS MICHALETZ; Man. Dirs Prof. Dr DIETRICH GÖTZE, JOLANDA L. VON HAGEN, BERNHARD LEWERICH.

Franz Steiner Verlag Wiesbaden GmbH: 7000 Stuttgart, Birkenwaldstr. 44, Postfach 101526; tel. (0711) 25820; telex 723636; fax (0711) 291450; f. 1949; archaeology, linguistics and philology, classical and oriental studies, history, geography, history of arts and sciences; periodicals; Man. Dirs Dr WOLFGANG WESSINGER, VINCENT SIEVEKING, REINHOLD HACK.

Dr Dietrich Steinkopff Verlag: 6100 Darmstadt 11, Saalbaustr. 12, Postfach 111442; tel. (06151) 26538; f. 1908; medical, chemical and scientific books and periodicals; Dir BERNHARD LEWERICH.

Lothar Stiehm Verlag: 6900 Heidelberg 1, Hausackerweg 16, Postfach 105802; tel. (06221) 21354; fax (06221) 12794; f. 1966; literature, bibliography; Dir L. STIEHM.

Stoytscheff Verlag: 6000 Frankfurt a.M. 1, Zeppelinalle 43, Postfach 970148; tel. (069) 793009-0; telex 4189621; f. 1949; law; Man. Dir NICO DE GIER.

Süddeutscher Verlag: 8000 München 2, Goethestr. 43; tel. (089) 51480; telex 522405; f. 1945; fiction, non-fiction, history, art, religion; Man. Dir Dr WOLFGANG REISTER.

Suhrkamp Verlag KG: 6000 Frankfurt a.M. 1, Lindenstr. 29–35, Suhrkamp Haus, Postfach 101945; tel. (069) 756010; telex 413972; fax (069) 75601522; f. 1950; modern German and foreign literature, philosophy, poetry; Dir Dr SIEGFRIED UNSELD.

Verlag Technik: 1020 Berlin, Oranienburgerstr. 13–14, Postfach 201; tel. (02) 28700; telex 112228; f. 1946; technical books, dictionaries and periodicals; Dir K. HIERONIMUS.

Verlag B. G. Teubner GmbH: 7000 Stuttgart 80, Industriestr. 15, Postfach 801069; tel. (0711) 789010; fax (0711) 78901-10; f. 1811; physics, mathematics, computer science, engineering, biology, geography, philology, sociology; Man. Dir HEINRICH KRÄMER.

Georg Thieme Verlag: 7000 Stuttgart 30, Rüdigerstr. 14; tel. (0711) 89310; telex 7252275; f. 1886; medicine and natural science; Man. Dirs Dr GÜNTHER HAUFF, ALBRECHT HAUFF.

K. Thienemanns Verlag: 7000 Stuttgart 1, Blumenstr. 36; tel. (0711) 210550; telex 723933; fax (0711) 2105539; f. 1849; picture books, children's books, juveniles; Dirs HANSJÖRG WEITBRECHT, GUNTER EHNI.

Jan Thorbecke Verlag: 7480 Sigmaringen, Karlstr. 10; tel. (07571) 728-100; telex 732534; fax (07571) 728-280; f. 1946; reference books; Dirs GEORG BENSCH, Dr JOACHIM BENSCH.

Tourist Verlag: 1020 Berlin, Neue Grünstr. 17; tel. (02) 2791002; telex 114488; f. 1977; maps, tourist guides and travel books; Man. KLAUS DAEHN.

transpress Verlagsgesellschaft mbH: 1086 Berlin, Französische Str. 13–14; tel. (02) 203410; telex 112229; f. 1960; specialized literature on transport, telecommunications, philately; Man. Dr H. BÖTTCHER.

Treptower Verlagshaus GmbH: 1193 Berlin, Am Treptower Park 28–30; tel. (02) 27100; telex 112611; f. 1990 (formerly the *Tribüne* trade union publishing house); Dirs D. BENSCH, K. HEINEMANN.

Verlag Ullstein GmbH: 1000 Berlin 61, Lindenstr. 76; tel. (030) 2591-3570; telex 183723; fax (030) 2591-3523; f. 1877; belles-lettres, biography, history, art, general and social science, politics; Man. Dir Dr HERBERT FLEISSNER.

Buchverlage Ullstein Langen Müller: 8000 München 22, Thomas-Wimmer-Ring 11; tel. (089) 235008-0; telex 5215045; fax (089) 235008-44; f. 1894; literature, art, music, theatre, contemporary history, biography; Publr Dr HERBERT FLEISSNER.

Verlag Eugen Ulmer GmbH & Co: 7000 Stuttgart 70, Wollgrasweg 41, Postfach 700561; tel. (0711) 45070; telex 723634; f. 1868; agriculture, horticulture, science, periodicals; Dir ROLAND ULMER.

Umschau Verlag Breidenstein GmbH: 6000 Frankfurt a.M. 1, Stuttgarter Str. 18–24, Postfach 110262; tel. (069) 26000; telex 411064; fax (069) 2600 222; f. 1950; picture books, non-fiction, geography, archaeology, food, military affairs, travel; Man. Dir HANS-JÜRGEN BREIDENSTEIN.

GERMANY
Directory

Union Verlag: 1080 Berlin, Charlottenstr. 79; tel. (02) 2202711; telex 114767; f. 1951; publications of the CDU; literature, art; Dir KLAUS-PETER GERHARDT.

Universitas Verlag: 8000 München 22, Thomas-Wimmer-Ring 11; tel. (089) 2350080; f. 1920; travel, history, fiction, biography; Dir Dr HERBERT FLEISSNER.

Urban & Schwarzenberg GmbH: 8000 München 2, Landwehrstr. 61; tel. (089) 5383-0; telex 523864; fax (089) 5383221; f. 1866; medicine, natural sciences; Man. Dir MICHAEL URBAN; brs in München, Vienna, Baltimore.

VCH Verlagsgesellschaft mbH: 6940 Weinheim, Pappelallee 3, Postfach 101161; tel. (06201) 602-0; telex 465516; fax (06201) 602-328; f. 1921; natural sciences, especially chemistry, biotechnology, materials science, information technology and physics, medicine, history, philosophy, history of art; Man. Dirs Prof. Dr HELMUT GRÜNEWALD, HANS DIRK KÖHLER.

Verlag Franz Vahlen GmbH: 8000 München 40, Wilhelmstr. 9; tel. (089) 381891; telex 5215085; fax (089) 38189398; f. 1870; law, economics; Man. Dir Dr HANS DIETER BECK.

Vandenhoeck & Ruprecht Verlag: 3400 Göttingen, Theaterstr. 13, Postfach 3753; tel. (0551) 54031; telex 965226; fax (0551) 46298; f. 1735; Protestant theology, economics, medical psychology, mathematics, philosophy, linguistics, history, classical studies, secondary school books, periodicals; Dirs Dr ARNDT RUPRECHT, Dr DIETRICH RUPRECHT.

Friedr. Vieweg & Sohn Verlagsgesellschaft mbH: 6200 Wiesbaden 1, Faulbrunnstr. 13, Postfach 5829; tel. (0611) 16020; telex 4186928; fax (0611) 160229; f. 1786; books on mathematics, natural sciences, architecture, medicine, philosophy, microcomputers, technics; scientific and technical periodicals; Man. Dir Dr FRANK LUBE.

Curt R. Vincentz-Verlag: 3000 Hannover 1, Schiffgraben 41–43, Postfach 6247; tel. (0511) 3499944; telex 923846; fax (0511) 3499999; f. 1893; science, trade, building, social welfare; Dir Dr LOTHAR VINCENTZ.

Verlag Klaus Wagenbach: 1000 Berlin 30, Ahornstr. 4; tel. (030) 2115060; fax (030) 2116140; f. 1964; literature, politics, periodicals, paperbacks; Dir Dr KLAUS WAGENBACH.

Ernst Wasmuth Verlag GmbH & Co: 7400 Tübingen, Fürststr. 133; tel. (07071) 33658; fax (07071) 35776; f. 1872; architecture, archaeology, art, history of art; Dirs ELSE WASMUTH, KARL-HEINZ SCHATTNER.

A. Weichert Verlag: 3000 Hannover 1, Tiestestr. 14; tel. (0511) 813068; telex 923872; f. 1872; children's books; Man. Dir ALFRED TRIPPO.

Weiss Verlag: 6072 Dreieich 3, Wildscheuerweg 1; tel. (030) 7817725; telex 4185381; f. 1945; fiction, popular science, children's books, science fiction, paperbacks; Propr ABRAHAM MELZER.

Westdeutscher Verlag: 6200 Wiesbaden 1, Faulbrunnstr. 13, Postfach 5829; tel. (0611) 160210; telex 4186928; fax (0611) 160229; f. 1947; history, economics, sociology, politics, psychology, law, periodicals; Man Dir Dr FRANK LUBE.

Georg Westermann Verlag: 3300 Braunschweig, Georg-Westermann-Allee 66, Postfach 3320; tel. (0531) 7080; telex (17) 622153; fax (0531) 708-127; f. 1838; cartography, education, science, technology, fiction, periodicals; Dir Dr JÜRGEN RICHTER.

Bruno Wilkens Verlag KG: 3000 Hannover 51, Hansinckstr. 11; tel. (0511) 5498811; f. 1922; medicine; Dir HELGA HOFMEISTER-WILKENS.

Carl Winter Universitätsverlag GmbH: 6900 Heidelberg, Lutherstr. 59; tel. (06221) 4149-0; telex 461660; f. 1822; university textbooks; Publr Dr CARL WINTER.

Verlag Die Wirtschaft Berlin GmbH: 1055 Berlin, Am Friedrichshain 22; tel. (02) 43870; telex 114566; fax (02) 4361249; f. 1946; specialist books, brochures and periodicals on economics, industrial management, statistics, economic planning, data processing, trade; Dir D. GRÜNEBERG.

Verlag Wissenschaft und Politik: 5000 Köln 1, Salierring 14–16; tel. (0221) 312878; fax (0221) 315787; f. 1961; politics, sociology, history, law, periodicals; Dirs BEREND VON NOTTBECK, CLAUS-PETER VON NOTTBECK.

Wissenschaftliche Verlagsgesellschaft mbH: 7000 Stuttgart 10, Birkenwaldstr. 44, Postfach 105339; tel. (0711) 25820; telex 723636; fax (0711) 291450; science, medicine, pharmacy; Dirs Dr WOLFGANG WESSINGER, VINCENT SIEVEKING, REINHOLD HACK.

Friedrich Wittig Verlag: 2000 Hamburg 61, In der Masch 6; tel. (040) 5535019; fax (040) 5531266; f. 1946; religion, children's, art books; Publishing Dir HENNING WENDLAND; Man. Dir FRIEDRICH HOLST.

Verlag Zeit im Bild: 8012 Dresden, Postfach 61; tel. (051) 48640; telex 2291; f. 1946; periodicals, politics, economics, foreign language; Man. K.-H. KAMENZ.

Ziemsen Verlag: 4600 Wittenberg Lutherstadt, Lucas-Cranach-Str. 21; tel. 2528; f. 1902; works on biology.

Paul Zsolnay Verlag GmbH: 6100 Darmstadt, Havelstr. 16; tel. (06151) 386301; f. 1948; poetry, non-fiction, fiction; Man. Dir GERHARD BECKMANN.

PRINCIPAL ASSOCIATION OF BOOK PUBLISHERS AND BOOKSELLERS

Börsenverein des Deutschen Buchhandels eV: 6000 Frankfurt a.M. 1, Postfach 100442, Grosser Hirschgraben 17–21; tel. (069) 1306-0; telex 413573; fax (069) 1306-201; f. 1825; Chair. DOROTHEE HESS-MAIER; Man. Dir Dr HANS-KARL VON KUPSCH (see Buchhändler-Vereinigung GmbH under Publishers).

Radio and Television

In 1991 there were an estimated 32m. radio receivers and 37.8m. television receivers in use in Germany.

Arbeitsgemeinschaft der öffentlich-rechtlichen Rundfunkanstalten der Bundesrepublik Deutschland (ARD) (Association of Public Law Broadcasting Organizations): 5000 Köln, Appellhofplatz 1, Postfach 101950; tel. (0221) 2201; telex 8882575; Chair. Intendant FRIEDRICH NOWOTTNY; the co-ordinating body of German Radio and Television organizations: Bayerischer Rundfunk, Hessischer Rundfunk, Norddeutscher Rundfunk, Radio Bremen, Saarländischer Rundfunk, Sender Freies Berlin, Süddeutscher Rundfunk, Südwestfunk, Westdeutscher Rundfunk, Deutsche Welle, Deutschlandfunk; RIAS Berlin is represented on the Council by an observer.

RADIO

Each of the members of ARD broadcasts 3–4 channels. Deutsche Welle and Deutschlandfunk broadcast programmes for Europe and overseas.

Deutsche Welle: 5000 Köln 1, Raderberggürtel 50, Postfach 100444; tel. (0221) 3890; telex 888485; fax (0221) 389-3000; German short-wave service; broadcasts 93 programmes daily in 34 languages; Dir-Gen. DIETER WEIRICH; Dir of Programmes JOSEF M. GERWALD; Dir of Television SIEGFRIED BERNDT; Tech. Dir GÜNTER ROESSLER; Dir of Administration GEBHARD BRAUN; Dir of Public Relations LOTHAR SCHWARTZ.

Deutschlandfunk: 5000 Köln 51, Raderberggürtel 40; tel. (0221) 3451; telex 8884920; fax (0221) 380766; 24 hours daily broadcasting from eight stations for Germany and Europe; Dir-Gen. EDMUND GRUBER; Dir of Programmes Dr DETTMAR CRAMER; Administrative Dir REINHARD HARTSTEIN; Technical Dir HELMUT HAUNREITER.

RIAS Berlin: 1000 Berlin 62, Kufsteiner Str. 69; tel. (030) 85030; telex 183790; fax (030) 8503390; broadcasts for US troops stationed in Germany; Chair. of US Supervisory Board VAN S. WUNDER; Dir Dr HELMUT DRÜCK.

The following radio stations broadcast in the area of the former GDR:

Berliner Rundfunk: 1160 Berlin, Nalepastr. 10–50; tel. (02) 6360; telex 112276; fax (02) 5589119; 9 medium-wave and 13 VHF transmitters, broadcasting 168 hours a week; Dir JÜRGEN ITZFELDT.

Radio aktuell: 1160 Berlin, Nalepastr. 10–50; tel. (02) 6363188; telex 112276; fax (02) 55891; broadcasts 168 hours a week on medium wave and VHF; Dir ALFRED EICHHORN.

Deutschlandsender Kultur: 1160 Berlin, Nalepastr. 18–50; tel. (02) 6360; telex 112276; one long-wave, four medium-wave, one short-wave and 12 VHF transmitters, broadcasting 168 hours a week; Dir MARTIN RADMANN.

Jugendradio DT 64: 1160 Berlin, Nalepastr. 10–50; tel. (02) 6364100; telex 112276; fax (02) 6362502; f. 1964; one medium-wave and 19 VHF transmitters, broadcasting 24 hours daily; Dir MICHAEL SCHIEWACK.

TELEVISION

There are three television channels. The autonomous regional broadcasting organizations combine to provide material for the First Programme which is produced by ARD. The Second Programme (Zweites Deutsches Fernsehen/ZDF) is completely separate and is controlled by a public corporation of all the Länder. It is partly financed by advertising. The Third Programme provides a cultural and educational service in the evenings only with contributions from several of the regional bodies.

Zweites Deutsches Fernsehen (ZDF): 6500 Mainz 1, Postfach 4040; tel. (06131) 701; telex 4187930; f. 1961 by the Länder Governments as a second television channel; 90 main transmitters; Dir-Gen. Prof. DIETER STOLTE; Dir of Programmes OSWALD RING;

GERMANY — Directory

Editor-in-Chief Klaus Bresser; Dir, International Affairs Hans Kimmel.

REGIONAL BROADCASTING ORGANIZATIONS

Antenne Brandenburg: 1561 Potsdam, Puschkinallee 4; tel. (033) 3200; telex 15553; fax (033) 23470; Dir Dr Jereczinsky.

Bayerischer Rundfunk: 8000 München 2, Rundfunkplatz 1; tel. (089) 5900-01; telex 521070; fax (089) 5900-2375; Chair. of Broadcasting Council Dr Wilhelm Fritz; Chair. of Administration Board Dr Franz Heubl.

Radio Bremen: 2800 Bremen 33, Bürgermeister-Spitta-Allee 45; tel. (0421) 2460; telex 245181; fax (0421) 246-1010; Dir-Gen. Karl-Heinz Klostermeier.

Hessischer Rundfunk: 6000 Frankfurt a.M. 1, Bertramstr. 8; tel. (069) 1551; telex 411127; fax (069) 1552900; Dir-Gen. Prof. Dr Hartwig Kelm; Chair. Admin. Council Eitel-Oskar Höhne; Chair. Broadcasting Council Ignatz Bubis.

Radio Mecklenburg-Vorpommern: 2500 Rostock, Richard-Wagner-Str. 7; tel. (081) 3980; telex 31102; fax (081) 22355; Dir Klaus-Peter Otto.

Norddeutscher Rundfunk (NDR): 2000 Hamburg 13, Rothenbaumchaussee 132–134; tel. (040) 4156-0; telex 2198910; fax (040) 447602; Dir-Gen. Dr Peter Schiwy.

Saarländischer Rundfunk: 6600 Saarbrücken, Funkhaus Halberg, Postfach 1050; tel. (0681) 6020; telex 4428977; fax (0681) 6023874; Chair. Broadcasting Council Rosemarie Keller; Dir-Gen. Dr Manfred Buchwald; Admin. Dir Fritz Raff.

Radio Sachsen-Anhalt: 4020 Halle, Waisenhausring 9; tel. (046) 37961; telex 4205; fax (046) 26106; Dir Michael Straube.

Sachsen Radio: 7022 Leipzig, Springerstr. 24; tel. (041) 51151; telex 512203; fax (041) 592421; Dir Manfred Müller.

Sender Freies Berlin: 1000 Berlin 19, Masurenallee 8–14; tel. (030) 30310; telex 182813; fax (030) 3015062; Chair. Broadcasting Council Gabriele Wiechatzek; Dir-Gen. Dr Günter von Lojewski; Admin. Dir Dirk Jens Rennefeld.

Süddeutscher Rundfunk: 7000 Stuttgart 10, Neckarstr. 230, Postfach 106040; tel. (0711) 2881; telex 723456; fax (0711) 2882600; f. 1924; Chair. Broadcasting Council Heinz Bühringer; Chair. Admin. Council Walter Ayass; Dir-Gen. Hermann Fünfgeld; Admin. Dir Margret Wittig-Terhardt.

Südwestfunk (SWF): 7570 Baden-Baden, Hans-Bredow-Str.; tel. (07221) 92-0; telex 787810; fax (07221) 2115-10; Chair. Broadcasting Council Rolf Weiler; Chair. Admin. Council Dr Robert Maus; Dir-Gen. Willibald Hilf; Admin. Dir Dr Hans-Joachim Lehmann.

Thüringer Rundfunk: 5300 Weimar, Humboldtstr. 36A; tel. (0621) 2451; telex 618921; fax (0621) 4365; Dir Hilmar Süss.

Westdeutscher Rundfunk (WDR): 5000 Köln 1, Appellhofplatz 1; tel. (0221) 2201; telex 8882575; Chair. Reinhard Grätz (Broadcasting Council), Dr Theodor Schwefer (Admin. Council); Doris Emons (School Broadcasting); Dir-Gen. Friedrich Nowottny; Admin. Dir Dr Norbert Seidel.

Europe 1: Europäische Rundfunk und Fernsehen AG, Europe 1, 6600 Saarbrücken, Postfach 111; tel. (0681) 30781; fax (0681) 372899; f. 1952; broadcasts in French; Dir Claude Fabre.

FOREIGN RADIO STATIONS

American Forces Network: 6000 Frankfurt/Main, Bertramstr. 6; tel. (069) 15688-123; fax (069) 15688-200; f. 1943; 10 stations, 52 AM/FM transmitters and four TV studios; Commanding Officer Col Zachary Fowler; Programme Dir Paul D. Van Dyke.

British Forces Broadcasting Service, Germany: 5 Köln-Marienburg, Postfach 510526; tel. (0221) 376990; telex 8881329; fax (0221) 376992; since April 1982 a division of the newly-formed Services Sound and Vision Corporation; 12 VHF radio transmitters and 45 low-powered TV transmitters; Senior Programme Dir Peter McDonagh.

Radio Free Europe/Radio Liberty Inc: Oettingenstr. 67, 8000 München 22; tel. (089) 21020; telex 523228; fax (089) 9101390; a non-profit-making private corporation, operating under American management and funded by congressional grants supplied through the Board for International Broadcasting, which also oversees the operations of both stations; transmitter facilities in Spain, Portugal and Germany. Radio Free Europe broadcasts to Bulgaria, Czechoslovakia, Estonia, Hungary, Latvia, Lithuania, Poland and Romania. Radio Liberty broadcasts to the USSR in Russian, Armenian, Azeri, Byelorussian, Georgian, Kazakh, Kirghiz, Tadzhik, Tatar-Bashkir, Turkestani, Ukrainian, Uzbek. Radio Free Afghanistan, a division of Radio Liberty, broadcasts in Dari and Pashtu. Pres. E. Eugene Pell; Dirs Dr A. Ross Johnson (RFE Div.), Dr S. Enders Wimbush (Radio Liberty Div.).

Radio Volga: 1500 Potsdam, Menzelstr. 5; operates one 200 kW transmitter on 1141 metres for Soviet forces in the former GDR; broadcasts for 18 hours a day with its own Russian language programmes and relays from Radio Moscow.

Voice of America (VOA Europe): 8000 München 22, Ludwigstr. 2; tel. (089) 286091; telex 523737; fax (089) 2809210; f. 1985; broadcasts in English on MW, VHF and cable to 23 European countries, mainly music, news and features on US life and culture; the Correspondents' Bureau provides VOA Washington headquarters with reports and feature programmes on newsworthy developments in Eastern and Western Europe and the USSR; Dir European Operations Earl Klitenic (acting).

Finance

(cap. = capital; p.u. = paid up; brs = branches; dep. = deposits; DM = Deutsche Mark; m. = million; res = reserves)

The Treaty Establishing a Monetary, Economic and Social Union, which took effect on 1 July 1990, stipulated that the FRG and the GDR (fully unified in October 1990) 'shall constitute a monetary union comprising a unified currency area and with the Deutsche Mark as the common currency. The Deutsche Bundesbank shall be the central bank in this currency area'. By late 1990 many of the large banks of the FRG had established representative branches in the area formerly constituting the GDR.

The Deutsche Bundesbank, the central bank of Germany, consists of the central administration in Frankfurt am Main (considered to be the financial capital of the country), 16 main offices (Landeszentralbanken) in the Länder, and over 200 branches. In carrying out its functions as determined by law, the Bundesbank is independent of the Federal Government, but is required to support the Government's general economic policy. All other credit institutions are subject to governmental supervision through the Federal Banking Supervisory Office (Bundesaufsichtsamt für das Kreditwesen) in Berlin.

Banks outside the central banking system are divided into three groups: private commercial banks, credit institutions incorporated under public law and co-operative credit institutions. All these commercial banks are 'universal banks', conducting all kinds of customary banking business. There is no division of activities. As well as the commercial banks there are a number of specialist banks, such as private or public mortgage banks.

The group of private commercial banks includes: those known as the 'Big Three' (the Deutsche Bank, the Dresdner Bank and the Commerzbank); all banks incorporated as a company limited by shares (Aktiengesellschaft—AG, Kommanditgesellschaft auf Aktien—KGaA) or as a private limited company (Gesellschaft mit beschränkter Haftung—GmbH) and those which are known as 'regional banks' because they do not usually function throughout Germany; and the private banks, which are established as sole proprietorships or partnerships and mostly have no branches outside their home town. Foreign banks are classed as regional banks. The main business of all private commercial banks is short-term lending. The private bankers fulfil the most varied tasks within the banking system.

The public law credit institutions are the savings banks (Sparkassen) and the Landesbanken. The latter act as central banks and clearing houses on a national level for the savings banks. Laws governing the savings banks limit them to certain sectors—credits, investments and money transfers—and they concentrate on the areas of home financing, municipal investments and the trades. In December 1984 there were 591 savings banks and 11 Landesbanken in the FRG.

The head institution of the co-operative system is the Deutsche Genossenschaftsbank. At the end of 1984 there were 3,707 industrial and agricultural credit co-operatives in the FRG, with a total of 19,587 offices.

Banking federations were established in the FRG in 1948. The federal association for the private commercial banks is the German Bankers' Association (Bundesverband deutscher Banken), which consists of provincial associations, the Association of German Mortgage Banks (Verband deutscher Hypothekenbanken) and the Association of German Shipping Banks (Verband deutscher Schiffsbanken). Other federal banking associations are the German Savings Banks Association (Deutscher Sparkassen- und Giroverband), the Association of German Industrial and Agricultural Credit Co-operatives (Bundesverband der Deutschen Volksbanken und Raiffeisenbanken) and the Association of Public-Law Credit Institutions (Verband öffentlicher Banken).

BANKS

The Central Banking System

Deutsche Bundesbank: 6000 Frankfurt 50, Wilhelm-Epstein-Str. 14; tel. (069) 158-1; telex 414431; fax (069) 5601071; f. 1957; to issue

GERMANY

bank notes, to regulate note and coin circulation and supply of credit; maintains head offices (Hauptverwaltungen) in each Land, known as Landeszentralbanken; required to support government economic policy, although it is independent of instructions from the Government. The Bank may advise on important monetary policy, and members of the Federal Government may take part in the deliberations of the Central Bank Council but may not vote; Pres. KARL OTTO PÖHL; Vice-Pres. Dr HELMUT SCHLESINGER.

Landeszentralbank in Baden-Württemberg: 7000 Stuttgart 1, Marstallstr. 3; tel. (0711) 20741; telex 723512; fax (0711) 296225; Pres. Board of Management Prof. Dr Dr h.c. NORBERT KLOTEN.

Landeszentralbank in Bayern: 8000 München 2, Postfach 20 16 05, Ludwigstr. 13; tel. (089) 2889-0; telex 524365; Pres. Board of Management LOTHAR MÜLLER.

Landeszentralbank in Berlin: 1000 Berlin 12, Leibnizstr. 9–10; tel. (030) 3404-1; telex 181653; Pres. Board of Management Dr DIETER HISS.

Landeszentralbank in Bremen: 2800 Bremen 1, Kohlhökerstr. 29; tel. (0421) 3291-0; telex 244810; Pres. Board of Management Prof. Dr KURT NEMITZ.

Landeszentralbank in der Freien und Hansestadt Hamburg: 2000 Hamburg 11, Ost-West-Str. 73; tel. (040) 3707-0; telex 21455450; fax (040) 3707-2205; Pres. Board of Management Dr WILHELM NÖLLING.

Landeszentralbank in Hessen: 6000 Frankfurt a.M. 1, Taunusanlage 5; tel. (069) 2388-0; telex (17) 6997404; fax (069) 2388-2130; Pres. Board of Management Dr KARL THOMAS.

Landeszentralbank in Niedersachsen: 3 Hannover, Georgsplatz 5; tel. (0511) 1233-1; telex 922651; Pres. Board of Management Prof. Dr HELMUT HESSE.

Landeszentralbank in Nordrhein-Westfalen: 4000 Düsseldorf, Berliner Allee 14; tel. (0211) 874-0; telex 8582774; Pres. Prof. Dr REIMUT JOCHIMSEN.

Landeszentralbank in Rheinland-Pfalz: 6500 Mainz, Hegelstr. 65; tel. (06131) 377-0; fax (06131) 381664; Pres. Dr HEINRICH SCHREINER.

Landeszentralbank im Saarland: 6600 Saarbrücken 1, Keplerstr. 18; tel. (0681) 5802-0; telex 4421258; Pres. HANS GLIEM.

Landeszentralbank in Schleswig-Holstein: 2300 Kiel, Fleethörn 26; tel. (0431) 990-0; telex 299803; fax (0431) 990119; Pres. Board of Management WERNER SCHULZ.

Staatsbank Berlin: 1086 Berlin, Charlottenstr. 33–33A; tel. (02) 230; telex 114671; f. 1948 as the State Bank of the GDR; re-formed as above in 1990; Pres. Dr WALTER KRÜGER.

Private Commercial Banks

Baden-Württembergische Bank AG: 7000 Stuttgart 1, Kleiner Schlossplatz 11, Postfach 106014; tel. (0711) 2094-0; telex 721881; fax (0711) 2094-712; f. 1977 by merger of Badische Bank, Handelsbank Heilbronn and Württembergische Bank; cap. DM 135m., dep. DM 13,490m. (Dec. 1989); 11 main brs, 108 brs and agencies.

Bank für Gemeinwirtschaft AG: 6000 Frankfurt a.M. 11, Theaterplatz 2; tel. (069) 2580; telex 4122154; fax (069) 2586838; f. 1958; cap. and res DM 2,517m. (Dec. 1989); Chair. PAUL WIEANDT; over 250 brs.

Bankers Trust GmbH: 6000 Frankfurt a.M. 1, Bockenheimer Landstr. 39, Postfach 100345; f. 1889; tel. (069) 71320; telex 411500; formerly Deutsche Unionbank GmbH, name changed in 1980; cap. DM 35.8m., dep. DM 2,963m. (Dec. 1989); Gen. Mans Dr WOLFGANG DIETRICH KUNZ, CECIL Baron VON HAHN, WOLFGANG ARGELANDER; 3 brs.

Bankhaus H. Aufhäuser: 8000 München 2, Löwengrube 18; tel. (089) 2393-1; telex 523154; fax (089) 2393-438; f. 1870; cap. DM 50.7m., res DM 46.2m. (Dec. 1989); Chair. Dr HANS PETER LINSS; Partners RUDOLF BAYER, RÜDIGER VON MICHAELIS, Dr HARALD RÜHL, HELMUT SCHREYER.

Bankhaus Bensel GmbH: 6800 Mannheim 1, Postfach 120251; tel (0621) 180080; telex 463271; fax (0621) 1708254; f. 1936; cap. DM 10m., dep. DM 158m. (Dec. 1989); Partner and Gen. Man. WOLFGANG KÖHN, Dr HARRO PETERSEN; Partner Baden-Württembergische Bank AG.

Bankhaus Gebrüder Bethmann: 6000 Frankfurt a.M. 1, Bethmannstr. 7–9, Postfach 100349; tel. (069) 2177-0; telex 411273; fax (069) 2177-283; f. 1748; commercial and investment bank; total assets DM 1,201.3m. (Dec. 1988); Partners WERNER CHROBOK, Dr CHRISTIAN HUMBERT, Dr WALTER SCHORR; 7 brs.

Bankhaus J. A. Krebs: 7800 Freiburg i. Br., Münsterplatz 4; tel. (0761) 31909-0; telex 772807; fax (0761) 31909-29; f. 1683; Proprs Dr WALTER KRÄMER, Dr STEFAN WALLRAVEN.

Bankhaus Gebr. Martin: 7320 Göppingen (Württemberg), Kirchstr. 35; tel. (07161) 6714-0; telex 727880; fax (07161) 6714-24;

Directory

f. 1912; Partners Dr RENATE HEES, SUSANNE MARTIN, ANDREAS HEES, WOLF MARTIN.

Bankhaus Neelmeyer AG: 2800 Bremen 1, Am Markt 14/16; tel. (0421) 36030; telex 244866; fax (0421) 325614; f. 1907; cap. DM 20m., dep. DM 1,022.4m. (Dec. 1989); Gen. Mans Dr UWE JANSSEN, Dr ROLF LATTREUTER, Dr FRIEDRICH-KARL VON STUDWITZ; 8 brs.

Bankhaus Carl F. Plump & Co: 2800 Bremen 1, Am Markt 19, Postfach 102507; tel. (0421) 36851; telex 244756; fax (0421) 3685269; f. 1828; private commercial bank; cap. DM 18.0m., dep. DM 329.4m. (Dec. 1989); Partners Fr. HOFFMANN, JAN FREYSOLDT.

Bayerische Hypotheken- und Wechsel-Bank AG (Hypo-Bank): 8000 München 2, Theatinerstr. 11, Postfach 200527; tel. (089) 9244-0; telex 52865-0; fax (089) 9244-0-2880; f. 1835; cap. and res DM 5,466m., dep. DM 99,062m., total assets DM 106,219m. (Dec. 1989); Chair. (Supervisory Board) Dr KLAUS GÖTTE; Chair. (Board of Management) Dr EBERHARD MARTINI; 489 brs.

Bayerische Vereinsbank AG: 8000 München 2, Kardinal-Faulhaber-Str. 1 and 14, Postfach 100101; tel. (089) 2132-1; telex 52861-0; fax (089) 2132-6415; f. 1869; cap. DM 4,900m., dep. DM 64,300m. (June 1990); Chair. (Board of Dirs) Dr ALBRECHT SCHMIDT.

Joh. Berenberg, Gossler & Co: 2000 Hamburg 36, Neuer Jungfernstieg 20; tel. (040) 34960; telex 215781; fax (040) 352132; f. 1590; cap. DM 105m., dep. DM 2,091m. (Dec. 1989); Partners JOACHIM H. WETZEL, PETER Freiherr VON KAP-HERR, JOACHIM VON BERENBERG-CONSBRUCH, CLAUS-G. BUDELMANN.

Berliner Bank AG: 1000 Berlin 12, Hardenbergstr. 32, Postfach 12 17 09; tel. (030) 3109-0; telex 182010; fax (030) 3109-2165; f. 1950; cap. DM 477m., res DM 860m., total assets DM 35,299m. (Dec. 1989); Chair. EDZARD REUTER; Man. Dir (International) GÜNTHER BERNT; Chief International Exec. CLAUDIO JARCZYK; 83 brs in Berlin, brs in Düsseldorf, Frankfurt, Hamburg, Hannover, Stuttgart and München, London, subsidiary in Luxembourg.

Berliner Commerzbank AG: 1000 Berlin 30, Potsdamerstr. 125, Postfach 110420; tel. (030) 26971; telex 183862; fax (030) 2697570; f. 1949; wholly-owned subsidiary of Commerzbank AG; cap. DM 162.5m., dep. DM 7,920m. (Dec. 1989); Mans SIEGFRIED ERNST, Dr HANS STRATHUS, PETER VON JENA; 60 brs in Berlin.

Berliner Handels- und Frankfurter Bank (BHF-Bank): 6000 Frankfurt a.M. 1, Bockenheimer Landstr. 10; tel. (069) 718-0; telex 411026; fax (069) 718-2296; f. 1856; cap. DM 272m., dep. DM 32,473m. (Dec. 1989); Man. Partners Dr W. GRAEBNER, Dr P. OPITZ, Dr W. RUPF, W. STRUTZ, K. SUBJETZKI, L. Graf VON ZECH.

Berliner Volksbank eG: 1000 Berlin 19, Kaiserdamm 86; tel. (030) 303061; telex 182803; fax (030) 30306-540; f. 1946; cap. DM 73.4m., dep. DM 4,005.9m. (Dec. 1988); Chair. HEINZ-DIETER PRÜSKE; 30 brs in Berlin.

Commerzbank AG: 6000 Frankfurt a.M., Neue Mainzer Str. 32-36; tel. (069) 13620; telex 4152530; fax (069) 285389; f. 1870; cap. and res DM 7,418m., dep. DM 115,687m. (Dec. 1989); Chair. (Supervisory Board) PAUL LICHTENBERG; Chair. Board of Man. Dirs Dr WALTER SEIPP; 779 domestic and 13 foreign brs.

Delbrück & Co: 1000 Berlin 30, Rankestr. 13; tel. (030) 8842880; fax (030) 88428818; 5000 Köln 1, Gereonstr. 15–23; tel. (0221) 16241; telex 8882605; fax (0221) 1624259; f. 1854; cap. DM 55m., dep. DM 1,115m. (Dec. 1989); 9 Man. Partners.

Deutsch-Skandinavische Bank AG: 6000 Frankfurt a.M., Alte Rothofstr. 8; tel. (069) 29830; telex 413413; fax (069) 284191; f. 1976; cap. DM 81m., dep. DM 2,246m. (Dec. 1989); Chair. JACOB PALMSTIERNA.

Deutsch-Südamerikanische Bank AG (Banco Germánico de la América del Sud): 2000 Hamburg 36, Neuer Jungfernstieg 16, Postfach 301246; tel. (040) 341070; telex 2142360; f. 1906; cap. DM 178m., dep. DM 6,797m. (Dec. 1989); Chair. JÜRGEN SARRAZIN; Gen. Mans ALBRECHT C. RÄDECKE, HELMUT FRÖHLICH, KURT ZIMMERLING.

Deutsche Bank AG: Central Office: 6000 Frankfurt a.M., Taunusanlage 12; tel. (069) 71500; telex 417300; f. 1870; cap. DM 1,988m., dep. DM 188,911m. (Dec. 1989); Hon. Pres. HERMANN J. ABS; Chair. of Supervisory Bd Dr F. WILHELM CHRISTIANS; 1,200 brs.

Deutsche Bank Berlin AG: 1000 Berlin 10, Otto-Suhr-Allee 6/16; tel. (030) 34070; telex 181433; fax (030) 34072788; f. 1949; wholly-owned subsidiary of Deutsche Bank AG; cap. DM 120m., dep. DM 8,721m. (Dec. 1989); Chair. Supervisory Board Dr HERBERT ZAPP.

Dresdner Bank AG: 6000 Frankfurt a.M. 11, Jürgen-Ponto-Platz 1; tel. (069) 2630; telex 415240; fax (069) 263-4831; f. 1872; cap. DM 1,243m., dep. DM 230m. (Dec. 1989); Chair. Board of Man. Dirs Dr WOLFGANG RÖLLER; 953 brs.

Dresdner Bank Berlin AG: 1000 Berlin 12, Uhlandstr. 9/11; tel. (030) 3196-1; telex 1-83875; fax (030) 3124041; f. 1949 as Berliner Bank für Handel und Industrie AG; in 1950 renamed Bank für

GERMANY

Handel und Industrie AG; in 1989 renamed as above; cap. DM 155m., res DM 744m., dep. DM 11,957m. (Dec. 1989); Man. Dirs Dr WOLFGANG POECK, RUDI PUCHTA, MANFRED TÜNGLER; 79 brs.

Grunelius & Co: 6000 Frankfurt a.M. 16, Untermainkai 26; tel. (069) 273905-0; telex 411723; fax (069) 27390523; f. 1824; cap. DM 5.7m., dep. 27.8m. (Dec. 1989); Partners Dr ERNST MAX VON GRUNELIUS, EDMUND KNAPP.

Georg Hauck & Sohn Bankiers KGaA: 6000 Frankfurt a.M. 1, Kaiserstr. 24; tel. (069) 21611; telex 411061; fax (069) 2161340; f. 1796; cap. DM 20m., res DM 38.6m. (Dec. 1989); Chair. Dr HEINRICH IRMLER; Partners MICHAEL HAUCK, AXEL SCHÜTZ.

Hesse Newman & Co: 2000 Hamburg 1, Ferdinandstr. 25-27, Postfach 103020; tel. (040) 33962-0; telex 2161942; fax (040) 33962-200; f. 1777; cap. DM 25m., dep. DM 202m. (June 1988); Man. PETER C. QUEITSCH.

Von der Heydt-Kersten & Söhne: 5600 Wuppertal-Elberfeld 1, Neumarkt 9; tel. (0202) 4870; telex 8591824; fax (0202) 487365; f. 1754; wholly-owned subsidiary of Commerzbank AG; Partners ADOLF HEDRICH, GERHARD WICHELHAUS.

Ibero-Amerika Bank AG: 2800 Bremen 1, Domshof 14/15, Postfach 104509; tel. (0421) 36300-0; telex 244899; fax (0421) 36300-60; f. 1949; cap. DM 10m., res DM 35.5m. (Dec. 1989); br. in Hamburg; Gen. Mans KLAUS F. MÜLLER-LEIENDECKER, ENNO E. VON MARCARD, HERBERT SCHOENNAGEL.

Kleinwort, Benson (Deutschland) GmbH & Co: 2800 Bremen 1, Langenstr. 15-21; tel. (0421) 36660; telex 244812; f. 1872, fmrly Bankhaus Martens & Weyhausen, name changed 1983; cap. DM 35m., res DM 7,037m., dep. DM 576m. (Dec. 1982); Mans WOLFGANG KUNZE, JENS-PETER KNOBLAUCH.

Kredietbank-Bankverein AG: 2800 Bremen 1, Wachtstr. 16; tel. (0421) 3684-1; telex 244816; fax (0421) 326286; f. 1863; cap. DM 15.5m., dep. DM 880m. (Dec. 1989); Mans GÜNTHER KÜCK, Dr W. J. ROELANTS; 1 br.

Marcard, Stein & Co: 2000 Hamburg 1, Ballindamm 36; tel. (040) 30990; telex 2165032; fax (040) 3099200; f. 1790; cap. DM 74.15m., dep. DM 1,214m. (Dec. 1988); 4 partners.

Merck Finck & Co: 8000 München 2, Pacellistr. 4; tel. (089) 21040; telex 522303; fax (089) 299814; f. 1870; cap. DM 124m., dep. DM 4,673m. (Dec. 1989); Partners AUGUST VON FINCK, WILHELM VON FINCK, ADOLF KRACHT, Dr iur. WILHELM WINTERSTEIN, Agricola Verwaltungsgesellschaft KG.

Metallbank GmbH: 6000 Frankfurt a.M. 1, Reuterweg 14, Postfach 101501; tel. (069) 1590; telex 416341; fax (069) 159-3674; f. 1980; cap. DM 40.0m., dep. DM 843.5m. (Sept. 1989); Chair. MEINHARD FORSTER; 3 brs.

B. Metzler seel. Sohn & Co KGaA Bankers: 6000 Frankfurt a.M. 1, Grosse Gallusstr. 18; tel. (069) 21040; telex 412724; f. 1674; cap. DM 100m., dep. DM 535m. (Dec. 1989); Partners CHRISTOPH VON METZLER, FRIEDRICH VON METZLER, Dr WOLFRAM NOLTE, HANS HERMANN RESCHKE, WERNER WANKE.

National-Bank AG: 4300 Essen 1, Theaterplatz 8; tel. (0201) 81151; telex 857811; fax (0201) 8115500; f. 1921; cap. DM 22m., dep. DM 1,618m. (Dec. 1988); Mans GÜNTER EHLEN, Dr HANS BRAUN, GUNTHER LANGE, GERHARD LEPPELMANN.

Oldenburgische Landesbank AG: 2900 Oldenburg, Stau 15-17; tel. (0441) 221-1; telex 25882; fax (0441) 221633; f. 1868; cap. DM 66.5m., dep. DM 6,035m. (Dec. 1989); Chair. Dr jur. CARL S. GROSS; Mans HERMANN CONRING, Dr HUBERT FORCH, H.-H. LUDEWIG.

Sal. Oppenheim Jr & Cie: 5000 Köln 1, Unter Sachsenhausen 4; tel. (0221) 145-01; telex 8882547; fax (0221) 1451512; 6000 Frankfurt/M., Bockenheimer Landstr. 20; tel. (069) 7134-0; telex 411016; f. 1789; cap. DM 200m., dep. DM 3,601m. (Dec. 1989); 8 partners.

Reuschel & Co: 8000 München 2, Maximiliansplatz 13; tel. (089) 2395-0; telex 523690; fax (089) 291180; f. 1947; cap. DM 174m., dep. DM 3,247m. (Dec. 1989); Partners Dr ERNST THIEMANN, Dr BERND VOSS, THOMAS KLINGELHÖFER.

Karl Schmidt Bankgeschäft: 8670 Hof/Saale, Ernst-Reuter-Str. 119, Postfach 1629, 1649; tel. (09281) 6010; telex 643880; fax (09281) 601324; f. 1828; cap. DM 120.6m., dep. DM 2,953.5m. (Dec. 1989); Partners Dr KARL-GERHARD SCHMIDT, GEORG BECHER, WERNER SCHMIDT, Dr REINER SCHMIDT, Dr KLAUS BECHER; 90 brs.

Otto M. Schröder: 2000 Hamburg 36, Alsterarkaden 27, tel. (040) 363141; telex 211119; fax (040) 363745; f. 1932; cap. DM 9m., dep. 101.5m. (Dec. 1989); Owner OTTO M. SCHRÖDER.

Schröder Münchmeyer Hengst & Co: 6000 Frankfurt a.M., Friedensstr. 6-10; tel. (069) 2179-0; telex 413756; fax (069) 2179511; f. 1969; majority shareholder is the Lloyds Bank group; cap. DM 140m. (1988); Man. Partners CHRISTOPH Graf VON HARDENBERG, ADOLF KRAUS, JOCHEN NEYNABER, ULRICH SCHÜTTE, Dr EBERHARD WEIERSHÄUSER; 5 brs.

Schweizerische Bankgesellschaft (Deutschland) AG: 6000 Frankfurt a.M., Bleichstr. 52, Postfach 102063; tel. (069) 1369-0; telex 412194; fax (069) 1369-1366; f. 1909; merchant bank; frmly Deutsche Länderbank AG; cap. DM 45m., res DM 134.6m. (Dec. 1989); Chair. Dr JÜRGEN-PETER KAVEN.

Schweizerische Kreditanstalt (Deutschland) AG: 6000 Frankfurt a.M., Kaiserstr. 30; tel. (069) 2691-0; telex 412127; fax (069) 2691-2444; f. 1969; cap. DM 165m., dep. DM 5,918.8m. (March 1988); Mans. K. MIESEL, F. HOYOS, K. J. ZAPF.

Simonbank AG: 4000 Düsseldorf 1, Martin-Luther-Platz 32; tel. (0211) 8793-0; telex 8587931; fax (0211) 134190; f. 1960; cap. DM 34m., dep. DM 1,639.5m. (Dec. 1989); Chair. PETER REIMPELL; Man. Dirs Dr OTTHEINZ JUNG-SENSSFELDER, PETER KLEVER.

J. H. Stein: 5000 Köln 1, Unter Sachsenhausen 10-20, Postfach 101748; telex 8882506; f. 1790; Partners JOHANN HEINRICH VON STEIN, Dr GERD HOLLENBERG, Dr HANS KASPAR Freiherr VON RHEINBABEN.

Trinkaus & Burkhardt KGaA: 4000 Düsseldorf 1, Königsallee 21-23; tel. (0211) 831-1; telex 8581490; fax (0211) 8312691; f. 1785; cap. DM 100m., dep. DM 4,939m. (Dec. 1989); Chair. HERBERT H. JACOBI; 5 brs.

Vereins- und Westbank: 2000 Hamburg 11, Alter Wall 22; tel. (040) 3692-01; telex 2151640; fax (040) 36922870; f. 1974 by merger; cap. and res DM 708m., dep. DM 13,608m. (Dec. 1989).

M. M. Warburg-Brinckmann, Wirtz & Co: 2000 Hamburg 1, Ferdinandstr. 75; tel. (040) 32820; telex 2162211; f. 1798; cap. DM 130m., dep. DM 3,248m. (Dec. 1989); Partners Dr C. OLEARIUS, MAX A. WARBURG.

Westfalenbank AG: 4630 Bochum 1, Huestr. 21–25; tel. (0234) 616-0; telex 825825; fax (0234) 616400; f. 1921; cap. DM 75m., dep. DM 5,349m. (Dec. 1989); 4 Dirs.

Public-Law Credit Institutions

Bayerische Landesbank Girozentrale: 8000 München 2, Brienner Str. 20; tel. (089) 217101; telex 5286270; fax (089) 2171-3579; f. 1972; cap. DM 1,250m., dep. DM 129,823m. (Dec. 1989).

Deutsche Girozentrale-Deutsche Kommunalbank: 6000 Frankfurt a.M. 1, Taunusanlage 10, Postfach 110542; tel. (069) 26930; telex 414168; fax (069) 2693-490; and 1000 Berlin 15, Kurfürstendamm 32; tel. (030) 8812096; telex 183353; fax (030) 8812606; f. 1918; cap. and res DM 785m., dep. DM 19,176m. (Dec. 1989); Chair. Board of Management ERNST-OTTO SANDVOSS.

Hamburgische Landesbank-Girozentrale: 2000 Hamburg 1, Gerhart-Hauptmann-Platz 50, Postfach 102820; tel. (040) 3333-0; telex 214510-0; f. 1938; cap. DM 672m., res DM 655m. (Dec. 1989); Chair. Dr H. FAHNING.

Hessische Landesbank-Girozentrale: 6000 Frankfurt a.M. 11, Junghofstr. 18–26, Postfach 110833; tel. (069) 132-01; telex 415291-0; fax (069) 291517; cap. and res DM 2,187m., dep. DM 66,081m. (Dec. 1989); CEO Dr HERBERT KAZMIERZAK.

Landesbank Rheinland-Pfalz Girozentrale: 6500 Mainz, Grosse Bleiche 54–56; tel. (06131) 130; telex 4187858; fax (06131) 132729; f. 1958; cap. and res DM 1,085m., total assets DM 49,116m. (Dec. 1989); Chair. KLAUS K. ADAM; Dep. Chair. HERMANN-JOSEPH BUNGARTEN.

Norddeutsche Landesbank Girozentrale (NORD/LB): 3000 Hannover 1, Georgsplatz 1; tel. (0511) 103-0; telex 921620; fax (0511) 103-2502; f. 1970 by merger of several north German banks; cap. and res DM 3,012m., total assets DM 78,398m. (Dec. 1989); Chair. Dr BERND THIEMANN; 202 brs.

Südwestdeutsche Landesbank Girozentrale: 7000 Stuttgart 10, Lautenschlagerstr. 2; tel. (0711) 127-0; telex 72519-0; fax (0711) 127-3278; cap. and res DM 1,953m., total assets DM 78,861m. (Dec. 1989); Chair. WERNER SCHMIDT; Deputy Chair. Dr KARL HEIDENREICH; 3 brs.

Westdeutsche Landesbank Girozentrale (WestLB): 4000 Düsseldorf 1, Herzogstr. 15, Postfach 1128; tel. (0211) 826-01; telex 8588216; fax (0211) 826-6120; f. 1969; cap. DM 2,815m., res DM 3,907m., dep. DM 154,317m. (Dec. 1989); Chair. F. NEUBER.

Central Bank of Co-operative Banking System

Deutsche Genossenschaftsbank: 6000 Frankfurt a.M. 1, Am Platz der Republik, Postfach 100651; tel. (069) 744701; telex 412291; fax (069) 74471685; f. 1949; cap. and res DM 3,575m., total assets DM 186,925m. (Dec. 1989); supports more than 3,000 local and five regional co-operative banks; Chair. BERND THIEMANN.

Specialist Banks

Deutsche Verkehrs-Kredit-Bank AG: 6000 Frankfurt a.M., Untermainkai 23–25; tel. (069) 2648-0; telex 416925; fax (069) 2648444; f. 1923; cap. p.u. DM 75m., res DM 172m., dep. DM 5,060m. (Dec. 1989); Mans A. GRUNHOLD, Dr K. J. MENCHE, Dr F. SCHLOSSNIKL.

Frankfurter Hypothekenbank AG: 6000 Frankfurt a.M., Junghofstr. 5–7; tel. (069) 29898-0; telex 411608; f. 1862; mortgage bank;

GERMANY

cap. DM 89.6m.; Gen. Mans Dr GERD KOIDL, Dr BERNT W. ROHRER, Dr HANS SCHUCK.

Industriekreditbank AG-Deutsche Industriebank: 4000 Düsseldorf 1, Karl-Theodor-Str. 6; tel. (0211) 8221-0; telex 8582791; fax (0211) 8221-559; and 1000 Berlin 12, Bismarckstr 105; tel. (030) 31009-0; telex 184376; f. 1949; cap. DM 240m., res DM 856m., dep. DM 20,799m. (March 1989); Chair. (Supervisory Board) Dr DIETER SPETHMANN; 7 brs.

Kreditanstalt für Wiederaufbau: 6000 Frankfurt a.M. 11, Postfach 111141; tel. (069) 74310; telex 4152560; fax (069) 7431-2944; f. 1948; cap. DM 1,000m., total assets DM 121,929m. (Dec. 1989); Chair. Bd of Dirs Dr THEO WAIGEL; Vice-Chair. Dr HELMUT HAUSSMANN.

Bankers' Organizations

Bundesverband deutscher Banken eV: 5000 Köln 1, Mohrenstr. 35-41, Postfach 100246; tel. (0221) 16631; telex 8882730; f. 1948; Pres. Dr WOLFGANG RÖLLER.

Bundesverband der Deutschen Volksbanken und Raiffeisenbanken eV: 5300 Bonn 1, Heussallee 5, Postfach 120440; tel. (0228) 509-0; telex 886779; fax (0228) 509201; f. 1971; Pres. WOLFGANG GRUEGER; Dir KARL-HARTMANN LUDWIG; 3,250 mems.

Deutscher Sparkassen- und Giroverband eV; 5300 Bonn, Simrockstr. 4, Postfach 1429; tel. (0228) 204-0; telex 886709; fax (0228) 204250; Pres. Dr HELMUT GEIGER; Mans HANS-MICHAEL HEITMÜLLER, Dr HANNES REHM.

STOCK EXCHANGES

Arbeitsgemeinschaft der Deutschen Wertpapierbörsen (Federation of German Stock Exchanges): 6000 Frankfurt a.M. 1, Biebergasse 6-10; tel. (069) 299903-0; fax (069) 29990330; f. 1986; responsible for all supraregional affairs of the German stock exchange system; Exec. Vice-Chair. Dr RÜDIGER VON ROSEN.

Frankfurt am Main: 6000 Frankfurt a.M., Wertpapierbörse, Postfach 100811; tel. (069) 2197-0; telex 411412; fax (069) 2197455; f. 1585; mems 198; Chair. FRIEDRICH VON METZLER; 3 Mans.

Berlin: Börse, 1000 Berlin 12, Fasanenstr. 3; tel. (030) 311091-0; fax (030) 311091-79; f. 1685; Pres. Dr GERNOT ERNST.

Bremen: Bremer Wertpapierbörse, 2800 Bremen 1, Obernstr. 2-12, Postfach 10 07 26; tel. (0421) 323037; telex 246331; fax (0421) 323123; mems 28 credit institutes; Pres. Dr ROLAND BELLSTEDT; Man. AXEL H. SCHUBERT.

Düsseldorf: Rheinisch-Westfälische Börse zu Düsseldorf, Ernst-Schneider-Platz 1; tel. (0211) 1389-0; telex 8582600; fax (0211) 133287; f. 1935; 106 mem. firms; Pres. ALFRED Freiherr VON OPPENHEIM.

Hamburg: 2000 Hamburg 11, Börse; tel. (040) 367444; telex 213228; 96 mem. firms; Pres. HANS-DIETER SANDWEG.

Hannover: Niedersächsische Börse zu Hannover, 3000 Hannover 1, Rathenaustr. 2; tel. (0511) 327661; fax (0511) 324915; f. 1787; mems 27; Pres. HORST RISSE; Man. Rechtsanwalt RUDOLF GROMMELT.

München: Bayerische Börse, 8000 München 2, Lenbachplatz 2A/1; tel. (089) 59900; telex 523515; mems 74; Chair. of Council WILHELM PFEIFFER.

Stuttgart: Baden-Württembergische Wertpapierbörse zu Stuttgart, 7000 Stuttgart 1, Hospitalstr. 12; tel. (0711) 290183; telex 721514; fax (0711) 290185; f. 1861; mems 49; Pres. Dr WOLFRAM FREUDENBERG; Man. Dir Rechtsanwalt HANS-JOACHIM FEUERBACH.

INSURANCE

German law specifies that property- and accident insurance may not be jointly underwritten with life-, sickness-, legal protection- or credit- insurance by the same company. Insurers are therefore obliged to establish separate companies to cover the different classes of insurance.

Aachener und Münchener Lebensversicherung AG: 5100 Aachen, Robert Schumann Str. 51; tel. (0241) 6001-0; telex 832346; fax (0241) 6001-138; f. 1868; Chair. Dr HELMUT GIES; Gen. Man. W. H. BÖRNER.

Albingia Versicherungs-AG: 2000 Hamburg 1, Ballindamm 39; tel. (040) 30220; telex 2161774; fax (040) 30222-585; f. 1901; Chair. H. SINGER; Gen. Man. V. BREMKAMP.

Allianz AG Holding: 8000 München 44, Postfach 440124; tel (089) 38000; telex 5230110; fax (089) 349941; f. 1890; Chair. Supervisory Bd Prof. Dr H. GRÜNEWALD; Chair. Bd of Mans Dr W. SCHIEREN.

Allianz Lebensversicherungs-AG: 7000 Stuttgart 10, Postfach 106002; tel. (0711) 663-0; telex 723571; fax (0711) 6632654; f. 1922; Chair. Dr W. SCHIEREN; Gen. Man. Dr U. HAASEN.

Colonia Lebensversicherung AG: 5000 Köln 80, Postfach 805060; tel. (0221) 690-02; telex 881585; fax (0221) 6902750; f. 1853; Chair. JEAN ARVIS; Gen. Man. DIETER WENDELSTADT.

Colonia Versicherung AG: 5000 Köln 80, Postfach 805050; tel. (0221) 69001; telex 8815-0; fax (0221) 6902740; f. 1839; Chair. JEAN ARVIS; Gen. Man. DIETER WENDELSTADT.

Continentale Krankenversicherung auf Gegenseitigkeit: 4600 Dortmund 1, Postfach 1343; tel. (0231) 12010; telex 822515; fax (0231) 1201-913; f. 1926; Chair. Dr J. LORSBACH; Gen. Man. Dr H. HOFFMANN.

Debeka Krankenversicherungsverein auf Gegenseitigkeit: 5400 Koblenz, Postfach 460; tel. (0261) 4980; fax (0261) 41402; f. 1905; Chair. H. LANGE; Gen. Man. P. GREISLER.

Deutsche Beamten-Lebensversicherungs-AG: 6200 Wiesbaden 1, Postfach 2109; tel. (0611) 3630; telex 6121946; fax (0611) 363359; f. 1872; Chair. Admin. Bd A. KRAUSE; Man. Dir M. BROSKA.

Deutsche Krankenversicherung AG: 5000 Köln 41, Aachener Str. 300, Postfach 100588; tel. (0221) 5780; telex 8881634; fax (0221) 5783694; f. 1927; Chair. K. WESSELKOCK; Gen. Man. H. G. TIMMER.

Deutscher Herold Lebensversicherungs-AG: 5300 Bonn 1, Postfach 1448; tel. (0228) 26801; telex 886653; f. 1921; Chair. W. SOBOTA; Speaker H. D. RITTERBEX, W. EWERT.

Frankfurter Versicherungs-AG: 6000 Frankfurt 1, Postfach 100201; tel. (069) 71261; telex 411376; fax (069) 728750; f. 1929; Chair. E. WUNDERLICH; Gen. Man. Dr H. SCHMEER.

Gerling-Konzern Allgemeine Versicherungs-AG: 5000 Köln 1, Postfach 100808; tel. (0221) 144-1; telex 88110; fax (0221) 1443319; f. 1918; Chair. G. VOGELSANG; Speaker A. WEILER.

Gothaer Versicherungsbank Versicherungsverein auf Gegenseitigkeit: 5000 Köln 1, Postfach 108026; tel. (0221) 5746-00; telex 221305; f. 1820; Chair. Prof. A. W. KLEIN; Gen. Man. Dr WOLFGANG PEINER.

Haftpflicht-Unterstützungs-Kasse kraftfahrender Beamter Deutschlands auf Gegenseitigkeit in Coburg (HUK-Coburg): 8630 Coburg, Bahnhofsplatz, Postfach 1802; tel. (09561) 96-0; telex 663414; fax (09561) 96-3636; f. 1933; Chair. Dr B. SCHRÖDER; Gen. Mans Dr G. SCHRAMM, F. BECK, R.-P. HOENEN, W. MICHEL, Dr W. WEILER.

Haftpflichtverband der Deutschen Industrie Versicherungsverein auf Gegenseitigkeit: 3000 Hannover 51, Postfach 510369; tel. (0511) 645-0; telex 922678; f. 1903; Chair. Dr H.-J. FONK; Gen. Man. Dipl. Ing. A. MORSBACH.

Hamburg-Mannheimer Versicherungs-AG: 2000 Hamburg 60, Postfach 601060; tel. (040) 6376-0; telex 2174600; fax (040) 63763302; f. 1899; Chair. Dr H. K. JANNOTT; Gen. Man. K. WESSELKOCK.

Iduna Vereinigte Lebensversicherung auf Gegenseitigkeit für Handwerk, Handel und Gewerbe: 2000 Hamburg 36, Postfach 302721; tel. (040) 41240; telex 17402052; f. 1914; Chair. G. WÄGER; Gen. Man. H. BECKER.

Landwirtschaftlicher Versicherungsverein Münster AG: 4400 Münster, Kolde-Ring 21, Postfach 6145; tel. (0251) 7020; telex 892560; f. 1896; Chair. H. OSTROP; Gen. Man. K.-A. LOSKANT.

Nordstern Allgemeine Versicherungs-AG: 5000 Köln 1, Gereonstr. 43-65, Postfach 101368; tel. (0221) 148-0; telex 8882714; fax (0221) 121461; f. 1866; direct and indirect underwriting of all classes of private insurance in Germany and abroad; life-, health-, credit- and legal protection-insurance through reinsurance only; Pres. Supervisory Bd JEAN ARVIS; Chair. C. KLEYBOLDT.

R+V Versicherungs-Gruppe: 6200 Wiesbaden, Taunusstr. 1, Postfach 4840; tel. (0611) 533-0; telex 4186819; fax (0611) 533-4500; f. 1922; group consists of 9 companies incl. R+V Allgemeine Versicherung AG, R+V Lebensversicherung AG and R+V Krankenversicherung AG; Chair. W. CROLL; Gen. Man. Dr PETER C. VON HARDER.

SIGNAL Krankenversicherung auf Gegenseitigkeit: 4600 Dortmund 1, Postfach 105052; tel. (0231) 135-0; telex 822231; fax (0231) 1354638; f. 1907; Chair. PAUL SCHNITKER; Gen. Man. H. FROMMKNECHT.

Vereinte Krankenversicherung AG: 8000 München 2, Postfach 202522; tel. (089) 6785-0; telex 5215721; fax (089) 67856523; f. 1925; Chair. Dr WERNER G. SEIFERT; Gen. Man. Dr H. K. JÄKEL.

Victoria Versicherungs-AG: 4000 Düsseldorf 1, Postfach 1116; tel. (0211) 82801; telex 8582984; fax (0211) 8282222; f. 1904; Chair. Dr E. OVERBECK; Gen. Man. Dr E. JANNOTT.

Victoria Lebensversicherung AG: 4000 Düsseldorf 1, Postfach 1116; tel. (0211) 82801; telex 8582984; fax (0211) 8282222; f. 1853; Chair. Dr E. OVERBECK; Gen. Man. Dr E. JANNOTT.

Volksfürsorge Deutsche Lebensversicherung AG: 2000 Hamburg 1, Postfach 106420; tel. (040) 2865-0; telex 2112440; fax (040) 28653369; f. 1912; Chair. Dr H. GIES; Gen. Man. Dr W. KASKE.

Württembergische Feuerversicherung AG; 7000 Stuttgart 10, Postfach 106042; tel. (0711) 6620; telex 723553; fax (0711) 6622520; f. 1828; Chair. O.-J. MAIER; Gen. Man. Dr G. BÜCHNER.

GERMANY   *Directory*

Reinsurance

Aachener Rückversicherungs-Gesellschaft AG: 5100 Aachen, Postfach 25; tel. (0241) 186-0; telex 832629; fax (0241) 186205; f. 1853; Chair. Supervisory Bd Dr jur. HELMUT GIES; Chair. Management Bd Dr A. MORENZ.

Bayerische Rückversicherung AG: 8000 München 22, Postfach 220010; tel. (089) 3844-0; telex 5215247; fax (089) 3844-279; f. 1911; Chair. Prof. Dr B. BÖRNER; Gen Man Dr P. FREY.

Deutsche Rückversicherung AG: 4000 Düsseldorf 30, Postfach 320269; tel. (0211) 4554-01; telex 8584560; fax (0211) 4554-199; f. 1952; Chair. Dr W. RIEGER; Gen. Man. G. HASSE.

Deutsche Versicherungs- und Rückversicherungs-AG (DARAG): 1020 Berlin, Inselstr. 1B; tel. 2700522; telex 114402; fax 2791890; f. 1957, re-formed 1990; marine cargo, aviation, engineering, machinery, fire reinsurance, technical insurance; Chair. H. GRAMER.

Frankona Rückversicherungs-AG: 8000 München 80, Maria-Theresia-Str. 35, Postfach 860380; tel. (089) 9228-0; telex 522531; fax (089) 9228395; f. 1886; Chair. Dr H. GERLING; Gen. Man. Dr A. KANN.

Gerling-Konzern Globale Rückversicherungs-AG: 5000 Köln 1, Postfach 100808; tel. (0221) 144-1; telex 88110; fax (0221) 1443718; f. 1954; Chair. R. SCHLENKER; Speaker Dr R. WOLTERECK.

Hamburger Internationale Rückversicherung AG: 2000 Hamburg 11, Postfach 111522; tel. (040) 37008-1; telex 2162938; fax (040) 367289; f. 1965; Chair. W. SCHWICKART; Gen. Man. R. SOLL.

Hannover Rückversicherungs-AG: 3000 Hannover 61, Karl-Wiechert-Allee 50, Postfach 610369; tel (0511) 5604-0; telex 922599; fax (0511) 5604188; f. 1966; Chair. Supervisory Board A. MORSBACH; Chair. Board of Mans R. C. BINGEMER.

Kölnische Rückversicherungs-Gesellschaft AG: 5000 Köln 1, Theodor-Heuss-Ring 11, Postfach 108016; tel. (0221) 7759-0; telex 8885231-0; fax (0221) 7759494; f. 1846; Chair. JEAN ARVIS; Gen. Man. Dr J. ZECH.

Münchener Rückversicherungs-Gesellschaft: 8000 München 40, Königinstr. 107; tel. (089) 3891-0; telex 5215233-0; fax (089) 399056; f. 1880; all classes of reinsurance; Chair. Supervisory Bd Prof. Dr D. SPETHMANN; Chair. Bd of Management Dr H. K. JANNOTT.

Rhein-Main Rückversicherungs-Gesellschaft AG: 6200 Wiesbaden 1, Sonnenberger Str. 44; tel. (0611) 525001; telex 4186473; fax (0611) 529610; f. 1935; all classes of reinsurance; Chair. W. CROLL; Gen. Man. Dr P. C. VON HARDER.

Principal Insurance Association

Gesamtverband der Deutschen Versicherungswirtschaft eV: 5000 Köln 1, Ebertplatz 1; tel. (0221) 7764-0; telex 8885255; fax (0221) 7764-153; f. 1948; affiliating 5 mem. asscns and 428 mem. companies; Pres. Dr GEORG BÜCHNER (Stuttgart); Vice-Pres. Dr U. HAASEN (Stuttgart), D. WENDELSTADT (Köln).

Trade and Industry

CHAMBERS OF INDUSTRY AND COMMERCE

Deutscher Industrie- und Handelstag (Association of German Chambers of Industry and Commerce): 5300 Bonn 1, Adenauerallee 148; tel. (0228) 1040; telex 886805; fax (0228) 104158; Pres. Dipl. Ing. HANS PETER STIHL; Sec.-Gen. Dr FRANZ SCHOSER; affiliates 84 Chambers of Industry and Commerce.

There are Chambers of Industry and Commerce in all the principal towns and also nine regional associations as follows:

Arbeitsgemeinschaft der Industrie- und Handelskammern in Baden-Württemberg, Vorort: Industrie- und Handelskammer Mittlerer Neckar Sitz Stuttgart: 7000 Stuttgart 1, Jägerstr. 30, Postfach 102444; tel. (0711) 2005-0; telex 722031; fax (0711) 2005-354; Chair. Dipl.-Ing. HANS PETER STIHL; Sec. PETER KISTNER.

Arbeitsgemeinschaft der Bayerischen Industrie- und Handelskammern: 8000 München 2, Max-Joseph-Str. 2; tel. (089) 5116-0; telex 523678; fax (089) 5116-306; Chair. Dr.-Ing. DIETER SOLTMANN; Sec. Dr WILHELM WIMMER; 10 mems.

Arbeitsgemeinschaft Hessischer Industrie- und Handelskammern: 6000 Frankfurt a.M. 1, Börsenplatz; tel. (069) 21970; telex 411255; fax (069) 2197-424; Chair. Dr HANS MESSER; Sec. RICHARD SPEICH; 12 mems.

Vereinigung der Niedersächsischen Industrie- und Handelskammern: 3000 Hannover 1, Königstr. 19, Postfach 3029; tel. (0511) 3481565; telex 922769; fax (0511) 3481525; f. 1899; Pres. Dr WERNER LOGES; Man. Dir Dr jur. CHRISTIAN AHRENS; 7 mems.

Vereinigung der Industrie- und Handelskammern in Nordrhein-Westfalen: 4000 Düsseldorf 1, Postfach 240120; tel. (0211) 352091; telex 8582680; fax (0211) 161012; Chair. Dr ALFRED VOSSSCHULTE; Sec. Ass. HANS G. CRONE-ERDMANN; 16 mems.

Kammergemeinschaft Öffentlichkeitsarbeit der Nordrhein-Westfälischen Industrie- und Handelskammern: 5000 Köln 1, Unter Sachsenhausen 10-26; tel. (0221) 1640-157; telex 8881400; fax (0221) 1640-123; Chair. Dr HEINZ MALANGRÉ; Sec. GÜNTER BOCK; 14 mems.

Arbeitsgemeinschaft der Industrie- und Handelskammern Rheinland-Pfalz: 6700 Ludwigshafen, Ludwigsplatz 2/3, Postfach 210744; tel. (0621) 59040; telex 6215942; fax (0621) 5904-166; Sec. Dr ANDREAS HERTING; 4 mems.

Verband der Industrie- und Handelskammern des Landes Schleswig-Holstein: 2300 Kiel 1, Lorentzendamm 24; tel. (0431) 5194-0; telex 299864; fax (0431) 5194-234; Chair. Dr FRITZ SÜVERKRÜP; Sec. WOLF-RÜDIGER JANZEN; 3 mems.

Arbeitsgemeinschaften der Norddeutschen Industrie- und Handelskammern: 2000 Hamburg 11, Börse; tel. (040) 366382; telex 211250; Chair. GUSTAV G. HEBOLD; Sec. Dr UWE CHRISTIANSEN.

EXPORT AND TRADE ASSOCIATIONS

Arbeitsgemeinschaft Aussenhandel der Deutschen Wirtschaft: 5000 Köln 51, Gustav-Heinemann-Ufer 84–88, Postfach 510548; tel. (0221) 37080; telex 8882601; fax (0221) 3708-730; Dir HEINZ TEMBRINK.

Bundesstelle für Aussenhandelsinformation (German Foreign Trade Information Office): 5000 Köln, Blaubach 13, Postfach 108007; tel. (0221) 2057-1; telex 8882735.

Bundesverband des Deutschen Gross- und Aussenhandels eV: 5300 Bonn, Kaiser-Friedrichstr. 13, Postfach 1349; tel. (0228) 26004-0; telex 886783; fax (0228) 26004-55; Pres. Konsul KLAUS RICHTER; 70 mem. asscns.

Hauptgemeinschaft des Deutschen Einzelhandels eV: 5000 Köln, Sachsenring 89; tel. (0221) 33980; telex 8881443; fax (0221) 3398-119; f. 1947; Chair. WOLFGANG HINRICHS; Exec. Dir KARL-HEINZ NIEHÜSER.

Zentralverband der Genossenschaftlichen Grosshandels- und Dienstleistungsunternehmen eV (Central Association of Co-operative Wholesale and Service Trade): 5300 Bonn 1, Postfach 120220; tel. (0228) 210011; Pres. HANS-JURGEN KLUSSMANN; c. 250,000 mems; 880 primary co-operatives; 13 central co-operatives.

INDUSTRIAL ASSOCIATIONS

Bundesverband der Deutschen Industrie eV (Federation of German Industry): 5000 Köln 51, Gustav-Heinemann-Ufer 84–88; tel. (0221) 3708-00; telex 8882601; fax (0221) 3708-730; Pres. Dipl.-Ing. HEINRICH WEISS; Dir-Gen. Dr LUDOLF-GEORG VON WARTENBERG; mems include some of the following asscns:

Arbeitsgemeinschaft Industriengruppe (General Industry): 7530 Pforzheim, Industriehaus, Postfach 470; tel. (07231) 33041; telex 783855; fax (07231) 355887; Chair. JOACHIM KÖHLE; Dir Dr ALFRED SCHNEIDER.

Arbeitsgemeinschaft Keramische Industrie eV (Ceramics): 6000 Frankfurt a.M. 97, Friedrich-Ebert-Anlage 38, Postfach 970171; tel. (069) 756082-0; fax (069) 75608212; Chair. (vacant); Dir R. A. REINFRIED VOGLER; 6 mem. asscns.

Bundesverband Bekleidungsindustrie eV (Clothing): 5000 Köln 1, Mevissenstr. 15; tel. (0221) 7744113; telex (17) 22150803; fax (0221) 7744128; Pres. GERD SOMBERG; Dirs-Gen. FRIEDHELM N. SARTORIS, RAINER MAUER.

Bundesvereinigung der Deutschen Ernährungsindustrie eV (Food): 5300 Bonn 2, Rheinallee 18; tel. (0228) 351051; telex 885679; fax (0228) 351992; f. 1949; Chair. Konsul HERMANN BAHLSEN; Chief Gen. Man. Dr GERHARD HEIN; 35 branch-organizations.

Bundesverband der Deutschen Luftfahrt-, Raumfahrt- und Ausrüstungsindustrie eV (BDLI) (German Aerospace Industries Asscn): 5300 Bonn 2, Konstantinstr. 90; tel. (0228) 849070; telex 885528; fax (0228) 330778; Pres. Dr-Ing. JOHANN SCHÄFFLER; Man. Dir Dr H. GEORG BRODACH.

Bundesverband Druck eV (Printing): 6200 Wiesbaden 1, Postfach 1869, Biebricher Allee 79; tel. (0611) 8030; telex 4186888; fax (0611) 803113; f. 1947; Pres. HANS-OTTO REPPEKUS; Man. Dir Dr WALTER HESSE; 12 mem. asscns.

Bundesverband Glasindustrie und Mineralfaserindustrie eV (Glass): 4000 Düsseldorf 1, Stresemannstr. 26, Postfach 8340; tel. (0211) 16894-0; telex 8587686; fax (0211) 16894-27; Chair. ERNST SCHNEIDER; Dir Dipl.-Vw. NORBERT ELL; 6 mem. asscns.

Bundesverband Steine und Erden eV (Building): 6000 Frankfurt a.M., Friedrich-Ebert-Anlage 38, Postfach 970171; tel. (069) 7560820; fax (069) 756082-12; f. 1948; Pres. Dipl. Kfm PETER SCHUHMACHER; Chief Dir Dipl.-Volksw. HANS-JÜRGEN REITZIG.

Deutscher Giessereiverband (Foundries): 4000 Düsseldorf, Sohnstr. 70, Postfach 8709; tel. (0211) 68710; telex 8586885; fax

GERMANY

(0211) 6871-333; Pres. Dipl.-Ing. EBERHARD MÖLLMANN; Man. Dir Dr KLAUS URBAT.

Deutsche Verbundgesellschaft eV (Electricity): 6900 Heidelberg 1, Ziegelhäuser Landstr. 5; tel. (06221) 4037-0; telex 461849; fax (06221) 4037-71; Chair. Dr HERMANN KRÄMER; Dir-Gen. Dipl.-Ing. HANS-GÜNTER BUSCH.

EBM Wirtschaftsverband (Metal Goods): 4000 Düsseldorf 30, Kaiserswerther Str. 135, Postfach 321230; tel. (0211) 454930; telex 8584985; fax (0211) 4549369; Pres. GÜNTER BECKER; Gen.-Man. Dipl.-Vw. KLAUS BELLWINKEL.

Gesamtverband kunststoffverarbeitende Industrie eV (GKV) (Plastics): 6000 Frankfurt a.M. 1, Am Hauptbahnhof 12; tel. (069) 271050; telex 411122; fax (069) 232799; f. 1949; Chair. LUDWIG EBERHARDT; Sec.-Gen. Dr REINHARD ACKERMANN; 950 mems.

Gesamtverband der Textilindustrie in der BRD (Gesamttextil) eV (Textiles): 6236 Eschborn, Frankfurter Str. 10–14; tel. (06196) 966-0; telex 4072561; fax (06196) 42170; Pres. WOLF DIETER KRUSE; Dir-Gen. Dr KONRAD NEUNDÖRFER.

Hauptverband der Deutschen Bauindustrie eV (Building): 6200 Wiesbaden, Abraham-Lincoln-Str. 30, Postfach 2966; tel. (06121) 7720; telex 4186147; 5300 Bonn 1, Am Hofgarten 9; tel. (0228) 267090; telex 886881; f. 1948; Pres. Prof. Dipl.-Ing. HERMANN BECKER; Dir-Gen. HORST FRANKE; 16 mem. asscns.

Hauptverband der Deutschen Holz und Kunststoffe verarbeitenden Industrie und verwandter Industriezweige eV (HDH) (Woodwork): 6200 Wiesbaden 1, An den Quellen 10; tel. (06121) 1709-0; telex 4186631; fax (06121) 378908; f. 1948; Pres. Senator HEINZ GOTSCHY; Gen. Exec. Man. HORST PRIESSNITZ; 28 mem. asscns, 4,000 mems.

Hauptverband der Papier, Pappe und Kunststoffe verarbeitenden Industrie eV (HPV) (Paper, Board and Plastic): 6000 Frankfurt a.M. 1, Arndtstr. 47; tel. (069) 740311; telex 411925; fax (069) 747714; f. 1948; 10 regional groups, 20 production groups; Pres. Dr ROBERT SIEGER; Dirs-Gen. Dr HORST KOHL, DIETER VON TEIN; 1,300 mems.

Mineralölwirtschaftsverband eV (Petroleum): 2000 Hamburg 1, Steindamm 71; tel. (040) 2854-0; telex 2162257; fax (040) 2854-53; f. 1946; Chair. HERBERT DETHARDING; Man. Dir Dr PETER SCHLÜTER.

Verband der Automobilindustrie eV (Motor Cars): 6000 Frankfurt a.M. 17, Westendstr. 61, Postfach 170563; tel. (069) 7570-0; telex 411293; fax (069) 7570-261; Pres. Dr ERIKA EMMERICH.

Verband der Chemischen Industrie eV (Chemical Industry): 6000 Frankfurt a.M. 1, Karlstr. 21; tel. (069) 2556-0; telex 411372; fax (069) 2556-471; f. 1877; Pres. HERMANN J. STRENGER; Dir-Gen. Dr WOLFGANG MUNDE; 1,500 mems.

Verband der Cigarettenindustrie (Cigarettes): 2000 Hamburg 13, Harvestehuder Weg 88; tel. (040) 414009-0; telex 215044; Chair. ULRICH HERTER; Dir-Gen. Dr HARALD KÖNIG.

Verband der deutschen feinmechanischen und optischen Industrie eV (Optical and Precision Instruments): 5000 Köln 1, Pipinstr. 16; tel. (0221) 219458; telex 8882226; f. 1949; Chair. Dipl.-Ing. GUNTER SIEGLIN; Dir Dipl.-Kfm. HARALD RUSSEGGER.

Verband Deutscher Maschinen- und Anlagenbau eV (VDMA) (Machinery and Plant Manufacture): 6000 Frankfurt a.M. 71 (Niederrad), Lyoner Str. 18, Postfach 710864; tel. (069) 66030; telex 411321; fax (069) 6603-511; f. 1892; Pres. Dr-Ing. BERTHOLD LEIBINGER; Gen. Man. Dr HANS-JÜRGEN ZECHLIN.

Verband Deutscher Papierfabriken eV (Paper): 5300 Bonn 1, Adenauerallee 55; tel. (0228) 26705-0; telex 886767; fax (0228) 2670562; Pres. CARL LUDWIG Graf VON DEYM; Dir-Gen. Dr OSCAR HAUS.

Verband für Schiffbau und Meerestechnik eV (Shipbuilding): 2000 Hamburg 1, An der Alster 1; tel. (040) 246205; telex 2162496; fax (040) 246287; Pres. Dr jur. NORBERT HENKE; Gen. Man. Dipl.-Kfm. WERNER FANTE.

Verein der Zuckerindustrie (Sugar): 5300 Bonn 1, Am Hofgarten 8, Postfach 2545; tel. (0228) 22850; telex 886718; fax (0228) 2285100; f. 1850; Chair. PETER NAMUTH; Dir-Gen. Dr DIETER LANGENDORF.

Wirtschaftsverband der Deutschen Kautschukindustrie eV (W.d.K.) (Rubber): 6000 Frankfurt a.M. 90, Zeppelinallee 69; tel. (069) 79360; telex 411254; f. 1894; Pres. GERT SILBER-BONZ; Gen. Man. KLAUS MOCKER; 94 mems.

Wirtschaftsverband Erdöl- und Erdgasgewinnung eV (Association of Crude Oil and Gas Producers): 3000 Hannover, Brühlstr. 9; tel. (0511) 327648; fax (0511) 321172; f. 1945; Pres. Prof. Dr-Ing. HEINO LÜBBEN; Gen. Man. LOTHAR MÖLLER.

Wirtschaftsverband Stahlbau und Energietechnik (SET) (Steel and Energy): 4000 Düsseldorf 30, Sternstr. 36, Postfach 300343; tel. (0211) 485006; telex 8584966; fax (0211) 4983428; Chair. Dipl.-Ing. FRITZ ADRIAN; Dir-Gen. Dipl.-Ing. A. SCHUMACHER.

Directory

Wirtschaftsverband Stahlverformung eV (Steelworks): 5800 Hagen-Emst, Goldene Pforte 1, Postfach 4009; tel. (02331) 51041; telex 823806; fax (02331) 51046; Pres. Dr-Ing. JOCHEN F. KIRCHHOFF; Dir-Gen. Dipl.-Phys. HANS-DIETER OELKERS.

Wirtschaftsvereinigung Bergbau eV (Mining): 5300 Bonn 1, Zitelmannstr. 9–11, Postfach 120280; tel. (0228) 540020; telex 8869566; fax (0228) 54002-35; Pres. Bergass. a.D. Dr-Ing. E.h. FRIEDRICH CARL ERASMUS; Gen. Mans FRIEDHELM OST, Dr-Ing. HARALD KLIEBHAN; 16 mem. asscns.

Wirtschaftsvereinigung Stahl (Steel): 4000 Düsseldorf 1, Breitestr. 69, Postfach 8705; tel. (0211) 8291; telex 8581811; fax (0211) 829231; Pres. Dr RUPRECHT VONDRAN; Dirs ALBRECHT KORMANN, GEORG MÜLLER.

Wirtschaftsvereinigung Metalle eV (Metal): 4000 Düsseldorf 30, Tersteegenstr. 28, Postfach 8706; tel. (0211) 45471-0; telex 8584721; fax (0211) 4547111; Pres. JÖRG STEGMANN; Dir-Gen. JÜRGEN ULMER.

Wirtschaftsvereinigung Ziehereien und Kaltwalzwerke eV (Metal): 4000 Düsseldorf 30, Drahthaus, Kaiserswerther Str. 137; tel. (0211) 4564-246; fax (0211) 4543-376; Chair. HANS MARTIN WÄLZHOLZ-JUNIUS; Gen.-Man. GÜNTER MÜLLER.

Zentralverband Elektrotechnik- und Elektronikindustrie (ZVEI) eV (Electrical and Electronic Equipment): 6000 Frankfurt a.M. 70, Stresemannallee 19, Postfach 701261; tel. (069) 6302-10; telex 411035; fax (069) 6302-317; f. 1918; Chair. Dr-Ing. KARLHEINZ KASKE; Dirs Prof. Dr RUDOLF SCHEID, Dr BODO BÖTTCHER (Economic and Commercial), Dipl.-Ing. INGO RÜSCH (Technical); 1,200 mems.

CONSULTATIVE ASSOCIATIONS

(See also under Bankers' Organizations, Chambers of Industry and Commerce, etc.)

Gemeinschaftsausschuss der Deutschen gewerblichen Wirtschaft (Joint Committee for German Industry and Commerce): 5000 Köln 51, Gustav-Heinemann-Ufer 84–88; tel. (0221) 3708-00; fax (0221) 3708-730; f. 1950; a discussion forum for the principal industrial and commercial organizations; Pres. Dr TYLL NECKER; 16 mem. organizations, including:

Centralvereinigung Deutscher Handelsvertreter- und Handelsmakler-Verbände (CDH): 5000 Köln 41, Geleniusstr. 1; tel. (0221) 514043; telex 8881743; fax (0221) 525767; Pres. NORBERT HOPF; Gen. Sec. ERNST H. HAUMANN; 31,000 mems in all brs.

Deutscher Hotel- und Gaststättenverband eV: 5300 Bonn 2, Kronprinzenstr. 46; tel. (0228) 820080; telex 885489; fax (0228) 8200846; f. 1949; Pres. LEO IMHOFF; Gen. Sec. Dr FRITHJOF WAHL; over 90,000 mems.

Zentralverband des Deutschen Handwerks: 5300 Bonn 1, Haus des Deutschen Handwerks, Johanniterstr. 1; tel. (0228) 545-0; telex 886338; f. 1949; Pres. Dipl. Ing. HERIBERT SPÄTH; Gen. Sec. HANNS-EBERHARD SCHLEYER; 56 mem. chambers, 52 asscns.

EMPLOYERS' ASSOCIATION

Bundesvereinigung der Deutschen Arbeitgeberverbände (Confederation of German Employers' Associations): 5000 Köln 51, Postfach 510508, Gustav-Heinemann Ufer 72; tel. (0221) 37950; telex 8881466; fax (0221) 3795-235; Pres. Dr KLAUS MURMANN; Dirs JÜRGEN HUSMANN, Dr FRITZ-HEINZ HIMMELREICH, Dr WERNER DOETSCH; affiliates 12 regional associations, and 46 trade associations, of which some are listed under industrial associations (see above).

Affiliated associations:

Arbeitgeberkreis Gesamttextil im Gesamtverband der Textilindustrie in der Bundesrepublik Deutschland eV (General Textile Employers' Organization): 6236 Eschborn, Frankfurter Strasse 10–14; tel. (06196) 966-0; telex 4072561; fax (06196) 42170; Chair. PETER FROWEIN; Dir Dr KLAUS SCHMIDT; 7 mem. asscns.

Arbeitgeberverband der Cigarettenindustrie (Employers' Association of Cigarette Manufacturers): 2000 Hamburg 13, Harvestehuder Weg 88; tel. (040) 41400902; telex 215044; fax (040) 41400910; f. 1949; Pres. Dr DORIS ANDRÉ; Dir LUTZ SANNIG.

Arbeitgeberverband der Deutschen Binnenschiffahrt eV (Employers' Association of German Inland Waterway Transport): 4100 Duisburg 13, Dammstr. 15–17; tel. (0203) 800060; telex 855692; fax (0203) 80006-21; Pres. Dr G. W. HULSMAN; Dir G. DÜTEMEYER.

Arbeitgeberverband Deutscher Eisenbahnen eV (German Railway Employers' Association): 5000 Köln, Volksgartenstr. 54A; tel. (0221) 313980; fax (0221) 325318; Pres. Dipl.-Ing. KLAUS-DIETER BOLLHÖFER; Dir Dr HELMUT DEPENHEUER.

Arbeitgeberverband des Privaten Bankgewerbes eV (Private Banking Employers' Association): 5000 Köln, Mohrenstr. 35-41;

tel. (0221) 131024; f. 1954; 164 mems; Pres. Klaus Müller-Gebel; Dir Dr Klaus Dutti.

Arbeitgeberverband der Versicherungsunternehmen in Deutschland (Employers' Association of Insurance Companies): 8000 München 81, Arabellastr. 29; tel. (089) 9220010; telex 524713; fax (089) 922001-50; Pres. Dr Peter von Blomberg; Dir-Gen. Dr Jürgen Willich.

Bundesarbeitgeberverband Chemie eV (Federation of Employers' Associations in the Chemical Industry): 6200 Wiesbaden, Abraham-Lincoln-Str. 24, Postfach 1280; tel. (0611) 719016; telex 4186646; fax (0611) 719010; Pres. Justus Mische; Dir Dr Karl Molitor; 12 mem. asscns.

Bundesvereinigung der Arbeitgeber im Bundesverband Bekleidungsindustrie eV (Confederation of Employers of the Clothing Industry): 5000 Köln 1, Mevissenstr. 15; tel. (0221) 7744110; telex (17) 22150803; fax (0221) 7744128; Pres. Gustav Adolf Pass; Dir Rainer Mauer; 10 mem. asscns.

Gesamtverband der Deutschen Land- und Forstwirtschaftlichen Arbeitgeberverbände eV (Federation of Agricultural and Forestry Employers' Associations): 5300 Bonn 2, Godesberger Allee 142–148, Postfach 200454; tel. (0228) 8198-248; telex 885586; fax (0228) 8198-231; Pres. Odal von Alten-Nordheim; Sec. Dipl.-Volksw. Dipl.-Landw. Martin Mallach.

Gesamtverband der metallindustriellen Arbeitgeberverbände eV (Federation of the Metal Trades Employers' Associations): 5000 Köln 1, Volksgartenstr. 54A; tel. (0221) 33990; telex 8882583; fax (0221) 3399-233; Pres. Dr Werner Stumpfe; Dir Dr Dieter Kirchner; 13 mem. asscns.

Vereinigung der Arbeitgeberverbände der Deutschen Papierindustrie eV (Federation of Employers' Associations of the German Paper Industry): 4000 Düsseldorf, Grafenberger Allee 368; tel. (0211) 666102; fax (0211) 660304; Pres. Dr Wolfgang Fromen; Dir Ass. Peter Karthäuser; 8 mem. asscns.

Vereinigung der Arbeitgeberverbände energie- und versorgungswirtschaftlicher Unternehmungen (Employers' Federation of Energy and Power Supply Enterprises): 3000 Hannover, Kurt Schumacher-Str. 24; tel. (0511) 323405; fax (0511) 13744; f. 1962; Pres. Ulrich Hartmann; Dir Gerhard M. Meyer; 6 mem. asscns.

Regional employers' associations:

Landesvereinigung Baden-Württembergischer Arbeitgeberverbände eV: 7000 Stuttgart, Löffelstr. 22–24, Postfach 700501; tel. (0711) 7682-0; telex 723651; fax (0711) 761675; Pres. Rolf Lenz; Dir Herfried Heisler; 43 mem. asscns.

Vereinigung der Arbeitgeberverbände in Bayern (Federation of Employers' Associations in Bavaria): 8000 München 2, Brienner Str. 7, Postfach 202527; tel. (089) 29079-0; fax (089) 222851; f. 1949; Pres. Hubert Stärker; Dir Karl Bayer; 77 mem. asscns.

Vereinigung der Unternehmensverbände in Berlin und Brandenburg eV (Federation of Employers' Associations in Berlin and Brandenburg): 1000 Berlin 12, Am Schillertheater 2; tel. (030) 310050; telex 184366; Pres. Klaus Osterhof; Dir Dr Hartmann Kleiner; 50 mem. asscns.

Vereinigung der Arbeitgeberverbände im Lande Bremen eV (Federation of Employers' Associations in the Land of Bremen): 2800 Bremen, Schillerstr. 10; tel. (0421) 36802-0; telex 244577; fax (0421) 36802-49; Pres. Dipl. Ing. Peter Kloess; Dir Eberhard Schodde; 14 mem. asscns.

Landesvereinigung der Arbeitgeberverbände in Hamburg eV (Federation of Employers' Associations in Hamburg): 2000 Hamburg 13, Feldbrunnenstr. 56; tel. (040) 414012-0; fax (040) 418004; Pres. Dieter Bonow; Gen. Man. Jürgen Meineke; 25 mem. asscns.

Vereinigung der Hessischen Unternehmerverbände eV (Federation of Employers' Associations in Hesse): 6000 Frankfurt a.M. 90, Lilienthalallee 4; tel. (069) 79050; telex 412136; fax (069) 7905-126; f. 1947; Pres. Hermann Habich; Dir and Sec. Dr Hubert Stadler; 52 mem. asscns.

Unternehmerverbände Niedersachsen eV (Federation of Employers' Associations in Lower Saxony): 3000 Hannover 1, Schiffgraben 36; tel. (0511) 85050; telex 0929912; fax (0511) 8505268; Pres. Hermann Bahlsen; Mans Gernot Preuss, Günter Seide, Dr Jürgen Wolfslast; 58 mem. asscns.

Landesvereinigung der Arbeitgeberverbände Nordrhein-Westfalen eV (North Rhine-Westphalia Federation of Employers' Associations): 4000 Düsseldorf 30, Uerdingerstr. 58–62; tel. (0211) 45730; telex 85856864; fax (0211) 4573209; Pres. Dr Ing. Jochen F. Kirchhoff; Dir Dr Hansjörg Döpp; 84 mem. asscns.

Landesvereinigung Rheinland-Pfälzischer Unternehmerverbände eV (Federation of Employers' Associations in the Rhineland Palatinate): 6500 Mainz, Hölderlinstr. 1; tel. (06131) 5575-0; fax (06131) 5575-39; f. 1963; Pres. Prof. Dr Rolf Fillibeck; Man. Dr Christoph Stollenwerk; 13 mem. asscns.

Vereinigung der Arbeitgeberverbände des Saarlandes eV (Federation of Employers' Associations in Saarland): 6600 Saarbrücken 6, Harthweg 15; tel. (0681) 51061; telex 4421229; fax (0681) 5847386; Pres. Dipl.-Ing. Edgar Stöber; Dir Dr Heiko Jütte; 17 mem. asscns.

Vereinigung der Schleswig-Holsteinischen Unternehmensverbände eV (Federation of Employers' Associations in Schleswig-Holstein): 2370 Rendsburg, Adolf-Steckel-Str. 17; tel. (04331) 59090; fax (04331) 25758; Pres. Dr Dietrich Schulz; Dir Jochen Hahne; 37 mem. asscns.

TRADE UNIONS

Following German unification in October 1990, the trade unions of the former GDR were absorbed into the 16 member unions of the DGB (see below).

Deutscher Gewerkschaftsbund (DGB): 4000 Düsseldorf 30, Hans-Böckler-Str. 39, Postfach 2601; tel. (0211) 43010; telex 8584822; fax (0211) 4301471; f. 1949; Pres. Heinz-Werner Meyer; Vice-Pres Ursula Engelen-Kefer, Ulf Fink.

The following unions, with a total of 7,797,077 (Dec. 1989) members, are affiliated to the DGB:

Industriegewerkschaft Bau-Steine-Erden (Building and Construction Trade): 6000 Frankfurt a.M., Bockenheimer Landstr. 73–77; tel. (069) 7437-0; telex 412826; fax (069) 7437278; Pres. Konrad Carl; 460,559 mems (Dec. 1989).

Industriegewerkschaft Bergbau und Energie (Mining and Energy): 4630 Bochum, Alte Hattingerstr. 19; tel. (0234) 3190; telex 825809; fax (0234) 319-514; f. 1889; Pres. Hans Berger; 600,000 mems (Dec. 1990).

Industriegewerkschaft Chemie- Papier- Keramik (Chemical, Paper and Ceramics): 3000 Hannover, Königsworther Platz 6; tel. (0511) 76310; telex 922608; fax (0511) 708473; Pres. Hermann Rappe; 725,000 mems (Nov. 1990).

Gewerkschaft der Eisenbahner Deutschlands (Railwaymen): 6000 Frankfurt a.M., Beethovenstr. 12–16; tel. (069) 75360; fax (069) 747892; Pres. Rudi Schäfer; 340,000 mems (Dec. 1987).

Gewerkschaft Erziehung und Wissenschaft (Education and Sciences): 6000 Frankfurt a.M. 90, Reifenbergerstr. 21; tel. (069) 78973-0; telex 412989; fax (069) 78973-201; Pres. Dr Dieter Wunder; 188,963 mems (June 1990).

Gewerkschaft Gartenbau, Land- und Forstwirtschaft (Horticulture, Agriculture and Forestry): 3500 Kassel 1, Druseltalstr. 51, Postfach 410180; tel. (0561) 34060; telex 99630; fax (0561) 315420; f. 1909; Pres. Günther Lappas; 43,817 mems (Dec. 1989).

Gewerkschaft Handel, Banken und Versicherungen (Commerce, Banks and Insurance): 4000 Düsseldorf 30, Tersteegenstr. 30; tel. (0211) 4582-0; telex 8584653; fax (0211) 4582-258; f. 1973; Pres. Lorenz Schwegler; 650,000 mems (Dec. 1990).

Gewerkschaft Holz und Kunststoff (Wood and Plastic-work): 4000 Düsseldorf, Sonnenstr. 14; tel. (0211) 7703-0; telex 2114218; fax (0211) 7703201; f. 1945; Pres. Horst Morich; 151,433 mems (Oct. 1990).

Gewerkschaft Leder (Leather): 7000 Stuttgart 1, Willi-Bleicher-Str. 20; tel. (0711) 295555; fax (0711) 293345; Pres. Werner Dick; 44,583 mems (Dec. 1989).

Industriegewerkschaft Medien (Media): 7000 Stuttgart 10, Friedrichstr. 15, Postfach 102451; tel. (0711) 2018-0; fax (0711) 2018-262; Pres. Erwin Ferlemann; 185,000 mems. (June 1990).

Industriegewerkschaft Metall (Metal Workers' Union): 6000 Frankfurt a.M., Wilhelm-Leuschner-Str. 79–85; tel. (069) 26470; telex 411115; fax (069) 2647843; Chair. Franz Steinkühler; c. 3,550,000 mems (Jan. 1991).

Gewerkschaft Nahrung- Genuss- Gaststätten (Food, Delicacies and Catering): 2000 Hamburg 1, Gertrudenstr. 9; tel. (040) 380130; telex 2161884; fax (040) 3892637; f. 1949; Pres. Heinz Günter Niebrügge; 271,291 mems (Dec. 1989).

Gewerkschaft Öffentliche Dienste, Transport und Verkehr (Public Services and Transport Workers' Union): 7000 Stuttgart 1, Theodor Heuss-Str. 2; tel. (0711) 2097-0; telex 723302; fax (0711) 2097-462; Chair. Dr Monika Wulf-Mathies; 2,300,000 mems (Jan. 1991).

Gewerkschaft der Polizei (Police Union): 4010 Hilden, Forststr. 3A; tel. (0211) 71040; telex 8581968; fax (0211) 7104222; f. 1950; Chair. Hermann Lutz; Sec. W. Dicke; 161,310 mems (Dec. 1989).

Deutsche Postgewerkschaft (Post and Telecommunications Union): 6000 Frankfurt a.M. 71, Rhonestr. 2; tel. (069) 66950; telex 412112; fax (069) 6695486; Pres. Kurt van Haaren; 472,145 mems (Dec. 1989).

GERMANY

Gewerkschaft Textil-Bekleidung (Textiles and Clothing): 4000 Düsseldorf 30, Ross Str. 94; Pres. WILLI ARENS; 250,783 mems (Dec. 1989).

The following are the largest unions outside the DGB:

Deutsche Angestellten-Gewerkschaft (DAG) (Clerical, Technical and Administrative Workers): 2000 Hamburg 36, Karl-Muck-Platz 1; tel. (040) 349150; telex 211642; f. 1945; Chair. ROLAND ISSEN; 494,126 mems (1987).

Deutscher Beamtenbund (Federation of Civil Servants): 5300 Bonn 2, Dreizehnmorgenweg 36; tel. (0228) 8110; fax (0228) 811171; f. 1918; Pres. WERNER HAGEDORN; 786,948 mems (1988).

TRADE FAIRS

More than 80 trade fairs take place annually in Germany. Fair organizers include:

Berlin: AMK Berlin Ausstellungs-Messe-Kongress-GmbH, Messedamm 22, 1000 Berlin 19; tel. (030) 30381; telex 182908; fax (030) 3038-2325; Man. Dirs Dr MANFRED BUSCHE, DONALD HELLSTEDT.

Düsseldorf: Düsseldorfer Messe GmbH—NOWEA, Postfach 320203, 4000 Düsseldorf 30; tel. (0211) 456001; telex 8584853; fax (0211) 439601.

Essen: Messe Essen GmbH, Norbertstr., Postfach 100165, 4300 Essen 1; tel. (0201) 7244-0; telex 8579647; fax (0201) 7244-248.

Frankfurt am Main: Messe Frankfurt GmbH, 6000 Frankfurt a.M. 1, Ludwig-Erhard-Anlage 1; tel. (069) 7575-0; telex 411558; fax (069) 7575-6433; f. 1907; Chair. EIKE MARKAU.

Friedrichshafen: Internationale Bodensee-Messe GmbH. Messegelände, 7990 Friedrichshafen 1; tel. (07541) 708-0; telex 734315; fax (07541) 708-10.

Hamburg: Hamburg Messe und Kongress GmbH, Jungiusstr. 13, 2000 Hamburg 36; tel. (040) 3569-0; telex 212609; fax (040) 3569-2180; f. 1973; multipurpose congress centre with 17 halls and conference rooms; Dir Conventions JOACHIM DIETERICH.

Hannover: Deutsche Messe- und Ausstellungs-AG, Messegelände, 3000 Hannover 82; tel. (0511) 89-31232; telex 922728; fax (0511) 89-32626.

Karlsruhe: Karlsruher Kongress- und Ausstellungs GmbH, Postfach 1208, 7500 Karlsruhe 1; tel. (0721) 37200; telex 7826240; fax (0721) 3720348.

Köln: Messe- und Ausstellungs GmbH, 5000 Köln 21, Postfach 210760; tel. (0221) 821-1; telex 8873426; fax (0221) 8210.

Leipzig: Leipziger Messe-Amt, 7010 Leipzig, Markt 11-15, Postfach 720; tel. (041) 71810; telex 512294; twice a year (March and September).

München: Münchener Messe- und Ausstellungs GmbH, Messegelände, Postfach 121009, 8000 München 12; tel. (089) 51070; telex 5212086; fax (089) 5107506.

Nürnberg: NMA Nürnberger Messe- und Ausstellungs GmbH, Messezentrum, 8500 Nürnberg 50; tel. (0911) 8606-0; telex 623613; fax (0911) 8606-228; f. 1974; Dir Dr HARTWIG HAUCK.

Offenbach: Offenbacher Messe GmbH, Postfach 101423, 6050 Offenbach/M. 1; tel. (069) 817091; telex 411298; fax (069) 8004261.

Saarbrücken: Saarmesse GmbH, Messegelände, 6600 Saarbrücken; tel. (0681) 53056; fax (0681) 53052.

Stuttgart: Stuttgarter Messe- und Kongress-GmbH, Am Kochenhof 16, Postfach 103252, 7000 Stuttgart 10; tel. (0711) 25890; telex 722584; fax (0711) 2589-440.

Wiesbaden: Heckmann GmbH, Kapellenstr. 47, 6200 Wiesbaden; tel. (0611) 58040; telex 4186518; fax (0611) 580417.

TRADE CENTRE

Internationales Handelszentrum (International Trade Centre): 1086 Berlin, Friedrichstr.; tel. (02) 20960; telex 114387; opened 1978; offices of foreign enterprises; provision of rooms and services for conferences, symposia, exhibitions and negotiations for the promotion of international trade; mediation of business contacts.

Transport

RAILWAYS

The treaty on German unification, signed in August 1990, envisaged the eventual incorporation of the Deutsche Reichsbahn (of the GDR) into the Deutsche Bundesbahn (Federal Railways). Until such time, the two rail networks would continue to operate separately.

In 1991 the total length of track in Germany was approximately 42,000 km (28,000 km in the former FRG and 14,000 km in the former GDR).

Deutsche Bundesbahn (DB) (German Federal Railways): 6000 Frankfurt a.M. 1, Friedrich-Ebert-Anlage 43–45; tel. (069) 2651; telex 414087; fax (069) 2656480; Pres. (vacant); Chair. H. WERTZ.

Deutsche Reichsbahn: Hauptverwaltung, 1130 Berlin, Ruschestr. 59; tel. (02) 4924247; telex 112564396; fax (02) 23727250.

Metropolitan Railway

Berliner Verkehrs-Betriebe (Berlin Transport Authority): 1000 Berlin 30, Potsdamer Str. 188; tel. (030) 2561; telex 183329; fax (030) 2164168; f. 1929; operates approximately 140 km of underground railway and 71.5 km of 'S-Bahn' railway; also runs bus services; Dirs Dipl. Ing. HELMUT DÖPFER, Dipl.-Kfm. KONRAD LORENZEN, HANS-BERNHARD LUDWIG, HARRO SACHSSE.

Stadtwerke München, Verkehrsbetriebe: 8000 München 80, Einsteinstr. 28, Postfach 202222; tel. (089) 2191-1; fax (089) 2191-2155; underground (57 km), tramway (85 km), omnibus (410 km); Dir Dipl.-Ing. DIETER BUHMANN.

Associations

BDE Bundesverband Deutscher Eisenbahnen, Kraftverkehre und Seilbahnen (Union of Non-Federal Railways, Bus-Services and Cable-Ways): 5000 Köln 1, Hülchrather Str. 17; tel. (0221) 77206-0; fax (0221) 77206-66; Pres. DIETER LUDWIG; Dir MANFRED MONTADA.

Verband Deutscher Verkehrsunternehem (VDV) (Association of Public Transport): 5000 Köln 1, Kamekestr. 37–39; tel. (0221) 525064; telex 8881718; fax (0221) 514272; f. 1895; Pres. Dipl.-Ing. D. BOLLHÖFER; Sec. Prof. Dr-Ing. GIRNAU.

ROADS

In December 1988 there were 496,652 km of classified roads in the FRG, including 8,721 km of motorway, 31,108 km of other main roads and 63,441 km of secondary roads. In the GDR, in 1988, there were 1,855 km of motorways, 11,263 km of trunk roads, 34,023 km of district roads and 77,400 km of roads in towns and villages (Kommunalstrassen).

Zentralarbeitsgemeinschaft des Strassenverkehrsgewerbes eV (ZAV) (Central Association of the Road Transport Industry): 6 Frankfurt a.M. 93, Breitenbachstr. 1, Haus des Strassenverkehrs; tel. (069) 775719; telex 411627; fax (069) 7919-300; Pres. HEINZ HERZIG; Gen. Sec. (vacant).

INLAND WATERWAYS

There are about 6,700 km of navigable inland waterways, and the Rhine-Main-Danube Canal, linking the North Sea and the Black Sea, is expected to be completed by 1992. Inland shipping accounts for about 20% of total freight traffic.

Abteilung Binnenschiffahrt und Wasserstrassen (Federal Ministry of Transport, Inland Waterways Dept): 5300 Bonn 2, Robert-Schuman-Platz 1; tel. (0228) 300-0; telex 885700; fax (0228) 300-3428; deals with construction, maintenance and administration of federal waterways and with national and international inland water transport.

Associations

Bundesverband der deutschen Binnenschiffahrt eV: 4100 Duisburg 13, Dammstr. 15–17; tel. (0203) 800060; telex 855692; fax (0203) 8000621; f. 1948; central Inland Waterway Association to further the interests of operating firms; Pres. Dr KARL HEINZ KÜHL; 4 Mans.

Deutsche Binnenreederei GmbH: 1017 Berlin, Alt Stralau 55–58; tel. (02) 55232100; telex 112703; fax (02) 5597638; f. 1990; Dir-Gen. Dr WOLFGANG HETTLER.

Hafenschiffahrtverband Hamburg eV: 2000 Hamburg 11, Mattentwiete 2; tel. 36128-0.

Verein für Binnenschiffahrt und Wasserstrassen eV (VBW): 4100 Duisburg 13, Dammstr. 15–17, Postfach 130 960; tel. (0203) 800060; telex 855692; fax (0203) 8000621; formerly Zentral-Verein für deutsche Binnenschiffahrt eV and Verein zur Wahrung der Rheinschiffahrtsinteressen eV; an organization for the benefit of all branches of the inland waterways; Pres. Dr H. ZÜNKLER; 6 Dirs.

SHIPPING

The principal seaports for freight are Bremen, Hamburg, Rostock-Überseehafen and Wilhelmshaven. Some important shipping companies are:

Christian F. Ahrenkiel GmbH & Co.: 2000 Hamburg 1, An der Alster 45; tel. (040) 28680; telex 2195580; tramp, shipowners and managers; 30 vessels, 523,000 grt.

Argo Reederei Richard Adler & Söhne: 2800 Bremen, Argo-Haus, Postfach 107529; tel. (0421) 3630725; telex 245206; Finland, UK; Propr MAX ADLER; 4 vessels, 15,300 grt.

GERMANY

Aug. Bolten Wm. Miller's Nachfolger: 2000 Hamburg 11, Mattentwiete 8; tel. (040) 3601-1; telex 211431; tramp; 6 vessels, 105,700 grt.

Bugsier- Reederei- und Bergungs-Gesellschaft mbH: 2000 Hamburg 11, Johannisbollwerk 10, Postfach 112273; tel. (040) 31110; telex 211228; fax (040) 313693; salvage, towage, tugs, ocean-going heavy lift cranes, submersible pontoons, harbour tugs; liner services between continent/Denmark and UK and Ireland; Chief Officers B. J. SCHUCHMANN, J. W. SCHUCHMANN, A. HUETTMANN; 6 vessels, 26,500 grt.

DAL Deutsche Afrika-Linien GmbH & Co: 2000 Hamburg, Palmaille 45; tel. (040) 380160; telex 212897-0; fax (040) 38016-663; Europe and South Africa; Man. Dirs R. BRENNECKE, H. VON RANTZAU, Dr E. VON RANTZAU.

Deutsche Schiffs-Revision und -Klassifikation: 1615 Zeuthen, Eichenallee 12; tel. (032982) 2633; telex 158721; fax (032982) 6788761; f. 1950; survey and classification of ships, approval of containers; Man. Dir Prof. Dr GÜNTER BOSSOW.

Deutsche Shell Tanker GmbH: 2000 Hamburg 60, Ueberseering 35, Postfach 600 440; tel. (040) 6341; telex 2163091; fax (040) 6319446; f. 1958; 8 vessels; 492,411 grt.

Döhle, Peter, Schiffahrts-KG (GmbH & Co): 2000 Hamburg 50, Palmaille 33, Postfach 500440; tel. (040) 381080; telex 214666; Man. Dirs PETER DÖHLE, H.-G. HÖLCK; shipbrokers, chartering agent for about 120 vessels, shipowners.

DSR-Lines, Deutsche/Seereederei Rostock GmbH: 2500 Rostock 1, Haus der Schiffahrt, POB 2188; tel. (081) 3660; telex 31381; fax (081) 36621831; shipping company; container ships, general cargo ships, bulk carriers, cargo trailer ships, special tankers; Chair. HARRY WENZEL.

John T. Essberger: 2000 Hamburg 50, Palmaille 49, Postfach 500429; tel. (040) 380160; telex 2163553; fax (040) 38016579; f. 1924; Man. Dirs L. V. RANTZAU-ESSBERGER, Dr E. VON RANTZAU, H. VON RANTZAU; 9 tankers, 12,792 grt.

Esso Tankschiff Reederei GmbH: 2000 Hamburg 60, Postfach 600640, Kapstadtring 2; tel. (040) 6393-0; telex 21700660; fax (040) 6393-3368; f. 1928; 7 tank barges.

Fisser & v. Doornum: 2000 Hamburg 13, Feldbrunnenstr. 43, Postfach 132265; tel. (040) 44186211; telex 212671; f. 1879; tramp; Man. Dirs Dr FRANK FISSER, WULF V. MOLTKE; 22 vessels, 79,600 grt.

Johs. Fritzen & Sohn GmbH: 2970 Emden 1, Neptunhaus; tel. (04921) 20011; telex 27821; fax (04921) 20013; f. 1919; port agents, Lloyd's sub-agents, bunker agents.

Hamburg-Südamerikanische Dampfschiffahrts-Gesellschaft Eggert & Amsinck: 2000 Hamburg 11, Ost-West-Str. 59, Hamburg-Süd-Haus; tel. (040) 37050; telex 21321699; worldwide service; 19 vessels, 342,697 grt.

Hapag-Lloyd AG: 2000 Hamburg 1, Ballindamm 25 and 2800 Bremen, Gustav-Deetjen-Allee 2-6; tel. (040) 3030; telex 217002; f. 1970; USA East Coast, Canada, North Pacific (Euro-Pacific), US Gulf/South Atlantic (Combi Line), West Indies (Carol), Mexico, Venezuela, Colombia and Costa Rica (Euro-Caribbean), Central America/West Coast (German Central America Service), Northern Brazil, South America/West Coast, Far East (Trio Service) and China, Indonesia, Australia, New Zealand (Australia, New Zealand, Europe Container Service), and the Canary Islands; Chair. H.-J. KRUSE; 20 vessels, 696,000 grt.

F. Laeisz Schiffahrts GmbH & Co: 2000 Hamburg 11, Trostbrücke 1, Postfach 111111; tel. (040) 36881; telex 403143; fax (040) 364876; Dir NIKOLAUS W. SCHÜES; Dir G. HEYENGA; 3 refrigerated vessels, 8 containers, 1 bulk carrier, 200,000 grt.

Moller, Walther & Co: 2000 Hamburg 50, Thedestr. 2; tel. (040) 389931; telex 211523; fax (040) 384935; 30 vessels.

Sloman Neptun Schiffahrts-AG: 2800 Bremen 1, Langenstr. 52+54, Postfach 1014 69; tel. (0421) 17630; telex 244421; fax (0421) 1763-313; f. 1873; Scandinavia, Western Europe, North Africa; gas carriers and heavy-lift vessels; seismic survey vessels; agencies, shipchandling, stevedoring; Mans WERNER KRIEGER, HERBERT JUNIEL; 17 vessels, 58,934 grt.

Oldenburg-Portugiesische Dampfschiffs-Rhederei GmbH: 2000 Hamburg 11, Postfach 110860; tel. (040) 361580; telex 211110; fax (040) 364431; f. 1882; Spain, Portugal, Mediterranean, Madeira, Algeria, Tunisia, Morocco, Canary Isles; Man. Dirs P. T. HANSEN, J. BERGMANN; 3 vessels, 6,000 grt; 5 vessels, 1,599 grt.

Egon Oldendorff: 2400 Lübeck, Fünfhausen 1; tel. (0451) 15000; telex 26411; fax (0451) 73522; Dirs H. OLDENDORFF, H. E. HELLMANN, G. ARNDT, W. DRABERT, W. SCHARNOWSKI; tramp; 29 vessels, 550,000 gross tonnage.

Rhein Maas und See Schiffahrtskontor GmbH. 4100 Duisburg 13, Krausstr 14, Postfach 130780; tel. (0203) 8040; telex 855700, fax (0203) 804330; 68 vessels.

Ernst Russ: 2000 Hamburg 36, Alsterarkaden 27; tel. (040) 36840; telex 2150090; f. 1893; Europe, Scandinavia, worldwide; tramps; Dir ERNST-ROLAND LORENZ-MEYER; 7 vessels, 110,856 grt.

Schiffsmaklerei AG: 2500 Rostock, Strandstr. 25; tel. (081) 383365; telex 31265; fax (081) 383568; f. 1958; international clearing and liner agency; agencies at Rostock, Wismar, Stralsund; branch office in Berlin; Dir ÉDUARD ZIMMERMANN.

Schiffsversorgung Rostock GmbH: 2540 Rostock-Überseehafen; tel. (081) 36631930; telex 31114; fax (081) 36621930; f. 1959; general ship supplies, provisions, technical equipment, nautical charts and handbooks, duty-free goods; Man. HORST SITZ.

Schlüssel Reederei KG: 2800 Bremen 1, Am Wall 58/60, Postfach 10 18 47; tel. (0421) 170561; telex 244520; fax (0421) 170565; f. 1950; ship owners, trampshipping, ship management.

H. Schuldt: 2000 Hamburg 1, Ballindamm 8; tel. (040) 309050; telex 2161900; f. 1868; ship management; services to the USA; Gen. Mans E. SIEH, B. TODSEN; 7 vessels, 88,000 grt.

Seehafen Rostock AG (Overseas port, Rostock): 2540 Rostock-Überseehafen; tel. (081) 366-0; telex 31264; fax (081) 36621932; f. 1960; Dir DIETER NOLL.

Seehafen Wismar GmbH (Wismar seaport): 2400 Wismar, Am alten Hafen; tel. (0824) 452300; telex 318882; fax (0824) 452595; f. 1946; Dir HORST LÜDEMANN.

Seereederei "Frigga" GmbH: 2000 Tangstedt, Hauptstr. 99; tel. (04109) 1408; telex 2180718; fax (04109) 6257; f. 1921; tramps; Dir E. EBERS; 2 vessels, 79,695 grt.

Hugo Stinnes Transozean Schiffahrt GmbH: 4330 Mülheim (Ruhr), Weseler Str. 60; telex 856714; liner service; Continent-West Africa; 9 vessels; 40,867 grt.

Stralsunder Hafen- und Lagerhausgesellschaft mbH (Stralsund seaport): 2300 Stralsund, Hafenstr. 15; tel. (0821) 692360; telex 31441-142; fax (0821) 692369; f. 1990; Dir HEINZ HAPP.

Tallierungs-GmbH: 2540 Rostock-Überseehafen; tel. (081) 36632131; telex 31347; fax (081) 36621839; tallying, checking, weighing, surveying, draught measurement, inspection and expertise; Dir MARGOT RECKLING.

Johs. Thode GmbH & Co: 2000 Hamburg 50, Köhlbrandtreppe 2; tel. (040) 3802040; telex 211375; fax (040) 3800245; 50 vessels.

Tietjen, Wilhelm: 2000 Hamburg 50, Palmaille 35; tel. (040) 381171; telex 211342; 43 vessels.

Unterweser Reederei GmbH: 2800 Bremen 1, Blumenthalstr. 16, Postfach 100867; tel. (0421) 3488-0; telex 244179; fax (0421) 3488100; f. 1890; Man. Dirs K. ESAU, M. SCHROIFF; 2 reduced draft supply vessels; 25 tugs.

Shipping Organizations

Verband Deutscher Küstenschiffseigner (German Coastal Shipowners Association): 2000 Hamburg-Altona, Grosse Elbstr. 36; tel. (040) 313435; telex 214444; fax (040) 315925; f. 1896; Pres. Dr H. J. STÖCKER; Man. Dipl. sc. pol. KLAUS KÖSTER.

Verband Deutscher Reeder eV (German Shipowners' Association): 2000 Hamburg 36, Esplanade 6, Postfach 305580; tel. (040) 350970; telex 211407; fax (040) 35097-211; Pres. Prof. DIETER ULKEN; Man. Dir Dr BERND KRÖGER.

Zentralverband der Deutschen Seehafenbetriebe eV (Federal Association of German Seaport Operators): 2000 Hamburg 50, Grosse Elbstr. 14; tel. (040) 311561; fax (040) 315714; f. 1932; Chair. HELMUTH KERN; Man. Dr LOTHAR L. V. JOLMES; approx. 850 mems.

CIVIL AVIATION

The major international airports are at Berlin (East and West), Köln-Bonn, Dresden, Düsseldorf, Frankfurt, Hamburg, Hannover, Leipzig, München and Stuttgart.

Aero Lloyd Flugreisen GmbH & Co Luftverkehrs-KG: 6370 Oberursel, Lessingstr. 7-9; tel. (06171) 6401; telex 410555; fax (06171) 641129; f. 1981; charter services; Gen. Mans Dr M. AKSMANOVIĆ, Dr W. SCHNEIDER; fleet of 3 Caravelle SE 210-10, 3 DC 9-32, 3 MD83, 2 MD-87.

Condor Flugdienst GmbH: 6078 Neu Isenburg 1, Hans-Boeckler-Str. 7; tel. (06102) 2450; telex 417697; fax (06102) 245261; f. 1955, wholly-owned subsidiary of Lufthansa; charter and inclusive-tour services; fleet of 3 DC-10-30, 7 B757-200, 9 B737-230, 3 Airbus A310; Man. Dirs Dr FRANZ SCHOIBER, Dr CLAUS GILLMANN, RUDOLF VON OERTZEN.

Deutsche Lufthansa AG: 5000 Köln 21, Von-Gablenz-Str. 2-6; tel. (0221) 8260; telex 8873531; fax (0221) 8262306; f. 1953; extensive world-wide network; Chair. Exec. Board HEINZ RUHNAU; Deputy Chair. Exec. Board Dipl. Ing. JÜRGEN WEBER; Chair. Supervisory Board GERD LAUSEN; fleet of 6 Boeing B747-400, 4 B747-400SCD, 12 B747-200SCD, 4 B747-200, 6 B747-200F, 10 DC10-30, 9 Airbus

GERMANY

A300-600, 12 A310, 7 A310-300, 15 A320, 15 B727-200, 40 B737-200, 27 B737-300, 2 B737-500.

DLT Deutsche Luftverkehrs-GmbH: 6239 Kriftel, Am Holzweg 26; tel. (06192) 407-0; telex 4072204; fax (06192) 407295; scheduled services; Exec. Mans HELMUT HORN, GERHARD SCHMID; fleet of 14 Fokker 50.

GCS German Cargo Services GmbH: 6092 Kelsterbach, Langer Kornweg 34, Postfach 1244; tel. (06107) 777698; telex 4189142; fax (06107) 777880; f. 1977; wholly-owned subsidiary of Lufthansa; freight-charter world-wide; Mans K.-H. KÖPFLE, J.-H. IRLE; fleet of 5 DC8-73 F, 2 B737F, 2 B747SF.

Germania Flug-GmbH: 5000 Köln 90, Flughafen; tel. (02203) 401; telex 8873712; f. 1978; charter and inclusive-tour services; Man. Dr HEINRICH BISCHOFF; fleet of 2 Boeing 727-100; 2 737-300.

Hapag-Lloyd Flug-GmbH: 3000 Hanover 42, Flughafen; tel. (0511) 73030; telex 9230136; f. 1972; charter and inclusive-tour services; Man. Dir CLAUS WÜLFERS; fleet of 5 Airbus A 300B4, 1 A300C4, 4 Boeing 737-200, 2 Boeing 727-200, 1 727-100.

Interflug, Gesellschaft für internationalen Flugverkehr mbH: 1189 Berlin-Schönefeld; tel. (02) 6720; telex 112891; fax (02) 6788390; f. 1955; the airline of the former GDR; flights throughout Europe and to the Middle, Near and Far East, Africa and Central America; Pres. Dr KLAUS HENKES; fleet of IL-62, IL-18, and TU-134 aircraft; 3 Airbus A-310-330.

LTU Lufttransport-Unternehmen GmbH & Co KG: 4000 Düsseldorf 30, Flughafen Halle 8; tel. (0211) 41520; telex 8585573; f. 1955; charter; Man. WERNER HUEHN; fleet of 10 TriStar.

LTU Lufttransport-Unternehmen Süd GmbH & Co Fluggesellschaft: 8000 München 87, Flughafen München-Riem; tel. (089) 9211-8950; telex 5214762; fax (089) 906270; f. 1983; charter; Dirs WERNER HUEHN, ULRICH REINHARDT; fleet of 7 Boeing 757, 3 Boeing 767.

Tourism

Germany's tourist attractions include spas, summer and winter resorts, mountains, medieval towns and villages. The North Sea coast, the Rhine Valley, the Black Forest, the mountains of Thuringia, the Erzgebirge and Bavaria are the most popular areas. In 1988/89 there were 38,102 hotels and guesthouses in the FRG, with 1,140,000 beds available for tourists. Overnight stays by foreign tourists totalled 33,600,000 in 1988/89, when the total number of foreign tourists visiting the FRG was more than 13m.

Deutsche Zentrale für Tourismus eV (DZT) (German National Tourist Board): 6000 Frankfurt a.M. 1, Beethovenstr. 69; tel. (069) 75720; fax (069) 751903; f. 1948; Dir GÜNTHER SPAZIER.

Atomic Energy

Bundesministerium für Forschung und Technologie (Federal Ministry for Research and Technology): 5300 Bonn 2, Heinemannstr. 2, Postfach 200240; tel. (0228) 591; telex 885674; fax (0228) 593601; f. 1955; Minister Dr HEINZ RIESENHUBER.

The Ministry is divided into five departments, the first dealing with administration and establishment, the second with basic research, co-ordination of research, and international co-operation, the third with energy, biology and ecology, the fourth with information and production engineering and research on working conditions, and the fifth with aerospace, raw materials and geosciences.

The Ministry's responsibility in the nuclear energy field is to promote nuclear research and nuclear engineering as well as to plan and co-ordinate the activities of all of these bodies.

Nuclear research and development is carried out by the research centres of the following institutions in co-operation with universities and industry:

1. Kernforschungszentrum Karlsruhe GmbH, Karlsruhe (KfK).
2. Kernforschungsanlage Jülich GmbH, Jülich (KFA).
3. Max-Planck-Institut für Plasmaphysik (IPP) Garching bei München.
4. Gesellschaft für Strahlen- und Umweltforschung mbH, München (GSF).
5. GKSS-Forschungszentrum, Geesthacht GmbH.
6. Hahn-Meitner Institut GmbH, Berlin (HMI).
7. Deutsches Elektronen-Synchrotron (DESY), Hamburg.
8. Gesellschaft für Schwerionenforschung mbH, Darmstadt (GSI).

Nuclear power made a contribution of 31.3% to electricity supply in the FRG in 1987. In December 1987 there were 21 nuclear power stations in operation in the FRG, with a total generating capacity of almost 19m. kW.

Nuclear power stations in operation in the FRG in 1986 were: the AVR Project at Jülich (Nordrhein-Westfalen), with a capacity of 15 MW; the KWO Project at Obrigheim/Neckar (Baden-Württemberg), with a capacity of 345 MW; the KWW Project at Würgassen/Weser (Nordrhein-Westfalen), with a capacity of 670 MW; the KKS Project at Stade/Elbe (Niedersachsen), with a capacity of 662 MW; the Biblis A and Biblis B Projects at Biblis/Rhein (Hessen), with respective capacities of 1,204 MW and 1,300 MW; the KKP Project at Philippsburg (Baden-Württemberg), with a capacity of 960 MW; the KKB Project at Brunsbuttel/Elbe (Schleswig-Holstein), with a capacity of 805 MW; the GKN I Project at Neckarwestheim/Neckar (Baden-Württemberg), with a capacity of 855 MW; the KNK II Project at Karlsruhe (Baden-Württemberg), with a capacity of 21 MW; the KKU Project at Esenshamm (Niedersachsen), with a capacity of 1,300 MW; the KKI I Project at Ohu/Isar (Bayern), with a capacity of 907 MW; the KKK Project at Krümmel (Schleswig-Holstein), with a capacity of 1,316 MW; the KWG Project at Grohnde (Niedersachsen), with a capacity of 1,361 MW; the KKG Project at Grafenrheinfeld (Bayern), with a capacity of 1,229 MW; the KRB IIB and C Projects at Gundremmingen (Bayern), with a capacity of 1,310 MW each; and the KBR Project at Brokdorf (Schleswig-Holstein), with a capacity of 1,365 MW.

Construction of the SNR-300 Project at Kalkar (Nordrhein-Westfalen), with a capacity of 327 MW, and of the Mulheim-Kärlich Project (Rheinland-Pfalz), with a capacity of 1,308 MW, was completed in the mid-1980s, but various problems have prevented their full operation. Four nuclear power plants were under construction in the FRG in 1987: the THTR-300 Project at Hamm-Uentrop (Nordrhein-Westfalen), with a capacity of 308 MW; the KKI II Project at Ohu/Isar (Bayern), with a capacity of 1,369 MW; the KKE Project at Emsland (Niedersachsen), with a capacity of 1,314 MW; and the GKN II Project at Neckarwestheim/Neckar (Baden-Württemberg), with a capacity of 1,300 MW.

In addition, 10 more nuclear power plants are due to be constructed and start operation by the year 2000. Sites have been chosen at Biblis, Neupotz (two plants), Wyhl, Hamm, Pfaffenhofen, Vahnum (two plants) and Borken. These will have a total capacity of about 15,600 MW. The following nuclear power stations, which were demonstration plants and started operation in the mid-1960s, have been closed down: the KRB Project at Gundremmingen (Bayern), with a capacity of 250 MW; the KWL Project at Lingen (Niedersachsen), with a capacity of 268 MW; and the VAK Project at Kohl/Main, with a capacity of 17 MW.

The use of nuclear energy has given rise to much controversy in the FRG and various protest groups have been formed. In 1975 the Government started an information campaign, which aims to provide the public with information on nuclear energy and all related energy questions, including energy conservation. The Government of Chancellor Helmut Kohl is strongly in favour of the continuation of the nuclear energy programme, and several new projects have been proposed.

Following the unification of the two German states in October 1990, the Staatliches Amt für Atomsicherheit und Strahlenschutz der DDR (Board of Nuclear Safety and Radiation Protection of the GDR) was amalgamated into the Bundesamt für Strahlenschutz (Federal Board for Radiation Protection). By mid-December 1990 both of the nuclear power stations in operation in the former GDR had been closed for reasons of safety.

GHANA

Introductory Survey

Location, Climate, Language, Religion, Flag, Capital

The Republic of Ghana lies on the west coast of Africa, with Côte d'Ivoire to the west and Togo to the east. It is bordered by Burkina Faso to the north. The climate is tropical, with temperatures generally between 21°C and 32°C (70°–90°F) and average annual rainfall of 2,000 mm (80 in) on the coast, decreasing inland. English is the official language, but there are eight major national languages. Many of the inhabitants follow traditional beliefs and customs. Christians make up an estimated 42% of the population. The national flag (proportions 3 by 2) has three equal horizontal stripes, of red, gold and green, with a five-pointed black star in the centre of the gold stripe. The capital is Accra.

Recent History

Ghana was formed by a merger of the Gold Coast, a former British colony, and the British-administered part of Togoland, a UN Trust Territory.

In the Gold Coast a new constitution was issued in 1950. The first general election to the new Legislative Assembly, held in 1951, resulted in an overwhelming victory for the Convention People's Party (CPP), led by Dr Kwame Nkrumah, who became Prime Minister in 1952. In 1956, at a UN-supervised plebiscite, British Togoland voted to join the Gold Coast in an independent state. Ghana was duly granted independence, within the Commonwealth, on 6 March 1957, and thus became the first British dependency in sub-Saharan Africa to achieve independence under majority rule. Dr Nkrumah established an authoritarian regime, aiming to lead Ghana towards 'African socialism', and played a leading role in the Non-Aligned Movement. Ghana became a republic on 1 July 1960, with Dr Nkrumah as President. In 1964 the country became a one-party state, with the CPP as the sole authorized party. President Nkrumah established close relations with the USSR and other communist countries. On 24 February 1966 Nkrumah, whose repressive policies and financial mismanagement had caused increasing resentment, was deposed by the army and police. The coup leaders established the National Liberation Council (NLC), led by Gen. Joseph Ankrah. In April 1969, following disputes within the ruling NLC, Gen. Ankrah was replaced by Brig. (later Lt-Gen.) Akwasi Afrifa, who introduced a new constitution, which established a non-executive presidency. In August an election for a new National Assembly was held, and the Progress Party (PP), led by Dr Kofi Busia, won 105 of the 140 seats. Dr Busia was appointed Prime Minister, and the PP Government took office on 1 October 1969. A three-man commission, formed by NLC members, held presidential power until 31 August 1970, when Edward Akufo-Addo was inaugurated as civilian President.

In reaction to increasing economic and political difficulties, the army seized power again in January 1972. The Constitution was abolished and all political institutions were replaced by a National Redemption Council (NRC) under the chairmanship of Lt-Col (later Gen.) Ignatius Acheampong. In 1975 supreme legislative and administrative authority was transferred from the NRC to a Supreme Military Council (SMC), also led by Gen. Acheampong. In 1976 Gen. Acheampong announced plans for a return to civilian rule without political parties, in the form of 'union' government, in which it was envisaged that the military should continue to play a role, and a programme for return to civilian government by June 1979 was announced. In March 1978 a referendum resulted in a vote of 54% in favour of 'union' government. This result was largely discredited, and in July Acheampong's deputy, Lt-Gen. Frederick Akuffo, assumed power in a bloodless coup. Akuffo declared that the return to a popularly elected government would take place in 1979, as planned, and he introduced a number of civilians into the NRC. The six-year ban on party politics was lifted in January 1979, and 16 new parties were subsequently registered.

Only a fortnight before the elections were due to take place in June 1979, however, a coup was staged by junior officers of the armed forces, led by Flight-Lt Jerry Rawlings. Their main grievance was that, despite economic mismanagement and corruption, Ghana's military leaders were immune from financial investigation, under the terms of the draft constitution. An Armed Forces Revolutionary Council (AFRC), under the leadership of Rawlings, assumed power and began to eradicate corruption. A 'Revolutionary Court' convicted Acheampong, Akuffo, Afrifa and six other senior officers on charges of corruption, and they were subsequently executed.

Although the return to civilian rule was postponed until September 1979, the elections took place in June. The People's National Party (PNP) gained a majority of parliamentary seats, and its leader, Dr Hilla Limann, was elected President, taking office on 24 September 1979. In 1980 the United National Convention (UNC) ended its alliance with the PNP, leaving the latter with a majority of only one seat in Parliament. In 1981 the UNC joined three other parties to form the All People's Party, a viable alternative to the PNP.

Dissatisfaction with the Government culminated in December 1981, when Flight-Lt Rawlings again seized power in a military coup, establishing a Provisional National Defence Council (PNDC), with himself as Chairman. The Council of State was abolished, the Constitution suspended, Parliament dissolved and political parties banned. In 1982 city and district councils were replaced by People's Defence Committees (PDCs), which were designed to allow the people a role in local government. They were renamed Committees for the Defence of the Revolution (CDRs) in 1984.

The PNDC's policies initially received strong support, but discontent with the regime and the apparent ineffectiveness of its economic policies was reflected in a series of attempted coups, widespread student unrest and alleged anti-Government conspiracies. In December 1985 the Chairman of the London-based Ghana Democratic Movement (GDM) was arrested in the USA, and was accused of involvement in a conspiracy to purchase weapons for shipment to dissidents in Ghana. In 1986 nine people were sentenced to death for their alleged involvement in a conspiracy to overthrow the Government, and a former minister and presidential candidate, Victor Owusu (leader of the disbanded Popular Front Party), was arrested for alleged subversion. In June 1987 it was announced that several people had been arrested and that weapons had been seized, following the discovery of another plot to overthrow the PNDC. In response to increasing tension, members of trade unions and PNDC organizations were ordered to register their firearms. In November the detention of seven people, including leaders of the pro-PNDC organizations, the New Democratic Movement (NDM) and the Kwame Nkrumah Revolutionary Guards (KNRG), was authorized in the interests of national security. In the same month two people were sentenced to 25 years' hard labour for their involvement in an attempted coup in 1983. The leader of the NDM was released from detention in December 1988.

In July 1987 the PNDC announced that elections for district assemblies would be held in late 1988. However, one-third of the 7,278 members of the district assemblies were to be selected by the Government, and the ban on political parties was to remain. These assemblies were to be 'the highest district political and administrative authorities', holding deliberative, political and executive power, and were regarded as the first stage in the development of a new political system of national democratic administration. In October and November 87% of eligible voters were registered for the forthcoming elections, and in April 1988 a further 0.4% of voters were registered in a supplementary registration exercise. In that month there was an extensive government reshuffle, in which a new post to co-ordinate the work of the CDRs was created, and new Secretaries for Information, Political Programmes and for the National Commission for Women and Development were appointed. The reshuffle was regarded as a move to prepare for the district assembly elections and as an attempt to further public acceptance of the Government's Economic Recovery Programme. During 1988 the number of districts was increased from 65 to 110, and in October districts were

GHANA

Introductory Survey

grouped within three electoral zones. Elections for the district assemblies in each zone were held in stages between December 1988 and February 1989. At the elections for district assemblies in the first zone, held on 6 December, an estimated 60% of registered voters participated, compared with an estimated 35% of the electorate in the elections held on 28 February in the third zone. Each district assembly was inaugurated 14 days after the declaration of the results.

On 24 September 1989 an attempted coup reportedly took place, involving a close associate of Rawlings, Maj. Courage Quashigah. Shortly afterwards, Lt-Gen. Arnold Quainoo was dismissed as Commander of the Armed Forces, although he remained a member of the PNDC. Rawlings himself assumed control of the armed forces until June 1990, when Maj.-Gen. Winston Mensa-Wood was appointed Commander. In October 1989 five senior members of the security forces, including Quashigah, were arrested in connection with an alleged conspiracy to assassinate Rawlings. The predominance of the Ewe ethnic group in government positions and other important posts, which had provoked discontent among other factions, was initially considered to be the cause of the revolt. In November, however, a board of enquiry, which investigated the allegations of treason, concluded that most of the conspirators were motivated by personal grievances and ambition. In January 1990 five more arrests were made in connection with the coup attempt. In August the human rights organization, Amnesty International, criticized the continued detention of Quashigah and six other members of the security forces, and claimed that they were imprisoned for political dissension. Amnesty also expressed concern over the death in custody of one of the alleged conspirators, Flight-Lt William Domie.

In August 1990 a pro-democracy organization, Movement for Freedom and Justice (MFJ), demanded a national referendum on the restoration of multi-party politics in Ghana. In September the Vice-Chairman of the MFJ, Johnny Hansen, accused the PNDC of intimidation, after the MFJ's inaugural rally was suppressed by security forces. Between July and October the PNDC organized a series of controlled debates on the subject of Ghana's political future, apparently in response to pressure from Western donors to increase democracy in return for continued aid. In October the PNDC pledged to accept the conclusions of any national consensus on future democracy in the country.

After the 1983 coup in Upper Volta (now Burkina Faso), which brought Capt. Thomas Sankara to power, the Ghanaian Government established close links with the neighbouring state. In 1986 Ghana and Burkina Faso agreed to establish a high-level political body, which would be responsible for preparing a 10-year timetable for the political union of the two countries. The countries also agreed to harmonize their currencies, energy, transport, trade and educational systems, and a joint military exercise, 'Teamwork 1986', was held. Further joint exercises were held in mid-1987. However, Capt. Sankara was overthrown and killed in a military coup in October. This development was condemned by Ghana, but relations with Burkina Faso improved following meetings between Rawlings and Capt. Blaise Compaoré, Sankara's successor, in early 1988. In December 1989, however, Ghana was accused of playing a role in an attempt to overthrow the Burkinabè Government. Burkina Faso claimed that the plot was organized in Ghana by a resident Burkinabè, Lt Boukary Kabore, and that Ghanaian mercenaries had been recruited. Ghana denied involvement in the attempted coup and condemned the allegations. In mid-January 1990 120 Ghanaians were deported from Burkina Faso without official explanation.

Relations with Togo deteriorated in 1986, after Ghanaian security forces captured a group of armed dissidents crossing the border from Togo. The Ghanaian Secretary for Foreign Affairs protested over the use of neighbouring territories as bases for subversive activities against Ghana. In September the Togolese Government claimed that the instigators of an attempted coup in Togo came from Ghanaian territory, and were trained in Ghana and Burkina Faso. In Lomé, the Togolese capital, tension between Ghanaian immigrants and the Togolese increased, and between October and early December 233 Ghanaians were deported from Togo. The common border between the two countries was closed in October, but was reopened by Togo in February 1987 and by Ghana in May. Relations between the two countries became strained again in January 1989, when Togo expelled 120 Ghanaians.

In September 1989 relations between Ghana and Liberia deteriorated sharply. It was rumoured that the Liberian Government planned to repatriate forcibly resident Ghanaians, following the return of over 400 Liberians from Ghana. The Ghanaian Government denied allegations that they had carried out a mass deportation of Liberian nationals. However, over 350 Ghanaians were expelled from Liberia in October and further deportations were expected. During the conflict in Liberia in 1990 (see chapter on Liberia), over 8,000 Ghanaian citizens resident in Liberia were evacuated. However, 2,000 Ghanaians were reported to have been taken hostage by a rebel faction, the National Patriotic Forces of Liberia (NPFL). In August 1990 Ghana sent troops to Liberia as part of the West African peacekeeping force (ECOMOG, see p. 134).

Government

Upon its accession to power on 31 December 1981, the Provisional National Defence Council (PNDC) dissolved Parliament, abolished the Council of State and suspended the 1979 Constitution. Executive and legislative powers are vested in the PNDC, which rules by decree. Ghana comprises 10 regions, each administered by a Regional Secretary. Within the regions, there is a total of 110 administrative districts. The basic unit of local democracy is the Committee for the Defence of the Revolution (CDR). In December 1988, and in January and February 1989, elections were held for district assemblies. Each district assembly has an elected chairman, while the District Secretary remains responsible for the routine administration of the district and continues to be appointed by the PNDC. Regional Co-ordinating Councils (RCCs) were inaugurated in August 1989.

Defence

In June 1990 Ghana had total armed forces of 12,200 (army 10,000, navy 1,400 and air force 800) and a paramilitary force of 5,000. Expenditure on defence in 1989 was 11,200m. cedis. The headquarters of the Defence Commission of the OAU is in Accra.

Economic Affairs

In 1989, according to estimates by the World Bank, Ghana's gross national product (GNP), measured at average 1987–89 prices, was US $5,503m., equivalent to $380 per head. During 1980–89, it was estimated, GNP increased, in real terms, at an average annual rate of 2.6%. GNP per head, however, declined by 0.8% annually. Over the same period, the population increased by an annual average of 3.4%. Ghana's gross domestic product (GDP) increased, in real terms, by an annual average of 2.1% in 1980–88. According to government estimates, GDP rose by only 2.7% in 1990 (compared to an increase of 6.1% in 1989).

Agriculture (including forestry and fishing) contributed 50% of GDP in 1989. An estimated 50.5% of the labour force were employed in the sector in 1989. The principal cash crops are cocoa (Ghana being one of the world's leading producers), coffee, bananas, oil palm, coconuts, limes, kola nuts and shea nuts. Timber production is also important. During 1980–88 agricultural production increased by an annual average of only 0.5%.

Industry (including mining, manufacturing, construction and power) contributed 16% of GDP in 1988, and employed 12.8% of the working population in 1984. During 1980–88 industrial production increased by an annual average of only 1.9%. However, the output of the industrial sector rose by 7.4% in 1989.

Mining employed 0.5% of the working population in 1984, and provided 1.1% of GDP in 1985. Gold and diamonds are the major minerals exported, although Ghana also possesses large reserves of bauxite and manganese ore. Following the rehabilitation of three gold mines, mineral production rose by 30% in 1988, and by 9% in 1989.

Manufacturing contributed 10% of GDP in 1988 and employed 10.9% of the working population in 1984. The most important sectors are food processing, textiles, vehicles, cement, paper, chemicals and petroleum. Manufacturing production increased by 8% in 1989, while the annual average growth rate in 1980–88 was 3.1%.

Energy is derived principally from hydroelectric power and petroleum. Imports of mineral fuels comprised 4.1% of the total value of imports in 1986. Solar power is exploited as an alternative source of energy.

In 1989 Ghana recorded a visible trade deficit of US $191.8m., and there was a deficit of $97.5m. on the current account of

GHANA   Introductory Survey, Statistical Survey

the balance of payments. In 1986 the principal source of imports was the United Kingdom (20%), while the principal market for exports was the USA (21%). Other major trading partners were the Federal Republic of Germany, the USSR, Nigeria, France and Japan. The principal exports in 1986 were cocoa (which accounted for 46.1% of total export earnings in 1987), timber and gold. The principal imports were capital goods, foodstuffs and mineral fuels.

In 1989 there was a budgetary surplus of 10,200m. cedis. Ghana's total external public debt in 1989 was US $3,099m. In 1988 the cost of debt-servicing was equivalent to 62.8% of exports of goods and services. The average annual rate of inflation was 37% in 1990.

Ghana is a member of the Economic Community of West African States (ECOWAS, see p. 133), which aims to promote co-operation and development.

Ghana's economy has been adversely affected by political instability and mismanagement. Since Ghana is primarily an agricultural country, the economy is also vulnerable to unfavourable weather conditions and to fluctuations in international commodity prices. A medium-term structural adjustment programme (1987-90) aimed to consolidate previous economic reforms. Despite substantial progress in the late 1980s, economic development deteriorated in 1990, owing, in part, to the increase in the price of petroleum following the crisis in the Gulf (see chapter on Iraq). In 1991 the Government implemented a further structural adjustment programme (1991-92), which was financed by the World Bank.

Social Welfare

The Government provides hospitals and medical care at nominal rates, and there is a government pension scheme. There were 293 hospitals, health centres and posts, and 60 private clinics, in 1982. In 1990 the number of physicians working in Ghana was estimated at 1,200. Ghana's shortage of foreign exchange has limited imports of medical equipment. Of projected total expenditure by the central Government in 1988, 12,879.5m. cedis (9.0%) was for health services, and a further 9,904.4m. cedis (6.9%) for social security and welfare. In 1990 the Government initiated two projects, financed by the International Development Association (IDA), which were designed to ensure the availability of vaccines, and to expand family-planning services.

Education

In April 1974 the NRC announced the introduction of a new educational structure, consisting of an initial phase of six years' primary education (beginning at six years of age), followed by three years' junior secondary education. Under the Junior Secondary School Programme, introduced in 1989, a levy of 500 cedis per pupil was charged to finance the rehabilitation of junior secondary schools. At the junior secondary schools pupils are examined to determine admission to senior secondary school courses, which lead to examinations at the 'Ordinary' level of the General Certificate of Education, and technical and vocational courses. In 1990 the Common Entrance Examination, which was previously used to select senior secondary pupils, was replaced by the Basic Education Certificate Examination (BECE). In 1987 enrolment at primary schools was equivalent to 71% of children in the relevant age-group (78% of boys; 63% of girls), while the comparable ratio at secondary schools was 40% (49% of boys; 32% of girls). There are three universities. Expenditure on education by the central Government in 1988 was estimated at 36,994.7m. cedis (25.7% of total spending). The Programme of Action to Mitigate the Social Costs of Adjustment (PAMSCAD), which was introduced in 1988, allocated 1,904m. cedis to education, to be invested in adult literacy programmes and the rehabilitation of school buildings. According to UNESCO estimates, the average rate of adult illiteracy in 1990 was 39.7% (males 30%; females 49%). In mid-1989 the Ministry of Education initiated a new campaign to improve teaching standards as part of the Educational Sector Adjustment Programme. In 1990 the Government introduced a five-year programme, financed by the USA, to improve conditions in primary schools.

Public Holidays

1991: 1 January (New Year's Day), 6 March (Independence Day), 29 March-1 April (Easter), 1 May (Labour Day), 5 June (Anniversary of the 1979 coup), 1 July (Republic Day), 25-26 December (Christmas), 31 December (Revolution Day).

1992: 1 January (New Year's Day), 6 March (Independence Day), 17-20 April (Easter), 1 May (Labour Day), 5 June (Anniversary of the 1979 coup), 1 July (Republic Day), 25-26 December (Christmas), 31 December (Revolution Day).

Weights and Measures

The metric system is in force.

Statistical Survey

Source (except where otherwise stated): Central Bureau of Statistics, POB 1098, Accra; tel. 66512.

Area and Population

AREA, POPULATION AND DENSITY

Area (sq km)	238,537*
Population (census results)	
1 March 1970	8,559,313
11 March 1984	
Males	6,063,848
Females	6,232,233
Total	12,296,081
Population (official estimates at mid-year)	
1985	12,717,000
1986	13,050,000
1987	13,391,000
Density (per sq km) at mid-1987	56.1

* 92,100 sq miles.

POPULATION BY REGION (1984 census)

Western	1,157,807
Central	1,142,335
Greater Accra	1,431,099
Eastern	1,680,890
Volta	1,211,907
Ashanti	2,090,100
Brong-Ahafo	1,206,608
Northern	1,164,583
Upper East	772,744
Upper West	438,008
Total	12,296,081

Principal Ethnic Groups (1960 census, percentage of total population): Akan 44.1, Mole-Dagbani 15.9, Ewe 13.0, Ga-Adangbe 8.3, Guan 3.7, Gurma 3.5.

GHANA

Statistical Survey

PRINCIPAL TOWNS (population at 1984 census)

Accra (capital)	867,459
Kumasi	376,249
Tamale	135,952
Tema	131,528
Takoradi	61,484
Cape Coast	57,224
Sekondi	31,916

BIRTHS AND DEATHS (UN estimates, annual averages)

	1970–75	1975–80	1980–85
Birth rate (per 1,000)	47.2	47.1	46.9
Death rate (per 1,000)	17.4	15.9	14.6

Source: UN, *World Population Prospects: Estimates and Projections as Assessed in 1984*.

ECONOMICALLY ACTIVE POPULATION (1984 census)

	Males	Females	Total
Agriculture, hunting, forestry and fishing	1,750,024	1,560,943	3,310,967
Mining and quarrying	24,906	1,922	26,828
Manufacturing	198,430	389,988	588,418
Electricity, gas and water	14,033	1,404	15,437
Construction	60,692	3,994	64,686
Trade, restaurants and hotels	111,540	680,607	792,147
Transport, storage and communications	117,806	5,000	122,806
Financing, insurance, real estate and business services	19,933	7,542	27,475
Community, social and personal services	339,665	134,051	473,716
Total employed	2,637,029	2,785,451	5,422,480
Unemployed	87,452	70,172	157,624
Total labour force	2,724,481	2,855,623	5,580,104

Source: ILO, *Year Book of Labour Statistics*.

Agriculture

PRINCIPAL CROPS ('000 metric tons)

	1987	1988	1989
Maize	598	751	749
Millet	173	192	180
Sorghum	206	178	245
Rice (paddy)	81	84	74
Sugar cane†	110	110	110
Cassava (Manioc)	2,726	2,788	3,327
Yams	1,185	902	782
Taro (Coco yam)†	1,012	907	1,063
Onions†	28	28	28
Tomatoes†	91	79	96
Eggplants (Aubergines)†	7	6	7
Pulses†	18	15	19
Oranges†	50	50	50
Lemons and limes†	30	30	30
Bananas†	4	4	4
Plantains†	1,078	1,135	1,036
Pineapples†	8	10	10
Palm kernels†	30	30	30
Groundnuts (in shell)†	191	230	200
Coconuts†	200	200	200
Copra†	7	7	7
Coffee (green)	1	n.a.	1†
Cocoa beans	184	289	300*
Tobacco (leaves)*	2	2	2

* Unofficial figure(s).   † FAO estimate(s).

Source: FAO, *Production Yearbook*.

LIVESTOCK ('000 head, year ending September)

	1987	1988	1989*
Horses	2	2	2
Asses	14	10	10
Cattle	1,170	1,144	1,150
Pigs	399	478	550
Sheep	1,989	2,046	2,200
Goats	1,901	2,007	2,000

* FAO estimates.

Poultry (million): 8 in 1987; 8 in 1988; 8 (FAO estimate) in 1989.

Source: FAO, *Production Yearbook*.

LIVESTOCK PRODUCTS (FAO estimates, '000 metric tons)

	1987	1988	1989
Beef and veal	16	16	16
Mutton and lamb	6	6	6
Goat meat	5	6	6
Pig meat	9	11	12
Poultry meat	9	9	10
Other meat	96	89	89
Cows' milk	10	9	9
Hen eggs	8.7	8.5	8.5
Cattle hides	2.0	2.0	2.0

Source: FAO, *Production Yearbook*.

Forestry

ROUNDWOOD REMOVALS ('000 cubic metres)

	1986	1987	1988
Sawlogs, veneer logs and logs for sleepers	720	720*	720*
Other industrial wood*	381	381	381
Fuel wood	15,483	15,724	15,924
Total	16,584	16,825	17,025

* FAO estimates.

Source: FAO, *Yearbook of Forest Products*.

SAWNWOOD PRODUCTION ('000 cubic metres)

	1986	1987	1988*
Total (incl. boxboards)	290	390	390

* FAO estimate.

Railway Sleepers ('000 cubic metres): 65 per year (1986–88).

Source: FAO, *Yearbook of Forest Products*.

Fishing

('000 metric tons, live weight)

	1986	1987	1988
Inland waters	53.0	54.0	57.6
Atlantic Ocean	267.7	328.0	302.9
Total catch	320.7	382.0	360.6

Source: FAO, *Yearbook of Fishery Statistics*.

GHANA

Statistical Survey

Mining

('000 metric tons, unless otherwise indicated)

	1986	1987	1988
Gold ore ('000 kg)	9.0	10.2	11.6
Diamonds ('000 carats)	599	442	216
Manganese ore	259	254	231
Bauxite	204	195	287

Crude petroleum ('000 metric tons): 10 in 1986 (Source: UN, *Industrial Statistics Yearbook*).

Industry

SELECTED PRODUCTS
('000 metric tons, unless otherwise indicated)

	1986	1987	1988
Wheat flour	62.8	71.4	95.2
Beer ('000 hectolitres)	546	589	614
Soft drinks ('000 crates)	959	1,355	1,277
Cigarettes (millions)	1,826	1,734	1,831
Motor spirit (petrol)	200.0	154.7	142.4
Kerosene	112.0	92.2	110.0
Diesel and gas oil	275.0	220.0	290.2
Cement	219.0	294.4	412.1
Electric energy (million kWh)	4,405.0	4,676.3	4,807.8

Aluminium (unwrought): 125,000 metric tons (primary metal) in 1986.

Finance

CURRENCY AND EXCHANGE RATES

Monetary Units
100 pesewas = 1 new cedi.

Denominations
Coins: ½, 1, 2½, 5, 10, 20 and 50 pesewas; 1 and 5 cedis.
Notes: 1, 2, 5, 10, 50, 100, 200 and 500 cedis.

Sterling and Dollar Equivalents (30 September 1990)
£1 sterling = 632.94 cedis;
US $1 = 337.84 cedis;
1,000 cedis = £1.580 = $2.960.

Average Exchange Rate (cedis per US $)
1987 153.73
1988 202.35
1989 270.00

GENERAL BUDGET (provisional, million cedis)

Revenue*	1986	1987	1988
Taxation	61,587	95,400	125,779
Taxes on income, profits, etc.	14,633	23,396	39,689
Employees' income tax	3,198	4,550	6,016
Self-employed income tax	1,492	3,579	5,080
Company tax	9,658	14,381	27,648
Domestic taxes on goods and services	19,858	26,990	36,318
General sales taxes	2,548	8,363	12,363
Excises	10,465	12,804	15,019
Petroleum tax	6,600	5,500	8,485
Taxes on international trade	27,096	45,015	49,772
Import duties	12,911	17,813	25,176
Export duties	14,170	27,019	24,465
Other current revenue	8,170	9,609	16,459
Total	**69,758**	**105,009**	**142,238**

* Excluding grants received, mainly from abroad (million cedis): 3,868 in 1986; 6,037 in 1987; 11,553 in 1988.

Expenditure†	1986	1987	1988
General public services	9,227	9,949	19,474
Defence	4,605	4,275	4,603
Public order and safety	4,038	6,118	8,581
Education	16,905	27,044	36,995
Health	5,854	9,502	12,880
Social security and welfare	3,777	6,554	9,904
Housing and community amenities	1,366	811	5,002
Recreational, cultural and religious affairs	1,192	2,245	2,195
Economic services	11,100	19,737	25,753
Agriculture, forestry and fishing	3,199	4,695	5,004
Mining, manufacturing and construction	1,094	1,884	1,617
Roads and waterways	2,669	8,589	12,444
Other transport and communications	2,706	2,745	2,535
Other purposes	12,597	15,901	18,511
Interest payments	11,341	10,587	11,961
Transfers to other levels of government	1,256	2,314	3,543
Total	**70,660**	**102,135**	**143,897**
Current	60,834	80,703	111,802
Capital	9,826	21,432	32,095

† Excluding net lending (million cedis): 2,667 in 1986; 4,852 in 1987; 5,983 in 1988.

1989 (projections, million cedis): Revenue and grants 204,617; Expenditure and net lending 196,191.

INTERNATIONAL RESERVES (US $ million at 31 December)

	1987	1988	1989
Gold*	81.5	77.5	78.3
IMF special drawing rights	15.9	0.3	29.9
Foreign exchange	179.2	221.0	317.4
Total	**276.6**	**298.8**	**425.6**

* National valuation.
Source: IMF, *International Financial Statistics*.

MONEY SUPPLY (million new cedis at 31 December)

	1985	1986	1987
Currency outside banks	21,896.9	31,240.2	46,116.5
Official entities' deposits with monetary authorities	784.5	2,034.5	3,693.5
Demand deposits at commercial banks	20,789.7	31,344.9	42,041.8
Total money	**42,686.6**	**64,619.6**	**91,851.8**

Source: Research Dept, Bank of Ghana.

COST OF LIVING (Consumer Price Index for Accra; average of monthly figures. Base: 1977 = 100)

	1986	1987	1988
Food	2,871.5	4,068.0	5,454.0
Clothing	5,205.8	8,069.6	9,993.1
Rent, fuel and light	3,380.8	5,059.8	7,305.7
All items (incl. others)	**4,262.8**	**6,156.0**	**8,073.9**

GHANA

NATIONAL ACCOUNTS (million new cedis at current prices)
National Income and Product

	1985	1986	1987
GDP in purchasers' values	343,048.4	511,372.7	745,999.8
Net factor income from abroad	−5,768.5	−12,576.0	−20,458.6
Gross national product	337,279.8	498,796.7	725,541.2
Less Consumption of fixed capital	16,338.8	29,267.1	47,679.8
National income in market prices	320,941.0	469,529.6	677,861.4
Other current transfers from abroad (net)	7,421.5	20,016.0	29,723.1
National disposable income	328,362.5	489,545.6	707,584.5

Expenditure on the Gross Domestic Product

	1985	1986	1987
Government final consumption expenditure	32,241.0	56,595.6	76,331.8
Private final consumption expenditure	284,621.0	421,849.4	608,801.4
Increase in stocks	138.9	340.1	554.1
Gross fixed capital formation	32,688.5	49,087.6	79,969.8
Total domestic expenditure	349,689.4	527,872.7	768,658.1
Exports of goods and services	33,185.0	98,148.0	153,836.7
Less Imports of goods and services	39,826.0	114,648.0	176,494.0
GDP in purchasers' values	343,048.4	511,372.7	745,999.8
GDP at constant 1975 prices	5,420.1	5,701.9	5,975.6

Source: Bank of Ghana.

BALANCE OF PAYMENTS (US $ million)

	1987	1988	1989
Merchandise exports f.o.b.	826.8	881.0	807.2
Merchandise imports f.o.b.	−951.5	−993.4	−999.0
Trade balance	−124.7	−112.4	−191.8
Exports of services	72.4	71.4	75.5
Imports of services	−237.5	−255.0	−272.6
Other income received	6.9	6.3	6.4
Other income paid	−138.8	−144.6	−130.2
Private unrequited transfers (net)	201.6	172.4	202.1
Official unrequited transfers (net)	123.2	196.1	213.1
Current balance	−96.9	−65.8	−97.5
Direct investment (net)	4.7	5.0	15.0
Other capital (net)	251.1	204.0	221.0
Net errors and omissions	−18.7	37.9	17.1
Overall balance	140.2	181.1	155.6

Source: IMF, *International Financial Statistics*.

External Trade

PRINCIPAL COMMODITIES ('000 cedis)

Imports	1984	1985	1986
Food and live animals	1,171,275	1,892,025	47,218,134
Beverages and tobacco	249,163	733,592	20,508
Crude materials (inedible) except fuels	472,515	827,424	7,104,389
Mineral fuels, lubricants, etc.	7,603,686	13,786,621	3,158,337
Animal and vegetable oils and fats	268,308	301,553	6,352
Chemicals	1,895,506	5,896,401	42,146
Basic manufactures	2,983,427	5,060,600	7,649,155
Machinery and transport equipment	5,321,655	12,436,517	11,084
Miscellaneous manufactured articles	629,748	4,890,961	114,122
Other commodities and transactions	1,291,977	1,329,592	12,081,922
Total	21,887,260	47,155,286	77,406,149

Exports	1986	1987	1988
Cocoa	41,895,579	67,872,726	n.a.
Logs	2,682,012	n.a.	n.a.
Sawn timber	1,995,159	n.a.	n.a.
Bauxite	547,412	851,442	2,351,894
Manganese ore	894,811	1,205,743	1,738,043
Diamonds	561,231	696,996	710,094
Gold	11,915,233	24,205,589	49,417,526
Total (incl. others)	76,948,000	147,275,000	n.a.

PRINCIPAL TRADING PARTNERS ('000 cedis)

Imports	1983	1984*	1985*
Canada	75,958	122,554	384,680
China, People's Republic	54,397	199,847	445,812
France	217,012	395,804	1,036,690
Germany, Federal Republic	1,456,783	2,510,000	5,394,777
Italy	558,702	867,633	1,561,173
Japan	475,059	838,011	2,845,424
Libya	56,085	1,339	7,433
Netherlands	340,383	700,980	1,216,629
Nigeria	529,861	6,964,148	10,601,454
Norway	57,026	75,224	201,533
United Kingdom	2,580,179	3,689,357	11,843,832
USA	1,000,741	1,247,423	2,725,773
Total (incl. others)	11,021,818	20,871,000	39,826,000

Exports	1983	1984	1985*
Germany, Federal Republic	688,173	1,291,156	2,035,879
Japan	6,990,046	1,913,942	3,249,391
Netherlands	932,170	237,472	3,400,444
USSR	813,721	1,917,849	2,156,475
United Kingdom	1,009,065	3,230,081	6,806,297
USA	628,230	883,882	2,743,024
Yugoslavia	n.a.	89,522	328,770
Total (incl. others)	8,851,000	20,161,000	33,185,000

* Provisional figures.
Source: Ghana High Commission, London.

GHANA

Transport

RAILWAYS (traffic)

	1986	1987	1988
Passengers carried ('000)	2,908	3,486	3,259
Freight carried ('000 metric tons)	600.2	593.4	744
Passenger-km (million)	255.1	566.8	389.3
Net ton-km (million)	100.0	106.2	125.5

ROAD TRAFFIC ('000 motor vehicles in use at 31 December)

	1983
Passenger cars	52,864
Buses and coaches	15,995
Goods vehicles	7,380

Source: International Road Federation, *World Road Statistics*.

INTERNATIONAL SEA-BORNE SHIPPING
(estimated freight traffic, '000 metric tons)

	1984	1985	1986
Goods loaded	1,377	1,410	1,432
Goods unloaded	3,341	3,390	3,422

Source: UN Economic Commission for Africa, *African Statistical Yearbook*.

CIVIL AVIATION (traffic on scheduled services)

	1983	1984	1985
Kilometres flown (million)	3.0	2.5	3.1
Passengers carried ('000)	271	261	253
Passenger-km (million)	338	276	278
Freight ton-km (million)	6.6	7.5	9.4
Mail ton-km (million)	0.4	2.2	0.6
Total ton-km (million)	37	34	37.0

Source: UN, *Statistical Yearbook*.

Tourism

	1985	1986	1987
Tourist arrivals ('000)*	54.3	55.1	41.2

* Excluding arrivals of Ghanaian nationals residing abroad (62,214 in 1987).

Source: Ghana High Commission, London.

Communications Media

('000 in use)

	1980	1987	1988
Radio receivers	1,700	4,000	4,140
Television receivers	57	171	178

Education

(1988)

	Institutions	Teachers	Students
Pre-primary	3,932	14,665	285,865
Primary	9,634	65,826	1,705,843
Secondary*	5,589†	45,429	793,388
Teacher training	39†	1,038	15,306
Technical and vocational	22†	1,279	14,915
University	3†	1,160‡	8,327‡

* Including Middle and Junior Secondary schools.
† 1984/85 figures.
‡ 1986 figures.

Source: mainly UNESCO, *Statistical Yearbook*.

Directory

The Constitution

The 1979 Constitution was suspended following the military coup of 31 December 1981.

The Government

(February 1991)

HEAD OF STATE

Chairman of the Provisional National Defence Council: Flight-Lt JERRY RAWLINGS (assumed power 31 December 1981).

PROVISIONAL NATIONAL DEFENCE COUNCIL

Flight-Lt JERRY RAWLINGS (Chairman and Chief of Defence Staff).
Justice DANIEL F. ANNAN (Vice-Chairman).
EBO TAWIAH.
Alhaji IDDRISU MAHAMA.
Capt. (retd) KOJO TSIKATA.
P. V. OBENG.
Lt-Gen. ARNOLD QUAINOO.
Maj.-Gen. WINSTON M. MENSA-WOOD.
Dr MARY GRANT.
Col JEFF ASMAH.

COMMITTEE OF SECRETARIES

Chairman of the Committee of Secretaries: P. V. OBENG.
Secretary for Fuel and Power: ATO AHWOI.
Secretary for Trade and Tourism: HUUDU YAHAYA.
Secretary for Local Government and Rural Development: KWAMENA AHWOI.
Secretary for Internal Affairs: NII OKAIJA ADAMAFIO.
Secretary for Education and Culture: Dr MARY GRANT (acting).
Secretary for Youth and Sports: K. SAARAH-MENSAH.
Secretary for Foreign Affairs: Dr OBED ASAMOAH.
Secretary for Information: Dr MUHAMMAD BEN ABDALLAH.
Secretary for Transport and Communications: KWAME PEPRAH.
Secretary for Works and Housing: KENNETH AMPRATWUM.
Secretary for Industry, Science and Technology: Capt. K. A. BUTAH.

GHANA

Secretary for Justice and Attorney General: G. E. K. AIKINS.
Secretary for Agriculture: Cdre (retd) STEVE OBIMPEH.
Secretary for Roads and Highways: Col RICHARD COMMEY.
Secretary for Finance and Economic Planning: Dr KWESI BOTCHWEY.
Secretary for Health: NANA AKUODO SARPONG.
Secretary for Lands and Natural Resources: J. A. DANSOH.
Secretary for Mobilization and Productivity: D. S. BOATENG.
Secretary of Chieftaincy Affairs: EMMANUEL TANOH.

PROVISIONAL NATIONAL DEFENCE COUNCIL SECRETARIAT

Secretary responsible for the Committees for the Defence of the Revolution: WILLIAM YEBOAH.
Secretary responsible for the State Committee for Economic Co-operation: E. G. DON-ARTHUR.
Secretary responsible for the Committee of Cocoa Affairs: I. K. ADJEI-MARFO.
Secretary responsible for the National Commission for Democracy: JOYCE ARYEE.
Secretary responsible for the National Commission for Women and Development: SELINA TAYLOR.
Secretaries responsible for Political Programmes: KOFI TOTOBI QUAKYI, ATO DADZIE, YAW AKRASI-SARPONG.

REGIONAL SECRETARIES

Greater Accra: Lt-Col (retd) W. A. THOMSON.
Eastern: F. OHENE-KENA.
Volta: Dr FRANCIS AGBLEH (acting).
Brong Ahafo: J. H. OWUSU-ACHEAMPONG.
Ashanti: Col (retd) E. M. OSEI-OWUSO.
Central: ATO AUSTIN.
Northern: JOHN BAWA.
Upper East: KUNDAB MOLBILA.
Upper West: YELIBORA ANTUMINI.
Western Region: J. R. E. AMENLEMAH.

SECRETARIATS

Secretariat for Agriculture: POB M37, Accra; tel. 665421.
Secretariat for Defence: Burma Camp, Accra; tel. 777611; telex 2077.
Secretariat for Education and Culture: POB M45, Accra; tel. 665421.
Secretariat for Finance and Economic Planning: POB M40, Accra; tel. 665421; telex 2132.
Secretariat for Foreign Affairs: POB M53, Accra; tel. 665421; telex 2001.
Secretariat for Fuel and Power: POB M212, Accra; tel. 665421.
Secretariat for Health: POB M44, Accra; tel. 665421.
Secretariat for Industry, Science and Technology: POB M47, Accra; tel. 665421.
Secretariat for Information: POB M41, Accra; tel. 228011; telex 2201.
Secretariat for Internal Affairs: POB M42, Accra; tel. 665421.
Secretariat for Lands and Natural Resources: POB M212, Accra; tel. 665421.
Secretariat for Local Government and Rural Development: POB M50, Accra; tel. 665421.
Secretariat for Mobilization and Productivity: POB M84, Accra; tel. 665421.
Secretariat for Roads and Highways: POB M43, Accra.
Secretariat for Trade and Tourism: POB M47, Accra; tel. 665421; telex 2105 (temporarily closed Nov. 1989).
Secretariat for Transport and Communications: POB M38, Accra; tel. 665421.
Secretariat for Works and Housing: POB M43, Accra; tel. 665421.
Secretariat for Youth and Sports: Accra; tel. 665421.

Legislature

Parliament was dissolved following the December 1981 coup.

Political Organizations

Following the coup in December 1981, all political parties were proscribed, as they had been in 1966–69 and 1972–79. Several political groups are active, some operating mainly from outside Ghana:

Campaign for Democracy in Ghana (CDG): London, England; advocates return to democracy as a conduit to development; Leader Maj. (retd) BOAKYE DJAN.

The Dawn Group: London, England; socialist.

Ghana Democratic Movement (GDM): London, England; f. 1983; advocates the restoration of a liberal democratic system; Leader JOSEPH H. MENSAH.

Kwame Nkrumah Revolutionary Guards (KNRG): Accra; African socialist; Sec.-Gen. JOHN NDEBUGRE (acting).

Movement for Freedom and Justice (MFJ): Accra; f. 1990; seeks restoration of multi-party political system and civilian rule; Chair. Prof. ADU BOAHEN (acting); Sec.-Gen. OBENG MANU.

New Democratic Movement (NDM): Accra; socialist; Chair. KWAME KARIKARI.

United Revolutionary Front (URF): London, England; coalition of Marxist-Leninist groups.

Diplomatic Representation

EMBASSIES AND HIGH COMMISSIONS IN GHANA

Algeria: F606/1, off Cantonments Rd, Christiansborg, POB 2747, Accra; tel. 776828; Ambassador: HAMID BOURKI.

Benin: C175 Odoi Kwao Crescent, POB 7871, Accra; tel. 225701; Chargé d'affaires: L. TONOUKOUIN.

Brazil: 5 Volta St, Airport Residential Area, POB 2918, Accra; tel. 777154; telex 2081; Ambassador: CARLOS NORBERTO DE OLIVEIRA PARES.

Bulgaria: 3 Kakramadu Rd, East Cantonments, POB 3193, Accra; tel. 774231; Ambassador: KOSTADIN GEORGIEV GYAUROV.

Burkina Faso: 772/3, Asylum Down, off Farrar Ave, POB 651, Accra; tel. 221988; telex 2108; Ambassador: EMILE GOUBA.

Canada: No. 46, Independence Ave, POB 1639, Accra; tel. 228555; telex 2024; High Commissioner: SANDELLE SCRIMSHAW.

China, People's Republic: No. 7, Agostinho Neto Rd, Airport Residential Area, POB 3356, Accra; tel. 777073; Ambassador: CUI JIE.

Côte d'Ivoire: House No. 9, 8th Lane, off Cantonments Rd, POB 3445, Christiansborg, Accra; tel. 774611; telex 2131; Ambassador: KONAN NDA.

Cuba: 10 Ridge Rd, Roman Ridge, Airport Residential Area, POB 9163 Airport, Accra; tel. 775842; Ambassador: NICOLÁS RODRÍGUEZ.

Czechoslovakia: C260/5, Kanda High Rd No. 2, POB 5226, Accra-North; tel. 223540; Ambassador: ILJA ULRICH.

Egypt: 27 Noi Fetreke St, Roman Ridge, POB 2508, Accra; Ambassador: BAHAA ELDIN MOSTAFA REDA.

Ethiopia: House No. 6, Adiembra Rd, East Cantonment, POB 1646, Accra; tel. 775928; Chargé d'affaires a.i.: BEIDE MELAKU.

France: 12th Rd, off Liberation Ave, POB 187, Accra; tel. 228571; Ambassador: JEAN-FRANÇOIS LIONNET.

Germany: Valldemosa Lodge, Plot No. 18, North Ridge Residential Area, 7th Ave Extension, POB 1757, Accra; tel. 221311; telex 2025; Ambassador: BURGHART NAGEL.

Guinea: 11 Osu Badu St, Dzorwulu, POB 5497, Accra-North; tel. 777921; Ambassador: DORE DIALE DRUS.

Holy See: Airport Residential Area, POB 9675, Accra; tel. 777759; Apostolic Pro-Nuncio: Most Rev. GIUSEPPE BERTELLO, Titular Archbishop of Urbisaglia.

Hungary: F582 A/1, Salem Rd, Christiansborg, POB 3027, Accra; tel. 774917; Ambassador: RAYMOND TÓTH.

India: 9 Ridge Rd, Roman Ridge, POB 3040, Accra; tel. 777916; telex 2154; fax 772176; High Commissioner: S. K. UPPAL.

Iran: 10 Agbaamo St, Airport Residential Area, POB 1260073, Accra; tel. 74474; telex 2117; Ambassador: SHAMEDDIN KHAREGHANI.

Italy: Jawaharlal Nehru Rd, POB 140, Accra; tel. 775621; telex 2039; Ambassador: MARIO FUGAZZOLA.

Japan: 8 Rangoon Ave, off Switchback Rd, POB 1637, Accra; tel. 775616; telex 2068; Ambassador: SHIGERU KUROSAWA.

Korea, Democratic People's Republic: 139 Roman Ridge, Ambassadorial Estate, Nortei Ababio Estate, POB 13874, Accra; tel. 777825; Ambassador: YI HAE-SOP.

GHANA

Korea, Republic: 3 Abokobi Rd, East Cantonments, POB 13700, Accra; tel. 777533; Ambassador: HONG-WOO NAM.

Lebanon: off Cantonments Rd, OSU RE, POB 562, Accra; tel. 776727; telex 2118; Ambassador: Dr MUHAMMAD ISSA.

Liberia: F675/1, off Cantonments Rd, Christiansborg, POB 895, Accra; tel. 775641; telex 2071; Ambassador: T. BOYE NELSON.

Libya: 14 Sixth St, Airport Residential Area, POB 6995, Accra; tel. 774820; telex 2179; Secretary of People's Bureau: ABDULLAH JIBRAN.

Mali: Crescent Rd, Block 1, POB 1121, Accra; tel. 666421; telex 2061; Ambassador: MUPHTAH AG HAIRY.

Netherlands: 89 Liberation Rd, Sankara Circle, POB 3248, Accra; tel. 221655; telex 2128; Chargé d'affaires a.i.: S. H. BLOEMBERGEN.

Nigeria: Rangoon Ave, POB 1548, Accra; tel. 776158; telex 2051; High Commissioner: T. A. OLU-OTUNLA.

Pakistan: 11 Ring Rd East, POB 1114, Accra; tel. 776059; telex 2426; High Commissioner: SHAFQAT ALI SHEIKH.

Poland: 2 Akosombo St, Airport Residential Area, POB 2552, Accra; tel. 775972; telex 2558; Chargé d'affaires a.i.: KLEMENS WALKOWIAK.

Romania: North Labone, Ward F, Block 6, House 262, POB M112, Accra; tel. 774076; telex 2027; Chargé d'affaires: GHEORGHE V. ILIE.

Saudi Arabia: F868/1, off Cantonments Rd, OSU RE, Accra; tel. 776651; Chargé d'affaires: ANWAR ABDUL FATTAH ABDRABBUH.

Singapore: Accra.

Spain: Airport Residential Area, Lamptey Ave Extension, POB 1218, Accra; tel. 774004; Ambassador: MANUEL MARÍA GONZÁLEZ-HABA.

Switzerland: 9 Water Rd S.I., North Ridge Area, POB 359, Accra; tel. 228125; telex 2197; Ambassador: H. STRAUCH.

Togo: Togo House, near Cantonments Circle, POB 4308, Accra; tel. 777950; telex 2166; Ambassador: LARBLI TCHINTCHIBIDJA.

USSR: F856/1, Ring Rd East, POB 1634, Accra; tel. 775611; Ambassador: YEVGENY D. OSTROVENKO.

United Kingdom: Osu Link, off Gamel Abdul Nasser Ave, POB 296, Accra; tel. 221665; telex 2323; High Commissioner: ANTHONY MICHAEL GOODENOUGH.

USA: Ring Road East, POB 194, Accra; tel. 775346; Ambassador: STEPHEN R. LYNE.

Yugoslavia: 47 Senchi St, Airport Residential Area, POB 1629, Accra; tel. 775761; Ambassador: LAZAR COVIĆ.

Judicial System

The civil law in force in Ghana is based on the Common Law, doctrines of equity and general statutes which were in force in England in 1874, as modified by subsequent Ordinances. Ghanaian customary law is, however, the basis of most personal, domestic and contractual relationships. Criminal Law is based on the Criminal Procedure Code, 1960, derived from English Criminal Law, and since amended. The Superior Court of Judicature consists of the Supreme Court, the Court of Appeal and the High Court of Justice; the Inferior Courts include the Circuit Courts, the District Courts and such other Inferior Courts as may be designated by law.

Supreme Court: The Supreme Court consists of the Chief Justice and not fewer than four other Justices of the Supreme Court. It is the final court of appeal in Ghana and has jurisdiction in matters relating to the enforcement or interpretation of the Constitution.

Chief Justice: E. N. P. SOWAH.

The Court of Appeal: The Court of Appeal consists of the Chief Justice and not fewer than five Judges of the Court of Appeal. It has jurisdiction to hear and determine appeals from any judgment, decree or order of the High Court.

The High Court: The High Court comprises the Chief Justice and not fewer than 12 Justices of the High Court. It exercises original jurisdiction in all matters, civil and criminal, other than those for offences involving treason. Trial by jury is practised in criminal cases in Ghana and the Criminal Procedure Code, 1960, provides that all trials on indictment shall be by a jury or with the aid of Assessors.

The Circuit Court: Circuit Courts exercise original jurisdiction in civil matters where the amount involved does not exceed C100,000. They also have jurisdiction with regard to the guardianship and custody of infants, and original jurisdiction in all criminal cases, except offences where the maximum punishment is death or the offence of treason. They have appellate jurisdiction from decisions of any District Court situated within its circuit.

District Courts: To each magisterial district is assigned at least one District Magistrate who has original jurisdiction to try civil suits in which the amount involved does not exceed C50,000. District Magistrates also have jurisdiction to deal with all criminal cases, except first-degree felonies, and commit cases of a more serious nature to either the Circuit Court or the High Court. A Grade I Circuit Court can impose a fine not exceeding C1,000 and sentences of imprisonment of up to two years and a Grade II Circuit Court may impose a fine not exceeding C500 and a sentence of imprisonment of up to 12 months. A District Court has no appellate jurisdiction, except in rent matters under the Rent Act.

Juvenile Courts: Jurisdiction in cases involving persons under 17 years of age, except where the juvenile is charged jointly with an adult. The Courts comprise a Chairman, who must be either the District Magistrate or a lawyer, and not fewer than two other members appointed by the Chief Justice in consultation with the Judicial Council. The Juvenile Courts can make orders as to the protection and supervision of a neglected child and can negotiate with parents to secure the good behaviour of a child.

National Public Tribunal: Considers appeals from the Regional Public Tribunals. Its decisions are final and are not subject to any further appeal. The Tribunal consists of at least three members and not more than five, one of whom acts as Chairman.

Regional Public Tribunals: Hears criminal cases relating to prices, rent or exchange control, theft, fraud, forgery, corruption or any offence which may be referred to them by the Provisional National Defence Council.

Special Military Tribunal: Hears criminal cases involving members of the armed forces. It consists of between five and seven members.

Religion

According to the 1960 census, the distribution of religious groups was: Christians 42.8%, traditional religions 38.2%, Muslims 12.0%, unclassified 7.0%. In August 1989 a law on the registration of religious bodies was introduced, specifying a requirement to make application to the Religious Affairs Committee of the National Commission for Culture.

CHRISTIANITY

Christian Council of Ghana: POB 919, Accra; tel. 776725; f. 1929; advisory body comprising 14 Protestant churches; Chair. Rt Rev. D. A. KORANTENG; Gen. Sec. Rev. D. A. DARTEY.

The Anglican Communion

Anglicans are adherents of the Church of the Province of West Africa, with six dioceses in Ghana. The Archbishop of the Province is the Bishop of Liberia.

Bishop of Accra: Rt Rev. FRANCIS W. B. THOMPSON, Bishopscourt, POB 8, Accra; tel. 662292.

Bishop of Cape Coast: (vacant), Bishopscourt, POB 38, Cape Coast.

Bishop of Koforidua: Rt Rev. ROBERT OKINE, POB 980, Koforidua.

Bishop of Kumasi: Rt Rev. EDMUND YEBOAH, Bishop's House, POB 144, Kumasi.

Bishop of Sekondi: Rt Rev. THEOPHILUS ANNOBIL, POB 85, Sekondi.

Bishop of Sunyani and Tamale: Rt Rev. JOSEPH KOBINA DADSON, Bishop's House, POB 110, Tamale.

The Roman Catholic Church

Ghana comprises two archdioceses and seven dioceses. At 31 December 1986 there were 1,935,492 adherents in the country.

Ghana Bishops' Conference: National Catholic Secretariat, POB 9712, Airport, Accra; tel. 776491; telex 2471; f. 1960; Pres. Rt Rev. PETER KWASI SARPONG, Bishop of Kumasi.

Archbishop of Cape Coast: Most Rev. JOHN KODWO AMISSAH, Archbishop's House, POB 112, Cape Coast; tel. 2593.

Archbishop of Tamale: Most Rev. PETER POREKU DERY, Gumbehini Rd, POB 42, Tamale; tel. 2425.

Other Christian Churches

African Methodist Episcopal Zion Church: POB 239, Sekondi; Pres. Rev. Dr ZORMELO.

Christian Methodist Episcopal Church: POB 3906, Accra; Pres. Rev. YEIDI BAWA.

Evangelical-Lutheran Church of Ghana: POB 197, Kaneshie; tel. 223487; telex 2134; Pres. Rev. PAUL KOFI FYNN; 6,600 mems.

GHANA

Directory

Evangelical-Presbyterian Church: POB 18, Ho; tel. 755; f. 1847; Moderator Rt Rev. D. A. KORANTENG; 294,848 mems.

Ghana Baptist Convention: POB 1979, Kumas; Pres. L. SARPONG-MENSAH.

Ghana Conference of Seventh-day Adventists: Cape Coast; 24,100 mems.

Mennonite Church: POB 5485, Accra; f. 1957; Moderator Rev. S. T. OKRAH; Sec. ABRAHAM K. WETSEH; 800 mems.

Methodist Church of Ghana: Liberia Rd, POB 403, Accra; tel. 228120; independent since 1961; Pres. Rt Rev. Prof. K. A. DICKSON; Sec. Rev. Dr EBENEZER H. BREW RIVERSON; 320,000 mems.

Presbyterian Church of Ghana: POB 1800, Accra; tel. 662511; telex 2525; f. 1828; Moderator Rt Rev. D. A. KORANTENG; Sec. Rev. I. K. FOKUO; 422,438 mems.

Western African Union Mission of Seventh-day Adventists: POB 1016, Accra; tel. 223720; telex 2119; f. 1943; Pres. P. K. ASAREH; Sec. SETH A. LARYEA.

The African Methodist Episcopal Church, the F'Eden Church, and the Society of Friends (Quakers) are also active in Ghana.

In June 1989 the activities of the Church of Jesus Christ of Latter-day Saints (Mormons) and the Jehovah's Witnesses were banned. The groups were alleged to have conducted themselves in a manner not conducive to public order.

ISLAM

There are a considerable number of Muslims in the Northern Region. The majority are Malikees.

Chief Imam: Alhaji MUKITAR ABASS.

The Press

In March 1989 a new newspaper licensing law was introduced. All publications were required to apply to the Secretariat for Information for a licence.

NEWSPAPERS

Daily

Daily Graphic: Graphic Rd, POB 742, Accra; tel. 228911; f. 1950; state-owned; Editor SAM CLEGG; circ. 40,000.

The Ghanaian Times: New Times Corpn, Ring Rd West, POB 2638, Accra; tel. 228282; f. 1958; state-owned; Editor CHRISTIAN AGGREY; circ. 40,000.

The Pioneer: Abura Printing Works Ltd, POB 325, Kumasi; tel. 2204; f. 1939; Editor KI OPUKU ACHEAMPONG; circ. 100,000.

Weekly

Business Weekly: Ring Rd, Industrial Area South, POB 2351, Accra; tel. 226037; f. 1966; Man. Editor MARK BOTSIO; circ. 5,000.

The Catholic Standard: POB 765, Accra; tel. 220165; f. 1938; Roman Catholic; Editor ANTHONY BONNAH KOOMSON; circ. 30,400; (licence revoked Dec. 1985).

Champion: POB 6828, Accra-North; tel. 229079; Man. Dir MARK D. N. ADDY; Editor FRANK CAXTON WILLIAMS; circ. 300,000.

Christian Messenger: Presbyterian Book Depot Bldg, POB 3075, Accra; tel. 662415; telex 2525; f. 1883; English, Twi and Ga edns; Editor G. B. K. OWUSU; circ. 60,000.

Echo: POB 5288, Accra; f. 1968; Sundays; Man. Editor J. K. TSIBOE; circ. 30,000.

Evening News: POB 7505, Accra; tel. 229416; Man. Editor OSEI POKU; circ. 30,000.

Graphic Sports: POB 742, Accra; tel. 228911; circ. 60,000.

The Mirror: Graphic Rd, POB 742, Accra; tel. 228911; telex 2475; f. 1953; state-owned; Sundays; Editor E. N. O. PROVENCAL (acting); circ. 60,000.

New Nation: POB 6828, Accra-North; Man. Dir MARK D. N. ADDY; Editor S. N. SASRAKU; circ. 300,000.

The Palaver Tribune: POB 5018, Accra; f. 1970; Editor-in-Chief CHRISTIAN ASHER; Editor BENJAMIN BAAH ARMAH; circ. 100,000; (publication suspended).

Punch: POB 6828, Accra-North; f. 1976; Man. Dir MARK D. N. ADDY; Editor PRINCE K. GOSWIN; circ. 280,000; (publication suspended).

Sporting News: POB 5481, Accra-North; f. 1967; Man. Editor J. OPPONG-AGYARE.

Star: Accra; Editor J. W. DUMOGA.

The Statesman: Accra; Man. Edito: W. K. DUMOGA (acting).

Weekly Spectator: New Times Corpn, Ring Road West, POB 2638, Accra; state-owned; f. 1963; Sundays; Editor J. D. ANDOH KESSON; circ. 165,000.

PERIODICALS

Fortnightly

Ideal Woman (Obaa Sima): POB 5737, Accra; tel. 221399; f. 1971; Editor KATE ABBAM.

Legon Observer: POB 11, Legon; f. 1966; publ. by Legon Society on National Affairs; Chair. J. A. DADSON; Editor EBOW DANIEL.

New Ghana: Information Services Dept, POB 745, Accra; English; political, economic and cultural affairs.

Monthly

African Woman: Ring Rd West, POB 1496, Accra.

Boxing and Football Illustrated: POB 8392, Accra; f. 1976; Editor NANA O. AMPOMAH; circ. 10,000.

Chit Chat: POB 7043, Accra; Editor ROSEMOND ADU.

Drum: POB 1197, Accra; general interest.

Ghana Journal of Science: Ghana Science Asscn, POB 7, Legon; Editor Dr A. K. AHAFIA.

Kpodoga: Tsito; f. 1976; rural community newspaper publ. by the Inst. of Adult Education of Univ. of Ghana; monthly in Ewe, 3 a year in English; Editor YAO ADUAMAH; circ. 2,000.

Police News: Police HQ, Accra; Editor S. S. APPIAH; circ. 20,000.

The Scope: POB 8162, Tema; Editor EMMANUEL DOE ZIORKLUI; circ. 10,000.

Students World: POB M18, Accra; tel. 774248; telex 2171; f. 1974; educational; Man. Editor ERIC OFEI; circ. 10,000.

The Teacher: Ghana National Association of Teachers, POB 209, Accra; tel. 221515; f. 1931.

The Ghana Information Services (POB 745, Accra; tel. 228011) publish the following periodicals:

Akwansosem: Akuapim Twi; Editor FOSTER APPIAH.

Ghana Digest: UN, OAU and agency reports; Editor S. IKOI-KWAKU; circ. 12,000.

Ghana News Bulletin: f. 1974; Editor E. A. AFRO; circ. 8,000.

Ghana Review: f. 1961; economic, social and cultural affairs; Editor J. OPPONG-AGYARE; circ. 18,000.

Kabaare: f. 1967; edited by ISD; circ. 2,000.

Kakyevole: Nzema; Editor T. E. KWESI; circ. 10,500.

Kasem Labie (Kasem): POB 57, Tamale; Editor A. C. AZIIBA.

Lahabili Tsugu: POB 57, Tamale; Dagbani; Editor T. T. SULEMANA.

Mansralo: Ga; Editor MARTIN NII-MOI.

Motabiala: Ewe; Editor K. GROPONE; circ. 10,000.

Nkwantabisa: Asante, Twi and Fante; Editors FOSTER APPIAH (Twi), E. N. S. EDUFUL (Fante); circ. 20,000.

The Post: f. 1980; current affairs and analysis; circ. 25,000.

Volta Review: f. 1976; edited by ISD; circ. 3,000.

Quarterly

Armed Forces News: General Headquarters, Directorate of Public Relations, Burma Camp, Accra; f. 1966; Editor A. ANKRAH-HOFFMAN; circ. 8,000.

Ghana Enterprise: c/o Ghana National Chamber of Commerce, POB 2325, Accra; tel. 662427; telex 2687; fax 662210; f. 1961; Editor J. B. K. AMANFU.

Ghana Manufacturer: c/o Asscn of Ghana Industries, POB 8624, Accra-North; tel. 777283; f. 1974; Editor (vacant); circ. 1,500.

Insight and Opinion: POB 5446, Accra; Editorial Sec. W. B. OHENE.

Radio and TV Times: Ghana Broadcasting Corpn, Broadcasting House, POB 1633, Accra; tel. 221161; telex 2114; f. 1960; Editor ERNEST ASAMOAH; circ. 5,000.

NEWS AGENCIES

Ghana News Agency: POB 2118, Accra; tel. 665135; telex 2400; f. 1957; Gen. Man. KWAO LOTSU; 10 regional offices, 110 district offices and 1 overseas office.

Foreign Bureaux

Associated Press (AP) (USA): POB 6172, Accra; Bureau Chief P. K. COBBINAH-ESSEM.

Telegrafnoye Agentstvo Sovetskovo Soyuza (TASS) (USSR): POB 9141, Accra; Agent IGOR AGEBEKOV.

United Press International (UPI) (USA): POB 9715, Accra; tel. 225436; telex 2340; Bureau Chief R. A. QUANSAH.

Xinhua (New China) News Agency (People's Republic of China): 2 Seventh St, Airport Residential Area, POB 3897, Accra; tel. 772042; telex 2314.

Publishers

Advent Press: POB 0102, Osu, Accra; tel. 777861; telex 2119; f. 1937; Gen. Man. EMMANUEL C. TETTEH.

Adwinsa Publications (Ghana) Ltd: Advance Press Bldg, 3rd Floor, School Rd, POB 92, Legoh Accra; tel. 221654; f. 1977; general, educational; Man. Dir KWABENA AMPONSAH.

Afram Publications: 72 Ring Rd East, POB M18, Accra; tel. 774248; telex 2171; f. 1974; textbooks and general; Man. Dir ERIC OFEI.

Africa Christian Press: POB 30, Achimota; tel. 225554; f. 1964; religious, biography, paperbacks; Gen. Man. RICHARD A. B. CRABBE.

Asempa Publishers: POB 919, Accra; tel. 221706; f. 1970; religion, social questions, African music, fiction, children's books; Gen. Man. Rev. EMMANUEL BORLABI BORTEY.

Baafour and Co: POB K189, Accra New Town; f. 1978; general; Man. B. KESE-AMANKWAA.

Benibengor Book Agency: POB 40, Aboso; fiction, biography, children's books and paperbacks; Man. Dir J. BENIBENGOR BLAY.

Black Mask Ltd: POB 7894, Accra North; tel. 229968; f. 1979; textbooks, plays, novels, handicrafts; Man. Dir YAW OWUSU ASANTE.

Editorial and Publishing Services: POB 5743, Accra; general, reference; Man. Dir M. DANQUAH.

Educational Press and Manufacturers Ltd: POB 9184; Airport-Accra; tel. 220395; f. 1975; textbooks, children's books; Man. G. K. KODUA.

Emmanuel Publishing Services: POB 5282, Accra; tel. 225238; f. 1978; educational and children's books; Dir EMMANUEL K. NSIAH.

Encyclopaedia Africana Project: POB 2797, Accra; tel. 776939; f. 1962; reference; Dir E. T. ASHONG.

Frank Publishing Ltd: POB M414, Accra; f. 1976; secondary school textbooks; Man. Dir FRANCIS K. DZOKOTO.

Ghana Publishing Corpn: PMB Tema; tel. 2921; f. 1965; textbooks and general fiction and non-fiction; Man. Dir F. K. NYARKO.

Ghana Universities Press: POB 4219, Accra; tel. 225032; f. 1962; scholarly and academic; Dir A. S. K. ATSU.

Goodbooks Publishing Co: POB 10416, Accra North; tel. 665629; f. 1968; children's books; Man. A. ASIRIFI.

Miracle Bookhouse: POB 7487, Accra North; tel. 226684; f. 1977; general; Man. J. APPIAH-BERKO.

Moxon Paperbacks: POB M160, Accra; tel. 665397; fax 773593; f. 1967; travel and guide books, Africana, fiction and poetry; quarterly catalogue of Ghanaian books and periodicals in print; Man. Dir JAMES MOXON.

Sedco Publishing Ltd: Sedco House, Tabon St, North Ridge, POB 2051, Accra; tel. 221332; telex 2456; fax 2201070; f. 1975; educational; Man. Dir COURAGE KWAMI SEGBAWU.

Sheffield Publishing Co: POB 4432, Accra; tel. 222689; f. 1970; religion, politics, economics, science, fiction; Publr RONALD MENSAH.

Unimax Publishers Ltd: 42 Ring Rd South Industrial Area, POB 10722, Accra-North; tel. 227443; telex 2515; atlases, educational and children's books; Dir EDWARD ADDO.

Waterville Publishing House: POB 195, Accra; tel. 663124; f. 1963; general fiction and non-fiction, textbooks, paperbacks, Africana; Man. Dir A. S. OBUAM.

Woeli Publishing Services: POB K601, Accra New Town; f. 1984; children's books, fiction; Dir W. A. DEKUTSEY.

PUBLISHERS' ASSOCIATIONS

Ghana Book Development Council: POB M430, Accra; tel. 229178; f. 1975; agency of Ministry of Education; promotes and co-ordinates writing, production and distribution of books; Exec. Dir D. A. NIMAKO.

Ghana Book Publishers' Association: c/o Ghana Universities Press, POB 4219, Accra; Sec. W. A. DEKUTSEY.

Radio and Television

In 1989 there were an estimated 4m. radio receivers in use. There are internal radio broadcasts in English, Akan, Dagbani, Ewe, Ga, Hausa and Nzema; there is an external service in English and French. There are two sound transmitting stations and 53 relay stations. In 1986 a new radio station was constructed at Bolgatanga.

The television service came into operation in 1965; there are two studios in Accra and four transmission stations: Ajangote about 32 km from Accra, Kissi in the Central Region, Jamasi in Ashanti and Bolgatanga in the Northern Region. In 1987 new colour television equipment was commissioned in Accra. In 1989 there were an estimated 175,000 television receivers in use.

Ghana Broadcasting Corporation: Broadcasting House, POB 1633, Accra; tel. 221161; telex 2114; f. 1935; Dir-Gen. GEORGE M. ARYEE; Dep. Dir-Gen. DAVID ANAGLATE; Dir of TV JAMES CROMWELL; Dir of Radio KWASI AMOAKO.

Finance

(cap. = capital; p.u. = paid up; res = reserves; dep. = deposits; m. = million; brs = branches; amounts in cedis)

BANKING
Central Bank

Bank of Ghana: Thorpe Rd, POB 2674, Accra; tel. 666902; telex 2052; fax 662996; f. 1957; cap. and res 1,116.1m., dep. 37,995.3m.; Chair. Dr GODFRIED KPORTUFE AGAMA.

State Banks

Agricultural Development Bank: C288/3 Ring Rd Central, POB 4191, Accra; tel. 228453; telex 2295; f. 1965; state-owned; credit facilities for farmers and commercial banking; cap. p.u. 100m. (1987); Chair. NATHAN QUAO; Man. Dir P. A. KURANCHIE.

Bank of Credit and Commerce Ghana: 4 Graphic Rd, POB 11011, Accra; tel. 220788; telex 2208; cap. 25m. (1988); Chair. Dr J. L. S. ABBEY; Man. Dir AQEEL AHMED SIDDIQUI.

Bank for Housing and Construction (BHC): 24 Kwame Nkrumah Ave, POB M1, Adabraka, Accra; tel. 666143; telex 2096; f. 1983; cap. p.u. 20m. (Sept. 1988); Chair. Mrs GLORIA NIKOI; Man. Dir YAW OSAFO-MAAFO.

Ghana Commercial Bank: POB 134, Accra; tel. 664914; telex 2034; f. 1953; state-owned; cap. 2,000m. (1988), dep. 48,266m. (1986); 141 brs; Chair. ISSIFU ALI; Man. Dir KWAME NINI OWUSU.

Ghana Co-operative Bank: Kwame Nkrumah Ave, POB 5292, Accra-North; tel. 228735; telex 2446; f. 1970; cap. 119m. (Dec. 1988), dep. 3,200m. (August 1989); Chair. W. M. ASIMA; Man. Dir OKO NIKOI OZANIE; 49 brs.

National Investment Bank (NIB): 37 Kwame Nkrumah Ave, POB 3726, Accra; tel. 221312; telex 2161; f. 1963; 75% state-owned; provides long-term investment capital and consultancy, joint venture promotion, consortium finance management and commercial banking services; cap. 39m. (1988), res 837.6m., dep 6,262.6m. (Dec. 1987); Chair. JOHN KOBINA RICHARDSON; Man. Dir J. G. AWUAH.

National Savings and Credit Bank: Ring Rd Central, Accra; tel. 228322; telex 2383; f. 1972; 75% state-owned; cap. 30m. (1987), dep. 2,398.6m. (Dec. 1986); Chair. and Man. Dir J. A. NUAMAH.

National Trust Holding Co: Dyson House, Kwame Nkrumah Ave, POB 9563, Airport, Accra; tel. 229664; f. 1976 to finance Ghanaian acquisitions of indigenous cos; also assists in their development and expansion, and carries out trusteeship business; cap. p.u. 11.7m. (1988); Chair. YAW OSAFO-MAAFO; Man. Dir E. J. A. ARYEE.

Social Security Bank (SSB): POB 13119, Accra; tel. 221726; telex 2209; f. 1976; cap. p.u. 460m. (Dec. 1987); Chair. K. O. SACKEY; Man. Dir PRYCE KOJO THOMPSON.

Merchant Banks

Ecobank Ghana (EBG): POB 16746, Accra North; tel. 229532; f. 1989; cap. p.u. 900m. (Nov. 1990); Chair. J. S. ADDO.

Merchant Bank (Ghana) Ltd: Swanmill, Kwame Nkrumah Ave, POB 401, Accra; tel. 666331; telex 2191; fax 667305; f. 1972; 30% state-owned; cap. and res 601.8m., dep. 8,625.2m. (Dec. 1988); Chair. YAW MANU SARPONG; Man. Dir KWAKU AGYEI-GYAMFI; 3 brs.

Foreign Banks

Barclays Bank of Ghana Ltd (UK): High St, POB 2949, Accra; tel. 664901; telex 24194; fax 667420; f. 1971; 40% state-owned; cap. and res 2,157.7m., dep. 16,049.7m. (Dec. 1988); Chair. Prof. SAMUEL SEY; Man. Dir DAVID BROOKES; 39 brs.

Standard Chartered Bank Ghana Ltd (UK): Standard Bank Bldg, High St, POB 768, Accra; tel. 664591; telex 667751; f. 1896; cap. and res 2,323.9m., dep. 17,352.4m. (Dec. 1988); Chair. DAVID ANDOH; Man. Dir S. A. FLEMING; 28 brs.

INSURANCE

Ghana Union Assurance Co Ltd: POB 1322, Accra; tel. 664421; telex 3027; fax 221085; f. 1973; Man. Dir KWADWO DUKU.

GHANA

Directory

The Great African Insurance Co Ltd: POB 12349, Accra North; tel. 227459; telex 3027; f. 1980; Man. Dir E. Akoto-Bamfo.

The State Insurance Corporation of Ghana: POB 2363, Accra; tel. 666961; telex 2171; f. 1962; state-owned; undertakes all classes of insurance; also engages in real estate and other investment; Man. Dir Joe Donkor.

Social Security and National Insurance Trust: POB M149, Accra; f. 1972; covers over 1.25m. employees; Chief Admin. A. Awuku.

Vanguard Assurance Co Ltd: Insurance Hall, Derby House, Derby Ave, POB 1868, Accra; tel. 666485; telex 2005; fax 668610; f. 1974; general accident, marine, motor and life insurance; Man. Dir Nana Awuah-Darko Ampem; 7 brs.

Several foreign insurance companies operate in Ghana.

Trade and Industry

PUBLIC BOARDS AND CORPORATIONS

Bast Fibres Development Board: POB 1992, Kumasi; f. 1970; promotes the commercial cultivation of bast fibres and their processing, handling and grading.

Food Production Corporation: POB 1853, Accra; f. 1971; state corpn providing employment for youth in large scale farming enterprises; controls 76,900 ha of land (16,200 ha under cultivation); operates 87 food farms on a co-operative and self-supporting basis, and rears poultry and livestock.

Ghana Cocoa Board (COCOBOD): POB 933, Accra; telex 2082; f. 1985 to replace the Cocoa Marketing Board; responsible for purchase, grading and export of cocoa, coffee and shea nuts, and encourages production and scientific research aimed at improving quality and yield of cocoa, coffee and shea nuts; CEO David Aninakwa.

Ghana Consolidated Diamond Co Ltd: POB M108, Accra; telex 2058; f. 1986, to replace Diamond Marketing Corpn, to grade, value and process diamonds, buy all locally won, produced or processed diamonds, promote the industry; responsible for securing the most favourable terms for purchase, grading, valuing, export and sale of local diamonds; Chair. Kofi Agyeman.

Ghana Cotton Co Ltd: f. 1986 to replace Cotton Development Board; ownership: govt 70%, private textile cos 30%; 15 regional offices; Chair. Harry Ganda.

Ghanaian Enterprises Development Commission: Accra; f. 1975; assists the indigenization of the economy; especially small and medium-scale industrial and commercial enterprises, by providing loans and advisory services.

Ghana Food Distribution Corporation: POB 4245, Accra; tel. 228428; f. 1971; buys, stores, preserves, distributes and sells foodstuffs through 10 regional centres; Man. Dir Dr P. A. Kuranchie.

Ghana Industrial Holding Corporation (GIHOC): POB 2784, Accra; tel. 664998; telex 2109; f. 1967; controls and manages 26 state enterprises, including steel, paper, bricks, paint, pharmaceuticals, electronics, metals, canneries, distilleries and boat-building factories; also has three wholly-owned subsidiaries and four joint ventures; managed by an Interim Superintending Secretariat from April 1989.

Ghana Investment Centre: Central Ministerial Area, POB M193, Accra; tel. 665125; telex 2229; f. 1981 to replace Capital Investments Board; negotiates new investments, approves projects, registers foreign capital and decides extent of govt participation; Chair. Sec. for Finance and Economic Planning.

Ghana National Manganese Corporation: POB M183, Ministry PO, Accra; telex 2046; f. 1975 following nationalization of African Manganese Co mine at Nsuta; Chair. P. O. Aggrey; Man. Dir Dr A. O. Barnafo.

Ghana National Petroleum Corporation: Private Mail Bag, Tema, Accra-North; tel. (0221) 6020; telex 2188; fax 712916; f. 1983; exploration, development, production and disposal of petroleum; Chair. Tsatsu Tsikata; Exec. Dirs Eric Cato-Browne (Marketing), A. K. Addae (Research and Development), Augustus O. Tanoh (Finance and Administration).

Ghana National Trading Corporation (GNTC): POB 67, Accra; tel. 664871; f. 1961; organizes exports and imports of selected commodities; over 500 retail outlets in 14 admin. dists.

Ghana Standards Board: c/o POB M245, Accra; tel. 662606; telex 2289; f. 1967; establishes and promulgates standards; promotes standardization, industrial efficiency and development and industrial welfare, health and safety; operates certification mark scheme; 301 mems; Dir Dr E. K. Marfo; Dep. Dir Sam Boateng.

Ghana Water and Sewerage Corporation: POB M194, Accra; f. 1966 to provide, distribute and conserve water for public, domestic and industrial use, and to establish, operate and control sewerage systems.

Grains and Legumes Development Board: POB 4000, Kumasi; tel. 4231; f. 1970; state-controlled; promotes and develops production of cereals and leguminous vegetables.

Minerals Commission: 10 Sixth St, Airport Residential Area, Accra; tel. 772783; telex 2545; fax 773324; f. 1984; supervises, promotes and co-ordinates the minerals industry.

Posts and Telecommunications Corporation: Posts and Telecommunications Bldg, Accra-North; tel. 221001; telex 3010; f. 1974; provides both internal and external postal and telecommunication services; Dir-Gen. M. K. Gbagonah.

State Construction Corporation: Ring Rd West, Industrial Area, Accra; f. 1966; state corpn with a labour force of 7,000; construction plans are orientated to aid agricultural production; Man. Dir J. A. Danso, Jr.

State Farms Corporation: Accra; undertakes agricultural projects in all regions but Upper Region; Man. Dir E. N. A. Thompson (acting).

State Fishing Corporation: POB 211, Tema; telex 2043; f. 1961; govt-sponsored deep-sea fishing, distribution and marketing (including exporting) org.; owns 12 deep-sea fishing trawlers.

State Gold Mining Corporation: POB 109, Tarkwa; Accra Office, POB 3634; tel. 775376; telex 2348; f. 1961; manages four gold mines; CEO F. Awua-Kyerematen.

State Hotels Corporation: POB 7542, Accra-North; tel. 664646; telex 2113; f. 1965; responsible for all state-owned hotels, restaurants, etc. in 10 major centres; Man. Dir S. K. A. Obeng; Gen. Man. Eben Amoah.

State Housing Construction Co: POB 2753, Accra; f. 1982 by merger; oversees govt housing programme.

Timber Export Development Board: POB 515, Takoradi; tel. 2921; telex 2189; f. 1985; promotes the sale and export of timber; CEO (vacant).

CHAMBER OF COMMERCE

Ghana National Chamber of Commerce: POB 2325, Accra; tel. 662427; telex 2687; fax 662210; f. 1961; promotes and protects industry and commerce, organizes trade fairs; 2,500 individual mems and 10 mem. chambers; Pres. Isaac E. Yamson; Exec. Sec. John B. K. Amanfu.

COMMERCIAL AND INDUSTRIAL ORGANIZATIONS

Ghana Export Promotion Council: Republic House, POB M146, Accra; tel. 228813; telex 2289; fax 668263; f. 1972; chair. and mems appointed by Ghana Mfrs' Assen, Ghana Nat. Chamber of Commerce, Ghana Export Co, Capital Investment Bd, Secr. for Trade, Secr. for Agriculture and Ghana Armed Forces; Exec. Sec. Kwesi Ahwoi.

The Indian Association of Ghana: POB 2891, Accra; tel. 776227; f. 1939; Pres. Atmaram Gokaldas.

Institute of Marketing (IMG): Accra; f. 1981; reorganized 1989; aims to promote professional competence; Chair. I. E. Yamson; Pres. Frank Appiah.

EMPLOYERS' ASSOCIATION

Ghana Employers' Association: Kojo Thompson Rd, POB 2616, Accra; tel. 228455; f. 1959; 374 mems; Pres. J. V. L. Phillips; Vice-Pres. Andrew Cathline.

Affiliated Bodies

Association of Ghana Industries: POB 8624, Accra-North; tel. 777283; telex 3027; f. 1957; Pres. John K. Richardson; Exec. Sec. Eddie Imbeah-Amoakuh.

Ghana Booksellers' Association: POB 10367, Accra-North; tel. 227148; Pres. Sampson Brako; Gen. Sec. Fred J. Reimmer.

The Ghana Chamber of Mines: POB 991, Accra; tel. 662719; telex 2036; f. 1928; Pres. Sam E. Jonah.

Ghana Electrical Contractors' Association: POB 1858, Accra.

Ghana National Contractors' Association: c/o J. T. Osei and Co, POB M11, Accra.

Ghana Port Employers' Association: c/o Ghana Cargo Handling Co Ltd, POB 488, Tema.

Ghana Timber Association (GTA): POB 246, Takoradi; f. 1952; promotes, protects and develops timber industry; Chair. Tetteh Nanor.

CO-OPERATIVES

The co-operative movement began in Ghana in 1928 among cocoa farmers, and evolved into the country's largest farmers' organization. In 1944 the co-operative societies were placed under government supervision. The movement was dissolved by the Nkrumah government in 1960, but was re-established after the coup in 1966. It is now under the direction of a government-appointed secretary-general. In 1986 there were 8,387 co-operative societies. The structure of the movement places the co-operative associations at the top, co-operative unions in a secondary position of seniority in the towns, and village co-operative societies at the base.

Department of Co-operatives: POB M150, Accra; tel. 666212; f. 1944; govt-supervised body, responsible for registration, auditing and supervision of co-operative socs; Registrar R. BUACHIE-APHRAM; Sec.-Gen. J. M. APPIAH.

Ghana Co-operatives Council Ltd: POB 4034, Accra; f. 1951; co-ordinates activities of all co-operative socs; comprises 15 nat. co-operative asscns and five central socs; Sec.-Gen. JOHN MARTIN APPIAH.

The 15 co-operative associations include the Ghana Co-operative Marketing Asscn Ltd, the Ghana Co-operative Credit Unions Asscn Ltd, the Ghana Co-operative Agricultural Producers and Marketing Asscn Ltd, and The Ghana Co-operative Consumers' Asscn Ltd.

TRADE UNIONS

Ghana Trades Union Congress: Hall of Trade Unions, POB 701, Accra; f. 1945; all chairmen, general secretaries and vice-chairmen of 17 affiliated unions, and the constitution of the TUC were suspended in March 1982; Chair. Interim Man. Cttee D. K. Y. VOMAWOK; Sec.-Gen. H. DANZERL (acting).

The following Unions are affiliated to the Congress (figures refer to membership in 1979):

Construction and Building Workers' Union (46,000); General Agricultural Workers' Union (127,000); General Transport, Petroleum and Chemical Workers' Union (12,504); Private Road Transport Workers' Union (21,700); Health Services Workers' Union (12,000); Industrial and Commercial Workers' Union (115,052); Local Government Workers' Union (38,933); Maritime and Dockworkers' Union (23,720); Mine-workers' Union (22,000); National Union of Seamen (5,000); Post and Telecommunications Workers' Union (11,500); Public Services Workers' Union (45,000); Public Utility Workers' Union (25,000); Railway Enginemen's Union (701); Railway and Port Workers' Union (13,216); Teachers' and Educational Workers' Union (34,000); Timber and Woodworkers' Union (22,000).

Transport

State Transport Corporation: Accra; f. 1965 to succeed Govt Transport Dept; Man. Dir Lt-Col AKYEA-MENSAH.

RAILWAYS

There were 947 km of railways in 1986, connecting Accra, Kumasi and Takoradi. In 1988 the Italian government agreed to provide US $30m., and the World Bank approved a loan of $9.4m., towards a project to rehabilitate the railway network. In 1990 Ghana received a further loan of $32m. from France. Work was due to be completed in July 1992.

Ghana Railway Corporation: POB 251, Takoradi; tel. 2181; telex 2297; f. 1977; responsible for the operation and maintenance of all railways; Gen. Man. AMPONSAH ABABIO.

ROADS

In 1985 there were about 28,300 km of classified roads in Ghana. Of this total, 14,140 km were trunk roads and 14,160 km were feeder roads. There were also some 6,000 km of unclassified tracks, owned and managed by private mining and timber companies. Of the total road network, 5,782 km were paved in 1985, including 150 km of motorway. A major five-year programme of road development and rehabilitation, costing US $828m., was initiated in 1988. The Ghana–Burkina Faso Road Transport Commission, based in Accra, was set up to implement the 1968 agreement on improving communications between the two countries. The road between Accra and Abidjan, Côte d'Ivoire, forms part of the planned Transafrica Highway. In 1991 the Government allocated a projected 10.3% of total expenditure to the rehabilitation of roads.

Ghana Highway Authority: POB 1641, Accra; tel. 666591; telex 2359; f. 1974 to plan, develop, classify and maintain roads and ferries; CEO H. O. A. QUAYNOR.

SHIPPING

The two main ports are Tema (near Accra) and Takoradi, both of which are linked with Kumasi by rail. The rehabilitation of the two ports, at an estimated cost of US $100m., was completed in 1990. The port was to be equipped with modern mechanical handling equipment to enable a quicker turn-round of ships. In 1983 goods loaded totalled an estimated 1.12m. metric tons, and goods unloaded an estimated 2.52m. tons.

Alpha (West Africa) Line Ltd: POB 451, Tema; telex 2184; operates regular cargo services to west Africa, the UK, the USA, the Far East and northern Europe; agents for Mercandia (West Africa) Line, Cameroon National Line, Pakistan National Lines, Uiterwyk West Africa Lines and Great South America Line; Man. Dir E. COLLINGWOODE-WILLIAMS.

Black Star Line Ltd: 4th Lane, Kuku Hill Osu, POB 2760, Accra; tel. 776161; telex 2019; f. 1957; state-owned; operates passenger and cargo services to Europe, the UK, Canada, the USA, the Mediterranean and west Africa; agents for Gold Star Line, Woermann Line, Zim West Africa Lines, Cie Maritime Belge, Seven Stars (Africa) Line, Société Ivoirienne de Transport Maritime (SITRAM), and Cie Maritime Zaïroise (CMZ); fleet of 5 freighters; displacement 59,495 g.r.t.; Man. Dir HERON R. BLAGOGEE.

Holland West-Afrika Lijn N.V.: POB 269, Accra; POB 216, Tema; and POB 18, Takoradi; cargo services to and from North America and the Far East; agents for Royal Interocean Lines and Dafra Line.

Liner Agencies (Ghana) Ltd: POB 66, Accra; tel. 222680; telex 2396; freight services to and from UK, Europe, USA, Canada, Japan and Far East; intermediate services between West African ports; agents for Barber W.A. Line, Elder Dempster Lines, Guinean Gulf Line, Kawasaki Kisen Kaisha, Mitsui OSK Lines, Nigerian National Shipping Line, Marine Chartering of San Francisco, A/S Bulkhandling of Oslo, Botany Bay Shipping Co, SITRAM, CMZ and Palm Line; Man. Dir M. N. ANKUMA.

Remco Shipping Lines Ltd: POB 3898, Accra; tel. 224609; displacement 11,880 g.r.t.

Scanship (Ghana) Ltd: CFAO Bldg, High St, POB 1705, Accra; tel. 664314; telex 2181; agents for Maersk Line, Splosna Plovba Line, Hoegh Line, Jadranska Slobodna Plovidba-Split, Keller Shipping, Polish Ocean Line, DSR Line, Estonian Shipping Co, Euro-Africa Line, Spliethoffs Shipping Corpn of India.

CIVIL AVIATION

The main international airport is at Kotoka (Accra). There are also airports at Takoradi, Kumasi, Sunyani and Tamale. In 1988 Ghana received a loan of US $12m. from France to finance the rehabilitation of Kotoka Airport (at a total cost of $55.5m.), which was due to start in 1991.

Gemini Airlines Ltd: America House, POB 7328, Accra-North; tel. 665785; f. 1974; operates once-weekly cargo flight between Accra and London; Dir V. OWUSU; Gen. Man. P. F. OKINE; fleet of one B-707F.

Ghana Airways Corporation: Ghana House, POB 1636, Accra; tel. 664856; telex 2489; fax 777675; f. 1958; state-owned; operates domestic services and international routes to west African destinations, Italy, the Federal Republic of Germany and the UK; Chair. W. A. ADDA; Man. Dir Wing-Commdr J. B. AZARIAH; fleet of one DC-10-30, two Fokker F28, one DC 9-50.

Tourism

Ghana's attractions include fine beaches, game reserves, traditional festivals, and old trading forts and castles. In 1989 there were 125,162 tourist arrivals and revenue from tourism totalled US $72.1m. In 1990 a government programme to expand tourism was initiated.

Ghana Tourist Board: Ministry of Trade and Tourism, 1st Floor, POB 3106, Accra; tel. 665441; telex 2143; f. 1968; Exec. Dir EDMUND Y. OFOSU-YEBOAH.

Ghana Association of Tourist and Travel Agencies: Ramia House, Kojo Thompson Rd, POB 7140, Accra; Pres. JOSEPH K. ANKUMAH; Sec. JOHNNIE MOREAUX.

Ghana Tourist Development Co Ltd: POB 8710, Accra; tel. 772084; telex 2714; fax 772093; f. 1974; develops tourist infrastructure, including hotels, restaurants and casinos; operates foreign exchange, duty-free and diplomatic shops; Man. Dir BETTY AKUFFO-AMOABENG.

Atomic Energy

Atomic Energy Commission: POB 80, Legon/Accra; construction of a nuclear reactor at Kwabenya, near Accra, which was begun in 1964, was suspended 1966–74; the Commission's present activities are mainly concerned with the applications of radio-isotopes in agriculture and medicine; Chair. Dr A. K. AHAFIA.

GREECE

Introductory Survey

Location, Climate, Language, Religion, Flag, Capital
The Hellenic Republic lies in south-eastern Europe. The country consists mainly of a mountainous peninsula between the Mediterranean Sea and the Aegean Sea, bounded to the north by Albania, Yugoslavia and Bulgaria, and to the east by Turkey. To the south, east and west of the mainland lie numerous Greek islands, of which the largest is Crete. The climate is Mediterranean, with mild winters and hot summers. The language is Greek, of which there are two forms—the formal language (katharevoussa) and the language commonly spoken and taught in schools (demotiki). Almost all of the inhabitants profess Christianity, and the Greek Orthodox Church, to which about 97% of the population adhere, is the established religion. The national flag (proportions 3 by 2) displays a white cross on a blue background. The capital is Athens.

Recent History
The liberation of Greece from the German occupation was followed by a civil war which lasted until 1949. The Communist forces were defeated, and the constitutional monarchy re-established. King Konstantinos (Constantine) acceded to the throne on the death of his father, King Paul, in 1964. A succession of weak governments and conflicts between the King and his ministers, and an alleged conspiracy involving military personnel who supported the Centre Union Party, resulted in a coup, led by right-wing army officers, in April 1967. An attempted counter-coup, led by the King, failed, and he went into exile. Colonel Georgios Papadopoulos emerged as the dominant personality in the new regime, becoming Prime Minister in December 1967 and Regent in March 1972. The regime produced nominally democratic constitutional proposals, but all political activity was banned and opponents of the regime were expelled from all positions of power or influence.

Following an abortive naval mutiny, said to be supported by the exiled King, Greece was declared a republic in June 1973. Papadopoulos was appointed President in July. Martial law was ended, and a civilian cabinet was appointed in preparation for a general election to be held by the end of 1973. A student uprising at the Athens Polytechnic in November 1973 was violently repressed by the army, and another military coup overthrew Papadopoulos. Lieut-Gen. Phaidon Ghizikis was appointed President, and a mainly civilian cabinet, led by Adamantios Androutsopoulos, was installed, but effective power lay with a small group of officers and the military police under Brig.-Gen. Demetrios Ioannides. As a result of the failure of the military junta's attempt to overthrow President Makarios of Cyprus and its inability to prevent the Turkish invasion of the island (see chapter on Cyprus), the Androutsopoulos Cabinet disintegrated in July 1974. President Ghizikis called Konstantinos Karamanlis, a former Prime Minister, back from exile to form a civilian Government of National Salvation. Martial law was ended, the press was freed from state control, and political parties, including the Communists, were allowed to emerge. A general election in November 1974 resulted in a decisive victory for Karamanlis' New Democracy (Nea Dimokratia—ND) party, which gained 54% of the votes cast and won 220 of the 300 seats in Parliament. A referendum in December 1974 rejected proposals for a return to constitutional monarchy, and in June 1975 a new republican constitution, providing for a parliamentary democracy, was promulgated. In the same month Prof. Konstantinos Tsatsos, a former cabinet minister, was elected President.

In the general election of November 1977 ND was re-elected with a reduced majority. In May 1980 Karamanlis was elected President and resigned as Prime Minister. The new leader of ND, Georgios Rallis, formed a government, reshuffling the previous Cabinet. He faced a growing challenge from the rising Panhellenic Socialist Movement (Panellinion Sosialistikon Kinema—PASOK). In the general election of October 1981 PASOK gained an absolute majority in Parliament. Its leader, Andreas Papandreou, became Prime Minister of the first socialist Government in Greek history, which was initially committed to withdrawal from the EEC, removal of US military bases, and to implementing an extensive programme of reform. By the end of 1982 domestic reforms included the lowering of the voting age to 18; legalization of civil marriage and divorce, while adultery was no longer to be a criminal offence; and a restructuring of the university system. Proposed radical 'socialization' of industry encountered widespread opposition and was largely limited to the introduction of worker participation in supervisory councils. Index-linking of wage increases to the rate of inflation, one of the first measures that the PASOK Government had introduced, was modified at the end of 1982 in an attempt to reduce inflation, and a 'freeze' on wages was imposed from January 1983. After a series of strikes in the first half of 1983, a controversial law was adopted in June, increasing worker participation in the public sector, but also limiting the right to strike: this measure was strongly opposed by the Communists, who had hitherto generally supported the Government's domestic policy. A prices and incomes policy, announced in December, provided for wage indexation in the public sector in 1984, and for price controls. The unions withdrew their demands for wage indexation in the private sector, and a back-dated general wage increase was agreed in February 1984. In the elections to the European Parliament, held in June 1984, PASOK slightly increased its percentage of the votes in comparison with the 1981 election, winning 10 of the 24 seats, while ND won nine.

In March 1985 Papandreou unexpectedly withdrew support for President Karamanlis' candidature for a further five-year term in office. The Prime Minister planned to amend the 1975 Constitution, proposing to relieve the President of all executive power and transfer it to the legislature, thus reducing the Head of State to a purely ceremonial figure. President Karamanlis resigned in protest at the proposed changes, and Parliament elected Christos Sartzetakis, a judge, as President, in a vote that was widely considered to be unconstitutional. A general election was held in June to enable the Government to secure support for the proposed constitutional changes. PASOK was returned to power, receiving 45.8% of the total votes (compared with 48% in 1981) and winning 161 seats in the 300-member Parliament. The main opposition party, ND, received 41% of the votes and secured 126 seats.

In October 1985 the Government introduced a stringent two-year programme of economic austerity, thus provoking widespread industrial unrest, which continued throughout Greece in 1986.

In March 1986 the Greek Parliament approved a series of constitutional amendments (denounced by ND as 'a step towards autocratic rule') limiting the powers of the President, whose executive powers were transferred to the legislature. The amendments limited the President's power to call a referendum and transferred to Parliament the right to declare a state of emergency. The President lost the right to dismiss the Prime Minister, and was to be permitted to dissolve Parliament only if the resignation of two governments in quick succession demonstrated the absence of political stability. However, the President was still allowed a substantial moderating role by the use of his right to object to legislation and to request Parliament to reconsider it or to approve it with an enlarged majority.

In an extensive government reshuffle in April 1986, Papandreou relinquished the portfolio of National Defence, and the Ministries of the Interior and of Public Order reverted to their separate status. At the local elections held throughout Greece in October 1986, the ruling PASOK lost substantial support to both ND and the Communist Party of Greece ('of the Exterior') (KKE—'Exterior'). Despite Papandreou's attempt to operate a tactical alliance between PASOK and the Communists, three ND candidates were elected as mayors in Greece's three largest cities—Athens, Piraeus and Thessaloniki. A government reshuffle in October, which reduced the Cabinet from 48 to 36 members, was widely criticized for failing to remove those ministers generally considered to be most responsible for PASOK's decline in popularity.

GREECE

In April 1987 the Government came into conflict with the Greek Orthodox Church when Parliament approved legislation allowing the State to expropriate about 140,000 ha of monastic land and to administer the Church's valuable urban assets. The Church (while agreeing in principle to the redistribution of its agricultural land) argued that the new law would destroy its autonomy, and threatened to sever its constitutional links with the State; it organized mass public demonstrations in opposition to the proposals. As a result, the Government withdrew the legislation in August, and in November an agreement was reached whereby the monastic land would be jointly administered by the Church and the State, and the Church would retain its urban property.

In May 1987, in response to numerous accusations made by ND of mismanagement and corruption on the part of the Government in the public sector, Papandreou sought and won (by 157 votes to 139) a parliamentary vote of confidence in his Government.

Opposition to the Government's economic austerity programme continued in 1987, with further strikes and demonstrations (supported by the principal trade union confederation, which had previously been loyal to the Government). The introduction of value-added tax in January proved to be particularly unpopular. Despite the scale of the opposition and the upheaval that the strikes caused in the towns, the Government's sole initial concession was to make a small adjustment of wages at the lower end of the salary scale in February. In November, however, Papandreou, confronted by continuing protests (and, according to some, with a view to regaining public support for PASOK in the forthcoming general election, due in 1989), modified the austerity programme by advancing the payment of 1988 wage increases from May to January; this prompted the resignation of the Minister of National Economy, who had been the main instigator of the programme.

Despite a series of disruptive strikes (in protest against a scarcity of resources and low levels of earnings) by teachers and doctors in early June 1988, a parliamentary motion expressing 'no confidence' in the Government proposed by the opposition parties, was rejected by 157 votes to 123. At the end of the month Papandreou carried out a cabinet reshuffle (which included the appointment of his son, Georgios Papandreou, as the new Minister of Education and Religion) in preparation for the next general election, due to take place in June 1989. However, the Government suffered a serious set-back in November 1988, when several leading members of the Cabinet were implicated in a major financial scandal involving the alleged embezzlement of large amounts of money from the Bank of Crete. As a result of these allegations, the Minister of Justice and the Minister of Public Order resigned from their posts. In an attempt to suppress opposition demands for the resignation of the entire Cabinet and the holding of an early general election, the Prime Minister carried out a further cabinet reshuffle, including the abolition of the important post of Deputy Prime Minister. Between November and December five more ministers either resigned or were dismissed, after denouncing government corruption. In December, however, Parliament approved the Government's 1989 budget proposals. This did not prevent the opposition parties from renewing their demand for immediate elections.

In January 1989 the Greek Left Party (Elliniki Aristera—EAR), led by Leonidas Kyrkos, formed an electoral alliance with the KKE ('Exterior'), under the leadership of Charilaos Florakis, to create the Left Coalition. Throughout the first half of 1989 a number of disruptive strikes were organized in protest against the Government's continuing policies of economic austerity and to demand wage increases. In early March ND introduced a parliamentary motion expressing 'no confidence' in the PASOK Government. The Government survived this attempt to force its resignation, despite abstentions by three senior PASOK members, who were subsequently expelled from the party. On the same day as the holding of the no-confidence vote, however, the Government suffered a further set-back as a result of the Bank of Crete affair, when Agamemnon Koutsogiorgas, the Minister to the Prime Minister and former Minister of Justice, resigned from his post, following allegations of his involvement in the embezzlement scandal. A few days later, in an apparent attempt to restore PASOK's waning popularity and to stem the increasing demands for his resignation, Papandreou implemented another cabinet reshuffle.

At the next general election, which was held on 18 June 1989 (coinciding with elections to the European Parliament), ND won the largest proportion of votes cast (44%, while PASOK and the Left Coalition gained 39% and 13% respectively), but failed to attain an overall majority in Parliament, thus rendering the election inconclusive. Following the failure of both ND and, then, PASOK to reach an agreement with the Left Coalition to form a coalition government, the President's mandate was automatically passed to Charilaos Florakis, the leader of the Left Coalition. In a development which surprised many observers, the Left Coalition agreed to form an interim coalition government with ND, on the condition that the ND leader, Konstantinos Mitsotakis, renounced his claim to the premiership. Accordingly, Tzannis Tzannetakis, an ND deputy for Athens, was appointed Prime Minister in a new 23-member cabinet, which included two Communist ministers (in charge of the Ministries of Justice and the Interior). The unprecedented Conservative-Communist coalition Government was sworn in on 2 July. The Government announced its intention to govern for about three months, during which time it would aim to implement a *katharsis* (campaign of purification), investigating and, if necessary, prosecuting officials of the former socialist Government, including Papandreou, who were alleged to have been participants in a number of scandals involving banking, armaments and financial transactions. Following the investigations, a fresh general election was to be held. At the end of September, Parliament ruled that Papandreou, who was recovering from a serious bout of ill health, and four of his former ministers should be tried before a special court for alleged involvement in the Bank of Crete affair, illegal telephone-tapping and illegal grain sales. In early October Tzannetakis and his Cabinet resigned from their posts, claiming that the Government's aim of initiating a *katharsis* of Greek politics had been fulfilled. A few days later, the President of the Supreme Court, Yannis Grivas, was appointed Prime Minister in a new 20-member interim cabinet composed of non-political personalities, which was to oversee the year's second general election. Once again, Greece was faced with a political impasse, however, following the election, which was held on 5 November, when the results showed only minor changes compared with the outcome in June (ND won 46% of the total votes, PASOK 41% and the Left Coalition 11%). The political crisis was temporarily resolved in mid-November when ND, PASOK and the Left Coalition, disregarding their differences, agreed to form an all-party coalition government that would administer the country until a further general election was held in April 1990 (subsequently scheduled to be held on 8 April). Xenofon Zolotas, a former Governor of the Bank of Greece, was appointed Prime Minister to lead the new 21-member interim Cabinet. However, following a dispute over military promotions in mid-February 1990, the all-party coalition Government collapsed, and the same non-political group of people who had overseen the November election was reinstated to govern as an 'ecumenical' cabinet until the general election. Attempts by Parliament, later in the month, to elect a Head of State by a two-thirds majority were unsuccessful, owing largely to a decision taken by the 148 ND representatives to abstain from voting, following the refusal of their candidate, Konstantinos Karamanlis, to take part in the election. In the first round of voting Christos Sartzetakis, the incumbent President, failed to be re-elected and was joined in defeat in the second round of voting by PASOK candidate Yannis Alevras. A third attempt to elect a President, in early March, also proved unsuccessful, as ND representatives continued to abstain, thereby denying any candidate the 60% support required for election in the third round of voting.

A general election took place on 8 April 1990, finally resolving the parliamentary deadlock which had resulted from elections held in June and November 1989. ND (which had campaigned on a platform of free-market economic policies, a severe reduction in government spending and the maintenance of US military bases in Greece) secured 46.9% of the votes cast and 150 seats in the 300-seat Parliament. Following the announcement of the results, Mitsotakis met Kostis Stefanopoulos, the leader of Democratic Renewal (Komma Dimokratikis Ananeosis—DIANA) and a former member of ND, who guaranteed, for the ND, the support of DIANA's one elected parliamentary representative, Theodoros Katsikis (who formally joined the ND in June 1990), thereby enabling Mitsotakis to form the first single-party Government since 1981. Losses by left-wing parties were compensated, to some extent, by the election of four independent candidates supported by PASOK and the Left Coalition. Two representatives of the Turkish Muslim population in Thrace and an ecologist candidate were also elected to Parliament.

In late April 1990 Parliament approved a motion of confidence in the Government, following reaffirmation by the new administration of its intention to implement widespread economic reforms, including the abolition of an index-linked incomes policy (in favour of collective bargaining) by the beginning of 1991, the introduction of measures to combat tax evasion and the halving of the country's huge public-sector deficit by 1992. Among provisions included in a series of emergency economic measures, introduced later in the month, were increases in the price of electricity, fuels, public transport and postal rates, a 2% increase in the lower rates of value-added tax, and surcharges of 7% on taxes paid in 1989 on professional income and non-reinvested company profits.

On 5 May 1990 Konstantinos Karamanlis took office as President for a five-year term, following his election in Parliament by an outright majority of 153 in a second round of voting held on the previous day.

The failure of interim governments to reach a consensus on comprehensive economic programmes, and the unpopularity of austerity measures introduced by the new Government, led to widespread industrial unrest. Throughout 1990 appeals by trade unions (particularly the Greek General Confederation of Labour—GSEE) for 24- and 48-hour general strikes were regularly supported by more than 1m. workers, seriously disrupting public services and industry. Public disaffection with economic policies pursued by the Government was exacerbated following the announcement, in May, of a programme of divestment and liquidation for 49 ailing state-owned companies, and the ratification, in July, of an economic development bill providing for the redundancy of thousands of workers employed by non-profit-making state-owned companies, the introduction of longer opening hours for shops and a fourth shift for workers, while encouraging private enterprise and foreign investment. In September 1990 further industrial action was undertaken in response to a social security reform bill, ratified at the end of the month, which sought to merge several ineffective pension funds into the state welfare organization (itself heavily indebted) and to raise the retirement age to 58 for women and to 60 for men by 1998. Further stoppages and demonstrations followed the announcement by the Government in December of plans to implement new legislation restricting the right to strike as part of a new programme to combat terrorist violence. Opponents maintained that the bill, which was later amended, was in contravention of international human rights agreements.

In August 1990 Nikos Athanasopoulos, a former PASOK Deputy Finance Minister, was found guilty by a specially-created criminal tribunal of criminal fraud and forgery through direct involvement in the re-sale of maize originating from Yugoslavia but marketed as Greek produce in order to avoid paying EEC duties, and was sentenced to three years' imprisonment. The head of a state-owned trading company and four Finance Ministry and customs officials were also found guilty of involvement in the affair. In October former PASOK Ministers of Public Order (Georgios Petsos) and Justice (Agamemnon Koutsogiorgas) were detained by the authorities, pending their trial in connection with alleged embezzlement from the Bank of Crete. Former PASOK Prime Minister Papandreou, who had been implicated in the embezzlement scandal, was also scheduled to stand trial before a 12-member tribunal of senior judges, in March 1991, for alleged corruption in office. Although Papandreou continued to refuse to recognize the need for him to testify, the Government, anxious to avoid a public confrontation with the former leader, was unlikely to endorse a forcible summons.

In December 1990 and January 1991 students and teachers' unions organized a series of demonstrations and illegal occupations of educational establishments, in protest at education reform proposals announced by the Government. The conflict intensified when a confrontation between rival groups resulted in the death of a teacher in Patras and when violent clashes with security forces occurred, following which four bodies were found in a building that had been set alight during the demonstrations. The intensity of opposition to the reforms forced the Minister of Education, Vassilios Kontoyiannopoulos, to resign and prompted his replacement, Georgios Souflias (the former Minister of Economy) to withdraw many of the proposals immediately. Talks aimed at settling the dispute had collapsed by mid-January 1991, however, and many elementary schools, high schools and universities continued to be disrupted by industrial action undertaken by teachers' unions.

Despite apparent public dissatisfaction with many policies instigated by the new administration, the ND were unexpectedly successful in municipal elections held in October 1990, winning in 136 of the 359 contested towns, including Thessaloniki and Athens (where a pro-ND independent candidate, Antonis Tritsis, was elected mayor, narrowly defeating former PASOK Minister for Culture, Melina Merkouri). PASOK and the Left Coalition, which presented joint candidates for many seats, won in a combined total of 213 towns, including Piraeus, Patras and Iraklion. In November 1990 reforms to the electoral law, proposed by the ND, which provided for a modified form of proportional representation in which a minimum of 3% of the national vote in a general election would be required by political parties wishing to appoint representatives to Parliament, were finally ratified. The new electoral system, which also contained procedural disincentives to the formation of political alliances to contest elections, gave rise to vehement opposition from left-wing parties, which considered the reforms to be unconstitutional.

The Government suffered a serious reversal in late December 1990, when proposals put forward by the Prime Minister for the release of 13 military officers, serving sentences of life imprisonment for seizing power in the 1967 military coup, elicited universal public and political condemnation and were immediately withdrawn.

The treaty of accession to the European Communities was signed in May 1979 and Greece became a full member in January 1981. Although originally critical of Greece's membership, the Socialist Government confined itself to seeking modification of the terms of accession, in order to take into account the under-developed Greek economy, and gave qualified assent to concessions proposed by the EEC in April 1983.

In September 1983, despite its pledge to remove US military bases, the Government signed a five-year agreement on defence and economic co-operation with the USA: the four existing US bases were to remain, and Greece was to receive US $300m.–$500m. worth of military aid annually. In November 1986 a Greek-US agreement on defence and industrial co-operation was signed. Under this five-year agreement, the USA agreed to help Greece to modernize its military industry and armed forces. A new defence co-operation agreement was signed in July 1990 between the Greek Minister of Foreign Affairs, Antonis Samaras, and the US Secretary of Defense, Richard Cheney. The agreement provided for the closure of two military bases (one at Hellenikon and the other a naval communications facility at Nea Makri) and the continuation of US annual military aid to Greece (at the level of US $345m. per year) as a form of rent for the two remaining bases, together with the provision of aircraft and naval destroyers worth $1,000m. in total. The new agreement, which was to be valid for eight years and replaced the 1983 Defence and Economic Co-operation Agreement (which had expired in December 1988 but had been extended at six-monthly intervals since then in view of the unstable political situation in Greece), encountered domestic opposition from left-wing parties anxious to curtail US involvement in Greece and external opposition from the Turkish Government, which expressed concern that a clause incorporated in the agreement guaranteeing US support for Greece in the event of acts of international aggression by a third party could seriously jeopardize the success of future negotiations regarding Cyprus.

A 10-year economic co-operation agreement with the USSR was signed in 1983. Proposals for the establishment of a Balkan nuclear-free zone were made by Greece in 1983, and in 1987 Greece issued joint appeals, with both the Bulgarian and Romanian Governments, for the elimination of nuclear and chemical weapons from the Balkan region. Aided by the recent easing of travel restrictions by the Soviet Government, about 5,000 Pontic Greek refugees arrived in Greece from the Black Sea area of the USSR between mid-1988 and January 1990. The Greek consular authorities in Moscow estimated that around 100,000 Pontic Greek refugees would have emigrated to Greece by 1993. The Greek Government was planning to resettle the majority of the refugees in Thrace, in northern Greece.

Relations with Turkey have been characterized by long-standing disputes concerning Cyprus (q.v.) and sovereignty over the continental shelf beneath the Aegean Sea. Having left the military structure of NATO in 1974, in protest at the Turkish occupation of northern Cyprus, Greece rejoined in 1980, but in 1981 the new Socialist Government demanded that NATO should guarantee protection against possible Turkish aggression, as a condition of continuing Greek membership; disputes with Turkey over air-space continued, and talks between the two countries' Ministers of Foreign Affairs made little progress. The difficulties in relations with Turkey were exacerbated by the unilateral declaration of an 'independent' Turkish-Cypriot state in Cyprus in November 1983, together with various minor sovereignty disputes over islands in the Aegean Sea, which led to Greece's withdrawal from NATO exercises in August 1984 and to a boycott of them in subsequent years. In June 1986 another UN peace initiative for Cyprus collapsed, and, despite several efforts by the UN, little progress was made in 1987. The Cyprus problem was exacerbated by the expansion of the Turkish forces on the island in 1987. However, distinct progress was made in September 1988, when the Greek Cypriot and Turkish Cypriot leaders began the first round of substantive direct negotiations, under UN auspices, in Nicosia. A target date of 1 June 1989 was, rather optimistically, designated for the conclusion of a comprehensive political settlement. Despite several rounds of intensive direct talks, under the supervision of the UN, in Nicosia and New York, it became apparent, by the end of June 1989, that no real progress had been achieved as a result of the discussions. A further session of UN-sponsored negotiations between the two respective leaders of the Greek and Turkish Cypriots began in New York in February 1990, but was abandoned in March. In February 1991 there appeared to be no immediate prospect of a resumption of discussions between the two sides.

In March 1987 a disagreement between Greece and Turkey over petroleum-prospecting rights in disputed areas of the Aegean Sea almost resulted in the outbreak of military conflict. In January 1988, however, the Greek and Turkish Prime Ministers held discussions at Davos, Switzerland, and agreed on measures to reduce tension and to improve bilateral relations. It was agreed that the two countries' Prime Ministers should meet annually (the Davos meeting was the first formal contact between Greek and Turkish Heads of Government for 10 years), and that joint committees should be established to negotiate peaceful solutions to disputes. In April, however, relations between Greece and Turkey deteriorated, when a meeting of the Turkish-EEC Association Council was postponed, following objections by the Turkish delegation to an attempt by the Greek delegates to include the Cyprus issue on the agenda of the meeting. In the following month the 'Davos spirit' was renewed, when the Greek and Turkish Ministers of Foreign Affairs met in Athens and formally pledged to respect each other's sovereignty in the Aegean region. In June Turgut Özal became the first Turkish Prime Minister to visit Greece for 36 years, when he arrived in Athens for a meeting with Papandreou. Relations with Turkey were placed under renewed strain in January 1990, when violent clashes occurred in Komotini, Thrace, between Greeks and some 1,500 resident Turkish Muslims (who were demonstrating on the anniversary of the 1988 Supreme Court ruling which had proscribed the use of the word 'Turkish' in domestic political contexts) resulted in 19 injuries. Three days earlier two Turkish Muslim parliamentary candidates had been found guilty of 'inciting violence and dissension' by including the word 'Turkish' in their campaign literature. In February the Turkish ambassador in Athens was temporarily recalled, and later in the month the Turkish consul-general in Komotini and the Greek consul-general in İstanbul were simultaneously expelled.

In August 1985 Greece and Albania reopened their borders, which had remained closed since 1940, and Greece formally annulled claims to North Epirus (southern Albania), where there is a sizeable Greek minority. In August 1987 the Greek Government put a formal end to a legal vestige of the Second World War by proclaiming that it no longer considered Greece to be at war with Albania. In April 1988 relations between Greece and Albania improved significantly when the two countries signed an agreement to promote trade between their border provinces. In January 1990, however, the situation deteriorated when several thousand Greeks marched to the Albanian embassy in Athens in a demonstration against the alleged ill-treatment of ethnic Greeks residing in Albania (numbering an estimated 300,000). During December an estimated 11,000 Albanians (many of them ethnic Greeks) seeking political asylum in Greece crossed the border illegally. Many refugees were sceptical of recently-announced proposals for a move towards democratization in Albania and feared the possibility of escalating violence and widespread revolt. The Greek Government expressed considerable concern at the magnitude of the exodus and urged ethnic Greeks in Albania to remain there and await the implementation of promised reforms and the legal relaxation of border restrictions. During a visit to Albania in January 1991 Prime Minister Mitsotakis met the Albanian President, Ramiz Alia, and secured from him a guarantee of safety for Albanian refugees who were prepared to return. By late January some 5,000 refugees had returned to Albania. While the Greek authorities insisted that those who had returned had done so voluntarily, Albanian reports suggested that they had been forcibly repatriated.

Government

Under the Constitution of June 1975, the President is Head of State and is elected by Parliament for a five-year term. The President appoints the Prime Minister and, upon his recommendation, the other members of the Cabinet. In March 1986 Parliament approved a series of constitutional amendments, divesting the President of his executive powers and transferring them to the legislature (see Recent History). The unicameral Parliament has 300 members, directly elected by universal adult suffrage for four years. In 1983 measures were introduced to devolve powers of local government (formerly confined almost exclusively to 55 representatives of the central Government) to local councils, which were eventually to be directly elected. In January 1987 it was announced that 13 administrative regions were to be created.

Defence

Greece returned to the military structure of NATO in October 1980, after an absence of six years. Military service is compulsory for all men between 18 and 40 years of age, and lasts 20–24 months. In 1978 women were given the right to volunteer for military service of 30–50 days' basic training and for specialized training. In June 1990 the armed forces numbered 162,500, of whom 126,800 were conscripts, and consisted of an army of 117,000, a navy of 19,500 and an air force of 26,000; in addition, there was a gendarmerie of 26,500 and a National Guard of 120,000. The defence budget for 1989 totalled 611,000m. drachmae.

Economic Affairs

In 1989, according to estimates by the World Bank, Greece's gross national product (GNP), measured at average 1987–89 prices, was US $53,626m., equivalent to $5,340 per head. During 1980–89, it was estimated, GNP increased, in real terms, at an average annual rate of 1.0%, while GNP per head grew by only 0.6% per year. Over the same period, the population increased by an annual average of 0.4%. Greece's gross domestic product (GDP) increased, in real terms, by an annual average of 1.4% in 1980–88.

Agriculture (including hunting, forestry and fishing) contributed an estimated 15.7% of GDP in 1988, and about 27% of the working population were employed in the sector in the same year. The principal cash crops are fruit and vegetables (which, together, accounted for around 11.3% of total export earnings in 1988) and tobacco. During 1980–88 agricultural production decreased by an annual average of 0.1%. The performance of the sector was adversely affected by severe drought in 1990.

Industry (including mining, manufacturing, power and construction) provided 28.5% of GDP in 1987, and employed 27.2% of the working population in 1988. During 1980–88 industrial production increased by an annual average of only 0.4%.

Mining contributed 1.8% of GDP in 1987, and employed 0.6% of the working population in 1988. Mineral fuels and lubricants, iron and steel, and aluminium and aluminium alloys are the major mineral/metal exports. Lignite, magnesite and marble are also mined. In addition, Greece has small reserves of uranium and natural gas.

Manufacturing provided an estimated 17.8% of GDP in 1988, and employed 19.3% of the working population in the same year. The most important branches, measured by the gross

GREECE

value of output, in 1983 were petroleum refineries, food products, textiles (particularly cotton), metals and metal products, and chemicals.

Energy is derived principally from petroleum and lignite. Petroleum and petroleum products accounted for 4.7% of the total cost of imports in 1988. Hydroelectric power resources are also being developed.

An important source of foreign exchange in Greece is tourism. In 1988 tourist arrivals totalled an estimated 8.3m., and in the same year receipts from the tourist sector amounted to about US $2,400m. In 1990 receipts from the tourist sector were estimated to have risen to $2,570m.

In 1989, according to IMF figures, Greece recorded a visible trade deficit of US $7,383m., and in 1990 there was a deficit of around $3,600m. on the current account of the balance of payments. In 1988 the principal source of imports (20.2%) was the Federal Republic of Germany, which was also the principal market for exports (25.1%). Other major trading partners are Italy, France, the USA and the United Kingdom. The principal exports in 1988 were clothing, fruit and vegetables, and textiles. The principal imports were machinery and transport equipment, food and live animals, and petroleum and petroleum products.

In 1989 there was an estimated budgetary deficit of 421,600m. drachmae. Greece's share of EEC aid under the 1985-91 Integrated Plan for the Mediterranean Region was to amount to 2,542m. ECUs (US $2,460m. at December 1982 values), of which 49% was for the development and diversification of agriculture. Greece's total public external debt was $17,482m. at the end of 1988. In that year the cost of debt-servicing was equivalent to more than 29% of earnings from exports of goods and services. In 1989 the average annual rate of inflation was 13.7%. About 6.5% of the labour force were unemployed in 1987.

Greece is a member of the EEC (see p. 135), and the Organisation for Economic Co-operation and Development (OECD, p. 186).

Greece's major economic problem is the increasing overall public-sector deficit, which exists despite the implementation of various austerity measures between 1985 and 1990. Much of the country's large public-sector deficit can be attributed to the inefficiency of the state sector, which continues to control about 65% of all economic activity. Greece's economic performance came under criticism from the OECD, the EEC and the IMF in 1990. Particular concern was expressed at the continuing public-sector deficit and the inefficiency of tax and social welfare systems. In January 1991, however, a new £1,700m. loan for Greece was provisionally agreed by EEC member states, although disbursement was expected to be dependent upon the fulfilment of stringent economic conditions.

Social Welfare

There is a state social insurance scheme for wage-earners, while voluntary or staff insurances provide for salaried staff. Every citizen is entitled to an old-age pension and sickness benefit. In 1981 Greece had 688 hospital establishments, with a total of 59,914 beds (equivalent to one for every 162 inhabitants), and there were 24,724 physicians working in the country. Of total expenditure by the central Government in 1981, about 86,700m. drachmae (10.1%) was for health, and a further 251,900m. drachmae (29.3%) for social security and welfare.

Education

Education is available free of charge at all levels, and is officially compulsory for all children between the ages of six and 15 years. Primary education begins at the age of six and lasts for six years. Secondary education, beginning at the age of 12, is generally for six years, divided into two equal cycles. In 1986 the total enrolment at primary and secondary schools was equivalent to 98% of the school-age population. Primary enrolment in that year included 97% of children in the relevant age-group, while the comparable ratio at secondary schools was 84%. In 1986/87 there were 13,642 pre-primary and primary schools, with a total estimated enrolment of 1,021,187 pupils, and 3,271 secondary schools, with an estimated 835,845 pupils. There was a total of 197,808 students in 82 higher education institutions (including 16 universities) in 1986/87. Between 1951 and 1981 the average rate of adult illiteracy declined from 72% to 10%. In 1990, according to estimates by UNESCO, the rate was only 6.8% (males 2.4%; females 10.9%).

The vernacular language (demotiki) has replaced the formal version (katharevoussa) in secondary education.

Public Holidays

1991: 1 January (New Year's Day), 6 January (Epiphany), 18 February (Clean Monday), 25 March (Independence Day), 5-8 April (Greek Orthodox Easter), 1 May (Labour Day), 27 May (Holy Spirit Day), 15 August (Assumption of the Virgin Mary), 28 October ('Ochi' Day, anniversary of Greek defiance of Italy's 1940 ultimatum), 25-26 December (Christmas).

1992: 1 January (New Year's Day), 6 January (Epiphany), 9 March (Clean Monday), 25 March (Independence Day), 24-27 April (Greek Orthodox Easter), 1 May (Labour Day), 4 June (Holy Spirit Day), 15 August (Assumption of the Virgin Mary), 28 October ('Ochi' Day, anniversary of Greek defiance of Italy's 1940 ultimatum), 25-26 December (Christmas).

Weights and Measures

The metric system is in force.

Statistical Survey

Source (unless otherwise stated): National Statistical Service of Greece, Odos Lycourgou 14-16, Athens; tel. (01) 3249302; telex 216734; fax (01) 3222205.

Area and Population

AREA, POPULATION AND DENSITY

Area (sq km)	131,957*
Population (census results)	
14 March 1971	8,768,641
5 April 1981	9,740,417
Population (official estimates at mid-year)	
1987	9,983,000
1988	10,010,000
1989	10,020,000
Density (per sq km) at mid-1989	75.9

* 50,949 sq miles.

PRINCIPAL TOWNS (population at 1981 census)

Athinai (Athens, the capital)	885,737	Larissa	102,426
Thessaloniki (Salonika)	406,413	Iraklion	102,398
		Volos	71,378
Piraeus	196,389	Kavala	56,705
Patras	142,163	Canea	47,451
		Serres	46,317

GREECE

Statistical Survey

BIRTHS, MARRIAGES AND DEATHS

	Registered live births		Registered marriages		Registered deaths	
	Number	Rate (per 1,000)	Number	Rate (per 1,000)	Number	Rate (per 1,000)
1981	140,953	14.5	71,178	7.3	86,261	8.9
1982	137,275	14.0	67,784	6.9	86,345	8.8
1983	132,608	13.5	71,143	7.2	90,586	9.2
1984	125,724	12.7	54,793	5.6	88,397	8.9
1985	116,481	11.7	63,709	6.4	92,886	9.3
1986	112,810	11.3	58,091	5.9	91,783	9.2
1987	106,392	10.6	66,166	6.6	95,656	9.5
1988	107,505	n.a.	47,873	n.a.	92,407	n.a.

ECONOMICALLY ACTIVE POPULATION (sample surveys, '000 persons aged 14 years and over, April–June)

	1986	1987	1988
Agriculture, hunting, forestry and fishing	1,026.0	970.7	972.0
Mining and quarrying	24.0	24.3	22.5
Manufacturing	717.6	715.6	706.5
Electricity, gas and water	35.5	34.9	34.9
Construction	235.2	232.1	231.7
Trade, restaurants and hotels	562.1	592.2	600.8
Transport, storage and communications	237.5	243.9	241.9
Finance, insurance, real estate and business services	139.0	145.6	160.4
Community, social and personal services	623.2	636.9	685.7
Activities not adequately defined	0.7	1.2	0.8
Total employed	3,600.8	3,597.4	3,657.2
Unemployed	286.9	286.2	303.5
Total labour force	3,887.8	3,883.6	3,960.8
Males	2,504.7	2,489.4	2,501.1
Females	1,383.0	1,394.2	1,459.7

Source: ILO, *Year Book of Labour Statistics*.

Agriculture

PRINCIPAL CROPS ('000 metric tons)

	1987	1988	1989
Wheat	2,213	2,183	2,005
Rice (paddy)	127	116	110
Barley	573	550	496
Maize	2,156	1,750	1,700
Oats	70	68	57
Potatoes	948	960	1,000†
Dry beans	27	29	29*
Other pulses	27	26	26*
Sunflower seed	140	60	40†
Cottonseed†	345	465	485
Cotton (lint)†	174	234	245
Olives*	1,420	1,500	1,500
Cabbages	183	174	175*
Tomatoes	1,665	1,655	2,180
Cucumbers and gherkins	161	168	156
Onions (dry)	141	158†	151†
Watermelons	627	550	600*
Melons	150	110	120*
Grapes	1,412†	1,720†	1,700*
Sugar beet	2,025	2,000	2,500†
Apples	303	267	260
Pears	120	91	93
Peaches and nectarines	575	591	582
Oranges	579	752	900†
Lemons and limes	119	160	190†
Apricots	107	154	97
Nuts	79.2	103.0	103.0*
Tobacco (leaves)	155	135	124*

* FAO estimate(s).   † Unofficial figure(s).
Source: FAO, *Production Yearbook*.

LIVESTOCK ('000 head, year ending 30 September)

	1987	1988	1989
Asses*	175	173	170
Buffaloes*	1	1	1
Cattle	761	741	731
Goats	6,600	5,876	5,970
Horses*	65	60	60
Mules*	83	82	81
Pigs	1,130	1,139	1,226
Sheep	11,032	10,816	10,376
Chickens*	31,000	31,000	31,000

* FAO estimate(s).
Source: FAO, *Production Yearbook*.

LIVESTOCK PRODUCTS ('000 metric tons)

	1987	1988	1989
Beef and veal	86	82†	85†
Mutton and lamb	84	85†	85†
Goat meat†	40	40	41
Pigmeat	164	160†	160†
Horsemeat*	3	3	3
Poultry meat	160	162	162
Other meat	5	5	5
Edible offals*	48	47	47
Cows' milk†	628	652	715
Sheep's milk	606†	642†	700†
Goats' milk	455†	482†	465*
Cheese	209.7	203.0*	221.0*
Butter	4.7	5.0†	4.0†
Hen eggs	117.2	124.0†	121.0*
Honey	11.5	11.6*	11.7*
Wool: greasy†	10	10	11
Wool: clean	6.0†	6.0†	6.5*
Cattle and buffalo hides*	7.9	7.6	7.7
Sheep skins*	13.0	13.7	13.7
Goatskins*	6.4	5.5	5.5

* FAO estimate(s).   † Unofficial figure(s).
Source: FAO, mainly *Production Yearbook*.

Forestry

ROUNDWOOD REMOVALS ('000 cubic metres, excl. bark)

	1986	1987	1988
Sawlogs, veneer logs and logs for sleepers	482	497	563
Pulpwood	210	220	220*
Other industrial wood	190	200	200*
Fuel wood	2,280	2,320	2,320*
Total	3,162	3,237	3,303*

* FAO estimate.
Source: FAO, *Yearbook of Forest Products*.

SAWNWOOD PRODUCTION
('000 cubic metres, incl. boxboards)

	1986	1987	1988
Coniferous (softwood)	290	201	180
Broadleaved (hardwood)	164	227	230
Total	454	428	410

Source: FAO, *Yearbook of Forest Products*.

GREECE

Fishing

('000 metric tons, live weight)

	1986	1987	1988
Inland waters	10.2	10.3†	10.0†
Atlantic Ocean	11.3	15.0	12.6
Mediterranean Sea*	101.5	106.5	103.8
Total catch*	123.0	131.8	126.4

* Excluding catches from vessels of less than 19 hp, estimated at 24,500 metric tons in 1986, 23,500 metric tons in 1987 and 22,500 metric tons in 1988.
† Provisional.

Mining

('000 metric tons, unless otherwise indicated)

	1985	1986	1987
Brown coal (incl. lignite)	35,888	38,096	44,612
Crude petroleum	1,250	1,253	1,149
Iron ore*	736	559	440†
Bauxite	2,454	2,231	2,477
Zinc concentrates*	21.1	22.5	20.7
Lead concentrates*	20.1	20.9	20.6
Chromium ore*	25	25	27†
Magnesite	884.4	944.0†	910.0†
Kaolin (raw)	76	86†	n.a.
Perlite (raw)	54.7	55.4	n.a.
Bentonite (raw)	182.7	328.2	n.a.
Salt (unrefined)	195	150†	150†
Marble ('000 cu m)	273	150†	150†
Natural gas (million cu m)	62	85	96

* Figures refer to the metal content of ores and concentrates.
† Estimate.
Source: mainly UN, *Industrial Statistics Yearbook*.

Industry

SELECTED PRODUCTS
('000 metric tons, unless otherwise indicated)

	1984	1985	1986
Edible fats	40	40	43
Olive oil (crude)	282	451	247
Raw sugar	218	318	288
Wine	312	308	283
Beer ('000 hectolitres)	2,969	3,262	3,103
Cigarettes (million)	25,699	27,635	28,500
Cotton yarn (pure)	125.3	123.6	n.a.
Woven cotton fabrics—pure and mixed (metric tons)	37,188	40,949	n.a.
Flax, hemp and jute yarn—pure and mixed (metric tons)	1,328	994	n.a.
Wool yarn—pure (metric tons)	10,076	9,223	n.a.
Woven woollen fabrics—pure and mixed (metric tons)[1]	2,816	2,959	n.a.
Yarn of artificial material (metric tons)	9,580	9,814	n.a.
Fabrics of artificial fibres (metric tons)	1,459	1,529	n.a.
Footwear—excl. rubber and plastic ('000 pairs)	11,180	11,305	11,430
Rubber footwear ('000 pairs)	410	394	1,049
Paper and paperboard	294	282	283
Sulphuric acid	1,155	1,609	892*
Hydrochloric acid (21° Bé)	49	54	44
Nitric acid (54% or 36.3° Bé)	478	501	490
Ammonia (anhydrous)	305	296	294
Caustic soda (Sodium hydroxide)	31	30	30
Nitrogenous fertilizers (single)	581	583	531

—continued	1984	1985	1986
Superphosphatic fertilizers (single)	80	79	60
Polyvinyl chloride	57.2	57	63
Liquefied petroleum gas	246	217	283
Naphthas	678	386	791
Motor spirit (petrol)	1,663	1,954	1,958
Jet fuels	1,465	1,341	1,936
Distillate fuel oils	3,798	3,231	3,741
Residual fuel oils	4,283	4,435	6,543
Cement	13,521	12,855	12,494
Crude steel (incl. alloys)	916	972	890*
Aluminium (unwrought)	189	145	127
Refined lead (unwrought)	9.1	13.1*	19.3*
Refrigerators—household ('000)	118	139	148
Washing machines—household ('000)	78	85	103
Television receivers ('000)	158	183	190
Lorries (number)[2]	4,685	3,076	3,092
Electric energy (million kWh)	24,820	27,740	28,237

1987 ('000 metric tons, unless otherwise indicated): Olive oil (crude) 273; Cigarettes (million) 28,900; Sulphuric acid 896*; Liquefied petroleum gas 303; Naphthas 753; Motor spirit (petrol) 2,423; Jet fuels 1,996; Distillate fuel oils 3,808; Residual fuel oils 6,303; Crude steel (incl. alloys) 908; Aluminium (unwrought) 132; Refined lead (unwrought) 2.7*; Electric energy (million kWh) 30,084. Source UN, *Industrial Statistics Yearbook*.

* Provisional.
[1] After undergoing finishing processes.
[2] Assembled wholly or mainly from imported parts.

Finance

CURRENCY AND EXCHANGE RATES

Monetary Units
100 leptae (singular: lepta) = 1 drachma.

Denominations
Coins: 10, 20 and 50 leptae; 1, 2, 5, 10 and 20 drachmae.
Notes: 50, 100, 500 and 1,000 drachmae.

Sterling and Dollar Equivalents (30 September 1990)
£1 sterling = 289.9 drachmae;
US $1 = 154.7 drachmae;
1,000 drachmae = £3.449 = $6.464.

Average Exchange Rate (drachmae per US $)
1987   135.43
1988   141.86
1989   162.42

BUDGET ESTIMATES (million drachmae)

Revenue	1987	1988	1989
Ordinary budget:			
Direct taxes	492,400	616,440	616,065
Excise duties	2,050	500	350
Indirect taxes	1,194,730	1,369,430	1,501,970
European Community	53,020	52,900	67,350
Credit receipts	—	656,530	1,051,800
Other	96,900	105,730	124,265
Sub-total	1,840,000	2,801,530	3,361,800
Extraordinary budget:			
Revenue from investments	6,000	6,500	9,000
Aid and loans from abroad	258,000	200,000	200,000
Revenue from NATO works	10,000	12,800	20,000
Increase in national debt	100,000	100,500	140,000
Receipts from EEC	—	63,000	81,000
Total	2,214,000	3,184,330	3,812,400

GREECE

Statistical Survey

Expenditure	1987	1988	1989
Ordinary budget:			
Political ministries	1,758,757	2,259,790	2,776,295
Defence	278,823	344,100	350,000
European Community	70,100	80,000	101,700
Police and other sectors	61,320	72,640	83,805
Sub-total	2,169,000	2,756,530	3,311,800
Provision for increase	50,000	45,000	50,000
Sub-total	2,219,000	2,801,530	3,361,800
Extraordinary budget:			
Expenditure on NATO works	10,000	12,800	20,000
Investments	364,000	370,000	430,600
Total	2,593,000	3,184,330	3,812,400

INTERNATIONAL RESERVES* (US $ million at 31 December)

	1987	1988	1989
Gold†	1,057.2	925.0	902.1
Reserve position in IMF	99.5	95.7	117.2
Foreign exchange	2,581.9	3,523.4	3,105.8
Total	3,738.6	4,544.1	4,125.1

* Figures exclude deposits made with the European Monetary Co-operation Fund.
† Gold reserves are valued at market-related prices.
Source: IMF, *International Financial Statistics*.

MONEY SUPPLY ('000 million drachmae at 31 December)

	1985	1986	1987
Currency outside banks	513.5	550.1	641.4
Private sector deposits at Bank of Greece	31.3	123.5	120.1
Demand deposits at commercial banks	198.5	222.5	238.5
Total money	743.3	896.0	1,000.0

Source: IMF, *International Financial Statistics*.

COST OF LIVING (Consumer Price Index. Base: 1982 = 100)

	1986	1987	1988
Foodstuffs	200.6	225.9	251.1
Alcohol, beverages and tobacco	196.4	227.2	300.6
Clothing and footwear	236.2	287.5	339.6
Housing	184.6	211.6	240.0
Household equipment	233.9	278.6	304.5
Medical and personal care	201.1	242.3	285.7
Education and recreation	230.1	284.3	329.2
Transport and communications	199.9	222.7	241.1
Miscellaneous	251.4	296.1	326.3
All items	209.0	243.3	276.2

NATIONAL ACCOUNTS
Expenditure on the Gross Domestic Product
('000 million drachmae at current prices)

	1987	1988	1989
Government final consumption expenditure	1,229.4	1,517.5	1,828.6
Private final consumption expenditure	4,332.4	5,116.0	6,096.7
Increase in stocks	25.4	29.2	85.8
Gross fixed capital formation	1,045.8	1,282.3	1,630.5
Statistical discrepancy	51.6	46.8	−27.3
Total domestic expenditure	6,684.6	7,991.8	9,614.3
Exports of goods and services	1,536.8	1,800.9	2,069.5
Less Imports of goods and services	1,993.4	2,290.7	2,839.5
GDP in purchasers' values	6,228.0	7,502.0	8,844.3
GDP at constant 1985 prices	4,658.9	4,830.4	4,981.9

Source: IMF, *International Financial Statistics*.

Gross Domestic Product by Economic Activity
(million drachmae at current prices)

	1986	1987*	1988†
Agriculture, hunting, forestry and fishing	745,513	844,047	1,014,753
Manufacturing	907,415	971,076	1,145,527
Wholesale and retail trade	802,934	886,131	1,008,620
Finance, insurance, etc.			
Public administration and defence	536,200	621,407	3,274,203
Other activities	1,846,194	2,126,483	
GDP at factor cost	4,838,256	5,449,144	6,443,103
Indirect taxes, *less* subsidies	642,036	806,450	1,003,120
GDP in purchasers' values	5,480,292	6,255,594	7,446,223

* Provisional. † Estimates.

BALANCE OF PAYMENTS (US $ million)

	1987	1988	1989
Merchandise exports f.o.b.	5,612	5,933	5,994
Merchandise imports f.o.b.	−11,112	−12,005	−13,377
Trade balance	−5,500	−6,072	−7,383
Exports of services	4,419	5,176	4,896
Imports of services	−1,736	−2,188	−2,424
Other income received	185	269	283
Other income paid	−1,626	−1,792	−1,928
Private unrequited transfers (net)	1,370	1,713	1,381
Government unrequited transfers (net)	1,665	1,936	2,602
Current balance	−1,223	−958	−2,573
Direct investment (net)	683	907	752
Other capital (net)	1,291	947	1,999
Net errors and omissions	223	41	−526
Overall balance	974	937	−348

Source: IMF, *International Financial Statistics*.

External Trade

PRINCIPAL COMMODITIES (million drachmae)

Imports c.i.f.	1986	1987	1988
Food and live animals	235,147	292,486	268,264
Meat and meat preparations	79,108	105,838	81,946
Fresh, chilled or frozen meat	76,046	101,002	53,433
Crude materials (inedible) except fuels	97,834	104,949	100,728
Textile fibres and waste	25,323	22,659	30,028

GREECE

Statistical Survey

Imports c.i.f.—*continued*	1986	1987	1988
Mineral fuels, lubricants, etc.	275,686	242,864	88,032
Petroleum and petroleum products	258,539	233,127	82,662
Crude petroleum	228,601	203,311	67,660
Petroleum products*	25,981	27,321	12,901
Chemicals	166,071	193,226	208,561
Chemical elements and compounds	46,967	54,522	52,960
Plastic materials, etc.	41,021	48,366	13,253
Basic manufactures	301,970	361,986	382,433
Textile yarn, fabrics, etc.	21,276	29,023	23,224
Iron and steel	73,918	69,786	79,054
Machinery and transport equipment	409,826	429,849	530,427
Non-electric machinery	143,280	164,803	216,101
Electrical machinery, apparatus, etc.	46,839	48,666	56,919
Transport equipment	187,239	188,081	218,662
Road motor vehicles and parts (excl. tyres, engines and electrical parts)	98,208	109,399	113,777
Ships and boats	79,534	75,797	101,908
Miscellaneous manufactured articles	71,572	98,281	134,660
Total (incl. others)	1,582,298	1,758,951	1,757,998

Exports f.o.b.	1986	1987	1988
Food and live animals	174,471	183,285	137,559
Fruit and vegetables	113,332	116,959	87,937
Fresh fruit and nuts (excl. oil nuts)†	34,472	31,494	22,844
Dried fruit†	18,847	19,317	19,053
Dried grapes (raisins)	17,722	16,059	10,545
Preserved or prepared vegetables	26,193	30,033	23,362
Beverages and tobacco	40,108	49,245	42,514
Tobacco and manufactures	30,589	38,435	34,767
Unmanufactured tobacco	29,856	37,251	32,781
Crude materials (inedible) except fuels	46,367	58,143	47,447
Mineral fuels, lubricants, etc.	51,833	58,905	40,251
Petroleum products*	51,027	48,097	33,161
Chemicals	26,021	27,434	30,376
Basic manufactures	216,488	230,777	217,714
Textile yarn, fabrics, etc.	76,813	85,043	67,517
Textile yarn and thread	46,190	51,067	40,017
Non-metallic mineral manufactures	33,822	34,035	32,947
Lime, cement, etc.	28,472	27,430	25,373
Cement	22,488	21,148	18,350
Iron and steel	43,444	35,725	39,308
Non-ferrous metals	25,335	35,015	41,913
Aluminium and aluminium alloys	18,361	27,688	31,188
Machinery and transport equipment	23,100	23,890	24,888
Miscellaneous manufactured articles	173,372	215,871	203,916
Clothing (excl. footwear)	151,855	194,981	176,183
Total (incl. others)	789,994	880,985	776,433

* Including partly refined petroleum.
† Dried citrus fruit and dried tropical fruit are included with 'fresh fruit and nuts'.

PRINCIPAL TRADING PARTNERS* (million drachmae)

Imports c.i.f.	1986	1987	1988
Austria	15,986	23,422	21,824
Belgium/Luxembourg	53,799	60,403	64,502
Brazil	11,882	15,280	21,930
Denmark	21,639	21,820	24,588
Egypt	16,717	5,145	6,064
France	127,885	137,574	140,808
German Democratic Republic	6,542	6,003	6,559
Germany, Federal Republic	335,592	389,888	355,065
Iran	7,046	4,053	1,879
Iraq	18,345	17,213	7,255
Italy	182,787	215,569	255,208
Japan	96,417	73,488	100,890
Netherlands	106,010	123,752	120,037
Romania	7,532	9,049	8,215
Saudi Arabia	102,460	66,879	4,263
Spain	20,042	25,162	37,084
Sweden	22,068	22,449	24,641
Switzerland	27,353	32,643	34,243
USSR	39,824	43,998	37,490
United Kingdom	65,735	85,790	86,875
USA	47,912	48,451	115,441
Yugoslavia	19,251	27,247	21,245
Total (incl. others)	1,582,299	1,758,951	1,757,998

* Imports by country of first consignment; exports by country of consumption.

Exports f.o.b.	1986	1987	1988
Belgium/Luxembourg	22,018	24,562	19,679
Bulgaria	8,229	5,689	4,802
Cyprus	11,938	13,037	19,971
Denmark	7,571	8,579	7,427
Egypt	18,909	16,447	10,702
France	74,872	75,909	66,907
Germany, Federal Republic	186,925	214,452	195,202
Hungary	2,581	2,541	1,507
Iraq	8,424	2,299	7,999
Italy	106,528	142,298	109,839
Japan	5,843	8,056	11,174
Lebanon	4,897	4,188	5,575
Libya	7,990	5,483	8,224
Netherlands	39,188	33,407	26,510
Romania	6,645	6,431	4,509
Saudi Arabia	22,162	17,521	9,562
Spain	7,194	12,234	10,434
Sweden	7,022	10,702	11,228
Switzerland	10,347	11,637	10,084
Syria	3,877	3,005	2,170
USSR	10,874	10,279	12,801
United Kingdom	53,772	75,522	59,838
USA	56,102	59,862	48,734
Yugoslavia	10,313	8,682	8,522
Total (incl. others)	789,995	880,985	776,433

Transport

RAILWAYS (estimated traffic)

	1986	1987	1988
Passenger-kilometres (million)	1,950.2	1,973.2	1,963.4
Net ton-kilometres (million)	702.4	598.8	604.4

ROAD TRAFFIC (motor vehicles in use at 31 December)

	1986	1987	1988*
Passenger cars	1,359,173	1,432,577	1,507,952
Buses and coaches	18,485	18,748	19,077
Goods vehicles	627,231	656,144	688,894
Motorcycles, etc.	179,281	188,840	203,582

* Provisional.

GREECE

SHIPPING
Merchant fleet (at 1 July)

	1988		1989	
	Vessels	Gross reg. tons	Vessels	Gross reg. tons
Cargo boats	974	12,114,894	900	11,651,136
Passenger boats	378	686,448	405	722,509
Tankers	331	9,015,348	340	8,839,094
Others	360	109,596	365	107,168

Freight traffic

	1985	1986	1987
Vessels entered ('000 net reg. tons)	151,530	173,315	192,330
Goods loaded ('000 metric tons)*	20,111	22,146	23,917
Goods unloaded ('000 metric tons)*	24,773	27,998	31,365

* International sea-borne shipping.

CIVIL AVIATION
(domestic and foreign flights of Olympic Airways)

	1986	1987	1988
Kilometres flown ('000)	48,501	51,317	51,976
Passenger-kilometres ('000)	6,382,020	7,121,478	7,530,881
Freight ton-kilometres ('000)	91,671	104,283	101,849
Mail ton-kilometres ('000)	9,617	9,810	10,460

Tourism

	1986	1987	1988
Number of visitors*	7,400,000	8,053,000	8,274,000
Receipts (US $'000)	1,834,218	2,268,123	2,396,083

* Estimates, including cruise passengers (465,435 in 1985).

TOURISTS BY COUNTRY OF ORIGIN
(foreign citizens, excluding cruise passengers)

Country	1983	1984	1985
Australia	83,230	96,953	121,894
Austria	195,381	237,918	282,468
Canada	72,540	82,226	102,552
Denmark	148,626	124,037	160,792
France	299,506	405,907	441,141
German Democratic Republic } Germany, Federal Republic }	728,478	864,000	1,050,078
Italy	327,610	328,598	364,177
Netherlands	153,672	192,879	280,309
Sweden	189,921	194,356	223,956
Switzerland	173,830	156,995	205,662
United Kingdom	888,991	1,043,363	1,329,259
USA	406,887	474,845	466,155
Yugoslavia	55,375	263,209	350,735
Others	1,050,767	1,055,746	1,194,319
Unspecified	3,663	2,160	496
Total	4,778,477	5,523,192	6,573,993

Communications Media

	1986	1987	1988
Radio receivers ('000 in use)	n.a.	4,100*	4,150*
Television receivers ('000 licensed)	n.a.	1,750*	1,755*
Telephones ('000 in use)	3,915.3	4,122.3	4,300.6
Newspapers:			
Daily	143	142	117
Non-daily	962	962	1,041
Other periodicals	778	777	800

* Source: UNESCO, *Statistical Yearbook*.

Book production: 4,651 titles (incl. pamphlets) in 1985.

Education
(1986/87)

	Institutions	Teachers	Students
Pre-primary	5,281	7,774	155,527
Primary	8,361	37,947	865,660
Secondary:			
General	2,765	43,797	717,408
Vocational	506	7,909	118,437
Higher:			
Universities	16	7,141	115,969
Other	66	5,209	81,839

Directory

The Constitution

A new constitution for the Hellenic Republic came into force on 11 June 1975. The main provisions of this Constitution, as subsequently amended, are summarized below.

Greece shall be a parliamentary democracy with a President as Head of State. All powers are derived from the people and exist for the benefit of the people. The established religion is that of The Eastern Orthodox Church of Christ.

EXECUTIVE AND LEGISLATIVE

The President

In March 1986 a series of amendments to the Constitution was approved by a majority vote of Parliament, which relieved the President of his executive power and transferred such power to the legislature, thus reducing the Head of State to a largely ceremonial figure.

The President is elected by Parliament for a period of five years. The re-election of the same person shall be permitted only once. The President represents the State in relations with other nations, is Supreme Commander of the armed forces and may declare war and conclude treaties. The President shall appoint the Prime Minister and, on the Prime Minister's recommendation, the other members of the Government. The President shall convoke Parliament once every year and in extraordinary session whenever he deems it reasonable. In exceptional circumstances the President may preside over the Cabinet, call the Council of the Republic, and suspend Parliament for a period not exceeding 30 days. In the amendment of March 1986, the President lost the right to dismiss the Prime Minister, his power to call a referendum was limited, and the right to declare a state of emergency was transferred to Parliament. The President can now dissolve Parliament only if the resignation of two Governments in quick succession demonstrates the absence of political stability. If no party has a majority in Parliament, the President must offer an opportunity to form a government to the leader of each of the four biggest parties in turn, strictly following the order of their parliamentary strengths. If no party leader is able to form a government, the President may try to assemble an all-party government; failing that, the President must appoint a caretaker cabinet, led by a senior judge, to hold office until a fresh election takes place. The Constitution continues to reserve a substantial moderating role for the President, however, in that he retains the right to object to legislation and may request Parliament to reconsider it or to approve it with an enlarged majority.

The Government

The Government consists of the Cabinet which comprises the Prime Minister and Ministers. The Government determines and directs the general policy of the State in accordance with the Constitution and the laws. The Cabinet must enjoy the confidence of Parliament and may be removed by a vote of no confidence. The Prime Minister is to be the leader of the party with an absolute majority in Parliament, or, if no such party exists, the leader of the party with a relative majority.

The Council of the Republic

The Council of the Republic shall be composed of all former democratic Presidents, the Prime Minister, the leader of the Opposition and the parliamentary Prime Ministers of governments which have enjoyed the confidence of Parliament, presided over by the President. It shall meet when the largest parties are unable to form a government with the confidence of Parliament and may empower the President to appoint a Prime Minister who may or may not be a member of Parliament. The Council may also authorize the President to dissolve Parliament.

Parliament

Parliament is to be unicameral and composed of not fewer than 200 and not more than 300 deputies elected by direct, universal and secret ballot for a term of four years. Parliament shall elect its own President, or Speaker. It must meet once a year for a regular session of at least five months. Bills passed by Parliament must be ratified by the President and the President's veto can be nullified by an absolute majority of the total number of deputies. Parliament may impeach the President by a motion signed by one-third and passed by two-thirds of the total number of deputies. Parliament is also empowered to impeach present or former members of the Government. In these cases the defendant shall be brought before an *ad hoc* tribunal presided over by the President of the Supreme Court and composed of 12 judges. Certain legislative work, as specified in the Constitution, must be passed by Parliament in plenum, and Parliament cannot make a decision without an absolute majority of the members present, which under no circumstances shall be less than one-quarter of the total number of deputies. The Constitution provides for certain legislative powers to be exercised by not more than two Parliamentary Departments. Parliament may revise the Constitution in accordance with the procedure laid down in the Constitution.

THE JUDICIAL AUTHORITY

Justice is to be administered by courts of regular judges, who enjoy personal and functional independence. The President, after consultations with a judicial council, shall appoint the judges for life. The judges are subject only to the Constitution and the laws. Courts are divided into administrative, civil and penal and shall be organized by virtue of special laws. They must not apply laws which are contrary to the Constitution. The final jurisdiction in matters of judicial review rests with a Special Supreme Tribunal.

Certain laws, passed before the implementation of this constitution and deemed not contrary to it, are to remain in force. Other specified laws, even if contrary to the Constitution, are to remain in force until repealed by further legislation.

INDIVIDUAL AND SPECIAL RIGHTS

All citizens are equal under the Constitution and before the law, having the same rights and obligations. No titles of nobility or distinction are to be conferred or recognized. All persons are to enjoy full protection of life, honour and freedom, irrespective of nationality, race, creed or political allegiance. Retrospective legislation is prohibited and no citizen may be punished without due process of law. Freedom of speech, of the Press, of association and of religion are guaranteed under the Constitution. All persons have the right to a free education, which the state has the duty to provide. Work is a right and all workers, irrespective of sex or other distinction, are entitled to equal remuneration for rendering services of equal value. The right of peaceful assembly, the right of a person to property and the freedom to form political parties are guaranteed under the Constitution. The exercise of the right to vote by all citizens over 18 years of age is obligatory. No person may exercise his rights and liberties contrary to the Constitution.

MOUNT ATHOS

The district of Mount Athos shall, in accordance with its ancient privileged status, be a self-governing part of the Greek State and its sovereignty shall remain unaffected.

The Government

HEAD OF STATE

President: KONSTANTINOS KARAMANLIS (took office 5 May 1990; term expires 5 May 1995).

THE CABINET
(February 1991)

Prime Minister and Minister of National Economy: KONSTANTINOS MITSOTAKIS.

Minister to the Prime Minister: MILTIADES EVERT.

Minister of National Defence: YANNIS VARVITZIOTIS.

Minister of Foreign Affairs: ANTONIS SAMARAS.

Minister of the Interior: SOTIRIS KOUVELAS.

Alternate Minister of the National Economy: EFTHYMIOS CHRISTODOULOU.

Minister of Finance: YANNIS PALEOKRASSAS.

Minister of Agriculture: MIHALIS PAPAKONSTANTINOU.

Minister of Labour: ARISTIDES KALATZAKOS.

Minister of Health, Welfare and Social Services: MARIETTA YANNAKOU.

Minister of Justice: ATHANASSIOS KANELLOPOULOS.

Minister of Education and Religion: GEORGIOS SOUFLIAS.

Minister of Public Order: YANNIS VASSILIADIS.

Minister of Macedonia and Thrace: GEORGIOS TZITZIKOSTAS.

Minister of Culture: TZANNIS TZANNETAKIS.

GREECE

Directory

Minister of Tourism: YANNIS KEFALOYANNIS.
Minister of the Aegean: GEORGIOS MISAILIDES.
Minister of the Environment and Town Planning and of Public Works: STEFANOS MANOS.
Minister of Industry, Energy and Technology: STAVROS DIMAS.
Minister of Commerce: ATHANASSIOS XARHAS.
Minister of Transport and Communications: NIKOLAOS GELESTHASIS.
Minister of Merchant Marine: ARISTOTLE PAVLIDES.
Minister without Portfolio: MIKIS THEODORAKIS.

MINISTRIES

Ministry to the President: Odos Zalokosta 10, Athens; tel. (01) 3630911; telex 216325.
Ministry to the Prime Minister: Leoforos Vassilissis Sophias 15, 106 74 Athens; tel. (01) 3646350; telex 214333.
Ministry of Agriculture: Odos Aharnon 2-6, Athens; tel. (01) 3291206; telex 215308.
Ministry of Commerce: Kanningos Sq., Athens; tel. (01) 3616251; telex 215282.
Ministry of Culture: Odos Aristidou 14, 101 86 Athens; tel. (01) 3243015; telex 216412.
Ministry of Education and Religion: Odos Metropoleos 15, Athens; tel. (01) 3230461; telex 216059.
Ministry of the Environment and Town Planning: Odos Amaliados 17, Athens; tel. (01) 6431461; telex 216374.
Ministry of Finance: Odos Karageorgi Servias 10, Athens; tel. (01) 3224071; telex 216373.
Ministry of Foreign Affairs: Odos Zalokosta 2, Athens; tel. (01) 3610581.
Ministry of Health, Welfare and Social Services: Odos Zalokosta 10, Athens; tel. (01) 3630911; telex 21625.
Ministry of Industry, Energy and Technology: Odos Mighlagopoulou 80, 101 92 Athens; tel. (01) 7700561; telex 215811; fax (01) 7772485.
Ministry of the Interior: Odos Stadiou 27, Athens; tel. (01) 3223521; telex 215776.
Ministry of Justice: Odos Zinonos 12, Athens; tel. (01) 5225903; telex 216352.
Ministry of Labour: Odos Pireos 40, Athens; tel. (01) 5233110; telex 216608.
Ministry of Merchant Marine: Odos Vassilissis Sophias 150, Piraeus; tel. (01) 4121211; telex 211232.
Ministry of National Defence: Holargos, Athens; tel. (01) 6465201.
Ministry of National Economy: Syntagma Sq., Athens; tel. (01) 3230911; telex 221086.
Ministry of Northern Greece: Odos El. Venizelou 48, Thessaloniki; tel. (031) 264321.
Ministry of Public Order: Katehaki 1, 101 77 Athens; tel. (01) 6928510; telex 216353.
Ministry of Public Works: Odos Har Trikoupi 182, Athens; tel. (01) 3618311; telex 216353.
Ministry of Transport and Communications: Leoforos Syngrou 49, Athens; tel. (01) 9233941; telex 216369.

Legislature

VOULI

President of Parliament: ATHANASSIOS TSALDARIS.

General Election, 8 April 1990

	Seats	Percentage of Votes
New Democracy (ND)	150	46.9
Panhellenic Socialist Movement (PASOK)	123	38.6
Left Coalition	19	10.3
Ecologist Alternative	1	0.8
Democratic Renewal (DIANA)	1	0.7
Independents	6*	1.7
Blank or spoiled votes	—	1.0
Total	**300**	**100.0**

* Includes four left-wing independents supported by PASOK and the Left Coalition, and two representatives of the Turkish Muslim population in Thrace.

Political Organizations

Democratic Centre Union (Enossi Dimokratikou Kentrou—EDIK): Odos Charilaou Trikoupi 18, 106 79 Athens; tel. (01) 3609711; telex 216689; fax (01) 3634412; f. 1974; democratic socialist party, merging Centre Union (f. 1961 by GEORGIOS PAPANDREOU) and New Political Forces (f. 1974 by Prof. IOANNIS PESMAZOGLOU and Prof. G. A. MANGAKIS); favours a united Europe; Pres. Dr IOANNIS G. ZIGHDIS.

Democratic Initiative Party: Athens; f. 1987; democratic socialist party; advocates decentralization, a mixed economy, and the removal of foreign military bases from Greece; at least 60% of its mems are ex-PASOK mems; Leader GERASIMOS ARSENIS.

Democratic Renewal (Komma Dimokratikis Ananeosis—DIANA): Odos 3 Septembriou 30, 104 32 Athens; tel. (01) 5240343; telex 216916; fax (01) 5242882; ; f. 1985 by former ND deputies; populist; advocates a moderate centre-right policy on economic and social matters and a pro-Western position on foreign affairs; Leader KOSTIS STEFANOPOULOS.

Democratic Socialist Party (KODISO): Odos Mavromichali 9, 106 79 Athens; tel. (01) 3600724; telex 224431; fax (01) 3607005; f. March 1979 by former EDIK deputies; favours membership of the EEC and political wing of NATO, decentralization and a mixed economy; Pres. CH. PROTOPAPAS.

Greek National Political Society (EPEN): Athens; f. 1984; rightwing; Leader Col GEORGIOS PAPADOPOULOS.

Hellenic Liberal Party: Vissarionos 1, 106 72 Athens; tel. (01) 3606111; telex 214886; f. 1910; aims to revive political heritage of fmr Prime Minister, Eleftherios Venizelos; 6,500 mems; Pres. NIKITAS VENIZELOS.

Left Coalition (Synaspismos): Athens; f. 1989 as an alliance between the Greek Left Party and the Communist Party of Greece ('of the Exterior'); Pres. CHARILAOS FLORAKIS.

  Communist Party of Greece ('of the Exterior') (KKE—'Exterior'): Leoforos Irakiou 145, 142 31 Athens; tel. (01) 2523543; telex 225402; f. 1918; banned 1947, reappeared 1974; Moscow-line communist party; Gen. Sec. ALEKA PAPARIGA.

  Greek Left Party (Elliniki Aristera—EAR): 1 Eleftherias Sq. and Odos Pireos, 105 53 Athens; tel. (01) 3219908; telex 224555; f. 1987; broadly-based socialist party comprising the former Greek Communist Party ('of the Interior'), splinter groups from the KKE ('Exterior') and PASOK, minority groups and independents; 15,000 mems; Sec.-Gen. LEONIDAS KYRKOS.

New Democracy Party (Nea Demokratia—ND): Odos Rigillis 18, 106 74 Athens; tel. (01) 7290071; telex 210856; fax (01) 7236429; f. 1974 by KONSTANTINOS KARAMANLIS; a broadly-based centre-right party that advocates social reform in the framework of a liberal economy; favours membership of the EEC and NATO, and supports European integration; Leader KONSTANTINOS MITSOTAKIS; Dir-Gen. ANTONIS SGARDELIS.

Panhellenic Socialist Movement (Panellinion Socialistikon Kinema—PASOK): Odos Charilaou Trikoupi 50, Athens; tel. (01) 3232049; telex 218763; f. 1974; incorporates Democratic Defence and Panhellenic Liberation Movement resistance organizations; favours socialization of the means of production, decentralization and self-management, aims at a Mediterranean socialist development through international co-operation; 500 local organizations, 30,000 mems; Leader ANDREAS PAPANDREOU.

Other parties include the People's Militant Unity Party (f. 1985 by PASOK splinter group), the Progressive Party (f. 1979, rightwing), the (Maoist) Revolutionary Communist Party of Greece (EKKE), the Panhellenic Unaligned Party of Equality (PAKI, f. 1988; Leader CHARALAMBOUS ALOMA TAMONTSIDES), Olympianism Party (pacifist; Leader GIORGOS ZOE), and the left-wing United Socialist Alliance of Greece (ESPE, f. 1984).

Terrorist organizations include the left-wing 17 November Revolutionary Organization (f. 1975; opposed to Western capitalism and the continuing existence of US military bases in Greece), the 1 May Revolutionary Organization, the Revolutionary People's Struggle (ELA), People's Revolutionary Solidarity, the Anti-State Struggle group, the Christos Tsoutsouvis Revolutionary Organization and the Revolutionary Praxis.

Diplomatic Representation

EMBASSIES IN GREECE

Albania: Odos Karachristou 1, Kolonaki, 115 21 Athens; tel. (01) 7234412; telex 210351; Ambassador: IZEDIN HAJDINI.

Algeria: Leoforos Vassileos Konstantinou 14, 116 35 Athens; tel. (01) 7518560; telex 210000; fax (01) 7018001; Ambassador: ORLIM BENKHELIL.

GREECE

Argentina: Leoforos Vassilissis Sofias 59, Athens; tel. (01) 7224753; telex 215218; Ambassador: Raúl Bercovich Rodríguez.
Australia: Odos Dimitriou Soutsou 37/Odos Tsoha, Athens; tel. (01) 6447303; telex 215815; Ambassador: Kevin Ian Gates.
Austria: Leoforos Alexandras 26, 106 83 Athens; tel. (01) 8211036; telex 215938; Ambassador: Dr Hellmuth Strasser.
Belgium: Odos Sekeri 3, 106 71 Athens; tel. (01) 3617886; telex 216422; fax (01) 3604289; Ambassador: Gilbert Loquet.
Brazil: Platia Philikis Etairias 14, 106 73 Athens; tel. (01) 7213039; telex 216604; Ambassador: Alcides da Costa Guimarães Filho.
Bulgaria: Odos Akademias 12, Athens; tel. (01) 3609411; Ambassador: Petar Iliev Slavtchev.
Canada: Odos Ioannou Ghennadiou 4, 115 21 Athens; tel. (01) 7239511; Ambassador: Ernest Hébert.
Chile: Leoforos Vasilissis Sofias 96, Athens; tel. (01) 7775017; Chargé d'affaires a.i.: Manuel Atria.
China, People's Republic: Odos Krinon 2A, Palaio Psychiko, 154 32 Athens; tel. (01) 6723282; telex 214383; fax (01) 6723819; Ambassador: Zhu Youwan.
Cuba: Odos Davaki 10, Athens; tel. (01) 6925367; Ambassador: M. F. Alfonso Rodríguez.
Cyprus: Odos Herodotou 16, Athens; tel. (01) 7232727; telex 215642; Ambassador: Demos Hadjimiltis.
Czechoslovakia: Odos Georges Seferis 6, Palaio Psychiko, 154 52 Athens; tel. (01) 6713755; telex 214146; fax (01) 9224915; Ambassador: Jan Lajka.
Denmark: Odos Philikis Etairias 15, Platia Kolonaki, 106 73 Athens; tel. (01) 7249315; telex 215586; Ambassador: Skjold Gustav Mellbin.
Egypt: Leoforos Vassilissis Sofias 3, Athens; tel. (01) 3618612; Ambassador: Ahmad Kadry Salamah.
Ethiopia: Odos Davaki 10, Erythros, 115 26 Athens; tel. (01) 6920483; telex 218548; Ambassador: Samuel Teferra.
Finland: Odos Eratosthenous 1, 116 35 Athens; tel. (01) 7011775; Ambassador: Erkki Tiilikainen.
France: Leoforos Vassilissis Sofias 7; tel. (01) 3611683; Ambassador: Jacques Thibau.
Germany: POB 61011, Leoforos Vassilissis Sofias 10, 151 24 Athens; tel. (01) 3694111; telex 215441; fax (01) 8020523; Ambassador: Werner Graf von der Schulenburg.
Holy See: Odos Mavili 2, Palaio Psychiko, 154 52 Athens; tel. (01) 6473598; Apostolic Pro-Nuncio: Most Rev. Giovanni Mariani, Titular Archbishop of Missua.
Honduras: Leoforos Vassilissis Sofias 86, 115 28 Athens; tel. (01) 7775802; telex 241890; Chargé d'affaires a.i.: Teodolinda Banegas de Makris.
Hungary: Odos Kalvou 16, Palaio Psychiko, 154 52 Athens; tel. (01) 6714889; Ambassador: László Kincses.
India: Odos Kleanthous 3, 106 74 Athens; tel. (01) 7216481; Ambassador: Harcharan Singh Dhody.
Iran: Odos Kalari 16, Palaio Psychiko, Athens; tel. (01) 6471436; Ambassador: Ahmad Ajallooeian.
Iraq: Odos Mazaraki 4, Palaio Psychiko, Athens; tel. (01) 6715012; Ambassador: Fetah al-Khezreji.
Ireland: Leoforos Vassileos Konstantinou 7, Athens; tel. (01) 7232771; telex 218111; fax (01) 7240217; Ambassador: Eamon Ryan.
Israel: Odos Marathonodromou 1, Palaio Psychiko, 154 52 Athens; tel. (01) 6719530; Chargé d'affaires a.i.: Arie Tenne.
Italy: Odos Sekeri 2, Athens; tel. (01) 3611722; Ambassador: Marco Pisa.
Japan: 21st Floor, Athens A Tower, Leoforos Messoghion 2-4, Ambelokipi, 115 27 Athens; tel. (01) 7758101; telex 214460; Ambassador: (vacant).
Jordan: Odos Palaio Zervou 30, Palaio Psychiko, 154 52 Athens; tel. (01) 6474161; telex 219366; Ambassador: Samir Khalifeh.
Korea, Republic: Odos Eratosthenous 1, 116 35 Athens; tel. (01) 7012122; telex 216202; Ambassador: Nam Kyun Park.
Kuwait: Odos Alex. Papanastassiou 55, Athens; tel. (01) 6473593; Ambassador: Saleh Mohamed al-Mohamed.
Lebanon: Leoforos Kifissias 26, 115 26 Athens; tel. (01) 7785158; Ambassador: Elias Ghosn.
Libya: Odos Vironos 13, Palaio Psychiko, Athens; tel. (01) 6472120; Ambassador: Abdalla Abumahara.
Mexico: Odos Diamandidou 73A, Palais Psychiko, 154 52 Athens; tel. (01) 6470852; telex 216172; fax (01) 6471506; Ambassador: Hugo Gutiérrez Vega.
Morocco: Odos Mousson 14, Palaio Psychiko, 154 52 Athens; tel. (01) 6474209; telex 210925; Ambassador: Larbi Mouline.
Netherlands: Leoforos Vassileos Konstantinou 5-7, 106 74 Athens; tel. (01) 7239701; telex 215971; fax (01) 7248900; Ambassador: H. A. L. Vijverberg.
New Zealand: An. Tsoha 15-17, Ambelokipi, 115 21 Athens; tel. (01) 6410311; telex 216630; Ambassador: Donald Harper.
Norway: Leoforos Vassileos Konstantinou 7, 106 74 Athens; tel. (01) 7246173; telex 215109; Ambassador: Tancred Ibsen.
Pakistan: Odos Loukianou 6, Athens; tel. (01) 7290122; Ambassador: Mohammad Rawal Veryamani.
Panama: Leoforos Vassilissis Sofias 21, Athens; tel. (01) 3631847; Ambassador: María Lakas Bahas.
Poland: Odos Chryssanthemon 22, Palaio Psychiko, 154 52 Athens; tel. (01) 6716917; Ambassador: Janusz Lewandowski.
Portugal: Odos Karneadou 44-46, 106 76 Athens; tel. (01) 7290096; telex 214903; fax (01) 7236784; Ambassador: Luís Navega.
Romania: Odos Emmanuel Benaki 7, Palaio Psychiko, Athens; tel. (01) 6718008; Ambassador: Nicolae Ecobescu.
Saudi Arabia: Odos Marathonodromou 71, Palaio Psychiko, 154 52 Athens; tel. (01) 6716911; Ambassador: Sheikh Abdullah Abdul-Rahman al-Malhooq.
South Africa: Leoforos Kifissias 124, 115 26 Athens; tel. (01) 6922125; telex 218165; Ambassador: Dr S. G. A. Golden.
Spain: Leoforos Vassilissis Sofias 29, Athens; tel. (01) 7214885; telex 215860; Ambassador: Enrique Mahou Stauffer.
Sweden: Leoforos Vassileos Konstantinou 7, 106 74 Athens; tel. (01) 7290421; telex 215646; fax (01) 7229953; Ambassador: Karl Anders Wollter.
Switzerland: Odos Iassiou 2, 115 21 Athens; tel. (01) 7230364; telex 216230; Ambassador: Charles Steinhäuslin.
Syria: Odos Marathonodromou 79, Palaio Psychiko, Athens; tel. (01) 6725577; Ambassador: Shahin Farah.
Thailand: Odos Taigetou 23, Palaio Psychiko, 154 58 Athens; tel. (01) 6717969; telex 225856; Ambassador: S. C. M. Sukri Gajaseni.
Tunisia: Odos Ethnikis Antistaseos 91, Chalandri, 152 31 Athens; tel. (01) 6717590; telex 223786; fax (01) 6474244; Ambassador: Férid Soudani.
Turkey: Odos Vassileos Gheorghiou B 8, 106 74 Athens; tel. (01) 7245915; telex 216334; Ambassador: Gündüz Aktan.
USSR: Odos Nikiforou Litra 28, Palaio Psychiko, Athens; tel. (01) 6725235; Ambassador: Anatoly A. Sliusar.
United Kingdom: Odos Ploutarchou 1, 106 75 Athens; tel. (01) 7236211; telex 216440; fax (01) 7241-872; Ambassador: Sir David Miers.
USA: Leoforos Vassilissis Sofias 91, 106 60 Athens; tel. (01) 7212951; telex 215548; fax (01) 7226724; Ambassador: Michael George Sotirhos.
Uruguay: Odos Likavitou I G, 106 72 Athens; tel. (01) 3613549; Ambassador: Carlos María Romero.
Venezuela: Leoforos Vassilissis Sofias 112, Athens; tel. (01) 7708769; Ambassador: José María Machin.
Yugoslavia: Leoforos Vassilissis Sofias 106, Athens; tel. (01) 7774344; Ambassador: Vladimir Sultanović.
Zaire: Odos Vassileos Konstantinou 2, 116 35 Athens; tel. (01) 7016171; telex 215994; Ambassador: Bomolo Lokoka.

Judicial System

The Constitution of 1975 provides for the establishment of a Special Supreme Tribunal. Other provisions in the Constitution provided for a reorganization of parts of the judicial system to be accomplished through legislation.

SUPREME ADMINISTRATIVE COURTS

Special Supreme Tribunal: Odos Patision 30, Athens; this court has final jurisdiction in matters of constitutionality.
Council of State: Old Palace Bldg, Athens; the Council of State has appellate powers over acts of the administration upon application by civil servants or other civilians.

SUPREME JUDICIAL COURT

Supreme Court: Leoforos Alexandros 121, Athens; this is the supreme court in the State, having also appellate powers. It consists of six sections, four Civil and two Penal, and adjudicates in quorum; Pres. Supreme Court Yannis Grivas.

COURTS OF APPEAL

These are 12 in number. They have jurisdiction in cases of Civil and Penal Law of second degree, and, in exceptional penal cases, of first degree.

GREECE
Directory

COURTS OF FIRST INSTANCE

There are 59 Courts of First Instance with jurisdiction in cases of first degree, and in exceptional cases, of second degree. They function both as Courts of First Instance and as Criminal Courts. For serious crimes the Criminal Courts function with a jury.

In towns where Courts of First Instance sit there are also Juvenile Courts. Commercial Tribunals do not function in Greece, and all commercial cases are tried by ordinary courts of law. There are, however, Tax Courts in some towns.

OTHER COURTS

There are 360 Courts of the Justice of Peace throughout the country. There are 48 Magistrates' Courts (or simple Police Courts).

In all the above courts, except those of the Justice of Peace, there are District Attorneys. In Courts of the Justice of Peace the duties of District Attorney are performed by the Public Prosecutor.

Religion

CHRISTIANITY

The Eastern Orthodox Church

The Orthodox Church of Greece: Odos Ioannou Gennadiou 14, 115 21 Athens; tel. (01) 7218381; f. 1850; 78 dioceses, 8,335 priests, 84 bishops, 9,025,000 adherents (1985).

The Greek branch of the Holy Eastern Orthodox Church is the officially established religion of the country, to which nearly 97% of the population profess adherence. The administrative body of the Church is the Holy Synod of 12 members, elected by the bishops of the Hierarchy.

Primate of Greece: Archbishop SERAPHIM of Athens.

Within the Greek State there is also the semi-autonomous Church of Crete, composed of seven Metropolitans and the Holy Archbishopric of Crete. The Church is administered by a Synod consisting of the seven Metropolitans under the Presidency of the Archbishop; it is under the spiritual jurisdiction of the Oecumenical Patriarchate of Constantinople, which also maintains a degree of administrative control.

Archbishop of Crete: Archbishop TIMOTHEOS (whose See is in Heraklion).

There are also four Metropolitan Sees of the Dodecanese, which are spiritually and administratively dependent on the Oecumenical Patriarchate and, finally, the peninsula of Athos, which constitutes the region of the Holy Mountain (Mount Athos) and comprises 20 monasteries. These are dependent on the Oecumenical Patriarchate of Constantinople, but are autonomous and are safeguarded constitutionally.

The Roman Catholic Church

Latin Rite

Greece comprises four archdioceses (including two directly responsible to the Holy See), four dioceses and one Apostolic Vicariate. In December 1988 there were an estimated 49,200 adherents in the country.

Archdiocese of Athens: Archbishopric, Odos Omirou 9, 106 72 Athens; tel. (01) 3624311; Archbishop Most Rev. NIKOLAOS FOSKOLOS.

Archdiocese of Rhodes: Archbishopric, Odos I. Dragoumi 5A, 851 00 Rhodes; tel. (0241) 21845; Apostolic Administrator Fr MICHEL PIERRE FRANZIDIS.

Metropolitan Archdiocese of Corfu, Zante and Cefalonia: Archbishopric, 491 00 Kerkyra; tel. (0661) 30277; Archbishop Mgr ANTONIOS VARTHALITIS.

Metropolitan Archdiocese of Naxos, Andros, Tinos and Myconos: Archbishopric, 842 00 Tinos (summer residence); tel. (0283) 22382; Naxos (winter residence); also responsible for the suffragan dioceses of Candia (Crete), Chios, Santorini and Syros and Milo; Archbishop Mgr JEAN PERRIS.

Apostolic Vicariate of Salonika (Thessaloniki): Leoforos Vassilissis Olgas 120B, 546 45 Thessaloniki; tel. (031) 835780; Apostolic Administrator Fr DEMETRIOS ROUSSOS.

Byzantine Rite

Apostolic Exarchate for the Byzantine Rite in Greece: Odos Acharnon 246, 112 53 Athens; tel. (01) 8677039; 2 parishes (Athens and Jannitsa, Macedonia); 12 secular priests, 17 religious sisters, 2,300 adherents (Dec. 1988); Exarch Apostolic Mgr ANDHARITHOS PRINTESIS, Titular Bishop of Gratianopolis.

Armenian Rite

Episcopacy of the Armenian Rite in Greece: Odos René Piot 2, 117 44 Athens; tel. (01) 9014089; 650 adherents (Dec. 1988); Bishop HOVANNES KOYOUNIAN.

Protestant Church

Greek Evangelical Church (Reformed): Odos Markon Botsari 24, 117 41 Athens; tel. (01) 9222684; f. 1858; comprises 30 organized churches; 5,000 adherents (1985); Moderator Rev. NIKOLAOS STAPHANIDES.

ISLAM

The law provides as religious head of the Muslims a Chief Mufti; the Muslims in Greece possess a number of mosques and schools.

JUDAISM

The Jewish population of Greece, estimated in 1943 at 75,000 people, was severely reduced as a result of the German occupation. In 1988 there were about 5,000 Jews in Greece.

Central Board of the Jewish Communities of Greece: Odos Sourmeli 2, 104 39 Athens; tel. (01) 8839953; telex 225110; fax (01) 8234488; f. 1945; officially recognized representative body of the communities of Greece; Pres. JOSEPH LOVINGER.

Jewish Community of Athens: Odos Melidoni 8, 105 53 Athens; tel. (01) 3252823; Rabbi JACOB D. ARAR.

Jewish Community of Larissa: Odos Kentavrou 27, Larissa; tel. (041) 220762; Rabbi ELIE SABETAI.

Jewish Community of Thessaloniki: Odos Tsimiski 24, 546 24 Thessaloniki; tel. (031) 275701; Pres. LEON BENMAYOR; Rabbi MOSHE HALEYOUVA.

The Press

In 1988 there were 117 daily newspapers and 1,041 non-daily newspapers. Afternoon papers are more popular than morning ones; in the Athens area in 1983 about 141,071 papers were sold each morning and up to 771,516 each afternoon.

PRINCIPAL DAILY NEWSPAPERS

Morning papers are not published on Mondays, nor afternoon papers on Sundays.

Athens

Acropolis: Odos Fidiou 12, 106 78 Athens; tel. (01) 3618811; telex 215733; f. 1881; morning; Independent-Conservative; Acropolis Publications SA; Publr G. LEVIDES; Dir MARNIS SKOUNDRIDAKIS; circ. 50,819.

Apogevmatini (The Afternoon): Odos Fidiou 12, 106 78 Athens; tel. (01) 3618811; telex 215733; f. 1956; independent; Publr GEORGIOS HATZIKONSTANTINOU; Editor J. MOSCHOVITIS; circ. 130,000.

Athens Daily Post: Odos Stadiou 57, Athens; tel. (01) 3249504; f. 1952; morning; English; Owner G. SKOURAS.

Athens News: Odos Lekka 23-25, 105 62 Athens; tel. (01) 3224253; f. 1952; morning; English; Publr-Propr JOHN HORN; circ. 10,000.

Athlitiki Icho (Athletics Echo): Odos Voulgari 11, 104 37 Athens; tel. (01) 5222524; f. 1945; morning; Editors and Proprs ATHAN SEMBOS, G. GEORGALAS; circ. 24,117.

Avghi (Dawn): Ag. Konstantiou 12, 104 31 Athens; tel. (01) 5231831; telex 222671; f. 1952; morning; publ. by the Greek Left Party; Dir GRIGORIS GIANNAROS; Editor L. VOUTSAS; circ. 55,000.

Avriani: Odos Dimitros 11, 177 78 Athens; tel. (01) 3424090; telex 218440; f. 1980; evening; Dir JOHN GAVRIELATOS; Publr and Editor G. A. KOURIS; circ. 115,000.

Dimokratikos Logos: Odos Dimitros 11, 177 78 Athens; tel. (01) 3424090; telex 218440; f. 1986; morning; Dir KOSTAS GERONIKOLOS; Publr and Editor G. A. KOURIS; circ. 12,000.

Eleftheri Ora: Odos Akadimias 32, 106 72 Athens; tel. (01) 3644128; f. 1981; evening; Publr J. MICHALOPOULOS; Dir G. MICHALOPOULOS; circ. 5,239.

Eleftherotypia: Odos Panepistimiou 57, Athens; f. 1974; evening; Publr CHR. TEGOPOULOS; Dir S. FYNTANIDIS; circ. 85,000.

Estia (Vesta): Odos Anthinou Gazi 7, 105 61 Athens; tel. (01) 3220631; f. 1898; afternoon; Publr and Editor ADONIS K. KYROU; circ. 7,978.

Ethnos (Nation): Odos Benaki, Metamorfosi Chalandriou, 152 35 Athens; tel. (01) 6580640; telex 2104415; f. 1981; evening; Publr GEORGE BOBOLAS; Dir G. A. FILIPPOPOULOS; circ. 150,000.

Express: Odos Halandri 65, Paradissos Amaroussiou, 151 25 Athens; tel. (01) 6827582; telex 219746; morning, financial; Publr Hellenews

1214

GREECE

Publications; Gen. Dir D. G. KALOFOLIAS; Editor-in-Chief T. MATSOUKIS; circ. 22,000.

Filathlos: Odos Dimitros 11, 177 78 Athens; tel. (01) 3424090; telex 218440; f. 1982; morning; Dir NICK KARAGIANNIDIS; Publr and Editor G. A. KOURIS; circ. 40,000.

Imerissia: Odos Geraniou 7A, 105 52 Athens; tel. (01) 5232159; f. 1947; morning; Publr A. MOTHONIOS and Co; circ. 11,000.

Kathmerini: Odos Stadiou 5, 105 62 Athens; tel. (01) 3220773; telex 226692; fax (01) 3229173; f. 1919; morning; Conservative; Editor NIKOS NIKOLAOU; circ. 90,000.

Mesimvrini (Midday): Odos Panepistimiou 10, 106 71 Athens; tel. (01) 3646010; telex 216495; f. 1980; evening; Publr ATHAN SEKERIS; Dir CH. PASSALARIS; circ. 24,701.

Naftemboriki (Daily Journal): Odos Lenorman 205, 104 42 Athens; tel. (01) 5130605; telex 221354; fax (01) 5146013; f. 1923; morning; non-political journal of finance, commerce and shipping; Dir N. ATHANASSIADIS; circ. 35,000.

Rizospastis (Radical): Leoforos N. Ionias 13B, Perissos, Athens; tel. (01) 2526434; telex 216156; morning; pro-Soviet Communist; Dir GRIGORIS FARAKOS; Editor G. TRIKALINOS; circ. 48,513.

Ta Nea (News): Odos Christou Lada 3, 102 39 Athens; tel. (01) 3230221; telex 210608; fax (01) 3228797; f. 1944; liberal; evening; Publr CHRISTOS LAMBRAKIS; Dir L. KARAPANAGIOTIS; circ. 155,000.

Vradyni (Evening Press): Odos Piraeus 9-11, 105 52 Athens; tel. (01) 5231001; telex 215354; f. 1923; evening; right-wing; Gen. Man. H. ATHANASIADOU; circ. 71,914.

Patras

Peloponnesos: Odos Alex. Ipsilandou 177, 262 25 Patras; tel. (061) 272452; f. 1886; independent conservative; Publr and Editor S. DOUKAS; circ. 6,000.

Thessaloniki

Ellinikos Vorras (Greek North): Odos Grammou-Vitsi 19, 551 34 Thessaloniki; tel. (031) 416621; telex 412213; f. 1935; morning; Publr TESSA LEVANTIS; Dir N. MERGIOS; circ. 14,467.

Makedonia: Odos Monastiriou 85, 546 27 Thessaloniki; tel. (031) 521621; f. 1911; morning; Propr Publishing Co of Northern Greece SA; Dir K. DIMADIS; Editor KATERINA VELIDES; circ. 47,989.

Thessaloniki: Odos Monastiriou 85, 546 27 Thessaloniki; tel. (031) 521621; f. 1963; evening; Propr Publishing Co of Northern Greece SA; Editor KATERINA VELIDES; circ. 36,040.

SELECTED PERIODICALS

Aktines: Odos Karytsi 14, 105 61 Athens; tel. (01) 3235023; f. 1938; monthly; current affairs, science, philosophy, arts; aims to promote a Christian civilization; Publr Christian Union; circ. 10,000.

The Athenian: Odos Peta 4, 105 58 Athens; tel. (01) 3222802; fax (01) 3223052; f. 1974; monthly; English; Publr SLOANE ELLIOTT; circ. 13,200.

Cosmopolitan: Leoforos Marathonas 14, Pallini, 153 00 Athens; tel. (01) 6665706; f. 1979; monthly; women's magazine; Publr P. ROKANAS; Dir K. KOSTOULIAS.

Deltion Diikiseos Epichiriseon (Business Administration Bulletin): Odos Rigilis 26, 106 74; Athens; tel. (01) 7235736; telex 29006; monthly; Editor J. PAPAMICHALAKIS; circ. 26,000.

Demosiografiki (Journalism): Prokopiou 7-9, 171 24 Athens; tel. (01) 9731338; f. 1987; monthly; Dir JOHN MENOÚNOS; circ. 2,000.

Ekonomicos Tachydromos (Financial Courier): Odos Christou Lada 3, 102 37 Athens; tel. (01) 3230221; telex 210608; fax (01) 3238740; f. 1926; weekly; Dir JOHN MARINOS; circ. 19,500.

Embros (Forward): Odos Christou Lada 7, Athens; tel. (01) 3228656; f. 1896; weekly; independent; Editor A. E. PARASCHOS.

Epikaira: Odos Voulis 17, Athens; Amaroussion Papyros Press Ltd; weekly; circ. 35,274.

Gynaika (Women): Fragklissias 7, Marousi, 151 25 Athens; tel. (01) 6826680; f. 1950; fortnightly; fashion, beauty, handicrafts, cookery, social problems, fiction, knitting, embroidery; Publr EVANGELOS TERZOPOULOS SA; circ. 94,654.

Hellenews: Halandriou 39, Paradissos Amaroussiou 151 25 Athens; tel. (01) 6827582; telex 219746; fax (01) 6825858; weekly; English; finance and business; Publr Hellenews Publications; Editor G. V. PAVLIDES.

Ikogeniakos Thesavros (Family Treasure): Athens; tel. (01) 5231033; f. 1967; weekly; women's and social matters; Publr KOSTANTINOS PAPAKRISTOPHILOU; Editor TAKIS AGELOPOULOS; circ. 31,180.

Makedoniki Zoi (Macedonian Life): Odos Mitropoleos 70, 546 22 Thessaloniki; tel. (031) 277700; monthly; Editor N. J. MERTZOS.

Pantheon: Odos Anaksagora 5, Athens; tel. (01) 5245433; fortnightly; Publr and Dir N. THEOFANIDES; circ. 74,141.

Politica Themata: Odos Ipsilantou 25, 106 75 Athens; tel. (01) 7218421; weekly; Publr J. CHORN; Dir C. KYRKOS; circ. 2,544.

Tachydromos (The Courier): Odos Christou Lada 3, 102 37 Athens; tel. (01) 3250810; telex 215904; f. 1953; weekly; illustrated magazine; Publr C. LAMBRAKIS SA; Dir ROULA MITROPOULOU; circ. 177,182.

Technika Chronika (Technical Times): Odos Karageorgi Servias 4, 105 62 Athens; tel. (01) 3234751; f. 1952; monthly; general edition on technical and economic subjects; Editor D. ROKOS; circ. 12,000.

To Vima (Tribune): Odos Christou Lada 3, 102 37 Athens; tel. (01) 3220221; telex 215904; fax (01) 3228797; f. 1922; weekly; liberal; Dir and Editor STAVROS R. PSYCHARIS; circ. 190,000.

Viomichaniki Epitheorissis (Industrial Review): Odos Zalokosta 4, 106 71 Athens; f. 1934; monthly; industrial and economic review; Publr S. VOVOLINIS; Editor D. KARAMANOS; circ. 25,000.

NEWS AGENCIES

Athenagence (ANA): Odos Pindarou 6, 106 71 Athens; tel. (01) 3639816; telex 215300; f. 1896; correspondents in leading capitals of the world and towns throughout Greece; Gen. Dir ANDREAS CHRISTODOULIDES.

Foreign Bureaux

Agence France-Presse (AFP): POB 3392, Odos Voukourestiou 18, 106 71 Athens; tel. (01) 3633388; telex 215595; Bureau Chief JEAN-PIERRE ALTIER.

Agencia EFE (Spain): Odos Zalokosta 4, 106 71 Athens; tel. (01) 3635826; telex 219561; Bureau Chief D. MARÍA-LUISA RUBIO; Correspondent JUAN JOSÉ FERNÁNDEZ ELORRIAGA.

Agenzia Nazionale Stampa Associata (ANSA) (Italy): Odos Valaoritou 9B, 106 71 Athens; tel. (01) 3605285; telex 221860; Correspondent GRAZIANO MOTTA.

Associated Press (AP) (USA): Odos Akadimias 27A, 106 71 Athens; tel. (01) 3602755; telex 215133.

Deutsche Press-Agentur (dpa) (Germany): Odos Achaeou 8, 106 75 Athens; tel. (01) 7230290; telex 215839; Correspondent URSULA DIEPGEN.

Informatsionnoye Agentstvo Novosti (IAN) (USSR): Odos Irodotou 9, 138 Athens; tel. (01) 7291016; telex 219601; Bureau Chief BORIS KOROLYOV; Correspondent J. KURIZIN.

Inter Press Service (IPS) (Italy): c/o ANA, Odos Pindarou 6, 106 71 Athens; tel. (01) 3639816; telex 215564.

Reuters News Agency (Hellas) SA (UK): 3rd Floor, Odos Voukourestiou 15, 106 71 Athens; tel. (01) 3647610; telex 215912; fax (01) 3604490.

Telegrafska Agencija Nova Jugoslavija (Tanjug) (Yugoslavia): Evrou 94-96, Ambelokipi, Athens; tel. (01) 7791545.

Telegrafnoye Agentstvo Sovetskovo Soyuza (TASS) (USSR): Odos Gizi 44, Palaio Psychiko, Athens; Correspondent ANATOLI TKACHUK.

United Press International (UPI) (USA): Odos Deligiori 55, 104 37 Athens; tel. (01) 5245385; telex 215572; fax (01) 5245384; Correspondent RALPH JOSEPH.

Xinhua (New China) News Agency (People's Republic of China): Odos Amarilidos 19, Palaio Psychiko, Athens; tel. (01) 6724997; telex 216235; Bureau Chief XIE CHENGHAO.

PRESS ASSOCIATIONS

Enossis Syntakton Imerission Ephimeridon Athinon (Journalists' Union of the Athens Daily Newspapers): Odos Akadimias 20, 106 71 Athens; telex 219467; fax (01) 3632608; f. 1914; Pres. DIMITRIOS MATHIOPOULOS; Gen. Sec. MANOLIS MATHIOUDAKIS; 1,100 mems.

Enossis Syntakton Periodikou Typou (Journalists' Union of the Periodical Press): Odos Valaoritou 9, Athens; Pres. ANDREAS KALOMARIS; 347 mems.

Foreign Press Association of Greece: Odos Akadimias 23, 134 Athens.

Publishers

Angyra Publications: Kifisou 85, Egaleo, 122 41 Athens; tel. (01) 3455276; telex 210804; fax (01) 3474732; f. 1932; general; Man. Dir DIMITRIOS PAPADIMITRIOU.

John Arsenidis Ekdotis: Odos Akademias 57, 106 79 Athens; tel. (01) 3629538; biography, literature, children's books, history, philosophy, social sciences; Man. Dir JOHN ARSENIDIS.

GREECE
Directory

Bergadi Editions: Odos Mavromichali 4, Athens; tel. (01) 3614263; academic, children's books; Dir MICHAEL BERGADIS.

Boukoumanis Editions: Odos Mavromichali 1, 106 79 Athens; tel. (01) 3618502; f. 1967; history, politics, sociology, psychology, belles-lettres, educational, arts, children's books, ecology; Man. ELIAS BOUKOUMANIS.

Ekdotike Athenon SA: Vissariones 1, 106 72 Athens; tel. (01) 3608911; fax (01) 3606157; f. 1961; history, archaeology, art; Man. Dirs GEORGE A. CHRISTOPOULOS, JOHN C. BASTIAS.

G. C. Eleftheroudakis SA: Odos Nikis 4, 105 63 Athens; tel. (01) 3222255; telex 219410; f. 1915; general, technical and scientific; Man. Dir VIRGINIA ELEFTHEROUDAKIS-GREGOU.

Etairia Ellinikon Ekdoseon: Odos Akademias 84, 142 Athens; tel. (01) 3630282; f. 1958; fiction, academic, educational; Man. Dir STAVROS TAVOULARIS.

Gnosis Publishing Co: Odos Zoodochou Pigis 29, 106 81 Athens; history, literature, art, children's books.

Hellenic Editions Co SA: Odos Akadimias 84, 106 78 Athens; tel. (01) 3607343; encyclopaedias; Editor-in-Chief J. ZAFIROPOULOS.

Kassandra M. Grigoris: Odos Solonos 71, 106 79 Athens; tel. (01) 3629684; f. 1967; Greek history, Byzantine archaeology, literature, theology; Man. Dir MICHEL GRIGORIS.

Denise Harvey and Co: Domos Publishing House, Mavromichali 16, 106 80 Athens; tel. (01) 3605532; f. 1972; modern Greek literature and poetry, belles-lettres, translations, selected general list (English and Greek); Man. Dir DENISE HARVEY.

I.D. Kollaros & Co SA: Odos Solonos 60, 106 72 Athens; tel. (01) 3635970; f. 1885; literature, history, textbooks, general; Gen. Dir MARINA KARAITIDIS.

Papazissis Publishers: Nikitara 2, 106 78 Athens; tel. (01) 3622496; telex 219807; f. 1929; economics, politics, law, history, school books; Man. Dir VICTOR PAPAZISSIS.

Patakis Editions: Odos Nikitara 3, 106 78 Athens; tel. (01) 3638362; fax (01) 3628950; literature, educational, philosophy, psychology, children's books.

D. and B. Saliveros: Arkadias and Teftidos 1, Peristeri, Athens; f. 1893; general and religious books, maps, diaries and calendars; Chair. D. SALIVEROS.

John Sideris: Odos Stadiou 44, Athens; tel. (01) 3229638; f. 1898; school textbooks, general; Man. J. SIDERIS.

J. G. Vassiliou: Odos Hippokratous 15, 106 79 Athens; tel. (01) 3623382; fax (01) 3623580; f. 1913; fiction, history, philosophy, dictionaries and children's books.

Government Publishing House

Government Printing House: Odos Kapodistriou 34, 104 32 Athens; tel. (01) 5248320.

PUBLISHERS' FEDERATIONS

Athens Federation of Publishers and Booksellers: Odos Themistokleus 54, 106 81 Athens; tel. (01) 3630029; Pres. V. GIANNIKOS; Sec. P. STATHATOS.

Hellenic Federation of Publishers and Booksellers: Odos Arachovis 61, 106 81 Athens; tel. (01) 3625458; fax (01) 3608789; f. 1961; Pres. DIMITRIS PANDELESKOS; Gen. Sec. ASSIMAKOPOULOS CHRISTOS.

Radio and Television

A television network of 17 transmitters is in operation. The Constitution of June 1975 placed radio and television under the direct supervision of the State. In 1987 there were an estimated 4.1m. radio receivers in use and 1.7m. television receivers were licensed. In the same year, 10 new municipal radio stations began to transmit programmes. By mid-1990 two privately-owned television companies, Mega-Channel and Antenna TV, had begun to broadcast programmes in Greece, thus ending the State's monopoly of television broadcasting.

Elliniki Radiophonia Tileorassi (ERT SA) (Greek Radio-Television): Leoforos Messoghion 432, 153 42 Athens; tel. (01) 6395970; telex 216066; fax (01) 6390652; state-controlled since 1938; Pres. and Man. Dir Prof. DIMITRIOS KORSOS.

Elliniki Tileorassi (Greek Television) **1 (ET 1):** Dir-Gen. NIKOS ALEVAS.

ET 2: Odos Messoghion 136, 115 25 Athens; tel. (01) 7701911; telex 210886; Dir-Gen. DEMETRIS PALEOTHODOROS. Dir-Gen. THANASSIS VALTINOS.

ET 3: Dir-Gen. NIKOS BAKOLAS.

Elliniki Radiophonia (ERA) (Greek Radio): Dir-Gen. NIKOS DIMOU.

Finance

(cap. = capital; p.u. = paid up; res = reserves; dep. = deposits; drs = drachmae; m. = million; br. = branch)

BANKING
Central Bank

Bank of Greece: Odos El. Venizelou 21, 102 50 Athens; tel. (01) 3201111; telex 215102; fax (01) 3232239; f. 1928; state bank of issue; cap. drs 3,877.0m., res drs 12,830.4m., dep. drs 3,897,034.1m. (Dec. 1989); Gov. DEMETRIOS CHALIKIAS; 27 brs.

Commercial Banks

Agricultural Bank of Greece: Odos Panepistimiou 23, 105 64 Athens; tel. (01) 3230521; telex 222160; fax (01) 3234386; f. 1929; a state agricultural bank, in 1990 the Government announced plans to transfer 49% of stock to private ownership; cap. drs 17,901.2m., res drs 66,218.4m., dep. drs 877,583.7m. (Dec. 1988); Gov. and Chair. THEODOROS G. DIMOPOULOS; 420 brs.

Bank of Attica: Odos Omirou 23, 106 72 Athens; tel. (01) 3646910; telex 223344; f. 1925; affiliated to Commercial Bank of Greece; cap. drs 432.5m., res drs 463.9m., dep. drs 16,018.7m. (Dec. 1986); Chair. and Gen. Man. KOSTAS KALYVIANAKIS; Vice-Chair. PANAYIOTIS POULIS; 12 brs.

Bank of Crete SA: Odos Voukourestiou 22, 106 71 Athens; tel. (01) 3606511; telex 218633; fax (01) 3644832; f. 1924 (reformed 1973); cap. drs 3,037.8m., res drs 1,427.0m., dep. drs 86,777.3m. (Dec. 1987); Chair. JOHN KAMARAS; 77 brs.

Bank of Piraeus: Odos Stadiou 34, 132 Athens; f. 1916; Chair. of Bd, Pres. and Gen. Man. KOSTAS LAMBRAKIS; Man. PETROS S. GREGOROPOULOS; 8 brs.

Commercial Bank of Greece: POB 16, Odos Sophokleous 11, 102 35 Athens; tel. (01) 3210911; telex 216545; fax (01) 3252131; f. 1907; cap. drs 12,609.5m., res drs 38,760.2m., dep. drs 1,020,548.0m. (Dec. 1989); Chair. and Man. Dir MICHAEL VRANOPOULOS; Gen. Man. GEORGE MICHELIS; 301 brs.

Credit Bank: Odos Stadiou 40, 102 52 Athens; tel. (01) 3260000; telex 218691; fax (01) 3224522; f. 1879, renamed 1972; cap. drs 13,200.0m., res drs 12,494.4m., dep. drs 543,291.8m. (Dec. 1989); Chair. and Gen. Man. YANNIS S. KOSTOPOULOS; 107 brs.

Ergobank SA: Odos Panepistimiou 36, 106 79 Athens; tel. (01) 3601011; telex 218826; f. 1975; cap. drs 3,100.8m., res drs 11,436.6m., dep. drs 194,999.8m. (Dec. 1989); Chair. C. S. KAPSASKIS; Gen. Man. Dr P. P. HAGGIPAVLOU; 55 brs.

General Hellenic Bank SA: Odos Panepistimiou 9, 102 29 Athens; tel. (01) 3241283; telex 215702; fax (01) 3222271; f. 1937 as Bank of the Army Share Fund, renamed 1966; cap. drs 3,928.7m., res drs 3,083.2m., dep. drs 182,510.3m. (Dec. 1989); Chair. D. DEMESTIHAS; Gen. Man. ACHILLEAS LAGIAS; 85 brs.

Investment Bank SA: Odos Korai 1, 105 64 Athens; tel. (01) 3230214; telex 214239; fax (01) 3239653; f. 1962; cap. drs 1,707.3m., res drs 1,635.6m., dep. drs 27,310.9m. (Dec. 1987); Chair. KONSTANTINOS J. LEVANTIS; Gen. Man. NIKOS P. THEODOSSIADES.

Ionian and Popular Bank of Greece: Odos Panepistimiou 45, 102 43 Athens; tel. (01) 3225501; telex 215269; fax (01) 3223814; f.1839; cap. drs 6,904.2m., res drs 13,558.8m., dep. drs 475,986.7m. (Dec. 1988); Chair. J. GLINIADAKIS; Gen. Man. P. ZACHAROPOULOS; 174 brs.

Macedonia Thrace Bank SA: Odos Ionos Dragoumi 5, 546 25 Thessaloniki; tel. (031) 542213; telex 418415; f, 1979; cap. drs 2,412.0m., res drs 5,255.0m., dep. drs 117,851.0m. (Dec. 1989); Pres. and Chair. ANTONIS S. ANEZINIS; 41 brs.

National Bank of Greece SA: Odos Aeolou 86, Cotzia Sq., 102 32 Athens; tel. (01) 3210411; telex 214931; f. 1841; cap. drs 54,980.6m., res drs 86,494.2m., dep. drs 3,711,930.7m. (Dec. 1989); Gov. MICHAEL VRANOPOULOS; 479 brs in Greece, 22 abroad.

National Mortgage Bank of Greece: POB 3667, Odos Panepistimiou 40, 102 10 Athens; tel. (01) 3648311; telex 221177; fax (01) 3605130; f. 1927; cap. drs 10,570.5m., res drs 30,413.8m., dep. drs 424,436.5m. (Dec. 1988); Gov. Prof. A. GEORGIADIS; 53 brs.

Traders' Credit Bank SA: Odos Santaroza 3, 105 64 Athens; tel. (01) 3218694; telex 223599; f. 1924, renamed 1952; affiliated to the National Bank of Greece; cap. drs 1,142.5m., res drs 2,284.7m., dep. drs 41,112.3m. (Dec. 1989); Chair. GEORGE A. ARCHONDIS; Gen. Man. KONSTANTIN MAVRAGANIS; 22 brs.

Development Banks

Hellenic Industrial Development Bank SA: Odos Panepistimiou 18, 106 72 Athens; tel. (01) 3237981; telex 215203; fax (01) 3621023; f. 1964; state-owned limited liability banking company; the major Greek institution in the field of industrial investment; cap. drs

GREECE

55,564m. (Sept. 1990), res drs 35,680.2m., dep. drs 320,165.8m. (Dec. 1988); Gov. EFTYCHIA PIPER-PYLARINOU; 11 brs.

National Investment Bank for Industrial Development SA: Leoforos Amalias 12-14, 102 36 Athens; tel. (01) 3242651; telex 216113; fax (01) 3296211; f. 1963; cap. drs 1,359.4m., res drs 16,077.2m., dep. drs 60,551.2m. (Dec. 1989); long-term loans, equity participation, promotion of co-operation between Greek and foreign enterprises; Chair. DEMETRIOS GERMIDES; Man. Dir BYRON N. BALLIS.

STOCK EXCHANGE

Athens Stock Exchange: Odos Sophokleous 10, 105 59 Athens; tel. (01) 3211301; telex 215820; fax (01) 3213938; f. 1876; Pres. NIKITAS A. NIARCHOS; Vice-Pres. GEORGE PERVANAS.

Agrotiki Hellenic General Insurance Co: Leoforos Syngrou 163, 171 21 Athens; tel. (1) 9358613; telex 223004; fax (1) 9358924.

PRINCIPAL INSURANCE COMPANIES

Alfa: Leoforos Kifissias 252-254, 152 31 Halandri; tel. (01) 6472411; telex 222693; f. 1977; Gen. Man. DEM. ATHINEOS.

Apollon: Leoforos Syngrou 39, 117 43 Athens; tel. (01) 9236362; Gen. Man. A. M. APOSTOLATOS.

Aspis Pronia: Odos Othonos 4, 105 57 Athens; tel. (01) 3224023; telex 215350; f. 1945; Man. Dir A. TAMBOURAS.

Astir: Odos Merlin 6, 106 71 Athens; tel. 3604111; telex 215383; f. 1930; Gen. Man. G. PAIPETIS.

Atlantiki Enosis: Odos Messoghion 71, 115 26 Athens; tel. (01) 7799211; telex 216822; f. 1970; Gen. Man. N. LAPATAS.

Cigna Insurance Co Hellas SA: Odos Phidippidou 2, 115 26 Athens; tel. (01) 7754731; telex 218339; fax (01) 7796719; Gen. Man. ANDREAS CHOURDAKIS.

Continental Hellas SA: Leoforos Syngrou 253, 171 22 Athens; tel. (01) 9429021; telex 222746; fax (01) 9425476; f. 1942; incorporating Plioktitai SA; Man. Dir SPYROS ALEXANDRATOS.

Cosmos: Odos Panepistimiou 25, 105 64 Athens; tel. (01) 3229273; f. 1942; Gen. Man. N. PLAKIDIS.

Crete Life Insurance Co SA: Odos Karageorghi Servias 4, 105 62 Athens; tel. (01) 3230981; telex 215379; f. 1940; Gen. Man. V. PLYTA.

Diana: Odos Tsimiski and I. Dragoumi 6, 546 24 Thessaloniki; tel. (031) 263729; telex 412526; f. 1975; Gen. Man. D. SPYRTOS.

Doriki: Odos Panepistimiou 58, 106 78 Athens; tel. (01) 36358121; telex 214326; f. 1972; Gen. Man. SPYROS NIKOLAIDES.

Dynamis SA: Leoforos Syngrou 106, 117 41 Athens; tel. (01) 9227255; telex 216678; f. 1977; Man. Dir NIKOLAS STAMATOPOULOS.

Ekonomiki: Odos Kapodistriou 38, 104 32 Athens; tel. (01) 5243374; Rep. D. NIKOLAYDIS.

Emporiki: Odos Philhellinon 6, 105 57 Athens; tel. (01) 3240093; telex 219218; fax (01) 3223835; f. 1940; Chair. PHOTIS P. KOSTOPOULOS; Exec. Dir MICHAEL P. PSALIDAS.

Estia Insurance and Reinsurance Co SA: Leoforos Syngrou 255, 171 22 Nea Smyrni, Athens; tel. (01) 9425513; telex 215833; f. 1943; Chair. ALKIVIADIS CHIONIS; Gen. Man. STAVROULA VAVAS-POLYCHRONOPOULOS.

Ethniki Insurance Co: Odos Karageorgi Servias 8, 102 10 Athens; tel. (01) 3222121; telex 215400; fax (01) 3236101; f. 1891; Dir L. KOKKINOS.

Ethnikon Idrima Asphalion tis Ellados: Odos Agiou Konstantinou 6, 101 Athens; f. 1933; Gen. Man. J. KYRIAKOS.

Europa Insurance Co SA: Leoforos Syngrou 70, 117 42 Athens; tel. (01) 9226077; telex 215268; Rep. I. MORFINOS.

Evropaiki Enosis: Odos Nikis 10, 105 63 Athens; tel. (01) 3249234; telex 214392; f. 1973; Gen. Man. PANOS MINETTAS.

Galaxias: Odos Panepistimiou 56, 106 78 Athens; tel. (01) 3639370; f. 1967; Gen. Man. I. TSOUPRAS.

Geniki Epagelmatiki: Odos Panepistimiou 56, 106 78 Athens; tel. (01) 3636910; f. 1967; Gen. Man. G. GIATRAKOS.

Gothaer Hellas: Odos Michalakopoulou 174, 115 27 Athens; tel. (01) 7750801; Gen. Man. S. GALANIS.

Halkyon: Odos Philonos 107-109, Piraeus; Man. Dir K. MARTINOS.

Hellas: Leoforos Kifissias 119, 151 24 Marousi; tel. (01) 8068501; telex 215226; f. 1973; Gen. Man. N. ADAMANTIADIS.

Hellenic Reliance Insurances S.A.: Odos Mavromichali 3, 185 03 Piraeus; tel. (01) 4115311; telex 212679; f. 1972; Gen. Man. M. N. LOURIDAS.

Hellenobretanniki General Insurances SA: Athens Tower 'B' Bldg, Odos Messogion 2-4, 115 27 Athens; tel. (01) 7755301; telex 216448; fax (01) 7714768; f. 1988; Gen. Man. D. J. PALEOLOGOS.

Hellinoelvetiki: Odos Hermou 6, 105 63 Athens; tel. (01) 3252106; telex 216936; f. 1943; Gen. Man. J. DELENDAS.

Directory

Hellinokypriaki A.E.G.A.: Leoforos Syngrou 102, 117 41 Athens; tel. (01) 9226094; telex 218722; Rep. PANOS PAPAYANNOPOULOS.

Hermes: Odos Christou Lada 2, 105 61 Athens; tel. (01) 3225602; f. 1940; general insurance; Gen. Man. N. NEGAS.

Horizon Insurance Co SA: Leoforos Amalias 26A, 105 57 Athens; tel. (01) 3227932; telex 216158; f. 1965; Gen. Mans THEODORE ACHIS, CHR. ACHIS.

Hydrogios: Odos Lagoumigi 6, 176 71 Athens; tel. (01) 9222749; Gen. Man. A. KASKARELIS.

Ikonomiki: Odos Kapodistriou 38, 102 Athens; f. 1968; Gen. Man. D. NIKOLAIDIS.

Ikostos Aion: Odos Kapodistriou 38, 104 32 Athens; tel. (01) 5243544; f. 1972; Gen. Man. N. KYLPASIS.

Ilios: Odos Mavromichali 10, 106 79 Athens; tel. (01) 3606410; telex 215834; f. 1941; Gen. Man. M. N. LOURIDAS; Chair J. PSOMAS.

Imperial Hellas SA: Leoforos Syngrou 253, 171 22 Athens; tel. (01) 9426352; fax (01) 9426202; f. 1971; Gen. Man. SAVVAS TZANIS.

Interamerican Insurance Co: Interamerican Plaza, Leoforos Kiffisias 117, 151 80 Maroussi, Athens; tel. (01) 8091111; telex 226177; fax (01) 8060820; f. 1971; Pres. and Man. Dir DIMITRI KONTOMINAS.

Interamerican Property and Casualty Insurance Co: Odos Agiou Konstantinou 59-61 and Leoforos Kifissias 117, 151 24 Maroussi, Athens; tel. (01) 9421222; telex 226177; f. 1975; Man. Dir G. ANTONIADIS.

Ioniki: Odos Korai 1, 105 64 Athens; tel. (01) 3236901; f. 1939; Gen. Man. E. DORKOFIKI.

Kykladiki: Odos Panepistimiou 59, 105 64 Athens; tel. (01) 3219184; telex 218560; f. 1919; Gen. Man. PAN. KATSIKOSTAS.

Laiki Insurance Company SA: Leoforos Syngrou 135, 171 21 N. Smyrni; tel. (01) 9332911; telex 215403; fax (01) 9335949; f. 1942; Gen. Man. N. MOURTZOUKOS.

Lloyd Hellenique SA: Odos Psaron 2 and Odos Agiou Konstantinou, 104 37 Athens; tel. (01) 5237168; telex 225397; f. 1942; Dir DOMINIQUE PRIGENT.

Makedonia Insurance Co: Odos Egnatia 1, 546 30 Thessaloniki; tel. (031) 526133; Gen. Man. K. EFTHIMIADIS.

Messoghios: Leoforos Syngrou 165, Athens; f. 1942; Gen. Man. E. TSAOUSIS.

National Insurance Institution of Greece: Odos Agiou Konstantinou 6, 104 31 Athens; tel. (01) 5223300; Rep. J. KYRIAKOS.

Olympic Ins. Co SA: Odos Tsimiski 21, 546 22 Thessaloniki; tel. (031) 239331; telex 415251; fax (031) 239264; f. 1972; Man. Dir GEORGE TARNATOROS-ANAGNOSTOU.

Omonia: Odos Agiou Konstantinou 2, Athens; Pres. F. TSOUKALAS.

Pagosmios Insurance SA: Leoforos Syngrou 194, 176 71 Athens; tel. (01) 9581341; telex 219319; f. 1975; Chair. L. FRANGOS; Gen. Man. G. FRANGOS.

Panellinios: Leoforos Syngrou 171, 171 21 Athens; tel. (01) 9352003; f. 1918; Gen. Man. A. VALYRAKIS.

Pegasus Insurance Co: Odos Stadiou 5, 105 62 Athens; tel. (01) 3227357; telex 214188; fax (01) 3246728; Gen. Man. M. PARASKAKIS.

Phoenix-General Insurance Co of Greece SA: Odos Omirou 2, 105 64 Athens; tel. (01) 322951; telex 215608; f. 1928; general insurance; Chair. P. I. LAMBROU; Gen. Man. Y. G. LINOS.

Piraiki: Odos Georges 10, 106 77 Athens; tel. (01) 3624868; telex 225921; f. 1943; Dir Gen. K. PAPAGEORGIOU.

Poseidon: Odos Karaiskou 163, 185 35 Piraeus; tel. (01) 4522685; fax (01) 4184337; f. 1972; Gen. Man. THANOS J. MELAKOPIDES.

Promitheus: Odos 3rd September 84, 104 Athens; tel. (01) 8827085; f. 1941; Gen. Man. C. GHONIS.

Proodos: Leoforos Syngrou 196, 176 71 Kallithea; tel. (01) 9593302; telex 214364; f. 1941; Gen. Man. N. DOIMAS.

Propontis-Merimna A.E.A.: Odos Agiou Konstantinou 6, 104 31 Athens; tel. (01) 5223300; f. 1917; Man. Dirs E. BALA-HILL, M. ARTAVANIS.

Prostasia: Leoforos Syngrou 253, 176 72 Athens; tel. (01) 9427091; Rep. A. PALMOS.

Skourtis GH: Odos Panepistimiou 58, 106 78 Athens; tel. (01) 3626081; Gen. Man. G. SKOURTIS.

Syneteristiki: Odos Gennadiou and Akadimias 8, 115 24 Athens; tel. (01) 3642611; Gen. Man. N. GEORGAKOPOULOS.

A large number of foreign insurance companies also operate in Greece.

Insurance Associations

Insurers' Union of Greece: Odos Voulis 22, 105 63 Athens; tel. (01) 3229395; Pres. J. KYRIAKOS; Man. CH. TSOUPIS; 39 mems.

GREECE

Association of Greek Insurance Companies: Odos Solonos 14, 106 73 Athens; tel. (01) 3610287; telex 226195; fax (01) 3644772; f. 1983; Chair. L. Kokkinos; 33 mems.

Association of Insurance Companies: Odos Xenophontos 10, 105 57 Athens; tel. (01) 3236733; telex 223522; 94 mems.

Trade and Industry

CHAMBERS OF COMMERCE

Athens Chamber of Commerce & Industry: Odos Akademias 7, 106 71 Athens; tel. (01) 3604815; telex 215707; f. 1919; Pres. Lazaros Efraimoglou; Sec.-Gen. Dim. Danilatos; 37,500 mems.

Handicraft Chamber of Athens: Odos Akademias 18, 106 71 Athens; tel. (01) 3630253; Pres. G. Kyriopoulos; Sec.-Gen. S. Papagelou; c. 60,000 mems.

Handicraft Chamber of Piraeus: Odos Karaiscou 111, 185 32 Piraeus; tel. (01) 4174152; f. 1925; Pres. Evag. Mytilineos; Sec.-Gen. Athan. Mystakidis; 18,500 mems.

Piraeus Chamber of Commerce & Industry: Odos Loudovikou, 185 31 Piraeus; tel. (01) 4177241; telex 212970; f. 1919; Pres. Manolis Niadas; Sec.-Gen. George Kassimatis.

Thessaloniki Chamber of Commerce and Industry: Odos Tsimiski 29, 546 24 Thessaloniki; tel. (031) 220920; telex 412115; f. 1919; Pres. Pantelis Konstantinidis; Sec.-Gen. John Mitatos; 11,500 mems.

INDUSTRIAL ASSOCIATIONS

Association of Industries of Northern Greece: POB 10709, 1 Morihovou Sq., 546 25 Thessaloniki; tel. (031) 539817, telex 418310; fax (031) 541491; f. 1914; Pres. Vassilios Panoutsos.

Federation of Greek Industries (SEB): Odos Xenophontos 5, 105 57 Athens; f. 1907; Pres. Stelios Argyros; 950 mems.

Hellenic Cotton Board: Leoforos Syngrou 150, 176 71 Athens; tel. (01) 9225011; telex 214556; f. 1931; state organization; Pres. Dimitrios Papaioannou.

Hellenic Organization of Small and Medium-size Industries and Handicrafts: Odos Xenias 16, 115 28 Athens; tel. (01) 7715002; telex 218819.

TRADE UNIONS

There are about 5,000 registered trade unions, grouped together in 82 federations and 86 workers' centres, which are affiliated to the Greek General Confederation of Labour (GSEE).

Greek General Confederation of Labour (GSEE): Odos Patission 69, Athens; tel. (01) 8834611; telex 226372; fax (01) 8229802; f. 1918; Pres. Lambros Kanellopoulos; Gen. Sec. Dimitrios Kostopoulos; 700,000 mems.

Pan-Hellenic Seamen's Federation: Livaros Building, Akti Miaouli 47-49, Piraeus; tel. (01) 4523589; f. 1920; confederation of 14 marine unions; Gen. Sec. Michel Zenzefilis.

TRADE FAIR

Helexpo: Odos Egnatia 154, 546 36 Thessaloniki; tel. (031) 239221; telex 412291; fax (031) 229116; f. 1926; official organizer of international fairs, exhibitions, festivals, cultural events and congresses (most notably the annual General Trade Fair of Thessaloniki, which takes place over two weeks starting on the first Sunday in September); Pres. George Athanassiades.

Transport

RAILWAYS

Ilektriki Sidirodromi Athinon-Pireos (ISAP) (Athens-Piraeus Electric Railways): Odos Athinas 67, 105 52 Athens; tel. (01) 3248311; telex 219998; fax (01) 3223935; Gen. Dir Konstantinos Kostoylas.

Organismos Sidirodromon Ellados (OSE) (Hellenic Railways Organization Ltd): Odos Karolou 1-3, 104 37 Athens; tel. (01) 5248395; telex 215187; fax (01) 5243290; f. 1971; state railways. Total length of track: 2,479 km (1988); Pres. Th. Rendis; Dir-Gen. D. Karapanos.

ROADS

In 1985 there were 34,492 km of roads in Greece. Of this total, 8,700 km were main roads, and 92 km were motorways.

INLAND WATERWAYS

There are no navigable rivers in Greece.

Corinth Canal: built 1893; over six km long, links the Corinthian and Saronic Gulfs. The Canal shortens the journey from the Adriatic to the Piraeus by 325 km; it is spanned by three single-span bridges, two for road and one for rail. The canal can be used by ships of a maximum draught of 22 ft and a width of 60 ft.

SHIPPING

In June 1989 the Greek merchant fleet totalled 2,010 vessels compared with 3,922 ships in 1980. The principal ports are Piraeus, Patras and Thessaloniki.

Union of Greek Shipowners: Karageorgis Bldg, Akti Kondyli, Piraeus; Pres. Stathis Gourdomichalis.

Among the largest shipping companies are:

Anangel Shipping Enterprises SA: Akti Miaouli 25, 185 35 Piraeus; tel. (01) 4112511; telex 213037; Dir A. Angelikousis; 47 vessels.

Bilinder Marine Corpn SA: Odos Diligrammi 59, Kifissia, 145 62 Athens; tel. (01) 8080211; telex 215394; fax (01) 8016681; 26 vessels.

Ceres Hellenic Shipping Enterprises Ltd: Akti Miaouli 69, 185 37 Piraeus; tel. (01) 4523612; telex 212257; Dir D. C. Hadjiantoniou; 74 vessels.

Chandris (Hellas) Inc: Akti Miaouli 95, 185 38 Piraeus; tel. (01) 4120932; telex 212218; fax (01) 4110891; Man. Dirs A. C. Piperas, M. G. Skordias; 18 vessels.

Costamare Shipping Co SA: Akti Miaouli 59, 185 36 Piraeus; tel. (01) 4521700; telex 211399; fax (01) 4527974; Dir V. C. Konstantakopoulos; 16 vessels.

European Navigation Inc: Odos Agiou Nikolaou 5-7, 185 10 Piraeus; tel. (01) 4522927; telex 211233; Dir P. Karnessis; 23 vessels.

Glafki (Hellas) Maritime Co: Odos Mitropoleos 3, Athens; tel. (01) 3244991; telex 214655; fax (01) 3228944; Dirs M. Fragoulis, G. Panagiotou; 23 vessels.

Golden Union Shipping Co SA: Odos Kolokotroni 126, 185 35 Piraeus; tel. (01) 4114511; telex 211190; fax (01) 4117553; Man. Dir Theodore Veniamis; 33 vessels.

Hellenic Mediterranean Lines Co Ltd: Electric Railway Station Building, POB 80057, 185 10 Piraeus; tel. (01) 4174341; telex 212517; fax (01) 4170090; f. 1929; Chair. Konst. A. Ringas; Man. Dir A. G. Yannoulatos; 5 passenger and car ferries.

Laskaridis Shipping Co Ltd: Akti Miaouli 91, 185 38 Piraeus; tel. (01) 4182551; telex 213876; fax (01) 4182388; Dirs C. P. Laskaridis, P. C. Laskaridis, A. C. Laskaridis; 23 vessels.

Marmaris Navigation Ltd: Odos Filellinon 4-6, Okeanion Bldg, 185 36 Piraeus; tel. (01) 4136613; telex 211234; Dir D. Diamantides; 23 vessels.

Mayamar Marine Enterprises SA: POB 80161, 185 34 Piraeus; tel. (01) 4115931; telex 213107; fax (01) 4116806; Dir J. C. Mavrakakis; 16 vessels.

Thenamaris (Ships Management) Inc: Odos Athinas 16, Kavouri, 166 71 Athens; tel. (01) 8969653; telex 210468; 51 vessels.

Tsakos Shipping and Trading SA: Akti Miaouli 85, 185 38 Piraeus; tel. (01) 4182111; telex 212670; fax (01) 4183116; Dirs E. Saroglou, E. N. Tsakos; 26 vessels.

United Shipping and Trading Co of Greece, SA: Odos Iassonos 6, 185 37 Piraeus; tel. (01) 4522511; telex 213014; fax (01) 4522564; Dir M. Zarbis; 14 vessels.

Varnima Corporation International SA: Marine Enterprises Bldg, Akti Miaouli 53-55, 185 36 Piraeus; tel. (01) 4522911; telex 212461; worldwide oil transportation; Chair. Vardis J. Vardinoyannis; Man. Dir G. J. Vardinoyannis; 10 vessels.

CIVIL AVIATION

There are international airports at Athens, Thessaloniki, Alexandroupolis, Corfu, Lesbos, Andravida, Rhodes, Kos and Heraklion/Crete, and 25 domestic airports. There are plans for a new international airport to be built at Spatsa, 48 km east of Athens.

Olympic Airways SA: Leoforos Syngrou 96-100, 117 41 Athens; tel. (01) 9292111; telex 216488; fax (01) 9219133; f. 1957; 51% state-owned, 49% of shares offered for transfer to private ownership in 1990; domestic services linking principal cities and islands in Greece, and international services to Albania, Australia, Austria, Belgium, Canada, Cyprus, Denmark, Egypt, France, Germany, Israel, Italy, Japan, Jordan, Kenya, Kuwait, Libya, the Netherlands, Saudi Arabia, Singapore, South Africa, Spain, Switzerland, Syria, Thailand, Turkey, the United Kingdom, the United Arab Emirates and the USA; fleet of 4 Boeing 747-200B, 3 Boeing 707-320C, 2 Boeing 707-320B, 6 Boeing 727-200, 11 Boeing 737-200 and 8 Airbus A300B4. Chair. V. Filias; Vice-Chair. Dr Dimitriu Bairaktaris.

GREECE

Tourism

The sunny climate, the natural beauty of the country and its great history and traditions attract tourists to Greece. There are numerous islands and other sites of archaeological interest. Tourism is expanding rapidly, with the improvement of transport and accommodation facilities. The number of tourists visiting Greece increased from 1m. in 1968 to an estimated 8.3m. in 1988. Receipts from tourism, which totalled US $120m. in 1968, reached $2,396.1m. in 1988.

Ellinikos Organismos Tourismou (EOT) (Greek National Tourist Organization): Odos Amerikis 2B, 105 64 Athens; tel. (01) 3223111; telex 215832; fax (01) 3224148; Pres. Prof. MARIOS RAPHAEL; Vice-Pres. NIKI GOULANDRIS.

Atomic Energy

Elliniki Epitropi Atomikis Energias (Greek Atomic Energy Commission): POB 60228, 153 10 Aghia Paraskevi, near Athens; tel. (01) 6514716; telex 218254; fax (01) 6533939; f. 1954; seven-member administrative cttee; Pres. Prof. CHARALAMBOS PROUKAKIS; Vice-Pres. Prof. P. MANAKOS.

National Center for Scientific Research 'Demokritos': POB 60228, 153 10 Aghia Paraskevi, near Athens; tel. (01) 6513110; telex 216199; fax (01) 6519180; institutes for: materials science, microelectronics, nuclear technology, radiation protection, nuclear physics, biology, physical chemistry, informatics and telecommunications, radio-isotopes and radiodiagnostic products; Dir Dr ION SIOTIS.

GRENADA

Introductory Survey

Location, Climate, Language, Religion, Flag, Capital

Grenada, a mountainous, heavily-forested island, is the most southerly of the Windward Islands, in the West Indies. The country also includes some of the small islands known as the Grenadines, which lie to the north-east of Grenada. The largest of these is the low-lying island of Carriacou. The climate is semi-tropical, with an average annual temperature of 28°C (82°F) in the lowlands. Annual rainfall averages about 1,500 mm (60 in) in the coastal area and 3,800 mm to 5,100 mm (150–200 in) in mountain areas. Most of the rainfall occurs between June and December. The majority of the population speak English, although a French patois is sometimes spoken. Most of the population profess Christianity, and the main denominations are Roman Catholicism (to which, it is estimated, more than 60% of the population adhere) and Anglicanism (about 20% of the population). The national flag (proportions 2 by 1) consists of a diagonally-quartered rectangle (yellow in the upper and lower segments, green in the right and left ones) surrounded by a red border bearing six five-pointed yellow stars (three at the upper edge of the flag, and three at the lower edge). There is a red disc, containing a large five-pointed yellow star, in the centre, and a representation of a nutmeg (in yellow and red) on the green segment near the hoist. The capital is St George's.

Recent History

Grenada was initially colonized by the French but was captured by the British in 1762. British control was recognized in 1783 by the Treaty of Versailles. Grenada continued as a British colony until 1958, when it joined the Federation of the West Indies, remaining a member until the dissolution of the Federation in 1962. Full internal self-government and statehood in association with the United Kingdom were achieved in March 1967. During this period, the political life of Grenada was dominated by Eric Gairy, a local trade union leader, who in 1950 founded the Grenada United Labour Party (GULP), with the support of an associated trade union. In 1951 GULP won a majority of the elected seats on the Legislative Council, but in 1957 it was defeated by the Grenada National Party (GNP), led by Herbert Blaize. Gairy was Chief Minister in 1961–62 but was removed from office by the British, and the Constitution suspended, after allegations of corruption. In the subsequent elections the GNP gained a majority of the elected seats, and Blaize became Chief Minister again. Gairy became Premier after the elections of 1967 and again after those of 1972, which he contested chiefly on the issue of total independence. Grenada became independent, within the Commonwealth, on 7 February 1974, with Gairy as Prime Minister. Opposition to Gairy within the country was expressed in demonstrations and a general strike, and the formation, by the three opposition parties, of the People's Alliance, which contested the 1976 general elections and reduced GULP's majority in the Lower House. The alliance comprised the GNP, the United People's Party and the New Jewel Movement (NJM).

The rule of Sir Eric Gairy, who was knighted in June 1977, was regarded by the opposition as increasingly autocratic and corrupt, and on 13 March 1979 he was replaced in a bloodless coup by the leader of the left-wing NJM, Maurice Bishop. The new People's Revolutionary Government (PRG) suspended the 1974 Constitution and announced the imminent formation of a People's Consultative Assembly to draft a new constitution. Meanwhile, Grenada remained a monarchy, with the British Queen as Head of State, represented in Grenada by a Governor-General. During 1980 and 1981 there was an increase in repression, against a background of mounting anti-Government violence and the PRG's fears of an invasion by US forces.

By mid-1982 relations with the USA, the United Kingdom and the more conservative members of CARICOM were becoming increasingly strained: elections had not been arranged, restrictions against the privately-owned press had been imposed, many detainees were still awaiting trial, and Grenada was aligning more closely with Cuba and the USSR. Cuba was supplying about 40% of the funds, and several hundred construction workers, for the airport at Point Salines, a project which further strengthened the US Government's conviction that Grenada was to become a major staging-post for Soviet manoeuvres in the area.

In March 1983 the PRG reiterated its fears that the USA was planning an invasion, and the armed forces were put on alert. The USA strenuously denied these allegations. In June Maurice Bishop sought to improve relations with the USA, and announced the appointment of a commission to draft a new constitution. This attempt at conciliation was not popular with the more left-wing members of the PRG regime, who regarded Bishop's actions as an ideological betrayal. This division within the Government erupted in October into a power struggle between Bishop and his deputy, Bernard Coard, the Minister of Finance and Planning. On 13 October Bishop was placed under house arrest, allegedly for his refusal to share power with Coard. Four days later, Gen. Hudson Austin, the commander of the People's Revolutionary Army (PRA), announced that Bishop had been expelled from the NJM. On 19 October thousands of Bishop's supporters, incensed by this news, stormed the house, freed Bishop from imprisonment, and demonstrated outside the PRA headquarters. Violence ensued, with PRA forces firing into the crowd. Later in the day, Bishop, three of his ministers and two trade union spokesmen were all executed by the PRA. A military coup had taken place, and the Government was replaced by a 16-man Revolutionary Military Council (RMC), led by Gen. Austin and supported by Coard and one other minister. The remaining NJM ministers were arrested and imprisoned, and a total curfew was imposed.

Regional and international outrage at the assassination of Bishop, plus fears of a US military intervention, were so intense that, after four days, the RMC relaxed the curfew, reopened the airport and promised to return to civilian rule as soon as possible. However, the Organization of Eastern Caribbean States (OECS, see p. 109) decided to intervene in an attempt to restore democratic order, and asked for help from the USA, which readily complied. (It is unclear whether the decision to intervene preceded or followed a request for help to the OECS by the Grenadian Governor-General, Sir Paul Scoon.) On 25 October 1983 about 1,900 US military personnel invaded the island, accompanied by 300 troops from Jamaica, Barbados and member-countries of the OECS. Fighting continued for some days, and the USA gradually increased its troop strength, with further reinforcements waiting off shore with a US naval task force. The RMC's forces were defeated, while Coard, Gen. Austin and others who had been involved in the coup were captured and imprisoned on the island, to await trial.

On 9 November 1983 Sir Paul Scoon appointed a non-political interim council to assume responsibility for the government of the country until elections could be held. Nicholas Braithwaite, a former Commonwealth official, was appointed chairman of this council in December. The 1974 Constitution was reinstated, and an electoral commission was created to prepare for elections. By mid-December the USA had withdrawn all its forces except 300 support troops, military police and technicians who were to help the 430 members of Caribbean forces who remained on the island. These numbers were maintained throughout 1984. A 550-member police force, trained by the USA and the United Kingdom, was established, including a paramilitary element which was to be the new defence contingent.

Several political parties, which had gone underground or into exile during the rule of the PRG, re-emerged and announced their intention of contesting the elections for a new House of Representatives. Sir Eric Gairy returned to Grenada in January 1984 to lead his GULP, although he stated that he would not stand as a candidate himself. In May three former NJM ministers formed the Maurice Bishop Patriotic Movement (MBPM) to contest the elections. A number of centre parties emerged or re-emerged, including the GNP, led by Herbert Blaize, the former Premier; the Grenada Democratic Movement

(GDM), led by Dr Francis Alexis; the National Democratic Party (NDP), led by George Brizan; and the Christian Democratic Labour Party (CDLP). Fears that a divided opposition would allow GULP to win a majority of seats in the new House led to negotiations between the centre parties to form an electoral alliance. After the failure of one attempt, and in response to US apprehension over growing support for GULP, a meeting between the GNP, GDM, NDP and CDLP was arranged at the end of August 1984 on Union Island, and attended by the Prime Ministers of Barbados, Saint Lucia and Saint Vincent and the Grenadines. The result was the agreed merger of the parties to form the New National Party (NNP), to be led by Herbert Blaize. The CDLP, however, soon left the new party, and there were some fears over the cohesion of the new grouping.

At the general election, held on 3 December 1984, the NNP achieved a convincing victory over its opponents by winning 14 of the 15 seats in the House of Representatives, and 59% of the popular votes. Both Sir Eric Gairy of GULP (which won 36% of the votes cast) and the MBPM claimed that the poll had been fraudulent, and the one successful GULP candidate, Marcel Peters, initially refused to take his seat in protest. He subsequently accepted the seat, but was expelled from the party and formed the Grenada Democratic Labour Party (GDLP). Blaize became Prime Minister, and appointed a seven-member cabinet, which included Brizan and Alexis. He also asked the remaining US and Caribbean troops on the island to stay, at least until March 1985, and stressed the need for national reconciliation. The last contingents of US and Caribbean troops left the island in September 1985.

The trial before the Grenada High Court of 19 detainees (including Coard, his wife and Austin), accused of murder and conspiracy against Bishop and six of his associates, had opened in November 1984. However, repeated adjournments prevented the start of proceedings. The approval by the House of Representatives of all the legislation that had been enacted during the rule of the PRG prevented an appeal by the detainees to the Judicial Committee of the Privy Council (based in the United Kingdom), and, in response to requests from the defence lawyers, further adjournments postponed the trial of 18 of the detainees until April 1986. One of the detainees agreed to give evidence for the State in return for a pardon. Eventually, verdicts on 196 charges of murder and conspiracy to murder were returned by the jury in December. Fourteen of the defendants were sentenced to death, three were given prison sentences of between 30 and 45 years, and one was found not guilty. Appeals by the accused were expected to be considered during 1988, but were delayed by procedural challenges and criticisms, and by the death of the President of the Appeal Court in December. Appeal hearings resumed in 1989, and continued into 1990.

The notable feature of the NNP's administration was the gradual disintegration of the party, owing to the divisions between the different groupings that comprised it. There were frequent disagreements between cabinet members, resentment at Blaize's authoritarian style of leadership and increasing acrimony over the question of who should succeed Blaize, particularly following his successive visits to the USA for medical treatment.

In 1986 the parliamentary strength of the NNP was reduced to 12 seats, following the resignation of two members who subsequently formed the Democratic Labour Congress (DLC). In April 1987 the NNP's majority in the House of Representatives was further reduced, and the coalition collapsed, when three more government members, including Alexis and Brizan (the former leaders of the GDM and NDP), resigned.

In July 1987 the three joined forces with the DLC and the GDLP to form a united opposition, with six seats in the House of Representatives. In October they formally launched a new political party, the National Democratic Congress (NDC). Brizan, who had earlier been appointed parliamentary opposition leader, was elected leader of the party. In January 1989, however, Brizan resigned as leader of the NDC in order to allow the election of Nicholas Braithwaite, head of the interim Government of 1983–84, to that post.

During 1988 and 1989 the actions of the Blaize Government, under provisions of the controversial Emergency Powers Act of 1987, gave rise to concerns among both regional neighbours and the opposition. Deportation orders and bans were enforced by the administration against prominent left-wing politicians and journalists from the region, and a variety of books and journals were proscribed.

A deterioration in Prime Minister Blaize's health coincided with a growing challenge to his administration from within the NNP throughout 1988. In January 1989 Blaize was replaced as leader of the ruling party by his cabinet colleague, Dr Keith Mitchell, but he remained Prime Minister. Blaize, however, appointed Ben Jones, the Minister of Foreign Affairs, as Deputy Prime Minister, and continued to distance Mitchell from the leadership of government. Furthermore, in July, pursuing allegations of corruption by the opposition NDC, Blaize appointed a commission of inquiry into the conduct of certain government departments and corporations, all of which were the responsibility of Mitchell. Only three days later, Blaize announced the dismissal of Mitchell and one of his supporters, the Chairman of the NNP, accusing them of violating the principles of cabinet government. Amid uncertainty as to whether the Blaize faction had formed a separate party, two more members of the Government resigned in protest. Thus, the Blaize Government retained the support of only five of the 15 members of the House of Representatives.

Blaize did not formally announce the formation of a new party, the National Party (TNP), until the end of August 1989. By then he had advised the acting Governor-General to prorogue Parliament. The Government thereby avoided being defeated in a motion of 'no confidence' (two had been proposed) or the prospect of a general election which would be consequent upon the immediate dissolution of Parliament. The term of the Parliament was due to expire at the end of December 1989, and a general election had to be held within three months. On 19 December, however, Prime Minister Blaize died. After consultations with the parliamentary opposition, the Governor-General appointed Ben Jones, the late Herbert Blaize's deputy and the new leader of TNP, as Prime Minister. At the general election, which was held on 13 March 1990, no party achieved an absolute majority. The NDC won seven of the 15 seats, the GULP, which had held no seats in the previous Parliament, won four, while TNP won only two, as did the NNP. The MBPM, which secured less than 2% of the total votes, failed to gain a single seat. Within a week, the NDC had achieved a working majority in Parliament, when Edzel Thomas, one of the GULP's successful candidates, announced his defection to the NDC. He was subsequently given a junior ministerial post in the Cabinet of the new Prime Minister, Nicholas Braithwaite. At the end of the month, the NDC's position was further strengthened when the two TNP members of the House of Representatives, Ben Jones and Alleyne Walker, expressed their support for the new Government by accepting Braithwaite's offer of cabinet posts.

In January 1991 Ben Jones resigned from his post as Minister of Foreign Affairs, to which he had been appointed from the Ministry of Agriculture in December 1990. (Alleyne Walker was also expected to resign from his junior ministerial position.) Jones's resignation followed a decision by TNP to withdraw its support from the Government after the announcement of a new taxation scheme in the 1991/92 budget. The opposition parties and trade unions believed that the scheme, which was to be introduced in an attempt to reduce the national debt, would adversely affect Grenadan businesses and their employees' standard of living.

As a member of the OECS, Grenada has been involved in discussions concerning the possible formation of a political union. Some islands displayed considerable reluctance and so, in 1988, four countries, Grenada, Dominica, Saint Lucia and Saint Vincent and the Grenadines, decided to proceed with their own plans for a political union. In 1989 the four countries of the Windward group agreed that any restrictions on travel between them should cease from 1 January 1990. At a meeting held by representatives of the four countries in St George's in late 1990, it was agreed that a constituent assembly would be convened to discuss the economic and political feasibilities of creating a federation. A mandate for such a federation was to be sought from the people of the Windward Islands in a referendum planned for May or June 1991. There was also a possibility that, despite early reservations, the three countries of the Leeward Islands, Antigua and Barbuda, Montserrat and Saint Christopher and Nevis, would be permitted to join the proposed federation.

GRENADA

Government

Grenada has dominion status within the Commonwealth. The British monarch is Head of State and is represented locally by a Governor-General. Executive power is held by the Cabinet, led by the Prime Minister. Parliament comprises the Senate, made up of 13 Senators appointed by the Governor-General on the advice of the Prime Minister and the Leader of the Opposition, and the 15-member House of Representatives, elected by universal adult suffrage. The Cabinet is responsible to Parliament.

Defence

A police force was formed in late 1983, modelled on the British system and trained by British officers. A paramilitary element, known as the Special Service Unit and trained by US advisers, acts as the defence contingent and participates in the Regional Security System, a defence pact with other East Caribbean states.

Economic Affairs

In 1989, according to estimates by the World Bank, Grenada's gross national product (GNP), measured at average 1987–89 prices, was US $179m., equivalent to US $1,900 per head. Between 1980 and 1989, it was estimated, the country's GNP per head increased, in real terms, by an average of 5.6% annually, and overall GNP by an annual average of 5.9%. Over the same period, population increased at an average rate of 0.8% per year. Gross domestic product (GDP), increased by an annual average of 5.5% between 1985 and 1989.

Agriculture (including forestry and fishing) contributed 21% of GDP in 1989, and it remains the principal activity for most of the islands' inhabitants. Agricultural output increased by 2.5% in 1989. Grenada, known as the Spice Island of the Caribbean, is the largest producer of nutmeg after Indonesia (which produces some 75% of the world's total), and in 1987 it supplied 23% of the world's nutmeg. In 1988 sales of nutmeg and mace (the pungent red membrane around the nut) accounted for 44.0% of Grenada's total export earnings of US $32.5m. In 1990, however, the price of nutmeg on the world market fell by 30%, due to the collapse of the cartel agreement between Grenada and Indonesia. The other principal cash crops are bananas (14.5% of exports in 1988), cocoa beans (9.8% of exports) and other fresh fruit and vegetables. In 1987 the agricultural sector accounted for more than 90% of exports. Livestock production, for domestic use, is important on Carriacou. There are extensive timber reserves on the island of Grenada, but forestry development is strictly controlled and involves a programme of reafforestation. Fishing was developed from the early 1980s, and by 1987 there were 1,749 fishermen with 635 locally-registered vessels.

Industry (manufacturing and construction) contributed 16.1% of GDP in 1989. Manufacturing, which contributed 5.5% of GDP, consists mainly of the processing of agricultural products and of cottage industries producing garments and spice-based items. Rum is the only significant industrial export, but in 1989, when total manufacturing output increased by 12.0%, the soft drinks and the tyre-retreading industries were also important. Construction, promoted by the Government's programme of infrastructural development, contributed 10.6% of GDP in 1989.

Grenada is dependent upon imports for its energy requirements, and in 1987 petroleum accounted for 5.8% of the total cost of imports. The Government intended to begin the construction of a hydro-electric power station on the Marquis river, in St Andrew's parish, in late 1990.

Government and tourist services contributed 25.1% of GDP in 1987. Although the hotels and restaurants sector accounted for only 6.5% of GDP, tourism is nevertheless an expanding industry. In 1989 tourist receipts were estimated to be some US $30.7m. Since 1984 the number of stop-over arrivals and cruise-ship visitors has more than doubled. In 1987, 32% of stop-over visitors were from CARICOM countries, 17.9% from the USA and 16.7% from Europe (mainly the United Kingdom). It was estimated in 1988 that some 25% of stop-over arrivals were Grenadans resident abroad.

The Caribbean Development Bank (CDB) reported that Grenada's trade deficit in 1988 was US $59.6m. This was recorded as an increase of 5.6% on the trade deficit for 1987, in which year there was a deficit of US $25.7m on the current account of the balance of payments. In 1987 the principal source of imports was the USA (26.2%). The EEC is the principal market for exports (68.6% in 1987), the main trading partner within it being the United Kingdom (which itself received some 34% of total exports in 1984). The EEC also provided 24.7% of imports in 1987. CARICOM, mainly Trinidad and Tobago, provided 20.4% of imports and received 14.4% of Grenada's exports in 1987. The principal exports are agricultural, notably nutmeg. The principal imports in 1984 were foodstuffs and basic manufactures. The trade deficit is partly offset by earnings from tourism, capital receipts and remittances from Grenadans working abroad.

For the financial year ending 30 April 1990 there was a projected surplus on the recurrent budget of EC $2.9m., the first surplus for more than 10 years. In 1989, however, the CDB warned that revenue receipts in Grenada were consistently overestimated. In the 1991/91 budget, recurrent expenditure was projected to total EC $196.0m. and capital expenditure EC $64.6m. Grenada's total external debt was EC $152.5m. at the end of March 1990. The average annual rate of inflation was 3.7% in 1989. Between 25% and 30% of the labour force were estimated to be unemployed in 1989.

Grenada is a member of CARICOM (see p. 108), and secured limited protection for some of its products when tariff barriers within the organization were removed in 1988. It is also a member of the Economic Commission for Latin America and the Caribbean (ECLAC, see p. 27), the Organization of American States (OAS, see p. 194), the Organization of Eastern Caribbean States (OECS, see p. 109) and is a signatory of the Lomé Conventions (see p. 151).

Grenada's economy was severely disrupted by the political troubles and military intervention of the early 1980s. Government attempts to diversify the economy and to encourage tourism and manufacturing have concentrated on the repair and development of infrastructure. Particularly with the cessation of US budgetary support in 1987, however, the Government has been hindered by its sizeable internal and external debts. In an attempt to reduce the debts, the Government announced the introduction of a new income tax in the 1991/92 budget. Grenada's economy remains dependent upon agriculture, which is vulnerable to adverse weather conditions and problems such as the banana disease, moko. The economy's susceptibility to the fluctuations in international commodity prices was demonstrated in 1990, when the price of nutmeg (Grenada's principal export commodity) on the world market decreased by 30%, following the breakdown of Grenada's cartel agreement with Indonesia (signed in 1987). The most promising and rapidly expanding sector of the Grenadan economy is tourism, and the island has encouraged considerable foreign investment, with the aim of expanding this industry. The European Investment Bank is helping to finance the development of the hotel sector, which hopes to have 2,000 rooms by 1994. Revenue from tourism was expected to increase by 10% per year from 1991 onwards.

Social Welfare

There was no system of social security payments in Grenada prior to 1979. New initiatives launched in that year included the Youth for Reconstruction Programme, to provide basic paramedical services and assistance to the elderly and disabled, a national milk distribution programme and the establishment of community-directed day care centres. A National Insurance Scheme began in 1983, and in 1988 had a total investment portfolio of EC $58m. In 1987 there were 42 physicians working in Grenada and the country had three hospitals, with a total of about 360 beds. There are six local health centres, all in the main towns. A mental hospital, destroyed by military action in 1983, was rebuilt with US financial aid.

Education

Education is free and compulsory for children between the ages of six and 14 years. The standard of education is high; primary education begins at five years of age and lasts for seven years. Secondary education, beginning at the age of 12, lasts for a further seven years, comprising a first cycle of five years and a second of two years. In 1987 a total of 20,976 children received public primary education in 63 schools. There were 18 public secondary schools, with 6,497 pupils registered, in 1987. In 1970 only 2.2% of the adult population had received no schooling. Technical Centres have been established in each parish, and there is a Technical and Vocational Institute in St George's. The Extra-Mural Department of the University of the West Indies has a branch in St George's, and there is also

GRENADA

a Teachers' Training College. A School of Medicine has been established at St George's, a School of Agriculture at Mirabeau and a School of Fishing at Victoria.

Public Holidays
1991: 1–2 January (New Year), 7 February (Independence Day), 29 March (Good Friday), 1 April (Easter Monday), 1 May (Labour Day), 20 May (Whit Monday), 30 May (Corpus Christi), 5–6 August (Emancipation Holidays), 25 October (Thanksgiving Day), 25–26 December (Christmas).

1992: 1–2 January (New Year), 7 February (Independence Day), 17 April (Good Friday), 20 April (Easter Monday), 1 May (Labour Day), 8 June (Whit Monday), 18 June (Corpus Christi), 3–4 August (Emancipation Holidays), 25 October (Thanksgiving Day), 25–26 December (Christmas).

Weights and Measures
The metric system is in use.

Statistical Survey

Source (unless otherwise stated): Central Statistical Office, Government of Grenada, Church Street, St George's; tel. (440) 3034.

AREA AND POPULATION
Area: 344.5 sq km (133.0 sq miles).
Population: 93,858 at census of 7 April 1970; 89,088 (males 42,943; females 46,145) at census of 30 April 1981; 94,118 (official estimate) at mid-1987.
Density (1987): 273.2 per sq km.
Principal Town: St George's (capital), population 7,500 (1980 estimate).
Births and Deaths (1987): Birth rate 32.1 per 1,000; Death rate 8.1 per 1,000.

AGRICULTURE, ETC.
Principal Crops ('000 metric tons, 1989): Roots and tubers 4*, Vegetables and pulses 3*, Coconuts 8*, Sugar cane 8*, Cocoa beans 1.4, Bananas 18*, Mangoes 2*, Avocados 2*, Other fruit 7*, Nutmeg and mace 3.2 (Source: mainly FAO, *Production Yearbook*).
* FAO estimates.
Livestock (FAO estimates, '000 head, year ending September 1989): Cattle 5, Pigs 11, Sheep 15, Goats 11, Asses 1 (Source: FAO, *Production Yearbook*).
Fishing (metric tons, live weight): Total catch 2,112 in 1986; 2,215 in 1987; 2,001 in 1988 (Source: FAO, *Yearbook of Fishery Statistics*).

INDUSTRY
Production (1986): Rum 71,943 gallons; Beer 15,000 hectolitres; Cigarettes 23m.; Electric energy (1987) 40.3 million kWh (Source: mainly UN, *Industrial Statistics Yearbook*).

FINANCE
Currency and Exchange Rates: 100 cents = 1 East Caribbean dollar (EC $). *Coins:* 1, 2, 5, 10, 25 and 50 cents. *Notes:* 1, 5, 20 and 100 dollars. *Sterling and US Dollar Equivalents* (30 September 1990): £1 sterling = EC $5.058; US $1 = EC $2.700; EC $100 = £19.77 = US $37.04. *Exchange Rate:* Fixed at US $1 = EC $2.70 since July 1976.
Budget (estimates, EC $ million): **1989/90:** *Revenue:* Recurrent 162.0, Grants 27.3. *Expenditure:* Recurrent 159.1, Capital 88.5. **1991/92:** Expenditure: Recurrent 196.0, Capital 64.6.
International Reserves (US $ million at 31 December 1989): Foreign exchange 15.89; Total 15.89 (Source: IMF, *International Financial Statistics*).
Money Supply (EC $ million at 31 December 1989): Currency outside banks 31.40; Demand deposits at deposit money banks 57.24; Total money 88.64 (Source: IMF, *International Financial Statistics*).
Cost of Living (Consumer Price Index; base: 1980 = 100): 146.7 in 1987; (base: 1987 = 100): 104.0 in 1988; 109.4 in 1989 (Source: UN, *Monthly Bulletin of Statistics*).
Gross Domestic Product (EC $ million in current purchasers' values): 311.2 in 1985; 347.6 in 1986; 375.7 in 1987 (Source: IMF, *International Financial Statistics*).
Balance of Payments (US $ million, 1988): Merchandise exports f.o.b. 32.81; Merchandise imports f.o.b. −94.50; *Trade balance* −61.69; Exports of services 52.34; Imports of services −31.50; *Balance on goods and services* −40.85; Private unrequited transfers (net) 15.30; Government unrequited transfers (net) 6.30; *Current balance* −19.25; Long-term capital (net) 23.16; Short-term capital (net) −9.81; Net errors and omissions −1.84; *Total* (net monetary movements) −7.74; Valuation changes (net) −0.11; Exceptional financing (net) 2.60; *Changes in reserves* −5.02 (Source: IMF, *International Financial Statistics*).

EXTERNAL TRADE
Principal Commodities (EC $ million, 1983): *Imports:* Food and live animals 35.4; Beverages and tobacco 3.3; Crude materials (inedible) except fuels 8.4; Mineral fuels, lubricants, etc. 17.2; Chemicals 12.1; Basic manufactures 39.2; Machinery and transport equipment 17.1; Total (incl. others) 154.5. *Exports:* Food and live animals 46.6 (Cocoa 11.0, Nutmeg 9.5, Bananas 8.7, Mace 2.3, Fresh fruit 12.8); Clothing 3.5; Total (incl. others) 50.7 (excl. re-exports 1.1).
1985 (EC $ million): Imports 187.0 (Food 24.8%); Exports 60.3.
1986 (EC $ million): Imports 225.5 (Food 21.9%); Exports 77.7.
1987 (EC $ million): Imports 239.4 (Food 24.2%); Exports 85.2.
Principal Trading Partners (EC million, 1984): *Imports:* Japan 10.4; Trinidad and Tobago 22.5; United Kingdom 27.6; USA 37.2; Total (incl. others) 151.1. *Exports* (incl. re-exports): Federal Republic of Germany 4.5; Netherlands 3.5; Trinidad and Tobago 16.7; United Kingdom 15.6; USA 2.4; Total (incl. others) 46.0.

TRANSPORT
Road Traffic (1987): Motor vehicles registered 11,250.
International Sea-borne Shipping: *Freight Traffic** (estimates, '000 metric tons, 1985): Goods loaded 27; Goods unloaded 52. *Ship Arrivals* (1987): 1,144. *Fishing vessels* (registered, 1987): 635.
* Source: UN, *Monthly Bulletin of Statistics*.
Civil Aviation (aircraft arrivals, 1987): 12,120.

TOURISM
Visitor Arrivals: 197,775 in 1988; 192,172 in 1989; 196,132 in 1990.
Cruise-ship Calls: 218 in 1989.
Receipts from Tourism (US $ million): 28.2 in 1988; 30.7 in 1989 (estimate).

COMMUNICATIONS MEDIA
Radio Receivers (licensed, 1988): 51,000 in use.
Television Receivers (official estimate, 1989): 30,000 in use.
Telephones (official estimate, 1988): 6,000 in use.
Newspapers (1987): 6 titles.
Book Production (1979): 10 titles (11,000 copies).

EDUCATION
Pre-primary (1986): 68 schools; 146 teachers; 3,283 pupils.
Primary (1987): 63 schools; 806 teachers; 20,976 pupils.
Secondary (1987): 18 schools*; 317 teachers; 6,497 pupils.
Higher (excluding figures for the Grenada Teachers' College, 1983): 53 teachers; 535 students.
Source: UNESCO, *Statistical Yearbook*.
* Government figure.

Directory

The Constitution

The 1974 independence Constitution was suspended in March 1979, following the coup, and almost entirely restored between November 1983, after the overthrow of the Revolutionary Military Council, and the elections of December 1984. The main provisions of this Constitution are summarized below:

The Head of State is the British monarch, represented in Grenada by an appointed Governor-General. Legislative power is vested in the bicameral Parliament, comprising a Senate and a House of Representatives. The Senate consists of 13 Senators, seven of whom are appointed on the advice of the Prime Minister, three on the advice of the Leader of the Opposition and three on the advice of the Prime Minister after he has consulted interests which he considers Senators should be selected to represent. The Constitution does not specify the number of members of the House of Representatives, but the country consists of 15 single-member constituencies, for which representatives are elected for up to five years, on the basis of universal adult suffrage.

The Cabinet consists of a Prime Minister, who must be a member of the House of Representatives, and such other Ministers as the Governor-General may appoint on the advice of the Prime Minister.

There is a Supreme Court and, in certain cases, a further appeal lies to Her Majesty in Council.

The Government

Head of State: HM Queen ELIZABETH II (succeeded to the throne 6 February 1952).

Governor-General: Sir PAUL SCOON (took office 1978).

THE CABINET
(February 1991)

Prime Minister and Minister of Home Affairs, Information, National Security, Personnel and Management, and Carriacou and Petit Martinique Affairs: NICHOLAS BRAITHWAITE.

Minister of Foreign Affairs: (vacant).

Minister of Finance, Trade and Industry: GEORGE BRIZAN.

Minister of Education, with Responsibility for Culture, Youth Affairs and Sport: CARLYLE GLEAN.

Minister of Works, with Responsibility for Communications and Public Utilities: KENNY LALSINGH.

Minister of Health, Housing and the Environment: MICHAEL ANDREWS.

Minister of Agriculture, with Responsibility for Lands, Forestry and Fisheries: PHINSLEY ST LOUIS.

Minister of Labour and Social Security, with Responsibility for Co-operatives and Community Development: EDZEL THOMAS.

Minister of Tourism, with Responsibility for Women's Affairs and Civil Aviation: JOAN PURCELL.

Attorney-General, with Responsibility for Legal Affairs and Local Government: FRANCIS ALEXIS.

MINISTRIES

All Ministries are in St George's.

Office of the Governor-General: Government House, St George's; tel. (440) 2401.

Office of the Prime Minister: Botanical Gardens, St George's; tel. (440) 2255; telex 3457; fax (440) 4116.

Ministry of Agriculture, Lands, Forestry and Fisheries: Treasury Bldg, St George's; tel. (440) 2248.

Ministry of Finance: Church St, St George's; tel. (440) 2731; telex 3418; fax (440) 4115.

Legislature

PARLIAMENT

Houses of Parliament: Church St, St George's; tel. (440) 2090; fax (440) 4138.

Senate

President: JOHN WATTS.

There are 13 appointed members.

House of Representatives

Speaker: Sir HUDSON SCIPIO.

General Election, 13 March 1990

Party	Seats
National Democratic Congress (NDC)	7
Grenada United Labour Party (GULP)	4*
The National Party (TNP)	2
New National Party (NNP)	2
Total	**15**

* In the week following the general election the NDC achieved an overall majority in the House of Representatives when one of the GULP members joined its ranks.

Political Organizations

Christian Democratic Labour Party (CDLP): St George's; f. 1984; Leader WINSTON WHYTE.

Grenada People's Movement: St George's; f. 1989 by former GULP mems; Chair. FENNIS AUGUSTINE; Leader Dr RAPHAEL FLETCHER.

Grenada United Labour Party (GULP): St George's; f. 1950; right-wing; Leader Sir ERIC GAIRY.

Maurice Bishop Patriotic Movement (MBPM): St George's; f. 1984 by former members of the New Jewel Movement; socialist; Leader TERRENCE MARRYSHOW.

National Democratic Congress (NDC): St George's; f. 1987 by former members of the NNP and merger of Democratic Labour Congress and Grenada Democratic Labour Party; centrist; Chair. KENNY LALSINGH; Leader NICHOLAS BRAITHWAITE; Gen. Sec. JEROME JOSEPH.

The National Party (TNP): St George's; f. 1989 by Prime Minister Herbert Blaize and his supporters, following a split in the New National Party; Chair. GEORGE MCGUIRE; Leader BEN JONES.

New National Party (NNP): St George's; f. 1984; merger of Grenada Democratic Movement, Grenada National Party and National Democratic Party; centrist; Chair. LAWRENCE JOSEPH; Leader Dr KEITH MITCHELL; Gen. Sec. JOHN MUNROE.

People's Party for Growth and Accountability: St George's; f. 1989; Leader DAVISON BUDHOO.

Diplomatic Representation

EMBASSIES AND HIGH COMMISSION IN GRENADA

China (Taiwan): POB 36, St George's; Ambassador: LIU PO-LUN.

United Kingdom: British High Commission, 14 Church St, St George's; tel. (440) 3222; telex 3419 (High Commissioner resident in Barbados).

USA: Point Salines, POB 54, St George's; tel. (440) 1731; fax (444) 4820; Ambassador: JAMES FORD COOPER.

Venezuela: Archibald Ave, POB 201, St George's; tel. (440) 1721; telex 3414; Ambassador: EFRAÍN SILVA MÉNDEZ.

Judicial System

Justice is administered by the Grenada Supreme Court, composed of a High Court of Justice and a two-tier Court of Appeal. The Court of Magisterial Appeals is presided over by the Chief Justice. The Itinerant Court of Appeal consists of three judges and sits twice a year; it hears appeals from the High Court and is the final court of appeal. There are also Magistrates' Courts which administer summary jurisdiction. In certain cases appeal lies to the Privy Council in the United Kingdom.

In 1988 the OECS excluded the possibility of Grenada's readmittance to the East Caribbean court system until after the conclusion of appeals by the defendants in the Maurice Bishop murder trial (see Recent History).

Chief Justice: Sir SAMUEL GRAHAM.

Puisne Judges: JAMES PATTERSON, LYLE G. ST PAUL.

Registrar of the Supreme Court: KEITH H. W. FRIDAY.

GRENADA

President of the Court of Appeal: Sir FREDERICK SMITH.
Office of the Attorney-General: St George's; tel. (440) 2050.

Religion

CHRISTIANITY
The Roman Catholic Church
Grenada comprises a single diocese, suffragan to the archdiocese of Castries (Saint Lucia). The Bishop participates in the Antilles Episcopal Conference (based in Kingston, Jamaica). At 31 December 1988 there were an estimated 67,563 adherents in the diocese.

Bishop of St George's in Grenada: Rt Rev. SYDNEY ANICETUS CHARLES, Bishop's House, Morne Jaloux, POB 375, St George's; tel. (443) 5299.

The Anglican Communion
Anglicans in Grenada are adherents of the Church in the Province of the West Indies. The country forms part of the diocese of the Windward Islands (the Bishop, the Rt Rev. PHILIP EDWARD RANDOLPH ELDER, resides in Kingstown, Saint Vincent).

Other Christian Churches
The Presbyterian, Methodist, Plymouth Brethren, Baptist and Seventh-day Adventist faiths are also represented.

The Press

NEWSPAPERS
Grenada Guardian: St George's; weekly; organ of GULP.
The Grenadian Voice: Melville St, POB 3, St George's; tel. (440) 1498; fax (440) 4117; weekly; Editor LESLIE PIERRE.
Government Gazette: St George's; weekly; official.
The Indies Times: Grenville St, St George's.
The Informer: Young St, St George's; tel. (440) 1530; fax (440) 4119; weekly; Editor CARLA BRIGGS.
The National: St George's.
The Tribune: St George's.
The West Indian: 45 Hillsborough St, St George's.

PRESS ASSOCIATION
Press Association of Grenada: St George's; f. 1986; Pres. LESLIE PIERRE.

Publishers

Grenada Publishers Ltd: Torchlight, Melville St, St George's; tel. (440) 2305.
West Indian Publishing Co Ltd: Hillsborough St, St George's; tel. (440) 2118; govt-owned.

Radio and Television

In 1988 there were an estimated 51,000 radio receivers in use, and in 1989 there were an estimated 30,000 television receivers in use.
Radio Grenada: POB 34, St George's; tel. (440) 3033; f. 1972; name changed in 1979, 1983 and 1984; housed in temporary studios since station destroyed in military intervention of 1983; govt-owned; Gen. Man. L. SMITH.
Discovery Television Ltd: St George's; f. 1986; bought by majority govt-owned Grenadan co in 1989; Man. LARRY UPTON.
Free Grenada Television: St George's; f. 1980; govt-owned and operated.
Grenada Television Service Ltd: Marne Jaloux, St George's; tel. (443) 5521; fax (443) 5054.

In October 1990 Parliament approved legislation providing for the transfer of Radio Grenada and Free Grenada Television to private ownership. Television programmes from Trinidad and from Barbados can be received on the island.

Finance

The Eastern Caribbean Central Bank (see p. 109), based in Saint Christopher, is the central issuing and monetary authority for Grenada.
Eastern Caribbean Central Bank—Grenada Office: 4 Camerhogne House, Church St, St George's; tel. (440) 3016.

BANKING
Grenada Bank of Commerce Ltd: Corner of Cross and Halifax Sts, POB 4, St George's; tel. (440) 3521; telex 3467; fax (440) 4153; f. 1983; cap. EC $5.5m., res EC $5.9m., dep. EC $92.2m. (Dec. 1989); Chair. LAURISTON WILSON; Man. MORRIS MATHLIN.
Grenada Co-operative Bank Ltd: 8 Church St, St George's; tel. (440) 2111; f. 1932; Man. Dir and Sec. G. V. STEELE; brs in St Andrew's and St Patrick's.
Grenada Development and Agriculture Bank: Treasury Bldg, The Carenage, St George's; tel. (440) 2382; f. 1976 after merger of the Grenada Agricultural Bank and the Grenada Development Corpn; Chair. SAMUEL GRAHAM; Man. RONALD CHARLES.
National Commercial Bank of Grenada Ltd: Corner of Halifax and Hillsborough Sts, POB 57, St George's; tel. (440) 3566; telex 3413; fax (440) 4140; f. 1979; govt-owned; total assets EC $110m. (1989); Gen. Man. MICHAEL B. ARCHIBALD; Dep. Gen. Man. DANIEL A. ROBERTS; 5 brs.
People's Bank (Grenada) Ltd: Grenville St, St George's; tel. (440) 3077; fax (440) 4141; f. 1988; cap. EC $34m.; Chair. GEORGE DE BOURG.

Foreign Banks
Bank of Nova Scotia (Canada): Halifax St, POB 194, St George's; tel. (440) 3274; telex 3452; Man. FITZROY O'NEALE.
Barclays Bank PLC (UK): Church and Halifax Sts, POB 37, St George's; tel. (440) 3232; telex 3421; fax (440) 4103; Man. L. E. POLLARD; 2 sub-brs in Carriacou and Grenville.
Caribbean Commercial Bank (Trinidad and Tobago): St George's; 1 br.

INSURANCE
Several foreign insurance companies operate in Grenada and the other islands of the group. Principal locally-owned companies include the following:
Grenada Insurance and Finance Co Ltd: Young St, POB 139, St George's; tel. (440) 3004.
Grenada Insurance Services Ltd: 12–14 Young St, POB 47, St George's; tel. (440) 2434.
Grenada Motor and General Insurance Co Ltd: Scott St, St George's; tel. (440) 3379.

Trade and Industry

Grenada Chamber of Industry and Commerce, Inc: Decaul Bldg, Mt Gay, POB 129, St George's; tel. (440) 2937; telex 3469; f. 1921, incorporated 1947; 189 mems; Pres. HUGH DOLLAND; Exec. Dir DAPHNE BROWN.
Grenada Cocoa Board: Scott St, St George's; tel. (440) 2234; telex 3444; f. 1987 (permanent from 1989) as merger of Cocoa Assen and Govt's Cocoa Rehabilitation Project; Chair. RAYMOND RUSH (acting).
Grenada Co-operative Banana Society: Scott St, St George's; tel. (440) 2486; f. 1955; a statutory body to control production and marketing of bananas; Chair. R. M. BHOLA.
Grenada Co-operative Nutmeg Association: POB 160, St George's; tel. (440) 2117; telex 3454; f. 1947; processes and markets all the nutmeg and mace grown on the island; Chair. NORRIS JAMES; Gen. Man. ROBIN S. RENWICK.
Grenada Electricity Services Ltd (Grenlec): POB 381, St George's; tel. (440) 2097; telex 3472; Man. G. C. BOWEN.
Grenada Industrial Development Corporation: Frequente Industrial Estate, St David's; tel. (444) 1035; fax (440) 4135; f. 1985; Chair. ALBERT XAVIER.
Grenada Manufacturers' Association: Grande Anse, POB 213, St David's; tel. (444) 4637; f. 1986; Pres. OSLYN WILLIAMS; Sec. ANN CAMPBELL.
Marketing and National Importing Board: Young St, St George's; tel. (440) 3191; telex 3435; fax (440) 4152; f. 1974; govt-owned; imports basic food items, incl. sugar, rice and milk; Chair. FINTON GEORGE DE BOURG; Gen. Man. STEPHEN JOHN.

EMPLOYERS' ORGANIZATION
Grenada Employers' Federation: POB 129, St George's; tel. (440) 1832.

There are several marketing and trading co-operatives, mainly in the agricultural sector.

TRADE UNIONS
Grenada Trade Union Council (GTUC): Green St, POB 405, St George's; tel (440) 3733; Pres. A. DE BOURG.

GRENADA

Commercial and Industrial Workers' Union: St George's; tel. (440) 3423; 492 mems; Pres. A. DE BOURG.

Grenada Union of Teachers (GUT): Marine Villa, St George's; f. 1913; Pres. (vacant); 1,300 mems.

Seamen and Waterfront Workers' Union: The Carenage, POB 154, St George's; tel. (440) 2573; f. 1952; Pres. ARTHUR RAMSEY; Gen. Sec. ERIC PIERRE; 350 mems.

Technical and Allied Workers' Union (TAWU): Green St, POB 405, St George's; tel. (440) 2231; f. 1958; Pres. (vacant).

Agricultural and General Workers' Union: St George's; Pres. GODWIN THOMAS.

Bank and General Workers' Union: St George's; tel. (440) 3563; Pres. DEREK ALLARD.

Grenada Manual, Maritime and Intellectual Workers' Union: St George's; associated with GULP; Pres. Sir ERIC GAIRY.

Public Workers' Union (PWU): POB 420, St George's; tel. (440) 2203; f. 1931; Pres. LAURET CLARKSON; Exec. Sec. GARTH D. GEORGE.

Transport

RAILWAYS

There are no railways in Grenada.

ROADS

In 1983 there were approximately 980 km (610 miles) of roads, of which 766 km (476 miles) were suitable for motor traffic. Many of these were severely damaged by military action in October 1983, and a major programme of repairs was undertaken over some years, often with US financial aid. Public transport is provided by small private operators, with a system covering the entire country.

SHIPPING

The main port is St George's, with accommodation for two ocean-going vessels of up to 500 ft. A number of shipping lines call at St George's. Grenville, on Grenada, and Hillsborough, on Carriacou, are used mostly by small craft.

Grenada Ports Authority: St George's; tel. (440) 3013; telex 3418.

CIVIL AVIATION

The Point Salines International Airport, 10 km (6 miles) from St George's, was opened in October 1984, and has scheduled flights to most East Caribbean destinations, including Venezuela, and to the United Kingdom and North America. There is an airfield at Pearls, 30 km (18 miles) from St George's, and Lauriston Airport, on the island of Carriacou, offers regular scheduled services to Grenada, Saint Vincent and Palm Island (Grenadines of Saint Vincent).

Grenada is a shareholder in the regional airline, LIAT (see under Antigua and Barbuda). In 1987 Air Antilles (based in Saint Lucia) was designated as the national carrier.

Grenada Airports Authority: Point Salines Int. Airport, St George's; tel. (444) 4101.

Tourism

Grenada has the attractions of both white sandy beaches and a scenic, mountainous interior with an extensive rain forest. There are also sites of historical interest, and the capital, St George's, is a noted beauty spot. In 1990 there were 196,132 tourist arrivals, of which almost 70% were cruise-ship passengers. There were approximately 2,080 hotel beds in 1988.

Grenada Hotel Association: POB 440, St George's; tel. (440) 1590; telex 3425; f. 1961; Pres. RICHARD CHERMAN.

Grenada Tourist Department: POB 293, St George's; tel. (440) 2001; telex 3422; Dir of Tourism DIANA TAYLOR (acting).

GUATEMALA

Introductory Survey

Location, Climate, Language, Religion, Flag, Capital

The Republic of Guatemala lies in the Central American isthmus, bounded to the north and west by Mexico, with Honduras and Belize to the east and El Salvador to the south. It has a long coastline on the Pacific Ocean and a narrow outlet to the Caribbean Sea. The climate is tropical in the lowlands, with an average temperature of 28°C (83°F), and more temperate in the central highland area, with an average temperature of 20°C (68°F). The official language is Spanish, but more than 20 indigenous languages are also spoken. Almost all of the inhabitants profess Christianity: the majority are Roman Catholics, while about 25% are Protestants. The national flag (proportions 3 by 2) has three equal vertical stripes, of blue, white and blue, with the national coat of arms (depicting a quetzal, the 'bird of freedom', and a scroll, superimposed on crossed rifles and sabres, encircled by a wreath) in the centre of the white stripe. The capital is Guatemala City.

Recent History

Under Spanish colonial rule, Guatemala was part of the Viceroyalty of New Spain. Independence was obtained from Spain in 1821, from Mexico in 1824 and from the Federation of Central American States in 1838. Subsequent attempts to revive the Federation failed and, under a series of dictators, there was relative stability, tempered by periods of disruption. A programme of social reform was begun by Juan José Arévalo (President in 1944-50) and his successor, Col Jacobo Arbenz Guzmán, whose policy of land reform evoked strong opposition from landowners. In 1954 President Arbenz was overthrown in a coup led by Col Carlos Castillo Armas, who invaded the country with US assistance. Castillo became President but was assassinated in July 1957. The next elected President, Gen. Miguel Ydigoras Fuentes, took office in March 1958 and ruled until he was deposed in March 1963 by a military coup, led by Col Enrique Peralta Azurdia. He assumed full powers as Chief of Government, suspended the Constitution and dissolved the legislature. A Constituent Assembly, elected in 1964, produced a new constitution in 1965. Dr Julio César Méndez Montenegro was elected President in 1966, and in 1970 the candidate of the Movimiento de Liberación Nacional (MLN), Col (later Gen.) Carlos Araña Osorio, was elected President. Despite charges of fraud in the elections of March 1974, Gen. Kjell Laugerud García of the MLN took office as President in July.

President Laugerud sought to discourage extreme right-wing violence and claimed some success, although in September 1979 Amnesty International estimated the number of lives lost in political violence since 1970 at 50,000–60,000. In March 1978 Gen. Fernando Romeo Lucas García was elected President. The guerrilla movement increased in strength in 1980-1981, while the Government was accused of the murder and torture of civilians and, particularly, persecution of the country's indigenous Indian inhabitants, who make up 60% of the population. An estimated 11,000 civilians were killed in 1981.

In the presidential and congressional elections of 7 March 1982, from which the left-wing parties were absent, the largest number of votes was awarded to the Government's candidate, Gen. Angel Aníbal Guevara, who was later confirmed as President by Congress. The other presidential candidates denounced the elections as fraudulent. Guevara was prevented from taking office in July by a coup on 23 March, in which a group of young right-wing military officers installed Gen. Efraín Ríos Montt (a candidate in the 1974 presidential elections) as leader of a three-man junta. Congress was closed, and the Constitution and political parties suspended. In June Gen. Ríos Montt dissolved the junta and assumed the presidency. He attempted to fight corruption, reorganized the judicial system and disbanded the secret police. The number of violent deaths diminished. However, after initially gaining the support of the national university, the Roman Catholic Church and the labour unions and hoping to enter into dialogue with the guerrillas, who refused to respond to an amnesty declaration in June, President Ríos Montt declared a state of siege, and imposed censorship of the press, in July. In addition, the war against the guerrillas intensified, and a civil defence force of Indians was established. The efficiency of the army increased. Whole villages were burnt, and many inhabitants killed, in order to deter the Indians from supporting the guerrillas. President Ríos Montt's increasingly corporatist policies alienated all groups, and his fragile hold on power was threatened in 1982 by several attempted coups, which he managed to forestall.

The US administration was eager to renew sales of armaments and the provision of economic and military aid to Guatemala, which had been suspended in 1977 as a result of serious violations of human rights. Several sales of spare parts for military equipment were made to Guatemala in 1982, despite restrictions by the US Congress. In January 1983 the US Government, satisfied that there had been a significant decrease in the abuse of human rights during Gen. Ríos Montt's presidency, announced the resumption of arms sales to Guatemala. However, independent reports claimed that the situation had deteriorated, and revealed that 2,600 people had been killed during the first six months of President Ríos Montt's rule. An estimated 100,000 refugees fled to Mexico during early 1983, and relations between Guatemala and Mexico were strained, following further incursions into Mexican territory by Guatemalan security forces, which resulted in the deaths of several refugees. In March the army was implicated in the massacre of 300 Indian peasants at Nahulá, and there was a resurgence in the activity of both left- and right-wing 'death squads'. The President declared a 30-day amnesty for guerrillas and political exiles, and lifted the state of siege which had been imposed in July 1982. Furthermore, he announced the creation of an electoral tribunal to organize and oversee a proposed transfer from military rule to civilian government. In April the army launched a new offensive, which made significant gains against the guerrillas, principally in the rebel stronghold of Petén and the province of El Quiché. In response, the Unidad Revolucionaria Nacional Guatemalteca (URNG), the main guerrilla grouping (formed in February 1982 in a new initiative seeking to end repression by the Government), announced a major change in tactics, which gave priority to attacks on economic targets instead of to direct confrontation with the army. The Government's pacification programme comprised three phases of aid programmes, combined with the saturation of the countryside by anti-guerrilla units. The 'guns and beans' policy provided food and medicine in exchange for recruitment to the Patrullas de Autodefensa Civil (PAC), a pro-Government peasant militia. (By 1985 these self-defence patrols numbered 900,000 men.) The 'roofs, bread and work' phase involved the development of 'model villages', and the 'Aid Programme for Areas in Conflict' (PAAC) was an ambitious rural development scheme.

By June 1983 opposition to the President was widespread, and several attempted coups were reported. On 29 June the air force and four army garrisons rebelled against the President. They demanded a return to constitutional rule and the dismissal of the President's advisers. Gen. Ríos Montt agreed to both demands but remained unconvincing on the issue of electoral reform. On 8 August 1983 Gen. Oscar Humberto Mejía Victores, the Minister of Defence, led a successful coup against President Ríos Montt.

The new President announced the abolition of the secret tribunals and ended press censorship. In addition, the Council of State was abolished. A 90-day amnesty for guerrillas was announced in October. The amnesty was extended throughout 1984. Urban and rural terrorism continued to escalate, however, and in November 1983 the Government was accused of directing a campaign of kidnappings against the Roman Catholic Church. Following the murder in northern Guatemala of six workers from the US Agency for International Development, the US House of Representatives suspended the US $50m. in aid which President Reagan had requested for Guatemala in 1984. Israel continued to supply weapons to Guatemala, and Israeli military advisers were reported to be active in the country. In October Gen. Mejía Victores acted to strengthen his position after rumours of his unpopularity among high-ranking officers. Supporters of Gen. Ríos Montt were sent into exile, and in January 1984 new army reforms were introduced. In accordance with the President's assurance of electoral reform, elections for a Constituent Assembly were scheduled for July 1984.

Under Gen. Mejía Victores, it was estimated that more than 100 political assassinations and 40 abductions occurred each month. The start of campaigning for elections to the Constituent Assembly heralded a new wave of political violence. Fifteen political parties planned to contest the election in July. Contrary to public forecasts, the centre groups, including the newly formed Unión del Centro Nacional (UCN), obtained the greatest number of votes. Under the system of proportional representation, however, the right-wing coalition of the MLN and the Central Auténtica Nacionalista (CAN) together obtained a majority of seats in the Assembly. In August a directive board, composed of representatives from the three major political parties, began drafting a new constitution.

In 1984 the Government continued to develop its controversial strategy of 'model villages', which entailed the construction of new settlements in isolated locations for Indian communities. Relations with neighbouring Mexico deteriorated in 1984, following an attack in April on a Guatemalan refugee camp situated in Mexico, during which six people were killed. By August 1984 the Organización del Pueblo en Armas (ORPA) had emerged as the most active of the guerrilla groups, operating in San Marcos and Quezaltenango.

Guatemala's new Constitution was promulgated in May 1985. In June President Mejía Victores confirmed that elections for the presidency, the National Congress and 331 mayoralties would be held in November. Prior to the elections, there was a substantial increase in rebel activity and political assassinations by 'death squads'. However, the principal threat to internal security before the elections occurred in September, when violent protests, led by students and trade unionists, broke out in reaction to a series of price increases which had been authorized by the Government in August. During the protests, several people were reported to have been killed and hundreds of demonstrators were arrested. The University of San Carlos in Guatemala City was temporarily occupied by soldiers.

Eight candidates participated in the presidential election in November 1985, but the main contest was between Jorge Carpio Nicolle, the candidate of the UCN, and Mario Vinicio Cerezo Arévalo, the candidate of the Partido Democracia Cristiana Guatemalteca (PDCG). As neither of the leading candidates obtained the requisite majority, a second round of voting was held in December, when Cerezo secured 68% of the votes cast. The PDCG formed the majority party in the new National Congress and won the largest proportion of mayoralties. Cerezo was believed to enjoy the support of the US administration, which increased its allocation of economic aid to US $104.4m. in 1986, and resumed military aid (of $5.1m.) to Guatemala, in support of the new civilian Government. In December 1986 the Guatemalan Government denied that Nicaraguan Contra rebels (supported by the USA) were being trained on Guatemalan territory. In 1987 only $3m. of non-lethal military aid was granted to Guatemala by the USA, and the amount was to be reduced to $2m. in 1988.

Immediately prior to the transfer of power in January 1986, the outgoing military Government decreed a general amnesty to encompass those suspected of involvement in murders and other abuses of human rights since March 1982. In February 1986, however, in an attempt to curb the continuing violence and to improve the country's bad record for the observance of human rights, the Department of Technical Investigations (DIT), which had been accused of numerous kidnappings and murders of citizens, was dissolved and replaced by a new criminal investigations unit. Cerezo's action was welcomed by the Grupo de Apoyo Mutuo (GAM), a grouping of the relatives of victims of repression, and by Amnesty International. Violence continued unabated, however, with 700 killings being recorded by human rights groups in the first six months of 1986 alone. President Cerezo claimed that not all murders were politically motivated, while his relations with the armed forces remained precarious. Meanwhile, the GAM attracted increasing support, and in August about 3,000 demonstrators took part in a protest to demand information on the fate of the thousands of *desaparecidos* ('disappeared'). In April 1987 the creation of a government commission to investigate disappearances was announced, and in May Amnesty International appealed to the President to fulfil his pledge to investigate abuses of human rights. Nevertheless, by mid-1988 there were frequent reports of torture and killings by right-wing 'death squads' as discontent with the Government's liberal policies increased. In June 1989 Amnesty International reported that the Guatemalan army and police continued to operate death, torture and abduction squads. In September the Consejo Nacional de Desplazados de Guatemala (CONDEG) was created to represent the 1m. refugees who had fled their homes since 1980. A report to the UN Commission for Human Rights in January 1990 stated that killings and disappearances were on the increase and that almost 3,000 complaints of human rights abuses had been lodged in 1989.

In June 1987 Guatemala was the venue for a meeting of Central American Presidents to discuss a peace proposal for the region. The country was a signatory of the agreed peace plan, signed in Guatemala City in August by the Presidents of Costa Rica, El Salvador, Guatemala, Honduras and Nicaragua. Although the plan was principally concerned with the conflicts in Nicaragua and El Salvador, it also referred to the long-standing guerrilla war in Guatemala. Subsequently, a Commission of National Reconciliation was formed in compliance with the terms of the accord. In October representatives of the Guatemalan Government and URNG guerrillas met in Spain to discuss the question of peace in Guatemala. Although the negotiations ended without agreement, the two sides did not exclude the possibility of holding further talks. The Government also presented to Congress legislation for an amnesty applicable to members of the URNG. Congress approved the amnesty law in November. Further talks between the two sides would be dependent on the guerrillas' acceptance of this amnesty. In December it was announced that an extreme right-wing coup attempt against President Cerezo had been foiled.

Right-wing pressure on the Government continued to force President Cerezo to postpone negotiations with the URNG, scheduled for March 1988. In May a further attempted coup, involving both civilians and members of the army, was foiled without incident, but led to a further postponement of negotiations with the URNG. Despite evident right-wing opposition to the policies of President Cerezo, the PDCG won 140 mayoralties out of 272 at municipal elections held in April. These were Guatemala's first elections in which voting was not compulsory, and, consequently, the level of participation was low (only an estimated 40% of the electorate). Despite his party's success, President Cerezo remained wary of discontent within the army. After another coup plot was discovered in July, President Cerezo rejected the URNG's proposal for a truce.

During 1989 the political situation in Guatemala became more unstable, as guerrilla activity by groups from both the right and the left intensified. In January a new leftist group emerged, the Comando Urbano Revolucionario, which joined the URNG guerrillas. Meanwhile, President Cerezo continued to refuse to negotiate with the URNG for as long as its members remained armed. In September the URNG made futher proposals for negotiations, following the signing of the Tela Agreement (the Central American peace plan accord, see p. 796), but the Guatemalan President adhered firmly to his conditions, and negotiations were again postponed.

In May 1989 a group of retired and active military officers attempted to stage a coup. However, the Government drew upon support within the army, and was able to foil the attempt without bloodshed. Nevertheless, there was growing discontent with government policies, as was reflected by a protracted strike by teachers in support of demands for increased pay. The strike, which began in late May, was supported by a series of one-day strikes by other public-sector workers. In August the dispute erupted into violent confrontations between demonstrators and members of the police and army until an agreement was finally reached in August.

During August and September 1989 a secret right-wing military organization perpetrated a series of terrorist attacks in an attempt to destabilize the Government. At the same time, the ruling party was undergoing a political crisis, following its internal presidential primary elections in August. The PDCG's choice of presidential candidate had been split between Alfonso Cabrera Hidalgo, the party's Secretary-General and former Minister of Foreign Affairs, and René de León Schlotter, the leader of the party's left wing and Minister of Urban and Rural Development. The most likely compromise candidate,

Danilo Barillas, had been assassinated a short while before the selection procedure, allegedly by the extreme right, which, by provoking disunity within the PDCG, hoped to give an advantage to its own candidates. In November 1989 the former military ruler, Gen. Efraín Ríos Montt, presented his candidacy for the presidential election that was to take place one year later. He was supported by the moderate Partido Institucional Democrático (PID) and the Frente de Unidad Nacional (FUN). A more progressive candidate for the right was Fernando Andrade Durán, who was supported by the Partido Democrático de Cooperación Nacional (PDCN) and the Partido Revolucionario (PR), while Manuel Ayau, an entrepreneur and independent candidate, was expected to win wide support.

During 1989 many political figures and labour leaders fled the country after receiving death threats from paramilitary groups. In October the Minister of the Interior, Roberto Valle, was replaced, as he had been unable to curb the recent wave of violence. Subsequently, in December, the Government launched a major counterinsurgency operation to combat the escalation in guerrilla activity. In the same month, President Cerezo accused the ruling party in El Salvador of supplying weapons to the right-wing death squads of Guatemala.

In August 1989 President Cerezo and the President of Mexico held a meeting, aimed at resolving the refugee problem and at establishing collaboration against drug-trafficking in the region. As Mexico had begun implementing measures to combat the problem of drug-trafficking within its borders, with some success, Guatemala was therefore developing as a new centre for heroin production and cocaine tran-shipments from Central America to the USA. In 1988 and 1989 the production of opium poppies had become widespread. Local efforts to confront the problem were largely ineffective, and a US $1m. programme dedicated mainly to the aerial spraying of poppy fields, financed by the USA, was hampered by ground-level retaliatory attacks.

Relations between Guatemala and the USA deteriorated considerably in 1990. In March the US ambassador was recalled, in protest at President Cerezo's continued failure to curb the growing incidence of violations of human rights in Guatemala. In June a US citizen and long-standing resident of Guatemala was found murdered by a roadside. Several arrests were made by the Government in an attempt to satisfy US demands that the perpetrators be brought to justice. However, in December the USA suspended US $2.8m. in military aid, as a result of the Government's failure to resolve the case.

Despite President Cerezo's promise to restrict the unlawful activities of the armed forces and right-wing death squads, the number of politically-motivated assassinations and 'disappearances' escalated in 1990, while the army continued to operate with virtual impunity. In December 13 peasants were massacred by army personnel in Santiago Atitlán. In the same month, the Guatemalan human rights commission reported that 585 people had been killed by security forces and paramilitary death squads in the first eight months of 1990. Among those murdered in December was a leader of the human rights organization GAM, Oscar Augusto Miranda, whose body was discovered outside Guatemala City.

In March 1990 the URNG and the National Reconciliation Commission (CNR) began discussions in Oslo, Norway, with a view to resolving the problem of reincorporating the armed movements into the country's political process. The talks, which constituted a preliminary stage towards initiating direct negotiations between the Government and the guerrillas, culminated in the signing of an agreement to continue the peace process. In June representatives of the CNR and of nine political parties, including the ruling PDCG, met for further talks with the URNG in Madrid, Spain. As a result of these negotiations, the URNG pledged not to disrupt the presidential and legislative elections scheduled for November, and agreed to participate in a constituent assembly to reform the Guatemalan Constitution. Further meetings were held in August, between representatives of the business community and the URNG in Ottawa, Canada, and in November in Metepec, Mexico, where the President of the CNR, Mgr Arnulfo Quezada, announced that a 'consensus of peace' had been reached and predicted that direct talks between the guerrillas and the Government would result.

In the period preceding the presidential, congressional and municipal elections of November 1990, public attention was increasingly drawn to the candidacy of a former military ruler, Gen. Efraín Ríos Montt. By October Gen. Ríos Montt had secured considerable support and, according to opinion polls, was the most popular presidential candidate. However, his attempt to regain the presidency was ended in mid-October, when he finally lost his protracted struggle with the courts, and his candidacy was declared invalid on constitutional grounds. Under the Constitution, anyone taking part in, or benefiting from, a military coup is disqualified from participating in elections. Of the 12 remaining presidential candidates (whose political allegiances ranged from the centre to the extreme right), the main contenders were considered to be Jorge Carpio Nicolle of the UCN (runner-up in the 1985 presidential election), Alvaro Arzú of the Plan por el Adelantamiento Nacional (PAN), Alfonso Cabrera of the ruling PDCG, and the candidate of the Movimiento de Acción Solidaria (MAS), Jorge Serrano Elías, an evangelist and a former member of the 1982 Ríos Montt Government, who secured the support of right-wing opinion which had backed Gen. Ríos Montt until his disqualification. As none of the candidates obtained an absolute majority in November, a second ballot took place on 6 January 1991, with voters choosing between the two leading candidates, Jorge Serrano and Jorge Carpio. Serrano secured 68% of the votes cast. The MAS failed to win a majority in Congress, however, with only 18 of the 116 contested seats. In an effort to offset the imbalance in Congress, Serrano invited members of the PAN and the Partido Socialista Democrático (PSD) to participate in the formation of a coalition government.

Until the return to civilian government in 1986, Guatemala remained steadfast in its claims to the neighbouring territory of Belize, a former British dependency. In protest at the UK's decision to grant independence to Belize, in accordance with a UN resolution of November 1980, Guatemala severed diplomatic relations with the UK. Guatemala's new Constitution, promulgated in May 1985, did not include Belize in its delineation of Guatemalan territory. In August 1986 consular links between Guatemala and the UK were restored. In December full diplomatic relations were resumed, and in 1987 a British Embassy was opened in Guatemala City. In May 1988 discussions were held in Miami, USA, between representatives of Guatemala, Belize and the UK. The participants decided to establish a permanent Joint Commission to formulate a draft treaty to resolve Guatemala's claims to Belize. In October the Commission announced the establishment of three subcommissions, to be responsible for drafting the treaty; the delimitation of the border; and the creation of a joint development zone, with the co-operation of the UK and the EEC. Approval of the treaty was to be decided by referendums, to be held in both Guatemala and Belize. Since the mid-1970s the UK has retained a garrison in Belize, numbering 1,500 soldiers in June 1990.

The removal of economic sanctions and trade restrictions from Belize in late 1986 opened the way to Guatemalan investment in that territory and to the possibility of joint development projects. Since much of Guatemala's foreign debt is owed to EEC members, President Cerezo was anxious to remain on good terms with the EEC countries. A settlement of the dispute over Belize is also important for Guatemala's Central American policy and for hopes of achieving peace in the region. Neighbouring countries do not support Guatemala in its claims to Belize.

Government

Guatemala is a republic comprising 22 departments. (In December 1986 Congress approved a preliminary law whereby the country was to be divided into eight regions.) Under the new Constitution, which took effect in January 1986, legislative power is vested in the unicameral National Congress, with 100 members elected for five years by universal adult suffrage. Of the total seats, 75 are filled by direct election and 25 on the basis of proportional representation. Executive power is held by the President (also directly elected for five years), assisted by a Vice-President and an appointed Cabinet.

Defence

In June 1990 the armed forces totalled 43,300, of whom 41,000 were in the army, 1,000 in the navy (including 600 marines) and 1,300 in the air force. In addition, there were paramilitary forces of 12,800. Military service is by conscription for at least two years. In the early 1980s the Patrullas de Autodefensa Civil (PAC), an anti-guerrilla peasant militia, was established. By 1985 these self-defence patrols numbered 900,000 men. Defence expenditure in 1990 was budgeted at 322.0m. quetzales.

GUATEMALA

Economic Affairs

In 1989, according to estimates by the World Bank, Guatemala's gross national product (GNP), measured at average 1987-89 prices, was US $8,205m., equivalent to $920 per head. During 1980-89, it was estimated, GNP increased, in real terms, at an average annual rate of 0.2%, although GNP per head declined by 2.6% per year. Over the same period, the population increased by an annual average of 2.9%. Guatemala's gross domestic product (GDP) decreased, in real terms, by an annual average of 0.2% in 1980-88.

Agriculture, including forestry and fishing, contributed 25.7% of GDP in 1990. In 1989 an estimated 58.1% of the working population were employed in this sector. The principal cash crops are coffee (which accounted for 26.4% of export earnings in 1990), bananas, sugar cane, cardamom and cotton. Exports of shrimps and fresh meat are also significant. During 1980-89 agricultural production increased by an annual average of 2.7%.

Industry, including mining, manufacturing, construction and power, contributed 20.3% of GDP in 1990. This sector employed 18.1% of the working population in 1989.

Mining contributed 0.3% of GDP in 1990, and employed 0.1% of the working population in 1989. The most important mineral export is petroleum, although this accounted for just 1.4% of total export earnings in 1990. In addition, antimony, lead, iron and tungsten are mined on a small scale.

Guatemala's industrial sector is the largest in Central America. Manufacturing contributed 14.9% of GDP in 1990, and employed 13.6% of the working population in 1989. The main branches of manufacturing are food processing, rubber, textiles, paper and pharmaceuticals.

In 1990 the services sector contributed 54.0% of GDP. In 1989 this sector employed 21.8% of the working population.

Energy is derived principally from mineral fuels and, to a lesser extent, hydroelectric power. Guatemala is a marginal producer of petroleum, with an average output of 2,000 b/d in 1988. However, imports of mineral fuels comprised 12.6% of the value of total imports in 1988.

In 1988 Guatemala recorded a visible trade deficit of US $339.9m., and there was a deficit of $414.0m. on the current account of the balance of payments. In 1988 the principal source of imports (37.2%) was the USA, which was also the principal market for exports (28.1%). Other major trading partners were the Federal Republic of Germany, Mexico, El Salvador, Japan and Venezuela. The main exports in 1990 were coffee, bananas, sugar, cardamom, fresh meat and cotton. The principal imports in 1988 were machinery and apparatus, chemical products, mineral products, base metals and manufactures, artificial resins and plastics.

In 1989 there was an estimated budgetary deficit of 310.0m. quetzales, equivalent to some 1.3% of GDP. By the end of 1988 Guatemala's total external public debt stood at US $2,131m. In 1988 the cost of debt-servicing was equivalent to 26.5% of export earnings. The average annual rate of inflation was 11.4% in 1989. An estimated 13% of the labour force were unemployed in 1989.

In early 1990 a rise in inflation and the depletion of reserves of foreign exchange led to the introduction of austerity measures by the Government. Owing to the abandonment of the International Coffee Organization's system of export quotas in 1989 (see p. 228), however, coffee exports rose dramatically. Coffee production was increased, and surplus stocks were cleared, virtually doubling sales between July 1989 and February 1990. At the end of 1989 Guatemala ceased its debt-service repayments to the World Bank. In mid-1990 the World Bank, in turn, halted disbursements of committed loans to Guatemala.

By September 1990 Guatemala's repayment arrears to the World Bank stood at US $43.3m., on a debt of $204.6m. By the end of 1990 the Government had succeeded in raising $368m. in loans from various sources, including $110m. from the Inter-American Development Bank. In January 1991 the newly-inaugurated President Serrano announced a 10% reduction in public expenditure as part of a programme of measures aimed at ensuring a balanced budget and confronting the problem of outstanding debt.

Social Welfare

Social security is compulsory, and all employers with five or more workers are required to enrol with the State Institute of Social Security. Benefits are available to registered workers for industrial accidents, sickness, maternity, disability, widowhood and hospitalization. In 1978 Guatemala had 107 hospitals, with a total of 12,217 beds, and in 1979 there were 819 physicians working in the government health service. A US $51m. project to improve health services, including two new hospitals in Guatemala City and one in Antigua, was announced in 1980. In 1986 a vaccination programme to benefit more than 1m. children was announced, in a campaign to combat infant mortality. In 1989 budgetary expenditure on health was estimated at 319.1m. quetzales (9.2% of total spending).

Education

Elementary education is free and, in urban areas, compulsory between seven and 14 years of age. Primary education begins at the age of seven and lasts for six years. Secondary education, beginning at 13 years of age, lasts for up to six years, comprising two cycles of three years each. In 1989 there were 3,097 pre-primary schools, 8,840 primary schools and 1,541 secondary schools. In 1983 an estimated 62% of children in the relevant age-group (boys 65%; girls 58%) attended primary schools. The comparable figure for secondary education in 1982 was 14%. In December 1988 the World Bank approved a loan of US $30m., which was intended to finance a programme to increase primary school enrolment to 80% by 1993. There are five universities. In 1981 a 'national literacy crusade' was launched by the Government, but in 1990, according to estimates by UNESCO, the average rate of adult illiteracy was 44.9% (males 36.9%; females 52.9%), the second highest level in the Western hemisphere. In 1989 budgetary expenditure on education was estimated at 538m. quetzales (15.5% of total spending).

Public Holidays

1991: 1 January (New Year's Day), 6 January (Epiphany), 29 March-1 April (Easter), 1 May (Labour Day), 30 June (Anniversary of the Revolution), 15 August (Assumption, Guatemala City only), 15 September (Independence Day), 12 October (Columbus Day), 20 October (Revolution Day), 1 November (All Saints' Day), 24-25 December (Christmas), 31 December (New Year's Eve).

1992: 1 January (New Year's Day), 6 January (Epiphany), 17-20 April (Easter), 1 May (Labour Day), 30 June (Anniversary of the Revolution), 15 August (Assumption, Guatemala City only), 15 September (Independence Day), 12 October (Columbus Day), 20 October (Revolution Day), 1 November (All Saints' Day), 24-25 December (Christmas), 31 December (New Year's Eve).

Weights and Measures

The metric system is in official use.

Statistical Survey

Sources (unless otherwise stated): Banco de Guatemala, 7a Avda 22-01, Zona 1, Apdo 365, Guatemala City; Dirección General de Estadística, Edif. América 4°, 8a Calle 9-55, Zona 1, Guatemala City; tel. (2) 26136.

Area and Population

AREA, POPULATION AND DENSITY

Area (sq km)	
Land	108,429
Inland water	460
Total	108,889*
Population (census results)†	
26 March 1973	5,160,221
26 March 1981	
Males	3,015,826
Females	3,038,401
Total	6,054,227
Population (official estimates at mid-year)	
1988	8,681,078
1989	8,935,395
1990	9,198,448
Density (per sq km) at mid-1990	84.5

* 42,042 sq miles.
† Excluding adjustments for underenumeration, estimated to have been 13.7% in 1981.

DEPARTMENTS (estimated population at mid-1990)

Alta Verapaz	573,741	Jutiapa	346,774
Baja Verapaz	179,582	Quezaltenango	542,556
Chimaltenango	334,109	Retalhuleu	231,896
Chiquimula	246,929	Sacatepéquez	174,979
El Petén	240,357	San Marcos	682,315
El Progreso	106,211	Santa Rosa	262,295
El Quiché	557,004	Sololá	234,652
Escuintla	526,249	Suchitepéquez	351,982
Guatemala	1,962,953	Totonicapán	289,124
Huehuetenango	693,809	Zacapa	158,657
Izabal	316,217		
Jalapa	186,057	**Total**	**9,198,448**

PRINCIPAL TOWNS (population at 1981 census)

Guatemala City (capital)	754,243	Puerto Barrios	46,882
Escuintla	75,442	Retalhuleu	46,652
Quezaltenango	72,922	Chiquimula	42,571
		Mazatenango	38,181

Source: CELADE.

BIRTHS, MARRIAGES AND DEATHS

	Registered live births		Registered marriages		Registered deaths	
	Number	Rate (per 1,000)	Number	Rate (per 1,000)	Number	Rate (per 1,000)
1983	288,502	38.3	30,422	4.0	74,462	9.9
1984	302,961	39.1	31,351	4.1	75,462	9.7
1985	322,994	40.6	38,199	4.8	68,955	8.7
1986	319,321	38.9	45,755	5.6	69,275	8.4
1987	324,784	38.5	44,440	5.3	66,703	7.9
1988	341,382	39.3	46,795	5.4	64,837	7.5

ECONOMICALLY ACTIVE POPULATION
(official estimates for 1989)

	Males	Females	Total
Agriculture, forestry, hunting and fishing	1,554,390	28,041	1,582,431
Mining and quarrying	2,685	39	2,724
Manufacturing	286,223	84,191	370,414
Construction	111,056	613	111,669
Electricity, gas, water and sanitary services	7,941	230	8,171
Commerce	134,016	64,809	198,825
Transport, storage and communications	66,406	1,685	68,091
Services	136,045	190,791	326,836
Activities not adequately described	41,833	12,640	54,473
Total	**2,340,595**	**383,039**	**2,723,634**

Agriculture

PRINCIPAL CROPS ('000 metric tons)

	1988	1989	1990*
Sugar cane	7,738	7,615	7,900
Cotton (lint)	48	45	52
Maize	1,414	1,373	1,440
Rice	75	49	65
Dry beans	100	99	110
Wheat	51	55	55
Coffee	195	206	236
Bananas ('000 stems)	16,327	17,958	17,160

* Estimates.

Source: *Cuentas Nacionales*, Banco de Guatemala.

LIVESTOCK ('000 head, year ending September)

	1987	1988	1989
Horses*	110	112	112
Cattle	2,004	2,010*	2,023
Sheep	666*	667*	660
Pigs	850*	820*	800
Goats*	76	76	76

Chickens (million): 15 in 1987; 15* in 1988; 15* in 1989.
* FAO estimate(s).

Source: FAO, *Production Yearbook*.

LIVESTOCK PRODUCTS ('000 metric tons)

	1987	1988	1989
Beef and veal	44	57	53
Pig meat	14	14*	15
Poultry meat†	57	58	59
Cheese†	15.9	16.1	16.1
Butter and ghee†	5.0	5.0	5.1
Hen eggs†	60.5	60.7	61.2
Cattle hides†	11.5	12.4	14.0

* Unofficial figure.   † FAO estimates.

Source: FAO, *Production Yearbook*.

GUATEMALA

Forestry

ROUNDWOOD REMOVALS ('000 cubic metres, excluding bark)

	1986	1987	1988
Sawlogs, veneer logs and logs for sleepers	104	104	104*
Other industrial wood	10	10	10
Fuel wood*	6,869	7,069	7,276
Total	6,983	7,183	7,390

* FAO estimate(s).
Source: FAO, *Yearbook of Forest Products*.

SAWNWOOD PRODUCTION ('000 cubic metres)

	1986	1987*	1988*
Coniferous (soft wood)	75	75	75
Broadleaved (hard wood)	8	8	8
Total	83	83	83

* FAO estimates.
Source: FAO, *Yearbook of Forest Products*.

Fishing

(metric tons, live weight)

	1986	1987	1988
Total catch	2,119	2,425	2,800

Source: FAO, *Yearbook of Fishery Statistics*.

Mining

SELECTED PRODUCTS (metric tons)

	1987	1988	1989
Antimony ore	3,083	2,160	2,182
Petroleum	179,640	180,215	178,295
Iron ore	10,706	8,092	6,541
Lead ore	92	100	150

Source: Ministry of Energy and Mines.

Industry

SELECTED PRODUCTS
('000 metric tons, unless otherwise indicated)

	1987	1988	1989
Cement	703	808	852
Sugar	677	711	731
Electricity (million kWh)	1,911	2,088	2,243
Cigarettes (million)	2,000	1,936	1,497

Source: *Cuentas Nacionales*, Banco de Guatemala.

Finance

CURRENCY AND EXCHANGE RATES

Monetary Units
100 centavos = 1 quetzal.

Denominations
Coins: 1, 5, 10 and 25 centavos.
Notes: 50 centavos; 1, 5, 10, 20, 50 and 100 quetzales.

Sterling and Dollar Equivalents (30 September 1990)
£1 sterling = 10.114 quetzales;
US $1 = 5.399 quetzales;
100 quetzales = £9.887 = $18.523.

Note: A multiple exchange rate system was introduced in November 1984. This system was modified in June 1986, since which time the official rate of US $1 = 1 quetzal has been applicable mainly to debt-service payments. There is also a banking market rate (introduced in 1984) and a regulated market rate. The banking market rate, applicable to private capital inflows and to 'invisible' transactions, was US $1 = 2.81 quetzales at 31 October 1989. The regulated market rate, which applies to most trade and capital transactions, was fixed at $1 = 2.50 quetzales from June 1986, when it replaced the previous auction market rate, until June 1988, when the rate was adjusted to $1 = 2.705 quetzales. It remained at this level until the end of 1988. The rate was fixed at $1 = 2.700 quetzales between January and August 1989, and at $1 = 2.780 between August and November 1989. The average value of the principal exchange rate (quetzales per US dollar) was: 2.5000 in 1987; 2.6196 in 1988; 2.8161 in 1989.

BUDGET (million quetzales)

Revenue	1987	1988	1989
Taxation	1,430.7	1,793.7	1,842.6
Treasury bills and foreign loans	472.2	690.4	736.4
Other receipts	427.1	505.3	591.3
Total	2,330.0	2,989.4	3,170.3

Expenditure	1987	1988	1989
Education	397.3	472.9	538.0
Health	201.3	291.2	319.1
Agriculture	91.1	139.4	156.4
Defence	351.8	387.1	416.2
Communications and public works	71.9	67.3	238.2
Transportation	131.7	195.4	254.0
Other items	1,095.8	1,322.0	1,558.4
Total	2,340.9	2,875.3	3,480.3

Source: Ministry of Finance.

INTERNATIONAL RESERVES
(US $ million at 31 December)

	1987	1988	1989
Gold*	22.1	22.1	22.9
IMF special drawing rights	1.7	0.2	0.7
Foreign exchange	286.1	201.0	306.0
Total	309.9	223.3	329.6

* Valued at US $42.22 per troy ounce.
Source: IMF, *International Financial Statistics*.

GUATEMALA

MONEY SUPPLY (million quetzales at 31 December)

	1987	1988	1989
Currency outside banks	931.2	1,069.0	1,329.2
Private sector deposits at Bank of Guatemala	26.5	34.4	43.0
Demand deposits at deposit money banks	807.9	915.6	1,065.6
Total money	1,765.6	2,019.0	2,437.8

Source: IMF, *International Financial Statistics*.

COST OF LIVING
(Consumer Price Index; base: March–April 1983 = 100)

	1987	1988	1989
Food and beverages	209.8	238.6	267.8
Domestic living expenses	141.6	155.6	187.1
Furniture, maintenance and equipment for the home	198.4	215.9	236.5
Clothing and footwear	224.4	241.7	263.6
Medical assistance	232.7	252.9	279.7
Education	146.8	155.1	170.9
Transport and communications	192.7	201.7	217.6
Reading and recreation	182.4	195.3	209.9
Others	218.7	235.8	254.4
All items	198.6	220.1	245.1

NATIONAL ACCOUNTS
Expenditure on the Gross Domestic Product
(million quetzales at current prices)

	1988	1989	1990*
Government final consumption expenditure	1,639.8	1,843.4	2,043.9
Private final consumption expenditure	17,288.9	19,831.9	28,846.7
Increase in stocks	67.3	−1.6	−121.4
Gross fixed capital formation	2,747.1	3,200.1	4,893.6
Total domestic expenditure	21,743.2	24,873.8	35,662.8
Exports of goods and services	3,308.5	4,125.0	7,821.4
Less Imports of goods and services	4,506.8	5,363.0	9,980.2
GDP in purchasers' values	20,544.9	23,635.8	33,504.0

* Estimates.

Gross Domestic Product by Economic Activity
(million quetzales at constant 1958 prices)

	1988	1989	1990
Agriculture, hunting, forestry and fishing	817.6	847.0	876.8
Mining and quarrying	8.7	9.1	9.5
Manufacturing	487.9	497.9	510.5
Electricity, gas and water	74.1	79.9	86.7
Construction	67.9	75.9	86.4
Trade, restaurants and hotels	776.2	807.3	832.2
Transport, storage and communications	230.4	247.7	264.8
Finance, insurance and real estate	121.4	127.1	134.7
Ownership of dwellings	164.2	167.7	233.5
General government services	218.5	225.6	209.6
Other community, social and personal services	195.9	202.8	171.4
Total	3,162.8	3,288.0	3,416.1

BALANCE OF PAYMENTS (US $ million)

	1986	1987	1988
Merchandise exports f.o.b.	1,043.8	977.9	1,073.3
Merchandise imports f.o.b.	−875.7	−1,333.2	−1,413.2
Trade balance	168.1	−355.3	−339.9
Exports of services	159.4	189.4	227.4
Imports of services	−420.2	−469.9	−525.8
Balance on goods and services	−92.7	−635.8	−638.3
Private unrequited transfers (net)	50.6	101.0	141.7
Government unrequited transfers (net)	24.5	92.3	82.6
Current balance	−17.6	−442.5	−414.0
Direct capital investment (net)	68.8	150.2	329.7
Other long-term capital (net)	−371.0	−302.7	105.0
Short-term capital (net)	−30.8	339.2	169.6
Net errors and omissions	67.3	−72.7	−2.3
Total (net monetary movements)	−283.3	−328.5	187.9
Valuation changes (net)	−11.0	−9.2	1.6
Exceptional financing (net)	392.2	274.5	−326.8
Official financing (net)	4.0	1.0	−2.5
Changes in reserves	101.9	−62.2	−139.7

Source: IMF, *International Financial Statistics*.

External Trade

PRINCIPAL COMMODITIES (US $ '000)

Imports c.i.f.	1986	1987	1988
Vegetable products	42,757.2	44,352.1	45,952.8
Animal and vegetable oils, fats and waxes	27,108.0	32,803.1	33,485.7
Food products, beverages and tobacco	24,452.4	46,834.1	50,915.5
Mineral products	162,367.0	229,601.4	196,933.2
Chemical products	200,877.5	236,672.1	266,142.4
Artificial resins and plastics, cellulose, etc.	58,335.8	93,383.8	118,433.0
Paper-making material, paper and manufactures	50,637.2	73,732.0	86,177.7
Textiles and manufactures	42,933.9	71,225.2	67,795.6
Base metals and manufactures	74,053.6	127,753.8	149,364.1
Machinery and apparatus, incl. electrical	137,619.1	267,988.9	280,397.8
Transport equipment	77,742.4	157,297.1	152,949.4
Total (incl. others)	959,496.4	1,473,618.3	1,556,974.5

Source: Las Aduanas de la República.

Exports f.o.b.	1988	1989	1990*
Coffee (incl. soluble)	386,900	380,000	334,100
Cotton	36,900	27,700	27,200
Fresh meat	14,800	24,500	35,500
Bananas	76,400	87,100	95,700
Sugar	78,000	92,100	153,400
Shellfish	14,500	15,400	16,000
Cardamom	37,600	27,500	37,800
Petroleum	12,000	16,400	17,800
Total (incl. others)	1,073,400	1,146,000	1,266,600

* Estimates.
Source: *Balanza de Pagos*, Banco de Guatemala.

GUATEMALA

PRINCIPAL TRADING PARTNERS (US $ '000)

Imports c.i.f.	1986	1987	1988
Costa Rica	27,960	43,504	54,117
El Salvador	46,045	73,557	81,134
Germany, Federal Republic	69,956	92,764	101,125
Honduras	4,105	11,489	10,168
Italy	10,123	50,621	49,556
Japan	54,205	94,836	98,305
Mexico	60,120	108,920	113,789
Netherlands	11,483	11,747	17,573
Netherlands Antilles	7,963	5,163	19,024
United Kingdom	13,858	28,306	31,152
USA	414,455	557,958	579,772
Venezuela	53,420	60,141	77,085
Total (incl. others)	959,496	1,447,178	1,556,975

Exports f.o.b.	1986	1987	1988
Costa Rica	52,955	60,583	62,863
El Salvador	100,869	133,934	127,982
Germany, Federal Republic	87,334	71,677	73,170
Honduras	21,800	24,903	33,688
Italy	32,257	35,498	43,587
Japan	41,189	18,418	26,507
Mexico	6,185	11,090	23,141
Netherlands	29,857	26,812	30,006
Nicaragua	9,419	11,137	11,908
United Kingdom	8,564	9,203	12,943
USA	483,183	399,081	301,383
Total (incl. others)	1,043,755	977,917	1,073,421

Source: *Balanza de Pagos*, Banco de Guatemala.

Transport

ROAD TRAFFIC ('000 motor vehicles in use)

	1987	1988	1989
Passenger cars	223.4	232.2	241.0
Commercial vehicles	70.0	72.6	75.2

Source: Ministry of Finance.

SHIPPING (freight traffic, '000 metric tons)

	1987	1988	1989
Goods loaded	1,381	1,417	1,355
Goods unloaded	2,307	2,231	2,608

CIVIL AVIATION (traffic on scheduled services)

	1983	1984	1985
Passengers carried ('000)	100	124	108
Passenger-km (million)	156	168	156
Freight ton-km (million)	6.3	8.1	9.0

Freight ton-km (million): 7.2 in 1986; 11.4 in 1987; 11.9 in 1988; 23.4 in 1989.

Tourism

	1987	1988	1989
Tourist arrivals	352,741	405,230	437,019
Receipts (US $ million)	102.9	118.2	151.9

Source: Instituto Guatemalteco de Turismo (INGUAT).

Education

(1989*)

	Schools	Teachers	Pupils
Pre-primary	3,097	4,979	165,303
Primary	8,840	33,666	1,235,509
Secondary	1,541	17,313	297,437

* Preliminary.

Source: Instituto Nacional de Estadística/USIPE, Ministerio de Educación.

Directory

The Constitution

In December 1984 the Constituent Assembly drafted a new constitution (based on that of 1965), which was approved in May 1985 and came into effect in January 1986. Its main provisions are summarized below:

Guatemala has a republican representative democratic system of government and power is exercised equally by the legislative, executive and judicial bodies. The official language is Spanish. Suffrage is universal and secret, obligatory for those who can read and write and optional for those who are illiterate. The free formation and growth of political parties whose aims are democratic is guaranteed. There is no discrimination on grounds of race, colour, sex, religion, birth, economic or social position or political opinions.

The State will give protection to capital and private enterprise in order to develop sources of labour and stimulate creative activity.

Monopolies are forbidden and the State will limit any enterprise which might prejudice the development of the community. The right to social security is recognized and it shall be on a national, unitary, obligatory basis.

Constitutional guarantees may be suspended in certain circumstances for up to 30 days (unlimited in the case of war).

CONGRESS

Legislative power rests with Congress, which is made up of 116 deputies, 87 of whom are elected directly by the people through universal suffrage. The remaining 29 deputies are elected on the basis of proportional representation. Congress meets on 15 January each year and ordinary sessions last four months; extraordinary sessions can be called by the Permanent Commission or the Executive. All Congressional decisions must be taken by absolute majority of the members, except in special cases laid down by law. Deputies are elected for five years; they may be re-elected after a lapse of one session, but only once. Congress is responsible for all matters concerning the President and Vice-President and their execution of their offices; for all electoral matters; for all matters concerning the laws of the Republic; for approving the budget and decreeing taxes; for declaring war; for conferring honours, both civil and military; for fixing the coinage and the system of weights and measures; for approving, by two-thirds majority, any international treaty or agreement affecting the law, sovereignty, financial status or security of the country.

PRESIDENT

The President is elected by universal suffrage, by absolute majority for a non-extendable period of five years. Re-election or prolongation of the presidential term of office are punishable by law. The

GUATEMALA

President is responsible for national defence and security, fulfilling the Constitution, leading the armed forces, taking any necessary steps in time of national emergency, passing and executing laws, international policy, nominating and removing Ministers, officials and diplomats, co-ordinating the actions of Ministers of State. The Vice-President's duties include presiding over Congress and taking part in the discussions of the Council of Ministers.

ARMY

The Guatemalan Army is intended to maintain national independence, sovereignty and honour, territorial integrity and peace within the Republic. It is an indivisible, apolitical, non-deliberating body and is made up of land, sea and air forces.

LOCAL ADMINISTRATIVE DIVISIONS

For the purposes of administration the territory of the Republic is divided into Departments and these into Municipalities, but this division can be modified by Congress to suit interests and general development of the Nation without loss of municipal autonomy.

JUDICIARY

Justice is exercised exclusively by the Supreme Court of Justice and other tribunals. Administration of Justice is obligatory, free and independent of the other functions of State. The President of the Judiciary, judges and other officials are elected by Congress for four years. The Supreme Court of Justice is made up of at least seven judges. The President of the Judiciary is also President of the Supreme Court. The Supreme Court nominates all other judges. Under the Supreme Court come the Court of Appeal, the Administrative Disputes Tribunal, the Tribunal of Second Instance of Accounts, Jurisdiction Conflicts, First Instance and Military, the Extraordinary Tribunal of Protection. There is a Court of Constitutionality presided over by the President of the Supreme Court.

The Government

HEAD OF STATE

President: Jorge Serrano Elías (took office 14 January 1991).

Vice-President: Gustavo Espina.

THE CABINET
(March 1991)

Minister of Foreign Affairs: Alvaro Arzú Irigoyen.

Minister of the Interior: Ricardo Méndez Ruiz.

Minister of National Defence: Gen. Luis Mendoza García.

Minister of Economy: Richard Aitkenhead Castillo.

Minister of Finance: Irma Raquel Zelaya Rosales.

Minister of Public Health and Social Assistance: Dr Miguel Angel Montepeque Contreras.

Minister of Communications, Transport and Public Works: Alvaro Heredia.

Minister of Agriculture: Adolfo Boppel Carrera.

Minister of Education: María Luisa Beltranena de Padilla.

Minister of Labour and Social Welfare: Dr Mario Solórzano Martínez.

Minister of Energy and Mines: Carlos Leonel Hurtarte Castro.

Minister of Urban and Rural Development: Manuel Benfeld Alejos.

Minister without Portfolio: Antulio Castillo Barajas.

MINISTRIES

All Ministries are situated in the Palacio Nacional, Guatemala City.

President and Legislature

PRESIDENT

Election, 11 November 1990

	Votes cast	Percentage of votes cast
Jorge Carpio Nicolle (UCN)	399,677	25.7
Jorge Serrano Elías (MAS)	374,931	24.1
Alfonso Cabrera Hidalgo (PDCG)	270,974	17.5
Alvaro Arzú Irigoyen (PAN)	268,656	17.3
Col Luis Ernesto Sosa Avila (MLN/FAN coalition)	74,779	4.8
René de León Schlotter (AP5/PSD coalition)	55,797	3.6
Angel Lee (PR)	33,405	2.2
José Fernández (PDCN)	32,311	2.1
Benedicto Lucas (MEC)	16,748	1.1
Fernando Leal (PNR)	11,049	0.7
Leonel Hernández (FUR)	7,954	0.5
Jorge Reyna (PD)	6,339	0.4

Since no candidate achieved the required overall majority, a second round of voting was held on 6 January 1991. At this election, Jorge Serrano Elías (MAS) received 68% of the valid votes cast, while Jorge Carpio Nicolle (UCN) won the remaining 32%.

CONGRESO NACIONAL

President: José Ricardo Gómez Gálvez.

Election, 11 November 1990

	Seats by National Listing	Seats by Departmental Representation	Total Seats
Unión del Centro Nacional (UCN)	8	33	41
Partido Democracia Cristiana Guatemalteca (PDCG)	6	22	28
Movimiento para Acción y Solidaridad (MAS)	8	10	18
Plataforma NO-Venta (PID/FRG/FUN coalition)	0	11	11
Plan por el Adelantamiento Nacional (PAN)	5	7	12
Movimiento de Liberación Nacional/Frente de Avance Nacional (MLN/FAN coalition)	1	3	4
Partido Revolucionario (PR)	0	1	1
Alianza Popular 5/Partido Socialista Democrático (AP5/PSD coalition)	1	0	1
Total	**29**	**87**	**116**

Political Organizations

Following the introduction of new legislation in 1983, all political parties were required to disband and reapply for registration. All political parties were legalized in May 1985.

Alianza Democrática: Guatemala City; f. 1983; centre party; Leader Leopoldo Urrutia.

Alianza Popular 5 (AP5): Sec.-Gen. Rolando Pineda Lam.

Central Auténtica Nacionalista (CAN): Guatemala City; f. 1980 from the CAO (Central Arañista Organizado); Leader Héctor Mayora Dawe.

Comité Guatemalteca de Unidad Patriota (CGUP) (Guatemalan Committee of Patriotic Unity): f. 1982; opposition coalition consisting of:

Frente Democrático contra la Represión (FDCR): Leader Rafael García.

Frente Popular 31 de Enero (FP-31): f. 1980; left-wing amalgamation of student, peasant and trade union groups; seized Brazilian Embassy, May 1982.

Frente de Avance Nacional (FAN): right-wing group.

Frente Cívico Democrático (FCD): Guatemala City; Leader Jorge González del Valle; formed electoral alliance with PDCG, January 1985.

Frente Demócrata Guatemalteco: Leader Clemente Marroquín Rojas.

GUATEMALA

Frente Republicano Guatemalteco (FRG): right-wing group.

Frente de Trabajadores: workers' front.

Frente Unido Revolucionario (FUR)*: f. 1985; electoral alliance formed by parties of the democratic left and consisting of:

Fuerza Nueva: Leader CARLOS RAFAEL SOTO.

Movimiento Humanista de Integración Demócrata: Guatemala City; f. 1983; Leader VICTORIANO ALVAREZ.

Movimiento 20 de Octubre: Leader MARCO ANTONIO VILLAMAR CONTRERAS.

Partido Socialista Democrático (PSD): 12 Calle 10-37 Zona 1, 01001, POB 1279, Guatemala City; tel. (2) 53-3219; fax (2) 20819; f. 1978; Pres. CARLOS GALLARDO FLORES; Sec.-Gen. MARIO SOLÓRZANO MARTÍNEZ.

Frente de Unidad Nacional (FUN): 7a Avda Sta Cecilia 27-51, Zona 8, Guatemala City; tel. (2) 71-4048; f. 1971; nationalist group; Leader GABRIEL GIRÓN ORTIZ.

Fuerza Democrática Popular: 11a Calle 4-13, Zona 1, Guatemala City; f. 1983; democratic popular force; Sec. Lic. FRANCISCO REYES IXCAMEY.

Fuerza Popular Organizada: popular organized force.

Movimiento para Acción y Solidaridad (MAS): centre-left.

Movimiento Emergente de Concordia (MEC)*: Guatemala City; f. 1983; Leaders DARÍO CHÁVEZ, ARTURO RAMÍREZ.

Movimiento de Liberación Nacional (MLN): 5a Calle 1-20, Zona 1, Guatemala City; f. 1960; extreme right-wing; 95,000 mems; Leader Lic. MARIO SANDÓVAL ALARCÓN.

Movimiento por la Recuperación de la Identidad Ideológica Demócrata Cristiana.

Pantinamit: f. 1977; represents interests of Indian population; Leader FERNANDO TEZAHUIC TOHÓN.

Partido Democracia Cristiana Guatemalteca (PDCG): 8a Avda 14-53, Zona 1, Guatemala City; f. 1968; 130,000 mems; Sec.-Gen. ALFONSO CABRERA HIDALGO; Leader of left-wing faction RENÉ DE LEÓN SCHLOTTER; right-wing faction led by Dr FRANCISCO VILLAGRÁN KRAMER.

Partido Democrático de Cooperación Nacional (PDCN)*: 4a Avda 4-05, Zona 1, Guatemala City; tel. (2) 24848; f. 1985; Sec.-Gen. Lic. ROLANDO BAQUIAX GÓMEZ.

Partido Institucional Democrático (PID): 2a Calle 10–73, Zona 1, Guatemala City; f. 1965; 60,000 mems; moderate conservative; Leader OSCAR HUMBERTO RIVAS GARCÍA; Dir DONALDO ALVAREZ RUIZ.

Partido Nacionalista Renovador (PNR)*: Guatemala City; first granted legal status in August 1979; 72,000 mems; Leader ALEJANDRO MALDONADO AGUIRRE; Sec.-Gen. RENÁN QUIÑÓNEZ SAGASTUME.

Partido Petenero: Guatemala City; f. 1983; defends regional interests of El Petén.

Partido Populista: populist party.

Partido Revolucionario (PR): Guatemala City; f. 1957; democratic party; 100,000 mems; Leaders JORGE GARCÍA GRANADOS, MARIO FUENTES PIERUCCINI.

Partido Revolucionario de los Trabajadores Centro-americanos (PRTC): Guatemala City.

Partido Social Cristiano: Guatemala City; f. 1983.

Partido Socialista Democrático (PSD): Guatemala City; f. 1980; Sec.-Gen MARIO SOLÓRZANO.

Partido de Unificación Anticomunista (PUA): Guatemala City; right-wing party; Leader LEONEL SISNIEGA OTERO.

Plan por el Adelantamiento Nacional (PAN): Leader and 1990 Presidential candidate ALVARO ARZÚ IRIGOYEN.

Unidad Revolucionaria Demócrata (URD).

Unión del Centro Nacional (UCN): f. 1984; centre party; Leader JORGE CARPIO NICOLLE; Sec.-Gen. RAMIRO DE LEÓN CARPIO.

Unión Popular: popular union.

* Ceased to be officially recognized in November 1990, owing to failure to secure the required minimum of 4% of the votes in the general election held that month.

In February 1982 the principal guerrilla groups unified to form the **Unidad Revolucionaria Nacional Guatemalteca (URNG)** (Guatemalan National Revolutionary Unity), which has links with the PSD. The political wing of the URNG is the **Representación Unitaria de la Oposición Guatemalteca (RUOG):** Leader RAÚL MOLINA MEJÍA. The URNG seeks a guarantee of basic human rights, truly representative government, and an end to repression and racial discrimination. Following a meeting between the URNG and the Commission of National Conciliation in March 1990, and a further meeting in Madrid in May with representatives of the leading Guatemalan political parties, the URNG pledged to end the armed struggle and join the political mainstream. At the beginning of 1991 the URNG consisted of:

Comando Urbano Revolucionario (CUR): joined URNG in January 1989.

Ejército Guerrillero de los Pobres (EGP): f. 1972; draws main support from Indians of western highlands; works closely with the **Comité de Unidad Campesina (CUC)** (Committee of Peasant Unity) and radical Catholic groups; mems 4,000 armed, 12,000 unarmed.

Fuerzas Armadas Rebeldes (FAR): formed early 1960s; originally military commission of CGT; associated with the CNT and CONUS trade unions; based in Guatemala City, Chimaltenango and El Petén; Commander NICOLÁS SIS.

Organización del Pueblo en Armas (ORPA): f. 1979; military group active in San Marcos province; originally part of FAR; Leader RODRIGO ASTURIAS ('Commdt GASPAR ILOM').

Partido Guatemalteco del Trabajo (PGT): communist party; divided into three armed factions: PGT-Camarilla (began actively participating in war in 1981); PGT-Núcleo de Conducción y Dirección; PGT-Comisión Nuclear; Gen. Sec. CARLOS GONZÁLEZ.

Other guerrilla groups are:

Comando de las Fuerzas Populares: f. 1981; left-wing.

Comando Guerrilleros del Pueblo (CGP): f. 1985; left-wing.

Comando Popular Revolucionario: f. 1988; fmrly part of URNG.

Ejército Secreto Anticomunista (ESA): right-wing guerrilla group.

Escuadrón de la Muerte (EM): right-wing death squad.

Frente Central de Resistencia-Partido Guatemalteco del Trabajo (FCR-PGT): f. 1988; left-wing.

Fuerza de Guerrilleros de los Pobres (FGP).

Octubre Revolucionario: f. 1987; Marxist organization.

Oficiales de la Montaña (Officers of the Mountain): extreme right-wing guerrilla group.

Diplomatic Representation

EMBASSIES IN GUATEMALA

Argentina: 2a Avda 11-04, Zona 10, Guatemala City; telex 5285; Ambassador: Dr ANGEL FERNANDO GIRARDI.

Austria: 6a Avda 20-25, Zona 10, Guatemala City; telex 5224; Commercial Attaché: Lic. BRUNO FREYTAG.

Belgium: Avda Reforma 13-70, Apdo 687-A, Zona 9, Guatemala City; tel. (2) 31-5608; telex 5137; Ambassador: PAUL VERMEIRSCH.

Bolivia: 12 Avda 15-37, Zona 10, Guatemala City; Chargé d'affaires a.i.: Dr JOSÉ GABINA VILLANUEVA G.

Brazil: 18 Calle 2-22, Zona 14, Guatemala City; tel. (2) 37-0949; telex 5200; Ambassador: HEITOR PINTO DE MOURA.

Canada: Galería España, 7 Avda y 12 Calle, Zona 9, Guatemala City; telex 5206; Ambassador: PIERRE TANGUAY.

Chile: 13 Calle 7-85, Zona 10, Guatemala City; telex 6162; Ambassador: SILVIO SALGADO RAMÍREZ.

China (Taiwan): Edif. Torrecafe, Of. 1030, 7a Avda 1-20, Zona 4, Guatemala City; telex 5107; Ambassador: MAO CHI-HSIEN.

Colombia: Edif. Gemini 10, 12 Calle, 1 Avda, Zona 10, Guatemala City; tel. (2) 32-0604; Ambassador: LAURA OCHOA DE ARDILLA.

Costa Rica: Edif. Galerías Reforma, Of. 320, Avda Reforma 8-60, Zona 9, Guatemala City; tel. (2) 32-5768; Chargé d'affaires: ROBERTO CHÁVEZ LIZANO.

Dominican Republic: 7a Calle 'A' 4-28, Zona 10, Guatemala City; Ambassador: PEDRO PABLO ALVAREZ BONILLA.

Ecuador: Oficina 602, Avda Reforma 12-01, Zona 10, Guatemala City; tel. (2) 31-2439; telex 6218; Ambassador: DIEGO PAREDES-PEÑA.

Egypt: 12a Calle 6-15, Zona 9, Guatemala City; telex 5157; Ambassador: MAHMOUD ABBAS.

El Salvador: 12 Calle 5-43, Zona 9, Guatemala City; tel. (2) 62-9385; telex 5418; Ambassador: AGUSTÍN MARTÍNEZ VARELA.

France: 16 Calle 4-53, Zona 10, Edif. Marbella, Guatemala City; tel. (2) 37-3639; telex 5963; Ambassador: JEAN MAZEO.

Germany: Edif. Plaza Maritima, 6 Avda 20-25, Zona 10, Guatemala City; tel. (2) 37-0028; telex 5209; Ambassador: Dr PETER BENSCH.

Holy See: 10a Calle 4-47, Zona 9, Guatemala City (Apostolic Nunciature); tel. (2) 32-4274; fax (2) 34-1918; Apostolic Nuncio: Most Rev. ORIANO QUILICI, Titular Archbishop of Tabla.

GUATEMALA

Honduras: 16 Calle 8-27, Zona 10, Apdo 730-A, 01909 Guatemala City; tel. (2) 37-3919; telex 5865; fax (2) 33-4629; Ambassador: GUILLERMO BOQUÍN V.
Israel: 13a Avda 14-07, Zona 10, Guatemala City; telex 5218; Ambassador: JACQUES YAACOV DECKEL.
Italy: 5 Avda 8-59, Zona 14, Guatemala City; tel. (2) 37-4557; telex 5129; Ambassador: FRANCESCO MARCELLO RUGGIRELLO.
Japan: Ruta 6, 8-19, Apdo 531, Zona 4, Guatemala City; tel. (2) 31-9666; telex 5926; fax (2) 31-5462; Ambassador: ONO SUMIO.
Korea, Republic: 15 Avda 24-51, Zona 13, Apdo 1649, Guatemala City; telex 5369; Ambassador: KEY-SUNG CHO.
Mexico: 16a Calle 0-51, Zona 14, Guatemala City; tel. (2) 68-0769; telex 5961; Ambassador: ABRAHAM TALAVERA LÓPEZ.
Nicaragua: 10 Avda 14-72, Zona 10, Guatemala City; telex 5653; Ambassador: RICARDO ZAMBRANA.
Paraguay: 7 Avda 7-78, 8°, Zona 4, Guatemala City.
Peru: 2a Avda 9-58, Zona 9, Guatemala City; Ambassador: ANDRÉS ARAMBURU ALVAREZ-CALDERÓN.
Portugal: 5 Avda 12-60, Zona 9, Guatemala City.
South Africa: 6 Avda 14-75, Zona 9, Guatemala City.
Spain: 10 Calle 6-20, Zona 9, Guatemala City; telex 5393; Ambassador: JUAN PABLO DE LA IGLESIA.
Sweden: 8a Avda 15-07, Zona 10, Guatemala City; tel. (2) 68-0621; telex 5916; Ambassador: PETER LANDELIUS.
Switzerland: 4a Calle 7-73, Zona 9, Apdo 1426, 01901 Guatemala City; tel. (2) 34-0743; telex 5257; fax (2) 31-8524; Ambassador: WILLY HOLD.
United Kingdom: Centro Financiero, Torre II, 7°, 7A Avda 5-10, Zona 4, Guatemala City; tel. (2) 32-1601; telex 5686; Ambassador: JUSTIN NASON.
USA: Avda La Reforma 7-01, Zona 10, Guatemala City; tel. (2) 31-1541; Ambassador: THOMAS STROOK.
Uruguay: 20a Calle 8-00, Apdo 2b, Zona 10, Guatemala City; Chargé d'affaires: HÉCTOR L. PEDETTI A.
Venezuela: 8a Calle 0-56, Zona 9, Guatemala City; telex 5317; Ambassador: Dr ROGELIO ROSAS GIL.

Judicial System

Corte Suprema: Centro Cívico, 21 Calle y 7a Avda, Guatemala City; tel. (2) 84323.
President of the Supreme Court: EDMUNDO VÁSQUEZ MARTÍNEZ.
Civil Courts of Appeal: 10 courts, 5 in Guatemala City, 2 in Quezaltenango, 1 each in Jalapa, Zacapa and Antigua. The two Labour Courts of Appeal are in Guatemala City.
Judges of the First Instance: 7 civil and 10 penal in Guatemala City, 2 civil each in Quezaltenango, Escuintla, Jutiapa and San Marcos, 1 civil in each of the 18 remaining Departments of the Republic.

Religion

Almost all of the inhabitants profess Christianity, with a majority belonging to the Roman Catholic Church. In recent years the Protestant Churches have attracted a growing number of converts.

CHRISTIANITY

The Roman Catholic Church

For ecclesiastical purposes, Guatemala comprises one archdiocese, eight dioceses, the Territorial Prelature of Escuintla, and the Apostolic Vicariates of El Petén and Izabal.

Bishops' Conference: Conferencia Episcopal de Guatemala, Secretariado General del Episcopado, Apdo 1698, 26a Calle 8-90, Zona 12, Guatemala City; tel. (2) 76-4727; f. 1973; Pres. RODOLFO QUEZADA TORUÑO, Bishop of Zacapa.
Archbishop of Guatemala City: PRÓSPERO PEÑADOS DEL BARRIO, Arzobispado, 7a Avda 6-21, Zona 1, Apdo 723, Guatemala City; tel. (2) 29707.

Protestant Churches

The Baptist Church: Convention of Baptist Churches of Guatemala, 12a Calle 9-54, Zona 1, Apdo 322, 01901 Guatemala City; tel. (2) 24227; f. 1946; Pres. Lic. JOSÉ ANGEL SAMOL GONZÁLEZ.
The Episcopal Church: Avda Castellana 40-06, Zona 8, Guatemala City; tel. (2) 72-0764; diocese founded 1967; Bishop of Guatemala: Rt Rev. ARMANDO GUERRA SORIA (Apdo 58A, Guatemala City); Cathedral Church of St James and six missions in Guatemala City, one mission in Quezaltenango, four missions in El Quiché and 17 rural missions in the Departments of Izabal and Zacapa.
Church of Jesus Christ of Latter-day Saints: 12a Calle 3-37, Zona 9, Guatemala City; 17 bishoprics, 9 chapels; Regional Rep. GUILLERMO ENRIQUE RITTSCHER.
The Lutheran Church: Consejo Nacional de Iglesias Luteranas, Apdo 1111, Guatemala City; tel. (2) 23401; 3,077 mems; Pres. Rev. DAVID RODRÍGUEZ U.
The Presbyterian Church: Iglesia Evangélica Presbiteriana Central, 6a Avda 'A' 4-68, Zona 1, Apdo 655, Guatemala City; tel. (2) 20791; f. 1882; 36,000 mems; Pastors: Rev. JUAN RENÉ GIRÓN T., Rev. JULIO CÉSAR PAZ PORTILLO, Rev. JOSÉ RAMIRO BOLAÑOS R.
The Union Church: 12 Calle 7-37, Plazuela España, Zona 9, Apdo 150A, 01909 Guatemala City; tel. (2) 31-6904; f. 1943; Pastor Rev. PHILIP TRUESDALE.

BAHÁ'Í FAITH

National Spiritual Assembly of the Bahá'ís: 3a Calle 4-54, Zona 1, 01001 Guatemala City; tel. (2) 29673; mems resident in 411 localities.

The Press

PRINCIPAL DAILIES

Diario de Centroamérica: 18a Calle 6-72, Zona 1, Guatemala City; tel. (2) 24418; f. 1880; morning; official; Dir LUIS MENDIZÁBAL; circ. 15,000.
El Gráfico: 14a Avda 9-18, Zona 1, Guatemala City; tel. (2) 51-0021; f. 1963; morning; Dir JORGE CARPIO NICOLLE; circ. 60,000.
Impacto: 9a Calle 1-56, Guatemala City; daily.
Imparcial: 7a Calle 10-54, Zona 1, Guatemala City; daily; circ. 25,000.
La Nación: 1 Avda 11-12, Guatemala City.
La Hora: 9a Calle 'A' 1-56, Zona 1, Guatemala City; tel. (2) 26864; telex 9259; fax (2) 51-7084; f. 1944; evening; independent; Dir OSCAR MARROQUÍN ROJAS; circ. 18,000.
Prensa Libre: 13a Calle 9-13, Zona 1, Guatemala City; tel. (2) 51-1838; f. 1951; morning; independent; Dir and Gen. Man. PEDRO JULIO GARCÍA; circ. 68,500.
La Tarde: 14 Avda 4-33, Guatemala City.

PERIODICALS

AGA: 9a Calle 3-43, Zona 1, Guatemala City; monthly; agricultural.
Gerencia: 10a Calle 3-17, Zona 10, Guatemala City; tel. (2) 31-1564; fmrly Otra Revista; official organ of the Association of Guatemalan Managers; Dir RICHARD AITKENHEAD CASTILLO.
Industria: 3a Avda 12-21, Zona 1, Guatemala City; monthly.
El Industrial: Ruta 6 No 9-21, Zona 4, Guatemala City; monthly; official organ of the Chamber of Industry.
Inforpress Centroamericana: 9 Calle 'A' 3-56, Zona 1, Guatemala City; tel. (2) 29432; f. 1972; weekly; Spanish; regional political and economic news and analysis; Dir ARIEL DELEON.
Panorama: 12 Calle 6-40, Guatemala City; economics, monthly.

PRESS ASSOCIATIONS

Asociación de Periodistas de Guatemala (APG): 14 Calle 3-29, Zona 1, Guatemala City; tel. (2) 21813; f. 1947; Pres. JESÚS ALVARADO MENDIZÁBAL.
Cámara Guatemalteca de Periodismo (CGP): Guatemala City; Pres. EDUARDO DÍAZ REINA.
Círculo Nacional de Prensa (CN): Guatemala City; Pres. JESÚS ABALCÁZAR LÓPEZ.

NEWS AGENCIES

Inforpress Centroamericana: 9a Calle 'A' 3-56, Zona 1, Guatemala City; tel. (2) 29432; f. 1972; independent news agency; publishes two weekly news bulletins, in English and Spanish.

Foreign Bureaux

ACAN-EFE (Central America): Edif. El Centro, 8°, 9a Calle y 7a Avda, Zona 1, Of. 8-21, Guatemala City; tel. (2) 51-9454; fax (2) 51-9484; Dir HAROLDO SÁNCHEZ.
Agenzia Nazionale Stampa Associata (ANSA) (Italy): Torre Norte, Edif. Geminis 10, Of. 805, Calle 12, No. 1-25, Zona 10, Guatemala City; tel. (2) 35-3039; telex 5251; Chief ALFONSO ANZUETO LÓPEZ.

GUATEMALA
Directory

Deutsche Presse-Agentur (dpa) (Germany): 5a Calle No 4–30, Apdo 2333, Zona 1, Guatemala City; tel. (2) 51-7505; telex 5227; Correspondent Julio César Anzueto.

Inter Press Service (IPS) (Italy): Edif. El Centro, 3°, Oficina 13, 7a Avda, 8-56, Zona 1, Guatemala City; tel. (2) 53-2727; telex 9246; Correspondent Gladys Calderón.

United Press International (UPI) (USA): 6a Calle 4-17, Zona 1, Guatemala City; tel. (2) 51-0440; telex 3729285; Correspondent Raúl Villatoro.

Publishers

Ediciones America: 12a Avda 14-55, Zone 1, Guatemala City; tel. (2) 51-4556; Man. Dir Rafael Escobar Argüello.

Ediciones Gama: 5a Avda 14-46, Zone 1, Guatemala City; tel. (2) 34-2331; Man. Dir Sara Monzón de Echeverría.

Ediciones Legales "Commercio e Industria": 12a Avda 14-78, Zone 1, Guatemala City; tel. (2) 53-5725; Man. Dir Luis Emilio Barrios.

Editorial Impacto: Via 6 3-14, Zone 4, Guatemala City; tel. (2) 32-2887; Man. Dir Iván Carpio.

Editorial del Ministerio de Educación: 15a Avda 3-22, Zona 1, Guatemala City.

Editorial Nueva Narrativa: 7a Avda 7-07, Zone 4, Edificio El Patio, Of. 106; Man. Dir Max Araújo A.

Editorial Oscar de León Palacios: 6a Calle 10-12, Zone 11, Guatemala City; tel. (2) 72-1636; educational texts; Man. Dir Oscar de León Palacios.

Editorial Palo de Hormigo: "o" Calle 16-40, Zone 15, colonia El Maestro; tel. 69-2080; Man. Dir Juan Fernando Cifuentes.

Editorial Universitaria: Universidad de San Carlos de Guatemala, Edif. de la Editorial Universitaria, Ciudad Universitaria, Zona 12, Guatemala City; tel. (2) 76-0790; literature, social sciences, health, pure and technical sciences, humanities, secondary and university educational textbooks; Editor Ivanova Alvarado de Ancheta.

Piedra Santa: 5a Calle 7-58, Zona 1, Guatemala City; tel. (2) 51-0231; telex 9225; fax (2) 51-0531; f. 1947; children's literature, incl. the magazine *Chiquirín* and text books; Man. Dir Oralia Díaz de Piedra Santa.

Seminario de Integración Social Guatemalteco: 11a Calle 4-31, Zona 1, Guatemala City; tel. (2) 29754; f. 1956; sociology, anthropology, social sciences, educational textbooks.

Radio and Television

In 1987 there were an estimated 550,000 radio receivers and 315,000 television receivers in use.

Dirección General de Radiodifusión y Televisión Nacional: Edif. Tipografía Nacional, 3°, 18 de Septiembre 6-72, Zona 1, Guatemala City; tel. (2) 53-2539; f. 1931; government supervisory body; Dir-Gen. Enrique Alberto Hernández Escobar.

RADIO

There are five government and six educational stations, including:

La Voz de Guatemala: 18 Calle 6-72, Zona 1, Guatemala City; tel. (2) 53-2539; government station; Dir Enrique Alberto Hernández Escobar.

Radio Cultural TGN: 4a Avda 30-09, Zona 3, Apdo 601, 01901 Guatemala City; tel. (2) 71-4378; f. 1950; religious and cultural station; programmes in Spanish and English, Cakchiquel, Kekchí and Mam; Dir Esteban Sywulka; Man. A. Wayne Berger.

There are 84 commercial stations, of which the most important are:

Emisoras Unidas de Guatemala: 7a Avda 6-45, Zona 9, Guatemala City; tel. (2) 34-7654; fax (2) 31-6315; Pres. Jorge Edgardo Archila; Vice-Pres. Rolando Archila.

La Voz de las Américas: 11a Calle 2-43, Zona 1, Guatemala City; Dir Augusto López S.

Radio Cinco Sesenta: 8a Calle 1-11, Zona 11, Guatemala City; Dir Edna Castillo Obregón.

Radio Continental: 15a Calle 3-45, Zona 1, Guatemala City; Dir R. Vizcaíno R.

Radio Nuevo Mundo: 6a Avda 10-45, Zona 1, Apdo 281, Guatemala City; Man. Alfredo González G.

Radio Panamericana: 1a Calle 25-48, Zona 7, Guatemala City; Dir María V. de Paniagua.

TELEVISION

Canal 3—Radio-Televisión Guatemala, SA: 30a Avda 3-40, Zona 11, Apdo 1367, 01901 Guatemala City; tel. (2) 94-7491; telex 5253; fax (2) 94-7492; f. 1956; commercial station; Pres. Lic. Max Kestler Farnés; Vice-Pres. J. F. Villanueva.

Tele Once: 20a Calle 5-02, Zona 10, Guatemala City; tel. (2) 68-2165; commercial; Dir A. Mourra.

Televisiete, SA: 3a Calle 6-24, Zona 9, Apdo 1242, Guatemala City; tel. (2) 62216; f. 1964; commercial station channel 7; Dir Dr J. Villanueva P.

Televisión Cultural Educativa: 4a Calle 18-38, Zona 1, Guatemala City; tel. (2) 53-1913; government station.

Trecevisión, SA: 3a Calle 10-70, Zona 10, Guatemala City; tel. (2) 63266; telex 6070; commerical; Dir Ing. Pedro Melgar R.; Gen. Man. Gilda Valladares Ortiz.

Finance

(cap. = capital; p.u. = paid up; res = reserves; dep. = deposits; m. = million; brs = branches; amounts in quetzales)

A stock exchange was established in Guatemala City in April 1987. The exchange was to be commonly owned (one share per associate) and was to trade stocks from private companies, government bonds, letters of credit and other securities.

BANKING

Superintendencia de Bancos: 7a Avda 22-01, Zona 1, Apdo 2306, Guatemala City; tel. (2) 53-4243; telex 5231; f. 1946; Superintendent Lic. Gustavo Ayestas Escobar; Gen. Sec. Lic. Douglas Borja Vielman.

Central Bank

Banco de Guatemala: 7a Avda 22-01, Zona 1, Apdo 365, Guatemala City; tel. (2) 53-4053; telex 5231; f. 1946; guarantee fund 94.8m. (Sept. 1987); Pres. Federico Linares; Man. Lic. Fabián Pira Arrivillaga.

State Commercial Bank

Crédito Hipotecario Nacional de Guatemala: 7a Avda 22-77, Zona 1, Apdo 242, 01901 Guatemala City; tel. (2) 82041; telex 5192; f. 1930; government-owned; cap. p.u. 15m., res 10.7m., dep. 1.9m. (June 1988); Pres. Lic. Víctor Manuel Moraga Miranda; Gen. Man. Lic. Ricardo Contreras Cruz; 2 brs.

Private Commercial Banks
Guatemala City

Banco Agrícola Mercantil, SA: 7a Avda 9-11, Zona 1, Guatemala City; tel. (2) 20601; telex 5347; f. 1946; cap. 5m., res 17.2m., dep. 387.0m. (Dec. 1989); Man. Lic. Armando González Campo; 2 brs.

Banco del Agro, SA: 9a Calle 5-39, Zona 1, Apdo 1443, Guatemala City; tel. (2) 51-4026; telex 4167; f. 1958; cap. 7.1m., res 11.0m., dep. 246.8m. (June 1988); Pres. Ricardo Rodríguez Paúl; Man. Aura Alicia Ayala de García.

Banco del Café, SA: Avda La Reforma 9-00, Zona 9, Apdo 831, Guatemala City; tel. (2) 31-1311; telex 5123; fax (2) 31-1480; f. 1978; cap. 12.5m., res 3.1m., dep. 314.3m. (June 1990); Pres. Eduardo M. González Rivera; Gen. Man. Lic. Manuel Eduardo González Castillo.

Banco de la Construcción, SA: 12 Calle 4-17, Zona 1, Apdo 999, Guatemala City; tel. (2) 53-9622; telex 5708; fax (2) 53-6091; f. 1983; cap. 12.5m., dep. 139.3m. (April 1990); Pres. Arq. Héctor Quezada Leonardo; Man. Ing. Lionel Toriello Nájera.

Banco del Ejército, SA: 5a Avda 6-06, Zona 1, Apdo 1797, Guatemala City; tel. (2) 51-0570; telex 5574; fax (2) 51-9105; f. 1972; cap. 9.8m., res 7.7m., dep. 222.7m. (May 1990); Pres. Col Gustavo Adolfo Rafael Rossito C.; Man. Col. José Ramiro Martínez O.

Banco de Exportación, SA: Avda La Reforma 11-49, Zona 10, Guatemala City; tel. (2) 37-3873; telex 5896; fax (2) 32-2879; f. 1985; cap. 7.5m., res 4.7m., dep. 128.1m. (Dec. 1989); Pres. Venancio Botrán Borja; Man. Ing. Rafael Viejo Rodríguez.

Banco Granai y Townson, SA: 7a Avda 1-86, Zona 4, Apdo 654, Guatemala City; telex 5159; fax (2) 34-7913; f. 1962; cap. 13.0m., res 6.9m., dep. 455.3m. (Dec. 1988); Pres. Mario Granai Arévalo; Gen. Man. Lic. Mario Asturias Arévalo; 22 brs.

Banco Industrial, SA: Edif. Centro Financiero, Torre 1, 7a Avda 5-10, Zona 4, Apdo 744, Guatemala City; tel. (2) 31-2323; telex 5236; fax (2) 31-9437; f. 1968 to promote industrial development; cap. 25m., res 19.1m., dep. 588.9m. (Dec. 1989); Pres. Juan Miguel

GUATEMALA *Directory*

Torrebiarte Lantzendorffer; Man. Lic. Norberto Rodolfo Castellanos Díaz.

Banco Inmobilario, SA: 8a Avda 10-57, Zona 1, Apdo 1181, Guatemala City; tel. (2) 51-9022; telex 6140; f. 1958; cap. 31.0m., res 0.5m., dep. 204.3m. (June 1988); Pres. Lic. Carlos Enrique Carrera Samayoa; Gen. Man. Dr Oscar Alvarez Morroquín; 15 brs.

Banco Internacional, SA: 7a Avda 11-20, Zona 1, Apdo 2588, Guatemala City; tel. (2) 51-2260; telex 4178; f. 1976; cap. 10.0m., res 4.5m., dep. 236.5m. (Dec. 1988); Pres. Lic. Jorge Skinner-Klée; Gen. Man. Julio Vielman Pineda.

Banco Metropolitano, SA: 5a Avda 8-24, Zona 1, Apdo 2688, Guatemala City; tel. (2) 25361; telex 5188; fax (2) 84073; f. 1978; cap. 15.2m., res 0.9m., dep. 193.4m. (June 1989); Pres. Ing. Francisco Alvarado Macdonald; Man. Eberto César Sigüenza López.

Banco Promotor, SA: 10 Calle 6-47, Zona 1, Apdo 930, Guatemala City; tel. (2) 51-2928; telex 9238; f. 1986; cap. 4.5m., dep. 75.8m. (June 1988); Pres. Lic. Julio Valladares Castillo; Man. Lic. Raúl Monterroso Rivera.

Banco del Quetzal, SA: Edif. El Roble, 6a Ave, No. 6-26, Zona 9, Apdo 1002, Guatemala City; tel. (2) 36-5452; telex 5893; f. 1984; cap. 4.4m., dep. 71.9m. (June 1988); Pres. Lic. Mario Roberto Leal Pivaral; Man. Ing. Juan Carlos Vercesi Galeani.

Banco de los Trabajadores: 8a Avda 9-41, Zona 1, Apdo 1956, Guatemala City; tel. (2) 24341; telex 9212; f. 1966; cap. 19.2m., dep. 61.4m. (June 1988); deals with loans for establishing and improving small industries as well as normal banking business; Pres. Lic. Juan José Alonzo Estrada; Man. Lic. Angel H. Mazariegos Rodas.

Quezaltenango

Banco de Occidente, SA: 7a Ave 11-15, Zona 1, Quezaltenango; tel. 53-1333; telex 5455; f. 1881; cap. 5.0m., res 23.0m., dep. 503.5m. (June 1988); Pres. Dr Luis Beltranena Valladares; Man. Ing. Manuel Angel Pérez Lara; 1 br.

State Development Banks

Banco Nacional de Desarrollo Agrícola—BANDESA: 9a Calle 9-47, Zona 1, Apdo 350, Guatemala City; tel. (2) 53-5222; telex 4122; f. 1971; cap. 10.5m., dep. 89.2m. (June 1988); agricultural development bank; Pres. Ing. Rodolfo Estrada Hurtarte; Man. Lic. José Miguel Argueta Bone.

Banco Nacional de la Vivienda—BANVI: 6a Avda 1-22, Zona 4, Apdo 2632, Guatemala City; tel. (2) 32-5782; telex 5371; f. 1973; cap. 30.6m., res 25.7m., dep. 258.3m. (April 1989); Pres. Lic. Edgar Guillermo Santos Maldonado.

Finance Corporations

Corporación Financiera Nacional—CORFINA: 8a Avda 10-43, Zona 1, Guatemala City; tel. (2) 83331; telex 5186; f. 1973; provides assistance for the development of industry, mining and tourism; cap. 34.3m., res 0.2m. (June 1988); Pres. Ing. Federico Moreno Hernández; Gen. Man. Edmundo Ruiz Sem.

Financiera Guatemalteca, SA—FIGSA: Avda Reforma 11-49, Zona 10, Apdo 2460, Guatemala City; tel. (2) 31-6051; telex 5896; fax (2) 32-2879; f. 1962; investment agency; cap. 4.7m., res 1.2m. (June 1988); Pres. Carlos González Barrios; Man. Lic. José Roberto Ortega Herrera.

Financiera Industrial y Agropecuaria, SA—FIASA: Avda La Reforma 10-00, Zona 9, Guatemala City; tel. (2) 31-0303; telex 5958; f. 1969; private development bank; medium- and long-term loans to private industrial enterprises in Central America; cap. 2.5m., res 16.7m. (June 1988); Pres. Jorge Castillo Love; Gen. Man. Lic. Federico Linares Martínez.

Financiera Industrial, SA (FISA): Torre No. 1 Centro Financiero, 7a Avda 5-10, Zona 4, Apdo 744, Guatemala City; tel. (2) 31-2323; telex 5236; fax (2) 31-9437; f. 1981; cap. 3m., res 2.2m. (Dec. 1989); Pres. Carlos Arías Masselli; Man. Lic. Carlos Humberto Alpírez Pérez.

Financiera de Inversión, SA: 10a Calle 3-17, Zona 10, Guatemala City; tel. (2) 31-1266; telex 3155; f. 1981; investment agency; cap. 2.7m. (June 1988); Pres. Lic. Mario Augusto Porras G.; Gen. Man. Lic. Antonio Sagastume Acevedo.

Foreign Banks

Bank of America, NT & SA: 5a Avda 10-55, Zona 1, Apdo 1335, Guatemala City; tel. (2) 51-2266; telex 5202; f. 1957; cap. 3m., res 2.9m., dep. 78.6m. (June 1988); Man. Michael Suárez.

Lloyds Bank PLC: 8a Avda 10-67, Zona 1, Apdo 1106, 01001 Guatemala City; tel. (2) 24651; telex 5263; f. 1959; cap. 13m., dep. 159.1m. (1990); Man. Philip V. Coggins ; 8 brs.

Banking Association

Asociación de Banqueros de Guatemala: Edif. Quinta Montúfar, 2°, 12a Calle 4-74, Zona 9, Guatemala City; tel. (2) 31-8211; f. 1961; represents all state and private banks; Pres. Dr Oscar Alvarez Marroquín.

INSURANCE
National Companies

La Alianza, Cía Anglo-Centroamericana de Seguros, SA: Edif. Etisa, 6°, Plazuela España, Zona 9, Guatemala City; tel. (2) 31-5475; telex 5551; f. 1968; Pres. F. Antonio Gándara García; Man. Ing. Rudy Gándara Merkle.

Aseguradora General, SA: 10a Calle 3-17, Zona 10, Guatemala City; tel. (2) 32-5933; telex 5441; f. 1968; Pres. Juan O. Niemann; Man. Enrique Neutze.

Aseguradora Guatemalteca de Transportes, SA: 5a Avda 6-06, Zona 1, 01001 Guatemala City; tel. (2) 51-9794; telex 5574; fax (2) 51-9105; f. 1978; Pres. Col Gustavo Adolfo Rafael Rossito Contreras; Man. César A. Ruano Sandoval.

Cía de Seguros Generales Granai & Townson, SA: 7a Avda 1-82, Zona 4, Guatemala City; tel. (2) 61361; telex 5955; f. 1947; Pres. Ernesto Townson R.; Gen. Man. Mario Asturias Arévalo.

Cía de Seguros Panamericana, SA: Avda La Reforma 9-00, Zona 9, Guatemala City; tel. (2) 32-5922; telex 5925; f. 1968; Pres. G. Frank Purvis, Jr; Gen. Man. J. Antonio González A.

Cía de Seguros El Roble, SA: 7a Avda 5-10, Zona 4, 01004 Guatemala City; tel. (2) 32-1702; telex 6094; fax (2) 32-1629; f. 1973; Pres. Federico Köng Vielman; Man. Ing. Ricardo Erales Cóbar.

Comercial Aseguradora Suizo-Americana, SA: 7a Avda 7-07, Zona 9, Apdo 132, 010009 Guatemala City; tel. (2) 32-0666; telex 5502; fax (2) 31-5495; f. 1946; Pres. Ernesto A. Piñero; Vice-Pres. William Bickford B.

Departamento de Seguros y Previsión del Crédito Hipotecario Nacional: 7a Avda 22-77, Zona 1, Guatemala City; tel. (2) 82041; telex 6065; f. 1935; Pres. Lic. Luis M. Montúfar Luna; Man. Lic. Ricardo Contreras Cruz.

La Seguridad de Centroamérica, SA: Avda La Reforma 12-01, Zona 10, Guatemala City; tel. (2) 31-7566; telex 5243; f. 1967; Pres. Edgardo Wagner D.; Vice-Pres. Marta de Toriello.

Seguros Cruz Azul, SA: Edif. Plaza Marítima 10, 6a Avda 20-25, Zona 10, Guatemala City; tel. (2) 37-2285; telex 5204; fax 37-2285; Gen. Man. Brian Murphy.

Seguros de Occidente, SA: 7a Calle 'A' 7-14, Zona 9, Guatemala City; tel. (2) 31-1222; telex 5605; f. 1979; Pres. Ing. Herculano Aguirre Montalvo; Gen. Man. Lic. Pedro Aguirre.

Seguros Universales, SA: 4a Calle 7-73, Zona 9, Apdo 1479, Guatemala City; tel. (2) 34-0733; telex 6104; fax (2) 32-3372; f. 1962; Pres. Francisco Javier Valls Planas; Man. Nolasco Sicilia García.

Insurance Association

Asociación Guatemalteca de Instituciones de Seguros—AGIS: Guatemala City; f. 1953; 8 mems; Pres. Enrique Neutze Aycinena; Man. Lic. Federico Piñol.

Trade and Industry
CHAMBERS OF COMMERCE AND INDUSTRY

Comité Coordinador de Asociaciones Agrícolas, Comerciales, Industriales y Financieras (CACIF): Edif. Cámara de Industria de Guatemala, Ruta 6, No 9-21, Zona 4, Guatemala City; tel. (2) 31-0651; telex 6133; co-ordinates work on problems and organization of free enterprise; mems: 6 chambers; Pres. Lic. Arturo Pellecer Arellano; Sec.-Gen. Rafael Pola.

Cámara de Comercio de Guatemala: 10a Calle 3-80, Zona 1, Guatemala City; tel. (2) 82681; telex 5478; fax (2) 51-4197; f. 1894; Man. Jonás Vásquez Alvarado.

Cámara de Industria de Guatemala: Ruta 6, 9-21, Zona 4, Apdo 214, Guatemala City; tel. (2) 34-0849; telex 5402; fax (2) 34-1090; f. 1958; Pres. Ing. Víctor Manuel Suárez Valdes; Gen. Man. Ing. Carlos Ramiro García Chiu.

DEVELOPMENT ORGANIZATIONS

Comisión Nacional del Petróleo: Diagonal 17, 29-78, Zona 11, Guatemala City; tel. (2) 46-0111; f. 1983; awards petroleum exploration licences.

Consejo Nacional de Planificación Económica: 9A Calle 10-44, Zona 1, Guatemala City; tel. (2) 53-9804; telex 533127; f.1954; prepares and supervises the implementation of the national economic development plan; Sec.-Gen. Ing. Marciano Castillo González.

Corporación Financiera Nacional—Corfina: see under Finance.

GUATEMALA   Directory

Dirección General de Hidrocarburos: Diagonal 17, 29-78, Zona 11, Apdo 1411, Guatemala City; tel. (2) 76-0679; f. 1983; control and supervision of petroleum and gas development.

Empresa Nacional de Fomento y Desarrollo Económico de El Petén (FYDEP): 11a Avda 'B' 32-46, Zona 5, Guatemala City; tel. (2) 31-6834; telex 6178; f. 1959; attached to the Presidency; economic development agency for the Department of El Petén; Dir Francisco Ángel Castellanos Góngora.

Instituto de Fomento de Hipotecas Aseguradas (FHA): 6a Avda 0-60, Zona 4, Guatemala City; f. 1961; insured mortgage institution for the promotion of house construction; Pres. Lic. Homero Augusto González Barillas; Man. Lic. José Salvador Samayoa Aguilar.

Instituto Nacional de Administración Pública (INAP): 5a Avda 12-65, Zona 9, Apto 2753, Guatemala City; tel. (2) 66339; f. 1964; provides technical experts to assist all branches of the Government in administrative reform programmes; provides in-service training for local and central government staff; has research programmes in administration, sociology, politics and economics; provides post-graduate education in public administration; Gen. Man. Dr Ariel Rivera Irías.

Instituto Nacional de Transformación Agraria (INTA): 14 Calle 7-14, Zona 1, Guatemala City; tel. (2) 80975; f. 1962 to carry out agrarian reform; current programme includes development of the 'Faja Transversal del Norte'; Pres. Ing. Jaime González; Vice-Pres. Ing. Francisco Morales.

PRODUCERS' ASSOCIATIONS

Asociación de Azucareros de Guatemala—ASAZGUA: Edif. Tívoli Plaza, 6a Calle 6-38, Zona 9, Guatemala City; telex 5248; fax (2) 31-8191; f. 1957; sugar producers' asscn; 19 mems; Gen. Man. Lic. Armando Boesche.

Asociación de Exportadores de Café: 11a Calle 5-66, 3°, Zona 9, Guatemala City; telex 5368; coffee exporters' asscn; 37 mems; Pres. Eduardo González Rivera.

Asociación General de Agricultores: 9a Calle 3-43, Zona 1, Guatemala City; f. 1920; general farmers' asscn; 350 mems; Pres. David Ordoñez; Man. Pedro Arrivillaga Rada.

Asociación Nacional de Avicultores—ANAVI: Edif. Galerías Reforma, 9°, Of. 904, Torre 2, Avda La Reforma 8-60, Zona 9, Guatemala City; tel. (2) 31-1381; telex 6215; fax (2) 34-7576; f. 1964; national asscn of poultry farmers; 60 mems; Pres. Ing. Mauricio Bonifasi; Dir Dr Mario A. Motta González.

Asociación Nacional de Fabricantes de Alcoholes y Licores (ANFAL): Km 16½ Carretera Roosevelt, Apdo 2065, Zona 10, Guatemala City; tel. (2) 92-0430; telex 5565; f. 1947; distillers' asscn; Pres. Felipe Botrán Merino; Man. Lic. Juan Guillermo Borja Mogollón.

Asociación Nacional del Café—Anacafé: Edif. Etisa, Plazuela España, Zona 9, Guatemala City; tel. (2) 36-7180; telex 5915; fax (2) 34-7023; f. 1960; national coffee asscn; Pres. Lic. James McSweeney.

Asociación de Agricultores Productores de Aceites Esenciales: 6a Calle 1-36, Zona 10, Apdo 272, Guatemala City; tel. (2) 34-7255; telex 5316; f. 1948; essential oils producers' asscn; 40 mems; Pres. José Luis Ralda; Man. Ing. Luis Alberto Asturias.

Cámara del Agro: 15a Calle 'A', No 7-65, Zona 9, Guatemala City; tel. (2) 61473; f. 1973; Man. César Bustamante Araúz.

Consejo Nacional del Algodón: 7a Avda 6-26, Zona 9, Guatemala City; tel. (2) 32-4540; f. 1964; consultative body for cultivation and classification of cotton; 125 mems; Pres Dieter Keller, Dr Moises Flores Pacheco; Man. Alfredo Gil Spillari.

Gremial de Huleros de Guatemala: Edif. Centroamericano, Of. 406, 7a Avda 7-78, Zona 4, Guatemala City; tel. (2) 31-4917; telex 5114; f. 1970; union of rubber producers; 125 mems; Pres. José Luis Ralda; Man. Lic. César Soto.

CO-OPERATIVES

The following federations group all Guatemalan co-operatives:

Federación de Cooperativas Artesanales.

Federación Nacional de Cooperativas de Ahorro y Crédito.

Federación Nacional de Cooperativas de Consumo

Federación Nacional de Cooperativas de Vivienda y Servicios Varios.

TRADE UNIONS

Trade union activity can now take place freely, having been severely restricted after repression in 1979 and 1980.

Frente Nacional Sindical (FNS) (National Trade Union Front): Guatemala City; f. 1968, to achieve united action in labour matters; affiliated are two confederations and 11 federations, which represent 97% of the country's trade unions and whose General Secretaries form the governing council of the FNS. The affiliated organizations include:

Comité Nacional de Unidad Sindical Guatemalteca—CONUS: Leader Miguel Ángel Solís; Sec.-Gen. Gerónimo López Díaz.

Confederación General de Sindicatos (General Trade Union Confederation): 18a Calle 5-50, Zona 1, Apdo 959, Guatemala City.

Confederación Nacional de Trabajadores (National Workers' Confederation): Guatemala City; Sec.-Gen. Miguel Ángel Albizúrez.

Consejo Sindical de Guatemala (Guatemalan Trade Union Council): 18a Calle 5-50, Zona 1, Apdo 959, Guatemala City; f. 1955; admitted to ICFTU and ORIT; Gen. Sec. Jaime V. Monge Donis; 30,000 mems in 105 affiliated unions.

Federación Autónoma Sindical Guatemalteca (Guatemalan Autonomous Trade Union Federation): Guatemala City; Gen. Sec. Miguel Ángel Solís.

Federación de Obreros Textiles (Textile Workers' Federation): Edif. Briz, Of. 503, 6a Avda 14-33, Zona 1, Guatemala City; f. 1957; Sec.-Gen. Facundo Pineda.

Federación de Trabajadores de Guatemala (FTG) (Guatemalan Workers' Federation): 5a Calle 4-33, Zona 1, Guatemala City; tel. (2) 26515; Promoter Adrian Ramírez.

A number of unions exist without a national centre, including the Union of Chicle and Wood Workers, the Union of Coca-Cola Workers and the Union of Workers of the Enterprise of the United Fruit Company.

Central Nacional de Trabajadores (CNT): 9a Avda 4-29, Zona 1, Apdo 2472, Guatemala City; f. 1972; cover all sections of commerce, industry and agriculture including the public sector; clandestine since June 1980; Sec.-Gen. Julio Celso de León; 23,735 mems.

Unidad de Acción Sindical y Popular (UASP): f. 1988; broad coalition of leading labour and peasant organizations; includes:

Comité de la Unidad Campesina (CUC) (Committee of Peasants' Unity).

Confederación General de Trabajadores de Guatemala (CGTG).

Confederación de Unidad Sindical de Trabajadores de Guatemala (CUSG): 5a Calle 4-33, Zona 1, Guatemala City; tel. (2) 26515; f. 1983; Sec.-Gen. Francisco Alfaro Mijangos.

Sindicato de Trabajadores de la Educación Guatemaltecos (STEG).

Sindicato de Trabajadores de la Industria de la Electricidad—STINDE.

Sindicato de Trabajadores del Instituto Guatemalteco de Seguro Social (STIGSS).

Unidad Sindical de Trabajadores de Guatemala—UNSITRAGUA.

Transport

RAILWAYS

Ferrocarriles de Guatemala—FEGUA: 9a Avda 18-03, Zona 1, Guatemala City; tel. (2) 83030; telex 5342; fax (2) 83807; f. 1968; government-owned; 782 km open from Puerto Barrios and Santo Tomás de Castilla on the Atlantic coast to Tecún Umán on the Mexican border, via Zacapa, Guatemala City and Santa María. Branch lines: Santa María–San José; Las Cruces–Champerico. From Zacapa another line branches southward to Anguiatú, on the border with El Salvador; owns the ports of Barrios (Atlantic) and San José (Pacific); Chair. F. A. Leal Estévez.

There are 102 km of plantation lines.

In 1990 plans were announced to rehabilitate a 231-km railway line running from El Salvador to the eastern coast of Guatemala. It was estimated that the project would cost US $9.6m. and take two years to complete.

ROADS

In 1989 there were 11,883 km of roads, of which 3,183 km were asphalted and 8,700 km gravel. The Guatemala section of the Pan-American highway is 518.7 km long and totally asphalted. The construction of a 1,500-km network of new highways, including a four-lane motorway from the capital to Palín Escuintla, began in 1981. A 44-km toll road linking Escuintla with San José was built in the mid 1980s, at a cost of US $18m. In 1990 a $49.1m project, supported by a loan of $21.5m from the World Bank, was begun

GUATEMALA

under which improvements were to be made to many secondary roads.

SHIPPING

Guatemala's major ports are Santo Tomás de Castilla and Puerto Quetzal. A major port reconstruction and expansion programme began in 1976, and in March 1983 the extension to the port of San José was opened.

Armadora Marítima Guatemalteca, SA: 14a Calle 8–14, Zona 1, Apdo 1008, Guatemala City; tel. (2) 53-7243; telex 5214; fax (2) 53-7464; cargo services; Pres. and Gen. Man. L. R. CORONADO CONDE.

Empresa Portuaria 'Quetzal': Edif. 74, 6°, 7a Avda y 4a Calle, Zona 9, Guatemala City; tel. (2) 31-4824; telex 6134; port and shipping co; Man. HUGO FRANCISCO MOTTA LEMUS.

Flota Mercante Gran Centroamericana, SA: Edif. Canella, 5°, 1a Calle 7-21, Zona 9, Guatemala City; tel. (2) 31-6666; telex 5211; f. 1959; services from Europe (in association with WITASS), Gulf of Mexico, US Atlantic and East Coast Central American ports; Pres. R. S. RAMÍREZ; Gen. Man. J. E. A. MORALES.

Líneas Marítimas de Guatemala, SA: 6a Avda 20–25, Edif. Plaza Marítima, 8°, Zona 10, Guatemala City; tel. (2) 37-0166; telex 5174; cargo services; Pres. J. R. MATHEAU ESCOBAR; Gen. Man. F. HERRERÍAS.

Several foreign lines link Guatemala with Europe, the Far East and North America.

CIVIL AVIATION

In 1982 a new international airport was completed at Santa Elena Petén.

Aerovías: Avda Hincapié, 18 Calle Interior, Aeropuerta 'La Aurora', Zona 13, Guatemala City; tel. (2) 31-6935; telex 5397; operates scheduled and charter cargo services; fleet: 3 Handley Page Herald, 1 Douglas DC-6.

AVIATECA—Empresa Guatemalteca de Aviación: Avda Hincapié, Aeropuerto 'La Aurora', Zona 13, Guatemala City; telex 5960; f. 1945; internal services and external services to the USA; transferred to private ownership in 1989; Pres. FREDERICK MELVILLE NOVELLA; Vice-Pres. Lic. ANDRÉS OLIVERO; fleet: 2 Boeing 727-100C and 727-200.

Tourism

As a result of violence in the country, the annual total of tourist arrivals declined from 504,000 in 1979, when tourist receipts were US $201m., to 192,000 in 1984 (receipts $56.6m.). Since 1985, however, the number of arrivals has risen and reached 437,019 in 1989, when receipts increased to $151.9m.

Guatemala Tourist Commission: Centro Cívico, 7a Avda 1–17, Zona 4, Guatemala City; tel. (2) 31-1333; telex 5532; fax (2) 31-8893; f. 1967; policy and planning council: 13 mems representing the public and private sectors; Pres. MARÍA ELISA FLORIDO; Dir JULIO CÉSAR FONSECA.

Asociación Guatemalteca de Agentes de Viajes (AGAV) (Guatemalan Association of Travel Agents): 6a Avda 8-41, Zona 9, Apdo 2735, Guatemala City; tel. (2) 31-0320; telex 5127; Pres. MARÍA DEL CARMEN FERNÁNDEZ O.

Atomic Energy

Dirección General de Energía Nuclear: Diagonal 17, 29–78, Zona 11, Apdo 1421, Guatemala City; tel. (2) 76-0679; telex 5516; programmes include the application of nuclear energy in agriculture and industry, nuclear medicine and the control of the import of radioactive materials; Dir Ing. RAÚL EDUARDO PINEDA GONZÁLEZ.

GUINEA

Introductory Survey

Location, Climate, Language, Religion, Flag, Capital

The Republic of Guinea lies on the west coast of Africa, with Sierra Leone and Liberia to the south, Senegal to the north, and Mali and Côte d'Ivoire inland to the east. The climate on the coastal strip is hot and moist, with temperatures ranging from about 17°C (62°F) in the dry season to about 30°C (86°F) in the wet season. The interior is higher and cooler. The official language is French, but Soussou, Manika and six other national languages are widely spoken. Most of the inhabitants are Muslims but some still adhere to traditional animist beliefs. Around 1% are Roman Catholics. The national flag (proportions 3 by 2) consists of three equal vertical stripes, of red, yellow and green. The capital is Conakry.

Recent History

Guinea was formerly French Guinea, part of French West Africa. It became the independent Republic of Guinea on 2 October 1958, after 95% of voters had rejected the Constitution of the Fifth Republic under which the French colonies became self-governing within the French Community. The new state was the object of punitive reprisals by the outgoing French authorities: all aid was withdrawn, and the administrative infrastructure destroyed. The administration was rebuilt on the basis of the Guinean Confédération général du travail and the Parti démocratique de Guinée (PDG), which in 1957 had secured 58 of the 60 seats in the Territorial Assembly. Its leader, Ahmed Sekou Touré, became President, and the PDG the sole political party. President Sekou Touré vigorously pursued a policy of socialist revolution, with emphasis on popular political participation.

There were attempted coups in 1961, 1965 and 1967. An abortive invasion by Portuguese troops and Guinean exiles in 1970 was followed by the arrest of prominent Guineans and foreigners who were suspected of involvement. Many executions took place, and, as a result, diplomatic relations with Senegal and the Federal Republic of Germany were severed in 1971, and with Côte d'Ivoire in 1973. This led to the country's virtual isolation, as dealings with the USSR had declined since the early 1960s. Reports of a 'permanent conspiracy' by foreign powers to overthrow the Touré Government continued to circulate, but in 1975 Guinea resumed normal relations with its African neighbours, with France and other Western powers, signing the Lomé Convention (see p. 151) and joining the Economic Community of West African States (ECOWAS, see p. 133).

All private trade was forbidden in 1975: transactions were conducted through official co-operatives under the supervision of an 'economic police'. In August 1977 demonstrations against the abolition of the traditional market, and the abuse of power by the 'economic police', were held by women in Conakry. Rioting broke out in other towns, as a result of which three state governors were killed. Sekou Touré yielded to many of the demands expressed, disbanded the 'economic police' and allowed limited private trading to recommence in July 1979.

Under Sekou Touré's regime, opposition was ruthlessly crushed and by 1983 almost 2m. Guineans were estimated to have fled the country. Allegations of widespread violations of human rights were repeatedly denied by the Government. In November 1978, at the 11th Congress of the PDG, the membership of the central organs of the party was increased, and the merging of the functions of party and state was announced. The country was renamed the People's Revolutionary Republic of Guinea. In December President Giscard d'Estaing made the first visit by a French President to independent Guinea, and plans for economic co-operation between the two countries were discussed. During 1979 Guinea furthered relations with other countries, and there was a general move away from rigid Marxism.

Legislative elections took place in January 1980, at which voters approved the PDG's list of 210 candidates to the National Assembly. In May 1982 Sekou Touré was returned unopposed for a fourth seven-year term of office as President, reportedly receiving 100% of the votes cast. Touré was re-elected Secretary-General of the PDG during the Party Congress of November 1983. A *rapprochement* with France resulted from the President's visit to Paris in 1982, despite protests by Guinean exiles.

In January 1984 a plot to overthrow the Government was discovered when a group of 20 mercenaries was arrested in southern Senegal. It was reported that thousands of Guineans were subsequently detained, accused of complicity in the coup plot. In March 1984, however, Sekou Touré died while undergoing heart surgery in the USA. On 3 April, before a permanent successor had been chosen by the PDG, the armed forces seized power in a bloodless coup. A Comité militaire de redressement national (CMRN) was appointed, headed by Col (later Gen.) Lansana Conté. The PDG and the National Assembly were dissolved, and the Constitution was suspended. The CMRN affirmed Guinea's support for the Organization of African Unity (OAU, see p. 190) and the country's principles of non-alignment, and pledged to restore democracy and to respect human rights. Some 250 political prisoners were released, and a relaxation of press restrictions was announced. A delegation led by the Prime Minister, Col Diarra Traoré, toured West African states to rally support from Guinea's neighbours. In May the country was renamed the Second Republic of Guinea, and in June Col Traoré visited several European countries in an effort to attract foreign investment and to consolidate relations, particularly with France. By July an estimated 200,000 Guinean exiles had returned to the country.

Trials of former politicians, most of whom had been detained since the coup in April, began in November 1984. In December an extensive reallocation of government portfolios was effected, as a result of which President Conté assumed the posts of Head of Government and Minister of Defence. The post of Prime Minister was abolished, and Col Traoré was demoted from that post to Minister of State for National Education. In early July 1985, while President Conté was chairing an ECOWAS conference in Togo, Col Traoré staged an attempted coup, seizing the radio station in Conakry. Troops loyal to Conté suppressed the revolt, during which 18 people were killed. Traoré was later arrested, along with many members of his family and more than 200 suspected sympathizers and followers. A series of attacks was subsequently aimed at the Malinke ethnic group, of which both Traoré and the late Sekou Touré were members.

In October 1985 President Conté began to implement the radical economic reforms that the World Bank and IMF had demanded as preconditions for the provision of structural aid. In December the Council of Ministers was reorganized to include a majority of civilians, and a CMRN Executive Committee was created. In addition, resident ministries were established in Guinea's four main natural regions. In May 1987 it was announced that 58 people, including nine former ministers, had been sentenced to death, following secret trials of more than 200 Guineans who had been detained either for crimes committed during the rule of Sekou Touré or for implication in the July 1985 coup attempt. The announcement did little to allay the beliefs held by international observers (and repeatedly denied by the Government) that many detainees had already been executed in the aftermath of the abortive coup. In December 1987 President Conté admitted publicly that Traoré had died in the hours following his detention. In January 1988 an amnesty for 67 political prisoners, including Sekou Touré's widow and son, was announced.

Reports of growing unrest within the armed forces caused Conté to postpone a proposed official visit to France in December 1987. In January 1988, following riots in Conakry as a result of the announcement of sharp increases in retail prices of staple goods, the Government was forced instead to announce a price 'freeze'. Later in the same month Conté reshuffled the Council of Ministers, removing his second-in-command, Maj. Kerfalla Camara, from the post of permanent secretary of the CMRN and allocating him instead to the resident Ministry for Upper Guinea, based in Kankan. Lt-Col Sory Doumbouya, previously Minister delegated to the

Presidency in charge of defence, was reassigned to the Middle Guinea region, while Maj. Faciné Touré, a former Minister of Foreign Affairs who had been appointed to the Forest Guinea Ministry in December 1985, returned to Conakry as Minister of Transport and Public Works. The demotion, in July 1988, of the Commander and Deputy Commander of the Presidential Guard was widely interpreted as a further attempt by Conté to consolidate his position. In September four government officials were given prison sentences, while the Norwegian honorary consul was fined, after having been found guilty of facilitating the dumping of toxic waste (which had been removed, at the request of the Conté Government, by a Norwegian cargo vessel) on Guinean territory in February 1988. An extensive reorganization of the Council of Ministers occurred in June 1989, as a result of which one of Conté's closest associates, Maj. Mamadou Baldet, was transferred from a regional ministry to a prominent ministerial post in Conakry, while Maj. Abou Camara, hitherto the Permanent Secretary of the CMRN, was appointed Resident Minister for Maritime Guinea.

In October 1988, in a speech to commemorate the 30th anniversary of the country's independence, Conté declared an amnesty for 39 political prisoners, including those who had been implicated in the 1985 coup attempt. At the same time, Conté proposed the establishment of a committee to draft a new constitution. In October 1989 President Conté announced that, following the approval of the document (in a national referendum that was to take place during 1990), the CMRN would be replaced by a new supreme political body, the Comité transitoire de redressement national (CTRN). The CTRN would be composed of both civilian and military officials, and would oversee a transitional period of not more than five years, at the end of which civilian rule, in the context of a two-party system, would be established. Thus, in the mid-1990s, elections would be held for the post of President of the Republic and Head of Government. This five-year mandate would be renewable only once. Moreover, a unicameral legislative body would be elected by universal suffrage. It was envisaged that the new Constitution would provide for a clear separation of the powers of the executive, legislative and judicial organs of state. In announcing plans for the establishment of a two-party system, Conté warned that no party that might jeopardize the country's ethnic harmony or undermine its democratic aspirations could be permitted to exist. In late 1989 members of the CMRN embarked upon a tour of the country, as part of a programme to inform the population about the proposed constitutional changes.

In late October 1989 the death, in police custody, of an alleged common-law offender provoked rioting in the Labé region; several protesters were killed, and many injuries were reported, following intervention by security forces. In December the Government denied allegations (which had been made by the human rights organization, Amnesty International) of the detention, in solitary confinement, and torture of six members of an opposition grouping, the Rassemblement populaire guinéen (RPG). In February 1990 an amnesty was announced for all political prisoners and exiles. Among those to benefit were former associates of Sekou Touré and those implicated in the July 1985 coup attempt.

In early March 1990 Conté effected a minor reorganization of the Council of Ministers, as a result of which Saliou Koumbassa (hitherto Minister of National Education and Scientific Research) and Lt-Col Jean Kolipé Lama (the Minister of Social Affairs and Employment) exchanged portfolios. The changes represented an apparent attempt to resolve a crisis in the education sector: in early 1990 schoolteachers had withdrawn their labour, in protest against inadequate pay and conditions. In mid-March the teachers resumed their duties, having received assurances that the Government would examine their grievances. In early November, however, the authorities ordered the closure of the University of Conakry, in response to a boycott of classes by students who were demanding the reform of the system for the allocation of grants, together with improved educational standards and facilities. Later in the same month, two students were killed, and others injured, when security forces acted to disperse a demonstration in support of the students' demands; several arrests were also made. Unrest continued, and in late November the Government, which claimed to have made considerable concessions to the protesters, ordered the resumption of classes. In early December, none the less, two demonstrators were killed by the security forces during further action (which had, moreover, been joined by schoolchildren).

Despite an appeal that was made by President Conté, in early November 1990, for the return to Guinea of political exiles, three members of the RPG were, later in the same month, given custodial sentences. One was convicted of forging official documents, while his co-defendants were found guilty of distributing banned newspapers on Guinean territory; all three had been detained since August, and had been classified as political prisoners by Amnesty International.

The draft Constitution was submitted for approval in a national referendum, as scheduled, on 23 December 1990. According to official results, the document received the support of 98.7% of those who voted (some 97.4% of the electorate), despite protests by Conté's opponents that the provisions of this *Loi fondamentale* were undemocratic. The period of transition to civilian rule was thus instigated, and in mid-January 1991 it was reported that the CMRN had been dissolved by presidential decree, and that the 37-member CTRN had been inaugurated under the chairmanship of President Conté. A reorganization of the Council of Ministers was announced in late February 1991.

By mid-1990 it was reported that about 130,000 refugees who had fled the civil conflict in Liberia were sheltering in Guinea. In April of that year President Conté denied suggestions that Guinean troops were supporting the incumbent regime in Liberia. In August Guinean armed forces were deployed along the border with Liberia, following a series of violent incursions by deserters from the Liberian army. Guinean army units also participated in the ECOWAS Monitoring Group that was dispatched to Liberia in that month (see p. 134).

Government

The 1982 Constitution, providing for a National Assembly elected by universal adult suffrage, was suspended following the coup in April 1984. A Comité militaire de redressement national (CMRN—Military Committee for National Recovery), with 25 (later 17) members, assumed power. On 23 December 1990 a new constitution (the *Loi fondamentale*) was approved in a national referendum. The new document provided for the dissolution of the CMRN and for the creation of a Comité transitoire de redressement national (CTRN). This new body was reported to have been inaugurated on 16 January 1991, following the dissolution of the CMRN. The function of the 37-member CTRN (which was to be composed of both civilian and military members) would be to oversee a transitional period, lasting not more than five years, at the end of which a two-party, civilian system was to be established, and a unicameral legislative body was to be elected by universal suffrage. In addition, the President of the Republic and Head of Government was to be elected for a five-year term of office, renewable only once.

Local administration is based on eight provinces, each under the authority of a provincial governor; there are 33 provincial prefectures. Provincial administrative councils meet every three months. Elections to district councils in the Conakry area were held in April 1986.

Defence

In June 1990 Guinea had an army of 8,500, a navy of 400 and an air force of 800. Paramilitary forces numbered 9,600, including a People's Militia of 7,000. Military service is compulsory and lasts for two years. Defence expenditure in 1982 was 1,850m. sylis. In November 1986 a non-aggression pact was signed with Sierra Leone and Liberia, Guinea's partners in the Mano River Union.

Economic Affairs

In 1989, according to estimates by the World Bank, Guinea's gross national product (GNP), measured at average 1987–89 prices, was US $2,372m., equivalent to $430 per head. Between 1980 and 1987, it was estimated, GNP per head declined at an average annual rate of 0.1%. The population increased by an annual average of 2.5% in 1980–89. During 1980–87 Guinea's gross domestic product (GDP) increased, in real terms, at an average annual rate of 2.1%.

Agriculture (including forestry and fishing) contributed 30% of GDP in 1989. About 74.9% of the labour force were employed in the agricultural sector in that year. The principal cash crops are fruits, coffee and the oil palm. Important staple crops include cassava, rice and other cereals and vegetables. Some 222,000 metric tons of cereals were imported into Guinea in 1988. The food supply is supplemented by the rearing of cattle and other livestock. Guinea has considerable forestry resources, and the Government hoped to enhance their commercial viability, while introducing measures to compensate for the earlier, excessive exploitation of timber in some regions, during the 1990s. Guinea's territorial waters contain significant stocks of fish; efforts to stimulate their development by Guinean interests were initiated in the late 1980s. During 1980–89 agricultural production increased by an annual average of 0.9%.

Industry (including mining, manufacturing, construction and power) contributed 32% of GDP in 1988. Less than 2% of the employed labour force were engaged in the industrial sector at the time of the 1983 census.

Mining contributed 10.8% of GDP in 1987. Only 0.7% of the employed labour force were engaged in extractive activities in 1983. Guinea is the world's second largest producer of bauxite ore, possessing about 30% of all known reserves of that mineral. In 1988 exports of bauxite and alumina provided an estimated 78.1% of export earnings. Diamonds of the highest quality are also extracted. Three joint-venture companies have been established, by the Guinean Government and foreign investors, to develop known deposits of gold. The exploitation of valuable reserves of high-grade iron ore, at Mt Nimba, was expected to commence in the early 1990s, following the conclusion, in 1989, of agreements with Liberia, regarding the establishment of a joint-venture company. The existence of reserves of granite, uranium, cobalt, nickel and platinum has been confirmed. Exploration for offshore petroleum was in progress in the late 1980s.

The manufacturing sector contributed 5% of GDP in 1988. In 1983 only 0.6% of the employed labour force were engaged in the manufacturing sector. An alumina smelter is in operation; other industrial companies are involved in the processing of agricultural products and in the manufacture of construction materials.

Guinea possesses considerable hydroelectric potential, and demand from the mining sector for electrical energy is great. Financing agreements have been concluded, with external creditors, for the construction of several hydroelectric installations. A total of 500m. kWh of electricity was generated in 1987. In 1988 imports of petroleum and related products accounted for an estimated 13.7% of the value of total imports.

In 1988 Guinea's visible trade surplus was estimated at US $502.2m., while there was an estimated deficit of $202.9m. on the current account of the balance of payments. The principal exports in 1988 were bauxite, alumina, diamonds and gold. The principal imports in that year were semi-manufactured goods, petroleum and petroleum products, food products and consumer goods. France and Belgium are Guinea's principal trading partners.

Guinea recorded a budget deficit of 91,000m. Guinea francs in 1989 (equivalent to 5.7% of GDP in that year), compared with a projected deficit of 69,900m. Guinea francs. Guinea's total external public debt was US $2,312m. at the end of 1988. In that year the cost of debt-servicing was equivalent to 21.9% of the value of exports of goods and services. Annual inflation averaged 55.1% in 1980–87.

Guinea is a member of the Economic Community of West African States (ECOWAS, see p. 133), of the Gambia River Basin Development Organization (OMVG, see p. 223), of the Mano River Union (see p. 224) and of the International Bauxite Association (see p. 228).

Guinea's potential for the attainment of wealth is substantial, owing to its valuable mineral deposits and to its favourable climate, which should facilitate the diversification of the primary sector. However, growth has been impeded by the dependence of the economy on the exploitation of bauxite, and thus by its vulnerability to fluctuations in international prices for that commodity. The attainment of self-sufficiency in foodstuffs remains a priority. The Conté Government's adjustment efforts, which have received the support of bilateral and multilateral creditors, have entailed a policy of retrenchment in the public sector, and the participation in the economy of private investors has been encouraged. Prospects for continued growth are dependent on the conclusion of further financing and debt-relief agreements with external creditors, and upon the continued tolerance, by the Guinean population, of the Government's austerity measures. Moreover, the influx, during 1990, of many thousands of refugees from Liberia (see Recent History) has imposed considerable strain on the Guinean economy, as funds have been diverted from development projects and natural resources have been over-exploited, in an attempt to accommodate those fleeing the civil conflict.

Social Welfare

Wages are fixed according to the Government Labour Code. A maximum working week of 48 hours is in force for industrial workers. In 1979 there were 248 hospitals and dispensaries, with a total of 6,858 beds. In 1981 there were only an estimated 100 physicians working in official medical services. Private medical care has been legally available since July 1984.

Education

Education is provided free of charge at every level. Primary education, beginning at seven years of age and lasting for six years, is officially compulsory. In 1988, however, only 23% of children in the relevant age-group were enrolled at primary schools (boys 31%; girls 15%). Secondary education, from the age of 13, lasts for a further seven years, comprising a first cycle of four years and a second of three years. In 1988 only 6% of children in the appropriate age-group were enrolled in secondary education (9% of boys; 3% of girls). There are universities at Conakry and Kankan. In 1990, according to estimates by UNESCO, the average rate of adult illiteracy was 76.0% (males 65.1%; females 86.6%). Under a six-year transitional education plan, announced in June 1984, ideological education was eliminated and French was adopted as the language of instruction in schools. Teaching of the eight national languages has been suspended. Private schools, which had been banned for 23 years under the Sekou Touré regime, were legalized in 1984.

Public Holidays

1991: 1 January (New Year's Day), 1 April (Easter Monday), 16 April* (Id al-Fitr, end of Ramadan), 1 May (Labour Day), 27 August (Anniversary of Women's Revolt), 21 September* (Mouloud, birth of Muhammad), 28 September (Referendum Day), 2 October (Republic Day), 1 November (All Saints' Day), 22 November (Day of 1970 Invasion), 25 December (Christmas).

1992: 1 January (New Year's Day), 4 April* (Id al-Fitr, end of Ramadan), 20 April (Easter Monday), 1 May (Labour Day), 27 August (Anniversary of Women's Revolt), 10 September* (Mouloud, birth of Muhammad), 28 September (Referendum Day), 2 October (Republic Day), 1 November (All Saints' Day), 22 November (Day of 1970 Invasion), 25 December (Christmas).

* These holidays are determined by the Islamic lunar calendar and may vary by one or two days from the dates given.

Weights and Measures

The metric system is in force.

GUINEA

Statistical Survey

Source (unless otherwise stated): Service de la Statistique Générale, Bureau du Premier Ministre, Conakry; tel. 44-21-48.

Area and Population

AREA, POPULATION AND DENSITY

Area (sq km)	245,857*
Population (census results)	
15 January–31 May 1955	2,570,219†
4–17 February 1983	4,533,240‡
Population (official estimates at mid-year)	
1986	4,794,000
1987	4,931,000
1988	5,071,000
Density (per sq km) at mid-1988	20.6

* 94,926 sq miles.
† Estimates for African population, based on results of sample survey.
‡ Excluding adjustment for underenumeration.

REGIONS (population at mid-1963)

Region	Area (sq km)	Population ('000)
Beyla	17,542	170
Boffa	6,003	90
Boké*	11,053	105
Conakry	308	172
Dabola	6,000	54
Dalaba	5,750	105
Dinguiraye	11,000	67
Dubréka*	5,676	86
Faranah*	12,397	94
Forécariah	4,265	98
Fria	n.a.	27
Gaoual	11,503	81
Guéckédou	4,157	130
Kankan	27,488	176
Kindia	8,828	152
Kissidougou	8,872	133
Kouroussa	16,405	93
Labé	7,616	283
Macenta	8,710	123
Mali	8,800	152
Mamou	6,159	162
N'Zérékoré	10,183	195
Pita	4,000	154
Siguiri	23,377	179
Télimélé	8,155	147
Tougué	6,200	75
Youkounkoun	5,500	55
Total	**245,857**	**3,360**

* The provinces of Boké, Dubréka and Faranah were abolished by presidential decree in January 1988.

PRINCIPAL TOWNS (population at December 1972)

Conakry (capital) 525,671 (later admitted to be overstated); Kankan 60,000.

BIRTHS AND DEATHS (UN estimates, annual averages)

	1975-80	1980-85	1985-90
Birth rate (per 1,000)	46.9	46.8	46.6
Death rate (per 1,000)	25.3	23.5	21.9

Source: UN, *World Population Prospects: 1988.*

ECONOMICALLY ACTIVE POPULATION
(persons aged 10 years and over, census of 1983)

	Males	Females	Total
Agriculture, hunting, forestry and fishing	856,971	566,644	1,423,615
Mining and quarrying	7,351	4,890	12,241
Manufacturing	6,758	4,493	11,251
Electricity, gas and water	1,601	1,604	3,205
Construction	5,475	3,640	9,115
Trade, restaurants and hotels	22,408	14,901	37,309
Transport, storage and communications	17,714	11,782	29,496
Finance, insurance, real estate and business services	2,136	1,420	3,556
Community, social and personal services	82,640	54,960	137,600
Activities not adequately defined*	101,450	54,229	155,679
Total labour force	**1,104,504**	**718,563**	**1,823,067**

* Includes 18,244 unemployed persons (not previously employed), whose distribution by sex is not available.

Source: International Labour Office, *Year Book of Labour Statistics.*

Mid-1989 (estimates in '000): Agriculture, etc. 2,280; Total labour force 3,043 (Source: FAO, *Production Yearbook*).

Agriculture

PRINCIPAL CROPS ('000 metric tons)

	1987	1988	1989
Maize	90*	80*	108
Millet	60*	60*	60†
Sorghum	34*	34*	34†
Rice (paddy)	515	521	525†
Other cereals	115*	115*	112†
Sweet potatoes	90*	100*	104
Cassava (Manioc)	420*	400*	358
Yams	80*	90*	100
Taro (Coco yam)	40*	50*	62
Pulses*	50	50	50
Coconuts†	18	18	18
Vegetables*	420	420	420
Sugar cane*	200	175	175
Citrus fruits*	163	163	163
Bananas*	107	110	110
Plantains*	350	350	350
Pineapples	25*	30*	36
Other fruits*	37	37	37
Palm kernels*	40	40	40
Groundnuts (in shell)*	60*	50*	45
Coffee (green)	18*	20*	24
Cocoa beans*	3	3	4
Tobacco (leaves)*	2	2	2

* FAO estimate(s). † Unofficial figure(s).
Source: FAO, *Production Yearbook.*

GUINEA

LIVESTOCK ('000 head, year ending September)

	1987	1988	1989
Cattle*	1,800	1,800	1,800
Sheep	490*	500*	506
Goats*	460	460	460
Pigs	38*	35*	33
Horses	2*	2*	2
Asses	2*	1*	1

* FAO estimate(s).
Poultry (FAO estimates, million): 13 in 1987; 13 in 1988; 13 in 1989.
Source: FAO, *Production Yearbook*.

LIVESTOCK PRODUCTS (FAO estimates, '000 metric tons)

	1987	1988	1989
Beef and veal	18	18	18
Poultry meat	18	18	18
Other meat	7	7	7
Cows' milk	42	42	42
Goats' milk	4	4	4
Hen eggs	13.9	13.9	13.9
Cattle hides	3.2	3.2	3.2

Source: FAO, *Production Yearbook*.

Forestry

ROUNDWOOD REMOVALS
(FAO estimates, '000 cubic metres, excluding bark)

	1986	1987	1988
Sawlogs, veneer logs and logs for sleepers*	180	180	180
Other industrial wood	434	445	456
Fuel wood	3,734	3,827	3,923
Total	4,348	4,452	4,559

* Assumed to be unchanged since 1972.
Source: FAO, *Yearbook of Forest Products*.

SAWNWOOD PRODUCTION
Total (incl. boxboards, FAO estimates): 90,000 cubic metres per year in 1972–88 (Source: FAO, *Yearbook of Forest Products*).

Fishing
(FAO estimates, '000 metric tons, live weight)

	1985	1986	1987
Freshwater fishes	2.0	2.5	3.0
Sardinellas	20.4	21.5	22.0
Other marine fishes	7.6	8.0	9.0
Total catch	30.0	32.0	34.0

1988: Catch as in 1987 (FAO estimates).
Source: FAO, *Yearbook of Fishery Statistics*.

Mining

	1985	1986	1987
Bauxite ('000 metric tons)*	13,956	14,835	16,282
Diamonds ('000 carats)†	132	204	175

* Data from *World Metal Statistics*, London.
† Estimates by the US Bureau of Mines.
Source: UN, *Industrial Statistics Yearbook*.
1988: Bauxite 16,834,000 metric tons (Source: UN, *Monthly Bulletin of Statistics*).

Industry

SELECTED PRODUCTS (estimated production; '000 metric tons, unless otherwise indicated)

	1985	1986	1987
Electric energy (million kWh)	489	497	500
Raw sugar	5	5*	n.a.
Palm oil†	45	46	n.a.
Plywood ('000 cubic metres)†	2	2	2
Alumina (calcined equivalent)‡	572	556	556

* Data from the International Sugar Organization, London (estimated figure for 1986).
† FAO estimates.
‡ Data from the US Bureau of Mines.
Source: UN, *Industrial Statistics Yearbook*.
Plywood ('000 cubic metres): 2 in 1988 (Source: FAO, *Yearbook of Forest Products*).

Finance

CURRENCY AND EXCHANGE RATES
Monetary Units
  100 centimes = 1 franc guineén (FG or Guinea franc).

Denominations
  Notes: 25, 50, 100, 500, 1,000 and 5,000 francs.

Sterling and Dollar Equivalents (30 September 1990)
  £1 sterling = 1,264.6 Guinea francs;
  US $1 = 675.0 Guinea francs;
  10,000 Guinea francs = £7.908 = $14.815.

Note: The Guinea franc was reintroduced in January 1986, replacing (at par) the syli. At the same time, the currency was devalued by more than 90%. The syli had been introduced in October 1972, replacing the original Guinea franc (at 10 francs per syli). In June 1975 the syli's value was linked to the IMF special drawing right at an exchange rate of SDR 1 = 24.6853 sylis. This remained in force until the syli's abolition. The average exchange rate of sylis per US dollar was: 22.366 in 1982; 23.095 in 1983; 24.090 in 1984. Some of the figures in this Survey are still in terms of sylis.

BUDGET ESTIMATES (million Guinea francs)

Revenue	1989	1990	1991
Receipts from mining	107,100	140,800	153,200
Other revenue	86,600	98,900	139,900
Grants	54,100	79,400	76,500
Total	247,800	319,100	369,600

Expenditure	1989	1990	1991
Current expenditure	158,800	202,500	216,100
Investment expenditure	158,900	195,600	233,900
Total	317,700	398,100	450,000

Source: *Marchés Tropicaux et Méditerranéens* (in *Africa Research Bulletin*).

GUINEA

NATIONAL ACCOUNTS
(million Guinea francs at current prices)

Expenditure on the Gross Domestic Product

	1985*	1986	1987
Government final consumption expenditure	3,060	80,400	80,300
Private final consumption expenditure	28,210	483,000	694,700
Increase in stocks	4,100	16,100	2,200
Gross fixed capital formation		99,300	161,500
Total domestic expenditure	35,370	678,800	938,700
Exports of goods and services	10,440	210,300	299,900
Less Imports of goods and services	12,500	228,100	321,800
GDP in purchasers' values	33,310	661,000	916,800
GDP at constant 1980 prices	24,968	24,371	26,094

* Estimates in million sylis.

Gross Domestic Product by Economic Activity

	1985*	1986	1987
Agriculture, hunting, forestry and fishing	16,040	203,500	273,900
Mining and quarrying	3,170	64,300	86,900
Manufacturing	950	39,100	50,900
Electricity, gas and water	70	4,900	7,400
Construction	510	31,600	49,400
Trade, restaurants and hotels	3,790	131,100	183,900
Transport, storage and communications	910	23,900	25,500
Finance, insurance, real estate and business services	630	22,200	31,300
Public administration and defence	2,050	42,900	53,700
Other services	280	23,200	44,900
GDP at factor cost	28,400	586,700	807,800
Indirect taxes, *less* subsidies	4,910	74,300	109,000
GDP in purchasers' values	33,310	661,000	916,800

* Estimates in million sylis.

Source: UN Economic Commission for Africa, *African Statistical Yearbook*.

External Trade

PRINCIPAL COMMODITIES (US $ million)

Imports	1986	1987	1988*
Food products	73.0	62.8	62.8
Consumer goods	88.8	69.4	61.9
Semi-manufactured goods	163.7	194.5	215.7
Petroleum and petroleum products	55.0	65.8	67.3
Capital goods	70.7	75.1	83.5
Total	451.2	467.6	491.2

Exports	1986	1987	1988*
Bauxite and alumina	461.8	479.3	428.2
Diamonds	50.9	59.3	59.4
Gold	11.2	17.8	24.5
Coffee	19.3	14.1	17.1
Fish	n.a.	n.a.	3.5
Total (incl. others)	554.5	583.9	548.1

* Estimates.

Source: *Africa Research Bulletin*.

PRINCIPAL TRADING PARTNERS

Imports (14 months, 1975–76): EEC 2,301 million sylis; USA 743 million sylis.

Exports (1973): EEC 1,260 million sylis, USA 545 million sylis.

Transport

RAILWAYS (traffic)

	1985	1986	1987
Freight ton-km (million)	534	542	559

Source: UN Economic Commission for Africa, *African Statistical Yearbook*.

INTERNATIONAL SEA-BORNE SHIPPING
(estimated freight traffic, '000 metric tons)

	1986	1987	1988
Goods loaded	9,879	10,493	9,920
Goods unloaded	482	493	690

Source: UN, *Monthly Bulletin of Statistics*.

CIVIL AVIATION (traffic on scheduled services, '000)*

	1981	1982
Kilometres flown	3,100	3,100
Passengers carried	128	131
Passenger-km	142,000	144,000
Freight ton-km	600	700

* UN estimates.

Source: UN, *Statistical Yearbook*.

Communications Media

	1986	1987	1988
Radio receivers ('000 in use)	200	210	220
Television receivers ('000 in use)	10	10	17
Daily newspapers:			
Number	1	n.a.	1
Average circulation ('000)	13	n.a.	13

Telephones (1987): 16,000 in use.

Source: mainly UNESCO, *Statistical Yearbook*.

Education

(1987/88)

	Institutions	Teachers	Pupils Males	Pupils Females	Pupils Total
Primary	2,315	7,239	199,516	89,398	288,914
Secondary General*	225	3,577	57,683	18,810	76,493
Teacher training	9	123	634	552	1,186
Vocational	26	635	3,327	1,347	4,674
Higher	10	1,033	5,220	695	5,915

* 1986/87 figures.

Source: Direction de la Statistique et de la Planification de l'Education, Conakry.

Directory

The Constitution

The Constitution of the People's Revolutionary Republic of Guinea, adopted in May 1982, was suspended in April 1984 by the Military Committee for National Recovery (CMRN), which had assumed power in a coup. The country's former name, the Republic of Guinea, was subsequently restored. A new constitution (the *Loi fondamentale*) was adopted in a national referendum on 23 December 1990.

The new Constitution defined a clear separation of the powers of the executive, legislative and judicial organs of state. Article 19 provided for the dissolution of the CMRN and for the creation, in its place, of a Transitional Committee for National Recovery (CTRN). The CTRN was to oversee a transitional period (of not more than five years), at the end of which civilian rule, in the context of a two-party political system, would be established. By the mid-1990s, therefore, elections would be held, on the basis of universal suffrage, for the post of President of the Republic and Head of Government, as well as for a unicameral legislative body.

The Government

HEAD OF STATE

President: Gen. LANSANA CONTÉ (took office 4 April 1984).

TRANSITIONAL COMMITTEE FOR NATIONAL RECOVERY

In accordance with the provisions of the December 1990 Constitution, a 37-member Transitional Committee for National Recovery (CTRN) was reported to have been inaugurated on 16 January 1991, to replace the Military Committee for National Recovery. The function of the CTRN (which was to be composed of both civilian and military members) would be to oversee a transitional period to civilian rule (see Constitution, above).

COUNCIL OF MINISTERS
(February 1991)

Head of Government, Minister of Defence, Security and Information: Gen. LANSANA CONTÉ.
Resident Minister for Maritime Guinea (Kindia): Maj. ABOU CAMARA.
Resident Minister for Upper Guinea (Kankan): Maj. KISSI CAMARA.
Resident Minister for Middle Guinea (Labé): Maj. HENRI TOFANI.
Resident Minister for Forest Guinea (N'Zérékoné): Maj. IBRAHIMA SORY DIALLO.
Minister of Foreign Affairs: Maj. JEAN TRAORÉ.
Minister delegated to the Presidency, in charge of National Defence: Maj. ABDOURAHMANE DIALLO.
Minister, Secretary-General of the Presidency: ALSENY RENÉ GOMEZ.
Minister delegated to the Presidency, in charge of Information, Culture and Tourism: HERVÉ VINCENT BANGOURA.
Minister delegated to the Presidency, in charge of Economic and Financial Control: Maj. HENRI FOULA.
Minister of Planning and International Co-operation: IBRAHIMA SYLLA.
Minister of Economy and Finance: EDOUARD BENJAMIN.
Minister of Administrative Reform and the Public Service: MAMOUNA BANGOURA.
Minister of the Interior and Decentralization: ALHASSANE CONDÉ.
Minister of Agriculture and Animal Resources: KOLY ABOUBACAR KOUROUMA.
Minister of Natural Resources and the Environment: Maj. MOHAMED LAMINE TRAORÉ.
Minister of Posts and Telecommunications: Capt. FASSOU JEAN-CLAUDE KOUROUMA.
Minister of Urban Development and Housing: BAHNA MBAYA SIDIBE.
Minister of Public Health and Population: Dr MADIGBE FOFANA.
Minister of Transport and Public Works: Maj. IBRAHIMA DIALLO.
Minister of National Education, in charge of Higher Education and Scientific Research: MAMADI DIAWARA.
Minister of Justice and Keeper of the Seals: Maj. FACINÉ TOURÉ.
Minister of Social Affairs and Employment: BASSIROU BARRY.
Minister of Youth, Sports and the Arts: Capt. JOSEPH GBAGBO ZOUMANIGUI.

There are also five Secretaries of State, with responsibility for Tourism and Hotels, Energy, Fisheries, Decentralization and Primary and Secondary Education.

MINISTRIES

Office of the President: Conakry; tel. 44-11-47; telex 623.
Permanent Secretariat of the CMRN: Conakry.
Ministry of Administrative Reform and the Public Service: Conakry.
Ministry of Agriculture and Animal Resources: BP 576, Conakry; tel. 44-19-66.
Ministry of Economy and Finance: Conakry; tel. 44-21-62; telex 2199.
Ministry of Foreign Affairs: Conakry; tel. 40-50-55; telex 634.
Ministry of the Interior and Decentralization: Conakry; telex 621.
Ministry of Justice: Conakry; tel. 44-16-04.
Ministry of National Education: Conakry; tel. 44-19-01; telex 631.
Ministry of Natural Resources and the Environment: Conakry.
Ministry of Planning and International Co-operation: BP 707, Conakry; tel. 44-16-37; telex 22311; fax 44-21-48.
Ministry of Posts and Telecommunications: Conakry.
Ministry of Public Health and Population: Conakry.
Ministry of Social Affairs and Employment: Conakry; tel. 44-33-05.
Ministry of Transport and Public Works: Conakry.
Ministry of Urban Development and Housing: BP 846, Conakry; tel. 46-41-40; telex 22352.
Ministry of Youth, Sports and the Arts: Conakry.

Legislature

ASSEMBLÉE NATIONALE

The National Assembly was dissolved by the Military Committee for National Recovery on 3 April 1984, following the military coup. A unicameral legislative body was to be elected, following the establishment, in the mid-1990s, of a two-party system.

Political Organizations

Following the military coup of April 1984, the country's sole political party, the Parti démocratique de Guinée (PDG), was dissolved. Although no political organizations have been formally active in Guinea since the coup, several groups oppose the Conté Government.

Mouvement pour le renouveau en Guinée (MRG): fmrly the Union du peuple guinéen (UPG); Pres. Maj. DIALLO THIERNO.
Organisation unifiée pour la libération de la Guinée (OULG): based mainly in Côte d'Ivoire; Pres. IBRAHIMA KAKE.
Rassemblement populaire guinéen (RPG): based in Guinea and France; Leader ALPHA CONDÉ.

Other opposition groupings, most of which are based in France, include the **Association de la jeunesse guinéenne en France (AJGF)**; **Groupe de réflexion des Guinéens (GRG)**; **Ligue guinéenne des droits de l'homme (LGDHC)**; **Regroupement de Guinéens de l'exterieur (RGE)**; **Solidarité guinéenne (SG)**; **Union des forces patriotiques guinéennes (UFPG)**.

Diplomatic Representation

EMBASSIES IN GUINEA

Algeria: BP 1004, Conakry; tel. 44-15-03; Chargé d'affaires a.i.: BOUGHDNIT NACBUN.

Benin: BP 707, Conakry; Ambassador: JONAS CROHOUNDIDI.

GUINEA

Canada: Corniche Sud, BP 99, Coleah, Conakry; tel. 46-36-26; telex 2170; Chargé d'affaires a.i.: ANDRÉE DUBOIS.
China, People's Republic: BP 714, Conakry; Ambassador: JIANG XIANG.
Congo: BP 178, Conakry; Ambassador: Mme C. ECKOMBAND.
Côte d'Ivoire: Conakry; telex 2126; Chargé d'affaires: ATTA YACOUBA.
Cuba: BP 71, Conakry; Ambassador: COLMAN FERREI.
Czechoslovakia: BP 1009 bis, Conakry; tel. 46-14-37; Ambassador: Dr ZDENKO HRČKA.
Egypt: BP 389, Conakry; Ambassador: HUSSEIN EL-NAZER.
France: BP 373, Conakry; tel. 44-16-55; telex 600; Ambassador: (vacant).
Germany: BP 540, Conakry; tel. 44-15-08; telex 22479; Ambassador: Dr HUBERT BEEMELMANS.
Ghana: BP 732, Conakry; Ambassador: LARRY BIMI.
Guinea-Bissau: BP 298, Conakry; Ambassador: ARAFAN ANSU CAMARA.
Iraq: Conakry; telex 2162; Chargé d'affaires: MUNIR CHIHAB AHMAD.
Italy: BP 84, Village Camayenne, Conakry; tel. 46-23-32; telex 636; Ambassador: FAUSTO MARIA PENNACCHIO.
Japan: BP 895, Conakry; tel. 44-36-07; telex 22482; Ambassador: TSUKASA ABE.
Korea, Democratic People's Republic: BP 723, Conakry; Ambassador: KIM CHANG-SOK.
Lebanon: BP 342, Conakry; telex 2106; Ambassador: MOHAMED ISSA.
Liberia: BP 18, Conakry; telex 2105; Chargé d'affaires: ANTHONY ZEZO.
Libya: BP 1183, Conakry; telex 645; Chargé d'affaires: MUFTAH MADI.
Mali: Conakry; telex 2154; Ambassador: KIBILI DEMBA DIALLO.
Morocco: BP 193, Conakry; telex 22422; Ambassador: MOHAMED AYOUCH.
Nigeria: BP 54, Conakry; telex 633; Ambassador: GBOKO YOUGH.
Romania: BP 348, Conakry; Ambassador: PETRU DESPOT.
Saudi Arabia: BP 611, Conakry; telex 2146; Chargé d'affaires: WAHEEB SHAIKHON.
Sierra Leone: BP 625, Conakry; Ambassador: Mrs MARIAM KAMARA.
Switzerland: BP 720, Conakry; tel. 46-26-12; telex 22416; Chargé d'affaires: PIERRE RIEM.
Syria: BP 609, Conakry; tel. 46-13-20; Chargé d'affaires: BECHARA KHAROUF.
Tanzania: BP 189, Conakry; tel. 46-13-32; telex 2104; Ambassador: NORMAN KIONDO.
USSR: BP 329, Conakry; Ambassador: VLADIMIR N. RAYEVSKY.
USA: BP 603, Conakry; tel. 44-15-20; Ambassador: DANE F. SMITH.
Viet-Nam: BP 551, Conakry; Ambassador: PHAM VAN SON.
Yugoslavia: BP 1154, Conakry; Ambassador: DANILO MILIĆ.
Zaire: BP 880, Conakry; telex 632; Ambassador: B. KALUBYE.

Judicial System

There is a High Court whose jurisdiction extends to political cases. The Cour d'appel, the Chambre des mises en accusation and the Tribunal supérieur de cassation are at Conakry. A Court of State Security and a military tribunal were established in August 1985 to try cases of crime against the internal and external security of the state.

Tribunaux du premier degré exist at Conakry and Kankan and have jurisdiction over civil and criminal cases and also act as industrial courts. A justice of the peace sits at N'Zérékoré.

Président, Cour d'Appel: FODÉ MAMADOU TOURÉ.

Religion

It is estimated that 95% of the population are Muslims and 1.5% Christians. In May 1967 President Sekou Touré ordered that all priests should be Guinea nationals.

ISLAM

Islamic League: Conakry; Sec.-Gen. El Hadj AHMED TIDIANE TRAORÉ.

CHRISTIANITY
The Anglican Communion

Anglicans in Guinea are adherents of the Church of the Province of West Africa, comprising 11 dioceses. The Archbishop of the Province is the Bishop of Liberia. The diocese of Guinea (formerly the Río Pongas), inaugurated in August 1985, is the first French-speaking diocese in the Province. The Bishop of Guinea also has jurisdiction over Guinea-Bissau.

Bishop of Guinea: (vacant), BP 105, Conakry.

The Roman Catholic Church

Guinea comprises the archdiocese of Conakry (with an estimated 20,000 adherents at 31 December 1977), the diocese of N'Zérékoré (22,000 adherents at 31 December 1988) and the Apostolic Prefecture of Kankan (46,954 adherents in 1968), of which the Archbishop of Conakry is Apostolic Administrator.

Bishops' Conference: Conférence Episcopale de la Guinée, BP 1006 bis, Conakry; Pres. Most Rev. ROBERT SARAH, Archbishop of Conakry.

Archbishop of Conakry: Most Rev. ROBERT SARAH, Archevêché, BP 1006 bis, Conakry; tel. 44-36-27.

There are also six Protestant mission centres active in Guinea: four operated by British and two by US societies.

The Press

Ecole Nouvelle: Conakry; monthly; education.
Fonike: BP 341, Conakry; sport and general; Dir IBRAHIMA KALIL DIARE.
Horoya (Liberty): BP 191, Conakry; weekly; Man. Dir MOHAMED MOUNIR CAMARA.
Journal Officiel de Guinée: BP 156, Conakry; fortnightly; govt.
La Guinéenne: Conakry; monthly; women's interest.
Le Travailleur de Guinée: Conakry; monthly; trade union organ.

NEWS AGENCIES

Agence Guinéenne de Presse: BP 1535, Conakry; tel. 46-54-14; telex 640; f. 1960; Man. Dir MOHAMED CONDÉ.

Foreign Bureaux

Informatsionnoye Agentstvo Novosti (IAN) (USSR): BP 414, Conakry; Dir VASILI ZUBKOV.
Xinhua (New China) News Agency (People's Republic of China): BP 455, Conakry; tel. 46-13-47; telex 2128; Correspondent ZHANG ZHENYI.

The BBC (UK), Reuters (UK), Agence France Presse and TASS (USSR) are also represented.

Publisher

Editions du Ministère de l'Education Nationale: Secrétariat à la Recherche scientifique, BP 561, Conakry; general and educational.

Radio and Television

In 1988 there were an estimated 220,000 radio receivers and 17,000 television receivers in use.

Radiodiffusion-Télévision Guinéenne (RTG): BP 391, Conakry; tel. 44-22-05; telex 22341; radio broadcasts in French, English, Créole-English, Portuguese, Arabic and local languages; television transmissions in colour; Dir-Gen. JUSTIN MOREL.

A network of rural radio stations was scheduled to begin broadcasts during the early 1990s.

Finance

(cap. = capital; m. = million; br. = branch; (amounts in Guinea francs unless otherwise stated).

BANKING
Central Bank

Banque Centrale de la République de Guinée: 12 blvd du Commerce, BP 692, Conakry; tel. 44-17-25; telex 22225; f. 1960; controls all banking activity; Gov. KERFALLA YANSANA; 4 brs.

GUINEA

Directory

Commercial Banks

Banque Internationale pour l'Afrique en Guinée (BIAG): blvd du Commerce, BP 1419, Conakry; tel. 44-44-42; telex 22180; fax 44-22-97; f. 1985; undergoing reorg. in 1990; cap. 10m. French francs (Dec. 1988); provides 'offshore' banking services; Pres. El Hadj CAMARA; Man. Dir JEAN MICHEL BAUDE.

Banque Internationale pour le Commerce et l'Industrie de la Guinée (BICI-GUI): ave de la République, BP 1484, Conakry; tel. 44-32-50; telex 22175; f. 1985; 39.6% state-owned, 15.4% by Banque Nationale de Paris (BNP); cap. 5,005m. (Dec. 1988); Pres. TAFSIR CAMARA; Man. Dir JEAN TABARIES; 12 brs.

Société Générale de Banques en Guinée: ave de la République, BP 1514, Conakry 1; tel. 44-17-41; telex 22212; fax 44-25-65; f. 1985; 34% owned by Société Générale (France); cap. 20m. French francs (Dec. 1989); Pres. P. DE GUILLEBON; Man. Dir CLAUDE SOULE.

Union Internationale de Banque en Guinée (UIBG): ave de la République, angle 5e blvd, BP 324, Conakry; tel. 44-20-96; telex 23135; fax 44-42-77; f. 1987, commenced activities Dec. 1988; 51% owned by Crédit Lyonnais (France); cap. 2,000m.; Pres. ALPHA AMADOU DIALLO; Man. Dir PIERRE OUTIN.

Islamic Bank

Banque Islamique de Guinée: ave de la République, BP 1247, Conakry; tel. 44-50-71; telex 22184; f. 1983; 51% owned by Dar al-Maal al-Islami (DMI); cap. US $1.9m. (Dec. 1986); provides Islamic banking services; Pres. Dr MAHMOUD EL HEW; Man. MOHAMED YAYA KOROMA.

INSURANCE

Société Nationale d'Assurances et de Réassurances de la République de Guinée (SNAR): BP 179, Conakry; Man. Dir OUSMANE SANOKO.

Union Guinéenne d'Assurances et de Réassurances (UGAR): Conakry; f. 1988; 60% state-owned, 40% by Union des Assurances de Paris; cap. 2,000m.

Trade and Industry

DEVELOPMENT AGENCY

Caisse Centrale de Coopération Economique (CCCE): Conakry; telex 780; French agency for economic co-operation; Dir in Guinea GUY TERRACOL.

CHAMBERS OF COMMERCE

Chambre de Commerce, d'Industrie et d'Agriculture de Guinée: BP 545, Conakry; tel. 44-44-95; telex 609; f. 1985; Chair. Capt. THIANA DIALLO; 70 mems.

Chambre Economique de Guinée: BP 609, Conakry.

TRADE ORGANIZATION

Entreprise Nationale Import-Export (IMPORTEX): BP 152, Conakry; tel. 44-28-13; telex 625; state-owned import and export agency; Dir MAMADOU BOBO DIENG.

NATIONALIZED INDUSTRIES

Under the regime of the late President Sekou Touré, a total of 35 state companies, responsible for all sectors of the economy, were established. By the end of 1988, 22 of the 24 state companies whose dissolution, restructuring or transfer to private ownership had been announced in 1986 (as part of a programme of economic and financial reform) had been transferred to private ownership.

TRADE UNIONS

Confédération des travailleurs de Guinée (CTG): BP 237, Conakry; f. 1984 to replace the Conféd. nat. des travailleurs de Guinée; Sec.-Gen. Dr MOHAMED SAMBA KÉBÉ.

Transport

RAILWAYS

There are 662 km of 1-m gauge track from Conakry to Kankan in the east of the country, crossing the Niger at Kouroussa. Three lines for the transport of bauxite link Sangaredi with the port of Kamsar in the west, and Conakry with Kindia and Fria, a total of 376 km. Arrangements have been made with the Liberian authorities for the use of the line linking the Nimba iron ore deposits with the port of Buchanan, and rehabilitation work is being carried out.

Office National des Chemins de Fer de Guinée (ONCFG): BP 589, Conakry; tel. 44-46-13; telex 22349; f. 1905; Man. Dir FOFANA M. KADIO.

ROADS

In 1985 there were 29,108 km of roads, including 4,000 km of main roads and 7,608 km of secondary roads; 4,366 km of the road network was paved. An 895-km cross-country road links Conakry to Bamako, in Mali, and the main highway connecting Dakar (Senegal) to Abidjan (Côte d'Ivoire) also crosses Guinea.

The second phase of a rehabilitation and maintenance project, covering 54% of Guinea's paved roads, began in 1984, financed by a loan of US $14m. from the International Development Association (IDA). The construction of a road linking Conakry to Mamou (the first section of a proposed road linking Conakry with N'Zérékoré) was completed in 1988. In June 1988 it was announced that 10,000 km of roads were to be improved, with the help of a $55m. credit from the IDA.

La Guinéenne-Marocaine des Transports (GUIMAT): Conakry; f. 1989; owned jtly by govt of Guinea and Hakkam (Morocco); operates national and regional transport services.

Office du Projet Routier: BP 581, Conakry.

Société Générale des Transports de Guinée (SOGETRAG): Conakry; f. 1984; state-owned; bus operator.

SHIPPING

Conakry and Kamsar are the international seaports. In 1987 3.1m. tons of bauxite were exported through Conakry and 9m. tons through Kamsar. A US $38m. port rehabilitation programme, supported by the World Bank and other donor agencies, was carried out in Conakry in 1983–87 and included the upgrading and extension of quays and storage facilities. A naval repair dockyard and deep-water port facilities were also to be constructed in Conakry, at a cost of $60m., as part of a further (1989–92) port extension programme. The merchant fleet (13 vessels in 1981) was also to be expanded. There are 2,450 m of quays providing nine alongside berths for ocean-going ships at Conakry.

Port Autonome de Conakry: BP 715, Conakry; tel. 44-27-37; telex 22276.

Port Autonome de Kamsar: Kamsar.

ENTRAT: BP 315, Conakry; state-owned stevedoring and forwarding co; Dir-Gen. DAOUDA DIAWARA.

Société Navale Guinéenne: BP 522, Conakry; telex 644; f. 1968; fmrly state-owned shipping co; agents for Cie Maritime des Chargeurs Réunis, Cie de Navigation Fraissinet et Cyprien Fabre, Delta Steamship Lines, Elder Dempster Line, Hanseatic Africa Line, Leif Hoëgh and Co A/S, Lloyd Triestino, Nouvelle Cie de Paquebots (NCP), Palm Line, Scandinavian West Africa Line, Société Navale de l'Ouest, United West Africa Service; Dir-Gen. NABY SYLLA.

SOTRAMAR: Kamsar; f. 1971; bauxite export from mines at Boké through port of Kamsar.

CIVIL AVIATION

There is an international airport at Conakry-Gbessia, and smaller airfields at Labé, Kankan and Faranah.

Air Guinée: ave de la République, BP 12, Conakry; f. 1960; international and internal services; flights to Bamako, Dakar, Freetown and Monrovia; Dir-Gen. NFA MOUSSA DIANE; fleet of 1 Ilyushin Il-18, 2 Antonov An-12B, 4 An-24, 1 Yak-40.

Air Mano: f. 1988, as a jt venture by the mems of the Mano River Union; services due to commence in the early 1990s; the participating countries each hold 7% of the total cap. (US $2.9m.), the balance being controlled by parastatal orgs, govt orgs and private interests; Chair. LLOYD DURING; fleet of 1 Boeing 737-200C, 1 Dash-7 (leased from Air Guinée).

Société de Gestion et d'Exploitation de l'Aéroport de Conakry (SOGEAC): Conakry; f. 1987 to manage Conakry international airport; 51% state-owned.

Tourism

Secrétariat d'Etat au Tourisme et à l'Hôtellerie: square des Martyrs, BP 1304, Conakry; tel. 44-26-06; f. 1989; state tourist office.

GUINEA-BISSAU

Introductory Survey

Location, Climate, Language, Religion, Flag, Capital

The Republic of Guinea-Bissau lies on the west coast of Africa, with Senegal to the north and Guinea to the east and south. The climate is tropical, although maritime and Sahelian influences are felt. The average temperature is 20°C (68°F). The official language is Portuguese, of which the locally spoken form is Creole (Crioulo). Other dialects are also widely spoken. The principal religious beliefs are animism and Islam. There is a small minority of Roman Catholics and other Christian groups. The national flag (proportions 2 by 1) has two equal horizontal stripes, of yellow and green, and a red vertical stripe, with a five-pointed black star at its centre, at the hoist. The capital is Bissau.

Recent History

Portuguese Guinea (Guiné) was settled by the Portuguese in the 15th century. Small nationalist groups began to form in the 1950s, and the Partido Africano da Independência da Guiné e Cabo Verde (PAIGC) was formed in 1956. Fighting broke out in the early 1960s, and by 1972 the PAIGC was in control of two-thirds of the country. In 1973 a National People's Assembly was elected in 'liberated' areas, and the independence of the Republic of Guinea-Bissau was proclaimed in September, with Luiz Cabral as President of the State Council. To combat the PAIGC's guerrilla campaign, about 40,000 Portuguese troops were operating in the territory. Portuguese forces began to sustain heavy losses in 1973–74, and this may have been a factor in the military coup in Portugal in April 1974. This coup brought the fighting to an end, and in August the new Portuguese Government and the PAIGC negotiated an agreement to end Portuguese rule. Accordingly, on 10 September 1974, Portugal recognized the independence of Guinea-Bissau.

The PAIGC regime introduced measures to lay the foundations for a socialist state. At elections in December 1976 and January 1977 voters chose regional councils from which a new National People's Assembly was later selected. In 1978 Francisco Mendes, who had been Chief State Commissioner since 1973, died; he was replaced by Commander João Vieira, the former State Commissioner for the Armed Forces and President of the National People's Assembly.

Until 1980 the PAIGC supervised both Cape Verde and Guinea-Bissau, the two constitutions remaining separate, but with a view to eventual unification. However, on 14 November, four days after the Government had approved a new constitution, President Cabral was deposed in a coup and Vieira was installed as Chairman of the Council of the Revolution. The National People's Assembly was dissolved.

At the PAIGC Congress in 1981, it was decided to preserve the single-party status of the PAIGC, with Vieira as Secretary-General, despite Cape Verde's withdrawal from the party. Diplomatic relations between the two countries were restored after the release of Cabral from detention in 1982. Vítor Saúde Maria, Vice-Chairman of the Council of the Revolution and former Minister of Foreign Affairs, was appointed Prime Minister in 1982, the post having been vacant since the 1980 coup; several ministers who were regarded as left-wing lost their portfolios.

In 1983 President Vieira established a commission, headed by the Minister of Justice, to examine plans for the revision of the Constitution and the electoral law. In 1984 President Vieira dismissed Saúde Maria from the premiership. Although the reason given for his dismissal was alleged involvement in a planned coup, it appeared that the principal reason was Saúde Maria's opposition to the proposed constitutional changes, which would concentrate more power in the hands of the President. Several other senior party members were subsequently accused of colluding with Saúde Maria and were expelled from the PAIGC. President Vieira formally assumed the role of Head of Government, and elections to the regional councils were held in April. The National People's Assembly was re-established, its members being chosen from the regional councillors. The Council of the Revolution was replaced by a 15-member Council of State, selected from the members of the National People's Assembly. Vieira was subsequently elected as President of the Council of State and Head of State. The National People's Assembly immediately ratified the new Constitution, and formally abolished the position of Prime Minister.

In August 1985 President Vieira launched a campaign against corruption, and many senior officials were dismissed or arrested. This campaign was apparently the cause of an attempted military coup which took place in November, led by Col Paulo Correia, the First Vice-President of the Council of State, and several senior army officers. By July 1986 six people who had been accused of involvement in the coup attempt had died in prison, leading to claims that they had been murdered. At the trial of the surviving defendants, which concluded in July, 12 alleged plotters were sentenced to death and 41 were sentenced to hard labour. Later in the month, six of those condemned to death, including Correia, were executed, but the six other plotters had their death sentences commuted. In December 1988 four plotters were released, under an amnesty to commemorate the 40th anniversary of the UN General Assembly's adoption of the Universal Declaration of Human Rights. In November 1989 it was announced that another eight of those serving prison sentences for their role in the coup had been released, while 11 others had been granted a reduction in their term of imprisonment. In January 1990 a further 22 were granted amnesty.

In July 1986 President Vieira enlarged the Council of Ministers from 15 to 19 members and created the posts of three resident Ministers for the Provinces. During the fourth PAIGC congress, held in November, delegates supported the liberalization of the economy, and re-elected President Vieira as Secretary-General of the PAIGC for a further four years. In February 1987 Vieira appointed Dr Vasco Cabral, the Minister of Justice, as Permanent Secretary of the Central Committee of the PAIGC, in an attempt to ensure that the programme of economic liberalization would receive the PAIGC's support. A minor government reshuffle ensued, which included the appointment of a new Minister of Justice, to replace Cabral, and the creation of two new Secretariats of State with responsibility for justice and foreign affairs. Following the devaluation of the peso in May, political tension increased, and the Government denied reports, published in a Lisbon magazine, that 20 army officers had been arrested for conspiring against Vieira. In August Vieira denied rumours that an attempted coup had been foiled during his visit to France for medical treatment in June and July. In July 1988 Bartolomeu Pereira, the Minister of Planning who had prepared Guinea-Bissau's structural adjustment programme with the IMF and the World Bank, was killed in a road accident. His post was assumed in November by Bernardino Cardoso, the Secretary of State for Economic Affairs and International Co-operation. In February 1989 a further minor government reshuffle was carried out, and in the same month it was announced that the PAIGC had established a six-member national commission to revise the Constitution. Regional elections were held in early June, with 95.8% of the 223,592 votes cast being in favour of the sole PAIGC list. It was reported that about 50% of the electorate participated. In mid-June the regional councils, in turn, elected the National Assembly, which subsequently elected the Council of State. Vieira was re-elected as President of the Council of State. In January 1990 President Vieira announced the creation of two commissions to review, respectively, the programme and statutes of the PAIGC and the laws on land ownership, in preparation for the fifth party congress to be held in November. In March an extensive government reshuffle took place, in which Vasco Cabral was appointed Second Vice-President, in charge of social affairs. Several ministries were restructured, and their number was increased from 19 to 24. In November the First Vice-President, Col Iafai Camara, was placed under house arrest, accused of supplying weapons to Senegalese separatists.

In April 1990 President Vieira announced his approval, in principle, of the introduction of a multi-party political system. In October a draft programme on the transition to a multi-party system was discussed at an international conference in Bissau. In December the central committee of the PAIGC decided that a multi-party system would be adopted, following a period of transition, and that a presidential election, involving a number of candidates, would be held in 1993. A second extraordinary congress was held in January 1991 to discuss the method of introducing the new system, and the number of political parties to be authorized.

Relations with Portugal deteriorated in October 1987, when six Portuguese vessels were seized for alleged illegal fishing in Guinea-Bissau's territorial waters. Portugal retaliated by suspending non-medical aid, but revoked its decision in early November, after the vessels were released. A few days later, however, the head of security at the embassy of Guinea-Bissau in Lisbon requested political asylum and disclosed the presence of explosive devices in the embassy, which, he alleged, were to be used to eliminate members of the opposition movement, Bafata, living in exile in Portugal, France, Senegal and Cape Verde. These allegations were vehemently denied by the Government of Guinea-Bissau. During a one-day visit to Portugal in October 1988, President Vieira discussed the issue of Portuguese-based members of Bafata with President Soares of Portugal. Vieira also invited Soares to visit Guinea-Bissau in early 1989. A four-day visit by the Portuguese Prime Minister, Aníbal Cavaco Silva, in March 1989 signified a distinct improvement in relations between the two countries. In November 1990 the mayor of Bissau, and ex-Prime Minister, Vítor Saúde María, was granted political asylum in Portugal, while there on an official mission.

Meanwhile, relations with Cape Verde, which had deteriorated after the coup in 1980, began to improve. In January 1988 the two countries signed a bilateral co-operation agreement and agreed to liquidate a joint shipping company, which had been founded before the 1980 coup. In September 1989 President Hosni Mubarak of Egypt and President Vieira signed a friendship and co-operation treaty.

In August 1989 a dispute arose between Guinea-Bissau and Senegal over the demarcation of maritime borders, which had been based on a 1960 agreement between the former colonial powers, Portugal and France. Guinea-Bissau began proceedings against Senegal in the International Court of Justice after rejecting an international arbitration tribunal's ruling in favour of Senegal. President Abdou Diouf of Senegal postponed a visit which he was to have made to Guinea-Bissau, although he met President Vieira in Dakar at the end of August. Guinea-Bissau requested direct negotiations with Senegal, and enlisted the aid of President Mubarak of Egypt (the President of the OAU) and President Soares of Portugal as mediators. In January 1990 Guinea-Bissau again urged the OAU, Portugal and also France to help in achieving a peaceful solution to the dispute. Guinea-Bissau and Senegal came close to military conflict in May 1990, when a Senegalese army reconnaissance platoon entered Guinea-Bissau territory. A military confrontation was avoided, however, with the withdrawal of the detachment. In August some 300 nationals of Guinea-Bissau fled the Senegalese region of Casamance, following clashes between the Senegalese army and Casamance separatists. In September more than 1,600 Senegalese sought refuge in Guinea-Bissau, having fled the Casamance region. The Government was expected to issue an international appeal for aid in order to cope with the influx of refugees.

Government

The Constitution of 1984 states that the PAIGC is the leading force in society and in the nation. The PAIGC's highest authority is the Party Congress, convened every five years. The Congress elects a Central Committee (70 members in November 1986) to supervise the Party's work. To direct its policy, the Central Committee elects from its members a Political Bureau (12 full members and four alternate members in November 1986). Legislative power is vested in the National People's Assembly, which has 150 members, chosen by the eight directly-elected regional councils from among their own members. The National People's Assembly, in turn, elects from among its members the 14-member Council of State, which assumes legislative functions between sessions of the National People's Assembly. The regional councils also elect, for a five-year term, the President of the Council of State (a post corresponding to that of President of the Republic), in whom executive power is vested. The President of the Council of State is also Head of Government, and appoints the Ministers and Secretaries of State.

Defence

In June 1990 the armed forces totalled 9,200 men (army 6,800, navy 300, air force 100 and paramilitary gendarmerie 2,000). Expenditure on defence in 1987 was 2,168m. Guinea pesos.

Economic Affairs

In 1989, according to estimates by the World Bank, Guinea-Bissau's gross national product (GNP), measured at average 1987–89 prices, was US $173m., equivalent to $180 per head. During 1980–89, it was estimated, GNP, measured at constant prices, increased by an annual average of 3.4%, although real GNP per head increased by only 1.5% per year. In 1980–89 the population increased by an annual average of 1.9%. Guinea-Bissau's gross domestic product (GDP) increased by 6.9% in 1988.

Agriculture (including forestry and fishing) contributed about 47% of GDP in 1989. An estimated 79.5% of the labour force were employed in the sector in 1988. The main cash crops are cashew nuts (which accounted for 53.1% of export earnings in 1986), palm kernels, groundnuts and cotton. Other crops produced include rice, maize, millet and sorghum. Livestock and timber production are also important. The fishing industry is rapidly becoming a major source of revenue.

Industry (including mining, manufacturing, construction and power) employed an estimated 3.5% of the labour force at mid-1980 and provided an estimated 12.9% of GDP in 1987. The mining sector is underdeveloped, although Guinea-Bissau possesses large reserves of bauxite and phosphate. Drilling of three offshore petroleum wells began in November 1989.

The sole branches of the manufacturing sector, which contributed 7.6% of GDP in 1987, are food-processing, brewing and cotton-processing, while there are plans to develop fish- and timber-processing.

Energy is derived principally from thermal and hydroelectric power. Imports of fuels and lubricants comprised 13.7% of the value of total imports in 1983.

In 1987 Guinea-Bissau recorded a trade deficit of US $32.3m., and there was a deficit of $16m. on the current account of the balance of payments. In 1984 the principal source of imports was Portugal (28.6%), which was also the principal market for exports in 1980 (26.5%). Other major trading partners include the USSR, France, the Federal Republic of Germany, the Netherlands, Spain and Switzerland. The principal exports in 1986 were palm kernels, groundnuts, cashew nuts, cotton, fish and timber. The principal imports in 1983 were foodstuffs, fuels, machinery and transport equipment.

In 1989 there was an estimated budgetary deficit of US $16.5m., and Guinea-Bissau's total external debt was $406m. In 1987 the cost of debt-servicing exceeded 37% of export earnings. The average annual rate of inflation was 17% in 1987/88.

Guinea-Bissau is a member of ECOWAS (see p. 133). In early 1990 Guinea-Bissau withdrew its application to join the Franc Zone. The application had been in place since 1987, but was withdrawn as a result of a series of agreements with Portugal to link the country's currency to the Portuguese escudo.

Guinea-Bissau is one of the world's poorest countries, and in the late 1970s suffered from growing external debt, decreasing exports and escalating inflation. Agriculture, the principal economic activity, is frequently affected by drought and plagues of locusts. A four-year Development Plan (1983–86) comprised a series of measures to liberalize the trading sector, to increase producer prices, and to encourage private enterprise, and was reinforced by a structural adjustment programme (SAP) (1987–89). A second Development Plan (1989–92) aims to consolidate progress. A five-year project, financed by the IDA, was introduced in 1990 to revitalize the economy through the rehabilitation of infrastructure. In September three financial agreements were signed with France, allocating more than 17m. French francs to development projects in Guinea-Bissau. The decentralization of banking activities, which began in 1989, continued throughout 1990, with the founding of the National Credit Bank, and into 1991, with the proposed creation of a Guinea Investment Company.

GUINEA-BISSAU

Social Welfare

Medical services are limited, owing to a severe shortage of facilities. The Government aims to establish one regional hospital in each of the eight regions. In 1981 there were 1,532 hospital beds. At mid-1989 there were 129 physicians and 235 qualified nurses working in the country. Of total budgetary expenditure by the central Government in 1987, 2,638.0m. pesos (5.4%) was for health services, and a further 4,272.7m. pesos (8.8%) for social security and welfare. In 1987 the IDA approved a credit of US $4.2m. for a health project involving the reorganization of the Ministry of Public Health, the rehabilitation of 25 health centres and the provision of drugs and other facilities, in an attempt to improve the level of primary health care. In 1988 Denmark provided a loan to build 13 health centres. However, in January 1989 the Government announced that hospital treatment would no longer be provided free of charge. A five-year health plan, due to be initiated in November 1989, aimed to review primary health care and to reduce transmissible diseases.

Education

Education is officially compulsory only for the period of primary schooling, which begins at seven years of age and lasts for six years. Secondary education, beginning at the age of 13, lasts for up to five years (a first cycle of three years and a second of two years). In 1987 the total enrolment at primary and secondary schools was equivalent to 35% of the school-age population (males 46%; females 23%), while enrolment at primary schools of children in the relevant age-group was equivalent to 53% (males 69%; females 37%). The comparable figure for secondary schools in 1987 was 6% (males 9%; females 3%). Expenditure on education by the central Government in 1987 was 2,541.1m. pesos (5.2% of total spending). In 1988 the IDA approved a credit of US $4.3m. for a project to expand the primary education system. Mass literacy campaigns have been launched: according to UNESCO estimates, the average rate of adult illiteracy in 1980 was 81.1% (males 75.4%; females 86.6%), but by 1990 the rate had declined to 63.5% (males 49.8%; females 76.0%). In January 1991 President Vieira announced the creation of the country's first university.

Public Holidays

1991: 1 January (New Year), 20 January (Death of Amílcar Cabral), 16 April* (Korité, end of Ramadan), 1 May (Labour Day), 23 June* (Tabaski, Feast of the Sacrifice), 3 August (Anniversary of the Killing of Pidjiguiti), 24 September (National Day), 14 November (Anniversary of the Movement of Readjustment), 25 December (Christmas Day).

1992: 1 January (New Year), 20 January (Death of Amílcar Cabral), 4 April* (Korité, end of Ramadan), 1 May (Labour Day), 11 June* (Tabaski, Feast of the Sacrifice), 3 August (Anniversary of the Killing of Pidjiguiti), 24 September (National Day), 14 November (Anniversary of the Movement of Readjustment), 25 December (Christmas Day).

* Religious holidays, which are dependent on the Islamic lunar calendar, may differ by one or two days from the dates shown.

Weights and Measures

The metric system is used.

Statistical Survey

AREA AND POPULATION

Area: 36,125 sq km (13,948 sq miles).

Population: 487,448 at census of 15 December 1970 (which covered only those areas under Portuguese control); 753,313 (males 362,589; females 390,724) at census of 16–30 April 1979; 943,000 (official estimate) at 1 January 1989. *By Region* (1979 census, provisional): Bafatá 116,032, Biombo 56,463, Bissau 109,214, Bolama/Bijagos 25,743, Cacheu 130,227, Gabú 104,315, Oio 135,114, Quinara 35,532, Tombali 55,099.

Density (January 1989): 26.1 per sq km.

Principal Towns (population at 1979 census): Bissau (capital) 109,214, Bafatá 13,429, Gabú 7,803, Mansôa 5,390, Catió 5,170, Cantchungo 4,965, Farim 4,468.

Births and Deaths (UN estimates, annual averages): Birth rate 40.9 per 1,000 in 1975–80, 40.7 per 1,000 in 1980–85, 40.8 per 1,000 in 1985–90; Death rate 21.9 per 1,000 in 1975–80, 21.7 per 1,000 in 1980–85, 20.0 per 1,000 in 1985–90. Source: UN, *World Population Prospects: 1988*.

Economically Active Population (ILO estimates, '000 persons at mid-1980): Agriculture, etc. 332 (males 174, females 158); Industry 14 (males 12, females 3); Services 57 (males 46, females 11); Total 403 (males 231, females 172). Source: ILO, *Economically Active Population Estimates and Projections, 1950–2025*.

AGRICULTURE, ETC.

Principal Crops ('000 metric tons, 1989): Rice (paddy) 162†, Maize 20*, Millet 25*, Sorghum 38†, Roots and tubers 40*, Groundnuts (in shell) 30†, Cottonseed 3*, Coconuts 25*, Copra 5*, Palm kernels 14*, Vegetables and melons 20*, Plantains 25*, Other fruits 17*, Sugar cane 6*, Cashew nuts 10*, Cotton (lint) 2*. * FAO estimate. † Unofficial figure. Source: FAO, *Production Yearbook*.

Livestock (FAO estimates, '000 head, year ending September 1989): Cattle 340, Pigs 290, Sheep 205, Goats 210.

Livestock Products (FAO estimates, '000 metric tons, 1989): Beef and veal 3; Pig meat 9; Cows' milk 10; Goats' milk 2.

Forestry (FAO estimates, '000 cubic metres, 1988): Roundwood removals 565 (sawlogs, etc. 40, other industrial wood 103, fuel wood 422); Sawnwood production 16.

Fishing (FAO estimates, metric tons, live weight, 1988): Fishes 3,202; Crustaceans and molluscs 298; Total catch 3,500.

INDUSTRY

Electric energy (1987): 14 million kWh.

FINANCE

Currency and Exchange Rates: 100 centavos = 1 Guinea peso. *Coins:* 5, 10, 20 and 50 centavos; 1, 2½, 5, 10 and 20 pesos. *Notes:* 50, 100 and 500 pesos. *Sterling and Dollar Equivalents* (30 September 1990): £1 sterling = 4,260.3 pesos; US $1 = 2,274.0 pesos; 10,000 Guinea pesos = £2.347 = $4.398. *Average Exchange Rate* (Guinea pesos per US dollar): 203.95 in 1986; 559.33 in 1987; 1,111.06 in 1988.

General Budget (estimates, million Guinea pesos, 1988): *Revenue:* Taxation 15,903 (Taxes on income of individuals 1,243, Excises 5,615, Import duties 2,999, Export duties 5,116, Poll taxes 600); Other current revenue 6,457; Capital revenue 14; Total 22,374. Figures exclude grants received from abroad (million pesos): 36,338. *Total Expenditure:* 84,101; *Expenditure* (1987): General public services 12,455.5; Defence 2,168.0; Public order and safety 958.0; Education 2,541.1; Health 2,638.0; Social security and welfare 4,272.7; Housing and community amenities 4,067.2; Recreational, cultural and religious affairs 197.6; Economic services 19,524.0 (Fuel and energy 751.4, Agriculture, forestry, fishing and hunting 9,823.0, Mining, manufacturing and construction 4,137.0, Transport and communications 3,895.6); Total 48,822.1 (Current 15,693.6, Capital 33,128.5). Figures exclude net lending (million pesos): 3,666.7. Source: IMF, *Government Finance Statistics Yearbook*.

Gross Domestic Product (million Guinea pesos at current prices): 46,973 in 1986; 92,375 in 1987; 171,949 in 1988. Source: UN, *Monthly Bulletin of Statistics*.

EXTERNAL TRADE

Principal Commodities (US $ million): *Imports* (1983): Food, beverages and tobacco 11.9, Fuels and lubricants 7.5, Machinery and equipment 2.6, Transport equipment 7.1, Total (incl. others) 54.9. *Exports* (1986): Palm kernels 1.0, Groundnuts (shelled) 0.7, Cashew nuts 5.1, Cotton 0.5, Fish 1.1, Timber 1.0, Total (incl. others) 9.6.

Principal Trading Partners (million pesos): *Imports* (1984): France 232.7, Germany, Fed. Repub. 213.7, Italy 110.4, Netherlands 215.6, Portugal 924.0, Senegal 362.0, Sweden 70.2, USSR 462.7, USA 192.4, Total (incl. others) 3,230.7. Source: Ministry of Planning, Bissau.
Exports (1980): Cape Verde 23.0, China, People's Repub. 14.6, Guinea 10.3, Netherlands 20.9, Portugal 101.3, Senegal 5.5, Spain 95.2, Switzerland 87.5, Total (incl. others) 382.3. Source: Direcção-Geral de Estatística, Bissau.

TRANSPORT

Road Traffic (vehicles in use, 1972): Cars 3,268, Lorries and buses 1,098, Motor cycles 758, Total 5,124.

International Sea-borne Shipping (estimated freight traffic, '000 metric tons, 1988): Goods loaded 32; Goods unloaded 285. Source: UN, *Monthly Bulletin of Statistics*.

Civil Aviation (traffic on scheduled services, 1985): Passengers carried ('000) 23; Passenger-km (million) 9. Source: UN, *Statistical Yearbook*.

COMMUNICATIONS MEDIA

Radio receivers (1988): 36,000 in use.
Telephones (1987): 7,000 in use.

EDUCATION

Pre-School (1987): 5 schools, 702 pupils, 26 teachers.
Primary (1987): 632 schools, 75,468 pupils, 3,065 teachers.
Secondary (1987): 5,468 pupils, 824 teachers (1986); 12 schools (1984/85).
Teacher Training (1987): 2 schools (1984/85), 337 pupils, 50 teachers.
Technical (1987): 2 schools (1984/85), 483 pupils, 54 teachers.
Source: UNESCO, *Statistical Yearbook*.

Directory

The Constitution

A new constitution for the Republic of Guinea-Bissau was approved by the National People's Assembly on 16 May 1984. Its main provisions are summarized below:

The Constitution defines Guinea-Bissau as an anti-colonialist and anti-imperialist Republic and a State of revolutionary national democracy, based on the people's participation in carrying out, controlling and directing public activities. The Constitution states that the party that fought against Portuguese colonialism, the Partido Africano da Independência da Guiné e Cabo Verde (PAIGC), shall be the leading political force in society and in the State. The PAIGC shall define the general bases for policy in all fields.

The economy of Guinea-Bissau shall be organized on the principles of state direction and planning. The State shall control the country's foreign trade.

The representative bodies in the country are the National People's Assembly and the regional councils. Other state bodies draw their powers from these. The members of the regional councils shall be directly elected. Members of the councils must be more than 18 years of age. The National Assembly shall have 150 members, who are to be elected by the regional councils from among their own members. All members of the National Assembly must be more than 21 years of age.

The National Assembly shall elect a 15-member Council of State, to which its powers are delegated between sessions of the Assembly. The Assembly also elects the President of the Council of State, who is also automatically Head of the Government and Commander-in-Chief of the Armed Forces. The Council of State will later elect two Vice-Presidents and a Secretary. The President and Vice-Presidents of the Council of State form part of the Government, as do Ministers, Secretaries of State and the Governor of the National Bank.

The Constitution can be revised at any time by the National People's Assembly on the initiative of the deputies themselves, or of the Council of State or the Government. Constitutional amendments providing for the operation of a multi-party political system were being considered in early 1991.

The Government

HEAD OF STATE

Head of Government, President of the Council of State and Commander-in-Chief of the Armed Forces: Commdr JOÃO BERNARDO VIEIRA (assumed power 14 November 1980; elected President of the Council of State 16 May 1984, and re-elected 19 June 1989).

COUNCIL OF STATE
(February 1991)

President: Commdr JOÃO BERNARDO VIEIRA.
First Vice-President: (vacant).
Second Vice-President: VASCO CABRAL.
Permanent Secretary: CARLOS CORREIA.

Members:
CARLOS CORREIA.
FILINTO DE BARROS.
JÚLIO SEMEDO.
FRANCISCA PEREIRA.
MÁRIO MENDES.
TEOBOLDO BARBOZA.
M'BANA MATCH.
CARMEN PEREIRA.
Col MANUEL MÁRIO MONTEIRO DOS SANTOS.
FATIMA FATI.
MAMADU FORE BALDE.

COUNCIL OF MINISTERS
(February 1991)

Head of Government, President of the Council of State, Commander-in-Chief of the Armed Forces, Minister of Defence and of the Interior: Commdr JOÃO BERNARDO VIEIRA.

First Vice-President of the Council of State and Minister of State for the Armed Forces: (vacant).

Second Vice-President of the Council of State and Minister of State for the Presidency, in charge of Social Affairs: VASCO CABRAL.

Minister of State for the Presidency: Dr FIDELES CABRAL D'ALMADA.

Minister of State for Rural Development and Agriculture: CARLOS CORREIA.

Minister of State for Economy and Finance: Col MANUEL MÁRIO MONTEIRO DOS SANTOS.

Minister of State for Social Affairs: CARMEN PEREIRA.

Minister of Natural Resources and Industry: FILINTO DE BARROS.

Minister of Foreign Affairs: JÚLIO SEMEDO.

Minister of Security and Public Order: (vacant).

Minister of Public Health: HENRIQUETA GODINHO GOMES.

Minister of Justice: MÁRIO CABRAL.

Minister of Education: MANUEL RAMBOUT BARCELOS.

Minister of Civil Service and Labour: NICANDRO PEREIRA BARRETO.

Minister of Trade and Tourism: LUÍS OLIVEIRA SANCA.

Minister for International Co-operation: BERNARDINO CARDOSO.

Minister of Women's Affairs: FRANCISCA PEREIRA.

Minister of Fishing: VÍTOR FREIRA MONTEIRO.

Minister of Transport: AVITO JOSÉ DA SILVA.

Minister of Public Works, Construction and Town Planning: ALBERTO LIMA GOMES.

Minister-Governor of the National Bank: Dr PEDRO A. GODINHO GOMES.

Minister of Information and Telecommunications: MOUSSA DJASSI.

Minister for the Northern Province: ZECA MARTINS.
Minister for the Eastern Province: MÁRIO MENDES.
Minister for the Southern Province: PAULO CARLOS MEDINA.
President of the Supreme Court: JOÃO AURIGEMA CRUZ PINTO.
There are 12 Secretaries of State.

MINISTRIES

All Ministries are in Bissau.

Ministry of Economy and Finance: Avda Amílcar Cabral, Bissau; tel. 213431.
Ministry of Information: Avda do Brasil, CP 248, Bissau.

Legislature

NATIONAL PEOPLE'S ASSEMBLY

A new National People's Assembly was inaugurated in June 1989. Its 150 members were selected from among the members of the eight directly-elected regional councils. All members are nominees of the PAIGC.

President: TIAGO ALELUIA LOPES.

Political Organizations

Partido Africano da Independência da Guiné e Cabo Verde (PAIGC): CP 106, Bissau; f. 1956; fmrly the ruling party in both Guinea-Bissau and Cape Verde; although Cape Verde withdrew from the PAIGC following the coup in Guinea-Bissau in Nov. 1980, Guinea-Bissau has retained the party name and initials; a meeting of the central cttee. in Dec. 1990 decided that a multi-party system would be adopted, following a period of transition; cen. cttee of 70 mems (60 full and 10 alt. mems) and political bureau of 16 mems (12 full and four alt.); Sec.-Gen. Commdr JOÃO BERNARDO VIEIRA; Perm. Sec. of Cen. Cttee VASCO CABRAL.

In November 1986 an opposition party, the **Guinea-Bissau Bafata Resistance Movement,** advocating a pluralist democratic system and led by DOMINGOS FERNANDES GOMES, was founded in Lisbon. The party maintains offices in Paris, Dakar (Senegal) and Praia (Cape Verde). A second opposition movement, the **Front for the Struggle of Guinea-Bissau Independence**, is also active outside Guinea-Bissau.

Diplomatic Representation

EMBASSIES IN GUINEA-BISSAU

Algeria: Rua 12 de Setembro 12, CP 350, Bissau; tel. 211522; Ambassador: R. BENCHIKH EL FEGOUN.
Brazil: Rua São Tomé Esquina/Avda Francisco Mendes, Bissau; tel. 201327; telex 245; Ambassador: MARCELO DIDIER.
Cape Verde: Bissau; Ambassador: ANTÓNIO LIMA.
China (Taiwan): Bissau.
Cuba: Rua Joaquim N'Com 1, Bissau; tel. 213579; Ambassador: DIOSDADO FERNÁNDEZ GONZÁLEZ.
Egypt: Rua 12 de Setembro, CP 72, Bissau; tel. 213642; Ambassador: FADEL FADEL ATTA.
France: Rua Eduardo Mondlane 67-A, Bissau; tel. 212633; Ambassador: JEAN THOMAS.
Germany: Avda Osvaldo Vieira 28, Bissau; tel. 212992; Ambassador: ERICH MESKE.
Guinea: Rua 14, no. 9, CP 396, Bissau; tel. 212681; Ambassador: GUIRANE NDIAYE.
Korea, Democratic People's Republic: Avda Domingos Ramos 42, Bissau; tel. 212885; Ambassador: SHIM JAE-DU.
Libya: Rua 16, CP 362, Bissau; tel. 212006; Representative: DOKALI ALI MUSTAFA.
Portugal: Rua de Lisboa 6, Bissau; tel. 213009; telex 248; fax 212777; Ambassador: AUGUSTO MARTINS GONÇALVES PEDRO.
Senegal: Bissau; tel. 212636; Ambassador: AHMED TIJANE KANE.
USSR: Rua Rui Djassi 17, Bissau; tel. 213535; Ambassador: ALEKSANDR P. BARYSHEV.
USA: Avda Domingos Ramos, 1067 Bissau Cedex; tel. 212816; Ambassador: WILLIAM L. JACOBSEN.

Judicial System

Under the provisions of the 1984 Constitution, judges of the Supreme Court are appointed by the President of the Council of State.

President of the Supreme Court: JOÃO AURIGEMA CRUZ PINTO.

Religion

About 54% of the population are animists, 38% are Muslims and 8% are Christians, mainly Roman Catholics.

CHRISTIANITY

The Roman Catholic Church

Guinea-Bissau comprises a single diocese, directly responsible to the Holy See. At 31 December 1989 there was an estimated 66,500 adherents in the country.

Bishop of Bissau: Mgr SETTIMIO ARTURO FERRAZZETTA, CP 20, 1001 Bissau; tel. 212469; fax 211880.

The Anglican Communion

Within the Church of the Province of West Africa, Guinea-Bissau forms part of the diocese of Guinea, inaugurated in August 1985. The Archbishop of the Province is the Bishop of Liberia. The Bishop of Guinea is resident in Conakry, Guinea.

The Press

In December 1989 a law defining the status and salary of journalists, as part of a new national policy on information, was approved by the Council of Ministers. It was later announced that all areas of the press were to be reorganized in 1990.

Nô Pintcha: Bissau; 3 a week; to become a daily in 1990; Dir Sra CABRAL; circ. 6,000.

Voz da Guiné: Bissau; daily; circ. 6,000.

NEWS AGENCIES

Agência Noticiosa da Guinea (ANG): CP 248, Bissau; tel. 212151; telex 96900.

Foreign Bureau

Informatsionnoye Agentstvo Novosti (IAN) (USSR): CP 11, Bissau; tel. 213433; telex 104; Correspondent A. KASSIMOV.

Radio and Television

There were 36,000 radio receivers in use in 1988. An experimental television service, funded by the Portuguese Government, Radiotelevisão Portuguesa and the Gulbenkian Foundation, started broadcasting in November 1989. Three regional radio stations were to be established, at Bafatá, Cantchungo and Catió, in 1990. In September 1990 Radio Freedom resumed transmission. The station, which broadcast on behalf of the PAIGC during Portuguese rule, ceased broadcasting in 1974, after independence.

Radiodifusão Nacional da República da Guiné-Bissau: CP 191, Bissau; govt-owned; broadcasts on short-wave, medium-wave and FM in Portuguese; Dir FRANCISCO BARRETO.

Finance

(cap. = capital; m. = million; brs = branches; amounts in Guinea pesos)

BANKING

In July 1990 the Guinea-Bissau Council of Ministers approved the creation of a National Credit Bank within the framework of the decentralization of banking activities, which began in 1989 with the founding of the International Bank and the transformation of the former National Bank into the Central Bank. It was announced that the National Credit Bank would have structural autonomy for a period of two years, during which time the operations of the former National Bank would be brought to a close, and an investment organization would be created.

Central Bank

Banco Nacional da Guiné-Bissau: Avda Amílcar Cabral, CP 38, Bissau; tel. 215433; telex 249; f. 1975; bank of issue; also operates as a commercial bank; cap. 100m.; Gov. Dr PEDRO A. GODINHO GOMES; 2 brs.

Other Banks

Banco Internacional da Guiné-Bissau: Avda Amílcar Cabral, CP 74, Bissau; tel. 213244; telex 204; fax 211072; f. Nov. 1989; joint banking institution with Portugal; cap. 3,260m.; owned by the Guinea-Bissau State (26%), Guinea-Bissau enterprises and businessmen (25%) and three Portuguese companies (49%); Chair. ARISTIDES MENEZES; Pres. CARLOS GOMES.

Caixa de Crédito da Guiné: Bissau; govt savings and loan institution.

Caixa Económica Postal: Avda Amílcar Cabral, Bissau; tel. 212999; telex 979; postal savings institution.

INSURANCE

In June 1979 it was announced that a single state-owned insurer would be set up to replace the Portuguese company Ultramarina.

GUINEA-BISSAU

Trade and Industry

Since independence the Government has been actively pursuing a policy of small-scale industrialization to compensate for the almost total lack of manufacturing capacity. It adopted a comprehensive programme of state control, and in late 1976 acquired 80% of the capital of a Portuguese company, **Ultramarina**, a large firm specializing in a wide variety of trading, ship-repairing and agricultural processing. The Government has also acquired major interests in the **CICER** brewery and created a joint-venture company with the Portuguese concern **SACOR** to sell petroleum products, following the construction of new storage facilities. Since 1975 three fishing companies have been formed with foreign participation: **GUIALP** (with Algeria), **Estrela do Mar** (with the USSR) and **SEMAPESCA** (with France). In December 1976 **SOCOTRAM**, an enterprise for the sale and processing of timber, was inaugurated. It operates a new factory in Bissau for the production of wooden tiles and co-ordinates sawmills and carpentry shops throughout the country. In 1979 the **Empresa de Automóveis da Guiné** opened a car-assembly plant at Bissau, capable of producing 500 vehicles per year. A plan to restructure several public enterprises was being implemented in early 1990, as part of the Government's programme to attract private investment. The restructuring of seven companies, including the **CICER** brewery, was to be completed in August 1990.

Empresa Nacional de Pesquisas e Exploração Petroliferas e Mineiras (PETROMINAS): Rua Eduardo Mondlane 58, Bissau; tel. 212279; state-owned; regulates all mineral prospecting; Dir-Gen. PIO GOMES CORREIA.

CHAMBER OF COMMERCE

Associacão Commercial e Industrial e Agricola da Guiné-Bissau: Bissau; f. 1987.

TRADE UNION

União Nacional dos Trabalhadores de Guiné (UNTG): 13 Avda Ovai di Vievra, CP 98, Bissau; tel. 212094; telex 900; Sec.-Gen. MÁRIO MENDES CORREA.

Transport

RAILWAYS

There are no railways in Guinea-Bissau.

ROADS

In 1989 there were about 3,500 km of roads, of which 540 km were tarred. A major road rehabilitation scheme is proceeding, and in 1989 donors provided US $31.3m. for road projects. An international road, linking Guinea-Bissau with The Gambia and Senegal, is planned. In August 1989 the Islamic Development Bank granted more than US $2m. towards the construction of a 111-km road linking north and south, and a 206-km road between Guinea-Bissau and Guinea. A five-year rehabilitation project, funded by international donors, was due to begin in April 1990. The programme included repair work on roads, the management and supply of equipment to transport companies, and town planning.

SHIPPING

Under a major port modernization project, the main port at Bissau was to be renovated and expanded, and four river ports were to be upgraded to enable barges to load and unload at low tide. The total cost of the project was estimated at US $47.4m., and finance was provided by the World Bank and Arab funds. In 1986 work began on a new river port at N'Pungda, which was to be partly funded by the Netherlands.

Empresa Nacional de Agências e Transportes Marítimos (Guinémar): Sociedade de Agências e Transportes da Guiné Lda, Rua Guerra Mendes, 4-4A, CP 244, Bissau; tel. 212675; telex 240; nationalized 1976; shipping agents and brokers; Gen. Man. MARCOS T. LOPES; Asst Gen. Man. NOËL CORREIA.

CIVIL AVIATION

There is an international airport at Bissalanca, which there are plans to expand, and 10 smaller airports serving the interior.

Transportes Aéreos da Guiné-Bissau (TAGB): Aeroporto Osvaldo Vieira, CP 111, Bissau; telex 268; f. 1977; domestic services and flights to France, Portugal, the Canary Islands (Spain), Guinea and Senegal; Dir Capt. EDUARDO PINTO LOPES; fleet of 1 BAe-748, 8 DC-3, 1 Dornier 228, several light aircraft.

Tourism

Centro de Informação e Turismo: CP 294, Bissau; state tourism and information service.

GUYANA

Introductory Survey

Location, Climate, Language, Religion, Flag, Capital

The Co-operative Republic of Guyana lies on the north coast of South America, between Venezuela to the west and Suriname to the east, with Brazil to the south. The narrow coastal belt has a moderate climate with two wet seasons, from April to August and from November to January, alternating with two dry seasons. Inland, there are tropical forests and savannah, and the dry season lasts from September to May. The average annual temperature is 27°C (80°F), with average rainfall of 1,520 mm (60 in) per year inland, rising to between 2,030 mm (80 in) and 2,540 mm (100 in) on the coast. English is the official language but Hindi, Urdu and Amerindian dialects are also spoken. The principal religions are Christianity (which is professed by about 50% of the population), Hinduism (about 33%) and Islam (less than 10%). The national flag (proportions 5 by 3 when flown on land, but 2 by 1 at sea) is green, with a white-bordered yellow triangle (apex at the edge of the fly) on which is superimposed a black-bordered red triangle (apex in the centre). The capital is Georgetown.

Recent History

Guyana was formerly British Guiana, a colony of the United Kingdom, formed in 1831 from territories finally ceded to Britain by the Dutch in 1814. A new constitution, providing for universal adult suffrage, was introduced in 1953. The elections of April 1953 were won by the left-wing People's Progressive Party (PPP), led by Dr Cheddi Jagan. In October, however, the British Government, claiming that a communist dictatorship was threatened, suspended the Constitution. An interim administration was appointed. The PPP split in 1955, and in 1957 some former members founded a new party, the People's National Congress (PNC), under the leadership of Forbes Burnham. The PNC draws its support mainly from the African-descended population, while PPP support comes largely from the (Asian-descended) 'East' Indian community. Both parties adhere to Marxist-Leninist ideology.

A revised constitution was introduced in December 1956 and fresh elections held in August 1957. The PPP won and Dr Jagan became Chief Minister. Another constitution, providing for internal self-government, was adopted in July 1961. The PPP won the elections in August and Dr Jagan was appointed Premier in September. In the elections of December 1964, held under the system of proportional representation that had been introduced in the previous year, the PPP won the largest number of seats in the Legislative Assembly, but not a majority. A coalition government was formed by the PNC and the United Force, with Burnham as Prime Minister. This coalition led the colony to independence, as Guyana, on 26 May 1966.

The PNC won elections in 1968 and in 1973, although the results of the latter, and every poll since, have been disputed by the opposition parties. Guyana became a Co-operative Republic on 23 February 1970, and Arthur Chung was elected non-executive President in March. In 1976 the PPP, which had boycotted the National Assembly since 1973, offered the Government its 'critical support'. Following a referendum in July 1978, which gave the Assembly power to amend the Constitution, elections to the Assembly were postponed for 15 months. The legislature assumed the role of a Constituent Assembly, established in November 1978, to draft a new constitution. In October 1979 elections were postponed for a further year. In October 1980 Forbes Burnham declared himself executive President of Guyana, and a new constitution was promulgated. Elections were announced for December.

Internal opposition to the PNC Government had increased after the assassination in June 1980 of Dr Walter Rodney, leader of the Working People's Alliance (WPA). The Government was widely believed to have been involved in the incident (an official inquest into Rodney's death was finally ordered in November 1987, but in 1988 it produced a verdict, rejected by the opposition, of death by misadventure). All opposition parties except the PPP and United Force urged their supporters to boycott the December 1980 elections to the National Assembly. The PNC, under Burnham, received 77.7% of the votes, according to official results, and won 41 of the 53 elective seats, although allegations of substantial electoral malpractice were made. The Government's international reputation was further diminished when an international observer team denounced the elections as fraudulent, but, on the basis of the voting for the Assembly, Burnham was declared to have been elected President. He was formally inaugurated in January 1981.

In 1981 arrests and trials of opposition leaders continued, and in 1982 the Government's relations with human rights groups, and especially the Christian churches, deteriorated further. Editors of opposition newspapers were threatened, political violence increased, and the Government was accused of interference in the legal process. Popular passive resistance to the Government took the form of economic non-co-operation, while the Government gave much publicity to rumours of an imminent invasion by Venezuela, in an attempt to divert attention from the internal crisis. Industrial unrest and public discontent continued in 1983, as Guyana's worsening economic situation increased opposition to the Government, and led to growing disaffection within the trade union movement and the PNC. Food shortages were exacerbated by government attempts to end the 'black market' in banned foodstuffs, which operated between Guyana and its neighbours. There were more strikes in 1984, and in December Burnham announced some concessions, including a rise in the daily minimum wage (virtually the only increase since 1979). There was also speculation about a possible government of national unity, formed by the PNC and the PPP to counter the threat of a right-wing military coup.

Forbes Burnham died in August 1985 and was succeeded as President by Desmond Hoyte, hitherto the First Vice-President and Prime Minister. President Hoyte's former posts were assumed by Hamilton Green, previously the First Deputy Prime Minister. At a general election, held in December, the PNC won 78% of the votes and 42 of the elective seats in the National Assembly. Desmond Hoyte was declared elected as President. Opposition groups, including the PPP and WPA, denounced the poll as fraudulent. In January 1986 five of the six opposition parties formed the Patriotic Coalition for Democracy (PCD).

President Hoyte's Government announced that its chief priority would be the revitalization of Guyana's rapidly deteriorating economy. Efforts were to be made to improve investment opportunities in Guyana. In addition, the ban on the import of wheat flour, imposed in 1982, was repealed, and the first shipments of flour from the USA arrived in September, as part of a new agreement on food aid. Further restrictions on several food items were rescinded in November.

The PCD refused to present candidates for the December 1986 municipal elections, and the 91 PNC candidates were declared winners by default. Hoyte reshuffled the Cabinet, and in January 1987 he announced his Government's intention to begin the 'roll-back of co-operative socialism'. Fuel shortages and interruptions to the electric power supply in Georgetown during October and November 1987, however, provoked protests by the opposition, which also demanded the implementation of the recommendations of an integrity commission, published in a report in August, for a legally enforceable code of conduct for persons in public life.

During 1988 the opposition expressed fears about the independence of the judiciary. In February the Government, prompted by a ruling of the Court of Appeal (in 1987) declaring invalid sections of the 1984 Labour (Amendment) Act, enacted a constitutional amendment which rescinded the court's jurisdiction in matters of labour legislation, particularly with regard to the Government's obligation to consult with trade unions and other organizations concerning such legislation. In addition, the amendment established that any legislation to be enacted by the National Assembly, including retrospective legislation, could not be deemed invalid on the grounds of inconsistency with former constitutions. Moreover, in April Keith Massiah retired as Chancellor of Justice, but, within one day, he was appointed to the Cabinet as Attorney-General, thereby causing controversy both in Guyana and other countries in the region. The opposition also claimed that the Government's continued recourse to the laws of libel against its critics was an abuse of the legal system.

In 1988 President Hoyte continued to hold negotiations with international financial agencies on an economic recovery plan acceptable to potential aid donors and, particularly, to the IMF. The successful implementation of an IMF-sponsored programme was also considered important to Hoyte's own position within the ruling PNC. Social unrest and industrial disruption, however, continued to hamper government efforts to reform the economy. Furthermore, the severity of austerity measures contained in the budget of March 1989, which included a devaluation of the currency, caused a six-week strike in the sugar and bauxite industries. Although a programme of IMF assistance was agreed in April (to take effect in 1990), the Government's difficulties in achieving its economic targets were compounded by widespread industrial unrest and the unexpected failure of a group of donor nations, co-ordinated by Canada, to provide sufficient aid. The viability of the Economic Recovery Programme (ERP), launched in April 1989, was, therefore, being increasingly questioned by early 1990.

Many of Guyana's economic problems, notably the emigration of skilled labour and industrial disruption, have been attributed to popular dissatisfaction at the political situation. In 1988 the Government suffered a further loss of control, following a division within the trade union movement. Seven unions withdrew from the Trades Union Congress (TUC) in September, alleging that elections for TUC officials were weighted in favour of PNC-approved candidates (it was reported that a faction within the PNC had resolved to re-establish the party's dominance within the TUC). The seven independent unions formed a separate congress, the Federation of Independent Trade Unions in Guyana (FITUG) in October 1988.

The Government refused to negotiate with FITUG, however, accusing it of being politically motivated. The FITUG unions were involved in several strikes during 1989, including protests against the budget and the continual failure of electricity supplies. The new federation suffered from some division itself, however, with one union withdrawing from FITUG, and tension arising between unions affiliated to the PPP and those influenced by the WPA. Negotiations in mid-1989 failed to secure agreement over adequate representation for independent unions at the TUC conference, and FITUG held its own conference in October 1989.

The main political issue of 1989 was that of electoral reform, the principal demands being the establishment of an independent electoral commission, the counting of votes at polling stations and the confinement to barracks of all military personnel on election day. PCD attempts to represent such demands were hampered by a failure to agree on a common leader or spokesperson, with an increase in WPA support, in particular, eroding Dr Jagan's position as the more pre-eminent opposition politician. The PCD parties did agree to boycott municipal elections in November 1989. Jagan met President Hoyte in December, but the discussions ended acrimoniously. In January 1990, however, the WPA generated some hope of political change following a meeting with Hoyte, at which the opposition party submitted a document detailing 31 discussion points, including electoral reform.

Outside the formal opposition of the political parties, the Government also experienced pressure from members of the Guyana Human Rights Association (whose demands include electoral reform, the abolition of the death sentence, an end to alleged police violence and an improvement in prison conditions), business leaders and prominent citizens such as the Anglican and Roman Catholic bishops. This culminated, in January 1990, in the formation of a movement for legal and constitutional change, Guyanese Action for Reform and Democracy (Guard). Hoyte, in an attempt to secure his position within the PNC, criticized some of Guard's leading members and condemned critics of the ERP. In June 1990 Guard initiated a series of mass protest rallies urging the Government to accelerate the process of democratic reform. To counter this civic movement, the PNC began mobilizing its own newly-established Committees to Re-elect the President (Creeps). Guard accused the Groups of adopting a confrontational stance, of orchestrating violent clashes at Guard's rallies, and of fomenting racial unrest in the country in an attempt to regain support from the Afro-Guyanese population.

In mid-October 1990 the former US President, Jimmy Carter, visited President Hoyte to discuss matters related to electoral reform. The most striking concessions made by the Government, as result of these discussions, were agreements to carry out a preliminary count of votes at polling stations (an opposition demand previously rejected by the PNC) and to compile a new electoral register, probably on a house-to-house basis. The original electors' list, drawn up by the Data Management Authority, had provoked popular outrage when it was found to include the names of several thousand dead people, while omitting thousands of eligible voters. Carter stated, after his visit, that he had been given assurances by the Guyanan Government that the forthcoming elections were to be conducted in a free and open manner, and that his Council for Freely-Elected Heads of Government would mount an observer mission to help guarantee this. However, the date of the general election seemed likely to be postponed, following the passage of a bill by the PNC in January 1991, extending the term of office of the National Assembly by two months after its official dissolution date of 2 February 1991, (in accordance with constitutional provisions, the general election was due to take place by 31 March). The Government stated that the delay was owing to the time required for the compilation of the new electoral register, a claim rejected by the increasingly impatient opposition parties.

Legislation approved by the National Assembly at the end of October 1990, provided for the formation of a Public Utilities Commission to oversee the transfer of state-owned enterprises to private ownership, and for a reduction in the number of cabinet positions, ministries and multiple Vice-Presidents. The number of ministries was to be reduced to 11 by May 1991.

Relations between the Government and the trade unions, which had hitherto been considerably strained, improved somewhat following the announcement in October 1990 of a 50% increase in wages for sugar workers.

Guyana has border disputes with its neighbours, Venezuela and Suriname, although relations with Brazil have continued to improve through trade and military agreements and the first visit to Guyana by a Brazilian Head of State, in 1989. Suriname restored diplomatic representation in Guyana in 1979, however, and bilateral meetings were resumed at the end of the year. In 1983 relations improved further as a result of increased trade links between the countries. In August 1989, following a visit to Suriname by President Hoyte, it was agreed that a joint commission would be established to examine the border dispute.

In 1962 Venezuela renewed its claim to 130,000 sq km (50,000 sq miles) of land west of the Essequibo river (nearly two-thirds of Guyanese territory). The area was accorded to Guyana in 1899, but Venezuela based its claim on a papal bull of 1493, referring to Spanish colonial possessions. The Port of Spain Protocol of 1970 put the issue in abeyance until 1982. Several border incidents were reported in 1982. After the failure of two rounds of negotiations in 1982, Guyana and Venezuela referred the dispute to the UN in 1983, but no immediate progress was made. A meeting between the Ministers of Foreign Affairs of the two countries in February 1985 led to a series of agreements on trade and the exchange of information and assistance. After further UN efforts, and a visit to Venezuela by President Hoyte, Guyana and Venezuela agreed to a mutually acceptable intermediary, suggested by the UN Secretary-General, in August 1989.

Guyana officially condemned the US-led invasion of Grenada in October 1983. This attitude, although popular in Guyana, led to a rapid deterioration in relations with the USA, which had already been adversely affected by the US Government's veto of anticipated loans to Guyana in September. Guyana's decision to dispense with seeking IMF financial support further compounded the country's increasing isolation among Western nations. To offset the fall in Western aid, Guyana sought to improve relations with socialist countries, such as Cuba, Libya, Yugoslavia and the Democratic People's Republic of Korea. After Hoyte became President, however, Guyana started to improve its relations with the USA and other Western countries. Hoyte sought to encourage investment in Guyana and emphasized policy changes during visits to North America in 1987, and to the United Kingdom and other European countries in 1988. The Government has also encouraged the development of Guyana's relations within CARICOM (see p. 108), and in

1989 it concluded agreements on fishing and technical assistance with Barbados. Guyana, traditionally, has close relations with the countries of the English-speaking Caribbean, but these were damaged by its defaulting on various debts in the early 1980s. In 1989 Hoyte committed Guyana to closer CARICOM integration.

Government

Under the 1980 Constitution, legislative power is held by the unicameral National Assembly, with 65 members: 53 elected for five years by universal adult suffrage, on the basis of proportional representation, and 12 regional representatives. Executive power is held by the President, who leads the majority party in the Assembly and holds office for its duration. The President appoints and heads a Cabinet, which includes a Prime Minister, and may include Ministers who are not elected members of the Assembly. The Cabinet is collectively responsible to the National Assembly. Guyana comprises 10 regions, each having a Regional Democratic Council which returns a representative to the National Assembly.

Defence

The armed forces are combined in a single service, the Combined Guyana Defence Force, consisting of 1,950 men (of whom 1,500 were in the army, 300 were in the air force and 150 in the navy) in June 1990. Paramilitary forces total 3,500, comprising a 2,000-strong People's Militia and 1,500 on National Service (established in 1974). Estimated defence expenditure in 1986 was US $65m.

Economic Affairs

According to estimates by the World Bank, in 1989 Guyana's gross national product (GNP), measured at average 1987–89 prices, was US $248m. Between 1980 and 1989, it was estimated, GNP declined, in real terms, at an average annual rate of 6.0%. GNP per head, equivalent to $310 in 1989, was estimated to have decreased at an average rate of 6.6% per year, in real terms, between 1980 and 1989. Over the same period, the population increased by an annual average of 0.6%. Guyana's gross domestic product (GDP) decreased, in real terms, by 23% between 1980 and 1989, according to the Inter-America Development Bank.

Agriculture (including forestry and fishing) contributed about 25% of GDP in the late 1980s, and employed an estimated 23.2% of the economically active population in 1988. The principal cash crops are sugar cane (sugar providing 37.7% of the value of total domestic exports in 1989) and rice (6.2%). The sugar industry alone accounted for 14.5% of GDP and, it was estimated, employed about one-half of the agricultural labour force in 1988. Vegetables and fruit are also cultivated for the local market, and livestock-rearing is being developed. During 1980–88 agricultural production increased by an annual average of 1.9%.

Timber resources in Guyana are extensive and underdeveloped. According to FAO estimates, some 83% of the country's total land area consists of forest and woodland. In 1988 timber shipments provided only 2.1% of total domestic exports. Fishing, which contributed 3.4% of GDP in 1988, is already being developed. The sector's principal export is shrimps, and in 1988 the value of the catch increased almost fourfold on that of the previous year, to constitute 9.4% of domestic exports.

Industry (including mining, manufacturing, construction and power) contributed 25.5% of GDP in 1988. The principal industry is mining, which contributed 10% of GDP in 1988 and employed 3.9% of the total labour force in 1980. Bauxite, which is used for the manufacture of aluminium, is one of Guyana's most valuable exports, and accounted for 32.8% of total domestic exports in 1988. Guyana's reserves of bauxite are extensive, but the industry has suffered from the effects of low international prices (in the early 1980s), a lack of investment and, particularly in the late 1980s, disruption by a labour force expressing economic and political dissatisfaction. The registered production of gold (7.6% of domestic exports in 1988) has increased since 1986, when the Government raised the price payable to miners in an effort to prevent smuggling. In late 1989 and early 1990, it was reported, there was a welcome increase in the number of gold prospectors, as a large influx of Brazilian *garimpeiros*, whose presence on the Yanomami Indian reserve had been declared illegal, crossed into Guyana. In 1990 the production of gold increased by 107%, compared with 1989, to reach 39,000 troy ounces, which represented the highest level of production since 1939. Diamonds constitute the country's other main mineral resource (in 1989, declared production was 7,842 metric carats, an increase of 85% on the figure for 1988), and there are some petroleum reserves.

Manufacturing (including power) accounted for 8.7% of GDP in 1988, and, according to the 1980 census, employed 11.7% of the total labour force. The main activities are the processing of bauxite, sugar, rice and timber. Rum is an important manufacture (earning 2.8% of total domestic exports in 1988), and in the late 1980s pharmaceuticals became an increasingly important export industry.

Energy requirements are almost entirely met by imported hydrocarbon fuels. In 1988 fuels and lubricants constituted 34.2% of the total value of imports (mainly from Venezuela and Trinidad and Tobago). Interruptions to electricity supplies, owing to ageing equipment and a shortage of generating capacity, are compounded by Guyana's repeated failure to pay for its imports of petroleum. Any expansion of industry is dependent upon an improvement in power supply, and, although there is considerable potential for hydroelectric schemes (there is one such project on the Upper Mazaruni river), any development in the energy sector is reliant upon the availability of investment.

In 1985 Guyana recorded a visible trade deficit of US $4.9m. (preliminary figures for 1988 indicated a small surplus), and a deficit of US $96.6m. on the current account of the balance of payments. In 1982 the principal source of imports was Trinidad and Tobago (42.3%), mainly on account of petroleum imports, and Venezuela also became an important trading partner during the 1980s. The USA, the United Kingdom and Canada are other important suppliers of imports. The United Kingdom is the principal market for exports (30.2% of total exports in 1987); the USA (25.7%), Venezuela, Canada, Germany and, within CARICOM, Trinidad and Tobago are also important markets. The principal exports are bauxite and sugar, and the principal imports are fuels and machinery.

In 1988 the Government estimated a budget deficit of $ G1,201.6m. on its current operations. By the end of 1988 Guyana's total debt was estimated to have risen to some US $1,800m., equivalent to 725% of annual GDP. Guyana's debt-service ratio in 1985 was only 9.5%, indicating that the country's main problem is with the large repayment arrears that have accrued. Debt-servicing was expected to cost some US $164m. in 1988. The average annual rate of inflation in 1988 was 10.0%. An estimated 3.4% of the labour force were unemployed in 1987, but Guyana's greater problem is a shortage of labour, particularly of managerial and technical personnel. The emigration rate remains high, at an estimated 13,500 per year, and compounds the existing economic difficulties.

Guyana is a founder member of CARICOM and of the International Bauxite Association (see p. 226). It is also a member of the Economic Commission for Latin America and the Caribbean (ECLAC, see p. 27) and of the International Sugar Organization (see p. 229).

Despite its extensive natural resources, Guyana has considerable economic difficulties. The country has large debts, mostly to the IMF (which declared Guyana ineligible for further loans in 1982), CARICOM and the major donor countries. Foreign investors also remain cautious of involvement in Guyana because of the state of its infrastructure, its record of extensive nationalization and state control of the economy, and the continuing political unrest. Particularly since President Hoyte assumed office, the Government has pursued policies of limited divestment of state-owned industries (officially denied), political moderation, financial reform and attempts to integrate the 'parallel economy' (which had an estimated annual turnover of between US $50m. and US $100m. in the late 1980s) into the formal economy. During 1990 various changes, aimed at revitalizing the economy, were introduced as part of the Economic Recovery Programme (ERP, launched, in April 1989), under which several state-owned industries, including the Guyana Telecommunications Corporation (GTC) and the Guyana Electricity Corporation, were to be transferred to private ownership (the GTC was bought by a US company in 1990). Guyana's economy was expected to benefit significantly from a gold mine in the Omai District of Essequibo province which was scheduled to start production towards the end of 1992. Its projected output of 255,000 troy ounces per year will make it one of the largest gold mines in South America and

GUYANA

will dramatically increase Guyana's gold production. Similarly, measures introduced to combat smuggling (which costs the country an estimated G $360m. annually) should also help Guyana to maximize earnings from gold. However, despite these developments, Guyana's economy, with its large agricultural sector, remains vulnerable to adverse weather conditions. This was illustrated in May 1990, when floods caused widespread damage to crops and destroyed almost one-half of the country's rice harvest. Similarly, sugar production decreased in 1989 and 1990 (as a result of industrial action coupled with problematic weather conditions).

Social Welfare

Improved water supplies, anti-tuberculosis campaigns and the control of malaria have steadily improved general health. A National Insurance Scheme, compulsory for most workers and employers, was established in 1969, and was subsequently extended to cover self-employed people. In 1979 there were 85 physicians in government service. In 1981 Guyana had 29 hospitals and 149 health centres. Of total expenditure by the central Government in 1984, $ G51.5m. (3.7%) was for health, and a further $ G36.8m. (2.7%) for social security and welfare.

Education

Education is officially compulsory, and is provided free of charge, for eight years between six and 14 years of age. In 1976 the Government assumed responsibility for all church and private schools. Primary education begins at six years of age and lasts for at least six years. Children receive secondary education either in a general secondary school for five years or stay on at primary school for a further three years. Enrolment at all primary and secondary schools in 1981 was equivalent to 80% of the school-age population, but the proportion fell to 70% in 1986. Primary enrolment in 1986 included an estimated 79% of children in the relevant age-group. The total number of pupils in all schools was 218,416 in 1985. There are also 15 technical, vocational, special and higher educational institutions. These include the University of Guyana in Georgetown and three teacher training colleges. In 1990, according to estimates by UNESCO, the average rate of adult illiteracy was only 3.6% (males 2.5%; females 4.6%), one of the lowest in the Western hemisphere. Expenditure on education by the central Government in 1988 was estimated at $ G114.7m., representing 6.4% of total spending.

Public Holidays

1991: 1 January (New Year's Day), 23 February (Mashramani, Republic Day), 29 March (Good Friday), 1 April (Easter Monday), 16 April* (Id al-Fitr, end of Ramadan), 1 May (Labour Day), 6 May (for Indian Heritage Day), 23 June* (Id al-Adha, feast of the Sacrifice), 1 July (Caribbean Day), 5 August (Freedom Day), 21 September* (Yum an-Nabi, birth of the Prophet), 25–26 December (Christmas).

1992: 1 January (New Year's Day), 23 February (Mashramani, Republic Day), 4 April* (Id al-Fitr, end of Ramadan), 17 April (Good Friday), 20 April (Easter Monday), 1 May (Labour Day), 4 May (Indian Heritage Day), 11 June* (Id al-Adha, feast of the Sacrifice), 29 June (Caribbean Day), 3 August (Freedom Day), 10 September* (Yum an-Nabi, birth of the Prophet), 25–26 December (Christmas).

* These holidays are dependent on the Islamic lunar calendar and may vary by one or two days from the dates given.

In addition, the Hindu festivals of Holi Phagwah (usually in March) and Divali (October or November) are celebrated. These festivals are dependent on sightings of the moon and their precise date is not known until two months before they take place.

Weights and Measures

The metric system has been introduced.

Statistical Survey

Sources (unless otherwise stated): Bank of Guyana, POB 1003, Georgetown; tel. (2) 63251; telex 2267.

AREA AND POPULATION

Area: 214,969 sq km (83,000 sq miles).

Population: 758,619 (males 375,481, females 382,778) at census of 12 May 1980; 811,000 (official estimate for 1988).

Density: 3.8 per sq km (1988).

Ethnic Groups (1980 census): 'East' Indians 389,760, Africans 231,330, Portuguese 2,975, Chinese 1,842, Amerindians 39,867, Mixed 83,763, Others 9,082; Total 758,619.

Capital: Georgetown, population 72,049 (metropolitan area 187,056) at mid-1976 (estimate).

Births and Deaths (1978 registrations, provisional): 23,200 live births (birth rate 28.3 per 1,000); 6,000 deaths (death rate 7.3 per 1,000).

Economically Active Population (persons between 15 and 65 years of age, 1980 census): Agriculture, forestry and fishing 48,603; Mining and quarrying 9,389; Manufacturing 27,939; Electricity, gas and water 2,772; Construction 6,574; Trade, restaurants and hotels 14,690; Transport, storage and communications 9,160; Financing, insurance, real estate and business services 2,878; Community, social and personal services 57,416; Activities not adequately defined 15,260; Total employed 194,681 (males 153,645; females 41,036); Unemployed 44,650 (males 26,439, females 18,211); Total labour force 239,331 (males 180,084, females 59,247).

AGRICULTURE, ETC.

Principal Crops (FAO estimates, '000 metric tons, 1989): Rice (paddy) 203, Maize 3, Roots and tubers 31, Coconuts 45, Sugar cane 3,100 (unofficial estimate), Pulses 2, Vegetables 12, Oranges 15, Bananas 18, Plantains 25, Other fruit 10 (Source: FAO, *Production Yearbook*).

Livestock (FAO estimates, '000 head, year ending September 1989): Cattle 210, Pigs 185, Sheep 120, Goats 77, Chickens 15,000 (Source: FAO, *Production Yearbook*).

Livestock Products (FAO estimates, '000 metric tons, 1989): Beef and veal 9, Mutton and lamb 1, Pig meat 1, Poultry meat 15, Cows' milk 48, Hen eggs 4.2 (Source: FAO, *Production Yearbook*).

Forestry (FAO estimates, '000 cubic metres, 1988): Roundwood removals: Sawlogs, veneer logs and logs for sleepers 188, Other industrial wood 21, Fuel wood 19, Total 228; Sawnwood production: Total (incl. boxboards) 57 (Source: FAO, *Yearbook of Forest Products*).

Fishing ('000 metric tons, live weight): Total catch 40.2 in 1986; 41.6 in 1987; 41.7 in 1988 (Source: FAO, *Yearbook of Fishery Statistics*).

MINING

Production (official figures, 1988): Bauxite 1.39m. metric tons; Gold 18,803 troy ounces; Diamonds 4,242 metric carats.

1989: Gold 18,841 troy ounces; Diamonds 7,842 metric carats.

1990: Gold 39,000 troy ounces.

INDUSTRY

Selected Products: Raw sugar (1988, '000 metric tons) 168, Rum (1984, '000 hectolitres) 154, Beer (1987, estimate, '000 hectolitres) 95, Cigarettes (1987, estimate, million) 477, Electric energy (1987, million kWh) 385 (Source: UN, *Industrial Statistics Yearbook*).

FINANCE

Currency and Exchange Rates: 100 cents = 1 Guyana dollar ($ G). *Coins:* 1, 5, 10, 25 and 50 cents. *Notes:* 1, 5, 10, 20 and 100 dollars. *Sterling and US Dollar Equivalents* (30 September 1990): £1 sterling = $ G84.31; US $1 = $ G45.00; $ G1,000 = £11.86 = US $22.22. *Average Exchange Rate:* ($ G per US $): 9.756 in 1987; 10.000 in 1988; 27.159 in 1989.

Budget (official estimates, $ G million, 1988): *Revenue:* Current revenue 1,642.5, Capital receipts 1.7, External grants 200.2; Total 1,844.4. *Expenditure:* Current expenditure on goods and services 2,844.1, Capital expenditure 1,074.2; Total 3,918.3.

International Reserves (US $ million at 31 December 1989): Foreign exchange 13.35; Total 13.35 (Source: IMF, *International Financial Statistics*).

GUYANA

Money Supply ($ G million at 31 December 1989): Currency outside banks 1,506, Demand deposits at commercial banks 1,410; Total money (including also private-sector deposits at the Bank of Guyana) 2,923 (Source: IMF, *International Financial Statistics*).

Cost of Living (Urban Consumer Price Index; base: 1985 = 100): 107.9 in 1986; 138.9 in 1987; 194.4 in 1988 (Source: IMF, *International Financial Statistics*).

Gross Domestic Product by Kind of Economic Activity ($ G million at current factor cost, 1987): Agriculture 884, Forestry and fishing 201, Mining and quarrying 360, Manufacturing (incl. power) 312, Distribution 290, Transport and communication 299, Engineering and construction 246, Rented dwellings 65, Financial services 185, Other services 125, Government 633, GDP at factor cost 3,600; Indirect taxes, *less* subsidies 538; GDP at market prices 4,138.

Balance of Payments (US $ million, 1985): Merchandise exports f.o.b. 214.0, Merchandise imports f.o.b. −209.1, *Trade Balance* 4.9; Exports of services 48.0, Imports of services −144.3, *Balance on Goods and Services* −91.4; Private unrequited transfers (net) −2.0, Government unrequited transfers (net) −3.2, *Current Balance* −96.6; Long-term capital (net) −36.0, Short-term capital (net) 2.3, Net errors and omissions −4.3, *Total* (net monetary movements) −134.6; Valuation changes (net) −10.9, Exceptional financing (net) 139.1, *Changes in Reserves* −6.4 (Source: IMF, *International Financial Statistics*).

EXTERNAL TRADE

Principal Commodities ($ G million, 1985): *Imports c.i.f.:* Consumer goods 76.5 (Food 16.0); Intermediate goods 660.6 (Fuels and lubricants 436.4, Chemicals 44.4); Capital goods 307.3 (Machinery 170.6, Transport equipment 92.6, Building materials 30.5); Total (incl. others) 1053.5. *Exports f.o.b.* Bauxite 421.6; Sugar 282.2; Rice 56.6; Shrimps 18.3; Rum 29.6; Gold 17.2; Total (incl. others) 883.6. (Figures exclude re-exports of $ G19.6 million).

Principal Trading Partners (US $ million, 1982): *Imports:* Canada 11.4; Trinidad and Tobago 122.8; United Kingdom 25.5; USA 55.2; Total (incl. others) 290.2. *Exports:* Trinidad and Tobago 27.6; United Kingdom 79.4; USA 93.6; Venezuela 56.0; Total (incl. others) 388.1.

TRANSPORT

Road Traffic ('000 vehicles in use, 1980): Passenger cars 32.5, Commercial vehicles 12.9 (Source: UN, *Statistical Yearbook*).

Shipping (international sea-borne freight traffic, estimates in '000 metric tons, 1985): Goods loaded 1,548; Goods unloaded 636 (Source: UN, *Monthly Bulletin of Statistics*).

Civil Aviation (1975): Passenger arrivals 42,210, departures 59,364; Freight loaded 2,438 tons, unloaded 1,297 tons.

COMMUNICATIONS MEDIA

Radio Receivers (1988): 365,000 in use (Source: UNESCO, *Statistical Yearbook*).

Television Receivers (1988): 16,000 in use (Source: UNESCO, *Statistical Yearbook*).

Telephones (1 January 1987): 33,000 in use (Source: UN, *Statistical Yearbook*).

Book Production (1983): 55 titles (16 books, 39 pamphlets) (Source: UNESCO, *Statistical Yearbook*).

EDUCATION

Pre-primary (1986): Institutions 349, Teachers 1,399 (1985), Students 25,316.

Primary (1986): Institutions 415, Teachers 3,948, Students 112,518.

Secondary (1985, excluding vocational courses): Teachers 2,087, Students 72,679.

Higher (1987): Teachers 509, Students 3,700.

Source: UNESCO, *Statistical Yearbook*.

Directory

The Constitution

Guyana became a republic, within the Commonwealth, on 23 February 1970. A new constitution was promulgated on 6 October 1980. Its main provisions are summarized below:

The Constitution declares the Co-operative Republic of Guyana to be an indivisible, secular, democratic sovereign state in the course of transition from capitalism to socialism. The bases of the political, economic and social system are political and economic independence, involvement of citizens and socio-economic groups, such as co-operatives and trade unions, in the decision-making processes of the State and in management, social ownership of the means of production, national economic planning and co-operativism as the principle of socialist transformation. Personal property, inheritance, the right to work, with equal pay for men and women engaged in equal work, free medical attention, free education and social benefits for old age and disability are guaranteed. Individual political rights are subject to the principles of national sovereignty and democracy, and freedom of expression to the State's duty to ensure fairness and balance in the dissemination of information to the public. Relations with other countries are guided by respect for human rights, territorial integrity and non-intervention.

THE PRESIDENT

The President is the supreme executive authority, Head of State and Commander-in-Chief of the armed forces, elected for a term of office, usually of five years' duration, with no limit on re-election. The successful presidential candidate is the nominee of the party with the largest number of votes in the legislative elections. The President may prorogue or dissolve the National Assembly (in the case of dissolution, fresh elections must be held immediately) and has discretionary powers to postpone elections for up to one year at a time for up to five years. The President may be removed from office on medical grounds, or for violation of the Constitution (with a two-thirds majority vote of the Assembly), or for gross misconduct (with a three-quarters majority vote of the Assembly if allegations are upheld by a tribunal).

The President appoints a First Vice-President and Prime Minister who must be an elected member of the National Assembly, and a Cabinet of Ministers, which includes non-elected members and is collectively responsible to the legislature. The President also appoints a Minority Leader, who is the elected member of the Assembly deemed by the President most able to command the support of the opposition.

THE LEGISLATURE

The legislative body is a unicameral National Assembly of 65 members; 53 members are elected by universal adult suffrage in a system of proportional representation, 10 members are elected by the 10 Regional Democratic Councils and two members are elected by the National Congress of Local Democratic Organs. The Assembly passes bills, which are then presented to the President, and may pass constitutional amendments.

LOCAL GOVERNMENT

Guyana is divided into 10 Regions, each having a Regional Democratic Council elected for a term of up to five years and four months, although it may be prematurely dissolved by the President. Local councillors elect from among themselves deputies to the National Congress of Democratic Organs. This Congress and the National Assembly together form the Supreme Congress of the People of Guyana, a deliberative body which may be summoned, dissolved or prorogued by the President and is automatically dissolved along with the National Assembly.

OTHER PROVISIONS

Impartial commissions exist for the judiciary, the public service and the police service. An Ombudsman is appointed, after consultation between the President and the Minority Leader, to hold office for four years.

Note: In February 1988 the National Assembly approved a constitutional amendment which ended the Government's obligation, as stipulated in the 1980 Constitution, to consult with trade unions and co-operative bodies on matters of labour legislation. The amendment also provided that any law enacted by the National Assembly could not be declared invalid on the grounds of inconsistency with previous constitutions.

GUYANA
Directory

The Government

HEAD OF STATE

President: HUGH DESMOND HOYTE (assumed office 6 August 1985; sworn in as elected President 12 December 1985).

CABINET
(February 1991)

President and Minister of Home Affairs and Public Information: HUGH DESMOND HOYTE.

Vice-Presidents

Prime Minister and First Vice-President: HAMILTON GREEN.
Deputy Prime Minister and Vice-President for Culture and Social Development: VIOLA BURNHAM.
Deputy Prime Minister and Vice-President in the Office of the President: RANJI CHANDISINGH.

Senior Ministers

Attorney-General and Minister of Justice: KEITH STANISLAUS MASSIAH.
Deputy Prime Minister and Minister of Planning and Development: WILLIAM HASLYN PARRIS.
Deputy Prime Minister and Minister of Public Utilities: ROBERT CORBIN.
Minister of Agriculture: Dr PATRICK MCKENZIE.
Minister of Communications and Works: JULES R. KRANENBURG.
Minister of Education: DERYCK BERNARD.
Minister of Finance: CARL B. GREENIDGE.
Minister of Foreign Affairs: (vacant).
Minister of Health and Public Welfare: NOEL BLACKMAN.
Minister of Regional Planning: JEFFREY THOMAS.
Minister of Trade and Tourism: WINSTON MURRAY.
Minister in the Ministry of Planning and Development: SEERAM PRASHAD.
Minister in the Office of the President: YVONNE HAREWOOD-BENN.

Ministers

Minister of Agriculture: VIBERT PARVATTAN.
Minister of Home Affairs and Public Information: STELLA ODIE-ALLI.
Minister of Public Services: Dr FAITH HARDING.
Minister of Labour and Co-operatives: PANDIT CHINTAMAN GOWKARRAN SHARMA.
Minister in the Ministry of Public Utilities: SHARAMDHEO SAWH.
Minister in the Ministry of Regional Planning: URMIA E. JOHNSON.

Minister of State

Ministry of Culture and Social Development: JEAN PERSICO.

MINISTRIES

Office of the President: New Garden St, Georgetown; tel. (2) 51330 telex 2205; fax (2) 63395.
Ministry of Agriculture: POB 1001, Regent and Vlissingen Rds, Georgetown; tel. (2) 69154.
Ministry of Communications and Works: Oranapai Towers, Wight's Lane, Kingston, Georgetown; tel. (2) 71511.
Ministry of Labour and Co-operatives: Homestretch Ave, D'Urban Park, Georgetown; tel. (2) 57070.
Ministry of Education and Social Development: 26 Brickdam, Stabroek, POB 1014, Georgetown; tel. (2) 54163.
Ministry of Energy and Mines: 41 Brickdam, Georgetown; tel. (2) 66549.
Ministry of Finance: Main and Urquhart Sts, Georgetown; tel. (2) 67241.
Ministry of Foreign Affairs: Takuba Lodge, 254 New Garden St and South Rd, Georgetown; tel. (2) 61606; telex 2220.
Ministry of Health and Public Welfare: Homestretch Ave, D'Urban Park, Georgetown; tel. (2) 65861.
Ministry of Home Affairs and Public Information: 6 Brickdam, Stabroek, Georgetown; tel. (2) 65861.
Ministry of Trade and Tourism: 95 Carmichael St, Georgetown; tel. (2) 62505; telex 2288.
Ministry of Justice and Office of Attorney-General: 95 Carmichael St, Georgetown; tel. (2) 62616.
Ministry of Labour and Co-operatives: Homestretch Ave, D'Urban Park, Georgetown; tel. (2) 57070.
Ministry of Regional Planning: 1 Water and Cornhill Sts, Stabroek, Georgetown; tel. (2) 56590.

Legislature

NATIONAL ASSEMBLY

Speaker: SASE NARAIN.

Election, 9 December 1985

Party	Votes	%	Seats
People's National Congress	228,718	78.55	42
People's Progressive Party	45,926	15.77	8
United Force	9,810	3.37	2
Working People's Alliance	4,176	1.43	1
Democratic Labour Movement	2,157	0.74	—
People's Democratic Movement	232	0.08	—
National Democratic Front	156	0.05	—
Total	291,175	100.00	53

In addition to the 53 elected members, the Assembly has 12 regional representatives.

Political Organizations

National Republican Party (NRP): Georgetown; f. 1990 after a split with URP; right-wing; Leader ROBERT GANGADEEN.

Patriotic Coalition for Democracy (PCD): Georgetown; f. 1986 by five opposition parties; the PCD campaigns for an end to alleged electoral malpractices; principal offices, including the chair of the collective leadership, rotate among the parties; now comprises the following four parties:

  Democratic Labour Movement (DLM): 34 Robb and King Sts, 4 floor, Lacytown, POB 10930, Georgetown; f. 1983; democratic-nationalist; Pres. PAUL NEHRU TENNASSEE; Gen. Sec. JAINARAYAN SINGH.

  People's Democratic Movement (PDM): Georgetown; tel. (2) 64707; f. 1973; centrist; Leader LLEWELLYN JOHN.

  People's Progressive Party (PPP): 41 Robb St, Georgetown; tel. (2) 72095; f. 1950; Marxist-Leninist; Gen. Sec. Dr CHEDDI B. JAGAN.

  Working People's Alliance (WPA): Walter Rodney House, 45 Croal St, Stabroek, Georgetown; originally popular pressure group, became political party 1979; independent Marxist; Collective Leadership: EUSI KWAYANA, Dr RUPERT ROOPNARINE.

People's National Congress (PNC): Congress Place, Sophia, POB 10330, Georgetown; tel. (2) 57850; f. 1955 after a split with the PPP; socialist; Leader HUGH DESMOND HOYTE; Gen. Sec. SEERAM PRASHAD.

United Force (UF): 96 Robb St, Bourda, Georgetown; right-wing; advocates rapid industrialization through govt partnership and private capital; Leader MARCELLUS FEILDEN SINGH.

United Republican Party (URP): Georgetown; f. 1985; right-wing.

In January 1989 a civic movement named **Guyanese Action for Reform and Democracy (Guard;** Leader LESLIE RAMSAMMY) was formed, committed to campaigning for constitutional and legal reforms and revised electoral practices.

Diplomatic Representation

EMBASSIES AND HIGH COMMISSIONS IN GUYANA

Brazil: 308 Church St, Queenstown, POB 10489, Georgetown; tel. (2) 57970; telex 2246; Ambassador: ADERBAL COSTA.

Canada: High and Young Streets, POB 10880, Georgetown; tel. (2) 72081; telex 2215; fax (2) 58380; High Commissioner: FRANK JACKMAN.

China, People's Republic: 108 Duke St, Kingston, Georgetown; tel. (2) 71651; tel. (2) 2251; Ambassador: YANG ZENGYE.

Colombia: 306 Church and Peter Rose Sts, Queenstown, Georgetown; tel. (2) 71410; telex 2200; Ambassador: BENILDO OSPINA CAICEDO.

GUYANA

Cuba: 46 High St, Kingston, Georgetown; tel. (2) 66732; telex 2272; Ambassador: LÁZARO CABEZAS GONZÁLEZ.

Germany: 70 Murray and Main Sts, Georgetown; tel. (2) 61089; telex 2273; Ambassador: (vacant).

India: 10 Ave of the Republic, Georgetown; tel. (2) 63996; telex 3025; High Commissioner: G. D. ATUK.

Jamaica: Camp St, Georgetown; tel. (2) 69517; telex 226; High Commissioner: (vacant).

Korea, Democratic People's Republic: 88 Premniranjan Place, Georgetown; tel. (2) 60266; telex 2228; Ambassador: CHONG JON-GYU.

Libya (People's Bureau): 375 Ganges St, Prashad Nagar, Georgetown; tel. (2) 61697; telex 2259; Chargé d'affaires: AHMED IBRAHIM EHIWASS.

Suriname: 304 Church St, POB 10508, Georgetown; tel. (2) 67844; telex 2282; Ambassador: JOHN KOLADER.

USSR: 48 Chandra Nagar St, Prashad Nagar, Georgetown; tel. (2) 72975; telex 2277; Ambassador: MIKHAIL A. SOBOLEV.

United Kingdom: 44 Main St, POB 10849, Georgetown; tel. (2) 65881; telex 2221; fax (2) 53555; High Commissioner: R. D. GORDON.

USA: 31 Main St, Georgetown; tel. (2) 54900; telex 2213; Ambassador: GEORGE JONES.

Venezuela: 296 Thomas St, Georgetown; tel. (2) 61543; telex 2237; Ambassador: ENRIQUE PEINADO BARRIOS.

Yugoslavia: 72 Brickdam, POB 10408, Georgetown; tel. (2) 71136; telex 2231; Ambassador: MARIN GERSKOVIĆ.

Judicial System

The Judicature of Guyana comprises the Supreme Court of Judicature, which consists of a Court of Appeal and a High Court (both of which are superior courts of record), and a number of Courts of Summary Jurisdiction.

The Court of Appeal, which came into operation in June 1966, consists of the Chancellor as President, the Chief Justice, and such number of Justices of Appeal as may be prescribed by the National Assembly.

The High Court of the Supreme Court consists of the Chief Justice as President of the Court and Puisne Judges. Its jurisdiction is both original and appellate. It has criminal jurisdiction in matters brought before it on indictment. A person convicted by the Court has a right of appeal to the Guyana Court of Appeal. The High Court of the Supreme Court has unlimited jurisdiction in civil matters and exclusive jurisdiction in probate, divorce and admiralty and certain other matters. Under certain circumstances, appeal in civil matters lies either to the Full Court of the High Court of the Supreme Court, which is composed of not less than two judges, or to the Guyana Court of Appeal.

A magistrate has jurisdiction to determine claims where the amount involved does not exceed a certain sum of money, specified by law. Appeal lies to the Full Court.

Chancellor of Justice: KENNETH M. GEORGE.

Chief Justice: RUDOLPH H. HARPER.

Attorney-General: KEITH STANISLAUS MASSIAH.

Religion

CHRISTIANITY

Guyana Council of Churches: 71 Murray St, Georgetown; tel. (2) 66610; f. 1967 by merger of the Christian Social Council (f. 1937) and the Evangelical Council (f. 1960); 15 mem. churches, 1 assoc. mem.; Chair. Rt Rev. RANDOLPH O. GEORGE (Anglican Bishop of Guyana); Sec. MICHAEL MCCORMACK.

The Anglican Communion

Anglicans in Guyana are adherents of the Church in the Province of the West Indies, comprising eight dioceses. The Archbishop of the Province is the Bishop of the North Eastern Caribbean and Aruba, resident in St John's, Antigua. The diocese of Guyana also includes French Guiana and Suriname. In 1986 the estimated membership in the country was 125,000.

Bishop of Guyana: Rt Rev. RANDOLPH OSWALD GEORGE, Austin House, Georgetown; tel. (2) 64183.

The Baptist Church

The Baptist Convention of Guyana: POB 101030, Georgetown; tel. (2) 60428; Chair. Rev. ALFRED JULIEN.

The Lutheran Church

The Lutheran Church in Guyana: 28–29 North and Alexander Sts, Lacytown, Georgetown; tel. (2) 64227; 14,147 mems; Pres. JAMES LOCHAN.

The Roman Catholic Church

Guyana comprises the single diocese of Georgetown, suffragan to the archdiocese of Port of Spain, Trinidad and Tobago. At 31 December 1988 there were an estimated 86,619 adherents in the country. The Bishop participates in the Antilles Episcopal Conference, based in Kingston, Jamaica.

Bishop of Georgetown: G. BENEDICT SINGH, Bishop's House, 27 Brickdam, POB 10720, Georgetown; tel. (2) 64469.

Other Christian Churches

Other denominations active in Guyana include the African Methodist Episcopal Church, the African Methodist Episcopal Zion Church, the Church of God, the Church of the Nazarene, the Ethiopian Orthodox Church, the Guyana Baptist Mission, the Guyana Congregational Union, the Guyana Presbyterian Church, the Hallelujah Church, the Methodist Church in the Caribbean and the Americas, the Moravian Church and the Presbytery of Guyana.

HINDUISM

Hindu Religious Centre: Maha Sabha, 162 Lamaha St, Georgetown; tel. (2) 57443; f. 1934; Hindus account for about one-third of the population; Pres. SASE NARAIN.

ISLAM

Guyana United Sad'r Islamic Anjuman: 157 Alexander St, Kitty, POB 10715, Georgetown; tel. (2) 69620; f. 1936; 120,000 mems; Pres. Haji ABDOOL RAHMAN; Sec. Haji S. M. YASEEN.

The Press

The Constitution does not provide for complete freedom of expression, and indirect press censorship is exercised by state control of newsprint.

DAILY

Guyana Chronicle: 2A Lama Ave, Bel Air Park, POB 11, Georgetown; tel. (2) 61576; fax (2) 60658; f. 1881; govt-owned; also produces weekly *Sunday Chronicle* (tel. (2) 63243); Editor-in-Chief RASCHID OSMAN; circ. 60,000 (weekdays), 100,000 (Sundays).

WEEKLIES AND PERIODICALS

The Catholic Standard: 293 Oronoque St, Queenstown, POB 10720, Georgetown; tel. (2) 61540; f. 1905; weekly; Editor Fr ANDREW MORRISON; circ. 10,000.

Diocesan Magazine: 144 Almond and Oronoque Sts, Queenstown, Georgetown; quarterly.

Guyana Business: 156 Waterloo St, POB 10110, Georgetown; tel. (2) 56451; f. 1889; organ of the Georgetown Chamber of Commerce and Industry; quarterly; Editor C. D. KIRTON.

Guynews: 18 Brickdam, Georgetown; monthly.

Labour Advocate: 61 Hadfield St, Werkenrust, Georgetown; weekly.

Mirror: Lot 8, Industrial Estate, Ruimveldt, Greater Georgetown; tel. (2) 62471; organ of the People's Progressive Party; owned by the New Guyana Co Ltd; Sundays; Editor JANET JAGAN; circ. 20,000.

New Nation: Sophia Exhibition Site, Georgetown; tel. (2) 68520; f. 1955; organ of the People's National Congress; weekly; Editor ADAM E. HARRIS; circ. 26,000.

The Official Gazette of Guyana: Guyana Public Communications Agency, 18–20 Brickdam, Georgetown; weekly; circ. 1,156.

Ratoon: 215 King St, Georgetown; monthly.

Stabroek News: 46–47 Robb St, Lacytown, Georgetown; tel. (2) 57473; f. 1986; 3 a week; pro-business independent; Editor DAVID DE CAIRES; circ. 17,000 (midweek), 22,000 (weekend).

Thunder: 41 Robb St, Georgetown; f. 1950; organ of the People's Progressive Party; quarterly; Editor CLINTON COLLYMORE; circ. 10,000.

NEWS AGENCIES

Guyana News Agency: Lama Ave, Bel Air Park, Georgetown; tel. (2) 54294; telex 2210; f. 1981; govt-operated; Editor-in-Chief W. HENRY SKERRETT.

GUYANA

Guyana Public Communications Agency: 18 Brickdam, Stabroek, Georgetown; tel. (2) 72025; telex 2210; fax (2) 60658; f. 1989; disseminates information about Guyana; Exec. Chair CHRISTOPHER NASCIMENTO; Dir, Information Services KESTER ALVES; Chief Admin Officer MELISSA HUMPHREY.

Foreign Bureaux

Inter Press Service (Italy): Suites 7 and 8, Federation Bldg, Croal St, Stabroek, Georgetown; tel. (2) 53213; Correspondent LINDSAY DAVIDSON.

Telegrafnoye Agentstvo Sovetskovo Soyuza (TASS) (USSR): Georgetown; Correspondent ALEKSANDR KAMISHEV.

United Press International (UPI) (USA): Georgetown; tel. (2) 65153; Correspondent DESIRÉE HARPER.

Xinhua (New China) News Agency (People's Republic of China): 52 Brickdam, Stabroek, Georgetown; tel. (2) 69965; Correspondent CHEN JING.

Associated Press (USA) is also represented.

PRESS ASSOCIATION

Guyana Press Association: Georgetown; revived in 1988; Pres. COURTNEY GIBSON.

Publisher

Guyana National Printers Ltd: 1 Public Rd, La Penitence, POB 10256, Greater Georgetown; tel. (2) 53623; telex 2212; f. 1939; govt-owned printers and publishers; Gen. Man. NOVEAR DEFREITAS.

Radio

In 1988 there were an estimated 365,000 radio receivers and 16,000 television receivers in use.

Guyana Broadcasting Corporation (GBC): St Phillips Green and High Sts, POB 10760, Georgetown; tel. (2) 58584; f. 1979; formed by merger of the Guyana Broadcasting Service and the Broadcasting Co Ltd (Radio Demerara) when the Government took over the assets of the latter; operates chanels GBC 1 (Coastal Service) and GBC 2 (National Service); Exec. Chair. J. L. PHILADELPHIA; Gen. Man. J. D. SYDNEY.

Guyana Television Corporation: Georgetown; govt-owned; limited service.

Two private stations relay US satellite television programmes.

Finance

(dep. = deposits; m. = million; brs = branches; amounts in Guyana dollars)

BANKING
Central Bank

Bank of Guyana: 1 Church St and Ave of the Republic, POB 1003, Georgetown; tel. (2) 63250; telex 2267; fax (2) 72965; f. 1965; assets $ G10,910.5m. (Dec. 1988); central bank of note issue; Gov. PATRICK E. MATTHEWS; Dep. Gov. ARCHIBALD L. MEREDITH.

Commercial Banks

Guyana Co-operative Agricultural and Industrial Development Bank: Lot 126, Parade and Barrack Sts, Kingston, Georgetown; tel. (2) 58808; fax (2) 68260; f. 1973; Man. Dir CYRIL K. HUNTE; 10 brs.

Guyana Co-operative Mortgage Finance Bank: 46 Main St, POB 1083, Georgetown; tel. (2) 68415; f. 1973; Man. Dir ALFRED E. O. BOBB.

Guyana National Co-operative Bank: 1 Lombard and Cornhill Sts, POB 242, Georgetown; tel. (2) 57810-9; telex 2235; fax (2) 60231; f. 1970; Man. Dir STEPHEN G. BACKER; Dep. Man. Dir JOHN ALLEYNE; 12 brs.

National Bank of Industry and Commerce: 38–40 Water St, POB 10440, Georgetown; tel. (2) 64095; telex 3044; fax (2) 72921; Man. Dir RAYMOND ACKLOO; 1 br.

Republic Bank for Trade and Industry Ltd: Water St, POB 10280, Georgetown; tel. (2) 68431; telex 2222; fax (2) 71612; f. 1990 by merger of Guyana Bank for Trade and Industry (frmly Barclays Bank) and Republic Bank (frmly Chase Manhattan Bank); Gen. Man. MARGUERITE DA SILVA; 2 brs.

Foreign Banks

Bank of Baroda (India): 10 Regent St and Ave of the Republic, POB 10768, Georgetown; tel. (2) 64005; telex 2243; f. 1908.

Bank of Nova Scotia (Canada): Alico Bldg, Regent and Hincks Sts, POB 10631; Georgetown; tel. (2) 64031; Man. RUBEN R. SALAZAR.

INSURANCE

Demerara Mutual Life Assurance Society Ltd: Demerara Life Bldg, 61 Ave of the Republic, POB 10409, Georgetown; tel. (2) 58991; fax (2) 58288; f. 1891; Chair. RICHARD B. FIELDS; Gen. Man. EAWAN E. DEVONISH.

Guyana Co-operative Insurance Service: 47 Main St, Georgetown; tel. (2) 68421; telex 2255; f. 1976; Chair. B. CLAUDE BONE; Gen. Man. HAROLD WILSON; Sec. D. COLE.

Guyana and Trinidad Mutual Life Insurance Co Ltd: Lots 27–29, Robb and Hincks Sts, Georgetown; tel. (2) 57912; fax (2) 59397; f. 1925; Chair. GEORGE U. JAIKARAN; Man. Dir R. E. CHEONG; affiliated company: Guyana and Trinidad Mutual Fire Insurance Co Ltd.

Hand-in-Hand Mutual Fire and Life Group: 1–4 Avenue of the Republic, POB 10188, Georgetown; tel. (2) 51867; fax (2) 57519; f. 1865; fire and life insurance; Chair. J. A. CHIN; Gen. Man. F. W. SPOONER.

There are also several foreign insurance companies operating in Guyana.

Insurance Association

Insurance Association of Guyana: 54 Robb St, Bourda, POB 10741, Georgetown; tel. (2) 63514; f. 1968.

STOCK EXCHANGE

In July 1989 the Government announced that it intended to establish a national securities exchange, with a view to becoming a member of the proposed regional stock exchange.

Trade and Industry

CHAMBER OF COMMERCE

Georgetown Chamber of Commerce and Industry: 156 Waterloo St, Cummingsburg, POB 10110, Georgetown; tel. (2) 56451; f. 1889; 104 mems; Pres. DENIS E. MOORE; Chief Exec. G. C. FUNG-ON.

PRODUCERS' ORGANIZATIONS

Consultative Association of Guyanese Industry Ltd: 78 Church and Carmichael Sts, POB 10730, Georgetown; tel. (2) 57170; f. 1962; 193 mems, 3 mem. asscns, 159 assoc. mems; Chair. H. B. DAVIS; Exec. Dir DAVID YANKANA.

Forest Products Association of Guyana: 6 Croal St and Manget Place, Georgetown; tel. (2) 69848; f. 1944; 43 mems; Pres. IDRIS DEEN; Exec. Officer WARREN PHOENIX.

Guyana Manufacturers' Association Ltd: 8 Church St, Company Path, Georgetown; tel. (2) 66791; fax (2) 66822; f. 1967; Pres. ALSTON AMIN KISSOON; Exec. Sec. NATHANIEL RAGNAUTH.

Guyana Rice Producers' Association: Lot 104 Regent St, Lacytown, Georgetown; tel. (2) 64411; f. 1946; c. 35,000 families; Pres. BUDRAM MAHADEO; Gen. Sec. PARIAG SUKHAI.

STATE AGENCIES AND MARKETING ORGANIZATIONS

Guyana's major industrial companies were nationalized during the 1970s, and the state sector predominates in the economy. Since 1982, however, the Government has transferred some industries to private ownership.

Bauxite Industry Development Company Ltd: 71 Main St, Georgetown; tel. (2) 57780; telex 2244; fax (2) 67413; f. 1976; holding company of Guyana Mining Enterprise Ltd; Chair. BERNARD CRAWFORD.

   Guyana Mining Enterprise Ltd (Guymine): East Bank, Berbice; tel. (3) 22336; telex 2245; f. 1977 by merger of Guyana Bauxite Co (Guybau) and Berbice Mining Enterprises; Chair. DUNSTAN BARROW.

Guyana Agency for the Environment: Georgetown; tel. (2) 57523; fax (2) 57524; f. 1988; f. 1988; monitors and formulates and implements policies on the environment; Dir Dr WALTER CHIN.

Guyana Electricity Corporation (GEC): 40 Main St, Georgetown; tel. (2) 62601; telex 2250; state-owned company (member of Guystac); responsible for the production, transmission, development and distribution of the public electricity supply; Gen. Man. NARVON PERSAUD.

Guyana Liquor Corporation: 8–11 Water and Schumaker Sts, Georgetown; tel. (2) 64404; telex 2284; fax (2) 50686; holding co for Demerara Distillers Ltd (f. 1700; taken over by Govt 1975); Exec. Chair. (vacant).

GUYANA
Directory

Demerara Distillers Ltd: 44 High St, Kingston, Georgetown; tel. (2) 61315; telex 2284; fax (2) 58686; Exec. Chair. YESU PERSAUD.

Guyana Marketing Corporation: Lombard St, Georgetown; tel. (2) 65846; Chair. Dr P. MCKENZIE; Gen. Man. KELVIN CRAIG.

Guyana National Engineering Corporation: see section on Shipping.

Guyana National Trading Corporation Ltd: see section on Shipping.

Guyana Natural Resources Agency (GNRA): 41 Brickdam and Boyle Pl., POB 1074, Stabroek, Georgetown; tel. (2) 66549; telex 3010; fax (2) 71211; f. 1986; management and development of natural resources; Exec. Chair. WINSTON M. KING; Dep. Chair. Dr BARTON SCOTLAND.

Guyana Oil Co Ltd: Providence, East Bank, Demerara; tel. (2) 62877; telex 2291.

Guyana Pharmaceutical Corporation Ltd: 1 Public Rd, La Penitence, Georgetown; tel. (2) 54700; telex 2203; fax (2) 57362; pharmaceuticals, chemicals, cosmetics; Exec. Chair. WILFRED A. (GUS) LEE; Finance Dir. CLYDE DOUGLAS.

Guyana Public Communications Agency: Georgetown; f. 1989, frmly Ministry of Information; Exec. Chair. KIT NASCIMENTO.

Guyana Rice Board: 1-2 Water St, Georgetown; tel. (2) 62480; telex 2266; f. 1973 to develop the rice industry and promote the expansion of its export trade, and to engage in industrial, commercial and agricultural activities necessary for the development of the rice industry; Exec. Chair. DARLENE HARRIS.

Guyana Stockfeeds Ltd: Farm, East Bank, Demerara; tel. (2) 63402; telex 2203; f. 1960; manufacture of poultry feeds.

Guyana Stores Ltd: 22 Church St, POB 10560, Georgetown; tel. (2) 66171; telex 2212; retailers and wholesalers; shares due to be sold in 1990; Chair. PAUL CHAN-A-SUE.

Guyana Sugar Corporation Ltd (Guysuco): 22 Church St, POB 10547, Georgetown; tel. (2) 66171; telex 2265; fax (2) 57274; f. 1976; Chair. HAROLD B. DAVIS; Sec. C. J. LAWRENCE.

Livestock Development Co Ltd: 58 High St, Georgetown; tel. (2) 61601.

DEVELOPMENT AGENCIES

Guyana-Libya Fishing Co: Houston, East Bank, Demerara; tel. (2) 54382; joint venture between the Govts of Guyana and Libya to develop fishing potential; Chair. F. G. DORWAY.

Guyana Manufacturing and Industrial Development Agency (Guymida): 237 Camp St, Cummingsburg, Georgetown; tel. (2) 62434; fax (2) 61492; f. 1984; provision of technical and managerial advice and assistance; development of entrepreneurial skills; identification of industrial potential; Exec. Dir. C. D. M. DUNCAN; Man, Industrial Operations M. MARIANO; Man, Admin C. WILSON; Man, Finance C. WADDY.

Mahaica-Mahaicony-Abary/Agricultural Development Authority (MMA-ADA): Onverwagt, West Coast, Berbice; tel. (2) 53591; telex 3055; f. 1977; aims to bring Berbice-Abary region into full agricultural production; Gen. Man. T. A. EARLE.

State Planning Commission: 229 South St, Lacytown, Georgetown; tel. (2) 68093; fax (2) 72499; Chief Planning Officer CLYDE ROOPCHAND.

CO-OPERATIVE SOCIETIES

Chief Co-operatives Development Officer: Ministry of Labour and Co-operatives, Homestretch Ave, D'Urban Park, Georgetown; tel. (2) 57070; M. G. EDGHILL.

In October 1988 there were 1,459 registered co-operative societies, mainly savings clubs and agricultural credit societies, with a total membership of over 100,000.

TRADE UNIONS

Federation of Independent Trade Unions in Guyana (FITUG): Georgetown; f. Oct. 1988 by seven independent unions that withdrew from the Trades Union Congress (see below); one union, the GPSU, withdrew in May 1989; Pres. GEORGE DANIELS; Sec. BIRCHMORE PHILADELPHIA.

Clerical and Commercial Workers' Union (CCWU): Clerico House, 140 Quamina St, South Cummingsburg, POB 101045, Georgetown; tel. (2) 52822; Gen. Sec. BIRCHMORE PHILADELPHIA.

Guyana Agricultural and General Workers' Union (GAWU): 104-106 Regent St, Lacytown, Georgetown; tel. (2) 72091; allied to the PPP; Gen. Sec. KOMAL CHAND; 20,000 mems.

Guyana Bauxite Supervisors' Union: Linden; Gen. Sec. LINCOLN LEWIS.

Guyana Mine Workers' Union: 784 Determa St, Mackenzie, Linden; tel. (4) 3146; Pres. ASHTON ANGEL; Gen. Sec. CHRISTOPHER JAMES; 5,800 mems.

National Association of Agricultural, Commercial and Industrial Employees: 64 High St, Kingston, Georgetown; tel. (2) 72301; f. 1946; Pres. B. KHUSIEL; Gen. Sec. NANDA K. GOPAUL; c. 2,000 mems.

University of Guyana Workers' Union: Turkeyen, Georgetown; supporter of Working People's Alliance; Pres. Fr MALCOLM RODRIGUES.

Trades Union Congress (TUC): Critchlow Labour College, Woolford Ave, Nonpareil Park, Georgetown; tel. (2) 61493; national trade union body; 17 affiliated unions; Pres. FRANK ANDREWS; Gen. Sec. JOSEPH POLLYDORE.

Amalgamated Transport and General Workers' Union: 46 Urquhart St, Georgetown; tel. (2) 66243; Pres. FRANK ANDREWS.

General Workers' Union: 106-107 Lamaha St, North Cummingsburg, Georgetown; tel. (2) 61185; f. 1954; terminated affiliation to People's National Congress in 1989; Pres. NORRIS WITTER; Gen. Sec. EDWIN JAMES; 3,000 mems.

Guyana Labour Union: 198 Camp St, Georgetown; tel. (2) 63275; Pres.-Gen. DESMOND HOYTE; 6,000 mems.

Guyana Postal and Telecommunication Workers' Union: 310 East St, POB 10352, Georgetown; tel. (2) 65255; Pres. SELWYN O. FELIX; Gen. Sec. ANJOU DANIELS.

Guyana Public Service Union (GPSU): 160 Regent Rd and New Garden St, Georgetown; tel. (2) 61770; founder mem. of FITUG in 1988; withdrew in May 1989; Pres. ADOLPH FARLEY; 11,600 mems.

Transport

RAILWAYS

There are no public railways in Guyana.

Guyana Mining Enterprise Railway: Mackenzie, Linden; tel. (4) 2484; bauxite transport; 48 km of line, Itumi to Linden; Superintendent R. C. KISSOON.

Port Kaituma-Matthews Ridge Railway: Port Kaituma; transport of minerals; 40 km, in north-west of country; Gen. Man. (vacant).

ROADS

The coastal strip has a well-developed road system. There are more than 3,000 miles (4,830 km) of paved and good-weather roads and trails. Construction of a long-delayed road link between Guyana and Brazil commenced in 1989; the first phase would connect Lethem (Guyana) with Kurupukari (Brazil). Germany was to provide a grant of US $3.5m. for road repairs as part of the Economic Recovery Programme, which was launched in April 1989.

Guyana Transport Services Ltd: Nelson Mandela Ave, Industrial Site, Ruimveldt, Greater Georgetown; tel. (2) 58261; f. 1971; transferred to private ownership 1989; provides road haulage and bus services; Gen Man. R VAN VELZEN.

SHIPPING

Guyana's principal ports are at Georgetown and New Amsterdam. A ferry service is operated between Guyana and Suriname. Communications with the interior are chiefly by river, although access is hindered by rapids and falls. There are 607 miles (1,077 km) of navigable rivers. The main rivers are the Mazaruni, the Potaro, the Essequibo, the Demerara and the Berbice.

John Fernandes Ltd: 24 Water St, Georgetown; tel. (2) 56294; telex 2226; ship agents and stevedore contractors; reps for West Indies Shipping Corpn (WISCO), Bernuth Lines, SMS, Caribbean Liners and Rambarran Shipping; Man. B. A. FERNANDES.

Shipping Association of Georgetown: 28 Main and Holmes Sts, Georgetown; tel. (2) 62632; f. 1952; Chair. F. A. GRIFFITH; Sec. and Man. W. V. BRIDGEMOHAN; members:

Caribbean Molasses Co Ltd: Mud Lots 1-2, Water St, POB 10208, Georgetown; tel. (2) 69238; telex 2274; exporters of molasses in bulk; Man. Dir N. F. COOPER.

Guyana National Engineering Corporation Ltd: 1-9 Lombard St, Charlestown, POB 10520, Georgetown; tel. (2) 63291; telex 2218; govt-owned; metal foundry, ship building and repair, agents for Saguenay Shipping Ltd, Tec Lines Ltd, W.I. Shipping Co Inc, Ivaran Lines, Linhas Brasileiras de Navegação, SA, Shipping Corpn of India Ltd, Flota Mercante Grancolombiana, SA; Exec. Chair. CLAUDE SAUL.

Guyana National Shipping Corporation Ltd: 5-9 Lombard St, La Penitence, POB 10988, Georgetown; tel. (2) 66171; telex 2232;

GUYANA

govt-owned; reps for Harrison and Mitsui OSK Lines, Samba and Resolve Maritime Corpn, airline reservations, and Lloyd Agencies; Exec. Chair. P. A. CHAN-A-SUE.

Guyana National Trading Corporation Ltd: 45–47 Water St, POB 10480, Georgetown; tel. (2) 61666; telex 2214; govt-owned, but transfer to private ownership pending in 1990; importers and distributors; reps for Nedlloyd Lines, Himmelman Supply Co, Smit-Lloyd, Atlantic Chartering and Trading Co and K-Line; travel agents for BWIA (Trinidad and Tobago) and Guyana Airways; Exec. Chair. F. A. GRIFFITH.

CIVIL AVIATION

The main airport is Timehri International, 42 km (26 miles) from Georgetown. The more important settlements in the interior have airstrips.

Guyana Airways Corporation: 32 Main St, POB 102, Georgetown; tel. (2) 59490; telex 2242; f. 1939 as British Guiana Airways; renamed as above 1963; govt-owned; operates internal scheduled services and to the Caribbean, the USA and Suriname; Gen. Man. Capt. GUY N. SPENCE; fleet of 1 Twin Otter, 1 Boeing 707-320B, 2 HS-748.

There is a weekly flight, via Georgetown, from Caracas (Venezuela) to Port of Spain (Trinidad and Tobago) and Suriname.

Tourism

Despite the beautiful scenery in the interior of the country, Guyana has limited tourist facilities, and began some encouragement of tourism only in the late 1980s.

Guyana Overland Tours: 48 Prince's and Russell Sts, Charlestown, POB 10173, Georgetown; tel. (02) 69876; f. 1968.

HAITI

Introductory Survey

Location, Climate, Language, Religion, Flag, Capital

The Republic of Haiti occupies the western part of the Caribbean island of Hispaniola (the Dominican Republic occupies the remaining two-thirds) and some smaller offshore islands. Cuba, to the west, is less than 80 km away. The climate is tropical but the mountains and fresh sea winds mitigate the heat. Temperatures vary little with the seasons, and the annual average in Port-au-Prince is about 27°C (80°F). The rainy season is from May to November. The official languages are French and Creole. About 80% of the population belong to the Roman Catholic Church, the country's official religion, and other Christian churches are also represented. A form of witchcraft, known as voodoo, is the folk religion. The national flag (proportions 2 by 1) has two equal vertical stripes, of blue and red. The state flag has, in addition, a white rectangular panel, containing the national coat of arms (a palm tree, surmounted by a Cap of Liberty and flanked by flags and cannons), in the centre. The capital is Port-au-Prince.

Recent History

Haiti was first colonized in 1659 by the French, who named the island Saint-Domingue. A successful uprising between 1791 and 1803 by African-descended slaves established the country in 1804 as an independent state, ruled by Jean-Jacques Dessalines, who proclaimed himself Emperor of Haiti. Hostility between the negro population and the mulattos continued throughout the 19th century until, after increasing political instability, the USA intervened militarily and ruled the country from 1915 to 1934. Thereafter, mulatto presidents were in power until 1946, when a negro president, Dusmarsais Estimé, was elected. He was overthrown in 1950 by a military coup, led by another negro, Gen. Paul Magloire, who was himself forced to resign in 1956. In 1957 Dr François Duvalier, a country physician, was elected President.

Despite a promising start, the Duvalier administration soon became a dictatorship, maintaining its authority by means of a notorious private army, popularly called the Tontons Macoutes (Creole for 'Bogeymen'), who used extortion and intimidation to crush all possible opposition to the President's rule. In 1964 Duvalier's tenure was changed to that of President-for-Life, and he retained almost total power over the country, by means of violence and voodoo threats, until his death in April 1971. In January 1971 the Constitution was amended to allow Duvalier to nominate his successor. He promptly named his son, Jean-Claude Duvalier, who became President, at 19 years of age, on the day of his father's death.

The release of political prisoners and an amelioration of conditions, including the appointment of more moderate cabinet ministers, indicated that the regime was slightly more humane than its predecessor, with the increasing need for international aid pressurizing the Government to be responsive to human rights agencies and critical donor countries. The regime was characterized by frequent cabinet changes and alternating policies of tentative liberalization and subsequent repression. Elections took place in February 1979 for the 58-seat National Assembly. As 57 of the seats were won by the official government party, the Parti de l'Unité Nationale (PUN), demonstrations occurred, in protest against alleged electoral malpractice.

In mid-1979 three illegal Christian Democratic opposition parties were formed by critics of the Duvalier regime. In October 1979 a new press law was introduced, banning any criticism of the President, or of government or security officials, and any articles or broadcasts deemed to be subversive. The rearrest in October 1980 of Sylvio Claude, the leader of the Parti Démocratique Chrétien d'Haïti (PDCH), for alleged subversion was followed in November and December by more than 400 arrests of opposition politicians, journalists and broadcasters. Leading opponents of the regime were deported. Claude was sentenced to 15 years' hard labour in August 1981. Foreign criticism forced a retrial at which the sentence was reduced to six years, and in September 1982 Claude was released into house arrest, from which he subsequently escaped.

The first municipal elections for 25 years were held in 1983. President Duvalier had promised in April 1982 that they would be 'free, honest and democratic'. In the event, all the opposition candidates for the politically sensitive Port-au-Prince posts were arrested just before the polls. In the provincial constituencies allegations of electoral fraud were made. On 27 August the Assembly was dissolved when the Constitution was amended, reaffirming, however, the Presidency-for-Life and Duvalier's right to name his successor. Elections for the Assembly were held on 12 February 1984. All 59 seats were won by the pro-Duvalier party, PUN, as no opposition candidates were allowed. Respect for human rights deteriorated further, as all political activity and opposition newspapers were banned. Rioting in May and June against government corruption resulted in the dismissal of ministers who were held responsible for the disturbances, and further government changes in August helped to strengthen the power of uncompromising elements within the Government, especially that of Dr Roger Lafontant, the Minister of State for the Interior and National Defence.

Demonstrations were organized by the Roman Catholic Church and other religious groups to protest against widespread poverty and corruption in Haiti. In April 1985 Duvalier announced a programme of constitutional reforms, including the eventual appointment of a Prime Minister and the formation of political parties, subject to certain limiting conditions. A popular referendum, held in June, to endorse these changes and the concept of the Life Presidency resulted in a 99.98% vote in favour. Opposition leaders alleged widespread electoral fraud, and denounced the Government's liberalization measures as an insincere gesture, designed for the benefit of foreign aid donors. In September Roger Lafontant, the minister most closely identified with the Government's acts of repression, was dismissed. Unrest in the northern areas of Haiti was again reported in December, after the deaths of four students in an anti-Government demonstration in Gonaïves. Duvalier dismissed four of his principal ministers and reduced the prices of basic commodities in an attempt to prevent an escalation of the disturbances. Further measures to curb continued disorder were adopted in January 1986. The university and schools were closed indefinitely, and radio stations were forbidden to report on current events. Finally, Duvalier imposed a state of siege and declared martial law.

On 7 February 1986, following intensified public protests, Duvalier and his family fled from Haiti to exile in France, leaving a five-member National Council of Government (CNG), led by the Army Chief of Staff, Gen. Henri Namphy, to succeed him. The interim military-civilian Council announced the appointment of a new cabinet. The National Assembly was dissolved, and the Constitution was suspended. Later in the month, the Tontons Macoutes were disbanded, educational establishments were reopened, the traditional blue and red flag was restored, while plans were made to recover and nationalize Duvalier's vast assets. Prisoners from Haiti's largest gaol were freed under a general amnesty. In March US $26m. of US aid, which had been withheld since January in protest against abuses of human rights, was released.

However, after the initial euphoria following the downfall of Duvalier, renewed rioting occurred to protest against the inclusion in the new Government of known supporters of the former dictatorship. Curfews lasting 16 hours per day were imposed to quell the disturbances. In March there was a cabinet reshuffle, following the resignations of three Duvalierist members of the CNG (only one of whom was replaced). The new three-member CNG comprised Gen. Namphy, Col Williams Régala (Minister of the Interior and National Defence) and Jacques François (then Minister of Finance).

In April Gen. Namphy showed signs of positive action in the announcement, firstly, of a road-building programme, expected to provide 6,000 jobs, and, secondly, of a proposed time-table for elections to restore constitutional government by February 1988. He also announced that he would not be a candidate in the presidential election. The first of these elections, to select

41 people (from 101 candidates) who would form part of the 61-member Constituent Assembly which was to revise the Constitution, took place in October 1986. However, the level of participation at the election was only about 5%, owing to the absence of democratic tradition in Haiti and to the lack of adequate organization and publicity.

The new Constitution was approved by 99.8% of voters in a referendum held on 29 March 1987. An estimated 50% of the electorate voted. An independent Provisional Electoral Council (CEP) was appointed to supervise the presidential and legislative elections, which were scheduled for 29 November.

There was continued unrest in the country, and in June 1987 general strikes were organized in protest against the Government's attempt to dissolve the country's principal trade union, the Centrale Autonome des Travailleurs Haïtiens (CATH), and its decision to limit the authority of the CEP. Violent confrontations continued prior to the elections. Two presidential candidates were murdered, while 12 other potential candidates were barred from taking part in the election because of their connections with the Duvalier regime. On 29 November the elections were cancelled three hours after voting had begun, owing to renewed violence and killings, for which former members of the Tontons Macoutes were believed to be responsible. The Government dissolved the CEP and took control of the electoral process. In December a new CEP was appointed by the Government, and elections were rescheduled for 17 January 1988. In protest at the removal from office of the independent electoral body, four prominent opposition candidates announced that they would boycott the new presidential election, and demanded the resignation of the CNG. Voting took place as planned, however, and a former university professor, Leslie Manigat of the Rassemblement des Démocrates Nationaux Progressistes (RDNP), with 50.3% of the total votes cast, was declared the winner. Legislative and municipal elections were held concurrently. It was officially estimated that 35% of the electorate had voted in the elections, although opposition leaders claimed that only 5% had participated, and alleged that there had been extensive fraud and malpractice. Although the result of the presidential election was widely discredited, Manigat took office on 7 February 1988.

President Manigat's new Government included no pro-Duvalier members, an omission which led to increasing protests by Duvalier's supporters, as they attempted to regain the political initiative. In June 1988, as a result of a dispute between President Manigat and Gen. Namphy over changes in the military hierarchy, the President dismissed Gen. Namphy from office. However, three days later, on 20 June, President Manigat was overthrown by disaffected members of the army. He was replaced by Gen. Namphy, who appointed a Cabinet composed entirely of members of the armed forces, and removed all restrictions on the appointment of Duvalier's supporters to the Government. The legislature was dissolved, and the Constitution of 1987 was formally abrogated; the new administration announced its intention to draft a new constitution. Under the new regime, widespread atrocities involving the Tontons Macoutes culminated, in September, in an attack by a gang of armed civilians on the congregation at a church in Port-au-Prince. Thirteen people died and more than 80 were injured in the attack, which provoked international condemnation.

On 18 September 1988 Gen. Namphy was ousted in a coup, led by Brig.-Gen. Prosper Avril (who became President) and non-commissioned officers from the Presidential Guard, who advocated the introduction of radical reforms. A purge of Duvalier's supporters within the armed forces included the removal from office of eight generals; only one representative of the armed forces was appointed to the new Cabinet. In October an attempted coup by pro-Duvalier members of the army was thwarted. In November an independent electoral body, the Collège Electoral d'Haïti (CEDA), was established to supervise future elections, to draft an electoral law and to ensure proper registration of voters. In November Col Jean-Claude Paul, the former commander of the Dessalines barracks and a leading figure in the September coup (who had been indicted, in March, for drug-trafficking offences by a court in the USA), died in mysterious circumstances. Colonel Paul's death removed one of the principal obstacles to the resumption of US aid to Haiti.

In January 1989 the CATH organized a one-day general strike in support of demands for a reduction in the prices of basic products and for an increase in the minimum wage. In addition, the union demanded that persons accused of violations of human rights be put on trial. The strike was declared illegal by the Government.

In March 1989 President Avril partially restored the Constitution of 1987 and restated his intention to hold democratic elections. In the following month the Government survived two coup attempts by the Leopard Corps, the country's élite anti-subversion squadron, and the Dessalines battalion, based in Port-au-Prince. The catalyst to the rebellion by the Leopard Corps was apparently the dismissal of four colonels from the Corps for their alleged role in drug-trafficking. The US Government had insisted in March that President Avril take measures against those involved in the drug trade as a prerequisite for the resumption of aid. Following the suppression of the Leopard Corps rebellion, the three leaders of the coup were deported from Haiti. Within two days the Government was threatened by a second coup, by the Dessalines battalion, which demanded the resignation of the President, the full restoration of the Constitution of 1987, and early elections. The Presidential Guard suppressed the uprising within a few days. Independent reports claimed that more than 30 soldiers and five civilians had been killed during the fighting. The two rebelling battalions were subsequently disbanded, and the strength of Haiti's armed forces was reduced from about 7,500 to around 6,000 men.

President Avril reshuffled the Cabinet in May 1989, dismissing two leading pro-Duvalier ministers. In June he restored a further suspended clause in the Constitution regarding the immunity of the armed forces from prosecution. Other minor concessions, including a reduction in the price of petrol, were granted following a transport strike in early July. President Avril also announced that 'available' state-owned lands would be leased for nine years to 'needy families'. The best land, however, was already in the possession of wealthy owners, thus limiting the significance of the measure. In September President Avril published a timetable for elections that had been drafted by the CEP. According to the proposals, local and regional elections were to be held in April 1990, to be followed by national and legislative elections, in two rounds, in July and August. The presidential election, also in two rounds, was scheduled to take place in October and November 1990. (President Avril's schedule was, however, revised under the interim presidency of Ertha Pascal-Trouillot.) The opposition parties began to form alliances in preparation for the elections. In August 1989 the conservative former Minister of Finance, Marc Bazin, and the leader of the Parti Nationaliste Progressiste Révolutionnaire (PANPRA), Serge Gilles, established the Alliance Nationale pour la Démocratie et le Progrès (ANDP), and 25 left-wing groups, led by the CATH, the Confédération d'Unité Démocratique (KID) and the Assemblée Populaire Nationale (APN), united to form the Front contre la Répression.

In late September 1989 the opposition parties and the trade unions, supported by the National Chamber of Commerce, organized a widely-observed general strike in protest against increases in taxation, which had been introduced in accordance with an IMF stand-by agreement, concluded earlier that month. At the beginning of November the Rassemblement National (RN), a broadly-based opposition coalition including conservative and left-wing political organizations, announced plans for peaceful protests against the Government. Three leaders of the RN were subsequently arrested and severely beaten in custody. The arrests prompted the CATH and the RN to call a 48-hour general strike, which was fully observed in Port-au-Prince and most of the provincial towns. In mid-December President Avril reshuffled the Cabinet, replacing eight of the 13 ministers with politicians holding more moderate views. In early January 1990 President Avril visited the People's Republic of China and Taiwan. During his absence the RN proposed another general strike and further demonstrations. On 20 January, following his return to Haiti, President Avril, in an attempt to restore order and to prevent the continuation of anti-Government activities (a colonel of the presidential guard had been murdered), imposed a 30-day state of siege. Entry visas for Haitians were introduced, more than 50 politicians were arrested, and several opposition leaders were deported from the country. However, the state of siege was ended after 10 days and the entry visa requirement was rescinded. In early February President Avril announced that the exiled opposition leaders were to be permitted to return to Haiti to participate in the forthcoming elections. At the same time it was announced that all political prisoners had been released.

President Avril resigned in March 1990, in response to sustained popular and political opposition, together with diplomatic pressure from the USA. Before entering temporary exile in the USA, Avril ceded power to the Chief of the General Staff, Gen. Hérard Abraham, who subsequently transferred authority to Ertha Pascal-Trouillot, a member of the Supreme Court. As President of a civilian interim government, Pascal-Trouillot shared power with a 19-member Council of State, whose principal function was to assist the interim Government in preparing for the elections that were to be held later in the year. Violence involving opponents of the reform movement and the largely anti-Duvalierist population resulted in many deaths in the aftermath of Avril's resignation. In May a new Provisional Electoral Council (CEP), with responsibility for the organization and supervision of the forthcoming elections, was established. Relations between the Government and the Council of State began to deteriorate in late May, when Pascal-Trouillot appointed Marie Violère Legagneur, a Duvalierist, to her Cabinet without the approval of the Council of State. While Pascal-Trouillot favoured a conciliatory approach towards the Duvalierists, the Council of State considered that the exclusion of the Duvalierists from political activity was an essential prerequisite to the conduct of free elections. Legagneur resigned in the following month.

In late June 1990 four gunmen opened fire at an emergency session of the Council of State, killing two members. In July two former members of the Duvalier regime, Roger Lafontant and Brig.-Gen. Williams Regala (who was widely believed to have been an instigator of the November 1987 election-day violence), returned from exile abroad, despite the existence of a warrant for their arrest. The warrant was, however, ignored by the security forces. A strike was organized by political leaders and business executives, in support of demands for the arrest of the two Duvalierists, who were considered to represent a threat to the planned free elections. Amid threats of further strikes, the Council of State issued an ultimatum to Pascal-Trouillot, demanding her resignation should she fail to have Lafontant and Regala arrested. Relations between the interim President and the Council of State deteriorated further in August, when the Council of State passed a motion of censure against the Government, accusing it of corruption and incompetence. Later in the same month five ministers resigned and were replaced without the consent of the Council of State. In September the CEP announced the postponement, until mid-December, of the elections, owing to a delay in the arrival of necessary funds and materials from donor countries. In October the UN announced that, in accordance with a request by the Haitian Government, it would be sending 390 observers to oversee the elections.

In November 1990 the CEP declared invalid the candidacies for the presidency of Lafontant, the representative of newly-formed Union pour la Réconciliation Nationale, and of former president Manigat, who had been allowed to return from exile to contest the forthcoming presidential election as the candidate of the Rassemblement des Nationaux-Progressistes. Fourteen other candidates were, none the less, approved by the CEP. Among the most popular candidates for the presidency was Fr Jean-Bertrand Aristide, a left-wing Catholic priest who represented the Front National pour le Changement et la Démocratie (FNCD). Shortly before the elections, at least seven people were killed and more than 50 injured, when an attack was perpetrated, allegedly by former members of the Tontons Macoutes, on a rally of the FNCD in Pétionville.

The presidential and legislative elections took place, as scheduled, on 16 December 1990. Voting was delayed in several areas when ballot papers failed to arrive; fears of a plot to disrupt the elections were, however, allayed when the interim Government extended the deadline for voting, to compensate for the delays. Preliminary results indicated an overwhelming victory in the presidential election for Aristide, who secured some 67% of the votes cast. His closest rival was Marc Bazin, the candidate of the centre-right Mouvement pour l'Instauration de la Démocratie en Haïti (MIDH), who received the support of about 14% of voters. However, the results of the concurrent legislative elections were less decisive. Fr Aristide's FNCD won five of the 27 seats in the Senate, and 18 (of 83) seats in the Chamber of Deputies, while the ANDP secured 16 seats in the lower house. Seven other seats in the Chamber of Deputies were distributed among other political parties. A second round of legislative voting, at which the distribution of the remaining seats was to be decided, was scheduled for 20 January 1991 (see below).

In early January 1991, one month before Aristide was due to be sworn in as President, a group of army officers, led by Roger Lafontant, seized control of the presidential palace, taking Pascal-Trouillot hostage and forcing her to announce her resignation. However, the army remained loyal to the Government and arrested those involved, thus thwarting Lafontant's attempt to impose martial law. More than 70 people were reported to have been killed during the rebellion and its suppression. In the aftermath of the incident, supporters of Aristide sought out and attacked opponents of the President-elect. Among their targets was the Roman Catholic Archbishop of Port-au-Prince, François-Wolff Ligondé. It was widely believed that Ligondé's outspoken condemnation of Aristide, at the beginning of January, might have acted as a catalyst for the Duvalierist rebellion. Ligondé was subsequently reported to have fled the country.

A high level of abstention in the second round of legislative voting, in January 1991, was attributed to popular unease as a result of the recent coup attempt. Preliminary results indicated that the FNCD had failed to secure an overall majority in the two legislative chambers.

Aristide was inaugurated as President of the Republic of Haiti on 7 February 1991. The new Head of State subsequently initiated proceedings to secure the extradition from France of former president Jean-Claude Duvalier. It was envisaged that, in the event of his return to Haiti, Duvalier would be charged with the embezzlement of state funds, the abuse of power and the murder of his political opponents. Aristide also undertook the reform of the armed forces, as a result of which several senior officers were obliged to relinquish their posts. In mid-February the new President nominated one of his close associates, René Préval, as prime minister, a choice that was endorsed by the two legislative chambers. Préval subsequently appointed his first Cabinet, in consultation with President Aristide.

International relations, although improved after 1971, continued to be strained because of Haiti's unpopular political regimes and government corruption. Relations between Haiti and its neighbour on the island of Hispaniola, the Dominican Republic, have traditionally been tense because of the use of the border area by anti-Government guerrillas, smugglers and illegal emigrants, resulting in the periodic closure of the border. In April 1987 the border was reopened to travellers, but not to trade. In June 1989 a fact-finding mission on behalf of the Caribbean Community (CARICOM) visited Haiti. This was followed, in August, by a visit from the Foreign Ministers of Jamaica, the Bahamas, Saint Lucia, and Trinidad and Tobago, who expressed support for the restoration of democracy in Haiti. However, they made no commitment to support Haiti's application for full membership of CARICOM or the African, Caribbean and Pacific (ACP) group of states. In 1989 the USA resumed aid to Haiti in recognition of the progress that President Avril had made towards the holding of democratic elections and his Government's efforts to combat drug-smuggling.

Following his election to the presidency, in December 1990, Fr Jean-Bertrand Aristide received assurances of political and economic support from external creditors, notably from the USA and France.

Government

The Constitution, approved by referendum in March 1987, provided for a bicameral legislature, comprising a 77-member Chamber of Deputies and a 27-member Senate. Executive power was held by the President, who was elected by universal adult suffrage for a five-year term and could not stand for immediate re-election. The President selected a Prime Minister from the political party commanding a majority in the legislature. The Prime Minister chose a cabinet in consultation with the President. However, the Constitution was rejected by the military Government that was installed after the coup in June 1988. Following a further coup in September 1988, the new President, Brig.-Gen. Prosper Avril, announced that his Government would respect the principles formulated in the 1987 Constitution until legislative elections were held, after which the newly-elected legislature, acting as a Constituent Assembly, would amend the Constitution. During the interim period, President Avril's Government was to rule by decree. Presidential and legislative elections took place in December 1990 and January 1991 (see Recent History).

There are nine Départements, subdivided into arrondissements and communes.

Defence

The size of Haiti's defence force was estimated at 7,400 men in June 1989. Included in the army (7,000 men) was the Leopard Corps, which, together with the Dessalines battalion, was disbanded in November 1989. The total strength of the armed forces was, as a consequence, reduced to about 6,000. In April 1990 the Presidential Guard (1,000 men) was also disbanded. The Haitian navy comprises a coastguard patrol of 250 men, and there is an air force of 150 men.

Economic Affairs

In 1989, according to estimates by the World Bank, Haiti's gross national product (GNP), measured at average 1987–89 prices, was US $2,556m., equivalent to $400 per head. During 1980–89, it was estimated, GNP increased, in real terms, at an average annual rate of 1.1%, while GNP per head declined by 0.7% per year. Over the same period, the population increased by an annual average of 1.8%. Haiti's gross domestic product (GDP) decreased, in real terms, by an annual average of 0.2% in 1980–88.

According to World Bank estimates, agriculture (including hunting, forestry and fishing) contributed 31% of GDP in 1988. About 66.2% of the employed labour force were engaged in agricultural activities in that year. The principal cash crops are coffee (which accounted for 21.6% of export earnings in 1988/89) and sugar. The other major export items are mangoes, cocoa, and oils for cosmetics and pharmaceuticals. The main food crops are maize, rice, bananas, and sweet potatoes.

Industry (including mining, manufacturing, construction and power) contributed 24.0% of GDP in 1988/89. About 8.9% of the employed labour force were engaged in the sector in 1988.

Mining contributed 0.1% of GDP in 1988/89. Less than 1% of the employed labour force were engaged in extractive activities in 1988. Marble, limestone and calcareous clay are mined. There are also unexploited copper and gold deposits. Bauxite mining ceased in 1983.

Manufacturing contributed 16.1% of GDP in 1988/89. About 6.5% of the employed labour force were engaged in the sector in 1988. The most important sectors in 1987, measured by gross value of output, were food products, metal products and machinery, and textiles.

Energy is derived principally from local timber and charcoal. Imports of fuel products accounted for 17.7% of the value of merchandise imports in 1988/89.

In 1988/89 Haiti recorded a visible trade deficit of US $100.6m., and there was a deficit of $62.6m. on the current account of the balance of payments. In 1988/89 the principal source of imports (46.9%) was the USA, which was also the principal market for exports (56.2%). Other major trading partners are Japan, Canada, Italy and France. The principal exports in 1988/89 were manufactured articles and coffee. The principal imports in that year were food and live animals, mineral fuels, machinery and transport equipment, and basic manufactures.

In the financial year ending 30 September 1989 there was an estimated budgetary deficit of US $60m. At the end of 1988, according to World Bank estimates, Haiti's total external public debt was $683m. In that year the cost of debt-servicing was equivalent to 8.8% of the value of exports of goods and services. The annual rate of inflation averaged 7.9% in 1980–88. Consumer prices declined by an annual average of 11.4% in 1987, but increased by 4.1% in 1988. An estimated 23.9% of the labour force were registered as unemployed in mid-1988.

Haiti is a member of the Latin-American Economic System (SELA, see p. 224) and the International Coffee Organization (see p. 228).

In terms of average income, Haiti is among the poorest countries in the Western hemisphere, and there is extreme inequality of wealth. Haiti is a major beneficiary of international aid organizations. The agricultural sector, which employs the majority of the working population, suffers from severe ecological problems, partly owing to the high population density. There is a very high level of unemployment, which has caused a large number of Haitians to emigrate to seek work. Political tensions in the late 1980s led to economic deterioration, which was exacerbated by the suspension of aid from the USA. Prospects for increased economic assistance from multilateral and bilateral creditors, appeared to be greatly improved during the early 1990s, owing to the transition to democratically-elected institutions in Haiti. Such assistance will prove vital to the country's economic adjustment efforts.

Social Welfare

Industrial and commercial workers are provided with free health care. In 1980 Haiti had 52 hospital establishments, with a total of only 3,964 beds, equivalent to one for every 1,264 inhabitants: the lowest level of provision in any country of the Western hemisphere. In 1984, according to World Bank estimates, there was one physician for every 7,180 people. Public health received an allocation of 89.5m. gourdes in 1984/85. Religious and other voluntary groups provide medical services in rural areas and in Port-au-Prince. In the late 1980s the AIDS virus reached epidemic proportions in Haiti. According to the WHO there were 2,337 reported AIDS cases at December 1989.

Education

Education is provided by the State, by the Roman Catholic Church and by other religious organizations, but many schools charge for tuition, books or uniforms. Learning is based on the French model, and French is used as the language of instruction. Primary education, which normally begins at six years and lasts for six years, is officially compulsory. Secondary education usually begins at 12 years of age and lasts for a further six years, comprising two cycles of three years each. In 1987 primary enrolment included only 44% of children in the relevant age-group (44% of boys; 44% of girls). Secondary education is provided by 21 public lycées and 123 private and religious schools. Enrolment at secondary schools in 1986 was equivalent to only 19% of children in the relevant age-group (20% of boys; 17% of girls). In 1985, according to estimates by UNESCO, the average rate of adult illiteracy was 62.4% (males 59.9%; females 64.7%), the highest national level in the Western hemisphere. The rate was even higher in rural areas (about 85%), where Creole is the popular language. Some basic adult education programmes, with instruction in Creole, were created in an attempt to redress the problem of adult illiteracy. In 1990, according to UNESCO estimates, the rate was 47.0% (males 40.9%; females 52.6%). Higher education is provided by 18 vocational training centres and 42 domestic science schools, and by the Université d'Etat d'Haïti, which has faculties of law, medicine, dentistry, science, agronomy, pharmacy, economic science, veterinary medicine and ethnology. Government expenditure on education in 1987 was 207.7m. gourdes.

Public Holidays

1991: 1 January (Independence Day), 2 January (Heroes of Independence), 11 February (Shrove Monday, half day), 12 February (Shrove Tuesday), 29 March (Good Friday), 14 April (Pan-American Day), 1 May (Labour Day), 18 May (Flag Day), 22 May (National Sovereignty), 15 August (Assumption), 24 October (United Nations Day), 2 November (All Souls' Day, half day), 18 November (Army Day and Commemoration of the Battle of Vertières), 5 December (Discovery Day), 25 December (Christmas Day).

1992: 1 January (Independence Day), 2 January (Heroes of Independence), 2 March (Shrove Monday, half-day), 3 March (Shrove Tuesday), 14 April (Pan-American Day), 17 April (Good Friday), 1 May (Labour Day), 18 May (Flag Day), 22 May (National Sovereignty), 15 August (Assumption), 24 October (United Nations Day), 2 November (All Souls' Day, half-day), 18 November (Army Day and Commemoration of the Battle of Vertières), 5 December (Discovery Day), 25 December (Christmas Day).

Weights and Measures

Officially the metric system is in force but many US measures are also used.

HAITI

Statistical Survey

Sources (unless otherwise stated): Banque de la République d'Haïti, Angle rue du Magasin d'État et rue des Miracles, Port-au-Prince; tel. (1) 2-4142; telex 0394; Ministère de l'Economie, des Finances et de l'Industrie, Port-au-Prince.

Area and Population

AREA, POPULATION AND DENSITY

Area (sq km)	27,750*
Population (census results)†	
31 August 1971	4,329,991
30 August 1982	
Males	2,448,370
Females	2,605,422
Total	5,053,792
Population (official estimates at mid-year)	
1987	5,438,000
1988	5,523,000
1989	5,609,000
Density (per sq km) at mid-1989	202.1

* 10,714 sq miles.
† Excluding adjustment for underenumeration.

DEPARTMENTS (provisional population figures, 1987)

Artibonite	789,019	North West	320,632
Central	393,217	South	526,420
Grande-Anse	514,962	South East	379,273
North	602,336	West	1,811,698
North East	197,669	**Total**	5,535,226

PRINCIPAL TOWN

Port-au-Prince (capital), estimated population 738,342 (including suburbs) at mid-1984.

BIRTHS AND DEATHS (UN estimates, annual averages)

	1975-80	1980-85	1985-90
Birth rate (per 1,000)	36.7	35.4	34.3
Death rate (per 1,000)	15.3	13.9	12.7

Source: UN, *World Population Prospects: 1988*.

ECONOMICALLY ACTIVE POPULATION
(official estimates, persons aged 10 years and over, mid-1988)

	Males	Females	Total
Agriculture, hunting, forestry and fishing	854,903	329,901	1,184,804
Mining and quarrying	8,989	8,646	17,635
Manufacturing	66,280	49,218	115,498
Electricity, gas and water	2,247	665	2,912
Construction	19,098	3,325	22,423
Trade, restaurants and hotels	65,157	195,551	260,708
Transport, storage and communications	14,604	1,995	16,599
Financing, insurance, real estate and business services	2,247	1,330	3,577
Community, social and personal services	62,909	52,544	115,453
Activities not adequately defined	26,961	21,948	48,909
Total Employed	1,123,395	665,123	1,788,518
Unemployed	265,041	296,743	561,784
Total labour force	1,388,436	961,866	2,350,302

Source: ILO, *Year Book of Labour Statistics*.

Agriculture

PRINCIPAL CROPS (FAO estimates, '000 metric tons)

	1987	1988	1989
Rice (paddy)	120	115	100
Maize	175*	145	130
Sweet potatoes	380	350	330
Beans	96	92	87
Sugar cane	3,000	3,000	3,000
Bananas	250*	230	225
Coffee (green)	30	32*	33*
Cocoa beans	2	2	2

* Unofficial figure.
Source: FAO, *Production Yearbook*.

LIVESTOCK
(FAO estimates, '000 head, year ending September)

	1987	1988	1989
Horses	430	430	432
Mules	84	85	86
Asses	216	216	217
Cattle	1,474	1,545	1,550
Pigs	750	900	950
Sheep	93	94	95
Goats	1,150	1,200	1,250

Chickens (FAO estimates, million): 12 in 1987; 13 in 1988; 14 in 1989.
Source: FAO, *Production Yearbook*.

LIVESTOCK PRODUCTS (FAO estimates, '000 metric tons)

	1987	1988	1989
Beef and veal	34	34	35
Goats' meat	5	5	5
Pig meat	15	16	18
Horse meat	5	5	5
Poultry meat	15	16	17
Cows' milk	23	23	23
Goats' milk	28	28	29
Hen eggs	4.0	4.0	4.0
Cattle hides	4.2	4.2	4.3

Source: FAO, *Production Yearbook*.

Forestry

ROUNDWOOD REMOVALS
(FAO estimates, '000 cubic metres)

	1986	1987	1988
Sawlogs, veneer logs and logs for sleepers*	224	224	224
Other industrial wood*	15	15	15
Fuel wood	5,188	5,288	5,390
Total	5,427	5,527	5,629

* Assumed to be unchanged since 1971.
Sawnwood production (FAO estimates): 12,000 cubic metres per year (1977-88) excluding railway sleepers (2,000 cubic metres per year in 1977-88).

Source: FAO, *Yearbook of Forest Products*.

HAITI

Fishing

(FAO estimates, '000 metric tons, live weight)

	1985	1986	1987
Freshwater fishes	0.3	0.3	0.3
Marine fishes	7.0	7.5	7.5
Caribbean spiny lobster	0.3	0.3	0.3
Total catch	7.5	8.0	8.1

1988: Catch as in 1987 (FAO estimate).
Source: FAO, *Yearbook of Fishery Statistics*.

Mining

('000 metric tons, year ending 30 September)

	1985/86	1986/87
Limestone	217.5	246.4
Calcareous clay	42.1	35.2

Industry

SELECTED PRODUCTS ('000 metric tons, unless otherwise indicated—year ending 30 September)

	1986/87	1987/88	1988/89
Wheat flour	91.8	106.2	99.5
Raw sugar	32.5*	30.4	n.a.
Cigarettes (million)	887.9	963.4	1,041.0
Soap	39.6†	43.9	47.9
Cement	253.0	265.3	235.6
Electric energy (million kWh)	481.8†	535.0	588.5

* Provisional.　† Estimate.

Finance

CURRENCY AND EXCHANGE RATES

Monetary Units
100 centimes = 1 gourde.

Denominations
Coins: 5, 10, 20 and 50 centimes.
Notes: 1, 2, 5, 10, 50, 100, 250 and 500 gourdes
(US currency notes also circulate).

Sterling and Dollar Equivalents (30 September 1990)
£1 sterling = 9.37 gourdes;
US $1 = 5.00 gourdes;
100 gourdes = £10.675 = $20.000.

Exchange Rate
Fixed at US $1 = 5 gourdes.

BUDGET (million gourdes, year ending 30 September)

Revenue	1984/85	1985/86	1986/87
Tax revenue	1,074.3	1,023.9	994.9
Taxes on income	180.9	153.3	137.4
Excises	259.7	293.1	274.8
Other taxes on goods and services	249.7	203.5	215.3
Import duties	251.2	256.0	229.4
Export duties	61.0	55.1	18.7
Other revenue*	855.4	572.9	267.4
Total	1,929.7	1,596.8	1,262.3

* Including grants from abroad.

Expenditure	1979/80	1980/81	1981/82
Goods and services		1,191.0	802.4
Interest payments	1,012.5	36.0	58.7
Other current expenditure		72.7	344.3
Capital expenditure	255.7	160.4	144.2
Total	1,268.2	1,460.1	1,349.6

Current expenditure (million gourdes): 1,406.8 in 1982/83; n.a. in 1983/84; 1,798.5 (goods and services 969.7, interest payments 58.6) in 1984/85; 1,780.4 (goods and services 958.6, interest payments 125.6) in 1985/86; 1,959.3 (goods and services 940.8) in 1986/87.
Source: IMF, *Government Finance Statistics Yearbook*.

INTERNATIONAL RESERVES (US $ million at 31 December)

	1987	1988	1989
Gold*	7.5	7.1	n.a.
IMF special drawing rights	—	—	0.1
Reserve position in IMF	0.1	0.1	0.1
Foreign exchange	16.9	12.9	12.4
Total	24.5	20.1	n.a.

* Valued at market-related prices.
Source: IMF, *International Financial Statistics*.

MONEY SUPPLY (million gourdes at 31 December)

	1986	1987	1988
Currency outside banks	829.1	979.5	205.0
Demand deposits at commercial banks	544.2	658.6	715.7

Source: IMF, *International Financial Statistics*.

COST OF LIVING
(Consumer Price Index for metropolitan area; base: 1980 = 100)

	1987	1988	1989
Food	125.9	133.6	144.4
Clothing	184.6	182.6	193.1
Rent, fuel and light	193.4	197.1	207.7
All items (incl. others)	141.3	147.1	158.1

HAITI

NATIONAL ACCOUNTS
(million gourdes at current prices, year ending 30 September)

Expenditure on the Gross Domestic Product

	1986/87	1987/88	1988/89
Final consumption expenditure	9,386	9,504	10,123
Increase in stocks	} 1,509	} 1,501	} 1,458
Gross fixed capital formation			
Total domestic expenditure	10,895	11,005	11,581
Exports of goods and services	2,086	1,817	1,763
Less Imports of goods and services	3,052	3,176	3,004
GDP in purchasers' values	9,929	9,646	10,340
GDP at constant 1975/76 prices	5,122	5,109	5,137

Gross Domestic Product by Economic Activity
(at constant 1975/76 prices)

	1986/87*	1987/88	1988/89
Agriculture, hunting, forestry and fishing	1,670	n.a.	n.a.
Mining and quarrying	5	5	6
Manufacturing	783	777	790
Electricity, gas and water	49	54	56
Construction	315	320	323
Trade, restaurants and hotels	899	892	886
Transport, storage and communication	99	105	108
Finance, insurance, real estate and business services	291	n.a.	n.a.
Government services	606	605	628
Other services	202	n.a.	n.a.
Sub-total	4,919	4,889	4,905
Import duties	222	220	232
GDP in purchasers' values	5,141	5,109	5,137

* Source: UN, *National Accounts Statistics*.

BALANCE OF PAYMENTS
(US $ million, year ending 30 September)

	1987	1988	1989
Merchandise exports f.o.b.	210.1	180.4	181.3
Merchandise imports f.o.b.	−311.2	−283.9	−282.0
Trade balance	−101.1	−103.5	−100.6
Exports of services	110.3	94.5	86.5
Imports of services	−190.5	−197.1	−188.8
Other income received	5.2	6.2	4.6
Other income paid	−26.1	−33.3	−30.1
Private unrequited transfers (net)	56.2	63.4	59.3
Government unrequited transfers (net)	114.8	129.5	106.6
Current balance	−31.2	−40.3	−62.6
Direct investment (net)	4.7	10.1	9.4
Other capital (net)	51.7	55.2	63.4
Net errors and omissions	−20.6	−28.5	−8.5
Overall balance	4.6	−3.5	1.7

Source: IMF, *International Financial Statistics*.

External Trade

PRINCIPAL COMMODITIES
(million gourdes, year ending 30 September)

Imports c.i.f.	1986/87	1987/88	1988/89
Food and live animals	350.0	349.0	324.9
Beverages and tobacco	31.5	20.0	19.0
Mineral fuels, lubricants, etc.	251.6	231.8	277.6
Crude materials (inedible) except fuels	41.0	53.9	34.1
Animal and vegetable oils and fats	179.1	153.1	132.6
Chemicals	192.0	170.0	144.7
Basic manufactures	298.2	270.2	220.1
Machinery and transport equipment	327.0	308.0	267.3
Total (incl. others)	1,884.3	1,719.5	1,568.7

Exports f.o.b.*	1986/87	1987/88	1988/89
Coffee	182.5	162.7	173.4
Cocoa	21.8	20.0	14.8
Essential oils	14.6	16.2	17.8
Light industrial products	68.7	49.0	43.6
Manufactured articles	668.9	577.4	498.4
Sisal	3.8	5.1	—
Molasses	1.9	2.6	1.8
Rope and cord	14.9	14.6	24.9
Total (incl. others)	1,053.2	899.1	802.8

* Excluding re-exports.

PRINCIPAL TRADING PARTNERS*
(million gourdes, year ending 30 September)

Imports c.i.f.	1986/87	1987/88	1988/89
Belgium	24.0	18.0	22.7
Canada	112.8	94.3	98.2
France	92.0	107.0	102.5
Germany, Federal Republic	65.3	62.0	65.1
Italy	18.9	13.4	16.0
Japan	130.1	110.0	106.3
Netherlands	58.4	54.1	50.4
United Kingdom	30.7	26.0	31.0
USA	859.1	786.0	736.0
Total (incl. others)	1,884.3	1,719.5	1,568.7

* Provisional.

Exports f.o.b.†	1986/87	1987/88	1988/89
Belgium	82.0	73.0	69.2
Canada	19.3	28.4	20.7
France	110.7	75.0	72.5
Germany, Federal Republic	36.5	29.4	24.1
Italy	123.0	106.5	90.3
Japan	4.8	11.2	9.0
Netherlands	17.3	13.3	15.0
United Kingdom	9.1	8.0	11.0
USA	531.5	485.7	416.1
Total (incl. others)	1,007.9	849.2	740.3

† Excluding re-exports.
Source: Administration Générale des Douanes.

Transport

ROAD TRAFFIC ('000 motor vehicles in use)

	1979	1980	1981
Passenger cars	24.9	21.8	21.8
Commercial vehicles	8.3	11.2	12.4

Source: UN, *Statistical Yearbook*.
1984: 50,000 vehicles.

INTERNATIONAL SEA-BORNE SHIPPING
(freight traffic, '000 metric tons)

	1986	1987	1988
Goods loaded	177	168	164
Goods unloaded	676	685	684

Source: UN, *Monthly Bulletin of Statistics*.

CIVIL AVIATION
International Flights, 1989: Passengers arriving 293,905; Passengers departing 311,643.

Tourism

VISITORS

	1986/87	1987/88	1988/89
Arrivals	130,047	90,710	79,277
Cruise passengers	70,515	122,746	105,460

Source: Office National du Tourisme.

Education

(1988/89)

	Schools	Teachers	Students
Primary	n.a.	24,900	889,500
Secondary	503	10,210	182,400

University of Haiti: c. 4,600 students (1986).

Directory

The Constitution

The Constitution of Haiti was approved by the electorate in a referendum held in March 1987. According to its provisions, a system of power-sharing between a President (who may not serve two consecutive five-year terms), a Prime Minister and a bicameral legislature was to be established. Former supporters of ex-President Jean-Claude Duvalier were to be barred from elective office for 10 years. Authority was to be distributed regionally by investing new powers in local government. The army and the police were no longer to be a combined force. The death penalty was abolished, and there was to be an independent judiciary. Official status was given to the Creole language spoken by Haitians and to the folk religion, voodoo. In June 1988 the Constitution was annulled by the military Government that was installed after a coup, but in September Brig.-Gen. Prosper Avril (who took office as President, following a further coup) announced that the principles of the 1987 Constitution would be respected by his administration. The Constitution was partially restored in March 1989. Following the resignation of Brig-Gen. Prosper Avril in March 1990, an interim President was installed, pending a presidential election (which took place in December 1990).

The Government

HEAD OF STATE

President: Fr JEAN-BERTRAND ARISTIDE (took office 7 February 1991).

CABINET
(February 1991)

Prime Minister, Minister of the Interior, and Minister of Defence: RENÉ PRÉVAL.
Minister of Economy and Finance: MARIE-MICHÈLE REY.
Minister of Foreign Affairs and Worship: MARIE-DENISE FABIEN JEAN-LOUIS.
Minister of Justice: BAYARD VINCENT.
Minister of Information and Co-ordination: MARID LAURENCE JOSSELYN-LASSEGUE.
Minister of Agriculture, Natural Resources and Rural Development: FRANÇOIS SÉVERIN.
Minister of Education, Youth and Sports: LESLY VOLTAIRE.
Minister of Health and Housing: DANIEL HENRYS.
Minister of Trade and Industry: SMARCK MICHEL.
Minister of Public Works, Transport and Communications: FRANTZ VERELLA.
Minister of Social Affairs: ERNST VERDIEU.
Minister of Planning, External Co-operation and Civil Service: RENAUD BERNARDIN.
Head of Commission for Overseas Haitians: (vacant).

MINISTRIES

Office of the President: Palais National, Port-au-Prince; tel. (1) 2-4020; telex 0068.
Ministry of Agriculture, Natural Resources and Rural Development: Damien, Port-au-Prince; tel. (1) 2-3457.
Ministry of Defence: Palais des Ministères, Port-au-Prince; tel. (1) 2-1714.
Ministry of Economy and Finance: Palais des Ministères, Port-au-Prince; tel. (1) 2-1628; telex 0207.
Ministry of Education, Youth and Sports: Blvd Harry Truman, Cité de l'Exposition, Port-au-Prince; tel. (1) 2-1036.
Ministry of Foreign Affairs and Worship: Blvd Harry Truman, Cité de l'Exposition, Port-au-Prince; tel. (1) 2-1647.
Ministry of Health and Housing: Palais des Ministères, Port-au-Prince; tel. (1) 2-1248.
Ministry of Information and Co-ordination: 300 route de Delmas, Port-au-Prince; tel. (1) 6-3229; telex 0238.
Ministry of the Interior: Palais des Ministères, Port-au-Prince; tel. (1) 2-1714.
Ministry of Justice: Blvd Harry Truman, Cité de l'Exposition, Port-au-Prince; tel. (1) 2-0718.
Ministry of Planning, External Co-operation and Civil Service: Port-au-Prince; tel. (1) 2-1027.
Ministry of Public Works, Transport and Communications: Palais des Ministères, BP 2002, Port-au-Prince; tel. (1) 2-0300; telex 0353.
Ministry of Social Affairs: rue de la Revolution, Port-au-Prince; tel. (1) 2-2400.
Ministry of Trade and Industry: Port-au-Prince.

HAITI

Directory

President and Legislature

PRESIDENT

On 10 March 1990 President Prosper Avril resigned and ceded power to the Chief of the General Staff, Gen. Hérard Abraham, who transferred authority to Ertha Pascal-Trouillot as provisional President pending free elections. Fourteen candidates contested the presidential election, which took place on 16 December. Preliminary results indicated that Fr Jean-Bertrand Aristide, the candidate of the Front National pour le Changement et la Démocratie (FNCD), secured some 67% of votes cast. Aristide's closest rival was Marc Bazin, the representative of the Mouvement pour l'Instauration de la Démocratie en Haïti (MIDH), who won about 14% of the votes. Aristide took office on 7 February 1991.

LEGISLATURE

The first round of voting for Haiti's two legislative chambers took place on 16 December 1990. The Front National pour le Changement et la Démocratie (FNCD) won five of the 27 seats in the Senate and 18 of the 83 seats in the Chamber of Deputies. The Alliance Nationale pour la Démocratie et le Progrés (ANDP) secured 16 seats in the Chamber of Deputies, while seven other seats in the lower house were distributed among other political parties. A second round of legislative voting, at which the apportionment of the remaining seats was to be decided, was conducted on 20 January 1991. Preliminary results indicated that the FNCD had failed to secure an overall majority in the two legislative chambers.

Political Organizations

Many political leaders returned to Haiti from exile, following the downfall of President Duvalier in February 1986. In August 1986 the National Council of Government issued a decree granting legal recognition to political parties on condition that they had at least 20 founding members and 2,000 sponsors. Many new political organizations were subsequently established.

Assemblée Populaire Nationale (APN): extreme left-wing.

Confédération d'Unité Démocratique (KID): Creole; grouping of popular organizations; Leader Evans Paul.

Front National pour le Changement et la Démocratie (FNCD): f. 1990; embraces 15 political organizations; Leader Fr Jean-Bertrand Aristide.

Front National de Concertation (FNC): f. 1987 to urge mobilization, organization and unity, while rejecting fascism and violence, in order to achieve democratic elections; consists of the 'Group of 57', 18 provincial co-ordinating committees and sectors of civilian society; moderate left-wing; Leader Gérard Gourgue; affiliated organizations include:

    Comité National du Congrès des Mouvements Démocratiques (KONACOM): Leader Victor Benoît.

Mobilisation pour le Développement National (MDN): c/o CHISS, 33 rue Bonne Foi, BP 2497, Port-au-Prince; tel. (1) 2-3829; f. 1986; Pres. Hubert de Ronceray.

Mouvement pour l'Instauration de la Démocratie en Haïti (MIDH): 114 Avda Jean Paul II, Port-au-Prince; tel. (1) 5-8377; f. 1986; centre-right; Pres. Marc Bazin.

Mouvement d'Organisation du Pays (MOP): centre party; Leader Gérard Philippe Auguste.

Parti Agricole et Industriel National (PAIN): f. 1956; Sec.-Gen. Louis Déjoie II.

Parti Démocratique Chrétien d'Haïti (PDCH): f. 1978; Christian Democrat party; Leader Sylvio Claude.

Parti Nationaliste Progressiste Démocratique Haïtien: left-wing.

Parti Nationaliste Progressiste Révolutionnaire (PANPRA): f. 1986; social-democratic; mem. of Socialist International; Leader Serge Gilles.

Parti Républicain Modéré Haïtien (PRMH): Pres. Nicolas Estiverne.

Parti Unifié des Communistes Haïtiens (PUCH): f. 1968; Sec.-Gen. René Théodore.

Parti pour l'Unité Nationale et Développement (PUND): f. 1988; Leader Dr Wisler Pierre-Louis.

Rassemblement des Démocrates Nationaux Progressistes (RDNP): f. 1979; centre party; Sec.-Gen. Leslie Manigat.

Union des Patriotes Démocratiques (UPD): f. 1988; Leader Rockefeller Guerre.

Union pour la Réconciliation Nationale (URN): f. 1990; Pres. Roger Lafontant.

Note: Several alliances were formed in late 1989, with a view to contesting the proposed legislative elections. The **Alliance Nationale pour la Démocratie et le Progrès** (ANDP) was formed by Marc Bazin, leader of the MIDH, and Serge Gilles, leader of the PANPRA; 25 left-wing parties, led by the CATH (see Trade Unions), the KID and the APN, united to form the **Front contre la Répression**.

Diplomatic Representation

EMBASSIES IN HAITI

Argentina: impasse Géraud, 20 Bourdon, Port-au-Prince; tel. (1) 2-2063; telex 0176; Chargé d'affaires: Antonio Meri.

Brazil: 387 ave John Brown, Bourdon, BP 808, Port-au-Prince; tel. (1) 5-6208; telex 0181; Ambassador: Aloysio M. D. Gomide.

Canada: 18 route de Delmas, Port-au-Prince; tel. (1) 2358; telex 0069; Ambassador: Anthony Malone.

Chile: 384 route de Delmas, entre rues 42 et 44, Port-au-Prince; Ambassador: Agustín Rodríguez Pulgar.

China (Taiwan): 2 rue Rivière, Port-au-Prince; Ambassador: Lee Nan Hsing.

Colombia: 384 route de Delmas, entre rues 42 et 44, Port-au-Prince; tel. (1) 6-2599; Ambassador: Juan Zapata Olivella.

Dominican Republic: Port-au-Prince; Ambassador: José del Carmen Acosta.

Ecuador: BP 2531, Port-au-Prince; tel. (1) 2-4576; telex 0195; Chargé d'affaires: Adolfo Alvarez.

France: 51 Place des Héros de l'Indépendance, Port-au-Prince; tel. (1) 2-0951; telex 0049; Ambassador: Jean-Raphaël Dufour.

Germany: 8 rue Mangonès, Pétion-Ville, BP 1147, Port-au-Prince; tel. (1) 7-0456; telex 0082; fax (1) 7-4131; Ambassador: Heinrich-Peter Rothmann.

Holy See: Morne Calvaire, Pétionville, BP 326, Port-au-Prince; tel. (1) 7-3411; Apostolic Nuncio: Most Rev. Giuseppe Leanza, Titular Archbishop of Lilibeo.

Israel: 1 Route Nationale, Chancerelles, Port-au-Prince; tel. (1) 3-8100; telex 0171; fax (1) 2-3767; Consul: Gilbert Bigio.

Italy: 1 impasse Brave, Delmas 60, BP 886, Port-au-Prince; tel. (1) 7-0424; telex 0447; Ambassador: Luigi Morrone.

Japan: Villa Bella Vista 2, impasse Tulipe, Desprez, Port-au-Prince; tel. (1) 5-3333; telex 0368; Ambassador: Aoki Satoshi.

Liberia: Port-au-Prince; tel. (1) 7-0692; Ambassador: Henry T. Hoff.

Mexico: Maison Roger Esper, 57A route de Delmas, Port-au-Prince; tel. (1) 6-2215; telex 0217; Ambassador: Sergio Romero Cuevas.

Panama: 29 rues Met. et Chavannes, Pétionville; tel. (1) 7-2260; Ambassador: (vacant).

Peru: 38 Débussy, Turgeau, POB 174, Port-au-Prince; tel. (1) 5-5425; Ambassador: S. E. M. Elmer Schialer-Figueroa.

Spain: 11 rue Oscar, Desprez, Port-au-Prince; tel. (1) 2-4410; Ambassador: José Francisco de Castro.

USA: blvd Harry Truman, Cité de l'Exposition, Port-au-Prince; tel. (1) 2-0200; telex 0157; Ambassador: Alvin Adams.

Venezuela: blvd Harry Truman, Cité de l'Exposition, BP 2158, Port-au-Prince; tel. (1) 2-0973; telex 0413; Ambassador: José Gregorio González-Rodríguez.

Judicial System

Law is based on the French Napoleonic Code, substantially modified during the presidency of Dr François Duvalier.

Courts of Appeal and Civil Courts sit at Port-au-Prince and the three provincial capitals: Gonaïves, Cap Haïtien and Port de Paix. In principle each commune has a Magistrates' Court.

Court of Cassation: Port-au-Prince; Pres. Gilbert Austin; Vice-Pres. Gabriel Voley.

Courts of Appeal. Civil Courts. Magistrates' Courts. Judges of the Supreme Courts and Courts of Appeal appointed by the President.

Religion

Roman Catholicism is the official religion, followed by 80% of the population. The folk religion is voodoo.

HAITI

CHRISTIANITY

The Roman Catholic Church

For ecclesiastical purposes, Haiti comprises two archdioceses and six dioceses.

Bishops' Conference: Conférence Episcopale de Haïti, Angle rues Piquant et Lamarre, BP 1572, Port-au-Prince; tel. (1) 2-4855; f. 1977; Pres. Most Rev. LÉONARD P. LAROCHE, Archbishop of Hinche.

Archbishop of Cap Haïtien: Most Rev. FRANÇOIS GAYOT, Archevêché, CP 22, rue 19–20 H, Cap Haïtien; tel. (3) 2-0071.

Archbishop of Port-au-Prince: (vacant); Archevêché, rue Dr Aubry, BP 538, Port-au-Prince; tel. (1) 2-2043.

The Episcopal Church

Bishop of Haiti: Rt Rev. Dr LUC GARNIER, Eglise Episcopale d'Haïti, BP 1309, Port-au-Prince.

Other Christian Churches

Baptist Convention: BP 20, Cap-Haïtien; tel. (3) 2-0567; Pres. Rev. ANDRÉ JEAN.

Lutheran Church: Petite Place Cuzeau, BP 13147, Delmas, Port-au-Prince; tel. (1) 6-3179; f. 1975; Minister BEN BICHOTTE.

Other denominations active in Haiti include Methodists and the Church of God 'Eben-Ezer'.

The Press

Following the downfall of President Duvalier in 1986, numerous new newspapers were established.

DAILIES

Artibonite Journal: Gonaïves.

Haïti Journal: BP 866, Port-au-Prince; circ. 2,000.

Le Jour: Port-au-Prince.

Le Journal Sud-Ouest: Jacmel.

Le Matin: 88 rue du Quai, Port-au-Prince; tel. (1) 2-2040; f. 1908; French; independent; Dir FRANK MAGLOIRE; circ. 5,000.

Le Nouvelliste: 198 rue du Centre, BP 1013, Port-au-Prince; tel. (1) 2-2114; f. 1896; evening; French; independent; Editor LUCIEN MONTAS; circ. 6,000.

L'Union: Cité de l'Exposition, Port-au-Prince.

Panorama: 27 rue du Peuple, Port-au-Prince; tel. (1) 2-2625; French; independent; Dir PAUL BLANCHET; circ. 2,500.

PERIODICALS

Balance: Port-au-Prince; weekly.

Haïti Observateur: Port-au-Prince; weekly; Editor RAYMOND JOSEPH.

Haïti Progrès: 11 rue Capois, Port-au-Prince; weekly; Editor BEN DUPUY.

Haiti Times: Port-au-Prince; monthly.

Le Journal de Commerce: 49 rue Traversière, BP 1569, Port-au-Prince; tel. (1) 7-3008; weekly; Dir GÉRARD ALLEN; circ. 4,000.

Le Messager du Nord-Ouest: Port de Paix; weekly.

Le Moniteur: BP 214 bis, Port-au-Prince; tel. (1) 2-1026; 2 a week; French; the official gazette; Dir MARCEL ELIBERT; circ. 2,000.

Optique: French Institute, BP 1316, Port-au-Prince; monthly; arts.

Le Petit Samedi Soir: Fontamara, Port-au-Prince; tel. (1) 4-0144; weekly; French; independent; Editor DIEUDONNÉ FARDIN; circ. 10,000.

Revue l'Educateur: Grande Rue, BP 164, Port-au-Prince; tel. (1) 2-2297; telex 0533; monthly; circ. 8,000.

Le Septentrion: Cap Haïtien; weekly; independent; Editor NELSON BELL; circ. 2,000.

FOREIGN NEWS BUREAUX

Agence France-Presse (AFP): 72 rue Pavée, BP 62, Port-au-Prince; tel. (1) 2-3759; telex 0379; Bureau Chief DOMINIQUE LEVANTI.

Associated Press (AP) (USA): BP 2443, Port-au-Prince; tel. (1) 7-4240; telex 0277; Correspondent MIKE NORTON.

Reuter (UK): Port-au-Prince; tel. (1) 5-0464.

United Press International (UPI) (USA) and Agencia EFE (Spain): 21 rue Gabart, Pétionville; tel. (1) 7-1628; telex 0480; Reps SONDRA SINGER BEAULIEU, SERGE BEAULIEU.

Publishers

Editions Caraïbes: Lalue, BP 2013, Port-au-Prince; tel. (1) 2-3179; telex 0198.

Editions Fardin: Fontamara, Port-au-Prince.

Editions du Soleil: BP 2471, rue du Centre, Port-au-Prince; tel. (1) 2-3147; telex 0001; education.

Maison Henri Deschamps: Grand rue, BP 164, Port-au-Prince; tel. (1) 3-2215; telex 0533; fax (1) 3-2216; f. 1893; education and literature; Man. Dir JACQUES DESCHAMPS.

Theodor: Imprimerie, rue Dantes, Destouches, Port-au-Prince.

Radio and Television

In 1988 there were an estimated 250,000 radio receivers and 27,000 television receivers in use. There are 29 radio stations and one television station.

Conseil National des Télécommunications (CONATEL): 16 Cité de l'Exposition, BP 2002, Port-au-Prince; tel. (1) 3-2929; telex 0353; fax (1) 3-0579; government communications licensing authority; Dir-Gen. ALIX LILAVOIS.

RADIO

Radio Antilles International: 175 rue du Centre, BP 2325, Port-au-Prince; tel. (1) 2-8797; f. 1984; independent; Dir-Gen. JACQUES SAMPEUR.

Radio Cacique: 5 Bellevue, BP 1480, Port-au-Prince; independent; Dir PATRICK DE LANDSHEER.

Radio Caraïbes: 23 ruelle Chavannes, Port-au-Prince; independent; Dir HARRY K. MULLER.

Radio Haïti Inter: Delmas 66A en face de Delmas 91, BP 737, Port-au-Prince; tel. (1) 7-3111; independent; Dir JEAN L. DOMINIQUE.

Radio Lumière: BP 1050, Port-au-Prince; tel. (1) 4-0330; f. 1959; Protestant; independent; Dir JOSEPH ROBINSON.

Radio MBC: 86 rue Américaine, BP 367, Port-au-Prince; independent; Dir-Gen. F. C. MAGLOIRE.

Radio Métropole: rue Pavée, BP 62, Port-au-Prince; Dir HERBERT WIDMAIER.

Radio Port-au-Prince: Stade Sylvio Cator, BP 81, Port-au-Prince; independent; Dir GEORGES J. HÉRARD.

Radio Soleil: BP 1362, Port-au-Prince; tel. (1) 2-3073; f. 1978; Catholic; independent; educational; broadcasts in Creole; Dir Fr ARNOUX CHERY.

Radio Télédiffusion Nationale: rue du Magasin de l'Etat, BP 1143, Port-au-Prince; tel. (1) 2-2421; government-operated; Dir Dr GEORGES MICHEL.

TELEVISION

Télé Haïti: ave Marie Jeanne 16A, BP 1126, Port-au-Prince; tel. (1) 2-3000; fax (1) 2-9140; f. 1959; independent; pay-cable station with 13 channels; in French, Spanish and English; Dir MARIE CHRISTINE BUSSENIUS.

Télévision Nationale d'Haïti: Delmas 33, BP 13400, Port-au-Prince; tel. (1) 6-0200; telex 0414; government-owned; cultural; 4 channels in Creole, French and Spanish; administered by four-mem. board; Dir HEROLD JEAN-FRANÇOIS.

Finance

(cap. = capital; m. = million; res = reserves; dep. = deposits; amounts in gourdes; brs = branches)

BANKING

Banque de la République d'Haïti: Angle rue du Magasin de l'Etat et rue des Miracles, BP 1570, Port-au-Prince; tel. (1) 2-4700; telex 0317; fax (1) 2-2607; f. 1911; fmrly Banque Nationale de la République d'Haïti; the central bank and bank of issue; cap. 52.1m., res 35.6m., dep. 1,474.0m. (Sept. 1989); Gen. Man. CHARLES A. BEAULIEU; 12 brs.

Banque Commerciale d'Haïti: Champ de Mars, Port-au-Prince; tel. (1) 2-3931.

Banque de Crédit Immobilier SA: 6 rue des Fronts Forts, Port-au-Prince; tel. (1) 2-2434; Dir-Gen. CLAUDE LEVY.

Banque Industrielle et Commerciale d'Haïti: BP 1007, Port-au-Prince; tel. (1) 2-1272; Dir-Gen. AMILCAR BLAISE.

Banque Nationale de Crédit: rue des Miracles et rue Américaine, BP 1320, Port-au-Prince; tel. (1) 2-0800; telex 0196; f. 1979; cap. 25m., dep. 729.9m. (Sept. 1989); Pres. ELIE JEAN-PHILIPPE.

HAITI

Banque Populaire Haïtienne: Angle rue Américaine et Fort Per, Port-au-Prince; tel. (1) 2-1800; telex 0406; f. 1955; state bank; cap. 5m.; Dir-Gen. SERGE PÉRODIN.

Banque de l'Union Haïtienne: Angle rue du Quai et rue Bonne Foi, BP 275, Port-au-Prince; tel. (1) 3-0491; telex 0173; fax (1) 2-4356; f. 1973; cap. 15m.; Pres. and Dir-Gen. MARCEL LÉGER; 5 brs.

Sogebank: Angle Rue des Miracles et Rue Magasin de l'Etat, BP 1315, Port-au-Prince; tel. (1) 2-4800; telex 0041; cap. 25m.; Pres. JEAN CLAUDE NADAL.

Sogebel: Rue des Miracles, BP 2409, Port-au-Prince; tel. (1) 3-9192; cap. 7.5m.; Dir-Gen. CHARLES CLERMONT.

Foreign Banks

Bank of Nova Scotia (Canada): rue des Miracles, Port-au-Prince; tel. (1) 2-0408; telex 0155; Dir-Gen. CHESTER HINKSON; 3 brs.

Banque Nationale de Paris (France): ave John Brown, Port-au-Prince; tel. (1) 2-2461; telex 0191; fax (1) 2-6720; Dir-Gen. MARCEL GARCÍA; 2 brs.

Citibank, NA (USA): route de Delmas, BP 1688, Port-au-Prince; tel. (1) 6-2600; telex 0124; Vice-Pres. GLADYS M. COUPET.

First National Bank of Boston (USA): rue des Miracles, BP 2216, Port-au-Prince; tel. (1) 2-1900; telex 0163; Dir-Gen. GUY CUVILLY; 3 brs.

Development Bank

Banque Nationale de Développement Agricole: Port-au-Prince; tel. (1) 2-1969; telex 0116; Dir-Gen. YVES LEREBOURS.

INSURANCE

National Companies

Compagnie d'Assurances d'Haïti: Delmas 21, Plaza 21, Etage Xerox, Port-au-Prince; Dir BRIAN HOGAN.

Office National d'Assurance Viellesse (ONA): Champ de Mars, Port-au-Prince; tel. (1) 3-1655; Dir ROBERT SIMON.

Foreign Companies

Global Insurance Centre SA (USA): Angle rues du Peuple et des Miracles, Etage Rhum Nazon, Port-au-Prince; tel. (1) 2-6695; fax (1) 3-0837; Dir FRITZ DE CATALOGNE.

Groupement Français d'Assurances (France): Etage Librairie à la Caravelle 26, rue Bonne Foi, Port-au-Prince; tel. (1) 2-0030; telex 0426; fax (1) 2-6677; Agent ALBERT A. DUFORT.

Dupuy & Merove-Pierre (USA): Angle rue des Miracles et rue Pétion 153, Port-au-Prince; tel. (1) 3-1058; fax (1) 3-1821; agents for Cigna International La Nationale d'Assurance SA; Dirs FRITZ DUPUY, RAOUL MÉROVÉ-PIERRE.

Preservatrices Foncières Assurances (France): Angle rue du Magasin de l'Etat et rue Eden, Place Geffrard 266 (Etage Stecher), Port-au-Prince; tel. (1) 2-4210; Dir PHILIPPE GATION.

Insurance Association

Association des Assureurs d'Haïti: 40 rue Lamarre, POB 2120, Port-au-Prince; tel. (1) 2-3082; fax (1) 3-8634; Pres. GERARD N. LEGER.

Trade and Industry

CHAMBERS OF COMMERCE

Chambre de Commerce et de l'Industrie d'Haïti (CCIH): BP 982, Port-au-Prince; tel. (1) 2-2475; fax (1) 2-0281; f. 1907; Pres. LUDOVIC LOUISDHON; Exec. Dir MICHAELE BERROUET.

Chambre de Commerce et d'Industrie Haïtiano-Américaine (HAMCHAM): Complexe 384, Delmas 42-44, Appt 6, Delmas, Port-au-Prince; f. 1979; tel. (1) 6-3164; fax (1) 6-0985; f. 1979; Pres. GLADYS COUPET.

Chambre Franco-Haïtienne de Commerce et d'Industrie: Holiday Inn, Le Plaza, Champ de Mars, Port-au-Prince; tel. (1) 3-8404; Pres. MARIE CHRISTINE BUSSENIUS.

COMMERCIAL, AGRICULTURAL AND INDUSTRIAL ORGANIZATIONS

Association des Industries d'Haïti (ADIH): Delmas 31 et 33, Etase Galerie 128, BP 2568, Port-au-Prince; tel. (1) 6-4509; telex 0071; fax (1) 6-2211; f. 1980; Pres. JURGEN ANDERSEN; Exec. Dir RAYMOND LAFONTANT, Jr.

Association Nationale des Distributeurs de Produits Pétroliers (ANADIPP): Dubois Shopping Centre, Route de Delmas, Bureau 401, Port-au-Prince; tel. (1) 6-1414; Pres. EDNER JEAN-FÉLIX.

Association Nationale des Importateurs et Distributeurs de Produits Pharmaceutiques (ANIDPP): c/o Maison Nadal, rue du Fort Per, Port-au-Prince; tel. (1) 2-1418; Pres. ANDRÉ NICOLAS.

Association des Producteurs Agricoles (APA): c/o Chambre de Commerce et d'Industrie d'Haïti, blvd Harry S. Truman, Cité de l'Exposition, Port-au-Prince; tel. (1) 2-0281; fax (1) 3-4717; f. 1985; Pres. REYNOLD BONNEFIL.

Association des Producteurs Nationaux (APRONA): c/o Masaïques Gardère, ave Hailé Sélassié, Port-au-Prince; tel. (1) 6-1890; Pres. FRANTZ GARDÈRE.

Association des Exporteurs de Café (ASDEC): c/o Usman, ave Somoza, BP B-65, Port-au-Prince; tel. (1) 2-2500; Pres. FRITZ BRANDT.

Centre de Promotion des Investissements et des Exportations Haïtiennes (PROMINEX): Angle rue Lamarre et ave John Brown, Port-au-Prince; tel. (1) 2-6381; Pres. CLAUDE LEVY.

DEVELOPMENT ORGANIZATIONS

Fonds de Développement Industriel: 43 rue des Miracles, BP 2597, Port-au-Prince; tel. (1) 2-7852; telex 0432; f. 1981; Dir ROLAND PIERRE.

Société Financière Haïtienne de Développement (SOFIHDES): BP 1399, blvd Harry S. Truman, Port-au-Prince; tel. (1) 2-8628; fax (1) 2-8997; f. 1983; accounting, data processing, management consultancy; cap. 1.5m. (1989); Dir-Gen. SERGE DEVIEUX; 1 br.

TRADE UNIONS

Centrale Autonome des Travailleurs Haïtiens (CATH): 93 rue des Casernes, Port-au-Prince; tel. (1) 2-4506; f. 1980; Sec. Gen. YVES ANTOINE RICHARD.

Confédération Ouvriers Travailleurs Haïtiens (KOTA): 155 rue des Césars, Port-au-Prince.

Confédération Nationale des Enseignants Haïtiens (CNEH): Angle Ruelle Berne et Lalue, Port-au-Prince; tel. (1) 5-4288.

Confederation des Travailleurs Haïtiens (CTH): f. 1986; Sec.-Gen. JEAN-CLAUDE LEBRUN.

Fédération Haïtienne de Syndicats Chrétiens (Haitian Federation of Christian Unions): BP 416, Port-au-Prince; Pres. LÉONVIL LEBLANC.

Fédération des Ouvriers Syndiques (FOS): Angle rues Dr Aubry et des Miracles 115, BP 371, Port-au-Prince; tel. (1) 2-0035; f. 1984; Pres. JOSEPH J. SÉNAT.

Organisation Générale Indépendante des Travailleurs Haïtiens (OGITH): Delmas 11, Port-au-Prince; tel. (1) 6-5317; f. 1988; admitted to ORIT; Gen. Sec. SCHILLER MARCELIN.

Syndicat des Employés de l'EDH (SEEH): c/o EDH, rue Joseph Janvier, Port-au-Prince; tel. (1) 2-3367.

Union Nationale des Ouvriers d'Haïti—UNOH (National Union of Workers of Haiti): Delmas 11, 121 bis, BP 3337, Cité de l'Exposition, Port-au-Prince; f. 1951; admitted to ORIT; Pres. MARCEL VINCENT; Sec.-Gen. FRITZNER ST VIL; 3,000 mems from 8 affiliated unions.

A number of unions are non-affiliated and without a national centre, including those organized on a company basis.

Transport

RAILWAYS

The only railway is used to transport sugar cane.

ROADS

There are 4,000 km of roads, of which about 600 km are paved. An all-weather road from Port-au-Prince to Cap Haïtien, on the northern coast, was completed in the late 1980s with finance from the World Bank. Another major road, connecting Port-au-Prince with Jacmel, has been built and financed by France.

SHIPPING

Many European and American shipping lines call at Haiti. The two principal ports are Port-au-Prince and Cap Haïtien. There are also 12 minor ports.

CIVIL AVIATION

The international airport, situated 16 km outside Port-au-Prince, is the country's principal airport, and is served by many international airlines linking Haiti with the USA and other Caribbean islands. There is an airport at Cap Haïtien, and smaller airfields at Jacmel, Jérémie, Les Cayes and Port-de-Paix.

HAITI

Air Haiti: 35 ave Marie-Jeanne, Port-au-Prince; tel. (1) 62722; f. 1969; began cargo charter operations 1970; scheduled cargo and mail services from Port-au-Prince to Cap Haïtien, San Juan (Puerto Rico), Santo Domingo (Dominican Republic), Miami and New York; Gen. Man. ERNEST CINEAS; fleet of 2 Curtiss C-46 Commando.

Haiti Air Freight: Aeroport International, Port-au-Prince; tel. (1) 62572; cargo carrier operating charter services from Port-au-Prince; fleet of 1 Convair 880, 1 DC-4, 1 Curtiss C-46.

Haiti Régional: Aeroport International, Port-au-Prince; f. 1988; a subsidiary of Haiti Air Freight; operates scheduled passenger service between Port-au-Prince and Santo Domingo and Charter flights; fleet of 2 Convair 440.

Tourism

Tourism was formerly Haiti's second largest source of foreign exchange. In 1985/86 the number of visitors totalled 208,092. As a result of subsequent political instability, the number of cruise ships visiting Haiti has declined considerably, causing a sharp decline in the number of tourist arrivals. In 1988/89 the number of visitors was 184,737.

Office National du Tourisme d'Haïti: ave Marie-Jeanne, Port-au-Prince; tel. (1) 2-1729; telex 0206; Dir ANTONIO FENELON.

Association Hotelière et Touristique d'Haïti: Hotel Montana, rue F. Cardozo, route de Pétionville, BP 2562, Port-au-Prince; tel. (1) 7-1920; telex 0493; fax (1) 7-6137; Pres. Mme R. DUNWELL; Exec. Dir JOËLLE L. COUPAND.

HONDURAS

Introductory Survey

Location, Climate, Language, Religion, Flag, Capital

The Republic of Honduras lies in the middle of the Central American isthmus. It has a long northern coastline on the Caribbean Sea and a narrow southern outlet to the Pacific Ocean. Its neighbours are Guatemala to the west, El Salvador to the south-west and Nicaragua to the south-east. The climate ranges from temperate in the mountainous regions to tropical in the coastal plains. The rainy season is from May to November. The national language is Spanish. Almost all of the inhabitants profess Christianity, and the overwhelming majority are adherents of the Roman Catholic Church. The national flag (proportions 3 by 2) has three horizontal stripes, of blue, white and blue, with five blue five-pointed stars, arranged in a diagonal cross, in the centre of the white stripe. The capital is Tegucigalpa.

Recent History

Honduras was ruled by Spain from the 16th century until 1821. In 1823 Honduras joined the short-lived Federation of Central America, which also comprised Costa Rica, El Salvador, Guatemala and Nicaragua. Honduras emerged as a sovereign state in 1838.

From 1939 the country was ruled as a dictatorship by Gen. Tiburcio Carías Andino, leader of the Partido Nacional (PN). In 1949 Gen. Andino was succeeded as President by Juan Manuel Gálvez, who was also a member of the PN. In 1954 the leader of the Partido Liberal (PL), Dr José Ramón Villeda Morales, was elected President but was immediately deposed by Julio Lozano Díaz, himself overthrown by a military junta in 1956. The junta organized elections in 1957, when the PL secured a majority in Congress and Dr Villeda Morales was re-elected President for a six-year term. He was overthrown in 1963 by Col (later Gen.) Oswaldo López Arellano, the Minister of Defence, who, following elections held on the basis of a new constitution, was appointed President in June 1965.

A presidential election in March 1971 was won by Dr Ramón Ernesto Cruz Uclés, the PN candidate, who took office in June. However, popular discontent over government austerity measures and delayed land reforms culminated in a bloodless coup, led by the former President, Gen. López Arellano, in December 1972. A group of young army officers, in favour of social reform, took control of the Supreme Council of the Armed Forces, and in March 1974 replaced President López Arellano as Commander-in-Chief of the Armed Forces by Col (later Gen.) Juan Melgar Castro, who was appointed President in April 1975. In 1976 the President postponed the 1977 elections until 1979. He was forced to resign by the Supreme Council of the Armed Forces in August 1978, being replaced by a military junta. The Commander-in-Chief of the Armed Forces, Gen. Policarpo Paz García, assumed the role of Head of State, and the junta promised that elections would take place.

Military rule was ended officially when, in April 1980, elections to a Constituent Assembly were held. The PL won 52% of the votes but was unable to assume power. Gen. Paz was appointed interim President for one year and, as the armed forces were allowed to nominate four members of the coalition Cabinet, the PL was in a minority. A general election in November 1981 resulted in a victory for the PL, led by Dr Roberto Suazo Córdova, which gained an absolute majority in the National Assembly. Dr Suazo was sworn in as President in January 1982. However, real power lay in the hands of Gen. Gustavo Alvarez, who was appointed Head of the Armed Forces in January 1982. In November 1982 Gen. Alvarez became Commander-in-Chief of the Armed Forces, having brought about an amendment to the Constitution in that month, whereby the posts of President and Commander-in-Chief of the Armed Forces, which had been merged under the rule of the military junta, were separated. During 1982 and 1983 Gen. Alvarez suppressed increasing political unrest by authorizing the arrests of trade union activists and left-wing sympathizers; 'death squads' were allegedly also used to eliminate 'subversive' elements of the population. In March 1984 Gen. Alvarez was deposed as Commander-in-Chief of the Armed Forces by a group of junior army officers. The General and several other high-ranking officers were subsequently sent into exile.

In March 1985 a constitutional crisis developed as a result of President Suazo's refusal to accept the appointment of five Supreme Court judges, who had been nominated by the National Assembly. At the same time, Suazo refused to support Efraín Bu Girón, the President of the National Assembly, as PL candidate in the presidential election that was scheduled to take place later in the same year. In May, however, an agreement was reached between representatives of the trade unions and the Assembly and members of the armed forces, whereby the judges originally appointed by the Government were permitted to complete their four-year term of office and the President's prerogative to designate the ruling party's presidential candidate was abolished. A new electoral law, adopted prior to the November 1985 presidential election, meant that, although the leading candidate of the PN, Rafael Leonardo Callejas, obtained 42% of the individual votes cast, the leading candidate of the PL, José Simeón Azcona del Hoyo (who had obtained only 27% of the individual votes cast), was declared the winner because the combined votes of the PL's candidates secured the requisite majority of 51% of the total votes cast. The result led to some dissent, but the transfer of power took place in January 1986, as planned.

In February 1988 a report by the human rights organization, Amnesty International, gave evidence of an increase in violations of human rights by the armed forces and by right-wing 'death squads'. In the same month three human rights activists were murdered. A Honduran human rights organization reported in 1988 that 263 'extra-judicial executions' had taken place during 1987, and claimed that the armed forces had been responsible for many of these deaths. In August 1988, and again in 1989, the Inter-American Court of Human Rights found the Honduran Government guilty of the 'disappearances' of Honduran citizens between 1981 and 1984, and ordered that compensation be paid to the families involved. In January 1989 Gen. Gustavo Alvarez, was killed by left-wing guerrillas in Tegucigalpa. It was widely alleged that Alvarez, as Commander-in-Chief of the Armed Forces during the early 1980s, had been responsible for many violations of human rights.

Throughout 1989 campaigns for the presidential, congressional and municipal elections (that were scheduled to be held in November) were conducted in an atmosphere of deteriorating economic conditions. Refusal to adopt several austerity measures proposed by the IMF, including the devaluation of the national currency, the lempira, resulted in failure to reach agreement on future loans and a *de facto* moratorium on all repayments. A wave of industrial unrest in the public sector and a strike by banana workers, in conjunction with demands by some 10,000 farmers for compensation for land appropriated by Nicaraguan 'Contras' (see below), forced the Government to rely more heavily on the help and recommendations of the United States Agency for International Development (USAID), including a plan for the immediate transfer of the state-owned forestry company, COHDEFOR, to private ownership.

Elections took place on 29 November 1989 for a new president, three vice-presidents, 128 members of the National Assembly and 289 municipal councillors. The presidential election was won by Rafael Leonardo Callejas, candidate for the right-wing opposition party, the PN, who received 51% of the votes cast, compared with 43% received by Carlos Flores Facussé, candidate for the governing PL.

Following his inauguration as President on 27 January 1990, Callejas promised to address Honduras' major domestic problems, which he identified as unemployment, food shortage and fluctuating oil supply. In March the new administration announced that it would adopt many of the austerity measures originally proposed by the IMF, including the devaluation of the lempira.

Beginning in the early 1980s, former Nicaraguan National Guards, regarded by the left-wing Sandinista Government of Nicaragua as counter-revolutionaries ('Contras'), established bases in Honduras, from which they conducted raids across the border between the two countries, allegedly with support from the Honduran armed forces. In 1982 Honduran plans for a major military offensive against Nicaragua were thwarted by opposition from the USA. In 1983, when Honduran foreign policy was controlled by the pro-US Gen. Gustavo Alvarez, Commander-in-Chief of the Armed Forces, US involvement in Honduras increased substantially. In February 1983 the USA and Honduras initiated 'Big Pine', a series of joint military manoeuvres on Honduran territory; these exercises continued throughout the 1980s, thus enabling the USA to construct permanent military installations in Honduras. In return for considerable military assistance from the USA, the Honduran Government permitted US military aid to be supplied to the Contras based in Honduras.

Following the overthrow of Gen. Alvarez, in March 1984, public opposition to the US military presence in Honduras increased, causing a temporary deterioration in relations between Honduras and the USA. In mid-1984 the Suazo Government indicated that it would review its policy of co-operation with the USA. In 1985 the USA declined to enter into a security pact with Honduras, but confirmed that it would take 'appropriate' measures to defend Honduras against any Communist aggression. In August of that year the Honduran Government announced that it would prevent the US Government from supplying further military aid to the Contras through Honduras. However, following a visit by President Azcona to the USA in 1986, the supply of aid was believed to have resumed.

In 1986 relations with Nicaragua deteriorated sharply, when Honduran troops were mobilized in an attempt to curb incursions across the Honduras-Nicaragua border by Nicaraguan government forces. In December, however, following revelations that the USA had secretly sold weapons to the Government of Iran and that the proceeds had been used to finance the activities of the Contra rebels, President Azcona requested the departure of the Contras from Honduras. Their presence in an area that had become known as 'Nueva Nicaragua' (New Nicaragua) was also adversely affecting the Honduran economy, as the region contained important coffee-growing land.

In August 1987 Honduras, Costa Rica, El Salvador, Guatemala and Nicaragua signed a Central American peace plan, known as the 'Esquipulas agreement' (see chapter on Costa Rica). However, the commitment of the Honduran Government to the accord, the provisions of which included an end to rebel forces' use of foreign territory as a base for attack, appeared to be only partial. Claiming that it no longer permitted the Nicaraguan Contras to maintain bases on its territory, the Honduran Government opposed a clause in the agreement providing for the establishment of a committee to monitor the dismantling of Contra bases in Honduras.

In March 1988 several thousand US troops were temporarily deployed in Honduras, in response to an incursion into Honduran territory by the Nicaraguan army. However, further violations of the border between Honduras and Nicaragua occurred during that year, as Nicaraguan troops forced at least 12,000 Contra rebels based in the border area into Honduras. In November President Azcona declared his opposition to the presence of the Contras in his country. In the following month it was announced that the International Court of Justice (ICJ) would consider an application that had been submitted by the Nicaraguan Government in 1986, in which Nicaragua held that Honduras had breached international law by allowing the Contras to operate from its territory. In response, the Honduran Govenment threatened to withdraw support from the Esquipulas agreement.

In February 1989 a summit meeting of the five Central American Presidents was convened at Costa del Sol, El Salvador. An agreement was reached, whereby the Nicaraguan Contra forces encamped in Honduras would demobilize, while President Ortega of Nicaragua guaranteed that free and fair elections would take place in his country by February 1990. At a further summit meeting of the five Central American Presidents, held in August 1989 at Tela, Honduras, the conditions for the demobilization of the Contras were expanded. The Honduran Government agreed to the establishment by the UN and the Organization of American States of a Comisión Internacional de Apoyo y Verificación (CIAV), to oversee the voluntary repatriation or removal to a third country of the rebel forces by December 1989; in return, the Nicaraguan Government agreed to abandon the action that it had initiated against Honduras at the ICJ. Following the announcement of the Tela agreement, Honduran troops were ordered to encircle the Contra encampments, in order to prevent the possibility of the rebel forces' moving deeper into Honduran territory.

Despite the initiatives towards peace which emerged during 1989, the Contra rebels continued to launch attacks against Nicaraguan troops during the latter part of that year, maintaining their positions in Honduras beyond the December deadline. In February 1990, following national elections in Nicaragua, the outgoing President Ortega of Nicaragua ordered his forces to observe an immediate unilateral cease-fire with the Contras. Contra raids into Nicaragua continued during early 1990; however, the rebel units officially disbanded and left Honduras in June.

Honduras has a long-standing dispute with El Salvador regarding the demarcation of the two countries' common border, and both Governments lay claim to the island of Meanguera, in the Gulf of Fonseca. In 1969 hostilities broke out between Honduras and El Salvador; although these soon subsided, the two countries only signed a peace treaty in 1980. In 1982 the Honduran armed forces were engaged against guerrilla forces in El Salvador, indicating an improvement in Honduran-Salvadorean relations. Honduran troops were also reportedly responsible for the deaths of several hundred Salvadorean refugees in Honduras, during that year. In 1984 the Government of Honduras suspended the training of Salvadorean troops by Honduran-based US military advisers, pending agreement on disputed territory. In 1986, however, the Governments of Honduras and El Salvador agreed that their conflicting territorial claims should be examined by the ICJ. During 1989 several border clashes occurred between Honduran and Salvadorean troops. In 1987 there were an estimated 27,000 Salvadorean refugees in Honduras.

Although Honduras has remained the USA's closest ally in the region, relations with the USSR improved during the late 1980s.

A trade agreement that Honduras signed with the USSR in 1987 was finally ratified in 1989; in October 1990 the two countries agreed to establish diplomatic relations.

Government

Under the provisions of the Constitution approved by the National Assembly in 1982, the President is elected by a simple majority of the voters. However, at the presidential and general elections in November 1985, the leading candidate of the political party that received the most votes was appointed President. The President holds executive power and has a four-year mandate. Legislative power is vested in the National Assembly, with 128 members elected by universal adult suffrage for a term of four years. The country is divided into 18 local Departments.

Defence

Military service is by conscription. Active service lasts eight months, with subsequent reserve training. In June 1990 the armed forces totalled 18,200 men, of whom 15,000 were in the army, 1,100 in the navy and 2,100 in the air force. Paramilitary forces numbered 5,000 men. In 1989 247.0m. lempiras were allocated to defence by the central Government. In 1990 US military aid to Honduras was almost halved, compared with the previous year, to US $20.2m. In mid-1990 some 300 US troops were based in Honduras (reduced from 1,500 at mid-1989).

Economic Affairs

In 1989, according to estimates by the World Bank, Honduras' gross national product (GNP), measured at average 1987–89 prices, was US $4,495m., equivalent to $900 per head. During 1980–89, it was estimated, GNP increased, in real terms, at an average annual rate of 2.3%, although GNP per head declined by 1.2% per year. Over the same period, the population increased by an annual average of 3.5%. Honduras' gross domestic product (GDP) increased, in real terms, by an annual average of 1.7% in 1980–88.

Agriculture (including forestry and fishing) contributed an estimated 20.6% of GDP in 1989. Some 42.6% of the labour force were employed in the sector in that year. The principal commercial products are coffee and bananas (which together accounted for an estimated 56.8% of all export earnings in 1989), sugar and shellfish. Timber production is also important. During 1980–88 agricultural production increased by an annual average of 1.1%.

Industry (including mining, manufacturing, construction and power) contributed an estimated 25.1% of GDP in 1989. During 1980–88 industrial production increased by an annual average of 0.8%.

Mining contributed an estimated 1.5% of GDP in 1989. Lead, zinc and silver are the major mineral exports. Gold, copper and low-grade iron ore are also mined. In addition, small quantities of petroleum derivatives are exported.

Manufacturing contributed an estimated 16.1% of GDP and employed 10.4% of the labour force in 1989. The most important sectors, measured by gross value of output, are food-processing, textiles and clothing, chemicals and machinery and transport equipment.

Energy production relies heavily upon imports of mineral fuels and lubricants (an estimated 14.9% of the value of total imports in 1989), although hydroelectric power is increasingly important and fuel wood remains a prime source of domestic energy.

In 1989 Honduras recorded a visible trade surplus of US $2.7m., while there was a deficit of $302.2m. on the current account of the balance of payments. In 1989 the principal source of imports (an estimated 38.8%) was the USA, which was also the principal market for exports (an estimated 64.8%). Other major trading partners are Japan, Germany, Mexico, Venezuela, Italy, Belgium and the Netherlands. The principal exports in 1989 were bananas, coffee, shellfish and minerals. The principal imports in that year were machinery and transport equipment, chemicals, basic manufactures and mineral fuels and lubricants. In the financial year ending 30 June 1989 there was an estimated budgetary deficit of 182.0m. lempiras. Honduras' total external public debt was US $2,739m. at the end of 1988. In that year the cost of debt-servicing was equivalent to 25.5% of the value of exports of goods and services. The annual rate of inflation averaged 4.7% in 1980–88; consumer prices increased by an average of 4.5% in 1988 and by 9.9% in 1989. An estimated 20% of the labour force were unemployed in 1988.

Honduras is a member of the Central American Common Market (CACM, see p. 110).

During the 1980s Honduras' agricultural development was adversely affected by fluctuations in world prices for coffee and bananas, competition from cheaper forestry products from Chile and the USA, and a dependence upon unreliable external funding for irrigation and agrarian reform programmes. The industrial sector suffered from insufficient investment and a shortage of foreign exchange. The economic costs of accommodating the Nicaraguan Contras, together with consistent failure to reach agreement with the IMF, led to the accumulation of large foreign debts and to a heavy reliance upon economic aid from the USA. In March 1990 the Government agreed to implement a programme of economic reforms that had been recommended by the IMF, including a devaluation of the national currency, a reduction in public expenditure and the transfer to private ownership of some state enterprises. In July of that year the IMF agreed to make available US $41m., in support of the reforms, and the USA released aid of $140m. for 1989, which it had previously suspended.

Social Welfare

The state-run system of social security provides benefits for sickness, maternity, orphans, unemployment and accidents. It also provides family and old-age allowances. A Labour Code affords guarantees for employees. In 1980 Honduras had 1,141 physicians. In 1988 there were 46 hospitals, 683 health centres and 5,639 hospital beds, cots and incubators. The 1990 budget allocated 280m. lempiras to the health sector. In July 1988 the USA made a $57.2m. donation to the Honduran health sector.

Education

Primary education, beginning at seven years of age and lasting for six years, is officially compulsory and is provided free of charge. Secondary education, which is not compulsory, begins at the age of 13 and lasts for up to five years, comprising a first cycle of three years and a second of two years. On completion of the compulsory period of primary education, every person is required to teach at least two illiterate adults to read and write. In 1990, according to estimates by UNESCO, adult illiteracy averaged 26.9% (males 24.5%; females 29.4%). In 1989 some 886,583 pupils were enrolled at 7,954 primary schools, while 148,004 pupils attended 475 secondary schools. In 1986 the enrolment at primary schools included an estimated 91% of children in the relevant age-group (compared with 74% in 1980), while the comparable ratio for secondary enrolment was only 21%. There are four universities, including an autonomous national university in Tegucigalpa. For 1990 the education budget was 469m. lempiras.

Public Holidays

1991: 1 January (New Year's Day), 29 March–1 April (Easter), 14 April (Pan-American Day/Bastilla's Day), 1 May (Labour Day), 15 September (Independence Day), 3 October (Morazán Day), 12 October (Discovery Day), 21 October (Army Day), 25 December (Christmas).

1992: 1 January (New Year's Day), 14 April (Pan-American Day/Bastilla's Day), 17–20 April (Easter), 1 May (Labour Day), 15 September (Independence Day), 3 October (Morazán Day), 12 October (Discovery Day), 21 October (Army Day), 25 December (Christmas).

Weights and Measures

The metric system is in force, although some old Spanish measures are used, including: 25 libras = 1 arroba; 4 arrobas = 1 quintal (46 kg).

HONDURAS

Statistical Survey

Source (unless otherwise stated): Department of Economic Studies, Banco Central de Honduras, 1a Calle, 6a y 7a Avda, Apdo 3165, Tegucigalpa; tel. 22-2270; telex 1121.

Area and Population

AREA, POPULATION AND DENSITY

Area (sq km)	
Land	111,888
Inland water	200
Total	112,088*
Population (census results)†	
17 April 1961	1,884,765
6 March 1974	
Males	1,317,307
Females	1,339,641
Total	2,656,948
Population (official estimates at mid-year)	
1987	4,051,400
1988	4,168,900
1989	4,289,800
Density (per sq km) at mid-1989	38.3

* 43,277 sq miles.
† Excluding adjustments for underenumeration, estimated to have been 10% at the 1974 census.

PRINCIPAL TOWNS
(Preliminary mid-1989 population estimate, excluding suburbs)

Tegucigalpa	608,100	Danlí	31,100
San Pedro Sula	300,900	Siguatepeque	28,900
La Ceiba	71,600	Tela	23,600
El Progreso	63,400	Juticalpa	20,600
Choluteca	57,400	Santa Rosa de	
Comayagua	39,600	Copán	20,300
Puerto Cortés	32,000	Olancho	14,600

BIRTHS AND DEATHS (UN estimates, annual averages)

	1975–80	1980–85	1985–90
Birth rate (per 1,000)	43.8	42.3	39.8
Death rate (per 1,000)	11.1	9.0	8.1

Expectation of life at birth: Males 61.9 years; females 66.1 years (1985–90).
Source: UN, *World Population Prospects: 1988*.

EMPLOYMENT ('000)

	1987	1988	1989
Agriculture, forestry, hunting and fishing	599.2	611.5	623.2
Mining and quarrying	2.8	2.8	2.8
Manufacturing	140.7	146.3	152.0
Construction	60.8	65.5	70.2
Electricity, gas, water and sanitary services	6.4	7.0	7.6
Transport, storage and communications	33.5	34.8	36.1
Wholesale and retail trade	116.1	122.6	129.1
Banking, insurance, etc.	19.0	20.9	22.8
Other services	345.1	381.7	418.4
Total	1,324.3	1,393.1	1,462.2

Agriculture

PRINCIPAL CROPS ('000 quintales*)

	1987	1988	1989†
Maize	8,798	9,522	10,980
Rice	1,256	1,046	1,450
Dry beans	992	511	1,306
Sorghum	800	1,019	1,221
Cotton	177	187	102
Tobacco	94	106	138
Coffee	1,761	2,069	2,179
Bananas	25,362	24,399	23,738
Sugar cane	58,620	55,201	58,576
Plantains	3,475	3,524	3,800
African palm	6,471	6,925	6,590

* Figures are in terms of the old Spanish quintal, equal to 46 kg (101.4 lb).
† Preliminary.

LIVESTOCK ('000 head)

	1987	1988	1989*
Cattle	2,870	3,046	3,259
Pigs	722	726	728
Horses and mules	298	296	295
Chickens	10,908	11,823	12,835

* Preliminary.

LIVESTOCK PRODUCTS ('000 metric tons)

	1987	1988	1989*
Beef and veal	74	80	81
Pig meat	10	10	11
Cows' milk ('000 litres)	283	298	317
Hen eggs ('000 eggs)	585	604	621

* Preliminary.

Forestry

ROUNDWOOD REMOVALS ('000 cubic metres, excluding bark)

	1986	1987	1988
Sawlogs, veneer logs and logs for sleepers	793	958	928
Other industrial wood*	15	15	15
Fuel wood*	4,704	4,859	5,014
Total	5,512	5,832	5,957

* FAO estimates.
Source: FAO, *Yearbook of Forest Products*.

SAWNWOOD PRODUCTION ('000 cubic metres)

	1987	1988	1989*
Coniferous (softwood)	898	859	732
Broadleaved (hardwood)	38	39	52
Total	936	898	784

* Preliminary.

HONDURAS

Fishing

(metric tons, live weight)

	1987	1988	1989*
Fishes	4,780	4,835	5,030
Shrimps and lobsters	4,668	5,574	5,710
Others	470	520	625
Total catch	9,918	10,929	11,365

* Preliminary.

Mining

(metric tons, unless otherwise indicated)

	1986	1987	1988*
Lead	8,584	2,087	13,643
Zinc	21,333	7,455	30,664
Silver	55	11	70
Gold (kg)	14	2	111

* Preliminary.

Industry

SELECTED PRODUCTS

	1987	1988	1989*
Raw sugar ('000 quintales)	4,121	3,729	4,130
Cement ('000 bags of 42.5 kg)	10,615	13,178	15,265
Cigarettes ('000 packets of 20)	104,565	115,961	127,990
Matches ('000 boxes of 50)	62,141	65,337	72,823
Beer ('000 12 oz bottles)	153,377	173,451	192,433
Soft drinks ('000 12 oz bottles)	586,704	681,066	723,975
Wheat flour ('000 quintales)	1,624	1,787	1,802
Fabric ('000 yards)	18,134	20,131	19,962
Rum ('000 litres)	1,684	1,892	2,046
Other alcoholic drinks ('000 litres)	4,219	4,435	4,427
Iron bars ('000 kg)	16,599	n.a.	n.a.
Pasteurized milk ('000 litres)	58,602	57,846	57,497
Vegetable oil ('000 lb)	15,174	18,506	22,336
Vegetable fat ('000 lb)	77,308	79,822	79,714

*Preliminary.

Finance

CURRENCY AND EXCHANGE RATES

Monetary Units
100 centavos = 1 lempira.

Denominations
Coins: 1, 2, 5, 10, 20 and 50 centavos.
Notes: 1, 2, 5, 10, 20, 50 and 100 lempiras.

Sterling and Dollar Equivalents (30 September 1990)
£1 sterling = 3.747 lempiras;
US $1 = 2.000 lempiras;
100 lempiras = £26.69 = $50.00.

Exchange Rate
The official rate is fixed at US $1 = 2.00 lempiras.

Note: A parallel exchange rate exists for certain transactions; the parallel exchange rate at 30 May 1990 was US $1 = 4.20 lempiras. The existence of the parallel exchange rate was legally recognized in March 1990, although the old official exchange rate of US $1 = 2.00 lempiras was retained for the purpose of foreign debt repayments.

BUDGET (million lempiras)

Revenue	1987	1988*	1989†
Current revenue	2,156.9	2,317.8	2,495.3
Taxes	1,151.7	1,241.1	1,358.1
Income tax	298.1	340.8	374.3
Property tax	26.6	70.0	82.4
Tax on production, domestic trade and transactions	382.9	415.6	457.1
Import taxes and duties	348.8	347.9	373.0
Export taxes and duties	94.3	65.3	70.1
Other taxes	1.0	1.5	1.2
Non-tax revenue	710.6	856.4	825.4
Transfers	0.8	0.9	2.2
Other receipts	293.8	219.4	309.8
Capital revenue	1,153.2	1,580.7	1,233.5
Internal borrowing	811.3	998.6	924.7
External borrowing	231.5	463.0	292.4
Capital transfers	110.4	119.1	66.4
Other	−69.4	−104.9	47.2
Total	3,240.7	3,793.6	3,776.0

Expenditure	1987	1988*	1989†
Current expenditure	2,089.2	2,273.1	2,531.0
Consumption expenditure	1,983.3	2,160.1	2,360.4
of which wages and salaries	1,102.7	1,193.5	1,321.7
Current transfers	106.3	113.0	170.6
Capital expenditure	474.9	597.5	601.8
Direct investment	455.7	541.1	553.2
of which real investment	424.8	547.2	558.1
Indirect investment	19.2	56.3	33.4
Net allowance on loans	103.2	67.9	118.1
Public debt servicing	571.5	865.8	536.5
Internal	462.0	202.0	133.7
External	109.5	663.8	402.8
Total	3,345.1	3,917.3	3,958.0

* Preliminary.
† Estimates.

CENTRAL BANK RESERVES (US $ million at 31 December)

	1987	1988	1989
Gold	1.05	1.05	1.05
Foreign exchange	106.00	50.00	21.10
Total	107.05	51.05	22.15

Source: IMF, *International Financial Statistics*.

MONEY SUPPLY (million lempiras at 31 December)

	1987	1988	1989
Currency outside banks	492	570	676
Private sector deposits at Central Bank	44	55	74
Demand deposits at commercial banks	583	628	774
Total money	1,119	1,253	1,524

Source: IMF, *International Financial Statistics*.

HONDURAS

COST OF LIVING
(Consumer Price Index for Urban Centres. Base: 1978 = 100)

	1987	1988	1989*
Food	167.0	179.5	201.9
Housing	221.3	229.2	245.2
Clothing	242.6	246.2	275.9
Medical care	197.3	203.6	215.2
Personal care	182.5	189.8	219.2
Beverages and tobacco	247.1	248.9	268.6
Transport	169.5	170.5	175.4
Miscellaneous	215.6	224.0	247.1
All items	**197.8**	**206.7**	**227.0**

* Preliminary.

NATIONAL ACCOUNTS (million lempiras at current prices)
Expenditure on the Gross Domestic Product

	1987	1988	1989*
Government final consumption expenditure	1,371	1,468	1,562
Private final consumption expenditure	5,869	6,541	7,187
Increase in stocks	161	25	−20
Gross fixed capital formation	1,035	1,141	1,278
Total domestic expenditure	**8,436**	**9,175**	**10,007**
Exports of goods and services	1,874	1,980	2,092
Less Imports of goods and services	2,182	2,242	2,329
GDP in purchasers' values	**8,128**	**8,913**	**9,770**

* Preliminary.

Gross Domestic Product by Economic Activity

	1987	1988*	1989†
Agriculture, hunting, forestry and fishing	1,518	1,630	1,779
Mining and quarrying	105	115	132
Manufacturing	1,055	1,230	1,390
Electricity, gas and water	236	242	255
Construction	311	343	395
Wholesale and retail trade	952	1,019	1,121
Transport, storage and communications	509	560	598
Finance, insurance and real estate	482	554	612
Owner-occupied dwellings	612	670	732
Public administration and defence	439	472	510
Other services	964	1,062	1,117
GDP at factor cost	**7,183**	**7,897**	**8,641**
Indirect taxes, *less* subsidies	945	1,016	1,129
GDP in purchasers' values	**8,128**	**8,913**	**9,770**

* Preliminary.
† Estimates.

BALANCE OF PAYMENTS (US $ million)

	1987	1988	1988
Merchandise exports f.o.b.	844.4	893.0	966.7
Merchandise imports f.o.b.	−893.9	−916.7	−964.0
Trade balance	**−49.5**	**−23.7**	**2.7**
Exports of services	125.6	123.6	125.8
Imports of services	−193.9	−201.9	−208.7
Other income received	12.0	12.2	12.9
Other income paid	−250.3	−274.2	−279.3
Private unrequited transfers (net)	16.0	17.5	16.0
Official unrequited transfers (net)	34.1	27.5	28.5
Current balance	**−306.1**	**−319.0**	**−302.2**
Direct investment (net)	38.8	46.8	37.4
Portfolio investment (net)	0.7	−0.3	0.1
Other capital (net)	80.0	15.2	−57.4
Net errors and omissions	27.1	22.4	−3.7
Overall balance	**−159.7**	**−234.8**	**−325.8**

Source: IMF, *International Financial Statistics*.

External Trade

PRINCIPAL COMMODITIES (million lempiras)

Imports c.i.f.	1987	1988*	1989†
Food and live animals	170.4	179.9	184.4
Mineral fuels, lubricants, etc.	238.5	229.8	292.9
Chemicals	388.8	406.6	417.8
Basic manufactures	339.1	373.1	384.6
Machinery and transport equipment	482.5	489.2	496.5
Miscellaneous manufactured articles	114.5	122.7	125.0
Total (incl. others)	**1,797.3**	**1,865.8**	**1,962.1**

Exports f.o.b.	1987	1988*	1989†
Bananas	643.6	690.7	686.1
Coffee	399.8	384.2	381.8
Wood	69.5	59.6	50.9
Lead and zinc	38.0	60.1	177.5
Silver	15.3	17.2	13.5
Frozen meat	45.2	40.8	38.1
Shellfish	116.8	164.0	158.6
Soap	1.6	1.6	2.6
Cotton	4.3	1.6	1.9
Tobacco	8.8	7.6	13.8
Total (incl. others)	**1,616.1**	**1,737.4**	**1,880.7**

* Preliminary.
† Estimates.

PRINCIPAL TRADING PARTNERS (million lempiras)

Imports c.i.f.	1987	1988*	1989†
Brazil	52.0	41.0	41.2
Canada	15.2	15.2	16.1
Costa Rica	37.8	25.4	33.8
France	36.2	37.5	39.0
Germany, Federal Republic	60.0	65.9	66.4
Guatemala	54.8	59.4	61.0
Japan	177.1	176.8	196.7
Mexico	97.2	102.7	105.6
Netherlands	92.1	77.0	95.8
United Kingdom	33.6	33.2	35.5
USA	705.3	738.6	761.4
Venezuela	82.7	105.9	108.6
Total (incl. others)	**1,797.3**	**1,865.8**	**1,962.1**

HONDURAS

Exports f.o.b.	1987	1988*	1989†
Belgium	67.2	95.2	90.4
Costa Rica	7.0	3.1	5.6
Germany, Federal Republic	168.7	183.5	196.9
Guatemala	21.3	20.2	28.5
Italy	90.3	109.5	112.2
Japan	79.2	122.8	112.4
Netherlands	32.4	42.9	42.0
Spain	26.9	29.4	31.5
Trinidad and Tobago	10.7	11.3	12.4
United Kingdom	25.0	28.0	29.6
USA	900.3	1,091.5	1,219.2
Total (incl. others)	1,616.1	1,737.4	1,880.7

* Preliminary.
† Estimates.

Transport

ROAD TRAFFIC (motor vehicles in use)

	1987	1988*	1989†
Passenger cars	28,791	31,845	35,539
Lorries and buses	65,843	70,377	79,660

* Preliminary.
† Estimates.

INTERNATIONAL SEA-BORNE SHIPPING
(freight traffic in '000 metric tons)

	1986	1987	1988*
Goods loaded	1,367	1,584	1,708
Goods unloaded	1,707	1,865	1,797

* Provisional figures.

CIVIL AVIATION (traffic on scheduled services)

	1983	1984	1985
Passengers carried ('000)	436	439	713
Passenger-km (million)	348	408	782
Freight ton-km (million)	1.9	2.2	1.0

Source: UN, *Statistical Yearbook*.

Tourism

	1987	1988	1989*
Number of visitors	192,426	218,253	249,761

* Preliminary.

Education

(1989)

	Institutions	Teachers	Students
Primary	7,954	24,378	886,583
Secondary	475	9,175	148,004
Teachers' training college	1	380	6,287
Universities	4	2,797	36,126

Directory

The Constitution

Following the elections of April 1980, the 1965 Constitution was revised. The new Constitution was approved by the National Assembly in November 1982. The following are some of its main provisions:

Honduras is constituted as a democratic Republic. All Hondurans over the age of 18 are citizens.

THE SUFFRAGE AND POLITICAL PARTIES

The vote is direct and secret. Any political party which proclaims or practises doctrines contrary to the democratic spirit is forbidden. A National Electoral Council will be set up at the end of each presidential term. Its general function will be to supervise all elections and to register political parties. A proportional system of voting will be adopted for the election of Municipal Corporations.

INDIVIDUAL RIGHTS AND GUARANTEES

The right to life is declared inviolable; the death penalty is abolished. The Constitution recognizes the right of habeas corpus and arrests may be made only by judicial order. Remand for interrogation may not last more than six days, and no-one may be held incommunicado for more than 24 hours. The Constitution recognizes the rights of free expression of thought and opinion, the free circulation of information, of peaceful, unarmed association, of free movement within and out of the country, of political asylum and of religious and educational freedom. Civil marriage and divorce are recognized.

WORKERS' WELFARE

All have a right to work. Day work shall not exceed eight hours per day or 44 hours per week; night work shall not exceed six hours per night or 36 hours per week. Equal pay shall be given for equal work. The legality of trade unions and the right to strike are recognized.

EDUCATION

The State is responsible for education, which shall be free, lay, and, in the primary stage, compulsory. Private education is liable to inspection and regulation by the State.

LEGISLATIVE POWER

Deputies are obliged to vote, for or against, on any measure at the discussion of which they are present. The National Assembly has power to grant amnesties to political prisoners; approve or disapprove of the actions of the Executive; declare part or the whole of the Republic subject to a state of siege; declare war; approve or withhold approval of treaties; withhold approval of the accounts of public expenditure when these exceed the sums fixed in the budget; decree, interpret, repeal and amend laws, and pass legislation fixing the rate of exchange or stabilizing the national currency. The National Assembly may suspend certain guarantees in all or part of the Republic for 60 days in the case of grave danger from civil or foreign war, epidemics or any other calamity. Deputies are elected in the proportion of one deputy and one substitute for every 35,000 inhabitants, or fraction over 15,000. Congress may amend the basis in the light of increasing population.

HONDURAS

EXECUTIVE POWER

Executive power is exercised by the President of the Republic, who is elected for four years, by a simple majority of the people. No President may serve more than one term.

JUDICIAL POWER

The Judiciary consists of the Supreme Court, the Courts of Appeal and various lesser tribunals. The nine judges and seven substitute judges of the Supreme Court are elected by the National Assembly for a period of four years. The Supreme Court is empowered to declare laws unconstitutional.

THE ARMED FORCES

The armed forces are declared by the Constitution to be essentially professional and non-political. The President exercises military power through a Commander-in-Chief who is designated for a period of three years by the National Assembly, and may be dismissed only by it by a two-thirds majority. Military service is obligatory.

LOCAL ADMINISTRATION

The country is divided into 18 Departments for purposes of local administration, and these are subdivided into autonomous Municipalities; the functions of local offices shall be only economic and administrative.

The Government

HEAD OF STATE

President: RAFAEL LEONARDO CALLEJAS (assumed office 27 January 1990).

Vice-Presidents: ROBERTO MARTÍNEZ LOZANO, JACOBO HERNÁNDEZ-CRUZ, MARCO TULIO CRUZ.

CABINET
(February 1991)

Minister of the Interior and Justice: FRANCISCO CARDONA.
Minister of Foreign Affairs: MARIO CARÍAS ZAPATA.
Minister of Public Education: JAIME MARTÍNEZ GUZMÁN.
Minister of Finance: BENJAMÍN VILLANUEVA.
Minister of Economy and Commerce: RAMÓN MEDINA LUNA.
Minister of Health and Social Security: CÉSAR CASTELLANOS.
Minister of Natural Resources: MARIO NUFIO GAMERO.
Minister of Labour and Social Affairs: RODOLFO ROSALES ABELLA.
Minister of Defence and Public Security: Col FRANCISCO ZEPEDA ANDINO.
Minister of Communications, Public Works and Transport: MAURO MEMBREÑO.
Minister of Culture, Tourism and Information: SONIA CANALES DE MENDIETA.
Secretary for Economic Planning: MANLIO MARTÍNEZ.
President of the Central Bank: RICARDO MADURO.
Director of the National Agrarian Institute (INA): JUAN RAMÓN MARTÍNEZ.

MINISTRIES

Office of the President: Casa Presidencial, 6a Avda, 1a Calle, Tegucigalpa; tel. 22-8287.
Ministry of Communications, Public Works and Transport: Barrio La Bolsa, Comayagüela, Tegucigalpa; tel. 33-7690.
Ministry of Culture, Tourism and Information: Costado Este del Palacio Legislativo, Tegucigalpa; tel. 22-6618.
Ministry of Defence and Public Security: Palacio de los Ministerios, Tegucigalpa; tel. 22-9521.
Ministry of Economy and Commerce: Edif. Salame, 5a Avda, 4a Calle, Tegucigalpa; tel. 22-3251; telex 1396.
Ministry of Finance: Palacio de Hacienda, Avda Cervantes, Tegucigalpa; tel. 22-8452.
Ministry of Foreign Affairs: Edif. Atala, Avda La Paz, Tegucigalpa; tel. 31-4209; telex 1129.
Ministry of Health and Social Security: 4a Avda, 3a Calle, Tegucigalpa; tel. 22-1386.
Ministry of the Interior and Justice: Palacio de los Ministerios, 2°, Tegucigalpa; tel. 22-8604.
Ministry of Labour and Social Affairs: 2a y 3a Avda, 7a Calle, Comayagüela, Tegucigalpa; tel. 22-8527.
Ministry of Natural Resources: Blvd Miraflores, Tegucigalpa; tel. 32-3141.
Ministry of Public Education: 1a Avda, 2a y 3a Calle, No 201, Comayagüela, Tegucigalpa; tel. 22-8573.

President and Legislature

PRESIDENT

Election, 26 November 1989

Candidate	Votes cast	Percentage of votes cast
RAFAEL LEONARDO CALLEJAS (PN)	917,168	50.97
CARLOS FLORES FACUSSÉ (PL)	776,983	43.18
ENRIQUE AGUILAR (PINU)	33,952	1.89
EFRAÍN DÍAZ (PDC)	25,433	1.42
Others	45,610	2.54
Total	1,799,146	100.00

ASAMBLEA NACIONAL

President: (vacant).

General Election, 26 November 1989

Party	Seats
Partido Liberal (PL)	71
Partido Nacional (PN)	55
Partido de Innovación y Unidad (PINU)	2
Total	128

Political Organizations

Asociación para el Progreso de Honduras (APROH): right-wing grouping of business interests and members of the armed forces; Vice-Pres. MIGUEL FACUSSÉ; Sec. OSWALDO RAMOS SOTO.

Francisco Morazán Frente Constitucional (FMFC): f. 1988; composed of labour, social, political and other organizations.

Frente Patriótico Hondureño (FPH): left-wing alliance comprising:

Partido Comunista de Honduras (PCH): f. 1954; gained legal status 1981; linked with DNU; Leader RIGOBERTO PADILLA RUSH.

Partido Comunista Marxista-Leninista.

Partido Socialista (Paso): Leaders MARIO VIRGILIO CARAS, ROGELIO MARTÍNEZ REINA.

Partido Demócrata Cristiano (PDC): legally recognized in 1980; Pres. EFRAÍN DÍAZ ARRIVILLAGA; Leader Dr HERNÁN CORRALES PADILLA.

Partido de Innovación y Unidad (PINU): Apdo 105, Tegucigalpa; f. 1970; legally recognized in 1978; Leader Dr MIGUEL ANDONIE FERNÁNDEZ.

Partido Liberal (PL): Tegucigalpa; tel. 32-0520; f. 1980; Liberal Party; factions within the party include the Alianza Liberal del Pueblo, the Movimiento Florista (Leader Ing. CARLOS ROBERTO FLORES FACUSSÉ), and the Movimiento Liberal Democrático Revolucionario (Pres. JORGE ARTURO REINA); Pres. Prof. RAFAEL PINEDA PONCE; Sec.-Gen. ROBERTO MICHELETTI BAIN.

Partido Nacional (PN): Tegucigalpa; f. 1902; traditional right-wing party; internal opposition tendencies include Movimiento Democratizador Nacionalista (Modena), Movimiento de Unidad y Cambio (MUC), Movimiento Nacional de Reivindicación Callejista (MONARCA) and Tendencia Nacionalista de Trabajo; Sec. MARIO AGUILAR GONZÁLEZ; Leader RAFAEL LEONARDO CALLEJAS.

Partido Revolucionario Hondureño (PRH): Apdo 1319, San Pedro Sula; f. 1977; not legally recognized; Sec.-Gen. FRANCISCO RODOLFO JIMÉNEZ CABALLERO.

Unión Revolucionaria del Pueblo (URP): f. 1980 from split in Communist Party; left-wing group, with peasant support.

In 1985 a broad-based opposition alliance, the Coordinadora Opositora Democrática Constitucional—Codeco, was formed by members of the PDC, PLH and PN.

In 1983 the guerrilla forces united to form the Directorio Nacional Unido (DNU), consisting of the following groups:

HONDURAS

Fuerzas Populares Revolucionarias (FRP) Lorenzo Zelaya.
Frente Morazanista para la Liberación de Honduras (FMLH).
Froylan Turcios.
Movimiento Popular de Liberación Cinchonero (MPLC).
Movimiento de Unidad Revolucionaria (MUR).
Partido Revolucionario de los Trabajadores Centroamericanos de Honduras (PRTCH).

Other guerrilla forces include the **Alianza por Acción Anticomunista (AAA)** and the **Frente Popular de Liberación, Nueve de Mayo (FPL)**.

Diplomatic Representation

EMBASSIES IN HONDURAS

Argentina: Colonia Rubén Darío 2 cuadras al sur del Cenáculo, Apdo 101-C, Tegucigalpa; tel. 32-3376; telex 1120; Ambassador: LUIS N. AUGUSTO SÁNCHEZ R.

Brazil: Plaza San Martín 501, Colonia Palmira, Apdo 341, Tegucigalpa; tel. 32-2021; telex 1151; Ambassador: CYRO GABRIEL DO ESPIRITO SANTO CARDOSO.

Chile: Edif. Interamericana frente Los Castaños, Blvd Morazán, Apdo 222, Tegucigalpa; telex 1195; Ambassador: VICTORIA EUGENIA MORALES ETCHEVERS.

China (Taiwan): Avda República de Panamá 2024, Colonia Palmira, Apdo 6-C, Tegucigalpa; tel. 32-9490; telex 1383; Ambassador: HUANG CHUAM-LI.

Colombia: Edif. Palmira, 4°, Colonia Palmira, Apdo 468, Tegucigalpa; tel. 32-9300; telex 1336; Ambassador: (vacant).

Costa Rica: Blvd Morazán, Colonia Palmira, 1a Calle 704, Apdo 512, Tegucigalpa; tel. 32-1768; telex 1154; Ambassador: MAXIMILIANO OREAMUNO BRENES.

Dominican Republic: Colonia La Granja 402, 4a Calle entre 4a y 5a Avda Comayagüela, Apdo 1460, Tegucigalpa; Ambassador: JUAN EMILIO CANÓ DE LA MOTA.

Ecuador: Avda Juan Lindo 122, Colonia Palmira, Apdo 358, Tegucigalpa; telex 1471; Ambassador: FERNANDO PROCEL GALLEGOS.

El Salvador: 2a Avda 205, Colonia San Carlos, Tegucigalpa; tel. 32-1344; telex 1301; Ambassador: SALVADOR TRIGUEROS.

France: Avda Juan Lindo, Colonia Palmira, Apdo 14-C, Tegucigalpa; tel. 32-1800; telex 1180; Ambassador: PIERRE DUMON.

Germany: Edif. Paysen, 3°, Blvd Morazán, Apdo 3145, Tegucigalpa; tel. 32-3161; telex 1118; Ambassador: Dr WALTER EICKHOFF.

Guatemala: Avda Juan Lindo 313, Colonia Palmira, Apdo 34-C, Tegucigalpa; tel. 32-5018; Ambassador: EUNICE LIMA.

Holy See: Palacio de la Nunciatura Apostólica, Colonia Palmira 412, Apdo 324, Tegucigalpa; tel. 32-8280; fax 31-4381; Apostolic Nuncio: Mgr FRANCISCO DE NITTIS.

Israel: Edif. Palmira, Apdo 1187, Tegucigalpa; Ambassador: SHLOMO COHEN.

Italy: Avda Principal Colonia Reforma 2062, Apdo 317, Tegucigalpa; telex 1332; Ambassador: Dr MARIO ALBERTO MONTECALVO.

Japan: 2a Avda, Colonia Reforma, Plaza del Guanacaste, Apdo 125-C, Tegucigalpa; telex 1141; Ambassador: KIICHI ITABASHI.

Mexico: Avda República del Brasil 2028, Apdo 769, Tegucigalpa; tel. 32-4039; telex 1143; fax 32-4224; Ambassador: MANUEL MARTÍNEZ DEL SOBRAL.

Nicaragua: Colonia Tepeyac, Bloque M-1, Apdo 392, Tegucigalpa; tel. 32-1209; telex 1274; Ambassador: Lic. FRANCISCO JOSÉ LACAYO.

Panama: Edif. Palmira, Apdo 397, Tegucigalpa; Ambassador: Dr CARLOS ALBERTO DE DIEGO SORIANO.

Peru: Edif. Palmira, 5°, Apdo 64-C, Tegucigalpa; Ambassador: JAIME CASTRO MENDIVIL.

Spain: Colonia Matamoros 801, Apdo 114-C, Tegucigalpa; tel. 32-1875; telex 1142; Ambassador: J. ALBI DE LA CUESTA.

United Kingdom: Edif. Palmira, 3°, Colonia Palmira, Apdo 290, Tegucigalpa; tel. 32-5429; telex 1234; fax 32-5480; Ambassador: PETER STREAMS.

USA: Avda La Paz, Apdo 26-C, Tegucigalpa; tel. 32-3120; fax 32-0027; Ambassador: CRESENCIO ARCOS.

Uruguay: Edif. Palmira, 4°, Apdo 329, Tegucigalpa; Ambassador: ALFREDO MENINI TERRA.

Venezuela: Colonia Palmira 2302, 4°, Calle República de Colombia, Apdo 775, Tegucigalpa; telex 1238; Ambassador: DIONSSIO TEODORO MARCANO.

Judicial System

There is a Supreme Court with nine judges. In addition, there are five Courts of Appeal, and departmental courts which have their own local jurisdiction.

Tegucigalpa has two Courts of Appeal which have jurisdiction (1) in the department of Francisco Morazán, and (2) in the departments of Choluteca Valle, El Paraíso and Olancho.

The Appeal Court of San Pedro Sula has jurisdiction in the department of Cortés. That of Comayagua has jurisdiction in the departments of Comayagua, La Paz and Intibucá; that of Santa Bárbara in the departments of Santa Bárbara, Lempira, Copán.

Supreme Court: 10a y 11a Avda, 3a Calle, Tegucigalpa; tel. 22-8790.

President of the Supreme Court of Justice: SALOMON JIMÉNEZ CASTRO.

Attorney-General: RUBÉN DARÍO ZEPEDA GUTIÉRREZ.

Religion

The majority of the population are Roman Catholics; the Constitution guarantees toleration to all forms of religious belief.

CHRISTIANITY

The Roman Catholic Church

Honduras comprises one archdiocese and six dioceses. In 1990 an estimated 85% of the population were adherents.

Bishops' Conference: Conferencia Episcopal de Honduras, Apdo 847, Tegucigalpa; tel. 32-4043; fax 32-7838; f. 1972; Pres. HÉCTOR ENRIQUE SANTOS HERNÁNDEZ, Archbishop of Tegucigalpa.

Archbishop of Tegucigalpa: HÉCTOR ENRIQUE SANTOS HERNÁNDEZ, Arzobispado, Apdo 106, Avda Jérez 11-13, Tegucigalpa; tel. 37-0353; fax 22-2337.

The Episcopal Church

Bishop of Honduras: Rt Rev. LEO FRADE, Apdo 586, San Pedro Sula; tel. 57-4009; fax 57-7803.

The Baptist Church

Baptist Convention of Honduras: Apdo 868, Tegucigalpa; tel. 22-7392; Pres. ALEXIS VIDES.

BAHÁ'Í FAITH

National Spiritual Assembly: Apdo 273, Tegucigalpa; tel. 33-1182; mems resident in 560 localities.

The Press

DAILIES

El Faro Porteño: Puerto Cortés.

La Gaceta: Tegucigalpa; f. 1830; morning; official govt paper; Dir MARCIAL LAGOS; circ. 3,000.

El Heraldo: Avda los Próceres, Frente Instituto del Tórax, Tegucigalpa; f. 1979; morning; independent; Dir JOSÉ FRANCISCO MORALES CÁLIX; circ. 45,000.

La Prensa: 3a Avda No 34, Apdo 143, San Pedro Sula; f. 1964; independent; Pres. AMILCAR SANTAMARÍA; circ. 50,000.

El Tiempo: Altos del Centro Comercial Miramontes, Colonia Miramontes, Tegucigalpa; f. 1970; liberal; Dir MANUEL GAMERO; circ. 42,000.

El Tiempo: 7a Avda No 6, Calle S.O. 55, Apdo 450, San Pedro Sula; f. 1970; left-of-centre; Dir EDMOND L. BOGRÁN; Editor MANUEL GAMERO; circ. 70,000.

La Tribuna: Apdo 1501, Tegucigalpa; f. 1977; morning; independent; Dir ADÁN ELVIR FLORES; circ. 60,000.

PERIODICALS

Cambio Empresarial: Apdo 4, Tegucigalpa; monthly; economic, political, social; Editor JOAQUÍN MEDINA OVIEDO.

El Comercio: Cámara de Comercio e Industrias de Tegucigalpa, Bulevar Centroamérica, Apdo 3444, Tegucigalpa; tel. 32-8210; telex 1537; fax 31-2049; f. 1970; monthly; commercial and industrial news; Man. JORGE MEJÍA ORTEGA.

Cultura para Todos: San Pedro Sula; monthly.

Espectador: San Pedro Sula; weekly.

Extra: Apdo 54, Tegucigalpa; tel. 37-2533; f. 1965; monthly; independent; current affairs; Editor VICENTE MACHADO VALLE.

HONDURAS

Directory

Hablemos Claro: Tegucigalpa; Editor Rodrigo Wong Arévalo.
Hibueras: Apdo 955, Tegucigalpa; Dir Raúl Lanza Valeriano.
Presente: Tegucigalpa; monthly.
Revista Ideas: Tegucigalpa; 6 a year; women's interest.
Revista Prisma: Tegucigalpa; quarterly; cultural; Editor María Luisa Castellanos.
Sucesos: Tegucigalpa; monthly.
Tragaluz: Apdo 1843, Tegucigalpa; every 2 months; cultural and literary review; Editor Helen Umaña; circ. 2,000.
Tribuna Sindical: Tegucigalpa; monthly.
El Trópico: Avda Atlántida, 3a Calle, La Ceiba; f. 1938; weekly; independent; general news; Editor Rodolfo Zavala.

PRESS ASSOCIATION

Asociación de Prensa Hondureña: 6a Calle (altos), Barrio Guanacaste, Apdo 893, Tegucigalpa; f. 1930; Pres. Mario Hernán Ramírez.

FOREIGN NEWS AGENCIES

Agence France-Presse (AFP) (France): Tegucigalpa; Correspondent Winston Calix.
Agencia EFE (Spain): Edif. Jiménez Castro, 5°, Of. 505, Tegucigalpa; tel. 22-0493; Bureau Chief Armando Enrique Cerrato Cortés.
Agenzia Nazionale Stampa Associata (ANSA) (Italy): 2da Avda B 434, Barrio Morazán, Tegucigalpa; tel. 22-0109; telex 1353; Correspondent Raúl Moncada.
Deutsche Presse-Agentur (dpa) (Germany): Edif. Jiménez Castro, Of. 203, 4a Calle y 5a Avda, Apdo 1501, Tegucigalpa; tel. 22-8883; Correspondent Wilfredo García Castro.
Inter Press Service (IPS) (Italy): Apdo 228, Tegucigalpa; tel. 32-5342; Correspondent Juan Ramón Durán.
Reuters (UK): Edif. Palmira frente Honduras Maya, 5°, Barrio Palmira, Tegucigalpa; tel. 31-5329.
United Press International (UPI) (USA): c/o Diario Tiempo, Barrio La Fuente, Tegucigalpa; tel. 31-0418; Correspondent Vilma Gloria Rosales.

Publishers

Compañía Editora Nacional, SA: 5a Calle Oriente No 410, Tegucigalpa.
Editora Cultural: 6a Avda Norte, 7a Calle, Comayagüela, Tegucigalpa.
Editorial Nuevo Continente: Avda Cervantes 123, Tegucigalpa; tel. 22-5073; Dir Leticia Silva de Oyuela.
Editorial Paulino Valladares, Carlota Vda de Valladares: 5a Avda, 5a y 6a Calle, Tegucigalpa.
Guaymuras: Apdo 1843, Tegucigalpa; tel. 37-5433; f. 1980; Dir Isolda Arita Melzer; Admin. Rosendo Antúnez.
Industria Editorial Lypsa: Apdo 167-C, Tegucigalpa; tel. 22-9775; Man. José Bennaton.
Universidad Nacional Autónoma de Honduras: Oficina de Relaciones Públicas, Carretera a Suyapa, Tegucigalpa; tel. 31-4601; telex 1289; f. 1847; Gen. Sec. Angel Valentín Aguilar.

Radio and Television

In 1988 there were 281 radio stations and nine main television stations. In that year there were an estimated 1,847,000 radio receivers and 330,000 television sets in use.

RADIO

Empresa Hondureña de Telecomunicaciones (Hondutel): Apdo 1794, Tegucigalpa; tel. 37-9802; telex 1343; fax 37-1111; Gen. Man. Col Manuel Suárez B.
Radio América: Apdo 259, Tegucigalpa; commercial station; 13 relay stations; Controller Liliana Andonie Medina.
Radio Nacional de Honduras: Apdo 403, Tegucigalpa; tel. 22-8042; telex 1147; f. 1976; official station, operated by the Govt; Dir Miguel Rafael Zavala.
La Voz de Centroamérica: Apdo 120, San Pedro Sula; commercial station; Gen. Man. Jorge Sikaffy.
La Voz de Honduras: Apdo 642, Tegucigalpa; commercial station; 23 relay stations; Gen. Man. Nahún Valladares.

TELEVISION

Compañía Televisora Hondureña, SA: Apdo 642, Tegucigalpa; tel. 32-7835; telex 1126; f. 1959; main station Channel 5; nine relay stations; Gen. Man. José Rafael Ferrari.
Corporación Centroamericana de Comunicaciones, SA de CV: Apdo 120, San Pedro Sula; Pres. J. J. Sikaffy.
Telesistema Hondureño, SA: Apdo 642, Tegucigalpa; tel. 32-0710; telex 1126; f. 1967; main station Channel 3; four relay stations; Gen. Man. Manuel Villeda Toledo; Asst Gen. Man. Lic. Ana María Villeda F.
Trecevisión: Apdo 393, Tegucigalpa; subscriber TV; one relay station in San Pedro Sula; Gen. Man. F. Pon Aguilar.
Voz y Imagen de Centro América: Apdo 120, San Pedro Sula; 2 relay stations; Pres. Jorge Sikaffy.

Finance

(cap. = capital; p.u. = paid up; res = reserves; dep. = deposits; m. = million; brs = branches; amounts in US dollars unless otherwise stated)

BANKING

Central Bank

Banco Central de Honduras—BANTRAL: 6a y 7a Avda, 1a Calle, Apdo 58-C, Tegucigalpa; tel. 22-2270; telex 1121; f. 1950; cap. and res $110.3m., dep. $590.0m. (March 1988); bank of issue; Pres. Ricardo Maduro; Man. Rigoberto Pineda S.; 3 brs.

Commercial Banks

Banco de el Ahorro Hondureño, SA (BANCAHORRO): Avda Colón 711, Apdo 78-C, Tegucigalpa; tel. 22-5161; telex 1184; f. 1960; cap. and res $5.3m., dep. $83.3m. (June 1984); Pres. and Gen. Man. Francisco Villars; 8 brs.
Banco Atlántida, SA (BANCATLAN): Blvd Miraflores, Plaza Bancatlán, Apdo 3164, Tegucigalpa; tel. 32-2854; telex 1106; fax 31-4127; f. 1913; cap. $12.5m., res $4.2m., dep. $297.6m. (Dec. 1989); Pres. Dr Paul Vinelli; 18 brs.
Banco Capitalizadora Hondureña, SA (BANCAHSA): 5a Avda 501, Apdo 344, Tegucigalpa; tel. 22-1171; telex 1162; f. 1948; cap. and res $7.2m., dep. $130.6m. (June 1987); Pres. and Gen. Man. Lic. Jorge Alberto Alvarado; 38 brs.
Banco del Comercio, SA (BANCOMER): 6a Avda, 1-2 Calle SO, Apdo 160, San Pedro Sula; tel. 54-3600; telex 5480; cap. and res $6.5m., dep. $28.3m. (June 1984); Pres. Rodolfo Córdoba Pineda; 4 brs.
Banco Continental, SA (BANCON): Edif Continental, 3a Avda 50, entre 2 y 3 Calle, Apdo 390, San Pedro Sula; tel. 53-2622; telex 5561; fax 52-2750; f. 1974; cap. and res $13.5m., dep. $50.3m. (Oct. 1989); Pres. Ing. Jaime Rosenthal Oliva; 7 brs.
Banco de las Fuerzas Armadas, SA (BANFFAA): Centro Comercial Los Castaños, Boulevard Morazan, Apdo 877, Tegucigalpa; tel. 32-8505; telex 1245; fax 31-3832; f. 1979; cap. and res 20.2m. lempiras, dep. 302.3m. lempiras (Dec. 1989); Gen. Man. Capt. Armando San Martín.
Banco de Honduras, SA: Edif. Midence Soto, Freute a Plaza Morázan, Apdo 3434, Tegucigalpa; tel. 37-1151; telex 1116; fax 22-3451; f. 1889; cap. and res $3.8m., dep. $31.3m. (June 1984); Gen. Man. Lic. María Lidia Solano; 3 brs.
Banco Mercantil, SA: 5a Calle, 10 Avda 924, Apdo 116, Tegucigalpa; tel. 22-6280; telex 1260; Pres. José Lamas; Gen. Man. Lic. Jacobo Atala.
Banco de Occidente, SA (BANCOCCI): Apdo 208, Calle Centenario, Santa Rosa de Copán; tel. 62-0232; telex 5533; f. 1951; cap. and res $8.1m., dep. $169.6m. (Dec. 1988); Pres. and Gen. Man. Lic. Jorge Bueso Arias; 14 brs.
Banco Sogerin, SA: 8a Avda, la Calle, Apdo 440, San Pedro Sula; tel. 53-3888; telex 5624; fax 57-2001; f. 1969; cap. and res 14.0m. lempiras, dep. 267.0m. lempiras (Dec. 1989); Pres. Reginaldo Panting P.; Gen. Man. Sidney José Panting; 23 brs.
Banco de los Trabajadores, SA (BANCOTRAB): 3a Avda, 13a Calle, El Obelisco, Apdo 139-C, Comayagüela; tel. 22-8723; telex 1202; f. 1967; cap. and res $7.1m., dep. $28.0m. (June 1984); Pres. Rolando del Cid V.; Man. Raúl Solís Dacosta; 13 brs.

Development Banks

Banco Centroamericano de Integración Económica: Apdo 772, Tegucigalpa; tel. 22-2230; telex 1103; f. 1961 to finance the economic development of the Central American Common Market and its member countries; mems Costa Rica, El Salvador, Guatemala,

HONDURAS

Directory

Honduras, Nicaragua; cap. and res $436.8m. (Dec. 1986); Pres. Lic. DANTE GABRIEL RAMÍREZ.

Banco Hondureño del Café (BANHCAFE, SA): 6a Avda 501, 5a Calle, Apdo 583, Tegucigalpa; tel. 22-4210; telex 1278; f. 1981 to help finance coffee production; cap. and res $17.4m., dep. $48.1m. (Dec. 1986); owned principally by private coffee producers; Pres. TITO ANTONIO SAGASTUME; Gen. Man. Lic. CARLOS CANIZALES.

Banco Municipal Autónomo (BANMA): 6a Avda, 6a Calle, Tegucigalpa; tel. 22-5963; f. 1963; cap. and res $25.2m., dep. $1.4m. (June 1984); Pres. Lic. JUSTO PASTOR CALDERÓN; 2 brs.

Banco Nacional de Desarrollo Agrícola (BANADESA): 13 Calle, 4-5 Avda Comayagüela, Apdo 212, Tegucigalpa; tel. 22-8505; telex 1105; f. 1980; cap. and res $37.5m., dep. $70m. (Oct. 1987); govt development bank (transfer to private ownership pending); loans to agricultural sector; Pres. Ing. ADOLFO LIONEL SEVILLA G.; 28 brs.

Financiera Centroamericana, SA (FICENSA): Edif. FICENSA, Blvd 'Los Castaños', Apdo 1432, Tegucigalpa; tel. 22-1035; telex 1200; f. 1974; private finance organization giving loans to industry, commerce and transport; cap. and res $3.9m., dep. $41.1m. (Dec. 1984); Pres. OSWALDO LÓPEZ ARELLANO; Gen. Man. JOSÉ ARTURO ALVARADO.

Financiera Nacional de la Vivienda—FINAVI: Apdo 1194, Tegucigalpa; f. 1975; housing development bank; cap. and res $5.3m. (July 1984); Exec. Pres. Lic. ELMAR LIZARDO.

Foreign Banks

Bank of America NT & SA (USA): Edif. Centro Comercial Los Castaños, Blvd Morazán, Apdo 199, Tegucigalpa; tel. 32-7350; telex 1101; cap. and res $1.5m., dep. $10.8m. (July 1983); Gen. Man. VÍCTOR PAZ.

Bank of London and Montreal Ltd (Bahamas): 5a Avda, 4a Calle, Apdo 29-C, Tegucigalpa; tel. 22-5151; telex 1117; Man. JULES P. GENASI; 6 brs.

Banking Association

Asociación Hondureña de Instituciones Bancarias (AHIBA): Edif. Bancahsa, 5°, Pieza 505, Apdo 1344, Tegucigalpa; tel. 37-7336; f. 1956; 14 mem. banks; Pres. Gen. OSWALDO LÓPEZ ARELLANO; Vice Pres. Lic. SALDOR GÓMEZ.

INSURANCE

El Ahorro Hondureño, SA, Compañía de Seguros: Edif. Trinidad, 5a Calle, 11a Avda, Apdo 3643, Tegucigalpa; tel. 37-8219; telex 1122; fax 37-4780; f. 1917; Pres. Lic. ARNULFO GUTIÉRREZ Z.; Gen. Man. Lic. HÉCTOR E. CHAVARRÍA R.

American Home Assurance Co: Edif. Los Castaños 4°, Blvd Morazán, Apdo 113-C, Tegucigalpa; tel. 32-1849; telex 1228; f. 1933; fmrly Hanover Insurance Co.; Gen. Man. O. REYNALDO RAMÍREZ C.

Aseguradora Hondureña, SA: Centro Comercial Plaza Miraflores 3°, Col. Miraflores, Apdo 312, Tegucigalpa; tel. 32-2729; telex 1246; f. 1954; Pres. and Gen. Man. ALBERTO AGURCIA.

Compañía de Seguros Interamericana, SA: Apdo 593, Colonia Los Castaños, Tegucigalpa; tel. 32-7614; telex 1362; f. 1957; Pres. SALOMÓN D. KAFATI; Gen. Man. RUBÉN ALVAREZ H.

Pan American Life Insurance Co: Edif. PALIC, Avda República de Chile 804, Tegucigalpa; tel. 32-8774; telex 1237; f. 1944; Gen. Man. Lic. FERNANDO RODRÍGUEZ.

Previsión y Seguros, SA: Apdo 770, Colonia Palmira, Edif. Maya, Tegucigalpa; tel. 32-4834; telex 1392; fax 313-2124; f. 1981; Gen. Man. Lic. FELIPE VINICIO ESPINOZA.

Seguros Continental, SA: 3a Avda 2 y 3, 7a Calle, Apdo 320, San Pedro Sula; tel. 53-1310; telex 5561; fax 52-2750; f. 1968; Pres. Ing. JAIME ROSENTHAL OLIVA; Man. MARIO R. SOLÍS.

Insurance Association

Cámara Hondureña de Aseguradores (CAHDA): Edif. JS, frente Iglesia la Guadalupe, Blvd Morazán, Apdo 183-C, Tegucigalpa; tel. 32-6020; Pres. Lic. FERNANDO J. RODRÍGUEZ; Sec. Lic. RUBÉN ALVAREZ H.

Trade and Industry

CHAMBERS OF COMMERCE

Cámara de Comercio e Industrias de Cortés: 17a Avda, 10a y 12a Calle, Apdo 14, San Pedro Sula; tel. 53-0761; f. 1931; 812 mems; Pres. Ing. FELIPE ARGÜELLO C.

Federación de Cámaras de Comercio e Industrias de Honduras (FEDECAMARA): Blvd Centroamérica, Apdo 3444, Tegucigalpa; tel. 32-8110; telex 1537; fax 31-2049; f. 1985; 1,423 mems; Exec. Sec. JORGE MEJÍA ORTEGA.

DEVELOPMENT ORGANIZATIONS

Consejo Hondureño de la Empresa Privada (COHEP): Avda Los Próceres 505, Apdo 133-C, Tegucigalpa; f. 1968; comprises 23 private enterprises; Pres. RICHARD ZABLAH; Exec. Sec. Ing. JOAQUÍN LUNA MEJÍA.

Corporación Financiera de Olancho: f. 1977 to co-ordinate and manage all financial aspects of the Olancho forests project; Pres. RAFAEL CALDERÓN LÓPEZ.

Corporación Hondureña de Desarrollo Forestal (COHDEFOR): Salida Carretera del Norte, Zona El Carrizal, Apdo 1378, Comayagüela; tel. 22-8810; telex 1172; f. 1974; semi-autonomous organization in charge of forestry management and control of the forestry industry; exports ceased in 1989 and all sawmills were expected to be transferred to private ownership by 1991; Gen. Man. Ing. JOSÉ SEGOVIA I.

Dirección General de Minas e Hidrocarburos (General Directorate of Mines and Hydrocarbons): Blvd Miraflores, Apdo 981, Tegucigalpa; tel. 32-7848; telex 1404; Dir-Gen. Ing. JOSÉ MAGIN LANZA V.

Instituto Hondureño del Café—IHCAFE: Apdo 40-C, Tegucigalpa; tel. 37-3131; telex 1167; f. 1970; coffee development programme; Gen. Man. Lic. RAMIRO RODRÍGUEZ LANZA.

Instituto Hondureño de Mercadeo Agrícola (IHMA): Apdo 727, Tegucigalpa; tel. 32-1629; telex 1138; agricultural development agency; Gen. Man. OSCAR ROBERTO GALLARDO.

Instituto Nacional Agrario (INA): Tegucigalpa; telex 1218; agricultural development programmes; Dir RAÚL FLORES GÓMEZ.

Secretaría Técnica del Consejo Superior de Planificación Económica (CONSUPLANE): Edif. Bancatlán 3°, Apdo 1327, Comayagüela; tel. 22-8738; telex 1222; f. 1965; national planning office; Exec. Sec. FRANCISCO FIGUEROA ZÚÑIGA.

PRODUCERS' ASSOCIATIONS

Asociación de Bananeros Independientes—ANBI (National Association of Independent Banana Producers): San Pedro Sula; tel. 22-7336; f. 1964; 62 mems; Pres. Ing. JORGE ALBERTO ALVARADO; Sec. CECILIO TRIMINIO TURCIOS.

Asociación Hondureña de Productores de Café (Coffee Producers' Association): 10a Avda, 6a Calle, Apdo 959, Tegucigalpa.

Asociación Nacional de Exportadores de Honduras (ANEXHON): Tegucigalpa; comprises 104 private enterprises; Pres. Dr RICHARD ZABLAH.

Asociación Nacional de Industriales (ANDI) (National Association of Manufacturers): Blvd Los Próceres No 505, Apdo 20-C, Tegucigalpa; Pres. HÉCTOR BULNES; Exec. Sec. DORCAS DE GONZALES.

Asociación Nacional de Pequeños Industriales (ANPI) (National Association of Small Industries): Apdo 730, Tegucigalpa; Pres. JUAN RAFAEL CRUZ.

Federación Nacional de Agricultores y Ganaderos de Honduras (FENAGH) (Farmers and Livestock Breeders' Association): Tegucigalpa; Pres. Ing. FERNANDO LARDIZÁBAL.

Federación Nacional de Cooperativas Cañeras (Fenacocal) (National Federation of Sugar Cane Co-operatives): Tegucigalpa.

TRADE UNIONS

Asociación Nacional de Empleados Públicos de Honduras (ANDEPH) (National Association of Public Employees of Honduras): Tegucigalpa.

Confederación de Trabajadores de Honduras—CTH (Workers' Confederation of Honduras): Barrio La Fuente, Calle Lempira, Casa 515, Apdo 720, Tegucigalpa; tel. 37-4243; f. 1964; affiliated to CTCA, ORIT, CIOSL, FIAET and ICFTU; Pres. LUIS SANTOS YANES; Sec.-Gen. FRANCISCO GUERRERO NUÑEZ; 200,000 mems; comprises the following federations:

Federación Central de Sindicatos Libres de Honduras (FECESITLIH) (Federation of Free Trade Unions): 1a Avda, 1a Calle, No 102, Apdo 621, Comayagüela; Pres. EMILIO GONZALES GARCÍA.

Federación Sindical de Trabajadores Nacionales de Honduras (FESITRANH) (Honduran Federation of Farmworkers): 10A Avda, 11A, Calle N.O., Bo. Los Andes, San Pedro Sula; f. 1957; Sec. Gen. ARMANDO GALDÁMEZ.

Sindicato Nacional de Motoristas de Equipo Pesado de Honduras (SINAMEQUIP) (National Union of HGV Drivers): Tegucigalpa.

Central General de Trabajadores (CGT) (General Confederation of Labour): Apdo 1236, Tegucigalpa; attached to Partido Demócrata Cristiano; Sec.-Gen. FELICITO AVILA.

HONDURAS

Federación Auténtica Sindical de Honduras (FASH): 1a Avda, 11a Calle No 1102, Comayagüela.

Federación de Trabajadores del Sur (FETRASUR) (Federation of Southern Workers): Choluteca.

Federación Unitaria de Trabajadores de Honduras (FUTH): 2a Avda entre 11 y 12 Calle, Casa 1127, frente a BANCAFE, Apdo 1663, Comayagüela, Tegucigalpa; tel. 37-6349; f. 1981; linked to left-wing electoral alliance Frente Patriótico Hondureño; Pres. HÉCTOR HERNÁNDEZ FUENTES; 50,000 mems.

Frente de Unidad Nacional Campesino de Honduras (FUNA-CAMH): f. 1980; group of farming co-operatives and six main peasant unions as follows:

Asociación Nacional de Campesinos de Honduras (ANACH) (National Association of Honduran Farmworkers): 8a Avda, 9a Calle SO, No 36, Blvd Lempira, San Pedro Sula; f. 1962; affiliated to ORIT; Pres. ANTONIO JULÍN MÉNDEZ; 80,000 mems.

Federación de Cooperativas Agropecuarias de la Reforma Agraria de Honduras (FECORAH).

Frente Nacional de Campesinos Independientes de Honduras.

Unión Nacional de Campesinos (UNC) (National Union of Farmworkers): Tegucigalpa; linked to CLAT; Leader ADÁN PALACIOS; Sec.-Gen. MARCEL CABALLERO; c. 25,000 mems.

Unión Nacional de Campesinos Auténticos de Honduras (UNCAH).

Unión Nacional de Cooperativas Populares de Honduras (UNACOOPH).

Transport

RAILWAYS

In 1989 there were 955 km of railways, all of which are in the north of the country and most of which are used for fruit cargo. A 97-km rail link was reportedly built between La Ceiba and San Pedro Sula in the mid-1980s.

Ferrocarril Nacional de Honduras (National Railway of Honduras): 1a Calle, Apdo 496, San Pedro Sula; tel. 53-3230; f. 1870; govt-owned; 128 km of track open; Gen. Man. P. R. ROMERO.

Tela Railroad Co: La Lima; tel. 56-2018; telex 8305; 344 km of track open; Pres. RONALD F. WALKER; Gen. Man. JOHN A. ORDMAN.

Vaccaro Railway: La Ceiba; 390 km of track open; Gen. Man. D. DEHORENZO.

ROADS

In 1988 there were 18,494 km of roads in Honduras, of which 2,262 km were paved, 7,133 km were passable in the summer only, and 9,099 km were passable throughout the year. Roads have been constructed by the Instituto Hondureño del Café and COHDEFOR in order to facilitate access to coffee plantations and forestry development areas.

Dirección General de Caminos: Tegucigalpa; highways board.

SHIPPING

Empresa Nacional Portuaria (National Port Authority): Apdo 18, Puerto Cortés; tel. 55-0987; telex 8007; fax 55-0367; f. 1965; has jurisdiction over all ports in Honduras; manages Puerto Cortés, Tela, La Ceiba, Trujillo/Castilla, Roatán, Amapala and San Lorenzo; a network of paved roads connects Puerto Cortés and San Lorenzo with the main cities of Honduras, and with the principal cities of Central America; Dir-Gen. ÁNGEL CASANOVA BORJAS.

There are several minor shipping companies. A number of foreign shipping lines call at Honduran ports.

CIVIL AVIATION

Local airlines in Honduras compensate for the deficiencies of road and rail transport, linking together small towns and inaccessible districts. There are three international airports. A new airstrip was opened at Roatán in 1988. In December 1988 the Spanish Govt and the IDB approved a loan of US $50m. to aid the construction of a new airport at Tegucigalpa, which would, it was estimated, cost $200m.

Servicio Aéreo de Honduras, SA (SAHSA): Apdo 129, Tegucigalpa; telex 321-1146; f. 1945; private company; operates domestic flights and also to the USA, Colombia, Nicaragua, Guatemala, Belize, Costa Rica and Panama; Pres. Gen. OSWALDO LÓPEZ ARELLANO; Gen. Man. Capt. ROLANDO FIGUEROA; fleet: 3 DC-3, 1 Boeing 727-100, 2 Boeing 737-200.

Aerovías Nacionales de Honduras, SA (ANHSA): c/o SAHSA; f. 1950; operates domestic service to the north coast and the east of the country; fleet: 2 DC-3.

Transportes Aéreos Nacionales, SA (TAN): Edif. TAN, Apdo 628, Tegucigalpa; tel. 28674; telex 848-5909; f. 1947; operates passenger and cargo services, internal and international to Belize, Mexico and the USA; Pres. Gen. OSWALDO LÓPEZ ARELLANO; Gen. Man. Capt. ROLANDO FIGUEROA; fleet: 1 Boeing 737-200-C, 2 L-188-A Electra.

Líneas Aéreas Nacionales, SA (LANSA): Apdo 35, La Ceiba; f. 1971; scheduled services within Honduras and to Islas de Bahía; Gen. Man. OSCAR M. ELVIR; fleet: 1 F27J, 4 DC-3, 1 Cessna 182, 1 Cessna 206.

Tourism

Tourists are attracted by the Mayan ruins, the fishing and boating facilities in Trujillo Bay and Lake Yojoa, near San Pedro Sula, and the beaches on the northern coast. Honduras received an estimated 249,761 tourists in 1989.

Instituto Hondureño de Turismo: Costado este del Palacio Legislativo, Apdo 154-C, Tegucigalpa; tel. 22-1183; telex 1322; f. 1975; department of the Secretaría de Cultura y Turismo; Dir-Gen. Lic. DEBORAH MILLS DE GOLDNER.

Atomic Energy

Comisión Hondureña de Energía Atómica: Apdo 104, Tegucigalpa; Pres. Dr RAFAEL TORRES FIALLOS.

HUNGARY

Introductory Survey

Location, Climate, Language, Religion, Flag, Capital

The Republic of Hungary (formerly the Hungarian People's Republic) lies in Eastern Europe, bounded to the north by Czechoslovakia, to the east by the USSR and Romania, to the south by Yugoslavia and to the west by Austria. Its climate is continental, with long, dry summers and severe winters. Temperatures in Budapest are generally between −3°C (27°F) and 28°C (82°F). The language is Hungarian (Magyar). There is a large Romany community (numbering between 500,000 and 700,000 people), and also Croat, German, Romanian, Serbian, Slovak, Slovene and Jewish minorities. Most of the inhabitants profess Christianity, and the largest single religious denomination is the Roman Catholic Church, claiming more than 6m. adherents. Other Christian groups are the Hungarian Reformed Church (a Presbyterian sect with about 2m. members), the Lutheran Church and the Hungarian Orthodox Church. The national flag (proportions 3 by 2) consists of three equal horizontal stripes, of red, white and green. The capital is Budapest.

Recent History

Hungary allied itself with Nazi Germany before the Second World War and obtained additional territory when Czechoslovakia was partitioned in 1938 and 1939. Having sought to break the alliance in 1944, Hungary was occupied by German forces. In January 1945 Hungary was liberated by Soviet troops and signed an armistice, restoring the pre-1938 frontiers. It became a republic in February 1946. Meanwhile, land distribution, under the March 1945 land reform, continued. Nationalization measures began in December 1946, despite opposition from the Roman Catholic Church under Cardinal József Mindszenty. In the 1947 elections the Communists became the largest single party, with 22.7% of the vote. By the end of that year the Communist Party had emerged as the leading political force. The Communists merged with the Social Democrats to form the Hungarian Workers' Party in June 1948. A People's Republic was established in August 1949.

Mátyás Rákosi became the leading figure as First Secretary of the Workers' Party. Opposition was subsequently removed by means of purges and political trials. Rákosi became Prime Minister in 1952 but, after the death of Stalin a year later, lost this post to the more moderate Imre Nagy, and a short period of liberalization followed. Rákosi, however, remained as First Secretary of the Party, and in 1955 Nagy was forced to resign. András Hegedüs, sponsored by Rákosi, was appointed Prime Minister. In-fighting between the Rákosi and Nagy factions increased in 1956 after the condemnation of Stalinism at the 20th Congress of the Communist Party of the Soviet Union in Moscow; in July Rákosi was forced to resign but was replaced by a close associate, Ernő Gerő.

The consequent discontent provoked demonstrations, and in October 1956 fighting broke out. Nagy was reinstated as Prime Minister and headed a series of governments. He promised various controversial reforms, but fighting continued. In November a new Soviet-supported government, led by János Kádár, was installed. Soviet troops, stationed in Hungary under the 1947 peace treaty, were asked to intervene and the uprising was suppressed. (In 1990 it was reported that some 2,500 Hungarian citizens had been killed in the uprising.) In June 1958 Nagy and four associates were executed for their part in the uprising. Kádár also became the leader of the newly-formed Hungarian Socialist Workers' Party (HSWP). He held the premiership until January 1958 and from September 1961 to July 1965 but, even when not formally in the Government, his Party leadership made him dominant in political life.

György Lázár became Chairman of the Council of Ministers (Prime Minister) in May 1975. In April 1978 Béla Biszku, who had been regarded as Kádár's deputy, was retired from the Secretariat of the Central Committee of the HSWP. At the Party Congress in March 1980 Kádár was re-elected First Secretary of the Central Committee. The June 1980 general election resulted in a 99.3% vote in favour of candidates of the Patriotic People's Front (the organization dominated by the HSWP and embracing all the legal political parties in Hungary). An extensive government reshuffle followed.

The 13th HSWP Congress was held in March 1985. János Kádár was re-elected leader of the Party, taking the new title of General Secretary of the Central Committee. Károly Németh, a member of the HSWP Politburo and of the Presidential Council, was elected to the newly-created post of Deputy General Secretary of the Party Central Committee. A new Politburo and Central Committee Secretariat were chosen, each containing three members elected for the first time. The Congress also reaffirmed the commitment to the country's economic reforms, the 'new economic mechanism', which had been introduced in 1968.

The legislative elections of June 1985 were the first to be held under the revised electoral law, giving voters a wider choice of candidates under the system of mandatory multiple nominations. The National Assembly again re-elected Pál Losonczi to the largely ceremonial post of President of the Presidential Council, which included seven new members. In June 1987 Losonczi was replaced by Károly Németh. Károly Grósz, a member of the Politburo and hitherto First Secretary of the Budapest HSWP Committee, was appointed Chairman of the Council of Ministers in place of György Lázár, who succeeded Németh as Deputy General Secretary of the Party Central Committee. In December the Council of Ministers underwent an extensive reorganization.

In March 1988, on the 140th anniversary of the 1848 Hungarian uprising against Austrian rule, some 10,000 people took part in an unofficial march through Budapest, demanding freedom of the press, freedom of association and the introduction of genuine reforms. The protest was not halted by the authorities (in contrast to demonstrations, held in February and March 1986, which had been suppressed by the police).

In April 1988 four prominent members of the HSWP, known for their advocacy of radical political and economic reforms, were expelled from the party. All four were associated with an unofficial political group, the Hungarian Democratic Forum (HDF, formally established later in 1988). At a special ideological conference of the HSWP, held in May 1988, major changes in party personnel and policy were approved. János Kádár was replaced as General Secretary of the Central Committee by Károly Grósz, the Chairman of the Council of Ministers. Kádár was promoted to the newly-created and purely ceremonial post of HSWP President, but lost his membership of the Politburo. About one-third of the members of the Central Committee (in particular, conservative associates of Kádár) were removed and replaced by younger politicians. The new Politburo included Imre Pozsgay (hitherto the Secretary-General of the Patriotic People's Front), a prominent advocate of reform and political pluralism, and Rezső Nyers, who had been largely responsible for the economic reforms initiated in 1968, but who had been removed from the Politburo in 1975. Grósz declared his commitment to radical economic and political reforms, although he excluded the immediate possibility of a multi-party political system. In June 1988 several changes were made within the Council of Ministers, including Pozsgay's appointment as a Minister of State, with special responsibility for political development. In the same month, Dr Brunó Ferenc Straub, who was not a member of the HSWP, was elected to the post of President of the Presidential Council, in succession to Károly Németh. In November 1988 Miklós Németh, hitherto the head of a department of the HSWP Central Committee, replaced Károly Grósz as Chairman of the Council of Ministers. Rezső Nyers was appointed a Minister of State, with special responsibility for economic development.

In the months following Grósz's appointment as leader of the HSWP, there was a relaxation of censorship laws, while a new free trade union, the Democratic Union of Scientific Workers (Hungary's first independent trade union for 40 years), as well as independent political groups, including the HDF, were founded. At a plenary session in July 1988, the Central Committee of the HSWP voted overwhelmingly in favour of an austere economic programme, designed to revitalize the economy within 10 years. This reform programme was given final approval by the National Assembly in October 1988. In January 1989 the work-force's right to strike was fully legalized. In the same month the National Assembly enacted two laws guaranteeing Hungarians the right to demonstrate freely, and to form associations and political parties independent of the HSWP. A separate law regulating the operation of such associations was approved by the National Assembly in October 1989. It was recognized that, as a consequence of the new law, the HSWP might not win a majority of seats in the National Assembly at the next general election, scheduled for mid-1990.

In February 1989 a special session of the HSWP Central Committee agreed to support the transition to a multi-party system. It was also agreed to abandon the clause in the Constitution guaranteeing the HSWP's leading role in society. In the same month the Government announced that the anniversary of the Russian Revolution of 1917 would no longer be celebrated in Hungary as a public holiday. In future, a public holiday would be celebrated on 15 March, the anniversary of the start of the 1848–49 uprising against Austrian rule. In March 1989, on the anniversary of this event, an estimated 100,000 people took part in a peaceful anti-Government demonstration in Budapest. Speeches were made by leaders of many of the newly-emerged opposition groups, in which they advocated democracy, free elections, the withdrawal of Soviet troops from Hungary, and an official commemoration of the 1956 uprising and the execution of Imre Nagy in 1958. In February 1989 the historical commission of the HSWP Central Committee had published a report, in which it was stated that the events of 1956 had been a 'popular uprising against the existing state power', and not a counter-revolution (the official designation hitherto). The report also stated that, following the Soviet military intervention, the uprising had been transformed into a 'national independence struggle'. In June 1989 Nagy was officially rehabilitated. In the same month the bodies of Nagy and four of his associates, who had also been executed in 1958, were reburied at a state funeral in Budapest, which was attended by an estimated 300,000 people.

During 1989 there was increasing evidence of dissension within the HSWP between conservative and reformist members. In the first three months of the year more than 20,000 members left the party (at least 100,000 members having tendered their resignation between late 1987 and early 1989). At a meeting of the Central Committee in April 1989 Grósz was re-elected General Secretary of the party. The entire membership of the Politburo resigned, and was replaced by a smaller body, consisting of seven former members and two new members. It was believed that the reorganization had been designed to remove more conservative elements in the Politburo. Also in April the Communist Youth Union (KISZ) voted to dissolve itself. A new organization, the Hungarian Democratic Youth Federation, was formed in its place, and declared itself independent of the HSWP. In May there was a reshuffle of the Council of Ministers, in which six posts were reallocated. The Chairman, Miklós Németh, declared that henceforth the Council would act independently of the HSWP, and that it would be answerable to the National Assembly before the HSWP. In May, two months before his death, Kádár was relieved of his post as President of the HSWP and of his membership of the Central Committee of the party. The official reason for his retirement was ill health, although it was also stated that he had been unable to accept the recent political changes taking place in Hungary. In June a radical restructuring of the HSWP was effected, following increasing dissatisfaction with Grósz's leadership by party members. Nyers was elected to the post of Chairman of the party. While Grósz remained as General Secretary, Nyers effectively emerged as the leading figure in the party. The Central Committee voted to establish a four-member Presidium to direct the party until the holding of the 14th HSWP Congress, set for October 1989. The Presidium comprised the four key figures in Hungarian politics, Nyers, Grósz, Németh and Pozsgay. It was also decided to expand the Politburo into an Executive Political Committee, with 21 members.

Round-table discussions were initiated between the HSWP and representatives of opposition groups in June 1989. The discussions centred on the holding of multi-party elections, changes to the presidential structure, amendments to the Constitution, and economic reforms. Evidence of the opposition's increasing strength was provided at a provincial by-election in July, when a joint candidate of three main opposition groups, the centre-right HDF, the liberal Alliance of Free Democrats (AFD) and the Federation of Young Democrats (FYD), defeated a candidate of the HSWP, thus becoming the first opposition deputy since 1947 to win representation in the National Assembly. Four of five further by-elections to the National Assembly were won by opposition candidates in July, August and September. In August some 2m. workers throughout the country went on strike in protest at planned price increases. It was the first instance of mass industrial action since 1956, and signalled growing popular discontent with the Government's economic management and the sharp deterioration of living standards. In August Grósz declared his intention to resign as General Secretary after the HSWP Congress in October. Meanwhile, a Reform Circles Alliance had been established within the HSWP. Pozsgay and Németh were both closely associated with the Alliance, the declared aims of which were the removal of anti-reformist members from important positions in the party, the renaming of the HSWP, and the acceleration of the economic reform process.

At the 14th HSWP Congress, held in October, delegates voted to dissolve the party and to reconstitute it as the Hungarian Socialist Party (HSP), to symbolize a break with the 'crimes, mistaken ideas and incorrect methods' of the HSWP. Nyers was elected Chairman of the HSP, and Pozsgay was nominated the party's candidate for the forthcoming presidential election. Nyers subsequently resigned from his post as Minister of State. The HSP named a 23-member Presidium, which was reported to comprise a majority of reformists, including Pozsgay, Németh and Gyula Horn, the Minister of Foreign Affairs. (Németh subsequently resigned from the Presidium, following disagreements on economic policy, thus separating the Council of Ministers from party leadership for the first time since 1949.) In the weeks following the establishment of the HSP it was rumoured that the party was close to collapse, since it had failed to attract a large membership. By mid-December the HSP had recruited only an estimated 67,000 members (compared with the 725,000 members of the HSWP before its dissolution). Furthermore, HSWP activists, meeting at a congress in December, declared that the HSWP had not been dissolved, and that it still retained a membership of around 80,000. At the congress, Gyula Thürmer was elected the HSWP President.

On 23 October 1989 (the anniversary of the 1956 uprising) the Republic of Hungary was proclaimed. (Since 1949 the country had been known as the Hungarian People's Republic.) In mid-October the National Assembly approved legislation enacting a number of radical reforms. These reforms had been determined in an agreement signed by the HSWP and members of the opposition at the conclusion, in September, of the round-table talks, initiated in June. Accordingly, the National Assembly approved fundamental amendments to the Constitution, including the removal of the clause guaranteeing one-party rule. A Constitutional Court, with 15 members, was subsequently established. A new electoral law was approved, which determined that elections to the National Assembly must be held before June 1990, and under which no seats were guaranteed to any party. The National Assembly also passed legislation to disband the HSP-controlled Workers' Militia. In a further development, it was agreed to dissolve the Presidential Council and to replace it with the post of President of the Republic. Mátyás Szűrös, the President of the National Assembly (Speaker), was named President of the Republic, on an acting basis. Szűrös was shortly afterwards replaced as President of the National Assembly, also on an acting basis, by István Fodor, hitherto a Deputy President of the Assembly. Following a referendum in late November, it was decided that a presidential election would take place after elections to the National Assembly, scheduled for March and April 1990. The existing Assembly was to be dissolved on 16 March. In mid-January 1990 it was revealed that the Ministry of the Interior had received regular reports on the activities of opposition groups and parties, by means of intercepted mail and telephone calls. In the ensuing so-called 'Danubegate' scandal, the Government ordered the Ministry's security apparatus to be disbanded, and the Minister of the Interior, István Horváth, resigned from his post.

The first free multi-party elections in Hungary since 1945 were held in two rounds, on 25 March and 8 April 1990. The elections were held under a mixed system of proportional and direct representation and were contested by a total of 28 parties and groups. The HDF won a clear majority of the total votes (42.7%) and gained 165 seats in the National Assembly. The Independent Smallholders' Party (ISP, which advocated the restoration to its original owners of land collectivized after 1947) and the Christian Democratic People's Party (CDPP), both of which contested the second round of the election in alliance with the HDF, secured 43 and 21 seats, respectively. The AFD secured the second largest proportion of the total votes (23.8%) and consequently gained 92 seats in the Assembly. The FYD, which was closely aligned with the AFD, obtained 21 seats. The HSP, winning 8.5% of the votes, secured 33 seats in the legislature. The hard-line HSWP failed to secure the 4% of the votes required for representation, as did the recently revived Social Democratic Party.

In mid-May 1990 a new, coalition government was formed, comprising members of the HDF (who held the majority of posts), together with members of the ISP, the CDPP and three independents. József Antall, the Chairman of the HDF, had earlier been elected to chair the new Council of Ministers. Among the declared aims of the new Government was to withdraw from the Warsaw Pact, to seek membership of the EEC, and to effect a full transition to a Western-style market economy. Severe economic hardships were anticipated during such a transitional period, including a sharp rise in the rates of unemployment and inflation, and a concomitant decline in living standards. In June, in line with the restoration of democracy in Hungary, the Patriotic People's Front voted to reorganize itself as a non-political federation of social associations.

In early May 1990, Árpád Göncz, a writer and member of the AFD, was elected President of the National Assembly. At the same time Göncz was elected President of Hungary, on an acting basis, pending a decision on the method of future presidential elections (whether by direct election or by decision of the National Assembly). In late July a nationwide referendum on the issue was held, but was invalidated by the extremely low participation of the electorate (less than 14% of whom voted, as opposed to the 50% required to validate the vote). Thus, in early August, Göncz was elected President by an overwhelming majority of the legislature. He was replaced as President of the National Assembly by György Szabad (formerly First Deputy President of the Assembly).

The three parties comprising the governing coalition suffered a severe set-back at by-elections held throughout Hungary in late September and early October 1990, which were designed to replace the Soviet-style council system with a system of multi-party self-governing local bodies. A coalition of the AFD and the FYD won control of Budapest and many other cities, while in the countryside, independent candidates gained an overwhelming majority of the votes. The governing coalition's poor result was attributed, in large part, to its failure to redress the recent sharp increase in the rates of inflation and unemployment. The Government faced a further crisis in late October, when taxi and lorry drivers blocked major roads, bridges and border crossings for three days in protest at the Government's decision to increase the price of petrol by 65%. This decision had been prompted by the sharp reduction in supplies of petroleum from the USSR earlier in the year, thus forcing Hungary to purchase petroleum on the world market at greatly increased prices, following Iraq's invasion and annexation of Kuwait in August. The situation was normalized when the Government agreed to reduce by 50% the increase in petrol prices.

In late November 1990 the Minister of Finance, Ferenc Rabár, resigned from his post, following disagreements within the Council of Ministers as regards economic policy. In the following month there was a minor ministerial reshuffle, in which, among other changes, Mihály Kupa was elected to the vacant post of Minister of Finance. Further government changes took place in January 1991.

Hungary pursues an active foreign policy, and relations with many Western nations improved steadily in the late 1980s, in line with the democratic changes taking place in Hungary. In 1988, following the liberalization of passport regulations, a record number of Hungarians travelled to Western countries. During 1987 János Kádár paid official visits to Sweden, the People's Republic of China and Belgium. In October 1987 Károly Grósz visited the Federal Republic of Germany, and in 1988, as HSWP General Secretary, he visited the United Kingdom, the USA, Canada, the USSR, Austria, Spain and France. In 1989 President Bush paid the first official visit to Hungary by a US President. In 1988 Hungary established diplomatic relations with the Republic of Korea, the first Eastern bloc country to do so. Full diplomatic relations were restored with Israel in 1989, and with the Holy See and Chile in 1990. Diplomatic relations were established with Guatemala, Oman and Qatar in 1990. In that year József Antall, the Chairman of the Council of Ministers, paid official visits to Italy, the Netherlands, the USA and the USSR. In November 1990 Hungary became a member of the Council of Europe (see p. 129), the first Eastern European country to do so.

Hungary has traditionally been aligned with the countries of Eastern Europe through its membership of the Warsaw Pact (see p. 211) and of the Council for Mutual Economic Assistance (CMEA, see p. 125). However, in late 1990 it was announced that the Warsaw Pact was to be dismantled in its entirety by the beginning of 1992, while the CMEA was to be replaced by a co-operative organization based on market economy principles. Hungary's relations with Romania and, to a lesser extent, with Czechoslovakia have been strained by the issue of the position of the large Hungarian minorities resident in those countries. In 1987 and 1988 Hungary received thousands of applications from Romanian citizens of Hungarian origin who wished to settle in Hungary, and by June 1989 about 15,000 such Romanians had received residence permits in Hungary. In June 1988 an estimated 50,000 people protested in Budapest against the Romanian Government's proposed destruction of some 7,000 villages in Romania, including 1,500 inhabited by ethnic Hungarians. Romania, apparently prompted by the officially tolerated demonstration, expelled the staff of the Hungarian consulate in Cluj, Transylvania. In August 1988 Grósz conferred with the then Romanian leader, Nicolae Ceauşescu, in an attempt to improve the treatment of the 1.7m. ethnic Hungarians in Romania. In 1989 three reception camps for Romanian refugees were established in Hungary. At a meeting between Rezső Nyers and President Ceauşescu in July 1989, the issue of the Hungarian minority in Romania was again discussed. The meeting was later described as 'totally unsuccessful', and the Hungarian Ministry of Foreign Affairs stated that relations between the two countries had reached a nadir. The situation deteriorated further in March 1990, following outbreaks of violence against ethnic Hungarians committed by Romanian nationalist activists, and the resultant arrival in Hungary of several hundred ethnic Hungarian refugees. In February 1991 Hungary signed a declaration of co-operation with Czechoslovakia and Poland, which pledged these countries' commitment to achieving 'total integration into the European political, economic, security and legislative order'.

Government

Legislative power is held by the unicameral National Assembly, comprising 386 members, who are elected for four years by universal adult suffrage under a mixed system of proportional and direct representation. The President of the Republic (Head of State) is elected by the National Assembly for a term of four years. The President, who is also Commander-in-Chief of the Armed Forces, may be re-elected for a second term. The Council of Ministers, the highest organ of state administration, is elected by the Assembly on the recommendation of the President. For local administrative purposes Hungary is divided into 19 counties and the capital city (with 22 districts).

Defence

Hungary was a founder member of the Warsaw Pact in 1955. (The Warsaw Pact was to have been dismantled by the beginning of 1992.) Military service starts at the age of 18 years and lasts for 12 months. In 1989 an alternative military service for conscientious objectors was introduced, the first of its kind in Eastern Europe. According to Western estimates, the total regular forces in June 1990 numbered 94,000 (including 50,500 conscripts): army 72,000 (including 42,500 conscripts) and air force 22,000 (including 8,000 conscripts). There is also an armed force of 18,000 border guards, although this was to be reduced to 9,000 by 1995. In October 1989 it was voted to disband the Workers' Militia, numbering 60,000 members. The 1990 defence budget totalled an estimated 44,620m. forint. In late 1989 it was announced that the army was to be reduced by more than 30% by the end of 1991. In 1989 a partial withdrawal of the 65,000 Soviet troops stationed in Hungary was commenced. Following negotiations between Hungary and the USSR in early 1990, it was agreed that all Soviet troops would be withdrawn by July 1991.

HUNGARY

Economic Affairs

In 1989, according to estimates by the World Bank, Hungary's gross national product (GNP), measured at average 1987–89 prices, was US $27,078m., equivalent to $2,560 per head. During 1980–89, it was estimated, GNP increased, in real terms, at an average annual rate of 1.3%, while GNP per head increased by 1.4% per year. Over the same period, the population decreased by an annual average of 0.1%. Hungary's gross domestic product (GDP) increased, in real terms, by an annual average of 1.6% in 1980–88. GDP decreased, in real terms, by 1.5% in 1989 and by 2% in 1990.

Agriculture (including forestry) contributed 16.3% of GDP in 1989. In that year about 18% of the working population were employed in agriculture. The principal crops are wheat, maize, barley, sugar beet and potatoes. Viticulture is also important. During 1980–88 agricultural production increased by an annual average of 2.4%. In 1988 agricultural production increased by 4.5%, compared with 1987.

Industry (including manufacturing, mining and power) employed 32% of the working population and contributed 35% of GDP in 1989. During 1980–88 industrial production increased by an annual average of 1.0%. In 1990, according to official estimates, industrial production declined by 6.8%, compared with 1989.

The principal branches of the manufacturing sector are engineering and chemicals. In 1988 the engineering industry provided 25% of industrial production. In 1987 the chemical industry provided 20% of total industrial production, and more than one-third of its output was exported. In 1989 manufacturing output declined by 3.4%.

Hungary's most important mineral resources are bauxite (production of which totalled 2.6m. metric tons in 1989) and brown coal (output reaching more than 12m. metric tons in 1989). Lignite and hard coal are also mined. In 1989 about 50% of total domestic energy requirements was met by imports of petroleum, natural gas and electricity from the USSR. In mid-1990 the USSR reduced its deliveries of petroleum by 30%. In 1988 about 31% of Hungary's electricity supply was generated from coal, 30% from hydrocarbons and 39% from nuclear power. In 1990, 22.2% of Hungary's total energy requirement was met by coal, 30.4% by mineral oil, 28.7% by natural gas, and 18.7% by other sources.

In 1989 Hungary recorded a visible trade surplus of US $1,043m., but there was a deficit of $573m. on the current account of the balance of payments. In 1990 there was a current account surplus of $156m. In 1989 the principal source of imports (22%) was the USSR, which was also the principal market for exports (25%). However, in line with the political and economic changes taking place in Eastern Europe, the EEC became Hungary's most important trading partner in 1990, accounting for some 36% of its total trade (imports plus exports).

In 1989 there was a budgetary deficit of 48,700m. forint. Hungary's total external debt was estimated to be US $20,000m. in mid-1990, the highest per head in Eastern Europe. By December 1990 the annual rate of inflation had risen to 35%. In the same month, 1.9% of the labour force were unemployed.

Hungary is a member of the Council for Mutual Economic Assistance (CMEA, see p. 125). This was to be replaced by a co-operative organization operating on market economy principles). Hungary is a contracting party to GATT (see p. 58), and in 1982 joined the IMF and the World Bank. In 1988 Hungary and the EEC signed an agreement, designed to promote the expansion of trade in the following 10 years. Hungary aimed to become a member of the EEC by 1995.

In 1968 a new system of economic management was introduced, aimed at developing a more market-oriented economy. Until then the economy had been based on the standard Soviet central planning system. Under the new scheme, industry was decentralized to a certain extent, with the aim of evolving a socialist market economy, with emphasis on monetarist policies. In 1989 state-related businesses accounted for around 90% of economic output. Among the changes to be introduced were the reform of personal and business taxation, liberalization of the structure of prices and wages, and the encouragement of private and co-operative ventures. Customs-free zones were established for joint ventures between Hungarian enterprises and foreign companies. The new Government, formed in mid-1990, pledged to effect a full transition to a Western-style market economy, and to this end initiated a comprehensive privatization programme. Within five years the Government hoped to have reduced the proportion of state-controlled companies from 90% to 40%.

In 1990 the economy experienced serious problems, such as increasingly high levels of inflation and unemployment, a large external debt and a deficit on the current account of the balance of payments. The deterioration of the economic situation had led to the Government's endorsement, in the late 1980s and early 1990, of austerity programmes, which incorporated sharp reductions in food and housing subsidies. As a result of these austerity measures, real income per person has decreased substantially. In late 1989 it was reported that about one-fifth of the population lived below the national subsistence level. Hungary's economic difficulties were compounded, in mid-1990, by the USSR's decision to reduce by 30% its deliveries of low-cost petroleum, thus forcing Hungary to purchase petroleum on the world market, at greatly increased prices, following Iraq's invasion and annexation of Kuwait in August 1990.

Social Welfare

The national insurance scheme is based largely on non-state contributions. Employees contribute between 3% and 15% of their earnings to the pension fund. Employers usually pay 40% of the earnings of each person employed. Publicly-financed employers pay 10%. The cost of health services and other social services is met by state subsidies and contributions from the place of work. The 1989 state budget allotted 74,700m. forint to health and social welfare, and a further 269,500m. forint to social security.

The implementation of the five-day working week was completed by 1985. A uniform system of retirement pensions was introduced in 1975: workers draw between 33% and 75% of their earnings, according to the number of years of service. Male workers are usually entitled to retirement pensions at the age of 60 and women at 55. In January 1989 unemployment benefit was introduced. There are also invalidity pensions, widows' pensions and orphans' allowances. Social insurance covers sickness benefits. Patients are entitled to sick pay, usually for one year, or two years in the case of tuberculosis, occupational disease and industrial accident. Most medical consultation and treatment is free, although a very small charge is generally made for medicines and between 15% and 50% for medical appliances. In January 1989, however, the price of medicines was increased by an average of 80%. In 1987 there were 33.4 physicians per 10,000 of the population, and in 1988 the total number of hospital beds was 104,832. The social insurance scheme also covers maternity benefits. Women are entitled to 24 weeks' maternity leave on full pay. A new child-care payment, in addition to the child-care allowance, was made available in 1985. In 1984 there were more than 3,600 private medical practices in Hungary, one-third of which were in Budapest.

Education

Children under the age of three years attend crèches (bölcsődék), and those between the ages of three and six years attend kindergartens (óvodák). They are not compulsory, but in 1986 about 92% of children in this age-group were attending. Compulsory education begins at six years of age, with the basic school (általános iskola). Basic education, comprising general subjects together with some practical training, continues until the child is 14. Provision is made in the basic school for talented children, particularly those who are linguistically inclined. In southern Hungary bilingual schools are being established to promote the languages of the national minorities. Children attend school until the age of 16 years. There are four types of secondary school, excluding special schools for the very gifted or, alternatively, the backward or abnormal child. The majority of children continue with their education after 16 years of age. The most popular types of secondary school are the grammar school (gimnázium) and the secondary vocational schools (technikum). The gimnázium provides a four-year course of mainly academic studies, although some vocational training does figure on the curriculum. The technikum offers full vocational training together with a general education, emphasis being laid on practical work. Apprentice training schools (ipari tanulók gyakorló iskolai) are attached to factories, agricultural co-operatives, etc., and lead to full trade qualifications. General education is less important as part of the curriculum in this type of school. Further education reform is being directed at revising the curricula and the method of

HUNGARY

assessing pupils. There are 57 higher institutes, including 10 universities and nine technical universities. Expenditure on education by all levels of government in 1988 was about 85,000m. forint (8.6% of total public spending).

Public Holidays

1991: 1 January (New Year's Day), 15 March (anniversary of 1848 uprising against Austrian rule), 1 April (Easter Monday), 1 May (Labour Day), 20 August (Constitution Day), 23 October (Day of the Proclamation of the Republic), 25–26 December (Christmas).

1992: 1 January (New Year's Day), 15 March (anniversary of 1848 uprising against Austrian rule), 20 April (Easter Monday), 1 May (Labour Day), 20 August (Constitution Day), 23 October (Day of the Proclamation of the Republic), 25–26 December (Christmas).

Weights and Measures

The metric system is in force.

Statistical Survey

Source (unless otherwise stated): Központi Statisztikai Hivatal (Hungarian Central Statistical Office), 1525 Budapest, Keleti Károly u. 5–7; tel. 202-4011; telex 22-4308.

Area and Population

AREA, POPULATION AND DENSITY

Area (sq km)	93,033*
Population (census results)	
1 January 1980	10,709,463
1 January 1990 (provisional)	
Males	4,987,300
Females	5,388,000
Total	10,375,300
Population (official estimates at 1 January)	
1988	10,604,400
1989	10,588,600
1990	10,375,300
Density (per sq km) at 1 January 1990	111.5

* 35,920 sq miles.

Languages (1980 census): Magyar (Hungarian) 98.8%; German 0.3%; Slovak 0.1%; Romany 0.3%; Croatian 0.2%; Romanian 0.1%.

ADMINISTRATIVE DIVISIONS (1 January 1990)

	Area (sq km)	Resident Population ('000)	Density (per sq km)	County Town (with population)
Counties:				
Baranya	4,487	419	93	Pécs (170,119)
Bács-Kiskun	8,362	545	65	Kecskemét (102,528)
Békés	5,632	412	73	Békéscsaba (67,621)
Borsod-Abaúj-Zemplén	7,247	762	105	Miskolc (196,449)
Csongrád	4,263	439	103	Szeged (175,338)
Fejér	4,373	421	96	Székesfehérvár (108,990)
Győr-Moson-Sopron	4,012	425	106	Győr (129,356)
Hajdú-Bihar	6,211	549	88	Debrecen (212,247)
Heves	3,637	335	92	Eger (61,908)
Jász-Nagykun-Szolnok	5,607	426	76	Szolnok (78,333)
Komárom-Esztergom	2,251	315	140	Tatabánya (74,271)
Nógrád	2,544	227	89	Salgótarján (47,826)
Pest	6,394	950	149	Budapest* (2,016,132)
Somogy	6,036	345	57	Kaposvár (71,793)
Szabolcs-Szatmár	5,938	572	96	Nyíregyháza (114,166)
Tolna	3,704	254	69	Szekszárd (36,865)
Vas	3,337	276	83	Szombathely (85,418)
Veszprém	4,689	382	81	Veszprém (63,902)
Zala	3,784	307	81	Zalaegerszeg (62,221)
Capital City				
Budapest*	525	2,016	3,840	—
Total	93,033	10,375	112	—

* Budapest has separate County status. The area and population of the city are not included in the larger County (Pest) which it administers.

PRINCIPAL TOWNS (population at 1 January 1990)

Budapest (capital)	2,016,132	Nyíregyháza	114,166
Debrecen	212,247	Székesfehérvár	108,990
Miskolc	196,449	Kecskemét	102,528
Szeged	175,338	Szombathely	85,418
Pécs	170,119	Szolnok	78,333
Győr	129,356	Tatabánya	74,271

BIRTHS, MARRIAGES AND DEATHS

	Registered live births		Registered marriages		Registered deaths	
	Number	Rate (per 1,000)	Number	Rate (per 1,000)	Number	Rate (per 1,000)
1982	133,559	12.5	75,550	7.1	144,318	13.5
1983	127,258	11.9	75,969	7.1	148,643	13.9
1984	125,359	11.8	74,951	7.0	146,709	13.8
1985	130,200	12.2	73,238	6.9	147,614	13.9
1986	128,204	12.1	72,434	6.8	147,089	13.8
1987	125,840	11.9	66,082	6.2	142,601	13.4
1988	124,296	11.7	65,907	6.2	140,042	13.2
1989	123,304	11.7	66,949	6.3	144,695	13.7

ECONOMICALLY ACTIVE POPULATION*
('000 persons at January each year)

	1987	1988	1989
Agriculture and forestry	942.7	911.5	887.8
Manufacturing, mining, electricity and water	1,605.4	1,576.8	1,543.9
Construction	341.5	345.4	339.3
Commerce	514.2	519.7	519.3
Transport and communications	404.3	400.0	400.3
Services (incl. gas and sanitary services)	1,077.1	1,091.4	1,132.1
Total	4,885.2	4,844.8	4,822.7

* Excluding persons seeking work for the first time.

HUNGARY

Statistical Survey

Agriculture

PRINCIPAL CROPS ('000 metric tons)

	1987	1988	1989
Wheat	5,748	7,026	6,540
Rice (paddy)	40	47	28
Barley	794	1,183	1,340
Maize	7,234	6,256	6,996
Rye	186	255	267
Oats	99	138	149
Potatoes	1,077	1,407	1,332
Pulses	272	386	433
Sunflower seed	803	716	699
Rapeseed	108	82	98
Sugar beet	4,258	4,511	5,301
Grapes	512	736	580
Apples	1,064	1,131	959
Tobacco (leaves)	20	16	15

LIVESTOCK ('000 head at December each year)

	1987	1988	1989
Cattle	1,664	1,690	1,598
Pigs	8,216	8,327	7,660
Sheep	2,336	2,216	2,069
Horses	88	76	75
Chickens	61,069	56,943	52,821
Ducks	1,906	2,005	1,868
Geese	1,109	1,519	2,125
Turkeys	1,076	1,361	1,750

LIVESTOCK PRODUCTS (metric tons)

	1987	1988	1989
Beef and veal	129,000	110,000	120,000*
Mutton and lamb	5,000	5,000	4,000†
Pig meat	1,037,000	1,022,000	1,010,000†
Poultry meat	463,000	478,000	430,000†
Edible offal	50,000	49,000	47,000
Edible pig fat	352,000	n.a.	n.a.
Cows' milk	2,816,000	2,873,000	2,812,000†
Sheep's milk	8,000	8,000	8,000*
Goats' milk	3,000	3,000	3,000*
Butter	32,788	34,924	37,909
Cheese	91,605	90,657	86,487
Hen eggs	235,376	254,703	236,300†
Honey	15,170	14,400	16,000*
Wool:			
greasy	10,050	9,631	9,000†
clean	4,146	4,027	3,000†
Cattle hides	13,267	9,908	11,000*

* FAO estimate. † Unofficial figure.
Source: mainly FAO, *Production Yearbook*.

Forestry

ROUNDWOOD REMOVALS ('000 cu metres)

	1987	1988	1989
Industrial wood	3,731	3,581	3,740
Fuel wood	2,936	2,820	2,738
Total	6,667	6,401	6,478

SAWNWOOD PRODUCTION ('000 cu metres)

	1987	1988	1989
Coniferous (soft wood)	361	354	313
Broadleaved (hard wood)	329	335	350
Total	690	689	663

Fishing

(metric tons, live weight)

	1987	1988	1989
Total catch	36,759	38,294	37,517

Mining

('000 metric tons, unless otherwise indicated)

	1987	1988	1989
Hard coal	2,360	2,255	2,127
Brown coal	13,261	12,986	12,020
Lignite	7,223	5,634	5,883
Crude petroleum	1,914	1,947	1,966
Bauxite	3,101	2,593	2,644
Natural gas (million cu metres)	7,126	6,272	6,176

Industry

SELECTED PRODUCTS
('000 metric tons, unless otherwise indicated)

	1987	1988	1989
Pig iron	2,107	2,093	1,954
Crude steel	3,621	3,583	3,356
Rolled steel	2,831	2,793	2,539
Aluminium	73.5	74.7	75.2
Cement	4,153	3,873	3,857
Nitrogenous fertilizers*	666.7	574.1	580.8
Phosphatic fertilizers†	282.8	237.9	215.1
Refined sugar	447.3	421.5	508.4
Buses and lorries (number)	14,362	13,737	12,773
Cotton fabrics ('000 sq metres)	311,466	311,602	262,726
Leather footwear ('000 pairs)	39,356	35,683	29,528
Electric power (million kWh)	29,693	29,183	29,580
Woollen cloth ('000 sq metres)	30,339	28,649	32,275
Television receivers ('000)	446	433	502

* Production in terms of nitrogen.
† Production in terms of phosphoric acid.

Finance

CURRENCY AND EXCHANGE RATES

Monetary Units
100 fillér = 1 forint.

Denominations
Coins: 10, 20 and 50 fillér; 1, 2, 5, 10 and 20 forint.
Notes: 20, 50, 100, 500 and 1,000 forint.

Sterling and Dollar Equivalents (30 September 1990)
£1 sterling = 116.70 forint;
US $1 = 62.29 forint;
1,000 forint = £8.569 = $16.054.

Average Exchange Rate (forint per US dollar)
1987 46.971
1988 50.413
1989 59.066

HUNGARY

Statistical Survey

STATE BUDGET ('000 million forint)

Revenue	1987	1988	1989
Payments made by enterprises (co-operatives) and agricultural co-operatives	469.4	423.6	443.2
Consumers' turnover tax	122.3	210.5	230.7
Payments made by the population	79.3	154.7	209.4
Payments made by organizations financed by state budget	63.7	80.9	138.8
Other receipts	25.9	28.5	41.6
Total revenue	**760.6**	**898.2**	**1,063.7**

Expenditure	1987	1988	1989
Investment	99.9	108.0	115.5
Industrial enterprises (co-operatives) and agricultural co-operatives	150.7	143.8	115.7
Supplement to consumers' prices	66.7	44.5	44.1
Budgetary institutions	242.7	304.4	386.5
Health and social welfare	42.2	55.1	74.7
Culture	73.5	93.0	127.6
Defence	45.4	59.0	62.0
Legal and security order	3.2	4.6	6.3
Administration	10.5	15.9	23.0
Economic tasks	54.5	64.3	71.2
Others	13.4	12.5	21.7
Social security	154.7	216.6	269.5
Others	80.3	91.1	181.1
Total expenditure	**795.0**	**908.4**	**1,112.4**

1991 (forecasts, '000 million forint): Revenue 852.9; Expenditure 931.7.

INTERNATIONAL RESERVES (US $ million at 31 December)

	1987	1988	1989
Gold*	525	510	479
Foreign exchange	1,634	1,467	1,246
Total	2,159	1,977	1,725

* National valuation.
Source: IMF, *International Financial Statistics*.

MONEY SUPPLY (million forint at 31 December)

	1987	1988	1989
Currency outside banks	153,700	164,400	180,500
Demand deposits at commercial and savings banks	143,100	129,600	163,300

COST OF LIVING (Consumer Price Index; base: 1980 = 100)

	1987	1988	1989
Food	151.1	175.0	206.0
Fuel and light	160.9	181.5	202.2
Clothing	175.6	210.7	249.0
Rent	216.8	247.2	264.5
All items (incl. others)	**159.1**	**183.8**	**215.0**

BALANCE OF PAYMENTS (US $ million)

	1987	1988	1989
Merchandise exports f.o.b.	9,967	9,989	10,492
Merchandise imports f.o.b.	−9,887	−9,406	−9,449
Trade balance	**80**	**583**	**1,043**
Services (net)	166	−180	−352
Other income received	247	240	232
Other income paid	−1,274	−1,332	−1,625
Private unrequited transfers (net)	105	117	130
Current balance	**−676**	**−572**	**−573**
Capital (net)	239	668	1,134
Overall balance	**−437**	**96**	**561**

Source: IMF, *International Financial Statistics*.

NATIONAL ACCOUNTS

Gross Domestic Product by Economic Activity ('000 million forint at current prices)

	1987	1988	1989
Industry*	402.3	430.1	508.5
Construction	92.3	96.8	108.2
Agriculture and forestry	189.2	209.5	239.7
Transport and communications	94.4	101.2	123.8
Wholesale and retail trade	128.1	125.8	159.9
Other material activities	30.4	30.7	38.2
Taxes on commodities (net) and price differences	116.0	195.4	239.6
Non-material services purchases by material sphere	173.7	220.0	288.1
Total	**1,226.4**	**1,409.5**	**1,706.0**

* Manufacturing, mining, electricity and gas.

External Trade

PRINCIPAL COMMODITIES
(distribution by SITC, million forint)

Imports c.i.f.	1987	1988	1989
Food and live animals	27,535	29,650	32,259
Coffee, tea, cocoa and spices	7,266	7,300	5,414
Animal feeding-stuff (excl. cereals)	9,355	13,564	15,518
Crude materials (inedible) except fuels	28,966	32,154	33,201
Cork and wood	4,858	5,604	5,928
Textile fibres and waste	6,235	7,824	7,337
Mineral fuels, lubricants, etc.	70,346	62,804	61,525
Coal, coke and briquettes	7,085	7,513	8,229
Petroleum, petroleum products, etc.	38,557	32,150	28,651
Gas (natural and manufactured)	15,184	13,685	14,449
Chemicals and related products	67,238	74,808	85,075
Organic chemicals	10,766	11,926	14,472
Inorganic chemicals	10,218	11,357	10,977
Artificial resins and plastic materials, etc.	9,995	10,830	12,064
Basic manufactures	73,866	79,355	91,815
Paper, paperboard and manufactures	8,365	8,975	10,888
Textile yarn, fabrics, etc.	15,228	15,474	16,965
Iron and steel	13,742	14,516	17,113
Non-ferrous metals	12,741	14,432	15,591
Other metal manufactures	7,571	8,561	10,792

HUNGARY

Statistical Survey

Imports c.i.f.—continued	1987	1988	1989
Machinery and transport equipment	139,769	142,826	175,008
Machinery specialized for particular industries	37,703	35,163	40,797
Metalworking machinery	8,009	7,736	9,797
Road vehicles and parts (excl. tyres, engines and electrical parts)	31,084	31,254	34,514
Miscellaneous manufactured articles	29,415	28,915	36,343
Total (incl. others)	443,956	460,894	523,507

Exports f.o.b.	1987	1988	1989
Food and live animals	70,839	86,625	105,976
Live animals	8,184	10,260	12,618
Meat and meat preparations	25,956	30,318	36,203
Cereals and cereal preparations	9,276	14,680	16,037
Vegetables and fruit	20,300	22,830	27,206
Beverages and tobacco	6,907	6,129	7,650
Crude materials (inedible) except fuels	16,740	20,631	23,663
Mineral fuels, lubricants, etc.	11,028	13,012	16,384
Petroleum, petroleum products, etc.	10,219	11,902	15,036
Chemicals and related products	49,506	59,136	70,615
Organic chemicals	8,508	9,885	11,580
Medicinal and pharmaceutical products	19,421	20,357	24,639
Basic manufactures	60,417	76,013	97,281
Textile yarn, fabrics, etc.	13,263	14,408	15,729
Iron and steel	14,369	19,865	26,719
Non-ferrous metals	9,999	14,548	20,955
Machinery and transport equipment	151,214	161,347	172,775
Machinery specialized for particular industries	30,917	32,189	33,854
Telecommunications and sound equipment	22,237	23,675	22,075
Other electrical machinery, apparatus, etc.	19,604	22,160	27,671
Road vehicles and parts (excl. tyres, engines and electrical parts)	45,502	45,662	44,734
Miscellaneous manufactured articles	53,959	55,310	60,148
Clothing and accessories (excl. footwear)	17,571	20,028	20,484
Footwear	7,446	6,468	7,020
Professional, scientific and controlling instruments and apparatus	14,356	13,266	13,880
Total (incl. others)	432,609	492,326	571,323

PRINCIPAL TRADING PARTNERS* (million forint)

Imports c.i.f.	1987	1988	1989
Austria	29,238	33,785	44,977
Belgium and Luxembourg	6,980	6,950	8,520
Brazil	5,143	8,179	6,890
Bulgaria	5,848	6,423	4,530
China, People's Republic	9,173	7,829	5,474
Czechoslovakia	24,835	23,695	26,966
Finland	2,751	3,786	4,021
France	8,813	9,323	11,517
German Democratic Republic	29,442	29,553	32,518
Germany, Federal Republic	62,571	64,893	83,917
Indonesia	2,172	2,076	1,596
Iran	53	67	51
Italy	12,393	14,518	17,000
Japan	5,686	6,666	6,400
Netherlands	6,808	8,252	10,752
Poland	18,370	19,194	17,222
Romania	8,498	8,189	8,501
Spain	1,726	1,793	2,083
Sweden	5,412	6,922	6,915
Switzerland and Liechtenstein	11,308	11,836	15,328
USSR	126,952	115,962	115,513
United Kingdom	7,641	8,494	11,560
USA	10,712	9,858	13,232
Yugoslavia	9,532	13,754	18,222
Total (incl. others)	443,956	460,894	523,507

* Imports by country of production; exports by country of last consignment.

Exports f.o.b.	1987	1988	1989
Algeria	3,187	3,133	2,309
Austria	21,967	28,202	37,109
Belgium and Luxembourg	3,072	3,982	4,984
Bulgaria	6,563	6,300	4,167
China, People's Republic	4,975	9,256	6,981
Cuba	2,280	2,516	2,810
Czechoslovakia	22,552	27,020	28,980
Egypt	3,094	2,707	3,152
Finland	2,849	4,534	5,822
France	8,356	9,733	13,655
German Democratic Republic	25,148	26,592	30,880
Germany, Federal Republic	43,233	54,293	68,010
Greece	2,428	3,123	4,772
Iran	4,985	4,718	5,128
Iraq	1,512	811	1,472
Italy	15,912	20,927	26,707
Japan	3,275	4,966	6,605
Libya	1,143	1,508	976
Netherlands	4,723	5,782	7,584
Nigeria	2,177	1,903	1,056
Poland	15,436	16,650	18,091
Romania	7,983	8,607	8,317
Sweden	4,465	6,021	7,479
Switzerland and Liechtenstein	6,394	9,003	9,449
Turkey	3,495	5,143	5,479
USSR	145,864	137,979	143,587
United Kingdom	6,055	8,814	10,299
USA	13,452	14,686	19,088
Yugoslavia	11,179	13,919	23,560
Total (incl. others)	432,609	492,326	571,323

Transport

RAILWAYS (traffic)

	1987	1988	1989
Passengers carried (million)	332.8	327.9	329.0
Passenger-kilometres (million)	12,262	12,437	12,741
Net ton-kilometres (million)	21,731	21,057	19,820

ROAD TRAFFIC (motor vehicles in use at 31 December)

	1987	1988	1989
Passenger cars	1,660,258	1,789,562	1,732,385
Goods vehicles	191,851	196,105	208,306
Buses	26,893	26,569	23,793
Motor cycles	405,690	412,390	n.a.

INLAND WATERWAYS (traffic)

	1987	1988	1989
Freight carried ('000 metric tons)	3,758	3,942	2,112
Freight ton-km (million)	2,046	2,188	2,100

HUNGARY

CIVIL AVIATION (traffic)

	1987	1988	1989
Kilometres flown	21,711,900	21,274,980	23,127,000
Passengers carried	1,320,311	1,309,635	1,500,000
Passenger-km ('000)	1,285,597	1,344,327	1,576,600
Cargo carried: metric tons	11,972	10,386	8,000
Cargo ton-km	15,880,000	14,264,000	10,600,000

Tourism

('000 arrivals)

	1987	1988	1989
Foreign tourists	11,826	10,563	14,236
Foreign visitors in transit	7,127	7,402	10,683
Total	18,953	17,965	24,919

TOURISTS BY COUNTRY OF ORIGIN
('000 arrivals, including visitors in transit)

	1987	1988	1989
Austria	3,264	3,844	4,554
Bulgaria	575	625	678
Czechoslovakia	4,870	3,505	3,708
German Democratic Republic	1,621	1,638	1,573
Germany, Federal Republic	1,097	1,278	1,612
Poland	3,253	2,820	4,481
Romania	421	271	236
USSR	529	683	2,266
Yugoslavia	2,228	2,023	4,416
Total (incl. others)	18,953	17,965	24,919

Communications Media

	1987	1988	1989
Television receivers*	279	277	279
Radio receivers†	512	n.a.	n.a.
Telephones in use	1,609,465	1,674,139	1,769,889
Books titles (including translations)	7,804	7,562	7,599
Daily newspapers	29	29	31
Average daily circulation	3,078,731	3,101,495	2,507,990

* Number of television receivers per 1,000 inhabitants.
† Estimated number of radio receivers per 1,000 inhabitants.

Education

(1989/90)

	Institutions	Teachers	Students
Nursery	4,748	33,835	392,273
Primary	3,527	90,602	1,183,573
Secondary	675	21,425	349,071
Higher	57	16,319	100,868

Directory

The Constitution

A new constitution was introduced on 18 August 1949, and the Hungarian People's Republic was established two days later. The Constitution was amended in April 1972 and December 1983. Further, radical amendments were made in October 1989. Shortly afterwards, the Republic of Hungary was proclaimed.

The following is a summary of the main provisions of the Constitution, as amended in October 1989.

GENERAL PROVISIONS

The Republic of Hungary is an independent, democratic constitutional state in which the values of civil democracy and democratic socialism prevail in equal measures. All power belongs to the people, which they exercise directly and through the elected representatives of popular sovereignty.

Political parties may, under observance of the Constitution, be freely formed and may freely operate in Hungary. Parties may not directly exercise public power. No party has the right to guide any state body. Trade unions and other organizations for the representation of interests safeguard and represent the interests of employees, members of co-operatives and entrepreneurs.

The State safeguards the people's freedom, the independence and territorial integrity of the country as well as the frontiers thereof, as established by international treaties. The Republic of Hungary rejects war as a means of settling disputes between nations and refrains from applying force against the independence or territorial integrity of other states, and from threats of violence.

The Hungarian legal system adopts the universally accepted rules of international law. The order of legislation is regulated by an Act of constitutional force.

The economy of Hungary is a market economy, availing itself also of the advantages of planning, with public and private ownership enjoying equal right and protection. Hungary recognizes and supports the right of undertaking and free competition, limitable only by an Act of constitutional force. State-owned enterprises and organs pursuing economic activities manage their affairs independently, in accordance with the mode and responsibility as provided by law.

The Republic of Hungary protects the institutions of marriage and the family. It provides for the indigent through extensive social measures, and recognizes and enforces the right of each citizen to a healthy environment.

GOVERNMENT

National Assembly

The highest organ of state authority in the Republic of Hungary is the National Assembly which exercises all the rights deriving from the sovereignty of the people and determines the organization, direction and conditions of government. The National Assembly enacts the Constitution and laws, determines the state budget, decides the socio-economic plan, elects the President of the Republic and the Council of Ministers, directs the activities of ministries, decides upon declaring war and concluding peace and exercises the prerogative of amnesty.

The National Assembly is elected for a term of four years and members enjoy immunity from arrest and prosecution without parliamentary consent. It meets at least twice a year and is convened by the President of the Republic or by a written demand of the Council of Ministers or of one-fifth of the Assembly's members. It elects a President, Deputy Presidents and Recorders from among its own members, and it lays down its own rules of procedure and agenda. As a general rule, the sessions of the National Assembly are held in public.

The National Assembly has the right of legislation which can be initiated by the President of the Republic, the Council of Ministers or any committee or member of the National Assembly. Decisions are valid only if at least half of the members are present, and they require a simple majority. Constitutional changes require a two-thirds majority. Acts of the National Assembly are signed by the President of the Republic.

The National Assembly may pronounce its dissolution before the expiry of its term, and in the event of an emergency may prolong its mandate or may be reconvened after dissolution. A new National Assembly must be elected within three months of dissolution and convened within one month of polling day.

Members of the National Assembly are elected on the basis of universal, equal and direct suffrage by secret ballot, and they are accountable to their constituents, who may recall them. All citizens of 18 years and over have the right to vote, with the exception of those who are unsound of mind, and those who are deprived of their civil rights by a court of law.

President of the Republic

The President of the Republic is the Head of State of Hungary. He/she embodies the unity of the nation and supervises the democratic operation of the mechanism of State. The President is also the Commander-in-Chief of the Armed Forces. The President is elected by the National Assembly for a period of four years, and may be re-elected for a second term. Any citizen of Hungary qualified to vote, who has reached 35 years of age before the day of election, may be elected President.

The President may issue the writ for general or local elections, convene the National Assembly, initiate legislation, hold plebiscites, direct local government, conclude international treaties, appoint diplomatic representatives, ratify international treaties, appoint higher civil servants and officers of the armed forces, award orders and titles, and exercise the prerogative of mercy.

Council of Ministers

The highest organ of state administration is the Council of Ministers, responsible to the National Assembly and consisting of a Chairman, Ministers of State and other Ministers who are elected by the National Assembly on the recommendation of the President of the Republic. The Council of Ministers directs the work of the ministries (listed in a special enactment) and ensures the enforcement of laws and the fulfilment of economic plans; it may issue decrees and annul or modify measures taken by any central or local organ of government.

Local Administration

The local organs of state power are the county, town, borough and town precinct councils, whose members are elected for a term of four years by the voters in each area. Local councils direct economic, social and cultural activities in their area, prepare local economic plans and budgets and supervises their fulfilment, enforce laws, supervise subordinate organs, maintain public order, protect public property and individual rights, and direct local economic enterprises. They may issue regulations and annul or modify those of subordinate councils. Local Councils are administered by an Executive Committee elected by and responsible to them.

JUDICATURE

Justice is administered by the Supreme Court of the Republic of Hungary, county and district courts. The Supreme Court exercises the right of supervising in principle the judicial activities and practice of all other courts.

All judicial offices are filled by election; Supreme Court, county and district court judges are all elected for an indefinite period; the President of the Supreme Court is elected by the National Assembly. All court hearings are public unless otherwise prescribed by law, and those accused are guaranteed the right of defence. An accused person must be considered innocent until proved guilty.

Public Prosecutor

The function of the Chief Public Prosecutor is to watch over the observance of the law. He is elected by the National Assembly, to whom he is responsible. The organization of public prosecution is under the control of the Chief Public Prosecutor, who appoints the public prosecutors.

RIGHTS AND DUTIES OF CITIZENS

The Republic of Hungary guarantees for its citizens the right to work and to remuneration, the right of rest and recreation, the right to care in old age, sickness or disability, the right to education, and equality before the law; women enjoy equal rights with men. Discrimination on grounds of sex, religion or nationality is a punishable offence. The State also ensures freedom of conscience, religious worship, speech, the Press and assembly. The right of workers to organize themselves is stressed. The freedom of the individual, and the privacy of the home and of correspondence are inviolable. Freedom for creative work in the sciences and the arts is guaranteed.

The basic freedoms of all workers are guaranteed and foreign citizens enjoy the right of asylum.

Military service (with or without arms) and the defence of their country are the duties of all citizens.

The Government
(February 1991)

HEAD OF STATE

President of the Republic: Árpád Göncz (elected 3 August 1990).

COUNCIL OF MINISTERS

A coalition of the Hungarian Democratic Forum (HDF), the Independent Smallholders' Party (ISP), the Christian Democratic People's Party (CDPP) and Independents.

Chairman: József Antall (HDF).
Minister of the Interior: Dr Péter Boross (Independent).
Minister of Agriculture: Dr Elemér Gergátz (ISP).
Minister of Defence: Lajos Für (HDF).
Minister of Justice: Dr István Balsai (HDF).
Minister of Industry and Trade: Péter Ákos Bod (HDF).
Minister of Environmental Protection and Urban Development: K. Sándor Keresztes (HDF).
Minister of Transport, Communications and Water Management: Csaba Siklós (HDF).
Minister of Foreign Affairs: Dr Géza Jeszenszky (HDF).
Minister of Labour: Dr Gyula Kiss (ISP).
Minister of Culture and Education: Dr Bertalan Andrásfalvy (HDF).
Minister of International Economic Relations: Dr Béla Kádár (Independent).
Minister of Social Welfare: Dr László Surján (CDPP).
Minister of Finance: Dr Mihály Kupa (Independent).
Ministers without Portfolio: Dr Ferenc Mádl (Independent), Katalin Botos (HDF), Dr András Gálszécsy (Independent), Dr Balázs Horváth (HDF), Ferenc József Nagy (ISP), Ernő Pungor (Independent).

MINISTRIES

Council of Ministers (Secretariat): 1055 Budapest, Kossuth Lajos tér 1/3; tel. 112-0600; telex 22-5547; fax 153-3622.

Ministry of Agriculture: 1055 Budapest, Kossuth Lajos tér 11; tel. 153-3000; telex 22-5445; fax 153-0518.

Ministry of Culture and Education: 1055 Budapest, Szalay u. 10/14; tel. 153-0600; telex 22-5935.

Ministry of Defence: 1055 Budapest, Pálffy György u. 7/11; tel. 132-2500; telex 22-5424.

Ministry of Environmental Protection and Urban Development: 1011 Budapest, Fő u. 44-50, POB 351; tel. 115-4840; telex 22-4879; fax 136-2198.

Ministry of Finance: 1051 Budapest, József Nádor tér 2/4; tel. 118-2066.

Ministry of Foreign Affairs: 1027 Budapest, Bem rkp. 47; tel. 156-8000; telex 22-5571.

Ministry of Industry and Trade: 1024 Budapest, Mártírok u. 85; tel. 132-6570; telex 22-5376.

Ministry of the Interior: 1051 Budapest, József Attila u. 2/4; tel. 112-1710; telex 22-5216.

Ministry of International Economic Relations: 1055 Budapest, Honvéd u. 13/15; tel. 153-0000; telex 22-5578; fax 153-2794.

Ministry of Justice: 1055 Budapest, Szalay u. 16; tel. 131-8922.

Ministry of Labour: 1051 Budapest, Roosevelt tér 7-8; tel. 132-2100.

Ministry of Social Welfare: 1051 Budapest, Arany János u. 6/8; tel. 132-3100; telex 22-4337; fax 153-4955.

Ministry of Transport, Communications and Water Management: 1400 Budapest, Dob u. 75/81, POB 87; tel. 122-0220; telex 22-5729; fax 122-8695.

Legislature

ORSZÁGGYÜLÉS
(National Assembly)

The unicameral National Assembly consists of 386 deputies, elected

HUNGARY

for a four-year term. At elections, held in March and April 1990, 176 deputies were elected directly to represent single-member constituencies, 152 according to a system of proportional representation of parties, while the remaining 58 were elected on a national list on the basis of a nationwide summary of surplus votes. An additional eight seats were reportedly to be reserved for one deputy each from Hungary's Romany, Croat, German, Romanian, Serbian, Slovak, Slovene and Jewish minorities.

President of the National Assembly: Dr GYÖRGY SZABAD.

Deputy Presidents: Dr ALAJOS DORNBACH, MÁTYÁS SZŰRÖS, VINCE VÖRÖS.

General election, 25 March and 8 April 1990

	%	Seats
Hungarian Democratic Forum (HDF)	42.74	165
Alliance of Free Democrats (AFD)	23.83	92
Independent Smallholders' Party (ISP)	11.13	43
Hungarian Socialist Party (HSP)	8.54	33
Federation of Young Democrats (FYD)	5.44	21
Christian Democratic People's Party (CDPP)	5.44	21
Others	2.88	11
Total	100.00	386

Political Organizations

Alliance of Free Democrats (AFD): 1051 Budapest, Mérleg u. 6; tel. 117-6911; fax 118-7944; f. 1988; 35,000 mems (1990); Chair. JÁNOS KIS.

Christian Democratic People's Party (CDPP): Budapest; re-formed 1989; Chair. LÁSZLÓ SURJÁN.

Federation of Young Democrats (FYD): 1394 Budapest, POB 368; tel. 112-1095; fax 131-9673; f. 1989; 10,000 mems; Leader VIKTOR ORBAN.

Green Party: Budapest; f. 1989; Co-Chair. KÁROLY SZITA, IVAN GYULAY, GYÖRGY ILOSVAY.

Hungarian Democratic Forum (HDF): 1538 Budapest, POB 579; tel. 115-9690; fax 156-8522; f. 1988; 25,000 mems (April 1990); Chair. JÓZSEF ANTALL.

Hungarian People's Party: Budapest; f. 1989; Chair. GYULA FEKETE.

Hungarian Socialist Party (HSP—Magyar Szocialista Párt): 1054 Budapest, Széchenyi rkp. 19; f. 1989 to replace the Hungarian Socialist Workers' Party; 67,000 mems (Dec. 1989); Chair. GYULA HORN.

Hungarian Socialist Workers' Party (HSWP—Magyar Szocialista Munkáspárt): 1092 Budapest, Köztelek u. 8; tel. 118-3100; f. 1956; dissolved and replaced by Hungarian Socialist Party in 1989; re-formed in 1989; approx. 80,000 mems (May 1990); Pres. GYULA THÜRMER.

Independent Smallholders' Party (ISP): 1051 Budapest, Aranyi János u. 10; tel. 111-2828; fax 155-1049; f. 1988; 70,000 mems (April 1990); Chair. FERENC NAGY.

Social Democratic Party (SDP): 1074 Budapest, Dohány u. 76; tel. 142-2385; f. 1980; absorbed by Communist Party in 1948; revived 1988; 15,000 mems (Nov. 1989); Chair. ANNA PETRASOVITS.

Diplomatic Representation

EMBASSIES IN HUNGARY

Afghanistan: 1062 Budapest, Lendvay u. 23; tel. 132-7187; Ambassador: SHER JAN MAZDORYAR.

Albania: 1068 Budapest, Bajza u. 26; tel. 122-7251; Ambassador: JANI POLENA.

Algeria: 1014 Budapest, Dísz tér 6; tel. 175-9884; telex 22-6916; Ambassador: BACHIR ROULS.

Argentina: 1068 Budapest, Rippl Rónai u. 1; tel. 122-8467; telex 22-4128; Ambassador: GUILLERMO MAGOUGH.

Australia: 1062 Budapest, Délibáb u. 30; tel. 153-4233; telex 22-7708; fax 153-4866; Ambassador: DOUGLAS TOWNSEND.

Austria: 1068 Budapest, Benczúr u. 16; tel. 122-9467; telex 22-4447; Ambassador: Dr FRANZ SCHMID.

Belgium: 1015 Budapest, Toldy Ferenc u. 13; tel. 115-2276; telex 22-4664; Ambassador: WILLEM VERKAMMEN.

Bolivia: Budapest II, Mártírok u. 43–45; tel. 116-3019; Chargé d'affaires: Dr MARIO PAZ-ZAMORA.

Brazil: 1118 Budapest, Somlói út 3; tel. 166-6044; telex 22-5795; Ambassador: IVAN VELLOSO DA SILVEIRA BATALHA.

Bulgaria: 1124 Budapest, Levendula u. 15–17; tel. 156-6840; telex 22-3032; Ambassador: VESSELIN FILEV.

Cambodia: 1122 Budapest, Ráth György u. 48; tel. 155-1128; Ambassador: UNG SEAN.

Canada: 1121 Budapest, Budakeszi út 32; tel. 176-7686; telex 22-4588; Ambassador: DEREK FRASER.

China, People's Republic: 1068 Budapest, Benczúr u. 17; tel. 122-4872; Ambassador: DAI BINGGUO.

Colombia: 1024 Budapest, Mártírok u. 43–45; tel. 135-2534; telex 22-6012; Ambassador: EDUARDO SUESCÚN-MONROY.

Costa Rica: Budapest; Chargé d'affaires: JOSÉ LUIS CALLACI LEGIZAMO.

Cuba: 1068 Budapest, Benczúr u. 26; tel. 121-4037; telex 22-4388; Ambassador: FAUSTINO MANUEL BEATO MOREJÓN.

Czechoslovakia: 1143 Budapest, Népstadion út 22; tel. 251-1700; telex 22-4744; Ambassador: RUDOLF CHMEL.

Denmark: 1122 Budapest, Határőr út 37; tel. 155-7320; telex 22-4137; fax 175-3803; Ambassador: OLE KOCH.

Ecuador: 1021 Budapest, Budakeszi út 55/D; tel. 176-7593; Ambassador: GALO RIVADENEIRA.

Egypt: 1016 Budapest, Bérc u. 16; tel. 166-8060; telex 22-5184; Ambassador: MOHAMED ALI EL-SHEREI.

Finland: 1118 Budapest, Kelenhegyi út 16a; tel. 185-0700; telex 22-4710; fax 185-0772; Ambassador: RISTO HYVÄRINEN.

France: 1062 Budapest, Lendvay u. 27; tel. 132-4980; telex 22-5143; Ambassador: CHRISTIANE MALITCHENKO.

Germany: 1146 Budapest, Izsó u. 5; tel. 122-4204; telex 22-5951; fax 160-1903; Ambassador: Dr ALEXANDER ARNOT.

Greece: 1063 Budapest, Szegfű u. 3; tel. 122-8004; telex 22-4113; Ambassador: EMMANUEL KALPADAKIS.

India: 1025 Budapest, Búzavirág u. 14; tel. 115-5211; telex 22-6374; Ambassador: SURINDER LAL MALIK.

Indonesia: 1068 Budapest, Gorkij fasor 26; tel. 142-8508; telex 22-5263; Ambassador: BUSTANUL ARIFIN.

Iran: 1062 Budapest, Délibáb u. 29; tel. 122-5038; telex 22-4129; Ambassador: KEYVAN IMANI.

Iraq: 1145 Budapest, Szántó Béla u. 13; tel. 122-6418; telex 22-6058; Ambassador: MOHAMMED GHANIM AL-ANAZ.

Italy: 1143 Budapest, Népstadion u. 95; tel. 121-2450; telex 22-5294; Ambassador: JOSEPH NITTI.

Japan: 1024 Budapest, Rómer Flóris u. 56–58; tel. 156-4533; telex 22-5167; Ambassador: EIJI SEKI.

Korea, Democratic People's Republic: 1068 Budapest, Benczúr u. 31; tel. 142-5174; telex 22-6721; Chargé d'affaires: BANG RYONG GAB.

Korea, Republic: 1368 Budapest, Hotel Fórum (Apáczai Csere J.u. 12–14); tel. 138-3388; Ambassador: HAN TAK-CHAE.

Libya: 1441 Budapest, POB 73; tel. 122-6076; telex 22-6940; Head of People's Bureau: FATHI M. AL-MISRATI.

Mexico: 1021 Budapest, Budakeszi út 55/D; tel. 176-7381; fax 176-7906; Ambassador: LUCIANO JOUBLANC.

Mongolia: 1125 Budapest, Istenhegyi út 59–61; tel. 155-7989; Ambassador: DANGASURENGIN SALDAN.

Morocco: 1026 Budapest, Törökvész Lejto 12/A; tel. 115-9251; telex 22-3580; Ambassador: MOHAMED CHAHID.

Netherlands: 1146 Budapest, Abonyi u. 31; tel. 122-8432; telex 22-5562; fax 141-6532; Ambassador: H. J. VAN OORDT.

Nicaragua: 1021 Budapest, Budakeszi út 55/D; tel. 176-7953; Chargé d'affaires a.i.: GUSTAVO CRUZ MORENO.

Norway: 1122 Budapest, Határőr út 35, POB 32; tel. 155-1811; telex 22-5867; fax 156-7928; Ambassador: LEIF EDWARD EDWARDSEN.

Pakistan: 1125 Budapest, Adonis u. 3/A; tel. 135-9183; Ambassador: HAMIDULLAH KHAN.

Peru: 1024 Budapest, Mártírok u. 43–45; tel. 115-0292; Ambassador: JOSÉ PABLO MORÁN VAL.

Philippines: Budapest, Hotel Buda Penta; tel. 156-6333; Chargé d'affaires: MARCIANO A. PAYNOR, Jr.

Poland: 1068 Budapest, Gorkij fasor 16; tel. 122-8437; Ambassador: TADEUSZ CZECHOWICZ.

Portugal: 1024 Budapest, Mártírok u. 43–45; tel. 115-5602; telex 22-6509; fax 115-4666; Ambassador: ZÓZIMO DA SILVA.

Romania: 1146 Budapest, Thököly út 72; tel. 142-6944; telex 22-5847; Ambassador: SIMION POP.

Spain: 1067 Budapest, Eötvös u. 11B; tel. 153-1011; telex 22-4130; Ambassador: LUIS DE LA TORRE.

Sweden: 1146 Budapest, Ajtósi Dürer sor 27/A; tel. 122-9880; telex 22-5647; Ambassador: STEN STRÖMHOLM.
Switzerland: 1143 Budapest, Népstadion út 107; tel. 122-9491; Ambassador: PAUL WIPFLI; Office of Israeli interests: 1026 Budapest, Fullánk u. 8; tel. 176-7897; Head of Office: SHLOMO MAROM.
Syria: 1026 Budapest, Harangvirág u. 3; tel. 176-7186; telex 22-6605; Ambassador: (vacant).
Thailand: 1025 Budapest, Józsefhegyi út 28-30 A/3; tel. 135-4590; telex 20-2706; fax 115-0606; Ambassador: SUTTISWAT KRIDAKON.
Turkey: 1014 Budapest, Úri u. 45; tel. 175-0609; Ambassador: HALIT GÜVENER.
USSR: 1062 Budapest, Bajza u. 35; tel. 132-0911; Ambassador: IVAN P. ABOIMOV.
United Kingdom: 1051 Budapest, Harmincad u. 6; tel. 118-2888; telex 22-4527; fax 118-0907; Ambassador: JOHN BIRCH.
USA: 1054 Budapest, Szabadság tér 12; tel. 112-6450; telex 22-4222; Ambassador: CHARLES THOMAS.
Uruguay: 1023 Budapest, Vérhalom u. 12–16; tel. 136-8333; Ambassador: JUAN B. ÓDDONE SILVEIRA.
Venezuela: 1023 Budapest, Vérhalom u. 12–16; tel. 135-3562; telex 22-6666; fax 115-3274; Ambassador: MORITZ EIRIS-VILLEGAS.
Viet-Nam: 1068 Budapest, Benczúr u. 18; tel. 142-9943; Ambassador: NGUYEN VAN QUY.
Yemen: Budapest, Hotel Duna Intercontinental; Chargé d'affaires: MARWAN NOMAN.
Yugoslavia: 1068 Budapest, Dózsa György u. 92/B; tel. 142-0566; Ambassador: RUDOLF-RUDI SOVA.

Judicial System

The system of court procedure in Hungary is based on an Act that came into effect in 1953 and has since been updated frequently. The system of jurisdiction is based on the local courts (district courts in Budapest, city courts in other cities), labour courts, county courts, the Metropolitan Court and the Supreme Court. In the legal remedy system of two instances, appeals against the decisions of city and district courts can be lodged with the competent county court and the Metropolitan Court of Budapest respectively. Against the judgment of first instance of the latter, appeal is to be lodged with the Supreme Court. The Chief Public Prosecutor and the President of the Supreme Court have the right to submit a protest on legal grounds against the final judgment of any court.

By virtue of the 1973 Act, effective 1974 and modified in 1979, the procedure in criminal cases is differentiated for criminal offences and for criminal acts. In the first instance, criminal cases are tried, depending on their character, by a professional judge; where justified by the magnitude of the criminal act, by a council composed of three members, a professional judge and two lay assessors, while in major cases the court consists of five members, two professional judges and three lay assessors. In the Supreme Court, second instance cases are tried only by professional judges. The President of the Supreme Court is elected by the National Assembly. Judges are appointed by the President of the Republic for an indefinite period. Assessors are elected by the local municipal councils.

In the interest of ensuring legality and a uniform application of the Law, the Supreme Court exercises a principled guidance over the jurisdiction of courts. In the Republic of Hungary judges are independent and subject only to the Law and other legal regulations.

The Minister of Justice supervises the general activities of courts. The Chief Public Prosecutor is elected by the National Assembly. The Chief Public Prosecutor and the Prosecutor's Office provide for the consistent prosecution of all acts violating or endangering the legal order of society, the safety and independence of the state, and for the protection of citizens.

The Prosecutors of the independent prosecuting organization exert supervision over the legality of investigations and the implementation of punishments, and assist with specific means in ensuring that legal regulations should be observed by state, economic and other organs and citizens, and they support the legality of court procedures and decisions.

President of the Supreme Court: PÁL SOLT.
Chief Public Prosecutor: KÁLMÁN GYÖRGYI.

Religion

National Council for Religious Affairs: Budapest; f. 1989 to replace State Office for Church Affairs; autonomous body, independent of the State.

CHRISTIANITY

Magyarországi Egyházak Ökuménikus Tanácsa (Ecumenical Council of Churches in Hungary): 1054 Budapest, Szabadság tér 2; tel. 111-4862; f. 1943; member churches: Reformed Church, Evangelical Lutheran, Baptist, Methodist, Hungarian Orthodox, Romanian Orthodox and Council of Free Churches; Pres. Bishop Dr KÁROLY TÓTH; Gen. Sec. Rev. LÁSZLÓ LEHEL.

The Roman Catholic Church

Hungary comprises three archdioceses, eight dioceses (including one for Catholics of the Byzantine rite) and one territorial abbacy (directly responsible to the Holy See). At 31 December 1988 the Church had 6,710,512 adherents in Hungary. There are 3,250 active churches.

Bishops' Conference: Magyar Püspöki Kar Konferenciája, 6301 Kalocsa, Szabadság tér 1; tel. 155; f. 1969; Pres. Cardinal Dr LÁSZLÓ PASKAI, Archbishop of Esztergom.

Latin Rite

Archbishop of Eger: Dr ISTVÁN SEREGÉLY, 3301 Eger, Széchenyi u. 1; tel. 13-259.
Archbishop of Esztergom: Cardinal Dr LÁSZLÓ PASKAI, Primate of Hungary, 2500 Esztergom, Berenyi Zsigmond u. 2; tel. 330-511.
Archbishop of Kalocsa: Dr LÁSZLÓ DANKÓ, 6301 Kalocsa, Szabadság tér 1; tel. 155.

Byzantine Rite

Bishop of Hajdudorog: SZILÁRD KERESZTES, 4401 Nyiregyháza, Bethlen u. 5, POB 60; tel. 42-17397; about 250,000 adherents; the Bishop is also Apostolic Administrator of the Apostolic Exarchate of Miskolc, with an estimated 22,800 Catholics of the Byzantine rite (Nov. 1988).

Protestant Churches

Evangélikus Egyház (Lutheran Church in Hungary) (Evangelical): 1088 Budapest, Puskin u. 12; tel. 138-2302; 430,000 mems (1985); Presiding Bishop Dr GYULA NAGY; Gen. Sec. Dr ÁGOSTON KARNER.
Magyarországi Baptista Egyház (Baptist Union of Hungary): 1062 Budapest, Aradi u. 48; tel. 132-2332; f. 1846; 12,250 mems; Pres. Rev. Dr JÁNOS VICZIÁN; Sec. Rev. KORNÉL GYŐRI.
Magyarországi Református Egyház (Reformed Church in Hungary) (Presbyterian): 1146 Budapest, Abonyi u. 21; tel. 122-7870; 2m. mems (1987); 1,306 churches; Pres. of Gen. Synod Bishop Dr KÁROLY TÓTH.

Orthodox Churches

Magyar Orthodox Egyház (Hungarian Orthodox Church): 1052 Budapest, Petőfi tér 2.1.2.; tel. 118-4813; Administrator Archpriest Dr FERIZ BERKI.
Görögkeleti Szerb Egyházmegye (Serbian-Orthodox Diocese): Szentendre; Parochus DUSÁN VUJICSICS.

The Russian (6,000 mems), Bulgarian and Romanian Orthodox Churches are also represented.

ISLAM

There are about 3,000 Muslims in Hungary. In 1987 it was announced that an Islamic centre was to be built in Budapest, with assistance from the Muslim World League.

JUDAISM

The Jewish community in Hungary is estimated to number between 80,000 and 100,000 people.

Magyar Izraeliták Országos Képviselete (Central Board of Hungarian Jews); **Budapesti Izraelita Hitközség** (Jewish Community of Budapest): 1079 Budapest, Síp u. 12; tel. 122-6475; 80,000 mems; 40 active synagogues; Orthodox and Conservative; Pres. GUSTÁV ZOLTAI; Chief Rabbi of Budapest GYÖRGY LANDESZMANN.

The Press

In 1988 the censorship laws were relaxed considerably, and in 1989 private ownership of publications was legalized. By late 1990 most of the former organs of political parties, trade unions, youth and social organizations had been transferred into full or partial private ownership.

In 1989 there were 31 dailies with an average total circulation of 2,507,990. These included more than 20 provincial dailies. Budapest dailies circulate nationally. In order of popularity they are: *Népszabadság*, *Népszava*, the evening *Esti Hírlap* and *Magyar Nemzet*. *Népszabadság*, the most important daily, was formerly the central organ of the Hungarian Socialist Workers' Party, but

HUNGARY

is now independent. The paper most respected for the quality of its news coverage and commentary is *Magyar Nemzet*.

Among the most popular periodicals are the illustrated weeklies, which include the satirical *Ludas Matyi*, the women's magazine *Nők Lapja*, the illustrated news journal *Képes Újság* and the political paper *Szabad Föld*. A news magazine giving a high standard of reporting and political discussion is *Magyarország*. Specialized periodicals include cultural, medical, scientific, agricultural and religious publications (including *Új Ember*, *Evangélikus Élet* and *Új Élet* for Catholic, Lutheran and Jewish congregations respectively).

PRINCIPAL DAILIES

Daily News: 1016 Budapest, Fém u. 5–7; tel. 175-6722; telex 22-4371; f. 1967; published by the Hungarian News Agency; in English and German; Editor-in-Chief Dr János Dobsa; circ. 15,000.

Esti Hirlap (Evening Journal): 1085 Budapest, Blaha Lujza tér 1–3; tel. 133-6130; telex 22-7040; 40% foreign-owned; Editor-in-Chief László Bernat; circ. 100,000.

Magyar Hirlap (Hungarian Journal): 1393 Budapest, POB 305; tel. 122-2400; telex 22-4268; f. 1968; 40% foreign-owned; Editor-in-Chief Zsolt Bajnok; circ. 96,000.

Magyar Nemzet (Hungarian Nation): 1073 Budapest, Erzsébet krt 9–11; tel. 122-2400; telex 22-4269; 45% foreign-owned; Editor (vacant); circ. 160,000.

Mai Nap (Today): 1087 Budapest, Kömyves K. krt 76; tel. 113-0284; telex 22-3634; fax 133-9153; f. 1988; Editor-in-Chief István Horváth; circ. 120,000.

Népsport (People's Sport): 1981 Budapest, Somogyi Béla u. 6; tel. 138-4366; telex 22-5245; fax 138-2463; Editor-in-Chief István Szekeres; circ. 250,000.

Népszabadság (People's Freedom): 1960 Budapest, Blaha Lujza tér 3; tel. 133-6130; telex 22-5551; f. 1942; independent; Editor-in-Chief Pál Eötvös; circ. 400,000.

Népszava (Voice of the People): 1964 Budapest, Rákóczi ut 54; tel. 122-4810; telex 22-4105; fax 122-2415; f. 1873; trade unions' daily; Editor András Deák; circ. 200,000.

WEEKLIES

Élet és Irodalom (Life and Literature); 1054 Budapest, Széchenyi u. 1; tel. 153-3122; f. 1957; literary and political; Editor Imre Bata; circ. 60,000.

Élet és Tudomány (Life and Science): 1073 Budapest, Erzsébet krt 5; tel. 142-0324; telex 22-7040; fax 138-3331; f. 1946; popular science; Editor-in-Chief Tamás Oláh; circ. 42,000.

Evangélikus Élet: 1088 Budapest, Puskin u. 12; tel. 114-2074; f. 1933; Evangelical/Lutheran Church newspaper; Editor László Lehel; circ. 12,000.

Film, Szinház, Muzsika (Films, Theatre, Music): 1073 Budapest, Erzsébet krt 9–11; tel. 122-2400; Editor Zoltán Iszlai; circ. 30,000.

Heti Világgazdaság (World Economics Weekly): 1133 Budapest, Vág u. 13; tel. 140-8776; telex 22-6676; f. 1979; Editor-in-Chief Mátyás Vince; circ. 141,000.

Képes Újság (Illustrated News): 1085 Budapest, Gyulai Pál u. 14; tel. 113-7660; f. 1960; Editor Mihaly Kovács; circ. 400,000.

Ludas Matyi: 1077 Budapest, Gyulai Pál u. 14; tel. 133-5718; satirical; Editor József Árkus; circ. 352,000.

L'udové Noviny: 1065 Budapest, Nagymező u. 49; tel. 131-9184; for Slovaks in Hungary; Editor Pál Kondács; circ. 1,700.

Magyar Ifjúság (Hungarian Youth): 1085 Budapest, Somogyi Béla u. 6; tel. 113-0460; telex 22-6423; Editor Lajos Gubcsi; circ. 207,000.

Magyar Mezőgazdaság (Hungarian Agriculture): 1355 Budapest, Kossuth Lajos tér 11; tel. 112-2433; telex 22-5445; f. 1946; Editor-in-Chief Dr Károly Fehér; circ. 24,000.

Magyar Nők Lapja (Hungarian Women's Journal): 1961 Budapest, Blaha Lujza tér 3; tel. and fax 138-4828; telex 225554; f. 1949; Editor-in-Chief Valeria Révai; circ. 550,000.

Magyarország (Hungary): 1085 Budapest, Gyulai Pál u. 14; tel. 138-4644; telex 22-6351; f. 1964; news magazine; Editor Dr József Pálfy; circ. 200,000.

Narodne Novine: 1396 Budapest, POB 495; tel. 112-4869; f. 1945; for Yugoslavs in Hungary; in Serbo-Croat and Slovene; Chief Editor Marko Marković; circ. 2,800.

Neue Zeitung: 1391 Budapest, Nagymező u. 49, Pf. 224; tel. 132-6334; f. 1957; for Germans in Hungary; Editor Peter Leipold; circ. 4,500.

Ország-Világ (Land and World): 1073 Budapest, Erzsébet krt 9–11; tel. 122-2400; f. 1957; Editor András Gál; circ. 208,000.

Directory

Rádió és Televízióújság (Radio and TV News): 1801 Budapest; tel. 138-7739; f. 1956; Editor János Boros; circ. 1,350,000.

Reform: 1443 Budapest, POB 222; tel. 142-4350; telex 22-3333; fax 122-4240; f. 1988; popular tabloid; 50% foreign-owned; Editor Péter Tőke; circ. 385,000.

Reformátusok Lapja: 1395 Budapest, POB 424; tel. 117-6809; f. 1957; Reformed Church paper for the laity; Editor-in-Chief and Publr Attila P. Komlós; circ. 40,000.

Szabad Föld (Free Soil): 1087 Budapest, Könyves Kálmán krt 76; tel. 133-6794; telex 22-5922; f. 1945; Editor Gyula Eck; circ. 750,000.

Szövetkezet (Co-operative): 1054 Budapest, Szabadság tér 14; tel. 131-3132; National Council of Hungarian Consumer Co-operative Societies; Editor-in-Chief Attila Kovács; circ. 85,000.

Tőzsde Kurir (Hungarian Stock Market Courier): 1074 Budapest, Rákóczi út 54; tel. 122-3273; fax 142-8356; business; Editor-in-Chief István Gábor Benedek.

Új Ember (New Man): 1053 Budapest, Kossuth Lajos u. 1; tel. 117-3638; fax 117-3471; f. 1945; religious weekly; Editor László Lukács; circ. 100,000.

Új Tükör (New Mirror): 1073 Budapest, Erzsébet krt 9–11; tel. 122-3058; f. 1976; illustrated cultural and sociological magazine; Deputy Editors László Gyurkó, Sándor Köröspataki Kiss; circ. 101,000.

Vasárnapi Hirek (Sunday News): 1979 Budapest, POB 14; tel. 138-4366; telex 22-3174; f. 1984; political; Editor Dr Zoltán Lőkös; circ. 300,000.

Világ (World): Budapest; f. 1989; survey of political and cultural events; circ. 50,000.

FORTNIGHTLIES

Foaia Noastra (Our Leaf): 1055 Budapest, Bajcsy Zs. u. 78; for Romanians in Hungary; Editor Sándor Hocopán; circ. 1,500.

Magyar Hirek (Hungarian News): 1068 Budapest, Benczúr u. 15; tel. 122-5616; telex 22-317; fax 122-2421; illustrated magazine primarily for Hungarians living abroad; Editor György Halász; circ. 70,000.

Pedagógusok Lapja (Teachers' Review): 1068 Budapest, Gorkij fasor 10; published by the Hungarian Union of Teachers; circ. 20,000.

Szövetkezeti Hírlap (Co-operative Herald): 1052 Budapest, Pesti Barnabás u. 6; tel. 117-0181; National Union of Artisans; Editor Mária Dolezsál; circ. 12,000.

Új Élet (New Life): 1075 Budapest, Síp u. 12; tel. 122-2829; for Hungarian Jews; Editor Dr István Domán; circ. 7,000.

OTHER PERIODICALS

(Published monthly unless otherwise indicated)

Állami Gazdaság (State Farming): General Direction of State Farming, 1054 Budapest, Akadémia u. 1–3; tel. 112-4617; fax 111-4877; f. 1946; Editor Mrs P. Görgényi.

Business Partner Hungary: 1051 Budapest, Dorottya u. 6; tel. 117-0850; telex 22-5646; fax 118-6483; f. 1986; quarterly; Hungarian, German and English; economic journal published by Institute for Economic, Market Research and Informatics (KOPINT-DATORG).

Cartactual: 1367 Budapest, POB 76; tel. 112-6480; telex 22-4964; f. 1965; every 2 months; map service periodical with supplement *Cartinform* (map bibliography); published in English, French, German and Hungarian; Editor-in-Chief Ernő Csáti.

Egyházi Krónika (Church Chronicle): 1052 Budapest, Petőfi tér 2.1.2; tel. 118-4813; f. 1952; every 2 months; Eastern Orthodox Church journal; Editor Archpriest Dr Feriz Berki.

Elektrotechnika (Electrical Engineering): 1055 Budapest, Kossuth Lajos tér 6–8; tel. 153-0117; telex 22-5792; fax 153-4069; f. 1908; organ of Electrotechnical Association; Editor Dr Tibor Kelemen; circ. 3,000.

Élelmezési Ipar (Food Industry): 1361 Budapest, POB 5; tel. 112-2859; f. 1947; Scientific Society for Food Industry; Editor Dr Ödön Vajda.

Energia és Atomtechnika (Energy and Nuclear Technology): 1055 Budapest, Kossuth Lajos tér 6–8; tel. 153-2751; telex 22-5792; fax 156-1215; f. 1947; every two months; Scientific Society for Energy Economy; Editor-in-Chief Dr G. Bőki.

Energiagazdálkodás (Energy Economy): 1055 Budapest, Kossuth Lajos tér 6; tel. 153-2894; Scientific Society for Energetics; Editor Dr Tamás Rapp.

Építésügyi Szemle (Building Review): 1054 Budapest, Beloiannisz u. 2–4; tel. 131-3180; building; Editor Dr József Kádár.

Ezermester (The Handyman): 1066 Budapest, Dessewffy u. 34; tel. 132-0542; telex 22-6423; f. 1957; do-it-yourself magazine; Editor J. Szücs; circ. 135,000.

Forum: Budapest; f. 1989; periodical of the Hungarian Socialist Party; Editor-in-Chief ISTVÁN SZERDAHELYI.

Gép (Machinery): 1027 Budapest, Fő u. 68; tel. 135-4175; telex 22-5792; fax 153-0818; f. 1949; Scientific Society of Mechanical Engineering; Editor Dr KORNÉL LEHOFER.

Hungarian Book Review: 1051 Budapest, Vörösmarty tér 1.X.1010; tel. 117-6222; f. 1958; quarterly review of Hungarian Publishers' and Booksellers' Association; in English, French and German; Editor-in-Chief GYULA KURUCZ.

Hungarian Business Herald: 1075 Budapest, Tanács krt 7.1.3; tel. 141-7270; f. 1970; quarterly review published in English and German by the Hungarian Chamber of Commerce; Editor-in-Chief Dr GERD BIRÓ; circ. 4,000.

Hungarian Digest: 1117 Budapest, Bölcső u. 3; tel. 181-1580; f. 1980; illustrated quarterly on political, economic and cultural issues; English; also in French as Revue de Hongrie, and in German as Ungarland; Editor TIBOR ZÁDOR; circ. 50,000.

Hungarian Economy: 1355 Budapest, Alkotmány u. 10; tel. 132-2186; telex 22-6613; fax 132-2990; f. 1972; quarterly; economic and business review; Editor-in-Chief Dr JÁNOS FOLLINUS; circ. 10,000

Hungarian Trade Union News: 1964 Budapest, Rákóczi út 54; tel. 122-4810; f. 1957; in six languages including English; Editor-in-Chief EMŐKE NÁNDORI.

Hungarian Travel Magazine: 1088 Budapest, Múzeum u. 11; tel. 138-4643; quarterly in English and German; illustrated journal of the Tourist Board for visitors to Hungary; Man. Editor JÚLIA SZ. NAGY.

Ipar-Gazdaság (Industrial Economy): 1371 Budapest, POB 433; tel. 135-4529; f. 1948; Editor Dr LÁSZLÓ LADÓ; circ. 4,000.

Jogtudományi Közlöny (Law Gazette): 1250 Budapest, Pf. 25, Országház u. 30; tel. 155-6894; f. 1866; law; Editor-in-Chief Dr JÓZSEF HALÁSZ; Editor Dr IMRE VÖRÖS; circ. 2,500.

Kortárs (Contemporary): 1054 Budapest, Széchenyi u. 1; tel. 112-1240; literary gazette; Editor ÁRPÁD THIERY; circ. 7,000.

Könyvtáros (The Librarian): 1135 Budapest, Frangepán u. 50-56; tel. 111-3279; f. 1951; Editor LÁSZLÓ BERECZKY; circ. 6,000.

Közgazdasági Szemle (Economic Review): 1112 Budapest, Budaörsi u. 43–45; tel. 185-0777; f. 1954; published by Cttee for Economic Sciences of Academy of Sciences; Editor KATALIN SZABÓ; circ. 15,000.

Look at Hungary: 1906 Budapest, POB 223; tel. 186-0133; f. 1980; quarterly photomagazine in English, Arabic, French and Portuguese; Editor-in-Chief GÁBOR VAJDA.

Made in Hungary: 1426 Budapest, POB 3; economics and business magazine published in English by MTI; Editor GYÖRGY BLASITS.

Magyar Jog (Hungarian Law): 1053 Budapest, Egyetem tér 1-3; tel. and fax 117-4930; f. 1953; law; Editor-in-Chief Dr JÁNOS NÉMETH; circ. 3,500.

Magyar Közlöny (Official Gazette): 1055 Budapest, Bajcsy Zs. u. 78; tel. 112-1236; Editor Dr ELEMÉR KISS; circ. 90,000.

Magyar Tudomány (Hungarian Science): Hungarian Academy of Sciences, 1051 Budapest, Nádor u. 7; tel. 117-9524; Editor-in-Chief BÉLA KÖPECZI.

Muzsika: 1073 Budapest, Erzsébet krt 9-11; tel. 121-5440; f. 1958; musical review; Editor-in-Chief MÁRIA FEUER; circ. 7,500.

Nagyvilág (The Great World): 1054 Budapest, Széchenyi u. 1; tel. 132-1160; f. 1956; review of world literature; Editor LÁSZLÓ KÉRY; circ. 12,000.

New Hungarian Quarterly: 1426 Budapest, POB 3; tel. 155-9573; fax 118-8297; f. 1960; illustrated quarterly in English; politics, economics, philosophy, education, culture, poems, short stories, etc.; Editor MIKLÓS VAJDA; circ. 3,500.

Református Egyház: 1146 Budapest, Abonyi u. 21; tel. 122-7870; f. 1949; official journal of the Hungarian Reformed Church; Editor-in-Chief FERENC DUSICZA; circ. 1,600.

Statisztikai Szemle (Statistical Review): 1525 Budapest, POB 51; tel. 115-5208; f. 1923; Editor-in-Chief MARIA VISI LAKATOS; circ. 1,500.

Társadalmi Szemle (Social Review): 1959 Budapest, Blaha Lujza tér 1-3; tel. 138-4262; theoretical-political review; Editor MIHÁLY BIHARI; circ. 35,000.

Technika (Technology): 1428 Budapest, POB 12; tel. 167-2148; f. 1957; general technical review; monthly in Hungarian, annually in English, German and Russian; Editor-in-Chief ÉMIL SZLUKA; circ. 15,000.

Turizmus (Tourism): 1088 Budapest, Múzeum u. 11; tel. 138-4638; telex 22-5297; Editor ZSOLT SZEBENI; circ. 8,000.

Új Technika (New Technology): 1014 Budapest, Szentháromság tér 1; tel. 155-7122; telex 22-6490; f. 1967; popular industrial quarterly; circ. 35,000.

Vigilia: 1364 Budapest, POB 111; tel. 117-7246; fax 117-4895; f. 1935; Catholic; Editor LÁSZLÓ LUKÁCS; circ. 11,500.

Villamosság (Electricity): 1055 Budapest, Kossuth Lajos tér 6–8; tel. 153-0117; organ of Electrotechnical Association; Gen. Editor FERENC KOVÁCS; circ. 3,000.

NEWS AGENCIES

Magyar Távirati Iroda (MTI) (Hungarian News Agency): 1016 Budapest, Fém u. 5–7; tel. 175-6722; telex 22-4371; f. 1880; 19 brs in Hungary; 23 bureaux abroad; Gen. Dir OTTO OLTVÁNYI.

Foreign Bureaux

Agence France-Presse (AFP): Budapest, Naphegy u. 1; tel. 183-6861; telex 22-3831; Correspondent PAL HERSKOVITS.

Agenzia Nazionale Stampa Associata (ANSA) (Italy): 1024 Budapest, Mártírok u. 43/45; tel. 135-2323; telex 22-4711; Bureau Chief NINO ALIMENTI.

Allgemeiner Deutscher Nachrichtendienst (ADN) (Germany): 1146 Budapest, Zichy Géza u. 5; tel. 121-0810; telex 22-4675; Bureau Chief BERND RUNGE.

Associated Press (AP) (USA): Budapest II, Riado u. 12; tel. 115-9490; Rep. ANDY TIMAR.

Československá tisková kancelář (ČTK) (Czechoslovakia): 1146 Budapest, Zichy Géza u. 5; tel. 142-7115; telex 22-5367; Correspondent STEFAN NÉMETH.

Informatsionnoye Agentstvo Novosti (IAN) (USSR): 1075 Budapest, Tanács Kőrút 9; tel. 132-0594; telex 61-224792; fax 142-3325; Bureau Chief A. POPOV.

Inter Press Service (IPS) (Italy): 1026 Budapest, Filler u. 26; tel. 136-3903; telex 22-4371; Rep. CATALINA WEINER.

Prensa Latina (Cuba): 1020 Budapest, Budakeszi u. 55/D, 7 p.; tel. 176-7474; telex 22-4800; Correspondent MIRIAM CASTRO CASO.

Reuters (UK): c/o Magyar Távirati Iroda, 1426 Budapest, POB 3.

Telegrafnoye Agentstvo Sovetskovo Soyuza (TASS) (USSR): 1023 Budapest, Vérhalom u. 12–16; Correspondent YEVGENI POPOV.

United Press International (UPI) (USA): 1137 Budapest, Pozsonyi u. 14; telex 22-5649; Bureau Chief Dr ANDREW L. SÜMEGHI.

Xinhua (New China) News Agency (People's Republic of China): 1068 Budapest, Benczur u. 39/A.1.4; tel. 122-8420; telex 22-5447; Chief Correspondent HOU FENGQING.

PRESS ASSOCIATIONS

Magyar Újságírók Országos Szövetsége (MUOSZ) (National Association of Hungarian Journalists): 1062 Budapest, Andrássy ut 101; tel. 122-1699; telex 22-5045; Chair. LÁSZLÓ ROBERT; Gen. Sec. GÁBOR BENCSIK; 4,700 mems.

Association of Hungarian Newspaper Publishers: Budapest; f. 1986 by four major newspaper publishing companies, MTI and local newspaper publrs; Chair. JÓZSEF BOCZ.

Publishers

PRINCIPAL PUBLISHING HOUSES

Akadémiai Kiadó: 1117 Budapest, Prielle Kornélia u. 19-35; tel. 181-2134; telex 22-6228; fax 166-6466; f. 1828; Publishing House of the Hungarian Academy of Sciences; humanities, social, natural and technical sciences, dictionaries, encyclopaedias, periodicals of the Academy and other institutions, issued partly in foreign languages; Man. Dir GYÖRGY HAZAI.

Corvina Kiadó: 1051 Budapest, Vörösmarty tér 1; tel. 117-6222; telex 22-4440; f. 1955; Hungarian works translated into foreign languages, art and educational books, fiction and non-fiction, tourist guides, cookery books, sport, musicology, juvenile and children's literature; Man. Dir ISTVÁN BART; Editorial Dir BÉLA REVICZKY.

Editio Musica Budapest: 1051 Budapest, Vörösmarty tér 1; tel. 118-4228; telex 22-5500; f. 1950; sheet music and books on musical subjects; Dir ISTVÁN HOMOLYA.

Európa Könyvkiadó: 1055 Budapest, Kossuth Lajos tér 13–15; tel. 131-2700; telex 22-5645; f. 1945; world literature translated into Hungarian; Man. LEVENTE OSZTOVITS.

Gondolat Könyvkiadó Vállalat: 1088 Budapest, Bródy Sándor u. 16; tel. 138-3777; popular scientific publications on natural and social sciences, art, encyclopaedic handbooks; Dir ILDIKÓ LENDVAI.

Helikon Kiadó: 1053 Budapest, Eötvös L. u. 8; tel. 117-4765; telex 22-7100; fax 117-4701; bibliophile books; Dir MAGDA MOLNAR.

Képzőművészeti Kiadó: 1051 Budapest, Vörösmarty tér 1; tel. 118-4981; telex 22-4405; fine arts; Man. PÉTER LÁTKI.

HUNGARY

Kossuth Könyvkiadó Vállalat: 1054 Budapest, Steindl u. 6; tel. 111-7440; f. 1944; sociological and popular publications; Man. ANDRÁS KOCSIS.

Közgazdasági és Jogi Könyvkiadó: 1054 Budapest, Nagy Sándor u. 6; tel. 112-6430; telex 22-6511; f. 1955; economic, sociological and juridical; Man. VILMOS DALOS.

Magvető Könyvkiadó: 1806 Budapest, Vörösmarty tér 1; tel. 118-5109; literature; Man. MIKLÓS JOVÁNOVICS.

Medicina Könyvkiadó: 1054 Budapest, Beloiannisz u. 8; tel. 112-2650; f. 1957; books on medicine, sport, tourism; Man. Prof. Dr ISTVÁN ÁRKY.

Mezőgazdasági Könyvkiadó: 1054 Budapest, Báthory u. 10; tel. 111-6650; telex 20-2536; fax 111-7270; ecology, natural sciences, environmental protection, food industry; Man. Dr CSABA GALLYAS.

Móra Ferenc Gyermek és Ifjúsági Könyvkiadó: 1146 Budapest, Május 1 u. 57–59; tel. 121-2390; telex 22-7027; fax 122-4276; f. 1950; children's books, science fiction; Man. JÁNOS SZILÁDI.

Műszaki Könyvkiadó: 1014 Budapest, Szentháromság tér 6; tel. 155-7122; telex 22-6490; fax 175-5713; f. 1955; scientific and technical, fiction and non-fiction; Man. PÉTER SZŰCS.

Népszava Lap-és Könyvkiadó Vállalat: 1553 Budapest, Rákóczi u. 54; tel. 122-4810; National Federation of Hungarian Trade Unions; Man. Dr JENŐ KISS.

Statisztikai Kiadó Vállalat: 1033 Budapest, Kaszásdülő u. 2; tel. 180-3311; telex 22-6699; fax 168-8635; f. 1954; publications on statistics, system-management and computer science; Dir BENEDEK BELECZ.

Szépirodalmi Könyvkiadó: 1073 Budapest, Erzsébet krt 9–11; tel. 122-1285; telex 22-6754; f. 1950; modern and classical Magyar literature; Man. SÁNDOR Z. SZALAI.

Tankönyvkiadó Vállalat: 1055 Budapest, Szalay u. 10–14; tel. 153-0600; f. 1949; school and university textbooks, pedagogical literature and language books; Man. ANDRÁS PETRÓ.

Zrinyi Katonai Kiadó: 1087 Budapest, Kerepesi u. 29; tel. 133-4750; military literature; Man. LÁSZLÓ NÉMETH.

CARTOGRAPHERS

Cartographia (Hungarian Company for Surveying and Mapping): 1443 Budapest, POB 132; tel. 163-4639; telex 22-6218; fax 163-4639; f. 1954; Dir GYÖRGY DOMOKOS.

Földmérési és Térképészeti Főosztály (Department of Geodesy and Cartography): 1055 Budapest, Kossuth Lajos tér 11; tel. 131-3736; telex 22-5445; fax 153-0518; f. 1954; Man. SÁNDOR ZSÁMBOKI.

PUBLISHERS' ASSOCIATION

Magyar Könyvkiadók és Könyvterjesztők Egyesülése (Hungarian Publishers' and Booksellers' Association): 1051 Budapest, Vörösmarty tér 1; POB 130; tel. 118-4758; f. 1878; most Hungarian publishers are members of the Association; Pres. GYÖRGY FEHÉR; Sec.-Gen. FERENC ZÖLD.

WRITERS' UNION

Magyar Írók Szövetsége (Association of Hungarian Writers): 1062 Budapest, Bajza u. 18; tel. 122-8840; f. 1945; Pres. ANNA JÓKAI; Sec.-Gen. SÁNDOR KOCZKÁS.

Radio and Television

In 1989 there were an estimated 6m. radio receivers and 4.2m. television receivers in use. Cable television systems are expanding, and in early 1985 were operating in 12 cities. In 1986 Hungary completed negotiations to receive TV programmes from a Western European satellite network. By the end of 1987 more than 25,000 homes in the city of Szekesfehervar were able to receive experimental satellite transmissions from the British Sky Channel. Programmes from the British-based Super Channel, the French TV-5 and the USA's CNN-Europe service were also available by 1988. In 1988 more than 40 areas (300,000 homes) were able to receive cable and satellite services.

RADIO

Magyar Rádió: 1800 Budapest, Bródy Sándor u. 5–7; tel. 138-8388; telex 22-5188; fax 138-7004; f. 1924; stations: Radio Kossuth (Budapest); Radio Petőfi (Budapest); Radio Bartók (Budapest, mainly classical music); 6 regional studios; external broadcasts: in English, German, Hungarian, Italian, Romanian, Russian, Slovak, Serbo-Croat, Spanish and Turkish; Pres. CSABA GOMBÁR.

Radio Danubius: f. 1986; commercial station; broadcasts news, music and information in Hungarian 21 hours a day; transmitting stations in Budapest, Lake Balaton region, Sopron, Szeged and Debrecen; Dir GYÖRGY VARGA.

TELEVISION

Magyar Televízió: 1810 Budapest, Szabadság tér 17; tel. 153-3200; telex 22-5568; fax 153-4568; f. 1957; first channel broadcasts about 85 hours a week and the second channel about 63 hours a week, every day, mostly colour transmissions; 100 high-capacity relay stations; Pres. ELEMÉR HANKISS.

Finance

The Hungarian financial system is being restructured. In January 1985 the functions of issue and credit at the National Bank were separated. Under reforms implemented in January 1987, the central banking and commercial banking functions were separated, and the banking system is now organized on three levels. The National Bank of Hungary, as the bank of issue, continues to participate in the formulation of economic policy. The 1987 reforms did not affect the National Bank's foreign exchange authority, nor alter substantially the Bank's total assets. At the second level are the commercial banks. These institutions have general and nation-wide authority, keep the accounts of enterprises, accept their deposits and extend credits to them. The commercial banks may participate in ventures and may provide banking services for their clients. They establish their own business policy and the terms and conditions of their contracts, within the limits of central banking regulations. The commercial banks (established from the units seceding from the National Bank of Hungary, the reorganization of the State Development Bank and the Creditbank of Budapest, and the General Banking and Trust Co Ltd) are: The General Banking and Trust and Co Ltd; Budapest Bank Rt.; Hungarian Creditbank Ltd; Hungarian Foreign Trade Bank; Commercial and Creditbank Ltd. At the third level of the banking system are the so-called specialized financial institutions. These small banks may establish deposit and credit links with economic entities, may participate in ventures and may provide banking services. Unlike the commercial banks, the specialized financial institutions may not keep the accounts of their clients.

Like the National Savings Bank (OTP), the Savings Co-operatives (Takarékszövetkezet) function as banks for the use of the general public, operating at the local level. Their main activity is the collection of deposits and the provision of credit to their members. Since January 1985, these co-operatives have been able to maintain accounts for small enterprises and private entrepreneurs, and can extend credit to them. They are also empowered to provide mortgage facilities to individuals. Minimum registered capital is 2.0m. forint at each co-operative. In early 1987 there were 260 such co-operatives in Hungary. Their interests are represented by SZÖVOSZ (National Federation of Consumer Co-operatives—see p. 1309).

Financial institutions with foreign capital shares may be founded with government permission. The first bank in Hungary to be founded with foreign capital involvement was the Central European International Bank (CIB), established in 1979. In 1985 a joint Hungarian-US commercial bank was established by the Central Exchange and Credit Bank of Budapest and Citibank of New York. It began operations in 1986, under the supervision of the National Bank of Hungary. Unicbank Rt., founded with 45% foreign capital, commenced operations in January 1987.

The issue of bonds, in order to finance housing and infrastructural projects, is of increasing significance. Offering a higher rate of interest than that of the National Savings Bank, bonds were first issued on a large scale in early 1983, available initially only to enterprises but later also to private individuals. In September 1984 the State Development Bank (now State Development Institution) began repurchasing and reselling bonds, thus giving rise to the existence of a domestic 'bond market'. By mid-1986 local councils and enterprises had issued 130 bonds to a total value of 8,000m. forint (equivalent to almost 3% of total Hungarian investment in 1985), about 70% of which had been purchased by private citizens. The bond market expanded rapidly in 1987, and by December 200 bonds, worth 24,320m. forint, were in circulation. In January 1988 the state guarantee for bonds was terminated, thus rendering the issue of bonds more difficult for less profitable organizations. The State also began to issue treasury bills in order to finance budget deficits. A national securities market opened in Budapest in January 1988, and a stock exchange in May 1990.

BANKING

(cap. = capital; res = reserves; dep. = deposits; m. = million; Ft = forint; brs = branches)

Central Bank

Magyar Nemzeti Bank (National Bank of Hungary): 1850 Budapest, Szabadság tér 8–9; tel. 153-2600; telex 22-5677; fax 132-4179;

HUNGARY

f. 1924; cap. 10,000m. Ft, res 11,596m. Ft, dep. 1,513,051m. Ft (Dec. 1989); issue of bank notes; transacts international payments business; supervises banking system; 18 brs; Pres. Dr GYÖRGY SURANYI; First Vice-Pres. Dr IMRE TARAFÁS.

Commercial Banks

Általános Értékforgalmi Bank Rt. (General Banking and Trust Co Ltd): 1093 Budapest, Szamuely u. 30-32; tel. 118-8688; telex 22-3578; fax 118-8695; f. 1923; commercial banking activities in Hungarian currency, deposit-taking and account-keeping in foreign currency, services for joint-venture companies; cap. 1,000m. Ft (Dec. 1988); Dir-Gen. ANTAL BESZÉDES.

Budapest Bank Rt.: 1052 Budapest, Deák Ferenc u. 5; tel. 118-1200; telex 22-3013; fax 118-1335; f. 1986; cap. 5,332m. Ft; Dir-Gen. OSZKÁR HEGEDŰS.

Dunabank Rt: 1054 Budapest, Báthori u. 12; tel. 111-1287; telex 22-3203; f. 1987 as Bank for Investment and Transactions; renamed 1989; cap. 1,000m. Ft; Chief Exec. KÁLMÁN DEBRECZENI; Chair. of Supervisory Bd ARANKA NOVÁK.

Közép-Európai Hitelbank Rt. (Central-European Credit Bank Ltd): 1364 Budapest, Váci utca 16; tel. 118-8377; telex 22-6104; fax 138-2273; f. 1988; fully-owned subsidiary of Central-European International Bank Ltd (CIB), for domestic business in the Hungarian market; cap. 360m. Ft, res 6,331m. Ft (Dec. 1989); Dirs GYÖRGY ZDEBORSKY, MICHAEL Graf VON MEDEM.

Magyar Hitel Bank Rt. (Hungarian Credit Bank Ltd): 1853 Budapest, Szabadság tér 5-6; tel. 153-2600; telex 22-3202; f. 1987; cap. 13,983m. Ft; activities include venture financing, securities trading, real estate investments, joint venture promotion and advisory services; Chair. ÁRPÁD BARTHA.

Magyar Külkereskedelmi Bank Rt. (Hungarian Foreign Trade Bank Ltd): 1821 Budapest, Szt. István tér 11; tel. 132-9360; telex 22-6941; fax 132-2568; f. 1950; cap. 6,003m. Ft (Dec. 1988); Chair. and Man. Dir GÁBOR ERDÉLY.

Merkantil Bank: 1365 Budapest, József A. u. 24, POB 676; tel. 118-2688; telex 20-2579; fax 117-2331; f. 1988; affiliated to Commercial and Creditbank Ltd; cap. 500m. Ft; Dir ÁDÁM KOLOSSVÁRY.

Országos Kereskedelmi és Hitelbank Rt. (Commercial and Credit Bank Ltd): 1851 Budapest, Arany János u. 24; tel. 112-5200; telex 22-3200; fax 111-3845; f. 1986; cap. 12,107m. Ft (Dec. 1989); Dir Dr GÉZA LENK; First Dep. Chief Exec. MIKLÓS SZIGETHY.

Development Financial Institution

Állami Fejlesztési Intézet (State Development Institution): 1052 Budapest, Deák F. u. 5; tel. 118-1200; telex 22-5672; fax 166-8643; f. 1987 to succeed the State Development Bank; finance of development projects dealing with company reorganization, privatization and investments; Chief Exec. BORBÁLA BÁGER; Dep. Chief Exec. ISTVÁN GOLDPERGER.

Specialized Financial Institutions

AGROBANK Rt. (Agricultural Innovation Bank Ltd): 1052 Budapest, Tanács krt 6; tel. 118-8933; telex 22-3111; fax 117-5650; f. 1984; joint-stock company; cap. 1,500m. Ft; 10 brs; Dir Dr PETER KUNOS.

Általános Vállalkozási Bank Rt. (General Bank for Venture Financing Ltd): 1055 Budapest, Stollár Béla u. 3A; tel. 132-6590; telex 22-3157; fax 131-3181; f. 1985; joint-stock company; cap. 2,200m. Ft; Gen. Man. ELEMÉR TERTÁK.

Építőipari Innovációs Bank Rt. (Innovation Bank for Construction Industry Ltd): 1063 Budapest, Szív u. 53; tel. 112-9010; telex 22-3743; fax 132-0567; f. 1985; joint stock company; cap. 1,160m. Ft; Man. Dir TAMÁS VARGA.

INNOFINANCE—Általános Innovációs Pénzintézet Rt. (General Financial Institution for Innovation Ltd): 1365 Budapest, POB 718; tel. 138-3366; telex 22-3182; fax 117-7800; f. 1980; joint-stock company; registered cap. 500m. Ft; Man. Dir ERZSÉBET BIRMAN.

Inter-Európa Bank Rt.: 1054 Budapest, Szabadság tér 15; tel. 132-0170; telex 20-7879; fax 153-4850; f. 1980 as INTERINVEST; associated mem. of San Paolo Group; cap. 2,807m. Ft; Man. Dir GYÖRGY IVÁNYI; Dep. Man. Dir ANDRÁS FELKAI.

INVESTBANK—Műszaki Fejlesztési Bank (Bank for Technical Development): 1053 Budapest, Képíró u. 9; tel. 118-4917; telex 22-3250; fax 118-4400; f. 1983; cap. 1,245m. Ft; Dir Dr ANNA TEMESI.

Ipari Fejlesztési Bank Rt. (Industrial Development Bank Ltd): 1054 Budapest, Hold u. 25; tel. 132-0320; telex 22-7351; fax 112-9552; f. 1988 (previously Magyar Iparbank Rt., f. 1987); cap. 3,200m. Ft; Gen. Man. Dr GYULA PÁZMÁNDI.

Iparbank Ltd (Industrial Bank Ltd): Budapest, Gerlóczy u. 5; tel. 117-6811; telex 22-3042; fax 117-1921; f. 1984; cap. 1,070.1m. Ft; Gen. Dir ISTVÁN KOLLÁR.

Kisvállalkozási Bank (Bank for Small Ventures): 1876 Budapest, Nádor u. 16; tel. 131-6940; telex 22-4280; f. 1986; affiliated to NSB; cap. 3,200m. Ft; Dir ÁRPÁD BACSÓKA.

Konzumbank Rt. (Consumers' Co-operative Societies Share Company): 1052 Budapest, Vitkovics M. u. 9; tel. 117-2600; telex 22-3305; fax 117-6721; f. 1986; cap. 1,042m. Ft; Dir Dr GÁBOR PÁL.

Mezőbank (National Banking Institution of Agricultural Co-operatives Corporation): 1025 Budapest, Áldás u. 5; tel. 135-9362; telex 22-7058; f. 1986; cap. 2,000m. Ft; Dir Dr GYULA KABAI.

Consortium Banks

Central-European International Bank Ltd (CIB): 1364 Budapest, Váci u. 16, POB 170; tel. 118-8377; telex 22-4759; fax 118-9415; f. 1979; shareholders: National Bank of Hungary (34%), Banca Commerciale Italiana, Bayerische Vereinsbank, Long-Term Credit Bank of Japan, Société Générale, Mitsui Taiyo Kobe Bank (13.2% each); an offshore bank conducting international banking business of all kinds; dep. $538m., total resources $605.3m. (Dec. 1989); Chair. Dr MARIO ARCARI; Man. Dir GYÖRGY ZDEBORSKY.

Citibank Budapest: 1052 Budapest, Váci u. 19–21; tel. 138-2666; telex 22-7822; f. 1986; joint-stock company; share cap. 1,000m. Ft; Gen. Man. ROBIN M. WINCHESTER.

Unicbank Rt.: 1052 Budapest, Váci u. 19–21; tel. 118-2088; telex 22-3123; fax 138-2836; f. 1986; cap. 1,000m. Ft; Man. Dir Dr PÉTER FELCSUTI; Shareholders: International Finance Corporation (IFC) (15%); Raiffeisen Zentralbank Österreich AG (RZB), Vienna (15%); DG Bank (Deutsche Genossenschaftsbank AG), Frankfurt (15%); Central Bank of Exchange and Credit Ltd (20%); National Savings Bank (11%); Association of Agricultural Co-operatives (6%); Association of Industrial Co-operatives (6%); Association of Service Co-operatives (6%); Association of Private Artisans (6%).

Savings Bank

Országos Takarékpénztár—OTP (National Savings Bank—NSB): 1876 Budapest, Nador u. 16; tel. 153-1444; telex 22-4432; f. 1949; cap. 1,300m. Ft, dep. 280,000m. Ft (Dec. 1988); savings deposits, credits, foreign transactions, lotteries; acts as estate agent; 598 brs; Gen. Man. Dr LÁSZLÓ TISZA.

Postabank és Takarékpénztár Rt. (Post Bank and Savings Corporation): 1920 Budapest, József nádor tér 1; tel. 118-0855; telex 22-3294; fax 117-1369; f. 1988; cap. 2,230m. Ft; Dir GÁBOR PRINCZ.

Financial Development Institution

Állami Fejlesztési Intézet (State Development Institution): 1052 Budapest, Deák Ferenc u. 5; tel. 118-1200; telex 22-5672; f. 1987; Gen. Dir BORBÁLA BÁGER.

Central Corporation

Pénzintézeti Központ (Central Corporation of Banking Companies): 1431 Budapest, Szamuely u. 38; tel. 117-1255; telex 22-6548; f. 1916; banking, property, rights and interests, deposits, securities, and foreign exchange management; cap. 1,000m. Ft; Dir-Gen. MIHÁLY BIRÓ.

STOCK EXCHANGE

In May 1990 a stock exchange began operations in Budapest.

Budapest Stock Exchange: Budapest; f. 1989; Pres. LAJOS BOKROS.

INSURANCE

In July 1986 the state insurance enterprise was divided into two companies, one of which retained the name of the former Állami Biztosító. Further companies have been founded since 1988.

Állami Biztosító (ÁB) (State Insurance Co): 1813 Budapest, Üllői u. 1; tel. 118-1866; telex 22-4550; fax 138-4741; f. 1949, reorganized 1986; handles life and property insurance, insurance of agricultural plants, co-operatives, foreign insurance, etc.; Gen. Man. Dr GABOR KEPECS.

Atlasz Utazási Biztosító (Atlasz Travel Insurance Co): 1052 Budapest, Deák F. u. 23; tel. 118-1999; telex 22-6725; fax 117-1529; f. 1988; cap. 1,000m. Ft; Gen. Man. GYÖRGY BORDÁS.

Garancia Biztosító Rt. (Garancia Insurance Co): 1052 Budapest, Semmelweis u. 17; tel. and fax 117-6226; f. 1988; cap. 1,050m. Ft; Gen. Man. OTTÓ GAÁL.

Hungária Biztosító Rt. (Hungária Insurance, Reinsurance and Export Credit Insurance Co): 1115 Budapest, Bánk bán utca 17/B; tel. 175-9211; telex 22-3104; f. 1986; handles international insurance, insurance of state companies and motor-car, marine, life, accident and liability insurance; cap. 3,000m. Ft; Man. Dir TAMÁS UZONYI.

Trade and Industry

CHAMBER OF COMMERCE

Magyar Gazdasági Kamara (Hungarian Chamber of Commerce): 1389 Budapest, POB 106; tel. 153-3333; telex 22-4745; fax 153-1285;

HUNGARY
Directory

f. 1848; develops trade with other countries; mediates between companies, etc.; mems: 2,100 industrial and foreign trade organizations; Pres. LAJOS TOLNAY; Gen. Sec. LÁSZLÓ FODOR.

SELECTED FOREIGN TRADE ORGANIZATIONS

Since 1980 Hungary's foreign trade organizations have been undergoing modernization. New regulations, introduced in 1988, permitted all business organizations to export products and to conduct business with foreign partners without the involvement of specialized traders. By early 1991 some 90% of all import activities had been liberalized and no special licences were required for foreign trading.

AÉV No 31: 1364 Budapest, POB 83; tel. 118-0511; telex 22-4928; fax 118-4082; f. 1951; state building factory; construction of industrial units, power plants, chemical combines, cement plants, etc.; undertakes building work abroad.

Agrária-Bábolna: 2943 Bábolna; tel. 34-69111; telex 226-555; fax 34-69002; f. 1789; turn-key poultry and pig farms with breeding stock and feed premixes; hatching eggs, breeding poultry, pigs, sheep and breeding jumping and riding horses; processed chicken; rodent and insect extermination services, etc.

Agrikon: 6001 Kecskemét, POB 43; tel. (76) 27-666; telex 26-493; Budapest office: 1364 Budapest 4, POB 167; tel. 118-9568; telex 22-5517; fax 117-2581; engineering and servicing for agricultural and food processing machines.

Agrimpex Trading Co Ltd: 1392 Budapest, POB 278; tel. 111-3800; telex 22-5751; fax 153-0658; f. 1948; agricultural products; Chair. and Gen. Man. ANDRÁS VERMES.

Agrober: 1502 Budapest, POB 94; tel. 162-0640; telex 22-5868; consulting engineers and contractors for the agriculture and food industry.

Agrotek: 1065 Budapest, POB 66; tel. 153-0555; telex 22-5651; fax 112-4896; export and import of agricultural machinery, including machinery for livestock breeding, and forestry equipment.

Artex: 1390 Budapest, POB 167; tel. 153-0222; telex 22-4951; fax 111-1295; f. 1949; furniture, carpets, porcelain, ceramics, gold and silver ware, applied arts, household and sports goods.

BHG Telecommunication Works: 1509 Budapest, POB 2; tel. 181-3300; telex 22-5933; fax 166-7433; telecommunications; Gen. Dir LÁSZLÓ MIKICS.

Bivimpex Trading Co: 1325 Budapest, POB 55; tel. 169-3522; telex 22-4279; fax 169-4716; f. 1971; raw hide and leather; Dir L. VERMES.

Börker: 1391 Budapest, POB 215; tel. 121-0760; telex 22-5543; fax 122-7095; f. 1949; trading company for basic materials and accessories for shoes, fancy leather goods, garments and furniture; Gen. Man. LAJOS ALSÓSZENTIVÁNYI.

BRG: 1300 Budapest, POB 43; tel. 168-2080; telex 22-5928; fax 168-9652; radio engineering.

Budaprint: 1300 Budapest, POB 111; tel. 188-8170; telex 22-4576; fax 169-9234; textile printing.

Budavox: 1392 Budapest, POB 267; tel. 186-8988; telex 22-5077; fax 161-1288; f. 1956; exports telecommunications equipment and systems; Gen. Man. IKLODY GÁBOR.

Chemokomplex: 1389 Budapest, POB 141; tel. 132-9980; telex 22-5158; machines and equipment for the chemical industry; Man. Dir FERENC NAGY.

Chemolimpex: 1805 Budapest, POB 121; tel. 118-3970; telex 22-4351; chemicals, agrochemicals, plastics, paints; Gen. Man. Dr PÉTER DOBROVITS.

Chinoin: 1325 Budapest, POB 110; tel. 169-0900; telex 22-4236; pharmaceutical and chemical works.

CIBINTRA International Trading Company Ltd: 1364 Budapest, Váci u.16, POB 170; tel. 118-8377; telex 22-6102; fax 118-5777; f. 1989; international trading house, with domestic activity also; Gen. Man. Dr MIKLÓS MARINOV.

Compack: 1441 Budapest, POB 42; tel. 121-1520; telex 22-4846; fax 122-4861; trading, food-processing and packing company.

Danubia Patent and Trademark Attorneys: 1368 Budapest, POB 198; tel. 118-1111; telex 22-5872; fax 138-2304; f. 1951; patent and trademark services; Dir M. LANTOS.

Délker: 1051 Budapest, POB 70; tel. 118-5888; telex 22-4428; company for trading of tropical fruits, foodstuffs, cosmetics and household goods.

Elektroimpex: 1392 Budapest, POB 296; tel. 132-8300; telex 22-5771; fax 131-0526; telecommunication and precision articles.

Elektromodul: 1390 Budapest, POB 158; tel. 149-5340; telex 22-5154; fax 140-2583; electro-technical components; Gen. Man. FERENC KIS KOVÁCS.

ERBE: 1361 Budapest, POB 17; tel. 112-3270; telex 22-3562; fax 153-4158; power plant investment company.

Factory and Machinery Erecting Enterprise: 1394 Budapest, POB 384; tel. 132-7360; telex 4783.

Fékon: 1475 Budapest, POB 67; tel. 157-2447; telex 22-5527; clothing company.

Ferunion: 1829 Budapest, POB 612; tel. 117-2611; telex 22-5054; fax 117-2594; tools, glassware, building materials, hardware.

FMV: 1475 Budapest, POB 215; tel. 252-0666; telex 22-4409; fax 183-5361; precision mechanics.

Folk-art: 1052 Budapest, Régiposta u. 12, POB 20; tel. 117-6138; telex 22-6814; fax 118-2154; f. 1948; foreign trade office of the Cooperative Enterprise for Folk Art and Handicraft; Dir Dr JUDITH LENDVAI.

Foreign Trade Company Ltd for Industrial Co-operation: 1367 Budapest, POB 111; tel. 142-4950; telex 22-4435; fax 132-6371; foreign trade office for co-operation and purchasing of licences in industry.

Gábor Áron Works: 1440 Budapest, POB 39; tel. 133-7970; telex 22-4127; engineering works.

Gamma Művek: 1519 Budapest, POB 330; tel. 185-0800; telex 22-4946; fax 166-5632; f. 1920; medical instruments, deep-bore logging and process control systems, elements for the instrumentation industry; Gen. Dir JÁNOS HENZ.

Ganz Danubius Shipyard and Crane Factory: Budapest XIII, Váci u. 202; tel. 149-6370; telex 22-4200; fax 140-1703; f. 1835.

Ganz Electric Works: 1525 Budapest, POB 63; tel. 175-3322; telex 22-5363; fax 156-2989; f. 1878; electric power generators, transformers, switchgear, electrical vehicles.

Ganz-Hunslet Rt.: 1087 Budapest, Vajda P. u. 12; tel. 113-8813; telex 20-2862; fax 114-3481; f. 1844; railway rolling stock, underground trains, trams (light rail rolling stock); CEO H. A. CODD.

Ganz Measuring Instrument Works: 1701 Budapest, POB 58; tel. 127-1025; telex 22-4395; fax 127-1025; all types of electrical measuring instrument.

Generalimpex: 1518 Budapest, POB 168; tel. 162-0200; telex 22-6758; f. 1980; permitted to import or export any product; Dir LÁSZLÓ NAGY.

Geominco: 1525 Budapest, POB 92; tel. 135-4580; telex 22-4442; geological and mining engineering; undertakes exploration and research.

Hungagent Ltd: 1374 Budapest, POB 542; tel. 188-6180; telex 22-4526; fax 188-8769; foreign representations agency; export-import.

Hungarian Aluminium Corporation (HUNGALU): 1387 Budapest, POB 30; tel. 149-4750; telex 22-5471; fax 140-2723; Gen. Man. Dr PÉTER KERESZTES.

Hungarian Deepfreezing Industry: 1364 Budapest, POB 12; tel. 118-3900; telex 22-4579.

Hungarocoop: 1370 Budapest, POB 334; tel. 153-1711; telex 22-4858; fax 153-3318; co-operative foreign trading company; import and export of consumer goods.

Hungarofilm: 1363 Budapest, POB 39; tel. 131-4746; telex 22-5768; fax 153-1850; f. 1956; film distribution; Pres. ISTVÁN VÁRADI.

Hungarofruct: 1394 Budapest, POB 386; tel. 131-7120; telex 22-5351; fax 132-1378; f. 1953; fresh and dehydrated fruit and vegetables.

Hungarotex: 1804 Budapest, POB 100; tel. 117-4555; telex 22-4751; f. 1953; textiles, garments, foodstuffs, etc; Gen. Man. LÁSZLÓ FÖLDVÁRI.

Hungexpo (Hungarian Foreign Trade Company for Fairs and Publicity): 1441 Budapest, POB 44; tel. 122-5008; telex 22-4525; fax 122-1021; advertising, publicity, public relations; printing; fairs, exhibitions; Dir JÁNOS HORVÁTH.

IDEX: 1011 Budapest, Fő u. 14–18, POB 24; tel. 115-0090; telex 22-4541; fax 135-1393; f. 1953; engineering, electronics, construction, oil and gas.

Ikarus: 1630 Budapest, POB 3; tel. 252-9666; telex 22-4766; fax 163-7066; f. 1895; construction and export of buses in complete state or in sets for assembly; Gen. Dir ANDRÁS SEMSEY; Tech. Dir ISTVÁN LEPSÉNYI.

Industria Ltd: 1117 Budapest, POB 272; commercial representation of foreign firms, technical consulting service, market research etc.

Interag Co Ltd: 1390 Budapest, Pannónia u. 11, POB 184; tel. 132-5770; telex 22-4776; fax 153-0736; represents foreign firms; conducts general export/import business, domestic trade.

Intercooperation Co Ltd: 1253 Budapest, POB 53; tel. 115-2220; telex 22-4242; establishment and carrying out of co-operation agreements, joint ventures and import and export deals.

IPV (Publishing and Promotion Co for Tourism): 1140 Budapest, POB 164; tel. 163-3652; telex 22-6074; fax 183-7320; publishing,

HUNGARY

publicity, film-making, exhibitions, advertising; Gen. Man ISTVÁN FAZEKAS.

KGyV Metallurgical Engineering Corpn: 1553 Budapest, POB 23; tel. 111-3612; telex 22-5920; fax 111-2274; f. 1951; manufacture of industrial furnaces and steel structures; Gen. Man. Dr SÁNDOR FARKAS.

Komplex Foreign Trade Co: 1807 Budapest, Andrássy ut 10, POB 125; tel. 111-7010; telex 22-5957; fax 111-7450; f. 1953; agricultural machinery, plant and equipment for food industry; Man. Dir ADOLF FÉDERER.

Konsumex: 1441 Budapest, POB 58; tel. 153-0511; telex 22-5151; fax 112-7281; f. 1959; consumer goods, household articles, etc.

Kopint-Datorg Institute for Economic and Market Research and Informatics: 1051 Budapest, Dorottya u. 6; tel. 118-6722; telex 22-5646; fax 118-6483.

Kultúra Hungarian Foreign Trading Co: 1389 Budapest, POB 149; tel. 201-4412; telex 22-4441; fax 115-0684; f. 1950; books, periodicals, works of art, sheet music, teaching aids; Gen. Man. JÓZSEF SZABÓ.

Labor Rt: Factory of Laboratory Instruments Co Ltd: 1450 Budapest, POB 33; tel. 133-9708; telex 22-4162; fax 134-0309; f. 1989; scientific instruments, laboratory equipment and engineering; Gen. Dir KÁROLY VARGA.

Lampart: 1475 Budapest, POB 41; tel. 157-0111; telex 22-5365; f. 1883; glass-lined processing equipment.

Lehel Hütőgépgyár: 5101 Jászberény, POB 64; tel. 12611; telex 02-3341; export of domestic refrigerators.

Licencia: 1368 Budapest, POB 207; tel. 118-1111; telex 22-5872; fax 138-2304; f. 1950; purchase and sale of patents and inventions; Gen. Dir LAJOS VEROSZTA; Dir FERENC GEBAUER.

Lignimpex: 1393 Budapest, POB 323; tel. 112-9850; telex 22-4251; timber, paper and fuel.

Magnesite Industry: 1475 Budapest, POB 11; tel. 157-1378; telex 22-5644; f. 1892; refractory products; Dir B. HAZAI.

Magyar Media Advertising Agency: 1392 Budapest 62, POB 279; tel. 132-5176; telex 22-3040.

MAHIR Hungarian Publicity Company: 1818 Budapest, POB 367; tel. 118-3444; telex 22-5341; fax 117-9032; advertising agency.

Masped: 1364 Budapest, Kristóf tér 2, POB 104; tel. 118-2922; telex 22-4471; fax 118-8343; international forwarding and carriage; Gen. Man. KÁLMÁN GELENCSÉR.

Medicor Trading Co Ltd: 1389 Budapest, POB 150; tel. 149-5130; telex 22-5051; fax 149-5957; medical instruments, X-ray apparatus and complete hospital installations; Chair. SZILVIA MÁDAI.

Medimpex: 1808 Budapest; tel. 118-3955; telex 22-5477; export and import of pharmaceutical and biological products, veterinary drugs, laboratory chemicals.

Mertcontrol: 1397 Budapest, POB 542; tel. 132-5300; telex 22-5777; fax 111-6897; f. 1951; quality control of import and export goods.

Metalimpex: 1393 Budapest, POB 330; tel. 118-7611; telex 22-5251; fax 142-9753; metals and metal products.

Metrimpex: 1391 Budapest, POB 202; tel. 112-5600; telex 22-5451; fax 153-4719; electronic, nuclear and other instruments and equipment.

Mineralimpex: 1062 Budapest, Andrássy ut 64; tel. 111-6470; telex 22-4651; fax 153-1779; oils and mining products; Dir-Gen. Dr JÓZSEF TÓTH.

Modex Trading Co Ltd: 1430 Budapest, POB 5; tel. 113-1489; telex 22-7525; fax 114-3896; ready-made clothing.

Mogürt: 1391 Budapest, POB 249; tel. 118-6044; telex 22-5357; fax 118-8895; f. 1946; motor vehicles; Gen. Man. PÁL ARDÓ.

MOM: 1525 Budapest, POB 52; tel. 156-4122; telex 22-4151; f. 1876; laboratory and optical instruments.

Monimpex Trading House: 1392 Budapest, POB 268; tel. 153-1222; telex 22-5371; fax 112-2072; wines, spirits, paprika, honey, sweets, ornamental plants.

MVMT: 1251 Budapest, POB 34; tel. 115-2600; telex 22-4382; fax 135-9524; electricity.

Nádex: 1525 Budapest, POB 14; tel. 135-0365; telex 22-6767; reed farming.

Nikex Trading Co Ltd: 1016 Budapest, Mészáros u. 48–54; tel. 156-0122; telex 22-4971; fax 175-5131; foreign trading co.

Novex: 1087 Budapest, Könyves Kálmán Krt. 76; tel. 133-8933; telex 22-3825; foreign trade; Man. Dir JÁNOS KOZMA.

Ofotért: 1917 Budapest; tel. 120-3669; telex 22-4418; f. 1949; optical and photographic articles; Gen. Dir JÁNOS SZIDÁUTH.

OMIKK Technoinform: 1428 Budapest, POB 12; tel. 118-3260; telex 22-4944; technical and economic information services.

OMKER: 1367 Budapest, POB 91; tel. 112-3000; telex 22-4683; fax 133-8718; f. 1950; medical instruments; Gen. Dir RÓBERT ZENTAI.

ORION: 1475 Budapest, POB 84; tel. 128-4830; telex 22-5798; fax 127-2490; f. 1913; radios, televisions and electrical goods; Gen. Dir L. KOVÁCS.

Pannonia-Csepel International Trading Co Ltd: 1051 Budapest, POB 354; tel. 132-938; telex 22-5128; fax 132-7318; metallurgical materials, welding electrodes, cast iron fittings, steel tubes and cylinders, bicycles, industrial sewing and pressing machinery and laundry equipment, complete tube manufacturing plants, bottle plants, etc.

Pharmatrade Hungarian Trading Co: 1367 Budapest, POB 126; tel. 118-5966; telex 22-6650; fax 118-5346; medicinal plants, cosmetics, medicinal muds and waters, food and feed additives, seeds, honey and bee products, fruit and vegetables, radioactive products.

Philatelia Hungarica: 1373 Budapest, POB 600; tel. 131-6146; telex 22-6508; fax 111-5421; f. 1950; stamps; wholesale only; Gen. Man. ISTVÁN ZALÁVÁRI.

Phylaxia: 1486 Budapest, POB 23; tel. 157-5311; telex 22-4549; vaccines, veterinary products.

Precision Fittings Factory: 3301 Eger, POB 2; tel. 11-911; telex 63-331; fax 11-112.

Prodinform: 1372 Budapest, POB 453; tel. 132-3770; telex 22-7750; fax 131-7578; technical and scientific information, technical consultations.

RÁBA (Hungarian Railway Carriage and Machine Works): 9002 Győr, POB 50; tel. 12-111; telex 02-4255; fax 14-311; f. 1896; commercial vehicles, diesel engines, agricultural tractors; Gen. Man. FERENC KÁRPÁTI.

Rekard: 9027 Győr, Kandó Kálmán u. 5–7; tel. (96) 13-122; telex 24-360; farm equipment.

Skála-Coop: 1450 Budapest, POB 60; tel. 133-6770; telex 22-5135; national co-operative company for purchase and disposal of goods including fine ceramics and glassware, industrial, agricultural and household metal ware, hand tools, electronic games, rubber and plastic products, cosmetics and chemicals, wood and paper industry products, leather and textile industry products, ready-to-wear clothing, vegetables and other foodstuffs; Gen. Man. ISTVÁN IMRE.

Tannimpex: 1395 Budapest, POB 406; tel. 112-3400; telex 22-4557; fax 153-2170; hides, leather, shoes, gloves, fancy goods and furs.

Tatabánya Mining Co: 2803 Tatabánya, POB 323; tel. (34) 10-144; telex 22-6206; fax (34) 11-061; f. 1894; production of mining equipment and machinery, preparation of industrial and drinking water, purification of waste waters, dewatering of sludges, tunnelling; Gen. Man. LÁSZLÓ VAS.

Taurus Hungarian Rubber Works: 1440 Budapest, POB 25; tel. 134-1140; telex 22-5312; fax 118-8754; f. 1882; rubber; Chief Exec. Dr LÁSZLÓ PALOTÁS.

Technoimpex: 1390 Budapest, POB 183; tel. 118-4055; telex 22-4171; fax 186-6418; exports machine tools, specialized machinery, equipment for the oil and gas industry, agricultural equipment; imports machine tools, machines for light industry; organizes barter deals, co-operation, leasing and joint ventures; Chair. and CEO ISTVÁN MÁTYÁS.

Temaforg: 1476 Budapest, POB 114; tel. 127-7880; telex 22-3456; textile and synthetic wastes, industrial wipers, geotextiles for agriculture, road and railway construction.

Terimpex: 1825 Budapest, POB 251; tel. 117-5011; telex 22-4551; cattle and agricultural products; Gen. Man. Dr LÁSZLÓ RÁNKY.

Terta, Telefongyár: 1956 Budapest, POB 16; tel. 252-6949; telex 22-4087; fax 252-9161; f. 1876; telecommunications and data teleprocessing systems.

Tesco: 1367 Budapest, POB 101; tel. 111-0850; telex 22-4642; fax 153-1852; f. 1962; organization for international technical and scientific co-operation; export and import of technical services world-wide; Gen. Man. ISTVÁN BENE.

Transelektro: 1394 Budapest, POB 377; tel. 132-0100; telex 22-4571; fax 153-0162; f. 1957; generators, power stations, cables, lighting, transformers, household appliances, catering equipment, etc.; Dir-Gen. PÁL KERTÉSZ.

TUNGSRAM Co Ltd: 1340 Budapest, Újpest 4; tel. 169-2800; telex 22-5058; fax 169-2868; f. 1896; light sources, lighting systems, vacuum engineering machinery, vacuum electronics, industrial electronics and components, etc.; Pres. and CEO GEORGE F. VARGA.

Vegyépszer Co Ltd: 1397 Budapest, POB 540; tel. 135-1125; telex 22-6930; fax 116-9470; building and assembling of chemical plant, supply of complete equipment, engineering, environment protection; Gen. Dir FERENC DERCZY.

VEPEX Ltd: 1370 Budapest, POB 308; tel. 142-5535; telex 22-4208; fax 142-5502; research, development and trading in biotechnology.

HUNGARY   Directory

Videoton Rt: 1398 Budapest, POB 557; tel. 121-0520; telex 22-4763; fax 142-1398; consumer electronics, computer technology; Gen. Dir ANDRÁS GEDE.

Volánpack: 1475 Budapest, POB 76; tel. 148-4300; telex 22-6935; fax 127-6031; forwarding and transport, packaging, warehousing, etc.; Gen. Dir MIKLÓS VAJDA.

Vörös Október MGTSZ, Ócsa: 1734 Budapest, POB 26; tel. 147-3759; telex 22-6156; agricultural co-operative.

TRADE FAIRS

Budapest International Fairs: Hungexpo, 1441 Budapest, POB 44; tel. 157-3555; telex 22-4188; f. 1968; technical goods (spring), consumer goods (autumn), and other specialized exhibitions and fairs; Dir JÁNOS HORVÁTH.

CO-OPERATIVE ORGANIZATIONS

Általános Fogyasztási Szövetkezetek Országos Szövetsége (ÁFEOSZ) (National Federation of Consumer Co-operatives): 1054 Budapest, Szabadság tér 14; tel. 153-4222; telex 22-4862; fax 111-3647; safeguards interests of Hungarian consumer co-operative societies, co-owner of co-op foreign trading companies and joint ventures; Pres. Dr PÁL SZILVASÁN; Gen. Sec. Dr ISTVÁN SZLAMENICKY; 3.5m. mems.

Ipari Szövetkezetek Országos Szövetsége (OKISZ) (National Federation of Industrial Co-operatives): 1146 Budapest, Thököly u. 58-60; tel. 141-5140; telex 22-7576; fax 141-5521; safeguards interests of over 3,000 member co-operatives; Pres. LAJOS KÖVESKUTI.

Országos Szövetkezeti Tanács (OSzT) (National Co-operative Council): 1373 Budapest, Szabadság tér 14; tel. 112-7467; telex 22-4862; Pres. Dr PÁL SZILVASÁN; Sec. Dr JÓZSEF PÁL.

Termelőszövetkezetek Országos Tanácsa (TOT) (National Council of Agricultural Co-operatives): 1054 Budapest, Akadémia u. 1-3; tel. 132-8167; telex 22-6810; f. 1967; Pres. ISTVÁN SZABÓ; Gen. Sec. Dr JÁNOS ELEKI; 1,280 co-operatives with 816,000 mems.

TRADE UNIONS

Magyar Szakszervezetek Országos Szövetsége (MSzOSz) (National Confederation of Hungarian Trade Unions): 1415 Budapest, Dózsa György u. 84B; tel. 153-2900; telex 22-5861; fax 141-4342; f. 1898, reorganized 1990; Pres. Dr SÁNDOR NAGY; 3,500,000 mems.

Affiliated Unions

Bányaipari Dolgozók Szakszervezeti Szövetsége (Federation of Mineworkers' Unions): 1068 Budapest, Gorkij fasor 46-48; tel. 122-1226; telex 22-7499; f. 1913; Pres. ISTVÁN HAVRÁN; Gen. Sec. ANTAL SCHALKHAMMER; 167,716 mems.

Bőripari Dolgozók Szakszervezete (Union of Leather Industry Workers): 1062 Budapest, Bajza u. 24; tel. 142-9970; f. 1868; Pres. LÁSZLÓ TURZO; Gen. Sec. TIBOR TRÉBER; 48,518 mems.

Egészségügyben Dolgozók Szakszervezeteinek Szövetsége (Union of Health Service Workers): 1051 Budapest, Nádor u. 32; tel. 132-7530; f. 1945; Pres. Dr ZOLTÁN SZABÓ; Gen. Sec. Dr PÁLNÉ KÁLLAY; 280,536 mems.

Élelmezésipari Dolgozók Szakszervezetek Szövetsége (Federation of Food Industry Workers' Unions): 1068 Budapest, Gorkij fasor 44; tel. 122-5880; f. 1905; Pres. ANDRAS GYENES; Gen. Sec. Dr LÁSZLÓ SZILÁGYI; 226,243 mems.

Építő-, Fa- és Épitőanyagipari Dolgozók Szakszervezeteinek Szövetsége (Federation of Building, Wood and Building Industry Workers' Unions): 1068 Budapest, Dózsa György u. 84A; tel. 142-5762; f. 1906; Pres. ISTVÁN GYÖNGYÖSI; Gen. Sec. GYULA SOMOGYI; 365,561 mems.

Helyiipari és Városgazdasági Dolgozók Szövetségének (Federation of Local Industry and Municipal Workers' Unions): 1068 Budapest, Benczur u. 43; tel. 111-6950; f. 1952; Pres. ZOLTAN FABOK; Gen. Sec. PÁL BAKÁNYI; 281,073 mems.

Kereskedelmi Szakszervezetek Szövetségének tagszervezeteiből (Federation of Commercial Workers' Unions): 1066 Budapest, Jókai u. 6; tel. 131-8970; f. 1948; Gen. Sec. JÁNOS VAS; 535,834 mems.

Közlekedési Szakszervezeteinek Szövetségének tagszervezeteiből (Federation of Transport Workers' Unions): 1428 Budapest, Köztársaság tér 3; tel. 113-9046; f. 1898; Pres. GÁBOR SCHLEMBACH; Gen. Sec. GYULA MOLDOVAN; 190,464 mems.

Magyar Közszolgálati Szakszervezetek Szövetsége (Federation of Hungarian Public Service Employees' Unions): 1088 Budapest, Puskin u. 4; tel. 118-8900; fax 118-7361; f. 1945; Pres. Dr ENDRE SZABÓ; 230,000 mems.

Magyar Pedagógusok Szakszervezete (Hungarian Union of Teachers): 1068 Budapest, Gorkij fasor 10; tel. 122-8456; fax 142-8122; f. 1945; Gen. Sec. ISTVÁNNÉ SZÖLLŐSI; 240,000 mems.

Magyar Postai és Hírközlési Dolgozók Szakszervezeti Szövetsége (Hungarian Federation of Trade Unions of Postal and Communications Employees): 1146 Budapest, Cházár András u. 13; tel. 142-8777; fax 121-4018; f. 1945; Pres. ENIKŐ HESZKY-GRICSER; 88,651 mems.

Magyar Textilipari Dolgozók Szakszervezete (Hungarian Union of Textile Workers): 1068 Budapest, Rippl-Rónai u. 2; tel. 142-8196; f. 1905; Pres. (vacant); Gen. Sec. TAMÁS KELETI; 110,953 mems.

Magyar Vas- Fém- és Villamosenergiaipari Szakszervezetek Szövetsége (Confederation of Hungarian Metal and Electric Energy Industry Workers' Unions): 1086 Budapest, Koltói Anna u. 5-7; tel. 113-5200; telex 22-4791; fax 133-8327; f. 1877; Pres. LÁSZLÓ PASZTERNÁK; 535,000 mems.

Mezőgazdasági, Erdészeti és Vizgazdálkodási Dolgozók Szakszervezeteinek Szövetsége tagszervezeteiből (Federation of Agricultural, Forestry and Water Conservancy Workers' Unions): 1066 Budapest, Jókai u. 2-4; tel. 131-4550; telex 22-7535; f. 1906; Pres. (vacant); Gen. Sec. TIBOR CZIRMAY; 389,569 mems.

Müvészeti és Tájékoztatási Szakszervezetek Szövetségének tagszervezeteiből (Federation of Hungarian Artists' and Telecommunication Workers' Unions): 1068 Budapest, Gorkij fasor 38; tel. 121-1120; f. 1957; Pres. IMRE VASS; Gen. Sec. KÁLMÁN PETŐ; 40,000 mems.

Nyomdadaipari Dolgozók Szakszervezete (Printers' Union): 1085 Budapest, Kölcsey u. 2; tel. 114-2413; telex 20-2612; fax 134-2524; f. 1862; Pres. ANDRÁS BÁRSONY; Vice-Pres JÁNOS ACZÉL, ZOLTÁN GODZSA; 49,436 mems.

Ruházatipari Dolgozók Szakszervezete (Union of Clothing Workers): 1077 Budapest, Almássy tér 2; tel. 142-2126; f. 1892; Pres. JULIANNA TÓTH; Gen. Sec. GÁBOR VERES; 37,117 mems.

Vasutasok Szakszervezete (Union of Railway Workers): 1068 Budapest, Benczúr u. 41; tel. 122-1895; telex 22-6819; f. 1945; Pres. PÁL PAPP; Gen. Sec. FERENC KOSZORUS; 196,698 mems.

Non-affiliated Unions

Democratic League of Independent Trade Unions (FSzDL): Budapest; f. 1989; 80,000 mems; Chair. PÁL FORGACS.

Magyar Vegyipari Dolgozók Szakszervezeti Szövetsége (Federation of Hungarian Chemical Industry Workers' Unions): 1068 Budapest, Benczúr u. 45; tel. 142-1778; telex 22-3420; fax 142-9975; f. 1897; Gen. Sec. LAJOS FŐCZE; 140,000 mems.

Tudományos Dolgozók Demokratikus Szakszervezete Szövetsége (TDDSZ) (Democratic Trade Union of Scientific Workers): Budapest; f. 1988; Chair. PÁL FORGACS.

Transport

Raabersped: 1531 Budapest, POB 33; tel. 175-1322; telex 22-5919; international forwarding agency (rail, road, air and sea); Dir Dr JÁNOS BERÉNYI.

Other forwarding agencies are Masped and Volánpack (see under Foreign Trade Organizations).

RAILWAYS

Magyar Államvasutak (MÁV) (Hungarian State Railways): 1940 Budapest, Andrássy ut 73-75; tel. 122-0660; telex 22-4342; fax 142-8596; state-owned since its foundation in 1868; total network 7,600 km, including 2,100 km of electrified lines; Gen Man. JÁNOS CSÁRÁDI.

Győr-Sopron-Ebenfurti-Vasut—Gysev-ROeEE (Railway of Győr-Sopron-Ebenfurt): 9401 Sopron, Matyas Kiraly u. 19; Hungarian-Austrian-owned railway; 84 km in Hungary, 82 km in Austria, all electrified; transport of passengers and goods; Dir-Gen. LÁSZLÓ OROSZVÁRY.

There is an underground railway in Budapest, with a network of 23 km in 1989; in that year 296m. passengers were carried.

ROADS

In late December 1988 the road network totalled 105,370 km, including 311 km of motorways, 6,379 km of main or national roads and 23,024 km of secondary roads. Construction of the Budapest ring motorway began in 1987, with financial assistance from the World Bank, and was scheduled for completion in 1990. There are extensive long-distance bus services. Road passenger and freight transport is provided by the state-owned VOLÁN companies and by individual (own account) operators.

Hungarocamion: 1442 Budapest, POB 108; tel. 157-3811; telex 22-5455; international road freight transport company; 17 offices in Europe and the Middle East; fleet of 1,800 lorries; Gen. Man. IMRE TORMA.

HUNGARY

Volán Vállalatok Központja (Centre of Volán Enterprises): 1391 Budapest, Erzsébet krt 96, POB 221; tel. 112-4290; telex 22-5177; centre of 25 Volán enterprises for inland and international road freight and passenger transport, forwarding, tourism; fleet of 17,000 lorries, incl. special tankers for fuel, refrigerators, trailers, 8,000 buses for regular passenger transport; 3 affiliates, offices and joint-ventures in Europe; Head KÁLMÁN GARAMI.

SHIPPING AND INLAND WATERWAYS

In 1987 the Hungarian merchant fleet comprised 15 vessels totalling 106,710 dwt.

MAHART—Magyar Hajózási Rt. (Hungarian Shipping Co): 1366 Budapest, POB 58; tel. 118-1880; telex 22-5258; carries passenger traffic on the Danube and Lake Balaton; cargo services on the Danube and its tributaries, Lake Balaton, and also Mediterranean and ocean-going services; operates port of Budapest (container terminal, loading, storage, warehousing, handling and packaging services); ship-building and ship-repair services; Dir-Gen. PÉTER MURADIN.

MAFRACHT: 1052 Budapest, Kristóf tér 2, POB 105; tel. 118-5276; telex 22-4471; shipping agency.

CIVIL AVIATION

The Ferihegy international airport is 16 km from the centre of Budapest. An expansion and development programme began in 1977, and the reconstruction work on the runway was completed in 1987. Ferihegy-2 opened in 1985. There are no public internal air services.

Légügyi Főigazgatóság (General Directorate of Civil Aviation): 1400 Budapest, Dob u. 75–81, POB 87; tel. 142-2544; telex 22-5729; controls civil aviation; Dir-Gen. ÖDÖN SKONDA.

Légiforgalmi és Repülőtéri Igazgatóság (LRI) (Air Traffic and Airport Administration): 1675 Budapest, POB 53; tel. 157-9123; telex 22-4054; fax 157-6982; f. 1973; controls civil air traffic and operates Ferihegy and Siófok Airports; Dir-Gen. TAMÁS ERDEI.

Magyar Légiközlekedési Vállalat—MALÉV (Hungarian Airlines): 1367 Budapest, Roosevelt tér 2, POB 122; tel. 118-9033; telex 22-4954; fax 117-2417; f. 1946; regular services from Budapest to Europe, North Africa and the Middle East; Gen. Dir LAJOS JAHODA; fleet of 1 Yak-40, 6 TU-134 and 12 TU-154; 3 Boeing 737-200 on lease.

Tourism

Tourism has developed rapidly and is an important source of foreign exchange. In 1990 convertible-currency income from tourism totalled some US $2,000m., 60% more than in 1989. Rouble receipts in 1990 reached 90m., considerably less than in 1989. Lake Balaton is the main holiday centre for boating, bathing and fishing. The cities have great historical and recreational attractions. The annual Budapest Spring Festival is held in March. Budapest has numerous swimming pools warmed by thermal springs, which are equipped with modern physiotherapy facilities. The first Budapest Grand Prix, the only Formula-1 motor race to be held in Eastern Europe, took place in August 1986. In 1990 there were 38m. foreign visitors (including visitors in transit), 25% more than in the previous year. There were 47,317 hotel beds in 1986, and a further 8,000–10,000 were to be created by 1994.

Országos Idegenforgalmi Hivatal (OIH) (Hungarian Tourist Board): 1051 Budapest, Vigadó u. 6; tel. 118-0750; telex 22-5182; fax 118-5241; f. 1968; Head Dr IMRE GELLAI.

Budapest Tourist (Budapest Travel Company): 1051 Budapest, Roosevelt tér 5; tel. 118-6663; telex 22-6448; fax 118-1658; f. 1916; runs tours, congresses and cultural programmes; provides accommodation; Dir IVÁN RÓNA.

COOPTOURIST—Co-operative Travel Agency: 1016 Budapest, Derék u. 2; tel. 175-0575; telex 22-5399; general tourism services for groups and individuals; branch offices throughout Hungary; Gen. Dir Dr SÁNDOR SIPOS.

DANUBIUS—Danubius Hotels: 1138 Budapest, Margitsziget; tel. 112-1000; telex 22-6850; fax 153-1883; Dir ISTVÁN PUSKÁS.

Express Utazási Iroda (Express Travel Bureau): 1054 Budapest, Szabadság tér 16; tel. 153-0660; telex 22-5384; fax 153-1715; f. 1957; package tours, study tours, vacation centres; Gen. Man. Dr GYULA TARCSI.

HungarHotels—Hungarian Hotel and Restaurant Company: 1052 Budapest, Petőfi Sándor u. 14; tel. 118-2033; telex 22-4209; fax 117-1374; f. 1956; Pres. TAMÁS BÚVÁRI.

IBUSZ—Idegenforgalmi, Beszerzési, Utazási és Szállítási Rt. (Hungarian Travel Agency): 1364 Budapest, Felszabadulás tér 5; tel. 118-1120; telex 22-4976; fax 117-7723; f. 1902; 24-hour service for individual travellers at: 1052 Budapest, Petőfi tér 3; tel. 118-5707; telex 22-4941; IBUSZ has 118 brs throughout Hungary; Gen. Man. ERIKA SZEMENKÁR.

Locomotiv Tourist: 1536 Budapest, Szilágyi Dezső tér 1, POB 241; tel. 115-9420; telex 22-4249; Dir Dr ADÁM MENYHÁRT.

Malév Air Tours: 1367 Budapest, Roosevelt tér 2, POB 122; tel. 118-3780; telex 22-5370; fax 118-7359; Dir ZSUZSA VÉRTESSY.

Máv Tours (Travel Bureau of Hungarian State Railways): 1378 Budapest, Guszev u. 1, POB 25; tel. 117-3723; telex 22-3251; Dir THOMAS LENGYEL.

Pannónia Hotels and Restaurants: 1088 Budapest, Puskin u. 6, POB 159; tel. 138-2187; telex 22-4561; fax 118-1344; f. 1949; owns 51 hotels; organizes through its Tourist Service Bureau tours, programmes, conferences etc. in Hungary, and Hungarian gastronomic festivals abroad; Gen. Man. GYULA HARBULA.

Pegazus Tours: 1053 Budapest, Károlyi Mihály u. 5; Dir MAUSZ GOTTHARD.

Volántourist Vállalat: 1066 Budapest, Teréz krt. 96; tel. 132-2905; telex 22-6722; fax 112-2298; f. 1970; Dir LAJOS CSETE.

Atomic Energy

Hungary's first nuclear power station at Paks (on the Danube, south of Budapest), built with Soviet assistance, began trial operations in December 1982, and was formally inaugurated in November 1983. Four units, each of 440 MW, were in operation by 1987. In 1988 a record output of 13,420m. kWh was achieved. Hungary has signed agreements for co-operation in the peaceful uses of atomic energy with Bulgaria, Cuba, Czechoslovakia, France, the former German Democratic Republic, India, Italy, Romania and the USSR. Hungary is a member of the International Atomic Energy Agency (based in Vienna), the Joint Institute for Nuclear Research (at Dubna, near Moscow) and the CMEA Standing Committee on Electricity and Nuclear Power.

Országos Atomenergia Bizottság (National Atomic Energy Commission): 1374 Budapest, POB 565; tel. 132-7172; telex 22-4907; fax 142-7598; f. 1956; Pres. ERNŐ PUNGOR.

Budapesti Műszaki Egyetem Nukleáris Technikai Intézet (Institute of Nuclear Techniques of the Technical University of Budapest): 1521 Budapest, POB 91; tel. 181-2564; telex 22-5931; fax 166-6808; f. 1971; Dir Prof. Dr G. CSOM.

Kossuth Lajos Tudományegyetem Kisérleti Fizikai Intézete (Institute for Experimental Physics of the Kossuth Lajos University): 4001 Debrecen, POB 105; tel. 15-222; telex 72-200; fax (52) 15-087; f. 1923; research in low-energy nuclear physics, neutron physics, and application of atomic and nuclear methods; Dir Prof. Dr J. CSIKAI.

Magyar Tudományos Akadémia Atommag Kutató Intézete—ATOMKI (Institute of Nuclear Research of the Hungarian Academy of Sciences): 4026 Debrecen, Bem tér 18/c; tel. 17-266; telex 72-210; fax 16-181; f. 1954; research in nuclear structure, reaction, ion-atom collisions, etc.; Dir Prof. Dr D. BERÉNYI.

Magyar Tudományos Akadémia Izotópkutató Intézete (Institute of Isotopes of the Hungarian Academy of Sciences): 1525 Budapest, POB 77, Konkoly Thege u. 29–33; tel. 169-6687; telex 22-5360; fax 156-5045; f. 1959; Dir Gen. Dr G. FÖLDIÁK.

Magyar Tudományos Akadémia Központi Fizikai Kutató Intézete—KFKI (Central Research Institute for Physics of the Hungarian Academy of Sciences): 1525 Budapest, POB 49; tel. 169-8566; telex 22-4722; fax 155-3894; f. 1950; research in computer science, nuclear, particle, reactor and solid state physics; Dir-Gen. ISTVÁN LOVAS.

Országos 'Frédéric Joliot-Curie' Sugárbiológiai és Sugáregészségügyi Kutató Intézet (National Research Institute for Radiobiology and Radiohygiene): 1775 Budapest, POB 101; f. 1957; tel. 226-0026; telex 22-5103; fax 226-6531; research on effects of ionizing and non-ionizing radiations, radiation protection, application of radiation and isotopes for medical purposes; Dir Gen. Dr L. B. SZTANYIK.

Paksi Atomerőmű Vállalat (PAV) (Paks Nuclear Power Plant): 7031 Paks, POB 71; tel. (75) 11-222; telex 14-440; fax 1551-332; f. 1976; electricity generation, foreign trade in training of nuclear power plant specialists, licences and auxiliary equipment for nuclear power plants; exports spent nuclear fuel; imports fresh nuclear fuel, nuclear power plant mountings; Dir Gen. JÓZSEF PÓNYA.

Villamosenergiaipari Kutató Intézet—VEIKI (Institute for Electric Power Research) 1368 Budapest, POB 233; tel. 118-3233; telex 22-5744; fax 117-9956; f. 1949; research on technology, safety, structure mechanics, control and instrumentation, water chemistry of nuclear power plants. Scientific divisions; Divisions of Nuclear and Heat Power Engineering, Systemtechnics, Chemical Engineering, Computer Engineering, Electrical Equipment and Combustion Engineering; Dir Dr GYÖRGY VAJDA.

ICELAND

Introductory Survey

Location, Climate, Language, Religion, Flag, Capital

The Republic of Iceland comprises one large island and numerous smaller ones, situated near the Arctic Circle in the North Atlantic Ocean. The main island lies about 300 km (190 miles) south-east of Greenland, about 1,000 km (620 miles) west of Norway and about 800 km (500 miles) north of Scotland. The Gulf Stream keeps Iceland warmer than might be expected, with average temperatures ranging from 10°C (50°F) in the summer to 1°C (34°F) in winter. Icelandic is the official language. Almost all of the inhabitants profess Christianity: the Evangelical Lutheran Church is the established church and embraces 93% of the population. The national flag (proportions 25 by 18) displays a red cross, bordered with white, on a blue background, the upright of the cross being to the left of centre. The capital is Reykjavík.

Recent History

Iceland became independent on 17 June 1944, when the Convention that linked it with Denmark, under the Danish throne, was terminated. Iceland became a founder-member of the Nordic Council (see p. 179) in 1952, and has belonged to both NATO (see p. 183) and the Council of Europe (see p. 129) since 1949.

From 1959 to 1971 Iceland was governed by a coalition of the Independence Party and the Social Democratic Party (SDP). In the general election of June 1971 there was a swing to the left, and Ólafur Jóhannesson, the leader of the Progressive Party, formed a coalition government with the People's Alliance and the Union of Liberals and Leftists. Elections held in June 1974 showed a swing back to the right, and in August the Independence and Progressive Parties formed a coalition led by Geir Hallgrímsson. Loss of popularity through its treatment of Iceland's economic problems, such as the perpetuation of rampant inflation by index-linked wage settlements, led to the Government's resignation in June 1978, following extensive election gains by the left-wing People's Alliance and SDP. Disagreements over economic measures, and over the People's Alliance's policy of withdrawal from NATO, led to two months of negotiations before a new government could be formed. In September 1978 Jóhannesson, the former Prime Minister, formed a coalition of his own Progressive Party with the People's Alliance and the SDP, but this Government, after addressing immediate economic necessities, resigned in October 1979, when the Social Democrats withdrew. An interim administration was formed by Benedikt Gröndal, the SDP leader. The results of a general election held in December were inconclusive, and in February 1980 Gunnar Thoroddsen of the Independence Party formed a coalition with the People's Alliance and the Progressive Party.

In June 1980 Vigdís Finnbogadóttir, a non-political candidate who was favoured by left-wing groups because of her opposition to the US military airbase in Iceland, achieved a narrow victory in the election for the mainly ceremonial office of President. She took office on 1 August 1980, becoming the world's first popularly-elected female Head of State, although her election had no direct effect on government policy. The coalition Government lost its majority in the Lower House of the Althing in September 1982, and a general election was held in April 1983. The Independence Party received the largest share (38.7%) of the votes, but there was a swing away from traditional parties, with two new parties (the Social Democratic Alliance and the Women's Alliance) together winning nearly 13% of the votes. A centre-right coalition was formed between the Independence and Progressive Parties, with Steingrímur Hermannsson, the Progressive Party leader and former Minister of Fisheries and Communications, as Prime Minister, and Geir Hallgrímsson, Prime Minister from 1974 to 1978 and leader of the Independence Party, as Minister for Foreign Affairs. In an attempt to halt the sharp increase in the rate of inflation, the Government discontinued the indexation of wages to the rate of inflation, extended existing wage agreements and devalued the króna in May 1983. Although these measures reduced inflation in 1984, there was considerable industrial unrest, in that year and in 1985, as a result of which large increases in wages for public-sector employees and fishermen were secured. There was also a further devaluation of the króna. In June 1985, to forestall the threat of further strikes, private-sector employers secured a no-strike agreement with the Icelandic Federation of Labour. In February 1986 a further wage settlement was agreed by the Government, the trade unions and the employers, and in 1987 another agreement, which restricted wage increases to less than the rate of inflation, were negotiated, although several unions chose to negotiate separate agreements.

In March 1987 Albert Guðmundsson resigned as Minister of Energy and Industry and as a member of the Independence Party, following accusations of tax evasion. He subsequently formed the Citizens' Party. A general election for an enlarged, 63-seat Althing was held in April. Both parties of the outgoing coalition suffered losses: the Independence Party's share of the seats was reduced from 24 to 18, and the Progressive Party lost one of its 14 seats. The newly-formed Citizens' Party won seven seats, while the Women's Alliance increased its number of seats from three to six. Ten seats were won by the SDP, which included former members of the Social Democratic Alliance, disbanded in 1986. Hermannsson tendered the resignation of his Government, but was requested to remain as leader of an interim administration until a new coalition was formed. Protracted negotiations took place, resulting in a coalition of the Independence, Progressive and Social Democratic Parties, formally constituted in July. Thorsteinn Pálsson, the leader of the Independence Party and the Minister of Finance in the outgoing Cabinet, was appointed Prime Minister.

In June 1988 President Finnbogadóttir (who had begun a second term in office in August 1984, no presidential election having been held, as her candidacy was unopposed) was elected for a third term. This was the first occasion on which an incumbent President seeking re-election had been challenged. Supported by all the main political parties, she received more than 90% of the votes and defeated her only rival, who had campaigned for a greater role for the Presidency.

In September 1988 the SDP and the Progressive Party withdrew from Prime Minister Pálsson's Government, following disagreements over economic policy. Later that month, the leader of the Progressives, Steingrímur Hermannsson (a former Prime Minister and the Minister for Foreign Affairs in the outgoing Government), became Prime Minister in a centre-left coalition with the SDP and the People's Alliance. The new Government committed itself to a series of devaluations of the króna, and introduced austerity measures, designed to lower inflation and to help the fishing industry.

Following the resignation of the founder of the right-wing Citizens' Party (CP), Albert Guðmundsson, from the party leadership in January 1989, relations between the CP and the left-wing parties improved, and in September a new government, based on a coalition agreement between the Progressive Party, the SDP, the People's Alliance, the CP and the Association for Equality and Social Justice, was formed. The new Government had a working majority of 11 seats. (Hitherto the coalition had only had a one-seat majority in the legislature as a whole and was actually in a minority in the lower house.) The CP's decision to join the Government caused a split in the party, and two members of the CP broke away to form a new party. Júlíus Sólnes, the new CP leader, was appointed Minister of Economic Planning and Nordic Co-operation, while the CP deputy leader, Oli Th. Guðbartsson, assumed the post of Minister of Justice and Ecclesiastical Affairs. After the formation of the new coalition Government, the Prime Minister, Steingrímur Hermannsson, affirmed that the Government would not change its policies. He emphasized the need to reduce inflation and to stimulate economic growth, as well as reiterating an earlier declaration of the Althing that no nuclear weapons would be located in Iceland.

In February 1990 a Ministry for the Environment was created, and Júlíus Sólnes became its first minister. The Prime

ICELAND

Minister once again took over the Economic Planning portfolio. The state of the economy continued to cause public dissatisfaction during 1990, and, as a result, voters at municipal elections held on 26 May favoured right-wing parties at the expense of left-wing groups.

The importance of fishing to Iceland's economy, and fears of excessive exploitation of the fishing grounds near Iceland by foreign fleets, caused the Icelandic Government to extend its territorial waters to 12 nautical miles (22 km) in 1964 and to 50 nautical miles (93 km) in September 1972. British opposition to these extensions resulted in two 'cod wars'. In October 1975 Iceland unilaterally introduced a fishing limit of 200 nautical miles (370 km), both as a conservation measure and to protect important Icelandic interests. The 1973 agreement on fishing limits between Iceland and the United Kingdom expired in November 1975, and failure to reach a new agreement led to the third and most serious 'cod war'. Casualties occurred, and in February 1976 Iceland temporarily severed diplomatic relations with Britain, the first diplomatic break between two NATO countries. In June 1976 the two countries reached an agreement, and in December the British trawler fleet withdrew from Icelandic waters. In June 1979 Iceland declared its exclusive rights to the 200-mile fishing zone.

In May 1985 the Althing unanimously approved a resolution declaring the country a 'nuclear-free zone', i.e. banning the entry of nuclear weapons. Iceland was host to a US-Soviet 'summit' meeting in October 1986. The country's membership of NATO is widely supported, although the military air-base at Keflavík is a cause of political controversy. In September 1988 the new Government declared that there would be no new military projects in Iceland.

Relations between Iceland and the USA were strained during July 1986, when the USA argued that, by approving the catch of 80 fin whales and 40 sei whales, Iceland was acting against a moratorium imposed by the International Whaling Commission (IWC), and the US Government threatened to impose a boycott on Icelandic fish products. Iceland declared that the catch of whales was for scientific purposes only and continued its programme, despite the sinking of two whaling ships in Reykjavík harbour by militant environmentalists. In 1987 Iceland reduced its catch by 20 sei whales, but threats of US sanctions resumed in August. The controversy raised doubts concerning the continuing use by US forces of the NATO base at Keflavík, and led to speculation that Iceland and Japan might withdraw from the IWC. Iceland reduced its catch quota for 1988. International pressure continued, and in August 1989 the Icelandic Government suspended for two years its programme of killing whales for research, thus ending an appeal by the environmental organization, Greenpeace, for a world-wide boycott of Icelandic products.

Government

According to the Constitution, executive power is vested in the President (elected for four years by universal adult suffrage) and the Cabinet, consisting of the Prime Minister and other Ministers appointed by the President. In practice, however, the President performs only nominally the functions ascribed in the Constitution to this office, and it is the Cabinet alone which holds real executive power. Legislative power is held jointly by the President and the Althing (Parliament), with 63 members elected by universal suffrage for four years (subject to dissolution by the President), using a mixed system of proportional representation. The Althing chooses 21 of its members to form the Upper House, the other 42 forming the Lower House. For some purposes the two Houses sit jointly as the United Althing. Electoral reforms, introduced in 1987, included the lowering of the minimum voting age from 20 to 18 years. The Cabinet is responsible to the Althing. Iceland has seven administrative districts.

Defence

Iceland has no defence forces of its own but is a member of NATO. There are units of US forces at Keflavík air base, which is used for observation of the North Atlantic Ocean, under an agreement made in 1951 between Iceland and NATO. The airfield at Keflavík is a base for the new US airborne early warning system. In June 1990 a total of 3,100 US military personnel (navy 1,800, air force 1,300) were stationed in Iceland. In July 1983 Iceland agreed to the construction of a military and civilian air-terminal at Keflavík, funded by the USA at a cost of US $120m.

Economic Affairs

In 1989, according to estimates by the World Bank, Iceland's gross national product (GNP), measured at 1987–89 prices, was US $5,351m., equivalent to $21,240 per head. During 1980–89, it was estimated, GNP increased, in real terms, at an average annual rate of 2.8%, and GNP per head increased by an annual average of 1.7%. In 1990, according to official estimates, Iceland's gross domestic product (GDP), measured at constant prices, declined by 0.3%. During 1975–90, however, GDP increased, in real terms, at an estimated average annual rate of 3.5%, and GDP per head increased by an annual average of 2.4%. Over the same period, the population increased by an annual average of 1.1%.

Agriculture (including forestry and fishing) contributed 13% of GDP in 1988. It was estimated that 5.1% of the labour force were employed in agriculture in 1988, while 11.9% were employed in fishing and fish-processing. The principal agricultural products are dairy produce and lamb, but they formed only 1.7% of export earnings in 1989. Fisheries products accounted for 72.3% of total export earnings in 1989. The total fish catch in 1989 was 13.6% lower than in 1988.

Industry (including mining, manufacturing, construction and power) contributed 33.3% of GDP in 1987. During 1985–90 industrial production increased by 8%. Mining is negligible.

Manufacturing contributed 20.3% of GDP in 1987, and employed 18.6% of the labour force in 1988. The most important sectors, measured by gross value of output (excluding fish-processing), are the production of aluminium, diatomite, fertilizer and ferro-silicon.

Iceland is potentially rich in hydroelectric and geothermal power. Electricity consumption was 4,200 GWh in 1989. However, fuels and lubricants totalling 6,878m. krónur were imported in 1989.

In 1989 Iceland recorded a visible trade surplus of US $134.2m., but there was a deficit of $93.3m. on the current account of the balance of payments. In 1989 the principal source of imports was the Federal Republic of Germany (13.1%), followed by the USA (11.0%) and the Netherlands (10.4%); the principal market for exports was the United Kingdom (20.8%), followed by the USA (14.3%). Other major trading partners are Japan, France, Portugal, Switzerland and Denmark. The principal imports were basic manufactures, machinery and transport equipment, and the principal exports were marine products, aluminium, ferro-silicon and diatomite.

Iceland forecast a budget deficit of 3,700m. krónur for 1991. Iceland's total external debt was 156,601m. krónur at the end of 1989. The debt-service ratio was 19.3% of GDP in that year. Inflation has been high, with an average increase in consumer prices of 20.3% in 1989 and 15.5% in 1990. Unemployment has been low, with only 1.6% of the total labour force unemployed in 1989.

Iceland is a member of the Nordic Council (p. 179), the Nordic Council of Ministers (see p. 180), the European Free Trade Association (p. 154), the Organisation for Economic Co-operation and Development (p. 186), and the Council of Europe (p. 129).

In 1988–90 the economy experienced a decline. GDP, which had increased by 8.7% in 1987 compared with 1986, declined by 0.8% in 1988, by 3.3% in 1989 and by 0.3% in 1990. In 1991, however, GDP was expected to increase by 1.6%. The economic crisis which occurred in 1988 was due largely to a drop in the export price of fish and to the weakness of the US dollar, coupled with high domestic inflation. Three devaluations of the króna were implemented in late 1988 and early 1989, leading to an improvement in the competitive position of the króna. According to an OECD report, the Icelandic economy should gradually recover, with an average annual growth rate of 1.5%–2.0% in the 1990s. The economy is vulnerable because of its dependence on fishing and the unpredictability of fish movements in the North Atlantic. Attempts to diversify into other activities have not yet been entirely successful.

Social Welfare

There is a comprehensive system of social security, providing a wide range of insurance benefits, including old-age pensions, family allowances, maternity grants, widows' pensions, etc. Contributions to the scheme are compulsory. Pensions and health insurance now apply to the whole population. Accident insurance applies to all wage and salary earners and self-employed persons—unless they request exemption—and unemployment insurance to the unions of skilled and unskilled

ICELAND

workers and seamen in all towns and villages of over 300 inhabitants, as well as to several unions in villages of less than 300 inhabitants. In 1980 there were 488 physicians working in Iceland, and the country had 46 hospital establishments, with a total of 3,730 beds, equivalent to one for every 61 inhabitants: one of the best ratios in the world. Of total expenditure by the central Government in 1989, 35,924m. krónur (41.7%) was for health and welfare.

Education

Education is compulsory and free for nine years between seven and 16 years of age. Primary education, beginning at the age of seven and lasting for six years, is available in day schools in urban regions, while in the more remote country districts pupils attend a state boarding-school. The total enrolment at primary schools in 1988 was equivalent to 102% of children in the relevant age-group. Secondary education begins at 13 years of age and lasts for up to seven years, comprising a first cycle of three years and a second of four years. Enrolment at secondary schools in 1988 was equivalent to 96% of children in the appropriate age-group. In 1974 the primary and lower secondary schools were formed into basic schools, leading to a national examination which gives access to further education. The matriculation examination at the end of four years at upper secondary school or at comprehensive school provides the qualification for university entrance. Iceland has four institutions of higher learning, but approximately two-thirds of the 2,500 students studying abroad, in 1988, were doing so at the tertiary level. Expenditure on education by the central Government in 1989 was 13,784m. krónur, representing 16.0% of total spending.

Public Holidays

1991: 1 January (New Year's Day), 28 March (Maundy Thursday), 29 March (Good Friday), 1 April (Easter Monday), 9 May (Ascension Day), 20 May (Whit Monday), 17 June (National Day), 5 August (Bank Holiday), 24–26 December (Christmas), 31 December (New Year's Eve).

1992: 1 January (New Year's Day), 16 April (Maundy Thursday), 17 April (Good Friday), 20 April (Easter Monday), 28 May (Ascension Day), 8 June (Whit Monday), 17 June (National Day), 3 August (Bank Holiday), 24–26 December (Christmas), 31 December (New Year's Eve).

Weights and Measures

The metric system is in force.

Statistical Survey

Sources (unless otherwise stated): Statistical Bureau of Iceland, Hverfisgata 8-10, 150 Reykjavík; tel. (1) 26699; National Economic Institute of Iceland, Reykjavík; tel. (1) 699500; Séđlabanki Íslands (Central Bank of Iceland), Kalkofnsvegur 1, 150 Reykjavík; tel. (1) 699600; telex 2020.

AREA AND POPULATION

Area: 103,000 sq km (39,769 sq miles).

Population: 204,578 at census of 1 December 1970; 253,500 (males 127,305; females 126,195 at 1 December 1989 (official estimate).

Density (per sq km): 2.5 (1989).

Principal Town: Reykjavík (capital), estimated population 96,708 at 1 December 1989.

Births, Marriages and Deaths (1989): Live births 4,560 (birth rate 18.0 per 1,000); Marriage rate 4.7 per 1,000; Deaths 1,715 (death rate 6.8 per 1,000).

Employment* (1988): Agriculture, forestry and fishing 12,948; Mining, quarrying and manufacturing 25,627; Construction 11,838; Trade, restaurants and hotels 20,412; Community, social and personal services 37,406; Total (incl. others) 127,779.

* Figures refer to the working population covered by compulsory social insurance.

AGRICULTURE, ETC.

Principal Crops (metric tons, 1989): Potatoes 8,382; Turnips 544.

Livestock (December 1989): Cattle 72,789; Sheep 560,920; Horses 69,238; Pigs 3,247; Poultry 281,997.

Livestock Products (metric tons, 1989): Mutton and lamb 9,623; Milk 99,868; Wool (unwashed) 1,200; Sheep skins 2,400; Eggs 2,900.

Fishing ('000 metric tons, live weight, 1989): Atlantic cod 353.6; Haddock 61.9; Saithe 79.8; Atlantic redfishes 92.9; Capelin 669.9; Atlantic herring 97.3; Crustaceans 28.7; Total (incl. others) 1,513.7.

INDUSTRY

Selected Products ('000 metric tons, unless otherwise indicated, 1989): Frozen fish 152; Salted, dried or smoked fish 88; Cement 104; Ferro-silicon 72.0; Aluminium (unwrought) 89.0; Electric energy 4,475 million kWh.

FINANCE

Currency and Exchange Rates: 100 aurar (singular: eyrir) = 1 new Icelandic króna (plural: krónur). *Coins:* 10 and 50 aurar; 1, 5, 10 and 50 krónur. *Notes:* 100, 500, 1,000 and 5,000 krónur. *Sterling and Dollar Equivalents* (30 September 1990): £1 sterling = 106.08 krónur; US $1 = 56.62 krónur; 1,000 krónur = 35.42T 017.00D. *Average Exchange Rate* (krónur per US $): 38.677 in 1987; 43.014 in 1988; 57.042 in 1989.

Budget (million krónur, 1989): *Revenue:* Direct taxes 13,252; Indirect taxes 61,240 (sales tax 34,179, taxes on alcohol and tobacco 5,374, excise tax 2,494, import duties 7,846, other indirect taxes 11,347); Non-tax revenue 5,509; Total 80,001. *Expenditure* (excluding net lending): General administration 8,211; Education 13,784; Health and welfare 35,924; Subsidies 4,663; Agriculture 3,839; Fisheries 2,295; Manufacturing 591; Power 826; Communications 5,730; Other purposes 10,193; Total 86,056.

International Reserves (US $ million at 31 December 1989): Gold 2.2; IMF special drawing rights 0.0; Reserve position in IMF 5.3; Foreign exchange 332.0; Total 339.5 (Source: IMF, *International Financial Statistics*).

Money Supply (million krónur at 31 December 1989): Currency outside banks 3,046; Demand deposits at commercial and savings banks 58,075; Total money 61,121 (Source: IMF, *International Financial Statistics*).

Cost of Living (consumer price index for Reykjavík; average of monthly figures; base: 1 February 1984 = 100): 256.53 in 1988; 310.73 in 1989; 356.84 in 1990.

Gross Domestic Product in purchasers' values (million krónur at current prices): 208,099 in 1987; 254,639 in 1988; 296,080 in 1989.

Balance of Payments (US $ million, 1989): Merchandise exports f.o.b. 1,401.5, Merchandise imports f.o.b. −1,267.3, *Trade balance* 134.2; Exports of services 540.0, Imports of services −764.5, *Balance of goods and services* −90.3; Private unrequited transfers (net) 0.9, Government unrequited transfers (net) −3.9, *Current balance* −93.3; Direct capital investment (net) −35.6, Other long-term capital (net) 296.3, Short-term capital (net) −135.7, Net errors and omissions 22.9, *Total* (net monetary movements) 54.6; Valuation change (net) −8.0, *Changes in reserves* 46.6 (Source: IMF, *International Financial Statistics*).

EXTERNAL TRADE

Principal Commodities (US $ million, distribution by SITC, 1989): *Imports c.i.f.:* Food and live animals 111.6; Crude materials (inedible) except fuels 73.4; Mineral fuels, lubricants, etc. 122.7; Chemicals and related products 116.1; Basic manufactures 256.3; Machinery and transport equipment 457.5; Miscellaneous manufactured articles 241.2; Total (incl. others) 1,406.9. *Exports f.o.b.:* Food and live animals 1,027.0 (Fish, crustaceans and molluscs, and preparations thereof 933.3); Basic manufactures 263.4 (Unwrought aluminium 239.2); Total (incl. others) 1,403.7.

Principal Trading Partners (million krónur, country of consignment, 1989): *Imports c.i.f.:* Australia 2,046, Denmark 7,263, Finland

1,618, France 2,496, Federal Republic of Germany 10,498, Italy 2,487, Japan 3,917, Netherlands 8,358, Norway 5,296, Sweden 6,592, USSR 3,383, United Kingdom 6,509, USA 8,823; Total (incl. others) 80,250. *Exports f.o.b.*: Denmark 2,927, France 4,595, Federal Republic of Germany 9,506, Italy 2,552, Japan 5,675, Norway 1,742, Portugal 3,447, Spain 2,698, Switzerland 4,410, USSR 2,490, United Kingdom 16,631, USA 11,435; Total (incl. others) 80,072.

TRANSPORT

Road Traffic (registered motor vehicles at 31 December 1989): Passenger cars 124,237; Buses and coaches 1,322; Goods vehicles 12,152.

Shipping: *Merchant fleet* (registered vessels, 31 December 1989): Fishing vessels 966 (displacement 126,000 grt); Passenger ships, tankers and other vessels 146 (displacement 64,000 grt). *International freight traffic* ('000 metric tons, 1989): Goods loaded 953; Goods unloaded 1,723.

Civil Aviation (scheduled external Icelandic traffic, '000, 1989): Kilometres flown 12,084, Passenger-kilometres 1,472,000, Cargo ton-kilometres 29,582, Mail ton-kilometres 3,720.

TOURISM

Foreign Visitors By Country of Origin (1989): Denmark 16,159, France 8,187, Federal Republic of Germany 18,316, Norway 9,061, Sweden 16,430, United Kingdom 11,990, USA 22,952; Total (incl. others) 130,498.

COMMUNICATIONS MEDIA

Radio Receivers (1989): 85,000 licensed.

Television Receivers (1989): 79,000 licensed.

Telephones (1989): 125,000 in use.

Books (production, 1989): 1,242 titles (incl. new editions).

Daily Newspapers (1989): 6 (combined circulation 100,000 copies per issue).

EDUCATION

Institutions (1988): Pre-primary, primary and secondary (lower level) 211; Secondary (higher level) 54; Tertiary (universities and colleges) 4.

Teachers (incl. part-time, 1988): Pre-primary, primary and secondary (lower level) 3,200.

Students (1989): Pre-primary 4,400; Primary 25,500; Secondary (lower level) 12,400; Secondary (higher level) 16,700; Tertiary 5,400.

Directory

The Constitution

A new constitution came into force on 17 June 1944, when Iceland declared its full independence. The main provisions of the Constitution are summarized below:

GOVERNMENT

The President is elected for four years by universal suffrage. All those qualified to vote who have reached the age of 35 years are eligible for the Presidency.

Legislative power is jointly vested in the Althing and the President. Executive power is exercised by the President and other governmental authorities in accordance with the Constitution and other laws of the land.

The President summons the Althing every year and determines when the session shall close. The President may adjourn meetings of the Althing but not for more than two weeks nor more than once a year. The President appoints the Ministers and presides over the State Council. The President may be dismissed only if a resolution supported by three-quarters of the Althing is approved by a plebiscite.

The President may dissolve the Althing. Elections must be held within two months and the Althing must reassemble within eight months.

The Althing is composed of 63 members, elected by eight proportionately represented constituencies for a period of four years. Substitute members are elected at the same time and in the same manner as Althing members. The Althing is divided into two houses, the Upper House (efri deild) and the Lower House (nedri deild); but sometimes both Houses work together as a United Althing. The Upper House consists of 21 of the members, whom the United Althing chooses from among the representatives, the remaining 42 forming the Lower House. Each House and the United Althing elects its own Speaker. The minimum voting age, both for local administrative bodies and for the Althing is 18 years and all citizens domiciled in Iceland may vote, provided they are of unblemished character and financially responsible.

The budget must be introduced in the United Althing but other bills may be introduced into either House. They must, however, be given three readings in each house and be approved by a simple majority before they are submitted to the President. If the President disapproves a bill, it nevertheless becomes valid but must be submitted to a plebiscite. Ministers may speak in either House, but may vote only in that of which they are members. The Ministers are responsible to the Althing and may be impeached by that body, in which case they are tried by the Court of Impeachment.

LOCAL GOVERNMENT

For purposes of local government, the country is divided into Provinces, Districts and Municipalities. The eight Urban Municipalities are governed by Town Councils, which possess considerable autonomy. The Districts also have Councils and are further grouped together to form the Provinces, over each of which a centrally appointed Chief Official presides. The franchise for municipal purposes is universal above the age of 18 years, and elections are conducted on a basis of proportional representation.

The Government

HEAD OF STATE

President: VIGDÍS FINNBOGADÓTTIR (took office 1 August 1980; began a second term 1 August 1984; re-elected for a third term, beginning 1 August 1988).

THE CABINET
(January 1990)

A coalition of the Progressive Party (PP), the Social Democratic Party (SDP), the People's Alliance (PA) and the Citizens' Party (CP).

Prime Minister and Minister for Economic Planning: STEINGRÍMUR HERMANNSSON (PP).

Minister for Foreign Affairs and Foreign Trade: JÓN BALDVIN HANNIBALSSON (SDP).

Minister of Finance: ÓLAFUR RAGNAR GRÍMSSON (PA).

Minister of Fisheries: HALLDÓR ÁSGRÍMSSON (PP).

Minister of Agriculture and Communications: STEINGRÍMUR SIGFÚSSON (PA).

Minister of Commerce and Industry: JÓN SIGURÐSSON (SDP).

Minister of Education and Culture: SVAVAR GESTSSON (PA).

Minister of Health and Social Security: GUÐMUNDUR BJARNASON (PP).

Minister of Social Affairs: JÓHANNA SIGURÐARDÓTTIR (SDP).

Minister of the Environment and Nordic Co-operation: JÚLÍUS SÓLNES (CP).

Minister of Justice and Ecclesiastical Affairs: OLI TH. GUÐBARTSSON (CP).

MINISTRIES

Prime Minister's Office: Stjórnarrádshúsid v/Lkæjartorg, 150 Reykjavík; tel. (1) 25000.

Ministry of Agriculture: Raudarárstíg 25, 150 Reykjavík; tel. (1) 609000; fax (1) 21160.

Ministry of Commerce: Arnarhváli, 150 Reykjavík; tel. (1) 609070; telex 2092; fax (1) 621289.

ICELAND

Ministry of Communications: Hafnarhúsinu við Tryggvagötu, 150 Reykjavík; tel. (1) 621700; fax (1) 621702.

Ministry of Education and Culture: Hverfisgötu 6, 150 Reykjavík; tel. (1) 25000; telex 2111.

Ministry of the Environment: Sölvholsgötu 4, 150 Reykjavík; tel. (1) 609650; fax (1) 624566.

Ministry of Finance: Arnarhváli, 150 Reykjavík; tel. (1) 609200; telex 2092; fax (1) 28280.

Ministry of Fisheries: Skúlagata 4, 150 Reykjavík; tel. (1) 609670; telex 2342; fax (1) 621853.

Ministry for Foreign Affairs: Hverfisgötu 115, 150 Reykjavík; tel. (1) 623000; telex 2225.

Ministry of Health: Laugavegi 116, 150 Reykjavík; tel. (1) 609000; fax (1) 19165.

Ministry of Industry: Arnarhváli, 150 Reykjavík; tel. (1) 25000.

Ministry of Justice and Ecclesiastical Affairs: Arnarhváli, 150 Reykjavík; tel. (1) 609010; telex 2224; fax (1) 27340.

Ministry of Social Affairs: Hafnarhúsinu við Tryggvagötu, 150 Reykjavík; tel. (1) 25000; telex 3000.

President

Presidential Election, 25 June 1988

	% of Votes
Vigdís Finnbogadóttir	92.7
Sigrún Thorsteinsdóttir	5.3

Legislature

ALTHING

Speaker of the United Althing: Guðrún Helgadóttir (PA).
Speaker of the Upper House: Jón Helgason (PP).
Speaker of the Lower House: Kjartan Jóhansson (SDP).
Secretary-General (Clerk) of the Althing: Fridrik Olafsson.

General Election, 25 April 1987

	% of Votes	Seats
Independence Party	27.2	18
Progressive Party	18.9	13
Social Democratic Party	15.2	10
People's Alliance	13.3	9
Citizens' Party	10.9	7
Women's Alliance	10.1	6
Others	4.4	1*
Total	**100.0**	**63**

* Independent member elected with 1.2% of the total votes.

Political Organizations

Althýdubandalag (People's Alliance—PA): Laugavegur 3, 101 Reykjavík; tel. (1) 217500; fax (1) 317599; f. 1956 by amalgamation of a section of the Social Democratic Party and the Socialist Unity Party, reorganized as a socialist party 1968; Chair. Ólafur Ragnar Grímsson; Parliamentary Leader Margrét Frímannsdóttir; Gen. Sec. Kristján Valdimarsson.

Althýduflokkurinn (Social Democratic Party—SDP): Althýduhusid, Hverfisgata 8-10, Reykjavík; tel. (1) 29244; f. 1916 with a moderate socialist programme; Chair. Jón Baldvin Hannibalsson; Parliamentary Leader Eidur Gudnason.

Borgaraflokkurinn (Citizens' Party): Reykjavík; f. 1987; adheres to the ideology of the Independence Party but with emphasis on the needs and rights of the individual; Leader Júlíus Sólnes.

Framsóknarflokkurinn (Progressive Party—PP): POB 5331, 105 Reykjavík; tel. (1) 674580; fax (1) 674825; f. 1916 with a programme of social and economic amelioration and co-operation; Chair. Steingrímur Hermannsson; Parliamentary Leader Páll Pétursson; Sec. Gudmundur Bjarnason.

Samtök um Kvennalista (Women's Alliance): Laugavegi 17, Reykjavík; tel. (1) 13725; fax (1) 27560; f. 1983; a non-hierarchical feminist movement to promote the interests of women and children; parliamentary leadership rotates.

Sjálfstaedisflokkurinn (Independence Party—IP): Háaleitisbraut 1, Reykjavík; tel. (1) 82900; f. 1929 by an amalgamation of the Conservative and Liberal Parties; its programme is social reform within the framework of private enterprise and the furtherance of national and individual independence; Leader Thorsteinn Pálsson.

Diplomatic Representation

EMBASSIES IN ICELAND

China, People's Republic: Víðimelur 29, POB 580, Reykjavík; telex 2148; Chargé d'affaires: Zhai Shixiong.

Czechoslovakia: Smáragata 16, POB 1443, 101 Reykjavík; tel. (1) 19823; Chargé d'affaires a.i.: (vacant).

Denmark: Hverfisgata 29, 101 Reykjavík; tel. (1) 621230; telex 2008; fax (1) 623316; Ambassador: Villads Villadsen.

Finland: Tungata 30, 101 Reykjavík; telex 2373; fax (1) 623880; Ambassador: Håkan Branders.

France: Túngata 22, Reykjavík; tel. (1) 17621; telex 2063; Ambassador: Jacques Mer.

Germany: Túngata 18, POB 400, 101 Reykjavík; tel. (1) 19535; telex 2002; fax (1) 25699; Ambassador: Hans Hermann Haferkamp.

Norway: Fjólugata 17, Reykjavík; telex 2163; Ambassador: Per Aasen.

Sweden: Lágmúla 7, 108 Reykjavík; telex 2087; Ambassador: Per Olof Forshell.

USSR: Garðastræti 33, Reykjavík; telex 2200; Ambassador: Igor Nikolayevich Krasavin.

United Kingdom: Laufásvegur 49, POB 460, 121 Reykjavík; tel. (1) 15883; telex 2037; fax (1) 27940; Ambassador: Sir Richard Best.

USA: Laufásvegur 21, Reykjavík; tel. (1) 29100; telex 3044; fax (1) 29139; Ambassador: Charles E. Cobb, Jr.

Judicial System

All cases are heard in Ordinary Courts except those specifically within the jurisdiction of Special Courts. The Ordinary Courts include both a lower division of urban and rural district courts presided over by the district magistrates, and the Supreme Court.

Justices of the Supreme Court are appointed by the President and cannot be dismissed except by the decision of a court. The Justices elect the Chief Justice for a period of two years.

SUPREME COURT

Chief Justice: Guðrún Erlendsdóttir.

Justices: Benedikt Blöndal, Bjarni K. Bjarnason, Gúdmundur Jónsson, Haraldur Henrysson, Hrafn Bragason, Hjörtur Torfason, Thor Vilhjálmsson.

Religion

There is complete religious freedom in Iceland.

CHRISTIANITY

Protestant Churches

Tjodkirkja Islands: (Evangelical Lutheran Church of Iceland): Biskupsstofa, Sudurgata 22, 150 Reykjavík; tel. (1) 621500; telex 3014; the national Church, endowed by the State; more than 93% of the population are members; Iceland forms one diocese, Reykjavík, with two suffragan sees; 284 parishes and 126 pastors; Bishop Ólafur Skúlason.

Fríkirkjan í Reykjavík (The Congregational Church in Reykjavík): POB 1671, 121 Reykjavík; tel. (1) 14579; f. 1899; Free Lutheran denomination; 5,500 mems; Head Cecil Haraldsson.

Óhádi söfnudurinn (Independent Congregation): Reykjavík; Free Lutheran denomination; 1,100 mems; Head Rev. Thórsteinn Ragnarsson.

Seventh-day Adventists: Sudurhlid 36, 105 Reykjavík; tel. (1) 679260; fax (1) 689460.

The Roman Catholic Church

Iceland comprises a single diocese, directly responsible to the Holy See. At 31 December 1988 there were an estimated 2,400 adherents in the country.

Bishop of Reykjavík: Rt Rev. Alfred Jólsön, Hávallagötu 14, POB 489, 121 Reykjavík; tel. (1) 11423; fax (1) 623878.

ICELAND

The Press

PRINCIPAL DAILIES

Althýdubladid (The Labour Journal): Ármúli 36, Reykjavík; tel. (1) 681866; fax (1) 82019; f. 1919; organ of the Social Democratic Party; Editor INGOLFUR MARGEIRSSON; circ. 8,500.

DV (Dagbladid-Vísir): Thverholt 11, POB 5380, Reykjavík; tel. (1) 27022; fax (1) 27079; f. 1910; independent; Editors JÓNAS KRISTJÁNSSON, ELLERT B. SCHRAM; circ. 39,000.

Dagur (The Day): Strandgata 31, POB 58, Akureyri; f. 1918; organ of the Progressive Party; Editors ÁSKELL THÓRISSON, BRAGI BERGMANN; circ. 6,400.

Morgunbladid (Morning News): Adalstræi 6, POB 1555, Reykjavík; tel. (1) 691100; telex 2127; fax (1) 681811; f. 1913; Independent; Editors MATTHÍAS JOHANNESSEN, STYRMIR GUNNARSSON; circ. 50,000.

Thjódviljinn (Will of the Nation): Sídumúla 6, POB 8020, 108 Reykjavík; tel. (1) 681333; f. 1936; organ of socialism, labour movement and national independence; Editor ÁRNI BERGMANN; circ. 12,000.

Timinn (The Times): Lyngháḷsi 9, Box 370, Reykjavík; tel. (1) 686300; f. 1917; organ of the Progressive Party; Editors INDRIDI G. THORSTEINSSON, INGVAR GISLASON; circ. 15,000.

WEEKLIES

Althýdumadurinn (Commoner): Strandgata 9, Akureyri; f. 1931; weekly; organ of Social Democratic Party; Editor (vacant); circ. 3,500.

Einherji: Siglufjordur; weekly; organ of the Progressive Party.

Íslendingur-Isafold (Icelander-Icecountry): Kaupangi v/Mýrarveg, 600 Akureyri; tel. (6) 21500; f. 1915; for North and East Iceland; Editor STEFÁN SIGTRYGGSSON.

Siglfirdingur: Siglufjordur; weekly; organ of the Independence Party.

Skutull: Isafjördur; weekly; organ of the Social Democratic Party.

PERIODICALS

ABC: Ármúla 18, 108 Reykjavík; tel. (1) 82300; fax (1) 689982; f. 1979; 8 a year; children; Editor HILDUR GISLADÓTTIR; circ. 10,000.

Ægir (The Sea): c/o Fiskifélag Íslands, Reykjavík; f. 1905; published by the Fisheries Asssociation, Reykjavík; monthly; Editor FRIDRIK FRIDRIKSSON; circ. 2,500.

Æskan (The Youth): POB 523, 121 Reykjavík; tel. (1) 10248; f. 1897; 10 a year; children's magazine; Editor KARL HELGASON.

Áfangar: Ármúla 18, 108 Reykjavík; tel. (1) 82300; f. 1979; quarterly; nature and travel; Editor VALTHÓR HLÖDVERSSON; circ. 8,000.

Atlantica: Höfdabakki 9, POB 8576, 128 Reykjavík 112; tel. (1) 84966; telex 2121; fax (1) 674066; 5 a year; in-flight magazine of Icelandair; Editor HARALDUR J. HAMAR.

Bíllinn: Ármúla 18, 108 Reykjavík; tel. (1) 82300; fax (1) 689982; f. 1982; 6 a year; cars and motorsport; Editor LEÓ M. JÓNSSON; circ. 10,000.

Bóndinn: Ármúla 18, 108 Reykjavík; tel. (1) 82300; fax (1) 689982; agriculture and farming; Editor LEÓ M. JÓNSSON; circ. 5,000.

Economic Statistics: Central Bank of Iceland, 150 Reykjavík; f. 1980; quarterly; published by the Economic Department of the Central Bank.

Eidfaxi: Ármúla 38, 108 Reykjavík; tel. (1) 685316; fax (1) 82019; monthly; horse-breeding and horsemanship; Editor ERLINGUR A. JÓNSSON; circ. 4,700.

Eimreidin (Progress): Sídumúli 12, Reykjavík; f. 1895; quarterly; literary and critical review.

Farvís (Travel-wise): Bolholti 4, 105 Reykjavík; tel. (1) 680699; fax (1) 76390; f. 1988; 3 or 4 a year; travel; Editor THORUNN GESTDÓTTIR.

Fiskifréttir: Bildshofda 18, 112 Reykjavík; tel. (1) 685380; fax (1) 689982; f. 1983; weekly; fishing; Editor GUDJÓN EINARSSON; circ. 6,000.

Freyr: POB 7080, 127 Reykjavík; tel. (1) 19200; fax (1) 628290; f. 1904; fortnightly; organ of the Icelandic Agriculture Society and the Farmers' Union; Editors MATTHÍAS EGGERTSSON, JÚLÍUS DANIELSSON; circ. 3,700.

Frjáls verzlun (Free Trade): Ármúla 18, POB 1193, 108 Reykjavík; tel. (1) 82300; f. 1939; monthly; business magazine; Editor HELGI MAGNÚSSON; circ. 8,500.

Gestgjafinn: Ármúla 18, 108 Reykjavík; tel. (1) 82300; fax (1) 689982; quarterly; food and drink; Editor IRIS ERLINGSDÓTTIR; circ. 12,000.

Gródur and Gardar: Ármúla 18, 108 Reykjavík; tel. (1) 82300; fax (1) 689982; f. 1984; 2 a year; gardening; Editor EIRIKUR EIRIKSSON; circ. 6000.

Hagtídindi: published by the Statistical Bureau of Iceland, Skuggasund 3, 150 Reykjavík; tel. (1) 609800; fax (1) 628865; f. 1914; monthly; Dir-Gen. HALLGRÍMUR SNORRASON.

Hár og fegurd (Hair and Beauty Magazine): Skúlagata 54, 105 Reykjavík; tel. (1) 628141; telex 3000; fax (1) 637059; f. 1980; 3 a year; hair, beauty, fashion; Editor PÉTUR MELSTED.

Heima Er Bezt: Tryggvabraut 18–20, Akureyri; tel. (6) 22500; fax (6) 2625; f. 1951; monthly; literary; Editor BOLLI GÚSTAFSSON; circ. 3,500.

Hús og híbýli: Háaleitisbraut 1, Reykjavík; tel. (1) 83122; fax (1) 680102; 6 a year; architecture, family and homes; Editor THÓRARINN J. MAGNÚSSON; circ. 15,000.

Húsfreyjan (The Housewife): Túngata 14, Reykjavík; tel. (1) 17044; f. 1950; quarterly; the organ of the Federation of Icelandic Women's Societies; Editor GRÉTA E. PÁLSDÓTTIR; circ. 5,400.

Iceland Review: Höfdabakki 9, POB 8576, 128 Reykjavík; tel. (1) 84966; telex 2121; fax (1) 674066; f. 1963; 4 a year; English; general; Editor HARALDUR J. HAMAR.

Ithróttabladid: Ármúla 18, 108 Reykjavík; tel. (1) 82300; fax (1) 689982; f. 1939; 6 a year; sport; Editor THORGRÍMUR THRÁINSSON; circ. 7,000.

Mannlif: Ármúla 18, 108 Reykjavík; tel. (1) 82300; fax (1) 689982; general interest; Editor ÁRNI THÓRARINSSON; circ. 17,000.

News from Iceland: Höfdabakki 9, POB 8576, 128 Reykjavík; tel. (1) 84966; telex 2121; fax (1) 674066; f. 1975; monthly; English; Editor HARALDUR J. HAMAR.

Nýtt Líf: Ármúla 18, 108 Reykjavík; tel. (1) 82300; fax (1) 689982; f. 1978; 8 a year; fashion; Editor GULLVEIG SÆMUNDSDÓTTIR; circ. 17,000.

Pressan (The Press): Ármúla 36, Reykjavík; tel. (1) 681866; fax (1) 82019; f. 1988; weekly; Editors GUNNAR SMÁRI EGILSSON, KRISTJÁN THORVALDSSON; circ. 20,000.

Rjettur: Reykjavík; monthly; left-wing magazine on politics and social problems; Editor EINAR OLGEIRSSON.

Samúel: Háaleitisbraut 1, 105 Reykjavík; tel. (1) 83122; fax (1) 680102; f. 1968; monthly; entertainment, sport and cars; Editor THÓRARINN J. MAGNÚSSON; circ. 12,700.

Sjávarfréttir: Ármúla 18, 108 Reykjavík; tel. (1) 685380; fax (1) 689982; f. 1973; quarterly; fishing and fishing-industry; Editor GUDJÓN EINARSSON; circ. 5,500.

Sjónvarpsvísir Stödvar 2: Ármúla 18, 108 Reykjavík; tel. (1) 82300; fax (1) 689982; f. 1987; monthly; Editor KJARTAN STEFÁNSSON; circ. 49,000.

Úrval (Digest): Thverholti 11, Reykjavík; tel. (1) 27022; fax (1) 27079; f. 1942; monthly; Editor SIGURDUR HREIDAR HREIDARSSON; circ. 6,500.

A veidum: Ármúla 18, 108 Reykjavík; tel. (1) 82300; fax (1) 689982; f. 1984; 2 a year; fishing and shooting; Editor EIRIKUR S. EIRÍKSSON; circ. 6,000.

Vid sem fljúgum: Ármúla 18 108 Reykjavík; tel. (1) 82300; fax (1) 689982; f. 1980; monthly; Icelandair in-flight magazine; Editor RAGNHEIDUR DAVIDSDÓTTIR; circ. 7,000.

Vikan (The Week): Háaleitisbraut 1, Reykjavík; tel. (1) 83122; fax (1) 680102; f. 1938; every 2 weeks; illustrated; Editor THÓRARINN J. MAGNÚSSON; circ. 13,500.

Víkingur (Seaman): Borgartúni 18, Reykjavík; 10 a year; Editor SIGURJÓN VALDIMARSSON.

Vinnan (Work): Grensásvegur 16, 108 Reykjavík; tel. (1) 83044; fax (1) 680093; monthly; f. 1943; publ. by Icelandic Federation of Labour; Editor SVERRIR ALBERTSSON; circ. 7,000.

NEWS AGENCIES

Foreign Bureaux

Agence France-Presse (AFP): Gardastraeti 13, 101 Reykjavík; tel. (1) 10586; Correspondent GÉRARD LEMARQUIS.

United Press International (UPI) (USA): Reykjavík; tel. (1) 84996; telex 2121; Correspondent BERNARD SCUDDER.

Publishers

Akranesútgáfan: Deildartúni 8, Akranes.

Almenna Bókafélagid: Austurstræti 18, Reykjavík; tel. (1) 25544; f. 1955; general; book club editions; Man. Dir KRISTJÁN JOHANNSSON.

ICELAND

Bókaforlag Odds Björnssonar: POB 558, Tryggvabraut 18–20, 600 Akureyri; tel. (6) 22500; f. 1897; general; Dir GEIR S. BJÖRNSSON.

Bókaútgáfa Æskunnar: POB 523, 121 Reykjavík; tel. (1) 10248.

Bókaútgáfa Gudjóns O. Gudjónssonar: Thverholti 13, Reykjavík; tel. (1) 27233.

Bókaútgáfan Björk: Háholti 7, Akranes; Man. DANIEL AGÚSTÍNUSSON.

Bókaútgáfan Hildur: Reykhólasveit 380, Króksfjarðarnes; tel. (3) 47757; Man. JON A. GUÐMUNDSSON.

Bókaútgáfan Hlidskjálf: Ingólfsstraeti 22, 101 Reykjavík; tel. (1) 17520.

Bókaverslun Sigfúsar Eymundssonar: Austurstræti 18, POB 340, 121 Reykjavík; tel. (1) 14255; fax (1) 13199; f. 1872; educational and general, import and export of books, maps of Iceland; Man. ÓLI BJÖRN KÁRASON.

Fjölvi: Hjallalandi 28, Reykjavík.

Forni: Kleppsvegi 4, 105 Reykjavík.

Fródi, hf: Ármúla 21, Reykjavík; Man. GISSUR EGGERTSSON.

Heimskringla: Laugavegi 18, Reykjavík, POB 392; tel. (1) 15199; telex 2265; f. 1932; Man. ARNI EINARSSON.

Hid íslenzka bókmenntafélag: Siðumúli, POB 8935, 128 Reykjavík, POB 1252; tel. (1) 679060; f. 1816; general; Pres. SIGURDUR LÍNDAL.

Hörpuútgáfan: Stekkjarholt 8-10, POB 25, 300 Akranes; Dir BRAGI THORDARSON.

Idunn: Bræðraborgarstígur 16, POB 294, 121 Reykjavík; tel. (1) 28555; telex 2308; fax (1) 28380; general; f. 1945; Man. Dir JÓN KARLSSON.

  Hladbud, hf: Bræðraborgarstígur 16, POB 294, 121 Reykjavík; tel. (1) 28555; telex 2308; f. 1944; mainly school books; Dir JÓN KARLSSON.

Ísafoldarprentsmidja, hf: Thingholtsstræti 5, POB 455, 121 Reykjavík; tel. (1) 17165; fax (1) 17226; f. 1877; Chair. and Gen. Man. LEÓ E. LÖVE.

Íslenzka Fornritafélag, Hid: Austurstræti 18, Reykjavík; f. 1928; Pres. J. NORDAL.

Jonsonn & Co (The English Bookshop): Hafnarstr 4/9, POB 1131, Reykjavík 101; tel. (1) 13133; f. 1927; general; Man. Dir BENEDIKT KRISTJÁNSSON.

Kynning: POB 1238, Reykjavík; tel. (1) 38456; f. 1966; natural science, books on Iceland, art, history; Man. H. HANNESSON.

Leiftur, hf: Höfðatúni 12, Reykjavík; tel. (1) 17554; Man. HJÖRTUR THORDARSON.

LITBRÁ-Offset: Höfðatúni 12, POB 999, 121 Reykjavík; tel. (1) 22930; fax (1) 622935.

Ljódhus Ltd: Laufásvegi 4, POB 1506, Reykjavík; Man. SIGFÚS DAÐASON.

Mál og Menning (Literary Book Club): Laugavegi 18, Reykjavík; tel. (1) 15199; telex 2265; f. 1937; 4,600 mems; Chair. THORLEIFUR EINARSSON; Man. ARNI EINARSSON; Editor HALLDOR GUÐMUNDSSON.

Menningarsjóður og Thjódvinafélag: Skálholtsstíg 7, POB 1398, Reykjavík; tel. (1) 621822; f. 1940; publishing dept of Cultural Fund; Dir EINAR LAXNESS.

Námsgagnastofnun (National Centre for Educational Materials): POB 5192, Reykjavík 125; tel. (1) 28088; telex 3000; fax (1) 624139; f. 1979; Dir (Publishing House) ASGEIR GUÐMUNDSSON.

Örn og Örlygur, hf: Síðumúli 11, 108 Reykjavík; tel. (1) 84866; telex 2197; fax 83995; f. 1966; general; book club editions; Owner and Man. Dir ÖRLYGUR HÁLFDANARSON.

Prenthusid: Barónsstíg 11B, Reykjavík.

Prentsmidja Árna Valdimarssonar: Brautarholti 16, Reykjavík.

Prentsmidjan Oddi, hf: Höfðabakka 7, POB 1305, 121 Reykjavík.

Rökkur: Flókagötu 15, Reykjavík; tel. (1) 18768.

Setberg: Freyjugatu 14, POB 619, 121 Reykjavík; tel. (1) 17667; telex 3000; fiction, cookery, juvenile and children's books; Dir ARNBJÖRN KRISTINSSON.

Siglufjardardrentsmidja: Suðurgötu 16, Siglufirði.

Skjaldborg Ltd: Ármúla 23, POB 8427, 128 Reykjavík; tel. (1) 672400.

Skuggsjá: Strandgötu 31, 222 Hafnarfjörður; tel. (01) 50045; general fiction; Dirs JÓHANNES OLIVERSSON, LILJA OLIVERSDÓTTIR.

Snaefell; Álfaskeiði 58, 220 Hafnarfirði; Man. THORKELL JOHANNESSON.

Stafafell: Laugavegi 1, Reykjavík; Man. MAGNÚS DANÍELSSON.

Steindórsprent, hf: Ármúla 5, POB 8495, 128 Reykjavík; tel. (1) 685200; fax (1) 678115.

Sudri: Kleppsvegi 2, 105 Reykjavík; tel. (1) 36384; Man. GUDJÓN ELÍASSON.

Thjódsaga: Thingholtsstræti 27, POB 147, 121 Reykjavík; tel. (1) 13510; fax (1) 627576; f. 1954; Icelandic folklore and history; Dir HAFSTEINN GUÐMUNDSSON.

Vaka-Helgafell Inc: Síðumúla 6, 108 Reykjavík; tel. (1) 688300; telex 3190; fax (1) 689733; general reference, non-fiction; Dir ÓLAFUR RAGNARSSON.

Vikingsútgáfan: Veghúsastíg 7, Reykjavík; Dir RAGNAR JONSSON.

Vikurútgáfan: Kleppsvegi 2, Reykjavík.

PUBLISHERS' ASSOCIATION

Félag íslenskra bókaútgefenda: Suðurlandsbraut 4A, 108 Reykjavík; tel. (1) 38020; fax (1) 678668; Pres. JÓN KARLSSON; Man. HEIMIR PÁLSSON.

Radio and Television

In 1989 there were some 155,000 radio receivers in use and 79,000 television receivers licensed.

Ríkisútvarpið (Icelandic National Broadcasting Service): Broadcasting Centre, Efstaleiti 1, 150 Reykjavík; tel. (1) 693000; telex 2066; fax (1) 693010; f. 1930; Dir-Gen. MARKÚS ÖRN ANTONSSON; Chair. of Programme Board INGA JÓNA THORDARDÓTTIR.

RADIO

Ríkisútvarpið: Radio Division, Efstaleiti 1, 150 Reykjavík; tel. (1) 693000; telex 2066; fax (1) 693010; f. 1930; Dir of Radio ELFA-BJÖRK GUNNARSDÓTTIR.

  Programme 1 has two long wave, 8 medium wave and 65 FM transmitters broadcasting 127 hours a week; Head MARGRÉT ODDSDÓTTIR.

  Programme 2 has 45 FM transmitters broadcasting 168 hours a week; Head STEFÁN JÓN HAFSTEIN.

Radio Bylgjan: Snorrabraut 54, 105 Reykjavík; privately-owned.

TELEVISION

Rikisútvarpið–Sjónvarp (Icelandic National Broadcasting Service —Television): Laugavegur 176, 105 Reykjavík; tel. (1) 693900; telex 2035; fax (1) 693988; f. 1966; covers 99% of the population; broadcasts daily, total 46 hours a week; Dir of Television PÉTUR GUÐFINNSSON.

Stöð 2: Krókhálsi 6, 110 Reykjavík; privately-owned.

The US Navy operates a radio station (24 hours a day), and a television service (80 hours a week), on the NATO base at Keflavík.

Finance

(cap. = capital; p.u. = paid up; res = reserves; dep. = deposits; m. = million; kr = krónur; brs = branches)

BANKING
Central Bank

Seðlabanki Íslands (Central Bank of Iceland): Kalkofnsvegur 1, 150 Reykjavík; tel. (1) 699600; telex 2020; f. 1961 to take over central banking activities of Landsbanki Íslands; cap. 1m. kr, res 3,418m. kr, dep. 18,281m. kr (1986); Govs Dr JÓHANNES NORDAL, TÓMAS ARNASON.

Commercial Banks

Búnaðarbanki Íslands (Agricultural Bank of Iceland): Austurstræti 5, 155 Reykjavík; tel. (1) 25600; telex 2383; fax (1) 621340; f. 1929; independent state-owned bank; res 2,417m. kr, dep. 21,741m. kr (1989); Chair. GUDNI AGUSTSSON; Man. Dirs STEFÁN PÁLSSON, JÓN ADOLF GUÐJONSSON, SOLON R. SIGURDSSON; 34 brs.

Íslandsbanki HF (National Bank of Iceland): Kringlunni 7, 155 Reykjavík; tel. (1) 608000; fax (1) 678711; f. 1990 by merger of Althýðubankinn hf, Iðnaðarbanki Íslands hf and Verslunarbanki Íslands with Landsbanki Íslands; Gen. Mans VALUR VALSSON, BJÖRN BJÖRNSSON, TRYGGVI PÁLSSON.

Samvinnubanki Íslands hf (Co-operative Bank of Iceland Ltd): Bankastræti 7, 101 Reykjavík; tel. (1) 20700; telex 3142; fax (1) 24989; f. 1962; cap. and res 587m. kr, dep. 589m. kr; Gen. Man. GEIR MAGNÚSSON; 22 brs.

INSURANCE

Tryggingastofnun Ríkisins (State Social Security Institution): Laugavegi 114, 150 Reykjavík; tel. (1) 604400; fax (1) 624535; f.

ICELAND

1936; Man. Dir EGGERT G. THORSTEINSSON; Chair. of Tryggingaráđ (Social Security Board) BOLLI HÉĐINSSON.

Private Companies

Iceland Insurance Co Ltd: Ármúla 3, 108 Reykjavík; tel. (1) 605060; telex 2103; fax (1) 605100; f. 1989; Chair. INGI R. HELGASON; Man. Dir AXEL GÍSLASON.

Íslenzk Endurtrygging (National Icelandic Reinsurance Co): Suđurlandsbraut 6, 108 Reykjavík; tel. (1) 681444; telex 2153; fax (1) 681282; f. 1939; cap. 60.2m. kr (1987); Gen. Man. BJARNI THORDARSON.

Líftryggingafélagiđ Andvaka (Andvaka Mutual Life Insurance Co): Ármúla 3, 108 Reykjavík; tel. (1) 605060; telex 2103; fax (1) 605100; f. 1949; Man. Dir AXEL GÍSLASON.

Samábyrgđ Íslands á fiskiskipum (Icelandic Mutual Fishing Craft Insurance): Lágmúli 9, 108 Reykjavík; tel. (1) 681400; telex 3163; fax (1) 84645; f. 1909; Man. Dir PÁLL SIGURDSSON.

Sjóvá-Almennar tryggingar hf (Iceland Marine Insurance Co): Kringlan 5, POB 3200, 123 Reykjavík; tel. (1) 692500; telex 2051; fax (1) 83718; f. 1988; share cap. 175m. kr (1989), res 3,858m. kr (1989); Chair. BENEDIKT SVEINSSON; Gen. Mans EINAR SVEINSSON, ÓLAFUR B. THORS.

Trade and Industry

CHAMBER OF COMMERCE

Verzlunarráđ Íslands (Chamber of Commerce); Hús verslunarinnar, 103 Reykjavík; tel. (1) 83088; telex 2316; fax (1) 686564; f. 1917; Chair. JÓHANN J. ÓLAFSSON; Gen. Sec. VILHJÁLMUR EGILSSON; 500 mems.

EMPLOYERS' ORGANIZATIONS

Federation of Icelandic Industries: POB 1407, 121 Reykjavík; tel. (1) 27577; fax (1) 25380; f. 1933; Chair. VIGLUNDUR THORSTEINSSON; Gen. Man. OLAFUR DAVIDSSON; 300 mems.

Vinnuveitendasamband Íslands (Employers' Federation): Garđastræti 41, POB 514, 121 Reykjavík; tel. (1) 25455; fax (1) 28421; f. 1934; Chair. E. O. KRISTJANSSON; Man. Dir THORARINN V. THORARINSSON.

FISHING INDUSTRY ASSOCIATIONS

Félag Íslenzkra Botnvörpuskipæigenda (Steam Trawler Owners' Association): Hafnarhuoll, Tryggvagötu, Reykjavík; tel. (1) 29500; telex 2090; f. 1916; Chair. THORHALLUR HELGASON; Sec.-Gen. ÁGÚST EINARSSON.

Fiskifélag Íslands (Fisheries Association): Reykjavík; f. 1911; conducts technical and economic research and services for fishing vessels; performs various functions for the fishing industry in accordance with Icelandic law or by arrangement with the Ministry of Fisheries; Man. THORSTEINN GISLASON.

Fiskveiđasjódur Íslands (Fisheries Loan Fund of Iceland): Suđurlandsbraut 4, 155 Reykjavík; tel. (1) 679100; fax (1) 689588; f. 1905; lends money for construction and purchase of fishing vessels, equipment and plant; financed by interest charges; loans granted 3,838m. kr (1989); Chair. BJÖRGVIN VILMUNDARSON; Gen. Man. MÁR ELÍSSON.

Landssamband Íslenzkra Utvegsmanna (Fishing Vessel Owners' Federation): POB 893, Reykjavík; f. 1939; Chair. K. RAGNARSSON; Man. KRISTJAN RAGNARSSON.

Sölusamband Íslenzkra Fiskframleidenda (Union of Icelandic Fish Producers): Adalstræti 6, POB 889, 121 Reykjavík; tel. (1) 11480; telex 2041; Dir MAGNÚS GUNNARSSON.

CO-OPERATIVE ASSOCIATION

Samband Íslenskra Samvinnufélaga (Federation of Icelandic Co-operative Societies): Samband House, 105 Reykjavík; tel. (1) 698100; telex 2023; fax (1) 678314; f. 1902; links 34 co-operative societies; Chair. SIGURDUR MARKUSSON; Dir-Gen. GUĐJÓN B. ÓLAFSSON; 44,895 mems.

TRADE UNIONS

Althýdusamband Íslands (ASÍ) (Icelandic Federation of Labour): Grensásveg 16A, 108 Reykjavík; fax (1) 680093; f. 1916; affiliated to ICFTU; Pres. ÁSMUNDUR STEFÁNSSON; 62,390 mems.

Menningar- og Fræđslusamband Althýdu (MFA) (Workers' Educational Association): Grensásveg 16A, 108 Reykjavík; Chair. KARL STEINAR GUĐNASON; Gen. Sec. TRYGGVI THÓR AĐALSTEINSSON.

Bandalag Starfsmanna Ríkis og Bæja (BSRB) (Municipal and Government Employees' Association): Grettisgötu 89, 105 Reykjavík; tel. (1) 626688; fax (1) 629106; f. 1942; Chair. ÖGMUNDUR JÓNASSON; 16,855 mems.

Bladamannafélag Íslands (Union of Icelandic Journalists): Síđumúla 23, Reykjavík; tel. (1) 39155; fax (1) 39177; f. 1897; Chair. LUDVÍK GEIRSSON; Sec. FRÍDA BJÖRNSDOTTIR; 400 mems.

Landssamband Idnadármanna (Federation of Icelandic Crafts and Industries): Hallveigarstigur 1, Reykjavík; tel. (1) 621590; fax (1) 12742; f. 1932; non-party; Chair. HARALDUR SUMARLIDASON; Gen. Sec. THÓRLEIFUR JÓNSSON; 3,200 mems.

Transport

RAILWAYS

There are no railways in Iceland.

ROADS

Much of the interior is uninhabited and the main road follows the coastline. Regular motor coach services link the main settlements. Development plans provide for new roads and harbour installations. At 31 December 1989 Iceland had 11,380 km of roads, of which 3,801 km were main roads.

Félag Sérleyfishafa (Icelandic Bus Routes Union): BSI bus terminal, Umferđarmiđstöđinni, Vatnsmýrarveg 10, 101 Reykjavík; tel. (1) 22300; telex 3082; fax (1) 29973; f. 1936; scheduled bus services throughout Iceland; also operates sightseeing tours and excursions; Chair. ÁGÚST HAFBERG.

SHIPPING

Heavy freight is carried by coastal shipping. The principal seaport for international shipping is Reykjavík.

Eimskip (Iceland Steamship Co): POB 220, Pósthússtræti 2, 101 Reykjavík; tel. (1) 697100; telex 2022; fax (1) 28216; f. 1914 as Eimskipafélag Íslands; transportation service incl. liner trade, general and bulk cargo between Iceland and the UK, Scandinavia, the Continent, the Baltic and the USA; also operates coastal services, warehousing and stevedores; Man. Dir HÖRĐUR SIGURGESTSSON; 13 vessels totalling 40,727 grt.

Nesskip hf: Nesskip's House, Austurstrond 1, 170 Seltjarnarnes; tel. (1) 625055; telex 2256; f. 1974; all shipping services; Chair. B. SVEINSSON; Man. Dir G. ASGEIRSSON; 7 vessels totalling 35,000 dwt (1988).

Skipaútgerd Ríkisins (Icelandic Shipping Dept): Hafnarhúsinu V, Tryggvagötu, Reykjavík 101; tel. (1) 28822; telex 3008; f. 1930; passenger and freight service round Iceland all the year; Gen. Man. GUĐMUNDUR EINARSSON.

Samband Íslenskra Samvinnufélaga (Samband Line): POB 1480, Kirkjusandur Samband House, 105 Reykjavík; tel. (1) 698300; telex 2101; fax (1) 678151; Iceland-Europe-USA-Far East; Dir OMAR JOHANNSSON; 8 cargo vessels, 1 tanker.

CIVIL AVIATION

Air transport is particularly important to Iceland and is used, for example, to transport agricultural produce from remote districts. There are regular air services between Reykjavík and outlying townships. There is an international airport at Keflavík, 47 km from Reykjavík.

Eagle Air (Arnarflug): POB 1046, Lágmúli 7, 108 Reykjavík; tel. (1) 29511; telex 2183; fax (1) 83575; f. 1976; privately owned, approx. 25 shareholders; internal network to 11 domestic airfields; external service to Amsterdam, Hamburg, Milan and Zürich; Chair. of Board HORDUR EINARSSON; Man. Dir KRISTINN SIGTRYGGSSON; fleet of 1 Piper Chieftain, 1 Boeing 737-200, 2 Cessna 402C, 1 Twin Otter; 1 Dornier DO-228 on order.

Icelandair (Flugleidir hf): Reykjavík Airport, 101 Reykjavík; tel. (1) 690100; telex 2021; fax (1) 690391; f. 1973 as the holding company for the two principal Icelandic airlines Flugfélag Íslands (f. 1937)

ICELAND

and Loftleidir (f. 1944); in 1979 all licences, permits and authorizations previously held by Flugfélag Íslands and Loftleidir were transferred to it; network centred in Reykjavík, to 10 domestic airfields, and scheduled external services to Sweden, Norway, Denmark, the United Kingdom, Germany, France, Luxembourg; the USA, Greenland and the Faroe Islands, and summer flights to Austria and Switzerland; Pres. and CEO Sigurður Helgason; fleet of 2 Boeing 757, 3 Boeing 737-400, 5 Fokker F27-200, 1 Boeing 737-400; 3 Fokker 50s on order.

Tourism

Iceland's main attraction for tourists lies in the ruggedness of the interior, with its geysers and thermal springs. In 1989 there were approximately 130,500 tourist arrivals, and receipts reached 9,373m. krónur.

Iceland Tourist Board: Laugavegur 3, 101 Reykjavík; tel. (1) 27488; telex 2248; fax (1) 624749; Gen. Man. Birgir Thorgilsson.

INDIA

Introductory Survey

Location, Climate, Language, Religion, Flag, Capital

The Republic of India forms a natural sub-continent, with the Himalaya mountain range to the north. Two sections of the Indian Ocean—the Arabian Sea and the Bay of Bengal—lie to the west and east, respectively. India's neighbours are the People's Republic of China, Bhutan and Nepal to the north, Pakistan to the north-west and Myanmar (formerly Burma) to the north-east, while Bangladesh is surrounded by Indian territory except for a short frontier with Myanmar in the east. Near India's southern tip, across the Palk Strait, is Sri Lanka. India's climate ranges from temperate to tropical, with an average summer temperature on the plains of approximately 27°C (85°F). Annual rainfall varies widely, but the summer monsoon brings heavy rain over much of the country in June and July. The official language is Hindi, spoken by about 30% of the population. English is used as an associate language for many official purposes. The Indian Constitution also recognizes 16 regional languages, of which the most widely spoken are Telugu, Bengali, Marathi, Tamil, Urdu and Gujarati. Many other local languages are also used. According to the 1981 census, about 80% of the population are Hindus and 11% Muslims. There are also Christians, Sikhs, Buddhists, Jains and other minorities. The national flag (proportions 3 by 2) has three equal horizontal stripes, of saffron, white and green, with the Dharma Chakra (Wheel of the Law), in blue, in the centre of the white stripe. The capital is New Delhi.

Recent History

After a prolonged struggle against British colonial rule, India became independent, within the Commonwealth, on 15 August 1947. The United Kingdom's Indian Empire was partitioned, broadly on a religious basis, between India and Pakistan (then in two sections, of which the eastern wing became Bangladesh in 1971). The principal nationalist movement opposing British rule was the Indian National Congress (later known as the Congress Party). At independence the Congress leader, Jawaharlal Nehru, became India's first Prime Minister. Sectarian violence, the movement of 12m. refugees, the integration of the former princely states into the Indian federal structure and a dispute with Pakistan over Kashmir presented major problems.

India became independent as a dominion, with the British monarch as Head of State, represented locally by an appointed Governor-General. In November 1949, however, the Constituent Assembly approved a republican constitution, providing for a President (with mainly ceremonial functions) to be Head of State. Accordingly, India became a republic on 26 January 1950, although remaining a member of the Commonwealth. France transferred sovereignty of Chandernagore to India in May 1950, and ceded its four remaining Indian settlements in 1954.

The lack of effective opposition to Congress policies expedited industrialization and social reform. In December 1961 Indian forces overran the Portuguese territories of Goa, Daman and Diu, which were immediately annexed by India. Border disputes with the People's Republic of China escalated into a brief military conflict in October 1962. Nehru died in May 1964 and was succeeded by Lal Bahadur Shastri, a former Minister of Home Affairs. India and Pakistan fought a second war over Kashmir in August–September 1965. Following mediation by the USSR, Shastri and President Ayub Khan of Pakistan signed a joint declaration, aimed at a peaceful settlement of the Kashmir dispute, on 10 January 1966. Shastri died on the following day, however, and Nehru's daughter, Mrs Indira Gandhi, formerly Minister of Information and Broadcasting, became Prime Minister. The Congress Party's majority was reduced at the 1967 general election.

Following the presidential election of August 1969, when two factions of Congress supported different candidates, the success of Indira Gandhi's candidate split the party. The Organization (Opposition) Congress, led by Morarji Desai, a former Deputy Prime Minister, emerged in November, but at the next general election to the lower house of the legislature, the Lok Sabha (House of the People), held in March 1971, Indira Gandhi's wing of Congress won 350 of the 515 elective seats where polling took place.

Border incidents led to a 12-day war with Pakistan in December 1971. The Indian army rapidly occupied East Pakistan, which India recognized as the independent state of Bangladesh. Indira Gandhi and President Zulfiqar Ali Bhutto of Pakistan held a 'summit' conference at Simla, India, in June–July 1972, when the two leaders agreed that their respective forces should respect the cease-fire line in Kashmir, and that India and Pakistan should resolve their differences through bilateral negotiations or other peaceful means. In 1975 the former protectorate of Sikkim became the 22nd state of the Indian Union, leading to tensions in India's relations with Nepal.

In June 1975 the Allahabad High Court found Indira Gandhi guilty of instigating electoral malpractice in 1971, and barred her from holding elective office for six years. She then declared a state of emergency, and arrested more than 900 political opponents. In November 1975 the Supreme Court declared her to be innocent of electoral malpractice. A general election to the Lok Sabha was held in March 1977, when the number of elective seats was increased to 542. The election resulted in victory for the Janata (People's) Party, chaired by Morarji Desai, who became Prime Minister. The Janata Party and an allied party, the Congress for Democracy, together received 43.2% of the total votes and won 298 of the 540 seats where polling took place. Congress received 34.5% of the votes and won 153 seats.

In January 1978 Indira Gandhi became leader of a new political group, the Congress (Indira) Party, known as Congress (I). A commission of inquiry, investigating the alleged excesses of her regime, found her guilty of corruption. In June Charan Singh, the Home Minister, and Raj Narain, the Health Minister, were dismissed for their criticism of Desai's Government. In November Indira Gandhi was elected to the Lok Sabha, but the House found her guilty of breach of privilege during the emergency rule, and she was expelled from the Lok Sabha.

In January 1979 Charan Singh returned to the Government as Minister of Finance and Desai's deputy. The Government's ineffectual approach to domestic problems provoked a wave of defections by Lok Sabha members of the Janata Party. Many joined Narain, who formed a new party, the Lok Dal, based on secularism. Congress (I) lost its position as official opposition party after defections from its ranks to the then official Congress party by members who objected to Indira Gandhi's authoritarianism. The resignation of Desai's Government in July was followed by the resignation from the party of Charan Singh, who became the leader of the Lok Dal and, shortly afterwards, Prime Minister in a coalition with both Congress parties. When Congress (I) withdrew its support in August, Singh's 24-day administration collapsed, and Parliament was dissolved. A general election to the Lok Sabha was held in January 1980, when polling took place in 525 of the 542 elective seats. Two more seats were decided in February. Altogether, Congress (I) received 42.7% of the total votes but won an overwhelming majority (352) of the elective seats. The Janata Party, with 18.9% of the votes, won only 31 seats, while the Lok Dal (9.4%) won 41 seats. Indira Gandhi was reinstated as Prime Minister. Presidential rule was imposed in nine states, ruled by opposition parties, in February. At state elections in June, Congress (I) gained majorities in eight of these nine states.

By-elections in June 1981 for the Lok Sabha and state assemblies were notable because of the landslide victory which Rajiv Gandhi, the Prime Minister's son and a former airline pilot, obtained in the former constituency of his late brother, Sanjay (who had been killed in an air crash in June 1980) and because of the failure of the fragmented Janata Party to win any seats. In January 1982 Indira Gandhi reshuffled the Council of Ministers, appointing a new Minister of Defence, a portfolio that she had previously held. In September there was a major reshuffle when Indira Gandhi appointed eight new ministers.

In February 1983 Rajiv Gandhi became a General Secretary of Congress (I).

Indira Gandhi's Government faced serious problems, as disturbances in several states, particularly in Assam, continued in 1982 and 1983, with violent protests against the presence of Bengali immigrants. Presidential rule in Assam was replaced by a Congress (I) government in February 1982, in an effort to quell dissent. To avert a constitutional crisis, further elections were held in Assam (and Meghalaya) in February 1983, amid scenes of great intercommunal violence, leading to several thousand deaths. In an effort to curtail the flow of Bengali immigrants, it was decided in July that the Assam/Bangladesh border should be fenced. Election defeats in Andhra Pradesh, Karnataka and Tripura in January 1983 represented a set-back for Indira Gandhi, who then reshuffled her Council of Ministers. There was also unrest in Jammu and Kashmir during local elections there in June 1983, and in July 1984, when the Chief Minister was deposed. Alleged police corruption and the resurgence of caste violence (notably in Bihar and Gujarat) caused further problems for the Government.

Another major problem was the widespread unrest in the Sikh community of Punjab, despite the election to the Indian presidency in July 1982 of Giani Zail Singh, the first Sikh to hold the position. There were demands for greater religious recognition, for the settlement of grievances over land and water rights, and over the sharing of the state capital at Chandigarh with Haryana, and also demands from a small minority for a separate Sikh state ('Khalistan'). In October 1983 the Punjabi Government was removed, and the state was brought under presidential rule, to prevent an escalation of violence between the Sikh and Hindu populations. However, the violence continued, and followers of an extremist Sikh leader, Jarnail Singh Bhindranwale, established a terrorist stronghold inside the Golden Temple (the Sikh holy shrine) at Amritsar. In June 1984 the Government sent in troops to dislodge the extremists. The armed assault on the Golden Temple resulted in the death of Bhindranwale and hundreds of his supporters, and serious damage to sacred buildings. A curfew was imposed in Punjab, and army personnel blockaded Amritsar. There were mutinies among Sikh troops in various parts of India.

In October 1984 Indira Gandhi was assassinated by militant Sikh members of her personal guard. Her son, Rajiv Gandhi, was immediately sworn in as Prime Minister, despite his lack of previous ministerial experience. There was widespread communal violence throughout India, with more than 2,000 deaths, which was curbed by the prompt action of the Government.

A general election to the Lok Sabha, which was due in January 1985 under the Constitution, was held in December 1984 throughout the country, apart from the states of Assam and Punjab, which were deemed by the Government to be too disturbed, as well as in two snowbound constituencies and five in which voting was postponed until January 1985. Congress (I), aided by the youthfulness of the electorate (68% of whom were between 21 and 40 years of age), the total disunity of the opposition and a large sympathy vote for Rajiv Gandhi, achieved a decisive victory, gaining the largest parliamentary majority in India's history. Including the results of the January 1985 polling, the party received 49.2% of the total votes and won 403 of the 513 contested seats. Rajiv Gandhi pledged to continue most of his mother's policies. At the state assembly elections of March 1985, however, Congress (I) performed less well than expected, suffering heavy defeats in Andhra Pradesh, Karnataka and Sikkim, and reduced majorities in other states.

In January 1986, in an attempt to revitalize Congress (I), Rajiv Gandhi appointed Arjun Singh, a former Governor of Punjab and hitherto Minister of Commerce, to the recently created post of Vice-President of the party (the post was abolished in October 1986), and two other senior Ministers as General Secretaries. In February there were mass demonstrations and strikes throughout India, in protest against government-imposed increases in the prices of basic commodities such as petroleum products, fertilizers, rice and wheat. The opposition parties united against Rajiv Gandhi's policies, and the entire parliamentary opposition boycotted the President's traditional address on the opening day of the budget session in Parliament. Congress (I) suffered considerable set-backs in the indirect elections to the upper house of the legislature, the Rajya Sabha (Council of States) in March, when its overall strength in the House declined to considerably less than the two-thirds majority necessary to enable constitutional amendments to be approved without the support of opposition members. In April Rajiv Gandhi expelled one senior member and suspended three others from Congress (I), in an attempt to purge the party of critics calling themselves 'Indira Gandhi loyalists'. In a major government reshuffle in May, the Prime Minister appointed Sikhs to two senior positions. Rajiv Gandhi survived an assassination attempt by three Sikhs in New Delhi in October.

In June 1986 Lal Denga, the leader of the Mizo National Front (MNF), signed a peace agreement with Rajiv Gandhi, thus ending Mizoram's 25 years of rebellion. The accord granted Mizoram limited autonomy in the drafting of local laws, independent trade with neighbouring foreign countries and a general amnesty for all Mizo rebels. Lal Denga led an interim coalition government, formed by the MNF and Congress (I), until February 1987, when the MNF won an absolute majority at elections to the state assembly. In the same month, Mizoram and Arunachal Pradesh were officially admitted as the 23rd and 24th states of India, respectively, and in May the Union Territory of Goa became India's 25th state.

During 1987 the Prime Minister and his party experienced a number of serious political set-backs. Congress (I) lost control of the Kerala state government at elections to the state assembly in March. It sustained further defeats in state elections in West Bengal in the same month, and in Haryana in June, but retained control of the Nagaland legislature at elections in November. For much of the early part of the year, political tensions were intensified by an open dispute between the Prime Minister and the outgoing President, Giani Zail Singh. Serious public concern was also aroused throughout 1987 by various accusations of corruption and financial irregularities, made against senior figures in Congress (I). Notable among these scandals was the 'Bofors affair', in which large payments were allegedly made to Indian agents by a Swedish company in connection with its sales of munitions to the Indian Government. The Prime Minister strongly denied any involvement in these matters, and a committee of inquiry, established by the Government in August 1987, subsequently exonerated him of any impropriety. However, following the state electoral defeats, the allegations of corruption and the declining popularity of Congress (I), five ministers and one deputy minister resigned from the Government between March and August. Among them was the Minister of Defence, Vishwanath Pratap Singh, who was also, with three other senior politicians, expelled from Congress (I) for 'anti-party activities'. V. P. Singh soon emerged as the leader of the Congress (I) dissidents, and in October formed a new political group, the Jan Morcha (People's Front), advocating fundamental socialist principles.

In 1988 a more confrontational style appeared to be adopted by the central administration towards non-Congress (I) state governments. In January Rajiv Gandhi dissolved the administration of Tamil Nadu and placed the state under presidential rule, in response to the outbreak of violent quarrels between rival factions of the ruling party, the All-India Anna Dravida Munnetra Kazhagam (AIADMK), following the death of the Chief Minister in December 1987. Elections for state assemblies were held in the north-eastern states of Tripura and Meghalaya in February 1988. In Tripura the ruling Communist-led Left Front coalition was narrowly defeated by Congress (I) and an allied local party, following a period of extreme separatist violence (see below). In Meghalaya Congress (I) lost its absolute majority, although remaining the largest single party, in the state assembly. Rajiv Gandhi then effected a major government reshuffle. Following a considerable number of resignations from the ruling Congress (I) party in Nagaland in August, the state government was dissolved, and presidential rule was declared. The number of states under direct rule increased to four in the following month, when President's rule was imposed in Mizoram, following a week of political instability.

In September 1988 the opposition forces attained a degree of unity when four major centrist parties, the Indian National Congress (S), the Jan Morcha, the Janata Party and the Lok Dal, and three major regional parties, the Asom Gana Parishad, the Dravida Munnetra Kazhagam (DMK) and the Telugu Desam, formed a coalition National Front (Rashtriya Morcha), to oppose Congress (I) at the next general election. In October three of the four centrist parties (Congress (S) withdrew at the last moment) formed a new political grouping, the Janata Dal (People's Party), which was to work in collaboration with the National Front. V.P. Singh, who was widely regarded as

Rajiv Gandhi's closest rival, was elected as President of the Janata Dal. In January 1989 Congress (I) was decisively defeated by the DMK in the elections to the state assembly in Tamil Nadu, but gained outright majorities over the regional parties in elections in the less significant states of Nagaland and Mizoram (where local factors operated). In late July the Government was faced with a potentially embarrassing situation, when all the opposition members of the Lok Sabha resigned and opposition members of the Rajya Sabha staged a mass walk-out in protest against alleged government corruption and incompetence regarding the notorious 'Bofors affair'. An anti-Government *bharat bandh* (nation-wide general strike), which was supported by all the main opposition groups, took place at the end of August, and was declared a success by the organizers.

A general election to the Lok Sabha was held between 22 and 26 November 1989 (two months earlier than scheduled) throughout the country, apart from the state of Assam, where there was considerable disruption, owing to tribal unrest (see below) and to the incomplete state of the electoral rolls. During the election, which attracted a turn-out of about 58%, more than 100 people died in election-related violence. Congress (I), which suffered its heaviest defeats in the northern states, lost its overall majority in the Lok Sabha. Of the 525 contested seats, Congress (I) won 193, the Janata Dal and its electoral allies in the National Front won 141 and three, respectively, and the Bharatiya Janata Party (BJP), aided by the wave of Hindu revivalism in the north of the country, won 88. A few days later, Rajiv Gandhi resigned from his post as Prime Minister, but was endorsed in his position as leader of Congress (I). The President asked him to remain as caretaker Prime Minister until the National Front, which had been promised the parliamentary support of the Communist parties and of the BJP, formed a new government. On 2 December V. P. Singh was sworn in as the new Prime Minister of India. He then appointed an 18-member Council of Ministers, the most noteworthy features of which were the appointment of Devi Lal, the populist Chief Minister of Haryana and President of Lok Dal (B), as Deputy Prime Minister, and the appointment of a Kashmiri Muslim, Mufti Mohammed Sayeed, to the post of Minister of Home Affairs. This latter appointment was widely regarded as a gesture of reconciliation to the country's Muslims and as reaffirmation of the Government's professed secular stance. A few weeks later, V. P. Singh's Government, which was the first minority government in Indian history, won a vote of confidence in the Lok Sabha, despite the abstention of all the Congress (I) members. In mid-January 1990, as part of a general purging process, the Government ordered the mass resignation of the country's state Governors. The President then appointed new ones. In late February elections to the state assemblies were held in Bihar, Gujarat, Madhya Pradesh, Manipur, Rajasthan, Arunachal Pradesh, Himachal Pradesh, Maharashtra, Orissa and the union territory of Pondicherry. All of the assemblies contested were formerly controlled by Congress (I). The elections were marred by violence, particularly in Bihar, where it was reported that about 80 people had been killed. Congress (I) lost power in eight of the 10 assemblies and there was a large increase in support for the right-wing Hindu nationalist BJP.

In mid-July 1990 the Government felt the strain of serious internal rifts when 13 members tendered their resignations in protest over the reinstatement (by his father, Devi Lal) of Om Prakash Chautala as Chief Minister of Haryana (he had been forced to resign from the post only seven weeks previously, following allegations of corruption and of instigating polling violence and electoral malpractice). Even the Prime Minister offered to resign, claiming that he had lost the trust of the people, but his resignation was refused by the leadership of the Janata Dal. The government crisis was quickly alleviated, however, when Devi Lal's son resigned from his post as Chief Minister of Haryana a few days later (although he remained as one of the General Secretaries of the Janata Dal). V. P. Singh refused the ministerial resignations, and normal government work was resumed. In early August Devi Lal was dismissed from his post as Deputy Prime Minister, for nepotism, disloyalty and for making unsubstantiated accusations of corruption against ministerial colleagues. In the following week a defiant Devi Lal demonstrated the strength of his rural following when about 250,000 farmers from northern India rallied in New Delhi to show their support for the veteran politician.

In August 1990 there were violent demonstrations in many northern Indian states, protesting against the Government's populist decision to implement the recommendations of the 10-year-old Mandal Commission and to raise the quota of government and public-sector jobs reserved for deprived sections of the population (particularly among the lower castes) from 22.5% to 49.5%. The majority of these demonstrations were organized by the student communtiy, which is dominated by upper castes. The violence escalated in September, with traffic blockades, attacks on government property, clashes between riot police and students (at least 70 people were killed) and about 20 occurrences of self-immolation. V.P. Singh came under increasing pressure from Congress (I), the BJP and from members of his own party to take action to resolve the crisis. The students, however, refused the Prime Minister's televised offer of talks with the Government. In an apparent attempt to broaden his party's electoral basis by creating a new caste alliance, V.P. Singh seemed to have alienated a large section of the urban élite. On 1 October the Supreme Court directed the Government to halt temporarily the implementation of the quota scheme (pending a decision on its constitutional validity) in an attempt to curb the growing caste violence. On the following day, however, a violent anti-quota demonstration, attended by an estimated 200,000 protesters, took place in New Delhi. About one week later, 47 commuters in Andhra Pradesh were burnt to death when their train was set on fire by extremists demonstrating their support for the Government's proposed scheme. Despite this incident and the growing number of suicides committed by people opposed to the scheme, V.P. Singh insisted that he was seeking to resolve the problems of injustice and poverty, and that he would rather resign than withdraw the scheme.

The Government's problems were seriously exacerbated in October 1990 by an increase in violence between Hindus and Muslims, throughout India, which was prompted by the threatened construction of a Hindu temple on the site of a disused 16th-century mosque in the holy town of Ayodhya, in Uttar Pradesh: this proposal was opposed by the Government, who believed that the dispute should be settled in court before any action was taken, but was vehemently supported by the Hindu fundamentalist party, the BJP. In addition, the critical situations in Punjab, Assam and Jammu and Kashmir showed no real signs of improvement. In mid-October the BJP withdrew its vital parliamentary support for the National Front, following the arrest (on the orders of V.P. Singh) of the President of the BJP, Lal Kishanchand Advani, as he led a controversial mass processsion of Hindu devotees to Ayodhya to begin the construction of a Hindu temple. According to the Prime Minister, the BJP leader had deliberately incited inter-communal hatred by exhorting tens of thousands of Hindu extremists throughout the country to join him in illegally tearing down the remains of the ancient mosque. About 20,000 paramilitary troops were dispatched to Ayodhya, and thousands of Hindu political activists were arrested, in an attempt to prevent a bloody Muslim-Hindu confrontation over the disputed religious site. However, at the end of the month, following repeated clashes between the police and crowds, Hindu extremists (many of them members of the Vishwa Hindu Parishad, the World Hindu Council) stormed and slightly damaged the mosque, and laid siege to it for several days.

The Prime Minister's hold on power seemed increasingly fragile in early November 1990, when one of his leading rivals within the Janata Dal, Chandra Shekhar (with the support of Devi Lal), formed his own dissident faction. Members of this breakaway faction, known as the Janata Dal (Socialist) or Janata Dal (S), were then expelled from the official Janata Dal. On 7 November the Lok Sabha convened for a special session, at which V.P. Singh's Government overwhelmingly lost a vote of confidence (346 votes against, 142 in favour). V.P. Singh immediately resigned, and President Venkataraman invited Rajiv Gandhi, as the leader of the party holding the largest number of seats in the Lok Sabha, to form a new government; the BJP and the Communists, who were also approached (as a formality), claimed that they did not have the requisite parliamentary support to form a government. Rajiv Gandhi refused the offer, in favour of Chandra Shekhar. Although the strength of the Janata Dal (S) in the Lok Sabha comprised only about 60 deputies, Congress (I) had earlier offered Shekhar unconditional parliamentary support (it refused, however, to form a coalition government with the rebel faction). On 10 November Chandra Shekhar, who had never previously held any government office (despite having had a long political career), was sworn in as India's new Prime Minister and appointed Devi Lal as Deputy Prime Minister. On the following day it was announced that Devi Lal was to be the President of the Janata Dal (S). A few days later, Shekhar won a vote of confidence (by 280 votes to 214) in the Lok Sabha. A new Council of Ministers was appointed later in the month, with Shekhar himself assuming a number of important portfolios, including that of defence and of the interior. The only non-Janata Dal (S) ministers to be appointed were the new Minister of Law and Justice and of Commerce, Dr Subramaniam Swamy, who had recently been made President of the original Janata Dal, and two members of the small Jharkhand Mukti Morcha party.

Although Shekhar succeeded in initiating a series of talks between the two sides involved in the Ayodhya dispute, violence between Hindus and Muslims increased throughout India (particularly in the northern states and in the southern city of Hyderabad) in December 1990, leaving more than 300 people dead. Senior officials described the violence as some of the worst seen in the country since India gained independence. The implementation of the controversial quota scheme remained postponed (the Supreme Court had not yet reached any final decision as regards the issue).

At the end of December 1990 a controversy arose over the exact nature of Congress (I)'s political role, when Rajiv Gandhi claimed that his party constituted the official opposition in Parliament, despite its being the main support of the Government. Congress (I) was, in fact, recognized as the main opposition in the Rajya Sabha, but not in the Lok Sabha (where the Speaker recognized the BJP as the official opposition).

In late January 1991 the Prime Minister dismissed the government of Tamil Nadu (allies of V.P. Singh), dissolved the state assembly and imposed direct rule on the southern state, claiming that this action was necessitated by the increased activity of Sri Lankan Tamil militants in the state, which had led to a breakdown in law and order. The Tamil Nadu government was also accused of harbouring Assamese militants. In the resultant riots that broke out in the state capital, Madras, more than 1,000 arrests were made by paramilitary troops.

The Government suffered a further set-back in February 1991. Five members of the Council of Ministers, including the Minister of External Affairs, were forced to resign when they lost their seats in the Lok Sabha for violating India's strict anti-defection laws: they had left the Janata Dal to join the Janata Dal (S). The fragility of the parliamentary alliance between the Janata Dal (S) and Congress (I) became apparent in early March when the Congress (I) deputies boycotted Parliament, following the revelation that Rajiv Gandhi's house had been kept under police surveillance. In an unexpected counter-move, Chandra Shekhar resigned on 6 March, but accepted the President's request that he remain in power as head of an interim government until the holding of a fresh general election (probably in April or May).

Intercommunal violence continued throughout the late 1980s and into the early 1990s. The violence in Goa, Assam, Karnataka and Tamil Nadu arose as a result of agitation over the official languages, and in Gujarat, Jammu and Kashmir, Rajasthan, Bihar, Uttar Pradesh and Madhya Pradesh as a result of Hindu-Muslim tension. The growth in Hindu fundamentalism (particularly in the northern states) was reflected in the rising popularity of the BJP and in the increasingly assertive stance adopted by certain Hindu groups, such as the Vishwa Hindu Parishad, which assumed a major role in the ongoing Ayodhya dispute (see above).

In 1986 the Gurkhas (of Nepalese stock) resident in West Bengal launched a campaign for a separate autonomous homeland in the Darjeeling region and the recognition of Nepali as an official language. The violent separatist campaign, led by the Gurkha National Liberation Front (GNLF), was prompted by the eviction, in March, of about 10,000 Nepalis from the state of Meghalaya, where the native residents had feared that they were becoming outnumbered by immigrants. When violent disturbances and a disruptive general strike were organized by the GNLF in West Bengal in June 1987, the central Government agreed to hold tripartite discussions with the GNLF's leader, Subhas Ghising, and the Chief Minister of West Bengal, Jyoti Basu. At these negotiations, which were held in Delhi in January 1988, the Prime Minister rejected outright the GNLF's demand for an autonomous Gurkha state.

However, the GNLF campaign for an independent homeland was ended in July, when Subhas Ghising agreed to the establishment of a semi-autonomous Darjeeling Hill Development Council, at a meeting with Jyoti Basu and the Minister of Home Affairs in Delhi. Under the formal peace agreement, which was signed in August, the GNLF was to cease all agitation and to surrender weapons, while the state government was to release all GNLF detainees. In addition, the Government agreed to grant Indian citizenship to all Gurkhas born or domiciled in India. Following the surrender of a large number of weapons by Gurkha separatists and the release of several hundred activists from prison, elections to the Darjeeling Hill Development Council were held in November. Although the GNLF won 26 of the 28 elective seats (the 14 remaining members of the 42-member Council were to be nominated), the prospects for the political situation in West Bengal continued to appear unsettled, since, despite the election results, Subhas Ghising (who was elected as Chairman of the Council) and his supporters continued to demand the establishment of a fully autonomous Gurkha state.

A similar, though more protracted, dispute was likewise resolved in Tripura. In the latter half of the 1970s a campaign was launched by the Tribal National Volunteers (TNV), demanding an autonomous state in part of Tripura. After more than 100 murders perpetrated by TNV guerrillas in 1986, the organization was declared illegal in January 1987. The violence intensified in January 1988, however, when a further 100 people were killed in guerrilla attacks. In an attempt to quell the violence, the central Government dispatched large numbers of paramilitary troops to Tripura and declared the state a disturbed area. Order was restored in the following month, when Congress (I), in alliance with a small local party, ousted the Marxists from power in the state assembly elections. In August the ethnic conflict was ended when an agreement was signed by the central Government and the TNV guerrillas, who agreed to disarm, disband and abandon their demands for an independent homeland. In return, the Government agreed to amend the Constitution to allow an increased participation of tribal representatives in local government and to restore alienated lands. The paramilitary troops were to be withdrawn following the implementation of the agreement.

In December 1985 an election for the state assembly in Assam took place, following the signing, in August, of an agreement between the central Government and two groups of Hindu activists, concluded after five years of sectarian violence, which limited the voting rights of immigrants to Assam: those foreigners (mainly Bangladeshis) who had arrived before 1966 were to be accorded full voting rights; those who had arrived between 1966 and 1971 were to be disenfranchised for 10 years; and those who had arrived after 1971 (the proclamation date of the independence of Bangladesh) were to be expelled from Assam. The election result was a victory for the Asom Gana Parishad (Assam People's Council), a newly-formed local party, which won 64 of the assembly's 126 seats, compared with 25 for its nearest rival, Congress (I), the former ruling party in Assam. The delayed voting for Assam's 14 seats in the Lok Sabha took place on the same day. Plans were revived in 1985 to erect a fence along the Assam/Bangladesh border, in an attempt to curb illegal immigration from Bangladesh. When the accord was announced in December, Bangladesh stated that it would not take back Bengali immigrants from Assam and denied that it had allowed any illegal refugees to cross its borders into Assam. The limited success of the rebel movements in West Bengal and Tripura apparently encouraged emulation by another disaffected Indian tribal group—the Bodos of Assam, led by the All-Bodo Students' Union, who demanded a separate state of Bodoland within India. In February 1989 the Bodos intensified their separatist campaign by organizing strikes, bombings and violent demonstrations. In response, the central Government dispatched armed forces into the state. In August the Bodo tribesmen agreed to suspend their campaign of violence, in which more than 500 people had been killed since 1986 and to hold peace talks with the state government and central government officials. At these talks, which were held in Delhi at the end of the month, the Bodos agreed to continue their suspension of violence, while the Assam Government agreed to suspend emergency security measures, which had been imposed in Bodo areas. The Assamese situation became more complicated in 1989, when a militant Maoist group, the United Liberation Front of Assam (ULFA), re-emerged. The ULFA (which was originally formed in 1979 and which belongs to a militant co-ordinating group, the Indo-Burma Revolutionary Front) demanded the outright secession of the whole of Assam from India. In 1990 the ULFA claimed responsibility for about 90 assassinations, abductions and bomb explosions. In late November, in an attempt to curb the separatist violence, which was seriously disrupting the state's tea industry (Assam accounts for about 65% of the country's total tea production), the central Government placed Assam under direct rule, dispatched paramilitary troops to the state and outlawed the ULFA. By late December the unrest seemed to have been substantially quelled as a result of the arrest of hundreds of militants and the seizure of large quantities of their weapons and ammunition.

The situation in Punjab has shown little sign of improvement since 1985, despite various attempts by successive governments to curb tensions and to end the violence. In September 1985 Rajiv Gandhi achieved a temporary solution to the unrest when a general election for the state assembly was held, following an agreement, signed in July, between the central Government and Harchand Singh Longowal, the moderate President of the main Sikh party, Shiromani Akali Dal. Despite the assassination of Longowal by Sikh extremists in August, the election was peaceful and resulted in a victory for Shiromani Akali Dal, which assumed power in the state after two years of presidential rule. On the same day as the state election, polling also took place for Punjab's 13 seats in the Lok Sabha, postponed from December 1984. An important element in the agreement that Rajiv Gandhi and Longowal negotiated in July 1985 was the proposed transfer of Chandigarh, since 1966 the joint capital of Punjab and Haryana, to Punjab alone. In return, Haryana was to benefit from the completion of the Sutlej-Yamuna canal, to bring irrigation water from Punjab to the dry south of the state, and the transfer of several Hindi-speaking border villages from Punjab to Haryana. Four commissions were established to organize the transfer, but each one failed to accomplish its task, and by early 1991 the transfer had still not taken place. Hindu-Sikh violence continued throughout 1986 (it was estimated that about 650 people were killed during the year) despite the replacement of the Governor of Punjab, after only three months in office, in April 1986, the dispatch of thousands of paramilitary reinforcements from New Delhi and the considerable improvement in the efficiency of the Punjab police force. A worrying development was that, after years of comparative quiescence among Punjab's Hindu minority (who comprise about 40% of the state's population), the extremist Hindu Shiv Sena ('Army of Shiva') group began to organize resistance against Sikh terrorism. Many Hindu families, on the other hand, left Punjab for Haryana, to escape the unrest. A steady flow of Sikh families began to enter Punjab from Haryana, where they feared retaliation from the Hindu majority. In January 1986 the Sikh extremist groups re-established a terrorist stronghold inside the Golden Temple complex at Amritsar. In mid-1986 the extremists separated from the ruling moderate Shiromani Akali Dal (Longowal) and formed several militant factions. In May 1987 Rajiv Gandhi dismissed the Chief Minister, Surjit Singh Barnala, and his government, suspended the state assembly and imposed President's rule in Punjab. Despite an increase in the number of arrests of Sikh terrorists and the resumption of discussions between the Government and the moderate Sikh leaders, the violence in Punjab worsened, and it was estimated that more than 2,700 people were killed during 1987 and 1988. Any progress made towards the resolution of the Punjab problem in 1989 was greatly hindered by the inability of the Akali Dal factions to agree among themselves (with extreme critics attacking any concessions offered by the central Government). In October 1990 V.P. Singh extended direct rule in Punjab for an eighth term (of a further six months) after failing to win the support of other political parties for holding elections in the state. The violence in Punjab reached an unprecedented level in 1990, with the Indian press reporting about 4,000 deaths in that year alone (although the official figure was much lower). In an effort to curb the violence, more than 200 Sikh political and religious leaders (including Simranjit Singh Mann, the President of the leading faction of the divided Akali Dal) were arrested in late November. A breakthrough occurred, however, in late December, when direct talks were held in New Delhi between the new Prime Minister, Chandra Shekhar, and Simranjit Singh Mann, despite opposition protest, concerning the crisis in Punjab. After the talks, Shekhar stated that the central Government was prepared to hold discussions with any group (including militants) that pledged to attempt to restore peace in Punjab, but stressed that it would make no compromise as regards the secesssionist violence. However, the killings showed no sign of abating in early 1991. The separatist movement in Punjab gained some cohesion in January 1991, as a result of the merger of the various factions of the Akali Dal to form a single party, the Shiromani Akali Dal, under the leadership of Simranjit Singh Mann.

In foreign affairs, the Janata Government of 1977–80 had initiated a policy of improving relations with all neighbouring countries, which successive governments continued. In 1982 India made an interim agreement with Bangladesh over the sharing of the Ganges waters, and in 1985 the two countries concluded an interim agreement which guaranteed Bangladesh's share of the Ganges' dry-season flow. In December 1986 India and Bangladesh signed an agreement on measures aimed at preventing cross-border terrorism. In September 1988 the two countries established a joint working committee to examine methods of averting the annual devastating floods in the Ganges delta.

Relations between India and Nepal deteriorated in early 1989, when India decided not to renew the two treaties determining trade and transit, insisting that a common treaty covering both issues be negotiated. Nepal refused, stressing the importance of keeping the treaties separate on the grounds that Indo-Nepalese trade issues are negotiable, whereas the right of transit is a recognized right of land-locked countries. India responded by closing most of the transit points through which most of Nepal's trade is conducted. It was widely believed that another matter aggravating the dispute was Nepal's recent acquisition of Chinese-made military equipment which, according to India, violated the Treaty of Peace and Friendship of 1950. However, in June 1990, following several rounds of high-level negotiations, India and Nepal signed an agreement restoring trade relations and reopening the transit points. Chandra Shekhar visited Kathmandu in February 1991 (the first official visit to Nepal by an Indian Prime Minister since 1977), shortly after it was announced that the first free elections there were to be held in May.

Relations with Pakistan had deteriorated in the late 1970s and early 1980s, owing to Pakistan's potential capability for the development of nuclear weapons and as a result of major US deliveries of armaments to that country. The Indian Government believed that such deliveries would upset the balance of power in the region and would precipitate an arms race. Pakistan's President, Gen. Mohammad Zia ul-Haq, visited India in December 1985, when he and Rajiv Gandhi announced their mutual commitment not to attack each other's nuclear installations and to negotiate the sovereignty of the disputed Siachin glacier region in northern Kashmir. By March 1986, however, relations had deteriorated again, and the two countries had resumed the exchange of widely-publicized diplomatic attacks (including India's allegations that Pakistan was harbouring and training Sikh extremists to infiltrate Punjab). Pakistan continued to demand a settlement of the Kashmir problem in accordance with earlier UN resolutions, prescribing a plebiscite under the auspices of the UN in the two parts of the state, now divided between India and Pakistan (the Pakistani-controlled sector is called Azad Kashmir). India, however, argued that the problem should be settled in accordance with the Simla agreement of 1972, which required that all Indo-Pakistani disputes be resolved through bilateral negotiations. The Indian decision to construct a barrage on the River Jhelum in Jammu and Kashmir, in an alleged violation of the 1960 Indus Water Treaty, has also created concern in Pakistan. In December 1988 Rajiv Gandhi visited Islamabad for discussions with Pakistan's new Prime Minister, Benazir Bhutto. At this meeting, which constituted the first official visit of an Indian Prime Minister to Pakistan for nearly 25 years, the two leaders signed three agreements, including a formal pledge not to attack each other's nuclear installations. Relations between India and Pakistan reached a crisis, however, in late 1989, when the outlawed Jammu and Kashmir National Liberation Front (JKNLF), led by Amanullah Khan, and several other militant Muslim groups intensified their campaigns of civil unrest, strikes and terrorism, demanding an independent Kashmir or unification with Pakistan. In an attempt to reduce the tension and violence, the central Government dispatched troops into Jammu and Kashmir (the only Indian state with a Muslim majority) in December and placed the entire Srinagar valley under an indefinite curfew. India claimed that the violence had largely been organized by militants trained and armed in Pakistan. Pakistan strenuously denied that it was officially involved in the uprising and stressed that the Muslim Kashmiris were fighting for self-determination. In mid-January 1990 the Chief Minister of Jammu and Kashmir, Dr Farook Abdullah, resigned from his post, the state assembly was suspended, and the state was placed under Governor's rule (with a new Governor appointed by the central Government). A few days later, following the murder of four members of the Indian air force by Muslim gunmen, thousands more Indian troops were sent into Jammu and Kashmir with orders to shoot insurgents on sight. At the same time, the local press was heavily censored, foreign journalists were temporarily detained, and communications were severed. By early February it was officially estimated that about 80 people (mainly civilians) had been killed in the resultant clashes between the troops and the protesters. Tension was heightened following reports that three Pakistani civilians had been killed by Indian soldiers when they attempted to cross into Indian-controlled Kashmir. Intense diplomatic efforts were immediately begun in order to alleviate what was seen as a potentially major confrontation between India and Pakistan. In mid-February the state Governor dissolved the state assembly of Jammu and Kashmir. A few days later, a peaceful mass demonstration of about 500,000 Muslims was held in Srinagar, demanding independence from India. In early March, however, the security forces opened fire on demonstrators, killing about 29 people. In May the principal Muslim religious figure in the Vale of Kashmir, Mirwaiz Maulvi Mohammad Farooq, was murdered (by an unknown assailant), and his funeral was the occasion for another major clash, in which at least 47 people died. The central Government imposed President's rule on Jammu and Kashmir in July, following the expiry of the six-month period of Governor's rule. In August and September there were reports of heavy skirmishing between Indian and Pakistani troops along the Kashmir border. Tension was eased somewhat in December, following discussions between the Ministers of External Affairs of the two countries, held in Islamabad, at which the agreement not to attack each other's nuclear installations (signed, but not ratified, in December 1988) was finalized. The agreement came into effect in January 1991.

Since 1983 India's relations with Sri Lanka have been dominated by tensions and conflicts between the island's Sinhalese and Tamil communities, in which India has sought to arbitrate. Negotiations and proposals by Indian mediators proved fruitless until July 1987, when Rajiv Gandhi and the Sri Lankan President, Junius Jayawardene, signed an accord aimed at settling the conflict. To help with the implementation of the accord, a 7,000-strong Indian Peace-Keeping Force (IPKF) was dispatched to Sri Lanka in August (the size of the IPKF had increased to an estimated 50,000 by February 1988). The IPKF encountered considerable resistance from the Tamil separatist guerrillas, especially during the siege of the Tamil stronghold in Jaffna in October 1987. Following the gradual implementation of the peace accord, however, several thousand IPKF troops were withdrawn from Sri Lanka in the latter half of 1988 and early 1989. In August 1989 an agreement between India and Sri Lanka was signed in Colombo, in which India stated that it would immediately cease hostilities against the Tamil guerrillas and that it would make 'all efforts' to withdraw its remaining 43,000 troops from Sri Lanka by 31 December. The complete withdrawal of Indian troops from Sri Lanka was, in fact, completed by the end of March 1990, yet violent conflict in the island flared up again very shortly afterwards. Following an escalation in the conflict in Sri Lanka later in that year, the flow of Sri Lankan refugees into Tamil Nadu increased considerably. By early 1991 the number of Sri Lankans living in refugee camps in Tamil Nadu totalled an estimated 150,000.

During 1981 there was a marked improvement in India's relations with the People's Republic of China, which had suffered a set-back after India's recognition of the Heng Samrin Government of Kampuchea (which has since reverted to its former name of Cambodia) in July 1980. Both countries agreed to find an early solution to their Himalayan border dispute (over about 128,000 sq km of land) and to seek to normalize relations. China was displeased, however, when Arunachal Pradesh was granted full statehood in February 1987. In that year both sides accused each other of troop concentrations on the disputed frontier and of border violations. No substantial progress was made during the eighth round of Sino-Indian negotiations, held in New Delhi in November. However, during Rajiv Gandhi's visit to China in December 1988 (the first visit to China by an Indian Prime minister for 34 years), the two countries agreed to establish a joint working group to negotiate the border dispute. This group met for discussions in July 1989 in Beijing. The first meeting of the Sino-Indian joint group on trade was held in New Delhi in September and the two sides made considerable progress in arranging for an expansion of commercial contracts. In the following month the highest-ranking Chinese official to visit India for almost 30 years, Deputy Prime Minister, Wu Xueqian, met Rajiv Gandhi for talks. Following this meeting, the Indian Prime Minister stated that prospects for the settlement of the border dispute had improved. The joint working group on this issue met for the second time in New Delhi in August 1990, and agreed to a mechanism whereby their military personnel were to meet periodically, to maintain peace in the border region. In February 1991 a major breakthrough in Sino-Indian relations occurred at the second meeting of the joint group on trade, held in Beijing, when a draft trade protocol for 1991/92, including the proposed resumption of border trade between the two countries for the first time in three decades, was signed. All six border posts had been closed since the brief border war between India and China in 1962.

The USSR is a major contributor of economic and military assistance to India (in 1986 it was estimated that about 70% of India's defence equipment was supplied by the USSR). The Indo-Soviet Chamber of Commerce and Industry was formally inaugurated in Delhi, to expand bilateral trade between the two countries, in June 1986, and Rajiv Gandhi held a successful series of meetings during a visit to Moscow in July 1987.

There are close ties between the USA and India in economic and scientific affairs, and political ties were further strengthened after Rajiv Gandhi's visit to the USA in October 1987. India remains uneasy, however, over the continued support, in aid and armaments, which is given to Pakistan by the USA, while the USA, in turn, remains concerned that its military or dual-use technology might be 'leaked' to the USSR through India, or diverted to an Indian programme to produce nuclear weapons.

Following the invasion and annexation of Kuwait by Iraq in August 1990, about 140,000 Indian expatriate workers were evacuated from the Persian (Arabian) Gulf region. When war broke out between Iraq and the multinational forces in January 1991, India stressed its neutrality (as a member of the Non-Aligned Movement) regarding the conflict, but in early February the Indian Government expressed 'grave concern' at civilian casualties resulting from the multinational forces' intensive aerial bombardment campaign. The Government's admission, in late January, that it was allowing US military transport aircraft to refuel in Bombay, on their way to the Gulf region from the Philippines, provoked widespread criticism from the general public and, notably, from Congress (I), which threatened to withdraw its support for Shekhar's minority Government if refuelling were not halted. As a result of these protests, the Government withdrew the US refuelling rights in February.

Government

India is a federal republic. Legislative power is vested in Parliament, consisting of the President and two Houses. The Council of States (Rajya Sabha) has 245 members, most of whom are indirectly elected by the State Assemblies for six years (one-third retiring every two years), the remainder being nominated by the President for six years. The House of the People (Lok Sabha) has 542 elected members, serving for five years (subject to dissolution). A small number of members of the Lok Sabha may be nominated by the President to represent the Anglo-Indian community, while the 542 members are directly elected by universal adult suffrage in single-member constituencies. The President is a constitutional Head of State, elected for five years by an electoral college comprising elected members of both Houses of Parliament and the state legislatures. The President exercises executive power on the advice of the Council of Ministers, which is responsible to Parliament. The President appoints the Prime Minister and, on the latter's recommendation, other Ministers.

India contains 25 self-governing states, each with a Governor (appointed by the President for five years), a legislature (elected for five years) and a Council of Ministers headed by the Chief Minister. Bihar, Jammu and Kashmir, Karnataka, Maharashtra and Uttar Pradesh have bicameral legislatures, the other 20 state legislatures being unicameral. Each state has its own legislative, executive and judicial machinery, corresponding to that of the Indian Union. In the event of the failure of constitutional government in a state, presidential rule can be imposed by the Union. There are also seven Union Territories, administered by Lieutenant-Governors or Administrators, all of whom are appointed by the President.

Defence

In June 1990 the estimated strength of India's armed forces was 1,262,000: an army of 1,100,000, a navy of 52,000 and an air force of 110,000. Military service has been voluntary but, under the amended Constitution, it is the fundamental duty of every citizen to perform national service when called upon. The proposed defence budget for 1990 was 157,500m. rupees.

Economic Affairs

In 1989, according to estimates by the World Bank, India's gross national product (GNP), measured at average 1987-89 prices, was US $287,383m., equivalent to $350 per head. During 1980-89, it was estimated, GNP increased, in real terms, at an average annual rate of 5.4%, while GNP per head grew by 3.2% per year. Over the same period, the population increased by an annual average of 2.1%. India's gross domestic product (GDP) increased, in real terms, by an annual average of 5.2% in 1980-88. Owing to favourable monsoon conditions and the resultant good harvests in 1988, GDP grew by a record 10% in 1988/89. GDP increased by an estimated 5.0% in 1989/90.

Agriculture (including forestry and fishing) contributed an estimated 32.6% of GDP in 1988/89. About 65% of the labour force are employed in agriculture. The principal cash crops are cotton (cotton fabrics and raw cotton accounted for an estimated 5.7% of total export earnings in 1988/89), tea, rice, spices and cashew nuts. Coffee and jute production are also important. During 1980-88 agricultural production increased by an annual average of 2.3%, despite the occurrence of devastating droughts and floods.

Industry (including mining, manufacturing, power and construction) contributed an estimated 28.1% of GDP in 1988/89. During 1980-88 industrial production increased by an annual average of 7.6%. In terms of output, India ranks among the 12 leading industrial nations in the world.

Mining contributed an estimated 2.3% of GDP in 1988/89, and employed 0.5% of the labour force in 1981. Iron ore and cut diamonds are the major mineral exports. Coal, limestone, zinc and lead are also mined. India has the fourth largest coal reserves in the world.

Manufacturing contributed an estimated 18.1% of GDP in 1988/89, and employed 10.3% of the labour force in 1981. The most important sectors are machinery and transport equipment, fabrics and garments, and chemicals.

Energy is derived principally from petroleum and coal. Imports of mineral fuels comprised 15.5% of the estimated cost of total imports in 1988/89.

In 1988/89 India recorded an estimated visible trade deficit of Rs 78,985m. and there was a record deficit of Rs 90,000m. on the current account of the balance of payments. In 1988/89 the principal source of imports (9.3%) was Japan, while the principal market for exports (18.4%) was the USA. Other major trading partners were the Federal Republic of Germany, the United Kingdom and the USSR. The principal exports in 1988/89 were gems and jewellery, engineering products, ready-made garments, and leather and leather manufactures. The principal imports were non-electric machinery, mineral fuels and lubricants, pearls, precious and semi-precious stones, and iron and steel.

In the financial year ending 31 March 1991 there was a projected budgetary deficit of Rs 72,060m. In 1988 India secured from its Western aid consortium financial aid commitments totalling US $6,300m. for 1988/89. India's total external public debt was $49,695m. at the end of 1988. In that year the cost of debt-servicing was equivalent to 21.8% of earnings from the exports of goods and services. The average annual rate of inflation, in the consumer price index, was an estimated 7% in 1989/90. In rural India the number of people wholly unemployed comprise about 6% of the potential labour force for adult males, but the proportion is around 23% when account is taken of underemployment.

India is a member of the Asian Development Bank (ADB, see p. 100) and of the South Asian Association for Regional Co-operation (SAARC, see p. 225).

The guidelines for the eighth Five Year Plan (1990-95) were approved in late 1988. The eighth Plan was to aim at an average annual GDP growth rate of 6%. It was projected, however, that this high growth rate would require an increase in levels of taxation and a reduction in government expenditure. A major problem in the Indian economy is a recurrent budget deficit. In the budget for 1990/91, interest payments comprised the largest single item of expenditure. The Gulf crisis, following the invasion and annexation of Kuwait by Iraq in August 1990, and the subsequent outbreak of war between Iraq and the multinational forces in January 1991, had an extremely adverse effect on the already fragile Indian economy. The price of petrol was raised substantially (a large proportion of India's imports of mineral fuels are provided by Gulf states), the rate of inflation surged, the balance-of-payments situation deteriorated, owing partly to the cessation of remittances from Indians working in the Gulf region (an evacuation by air of about 140,000 Indian expatriate workers had been conducted in late 1990), and the budget deficit increased. In an attempt to resolve the economic crisis, the new Prime Minister, Chandra Shekhar, announced in December 1990 that the Government planned to introduce limited privatization measures, to reduce public expenditure, and to impose new taxes. In January 1991 India obtained two credits from the IMF, totalling US $1,800m., to be repaid over five years and with the first repayment not due for three years.

Social Welfare

Health programmes are primarily the responsibility of the state governments, but the Union Government provides finance for improvements in public health services. The structure of the health system is based on a network of primary health centres. In 1977 there were 5,372 such centres and 37,745 sub-centres in rural areas. In 1981 India had 1,066,164 hospital beds and 268,712 physicians. Various national health programmes aim to combat leprosy, malaria and tuberculosis. Smallpox was declared eradicated in 1977. The family planning programme was launched in 1952 and the emphasis now is on advice and education through Family Welfare Centres. A new approach to family planning was introduced in 1986, with the aim of reducing India's rate of population growth from 2.3% to 1.2% per year, so that the population does not exceed 1,000m. by the year 2000. Expenditure on health by all levels of government in the financial year 1986/87 was about Rs27,680m. (3.8% of total government spending).

Education

Education is primarily the responsibility of the individual state governments. Elementary education for children up to 14 years of age is theoretically compulsory in all states except Nagaland and Himachal Pradesh. Lower primary education, for children aged six to 11, is free in all states. Upper primary education, for children aged 11-14, is free in 12 states. Enrolment at the first level of education in 1988 was equivalent to 99% of children aged six to 10 years (114% of boys; 83% of girls). Secondary enrolment in 1988 was equivalent to 41% of those aged 11 to 17 (52% of boys; 29% of girls). A new pattern of education, consisting of 10 years' elementary education, two years at higher secondary level and three years for the first degree course, had been introduced in the majority of states by 1985/86. In 1978 the National Board for Adult Education launched a massive programme to combat illiteracy. Of the total population, 36.17% were literate in 1981, compared with 15.67% in 1961. However, female literacy was only 24.88% in 1981, and women's education, especially in rural areas, has made few advances. In 1990, according to UNESCO estimates, the rate of literacy had risen to 48.2% (61.8% males, 33.7% females). Government expenditure on education in 1987 was about Rs106,434m. (8.5% of total government spending).

Public Holidays

The public holidays observed in India vary locally. The dates given below apply to Delhi (unless otherwise indicated). As religious feasts depend on astronomical observations, holidays are usually declared at the beginning of the year in which they will be observed. It is not possible, therefore, to indicate more than the month in which some of the following holidays will occur.

INDIA

1991: January (Pongal), 26 January (Republic Day), 12 February* (Maha Shrivratri), 1 March (Holi), 28 March (Mahabir Jayanti), 29 March (Good Friday), April (Ram Navami), 16 April (Id al-Fitr, end of Ramadan), 28 May (Buddha Purnima), 23 June (Id-uz-Zuha, Feast of the Sacrifice), June/July (Rath Yatra), 13 July (Muharram, Islamic New Year), 15 August (Independence Day), August/September (Onam), 2 September (Janmashtami), 21 September (Birth of the Prophet), 2 October (Mahatma Gandhi's Birthday), 16 October (Maha Ashtami and Dussehra*), 7 November* (Diwali), 21 November (Guru Nanak Jayanti), 25–26 December (Christmas).

1992: January (Pongal), 26 January (Republic Day), January/February/March (Maha Shrivratri and Holi), March/April (Ram Navami and Mahabir Jayanti), 4 April (Id al-Fitr, end of Ramadan), 17 April (Good Friday), May (Buddha Purnima), 11 June (Id-uz-Zuha, Feast of the Sacrifice), June/July (Rath Yatra), 2 July (Muharram, Islamic New Year), 15 August (Independence Day), 10 September (Birth of the Prophet), August/September/October (Janmashtami, Onam and Maha Ashtami), September/October/November (Dussehra, Diwali and Guru Nanak Jayanti), 2 October (Mahatma Gandhi's Birthday), 25–26 December (Christmas).

* Date applies to Bombay.

Weights and Measures

The metric system has been officially introduced. The imperial system is also still in use, as are traditional Indian weights and measures, including:
1 tola = 11.66 grams
1 seer = 933.1 grams
1 maund = 37.32 kg
1 lakh = (1,00,000) = 100,000
1 crore = (1,00,00,000) = 10,000,000

Statistical Survey

Source (unless otherwise stated): Central Statistical Organization, Ministry of Planning, Sardar Patel, Bhavan, Parliament St, New Delhi 110 001; tel. (11) 353626.

Area and Population

AREA, POPULATION AND DENSITY*

Area (sq km)	3,287,263†
Population (census results)‡	
1 April 1971	548,159,652
1 March 1981§	
Males	354,397,884
Females	330,786,808
Total	685,184,692
Population (official estimates at mid-year)	
1987	781,374,000
1988	796,596,000
1989	811,817,000
Density (per sq km) at mid-1989	247.0

* Including Sikkim (incorporated into India on 26 April 1975) and the Indian-held part of Jammu and Kashmir.
† 1,269,219 sq miles.
‡ Excluding adjustment for underenumeration, estimated at 1.67% in 1971 and 1.7% in 1981.
§ Including estimates for Assam.
Source: Registrar General of India.

STATES AND TERRITORIES

			Population	
	Capital	Area (sq km)	April 1971	March 1981
States				
Andhra Pradesh	Hyderabad	275,068	43,502,708	53,549,673
Arunachal Pradesh[1]	Itanagar	83,743	467,511	631,839
Assam	Dispur	78,438	14,625,152	19,896,843*
Bihar	Patna	173,877	56,353,369	69,914,734
Goa[5]	Panaji	3,702	n.a.	1,007,749
Gujarat	Gandhinagar	196,024	26,697,475	34,085,799
Haryana	Chandigarh[2]	44,212	10,036,808	12,922,618
Himachal Pradesh	Simla	55,673	3,460,434	4,280,818
Jammu and Kashmir[3]	Srinagar	222,236	4,616,632	5,987,389
Karnataka	Bangalore	191,791	29,299,014	37,135,714
Kerala	Thiruvananthapuram (Trivandrum)	90,060	21,347,375	25,453,680
Madhya Pradesh	Bhopal	443,446	41,654,119	52,178,844
Maharashtra	Bombay	307,690	50,412,235	62,784,171
Manipur	Imphal	22,327	1,072,753	1,420,953
Meghalaya	Shillong	22,429	1,011,699	1,335,819
Mizoram[4]	Aizawl	21,081	332,390	493,757
Nagaland	Kohima	16,579	516,449	774,930
Orissa	Bhubaneswar	155,707	21,944,615	26,370,271
Punjab	Chandigarh[2]	50,362	13,551,060	16,788,915
Rajasthan	Jaipur	342,239	25,765,806	34,261,862
Sikkim	Gangtok	7,096	209,843	316,385
Tamil Nadu	Madras	130,058	41,199,168	48,408,077
Tripura	Agartala	10,486	1,556,342	2,053,058
Uttar Pradesh	Lucknow	294,411	88,341,144	110,862,013
West Bengal	Calcutta	88,752	44,312,011	54,580,647
Territories				
Andaman and Nicobar Islands	Port Blair	8,249	115,133	188,741
Chandigarh[2]	Chandigarh	114	257,251	451,610
Dadra and Nagar Haveli	Silvassa	491	74,170	103,676
Delhi	Delhi	1,483	4,065,698	6,220,406
Daman and Diu[5]	Daman	112	n.a.	78,981
Lakshadweep	Kavaratti	32	31,810	40,249
Pondicherry	Pondicherry	492	471,707	604,471

* Estimate.
[1] Arunachal Pradesh was granted statehood in February 1987.
[2] Chandigarh forms a separate Union Territory, not within Haryana or Punjab. As part of a scheme for a transfer of territory between the two states, Chandigarh was due to be incorporated into Punjab on 26 January 1986, but the transfer has been postponed.
[3] The area figure refers to the whole of Jammu and Kashmir State, of which 78,114 sq km (Azad Kashmir) is occupied by Pakistan. The population figures refer only to the Indian-held part of the territory.
[4] Mizoram was granted statehood in February 1987.
[5] Goa was granted statehood in May 1987. Daman and Diu remain a Union Territory. The population of Goa, Daman and Diu was 857,771 at the 1971 census.

Source: *Census of India*, Part II–B(i) Primary Census Abstract of General Population 1981.

INDIA

Statistical Survey

PRINCIPAL TOWNS (population at 1981 census*)

Greater Bombay	8,243,405	Sholapur	514,860	
Delhi	4,884,234	Jodhpur	506,345	
Calcutta	3,305,006	Thiruvananthapuram		
Madras	3,276,622	(Trivandrum)	499,531	
Bangalore	2,628,593	Ranchi	489,626	
Hyderabad	2,187,262	Mysore	479,081	
Ahmedabad	2,159,127	Vijaywada		
Kanpur (Cawnpore)	1,486,522	(Vijayavada)	461,772	
Nagpur	1,219,461	Jamshedpur	457,061	
Pune (Poona)	1,203,351	Rajkot	445,076	
Jaipur (Jeypore)	977,165	Meerut	417,395	
Lucknow	916,954	Jalandhar	408,196	
Indore	829,327	Bareilly	394,938	
Madurai	820,891	Kozhikode (Calicut)	394,447	
Patna	813,963	Chandigarh	379,660	
Surat	776,876	Ajmer	375,593	
Howrah	744,429	Guntur	367,699	
Vadodara (Baroda)	734,473	Tiruchirapalli	362,045	
Varanasi (Banaras)	720,755	Salem	361,394	
Coimbatore	704,514	Kota	358,241	
Agra	694,191	Kolhapur	340,625	
Bhopal	671,018	Raipur	338,245	
Jabalpur		Warangal	335,150	
(Jubbulpore)	649,085	Faridabad	330,864	
Allahabad	619,628	Moradabad	330,051	
Ludhiana	607,052	Aligarh	320,861	
Amritsar	594,844	Bhilainagar	319,450	
Srinagar	594,775	Durgapur	311,798	
Visakhapatnam	584,166	Thane	309,897	
Kochi (Cochin)	551,567	Bhavnagar	308,642	
Gwalior	539,015	Gorakhpur	307,501	
Hubli-Dharwar	527,108			

* Figures refer to the city proper in each case. For urban agglomerations, the following populations were recorded: Calcutta 9,194,018; Delhi 5,729,283; Madras 4,289,347; Bangalore 2,921,751; Ahmedabad 2,548,057; Hyderabad 2,545,836; Pune (Poona) 1,686,109; Kanpur 1,639,064; Nagpur 1,302,066; Jaipur 1,015,160; Lucknow 1,007,604; Coimbatore 920,355; Patna 918,903; Surat 913,806; Madurai 907,732; Varanasi (Banaras) 797,162; Jabalpur 757,303; Agra 747,318; Vadodara (Baroda) 744,881; Kochi (Cochin) 685,836; Dhanbad 678,069; Jamshedpur 669,580; Allahabad 650,070; Ulhasnagar 648,671; Tiruchirapalli 609,548; Srinagar 606,022; Visakhapatnam 603,630; Gwalior 555,862; Kozhikode (Calicut) 546,058; Vijayawada 543,008; Meerut 536,615; Thiruvananthapuram (Trivandrum) 520,125; Salem 518,615; Sholapur 514,860; Ranchi 502,771.

Capital: New Delhi, population 273,036 in 1981.

BIRTHS AND DEATHS
(estimates, based on Sample Registration Scheme)

	1986/87	1987/88	1988/89
Birth rate (per 1,000)	32.6	32.2	31.3
Death rate (per 1,000)	11.1	10.9	10.9

ECONOMICALLY ACTIVE POPULATION
(1981 census, excluding Assam)*

	Males	Females	Total
Agriculture, hunting, forestry and fishing	116,482,682	36,532,504	153,015,187
Mining and quarrying	1,100,931	163,158	1,264,089
Manufacturing	21,480,943	3,662,094	25,143,037
Electricity, gas and water	949,663	24,135	973,799
Construction	3,207,287	358,121	3,565,408
Trade, restaurants and hotels	11,356,083	808,674	12,164,757
Transport, storage and communications	5,898,901	170,432	6,069,332
Finance, insurance, real estate and business services	1,656,407	107,830	1,764,237
Community, social and personal services	15,410,505	3,146,217	18,556,722
Activities not adequately defined†	3,536,806	18,551,606	22,088,411
Total	181,080,208	63,524,771	244,604,979

* Figures are based on a 5% sample tabulation of census returns. As each figure is estimated independently, the totals shown may differ from the sum of the component parts.

† The figures refer to marginal workers and persons who were unemployed or seeking work for the first time.

Agriculture

PRINCIPAL CROPS ('000 metric tons, year ending 30 June)

	1987/88	1988/89	1989/90
Rice (milled)	56,860	70,489	74,053
Sorghum (Jowar)	12,200	10,170	12,915
Cat-tail millet (Bajra)	3,300	7,780	6,620
Maize	5,720	8,230	9,409
Finger millet (Ragi)	2,320	2,410	2,781
Small millets	1,250	1,164	1,112
Wheat	46,170	54,110	49,652
Barley	1,577	1,722	1,469
Total cereals	129,390	156,073	158,012
Chick-peas (Gram)	3,626	5,129	4,232
Pigeon-peas (Tur)	2,282	2,718	2,723
Dry beans, dry peas, lentils and other pulses	5,054	6,003	5,659
Total food grains	140,354	169,922	170,627
Groundnuts (in shell)	6,844	9,659	6,088
Sesame seed	583	682	715
Rapeseed and mustard	3,455	4,377	4,123
Linseed	393	361	342
Castor beans	480	416	508
Total edible oil seeds (incl. others)	n.a.	18,033	16,750
Cotton lint*	6,382	8,744	11,414
Jute†	5,793	6,710	7,112
Kenaf (Mesta)†	985	1,149	1,239
Tea (made)	673	706	703
Sugar cane:			
production gur	19,700	20,400	22,300
production cane	196,737	203,037	222,628
Tobacco (leaves)	367	491	n.a.
Potatoes	14,046	14,857	15,137
Chillies (dry)	580	680	783

* Production in '000 bales of 170 kg each.
† Production in '000 bales of 180 kg each.

Source: Directorate of Economics and Statistics, Ministry of Agriculture and Ministry of Commerce (for tea).

INDIA

LIVESTOCK (FAO estimates, '000 head year ending September)

	1987	1988	1989
Cattle*	199,300	193,000	195,500
Sheep*	55,482	51,684	53,486
Goats*	103,500	105,000	107,000
Pigs	10,200	10,300	10,300
Horses	950	953	955
Asses	1,300	1,328	1,400
Mules	134	135	138
Buffaloes*	74,230	72,000	73,700
Camels	1,350	1,390	1,400

* Unofficial figures.

Poultry (FAO estimates, million): 215 in 1987; 260 in 1988; 270 in 1989.

Source: FAO, *Production Yearbook*.

LIVESTOCK PRODUCTS ('000 metric tons)

	1987	1988	1989
Beef and veal†	239	232	234
Buffalo meat†	207	290	355
Mutton and lamb†	162	148	158
Goats' meat†	380	378	385
Pig meat†	80	86	86
Poultry meat†	193	225	240
Cows' milk*	19,300	22,000	23,000
Buffaloes' milk*	25,200	24,500	25,500
Goats' milk*	1,400	1,500	1,500
Butter and ghee*	750	800	840
Hen eggs*	952	980	1,072
Wool:			
greasy	43.7	44.3	29.0*
clean	29.3*	29.7*	22.0†
Cattle and buffalo hides (fresh)†	838.9	832.9	844.7
Sheep skins (fresh)†	48.6	45.0	45.0
Goat skins (fresh)†	88.2	87.3	89.1

* Unofficial figure(s).   † FAO estimate(s).

Source: FAO, *Production Yearbook*.

Forestry

ROUNDWOOD REMOVALS (FAO estimates, '000 cu metres)

	1986	1987	1988
Sawlogs, veneer logs and logs for sleepers	18,350	18,350	18,350
Pulpwood*	1,208	1,208	1,208
Other industrial wood	4,479	4,575	4,670
Fuel wood	230,352	235,268	240,184
Total	254,389	259,401	264,412

* Assumed to be unchanged since 1978.

Source: FAO, *Yearbook of Forest Products*.

SAWNWOOD PRODUCTION (FAO estimates, '000 cu metres)

	1983	1984	1985
Coniferous sawnwood (incl. boxboards)	1,965	2,160	2,374
Broadleaved sawnwood (incl. boxboards)	12,278	13,495	14,834
Sub-total	14,243	15,655	17,208
Railway sleepers*	252	252	252
Total	14,495	15,907	17,460

* Assumed to be unchanged since 1979.

1986–88: Annual production as in 1985 (FAO estimates).

Source: FAO, *Yearbook of Forest Products*.

Fishing

('000 metric tons, live weight)

	1987	1988	1989
Indian Ocean:			
Bombay-duck (Bummalo)	88.9	115.7	135.6
Marine catfishes	59.4	68.2	69.9
Croakers and drums	169.6	164.8	229.9
Indian oil-sardine (sardinella)	246.4	228.0	288.0
Anchovies	58.1	66.2	64.3
Hairtails and cutlass fishes	72.2	49.5	70.0
Indian mackerel	66.0	66.7	170.1
Other marine fishes (incl. unspecified)	918.1	1,073.4	1,218.6
Total sea-fish	1,678.7	1,832.5	2,246.4
Shrimps and prawns	197.2	232.8	238.4
Other marine animals	64.8	64.1	83.5
Total sea catch	1,940.7	2,129.4	2,568.3
Inland waters:			
Freshwater fishes	1,229.0	1,319.0	1,371.3
Total catch	3,169.7	3,448.4	3,939.6

Source: Department of Agriculture and Co-operation (Fisheries Division), Ministry of Agriculture.

Mining

('000 metric tons, unless otherwise indicated)

	1987/88	1988/89	1989/90
Coal	179,844	194,376	199,596
Lignite	8,496	8,280	12,636
Iron ore*	48,972	49,284	51,657
Manganese ore*	1,284	1,284	1,305
Bauxite	2,496	4,272	4,480
Chalk (Fireclay)	552	612	507
Kaolin (China clay)	660	552	576
Dolomite	2,136	2,136	2,448
Gypsum	1,704	1,440	1,567
Limestone	56,328	62,952	63,805
Crude petroleum	30,360	32,040	34,080
Sea salt	9,828	8,316	10,599
Chromium ore*	660	936	1,032
Phosphorite	624	696	713
Kyanite	36	40	37
Magnesite	432	528	476
Steatite	360	396	415
Copper ore*	5,064	5,124	5,211
Lead concentrates (metric tons)*	43,596	41,916	44,233
Zinc concentrates (metric tons)*	104,892	122,904	127,493
Mica—crude (metric tons)	3,600	4,800	4,200
Gold (kilograms)	1,872	2,016	1,754
Diamonds (carats)	17,304	13,632	16,605
Natural gas (million cu m)†	7,968	9,252	10,944

* Figures refer to gross weight. The estimated metal content is: Iron 63%; Manganese 40%; Chromium 30%; Copper 1.2%; Lead 70%; Zinc 60%.

† Figures refer to gas utilized.

Source: Indian Bureau of Mines.

INDIA
Statistical Survey

Industry

SELECTED PRODUCTS
('000 metric tons, unless otherwise indicated)

	1987/88	1988/89	1989/90
Refined sugar*	9,108	8,748	9,422
Cotton cloth (million metres)	9,401	8,964	n.a.
Jute manufactures	1,192	1,388	1,302
Paper and paper board	1,998	2,072	2,210
Soda ash	955	1,190	1,369
Fertilizers	7,476	8,904	8,624
Petroleum products	44,640	45,696	n.a.
Cement	39,576	44,292	n.a.
Pig iron	10,871	11,873	11,974
Finished steel	10,638	11,118	10,534
Aluminium (metric tons)	244,752	331,536	430,003
Diesel engines (number)	1,898,400	1,854,000	1,778,400
Sewing machines (number)	327,600	237,600	n.a.
Radio receivers (number)	984,000	1,044,000	666,000
Electric fans (number)	6,060,000	6,456,000	4,704,000
Passenger cars and jeeps (number)	171,684	201,936	223,831
Passenger buses and trucks (number)	119,868	115,788	125,836
Motor cycles and scooters (number)	1,505,304	1,666,920	1,753,766
Bicycles (number)	6,672,000	6,672,000	6,680,000

* Figures relate to crop year (beginning November) and are in respect of cane sugar only.

Finance

CURRENCY AND EXCHANGE RATES

Monetary Units
100 paise (singular: paisa) = 1 Indian rupee.

Denominations
Coins: 5, 10, 20, 25 and 50 paise; 2 rupees.
Notes: 1, 2, 5, 10, 20, 50, 100 and 500 rupees.

Sterling and Dollar Equivalents (30 September 1990)
£1 sterling = 33.850 rupees;
US $1 = 18.068 rupees;
1,000 Indian rupees = £29.54 = US $55.35.

Average Exchange Rate (rupees per US $)
1987   12.962
1988   13.917
1989   16.226

BUDGET (estimates, million rupees, year ending 31 March)

Revenue	1989/90	1990/91
Tax revenue	471,637.9	555,411.9
Customs	178,769.9	214,603.8
Union excise duties	221,034.2	249,519.6
Corporation tax	47,550.0	60,890.0
Income tax	10,778.1	13,616.9
Estate duty	40.0	35.0
Wealth tax	1,600.0	1,750.0
Gift tax	90.0	90.0
Expenditure tax	660.0	720.0
Taxes from Union Territories	9,387.6	12,058.5
Other taxes	1,728.1	2,128.1
Non-tax revenue	311,403.5	322,274.8
Fiscal services	8,432.4	5,652.2
Interest receipts	86,650.9	95,190.9
Dividends and profits	7,164.3	7,208.9
General services	14,707.9	16,084.9
Social and community services	2,995.4	3,080.2
Economic services	181,075.2	185,740.9
Grants in aid and contributions	9,124.8	8,077.3
Non-tax revenue from Union Territories	1,252.6	1,239.5
Total	**783,041.4**	**877,686.7**

Expenditure	1989/90	1990/91
General services	348,316.9	389,399.7
Organs of state	4,724.3	3,639.7
Fiscal services	11,707.0	11,331.7
Interest payments and debt-servicing	177,100.0	208,500.0
Administrative services	20,616.4	23,499.1
Pensions and miscellaneous general services	27,807.5	28,875.0
Defence services	106,361.7	113,554.2
Social services	28,670.4	33,107.7
Economic services	334,826.8	354,133.3
Agriculture and related activities	41,720.6	48,689.6
Rural development	24,972.3	25,100.2
Irrigation and flood control	848.8	1,017.9
Special areas programmes	78.1	150.7
Energy	8,876.2	9,168.7
Industry and minerals	58,277.0	46,853.4
Transport	123,421.4	130,696.4
Communications	39,330.1	50,184.1
Science, technology and the environment	10,504.8	12,284.5
General economic services	26,797.5	29,987.8
Grants in aid and contributions	183,578.1	218,084.1
Grants in aid to state governments	87,959.8	113,089.3
Grants in aid to Union Territories	780.3	1,143.5
Payment of states' share of Union excise duties	93,101.1	101,883.7
Technical and economic co-operation with other countries	1,621.6	1,901.6
Aid materials and equipment	115.3	66.0
Disbursements by Union Territories	12,010.9	13,275.5
Total	**907,403.1**	**1,008,000.3**

Source: Government of India, Annual Budget Papers, 1990/91.
Revised totals (million rupees, year ending 31 March): Revenue 759,460 in 1989/90, 873,290 in 1990/91; Expenditure 876,960 in 1989/90, 945,350 in 1990/91.
Eighth Five-Year Plan (1990–95) (estimates, million rupees): total expenditure 6,100,000; public sector outlay 3,350,000; private sector outlay 2,750,000.

INTERNATIONAL RESERVES (US $ million at 31 December)

	1987	1988	1989
Gold*	213	183	161
IMF special drawing rights	159	96	113
Reserve position in IMF	691	656	640
Foreign exchange	5,603	4,148	3,105
Total	**6,666**	**5,083**	**4,019**

* National valuation, based on cost of acquisition.
Source: IMF, *International Financial Statistics*.

MONEY SUPPLY
(million rupees, last Friday of year ending 31 March)

	1987/88	1988/89	1989/90
Currency with the public	336,500	384,150	465,640
Demand deposits with banks	238,550	277,300	342,390
Other deposits with reserve bank	2,970	4,620	8,060
Total money	**578,020**	**666,070**	**816,090**

Source: Reserve Bank of India.

INDIA

COST OF LIVING
(Consumer Price Index for industrial workers; base: 1980 = 100)

	1987	1988	1989
Food	184.7	202.7	214.7
Fuel and light	200.6	216.9*	235.6
Clothing	158.0	167.5*	184.4
Rent	190.4	211.5*	224.3
All items (incl. others)	184.4	201.8	216.2

* Average for January–September.
Source: ILO, mainly *Year Book of Labour Statistics*.

NATIONAL ACCOUNTS
('000 million rupees at current prices, year ending 31 March)

National Income and Product

	1986/87	1987/88	1988/89
Domestic factor incomes*	2,305.13	2,605.32	3,094.41
Consumption of fixed capital	299.29	338.76	394.55
Gross domestic product at factor cost	2,604.42	2,944.08	3,488.96
Indirect taxes	427.14	499.62	565.25
Less Subsidies	97.95	118.17	142.63
GDP in purchasers' values	2,933.61	3,325.53	3,911.58
Factor income from abroad	6.63	6.03	6.03†
Less Factor income paid abroad	24.68	32.22	32.22†
Gross national product	2,915.56	3,299.34	3,885.39
Less Consumption of fixed capital	299.29	338.76	394.55
National income in market prices	2,616.27	2,960.58	3,490.84
Other current transfers from abroad	29.91	35.33	35.33†
Less Other current transfers paid abroad	0.15	0.34	0.34†
National disposable income	2,646.03	2,995.57	3,525.83

* Compensation of employees and the operating surplus of enterprises.
† Assumed to be unchanged from 1987/88.

Expenditure on the Gross Domestic Product

	1986/87	1987/88	1988/89
Government final consumption expenditure	346.25	410.34	463.61
Private final consumption expenditure	1,964.44	2,210.17	2,549.85
Increase in stocks	92.86	86.89	151.82
Gross fixed capital formation	620.22	674.51	801.98
Total domestic expenditure	3,023.77	3,381.91	3,967.26
Exports of goods and services	165.43	203.48	
Less Imports of goods and services	223.59	254.14	−55.68
Statistical discrepancy	−32.00	−5.72	
GDP in purchasers' values	2,933.61	3,325.53	3,911.58

Gross Domestic Product by Economic Activity
(at current factor cost)

	1986/87*	1987/88†	1988/89†
Agriculture	694.59	837.27	1,051.91
Forestry and logging	47.27	51.02	54.41
Fishing	20.58	28.26	31.09
Mining and quarrying	61.14	71.13	79.82
Manufacturing	423.52	541.60	629.91
Electricity, gas and water	25.84	62.68	71.75
Construction	138.93	170.32	198.56
Trade, restaurants and hotels	319.64	372.25	437.14
Transport, storage and communications	115.17	199.22	240.44
Banking and insurance	89.02	111.41	132.27
Real estate and business services	88.49	137.35	150.67
Public administration and defence	136.03	179.29	205.11
Other services	147.93	182.28	205.88
Total	2,308.15	2,944.08	3,488.96

* Figures refer to net domestic product.
† Estimates.

BALANCE OF PAYMENTS (US $ million)

	1985	1986	1987
Merchandise exports f.o.b.	9,465	10,248	11,884
Merchandise imports f.o.b.	−15,081	−15,686	−17,661
Trade balance	−5,616	−5,438	−5,777
Exports of services	3,913	3,746	3,813
Imports of services	−5,250	−5,526	−6,235
Balance on goods and services	−6,953	−7,218	−8,199
Private unrequited transfers (net)	2,456	2,223	2,636
Government unrequited transfers (net)	320	399	370
Current balance	−4,177	−4,597	−5,192
Long-term capital (net)	3,341	4,496	4,511
Short-term capital (net)	−60	−504	1,223
Net errors and omissions	500	197	−409
Total (net monetary movements)	−397	−409	133
Monetization of gold (net)	13	22	—
Valuation changes (net)	429	93	165
Exceptional financing (net)	37	30	21
Changes in reserves	82	−263	318

Source: IMF, *International Financial Statistics*.

External Trade

PRINCIPAL COMMODITIES
(million rupees, year ending 31 March)

Imports c.i.f.	1986/87	1987/88	1988/89*
Wheat	372.7	89.9	3,781.6
Milk and cream	84.5	641.0	775.0
Fruit and nuts (excl. cashew nuts)	592.1	635.8	639.5
Sugar	2,052.4	1,930.7	n.a.
Pulp and waste paper	2,084.3	2,385.4	2,528.0
Synthetic and regenerated fibres	441.1	331.4	374.3
Wool (raw)	558.7	1,318.7	1,575.3
Crude rubber (incl. synthetic and reclaimed)	807.4	1,204.1	1,726.4
Crude fertilizers	1,311.0	1,398.4	1,850.9
Manufactured fertilizers	4,951.3	1,878.7	4,929.5
Sulphur and unroasted iron pyrites	1,473.1	1,803.1	2,405.9
Other crude minerals	644.0	801.0	1,210.8
Metalliferous ores and metal			

INDIA

Imports c.i.f.—continued	1986/87	1987/88	1988/89*
scrap	3,677.1	4,424.6	6,774.2
Mineral fuels, lubricants, etc.	27,966.8	40,427.9	43,740.4
Edible vegetable oil	6,119.6	9,687.7	7,270.1
Organic chemicals	5,044.1	6,761.1	11,270.1
Inorganic chemicals	5,312.6	4,057.1	8,128.3
Chemical materials and products	1,196.2	1,913.0	2,040.9
Artificial resins, plastic materials	4,358.9	5,670.7	8,101.4
Medicinal and pharmaceutical products	1,580.3	1,678.0	2,020.9
Paper, paperboard and manufactures	1,948.1	2,700.3	3,057.0
Textile yarn, fabrics, etc.	1,247.2	1,867.0	2,873.4
Pearls, precious and semi-precious stones	14,954.8	20,184.4	31,752.1
Other non-metallic mineral manufactures	851.3	1,048.0	1,658.3
Iron and steel	14,496.9	13,197.1	19,372.6
Non-ferrous metals	4,149.1	6,389.1	7,858.2
Other metal manufactures	1,991.4	1,605.2	1,938.5
Non-electric machinery	37,139.0	45,519.3	43,709.0
Electrical machinery	8,774.5	10,932.9	16,080.2
Transport equipment	6,768.4	7,598.9	7,666.0
Professional, scientific and controlling instruments, photographic and optical goods, watches and clocks	4,556.2	4,997.5	6,957.4
Total (incl. others)	202,006.5	222,437.4	281,936.5

* Provisional.

Source: Ministry of Commerce, *Annual Report 1987/88, 1988/89, 1989/90*.

Exports f.o.b.	1986/87	1987/88*	1988/89*
Marine products	5,389.7	5,251.1	6,325.0
Meat and meat preparations	754.6	855.4	944.7
Rice	1,973.3	3,245.7	3,314.7
Wheat	347.1	354.6	29.9
Cashew kernels	3,275.5	3,067.0	2,772.0
Other vegetables and fruit	1,558.2	1,507.9	1,644.0
Coffee and coffee substitutes	2,967.0	2,632.2	2,797.1
Tea and maté	5,767.8	5,923.7	5,989.6
Spices	2,790.3	3,092.9	2,508.0
Oil cakes	1,897.7	1,732.8	3,704.3
Unmanufactured tobacco, tobacco refuse	1,453.6	1,093.2	1,029.3
Cotton (raw)	2,046.6	954.9	280.2
Cotton fabrics	6,372.5	10,637.8	11,313.0
Ready-made garments	13,305.1	17,920.6	20,975.3
Jute manufactures	2,440.2	2,428.2	2,499.1
Carpets (hand-made)	2,827.2	3,914.3	4,695.6
Leather and leather manufactures	9,224.1	11,485.2	14,895.0
Gems and jewellery	20,743.1	26,136.0	43,989.9
Works of art	1,905.5	2,483.8	3,256.2
Iron ore	5,466.1	5,427.6	6,725.0
Other ores and minerals	1,509.5	1,373.2	3,133.0
Engineering products	11,327.3	14,330.4	23,216.6
Chemicals and allied products	5,458.8	7,742.9	14,369.1
Mineral fuels, lubricants, etc.	4,112.3	6,487.5	5,049.6
Total (incl. others)	124,523.6	157,412.3	202,951.5

* Provisional.

Source: Ministry of Commerce, *Annual Report 1987/88, 1988/89, 1989/90*.

PRINCIPAL TRADING PARTNERS
(million rupees, year ending 31 March)

Imports c.i.f.	1986/87	1987/88	1988/89*
Australia	4,310.3	5,033.6	7,018.4
Belgium	10,897.7	13,706.7	20,376.8
Brazil	2,807.0	3,556.5	3,331.1
Canada	3,803.7	2,987.4	4,269.3
Egypt	3,013.0	984.6	733.7
France	6,696.4	7,975.7	8,216.0
Germany, Democratic Republic	896.5	932.7	1,333.9
Germany, Federal Republic	19,378.8	21,586.2	24,719.1
Hong Kong	4,092.0	1,200.7	1,752.5
Iran	1,405.3	1,440.5	1,291.5
Iraq	1,261.5	6,110.8	1,938.4
Italy	4,902.2	5,126.0	5,032.2
Japan	25,589.2	21,262.0	26,335.4
Jordan	1,343.7	1,230.6	1,958.9
Korea, Republic	3,223.2	3,334.1	4,332.3
Kuwait	2,903.1	4,715.2	5,215.8
Malaysia	5,521.5	8,405.5	7,921.4
Morocco	2,259.3	1,686.0	3,055.7
Netherlands	3,853.5	4,424.5	5,360.7
Poland	1,094.3	568.8	664.5
Romania	1,058.1	580.1	717.5
Saudi Arabia	8,625.3	7,654.8	18,945.2
Singapore	3,606.0	4,192.7	6,275.0
Spain	2,120.5	1,792.3	1,398.4
Sweden	3,533.0	3,037.7	2,354.7
Switzerland	3,485.3	2,362.9	2,851.4
USSR	10,147.9	16,077.7	12,580.6
United Arab Emirates	3,605.3	7,628.7	8,812.8
United Kingdom	16,232.5	18,284.9	24,006.0
USA	19,610.8	20,016.8	31,965.3
Yugoslavia	1,022.9	1,700.0	1,513.2
Zambia	703.1	1,410.3	1,776.4

* Provisional.

Source: Ministry of Commerce, *Annual Report 1987/88, 1988/89, 1989/90*.

Exports f.o.b.	1986/87	1987/88*	1988/89*
Australia	1,460.8	1,811.0	2,660.3
Bangladesh	1,639.6	1,868.1	2,619.3
Belgium	3,425.4	4,844.2	8,859.1
Canada	1,367.7	1,704.1	1,972.2
Czechoslovakia	736.1	1,025.4	1,849.5
Egypt	809.7	782.6	855.0
France	2,712.9	3,752.4	4,319.1
Germany, Democratic Republic	876.8	1,063.3	1,830.5
Germany, Federal Republic	7,332.4	10,619.1	12,366.0
Hong Kong	4,102.0	4,531.5	8,205.9
Iran	472.6	1,386.3	893.6
Italy	3,105.1	5,023.8	5,405.8
Japan	13,338.5	16,149.2	21,622.6
Kuwait	927.2	1,056.5	1,553.6
Malaysia	848.3	891.7	1,303.3
Nepal	1,028.3	936.8	986.1
Netherlands	2,258.4	2,824.5	4,041.1
Poland	1,216.7	2,012.0	1,459.0
Romania	803.1	689.8	376.7
Saudi Arabia	2,135.6	2,959.1	3,261.8
Singapore	2,159.1	2,753.5	3,255.1
Sri Lanka	868.4	1,016.3	1,470.3
Switzerland	1,593.5	2,049.1	2,711.3
USSR	18,672.0	19,714.9	26,092.1
United Arab Emirates	2,871.2	3,141.4	4,260.0
United Kingdom	7,000.5	10,333.8	11,648.9
USA	23,317.4	29,076.3	37,362.8

* Provisional.

Source: Ministry of Commerce, *Annual Report 1987/88, 1988/89, 1989/90*.

INDIA
Statistical Survey

Transport

RAILWAYS (million, year ending 31 March)

	1987/88	1988/89	1989/90
Passengers	3,827	3,500	3,655
Passenger-km	269,389	263,731	276,564
Freight (metric tons)	288	300	310
Freight (metric ton-km)	218,364	221,760	229,020

Source: Railway Board, Ministry of Railways.

ROAD TRAFFIC ('000 motor vehicles in use at 31 March)

	1987	1988	1989*
Private cars	1,484	1,675	
Jeeps	297	371	2,481
Taxis	189	193	
Buses and coaches	239	261	294
Goods vehicles	962	1,072	1,197
Motor cycles and scooters	7,694	9,228	10,617
Others	1,670	1,838	2,104
Total	12,534	14,639	16,693

* Provisional

Source: Transport Research Division, Ministry of Surface Transport.

INTERNATIONAL SEA-BORNE SHIPPING (year ending 31 March)

	1983/84	1984/85	1985/86
Vessels* ('000 net regd tons):			
Entered	24,786	31,036	35,566
Cleared	23,002	26,766	26,924
Freight† ('000 metric tons):			
Loaded	29,040	31,720	36,730
Unloaded	38,740	36,846	45,818

Freight† ('000 metric tons): Loaded 39,789 in 1986/87, 40,147 in 1987/88; Unloaded 43,576 in 1986/87; 49,953 in 1987/88.

* Excluding minor and intermediate ports.
† Including bunkers.

Source: Directorate General of Commercial Intelligence and Statistics.

CIVIL AVIATION (traffic)

	1987/88	1988/89	1989/90
Kilometres flown ('000)	125,544	114,840	117,445
Passenger-km ('000)	17,648,916	17,114,940	17,880,192
Freight ton-km ('000)	647,652	645,636	677,918
Mail ton-km ('000)	27,408	26,412	26,136

Source: Directorate General of Civil Aviation.

Tourism

FOREIGN VISITORS BY COUNTRY OF ORIGIN*

	1987	1988	1989
Australia	32,883	31,462	30,443
Canada	37,677	37,498	40,306
France	64,432	69,799	78,001
Germany, Federal Republic	70,697	76,371	78,431
Iran	23,571	20,215	19,363
Italy	41,151	47,612	50,751
Japan	46,240	49,244	58,707
Malaysia	28,480	29,635	33,120
Saudi Arabia	24,475	22,612	19,622
Singapore	26,380	27,565	29,377
Sri Lanka	74,351	70,640	67,680
Switzerland	27,791	31,147	32,034
USSR	27,968	33,739	36,940
United Arab Emirates	31,180	29,385	31,479
United Kingdom	166,590	200,509	229,496
USA	134,876	122,888	134,314
Total (incl. others)	1,163,774	1,239,992	1,337,232

* Figures exclude nationals of Bangladesh and Pakistan. Including these, the total was 1,736,093 in 1989.

Source: Ministry of Tourism and Civil Aviation.

Receipts from tourism (million rupees, year ending 31 March): 18,560 in 1987/88; 21,030 in 1988/89; 24,560 in 1989/90.

Communications Media

	1985	1986	1987
Television receivers*	n.a.	12,500,000	n.a.
Telephones*	n.a.	4,044,000	4,408,000
Daily newspapers*	1,802	1,978	2,151
Non-daily newspapers*	20,846	21,638	22,478
Other periodicals			

Licensed television receivers: 6 million in 1988.
Radio receivers in use (million): 62 in 1987; 63.5 in 1988.

* Figures refer to year ending 31 March.

Sources: Ministry of Communications; Registrar of Newspapers for India; Ministry of Information and Broadcasting; UNESCO, *Statistical Yearbook*.

Education

(1988/89)

	Institutions	Teachers	Students
Primary	548,059	1,603,058	95,739,976
Middle	144,145	1,032,534	30,940,062
Secondary (High School)	56,543	787,974	13,149,351
Higher secondary (New pattern)	12,122	447,556	3,080,591

Source: Ministry of Human Resources Development.

Directory

The Constitution

The Constitution of India, adopted by the Constituent Assembly on 26 November 1949, was inaugurated on 26 January 1950. The Preamble declares that the People of India solemnly resolve to constitute a Sovereign Democratic Republic and to secure to all its citizens justice, liberty, equality and fraternity. There are 397 articles and nine schedules, which form a comprehensive document.

UNION OF STATES

The Union of India comprises 25 states and seven Union Territories. There are provisions for the formation and admission of new states.

The Constitution confers citizenship on a threefold basis of birth, descent, and residence. Provisions are made for refugees who have migrated from Pakistan and for persons of Indian origin residing abroad.

FUNDAMENTAL RIGHTS AND DIRECTIVE PRINCIPLES

The rights of the citizen contained in Part III of the Constitution are declared fundamental and enforceable in law. 'Untouchability' is abolished and its practice in any form is a punishable offence. The Directive Principles of State Policy provide a code intended to ensure promotion of the economic, social and educational welfare of the State in future legislation.

THE PRESIDENT

The President is the head of the Union, exercising all executive powers on the advice of the Council of Ministers responsible to Parliament. He is elected by an electoral college consisting of elected members of both Houses of Parliament and the Legislatures of the States. The President holds office for a term of five years and is eligible for re-election. He may be impeached for violation of the Constitution. The Vice-President is the ex officio Chairman of the Rajya Sabha and is elected by a joint sitting of both Houses of Parliament.

THE PARLIAMENT

The Parliament of the Union consists of the President and two Houses: the Rajya Sabha (Council of States) and the Lok Sabha (House of the People). The Rajya Sabha consists of 245 members, of whom a number are nominated by the President. One-third of its members retire every two years. Elections are indirect, each state's legislative quota being elected by the members of the state's legislative assembly. The Lok Sahba has 542 members elected by adult franchise; not more than 17 represent the Union Territories. It may also include a number of members nominated by the President.

GOVERNMENT OF THE STATES

The governmental machinery of states closely resembles that of the Union. Each of these states has a governor at its head appointed by the President for a term of five years to exercise executive power on the advice of a council of ministers. The states' legislatures consist of the Governor and either one house (legislative assembly) or two houses (legislative assembly and legislative council). The term of the assembly is five years, but the council is not subject to dissolution.

LANGUAGE

The Constitution provides that the official language of the Union shall be Hindi. (The English language will continue to be an associate language for many official purposes.)

LEGISLATION—FEDERAL SYSTEM

The Constitution provides that bills, other than money bills, can be introduced in either House. To become law, they must be passed by both Houses and receive the assent of the President. In financial affairs, the authority of the Lower House is final. The various subjects of legislation are enumerated on three lists in the seventh schedule of the Constitution: the Union List, containing nearly 100 entries, including external affairs, defence, communications and atomic energy; the State List, containing 65 entries, including local government, police, public health, education; and the Concurrent List, with over 40 entries, including criminal law, marriage and divorce, labour welfare. The Constitution vests residuary authority in the Centre. All matters not enumerated in the Concurrent or State Lists will be deemed to be included in the Union List, and in the event of conflict between Union and State Law on any subject enumerated in the Concurrent List the Union Law will prevail. In time of emergency Parliament may even exercise powers otherwise exclusively vested in the states. Under Article 356, 'If the President on receipt of a report from the government of a state or otherwise is satisfied that a situation has arisen in which the Government of the state cannot be carried on in accordance with the provisions of this Constitution, the President may by Proclamation: (a) assume to himself all or any of the functions of the government of the state and all or any of the powers of the governor or any body or authority in the state other than the Legislature of the state; (b) declare that the powers of the Legislature of the state shall be exercisable by or under the authority of Parliament; (c) make such incidental provisions as appear to the President to be necessary': provided that none of the powers of a High Court be assumed by the President or suspended in any way. Unless such a Proclamation is approved by both Houses of Parliament, it ceases to operate after two months. A Proclamation so approved ceases to operate after six months, unless renewed by Parliament. Its renewal cannot be extended beyond a total period of three years. An independent judiciary exists to define and interpret the Constitution and to resolve constitutional disputes arising between states, or between a state and the Government of India.

OTHER PROVISIONS

Other Provisions of the Constitution deal with the administration of tribal areas, relations between the Union and states, inter-state trade and finance.

AMENDMENTS

The Constitution is flexible in character, and a simple process of amendment has been adopted. For amendment of provisions concerning the Supreme Courts and the High Courts, the distribution of legislative powers between the Union and the states, the representation of the states in Parliament, etc., the amendment must be passed by both Houses of Parliament and must further be ratified by the legislatures of not less than half the states. In other cases no reference to the state legislatures is necessary.

Numerous amendments were adopted in August 1975, following the declaration of a state of emergency in June. The Constitution (39th Amendment) Bill laid down that the President's reasons for proclaiming an emergency may not be challenged in any court. Under the Constitution (40th Amendment) Bill, 38 existing laws may not be challenged before any court on the ground of violation of fundamental rights. Thus detainees under the Maintenance of Internal Security Act could not be told the grounds of their detention and were forbidden bail and any claim to liberty through natural or common law. The Constitution (41st Amendment) Bill provided that the President, Prime Minister and state Governors should be immune from criminal prosecution for life and from civil prosecution during their term of office.

In November 1976 a 59-clause Constitution (42nd Amendment) Bill was approved by Parliament and came into force in January 1977. Some of the provisions of the Bill are that the Indian Democratic Republic shall be named a 'Democratic Secular and Socialist Republic'; that the President 'shall act in accordance with' the advice given to him by the Prime Minister and the Council of Ministers, and, acting at the Prime Minister's direction, shall be empowered for two years to amend the Constitution by executive order, in any way beneficial to the enforcement of the whole; that the term of the Lok Sabha and of the State Assemblies shall be extended from five to six years; that there shall be no limitation on the constituent power of Parliament to amend the Constitution, and that India's Supreme Court shall be barred from hearing petitions challenging Constitutional amendments; that strikes shall be forbidden in the public services and the Union Government have the power to deploy police or other forces under its own superintendence and control in any state. Directive Principles are given precedence over Fundamental Rights: 10 basic duties of citizens are listed, including the duty to 'defend the country and render national service when called upon to do so'.

The Janata Party Government, which came into power in March 1977, promised to amend the Constitution during the year, so as to 'restore the balance between the people and Parliament, Parliament and the judiciary, the judiciary and the executive, the states and the centre, and the citizen and the Government that the founding fathers of the Constitution had worked out'. The Constitution (43rd Amendment) Bill, passed by Parliament in December 1977, the Constitution (44th Amendment) Bill, passed by Parliament in December 1977 and later redesignated the 43rd

INDIA

Amendment, and the Constitution (45th Amendment) Bill, passed by Parliament in December 1978 and later redesignated the 44th Amendment, reversed most of the changes enacted by the Constitution (42nd Amendment) Bill. The 44th Amendment is particularly detailed on emergency provisions: An emergency may not be proclaimed unless 'the security of India or any part of its territory was threatened by war or external aggression or by armed rebellion.' Its introduction must be approved by a two-thirds majority of Parliament within a month, and after six months the emergency may be continued only with the approval of Parliament. Among the provisions left unchanged after these Bills were a section subordinating Fundamental Rights to Directive Principles and a clause empowering the central government to deploy armed forces under its control in any state without the state government's consent. In May 1980 the Indian Supreme Court repealed sections 4 and 55 of the 42nd Amendment Act, thus curtailing Parliament's power to enforce directive principles and to amend the Constitution. The death penalty was declared constitutionally valid. The 53rd Amendment to the Constitution, approved by Parliament in August 1986, granted statehood to the Union Territory of Mizoram; the 55th Amendment, approved in December 1986, granted statehood to the Union Territory of Arunachal Pradesh; and the 57th Amendment, approved in May 1987, granted statehood to the Union Territory of Goa (Daman and Diu remain, however, as a Union Territory). The 59th Amendment, approved in March 1988, empowered the Government to impose a state of emergency in Punjab, on the grounds of internal disturbances. In December 1988 the minimum voting age was lowered from 21 to 18 years.

THE PANCHAYAT RAJ SCHEME

This scheme is designed to decentralize the powers of the Union and State Governments. It is based on the Panchayat (Village Council) and the Gram Sabha (Village Parliament) and envisages the gradual transference of local government from state to local authority. Revenue and internal security will remain state responsibilities at present. By 1978 the scheme had been introduced in all the states except Meghalaya, Nagaland and 23 out of 31 districts in Bihar. The Panchayat operated in all the Union Territories except Lakshadweep, Mizoram (which became India's 23rd state in February 1987) and Pondicherry.

The Government

President: RAMASWAMY VENKATARAMAN (sworn in 25 July 1987).
Vice-President: Dr SHANKAR DAYAL SHARMA (sworn in 3 September 1987).

COUNCIL OF MINISTERS*
(February 1991)

Prime Minister and Minister of Defence, of Home Affairs, of Industry, of Information and Broadcasting, of Labour, of Welfare, of Ocean Development, of Personnel, Public Grievances and Pensions, of Atomic Energy, of Planning, of Programme Implementation, and of Science and Technology, and Minister of State: CHANDRA SHEKHAR.
Deputy Prime Minister and Minister of Agriculture and of Tourism: DEVI LAL.
Minister of External Affairs: (vacant).
Minister of Energy: KALYAN SINGH KALVI.
Minister of Commerce and of Law and Justice: Dr SUBRAMANIAN SWAMY.
Minister of Finance: YASHWANT SINHA.
Minister of Food and Civil Supplies: RAO BIRENDRA SINGH.
Minister of Health and Family Welfare: (vacant).
Minister of Human Resources Development: RAJMANGAL PANDE.
Minister of Petroleum and Chemicals and of Parliamentary Affairs: SATYA PRAKASH MALVIYA.
Minister of Railways: JANESHWAR MISHRA.
Minister of Steel and Mines: ASHOKE KUMAR SEN.
Minister of Textiles and of Food-Processing Industries: HUKUMDEO NARYAN YADAV.
Minister of Urban Development: DAULAT RAM SARAN.
Minister of Water Resources and of Surface Transport: MANUBHAI KOTADIA.
Minister of State for Civil Aviation: HARMOHAN DHAWAN.

* Following the collapse of the parliamentary alliance between the Janata Dal (S) and Congress (I), Chandra Shekhar resigned on 6 March 1991, but, at the President's request, agreed to head an interim government until the holding of a fresh general election (probably in April or May).

Minister of State for Communications: Dr SANJAY SINGH.
Minister of State for the Environment and Forests: MANEKA GANDHI.

In addition, there are 12 Ministers of State and four Deputy Ministers.

MINISTRIES

President's Office: Rashtrapati Bhavan, New Delhi 110 004; tel. (11) 3015321; telex 3166427.
Vice-President's Office: 6 Maulana Azad Rd, New Delhi 110 011; tel. (11) 3016344.
Prime Minister's Office: South Block, New Delhi 110 011; tel. (11) 3012312.
Ministry of Agriculture: Krishi Bhavan, Dr Rajendra Prasad Rd, New Delhi 110 001; tel. (11) 388911; telex 3165423.
Ministry of Civil Aviation: Sardar Patel Bhavan, New Delhi 110 001; tel. (11) 351700; telex 3165976.
Ministry of Commerce and Tourism: Transport Bhavan, Parliament St, New Delhi 110 001; tel. (11) 37117890; telex 3166527; fax (11) 3710518.
Ministry of Communications: Sanchar Bhavan, 20 Asoka Rd, New Delhi 110 001; tel. (11) 3710448; telex 314422.
Ministry of Defence: South Block, New Delhi 110 011; tel. (11) 3012380; telex 3162679.
Ministry of Electronics: Lok Nayak Bhavan, Khan Market, New Delhi 110 003; tel. (11) 698713.
Ministry of Energy: Shastri Bhavan, New Delhi 110 001; tel. (11) 3710271.
Ministry of the Environment and Forests: Paryavaran Bhavan, CGO Complex Phase II, Lodi Rd, New Delhi 110 003; tel. (11) 360721.
Ministry of External Affairs: South Block, New Delhi 110 011; tel. (11) 3012318; telex 3161880.
Ministry of Finance: North Block, New Delhi 110 001; tel. (11) 3012611; telex 3166562.
Ministry of Food and Civil Supplies: Krishi Bhavan, New Delhi 110 001; tel. (11) 382349; telex 3166505.
Ministry of Food-Processing Industries: Transport Bhavan, Parliament St, New Delhi 110 001; tel. (11) 3711945.
Ministry of Health and Family Welfare: Nirman Bhavan, New Delhi 110 011; tel. (11) 3018863.
Ministry of Home Affairs: Room 26, North Block, New Delhi 110 001; tel. (11) 3012951; telex 3166724.
Ministry of Human Resources Development: Shastri Bhavan, New Delhi 110 001; tel. (11) 386995; telex 3161336.
Ministry of Industry: Udyog Bhavan, New Delhi 110 011; tel. (11) 3011815; telex 3166294.
Ministry of Information and Broadcasting: Shastri Bhavan, New Delhi 110 001; tel. (11) 382639; telex 3166349.
Ministry of Labour: Shram Shakti Bhavan, Rafi Marg, New Delhi 110 001; tel. (11) 3710265; telex 3161131.
Ministry of Law and Justice: Shastri Bhavan, Dr Rajendra Prasad Rd, New Delhi 110 001; tel. (11) 384777.
Ministry of Ocean Development: Block 12, CGO Complex, Lodi Rd, New Delhi 110 003; tel. (11) 360874.
Ministry of Parliamentary Affairs: Parliament House, New Delhi 110 001; tel. (11) 3017663.
Ministry of Personnel, Public Grievances and Pensions: Block 3, CGO Complex, New Delhi 110 003; tel. (11) 3014848.
Ministry of Petroleum and Chemicals: Shastri Bhavan, New Delhi 110 001; tel. (11) 383501; telex 3166235.
Ministry of Planning: Sardar Patel Bhavan, Parliament St, New Delhi 110 001; tel. (11) 350150.
Ministry of Programme Implementation: Sardar Patel Bhavan, New Delhi 110 001; tel. (11) 3012787; telex 3163195.
Ministry of Railways: Rail Bhavan, Raisina Rd, New Delhi 110 001; tel. (11) 388931; telex 313561.
Ministry of Science and Technology: CSIR Bldg, Rafi Marg, New Delhi 110 001; tel. (11) 3711744.
Ministry of Space: 3 Lok Nayak Bhavan, New Delhi 110 003; tel. (11) 698313.
Ministry of Steel and Mines: Udyog Bhavan, New Delhi 110 011; tel. (11) 3015489; telex 3161483.
Ministry of Surface Transport: 1 Transport Bhavan, Parliament St, New Delhi 110 001; tel. (11) 3714938; telex 3161159.
Ministry of Textiles: Udyog Bhavan, New Delhi 110 011; tel. (11) 3011769.

INDIA
                        Directory

Ministry of Urban Development: Nirman Bhavan, New Delhi 110 011; tel. (11) 3019377.
Ministry of Water Resources: Shram Shakti Bhavan, Rafi Marg, New Delhi 110 001; tel. (11) 3710305; telex 3166568.
Ministry of Welfare: Shastri Bhavan, New Delhi 110 001; tel. (11) 382683; telex 3166256.

Legislature

PARLIAMENT

Rajya Sabha
(Council of States)

Most of the members of the Rajya Sabha are indirectly elected by the State Assemblies for six years, with one-third retiring every two years. The remaining members are nominated by the President.

Chairman: YASHWANT SINHA.

Distribution of Seats, August 1990

Party	Seats
Congress (I)	108
Janata Dal	39
Communist (CPI–Marxist)	17
Telugu Desam	10
Bharatiya Janata Party	17
All India Anna Dravida Munnetra Kazhagam	4
Communist (CPI)	3
Dravida Munnetra Kazhagam	10
Asom Gana Parishad	5
Revolutionary Socialist Party	2
Jammu and Kashmir National Conference (F)	2
Independents and others	12
Nominated	5
Vacant	11
Total	**245**

Lok Sabha
(House of the People)

Speaker: RABI RAY.
Deputy Speaker: SHIVRAJ PATIL.

General Election, 22, 24 and 26 November 1989*

Party	Number of votes (million)	Seats
Congress (I)	115	193
Telugu Desam	10	2
Communist (CPI–Marxist)	19	32
All India Anna Dravida Munnetra Kazhagam (AIADMK)	4.5	11
Janata Dal	50	141
Bahujan Samaj Party	5.7	3
Communist (CPI)	7.5	12
Jharkhand Mukti Morcha	n.a.	3
Jammu and Kashmir National Conference (F)	n.a.	3
Revolutionary Socialist Party	1.8	4
Akali Dal (Mann)	2.3	6
Forward Bloc	1.2	3
Bharatiya Janata Party	33	88
Indian Union Muslim League	n.a.	2
Unattached, independents and others	n.a.	22
Nominated	—	2†
Vacant	—	18
Total	n.a.	**545**

* Elections were countermanded in four seats because of the deaths of candidates, and polling for the 14 seats in Assam was postponed.
† Nominated by the President to represent the Anglo-Indian community.

State Governments
(February 1991)

ANDHRA PRADESH
(Capital—Hyderabad)

Governor: KRISHNA KANT.
Chief Minister: N. JANARDHAN REDDY (Congress—I).
Legislative Assembly: 294 seats (Congress—I 183, Telugu Desam Party 74, Communist—CPI—M 6, Communist—CPI 8, Majlis-Ittehad-ul-Muslimeen 4, Bharatiya Janata Party 5, independents and others 13, vacant 1).

ARUNACHAL PRADESH
(Capital—Itanagar)

Governor: D. D. THAKUR.
Chief Minister: GEGONG APANG (Congress—I).
Legislative Assembly: 60 seats (Congress—I 37, Janata Dal 11, Janata Party 1, independents and others 11).

ASSAM
(Capital—Dispur)

Governor: DEVI DAS THAKUR.
Chief Minister: (vacant).
Legislative Assembly: 126 seats (Asom Gana Parishad 72, Congress—I 23, United Minorities Front 17, Congress—S 4, Plains Tribal Council of Assam 3, Communist—CPI—M 2, independents and others 3, vacant 2).

The state government was dismissed, and the Assembly was suspended, when Assam was placed under President's rule in November 1990.

BIHAR
(Capital—Patna)

Governor: B. SATYA NARAIN REDDY.
Chief Minister: LALLU PRASAD YADAV (Janata Dal).
Legislative Assembly: 380 seats (Janata Dal 116, Congress—I 71, Lok Dal 46, Communist—CPI 33, Bharatiya Janata Party 29, Janata Party 3, Jharkhand Mukti Morcha 19, Communist—CPI—M 6, Indian People's Front 7, independents and others 49, vacant 1).
Legislative Council: 96 seats.

GOA
(Capital—Panaji)

Governor: KHURSHID ALAM KHAN.
Chief Minister: RAVI S. NAIK (Maharashtrawadi Gomantak Party).
Legislative Assembly: 40 seats (Congress—I 18, Maharashtrawadi Gomantak Party 18, others 1, vacant 3).

GUJARAT
(Capital—Gandhinagar)

Governor: Dr SARUP SINGH.
Chief Minister: CHIMANBHAI PATEL (Janata Dal—S).
Legislative Assembly: 182 seats (Congress—I 33, Janata Dal—S 65, Bharatiya Janata Party 66, Janata Dal 6, independents 12).

HARYANA
(Capital—Chandigarh)

Governor: DHANIK LAL MANDAL.
Chief Minister: HUKAM SINGH (Janata Dal).
Legislative Assembly: 90 seats (Congress—I 5, Janata Dal—S 41, Bharatiya Janata Party 16, Janata Dal 16, independents and others 10, vacant 2).

HIMACHAL PRADESH
(Capital—Simla)

Governor: VIRENDRA VERMA.
Chief Minister: SHANTA KUMAR (Bharatiya Janata Party).
Legislative Assembly: 68 seats (Congress—I 8, Bharatiya Janata Party 46, Janata Dal 3, Janata Dal—S 7, independents and others 4).

JAMMU AND KASHMIR
(Capitals—Srinagar (Summer), Jammu (Winter))

Governor: GIRISH CHANDRA SAKSENA.
Chief Minister: (vacant).
Legislative Assembly: 76 seats.
Legislative Council: 36 seats.

The Chief Minister resigned, and the Assembly was suspended, when Jammu and Kashmir was placed under Governor's rule in January 1990. The Assembly was dissolved in February 1990. The state was placed under President's rule in July 1990.

KARNATAKA
(Capital—Bangalore)

Governor: KHURSHID ALAM KHAN (acting).

Chief Minister: S. BANGARAPPA (Congress–I).
Legislative Assembly: 224 seats (Congress–I 177, Janata Dal 24, Bharatiya Janata 4, independents and others 17, vacant 2).
Legislative Council: 75 seats.

KERALA
(Capital—Thiruvananthapuram)
Governor: BASAVAIAH RACHIAH.
Chief Minister: EZHAMBALA KRISHNAN NAYANAR (Communist–CPI–M).
Legislative Assembly: 140 seats (Communist–CPI–M 38, Communist–CPI 16, Congress–I 33, Muslim League 15, Kerala Congress 5, Kerala Congress (M) 4, Congress–S 6, Janata Party 7, Revolutionary Socialist Party 5, independents 9, Lok Dal 1, vacant 1).

MADHYA PRADESH
(Capital—Bhopal)
Governor: KUNWAR MAHMOOD ALI.
Chief Minister: SUNDERLAL PATWA (Bharatiya Janata Party).
Legislative Assembly: 320 seats (Congress–I 56, Bharatiya Janata 220, Janata Dal 16, Janata Dal–S 12, independents and others 15, vacant 1).

MAHARASHTRA
(Capital—Bombay)
Governor: C. SUBRAMANIAM.
Chief Minister: SHARAD PAWAR (Congress–I).
Legislative Assembly: 288 seats (Congress–I 141, Janata Dal 24, Shiv Sena 52, Bharatiya Janata Party 42, independents and others 16, People and Workers' Party 8, Communist–CPI 2, Communist–CPI–M 3).
Legislative Council: 78 seats.

MANIPUR
(Capital—Imphal)
Governor: CHINTAMANI PANIGRAHI.
Chief Minister: R. K. RANVIR SINGH (Manipur People's Party).
Legislative Assembly: 60 seats (Manipur People's Party 10, Congress–I 26, Janata Dal 10, Congress–S 6, Communist–CPI 3, others 3, vacant 2).

MEGHALAYA
(Capital—Shillong)
Governor: MADHUKAR DIGHE.
Chief Minister: B. B. LYNGDOH (United Meghalaya Parliamentary Party).
Legislative Assembly: 60 seats (Congress–I 22, Hill People's Union 18, Hills State People's Democratic Party 4, independent 9, others 5, vacant 2).

MIZORAM
(Capital—Aizawl)
Governor: SWARAJ KAUSHAL.
Chief Minister: LALTHANHAWLA (Congress–I).
Legislative Assembly: 40 seats (Mizo National Front 14, Congress–I 22, others 3, vacant 1).

NAGALAND
(Capital—Kohima)
Governor: M. M. THOMAS.
Chief Minister: VAMUZO (Nagaland People's Council).
Legislative Assembly: 60 seats (Congress–I 23, Nagaland People's Council 22, vacant 15).

ORISSA
(Capital—Bhubaneswar)
Governor: YAGYA DUTT SHARMA.
Chief Minister: BIJU PATNAIK (Janata Dal).
Legislative Assembly: 147 seats (Congress–I 10, Janata Dal 123, Communist–CPI 5, Communist–CPI–M 2, Bharatiya Janata Party 2, independents 5).

PUNJAB
(Capital—Chandigarh)
Governor: Gen. (retd.) OM PRAKASH MALHOTRA.
Chief Minister: (vacant).
Legislative Assembly: 117 seats.
The Chief Minister and the Cabinet were dismissed, and the Assembly was dissolved, when Punjab was placed under President's rule in May 1987.

RAJASTHAN
(Capital—Jaipur)
Governor: Dr DEBI PRASAD CHATTOPADHYAY.
Chief Minister: BHAIRON SINGH SHEKHAWAT (Bharatiya Janata Party).
Legislative Assembly: 200 seats (Congress–I 32, Bharatiya Janata Party 65, Janata Dal 47, Janata Dal–S 23, independents and others 27, vacant 6).

SIKKIM
(Capital—Gangtok)
Governor: Adm. (retd) RADHAKRISHAN HARIRAM TAHILIANI.
Chief Minister: NAR BAHADUR BHANDARI (Sikkim Samgram Parishad).
Legislative Assembly: 32 seats (Sikkim Samgram Parishad 32).

TAMIL NADU
(Capital—Madras)
Governor: BHISHMA NARAIN SINGH.
Chief Minister: (vacant).
Legislative Assembly: 234 seats.
The state government was dismissed, and the Assembly was dissolved, when Tamil Nadu was placed under the President's rule in January 1991.

TRIPURA
(Capital—Agartala)
Governor: RAGHUNATH REDDY.
Chief Minister: SUDHIR RANJAN MAJUMDAR (Congress–I).
Legislative Assembly: 60 seats (Communist–CPI–M 26, Congress–I 24, Tripura Upajati Juba Samity 7, Revolutionary Socialist Party 2, vacant 1).

UTTAR PRADESH
(Capital—Lucknow)
Governor: B. SATYA NARAIN REDDY.
Chief Minister: MULAYAM SINGH YADAV (Janata Dal–S).
Legislative Assembly: 425 seats (Congress–I 94, Bahujan Samaj Party 13, Lok Dal (B) 2, Bharatiya Janata Party 57, Janata Dal–S 120, Janata Dal 80, Communist–CPI 6, Communist–CPI–M 2, independents and others 47, vacant 4).
Legislative Council: 108 seats.

WEST BENGAL
(Capital—Calcutta)
Governor: NURUL HASAN.
Chief Minister: JYOTI BASU (Communist–CPI–M).
Legislative Assembly: 294 seats (Communist–CPI–M 184, Congress–I 40, Forward Bloc 26, Revolutionary Socialist 17, Communist–CPI 11, others 12, vacant 4).

UNION TERRITORIES

Andaman and Nicobar Islands (Headquarters—Port Blair):
Lt-Gov.: SURJEET SINGH BARNALA (acting).
Chandigarh (Headquarters—Chandigarh):
Administrator: Gen. (retd) OM PRAKASH MALHOTRA.
Chandigarh was to be incorporated into Punjab state on 26 January 1986, but the transfer was postponed.
Dadra and Nagar Haveli (Headquarters—Silvassa):
Administrator: KHURSHID ALAM KHAN.
Daman and Diu (Headquarters—Daman):
Administrator: KHURSHID ALAM KHAN.
Delhi (Headquarters—Delhi):
Lt-Gov.: MARKANDEY SINGH.
Metropolitan Council: 61 seats.
Lakshadweep (Headquarters—Kavaratti):
Administrator: J. SAGAR.
Pondicherry (Capital—Pondicherry):
Lt-Gov.: Dr HAR SARUP SINGH.
Chief Minister: (vacant).
Assembly: 30 seats (DMK 9, AIADMK 3, Congress–I 11, Janata Dal 4, Communist–CPI 2, independent 1).
The Assembly was suspended when Pondicherry was placed under President's rule in January 1991.

Political Organizations
MAJOR NATIONAL POLITICAL ORGANIZATIONS

Prior to independence in 1947, the leading nationalist group was the Congress Party, established in 1885. In 1907 Congress split

INDIA

Directory

into two factions: the Extremists and the Moderates. In 1969 Congress again split into two distinct organizations, with Indira Gandhi's Government continuing in office, while the Indian National Congress (Organization) became India's first recognized opposition party. Further splits occurred in January 1978, when Indira Gandhi formed a breakaway group, the Indian National Congress (I), and again in 1981, when the Indian National Congress (Socialist) was formed. In July 1981 a Supreme Court ruling confirmed Congress (I) as the official Congress party. In December 1986 Congress (S) split, the majority faction voting to rejoin Congress (I) while the remaining members decided to continue as Congress (S).

All India Congress Committee (I): 24 Akbar Rd, New Delhi 110 011; tel. (11) 3019080; f. 1978, as Indian National Congress (I), as a breakaway group under Indira Gandhi; Pres. RAJIV GANDHI; Gen. Secs Dr BALRAM JAKHAR, H. K. L. BHAGAT, Mrs RAJENDRA KUMARI BAJPAI, JANARDHAN POOJARI, GHULAM NABI AZAD, VITHAL NARWAL GADGIL.

Bharatiya Janata Party (BJP): (Indian People's Party): 11 Ashok Rd, New Delhi 110 001; tel. (11) 383349; f. 1980 as a breakaway group from Janata Party; radical right-wing Hindu party; Pres. Dr MURLI MANOHAR JOSHI; Vice-Pres. SUNDERSINH BHANDARI; Dep. Vice-Pres. VIJAYA RAJA SCINDIA; Gen. Secs KUSHABHAU THAKRE, O. RAJGOPAL, SURAJ BHAN, GOVINDACHARYA.

Communist Party of India (CPI): Ajoy Bhavan, Kotla Marg, New Delhi 110 002; tel. (11) 3315546; f. 1925; advocates the establishment of a socialist society led by the working class, and ultimately of a communist society; Gen. Sec. INDRAJIT GUPTA; 467,539 mems.

Communist Party of India—Marxist (CPI—M): 14 Ashoka Rd, New Delhi 110 001; tel. (11) 3711870; telex 3165729; f. 1964 as pro-Beijing breakaway group from the CPI; declared its independence of Beijing in 1968 and is managed by a central committee of 65 mems and a politburo of 11 mems; Leaders JYOTI BASU, M. BASAVAPUNNAIAH, HARKISHAN SINGH SURJEET; Gen. Sec. E. M. SANKARAN NAMBOODIRIPAD; 564,000 mems.

Indian National Congress (S)*: 3 Raisina Rd, New Delhi 110 001; tel. (11) 382478; f. 1981; aims include the establishment by peaceful means of a socialist, co-operative commonwealth; advocates govt control of large-scale industries and services, co-operativism in industry and agriculture, and a neutral foreign policy; 4m. mems; Pres. SARAT CHANDRA SINHA; Gen. Secs K. P. UNNIKRISHNAN, V. KISHORE CHANDRA S. DEO.

Janata Dal* (People's Party): 7 Jantar Mantar Rd, New Delhi 110 001; tel. (11) 3321833; f. 1988 as a merger of parties within the Rashtriya Morcha; advocates immediate cease-fire and negotiated settlement in Sri Lanka, non-alignment, the eradication of poverty, unemployment and wide disparities in wealth, and the protection of minorities; 136-mem. National Executive; Pres. SOMAPPA RAYAPPA BOMMAI; Gen. Secs JAIPAL REDDY, PURUSHOTTAM KAUSHIK, GOPAL PACHERWAL.

Janata Dal (S): New Delhi; f. 1990 as a breakaway group from Janata Dal; Pres. DEVI LAL; Gen. Secs OM PRAKASH CHAUTALA, SATYA PRAKASH MALVIYA, MAHFOOZ A. KHAN.

Janata Party* (People's Party): 5 Pandit Pant Marg, New Delhi 110 001; tel. (11) 3782444; f. May 1977 by the merger of the Indian National Congress (Organization), the Bharatiya Lok Dal (BLD), the Bharatiya Jan Sangh (People's Party of India) and the Socialist Party, which had combined as the Janata Party to contest the March 1977 general election; Congress for Democracy, a party formed in February 1977, merged with the Janata Party in May 1977; the Rashtriya Sanjay Manch and the Lok Dal (A), one of the two factions in the Lok Dal, merged with the Janata Party in April 1988; aims to achieve, by democratic and peaceful means, a socialist society, free from social, political and economic exploitation; Pres. Dr SUBRAMANIAN SWAMY.

Lok Dal* (People's Party): 15 Windsor Place, New Delhi 110 001; tel. (11) 388925; f. 1984 by merger of the Lok Dal (a splinter group from the Janata Party) with the Democratic Socialist Party and the Janavadi Dal; advocates secularism, the cause of the poor and underprivileged, the primacy of agriculture and small industry; in 1987 split into two factions, of which the larger was Lok Dal (B); Lok Dal (A) merged with the Janata Party in 1988.

Rashtriya Morcha (National Front): f. 1988 as a seven-party united opposition front; Chair. NANDMURI TARAK RAMARAO; Convener and CEO VISHWANATH PRATAP SINGH.

MAJOR REGIONAL POLITICAL ORGANIZATIONS

Akhil Bharat Hindu Mahasabha: Hindu Mahasabha Bhavan, Mandir Marg, New Delhi 110 001; tel. (11) 343105; f. 1915; seeks the establishment of a democratic Hindu state; Pres. ACHARYA BALARAO SAVARKAR; Gen. Sec. GOPAL V. GODSE; 5.1m. mems.

All-India Anna Dravida Munnetra Kazhagam (AIADMK) (All-India Anna Dravidian Progressive Asscn): Lloyd's Rd, Madras 600 004; f. 1972; breakaway group from the DMK; Leader C. JAYALALITHA JAYARAM.

All India Forward Bloc: 28 Gurdwara Rakabganj Rd, New Delhi 110 001; tel. (11) 384576; f. 1940 by Netaji Subhash Chandra Boase; socialist aims, including nationalization of major industries, land reform and redistribution; Chair. P. D. PALIWAL; Gen. Sec. CHITTA BASU; 900,000 mems.

Asom Gana Parishad (AGP)* (Assam People's Council): Golaghat, Assam; f. 1985; draws support from the All-Assam Gana Sangram Parishad and the All-Assam Students' Union (Pres. KESHAB MAHANTA; Gen. Sec. ATUL BORA); advocates the unity of India in diversity and a united Assam; Leader PRAFULLA KUMAR MAHANTA.

Bahujan Samaj Party: promotes the rights of the *Harijans* ('Untouchables') of India; Leader KANSHI RAM.

Dravida Munnetra Kazhagam (DMK)*: Royapuram, Madras 600 013; f. 1949; aims at full autonomy for Tamil Nadu within the Union, to establish regional languages as state languages and English as the official language; Pres. MUTHUVEL KARUNANIDHI; Gen. Sec. NANJIL K. MANOGARAN; over 1.6m. mems.

Hind National Party: f. 1990; advocates abolition of all reservations and segregative laws; Pres. RAM CHANDRA JAIN (acting).

Jammu and Kashmir National Conference (JKNC): Mujahid Manzil, Srinagar 190 002; tel. 71500; fmrly All Jammu and Kashmir National Conference, f. 1931, renamed 1939, reactivated 1975; state-based party campaigning for internal autonomy and responsible self-govt; Leader Dr FAROOQ ABDULLAH; Gen. Sec. SHEIKH NAZIR AHMED; 1m. mems.

Peasants' and Workers' Party of India: Mahatma Phule Rd, Naigaum, Bombay 400 014; f. 1949; Marxist; seeks to nationalize all basic industries, to promote industrialization, and to establish a unitary state with provincial boundaries drawn on a linguistic basis; Gen. Sec. DAJIBA DESAI; c. 10,000 mems.

Republican Party of India (RPI): Azad Maidan, Fort, Bombay 400 001; main aim is to realize the aims and objects set out in the preamble to the 1950 Constitution; Pres. BALA SAHIB PRAKASH; Gen. Sec. Mrs J. ISHWARIBAI.

Shiromani Akali Dal: Baradan Shri Darbar Sahib, Amritsar; f. 1920; merged with Congress Party 1958–62; moderate Sikh party; opposes govt intervention in Sikh affairs; seeks autonomy for all states, equal rights for all and safeguards for minorities; Pres. SIMRANJIT SINGH MANN; Gen. Sec. ONKAR SINGH THAPAR; 1m. mems.

Telugu Desam* (Telugu Nation): 3-5-910, Himayatnagar, Hyderabad 500 029; tel. (842) 227070; f. 1982; state-based party (Andhra Pradesh); campaigns against rural poverty and social prejudice; Founder and Pres. NANDMURI TARAK RAMA RAO; Gen.-Sec. P. UPENDRA; 1,184,595 mems.

* Member of Rashtriya Morcha.

Diplomatic Representation

EMBASSIES AND HIGH COMMISSIONS IN INDIA

Afghanistan: 5/50F Shanti Path, Chanakyapuri, New Delhi 110 021; tel. (11) 603331; Ambassador: AHMAD SARWAR.

Algeria: 15 Anand Lok, New Delhi 110 049; tel. (11) 6465970; telex 3162258; fax (11) 6465966; Ambassador: MUSTAPHA BENAMAR.

Argentina: B-8/9 Vasant Vihar, Paschimi Marg, New Delhi 110 057; tel. (11) 671345; telex 3161110; Ambassador: TERESA HORTENCIA INÉS FLOURET.

Australia: 1/50-G Shanti Path, Chanakyapuri, New Delhi 110 021; tel. (11) 601336; telex 3161156; fax (11) 675088; High Commissioner: DAVID WYKE EVANS.

Austria: EP/13 Chandragupta Marg, Chanakyapuri, New Delhi 110 021; tel. (11) 601555; telex 3161699; Ambassador: Dr CHRISTOPH COMARO.

Bangladesh: 56M Ring Rd, Lajpat Nagar-III, New Delhi 110 024; tel. (11) 6834668; telex 3175218; High Commissioner: FARUQ AHMED CHOUDHURY.

Belgium: 50N, Plot 4, Shanti Path, Chanakyapuri, New Delhi 110 021; tel. (11) 608195; telex 3161487; Ambassador: KAMIEL CRIEL.

Bhutan: Chandragupta Marg, Chanakyapuri, New Delhi 110 021; tel. (11) 609217; telex 3162263; Ambassador: Dasho KARMA LETHO.

Brazil: 8 Aurangzeb Rd, New Delhi 110 011; tel. (11) 3017301; telex 3165277; fax (11) 3015086; Ambassador: OCTAVIO RAINHO DA SILVA NEVES.

Bulgaria: 16/17 Chandragupta Marg, Chanakyapuri, New Delhi 110 021; tel. (11) 607411; telex 3161490; Ambassador: ALEXANDER STENOEV TONEV.

Cambodia: E-23 Defence Colony, New Delhi 110 024; tel. (11) 693417; Ambassador: SOK SATH.

Canada: 7/8 Shanti Path, Chanakyapuri, New Delhi 110 021; tel. (11) 6876500; telex 3166346; High Commissioner: JOHN L. PAYNTER.
Chile: 1/13 Shanti Niketan, New Delhi 110 021; tel. (11) 671363; telex 3166097; Ambassador: EDUARDO ORTIZ.
China, People's Republic: 50D Shanti Path, Chanakyapuri, New Delhi 110 021; tel. (11) 600328; telex 3162250; Ambassador: TU GUOWEI.
Colombia: 82D Malcha Marg, Chanakyapuri, New Delhi 110 021; tel. (11) 3012771; telex 3163090; Ambassador: LUIS GUILLERMO PARRA.
Cuba: 4 Munirka Marg, Vasant Vihar, New Delhi 110 057; tel. (11) 600508; telex 3171395; fax (11) 615338; Ambassador: SONIA DÍAZ LLERA.
Cyprus: 52 Jor Bagh, New Delhi 110 003; tel. (11) 697503; telex 3161788; High Commissioner: ANTONIOS J. VAKIS.
Czechoslovakia: 50M Niti Marg, Chanakyapuri, New Delhi 110 021; tel. (11) 608215; telex 3172234; Ambassador: Dr MILOSLAV JEZIL.
Denmark: 2 Golf Links Area, New Delhi 110 003; tel. (11) 616273; telex 3166160; Ambassador: JENS OSTENFELD.
Egypt: 1/50M Niti Marg, New Delhi 110 021; tel. (11) 608904; telex 3162611; Ambassador: MOHAMMED AHMED EL-ZOEIBY.
Ethiopia: 7/50G Satya Marg, Chanakyapuri, New Delhi 110 021; tel. (11) 604407; telex 3172358; Ambassador: GEBEYEHU ALEMNEH.
Finland: E-3 Nyaya Marg, Chanakyapuri, New Delhi 110 021; tel. (11) 605409; telex 3165030; fax (11) 671380; Ambassador: JYRKI AIMONEN.
France: 2/50E Shanti Path, Chanakyapuri, New Delhi 110 021; tel. (11) 604004; telex 3172351; Ambassador: ANDRÉ LEWIN.
Germany: 6 Block 50G, Shanti Path, Chanakyapuri, New Delhi 110 021; tel. (11) 604861; telex 3165670; fax (11) 6873117; Ambassador: Dr HANS-GEORG WIECK.
Ghana: A-42 Vasant Marg, Vasant Vihar, New Delhi 110 057; tel. (11) 670788; High Commissioner: (vacant).
Greece: 16 Sundar Nagar, New Delhi 110 003; tel. (11) 617800; telex 3165232; Ambassador: ALEXANDER PHILON.
Guyana: 85 Poorvi Marg, Vasant Vihar, New Delhi 110 057; tel. (11) 674194; telex 3172167; fax (11) 6874286; High Commissioner: BALRAM RAGHUBIR.
Holy See: 50C Niti Marg, Chanakyapuri, New Delhi 110 021 (Apostolic Nunciature); tel. (11) 606520; Pro-Nuncio: Most Rev. GEORGE ZUR, Titular Archbishop of Sesta.
Hungary: Plot 2, 50M Niti Marg, Chanakyapuri, New Delhi 110 021; tel. (11) 608414; telex 3166038; Ambassador: Dr ANDRÁS BALOGH.
Indonesia: 50A Chanakyapuri, New Delhi 110 021; tel. (11) 602352; telex 3165709; Ambassador: IDA BAGUS MANTRA.
Iran: 5 Barakhamba Road, New Delhi 110 001; tel. (11) 3329600; telex 3166421; Ambassador: EBRAHIM RAHIMPOUR.
Iraq: 169–171 Jor Bagh, New Delhi 110 003; tel. (11) 618011; telex 3166253; Ambassador: ABDUL WADUD ASH-SHEKHALI.
Ireland: 13 Jor Bagh, New Delhi 110 003; tel. (11) 617435; telex 3165546; fax (11) 6382936; Ambassador: PAUL DEMPSEY.
Italy: 50E Chandragupta Marg, New Delhi 110 021; tel. (11) 6873840; telex 3166020; Ambassador: GABRIELE MENEGATTI.
Japan: Plots 4–5, 50G Shanti Path, Chanakyapuri, New Delhi 110 021; tel. (11) 604071; telex 3172364; fax (11) 670928; Ambassador: SHUNJI KOBAYASHI.
Jordan: 35 Malcha Marg, Chanakyapuri, New Delhi 110 021; tel. (11) 3013495; telex 3161963; Ambassador: Dr SULEIMAN DAJANI.
Kenya: E-66 Vasant Marg, Vasant Vihar, New Delhi 110 057; tel. (11) 6876538; telex 3172166; High Commissioner: BENJAMIN BETTS BORE.
Korea, Democratic People's Republic: 42/44 Sundar Nagar, New Delhi 110 003; tel. (11) 617140; telex 3165059; Ambassador: YU TAE-SOP.
Korea, Republic: 9 Chandragupta Marg, Chanakyapuri, New Delhi 110 021; tel. (11) 601601; telex 315537; Ambassador: KIM TAEZHEE.
Kuwait: 5A Shanti Path, Chanakyapuri, New Delhi 110 021; tel. (11) 600791; telex 3172211; Ambassador: ALI ZAKARIA AL-ANSARI.
Laos: New Delhi; Ambassador: CHANPHENG SIHAPHOM.
Lebanon: 10 Sardar Patel Marg, Chanakyapuri, New Delhi 110 021; tel. (11) 3013174; telex 3161161; Ambassador: ALEXANDER AMMOUN.
Liberia: 79 Poorvi Marg, Vasant Vihar, New Delhi 110 057; tel. (11) 602800; telex 3166686; Ambassador: RUDOLFF KOLACO.
Libya: 22 Golf Links, New Delhi 110 003; tel. (11) 697717; telex 3165193; Secretary of People's Bureau: OMAR AHMAD JADOLLAH AL-AUKALI.

Malaysia: 50M Satya Marg, Chanakyapuri, New Delhi 110 021; tel. (11) 601291; telex 3165096; High Commissioner: MOHAMMED AMIR JAFFAR.
Maldives: New Delhi; High Commissioner: MOHAMED MUSTHAFA HUSSAIN.
Mauritius: 5 Kautilya Marg, Chanakyapuri, New Delhi 110 021; tel. (11) 3011112; telex 3166045; fax (11) 3019925; High Commissioner: Dr BOODHUM TEELOCK.
Mexico: 10 Jor Bagh, New Delhi 110 003; tel. (11) 697991; telex 3166121; Ambassador: PEDRO GONZÁLEZ-RUBIO S.
Mongolia: 34 Archbishop Makarios Marg, New Delhi 110 003; tel. (11) 618921; Ambassador: DASHDAVAAGIIN CHULUUNDORJ.
Morocco: 33 Archbishop Makarios Marg, New Delhi 110 003; tel. (11) 611588; telex 3166118; Ambassador: AHMED BOURZAIM.
Myanmar: Burma House, 3/50F Nyaya Marg, Chanakyapuri, New Delhi 110 021; tel. (11) 600251; telex 3172224; Ambassador: Dr KHIN MAUNG WIN.
Nepal: Barakhamba Rd, New Delhi 110 001; tel. (11) 3328191; telex 3166283; Ambassador: Ms BINDHESWARI SHAH.
Netherlands: 6/50F Shanti Path, Chanakyapuri, New Delhi 110 021; tel. (11) 609571; telex 3165070; fax (11) 609327; Ambassador: Ms E. M. SCHOO.
New Zealand: 25 Golf Links, New Delhi 110 003; tel. (11) 697592; telex 3165100; High Commissioner: PRISCILLA WILLIAMS.
Nicaragua: E-514 Greater Kailash-II, New Delhi 110 048; tel. (11) 6442083; telex 3166034; Ambassador: CÉSAR A. AROSTEGUI.
Nigeria: 21 Palam Marg, Vasant Vihar, New Delhi 110 057; tel. (11) 670405; telex 3165195; High Commissioner: MUSA M. BELLO.
Norway: 50C Shanti Path, Chanakyapuri, New Delhi 110 021; tel. (11) 605982; telex 3165397; Ambassador: JON ATLE GAARDER.
Oman: 16 Palam Marg, New Delhi 110 057; tel. (11) 670215; telex 3172342; Ambassador: AHMED YOUSUF AL-HARITHY.
Pakistan: 2/50G Shanti Path, Chanakyapuri, New Delhi 110 021; tel. (11) 600603; telex 3165270; High Commissioner: ABDUL SATTAR.
Panama: D-129 Panchsheel Enclave, New Delhi 110 017; tel. (11) 6438620; telex 3117094; Ambassador: HORACIO J. BUSTAMANTE.
Peru: D-1/39, Vasant Vihar, New Delhi 110 057; tel. (11) 673937; telex 3165274; fax (11) 6876427; Ambassador: FERNANDO GUILLÉN.
Philippines: 50N Nyaya Marg, Chanakyapuri, New Delhi 110 021; tel. (11) 601120; telex 3172397; fax (11) 6876401; Ambassador: PABLO A. ARAQUE.
Poland: 50M Shanti Path, Chanakyapuri, New Delhi 110 021; tel. (11) 608321; telex 3161894; Ambassador: JULIUSZ BIALY.
Portugal: B-76 Greater Kailash-I, New Delhi 110 048; tel. (11) 6441206; telex 3171163; Ambassador: ANTÓNIO TELCO DE ALMEIDA DE MAGHALHÃES COLACO.
Qatar: A-3 West End Colony, New Delhi 110 021; tel. (11) 601240; telex 3172304; Ambassador: (vacant).
Romania: A-52 Vasant Marg, Vasant Vihar, New Delhi 110 057; tel. (11) 670700; telex 3172204; Ambassador: N. FINANTU.
Saudi Arabia: S-347 Panchshila Park, New Delhi 110 017; tel. (11) 6445419; telex 3171397; Ambassador: Shaikh FOUAD S. MOUFTI.
Senegal: New Delhi; Ambassador: AHMED EL MANSOUR DIOP.
Singapore: E-6 Chandragupta Marg, Chanakyapuri, New Delhi 110 021; tel. (11) 604162; telex 3172169; fax (11) 677798; High Commissioner: MICHAEL CHEOK PO CHUAN.
Somalia: New Delhi; Ambassador: MOHAMED OSMAN OMAR.
Spain: 12 Prithviraj Rd, New Delhi 110 011; tel. (11) 3013834; telex 3161488; Ambassador: SANTIAGO SALAS.
Sri Lanka: 27 Kautilya Marg, Chanakyapuri, New Delhi 110 021; tel. (11) 3010201; telex 3161162; fax (11) 3015295; High Commissioner: Dr F. S. C. P. KALPAGÉ.
Sudan: New Delhi; Ambassador: (vacant).
Sweden: Nyaya Marg, Chanakyapuri, New Delhi 110 021; tel. (11) 604961; telex 3162282; fax (11) 676401; Ambassador: PER KETTIS.
Switzerland: Nyaya Marg, Chanakyapuri, New Delhi 110 021; tel. (11) 604225; telex 3172350; fax (11) 6873093; Ambassador: JEAN-PIERRE ZEHNDER.
Syria: 28 Vasant Marg, Vasant Vihar, New Delhi 110 057; tel. (11) 670233; telex 3172360; Ambassador: MOHAMMAD KHODAR.
Tanzania: 27 Golf Links, New Delhi 110 003; tel. (11) 694351; telex 3162977; High Commissioner: ONESIPHORUS HENRY TOSHA.
Thailand: 56N Nyaya Marg, Chanakyapuri, New Delhi 110 021; tel. (11) 605985; Ambassador: NIKORN PRAISAENGPETCH.
Trinidad and Tobago: 121 Jor Bagh, New Delhi 110 003; tel. (11) 618100; telex 3162481; fax (11) 4624581; High Commissioner: PREMCHAND JAGDEO DASS.

INDIA — *Directory*

Tunisia: 23 Palam Marg, Vasant Vihar, New Delhi 110 057; tel. (11) 676204; telex 3172162; fax (11) 674385; Ambassador: ALI TEKAIA.

Turkey: 50N Nyaya Marg, Chanakyapuri, New Delhi 110 021; tel. (11) 601921; telex 3172408; Ambassador: YALIM ERALP.

Uganda: 61 Golf Links, New Delhi 110 003; tel. (11) 693584; telex 3166243; High Commissioner: JAMES JUUCO.

USSR: Shanti Path, Chanakyapuri, New Delhi 110 021; tel. (11) 606026; telex 312802; Ambassador: VIKTOR FEDOROVICH ISAKOV.

United Arab Emirates: EP-12 Chandragupt Marg, New Delhi 110 021; tel. (11) 670830; telex 3172325; Ambassador: AHMED ABDULLAH AL-MUSALLY.

United Kingdom: Shanti Path, Chanakyapuri, New Delhi 110 021; tel. (11) 601371; telex 3165125; fax (11) 6872882; High Commissioner: Sir DAVID GOODALL.

USA: Shanti Path, Chanakyapuri, New Delhi 110 021; tel. (11) 600651; telex 3165269; Ambassador: WILLIAM CLARK.

Venezuela: N-114 Panchshila Park, New Delhi 110 017; tel. (11) 6436783; telex 3171393; fax (11) 6435264; Ambassador: Dr FRANK BRACHO.

Viet-Nam: 17 Kautilya Marg, Chanakyapuri, New Delhi 110 021; tel. (11) 3018059; Ambassador: VU XUAN ANG.

Yemen: B-70 Greater Kailash-I, New Delhi 110 048; tel. (11) 6414623; telex 3165567; Ambassador: MOHAMED BIN MOHAMED AL-HUBEISHI.

Yugoslavia: 3/50G Niti Marg, Chanakyapuri, New Delhi 110 021; tel. (11) 6872073; telex 3172365; Ambassador: Dr ERNEST PETRÍC.

Zaire: 160 Jor Bagh, New Delhi 110 003; tel. (11) 619455; telex 3166275; Ambassador: BELTCHIKA KALUBYE.

Zambia: 14 Jor Bagh, New Delhi 110 003; tel. (11) 619328; telex 3166084; High Commissioner: E. B. MONGA (acting).

Zimbabwe: B-8 Anand Niketan, New Delhi 110 021; tel. (11) 677460; telex 3172289; High Commissioner: TIRIVAFI JOHN KANGAI.

Judicial System

THE SUPREME COURT

The Supreme Court, consisting of a Chief Justice and not more than 25 judges appointed by the President, exercises exclusive jurisdiction in any dispute between the Union and the states (although there are certain restrictions where an acceding state is involved). It has appellate jurisdiction over any judgment, decree or order of the High Court where that Court certifies that either a substantial question of law or the interpretation of the Constitution is involved.

Provision is made for the appointment by the Chief Justice of India of judges of High Courts as ad hoc judges at sittings of the Supreme Court for specified periods, and for the attendance of retired judges at sittings of the Supreme Court. The Supreme Court has advisory jurisdiction in respect of questions which may be referred to it by the President for opinion. The Supreme Court is also empowered to hear appeals against a sentence of death passed by a State High Court in reversal of an order of acquittal by a lower court, and in a case in which a High Court has granted a certificate of fitness.

The Supreme Court also hears appeals which are certified by High Courts to be fit for appeal, subject to rules made by the Court. Parliament may, by law, confer on the Supreme Court any further powers of appeal.

The judges hold office until the age of 65 years.

Supreme Court: New Delhi; tel. (11) 387954; telex 3166023.

Chief Justice of India: RANGANATH MISHRA.

Judges of the Supreme Court: B. C. RAY, LALIT MOHAN SHARMA, M. N. VENKATACHALIAH, S. RANGANATHAN, N. D. OJHA, KAMAL NARAIN SINGH, MADHUKAR HIRALAL KANIA, KALMANJE JAGANNATHA SHETTY, Dr THAMARAPALLI KOCHU THOMMEN, AZIZ MUSHABBER AHMADI, KULDIP SINGH, S. RATNAVEL PANDIAN, KHAGENDRA NATH SAIKIA, V. RAMASWAMY, P. B. SAWANT, N. M. KASLIWAL, M. M. PUNCHHI, K. RAMASWAMY, MEERA SAHIB FATHIMA BEEVI, K. JAYACHANDRA REDDY, SURESH CHANDRA AGRAWAL, RAM MANOHAR SAHAI, J. S. VERMA.

Attorney-General: G. RAMASWAMY.

HIGH COURTS

The High Courts are the Courts of Appeal from the lower courts, and their decisions are final except in cases where appeal lies to the Supreme Court.

LOWER COURTS

Provision is made in the Code of Criminal Procedure for the constitution of lower criminal courts called Courts of Session and Courts of Magistrates. The Courts of Session are competent to try all persons duly committed for trial, and inflict any punishment authorized by the law. The President and the local government concerned exercise the prerogative of mercy.

The constitution of inferior civil courts is determined by regulations within each state.

Religion

INDIAN FAITHS

Buddhism: The Buddhists in Ladakh (Jammu and Kashmir) are followers of the Dalai Lama. Head Lama of Ladakh: KAUSHAK SAKULA, Dalgate, Srinagar, Kashmir. In 1981 there were 4.72m. Buddhists in India, representing 0.70% of the population.

Hinduism: 549.8m. Hindus (1981 census), representing 80.25% of the population.

Islam: Muslims are divided into two main sects, Shi'as and Sunnis. Most of the Indian Muslims are Sunnis. At the 1981 census Islam had 75.4m. adherents (11% of the population).

Jainism: 3.2m. adherents (1981 census), 0.46% of the population.

Sikhism: 13.1m. Sikhs (comprising 1.91% of the population at the 1981 census), the majority living in the Punjab.

Zoroastrians: More than 120,000 Parsis practise the Zoroastrian religion.

CHRISTIANITY

National Council of Churches in India: Christian Council Lodge, Civil Lines, Nagpur 440 001, Maharashtra; tel. (712) 531312; f. 1953; mems: 24 reformed and three orthodox churches, 14 regional Christian councils, 12 All-India ecumenical orgs and seven related agencies; represents c. 8m. mems; Pres. Rt Rev. S. K. PARMAR; Gen. Sec. Rev. K. LUNGMUANA.

Orthodox Churches

Malankara Orthodox Syrian Church: Catholicate Palace, Devalokam, Kottayam 686 038, Kerala; tel. 8500; c. 1.6m. mems (1985); Catholicos of the East and Malankara Metropolitan: HH BASELIUS MARTHOMA MATHEWS I; Sec. M. T. PAUL.

Mar Thoma Syrian Church of Malabar: Mar Thoma Sabha Office, Poolatheen, Tiruvalla 689 101, Kerala; tel. (47811) 2449; c. 700,000 mems (1988); Metropolitan: Most Rev. Dr ALEXANDER MAR THOMA; Sec. Rev. Dr K. V. MATHEW.

The Malankara Jacobite Syrian Orthodox Church is also represented.

Protestant Churches

Church of North India (CNI): CNI Bhavan, 16 Pandit Pant Marg, New Delhi 110 001; tel. (11) 3716513; telex 3166763; f. 1970 by merger of the (Anglican) Church of India, the Council of the Baptist Churches in Northern India, the Methodist Church (British and Australasian Conferences), the United Church of Northern India (a union of Presbyterians and Congregationalists, f. 1924), the Church of the Brethren and the Disciples of Christ; comprises 23 dioceses; c. 1m. mems (1989); Moderator Most Rev. JOHN ELLIOT GHOSE, Bishop of Darjeeling; Gen. Sec. Rev. NOEL S. SEN.

Church of South India (CSI): Cathedral Rd, POB 4906, Madras 600 086; tel. (44) 471266; f. 1947 by merger of the Methodist Church in South India, the South India United Church (itself a union of churches in the Congregational and Presbyterian/Reformed traditions) and the four southern dioceses of the (Anglican) Church of India; comprises 21 dioceses (incl. one in Sri Lanka); c. 2.2m. mems (1988); Moderator Most Rev. Dr P. VICTOR PREMASAGAR, Bishop in Medak; Gen. Sec. Prof. GEORGE KOSHY.

Methodist Church in India: Methodist Centre, 21 YMCA Rd, Bombay 400 008; tel. (22) 374137; 473,000 mems (1985); Gen. Sec. Rev. JAMES C. LAL.

Samavesam of Telugu Baptist Churches: C. A. M. Compound, Nellore 524 003, Andhra Pradesh; tel. 5122; f. 1962; comprises 717 independent Baptist churches; 425,000 mems (1989); Gen. Sec. Dr S. BENJAMIN.

United Church of North India and Pakistan: Church House, Mhow, Madhya Pradesh; Sec. (vacant).

United Evangelical Lutheran Churches in India: 1 First St, Haddows Rd, Madras 600 006; tel. (44) 471676; telex 416613; f. 1975; nine constituent denominations: Andhra Evangelical Lutheran Church, Arcot Lutheran Church, Evangelical Lutheran Church in Madhya Pradesh, Gossner Evangelical Lutheran Church, India Evangelical Lutheran Church, Jeypore Evangelical Lutheran Church, Northern Evangelical Lutheran Church, South Andhra Lutheran Church and Tamil Evangelical Lutheran Church; c. 1.5m.

mems (1985); Pres. Rev. Dr JAYASEELAN JACOB; Exec. Sec. Dr K. RAJARATNAM.

Other denominations active in the country include the Assembly of the Presbyterian Church in North East India, the Bengal-Orissa-Bihar Baptist Convention (6,000 mems), the Chaldean Syrian Church of the East, the Convention of the Baptist Churches of Northern Circars, the Council of Baptist Churches of North East India, the Council of Baptist Churches of Northern India, the Hindustani Convent Church and the Mennonite Church in India.

The Roman Catholic Church

India comprises 19 archdioceses, 103 dioceses and one Apostolic Prefecture. These include two archdioceses and 21 dioceses of the the Syro-Malabarese rite, and one archdiocese and three dioceses of the Syro-Malankarese rite. The archdiocese of Goa and Damão, the seat of the Patriarch of the East Indies, is directly responsible to the Holy See. The remaining archdioceses are metropolitan sees. In December 1987 there were an estimated 11,845,238 adherents in the country.

Catholic Bishops' Conference of India (CBCI): CBCI Centre, Ashok Place, nr Goldakkhana, New Delhi 110 001; tel. (11) 344695; telex 3161366; fax (11) 345926; f. 1944; Pres. Most Rev. ALPHONSUS MATHIAS, Archbishop of Bangalore; Sec.-Gen. Rt Rev. LAWRENCE MAR EPHRAEM, Auxiliary Bishop of Thiruvananthapuram.

Latin Rite

Patriarch of the East Indies: Most Rev. RAUL NICOLAU GONSALVES (Archbishop of Goa and Damão), Paço Patriarcal, POB 216, Altinho, Panjim, Goa 403 001; tel. (832) 3353.

Archbishop of Agra: Most Rev. CECIL DE SA, Archbishop's House, Wazirpura Rd, Agra 282 003, Uttar Pradesh; tel. (562) 73330.

Archbishop of Bangalore: Most Rev. ALPHONSUS MATHIAS, Archbishop's House, 18 Miller's Rd, Bangalore 560 046, Karnataka; tel. (812) 330438.

Archbishop of Bhopal: Most Rev. EUGENE D'SOUZA, Archbishop's House, 33 Ahmedabad Palace Rd, Bhopal 462 001, Madhya Pradesh; tel. (755) 540829.

Archbishop of Bombay: Cardinal SIMON IGNATIUS PIMENTA, Archbishop's House, 21 Nathalal Parekh Marg, Bombay 400 039, Maharashtra; tel. (22) 2021093.

Archbishop of Calcutta: Most Rev. HENRY SEBASTIAN D'SOUZA, Archbishop's House, 32 Park St, Calcutta 700 016; tel. (33) 444666.

Archbishop of Cuttack-Bhubaneswar: Most Rev. RAPHAEL CHEENATH, Archbishop's House, Satya Nagar, Bhubaneswar 751 007, Orissa.

Archbishop of Delhi: Most Rev. ALAN DE LASTIC, Archbishop's House, Ashok Place, New Delhi 110 001; tel. (11) 343457.

Archbishop of Hyderabad: Most Rev. SAMININI ARULAPPA, Archbishop's House, Sardar Patel Rd, Secunderabad 500 003, Andhra Pradesh; tel. (842) 75545.

Archbishop of Madras and Mylapore: Most Rev. GNANADICKAM CASIMIR, Archbishop's House, 21 San Thome High Rd, Madras 600 004, Tamil Nadu; tel. (44) 71102.

Archbishop of Madurai: Most Rev. MARIANUS AROKIASAMY, Archdiocesan Curia, Madurai 625 008, Tamil Nadu; tel. (452) 41408.

Archbishop of Nagpur: Most Rev. LEOBARD D'SOUZA, Archbishop's House, Mohan Nagar, Nagpur 440 001, Maharashtra; tel. (712) 533239.

Archbishop of Pondicherry and Cuddalore: Most Rev. VENMANI S. SELVANATHER, Archbishop's House, POB 2, Pondicherry 605 001; tel. (413) 24748.

Archbishop of Ranchi: Most Rev. TELESPHORE P. TOPPO, Archbishop's House, Purulia Rd, POB 5, Ranchi 834 001, Bihar; tel. (651) 22226.

Archbishop of Shillong-Guwahati: Most Rev. HUBERT D'ROSARIO, Archbishop's House, POB 37, Shillong 793 003, Meghalaya; tel. (364) 23355.

Archbishop of Verapoly: Most Rev. CORNELIUS ELANJIKAL, Latin Archbishop's House, POB 2581, Kochi 682 031, Kerala; tel. (484) 352892.

Syro-Malabarese Rite

Archbishop of Changanacherry: Most Rev. JOSEPH POWATHIL, Metropolitan Curia, POB 20, Changanacherry 686 101, Kerala; tel. (4824) 20040.

Archbishop of Ernakulam: Cardinal ANTHONY PADIYARA, Archdiocesan Curia, POB 2580, Ernakulam, Kochi 682 031, Kerala; tel. (484) 352629.

Syro-Malankarese Rite

Archbishop of Thiruvananthapuram: Most Rev. BENEDICT MAR GREGORIOS, Archbishop's House, Pattom, Thiruvananthapuram 695 004, Kerala; tel. (471) 77642.

BAHÁ'Í FAITH

National Spiritual Assembly: Bahá'í House, 6 Canning Rd, POB 19, New Delhi 110 001; tel. (11) 389326; telex 3163171; c. 1m. mems; Gen. Sec. R. N. SHAH.

The Press

Freedom of the Press was guaranteed under the 1950 Constitution. A measure giving the Press the right to publish proceedings of Parliament without being subjected to censorship or the fear of civil or criminal action, popularly known as the 'Feroz Gandhi Act', was withdrawn when the Government declared a state of emergency in June 1975 and article 19 of the Constitution, which guaranteed the right to freedom of speech and expression, was suspended. In order to facilitate news censorship, the existing news agencies were merged to form Samachar, a state news agency. Although pre-censorship was disallowed by the courts in 1975, and censorship of foreign correspondents ended in 1976, the Prevention of Publication of Objectionable Matter Act, approved by Parliament in early 1976, still greatly restricted press freedom.

In April 1977 the Government introduced bills to repeal the Prevention of Publication of Objectionable Matter Act and to restore the rights of the 'Feroz Gandhi Act', which were both subsequently approved by Parliament. The right to report parliamentary proceedings was further guaranteed under the Constitution (45th amendment) Bill of December 1978, later redesignated the 44th amendment. In April 1978 Samachar was disbanded and the original agencies were re-established.

In March 1979 a Press Council was set up (its predecessor was abolished in 1975). Its function is to uphold the freedom of the press and maintain and improve journalistic standards. In 1980 a second Press Commission was appointed to inquire into the growth and status of the press since the first commission gave its report.

The growth of a thriving press has been inhibited by cultural barriers caused by religious, social and linguistic differences. Consequently the English-language press, with its appeal to the educated middle-class urban readership throughout the states, has retained its dominance. The English-language metropolitan dailies, such as the *Times of India* (published in seven cities), *Indian Express* (published in 14 cities), the *Hindu* (published in seven cities) and the *Statesman* (published in two cities), are some of the widest circulating and most influential newspapers. In December 1987 there were 24,629 newspapers (incl. 2,151 dailies) and magazines. The readership of daily newspapers is just over 21 per thousand, and in 1987 they were published in 92 languages. On 31 December 1985 the total circulation of newspapers and periodicals was 61,981,000.

The main Indian language dailies, such as the *Navbharat Times* (Hindi), *Malayala Manorama* (Malayalam), the *Punjab Kesri*, the *Jugantar* (Bengali) and *Ananda Bazar Patrika* (Bengali), by paying attention to rural affairs, cater for the increasingly literate non-anglophone provincial population. Most Indian-language papers have a relatively small circulation.

The more popular weekly and fortnightly periodicals include the cultural Tamil publications *Kumudam*, *Kalki*, *Vaarantari Rani* and *Ananda Vikatan*, the Malayalam fortnightly *Vanitha*, the English *Illustrated Weekly of India*, *India Today*, *Sunday* and the sensationalist *Blitz News Magazine*, published in English, Hindi, Marathi and Urdu. The main monthly periodicals are the *Reader's Digest* and the Hindi *Manohar Kahaniyan*.

The majority of publications in India are under individual ownership (61% in 1984), and they claim a large part of the total circulation (39.6% in 1986). The most powerful groups, owned by joint stock companies, publish most of the large English dailies and frequently have considerable private commercial and industrial holdings. Four of the major groups are as follows:

Times of India Group (controlled by ASHOK JAIN and family): dailies: the *Times of India, Economic Times*, the Hindi *Navbharat Times*, the *Maharashtra Times* (Bombay); periodicals: the *Illustrated Weekly of India, Career and Competition Times, 2001*, the Hindi weekly *Dharmayug*, the Hindi fortnightly *Dinaman*, the English fortnightlies *Femina* and *Filmfare* and Hindi pubs including *Parag* and *Sarita*.

Indian Express Group (controlled by the RAMNATH GOENKA family): publishes nine dailies including the *Indian Express*, the Marathi *Lokasatta*, the Tamil *Dinamani*, the Telugu *Andhra Prabha*, the Kannada *Kannada Prabha* and the English *Financial Express*; six periodicals including the English weeklies the *Indian Express* (Sunday edition), *Screen*, the Telugu *Andhra Prabha Illustrated Weekly* and the Tamil *Dinamani Kadir* (weekly).

Hindustan Times Group (controlled by the K. K. BIRLA family): dailies: the *Hindustan Times* (Delhi and Patna), *Pradeep* (Patna) and the Hindi *Hindustan* (Delhi); periodicals: the weeklies the

INDIA   *Directory*

Overseas Hindustan Times, the Hindi *Saptahik Hindustan* (Delhi) and the Hindi monthly *Nandan* and *Kadambini* (New Delhi).

Ananda Bazar Patrika Group (controlled by AVEEK SARKAR and family): dailies: the *Ananda Bazar Patrika* (Calcutta) and the English *Business Standard* and *The Telegraph*; periodicals include: the English weeklies *Sunday* and *Sportsworld*, the English fortnightly *Business World*, Bengali weekly *Desh*, Bengali monthly *Anandamela*, Bengali fortnightly *Anandalok* and the Bengali monthly *Sananda*.

PRINCIPAL DAILIES
Delhi (incl. New Delhi)

The Business and Political Observer: Vijaya, 17 Barakhamba Rd, New Delihi 110 001; tel. (11) 3713200; telex 3166893; fax (11) 3327065; f. 1990; Chair. of Editorial Board R. K. MISHRA.

Daily Milap: 8A Bahadur Shah Zafar Marg, New Delhi 110 002; tel. (11) 3317737; f. 1923; Urdu; nationalist; also publ. from Jullundur and Hyderabad; Man. Editor PUNAM SURI; Chief Editor NAVIN SURI; circ. (Delhi) 22,000.

Daily Pratap: Pratap Bhawan, 5 Bahadur Shah Zafar Marg, New Delhi 110 002; tel. (11) 3317938; f. 1919; Urdu; Editor K. NARENDRA; circ. 26,700.

The Economic Times: Bahadur Shah Zafar Marg, New Delhi 110 002; tel. (11) 3312277; telex 3161339; fax (11) 3323346; f. 1961; English; also publ. from Calcutta, Ahmedabad, Bangalore and Bombay; Editor T. N. NINAN; combined circ. 101,600, circ. (Delhi) 33,400.

Financial Express: Bahadur Shah Zafar Marg, New Delhi 110 002; tel. (11) 3311111; telex 3165803; f. 1961; morning; English; also publ. from Bombay, Bangalore and Madras; Editor A. M. KHUSRO; combined circ. 37,400.

Hindustan: 18/20 Kasturba Gandhi Marg, New Delhi 110 001; tel. (11) 3318201; telex 3166310; fax (11) 3321189; f. 1936; morning; Hindi; also publ. from Patna; Editor HARI NARAYAN NIGAM; circ. (Delhi) 140,321.

The Hindustan Times: 18/20 Kasturba Gandhi Marg, New Delhi 110 001; tel. (11) 3318201; telex 3166310; f. 1923; morning; English; also publ. from Patna; Editor H. K. DUA; circ. (Delhi) 323,700.

Indian Express: Bahadur Shah Zafar Marg, New Delhi 110 002; tel. (11) 3311111; telex 3165908; f. 1953; English; also publ. from Bombay, Chandigarh, Cochin, Bangalore, Ahmedabad, Madras, Madurai, Hyderabad, Vizianagaram and Vijayawada; Editor N. S. JAGANNATHAN; combined circ. 576,200, circ. (Delhi) 89,100.

Janasatta: 9/10 Bahadur Shah Zafar Marg, New Delhi 110 002; f. 1983; Hindi; tel. (11) 3311111; telex 3165803; also publ. from Chandigarh and Bombay; Editor-in-Chief PRABHASH JOSHI; combined circ. 109,700.

National Herald: Herald House, Bahadur Shah Zafar Marg, New Delhi 110 002; tel. (11) 3319014; telex 3165821; f. 1938; English; nationalist; also publ. from Lucknow; Editor S. BHATTACHARJEE; combined circ. 74,400.

Navbharat Times: 7 Bahadur Shah Zafar Marg, New Delhi 110 002; tel. (11) 3312277; telex 3161337; fax (11) 3323346; f. 1947; Hindi; also publ. from Bombay, Lucknow, Jaipur and Patna; Editor RAJENDRA MATHUR; combined circ. 478,200, circ. (Delhi) 264,300.

Patriot: Link House, Bahadur Shah Zafar Marg, New Delhi 110 002; tel. (11) 3311056; f. 1963; English; Editor SITANSHU DAS; circ. 33,000.

Sandhya Times: 7 Bahadur Shah Zafar Marg, New Delhi 110 002; tel (11) 262071; telex 3173300; f. 1979; Hindi; evening; Editor SAT SONI; circ. 63,400.

The Statesman: Connaught Circus, New Delhi 110 001; tel. (11) 315911; telex 3166324; f. 1875; morning; English; also publ. from Calcutta; Delhi Editor D. P. KUMAR; combined circ. 155,900.

Times of India: 7 Bahadur Shah Zafar Marg, Delhi 110 002; tel. (11) 3312277; telex 3173300; English; also publ. from Bombay, Jaipur, Bangalore, Ahmedabad, Lucknow and Patna; Editor DILEEP PADGAONKAR; circ. (Delhi) 165,200.

Andhra Pradesh
Hyderabad

Deccan Chronicle: 36 Sarojini Devi Rd, Hyderabad 500 003; tel. (842) 72126; telex 4256644; f. 1938; English; Editor T. VENKATRAM REDDY; circ. 63,700.

Eenadu: Somajiguda, Hyderabad 500 482; tel. (842) 223422; telex 4256521; fax (842) 228787; f. 1974; Telugu; also publ. from Tirupati, Visakhapatnam and Vijayawada; Chief Editor RAMOJI RAO; combined circ. 289,800.

Newstime: 6-3-570 Somajiguda, Hyderabad 500 482; tel. (842) 223422; telex 4256521; f. 1984; also publ. from Vijaywada and Visakhapatnam; Editor RAMOJI RAO; circ. 60,000.

Rahnuma-e-Deccan Daily: 5-3-831, Shankar Bagh, Hyderabad 500 012; tel. (842) 43210; f. 1949; morning; Urdu; independent; Gen. Man. MIR ALI HYDER HUSSAINI; Editor SYED VICARUDDIN; circ. 18,900.

Siasat Daily: Jawaharlal Nehru Rd, Hyderabad 500 001; tel. (842) 44180; telex 4256579; fax (842) 44188; f. 1949; morning; Urdu; Editor ABID ALI KHAN; circ. 36,800.

Vijayawada

Andhra Jyoti: Andhra Jyoti Bldg, POB 712, Vijayawada 520 010; tel. (866) 474532; telex 475217; f. 1960; Telugu; also publ. from Hyderabad and Tirupati; Editor NANDURI RAMAMOHAN RAO; combined circ. 158,100.

Andhra Patrika: POB 534, Gandhinagar, Vijayawada 520 003; tel. (866) 61247; f. 1914; Telugu; also publ. from Hyderabad; Editor S. RADHAKRISHNA; combined circ. 20,000.

Andhra Prabha: 16-1-28, Kolandareddy Rd, Vijayawada 520 016; tel. (866) 61351; telex 475231; f. 1935; Telugu; also publ. from Bangalore, Hyderabad, Madras and Vijianagram; Editor P. V. RAO; combined circ. 64,400.

Indian Express: George Oakes Building, Besant Rd, Vijayawada 520 003; English; also publ. from Bangalore, Madras, Cochin, Hyderabad, Vijianagram and Madurai; Editor N. S. JAGANNATHAN; combined circ. 284,900.

Assam
Guwahati

Assam Tribune: Tribune Bldgs, Chandmari, Guwahati 781 003; tel. 23251; telex 2352417; f. 1939; English; Man. Partner P. G. BARUAH; Editor R. N. BOROOAH; circ. 39,600.

Dainik Asam: Tribune Bldgs, Guwahati 781 003; tel. 23251; f. 1965; Assamese; Editor P. C. BORUA; circ. 34,500.

Jorhat

Dainik Janambhoomi: Nehru Park Rd, Jorhat 785 001; tel. 20033; f. 1972; Assamese; Editor J. K. BORGOHAIN; circ. 37,400.

Bihar
Patna

Aryavarta: Mazharul Haque Path, Patna 800 001; tel. (612) 22130; telex 267; f. 1940; morning; Hindi; Chief Editor S. N. JHA; circ. 72,000.

Hindustan Times: Buddha Marg, Patna 800 001; tel. (612) 23434; f. 1918; morning; English; Editor H. K. DUA; circ. 36,200.

The Indian Nation: Mazharul Haque Path, Patna 800 001; tel. (612) 22130; telex 267; f. 1930; morning; English; Editor DEENA NATH JHA; circ. 40,000.

Ranchi

Ranchi Express: 55 Baralal St, Ranchi 834 001; tel. 22111; f. 1963; Hindi; Editor BALBIR DUTT; circ. 56,800.

Goa
Panaji

Gomantak: Gomantak Bhavan, St Inez, Goa 403 001; tel. 3212; f. 1962; morning; Marathi; Editor NARAYAN G. ATHAWALAY; circ. 16,800.

Navhind Times: Navhind Bhavan, Rua Ismael Gracias, Panjim, Goa 403 001; tel. 5684; telex 194217; fax 5098; f. 1963; morning; English; Editor M. M. MUDALIAR; circ. 22,500.

Gujarat
Ahmedabad

Gujarat Samachar: Gujarat Samachar Bhavan, Khanpur, Ahmedabad 380 001; tel. (272) 22821; telex 1216642; f. 1932; morning; Gujarati; also publ. from Surat, Baroda and Bombay; Man. Editor SHREYANS SHAH; combined circ. 387,000.

Indian Express: Janasatta Bldg, Mirzapur Rd, Ahmedabad; f. 1968; English; Editor N. S. JAGANNATHAN; circ. (Ahmedabad) 21,400.

Lokasatta—Janasatta: Mirzapur Rd, POB 188, Ahmedabad 380 001; tel. (272) 350300; telex 1216429; f. 1953; morning; Gujarati; also publ. from Rajkot and Vadodara; Co ordinating Editor DIGANT OZA; combined circ. 75,473.

Sandesh: Sandesh Bldg, Cheekanta Rd, Ahmedabad 380 001; tel. (272) 24241; telex 1216532; f. 1923; Gujarati; also publ. from Vadodara, Rajkot and Surat; Editor C. S. PATEL; combined circ. 300,000.

Times of India: 139 Ashram Rd, POB 4046, Ahmedabad 380 009; tel. (272) 402151; telex 121490; f. 1968; English; also publ. from Bombay, Delhi, Bangalore, Jaipur, Patna and Lucknow; Editor DILEEP PADGAONKAR; Resident Editor HARISH KHARE; circ. (Ahmedabad) 43,700.

INDIA

Western Times: Sanskar Kendra, Paldi, Ahmedabad 380 006; tel. (272) 77116; f. 1967; English and Gujarati edns; Man. Editor Nikunj Patel; Editor Ramu Patel; circ. 14,000 (English), 21,100 (Gujarati).

Rajkot

Jai Hind: POB 59, Sharda Baug, Rajkot 360 001; tel. (281) 40511; f. 1948; morning and evening (in Rajkot as *Sanj Samachar*); Gujarati; also publ. from Ahmedabad; Editor Y. N. Shah; combined circ. 61,300.

Phulchhab: Phulchhab Bhavan, Mahatma Gandhi Rd, POB 118, Rajkot 360 001; tel. (281) 44611; f. 1950; morning; Gujarati; Man. Mansukh C. Joshi; Editor Harsukh M. Sanghani; circ. 89,800.

Surat

Gujaratmitra and Gujaratdarpan: Gujaratmitra Bhavan, nr Old Civil Hospital, Sonifalia, Surat 395 003; tel. (261) 23283; telex 188261; f. 1863; morning; Gujarati; Editor B. P. Reshamwala; circ. 79,485.

Jammu and Kashmir
Jammu

Kashmir Times: Residency Rd, Jammu 180 001; tel. 44777; f. 1955; morning; English; Editor V. Bhasin; circ. 42,000.

Srinagar

Srinagar Times: Badshah Bridge, Srinagar; f. 1969; Urdu; Editor Gulam Muhammad Sofi; circ. 14,000.

Karnataka
Bangalore

Deccan Herald: 66 Mahatma Gandhi Rd, Bangalore 560 001; tel. (812) 573291; telex 845339; f. 1948; morning; English; also publ. from Hubli-Dharwar; Editor-in-Chief K. N. Hari Kumar; circ. 140,300.

Indian Express: 1 Queen's Rd, Bangalore 560 001; tel. (812) 76894; telex 845597; f. 1965; English; also publ. from Kochi, Hyderabad, Madras, Madurai, Vijayawada and Vizianagaram; Editor N. S. Jagannathan; combined circ. 284,900.

Kannada Prabha: 1 Queen's Rd, Banglalore 560 001; tel. (812) 76893; Kannada; Editor Khadri Shamanna; circ. 76,200.

Prajavani: 66 Mahatma Gandhi Rd, Bangalore 560 001; tel. (812) 573291; telex 845339; f. 1948; morning; Kannada; also publ. from Hubli-Dharwar; Editor-in-Chief K. N. Harikumar; Editor M. B. Singh; combined circ. 231,100.

Hubli-Dharwar

Sanjukta Karnataka: Koppikar Rd, Hubli 580 020; tel. 64858; telex 865220; f. 1933; Kannada; also publ. from Bangalore; Man. Editor K. Shama Rao; combined circ. 68,700.

Manipal

Udayavani: Udayavani Bldg, Press Corner, Tile Factory Rd, Manipal 576 119; tel. 20843; telex 833207; f. 1970; Kannada; Editor T. Satish U. Pai; circ. 80,300.

Kerala
Kozhikode

Deshabhimani: 11/127 Convent Rd, Kozhikode 673 032; tel. (495) 77286; f. 1946; morning; Malayalam; publ. by the CPI-M; also publ. from Kochi and Thiruvananthapuram; Chief Editor S. Ramachandran Pillai; combined circ. 104,400.

Mathrubhumi: Mathrubhumi Bldgs, Robinson Rd, Kozhikode 673 001; tel. (495) 63651; f. 1923; Malayalam; Chief Editor Vasudevan Nair; also publ. from Thiruvananthapuram and Kochi; combined circ. 442,200.

Kottayam

Deepika: POB 7, Kottayam 686 001; tel. (481) 3706; telex 888203; fax (481) 5048; f. 1887; Malayalam; independent; also publ. from Trichur; Man. Dir Joseph Kurian; Chief Editor Dr Victor Z. Narively; combined circ. 63,000.

Malayala Manorama: Malayala Manorama, K. K. Rd, POB 26, Kottayam 686 001; tel. (481) 3615; telex 888201; fax (481) 2479; f. 1888; also publ. from Kozhikode, Thiruvananthapuram and Kochi; morning; Malayalam; Man. Dir and Editor Mammen Mathew; Chief Editor K. M. Mathew; combined circ. 612,222.

Thiruvananthapuram

Kerala Kaumudi: POB 77, Pettah, Thiruvananthapuram 605 024; tel. (471) 71050; telex 435214; f. 1911; Malayalam; also publ. from Kozhikode; Editor-in-Chief M. S. Mani; combined circ. 136,000.

Trichur

Express: POB 15, Trichur 680 001; tel. 21830; f. 1944; Malayalam; Editor K. Balakrishnan; circ. 68,200.

Madhya Pradesh
Bhopal

Dainik Bhaskar: 6 Dwarka Sadan, Habibganj, Bhopal; tel. (755) 65163; f. 1958; morning; Hindi; also publ. from Indore, Jabalpur and Gwalior; Editor R. C. Agrawal; combined circ. 132,000.

Indore

Nai Dunia: 60/1 Babu Labhchand, Chhajlani Marg, Indore 452 009; tel. (731) 62061; telex 735342; f. 1947; morning; Hindi; also publ. from Bhopal; Man. Editor Basantilal Sethia; combined circ. 127,600.

Raipur

Deshbandhu: Deshbandhu Complex, Ramsagarpara Layout, Raipur 492 001; tel. 27563; Hindi; also publ. from Jabalpur, Satna and Bhopal; Chief Editor Maya Ram Surjan; circ. 40,000 (Raipur), 15,900 (Satna).

Maharashtra
Bombay

Bombay Samachar: Red House, Syed Abdulla Brelvi Rd, Fort, Bombay 400 001; tel. (22) 2045531; telex 114237; f. 1822; morning and Sunday; Gujarati; political and commercial; Editor Jehan D. Daruwala; circ. 129,600.

The Daily: West View, 87 Nathalal Parekh Marg, Colaba, Bombay 400 005; tel. (22) 216831; telex 1186146; fax (22) 2871236; f. 1981; Editor Rajat Sharma.

The Economic Times: Head Office, POB 213, Bombay 400 001; tel. (22) 4150271; telex 1173300; f. 1961; also publ. from New Delhi, Calcutta and Bangalore; English; Editor T. N. Ninan; combined circ. 101,600.

Financial Express: Express Towers, Nariman Point, Bombay 400 021; tel. (22) 2022627; telex 112585; f. 1961; morning; English; also publ. from New Delhi and Madras; Editor A. M. Khusro; combined circ. 37,400.

Free Press Journal: Free Press House, 215 Free Press Journal Rd, Nariman Point, Bombay 400 021; tel. (22) 2874566; telex 112570; f. 1930; English; also publ. from Indore; Editor Janardan Thakur; combined circ. 40,000.

The Independent: 121 D.N. Rd, Bombay 400 001; tel. (22) 2620271; telex 1186054; fax (22) 2620080; f. 1989; Editor Pritish Nandy.

Indian Express: Express Towers, Nariman Point, Bombay 400 021; tel. (22) 2022627; telex 112276; f. 1940; English; also publ. from Pune; Editor N. S. Jagannathan; combined circ. 139,000.

Inquilab: 156D J. Dadajee Rd, Tardeo, Bombay 400 034; tel. (22) 4942586; telex 1175624; f. 1938; Urdu; Editor Riyaz Ahmed Khan; circ. 22,100.

Janmabhoomi: Janmabhoomi Bhavan, Ghoga St, Fort, Bombay 400 001; tel. (22) 2870831; telex 116859; f. 1934; evening; Gujarati; Propr Saurashtra Trust; Editor Harindra Dave; circ. 35,600.

Janmabhoomi-Pravasi: Janmabhoomi Bhavan, Ghoga St, Fort, Bombay 400 001; tel. (22) 2870831; telex 116859; f. 1939; morning; Gujarati; Propr Saurashtra Trust; Editor Harindra Dave; circ. 23,300.

Lokasatta: Express Towers, Nariman Point, Bombay 400 021; tel. (22) 2022627; f. 1948; morning (except Sunday); Marathi; also publ. from Pune; Editor Madhavrao Gadkari; combined circ. 258,500.

Maharashtra Times: Dr Dadabhai Naoroji Rd, POB 213, Bombay 400 001; tel. (22) 4150271; telex 1173300; f. 1962; Marathi; Editor G. S. Talwalkar; circ. 158,100.

Mid-Day: 156 D. J. Dadajee Rd, Tardeo, Bombay 400 034; tel. (22) 4942586; telex 1175624; f. 1979; daily and Sunday; English; Editor-in-Chief Nikhil Lakshman; circ. 60,393.

Navakal: 13 Shenviwadi, Khadilkar Rd, Girgaun, Bombay 400 004; tel. (22) 353585; f. 1923; Marathi; Editor N. Y. Khadilkar; circ. 108,300.

Navbharat Times: Dr Dadabhai Naoroji Rd, Bombay 400 001; tel. (22) 4150271; telex 1173300; f. 1950; Hindi; also publ. from New Delhi and Lucknow; circ. (Bombay) 107,800.

Navshakti: Free Press House, 215 Nariman Point, Bombay 400 021; tel. (22) 2874566; telex 112570; f. 1932; Marathi; Editor Atmaram Sawant; circ. 65,000.

Sakal: Dr N. B. Parulekar Rd, Prabhadevi, Bombay 400 025; tel. (22) 4304387; f. 1970; daily; Marathi; also publ. from Pune and Kolhapur; combined circ. 209,500.

The Times of India: Dr Dadabhai Naoroji Rd, Bombay 400 001; tel. (22) 4150271; telex 1173300; f. 1838; morning; English; also

INDIA

publ. from Delhi, Ahmedabad, Bangalore, Jaipur, Patna and Lucknow; Editor DILEEP PADGAONKAR; circ. (Bombay) 307,100.

Kolhapur

Pudhari: 2318, 'C' Ward, Kolhapur 416 002; tel. 22551; f. 1974; Marathi; Editor P. G. JADHAV; circ. 58,800.

Nagpur

Hitavada: Wardha Rd, Nagpur; tel. (712) 23155; f. 1911; morning; English; also publ. from Bhopal; Editor M. Y. BODHANKAR; combined circ. 31,000.

Nagpur Times: 37 Farmland, Ramdaspeth, Nagpur 440 010; tel. (712) 34483; telex 715235; f. 1933; English; Editor NARESH GADRE; circ. 20,000.

Nava Bharat: Nava Bharat Bhavan, Cotton Market, POB 382, Nagpur 440 018; tel. (712) 46145; telex 715453; f. 1938; morning; Hindi; also publ. from Bhopal, Jabalpur, Bilaspur, Indore and Raipur; Editor-in-Chief R. G. MAHESWARI; combined circ. 215,700.

Tarun Bharat: 28 Farmland, Ramdaspeth, Nagpur 440 010; tel. (712) 25052; f. 1944; Marathi; independent; also publ. from Pune and Belgaum; Editor L. T. JOSHI; combined circ. 95,451.

Pune

Kesari: 568 Narayan Peth, Pune 411 030; tel. (212) 449250; f. 1881; Marathi; also publ. from Solapur, Kolhapur, Ahmednagar and Sangli; Editor Dr SHARATCHANDRA GOKHALE; combined circ. 87,200.

Sakal: 595 Budhwar Peth, Pune 411 002; tel. (212) 448403; telex 145504; f. 1932; daily; Marathi; also publ. from Bombay, Nashik and Kolhapur; Editor VIJAY KUVALEKAR; Gen. Man. K. M. BHIDE; combined circ. daily more than 220,100.

Orissa

Cuttack

Samaj: Gopabandhu Bhawan, Buxibazar, Cuttack 753 001; tel. (671) 20994; telex 676267; f. 1919; Oriya; Editor R. N. RATH; circ. 112,500.

Punjab

Jalandhar

Ajit: Ajit Bhavan, Nehru Garden Rd, Jalandhar 144 001; f. 1955; Punjabi; tel. 75961; telex 385265; Man. Editor S. BARJINDER SINGH; circ. 149,600.

Hind Samachar: Civil Lines, Jalandhar 144 001; tel. (181) 58881; telex 385221; fax (181) 58889; f. 1948; morning and Sunday; Urdu; Editor VIJAY KUMAR CHOPRA; circ. 51,757.

Jag Bani: Civil Lines, Jalandhar 144 001; tel. (181) 58881; telex 385221; fax (181) 58889; f. 1978; morning and Sunday; Punjabi; publ. by Hind Samachar Ltd; Editor VIJAY KUMAR CHOPRA; circ. 48,284.

Punjab Kesari: Civil Lines, Jalandhar 144 001; tel. (181) 58881; telex 385221; fax (181) 58889; f. 1965; morning and Sunday; Hindi; also publ. from Delhi; Editor VIJAY KUMAR CHOPRA; combined circ. 540,952.

Chandigarh

The Tribune: 29C Chandigarh 160 020; tel. (172) 41035; telex 395285; f. 1881; English, Hindi and Punjabi; Editor-in-Chief (all edns) V. N. NARAYANAN; Editor (Hindi edn) VIJAY SAIHGAL (acting); Editor (Punjabi edn) HARBHAJAN SINGH HALWARVI; circ. 159,600 (English), 53,000 (Hindi), 60,000 (Punjabi).

Rajasthan

Jaipur

Rajasthan Patrika: Kesargarh, Jawahar Lal Nehru Marg, Jaipur 302 004; tel. (141) 561582; telex 3652435; f. 1956; Hindi; English; also publ. from Jodhphur, Bikaner, Udaipur and Kota; Editor VIJAY BHANDARI; combined circ. (Hindi) 237,600, (English) 2,900.

Rashtradoot: M.I. Rd, POB 30, Jaipur 302 001; tel. (141) 72634; f. 1951; Hindi; also publ. from Kota and Bikaner; Chief Editor RAJESH SHARMA; circ. 126,000 (Jaipur), 45,000 (Kota), 35,000 (Bikaner).

Tamil Nadu

Madras

Daily Thanthi: 46 E.V.K. Sampath Rd, POB 467, Madras 600 007; tel. (44) 587731; telex 418101; f. 1942; Tamil; also publ. from Bangalore, Coimbatore, Cuddalore, Madurai, Salem, Tiruchi, Tirunelveli and Vellore; Chief Gen. Man. R. SOMASUNDARAM; Editor R. THIRUVADI; combined circ. 301,100.

Dinakaran: 106/107 Kutchery Rd, Mylapore, Madras 600 004; tel. (44) 71006; telex 416065; f. 1977; Tamil; also publ. from Madurai, Trichy, Vellore. Tirunelveli, Salem and Coimbatore; Editor K. KESAVAN; combined circ. 201,000.

Dinamani: Express Estates, Mount Rd, Madras 600 002; tel. (44) 860551; telex 418222; f. 1934; morning; Tamil; also publ. from Madurai and Bangalore; Editor IRAVATHAM MAHADEVAN; combined circ. 154,000.

The Hindu: 859/860 Anna Salai, Madras 600 002; tel. (44) 566567; telex 41358; fax (44) 835325; f. 1878; morning; English; independent; also publ. from Bangalore, Coimbatore, Hyderabad, Gurgaon, Visakhapatnam and Madurai; Editor N. RAVI; combined circ. 424,100.

Indian Express: Express Estates, Mount Rd, Madras 600 002; tel. (44) 860551; telex 41222; fax (44) 8254500; also publ. from Delhi, Bombay, Chandigarh, Cochin, Bangalore, Ahmedabad, Madurai, Hyderabad, Vizianagaram and Vijayawada; Editor N. S. JAGANNATHAN; circ. 284,900 (Madras, Madurai, Bangalore, Cochin, Hyderabad, Vijayawada and Vizianagaram).

Murasoli: 93 Kodambakkam High Rd, Madras 600 034; tel. (44) 470044; f. 1960; Tamil; Editor MURASOLI MARAN; circ. 54,000.

Tripura

Agartala

Dainik Sambad: 11 Jagannath Bari Rd, Agartala 799 001; tel. 3928; telex 604204; f. 1966; Bengali; Editor B. C. DUTTA BHAUMIK.

Uttar Pradesh

Agra

Amar Ujala: Sikandara Rd, Agra 282 007; tel. (562) 72408; telex 565255; f. 1948; Hindi; also publ. from Bareilly, Moradabad and Meerut; Editor AJAI K. AGARWAL; circ. 78,000 (Agra), 52,900 (Bareilly), 35,000 (Moradabad), 51,100 (Meerut).

Allahabad

Amrita Prabhat: 10 Edmonstone Rd, Allahabad 211 001; tel. (532) 52620; f. 1977; Hindi; Chief Editor TUSHAR KANTI GHOSH; Editor KAMLESH BIHARI MATHUR; circ. 44,000.

Northern India Patrika: 10 Edmonstone Rd, Allahabad 211 001; tel. (532) 52665; f. 1959; English; Chief Editor TUSHAR KANTI GHOSH; Editor S. KAUSER HUSAIN (acting); circ. 46,000.

Kanpur

Daily Jagran: 2 Sarvodaya Nagar, Kanpur 208 005; tel. 216161; telex 325289; f. 1942; Hindi; also publ. from Gorakhpur, Jhansi, Lucknow, Meerut, Agra, Varanasi (Allahabad), Bareilly and New Delhi; Editor NARENDRA MOHAN; combined circ. 580,000.

Vyapar Sandesh: 48/12 Lathi Mohal Lane, Kanpur, 208 001; tel. (512) 69889; f. 1958; Hindi; commercial news and economic trends; Editor HARI SHANKAR SHARMA; circ. 17,000.

Lucknow

National Herald: 1 Bisheshwar North Rd, Lucknow 226 001; f. 1938 Lucknow, 1968 Delhi; English; Editor A. N. DAR.

The Pioneer: 20 Vidhan Sabha Marg, Lucknow 226 001; tel. (522) 240516; f. 1865; English; also publ. from Varanasi and Kanpur; Editor SOMNATH SAPRU; combined circ. 104,000.

Swatantra Bharat: Pioneer House, 20 Vidhan Sabha Marg, Lucknow 226 001; tel. (522) 36516; f. 1947; Hindi; also publ. from Varanasi; Editor RAJ NATH SINGH; combined circ. 119,800.

Varanasi

Aj: Sant Kabir Rd, Kabirchaura, POB 1007 & 1052, Varanasi 221 001; tel. (542) 62061; telex 545213; f. 1920; Hindi; also publ. from Gorakhpur, Patna, Allahabad, Ranchi, Agra, Bareilly, Lucknow, Dhanbad, Jamshedpur and Kanpur; Editor S. V. GUPTA; circ. 159,800 (Varanasi, Allahabad and Gorakhpur), 54,000 (Kanpur and Agra), 130,000 (Patna and Ranchi).

West Bengal

Calcutta

Aajkaal: 96 Raja Rammohan Sarani, Calcutta 700 009; tel. (33) 353671; telex 212216; f. 1981; morning; Bengali; Chief Editor PRATAP K. ROY; circ. 177,600.

Amrita Bazar Patrika: 41A Acharya J. C. Bose Rd, Calcutta 700 017; tel. (33) 296055; telex 217245; f. 1868; morning; English; nationalist; also published from Jamshedpur (Bihar); Editor T. K. GHOSH; combined circ. 128,000.

Anandabazar Patrika: 6 Prafulla Sarkar St, Calcutta 700 001; tel. (33) 274880; telex 215468; fax (33) 270995; f. 1922; morning; Bengali; Editor AVEEK SARKAR; circ. 400,676.

Bartaman: 76A Acharya J.C. Bose Rd, Calcutta 700 014; tel. (33) 243907; telex 217380; f. 1984; Editor BARUN SENGUPTA; circ. 111,700.

INDIA *Directory*

Business Standard: 6 Prafulla Sarkar St, Calcutta 700 001; tel. (33) 243907; telex 215468; f. 1975; morning; English; Editor AVEEK SARKAR (acting); circ. 22,700.
Dainik Basumati: 166 Bepin Behari Ganguly St, Calcutta 700 012; tel. (33) 359462; f. 1914; Bengali; independent nationalist; Editor ASHIM SHOME; circ. 26,000.
The Economic Times: 105/7A, S. N. Banerjee Rd, Calcutta 700 014; tel. (33) 294232; telex 215946; English; also publ. from Ahmedabad, Delhi, Bangalore and Bombay; circ. (Calcutta) 13,500.
Evening Brief: 164 Lenin Sarani, Calcutta 700 013; tel. (33) 276231; f. 1986; English; Editor S. C. TALUKDAR; circ. 38,000.
Himalchuli: 7 Old Court House St, Calcutta 700 001; tel. (33) 206663; f. 1982; Nepali; Editor S. C. TALUKDAR; circ. 34,000.
Ganashakti: 31 Alimmuddin St, Calcutta 700 016; tel. (33) 249533; telex 215904; f. 1965; morning; Bengali; Chief Editor ANIL BISWAS.
Jugantar: 41A Acharya J. C. Bose Rd, Calcutta 700 017; tel. (33) 296055; telex 217245; f. 1936; Bengali; Editor T. K. GHOSH; circ. 302,000.
Kolkata: 164 Lenin Sarani, Calcutta 700 013; tel. (33) 276231; f. 1988; Bengali; Editor S. C. TALUKDAR; circ. 85,000.
Paigam: 26/1 Market St, Calcutta 700 087; tel. (33) 246040; f. 1948; Bengali; morning; Editor MARJINA TARAFDAR; circ. 14,200.
Paschim Banga Sambad: 7 Old Court House St, Calcutta 700 001; tel. (33) 206663; f. 1982; Bengali; Editor S. C. TALUKDAR; circ. 38,000.
Sanmarg: 160C Chittaranjan Ave, Calcutta 700 007; tel. (33) 315301; f. 1948; Hindi; Editor RAMAWTAR A. GUPTA; circ. 62,700.
The Statesman: Statesman House, 4 Chowringhee Sq., Calcutta 700 001; tel. (33) 271000; telex 214509; f. 1875; morning; English; independent; also publ. from New Delhi; Editor SUNANDA K. DATTA-RAY; combined circ. 155,900.
The Telegraph: 6 Prafulla Sarkar St, Calcutta 700 001; tel. (33) 278000; telex 215468; f. 1982; English; Editor AVEEK SARKAR; circ. 129,000.
Uttar Banga Sambad: 7 Old Court House St, Calcutta 700 001; tel. (33) 206663; f. 1980; Bengali; Editor S. C. TALUKDAR; circ. 56,000.
Vishwamitra: 74 Lenin Sarani, Calcutta 700 013; tel. (33) 241139; telex 215882; f. 1916; morning; Hindi; commercial; also publ. from Bombay; Editor PRAKASH CHANDRA AGRAWALLA; combined circ. 81,100.

SELECTED PERIODICALS
Delhi and New Delhi

Alive: Delhi Press Bldg, E-3, Jhandewala Estate, Rani Jhansi Rd, Delhi 110 055; tel. (11) 526311; telex 3163053; f. 1940; fortnightly; English; political and cultural; Editor VISHWA NATH; circ. 12,500.
Bal Bharati: Patiala House, Publications Division, Ministry of Information and Broadcasting, Delhi; tel. (11) 387038; f. 1948; monthly; Hindi; for children; Editor P. K. BHARGAVA; circ. 30,000.
Bano: 13/14 Asaf Ali Rd, New Delhi 110 002; tel. (11) 732666; telex 3161601; fax (11) 736539; f. 1947; monthly; Urdu; women's interests; Editor SADIA DEHLVI; circ. 38,000.
Biswin Sadi: 3583 Netaji Subash Marg, Darya Ganj, POB 7013, New Delhi 110 002; tel. (11) 271637; f. 1937; monthly; Urdu; Editor Z. REHMAN NAYYAR; circ. 36,000.
Career and Competition Times: c/o Times of India, 10 Daryaganj, New Delhi 110 002; tel. (11) 3276567; telex 3161337; fax (11) 3323346; f. 1981; monthly; English; Editor BIDYUT SARKAR; circ. 57,000.
Careers Digest: 21 Shankar Market, Delhi 110 001; tel. (11) 44726; f. 1963; monthly; English; Editor O. P. VARMA; circ. 35,000.
Catholic India: CBCI Centre, 1 Ashok Place, Goldakkhana, New Delhi 110 001; tel. (11) 344470; telex 3161366; quarterly.
Champak: Delhi Press Bldg, E-3, Jhandewala Estate, Rani Jhansi Rd, Delhi 110 055; tel. (11) 526311; telex 3163053; f. 1969; fortnightly; Hindi, also in English, Gujarati and Marathi; Editor VISHWA NATH; circ. 65,500.
Children's World: Nehru House, 4 Bahadur Shah Zafar Marg, New Delhi 110 002; tel. (11) 3316970; f. 1968; monthly; English; Exec. Editor K. RAMAKRISHNAN; Editor VAIJAYANTI TONPE; circ. 25,000.
Competition Refresher: 1525 Nai Sarak, Delhi 110 006; f. 1984; monthly; English; Chief Editor D. SARNA; circ. 103,100.
Competition Success Review: 604 Prabhat Kiran, Rajendra Place, Delhi 110 008; tel. (11) 5712898; monthly; English; f. 1963; Editor S. K. SACHDEVA; circ. 258,400.
Cricket Samrat: L-1 & 2, Kanchan House, Najafgarh Rd, Commercial Complex, New Delhi 110 015; tel. (11) 591175; f. 1978; monthly; Hindi; Editor ANAND DEWAN; circ. 84,600.

Dinaman Times: 10 Daryaganj, New Delhi 110 002; tel. (11) 271911; f. 1965; every Sunday; Hindi; news; Editor GHANSHYAM PANKAJ.
Dost Aur Dosti: 13/14 Asaf Ali Rd, New Delhi 110 002; tel. (11) 732666; telex 3161601; fax (11) 736539; f. 1988; monthly; Hindi; youth; Editor M. YUNUS DEHLVI; circ. 50,000.
Employment News: Government of India, East Block IV, Level 7, R. K. Puram, New Delhi 110 066; tel. (11) 603856; f. 1976; weekly; Hindi, Urdu and English edns; Gen. Man. and Chief Editor NAGENDRA MISHRA; combined circ. 405,000.
Film Mirror: 26F Connaught Place, Delhi 110 001; tel. (11) 3312329; f. 1964; monthly; English; Editor HARBHAJAN SINGH; circ. 33,200.
Filmi Duniya: 16 Darya Ganj, New Delhi 110 002; tel. (11) 3278087; f. 1958; monthly; Hindi; Chief Editor NARENDRA KUMAR; circ. 109,100.
Filmi Kaliyan: 16/39 Subhash Nagar, New Delhi 110 027; tel. (11) 272080; f. 1969; monthly; English; cinema; Editor-in-Chief V. S. DEWAN; circ. 102,700.
Grih Shobha: Delhi Press Bldg, E-3 Jhandewala Estate, Rani Jhansi Rd, New Delhi 110 055; tel. (11) 526311; telex 3163053; f. 1979; monthly; Marathi and Gujarati edns; Editor VISHWA NATH; circ. 320,100.
India Perspectives: Room 137, 'A' Wing, Shastri Bhavan, New Delhi 1; tel. (11) 389471; f. 1988; Chief Editor DALIP SINGH.
India Today: F 14/15, Connaught Place, New Delhi 110 001; tel. (11) 3315801; telex 3161245; fax (11) 3316180; f. 1975; fortnightly; English and Hindi; Editor AROON PURIE; circ. 368,700 (English), 232,700 (Hindi).
Indian Horizons: Azad Bhavan, Indraprastha Estate, New Delhi 110 002; tel. (11) 3318647; telex 314904; f. 1951; quarterly; English; publ. by the Indian Council for Cultural Relations; Editor A. SRINIVASAN; circ. 1,900.
Indian Observer: 26F Connaught Place, Delhi 110 001; tel. (11) 3312329; f. 1958; monthly; English; Editor HARBHAJAN SINGH; circ. 26,500.
Indian Railways: POB 467, New Delhi 110 001; tel. (11) 383522; telex 313561; f. 1956; monthly; English; publ. by the Ministry of Railways (Railway Board); Editor MANOHAR D. BANERJEE; circ. 12,000.
Intensive Agriculture: Ministry of Agriculture and Rural Development, Directorate of Extension, New Delhi 110 066; tel. (11) 600591; f. 1955; monthly; English; Editor SHUKLA HAZRA; circ. 15,000.
Jagat (Hindi) Monthly: 8/818 Ajmeri Gate, Delhi 110 006; f. 1958; Hindi; popular and family magazine; Editor PREM CHAND VERMA; circ. 18,000.
Jagat Weekly: 8/818 Ajmeri Gate, Delhi 110 006; tel. (11) 664847; f. 1956; Urdu; progressive; Editor PREM CHAND VERMA; circ. 11,000.
Journal of Industry and Trade: Ministry of Commerce and Supply, Delhi 110 011; tel. (11) 3016664; f. 1952; monthly; English; Man. Dir A. C. BANERJEE; circ. 2,000.
Kadambini: Hindustan Times House, Kasturba Gandhi Marg, New Delhi 110 001; tel. (11) 3318201; telex 3166310; f. 1960; monthly; Hindi; Editor RAJENDRA AWASTHY; circ. 63,400.
Krishak Samachar: Bharat Krishak Samaj, Dr Panjabrao Deshmukh Krishak Bhavan, A-1 Nizamuddin West, New Delhi 110 013; tel. (11) 619508; f. 1957; monthly; English and Hindi edns; agriculture; Editor K. PRABHAKAR REDDY; circ. (English) 12,000, (Hindi) 30,000.
Kurukshetra: Krishi Bhavan, Delhi 110 001; monthly; English; rural development; Editor RATNA JUNEJA; circ. 13,000.
Lalita: 92 Daryaganj, Delhi 110 002; tel. (11) 272482; f. 1959; monthly; Hindi; Editor L. RANIGUPTA; circ. 20,000.
Link Indian News Magazine: Link House, Bahadurshah Zafar Marg, New Delhi 110 002; tel. (11) 3311056; telex 3162384; f. 1958; weekly; independent; Editor SITANSHU DAS; circ. 11,000.
Mayapuri: A-5, Mayapuri, New Delhi 110 064; tel. (11) 591439; telex 3176125; f. 1974; weekly; Hindi; cinema; Editor A. P. BAJAJ; circ. 151,235.
Mujrim: 13/14 Asaf Ali Rd, New Delhi 110 002; tel. (11) 732666; telex 3161601; f. 1959; monthly; Urdu; detective fiction; Editor M. YUNUS DEHLVI; circ. 35,000.
Mukta: Delhi Press Bldg, E-3 Jhandewala Estate, Rani Jhansi Rd, New Delhi 110 055; tel. (11) 526391; telex 3163053; f. 1961; fortnightly; Hindi; youth; Editor VISHWA NATH; circ. 25,000.
Nandan: Hindustan Times House, Kasturba Gandhi Marg, New Delhi 110 001; tel. (11) 3318201; telex 3166317; f. 1963; monthly; Hindi; Editor JAI PRAKASH BHARTI; circ. 186,000.
Nav Chitrapat: 92 Daryaganj, Delhi 110 002; tel. (11) 272482; f. 1932; monthly; Hindi; Editor SATYENDRA SHYAM; circ. 36,000.

INDIA

New Age: 15 Kotla Rd, Delhi 110 002; tel. (11) 3310762; telex 3165982; f. 1953; main organ of the Communist Party of India; weekly; English; Editor PAULY V. PARAKAL; circ. 215,000.

Organiser: 29 Rani Jhansi Rd, Delhi 110 055; tel. (11) 529595; f. 1947; weekly; English; Editor V. P. BHATIA; circ. 44,100.

Overseas Hindustan Times: Hindustan Times House, Kasturba Gandhi Marg, Delhi 110 001; weekly; English.

Panchajanya: 29 Rani Jhansi Marg, New Delhi 110 055; tel. (11) 529595; f. 1948; weekly; Hindi; Gen. Man. S. D. BATRA; Editor TARUN VIJAY; circ. 72,000.

Parag: 10 Daryaganj, New Delhi 110 002; tel. (11) 277360; f. 1958; children's monthly; Hindi; Editor HARI KRISHNA DEVSARE; circ. 60,000.

Priya: 92 Daryaganj, Delhi 110 002; f. 1960; monthly; Hindi; Editor SATYENDRA SMYAM; circ. 28,000.

Punjabi Digest: 209 Hemkunt House, 6 Rajendra Place, POB 2549, New Delhi 110 008; tel. (11) 5715225; f. 1971; literary monthly; Gurmukhi; Chief Editor Sardar J. B. SINGH; circ. 75,600.

Rangbhumi: 5A/15 Ansari Rd, Darya Ganj, Delhi 110 002; tel. (11) 274667; f. 1941; Hindi; films; Editor S. K. GUPTA; circ. 30,000.

Ruby Magazine: 3583 Netaji-Subash Marg, Darya Ganj, POB 7014, New Delhi 110 002; tel. (11) 271637; f. 1966; monthly; Urdu; Editor REHMAN NAYYAR; circ. 23,000.

Sainik Samachar: Block L-1, Church Rd, New Delhi 110 001; tel. (11) 3019668; f. 1909; pictorial weekly for India's armed forces; English, Hindi, Urdu, Tamil, Punjabi, Telugu, Marathi, Kannada, Gorkhali, Malayalam, Bengali, Assamese and Oriya edns; Editor-in-Chief BIBEKANANDA RAY; circ. 18,000.

Saptahik Hindustan: 18–20 Kasturba Gandhi Marg, Delhi 110 001; tel. (11) 3318201; telex 3166310; f. 1950; weekly; Hindi; Editor MRINAL PANDE; circ. 32,100.

Sarita: Delhi Press Bldg, E-3, Jhandewala Estate, Rani Jhansi Rd, Delhi 110 055; tel. (11) 526311; telex 3163053; f. 1946; fortnightly; Hindi; Editor VISHWA NATH; circ. 243,400.

Shama: 13/14 Asaf Ali Rd, New Delhi 110 002; tel. (11) 732666; telex 3161601; fax (11) 736539; f. 1939; monthly; Urdu; art and literature; Editors M. YUNUS DEHLVI, IDREES DEHLVI, ILYAS DEHLVI; circ. 65,000.

Sher-i-Punjab: Hemkunt House, 6 Rajendra Place, New Delhi 110 008; tel. (11) 5715225; f. 1911; weekly news magazine; Chief Editor Sardar JANG BAHADUR SINGH; circ. 15,000.

South Asia Journal: Sage Publications India (Pvt) Ltd, M-32 Market, Greater Kailash-1, POB 4215, New Delhi 110 048; tel. (11) 6419884; f. 1987; quarterly; journal of the Indian Council for South Asian Co-operation (ICSAC); Chair. DINESH SINGH; Editor-in-Chief BIMAL PRASAD.

Suman Saurabh: Delhi Press Bldg, E-3 Jhandewala Estate, Rani Jhansi Rd, New Delhi 110 055; tel. (11) 526311; telex 3163053; f. 1983; monthly; Hindi; children; Editor VISHWA NATH; circ. 47,200.

The Sun: 8B Bahadur Shah Zafar Marg, POB 7164, Delhi 110 002; tel. (11) 3319286; telex 3165931; f. 1977; weekly; English; Editor V. B. GUPTA; circ. 22,400.

Sunday Mail (English): C-43 Neeti Bagh, New Delhi 110 049; tel. (11) 663243; fax (11) 6862017; f. 1986; weekly; also publ. from Bombay, Calcutta and Madras; Editor-in-Chief T. V. R. SHENOY; combined circ. 55,000.

Sunday Mail (Hindi): E-595, Greater Kailash-II, New Delhi 110 048; tel. (11) 6460140; f. 1989; weekly; also publ. from Calcutta; Editor-in-Chief K. L. NANDAN; combined circ. 155,000.

The Sunday Observer: Vijaya, 17 Barakhamba Rd, New Delhi 110 001; tel. (11) 3713200; telex 3166893; fax (11) 3327065; f. 1981; weekly; English and Hindi edns; also publ. from Bombay; Editor CHANDAN MITRA; combined circ. 61,800.

Surya India: Kanchenjunga Bldg, 18 Barakhamba Rd, Delhi; tel. (11) 3310202; telex 3162997; f. 1977; monthly; English; political and social news; Editor Dr J. K. JAIN.

Sushama: 13/14 Asaf Ali Rd, New Delhi 110 002; tel. (11) 732666; telex 3161601; fax (11) 736539; f. 1959; monthly; Hindi; art and literature; Editors IDREES DEHLVI, ILYAS DEHLVI, YUNUS DEHLVI; circ. 80,000.

Sushmita: 13/14 Asaf Ali Rd, New Delhi 110 002; tel. (11) 732666; telex 3161601; fax (11) 736539; f. 1989; weekly; Hindi; literature, films and television; Editors M. YUNUS DEHLVI, IDREES DEHLVI, ILYAS DEHLVI; circ. 50,000.

Vigyan Pragati: PID Bldg, Hillside Rd, New Delhi 110 012; tel. (11) 585359; f. 1952; monthly; Hindi; popular science; Editor DEEKSHA BIST; circ. 100,000.

Woman's Era: Delhi Press Bldg, E-3, Jhandewala Estate, Rani Jhansi Rd, Delhi 110 055; tel. (11) 526311; telex 3163053; f. 1973; fortnightly; English; Editor VISHWA NATH; circ. 106,700.

Yojana: Yojana Bhavan, Parliament St, Delhi 110 001; tel. (11) 3710473; f. 1957; fortnightly; English, Tamil, Bengali, Marathi, Gujarati, Assamese, Malayalam, Telugu, Kannada, Punjabi, Urdu and Hindi edns; Chief Editor D. K. BHARADWAJ; circ. 80,000.

Andhra Pradesh
Hyderabad

Islamic Culture: Opposite Osmania University Post Office, Hyderabad 7; f. 1927; quarterly; English; Editor Prof. SYED SIRAJUDDIN; circ. 700.

Vijayawada

Andhra Jyoti Sachitra Vara Patrika: Vijayawada 520 010; tel. (866) 74532; f. 1967; weekly; Telugu; Editor PURANAM SUBRAMANYA SARMA; circ. 71,000.

Bala Jyoti: Labbipet, Vijayawada 520 010; tel. (866) 474532; telex 475217; f. 1980; monthly; Telugu; Assoc. Editor A. SASIKANT SATAKARNI; circ. 32,600.

Jyoti Chitra: Andhra Jyoti Bldgs, Vijayawada 520 010; tel. (866) 474332; f. 1977; weekly; Telugu; Editor T. KUTUMBA RAO; circ. 52,600.

Vanita Jyoti: Labbipet, Vijayawada 520 010; tel. (866) 74532; f. 1978; monthly; Telugu; Asst Editor J. SATYANARAYANA; circ. 25,400.

Assam
Guwahti

Asam Bani: Tribune Bldg, Guwahti 781 003; tel. 23251; f. 1955; weekly; Assamese; Editor TILAK HAZARIKA; circ. 29,400.

Bihar
Patna

Anand Digest: Govind Mitra Rd, Patna 800 004; tel. 50341; f. 1981; monthly; Hindi; family magazine; Editor Dr S. S. SINGH; circ. 55,900.

Balak: Govind Mitra Rd, POB 5, Patna 800 004; tel. 50341; f. 1926; monthly; Hindi; children's; Editor S. R. SARAN; circ. 32,000.

Jyotsana: Rajendranagar, Patna; f. 1947; monthly; Hindi; Editor S. NARAYAN; circ. 11,000.

Nar Nari: Nari Prakashan, Patna 800 004; f. 1949; monthly; Hindi; Editor V. VATSYAYAN; circ. 10,000.

Gujarat
Ahmedabad

Aaspas: nr Khanpur Gate, Khanpur, Ahmedabad 380 001; tel. (272) 391131; f. 1976; weekly; Gujarati; Editor GUNVANT C. SHAH; circ. 100,373.

Akhand Anand: Swami Akhandanand Marg, POB 50, Bhadra, Ahmedabad; tel. (272) 391798; f. 1947; monthly; Gujarati; Pres. H. M. PATEL; Editor RAMANLAL MANEKLAL BHATT; circ. 30,878.

Chitralok: Gujarat Samachar Bhavan, Khanpur, POB 254, Ahmedabad; f. 1952; weekly; Gujarati; films; Editor SHREYANS SHAH; circ. 18,900.

Sakhi: Sakhi Publications, Jai Hind Press Bldg, nr Gujarat Chamber, Ashram Rd, Navrangpura, Ahmedabad 380 009; tel. (272) 407052; f. 1984; monthly; Gujarati; women's; Editor Y. N. SHAH; circ. 14,000.

Stree: Sandesh Bhavan, Gheekanta, POB 151, Ahmedabad 380 001; tel. (272) 24243; telex 1216532; f. 1962; weekly; Gujarati; Editor LILABEN PATEL; circ. 72,600.

Zagmag: Gujarat Samachar Bhavan, Khanpur, Ahmedabad 380 001; tel. (272) 22821; telex 1216642; f. 1952; weekly; Gujarati; for children; Editor BAHUBALI S. SHAH; circ. 38,000.

Rajkot

Amruta: Sharda Baug, Rajkot 360 001; tel. (281) 40513; f. 1967; weekly; Gujarati; films; Editor Y. N. SHAH; circ. 26,900.

Niranjan: Niranjan Publications, Jai Hind Press Bldg, Sharda Baug, Rajkot 360 001; tel. (281) 40517; f. 1971; fortnightly; Gujarati; children's; Editor N. R. SHAH; circ. 25,000.

Parmarth: Sharda Baug, Rajkot 360 001; tel. (281) 40511; monthly; Gujarati; philosophy and religion; Editor Y. N. SHAH; circ. 30,000.

Phulwadi: Sharda Baug, Rajkot 360 001; tel. (281) 40513; weekly; Gujarati; for children; Editor Y. N. SHAH; circ. 31,700.

Karnataka
Bangalore

Mayura: 66 Mahatma Gandhi Rd, Bangalore 560 001; tel. (812) 573291; telex 8452339; f. 1968; monthly; Kannada; Editor-in-Chief K. N. HARI KUMAR; circ. 76,300.

INDIA

Directory

New Leader: 93 North Rd, St Mary's Town, Bangalore 560 005; f. 1887; weekly; English; Editor Rt Rev. HERMAN D'SOUZA; circ. 10,000.

Prajamata: North Anjaneya Temple Rd, Basavangudi, Bangalore 560 004; tel. (812) 602634; f. 1931; weekly; Kannada; news and current affairs; Chief Editor G. V. ANJI; circ. 58,500.

Sudha: 66 Mahatma Gandhi Rd, Bangalore 560 001; tel. (812) 573291; telex 845339; fax (812) 571096; f. 1965; weekly; Kannada; Editor-in-Chief K. N. HARI KUMAR; circ. 163,200.

Manipal

Taranga: Udayavani Bldg, Press Corner, Manipal 576 119; tel. 20841; f. 1983; weekly; Kannada; Editor S. K. GULVADI; circ. 148,500.

Kerala
Kottayam

Balarama: MM Publications Ltd, POB 226, Erayilkadavu, Kottayam 686 001; tel. (481) 3721; telex 888201; fax (481) 2479; f. 1972; children's fortnightly; Malayalam; Chief Editor BINA PHILIP MATHEW; circ. 181,100.

Malayala Manorama: K. K. Rd, POB 26, Kottayam 686 001; tel. (481) 3615; telex 888201; fax (481) 2479; f. 1937; weekly; Malayalam; also publ. from Kozhikode; Man. Dir and Editor MAMMEN MATHEW; Chief Editor MAMMEN VARGHESE; combined circ. 1,216,626.

Vanitha: MM Publications Ltd, POB 226, Erayilkadavu, Kottayam 686 001; tel.(481) 3721; telex 888201; fax (481) 2479; f. 1975; women's fortnightly; Malayalam; Chief Editor Mrs K. M. MATHEW; circ. 218,206.

The Week: Malayala Manorama Co Ltd, K. K. Rd, POB 26, Kottayam 686 001; tel. (481) 3615; telex 888201; fax (481) 2479; f. 1982; weekly; English; current affairs; Chief Editor MAMMEN MATHEW; circ. 44,500.

Kozhikode

Grihalakshmi: The Mathrubhumi Bldg, Kozhikode 673 001; tel. 63651; f. 1979; monthly; Malayalam; Editor M. T. VASUDEVAN NAIR; circ. 90,900.

Mathrubhumi Illustrated Weekly: Mathrubhumi Bldg, K. P. Kesava Menon Rd, Kozhikode 673 001; tel. 63651; f. 1923; weekly; Malayalam; Editor N. V. KRISHNA WARRIOR; circ. 78,600.

Quilon

Karala Sabdam: Thevally, Quilon 691 009; tel. 2403; telex 886296; f. 1962; weekly; Malayalam; Man. Editor B. A. RAJAKRISHNAN; circ. 84,200.

Nana: Therally, Quilon 691 009; tel. 2403; telex 886296; weekly; Malayalam; Man. Editor B. A. RAJAKRISHNAN; circ. 63,200.

Thiruvananthapuram

Kala Kaumudi: Kaumudi Bldg, Pettah, Thiruvananthapuram 695 024; telex 435214; weekly; Malayalam; Editor S. J. NAIR; circ. 57,700.

Madhya Pradesh

Krishak Jagat: 43 Fire Brigade St, Sultaniya Rd, POB 3, Bhopal 462 001; tel. (755) 542466; f. 1946; weekly; Hindi; also Marathi edn; agriculture; Chief Editor SURESH CHANDRA GANGRADE; Editor VIJAY KUMAR BONDRIYA; circ. 14,486.

Maharashtra
Bombay

Abhiyan: Shakti Publications (Pvt) Ltd, Bombay; tel. (22) 6884435; f. 1986; weekly; Gujarati; Editor SHEELA BHATT; circ. 112,400.

Bhavan's Journal: Bharatiya Vidya Bhavan, Bombay 400 007; tel. (22) 8114462; f. 1954; fortnightly; English; literary; Man. Editor J. H. DAVE; Editor S. RAMAKRISHNAN; circ. 25,000.

Blitz News Magazine: 17/17H Cawasji Patel St, Bombay 400 001; tel. (22) 2047166; telex 1186801; f. 1941; weekly; English, Hindi, Marathi and Urdu edns; Editor-in-Chief R. K. KARANJIA; combined circ. 419,000.

Bombay: 28 A&B Jolly Maker Chambers-II, Nariman Point, Bombay 400 021; tel. (22) 2026152; telex 1185373; fax (22) 2026164; f. 1979; fortnightly; English; Editor ARUN KATIYAR; circ. 18,851.

Business India: Nirmal, 18th Floor, Nariman Point, Bombay 400 021; tel. (22) 2024422; telex 1183557; f. 1978; fortnightly; English; Publr ASHOK H. ADVANI; circ. 79,100.

Business World: 145 Atlanta, 209 Ceremonial Blvd, Nariman Point, Bombay 400 021; tel. (22) 240581; telex 112354; f. 1980; fortnightly; English; Editor R. JAGANNATHAN; circ. 35,100.

Chitralekha: 62 Vaju Kotak Marg, Fort, Bombay 400 001; tel. (22) 2611526; telex 1178298; fax (22) 2615895; f. 1950; weekly; Gujarati; Editors Mrs M. V. KOTAK, H. MEHTA; circ. 325,000.

Cine Blitz: 17/17H Cowasji Patel St, Bombay 400 001; tel. (22) 2043546; telex 116801; f. 1974; monthly; English; films; Editor RITA K. MEHTA; circ. 81,000.

Current Weekly: Nariman Bhavan, 15th Floor, Nariman Point, Bombay 400 021; tel. (22) 2024067; f. 1949; English; Editor AYUB SYED; circ. 80,000.

Debonair: 41A Dr E. Moses Rd, Bombay 400 018; tel. (22) 4941601; f. 1972; English; monthly; Exec. Editor AMRITA SHAH; circ. 87,500.

Dharmayug: Dr Dadabhai Naoroji Rd, Bombay 400 001; tel. (22) 2620271; telex 1173504; fax (22) 2620401; f. 1950; weekly; Hindi; Editor GANESH MANTRI; circ. 70,700.

Economic and Political Weekly: Hitkari House, 284 Shahid Bhagatsingh Rd, Bombay 400 038; tel. (22) 2616072; f. 1966; English; Editor KRISHNA RAJ; circ. 12,000.

The Economic Scene: Orient House, Mangalore St, Ballard Estate, Bombay 400 038; tel. (22) 267621; telex 112618; f. 1976; monthly; English; Editor ACHYUT VAZE.

Eve's Weekly: J. K. Somani Bldg, Bombay Samachar Marg, Bombay 400 023; tel. (22) 271444; f. 1947; English; Editor SHOLA RAMACHANDRAN; circ. 40,000.

Femina: Times of India Bldg, Dr Dadabhai Naoroji Rd, Bombay 400 001; tel. (22) 2620271; telex 1182699; f. 1959; fortnightly; English and Gujarati; Editor VIMLA PATIL; circ. 64,000.

Filmfare: Times of India Bldg, Dr Dadabhai Naoroji Rd, Bombay 400 001; tel. (22) 4150271; telex 1173504; f. 1952; fortnightly; English and Hindi; Editor RAUF AHMED; circ. 62,800 (English), 43,700 (Hindi).

Gentleman: 920 Tulsiani Chambers, Nariman Point, Bombay 400 021; tel. (22) 2872142; f. 1980; monthly; English; Editor MANECK DANAR; circ. 82,000.

Illustrated Weekly of India: Dr Dadabhai Naoroji Rd, Bombay 400 001; tel. (22) 4150271; telex 1173504; f. 1929; weekly; English; Editor PRITISH NANDY; circ. 81,900.

Indian and Eastern Engineer: Piramal Mansion, 235 Dr Dadabhai Naoroji Rd, Bombay 400 001; tel. (22) 2613223; telex 113599; fax (22) 2024548; f. 1858; monthly; English; Editor S. K. GHASWALA; circ. 7,000.

Indian PEN: Theosophy Hall, 40 New Marine Lines, Bombay 400 020; tel. (22) 292175; f. 1934; quarterly; organ of Indian Centre of the International PEN; Editor NISSIM EZEKIEL.

Janmabhoomi Pravasi: Janmabhoomi Bhavan, Ghoga St, Fort, Bombay 400 001; tel. (22) 2870831; telex 116859; f. 1939; weekly; Gujarati; Editor HARINDRA J. DAVE; circ. 100,600.

JEE: 62 Vaju Kotak Marg, Fort, Bombay 400 001; tel. (22) 2611526; fortnightly; Gujarati and Marathi; Editor MADHURI KOTAK; circ. 106,400.

Meri Saheli: 160 D.N. Rd, Bombay 400 001; f. 1987; monthly; Hindi; Editor HEMA MALINI; circ. 89,600.

Mirror: J. K. Somani Bldg, Samachar Marg, Bombay 400 023; tel. (22) 271444; f. 1961; monthly; English; Editor PRABHA GOVIND; circ. 54,000.

Movie: 412 Tulsiani Chambers, 212 Nariman Point, Bombay 400 021; tel. (22) 233124; f. 1981; monthly; English; Editor DINESH RAHEJA; circ. 71,100.

Onlooker: Free Press House, 215 Free Press Journal Marg, Nariman Point, Bombay 400 021; tel. (22) 2874566; telex 112570; f. 1939; fortnightly; English; news magazine; Editor K. GOPALAKRISHNAN; circ. 61,000.

Parade: Esperanca, Shahid Bhagat Singh Rd, Bombay 400 039; tel. (22) 2024181; telex 112029; f. 1988; monthly; English; Editor RAJENDRA MENON; circ. 77,400.

Pravasi: Janmabhoomi Bhavan, Ghoga St, Fort, Bombay 400 001; tel. (22) 2870831; telex 116859; f. 1939; weekly; Gujarati; Propr Saurashtra Trust; Editor HARINDRA DAVE; circ. 100,600.

Reader's Digest: Orient House, Mangalore St, Ballard Estate, Bombay 400 038; tel. (22) 2617291; telex 1183406; f. 1954; monthly; English; Man. Dir and Publr ANIL GORE; Editor ASHOK MAHADEVAN; circ. 362,713.

Savvy: Esperanca, 7th Floor, Shahid Bhagat Singh Rd, Bombay 400 039; tel. (22) 2024135; telex 112029; f. 1984; monthly; English; Editor INGRID ALBOURQUE; circ. 57,100.

Screen: Express Towers, Nariman Point, Bombay 400 021; tel. (22) 2022627; f. 1951; film weekly; English; Editor UDAYA TARA NAYAR; circ. 84,000.

Shree: 40 Cawasji Patel St, Bombay 400 023; tel. (22) 2044171; telex 1170044; f. 1967; weekly; Marathi; Editor KAMLESH D. MEHTA; circ. 61,700.

Shreewarsha: 40 Cawasji Patel St, Bombay 400 023; f. 1980; weekly; Hindi; Editor and Man. Dir R. M. BHUTTA; circ. 50,000.

INDIA *Directory*

Society: Esperanca, 7th Floor, Shahid Bhagat Singh Rd, Bombay 400 039; tel. (22) 2024181; telex 1182029; f. 1979; monthly; English; Editor SUMA VARUGHESE; circ. 56,800.

Star and Style: J. K. Somani Bldg, Bombay Samachar Marg, Bombay 400 023; tel. (22) 271444; f. 1965; fortnightly; English; film and fashion; Editor BHARATHI S. PRADHAN; circ. 87,000.

Stardust: Esparanca, 7th Floor, Shahid Bhagat Singh Rd, Bombay 400 039; tel. (22) 2024181; telex 112029; f. 1971; monthly; English; Editor NISHI PREM; circ. 160,900.

2001: Times of India Bldg, Dr Dadabhai Naoroji Rd, Bombay 400 001; tel. (22) 2621692; telex 1182699; fax (22) 2620144; f. 1966; monthly; English; Editor MUKUL SHARMA; circ. 20,600.

Vyapar: Janmabhoomi Bhavan, Janmabhoomi Marg, Fort, Bombay 400 001; tel. (22) 2870831; telex 116859; f. 1949; Gujarati (2 a week) and Hindi (weekly); commerce; Propr Saurashtra Trust; Editor S. J. VASANI; circ. 34,300 (Gujarati), 20,400 (Hindi).

Yuvdarhsan: c/o Warsha Publications Pvt Ltd, Warsha House, 6 Zakaria Bunder Rd, Sewri, Bombay 400 015; tel. (22) 441843; f. 1975; weekly; Gujarati; Editor and Man. Dir R. M. BHUTTA; circ. 23,800.

Nagpur

All India Reporter: AIR Ltd, Congress Nagar, POB 209, Nagpur 440 012; tel. (712) 34321; f. 1914; monthly; English; law journal; Chief Editor V. R. MANOHAR; circ. 36,000.

Pune (Poona)

Swaraj: 467A Shaniwar peth, Pune 411 030; tel. (212) 435555; f. 1936; weekly; Marathi; Man. M. D. GOKHALE; circ. 28,800.

Rajasthan
Jaipur

Rashtradoot Saptahik: HO, M.I. Rd, POB 30, Jaipur 302 001; tel. (141) 72634; f. 1983; Hindi; also publ. from Kota and Bikaner; Chief Editor and Man. Editor RAJESH SHARMA; CEO SOMESH SHARMA; combined circ. 167,500.

Tamil Nadu
Madras

Ambulimama: 188 N. S. K. Salai, Vadapalani, Madras 600 026; f. 1947; monthly; Tamil; Editor NAGI REDDI; circ. 68,000.

Ambuli Ammavan: 188 N. S. K. Salai, Vadapalani, Madras 600 026; f. 1970; children's monthly; Malayalam; Editor NAGI REDDI; circ. 15,000.

Ananda Vikatan: 757 Mount Rd, Madras 600 002; tel. (44) 82074; f. 1924; weekly; Tamil; Editor S. BALASUBRAMANIAN; circ. 200,700.

Andhra Prabha Illustrated Weekly: Express Estates, Mount Rd, Madras 600 002; f. 1952; weekly; Telugu; Editor POTTURI VENKATESWARA RAO; circ. 57,500.

Chandamama: 188 N. S. K. Salai, Vadapalani, Madras 600 026; f. 1947; children's monthly; Hindi, Gujarati, Telugu, Kannada, English, Bengali, Assamese; Editor NAGI REDDI; combined circ. 420,000.

Chandoba: 188 N. S. K. Salai, Vadapalani, Madras 600 026; f. 1952; monthly; Marathi; Editor NAGI REDDI; circ. 110,000.

Devi: 727 Anna Salai, Madras 600 006; tel. (44) 861428; f. 1983; weekly; Tamil; Editor B. RAMACHANDRA ADITYAN; circ. 117,800.

Dinamani Kadir: Express Estate, Mount Rd, Madras 600 002; weekly; Editor G. KASTURI RANGAN (acting); circ. 55,000.

Frontline: 859/860 Anna Salai, Madras 600 002; tel. (44) 835067; telex 416655; fax (44) 835325; f. 1984; English; fortnightly; Editor N. RAM; circ. 68,500.

Hindu International Edition: 859/860 Anna Salai, Madras 600 002; tel. (44) 835067; telex 416655; fax (44) 835325; f. 1975; weekly; Editor GOPALAN KASTURI; circ. 5,950.

Jahnamamu (Oriya): 188 N. S. K. Salai, Vadapalani, Madras 600 026; f. 1972; children's monthly; Editor NAGI REDDI; circ. 110,000.

Junior Vikatan: 757 Anna Salai, Madras 600 002; tel. (44) 864054; f. 1983; weekly; Tamil; Editor S. BALASUBRAMANIAN; circ. 191,200.

Kalai Magal: POB 604, Madras 600 004; tel. (44) 76011; f. 1932; monthly; Tamil; literary and cultural; Editor R. NARAYANASWAMY; circ. 22,700.

Kalkandu: 151 Purasawalkam High Rd, Madras; f. 1948; weekly; Tamil; Editor TAMIL VANAN; circ. 170,500.

Kalki: 84/1C Race Course Rd, Guindy, Madras 600 032; tel. (48) 431543; f. 1941; weekly; Tamil; literary and cultural; Editor K. RAJENDRAN; circ. 88,200.

Kumudam: 151 Purasawalkam High Rd, Madras 600 010; tel. (44) 662146; telex 41462; f. 1947; weekly; Tamil; Editor S. A. P. ANNAMALAI; circ 485,200.

Malaimathi: Madras; f. 1958; weekly; Tamil; Editor P. S. ELANGO; circ. 84,000.

Muththaram: 93A Kogambakkam High Rd, Madras 600 034; tel. (44) 476306; f. 1980; weekly; Tamil; Editor Sri PARASAKTHI; circ. 60,300.

Pesum Padam: 325 Arcot Rd, Madras 600 024; tel. (44) 422064; f. 1942; monthly; Tamil; films; Man. Editor K. NATARAJAN; circ. 36,100.

Picturpost: 325 Arcot Rd, Madras 600 024; tel. (44) 422064; f. 1943; monthly; English; films; Man. Editor K. NATARAJAN; circ. 11,000.

Rani Muthu: 46C E. V. K. Sampath Rd, Madras 600 007; tel. (44) 580495; f. 1969; monthly; Tamil; Editor A. MA. SAMY; circ. 124,400.

Rani Weekly: 1091 Periyar E.V.R. High Rd, Madras 600 007; tel. (44) 38471; f. 1962; Tamil; Editor A. MA. SAMY; circ. 257,400.

Sportstar: 859/860 Anna Salai, Madras 600 002; tel. (44) 835067; telex 416655; fax (44) 835325; f. 1978; English; weekly; Editor N. RAM; circ. 86,600.

Thuglak: 5 Bishops Wallers Ave, C.I.T. Colony, Madras 600 004; tel. (44) 74222; f. 1970; fortnightly; Tamil; Editor CHO S. RAMASWAMY; circ. 197,300.

Vellore

Mathajothidam: 3 Arasamaram, Vellore; f. 1949; monthly; Tamil; astrology; Editor V. K. V. SUBRAMANYAM; circ. 28,000.

Uttar Pradesh
Allahabad

Alokpaat: Mitra Prakashan (Pvt) Ltd, 281 Muthiganj, Allahabad 211 003; tel. (532) 51042; telex 540280; f. 1986; monthly; Bengali; Editor ALOKE MITRA; circ. 62,500.

Jasoosi Duniya: 5 Kolhan Tola St, Allahabad; f. 1953; monthly; Urdu and Hindi edns; Editor S. ABBAS HUSAINY; combined circ. 70,000.

Manohar Kahaniyan: Mitra Prakashan (Pvt) Ltd, 281 Muthiganj, Allahabad 211 003; tel. (532) 51042; telex 540280; f. 1940; monthly; Hindi; Editor ALOKE MITRA; circ. 368,600.

Manorama: Mitra Parkashan (Pvt) Ltd, 281 Muthiganj, Allahabad 211 003; tel. (532) 51042; telex 540280; f. 1924 (Hindi), 1986 (Bengali); fortnightly (Hindi), monthly (Bengali); Editor ALOKE MITRA; circ. 215,200 (Hindi), 61,000 (Bengali).

Maya: Mitra Prakashan (Pvt) Ltd, 281 Muthiganj, Allahabad 211 003; tel. (532) 51042; telex 540280; f. 1929; fortnightly; Hindi; Editor ALOKE MITRA; circ. 224,000.

Nutan Kahaniyan: 15 Sheocharan Lal Rd, Allahabad 211 003; tel. (532) 56612; f. 1975; Hindi; monthly; Editor N. P. SINGH; circ. 167,500.

Probe India: Mitra Prakashan (Pvt) Ltd, 281 Muthiganj, Allahabad 211 003; tel. (532) 53681; telex 540280; f. 1979; monthly; English; Editor ALOKE MITRA; circ. 35,600.

Satyakatha: Mitra Prakashan (Pvt) Ltd, 281 Muthiganj, Allahabad 211 003; tel. (532) 51042; telex 540280; f. 1974; monthly; Hindi; Editor ALOKE MITRA; circ. 150,500.

Dehra Dun

Current Events: 15 Rajpur Rd, Dehra Dun; f. 1955; quarterly review of national and international affairs; English; Editor DEV DUTT; circ. 5,000.

Kanpur

Kanchan Prabha: Rajendra Nagar (East), Kanpur 226 004; f. 1974; Hindi; monthly; Man. Editor P. C. GUPTA; Editor Y. M. GUPTA; circ. 26,000.

West Bengal
Calcutta

All India Appointment Gazette: 7 Old Court House St, Calcutta 700 001; tel. (33) 206663; f. 1973; every two weeks; English; Editor S. C. TALUKDAR; circ. 170,000.

Anandalok: 6 Prafulla Sarkar St, Calcutta 700 001; tel. (33) 278000; telex 215468; f. 1975; fortnightly; Bengali; film; Editor SEVABRATA GUPTA; circ. 64,100.

Anandamela: 6 Prafulla Sarkar St, Calcutta 700 001; tel. (33) 278000; telex 215468; f. 1975; monthly; Bengali; juvenile; Editor AVEEK SARKAR, (acting); circ. 54,000.

Capital: 1/2 Old Court House Corner, POB 14, Calcutta 700 001; tel. (33) 200099; telex 217172; f. 1888; fortnightly; English; financial; Editor S. BANERJEE, (acting); circ. 8,000.

Competition Leader: 7 Old Court House St, Calcutta 700 001; f. 1977; monthly; English; Editor S. C. TALUKDAR; circ. 97,000.

Desh: 6 Prafulla Sarkar St, Calcutta 700 001; tel. (33) 274880; telex 215468; f. 1933; weekly; Bengali; literary; Editor S. GHOSH; circ. 81,200.

INDIA

Engineering Times: Wachel Molla Mansion, 8 Lenin Sarani, Calcutta 700 072; f. 1955; weekly; English; Editor E. H. TIPPOO; circ. 19,000.

Karmasangsthaan: 7 Old Court House St, Calcutta 700 001; tel. (33) 207618; f. 1988; weekly; Bengali; Editor S. C. TALUKDAR; circ. 40,000.

Khela: 96 Raja Rammohan Sarani, Calcutta 700 009; tel. (33) 355302; telex 212216; f. 1981; weekly; Bengali; sports; Editor ASOKE DASGUPTA; circ. 18,900.

Naba Kallol: 11 Jhamapookur Lane, Calcutta 700 009; tel. (33) 354294; f. 1960; monthly; Bengali; Editor P. K. MAZUMDAR; circ. 43,000.

Neetee: 4 Sukhlal Johari Lane, Calcutta; f. 1955; weekly; English; Editor M. P. PODDAR.

Prabuddha Bharata (Awakened India): 5 Dehi Entally Rd, Calcutta 700 014; tel. (33) 290898; monthly; circ. 8,000.

Sananda: 6 Prafulla Sarkar St, Calcutta 700 001; tel. (33) 278000; telex 215468; f. 1986; fortnightly; Bengali; Editor APARNA SEN; circ. 74,400.

Screen: P-5, Kalakar St, Calcutta 700 070; f. 1960; weekly; Hindi; Editor M. P. PODDAR; circ. 58,000.

Sportsworld: 6 Prafulla Sarkar St, Calcutta 700 001; tel. (33) 278000; telex 215468; weekly; English; Editor MANSUR ALI KHAN PATAUDI; circ. 50,000.

Statesman: Statesman House, 4 Chowringhee Sq., Calcutta 700 001; tel. (33) 271000; telex 215303; f. 1875; overseas weekly; English; Editor SUNANDA KUMAR DATTA-RAY.

Suktara: 11 Jhamapooker Lane, Calcutta 700 009; tel. (33) 355294; f. 1948; monthly; Bengali; juvenile; Editor M. MAJUMDAR; circ. 61,300.

Sunday: 6 Prafulla Sarkar St, Calcutta 700 001; tel. (33) 274880; telex 215468; f. 1973; weekly; English; Editor VIR SINGHVI; circ. 126,500.

Tea Journal: 164 Lenin Sarani, Calcutta 700 013; tel. (33) 276231; f. 1988; monthly; English; Editor S. C. TALUKDAR; circ. 23,000.

NEWS AGENCIES

Press Trust of India Ltd: 357 Dr Dadabhai Naoroji Rd, Bombay 400 001; tel. (22) 2872371; telex 112343; fax (22) 2024815; f. 1947, re-established 1978; Chair. AVEEK SARKAR; Exec. Dir P. UNNIKRISHNAN.

United News of India (UNI): 9 Rafi Marg, New Delhi 110 001; tel. (11) 3710313; telex 3166305; f. 1961; Indian language news; World TV News Service (UNISCAN); special services covering banking, business, economic affairs, agriculture, overseas news and features; brs in 90 centres in India; Chair. ADHIP KUMAR SARKAR; Gen. Man. and Chief Editor K. P. K. KUTTY.

Foreign Bureaux

Agence France-Presse (AFP): 204 Surya Kiran Bldg, 19 Kasturba Gandhi Marg, New Delhi 110 001; tel. (11) 3322881; telex 3165075; Bureau Chief MARIE-FRANCE ROUZE.

Agentstvo Pechati Novosti (USSR): 2/8 Shantiniketan, New Delhi 110 021; tel. (11) 674347; Correspondent ALEKSANDR V. YELEZNOV.

Agenzia Nazionale Stampa Associata (ANSA) (Italy): A-293 New Friends Colony, New Delhi 110 065; tel. (11) 634402; telex 3165381; Chief Rep. Dr ELIO CRISCUOLI.

Allgemeiner Deutscher Nachrichtendienst (ADN) (Germany): C-64 Anand Niketan, New Delhi 110 021; tel. (11) 671864; telex 3166860; Correspondent GÜNTER CASCHUBE.

Associated Press (AP) (USA): 6B Jor Bagh Lane, New Delhi 110 003; tel. (11) 698775; telex 3174132; Bureau Chief EARLEEN FISHER.

Československá tisková káncelář (ČTK) (Czechoslovakia): C-59 Anand Niketan, New Delhi 110 021; tel. (11) 672276; telex 3162462; Correspondent JIŘÍ CHRÁST.

Deutsche Presse-Agentur (dpa) (Germany): B-1/44 Amrita Shergil Marg, New Delhi 110 003; tel. (11) 617792; telex 3162331; Chief Rep. Dr HEINZ-RUDOLF OTHMERDING.

Inter Press Service (IPS) (Italy): 49, 1st Floor, Defence Colony Market, New Delhi 110 024; tel. (11) 624725; telex 310555; fax (11) 941111; Correspondent RAJIV TIWARI.

Islamic Republic News Agency (IRNA) (Iran): B-159 Greater Kailash-I, New Delhi 110 048; tel. (11) 6446866; telex 3166041; Bureau Chief MOHAMMAD KHODDADI.

Jiji Tsushin-sha (Japan): B-87 Greater Kailash I, New Delhi 110 048; tel. (11) 6445296; telex 3165590; fax (11) 6463873; Correspondent FUMIHIKO SUGIYAMA.

Kyodo News Service (Japan): PTI Bldg, 1st Floor, 4 Parliament St, New Delhi 110 001; tel. (11) 381954; telex 3165016; Bureau Chief KAZUHISA INOUYE.

Magyar Távirati Iroda (MTI) (Hungary): F-3/17 Vasant Vihar, New Delhi 110 057; tel. (11) 677397; telex 3172373; Correspondent JENŐ ERDÉSZ.

Novinska Agencija Tanjug (Yugoslavia): 14 Palam Marg, Vasant Vihar, New Delhi 110 057; tel. (11) 672649; Correspondent BOZIDAR FRANCUSKI.

Reuters (UK): 1 Kautilya Marg, Chanakyapuri, New Delhi 110 021; tel. (11) 3014654; telex 3166423; fax (11) 3014043; Chief Correspondent (India) MICHAEL BATTYE.

Telegrafnoye Agentstvo Sovetskovo Soyuza (TASS) (USSR): A-10/6 Vasant Vihar, New Delhi 110 057; tel. (11) 672351; telex 3166092; Bureau Chief SERGEI V. KARMALITO.

United Press International (UPI) (USA): Ambassador Hotel, Suite 202–204, Sujan Singh Park, New Delhi 110 003; tel. (11) 698991; telex 3162846; Bureau Chief DAVID ALEXANDER.

Xinhua (New China) News Agency (People's Republic of China): 50D, Shanti Path, Chanakyapuri, New Delhi 110 021; tel. (11) 601394; telex 3162250; Chief TAN RENXIA.

The following agencies are also represented: Associated Press of Pakistan, Bangladesh Sangbad Sangstha, BTA (Bulgaria), PAP (Poland) and Viet-Nam News Agency.

CO-ORDINATING BODIES

Press Information Bureau: Shastri Bhavan, Dr Rajendra Prasad Rd, New Delhi 110 001; tel. (11) 383643; f. 1946 to co-ordinate press affairs for the govt; represents newspaper managements, journalists, news agencies, parliament; has power to examine journalists under oath and may censor objectionable material; Prin. Information Officer I. RAMAMOHAN RAO.

Registrar of Newspapers for India: Ministry of Information and Broadcasting, West Block 8, Wing 2, Ramakrishna Puram, New Delhi 110 066; tel. (11) 698758; f. 1956 as a statutory body to collect press statistics; maintains a register of all Indian newspapers; Registrar P. B. RAY.

PRESS ASSOCIATIONS

All-India Newspaper Editors' Conference: 36–37 Northend Complex, Rama Krishna Ashram Marg, New Delhi 110 001; tel. (11) 344519; f. 1940; 450 mems; Pres. VISHWA BANDHU GUPTA; Sec.-Gen. R. KRISHNAMURTHY.

Editors' Guild of India: A2 First Floor, 28 Feroz Shah Rd, New Delhi 110 001; f. 1977; Pres. NIKHIL CHAKRAVARTY; Sec.-Gen. RAJENDRA MATHUR.

The Foreign Correspondents' Association of South Asia: c/o Los Angeles Times, F-160 Malcha Marg, New Delhi 110 021; tel. (11) 3011374; 142 mems; Pres. DAVID HOUSEGO; Sec. S. GOPAL.

Indian Federation of Working Journalists: F-101, Curzon Rd M.S. Apts, Kasturba Gandhi Marg, POB 571, New Delhi 110 001; tel. (11) 384650; f. 1950; 22,000 mems; Pres. K. VIKRAM RAO; Sec.-Gen. MANOHAR P. ANDHARE.

Indian Languages Newspapers' Asscn: Janmabhoomi Bhavan, Janmabhoomi Marg, POB 10029, Fort, Bombay 400 001; tel. (22) 2870537; f. 1941; 340 mems; Pres. KIRAN SHETH; Gen. Secs G. W. DESHPANDE, V. K. BONDRIYA, CHANDRAKANT BHAVE.

Indian Newspaper Society: INS Bldgs, Rafi Marg, New Delhi 110 001; tel. (11) 3715401; telex 3166312; f. 1939; 630 mems; Pres. NARESH MOHAN; Sec. S. BHUSHAN JAIN.

National Union of Journalists (India): 7 Jantar Mantar Rd, 2nd Floor, New Delhi 110 001; tel. (11) 3321610; f. 1972; 10,000 mems; Pres. B. K. DHAL; Sec.-Gen. A. N. MISHRA.

Press Institute of India/Research Institute for Newspaper Development: Sapru House Annexe, Barakhamba Rd, New Delhi 110 001; tel. (11) 3318066; f. 1963; 31 mem. newspapers and other orgs; Chair. AVEEK KUMAR SARKAR; Dir K. S. RAMAKRISHNAN.

Publishers

Delhi and New Delhi

Affiliated East West Press (Pvt) Ltd: 104 Nirmal Tower, Barakhamba Rd, New Delhi 110 001; tel. (11) 3315398; telex 3163421; fax (11) 3312830; textbooks; Man. Dir K. S. PADMANABHAN.

Allied Publishers (Pvt) Ltd: 13/14 Asaf Ali Rd, New Delhi 110 002; tel. (11) 732001; telex 3162953; academic and general; Man. Dir S. M. SACHDEV.

Amerind Publishing Co (Pvt) Ltd: 66 Janpath, New Delhi 110 001; tel. (11) 3324578; telex 3161990; fax (11) 3322639; f. 1970; offices at Calcutta, Bombay and New York; scientific and technical; Dirs G. PRIMLANI, M. PRIMLANI.

Arnold Publishers India (Pvt) Ltd: AB/9 Safdarjung Enclave, New Delhi 110 029; tel. (11) 607806; telex 3166417; literature and general; Man. Dir G. A. VAZIRANI.

INDIA

Atma Ram and Sons: Kashmere Gate, POB 1429, Delhi 110 006; tel. (11) 2523082; f. 1909; scientific, technical, humanities, medical; Dir S. PURI; Man. Dir ISH K. PURI.

B.R. Publishing Corpn: 29/9, Nangia Park, Shakti Nagar, Delhi 110 007; tel. (11) 7120113; telex 3166778; a division of D. K. Publishers Distributors (Pvt) Ltd; Dir PRAVEEN MITTAL.

Cambridge Publishing House: D-36 South Extension, Part 1, New Delhi 110 049; tel. (11) 619125; juvenile; Propr ARUN KUMAR GUPTA.

S. Chand and Co (Pvt) Ltd: Ram Nagar, POB 5733, New Delhi 110 055; tel. (11) 772081; telex 3161310; f. 1917; educational and general in English and Hindi; also book exports and imports; Dir RAVINDRA KUMAR GUPTA; Man. Dir RAJENDRA KUMAR GUPTA.

Children's Book Trust: Nehru House, 4 Bahadur Shah Zafar Marg, New Delhi 110 002; tel. (11) 3316970; f. 1957; children's books in several languages; Exec. Editor K. RAMAKRISHNAN.

Concept Publishing Co: A/15-16, Commercial Block, Mohan Garden, New Delhi 110 059; tel. (11) 5554042; f. 1975; geography, rural and urban development, education, sociology, economics, anthropology, agriculture, religion, history, law, philosophy, information sciences, ecology; Man. Dir ASHOK KUMAR MITTAL; Man. Editor ARVIND KUMAR MITTAL.

Eurasia Publishing House (Pvt) Ltd: Ram Nagar, New Delhi 110 055; tel (11) 772080; f. 1964; educational in English and Hindi; Man. Dir S. L. GUPTA.

Heritage Publishers: 4C Ansari Rd, Darya Ganj, New Delhi 110 002; tel. (11) 3266258; f. 1973; social sciences, art and architecture, economics, commerce, literature; Dir B. R. CHAWLA.

Hind Pocket Books (Pvt) Ltd: G. T. Rd, Shahadara, Delhi 110 032; tel. (11) 2282046; f. 1958; fiction and non-fiction paperbacks in English, Hindi, Punjabi and Urdu; Man. Dir DINANATH MALHOTRA; Editorial Dir MADHVI MALHOTRA.

Hindustan Publishing Corpn: 6 U.B. Jawahar Nagar, Delhi 110 007; tel. (11) 2915059; archaeology, pure and applied sciences, sociology, anthropology, economics; Dir S. K. JAIN.

Inter-India Publications: D-17, Raja Garden, New Delhi 110 015; tel. (11) 5413145; f. 1977; academic and research works; Dir MOOL CHAND MITTAL.

Lancers Books: POB 4236, New Delhi 110 048; tel. (11) 6414617; f. 1977; politics (with special emphasis on north-east India), defence; Propr S. KUMAR.

Motilal Banarsidass: 41 UA Bungalow Rd, Jawahar Nagar, Delhi 110 007; tel. (11) 2911985; telex 3166053; f. 1903; Indology, in English and Sanskrit; Dirs N. P. JAIN, J. P. JAIN, R. P. JAIN, S. L. JAIN.

Munshiram Manoharlal Publishers (Pvt) Ltd: 54 Rani Jhansi Rd, POB 5715, New Delhi 110 055; tel. (11) 771668; telex 3165233; fax (11) 512745; f. 1952; Indian art, architecture, archaeology, religion, music, dance, dictionaries, history, politics; Man. Dir DEVENDRA JAIN.

National Book Trust: A-5 Green Park, New Delhi 110 016; tel. (11) 664667; telex 3173034; f. 1967; autonomous organization established by the Ministry of Human Resources Development to produce and encourage the production of good literary works; Chair. ANAND SWARUP.

Oxford and IBH Publishing Co (Pvt) Ltd: 66 Janpath, New Delhi 110 001; tel. (11) 3324578; telex 3161990; fax (11) 3322639; f. 1964; science, technology and reference in English; Dirs GULAB PRIMLANI, MOHAN PRIMLANI.

Oxford University Press: YMCA Library Bldg, 1st Floor, Jai Singh Rd, POB 43, New Delhi 110 001; tel. (11) 350490; telex 3161108; educational, scientific, medical, general and reference; Gen. Man. S. K. MOOKERJEE; 4 brs.

Penguin Books India (Pvt) Ltd: B4/246 Safdarjung Enclave, New Delhi 110 029; tel. (11) 673538; telex 3162062; fax (11) 6875611; f. 1985; Indian literature in English; Chair. PATRICK WRIGHT; Man. Dir AVEEK SARKAR.

People's Publishing House (Pvt) Ltd: 5E Rani Jhansi Rd, New Delhi 110 055; tel. (11) 523349; f. 1947; Marxism, Leninism, peasant movt; Gen. Man. P. P. C. JOSHI.

Prentice-Hall of India (Pvt) Ltd: M-97 Connaught Circus, New Delhi 110 001; tel. (11) 3321779; telex 3161808; f. 1963; university-level text and reference books; Man. Dir A. K. GHOSH.

Rajkamal Prakashan (Pvt) Ltd: 1B Netaji Subhas Marg, New Delhi 110 002; tel. (11) 274463; f. 1946; Hindi; literary; also literary journal and monthly trade journal; Man. Dir SHEILA SANDHU.

Rajpal and Sons: 1590 Madarsa Rd, Kashmere Gate, Delhi 110 006; tel. (11) 2519104; f. 1891; humanities, social sciences, art, juvenile; Hindi; Man. Partner VISHWANATH MALHOTRA.

RIS (Research and Information System) Publications: 40B Lodhi Estate, New Delhi 110 003; tel. (11) 617403; fax (11) 3313411; f. 1984; current and economic affairs involving non-aligned and developing countries; Dir Dr V. R. PANCHAMUKHI.

Rupa & Co: 3831 Pataudi House Rd, Daryaganj, New Delhi 110 002; tel. (11) 272161; f. 1936.

Sage Publications India (Pvt) Ltd: M-32 Market, Greater Kailash-1, POB 4215, New Delhi 110 048; tel. (11) 6419884; social science; Man. Dir TEJESHWAR SINGH.

Sahgal, N. D., and Sons: Dariba Kalan, Delhi; f. 1917; politics, history, general knowledge, sport, fiction and juvenile in Hindi; Man. G. SAHGAL.

Shiksha Bharati: Madrasa Rd, Kashmere Gate, Delhi 110 006; tel. (11) 2523904; f. 1955; textbooks, popular science and juvenile in Hindi and English; Man. Partner VEENA MALHOTRA.

Sterling Publishers (Pvt) Ltd: L-10 Green Park Extension, New Delhi 110 016; tel. (11) 660904; telex 3165625; fax (11) 6444169; f. 1965; academic books on the humanities and social sciences, paperbacks; Chair. O. P. GHAI; Man. Dir S. K. GHAI.

Tata McGraw-Hill Publishing Co Ltd: 4/12 Asaf Ali Rd, 3rd Floor, New Delhi 110 002; tel. (11) 3278251; telex 3161979; fax (11) 3278253; f. 1970; engineering, sciences, management, humanities, social sciences; Dir R. RADHAKRISHNAN.

Technical and Commercial Book Co: 75 Gokhale Market, Tis Hazari, Delhi 110 054; tel. (11) 228315; telex 112651; f. 1913; technical; Propr D. N. MEHRA; Man. RAMAN MEHRA.

Vikas Publishing House (Pvt) Ltd: 576 Masjid Rd, Jangpura, New Delhi 110 014; tel. (11) 624605; telex 31592252; medicine, sciences, engineering, textbooks, academic, fiction, women's studies; Man. Dir NARENDRA KUMAR.

Wiley Eastern Ltd: 4835/24 Ansari Rd, New Delhi 110 002; tel. (11) 3276802; telex 3166507; fax (11) 3312601; f. 1966; Man. Dir A. MACHWE.

Bombay

Allied Publishers (Pvt) Ltd: 15 J. N. Heredia Marg, Ballard Estate, Bombay 400 038; tel. (22) 2617926; telex 1186506; f. 1934; economics, medicine, politics, history, philosophy, science, mathematics and fiction; Man. Dir S. M. SACHDEV.

Asia Publishing House (Pvt) Ltd: 18/20 K. Dubash Marg, Bombay 400 023; tel. (22) 225353; telex 1171665; f. 1981; humanities, social sciences, science, inflight magazines and general; English; Man. Dir ANANDA JAISINGH.

Bharatiya Vidya Bhavan: Munshi Sadan, Kulapati K. M. Munshi Marg, Bombay 400 007; tel. (22) 8114463; f. 1938; art, literature, culture, philosophy, religion, history of India in English, Hindi, Sanskrit and Gujarati; various periodicals; Pres. C. SUBRAMANIAM; Sec.-Gen. S. RAMAKRISHNAN.

Blackie and Son (Pvt) Ltd: Blackie House, 103–105 Walchand Hirachand Marg, POB 381, Bombay 400 001; tel. (22) 261410; f. 1901; educational, scientific and technical, general and juvenile; Man. Dir D. R. BHAGI.

Himalaya Publishing House: 'Ramdoot', Dr Bhalerao Marg (Kelewadi), Girgaon, Bombay 400 004; tel. (22) 360170; f. 1976; textbooks; Dir D. P. PANDEY.

India Book House (Pvt) Ltd: 412 Tulsiani Chambers, Nariman Point, Bombay 400 021; tel. (22) 240626; telex 116297; Chair. G. L. MIRCHANDANI.

International Book House (Pvt) Ltd: Indian Mercantile Mansions Extension, Madame Cama Rd, Bombay 400 039; tel. (22) 2021634; f. 1941; general, educational, scientific and law; Man. Dir S. K. GUPTA; Gen. Man. C. V. THAMBI.

Jaico Publishing House: 121-125 Mahatma Gandhi Rd, Bombay 400 023; tel. (22) 276702; telex 113369; fax (22) 2041673; f. 1947; general paperbacks; imports scientific, medical, technical and educational books; Chair. JAMAN H. SHAH; Man. Dir ASHWIN J. SHAH.

Popular Prakashan (Pvt) Ltd: 35C Pandit Madan Mohan Malaviya Marg, Tardeo, Popular Press Bldg, opp. Roche, Bombay 400 034; tel. (22) 4941656; f. 1968; sociology, biographies, current affairs, medicine, history, politics and administration in English and Marathi; Man. Dir R. G. BHATKAL.

Somaiya Publications (Pvt) Ltd: 172 Mumbai Marathi Grantha Sangrahalaya Marg, Dadar, Bombay 400 014; tel. (22) 4130230; telex 112723; f. 1967; economics, sociology, history, politics, mathematics, sciences, language, literature, education, psychology, religion, philosophy, logic; Chair. Dr S. K. SOMAIYA.

Taraporevala, Sons and Co (Pvt) Ltd D.B.: 210 Dr Dadabhai Naoroji Rd, Fort, Bombay 400 001; tel. (22) 2041433; f. 1864; Indian art, culture, history, sociology, scientific, technical and general in English; Pres. R. J. TARAPOREVALA.

N. M. Tripathi (Pvt) Ltd: 164 Samaldas Gandhi Marg, Bombay 400 002; tel. (22) 313651; f. 1888; law and general in English and Gujarati; Chair. D. M. TRIVEDI.

INDIA — Directory

Calcutta

Academic Publishers: 12/1A Bankim Chatterjee St, POB 12341, Calcutta 700 073; tel. (33) 324697; fax (33) 326059; f. 1958; textbooks; Man. Partner B. K. DHUR.

Advaita Ashrama: 5 Dehi Entally Rd, Calcutta 700 014; tel. (33) 290898; f. 1899; religion, philosophy, spiritualism, Vendanta; publication centre of Ramakrishna Math and Ramakrishna Mission; Pres. Swami SWANANDA; Publication Man. Swami BODHASARA-NANDA.

Allied Book Agency: 18A Shyama Charan De St, Calcutta 700 073; tel. (33) 312594; general and academic; Dir B. SARKAR.

Ananda Publishers (Pvt) Ltd: 45 Beniatola Lane, Calcutta 700 009; tel. (33) 314352; literature, general; Dir A. SARKAR.

Assam Review Publishing Co: 29 Waterloo St, Calcutta 700 069; tel. (33) 282251; f. 1926; publrs of *Tea Plantation Directory* and *Tea News*; Partners G. L. BANERJEE, S. BANERJEE.

Book Land (Pvt) Ltd: 1 Shankar Ghosh Lane, Calcutta 700 007; economics, politics, history and general; Man. Dir J. N. BASU.

Chuckerverty, Chatterjee and Co Ltd: 15 College Sq., Calcutta 700 012; Dir BINODELAL CHAKRAVARTI.

Eastern Law House (Pvt) Ltd: 54 Ganesh Chandra Ave, Calcutta 700 013; tel. (33) 274989; fax (33) 943333; f. 1918; legal, commercial and accountancy; Dir ASOK DE; br in New Delhi.

Firma KLM Private Ltd: 257B B. B. Ganguly St, Calcutta 700 012; tel. (33) 274391; f. 1950; Indology, scholarly in English, Bengali, Sanskrit and Hindi; Man. Dir R. N. MUKERJI.

Intertrade Publications (India) (Pvt) Ltd: 55 Gariahat Rd, POB 10210, Calcutta 700 019; tel. (33) 474872; f. 1954; economics, medicine, law, history and trade directories; Man. Dir Dr K. K. ROY.

A. Mukherjee and Co (Pvt) Ltd: 2 Bankim Chatterjee St, Calcutta 700 073; tel. (33) 341606; f. 1940; educational and general in Bengali and English; Man. Dirs RAJEEV NEOGI, RANJAN SENGUPTA.

Naya Prokash: 206 Bidhan Sarani, POB 11468, Calcutta 700 006; tel. (33) 316009; fax (33) 943333; f. 1960; agriculture, horticulture, Indology, history, political science, defence studies; Partners BARINDRA MITRA, PARTHA SANKAR BASU.

New Era Publishing Co: 31 Gauri Bari Lane, Calcutta 700 004; f. 1944; Propr Dr P. N. MITRA; Man. S. K. MITRA.

W. Newman and Co Ltd: 3 Old Court House St, Calcutta 700 069; f. 1851; general; Man. Dir P. N. BHARGAVA.

Punthi Pustak: 136/4B Bidhan Sarani, Calcutta 700 004; tel. (33) 558473; religion, history, philosophy; Propr S. K. BHATTACHARYA.

Renaissance Publishers (Pvt) Ltd: 15 Bankim Chatterjee St, Calcutta 700 012; f. 1949; politics, philosophy, history; Man. Dir J. C. GOSWAMI.

Saraswati Library: 206 Bidhan Sarani, Calcutta 700 006; tel. (33) 345492; f. 1914; history, philosophy, religion, literature; Man. Partner B. BHATTACHARJEE.

M. C. Sarkar and Sons (Pvt) Ltd: 14 Bankim Chatterjee St, Calcutta 700 073; tel. (33) 341782; f. 1910; reference; Dirs SUPRIYA SARKAR, SAMIT SARKAR.

Thacker's Press and Directories: POB 2512, Calcutta 700 001; industrial pubs and directories; Chair. JUTHIKA ROY; Dirs B. B. ROY, A. BOSE.

Visva-Bharati: 6 Acharya Jagadish Bose Rd, Calcutta 700 017; tel. (33) 449868; f. 1923; literature; Dir JAGADINDRA BHOWMICK.

Madras

Higginbothams Ltd: 814 Anna Salai, POB 311, Madras 600 002; tel. (44) 831841; telex 417038; fax (44) 562590; f. 1844; general; Gen. Man. S. CHANDRASEKHAR.

B. G. Paul and Co: 4 Francis Joseph St, Madras; f. 1923; general, educational and oriental; Man. K. NILAKANTAN.

T. R. Publications: 32 II Main Rd, C.I.T. East, Madras 600 035; tel. (44) 441246; telex 416643.

Thompson and Co (Pvt) Ltd: 33 Broadway, Madras 600 001; f. 1890; directories in English, Tamil, Telugu and Malayalam; Man Dir K. M. CHERIAN.

Other Towns

Bharat Bharti Prakashan: Western Kutchery Rd, Meerut 250 001; tel. 73748; f. 1952; textbooks; Man. Dir RAJENDRA AGARWAL.

Bharati Bhawan: Thakurbari Rd, Kadamkuan, Patna 800 003; tel. (612) 50325; f. 1942; educational and juvenile; other brs in Muzaffarpur, Ranchi, Darbhanga and Calcutta; Partners T. K. BOSE, DOLLY BOSE, SUROJIT BOSE and SANJIB BOSE.

Bishen Singh Mahendra Pal Singh: 23A Connaught Place, POB 137, Dehra Dun 248 001; tel. (935) 24048; f. 1957; botany; Dir GAJENDRA SINGH.

Catholic Press: Ranchi 834 001, Bihar; f. 1928; books and periodicals; Dir WILLIAM TIGGA.

Chugh Publications: 2 Strachey Rd, POB 101, Allahabad; tel. (532) 21589; sociology, economics, history, general; Propr RAMESH KUMAR.

Geetha Book House: K. R. Circle, Mysore 570 001; tel. (821) 33589; f. 1959; general; Dirs M. GOPALA KRISHNA, M. GURURAJA RAO.

Goel Publishing House: Subhash Bazar, Meerut 250 001; tel. 27843; textbooks; Dir KAMAL K. RASTOGI.

Kalyani Publishers: 1/1 Rajinder Nagar, Ludhiana, Punjab; tel. (161) 50221; textbooks; Dir RAJ KUMAR.

Kitabistan: 30 Chak, Allahabad 211 003; tel. (532) 51885; f. 1932; general, agriculture, govt pubs in Urdu, Farsi and Arabic; Partners A. U. KHAN, SULTAN ZAMAN, NASEEM FAROOQI.

The Law Book Co (Pvt) Ltd: 18B Sardar Patel Marg, Civil Lines, POB 1004, Allahabad 211 001; tel. (532) 2415; f. 1929; legal texts in English; Man. Dir L. R. BAGGA; Dirs RAJEEV R. BAGGA, DEEPAK BAGGA, ANIL BAGGA, RAKESH BAGGA.

Macmillan India Ltd: 315/316 Raheja Chambers, 12 Museum Rd, Bangalore 560 001; tel. (532) 573478; telex 8452615; scholarly monographs in English and Hindi, textbooks and general; Pres. and Man. Dir S. G. WASANI.

Navajivan Publishing House: PO Navajivan, Ahmedabad 380 014; tel. (272) 447635; f. 1919; Gandhiana and related social science; in English, Hindi and Gujarati; Man. Trustee JITENDRA DESAI.

Nem Chand and Bros: Civil Lines, Roorkee 247 667; tel. 2258; f. 1951; engineering textbooks and journals.

Orient Longman Ltd: 3-6-272 Himayatnagar, Hyderabad 500 029; tel. (842) 240305; telex 4256803; f. 1948; educational, technical, general and children's in almost all Indian languages; Chair. J. RAMESHWAR RAO.

Publication Bureau: Panjab University, Chandigarh 160 014; tel. (172) 22782; f. 1948; textbooks and general; Head of Bureau and Sec. R. K. MALHOTRA.

Ram Prasad and Sons: Hospital Rd, Agra 282 003; tel. (562) 73418; f. 1905; agricultural, arts, history, commerce, education, general, pure and applied science, economics, sociology; Dirs R. N., B. N. and Y. N. AGARWAL; Man. S. N. AGARWAL.

Upper India Publishing House (Pvt) Ltd: Aminabad, Lucknow 226 018; tel. (522) 42711; f. 1921; Indian history, religion, art and science; English and Hindi; Man. Dir S. BHARGAVA.

Government Publishing House

Publications Division: Ministry of Information and Broadcasting, Govt of India, Patiala House, New Delhi 110 001; tel. (11) 387983; f. 1941; culture, art, literature, planning and development, general; also 20 magazines in English and several Indian languages; Dir Dr S. S. SHASHI.

PUBLISHERS' ASSOCIATIONS

Delhi State Booksellers' and Publishers' Association: C-27/1 Connaught Place, New Delhi 110 001; tel. (11) 3713671; 325 mems; Pres. M. G. ARORA; Sec. J. GURWARA.

Federation of Indian Publishers: Federation House, 18/1C Institutional Area, JNU Rd, New Delhi 110 067; tel. (11) 654847; 11 affiliated asscns; 250 mems; Pres. GULAB VAZIRANI; Gen. Sec. S. BALWANT.

Federation of Publishers and Booksellers Associations in India: 4833/24 Govind Lane, 1st Floor, Ansari Rd, New Delhi 110 002; tel. (11) 272845; 17 affiliated asscns; 680 mems; Pres. N. K. MEHRA; Sec. S. C. SETHI.

Publishers' and Booksellers' Guild: 5A Bhawani Dutta Lane, Calcutta 700 073; tel. (33) 311541; fax (33) 326059; 50 mems; Pres. DWIJENDRANATH BASU; Sec. SUPROKASH BASU.

Radio and Television

Radio broadcasting in India began in 1927 and came under government control in 1930. A television station was established in Delhi, on an experimental basis, in 1959, and the first general service began in Delhi in 1965. In 1976 television broadcasting became independent of All India Radio, under the name Doordarshan India. Colour transmissions began in 1981. To maximize broadcasting coverage, the Government installs and maintains radio and television sets in community centres. Both radio and television carry commercial advertising.

In 1988 there were an estimated 63.5m. radio receivers in use, and in 1990 there were 12.5m. television receivers in use.

In August 1990 the Lok Sabha unanimously passed the Prasar Bharati Corporation Bill granting autonomy to the state-operated

INDIA

Directory

national radio and television networks. In February 1991 the Government announced that implementation of the Bill was to be delayed in order to incorporate some amendments, following a public debate.

RADIO

All India Radio (AIR): Akashvani Bhavan, Parliament St, New Delhi 110 001; tel. (11) 3710006; telex 3165585; broadcasting is controlled by the Ministry of Information and Broadcasting and is govt-financed; operates a network of 102 broadcasting centres, covering 95% of the population and about 83% of the total area of the country; Dir-Gen. A. R. SHINDE; Dir of Programmes (Devt) S. S. KAPUR.

The News Services Division of AIR, centralized in New Delhi, is one of the largest news organizations in the world. It has 42 regional news units, which broadcast 273 bulletins daily in 24 languages and 36 dialects. Eighty-one bulletins in 19 languages are broadcast in the Home Services and 64 bulletins in 24 languages in the External Services.

Radio broadcasting stations are grouped into four zones:

East: Agartala, Aizawl, Bhagalpur, Calcutta, Cuttack, Darbhanga, Dibrugarh, Gangtok, Guwahati, Imphal, Itanagar, Jeypore, Keonjhar, Kohima, Kurseong, Pasighat, Patna, Ranchi, Sambalpur, Shillong, Silchar, Siliguri, Tawang, Tezu and Tura.

North: Agra, Ajmer, Allahabad, Almora, Bikaner, Chandigarh, Delhi, Gorakhpur, Jaipur, Jammu, Jodhpur, Jullundur, Kanpur, Kota, Leh, Lucknow, Mathura, Najibabad, Rampur, Rohtak, Simla, Srinagar, Suratgarh, Udaipur and Varanasi.

South: Adlibad, Alleppey, Bangalore, Bhadravati, Coimbatore, Cuddapah, Dharwar, Gulbarga, Hyderabad, Kochi, Kothagudam, Kozhikode, Madras, Madurai, Mangalore, Mysore, Nagar-Coil, Pondicherry, Port Blair, Thiruvananthapuram, Tiruchirapalli, Tirunelveli, Trichur, Vijayawada, Vishakhapatnam and Warrangal.

West: Ahmedabad, Ambikapur, Aurangabad, Bhopal, Bhuj, Bombay, Chhatarpur, Gwalior, Indore, Jabalpur, Jagdalpur, Jalgaon, Nagpur, Panaji, Parbhani, Pune, Raipur, Rajkot, Ratnagiri, Rewa, Sangli, Sholapur and Vadodara (Baroda).

TELEVISION

Doordarshan India (Television India): Mandi House, Doordarshan Bhavan, Copernicus Marg, New Delhi 110 001; tel. (11) 382094; telex 3166143; f. 1976; broadcasting is controlled by the Ministry of Information and Broadcasting and is govt-financed; programmes: 280 hours weekly; Dir-Gen. SHIV SHARMA.

In December 1988 there were 17.3m. television receivers. In April 1989, 51.8% of the country's area and 73.7% of the population were covered by the TV network. There were 520 transmitters in operation in March 1990.

There are 18 television stations, located at Ahmedabad, Bangalore, Bombay, Calcutta, Cuttack, Delhi, Gauhati, Gorakhpur, Hyderabad, Jaipur, Jalandhar, Lucknow, Madras, Nagpur, Rajkot, Ranchi, Srinagar and Thiruvananthapuram. There are also nine relay centres, situated at Amritsar, Asansol, Bhatinda, Chandigarh, Kanpur, Kochi, Kozhikode, Kurseong and Murshidabad.

Finance

(cap. = capital; p.u. = paid up; res = reserves; dep. = deposits; m. = million; brs = branches; amounts in rupees)

BANKING

State Banks

Reserve Bank of India: Central Office, Shahid Bhagat Singh Rd, POB 406, Bombay 400 023; tel. (22) 2861602; telex 114222; f. 1935; nationalized 1949; sole bank of issue; cap. and res 1,550m. (1988); Gov. S. VENKITARAMANAN; Exec. Dirs IRIS VAZ, M. L. T. FERNANDES, V. VISVANATHAN; 11 brs.

State Bank of India: Madame Cama Rd, POB 10121, Bombay 400 021; tel. (22) 2022426; telex 112995; f. 1955; cap. p.u. 1,500m., res 8,751.7m., dep. 435,152.6m. (March 1990); subsidiaries in Bikaner and Jaipur, Hyderabad, Indore, Mysore, Patila, Saurashtra and Travancore; controls 28 state co-operative banks and 349 dist. cooperative banks; 34 private-sector banks and 194 regional rural banks; rep. brs and offices world-wide; Chair. M. N. GOIPORIA; Man. Dirs T. K. SINHA, V. MAHADEVAN; 8,379 brs.

Commercial Banks

Fourteen of India's major commercial banks were nationalized in 1969 and a further six in 1980. They are managed by 15-mem. boards of directors (two directors to be appointed by the central Government, one employee director, one representing employees who are not workmen, one representing depositors, three representing farmers, workers, artisans, etc., five representing persons with special knowledge or experience, one Reserve Bank of India official and one Government of India official). The Department of Banking of the Ministry of Finance controls all banking operations.

There were 59,698 branches of public sector and other commercial banks in March 1990.

Aggregate deposits of all scheduled commercial banks amounted to Rs 1,727,590m. in March 1990.

Allahabad Bank: 2 Netaji Subhas Rd, Calcutta 700 001; tel. (33) 209258; telex 217547; f. 1865; cap. p.u. 575m., dep. 52,536m. (March 1990); Chair. and Man. Dir R. L. WADHWA; 1,766 brs.

Andhra Bank: Andhra Bank Bldg, Sultan Bazar, Hyderabad 500 001; tel. (842) 40141; telex 1556283; f. 1923; nationalized 1980; cap. p.u. 220m., dep. 32,257m. (March 1990); Chair. and Man. Dir K. R. NAYAK; Exec. Dir A. T. AKOLKAR; 1,055 brs.

Bank of Baroda: 3 Walchand Hirachand Marg, Ballard Pier, POB 10046, Bombay 400 038; tel. (22) 260341; telex 116345; f. 1908; cap. p.u. 964m., dep. 130,335m. (March 1990); Chair. and Man. Dir Dr A. C. SHAH; 2,154 brs (world-wide).

Bank of India: Express Towers, Nariman Point, POB 234, Bombay 400 021; tel. (22) 2023020; telex 112281; f. 1906; cap. p.u. 2,590m., dep. 155,085m. (March 1990); Chair. and Man. Dir R. SRINIVASAN; 2,250 brs (world-wide).

Bank of Maharashtra: 'Lokmangal', 1501 Shivajinagar, Pune 411 005; tel. (212) 52731; telex 145207; f. 1935; cap. and res 936m., dep. 32,342.5m. (March 1990); Chair. and Man. Dir T. K. K. BHAGVAT; 1,116 brs.

Canara Bank: 112 Jayachamarajendra Rd, POB 6648, Bangalore 560 002; tel. (812) 76851; telex 845205; f. 1906; cap. p.u. 579m., dep. 109,227m. (March 1990); Chair. and Man. Dir N. D. PRABHU; 2,006 brs.

Central Bank of India: Chandermukhi, Nariman Point, Bombay 400 021; tel. (22) 2026428; telex 112909; f. 1911; cap. 1,330m., res 440m., dep. 114,566m. (March 1990); Chair. and Man. Dir N. M. MISTRY; 2,907 brs.

Corporation Bank: Mangaladevi Temple Rd, POB 88, Mangalore 575 001; tel. (824) 26416; telex 842228; f. 1906; nationalized 1980; cap. p.u. 120m., dep. 15,306m. (March 1990); Chair. and Man. Dir Y. S. HEGDE; Exec. Dir K. R. RAMAMOORTHY; 437 brs.

Dena Bank: 17 Horniman Circle, Fort, POB 41, Bombay 400 023; tel. (22) 2860746; telex 112511; f. 1938; cap. p.u. 720m., dep. 30,009m. (March 1990); Chair. and Man. Dir G. S. DAHOTRE; Exec. Dir S. DORESWAMY; 1,092 brs.

Indian Bank: 31 Rajaji Salai, POB 1866, Madras 600 001; tel. (44) 514151; telex 418307; fax (44) 521490; f. 1907; cap. p.u. 560m., dep. 70,586m. (March 1990); Chair. and Man. Dir M. GOPALAKRISHNAN; Gen. Man. K. SUBRAMANIAN; 1,367 brs.

Indian Overseas Bank: 151 Anna Salai, POB 3765, Madras 600 002; tel. (44) 864141; telex 416290; fax (44) 8253395; f. 1937; cap. p.u. 2,500m., dep. 66,533m. (March 1990); Chair. and Man. Dir P. S. GOPALAKRISHNAN; 1,200 brs (world-wide).

New Bank of India: 1 Tolstoy Marg, New Delhi 110 001; tel. (11) 3311452; telex 3166920; f. 1936; nationalized 1980; cap. p.u. 560m., dep. 20,426m. (March 1990); Chair. and Man. Dir J. SETHI (acting); 581 brs.

Oriental Bank of Commerce: Harsha Bhavan, E Block, Connaught Place, POB 329, New Delhi 110 001; tel. (11) 3321459; telex 3165462; f. 1943; nationalized 1980; cap. p.u. 280m., dep. 24,708m. (March 1990); Chair. and Man. Dir S. K. SONI; 528 brs.

Punjab and Sind Bank: 21 Bank House, Rajendra Place, New Delhi 110 008; tel. (11) 5720849; telex 3166456; f. 1908; nationalized 1980; cap. 725m., dep. 24,406m. (March 1990); Chair. and Man. Dir M. S. CHAHAL; 657 brs.

Punjab National Bank: 7 Bhikaiji Cama Place, Africa Ave, POB 274, New Delhi 110 066; tel. (11) 602303; telex 3161906; f. 1895; cap. 1000m., dep. 125,610m. (March 1990); Chair. and Man. Dir RASHID JILANI; 2,960 brs.

Syndicate Bank: POB 1, Manipal 576 119; tel. 8261; telex 82242; f. 1925; cap. 740m., dep. 67,916m. (March 1990); Chair. and Man. Dir P. S. V. MALLYA; 1,528 brs.

UCO Bank (United Commercial Bank): 10 Biplabi Trailokya Maharaj Sarani (Brabourne Rd), POB 2455, Calcutta 700 001; tel. (33) 260120; telex 214323; fax (33) 304482; f. 1943; dep. 72,880m. (1989); Chair. and Man. Dir HARBHAJAN SINGH (acting); 1,747 brs.

Union Bank of India: Union Bank Bhavan, 239 Vidhan Bhavan Marg, Nariman Point, Bombay 400 021; tel. (22) 2024647; telex 1185156; fax (22) 274135; f. 1919; cap. 500m., dep. 63,011m. (March 1990); Chair. and Man. Dir S. P. TALWAR; 1,837 brs.

United Bank of India: 16 Old Court House St, Calcutta 700 001; tel. (33) 237471; telex 217387; f. 1950; cap. p.u. 2,630m., dep. 45,740m. (March 1990); Chair. and Man. Dir J. V. SHETTY; 1,301 brs.

INDIA

Vijaya Bank: 41/42 Mahatma Gandhi Rd, Bangalore 560 001; tel. (812) 573341; telex 8452428; f. 1931; nationalized 1980; cap. 270m., dep. 23,571m. (March 1990); Chair. and Man. Dir K. SADANANDA SHETTY; 719 brs.

Principal Private Banks

Bank of Madura Ltd: 758 Anna Salai, POB 5225, Madras 600 002; tel. (44) 863456; telex 417807; cap. p.u. 10m., dep. 3,501m. (March 1990); Chair. S. P. SABAPATHY; 252 brs.

Bombay Mercantile Co-operative Bank Ltd: 78 Mohammed Ali Rd, Bombay 400 003; tel. (22) 325961; telex 1173727; f. 1939; cap. p.u. 30.7m., dep. 3,691.5m. (March 1990); Chair. EDULJI H. TUREL; Chief. Gen. Man. J. T. BASRAI; 36 brs.

Karnataka Bank Ltd: POB 716, Kodialbail, Mangalore 575 003; tel. (824) 33701; telex 8832280; f. 1924; cap. p.u. 45m., dep. 5,025.3m. (March 1990); Chair. H. M. RAMA RAO; Gen. Mans M. S. KRISHNA BHAT, T. GOPAL KRISHNA RAO; 273 brs.

The Sangli Bank Ltd: Rajwada Chowk, POB 158, Sangli 416 416; tel. 3611; telex 193211; f. 1916; cap. p.u. 4.4m. (1989), dep. 4,188m. (1990); Chair. and CEO A. B. ARADHYE; Gen. Man. G. K. MUNGALE; 169 brs.

United Western Bank Ltd: 172/4 Raviwar Peth, Shivaji Circle, POB 2, Satara 415 001; tel. 2523; telex 147212; f. 1936; cap. 7.5m., dep. 3,596m. (1989); Chair. K. B. DAMLE; Jt Gen. Mans P. V. KULKARNI, S. T. MODAK; 176 brs.

Foreign Banks

In September 1989 the Reserve Bank of India announced that foreign banks opening branches in India would henceforth require a minimum capital of 150m. rupees. At that time there were 21 foreign banks (with 137 branches) accepting deposits and making loans locally, while a further 18 foreign banks had branch offices. Among the most important foreign banks operating in India are:

Abu Dhabi Commercial Ltd (UAE): Rehmat Manzil, 75 Veer Nariman Rd, Bombay; tel. (22) 223866; telex 115481; Man. EBRAHIM ABDUL RAHMAN.

Algemene Bank Nederland NV (Netherlands): 14 Veer Nariman Rd, Bombay 400 023; tel. (22) 2042331; telex 113246; Gen. Man. (India) A. KAPUR; 3 brs.

American Express International Banking Corpn (USA): Dalamal Towers, First Floor 211, Nariman Point, Bombay 400 021; tel. (22) 233230; telex 113808; Vice-Pres. (India) JOHN FILMERIDIS; 3 brs.

ANZ Grindlays Bank (UK): 90 Mahatma Gandhi Rd, POB 725, Bombay 400 023; tel. (22) 271295; telex 114792; CEO Dr ROBERT JOHN EDGAR; 54 brs.

Banca Nazionale del Lavoro (Italy): 61 Maker Chambers VI, 6th Floor, Nariman Point, Bombay 400 021; tel. (22) 2043736; telex 114053; fax (22) 2043482; Rep. L. S. AGARWAL.

Bank of America National Trust and Savings Association (USA): Express Towers, Ground Fl., Nariman Point, Bombay 400 021; tel. (22) 2023431; telex 112152; Vice-Pres. and Country Man. VIKRAM TALWAR; 4 brs.

The Bank of Bahrain and Kuwait BSC: Embassy Centre, 207 Nariman Point, Bombay 400 021; tel. (22) 2041838; telex 115101; Gen. Man. and CEO M. G. RAMAKRISHNA.

Bank of Credit and Commerce International (Overseas) Ltd (Cayman Islands): Marker Chambers III, Nariman Point, Bombay 400 021; tel. (22) 241091; telex 115839; Gen. Man. (India) B. N. CHOUDHURY; 1 br.

Bank of Oman Ltd: Air India Bldg, Nariman Point, Bombay 400 021; tel. (22) 2026096; telex 115936; CEO M. V. KULKARNI.

Bank of Tokyo Ltd (Japan): Jeevan Prakash, Sir P. Mehta Rd, Bombay 400 001; tel. (22) 2860564; telex 112155; Gen. Man. MOTAOKI TSURUNO; 3 brs.

Banque Nationale de Paris (France): French Bank Bldg, 62 Homji St, Fort, POB 45, Bombay 400 001; tel. (22) 2860943; telex 112341; Man. P. GRANDAMY; 5 brs.

Barclays Bank PLC (UK): 21-23 Maker Chambers VI, 2nd Floor, Nariman Point, Bombay 400 021; tel. (22) 2044353; telex 1182073; fax (22) 2043238; Chief Man. (India) C. J. MIDDLETON; 1 br.

British Bank of the Middle East (Hong Kong): 16 Veer Nariman Rd, Fort, POB 876, Bombay 400 023; tel. (22) 2048203; telex 1185956; fax (22) 2046077; Man. L. J. SALDANHA.

Citibank, N.A. (USA): Sakhar Bhavan, 230 Backbay Reclamation, Nariman Point, Bombay 400 021; tel. (22) 2860871; telex 115379; CEO J. RAO; 4 brs.

Deutsche Bank AG (Germany): Tulsiani Chambers, Nariman Point, POB 9995, Bombay 400 021; tel. (22) 223262; telex 1184042; fax (22) 2045047; CEO JÜRGEN HINRICH FRESE; 2 brs.

Hongkong and Shanghai Banking Corpn Ltd (Hong Kong): 52-60 Mahatma Gandhi Rd, POB 128, Bombay 400 001; tel. (22) 274921; telex 1182223; fax (22) 2028291; CEO G. C. DOBBY; 20 brs.

Midland Bank (UK): 152 Maker Chamber No. IV, 14th Floor, 222 Nariman Point, Bombay 400 021; tel. (22) 2024973; telex 115478; fax (22) 2024954; Rep. JOHN W. RAE.

Mitsui Bank Ltd (Japan): 6 Wallace St, Bombay 400 001; tel. (22) 2043931; telex 112987; Gen. Man. and CEO S. YAMAMOTO; 1 br.

Oman International Bank (Oman): 1A Mittal Court, Nariman Point, Bombay 400 021; tel. (22) 2047444; telex 113569; CEO V. V. CHANDY.

Royal Bank of Canada: N-104 Panchshila Park, New Delhi 110 017; tel. (11) 6410785; telex 3162927; Regional Rep. COLIN D. LIPTROT.

Sanwa Bank Ltd (Japan): World Trade Centre, 5th Floor, Barakhamba Lane, New Delhi 110 001; tel. (11) 3318008; telex 3162961; Gen. Man. MICHIHIRO SHINOHARA.

Société Générale (France): Maker Chambers IV, Ground Floor, Bajaj Marg, Nariman Point, POB 11635, Bombay 400 021; tel. (22) 243403; telex 1182635; fax (22) 2045459; Gen. Man. DANIEL MOLLE.

Sonali Bank (Bangladesh): 15 Park St, Calcutta 700 016; tel. (33) 297998; telex 212727; Dep. Gen. Man. SIRAJUDDIN AHMED; 1 br.

Standard Chartered Bank (UK): 23-25 Mahatma Gandhi Rd, Fort, POB 558, Bombay 400 023; tel. (22) 257198; telex 112230; Chief Man. P. S. NAT; 24 brs.

Banking Organizations

Indian Banks' Association: Stadium House, 81-83 Veer Nariman Rd, Churchgate, Bombay 400 020; tel. (22) 222365; telex 115146; 85 mems; Chair. M. N. GOIPORIA; Sec. A. K. BAKHSHY.

Indian Institute of Bankers: 'The Arcade', World Trade Centre, 2nd Floor, East Wing, Cuffe Parade, Bombay 400 005; tel. (22) 217003; telex 113524; f. 1928; 341,232 mems; Pres. R. N. MALHOTRA; Chief Sec. R. D. PANDYA.

National Institute of Bank Management: Kondhwe Khurd, Post Bag No. 1, Pune 411 022; tel. (212) 673080; telex 145256; f. 1969; Dir B. K. GHOSE.

DEVELOPMENT FINANCE ORGANIZATIONS

Agricultural Finance Consultants Ltd: Dhanraj Mahal, 1st Floor, Chhatrapati Shivaji Maharaj Marg, Bombay 400 039; tel. (22) 2028924; telex 115849; f. 1968; fmrly Agricultural Finance Corpn Ltd; renamed 1989; a consortium of commercial banks, set up to help member commercial banks participate in the financing of agriculture and rural development projects; provides project consultancy services to commercial banks, Union and State govts, public sector corpns, the World Bank, the ADB, FAO, the International Fund for Agricultural Development and other institutions and to individuals; undertakes techno-economic and investment surveys in agriculture and agro-industries etc.; regional offices in Calcutta, Lucknow and Bangalore; project office in New Delhi; br. offices in Ahmedabad, Bhopal, Guwahati, Hyderabad, Madras, Patna and Thiruvananthapuram; cap. p.u. 100m. (March 1989); Chair. Dr. G. V. K. RAO; Man. Dir B. VENKATA RAO.

Credit Guarantee Corpn of India Ltd: Bombay; f. 1971; promoted by the Reserve Bank of India; guarantees loans and other credit facilities extended by (i) scheduled and non-scheduled commercial banks to small traders, farmers and self-employed persons and small borrowers under a differential interest rates scheme; (ii) scheduled and non-scheduled commercial banks and state financial corpns to small transport and business enterprises; (iii) scheduled commercial banks and certain state and central co-operative banks to service co-operative socs assisting their mems engaged in industrial activity; Chair. Dr R. K. HAZARI; Man. C. S. SUBRAMANIAM.

Industrial Credit and Investment Corpn of India Ltd: 163 Backbay Reclamation, Bombay 400 020; tel. (22) 2022535; telex 1183062; fax (22) 2046582; f. 1955 to assist industrial enterprises by providing finance in both rupee and foreign currencies in the form of long- or medium-term loans or equity participation, sponsoring and underwriting new issues of shares and securities, guaranteeing loans from other private investment sources, furnishing managerial, tech. and admin. advice to industry; also offers suppliers' and buyers' credit, export development capital, asset credit, technology finance, merchant banking services, instalment sales and equipment leasing facilities; regional offices at Calcutta, Madras and New Delhi; development office at Guwahati (Assam); share cap. 915.6m., res 1,947.6m. (March 1990); Chair. and Man. Dir N. VAGHUL.

Industrial Development Bank of India (IDBI): IDBI Tower, Cuffe Parade, Colaba, Bombay 400 005; tel. (22) 214450; telex 116866; f. 1964, reorg. 1976; the main financial institution for co-ordinating and supplementing the working of other financial institutions and also for promoting and financing industrial development; 5 regional offices and 21 br. offices; cap. p.u. 6,370m., res 11,020m. (March 1990); Chair. and Man. Dir SURESH S. NADKARNI.

INDIA   *Directory*

Industrial Finance Corpn of India: Bank of Baroda Bldg, 16 Sansad Marg, POB 363, New Delhi 110 001; tel. (11) 3322052; telex 3166123; fax (11) 3320245; f. 1948 to provide medium- and long-term finance to cos and co-operative socs in India, engaged in manufacture, preservation or processing of goods, shipping, mining, hotels and power generation and distribution; promotes industrialization of less developed areas, and sponsors training in management techniques and development banking; cap. p.u. 1,000m., res 3,270m. (March 1990); Chair. D. N. DAVAR; 8 regional offices and 11 br. offices.

National Bank for Agriculture and Rural Development: Sterling Centre, Dr Annie Besant Rd, Worli, POB 6552, Bombay 400 018; tel. (22) 4924306; telex 1173770; f. 1982 to provide credit for agricultural and rural development through commercial, co-operative and regional rural banks; cap. and res 3,276.7m. (1986); held 50% each by the cen. govt and the Reserve Bank; Chair. P. R. NAYAK; Man. Dir P. KOTAIAH; 16 regional offices and 7 sub-offices.

STOCK EXCHANGES

There are 19 stock exchanges (with a total of more than 6,250 listed companies) in India, including:

Ahmedabad Share and Stock Brokers' Association: Manek Chowk, Ahmedabad 380 001; tel. (272) 347149; telex 1216789; f. 1894; 296 mems; Pres. CHANDRAKANT BAPUBHAI DESAI; Exec. Dir M. L. SONEJI.

Bangalore Stock Exchange Ltd: Unity Bldg, 'M' Block, J.C. Rd, Bangalore 560 002; tel. (812) 237238; telex 2874; 130 mems; Pres. R. JAGADISH KUMAR; Sec. M. RAGHAVENDRA RAO.

Bombay Stock Exchange: Phiroze Jeejeebhoy Towers, 25th Floor, Dalal St, Bombay 400 001; tel. (22) 275860; telex 1185925; fax (22) 2028121; f. 1875; 556 mems; Pres. GOVINDBHAI B. DESAI; Exec. Dir M. R. MAYYA.

Calcutta Stock Exchange Association Ltd: 7 Lyons Range, Calcutta 700 001; tel. (33) 203335; telex 217414; f. 1908; 645 mems; Pres. C. L. CHANGOIWALA; Exec. Dir D. J. BISWAS.

Delhi Stock Exchange Association Ltd: 3 & 4/4B Asaf Ali Rd, New Delhi 110 002; tel. (11) 3271302; telex 3165317; f. 1947; 125 mems; Pres. HARISH C. BHASIN; Exec. Dir R. K. PANDEY.

Ludhiana Stock Exchange Association Ltd: Lajpatrai Market, Ludhiana 141 008; tel. 32748; telex 386429; f. 1984; 220 mems; Pres. VISHWANATH DHIRI; Sec. P. S. BATHLA.

Madras Stock Exchange Ltd: Exchange Bldg, 11 Second Line Beach, POB 183, Madras 600 001; tel. (44) 521071; telex 418059; f. 1937; 168 mems; Pres. S. P. SIVAPRAKASAM; Exec. Dir S. RAMANATHAN.

Uttar Pradesh Stock Exchange Association: 14/113 Civil Lines, Kanpur 208 001; tel. (512) 210822; telex 325420; 500 mems; Pres. PADAM KUMAR JAIN; Exec. Sec. G. L. SHARMA.

The other recognized stock exchanges are: Hyderabad, Madhya Pradesh (Indore), Kochi, Pune, Guwahati, Jaipur, Kanara (Mangalore), Bhubaneswar (Orissa), and Magadh (Patna).

INSURANCE

In January 1973 all Indian and foreign insurance companies were nationalized. The general insurance business in India is now transacted by only four companies, subsidiaries of the General Insurance Corpn of India.

General Insurance Corpn of India (GIC): Industrial Assurance Bldg, 4th Floor, Churchgate, Bombay 400 020; tel. (22) 220046; telex 113833; fax (22) 241109; f. 1973 by the reorg. of 107 private life and non-life insurance cos (incl. brs of foreign cos operating in the country) as the four subsidiaries listed below; Chair. S. V. MONY; Man. Dir A. S. MITRA.

National Insurance Co Ltd: 3 Middleton St, Calcutta 700 071; tel. (33) 292131; telex 215906; fax (33) 294569; Chair. and Man. Dir Y. D. PATIL.

New India Assurance Co Ltd: New India Assurance Bldg, Mahatma Gandhi Rd, Fort, Bombay 400 023; tel. (22) 274617; telex 1182423; fax (22) 2615033; f. 1919; Chair. and Man. Dir S. V. MONY.

The Oriental Insurance Co Ltd: Oriental House, A-25/27 Asaf Ali Rd, New Delhi 110 002; tel. (11) 3279221; telex 3162583; fax (11) 3263175; Chair. and Man. Dir G. V. RAO.

United India Insurance Co Ltd: 24 Whites Rd, Madras 600 014; tel. (44) 810061; telex 416141; cap. and res 966m.; Chair. and Man. Dir M. M. BHAGAT.

Life Insurance Corpn of India (LIC): Jeevan Bima Marg, Bombay 400 021; tel. (22) 2021383; telex 1182327; fax (22) 2022151; f. 1956; controls all life insurance business; Chair. M. G. DIWAN; Man. Dir K. P. NARASIMHAN; 1,279 brs.

Trade and Industry
CHAMBERS OF COMMERCE

There are chambers of commerce in most commercial and industrial centres. The following are among the most important:

Associated Chambers of Commerce and Industry of India (ASSOCHAM): 2nd Floor, Allahabad Bank Bldg, 17 Parliament St, New Delhi 110 001; tel. (11) 310704; telex 3161754; fax (11) 312193; f. 1921; a central org. of 350 chambers of commerce and industry and industrial assens representing more than 52,000 cos throughout India; 6 promoter chambers, 100 ordinary mems, 15 patron mems and 400 corporate associates; Pres. AVIJIT MAZUMDAR; Sec.-Gen. B. P. GUNAJI.

Federation of Indian Chambers of Commerce and Industry: Federation House, Tansen Marg, New Delhi 110 001; tel. (11) 3319251; telex 3162521; f. 1927; 470 ordinary mems, 1,058 assoc. mems, 72 cttee mems; Pres. SUDARSHAN KUMAR BIRLA; Sec.-Gen. D. H. PAI PANANDIKER.

Indian National Committee of International Chambers of Commerce: Federation House, Tansen Marg, New Delhi 110 001; tel. (11) 3319251; telex 3162521; f. 1929; 46 org. mems, 180 assoc. mems, 68 cttee mems; Pres. RAUNAQ SINGH; Sec.-Gen. D. H. PAI PANANDIKER.

Bengal Chamber of Commerce and Industry: 6 Netaji Subhas Rd, Calcutta 700 001; tel. (33) 208393; telex 217369; f. 1853; 221 mems; Pres. A. SEN; Sec. PRADIP DAS GUPTA.

Bengal National Chamber of Commerce and Industry: 23 R. N. Mukherjee Rd, Calcutta 700 001; telex 212189; f. 1887; 350 mems, 30 affiliated industrial and trading assens; Pres. D. K. ROY; Sec. SUNIL BANIK.

Bharat Chamber of Commerce: 28 Hemanta Basu Sarani, Calcutta 700 001; tel. (33) 208286; f. 1900; 692 mems; Pres. D. D. KOTHARI; Sec. B. S. SARKAR.

Bihar Chamber of Commerce: Judges' Court Rd, POB 71, Patna 800 001; tel. (612) 53505; f. 1926; 700 ordinary mems, 50 asscn mems; Pres. P. MUKERJI; Sec.-Gen. K. P. S. KESHRI.

Bombay Chamber of Commerce and Industry: Mackinnon Mackenzie Bldg, 4 Shoorji Vallabhdas Marg, Ballard Estate, POB 473, Bombay 400 001; tel. (22) 2614681; telex 1173571; f. 1836; 694 ordinary mems, 482 assoc. mems, 47 hon. mems, 8 special category mems; Pres. Dr N. M. DHULDHOYA; Sec. VIVEK S. DATE.

Calcutta Chamber of Commerce: 18H Park St, Stephen Court, Calcutta 700 071; tel. (33) 290758; 460 mems; Pres. P. M. SINGHVI; Sec. Dr P. KHAITAN.

Federation of Andhra Pradesh Chambers of Commerce and Industry: 11-6-841, Red Hills, Hyderabad 500 004; tel. (842) 33658; telex 4256038; 1,327 mems; Pres. C. H. VENKATESHWAR RAO; Sec. M. VENKATA RAO.

Federation of Karnataka Chambers of Commerce and Industry: Kempegowda Rd, Bangalore 560 009; tel. (812) 29255; telex 8452115; f. 1916; 2,000 mems; Pres. N. VENKATESHIAH; Sec. RAGHAVENDRA RAO.

Federation of Madhya Pradesh Chambers of Commerce and Industry: Udyog Bhavan, 129A Malviya Nagar, Bhopal 462 003; tel. (755) 551472; f. 1975; 358 ordinary mems, 58 asscn mems; Pres. D. P. MANDELIA; Sec.-Gen. SURESH BHARGAVA.

Goa Chamber of Commerce: Goa Chamber Bldg, Rua de Ormuz, POB 59, Panjim; tel. 4223; f. 1908; 511 mems; Pres. P. S. ANGLE; Sec. O. L. DA LAPA-SOARES.

Gujarat Chamber of Commerce and Industry: Gujarat Chamber Bldg, Ashram Rd, POB 4045, Ahmedabad 380 009; tel. (272) 402301; f. 1949; 6,426 mems; Pres. JAGDISH S. JHAVERI; Sec.-Gen. I. N. KANIA.

Indian Chamber of Commerce: India Exchange, 4 India Exchange Place, Calcutta 700 001; tel. (33) 203243; telex 217432; fax (33) 204495; f. 1925; 250 ordinary mems, 50 assoc. mems, 20 affiliated asscns; Pres. SANJIV GOENKA; Sec.-Gen. B. K. AGRAWAL.

Indian Merchants' Chamber: IMC Marg, Bombay 400 020; tel. (22) 2046633; telex 115195; f. 1907; 168 asscn mems, 2,100 mem. firms; Pres. MAHENDRA KUMAR SANGHI; Sec.-Gen. RAMU PANDIT.

Indo-American Chamber of Commerce: 1C Vulcan Insurance Bldg, Veer Nariman Rd, Bombay 400 020; tel. (22) 221413; telex 113891; 1,700 mems; Pres. BINAY KUMAR; Sec.-Gen. V. RANGARAJ.

Indo-French Chamber of Commerce and Industry: Bakhtawar, Nariman Point, Bombay 400 021; tel. (22) 2023540; telex 113599; 350 mems; Pres. HARISH MAHINDRA; Sec.-Gen. MINOO P. VAZIFDAR.

Indo-German Chamber of Commerce: Maker Towers 'E', Cuffe Parade, Bombay 400 005; tel. (22) 216131; telex 114254; 3,600 mems; Pres. Dr D. C. KOTHARI; Exec. Dir Dr G. KRUEGER.

Karnataka Chamber of Commerce and Industry: Karnataka Chamber Bldg, Hubli 580 020; tel. 63102; f. 1929; 1,600 mems; Pres K. B. DESAI; Sec. G. B. GOUDAPPAGOL.

Kochi Chamber of Commerce and Industry: Bristow Rd, Willingdon Island, Kochi 682 003; tel. 6348; telex 8856371; 125 mems; Pres. PAMELA ANNA MATHEW; Sec. P. SETHURAM.

Madras Chamber of Commerce and Industry: Karumuttu Centre, 498 Anna Salai, Madras 600 035; tel. (44) 451452; telex 417036; fax (44) 451264; f. 1836; 194 mem. firms, 32 assoc., 10 affiliated and 11 hon.; Chair. V. CHIDAMBARAM; Sec. N. KANNAN.

Maharashtra Chamber of Commerce: Oricon House, 6th Floor, 12 K. Dubhash Marg (Rampart Row), Fort, Bombay 400 023; tel. (22) 244548; telex 113527; f. 1927; c. 2,000 mems; Pres. SUBHASH D. DANDEKAR; Sec.-Gen. S. S. PINGLE.

Mahratta Chamber of Commerce and Industry: Tilak Rd, Pune 411 002; tel. (212) 440371; telex 145333; 2,100 mems; Pres. H. K. FIRODIA; Sec. Dr B. R. SABADE.

Merchants' Chamber of Commerce and Industry: 14 Old Court House St, Calcutta 700 001; tel. (33) 281502; 600 mems; Pres. AMITAV KOTHARI; Chief Exec. H. R. BOSE.

Merchants' Chamber of Uttar Pradesh: 14/76 Civil Lines, Kanpur 208 001; tel. (532) 246874; f. 1932; 200 mems; Pres. RAMESH MOROLIA; Sec. B. K. PARIEK.

North India Chamber of Commerce and Industry: 9 Gandhi Rd, Dehra Dun, Uttar Pradesh; tel. (935) 23479; f. 1967; 105 ordinary mems, 29 asscn mems, 7 mem. firms, 91 assoc. mems; Pres. DEV PANDHI; Hon. Sec. ASHOK K. NARANG.

Oriental Chamber of Commerce: 6 Dr Rajendra Prasad Sarani (Clive Row), Calcutta 700 001; tel. (33) 203609; f. 1932; 248 ordinary mems, 4 assoc. mems; Pres. SHAHANSHAH JEHANGIR; Sec. KAZI ABU ZOBER.

PHD Chamber of Commerce and Industry: PHD House, Thapar Floor, 4/2 Siri Institutional Area, opp. Asian Games Village, POB 130, New Delhi 110 016; tel. (11) 6863801; telex 3173058; fax (11) 6863135; f. 1905; more than 1,180 mems, 70 asscn mems; Pres. S. S. KANWAR; Sec.-Gen. M. L. NANDRAJOG.

Rajasthan Chamber of Commerce and Industry: Rajasthan Chamber Bhavan, M.I. Rd, Jaipur 302 003; tel. (141) 76663; 550 mems; Pres. S. K. MANSINGHKA; Sec.-Gen. K. L. JAIN.

Southern India Chamber of Commerce and Industry: Indian Chamber Bldgs, Esplanade, POB 1208, Madras 600 108; tel. (44) 562228; telex 416689; f. 1909; 1,158 mems; Pres. M. A. ALAGAPPAN; Sec. J. PRASAD DAVIDS.

Upper India Chamber of Commerce: 14/113 Civil Lines, POB 63, Kanpur 208 001; tel. (512) 210684; f. 1888; 134 mems; Pres. D. N. DIKSHIT; Sec. K. K. GANGADHARAN.

Utkal Chamber of Commerce and Industry Ltd: Cantonment Rd, Cuttack 753 001; tel. 22311; 115 mems; Pres. SUKUMAR SEN; Sec. JAGDISH LAL.

Uttar Pradesh Chamber of Commerce: 15/197 Civil Lines, Kanpur 208 001; tel. 211696; f. 1914; 200 mems; Pres. Dr B. K. MODI; Sec. AFTAB SAMI.

FOREIGN TRADE CORPORATIONS

Cashew Corpn of India Ltd: Jawahar Vyapar Bhavan, Tolstoy Marg, New Delhi 110 001; tel. (11) 3313177; telex 3165181; imports raw cashew nuts for distribution to the export-orientated sector of the cashew processing industry; also undertakes exports of cashew kernels; cap. p.u. Rs15m., res and surplus Rs104.7m. (1988); Chair. P. K. SHUNGLU.

Export Credit Guarantee Corpn of India Ltd: Express Towers, 10th Floor, Nariman Point, POB 373, Bombay 400 021; tel. (22) 2023023; telex 1183231; fax (22) 2045253; f. 1957 to insure for risks involved in exports on credit terms and to supplement credit facilities by issuing guarantees, etc.; cap. Rs60m., res Rs249m. (1987); Chair. and Man. Dir J. G. KANGA; Gen. Man. N. M. CHORDIA.

Handicrafts and Handlooms Exports Corpn of India Ltd: Lok Kalyan Bhavan, 11A Rouse Ave Lane, New Delhi 110 002; tel. (11) 3311086; telex 3161522; fax (11) 3315351; f. 1958; govt undertaking dealing in export of handicrafts, handloom goods, ready-to-wear clothes, carpets and precious jewellery, while promoting exports and trade development; subsidiary of the State Trading Corpn of India Ltd; cap. p.u. Rs75m. (1988); Chair. and Man. Dir B. B. BHASIN.

Minerals and Metals Trading Corpn of India Ltd: Scope Complex, Core 1, 7 Lodi Rd, New Delhi 110 003; tel. (11) 362200; telex 3161045; fax (11) 362077; f. 1963; export of iron and manganese ore, ferro-manganese, finished stainless steel products, mica, coal and other minor minerals, import of steel, non-ferrous metals, rough diamonds, fertilizers, etc. for supply to industrial units in the country; cap. p.u. Rs350m., res and surplus Rs 2,128.5m. (March 1989); 10 regional offices in India, foreign offices in Japan and Romania; Chair. I. G. JHINGRAN; Man. Dir S. K. AGRAWAL.

Projects and Equipment Corpn of India Ltd: Hansalaya, 15 Barakhamba Rd, New Delhi 110 001; tel. (11) 3313351; telex 3165256; fax (11) 3315279; f. 1971; export of engineering, industrial and railway equipment; undertakes turnkey and other projects and management consultancy abroad; cap. p.u. Rs15m., res and surplus Rs131.7m. (1989); Chair. and Man. Dir S. N. MALIK.

State Trading Corpn of India Ltd: Jawahar Vyapar Bhavan, Tolstoy Marg, New Delhi 110 001; tel. (11) 3313177; telex 3165734; fax (11) 3326741; f. 1956; govt undertaking dealing in exports and imports; cap. p.u. Rs300m., res and surplus Rs2,560m. (1989); 19 regional brs and 19 offices overseas; Chair. and Man. Dir S. C. VAISH.

Trade Development Authority: Bank of Baroda Bldg, 16 Parliament St, POB 767, New Delhi 110 001; tel. (11) 3320214; telex 3165155; f. 1970 to promote selective development of exports of high quality products; arranges investment in export-orientated ventures undertaken by India with foreign collaboration; brs in Frankfurt, New York, Tokyo, Harare, Dubai, Los Angeles and Kuala Lumpur; Chair. A. N. VERMA; Exec. Dir K. KIPGEN.

INDUSTRIAL AND AGRICULTURAL ORGANIZATIONS

Organizations engaged in the financing of agricultural and industrial development are listed under Finance. There are also industrial development corporations in the separate states. The following are among the more important industrial and agricultural organizations.

Coal India Ltd: 10 Netaji Subhas Rd, Calcutta 700 001; tel. (33) 202103; telex 217180; fax (33) 283373; cen. govt holding co with seven subsidiaries; responsible for almost total (more than 90%) exploration for, planning and production of coal mines; marketing of coal and its products; cap. p.u. Rs47,641.6m., turnover Rs56,001m. (1988/89); Chair. Dr M. P. NARAYANAN.

Cotton Corpn of India Ltd: Air India Bldg, 12th Floor, Nariman Point, Bombay 400 021; tel. (22) 2024363; telex 113463; fax (22) 2025130; f. 1970 as an agency in the public sector for the purchase, sale and distribution of home-produced cotton and imported cotton staple fibre; exports long staple cotton; cap. p.u. Rs230m. (March 1989); Chair. and Man. Dir M. B. LAL.

Fertilizer Corpn of India Ltd: Madhuban, 55 Nehru Place, New Delhi 110 019; tel. (11) 6439694; telex 3162797; f. 1961; fertilizer factories at Sindri, Gorakhpur, Talcher and Ramagundam, producing nitrogenous, phosphatic and some industrial products; cap. p.u. Rs5,819m., res and surplus Rs200m. (March 1989); Chair. and Man. Dir R. GUPTA.

Fertilizers and Chemicals (Travancore) Ltd: POB 14, Udyogamandal 683 501, Via Cochin, Kerala; tel. (481) 856101; telex 8855004; fax (481) 852125; f. 1943; cap. p.u. Rs3,227.7m., res and surplus Rs299m. (March 1989). Major shareholdings were acquired by Govt in 1963; mfrs of fertilizers and chemicals of different qualities. Chair. and Man. Dir S. M. JAIN (acting).

Food Corpn of India: 16–20 Barakhamba Lane, New Delhi 110 001; tel. (11) 3316871; telex 3166234; f. 1965 to undertake trading in food grains on a commercial scale but within the framework of an overall govt policy; to provide farmers an assured price for their produce; to supply food grains to the consumer at reasonable prices; also purchases, stores, distributes and sells food grains and other foodstuffs and arranges imports and handling of food grains and fertilizers at the ports; distributes sugar in a number of states and has set up rice mills; cap. p.u. Rs8,336.7m., res and surplus Rs142.7m. (March 1988); Chair. J. C. LYNN; Man. Dir J. M. LYNGDOH.

Hindustan Fertilizer Corpn Ltd: Madhuban, 55 Nehru Place, New Delhi 110 019; tel. (11) 6419771; telex 3163147; cap. p.u. Rs6,152.2m., res and surplus Rs51.3m. (March 1989); Operates Barauni, Durgapur, Haldia and Namrup fertilizer plants. Chair. and Man. Dir M. L. SHARMA.

Housing and Urban Development Corpn Ltd: HUDCO House, Lodhi Rd, New Delhi 110 003; tel. (11) 699534; telex 3161037; fax (11) 625308; f. 1970; to finance and undertake housing and urban development programmes including the setting-up of new or satellite towns and building material industries; cap. Rs980m., res and surplus Rs1,107m. (March 1988); six brs; Chair. and Man. Dir S. K. SHARMA.

Indian Dairy Corpn: Suraj Plaza II, Sayajigunj, Baroda 390 005; tel. (265) 66637; telex 175239; aims to promote dairying in India; to execute the IDA/EEC/Govt of India dairy development programme 'Operation Flood' which aims at covering 155 districts for dairy development to link them to major urban centres for milk marketing to enable the organized dairy sector to obtain a commanding share of these markets, to set up a nat. milk herd and a nat. milk network; cap. p.u. Rs10m., res and surplus Rs1,344m. (March 1988); Chair. Dr VERGHESE KURIEN; Man. Dir R. P. ANJA.

Jute Corpn of India Ltd: 1 Shakespeare Sarani, Calcutta 700 071; tel. (33) 228829; telex 217266; f. 1971; objects: (i) to undertake price support operations in respect of raw jute; (ii) to ensure remunerative prices to producers through efficient marketing; (iii) to operate a buffer stock to stabilize raw jute prices; (iv) to handle the import and export of raw jute; (v) to promote the export of jute goods; cap. p.u. Rs50m. (March 1989); Chair. and Man. Dir A. MAJUMDAR.

National Co-operative Development Corpn: 4 Siri Institutional Area, Hauz Khas, New Delhi 110 016; tel. (11) 669246; telex 3173059; f. 1963 to plan, promote and finance country-wide programmes through co-operative societies for the production, processing, marketing, storage, export and import of agricultural produce, foodstuffs and notified commodities; also programmes for the development of poultry, dairy, fish products, coir, handlooms, distribution of consumer articles in rural areas and minor forest produce in the co-operative sector; seven regional and eight project offices; Pres. DEVI LAL; Man. Dir J. K. ARORA.

National Industrial Development Corpn Ltd: Chanakya Bhavan, Africa Ave, Chanakyapuri, POB 5212, New Delhi 110 021; tel. (11) 670154; telex 3172252; f. 1954; consultative engineering services to cen. and state govts, public and private sector enterprises, the UN and overseas investors; cap. p.u. Rs7.2m. (March 1988); Chair. and Man. Dir ARUN PRASADA.

National Mineral Development Corpn Ltd: Khanij Bhavan, 10-3-311/A Castle Hills, Masab Tank, POB 1352, Hyderabad 500 028; tel. (842) 222071; telex 4256432; fax (842) 222236; f. 1958; cen. govt undertaking under the Ministry of Steel and Mines; to exploit minerals (excluding coal, atomic minerals, lignite, petroleum and natural gas) in public sector; may buy, take on lease or otherwise acquire mines for prospecting, development and exploitation; iron ore mines at Bailadila-11C, Bailadila-14 and Bailadila-5 in Madhya Pradesh, and at Donimalai in Karnataka State, and diamond mines at Panna in Madhya Pradesh; research and development laboratories and consultancy wing at Hyderabad; investigates mineral projects; iron ore production in 1989/90 was 10m. metric tons, diamond production 16,071 carats; cap. p.u. Rs1,193.2m., res and surplus Rs33.1m. (March 1989); Chair. and Man. Dir P. C. GUPTA.

National Productivity Council: Utpadakta Bhavan, Lodi Rd, New Delhi 110 003; tel. (11) 690331; telex 3166059; f. 1958 to increase productivity and to improve quality by improved techniques which aim at efficient and proper utilization of available resources; autonomous body representing national orgs of employers and labour, govt ministries, professional orgs, local productivity councils, small-scale industries and other interests; 75 mems; Chair. OTIMA BORDIA; Dir-Gen. Dr G. K. SURI.

National Research Development Corpn: 20–22 Zamroodpur Community Centre, Kailash Colony Extension, New Delhi 110 048; tel. (11) 6419945; telex 317138; fax (11) 6449401; f. 1953 to stimulate development and commercial exploitation of new inventions with financial and technical aid; finances development projects to set up demonstration units in collaboration with industry; exports technology; cap. p.u. Rs21.8m. (March 1988); Man. Dir N. K. SHARMA.

National Seeds Corpn Ltd: Beej Bhavan, Pusa, New Delhi 110 012; tel. (11) 5712292; telex 3177305; f. 1963 to improve and develop the seed industry; cap. p.u. Rs155.3m., res and surplus Rs5.9m. (March 1989); Chair. and Man. Dir S. SATYABHAMA.

The National Small Industries Corpn Ltd: Laghu Udyog Bhavan, Okhla Industrial Estate, New Delhi 110 020; tel. (11) 6837071; telex 3162376; fax (11) 6837669; f. 1955 to aid, advise, finance, protect and promote the interests of small industries; cap. p.u. Rs426.9m. (March 1990); all shares held by the Govt; Chair. Dr J. S. JUNEJA.

Rashtriya Chemicals and Fertilizers Ltd: Priyadarshini, Eastern Express Highway, Bombay 400 022; tel. (22) 5512854; telex 1171228; fax (22) 4070386; cap. p.u. Rs5,517, res and surplus Rs1,583.7m. (March 1989); Operates Trombay fertilizer plant; expansion projects and proposed new projects. Chair. and Man. Dir R. CHANDRASEKARAN (acting).

Rehabilitation Industries Corpn Ltd: 25 Mirza Ghalib St, Calcutta 700 016; tel. (33) 241181; telex 215926; f. 1959 to create employment opportunities through multi-product industries, ranging from consumer goods to engineering products and services, for refugees from Bangladesh and migrants from Pakistan, repatriates from Myanmar and Sri Lanka, and other immigrants of Indian extraction; cap. p.u. Rs47.6m. (March 1989); Chair. and Man. Dir RAJAT BARUA.

State Farms Corpn of India Ltd: Farm Bhavan, 14–15 Nehru Place, New Delhi 110 019; tel. (11) 6446901; f. 1969 to administer the central state farms; activities include the production of quality seeds of high-yielding varieties of wheat, paddy, maize, bajra and jowar; advises on soil conservation, reclamation and development of waste and forest land; consultancy services on farm mechanization; cap. p.u. Rs191m., res and surplus Rs29m. (March 1989); Chair. A. R. MALLU; Man. Dir M. ALI KHAN.

Steel Authority of India Ltd: Ispat Bhavan, Lodi Rd, POB 3049, New Delhi 110 003; tel. (11) 690481; telex 3162689; fax (11) 625051; f. 1973 to provide co-ordinated development of the steel industry in both the public and private sectors; steel plants at Bhilai, Bokaro, Durgapur, Rourkela; alloy steel plants at Durgapur and Salem; subsidiaries: Visvesvaraya Iron and Steel Ltd, Maharashtra Elektrosmelt Ltd, Iisco-ujjain Pipe and Foundry Co Ltd, and Indian Iron and Steel Corpn Ltd, Burnpur; combined ingot steel capacity is 10.9m. metric tons annually; cap. p.u. Rs39,859m., res Rs5,192.4m. (March 1990); Chair. S. R. JAIN.

Tea Board of India: 14 Brabourne Rd, POB 2172, Calcutta 700 001; tel. (33) 260210; telex 214527; f. to provide financial assistance to tea research stations; sponsors and finances independent research projects in universities and tech. institutions to supplement the work of tea research establishments; also promotes tea production and export; Chair. PRANAB KUMAR BORA.

PRINCIPAL INDUSTRIAL ASSOCIATIONS

Ahmedabad Textile Mills' Association: Ranchhodlal Marg, Navrangpura, POB 4056, Ahmedabad 380 009; tel. (272) 402273; telex 126227; f. 1891; 36 mems; Pres. MANUBHAI H. PATEL; Exec. Dir M. D. RAJPAL.

All India Federation of Master Printers: E-14, South Extn Market Part II, 3rd Floor, New Delhi 110 049; tel. (11) 6449855; f. 1954; 31 affiliates, 6,000 mems; Pres. H. M. ANANTHARAM; Gen. Sec. C. R. JANARDHAN.

All India Manufacturers' Organization (AIMO): Jeevan Sahakar, 4th Floor, Sir P.M. Rd, Fort, Bombay 400 001; tel. (22) 2861016; telex 1186179; f. 1941; 1,500 mems; Pres. KAMAL M. MORARKA; Sr Vice-Pres. VIJAY G. KALANTRI.

Association of Indian Automobile Manufacturers: 148 M.G. Rd, Bombay 400 023; tel. (22) 242416; telex 1184869; f. 1960; 29 mems; Pres. ABHAY FIRODIA; Sec. S. G. SHAH.

Association of Man-made Fibre Industry of India: Resham Bhavan, 78 Veer Nariman Rd, Bombay 400 020; tel. (22) 2040009; telex 113925; f. 1954; 9 mems; Pres. INDU PAREKH; Sec.-Gen. D. H. VORA.

Automotive Component Manufacturers' Association of India: S-253 Greater Kailash-I, New Delhi 110 048; tel. (11) 6426186; telex 3161825; 178 mems; Pres. T. K. BALAJI; Exec. Dir N. SRINIVASAN.

Automotive Tyre Manufacturers' Association: 9A Connaught Place, New Delhi 110 001; tel. (11) 3325812; telex 3161762; 11 mems; Chair. V. K. MODI; Sec.-Gen. D. RAVINDRAN.

Bharat Krishak Samaj (Farmers' Forum, India): Dr Panjabrao Deshmukh Krishak Bhavan, A-1 Nizamuddin West, New Delhi 110 013; tel. (11) 619508; f. 1954; national farmers' org.; Pres. (ex-officio) Minister of Agriculture; 1m. ordinary mems, 43,000 life mems; Chair. Dr BAL RAM JAKHAR; Gen. Sec. S. L. SHAH.

Bombay Metal Exchange Ltd: 88/90 Kika St, Bombay 400 004; tel. (22) 8550964; 330 mems; Pres. SEVANTILAL M. MORAKHIA; Sec. S. M. SANGHVI.

Bombay Millowners' Association: Elphinstone Bldg, 10 Veer Nariman Rd, Fort, POB 95, Bombay 400 001; tel. (22) 2040411; telex 1185372; f. 1875; 36 mem. cos; Chair. NUSLI N. WADIA; Sec.-Gen. R. L. N. VIJAYANAGAR.

Bombay Motor Merchants' Association Ltd: Sukh Sagar, 3rd Floor, Sandhurst Bridge, Bombay 400 007; tel. (22) 8112769; 405 mems; Pres. S. TARLOCHAN SINGH ANAND; Gen. Sec. MANMOHAN S. CHADHA.

Bombay Piece-Goods Merchants' Mahajan: 250 Shaikh Memon St, Bombay 400 002; tel. (22) 255750; f. 1881; 1,770 mems; Pres. SURENDRA TULSIDAS SAVAI; Hon. Secs P. P. NARSANA, D. M. MEHTA.

Bombay Shroff Association: 233 Shroff Bazar, Bombay 400 002; tel. (22) 325588; 430 mems; Pres. CHANDRAKANT P. JERAJANI; Chief Exec. KISORE J. SHAH.

Calcutta Baled Jute Association: 6 Netaji Subhas Rd, Calcutta 700 001; tel. (33) 208393; telex 217369; f. 1892; 49 mems; Chair. PURANMULL KANKARIA; Sec. A. E. SCOLT.

Calcutta Flour Mills Association: 6 Netaji Subhas Rd, Calcutta 700 001; tel. (33) 208393; telex 217369; f. 1932; 22 mems; Chair. D. N. JATIA; Sec. PROSENJIT DAS GUPTA.

Calcutta Tea Traders' Association: 6 Netaji Subhas Rd, Calcutta 700 001; tel. (33) 208393; telex 217369; f. 1886; 1,173 mems; Chair. Ms AFROZE RANDERIAN; Sec. PROSENJIT DASGUPTA.

Cement Manufacturers' Association: Vishnu Kiran Chamber, 2142-47, Gurdwara Rd, New Delhi 110 005; tel. (11) 5713268; telex 3162230; 58 mems; Pres. M. H. DALMIA; Sec.-Gen. S. M. CHAKRAVARTY.

Confederation of the Engineering Industry (CEI): 23–26 Institutional Area, Lodi Rd, New Delhi 110 003; tel. (11) 615115; telex

3166655; fax (11) 694298; f. 1986; 2,551 mem. cos, 35 affiliated asscns; Pres. V. SRINIVASAN; Dir-Gen. TARUN DAS.

East India Cotton Association Ltd: Cotton Exchange, Marwari Bazar, Bombay 400 002; tel. (22) 314876; telex 1183152; f. 1921; 366 mems; Pres. CHANDRASINH H. MIRANI; Secs HEMANT MULKY, S. S. BARODIA.

Federation of Gujarat Mills and Industries: Federation Bldg, Sampatrao Colony, R. C. Dutt Rd, Baroda 390 005; tel. (265) 325101; f. 1918; 300 mems; Pres. JAL PATEL; Sec. Dr PARESH RAVAL.

Federation of Indian Export Organizations: PHD House, 3rd Floor, Siri Institutional Area, Hauz Khas, opposite Asian Games Village, New Delhi 110 016; tel. (11) 666582; telex 3173194; f. 1965; 1,650 mems; Pres. RAMU S. DEORA; Sec.-Gen. CHANDRAKANT G. RAO.

Grain, Rice and Oilseeds Merchants' Association: Grainseeds House, 72/80 Yusef Meheralli Rd, Bombay 400 003; tel. (22) 8554021; f. 1899; 950 mems; Pres. SHARADKUMAR DEVRAJ; Secs A. SHAMJI, Z. LALJI.

Indian Chemical Manufacturers' Association: Phelps Bldg, 9A Connaught Place, New Delhi 110 001; tel. (11) 3327421; f. 1938; 240 mems; Pres. ATMARAM SARAOGI; Chief Exec. R. PARTHASARATHY.

Indian Drug Manufacturers' Association: 102B Poonam Chambers, Dr A. B. Rd, Worli, Bombay 400 018; tel. (22) 4926308; telex 1176239; 800 mems; Pres. N. I. GANDHI; Sec.-Gen. I. A. ALVA.

Indian Jute Mills Association: Royal Exchange, 6 Netaji Subhas Rd, Calcutta 700 001; tel. (33) 209918; telex 217369; sponsors and operates export promotion, research and product development; regulates labour relations; 35 mems; Chair. H. V. KANORIA; Sec. S. RAY.

Indian Leather Products Association: India Exchange, 4 India Exchange Place, Calcutta 700 001; tel. (33) 207763; telex 217239; 175 mems; Pres. S. S. SAWHNEY; Exec. Dir S. K. GUPTA.

Indian Mining Association: 6 Netaji Subhas Rd, Calcutta 700 001; tel. (33) 263861; telex 217369; f. 1892; 50 mems; Sec. K. MUKERJEE.

Indian Mining Federation: 135 Biplabi Rashbehari Basu Rd, Calcutta 700 001; tel. (33) 250484; f. 1913; 33 mems; Chair. H. S. CHOPRA; Sec. S. K. GHOSE.

Indian Motion Picture Producers' Association: Imppa House, Dr Ambedkar Rd, Bombay 400 050; tel. (22) 6486344; f. 1938; 1,200 mems; Pres. SHAKTI SAMANTA; Sec. ANIL NAGRATH.

Indian National Shipowners' Association: 22 Maker Tower, F, Cuffe Parade, Bombay 400 005; tel. (22) 212103; telex 1184611; f. 1929; 23 mems; Pres. SHASHIKANT N. RUIA; CEO B. V. NILKUND.

Indian Oil & Produce Exporters' Association: 78/79 Bajaj Bhavan, Nariman Point, Bombay 400 021; tel. (22) 2023225; telex 115637; 200 mems; Chair. H. V. MARIWALA; Sec. G. CHANDRASHEKHAR.

Indian Paper Mills Association: India Exchange, 8th Floor, India Exchange Place, Calcutta 700 001; tel. (33) 203242; telex 217432; f. 1939; 37 mems; Pres. N. D. MOHTA; Sec. B. GHOSH.

Indian Refractory Makers' Association: Royal Exchange, 6 Netaji Subhas Rd, Calcutta 700 001; tel. (33) 208393; telex 217369; 95 mems; Pres. R. H. DALMIA.

Indian Soap and Toiletries Makers' Association: 614 Rahela Centre, Free Press Journal Marg, Bombay 400 021; tel. (22) 224115; 67 mems; Pres. P. M. SINHA; Sec. K. H. BHAGELA.

Indian Sugar Mills Association: 'Sugar House', 39 Nehru Place, New Delhi 110 019; tel. (11) 6416601; telex 3162654; f. 1932; 170 mems; Pres. S. V. BALASUBRAMANIAM; Sec.-Gen. S. L. JAIN.

Indian Tea Association: Royal Exchange, 6 Netaji Subhas Rd, Calcutta 700 001; tel. (33) 208393; telex 217369; f. 1881; 63 mem. cos; 249 tea estates; Chair. NARENDRA KUMAR; Sec.-Gen. M. K. CHOUDHURI.

Indian Woollen Mills' Federation: Churchgate Chambers, 5 New Marine Lines, Bombay 400 020; tel. (22) 298075; telex 1183067; f. 1963; 47 ordinary mems, 25 assoc. mems; Chair. K. C. BOTHRA; Sec.-Gen. A. C. CHAUDHURI.

Industries and Commerce Association: ICO Association Rd, POB 70, Dhanbad 826 001; tel. (326) 2639; f. 1933; 50 mems; Pres. D. K. AGARWALLA; Sr Vice-Pres. UMESH CHAND.

Jute Balers' Association: 12 India Exchange Place, Calcutta 700 001; tel. (33) 201491; f. 1909; 276 mems; represents all Indian jute balers; Chair. SATYANARAYAN TOSHNIWAL; Sec. SUJIT CHOUDHURY.

Maharashtra Motor Parts Dealers' Association: 13 Kala Bhavan, 3 Mathew Rd, Bombay 400 004; tel. (22) 8114468; 390 mems; Pres. K. C. KHANDELWAL; Sec. PRAVIN V. SHAH.

Master Stevedores' Association: Royal Exchange, 6 Netaji Subhas Rd, Calcutta 700 001; tel. (33) 208393; telex 217369; f. 1934; 11 mems; Pres. D. S. BOSE; Sec. ALBAN E. SCOLT.

Organization of Pharmaceutical Producers of India (OPPI): Cook's Blg, 324 Dr D.N. Rd, Bombay 400 001; tel. (22) 2045509; telex 113880; 63 mems; Pres. Dr S. AGARWALA; Sec. R. D. JOSHI.

Silk and Art Silk Mills' Association Ltd: Resham Bhavan, 78 Veer Nariman Rd, Bombay 400 020; tel. (22) 2041006; f. 1939; 345 mems; Chair. M. H. DOSHI; Sec. K. A. SAMUEL.

Southern India Mills' Association: Racecourse, Coimbatore 641 018, Tamil Nadu; f. 1933; 200 mems; Chair. D. LAKSHMINARAYANASWAMY; Sec. T. RANGASWAMY.

United Planters' Association of Southern India (UPASI): Glenview, POB 11, Coonoor 643 101; tel. 20270; telex 853211; f. 1893; 800 mems; Pres. G. G. MUTHANNA; Sec. B. SIVARAM.

EMPLOYERS' FEDERATIONS

Council of Indian Employers: Federation House, Tansen Marg, New Delhi 110 001; tel. (11) 3319251; telex 3161768; f. 1956; Sec. R. C. PANDE; comprises:

All India Organization of Employers (AIOE): Federation House, Tansen Marg, New Delhi 110 001; tel. (11) 3319251; telex 3161768; fax (11) 3320714; f. 1932; 62 industrial asscn mems and 164 corporate cos; Pres. CHIRAYU R. AMIN; Sec.-Gen. D. H. PAI PANANDIKER.

Employers' Federation of India (EFI): Army and Navy Bldg, 148 Mahatma Gandhi Rd, Bombay 400 023; tel. (22) 244232; telex 1182529; f. 1933; 31 asscn mems, 183 co mems, 19 hon. mems; Pres. KESHUB MAHINDRA; Sec.-Gen. S. K. NANDA.

Standing Conference of Public Enterprises (SCOPE): SCOPE Complex, 7 Lodhi Rd, New Delhi 110 003; tel. (11) 360101; telex 3174057; f. 1973; representative body of all central public enterprises in India; advises the Govt and public enterprises on matters of major policy and co-ordination; trade enquiries, regarding imports and exports of commodities, carried out on behalf of mems; 200 mems; Chair. MOOSA RAZA; Sec.-Gen. WARIS RASHEED KIDWAI.

Employers' Association of Northern India: 14/113 Civil Lines, POB 344, Kanpur 208 001; tel. (512) 210513; f. 1937; 179 mems; Chair. Dr K. B. AGARWAL; Sec.-Gen. S. C. SAXENA.

Employers' Federation of Southern India: Karumuttu Centre, 498 Anna Salai, Madras 600 035; tel. (44) 451452; telex 417036; fax (44) 451264; f. 1920; 265 mem. firms; Pres. RAVI BHOOTHALINGAM; Sec. N. KANNAN.

TRADE UNIONS

In the absence of compulsory registration and the need to file returns, a precise estimate of the aggregate trades-union membership in India is not available, but in 1986 it was believed that only about 10m. workers, out of a labour force of 222.5m., belonged to unions.

Indian National Trade Union Congress (INTUC): 1B Maulana Azad Rd, New Delhi 110 011; tel. (11) 3018150; f. 1947; the largest and most representative trade union org. in India; 4,408 affiliated unions with a total membership of 5,179,572; affiliated to ICFTU; 26 state brs and 28 nat. industrial feds; Pres. G. RAMANUJAM; Gen. Sec. Shri GOPESHWAR.

Bharatiya Mazdoor Sangh: Ram Naresh Bhavan, Tilak Gali, New Delhi 110 055; tel. (11) 523644; f. 1955; 3,890,013 mems; 24 state brs; 27 nat. feds; Pres. R. B. JOSHI; Gen. Sec. G. PRABHAKAR.

Centre of Indian Trade Unions: 6 Talkatora Rd, New Delhi 110 001; tel. (11) 384071; f. 1970; 1.8m. mems; 20 state brs; over 3,000 affiliated unions; Pres. E. BALANANDAN; Gen. Sec. SAMAR MUKHERJEE.

National industrial federations:

All India Council of Atomic Energy Employees: Tel Rasayan Bhavan, Tilak Rd, Dadar, Bombay 400 014; f. 1981; 3,000 mems; Pres. RAJA KULKARNI; Gen. Sec. MARY EMMANUEL.

Indian National Cement Workers' Federation: Mazdoor Karyalaya, Congress House, Bombay 400 004; tel. (22) 351809; 76,816 mems; 49 affiliated unions; Pres. H. N. TRIVEDI; Gen. Sec. N. NANJAPPAN.

Indian National Chemical Workers' Federation: Tel Rasayan Bhavan, Tilak Rd, Dadar, Bombay 400 014; tel. (22) 4121742; Pres. RAJA KULKARNI; Gen. Sec. K. H. DASTOOR.

Indian National Electricity Workers' Federation: 19 Mazdoor Maidan, Power House, Jaipur 302 006; tel. (141) 76175; 124,600 mems; 17 affiliated unions; Pres. DALIP SINGH AZAD; Gen. Sec. DAMODAR MAURYA.

Indian National Metal Workers' Federation: 26 K Rd, Jamshedpur 831 001; tel. (657) 3506; Pres. V. G. GOPAL; Gen. Sec. S. GOPESHWAR.

Indian National Mineworkers' Federation: Michael John Smriti Bhawan, Rajendra Path, Dhanbad, Bihar; tel. 3506;

INDIA

f. 1949; 351,454 mems in 139 affiliated unions; Pres. KANTI MEHTA; Gen. Sec. S. DAS GUPTA.

Indian National Paper Mill Workers' Federation: Ballarpur, Chanda; Pres. G. SANJEEVA REDDY; Gen. Sec. P. J. NAIR.

Indian National Port and Dock Workers' Federation: POB 87, Vasco-da-Gama 403 802, Goa; f. 1954; 18 affiliated unions; 81,000 mems; Pres. S. R. KULKARNI; Gen. Sec. JANAKI MUKHERJEE.

Indian National Press Workers' Federation: 162 South Ave, New Delhi 110 011; Pres. S. W. DHABE.

Indian National Sugar Mills Workers' Federation: 19 Lajpatrai Marg, Lucknow; tel. (522) 47638; 100 affiliated unions; 40,000 mems; Pres. C. SINGH; Gen. Sec. RAM YASH SINGH.

Indian National Textile Workers' Federation: Mazdoor Manzil, G. D. Ambekar Marg, Parel, Bombay 400 012; tel. (22) 4123713; f. 1948; 430 affiliated unions; 484,879 mems; Pres. P. L. SUBBIAH; Gen. Sec. H. J. NAIK.

Indian National Transport Workers' Federation: Sham Shivir, Tansen Marg, Gwalior 474 002; Pres. T. S. VIYOGI; Gen. Sec. K. S. VERMA.

National Federation of Petroleum Workers: Tel Rasayan Bhavan, Tilak Rd, Dadar, Bombay 400 014; tel. (22) 4121742; f. 1959; 22,340 mems; Pres. RAJA KULKARNI.

Assam Chah Karmachari Sangha: POB 13, Dibrugarh 786 001; tel. (33) 20870; 12,039 mems; 20 brs; Pres. BIJOY CHANDRA BHAGAVATI; Gen. Sec. A. K. BHATTACHARYA.

All India Trade Union Congress (AITUC): 24 Canning Lane, New Delhi 110 001; tel. (11) 386427; f. 1920; affiliated to WFTU; more than 3.4m. mems, c. 4,000 affiliated unions; 22 state brs, 10 national federations; Pres. M. S. KRISHNAN; Sec. HOMI DOJI.

Major affiliated unions:

  Annamalai Plantation Workers' Union: Valparai, Via Pollachi, Tamil Nadu; over 21,000 mems.

  Zilla Cha Bagan Workers' Union: Mal, Jalpaiguri, West Bengal; 15,000 mems; Pres. NEHAR MUKHERJEE; Gen. Sec. BIMAL DAS GUPTA.

United Trades Union Congress (UTUC): 249 Bepin Behari Ganguly St, Calcutta 700 012; tel. (33) 275609; f. 1949; 963,023 mems from 803 affiliated unions; 10 state brs and 6 nat. feds; Pres. C. BABY JOHN; Gen. Sec. JATIN CHAKRABORTY.

Major affiliated unions:

  All India Farm Labour Union: c/o UTUC Jakkanpur New Area, Patna 800 001, Bihar; c. 35,000 mems; Pres. MAHENDRA SINGH TIKAIT.

  Bengal Provincial Chatkal Mazdoor Union: Calcutta; textile workers; 28,330 mems.

Hind Mazdoor Sabha (HMS): Nagindas Chambers, 167 P. D'Mello Rd, Bombay 400 001; tel. (22) 2612185; f. 1948; affiliated to ICFTU; 2.8m. mems from 1,724 affiliated unions; 18 state brs; 18 nat. industrial feds; Pres. SAMARENDRA KUNDU; Gen. Sec. UMRAOMAL PUROHIT.

Major affiliated unions:

  Bombay Port Trust Employees' Union: Pres. Dr SHANTI PATEL; Gen. Sec. S. K. SHETYE.

  Colliery Mazdoor Congress, Asansol (Coalminers' Union): Pres. MADHU DANDAVATE; Gen. Sec. JAYANTA PODDER.

  Koyala Ispat Mazdoor Panchayat, Jharia (Steel Workers' Union): Gen. Sec. HIT NARAYAN SINGH.

  Oil and Natural Gas Commission Employees' Mazdoor Sabha: Vododara; 4,000 mems; Pres. R. DULARE; Gen. Sec. G. G. PARADKAR.

  South Central Railway Mazdoor Union: 7C Railway Bldg, Accounts Office Compound, Secunderabad 500 371; tel. (842) 6994; f. 1966; 73,150 mems; Pres. K. S. N. MURTHY; Gen. Sec. N. SUNDARESAN; 126 brs.

  West Bengal Cha Mazdoor Sabha: Cha Shramik Bhavan, Jalpaiguri 735 101, West Bengal; tel. 349; f. 1947; 45,000 mems; Pres. SRIRAM SINGH; Gen. Sec. SAMIR ROY.

Confederation of Central Government Employees and Workers: New Delhi 110 060; tel. (11) 587804; 1.2m. mems; Pres. S. MADHUSUDAN; Sec.-Gen. S. K. VYAS.

Affiliated union:

  National Federation of Post, Telephone and Telegraph Employees (NFPTTE): C-1/2 Baird Rd, New Delhi 110 001; tel. (11) 322545; f. 1954; 221,880 mems (est.); Pres. R. G. SHARMA; Gen. Sec. O. P. GUPTA.

All India Bank Employees' Association (AIBEA): New Delhi; Pres. D. P. CHADDA; Gen. Sec. TARAKESWAR CHAKRAVARTY.

All India Defence Employees' Federation (AIDEF): 70 Market Rd, Kirkee, Pune 411 003; tel. (212) 58761; 325 affiliated unions; 409,000 mems; Pres. SAMUEL AUGUSTINE; Gen. Sec. K. M. MATHEW.

All India Port and Dock Workers' Federation: 9 Second Line Beach, Madras 600 001; tel. (44) 25983; f. 1948; 100,000 mems in 26 affiliated unions; Pres. S. R. KULKARNI; Gen. Sec. S. C. C. ANTHONY PILLAI.

All India Railwaymen's Federation (AIRF): 4 State Entry Rd, New Delhi 110 055; tel. (11) 343493; f. 1924; 934,412 mems; 16 affiliated unions; Pres. UMRAOMAL PUROHIT; Gen. Sec. J. P. CHAUBEY.

National Federation of Indian Railwaymen (NFIR): 3 Chelmsford Rd, New Delhi 110 055; tel. (11) 352013; f. 1952; 20 affiliated unions; 828,493 mems; Pres. KESHAV H. KULKARNI; Gen. Sec. SASHI BHUSAN RAO.

Transport

RAILWAYS

India's railway system is the largest in Asia and the fourth largest in the world. The total length of Indian railways in 1988/89 was 61,990 route-km. The Government exercises direct or indirect control over all railways through the Railway Board.

A 16.43-km underground railway for Calcutta was scheduled for completion by 1988. In 1986 the underground network covered a total of 10 km, in two sections. When completed, it is expected to carry more than 1m. people daily.

Indian Government Administration (Ministry of Railways, Railway Board): Rail Bhavan, Raisina Rd, New Delhi; tel. (11) 388931; telex 313561; Chair. RICHARD DAVID KITSON.

Zonal Railways

The railways are grouped into nine zones:

Central: Victoria Terminus, Bombay 400 001; tel. (22) 4151551; telex 1173819; Gen. Man. A. N. SHUKLA.

Eastern: 17 Netaji Subhas Rd, Calcutta 700 001; tel. (33) 226811; Gen. Man. M. K. RAO.

North Eastern: Gorakhpur 273 012; tel. (551) 3041; Gen. Man. GAURI SHANKAR.

Northeast Frontier: Maligaon, Guwahati 781 011; tel. 88422; telex 2352336; f. 1958; Gen. Man. K. RAMAKRISHNAN.

Northern: Baroda House, New Delhi 110 001; tel. (11) 387227; Gen. Man. S. M. VAISH.

South Central: Rail Nilayam, Secunderabad 500 371; tel. (842) 74848; Gen. Man. R. NARASIMHAN.

South Eastern: Calcutta 700 043; tel. (33) 451741; Gen. Man. S. P. JAIN.

Southern: Park Town, Madras 600 003; tel. (44) 564141; Gen. Man. N. VENKATASUBRAMANIAN.

Western: Churchgate, Bombay 400 020; tel. (22) 291502; Gen. Man. M. V. SRINIVASAN.

ROADS

In October 1989 there were about 2m. km of roads in India, 36,112 km of which were national highways.

Ministry of Surface Transport (Roads Wing): 1 Transport Bhavan, Parliament St, New Delhi 110 001; tel. (11) 3714938; telex 312448; responsible for the maintenance of India's system of national highways, with a total length of 36,112 km in 1989, connecting the state capitals and major ports and linking with the highway systems of neighbouring countries. This system includes 63 highways which constitute the main trunk roads of the country.

Border Roads Development Board: f. 1960 to accelerate the economic development of the north and north-eastern border areas; it has constructed and improved 20,449 km of roads and maintains about 18,000 km (1988).

INLAND WATERWAYS

About 15,655 km of rivers are navigable by power-driven craft, and 3,490 km by large country boats. Services are mainly on the Ganga and Brahmaputra and their tributaries, the Godavari, the Mahanadi, the Narmada, the Tapi and the Krishna.

Central Inland Water Transport Corpn Ltd: 4 Fairlie Place, Calcutta 1; tel. (33) 202321; telex 212779; f. 1967; inland water transport services in Bangladesh and the north-east Indian states; also shipbuilding and repairing, general engineering, dredging, lightening of ships and barge services; Chair. and Man. Dir S. K. BHOSE.

SHIPPING

In July 1984 India was 16th on the list of principal merchant fleets of the world. In December 1990 the fleet had 405 vessels, with a total displacement of 5.92m. grt. There are some 55 shipping companies in India. The major ports are Bombay, Calcutta, Haldia, Kandla, Kochi, Madras, Mormugao, New Mangalore, Paradip (Paradeep), Tuticorin and Visakhapatnam. An auxiliary port to Calcutta at Haldia was opened to international shipping in 1977 and has since undergone further modernization. A new port (named Jawaharlal Nehru Port) at Nhava Sheva, near Bombay, was commissioned in 1989.

Bombay

Bharat Line Ltd: Bharat House, 104 Apollo St, Fort, Bombay 400 001; Chair. and Man. Dir GUNVANTRAI T. KAMDAR; brs in Calcutta, Bhavnagar and Madras.

Chowgule Steamships Ltd: Bakhtawar, 3rd Floor, Nariman Point, POB 11596, Bombay 400 021; tel. (22) 2026822; telex 112409; f. 1963; eight bulk carriers and one tanker totalling 381,215 dwt; Chair. VISHWASRAO DATTAJI CHOWGULE; Man. Dir SHIVAJIRAO DATTAJI CHOWGULE.

Great Eastern Shipping Co Ltd: Hong Kong Bank Bldg, 60 Mahatma Gandhi Rd, Bombay 400 001; tel. (22) 274869; telex 112824; f. 1948; cargo services; 33 vessels; Chair. VASANT J. SHETH; Dep. Chair. and Man. Dir K. M. SHETH; br. in New Delhi.

Scindia Steam Navigation Co Ltd: Scindia House, Narottam Morarjee Marg, Ballard Estate, Fort, Bombay 400 038; tel. (22) 2618162; telex 1173519; fax (22) 2618160; f. 1919; cargo services; 13 vessels (incl. three bulk carriers) totalling 361,914 dwt; Chair. N. S. PARULEKAR; Man. Dir V. M. PAREKH; br. in Calcutta.

Shipping Corpn of India Ltd: Shipping House, 245 Madame Cama Rd, Bombay 400 021; tel. (22) 2026666; telex 1182371; f. 1961 as a govt undertaking; fleet of 125 vessels consisting of tankers, freighters, VLCCs, combination carriers, product carriers, passenger-cum-cargo ships, bulk carriers totalling 4.9m. dwt; brs in Calcutta, New Delhi, Mombasa and London; Chair. and Man. Dir JAGDISH C. SHETH.

South-East Asia Shipping Co Ltd: 402–406 Himalaya House, Dr Dadabhoy Naoroji Rd, Bombay 400 001; tel. (22) 269231; telex 112753; f. 1948; world-wide cargo services; five vessels totalling 61,259 dwt; Chair. N. H. DHUNJIBHOY; CEO D. P. ADENWALLA.

Calcutta

India Steamship Co Ltd: 21 Hemanta Basu Sarani, POB 2090, Calcutta 700 001; tel. (33) 281171; telex 212549; f. 1928; cargo services; 25 vessels totalling 531,562 dwt; Chair. K. K. BIRLA; Man. Dir L. M. S. RAJWAR; brs in Bombay, Delhi and London.

Surrendra Overseas Ltd: Apeejay House, 15 Park St, Calcutta 700 016; tel. (33) 295455; telex 213485; cargo services; nine vessels totalling 274,000 dwt; Dir JIT PAUL.

Madras

South India Shipping Corpn Ltd: Chennai House, 7 Esplanade Rd, POB 234, Madras 600 108; tel. (44) 30141; telex 41371; nine vessels; Chair. J. H. TARAPORE; Man. Dir F. G. DASTUR.

CIVIL AVIATION

There are four international airports in India: Bombay Airport, Calcutta Airport, Delhi Airport and Madras Airport. There are about 90 other airports. In September 1989 it was announced that Ahmedabad Airport was to be upgraded to an international airport.

Air India: Air India Bldg, Nariman Point, Bombay 400 021; tel. (22) 2024142; telex 1178327; fax (22) 2023686; f. 1932 as Tata Airlines; renamed Air India in 1946; in 1953 became a state corpn responsible for international flights; services to 38 online stations in 24 countries covering four continents; Chair. and Man. Dir SUBHASH GUPTA (acting); fleet of 10 Boeing 747-200B, 3 Airbus A300-B4, 8 Airbus A310-300, 2 Boeing 747-300C.

Indian Airlines: Airlines House, 113 Gurudwara Rakabganj Rd, Parliament St, New Delhi 110 001; tel. (11) 3718951; telex 3166110; fax (11) 381730; f. 1953; state corpn responsible for regional and domestic flights; services to 67 cities throughout India and in Afghanistan, Bangladesh, Maldives, Nepal, Pakistan, Singapore, Sri Lanka and Thailand; Chair. and Man. Dir Air Marshal S. S. RAMDAS; fleet of 30 Boeing 737, 11 Airbus 300, 14 Airbus 320, 3 HS 748, 4 F-27.

Vayudoot Private Ltd: Safdarjung Airport, New Delhi 110 003; tel. (11) 693851; telex 3161052; fax (11) 3295312; f. 1981 to connect the smaller towns of north-western and eastern India; links 78 airfields with Calcutta, Delhi, Hyderabad and Bombay; jtly owned by Indian Airlines and Air India; Chair. and Man. Dir Air Marshal S. S. RAMDAS; fleet of 11 HAL 748, 4 F-27-100, 11 Dornier 228.

Tourism

The tourist attractions of India include its scenery, its historic forts, palaces and temples, and its rich variety of wild life. Tourist infrastructure has recently been expanded by the provision of more luxury hotels and improved means of transport. In 1989 there were 1,736,093 foreign visitors to India, and in 1989/90 revenue from tourism totalled Rs 24,560m.

Department of Tourism of the Government of India: Ministry of Commerce and Tourism, Transport Bhavan, Parliament St, New Delhi 110 001; tel. (11) 37117890; telex 3166527; fax (11) 3710518; formulates and administers govt policy for promotion of tourism; plans the organization and development of tourist facilities; operates tourist information offices in India and overseas; Dir-Gen. YOGESH CHANDRA.

India Tourism Development Corpn Ltd: Scope Complex, Core VIII, 7 Lodi Rd, New Delhi 110 003; tel. (11) 360303; telex 3174074; fax (11) 360233; f. 1966; operates hotels (largest hotel chain owner), resort accommodation, tourist transport services, duty-free shops and a travel agency and provides consultancy and management services; Chair. and Man. Dir YOGESH CHANDRA.

Atomic Energy

There are three operating nuclear power stations, at Tarapur near Bombay, at Kalpahkam (Tamil Nadu) and at Kota (Rajasthan). Four more stations are being built at Narora (Uttar Pradesh), Kakrapar (Gujarat), Kaiga (Karnataka), and Rawatbhata (Rajasthan). India has six heavy water plants in operation and two more are under construction. A nuclear fuel complex at Hyderabad (Andhra Pradesh) produces the fuel required by the nuclear power stations.

Department of Atomic Energy: South Block, New Delhi 110 011; tel. (11) 3011773; telex 3166182; fax (11) 3013843; Dr P. K. IYENGAR.

Atomic Energy Commission: Anushakti Bhavan, Chatrapati Shivaji Mharaj Marg, Bombay 400 039; tel. (22) 2022543; telex 112355; fax (22) 2048476; organizes research on the use of atomic energy for peaceful purposes; Chair. Dr P. K. IYENGAR; Sec. S. RAJAGOPAL.

Bhabha Atomic Research Centre (BARC): Trombay, Bombay 400 085; tel. (22) 5518700; telex 1171017; f. 1957; national centre for research in and development of nuclear energy for peaceful uses; Dir Dr R. CHIDAMBARAM; five research reactors:

APSARA: 1 MW, research and isotope production, criticality 1956.

CIRUS: 40 MW, isotope production and material testing, criticality 1960.

ZERLINA: Zero Energy Reactor for Lattice Investigations and New Assemblies, criticality 1961, decommissioned 1983.

PURNIMA: criticality 1972, originally Plutonium Oxide fuelled fast critical facility, modified as PURNIMA II with Uranium 233 in the form of Uranyl nitrate solution as fuel, criticality 1984. Modified as PURNIMA III to mock-up the core of the KAMINI reactor, which is under construction at Igcar, Kalpakkam.

DHRUVA: 100 MW, research, isotope production, material and reactor components testing, criticality 1985.

Other major facilities include:

ISOMED: for radiation sterilization of medical products.

FRP: Fuel reprocessing plants at Trombay to reprocess irradiated fuel from CIRUS and DHRUVA, and at Tarapur for power reactor fuel reprocessing.

Van de Graaff: 5.5-MV accelerator for studies in nuclear reactions, ion implantation etc.

Radio Metallurgy Laboratories: with facility to fabricate uranium oxide and plutonium oxide MOX fuel.

Reactor Engineering Laboratories: for analysing and testing both power and research reactor components.

Waste Management: research and development plants at Trombay and Tarapur.

INDONESIA

Introductory Survey

Location, Climate, Language, Religion, Flag, Capital
The Republic of Indonesia consists of a group of about 13,700 islands, lying between the mainland of South-East Asia and Australia. The archipelago is the largest in the world, and it stretches from the Malay peninsula to New Guinea. The principal islands are Java, Sumatra, Kalimantan (Borneo), Sulawesi (Celebes), Irian Jaya (West New Guinea), the Moluccas and Timor. Indonesia's only land frontiers are with Papua New Guinea, to the east of Irian Jaya, and with the Malaysian states of Sarawak and Sabah, which occupy northern Borneo. The climate is tropical, with an average annual temperature of 26°C (79°F) and heavy rainfall during most seasons. The official language is Bahasa Indonesia (a form of Malay) but some 25 local languages (mainly Javanese) and more than 250 dialects are also spoken. An estimated 87% of the inhabitants profess adherence to Islam. About 10% of the population are Christians, while most of the remainder are either Hindus or Buddhists. The national flag (proportions 3 by 2) has two equal horizontal stripes, of red and white. The capital is Jakarta, on the island of Java.

Recent History
Indonesia was formerly the Netherlands East Indies, except for the former Portuguese colony of East Timor (see below).

Dutch occupation began in the 17th century and gradually extended over the whole archipelago. Nationalist opposition to colonial rule began in the early 20th century. During the Second World War the territory was occupied by Japanese forces from March 1942. On 17 August 1945, three days after the Japanese surrender, a group of nationalists proclaimed the independence of Indonesia. The first President of the self-proclaimed republic was Dr Sukarno, a leader of the nationalist movement since the 1920s. The declaration of independence was not recognized by the Netherlands, which attempted to restore its pre-war control of the islands. After four years of intermittent warfare and negotiations between the Dutch authorities and the nationalists, agreement was reached on a formal transfer of power. On 27 December 1949 the United States of Indonesia became legally independent, with Dr Sukarno continuing as President. Initially, the country had a federal constitution which gave limited self-government to the 16 constituent regions. In August 1950, however, the federation was dissolved and the country became the unitary Republic of Indonesia. The 1949 independence agreement excluded West New Guinea (now Irian Jaya), which remained under Dutch control until October 1962; following a brief period of UN administration, however, it was transferred to Indonesia in May 1963.

Dr Sukarno followed a policy of extreme nationalism, and his regime became increasingly dictatorial. His foreign policy was sympathetic to the People's Republic of China but, under his rule, Indonesia also played a leading role in the Non-Aligned Movement (see p. 237). Inflation and widespread corruption eventually provoked opposition to Dr Sukarno's regime; in September–October 1965 there was an abortive military coup, in which the Indonesian Communist Party (PKI) was strongly implicated. A mass slaughter of alleged PKI members and supporters ensued. In March 1966 Dr Sukarno was forced to transfer emergency executive powers to military commanders, led by Gen. Suharto, Chief of Staff of the Army, who outlawed the PKI. In February 1967 Dr Sukarno transferred full power to Gen. Suharto. In March the People's Consultative Assembly removed Sukarno from office and named Gen. Suharto acting President. He became Prime Minister in October 1967 and, following his election by the Assembly, he was inaugurated as President in March 1968. In July 1971, in the first general election since 1955, the government-sponsored Sekretariat Bersama Golongan Karya (Joint Secretariat of Functional Groups), known as Sekber Golkar, won a majority of seats in the House of Representatives. Gen. Suharto was re-elected to the presidency in March 1973.

Under Gen. Suharto's 'New Order', real power passed from the legislature and Cabinet to a small group of army officers and to the Operation Command for the Restoration of Order and Security (Kopkamtib), the internal security organization. Left-wing movements were suppressed, and a liberal economic policy adopted. A general election in May 1977 gave Golkar a majority in the legislature, and Gen. Suharto was re-elected President (unopposed) in March 1978. Despite criticism of the Government (most notably a petition signed by 50 prominent citizens in 1980), Golkar won an increased majority in the elections in May 1982, although the campaign was marred by considerable violence. In March 1983 Gen. Suharto was re-elected, again unopposed, as President.

During 1984 Gen. Suharto's attempt to introduce legislation requiring all political, social and religious organizations to adopt Pancasila, the five-point state philosophy (belief in a supreme being; humanitarianism; national unity; democracy by consensus; social justice), as their only ideology encountered opposition, particularly from the Petition of 50 (the signatories of the 1980 protest). Serious rioting and a series of bombings and arson attempts in and around Jakarta were allegedly instigated by Muslim opponents of the proposed legislation, and many Muslims were tried and sentenced to long terms of imprisonment. The law concerning mass organizations was enacted in June 1985, and all the political parties had accepted Pancasila by July. In 1986 and 1987 several factors gave rise to widespread criticism of Gen. Suharto and his Government within Indonesia and abroad: the publication, in an Australian newspaper, of a report accusing the Suharto family of corrupt practices; allegations of abuses of human rights in East Timor (see below); the execution of nine former PKI members (imprisoned for their alleged involvement in the 1965 coup attempt) in February 1987; and the Government's subsequent refusal to allow lawyers of the International Federation of Human Rights into the country, amid further reports of abuses of human rights. In the April 1987 general election, however, Golkar won 299 of the 500 seats in the House of Representatives. Moreover, for the first time the party achieved an overall majority of seats in each of Indonesia's 27 provinces.

In February 1988 new legislation reaffirmed the 'dual (i.e. military and socio-economic) function' of the Indonesian Armed Forces (ABRI). Shortly afterwards, Gen. Try Sutrisno (hitherto Chief of Staff of the Army) replaced Gen. L. B. Murdani as Commander-in-Chief of the Armed Forces. In March Gen. Suharto was again re-elected unopposed as President. At the subsequent vice-presidential election, in a departure from previous procedure, Gen. Suharto did not recommend a candidate, but encouraged the People's Consultative Assembly to choose one. However, Lt-Gen. (retd) Sudharmono, the Chairman of Golkar, and Dr Jailani Naro, the leader of the United Development Party (PPP), were both nominated for the post, and Gen. Suharto was obliged to indicate his preference for Sudharmono before Dr Naro withdrew his candidacy and Sudharmono was elected unopposed. During the electoral process, a senior member of ABRI, Brig.-Gen. Ibrahim Salim, suggested that the nomination procedure for the vice-presidency was unfair. He was prevented from completing his speech and subsequently lost his seat in the People's Consultative Assembly. ABRI disapproved of Sudharmono's appointment as, under his chairmanship of Golkar, there had been a shift away from military dominance in the grouping and he was suspected of having left-wing sympathies. A cabinet reshuffle took place in March, and 19 new ministers were appointed.

ABRI's influence was further eroded in September by the replacement of Kopkamtib, commanded by Gen. Murdani, by the Co-ordinating Board for the Development of National Stability (Bakorstanas), led by Gen. Sutrisno. Kopkamtib had been a military organization, whose chief responsibility was the suppression of left-wing movements, whereas Bakorstanas included representatives from the Cabinet and non-military government departments, and its main task was to expose corruption. In October Sudharmono resigned as Chairman of Golkar and was replaced by Gen. (retd) Wahono, who was acceptable both to ABRI and the developing bureaucratic élite. By January 1989 an anti-communist campaign had resulted in the expulsion of three senior officials from Golkar and the execution of two former members of the armed forces, convicted in 1968 for their involvement in the 1965 attempted coup. The lack of evidence of any genuine communist re-emergence led to the belief that the campaign was organized by ABRI to discredit Sudharmono.

In early 1989 tension arising from land disputes produced social unrest in three areas of Java and on the eastern island of Sumbawa. The most serious incident took place in February in southern Sumatra, where between 30 and 100 people were killed as a result of clashes between the armed forces and dissenting villagers. The first student demonstrations since 1978 were held to protest against the Government's expropriation of land without sufficient indemnification for those subject to relocation. The armed forces did not attempt to suppress the student protests. This implicit criticism of the regime and discussions about democratization and reform had been encouraged by speculation over Gen. Suharto's successor. This speculation began as a result of comments made by Gen. Suharto in the previous April, suggesting that other candidates might contest the presidential election in 1993. In early May, however, Gen. Suharto warned officials to dismiss the topic of the succession. In September it appeared likely that Gen. Suharto would seek election for a sixth term, when the minority Indonesian Democratic Party announced that it would support his candidacy. In August 1990 a group of 58 prominent Indonesians, comprising many of the original Petition of 50, issued a public demand to Gen. Suharto to retire from the presidency at the end of his current term of office and to permit greater democracy in Indonesia. In a speech two days later, Gen. Suharto alluded to political reform, recommended greater freedom of expression and implied that he would seek a further term as President. In late August the Government announced that censorship of both the local and foreign press was to be relaxed and that the authorities would no longer revoke the publishing licences of newspapers that violated legislation governing the press. In October, however, a tabloid newspaper was banned, following several days of protest by Muslims who considered an opinion poll that was published in the newspaper to have been blasphemous.

The Government had, for some time, been seeking to win the support of the Muslim electorate in preparation for the presidential elections in 1993. In 1989 Gen. Suharto promoted legislation whereby decisions by Islamic courts no longer required confirmation by civil courts. In December 1990 Gen. Suharto opened the symposium of the newly-formed Association of Muslim Intellectuals (ICMI), an organization which united a broad spectrum of Islamic interests. ICMI was widely expected either to develop into a new Islamic political movement or to become the basis of support for Gen. Suharto's presidential candidacy in 1993. ABRI was opposed to the establishment of ICMI because it regarded the polarization of politics by religion as a threat to stability. During 1990 the nature of ABRI's dual function had been queried from within the armed forces, with some support evinced for a lessening of its political role. However, pressure from ABRI was widely believed to have led to Gen. Suharto's gestures towards democratization.

In April 1990 a series of armed attacks on police posts took place in the province of Aceh, in northern Sumatra. The rebellion, led by a separatist group calling itself the National Liberation Front Aceh Sumatra (which was perhaps related to Aceh Merdeka, a group that declared Aceh's independence from Indonesia in 1977), rapidly gathered support amongst the Acehnese. Traditional Acehnese hostility towards central government had been inflamed by the fact that the local population had not benefited from the exploitation of Aceh's rich mineral resources and also by resentment towards the thousands of Javanese resettled in the province under the Government's transmigration programme. In June an extensive military operation was launched against the rebels, who were referred to by the Indonesian authorities as the Security Disturbance Movement (GPK). The rebellion reached a peak in July and August. In November an estimated 8,000–12,000 government troops were active in the province. Reports of burned villages and the torture of suspects by the armed forces remained unconfirmed. By the end of 1990 there were alleged to be several hundred casualties.

In 1975 Portugal withdrew from its colony of East Timor. The territory's capital, Dili, was occupied by the forces of the left-wing Frente Revolucionário de Este Timor Independente (Fretilin), which advocated independence for East Timor. To prevent Fretilin from gaining full control, Indonesian troops intervened and set up a provisional government. In July 1976 East Timor was fully integrated as the 27th province of Indonesia. Human rights organizations claim that as many as 200,000 people, from a total population of 650,000, may have been killed by the Indonesian armed forces during the annexation. In February 1983 the UN Commission on Human Rights adopted a resolution affirming East Timor's right to independence and self-determination, and in 1990 the UN continued to withhold recognition of Indonesia's absorption of the territory. In September 1983, following a five-month cease-fire during which government representatives negotiated with Fretilin, the armed forces launched a major new offensive. During 1984 conditions in East Timor worsened, with widespread hunger, disease and repression among civilians, and continuing battles between rebels and Indonesian troops. The rebels suffered a serious set-back in August 1985, when the Australian Government recognized Indonesia's incorporation of East Timor. In November 1988 Gen. Suharto visited East Timor, prior to announcing that travel restrictions (in force since the annexation in 1976) were to be withdrawn. The territory was opened to visitors in late December. This development may have been prompted by Indonesia's failure to gain the chairmanship of the Non-Aligned Movement in 1988; conditions in East Timor were cited by those countries who refused to support Indonesia's claim. In October 1989 the Pope visited East Timor, as part of a tour of Indonesia, and made a plea to the Government to halt violations of human rights. Following a mass conducted by the Pope in the provincial capital, Dili, anti-Government protesters clashed with security guards. In January 1990 a visit to East Timor by the US Ambassador to Indonesia prompted further protest demonstrations, which were violently suppressed by the armed forces. In October student protests led to the occupation of two schools by the armed forces and to the arrest, and alleged torture, of nearly 100 students. In November the Government rejected proposals by the military commander of Fretilin, José Xanana Gusmão, for unconditional peace negotiations aimed at ending the armed struggle in East Timor.

In May 1977 there was a rebellion in Irian Jaya, said to have been organized by the Organisasi Papua Merdeka (OPM), or Free Papua Movement, which seeks unification with Papua New Guinea. Fighting continued until December 1979, when Indonesia and Papua New Guinea finalized a new border administrative agreement. Since then, however, there have been frequent border incidents, and in early 1984 fighting broke out in Jayapura, the capital of Irian Jaya. As a result, about 10,000 refugees fled over the border into Papua New Guinea. In October 1984 Indonesia and Papua New Guinea signed a five-year agreement establishing a joint border security committee; by the end of 1985 Indonesians were continuing to cross into Papua New Guinea, but a limited number of repatriations took place in 1986. There was also concern among native Irian Jayans (who are of Melanesian origin) at the introduction of large numbers of Javanese into the province, under the Government's transmigration scheme. This was interpreted as an attempt to reduce the Melanesians to a minority and thus to stifle opposition. In 1986 it was announced that the Government intended to resettle 65m. people over 20 years, in spite of protests from human rights and conservation groups that the scheme would cause ecological damage and interfere with the rights of the native Irian Jayans. Relations with Papua New Guinea improved when the Prime Minister, Paias Wingti, visited Gen. Suharto in January 1988. However, a series of cross-border raids by the Indonesian armed forces in October and November, in an attempt to capture Melanesian separatists operating on the border, led to renewed tension between the two countries. Following a further round of bilateral discussions on border issues in July 1989, however, it was announced that Papua New Guinea would establish a consulate in the capital of Irian Jaya, Jayapura, and that an Indonesian consulate would be opened in the border town of Vanimo. In October 1990 a renewal of the basic accord on border arrangements, signed by both Governments, included an agreement on the formation of a joint defence committee and formal commitment to share border intelligence.

Under Gen. Suharto, Indonesia's foreign policy is one of non-alignment, although the country maintains close relations with the West. In the mid-1980s Indonesia improved its relations with the USSR. In September 1989 President Suharto visited

INDONESIA

the USSR and discussed the problem of Cambodia with the Soviet leader. Indonesia is a member of the Association of South East Asian Nations (ASEAN, see p. 103) and supported that organization's opposition to Viet-Nam's military presence in Cambodia. Indonesia played a prominent role in attempts to find a political solution to the situation in Cambodia (see p. 613), hosting four informal meetings in Jakarta, in July 1988, February 1989 and February and September 1990. The Indonesian Minister of Foreign Affairs, Ali Alatas, and his French counterpart were appointed Co-Chairmen of the Paris International Conference on Cambodia, which first met in August 1989. In this role he also attended a meeting in Paris in December 1990 of the newly-formed Supreme National Council of Cambodia.

In July 1985 Indonesia and the People's Republic of China signed a memorandum of understanding on the resumption of direct trade links, which had been suspended since 1967. In April 1988 the Indonesian Government indicated its readiness to re-establish full diplomatic relations with the People's Republic, subject to an assurance that China would not seek to interfere in Indonesia's internal affairs; previously, Suharto had insisted that China acknowledge its alleged complicity in the 1965 attempted coup. Diplomatic relations were finally restored in August 1990, following an Indonesian undertaking to settle financial debts incurred with China by the Sukarno regime. In November Gen. Suharto visited China and Viet-Nam (the first Indonesian leader to do so since 1964 and 1975 respectively). Gen. Suharto subsequently announced that former Indonesian communists living in exile would be permitted to return home, although they risked imprisonment.

For a limited period in September 1988, Indonesia closed the straits of Sunda and Lombok to international shipping, owing to 'live firing exercises'. The USA, Australia and the Federal Republic of Germany expressed concern at this contravention of the Law of the Sea, whereby foreign vessels are allowed 'innocent passage' through the straits. In October the Australian Minister for Foreign Affairs and Trade, Gareth Evans, visited Indonesia. Despite tensions between the two countries concerning Indonesian incursions into Papua New Guinea and the temporary closure of the straits, a joint communiqué, confirming co-operation in the formerly disputed Timor Gap area, was issued. In December 1989 Indonesia and Australia concluded a temporary agreement providing for joint exploration for petroleum and gas in the Timor Gap, which had been a disputed area since 1978. However, no permanent sea boundary was approved. In April 1990 the two countries restored defence co-operation links, following a four-year disruption.

Government

The highest authority of the state is the People's Consultative Assembly, with 1,000 members who serve for five years. The Assembly includes 500 members of the House of Representatives, the country's legislative organ. The House has 100 appointed members and 400 directly elected representatives. The remaining 500 seats in the Assembly are allocated to regional representatives, members of the Armed Forces belonging to Sekber Golkar (the governing alliance), and delegates of other organizations, selected in proportion to their elected seats in the House. Executive power rests with the President, elected for five years by the Assembly. He governs with the assistance of an appointed Cabinet, responsible to him.

There are 27 provinces, and local government is through a three-tier system of Provincial, Regency and Village Assemblies. Provincial Governors are appointed by the President.

Defence

In June 1990 the total strength of the armed forces was 283,000 men: army 215,000, navy 43,000 and air force 25,000. There was also a paramilitary force of some 115,000. Military service is selective. Defence expenditure for 1990 was budgeted at 2,674,000m. rupiahs.

Economic Affairs

In 1988, according to estimates by the World Bank, Indonesia's gross national product (GNP), measured at average 1986–88 prices, was US $75,960m., equivalent to $430 per head. During 1980–88, it was estimated, overall GNP increased, in real terms, at an average rate of 3.8% per year, while GNP per head expanded by 1.7% annually. Over the same period the population grew by an annual average of 2.1%. Indonesia's gross domestic product (GDP) increased, in real terms, by an annual average of 5.1% in 1980–88.

Agriculture (including forestry and fishing) contributed an estimated 24.1% of GDP, and employed 55.8% of the working population, in 1988. About two-thirds of Indonesia's land area is covered by tropical rain forests. Despite a 1985 ban on exports of logs, forestry exports accounted for about 13% of total exports in 1988. In 1988 the World Bank estimated that deforestation was taking place at a rate of 900,000 ha annually. In the late 1980s Indonesia remained the world's second largest producer of natural rubber. Export earnings from crude rubber accounted for an estimated 4.9% of total export revenue in 1989. Oil palm, coffee, sugar cane, tea, coconuts and tobacco are among the country's other principal cash crops. Rice is the main food crop. During 1980–88 agricultural production increased by an annual average of 3.1%.

Industry (including mining, manufacturing, construction and power) employed 13.4% of the working population in 1985, and provided an estimated 35.7% of GDP in 1988. During 1980–88 industrial production increased by an annual average of 5.1%.

Mining employed only 0.7% of the working population in 1985, but contributed 11.6% of GDP in 1988. Indonesia's principal mineral resource is petroleum, and the country is the world's leading exporter of liquefied natural gas. Tin, bauxite, nickel, copper, gold and coal are also mined.

In 1988 manufacturing contributed 18.5% of GDP and employed 8.6% of the working population. Apart from petroleum refineries, the main branches of the sector (in terms of output) are food products, tobacco, textiles, chemicals and wood products. During 1980–88 manufacturing production increased by an annual average of 13.1%.

Petroleum provided 61.6% of total energy requirements in 1989/90, gas 23.5%, hydroelectric power 7.5%, coal 6.8% and geothermal power 0.6%. Further diversification, away from reliance on petroleum and gas, was envisaged. In 1988 the cost of energy imports was equivalent to 14% of revenue from merchandise exports.

In 1988 services (including trade, transport and communications, finance and tourism) contributed an estimated 40.2% of GDP and employed 29.6% of the working population. Trade, hotels and restaurants contributed about 17.3% of GDP in that year. Tourism is one of the principal sources of foreign exchange. In 1988 a total of 136.9m. metric tons of freight for international traffic were loaded and discharged in Indonesian ports. During 1980–88 the services sector expanded by an annual average of 6.4%.

In 1989 Indonesia recorded a visible trade surplus of US $5,666m. There was, however, a deficit of $1,108m. on the current account of the balance of payments in that year. In 1989 the principal source of imports (23.0%) and the principal market for exports (an estimated 43.3%) was Japan. Other major trading partners are the USA, Singapore, Germany, Taiwan and the Republic of Korea. The principal exports in 1989 were petroleum and petroleum products (27%), wood and wood products (13%) and natural and manufactured gas (11%). The principal imports were machinery, transport and electrical equipment, and chemical and mineral products.

In the financial year ending 31 March 1990 there was a budgetary deficit of 3,580,000m. rupiahs. Indonesia's total external public debt at the end of 1988 was estimated at US $41,258m., with the cost of debt-servicing in that year being equivalent to 34.1% of revenue from exports of goods and services. The annual rate of inflation averaged 8.5% in 1980–88, 6.3% in 1989 and 9.6% in 1990. In 1988 about 2.8% of the labour force were unemployed.

Indonesia is a member of ASEAN (see p. 103), which aims to accelerate economic progress in the region, and of OPEC (see p. 200).

The decline in international petroleum prices after 1982 adversely affected Indonesia's export revenues, necessitating diversification into non-oil and -gas resources. In an attempt to increase efficiency and international competitiveness, a series of financial and trade reforms was introduced from 1983 onwards. Repelita V was the second Five-Year Plan (1989–94), aiming to promote the expansion of the manufacturing sector both as a potential source of export earnings and to absorb the increase in the labour force (predicted to expand at an annual average rate of 3% over the duration of the Plan). Indonesia's development plans are largely financed by foreign aid, much of which is donated regularly by the Inter-Govern-

INDONESIA

mental Group for Indonesia. In 1990 the Indonesian economy continued to expand rapidly, as deregulatory reforms took effect and the influx of foreign investment remained high (US $4,800m. in 1989). In response to growing concern about the disparity of wealth, the Government was considering limited plans to ensure a more equitable distribution of income. Stricter monetary controls were imposed in an attempt to curb the resurgence of inflation. Rises in consumer prices were due to an increase in the demand for funds and increases in petroleum prices in the second half of 1990, following Iraq's forcible annexation of Kuwait in August. Indonesia would benefit from a further short-term increase in petroleum prices in 1991, but a sustained increase in prices, causing an international recession, would impede its economic growth based on non-oil and -gas exports.

Social Welfare

About 10% of the population benefit from a state insurance scheme. Benefits include life insurance and old-age pensions. In addition, there are two social insurance schemes, administered by state corporations, providing pensions and industrial accident insurance. In 1988/89 Indonesia had 1,474 hospitals (with a total of 114,846 beds). About one-half of the hospitals are privately administered. In 1987/88 there were 5,639 public health centres and 17,382 sub-centres, and 23,084 physicians working in the country. In the 1989/90 budget, about 3.3% (434,000m. rupiahs) of proposed development expenditure was allocated to health, family planning and social welfare.

Education

Education is mainly under the control of the Ministry of Education and Culture, but the Ministry of Religious Affairs is in charge of Islamic religious schools at the primary level. Primary education, beginning at seven years of age and lasting for six years, was made compulsory in 1987. Secondary education, which is not compulsory, begins at 13 years of age and lasts for a further six years, comprising two cycles of three years each. Secondary enrolment was 53.5% of the school-age population at junior high school (age 13–15) and 34.8% at senior high school (age 16–18) in 1987/88. In 1988/89 about 26.7m. pupils were enrolled at 145,571 primary schools, while 9.0m. were receiving general secondary education. In 1988/89 a total of 1,281,213 students attended 3,184 technical and vocational schools. In 1987/88 there were 48 state and 744 private universities, with a total enrolment of 326,877 and 852,612 students respectively. For 1991/92 about 2,500,000m. rupiahs, representing 12.5% of total development expenditure was allocated to education. In 1985, according to estimates by UNESCO, the rate of adult illiteracy was 25.9% (males 17.0%; females 34.6%).

Public Holidays

1991: 1 January (New Year's Day), 12 February* (Ascension of the Prophet Muhammad), 29 March (Good Friday), 16 April* (Id al-Fitr, end of Ramadan), 9 May (Ascension Day), 23 June* (Id al-Adha, Feast of the Sacrifice), 13 July* (Muharram, Islamic New Year), 17 August (Indonesian National Day), 21 September* (Mouloud, Prophet Muhammad's Birthday), 25 December (Christmas Day).

1992: 1 January (New Year's Day), 1 February* (Ascension of the Prophet Muhammad), 4 April* (Id al-Fitr, end of Ramadan), 17 April (Good Friday), 28 May (Ascension Day), 11 June (Id al-Adha, Feast of the Sacrifice), 2 July* (Muharram, Islamic New Year), 17 August (Indonesian National Day), 10 September* (Mouloud, Prophet Muhammad's Birthday), 25 December (Christmas Day).

* These holidays are dependent on the Islamic lunar calendar and may vary by one or two days from the dates given.

Weights and Measures

The metric system is in force.

Statistical Survey

Source (unless otherwise stated): Central Bureau of Statistics, 8 Jalan Dokter Sutomo, POB 3, Jakarta; tel. (021) 363366; telex 45159.

Note: Unless otherwise stated, figures for the disputed former Portuguese territory of East Timor (annexed by Indonesia in July 1976) are not included in the tables.

Area and Population

AREA, POPULATION AND DENSITY

Area (sq km)	
Indonesia	1,904,569*
East Timor	14,874†
Population (census results)	
31 October 1980	
Indonesia	146,934,948
East Timor	555,350
31 October 1985 (inter-censal survey)	
Indonesia	
Males	81,321,445
Females	82,094,867
Total	163,416,312
East Timor	
Males	322,667
Females	308,009
Total	630,676
Population (official estimates at mid-year)	
Indonesia	
1987	171,335,457
1988	174,893,781
1989	178,421,263
East Timor	
1987	674,083
1988	695,055
1989	714,847
Density (per sq km) at mid-1989	
Indonesia	93.7
East Timor	48.1

* 735,358 sq miles.   † 5,743 sq miles.

INDONESIA

Statistical Survey

ISLANDS (estimated population at mid-1989)*

	Area (sq km)	Population	Density (per sq km)
Jawa (Java) and Madura	132,187	107,513,798	813.3
Sumatera (Sumatra)	473,606	36,881,990	77.9
Kalimantan (Borneo)	539,460	8,677,459	16.1
Sulawesi (Celebes)	189,216	12,507,650	66.1
Bali	5,561	2,782,038	500.3
Nusa Tenggara†	68,053	6,688,496	98.3
Maluku (Moluccas)	74,505	1,814,150	24.3
Irian Jaya (West Irian)	421,981	1,555,682	3.7
Indonesia	1,904,569	178,421,263	93.7
Timor Timur (East Timor)	14,874	714,847	48.1
Total	1,919,443	179,136,110	93.3

* Figures refer to provincial divisions, each based on a large island or group of islands but also including adjacent small islands.

† Comprising most of the Lesser Sunda Islands, principally Flores, Lombok, Sumba, Sumbawa and part of Timor.

PRINCIPAL TOWNS (population)

	1980 Census	1983*
Jakarta (capital)	6,503,449	7,347,800
Surabaya	2,027,913	2,223,600
Bandung	1,462,637	1,566,700
Medan	1,378,955	1,805,500
Semarang	1,026,671	1,205,800
Palembang	787,187	873,900
Ujung Pandang (Makassar)	709,038	840,500
Malang	511,780	547,100
Padang	480,922	656,800
Surakarta	469,888	490,900
Yogyakarta	398,727	420,700
Banjarmasin	381,286	423,600
Pontianak	304,778	342,700

* Revised official estimates for 31 December.

BIRTHS AND DEATHS (UN estimates, annual averages)

	1975-80	1980-85	1985-90
Birth rate (per 1,000)	35.4	32.2	27.4
Death rate (per 1,000)	15.1	12.6	11.2

Source: UN, *World Population Prospects: 1988*.

1985 (incl. East Timor): Registered live births 5,400,562 (birth rate 32.8 per 1,000); Registered deaths 1,846,431 (death rate 11.2 per 1,000).

1987 (incl. East Timor): Registered live births 4,884,124 (birth rate 28.4 per 1,000); Registered deaths 1,344,410 (death rate 7.8 per 1,000).

Marriages (incl. East Timor): 1,158,318 (marriage rate 7.2 per 1,000) in the fiscal year ending 31 March 1984.

ECONOMICALLY ACTIVE POPULATION
(ISIC Major Divisions, persons aged 10 years and over, survey of 31 October 1985, including East Timor)

	Males	Females	Total
Agriculture, hunting, forestry and fishing	22,074,219	12,067,590	34,141,809
Mining and quarrying	346,157	69,355	415,512
Manufacturing	3,170,142	2,625,777	5,795,919
Electricity, gas and water	64,966	4,749	69,715
Construction	2,043,370	52,207	2,095,577
Trade, restaurants and hotels	4,577,378	4,767,832	9,345,210
Transport, storage and communications	1,933,707	24,626	1,958,333
Financing, insurance, real estate and business services	201,497	48,984	250,481
Community, social and personal services	5,506,915	2,810,370	8,317,285
Activities not adequately defined	32,243	35,054	67,297
Total employed	39,950,594	22,506,544	62,457,138
Unemployed	898,057	470,420	1,368,477
Total labour force	40,848,651	22,976,964	63,825,615

August 1988 (survey, persons aged 10 years and over, including East Timor): Agriculture 40,475,109; Manufacturing 6,259,965; Trade 10,328,247; Other services 11,161,423; Total employed (incl. others) 72,538,549.

Agriculture

PRINCIPAL CROPS ('000 metric tons)

	1987	1988	1989
Rice (paddy)	40,078	41,676	43,566
Maize	5,155	6,652	6,324
Potatoes	417	418	455*
Sweet potatoes	2,013	2,159	2,106
Cassava (Manioc)	14,356	15,471	16,581
Other roots and tubers	263	220	220*
Pulses*	334	354	334
Soybeans	1,161	1,254	1,253
Groundnuts (in shell)	760	589	594
Coconuts*	12,000	12,100	12,300
Copra†	1,250	1,270	1,340
Palm kernels	297	314	298
Vegetables	3,680	3,147*	3,343*
Bananas	2,281	2,308	2,350*
Other fruit	3,938	3,990	3,862*
Sugar cane	26,131	24,825	24,416
Coffee (green)	358	384	390†
Tea (made)	156	144	135†
Tobacco (leaves)	114	147†	145†
Natural rubber	1,132	1,235	1,140*

* FAO estimate(s).   † Unofficial estimate(s).

Source: FAO, *Production Yearbook*.

LIVESTOCK ('000 head, year ending September)

	1987	1988	1989*
Cattle	9,742	10,006	10,050
Sheep	5,364	5,445	5,500
Goats	10,393	10,555	10,600
Pigs	6,339	6,464	6,700
Horses	659	664	725
Buffaloes	3,296	3,297	3,300

Chickens (million): 434 in 1987; 435* in 1988; 444* in 1989.
Ducks (million): 26 in 1987; 25 in 1988; 29* in 1989.

* FAO estimate.   † Unofficial estimate.

Source: FAO, *Production Yearbook*.

INDONESIA

LIVESTOCK PRODUCTS ('000 metric tons)

	1987	1988	1989
Beef and veal*	214	232	230
Buffalo meat*	45	47	40
Mutton and lamb	43†	45†	45*
Goats' meat	51†	53†	53*
Pig meat	159	165	170*
Poultry meat	390	445	447*
Edible offals*	86	91	91
Cows' milk	227	250	252*
Hen eggs	372	434	435
Other poultry eggs	88.0	90.0	92.5
Cattle and buffalo hides*	31.7	34.1	33.9

Note: Figures for meat refer to inspected production only, i.e. from animals slaughtered under government supervision.

* FAO estimate(s).   † Unofficial estimate.

Source: FAO, *Production Yearbook* and *Quarterly Bulletin of Statistics*.

Forestry

ROUNDWOOD REMOVALS ('000 cubic metres, excluding bark)

	1986	1987	1988
Sawlogs, veneer logs and logs for sleepers:			
Coniferous*	351	464	464
Non-coniferous	27,400†	36,226*	36,226*
Pulpwood*	200	200	200
Other industrial wood*	2,630	2,676	2,720
Fuel wood*	129,641	131,845	133,989
Total	160,224	171,411	173,599

* FAO estimate(s).   † Unofficial estimate.

Source: FAO, *Yearbook of Forest Products*.

SAWNWOOD PRODUCTION
('000 cubic metres, including boxboards)

	1986	1987	1988
Coniferous (soft wood)*	13	13	13
Broadleaved (hard wod)	7,442	9,750	10,173
Total	7,455	9,763	10,186

* FAO estimates.

Railway sleepers (FAO estimates, '000 cubic metres): 7 per year.

Source: FAO, *Yearbook of Forest Products*.

Fishing
('000 metric tons, live weight)

	1986	1987	1988
Carps, barbels, etc.	152.6	164.3	184.9
Other freshwater fishes (incl. unspecified)	288.5	299.5	313.2
Milkfish	103.6	105.9	117.2
Other diadromous fishes	20.2	21.5	22.6
Scads	163.4	145.3	147.8
Goldstripe sardinella	120.6	118.3	119.4
Bali sardinella	51.4	61.5	63.3
'Stolephorus' anchovies	108.0	118.0	118.9
Skipjack tuna	85.2	102.6	104.3
Other tunas, bonitos, billfishes, etc.	206.7	215.5	220.9
Indian mackerels	124.2	121.3	121.4
Other marine fishes (incl. unspecified)	790.1	834.3	867.7
Total fish	2,214.4	2,308.1	2,401.6
Marine shrimps, prawns, etc.	157.3	186.9	202.3
Other crustaceans	24.0	27.6	33.0
Molluscs	46.6	52.1	53.9
Other aquatic animals	14.7	10.3	12.5
Total catch	2,457.1	2,585.0	2,703.3
Inland waters	607.1	653.0	714.5
Indian Ocean	343.5	382.4	401.9
Pacific Ocean	1,506.5	1,549.5	1,586.9

Crocodiles (number): 15,102 in 1988.
Corals (metric tons): 307 in 1986; 205 in 1987; 205 (FAO estimate) in 1988.
Aquatic plants ('000 metric tons): 72.8 in 1986; 85.4 in 1987; 91.3 in 1988.

Source: FAO, *Yearbook of Fishery Statistics*.

Mining
(metric tons, unless otherwise indicated)

	1987	1988	1989
Crude petroleum ('000 barrels)	479,058	491,511	514,185
Natural gas ('000 million cu ft)	1,732,052	1,846,861	1,805,416
Bauxite	635,309	517,891	826,313
Coal	2,813,533	4,094,629	8,092,888
Nickel ore*	1,860,464	1,733,208	2,020,917
Copper concentrate*	258,836	293,711	324,624
Tin	26,209	29,568	31,263
Gold (kg)	3,752	4,731	n.a.
Silver (kg)	50,485	61,538	n.a.

* Figures refer to gross weight. In 1987 the metal content (in metric tons) was: Nickel 43,385; Copper 82,600.

INDONESIA

Industry

SELECTED PRODUCTS
('000 metric tons, unless otherwise indicated)

	1985	1986	1987
Wheat flour	1,191	1,151	1,182
Refined sugar	1,677	1,874	2,123
Cotton yarn (pure and mixed)	259.7	306.7	n.a.
Nitrogenous fertilizers*	1,749.1	1,971.1	1,978.9
Cement	10,477	11,088	11,814
Cigarettes (million)	119,236	114,312	124,432
Tyres ('000)†	3,899	4,480	4,751
Kerosene ('000 barrels)	38,382.9	43,043.3	41,407
Jet fuel ('000 barrels)	3,845.3	1,561.4	5,520
Distillate fuel oils ('000 barrels)	50,059.9	55,846.3	61,950
Residual fuel oils ('000 barrels)	44,716.5	47,814.4	65,600
Aluminium (unwrought)	216.8	220.0	202.7
Radio receivers ('000)	1,014	966	997
Television receivers ('000)	565	539	575
Motor vehicles—assembly ('000)	142	168	159

* Estimated production in terms of nitrogen. † For motor cars only.

Palm oil ('000 metric tons): 1,345 in 1987; 1,441 in 1988; 1,377 in 1989 (Source: FAO).

Motor spirit ('000 metric tons): 3,240 (estimate) in 1986; 3,487 in 1987; 3,765 in 1988 (Source: UN, *Monthly Bulletin of Statistics*).

Tin (primary metal, metric tons): 24,200 in 1987; 28,365 in 1988; 29,916 in 1989 (Source: International Tin Council).

Finance

CURRENCY AND EXCHANGE RATES

Monetary Units
100 sen = 1 rupiah (Rp.).

Denominations
Coins: 5, 10, 25, 50 and 100 rupiahs.
Notes: 100, 500, 1,000, 5,000 and 10,000 rupiahs.

Sterling and Dollar Equivalents (30 September 1990)
£1 sterling = 3,492.2 rupiahs;
US $1 = 1,864.0 rupiahs;
10,000 rupiahs = £2.864 = $5.365.

Average Exchange Rate (rupiahs per US $)
1987 1,643.8
1988 1,685.7
1989 1,770.1

BUDGET
('000 million rupiahs, year ending 31 March)

Revenue	1987/88	1988/89	1989/90*
Petroleum and natural gas	10,047	9,527	7,899.7
Other tax receipts	8,779	11,908	14,909.6
Income tax	2,663	3,949	4,947.6
Sales tax	3,390	4,505	5,830.9
Import tax and excise tax	2,044	2,582	2,908.2
Export tax	184	156	159.8
Other taxes	498	716	1,063.1
Non-tax receipts	1,977	1,569	2,440.5
Total domestic receipts	20,803	23,004	25,249.8
Foreign aid receipts	6,158	9,991	11,325.1
Programme aid	728	2,041	1,798.9
Project aid and export credits	5,430	7,950	9,526.2
Total	26,961	32,995	36,574.9

* Estimates.

Expenditure	1987/88	1988/89	1989/90*
Personal emoluments	4,617	4,998	5,966.5
Salaries and pensions	3,561	3,833	4,607.8
Rice allowances	451	518	616.4
Food allowances	299	327	370.7
Other remunerations	176	185	206.6
Missions abroad	130	135	165.0
Purchases of goods	1,329	1,492	1,476.6
Domestic products	1,239	1,378	1,435.0
Foreign products	90	114	131.6
Regional subsidies	2,816	3,038	3,594.1
Personal	2,592	2,779	3,340.6
Non-personal	224	259	253.5
Debt servicing	8,205	10,940	12,236.8
Domestic debts	39	77	148.8
Foreign debts	8,166	10,863	12,088.0
Others	515	271	171.0
Total ordinary budget	17,482	20,739	23,445.0
Total development budget	9,477	12,251	13,129.9
Locally financed	4,047	4,301	3,603.7
Project aid	5,430	7,950	9,526.2
Total	26,959	32,990	36,574.9

* Estimates.

Source: Ministry of Finance.

DEVELOPMENT EXPENDITURE
('000 million rupiahs, year ending 31 March)

	1987/88	1988/89	1989/90*
Agriculture and irrigation	1,361	527	1,994.2
Industry and mining	37	232	341.8
Electric power	348	177	1,614.7
Tourism and transport	753	586	2,522.1
Trade and co-operatives	156	179	199.9
Manpower and transmigration	138	168	335.3
Regional, rural and urban development	926	1,092	1,552.3
Religious affairs	17	16	264
Education, culture and youth	463	370	1,683.2
Health, family planning and social welfare	188	240	434.0
Housing and sanitation	159	82	620.1
Law enforcement	20	27	28.9
National defence and security	169	175	812.6
Information and communications	15	14	46.2
Science and technology	76	149	278.9
Armed forces and civil service	113	149	99.2
Investment through banking system	51	25	291.8
Natural resources and living conditions	64	93	248.8
Total	5,054	4,301	13,129.9

* Estimates.

Source: Ministry of Finance.

INTERNATIONAL RESERVES (US $ million at 31 December)

	1987	1988	1989
Gold*	1,319	1,158	1,044
IMF special drawing rights	6	3	1
Reserve position in IMF	103	97	95
Foreign exchange	5,483	4,948	5,357
Total	6,611	6,206	6,206

* Valued at market-related prices.

Source: IMF, *International Financial Statistics*.

INDONESIA

Statistical Survey

MONEY SUPPLY ('000 million rupiahs at 31 December)

	1987	1988	1989
Currency outside banks	5,802	6,245	7,908
Demand deposits at deposit money banks	6,776	8,032	12,477

Source: IMF, *International Financial Statistics*.

COST OF LIVING (Consumer Price Index—average of monthly figures. Base: April 1977–March 1978 = 100)

	1987	1988	1989
Food	275.1	310.7	335.6
Housing	311.5	327.7	348.2
Clothing	263.7	276.3	288.3
Miscellaneous	291.7	303.3	316.4
All items	287.3	310.4	330.3

NATIONAL ACCOUNTS ('000 million rupiahs at current prices)

National Income and Product

	1986	1987	1988*
Domestic factor incomes†	90,889.9	111,128.8	124,368.7
Consumption of fixed capital	5,127.3	6,226.9	6,972.6
Gross domestic product at factor cost	96,017.2	117,355.7	131,341.3
Indirect taxes, *less* subsidies	6,528.7	7,183.2	8,110.9
GDP in purchasers' values	102,545.9	124,538.9	139,452.2
Net factor income from abroad	−4,192.5	−6,017.3	−6,737.6
Gross national product	98,353.4	118,521.6	132,714.5
Less Consumption of fixed capital	5,127.3	6,226.9	6,972.6
National income in market prices	93,226.1	112,294.7	125,741.9

* Preliminary figures.
† Compensation of employees and the operating surplus of enterprises. The amount is obtained as a residual.

Expenditure on the Gross Domestic Product

	1986	1987	1988*
Government final consumption expenditure	11,328.7	11,763.5	12,755.8
Private final consumption expenditure	63,355.3	71,988.9	80,995.9
Increase in stocks	4,106.3	7,850.9	8,180.6
Gross fixed capital formation	24,781.9	30,980.2	33,907.0
Total domestic expenditure	103,572.2	122,583.5	135,839.3
Exports of goods and services	20,009.9	29,894.7	34,621.9
Less Imports of goods and services	21,036.2	27,939.3	31,009.1
GDP in purchasers' values	102,545.9	124,538.9	139,452.2

* Preliminary figures.

Gross Domestic Product by Economic Activity

	1986	1987	1988*
Agriculture, forestry and fishing	24,750.5	29,016.0	33,597.8
Mining and quarrying	11,502.8	17,266.8	16,184.9
Manufacturing	17,184.7	21,150.4	25,821.0
Electricity, gas and water	647.1	746.9	836.9
Construction	5,313.8	6,087.4	6,988.4
Trade, hotels and restaurants	17,083.4	20,870.2	24,167.2
Transport and communications	6,406.9	7,414.1	8,059.3
Finance, insurance and real estate	4,058.8	4,823.7	5,263.4
Government services	4,314.6	4,902.5	5,351.0
Ownership of dwellings	2,976.0	3,349.1	3,736.0
Public administration	8,307.3	8,911.8	9,446.2
Total	102,545.9	124,538.9	139,452.1

* Preliminary figures.

BALANCE OF PAYMENTS (US $ million)

	1987	1988	1989
Merchandise exports f.o.b.	17,206	19,509	22,974
Merchandise imports f.o.b.	−12,532	−13,831	−16,310
Trade balance	4,674	5,678	6,664
Exports of services	1,626	1,861	2,437
Imports of services	−8,655	−9,190	−10,548
Balance on goods and services	−2,355	−1,651	−1,447
Private unrequited transfers (net)	86	99	167
Government unrequited transfers (net)	171	155	172
Current balance	−2,098	−1,397	−1,108
Direct capital investment (net)	385	576	682
Other long-term capital (net)	2,046	1,233	2,334
Short-term capital (net)	970	408	−98
Net errors and omissions	−673	−933	−1,361
Total (net monetary movements)	630	−113	449
Valuation changes (net)	247	−338	−29
Changes in reserves	876	−451	420

Source: IMF, *International Financial Statistics*.

FOREIGN AID (US $ million)*

	1984/85	1985/86
Concessionary loans from IGGI†	2,228.3	2,148.8
Bilateral	710.0	601.4
Belgium	—	6.0
Canada	21.7	—
France	26.2	23.3
Germany, Fed. Repub.	73.1	29.8
Italy	—	—
Japan	486.4	489.2
Netherlands	24.0	22.4
Switzerland	—	21.2
USA	78.6	9.5
Multilateral (international agencies)	1,518.3	1,547.4
IBRD	964.9	1,234.1
ADB	553.4	313.3
Semi-concessionary loans and commercial loans, including export credit for projects	1,260.7	951.7
Cash loans	705.1	1,864.2
Total	4,194.1	4,964.7

* Figures refer to agreed commitments to provide aid, rather than to actual disbursements.
† Inter-Governmental Group for Indonesia.
Source: Bank Indonesia.

INDONESIA

External Trade

PRINCIPAL COMMODITIES (US $ million)

Imports c.i.f.	1987	1988	1989
Food and live animals	623.8	639.8	910.9
Cereals and cereal preparations	306.4	264.1	385.9
Beverages and tobacco	32.6	34.4	33.6
Crude materials (inedible) except fuels	990.6	1,203.3	1,673.9
Textile fibres and waste	357.8	385.2	490.6
Mineral fuels, lubricants, etc.	1,144.0	948.5	1,252.6
Petroleum and petroleum products	1,067.9	898.6	1,180.4
Crude petroleum	505.1	468.9	576.0
Petroleum products, refined	n.a.	380.2	526.4
Animal and vegetable oils, fats and waxes	96.9	176.7	150.5
Chemicals and related products	2,325.9	2,532.3	2,873.3
Chemical elements and compounds	978.9	1,104.1	1,272.5
Plastic materials, etc.	623.7	705.7	719.6
Polymers of ethylene, primary forms	n.a.	269.0	200.4
Basic manufactures	1,784.9	2,070.2	2,638.0
Textile yarn, fabrics, etc.	213.0	307.7	510.7
Iron and steel	693.8	882.2	995.6
Tubes, pipes, hollow profile, pipe fittings	n.a.	172.8	262.5
Machinery and transport equipment	4,818.7	5,097.0	6,181.9
Non-electric machinery	3,183.7	3,579.5	4,558.6
Electrical machinery, apparatus, etc.	592.6	466.4	601.1
Transport equipment	1,042.4	1,051.1	1,372.0
Road motor vehicles and parts*	710.4	772.0	849.5
Miscellaneous manufactured articles	469.6	534.2	633.6
Precision instruments	284.5	225.2	258.8
Other commodities and transactions	83.3	12.0	11.2
Total	12,370.3	13,248.5	16,359.6

* Excluding tyres, engines and electrical parts.

Exports f.o.b.	1987	1988	1989*
Food and live animals	1,683.8	2,000.6	2,185.3
Fish and fish preparations	432.6	652.3	n.a.
Coffee, tea, cocoa and spices	963.4	981.5	n.a.
Coffee (incl. extracts, etc.)	538.7	551.9	545.7
Beverages and tobacco	71.9	69.2	127.4
Crude materials (inedible) except fuels	1,925.9	2,660.9	2,440.0
Crude rubber	957.8	1,243.1	1,071.5
Wood	399.4	576.3	n.a.
Metalliferous ores and metal scrap	308.4	640.6	n.a.
Non-ferrous ores and concentrates	305.9	n.a.	n.a.
Mineral fuels, lubricants, etc.	8,581.9	7,723.2	7,879.3
Petroleum and petroleum products	6,156.9	5,189.0	5,980.7
Crude petroleum	5,040.4	4,234.5	5,046.1
Petroleum products	1,116.5	954.5	934.6
Residual fuel oils	765.0	n.a.	n.a.
Gas (natural and manufactured)	2,399.1	2,492.6	2,465.4
Animal and vegetable oils, fats and waxes	290.2	539.4	963.4
Fixed vegetable oils and fats	234.3	460.1	n.a.
Chemicals and related products	251.0	345.7	617.5

Exports f.o.b.—continued	1987	1988	1989*
Basic manufactures	3,267.2	4,281.0	5,733.5
Wood and cork manufactures (excl. furniture)	1,922.8	2,297.4	n.a.
Plywood and similar laminated wood products	1,759.3	2,073.7	2,178.3
Textile yarn, fabrics, etc.	468.7	680.4	754.5
Non-ferrous metals	412.1	542.7	n.a.
Machinery and transport equipment	57.1	126.2	180.4
Miscellaneous manufactured articles	731.8	1,154.3	1,558.9
Clothing (excl. footwear)	595.8	796.7	1,066.7
Other commodities and transactions	274.8	318.0	339.9
Gold (non-monetary)	274.7	317.5	n.a.
Total	17,135.6	19,218.5	22,025.6

PRINCIPAL TRADING PARTNERS (US $ million)

Imports	1987	1988	1989
Australia	462.7	578.4	924.8
Canada	303.0	274.1	310.5
China, People's Republic	408.4	438.7	527.4
France	392.0	464.8	406.1
Germany, Fed. Republic	836.0	886.6	920.4
Italy	236.7	247.6	348.2
Japan	3,596.1	3,385.6	3,766.7
Korea, Republic	268.4	376.3	562.3
Malaysia	138.9	276.1	369.0
Netherlands	316.1	258.4	247.7
Saudi Arabia	630.5	565.2	223.1
Singapore	946.8	895.5	1,122.1
Taiwan	458.8	624.9	977.5
United Kingdom	324.8	339.9	359.6
USA	1,415.1	1,735.7	2,217.9
Total (incl. others)	12,370.3	13,248.5	16,359.6

Exports	1987	1988	1989*
Australia	309.8	293.3	386.9
China, People's Republic	343.0	491.8	n.a.
Germany, Fed. Republic	361.1	455.5	495.5
Hong Kong	419.6	554.4	570.2
Italy	174.9	220.5	202.9
Japan	7,393.3	8,018.3	9,535.2
Korea, Republic	673.3	840.3	n.a.
Malaysia	93.8	184.0	225.8
Netherlands	493.4	646.3	594.3
Singapore	1,449.2	1,653.2	1,786.8
Taiwan	473.7	478.0	n.a.
Thailand	87.2	151.4	251.5
United Kingdom	212.4	348.8	348.1
USA	3,348.7	3,073.7	3,420.6
Total (incl. others)	17,135.6	19,218.5	22,025.6

* Provisional estimates.

Transport

RAILWAYS (traffic)

	1985	1986	1987
Passenger-km (million)	6,774	7,327	7,898
Freight ton-km (million)	1,333	1,465	1,808

INDONESIA

ROAD TRAFFIC (motor vehicles registered at 31 December)

	1986	1987	1988
Passenger cars	1,063,959	1,170,103	1,073,106
Lorries and trucks	882,331	953,694	892,581
Buses and coaches	256,574	303,378	385,731
Motor cycles	5,118,907	5,554,305	5,419,531

INTERNATIONAL SEA-BORNE SHIPPING

	1986	1987	1988
Goods loaded ('000 metric tons)	148,094	134,249	115,381
Goods unloaded ('000 metric tons)	19,250	23,081	21,517

Merchant shipping fleet ('000 grt at 30 June): 2,126 in 1988; 2,035 in 1989.

CIVIL AVIATION (traffic on scheduled services)

	1985	1986	1987
Kilometres flown (million)	120.2	189.4	135.1
Passengers carried ('000)	6,285	6,764	7,408
Passenger-km (million)	9,529	11,136	11,539
Freight ton-km (million)	146.2	211.5	333.5

Tourism

	1982	1983	1984
Visitors ('000)	592.0	638.9	683.0
Receipts (US $ million)	358.8	440.0	519.0

Source: Directorate-General of Tourism.

1987: 1,060,347 visitors; **1988**: 1,357,244 visitors; **1989**: 1,620,000 visitors.

Communications Media

	1986	1987	1988
Television receivers (registered)	6,103,579	5,842,723	5,814,262
Telephones (registered)	784,836	864,372*	n.a.

* Estimate.

Education

(1988/89)

	Institutions	Teachers	Pupils and Students
Primary schools	145,571	1,134,089	26,725,364
Junior high schools	20,334	412,412	6,446,966
Senior high schools	404	200,509	2,600,053
Technical and vocational schools	3,184	88,334	1,281,213
Teacher training	617	17,616	191,677
Universities*			
State	48	55,059	326,877
Private	744	60,300	852,612

* 1987/88.

Source: Department of Education and Culture.

Directory

The Constitution

Indonesia had three provisional constitutions: in August 1945, February 1950 and August 1950. In July 1959 the Constitution of 1945 was re-enacted by presidential decree. The General Elections Law of 1969 supplemented the 1945 Constitution, which has been adopted permanently by the People's Consultative Assembly. The following is a summary of its main provisions:

GENERAL PRINCIPLES

The 1945 Constitution consists of 37 articles, four transitional clauses and two additional provisions, and is preceded by a preamble. The preamble contains an indictment of all forms of colonialism, an account of Indonesia's struggle for independence, the declaration of that independence and a statement of fundamental aims and principles. Indonesia's National Independence, according to the text of the preamble, has the state form of a Republic, with sovereignty residing in the People, and is based upon the *Pancasila*:

1. Belief in the One Supreme God.
2. Just and Civilized Humanity.
3. The Unity of Indonesia.
4. Democracy led by the wisdom of deliberations (*musyawarah*) among representatives.
5. Social Justice for all the people of Indonesia.

STATE ORGANS

Majelis Permusyawaratan Rakyat—MPR (People's Consultative Assembly)

Sovereignty is in the hands of the People and is exercised in full by the People's Consultative Assembly as the embodiment of the whole Indonesian People. The Consultative Assembly is the highest authority of the State, and is to be distinguished from the legislative body proper (Dewan Perwakilan Rakyat, see below) which is incorporated within the Consultative Assembly. The Consultative Assembly, with a total of 1,000 members, is composed of all members of the Dewan, augmented by delegates from the regions, members of political organizations (including members of the armed forces belonging to Golkar), and representatives of other groups. The Assembly sits at least once every five years, and its primary competence is to determine the constitution and the broad lines of the policy of the State and the Government. It also elects the President and Vice-President, who are responsible for implementing that policy. All decisions are taken unanimously in keeping with the traditions of *musyawarah*.

The President

The highest executive of the Government, the President, holds office for a term of five years and may be re-elected. As Mandatory of the MPR he must execute the policy of the State according to the Decrees determined by the MPR during its Fourth General and Special Sessions. In conducting the administration of the State, authority and responsibility are concentrated in the President. The Ministers of the State are his assistants and are responsible only to him.

Dewan Perwakilan Rakyat—DPR (House of Representatives)

The legislative branch of the State, the House of Representatives, sits at least once a year. It has 500 members: 100 nominated by

INDONESIA

the President and 400 directly elected. Every statute requires the approval of the DPR. Members of the House of Representatives have the right to submit draft bills which require ratification by the President, who has the right of veto. In times of emergency the President may enact ordinances which have the force of law, but such Ordinances must be ratified by the House of Representatives during the following session or be revoked.

Dewan Pertimbangan Agung—DPA (Supreme Advisory Council)
The DPA is an advisory body assisting the President who chooses its members from political parties, functional groups and groups of prominent persons.

Mahkamah Agung (Supreme Court)
The judicial branch of the State, the Supreme Court and the other courts of law are independent of the Executive in exercising their judicial powers.

Badan Pemeriksa Keuangan (Supreme Audit Board)
Controls the accountability of public finance, enjoys investigatory powers and is independent of the Executive. Its findings are presented to the DPR.

The Government

HEAD OF STATE
President: SUHARTO (inaugurated 27 March 1968; re-elected March 1973, March 1978, March 1983 and March 1988).
Vice-President: Gen. SUDHARMONO.

CABINET
(January 1991)

Minister of Home Affairs, concurrently Chairman of the Election Committee: Gen. RUDINI.
Minister of Foreign Affairs: ALI ALATAS.
Minister of Defence and Security: Gen. L. B. MURDANI.
Minister of Justice: ISMAIL SALEH.
Minister of Information: HARMOKO.
Minister of Finance: Prof. Dr JOHANNES B. SUMARLIN.
Minister of Trade: Dr ARIFIN M. SIREGAR.
Minister of Co-operatives: BUSTANIL ARIFIN.
Minister of Agriculture: Dr WARDOYO.
Minister of Forestry: Dr HASRUL HARAHAP.
Minister of Industry: HARTARTO.
Minister of Mining and Energy: Dr GINANDJAR KARTASASMITA.
Minister of Public Works: RADINAL MOCHTAR.
Minister of Communications: AZWAR ANAS.
Minister of Tourism, Posts and Telecommunications: Gen. SUSILO SUDARMAN.
Minister of Manpower: COSMAS BATUBARA.
Minister of Transmigration: Lt-Gen. SUGIARTO.
Minister of Education and Culture: Prof. FUAD HASSAN.
Minister of Health: ADHYATMA.
Minister of Religious Affairs: Haji MUNAWIR SJADZALI.
Minister of Social Affairs: Mrs HARYATI SUBADIO.
Minister-Co-ordinator for Political Affairs and Security: SUDOMO.
Minister-Co-ordinator for the Economy, Finance, Industry and Development Supervision: RADIUS PRAWIRO.
Minister-Co-ordinator for Public Welfare: SUPARDJO RUSTAM.
Minister of State and State Secretary: Maj.-Gen. MURDIONO.
Minister of State for National Development Planning, concurrently Chairman of the National Development Planning Board (Bappenas): Dr SALEH AFIF.
Minister of State for Research and Technology, concurrently Chairman of the Board for the Study and Application of Technology: Prof. Dr BUCHARUDDIN JUSUF HABIBIE.
Minister of State for Population and the Environment: Prof. Dr EMIL SALIM.
Minister of State for Public Housing: SISWONO JUDO HUSODO.
Minister of State for Youth and Sports: AKBAR TANJUNG.
Minister of State for State Administrative Reforms, concurrently Vice-Chairman of the National Development Planning Board: SARWONO KUSUMAATMADJA.
Minister of State for Women's Affairs: Mrs A. SULASIKIN MURPRATOMO.
Junior Minister and Cabinet Secretary: SAADILAH MURSJID.

There are five other Junior Ministers.

Officials with the rank of Minister of State:
Attorney-General: AGUNG SINGGIH.
Governor of Bank Indonesia: ADRIANUS MOOY.
Commander-in-Chief of the Indonesian Armed Forces: Gen. TRY SUTRISNO.

MINISTRIES

Office of the President: Istana Merdeka, Jakarta; tel. (021) 331097.
Office of the Vice-President: Jalan Merdeka Selatan 6, Jakarta; tel. (021) 363539.
Office of the Attorney-General: Jalan Sultan Hasanuddin 1, Jakarta; tel. (021) 773557.
Office of the Cabinet Secretary: Jalan Veteran 18, Jakarta Pusat; tel. (021) 3810973.
Office of Co-ordinating Minister for Political Affairs and Security: Jalan Merdeka Barat 15, Jakarta; tel. (021) 376004.
Office of the Co-ordinating Minister for People's Welfare: Jalan Merdeka Barat 3, Jakarta Pusat; tel. (021) 353055.
Office of the Minister of State for the Role of Women: Jalan Merdeka Barat 15, Jakarta Pusat 10110; tel. (021) 3805563.
Office of the State Secretary: Perpustakaan, Dewan Perwakilan Rakyat-R.I., Jalan Gatot Subroto, Senayan, Jakarta 10270; tel. (021) 5001223.
Ministry of Agriculture: Jalan Harsono Room 3, Ragunan Pasar Minggu, Jakarta Selatan; tel. (021) 783006.
Ministry of Communications: Jalan Merdeka Barat 8, Jakarta 10110; tel. (021) 366332; telex 46116.
Ministry of Co-operatives: Jalan H. R. Rasuna Said, Kav. 3–5, POB 177, Jakarta; tel. (021) 5204368; telex 62843.
Ministry of Defence and Security: Jalan Merdeka Barat 13, Jakarta 10110; tel. (021) 374408.
Ministry of the Economy, Finance, Industry and Development Supervision: Jalan Lapangan Banteng Timur 4, Jakarta; tel. (021) 365079.
Ministry of Education and Culture: Jalan Jenderal Sudirman, Senayan, Jakarta Pusat; tel. (021) 581618.
Ministry of Finance: Jalan Lapangan Banteng Timur 4, Jakarta Pusat; tel. (021) 348938.
Ministry of Foreign Affairs: Jalan Taman Pejambon 6, Jakarta Pusat; tel. (021) 368014.
Ministry of Forestry: Jalan Gatot Subroto, Jakarta 10270; tel. (021) 581820; telex 45996; fax (021) 5700226.
Ministry of Health: Jalan H. R. Rasuna Said Blx 5, Kav. 49, Jakarta Pusat; tel. (021) 5201595.
Ministry of Home Affairs: Jalan Merdeka Utara 7, Jakarta Pusat; tel. (021) 373908.
Ministry of Industry: Jalan Jenderal Gatot Subroto, Kav. 52–53, Jakarta; tel. (021) 511661; telex 62444; fax (021) 512720.
Ministry of Information: Jalan Merdeka Barat 9, Jakarta Pusat; tel. (021) 377408; telex 44264.
Ministry of Justice: Jalan H. R. Rasuna Said, Kav. 4/5, Jakarta Pusat; tel. (021) 513004.
Ministry of Manpower: Jalan Jenderal Gatot Subroto, Jakarta Pusat; tel. (021) 515717.
Ministry of Mining and Energy: Jalan Merdeka Selatan 18, Jakarta Pusat; tel. (021) 360232.
Ministry of National Development Planning: Jalan Taman Suropati 2, Jakarta Pusat; tel. (021) 336207; telex 61623.
Ministry for Population and the Environment: Jalan Medan Merdeka Barat 15, Jakarta Pusat; tel. (021) 371295; telex 46143.
Ministry of Public Housing: Jalan Kebon Sirih 31, Jakarta 10340; tel. (021) 333649; telex 61257; fax (021) 327430.
Ministry of Public Works: Jalan Pattimura 20, Kebayoran Baru, 12110 Jakarta Selatan; tel. (021) 717564; telex 47247.
Ministry of Religious Affairs: Jalan M. H. Thamrin 6, Jakarta Pusat; tel. (021) 320135.
Ministry of Research and Technology: Gedung Menara Patra, 3rd Floor, Jalan M. H. Thamrin 8, Jakarta Pusat; tel. (021) 324767.
Ministry of Social Affairs: Jalan Ir H. Juanda 36, Jakarta Pusat; tel. (021) 341329.
Ministry for State Administrative Reforms: Jalan Taman Suropati 2, Jakarta; tel. (021) 334811.

INDONESIA

Ministry of Tourism, Posts and Telecommunications: Jalan Kebon Sirih 36, Jakarta; tel. (021) 346855.

Ministry of Trade: Jalan Mohammed Ikhwan Ridwan Rais 5, Jakarta; tel. (021) 348667.

Ministry of Transmigration: Jalan Letjen. Haryono MT, Cikoko, Jakarta Selatan; tel. (021) 794682.

Ministry of Youth and Sports: Jalan Jenderal Sudirman, Senayan, Jakarta Pusat; tel. (021) 581986.

Directorate-General of Tourism: Jalan Kramatraya 81; tel. (021) 359001.

Legislature

MAJELIS PERMUSYAWARATAN RAKYAT—MPR
(People's Consultative Assembly)

The Assembly consists of the members of the House of Representatives, regional delegates, members of political organizations (including members of the Armed Forces belonging to Golkar), and representatives of other groups. In 1987 the membership of the Assembly was expanded to 1,000.

Chairman: KHARIS SUHUD.

	Seats
Members of the House of Representatives	500
Regional representatives*	147
Political organizations†	253
Others	100
Total	1,000

* To be a minimum of four, and a maximum of eight, representatives from each region.
† Including members of the Armed Forces belonging to Golkar. Organizations are represented on a proportional basis, according to the composition of the House of Representatives.

Dewan Perwakilan Rakyat—DPR
(House of Representatives)

In March 1960 a presidential decree prorogued the elected Council of Representatives and replaced it by a nominated House of 283 members (increased to 460 in 1968). Subsequently, the number of appointed members was reduced to 96. The remaining 364 were directly elected. In 1987, as a result of an increase in the size of the electorate, the House of Representatives was expanded from 460 to 500 members; of these, 100 members were nominated by the President and 400 directly elected.

Speaker: KHARIS SUHUD.

General Election, 23 April 1987

	Seats
Golkar	299
Partai Persatuan Pembangunan	61
Partai Demokrasi Indonesia	40
Appointed members*	100
Total	500

* Members of the political wing of the Indonesian Armed Forces (ABRI).

Political Organizations

A presidential decree of January 1960 enables the President to dissolve any party whose membership does not cover one-quarter of Indonesia, or whose policies are at variance with the aims of the State.

The following parties and groups participated in the general election held in April 1987:

Sekretariat Bersama Golongan Karya (Sekber Golkar) (Joint Secretariat of Functional Groups): Jalan Anggrek Nelimurni, Jakarta 11480; tel. (021) 5481618; telex 62147; f. 1964; reorg. 1971; the governing alliance of groups representing farmers, fishermen and the professions; Pres. and Chair. of Advisory Bd SUHARTO; Gen. Chair. Gen. (retd) WAHONO; Sec.-Gen. RACHMAT WITOELAR.

Partai Demokrasi Indonesia (PDI) (Indonesian Democratic Party): Jalan Diponegoro 58, Jakarta 10310; tel. (021) 336331; f. 1973 by the merger of five* nationalist and Christian parties; Gen. Chair. SOERJADI; Sec.-Gen. NICO DARYANTO.

Partai Persatuan Pembangunan (PPP) (United Development Party): Jalan Diponegoro 60, Jakarta; tel. (021) 356381; f. 1973 by the merger of four* Islamic parties (Nahdatul Ulama—NU, Sarikat Islam, Perti and Muslimin Indonesia—MI); Pres. ISMAEL HASSAN METAREUM; Sec.-Gen. MARDINSYAH.

* In May 1990 it was reported that these nine parties had regrouped to form an opposition alliance, which advocated a return to multi-party democracy and a restriction of the army's role in politics.

The following groups are in conflict with the Government:

Frente Revolucionário de Este Timor Independente (Fretilin): based in East Timor; f. 1974; seeks independence for East (fmrly Portuguese) Timor; entered into alliance with the UDT in 1986; c. 13,000 mems in 1987; Sec. for International Relations JOSÉ RAMOS HORTA; Mil. Commdr JOSÉ XANANA GUSMÃO.

National Liberation Front Aceh Sumatra: based in Aceh; f. 1990; seeks independence from Indonesia.

Organisasi Papua Merdeka (OPM) (Free Papua Movement): based in Irian Jaya; f. 1963; seeks unification with Papua New Guinea; Leader ELKY BEMEI.

União Democrática Timorense (UDT): based in Dili, East Timor; f. 1974; advocates self-determination for East Timor through a gradual process in which ties with Portugal would be maintained; allied itself with Fretilin in 1986.

Diplomatic Representation

EMBASSIES IN INDONESIA

Afghanistan: Jalan Dr Kusuma Atmaja 15, Jakarta; tel. (021) 333169; Chargé d'affaires: ABDUL GHAFUR BAHER.

Algeria: Jalan H. R. Rasuna Said, Kav. 10-1, Kuningan, Jakarta; tel. (021) 514719; Ambassador: MUHAMMAD KESSOURI.

Argentina: Jalan Duren Ban Ka 22, Jakarta 12730; tel. (021) 338088; telex 45529; Ambassador: GASPAR TABOADA.

Australia: Jalan M. H. Thamrin 15, Jakarta; tel. (021) 323109; Ambassador: BILL MORRISON.

Austria: Jalan Diponegoro 44, Jakarta 10310; tel. (021) 338101; telex 46387; Ambassador: Dr HERBERT KRÖLL.

Bangladesh: Jalan Mendut 3, Jakarta; tel. (021) 324850; Ambassador: Maj.-Gen. MOINUL HUSSEIN CHOWDHURY.

Belgium: Wisma BCA, 15th Floor, Jalan Jenderal Sudirman 22–23, Jakarta 12920; tel. (021) 5780510; telex 44413; fax (021) 5700676; Ambassador: NESTOR COCKX.

Brazil: Jalan Cik Ditiro 39, Menteng, Jakarta 10310; tel. (021) 358378; telex 45657; Ambassador: ANDRÉ GUIMARÃES.

Brunei: Jakarta; Ambassador: Dato Paduka Haji AWANG YAHYA BIN Haji HARRIS.

Bulgaria: Jalan Imam Bonjol 34/36, Jakarta 10310; tel. (021) 346725; telex 45106; Ambassador: OGNYAN MITEV.

Canada: Wisma Metropolitan, 5th Floor, Jalan Jenderal Sudirman 29, POB 52/JKT, Jakarta; tel. (021) 510709; telex 62131; Ambassador: JACK WHITTLETON.

Chile: Bina Mulia Bldg (Revlon), 7th Floor, Jalan H. R. Rasuna Said, Kav 10, Jakarta 12950; tel. (021) 5201131; telex 62587; Ambassador: RAÚL SCHMIDT DUSSAILLANT.

China, People's Republic: Jakarta; Ambassador: QIAN YONGNIAN.

Czechoslovakia: Jalan Prof. Mohammed Yamin 29, POB 1319, Jakarta; tel. (021) 344994; fax (021) 3101180; Ambassador: IZIDOR POCIATEK.

Denmark: Denmark House, Jalan Abdul Muis 34, POB 2329, Jakarta Pusat; tel. (021) 346615; telex 44188; Ambassador: MICHAEL BENDIX.

Egypt: Jalan Teuku Umar 68, Jakarta; tel. (021) 331141; Ambassador: MUHAMMAD ALI KAMEL.

Finland: Bina Mulia Bldg, 10th Floor, Jalan H. R. Rasuna Said, Kav. 10, Kuningan, Jakarta 12950; tel. (021) 516980; telex 62128; Ambassador: ERIK HEINRICHS.

France: Jalan M. H. Thamrin 20, Jakarta 10310; tel. (021) 332807; telex 61439; fax (021) 3100504; Ambassador: PATRICK O'CORNESSE.

Germany: Jalan M. H. Thamrin 1, Jakarta; tel. (021) 323908; telex 44333; Ambassador: THEODOR WALLAU.

Holy See: Jalan Merdeka Timur 18, POB 4227, Jakarta (Apostolic Nunciature); tel. (021) 341142; Apostolic Pro-Nuncio: FRANCESCO CANALINI.

Hungary: 36 Jalan H. R. Rasuna Said, Kav X/3, Kuningan, Jakarta 12950; tel. (021) 5203459; fax (021) 5203461; Ambassador: ISTVAN DEBRECENI.

India: Jalan H. R. Rasuna Said, Kav. S-1, Kuningan, Jakarta; tel. (021) 5204150; telex 44260; fax (021) 5204160; Ambassador: R. S. KALHA.

INDONESIA

Iran: Jalan Hos Cokroaminoto 110, Jakarta; tel. (021) 330623; telex 44433; Ambassador: MIR FAKHAR.

Iraq: Jalan Teuku Umar 38, Jakarta; tel. (021) 355017; telex 46280; Ambassador: ZAKI ABDULHAMID AL-HABBA.

Italy: Jalan Diponegoro 45, Jakarta; tel. (021) 337440; telex 61546; Ambassador: MICHELE MARTINEZ.

Japan: Jalan Mohammad Hoesni Thamrin 24, Jakarta; tel. (021) 324308; Ambassador: SUMIO EDAMURA.

Korea, Democratic People's Republic: Jalan Teuku Umar 72/74, Jakarta; tel. (021) 3100707; Ambassador: HAN PONG-HA.

Korea, Republic: Jalan Jenderal Gatot Subroto 57, Jakarta Selatan; tel. (021) 512309; Ambassador: YOUNG-SUP KIM.

Laos: Jakarta; Ambassador: PHANTHONG PHOMMAHASAI.

Malaysia: Jalan Imam Bonjol 17, Jakarta 10310; tel. (021) 336438; telex 61445; Ambassador: Dato' ABDULLAH ZAWAWI BIN Haji MOHAMMED.

Mexico: Jalan M. H. Thamrin 59, Jakarta; tel. (021) 337974; telex 61140; Ambassador: GUILLERMO CORONA MUÑOZ.

Myanmar: Jalan Haji Agus Salim 109, Jakarta; tel. (021) 320440; telex 61295; Ambassador: U THAN HLA.

Netherlands: Jalan H. R. Rasuna Said, Kav. S-3, Kuningan, Jakarta 12950; tel. (021) 511515; telex 62411; fax (021) 5700734; Ambassador: Baron G. W. DE VOS VAN STEENWIJK.

New Zealand: Jalan Diponegoro 41, Menteng, POB 2439, Jakarta; tel. (021) 330680; telex 46109; fax (021) 3104866; Ambassador: GORDON PARKINSON.

Nigeria: 15 Jalan Imam Bonjol, POB 3649, Jakarta; tel. (021) 327838; telex 61607; Ambassador: ADO SANUSI.

Norway: Bina Mulia Bldg, 4th Floor, Jalan H. R. Rasuna Said, Kav. 10, Jakarta 12950; tel. (021) 511990; telex 62127; fax (021) 5207365; Ambassador: TOROLF RAA.

Pakistan: Jalan Teuku Umar 50, Jakarta; tel. (021) 350576; Ambassador: MATAHAR HUSEIN.

Papua New Guinea: Panin Bank Centre, 1 Jalan Jenderal Sudirman, Jakarta; tel. (021) 711225; Ambassador: SEBULON KULU.

Philippines: Jalan Imam Bonjol 6-8, Jakarta; tel. (021) 3100334; Ambassador: Brig.-Gen. RAMON FAROLAN.

Poland: Jalan Diponegoro 65, Jakarta; tel. (021) 320509; Ambassador: PAWEŁ CIEŚLAR.

Romania: Jalan Cik Ditiro 42A, Jakarta; tel. (021) 3106240; telex 61208; Ambassador: VALERIU GEORGESCU.

Saudi Arabia: Jalan Imam Bonjol 3, Jakarta; tel. (021) 346342; Ambassador: MUHAMMAD SAID BASRAWI.

Singapore: Block X/4, Jalan H. R. Rasuna Said, Kav. 2, Kuningan, Jakarta 12950; tel. (021) 5201489; telex 62213; fax (021) 5201486; Ambassador: BARRY DESKER.

Spain: Wisma Kosgoro 12A, Jalan M. H. Thamrin 53, Jakarta; tel. (021) 325996; telex 45667; Ambassador: LEOPOLDO STAMPA.

Sri Lanka: Jalan Diponegoro 70, Jakarta; tel. (021) 321018; Ambassador: RUDRA S. RAJASINGHAM.

Sweden: Bina Mulia Bldg, 7th Floor, Jalan H. R. Rasuna Said, Kav. 10; POB 2824, Jakarta 10001; tel. (021) 5201551; telex 62714; fax (021) 512652; Ambassador: LARS-ERIK WINGREN.

Switzerland: Blok X 3/2, Jalan H. R. Rasuna Said, Kuningan 12950 Jakarta Selatan; tel. (021) 516061; telex 44113; Ambassador: BERNARD FREYMOND.

Syria: Jalan Gondangdia Lama 38, Jakarta; tel. (021) 359261; Ambassador: NADIM DOUAY.

Thailand: Jalan Imam Bonjol 74, Jakarta; tel. (021) 343762; Ambassador: RONGPET SUBHARITIKUL.

Turkey: Jalan R. S. Kuningan, Kav. I, Kuningan, Jakarta; tel. (021) 516258; telex 62506; Ambassador: SENCER ASENA.

USSR: Jalan M. H. Thamrin 13, Jakarta; tel. (021) 322162; Ambassador: VALERY V. MALYGIN.

United Kingdom: Jalan M. H. Thamrin 75, Jakarta 10310; tel. (021) 330904; telex 61166; fax (021) 321824; Ambassador: ROGER CARRICK.

USA: Jalan Merdeka Selatan 5, Jakarta; tel. (021) 360360; telex 44218; Ambassador: JOHN CAMERON MONJO.

Venezuela: Central Plaza Bldg, 17th Floor, Jalan Jenderal Sudirman, Jakarta; tel. (021) 516885; telex 62701; fax (021) 512487; Ambassador: JESÚS GARCÍA CORONADO.

Viet-Nam: Jalan Teuku Umar 25, Jakarta; tel. (021) 347325; Ambassador: DO NGOC DUONG.

Yugoslavia: Jalan Hos Cokroaminoto 109, Jakarta 10310; tel. (021) 333593; telex 45149; Ambassador: VJEKOSLAV KOPRIVNJAK.

Judicial System

There is one codified criminal law for the whole of Indonesia. In December 1989 the Islamic Judicature Bill, giving wider powers to Shariah courts, was approved by the House of Representatives. The new law gave Muslim courts authority over civil matters, such as marriage. Muslims may still choose to appear before a secular court. Europeans are subject to the Code of Civil Law published in the State Gazette in 1847. Alien orientals (i.e. Arabs, Indians, etc.) and Chinese are subject to certain parts of the Code of Civil Law and the Code of Commerce. The work of codifying this law has started, but, in view of the great complexity and diversity of customary law, it may be expected to take a considerable time to achieve.

Supreme Court: The final court of appeal.

Chief Justice: Lt-Gen. ALI SAID.

High Courts in Jakarta, Surabaya, Medan, Ujungpandang (Makassar), Banda Aceh, Padang, Palembang, Bandung, Semarang, Banjarmasin, Menado, Denpasar, Ambon and Jayapura deal with appeals from the District Courts.

District Courts deal with marriage, divorce and reconciliation.

Religion

All citizens are required to state their religion. According to a survey in 1985, 86.9% of the population were Muslims, while 9.6% were Christians, 1.9% were Hindus, 1.0% were Buddhists and 0.6% professed adherence to tribal religions.

ISLAM

In 1989 there were an estimated 150m. Muslims in Indonesia, giving it the world's largest Islamic population.

Indonesian Ulama Council (MUI): Central Muslim organization; Chair. HASAN BASRI.

CHRISTIANITY

Persekutuan Gereja-Gereja di Indonesia (Communion of Churches in Indonesia): Jalan Salemba Raya 10, Jakarta 10430; tel. (021) 8581321; fax (021) 8581323; f. 1950; 54 mem. churches; Chair. Rev. Dr S. SOPATER; Gen. Sec. Rev. Dr JOSEPH M. PATTIASINA.

The Roman Catholic Church

Indonesia (excluding East Timor) comprises eight archdioceses and 25 dioceses. At 31 December 1988 there were an estimated 4.53m. adherents in the country, representing about 2.6% of the total population.

Bishops' Conference: Konperensi Waligeraja Indonesia, Taman Cut Mutiah 10, Jakarta 10340; tel. (021) 336422; telex 61522; f. 1973; Pres. Most Rev. JULIUS RIYADI DARMAATMADJA, Archbishop of Semarang.

Archbishop of Ende: Most Rev. DONATUS DJAGOM, Keuskupan Agung, Tromol Pos 210, Ende, Flores; tel. 176.

Archbishop of Jakarta: Most Rev. LEO SOEKOTO, Jalan Katedraal 7, Jakarta 10710; tel. (021) 362392.

Archbishop of Kupang: Most Rev. GREGORIUS MANTEIRO, Keuskupan Agung, Jalan Ahmad Yani 43, Kupang, Timor; tel. 21031.

Archbishop of Medan: Most Rev. ALFRED GONTI PIUS DATUBARA, Jalan Imam Bonjol 39, 20152 Medan, Sumatra Utara; tel. (061) 516647.

Archbishop of Merauke: Most Rev. JACOBUS DUIVENVOORDE, Keuskupan Agung, Merauke 99602, Irian Jaya; tel. (0971) 21011.

Archbishop of Pontianak: Most Rev. HIERONYMUS HERCULANUS BUMBUN, POB 120, Jalan A. R. Hakim 92A, Pontianak 78001, Kalimantan Barat; tel. (0561) 2382.

Archbishop of Semarang: Most Rev. JULIUS RIYADI DARMAATMADJA, Keuskupan Agung, Jalan Pandanaran 13, 50231 Semarang; tel. (024) 312276.

Archbishop of Ujung Pandang: Most Rev. FRANCIS VAN ROESSEL, Keuskupan Agung, Jalan Thamrin 5-7, Ujung Pandang; tel. (0411) 5744.

East Timor comprises the single diocese of Dili, directly responsible to the Holy See. At 31 December 1988 the territory had an estimated 566,301 Roman Catholics (about 80% of the total population).

Bishop of Dili: Rt Rev. CARLOS FILIPE XIMINES BELO, Uskupan Lecidere, K. P. 250, Dili 8800; tel. 21331.

Other Christian Churches

Protestant Church in Indonesia (Gereja Protestan di Indonesia): Jalan Medan Merdeka Timur 10, Jakarta Pusat; tel. (021) 342895;

INDONESIA

merger of eight churches of Calvinist tradition; 2,287,000 mems, 2,896 congregations, 1,920 pastors (1985); Chair. Rev. D. J. LUMENTA.

Numerous other Protestant communities exist throughout Indonesia, mainly organized on a local basis. The largest of these (1985 memberships) are: the Batak Protestant Christian Church (1,875,143); the Christian Church in Central Sulawesi (100,000); the Christian Evangelical Church in Minahasa (730,000); the Christian Protestant Church in Indonesia (210,924); the East Java Christian Church (123,850); the Evangelical Christian Church in West Irian (360,000); the Evangelical Christian Church of Sangir-Talaud (190,000); the Indonesian Christian Church/Huria Kristen Indonesia (316,525); the Javanese Christian Churches (121,500); the Kalimantan Evangelical Church (182,217); the Karo Batak Protestant Church (164,288); the Nias Protestant Christian Church (250,000); the Protestant Church in the Moluccas (575,000); the Protestant Evangelical Church in Timor (700,000); the Simalungun Protestant Christian Church (155,000); and the Toraja Church (250,000).

The Press

PRINCIPAL DAILIES

Bali

Harian Pagi Umum (Bali Post): Jalan Kepudang 67A, Denpasar 80232; f. 1948; daily (Indonesian edn), weekly (English edn); Editor K. NADHA; circ. 25,000.

Java

Bandung Post: Jaan Naripan 7, Bandung.

Berita Buana: Jalan Tanah Abang Dua 33–35, Jakarta Pusat 10110; tel. (021) 340011; telex 46472; f. 1970; relaunched 1990; Indonesian; circ. 150,000.

Berita Yudha: Jalan Bangka II/2, 2nd Floor, Kebayoran Baru, Jakarta; tel. (021) 75286; f. 1971; Indonesian; Editor SUNARDI; circ. 50,000.

Bisnis Indonesia: Jalan Kramat V/8, Jakarta 10430; tel. (021) 342191; f. 1985; Indonesian; Editor AMIR DAUD; circ. 30,000.

Harian Indonesia (Indonesia Rze Pao): Jalan Toko Tiga Seberang 21, POB 534, Jakarta Kota; tel. (021) 6295984; fax (021) 6297830; f. 1966; Chinese; Editor W. D. SUKISMAN; Dir HADI WIBOWO; circ. 42,000.

Harian Terbit: Jalan Pulogadung 15, Jakarta 13260; tel. (021) 4713347; fax (021) 4896630; f. 1971; Indonesian; Editor R. H. S. HADIKAMAJAYA; circ. 70,000.

Harian Umum AB: CTC Bldg, 2nd Floor, Kramat Raya 94, Jakarta Pusat; f. 1965; official armed forces journal; Dir GOENARSO; Editor-in-Chief N. SOEPANGAT; circ. 80,000.

The Indonesia Times: Jalan Letjen. S. Parman, Kav. 72, POB 224, Slipi, Jakarta; tel. (021) 592403; telex 46968; f. 1974; English; Vice-Chief Editor T. S. S. SUTANTO; circ. 35,000.

Indonesian Daily News: Surabaya; f. 1957; English; Editor HOS. NURYAHYA; circ. 10,000.

Indonesian Observer: Jalan A. M. Sangaji 11, POB 2211, 10001 Jakarta; tel. (021) 352664; f. 1955; English; independent; Editor (vacant); circ. 25,000.

Jakarta Post: Jalan Palmerah Selatan 15B/C, Jakarta Pusat 10270; tel. (021) 5483948; fax (021) 5492685; f. 1983; English; Gen. Man. RAYMOND TORUAN; Editor SABAM SIAGIAN; circ. 21,500.

Jawa Pos: Jalan Kembang Jepun 167, Surabaya; tel. (031) 22778; telex 31988; f. 1949; Indonesian; Chief Editor DAHLAN ISKAN; circ. 120,000.

Kedaulatan Rakyat: Jalan P. Mangkubumi 40–42, Yogyakarta; f. 1945; Indonesian; independent; Editor IMAN SUTRISNO; circ. 50,000.

Kompas: Jalan Gajah Mada 104, Jakarta 11140; tel. (021) 6297809; telex 41216; fax (021) 6297742; f. 1965; Indonesian; Editor Drs JAKOB OETAMA; circ. 523,453.

Masa Kini: Jalan Suroto 16, Yogyakarta 55224; f. 1966; tel. (0274) 86662; Chief Editor H. DJARNAWI HADIKUSUMA; circ. 25,000.

Merdeka: Jalan A. M. Sangaji 11, Jakarta; tel. (021) 364858; f. 1945; Indonesian; independent; Dir and Chief Editor B. M. DIAH; circ. 130,000.

Pelita (Torch): Jalan Diponegoro 60, Jakarta; f. 1974; Indonesian; Muslim; Editor AKBAR TANJUNG; circ. 80,000.

Pewarta Surabaya: Jalan Karet 22, POB 85, Surabaya; f. 1995; Indonesian; Editor RADEN DJAROT SOEBIANTORO; circ. 10,000.

Pikiran Rakyat: Jalan Asia-Afrika 77, Bandung 40111; tel. (022) 51216; telex 28385; f. 1950; Indonesian; independent; Editor BRAM M. DARMAPRAWIRA; circ. 150,000.

Pos Kota: Jalan Gajah Mada 100, Jakarta; tel. (021) 6290874; telex 41171; f. 1970; Indonesian; Editor H. SOFYAN LUBIS; circ. 500,000.

Suara Karya: Jalan Bangka 11/2, Kebayoran Baru, Jakarta; f. 1971; Indonesian; Editor SYAMSUL BASRI; circ. 100,000.

Suara Merdeka: Jalan Pandanaran 30, Semarang; tel. (024) 26544; telex 22269; fax (024) 20199; f. 1950; Indonesian; Publr BUDI SANTOSO; Editor SUWARNO; circ. 160,000.

Suara Pembaruan: Jalan Dewi Sartika 136/D, Jakarta 13630; tel. (021) 8093208; telex 48202; fax (021) 8091652; f. 1987; fmrly known as Sinar Harapan (Ray of Hope); Publr ALBERT HASIBUAN; Editor STIADI TRYMAN.

Surabaya Post: Jalan Taman Ade Irma Nasution 1, Surayaba; tel. (031) 45523; telex 31158; fax (031) 45394; f. 1953; independent; Publr Mrs TUTY AZIS; Editor IMAM PUJONO; circ. 115,000.

Kalimantan

Banjarmasin Post: Jalan Pasar Baru 222, Banjarmasin; f. 1971; Indonesian; Chief Editor H. J. DJOK MENTAYA; circ. 50,000.

Gawi Manuntung: Jalan Pangeran Samudra 97B, Banjarmasin; f. 1972; Indonesian; Editor M. ALI SRI INDRADJAYA; circ. 5,000.

Sulawesi

Pedoman Rakyat: Jalan H. A. Mappanyukki 28, Ujungpandang; f. 1947; independent; Editor M. BASIR; circ. 30,000.

Suluh Merdeka: Jalan Haryane MT, Menado.

Sumatra

Analisa: Jalan Jenderal A. Yani 37–43, Medan; tel. (061) 326655; telex 51326; fax (061) 514031; f. 1972; Indonesian; Editor SOFFYAN; circ. 75,000.

Haluan: Jalan Damar 57 C/F, Padang; f. 1948; Editor-in-Chief RIVAI MARLAUT; circ. 40,000.

Mimbar Umum: Merah; tel. (061) 517807; telex 51905; f. 1947; Indonesian; independent; Editor MOHD LUD LUBIS; circ. 55,000.

Sinar Indonesia Baru: Jalan Brigjen. Katamso 54, Medan; f. 1970; Indonesian; Chief Editor G. M. PANGGABEAN; circ. 150,000.

Suara Rakyat Semesta: Jalan K. H. Ashari 52, Palembang; Indonesian; Editor DJADIL ABDULLAH; circ. 10,000.

Waspada: Jalan Jenderal Sudirman, Brigjen Katamso 1, Medan; tel. (061) 520858; telex 51347; fax (061) 510025; f. 1947; Indonesian; Chief Editor ANI IORUS; circ. 60,000 (daily), 55,000 (Sunday).

PRINCIPAL PERIODICALS

Amanah: Jalan Garuda 69, Kemayoran, Jakarta; tel. (021) 410254; fortnightly; Muslim current affairs; Indonesian; Man. Dir MASKUN ISKANDAR; circ. 180,000.

Basis: POB 299 yk, Yogyakarta 55001; tel. (0274) 88283; f. 1951; monthly; cultural; Editor DICK HARTOKO; circ. 3,000.

Berita Negara: Jalan Pertjetakan Negara 21, Kotakpos 2111, Jakarta; tel. (021) 4207251; f. 1951; 2 a week; official gazette.

Bobo: PT Gramedia, Jalan Kebahagiaan 4-14, Jakarta 11140; tel. (021) 6297809; telex 41216; fax (021) 6390080; f. 1973; weekly; children's magazine; Editor TINEKE LATUMETEN; circ. 240,000.

Bola: Jalan Palmerah Selatan 17, Jakarta 10270; tel. (021) 5483008; fax (021) 5483008; weekly; Friday; sports magazine; Indonesian; Editor HIKMAT KUSUMANINGRAT; circ. 407,850.

Buana Minggu: Jalan Tanah Abang Dua 33, Jakarta Pusat 10110; tel. (021) 364190; telex 46472; weekly; Sunday; Indonesian; Editor WINOTO PARARTHO; circ. 193,450.

Budaja Djaja: Jalan Gajah Mada 104–110A, Jakarta Barat; f. 1968; cultural; independent; Editor AJIP ROSIDI; circ. 4,000.

Business News: Jalan H. Abdul Muis 70, Jakarta 10160; tel. (021) 348207; fax (021) 354280; f. 1956; 3 a week (Indonesian edn), 2 a week (English edn); Chief Editor SANJOTO SASTROMIHARDJO; circ. 15,000.

Depthnews Indonesia: Jalan Jatinegara Barat III/6, Jakarta 13310; tel. (021) 8194994; fax (021) 8195501; f. 1972; weekly; publ. by Press Foundation of Indonesia; Editor SUMONO MUSTOFFA.

Dunia Wanita: Jalan Brigjen. Katamso 1, Medan; tel. (061) 520858; fax (061) 510025; f. 1949; fortnightly; Indonesian; women's magazine; Chief Editor Dr RAYATI SYAFRIN; circ. 10,000.

Economic Review: c/o BNI 1946, Jalan Jenderal Sudirman, Kav. 1, POB 2955, Jakarta 10001; tel. (021) 5701001; telex 45524; fax (021) 5700926; f. 1947; 6 a year; English.

Economics and Finance in Indonesia: Institute for Economic and Social Research, University of Indonesia, Jalan Raya Salemba 4, Jakarta 10400; tel. (021) 330225; fax (021) 334310; f. 1948; quarterly; circ. 4,000.

Ekonomi Indonesia: Jalan Merdeka, Timur 11–12, Jakarta; tel. (021) 494458; monthly; English; economic journal; Editor Z. ACHMAD; circ. 20,000.

INDONESIA

Femina: Blok B, Jalan H. R. Rasuna Said, Kav. 32–33, Jakarta Selatan; tel. (021) 513816; telex 62338; fax (021) 513041; f. 1972; weekly; women's magazine; Publisher SOFJAN ALISJAHBANA; circ. 130,000.

Gema Jusani: Jalan Salemba Tengah 47, Jakarta Pusat; f. 1981; monthly; Indonesian; journal of Corps of Invalids; Editor H. ANWAR BEY; circ. 20,000.

Hai: Jalan Palmerah Selatan 22, Jakarta 10270; tel. (021) 5483008; telex 41216; fax (021) 6390080; f. 1973; weekly; youth magazine; Editor ARSWENDO ATMOWILOTO.

Horison: Jalan Gajah Mada 104–110A, Jakarta Barat; f. 1966; monthly; literary and cultural; independent; Editors MOCHTAR LUBIS, H. B. JASSIN, TAUFIC ISMAEL; circ. 4,000.

Hukum & Keadilan: Jalan Gajah Mada 110A, Jakarta Barat; f. 1974; fortnightly; independent law journal; Editors SUARDI TASRIF, SOENARDI, ADNAN BUYUNG NASUTION; circ. 3,000.

Indonesia Magazine: 20 Jalan Merdeka Barat, Jakarta; tel. (021) 352015; telex 46655; f. 1969; monthly; English; Chair. G. DWIPAYANA; Editor-in-Chief HADELY HASIBUAN; circ. 15,000.

Intisari (Digest): Jalan Palmerah Selatan 24, POB 291/JKB, Jakarta 11001; tel. (021) 5483008; telex 46327; fax (021) 5486085; f. 1963; monthly; investment and trading; Editors IRAWATI, Drs J. OETAMA; circ. 141,000.

Keluarga: Jalan Sangaji 11, Jakarta; fortnightly; women's and family magazine; Editor S. DAHONO.

Majalah Ekonomis: Jakarta; monthly; English; business; Chief Editor S. ARIFIN HUTABARAT; circ. 20,000.

Majalah Kedokteran Indonesia (Journal of the Indonesian Medical Asscn): Jalan Kesehatan 111/29, Jakarta 11/16; f. 1951; monthly; Indonesian, English.

Manglé: Jalan Lodaya 19–21, 40262 Bandung; tel. (022) 411438; f. 1957; weekly; Sundanese; Chief Editor Drs OEJANG DARAJATOEN; circ. 74,000.

Matra: Jalan H. R. Rasuna Said, Kav. 62, Jakarta; tel. (021) 515952; telex 46777; f. 1986; monthly; men's magazine; general interest and current affairs; Editor-in-Chief FIKRI JUFRI; circ. 100,000.

Mimbar Kabinet Pembangunan: Jalan Merdeka-Barat 7, Jakarta; f. 1966; monthly; Indonesian; publ. by Dept of Information.

Mutiara: Jalan Dewi Sartika 136D, Cawang, Jakarta Timur; general interest; Publr H. G. RORIMPANDEY.

Nova: PT Gramedia, Jalan Kebahagiaan 4-14, Jakarta 11140; tel. (021) 6297809; telex 41216; fax (021) 6390080; weekly; Sunday; women's interest; Indonesian; Editor EVIE FADJARI; circ. 220,000.

Peraba: Bintaran Kidul 5, Yogyakarta; weekly; Indonesian and Javanese; Roman Catholic; Editor W. KARTOSOEHARSONO.

Pertani PT: Jalan Pasar Minggu, Kalibata, POB 247 KBY, Jakarta Selatan; tel. (021) 793108; telex 47249; f. 1974; Indonesian; agricultural; Pres. Dir Ir RUSLI YAHYA.

Rajawali: Jakarta; monthly; Indonesian; civil aviation and tourism; Dir R. A. J. LUMENTA; Man. Editor KARYONO ADHY.

Selecta: Kebon Kacang 29/4, Jakarta; fortnightly; illustrated; Editor SAMSUDIN LUBIS; circ. 80,000.

Sinar Jaya: Jalan Sultan Agung 67A, Jakarta Selatan; bi-weekly; agriculture; Chief Editor Ir SURYONO PROJOPRANOTO.

Tempo: Gedung Tempo, 8th Floor, Jalan H. R. Rasuna Said, Kav. C-17, Jakarta; tel. (021) 5201022; telex 46777; fax (021) 5204121; f. 1971; weekly; Indonesian; current affairs; Editor GOENAWAN MOHAMAD; circ. 162,000.

NEWS AGENCIES

Antara (Indonesian National News Agency): Wisma Antara, 19th and 20th Floors, 17 Jalan Merdeka Selatan, POB 257, Jakarta 10002; tel. (021) 344379; telex 44305; fax (021) 343052; f. 1937; state radio, TV and 54 newspaper subscribers in 1989; 27 brs in Indonesia, three overseas brs; nine bulletins in Indonesian and seven in English; one European edn, one Asian edn; monitoring service of stock exchanges world-wide; photo service; Man. Dir/Editor-in-Chief HANDJOJO NITIMIHARDJO.

Kantorberita Nasional Indonesia (KNI News Service): Jalan Jatinegara Barat III/6, Jakarta Timur 13310; tel. (021) 811003; fax (021) 8195501; f. 1966; independent national news agency; foreign and domestic news in Indonesian and English; Dir and Editor-in-Chief Drs SUMONO MUSTOFFA; Exec. Editor ANWAR BEY.

Foreign Bureaux

Agence France-Presse (AFP): Jalan Indramayu 18, Jakarta Pusat 10310; tel. (021) 334877; Chief Correspondent ALAIN BOEBION.

Agencia EFE (Spain): J. L. Cilandak VI/37, Kebayoran Baru, Jakarta; Bureau Chief MIRIAM PADILLA.

Agenzia Nazionale Stampa Associata (ANSA) (Italy): Jalan Taman Setiabudi Timur, Jakarta 12910; tel. (021) 511164; Correspondent LOUISE WANANDAR.

Associated Press (AP) (USA): 18th Floor, Wisma Antara, Suite 1806, 17 Jalan Medan Selatan, Jakarta 10110; tel. (021) 367690; telex 46439; Correspondent GHAFUR FADYL.

Inter Press Service (IPS) (Italy): 4th Floor, Gedung Dewan Pers, Jalan Kebon Sirah 34, Jakarta 10110; tel. (021) 353131; Chief Correspondent KALAYANAMITRA.

Jiji Tsushin-sha (Japan): Jalan Raya Bogor 109B, Jakarta; tel. (021) 8090509; Correspondent MARGA RAHARJA.

Kyodo Tsushin (Japan): Skyline Bldg, 11th Floor, M. H. Thamrin 9, Jakarta Pusat; tel. (021) 345012; Correspondent MASAYUKI KITAMURA.

Reuters (UK): 11th Floor, Wisma Antara, Jalan Medan Merdeka Selatan 17, POB 2318, Jakarta Pusat; tel. (021) 345011; telex 45373; Correspondent JONATHAN THATCHER.

Telegrafnoye Agentstvo Sovetskovo Soyuza (TASS) (USSR): 7 Surabaya, Jakarta; Correspondent YURI SAGAJDA.

United Press International (UPI) (USA): Wisma Antara, 14th Floor, Jalan Medan Merdeka Selatan 17, Jakarta; tel. (021) 341056; telex 44305; Bureau Chief JOHN HAIL.

PRESS ASSOCIATIONS

Persatuan Wartawan Indonesia (Indonesian Journalists' Asscn): Gedung Dewan Pers, 4th Floor, 34 Jalan Kebon Sirih, Jakarta 10110; tel. (021) 353175; f. 1946; 5,000 mems (Sept. 1989); Exec. Chair. M. SOEGENG WIDJAJA; Gen. Sec. H. SOFJAN LUBIS.

Serikat Penerbit Suratkabar (SPS) (Indonesian Newspaper Publishers' Asscn): Gedung Dewan Pers, Floor 6, Jalan Kebonsirih 34, Jakarta Pusat; f. 1946; tel. (021) 359671; Chair. D. M. SUNARDI; Sec.-Gen. MUHAMMAD CHUDORI.

Yayasan Pembina Pers Indonesia (Press Foundation of Indonesia): Jalan Jatinegara Barat III/6, Jakarta Timur; tel. (021) 8194994; f. 1967; Chair. SUGIARSO SUROYO, MOCHTAR LUBIS.

Publishers

Jakarta

Aries Lima: Blok B/2, Komplex Maya Indah II, Jalan Kramat Raya 3E, Jakarta Pusat; tel. (021) 367038; f. 1974; general and children's; Pres. TUTI SUNDARI AZMI.

Aya Media Pustaka PT: Blok C/2, Jalan Dharmawangsa III, Jakarta 12160; tel. (021) 7206903; telex 47477; fax (021) 7201401; children's; Dir Drs ARIANTO TUGIYO.

Balai Pustaka: Jalan Dr Wahidin 1, POB 29, Jakarta; tel. (021) 361701; telex 45905; f. 1908; children's, literary, scientific pubis and periodicals; CEO/Pres. Drs ZAKARIA IDRIS.

Bhratara Karya Aksara: Jalan Rawabali II/5, Kawasan Industri Pulogadung, Jakarta 13001; tel. (021) 4890280; telex 49283; f. 1975; university and educational textbooks; Man. Dir HADI TOPOBROTO.

Bulan Bintang: Jalan Kramat Kwitang 1/8, Jakarta 10420; tel. (021) 342883; f. 1954; religious, social science, natural and applied sciences, art; Pres. AMRAN ZAMZAMI; Man. Dir FAUZI AMELZ.

C. V. Haji Masagung: Jalan Kwitang 8, POB 2260, Jakarta 10002; tel. (021) 362909; telex 45255; f. 1953; general, religious, textbooks, science; Pres. Haji MASAGUNG.

Djambatan: Jalan Kramat Raya 152, Tromolpos 1116, Jakarta 10011; tel. (021) 324332; f. 1954; children's, textbooks, social sciences, fiction; Dir ROSWITHA PAMOENTJAK SINGGIH.

Dunia Pustaka Jaya: Jalan Kramat Raya 5K, Jakarta 10450; tel. (021) 367339; f. 1971; fiction, religion, essays, poetry, drama, criticism, art, philosophy and children's; Man. YUS RUSAMSI.

EGC CV: Jalan Agung Jaya III/2 Sunter Agung Podomoro, Jakarta 14350; tel. (021) 682223; fax (021) 684546; medical and public health, psychology.

Erlangga: Jalan Kramat IV/11, Jakarta 10420; tel. (021) 356593; f. 1952; secondary school and university textbooks; Man. Dir M. HUTAURUK.

Gaya Favorit Press: Blok B, Jalan H. R. Rasuna Said, Kav. 32–33, Jakarta 12910; tel. (021) 513816; telex 62338; f. 1971; fiction, popular science and children's; Man. Dir NY MIRTA KARTOHADIPRODJO.

Ghalia Indonesia: Jalan Pramuka Raya 4, Jakarta Timur; tel. (021) 884814; f. 1972; children's and general science, textbooks; Man. Dir LUKMAN SAAD.

Gramedia: Jalan Palmerah Selatan 22, Lantai IV, POB 615, Jakarta Pusat; tel. (021) 5483008; telex 46327; f. 1973; university textbooks, general non-fiction, children's and magazines; Gen. Man. ALFONS TARYADI.

Gunung Mulia: Jalan Kwitang 22, Jakarta Pusat; tel. (021) 372208; f. 1951; general, children's, religious, home economics; Man. LIEM KIE DJIAN.

Hidakarya Agung PT: Jalan Kebon Kosong F74, Kemayoran, Jakarta Pusat; tel. (021) 411074; Dir CHAIRI MACHMUD.

Ichtiar: Jalan Majapahit 6, Jakarta Pusat; tel. (021) 341226; f. 1957; textbooks, law, social sciences, economics; Dir JOHN SEMERU.

Indira PT: Jalan Borobudur 20, Jakarta Pusat; tel. (021) 882754; telex 48211; f. 1953; general science and children's; Man. Dir WAHYUDI DJOJOADINOTO.

Kinta CV: Jalan Kemanggisan Ilir V/110, Pal Merah, Jakarta Barat; tel. (021) 5494751; f. 1950; textbooks, social science, general; Man. Drs MOHAMAD SALEH.

Mutiara Sumber Widya PT: Jalan Salemba Tengah 36–38 Jakarta; tel. (021) 882441; telex 46709; f. 1951; textbooks, religious, social sciences, general and children's; Pres. FAHMI OEMAR.

Penerbit Universitas Indonesia: Jalan Salemba Raya 4, Jakarta; tel. (021) 335373; f. 1969; science; Man. Dr EDI SWASONO.

Pradnya Paramita PT: Jalan Bunga 8–8A, Matraman, Jakarta 13140; tel. (021) 8504944; f. 1973; children's, general, educational, technical and social science; Pres. Dir SOEHARDJO.

Pustaka Antara PT: Jalan Teluk Betung 55, Jakarta Pusat 10230; tel. (021) 326510; f. 1952; textbooks, political, religious, children's and general; Man. Dir AIDA JOESOEF AHMAD.

Pustaka Sinar Harapan: Jalan Dewi Sartika 136D, Jakarta 13630; tel. (021) 8093208; telex 48202; f. 1981; general science, fiction, comics, children's; Dir ARISTIDES KATOPPO.

Rineka Cipta: Blok B/5, Jalan Jenderal Sudirman, Kav. 36A, Bendungan Hilir, Jakarta; tel. (021) 586640; f. 1990 by merger of Aksara Baru (f. 1972) and Bina Aksara; general science and university texts; Dir DRS SUARDI.

Sastra Hudaya: Jalan Kalasan 1, Jakarta Pusat; tel. (021) 882321; f. 1967; religious, textbooks, children's and general; Man. ADAM SALEH.

Tintamas Indonesia: Jalan Kramat Raya 60, Jakarta Pusat 10420; tel. (021) 3107148; f. 1947; history, modern science and culture, especially Islamic; Man. Miss MARHAMAH DJAMBEK.

Widjaya: Jalan Pecenongan 48C, Jakarta Pusat; tel. (021) 363446; f. 1950; textbooks, children's, religious and general; Man. DIDI LUTHAN.

Yasaguna: Jalan Minangkabau 44, POB 422, Jakarta Selatan; tel. (021) 820422; f. 1964; agricultural, children's, handicrafts; Dir HILMAN MADEWA.

Bandung

Alma'arif: Jalan Tamblong 48–50, Bandung; tel. (022) 50708; f. 1949; textbooks, religious and general; Man. H. M. BAHARTHAH.

Alumni: Jalan Dr Djundjunan 190, POB 272, Bandung; tel. (022) 87672; telex 28460; f. 1968; university and school textbooks; Dir EDDY DAMIAN.

Angkasa: Jalan Merdeka 6, POB 354, Bandung; tel. (022) 51795; telex 28530; Dir FACHRI SAID.

Binacipta: Jalan Ganesya 4, Bandung; tel. (022) 84319; f. 1967; textbooks, scientific and general; Dir Mrs R. BARDIN.

Diponegoro Publishing House: Jalan Mohammad Toha 44–46, Bandung 40252; tel. (022) 471215; f. 1963; religious, textbooks, fiction, non-fiction, general; Man. H. A. A. DAHLAN.

Eresco PT: Jalan Ciateul 40, Bandung; tel. (022) 472529; f. 1957; scientific and general; Man. Dr ARFAN ROZALI.

Orba Sakti: Jalan Pandu Dalam 3/67, Bandung; tel. (022) 614718; Dir H. HASBULLOH.

Remaja Rosdakarya: Jalan Ciateul 34–36, POB 284, Bandung 40252; tel. (022) 470287; textbooks and children's fiction; Man. ROZALI USMAN.

Tarsito: Jalan Guntur 20, Bandung; tel. (022) 421915; Dir T. SITORUS.

Tira Pustaka: Jalan Cemara Raya 1, Kav. 10D, Jaka Permai Jakasampurna, Bekasi Jawa Barat, Bandung; tel. (0219) 71276; telex 62612; Dir WILLIE KOEN.

Flores

Penerbit Nusa Indah: Jalan Katedral 5, Ende 86312, Flores; tel. 81; f. 1970; religious and general; Dir HENRI DAROS.

Kudus

Menara Kudus: Jalan Menara 2, Kudus; tel. 143527; f. 1958; religious; Man. HILMAN NAJIB.

Medan

Hasmar: Jalan Letjen Haryono M.T. 1, POB 446, Medan; tel. (061) 24181; primary school textbooks; Dir HASBULLAH LUBIS; Man. AMRAN SAID RANGKUTI.

Islamiyah: Jalan Sutomo 328–329, Kotakpos 11, Medan; tel. (061) 25426; f. 1954.

Madju: Jalan Sisingamangaraja Raja 25, Medan; tel. (061) 26550; f. 1950; textbooks, children's and general; Pres. and Dir H. MOHAMED ARBIE.

Semarang

Effhar COY PT: Jalan Dorang 7, Semarang; tel. (024) 23518; f. 1974; school textbooks; Dir DARADJAT HARAHAP.

Intan Pariwara: Jalan Macanan, Ketandan, Klaten, Jawa-Tengah; tel. (0272) 21641; Pres. SOETIKNO.

Surabaya

Airlangga University Press: Dharmahusada 47, Surabaya; tel. (031) 472719; Dir Drs SOEDHARTO.

Assegaff: Jalan Panggung 136, Surabaya; tel. (031) 22971; f. 1951; religion, languages, primary school textbooks; Man. HASSAN ASSEGAFF.

Bina Ilmu PT: Jalan Tunjungan 53E, Surabaya 60275; tel. (031) 472214; fax (031) 515421; f. 1973; school textbooks; Pres. ARIEFIN NOOR.

Bintang: Jalan Potroagung III/1A, Surabaya; tel. (031) 315941; Dir AGUS WINARNO.

Grip: Jalan Kawung 2, POB 129, Surabaya; tel. (031) 22564; f. 1958; textbooks and general; Man. Mrs SURIPTO.

Institut Dagang Muchtar: Jalan Embong Wungu 8, Surabaya; tel. (031) 42973; textbooks for business colleges; Pres. Z. A. MOECHTAR.

Jaya Baya: Jalan Embong Malang 69H, POB 250, Surabaya 60001; tel. (031) 41169; f. 1945; religion, philosophy and ethics; Man. TADJIB ERMADI.

Karunia: Jalan Peneleh 18, Surabaya; tel. (031) 44120; f. 1970; textbooks and general; Man. HASAN ABDAN.

Marfiah: Jalan Kalibutuh 131, Surabaya; reference and primary school textbooks; Man. S. WAHYUDI.

Sinar Wijaya: Komplek Terminal Jembatan Merah, Stand C33-37, Surabaya; tel. (031) 270284; Dir DULRADJAK.

Ujungpandang

Bhakti Centra Baru PT: Jalan Jend. Akhmad Yani 15, Ujungpandang 90174; tel. (0411) 5192; telex 71276; f. 1972; textbooks, religion and general; Gen. Man. MOHAMMAD ALWI HAMU.

Yogyakarta

Centhini Yayasan: Jalan Dr Sutomo 9, Yogyakarta 55211; tel. (0274) 3010; f. 1984; Javanese Culture; Chair H. KARKONO KAMAJAYA.

Indonesia UP: Jalan Dr Sutomo 9, Yogyakarta 55211; tel. (0274) 3010; f. 1950; general science; Dir H. KARKONO KAMAJAYA.

Kedaulatan Rakyat PT: Jalan P. Mangkubumi 40–42, Yogyakarta; tel. (0274) 2163; telex 25176; Dir DRONO HARDJUSUWONGSO.

Yayasan Kanisius: Jalan Cempaka 9, Deresan, Yogyakarta 55281; tel. (0274) 88783; telex 25143; f. 1922; textbooks, religious and general; Man. R. P. S. PADMOBUSONO.

Government Publishing House

Balai Pustaka (State Publishing and Printing House): Jalan Dr Wahadin 1, Jakarta; history, anthropology, politics, philosophy, medical, arts and literature.

PUBLISHERS' ASSOCIATION

Ikatan Penerbit Indonesia (IKAPI) (Asscn of Indonesian Book Publishers): Jalan Kalipasir 32, Jakarta 10330; tel. (021) 321907; f. 1950; 293 mems; Pres. ROZALI USMAN SH; Sec.-Gen. SETIA DHARMA MADJID.

Radio and Television

In 1986 there were an estimated 32.8m. radio receivers in use. There were 5.8m. registered television receivers in use in 1988. In March 1989 Indonesia's first private commercial television station began broadcasting to the Jakarta area. By mid-1990 there were two privately-owned television stations in operation.

Directorate-General of Posts and Telecommunications: Jalan Kebon Sirih 37, Jakarta; tel. (021) 346000; telex 44407; Dir-Gen. S. ABDULRACHMAN.

RADIO

Radio Republik Indonesia (RRI): Jalan Merdeka Barat 4–5, POB 157, Jakarta 10110; tel. (021) 349091; telex 44349; fax (021) 367132; f. 1945; 49 stations; Dir ARSYAD SUBIK; Dep. Dirs FACHRUDDIN

INDONESIA

SOEKARNO (Overseas Service), SURYANTA SALEH (Programming), CHAIRUL ZEN (Programme Development), SAMSUL MUIN HARAHAP (Administration).

Voice of Indonesia: Medan Merdeka Barat 4-5, Jakarta; (021) 366811; foreign service; daily broadcasts in Arabic, English, French, German, Indonesian, Japanese, Bahasa Malaysia, Mandarin, Spanish and Thai.

TELEVISION

Rajawali Citra Televisi Indonesia (RCTI): Jalan Raya Pejuangan, Kebon Jeruk, Jakarta 11530; tel. (021) 5493960; fax (021) 5493846; f. 1989; first private channel; 20-year licence; Pres. Dir J. P. SOEBANDONO.

Yayasan Televisi Republik Indonesia (TVRI): TVRI Senayan, Jalan Gerbang Pemuda, Senayan, Jakarta; tel. (021) 581125; telex 46154; f. 1962; state-controlled; Dir Dr ISHADI.

Finance

(cap. = capital; auth. = authorized; p.u. = paid up; res = reserves; dep. = deposits; m. = million; brs = branches; amounts in rupiahs)

BANKING

Until 1988 the Indonesian banking sector was dominated by five state commercial banks and one state savings bank, although 112 other banks, with 1,800 branches, were in operation. Following the introduction of extensive financial-sector reforms in October 1988, licences were granted to 14 new foreign joint-venture banks, 26 commercial banks and about 250 secondary banks before the end of 1989. In addition, 700 new branches were established by existing banks during that period.

In mid-June 1990 total bank deposits stood at 63,010,000m. rupiahs.

Central Bank

Bank Indonesia: Jalan M. H. Thamrin 2, Jakarta; tel. (021) 372408; telex 44164; f. 1828; nationalized 1951; central bank since 1953; cap. and res 447,000m., dep. 3,406,000m. (March 1986); Gov. ADRIANUS MOOY; Pres. T. M. ZAHIRSJAH.

State Banks

Bank Bumi Daya: Jalan Imam Bonjol 61, POB 106, Jakarta 10002; tel. (021) 333721; telex 61117; fax (021) 330153; f. 1959; commercial and foreign exchange bank, specializes in credits to the plantation and forestry sectors; cap. and res 365,458m., dep. 7,408,354m. (June 1988); Pres. Dir H. SURASA; 82 brs, 17 sub-brs.

Bank Dagang Negara: Jalan M. H. Thamrin 5, POB 338/JKT, Jakarta; tel. (021) 321707; telex 61628; fax (021) 323618; f. 1960; auth. foreign exchange bank; specializes in credits to the mining sector; cap. p.u. 250m., dep. 5,028,041m. (Dec. 1987); Pres. H. M. WIDARSADIPRADJA; 127 brs.

Bank Ekspor Impor Indonesia: Jalan Lapangan Setasiun 1, POB 32, Jakarta Kota; tel. (021) 673122; telex 42702; fax (021) 674734; f. 1968; commercial and foreign exchange bank; specializes in credits for manufacture and export; cap. 200m., dep. 3,801,806m. (Dec. 1988); Pres. MOELJOTO DJOJOMARTONO; 56 brs.

Bank Negara Indonesia 1946: Jalan Jenderal Sudirman, Kav 1, POB 2955, Jakarta 10001; tel. (021) 5701001; telex 44303; fax (021) 5700980; f. 1946; commercial bank; specializes in credits to the industrial sector; cap. and res 598,803m., dep. 17,015,516m. (Dec. 1989); Pres. A. KUKUH BASUKI; 291 domestic brs, 5 overseas brs.

Bank Rakyat Indonesia; Jalan Jenderal Sudirman, Kav. 44-46, POB 94, Jakarta 10210; tel. (021) 5704313; telex 44574; fax (021) 5704154; f. 1895, present name since 1946; commercial and foreign exchange bank; specializes in credits to co-operatives in agriculture and fisheries, in rural credit generally and international business; cap. 300m., res 582,072m., dep. 14,161,929m. (Dec. 1989); Pres. KARMARDY ARIEF; 295 brs.

Bank Tabungan Negara (State Savings Bank): Jalan H. R. Rasuna Said, Kav. C-17, Jakarta Selatan; tel. (021) 5781210; telex 62313; f. 1964; savings bank; cap. p.u. 100m., dep. 810,033m. (June 1986); Pres. SASONOTOMO; 14 brs.

Selected National Private Banks

PT Bank Bali: Jalan Hayam Wuruk 84-85, Jakarta 11160; tel. (021) 6498006; telex 42724; f. 1954; foreign exchange bank; cap. p.u. 7,088m., dep. 255,871m. (March 1986); Pres. G. KARYADI; Chair. P. H. SUGIRI; 5 brs, 3 sub-brs.

PT Bank Buana Indonesia: Jalan Asemka 32-35, Jakarta; tel. (021) 672901; telex 42042; fax (021) 676916; f. 1956; foreign exchange bank; cap. p.u. 10,000m., dep. 595,453m. (Dec. 1989); Pres. HENDRA SURYADI; 23 brs, 79 sub-brs.

PT Bank Central Asia: Jalan Jenderal Sudirman, Kav. 22-23, Jakarta; tel. (021) 671771; telex 42860; fax (021) 6901828; f. 1957; cap. p.u. 47,000m., dep. 1,722,833m. (Dec. 1988); Pres. A. ALI; CEO Dir MOCHTAR RIADY; 20 brs, 15 sub-brs, repr. office 1.

PT Bank Danamon: Jalan Kebon Sirih 15, Jakarta 10002; tel. (021) 3805056; telex 61342; fax (021) 325601; f. 1956; cap. 7,840m., dep. 382,527m. (Dec. 1988); Pres. R. BIENTARNO; Gen. Man. HERMAN TANUWIDJAJA.

PT Bank Duta: Jalan Kebon Sirih 12, Jakarta 10110; tel. (021) 3800900; telex 48308; f. 1966; foreign exchange bank; placed under the control of Bank Indonesia in September 1990, owing to 'improper foreign exchange dealings'; cap. p.u. 10,000m., dep. 352,104m. (March 1986); 7 brs, 2 sub-brs.

PT Bank Niaga: Jalan Gajah Mada 18, Jakarta; tel. (021) 377809; telex 45894; f. 1955; foreign exchange bank; cap. p.u. 9,896m., dep. 271,515m. (March 1986); Pres. Dir ROBBY DJOHAN; Man. Dirs I. JONOSEWOJO, WIJATNO SOEPENADIE; 16 brs, 4 sub-brs.

PT Bank NISP: Jalan Taman Cibeunying Selatan 31, Bandung; tel. (022) 57926; telex 28269; fax (022) 73959; f. 1941; cap. p.u. 5,004m., dep. 195,788m. (June 1990); Pres. KARMAKA SURJAUDAJA; Man. Dirs PETER EKO SUTIOSO, ANWARY SURJAUDAJA; 16 brs.

PT Bank Pacific: Jalan K. H. Samanhudi 17-19, Jakarta; tel. (021) 376408; telex 44818; f. 1958; foreign exchange bank; cap. p.u. 12,000m., dep. 82,974m. (March 1986); Pres. M. HATTA ABDULAH; Man. Dirs OEMAR SAID, ABDUL FIRMAN, H. P. TOAR; 5 brs, 3 sub-brs.

PT Bank Perdania: Jalan Raya Mangga Besar 7-11, Jakarta; tel. (021) 621708; telex 41120; fax (021) 6592164; f. 1956; foreign exchange bank; Pres. ISMED SIREGAR; 1 br., 1 sub-br.

PT Bank Umum Nasional: Jalan Prapatan 50, Jakarta; tel. (021) 365563; telex 46034; f. 1952; foreign exchange bank; cap. p.u. 28,222m., dep. 695,698m. (Dec. 1987); Pres. Dir KAHARUDIN ONGKO, S. RANTY, V. U. KULIH; Exec. Dir M. DJAILANI; 15 brs, 4 sub-brs.

PT Bank Yudha Dhakti: Jakarta; f. 1990; established and wholly-owned by the Indonesian armed forces; Pres. SOLATI SIREGAR.

PT Overseas Express Bank: Jalan Pecenongan 84, POB 471 Jakarta 10120; tel. (021) 358103; telex 46350; f. 1974; foreign exchange bank; cap. p.u. 6,000m., dep. 443,888m. (June 1990); Chair. I NYOMAN MOENA; 9 brs.

PT Pan Indonesia (Panin) Bank: Panin Bank Centre, Jalan Jen. Sudirman, Senayan, Jakarta; tel. (021) 7394545; telex 47394; f. 1971; foreign exchange bank; cap. p.u. 16,000m., dep. 437,367m. (Sept. 1988); Pres. PRIJATNA ATMADJA; 14 brs, 12 sub-brs.

PT Sejahtera Bank Umum: Jalan Tiang Bendera 15, Jakarta Barat; tel. (021) 673804; telex 42760; f. 1952; cap. p.u. 10,000m., dep. 253,135m. (June 1989); Pres. LESMANA BASUKI; Man. Dir STEPHANUS SOEARTO; 7 brs, 1 sub-br.

PT South East Asia Bank Ltd: Jalan Asemka 16-17, Jakarta; tel. (021) 672197; telex 42731; f. 1957; cap. p.u. 4,000m., dep. 24,110m. (June 1986); Pres. Dir AGUS SALIM; Man. Dirs Drs B. SURYADI, TRISNO HARIANTO, HARIONO; 2 brs.

PT United City Bank: Jalan Hayam Wuruk 121, Jakarta; tel. (021) 6293508; telex 41165; f. 1968; cap. p.u. 18,203m., dep. 31,316m. (Dec. 1986); Pres. TJOKROPRANOLO; 3 brs, 2 sub-brs.

Development Bank

Bank Pembangunan Indonesia (BAPINDO) (Development Bank of Indonesia): Jalan Gondangdia Lama 2-4, POB 140, Jakarta 10002; tel. (021) 321908; telex 44214; f. 1960; state bank; provides medium- and long-term investment loans to new and existing business enterprises; equity financing and general banking services; and non-financial assistance, industrial research, and technical consultancy services; cap. p.u. 49,981m., total resources 1,459,900m. (Dec. 1986); Pres. SUBEKTI ISMAUN; 21 brs.

Selected Finance Corporations

PT Bahana Pembinaan Usaha Indonesia (BAHANA): Jalan Teuku Cik Ditiro 23, POB 3228, Jakarta 10350; tel. (021) 325207; telex 45332; fax (021) 326970; f. 1973; cap. p.u. 10,000m.; Pres. BAHAUDDIN DARUS.

PT Inter-Pacific Financial Corpn: Jalan Jenderal Sudirman, Kav. 31, Jakarta 12920; tel. (021) 5781095; telex 46289; fax (021) 5781084; f. 1973; cap. p.u. 3,000m.; Pres. and Dir SUPARI DHIRDJOPRAWIRO.

PT Multinational Finance Corpn (MULTICOR): Wisma BCA, 12th Floor, Jalan Jenderal Sudirman, Kav. 22-23, Jakarta 12920; tel. (021) 5781450; telex 44932; f. 1974; cap. p.u. 1,000m.; Pres. and Dir K. R. WYNN.

PT Mutual International Finance Corpn: Nusantara Bldg, 17th Floor, Jalan M. H. Thamrin 59, Jakarta 10350; tel. (021) 331108;

telex 61390; f. 1973; cap. p.u. 1,200m.; Pres. Dir ROCHMAT TANUSEPUTRA; Dep. Pres. Dir T. MARUYAMA.

PT Private Development Finance Co of Indonesia: Jalan Abdul Muis 60, Jakarta; tel. (021) 366608; telex 46778; f. 1973; cap. p.u. 4,539m.; Chair. and CEO SUDIARSO.

PT Usaha Pembiayaan Pembangunan Indonesia (PT Indonesian Development Finance Co): UPPINDO Bldg, Jalan H. R. Rasuna Said, Jakarta 12940; tel. (021) 8296970; fax (021) 8298536; f. 1972; cap. p.u. 26,103m. (Aug. 1990); Chair. HENDROBUDIYANTO; Pres. SARWONO WISHNUWARDHANA.

Foreign Banks

Algemene Bank Nederland NV (Netherlands): Jalan Ir H. Juanda 23–24, POB 2950, Jakarta 10001; tel. (021) 362309; telex 44124; Man. LEN H. STEFFEN.

Bangkok Bank Ltd (Thailand): Jalan M. H. Thamrin 3, POB 1165, Jakarta; tel. (021) 366008; telex 46193; f. 1968; Gen. Man. and Sr Vice-Pres. PHAIBUL INGKHAVAT; Br. Man. SAKSITH TEJASAKULSIN.

Bank of America NT & SA (USA): Wisma Antara, 1st Floor, Jalan Medan Merdeka Selatan 17, POB 195, Jakarta; tel. (021) 348031; telex 44374; f. 1968; Vice-Pres. and Man. Z. MISSERLIAN.

Bank of Tokyo Ltd (Japan): Midplaza Bldg, Jalan Jenderal Sudirman Kav. 10–11, POB 2711, Jakarta 10220; tel. (021) 5780709; telex 62467; fax (021) 581927; Gen. Man. KAZUTERU TANAKA.

The Chase Manhattan Bank, NA (USA): Chase Plaza, Jalan Jenderal Sudirman, Kav. 21, POB 311/JKT, Jakarta; tel. (021) 5782213; telex 62152; fax (021) 5780958; Country Man. KENNETH S. PATTON.

Citibank, NA (USA): Jalan Jenderal Sudirman 1, Jakarta 12930; tel. (021) 5782007; telex 44368; f. 1912; Vice-Pres JAMES F. HUNT, EDWIN GERUNGAN, ROBERT THORNTON.

Deutsche Bank (Asia) (Germany): Jalan Imam Bonjol 80, POB 135, Jakarta 10001; tel. (021) 331092; telex 61524; fax (021) 335252; Gen. Man. JÜRGEN MARZINIAK.

Hongkong and Shanghai Banking Corpn Ltd (Hong Kong): Wisma Metropolitan II, Jalan Jenderal Sudirman, Kav. 31, POB 2307, Jakarta 10001; tel. (021) 5780075; telex 44160; fax (021) 5781915; Man. K. R. WHITSON.

Standard Chartered Bank (UK): Wisma Kosgoro, Jalan M. H. Thamrin 53, POB 57/JKWK, Jakarta 10350; tel. (021) 325008; telex 61179; fax (021) 323619; Man. S. J. PARKER; 3 brs.

Westpac Banking Corpn (Australia): 17th Floor, BNI Bldg, Jalan Jenderal Sudirman, Jakarta; tel. (021) 5705137; telex 44277; fax (021) 5705138; f. 1972; Chief Rep. MICHAEL J. BURNS.

Banking Association

Indonesian National Private Banks Association (Perhimpunan Bank-Bank Nasional Swasta—PERBANAS): Jalan Perbanas, Karet Kuningan, Setiabudi, Jakarta 12940; tel. (021) 515731; telex 41467; fax (021) 513887; f. 1952; 101 mems; Chair. ABDULGANI; Sec.-Gen. THOMAS SUYATNO.

STOCK EXCHANGES

In 1990, 76 companies were listed on the Jakarta Stock Exchange, compared with only 24 in 1988. The rapid increase was due to the introduction of financial reforms in October 1988.

Badan Pelaksana Bursa Komoditi (Indonesian Commodity Exchange Board—ICEB): Bursa Bldg, 2nd and 4th Floors, Jalan Medan Merdeka Selatan 14, Jakarta 10110; tel. (021) 371921; telex 44194; fax (021) 3804426; trades in rubber, coffee and auction for transfer of textile quota; Chair. RUDY LENGKONG.

Jakarta Stock Exchange: Jalan Merdeka Selatan 14, Jakarta Pusat; transferred to the private sector in January 1991.

Regulatory Authority

Badan Pelaksana Pasar Modal (BAPEPAM) (Capital Market Executive Agency): Jalan Medan Merdeka Selatan 14, Jakarta 10110; tel. (021) 365509; telex 45604; Chair. MARZUKI USMAN; Exec. Sec. AGOESTIAR ZOEBIER.

INSURANCE

In accordance with Ministry of Finance regulations, all 12 non-life foreign insurance companies had merged by 1980 with one or more domestic companies to form joint ventures. In 1982 a new regulation allowed foreign companies to form joint ventures in the life insurance sector.

In 1988 there were 105 insurance companies, comprising 12 non-life joint venture companies, 58 non-life companies, 24 life companies, four reinsurance companies, five social insurance companies, and two life joint venture company.

Insurance Supervisory Authority of Indonesia: Directorate of Financial Institutions, Ministry of Finance, Jalan Lapangan Banteng Timur 2–4, Jakarta Pusat; tel. (021) 360298; telex 46415; Dir Dr BAMBANG SUBIANTO.

Selected Life Insurance Companies

PT Asuransi Jiwa Buana Putra: Jalan Salemba Tengah 23, Jakarta Pusat; tel. (021) 8582481; telex 44338; f. 1974; Pres. SOEBAGYO SOETJITRO.

PT Asuransi Jiwa Central Asia Raya: Jalan Gajah Mada 3–5, Jakarta 10130; tel. (021) 348512; telex 46414; fax (021) 3806972; Man. Dir DJONNY WIGUNA.

PT Asuransi Jiwa Ikrar Abadi: Jalan Letjen. S. Parman 108, POB 3562, Jakarta 11440; tel. (021) 591335; f. 1975; Pres. Dir HARRY HARMAIN DIAH.

PT Asuransi Jiwa Iman Adi: Jalan Matraman Raya 102, Slipi, Jakarta; Man. B. W. DUMALANG.

PT Asuransi Jiwa Jiwasraya: Jalan H. Juanda 34, POB 240, Jakarta Pusat; tel. (021) 345031; telex 45601; f. 1959; Pres. RUCHIMAT BRATASASMITA.

PT Asuransi Jiwa 'Panin Putra': Jalan Pintu Besar Selatan 52A, Jakarta 11110; tel. (021) 672586; telex 63824; fax (021) 676354; f. 1974; Pres. Dir SUJONO SOEPENO; Chair. NUGROHO TJOKROWIRONO.

PT Asuransi Pensiun Bumiputera 1974: Jalan HOS Cokroaminoto 85, POB 3504, Jakarta; tel. (021) 344347; telex 44494; f. 1974; Gen. Man. SUDIBYO SUTOWIBOWO.

Bumi Asih Jaya Life Insurance Co: Jalan Matraman Raya 165–167, Jakarta 13140; tel. (021) 8582268; telex 48278; fax (021) 8582287; f. 1967; Pres. K. M. SINAGA.

Bumiputera 1912 Mutual Life Insurance Co: Wisma Bumiputera, Floors 18–21, Jalan Jenderal Sudirman, Kav. 75, Jakarta 12910; tel. (021) 5782717; telex 44494; f. 1912; Pres. SUGIARTO.

PT Mahkota Jaya Abadi (Life Insurance Ltd): Jakarta; Man. WIDODO SUKARNO.

Selected Non-Life Insurance Companies

PT Asuransi Bintang: Jalan Hayam Wuruk 4CX, Jakarta 10120; tel. (021) 372908; telex 45648; fax (021) 357463; f. 1955; general insurance; Man. Dir B. MUNIR SYAMSOEDDIN; Gen. Man. SUDIRMAN NOORDEEN.

PT Asuransi Central Asia: Jalan Gajah Mada 3, Jakarta Pusat; tel. (021) 373073; telex 46569; Pres. ANTHONY SALIM.

PT Asuransi Indrapura: Wisma Metropolitan 2, 11th Floor, Jalan Jenderal Sudirman, POB 3738, Jakarta 12920; tel. (021) 5703729; telex 62641; fax (021) 5705000; f. 1954; Presiding Dir ROBERT TEGUH.

PT Asuransi Jasa Indonesia: Jalan Letjen. M. T. Haryono, Kav. 61, Jakarta Selatan; tel. (021) 7994508; telex 47365; Pres. IWA SEWAKA.

PT Asuransi 'Ramayana': Jalan Kebon Sirih 49, Jakarta Pusat; tel. (021) 337148; telex 61670; fax (021) 334825; f. 1956; Pres. R. G. DOERIAT; Dirs SADIJONO HARJOKUSUMO, F. X. WIDIASTANTO.

PT Asuransi Wahana Tata: Jalan H. R. Rasuna Said, Kav. C-4, Jakarta 12920; tel. (021) 5203145; telex 62304; fax (021) 5203149; Pres. RUDY WANANDI.

PT Maskapai Asuransi Indonesia: Jalan Sultan Hasanuddin 53–54, Kebayoran Baru, Jakarta Selatan; tel. (021) 710708; telex 47290; fax (021) 7398497; Dirs P. L. KESUMA, JAN F. H. NINKEULA, WINIFRIED HARAHAP.

PT Maskapai Asuransi Timur Jauh: Jalan Medan Merdeka Barat 1, Jakarta Pusat; tel. (021) 370266; telex 44828; f. 1954; Pres. Dir BUSTANIL ARIFIN; Dirs V. H. KOLONDAM, SOEBAKTI HARSONO.

PT Perusahaan Maskapai Asuransi Murni: Jalan Roa Malaka Selatan 21–23, Jakarta Barat; tel. (021) 679968; telex 42851; f. 1953; Dirs HASAN DAY, HOED IBRAHIM, R. SOEGIATNA PROBOPINILIH.

PT Tugu Pratama Indonesia: Wisma Tugu, Jalan H. R. Rasuna Said, Kav. C-8-9, Jakarta 12940; tel. (021) 8299575; telex 62809; fax (021) 8291170; general insurance; Pres. SONNI DWI HARSONO.

Joint Ventures

PT Asuransi Insindo Taisho: Nusantara Bldg, 20th Floor, Jl. M. H. Thamrin 59, Jakarta 10350; tel. (021) 336101; telex 61409; Pres. Dir PUTU WIDNYANA, Vice-Pres. KOICHI NEMOTO.

PT Asuransi Jayasraya: Jalan M. H. Thamrin 9, Jakarta; tel. (021) 324207; Dirs SUPARTONO, SADAO SUZUKI.

PT Asuransi New Hampshire Agung: Wisma American International, Jalan K H Hasyim Ashari 35, Jakarta; tel (021) 356581; Pres. Dir PETER MEYER; Vice-Pres. Dir HERMAN EFFENDI.

PT Asuransi Royal Indrapura: Chase Plaza, 6th Floor, Jalan Jenderal Sudirman Kav. 21, Jakarta 12920; tel. (021) 5782364; telex 62137; Dirs F. LAMURY, R. J. BROADHURST.

INDONESIA

Insurance Association

Dewan Asuransi Indonesia (Insurance Council of Indonesia): Jalan Majapahit 34, Blok V/29, Jakarta 10160; tel. (021) 363264; telex 44981; fax (021) 354307; f. 1957; Chair. PURWANTO; Gen. Sec. SOEDJIWO.

Trade and Industry

National Development Planning Agency (Bappenas): Jalan Taman Suropati 2, Jakarta; tel. (021) 348990; formulates Indonesia's national economic development plans; Chair. Dr SALEH AFIF; Vice-Chair. SARWONO KUSUMAATMADJA.

CHAMBER OF COMMERCE

Kamar Dagang dan Industri Indonesia (KADIN) (Indonesian Chamber of Commerce and Industry): Chandra Bldg, 3rd–5th Floors, Jalan M. H. Thamrin 20, Jakarta 10350; tel. (021) 32400; telex 61262; f. 1969; 27 regional offices throughout Indonesia; Chair. SOTION ARDJANGGI; Sec.-Gen. IBNOE SOEDJONO.

TRADE AND INDUSTRIAL ORGANIZATIONS

Association of State-Owned Companies: CTC Bldg, Jalan Kramat Raya 94–96, Jakarta; tel. (021) 346071; telex 44208; co-ordinates the activities of state-owned enterprises; Pres. ODANG.

Association of Indonesian Coffee Exporters (AEKI): Jakarta; Chair. DHARYONO KERTOSASTRO.

Badan Koordinasi Penanaman Modal (BKPM) (Investment Co-ordinating Board): Jalan Jenderal Gatot Subroto 44, POB 3186, Jakarta; tel. (021) 512008; telex 45651; f. 1976; Chair. SANYOTO SASTROWARDOYO.

CAFI (Commercial Advisory Foundation in Indonesia): Jalan Probolinggo 5, POB 249, Jakarta 10002; tel. 324487; f. 1958; information, consultancy and translation services; Chair. Dr R. Ng. S. SOSROHADIKOESOEMO; Man. Dir BENNY SUDIBJO PONTJOSOEGITO.

Export Arbitration Board: Jalan Kramat Raya 4–6, Jakarta; Chair. Ir R. M. SOSROHADIKUSUMO; Vice-Chair. SANUSI.

Gabungan Perusahaan Ekspor Indonesia (Indonesian Exporters' Federation): Jalan Kramat Raya 4–6, Jakarta; Pres. NAAFII; Sec. A. SOFYAN MUNAF.

GINSI (Importers' Assen of Indonesia): Jalan Kesejahteraan 98, Pintu Timur, Arena Pekan Raya, POB 2744/JKT, Jakarta 10110; tel. (021) 360643; telex 46793; f. 1956; 3,000 mems; Chair. DARYATMO; Sec.-Gen. SOEHARLY.

Indonesian Palm Oil Producers' Association: Jakarta; Chair. NUKMAN NASUTION.

Indonesian Textile Association (API): Panin Bank Centre, 3rd Floor, Jalan Jenderal Sudirman 1, Jakarta Pusat 10270; tel. (021) 7396094; telex 47228; fax (021) 7396341; f. 1974; Sec.-Gen. DANANG D. JOEDONAGORO.

Indonesian Tobacco Association: Jalan H. Agus Salim 85, Jakarta; tel. (021) 320627; telex 31357; fax (021) 325181; Pres. H. A. ISMAIL.

Masyarakat Perhutanan Indonesia (MPI) (Indonesian Forestry Community): Gedung Manggala Wanabakti, 9th Floor, Wing C/Blok IV, Jalan Jenderal Gatot Subroto, Jakarta Pusat 10270; tel. (021) 583010; telex 46977; f. 1974; nine mems; Pres. M. HASAN.

National Board of Arbitration (BANI): Jalan Merdeka Timur 11, Jakarta; f. 1977; resolves company disputes; Chair. Prof. R. SUBEKTI.

Rubber Association (Gapkinde): Jakarta; Pres. SUTRISNO BUDIMAN.

Shippers' Council of Indonesia: Jalan Kramat Raya 4–6, Jakarta; Pres. R. S. PARTOKUSUMO.

STATE TRADING ORGANIZATIONS

General Management Board of the State Trading Corporations (BPU-PNN): Jakarta; f. 1961; Pres. Col SUHARDIMAN.

PT Aneka Tambang: Jalan Bungur Besar 24, POB 2513, Jakarta; tel. (021) 410108; telex 49147; f. 1968; minerals; Pres. Ir KOSIM GANDATARUNA.

PT Dharma Niaga Ltd: Jalan Abdul Muis 6/8/10, POB 2028, Jakarta 10160; tel. (021) 349978; telex 44312; fax (021) 3810434; f. 1970; import, export, distribution, installation, after sales service; Pres. Drs BENARTO.

PT Indosat: Jalan Merdeka Barat 21, Jakarta 10110; tel. (021) 3802614; telex 44383; telecommunications.

PT Nurtanio: BPP Teknologi Bldg, Jalan M. H. Thamrin 8, Jakarta; tel. (021) 322395; telex 44331; aerospace; Chair. Dr B. J. HABIBIE.

Perum Perhutani (State Forest Corpn): Gedung Manggala Wanabakti, Blok IV/Lantai 4, Jalan Gatot Subroto Senayan, POB 19/JKWB, Jakarta Pusat; tel. (021) 587090; telex 46283; f. 1973; Pres. Dir Ir HARTONO WIRJODARMODJO.

Perum Pos dan Giro: Jalan Cilaki 73, Bandung 40115; tel. (022) 431050; telex 28174; fax (022) 52717; provides postal and giro services; CEO MARSOEDI.

Perum Tambang Batubara: Jalan Prof. Dr Supomo SH 10, Jakarta 12870; tel. (021) 8295608; telex 48203; fax (021) 8297642; f. 1968; coal-mining; Pres. SAPARI SUTISNAWINATA.

Perusahaan Pertambangan Minyak & Gas Bumi Negara (PERTAMINA): Jalan Merdeka Timur 1A, POB 12, Jakarta; tel. (021) 3031; telex 44152; f. 1957; state-owned petroleum and natural gas mining enterprise; Pres. and Dir FAISAL ABDA'OE.

Perusahaan Umum Telekomunikasi (Perumtel): Jalan Cisanggarung 2, 40114 Bandung; tel. (022) 436100; telex 28220; domestic telecommunications; CEO Ir W. MOENANDIR.

PT Tambang Timah (Persero): Jalan Jenderal Gatot Subroto, Jakarta; tel. (021) 510731; telex 62404; tin; Gen. Man. SUDJATMIKO.

PT Tjipta Niaga: Jalan Kalibesar Timur IV/1, POB 1314/JAK, Jakarta; tel. (021) 673923; telex 42747; f. 1964; import and distribution of basic goods, bulk articles, sundries, provisions and drinks, and export of Indonesian produce; Pres. Drs E. SIMANDJUNTAK.

TRADE UNION FEDERATIONS

All-Indonesia Union of Workers (SPSI): Jalan M. H. Thamrin 20, Gedung Chandra Lantai VI, Jakarta; tel. (021) 323872; f. 1973, renamed 1985; comprises 10 national industrial unions; Chair. IMAM SUDARWO; Vice-Chair. Drs SUKARNO; Gen. Sec. ARIEF SOEMADJI.

Setia Kawan (Solidarity) Free Trade Union: Jakarta; f. 1990 by the Indonesian Institute for the Defence of Human Rights; not granted recognition by the Government; Chair. H. J. C. PRINCEN.

Transport

RAILWAYS

There are railways on Java, Madura and Sumatra, totalling 6,521 km (4,049 miles) in 1987, of which 110 km (68.31 miles) were electrified.

Perusahaan Jawatan Kereta Api (Indonesian State Railways): Jalan Perintis Kermedekaan 1, Bandung 40113, Java; tel. (022) 430031; telex 28263; fax (022) 50342; six regional offices; controls 6,458 km of track on Java and Sumatra, of which 125 km are electrified (1987); Chief Dir Ir SUHARSO.

ROADS

There is an adequate road network on Java, Sumatra, and Bali, but on most of the other islands traffic is by jungle track or river boat. Total length of roads in 1986 was 219,009 km, of which 12,942 km were main or national roads and 198 km were motorway. In 1986 plans for a three-island tunnel and bridge link-up between Sumatra, Java and Bali were approved. In 1987 the ADB approved a US $150m. loan for the ninth road (maintenance) sector project, which was scheduled for completion by 1991 and aimed to repair 4,000 km of roads and to replace 80 bridges in 10 provinces.

Directorate General of Highways: Ministry of Public Works, Jalan Pattimura 20, Kebayoran Baru Jakarta; tel. (021) 7203165; Dir Gen. Ir SURYATIN SASTROMIJOYO.

SHIPPING

The Ministry of Communications controls 392 ports, of which the four main ports of Tanjung Priok (near Jakarta), Tanjung Perak (near Surabaya), Belawan (near Medan) and Ujung Pandang (in South Sulawesi) have been designated gateway ports for nearly all international shipping to deal with Indonesia's exports and are supported by 15 collector ports. A six-year port modernization programme, costing US $186.5m., began in 1985. Among the ports to be upgraded was Surabaya's Tanjung Perak, which was to have expanded container facilities. Panjang Port, on Sumatra, was to be expanded between 1987 and 1989. In February 1989 the Asian Development Bank approved a loan of US $20m. for the modernization of eight ports: Samarinda, Tarakan, Toli Toli, Pare Pare, Pantoloan, Old Martapura, Kampung Baru and Belangbelang. In 1986 the total merchant fleet (inter-island and ocean-going) was 6,757 vessels, including 35 ocean-going cargo vessels and 78 bulk carriers.

Inter-island shipping is conducted by state-owned and private shipping lines, and there are numerous small craft.

Directorate General of Sea Communications: Ministry of Communications, Jalan Medan Merdeka Timur 5, Jakarta; tel. (021) 363009; telex 46117; Dir-Gen. J. E. HABIBIE.

INDONESIA

Indonesian National Ship Owners' Association (INSA): Jalan Tanah Abang III/10, Jakarta; tel. (021) 375682; telex 46428; Pres. BOED IHAROJO SASTROHADIWIRJO.

Indonesian Oriental Lines, PT Perusahaan Pelayaran Nusantara: Jalan Raya Pelabuhan Nusantara, POB 2062, Jakarta 10001; tel. (021) 494344; telex 44233; 6 ships; Pres. Dir A. J. SINGH.

PT Jakarta Lloyd: Jalan Agus Salim 28, Jakarta Pusat 10340; tel. (021) 331301; telex 44375; fax (021) 333514; f. 1950; services to USA, Europe, Japan, Australia and the Middle East; 5 semi-containers, 3 full containers, 3 general cargo vessels; Pres. Dir Drs M. MUNTAQA.

PT Karana Line: Jalan Kali Besar Timur 30, POB 30, Jakarta Kota; tel. (021) 679103; telex 42727; 6 ships; Pres. Dir HAPOSAN PANGGABEAN.

PT Pelayaran Bahtera Adhiguna: Jalan Kalibesar Timur 10–12, POB 1313 Jakarta 11110; tel. (021) 676547; telex 42854; f. 1971; 8 ships; Pres. H. DJAJASUDHARMA.

PT Pelayaran Nasional Indonesia (PELNI): Jalan Angkasa 18, POB 115, Jakarta; tel. (021) 417817; telex 44301; state-owned; national shipping co; 4 passenger ships, 34 cargo vessels; Pres. Dir SOEDHARNO MUSTAFA.

PT Pengembangan Armada Niaga Nasional: Pann Bldg, Jalan Cikini IV/II, Jakarta 10330; tel. (021) 322003; telex 61580; fax (021) 322980; state-controlled; 34 ships; Pres. Dir W. NAYOAN; Dir RACHMAN PASHA.

PT Perusahaan Pelayaran Nusantara 'Nusa Tenggara': Kantor Pusat, Jalan Diponegoro 115 Atas, POB 69, Denpasar 80001, Bali; tel. (0361) 35402; telex 35210; fax (0361) 35402; 6 ships; Man. Dir KETUT DERESTHA.

PT Perusahaan Pelayaran Samudera Admiral Lines: Jalan Gunung Sahari 79-80, POB 1476, Jakarta Pusat; tel. (021) 417908; telex 49122; fax (021) 415751; 9 ships; Pres. H. J. WAGIMAN.

PT Perusahaan Pelayaran Samudera Gesuri Lloyd: Gesuri Lloyd Bldg, Jalan Tiang Bendera 45, POB 289/JKT, Jakarta 11220; tel. (021) 6904000; telex 42043; f. 1963; 7 cargo vessels, 5 charter ships; Pres. Dir ADIL NURIMBA.

PT Perusahaan Pelayaran Samudera 'Samudera Indonesia': Jalan Kali Besar Barat 43, POB 1244, Jakarta Kota; tel. (021) 671093; telex 42753; 4 ships; Pres. Dir S. SASTROSATAMO.

PT Perusahaan Pelayaran Samudera Trikora Lloyd: Jalan Malaka 1, POB 1076/JAK, Jakarta 11001; tel. (021) 671751; telex 42061; f. 1964; 5 ships; Pres. Dir B. SASTROHADIWIRYO; Man. Dir M. HARJONO KARTOHADIPRODJO.

PT Perusahaan Pertambangan Minyak dan Gas Bumi Negara (PERTAMINA): Directorate for Shipping and Telecommunications, Jalan Jos Sudarso 32–34, POB 265, Tanjung Priok, Jakarta; tel. (021) 494309; telex 42753; state-owned; tanker services; 80 tankers and 380 small vessels; Pres. and Chair. ABDUL RACHMAN RAMLY.

CIVIL AVIATION

The first stage of a new international airport, the Sukarno-Hatta Airport, at Cengkareng, near Jakarta, was opened in April 1985, to complement Halim Perdanakusuma Airport which was to handle charter and general flights only. Construction of an international passenger terminal at the Frans Kaisepo Airport, in Irian Jaya, was completed in 1988. Other international airports include Polonia Airport in Medan (North Sumatra), Ngurah Rai Airport at Denpasar (Bali), Juanda Airport, near Surabaya (East Java), Sam Ratulangi Airport, in Manado (North Sulawesi) and Hasanuddin Airport, near Ujung Pandang (South Sulawesi). Domestic air services link the major cities, and international services are provided by the state airline, PT Garuda Indonesia, by its subsidiary, PT Merpati Nusantara Airlines, and by numerous foreign airlines. In December 1990 it was announced that private airlines equipped with jet-engined aircraft would be allowed to serve international routes.

Directorate General of Air Communications: Ministry of Communications, Jalan Angkasa I/2, Jakarta; tel. (021) 416321; telex 49482; Dir-Gen. SOBIRIN MISBACH.

PT Bali International Air Service: Jalan Angkasa 1-3, POB 2965, Jakarta; tel. (021) 6295388; telex 41247; f. 1970; private company; subsidiary of BIA; charter services; Pres. J. A. SUMENDAP; Gen. Man. G. B. RUNGKAT; fleet of 4 Trislander, 2 BN Islander, 1 Cessna 404, 1 HS 748.

PT Bouraq Indonesia Airlines (BOU): Jalan Angkasa 1-3, POB 2965, Jakarta; tel. (021) 6295364; telex 41247; f. 1970; private company; scheduled domestic passenger and cargo services linking Jakarta with points in Java, Kalimantan, Sulawesi, Bali, Timor and Tawau (Malaysia); Pres. J. A. SUMENDAP; fleet of 16 HS-748, 4 VC8.

PT Garuda Indonesia: Jalan Medan Merdeka Selatan 13, POB 164, Jakarta 10110; tel. (021) 3801901; telex 49113; f. 1949; state airline; operates domestic, regional and international services to Australia, Austria, Belgium, Egypt, France, Germany, Hawaii, Hong Kong, Italy, Japan, the Republic of Korea, Malaysia, the Netherlands, New Zealand, the Philippines, Singapore, Switzerland, Taiwan, Thailand, the USSR, the United Arab Emirates, the United Kingdom, the USA and Viet-Nam; Pres. Dir M. SOEPARNO; fleet of 6 Boeing 747, 34 Fokker-28, 18 DC-9, 6 DC-10, 9 Airbus A-300, 5 Boeing 737-300.

PT Mandala Airlines: Jalan Veteran I/34, POB 3706, Jakarta; tel. (021) 368107; f. 1969; privately-owned; passenger and cargo services from Jakarta to Medan, Padang, Semarang, Surabaya, Ujungpadang, Ambon, Denpasar and Menado; Pres. Dir SANTOSO; fleet of 3 L-188 Electra, 2 Viscount 800.

PT Merpati Nusantara Airlines: Jalan Angkasa 2, POB 1323, Jakarta 10013; tel. (021) 413608; telex 49154; fax (021) 4207311; f. 1962; subsidiary of PT Garuda Indonesia; domestic and regional services to Australia and Malaysia; Pres. Capt. F. H. SUMOLANG; fleet of 15 F-27, 2 HS-748, 11 DHT, 18 CN-212, 2 Hercules L-100, 27 F-28, 8 DC-9.

PT Sempati Air Transport: Jalan Medan Merdeka Timur 7, POB 2068, Jakarta; tel. (021) 343323; telex 45132; f. 1968; subsidiary of PT Tri Usaha Bhakti; passenger and cargo services throughout ASEAN countries; Pres. Capt. DOLF LATUMAHINA; fleet of 7 Fokker F-27.

Tourism

Indonesia's tourist industry is based mainly on the islands of Java, famous for its volcanic scenery and religious temples, and Bali, renowned for its traditional dancing and religious festivals. In 1989 a total of 1.62m. tourists visited Indonesia, an increase of about 25% over 1988 arrivals.

Direktorat Jenderal Pariwisata (Directorate-General of Tourism): 81 Jalan Kramat Raya, Jakarta 10450; tel. (021) 3103088; telex 45625; f. 1957; private body to promote national and international tourism; Chair. HAMENGKU BUWONO; Vice-Chair. Sri BUDOYO; Dir-Gen. JOOP AVE.

Atomic Energy

In July 1989 it was announced that Indonesia would proceed with plans for the construction of its first nuclear power plant. The plant, scheduled to become operational by the year 2000, was to be constructed in central Java and to have a generating capacity of 600 MW.

National Atomic Energy Agency (Badan Tenaga Atom Nasional—BATAN): Jalan K. H. Abdul Rachim, Kuningan Barat, Mampang Prapatan, POB 85/KBY, Jakarta Selatan; tel. (021) 511109; telex 46354; f. 1958; Dir-Gen. Ir DJALI AHIMSA.

IRAN

Introductory Survey

Location, Climate, Language, Religion, Flag, Capital

The Islamic Republic of Iran lies in western Asia, bordered by the USSR to the north, by Turkey and Iraq to the west, by the Persian (Arabian) Gulf and the Gulf of Oman to the south, and by Pakistan and Afghanistan to the east. The climate is one of great extremes. Summer temperatures of more than 55°C (131°F) have been recorded, but in the winter the great altitude of much of the country results in temperatures of −18°C (0°F) and below. The principal language is Farsi (Persian), spoken by about 50% of the population. Turkic-speaking Azerbaizhanis form about 27% of the population, and Kurds, Arabs, Baluchis and Turkomans form less than 25%. The great majority of Persians and Azerbaizhanis are Shi'i Muslims, while the other ethnic groups are mainly Sunni Muslims. There are also small minorities of Christians (mainly Armenians), Jews and Zoroastrians. The Bahá'í faith, which originated in Iran, has been severely persecuted. The national flag (proportions 3 by 1) has three horizontal stripes, of green, white and red, with the emblem of the Islamic Republic centrally positioned in red and the inscription 'Allaho Akbar' ('God is Great') repeated 22 times at the top and bottom. The capital is Teheran.

Recent History

Iran, called Persia until 1935, was formerly a monarchy, ruled by a Shah (Emperor). The country adopted its first imperial constitution in 1906, when the Qajar dynasty was in power. In 1921 Reza Khan, a Cossack officer, staged a military coup and became Minister of War. In 1923 he became Prime Minister, and in 1925 the National Assembly deposed the Shah and handed full power to Reza Khan. He was subsequently elected Shah, taking the title Reza Shah Pahlavi, and began the modernization of the country. During the Second World War Reza Shah favoured Nazi Germany. British and Soviet forces entered Iran in 1941, forcing the Shah to abdicate in favour of his son, Muhammad Reza Pahlavi.

After the war, British and US forces left Iran, although Soviet forces remained in Azerbaizhan until 1946. The Majlis (National Consultative Assembly) approved the nationalization of the petroleum industry in March 1951. The leading advocate of this measure was Dr Muhammad Mussadeq, leader of the National Front, who became Prime Minister in April 1951. After internal disturbances, Mussadeq was deposed in August 1953 in a coup supported by the USA and other Western countries. The dispute over nationalization was settled in August 1954, when an agreement was reached with foreign interests whereby concessions for petroleum drilling were granted to a consortium of eight companies. The Shah assumed total control of government in 1963, when he began an extensive redistribution of large estates to small farmers. In 1965 the Prime Minister, Hassan Ali Mansur, was assassinated, reportedly by a follower of the Ayatollah Ruhollah Khomeini, a Shi'ite Muslim religious leader (exiled in 1964) who opposed the Shah's 'White Revolution' because it conflicted with traditional Islamic customs. The next Prime Minister was Amir Abbas Hoveida, who held office until 1977.

Between 1965 and 1977 Iran enjoyed political stability and considerable economic growth, based on petroleum revenues. In March 1975 the Shah introduced a single-party system, based on the Iran National Resurgence Party (Rastakhiz). Opposition grew, however, and during 1977 and 1978 demonstrations and strikes against the Shah and his secret police (SAVAK) rose to crisis level. The most effective opposition came from the exiled religious leader, Ayatollah Khomeini, who conducted his campaign from France, where he had arrived in October 1978 after 14 years of exile in Iraq. Khomeini demanded a return to the principles of Islam, and the response to this call in Iran was so great that the Shah felt compelled to leave the country in January 1979. Khomeini arrived in Teheran shortly afterwards, and effectively took power on 11 February. A 15-member Islamic Revolutionary Council (IRC) was formed.

Iran quickly severed its links with the Central Treaty Organization (CENTO) and aligned itself with the Arab world against Israel. Khomeini declared Iran an Islamic Republic on 1 April 1979, and introduced a constitution which vested supreme authority in the Wali Faqih, a religious leader (initially Khomeini) appointed by the Shi'ite clergy, with no fixed term of office, while the elected President was to be chief executive. A presidential election in January 1980 resulted in a win for Abolhasan Bani-Sadr, who received about 75% of the votes. In February he was sworn in as President, and also became Chairman of the IRC. Elections to the 270-seat Majlis (National Assembly) followed, and resulted in a clear win for the Islamic Republican Party (IRP), which was identified with Khomeini.

After the Majlis began its first session in May 1980, the IRC was dissolved. It was clear that a rift was developing between President Bani-Sadr and the more extreme element in the IRP, and in June Khomeini dismissed Bani-Sadr as Commander-in-Chief of the Armed Forces and as President. Bani-Sadr fled to France, where he formed a 'National Council of Resistance' in alliance with Massoud Rajavi, the leader of the Iranian Mujahidin-e-Khalq (an Islamic guerrilla group), who had also fled to France. Bani-Sadr left the council in April 1984 because of his objection to Rajavi's increasing co-operation with the Iraqi Government. Rajavi himself left Paris in June 1986 for Baghdad, Iraq.

In November 1979 Iranian students seized 63 hostages in the US Embassy in Teheran. The original purpose of the seizure was to give support to a demand for the return of the Shah (then in the USA) to Iran to face trial. The problem was not resolved by the death of the Shah in Egypt in July 1980, as the Iranians made other demands, the most important of which was for a US undertaking not to interfere in the affairs of Iran. Intense diplomatic activity finally resulted in the release of the 52 remaining US hostages in January 1981.

Meanwhile, political chaos developed. A three-man Presidential Council replaced Bani-Sadr until a new presidential election in July 1981. In late June, however, a bomb exploded at the headquarters of the IRP, killing Ayatollah Beheshti (the Chief Justice of Iran and leader of the IRP), four government ministers, six deputy ministers and 20 members of the Majlis.

The presidential election in July 1981 resulted in a win for the Prime Minister, Muhammad Ali Rajai. Muhammad Javad Bahonar then became Prime Minister. A further bomb attack occurred in late August, killing both the President and the Prime Minister. Ayatollah Muhammad Reza Mahdavi Kani became Prime Minister in September, and another presidential election took place on 2 October. Hojatoleslam Ali Khamenei, a leading figure in the IRP, was elected President, winning more than 16m. of the 16.8m. votes cast. Later in October, Mir Hussein Moussavi, who had been Minister of Foreign Affairs since July, was appointed Prime Minister. A new Council of Experts was elected in December 1982 to choose a successor to Ayatollah Khomeini.

War broke out with Iraq in September 1980, when Iraq invaded Iran over a front of 500 km (300 miles) after a border dispute. The Iran–Iraq War soon degenerated into a conflict of attrition, with neither side able to launch a decisive offensive. When, beginning in October 1983, Iran staged a series of offensives across its northern border with Iraq, threatening the only remaining outlet for Iraqi petroleum exports through the Kirkuk pipeline, Iraq intensified its attacks on Iranian towns and on Iran's petroleum industry, centred on Kharg Island in the Gulf. Iran threatened to make the Gulf impassable to all shipping if Iraqi military action destroyed its ability to export oil by that route.

In February and March 1984 a further Iranian offensive led to the capture of marshlands around the man-made Majnoun Islands in southern Iraq, the site of petroleum reserves estimated at 8,000m. barrels. Iraq failed to recapture the territory and was censured internationally for its alleged use of mustard gas in the fighting. A long hiatus ensued, during which Iraq constructed a formidable defensive network along the southern front.

Although it had declared a maritime exclusion zone at the north-east end of the Persian Gulf, enclosing Kharg Island, in August 1982 and made spasmodic attacks against shipping (not only oil tankers), Iraq refrained from attacking tankers using the Kharg terminal until May 1984. Iran retaliated by attacking Saudi Arabian and Kuwaiti tankers in the Gulf. A sporadic series of attacks on shipping by both Iran and Iraq continued, while Iraqi fighter aircraft damaged the Kharg Island oil terminal in sporadic raids, dating from the end of February 1984. Through a limited offensive in the central sector of the war front in October 1984, Iran expelled the Iraqis from all of its territory.

In August 1983 the resignation of the Ministers of Commerce and of Labour, followed shortly afterwards by the dismissal of three other Ministers, was the result of factional strife within the Government. The outgoing Ministers were right-wing 'bazaaris', the merchant class, who opposed, on grounds of religion and self-interest, the programme of nationalization and land reform advocated by technocrats in the Council of Ministers. Prime Minister Moussavi nominated five replacements from the latter group but, in the case of three of them, had to make alternative choices before all the posts were filled by candidates acceptable to the predominantly conservative, clerical Majlis, whose approval is necessary for government appointments. The Majlis has also obstructed basic policy initiatives, particularly in the field of economic reform.

Elections to the second Majlis were held on 15 April and 17 May 1984, and a high proportion of the 1,230 or more candidates were professional people. The elections were boycotted by the Liberation Movement (the sole officially-recognized opposition party), led by Dr Mehdi Bazargan (who had been Prime Minister from February to November 1979), in protest at the allegedly undemocratic conditions prevailing in Iran. Some 60%–70% of the electorate (totalling 24m.–25m.) voted in the elections. When the second Majlis assembled on 28 May, it was estimated that more than 50% of the seats were filled by new members, raising hopes that Prime Minister Moussavi might have greater success in implementing economic reforms. However, the Council of Guardians, which exists to determine whether legislation approved by the Majlis is both constitutional and conforms to Islamic law, remained of a conservative, clerical cast and continued to impede socialist economic reforms.

Moussavi's Council of Ministers suffered a reverse in August 1984, when, under the provisions of new legislation requiring a separate vote of confidence for each Minister, five of its members failed to win the approval of the Majlis and were replaced.

Widespread active popular opposition to the Islamic regime was not conspicuous until 1985. Dissatisfaction with the conduct of the war with Iraq, and with austere economic conditions, precipitated demonstrations and rioting in several Iranian cities, including Teheran. Suppression of opposition to the Islamic regime continues. A report by the UN Human Rights Commission, published in February 1987, estimated the number of executions by the Government at a minimum of 7,000 between 1979 and 1985. The Mujahidin-e-Khalq (the most prominent opposition guerrilla group in Iran) assess the number of executions at more than 70,000 since June 1981. In October 1989 the human rights organization, Amnesty International, claimed that at least 1,200 people had been executed in Iran during the previous 12 months, and that many of these, who had been convicted of serious drugs offences, were in fact political dissidents. In January 1990 a delegation from the UN Human Rights Commission visited Iran, for the first time since 1979, to investigate the alleged abuse of human rights. This was subsequently confirmed in two reports by a special representative of the UN. A highly condemnatory report, published in December 1990 by Amnesty International, added further weight to their conclusions, and in the same month the UN Human Rights Commission drafted a resolution criticizing Iran's human rights record.

Only three candidates, including President Khamenei, contested the August 1985 presidential election. The Council of Guardians rejected the candidacy of nearly 50 people who had applied to stand in the election, including Dr Mehdi Bazargan, leader of the Liberation Movement of Iran, who opposed the continuation of the war with Iraq. Ali Khamenei was re-elected President for a second four-year term, with 85.7% of the total (14,244,630) votes being cast in his favour.

Although 99 deputies either voted against him or abstained, Hussein Moussavi was confirmed as Prime Minister by the Majlis on 13 October 1985. A dispute over the composition of Moussavi's new Council of Ministers, which President Khamenei considered to be too radical (withholding his approval from half of Moussavi's appointees), was not resolved until the intervention of Ayatollah Khomeini on Moussavi's behalf.

In the continuing war with Iraq the Government of Iran had ignored Iraqi terms for a cease-fire, insisting that only the removal of the regime of Saddam Hussain, the withdrawal of all Iraqi forces from Iran (which was achieved by Iranian military action) and Iraqi settlement of Iranian claims for US $350,000m. in war damages (as calculated in March 1985) could bring an end to hostilities. The UN had painstakingly engineered an agreement between Iran and Iraq in June 1984, halting attacks on civilian targets, but, after the failure of an Iranian offensive in March 1985 (and with the war on the ground once more in deadlock), Iraq declared Iranian airspace a war zone and resumed the bombardment of Iranian cities. Making full use of its air superiority, Iraq struck more than 30 Iranian population centres in the first half of 1985. President Saddam Hussain's stated intention was to take the war to every part of Iran until the Iranian leadership decided to begin negotiating.

Between August 1985 and January 1986 Iraq made a series of some 60 raids on Kharg Island. During this period Iranian oil shipments from the terminal were minimal, while the overall rate of exports of crude petroleum fell to 1.2m. b/d in February 1986. In that month Iraq announced an expansion of the area of the Gulf from which it would try to exclude Iranian shipping. Previously confined to the waters around Iran's Gulf ports, the area was broadened to include the coast of Kuwait. Attacks on tankers and other commercial vessels in the Gulf were increased by both sides during 1986, and Iran intensified its practice of intercepting merchant vessels in the Gulf and confiscating goods which it believed to be destined for Iraq. Iraqi forces were successful in damaging the alternative oil export facilities which Iran established at the islands of Sirri and Larak. However, despite extensive damage to the Kharg terminal, Iran sustained its petroleum exports by exploiting the ample spare capacity available there, and by the transhipment of petroleum to the floating terminals at Sirri and Larak.

In February 1986 Iran began the Wal-Fajr (Dawn) 8 offensive, so called to commemorate the month of Ayatollah Khomeini's return to Iran in 1979. Massed Iranian forces crossed the Shatt al-Arab waterway and occupied the disused Iraqi port of Faw, on the Persian Gulf, and, according to Iran, about 800 sq km of the Faw peninsula. From this position, within sight of the Kuwaiti island of Bubiyan (commanding the Khawr Abdullah channel between the peninsula and the island), Iran threatened Iraq's only access to the Gulf. However, the difficulty of the terrain to the west prevented further Iranian gains, and the position on the Faw peninsula was not easily defensible. To divert Iraqi forces, Iran had begun a complementary assault along the Faw–Basra road. When Iraq launched a counter-offensive on Faw in mid-February, Iran opened up a second front (the Wal-Fajr 9 offensive) in Iraqi Kurdistan, several hundred kilometres to the north. Iraq's counter-offensive failed to dislodge an estimated 30,000 Iranian troops from in and around Faw. At the end of February the UN Security Council, while urging the combatants to agree on a cease-fire, implicitly blamed Iraq for starting the war.

In May 1986 Iraq made its first armed incursions into Iran since withdrawing its forces from Iranian territory in 1982. Iranian forces counter-attacked and drove the Iraqis out of the country in July. Also in May, Iraqi aircraft raided Teheran for the first time since June 1985, initiating a new wave of reciprocal attacks on urban and industrial targets in Iran and Iraq, in particular on petroleum-related installations, which continued for the remainder of 1986 and into 1987.

In November 1986 it emerged that the USA, despite its discouragement of arms sales to Iran by other countries, had been conducting secret negotiations with the Islamic Republic since July 1985 and had made three shipments of weapons and spare parts to Iran through Israeli intermediaries, in September 1985 and July and October 1986. These were allegedly in exchange for Iranian assistance in releasing American hostages who had been detained by Shi'ite groups in Lebanon, and an Iranian undertaking to relinquish involvement in international terrorism. The talks were reportedly conducted by the Speaker of the Majlis, Hojatoleslam Hashemi Rafsanjani, with Ayatollah Khomeini's consent but unbeknown to other senior government figures.

In late 1986 and early 1987 Iranian forces mounted offensives against Basra, and, after suffering heavy casualties, advanced to within 10 km of the city. Further offensives were launched in 1987, but Iranian forces failed to capture Basra.

During 1986 and 1987 the waters of the Gulf increasingly became the focus of international attention. Iran had begun to attack Kuwaiti shipping, and neutral shipping using Kuwait, because of Kuwait's support for Iraq. Kuwait then chartered Soviet tankers, and in May the USA agreed to re-register 11 Kuwaiti tankers under the US flag, entitling them to US naval protection. The *USS Stark* was mistakenly attacked by an Iraqi fighter aircraft in May 1987.

On 20 July 1987, in response to this escalation of tension, the UN Security Council adopted Resolution 598, urging an immediate cease-fire, the withdrawal of military forces to international boundaries, and the co-operation of Iran and Iraq in mediation efforts to achieve a peace settlement. However, by early 1988, despite intervention by the League of Arab States and a visit by the UN Secretary-General to Iran and Iraq, no success had been achieved in the implementation of the resolution.

Meanwhile, on 24 July 1987, the re-registered Kuwaiti tanker *USS Bridgeton* struck a mine while under US naval escort in the Gulf, and in August the United Kingdom and France dispatched minesweepers to the Gulf region, followed in September by vessels from the Netherlands, Belgium and Italy. Iraqi air attacks on tankers transporting Iranian oil, and Iranian reprisals against merchant shipping involved in trade with Iraq, continued.

In January and February 1988 the intervention of Ayatollah Khomeini, regarding two important questions of government, was believed to have strengthened the hand of 'reformers', identified with Hashemi Rafsanjani, the Speaker of the Majlis, and Prime Minister Moussavi; and to have dealt a blow to the conservative clerical faction within the Iranian leadership. Elections to the third Majlis in April and May provided a further boost for the 'reformers' in the Government by producing an assembly strongly representative of their views. In June Hashemi Rafsanjani was re-elected as Speaker of the Majlis and Hossein Moussavi was overwhelmingly endorsed as Prime Minister.

In March the Mujahidin Iranian National Liberation Army (NLA), supported by Iraq, mounted its first major offensive since its creation in 1987. In mid-April Iraqi forces recaptured the Faw peninsula, and in May drove Iranian forces across the Shatt al-Arab into Iran. The appointment of Hojatoleslam Hashemi Rafsanjani as acting Commander-in-Chief of the armed forces in June failed to prevent further Iranian defeats, despite the creation of a general command headquarters to rationalize the disjointed military command structure. In mid-June Iraq recaptured Majnoun Island and the surrounding area on the southern front.

In early July 1988 the *USS Vincennes* shot down an Iran Air Airbus A300B over the Strait of Hormuz, having mistakenly assumed the airliner to be an attacking F-14 fighter-bomber. All 290 passengers and crew were killed. This was regarded as a set-back to Majlis Speaker Rafsanjani, who sought to end Iran's diplomatic isolation, and a boost to Iran's conservative mullahs, who were thought to favour the continuation of the war with Iraq.

In July Iraqi troops crossed into Iranian territory for the first time since 1986, capturing the border town of Dehloran. In mid-July the last Iranian troops occupying territory in southern Iraq were dislodged. On 18 July 1988 Iran unexpectedly announced its official and unconditional acceptance of the UN Security Council's Resolution 598. The first clause of the resolution required the combatants to withdraw to international borders and to observe a cease-fire, which finally came into force on 20 August. Negotiations between Iran and Iraq for a comprehensive peace settlement began in Geneva on 25 August, under the aegis of the UN. However, the negotiations soon became deadlocked in disputes concerning sovereignty over the Shatt al-Arab, the right of navigation in the waterway and the Gulf, the exchange of prisoners of war, and the withdrawal of troops to within international borders. In November, in an attempt to break the deadlock, the UN sought to persuade both sides to agree to an exchange of prisoners. Iran and Iraq agreed to the repatriation of all sick and wounded prisoners, and the first exchange was reported to have occurred on 24 November. However, attempts to effect a comprehensive exchange collapsed almost immediately. In February 1989 the UN sought to persuade representatives of the Iranian and Iraqi Governments to accelerate confidence-building measures in order to break the deadlock in the negotiations. In November, in an attempt to achieve this, Iran proposed an immediate exchange of prisoners of war, accompanied by the withdrawal of troops to within international borders. By the end of 1989, however, the cease-fire remained the only element of Resolution 598 to have been successfully implemented.

In July 1990 the Iraqi and Iranian Ministers of Foreign Affairs conferred at the UN's European headquarters in Geneva. It was the first such direct meeting between them since the cease-fire in the war had taken effect, and it had been facilitated by an exchange of letters between Presidents Saddam Hussain and Rafsanjani in May of that year. It was hoped that the discussions in Geneva might lead to a 'summit' meeting between the two leaders, but this breakthrough in the peace process was quickly overtaken by the consequences of Iraq's invasion and annexation of Kuwait in August.

On 16 August 1990 Saddam Hussain sought an immediate, formal peace with Iran, accepting all the claims that Iran had pursued since the declaration of a cease-fire (including the reinstatement of the Algiers Agreement of 1975, dividing the Shatt al-Arab). While these concessions were evidently dictated by expediency (on 17 August 1990 Iraq began to redeploy in Kuwait troops hitherto positioned on its border with Iran), and thus left the issues underlying the war unresolved, they were welcomed by Iran. Exchanges of prisoners of war commenced on 17 August, and on 18 August Iraq began to withdraw troops from the central border areas of Ilam, Meymak, Mehran and Naft Shahr. A dispute regarding the precise number of prisoners of war led to the suspension of the exchanges in September. In October Iran and Iraq restored diplomatic relations and announced their intention to establish a joint commission (in conjunction with the International Committee of the Red Cross) to supervise the resumption of the exchanges. In January 1991 an Iraqi delegation visited Teheran, and negotiations were reported to have culminated in the conclusion of agreements concerning, among other issues, arrangements for the exchange of remaining prisoners of war and the creation of a demilitarized zone along the Iran–Iraq border.

Iran consistently opposed Iraq's occupation of Kuwait, and repeatedly demanded that Iraqi troops be withdrawn from that state. At the same time, Iran impugned the deployment of a multinational armed force in Saudi Arabia, especially the presence there of US armed forces. In November 1990 Iran was reported to have proposed to the Gulf States a new regional security plan, to be guaranteed by Iran, and this was interpreted as an indication of Iranian anxiety at the possibility of a US-dominated security arrangement for the region after the resolution of the Gulf crisis. In December Iran increased its diplomatic efforts to avert war in the Gulf, but, following a meeting of the National Security Council, the Government declared that it would remain neutral in the event of military conflict. The Iraqi delegation which visited Iran in early January 1991 was believed to have sought guarantees of Iranian support in such an event. At the outbreak of hostilities between the multinational forces (acting in accordance with resolutions of the UN Security Council) and Iraq on 16 January, however, there was no indication of any change in the Iranian policy of neutrality.

In late January 1991 it was reported that as many as 100 Iraqi combat and reconnaissance aircraft had landed in Iran since the outbreak of hostilities in the Gulf. Iran did not appear to be collaborating in the Iraqi war effort. From the arrival of the first aircraft, it repeated its commitment to neutrality in the conflict and stated that the Iraqi planes would be impounded for the duration of hostilities, as would any military aircraft of other nationalities if they landed in Iran. There was thus speculation that the pilots of the Iraqi planes might have defected from Iraq, or that the landings might have been made deliberately in order to preserve the aircraft from destruction in combat. Iran was reported to have made a formal protest to the Iraqi chargé d'affaires in Teheran at the violation of its airspace.

Iran criticized the UN multinational force for launching a ground offensive against Iraqi forces in Kuwait and southern

Iraq during the night of 23–24 February 1991. The Iranian Government claimed, through its diplomacy, to have been on the verge of obtaining an unconditional withdrawal of Iraqi forces from Kuwait. It expressed concern at the number of Iraqi civilian casualties in the continuing bombing campaign by the multinational force, and at the possibility of a prolonged US military presence in the region.

The swift defeat of the Iraqi army by the multinational force appeared likely to increase Iran's regional influence, and the country was expected to urge the UN to grant it a bigger role in future regional security arrangements, on the basis of UN Security Council Resolution 598. At the conclusion of hostilities, some 160 Iraqi civilian and military aircraft had been impounded by Iran. It remained unclear whether the Government had colluded with Iraq in allowing them to land on Iranian territory. There was speculation that Iran might seek to trade the aircraft for a formal, written peace treaty with Iraq; or that it might claim possession of the aircraft outright in lieu of war reparations.

The cease-fire of August 1988 stimulated new conflicts and exacerbated existing tensions within the Government. In September Ayatollah Khomeini acted to avert a rift in the leadership, regarding Iran's future political and economic direction, which focused on the extent to which ties with Western countries should be restored. In February 1989 Khomeini referred explicitly to a division in the Iranian leadership (between 'reformers', who sought Western participation in Iran's post-war reconstruction, and 'conservatives', who opposed such involvement), and declared that he would never allow the 'reformers' to prevail. His intervention was regarded as having decisively strengthened the 'conservative' cause and was reportedly prompted by Hashemi Rafsanjani's announcement, on 13 February, of his intention to stand as a candidate in the presidential election scheduled for mid-1989. In March and April prominent 'reformers' within the leadership, including Ayatollah Montazeri (who had been elected as successor to Ayatollah Khomeini by the Council of Experts in 1985) announced their resignation. In early April 1989 it was reported that the Council of Experts had established a five-member leadership council to replace Montazeri as Khomeini's successor. On 24 April a 20-member council (the Council for the Study and Codification of the Amendment to the Constitution) was appointed by Ayatollah Khomeini to draft amendments to the Iranian Constitution.

Ayatollah Khomeini died on 3 June 1989. In an emergency session on 4 June the Council of Experts elected President Khamenei to succeed Khomeini as Iran's spiritual leader (Wali Faqih), and on 5 June the Prime Minister, Hossein Moussavi, declared his support, and that of all government institutions, for Khamenei. On 8 June Hojatoleslam Hashemi Rafsanjani was re-elected for a further one-year term as Speaker of the Majlis. The presidential election, which had originally been scheduled to take place on 18 August, was brought forward to 28 July, to be held simultaneously with a referendum on proposed amendments to the Constitution. By mid-July both 'conservatives' and 'reformers' within the leadership had apparently united in support of the candidacy of Rafsanjani for the presidency. The presidential election was ultimately contested by only Rafsanjani and Abbas Sheibani, a former minister, who was widely regarded as a 'token' candidate. According to official figures, of the total 16.2m. votes cast, 15,551,570 (95.9%) were for Rafsanjani, and 632,247 (3.9%) for Sheibani. A total of 24m. people had been eligible to vote. At the same time, 95% of those who voted approved the 45 proposed amendments to the Constitution, the most important of which were the elevation of the President to the Government's Chief Executive and the abolition of the post of Prime Minister. On 15 August Rafsanjani resigned as Speaker of the Majlis, and on the following day Ayatollah Mahdi Karrubi was elected by the Majlis as his successor.

Rafsanjani was sworn in as President on 17 August 1989. On 29 August, following a three-day debate, the Majlis approved Rafsanjani's 22 ministerial nominations. The new Council of Ministers was regarded as a balanced coalition of 'conservatives', 'reformers' and technocrats, and its endorsement by the Majlis was viewed as a mandate for Rafsanjani to conduct a more conciliatory foreign policy towards the West.

Despite the smooth transition to the 'post-Khomeini era', political tension between 'conservatives' and 'reformers' remained high throughout the remainder of 1989. In January 1990, following demonstrations by supporters of 'conservatives' in the Government against the leading 'reformer', Grand Ayatollah Hossein Ali Montazeri, who had been dismissed from his position as the designated successor to Ayatollah Khomeini in March 1989, Ayatollah Ali Khamenei ordered members of the Majlis not to undermine the Government through their continuous criticism of public institutions. This 'warning' was followed by pledges of support from the Majlis, notably from its Speaker, Mahdi Karrubi, for the policies of President Rafsanjani. Elections to the 83-member Council of Experts in October 1990 were nevertheless preceded by a lengthy and acrimonious debate regading changes to the criteria governing the selection of candidates. Those who opposed the Government's economic and diplomatic policies alleged that the changes amounted to an attempt by Rafsanjani and his supporters to reduce their influence within government institutions. In early October, however, Ayatollah Ali Khamenei intervened decisively in the debate, in support of the changes and against a movement within the Majlis to postpone the elections, which were subsequently held, as scheduled, on 8 October. By the end of 1990 President Rafsanjani, buoyed by economic successes, had achieved considerable success in his pursuit of improved relations with the West.

In February 1989 Ayatollah Khomeini ordered that a British author, Salman Rushdie, be killed for writing material offensive to Islam in his novel, *The Satanic Verses*. Khomeini's religious edict led to a sharp deterioration in relations between Iran and the United Kingdom and other Western countries. High-level diplomatic contacts between the EEC member states and Iran were suspended, while the United Kingdom announced the withdrawal of all diplomatic representatives and staff in Teheran. Iran, in turn, announced the withdrawal of all diplomatic representatives and staff in EEC countries, and on 7 March severed diplomatic relations with the United Kingdom. Since Rafsanjani's election to the presidency in August 1989, however, there has been a gradual thaw in relations with the West, dictated by Western needs to secure Iranian assistance to obtain the release of Western hostages held captive by pro-Iranian Shi'ite groups in Lebanon, and by Iran's need to restore economic links with Western countries. After Iraq's occupation of Kuwait in August 1990, the process received the fillip of Iran's adherence to the UN-sponsored policy of imposing economic sanctions on Iraq, together with Iran's declared neutrality at the outbreak of hostilities in the Gulf in January 1991. In September 1990, after the British Government accepted that *The Satanic Verses* had caused offence to Muslims and stated that it had no wish to insult Islam, Iran and the United Kingdom restored full diplomatic relations. In October the EEC revoked the ban that had been imposed on high-level diplomatic contacts with Iran in February 1989, and in November 1990 that organization announced plans to establish permanent representation in Teheran.

In June 1989 Rafsanjani visited the USSR, where he and the Soviet leader, Mikhail Gorbachev, signed a 'declaration on the principles of relations' between Iran and the USSR. In January 1990 the Soviet authorities agreed to allow greater freedom of movement for ethnic Azerbaizhanis between northern Iran and the Azerbaizhani enclave of Nakhichevan in the USSR. In the same month, however, tension developed between Iran and the USSR, when the USSR used force in an attempt to subdue Azeri separatism in the Azerbaizhani SSR.

In July 1989 the USA unexpectedly offered to pay compensation for each of the 290 passengers and crew of the Iran Air Airbus A300B mistakenly shot down by the *USS Vincennes* in July 1988. However, the fragility of Iran's relations with the USA was underlined in early August when, in response to the abduction by Israeli forces of the Lebanese Shi'ite Muslim leader, Sheikh Abdul Karim Obeid, a US hostage in Lebanon, Lt-Col William Higgins, was purportedly executed by his captors. While denying any involvement in the alleged killing, Iran was widely suspected of complicity. In November 1989 the USA agreed to release US $567m. of the total $810m. of Iranian assets seized 10 years previously, at the time of the siege of the US Embassy in Teheran, in order to secure US bank claims on Iran. At the same time, while denying that the release of the assets was linked to the question of US hostages in Lebanon, the USA expressed the hope that Iran would use its influence with pro-Iranian groups in Lebanon to facilitate their release.

Relations between the USA and Iran remained stable during 1990, in contrast with the noticeable improvement in Iran's relations with the United Kingdom and other European countries. The USA expressed gratitude for the likely role of Iranian diplomacy in securing the release, in mid-1990, of some Western hostages who had been held captive in Lebanon, and in September it agreed to pay Iran $200m. in compensation for undelivered military equipment. There was speculation that Iran's observance of the economic sanctions imposed on Iraq by the UN in August (when it could have done much to undermine them) was partly responsible for the USA's decision, in late 1990, to end its ban on imports of Iranian petroleum. In early 1991, however, Iran remained vehemently opposed to the presence of US armed forces in the Gulf.

Relations between Iran and Saudi Arabia became increasingly strained after an incident in Mecca in July 1987, when 402 people, including 275 Iranian pilgrims, lost their lives. In late 1989 there were signs of an incipient 'proxy war' between Iran and Saudi Arabia in Lebanon, when a Saudi Arabian embassy employee was assassinated by members of the pro-Iranian 'Islamic Jihad' in west Beirut. In July 1990, having boycotted the *Hajj* (annual pilgrimage to Mecca) for a third successive year, Iran accused Saudi Arabia of being unfit to administer its Islamic shrines, following an incident in which more than 1,400 Muslim pilgrims were trampled to death during a stampede in a tunnel near Mecca. There have been indications, however, of an improvement in relations since Iraq's occupation of Kuwait in August 1990: in September Iran and Saudi Arabia issued a joint communiqué condemning the occupation. Iran has also sought to achieve a common stance with Syria over the crisis in the Gulf, and in January 1991 Jordan announced its intention to re-establish diplomatic relations with Iran, after an 11-year rift.

Government

Legislative power is vested in the Islamic Consultative Assembly (Majlis), with 270 members. The chief executive of the administration is the President. The Majlis and the President are both elected by universal adult suffrage for a term of four years. A 12-member Council of Guardians supervises elections and ensures that legislation is in accordance with the Constitution and with Islamic precepts. The Committee to Determine the Expediency of the Islamic Order, created in February 1988, and formally incorporated into the Constitution in July 1989, rules on legal and theological disputes between the Majlis and the Council of Guardians. The executive, legislative and judicial wings of state power are subject to the authority of the Wali Faqih.

Defence

In June 1990 Iran's regular armed forces totalled 504,000 (army 305,000, Revolutionary Guard Corps (Pasdaran) about 150,000, navy 14,500, air force 35,000). Including active paramilitary forces, however, the total strength could be up to 2m. There were 350,000 army reserves and more than 2.5m. in paramilitary forces, including 2.5m. in the Home Guard (Hezbollahi, 'of the party of God'). There is a 24-month period of military service. Defence expenditure for 1990/91 was estimated at IR 615,000m.

Economic Affairs

In the year ending 20 March 1987, according to estimates by the United Nations, Iran's gross domestic product (GDP), measured at current prices, was US $183,843m., equivalent to $3,716 per head. During 1980–86, in terms of constant prices, GDP increased by an estimated annual average rate of 4.3%, while GDP per head increased by an annual average of 1.4%.

Agriculture (including forestry and fishing) contributed 23.5% of GDP in 1986/87. About 28% of the labour force were employed in agriculture in 1989. The principal cash crop is fresh and dried fruit, which accounted for about 24% of non-petroleum export earnings in 1985/86. The principal subsistence crops are wheat, barley, sugar beet and sugar cane. Production of beef, and of mutton and lamb, is also important. According to FAO statistics, agricultural production increased by an annual average of 1.7% during 1980–89.

Industry (including mining, manufacturing, construction and power) contributed 18.8% of GDP in 1986/87.

Mining contributed 5.3% of GDP in 1986/87. Metal ores are the major non-hydrocarbon mineral exports, and coal, magnesite and gypsum are also mined. In January 1990 Iran's reserves of petroleum were estimated at 93,000m. barrels, sufficient to maintain the 1989 level of production for 89 years. Iran's reserves of natural gas are the second largest in the world, after those of the USSR. Manufacturing contributed 6.4% of GDP in 1986/87. During 1977–84 the output of the manufacturing sector (excluding petroleum refineries) increased at an average rate of 5.2% per year. The most important sectors, in terms of value added, are textiles, food processing and transport equipment.

Principal sources of energy are natural gas, reserves of which were estimated at 14,200,000m. cu m at 1 January 1989, and coal. Imports of mineral fuels comprised only 2% of the value of total imports in 1984/85.

The banking and insurance industries are nationalized, and an Islamic banking system has been in force since 1984. More than 10% of short- and medium-term private deposits are subject to Islamic rules, and in 1985 all bank loans and advances were Islamized.

In 1987/88 Iran recorded a visible trade deficit of US $558m., and there was a deficit of $2,476m. on the current account of the balance of payments. In 1987/88 the principal source of imports (19.2%) was the Federal Republic of Germany, which was also the principal market for exports (30.7%). Other major trading partners are Japan, Brazil, the United Kingdom, Italy and the United Arab Emirates. The principal exports in 1984/85 were petroleum and petroleum products (which accounted for almost 98% of their total value). Other important exports are agricultural and traditional goods and metal ores. The principal imports were machinery and motor vehicles, paper, textiles, iron and steel and mineral products, and food and live animals.

For the financial year ending 20 March 1992 the Government drafted a budget which provided for expenditure of IR 8,188,000m., and for revenues of IR 7,088,000m. The average annual rate of inflation was 22.3% in 1989, declining (according to official estimates) to less than 20% in mid-1990. An estimated 28.6% of the total labour force were unemployed during the first half of 1987.

The outbreak of military conflict in the Gulf in January 1991 raised questions regarding the potential effect of the hostilities on the international petroleum market, on Iranian domestic politics, and on Iran's relations with the Western countries participating in the war against Iraq, all of which will influence Iran's future economic reconstruction. The main focus of Iran's Five-Year Development Plan (1990/91–1994/95) is the rehabilitation of the country's petroleum industry. Foreign investment is regarded as vital to this project. As relations with Europe and, to a lesser extent, the USA improved during 1990, so the flow of foreign finance increased. The position of President Rafsanjani and those Iranian leaders who advocate increased interaction with the West as a means to achieve economic reconstruction appeared, during the initial stages of the crisis in the Gulf, to have been strengthened, but since the outbreak of hostilities there has been increasing evidence of opposition to the forces, especially the USA, ranged against Iraq. Sustained, reliable earnings from petroleum are the most important factor in Iran's future economic success.

Social Welfare

Under Article 29 of the 1979 Constitution, the Government has a duty to provide every citizen with insurance benefits covering illness, unemployment and retirement. In 1984 Iran had 589 hospital establishments, with a total of 70,000 beds. In 1983 there were 15,945 physicians working in the country. Of total expenditure by the central Government in the financial year 1986/87 about IR 208,000m. (6.0%) was for health services, and a further IR 491,900m. (14.3%) was for social security and welfare.

Education

Education is officially compulsory for eight years, between six and 14 years of age, but this has not been fully implemented in rural areas. Primary education, which is provided free of charge, begins at the age of six and lasts for five years. Secondary education, from the age of 11, lasts for up to seven years: a first cycle of three years and a second of four years. In 1987 the total enrolment at primary and secondary schools was equivalent to 79% of the school-age population (87% of boys; 70% of girls), while primary enrolment included 94% of children in the relevant age-group (98% of boys; 89% of girls). There are 21 universities, including nine in Teheran, which were closed by the Government in 1980 but have been reopened gradually since 1983. There were 145,047 students enrolled at Iran's universities and equivalent institutions in 1986. According to the census of October 1986, the rate of adult illiteracy among the settled population averaged 47.7% (males 36.8%; females 59.0%). Expenditure on education by the central Government in the financial year 1986/87 was IR 674,400m. (19.6% of total spending). Post-revolutionary policy has been to eliminate mixed-sex schools and to reduce instruction in art and music, while greater emphasis has been placed on agricultural and vocational programmes in higher education. According to the Government, 24,000 new schools were built between the revolution, in 1979, and 1984.

Public Holidays

The Iranian year 1370 runs from 21 March 1991 to 20 March 1992, and the year 1371 runs from 21 March 1992 to 20 March 1993.

1991: 11 February (National Day—Fall of the Shah), 12 February (Leilat al-Meiraj, ascension of Muhammad), 20 March (Oil Nationalization Day), 21–24 March (Now Ruz, the Iranian New Year), 1 April (Islamic Republic Day), 2 April (Revolution Day), 16 April (Id al-Fitr, end of Ramadan), 9 June (Birthday of Twelfth Imam), 23 June (Id al-Adha, feast of the Sacrifice), 14 July (Martyrdom of Imam Ali), 22 July (Ashoura), 21 September (Mouloud, Birth of Muhammad).

1992: 1 February (Leilat al-Meiraj, ascension of Muhammad), 11 February (National Day—Fall of the Shah), 20 March (Oil Nationalization Day), 21–24 March (Now Ruz, the Iranian New Year), 1 April (Islamic Republic Day), 2 April (Revolution Day), 4 April (Id al-Fitr, end of Ramadan), 9 June (Birthday of Twelfth Imam), 11 June (Id al-Adha, feast of the Sacrifice), 11 July (Ashoura), 14 July (Martyrdom of Imam Ali), 10 September (Mouloud, Birth of Muhammad).

Weights and Measures

The metric system is in force, but some traditional units are still in general use.

Statistical Survey

The Iranian year runs from 21 March to 20 March.

Source (except where otherwise stated): Statistical Centre of Iran, Dr Fatemi Ave, Cnr Rahiye Moayeri, Opposite Sazeman-e-Ab, Teheran 14144; tel. 655061; telex 213233.

Area and Population

AREA, POPULATION AND DENSITY

Area (sq km)	1,648,000*
Population (census results)†	
1 November 1976	33,708,744
8 October 1986	
Males	25,280,961
Females	24,164,049
Total	49,445,010
Population (official estimates at mid-year)	
1988	52,522,000
1989	54,203,000
Density (per sq km) at mid-1989	32.9

* 636,296 sq miles.
† Excluding adjustment for underenumeration, estimated to have been 2.28% in 1976.

PRINCIPAL TOWNS (population at 1986 census)

Tehran (Teheran, the capital)	6,042,584	Zahedan	281,923
Mashad (Meshed)	1,463,508	Karaj	275,100
Esfahan (Isfahan)	988,753	Hamadan	273,499
Tabriz	971,482	Arak	265,349
Shiraz	848,289	Kerman	257,284
Ahwaz	579,826	Qazvin	248,591
Bakhtaran (Kermanshah)	560,514	Yazd	230,483
		Zanjan	215,261
Qom	543,139	Eslamshahr (Islam Shahr)	215,129
Orumiyeh	300,746	Khorramabad	208,592
Rasht	290,897	Sanandaj	204,537
Ardabil (Ardebil)	281,973	Bandar-e-Abbas	201,642

BIRTHS AND DEATHS (UN estimates, annual averages)

	1975–80	1980–85	1985–90
Birth rate (per 1,000)	43.1	41.9	42.4
Death rate (per 1,000)	11.9	9.7	8.0

Source: UN, *World Population Prospects: 1988*.

1986: Registered live births 2,033,285 (birth rate 40.9 per 1,000); Registered deaths 190,061 (death rate 3.8 per 1,000).
1987: Registered live births 1,977,129 (birth rate 38.6 per 1,000); Registered deaths 202,266 (death rate 3.9 per 1,000).
1988: Registered live births 1,832,089 (birth rate 34.9 per 1,000); Registered deaths 204,220 (death rate 3.9 per 1,000).
Note: Registration is incomplete.

ECONOMICALLY ACTIVE POPULATION
(October 1986 census)

	Males	Females	Total
Agriculture, forestry, hunting and fishing	2,931,731	259,030	3,190,761
Mining and quarrying	31,833	537	32,370
Manufacturing	1,240,543	210,787	1,450,330
Construction	1,196,945	9,319	1,206,264
Electricity, gas, water supply	88,793	2,251	91,044
Commerce	860,777	14,681	875,458
Transport, storage and communications	621,994	8,552	630,546
Services	2,739,414	424,627	3,164,041
Others (not adequately defined)	314,200	45,521	359,721
Total	10,026,230	975,305	11,001,535

IRAN

Agriculture

PRINCIPAL CROPS ('000 metric tons)

	1987	1988	1989
Wheat	7,600	7,265	5,800
Rice (paddy)	1,803	1,419	1,200
Barley	2,731	2,600	2,600
Maize	60†	55*	40*
Potatoes	2,348	1,433	1,400*
Pulses	370	379*	386*
Soybeans	90†	90†	90*
Cottonseed	225	201	260†
Cotton (lint)	104†	94	122†
Tomatoes*	780	780	690
Onions (dry)	922	297	500*
Other vegetables*	1,690	1,700	1,710
Watermelons*	960	960	925
Melons*	452	450	440
Grapes	1,520	1,360*	950*
Dates	524	440*	440*
Apples	1,238	1,010*	1,010*
Pears	107	71*	71*
Oranges*	180	180	150
Other citrus fruits*	91	91	92
Apricots*	56	57	57
Other fruits*	919	644	645
Sugar cane	1,575	1,120*	1,357*
Sugar beets	4,456	3,669	3,353*
Almonds	63.2	56*	56*
Pistachios	113.7	97.6*	105*
Walnuts	33.0	30*	30*
Tea (made)	46	56	46*
Tobacco (leaves)*	23	19	19

* FAO estimate(s).   † Unofficial estimate.
Source: FAO, *Production Yearbook*.

LIVESTOCK (FAO estimates, '000 head, year ending September)

	1987	1988	1989
Horses	271	270	270
Mules	127	127	126
Asses	1,780	1,760	1,740
Cattle	8,350	8,350	8,000
Buffaloes	230	230	230
Camels	27	27	27
Sheep	34,500	34,500	34,000
Goats	13,600	13,620	13,500

Chickens (FAO estimates, million): 105 in 1987; 110 in 1988; 115 in 1989.
Source: FAO, *Production Yearbook*.

LIVESTOCK PRODUCTS (FAO estimates, '000 metric tons)

	1987	1988	1989
Beef and veal	169	169	180
Buffalo meat	10	10	10
Mutton and lamb	234	234	241
Goats' meat	46	46	46
Poultry meat	250	255	260
Other meat	17	22	18
Cows' milk	1,754	1,754	1,680
Buffaloes' milk	38	38	38
Sheep's milk	725	725	725
Goats' milk	269	270	267
Cheese	114.3	114.6	112.3
Butter	73.3	73.3	71.2
Hen eggs	240	250	260
Honey	6.1	6.2	6.2
Wool*:			
greasy	32	32	32
clean	17.6	17.6	17.6
Cattle and buffalo hides	35.3	35.3	37.5
Sheep skins	39.0	39.0	40.2
Goat skins	9.1	9.1	9.3

* Unofficial estimates.
Source: FAO, *Production Yearbook*.

Forestry

ROUNDWOOD REMOVALS (FAO estimates, '000 cu metres)

	1986	1987	1988
Sawlogs, veneer logs and logs for sleepers*	369	369	369
Other industrial wood†	4,007	4,007	4,007
Fuel wood	2,411	2,423	2,441
Total	6,787	6,799	6,817

* Assumed to be unchanged since 1977.
† Assumed to be unchanged since 1974.
Source: FAO, *Yearbook of Forest Products*.

SAWNWOOD PRODUCTION ('000 cu metres)

	1975	1976	1977
Sawnwood (incl. boxboards)*	90	90	90
Railway sleepers	80	54	73
Total	170	144	163

* FAO estimate (production assumed to be unchanged since 1974).
1978-88: Annual production as in 1977 (FAO estimate).
Source: FAO, *Yearbook of Forest Products*.

Fishing

('000 metric tons, live weight)

	1986	1987*	1988*
Freshwater fishes	20.3	20.1	20.1
Diadromous fishes	6.9	6.9	6.9
Marine fishes	118.2	116.1	122.3
Marine crustaceans and molluscs	6.7	6.7	6.7
Total catch	152.1	149.8	156.0
Inland waters	30.3	30.0	30.0
Indian Ocean	121.8	119.8	126.0

* FAO estimates.
Source: FAO, *Yearbook of Fishery Statistics*.
Production of caviar (metric tons, year ending 20 March): 222 in 1982/83; 170 in 1983/84; 248 in 1984/85 (Source: Iran Fishery Co).

Mining

CRUDE PETROLEUM (net production, '000 barrels per day)

	1983/84	1984/85	1985/86
Southern oilfields	2,454	2,113	2,265
Naftshahr oilfield	0	0	0
Offshore oilfields	255	258	239
Doroud-Forouzan-Abouzar-Soroush	63	70	72
Bahregansar-Nowruz	0	0	0
Salman-Rostam	172	168	144
Sirri	20	20	23
Total	2,709	2,371	2,504

Source: Ministry of Oil.
Production ('000 metric tons): 93,380 in 1986; 115,510 in 1987; 112,920 in 1988; 147,490 in 1989. Source: UN, *Monthly Bulletin of Statistics*.

IRAN

NATURAL GAS (million cu metres)

	1985/86	1986/87	1987/88
Consumption (domestic)*	24,100	15,560	20,434
Flared	10,300	9,720	10,600
Total production	34,400	25,300	32,035

* Includes gas reinjected to maintain oilfield pressure.

OTHER MINERALS ('000 metric tons, year ending 20 March)*

	1984/85	1985/86	1986/87
Hard coal†	850	900	722
Iron ore‡	1,354	1,483	1,156
Copper ore‡	43.3	50.0	50.0
Lead ore‡	19.9	21.6	25.0
Zinc ore‡	47.1	50.0	17.0
Chromium ore‡§	38	38	30
Magnesite (crude)	2,240.0	2,240.8	n.a.
Native sulphur	30	30	30
Barytes	91	91	41
Salt (unrefined)	691	703	570
Gypsum (crude)†	9,666	8,384	6,082

* Figures for 1984/85 and 1985/86 refer to estimated production, based on data from the US Bureau of Mines.
† Figures refer to calendar years 1984, 1985 and 1986.
‡ Figures refer to the metal content of ores.
§ Year ending 30 June.

Industry

PETROLEUM PRODUCTS ('000 metric tons)

	1985	1986	1987
Liquefied petroleum gas*†	1,200	1,000	985
Naphtha	142	140	140
Motor spirit (petrol)	4,547	3,950	3,996
Aviation gasoline	90	80	90
Kerosene	3,100	2,900	3,126
White spirit*	80	70	70
Jet fuel	350	300	365
Distillate fuel oils	11,359	7,300	8,930
Residual fuel oils	11,683	10,100	10,207
Lubricating oils	394	400	119
Petroleum bitumen (asphalt)*	1,624	1,610	1,350

* Estimated production.
† Includes production from natural gas plants ('000 metric tons): 600 in 1985; 500 in 1986; and from petroleum refineries: 600 in 1985; 500 in 1986.

1988 (estimate, '000 metric tons): Motor spirit 4,300 (Source: UN, *Monthly Bulletin of Statistics*).

OTHER PRODUCTS (year ending 20 March)

	1984/85	1985/86	1986/87
Refined sugar ('000 metric tons)	477	497	511
Cigarettes (million)	16,154	16,168	15,239
Paints ('000 metric tons)	70	48	27
Cement ('000 metric tons)	12,064	11,954	13,124
Refrigerators ('000)	726	721	411
Gas stoves ('000)	1,283	1,089	938
Telephone sets ('000)	328	331	259
Radios and recorders ('000)	208	312	245
Television receivers ('000)	530	488	411
Motor vehicles (assembled) ('000)	365	299	166
Footwear (million pairs)	66	62	61
Machine-made carpets ('000 sq m)	8,703	10,442	7,103

Production of Electricity (estimates, million kWh): 36,594 in 1984/85; 39,220 in 1985/86 (Source: Ministry of Energy).

Finance

CURRENCY AND EXCHANGE RATES

Monetary Units
100 dinars = 1 Iranian rial (IR).

Denominations
Coins: 1, 2, 5, 10, 20 and 50 rials.
Notes: 100, 200, 500, 1,000, 2,000, 5,000 and 10,000 rials.

Sterling and Dollar Equivalents (30 September 1990)
£1 sterling = 124.18 rials;
US $1 = 66.28 rials;
1,000 Iranian rials = £8.053 = $15.087.

Average Exchange Rate (rials per US $)
1987 71.460
1988 68.683
1989 72.015

Note: The data on exchange rates refer to the official rate of the Central Bank, applicable to all foreign exchange transactions since December 1984, and to almost all transactions prior to that date. Since 22 May 1980 this valuation of the Iranian rial has been linked to the IMF's special drawing right (SDR) at a mid-point rate of SDR 1 = 92.30 rials. Prior to December 1984, a system of multiple exchange rates was in operation, with a preferential rate, applicable to proceeds from non-oil exports, and another rate applicable to sales of foreign exchange for tourism.

GOVERNMENT BUDGET ESTIMATES
(million rials, year ending 20 March)

Revenue	1985/86	1986/87
General revenue	3,780,400	3,574,700
Income from taxation	1,138,200	1,169,800
Oil	1,867,000	1,600,000
Sales of foreign exchange	119,000	111,000
Other	396,300	424,200
Special income	259,900	269,700
Deficit finance	354,400	475,000
Total	4,134,800	4,049,700

Expenditure	1985/86	1986/87
Expenditure	3,874,900	3,780,000
War expenditure	400,000	430,000
War reconstruction	50,000	35,000
Fixed investment	1,085,800	949,200
Repayment of foreign loans	33,800	24,500
Current expenditure	2,305,300	2,341,300
From special income	259,900	269,700
Total	4,134,800	4,049,700

CENTRAL BANK RESERVES (US $ million at 31 December)

	1980	1981	1982
Gold*	220	247	229
IMF special drawing rights	307	339	331
Reserve position in IMF	299	165	84
Foreign exchange*	9,617	1,102	5,287
Total	10,443	1,853	5,931

* Figures refer to 20 December. Gold is valued at 35 SDRs per troy ounce.

Source: IMF, *International Financial Statistics*.

IRAN

Statistical Survey

MONEY SUPPLY ('000 million rials at 20 December)

	1981	1982	1983
Currency outside banks	1,248.3	1,465.4	1,756.9
Official entities' deposits at Central Bank	166.5	329.1	335.0
Demand deposits at commercial banks	1,222.1	1,498.6	1,830.1
Total	2,636.9	3,293.1	3,922.0

Source: IMF, *International Financial Statistics*.

COST OF LIVING (Consumer Price Index; base: 1980 = 100)

	1983	1984	1985
Food	179.5	195.6	205.8
Fuel and light	140.8	146.3	151.9
Clothing	193.0	221.5	227.2
Rent	130.2	145.1	163.8
All items (incl. others)	176.6	198.6	207.4

Source: ILO, *Year Book of Labour Statistics*.

NATIONAL ACCOUNTS
('000 million rials at current prices, year ending 20 March)

National Income and Product*

	1983/84	1984/85	1985/86
Domestic factor incomes†	12,538.4	13,641.0	13,893.9
Consumption of fixed capital	932.9	1,062.0	1,097.6
Gross domestic product (GDP) at factor cost	13,471.3	14,703.0	14,991.5
Indirect taxes	416.8	481.6	501.8
Less Subsidies	138.6	155.0	187.5
GDP in purchasers' values	13,749.5	15,029.6	15,305.8
Factor income from abroad	108.4	90.7	60.8
Less Factor income paid abroad	115.1	102.1	94.4
Gross national product (GNP)	13,742.8	15,018.2	15,272.2
Less Consumption of fixed capital	932.9	1,062.0	1,097.6
National income in market prices	12,809.9	13,956.2	14,174.6

* Figures are provisional. Revised totals (in '000 million rials) are: GDP in purchasers' values 14,027 in 1983/84, 15,162 in 1984/85, 16,556 in 1985/86; GNP 14,021 in 1983/84, 15,151 in 1984/85, 16,522 in 1985/86.
† Compensation of employees and the operating surplus of enterprises.

Source: UN, *National Accounts Statistics*.

Expenditure on the Gross Domestic Product

	1985/86	1986/87	1987/88
Government final consumption expenditure	2,443	2,371	2,707
Private final consumption expenditure	9,627	10,439	12,226
Increase in stocks	177	1,794	2,358
Gross fixed capital formation	2,841	2,606	2,658
Statistical discrepancy	1,483	1,298	1,578
Total domestic expenditure	16,571	18,508	21,527
Exports of goods and services	1,251	553	837
Less Imports of goods and services	1,266	935	1,094
GDP in purchasers' values	16,556	18,126	21,270
GDP at constant 1974/75 prices	3,651	3,344	3,307

Source: IMF, *International Financial Statistics*, and UN, *Monthly Bulletin of Statistics*.

Gross Domestic Product by Economic Activity (at factor cost)*

	1984/85	1985/86	1986/87
Agriculture, hunting, forestry and fishing	2,493.9	2,927.6	3,732.9
Mining and quarrying	1,696.4	1,493.6	846.6
Manufacturing	1,167.3	1,174.3	1,014.6
Electricity, gas and water	107.0	113.7	138.5
Construction	1,115.2	1,020.2	999.8
Trade, restaurants and hotels	3,205.4	3,040.5	3,499.1
Transport, storage and communications	1,138.4	1,138.1	1,092.6
Finance, insurance, real estate and business services	1,867.2	1,938.3	2,072.6
Government services	1,189.8	1,355.2	1,357.9
Other services	975.1	1,059.8	1,160.2
Sub-total	14,955.7	15,261.3	15,914.8
Less Imputed bank service charge	252.7	269.8	149.5
Total	14,703.0	14,991.5	15,765.3

* Figures are provisional.

BALANCE OF PAYMENTS (US $ million, year ending 20 March)

	1985/86	1986/87	1987/88
Merchandise exports f.o.b.	14,175	7,171	10,639
Merchandise imports f.o.b.	−12,006	−10,585	−11,197
Trade balance	2,169	−3,414	−558
Exports of services	763	607	437
Imports of services	−3,408	−2,348	−2,355
Current balance	−476	−5,155	−2,476
Long-term capital (net)	−160	802	719
Short-term capital (net)	704	2,325	1,378
Net errors and omissions	487	814	155
Total (net monetary movements)	555	−1,214	−224
Valuation changes (net)	58	60	42
Changes in reserves	613	−1,154	−182

Source: IMF, *International Financial Statistics*.

External Trade

PRINCIPAL COMMODITIES
(US $ million, year ending 20 March)

Imports c.i.f.	1983/84	1984/85	1985/86
Food and live animals	2,368	2,070	1,538
Beverages and tobacco	90	82	99
Crude materials (inedible) except fuels	802	522	314
Mineral fuels, lubricants, etc.	205	299	247
Animal and vegetable oils and fats	338	361	310
Chemicals and chemical products	2,084	1,768	1,163
Paper, textiles, iron and steel, mineral products, etc.	5,326	3,561	3,356
Machinery and motor vehicles	6,317	5,452	3,896
Miscellaneous manufactured articles	530	358	293
Other commodities	43	21	773
Total	18,103	14,494	11,989

IRAN

Exports f.o.b. (excl. petroleum and gas)	1983/84	1984/85	1985/86
Agricultural and traditional goods	318.1	295.0	371.0
Carpets	88.9	89.8	115.1
Fruit (fresh and dried)	125.5	79.8	113.3
Animal skins and hides, and leather	34.6	48.7	60.5
Caviar	19.0	21.9	19.8
Casings	13.6	11.4	12.5
Others	36.5	43.4	49.8
Metal ores	12.5	38.8	30.0
Industrial manufactures	26.0	27.3	64.0
Shoes	2.8	2.6	3.0
Biscuits and pastries	1.3	0.3	0.8
Textile manufactures	10.0	14.3	8.8
Cements	3.1	1.1	0.8
Motor vehicles	1.4	0.2	0.3
Others	7.2	6.6	45.8
Total	356.6	361.1	465.0

PETROLEUM EXPORTS
('000 barrels per day, year ending 20 March)

	1985/86	1986/87	1987/88
Crude petroleum	1,400	1,253	1,545
Refined oil products	27	3	—

Source: Ministry of Oil.

Value of crude petroleum exports ('000 million rials, year ending 20 December; estimates): 731.5 in 1981; 1,508.3 in 1982; 1,621.0 in 1983; 1,065.9 in 1984; 1,364.0 in 1985; 997.0 in 1986 (Source: IMF, *International Financial Statistics*).

Total Exports ('000 million rials, year ending 20 December; estimates): 980.8 in 1981; 1,632.4 in 1982; 1,684.7 in 1983 (Source: IMF, *International Financial Statistics*).

PERCENTAGE GEOGRAPHICAL DISTRIBUTION OF CRUDE PETROLEUM EXPORTS

	1985	1986	1987
Western Europe	53.8	50.9*	49.0*
Japan	14.6	15.2	12.7
Asia (excluding Japan)	20.9	23.3	13.4
Africa	0.8	2.4	—
South America	1.4	1.7	17.3
Eastern Europe	8.5	6.5	7.6

* Figures include data for the USA and Canada.
Source: Ministry of Oil.

PRINCIPAL TRADING PARTNERS
(US $ million, year ending 20 March)

Imports c.i.f.	1985/86	1986/87	1987/88
Argentina	472	218	298
Australia	315	208	255
Austria	250	140	114
Belgium	347	291	247
Brazil	239	210	432
Germany, Fed. Republic	1,900	1,460	1,402
Italy	553	521	444
Japan	1,609	1,085	823
Korea, Republic	292	200	189
Netherlands	289	250	182
New Zealand	238	138	129
Romania	398	73	75
Spain	210	114	82
Sweden	192	122	70
Switzerland	970	196	166
Turkey	898	502	370
United Arab Emirates	350	459	305
United Kingdom	077	542	430
Total (incl. others)	11,505	8,001	7,900

Exports f.o.b.*	1985/86	1986/87	1987/88
Bulgaria	6.9	5.1	2.5
France	4.3	14.4	22.6
German Democratic Republic	13.6	15.4	7.8
Germany, Fed. Republic	113.6	240.9	276.3
Hungary	16.6	5.4	4.4
Italy	54.1	58.5	90.0
Japan	3.9	10.9	24.7
Korea, Republic	3.8	0.8	2.6
Kuwait	5.0	4.6	1.5
Lebanon	1.8	1.9	1.3
Netherlands	4.0	17.2	20.4
Saudi Arabia	3.7	4.3	1.7
Switzerland	34.1	47.2	7.3
Turkey	11.0	5.2	8
USSR	30.3	18.7	70.6
United Arab Emirates	65.2	138.9	120.4
United Kingdom	16.3	17.3	19.5
Total (incl. others)	465.0	778.7	901.3

* Excluding petroleum products and hydrocarbon solvents obtained from petroleum.

Transport

RAILWAYS (traffic)

	1985	1986	1987
Passenger-km (million)	5,585	4,638	3,674
Freight ton-km (million)	6,888	7,316	8,625

ROAD TRAFFIC ('000 vehicles in use)

	1985	1986	1987
Cars	1,897	1,936	1,966
Buses	67	71	73
Trucks	372	379	382
Ambulances	1,208	1,340	1,531
Motor cycles	523	552	578

MERCHANT SHIPPING FLEET
('000 gross registered tons at 30 June)

	1985	1986	1987
Oil tankers	120	120	120
Other vessels	1,883	1,977	1,973
Total	2,003	2,097	2,093

INTERNATIONAL SEA-BORNE SHIPPING
(estimated freight traffic, '000 metric tons)

	1986	1987	1988
Goods loaded	79,505	81,341	87,392
Crude petroleum and petroleum products	79,418	81,256	87,162
Goods unloaded	13,153	13,612	13,782
Petroleum products	3,109	2,845	2,930

Source: UN, *Monthly Bulletin of Statistics*.

CIVIL AVIATION (traffic on scheduled services)

	1983	1984	1985
Kilometres flown (million)	23.5	28.6	25.9
Passengers carried ('000)	3,191	4,088	3,422
Passenger-km (million)	3,021	4,089	4,090
Freight ton-km (million)	74.1	90.0	104.0

Source: UN, *Statistical Yearbook*.

Tourism

	1980	1981	1982
Visitors	156,380	185,756	62,373

1984: Total number of visitors 157,000 (estimate).
1986/87: Total number of visitors 171,837 (85,801 tourists).

Education

('000 students)

	1986/87*	1987/88*
Kindergartens	123	146
Primary schools	7,233	7,758
Junior high schools	2,299	2,467
High schools	1,077	1,174
Technical and vocational schools	201	203
Colleges and teacher training colleges	62	62
Others†	180	194
Total	11,175	12,011
Number of institutions	71,099	74,039
Number of teachers‡	546,923	563,496

* The Iranian year runs from 21 March to 20 March. The year 1986/87 corresponds to the Iranian year 1365; 1987/88 to 1366.
† Includes students at schools for exceptional children and on general adult courses.
‡ Includes kindergartens, primary, junior high, and high schools.

Directory

The Constitution

A draft constitution for the Islamic Republic of Iran was published on 18 June 1979. It was submitted to a 'Council of Experts', elected by popular vote on 3 August 1979, to debate the various clauses and to propose amendments. The amended Constitution was approved by a referendum on 2-3 December 1979. A further 45 amendments to the Constitution were approved by a referendum on 28 July 1989.

The Constitution states that the form of government of Iran is that of an Islamic Republic, and that the spirituality and ethics of Islam are to be the basis for political, social and economic relations. Persians, Turks, Kurds, Arabs, Baluchis, Turkomans and others will enjoy completely equal rights.

The Constitution provides for a President to act as chief executive. The President is elected by universal adult suffrage for a term of four years. Legislative power is held by the Majlis (Islamic Consultative Assembly), with 270 members who are similarly elected for a four-year term. Provision is made for the representation of Zoroastrians, Jews and Christians.

All legislation passed by the Islamic Consultative Assembly must be sent to the Council for the Protection of the Constitution (Article 94), which will ensure that it is in accordance with the Constitution and Islamic legislation. The Council for the Protection of the Constitution consists of six religious lawyers appointed by the Faqih (see below) and six lawyers appointed by the High Council of the Judiciary and approved by the Islamic Consultative Assembly. Articles 19-42 deal with the basic rights of individuals, and provide for equality of men and women before the law and for equal human, political, economic, social and cultural rights for both sexes.

The press is free, except in matters that are contrary to public morality or insult religious belief. The formation of religious, political and professional parties, associations and societies is free, provided they do not negate the principles of independence, freedom, sovereignty and national unity, or the basis of Islam.

The Constitution provides for a *Wali Faqih* (religious leader) who, in the absence of the Imam Mehdi (the hidden Twelfth Imam), carries the burden of leadership. The amendments to the Constitution that were approved in July 1989 increased the powers of the Presidency by abolishing the post of Prime Minister, formerly the Chief Executive of the Government.

PROVINCIAL DIVISIONS

According to the state division of May 1977, Iran was divided into 23 provinces (Ostans), 472 counties (shahrestan) and 499 municipalities (bakhsh).

The Government

WALI FAQIH (RELIGIOUS LEADER)

Ayatollah SAYED ALI KHAMENEI.

HEAD OF STATE

President: Hojatoleslam ALI AKBAR HASHEMI RAFSANJANI (took office 17 August 1989).

First Vice-President and President of the Council of Ministers: Dr HASSAN IBRAHIM HABIBI.

Second Vice-President in charge of Judicial and Parliamentary Affairs: SAYED ATTAOLLAH MOHADJERANI.

Third Vice-President in charge of Executive Affairs: HAMID MERZADEH.

COUNCIL OF MINISTERS
(January 1991)

Minister of Foreign Affairs: Dr ALI AKBAR VELAYATI.
Minister of Education and Training: MUHAMMAD ALI NAJAFI.
Minister of Culture and Islamic Guidance: Hojatoleslam Dr SAYED MUHAMMAD KHATAMI.
Minister of Information: ALI FALAHIAN.
Minister of Commerce: ABDOLHOSSEIN VAHADJI.
Minister of Health: IRADJ FAZEL.
Minister of Posts, Telegraphs and Telephones: Eng. SAYED MUHAMMAD GHARAZI.
Minister of Justice: ISMAÏL CHOUCHTARI.
Minister of Defence and Logistics: AKBAR TORKAN.
Minister of Roads and Transport: Eng. MUHAMMAD SAYEDIKIYA.
Minister of Industries: MUHAMMAD REZA NEEMATZADEH.
Minister of Heavy Industry: MUHAMMAD HADI NEJAD HOSSEINIAN.
Minister of Higher Education: MOSTAPHA MOUÏNE.
Minister of Mines and Metals: HOSSEIN MAHLOUDJI.
Minister of Labour: HOSSEIN KAMALI.
Minister of the Interior: ABDOLLAH NOURI.
Minister of Agriculture: ISA KALANTARI.
Minister of Housing and Urban Development: Eng. SERAG ED-DIN KAZEROUNI.
Minister of Energy: NAMDAR ZANGANEH.
Minister of Oil: GHOLAMREZA AQAZADEH.
Minister of Economic Affairs and Finance: MOHSEN NOURBAKHCH.
Minister of Construction Jihad: GHOLAMREZA FOROUZESH.

MINISTRIES

Ministry of Mines and Metals: 248 Somayeh Ave, Teheran; tel. (021) 836051; telex 212718.

Ministry of Roads and Transport: 49 Taleghani Ave, Teheran; tel. (021) 646770.

All ministries are in Teheran. The Plan and Budget Organization, which was made a ministry, was returned to its former status, under the Presidency, in 1989.

President and Legislature

PRESIDENT

Election, 28 July 1989

Candidates	Votes	%
Hojatoleslam ALI AKBAR HASHEMI RAFSANJANI	15,551,570	95.9
ABBAS SHEIBANI	632,247	3.9
Invalid	32,445	0.2
Total	16,216,262	100.0

MAJLIS-E-SHURA E ISLAMI—ISLAMIC CONSULTATIVE ASSEMBLY

Elections to the third Majlis took place in two rounds, on 8 April and 13 May 1988. These were the first elections not to be contested by political parties. The Islamic Republican Party, which had won a clear majority of seats in the elections to the Majlis in 1980 and 1984 (as the larger of only two parties permitted to participate), was disbanded in June 1987. In the 1988 elections the 270 seats were contested by some 1,600 candidates, recommended by political groups and approved by local screening committees.

Speaker: Hojatoleslam MAHDI KARRUBI.

Deputy Speakers: Hojatoleslam HOSSEIN HASHEMIAN, ASADOLLAH BAYAT.

NATIONAL SECURITY COUNCIL

Formed in July 1989 to co-ordinate defence and national security policies, the political programme and intelligence reports, and social, cultural and economic activities related to defence and security. The Council comprises the heads of the three branches of the Government; the chief of the supreme command council of the armed forces; the head of the Plan and Budget Organisation; two representatives appointed by the Wali Faqih; the ministers of foreign affairs, the interior and information; and the commander of the armed forces.

Chairman: ABDOLLAH NOURI.

COUNCIL OF EXPERTS

Elections were held on 10 December 1982 to appoint a Council of Experts which was to choose an eventual successor to the Wali Faqih, Ayatollah Khomeini, after his death. The Constitution provides for a three- or five-man body to assume the leadership of the country if there is no recognized successor on the death of the Wali Faqih. The Council comprises 83 clerics. Elections to a second term of the Council were held on 8 October 1990.

Chairman: Ayatollah ALI MESHKINI.

Deputy Chairman: Ayatollah IBRAHIM AMINI.

Secretaries: Mr TAHERI, Mr KHORRAMABADI, MUHAMMAD MOMEN.

SHURA-E-NIGAHBAN—COUNCIL OF GUARDIANS

The Council of Guardians, composed of six qualified Muslim jurists and six lay Muslim lawyers, appointed by Ayatollah Khomeini and the Supreme Judicial Council, respectively, was established in 1980 to supervise elections and to examine legislation adopted by the Majlis, ensuring that it accords with the Constitution and with Islamic precepts.

Chairman: Ayatollah MUHAMMAD MUHAMMADI GUILANI.

COMMITTEE TO DETERMINE THE EXPEDIENCY OF THE ISLAMIC ORDER

Formed in February 1988, by order of Ayatollah Khomeini, to arbitrate on legal and theological questions in legislation passed by the Majlis, in the event of a dispute between the latter and the supervisory Council of Guardians. The Committee comprises the six qualified religious jurists on the Council of Guardians and seven leading government officials.

Political Organizations

The Islamic Republican Party was founded in 1978 to bring about the Islamic Revolution under the leadership of Ayatollah Khomeini. After the revolution the IRP became the ruling party in what was effectively a one-party state. In June 1987 Ayatollah Khomeini officially disbanded the IRP at the request of party leaders, who said that it 'had achieved its purpose and might only provide an excuse for discord and factionalism' if it were not dissolved. Of the parties listed below, only the Nelzat-Azadi (Liberation Movement of Iran) has enjoyed official recognition and been allowed to participate in elections.

Democratic Party of Iranian Kurdistan: Mahabad; f. 1945; seeks autonomy for Kurdish area; mem. of the National Council of Resistance; 54,000 mems; Sec.-Gen. Dr ABD AR-RAHMAN QASSEMLOU.

Fedayin-e-Khalq (Warriors of the People): urban Marxist guerrillas.

Hezb-e-Komunist Iran (Communist Party of Iran): f. 1979 on grounds that Tudeh Party was Moscow-controlled; Sec.-Gen. 'AZARYUN'.

Komala: f. 1969; Kurdish wing of the Communist Party of Iran; Marxist-Leninist; Leader IBRAHIM ALIZADEH.

Mujahidin-e-Khalq (Holy Warriors of the People): Islamic guerrilla group; since June 1987 comprising the National Liberation Army; mem. of the National Council of Resistance; Leaders MASSOUD RAJAVI and MARYAM RAJAVI (in Baghdad 1986–).

Muslim People's Republican Party: Tabriz; over 3.5m. members (2.5m. in Azerbaizhan); Sec.-Gen. HOSSEIN FARSHI.

National Democratic Front: f. March 1979; Leader HEDAYATOLLAH MATINE-DAFTARI (in Paris, January 1982–).

National Front (Union of National Front Forces): comprises Iran Nationalist Party, Iranian Party, and Society of Iranian Students.

Nelzat-Azadi (Liberation Movement of Iran): f. 1961; emphasis on basic human rights as defined by Islam; Gen. Sec. Dr MEHDI BAZARGAN; Principal Officers Prof. SAHABI, Dr YAZDI, S. SADR, Dr SADR, Eng. SABAGHIAN, Eng. TAVASSOLI.

Pan-Iranist Party: extreme right-wing; calls for a Greater Persia; Leader MOHSEN PEZESHKPOUR.

Sazmane Peykar dar Rahe Azadieh Tabaqe Kargar (Organization Struggling for the Freedom of the Working Class): Marxist-Leninist.

Tudeh Party (Communist): f. 1941; declared illegal 1949; came into open 1979, banned again April 1983; pro-Moscow; First Sec. Cen. Cttee ALI KHAVARI.

The National Council of Resistance (NCR) was formed in Paris in October 1981 by former President ABOLHASAN BANI-SADR and the Council's current leader, MASSOUD RAJAVI, the leader of the Mujahidin-e-Khalq in Iran. In 1984 the Council comprised 15 opposition groups, operating either clandestinely in Iran or from exile abroad. BANI-SADR left the Council in 1984 because of his objection to RAJAVI's growing links with the Iraqi Government. The French Government asked RAJAVI to leave Paris in June 1986 and he is now based in Baghdad, Iraq. On 20 June 1987 RAJAVI, Secretary of the NCR, announced the formation of a National Liberation Army (10,000–15,000-strong) as the military wing of the Mujahidin-e-Khalq. There is also a National Movement of Iranian Resistance, led by a former Prime Minister, Dr SHAPOUR BAKHTIAR. Dissident members of the Tudeh Party founded the Democratic Party of the Iranian People in Paris in February 1988.

Diplomatic Representation

EMBASSIES IN IRAN

Afghanistan: Abbas Abad Ave, Pompe Benzine, Corner of 4th St, Teheran; tel. (021) 627531; Ambassador: MOHAMMAD HAMID ANSARI.

Algeria: Vali Asr Ave, Ofogh St, No. 26, Teheran; tel. (021) 293482; telex 212393; Ambassador: MOHAMMED LARBI OULD KHELIFA.

Argentina: POB 98-164, Ave Mossadegh, Blvd Nahid, No. 35, Tajrish, Teheran; Chargé d'affaires a.i.: EDELBERTO J. LEMOS.

Australia: 123 Khaled al-Islambuli Ave, POB 15875-4334, Teheran 15138; tel. (021) 626202; telex 212459; Ambassador: MICHAEL LANDLE.

Austria: Taleghani Ave, Corner Forsat Ave No. 140, Teheran; tel. (021) 828431; telex 212872; Ambassador: HERBERT TRAXL.

Bahrain: Park Ave, 31st St, No. 16, Teheran; Ambassador: YACOUB YOUSUF ABDULLA.

Bangladesh: Gandhi Ave, 5th St, Building No. 14, POB 11365-3711, Teheran; tel. (021) 682979; telex 212303; Ambassador: M. M. REZAUL KARIM.

Belgium: Fereshteh Ave, Shabdiz Lane, 3 Babak St, POB 11365-115, Teheran 19659; tel. (021) 294574; telex 212446; Ambassador: RAYMOND SCHRIJVERS.

Brazil: Vanak Sq., Vanak Ave No. 58, Teheran 19964; tel. (021) 685175; telex 212392; Ambassador: RONALD LESLIE MORAES SMALL.

Bulgaria: Vali Asr Ave, Tavanir St, Nezami Ganjavi St, No. 82, POB 11365-7451, Teheran; tel. (021) 650002; telex 212700; Ambassador: STEFAN POLENDAKOV.

IRAN

Canada: POB 11365-4647, 57 Shahid Sarafraz St; tel. 622623; fax 623202; Chargé d'affaires: SCOTT MULLIN.

China, People's Republic: Pasdaran Ave, Golestan Ave 1, No. 53, Teheran; Ambassador: WANG BENZUO.

Colombia: Teheran; Ambassador: ANTONIO BAYONA.

Cuba: Africa Ave, Amir Parviz St, No. 1/28, Teheran; tel. (021) 632953; Ambassador: LUIS MARISY FIGUEREDO.

Czechoslovakia: Enghelab Ave, Sarshar St, No. 61, POB 11365-4457, Teheran; tel. (021) 828168; Ambassador: MILAN MÁCHA.

Denmark: Intersection Africa and Modaress Expressway, Bidar St, No. 40, POB 11365-158, Teheran; tel. (021) 297371; telex 212784; Ambassador: HANS GRUNNET.

Finland: Vali Asr Ave, Vanak Sq., Nilov St, POB 15115-619, Teheran; tel. (021) 684985; telex 212930; Ambassador: TAPANI BROTHEROUS.

France: ave de France No. 85, Teheran; Ambassador: CHRISTIAN GRAEFF.

Gabon: POB 337, Teheran; tel. (021) 823828; telex 215038; Ambassador: J. B. ESSONGUE.

Germany: 324 Ferdowsi Ave, POB 11365-179, Teheran; tel. 314111; telex 212488; Ambassador: Dr ARMIN FREITAG.

Ghana: Ghaem Magham Farahani Ave, Varahram St No. 12, Teheran; Chargé d'affaires a.i.: HUMPHREY OKPOTI LARSEY.

Greece: Afrigha Expressway (Ex. Jordan Ave), Niloufar St No. 20, POB 11365-8151, Teheran 19677; tel. (021) 4272384; Ambassador: DIMITRI ARGYRIADES.

Holy See: Apostolic Nunciature, Razi Ave, No. 97, ave de France Crossroad, POB 11365-178, Teheran; tel. (021) 6403574; Apostolic Pro-Nuncio: Most Rev. GIOVANNI V. BULAITIS, Titular Archbishop of Narona.

Hungary: Abbas Abad Park Ave, 13th St, No. 18, Teheran; tel. (021) 622800; Ambassador: Dr ZSIGMOND KÁZMÉR.

India: Saba-e-Shomali Ave, No. 166, POB 11365-6573, Teheran; tel. (021) 894554; telex 212858; Ambassador: RAMISA CHANDER ARORA.

Indonesia: Ghaem Magham Farahani Ave, No. 210, POB 11365-4564, Teheran; tel. (021) 626865; telex 212049; Ambassador: MOHAMMAD SABIR.

Iraq: Vali Asr Ave, No. 494, Teheran.

Ireland: 8 Mirdamad Ave, North Razan St, Teheran; tel. (021) 222731; telex 213865; Ambassador: NOËL PURCELL-O'BYRNE.

Italy: 81 ave de France, Teheran; tel. (021) 672107; telex 214171; Ambassador: VITTORIO AMEDEO FARINELLI.

Japan: Bucharest Ave, N.W. Corner of 5th St, POB 11365-814, Teheran; tel. (021) 623396; telex 212757; Ambassador: YUHIRO FUJIMOTO.

Jordan: Teheran.

Korea, Democratic People's Republic: Fereshteh Ave, Sarvestan Ave, No. 11, Teheran; Ambassador: CHO KYU-IL.

Korea, Republic: 37 Bucharest Ave, Teheran; tel. (021) 621125; Chargé d'affaires a.i.: SUNG KU KANG.

Kuwait: Dehkadeh Ave, 3-38 Sazman-Ab St, Teheran; tel. (021) 636712; Ambassador: AHMAD ABD AL-AZIZ AL-JASSIM.

Lebanon: Teheran; Ambassador: JA'FAR MA'AWI.

Libya: Ostad Motahhari Ave, No. 163, Teheran; Sec.-Gen. Committee of People's Bureau: MAHDI AL-MABIRASH.

Malaysia: Bucharest Ave, No. 8, Teheran; tel. (021) 629523; Chargé d'affaires a.i.: SOPIAN BIN AHMAD.

Mauritania: Teheran.

Netherlands: POB 11365-138, Vali Asr Ave, Ostad Motahhari Ave, Sarbederan St, Jahansouz Alley, No. 36, Teheran; tel. (021) 896011; telex 212788; Ambassador: Dr J. M. J. B. HORAK.

New Zealand: Mirza-e-Shirazi Ave, Kucheh Mirza Hassani, No. 29, POB 11365-436, Teheran; tel. (021) 625061; telex 212078; Ambassador: D. F. L. MARKES.

Nicaragua: Teheran; Ambassador: GONZALO MURILLO.

Nigeria: Khaled Islamboli Ave, 31st St, No. 9, POB 11365-7148, Teheran; tel. (021) 684936; telex 213151; Ambassador: U. B. WALI.

Norway: Bucharest Ave, 6th St, No. 23, POB 15875-4891, Teheran 15146; tel. (021) 624644; telex 213009; Ambassador: JAN NAERBY.

Oman: Pasdaran Ave, Golestan 9, No. 5 and 7, POB 41-1586, Teheran; tel. (021) 243199; telex 212835; Chargé d'affaires a.i.: RASHID BIN MUBARAK BIN RASHID AL-ODWALI.

Pakistan: Dr Fatemi Ave, Jamshidabad Shomali, Mashal St, No. 1, Teheran; tel. (021) 934331; TANVIR AHMAD KHAN.

Philippines: 22 Kayhan St, Moghaddas Ardebili Ave, Zafaranieh, POB 19395-4797, Teheran; tel. (021) 295840; Ambassador SUROTANI P. USODAN.

Poland: Africa Expressway, Piruz St, No. 1/3, Teheran; tel. (021) 227262; Ambassador: STEFAN SZYMCZYKIEWICZ.

Portugal: Mossadegh Ave, Tavanir Ave, Nezami Ghanjavi Ave, No. 30, Teheran; tel. (021) 681380; telex 212588; Ambassador: FERNANDO PINTO DOS SANTOS.

Qatar: Africa Expressway, Golazin Ave, Parke Davar, No. 4, Teheran; tel. (021) 221255; telex 212375; Chargé d'affaires a.i.: I. MUHAMMAD AL-QAYED.

Romania: Fakhrabad Ave 22-28, Teheran; tel. (021) 759841; telex 212791; Ambassador: ILIE CASU.

Senegal: Vozara Ave, 4 8th St, BP 3217, Teheran; tel. (021) 624142.

Somalia: Shariati Ave, Soheyl Ave, No. 20, Teheran; Chargé d'affaires a.i.: MUHAMMAD SHEIKH AHMAD.

Spain: Ghaem Magham Farahani Ave, Varahram St, No. 14, Teheran; tel. (021) 624575; telex 212980; Ambassador: JOSÉ MARÍA SIERRA.

Sudan: Khaled Islambouli Ave, 23rd St, No. 10, Teheran; tel. (021) 628476; telex 213372; Ambassador: IBRAHIM AHMAD OTHMAN HAMRA.

Sweden: POB 15875-4313, 78 Africa Sq., Teheran; tel. (021) 620514; telex 212822; Ambassador: HÅKAN GRANQVIST.

Switzerland: POB 19395-4683, 13 Boustan Ave, Teheran; tel. (021) 268227; telex 212851; fax 269448; Ambassador: ANTON GREBER.

Syria: Bucharest Ave, 10th St, No. 42, Teheran; Ambassador: IBRAHIM YUNIS.

Thailand: Baharestan Ave, Parc Amin ed-Doleh, No. 4, POB 11495-111, Teheran; tel. (021) 301433; telex 214140; Ambassador: WAIPOTE SUWANAMOLI.

Tunisia: Teheran.

Turkey: Ferdowsi Ave, No. 314, Teheran; tel. (021) 315299; Ambassador: VULKAN VURAL.

USSR: 39 Neauphle-le-Château St, Teheran; Ambassador: VLADIMIR GUDEV.

United Arab Emirates: Zafar Ave, No. 355-7, Teheran; tel. (021) 221333; telex 212697; Chargé d'affaires a.i.: T. AHMAD AL-HAIDAN.

United Kingdom: Ferdowsi Ave, Teheran; Chargé d'affaires a.i.: DAVID REDDAWAY.

Venezuela: Bucharest Ave, 9th St, No. 31, POB 15875-4354, Teheran; tel. (021) 625185; telex 213790; Ambassador: Dr JOSÉ RAFAEL ZANONI.

*Yemen Arab Republic: Bucharest Ave, No. 26, Teheran; Chargé d'affaires a.i.: ABDULLAH AR-RAZI.

*Yemen, People's Democratic Republic: Bucharest Ave, 10th St, No. 41, Teheran; Ambassador: KHADIR SALIH AL-HAMZAH.

Yugoslavia: Vali Asr Ave, Fereshteh Ave, Amir Teymour Alley, No. 12, Teheran; tel. (021) 294127; telex 214235; Ambassador: MIRKO ZARIĆ.

Zaire: Vali Asr Ave, Chehrazi St, No. 68, POB 11365-3167, Teheran; tel. (021) 222199; Chargé d'affaires a.i.: N'DJATE ESELE SASA.

* Merged to form the Republic of Yemen in May 1990.

Judicial System

In August 1982 the Supreme Court revoked all laws dating from the previous regime which did not conform with Islam. In October 1982 all courts set up prior to the Islamic Revolution were abolished. In June 1987 Ayatollah Khomeini ordered the creation of clerical courts to try members of the clergy opposed to government policy. A new system of qisas (retribution) is being established, where the emphasis is on speedy justice. Islamic codes of correction were introduced in 1983, including the dismembering of a hand for theft, flogging for fornication and violations of the strict code of dress for women, and stoning for adultery. One hundred and nine offences may be punished by the death penalty. More than 1,000 itinerant justices have been appointed to tour the country, deciding cases in each locality and dispensing immediate punishment. The aim is to keep imprisonment to a minimum. In January 1983, however, investigative teams were formed to ensure that the judiciary did not exceed its authority. In 1984 there was a total of 2,200 judges. The new Supreme Court has 16 branches.

SUPREME COURT

Chief Justice: Hojatoleslam MUHAMMAD YAZDI.

Prosecutor-General: Hojatoleslam MUHAMMADI REYSHAHRI.

Religion

According to the 1979 Constitution, the official religion is Islam of the Ja'fari sect (Shi'ite), but other Islamic sects, including Zeydi,

Hanafi, Maleki, Shafe'i and Hanbali, are valid and will be respected. Zoroastrians, Jews and Christians will be recognized as official religious minorities. According to the 1976 census, there were then 310,000 Christians (mainly Armenian), 80,000 Jews and 30,000 Zoroastrians.

ISLAM

The great majority of the Iranian people are Shi'a Muslims, but there is a minority of Sunni Muslims. Persians and Azerbaizhanis are mainly Shi'i, while the other ethnic groups are mainly Sunni.

During 1978 there was a revival of the influence of the Ayatollahs (or senior Shi'ite divines). The late Ayatollah RUHOLLAH KHOMEINI of Qom, who had been exiled to Iraq in 1964 and moved to near Paris in October 1978, conducted a campaign of opposition to the Shah, returning to Iran in February 1979 and bringing about the downfall of the Shah's regime. Other important Ayatollahs include Ayatollah ABD AL-KARIM MOUSSAVI ARDEBILI, Ayatollah AHMAD AZARI-QOMI, Ayatollah HOSSEIN ALI MONTAZERI of Teheran, Ayatollah ABOLGHASSEM KHOI of Najaf, Iraq, and the Ayatollahs SHAHABOLDIN MARASHI NAJAFI and MUHAMMAD REZA GOLPAYEGHANI of Qom.

CHRISTIANITY
The Roman Catholic Church

At 31 December 1988 there were an estimated 12,290 adherents in Iran, comprising 8,090 of the Chaldean Rite, 2,200 of the Armenian Rite and 2,000 of the Latin Rite.

Armenian Rite
Bishop of Isfahan: Dr VARTAN TEKEYAN, Armenian Catholic Bishopric, Khiaban Ghazzali 22, Teheran; tel. (031) 677204; diocese founded 1934.

Chaldean Rite
Archbishop of Ahwaz: HANNA ZORA, Archbishop's House, POB 61956, Naderi St, Ahwaz; tel. (061) 24890.
Archbishop of Teheran: YOUHANNAN SEMAAN ISSAYI, Archevêché, Forsat Ave 91, Teheran 15819; tel. (021) 823549.
Archbishop of Urmia (Rezayeh) and Bishop of Salmas (Shahpour): THOMAS MERAM, Khalifagari Kaldani Katholiq, POB 338, Orumiyeh 57135; tel. (0441) 22739.

Latin Rite
Archbishop of Isfahan: IGNAZIO BEDINI, Consolata Church, POB 11365-445, 75 France Ave, Teheran; tel. (031) 673210.

The Anglican Communion

Anglicans in Iran are adherents of the Episcopal Church in Jerusalem and the Middle East, formally inaugurated in January 1976. The Rt Rev. HASSAN DEHQANI-TAFTI, the Bishop in Iran from 1961, was President-Bishop of the Church from 1976 to 1986. Following an assassination attempt against him in October 1979, the Bishop went into exile (he now resides in the United Kingdom and has been Assistant Bishop of Winchester, in the Church of England, since 1982).
Bishop in Iran: Rt Rev. IRAJ MOTTAHEDEH, Abbas-abad, POB 81465-135, Isfahan; tel. (031) 34675; diocese founded 1912.

Presbyterian Church

Synod of the Evangelical (Presbyterian) Church in Iran: Assyrian Evangelical Church, Khiaban-i Hanifnejad, Khiaban-i Aramanch, Teheran; Moderator Rev. ADEL NAKHOSTEEN.

ZOROASTRIANS

There are about 30,000 Zoroastrians, a remnant of a once widespread sect. Their religious leader is MOUBAD.

OTHER COMMUNITIES

Communities of Armenians, and somewhat smaller numbers of Jews (an estimated 30,000 in 1986), Assyrians, Greek Orthodox Christians, Uniates and Latin Christians are also found as officially recognized faiths. The Bahá'í faith, which originated in Iran, has about 300,000 Iranian adherents, although at least 10,000 are believed to have fled since 1979 in order to escape persecution. The Government banned all Bahá'í institutions in August 1983.

The Press

Teheran dominates the press scene as many of the daily papers are published there and the bi-weekly, weekly and less frequent publications in the provinces generally depend on the major metropolitan dailies as a source of news. A press law which was announced in August 1979 required all newspapers and magazines to be licensed and imposed penalties of imprisonment for insulting senior religious figures. Offences against the Act will be tried in the criminal courts. In the Constitution which was approved in December 1979, the press is free, except in matters that are contrary to public morality, insult religious belief or slander the honour and reputation of individuals. Many of the papers which were published under the Shah's regime ceased publication after the revolution. In August 1980 Ayatollah Khomeini issued directives which indicated that censorship would be tightened up, and several papers were closed down in 1981. The radical daily *Azadegan* (Morning of the Liberated) was closed by the Prosecutor-General in June 1985 and reappeared under a different title, *Abrar* (Rightly Guided), after complaints from deputies in the Majlis of its criticism of conservative members of the assembly. Later in 1985, however, a policy of relative liberalization of the press was introduced. Ayatollah Khomeini told journalists in September and October that criticism of the government was permissible if it was constructive and not designed to arouse dissent.

PRINCIPAL DAILIES

Abrar (Rightly Guided): Apadan Ave 198, Abbasabad, Teheran; tel. (021) 859971; f. 1985 after closure of *Azadegan* by order of the Prosecutor-General; morning; Farsi; circ. 30,000.

Alik: POB 11365-953, Jomhoori Islami Ave, Alik Alley, Teheran 11357; tel. (021) 676671; f. 1931; afternoon; political and literary; Armenian; Propr A. AJEMIAN.

Bahari Iran: Khayaban Khayham, Shiraz; tel. 33738.

Ettela'at (Information): Khayyam St, Teheran; tel. (021) 311071; telex 212336; f. 1925; evening; Farsi; political and literary; owned and managed by Mostazafin Foundation from October 1979 until 1 January 1987, when it was placed under the direct supervision of *Wilayat-e-Faqih* (religious jurisprudence); Editor Mr SHIRANI; circ. 250,000.

Jomhoori Islami (Islamic Republic): Teheran; was organ of the Islamic Republican Party until it was dissolved in 1987; continues to appear; circ. 30,000.

Kayhan (Universe): Ferdowsi Ave, Teheran; tel. (021) 310251; telex 212467; f. 1941; evening; Farsi; political; also publishes *Kayhan International* (f. 1959; daily and weekly; English; Editor HOSSEIN RAGHFAR), *Kayhan Arabic* (f. 1980; daily and weekly; Arabic), *Kayhan Persian* (f. 1942; daily; Persian), *Kayhan Turkish* (f. 1984; monthly; Turkish), *Kayhan Havaie* (f. 1950; weekly for Iranians abroad; Farsi), *Kayhan Andishe* (World of Religion; f. 1985; 6 a year; Farsi), *Zan-e-Ruz* (Woman Today; f. 1964; weekly; Farsi), *Kayhan Varzeshi* (World of Sport; f. 1955; weekly; Farsi), *Kayhan Bacheha* (Children's World; f. 1956; weekly; Farsi), *Kayhan Farhangi* (World of Culture; f. 1984; monthly; Farsi); *Kayhan Yearbook* (yearly; Farsi); *Period of 40 Years*, *Kayhan* (series of books; Farsi); owned and managed by Mostazafin Foundation from October 1979 until 1 January 1987, when it was placed under the direct supervision of *Wilayat-e-Faqih* (religious jurisprudence); Chief Editor SAYED MOHAMMAD ASGHARY; circ. 350,000.

Khorassan: Meshed; Head Office: Khorassan Daily Newspapers, 14 Zohre St, Mobarezan Ave, Teheran; f. 1948; Propr MUHAMMAD SADEGH TEHERANIAN; circ. 40,000.

Mojahed: organ of the Mujaheddin Khalq; ceased publication June 1986.

Rahnejat: Darvazeh Dowlat, Isfahan; political and social; Propr N. RAHNEJAT.

Risala'at (The Message): Teheran; organ of right-wing group of the same name; political; Propr Ayatollah AHMAD AZARI-QOMI; circ. 40,000.

Teheran Times: Nejatullahi Ave, 32-Kouche Bimch, Teheran; tel. (021) 839900; telex 213662; f. 1979; independent; English; Editor-in-Chief M. B. ANSARI.

PRINCIPAL PERIODICALS

Acta Medica Iranica: Faculty of Medicine, Enghelab Ave, Teheran Medical Sciences Univ., Teheran 14-174; tel. (021) 6112743; f. 1960; quarterly; English, French, German; under the supervision of the Research Vice-Dean (G. POURMAND) and the Editorial Board; Editor-in-Chief PARVIZ JABAL-AMELI (Dean, Faculty of Medicine); circ. 2,000.

Al-Akha: Khayyam Ave, Tehran; telex 212336; f. 1960; weekly; Arabic; Editor NAZIR FENZA.

Akhbar-e-Pezeshki: 86 Ghaem Magham Farahani Ave, Teheran; weekly; medical; Propr Dr T. FORUZIN.

Armaghan: Baghe Saba, 127 Salim Street, Teheran 16137; tel. (021) 750698; f. 1910; monthly; literary and historical; Propr Dr MUHAMMAD VAHID-DASTGERDI; circ. 3,000.

Ashur: Ustad Motahhari Ave, 11-21 Kuhe Nour Ave, Teheran; tel. (021) 622111; f. 1985; Assyrian; monthly; Founder and Editor Dr W. BET-MANSOUR; circ. 8,000.

IRAN

Auditor: 77 Ferdowsi Ave North, Teheran; quarterly; financial and managerial studies.

Ayandeh: POB 19575-583, Niyavaran, Teheran; tel. (021) 283254; monthly; Iranian literary, historical and book review journal; Editor Prof. IRAJ AFSHAR.

Bulletin of the National Film Archive of Iran: POB 5158, Baharestan Sq., Teheran 11365; tel. 311242; telex 214283; f. 1989; English periodical; Editor M. H. KHOSHNEVIS.

Daneshkadeh Pezeshki: Faculty of Medicine, Teheran Medical Sciences University; tel. (021) 6112743; f. 1947; 10 a year; medical magazine; Propr Dr HASSAN AREFI; circ. 1,500.

Daneshmand: POB 15875-3649, Teheran; tel. (021) 854969; f. 1963; monthly; scientific and technical magazine; Editor ALI MIRZAEI.

Dokhtaran and Pesaran: Khayyam Ave, Teheran; f. 1947; weekly teenage magazine; Editor NADER AKHAVAN HAYDARI.

Donaye Varzesh: Khayyam Ave, Ettela'at Bldg, Teheran; telex 212336; weekly; sport; Editor Mr SAMIMI; circ. 100,000.

Echo of Islam: POB 14155-3987, Teheran; monthly; English; published by the Foundation of Islamic Thought.

Ettela'at Banovan: 11 Khayyam St, Teheran; telex 212336; weekly; women's magazine; Editor Mrs RAHNAWARD; circ. 85,000.

Ettela'at Haftegi: 11 Khayyam St, Teheran; telex 212336; weekly; Editor Mr NAYYERI; circ. 60,000.

Farhang-e-Iran Zamin: POB 19575-583, Niyavaran, Teheran; tel. (021) 283254; annual; Iranian studies; Editor Prof. IRAJ AFSHAR.

Faza: Enghelab Ave, Teheran; aviation; Propr H. KAMALI-TAQARI.

Film: POB 5875, Teheran 11365; tel. 679373; f. 1982; monthly in Farsi with an English supplement; Editor M. MEHRABI.

Honar va Memar: Enghelab Ave No. 256, Teheran; monthly; scientific and professional; Propr A. H. ECHRAGH.

Iran Press Digest (Economic): Hafiz Ave, 4 Kucheh Hurtab, POB 11365-5551, Teheran; tel. (021) 668114; telex 212300; weekly; Editor J. BEHROUZ.

Iran Press Digest (Political): Hafiz Ave, 4 Kucheh Hurtab, POB 11365-5551, Teheran; tel. (021) 668114; telex 212300; weekly.

Iran Trade and Industry: POB 1228, Hafiz Ave, Teheran; monthly; English.

Iran Tribune: POB 111244, Teheran; monthly; English.

Iranian cinema: POB 5158, Baharestan Sq., Teheran 11365; tel. 311242; f. 1985; annually; English; Editor B. REYPOUR.

Jam: POB 1871, Jomhoori Islami Ave, Sabuhi Bldg, Teheran; monthly; arts; Propr A. VAKILI.

Jame'e Dandan-Pezeshki Iran: 2 Ex-Shahi Alley, Shahid Dr Abbaspour St, Vali Asr Ave, POB 14155-3695, Teheran; tel. (021) 686508; telex 212918; monthly; medical; organ of Iranian Dental Assen; Propr Dr HAMID ADELI-NAJAFI.

Javanan Emrooz: 11144 Khayyam Ave, POB 11335-9365, Ettela'at, Teheran; tel. (021) 311205, telex 212336; f. 1966; weekly; youth; Editor ALI AGHA MUHAMMADI.

Javaneh: POB 15875-1163, Motahhari Ave, Cnr Mofatteh St, Teheran; tel. (021) 839051; published by Soroush Press; quarterly.

Kayhan Bacheha (Children's World): Shahid Shahsheragi Ave, Teheran; tel. (021) 310251; telex 212467; f. 1956; weekly; Editor AMIR HOSSEIN FARDI; circ. 150,000.

Kayhan Varzeshi (World of Sport): Ferdowsi Ave, Teheran; tel. (021) 310251; telex 212467; f. 1955; weekly; Dir MAHMAD MONSETI; circ. 125,000.

Mahjubah: POB 14155-3897, Teheran; Islamic women's magazine; published by the Islamic Thought Foundation.

Majda: 2 Ex-Shahi Alley, Shahid Dr Abaspour St, Vali-Asr Ave, Teheran; tel. (021) 686508; telex 212918; f. 1963; three a year; medical; journal of the Iranian Dental Association.

Mokhtarein va Mobtakerin: Motahhari Ave, Cnr Mofatteh St, POB 15875-1163, Teheran; tel. (021) 839051; quarterly; Farsi; published by Soroush Press; Iranian technological innovations.

Music Iran: 1029 Amiriye Ave, Teheran; f. 1951; monthly; Editor BAHMAN HIRBOD; circ. 7,000.

Nameh-e-Mardom: Teheran; organ of the Tudeh Party.

Neda-e-Nationalist: W. Khayaban Hafiz (Khayaban Rish Kutcha Bostan), POB 1999, Teheran.

Negin: Vali Asr Ave, Adl St 52, Teheran; monthly; scientific and literary; Propr and Dir M. ENAYAT.

Pars: Alley Dezhban, Shiraz; f. 1941; irregular; Propr and Dir F. SHARGHI; circ. 10,000.

Pezhuhshgar: Vali Asr Ave, Teheran; scientific; Propr Dr R. OLUMI.

Salamate Fekr: M.20, Kharg St, Teheran; tel. (021) 223034; f. 1958; monthly; organ of the Mental Health Soc.; Editors Prof. E. TCHEHRAZI, ALI REZA SHAFAI.

Sepid va Siyah: Ferdowsi Ave, Teheran; monthly; popular; Editor Dr A. BEHZADI; circ. 30,000.

Setareye Esfahan: Isfahan; weekly; political; Propr A. MIHANKHAH.

Sokhan: Hafiz Ave, Zomorrod Passage, Teheran; f. 1943; Khanlari; monthly; literary and art; Propr PARVIZ NATEL-KHANLARY.

Soroush: Motahhari Ave, Corner Mofatteh St, POB 15875-1163, Teheran; tel. (021) 830771; f. 1972; weekly in Farsi, monthly in English, French and Arabic; cultural magazine; Editor M. FIROOZAN.

Tarikh-e-Islam: Amiriyeh 94 Ku, Ansari, Teheran; monthly; religious; Propr A. A. TASHAYYOD.

Tebb-o-Daru: POB 3033, Inqilah Ave, Teheran; medical; Man. Dr SH. ASSADI ZADEH.

Teheran Mossavar: Lalezar Ave, Teheran; weekly; political and social.

Vahid: 55 Jomhoori Islami Ave, Jam St, Teheran; weekly; literature; Propr Dr S. VAHIDNIA.

Yaghma: 15 Khanequah Ave, Teheran; tel. (021) 305344; f. 1948; monthly; literature; Propr HABIB YAGHMAIE.

Zan-e-Ruz (Woman Today): Ferdowsi Ave, Teheran; telex 212467; f. 1964; weekly; women's; circ. over 100,000.

NEWS AGENCIES

Islamic Republic News Agency (IRNA): 873 Vali Asr Ave, POB 764, Teheran; tel. (021) 892050; telex 212827; f. 1936; Man. Dir HOSSEIN NASIRI.

Foreign Bureaux

Agence France-Presse (AFP): POB 1535, Ghaen St, Teheran; tel. (021) 314190; telex 2479; Correspondent JACQUES CHARMELOT.

Agenzia Nazionale Stampa Associata (ANSA) (Italy): 7 East Africa St, Nahid Blvd, Teheran; tel. (021) 009821; telex 213629; Correspondent (vacant).

Anatolian News Agency (Turkey): Teheran.

Kyodo Tsushin (Japan): No. 23, First Floor, Couche Kargozar, Couche Sharsaz Ave, Zafar, Teheran; tel. (021) 220448; telex 214058; Correspondent MASARU IMAI.

Novinska Agencija Tanjug (Yugoslavia): Teheran.

Reuters (UK): POB 15875-1193, Teheran; tel. (021) 847700; telex 212634; (Correspondent, HUGH POPE, expelled from Iran in July 1986 for allegedly revealing military secrets).

Telegrafnoye Agentstvo Sovetskovo Soyuza (TASS) (USSR): Kehyaban Hamid, Kouche Masoud 73, Teheran; Correspondent (vacant).

Xinhua (New China) News Agency (People's Republic of China): 75 Golestan 2nd St, Pasdaran Ave, Teheran; tel. (021) 241852; telex 212399; Correspondent XU BOYUAN.

Publishers

Ali Akbar Elmi: Jomhoori Islami Ave, Teheran; Dir ALI AKBAR ELMI.

Amir Kabir: 28 Vessal Shirazi St, Teheran; f. 1950; historical, social, literary and children's books; Dir ABD AR-RAHIM JAFARI.

Boroukhim: Ferdowsi Ave, Teheran; dictionaries.

Danesh: 357 Nasser Khosrow Ave, Teheran; f. 1931 in India, transferred to Iran in 1937; literary and historical (Persian); imports and exports books; Man. Dir NOOROUAH IRANPARAST.

Ebn-e-Sina: Meydane 25 Shahrivar, Teheran; f. 1957; educational publishers and booksellers; Dir EBRAHIM RAMAZANI.

Eghbal Printing & Publishing Organization: 15 Booshehr St, Dr Shariati Ave, Teheran; tel. (021) 768113; f. 1903; Man. Dir DJAVAD EGHBAL.

Iran Chap Co: Khayam Ave, Teheran; tel. 3281; telex 212336; fax 315530; f. 1966; newspapers, books, magazines, book binding, colour printing and engraving; Man. Dir M. DOAEI.

Iran Exports Publication Co Ltd: POB 15815-3373, Teheran 11456; tel. (021) 899461; telex 215017; f. 1987; business and trade.

Kanoon Marefat: 6 Lalezar Ave, Teheran; Dir HASSAN MAREFAT.

Khayyam: Jomhoori Islami Ave, Teheran; Dir MOHAMMAD ALI TARAGHI.

Majlis Press: Ketab-Khane Majlis-e-Showraie Eslami No. 1, Baharistan Sq., Teheran 11564; tel. (021) 393257; f. 1924; Dir ABD AL-HOSSEIN HAIERI; Ketab Khane Majlis-e-Showraie Eslami No. 2, Imam Khomeini Ave, Teheran 13174; tel. (021) 662906; f. 1950; Dir ABD AL-HOSSEIN HAIERI.

Safiali Shah: Baharistan Sq., Teheran; Dir MANSOUR MOSHFEGH.

IRAN
Directory

Sahab Geographic and Drafting Institute: 30 Somayeh St, Hoquqi Crossroad, Dr Ali Shariati Ave, POB 11365-617, Teheran 16517; tel. (021) 765691; telex 222584; fax (021) 855443; maps, atlases, and books on geography, science, history and Islamic art; Founder and Pres. ABBAS A. SAHAB.

Scientific and Cultural Publications Co: Ministry of Higher Education and Culture, POB 5433-5437, Teheran; tel. (021) 686317; f. 1974; Iranian and Islamic studies and scientific and cultural books; Pres. M. BOROUJERDI.

Taban Press: Nassir Khosrow Ave, Teheran; f. 1939; Propr A. MALEKI.

Teheran Economist: 99 Sargord Sakhaie Ave, Teheran-11.

Teheran University Press: 16 Kargar Shomali Ave, Teheran; tel. (021) 632062; f. 1944; university textbooks; Man. Dir Dr FIRUZ HARIRCHI.

Towfigh: Jomhoori Islami Ave, Teheran; publishes humorous Almanac and pocket books; distributes humorous and satirical books; Dir Dr FARIDEH TOWFIGH.

Zawar: Jomhoori Islami Ave, Teheran; Dir AKBAR ZAWAR.

Radio and Television

There were 11.5m. radio receivers and 2.3m. television sets in use in 1990.

Islamic Republic of Iran Broadcasting (IRIB): Mossadegh Ave, Jame Jam St, POB 19395-1774, Teheran; tel. (021) 21961; telex 212431; semi-autonomous government authority; non-commercial; operates two national television and three national radio channels, as well as local provincial radio stations throughout the country; Dir-Gen. Hojatoleslam SAYED MUHAMMAD HASHEMI.

RADIO

Radio Network 1 (Voice of the Islamic Republic of Iran): there are three national radio channels: Radio Networks 1 and 2 and Radio Quran, which broadcasts recitals of the Quran (Koran) and other programmes related to it; covers whole of Iran and reaches whole of Europe, SW USSR, whole of Asia, Africa and part of USA; medium-wave regional broadcasts in local languages; Arabic, Armenian, Assyrian, Azerbaizhani, Baluchi, Bandari, Dari, Farsi, Kurdish, Mazandarani, Pashtu, Turkoman, Turkish and Urdu; external broadcasts in English, French, German, Spanish, Turkish, Arabic, Kurdish, Urdu, Pashtu, Armenian, Bengali, Russian and special overseas programme in Farsi; 53 transmitters.

TELEVISION

Television (Vision of the Islamic Republic of Iran): 625-line, System B; Secam colour; two production centres in Teheran producing for two networks and 28 local TV stations.

Finance

(cap. = capital; p.u. = paid up; dep. = deposits; res = reserves; brs = branches; m. = million; amounts in rials)

BANKING

Prior to the Islamic Revolution, the banking system comprised 36 banks. Banks were nationalized in June 1979 and a revised banking system has been introduced consisting of nine banks. Three banks were reorganized, two (Bank Tejarat and Bank Mellat) resulted from mergers of 22 existing small banks, three specialize in industry and agriculture and one, the Islamic Bank (now Islamic Economy Organization), set up in May 1979, was exempt from nationalization. A change-over to an Islamic banking system, with interest being replaced by a 4% commission on loans, began on 21 March 1984.

Although the number of foreign banks operating in Iran has fallen dramatically since the Revolution, some 30 are still represented. Since the exclusion of French banks from the Iranian market at the end of 1983, German, Swiss, Japanese and British banks have been responsible for about 30% of total trade financing.

Central Bank

Bank Markazi Jomhouri Islami Iran (Central Bank): Ferdowsi Ave, POB 1136-58551, Teheran; tel. (021) 310101; telex 212359; f. 1960; Bank Markazi Iran until Dec. 1983; central note-issuing bank of Iran, government banking; cap. p.u. 125,000m., dep. 6,839,029m., res 72,431m., total assets 7,198,215m. (March 1985); Gov. MUHAMMAD HOSSEIN ADELI.

Commercial Banks

Bank Keshavarzi (Agricultural Bank): 129 Patrice Lumumba Ave, Jalal al-Ahmad Expressway, POB 14155-6395, Teheran; tel. (021) 9121; telex 212058; f. 1979 as merger of the Agricultural Development Bank of Iran and the Agricultural Co-operative Bank of Iran; State-owned; cap. 156,395m., dep. 214,004m. (August 1990); 422 brs; Man. Dir SAYED ALI MILANI HOSSIENI.

Bank Mellat (Nation's Bank): Park Shahr, Varzesh Ave, POB 11365-5964, Teheran; tel. (021) 674357; telex 212619; f. 1980 as merger of the following: International Bank of Iran, Bank Bimeh Iran, Bank Dariush, Distributors' Co-operative Credit Bank, Iran Arab Bank, Bank Omran, Bank Pars, Bank of Teheran, Foreign Trade Bank of Iran, Bank Farhangian; State-owned; cap. p.u. 33,500m., dep. 2,024,772m., total assets 2,451,230m. (March 1989); 1,209 brs throughout Iran and 3 brs abroad; Chair. and Man. Dir Dr M. BAGHERI.

Bank Melli Iran (The National Bank of Iran): Ferdowsi Ave, POB 11365-171, Teheran; tel. (021) 3231; telex 212890; f. 1928; State-owned; cap. 25,000m., dep. 12,400m., dep. 4,095,145m., total assets 4,825,995m. (March 1989); 1,914 brs throughout Iran, 21 brs abroad; Chair. and Man. Dir ASSADOLLAH AMIRASLANI.

Bank Refah Kargaran: POB 15815/1866, 125 Ayatollah Shahid Dr Moffateh Ave, Teheran; tel. (021) 825000; telex 213786; f. 1960; State-owned; cap. p.u. 10,000m., dep. 522,701m. (March 1989); 140 brs throughout Iran.

Bank Saderat Iran (The Export Bank of Iran): 3 Corner of Fajr St, Ghaem Magham Farzhani Ave, Teheran; tel. (021) 837006; telex 213077; fax (021) 836095; f. 1952, reorganized 1979; State-owned; cap. p.u. and res. 21,300.4m., dep. 2,408,564.4m., total assets 2,932,084.7m. (March 1988); 2,560 brs in Iran, 20 foreign brs; Man. Dir VALIOLLAH SEIF.

Bank Sepah (Army Bank): Imam Khomeini Sq, Teheran; tel. (021) 311091; telex 212462; f. 1925, reorganized 1979; State-owned; cap. p.u. 8,000m., total assets 2,064,362m. (March 1989); 933 brs throughout Iran and 5 brs abroad; Chair. and Man. Dir ABOLGHASEM DJAMSHIDI.

Bank Tejarat (Commercial Bank): 130 Taleghani Ave, POB 11365-5416, Teheran; tel. (021) 890130; telex 212077; fax (021) 828215; f. 1979 as merger of the following: Irano-British Bank, Bank Etebarate Iran, The Bank of Iran and the Middle East, Mercantile Bank of Iran and Holland, Bank Barzagani Iran, Bank Iranshahr, Bank Sanaye Iran, Bank Shahriar, Iranians' Bank, Bank Kar, International Bank of Iran and Japan, Bank Russo-Iran; State-owned; cap. p.u. 39,120m., dep. 1,452,548m., total assets 2,163,813m. (March 1989); 1,000 brs; Chair. and Man. Dir MUHAMMAD JAFAR EFTEKHAR.

Islamic Economy Organization (formerly Islamic Bank of Iran): Ferdowsi Ave, Teheran; f. February 1980; cap. 2,000m.; provides interest-free loans and investment in small industry.

Development Bank

Bank Sanat va Madan (Bank of Industry and Mines): 593 Hafiz Ave, POB 11365/4978, Teheran; tel. (021) 893271; telex 212816; f. 1979 as merger of the following: Industrial Credit Bank (ICB), Industrial and Mining Development Bank of Iran (IMDBI), Development and Investment Bank of Iran (DIBI), Iranian Bankers Investment Company (IBICO); cap. p.u. 40,980m., res 97,953m., total assets 606,267m. (1984); Chair. and Man. Dir MORTEZA ARAMY PARCHEBAF.

Housing Bank

Bank Maskan (Housing Bank): Ferdowsi Ave, Teheran; tel. (021) 675021; telex 213904; f. 1980; State-owned; cap. p.u. 42,663.8m., dep. 221,153.4m., total assets 1,313,708m. (June 1985); provides mortgage and housing finance; 187 brs; Chair. and Man. Dir ABDULLAH EBTEHAJ.

STOCK EXCHANGE

Teheran Stock Exchange: Taghinia Bldg, 521 South Saadi Ave, Teheran 11447; tel. (021) 311149; f. 1966; Chair. of Council M. NOURBAKHSH.

INSURANCE

The nationalization of insurance companies was announced on 25 June 1979.

Bimeh Alborz (Alborz Insurance Co): POB 4489-15875, Alborz Bldg, 234 Sepahbod Garani Ave, Teheran; tel. (021) 893201; telex 214134; fax (021) 898088; state-owned insurance company; all types of insurance; Man. Dir AHMAD-REZA RAFIEE.

Bimeh Asia (Asia Insurance Co): POB 1365-5366, Asia Insurance Bldg, 297-299 Taleghani Ave, Teheran; tel. (021) 836040; telex 213664; fax (021) 827196; all types of insurance; Man. Dir MASOUM ZAMIRI.

Bimeh Dana (Dana Insurance Co): POB 11365-7413, Dana Insurance Bldg, 315 Engelab Ave, Teheran; tel. (021) 673041, inc, personal accident and health insurance; Man. Dir. M. TEHRANI.

IRAN

Bimeh Iran (Iran Insurance Co): POB 11365-9153, Saadi Ave, Teheran; tel. (021) 304026; telex 212782; fax (021) 313510; all types of insurance; Man. Dir GHOLAMHOSEIN DELJOU.

Bimeh Markazi Iran (Central Insurance of Iran): POB 15875-4345, 149 Taleghani Ave, Teheran; tel. (021) 6409912; telex 212888; fax (021) 6405729; supervises the insurance market and tariffs for new types of insurance cover; the sole state reinsurer for domestic insurance companies, which are obliged to reinsure 50% of their direct business in life insurance and 25% of business in non-life insurance with Bimeh Markazi Iran; Pres. AHMAD GERANMAYEH.

Trade and Industry

CHAMBER OF COMMERCE

Iran Chamber of Commerce, Industries and Mines: 254 Taleghani Ave, Teheran; tel. (021) 836031; telex 213382; fax (021) 825111; supervises the affiliated 20 Chambers in the provinces.

STATE ENTERPRISES

Iranian Offshore Oil Co (IOOC): 339 Dr Beheshti Ave, POB 15875-4546, Teheran; tel. (021) 624102; telex 212707; wholly owned subsidiary of NIOC; f. 1980; development, exploitation and production of crude oil, natural gas and other hydrocarbons in all offshore areas of Iran in Persian Gulf; Chair. M. HASHEMIAN; Man. Dir S. M. KHOEE.

National Iranian Copper Industries Co (NICEC).

National Iranian Drilling Co: Chair. MANSOUR PARVINIAN.

National Iranian Gas Co (NIGC): Man. Dir MOHAMMAD ISMAIL KARACHIAN.

National Iranian Industries Organization (NIIO): POB 14155-3579, 133 Dr Fatemi Ave, Teheran; tel. (021) 656031-40; telex 214176; fax (021) 658070; f. 1979; owns 500 factories in Iran.

National Iranian Industries Organization Export Co (NECO): No. 8, Second Alley, Bucharest Ave, Teheran 15944; tel. (021) 4162384; telex 212429.

National Iranian Lead and Zinc Co (NILZC).

National Iranian Mines and Metal Smelting Co (NIMMSC).

National Iranian Mining Explorations Co (NIMEC).

National Iranian Oil Co (NIOC): Taleghani Ave (POB 1863), Teheran; tel. (021) 6151; telex 212514; a State organization controlling all petroleum, petrochemical and natural gas operations in Iran; incorporated April 1951 on nationalization of oil industry to engage in all phases of oil operations; in February 1979 it was announced that in future Iran would sell oil direct to the oil companies and in September 1979 the Ministry of Oil took over control of the National Iranian Oil Company, and the Minister of Oil took over as Chairman and Managing Director; Chair. of Board and Gen. Man. Dir GHOLAMREZA AQAZADEH (Minister of Oil); Directors: M. NEJAD HOSSAINIAN (Engineering), A. SALEHIFROOZ (Refining), H. MUHAMMAD NEJAD (Distribution and Pipelines), G. HASSANTASH (Administration), M. KESHAVARZ (Legal Affairs), S. M. HEDAYATZADEH (International Affairs), H. KHERADMAND (Corporate Planning Affairs), M. KARBAUSIAN (Commercial Affairs), M. PARVINIAN (Oil Production).

National Iranian Petrochemical Co (NIPC): POB 7484, Karimkhan Zand Blvd, Teheran; tel. (021) 839060-74; telex 213520; fax (021) 822087; f. 1964; wholly owned by Iranian Govt; Pres. AHMAD RAHGOZAR.

National Iranian Steel Co (NISC): Teheran; Man. Dir MOHAMMED TAQI BANKI.

CO-OPERATIVES

Central Organization for Co-operatives of Iran: Teheran; in October 1985 there were 4,598 labour co-operatives, with a total membership of 703,814 and capital of 2,184.5m. rials, and 9,159 urban non-labour co-operatives, with a total membership of 262,118 and capital of 4,187.5m. rials.

Central Organization for Rural Co-operatives of Iran (CORC): Teheran; Man. Dir SAYED HASSAN MOTEVALLI-ZADEH.

The CORC was founded in 1963, and the Islamic Government of Iran has pledged that it will continue its educational, technical, commercial and credit assistance to rural co-operative societies and unions. At the end of the Iranian year 1363 (1984/85) there were 3,104 Rural Co-operative Societies with a total membership of 3,925,000 and share capital of 25,900m. rials. There were 181 Rural Co-operative Unions with 3,097 members and capital of 7,890m. rials.

TRADE FAIR

Export Promotion Centre of Iran: POB 11-48, Tajrish, Teheran; tel. (021) 21911; telex 212896; international trade fairs and exhibitions; Pres. HOSSEIN KHABBAZAN.

Transport

RAILWAYS

Iranian Islamic Republic Railway: Shahid Kalantary Bldg, Rahe-Ahan Sq., Teheran 13185; tel. (021) 555120; telex 213103; f. 1934; Pres. Eng. SADEGH AFSHAR; Vice-Pres. E. MUHAMMAD (Admin. and Finance), Vice-Pres. NASSER POURMIRZA (Technical and Operations), Vice-Pres. REZA IRANKHAH (Planning and Technical Studies), Vice-Pres. Eng. VAHAB JAMSHIDI (Construction and Renovation).

The total length of main lines in the Iranian railway system, which is generally single-tracked, is 4,567 km (4,473 km of 1,435 mm gauge and 94 km of 1,676 mm gauge). The system includes the following main routes:

Trans-Iranian Railway runs 1,392 km from Bandar Turkman on the Caspian Sea in the north, through Teheran, and south to Bandar Imam Khomeini on the Persian Gulf.

Southern Line links Teheran to Khorramshahr via Qom, Arak, Doroud, Andimeshk and Ahwaz; 937 km.

Northern Line links Teheran to Gorgan via Garmsar, Firooz Kooh and Sari; 499 km.

Teheran–Kerman Line via Kashan, Yazd and Zarand; 1,106 km.

Teheran–Tabriz Line linking with the Azerbaizhan Railway; 736 km.

Tabriz–Djulfa Electric Line: 146 km.

Garmsar–Meshed Line connects Teheran with Meshed via Semnan, Damghan, Shahrud and Nishabur; 812 km.

Qom–Zahedan Line when completed will be an intercontinental line linking Europe and Turkey, through Iran, with India. Zahedan is situated 91.7 km west of the Baluchistan frontier, and is the end of the Pakistani broad gauge railway. The section at present links Qom to Kerman via Kashan, Sistan, Yazd, Bafq and Zarand; 1,005 km. A branch line from Sistan was opened in 1971 via Isfahan to the steel mill at Zarrin Shahr; 112 km. A broad-gauge (1,976-mm) track connects Zahedan and Mirjaveh, on the border with Pakistan; 94 km.

Zahedan–Quetta (Pakistan) Line: 685km; not linked to national network.

Ahwaz–Bandar Khomeini Line connects Bandar Khomeini with the Trans-Iranian railway at Ahwaz; this line is due to be double-tracked; 112 km.

Azerbaizhan Railway extends from Tabriz to Djulfa (146.5 km), meeting the Caucasian railways at the Soviet frontier. Electrification works for this section have been completed and the electrified line was opened in April 1982. A standard gauge railway line (139 km) extends from Tabriz (via Sharaf-Khaneh) to the Turkish frontier at Razi.

A 730-km line to link Bandar Abbas and Bafq has been under construction since 1982, and was due to be electrified by 1990.

Underground Railway. An agreement was signed in March 1976 between the Municipality of Teheran and French contractors for the construction of a subway. Four lines are to be built with a total length of 143 km. Construction began during 1978, but the project was suspended after the revolution in 1979. Work on two of the lines resumed in September 1986 and was due to be completed in mid-1992, when work on the remaining two lines will begin.

ROADS

In 1989 there were 490 km of motorways, 18,044 km of paved main roads, 33,275 km of paved feeder roads, 49,398 km of gravel roads and 52,120 km of earth roads. There is a paved highway (A1, 2,089 km) from Bazargan on the Turkish border to the Afghanistan border. The A2 highway runs 2,473 km from the Iraqi border to Mir Javeh on the Pakistan border, 2,422 km of the A2 has been completed, and the remaining 51 km are under construction.

Ministry of Roads and Transport: 49 Taleghani Ave, Teheran; tel. (021) 661034; telex 213381.

INLAND WATERWAYS

Principal waterways:

Lake Rezaiyeh (Lake Urmia) 80 km west of Tabriz in North-West Iran; and River Karun flowing south through the oilfields into the River Shatt al-Arab, thence to the head of the Persian Gulf near Abadan.

Lake Rezaiyeh: From Sharafkhaneh to Golmankhaneh there is a twice-weekly service of tugs and barges for transport of passengers and goods.

River Karun: Regular cargo service is operated by the Mesopotamia-Iran Corpn Ltd. Iranian firms also operate daily motorboat services for passengers and goods.

SHIPPING

Persian Gulf: The main oil terminal is at Kharg Island. The principal commercial non-oil ports are Bandar Shahid Rajai (which was officially inaugurated in 1983 and handles 9m. of the 12m. tons of cargo passing annually through Iran's Persian Gulf ports), Bandar Khomeini, Bushehr, Bandar Abbas and Chah Bahar. A project to develop Bandar Abbas port, which pre-dates the Islamic Revolution and was originally to cost IR 1,900,000m., is now in progress. Khorramshahr, Iran's biggest port, was put out of action in the war with Iraq, and Bushehr and Bandar Khomeini also sustained war damage, which has restricted their use. In August 1988 the Iranian news agency (IRNA) announced that Iran was to spend $200m. on the construction of six 'multi-purpose' ports on the Arabian and Caspian Seas, while ports which had been damaged in the war were to be repaired. During 1988 Iran signed a contract with the USSR for two cargo ships which will provide the basis of a new shipping line between the ports of Anzali and Noshahr, on the Caspian Sea, and Baku, in the USSR.

Caspian Sea: Principal port Bandar Anzali (formerly Bandar Pahlavi) and Bandar Nowshahr.

Iranian National Tanker Co: 67 Shahid Atefi St, Africa Ave, POB 16765-947, Teheran; tel. (021) 296041; telex 213938; fleet of 28 tankers, 35 chartered tankers and 34 other vessels; support fleet of 32 tugs and supply boats; Chair. and Man. Dir MUHAMMAD SOURI.

Irano–Hind Shipping Co: No. 3, 13th St, Miremad Ave, Dr Beheshti Ave, Teheran; tel. (021) 850213; telex 215233; joint venture between the Islamic Republic of Iran and the Shipping Corpn of India; fleet of 9 vessels, including two refrigerated cargo ships; Chair. M. H. DAJMAR; Vice-Chair. J. C. SHETH; Man. Dir K. R. SACHAR.

Islamic Republic of Iran Shipping Lines (IRISL): POB 15875-4646, Arya Building, 127 Ghaem Magham Farahani Ave, Teheran 15896; tel. (021) 833061; telex 212794; f. 1967; affiliated to the Ministry of Commerce Jan. 1980; fleet of 95 vessels; liner services between the Persian Gulf and Europe, the Far East and South America; Chair. and Man. Dir MUHAMMAD HOSSEIN DAJMER.

Ports and Shipping Organization: 751 Enghelab Ave, Teheran; tel. (021) 837041; telex 212271; Man. Dir Eng. MUHAMMAD MADAD.

CIVIL AVIATION

The two main international airports are Mehrabad (Teheran) and Abadan. An international airport was opened at Isfahan in July 1984 and the first international flight took place in March 1986. Work on a new international airport, 40 km south of Teheran, abandoned in 1979, resumed in the mid-1980s, and work on three others, at Tabas, Ardebil and Ilam was under way in mid-1990. The airports at Urumiyeh, Ahwaz, Bakhtaran, Sanandaz, Abadan, Hamadan and Shiraz were to be modernized and smaller ones constructed at Lar, Lamard, Rajsanjan, Barm, Kashan, Maragheh, Khoy, Sirjan and Abadeh.

Iran Air (Airline of the Islamic Republic of Iran): Iran Air Bldg, Mehrabad Airport, Teheran; tel. 9111; telex 212795; f. 1962; Chair. and Man. Dir S. H. SHAFTI; serves Persian Gulf area*, Athens, Beijing, Bombay, Damascus*, Frankfurt, Geneva, Istanbul, Karachi, Kuala Lumpur, Larnaca, London, Paris, Rome, Tokyo, Vienna and, from 1988, Lagos, Cotonou and Accra; fleet of 4 Airbus A-300B2, 4 Boeing 747SP, 3 747 100/200, 1 747F, 3 707, 1 707F, 4 727-200, 2 727-100, 3 737-200, 1 737-200 VIP.

* In January 1991 Iran Air suspended flights to Damascus, to Doha, in Qatar, and to Dubai and Sharjah, in the United Arab Emirates.

Iran Asseman Airlines: POB 13145-1476, Mehrabad Airport, Teheran; tel. (021) 661967; telex 212575; fax (021) 6404318; f. after Islamic Revolution as result of merger of Air Taxi Co (f. 1958), Pars Air (f. 1969), Air Service Co (f. 1962) and Hoor Asseman; Man. Dir ALI ABEDZADEH; domestic routes and charter services; fleet of 3 Fairchild FH-227B, 2 Fokker F28-4000, 4 Falcon 20, 6 Turbo Commander, 2 Aero Commander, 7 Shrike Commander, 2 Piper Chieftain, 2 Islander.

Tourism

Tourism has been adversely affected by political upheaval since the revolution. Iran's chief attraction for the tourist is its wealth of historical sites, notably Isfahan, Rasht, Tabriz, Susa and Persepolis. There were 89,400 visitors to Iran in 1985, compared with 185,756 in 1981. The total rose to 171,837 during the Iranian year 21 March 1986–20 March 1987.

Atomic Energy

Atomic Energy Organization of Iran: POB 14155-1339, Teheran; tel. (021) 61381; telex 213383; f. 1973; originally set up to produce nuclear power to provide for the base load electricity needs of the country; main aim now is the exploration and exploitation of uranium (deposits have been found in several regions of Iran in commercially viable quantities); to utilize nuclear technology in industry, agriculture and medicine; to provide research and development work and training for greater national self-sufficiency in nuclear science and technology; work on Bushehr nuclear power plant, a pressurized water reactor (two 1,200 MW units), which was being built by Kraftwerk Union AG of the Federal Republic of Germany, and was 85% completed by 1979, had not been resumed by mid-1990; Pres. REZA AMROLLAHI.

Isfahan Nuclear Technology Centre (INTC): POB 81465-1589, Isfahan; tel. (031) 58081; telex 312351; f. 1979; applied engineering research in areas related to nuclear reactor technology.

Teheran University Nuclear Centre: Institute of Nuclear Science and Technology, POB 2989, Teheran; f. 1958; research in nuclear physics, electronics, nuclear chemistry, radiobiology and nuclear engineering; training and advice on nuclear science and the peaceful applications of atomic energy; a 5-MW pool-type research reactor on the new campus of Teheran University went critical in November 1967; a 3-MeV Van de Graaff-type accelerator became operational in 1972; Dir Dr J. MOGHIMI.

IRAQ

Introductory Survey

Location, Climate, Language, Religion, Flag, Capital

The Republic of Iraq is an almost land-locked state in western Asia, with a narrow outlet to the sea on the Persian (Arabian) Gulf. Its neighbours are Iran to the east, Turkey to the north, Syria and Jordan to the west, and Saudi Arabia and Kuwait to the south. The climate is extreme, with hot, dry summers, when temperatures may exceed 43°C (109°F), and cold winters, especially in the highlands. Summers are humid near the Persian Gulf. The official language is Arabic, spoken by about 80% of the population. About 15% speak Kurdish, while there is a small Turkoman-speaking minority. About 95% of the population are Muslims, of whom more than 50% belong to the Shi'i sect. However, the regime that came to power in 1968 has been dominated by members of the Sunni sect. The national flag (proportions 3 by 2) has three equal horizontal stripes, of red, white and black, with three five-pointed green stars on the central white stripe. The inscription 'Allahu Akhbar' ('God is Great') was added to the flag in January 1991. The capital is Baghdad.

Recent History

Iraq was formerly part of Turkey's Ottoman Empire. During the First World War (1914–18), when Turkey was allied with Germany, the territory was captured by British forces. In 1920 Iraq was placed under a League of Nations mandate, administered by the United Kingdom (UK). In 1921 Amir Faisal ibn Hussain, a member of the Hashimi (Hashemite) dynasty of Arabia, was proclaimed King of Iraq, and his brother, Abdullah, was proclaimed Amir (Emir) of neighbouring Transjordan (later renamed Jordan), also administered by the UK under a League of Nations mandate. The two new monarchs were sons of Hussain (Hussein) ibn Ali, the Sharif of Mecca, who had proclaimed himself King of the Hijaz (now part of Saudi Arabia) in 1916. The British decision to nominate Hashemite princes to be rulers of Iraq and Transjordan was a reward for Hussain's co-operation in the wartime campaign against Turkey.

During its early years the new kingdom was faced by Kurdish revolts (1922–32) and by border disputes in the south. The leading personality in Iraqi political life under the monarchy was Gen. Nuri as-Said, who became Prime Minister in 1930 and held the office for seven terms, over a period of 28 years. He strongly supported Iraq's friendship with the UK and with the West in general. After prolonged negotiations, a 25-year Anglo-Iraqi Treaty of Alliance was signed in 1930. The British mandate ended on 3 October 1932, when Iraq became fully independent.

King Faisal I died in 1933 and was succeeded by his son, Ghazi. In 1939, however, King Ghazi was killed in a motor accident. The new king, Faisal II, was an infant at the time of his accession, and his uncle, Prince Abd al-Ilah, acted as regent until 1953, when the king assumed full powers. Like Gen. Nuri, Prince Abd al-Ilah was pro-Western in outlook. An attempted pro-Nazi coup in May 1941 was thwarted by the intervention of British forces. Despite nationalist opposition, Iraq declared war on Germany and Italy in January 1943. British troops were withdrawn in October 1947, although a British air base remained until 1959. Iraqi forces participated in the Arab–Israeli war of 1948–49. The Constitutional Union Party, founded by Gen. Nuri in 1949, became the sole legal party in 1953, after all opposition groups were banned. In 1955 Iraq signed the Baghdad Pact, an agreement on collective regional security against a possible threat from the USSR.

In February 1958 Iraq and Jordan formed an Arab Federation, with King Faisal of Iraq as its Head of State. In March Gen. Nuri resigned as Iraqi Prime Minister to become Prime Minister of the new union. On 14 July, however, a military revolution overthrew the Iraqi monarchy. King Faisal, Prince Abd al-Ilah and Gen. Nuri were all killed. The victorious rebels abolished the 1925 Constitution, dissolved the legislature and proclaimed a republic, with Brig. (later Lt-Gen.) Abd al-Karim Kassem at the head of a left-wing nationalist regime. Iraq withdrew from the Baghdad Pact in March 1959. For more than four years, Kassem maintained a precarious and increasingly isolated position, opposed by Pan-Arabs, Kurds and other groups. In February 1963 the Pan-Arab element in the armed forces staged a coup in which Kassem was killed. A new government was formed under Col (later Field Marshal) Abd as-Salem Muhammad Aref, who initiated a policy of closer relations with the United Arab Republic (Egypt). Martial law, in force since 1958, was ended in January 1965, and a civilian government was inaugurated in September 1965. President Aref was killed in an air accident in March 1966, and was succeeded by his brother, Major-Gen. Abd ar-Rahman Muhammad Aref. Iraq declared war on Israel at the outbreak of the Six-Day War in June 1967, but Iraqi forces were not involved in the conflict. The second President Aref was ousted by members of the Arab Socialist Renaissance (Baath) Party on 17 July 1968. Major-Gen. (later Field Marshal) Ahmad Hassan al-Bakr, a former Prime Minister, became President and Prime Minister, and supreme authority was vested in the Revolutionary Command Council (RCC), of which President al-Bakr was also Chairman. Provisional constitutions, proclaiming socialist principles, were introduced in September 1968 and July 1970. A National Charter, to be the basis of a permanent constitution, was issued in November 1971. This envisaged an elected National Assembly but, until the Assembly's formation, power remained with the RCC.

Relations with the Syrian Government deteriorated after a younger generation of Baathists seized power in Syria in 1970. A bitter rivalry has since existed between Syrian and Iraqi Baathists. Relations with Syria dramatically improved in October 1978, when President Assad of Syria visited Baghdad. Plans were announced for eventual complete political and economic union of the two countries. Economic difficulties, such as the dispute over water from the Euphrates river, were soon settled but progress on political union was slow. On 16 July 1979 the Vice-Chairman of the RCC, Saddam Hussain, who had long been the real power in Iraq, replaced Bakr as Chairman, and as President of Iraq. A few days later, an attempted coup was reported and several members of the RCC were executed for their alleged part in the plot. The suspicion of Syrian implication put an end to all further talk of political union between Iraq and Syria, but economic co-operation continued.

Since the cease-fire in the Iran-Iraq War in August 1988, Iraq has been fighting a 'proxy war' against Syrian domination of Lebanon by supplying money and arms to the Christian Lebanese Forces. Iraq supported the interim military administration that was appointed by former President Gemayel and opposed by Syria. After March 1989, when the 'war of liberation' waged by the Lebanese army against Syrian forces in Lebanon began, Iraq became the principal supplier of arms to the Lebanese army.

During 1979 the National Progressive Front, an alliance of Baathists and Communists, broke up amid accusations that the Baathists were conducting a 'reign of terror'. In February 1980 President Hussain announced his National Charter, re-affirming the principles of non-alignment. In June elections, the first since the 1958 revolution, were held for a 250-member, legislative National Assembly, followed in September by elections for a 50-member Kurdish Legislative Council.

Relations with Iran, precarious for many years, developed into full-scale war in September 1980. Prior to 1975, Iran had been supporting a rebellion by Kurds in northern Iraq. The Algiers Agreement between Iran and Iraq, signed in 1975, defined the southern border between the two countries as a line along the middle of the Shatt al-Arab waterway, and also virtually ended the Kurdish rebellion by depriving it of Iranian support. In the years after 1975, however, Iraq grew increasingly dissatisfied with the 1975 agreement. Iraq also wanted the withdrawal of Iranian forces from Abu Musa and Tumb islands, which Iran occupied in 1971.

The Iranian revolution of 1979 exacerbated these grievances. Conflict soon developed over Arab demands for autonomy in Iran's Khuzestan region (named 'Arabistan' by Arabs), which Iran accused Iraq of encouraging. Iraq's Sunni leadership was suspicious of Shi'ite Iran, and feared that trouble might arise from its own Shi'ites, who form more than 50% of the population. Border disputes occurred in the summer of 1980, and more extensive fighting began after Iran ignored Iraqi diplomatic efforts, demanding the withdrawal of Iranian forces from the border area of Zain ul-Qos in Diali province. Iraq maintained that this area should have been returned under the 1975 agreement, which Iraq then abrogated on 16 September 1980. Iraqi advances into Iran began on 22 September along a front of 500 km (300 miles). Fierce Iranian resistance brought about a stalemate, which lasted until the spring of 1982, when Iranian counter-offensives led to the retaking of the port of Khorramshahr in May and the withdrawal of Iraqi troops from the territory which they had taken in 1980. In July 1982 the Iranian army crossed into Iraq. (For a full account of the Iran-Iraq War (1980–88), see Iran, *Recent History*, p. 1381.)

In 1984 the balance of military power in the continuing war with Iran moved in Iraq's favour, and its financial position improved, as the USA and the USSR, both officially neutral, provided aid. The USSR increased its military aid following a *rapprochement* in March, precipitated by Iran's anti-Soviet stance. (At the end of 1987 it was estimated that the USSR had supplied Iraq with military aid worth $10,000m. since ending a ban on sales of weapons in 1982.) The USA assisted Iraq with the financing of crucial projects for the construction of pipelines to carry petroleum exports, and an increasing allocation of commodity credits, which totalled $2,500m. between 1981 and 1985. (Iraq and the USA re-established full diplomatic relations on 26 November 1984, more than 17 years after they had been severed by Iraq following the Arab–Israeli war of 1967.) Egypt was estimated to have provided military supplies worth more than US $2,000m., and Brazil, Chile and the People's Republic of China also sold arms to Iraq.

Saddam Hussain retained his positions as Chairman of the RCC and Regional Secretary of the Baath Party, following its regional Congress in June 1982. In fact, a subsequent purge throughout the administration left him more firmly in control than before. Kurdish rebels became active again in northern Iraq, occasionally supporting Iranian forces. Another threat was posed by the Supreme Council of Iraqi Opposition Groups, formed in Teheran in November 1982 by the exiled Shi'ite leader, Hojatoleslam Muhammad Baqir al-Hakim.

In July 1986 the ruling Arab Baath Socialist Party held an extraordinary regional conference, the first since June 1982. Three new members were elected to the party's Regional Command (RC), increasing its number to 17. Naim Haddad, who had been a member of the RC and of the ruling Revolutionary Command Council (RCC) since their formation in 1968, was not re-elected to the RC, and was subsequently removed from the RCC, on which he was replaced by Sa'adoun Hammadi, the Chairman of the National Assembly. These changes strengthened Saddam Hussain's position as party leader.

An attempted coup was believed to have taken place in Baghdad in October 1983, led by the recently dismissed head of intelligence, Barzan Takriti (the President's half-brother), and a number of senior army officers, who were later reported to have been executed. Iraq's Shi'ite community was not attracted by the Islamic fundamentalism of Ayatollah Khomeini of Iran, remaining loyal to Iraq and its Sunni President, while the opposition of Iranian-backed terrorist groups (such as the Shi'ite fundamentalist Dawa group, which repeatedly attempted to assassinate Hussain) had no significant effect. While the cease-fire in the Iran-Iraq War of August 1988, which was precipitated by Iraqi military successes, strengthened Hussain's position, it also allowed domestic conflicts to find expression again. Hussain's regime is widely regarded as one of the most autocratic in the Arab world, and in February 1989 there were reports of a further attempt by senior army officers to stage a coup. In November 1988 Hussain announced a programme of political reforms, including the introduction of a multi-party political system, and in January 1989 he declared that these would be incorporated into a new constitution. This development was regarded as an attempt to retain the loyalty of Iraq's Shi'ite community, which sought a liberalization of Iraqi society as a reward for its role in the war against Iran.

In April 1989 elections were held to the 250-member National Assembly for the third time since its creation in 1980. The 250 seats were reportedly contested by 911 candidates, one quarter of whom were members of the Baath Party. The remaining candidates were reported to be either independent or members of the National Progressive Front. It was estimated that 75% of Iraq's electorate (totalling about 8m.) voted in the elections, and that more than 50% of the newly-elected deputies were members of the Baath Party. A new draft Constitution was completed in January 1990, and approved by the National Assembly in July, when its provisions were published in the Iraqi press. It allows for a multi-party political system, and there has been speculation that defunct political parties, such as the National Democratic Party, will be permitted to re-form and participate in future elections. Under the terms of the draft Constitution, a 50-member Consultative Assembly is to be established. Half of its members are to be appointed by the President, and the other half elected by direct, secret ballot. The Consultative Assembly, together with the National Assembly, will assume the duties of the RCC, which is to be abolished after a presidential election has taken place. (In an amendment to the published draft of the Constitution, the National Assembly recommended that Saddam Hussain be elected for life.) Following its approval by the National Assembly, the draft Constitution was to be subjected to a popular referendum for approval before ratification by the President. In Sept. 1989 elections were held to the 50-member Legislative Council of the Kurdish Autonomous Region.

The problem of autonomy for Iraq's 2.5m.–3m. Kurds (currently in limited operation in three provinces) remains unresolved. Resources were repeatedly diverted from the war with Iran to control Kurdish rebellion in the north-east of the country. Hussain sought an accommodation with the Kurds, and a series of discussions began in December 1983, after a cease-fire had been agreed with Jalal Talibani, the leader of the main Kurdish opposition party in Iraq, the Patriotic Union of Kurdistan (PUK). These discussions did not include the other main Kurdish group, the Democratic Party of Kurdistan (DPK), led by Masoud Barzani. The breakdown of the talks in May 1984 frustrated hopes for a government of national unity, including the PUK and the Communist Party of Iraq. However, it was reported that Hussain persisted, informally, in trying to persuade the PUK to join the National Progressive Front. Negotiations on Kurdish autonomy collapsed again in January 1985. After a cease-fire lasting 14 months, fighting broke out in Kurdistan between PUK guerrillas and government troops. The PUK blamed the Government's continued persecution and execution of Kurds; its refusal to permit consideration in autonomy talks of the one-third of Kurdistan which, in Kirkuk province, contains some of Iraq's main oilfields; and an agreement with Turkey to act jointly to quell Kurdish resistance, which had been made in October 1984. Then, in February 1985, the PUK rejected the offer of an amnesty for President Hussain's political opponents, at home and abroad, and fighting continued, with Kurdish and Iranian forces repeatedly collaborating in raids against Iraqi military and industrial targets.

Since 1987, when the Iranian military threat began to recede, Iraq had concentrated more resources in the north of the country to counter the activities of the Kurdish separatist movement, which claimed to control a 'liberated zone' of 10,000 sq km. In May 1988 the DPK and the PUK announced the formation of a coalition of six organizations to continue the struggle for Kurdish self-determination and to co-operate militarily with Iran. The cease-fire in the Iran-Iraq War in August 1988 allowed Iraq to divert more troops and equipment to Kurdistan, and to launch a new offensive to overrun guerrilla bases near the borders with Iran and Turkey, during which chemical weapons were allegedly used, forcing Kurdish civilians and fighters to escape into Iran and Turkey. By mid-September, more than 100,000 Kurdish refugees were believed to have escaped into Turkey, while Iraqi Kurds seeking refuge in Iran joined an estimated 100,000 of their countrymen, 40,000 of whom had escaped from Halabja, after attacks with chemical weapons on the city in March.

On 26 September 1988 the UN Security Council adopted a resolution (No. 620) unanimously condemning the use of chemical weapons in the Iran-Iraq War. However, Iraq continued to deny that it was using chemical weapons against the Kurds, despite what the USA described as compelling evidence to the contrary. On 6 September, with its army effectively in control of the border with Turkey, the Iraqi Government offered a full amnesty to all Iraqi Kurds inside and outside the country, excluding only Jalal Talibani, the leader of the PUK. However, the offer was generally dismissed by Kurds as a propaganda ploy, although the Government subsequently claimed that more than 60,000 Kurdish refugees had taken advantage of the amnesty to return to Iraq.

On 17 September 1988 the Government began to evacuate inhabitants of the Kurdish Autonomous Region to the interior of Iraq, as part of a plan to create a 30-km.-wide uninhabited 'security zone' along the whole of Iraq's border with Iran and Turkey. In June 1989 Kurdish opposition groups appealed for international assistance to halt the evacuations, claiming that they were, in fact, forcible deportations of Kurds to areas more susceptible to government control, and that many of the evacuees (reported to number 300,000 by August 1989) did not reside in the border strip which was to be incorporated into the 'security zone', but in other areas of the Kurdish Autonomous Region. By October 1989, despite international censure of the evacuation programme, the 'security zone' was reported to be in place, prompting the PUK to announce a campaign of urban guerrilla warfare against the Government throughout Iraq.

In March 1985 King Hussein of Jordan and President Mubarak of Egypt made an unexpected visit to Baghdad to demonstrate their support for Saddam Hussain, despite the fact that full diplomatic relations had not existed between Egypt and Iraq since Egypt's signing of the peace treaty with Israel in 1979.

In April 1985 the UN Secretary-General, Javier Pérez de Cuéllar, visited both Teheran and Baghdad, in an attempt to establish a basis on which peace negotiations between Iran and Iraq could begin. Iraq made it clear that it was interested only in a permanent cease-fire and immediate, direct negotiations with Iran; while Iran continued to insist on the removal of Saddam Hussain, an Iraqi admission of responsibility for starting the war, and the payment of reparations.

Following an extraordinary meeting of the League of Arab States (which unanimously condemned Iran for prolonging the war with Iraq, deplored its occupation of Arab (i.e. Iraqi) territory, and urged it to implement the UN Security Council's Resolution 598—see chapter on Iran, *Recent History*, p. 1381) in Amman, Jordan, in November 1987, the Iraqi Government, in common with eight other Arab countries, re-established diplomatic relations with Egypt. Meanwhile, during the meeting, contacts between President Hussain and President Assad revived speculation of a *rapprochement* between Iraq and Syria, which had supported Iran in the Iran-Iraq War. President Assad, however, had obstructed the League's adoption of an Iraqi proposal that member states should sever their diplomatic links with Iran, and Syria subsequently averred that the good relations between Syria and Iran were unchanged.

During 1987/88, for the first time in six years, owing to disorganization and a shortage of volunteers, Iran was unable to launch a major winter offensive. Iraqi forces advanced along the length of the war front, but not before Kurdish guerrillas had, in February 1988, made inroads into government-controlled territory in Iraqi Kurdistan, where Iranian forces, with Kurdish assistance, had earlier established bridgeheads. This was the largest Kurdish offensive since 1974/75, uniting forces from the DPK and the PUK. In March 1988 Iraq retaliated, using chemical weapons against the captured town of Halabja.

In mid-April 1988 Iraqi forces regained control of the Faw peninsular, and in May they recaptured the Shalamcheh area, driving the Iranians across the Shatt al-Arab. In mid-June they recaptured Majnoon Island, and at the end of the month expelled Iranian forces from Iraqi territory in Kurdistan. On 13 July Iraqi forces crossed into Iranian territory for the first time since 1986. Remaining pockets of Iranian resistance in southern Iraq had collapsed by mid-July, and on 18 July, to universal surprise, Iran officially announced its unconditional acceptance of Resolution 598. However, the implementation of a cease-fire was delayed by Iraq's demand for the initiation of direct peace talks with Iran, under UN auspices, prior to the cessation of hostilities. Iraq eventually withdrew this demand, and on 20 August a cease-fire came into force, monitored by a specially-created UN observer force of 350 officers, the UN Iran-Iraq Military Observer Group (UNIIMOG).

Negotiations between Iran and Iraq for a comprehensive peace settlement, based on the full implementation of Resolution 598, began at ministerial level in Geneva on 25 August 1988, under the aegis of the UN. However, deadlock soon arose over the question of the location of frontiers, in particular the southern border through the Shatt al-Arab waterway. This and other disputes, mostly concerning issues for which there was no provision in Resolution 598, delayed the implementation of the resolution beyond the introduction of a cease-fire. Clause Three, for example, urged the repatriation of prisoners of war. In November Iran and Iraq agreed to exchange all sick and wounded prisoners of war. The first exchanges took place in the same month, but the arrangements collapsed shortly afterwards, following a dispute over the number of prisoners involved. Resolution 598 also envisaged the creation of an impartial judicial body to determine who was responsible for starting the war. Its conclusions, when reached, seemed likely to prove to be a major obstacle to a peace settlement. While it was generally accepted that Iraq had initiated the conflict by invading Iran on 22 September 1980, Iraq maintained that the war began on 4 September with Iranian shelling of Iraqi border posts.

In February 1989 the negotiations for a peace settlement, which had been in suspension since November 1988, were renewed. By the end of April, however, after four sessions of talks, positions remained deadlocked, owing to Iran's demand that Iraqi forces withdraw to international borders, and Iraq's refusal to do so until the Shatt-al-Arab became freely navigable again. In November 1989, in an attempt to unblock the negotiations, Iran proposed an immediate exchange of prisoners of war, accompanied by the withdrawal of troops to within international borders. By the end of 1989, however, the cease-fire remained the only element of Resolution 598 to have been successfully implemented. In early 1990 Iraq proposed the resumption of direct peace negotiations with Iran (under UN auspices) and the immediate exchange of sick and wounded prisoners of war. At the same time, at the invitation of the Soviet Ministry of Foreign Affairs, Iran and Iraq agreed to resume negotiations in the USSR, although Soviet officials emphasized that this initiative was not a substitute for UN peace efforts in the region.

In July 1990 the Iraqi and Iranian Ministers of Foreign Affairs conferred at the UN's European headquarters in Geneva. It was the first such direct meeting between them since the cease-fire in the Iran-Iraq War had taken effect, and had been facilitated by an exchange of letters between Presidents Saddam Hussain and Rafsanjani in May. It was hoped that the talks in Geneva might lead to a 'summit' meeting between the two leaders, but this breakthrough in the peace process was quickly overtaken by the consequences of Iraq's invasion and annexation of Kuwait in August 1990. On 16 August Saddam Hussain abruptly sought an immediate, formal peace with Iran by accepting all the claims that Iran had pursued since the declaration of a cease-fire, including the reinstatement of the Algiers Agreement of 1975, dividing the Shatt al-Arab. While these concessions were welcomed by Iran, it insisted that the issue of peace with Iraq was separate from that of Iraq's occupation of Kuwait. Exchanges of prisoners of war commenced on 17 August, and on 18 August Iraq began to withdraw troops from the central border areas of Ilam, Meymak, Mehran and Naft Shahr.

From late 1989 there was increased concern in Western countries about the scale of a military expansion programme apparently under way in Iraq; about the involvement of Western companies in the programme; and about covert attempts by Iraq to obtain advanced military technology from the West. International attention focused on Iraq in September 1989, following an explosion at an Iraqi defence industry complex, which was thought to be a major installation in an Iraqi missile development programme.

In March 1990 Iraq's conviction for espionage, and subsequent execution, of an Iranian-born UK journalist, Farzad Bazoft, provoked international outrage and damaged relations with the UK. At the end of March 1990 the UK Government claimed to have thwarted attempts by Iraq to import prohibited military devices from the UK, and in April it alleged that steel tubes which Iraq had ordered from a British company were to be used to construct a 'supergun'. In April the US President, George Bush, also urged Iraq to abandon production of chemical weapons, and in June the US media alleged that France had helped to extend the range, and to improve the accuracy, of Iraqi missiles. At the end of July the US Congress voted to impose sanctions, which formally prohibited sales of weapons and military techology to Iraq.

As its relations with the West deteriorated, Iraq's standing in the Arab world improved. The outrage that was provoked by Iraq's execution of Farzad Bazoft, together with more general attacks in Western media on its human rights record, elicited expressions of support for Iraq from the Arab League and from individual Arab states. In April 1990, after Saddam Hussain had referred to Iraq's chemical weapons as a deterrent against a nuclear attack by Israel, there were further expressions of support, even from Iraq's staunchest Arab rival, Syria, for Iraq's right to defend itself.

Prior to a meeting of the OPEC ministerial council in Geneva on 25 July 1990, Iraq had implied that it might take military action against countries which continued to flout their OPEC production quotas. It had also accused Kuwait of violating the Iraqi border in order to steal Iraqi oil resources worth $2,400m., and suggested that Iraq's debt to Kuwait, accumulated largely during the Iran-Iraq War, should be waived. On the eve of the OPEC meeting in Geneva, Iraq stationed two armoured divisions on its borders with Kuwait.

The Iraqi threat and military mobilization led to a sharp increase in regional tension. Before the OPEC meeting in Geneva on 25 July 1990, President Mubarak of Egypt and Chedli Klibi, the Secretary-General of the Arab League, travelled to Baghdad in an attempt to calm the situation. The USA, meanwhile, placed on alert its naval forces stationed in Bahrain. At the conclusion of the meeting, however, the threat of Iraqi military action appeared to recede: both Kuwait and the UAE agreed to reduce their petroleum production, while OPEC agreed to raise its 'benchmark' price of crude petroleum from US $18 per barrel to $21 per barrel.

Direct negotiations between Iraq and Kuwait commenced in Saudi Arabia at the end of July 1990, with the aim of resolving disputes over territory, petroleum pricing and Iraq's debt to Kuwait. Kuwait was expected to accede to Iraqi demands for early negotiations to draft a border demarcation treaty, and Iraq was expected to lay claim to the islands of Bubiyan and Warbah, situated at the mouth of the Shatt al-Arab. (After Kuwait obtained independence in 1961—it had formerly been under the protection of the UK—Iraq claimed sovereignty over the country. Kuwait was placed under the protection of British troops, who were later withdrawn and replaced by Arab League forces. On 4 October 1963 the Iraqi Government formally recognized Kuwait's complete independence and sovereignty within its present borders. On 1 August, however, the talks collapsed, and on 2 August Iraq invaded Kuwait, taking control of the country and establishing a provisional Free Government. There was no evidence at all to support Iraq's claim that its forces had entered Kuwait at the invitation of insurgents, who had overthrown the Kuwaiti Government. The invasion appeared more likely to have been motivated by Iraq's financial difficulties in the aftermath of the Iran-Iraq War; by strategic interests—Iraq had long sought the direct access to the Persian Gulf which it gained by occupying Kuwait; and by Iraq's pursuit of regional hegemony.

The immediate response, on 2 August 1990, of the UN Security Council to the invasion of Kuwait was to convene and to adopt unanimously a resolution (No. 660), which condemned the Iraqi invasion of Kuwait; demanded the immediate and unconditional withdrawal of Iraqi forces from Kuwait; and appealed for a negotiated settlement of the conflict. On 6 August the UN Security Council convened again and adopted a further resolution (No. 661), which imposed mandatory economic sanctions on Iraq and occupied Kuwait, affecting all commodities with the exception of medical supplies and foodstuffs 'in humanitarian circumstances'.

As early as 3 August 1990, it was feared that the economic sanctions imposed on Iraq and Kuwait would be superseded international military conflict. On 3 August Iraqi troops began to deploy along Kuwait's border with Saudi Arabia, and the USA and the UK announced that they were sending naval vessels to the Gulf. On 7 August, at the request of King Fahd of Saudi Arabia, the USA dispatched combat troops and aircraft to Saudi Arabia, in order to secure the country's border with Kuwait against a possible attack by Iraq. US troops began to occupy positions in Saudi Arabia on 9 August, one day after Iraq announced its formal annexation of Kuwait. On the same day, the UN Security Council convened and adopted a unanimous resolution (No. 662), which declared the annexation of Kuwait to be null and void, and urged all states and institutions not to recognize it.

The dispatch of US troops signified the beginning of 'Operation Desert Shield' for the defence of Saudi Arabia, in accordance with Article 51 of the UN Charter. At the beginning of January 1991, two weeks before 'Operation Desert Storm' (see below) for the liberation of Kuwait commenced, some 30 countries had contributed ground troops, aircraft and warships to the multinational force in Saudi Arabia and the Gulf region. By far the biggest contributor was the USA, which, it was estimated, had deployed some 430,000 ground troops, 1,300 fighter and support aircraft, 2,000 tanks and 55 warships by 15 January 1991. Arab countries participating in the multinational force were Egypt, Syria, Morocco and the members of the Co-operation Council for the Arab States of the Gulf—Bahrain, Kuwait, Oman, Qatar, Saudi Arabia and the UAE. It was estimated that Iraq had deployed some 510,000 ground troops, 500 fighter and support aircraft, 4,000 tanks and 15 warships in Kuwait and southern Iraq by 15 January 1991.

Iraq's invasion and annexation of Kuwait altered the pattern of relations prevailing in the Arab world. In the immediate aftermath of the invasion, individual Arab states condemned Iraq's action, and on 3 August 1990 a hastily-convened meeting of the Arab League in Cairo agreed a resolution (endorsed by 14 of the 21 member states and opposed by Iraq, Jordan, Mauritania, Sudan, Yemen and the PLO) which condemned the invasion of Kuwait and demanded the immediate and unconditional withdrawal of Iraqi forces. At a 'summit' meeting of Arab League Heads of State, held in Cairo on 10 August, the demand for Iraq to withdraw from Kuwait was reiterated, and 12 of the 20 members participating in the meeting voted to send an Arab deterrent force to the Gulf in support of the UN's effort to deter potential aggression against Saudi Arabia.

As a crisis in the Gulf developed, Western diplomacy strove to maintain Iraq's isolation. The invasion of Kuwait had provoked widespread popular support for Iraq, notably in Jordan, where there is a huge Palestinian population, and also in the Maghreb States. Although conducted with the authority of the UN, in pursuit of aims formulated in specific UN resolutions, and with the active support of Egypt, Syria, Morocco and the Gulf States, both 'Operation Desert Shield' and 'Operation Desert Storm' were widely perceived, in parts of the Arab world, to be US-led campaigns to secure US interests in the Gulf region.

On 12 August 1990 Saddam Hussain proposed an initiative for the resolution of the conflict in the Gulf, linking Iraq's occupation of Kuwait with other conflicts in the Middle East, in particular the continuing Israeli occupation of the West Bank of Jordan and the Gaza Strip, and the Palestinian question. This was the first explicit example of so-called 'linkage' in diplomatic efforts to resolve the crisis in the Gulf. Practically, 'linkage' would have amounted to the trading of an Iraqi withdrawal from Kuwait for, at least, the convening of an international conference on the Palestinian issue, and it was repeatedly rejected by the USA, which considered that 'linkage' would reward Iraq's aggression and enhance its reputation in the Arab world.

The authority for the deployment of a multinational force for the defence of Saudi Arabia was contained in Article 51 of the UN Charter, which affirms 'the inherent right of individual or collective self-defence if an armed attack occurs against a member of the United Nations, until the Security Council has taken measures necessary to maintain international peace and security'. The UN Security Council warned, however, that its authorization would be necessary for the use of force to implement the economic sanctions imposed on Iraq and Kuwait. Article 42 of the UN Charter provided for the taking of 'such action by air, sea or land forces as may be necessary to maintain international peace and security', including the use of a blockade. In order to clarify its provisions, the USA drafted a resolution which would allow the UN to use legitimately the force necessary to maintain a blockade against Iraq. On 25 August 1990 the UN Security Council adopted a resolution (No. 665) which requested, with immediate effect, member states deploying maritime forces in the area to use 'such measures commensurate to the specific circumstances as may be necessary under the authority of the Security Council to halt all inward and outward maritime shipping in order to inspect and verify the cargoes and destinations' and ensure the implementation of the mandatory economic sanctions against Iraq and Kuwait. The resolution also invited all states to co-operate by political and diplomatic means to ensure compliance with sanctions.

Successive diplomatic efforts to achieve a peaceful solution to the crisis in the Gulf—undertaken, at different times, by the UN and by numerous individual countries—between August 1990 and mid-January 1991 foundered, virtually without exception, on Iraq's steadfast refusal to withdraw its forces from Kuwait. Diplomacy was initially complicated by the treatment of Western citizens residing in Iraq and Kuwait. On 9 August 1990 Iraq closed its borders to foreigners, and on 10 August all US and UK nationals in Kuwait were ordered to assemble at hotels prior to their removal to Iraq. Iraq subsequently announced that Westerners would be housed near military locations in order to deter an attack on Iraq by the multinational force in Saudi Arabia. On 28 August, however, Iraq announced that all foreign women and children were free to leave Iraq and Kuwait, extending this permission to all foreigners on 6 December.

On 29 November 1990 the UN Security Council convened and adopted a resolution (No. 678), drafted by the USA, which, with reference to its previous resolutions regarding Iraq's occupation of Kuwait, authorized 'all member states co-operating with the Government of Kuwait, unless Iraq on or before 15 January 1991, fully implements... the foregoing resolutions, to use all necessary means to uphold and implement Security Council Resolution 660 and all subsequent relevant resolutions and to restore international peace and security in the area'. Iraq denounced Resolution 678, the first UN resolution since 1950 which authorized the use of force, as a threat, and reiterated its demand for the UN Security Council to address equally all the problems of the Middle East.

'Operation Desert Storm'—in effect, war with Iraq—in pursuance of the liberation of Kuwait, as demanded by UN Resolution 660, commenced on the night of 16–17 January 1991. It was preceded by intense diplomatic activity to achieve a peaceful solution to the crisis in the Gulf, in particular a visit, on 10 January, by the UN Secretary-General, Javier Pérez de Cuéllar, to Baghdad for talks with Saddam Hussain. The failure of this mission was widely regarded as signalling the inevitability of military conflict. On 14 January Iraq's National Assembly approved a resolution which afforded the President all constitutional powers to respond to any 'US-led' attack.

The declared aim of the multinational force in Saudi Arabia, in the initial phase of 'Operation Desert Storm', was to gain air superiority, and then air supremacy, over Iraqi forces, in order to facilitate air attacks on Iraqi military and industrial installations. Hostilities commenced with air raids on Baghdad, and more than 110,000 attacking air missions were flown over Iraq and Kuwait by the multinational air forces before the suspension of hostilities on 28 February 1991.

The multinational force claimed air supremacy over Iraq and Kuwait on 30 January 1991, and air attacks were refocused on the fortified positions of Iraqi ground troops in Kuwait, in preparation for a ground offensive. During the initial phase of the air campaign, the Iraqi air force appeared to have offered surprisingly little resistance. Indeed, by 8 February it was reported that more than 100 Iraqi fighter aircraft had sought refuge in Iran, and the apparent good faith of Iran's reaffirmation of its neutrality in the conflict prompted speculation that they had been directed there deliberately in an attempt to prevent the total destruction of the Iraqi air force.

Iraq's most serious response to the military campaign waged against it was attacks with *Scud* missiles on Israel. While these were of little military significance, they threatened to provoke Israeli retaliation against Iraq and the consequent disintegration of the multinational force, since it would be politically impossible for any Arab state to fight alongside Israel against Iraq. US diplomacy, together with the installation in Israel of advanced US air defence systems, appeared to avert the threat of Israeli retaliation for the attacks by the missiles, 37 of which had been launched by late February 1991. In addition, Iraq launched 35 *Scud* missiles against Saudi Arabia.

On 6 February 1991 Iraq formally severed diplomatic relations with the USA, the UK, France, Italy, Egypt and Saudi Arabia. Between August 1990 and January 1991 many foreign embassies in Baghdad had closed, and most countries had withdrawn their diplomatic staff before the outbreak of hostilities in the Gulf.

On 15 February 1991 the Iraqi Government abruptly expressed its willingness to 'deal with' the UN Security Council resolutions pertaining to its occupation of Kuwait. However, its offer to do so was conditional upon the fulfilment of a long list of requirements (including an assurance that the as-Sabah family would not be restored to power in Kuwait) and was accordingly unacceptable to the multinational force. The offer to 'deal with' the UN resolutions was nevertheless thought to indicate a new flexibility on the part of the Iraqi leadership.

Soviet diplomacy came to the fore in seeking to persuade Iraq to alter its offer to withdraw from Kuwait into one which the multinational force could accept. On 21 February 1991 Iraq agreed to an eight-point Soviet peace plan which stipulated that: Iraq should make a full and unconditional withdrawal from Kuwait; that the withdrawal was to begin on the second day of a cease-fire; that the withdrawal should take place within a fixed time-frame; that, after two-thirds of Iraq's forces had withdrawn from Kuwait, the UN-sponsored economic sanctions were to be repealed; that the relevant UN Security Council resolutions should be waived following Iraq's withdrawal; that all prisoners of war were to be released following a cease-fire; that the withdrawal was to be monitored by observers from neutral countries following a cease-fire; that other details were to be discussed at a later stage.

The eight-point Soviet peace plan remained unacceptable to the multinational force, not least because it stipulated that a cease-fire should take effect before Iraq began to withdraw from Kuwait. On 22 February 1991, in response, the USA, representing the multinational force, demanded that Iraq commence a large-scale withdrawal of its forces from Kuwait by noon (US Eastern Standard Time) on 23 February, and that the withdrawal should be completed within one week. In response to this ultimatum, the USSR proposed a further plan for peace, this time containing six points—subsequently formally approved by Iraq—in a final attempt to avert a ground war in Kuwait and Iraq. However, once again the plan was rejected by the multinational force because it did not amount to the unconditional withdrawal of Iraqi forces from Kuwait which UN Security Council Resolution 660 demanded.

During the night of 23–24 February 1991 the multinational force launched a ground offensive for the liberation of Kuwait. Iraqi troops defending Kuwait's border with Saudi Arabia were quickly defeated, offering little resistance to the multinational force. One of the biggest problems which confronted the multinational force was that of coping with the very large number of Iraqi troops who surrendered at the onset of the ground war.

A flanking movement, far to the west, by French units and elements of the 101st US Airborne Division succeeded in severing the main road west from Basra, while the road leading north from Basra was breached by repeated bombing. Divisions of Iraq's élite Republican Guards in the Kuwait area were thus isolated to the south of the Tigris and Euphrates rivers and prevented from retreating towards Baghdad. On 28 February President Bush announced that the war to liberate Kuwait had been won and declared a cease-fire. Iraq had agreed to renounce its claim to Kuwait, and to release all the prisoners of war whom it was holding. It also indicated that it would comply with the remaining relevant UN Security Council resolutions.

On 3 March 1991 Iraq accepted the cease-fire terms dictated, at a meeting with Iraqi military commanders, by the commander of the multinational force, Gen. Norman Schwarzkopf of the US Army. On the following day it was reported that the southern city of Basra had been captured by Iraqi rebel forces, including Shi'ite Muslims and disaffected soldiers returning from Kuwait. The southern cities of Amarah, Diwaniyah, Samawah and Nasiriyah were also reported to have fallen under rebel control, while in the north Kurdish separatists overran a large area of Kurdistan. By 6 March the rebellion in Basra had apparently been crushed by Republican Guards loyal to Saddam Hussain. On 10 March the US Government indicated that it might be prepared to resume air attacks on Iraqi forces loyal to Saddam Hussain if they resorted to chemical weapons in their attempt to defeat the rebel forces.

Government

Power rests with the President and a Revolutionary Command Council (RCC), which in early 1991 comprised eight members (including the Chairman and Vice-Chairman). Considerable influence is exercised by the Iraq Regional Command of the Baath Party, while the routine administration of the country is undertaken by an appointed Council of Ministers. Legislative responsibility is shared between the RCC and the National Assembly, with 250 members elected by universal adult suffrage for four years. The country is divided into 15 Provinces and three Autonomous Regions. A Kurdish Autonomous Region has been created, and elections to a 50-member Kurdish Legislative Council were held for the first time in September 1980.

Defence

Military service is compulsory for all men at the age of 18 years, and lasts between 21 months and two years, extendable in wartime. The extension of the lower-age limit to include 17-year-olds was announced in December 1990. In June 1990 the armed forces totalled 1m. regular members; the army had a total strength of 955,000 (including an estimated 480,000 active reserves); the air force had a strength of 40,000, and the navy 5,000. Budgeted defence expenditure in 1990 was ID 4,150m. (US $13,300m.).

Economic Affairs

In 1990, according to the Central Statistical Organization of Iraq, the country's gross domestic product (GDP), measured in current prices, was US $63,693m., equivalent to $3,654 per head. During 1980–88, according to UN estimates, GDP declined, in real terms, at an average rate of 1.5% per year, with real GDP per head falling by 4.9% annually. Over the same period, the population increased by an annual average of 3.4%.

Agriculture (including forestry and fishing) contributed 15.4% of GDP in 1986. Around 21% of the labour force were employed in agriculture in 1989. Dates are the principal cash crop. Other crops include wheat, barley, rice, sugar beet and cane and melons. Production of eggs and poultry meat is also important. During 1980–89 agricultural production increased by an annual average of 3.5%.

Industry (including mining, manufacturing, construction and power) contributed 35.1% of GDP in 1986.

Mining (including production of crude petroleum and gas) contributed 17.8% of GDP in 1986, although the sector employed only 1.2% of the labour force in 1989. The principal mineral exports are crude petroleum and petroleum products, sulphur and phosphate-based fertilizers. In addition, Iraq has substantial reserves of natural gas.

Manufacturing contributed 8.6% of GDP in 1986 and employed 7.1% of the labour force in 1987. Measured by the value of output, chemical, petroleum, coal, rubber and plastic products accounted for 35.2% of manufacturing activity in 1986. Other important branches of the sector in that year were food products (providing 15.8% of manufacturing output), non-metallic mineral products (12.6%) and textiles (6.1%).

Energy is derived principally from hydroelectric power, and there is also an oil-fired power station.

All banks are nationalized and are few in number in comparison with other Arab countries. Rafidain Bank, the only commercial bank, is the biggest Arab commercial bank in terms of deposits and gross assets. There are three specialized banks: the Agricultural Co-operative Bank, the Industrial Bank and the Real Estate Bank.

In 1987 Iraq recorded a trade surplus of US $1,599m. In 1985 the principal source of imports was Japan (15.5%), while the principal market for exports (excluding crude petroleum and petroleum products) was Turkey. Other major trading partners are the Federal Republic of Germany, the USA, Brazil, Italy and France. Crude petroleum is by far the most important export, accounting for 98.62% of total exports in 1983. Dates are the second most important export commodity.

Proposed budget allocations for 1990 envisaged total expenditure of 24,400m. Iraqi dinars. The overall budget reportedly included a deficit of 6,600m. Iraqi dinars. Iraq's total external debt (including war reparation payments, compensation for damage to petroleum facilities and indemnities to foreign workers' forced to leave Kuwait) was estimated at $200,000m. in early 1991. Some $3,000m. per year is required merely to service the Western portion of the foreign debt. The average rate of inflation in 1987 was 10%.

Iraq is a member of the Arab Fund for Economic and Social Development (see p. 97), the Arab Monetary Fund (p. 98), the Council of Arab Economic Unity (p. 127), the Islamic Development Bank (p. 170), the Organization of Arab Petroleum Exporting Countries (p. 197), the Organization of the Petroleum Exporting Countries (p. 200) and the Arab Co-operation Council (p. 222).

Following the cease-fire in the Iran-Iraq War in August 1988, the Government's economic priority was to expand the industrial sector in order to reduce the economy's virtually total dependence on exported petroleum. Foreign assistance was sought for numerous development projects, and Iraq hosted a large foreign labour force. The country's most serious economic problem was the size of its foreign debt—estimated at some US $75,000m., excluding the payment of war reparations to Iran and Kuwait. If, however, Iraq could continue to reschedule the repayment of existing loans and secure new credit, the prospects for development were favourable, since the country possesses large petroleum reserves (second only to those of Saudi Arabia), a well-educated labour force, abundant water and fertile farming land.

Since 6 August 1990, when the UN imposed mandatory economic sanctions on Iraq, exports of crude and refined petroleum have ceased, and the consequent loss of revenue is likely to cut deeply into Iraq's reserves of foreign exchange. According to the IMF, Iraq's imports declined from ID 260m. in July 1990 to only ID 0.7m. in September. In February 1991, following the outbreak of hostilities between Iraq and the multinational force in Saudi Arabia, it was reported that almost all of Iraq's petroleum refining capacity had been either destroyed or severely damaged. It was estimated that it could take as long as three years and cost US $10,000m.–$20,000m. to restore the facilities. Iraq's industrial plant and transport network were also reported to have sustained heavy damage as a result of the hostilities.

It has been estimated that the development programme under way in Iraq after the war with Iran may have been set back by as much as 15 years as a result of the renewed hostilities in the Gulf. The speed of Iraq's recovery will depend on the extent of the damage to its infrastructure at the conclusion of hostilities, and on the length of time that the UN's economic sanctions remain in force. In view of the size of Iraq's existing foreign debt and its impaired relations with major creditors such as Saudi Arabia, additional foreign finance is likely to be difficult to obtain. While the USA has spoken cautiously of its willingness to assist in the reconstruction of Iraq after the liberation of Kuwait has been achieved, the survival of Saddam Hussain in power is likely to preclude such assistance.

Social Welfare

A limited Social Security Scheme was introduced in 1957 and extended in 1976. Benefits are given for old age, sickness, unemployment, maternity, marriage and death. Health services are provided free of charge. Many of the new health facilities that were scheduled under the 1981–85 Five-Year Plan were completed in spite of the war with Iran. More than $1,500m. was spent on building more than 30 new hospitals, providing about 11,500 beds. By the end of 1986, as a result of these additions, Iraq had 228 hospital establishments, with a total of 32,166 beds. There were reportedly 6,074 physicians working in the country at the end of 1986.

Education

Education is free, and primary education, beginning at six years of age and lasting for six years, has been made compulsory in an effort to reduce illiteracy. Enrolment at primary schools of children in the relevant age-group reached 100% in 1978, but the proportion had fallen to 84% by 1988. Secondary education begins at 12 years of age and lasts for up to six years, divided into two cycles of three years each. An estimated 39% of children in the appropriate age-group (48% of boys; 31% of girls) attended secondary schools in 1988. There are 47 teacher-training institutes, 19 technical institutes and eight universities. In the 1990/91 academic year 47,800 students were reported to have enrolled in courses of higher education.

Public Holidays

1991: 1 January (New Year's Day), 6 January (Army Day), 8 February (14 Ramadan Revolution, anniversary of the 1963 coup), 12 February* (Leilat al-Meiraj, ascension of Muhammad), 16 April* (Id al-Fitr, end of Ramadan), 23 June* (Id al-Adha, Feast of the Sacrifice), 13 July* (Islamic New Year), 14 July (Republic Day, anniversary of the 1968 coup), 22 July* (Ashoura), 21 September* (Mouloud, Birth of Muhammad).

1992: 1 January (New Year's Day), 6 January (Army Day), 1 February* (Leilat al-Meiraj, ascension of Muhammad), 8 February (14 Ramadan Revolution, anniversary of the 1963 coup), 4 April* (Id al-Fitr, end of Ramadan), 11 June* (Id al-Adha, Feast of the Sacrifice), 2 July* (Islamic New Year), 11 July* (Ashoura), 14 July (Republic Day, anniversary of the 1968 coup), 10 September* (Mouloud, Birth of Muhammad).

* These holidays are dependent on the Islamic lunar calendar and may vary by one or two days from the dates given.

Weights and Measures

The metric system is in force. Local measurements are also used, e.g. 1 meshara or dunum = 2,500 sq metres (0.62 acre).

Statistical Survey

Source: Central Statistical Organization, Ministry of Planning, Karradat Mariam, ash-Shawaf Sq., Baghdad; tel. 537-0071; telex 212218.

Area and Population

AREA, POPULATION AND DENSITY

Area (sq km)	438,317*
Population (census results)†	
17 October 1977	12,000,497
17 October 1987	
Males	8,364,873
Females	7,913,443
Total	16,278,316
Population (official estimates at October)†	
1985	15,585,000
1986	16,110,000
1988	17,250,000
Density (per sq km) at October 1988	39.4

* 169,235 sq miles. This figure includes 924 sq km (357 sq miles) of territorial waters but excludes the Neutral Zone, of which Iraq's share is 3,522 sq km (1,360 sq miles). The Zone lies between Iraq and Saudi Arabia, and is administered jointly by the two countries. Nomads move freely through it but there are no permanent inhabitants.

† Figures exclude Iraqis abroad, estimated at 129,000 in 1977. Estimates have not been adjusted to take account of the 1987 census results.

GOVERNORATES (estimated population at October 1986)

	Area* (sq km)	Population ('000)	Density (per sq km)
Nineveh	37,698	1,393	37.0
Salah ad-Din	29,004	454	15.7
At-Ta'meem	10,391	674	64.9
Diala	19,292	706	36.6
Baghdad	5,159	4,868	943.6
Al-Anbar	137,723	598	4.3
Babylon	5,258	759	144.4
Karbala	5,034	337	66.9
An-Najaf	27,844	484	17.4
Al-Qadisiya	8,507	524	61.6
Al-Muthanna	51,029	259	5.1
Thi-Qar	13,626	741	54.4
Wasit	17,308	494	28.5
Maysan	14,103	417	29.6
Basrah (Basra)	19,070	1,346	70.6
Autonomous Regions:			
D'hok	6,120	343	56.0
Arbil	14,471	774	53.5
As-Sulaimaniya	15,756	939	59.6
Total	437,393†	16,110	36.8

* Excluding territorial waters (924 sq km).
† Total area, including territorial waters: 438,317 sq km.

Population (at census of 17 October 1987): 1,507,926 in Nineveh governorate; 1,108,773 in Babylon governorate; more than 750,000 in each of five other governorates (Diala, al-Anbar, Thi-Qar, Basrah and as-Sulaimaniya).

PRINCIPAL TOWNS (population at 1977 census)

Baghdad (capital)	3,236,000*	Mosul	1,220,000
Basrah (Basra)	1,540,000	Kirkuk	535,000

* The population of Baghdad at the 17 October 1987 census was 3,844,608.

BIRTHS AND DEATHS (UN estimates, annual averages)

	1975–80	1980–85	1985–90
Birth rate (per 1,000)	46.7	44.4	42.6
Death rate (per 1,000)	9.4	8.7	7.8

Source: UN, *World Population Prospects: 1988*.

ECONOMICALLY ACTIVE POPULATION*
(persons, aged 7 years and over, 1987 census)

	Males	Females	Total
Agriculture, forestry and fishing	422,265	70,741	493,006
Mining and quarrying	40,439	4,698	45,137
Manufacturing	228,242	38,719	266,961
Electricity, gas and water	31,786	4,450	36,236
Construction	332,645	8,541	341,186
Trade, restaurants and hotels	191,116	24,489	215,605
Transport, storage and communications	212,116	12,155	224,271
Financing, insurance, real estate and business services	16,204	10,811	27,015
Community, social and personal services	1,721,748	233,068	1,954,816
Activities not adequately defined	146,616	18,232	167,848
Total labour force	3,346,177	425,904	3,772,081

* Figures exclude persons seeking work for the first time, totalling 184,264 (males 149,938, females 34,326), but include other unemployed persons.

Source: ILO, *Year Book of Labour Statistics*.

Agriculture

PRINCIPAL CROPS ('000 metric tons)

	1987	1988	1989
Wheat	722	929	491†
Rice (paddy)	196	141	140*
Barley	743	1,437	663†
Maize	61	77	70*
Potatoes	168	144	160*
Dry broad beans	9	6	10*
Sunflower seed	9	10	11*
Sesame seed	9	11	13*
Cabbages	7	14	11*
Tomatoes	595	558	650†
Pumpkins, etc.	48	52	53*
Cucumbers	323	291	345†
Aubergines	168	207	210*
Green peppers	27	30	35*
Onions (dry)	88	122	130*
Carrots	9	22	20*
Watermelons	588	483	585†
Melons	273	260	412†
Grapes†	440	445	450
Dates	324	356	375†
Sugar cane	60	30	60*

IRAQ

—continued

	1987	1988	1989
Apples	65	70*	75*
Peaches and nectarines	28	28*	28*
Plums*	32	33	33
Oranges†	160	165	175
Tangerines, etc.*	70	72	75
Apricots	31	32*	33
Tobacco (leaves)	9	2	2
Seed cotton	14	12	15

* FAO estimates.   † Unofficial figures.
Source: FAO, *Production Yearbook*.

LIVESTOCK ('000 head, year ending September)

	1987	1988	1989*
Horses	55*	55*	58
Mules	25*	26*	26
Asses	400*	410*	415
Cattle	1,580*	1,600†	1,650
Buffaloes	140*	141†	145
Camels	55*	55*	58
Sheep	9,000	9,000†	9,500
Goats	1,500*	1,550*	1,600

Poultry (million): 75* in 1987; 76* in 1988; 77* in 1989.
* FAO estimates.   † Unofficial figures.
(Source: FAO, *Production Yearbook*).

LIVESTOCK PRODUCTS ('000 metric tons)

	1987	1988	1989
Beef and veal	45*	47	48*
Buffalo meat	3*	3	3
Mutton and lamb	19*	20	21*
Goats' meat	8*	8	8*
Poultry meat	211	173	214†
Cows' milk	293†	297†	298*
Buffalo milk*	24	25	26
Sheep's milk*	167	170	172
Goats' milk*	69	70	73
Cheese*	32.7	33.1	33.8
Butter*	7.7	7.9	8.0
Hen eggs*	74.1	61.4	60.0
Wool:			
greasy	16.2†	15.9†	16.3*
clean	8.9	8.8	9.0*
Cattle and buffalo hides*	6.5	6.8	7.0
Sheep skins	3.6	3.8	3.9
Goat skins	1.6	1.6	1.6

* FAO estimates.   † Unofficial figure.
Source: FAO, *Production Yearbook*.

Forestry

ROUNDWOOD REMOVALS
(FAO estimates, '000 cubic metres, excluding bark)

	1986	1987	1988
Sawlogs, veneer logs and logs for sleepers	20	20	20
Other industrial wood	30	30	30
Fuel wood	93	93	99
Total	143	143	149

Source: FAO, *Yearbook of Forest Products*.

Fishing

('000 metric tons, live weight)

	1986*	1987*	1988
Inland waters	15.6	15.5	13.0
Indian Ocean	5.0	5.0	5.0*
Total catch	20.6	20.5	18.0*

* FAO estimate(s).
Source: FAO, *Yearbook of Fishery Statistics*.

Mining

('000 metric tons, unless otherwise indicated)

	1985	1986	1987
Crude petroleum	68,778	82,667	101,816
Natural gas (petajoules)	31	62	146
Native sulphur*	500	600	620

* Estimates by the US Bureau of Mines.
Source: UN, *Industrial Statistics Yearbook*.

Crude petroleum ('000 metric tons): 130,509 in 1988; 142,120 in 1989 (Source: UN, *Monthly Bulletin of Statistics*).

Industry

SELECTED PRODUCTS
('000 metric tons, unless otherwise indicated)

	1985	1986	1987
Cigarettes (million)	7,000	7,000	7,000*
Cement	8,000*	7,992	9,780*
Liquefied petroleum gas*†	400	390	410
Naphtha	500	450	600
Motor spirit (petrol)	1,650	1,650	1,740
Kerosene	750	750	790
Jet fuel	380	375	410
Distillate fuel oils	3,900	3,700	4,000
Residual fuel oils	5,100	5,100	6,000
Lubricating oils	100	100	150
Paraffin wax*	60	70	80
Petroleum bitumen (asphalt)	400	400	410
Electric energy (million kWh)	20,994	22,297	22,860

* Estimated production.
† Includes estimated production ('000 metric tons) from natural gas plants: 200 in 1985; 210 in 1986; 200 in 1987; and from petroleum refineries: 200 in 1985; 180 in 1986; 210 in 1987.

Footwear (excluding rubber): 3,305,000 pairs in 1986.
Source: UN, *Industrial Statistics Yearbook*.

1988 (estimates, '000 metric tons): Motor spirit 1,760; Kerosene and jet fuel 1,210; Distillate fuel oil 4,000; Residual fuel oils 6,100.
Source: UN, *Monthly Bulletin of Statistics*.

IRAQ

Finance

CURRENCY AND EXCHANGE RATES

Monetary Units
1,000 fils = 20 dirhams = 1 Iraqi dinar (ID).

Denominations
Coins: 1, 5, 10, 25, 50 and 100 fils; 1 dinar.
Notes: 250 and 500 fils; 1, 5 and 10 dinars.

Sterling and Dollar Equivalents (30 September 1990)
£1 sterling = 582.39 fils;
US $1 = 310.86 fils;
100 Iraqi dinars = £171.71 = $321.69.

Exchange Rate
From February 1973 to October 1982 the Iraqi dinar was valued at US $3.3862. Since October 1982 it has been valued at $3.2169. The dinar's average value in 1982 was $3.3513.

BUDGET ESTIMATES (ID million)

Revenue	1981	1982
Ordinary	5,025.0	8,740.0
Economic development plan	6,742.8	7,700.0
Autonomous government agencies	7,667.8	n.a.
Total	19,434.9	n.a.

Petroleum revenues (estimates, US $ million): 9,198 in 1981; 10,250 in 1982; 9,650 in 1983; 10,000 in 1984; 11,900 in 1985; 6,813 in 1986; 11,300 in 1987.

Expenditure	1981	1982
Ordinary	5,025.0	8,740.0
Economic development plan	6,742.0	7,700.0
Autonomous government agencies	7,982.4	n.a.
Total	19,750.2	n.a.

CENTRAL BANK RESERVES
(US $ million at 31 December)

	1975	1976	1977
Gold	168.0	166.7	176.1
IMF special drawing rights	26.9	32.5	41.5
Reserve position in IMF	31.9	31.7	33.4
Foreign exchange	2,500.5	4,369.8	6,744.7
Total	2,727.3	4,600.7	6,995.7

IMF special drawing rights (US $ million at 31 December): 132.3 in 1981; 81.9 in 1982; 9.0 in 1983; 0.1 in 1984; 7.2 in 1987.
Reserve position in IMF (US $ million at 31 December): 130.3 in 1981; 123.5 in 1982.
Note: No figures for gold or foreign exchange have been available since 1977.
Source: IMF, *International Financial Statistics*.

COST OF LIVING
(Consumer Price Index; base: 1979 = 100)

	1986	1987	1988
Food	203.3	250.2	309.0
Fuel and light	158.9	169.0	169.0
Clothing	213.8	217.6	246.5
Rent	206.8	222.5	246.4
All items (incl. others)	201.6	229.8	278.9

Source: ILO, *Year Book of Labour Statistics*.

NATIONAL ACCOUNTS (ID million at current prices)
Gross Domestic Product by Economic Activity

	1984	1985	1986*
Agriculture, hunting, forestry and fishing	1,941.9	2,265.7	2,186.1
Mining and quarrying	3,565.5	3,596.4	2,537.2
Manufacturing	1,255.4	1,416.2	1,227.4
Electricity, gas and water†	163.3	172.4	219.9
Construction	1,416.8	1,094.6	1,006.4
Trade, restaurants and hotels†	1,854.9	1,597.6	1,601.4
Transport, storage and communications	807.9	783.0	923.3
Finance, insurance and real estate‡	1,534.9	1,192.0	1,497.8
Government services	2,434.6	2,507.8	2,853.8
Other services	165.8	158.1	165.8
Sub-total	15,141.0	14,783.8	14,219.1
Less Imputed bank service charge	720.9	478.6	643.3
GDP at factor cost	14,420.1	14,305.2	13,575.8
Indirect taxes	678.0	614.0	n.a.
Less Subsidies	307.0	373.0	n.a.
GDP in purchasers' values	14,791.1	14,546.2	n.a.

* Figures are provisional.
† Gas distribution is included in trade.
‡ Including imputed rents of owner-occupied dwellings.
Source: UN, *National Accounts Statistics*.

External Trade

PRINCIPAL COMMODITIES (ID million)

Imports c.i.f.	1976	1977*	1978
Food and live animals	159.6	154.0	134.5
Cereals and cereal preparations	70.0	79.9	74.9
Sugar, sugar preparations and honey	37.2	24.1	10.2
Crude materials (inedible) except fuels	33.7	20.5	25.1
Chemicals	58.5	47.4	58.7
Basic manufactures	293.3	236.7	285.2
Textile yarn, fabrics, etc.	44.3	69.4	72.7
Iron and steel	127.5	44.3	73.2
Machinery and transport equipment	557.4	625.8	667.4
Non-electric machinery	285.4	352.5	368.1
Electrical machinery, apparatus, etc.	106.9	120.2	160.5
Transport equipment	165.2	153.1	138.8
Miscellaneous manufactured articles	33.2	49.4	51.7
Total (incl. others)	1,150.9	1,151.3	1,244.1

* Provisional. Revised total is ID 1,323.2 million.
Total imports (official estimates, ID million): 1,738.9 in 1979; 2,208.1 in 1980; 2,333.8 in 1981.
Total imports (IMF estimates, ID million): 6,013.0 in 1981; 6,321.4 in 1982; 3,086.2 in 1983; 2,978.8 in 1984; 3,199.0 in 1985; 2,659.8 in 1986; 2,196.0 in 1987; 2,809.8 in 1988; 3,191.0 in 1989 (Source: IMF, *International Financial Statistics*).

IRAQ   Statistical Survey

Exports f.o.b.*	1976	1977	1978
Mineral fuels, lubricants, etc.	2,595.6	2,557.3	3,223.1
Petroleum and petroleum products	2,595.6	2,557.3	3,222.9
Crude and partly refined petroleum	2,564.2	2,541.1	3,204.4
Petroleum products	31.4	16.2	18.5
Total (incl. others)	2,626.5	2,583.8	3,267.3

* Figures are provisional. Revised totals (ID million) are: 2,738.1 in 1976; 2,849.6 in 1977; 3,266.4 in 1978; 6,329.0 in 1979; 7,760.4 in 1980.

Exports of crude petroleum (estimates, ID million): 6,089.6 in 1981; 5,982.4 in 1982; 5,954.8 in 1983; 6,937.0 in 1984; 8,142.5 in 1985; 5,126.2 in 1986; 6,988.9 in 1987; 7,245.8 in 1988.

Source: IMF, *International Financial Statistics*.

PRINCIPAL TRADING PARTNERS (ID million)

Imports	1983	1984	1985
Australia	10.7	35.2	45.7
Austria	33.7	49.0	53.3
Brazil	32.7	67.0	118.9
China, People's Republic	22.1	11.5	40.5
France	118.7	117.1	112.5
Germany, Fed. Republic	323.6	236.3	211.0
Italy	162.9	116.5	128.2
Japan	369.4	258.3	352.1
Jordan	18.0	50.2	34.2
Korea, Republic	54.1	39.5	68.8
Malaysia	35.0	16.9	49.9
Netherlands	42.7	57.9	37.2
Sweden	52.0	37.7	46.2
Switzerland	55.2	26.8	36.5
Turkey	101.7	218.6	259.2
United Kingdom	118.6	118.2	109.8
USA	45.1	153.6	126.0
Yugoslavia	40.8	50.8	71.0
Total (incl. others)	2,062.8	2,080.7	2,266.0

Exports (excl. petroleum)	1983	1984	1985
China, People's Repub.	—	—	0.9
Hong Kong	—	—	0.7
India	1.7	0.8	0.6
Japan	—	0.3	0.5
Jordan	3.4	2.1	6.8
Kuwait	5.3	4.0	2.0
Saudi Arabia	1.0	0.7	0.5
Turkey	8.2	16.5	21.8
United Arab Emirates	2.5	0.4	2.3
United Kingdom	0.9	0.5	0.8
Total (incl. others)	81.8	82.7	46.9

Note: Since 1975 no official figures have been available for the destination of petroleum exports.

Transport

RAILWAYS (traffic)

	1987	1988	1989
Passenger-km (million)	1,150	1,570	1,643
Freight ton-km (million)	1,584	2,079	2,678

ROAD TRAFFIC (motor vehicles in use at 31 December)

	1987	1988	1989
Passenger cars	573,990	630,319	672,205
Buses and coaches	50,877	43,005	47,200
Goods vehicles*	117,630	117,100	128,550

* Including vans.
Source: International Road Federation, *World Road Statistics*.

SHIPPING (movement of cargo vessels in Iraqi ports)

	1978	1979	1980
Number of vessels			
Entered	1,127	1,664	1,446
Cleared	1,136	1,124	1,485
Gross registered tons ('000)			
Entered	13,841	14,006	18,187
Cleared	13,871	n.a.	n.a.
Cargo ('000 metric tons, excl. crude petroleum)			
Entered	4,191	6,717	6,535
Cleared	897	1,335	1,097

CIVIL AVIATION (revenue traffic on scheduled services)

	1983	1984	1985
Kilometres flown (million)	15.7	13.4	15.1
Passengers carried ('000)	454	435	540
Passenger-km (million)	1,249	1,200	1,525
Freight ton-km (million)	44.3	52.0	54.6

Source: UN, *Statistical Yearbook*.

Tourism

ARRIVALS OF VISITORS BY COUNTRY OF ORIGIN ('000)

	1982	1983	1984
Egypt	619.3	389.7	547.2
Germany, Federal Republic	29.0	19.6	16.9
India	63.6	35.9	33.5
Saudi Arabia	29.4	18.6	28.3
Turkey	405.9	357.0	614.3
United Kingdom	21.9	30.6	8.3
Yugoslavia	59.1	47.5	45.7
Other Middle East	443.6	237.1	279.1
Total (incl. others)	2,020.1	1,377.5	1,811.5

Source: UN, *Statistical Yearbook*.

Education

	Teachers		Pupils/Students	
	1987	1988	1987	1988
Pre-primary	4,572	4,654	76,558	85,096
Primary	119,280	130,777	2,996,953	3,023,132
Secondary:				
General	40,438	42,829	985,123	981,409
Teacher training	1,300	1,367	27,965	25,172
Vocational	8,316	9,741	150,606	160,278
Higher	10,365	11,072	183,608	209,818

Schools: Pre-primary: 594 in 1987; 614 in 1988. Primary: 7,954 in 1987; 8,052 in 1988.

Source: UNESCO, *Statistical Yearbook*.

Directory

The Constitution

The following are the principal features of the Provisional Constitution, issued on 22 September 1968:

The Iraqi Republic is a popular democratic and sovereign state. Islam is the state religion.

The political economy of the State is founded on socialism.

The State will protect liberty of religion, freedom of speech and opinion. Public meetings are permitted under the law. All discrimination based on race, religion or language is forbidden. There shall be freedom of the Press, and the right to form societies and trade unions in conformity with the law is guaranteed.

The Iraqi people is composed of two main nationalities: Arabs and Kurds. The Constitution confirms the nationalistic rights of the Kurdish people and the legitimate rights of all other minorities within the framework of Iraqi unity.

The highest authority in the country is the Council of Command of the Revolution (or Revolutionary Command Council—RCC), which will promulgate laws until the election of a National Assembly. The Council exercises its prerogatives and powers by a two-thirds majority.

Two amendments to the Constitution were announced in November 1969. The President, already Chief of State and head of the government, also became the official Supreme Commander of the Armed Forces and President of the Command Council of the Revolution. Membership of the latter body was to increase from five to a larger number at the President's discretion.

Earlier, a Presidential decree replaced the 14 local government districts by 16 governorates, each headed by a governor with wide powers. In April 1976 Tekrit (Saladin) and Karbala became separate governorates, bringing the number of governorates to 18, although three of these are designated Autonomous Regions.

The 15-article statement which aimed to end the Kurdish war was issued on 11 March 1970. In accordance with this statement, a form of autonomy was offered to the Kurds in March 1974, but some of the Kurds rejected the offer and fresh fighting broke out. The new Provisional Constitution was announced in July 1970. Two amendments were introduced in 1973 and 1974, the 1974 amendment stating that 'the area whose majority of population is Kurdish shall enjoy autonomy in accordance with what is defined by the Law'.

The President and Vice-President are elected by a two-thirds majority of the Council. The President, Vice-President and members of the Council will be responsible to the Council. Vice-Presidents and Ministers will be responsible to the President.

Details of a new, permanent Constitution were announced in March 1989. The principal innovations proposed by the permanent Constitution, which was approved by the National Assembly in July 1990, were the abolition of the RCC, following a presidential election, and the assumption of its duties by a 50-member Consultative Assembly and the existing National Assembly; and the incorporation of the freedom to form political parties. The new, permanent Constitution is to be submitted to a popular referendum for approval.

In July 1973 President Bakr announced a National Charter as a first step towards establishing the Progressive National Front. A National Assembly and People's Councils are features of the Charter. A law to set up a 250-member National Assembly and a 50-member Kurdish Legislative Council was adopted on 16 March 1980, and the two Assemblies were elected in June and September 1980 respectively.

The Government

HEAD OF STATE

President: SADDAM HUSSAIN (assumed power 16 July 1979).
Vice-President: TAHA MOHI ED-DIN MARUF.

REVOLUTIONARY COMMAND COUNCIL

Chairman: SADDAM HUSSAIN.
Vice-Chairman: IZZAT IBRAHIM.
Secretary-General: KHALED ABD AL-MONEIM RASHID.

Other Members:
TAHA YASSIN RAMADAN
TAREQ AZIZ
HASSAN ALI NASSAR AL-AMIRI
Dr SA'ADOUN HAMMADI
TAHA MOHI ED-DIN MARUF

COUNCIL OF MINISTERS
(March 1991)

President and Prime Minister: SADDAM HUSSAIN.
First Deputy Prime Minister: TAHA YASSIN RAMADAN.
Deputy Prime Minister: Dr SA'ADOUN HAMMADI.
Deputy Prime Minister and Minister of Foreign Affairs: TAREQ AZIZ.
Minister of Defence: Gen. SAADI TUMA ABBAS.
Minister of Transport and Communications: MUHAMMAD HAMZA AZ-ZUBAIDI.
Head of Presidency Diwan (Presidential Cabinet): AHMAD HUSSAIN AS-SAMARRAI.
Minister of the Interior: ALI HASSAN AL-MAJID.
Minister of Education: ABD AL-QADIR IZZUDIN HAMMUDI.
Minister of Higher Education and Scientific Research: Dr MUNDHIR IBRAHIM.
Minister of Youth Affairs: ABD AL-FATTAH MUHAMMAD AMIN.
Minister of Justice: AKRAM ABD AL-QADR ALI.
Minister of Housing and Construction: TAHER MUHAMMAD HASSOUN AL-MARZOUK.
Minister of Planning: SAMAL MAJID FARAJ.
Minister of Health: ABD AS-SALEM MUHAMMAD SAEED.
Minister of Trade and acting Minister of Finance: MUHAMMAD MAHDI SALIH.
Minister of Agriculture and Irrigation: ABD AL-WAHAB MAHMOUD ABDULLAH.
Minister of Culture and Information: LATIF NASIF AL-JASIM.
Minister of Labour and Social Affairs: UMEED MADHAT MUBARAK.
Minister of Awqaf (Religious Endowments) and Religious Affairs: ABDULLAH FADEL-ABBAS.
Minister of Local Government: (vacant).
Minister of Industry, Military Industrialization and acting Minister of Oil: Brig-Gen. HUSSAIN KAMEL.
Minister of State for Foreign Affairs: MUHAMMAD SAEED AS-SAHAF.
Minister of State for Military Affairs: Gen. ABD AL-JABBAR KHALIL ASH-SHANSHAL.
Minister of State at the President's Office: HASHIM AQRAWI SUBHI.
Advisers to President (with status of Minister): SUBHI YASIN KHUDAIR, ABD AL-GHANI ABD AL-GHAFUR, SAMIR MUHAMMAD ABD AL-WAHHAB, ABD AL-HASAN RAHI FIR'AWN, SAADI MAHDI SALIH, MAZBAN KADR HADI, KHALED ABD AL-MONEIM.
Minister of State: ARSHAD AHMAD MUHAMMAD AZ-ZIBARI.

MINISTRIES*

Office of the President: Presidential Palace, Karradat Mariam, Baghdad.
Office of the First Deputy Prime Minister: Karradat Mariam, Baghdad.
Ministry of Agriculture and Irrigation: Khulafa St, Khullani Sq., Baghdad; tel. 887-3251; telex 212222.
Ministry of Awqaf and Religious Affairs: North Gate, St opposite College of Engineering, Baghdad; tel. 888-9561; telex 212785.
Ministry of Culture and Information: Nr an-Nusoor Sq., fmrly Qasr as-Salaam Bldg, Baghdad; tel. 551-4333; telex 212800.
Ministry of Defence: North Gate, Baghdad; tel. 888-9071; telex 212202.
Ministry of Education: POB 258, Baghdad; tel. 886-0000; telex 2259.
Ministry of Finance: Khulafa St, Nr ar-Russafi Sq., Baghdad; tel. 887-4871; telex 212459.
Ministry of Foreign Affairs: Opposite State Org. for Roads and Bridges, Karradat Mariam, Baghdad; tel. 537-0091; telex 212201.

IRAQ *Directory*

Ministry of Industry and Military Industrialization: Nidhal St, Nr Sa'adoun Petrol Station, Baghdad; tel. 887-2006; telex 212205.

Ministry of Labour and Social Affairs: Khulafa St, Khullani Sq., Baghdad; tel. 887-1881; telex 212621.

Ministry of Local Government: Karradat Mariam, Baghdad; tel. 537-0031; telex 212568.

Ministry of Oil: POB 6178, al-Mansour, Baghdad; tel. 541-0031; telex 212216.

Ministry of Planning: Karradat Mariam, ash-Shawaf Sq., Baghdad; tel. 537-0071; telex 212218.

Ministry of Trade: Khulafa St, Khullani Sq., Baghdad; tel. 887-2682; telex 212206.

Ministry of Transport and Communications: Nr Martyr's Monument, Karradat Dakhil, Baghdad; tel. 776-6041; telex 212020.

* In January 1991 the Government announced its intention to relocate the principal ministries to the city of Ramadi, west of Baghdad.

KURDISH AUTONOMOUS REGION

Executive Council: Acting Chair. MUHAMMAD AMIN MUHAMMAD.

Legislative Council: Chair. AHMAD ABD AL-QADIR AN-NAQSHABANDI.

Legislature

NATIONAL ASSEMBLY

No form of National Assembly existed in Iraq between the 1958 revolution, which overthrew the monarchy, and June 1980. (The existing provisional constitution contains provisions for the election of an assembly at a date to be determined by the Government. The members of the Assembly are to be elected from all political, social and economic sectors of the Iraqi people.) In December 1979 the RCC invited political, trade union and popular organizations to debate a draft law for setting up a 250-member National Assembly (elected from 56 constituencies) and a 50-member Kurdish Legislative Council, both to be elected by direct, free and secret ballot. Elections for the first National Assembly took place on 20 June 1980, and for the Kurdish Legislative Council on 11 September 1980, 13 August 1986 and 9 September 1989. The Assembly is dominated by members of the ruling Baath Party.

Elections for the second National Assembly were held on 20 October 1984. The total number of votes cast was 7,171,000 and Baath Party candidates won 73% (183) of the 250 seats, compared with 75% in the previous Assembly. The number of women elected rose to 33.

Elections for the third National Assembly, which were originally scheduled to be held in late August 1988 but were subsequently postponed on three occasions, were held on 1 April 1989. It was estimated that 75% of Iraq's 8m.-strong electorate participated in the elections, and that Baath Party candidates won more than 50% of the 250 seats.

Chairman: SAADI MAHDI SALIH.

Chairman of the Kurdish Legislative Council: AHMAD ABD AL-QADIR AN-NAQSHABANDI.

Political Organizations

National Progressive Front: Baghdad; f. July 1973, when Arab Baath Socialist Party and Iraqi Communist Party signed a joint manifesto agreeing to establish a comprehensive progressive national and nationalistic front. In 1975 representatives of Kurdish parties and organizations and other national and independent forces joined the Front; the Iraqi Communist Party left the National Progressive Front in mid-March 1979; Sec.-Gen. NAIM HADDAD (Baath).

Arab Baath Socialist Party: POB 6012, al-Mansour, Baghdad; revolutionary Arab socialist movement founded in Damascus in 1947; has ruled Iraq since July 1968, and between July 1973 and March 1979 in alliance with the Iraqi Communist Party in the National Progressive Front; founder and Sec.-Gen. MICHAEL AFLAQ; Regional Command Sec. SADDAM HUSSAIN; Deputy Regional Command Sec. IZZAT IBRAHIM; mems. of Regional Command: TAHA YASSIN RAMADAN, HASSAN ALI AL-AMIRI, SA'ADOUN SHAKER, TAREQ AZIZ, MUHAMMAD HAMZAH AZ-ZUBAYDI, ABD AL-GHANI ABD AL-GHAFUR, SAMIR MUHAMMAD ABD AL-WAHHAB, ABD AL-HUSAIN RAHI MIN'AWI, SA'DI MAHDI SALIH, SHA'BOUN HAMMADI MIRDAN KHADR HADI, ALI HASSAN AL-MAJID, KAMIL YASSIN RASHID and LATIF NASIF AL-JASIM; approx. 100,000 mems.

Kurdistan Democratic Party: Aqaba bin Nafi's Sq., Baghdad; f. 1946; Kurdish Party; supports the National Progressive Front; Sec.-Gen. MUHAMMAD SAEED AL-ATRUSHI.

Kurdistan Revolutionary Party: f. 1972; succeeded Democratic Kurdistan Party; admitted to National Progressive Front 1974; Sec.-Gen. ABD AS-SATTAR TAHER SHAREF.

There are several illegal opposition groups, including:

Ad-Da'wa al-Islamiya (Voice of Islam): f. 1968; Mem. Supreme Council of the Islamic Revolution of Iraq; guerrilla group; Leader MUAFFAQ RUBAIE (ABU ALI).

Iraqi Communist Party: Baghdad: f. 1934; became legally recognized in July 1973 on formation of National Progressive Front; left National Progressive Front March 1979; proscribed as a result of its support for Iran during the Gulf War; First Sec. AZIZ MUHAMMAD.

Umma (Nation) Party: f. 1982; opposes Saddam Hussain's regime; Leader SAAD SALEH JABR.

There is also a Democratic Party of Kurdistan (DPK; f. 1946), in opposition to the Iraqi Government (Leader MASOUD BARZANI); a Patriotic Union of Kurdistan (PUK; f. 1975; Leader JALAL TALIBANI); a Socialist Party of Kurdistan (SPK; f. 1975; Leader RASSOUL MARMAND); a United Socialist Party of Kurdistan (USPK) (Leader MAHMOUD OSMAN), a breakaway group from the PUK; and the Kurdish Hezbollah (party of God; f. 1985; Leader Sheikh MUHAMMAD KALED), a breakaway group from the DPK and a member of the Supreme Council of the Islamic Revolution (SCIR), which is based in Teheran under the leadership of the exiled Iraqi Shi'ite leader, Hojatoleslam MUHAMMAD BAQIR AL-HAKIM.

Various alliances of political and religious groups have been formed to oppose the regime of Saddam Hussain in recent years. The most recent, the Iraqi National Joint Action Committee, was formed in Damascus in December 1990, grouping together some 17 organizations, including the SCIR, the SPK, Ad-Da'wa al-Islamiya and the Umma Party.

Diplomatic Representation

EMBASSIES IN IRAQ*

Afghanistan: Maghrib St, ad-Difa'ie, 27/1/12 Waziriya, Baghdad; tel. 5560331; Ambassador: MOHAMMAD SA'ED.

Albania: Baghdad; Ambassador: GYLANI SHEHU.

Algeria: ash-Shawaf Sq., Karradat Mariam, Baghdad; tel. 537-2181; Ambassador: AL-ARABI SI AL-HASSAN.

Argentina: Hay al-Jamia District 915, St 24, No. 142, POB 2443, Baghdad; tel. 776-8140; telex 213500; Ambassador: GERÓNIMO CORTES-FUNES.

Australia: Masba 39B/35, POB 661, Baghdad; tel. 719-3434; telex 212148; Ambassador: P. LLOYD.

Austria: POB 294, Hay Babel 929/2/5 Aqaba bin Nafi's Sq., Masbah, Baghdad; tel. 719-9033; telex 212383; Ambassador: Dr ERWIN MATSCH.

Bahrain: al-Mansour, Hay al-Watanabi, POB 27117, Mah. 605, Zuqaq 7, House 4/1/44, Baghdad; tel. 5423656; telex 213364; Ambassador: ABD AR-RAHMAN AL-FADHIL.

Bangladesh: 75/17/929 Hay Babel, Baghdad; tel. 7196367; telex 2370; Ambassador: MUFLEH R. OSMARRY.

Belgium: Hay Babel 929/27/25, Baghdad; tel. 719-8297; telex 212450; Ambassador: MARC VAN RYSSELBERGHE.

Brazil: 609/16 al-Mansour, Houses 62/62-1, Baghdad; tel. 5411365; telex 2240; Ambassador: MAURO SERGIO CONTO.

Bulgaria: Ameriya, New Diplomatic Quarter, POB 28022, Baghdad; tel. 556-8197; Ambassador: ASSEN ZLATANOV.

Canada: 47/1/7 al-Mansour, Baghdad; tel. 542-1459; telex 212486; Ambassador: DAVID KARSGAARD.

Central African Republic: 208/406 az-Zawra, Harthiya, Baghdad; tel. 551-6520; Chargé d'affaires: RENÉ BISSAYO.

Chad: 97/4/4 Karradat Mariam, POB 8037, Baghdad; tel. 537-6160; Ambassador: MAHAMAT DJIBER AHNOUR.

China, People's Republic: New Embassy Area, International Airport Rd, Baghdad; tel. 556-2740; telex 212195; Ambassador: ZHANG DAYONG.

Cuba: St 7, District 929 Hay Babel, al-Masba Arrasat al-Hindi; tel. 719-5177; telex 212389; Ambassador: JUAN ALDAMA LUGONES.

Czechoslovakia: Dijlaschool St, No. 37, Mansour, Baghdad; tel. 541-7136; Ambassador: Dr MIROSLAV KOTORA.

Denmark: Zuqak No. 34, Mahallat 902, Hay al-Wahda, House No. 18/1, POB 2001, Alwiyah, Baghdad; tel. 719-3036; telex 212400; Ambassador: TORBEN G. DITHMER.

IRAQ *Directory*

Djibouti: POB 6223, al-Mansour, Baghdad; tel. 551-3805; Ambassador: ABSEIA BOOH ABDULLA.

Finland: POB 2041, Alwiyah, Baghdad; tel. 776 6271; telex 212454; Ambassador: HENRY SÖDERHOLM.

Germany: Zuqaq 2, Mahala 929, Hay Babel (Masbah Square), Baghdad; tel. 719-2037; telex 212262; Ambassador: Dr RICHARD ELLERKMANN.

Greece: 63/3/913 Hay al-Jamia, al-Jadiriya, Baghdad; tel. 776-9511; telex 212479; Ambassador: EPAMINONDAS PEYOS.

Holy See: as-Sa'adoun St 904/2/46, POB 2090, Baghdad (Apostolic Nunciature); tel. 719-5183; Apostolic Pro-Nuncio: Most Rev. MARIAN OLEŚ, Titular Archbishop of Ratiaria.

Hungary: Abu Nuwas St, az-Zuwiya, POB 2065, Baghdad; tel. 776-5000; telex 212293; Ambassador: TAMÁS VARGA.

India: Taha St, Najib Pasha, Adhamiya, Baghdad; tel. 422-2014; telex 212248; Ambassador: K. N. BAKSHI.

Indonesia: 906/2/77 Hay al-Wahda, Baghdad; tel. 719-8677; telex 2517; Ambassador: A. A. MURTADHO.

Iran: Karradat Mariam, Baghdad; Ambassador: (vacant).

Ireland: 913/28/101 Hay al-Jamia, Baghdad; tel. 7768661; Ambassador: PATRICK MCCABE.

Japan: 929/17/70 Hay Babel, Masba, Baghdad; tel. 719-3840; telex 212241; Ambassador: TAIZO NAKAMARA.

Jordan: House No. 1, St 12, District 609, al-Mansour, POB 6314, Baghdad; tel. 541-2892; telex 2805; Ambassador: HILMI LOZI.

Korea, Republic: 915/22/278 Hay al-Jamia, Baghdad; tel. 7765496; Ambassador: BONG RHUEM CHEI.

Lebanon: Iwadia Askary St, House 5, Baghdad; tel. 416-8092; telex 2263; Ambassador: HEKMAT AOUAD.

Libya: Baghdad; Head of the Libyan People's Bureau: ABBAS AHMAD AL-MASSRATI (acting).

Malaysia: 6/14/929 Hay Babel, Baghdad; tel. 7762622; telex 2452; Ambassador: K. N. NADARAJAH.

Mauritania: al-Mansour, Baghdad; tel. 551-8261; Ambassador: MUHAMMAD YEHYA WALAD AHMAD AL-HADI.

Mexico: 601/11/45 al-Mansour, Baghdad; tel. 719-8039; telex 2582; Chargé d'affaires: VÍCTOR M. DELGADO.

Morocco: Hay al-Mansour, POB 6039, Baghdad; tel. 552-1779; Ambassador: ABOLESLAM ZENINED.

Netherlands: 29/35/915 Jadiriya, POB 2064, Baghdad; tel. 776-7616; telex 212276; Ambassador: Dr N. VAN DAM.

New Zealand: 2D/19 az-Zuwiya, Jadiriya, Baghdad; POB 2350, Alwiyah, Baghdad; tel. 776-8177; telex 212433; Ambassador: JOHN CLARKE.

Nigeria: 2/3/603 Mutanabi, al-Mansour, POB 5933, Baghdad; tel. 5421750; telex 212474; Ambassador: A. G. ABDULLAHI.

Norway: 20/3/609 Hay al-Mansour, Baghdad; tel. 5410097; telex 212715; Ambassador: HARALD LONE.

Oman: POB 6180, 213/36/15 al-Harthiya, Baghdad; tel. 551-8198; telex 212480; Ambassador: KHALIFA BIN ABDULLA BIN SALIM AL-HOMAIDI.

Pakistan: 14/7/609 al-Mansour, Baghdad; tel. 541-5120; Ambassador: KHALID MAHMOUD.

Philippines: Hay Babel, Baghdad; tel. 719-3228; telex 3463; Ambassador: AKMAD A. SAKKAN.

Poland: 30 Zuqaq 13, Mahalla 931, Hay Babel, POB 2051, Baghdad; tel. 719-0296; Ambassador: Dr WITOLD JURASZ.

Portugal: 66/11 al-Karada ash-Sharqiya, Hay Babel, Sector 925, St 25, No. 79, POB 2123, Alwiya, Baghdad; tel. 776-4953; telex 212716; Ambassador: GABRIEL MESQUITO DE BRITO.

Qatar: 152/406 Harthiya, Hay al-Kindi, Baghdad; tel. 551-2186; telex 2391; Ambassador: MUHAMMAD RASHID KHALIFA AL-KHALIFA.

Romania: Arassat al-Hindia, Hay Babel, Mahalla 929, Zukak 31, No 452/A, Baghdad; tel. 7762860; telex 2268; Ambassador: IONEL MIHAIL CETATEANU.

Senegal: 569/5/10, Hay al-Mansour Baghdad; tel. 5420806; Ambassador: DOUDOU DIOP.

Somalia: 603/1/5 al-Mansour, Baghdad; tel. 551 0000; Ambassador: ISSA ALI MOHAMMED.

Spain: ar-Riyad Quarter, District 908, Street No. 1, No. 21, POB 2072, Alwiya, Baghdad; tel. 719-2852; telex 212239; Ambassador: JUAN LÓPEZ DE CHICHERI.

Sri Lanka: 07/80/904 Hay al-Wahda, POB 1094, Baghdad; tel. 719-3040; Ambassador: N. NAVARATNARAJAH.

Sudan: 38/15/601 al-Imarat, Baghdad; tel. 542-4889; Ambassador: ALI ADAM MUHAMMAD AHMAD.

Sweden: 15/41/103 Hay an-Nidhal, Baghdad; tel. 719-5361; telex 212352; Ambassador: HENRIK AMNEUS.

Switzerland: Hay Babel, House No. 41/5/929, POB 2107, Baghdad; tel. 719-3091; telex 212243; Ambassador: HANS-RUDOLF HOFFMANN.

Thailand: 1/4/609, POB 6062, al-Mansour, Baghdad; tel. 5418798; telex 213345; Ambassador: CHEUY SUETRONG.

Tunisia: Mansour 34/2/4, POB 6057, Baghdad; tel. 551-7786; Ambassador: LARBI HANTOUS.

Turkey: 2/8 Waziriya, POB 14001, Baghdad; tel. 422-2768; telex 214145; Ambassador: SÖNMEZ KÖKSAL.

Uganda: 41/1/609 al-Mansour, Baghdad; tel. 551-3594; Ambassador: SWAIB M. MUSOKE.

USSR: 4/5/605 al-Mutanabi, Baghdad; tel. 541-4749; Ambassador: VIKTOR J. MININ.

United Arab Emirates: al-Mansour, 50 al-Mansour Main St, Baghdad; tel. 551-7026; telex 2285; Ambassador: HILAL SA'ID HILAL AZ-ZU'ABI.

Venezuela: al-Mansour, House No. 12/79/601, Baghdad; tel. 552-0965; telex 2173; Ambassador: FREDDY RAFAEL ALVAREZ YANES.

Viet-Nam: 29/611 Hay al-Andalus, Baghdad; tel. 551-1388; Ambassador: TRAN KY LONG.

†Yemen Arab Republic: Jadiriya 923/28/29, Baghdad; tel. 776-0647; Ambassador: MOHAMMED ABDULLAH ASH-SHAMI.

†Yemen, People's Democratic Republic: 906/16/8, Hay al-Wahda, Baghdad; tel. 719-6027; telex 213542; Ambassador: MUHAMMAD AHMAD SALMAN.

Yugoslavia: 16/35/923 Hay Babel, Jadiriya, POB 2061, Baghdad; tel. 776-7887; telex 213521; Ambassador: STOJAN ANDOV.

* Prior to the outbreak of hostilities between Iraq and the multinational force in Saudi Arabia in January 1991, many countries evacuated their diplomatic personnel from Iraq. In early January Iraq proposed that all foreign embassies should relocate from Baghdad to the city of Ramadi.

† Merged to form the Republic of Yemen in May 1990.

Judicial System

Courts in Iraq consist of the following: The Court of Cassation, Courts of Appeal, First Instance Courts, Peace Courts, Courts of Sessions, Shari'a Courts and Penal Courts.

The Court of Cassation: This is the highest judicial bench of all the Civil Courts; it sits in Baghdad, and consists of the President and a number of vice-presidents and not fewer than 15 permanent judges, delegated judges and reporters as necessity requires. There are four bodies in the Court of Cassation, these are: (a) the General body, (b) Civil and Commercial body, (c) Personal Status body, (d) the Penal body.

Courts of Appeal: The country is divided into five Districts of Appeal: Baghdad, Mosul, Basra, Hilla, and Kirkuk, each with its Court of Appeal consisting of a president, vice-presidents and not fewer than three members, who consider the objections against the decisions issued by the First Instance Courts of first grade.

Courts of First Instance: These courts are of two kinds: Limited and Unlimited in jurisdiction.

Limited Courts deal with Civil and Commercial suits, the value of which is five hundred Dinars and less; and suits, the value of which cannot be defined, and which are subject to fixed fees. Limited Courts consider these suits in the final stage and they are subject to Cassation.

Unlimited Courts consider the Civil and Commercial suits irrespective of their value, and suits the value of which exceeds five hundred Dinars with first grade subject to appeal.

First Instance Courts consist of one judge in the centre of each *Liwa*, some *Qadhas* and *Nahiyas*, as the Minister of Justice judges necessary.

Revolutionary Courts: These deal with major cases that would affect the security of the State in any sphere: political, financial or economic.

Courts of Sessions: There is in every District of Appeal a Court of Sessions which consists of three judges under the presidency of the President of the Court of Appeal or one of his vice-presidents. It considers the penal suits prescribed by Penal Proceedings Law and other laws. More than one Court of Sessions may be established in one District of Appeal by notification issued by the Minister of Justice mentioning therein its headquarters, jurisdiction and the manner of its establishment.

Shari'a Courts: A Shari'a Court is established wherever there is a First Instance Court; the Muslim judge of the First Instance

IRAQ
Directory

Court may be a *Qadhi* to the Shari'a Court if a special *Qadhi* has not been appointed thereto. The Shari'a Court considers matters of personal status and religious matters in accordance with the provisions of the law supplement to the Civil and Commercial Proceedings Law.

Penal Courts: A Penal Court of first grade is established in every First Instance Court. The judge of the First Instance Court is considered as penal judge unless a special judge is appointed thereto. More than one Penal Court may be established to consider the suits prescribed by the Penal Proceedings Law and other laws.

One or more Investigation Court may be established in the centre of each *Liwa* and a judge is appointed thereto. They may be established in the centres of *Qadhas* and *Nahiyas* by order of the Minister of Justice. The judge carries out the investigation in accordance with the provisions of Penal Proceedings Law and the other laws.

There is in every First Instance Court a department for the execution of judgments presided over by the Judge of First Instance if a special president is not appointed thereto. It carries out its duties in accordance with the provisions of Execution Law.

Religion

ISLAM

About 95% of the population are Muslims, more than 50% of whom are Shi'ite. The Arabs of northern Iraq, the Bedouins, the Kurds, the Turkomans and some of the inhabitants of Baghdad and Basra are mainly of the Sunni sect, the remaining Arabs south of the Diyali belong to the Shi'i sect.

CHRISTIANITY

There are Christian communities in all the principal towns of Iraq, but their principal villages lie mostly in the Mosul district. The Christians of Iraq comprise three groups: (*a*) the free Churches, including the Nestorian, Gregorian and Syrian Orthodox; (*b*) the churches known as Uniate, since they are in union with the Roman Catholic Church, including the Armenian Uniates, Syrian Uniates and Chaldeans; (*c*) mixed bodies of Protestant converts, New Chaldeans and Orthodox Armenians.

Roman Catholic Church:

Latin Rite: Archbishop of Baghdad: HE Mgr PAUL DAHDAH, Archevêché Latin, Wahdah 904/8/44, POB 2090, Baghdad; tel. 719-9537; approx. 3,500 adherents.

Armenian Rite: Archbishop of Baghdad: Most Rev. PAUL COUSSA, POB 2344, Baghdad; tel. 719-1827; approx 2,200 adherents.

Chaldean Rite: Archbishop of Mosul: Most Rev. GEORGES GARMO, Archevêché Chaldéen, Mosul; tel. 762149; Patriarch of Babylon of the Chaldeans: His Beatitude RAPHAEL I BIDAWID Patriarcat Chaldéen Catholique, Baghdad; tel. 537-8511; with 18 archbishops and bishops in Iraq, Iran, Syria, Turkey, Egypt, USA and Lebanon; approx. 450,000 adherents.

Syrian Rite: Archbishop of Mosul: Most Rev. CYRIL EMANUEL BENNI, Archevêché Syrien Catholique, Mosul; tel. 762160; Archbishop of Baghdad: Most Rev. ATHANASE MATTI SHABA MATOKA, Archevêché Syrien Catholique, Baghdad; tel. 719-1850; approx. 24,000 adherents.

Orthodox Syrian Community: 12,000 adherents.

Armenian Orthodox (Apostolic) **Community:** Bishop AVAK ASADOURIAN, Primate of the Armenian Diocese of Iraq, Younis as-Saba'awi Sq., Baghdad; tel. 885-5066; nine churches (four in Baghdad); 23,000 adherents, mainly in Baghdad.

JUDAISM

Unofficial estimates assess the present size of the Jewish community at 2,500, almost all residing in Baghdad.

OTHERS

About 30,000 Yazidis and a smaller number of Turkomans, Sabeans and Shebeks reside in Iraq.

Sabean Community: 20,000 adherents; Head Sheikh DAKHIL, Nasiriyah; Mandeans, mostly in Nasiriyah.

Yazidis: 30,000 adherents; Leader TASHIN BAIK, Ainsifni.

The Press

DAILIES

Al-Baath ar-Riyadhi: Baghdad; sports; Propr and Editor UDAI SADDAM HUSSAIN.

Baghdad Observer: POB 624, Karantina, Baghdad; f. 1967; English; State-sponsored; Editor-in-Chief NAJI AL-HADITHI; circ. 22,000.

Al-Iraq: POB 5717, Baghdad; f. 1976; Kurdish; formerly *Al-Ta'akhi*; organ of the National Progressive Front; Editor-in-Chief SALAHUDIN SAEED; circ. 30,000.

Al-Jumhuriya (The Republic): POB 491, Waziriya, Baghdad; f. 1963, re-founded 1967; Arabic; Editor-in-Chief SAMI MAHDI; circ. 150,000.

Ar-Riyadhi (Sportsman): POB 58, Jadid Hassan Pasha, Baghdad; f. 1971; Arabic; published by Ministry of Youth; circ. 30,000.

Tariq ash-Sha'ab (People's Path): as-Sa'adoun St, Baghdad; Arabic; organ of the Iraqi Communist Party; Editor ABD AR-RAZZAK AS-SAFI.

Ath-Thawra (Revolution): Aqaba bin Nafi's Square, POB 2009, Baghdad; tel. 719-6161; f. 1968; Arabic; organ of Baath Party; Editor-in-Chief HAMEED SAEED; circ. 250,000.

WEEKLIES

Alif Baa (Alphabet): POB 491, Karantina, Baghdad; Arabic; Editor-in-Chief KAMIL ASH-SHARQI; circ. 150,000.

Al-Idaa'a wal-Television (Radio and Television): Iraqi Broadcasting and Television Establishment, Karradat Mariam, Baghdad; tel. 537-1161; telex 212246; radio and television programmes and articles; Arabic; Editor-in-Chief KAMIL HAMDI ASH-SHARQI; circ. 40,000.

Majallati: Children's Culture House, POB 8041, Baghdad; telex 212228; Arabic; children's newspaper; Editor-in-Chief FAROUQ SALLOUM; circ. 35,000.

Ar-Rased (The Observer): Baghdad; Arabic; general.

Sabaa Nisan: Baghdad; f. 1976; Arabic; organ of the General Union of the Youth of Iraq.

Sawt al-Fallah (Voice of the Peasant): Karradat Mariam, Baghdad; f. 1968; Arabic; organ of the General Union of Farmers Societies; circ. 40,000.

Waee ul-Ummal (The Workers' Consciousness): Headquarters of General Federation of Trade Unions in Iraq, Gialani St, Senak, POB 2307, Baghdad; Arabic; Iraq Trades Union organ; Chief Editor KHALID MAHMOUD HUSSEIN; circ. 25,000.

PERIODICALS

Afaq Arabiya (Arab Horizons): Aqaba bin Nafi's Sq., POB 2009, Baghdad; monthly; Arabic; literary and political; Editor-in-Chief Dr MOHSIN J. AL-MUSAWI.

Al-Aqlam (Pens): Adamiya, POB 4032, Baghdad; tel. 443-3644; telex 214135; f. 1964; publ. by the Ministry of Culture and Information; monthly; Arabic; literary; Editor-in-Chief Dr ALI J. AL-ALLAQ; circ. 7,000.

Bagdad: Dar al-Ma'mun for Translation and Publishing, Karradat Mariam, POB 24015, Baghdad; tel. 538-3171; telex 212984; fortnightly; French; cultural and political.

Al-Funoon al-Ida'iya (Fields of Broadcasting): Cultural Affairs House, Karradat Mariam, Baghdad; quarterly; Arabic; supervised by Broadcasting and TV Training Institute; engineering and technical; Chief Editor MUHAMMAD AL-JAZA'RI.

Gilgamesh: Dar al-Ma'mun for Translation and Publishing, Karradat Mariam, POB 24015, Baghdad; tel. 538-3171; telex 212984; quarterly; English; cultural.

Hurras al-Watan: Baghdad; Arabic.

L'Iraq Aujourd'hui: Aqaba bin Nafi's Sq, POB 2009, Baghdad; f. 1976; bi-monthly; French; cultural and political; Editor NADJI AL-HADITHI; circ. 12,000.

Iraq Oil News: al-Mansour, POB 6178, Baghdad; tel. 541-0031; telex 2216; f. 1973; monthly; English; publ. by the Information and Public Relations Div. of the Ministry of Oil.

Journal of the Faculty of Medicine, The: College of Medicine, University of Baghdad, Jadiriya, Baghdad; tel. 93091; f. 1935; quarterly; Arabic and English; medical and technical; Editor Prof. YOUSUF D. AN-NAAMAN.

Majallat al-Majma' al-'Ilmi al-'Iraqi (Iraqi Academy Journal): Iraqi Academy, Waziriya, Baghdad; f. 1947; quarterly; Arabic; scholarly magazine on Arabic Islamic culture; Gen. Sec. Dr NURI HAMMOUDI AL-QAISI.

Majallat ath-Thawra az-Ziraia (Magazine of Iraq Agriculture): Baghdad; quarterly; Arabic; agricultural; published by the Ministry of Agriculture.

Al Maskukat (Coins): State Organization of Antiquities and Heritage, Karkh Salihiya St, Baghdad; tel. 537-6121; f. 1969; annually; the journal of numismatics in Iraq; Chair. of Ed. Board Dr MUAYAD SA'ID DAMERJI.

IRAQ   Directory

Al-Masrah wal-Cinema: Iraqi Broadcasting, Television and Cinema Establishment, Salihiya, Baghdad; monthly; Arabic; artistic, theatrical and cinema.

Al-Mawrid: Aqaba bin Nafi's Sq, POB 2009, Baghdad; f. 1971; monthly; Arabic; cultural.

Al-Mu'allem al-Jadid: Ministry of Education, al-Imam al-A'dham St, A'dhamaiya, Nr Antar Sq., Baghdad; tel. 422-2594; telex 212259; f. 1935; quarterly; Arabic; educational, social, and general; Editor in Chief KHALIL I. HAMASH; circ. 190,000.

An-Naft wal-Aalam (Oil and the World): publ. by the Ministry of Oil, POB 6178, Baghdad; f. 1973; monthly; Arabic; Editor-in-Chief QASIM AHMAD TAQI AL-URAIBI (Minister of Oil).

Sawt at-Talaba (The Voice of Students): al-Maghreb St, Waziriyah, Baghdad; f. 1968; monthly; Arabic; organ of National Union of Iraqi Students; circ. 25,000.

As-Sina'a (Industry): POB 5665, Baghdad; every 2 months; Arabic and English; publ. by Ministry of Industry and Minerals; Editor-in-Chief ABD AL-QADER ABD AL-LATIF; circ. 16,000.

Sumer: State Organization of Antiquities and Heritage, Karkh, Salihiya St, Baghdad; tel. 537-6121; f. 1945; annually; archaeological, historical journal; Chair. of Ed. Board Dr MUAYAD SA'ID DAMERJI.

Ath-Thaquafa (Culture): Place at-Tahrir, Baghdad; f. 1970; monthly; Arabic; cultural; Editor-in-Chief SALAH KHALIS; circ. 5,000.

Ath-Thaquafa al-Jadida (The New Culture): Baghdad; f. 1969; monthly; pro-Communist; Editor-in-Chief SAFA AL-HAFIZ; circ. 3,000.

At-Turath ash-Sha'abi (Popular Heritage): Aqaba bin Nafi's Sq., POB 2009, Baghdad; monthly; Arabic; specializes in Iraqi and Arabic folklore; Editor-in-Chief LUTFI AL-KHOURI; circ. 15,000.

Al-Waqai al-Iraqiya (Official Gazette of Republic of Iraq): Ministry of Justice, Baghdad; f. 1922; Arabic and English weekly editions; circ. Arabic 10,500, English 700; Dir HASHIM N. JAAFER.

NEWS AGENCIES

Iraqi News Agency (INA): 28 Nissan Complex—Baghdad, POB 3084, Sadoun; tel. 5383199; telex 2267; f. 1959; Dir-Gen. ADNAN AL-JUBOURI.

Foreign Bureaux

Agence France-Presse (AFP): Apt 761-91-97, POB 190, Baghdad; tel. 551-4333; Corresp. FAROUQ CHOUKRI.

Allgemeiner Deutscher Nachrichtendienst (ADN) (German Democratic Republic): Zukak 24, Mahalla 906, Hay al-Wahda, Beit 4, Baghdad; Correspondent HANS DAHNE.

Associated Press (AP) (USA): Hay al-Khadra 629, Zuqaq No. 23, Baghdad; tel. 555-9041; telex 213324; Corresp. SALAH NASRAWI.

Deutsche Presse-Agentur (dpa) (Federal Republic of Germany): POB 5699, Baghdad; Correspondent NAJHAT KOTANI.

Reuters (UK): House No. 8, Zuqaq 75, Mahalla 903, Hay al-Karada, Baghdad; tel. 719-1843; telex 213777; Corresp. SUBHY HADDAD.

Telegrafnoye Agentstvo Sovetskovo Soyuza (TASS) (USSR): 67 Street 52, Alwiya, Baghdad; Correspondent ANDREI OSTALSKY.

Xinhua (New China) News Agency (People's Republic of China): al-Mansour, Adrus District, 611 Small District, 5 Lane No. 8, Baghdad; tel. 541-8904; telex 213253; Corresp. ZHU SHAOHUA.

ANSA (Italy) also has an office in Baghdad (POB 5602; tel. 776-2558).

Publishers

National House for Publishing, Distribution and Advertising: Ministry of Culture and Information, al-Jumhuriya St, POB 624, Baghdad; tel. 425-1846; telex 212392; f. 1972; publishes books on politics, economics, education, agriculture, sociology, commerce and science in Arabic and other Middle Eastern languages; sole importer and distributor of newspapers, magazines, periodicals and books; controls all advertising activities, inside Iraq as well as outside; Dir-Gen. M. A. ASKAR.

Afaq Arabiya Publishing House: Adamiya, POB 4032, Baghdad; tel. 443-6044; telex 214135; fax 4448760; publisher of literary monthlies, *Al-Aqlam* and *Afaq Arabiya*, periodicals, *Foreign Culture*, *Art*, *Folklore*, and cultural books; Chair. Dr MOHSIN AL-MUSAWI.

Dar al-Ma'mun for Translation and Publishing: Karradat Mariam, POB 24015, Baghdad; tel. 538-3171; telex 212984; publisher of newspapers and magazines including: *The Baghdad Observer* (daily newspaper), *Bagdad* (monthly magazine), *Gilgamesh* (quarterly magazine).

Al-Hurriyah Printing Establishment: Karantina, Sarrafia, Baghdad; tel. 69721; telex 212228; f. 1970; largest printing and publishing establishment in Iraq; State-owned; controls *Al-Jumhuriyah* (see below).

Al-Jamaheer Press House: Sarrafia, POB 491, Baghdad; tel. 416-9341; telex 212363; fax 416-1875; f. 1963; publisher of a number of newspapers and magazines, *Al-Jumhuriyah*, *Baghdad Observer*, *Alif Baa*, *Yord Weekly*; Pres. SAAD QASSEM HAMMOUDI.

Al-Ma'arif Ltd: Mutanabi St, Baghdad; f. 1929; publishes periodicals and books in Arabic, Kurdish, Turkish, French and English.

Al-Muthanna Library: Mutanabi St, Baghdad; f. 1936; booksellers and publishers of books in Arabic and oriental languages; Man. ANAS K. AR-RAJAB.

An-Nahdah: Mutanabi St, Baghdad; politics, Arab affairs.

Kurdish Culture Publishing House: Baghdad; f. 1976; attached to the Ministry of Culture and Information.

Ath-Thawra Printing and Publishing House: Aqaba bin Nafi's Sq., POB 2009, Baghdad; tel. 719-6161; telex 212215; f. 1970; state-owned; Chair. TARIQ AZIZ.

Thnayan Printing House: Baghdad.

Radio and Television

In 1988 there were an estimated 3.5m. radio receivers and 1.2m. television receivers in use.

RADIO

State Organization for Broadcasting and Television: Broadcasting and Television Bldg, Salihiya, Karkh, Baghdad; tel. 537-1161; telex 212246.

Iraqi Broadcasting and Television Establishment: Salihiya, Baghdad; tel. 31151; telex 2446; f. 1936; radio broadcasts began 1936; home service broadcasts in Arabic, Kurdish, Syriac and Turkoman; foreign service in French, German, English, Russian, Azeri, Hebrew and Spanish; there are 16 medium-wave and 30 short-wave transmitters; Dir-Gen. HAMID SAID; Dir-Gen. of Radio ADNAN RASHID SHUKR; Dir of Engineering and Technical Affairs MUHAMMAD FAKHRI RASHID.

Idaa'a Baghdad (Radio Baghdad): f.1936; 22 hours daily.

Idaa'a Sawt al-Jamahir: f. 1970; 24 hours.

Other stations include **Idaa'a al-Kurdia**, **Idaa'a al-Farisiya** (Persian).

TELEVISION

Baghdad Television: Ministry of Culture and Information, Iraqi Broadcasting and Television Establishment, Salihiya, Karkh, Baghdad; tel. 537-1151; telex 212446; f. 1956; government station operating daily on two channels for 9 hours and 8 hours respectively; Dir-Gen. Dr MAJID AHMAD AS-SAMARRIE.

Kirkuk Television: f. 1967; government station; 6 hours daily.

Mosul Television: f. 1968; government station; 6 hours daily.

Basra Television: f. 1968; government station; 6 hours daily.

Missan Television: f. 1974; government station; 6 hours daily.

Kurdish Television: f. 1974; government station; 8 hours daily.

There are 18 other TV stations operating in the Iraqi provinces.

Finance

(cap. = capital; p.u. = paid up; dep. = deposits; res = reserves; brs = branches; m. = million; amounts in Iraqi dinars)

All banks and insurance companies, including all foreign companies, were nationalized in July 1964. The assets of foreign companies were taken over by the State.

BANKING

Central Bank

Central Bank of Iraq: Rashid St, POB 64, Baghdad; tel. 8865171; telex 212203; f. 1947 as National Bank of Iraq; name changed as above 1956; has the sole right of note issue; cap. and res 125m. (Sept. 1988); Gov. SUBHI N. FRANKOOL; brs in Mosul and Basra.

Commercial Banks

Rafidain Bank: New Banks' St, POB 11360 Massarif, Baghdad; tel. 887-0521; telex 2211; f. 1941; state-owned; cap. p.u. 100m., res 710.4m., dep. 14,962m., total assets 66,537m. (Dec. 1988); Pres. and Chair. TARIQ H. AL-KHATEEB; 113 brs in Iraq.

Rashid Bank: 7177 Haifa St, Baghdad; tel. 5385085; telex 214121; f. 1988; state-owned; cap. 100m., res 707,000 dep. 559.7m., total assets 756.2 (Dec. 1988); Dir-Gen. ABDEL MAJID AL-ANI; 3 brs.

Specialized Banks

Agricultural Co-operative Bank of Iraq: Rashid St, POB 5112, Baghdad; tel. 888-9081; f. 1936; State-owned; cap. p.u. 295.7m., res 14m., dep 10.5., total assets 351.6m. (Dec. 1988); Dir Gen. HDIYA H. AL-KHAYOUN; 32 brs.

Industrial Bank of Iraq: al-Khullani Sq., POB 5825, Baghdad; tel. 887-2181; telex 2224; f. 1940; State-owned; cap. p.u. 59.7m., dep. 77.9m. (Dec. 1988); Dir-Gen. BASSIMA ABD AL-HADDI ADH-DHAHIR; 5 brs.

Real Estate Bank of Iraq: Yaffa St, al-Salhiya, POB 14185, Baghdad; tel. 537-5165; telex 2635; f. 1949; State-owned; gives loans to assist the building industry; cap. p.u. 800m., res 11m., total assets 2,593.6m. (Dec. 1988); acquired the Co-operative Bank in 1970; Dir Gen. ABD AR-RAZZAK AZZIZ; 18 brs.

INSURANCE

Iraqi Life Insurance Co: Aqaba Bin Nafie Sq, Khalid Bin Wileed St, POB 989, Baghdad; tel. 7192184; telex 213818; f. 1959; Chair. and Gen. Man. ABD AL-KHALIQ RAUF KHALIL.

Iraq Reinsurance Company: Aqaba bin Nafi's Sq., Khalid bin al-Waleed St, POB 297, Baghdad; tel. 719-5131; telex 214407; fax 791497; f. 1960; transacts reinsurance business on the international market; total assets 93.2m. (1985); Chair. and Gen. Man. K. M. AL-MUDARIES.

National Insurance Co: Al-Khullani St, POB 248, Baghdad; tel. 886-0730; telex 2397; f. 1950; cap. p.u. 20m.; state monopoly for general business and life insurance; Chair. and Gen. Man. MOWAFAQ H. RIDHA.

STOCK EXCHANGE

Capital Market Authority: Baghdad; Chair. MUHAMMAD HASSAN FAG EN-NOUR.

Trade and Industry

CHAMBERS OF COMMERCE

Federation of Iraqi Chambers of Commerce: Mustansir St, Baghdad; tel. 888-6111; f. 1969; all Iraqi Chambers of Commerce are affiliated to the Federation; Chair. ABD AL-MOHSEN A. ABU ALKAHIL; Sec.-Gen. FUAD H. ABD AL-HADI.

EMPLOYERS' ORGANIZATION

Iraqi Federation of Industries: Iraqi Federation of Industries Bldg, al-Khullani Sq., Baghdad; f. 1956; 6,000 mems; Pres. HATAM ABD AR-RASHID.

INDUSTRIAL ORGANIZATIONS

In 1987 and 1988, as part of a programme of economic and administrative reform, to increase efficiency and productivity in industry and agriculture, many of the state organizations previously responsible for various industries were abolished or merged, and new state enterprises or mixed-sector national companies were established to replace them. For example, all the state organizations within the Ministries of Industry and of Heavy Industries were abolished and their functions and responsibilities combined in a smaller number of state enterprises; the five state organizations, grouped under the Ministry of Irrigation, were replaced by 14 national companies; and the number of state enterprises serving the farming sector was halved to six (see Agricultural Organizations). In 1987 and 1988 (up to June) 811 state organizations and departments were abolished. In August 1988 some 32 state enterprises were attached to the newly created Ministry of Industry and Military Industrialization, in addition to 11 under the aegis of the Military Industries Commission (MIC), which is, itself, attached to the new ministry. Newly created state enterprises include the following:

Iraqi State Enterprise for Cement: f. 1987 by merger of central and southern state cement enterprises.

National Company for Chemical and Plastics Industries: Dir-Gen. RAJA BAYYATI.

The Rafidain Company for Building Dams: f. 1987 to replace the State Org. for Dams.

State Enterprise for Battery Manufacture. f. 1987, Dir-Gen. ADEL ABBOUD.

State Enterprise for Communications and Post: f. 1987 from state org. for post, telegraph and telephones, and its subsidiaries.

State Enterprise for Construction Industries: f. 1987 by merger of state orgs for gypsum, asbestos, and the plastic and concrete industries.

State Enterprise for Cotton Industries: f. 1988 by merger of state org. for cotton textiles and knitting, and the Mosul State org. for textiles.

State Enterprise for Drinks and Mineral Water: f. 1987 by merger of enterprises responsible for soft and alcoholic drinks.

State Enterprise for the Fertilizer Industries: f. by merger of Basra-based and central fertilizer enterprises.

State Enterprise for Generation and Transmission of Electricity: f. 1987 from State Org. for Major Electrical Projects.

State Enterprise for Import and Export: f. 1987 to replace the five state organizations responsible to the Ministry of Trade for productive commodities, consumer commodities, grain and food products, exports and imports.

State Enterprise for Leather Industries: f. 1987; Dir Gen. MUHAMMAD ABD AL-MAJID.

State Enterprise for Sugar Beet: f. 1987 by merger of sugar enterprises in Mosul and Sulaimaniya.

State Enterprise for Textiles: f. 1987 to replace the enterprise for textiles in Baghdad, and the enterprise for plastic sacks in Tikrit.

State Enterprise for Tobacco and Cigarettes.

State Enterprise for Woollen Industries: f. by merger of state orgs for textiles and woollen textiles and Arbil-based enterprise for woollen textiles and women's clothing.

AGRICULTURAL ORGANIZATIONS

The following bodies are responsible to the Ministry of Agriculture and Agrarian Reform:

State Agricultural Enterprise in Dujaila.

State Enterprise for Agricultural Supplies: Dir-Gen. MUHAMMAD KHAIRI.

State Enterprise for Developing Animal Wealth.

State Enterprise for Fodder.

State Enterprise for Grain Trading and Processing: Dir-Gen. ZUHAIR ABD AR-RAHMAN.

State Enterprise for Poultry (Central and Southern Areas).

State Enterprise for Poultry (Northern Area).

State Enterprise for Sea Fisheries: POB 260, Basra; telex 7011; Baghdad office: POB 3296, Baghdad; tel. 92023; telex 212223; fleet of 3 fish factory ships, 2 fish carriers, 1 fishing boat.

TRADE UNIONS

General Federation of Trade Unions of Iraq: POB 3049, Tahrir Sq, Rashid St, Baghdad; tel. 887-0810; telex 212457; f. 1959; 6 vocational trade unions and 18 local trade union federations in the governorates of Iraq. Number of workers in industry is 536,245, in agriculture 150,967 (excluding peasants) and in other services 476,621 (1986); GFTU is a member of the International Confederation of Arab Trade Unions and of the World Federation of Trade Unions; Pres. FADHIL MAHMOUD GHAREB.

Union of Teachers: Al-Mansour, Baghdad; Pres. Dr ISSA SALMAN HAMID.

Union of Palestinian Workers in Iraq: Baghdad; Sec.-Gen. SAMI ASH-SHAWISH.

There are also unions of doctors, pharmacologists, jurists, artists, and a General Federation of Iraqi Women (Chair. MANAL YOUNIS).

CO-OPERATIVES

At the end of 1986 there were 843 agricultural co-operatives, with a total of 388,153 members. At the end of 1985 there were 67 consumer co-operatives, with 256,522 members.

PEASANT SOCIETIES

General Federation of Peasant Societies: Baghdad; f. 1959; has 734 affiliated Peasant Societies.

PETROLEUM AND GAS

Ministry of Oil: POB 6178, al-Mansour City, Baghdad; tel. 551-0031; telex 212216; solely responsible until mid-1989 for petroleum sector and activities relevant to it; since mid-1989 these responsibilities have been shared with the Technical Corpn for Special Projects of the Ministry of Industry and Military Industrialization; the Ministry was merged with INOC in May 1987; the state organizations responsible to the ministry for oil refining and gas processing, for oil products distribution, for oil training, and for gas were simultaneously abolished, and those for northern and southern oil, for oil equipment, for oil and gas exploration, for oil tankers, and for oil projects were converted into companies, as part of a plan to streamline the oil industry and make it more efficient; Acting Minister of Oil Brig-Gen. HUSSAIN KAMEL.

Iraq National Oil Company (INOC): al-Khullani Sq., POB 476, Baghdad; tel. 887-1115; telex 212204; f. in 1964 to operate the petroleum industry at home and abroad; when Iraq nationalized its petroleum, structural changes took place in INOC and it became solely responsible for exploration, production, transportation and marketing of Iraqi crude petroleum and petroleum products. INOC was merged with the Ministry of Oil in 1987, and the functions of some of the organizations under its control were transferred to newly created ministerial departments or to companies responsible to the ministry.

Iraqi Oil Drilling Co: f. 1990.

Iraqi Oil Tankers Company: POB 37, Basra; tel. 319990; telex 207007; fmrly the State Establishment for Oil Tankers; reformed as a company in 1987; responsible to the Ministry of Oil for operating a fleet of 17 oil tankers; Chair. MUHAMMAD A. MUHAMMAD.

National Company for Distribution of Oil Products and Gas: Rashid St, POB 3, South Gate, Baghdad; tel. 888-9911; telex 212247; fmrly a State organization; reformed as a company in 1987; fleet of 6 tankers; Dir-Gen. HAZIM ALI AT-TALIB.

National Company for Manufacturing Oil Equipment: fmrly a State organization; reformed as a company in 1987.

National Company for Oil and Gas Exploration: INOC Building, POB 476, al-Khullani Sq, Baghdad; fmrly the State Establishment for Oil and Gas Exploration; reformed as a company in 1987; responsible for exploration and operations in difficult terrain such as marshes, swamps, deserts, valleys and in mountainous regions; Chair. Dr HASHIM AL-KHURSAN.

Northern Petroleum Company (NPC): POB 1, at-Ta'meem Governorate; f. 1987 by the merger of the fmr Northern and Central petroleum organizations to carry out petroleum operations in northern Iraq; Dir-Gen. Dr SAMI SHARIF.

Southern Petroleum Company (SPC): POB 240, Basra; fmrly the Southern Petroleum Organization; reformed as the SPC in 1987 to undertake petroleum operations in southern Iraq; Dir-Gen. MOUJID ABD AZ-ZAHRA AL-UBAIDA.

State Company for Oil Projects (SCOP): POB 198, Oil Compound, Baghdad; tel. 774-1310; telex 212230; fmrly the State Org. for Oil Projects; reformed as a company in 1987; responsible for construction of petroleum projects, mostly inside Iraq through direct execution, and also for design supervision of the projects and contracting with foreign enterprises, etc.; Dir-Gen. ALI H. IJAM.

State Enterprise for Oil and Gas Industrialization in the South: f. 1988 by merger of enterprises responsible for the gas industry and oil refining in the south.

State Enterprise for Petrochemical Industries.

Transport

RAILWAYS

The metre-gauge line runs from Baghdad, through Khanaqin and Kirkuk, to Arbil. The standard gauge line covers the length of the country, from Rabia, on the Syrian border, via Mosul, to Baghdad (534 km), and from Baghdad to Basra and Umm Qasr (608 km), on the Arabian Gulf. A 404-km standard-gauge line linking Baghdad to Husaibah, near the Iraqi-Syrian frontier, was completed in 1983. The 638-km line from Baghdad, via al-Qaim (on the Syrian border), to Akashat, and the 252-km Kirkuk-Baiji-Haditha line, which was designed to serve industrial projects along its route, were opened in 1986. The 150-km line linking the Akashat phosphate mines and the fertilizer complex at al-Qaim was formally opened in January 1986 but had already been in use for two years. Lines totalling some 2,400 km were planned at the beginning of the 1980s, but by 1988 only 800 km had been constructed. All standard-gauge trains are now hauled by diesel-electric locomotives, and all narrow-gauge (one-metre) line has been replaced by standard gauge (1,435 mm). As well as the internal service, there is a regular international service between Baghdad and Istanbul. A rapid transit transport system is to be established in Baghdad, with work to be undertaken as part of the 1987-2001 development plan for the city.

Responsibility for all railways, other than the former Iraq Republic Railways (see below), and for the design and construction of new railways, which was formerly the province of the New Railways Implementation Authority, was transferred to the newly created State Enterprise for Implementation of Transport and Communications Projects.

State Enterprise for Iraqi Railways: Baghdad Central Station Bldg, Damascus Sq., Baghdad; tel. 537-30011; telex 212272; fmrly the Iraqi Republic Railways, under the supervision of State Org. for Iraqi Railways; reformed as a State Enterprise in 1987, under the Ministry of Transport and Communications; total length of track (1986): 2,029 km, consisting of 1,496 km of standard gauge, 533 km of one-metre gauge; Dir-Gen. MUHAMMAD Y. AL-AHMAD.

New Railways Implementation Authority: POB 17040, al-Hurriya, Baghdad; tel. 537-0021; telex 2906; f. to design and construct railways to augment the standard-gauge network and to replace the metre-gauge network; Sec.-Gen. R. A. AL-UMARI.

ROADS

At the end of 1989, according to the Central Statistical Organization, there were 36,438 km of new paved roads; 10,776 km of earth roads; and 4,039 km of roads under construction.

The most important roads are: Baghdad-Mosul-Tel Kotchuk (Syrian border), 521 km; Baghdad-Kirkuk-Arbil-Mosul-Zakho (border with Turkey), 544 km; Kirkuk-Sulaimaniya, 160 km; Baghdad-Hilla-Diwaniya-Nasiriya-Basra, 586 km; Baghdad-Kut-Nassirya, 186 km; Baghdad-Ramadi-Rurba (border with Syria), 555 km; Baghdad-Kut-Umara-Basra-Safwan (border with Kuwait), 660 km; Baghdad-Baqaba-Kanikien (border with Iran). Most sections of the six-lane 1,264-km international Express Highway, linking Safwan (on the Kuwaiti border) with the Jordanian and Syrian borders, had been completed by June 1990. The Diwaniya-Nasiriya section remains under construction, and is due to be completed in 1993. Studies have been completed for a second, 525-km Express Highway, linking Baghdad and Zakho on the Turkish border. The estimated cost of the project is more than $4,500m. and is likely to preclude its implementation in the immediate future. An elaborate network of roads was constructed behind the war front with Iran in order to facilitate the movement of troops and supplies during the 1980-88 conflict.

Iraqi Land Transport Co: Baghdad; f. 1988 to replace State Organization for Land Transport; fleet of more than 1,000 large trucks; Dir Gen. AYSAR AS-SAFI.

Joint Land Transport Co: Baghdad; joint venture between Iraq and Jordan; operates a fleet of some 750 trucks.

State Enterprise for Implementation of Expressways: f. 1987; Dir-Gen. FAIZ MUHAMMAD SAID.

State Enterprise for Roads and Bridges: Karradat Mariam, Karkh, POB 917, Baghdad; tel. 32141; telex 212282; responsible for road and bridge construction projects to the Ministry of Housing and Construction.

SHIPPING

The ports of Basra and Umm Qasr are usually the commercial gateway of Iraq. They are connected by various ocean routes with all parts of the world, and constitute the natural distributing centre for overseas supplies. The Iraqi State Enterprise for Maritime Transport maintains a regular service between Basra, the Gulf and north European ports. The Iran-Iraq War caused the closure of the port of Basra. There is also a port at Khor az-Zubair, which came into use during 1979, though it too has been closed, owing to the war.

At Basra there is accommodation for 12 vessels at the Maqal Wharves and accommodation for 7 vessels at the buoys. There is 1 silo berth and 2 berths for oil products at Muftia and 1 berth for fertilizer products at Abu Flus. There is room for 8 vessels at Umm Qasr. There are deep-water tanker terminals at Khor al-Amaya and Faw for 3 and 4 vessels respectively. The latter port, however, was abandoned during the early part of the Iran-Iraq War.

For the inland waterways, which are now under the control of the General Establishment for Iraqi Ports, there are 1,036 registered river craft, 48 motor vessels and 105 motor boats.

General Establishment for Iraqi Ports: Maqal, Basra; tel. 413211; telex 207008; f. 1987 when State Org. for Iraqi Ports was abolished; fleet of 26 vessels (incl. 17 dredgers, 6 crane ships, 2 pilot ships and 1 cargo/training ship); Dir-Gen. ABD AR-RAZZAQ ABD AL-WAHAB.

State Enterprise for Iraqi Water Transport: Airport St, al-Furat Quarter, POB 23016, Baghdad, telex 212565; f. 1987 when State Org. for Iraqi Water Transport was abolished; responsible for the planning, supervision and control of six nat. water transportation enterprises incl:

State Enterprise for Maritime Transport (Iraqi Line): al-Jadiriya al-Hurriya Ave, POB 13038, Baghdad; tel. 776-3201; telex 212565; Basra office: 14 July St, POB 766, Basra; tel. 210206; telex 207052; f. 1952; fleet of 21 vessels (incl. 16 general cargo vessels, 4 barges and 1 tanker); Dir-Gen. JABER Q. HASSAN; Operations Man. M. A. ALI.

IRAQ

Shipping Company
Arab Bridge Maritime Navigation Co: Aqaba, Jordan; tel. (03) 316307; telex 62354; fax (03) 316313; f. 1987; joint venture by Egypt, Iraq and Jordan to improve economic co-operation; an expansion of the company that established a ferry link between the ports of Aqaba, Jordan, and Nuweibeh, Egypt, in 1985; cap. US $6m.; Chair. NABEEH AL-ABWAH.

CIVIL AVIATION
There are international airports near Baghdad, at Bamerni, and at Basra. A new airport, Saddam International, is under construction at Baghdad. Internal flights connect Baghdad to Basra and Mosul.

National Company for Civil Aviation Services: al-Mansour, Baghdad; tel. 551-9443; telex 212662; f. 1987 following the abolition of the State Organization for Civil Aviation; responsible for the provision of aircraft, and for airport and passenger services.

Iraqi Airways Co: Saddam International Airport, Baghdad; tel. 551-9999; telex 212297; f. 1948; Dir-Gen. NOUR ED-DIN AS-SAFI; formerly Iraqi Airways, prior to privatization in September 1988; regular services from Baghdad to Abu Dhabi, Algiers, Amman, Amsterdam, Athens, Bahrain, Bangkok, Basra, Beirut, Belgrade, Berlin, Bombay, Bucharest, Budapest, Cairo, Casablanca, Copenhagen, Damascus, Dhahran, Doha, Dubai, Frankfurt, Geneva, Istanbul, Jeddah, Karachi, Khartoum, Kuala Lumpur, Kuwait, London, Madrid, Moscow, Mosul, Munich, New Delhi, Paris, Prague, Rome, Sofia, Tripoli, Tunis, Vienna, Warsaw; fleet: 3 Boeing 747-200C, 2 Boeing 707-320C, 6 Boeing 727-200, 2 Boeing 737-200, 1 Boeing 747SP, 30 Ilyushin Il-76T/M, 5 Antonov An-12, 3 Antonov An-24, 6 JetStar II, 4 Falcon 50, 2 Falcon 20F, 4 Piaggio P.166.

Tourism

The Directorate-General for Tourism was abolished in August 1988 and the various bodies under it and the services that it administered were offered for sale or lease to the private sector. The directorate was responsible for 21 summer resorts in the north, and for hotels and tourist villages throughout the country. These were to be offered on renewable leases of 25 years or sold outright.

Atomic Energy

Iraqi nuclear facilities, as inspected by the International Atomic Energy Agency in November 1990, consisted of three nuclear reactor sites and at least four nuclear research laboratories. All three reactors, sited in the city of Tuwaitha, were used exclusively for research purposes, rather than to generate power. The largest, Tammaz-1, originally had a capacity of 40 MW, but it was damaged in an attack by the Israeli air force in June 1981 and was not fully rebuilt. A second reactor, Tammaz-2, was a French model and used fuel from Tammaz-1 to generate 500 kW–800 kW of energy. The third reactor, the IRT-5000, generated 5 MW–10 MW of energy.

IRELAND

Introductory Survey

Location, Climate, Language, Religion, Flag, Capital

The Republic of Ireland consists of 26 of the 32 counties which comprise the island of Ireland. The remaining six counties, in the north-east, form Northern Ireland, which is part of the United Kingdom. Ireland lies in the Atlantic Ocean, about 80 km (50 miles) west of Great Britain. The climate is mild and equable, with temperatures generally between 0°C (32°F) and 21°C (70°F). Irish is the official first language, but its use as a vernacular is now restricted to certain areas, collectively known as the Gaeltacht, mainly in the west of Ireland. English is universally spoken. Official documents are printed in English and Irish. Almost all of the inhabitants profess Christianity: about 95% are Roman Catholics and 5% Protestants. The national flag (proportions 2 by 1) consists of three equal vertical stripes, of green, white and orange. The capital is Dublin.

Recent History

The whole of Ireland was formerly part of the United Kingdom. In 1920 the island was partitioned, the six north-eastern counties remaining part of the United Kingdom, with their own government. On 6 December 1922 the 26 southern counties achieved dominion status, under the British Crown, as the Irish Free State. The dissolution of all remaining links with Great Britain culminated in the adoption, by plebiscite, of a new constitution, which gave the Irish Free State full sovereignty within the Commonwealth as from 29 December 1937. Formal ties with the Commonwealth were ended on 18 April 1949, when the 26 southern counties became a republic. The partition of Ireland remained a contentious issue, and from 1969 a breakaway group from a volunteer force, the Irish Republican Army (IRA—see Northern Ireland, Vol II), calling itself the Provisional IRA, conducted a violent campaign to achieve reunification.

In the general election of February 1973, Fianna Fáil, Ireland's traditional ruling party with 44 years in office, was defeated. Jack Lynch, who had been Prime Minister since 1966, resigned, and Liam Cosgrave formed a coalition between his own party, Fine Gael, and the Labour Party. The Irish Government remained committed to power-sharing in the six counties, but resisted any British military withdrawal from Northern Ireland (see Northern Ireland, Vol. II).

Following the assassination of the British Ambassador to Ireland by the Provisional IRA in July 1976, the Irish Government introduced stronger measures against terrorism. President Carroll O'Daly resigned in October 1976, and Dr Patrick Hillery of Fianna Fáil, the only candidate nominated for the presidency, took office in December. Fianna Fáil won the general election of June 1977 and Jack Lynch again became Prime Minister, maintaining the improved relations with the British Government which had been achieved by the Cosgrave administration; he aimed at devolved government in Northern Ireland, rather than a totally united Ireland, a policy which aroused criticism from within Fianna Fáil. After the murder by the IRA in August 1979 of Admiral of the Fleet the Earl Mountbatten of Burma, a prominent British public figure, at Mullaghmore, County Sligo, and the massacre on the same day of 18 British soldiers at Warrenpoint in Northern Ireland, Lynch agreed to increase border security. In December Lynch resigned as Prime Minister and was succeeded by Charles Haughey, formerly Minister for Health, who pursued the aim of a united Ireland with a measure of autonomy for the six northern counties, provided that a power-sharing executive be maintained.

In June 1981, following an early general election, Dr Garret FitzGerald, who had been Minister for Foreign Affairs in 1973-77, became Prime Minister. He formed a coalition government between his own party, Fine Gael, and the Labour Party. However, the rejection by the Dáil of the coalition's budget proposals precipitated a further general election in February 1982. Haughey was returned to power, with the support of three Workers' Party members and two independents. The worsening economic situation, however, made the Fianna Fáil Government increasingly unpopular, and in November Haughey lost the support of the independents over proposed public expenditure cuts. In the subsequent general election Fianna Fáil failed to gain an overall majority and Dr FitzGerald again became Prime Minister. In December he formed a coalition with the Labour Party, and included four of its members in the Cabinet. In September 1983 a controversial referendum approved a constitutional amendment to ban abortion. At elections to the European Parliament in June 1984, Fianna Fáil won eight of the 15 seats allotted to Ireland, while Fine Gael won six. The Labour Party lost all four of the seats that it had previously held.

During 1986 Dr FitzGerald's Government lost popularity, partly due to the formation, in December 1985, of a new party, the Progressive Democrats, by former members of Fianna Fáil. In early June a controversial government proposal to end a 60-year constitutional ban on divorce was defeated by national referendum, and shortly afterwards, as a result of a series of defections, the Government lost its parliamentary majority. In January 1987 Labour members of the Dáil refused to support Fine Gael's budget proposals envisaging reductions in planned public expenditure, and the coalition collapsed. At a general election held on 17 February, Fianna Fáil, led by Charles Haughey, won 81 of the 166 seats in the Dáil, with 44% of the first-preference votes, while the Progressive Democrats, contesting their first election, won 14 seats and almost 12% of the votes. Fine Gael's strength declined from 68 to 51 seats. Sinn Fein (the political wing of the IRA) failed to secure any seats in the election. In November 1986 it had abandoned its policy of abstentionism from Parliament, which it had pursued since 1922. In March 1987 Charles Haughey became Prime Minister for the third time. Haughey retained popular support, despite instituting an unprecedented programme of economic austerity. As a minority government, the Fianna Fáil administration was dependent on opposition support to secure approval for its budget proposals. Since the policy of austerity that Haughey adopted was similar to that initially envisaged by Fine Gael, this did not present a problem. Massive reductions in public expenditure in 1987 and 1988 led to an encouraging economic recovery, so that all parties in the Dáil united in support of the 1989 budget proposals, announced in January, which increased welfare payments and eased the tax burden on low-paid workers.

In May 1989, following a parliamentary defeat for the Government over compensation for haemophiliacs who had contracted AIDS (the sixth minor defeat for the administration), Haughey asked the President to dissolve the Dáil. In an attempt to secure an overall majority, Haughey announced a premature general election for 15 June, to coincide with elections to the European Parliament. Fine Gael and the Progressive Democrats subsequently concluded an electoral pact to oppose Fianna Fáil. Although the Haughey administration had achieved significant economic improvements, severe reductions in public expenditure and continuing problems of unemployment and emigration adversely affected Fianna Fáil's support in the election. Fianna Fáil received 44% of first-preference votes (as in 1987) but won only 77 of the 166 seats in the Dáil (compared with 81 in 1987), while Fine Gael increased its representation to 55 seats, the Progressive Democrats won only six seats (compared with 14 in 1987) and the Labour Party and the Workers' Party both made significant gains.

At the end of June 1989 the Dáil reconvened to elect the Prime Minister. The Progressive Democrats voted in favour of Alan Dukes, the leader of Fine Gael, in accordance with their pre-election pact, despite attempts by Fianna Fáil to gain the Progressive Democrats' support for Haughey's candidacy. Haughey was rejected by 86 votes to 78. Dukes and Richard Spring, the leader of the Labour Party, also failed to be elected. Haughey was forced to resign (on the insistence of the opposition parties, who claimed that his remaining as Prime Minister would be unconstitutional), although continuing to lead an interim administration. The Dáil was adjourned three times, owing to successive failures to elect a Prime Minister. This was largely due to Haughey's preference for a minority government and his reluctance to concede any cabinet posts in a coalition agreement, although both Fine Gael and the Progressive Democrats stipulated the granting of portfolios as a condition of any agreement. After nearly four weeks of negotiations, however, Fianna Fáil formed an 'alliance' with the Progressive Democrats and included two of the latter's members in a new cabinet. Fianna Fáil also conceded a junior portfolio to the Progressive Democrats. The coalition parties negotiated a policy document whose provisions included a reduction in rates of income tax, an emphasis on the creation of employment opportunities, a programme to reduce hospital waiting-lists and the allocation of I£1m. to haemophiliacs who had contracted AIDS. On 12 July 1989 Haughey was finally elected Prime Minister by a majority of 84 to 79, with two abstentions. In accordance with the policy agreement, the Government's proposals for the 1990 budget, announced in January of that year, included a reduction in the standard rate, and in the highest rate, of income tax.

In April 1990 the Government published draft legislation proposing the formal abolition of the death penalty in Ireland. Although the death penalty had been retained for some categories of murder, it had not been invoked since 1954.

In October 1990 Brian Lenihan, the Deputy Prime Minister and Minister of Defence, was accused of contacting the President in an attempt to avert a general election following the collapse of the Fine Gael/Labour Party coalition Government in 1982. Lenihan denied the accusation, despite the subsequent release of tape-recordings which featured Lenihan referring to the alleged incident. The opposition parties proposed a motion of 'no confidence' in Lenihan and the Government. The Progressive Democrats demanded Lenihan's resignation in return for their continued support. Following Haughey's dismissal of Lenihan, the coalition Government defeated the no-confidence motion by 83 votes to 80. Lenihan voted in favour of the Government and was retained as Fianna Fáil's presidential candidate, with Haughey's support.

The presidential election was held on 7 November 1990, using the Irish system of proportional representation, i.e. the single transferable vote. Lenihan had been expected to win by a wide margin. His reputation was, however, adversely affected by his alleged mendacity, which had led to his dismissal from the Government. Lenihan secured 44.1% of the first-preference votes, while Mary Robinson, a liberal lawyer associated with human rights (who was supported by the Labour Party and the Workers' Party), obtained 38.9%, and Austin Currie, the Fine Gael candidate, 17.0%. Following the redistribution of Austin Currie's supporters' second-preference votes, Robinson won the election with 51.9% of the votes. She took office as President in December.

In November 1990 Haughey appointed John Wilson, the Minister for the Marine, as Deputy Prime Minister. Following Fine Gael's poor performance in the presidential election, Alan Dukes resigned the party leadership in the same month, pre-empting a motion of 'no confidence' in his performance. He was replaced by John Bruton, hitherto the deputy leader of Fine Gael. In December 1990, in response to the popularity of Robinson's liberal policies, Haughey announced plans to modernize Irish society, including changes in legislation covering marital breakdown and homosexuality. In February 1991 Brendan Daly, who was briefly the Minister for the Marine, was appointed Minister for Defence.

Regular discussions between the British and Irish heads of government, initiated in May 1980, led to the formation in November 1981 of an Anglo-Irish Intergovernmental Council, intended to meet at ministerial and official levels. Anglo-Irish relations were damaged by Ireland's neutral stance over the Argentine invasion of the Falkland Islands in 1982, but formal discussions by the heads of government were resumed in November 1983.

In May 1983 representatives of the three main political parties in the Republic, and of the Social Democratic and Labour Party of Northern Ireland, initiated the New Ireland Forum to discuss the future of Ireland and Northern Ireland. The Forum's report was rejected by the United Kingdom Government, but discussions between the United Kingdom and Ireland continued, and in November 1985 resulted in the signing of the Anglo-Irish Agreement. The Agreement provided for regular participation in Northern Ireland affairs by the Irish Government on political, legal, security and cross-border matters. The involvement of the Government of Ireland was to be through an Intergovernmental Conference. The Agreement maintained that no change in the status of Northern Ireland would be made without the assent of the majority of its population. The terms of the Agreement were approved by both the Irish and the British Parliaments, although in Northern Ireland many Protestants expressed strong disapproval.

Under the provisions of the Anglo-Irish Agreement, the Irish Government pledged co-operation in the implementation of new measures to improve cross-border security, in order to suppress IRA operations. It also promised to participate in the European Convention on the Suppression of Terrorism, which it subsequently signed in February 1986. The Convention had not been signed by the Irish Government previously, because it was thought to contravene a provision in the Constitution which prevented extradition for political offences.

In March 1987 the new Haughey Government pledged to honour the Anglo-Irish Agreement and to co-operate with the United Kingdom in its efforts to suppress terrorism. Relations between the two countries were strained, however, when the Irish Government repeated its requests for reform in the emergency provisions whereby some alleged offences in Northern Ireland are tried by a single judge, without a jury. In November the discovery of an illegal shipment of armaments from Libya, intended for the IRA, and the perpetration of a bombing outrage (resulting in the deaths of 11 civilians) by the IRA at Enniskillen, Northern Ireland, increased pressure on the Irish Government to approve new extradition procedures. In December the Government approved amendments to the 1965 Extradition Act, whereby the European Convention on the Suppression of Terrorism was ratified, but controversial measures were also introduced, without consulting the British Government, granting the Irish Attorney-General the right to approve or reject warrants for extradition of suspected IRA terrorists to the United Kingdom. In January 1988, however, the Irish Supreme Court ruled that members of the IRA could not be protected from extradition to Northern Ireland on the grounds that their offences were politically motivated. In May the British Government accepted the conditions imposed by the amendments. The first application for the extradition of an IRA suspect under the new agreement failed, however, because of a technical defect in the warrant. In December the Irish Attorney-General, John Murray, refused to grant the extradition of an alleged terrorist, Patrick Ryan, who was repatriated to Ireland in November, following a similar refusal by the Belgian authorities. The Irish decision was based on allegations that Ryan would not receive a fair trial in the United Kingdom because publicity had prejudiced his case. Owing to the hostility of the British reaction to this decision, Haughey cancelled a planned meeting with the British Prime Minister, Margaret Thatcher, at the EEC 'summit' conference in Rhodes, Greece, in December. The British Government was subsequently invited to invoke the 1976 Criminal Law Jurisdiction Act, whereby suspects may be tried in Ireland for alleged crimes committed elsewhere. In October 1989, however, the Irish Director of Public Prosecutions announced that there was insufficient evidence against Ryan to justify prosecution.

Relations between the Irish and British Governments were strained in 1988. Irish confidence in the impartiality of the British system of justice was severely undermined by proposed legislation to combat terrorism in Northern Ireland (see Northern Ireland, Vol. II) and by the decision, in January 1988, not to prosecute members of the Royal Ulster Constabulary (RUC) allegedly implicated in a policy of shooting terrorist suspects, without attempting to apprehend them, in Northern Ireland in 1982. Moreover, the British Government refused to publish the findings of an official inquiry into these allegations. Strained relations with the United Kingdom did not, however, present a threat to the Anglo-Irish Agreement, and the co-ordination between the Garda (Irish police force) and the RUC, established under the agreement, resulted in an unprecedentedly high level of co-operation on cross-border security in 1988.

In February 1989 a permanent joint consultative assembly, comprising 25 British and 25 Irish MPs, was established. The representatives were selected in October. The assembly's meetings, the first of which began in February 1990, were to take place twice a year, alternately in Dublin and London.

In September 1989 the Irish Government demanded a full review of the Ulster Defence Regiment (UDR), the largely Protestant volunteer force forming part of the security forces in Northern Ireland (see Northern Ireland, Vol. II).

IRELAND

In January 1990 an initiative was launched by Peter Brooke, the British Secretary of State for Northern Ireland, to convene meetings between representatives from the major political parties in Northern Ireland, and the British and Irish Governments, to discuss devolution in Northern Ireland. In response to demands from Northern Ireland's Democratic Unionist Party and Ulster Unionist Party, the Irish and British Governments publicly stated that they were prepared to consider an alternative to the Anglo-Irish Agreement. Other Unionist preconditions for the opening of discussions were the suspension of regular meetings under the Anglo-Irish Agreement for the duration of the talks, and the suspension of the Anglo-Irish Secretariat. The Unionists subsequently compromised on these demands, accepting that the time-lapse between meetings of the Anglo-Irish Conference could be utilized to open negotiations and that the Anglo-Irish Secretariat, while not servicing Conference meetings, would continue other work for the duration of the talks.

In May 1990 the Unionists agreed to hold direct discussions with the Irish Government, a concession previously withheld because it lent credence to the Irish claim to a right to be involved in Northern Ireland's affairs. Disagreement remained, however, on the timing of Ireland's entry to the talks. The Irish Government argued that, as a signatory to an international agreement (the Anglo-Irish Agreement) which the Unionists were trying to replace, it should be involved from the beginning. The Unionists were prepared to hold discussions with Ireland only after the political parties in Northern Ireland had reached agreement on a devolved administration in Northern Ireland.

In June 1990 Brooke announced plans for a three-tiered structure of interlocking talks: inter-party talks in Northern Ireland; discussions between the Irish and British Governments; and talks between the Northern Ireland parties and the Irish Government. By July 1990 the timing of the Irish Government's involvement in the process remained unresolved and the Unionists had announced that they were prepared to meet Irish representatives only as part of a UK delegation. This was unacceptable to the Irish Government and Northern Ireland's Social Democratic and Labour Party. Talks were adjourned and little progress was made when they recommenced in September. In February 1991 the Irish Government submitted proposals to Brooke, which were designed to allay Unionist concerns, using a formula omitting the term UK (see Northern Ireland, Vol. II).

In March 1990 the Irish Supreme Court rejected an attempt by Ulster Unionists to have the Anglo-Irish Agreement declared contrary to Ireland's Constitution, which claims jurisdiction over Northern Ireland. In the same month the Supreme Court ruled against the extradition to the UK of two IRA prisoners, who escaped from detention in Northern Ireland, on the grounds that they risked being assaulted by prison staff. This adversely affected relations with the UK, although Brooke attempted to minimize the impact of the ruling. In July 1990, however, Desmond Ellis, an IRA member charged with terrorist offences in the UK, lost his appeal against extradition in the High Court in Dublin. It was the first case to be considered under the 1987 Extradition Act, based on the European Convention on the Suppression of Terrorism. In November the Supreme Court upheld the ruling, and Ellis was extradited to stand trial in the UK.

Ireland has been a member of the EEC since 1973. In May 1987 the country affirmed its commitment to the EEC when, in a referendum, 69.9% of Irish voters supported adherence to the Single European Act, which aimed to secure closer economic and political co-operation between EEC member-states and to provide a common European foreign policy.

Government

Legislative power is vested in the bicameral National Parliament, comprising a Senate (with restricted powers) and a House of Representatives. The Senate (Seanad Éireann) has 60 members, including 11 nominated by the Prime Minister and 49 indirectly elected for five years. The House (Dáil Éireann) has 166 members, elected by universal adult suffrage for five years (subject to dissolution) by means of the single transferable vote, a form of proportional representation.

The President is a constitutional Head of State, elected by direct popular vote for seven years. Executive power is effectively held by the Cabinet, led by the Taoiseach (Prime Minister), who is appointed by the President on the nomination of the Dáil. The President appoints other Ministers on the nomination of the Prime Minister with the previous approval of the Dáil. The Cabinet is responsible to the Dáil.

Defence

In June 1990 the regular armed forces totalled 13,000. The army comprised 11,200, the navy 1,000 and the air force 800. There was also a reserve of 16,100. The defence budget for 1990 was estimated at I£292.0m. Military service is voluntary.

Economic Affairs

In 1989, according to estimates by the World Bank, Ireland's gross national product (GNP), measured at average 1987-89 prices, was US $30,054m., equivalent to $8,500 per head. During 1980-89, it was estimated, GNP increased, in real terms, at an average annual rate of 1.2%, and real GNP per head increased by 0.8% per year. Over the same period, the population increased by an annual average of 0.4%. Ireland's gross domestic product (GDP) increased, in real terms, by an annual average of 1.7% in 1986-88.

Agriculture (including forestry and fishing) contributed 10.5% of GDP in 1989. An estimated 14.7% of the working population were employed in the sector in 1990. Beef and dairy production, which, in 1989, accounted for an estimated 5.1% and 5.4% of total exports respectively, dominate Irish agriculture. Principal crops include barley, sugar beet, potatoes and wheat. During 1980-87 agricultural production increased by an estimated annual average of 0.3%.

Industry (comprising mining, manufacturing, construction and utilities) provided 35.2% of GDP in 1989, and employed about 28.8% of the working population in 1990. During 1980-87 industrial production increased by an estimated annual average of 1.7%.

Mining (including quarrying and turf production) was estimated to employ 0.7% of the working population in 1990. Ireland possesses substantial deposits of lead-zinc ore and recoverable peat, both of which are exploited. Natural gas, mainly from the Kinsale field, and small quantities of coal are also extracted. Offshore reserves of petroleum have been located.

Manufacturing was estimated to employ 20% of the working population in 1990. The manufacturing sector comprises many high-technology, largely foreign-owned, capital-intensive enterprises. The electronics industry employed about 2.4% of the working population in 1989, and accounted for 29% of the value of exports.

Energy is derived principally from gas, which provided 54% of total requirements in 1984, while petroleum provided 20%, peat 18%, hydroelectric power 7% and coal 1%. In 1988 energy imports were equivalent to 5% of merchandise exports.

Service industries (including commerce, tourism, finance, transport and communications) contributed 54.3% of GDP in 1989 and employed an estimated 57.0% of the working population. The financial sector is of increasing importance to Ireland. International banking business totalled US $16,200m. in 1989. An international financial services centre was completed in 1990. Tourism is one of the principal sources of foreign exchange. It accounted for more than 6% of export earnings from goods and services in 1989.

In 1989, according to government estimates, Ireland recorded a visible trade surplus of I£2,309m. and there was a surplus of I£371m. on the current account of the balance of payments. In 1989 the principal source of imports (41%) was the UK, which was also the principal market for exports (34%). Other major trading partners are the USA and the Federal Republic of Germany, which, in 1989, accounted for about 12% and 10% of total trade respectively. In 1989 principal imports included petroleum products, machinery and transport equipment and chemicals. Principal exports included electronic goods, beef and dairy products.

In 1990 there was an estimated budgetary deficit of I£282m. In 1990 Ireland's total national debt was I£25,000m. In 1988 the cost of servicing the debt was equivalent to 10.8% of exports of goods and services. The average annual rate of inflation was 8.0% in 1980-88, 4% in 1989 and 3.4% in 1990. An estimated 18.5% of the labour force were unemployed in January 1991.

Ireland became a member of the European Communities (see p. 135) in 1973.

During the 1980s the Irish economy suffered from high levels of unemployment and emigration, high inflation and a stagnation in real output. Following a strict austerity programme instituted in 1987, however, economic growth resumed, inflation was significantly reduced, unemployment started to decrease and government borrowing was reduced. As one of the less-developed members of the EEC, Ireland has received substantial assistance from the Community's Regional Fund. In 1991 the future of Irish agricultural exports was, however, expected to be adversely affected by EEC surpluses in beef and dairy products and reductions in subsidies. (Irish receipts from the Common Agricultural Policy were estimated at £1,500m. in 1989.) In 1991 unemployment was beginning to rise again as the Irish economy was affected by recessionary trends, particularly in its principal market, the UK. The Government plans to facilitate trade with other European countries through improved links to air- and sea-ports, and to develop Dublin as a financial services centre. In early 1991 the Government initiated a 10-year 'programme for economic and social progress', which included agreements restricting pay increases to less than 4% per year in the following three years.

Social Welfare

Social welfare benefits in Ireland may be grouped into two broad categories: those receivable under compulsory insurance schemes by contributors and their dependants; and those receivable on a non-contributory basis by people of inadequate means. Child benefit is payable to all households for each child.

Social Insurance is compulsory for both employees and the self-employed. The social insurance scheme provides for orphans' benefits, widows', retirement and old-age pensions; unemployment, disability, maternity, deserted wives', invalidity, and dental and optical benefits; and death grants. An occupational injuries benefit scheme is also in operation. The cost of the social insurance scheme is shared by the employer, the employee, the self-employed and the State. Varying rates of social insurance are payable, and the rate payable determines the range of benefits available. Private-sector employees contribute the highest rate and have cover for all benefits; the contributions of the self-employed provide funds for old age, widows' and orphans' benefits; permanent and pensionable employees in the state sector have cover mainly for widows' and orphans' benefits.

People of inadequate means who are not entitled to benefit under these contributory schemes may receive non-contributory pensions or other benefits from the State or other public funds. These benefits include lone parents' allowance, old-age and blindness pensions, carers' allowance, supplementary welfare allowance, unemployment assistance and family income supplement. Expenditure on social welfare in 1989 was estimated at I£2,800m.

Health services are provided by eight health boards, under the administration of the Department of Health. There are three categories of entitlement, with people on low incomes qualifying for the full range of health services free of charge, and people in two higher bands of income qualifying for progressively fewer free services.

Drugs and medicines are available free of charge to all people suffering from specified long-term ailments. Hospital in-patient and out-patient services are free of charge to all children under 16 years of age, suffering from specified long-term ailments. Immunization and diagnostic services, as well as hospital services, are free of charge to everyone suffering from an infectious disease. A maintenance allowance is also payable in certain cases. Government expenditure on health was projected to be I£1,148m. in 1990. In addition, there are various community welfare services for the chronically sick, the elderly, the disabled and families under stress. In 1980 Ireland had 209 hospital establishments, with a total of 33,028 beds, and in 1988 there were 5,590 physicians, aged under 65 years, resident in the country.

Education

Education in Ireland is compulsory for nine years between six and 15 years of age. Primary education may begin at the age of four and lasts for eight years. Most children attend a national school until the age of 12, when they transfer to a post-primary school. In 1988/89 the total enrolment at primary and secondary schools was equivalent to 96% of the school-age population.

Post-primary education takes place in four types of school and lasts for up to six years, comprising a first cycle of three years, an optional transition year in some schools and a second cycle of two years. Secondary schools are private institutions, administered by boards of governors or religious communities, but they are subsidized by the Department of Education. Pupils take the Intermediate Certificate examination at 15 or 16 years of age, and may proceed to a two-year course leading to the Leaving Certificate at 17 or 18. In 1988/89 there were 251 vocational schools, providing primary school leavers with a general course which is similar to that for pupils in secondary schools, but with a greater emphasis on non-academic subjects. In 1988/89 there were 16 state comprehensive schools, offering academic and technical subjects, structured to the needs, abilities and interests of the pupils, and leading to examinations for the Intermediate Certificate or the Leaving Certificate. The 47 community schools offer a similar curriculum. They were originally intended to replace existing vocational and secondary schools in rural areas, but since 1985 they have also been established in new city areas. In 1988/89 an estimated 84% of children in the post-primary group were receiving post-primary education.

Six technical colleges in Dublin and nine regional technical colleges provide a range of craft, technical, professional and other courses. The majority of courses lead to academic awards granted by the National Council for Educational Awards at Certificate, diploma, degree and postgraduate levels.

The gaining of certain successes in the Leaving Certificate examination qualifies for entrance to the four universities: the University of Dublin (Trinity College), which offers a full range of courses; the National University of Ireland, which comprises the University Colleges of Cork, Dublin and Galway; and the Dublin City University and the University of Limerick (former National Institutes of Higher Education which were granted university status in 1989). Universities are self-governing, although they receive annual state grants. The Department of Education provides grants to more than one-third of students in further education.

In the 1990 budget an estimated I£1,138m. was allocated to education.

Public Holidays

1991: 1 January (New Year), 18 March (for St Patrick's Day), 29 March (Good Friday), 1 April (Easter Monday), 3 June (June Bank Holiday), 5 August (August Bank Holiday), 28 October (October Bank Holiday), 25–26 December (Christmas).

1992: 1 January (New Year), 17 March (St Patrick's Day), 17 April (Good Friday), 20 April (Easter Monday), 1 June (June Bank Holiday), 3 August (August Bank Holiday), 26 October (October Bank Holiday), 25–26 December (Christmas).

Weights and Measures

The imperial system of weights and measures is in force, but metrication is being introduced gradually.

Statistical Survey

Source (unless otherwise stated): Central Statistics Office, St Stephen's Green House, Earlsfort Terrace, Dublin 2; tel. (01) 767531.

Area and Population

AREA, POPULATION AND DENSITY

Area (sq km)	
Land	68,895
Inland waters	1,388
Total	70,283*
Population (census results)	
5 April 1981	3,443,405
13 April 1986†	
Males	1,769,690
Females	1,770,953
Total	3,540,643
Population (official estimates at 15 April)	
1988	3,538,000
1989	3,515,000
1990	3,503,000
Density (per sq km) at April 1990	49.8

* 27,136 sq miles.
† Source: *Census of the Population of Ireland, 1986—Summary Population Report*.

PROVINCES (1986 census)

	Land area (sq km)	Population	Density (per sq km)
Connaught	17,122	431,409	25.2
Leinster	19,633	1,852,649	94.4
Munster	24,127	1,020,577	42.3
Ulster (part)	8,012	236,008	29.5
Total	68,895	3,540,643	51.4

PRINCIPAL TOWNS
(population, including suburbs or environs, at 1986 census)

Dublin (capital)*	920,956	Galway	47,104
Cork	173,694	Waterford	41,054
Limerick	76,557		

* Greater Dublin area, including Dún Laoghaire (population 54,715 in 1986).

BIRTHS, MARRIAGES AND DEATHS (rates per 1,000)

	Birth rate	Marriage rate	Death rate
1982	20.4	5.8	9.3
1983	19.2	5.6	9.4
1984	18.2	5.2	9.1
1985	17.6	5.3	9.4
1986	17.4	5.2	9.5
1987	16.5	5.2	8.9
1988	15.4	5.2	8.9
1989*	14.7	5.1	8.8

* Provisional figures.

ECONOMICALLY ACTIVE POPULATION
(estimates, '000 persons, excluding unemployed)

	1988	1989	1990*
Agriculture, forestry and fishing	166	163	165
Mining, quarrying and turf production	7	7	8
Manufacturing	209	215	224
Construction	70	70	77
Electricity, gas and water	14	14	13
Commerce, insurance and finance	222	222	224
Transport and communications	64	66	68
Public administration and defence	70	67	64
Other economic activities	270	266	277
Total	1,091	1,090	1,120

* Preliminary estimates.

Agriculture

PRINCIPAL CROPS ('000 metric tons)

	1987	1988	1989
Wheat	402	475	477
Oats	106	113	99
Barley	1,599	1,606	1,474
Potatoes	697	694	581
Sugar beet*	1,623	1,334	1,451

* Figures relate to quantities delivered to factories.

LIVESTOCK ('000 head)

	1987	1988	1989
Cattle	6,647	6,604	6,801
Sheep	5,595	6,656	7,698
Pigs	999	979	996

LIVESTOCK PRODUCTS ('000 metric tons)

	1987	1988	1989
Beef and veal	477.4	458.0	431.6
Mutton and lamb	47.5	48.8	63.3
Pig meat	143.1	147.5	144.0
Poultry meat	69	78	72
Edible offals*	81	77	80
Cows' milk†	5,390	5,197	5,248
Butter‡	134.4	123.9	139.1
Cheese‡	65.2	74.6	73.6
Dry milk	167	138	165
Hen eggs	39	38	34
Cattle hides*	40.4	38.0	39.0
Sheep skins*	7.3	7.6	8.1

* FAO estimates (Source: FAO, *Production Yearbook* and *Quarterly Bulletin of Statistics*).
† Figures refer to deliveries. Estimated production of cows' milk (in '000 metric tons) was: 5,521 in 1987; 5,323 in 1988; 5,375 in 1989.
‡ Figures refer to factory production. Total production of cheese (in '000 metric tons) was: 67 in 1987; 80 in 1988; 76 in 1989.

IRELAND

Forestry

ROUNDWOOD REMOVALS ('000 cubic metres, including bark)

	1987	1988	1989
Sawlogs, veneer logs and logs for sleepers	784	854	855
Pulpwood	613	578	600
Fuel wood	49	46	50
Total	1,446	1,478	1,505

SAWNWOOD PRODUCTION
('000 cubic metres, including boxboards)

	1987	1988	1989
Coniferous (soft wood)	317	353	353
Broadleaved (hard wood)*	11	13	15
Total	328	366	368

* Estimated production.

Fishing

SEA FISH (landings in metric tons)

	1987	1988
European plaice	3,078	3,251
Atlantic cod	7,711	8,625
Haddock	3,264	2,996
Whiting	9,471	9,896
Dogfish	7,940	5,125
Atlantic herring	39,567	41,345
Atlantic mackerel	75,238	67,547
Horse mackerel	31,539	39,315
Blue whiting	3,706	4,646
Argentines	0	3,040
Total fish (incl. others)	197,550	203,473
Crabs	3,330	3,650
Norway lobster	4,435	3,147
Mussels	14,893	12,648
Total shellfish (incl. others)	25,863	22,783
Total catch	223,413	226,256

INLAND FISH (catch in metric tons)

	1985	1986	1987
Atlantic salmon	1,493	1,655	1,254
Sea trout	22	22	23
European eel	87	87	n.a.

Mining

('000 metric tons, unless otherwise indicated)

	1987	1988	1989
Coal	45	42	43
Natural gas (terajoules)	62,362	75,795	85,876
Lead*	33.8	32.0	32.1
Zinc*	177.0	173.2	168.8
Silver (kilograms)*	7,200	5,500	7,200
Peat	6,251	4,847	8,389

* Figures refer to the metal content of ores mined.

Industry

SELECTED PRODUCTS
(provisional, '000 metric tons, unless otherwise indicated)

	1987	1988	1989
Flour	157.4	162	161
Margarine	22	22	25
Cigarettes (million)	6,659	6,420	6,161
Wool yarn	8.7	9.3	9.1
Woven woollen fabrics (million sq m)	1.7	1.7	1.8
Footwear ('000 pairs)	2,200	2,100	1,913
Nitrogenous fertilizers*	255.4	285.9	268.0
Phosphate fertilizers*	3.0	3.0	n.a.
Motor spirit (petrol)	298	295	340
Distillate fuel oils	533	503	532
Residual fuel oils	559	489	508
Cement	1,448	n.a.	n.a.
Electric energy (million kWh)	12,866	13,068	13,640
Manufactured gas (terajoules)	106	n.a.	n.a.

* Source: FAO, *Quarterly Bulletin of Statistics*. Figures are in terms of nitrogen or phosphoric acid, and refer to estimated production during the 12 months ending 30 June of the year stated.

Finance

CURRENCY AND EXCHANGE RATES

Monetary Units:
100 pence = 1 Irish pound (I£ or punt).

Denominations:
Coins: 1, 2, 5, 10, 20 and 50 pence.
Notes: 1, 5, 10, 20, 50 and 100 pounds.

Sterling and Dollar Equivalents (30 September 1990)
£1 sterling = I£1.0915;
US $1 = 58.39 pence;
I£100 = £91.62 sterling = $171.25.

Average Exchange Rate (US $ per Irish pound)
1987 1.4881
1988 1.5261
1989 1.4190

BUDGET (I£ million)

Revenue	1988*	1989*	1990†
Customs	108	132	147
Excise	1,481	1,638	1,684
Capital taxes	62	60	64
Income tax	3,055	2,810	2,920
Corporation tax	334	303	338
Motor vehicle duties	140	148	149
Stamp duties	198	279	286
Value added tax	1,805	1,943	2,015
Employment and training levy	126	117	124
EEC agricultural levies	13	13	13
Total (incl. others)	7,690	7,756	8,130

* Out-turn. † Post-budget estimate.

IRELAND

Statistical Survey

Expenditure	1988*	1989*	1990†
Debt service	2,141	2,141	2,310
Agriculture, fisheries and forestry	256	288	257
Defence	296	302	330
Justice (incl. police)	367	374	412
Education	1,073	1,146	1,138
Social welfare	1,606	1,585	1,551
Health	1,001	1,069	1,148
Housing	32	24	20
Industry and labour	214	199	214
Total (incl. others)	7,989	8,050	8,412

* Out-turn. † Post-budget estimate.

GOLD RESERVES AND CURRENCY IN CIRCULATION
(I£ million at 31 December)

	1987	1988	1989
Official gold reserves	83.0	75.3	69.8
Coin and bank notes in circulation	1,214.0	1,346.5	1,459.2

COST OF LIVING
(Consumer Price Index; base: November 1968 = 100)

	1988	1989	1990
Food	744.6	779.5	792.9
Alcoholic drink	893.8	929.8	957.3
Tobacco	837.0	862.1	858.5
Clothing and footwear	616.9	629.1	638.1
Fuel and light	1,019.7	1,047.5	1,076.4
Housing	503.0	544.1	625.9
Durable household goods	585.5	602.7	615.0
Other goods	870.3	910.1	926.9
Transport	1,001.2	1,035.4	1,072.6
Services and related expenditure	996.8	1,041.2	1,080.6
All items	803.6	836.4	864.2

NATIONAL ACCOUNTS (I£ million at current prices)
National Income and Product

	1987	1988	1989
Gross domestic product at factor cost	17,933.4	19,332	20,923
Net factor income from the rest of the world*	−1,957.0	−2,542	−3,039
Gross national product at factor cost	15,976.4	16,790	17,884
Less Consumption of fixed capital	1,994.0	2,129	2,337
Net national product at factor cost	13,982.4	14,661	15,547
of which:			
Compensation of employees	10,637.8	11,140	11,869
Other domestic income	3,344.5	3,520	3,677
Indirect taxes, less subsidies	2,107.9	2,151	2,996
Net national product at market prices	16,090.2	16,811	18,542
Consumption of fixed capital	1,994.0	2,129	2,337
Gross national product at market prices	18,084.2	18,940	20,879
Less Net factor income from the rest of the world*	−1,957.1	−2,542	−3,039
Gross domestic product at market prices	20,041.3	21,482	23,918
Balance of exports and imports of goods and services*	−1,316.8	−1,967	−2,302

National Income and Product—*continued*

	1987	1988	1989
Available resources	18,724.5	19,515	21,616
of which:			
Private consumption expenditure	11,783	12,376	13,523
Government consumption expenditure	3,577	3,595	3,683
Gross fixed capital formation	3,337.8	3,627	4,320
Increase in stocks	26.7	−83	90

* Excludes transfers between Ireland and the rest of the world.

Gross Domestic Product by Economic Activity (at factor cost)

	1987	1988	1989
Agriculture, forestry and fishing	1,925.1	2,207	2,311
Mining, manufacturing, electricity, gas, water and construction	6,568.1	6,951	7,741
Public administration and defence	1,189.6	1,190	1,238
Transport, communications and trade	3,161.7	3,522	3,691
Other services	5,973.3	6,429	7,000
Sub-total	18,817.8	20,299	21,981
Adjustment for financial services	−884.4	−967	−1,058
Total	17,933.4	19,332	20,923

BALANCE OF PAYMENTS (I£ million)

	1987	1988	1989
Current Receipts:			
Merchandise exports (f.o.b.)*	10,447	12,073	14,358
Tourism and travel	564	655	751
Trading and investment income	766	920	1,256
International transfers	1,322	1,408	1,526
Other items	791	821	897
Total	13,890	15,877	18,788
Current Expenditure:			
Merchandise imports (c.i.f.)*	9,137	10,048	12,114
Tourism and travel	556	630	698
Foreign trading and investment income	2,740	3,478	4,311
International transfers	443	397	418
Other items	775	887	876
Total	13,651	15,440	18,417
Current balance	239	437	371

* Adjusted for balance-of-payments purposes.

External Trade

PRINCIPAL COMMODITIES (distribution by SITC, I£'000)

Imports c.i.f.	1987†	1988	1989†
Food and live animals	985,469	1,066,239	1,153,931
Cereals and cereal preparations	180,729	181,677	182,254
Vegetables and fruit	187,905	188,784	213,646
Animal feeding-stuff (excl. cereals)	185,307	213,462	243,727
Crude materials (inedible) except fuels	257,351	294,623	343,353

IRELAND — Statistical Survey

Imports c.i.f.—continued	1987†	1988	1989†
Mineral fuels, lubricants, etc.	676,514	568,001	674,301
Petroleum, petroleum products, etc.	511,739	388,336	493,888
Crude petroleum oils, etc.	144,412	100,896	141,357
Refined petroleum products	353,315	378,082	337,623
Motor spirit (petrol) and other light oils	80,965	73,621	93,720
Motor spirit (incl. aviation spirit)	76,045	69,231	82,883
Gas oils (distillate fuels)	110,048	98,662	127,284
Other fuel oils	90,267	37,484	39,412
Chemicals and related products	1,126,241	1,292,151	1,524,802
Organic chemicals	201,624	213,261	270,583
Medicinal and pharmaceutical products	174,733	207,686	240,889
Manufactured fertilizers	139,172	136,969	161,779
Artificial resins and plastic materials, etc.	247,744	193,281	218,176
Products of polymerization, etc.	163,555	111,225	129,055
Basic manufactures	1,442,726	1,637,605	1,847,176
Paper, paperboard, etc.	298,763	347,555	382,597
Paper and paperboard	182,762	221,622	242,805
Textile yarn, fabrics, etc.	342,171	373,242	378,930
Non-metallic mineral manufactures	131,346	137,768	173,948
Iron and steel	155,636	208,116	252,985
Machinery and transport equipment	3,065,335	3,516,580	4,649,829
Power generating machinery and equipment	174,398	261,761	356,786
Machinery specialized for particular industries	281,146	350,989	440,832
General industrial machinery, equipment and parts	296,726	308,818	367,903
Office machines and automatic data processing equipment	1,006,446	979,419	1,285,026
Parts and accessories for office machines, etc.	716,337	690,398	895,311
Telecommunications and sound equipment	157,624	175,009	212,660
Other electrical machinery, apparatus, etc.	603,286	789,957	1,032,431
Road vehicles and parts (excl. tyres, engines and electrical parts)	399,417	529,201	756,536
Passenger motor cars (excl. buses)	230,596	304,095	422,386
Miscellaneous manufactured articles	1,172,788	1,345,892	1,552,922
Clothing and accessories (excl. footwear)	379,335	415,736	455,329
Total (incl. others)*	9,155,207	10,214,758	12,287,833

* Including transactions not classified by commodity (I£'000): 280,373 in 1987; 317,664 in 1988; 346,161 in 1989. These amounts include imports through Shannon Free Airport (I£'000): 87,430 in 1987; 107,028 in 1988; 120,999 in 1989. The total also includes imports of non-monetary gold (I£'000): 5,380 in 1987; 6,752 in 1988; 6,853 in 1989.
† Provisional.

Exports f.o.b.	1987†	1988	1989†
Food and live animals	2,676,203	2,900,560	3,208,932
Live animals	173,893	229,266	194,948
Bovine animals	115,668	151,247	110,870
Meat and meat preparations	763,031	764,180	888,493
Fresh, chilled or frozen meat	712,764	706,812	813,806
Meat of bovine animals	590,081	566,048	629,318
Dairy products and birds' eggs	620,227	680,947	795,475
Milk and cream	180,317	147,565	236,658
Preserved, concentrated or sweetened milk and cream	173,721	139,945	231,791
Butter	322,465	334,643	368,438
Beverages and tobacco	236,745	251,270	297,870
Beverages	205,595	222,187	265,826
Crude materials (inedible) except fuels	439,637	551,942	629,275

Exports f.o.b.—continued	1987†	1988	1989†
Chemicals and related products	1,307,169	1,612,583	2,084,847
Organic chemicals	582,048	671,912	903,271
Organo-inorganic and heterocyclic compounds	430,264	481,693	632,752
Heterocyclic compounds (incl. nucleic acids)	400,291	610,760	457,426
Basic manufactures	942,246	1,036,052	1,148,765
Textile yarn, fabrics, etc.	314,702	339,024	345,612
Machinery and transport equipment	3,364,528	3,840,390	4,652,376
General industrial machinery, equipment and parts	253,337	291,676	329,227
Office machines and automatic data processing equipment	2,242,727	2,264,022	2,903,130
Automatic data processing machines and units	1,484,607	1,206,525	1,544,467
Complete digital data processing machines	1,220,457	737,304	887,221
Electrical machinery, apparatus, etc.	613,962	810,144	911,375
Miscellaneous manufactured articles	1,304,260	1,606,562	1,965,651
Clothing and accessories (excl. footwear)	211,233	218,571	241,955
Professional, scientific and controlling instruments and apparatus	354,228	377,758	403,576
Total (incl. others)*	10,723,498	12,304,847	14,596,912

* Including transactions not classified by commodity (I£'000): 360,885 in 1987; 427,811 in 1988; 526,018 in 1989. These amounts include exports through Shannon Free Airport (I£'000): 241,145 in 1987; 279,767 in 1988; 333,600 in 1989. The total also includes exports of non-monetary gold (I£'000): 1,202 in 1987; 1,585 in 1988; 1,579 in 1989.
† Provisional.

PRINCIPAL TRADING PARTNERS* (I£'000)

Imports c.i.f.	1987†	1988	1989†
Belgium/Luxembourg	197,489	213,988	267,445
Canada	85,841	94,442	94,592
Denmark	85,158	93,469	114,009
Finland	82,958	99,586	103,128
France	401,238	417,011	503,228
Germany, Federal Republic	764,584	880,811	1,074,842
Italy	224,955	259,458	324,179
Japan	397,643	496,898	718,929
Netherlands	338,787	407,479	508,516
Spain	117,966	118,359	151,522
Sweden	139,532	160,136	198,677
Switzerland	68,374	71,692	78,684
United Kingdom	3,815,917	4,303,581	5,027,495
USA	1,555,414	1,623,325	1,973,240
Total (incl. others)	9,155,207	10,214,758	12,287,833

* Imports by country of origin; exports by country of final destination. The distribution excludes trade through Shannon Free Airport (see previous tables) except for Canada, the USA and the EEC.
† Provisional.

IRELAND

Exports f.o.b.	1987†	1988	1989†
Belgium/Luxembourg	512,829	544,973	661,245
Canada	110,010	121,317	96,969
Denmark	97,650	95,726	131,740
Egypt	70,646	79,903	74,515
France	994,372	1,120,970	1,455,042
Germany, Federal Republic	1,202,610	1,368,785	1,610,411
Italy	392,478	464,530	646,596
Netherlands	778,271	860,971	1,031,106
Nigeria	41,120	51,378	35,167
Spain	164,160	209,612	286,852
Sweden	205,367	231,594	269,106
United Kingdom	3,662,630	4,349,718	4,896,095
USA	833,806	949,518	1,153,447
Total (incl. others)	10,723,498	12,304,848	14,596,912

Transport

RAILWAYS (traffic, '000)

	1986	1987	1988
Passengers carried	21,735	24,895	24,043
Passenger train-km	9,655	9,692	9,288
Freight tonnage	3,126	3,014	3,010
Freight train-km	4,239	4,232	3,942

ROAD TRAFFIC (licensed motor vehicles at 30 September)

	1986	1987	1988
Private cars	712,475	737,980	750,767
Goods vehicles	101,475	111,023	118,764
Public service vehicles	8,132	8,347	8,653
Motor cycles	25,735	25,828	24,877

1988: Goods vehicles 118,764; Motor cycles 24,877.

SHIPPING (sea-borne freight traffic, '000 net registered tons)*

	1987	1988	1989
Displacement	22,557	25,630	25,940

* Figures refer to vessels engaged in both international and coastal trade.

CIVIL AVIATION

	1987/88	1988/89	1989/90
Kilometres flown ('000)	28,177	36,179	41,517
Passengers carried	2,669,671	3,522,905	4,069,397
Freight carried (tons)	38,771	43,278	47,389
Mail carried (tons)	1,720	2,079	2,793
Passenger-km ('000)*	2,881,335	3,386,046	4,005,178
Freight ton-km ('000)	88,446	106,679	122,325

* Scheduled services only.

Tourism

FOREIGN TOURIST ARRIVALS BY ORIGIN ('000)*

	1987	1988	1989
Great Britain	1,236	1,508	1,716
Northern Ireland	566	582	680
France	113	111	138
Germany, Federal Republic	103	113	154
Netherlands	40	38	46
Other continental Europe	134	146	209
United States	367	385	385
Canada	31	34	42
Other areas	74	90	114
Total	2,664	3,007	3,484

* Excluding excursionists ('000): 7,368 in 1987; 7,348 in 1988.

Communications Media

	1987	1988	1989
Television licences	787,501	759,711	781,795
Telephones in use	789,000	843,000	902,567
Daily newspapers	8	8	8

Radio receivers (estimate, 1988): 2,125,000 in use.
Television receivers (1989): 870,763 declared.
Book production (1985): 2,679 titles (including 2,051 pamphlets).
Source: UNESCO, *Statistical Yearbook*.

Education

(1988/89)

	Institutions	Teachers (full-time)	Students (full-time)
National schools*	3,364	20,362	560,116
Secondary schools	496	11,698	213,640
Vocational schools	251	4,867	84,442
Comprehensive schools	16	491	8,837
Community schools	47	1,846	31,651
Teacher (primary) training colleges	5	130	1,402
Preparatory colleges	1		27
Technical colleges†	9	1,088	13,886
Technology colleges†	11	872	9,382
Universities and Institutes	7	1,974	35,820

* National schools are state-aided primary schools.
† Third-level pupils only.

Sources: Department of Education, Dublin 1; Higher Education Authority.

Directory

The Constitution

The original Constitution of the Irish Free State came into operation on 6 December 1922. Certain provisions which were regarded as contrary to national sentiments were gradually removed by successive amendments, with the result that by 1937 the text differed considerably from that of the original document. It was superseded by an entirely new Constitution, which was approved by Parliament on 14 June 1937, and enacted by the people by means of a plebiscite on 1 July. This new Constitution came into operation on 29 December 1937. Ireland became a republic on 18 April 1949. The following is a summary of the Constitution's main provisions:

TITLE OF THE STATE

The title of the State is Éire or, in the English language, Ireland.

NATIONAL STATUS

The Constitution declares that Ireland is a sovereign, independent, democratic State. It affirms the inalienable, indefeasible and sovereign right of the Irish nation to choose its own form of government, to determine its relations with other nations, and to develop its life, political, economic and cultural, in accordance with its own genius and traditions.

The Constitution applies to the whole of Ireland, but, pending the re-integration of the national territory, the laws enacted by the Parliament established by the Constitution have the same area and extent of application as those of the Irish Free State.

THE PRESIDENT

At the head of the State is the President, elected by direct suffrage, who holds office for a period of seven years. He, on the advice of the Government or its head, summons and dissolves Parliament, signs and promulgates laws and appoints judges; on the nomination of the Dáil he appoints the Prime Minister and, on the nomination of the Prime Minister with the previous approval of the Dáil, he appoints the other members of the Government. The supreme command of the Defence Forces is vested in him, its exercise being regulated by law.

In addition, the President has the power to refer certain Bills to the Supreme Court for decision on the question of their constitutionality; and also, at the instance of a prescribed proportion of the members of both Houses of Parliament, to refer certain Bills to the people for decision at a referendum.

The President, in the exercise and performance of certain of his constitutional powers and functions, has the aid and advice of a Council of State.

PARLIAMENT

The Oireachtas, or National Parliament, consists of the President and two Houses, viz. a House of Representatives called Dáil Éireann, and a Senate, called Seanad Éireann. The Dáil consists of 166 members, who are elected for a five-year term by adult suffrage on the system of proportional representation by means of the single, transferable vote. Of the 60 members of the Senate, 11 are nominated by the Prime Minister, six are elected by the universities, and 43 are elected from five panels of candidates established on a vocational basis, representing: national language and culture, literature, art, education and such professional interests as may be defined by law for the purpose of this panel; agriculture and allied interests, and fisheries; labour, whether organized or unorganized; industry and commerce, including banking, finance, accountancy, engineering and architecture; and public administration and social services, including voluntary social activities.

A maximum period of 90 days is afforded to the Senate for the consideration or amendment of Bills sent to that House by the Dáil, but the Senate has no power to veto legislation.

EXECUTIVE

The Executive Power of the State is exercised by the Government, which is responsible to the Dáil and consists of not fewer than seven and not more than 15 members. The head of the Government is the Prime Minister.

FUNDAMENTAL RIGHTS

The State recognizes the family as the natural, primary and fundamental unit group of Society, possessing inalienable and imprescriptible rights antecedent and superior to all positive law. It acknowledges the right to life of the unborn and guarantees in its laws to defend and vindicate that right. It acknowledges the right and duty of parents to provide for the education of their children, and, with due regard to that right, undertakes to provide free education. It pledges itself also to guard with special care the institution of marriage.

The Constitution contains special provision for the recognition and protection of the fundamental rights of citizens, such as personal liberty, free expression of opinion, peaceable assembly, and the formation of associations and unions.

Freedom of conscience and the free practice and profession of religion are, subject to public order and morality, guaranteed to every citizen. No religion may be endowed or subjected to discriminatory disability. Since December 1972, when a referendum was taken on the issue, the Catholic Church has no longer enjoyed a special, privileged position.

SOCIAL POLICY

Certain principles of social policy intended for the general guidance of Parliament, but not cognizable by the courts, are set forth in the Constitution. Among their objects are the direction of the policy of the State towards securing the distribution of property so as to subserve the common good, the regulation of credit so as to serve the welfare of the people as a whole, the establishment of families in economic security on the land, and the right to an adequate means of livelihood for all citizens.

The State pledges itself to safeguard the interests, and to contribute where necessary to the support, of the infirm, the widow, the orphan and the aged, and shall endeavour to ensure that citizens shall not be forced by economic necessity to enter occupations unsuited to their sex, age or strength.

AMENDMENT OF THE CONSTITUTION

No amendment to the Constitution can be effected except by the decision of the people given at a referendum.

The Government

HEAD OF STATE

President: MARY ROBINSON (assumed office 3 December 1990).

THE CABINET
(February 1991)

A coalition of Fianna Fáil and the Progressive Democrats.

Taoiseach (Prime Minister) and Minister for the Gaeltacht: CHARLES J. HAUGHEY.
Tánaiste (Deputy Prime Minister) and Minister for the Marine: JOHN P. WILSON.
Minister for Defence: BRENDAN DALY.
Minister for Industry and Commerce: DESMOND J. O'MALLEY*.
Minister for the Environment: PÁDRAIG FLYNN.
Minister for Foreign Affairs: GERARD COLLINS.
Minister for Tourism and Transport: SEAMUS BRENNAN.
Minister for Energy: ROBERT M. MOLLOY*.
Minister for Finance: ALBERT REYNOLDS.
Minister for Health: RORY O'HANLON.
Minister for Social Welfare: Dr MICHAEL WOODS.
Minister for Agriculture and Food: MICHAEL O'KENNEDY.
Minister for Justice and for Communications: RAY BURKE.
Minister for Education: MARY O'ROURKE.
Minister for Labour: BERTIE AHERN.

* Member of Progressive Democrats. All other Ministers belong to Fianna Fáil.

MINISTRIES

Office of the President: Áras an Uachtaráin, Phoenix Park, Dublin 8; tel. (01) 772815; fax (01) 710529.
Department of the Taoiseach: Government Bldgs, Upper Merrion St, Dublin 2; tel. (01) 689333; telex 93938; fax (01) 789791.
Department of Agriculture and Food: Kildare St, Dublin 2; tel. (01) 789011; telex 93607; fax (01) 612890.

IRELAND

Department of Communications: Scotch House, Hawkins St, Dublin 2; tel. (01) 718211; telex 93736; fax (01) 6798834.

Department of Defence: Parkgate, Dublin 8; tel. (01) 771881; telex 25250; fax (01) 796097.

Department of Education: Marlborough St, Dublin 1; tel. (01) 734700; telex 31136; fax (01) 729553.

Department of Energy: 25 Clare St, Dublin 2; tel. (01) 715233; telex 90335; fax (01) 773169.

Department of the Environment: Custom House, Dublin 1; tel. (01) 793377; telex 31014; fax (01) 742710.

Department of Finance: Government Bldgs, Upper Merrion St, Dublin 2; tel. (01) 767571; telex 30357; fax (01) 789936.

Department of Foreign Affairs: 80 St Stephen's Green, Dublin 2; tel. (01) 780822; fax (01) 780628.

Department of the Gaeltacht: 1 Lower Grand Canal St, Dublin 2; tel. (01) 764751; telex 30782; fax (01) 764755.

Department of Health: Hawkins House, Dublin 2; tel. (01) 714711; telex 33451; fax (01) 711947.

Department of Industry and Commerce: Kildare St, Dublin 2; tel. (01) 614444; telex 93478; fax (01) 762654.

Department of Justice: 72–76 St Stephen's Green, Dublin 2; tel. (01) 789711; fax (01) 615461.

Department of Labour: Davitt House, 65A Adelaide Rd, Dublin 2; tel. (01) 765861; telex 93435; fax (01) 769047.

Department of the Marine: Leeson Lane, Dublin 2; tel. (01) 785444; telex 91798; fax (01) 618214.

Department of Social Welfare: Áras Mhic Dhiarmada, Dublin 1; tel. (01) 786444; telex 32969; fax (01) 741709.

Department of Tourism and Transport: Kildare St, Dublin 2; tel. (01) 789522; telex 91806; fax (01) 763350.

Legislature

OIREACHTAS (PARLIAMENT)

Parliament comprises two Houses—Dáil Éireann (House of Representatives), with 166 members, and Seanad Éireann (Senate), with 60 members, of whom 11 are nominated by the Taoiseach and 49 elected (six by the universities and 43 from specially constituted panels).

Dáil Éireann

Speaker: SEAN TREACY.

General Election, 15 June 1989

Party	Votes*	% of votes*	Seats
Fianna Fáil	731,472	44.15	77
Fine Gael	485,307	29.29	55
Labour Party	156,989	9.48	15
Workers' Party	82,263	4.97	7
Progessive Democrats	91,013	5.49	6
Others	109,769	6.63	6
Total	**1,656,813**	**100.00**	**166**

* The election was conducted by means of the single transferable vote. Figures refer to first-preference votes.

Seanad Éireann

Speaker: TRAS HONAN.

Election, August 1989 (11 members nominated)

Party	Seats at election
Fianna Fáil	32
Fine Gael	15
Labour	4
Progessive Democrats	3
Others	6

Political Organizations

Comhaontas Glas (The Green Party): 5A Upper Fownes St, Dublin 2; tel. (01) 771436; fmrly The Ecology Party; desires a humane, ecological society, freedom of information and political decentralization; Co-ordinators MARY BOWERS, STEPHEN RAWSON.

Communist Party of Ireland: James Connolly House, 43 East Essex St, Dublin 2; tel. (01) 711943; f. 1933; its aim is a united, socialist, independent Ireland; Chair. MICHAEL O'RIORDAN; Gen. Sec. JAMES STEWART.

Democratic Socialist Party: Dublin; f. 1982 by merger of Socialist Party (f. 1970) and Limerick Socialist Organization; aims to create a democratic socialist Ireland, opposes Irish nationalist claim to Northern Ireland; Pres. JAMES KEMMY; Sec. JOE HOLOHAN.

Fianna Fáil (literally, Soldiers of Destiny—The Republican Party): 13 Upper Mount St, Dublin 2; tel. (01) 761551; fax (01) 785690; f. 1926; supports the peaceful reunification of Ireland; Pres. CHARLES HAUGHEY; Gen. Sec. FRANK WALL.

Fine Gael (United Ireland Party): 51 Upper Mount St, Dublin 2; tel. (01) 761573; telex 31569; fax (01) 609168; f. 1933; mem. of the European People's Party (Christian Democratic Group) in the European Parliament; Leader JOHN BRUTON; Nat. Exec. Chair. SEAN BARRETT; Gen. Sec. EDWARD O'REILLY.

Irish Republican Socialist Party: Dublin; f. 1974; political wing of INLA (see Northern Ireland, Vol. II); aims to establish a united 32-county democratic socialist republic in Ireland; Chair. JIM LAINE; Gen. Sec. FRANCIS BARRY.

The Labour Party: 16 Gardiner Place, Dublin 1; tel. (01) 788411; fax (01) 745479; originated with the addition of political functions to the Trade Union Congress in 1912; at the end of 1930 it was decided to separate the political and industrial functions of the Party, and the TUC and the Labour Party became separate bodies; Chair. MERVYN TAYLOR; Vice-Chair. NIAMH BHREATHNAOH; Leader of Parl. Labour Party RICHARD SPRING; Gen. Sec. RAYMOND KAVANAGH.

Progressive Democrats: 25 South Frederick St, Dublin 2; tel. (01) 794399; fax (01) 794757; f. 1985; represents a break with Fianna Fáil and Fine Gael; desires a peaceful approach to the Northern Ireland situation; tax reforms; the encouragement of private enterprise; a clear distinction between church and state; and constitutional reform, including the abolition of the Senate and a pluralist Republican Constitution; Leader DESMOND O'MALLEY; Gen. Sec. DAVID O'KEEFFE.

Republican Sinn Fein: f. 1986 by disaffected members of Sinn Fein; supports military resistance to British rule in Northern Ireland; Chair. DAITHI O'CONNELL.

Sinn Fein ('Ourselves Alone'): 44 Parnell Sq., Dublin 1; tel. (01) 726932; fax (01) 733074; f. 1905; advocates the complete overthrow of British rule in Ireland; seeks the reunification of Ireland by revolutionary means, and the establishment of a 32-county democratic socialist republic; Pres. GERARD ADAMS.

The Workers' Party (WP): 30 Gardiner Place, Dublin 1; tel. (01) 740716; telex 31490; fax (01) 789119; f. 1905; formerly Sinn Fein The Workers' Party; aims to establish an All-Ireland Unitary Socialist State; Pres. PROINNSIAS DE ROSSA; Gen. Sec. SEAN GARLAND.

Diplomatic Representation

EMBASSIES IN IRELAND

Argentina: 15 Ailesbury Drive, Dublin 4; tel. (01) 691546; telex 90564; Ambassador: NICOLÁS A. SONSCHEIN.

Australia: 2nd Floor, Fitzwilton House, Wilton Terrace, Dublin 2; tel. (01) 761517; fax (01) 685266; Ambassador: BRIAN BURKE.

Austria: 15 Ailesbury Court, 93 Ailesbury Rd, Dublin 4; tel. (01) 694577; telex 30366; Ambassador: Dr HELGA WINKLER-CAMPAGNA.

Belgium: 2 Shrewsbury Rd, Dublin 4; tel. (01) 692082; telex 93322; fax (01) 838488; Ambassador: LUC PUTMAN.

Canada: 65–68 St Stephen's Green, Dublin 2; tel. (01) 781988; telex 93803; fax (01) 781285; Ambassador: M. A. WADSWORTH.

China, People's Republic: 40 Ailesbury Rd, Dublin 4; tel: (01) 691707; telex 30626; Ambassador: HAN LILI.

Denmark: 121–122 St Stephen's Green, Dublin 2; tel. (01) 756404; telex 93523; fax (01) 784536; Chargé d'affaires a.i.: CHRISTOFFER BERTELSEN.

Egypt: 12 Clyde Rd, Ballsbridge, Dublin 4; tel. (01) 606566; telex 33202; Ambassador: HUSSEIN A. MESHARAFA.

Finland: Russell House, Stokes Place, St Stephen's Green, Dublin 2; tel. (01) 781344; telex 92308; fax (01) 783727; Ambassador: OSMO LARES.

France: 36 Ailesbury Rd, Dublin 4; tel. (01) 694777; Ambassador: MICHEL COMBAL.

Germany: 31 Trimleston Ave, Booterstown, Blackrock, Co Dublin; tel. (01) 693011; telex 93809; Ambassador: Dr HELMUTH RUECK-RIEGEL.

Greece: 1 Upper Pembroke St, Dublin 2; tel. (01) 767254; telex 30878; Ambassador: Panayotis A. Tsounis.
Holy See: 183 Navan Rd, Dublin 7 (Apostolic Nunciature); tel. (01) 309344; fax (01) 304561; Apostolic Nuncio: Most Rev. Emanuele Gerada, Titular Archbishop of Nomentum.
India: 6 Leeson Park, Dublin 6; tel. (01) 970843; telex 30670; Ambassador: Prem Shunker.
Iran: 72 Mount Merrion Ave, Blackrock, Co Dublin; tel. 880252; telex 90336; Ambassador: Bahram Ghasemi.
Italy: 63/65 Northumberland Rd, Dublin 4; tel. (01) 601744; telex 93950; fax (01) 682759; Ambassador: Dr Marcello Salimei.
Japan: 22 Ailesbury Rd, Dublin 4; tel. (01) 694244; Ambassador: Y. Hatano.
Korea, Republic: 20 Clyde Rd, Ballsbridge, Dublin 4; tel. (01) 608800; telex 91776; fax (01) 608716; Ambassador: Hyung-ki Min.
Netherlands: 160 Merrion Rd, Ballsbridge, Dublin 4; tel. (01) 693444; telex 93561; fax (01) 839690; Ambassador: E. F. C. Niehe.
Nigeria: 56 Leeson Park, Dublin 6; tel. (01) 604366; telex 24163; Ambassador: A. D. J. Blankson.
Norway: Hainault House, 69/71 St Stephen's Green, Dublin 2; tel. (01) 783133; telex 90173; Ambassador: Kirsten Ohm.
Portugal: Knocksinna House, Knocksinna, Foxrock, Dublin 18; tel. (01) 893375; telex 30777; fax (01) 892849; Ambassador: Pedro José Ribeiro de Menezes.
Spain: 17A Merlyn Park, Dublin 4; tel. (01) 691640; telex 93826; Ambassador: José A. de Yturriaga.
Sweden: Sun Alliance House, 13-17 Dawson St, Dublin 2; tel. (01) 715822; telex 93341; fax (01) 6796718; Ambassador: Margareta Hegardt.
Switzerland: 6 Ailesbury Rd, Ballsbridge, Dublin 4; tel. (01) 692515; telex 93299; fax (01) 830344; Ambassador: Charles Hummel.
Turkey: 11 Clyde Rd, Ballsbridge, Dublin 4; tel. (01) 685240; telex 31563; fax (01) 685014; Ambassador: Halil Dag.
USSR: 184-186 Orwell Rd, Rathgar, Dublin 6; tel. (01) 975748; telex 33622; Ambassador: Gennadi Vasilevich Uranov.
United Kingdom: 31-33 Merrion Rd, Dublin 4; tel. (01) 695211; telex 93717; fax (01) 838423; Ambassador: Sir Nicholas Fenn.
USA: 42 Elgin Rd, Ballsbridge, Dublin 4; tel. (01) 688777; telex 93684; Ambassador: Richard Moore.

Judicial System

Justice is administered in public by Judges appointed by the President on the advice of the Government. The Judges of all Courts are completely independent in the exercise of their judicial functions. The jurisdiction and organization of the Courts are dealt with in the Courts (Establishment and Constitution) Act, 1961, and the Courts (Supplemental Provisions) Acts, 1961 to 1981.

Attorney-General: John Murray.

SUPREME COURT

The Supreme Court: Four Courts, Morgan Place, Dublin 7; tel. (01) 725555; consisting of the Chief Justice and four other Judges, has appellate jurisdiction from all decisions of the High Court. The President of Ireland may, after consultation with the Council of State, refer a Bill which has been passed by both Houses of the Oireachtas (other than a Money Bill or certain others), to the Supreme Court to establish whether it or any other provisions thereof are repugnant to the Constitution.

Chief Justice: Thomas A. Finlay.

Judges:
Francis Griffin.
Anthony Hederman.
Niall McCarthy.
Hugh James O'Flaherty.

COURT OF CRIMINAL APPEAL

The Court of Criminal Appeal, consisting of the Chief Justice or an ordinary Judge of the Supreme Court and two Judges of the High Court, deals with appeals by persons convicted on indictment, where leave to appeal has been granted. The decision of this Court is final unless the Court or Attorney-General or the Director of Public Prosecutions certifies that a point of law involved should, in the public interest, be taken to the Supreme Court.

HIGH COURT

The High Court, consisting of the President of the High Court and 15 ordinary Judges, has full original jurisdiction in, and power to determine, all matters and questions whether of law or fact, civil or criminal. The High Court on circuit acts as an appeal court from the Circuit Court. The Central Criminal Court sits as directed by the President of the High Court to try criminal cases outside the jurisdiction of the Circuit Court. The duty of acting as the Central Criminal Court is assigned, for the time being, to a Judge of the High Court.

President: Liam Hamilton.

Judges:
Sean Gannon, Declan Costello, Ronan Keane, Mella Carroll, Rory O'Hanlon, Henry D. Barron, Francis D. Murphy, Kevin Lynch, Seamus Egan, Robert Barr, Gerard Lardner, John J. Blayney, John J. P. Mackenzie, Richard Johnson, Vivian Lavan.

CIRCUIT AND DISTRICT COURTS

The civil jurisdiction of the Circuit Court is limited to £15,000 in contract and tort and in actions founded on hire-purchase and credit-sale agreements and to a rateable value of £200 in equity, and in probate and administration, but where the parties consent the jurisdiction is unlimited. In criminal matters the Court has jurisdiction in all cases except murder, treason, piracy and allied offences. One Circuit Judge is permanently assigned to each circuit outside Dublin and five to the Dublin circuit. In addition there is one permanently unassigned Judge. The Circuit Court acts as an appeal court from the District Court, which has a summary jurisdiction in a large number of criminal cases where the offence is not of a serious nature. In civil matters the District Court has jurisdiction in contract and tort (except slander, libel, seduction, slander of title, malicious prosecution and false imprisonment) where the claim does not exceed £2,500 and in actions founded on hire-purchase and credit-sale agreements.

All criminal cases except those dealt with summarily by a Justice in the District Court are tried by a Judge and a jury of 12 members. Juries are also used in very many civil cases in the High Court. In a criminal case the jury must be unanimous in reaching a verdict but in a civil case the agreement of nine members is sufficient.

Religion

CHRISTIANITY

The organization of the churches takes no account of the partition of Ireland into two separate political entities. Thus the Republic of Ireland and Northern Ireland are subject to a unified jurisdiction for ecclesiastical purposes. The Roman Catholic Primate of All Ireland and the Church of Ireland (Protestant Episcopalian) Primate of All Ireland now have their seats in Northern Ireland, at Armagh, and the headquarters of the Presbyterian Church in Ireland is at Belfast, Northern Ireland.

At 31 December 1988 the Roman Catholic population of Ireland was estimated to be 3,986,155. In 1984 people belonging to the Presbyterian Church numbered just over 347,000.

Irish Council of Churches: Inter-Church Centre, 48 Elmwood Ave, Belfast, BT9 6AZ, Northern Ireland; tel. (0232) 663145; fax (0232) 381737; f. 1922 (present name adopted 1966); eight mem. churches; Pres. C. M. Barkley; Gen. Sec. David Bleakley.

The Roman Catholic Church

Ireland (including Northern Ireland) comprises four archdioceses and 23 dioceses.

Archbishop of Armagh and Primate of All Ireland: Most Rev. Cahal Daly, Ara Coeli, Cathedral Rd, Armagh, BT61 7QY, Northern Ireland; tel. (0861) 522045.

Archbishop of Cashel and Emly: Most Rev. Dermot Clifford, Archbishop's House, Thurles, Co Tipperary; tel. (0504) 21512.

Archbishop of Dublin and Primate of Ireland: Most Rev. Desmond Connell, Archbishop's House, Drumcondra, Dublin 9; tel. (01) 373732.

Archbishop of Tuam: Most Rev. Joseph Cassidy, St Jarlath's, Tuam, Co Galway; tel. (093) 24166.

Besides the hierarchy, the Roman Catholic Church has numerous religious orders strongly established in the country. These play an important role, particularly in the spheres of education, health and social welfare.

Church of Ireland
(The Anglican Communion)

Ireland (including Northern Ireland) comprises two archdioceses and 10 dioceses.

IRELAND   Directory

Central Office of the Church of Ireland: Church of Ireland House, Church Ave, Rathmines, Dublin 6; tel. (01) 978422; fax (01) 978821; 410,000 mems; Chief Officer and Sec. to the Representative Church Body R. H. SHERWOOD.
Archbishop of Armagh and Primate of All Ireland: Most Rev. ROBERT HENRY ALEXANDER EAMES, The See House, Cathedral Close, Armagh, BT61 7EE, Northern Ireland; tel. (0861) 522851.
Archbishop of Dublin and Primate of Ireland: Most Rev. DONALD CAIRD, The See House, 17 Temple Rd, Milltown, Dublin 6; tel. (01) 977849.

Protestant Churches

Baptist Union of Ireland: 117 Lisburn Rd, Belfast, BT9 7AF; tel. (0232) 663108; fax (0232) 663616; Pres. Pastor R. C. McMULLAN; Sec. Pastor J. R. GRANT.
Lutheran Church: 21 Merlyn Park, Dublin 4; tel. 692529; Rev. PAUL G. FRITZ.
Methodist Church in Ireland: 1 Fountainville Ave, Belfast, BT9 6AN; tel. (0232) 324554; Sec. Rev. EDMUND T. I. MAWHINNEY; Pres. Rev. WILLIAM T. BUCHANAN, Rathcoole Drive, Newtownabbey, BT37 9AQ; tel. (0232) 852546.
Non-Subscribing Presbyterian Church of Ireland: 102 Carrickfergus Rd, Larne, Co Antrim; tel. (0574) 72600; Clerk to Gen. Synod Rev. Dr JOHN W. NELSON.
Presbyterian Church in Ireland: Church House, Fisherwick Place, Belfast, BT1 6DW; tel. (0232) 322284; Moderator of the General Assembly Rt Rev. Dr R. F. G. HOLMES; Clerk of Assembly and Gen. Sec. Rev. S. HUTCHINSON.
The Religious Society of Friends: Swanbrook House, Morehampton Rd, Dublin 4; tel. 683684; Registrar SARAH JACKSON.

BAHÁ'Í FAITH

National Spiritual Assembly: 24 Burlington Rd, Dublin 4; tel. 683150.

JUDAISM

Chief Rabbi: Very Rev. EPHRAIM MIRVIS, Herzog House, Zion Rd, Rathgar, Dublin 6; tel. (01) 967351; fax (01) 967599.

The Press

The Constitution of Ireland provides for the recognition and protection of the fundamental rights of the citizen, including free expression of opinion. Despite the powerful position of the Roman Catholic Church in Ireland there is open discussion on controversial issues. The right of a journalist's professional secrecy is not recognized by the Irish Courts.

Ireland has seven daily newspapers, five in Dublin and two in Cork, including four morning papers which are distributed nationally. There are four national Sunday papers.

DAILIES
Cork

Cork Evening Echo: 95 Patrick St, Cork; tel. (021) 963300; telex 6014; f. 1892; Editorial Dir D. CROSBIE; Editor JAMES O'SULLIVAN; circ. 36,250.
Cork Examiner: 95 Patrick St, Cork; tel. (021) 963300; telex 6014; f. 1841; national; Editor F. O'CALLAGHAN; circ. 63,560.

Dublin

Evening Herald: Independent House, 90 Middle Abbey St, Dublin 1; tel. (01) 731333; f. 1891; independent national; Editor MICHAEL BROPHY; circ. 132,314.
Evening Press: Tara House, Tara St, Dublin 2; tel. (01) 713333; fax (01) 713097; f. 1954; Editor SEAN WARD; circ. 101,962.
Irish Independent: Independent House, 90 Middle Abbey St, Dublin 1; tel. (01) 731666; telex 33472; fax (01) 720304; f. 1905; non-party; Editor VINCENT DOYLE; circ. 154,586.
Irish Press: Tara House, Tara St, Dublin 2; tel. (01) 713333; telex 93752; f. 1931; independent; Editor H. LAMBERT; circ. 86,655.
The Irish Times: 11-15 D'Olier St, Dublin 2; tel. (01) 6792022; telex 93639; fax (01) 6793910; f. 1859; independent national; Editor CONOR BRADY; circ. 93,187.

WEEKLY AND OTHER NEWSPAPERS

An Phoblacht (Republican News): 58 Parnell Sq., Dublin 1; tel. (01) 733611; fax (01) 733074; weekly; party newspaper of Sinn Fein; circ. 43,000.
Anglo-Celt: Anglo-Celt Place, Cavan; tel. (049) 31100; f. 1846; Friday; nationalist; Editor J. F. O'HANLON; circ. 16,768 (incl. USA and Canada).
Argus: Argus Newspapers Ltd, Jocelyn St, Dundalk; tel. (042) 31500; fax (042) 31643; f. 1835; Thursday; Editor KEVIN MULLIGAN; circ. 10,000.
Cavan Leader: 21 Farnham St, Cavan; tel. (049) 32777; fax (049) 32026; Wednesday; Editor EUGENE McGEE; circ. 10,500.
Clare Champion: O'Connell St, Ennis, Co Clare; tel. (065) 28105; fax (065) 20374; f. 1903; Thursday; independent; Editor J. F. O'DEA; Man. Dir F. GALVIN; circ. 21,040.
Connacht Tribune: Market St, Galway; tel. (091) 67251; fax (091) 67970; f. 1909; Friday; nationalist; Editor J. CUNNINGHAM; circ. 29,712.
Connaught Telegraph: Ellison St, Castlebar, Co Mayo; tel. (094) 21711; f. 1828; Wednesday; Man. Dir J. CONNOLLY; Editor TOM COURELL; circ. 12,000.
Derry People and Donegal News: Crossview House, High Rd, Letterkenny, Co Donegal; tel. (074) 21014; f. 1902; Saturday; nationalist; Editor T. QUIGLEY.
Donegal Democrat: Donegal Rd, Ballyshannon, Co Donegal; tel. (072) 51201; fax (072) 51945; f. 1919; Friday; Man. Dir CECIL J. KING; Editor JOHN BROMLEY; circ. 19,031.
Drogheda Independent: 9 Shop St, Drogheda, Co Louth; tel. (041) 38658; f. 1884; Thursday; Editor PAUL MURPHY; circ. 16,491.
Dundalk Democrat: 3 Earl St, Dundalk, Co Louth; tel. (042) 34058; fax (042) 31399; f. 1849; Saturday; independent; Editor T. P. ROE; circ. 18,400.
East Cork News: 25 Michael St, Waterford; tel. (051) 74951; f. 1981; Wednesday; Editor PETER DOYLE.
Echo and South Leinster Advertiser: Mill Park Rd, Enniscorthy, Co Wexford; tel. (054) 33231; fax (054) 33506; f. 1902; Wednesday; independent; Editor JAMES GAHAN; circ. 21,500.
The Guardian: The People Newspapers Ltd, 1 North Main St, Wexford; tel. (053) 22155; f. 1881; Friday; Man Dir MICHAEL ROCHE; circ. 37,141.
Iris Oifigiuil (Dublin Gazette): Stationery Office, Dublin 8; tel. (01) 781666; fax (01) 780645; f. 1922; Tuesday and Friday; official paper publ. under government authority; Editor The Controller.
Irish Catholic: 55 Lower Gardiner St, Dublin 1; tel. (01) 747538; fax (01) 364805; f. 1888; Thursday; Editor NICK LUNDBERG; circ. 40,100.
The Kerryman (The Corkman): Clash Industrial Estate, Tralee, Co Kerry; tel. (066) 21666; telex 28100; fax (066) 21608; f. 1904; Thursday; independent; Editor BRIAN LOONEY; circ. 36,594.
Kilkenny People: 34 High St, Kilkenny; tel. (056) 21015; fax (056) 21414; f. 1892; independent nationalist weekly; Editor and Man. Dir JOHN E. KERRY KEANE; circ. 17,825.
Leinster Express: Dublin Rd, Portlaoise, Co Laois; tel. (0502) 21666; fax (0502) 20491; f. 1831; Wednesday for Saturday; Editor TEDDY FENNELLY; circ. 17,050.
Leinster Leader: 19 South Main St, Naas, Co Kildare; tel. (045) 97302; f. 1880; Saturday; nationalist; Editor S. CARROLL; circ. 14,000.
Leitrim Observer: St George's Terrace, Carrick-on-Shannon, Co Leitrim; tel. (078) 20025; fax (078) 20112; f. 1889; Wednesday; national; Editor G. DUNNE; circ. 11,400.
Limerick Chronicle: 54 O'Connell St, Limerick; tel. (061) 45233; fax (061) 314804; f. 1766; Tuesday; independent; Editor BRENDAN HALLIGAN; circ. 8,000.
Limerick Echo and Shannon News: 51 O'Connell St, Limerick; tel. (061) 49966; f. 1897; Thursday; independent; Editor MARTIN BYRNES; circ. 12,500.
Limerick Leader: 54 O'Connell St, Limerick; tel. (061) 315233; fax (061) 314804; f. 1889; 3 a week; independent; Editor BRENDAN HALLIGAN; circ. Monday and Wednesday 3,788, Friday 33,901.
Longford Leader: Market Sq., Longford; tel. (043) 45241; fax (043) 41489; f. 1897; Friday; independent; Editor EUGENE McGEE; circ. 19,500.
Mayo News: The Fairgreen, Westport, Co Mayo; tel. (098) 25365; fax (098) 26108; f. 1892; Wednesday; independent; Man. Editor SEAN STAUNTON; circ. 12,000.
Meath Chronicle and Cavan and Westmeath Herald: 12 Market Sq., Navan, Co Meath; tel. (046) 21442; fax (046) 23565; f. 1897; Saturday; Man. Dir JOHN T. DAVIS; Editor JAMES DAVIS; circ. 17,500.
Midland Tribune: Emmet St, Birr, Co Offaly; tel. (0509) 20003; f. 1881; Wednesday; national; Editor J. I. FANNING; circ. 10,000.
The Munster Express: 37 The Quay and 1-6 Hanover St, Waterford; tel. (051) 72141; fax (051) 77285; f. 1859; independent; 2 a week; Editor and Gov. Dir J. J. WALSH; circ. 19,125.
Nationalist and Leinster Times: 42 Tullow St, Carlow, Co Carlow; tel. (0503) 31731; telex 31442; f. 1883; Wednesday for Friday;

IRELAND

independent; Man. Dir Tom Geoghegan; Editor Tom Mooney; circ. 18,909.

Nationalist and Munster Advertiser: Nationalist Newspaper Co Ltd, Queen St, Clonmel, Tipperary; tel. (052) 22211; f. 1890; Thursday for Saturday; nationalist; Editor Brendan Long; circ. 14,484.

New Ross Standard: 1 North Main St, Wexford; tel. (053) 22155; f. 1880; Friday; Proprs The People Newspapers Ltd; Man. Dir Michael Roche; circ. 37,141.

The Northern Standard: The Diamond, Monaghan; tel. (047) 82188; fax (047) 84070; f. 1839; Friday; county newspaper of Co Monaghan; Editor P. Smyth; circ. 13,250.

Offaly Express: Harbour St, Tullamore, Co Offaly; tel. (0506) 21744; Editor Teddy Fennelly; circ. 5,845.

Roscommon Champion: Church St, Roscommon; tel. (0903) 25051; fax (0903) 25053; f. 1927; weekly; news, features and sport; Editor Seamus Dooley; circ. 10,000.

Sligo Champion: Wine St, Sligo; tel. (071) 69222; fax (071) 69040; f. 1836; Wednesday; nationalist; Editor S. Finn; circ. 26,519.

Southern Star: Skibbereen, Co Cork; tel. (028) 21200; f. 1889; Saturday; non-political; Editor W. J. O'Regan; circ. 17,408.

Sunday Independent: Independent House, 90 Middle Abbey St, Dublin; tel. (01) 731666; telex 33472; fax (01) 720304; f. 1905; non-party; Editor Aengus Fanning; circ. 238,000.

The Sunday Press: Tara House, Tara St, Dublin 2; tel. (01) 713333; telex 25353; fax (01) 713097; f. 1949; independent; Editor Michael Keane; circ. 207,000.

Sunday Tribune: 15 Lower Baggot St, Dublin 2; tel. (01) 615555; telex 90995; fax (01) 615302; f. 1980; Editor Vincent Browne.

Sunday World: Newspaper House, 18 Rathfarnham Rd, Terenure, Dublin 6; tel. (01) 901980; telex 24886; fax (01) 901838; f. 1973; Editor Colin McClelland; circ. 327,104.

Tipperary Star: Friar St, Thurles, Co Tipperary; tel. (0504) 21122; f. 1909; Saturday; independent; Editor Michael Dundon; circ. 10,983.

Tullamore Tribune: Church St, Tullamore, Co Offaly; tel. (0506) 21152; fax (0506) 21927; f. 1978; Wednesday; Editor G. V. Oakley; circ. 5,000.

Waterford News & Star: 25 Michael St, Waterford; tel. (051) 74951; f. 1848; Thursday; Editor P. Doyle; circ. 18,621.

Western People: Francis St, Ballina, Co Mayo; tel. (096) 21188; fax (096) 70208; f. 1883; Tuesday; independent nationalist; Editor Terence Reilly; Gen. Man. Gerry Walsh; circ. 28,242.

Westmeath Examiner: 19 Dominick St, Mullingar, Co Westmeath; tel. (044) 48426; fax (044) 48426; f. 1882; weekly; Man. Dir Nicholas J. Nally; circ. 13,135.

Westmeath Independent and Offaly Independent: Gleeson St, Athlone, Co Westmeath; tel. (0902) 72003; fax (0902) 72003; f. 1846; Thursday; Editor Margaret Grennan; circ. 13,180.

Wicklow People: Independent House, 90 Middle Abbey St, Dublin 1; tel. (01) 731666; f. 1883; Friday; Proprs The People Newspapers Ltd; Man. Dir Ray Doyle; Editor Dermot Walsh; circ. 36,536.

SELECTED PERIODICALS

Aspect: POB 15, New Rd, Greystones, Co Wicklow; tel. (0404) 875514; fax (0404) 760773; f. 1982; monthly; current affairs; Editor John O'Neill.

Banking Ireland: Belenos Publications, 50 Fitzwilliam Sq., Dublin 2; tel. (01) 764587; fax (01) 619781; f. 1898; quarterly; journal of the Institute of Bankers in Ireland; Editor Gerry Lawlor; circ. 13,000.

Business & Finance: 50 Fitzwilliam Sq., Dublin 2; tel. (01) 764587; fax (01) 764587; f. 1964; weekly; Editor Brian O'Connor; Man. Editor W. Ambrose; circ. 11,355.

Caritas (1934) Ireland: St Augustine's, Blackrock, Co Dublin; tel. (01) 885518; quarterly; publ. by The Hospitaller Brothers of St John of God; covers the Order's health services in Ireland.

Horizon: 2-6 Tara St, Dublin 2; tel. (01) 713500; fax (01) 713074; bimonthly; publ. by Jude Publications Ltd; circ. 8,000.

Hot Press: 13 Trinity St, Dublin 2; tel. (01) 6795077; fax (01) 6795097; fortnightly; music, leisure, current affairs; Editor Niall Stokes; circ. 21,500.

In Dublin: 129 Lower Baggot St, Dublin 2; tel. (01) 785411; fax (01) 785536; f. 1976; fortnightly; listings and reviews of theatre, music, restaurants, exhibitions, news and current affairs; Editor Damian Corless; circ. 15,000.

Industry and Commerce: 2-6 Tara St, Dublin 2; tel. (01) 713500; fax (01) 713074; monthly; publ. by Jude Publications Ltd; circ. 10,000.

Ireland of the Welcomes: Baggot St Bridge, Dublin 2; tel. (01) 765871; fax (01) 764764; f. 1952; every 2 months; publ. by Irish Tourist Board; Irish cultural items; Publr Trevor Byne; Editor Peter Harbison; circ. 125,000.

Ireland's Own: North Main St, Wexford; tel. 22155; f. 1902; weekly; stories, articles, serials, cartoons, family reading; Editor Austin Channing; circ. 52,341.

Irish Business: 128 Lower Baggot St, Dublin 2; tel. (01) 619236; fax (01) 612417; f. 1975; monthly; Editor Andrew Whittaker; circ. 9,687.

Irish Doctor: 2-6 Tara St, Dublin 2; tel. (01) 713500; fax (01) 713074; f. 1987; publ. by Jude Publications Ltd; Editor Dr Aidan Meade; circ. 6,500.

The Irish Exporter: 2-6 Tara St, Dublin 2; tel. (01) 713500; fax (01) 713074; monthly; publ. by Jude Publications Ltd; circ. 8,500.

Irish Farmers' Journal: The Irish Farm Centre, Bluebell, Dublin 12; tel. (01) 501166; fax (01) 520876; f. 1948; weekly; Editor Matthew Dempsey; circ. 71,424.

Irish Field: POB 74, 11-15 D'Olier St, Dublin 2; tel. (01) 6792022; fax (01) 6793029; f. 1870; Saturday; horse-racing, show-jumping and breeding; Proprs The Irish Times Ltd; Man. Editor V. Lamb; circ. 11,210.

Irish Journal of Medical Science: Royal Academy of Medicine in Ireland, 6 Kildare St, Dublin 2; tel. (01) 767650; fax (01) 611684; f. 1832; monthly; organ of the Royal Academy of Medicine; Editor Dr John F. Murphy.

Irish Law Reports Monthly: The Round Hall Press, Kill Lane, Blackrock, Co Dublin; tel. (01) 892922; fax (01) 893072; f. 1981; Sr Editor Bart Daly.

Irish Law Times: The Round Hall Press, Kill Lane, Blackrock, Co Dublin; tel. (01) 2892922; fax (01) 2893072; f. 1867; monthly; Editor Bart Daly.

Irish Marketing Journal: 59 Upper Georges St, Dun Laoghaire, Co Dublin; tel. (01) 800692; fax (01) 802226; f. 1974; monthly; Editor Norman Barry; circ. 5,300.

IT-Irish Tatler: 46 Lower Leeson St, Dublin 2; tel. (01) 611811; fax (01) 612830; f. 1890; Man. Editor Nell Stewart-Liberty; circ. 27,138.

Magill: 15 Lower Baggot St, Dublin 2; tel. (01) 606055; f. 1977; 14 issues a year; deals with Irish current affairs; Publr Vincent Browne; Editor (vacant); circ. 20,500.

Management: Jemma Publications Ltd, 22 Brookfield Ave, Blackrock, Co Dublin; tel. (01) 886946; telex 90169; f. 1954; monthly; Editor Frank Corr; circ. 7,500.

Motoring Life: G. P. Publications, 48 North Great George's St, Dublin 1; tel. (01) 721636; f. 1946; monthly; Editor Fergal K. Herbert; circ. 12,000.

The Pioneer: 27 Upper Sherrard St, Dublin 1; tel. (01) 749464; f. 1948; monthly; official organ of Pioneer Total Abstinence Association of the Sacred Heart; Editor Rev. J. C. Smyth; circ. 20,000.

RTE Guide: Radio Telefís Éireann, Donnybrook, Dublin 4; tel. (01) 642720; weekly programme of the Irish broadcasting service; Editor John Walsh; circ. 123,041.

Reality: Redemptorist Publications, 75 Orwell Rd, Rathgar, Dublin 6; tel. (01) 961688; f. 1936; Christian monthly; Editor Rev. Kevin H. Donlon; circ. 20,000.

Social and Personal: 46 Lower Leeson St, Dublin 2; tel. (01) 611811; fax (01) 612830; Man. Editor Nell Stewart-Liberty; circ. 10,000.

Studies: 35 Lower Leeson St, Dublin 2; tel. (01) 766785; f. 1912; quarterly review of letters, history, religious and social questions; Editor Noel Barber.

U Magazine: 126 Lower Baggot St, Dublin 2; tel. (01) 608264; f. 1979; monthly; women's interest; Editor Marlene Lyng; circ. 25,915.

Woman's Way: 126 Lower Baggot St, Dublin 2; tel. (01) 608264; f. 1963; weekly; Editor Celine Naughton; circ. 70,800.

NEWS AGENCIES

There is no national news agency.

Foreign Bureaux

Agenzia Nazionale Stampa Associata (ANSA) (Italy): 4 Idrone Close, Templeogue, Dublin 16; tel. 766662; Bureau Chief Enzo Farinella.

Reuters Ltd (UK): Kestrel House, Clanwilliam Place, off Lower Mount St, Dublin 2; tel. (01) 603377; fax (01) 603840; Correspondent Paul Majendie.

Telegrafnoye Agentstvo Sovetskovo Soyuza (TASS) (USSR): 59 Glenbrook Park, Dublin 14; Correspondent Igor Ponomarev.

PRESS ORGANIZATION

Provincial Newspapers Association of Ireland: 33 Parkgate St, Dublin 8; tel. (01) 6793679; f. 1917; 37 mems; association of Irish

IRELAND   Directory

provincial newspapers; Pres. B. G. CUNNINGHAM; Sec. UNA SHERIDAN.

Publishers

Anvil Books Ltd: 45 Palmerston Rd, Dublin 6; tel (01) 973628; f. 1964; imprint: The Children's Press; biography, Irish history, folklore, sociology, children's; Man. Dir R. DARDIS.

Arlen House—The Women's Press: Kinnear Court, 16-20 South Cumberland St, Dublin 2; tel. (01) 717383; f. 1977; fiction, biography, classics, poetry and women's studies; Chief Exec. CATHERINE ROSE.

The Blackwater Press: c/o Folens & Co Ltd, Airton Rd, Tallaght, Dublin 24; tel. (01) 515311; fax (01) 515306; fiction, political, sport, history, Irish; Man. Dir JOHN O'CONNOR.

Boole Press Ltd: POB 5, Dún Laoghaire, Co Dublin; tel. (01) 808025; fax (01) 802523; f. 1979; scientific, technical, medical, scholarly; Chair M. O'REILLY.

Comhairle Bhéaloideas Éireann: University College, Belfield, Dublin 4; University College Dublin Press.

The Dolmen Press Ltd: f. 1951; poetry, literary; Publr LIAM MILLER.

Duffy, James & Co Ltd: 21 Shaw St, Dublin 2; f. 1830; official Catholic publications, religious books, works of Irish interest, plays; Man. Dir EOIN O'KEEFFE.

Dundalgan Press (W. Tempest) Ltd: Francis St, Dundalk; tel. (042) 34013; fax (042) 32351; f. 1859; historical and biographical works; Sec. BRIAN A. MCQUAID.

Eason & Son Ltd: 66 Middle Abbey St, Dublin 1; tel. (01) 733811; telex 32566; fax (01) 730620; f. 1886; general Irish interest; Chair. W. H. CLARKE.

Educational Co of Ireland Ltd: POB 43A, Ballymount Rd, Walkinstown, Dublin 12; tel. (01) 500611; fax (01) 500993; f. 1877, inc. 1910; school textbooks; Dirs F. MAGUIRE, S. O'NEILL, URSULA NÍ DHÁLAIGH.

C. J. Fallon Ltd: POB 1054, Lucan Rd, Palmerstown, Dublin 20; tel. (01) 265777; f. 1927; educational; Man. Dir H. J. MCNICHOLAS.

Folens and Co Ltd: Airton Rd, Tallaght, Co Dublin; tel. (01) 515311; educational; Man. Dir D. FOLENS.

Four Courts Press: Kill Lane, Blackrock, Co Dublin; tel. (01) 892922; fax (01) 893072; f. 1977; philosophy, theology; Man. Dir MICHAEL ADAMS.

Gallery Press: Loughcrew, Oldcastle, Co Meath; tel. (049) 41779; f. 1970; poetry, plays, prose by Irish authors; Chief Execs PETER FALLON, JEAN BARRY.

Gill and Macmillan Ltd: Goldenbridge, Inchicore, Dublin 8; tel. (01) 531005; telex 92197; fax (01) 541688; f. 1968; literature, biography, history, social sciences, theology, philosophy and textbooks; Man. Dir M. H. GILL.

Irish Academic Press: Kill Lane, Blackrock, Co Dublin; tel. (01) 2892922; fax (01) 2893072; f. 1974; imprints: Irish University Press, Irish Academic Press, Ecclesia Press; history, travel, literature, bibliography; Man. Dir MICHAEL ADAMS.

Mercier Press Ltd: 4 Bridge St, POB 5, Cork; tel. (021) 504022; telex 75463; fax (021) 504216; f. 1946; Irish folklore, history, law, music, bibliography, religious; Man. Dir JOHN SPILLANE.

The O'Brien Press: 20 Victoria Rd, Rathgar, Dublin 6; tel. (01) 979598; fax (01) 979274; f. 1974; fiction, biography, history, general, children's; Man. Dir MICHAEL O'BRIEN; Gen. Editor IDE NÍ LAOGHAIRE.

Phoenix Publishing Co Ltd: 20 Parnell Sq., Dublin 1; tel. (01) 749215; educational; Dirs W. SHORTLAND, R. WALKER.

Poolbeg Press Ltd: Knocksedan House, Forrest Great, Swords, Co Dublin; tel. (01) 407433; fax (01) 403753; f. 1976; general; Editor JO O'DONOGHUE.

The Round Hall Press: Kill Lane, Blackrock, Co Dublin; tel. (01) 892922; fax (01) 893072; law books and journals; Man. Dir BART DALY.

Runa Press: 2 Belgrave Terrace, Monkstown, Co Dublin; tel. (01) 801869; f. 1942; belles-lettres, educational (university), essays, poetry, science, philosophy; Dir RHODA HANAGHAN.

Veritas Publications: Veritas House, 7-8 Lower Abbey St, Dublin 1; tel. (01) 788177; fax (01) 786507; f. 1900; general, religion, school textbooks, audio, video tapes, multi-media education kits; Dir Rev. MARTIN TIERNEY.

Wolfhound Press: 68 Mountjoy Sq., Dublin 1; tel. 740354; f. 1974; literature, biography, art, children's, fiction, history; Publr SEAMUS CASHMAN.

Government Publishing House
Stationery Office: Bishop St, Dublin 8; tel. (01) 781666.

PUBLISHERS' ASSOCIATION

Cumann Leabharfhoilsitheoirí Éireann (CLÉ) (Irish Book Publishers' Association): Book House Ireland, 65 Middle Abbey St, Dublin 1; tel. (01) 730108; f. 1970; 55 mems; Pres. ALEX MILLER; Admin. CECILY GOLDEN.

Radio and Television

There were an estimated 2,125,000 radio receivers in use in 1988, and 870,763 licensed television receivers in use in 1989. Under the Radio and Television Act of 1988, provision was made for an independent television station, an independent national radio service and a series of 23 regional stations.

Radio Telefís Éireann (RTE): Donnybrook, Dublin 4; tel. (01) 693111; telex 93700; fax (01) 838140; autonomous statutory corporation, f. 1960 under the Broadcasting Authority Act; controls and operates radio and television in the Republic; operations are financed by repayable state loans to a permitted limit of I£25m. and surpluses earned on the operating account, and the current expenditure by net licence revenue and sale of advertising time; governed by Authority of nine, appointed by the Government; Chair. of Authority JAMES P. CULLITON; Dir-Gen. VINCENT FINN; Dir of Programmes (Television) BOB COLLINS; Dir of Programmes (Radio) KEVIN HEALY.

The Independent Radio and Television Commission (IRTC): Marine House, Clanwilliam Court, Dublin 2; tel (01) 760966; fax (01) 760948; f. 1988; established by the Government to ensure the creation, development and monitoring of independent broadcasting in Ireland; operations are financed by franchise levies paid by franchised stations; Chair. SEAMUS HENCHY; Sec. MICHAEL O'KEEFFE.

RADIO

RTE broadcasts on two channels (Radio 1 and Radio 2) approx. 262 hours a week, Cork local radio 13 hours a week and community radio 8-9 hours a week. Advertising is limited to 10% of transmission time.

Raidió na Gaeltachta: Casla, Connamara, Co Galway; tel. (091) 72235; telex 50815; f. 1972; broadcasts a minimum of 74 hours per week for Irish-speaking communities; financed by RTE; Controller BREANDÁN FEIRITÉAR; c. 60,000 listeners.

Century Radio: 1 Christchurch Sq., High St, Dublin 8; tel. (01) 533666; fax (01) 537922; national independent radio franchise; Controller BOB HOPTON.

TELEVISION

Reception of both RTE-1, from seven main transmitters, and of RTE-2 is available to 98% of the population. Advertising is limited to 10% of transmission time. Regular transmissions: c. 3,400 hours yearly on RTE-1, 2,300 hours on RTE-2.

TV3: 4 Windmill Lane, Dublin 2; tel. (01) 713444; fax (01) 718413; awarded the franchise for an independent television channel in April 1989; scheduled to begin broadcasting in late 1991; Man. Dir JAMES MORRIS.

Finance

(cap. = capital; p.u. = paid up; auth. = authorized; res = reserves; dep. = deposits; m. = million; brs = branches; amounts in Irish pounds unless otherwise stated)

BANKING

Bank Ceannais na hÉireann (Central Bank of Ireland): POB 559, Dame St, Dublin 2; tel. (01) 716666; telex 31041; fax (01) 716561; f. 1942; sole issuer of Irish currency in the State; cap. and res I£894.0m., dep. I£1,503.6m. (Dec. 1987); Gov. M. F. DOYLE; Gen. Man. TIMOTHY O'GRADY-WALSHE.

Principal Banks

AIB Capital Markets PLC: Bankcentre, Ballsbridge, Dublin 4; tel. (01) 604733; telex 93917; fax (01) 604773; f. 1966; formerly Allied Irish Investment Bank PLC; merchant banking, corporate finance and investment management; cap. p.u. I£8m., dep. I£833.6m. (Feb. 1989); Man. Dir THOMAS P. MULCAHY; Sec. D. COVENEY.

AIB Group: POB 452, Bankcentre, Ballsbridge, Dublin 4; tel. (01) 600311; telex 93768; fax (01) 604773; f. 1966; formerly Allied Irish

IRELAND

Directory

Banks PLC; mem. of Associated Banks; cap. p.u. I£252.8m., dep. I£14,304m. (March 1990); Chair. PETER SUTHERLAND; Group CEO GERALD B. SCANLAN; 253 brs and sub-brs in the Republic of Ireland, 73 brs in Northern Ireland and Great Britain, 5 overseas brs and 1 rep. office.

Algemene Bank Nederland (Ireland) Ltd: 121-122 St Stephen's Green, Dublin 2; tel. (01) 717333; telex 93473; fax (01) 717689; f. 1972; wholly-owned subsidiary of Algemene Bank Nederland NV, Amsterdam; cap. I£11.4m., dep. I£435.4m. (Dec. 1989); Chair. D. E. WILLIAMS; Chief Exec. G. D. WOODS.

Anglo Irish Bank Corporation PLC: Stephen Court, 18-21 St Stephen's Green, Dublin 2; tel. (01) 763225; f. 1964; merchant bank concerned primarily with retail banking, instalment credit, leasing and treasury; acquired by City of Dublin Bank Group 1978; cap. auth. I£60m., issued I£29.1m., assets I£350m. (1989); Chair. A. G. MURPHY; CEO SEAN FITZPATRICK.

Ansbacher & Co Ltd: 52 Lower Leeson St, Dublin 2; tel. (01) 613699; telex 93241; fax (01) 600604; f. 1950; cap. p.u. I£5m., dep. I£117.6m. (Dec. 1989); Chair. J. LIPPER; Man. Dir G. J. MOLONEY.

Bank of America NT & SA: Russell Court, St Stephen's Green, Dublin 2; tel. (01) 781222; telex 93817; fax (01) 755906; Vice-Pres. and Country Man. PETER STRATFORD.

Bank of Ireland: Head Office: Lower Baggot St, Dublin 2; tel. (01) 615933; telex 93427; fax (01) 615671; 54 Donegall Place, Belfast BT1 5BX; tel. (0232) 244901; telex 74327; fax (0232) 248705; 36 Queen St, London EC4R 1BN; tel. (01) 3274500; fax (01) 4891886; f. 1783; cap. I£249m.; dep. I£9,986m. (1989); mem. of Associated Banks; Gov. Dr W. J. L. RYAN; CEO PATRICK MOLLOY; brs in Britain, Northern Ireland, Jersey, Hong Kong, New York and Cayman Islands, rep. offices in Brussels and Frankfurt.

Banque Nationale de Paris (Ireland) Ltd: 111 St Stephen's Green West, Dublin 2; tel. (01) 712811; telex 90641; fax (01) 713884; cap. p.u. I£8.6m., dep. I£577.1m.; Chair. E. PHILIPPON; Gen. Man. PAUL-FRANÇOIS GAUVIN.

Barclays Bank PLC: 47/48 St Stephen's Green, Dublin 2; tel. (01) 611777; telex 30427; fax (01) 600139; Gen. Man. for Ireland J. D. C. BURKE.

Chase Bank (Ireland) PLC: 10-11 South Leinster St, Dublin 2; tel. (01) 763788; fax (01) 763051; wholly-owned subsidiary of Chase Manhattan Overseas Banking Corpn; cap. I£2m., dep. I£0.2m. (Dec. 1989); Man. Dir DOUGLAS K. BONNAR; Sec. D. WHITE.

Guinness and Mahon Ltd: 17 College Green, Dublin 2; tel. (01) 6796944; telex 93667; fax (01) 720642; f. 1836; affiliated to Guinness, Mahon and Co Ltd, London; cap. auth. I£7.3m., dep. I£147m.; Chair. CHARLES T. G. DILLON; Chief Exec. MICHAEL J. PENDER.

Hill Samuel Bank (Ireland) Ltd: Hill Samuel House, Adelaide Rd, Dublin 2; tel. (01) 760444; telex 93760; f. 1964; wholly-owned subsidiary within the TSB group; cap. I£8.5m., res I£10.9m., dep. I£401m. (Oct. 1989); Chair. E. A. EMERSON; Man. Dir S. O'SHEA.

Industrial Credit Corporation PLC: 32-34 Harcourt St, Dublin 2; tel. (01) 720055; telex 93220; fax (01) 717797; f. 1933; state-owned; industrial and commercial financing; cap. I£11.9m., dep. I£603m. (Dec. 1989); Chair. J. T. BARTON; Man. Dir F. A. CASEY.

Investment Bank of Ireland Ltd: 26 Fitzwilliam Place, Dublin 2; tel. (01) 616433; telex 93811; fax (01) 616688; f. 1966; merchant bank; subsidiary of Bank of Ireland; cap. p.u. I£6m., dep. I£2,004.1m. (March 1990); Chair. M. A. KEANE.

Irish Bank of Commerce Ltd: 52/53 Harcourt St, Dublin 2; tel. (01) 756411; telex 90880; fax (01) 751795; f. 1973; merchant bank; subsidiary of Crédit Commercial de France; cap. I£2m., res I£977,000, dep. I£114.5m. (1986); Chair. A. G. MURPHY; CEO GERARD A. E. WATSON.

Irish Intercontinental Bank Ltd: 91 Merrion Sq., Dublin 2; tel. (01) 760291; telex 33322; fax (01) 785034; f. 1973; subsidiary of Kredietbank NV, Antwerp, Belgium; merchant bank; cap. issued I£7m.; dep. I£584.3m. (Dec. 1988); Chair. D. MCALEESE; CEO PATRICK MCEVOY.

National Irish Bank Financial Services Co Ltd: 7-8 Wilton Terrace, Dublin 2; tel. (01) 785066; fax (01) 785269; f. 1989; nominal cap. I£250,000; Chief Exec. J. LACEY; Man. N. D'ARCY.

National Irish Investment Bank Ltd: 7 Wilton Terrace, Dublin 2; tel. (01) 785066; telex 93347; fax (01) 614165; f. 1969; merchant bank; subsidiary of the National Irish Bank Ltd; cap. issued I£9.75m. (Dec. 1987); Chair. J. LACEY; Gen. Man. N. FROST.

Smurfit Paribas Bank Ltd: 94 St Stephen's Green, Dublin 2; tel. (01) 774573; telex 90951; fax (01) 783435; f. 1983; merchant bank; Chair. IVOR KENNY; CEO RAY CURRAN.

UDT Bank Ltd: 13-16 Fleet St, Dublin 2; tel. (01) 713311; telex 91110; Chair. DON C. MCCRICKARD.

Ulster Bank Ltd: 33 College Green, Dublin 2; tel. (01) 777623; telex 747334; fax (01) 322097; and 47 Donegall Place, Belfast, BT1 5AU; tel. (0232) 320222; telex 747334; fax (0232) 322097; subsidiary of National Westminster Bank PLC (United Kingdom); cap. p.u. I£20m., dep. I£2,933m. (Dec. 1989); Chair. Dr W. G. H. QUIGLEY; CEO DAVID WENT; 157 brs.

Ulster Investment Bank Ltd: 2 Hume St, Dublin 2; tel. (01) 613444; telex 93980; fax (01) 763021; f. 1973; mem. of National Westminster Bank Group; cap. I£3m.; res I£34.1m., dep. I£1,087m. (Sept. 1989); Chair. MARTIN RAFFERTY; CEO BRIAN MCCONNELL.

Westdeutsche Landesbank (Ireland) Ltd: 18 Dawson St, Dublin 2; tel. (01) 776951; telex 93926; fax (01) 712234; f. 1978; Standard Chartered Bank Ireland Ltd until 1990; cap. I£5m.; Chair. J. ROCHE; Man. Dir N. J. HUME.

Woodchester Investment Bank Ltd: Woodchester House, Golden Lane, Dublin 8; tel. (01) 796811; telex 93243; fax (01) 796420; f. 1972; merchant bank; formerly Trinity Bank; wholly-owned subsidiary of Woodchester Investments PLC; cap. p.u. I£3.1m., res I£1.3m., dep. I£43.8m. (March 1989); Chair. CRAIG MCKINNEY; Man. Dir PAUL CRAN.

Savings Banks

Post Office Savings Bank: College House, Townsend St, Dublin 2; tel. (01) 728888; telex 33444; fax (01) 6795765; dep. I£1,831m. (Dec. 1989); f. 1861; Man. of Savings R. MCDONNELL; over 1,400 brs.

Association of Trustee Savings Banks in Ireland: Administration Centre, Douglas, Cork; tel. (021) 361301; telex 75347; fax (021) 364703; f. 1817; total assets exceed I£800m.; Jt Secs M. N. CONLON, G. F. WALSH.

Banking Associations

The Institute of Bankers in Ireland: Nassau House, Nassau St, Dublin 2; tel. (01) 6793311; fax (01) 6793504; f. 1898; Pres. G. B. SCANLAN; CEO and Sec. PATRICK J. ROCK.

Irish Bankers' Federation: Nassau House, Nassau St, Dublin 2; tel. (01) 715311; telex 93957; fax (01) 6796680; Dir-Gen. JAMES A. BARDON; Pres. GERALD B. SCANLAN.

STOCK EXCHANGE

The Stock Exchange (Irish Unit): 24-28 Anglesea St, Dublin 2; tel. (01) 778808; telex 93437; f. 1799 as the Dublin Stock Exchange; merged in 1971 with the Cork Stock Exchange to form the Irish Stock Exchange; amalgamated in 1973 with the United Kingdom stock exchanges to form The Stock Exchange, centred in London; Pres. K. BEATON; Gen. Man. TOM HEALY; 99 mems.

Irish Futures and Options Exchange: Segrave House, Earlsfort Terrace, Dublin 2; tel. (01) 1767413; f. 1989; Chief Exec. DIARMUID BRADLEY; 24 mems.

INSURANCE
Principal Companies

Abbey Life Assurance (Ireland) Ltd: Abbey Life House, Temple Rd, Blackrock, Co Dublin; tel. (01) 832377; fax (01) 832036; f. 1981; Chair. P. A. C. SEYMOUR; Gen. Man. J. L. RENNIE.

Cornhill Insurance PLC: Russell Court, St Stephen's Green, Dublin 2; tel. (01) 730622; fax (01) 781327; Man. B. J. GLASCOTT.

Eagle Star Insurance Co Ltd: Shield House, 45-47 Pembroke Rd, Ballsbridge, Dublin 4; tel. (01) 683943; telex 30737; fax (01) 684897.

Guardian Royal Exchange Assurance PLC: 35-38 St Stephen's Green, Dublin 2; tel. (01) 61500; fax (01) 615523; f. 1968; Chair. J. E. H. COLLINS; Man. Dir P. R. DUGDALE.

Hibernian Insurance Co Ltd: Haddington Rd, Dublin 4; tel. (01) 608288; telex 30872; f. 1908; Hibernian Fire and General Insurance Co Ltd; fire and general; cap. p.u. 2m.; Chair. D. EDMUND WILLIAMS; Dir and Gen. Man. E. F. WALSH.

Insurance Corporation of Ireland PLC: Burlington House, Burlington Rd, Dublin 4; tel. (01) 601377; telex 93618; fax (01) 609220; wholly-owned by Assurances Générales de France; Chief Exec. A. J. G. BANKS; Gen. Man. J. R. O'HANLON.

Irish Life Assurance PLC: Irish Life Centre, Lower Abbey St, Dublin 1; tel. (01) 720288; fax (01) 787250; f. 1939; cap. p.u. 500,000; industrial and life assurance, annuity group assurance and pension schemes; Chair. JOHN REIHILL; Man. Dir T. D. KINGSTON; Sec. L. G. ANDREWS.

Irish National Insurance Co PLC: 9-10 Dawson St, Dublin 2; tel. (01) 776881; telex 30460; fax (01) 776161; f. 1919; fire, engineering, third party, employers' liability, motor, general, accident, burglary, bonds, livestock, reinsurance, contractors all risks; brs in London and Paris; member of New Ireland Holdings PLC Group; Chair. MAIRTIN MCCULLOUGH; Man. Dir A. J. HATCH.

Irish Public Bodies Mutual Insurances Ltd: 1 Westmoreland St, Dublin 2; tel. (01) 778000; telex 93290; fax (01) 778590; f. 1926; fire

IRELAND

and accident; Chair. JOSEPHINE QUINLAN; Gen. Man. B. DOYLE; Sec. ROSEMARY REILLY.

New Ireland Assurance Co PLC: 11–12 Dawson St, Dublin 2; tel. (01) 717077; telex 90692; fax (01) 797313; f. 1924; auth. cap. I£7.6m.; Chair. J. DESMOND TRAYNOR; Man. Dir JOHN F. CASEY; Sec. E. O'BRIEN.

Norwich Union Life Insurance Society and **Norwich Union Fire Insurance Society Ltd:** 60/63 Dawson St, Dublin 2; tel. (01) 717181; telex 93426; fax (01) 710678; f. 1797, in Ireland 1816; Chair. M. D. CORBETT.

PMPA Insurance PLC: Wolfe Tone House, Wolfe Tone St, Dublin 1; tel. (01) 726444; telex 31003; fax (01) 724652; Chief Exec. JIM QUIGLEY.

Shield Insurance Co Ltd: Shield House, 45–47 Pembroke Rd, Ballsbridge, Dublin 4; tel. (01) 683943; telex 30737; fax (01) 684897; f. 1950; general, excluding life; Chair. J. G. RONAN.

Standard Life Assurance Co: 90 St Stephen's Green, Dublin 2; tel. (01) 757411; fax (01) 751903; est. in Scotland 1825, operating in Ireland since 1834; life assurance and annuities; assets exceed £18,000m. (sterling); Chair. (in Edinburgh) NORMAN LESSELS; Man. Dir A. SCOTT BELL.

Zurich Insurance Co: Stephen Court, 18–21 St Stephen's Green, Dublin 2; tel. (01) 764276; fax (01) 761494; Man. E. O. BAILY.

Insurance Associations

Insurance Institute of Ireland: Office and Library: 32 Nassau St, Dublin 2; tel. 772753; f. 1885; Pres. R. P. POWER; Sec.-Gen. P. F. MCGOVERN; 4,000 mems.

Irish Insurance Federation: Russell House, Russell Court, Stephen's Green, Dublin 2; tel. (01) 782499; fax (01) 782435; Sec. A. CASSELLS.

Trade and Industry

CHAMBERS OF COMMERCE

Association of Western Chambers of Commerce of Ireland: James St, Westport; mem. chambers: Ballina, Ballyshannon, Castlebar, Ennis, Galway, Letterkenny, Limerick, Sligo, Westport; Chair. CHARLES N. RABBITT; Sec. MICHAEL BROWNE.

The Chambers of Commerce of Ireland: 7 Clare St, Dublin 2; tel. (01) 612888; telex 90716; fax (01) 766043; f. 1923; Pres. MARY BENNETT; Deputy Pres. JAMES KENNEDY; Dir. P. SKEHAN; 48 mems.

EMPLOYERS' ASSOCIATIONS

Confederation of Irish Industry: Confederation House, Kildare St, Dublin 2; tel. (01) 779801; telex 93502; fax (01) 777823; f. 1932; 2,000 mems; Pres. PATRICK J. WRIGHT; Dir-Gen. LIAM CONNELLAN; Sec. GERARD SHEEHY.

Federation of Irish Employers: Baggot Bridge House, 84–86 Lower Baggot St, Dublin 2; tel. (01) 601011; telex 93806; fax (01) 601717; 3,500 mems; Pres. LIAM DOWNEY; Dir-Gen. JOHN DUNNE; Sec. JOHN CASEY.

TRADE UNIONS

Irish Congress of Trade Unions: 19 Raglan Rd, Dublin 4; tel. (01) 680641; fax (01) 609027; f. 1959; represents 679,000 workers in the Republic and Northern Ireland; Gen. Sec. PETER CASSELLS; 78 affiliated unions (July 1990).

Principal affiliated unions:

*These unions have their head office in the United Kingdom and the membership figure given is for the Republic of Ireland and Northern Ireland together.

*Amalgamated Transport and General Workers' Union: Transport House, 102 High St, Belfast, BT1 2DL; tel. (0232) 232381; telex 747202; fax (01) 734602; Irish Sec. J. FREEMAN; 100,000 mems.

*Amalgamated Union of Engineering Workers—Engineering Section: 26–34 Antrim Rd, Belfast, BT15 2AA; tel. (0232) 743271; Sec. J. BLAIR; 26,812 mems (1983).

*Amalgamated Union of Engineering Workers, Technical, Administrative and Supervisory Section: 26–34 Antrim Rd, Belfast, BT15 2AA; tel. (0232) 746189; Irish Rep. J. BOWERS; 6,350 mems.

*Association of Professional, Executive, Clerical and Computer Staff: 291 Antrim Rd, Belfast, BT15 2GZ; tel. (0232) 748678; Area Sec. P. A. MCCARTAN; 4,000 mems.

Directory

Automobile, General Engineering and Mechanical Operatives' Union: 22 North Frederick St, Dublin 1; tel. (01) 744233; Gen. Sec. LAURENCE DOYLE; 3,500 mems.

Bakery and Food Workers' Amalgamated Union: 12 Merrion Sq., Dublin 2; tel. (01) 619457; f. 1889; Gen. Sec. PATRICK SHANLEY; 4,000 mems.

Building and Allied Trades' Union: Arus Hibernia, 13 Blessington St, Dublin 7; tel. (01) 301911; fax (01) 304869; incorporating National Union of Woodworkers and Woodcutting Machinists and the Ancient Guild of Incorporated Brick and Stonelayers and Allied Trades' Union; Gen. Sec. PATRICK O'SHAUGHNESSY.

Civil and Public Service Union: 72 Lower Leeson St, Dublin 2; tel. (01) 765394; Gen. Sec. JOHN O'DOWD; 12,003 mems.

Communications Union of Ireland: 575–577 North Circular Rd, Dublin 1; tel. (01) 743402; f. 1922; Gen. Sec. SEAMUS DEPAOR; 9,000 mems (1985).

*Confederation of Health Service Employees: 27 Ulsterville Ave, Lisburn Rd, Belfast, BT9 7AS; tel. (0232) 662994; Irish Rep. W. F. JACKSON; 19,000 mems.

*Electrical, Electronic, Telecommunication and Plumbing Union: AUEW House, 1A Adela St, Belfast, BT14 6AW; tel. (0232) 740244; Irish Rep. C. C. LOWRY.

Electrical Trades Union: 5 Cavendish Row, Dublin 1; tel. (01) 747047; fax (01) 747048; f. 1923; Gen. Sec. FRANK O'REILLY; 11,533 mems.

Electricity Supply Board Officers' Association: 43 East James's Place, Lower Baggot St, Dublin 2; tel. (01) 767444; f. 1959; Gen. Sec. JOHN HALL; Pres. EAMON KELLY; 3,035 mems.

*Furniture, Timber and Allied Trades Union: 52 Peter's Hill, Belfast, BT13 2AB; tel. (0232) 243588; District Organizer J. WILLEY; 1,302 mems (1986).

*General, Municipal, Boilermakers and Allied Trades Union: 102 Lisburn Rd, Belfast, BT9 6AG; tel. (0232) 681421; T. D. DOUGLAS; 15,500 mems.

Ireland Association of Secondary Teachers: 36 Lower Baggot St, Dublin 2; tel. (01) 607444; fax (01) 607403; f. 1909; Gen. Sec. KIERAN MULVEY; 12,000 mems.

Irish Distributive and Administrative Trade Union (IDATU): O'Lehane House, 9 Cavendish Row, Dublin 1; tel. (01) 746321; fax (01) 729581; f. 1901; Gen. Sec. HUGH M. POLLOCK; 21,000 mems.

Irish Federation of Musicians and Associated Professions: Cecilia House, 63 Lower Gardiner St, Dublin 1; tel. (01) 744645; Gen. Sec. P. PRINGLE; 1,000 mems.

Irish Medical Organization: 10 Fitzwilliam Place, Dublin 2; tel. (01) 767273; fax (01) 612758; Sec. Gen. MICHAEL B. MCCANN; Deputy Sec.-Gen. ED MADDEN; 4,000 mems.

Irish Municipal Employees' Trade Union: 8 Gardiner Place, Dublin 1; tel. (01) 743362; Gen. Sec. SEAN REDMOND; 3,000 mems.

Irish National Painters and Decorators' Trade Union: 76 Aungier St, Dublin 2; tel. (01) 751720; Gen. Sec. GERARD FLEMING; 3,010 mems.

Irish National Teachers' Organization: 35 Parnell Sq., Dublin 1; tel. (01) 722533; fax (01) 722462; f. 1868; Pres. J. WHITE; Sec. E. G. QUIGLEY; 24,500 mems (1989/90).

Irish National Union of Vintners', Grocers' and Allied Trades Assistants: 20 Parnell Sq., Dublin 1; tel. (01) 746634; f. 1917; Gen. Sec. J. CAGNEY; 4,680 mems.

Local Government and Public Services Union: 9 Gardiner Place, Dublin 1; tel. (01) 728899; fax (01) 728715; Gen. Sec. P. FLYNN; 18,000 mems (1987).

Manufacturing, Science and Finance Union: 545 Antrim Rd, Belfast, BT15 3BY; tel. (0232) 370551; fax (0232) 370687; Regional Officers J. BOWERS, J. NICHOLL, E. OAKES; 15 Merrion Sq., Dublin 2; tel. (01) 611063; fax (01) 611738; National Officer B. ANDERSON.

Marine, Port and General Workers' Union: 14 Gardiner Place, Dublin 1; tel. (01) 726566; Gen. Sec. SEAMUS REDMOND; 7,000 mems.

National Engineering and Electrical Trade Union: 6 Gardiner Row, Dublin 1; tel. (01) 745935; f. 1966 as result of merger between National Engineering Union, National Union of Scalemakers and Irish Engineering Industrial and Electrical Trade Union; Jt Gen. Secs K. M. P. MCCONNELL (Financial), I. J. MONELEY (Industrial); 10,000 mems.

*National Graphical Association (1982): Graphic House, 107 Clonskeagh Rd, Dublin 6; tel. (01) 697788; fax (01) 839977; Gen. Sec. A. D. DUBBINS; Regional Officer N. S. BROUGHALL; 5,176 mems.

IRELAND

*National Union of Journalists (Irish Council): Liberty Hall, Dublin 1; tel. (01) 748694; fax (01) 749250; Chair. ANN CAHILL; National Exec. mems MICHAEL FOLEY, BARRY MCCALL (Republic of Ireland), JOHN MCANULTY (Northern Ireland); 2,943 mems (1989).

*National Union of Public Employees: 523 Antrim Rd, Belfast, BT15 6BS; tel. (0232) 23988; Irish Rep. Ms I. MCCORMACK; 12,000 mems.

*National Union of Tailors and Garment Workers: Irish Divisional Office, 44 Elmwood Ave, Belfast, BT9 6BB; tel. (0232) 381942; fax (0232) 662343; Irish Rep. MARTIN DUMMIGAN; 10,200 mems.

Postal and Telecommunications Workers' Union: 53 Parnell Sq., Dublin 1; tel. (01) 726911; f. 1923; Gen. Sec. DAVID T. BEGG; 10,000 mems.

Public Service Executive Union: 30 Merrion Square, Dublin 2; tel. (01) 767271; fax (01) 615777; f. 1890; Gen. Sec. D. MURPHY; 6,000 mems.

Services, Industrial, Professional and Technical Union: 10 Palmerston Park, Dublin 6; tel. (01) 733977; fax (01) 975008; formed following the merging of the Federated Workers' Union of Ireland with the Irish Transport and General Workers' Union in 1990; Jt Gen. Pres WILLIAM A. ATTLEY, EDMUND D. BROWNE; 200,000 mems.

Teachers' Union of Ireland: 73 Orwell Rd, Rathgar, Dublin 6; tel. (01) 961588; fax (01) 961853; f. 1955; Gen. Sec. JAMES DORNEY; 7,000 mems.

*Transport Salaried Staffs' Association: 7 Gardiner Place, Dublin 1; tel. (01) 743467; f. 1897; Sec. D. CASEY; 3,025 mems.

*Union of Construction, Allied Trades and Technicians: 56 Parnell Sq. West, Dublin 1; tel. (01) 731599; Republic of Ireland Rep. NOEL O'NEILL; 18,178 mems.

Union of Professional and Technical Civil Servants: 16 Earlsfort Terrace, Dublin 2; tel. (01) 789855; f. 1919; Gen. Sec. G. MAXWELL; 6,000 mems.

*Union of Shop, Distributive and Allied Workers: 40 Wellington Park, Belfast, BT9 6DN; tel. (0232) 663773; Sec. ALAN WHITE; 6,905 mems.

Principal unaffiliated unions:

Institute of Journalists (Irish Region): The Lodge, Glendalough, Co Wicklow; tel. (0404) 5196; Chair. GEORGE PECHE; Education Officer VALERIE COX.

Irish Bank Officials' Association: 93 St Stephen's Green, Dublin 2; tel. (01) 722255; telex 90746; fax (01) 780567; f. 1917; Gen. Sec. CIARAN RYAN.

National Busworkers' Union: 54 Parnell Sq., Dublin 1; tel. (01) 744205; Gen. Sec. THOMAS DARBY.

Post Office Officials' Association: Lismullen, Navan; tel. (046) 378178; Gen. Sec. EOGHAN O'NEILL.

DEVELOPMENT ORGANIZATIONS

Córas Tráchtála (Irish Export Board): Merrion Hall, Strand Rd, Sandymount, Dublin 4; tel. (01) 695011; telex 93678; fax (01) 695820; f.1959; promotion and development of exports and aid for Irish exporters and a comprehensive service to foreign buyers, financed by a grant-in-aid; 24 overseas offices; Chair. C. MCCARTHY; CEO A. P. MCCARTHY.

Industrial Development Authority of Ireland: Wilton Park House, Wilton Place, Dublin 2; tel. (01) 686633; telex 93431; f. 1949; autonomous state-sponsored organization with national responsibility for industrial development; administers financial incentive schemes for new industrial investment; aims (i) to promote investment in manufacturing and internationally-traded services (including financial services); (ii) to develop indigenous industry; (iii) to stimulate entrepreneurial and small-scale industries; 19 overseas offices; Man. Dir KIERAN MCGOWAN; Exec. Dirs DAN FLINTER, SEAN DONNELLY, P. J. DALY.

Irish Co-operative Organization Society Ltd: The Plunkett House, 84 Merrion Sq., Dublin 2; tel. (01) 764783; telex 30379; fax (01) 681784; f. 1894 as co-ordinating body for agricultural co-operative movement; Pres. WILLIAM R. NAGLE; Dir-Gen. JOHN TYRRELL; mems: 200 co-operatives, approx. 140,000 farmers.

Irish Goods Council: Merrion Hall, Strand Rd, Dublin 4; tel. (01) 696011; fax (01) 696251; serves industry in the home market; Chair. TOM HARDIMAN; CEO JOHN CORRIGAN.

PRINCIPAL NATIONALIZED INDUSTRIES

An Post (The Post Office): College House, Townsend St, Dublin 2; tel. (01) 720000, telex 80111, fax (01) 705705, f. 1984; provides national postal, savings and agency services through 2,100 outlets; 7,865 employees; Chair. VIVIAN MURRAY; CEO JOHN HYNES.

Directory

Bord Gais Éireann (BGE) (The Irish Gas Board): POB 51, Inchera, Little Island, Co Cork; tel. (021) 509199; telex 75087; fax (021) 353487; 24A D'Olier St, Dublin 2; tel. (01) 6792311; telex 32888; fax (01) 6792386; f. 1975; state gas transmission company; Chair. M. N. CONLON; CEO J. J. LYNCH.

Bord na Móna (Irish Peat Board): Lower Baggot St, Dublin 2; tel. (01) 688555; telex 30206; fax (01) 601800; f. 1946; develops Ireland's peat resources, produces milled peat and machine turf for electricity generation, machine turf and briquettes for general, industrial and domestic use and horticultural moss peat products for gardeners; 2,500 employees; Chair. B. HALLIGAN; Man. Dir E. O'CONNOR.

Bord Solathair an Leictreachais (Electricity Supply Board): 27 Lower Fitzwilliam St, Dublin 2; tel. (01) 771821; telex 25313; f. 1927; controls 11 generating stations operating on peat, 2 oil stations, 2 oil or gas stations, 2 gas stations, 10 hydro stations and 2 coal-fired stations; 12,454 employees; Chair. Prof. C. T. G. DILLON; CEO P. J. MORIARTY.

Comhlucht Groighe Naísiunta Na h-Éireann Teoranta (Irish National Stud Co Ltd): Tully, Kildare; tel. (045) 21251; telex 60706; fax (045) 22129; f. 1946 primarily for the running of a stud farm for thoroughbred horses at the National Stud and in particular to provide the services of first-class stallions; advisory service to breeders; farming activities such as raising cattle, hay etc.; cap. issued I£3.4m. held by minister of finance; 54 employees; Chair. JOHN M. OXX; Man. JOHN CLARKE.

Irish Steel Ltd: Haulbowline, Cobh, Co Cork; tel. (021) 811731; fax (021) 811347; f. 1947; steelmaking, rolling and galvanized sheetmaking; auth. cap. I£125m.; 633 employees; Chair. W. HUGH O'CONNOR; CEO L. S. COUGHLAN.

Nitrigin Éireann Teoranta (NET): Dublin; f. 1961; production of nitrogenous fertilizers and complete fertilizers; cap. auth. I£77.5m.; 800 employees; Chair. S. MACHALE; Man. Dir T. A. JAGO.

Siuícre Éireann Cpt (Irish Sugar PLC): St Stephen's Green House, Dublin 2; tel. (01) 767501; telex 30662; fax (01) 767624; f. 1933; processing of sugar beet grown by 7,000 Irish farmers for domestic and industrial purposes, formulation of other food products, production of animal feedstuffs, manufacture of specialized machinery, and production and distribution of ground limestone; 1,556 employees; Chair. B. M. CAHILL; Man. Dir C. K. COMERFORD.

Erin Foods Ltd: St Stephen's Green House, Dublin 2; tel. (01) 767501; telex 25352; fax (01) 767624; f. 1958; a division of Irish Sugar PLC; processing of vegetables, manufacture of soups and formulated products; Group Chair. JAMES E. FITZPATRICK; Man. Dir MAURICE SHEEHY.

Telecom Éireann: St Stephen's Green West, Dublin 2; tel. (01) 714444; telex 91111; fax (01) 716916; f. 1984; provides telecommunications services; 15,000 employees; Chair. M. W. J. SMURFIT.

In addition to these there exist numerous smaller state-sponsored bodies. Among those not mentioned elsewhere in this chapter are: The Irish Livestock and Meat Board, The Voluntary Health Insurance Board, The Hospitals Trust Board and the Institute for Industrial Research and Standards.

Transport

Córas Iompair Éireann (CIE) (The Irish Transport Co): Heuston Station, Dublin 8; tel. (01) 771871; telex 25153; fax (01) 771350; f. 1945; government-appointed; controls the railways, inland waterways and road transport services; Chair. and CEO G. T. PAUL CONLON.

RAILWAYS

In 1988 there were 1,947 km of track, of which 38 km were electrified, controlled by Iarnród Éireann. The Dublin Area Rapid Transit (DART) was built at a cost of I£113m., to provide extra passenger capacity.

Iarnród Éireann (Irish Rail): Connolly Station, Dublin 1; tel. (01) 363333; telex 31638; fax (01) 364760; Chair. G. T. CONLON; Man. Dir D. WATERS.

INLAND WATERWAYS

The commercial canal services of CIE have been discontinued. However, the Grand Canal and the canal link into the Barrow Navigation System are maintained by the CIE for use by pleasure craft. The River Shannon is navigable for 241 km (150 miles). Other inland waterways are estimated at 188 km (117 miles).

ROADS

At 31 December 1989 there were 92,303 km (57,354 miles) of roads of which 5,255 km (3,265 miles) were main roads. About 94% of all roads were surfaced.

IRELAND

SHIPPING

The principal sea ports are Dublin, Duń Laoghaire, Cork, Waterford, Rosslare, Limerick, Foynes, Galway, New Ross, Drogheda, Dundalk, Fenit and Whiddy Island.

B+I Line PLC (British & Irish Steam Packet Co Ltd): Ferryport, Alexandra Rd, Dublin 1; tel. (01) 788077; telex 33303; fax (01) 788490; f. 1836; drive on/drive off car ferry and roll on/roll off freight services between Dublin and Holyhead, and Rosslare and Pembroke; roll-on/roll-off freight service between Dublin and Liverpool; groupage and roll-on/roll-off from all parts of Britain to and from Ireland; unit load freight service between Dublin and Le Havre, Rotterdam and Antwerp; agents in Ireland for C.M.A.; Chief Exec. J. J. KENNEDY; Sec. PAT RYAN; 6 vessels and other vessels on charter.

Celtic Coasters Ltd: Beech Hill, Clonskeagh, Dublin 4; tel. (01) 694300; telex 93793; f. 1958; shipowners/ship-agents; also in Cork; associate company of Dublin Shipping Ltd; Chair. L. ST J. DEVLIN; Gen. Man. E. CONNOR; 1 tanker.

Dublin Shipping Ltd: 6 Beech Hill, Clonskeagh, Dublin 4; tel. (01) 696477; telex 93793; fax (01) 839361; Chair. C. JONES; Man. Dir E. CONNOR; 5 tankers.

Irish Shipping Ltd: Merrion Hall, Strand Rd, Dublin 4; tel. (01) 695522; telex 25126; f. 1941; world-wide tramping service; Dir and Gen. Man. W. A. O'NEILL; 10 carriers.

Sealink Stena Line: Adelaide House, 7 Haddington Terrace, Dun Laoghaire, Co Dublin; tel. (01) 807777; telex 30847; fax (01) 808141; services between Duń Laoghaire and Holyhead, Rosslare and Fishguard, Larne and Stranraer, passengers, drive-on/drive-off car ferry, roll-on/roll-off services.

CIVIL AVIATION

There are international airports at Shannon, Dublin, Cork and Knock (Horan International), but only Shannon and Knock are used for transatlantic flights. The national airline is Aer Lingus.

Aer Rianta (Irish Airports): Dublin Airport, Dublin; tel. (01) 379900; telex 31266; fax (01) 427975; responsible for the management and development of Dublin, Shannon and Cork airports; Chair. D. F. DESMOND; CEO DEREK KEOGH.

Airlines

Aer Lingus PLC: POB 180, Dublin Airport, Dublin; tel. (01) 370011; telex 31404; fax (01) 420801; f. 1936; incorporated Aerlinte Eíreann 1947; regular services to 29 cities in Europe, the USSR and the USA; Chair. BRIAN A. SLOWEY; Chief Exec. CATHAL MULLAN; fleet of 3 Boeing 747, 5 737-200, 4 737-200C, 5 737-200ADV, 4 One-Eleven 200, 5 737-400, 2 737-300.

Aer Turas Teoranta: Corballis Rd South, Dublin Airport, Dublin; tel. (01) 379131; telex 33393; fax (01) 420910; f. 1962; world-wide cargo charter services; CEO P. J. COUSINS; fleet of 1 Douglas DC8-63FQN, 1 Canadair CL-44J.

Ryanair: College Park House, Nassau St, Dublin 2; tel. (01) 6797444; telex 91608; fax (01) 770957; f. 1986; scheduled carrier; Chair. ARTHUR WALLS; CEO P. J. MCGOLDRICK; fleet of 6 Rombac 1-11-500, 3 ATR 42.

Tourism

Intensive marketing campaigns have been undertaken in recent years to develop new markets for Irish tourism. The country has numerous beauty spots, notably the Killarney Lakes and the west coast. In 1989 a total of 3,484,000 foreign tourists (excluding excursionists) visited the Republic and projected revenue from tourism was US $1,360m.

Bord Faílte Eíreann (Irish Tourist Board): Baggot St Bridge, Dublin 2; tel. (01) 765871; telex 93755; fax (01) 764764; f. 1955; Chair. and Chief Exec. MARTIN DULLY; Sec. NIALL REDDY.

Dublin and Eastern Regional Tourism Organization Ltd: 1 Clarinda Park North, Dun Laoghaire, Co Dublin; tel. (01) 808571; telex 93560; Chair. T. ELMORE; Man. MATT MCNULTY.

ISRAEL

Introductory Survey

Location, Climate, Language, Religion, Flag, Capital

The State of Israel lies in western Asia, occupying a narrow strip of territory on the eastern shore of the Mediterranean Sea. The country also has a narrow outlet to the Red Sea at the northern tip of the Gulf of Aqaba. All of Israel's land frontiers are with Arab countries, the longest being with Egypt to the west and with Jordan to the east. Lebanon lies to the north, and Syria to the north-east. The climate is Mediterranean, with hot, dry summers, when the maximum temperature in Jerusalem is generally between 30°C and 35°C (86°F to 95°F), and mild, rainy winters, with a minimum temperature in Jerusalem of about 5°C (41°F). The climate is sub-tropical on the coast but more extreme in the Negev Desert, in the south, and near the shores of the Dead Sea (a lake on the Israeli-Jordanian frontier), where the summer temperature may exceed 50°C (122°F). The official language of Israel is Hebrew, spoken by about two-thirds of the population, including most Jews. About 15% of Israeli residents, including Muslim Arabs, speak Arabic (which is also the language spoken by the inhabitants of the Occupied Territories), while many European languages are also spoken. About 82% of the population profess adherence to Judaism, the officially recognized religion of Israel, while almost 14% are Muslims. The national flag (proportions 250 by 173) has a white background, with a six-pointed blue star composed of two overlapping triangles (the 'Shield of David') between two horizontal blue stripes near the upper and lower edges. The Israeli Government has designated the city of Jerusalem (part of which is Jordanian territory annexed by Israel in 1967) as the country's capital, but this is not recognized by the United Nations, and most foreign governments maintain their embassies in Tel-Aviv.

Recent History

The Zionist movement, launched in Europe in the 19th century, aimed at the re-establishment of an autonomous community of Jews in their historic homeland of Palestine (the 'Promised Land'). The growth of Zionism was partly due to the insecurity that was felt by Jewish minorities in many European countries as a result of racial and religious hostility, known as anti-semitism, which sometimes included discrimination, persecution and even massacre.

Palestine, for long inhabited by Arabs, became a part of Turkey's Ottoman Empire in the 16th century. During the First World War (1914–18), when Turkey was allied with Germany, the Arabs under Ottoman rule rebelled. Palestine was occupied by British forces in 1917–18, when the Turks withdrew. Meanwhile, in November 1917, the British Foreign Secretary, Arthur Balfour, declared British support for the establishment of a Jewish national home in Palestine, on condition that the rights of 'the existing non-Jewish communities' there were safeguarded. The Balfour Declaration, as it is known, was confirmed by the governments of other countries then at war with Turkey.

British occupation of Palestine continued after the war, when the Ottoman Empire was dissolved. In 1920 the territory was formally placed under British administration by a League of Nations mandate, which incorporated the Balfour Declaration. British rule in Palestine was hampered by the conflict between the declared obligations to the Jews and the rival claims of the indigenous Arab majority. In accordance with the mandate, Jewish settlers were admitted to Palestine (whose population in 1919 was almost entirely Arab), but only on the basis of limited annual quotas. Serious anti-Jewish rioting by Arabs occurred in 1921 and 1929. Attempts to restrict immigration led to Jewish-sponsored riots in 1933. The extreme persecution of Jews by Nazi Germany caused an increase in the flow of Jewish immigrants, both legal and illegal, but this intensified the unrest in Palestine. In 1937 a British proposal to establish separate Jewish and Arab states, while retaining a British-mandated area, was accepted by most of the Zionists but rejected by the Arabs, and by the end of that year the conflict between the two communities had developed into open warfare, which continued throughout 1938. A British offer of eventual independence for a bi-communal Palestinian state, made in 1939, led to further incidents, but the scheme was postponed because of the Second World War (1939–45). During the war the Nazis caused the deaths of an estimated 6m. Jews in central and eastern Europe, more than one-third of the world's total Jewish population. The enormity of this massacre, known as the Holocaust, greatly increased international sympathy for Jewish claims to a homeland in Palestine.

After the war, there was strong opposition by Palestinian Jews to continued British occupation. Numerous terrorist attacks were made by Jewish groups against British targets. In November 1947 the UN approved a plan for the partition of Palestine into two states, one Jewish (covering about 56% of the area) and one Arab. The plan was, however, rejected by Arab states and by the leadership of the Palestinian Arabs. Meanwhile, the conflict between the two communities in Palestine escalated into full-scale war.

On 14 May 1948 the United Kingdom (UK) terminated its Palestine mandate, and Jewish leaders immediately proclaimed the State of Israel, with David Ben-Gurion as Prime Minister. Although the new nation had no agreed frontiers, it quickly received wide international recognition. Neighbouring Arab states sent forces into Palestine in an attempt to crush Israel. Fighting continued until January 1949. The cease-fire agreements left Israel in control of 75% of Palestine, including West Jerusalem. The *de facto* territory of Israel was thus nearly one-third greater than the area that had been assigned to the Jewish state under the UN partition plan. Most of the remainder of Palestine was controlled by Jordanian forces. This area, known as the West Bank (or, to Israelis, as Judaea and Samaria), was annexed by Jordan in December 1949 and, following a referendum, fully incorporated in April 1950. No independent Arab state was established in Palestine, and the independence of Israel was not recognized by any Arab government until 1980.

When the British mandate ended, the Jewish population of Palestine was about 650,000 (or 40% of the total), compared with 56,000 in 1920. With the establishment of the new state encouraged further Jewish immigration. The Law of Return, adopted in July 1950, established a right of immigration for all Jews. The rapid influx of Jewish settlers enabled Israel to consolidate its specifically Jewish character. At the same time, many former Arab residents of Palestine had become refugees in neighbouring countries, mainly Jordan and Lebanon. About 400,000 Arabs had evacuated their homes prior to May 1948, and another 400,000 fled subsequently. In 1964 some exiled Palestinian Arabs formed the Palestine Liberation Organization (PLO), with the aim, at that time, of the overthrow of Israel.

In July 1956 the Egyptian Government announced the nationalization of the company that operated the Suez Canal. In response, Israel launched an attack on Egypt in October, occupying the Gaza Strip (part of Palestine under Egyptian occupation since 1949) and the Sinai Peninsula. After pressure from the UN and the USA, Israeli forces evacuated these areas in 1957, when a UN Emergency Force (UNEF) was established in Sinai. In May 1967 the United Arab Republic (Egypt) secured the withdrawal of UNEF from its territory. Egyptian forces immediately reoccupied the garrison at Sharm esh-Sheikh, near the southern tip of Sinai, and closed the Straits of Tiran to Israeli shipping, effectively blockading the Israeli port of Eilat, situated at the head of the Gulf of Aqaba. In retaliation, Israel attacked Egypt and other Arab countries in June. Israeli forces quickly overcame opposition and made substantial territorial gains. The Six-Day War, as it is known, left Israel in possession of all Jerusalem, the West Bank area of Jordan, the Sinai Peninsula in Egypt, the Gaza Strip and the Golan Heights in Syria. East Jerusalem was almost immediately integrated into the State of Israel, while the other conquered areas were regarded as Occupied Territories.

Ben-Gurion resigned in June 1963 and was succeeded by Levi Eshkol. Three of the parties in the ruling coalition merged to form the Israel Labour Party in 1968. On the death of Eshkol in February 1969, Golda Meir was elected Prime Minister by the Labour Party executive. She continued in office following the general elections of October 1969 and December 1973. A cease-fire between Egypt and Israel was arranged in August 1970, so ending the two years of war of attrition in the Suez Canal zone, but other Arab States and Palestinian Arab guerrilla, mainly PLO, groups continued their hostilities. Another war between the Arab states and Israel broke out on 6 October 1973, coinciding with Yom Kippur (the Day of Atonement), the holiest day of the Jewish year. In simultaneous attacks on Israeli-held territory, Egyptian forces crossed the Suez Canal and reoccupied part of Sinai, while Syrian troops launched an offensive on the Golan Heights. Israel made cease-fire agreements with Egypt and Syria on 24 October. A disengagement agreement with Syria was signed in May 1974. A further disengagement agreement between Israel and Egypt was signed in September 1975.

General Itzhak Rabin had succeeded Golda Meir as Prime Minister of a Labour Alignment coalition after her resignation in June 1974. In December 1976 Rabin lost the support of the National Religious Party (NRP) and subsequently resigned, continuing in office in a caretaker capacity until May 1977, when the Labour Alignment was unexpectedly defeated in a general election. The Likud (Consolidation) bloc, led by Menachem Begin of the Herut (Freedom) Party, was able to form a government in June 1977 with the support of minority parties.

In November 1977 President Anwar Sadat of Egypt visited Israel, indicating a tacit recognition by Egypt of the State of Israel. In September 1978 President Carter of the USA, President Sadat and Prime Minister Begin met at Camp David, in the USA, and drew up two agreements. The first was a 'framework for peace in the Middle East', providing for autonomy for the West Bank and the Gaza Strip after a transitional period of five years, and the second was a 'framework for the conclusion of a peace treaty between Egypt and Israel', which was subsequently signed in Washington on 26 March 1979. In February 1980 Egypt became the first Arab country to grant diplomatic recognition to Israel. Israel's phased withdrawal from Sinai was completed in April 1982. The approval in July 1980 of legislation which stated explicitly that Jerusalem should be for ever the undivided capital of Israel, and Israel's formal annexation of the Golan Heights in December 1981, subsequently inhibited prospects of agreement on Palestinian autonomy.

In June 1982 a major crisis developed when Israeli forces launched 'Operation Peace for Galilee', advanced through Lebanon and surrounded West Beirut, trapping 6,000 PLO fighters. Egypt withdrew its ambassador from Tel-Aviv in protest at the Israeli action. Intensive diplomatic efforts resulted in the evacuation of 14,000–15,000 PLO and Syrian fighters from Beirut to various Arab countries at the end of August 1982. With Israeli troops in effective control of Beirut, a massacre took place in the Palestinian refugee camps of Sabra and Chatila in mid-September; Israel finally acknowledged a figure of 700–800 dead. The Israeli Government instituted an enquiry, which blamed Lebanese Phalangists for the actual killing, but concluded that Israel's political and military leaders bore indirect responsibility through their negligence. General Ariel Sharon was forced to resign as Minister of Defence.

Lengthy talks between Israel and Lebanon, begun in December 1982, culminated in the signing on 17 May 1983 of a 12-article agreement, formulated by the US Secretary of State, George Shultz, declaring an end to hostilities and calling for the withdrawal of all foreign forces from Lebanon within three months. Syria rejected the agreement, leaving some 30,000 troops and 7,000 PLO men in the north-east of Lebanon, and Israel consequently refused to withdraw from the south. In September 1983 Israel redeployed its forces south of Beirut along the Awali river.

In January 1981 Begin called an early general election for June. Begin's belligerent stance over the threat of Syrian missiles in Lebanon in June, and the efforts of a new Minister of Finance, Yoram Aridor, to curb the rise in the cost of living, resulted in an unexpected swing in his favour; and by making an agreement with the religious parties, Begin was able to form a new coalition government in early August. When Israeli forces moved into Lebanon in June 1982, support for Begin continued until the operation escalated into a full-scale war.

By the summer of 1983, the Government's prestige had been damaged by the Beirut massacres and by a capitulation to wage demands by the country's doctors. Begin announced his resignation on 30 August 1983. Itzhak Shamir, the Minister of Foreign Affairs since 1980, succeeded him as leader of the Likud bloc and as Prime Minister, his Likud grouping having a theoretical majority of seven seats in the Knesset, with the support of minority religious parties.

Problems with the economy troubled the Government during the second half of 1983, and the Labour Party was able to force a general election in July 1984. Neither the Labour Alignment (which won 44 of the 120 seats in the Knesset) nor Likud (41 seats) could form a viable coalition government, and therefore the President, Chaim Herzog, invited the Labour leader, Shimon Peres, to form a 'Government of national unity' with Likud. An agreement was reached whereby Peres was to be Prime Minister for two years and one month from September 1984, while Itzhak Shamir was to be Deputy Prime Minister and Minister of Foreign Affairs, after which time they were to exchange their respective posts for a further two years and one month.

Israeli forces in Lebanon had withdrawn to the Awali river in September 1983. Responsibility for policing the occupied southern area fell increasingly on an Israeli-controlled militia, the so-called 'South Lebanon Army' (SLA). The Israeli 'Government of national unity' was pledged to withdraw from Lebanon, and completed a three-phased withdrawal in June 1985, leaving a 10–20 km buffer zone on the Lebanese side of the border, controlled by the SLA, in which Israel continued to have influence. During 1986 rocket attacks on settlements in northern Israel were resumed by Palestinian guerrillas, who had re-established mobile bases in the south of Lebanon following the Israeli withdrawal. Israeli air attacks on Palestinian targets in southern Lebanon have continued since then.

In the late 1980s there was growing support among Lebanese Muslims for the Shi'ite fundamentalist Hezbollah (Party of God), which intensified resistance against the Israeli-controlled SLA with attacks on positions within the buffer zone in southern Lebanon. The conflict between Israel and Hezbollah escalated following the abduction, in July 1989, of Sheikh Obeid, a local Shi'a Muslim leader, by Israeli agents. A series of retaliatory attacks by Hezbollah, leading, in turn, to Israeli counter-attacks, took place in August and September.

From 1984 onwards, numerous attempts were made, both by the parties immediately concerned (Israel and the Arabs), and by other powers (including the USA, the USSR, the UN and the EEC), to find a solution to the most pressing problem in the Middle East—the desire of Palestinians for an independent state. A situation of virtual deadlock had arisen because the PLO would not recognize Israel's right to exist, and Israel, convinced that the PLO was a terrorist organization, refused any direct talks with the PLO: repeated proposals by King Hussein of Jordan for an international peace conference, to be convened by the UN, were rejected by Israel on the grounds that the PLO would be represented.

Towards the end of 1988 there were signs that this deadlock might soon be broken. In December 1987, following the deaths of four Palestinians in a collision with an Israeli army truck at a military checkpoint in the Gaza Strip, demonstrations and civil disobedience against Israeli rule had intensified and soon spread to the other Occupied Territories. The uprising (intifada) apparently began as a spontaneous expression of frustration at occupation and depressed living conditions. An underground leadership calling itself the Unified National Leadership of the Uprising (UNLU) emerged, comprising elements from across the Palestinian political spectrum (the PLO, the Communist Party and Islamic Jihad). Israeli forces attempted to crush the uprising with increasing severity, for which they were condemned by world opinion. By December 1990 the number of people killed since the uprising began in December 1987 had risen to 743 Palestinians and 55 Israelis.

Against the background of escalating violence in the Occupied Territories, other developments were taking place which were creating circumstances under which Israel might be stimulated into seeking, or accepting, a solution. At the end of July 1988 King Hussein abrogated Jordan's legal and administrative responsibilities in the West Bank, cancelled the Jordanian programme of investment there (launched in 1986), and declared that he was no longer prepared to act as the representative of the Palestinians in any international conference on the Palestinian question. This undermined Israel's Palestine policy, and greatly strengthened the negotiating position of the PLO.

In November 1988, at a meeting of the Palestine National Council in Algiers, the PLO declared an independent Palestinian State (notionally in the West Bank and the Gaza Strip), and endorsed UN Security Council Resolution 242, thereby implicitly granting recognition to Israel. In December, in Stockholm, Yasser Arafat stated explicitly that 'the Palestine National Council accepted two States, a Palestinian State, and a Jewish State, Israel'. Later in December, before the UN General Assembly in Geneva, Arafat presented a three-point peace initiative, including an international conference under UN auspices, a UN peace-keeping force to supervise Israeli withdrawal from the Occupied Territories, and a comprehensive settlement based on UN Security Council Resolutions 242 and 338. Although the USA refused to accept the PLO proposals, alleging ambiguities, the PLO's explicit rejection of terrorism caused the US Government to decide to open a dialogue with the PLO, thus changing the direction of US-Israeli policy over Palestine. The UK, among other countries, urged Israel to make a positive response to the change in the PLO's position.

Israel's Prime Minister, Itzhak Shamir, however, declared that he would not negotiate with the PLO, distrusting its undertaking to abandon violence. Instead, he appeared to favour the introduction of limited self-rule for the Palestinians of the West Bank and Gaza Strip, as outlined in the 1978 US-sponsored Camp David accords with Egypt. Meanwhile, intense international pressure for the convening of a Middle East peace conference developed at the end of 1988, with both the USA and the USSR increasing diplomatic efforts to bring Israel and the PLO to negotiations.

At the general election which was held on 1 November 1988, as in 1984, neither Likud (40 seats) nor Labour (39 seats) secured enough seats to be able to form a coalition with groups of smaller parties. The religious parties won 18 seats in the election, gaining potential significance in the formation of a government either by Likud or Labour. After two changes of direction, Peres and the Labour Party eventually agreed to the formation in December of another 'Government of national unity' under the Likud leader, Itzhak Shamir, with Peres as Deputy Prime Minister and Minister of Finance. In the coalition accord, no mention was made of an international Middle East peace conference, nor were any new proposals advanced for solving the Arab–Israeli problem.

In April 1989 Shamir presented a four-point proposal for peace, which included a reaffirmation by Egypt, Israel and the USA of their dedication to the Camp David accords and free democratic elections in the West Bank and Gaza to elect Palestinian delegates who could negotiate self-rule under Israeli authority. This initiative was reaffirmed in late July, after an unsuccessful attempt by the Likud Central Committee to attach stringent conditions to the proposal. The USA exerted pressure on the PLO to consider the Israeli plans for the holding of elections, but in August a senior PLO spokesman stated that the PLO did not consider that elections could establish the basis for a political settlement. In mid-September President Mubarak of Egypt invited Israeli clarification on 10 points connected with Shamir's election plans and, at the same time, offered to convene an Israeli-Palestinian meeting in Cairo to discuss details about the proposed elections. Mubarak's 10-Point Plan was accepted by the Labour Party members of the inner cabinet, but was vetoed in early October by the Likud ministers on the grounds that they did not want any direct contact with PLO delegates. In early November the inner cabinet provisionally accepted a five-point initiative proposed by the US Secretary of State, James Baker, regarding a preliminary Israeli-Palestinian meeting to discuss the holding of elections in the West Bank and Gaza Strip, on the condition that Israel would not be required to negotiate with PLO delegates, and that the talks would be concerned only with Israel's election proposals. However, the PLO continued to demand a direct role in talks with the Israelis, and, thus, it appeared by January 1990 that the Baker initiative was in jeopardy.

In January 1990 Shamir's dismissal from the Government of Ezer Weizman, the Labour Minister of Science and Technology, for unauthorised contact with the PLO, endangered the fragile Likud-Labour coalition. The coalition was further undermined at the end of the month, when five disaffected members of the Knesset split from Likud to form an independent party, the Movement for the Advancement of the Zionist Idea (MAZI).

In February 1990 Ariel Sharon launched a campaign for the premiership, after resigning the post of Minister of Trade and Industry in protest at Shamir's peace policy and the Government's failure to suppress the *intifada*. Meanwhile, the USA attempted to apply further pressure on Israel to accelerate the pace of the peace process. At the beginning of March the US President, George Bush, opposed the grant to Israel of a $400m. loan for the housing of Soviet immigrants because Israel would not guarantee that the housing in question would not be in the Occupied Territories, including East Jerusalem.

On 11 March 1990 Shimon Peres and five Labour colleagues withdrew from a cabinet meeting, in protest at further delays of a proposed vote on US plans for talks between an Israeli and a Palestinian delegation. Two days later, Shamir dismissed Peres from the Government, prompting the resignation of all the Labour ministers. On 15 March the Knesset approved a motion expressing 'no confidence' in Shamir, the first such vote against an Israeli government to have succeeded. Shamir nevertheless retained authority in a transitional administration. On 20 March President Herzog invited Peres to form a new coalition government, after Peres had received assurances of support from five members of the Knesset belonging to Agudat Israel. However, there ensued a two-month period of political bargaining, during which both Likud and the Labour Party tried to establish a viable coalition government by soliciting the support of the minor religious parties represented in the Knesset. On 25 April Peres acknowledged that he had failed to form a new government. President Herzog accordingly invited Shamir to form an administration, within 21 days. On 14 May Shamir was granted a 21-day extension of his mandate, owing to disputes with potential coalition partners over the distribution of cabinet posts.

Violence erupted throughout Israel and the Occupied Territories on 19 May 1990, when seven Palestinians were murdered by an Israeli civilian gunman at Rishon LeZiyyon. During the ensuing three days of rioting, a further 21 Palestinians died. On 30 May an attack by members of the Palestine Liberation Front (PLF), one of the groups within the PLO, on a beach near Tel-Aviv led the USA to demand that the PLO condemn the attack. When it failed to do so in terms satisfactory to the USA, the USA suspended its dialogue with the PLO. On 31 May the USA vetoed a UN Security Council resolution urging that international observers be dispatched to the Occupied Territories.

On 8 June 1990 Shamir announced the formation of a new government, following the signing of a coalition agreement which gave him the support of 62 of the 120 members of the Knesset. In a policy document Shamir emphasized the right of Jews to settle in all parts of 'Greater Israel'; his opposition to the creation of an independent Palestinian state; and his refusal to negotiate with the PLO, indeed with any Palestinians other than those resident in the Occupied Territories (excluding East Jerusalem). On 11 June the new Government won a vote of confidence in the Knesset, by 62 votes to 57, with one abstention. The Government thus empowered was a narrow, right-wing coalition of Likud and five small parties (the MAZI, the NRP, Shas and the Tzomet and Tehiya parties), together with three independent members of the Knesset.

On 18 June 1990 Shamir invited President Assad of Syria to visit Israel for the purpose of peace negotiations, and on 22 June Jean-Claude Aimé, the special envoy of the UN Secretary-General, visited Israel to discuss issues related to the Occupied Territories. Shamir was thought to be seeking to appease the USA after the US Secretary of State, James Baker, had expressed impatience at the lack of progress in the peace process. However, on 27 June Shamir wrote to US President Bush, rejecting the principal elements of US proposals for direct talks between Israeli and Palestinian delegations.

Iraq's invasion of Kuwait on 2 August 1990 led to improved relations between Israel and the USA, because it was vital, if a broad coalition of Western and Arab powers opposed to Iraq were to be maintained, that Israel did not become actively involved in the new conflict in the region of the Persian (Arabian) Gulf. On 12 August President Saddam Hussain of Iraq offered to withdraw his forces from Kuwait if Israel would withdraw from the Occupied Territories. Israel firmly rejected any analogy between the occupation of Kuwait and its presence in the Occupied Territories. As a crisis developed in the Gulf region, as a result of Iraq's invasion and annexation of Kuwait, there was support for Iraq from both Palestinians resident in the Occupied Territories and from the PLO. The PLO's support for Iraq led left-wing Israeli groups to cancel scheduled meetings with PLO representatives and other Palestinian leaders.

The improvement taking place in US-Israeli relations was seriously jeopardized in October 1990, when Israeli police shot and killed at least 18 Palestinians on the Temple Mount in Jerusalem, after they had clashed with Jewish worshippers there. The killings provoked international outrage and lent weight to the arguments of those who, like Saddam Hussain, sought to link Iraq's occupation of Kuwait with the Israeli presence in the Occupied Territories in any solution to the crisis in the Gulf. There was intense pressure on the UN to respond to this outrage, since it was with UN authority that a multinational force had been deployed in Saudi Arabia for the protection of the Kingdom. To many Arabs, the disparity between the vigour with which the UN was seeking to implement successive resolutions pertaining to the occupation of Kuwait and its long-standing impotence with regard to successive resolutions pertaining to the Occupied Territories was now more conspicuous than before.

The UN Security Council voted to send a mission to the Occupied Territories to investigate the Temple Mount killings, but the Israeli Cabinet announced that it would not co-operate with any such UN delegation and rejected the UN's criticism of its decision. In early November 1990 the UN Secretary-General asked the Security Council to request the convening of an unprecedented international conference, with the aim of forcing Israel to accept that Palestinians in the Occupied Territories were protected by the provisions of the Fourth Geneva Convention (concerning the protection of civilians during wartime). On 13 November the Israeli Government announced that it would permit a UN emissary to visit Israel to discuss the situation in the Occupied Territories.

In late November 1990 there was increased concern in Israel about the security of its borders with Lebanon and Jordan, and about improvements in relations between the USA and Syria, which, it was feared, might damage Israel's interests.

In mid-December 1990 the USA resisted attempts by the UN Security Council to draft a resolution advocating the convening of a Middle East peace conference and an increase in the UN presence in the Occupied Territories. The USA feared that the holding of a peace conference, at this time, could be construed as a concession to Saddam Hussain's concept of 'linkage'.

In mid-December 1990 Shamir visited the USA to confer with President Bush. He was reported to have sought, and received, assurances from President Bush that any diplomatic solution of the crisis in the Gulf would protect Israeli interests. Nevertheless, only days later, the USA proposed a UN Security Council resolution condemning Israel's reinstatement of a policy of deporting Palestinians, in response to violence in the Occupied Territories, as a violation of the Fourth Geneva Convention. The USA also supported further criticism by the UN of Israel's treatment of the Palestinian population in the Occupied Territories and supported a separate UN appeal for an 'active negotiating process' in the Middle East 'at an appopriate time'. However, in view of the crisis in the Gulf, the USA did not believe that such a time had arrived.

Attacks on Israel by Iraqi *Scud* missiles, beginning on 18 January 1991, created the most serious threat to the integrity of the multinational force which had commenced hostilities against Iraq on 16–17 January. It was widely expected that Israel would retaliate immediately, so risking the withdrawal of Arab countries from the multinational force. While Egypt implied that it would accept a measured degree of retaliation, Syria stated bluntly that it would change sides in response to any Israeli attack on Iraq which violated Jordanian airspace. Graver still was the possibility of Iranian involvement on the side of Iraq in response to Israeli military action. US diplomacy, supported by the installation in Israel of advanced US air defence systems, succeeded in averting an immediate Israeli military response, although Israel vowed that it would, ultimately, retaliate for the attacks. By late February Iraq had launched 37 *Scud* missiles, in 16 separate attacks, against Israel. The attacks had killed two people directly and injured more than 300.

Wider strategic considerations apart, a policy of restraint appeared to be in Israel's best interest. The Iraqi missile attacks, together with fears that similar attacks using chemical warheads might be launched, provoked a rare, open outburst of international sympathy for Israel. They also strengthened the Israeli case for rejecting any 'linkage' between the occupation of Kuwait and the Occupied Territories and undermined the PLO's claim to be the only credible interlocutor in a future dialogue with the Israeli Government. In response to the widespread support, expressed by ordinary Palestinians and in the official policy of the PLO, for Saddam Hussain, the attitude of the Israeli Government hardened. Its new mood was symbolized by the appointment by Shamir, in February 1991, of Gen. Rechavam Ze'evi, the leader of the Moledet (Homeland) Party, as Minister without Portfolio and a member of the policy-making 'inner cabinet'. The appointment was strongly opposed by some cabinet members, as Ze'evi was known to advocate a policy of 'transfer' (i.e. the forcible, mass deportation of Palestinians) as a solution to the Arab-Israeli conflict. In early February, in a speech to the Knesset, Shamir again rejected, with more authority than he had been able to muster for many months, proposals for convening an international conference on the Palestinian issue, and promoted his own peace plan, formulated in 1989 (see above), as the only starting-point for any peace dialogue involving the Israeli Government.

In late February 1991 Israel viewed with alarm the likelihood of a successful, Soviet-inspired diplomatic attempt to bring about a cease-fire in the war between the multinational force and Iraq, since such a conclusion to the hostilities would leave Saddam Hussain in power, with much of his military strength intact. Israel openly urged the USA to remove Saddam Hussain from power, even though the legality of such action, with reference to the UN Security Council's Resolution 660, was questionable.

Israeli relations with African countries, the USSR and Eastern Europe improved significantly in late 1989. In September Hungary became the first Eastern bloc country to restore diplomatic relations with Israel, which had been severed in 1967. In January 1990 the USSR upgraded diplomatic links with both Israel and the PLO. Some 200,000 Soviet Jews emigrated to Israel during 1990, owing to the easing of emigration restrictions in the USSR. The Israeli Government has forecast that as many as 1m. Soviet Jews will emigrate to Israel by 1992, altering the demographic character of the country and presenting a major challenge to the economy. Their absorption, in particular the question of where they are entitled to settle, is also likely to be politically controversial. Israel restored diplomatic relations with Poland and Czechoslovakia in February 1990.

Government

Supreme authority in Israel rests with the Knesset (Assembly), with 120 members elected by universal suffrage for four years (subject to dissolution), on the basis of proportional representation. The President, a constitutional Head of State, is elected by the Knesset for five years. Executive power lies with the Cabinet, led by the Prime Minister. The Cabinet takes office after receiving a vote of confidence in the Knesset, to which it is responsible. Ministers are usually members of the Knesset, but non-members may be appointed.

The country is divided into six administrative districts. Local authorities are elected at the same time as elections to the Knesset. There are 31 municipalities (including two Arab towns), 115 local councils (46 Arab and Druze) and 49 regional councils (one Arab) comprising representatives of 700 villages.

Defence

The Israel Defence Forces consist of a small nucleus of commissioned and non-commissioned regular officers, a contingent called up for national service, and a large reserve. Men are called up for 36 months of military service, and women for 24 months. Military service is compulsory for Jews and Druzes, but voluntary for Christians and Arabs. Total regular armed forces numbered 141,000 (including 110,000 conscripts) in June 1990, and full mobilization to 645,000 can be quickly achieved with reserves of 504,000. The armed forces are divided into an army of 104,000, a navy of 9,000 and an air force of 28,000. The defence budget for 1990 was 12,430m. new shekels (US $6,320m.).

Economic Affairs

In 1989, according to estimates by the World Bank, Israel's gross national product (GNP), measured at average 1987–89 prices, was US $44,131m., equivalent to $9,750 per head. During 1980–89, it was estimated, GNP increased, in real terms, at an average annual rate of 3.2%, while GNP per head grew by 1.4% per year. Over the same period, the population increased by an annual average of 1.7%. Israel's gross domestic product (GDP) increased, in real terms, by an annual average of 3.2% in 1980–88. GDP increased by 1% in 1989.

Agriculture (including hunting, forestry and fishing) contributed 4.8% of net domestic product (NDP) in 1987, and employed 4.6% of the working population in 1989, the majority of whom lived in large co-operatives (*kibbutzim*), of which there were 269 at December 1986, or co-operative smallholder villages (*moshavim*), of which there were 456 at December 1987. Israel is largely self-sufficient in foodstuffs. Citrus fruits constitute the main export crop. Other important crops are vegetables (particularly potatoes), wheat, melons, pumpkins and avocados. Poultry, livestock and fish production are also important. Agricultural output increased at an average rate of 2.8% in 1980–87. However, it fell by 10.3% in 1988 and rose by only 0.6% in 1989.

Industry (including manufacturing, power, construction and mining) contributed 28.1% of NDP in 1987, and employed 27.4% of the working population in 1989. The State plays a major role in all sectors of industry, and there is a significant co-operative sector. Industrial production declined by 2% in 1989.

The mining and quarrying sector employed 0.3% of the working population in 1989. There were 33 producing oil wells by 1987, and some natural gas is produced. Potash, bromides, magnesium and other salts are mined. Israel is the world's largest exporter of bromine. There are also proven reserves of 20m. metric tons of low-grade copper ore, and gold, in potentially commercial quantities, was discovered in 1988.

Manufacturing and mining contributed 20.7% of NDP in 1987. Manufacturing employed 21.2% of the working population in 1989. The principal branches of manufacturing, measured by gross revenue, in 1987 were food products, beverages and tobacco (accounting for 21.4% of the total), electrical machinery (14.1%), chemical, petroleum and coal products (10.6%), metal products (10.2%) and textiles and clothing (9.9%). Diamond polishing is also an important activity.

Energy is derived principally from imported petroleum and petroleum products. Imports of mineral fuels comprised 8.4% of the total value of imports in 1988.

Tourism is an important source of revenue. In 1989 a total of 1,424,000 tourists visited Israel, and receipts from the tourist sector totalled US $1,800m. Like all its counterparts in the Middle East and North Africa, the Israeli tourist industry will suffer as a result of the war between Iraq and the multinational forces in Saudi Arabia.

The Israeli banking system is highly developed. The subsidiaries of the three major Israeli bank-groups are represented in many parts of the world.

In 1989 Israel recorded a visible trade deficit of US $1,819m., and there was a deficit of $1,148m. on the current account of the balance of payments. In 1988 the principal source of imports was the USA, which was also the principal market for exports. Other major trading partners are the UK, Germany, Belgium and Japan. The principal exports in 1988 were worked diamonds, machinery and parts, chemical products, and fruit and vegetables. The principal imports were rough diamonds, machinery and parts, chemicals and related products, vehicles and crude petroleum and petroleum products.

The budget for 1989/90 envisaged revenue and expenditure balancing at 53,449m. new shekels. Government revenue each year normally includes some US $3,000m. in economic and military aid from the USA. In early 1991 the Government stated that it might require an additional $10,000m. in grants and loan guarantees from the USA in order to compensate for losses arising from the Gulf War by mid-February 1991; and to finance the absorption of an estimated 1m. Soviet Jewish immigrants by the end of 1992. Israel's nominal external debt amounted to about $10,000m. in 1990, equivalent to approximately 35% of annual GNP. Consumer prices rose by 20.7% in the 12 months to December 1989. An estimated 10% of the labour force were unemployed in the second quarter of 1990.

Assuming a conclusion to the war between Iraq and the multinational forces in Saudi Arabia which is favourable to the long-term security of Israel, the biggest challenge expected to confront the Israeli economy in the period 1990–95 is the absorption of an estimated 1m. Jewish immigrants from the USSR. This will require the restructuring of the labour market to create some 550,000 new jobs; and new investment estimated at US $40,000m.

In late 1990 the Government approved proposals by the Minister of Finance and the Governor of the Bank of Israel to reduce the State's traditional close involvement in the economy, as a response to the challenge of immigration. The proposals included plans for the liberalization of financial markets and a major reduction in import barriers. They would allow virtually free imports of foreign capital, while, as a consequence of deregulation, the domestic capital market would become a major source of funds for new investment. The proposals envisaged a more trade-orientated Israeli economy, since, if their objectives are to be fulfilled, Israeli exports will have to increase by an annual average of 13%.

By 1990 the deleterious effects of the *intifada* on the economy appeared to have diminished. The Bank of Israel calculated that, in terms of lost output, the uprising in the Occupied Territories cost the economy about 2% of GNP in 1988 and 0.5%–1% of GNP in 1989.

Social Welfare

There is a highly advanced system of social welfare. Under the National Insurance Law, the State provides retirement pensions, benefits for industrial injury and maternity, and allowances for large families. The Histadrut (General Federation of Labour), to which more than 90% of all Jewish workers in Israel belong, provides sickness benefits and medical care. The Ministry of Social Welfare provides for general assistance, relief grants, child care and other social services. In 1983 Israel had 11,895 physicians, equivalent to one for every 339 inhabitants, one of the best doctor-patient ratios in the world. In 1988 there were 161 hospitals (of which 64 were private) and 27,842 beds. In 1989/90 about 15% of total government expenditure was allocated to housing amenities, labour, social welfare and health.

Education

Israel has European standards of literacy and educational services. Free compulsory primary education is provided for all children between five and 15 years of age. There is also secondary, vocational and agricultural education. Post-primary education is also free, and it lasts six years, of which four are compulsory. Enrolment at primary and secondary schools in 1987 was equivalent to 92% of children aged six to 17. There are six universities, one institute of technology and one institute of science (the Weizmann Institute), which incorporates a graduate school of science. In 1989/90, 10.25% of government expenditure was allocated to education and culture.

Public Holidays

The Sabbath starts at sunset on Friday and ends at nightfall on Saturday. The Jewish year 5752 begins on 9 September 1991, and the year 5753 on 28 September 1992.

1991: 30 March–5 April (Passover—public holidays on first and last days of festival), 18 April (Independence Day), 19 May (Shavuot), 9–10 September (Rosh Hashanah, Jewish New Year), 18 September (Yom Kippur), 23 September (Succot), 30 September (Simhat Torah).

1992: 18–24 April (Passover—see 1991), 7 May (Independence Day), 7 June (Shavuot), 28–29 September (Rosh Hashanah, Jewish New Year), 7 October (Yom Kippur), 12 October (Succot), 19 October (Simhat Torah).

(The Jewish festivals and fast days commence in the evening of the dates given.)

Islamic holidays are observed by Muslim Arabs, and Christian holidays by the Christian Arab community.

Weights and Measures

The metric system is in force.

1 dunum = 1,000 sq metres.

Statistical Survey

Source: Central Bureau of Statistics, Hakirya, Romema, POB 13015, Jerusalem 91130; tel. (02) 211400.

Area and Population

AREA, POPULATION AND DENSITY

Area (sq km)	
Land	21,501
Inland water	445
Total	21,946*
Population (*de jure*; census results)†	
20 May 1972	3,147,683
4 June 1983	
Males	2,011,590
Females	2,026,030
Total	4,037,620
Population (*de jure*; official estimates at 31 December)†	
1986	4,331,300
1987	4,406,500
1988	4,476,800
Density (per sq km) at 31 December 1988	204.0

* 8,473.4 sq miles. Area includes East Jerusalem, annexed by Israel in June 1967.
† Including the population of East Jerusalem and Israeli residents in certain other areas under Israeli military occupation since June 1967. Beginning in 1981, figures also include non-Jews in the Golan sub-district, an Israeli-occupied area of Syrian territory. Census results exclude adjustment for underenumeration.

Mid-1989: Estimated population 4,509,000.

ADMINISTERED TERRITORIES*

	Area (sq km)	Estimated population (31 December 1988)
Golan	1,176	24,300
Judaea and Samaria	5,879	895,000
Gaza Area†	378	589,000
Total	7,433	1,508,300

The area figures in this table refer to 1 October 1973. No later figures are available.

* The area and population of the Administered Territories have changed as a result of the October 1973 war.
† Not including El-Arish and Sinai which, as of April 1979 and April 1982 respectively, were returned to Egypt.

POPULATION BY RELIGION (estimates, 31 December 1988)

	Males	Females	Total	%
Jews	1,819,500	1,839,500	3,659,000	81.7
Muslims	322,300	312,300	634,600	14.2
Christians	51,200	53,800	105,000	2.3
Druze and others	39,900	38,200	78,100	1.7
Total	2,232,900	2,243,900	4,476,800	100.0

PRINCIPAL TOWNS (estimated population at 31 December 1988)

Jerusalem (capital)	493,500*	Rishon LeZiyyon	123,800
Tel-Aviv–Jaffa	317,800	Netanya	117,800
Haifa	222,600	Ramat Gan	115,700
Holon	146,100	Beersheba	113,200
Petach-Tikva	133,600	Bene Beraq	109,400
Bat Yam	133,100		

* Including East Jerusalem, annexed in June 1967.

BIRTHS, MARRIAGES AND DEATHS*

	Registered live births		Registered marriages		Registered deaths	
	Number	Rate (per 1,000)	Number	Rate (per 1,000)	Number	Rate (per 1,000)
1981	93,308	23.6	29,652	7.5	26,085	6.6
1982	96,695	24.0	29,555	7.4	27,780†	6.9
1983	98,724	24.0	31,096	7.6	27,731	6.8
1984	98,478	23.7	29,871	7.2	27,805	6.7
1985	99,376	23.5	29,158	6.9	28,093	6.6
1986	99,341	23.1	30,113	7.0	29,415	6.8
1987	99,022	22.7	30,116	6.9	29,191	6.7
1988	100,454	22.6	31,070	7.0	29,410	6.6

* Including East Jerusalem.
† Excluding casualties of war.

1989 (provisional): Live births 100,500 (birth rate 22.3 per 1,000); Deaths 28,600 (death rate 6.3 per 1,000).

IMMIGRATION*

	1986	1987	1988
Immigrants:			
on immigrant visas	2,928	5,924	6,306
on tourist visas†	1,014	1,231	1,293
Potential immigrants:			
on potential immigrant visas	4,330	4,682	4,464
on tourist visas†	1,233	1,128	971
Total	9,505	12,965	13,034

* Excluding immigrating citizens (1,764 in 1986; 1,833 in 1987; 1,800 in 1988) and Israeli residents returning from abroad.
† Figures refer to tourists who changed their status to immigrants or potential immigrants.

ECONOMICALLY ACTIVE POPULATION (annual averages, '000 persons aged 15 years and over, excluding armed forces)

	1987	1988	1989
Agriculture, forestry and fishing	72.0	66.6	67.6
Mining and quarrying	4.7	3.6	4.2
Manufacturing	323.7	318.0	309.5
Electricity and water	13.6	14.5	14.4
Construction	67.7	73.7	71.6
Trade, restaurants and hotels	193.4	206.5	211.4
Transport, storage and communications	91.6	94.8	93.0
Financing and business services	134.3	146.5	144.5
Public and community services	404.3	421.4}	536.6
Personal and other services	89.1	97.2}	
Activities not adequately defined	9.3	9.4	8.4
Total employed	1,403.7	1,453.1	1,461.2
Unemployed	90.4	99.9	142.5
Total civilian labour force	1,494.1	1,553.0	1,603.7
Males	908.6	938.6	956.0
Females	585.5	614.4	647.7

ISRAEL

Agriculture

PRINCIPAL CROPS ('000 metric tons)

	1986	1987	1988
Wheat	168.5	298.0	211.0
Barley	11.2	20.5	10.0
Corn on the cob	89.6	106.5	105.3
Potatoes	206.5	218.3	215.7
Groundnuts (in shell)	23.0	21.1	18.9
Cottonseed	115.9	97.7	103.9
Cotton (lint)	68.9	59.2	63.0
Olives	38.0	25.0	39.0
Cabbages	38.8	46.3	37.5
Tomatoes	282.1	264.0	245.3
Cucumbers	60.4	60.7	64.5
Peppers (green)	50.5	47.6	36.0
Onions (dry)	50.3	42.2	43.0
Carrots	67.7	80.3	72.7
Watermelons	92.1	107.8	116.7
Melons	43.7	46.5	43.8
Grapes (table)	51.5	50.1	48.0
Grapes (wine)	30.8	37.8	36.4
Apples	115.7	111.3	111.7
Peaches	32.2	29.7	35.5
Clementines and tangerines	126.4	143.6	113.6
Lemons	58.1	69.0	46.8
Grapefruit	376.6	392.2	314.3
Other citrus fruit*	747.5	903.5	651.5
Avocados	68.0	134.7	35.8
Bananas	95.5	101.0	69.1
Strawberries	11.0	13.1	12.2

* Including oranges ('000 metric tons): 897 in 1987; 638 in 1988.

LIVESTOCK ('000 head)

	1986	1987	1988
Cattle	325	345	357
Poultry	24,310	25,790	25,240
Sheep	306	372	394
Goats	126.5	116	125

Milk production (million litres): 870 in 1986; 907 in 1987; 890 in 1988.

Fishing

('000 metric tons, live weight)

	1986	1987	1988*
Inland waters	13.3	15.0	15.0
Mediterranean and Black Sea*	5.0	4.8	4.8
Atlantic Ocean	2.8	8.5	8.5
Indian Ocean*	0.2	0.2	0.2
Total catch	21.2	28.4	28.4

* FAO estimates.
Source: FAO, *Yearbook of Fishery Statistics*.

Mining

	1986	1987	1988
Crude petroleum (million litres)	14	17	21
Natural gas (million cu m)	40	45	41
Phosphate rock ('000 metric tons)	2,518	2,731	2,548
Potash ('000 metric tons)	2,035	2,057	2,041

Industry

SELECTED PRODUCTS
('000 metric tons, unless otherwise stated)

	1986	1987	1988
Wheat flour	514	529	528
Refined vegetable oils (metric tons)	79,640	76,876	69,597
Margarine	33.7	32.6	30.9
Wine ('000 litres)	17,381	16,995	15,670
Beer ('000 litres)	52,281	53,638	55,572
Cigarettes (metric tons)	6,723	6,888	5,882
Cotton yarn (metric tons)	14,914	16,132	13,543
Newsprint (metric tons)	1,148	2,028	1,940
Writing and printing paper (metric tons)	64,930	65,119	60,257
Other paper (metric tons)	35,752	36,737	44,950
Cardboard (metric tons)	54,468	61,636	71,087
Rubber tyres ('000)	744	920	573
Ammonia (metric tons)	89,400	97,056	89,223
Ammonium sulphate (metric tons)	46,251	40,843	40,855
Sulphuric acid	182	143	164
Chlorine (metric tons)	29,844	32,901	33,804
Caustic soda (metric tons)	26,991	29,717	29,717
Polyethylene (metric tons)	76,881	90,323	94,305
Liquefied petroleum gas (metric tons)	168,261	191,867	197,517
Paints (metric tons)	40,609	43,391	32,227
Cement	1,624	2,226	2,326
Commercial vehicles (number)	1,152	971	615
Electricity (million kWh)	15,503	17,102	18,761

Finance

CURRENCY AND EXCHANGE RATES

Monetary Units
100 agorot (singular: agora) = 1 new shekel (sheqel).

Denominations
Coins: 1 agora, 5, 10 and 50 agorot; 1 new shekel.
Notes: 1, 5, 10, 50 and 100 new shekels.

Sterling and Dollar Equivalents (30 September 1990)
£1 sterling = 3.854 new shekels;
US $1 = 2.057 new shekels;
100 new shekels = £25.95 = $48.61.

Average Exchange Rate (new shekels per US $)
1987   1.5946
1988   1.5989
1989   1.9164

Note: The new shekel, worth 1,000 of the former units, was introduced on 1 January 1986.

ISRAEL

CENTRAL GOVERNMENT BUDGET ESTIMATES
(million new shekels, year ending 31 March)

Revenue	1988/89	1989/90
Ordinary budget	31,161.0	36,857.0
Income tax and property tax	11,062.2	13,250.1
Customs and excise	1,187.2	711.3
Purchase tax	2,692.3	3,158.6
Employers' tax	588.9	578.7
Value added tax	6,213.5	7,603.6
Other taxes	1,819.8	2,539.5
Interest	539.1	774.0
Transfer from development budget	5,827.1	6,962.3
Other receipts	1,411.6	1,278.9
Development budget	19,289.0	14,033.0
Foreign loans	6,172.5	6,850.9
Internal loans	37,514.2	12,103.5
Transfer to ordinary budget	−5,827.2	−6,963.2
Other receipts	1,938.5	2,041.8
Total	50,450.0	50,890.0

Revised budget estimates (million new shekels, year ending 31 March): 1987/88: Revenue and Expenditure 41,257; 1988/89: Revenue and Expenditure 53,088; 1989/90: Revenue and Expenditure 53,449.

Expenditure*	1988/89	1989/90
Ordinary account	31,161.0	36,857.0
Ministry of finance	227.5	294.9
Ministry of defence	9,024.2	10,586.4
Ministry of health	448.7	560.2
Ministry of education and culture	3,003.9	3,777.8
Ministry of police	648.2	810.8
Ministry of labour and social welfare	3,807.9	4,883.6
Other ministries†	894.3	1,533.3
Interest	7,054.9	8,182.3
Pensions and compensations	872.5	1,138.9
Transfers to local authorities	570.3	670.8
Subsidies	1,654.7	1,621.7
Reserves	1,919.5	1,776.5
Other expenditures	1,028.3	1,017.3
Development budget	19,289.0	14,033.0
Agriculture	125.4	144.5
Industry, trade and tourism	555.5	662.4
Housing	408.9	512.2
Public buildings	150.5	192.3
Development of energy resources	38.6	44.9
Debt repayment	17,533.7	11,937.9
Other expenditures	476.4	538.9
Total	50,450.0	50,890.0

* Does not include the entire defence budget.
† Includes the President, Prime Minister, State Comptroller and the Knesset.

CENTRAL BANK RESERVES (US $ million at 31 December)

	1987	1988	1989
Gold*	50.5	47.9	46.8
IMF special drawing rights	0.1	0.1	0.1
Foreign exchange	5,876.0	4,015.5	5,276.1
Total	5,926.6	4,063.5	5,323.0

* Valued at 35 SDRs per troy ounce.
Source: IMF, *International Financial Statistics*.

MONEY SUPPLY (million new shekels at 31 December)

	1987	1988	1989
Currency outside banks	1,365	1,643	2,224
Demand deposits at deposit money banks	1,922	2,012	3,079

Source: IMF, *International Financial Statistics*.

COST OF LIVING
(Consumer Price Index, annual averages; base: 1980 = 100)

	1987	1988	1989
Food	38,909	46,029	55,484
Fuel and light	25,482	27,979	39,472
Clothing	35,521	39,429	41,027
Rent	41,307	48,329	63,944
All items (incl. others)	39,938	46,447	55,833

Source: International Labour Office, *Year Book of Labour Statistics*.

NATIONAL ACCOUNTS (million new shekels at current prices)
National Income and Product (provisional)

	1985	1986	1987
Compensation of employees	13,946	22,246	29,222
Operating surplus	7,289	8,591	10,726
Domestic factor incomes	21,235	30,837	39,948
Consumption of fixed capital	4,753	7,145	8,805
Statistical discrepancy	12	1,143	540
Gross domestic product at factor cost	26,000	39,125	49,293
Indirect taxes	5,944	9,988	13,192
Less Subsidies	1,858	1,935	2,372
GDP in purchasers' values	30,086	47,178	60,113
Factor income received from abroad	1,322	1,385	1,522
Less Factor income paid abroad	3,662	4,581	5,165
Gross national product	27,746	43,982	56,470
Less Consumption of fixed capital	4,753	7,145	8,805
National income in market prices	22,993	36,837	47,665

Source: UN, *National Accounts Statistics*.

Expenditure on the Gross Domestic Product

	1986	1987	1988
Government final consumption expenditure	13,865	19,610	22,308
Private final consumption expenditure	27,388	35,636	42,324
Increase in stocks	804	60	−60
Gross fixed capital formation	7,872	10,910	12,314
Total domestic expenditure	49,929	66,216	76,886
Exports of goods and services	17,219	21,996	24,159
Less Imports of goods and services	23,292	32,572	34,087
GDP in purchasers' values	43,856	55,640	66,958
GDP at constant 1985 prices	29,007	31,054	31,609

Source: IMF, *International Financial Statistics*.

ISRAEL

Net Domestic Product by Economic Activity (at factor cost)

	1985	1986	1987
Agriculture, hunting, forestry and fishing	1,062	1,565	2,020
Manufacturing, mining and quarrying	4,742	6,847	8,661
Electricity, gas and water	424	666	953
Construction	924	1,454	2,153
Wholesale and retail trade, restaurants and hotels	2,971	4,151	5,284
Transport, storage and communications	1,599	2,387	3,191
Finance, insurance, real estate and business services	4,771	6,284	8,513
Government services	4,800	7,336	9,420
Other community, social and personal services	580	1,116	1,681
Statistical discrepancy	777	630	688
Sub-total	22,650	32,436	42,564
Less Imputed bank service charge	1,414	1,600	2,614
Other adjustments (incl. errors and omissions)	12	1,143	540
Total	21,248	31,979	40,490

Source: UN, *National Accounts Statistics*.

BALANCE OF PAYMENTS (US $ million)

	1987	1988	1989
Merchandise exports f.o.b.	9,140	10,111	10,917
Merchandise imports f.o.b.	12,898	13,158	12,736
Trade balance	−3,758	−3,047	−1,819
Export of services	4,774	5,201	5,750
Import of services	6,724	7,340	7,659
Balance on goods and services	−5,708	−5,186	−3,728
Private unrequited transfers (net)	1,369	1,145	1,566
Government unrequited transfers (net)	3,471	3,418	3,310
Current balance	−868	−623	1,148
Long-term capital (net)	559	−573	−115
Short-term capital (net)	565	−59	−898
Net errors and omissions	388	93	1,254
Total (net monetary movements)	644	−1,162	1,389
Valuation changes (net)	438	−63	3
Changes in reserves	1,082	−1,225	1,392

Source: IMF, *International Financial Statistics*.

External Trade

PRINCIPAL COMMODITIES (US $ '000)

Imports c.i.f.*	1986	1987	1988
Diamonds, rough	1,522,000	1,837,000	2,414,900
Machinery and parts	1,413,200	1,708,100	1,654,100
Electrical machinery and parts	575,400	680,600	663,600
Iron and steel	297,900	318,500	382,600
Metal products n.i.e.	225,100	264,900	248,500
Vehicles	586,100	915,300	1,017,200
Chemicals and related products	835,100	1,040,100	1,184,200
Crude petroleum and petroleum products	786,200	1,032,700	951,400
Cereals	251,100	233,600	288,300
Textiles and textile articles	331,000	392,000	367,000
Total (incl. others)	9,635,200	11,916,400	12,959,700

* Figures exclude military goods. Total imports in 1988 were $15,021 million.

1989 (US $ million): Total imports 13,196.9, excluding military goods (1,192).

Exports f.o.b.	1986	1987	1988
Diamonds, worked	1,879,400	2,301,900	2,837,100
Clothing	282,200	344,800	375,700
Textiles and textile articles	151,900	209,400	224,500
Fruit and vegetables	523,100	636,200	666,500
Fertilizers	158,900	184,100	228,700
Organic chemicals	266,100	307,900	373,300
Inorganic chemicals	178,800	208,000	247,800
Chemical products	491,400	684,500	746,300
Transport equipment	242,400	291,700	292,900
Machinery and parts	766,700	882,900	1,688,900
Electrical machinery and parts	279,300	345,400	496,300
Metals and metal products	875,100	863,600	333,400
Total (incl. others)	7,154,300	8,475,400	9,739,300

PRINCIPAL TRADING PARTNERS (US $ '000)

Imports (excl. military goods)	1986	1987	1988
Argentina	27,100	37,600	39,000
Australia	58,100	50,000	83,700
Austria	56,400	59,800	59,500
Belgium/Luxembourg	1,258,400	1,695,600	1,966,700
Brazil	22,700	17,500	46,100
Canada	80,400	113,200	92,300
Denmark	48,700	60,000	57,400
Finland	56,000	70,400	88,800
France	385,600	545,900	545,500
Germany, Fed. Rep.	1,213,500	1,539,100	1,468,400
Greece	24,800	48,100	56,900
Hong Kong	51,800	86,700	98,000
India	21,600	39,700	85,600
Ireland	21,900	50,700	32,900
Italy	559,800	755,200	795,000
Japan	307,400	401,000	478,300
Netherlands	301,700	381,200	448,400
Romania	28,800	30,600	34,100
Singapore	19,700	28,200	32,300
South Africa	202,900	221,300	204,900
Spain	125,700	125,800	125,300
Sweden	106,800	172,000	160,100
Switzerland	774,100	879,800	1,162,100
Turkey	18,500	19,900	34,600
United Kingdom	985,000	1,117,500	1,208,800
USA	1,788,600	1,932,400	2,153,200
Uruguay	16,400	24,800	32,300

ISRAEL

Statistical Survey

Exports	1986	1987	1988
Australia	56,600	71,200	104,500
Austria	41,700	41,900	50,000
Belgium/Luxembourg	265,500	278,200	393,900
Brazil	44,300	47,300	51,300
Canada	78,100	85,300	95,200
France	313,100	386,600	383,200
Germany, Fed. Rep.	373,400	473,600	521,100
Greece	44,600	96,700	125,700
Hong Kong	273,300	378,900	513,000
Italy	251,700	306,900	382,100
Japan	323,300	494,600	657,100
Netherlands	309,200	384,900	461,000
Singapore	40,100	37,000	54,700
South Africa	63,800	81,600	106,600
Spain	55,800	99,300	123,700
Sweden	43,500	51,900	51,300
Switzerland	178,900	197,600	237,800
Turkey	34,000	34,300	42,900
United Kingdom	513,300	656,600	769,600
USA	2,348,700	2,758,900	2,986,800
Venezuela	27,000	22,100	45,200

Transport

RAILWAYS (traffic)

	1986	1987	1988
Passengers ('000)	2,516	2,544	2,495
Freight ('000 metric tons)	6,406	6,851	6,589

ROAD TRAFFIC, 1988 (motor vehicles)

Private cars (incl. station wagons)	753,450
Trucks, trailers	143,805
Buses	8,693
Taxis	7,956
Motor cycles, motor scooters	35,133
Other vehicles	3,749
Total	952,786

SHIPPING
(international sea-borne freight traffic, '000 metric tons)*

	1986	1987	1988
Goods loaded	7,336	8,052	7,737
Goods unloaded	9,712	11,324	11,702

* Excluding petroleum.

CIVIL AVIATION (El Al revenue flights only, '000)

	1986	1987	1988
Kilometres flown	42,581	45,184	44,407
Revenue passenger-km	6,931,000	7,558,000	6,953,000
Mail (tons)	1,083	1,247	1,222

Tourism

	1987	1988	1989
Tourist arrivals	1,378,742	1,169,582	1,424,000

Communications Media

	1986	1987	1988
Radio receivers ('000 in use)	2,000	2,050	2,074
Television receivers ('000 in use)	1,125	1,150	1,175
Telephones ('000 in use)	1,890	2,065	2,190
Daily newspapers	27	n.a.	30

Book production (1985): 2,214 titles; 8,872,000 copies.
Non-daily newspapers (1985): 83.
Other periodicals (1985): 807.
Source: mainly UNESCO, *Statistical Yearbook*.

Education

(1988/89)

	Schools	Pupils	Teachers
Jewish			
Kindergarten	n.a.	277,200	n.a.
Primary schools	1,323	493,649	35,364
Intermediate schools	304	120,339	13,274
Secondary schools	536	202,261	24,649
Vocational schools	315	94,454	n.a.
Agricultural schools	25	5,022	n.a.
Teacher training colleges	27	11,574	n.a.
Others (handicapped)	191	11,434	3,152
Arab			
Kindergarten	n.a.	21,900	n.a.
Primary schools	327	139,220	6,644
Intermediate schools	63	27,230	1,868
Secondary schools	84	38,237	2,542
Vocational schools	42	6,516	n.a.
Agricultural schools	2	718	n.a.
Teacher training colleges	2	568	n.a.
Others (handicapped)	15	1,146	220

Directory

The Constitution

There is no written constitution. In June 1950 the Knesset voted to adopt a state constitution by evolution over an unspecified period. A number of laws, including the Law of Return (1950), the Nationality Law (1952), the State President (Tenure) Law (1952), the Education Law (1953) and the 'Yad-va-Shem' Memorial Law (1953), are considered as incorporated into the State Constitution. Other constitutional laws are: The Law and Administration Ordinance (1948), the Knesset Election Law (1951), the Law of Equal Rights for Women (1951), the Judges Act (1953), the National Service and National Insurance Acts (1953), and the Basic Law (The Knesset) (1958). The provisions of constitutional legislation that affect the main organs of government are summarized below:

THE PRESIDENT

The President is elected by the Knesset for a maximum of two five-year terms.

Ten or more Knesset Members may propose a candidate for the Presidency.

Voting will be by secret ballot.

The President may not leave the country without the consent of the Government.

The President may resign by submitting his resignation in writing to the Speaker.

The President may be relieved of his duties by the Knesset for misdemeanour.

The Knesset is entitled to decide by a two-thirds majority that the President is too incapacitated owing to ill health to fulfil his duties permanently.

The Speaker of the Knesset will act for the President when the President leaves the country, or when he cannot perform his duties owing to ill health.

THE KNESSET

The Knesset is the parliament of the State. There are 120 members.

It is elected by general, national, direct, equal, secret and proportional elections.

Every Israeli national of 18 years or over shall have the right to vote in elections to the Knesset unless a court has deprived him of that right by virtue of any law.

Every Israeli national of 21 and over shall have the right to be elected to the Knesset unless a court has deprived him of that right by virtue of any law.

The following shall not be candidates: the President of the State; the two Chief Rabbis; a judge (shofet) in office; a judge (dayan) of a religious court; the State Comptroller; the Chief of the General Staff of the Defence Army of Israel; rabbis and ministers of other religions in office; senior State employees and senior Army officers of such ranks and in such functions as shall be determined by law.

The term of office of the Knesset shall be four years.

The elections to the Knesset shall take place on the third Tuesday of the month of Cheshven in the year in which the tenure of the outgoing Knesset ends.

Election day shall be a day of rest, but transport and other public services shall function normally.

Results of the elections shall be published within 14 days.

The Knesset shall elect from among its members a Chairman and Vice-Chairman.

The Knesset shall elect from among its members permanent committees, and may elect committees for specific matters.

The Knesset may appoint commissions of inquiry to investigate matters designated by the Knesset.

The Knesset shall hold two sessions a year; one of them shall open within four weeks after the Feast of the Tabernacles, the other within four weeks after Independence Day; the aggregate duration of the two sessions shall not be less than eight months.

The outgoing Knesset shall continue to hold office until the convening of the incoming Knesset.

The members of the Knesset shall receive a remuneration as provided by law.

THE GOVERNMENT

The Government shall tender its resignation to the President immediately after his election, but shall continue with its duties until the formation of a new government. After consultation with representatives of the parties in the Knesset, the President shall charge one of the Members with the formation of a government. The Government shall be composed of a Prime Minister and a number of ministers from among the Knesset Members or from outside the Knesset. After it has been chosen, the Government shall appear before the Knesset and shall be considered as formed after having received a vote of confidence. Within seven days of receiving a vote of confidence, the Prime Minister and the other ministers shall swear allegiance to the State of Israel and its Laws and undertake to carry out the decisions of the Knesset.

The Government

HEAD OF STATE

President: Gen. CHAIM HERZOG (took office 5 May 1983; re-elected 23 February 1988).

THE CABINET
(February 1991)

Prime Minister, Minister of Labour and Minister of Environment: ITZHAK SHAMIR (Likud).

Deputy Prime Minister and Minister of Foreign Affairs: DAVID LEVY (Likud).

Deputy Prime Minister and Minister of Trade and Industry: MOSHE NISSIM (Likud).

Minister of Defence: MOSHE ARENS (Likud).

Minister of Finance: ITZHAK MODAI (MAZI).

Minister of Housing: ARIEL SHARON (Likud).

Minister of Justice: DAN MERIDOR (Likud).

Minister of Police: RONNI MILO (Likud).

Minister of Transport: MOSHE KATZAV (Likud).

Minister of Economy and Planning: DAVID MAGEN (Likud).

Minister of Health: EHUD OLMERT (Likud).

Minister of Tourism: GIDEON PATT (Likud).

Minister of Immigration Absorption: ITZHAK PERETZ (Independent).

Minister of Interior: ARYE DERI (Shas).

Minister of Education and Culture: ZEVULUN HAMMER (NRP).

Minister for Religious Affairs: AVNER SHAKI (National Religious Party).

Minister for Agriculture: RAFAEL EITAN (Tzomet).

Minister for Science, Technology and Energy: YUVAL NEEMAN (Tehiya).

Minister of Communications: RAFAEL PINHASI (Shas).

Minister without Portfolio: Gen. RECHAVAM ZE'EVI.

MINISTRIES

Office of the Prime Minister: Hakirya, Ruppin St, Jerusalem.

Ministry of Agriculture: POB 7011, Hakirya, Tel-Aviv 61070; tel. 03-255473; telex 361496; fax 03-211217.

Ministry of Communications: 23 Rehov Yafo, Jerusalem 91999; tel. 02-230222; fax 02-240621.

Ministry of Defence: Kaplan St, Hakirya, Tel-Aviv 67659; tel. 03-205144; telex 33722; fax 03-217915.

Ministry of Economics and Planning: 3 Rehov Kaplan, Kiryat Ben-Gurion, Jerusalem 91950; tel. 02-535178; fax 02-789424.

Ministry of Education and Culture: Hakirya, 14 Klausner St, Tel-Aviv; tel. 03-414155.

Ministry of Energy and Infrastructure: 234 Rehov Yafo, Jerusalem 91130; tel. 02-551211; fax 02-534828.

Ministry of the Environment: 2 Kaplan St, Kiryat Ben-Gurion, POB 6158, Jerusalem 91061; tel. 02-660151.

Ministry of Finance: 1 Kaplan St., Kiryat Ben-Gurion, POB 883, Jerusalem; tel. 02-558111; telex 25216; fax 02-558359.

Ministry of Foreign Affairs: Hakirya, Romema, Jerusalem 91950; tel. 02-303111; telex 25223; fax 02-303367.

Ministry of Health: 2 Ben Tabai St, Jerusalem 91010; tel. 02-705705; telex 26138; fax 02-781456.

Ministry of Housing and Construction: 2 Clermont-Ganneau St, POB 13198, Jerusalem 91131; tel. 02-277211; fax 02-823532.

ISRAEL

Ministry of Immigrant Absorption: 1 Rehov Kaplan, Kiryat Ben-Gurion, Jerusalem 91006; tel. 02-695611.

Ministry of the Interior: 2 Kaplan St, Kiryat Ben-Gurion, POB 6158, Jerusalem 91061; tel. 02-660151.

Ministry of Justice: 29 Rehov Salahadin, Jerusalem 91010; tel. 02-270111; fax 02-869473.

Ministry of Labour and Social Affairs: 2 Rehov Kaplan, Kiryat Ben-Gurion, Jerusalem 91008; tel. 02-694211; fax 02-699427.

Ministry of Police: 3 Sheikh Jarrah, Kiryat Hamemshala, Jerusalem 91181; tel. 02-277211; fax 02-826769.

Ministry of Religious Affairs: 236 Rehov Yafo, Jerusalem 91130; tel. 02-532140; fax 02-551146.

Ministry of Science: Kiryat Hamemshala, Bldg 3, Jerusalem 91181; tel. 02-277096; fax 02-820691.

Ministry of Tourism: 24 Rehov King George, POB 1018, Jerusalem; tel. 02-237311; fax 02-382148.

Ministry of Trade and Industry: 30 Rehov Agron, Jerusalem 94190; tel. 02-210111; fax 02-245110.

Ministry of Transport: Klal Bldg, 97 Rehov Yafo, Jerusalem 91000; tel. 02-229211; fax 02-229206.

Legislature

KNESSET

Speaker: Dov Shilansky.

General Election, 1 November 1988

Party	Votes	Seats
Likud	709,305	40
Labour	685,363	39
Shas	107,709	6
Ratz	97,513	5
National Religious Party	89,720	5
Agudat Israel	102,714	5
Hadash	84,032	4
Tehiya	70,370	3
United Workers Party (Mapam)	56,345	3
Shinui	39,538	2
Moledet	44,174	2
Degal Hatora	34,279	2
Tzomet	45,489	2
Arab Democratic Party	27,012	1
Progressive List for Peace	33,695	1
Others (12 parties)	55,874	—
Total	**2,283,132**	**120**

Political Organizations

Agudath Israel: POB 513, Jerusalem; tel. 02-385251; fax 02-385145; orthodox Jewish party; stands for strict observance of Jewish religious law; Leaders Moshe Feldman, Menachem Porush.

Agudat Israel World Organization (AIWO): Hacherut Sq., POB 326, Jerusalem 91002; tel. 02-384357; f. 1912 at Congress of Orthodox Jewry, Kattowitz, Germany (now Katowice, Poland), to help solve the problems facing Jewish people all over the world; more than 500,000 mems in 25 countries; Pres. Rabbi Dr I. Lewin (New York); Chair. Rabbi J. M. Abramowitz (Jerusalem), Rabbi M. Sherer (New York); Gen. Sec. Abraham Hirsch (Jerusalem).

Arab Democratic Party: Nazareth; tel. 06-560937; f. 1988; aims: to unify Arab political forces so as to influence Palestinian and Israeli policy; international recognition of the Palestinian people's right to self-determination; the holding of an international peace conference in the Middle East, with the participation of all parties to the conflict, including the PLO, as sole representative of the Palestinian people, on an equal footing; the withdrawal of Israel from all territories occupied in 1967; Chair. Abd al-Wahab Darawshah.

Centre Party (Shinui): 22 Rehov Mikveh Yisrael, Tel-Aviv; tel. 03-614737; f. 1988; as a merger of dissidents from the Labour Alignment and Likud blocs with the Shinui party, led by Amnon Rubinstein, which withdrew from the coalition govt of nat. unity in May 1987; mems included Moshe Amirav, expelled from Herut Central Cttee for holding indirect talks with PLO.

Council for Peace and Security: f. 1988 by four retd Israeli generals: Maj.-Gen. Aharon Yariv, Maj.-Gen. Ori Orr, Brig.-Gen. Yoram Agmon and Brig.-Gen. Ephraim Sneh; Moshe Amirav of Centre Party a founder mem.; aims: an Israeli withdrawal from the Occupied Territories in return for a peace treaty with the Arab nations.

Degel Hatora: 103 Rehov Beit Vegan, Jerusalem; tel. 02-422069; f. 1988 as breakaway from Agudat Israel; orthodox Western Jews; Sec.-Gen. Haim Epstein.

Gush Emunim (Bloc of the Faithful): f. 1967; engaged in unauthorized establishment of Jewish settlements in the occupied territories; Leader Rabbi Moshe Levinger.

Hadash (Democratic Front for Peace and Equality): 3 Rehov Hashikma, POB 26205, Tel-Aviv; tel. 03-827492; descended from the Socialist Workers' Party of Palestine (f. 1919), renamed Communist Party of Palestine 1921, Communist Party of Israel (Maki) 1948; pro-Soviet anti-Zionist group formed New Communist Party of Israel (Rakah) 1965; Jewish Arab membership; aims for a socialist system in Israel, a lasting peace between Israel and the Arab countries and the Palestinian Arab people, favours full implementation of UN Security Council Resolutions 242 and 338, Israeli withdrawal from all Arab territories occupied since 1967, formation of a Palestinian Arab state in the West Bank and Gaza Strip, recognition of national rights of State of Israel and Palestine people, democratic rights and defence of working class interests, and demands an end of discrimination against Arab minority in Israel and against oriental Jewish communities. Contested 1988 general election as Hadash (Democratic Front for Peace and Equality), an alliance with the Black Panther movement of Oriental Jews, winning 4 seats in the Knesset; Sec.-Gen. Meir Vilner.

Israel Labour Party: 110 Ha'yarkon St, Tel-Aviv 61032; tel. 03-209222; fax 03-5271744; f. 1968 as a merger of the three Labour groups, Mapai, Rafi and Achdut Ha'avoda; a Zionist democratic socialist party, was in government from 1948 to 1977; with the United Workers' Party (Mapam), formed the main opposition bloc under name of Labour-Mapam Alignment until elections of July 1984; formed National Unity government with Likud in 1984 and again in 1988; Yahad (Together) (f. 1984; advocates a peace settlement with the Arab peoples and the Palestinians; Leader Ezer Weizmann) joined the Labour bloc in Jan. 1987; Chair. of Israel Labour Party Shimon Peres; Sec.-Gen. Micha Harish.

Kach (Thus): 111 Agripas St, Jerusalem; tel. 02-247202; f. 1977; right-wing religious nationalist party; advocates creation of a Torah state and expulsion of all Arabs from Israel and the Occupied Territories; not permitted to contest the 1988 general election; Leader (vacant).

Likud (Consolidation): 38 Rehov King George, Tel-Aviv 61231; tel. 03-5630666; fax 03-283560; f. September 1973; is a parliamentary bloc of Herut (Freedom; f. 1948; Leader Itzhak Shamir; Sec.-Gen. Moshe Arens), the Liberal Party of Israel (f. 1961; Chair. Avraham Sharir), Laam (For the Nation) (f. 1976; fmrly led by Yigael Hurwitz, who left the coalition to form his own party, Ometz, before the 1984 general election), Ahdut (a one-man faction, Hillel Seidel), Tami (f. 1981; represents the interests of Sephardic Jews; Leader Aharon Uzan), which joined Likud in June 1987 and an independent faction with five Knesset members (f. 1990; Leader Itzhak Modai), reportedly the nucleus of a new Party for the Advancement of the Zionist Idea; Herut and the Liberal Party formally merged in August 1988 to form the Likud-National Liberal Movement; aims: territorial integrity (advocates retention of all the territory of post-1922 mandatory Palestine); absorption of newcomers; a social order based on freedom and justice, elimination of poverty and want; development of an economy that will ensure a decent standard of living; improvement of the environment and the quality of life. Likud was the sole government party from June 1977 until September 1984 when it formed the National Unity government with Likud; a new National Unity government was formed after the 1988 election; Leader of Likud Itzhak Shamir.

Moledet (Homeland): 14 Rehov Yehuda Halevi, Tel-Aviv; tel. 03-654580; f. 1988; right-wing nationalist party; aims: the expulsion ('transfer') of the 1.5m. Palestinians living in the West Bank and Gaza Strip; Leader Gen. Rechavam Ze'evi.

Morasha (Heritage): Tel-Aviv; merged with National Religious Party faction in the Knesset July 1986.

Movement for the Advancement of the Zionist Idea (MAZI): f. 1990 as breakaway group of Likud; Leader Itzhak Modai.

National Religious Party (NRP): 166 Ibn Gavirol St, Kastel Bldg, Tel-Aviv; tel. 03-444151; fax 03-5468942; f. 1956; stands for strict adherence to Jewish religion and tradition, and strives to achieve the application of religious precepts of Judaism in everyday life; it is also endeavouring to establish the Constitution of Israel on Jewish religious law (the Torah); withdrew from (Labour) government coalition in December 1976 and before the 1984 general election supported the Likud coalition; 135,000 mems; Leader Prof. Avner Shaki.

New Liberal Party: Tel-Aviv; f. 1987 as a merger of three groups: Shinui-Movement for Change (f. 1974 and restored 1978, when

ISRAEL

Democratic Movement for Change split into two parties; centrist; Leader AMNON RUBINSTEIN), the Centre Liberal Party (f. 1986 by members of the Liberal Party of Israel; Leader ITZHAK BERMAN), and the Independent Liberal Party (f. 1965 by 7 Liberal Party of Israel Knesset mems, after the formation of the Herut Movement and Liberal Party of Israel bloc; 20,000 mems; Chair. MOSHE KOL; Gen. Sec. NISSIM ELIAD); Leaders AMNON RUBINSTEIN, ITZHAK BERMAN and MOSHE KOL.

Poale Agudat Israel: f. 1924; working-class Orthodox Judaist party; Leader Dr KALMAN KAHANE.

Political Zionist Opposition (Ometz): f. 1982; one-man party, YIGAEL HURWITZ.

Progressive List for Peace: 5 Simtat Lane, Nes Tziona, Tel-Aviv; tel. 03-662457; fax 03-659474; f. 1984; Jewish-Arab; advocates recognition of the PLO and the establishment of a Palestinian state in the West Bank and the Gaza Strip; Leader MUHAMMAD MI'ARI.

Ratz (Civil Rights and Peace Movement): 21 Tchernihovsky St, Tel-Aviv 63291; tel. 03-5101847; fax 03-661943; f. 1973; concerned with human and civil rights, opposes discrimination on basis of religion, gender or ethnic identification and advocates a peace settlement with the Arab countries and the Palestinians; Leader Mrs SHULAMIT ALONI.

Religious Zionism Party (Matzad): Tel-Aviv; f. 1983; breakaway group from the National Religious Party; also known as Morasha (Heritage); Leader Rabbi HAIM DRUCKMAN.

Shas (Sephardic Torah Guardians): Beit Abodi, Rehov Hahida, Bene Beraq; tel. 03-579776; f. 1984 by splinter groups from Agudat Israel; ultra-orthodox Jewish party; Spiritual Leader Rabbi ELIEZER SHACH.

Tami: f. 1981; represents the interests of Sephardic Jews; Leader AHARON UZAN.

Tehiya—Zionist Revival Movement: 34 Rehov Hahaluts, POB 355, Jerusalem; tel. 02-259385; f. 1979; aims: Israeli sovereignty over Judaea, Samaria, Gaza; extensive settlement programme; economic independence; uniting of religious and non-religious camps; opposes Camp David accords; Leaders YUVAL NE'EMAN, GERSHON SHAFAT, GEULA COHEN, ELYAKIM HAEZNI, DAMI DAYAN.

Telem—State Renewal Movement: f. 1981 by the late MOSHE DAYAN; proposes the administration of a unilateral Palestinian autonomy in Judaea and Samaria, against the annexation of territories to Israel; supports Likud coalition; Leader MORDECHAI BEN-PORAT.

Tzomet Party: 22 Rehov Huberman, Tel-Aviv; tel. 03-204444; f. 1988; right-wing nationalist party; breakaway group from Tehiya party; Leader RAFAEL EITAN.

United Arab List: Arab party affiliated to Labour Party.

United Workers' Party (Mapam): 4 Rehov Itama Ben-Avi, POB 1777, Tel-Aviv 61016; tel. 03-266245; telex 33499; fax 03-210154; f. 1948; left-wing socialist-Zionist Jewish-Arab party; grouped in Labour-Mapam Alignment with Israel Labour Party from January 1969 until Sept. 1984 when it withdrew in protest over Labour's formation of a national government with Likud; member of the Socialist International; 77,000 mems; Sec.-Gen. ELIAZAR GRANOT.

Yahad (Together): f. 1984; advocates a peace settlement with the Arab peoples and the Palestinians; joined the Labour Party parliamentary bloc in January 1987; Leader EZER WEIZMANN.

Diplomatic Representation

EMBASSIES IN ISRAEL

Argentina: 112 Rehov Hayarkon, 2nd Floor, Tel-Aviv; tel. 03-5271313; telex 33730; fax 03-9271150; Ambassador: ALBERTO E. HAM.

Australia: Beit Europa, 37 Shaul Hamelech Blvd, Tel-Aviv 64928; tel. 03-250451; telex 33777; Ambassador: JOHN BRUCE CAMBELL.

Austria: 11 Rehov Herman Cohen, POB 11095, Tel-Aviv 61110; tel. 03-246186; telex 33435; fax 03-5244039; Chargé d'affaires: Dr KURT HENGL.

Belgium: 266 Rehov Hayarkon, Tel-Aviv 63504; tel. 03-454164; telex 342211; Ambassador: MICHEL ADAM.

Bolivia: 73A Rehov Nordau, Herzliya 'B' 46582; tel. 052-582261; Ambassador: SIMÓN SEJAS TORDOYA.

Brazil: 14 Rehov Hei Beiyar, Kikar Hamedina, 5th Floor, Tel-Aviv 62093; tel. 03-219292; telex 33752; Ambassador: ASDRUBAL PINTO DE ULYSSEA.

Bulgaria: Tel-Aviv.

Cameroon: Dan Panorama Hotel, 10 Rehov Kaufmann, POB 50252, Tel-Aviv 61500; Chargé d'affaires a.i.: ETONNDI ESSOMBA.

Directory

Canada: 220 Rehov Hayarkon, Tel-Aviv 63405; tel. 03-228122; telex 341293; Ambassador: JAMES K. BARTLEMAN.

Chile: 54 Rehov Pinkas, Apt 45, Tel-Aviv 62261; tel. 03-440414; telex 342189; Ambassador: JORGE MASSA.

Colombia: 52 Rehov Pinkas, Apt 26, Tel-Aviv 62261; tel. 03-449616; telex 342165; Ambassador: EDMUNDO ESQUENAZI.

Costa Rica: 13 Diskin St, Apt 1, POB 1316, Jerusalem 91012; tel. 02-666197; telex 33533; fax 02-638469; Ambassador: LAUREANO ALBÁN.

Côte d'Ivoire: Dubnov Tower, 3 Rehov Daniel Frisch, POB 14371; Tel-Aviv 64371; tel. 03-262211; telex 341143; fax 03-262008; Ambassador: JEAN-PIERRE BONI.

Czechoslovakia: POB 16361, Tel-Aviv 61664; tel. 03-218282; fax 03-218286; Ambassador: MILOS POJAR.

Denmark: 23 Rehov Bnei Moshe, POB 21080, Tel-Aviv 62308; tel. 03-5442144; telex 33514; fax 03-5465502; Ambassador: ELLEN MARGRETHE LOJ.

Dominican Republic: 4 Sderot Shaul Hamelech, Apt 81, Tel-Aviv 64733; tel. 03-257580; Ambassador: ALFREDO LEBRON PUMAROL.

Ecuador: 'Asia House', 4 Rehov Weizman, POB 30, Tel-Aviv 64239; tel. 03-258073; telex 342179; fax 03-269437; Ambassador: PATRICIO PALACIOS.

Egypt: 54 Rehov Bazel, Tel-Aviv 62744; tel. 03-5464151; telex 361289; fax 03-5441615; Ambassador: MUHAMMAD BASSIOUNI.

El Salvador: 16 Kovshei Katamon, POB 4005, Jerusalem 93663; tel. 02-633575; Ambassador: ENRIQUE GUTTFREUND HANCHEL.

Finland: Beith Eliahu, 2 Rehov Ibn Gvirol, Tel-Aviv 64077; tel. 03-250527; telex 33552; Ambassador: PEKKA J. KORVENHEIMO.

France: 112 Tayelet Herbert Samuel, Tel-Aviv; tel. 03-245371; telex 33662; fax 03-5440062; Ambassador: ALAIN PIERRET.

Germany: 3 Rehov Daniel Frish, POB 16038, Tel-Aviv 64731; tel 03-5421313; telex 33621; fax 03-269217; Ambassador: WILHELM HAAS.

Greece: 65 Shderot Shaul Hamelech, Tel-Aviv; tel. 03-259704; telex 341227; Ambassador: PETROS ANGHELAKIS.

Guatemala: 74 Rehov Hei Beiyar, Apt 6, Tel-Aviv 62198; tel. 03-5467372; Ambassador: STELLA R. DE GARCÍA-GRANADOS.

Haiti: 16 Rehov Bar Giora, Tel-Aviv 64336; tel. 03-280285; Ambassador: FRANCK M. JOSEPH.

Honduras: 46 Rehov Hei Beiyar, Apt 3, Kikar Hamedina, Tel-Aviv 62093; tel. 03-5469506; telex 361499; Ambassador: MOISES STARKMAN.

Hungary: Tel-Aviv.

Italy: 'Asia House', 4 Rehov Weizman, Tel-Aviv 64239; tel. 03-264223; telex 342664; Ambassador: ALBERTO LEONCINI-BARTOLI.

Japan: 'Asia House', 4 Rehov Weizman, Tel-Aviv 64239; tel. 03-257292; telex 242202; fax 03-265069; Ambassador: SADAKAZU TANIGUCHI.

Liberia: 6 Shimeon Frug, Ramat-Gan; tel. 03-728525; telex 361637; Ambassador: Maj. SAMUEL B. PEARSON, Jr.

Mexico: 3 Rehov Bograshov, Tel-Aviv 63808; telex 32352; fax 03-5237399; Ambassador: ROGELIO MARTÍNEZ.

Myanmar: 19 Rehov Yona, Ramat Gan 52376; tel. 03-783151; Chargé d'affaires a.i.: U BA YIN.

Netherlands: 'Asia House', 4 Rehov Weizman, Tel-Aviv 64239; tel. 03-257377; telex 342180; Ambassador: J. H. R. D. VAN ROIJEN.

Norway: 40 Rehov Namal Tel-Aviv, Tel-Aviv 63506; tel. 03-5442030; telex 33417; fax 03-5442034; Ambassador: JOHN GRIEG.

Panama: 10 Rehov Hei Beiyar, Kikar Hamedina, Tel-Aviv 62998; tel. 03-256711; Ambassador: Maj. RODOLFO CASTRELLÓN.

Peru: 52 Rehov Pinkas, Apt 31, 8th Floor, Tel-Aviv 62261; tel. 03-454065; telex 371351; Ambassador: GUILLERMO FERNÁNDEZ-CORNEJO.

Philippines: Textile Centre Bldg, 13th Floor, 2 Rehov Kaufmann, POB 50085, Tel-Aviv; tel. 03-5102231; telex 32104; fax 03-5102229; Ambassador: AMANTE MANZANO (designate).

Poland: Tel-Aviv; Ambassador: (vacant).

Romania: 24 Rehov Adam Hacohen, Tel-Aviv 64585; tel. 03-247379; Ambassador: IULIAN BITULEANU.

South Africa: 2 Rehov Kaplan, 9th Floor, Tel-Aviv 64734; tel. 03-256147; telex 361208; Ambassador: JOHAN L. VILJOEN.

Spain: Dubnov Tower, 3 Rebov Daniel Frisch, 16th Floor, Tel-Aviv 64731; tel. 03-265210; telex 361415; fax 252505; Ambassador: PEDRO LÓPEZ DE AGUIRREBENGOA.

Sweden: 'Asia House', 4 Rehov Weizman, Tel-Aviv 64239; tel. 03-258111; telex 33650; Ambassador: MATS BERGQUIST.

Switzerland: 228 Rehov Hayarkon, Tel-Aviv 63405; tel. 03-5464455; telex 342237; Ambassador: JEAN OLIVIER QUINCHE.

ISRAEL

Togo: Beit Hatassianim, 29 Rehov Hamered, POB 50222, Tel-Aviv 68125; tel. 03-652206; Ambassador: Koffi-Mawuenam Kowouvi.

Turkey: 34 Rehov Amos, Tel-Aviv 62495; tel. 03-442315; Chargé d'affaires a.i.: Ekrem Esat Güvendiren.

United Kingdom: 192 Rehov Hayarkon, Tel-Aviv 63405; tel. 03-5249171; telex 33559; fax 03-291699; Ambassador: Mark Elliott.

USA: 71 Rehov Hayarkon, Tel-Aviv 63903; tel. 03-654338; telex 33376; Ambassador: William A. Brown.

Uruguay: 52 Rehov Pinkas, Apt. 10, 2nd Floor, Tel-Aviv 62261; tel. 03-440411; telex 342669; Ambassador: Juan Andrés Pacheco.

Venezuela: Textile Center, 2 Rehov Kaufmann, 16th Floor, Tel-Aviv 61500; tel. 03-656287; telex 342172; Ambassador: Nestor Coll Blasini.

Zaire: 60 Hei Beiyar, Kikar Hamedina, Tel-Aviv 62198; tel. 03-452681; telex 371239; Ambassador: Gen. Eluki Monga Aundu.

The Jewish Agency for Israel

POB 92, Jerusalem 91920; tel. 02-202222; fax 02-202303.

Organization: The governing bodies are the Assembly which determines basic policy, the Board of Governors which sets policy for the Agency between Assembly meetings and the Executive responsible for the day to day running of the Agency.

Chairman of Executive: Simcha Dinitz.

Chairman of Board of Governors: Mendel Kaplan.

Director-General: Moshe Nativ.

Secretary-General: Howard Weisband.

Functions: According to the Agreement of 1971, the Jewish Agency undertakes the immigration and absorption of immigrants in Israel, including absorption in agricultural settlement and immigrant housing; social welfare and health services in connection with immigrants; education, youth care and training; neighbourhood rehabilitation through project renewal.

Budget (1990/91): US $606m.

Judicial System

The law of Israel is composed of the enactments of the Knesset and, to a lesser extent, of the acts, orders-in-council and ordinances that remain from the period of the British Mandate in Palestine (1922–48). The pre-1948 law has, largely, been replaced, amended or reorganized, in the interests of codification, by Israeli legislation. This legislation generally follows a pattern which is very similar to that operating in England and the USA.

Attorney-General: Joseph Harish.

CIVIL COURTS

The Supreme Court: 6 Heshin St, Jerusalem 95156; tel. 02-706411; fax 02-224115. This is the highest judicial instance in the State. It has jurisdiction as an Appellate Court from the District Courts in all matters, both civil and criminal (sitting as a Court of Civil Appeal or as a Court of Criminal Appeal), and as a Court of First Instance (sitting as a High Court of Justice) in matters in which it considers it necessary to grant relief in the interests of justice and which are not within the jurisdiction of any other court or tribunal. This includes applications for orders in the nature of *habeas corpus*, *mandamus*, prohibition and *certiorari*, and enables the court to review the legality of acts of administrative authorities of all kinds.

President of the Supreme Court: Meir Shamgar.

Vice-President of the Supreme Court: Menachem Eylon.

Justices of the Supreme Court: A. Barak, M. Bejski, Sh. Levin, D. Levin, G. Bach, S. Netanyahu, E. Goldberg, Y. Malz, T. Or.

Chief Registrar: Judge S. Tzur (magistrate).

The District Courts: Jerusalem, Tel-Aviv, Jaffa, Haifa, Beersheba, Nazareth. They have unlimited jurisdiction as Courts of First Instance in all civil and criminal matters not within the jurisdiction of a Magistrates' Court, all matters not within the exclusive jurisdiction of any other tribunal, and matters within the concurrent jurisdiction of any other tribunal so long as such tribunal does not deal with them, and as an Appellate Court in appeals from judgments and decisions of Magistrates' Courts and judgments of Municipal Courts and various administrative tribunals.

Magistrates' Courts: There are 28 Magistrates' Courts, having criminal jurisdiction to try contraventions, misdemeanours and certain felonies, and civil jurisdiction to try actions concerning possession or use of immovable property, or the partition thereof whatever may be the value of the subject matter of the action, and other civil actions on a limited basis.

Labour Courts: Established in 1969. Regional Labour Courts in Jerusalem, Tel-Aviv, Haifa, Beersheba and Nazareth, composed of Judges and representatives of the public. A National Labour Court in Jerusalem, presided over by Judge M. Goldberg. The Courts have jurisdiction over all matters arising out of the relationship between employer and employee; between parties to a collective labour agreement; matters concerning the National Insurance Law and the Labour Law and Rules.

RELIGIOUS COURTS

The Religious Courts are the Courts of the recognized religious communities. They are competent in certain defined matters of personal status concerning members of their community. Where any action of personal status involves persons of different religious communities the President of the Supreme Court will decide which Court shall have jurisdiction. Whenever a question arises as to whether or not a case is one of personal status within the exclusive jurisdiction of a Religious Court, the matter must be referred to a Special Tribunal composed of two Justices of the Supreme Court and the President of the highest court of the religious community concerned in Israel. The judgments of the Religious Courts are executed by the process and offices of the Civil Courts.

Jewish Rabbinical Courts: These Courts have exclusive jurisdiction in matters of marriage and divorce of Jews in Israel who are Israeli citizens or residents. In all other matters of personal status they have concurrent jurisdiction with the District Courts with the consent of all parties concerned.

Muslim Religious Courts: These Courts have exclusive jurisdiction in matters of marriage and divorce of Muslims who are not foreigners, or who are foreigners subject by their national law to the jurisdiction of Muslim Religious Courts in such matters. In all other matters of personal status they have concurrent jurisdiction with the District Courts with the consent of all parties concerned.

Christian Religious Courts: The Courts of the recognized Christian communities have exclusive jurisdiction in matters of marriage and divorce of members of their communities who are not foreigners. In all other matters of personal status they have concurrent jurisdiction with the District Courts with the consent of all parties concerned. But neither these Courts nor the Civil Courts have jurisdiction to dissolve the marriage of a foreign subject.

Druze Courts: These Courts, established in 1963, have exclusive jurisdiction in matters of marriage and divorce of Druze in Israel, who are Israeli citizens or residents, and concurrent jurisdiction with the District Courts in all other matters of personal status of Druze with the consent of all parties concerned.

Religion

JUDAISM

Judaism, the religion of the Jews, is the faith of the majority of Israel's inhabitants. On 31 December 1988 Judaism's adherents totalled 3,659,000, equivalent to 81.7% of the country's population. Its basis is a belief in an ethical monotheism.

There are two main Jewish communities: the Ashkenazim and the Sephardim. The former are the Jews from Eastern, Central, or Northern Europe, while the latter originate from the Balkan countries, North Africa and the Middle East.

There is also a community of about 10,000 Falashas (Ethiopian Jews) who have been airlifted to Israel at various times since the fall of Emperor Haile Selassie in 1974.

The supreme religious authority is vested in the Chief Rabbinate, which consists of the Ashkenazi and Sephardi Chief Rabbis and the Supreme Rabbinical Council. It makes decisions on interpretation of the Jewish law, and supervises the Rabbinical Courts. There are 8 regional Rabbinical Courts, and a Rabbinical Court of Appeal presided over by the two Chief Rabbis.

According to the Rabbinical Courts Jurisdiction Law of 1953, marriage and divorce among Jews in Israel are exclusively within the jurisdiction of the Rabbinical Courts. Provided that all the parties concerned agree, other matters of personal status can also be decided by the Rabbinical Courts.

There are 195 Religious Councils, which maintain religious services and supply religious needs, and about 405 religious committees with similar functions in smaller settlements. Their expenses are borne jointly by the State and the local authorities. The Religious Councils are under the administrative control of the Ministry of Religious Affairs. In all matters of religion, the Religious Councils are subject to the authority of the Chief Rabbinate. There are 365 officially appointed rabbis. The total number of synagogues is about 7,000, most of which are organized within the framework of the Union of Israel Synagogues.

ISRAEL

Head of the Ashkenazi Community: The Chief Rabbi AVRAHAM SHAPIRO.

Head of the Sephardic Community: Jerusalem; tel. 02-244785; The Chief Rabbi MORDECHAI ELIAHU.

Two Jewish sects still loyal to their distinctive customs are:

The Karaites, a sect which recognizes only the Jewish written law and not the oral law of the Mishna and Talmud. The community of about 12,000, many of whom live in or near Ramla, has been augmented by immigration from Egypt.

The Samaritans, an ancient sect mentioned in 2 Kings xvii, 24. They recognize only the Torah. The community in Israel numbers about 500; about half of them live in Holon, where a Samaritan synagogue has been built, and the remainder, including the High Priest, live in Nablus, near Mt Gerizim, which is sacred to the Samaritans.

ISLAM

The Muslims in Israel are mainly Sunnis, and are divided among the four rites of the Sunni sect of Islam: the Shafe'i, the Hanbali, the Hanafi and the Maliki. Before June 1967 they numbered approx. 175,000; in 1971, approx. 343,900. On 31 December 1988 the total Muslim population of Israel was 634,600.

Mufti of Jerusalem: POB 19859, Jerusalem; tel. 02-283528; Sheikh SAAD ED-DIN AL-ALAMI (also Chair. Supreme Muslim Council for Jerusalem).

There was also a total of 78,100 Druzes in Israel at 31 December 1988.

CHRISTIANITY

The total Christian population of Israel (including East Jerusalem) at 31 December 1988 was 105,000.

United Christian Council in Israel: POB 116, Jerusalem 91000; f. 1956; 21 mems (churches and other bodies); Pres. CHARLES KOPP; Gen. Sec. Dr ALVIN MARTIN.

The Roman Catholic Church

Armenian Rite

The Armenian Catholic Patriarch of Cilicia is resident in Beirut, Lebanon.

Patriarchal Vicariate of Jerusalem: Via Dolorosa, Third Station, POB 19546, Jerusalem; tel. 02-284262; f. 1856; Vicar Patriarchal Fr JOSEPH ROUBIAN.

Chaldean Rite

The Chaldean Patriarch of Babylon is resident in Baghdad, Iraq.

Patriarchal Vicariate of Jerusalem: Chaldean Patriarchal Vicariate, Saad and Said Quarter, Nablus Rd, Jerusalem; Vicar Patriarchal HENRI GOUILLON.

Latin Rite

The Patriarchate of Jerusalem covers Palestine, Jordan and Cyprus. At 31 December 1988 there were an estimated 62,868 adherents.

Bishops' Conference: Conférence des Evêques Latins dans les Régions Arabes, Patriarcat Latin, POB 14152, Jerusalem; tel. 02-282323; f. 1967; Pres. His Beatitude MICHEL SABBAH; Patriarch of Jerusalem.

Patriarchate of Jerusalem: Patriarcat Latin, POB 14152, Jerusalem; tel. 02-282323; Patriarch: His Beatitude MICHEL SABBAH; Vicar General for Israel: Mgr HANNA KALDANY (Titular Bishop of Gaba), Vicariat Patriarcal Latin, Nazareth.

Maronite Rite

The Maronite community, under the jurisdiction of the Maronite Patriarch of Antioch (resident in Lebanon), has about 7,000 members.

Patriarchal Vicariate of Jerusalem: Vicariat Maronite, Maronite St 25, Jerusalem; tel. 02-282158; Vicar Patriarchal AUGUSTIN HARFOUCHE (also representing the Archbishop of Tyre, Lebanon, as Vicar General for Israel).

Melkite Rite

The Greek-Melkite Patriarch of Antioch (Maximos V Hakim) is resident in Damascus, Syria.

Patriarchal Vicariate of Jerusalem: Vicariat Patriarcal Grec-Melkite Catholique, POB 14130, Jerusalem 91141; tel. 02-282023; about 3,000 adherents (1988); Vicars Patriarchi Mgr HILARION CAPUCCI (Titular Archbishop of Caesarea in Palestine), Mgr LUTFI LAHAM (Titular Archbishop of Tarsus).

Archbishop of Akko (Acre): Most Rev. MAXIMOS SALLOUM, Archevêché Grec-Catholique, 33 Hagefen St, POB 279, Haifa; tel. 04-523114; about 41,000 adherents (1987).

Syrian Rite

The Syrian Catholic Patriarch of Antioch is resident in Beirut, Lebanon.

Patriarchal Vicariate of Jerusalem: Vicariat Patriarcal Syrien Catholique, Nablus Rd, POB 19787, Jerusalem; tel. 02-282657; fax 02-284217; about 960 adherents in Palestine and Jordan (Dec. 1988); Vicar Patriarchal Mgr PIERRE ABD AL-AHAD.

The Armenian Apostolic (Orthodox) Church

Patriarch of Jerusalem: TORKOM MANOOGIAN, St James's Cathedral, Jerusalem.

The Greek Orthodox Church

The Patriarchate of Jerusalem contains an estimated 260,000 adherents throughout the Middle East.

Patriarch of Jerusalem: DIODOROS I, Greek Orthodox Patriarchate St, Old City, POB 19632-633, Jerusalem; tel. 02-284917.

The Anglican Communion

Episcopal Church in Jerusalem and the Middle East: St George's Close, POB 1248, Jerusalem; President-Bishop Rt Rev. SAMIR KAFITY, Bishop in Jerusalem.

Other Christian Churches

Other denominations include the Coptic Orthodox Church (700 members), the Russian Orthodox Church, the Ethiopian Orthodox Church, the Romanian Orthodox Church, the Lutheran Church and the Church of Scotland.

The Press

Tel-Aviv is the main publishing centre. Largely for economic reasons there has developed no local press away from these cities; hence all papers regard themselves as national. Friday editions, Sabbath eve, are increased to up to twice the normal size by special weekend supplements, and experience a considerable rise in circulation. No newspapers appear on Saturday.

Most of the daily papers are in Hebrew, and others appear in Arabic, English, French, Polish, Yiddish, Hungarian and German. The total daily circulation is 500,000–600,000 copies, or 21 papers per hundred people, although most citizens read more than one daily paper.

Most Hebrew morning dailies have strong political or religious affiliations. *Al-Hamishmar* is affiliated to Mapam, *Hatzofeh* to the National Religious Front—World Mizrahi. *Davar* is the long-established organ of the Histadrut. Most newspapers depend on subsidies from political parties, religious organizations or public funds. The limiting effect on freedom of commentary entailed by this party press system has provoked repeated criticism.

The Jerusalem Arabic daily *Al-Anba* has a small circulation (10,000) but an increasing number of Israeli Arabs are now reading Hebrew dailies. The daily, *Al-Quds*, was founded in 1968 for Arabs in Jerusalem and the West Bank; the small indigenous press of occupied Jordan has largely ceased publication or transferred operations to Amman. Two of the four Arabic newspapers which are published in occupied East Jerusalem, the daily, *Al-Mithaq*, and the weekly, *Al-Ahd*, were closed by the Israeli authorities in August 1986. It was alleged that they were financed and managed by the Popular Front for the Liberation of Palestine. The Palestinian news agency in the West Bank town of Nablus was closed for two years in October 1987. Since the Palestinian uprising in the Occupied Territories began in December 1987, further action has been taken by the Israeli authorities to curb allegedly pro-PLO press activities. In February 1988 the left-wing newspaper, *Derech Hanitzotz*, was closed by the Israelis for its alleged links with the Democratic Front for the Liberation of Palestine; in March the Palestine Press Service in East Jerusalem (the only remaining Arab news agency in the Occupied Territories) was closed by military order for six months; and in April the minor weekly magazine *Al-Awdah* (The Return) (also based in East Jerusalem) was closed, on the grounds that it was being funded by the PLO.

There are around 400 other newspapers and magazines including some 50 weekly and 150 fortnightly; over 250 of them are in Hebrew, the remainder in eleven other languages.

The most influential and respected dailies, for both quality of news coverage and commentary, are *Ha'aretz* and the trade union paper, *Davar*, which frequently has articles by government figures. These are the most widely read of the morning papers, exceeded only by the popular afternoon press, *Ma'ariv* and *Yedioth Aharonoth*. The *Jerusalem Post* gives detailed and sound news coverage in English.

The Israeli Press Council (Chair. JOSHUA ROTENSTREICH), established in 1963, deals with matters of common interest to the Press such as drafting the code of professional ethics which is binding on all journalists.

ISRAEL

The Daily Newspaper Publishers' Association represents publishers in negotiations with official and public bodies, negotiates contracts with employees and purchases and distributes newsprint.

DAILIES

Al-Anba (The News): POB 428, 37 Hillel St, Beit Agron, Jerusalem; f. 1968; Arabic; published by Jerusalem Publications Ltd; Editor and Man. Dir OVADIA DANON; circ. 10,000.

Davar (The Word): POB 199, 45 Sheinkin St, Tel-Aviv; tel. 03-286141; telex 33807; fax 03-294783; f. 1925; morning; Hebrew; official organ of the General Federation of Labour (Histadrut); Editor HANNAH ZEMER; circ. 39,000; there are also weekly magazine editions.

Al-Fajr (The Dawn): Jerusalem; tel. 02-289175; telex 26467; fax 02-283336; Arabic; Publr PAUL AJILOUNY; Editor HANNAH SINIORA.

Ha'aretz (The Land): 21 Salman Schocken St, POB 233, Tel-Aviv; tel. 03-5121212; telex 33748; fax 03-810012; f. 1918; morning; Hebrew; liberal, independent; Editor GERSHOM G. SCHOCKEN; circ. 55,000 (weekdays), 75,000 (weekends).

Hadashot (The News): Tel-Aviv; late morning; Hebrew.

Al-Hamishmar (The Guardian): 2 Rehov Choma Umigdal, Tel-Aviv 67771; tel. 03-378833; telex 341652; fax 03-5370037; f. 1943; morning; Hebrew; organ of the United Workers' Party (Mapam); Editor ZVI TIMOR; circ. 20,000.

Hamodia (The Informer): Yehuda Hamackabbi 3, POB 1306, Jerusalem; fax 02-539108; morning; Hebrew; organ of Agudat Israel; Editors M. A. DRUCK, H. M. KNOPF; circ. 15,000.

Hatzofeh (The Watchman): 66 Hamasger St, Tel-Aviv; tel. 03-5622951; fax 03-5621502; f. 1938; morning; Hebrew; organ of the National Religious Party; Editor M. ISHON; circ. 16,000.

Israel Nachrichten (News of Israel): 52 Harakevet St, Tel-Aviv; tel. 03-370011; f. 1974; morning; German; Editor S. HIMMELFARB; circ. 20,000.

Israelski Far Tribuna: 113 Givat Herzl St, Tel-Aviv; tel. 03-3700; f. 1952; Bulgarian; circ. 6,000.

Al-Ittihad (Unity): POB 104, Haifa; tel. 04-511296; f. 1944; Arabic; organ of the Israeli Communist Party (Rakkah); Chief Editor EMILE HABIBY.

The Jerusalem Post: POB 81, Romema, 91000, Jerusalem; tel. 02-551616; telex 26121; fax 02-389527; f. 1932; morning; English; independent; Pres. and Pblr YEHUDA LEVY; Editor DAVID GROSS; circ. 30,000 (weekdays), 50,000 (weekend edition); there is also a weekly international edition, circ. 60,000.

Le Journal d'Israel: 26 Agra St, POB 28330, Tel-Aviv; f. 1971; French; independent; Chief Editor J. RABIN; circ. 10,000; also overseas weekly selection; circ. 15,000.

Letzte Nyess (Late News): 52 Harakevet St, POB 28034, Tel-Aviv; f. 1949; morning; Yiddish; Editor S. HIMMELFARB; circ. 23,000.

Ma'ariv (Evening Prayer): 2 Carlebach St, Tel-Aviv 61200; tel. 03-5632111; telex 33735; fax 03-5610614; f. 1948; mid-morning; Hebrew; independent; published by Modiin Publishing House; Editor IDO DISSENTSHIK; circ. daily 130,000, weekend 240,000.

Mabat: Tel-Aviv; f. 1971; morning; economic and social; Editor S. YARKONI.

Al-Mawqif: Jerusalem; Arabic; owned by the Arab Council for Public Affairs.

Al-Mithaq (The Covenant): Jerusalem; Arabic; Editor MAHMOUD KHATIB; (closed down by Israeli authorities August 1986).

An-Nahar (Day): Jerusalem; Arabic; pro-Jordanian; Editor OTHMAN HALLAQ.

The Nation: Jerusalem; f. 1988; English; Editor and Publr HESH KESTIN.

Nowiny i Kurier: 52 Harakevet St, Tel-Aviv; f. 1952; morning; Polish; Editor S. HIMMELFARB; circ. 15,000.

Al-Quds (Jerusalem): POB 19788, Jerusalem; tel. 02-284061; telex 02-282475; f. 1968; Arabic; Publr MAHMOUD ABU ZALAF; Editor-in-Chief WALID ABU ZALAF; circ. 40,000.

Ash-Sha'ab (The People): Jerusalem; f. 1972; Arabic; circ. 15,000; Editor SALAH ZUHAIKA.

Sha'ar: 52 Harakevet St, Tel-Aviv 64284; Hebrew; economy and finance; Editor S. HIMMELFARB.

Shearim (The Gates): 64 Frishman St, Tel-Aviv; tel. 03-242126; organ of Poale Agudat Israel; Editor MAIER HALACHMI; circ. 15,000.

Uj Kelet: 52 Harakevet St, Tel-Aviv; f. 1918; morning; Hungarian; independent; Editor S. HIMMELFARB; circ. 20,000.

Viata Noastra: 52 Harakevet St, Tel-Aviv; f. 1950; morning; Romanian; Editor S. HIMMELFARB; circ. 30,000.

Yedioth Aharonoth (The Latest News): 2 Rehov Mozes, Tel-Aviv 61000; tel. 03-212212; telex 33847; fax 03-253950; f. 1939; evening; independent; Editor-in-Chief MOSHE VARDI; circ. 300,000, Friday 600,000.

WEEKLIES AND FORTNIGHTLIES

Al-Ahd (Sunday): Jerusalem; weekly; Arabic; (closed down by Israeli authorities August 1986).

Al-Awdah (The Return): East Jerusalem; weekly; Arabic and English; Proprs IBRAHIM QARA'EEN, Mrs RAYMONDA TAWIL; circ. 10,000; (closed down by Israeli authorities April 1988).

Bama'alah: POB 303, Tel-Aviv; Hebrew; journal of the young Histadrut Movement; Editor N. ANAELY.

Bamahane (In the Camp): Military POB 1013, Tel-Aviv; f. 1948; military, illustrated weekly of the Israel Armed Forces; Hebrew; Editor-in-Chief YOSSEF ESHKOL; circ. 70,000.

Bitaon Heyl Ha'avir (Air Force Magazine): Doar Zwai 1560, Zahal; tel. 03-5610948; f. 1948; fortnightly; Hebrew; Man. Editor D. MOLAD; Editor-in-Chief AHARON LAPIDOT; Technical Editor RAM AVRAHAMI; circ. 30,000.

Davar Hashavua (The Weekly Word): 45 Shenkin St, Tel-Aviv; tel. 02-286141; f. 1946; weekly; Hebrew; popular illustrated; published by Histadrut, General Federation of Labour; Editor TUVIA MENDELSON; circ. 43,000.

Derech Hanitzotz/Tariq a-Sharara (The Shining Way): Hanitzotz Publishing House, POB 1575, Jerusalem; tel. 02-225382; fax 02-251614; twice weekly; left-wing; Hebrew and Arabic; published by Nitzotz-Ashara Organization; circ. Hebrew edition 800, Arabic edition 1,500; (closed down by Israeli authorities in February 1988).

Ethgar (The Challenge): 75 Einstein St, Tel-Aviv; twice weekly; Hebrew; Editor NATHAN YALIN-MOR.

Gesher (The Bridge): Jerusalem; fortnightly; Hebrew; Editor ZIAD ABU ZAYAD.

Glasul Populurui: Tel-Aviv; weekly of the Communist Party of Israel; Romanian; Editor MEÏR SEMO.

Haolam Hazeh (This World): POB 136, 3 Gordon St, Tel-Aviv 61001; tel. 03-5376804; fax 03-5376811; f. 1937; weekly; independent; illustrated news magazine; Editor-in-Chief RAFFI GINAT.

Harefuah (Medicine): 39 Shaul Hamelech Blvd, Tel-Aviv 64928; f. 1920; fortnightly journal of the Israeli Medical Association; Hebrew with English summaries; Editor I. SUM; circ. 7,500.

Hotam: Al-Hamishmar House, Choma U'Migdal St, Tel-Aviv; weekly of the United Workers' Party (Mapam); Hebrew.

Al-Hurriya (Freedom): 38 King George St, Tel-Aviv; Arabic weekly of the Herut Party.

Illustrirte Weltwoch: Tel-Aviv; f. 1956; weekly; Yiddish; Editor M. KARPINOVITZ.

Jerusalem Post International Edition: POB 81, Romema, Jerusalem 91000; tel. 02-551616; telex 26121; f. 1959; weekly; English; overseas edition of the *Jerusalem Post* (q.v.); circ. 60,000 to 95 countries.

Kol Ha'am (Voice of the People): Tel-Aviv; f. 1947; Hebrew; organ of the Communist Party of Israel; Editor B. BALTI.

Laisha (For Women): 35 Bnei Brak St, POB 28122, Tel-Aviv 67132; tel. 03-371464; fax 03-378071; f. 1946; Hebrew; women's magazine; Editor ZVI ELGAT.

Ma'ariv Lanoar: 2 Carlebach St, Tel-Aviv 67132; tel. 03-5632111; f. 1957; weekly for youth; Hebrew; Editor AMNON BEI-RAV; circ. 100,000.

Magallati (My Magazine): Arabic Publishing House, POB 28049, Tel-Aviv; tel. 03-371438; f. 1960; young people's fortnightly; Man. JOSEPH ELIAHOU; Editor-in-Chief IBRAHIM MUSA IBRAHIM; Editors GAMIL DAHLAN, MISHEL HADDAD; circ. 5,000.

MB (Mitteilungsblatt): POB 1480, Tel-Aviv; tel. 03-664461; fax 03-664435; f. 1932; German monthly journal of the Irgun Olei Merkas Europa (Settlers from Central Europe); Editor ZEEV ESTREICHER.

Al-Mirsad (The Telescope): POB 1777, Tel-Aviv; tel. 03-266244; fax 03-664463; f. 1948; Arabic; Mapam.

Reshumot: Ministry of Justice, Jerusalem; f. 1948; Hebrew, Arabic and English; official government gazette.

Sada at-Tarbia (The Echo of Education): published by the Histadrut and Teachers' Association, POB 2306, Rehovot; f. 1952; fortnightly; Arabic; educational; Editor TUVIA SHAMOSH.

OTHER PERIODICALS

Ariel: Cultural and Scientific Relations Division, Ministry for Foreign Affairs, Jerusalem; Publishers, Editorial and Distribution: Jerusalem Post Publications Ltd, POB 3349, Jerusalem 91002; tel. 02-381515; fax 02-385076; f. 1962; quarterly review of the arts and letters in Israel; regular edns in English, Spanish, French, German and Russian; occasional edns in several other languages; Editor ASHER WEILL; Asst Editor ALOMA HALTER; circ. 25,000.

ISRAEL

Avoda Urevacha Ubituach Leumi: POB 915, Jerusalem; f. 1949; monthly review of the Ministry of Labour and Social Affairs, and the National Insurance Institute, Jerusalem; Hebrew; Chief Editor AVNER MICHAELI; Editor MICHAEL KLODOVSKY; circ. 2,500.

Bakalkala Ubamishar (Economics and Trade): POB 20027, Tel-Aviv 61200; tel. 03-5612444; telex 33484; fax 03-5612614; f. 1919; monthly; Hebrew; published by Federation of Israeli Chambers of Commerce; Editor Z. AMIT.

Al-Bushra (Good News): POB 6088, Haifa; f. 1935; monthly; Arabic; organ of the Ahmadiyya movement; Editor FALAHUD DIN O'DEH.

Business Diary: 37 Hanamal St, Haifa; f. 1947; weekly; English, Hebrew; shipping movements, import licences, stock exchange listings, business failures, etc.; Editor G. ALON.

Christian News from Israel: 30 Jaffa Rd, Jerusalem; f. 1949; half-yearly; English, French, Spanish; issued by the Ministry of Religious Affairs; Editor SHALOM BEN-ZAKKAI; circ. 10,000.

Di Goldene Keyt: 30 Weizmann St, Tel-Aviv; f. 1949; literary quarterly; Yiddish; published by the Histadrut; Man. Editor MOSHE MILLIS; Editor A. SUTZKEVER.

Divrei Haknesset: c/o The Knesset, Jerusalem; f. 1949; Hebrew; records of the proceedings of the Knesset; published by the Government Printer, Jerusalem; Editor DVORA AVIVI (acting); circ. 350.

Doing Business with Israel: POB 20027, Tel-Aviv; published by Federation of Israeli Chambers of Commerce; Editor ZVI SEGAL.

Etgar (Challenge): POB 1575, Jerusalem; tel. 02-225382; fax 02-251614; f. 1989; monthly in Hebrew, quarterly in English; circ. Hebrew edition 1,000, English edition 1,000.

The Family Physician: 101 Arlosoroff St, POB 16250, Tel-Aviv 62098; tel. 03-433388; fax 03-433474; f. 1970; three times a year; Hebrew with English summaries; medical; Editor Prof. MAX R. POLLIACK; circ. 4,500.

Folk un Zion: POB 7053, Tel-Aviv 61070; tel. 03-5423317; f. 1950; bi-monthly; current events relating to Israel and World Jewry; circ. 3,000; Editor MOSHE KALCHHEIM.

Frei Israel: POB 8512, Tel-Aviv; progressive monthly; published by Asscn for Popular Culture; Yiddish.

Gazit: 8 Zvi Brook St, POB 4190, Tel-Aviv; f. 1932; monthly; Hebrew and English; art, literature; Publisher G. TALPHIR.

Hameshek Hahaklai: 21 Melchett St, Tel-Aviv; f. 1929; Hebrew; agricultural; Editor ISRAEL INBARI.

Al-Hamishmar (The Guardian): 4 Ben Avigdor St, Tel-Aviv; Bulgarian monthly of United Workers' Party.

Hamizrah Hehadash (The New East): Israel Oriental Society, The Hebrew University, Mount Scopus, Jerusalem 91905; tel. 02-883633; f. 1949; annual of the Israel Oriental Society; Middle Eastern, Asian and African Affairs; Hebrew with English summary; Editor AHARON LAYISH; circ. 1,500–2,000.

Hamionai (The Hotelier): POB 11586, Tel-Aviv; f. 1962; monthly of the Israel Hotel Association; Hebrew and English; Editor Z. PELTZ.

Hapraklit: 8 Wilson St, POB 14152, Tel-Aviv 61141; tel. 03-5614695; fax 03-561476; f. 1943; quarterly; Hebrew; published by the Israel Bar Association; Editor-in-Chief A. POLONSKI; Editor ARNAN GAVRIELI; circ. 9,000.

Hassadeh Quarterly: 8 Shaul Hamelech Blvd, POB 40044, Tel-Aviv 61400; tel. 03-5429024; fax 03-252045; f. 1920; monthly; review of Israeli agriculture; English; Editor-in-Chief J. M. MARGALIT; circ. 10,000.

Hed Hagan: 8 Ben Saruk St, Tel-Aviv 62969; tel. 03-5432958; f. 1935; Hebrew; educational; Editor Mrs ZIVA PEDAHZUR; circ. 6,300.

Hed Hahinukh: 8 Ben Saruk St, Tel-Aviv 62969; tel. 03-5432911; fax 03-5432928; f. 1926; monthly; Hebrew; educational; published by the Israeli Teachers' Union; Editor ORA GADELL; circ. 40,000.

Innovation: POB 7422, Haifa 31070; tel. 04-255104; f. 1975; monthly; English; industrial research and development in Israel; published by A. G. Publications Ltd; Editor A. GREENFIELD.

Israel Business: POB 7422, Haifa 31070; tel. 04-255104; f. 1961; monthly; English; business news and economic devt; published by A.G. Publications Ltd; Editor A. GREENFIELD.

Israel Economist: 6 Hazanowitz St, POB 7052, Jerusalem 91070; tel. 02-234131; fax 02-246569; f. 1945; monthly; English; independent; political and economic; Editor BEN MOLLOV; Publisher ISRAEL KELMAN; also publishes *Keeping Posted* (diplomatic magazine), *Mazel and Brucha* (jewellers' magazine), annuals: *Travel Agents' Manual, Electronics, International Conventions in Israel, Arkia, In Flight,* various hotel magazines.

Israel Environment Bulletin: Ministry of the Environment, POB 6234, Jerusalem 91061; tel. 02-701606; telex 25629; fax 02-385638; f. 1973; Editor SHOSHANA GABBAY; circ. 2,000.

Israel Export and Trade Journal: POB 11586, Tel-Aviv; f. 1949; monthly; English; commercial and economic; published by Israel Periodicals Co Ltd; Man. Dir ZALMAN PELTZ.

Israel Journal of Medical Sciences: 2 Etzel St, French Hill, 97853 Jerusalem; tel. 02-817727; fax 02-815722; f. 1965; monthly; Editor-in-Chief Dr M. PRYWES; Man. Mrs S. TOLEDANO; circ. 5,500.

Israel Journal of Psychiatry and Related Sciences: Gefen Publishing House Ltd, POB 6056, Jerusalem 91060; tel. 02-380247; fax 02-388423; f. 1963; quarterly; Editor-in-Chief E. L. EDELSTEIN.

Israel Journal of Veterinary Medicine: POB 3076, Rishon Le-Zion 75130; f. 1943; quarterly of the Israel Veterinary Medical Asscn; formerly *Refuah Veterinarith*; Editor Prof. N. AYALON.

Israel Scene: POB 92, Jerusalem 91920; tel. 02-527156; telex 26436; fax 02-533542; f. 1980 as continuation of *Israel Digest*; monthly; English; published by the World Zionist Organization; news, features and analysis; circ. 50,000; Editor ASHER WEILL.

Israel-South Africa Trade Journal: POB 11587, Tel-Aviv; f. 1973; bi-monthly; English; commercial and economic; published by Israel Publications Corpn Ltd; Man. Dir Z. PELTZ.

Israels Aussenhandel: POB 11586, Tel-Aviv 61114; tel. 03-5280215; telex 341118; f. 1967; monthly; German; commercial; published by Israel Periodicals Co Ltd; Editor PELTZ NOEMI; Man. Dir ZALMAN PELTZ.

Al-Jadid (The New): POB 104, Haifa; f. 1951; literary monthly; Arabic; Editor SALEM JUBRAN; circ. 5,000.

Kalkalan: 8 Akiva St, POB 7052, Jerusalem; f. 1952; monthly; independent; Hebrew commercial and economic; Editor J. KOLLEK.

Kibbutz Currents: 10 Dubnov, Tel-Aviv 64732; tel. 03-342513; quarterly; English journal of the Kibbutz Movement; Editor JOEL MAGID; circ. 2,000.

Kiryat Sefer: POB 503, Jerusalem; tel. 02-585019; telex 25307; fax 02-666804; f. 1924; bibliographical quarterly of the Jewish National and University Library, Jerusalem; Hebrew; Editor Dr A. SHINAN.

Labour in Israel: 93 Arlosorof St, Tel-Aviv 62098; tel. 03-431111; telex 342488; fax 03-269906; quarterly; English, French, German and Spanish; bulletin of the Histadrut (General Federation of Labour in Israel); circ. 28,000.

Leshonenu: Academy of the Hebrew Language, POB 3449, Jerusalem 91034; tel. 02-632242; f. 1929; 4 a year; for the study of the Hebrew language and cognate subjects; Editor J. BLAU.

Leshonenu La'am: Academy of the Hebrew Language, POB 3449, Jerusalem 91034; tel. 02-632242; fax 02-666804; f. 1945; popular Hebrew philology; Editors S. BAHAT, Y. YANNAY, Y. OFER.

Ma'arachot (Campaigns): Hakirya, 3 Mendler St, POB 7026, Tel-Aviv; tel. 03-5694345; f. 1939; military and political bi-monthly; Hebrew; periodical of Israel Defence Force; Editors Lt Col YISHAI CORDOVA, Lt Col R. ROJANSKI.

Melaha Vetaassiya (Trade and Industry): POB 11587, Tel-Aviv; f. 1969; bi-monthly review of the Union of Artisans and Small Manufacturers of Israel; Hebrew; Man. Dir Z. PELTZ.

Mibifnim (From Within): 3 Ta'as St, Ramath-Gan, POB 40016, Tel-Aviv 61400; tel. 03-7514938; f. 1923; quarterly of the United Kibbutz Movement (TKM); Hebrew; Editor DANI HADARI; circ. 5,000.

Molad: POB 1165, Jerusalem 91010; f. 1948; annual; Hebrew; independent political and literary periodical; published by Miph'ale Molad Ltd; Editor EPHRAIM BROIDO.

Monthly Bulletin of Statistics: Israel Central Bureau of Statistics, POB 13015, Jerusalem 91130; tel. 02-553400; fax 02-553325; f. 1949.

  Foreign Trade Statistics: f. 1950; Hebrew and English; appears annually, 2 vols; imports/exports.

  Foreign Trade Statistics Quarterly: f. 1950; Hebrew and English.

  Judea, Samaria and Gaza Area Statistics: f. 1971; irregular; Hebrew and English.

  Tourism and Hotel Services Statistics Quarterly: f. 1973; Hebrew and English.

  Price Statistics Monthly: f. 1959; Hebrew.

  Transport Statistics Quarterly: f. 1974; Hebrew and English.

  Agricultural Statistics Quarterly: f. 1970; Hebrew and English.

  New Statistical Projects: quarterly; Hebrew.

Moznaim (Balance): POB 7098, Tel-Aviv; tel. 03-253256; f. 1929; monthly; Hebrew; literature and culture; Editors ORTSION BARTANA, ZVI ATZMON; circ. 3,000.

Na'amat-Urim Lahorim: 93 Arlozorov St, Tel-Aviv 62098; f. 1934; monthly journal of the Council of Women Workers of the Histadrut; Hebrew; Editor ZIVIA COHEN; circ. 10,500.

Nekuda: Hebrew; organ of the Jewish settlers of the West Bank and Gaza Strip.

ISRAEL

New Outlook: 9 Gordon St, Tel-Aviv 63458; tel. 03-236496; fax 03-232252; f. 1957; monthly; Israeli and Middle Eastern Affairs; dedicated to the quest for Arab-Israeli peace; Editor-in-Chief CHAIM SHUR; Senior Editor DAN LEON; circ. 10,000.

Newsletter on Freedom of the Press: POB 1575, Jerusalem; tel. 02-225382; fax 02-251614; f. 1988, following closure of Derech Hanitzotz/Tariq a-Sharara; monthly; circ. 300.

Proche-Orient Chrétien: POB 19079, Jerusalem 91190; tel. 02-283285; f. 1951; quarterly on churches and religion in the Middle East; circ. 800.

Quarterly Review of the Israel Medical Association (Mif'al Haverut Hutz—World Fellowship of the Israel Medical Association): 39 Shaul Hamelech Blvd, POB 33289, Tel-Aviv 61332; tel. (03) 255521; fax 03-256103; quarterly; English; Editor-in-Chief YEHUDA SHOENFELD.

Scopus: Hebrew University of Jerusalem, Mount Scopus, Jerusalem 91905; tel. 02-882837; telex 26458; fax 02-322556; f. 1946; annual; English; published by Division for Development and Public Relations, Hebrew University of Jerusalem; Editor V. LONDON; circ. 17,000.

The Sea: Hane'emanim 8, POB 33706, Haifa; tel. 04-529818; every six months; published by Israel Maritime League; review of marine problems; Pres. M. POMROCK; Chief Editor M. LITOVSKI; circ. 5,000.

Shdemot: 10 Dubnov, Tel-Aviv 64732; tel. 03-342513; three a year; Hebrew; Editor JOEL MAGID; circ. 2,500.

Shituf (Co-operation): 24 Ha'arba St, POB 7151, Tel-Aviv; f. 1948; bi-monthly; Hebrew; economic, social and co-operative problems in Israel; published by the Central Union of Industrial, Transport and Service Co-operative Societies; Editor L. LOSH; circ. 12,000.

Sinai: POB 642, Jerusalem; tel. 02-526231; f. 1937; Hebrew; Torah science and literature; Editor Dr YITZCHAK RAPHAEL.

Sindibad: POB 28049, Tel-Aviv; f. 1970; children's monthly; Hebrew; Man. JOSEPH ELIAHOU; Editor WALID HUSSEIN; circ. 7,000.

Spectrum: Jerusalem; monthly of the Israel Labour Party; Editor DAVID TWERSKY.

At-Ta'awun (Co-operation): 93 Arlosoroff St, POB 303, Tel-Aviv 62098; tel. 03-431813; telex 342488; fax 03-267368; f. 1961; Arabic; published by the Arab Workers' Dept of the Histadrut; co-operatives irregular; Editor ZVI HAIK.

Terra Santa: POB 186, Jerusalem 91001; tel. 02-282354; f. 1921; every two months; published by the Custody of the Holy Land (the official custodians of the Holy Shrines); Italian, Spanish, French, English and Arabic editions published in Jerusalem, by the Franciscan Printing Press, German edition in Munich, Maltese edition in Valletta.

Tmuroth: 48 Hamelech George St, POB 23076, Tel-Aviv; f. 1960; monthly; Hebrew; organ of the Liberal Labour Movement; Editor S. MEIRI.

WIZO Review: Women's International Zionist Organization, 38 Sderot David Hamelekh, Tel-Aviv 64237; tel. 03-5421805; telex 35770; fax 03-258267; f. 1947; six per year; English edition (quarterly), Spanish and German editions (two a year); Editor JACQUELINE HAHN-EFRATI; circ. 20,000.

Zion: POB 4179, Jerusalem 91041; tel. 02-637171; fax 02-662135; f. 1935; quarterly; Hebrew, with English summaries; research in Jewish history; Editors H. BEINART, I. GUTMAN, S. ALMOG, I. EFAL, J. HACKER.

Zraim: 7 Dubnov St, POB 40027, Tel-Aviv; f. 1953; Hebrew; journal of the Bnei Akiva (Youth of Tora Va-avoda) Movement; Editor ELYAHU DAVID.

Zrakor: Haifa; f. 1947; monthly; Hebrew; news digest, trade, finance, economics, shipping; Editor G. ALON.

The following are all published by Weizmann Science Press of Israel, 8A Horkania St, POB 801, Jerusalem 91007; tel. 02-663203; telex 26144.

Israel Journal of Botany: f. 1951; quarterly; Editor Prof. A. HALEVI.

Israel Journal of Chemistry: f. 1951; quarterly; Editor Prof. H. LEBANON.

Israel Journal of Earth Sciences: f. 1951; quarterly; Editors Dr Y. BARTOV, Prof. A. FLEXER.

Israel Journal of Mathematics: f. 1951; monthly, 3 vols of 4 issues per year; Editor Prof. A. LUBOTZKY.

Israel Journal of Technology: f. 1951; quarterly; Editor Prof. D. ABIR.

Israel Journal of Zoology: f. 1951; quarterly; Editor Prof. J. HELLER.

Journal d'Analyse Mathématique: f. 1955; two vols per year; Editor Prof. L. ZALCMAN.

Lada'at (Science for Youth): f. 1971; Hebrew; ten issues per vol.; Editor Dr M. ALMAGOR.

Mada (Science): 8A Horkanya St, POB 801, Jerusalem 91007; tel. 02-783203; fax 02-783784; f. 1955; popular scientific bi-monthly in Hebrew; Editor-in-Chief Dr YACHIN UNNA; circ. 10,000.

PRESS ASSOCIATIONS

Daily Newspaper Publishers' Association of Israel: 74 Petach Tikva Rd, POB 51202, Tel-Aviv 61200; fax 03-5617938; safeguards professional interests and maintains standards, supplies newsprint to dailies; negotiates with trade unions, etc.; mems all daily papers; affiliated to International Federation of Newspaper Publishers; Pres. SHABTAI HIMMELFARB; Gen. Sec. BETZALEL EYAL.

Foreign Press Association: Beit Sokolov, 9 Rehov Itamar Ben Avi, Tel-Aviv; tel. 03-216143; fax 03-210931; Pres. B. SLATER.

Israel Press Association: Sokolov House, 4 Kaplan St, Tel-Aviv.

NEWS AGENCIES

Jewish Telegraphic Agency (JTA): Israel Bureau, Jerusalem Post Building, Romema, Jerusalem; Dir DAVID LANDAU.

ITIM, News Agency of the Associated Israel Press: 10 Tiomkin St, Tel-Aviv; f. 1950; co-operative news agency; Dir and Editor ALTER WELNER.

Palestine Press Service: Salah ad-Din St, East Jerusalem; Proprs IBRAHIM QARA'EEN, Mrs RAYMONDA TAWIL; only Arab news agency in the Occupied Territories; (closed down by Israeli authorities for six months, March 1988).

Foreign Bureaux

Agence France-Presse: 34 Ben Yehuda St, 17th floor, POB 1507, Jerusalem; tel. 02-226542; telex 26401; Correspondent DAVID DAURE.

Agencia EFE (Spain): POB 3279, Avizohar 2, Apt 9, Bet Ha'Kerem, Jerusalem 91032; tel. 02-436658; telex 26446; Correspondent ELÍAS-SAMUEL SCHERBACOVSKY.

Agenzia Nazionale Stampa Associata (ANSA) (Italy): Industry House, 29 Hamered St, Tel-Aviv 68125; tel. 03-656279; telex 341704; Bureau Chief GRAZIANO MOTTA: 7 Marcus St, Jerusalem 92233; tel. 02-666098; telex 26420; Correspondent GIORGIO RACCAH.

Associated Press (AP) (USA): 30 Ibn Gavirol St, POB 20220, Tel-Aviv 61201; tel. 03-262283; telex 341411; POB 1625, 18 Shlomzion Hamalcha, Jerusalem; tel. 02-224632; telex 25258; Chief of Bureau NICHOLAS TATRO.

Deutsche Presse-Agentur (dpa) (Federal Republic of Germany): 30 Ibn Gavirol St, POB 16231, Tel-Aviv 61161; tel. 03-254268; telex 33416; Correspondents GIDEON BERLI, CHRISTIAN FÜRST.

Jiji Tsushin-Sha (Japan): 88A Herzl Ave, Jerusalem 96344; tel. (02) 532605; Correspondent HIROKAZU OIKAWA.

Kyodo News Service (Japan): 19 Lessin St, Tel-Aviv; tel. 03-258185; telex 361568; Correspondent HIDEO MIYAWAKI.

Reuters (UK): 38 Hamasger St, Tel-Aviv 67211; tel. 03-5372211; telex 361567; fax 03-5372045; 16c King George St, Jerusalem 94229; tel. 02-243805; telex 26189; fax 02-224633.

United Press International (UPI) (USA): 138 Petah Tikva Rd, Tel-Aviv; Bureau Man. BROOKE W. KROEGER; Bureau Man. in Jerusalem LOUIS TOSCANO.

The following is also represented: TASS (USSR).

Publishers

Achiasaf Ltd: 13 Yosef Hanassi St, POB 4810, Tel-Aviv 65236; tel. 03-5283339; telex 341730; fax 03-5286705; f. 1933; general; Man. Dir MATAN ACHIASAF.

Am Hassefer Ltd: 9 Bialik St, Tel-Aviv; tel. 03-53040; f. 1955; Man. Dir DOV LIPETZ.

'Am Oved' Ltd: 22 Mazah St, POB 470, Tel-Aviv; tel. 03-291526; fax 03-298911; f. 1942; fiction, non-fiction, reference books, school and university textbooks, children's books, poetry, classics, science fiction; Man. Dir AHARON KRAUS.

Amichai Publishing House Ltd: 5 Yosef Hanassi St, Tel-Aviv 65236; tel. 03-284990; f. 1948; Man. Dir YITZHAK ORON.

Arabic Publishing House: 17A Hagra St, POB 28049, Tel-Aviv; tel. 03-371438; f. 1960; established by the Histadrut (trade union) organization; periodicals and books; Dir JOSEPH ELIAHOU; Editor-in-Chief IBRAHIM M. IBRAHIM.

Carta, The Israel Map and Publishing Co Ltd: Yad Haruzim St, POB 2500, Jerusalem 91024; tel. 02-733501; telex 26587; fax 02-734882; f. 1958; the principal cartographic publisher; Chair. EMANUEL HAUSMAN; Pres. and CEO SHAY HAUSMAN.

ISRAEL

Dvir Publishing Co Ltd, The: 32 Schocken St, POB 149, Tel-Aviv; tel. 03-826138; f. 1924; literature, science, art, education; Publrs O. ZMORA, A. BITAN.

Eked Publishing House: 29 Bar-Kochba St, POB 11138, Tel-Aviv; tel. 03-283648; f. 1959; poetry, belles lettres, fiction; Man. Dir MARITZA ROSMAN.

Encyclopedia Publishing Co: 29 Jabotinski St, Jerusalem; tel. 02-632310; telex 26144; f. 1947; Hebrew Encyclopedia and other encyclopaedias; Chair. ALEXANDER PELI.

Rodney Franklin Agency: 5 Karl Netter St, POB 37727, Tel-Aviv 61376; tel. 03-5288948; telex 361579; fax 03-623010; exclusive representative of various British and USA publishers; Dir RODNEY FRANKLIN.

Gazit: 8 Zvi Brook St, POB 4190, Tel-Aviv; tel. 03-53730; art publishers; Editor GABRIEL TALPHIR.

Hakibbutz Hameuchad Publishing House Ltd: 15 Nehardea St, POB 40015, Tel-Aviv; tel. 03-751483; f. 1940; general; Dir UZI SHAVIT.

Israeli Music Publications Ltd: 25 Keren Hayesod St, POB 7681, Jerusalem 91076; tel. 02-241377; f. 1949; books on music and musical works; Dir STANLEY SIMMONDS.

Izre'el Publishing House Ltd: 76 Dizengoff St, Tel-Aviv; tel. 03-285350; f. 1933; Man. ALEXANDER IZRE'EL.

The Jerusalem Publishing House Ltd: 39 Tchernechovski St, POB 7147, Jerusalem 91071; tel. 02-636511; fax 02-634266; f. 1967; biblical research, history, encyclopaedias, archaeology, arts of the Holy Land, cookbooks, guide books, economics, politics; Dir SHLOMO S. GAFNI; Man. Editor RACHEL GILON.

Jewish History Publications (Israel 1961) Ltd: 29 Jabotinski St, Jerusalem; tel. 02-632310; telex 26144; f. 1961; encyclopaedias, World History of the Jewish People series; Chair. ALEXANDER PELI; Editor-in-Chief Prof. J. PRAWER.

Karni Publishers Ltd: 32 Schocken St, POB 149, Tel-Aviv 61001; tel. 03-812244; fax 03-826138; f. 1951; children's and educational books; Publrs O. ZMORA, A. BITAN.

Keter Publishing House Jerusalem Ltd: POB 7145, Givat Shaul B, Jerusalem 91071; tel. 02-521201; telex 25275; fax 02-536811; f. 1959; original and translated works in all fields of science and humanities, published in English, French, German, other European languages and Hebrew; publishing imprints: Israel Program for Scientific Translations, Israel Universities Press, Keter Books, Encyclopedia Judaica; Man. Dir OREN MOST.

Kiryat Sefer: 15 Arlosoroff St, Jerusalem; tel. 02-521141; f. 1933; concordances, dictionaries, textbooks, maps, scientific books; Dir AVRAHAM SIVAN.

Magnes Press, The: The Hebrew University, Jerusalem; tel. 02-660341; telex 25391; fax 02-666804; f. 1929; biblical studies, Judaica, and all academic fields; Dir DAN BENOVICI.

Rubin Mass Ltd: 11 Marcus St, POB 990, Jerusalem 91009; tel. 02-632565; telex 26144; fax 02-290774; f. 1927; Hebraica, Judaica, export of all Israeli publications; Dir OREN MASS.

Massada Press Ltd: 29 Jabotinski St, Jerusalem; tel. 02-632310; telex 26144; f. 1961; encyclopaedias, Judaica, the arts, educational material, children's books; Chair. ALEXANDER PELI; Man. Dir NATHAN REGEV.

Ministry of Defence Publishing House: 27 David Elazar St, Hakiriya, Tel-Aviv 67673; tel. 03-217940; fax 03-205509; f. 1939; military literature, Judaism, history and geography of Israel; Dir SHALOM SERI.

M. Mizrachi Publishers: 67 Levinsky, Tel-Aviv; tel. 03-625652; f. 1960; children's books, novels; Dir MEIR MIZRACHI.

Mosad Harav Kook: POB 642, Jerusalem; tel. 02-526231; f. 1937; editions of classical works, Torah and Jewish studies; Dir Rabbi M. KATZENELENBOGEN.

Otsar Hamoreh: 8 Ben Saruk, POB 303, Tel-Aviv; tel. 03-260211; f. 1951; educational.

Alexander Peli Jerusalem Publishing Co Ltd: 29 Jabotinski St, Jerusalem; tel. 02-632310; telex 26144; f. 1977; encyclopaedias, Judaica, history, the arts, educational material; Chair. ALEXANDER PELI; Man. Dir NATHAN REGEV.

Schocken Publishing House Ltd: 3 Rehov Nafcha, POB 2316, Tel-Aviv 61022; tel. 03-200127; telex 342449; fax 03-294147; f. 1938; general; Dir Mrs RACHELI EDELMAN.

Shikmona Publishing Co Ltd: Givat Shaul B, POB 7145, Jerusalem 91071; tel. 02-521201; telex 25275; fax 02-536811; f. 1965; Zionism, archaeology, art, guide-books, fiction and non-fiction.

Sifriat-Ma'ariv Ltd: Derech Petach Tikva 72A, POB 20208, Tel-Aviv 61201; f. 1954; Man. Dir IZCHAK YACHIN; Editor-in-Chief MIID HIM

Sifriat Poalim Ltd: 2 Choma Umigdal St, Tel-Aviv 67771; tel. 03-376845; f. 1939; general literature; Gen. Man. NATHAN SHAHAM.

Sinai Publishing Co: 72 Allenby St, Tel-Aviv 65172; tel. 03-663672; f. 1853; Hebrew books and religious articles; Dir MOSHE SCHLESINGER.

World Zionist Organization Torah Education Dept: POB 7044, Jerusalem 91070; tel. 02-632584; telex 25236; fax 02-202697; f. 1945; education, Jewish philosophy, studies in the Bible, children's books published in Hebrew, English, French, Spanish, German, Swedish and Portuguese.

Weizmann Science Press of Israel: 8A Horkanya St, POB 801, Jerusalem 91007; tel. 02-783203; fax 02-793784; f. 1955; publishes scientific books and periodicals; Publr HAIM TESSLER.

Yachdav United Publishers Co Ltd: 29 Carlebach St, POB 20123, Tel-Aviv; tel. 03-5614121; telex 341118; fax 03-5611996; f. 1960; educational; Chair. EPHRAIM BEN-DOR; Exec. Dir ARIE FRIEDLER.

Yavneh Publishing House Ltd: 4 Mazeh St, Tel-Aviv 65213; tel. 03-297856; telex 35770; f. 1932; general; Dir AVSHALOM ORENSTEIN.

S. Zack and Co: 2 King George St, Jerusalem 94429; tel. 02-227819; fax 02-252493; f. c. 1930; fiction, science, philosophy, religion, children's books, educational and reference books, dictionaries; Dir MICHAEL ZACK.

PUBLISHERS' ASSOCIATION

Israel Book Publishers Association: 29 Carlebach St, POB 20123, Tel-Aviv 67132; tel. 03-5614121; telex 341118; fax 03-5611996; f. 1939; mems: 84 publishing firms; Chair. RACHELI EIDELMAN; Man. Dir ARIE FRIEDLER.

Radio and Television

In 1988 there were an estimated 2,074,000 radio receivers and 1,175,000 television receivers in use.

RADIO

Israel Broadcasting Authority (IBA) (Radio): POB 6387, Jerusalem; tel. 02-222121; telex 26488; f. 1948; station in Jerusalem with additional studios in Tel-Aviv and Haifa. IBA broadcasts six programmes for local and overseas listeners on medium, shortwave and VHF/FM in 16 languages: Hebrew, Arabic, English, Yiddish, Ladino, Romanian, Hungarian, Moghrabit, Persian, French, Russian, Bucharian, Georgian, Portuguese, Spanish and Ethiopian; Chair. MICHA YINON; Dir-Gen. URI PORAT; Dir of Radio (vacant); Dir External Services VICTOR GRAJEWSKY.

Galei Zahal: POB MPO 01005, Zahal; tel. 814888; f. 1951; Israeli defence forces broadcasting station, Tel-Aviv, with studios in Jerusalem; broadcasts music, news and other programmes on mediumwave and FM stereo in Hebrew; Dir NACHMAN SHAI; Dir of Engineering S. KASIF.

TELEVISION

Israel Broadcasting Authority (IBA): POB 7139, Jerusalem 91071; tel. 02-557111; telex 25301; broadcasts began in 1968; station in Jerusalem with additional studios in Tel-Aviv; one colour network (VHF with UHF available in all areas); broadcasts in Hebrew and Arabic; Dir of Television T. SA'AR; Dir of Engineering YAAKOV SVIRY.

Israel Educational Television: Ministry of Education and Culture, 14 Klausner St, Tel-Aviv; tel. 03-5434343; telex 342325; fax 03-427091; f. 1966 by Hanadiv (Rothschild Memorial Group) as Instructional Television Trust; began transmission in 1966; school programmes form an integral part of the syllabus in a wide range of subjects; also adult education; Gen. Man. YAAKOV LORBERBAUM; Dir of Engineering A. KAPLAN.

In September 1986 the Government approved the establishment of a commercial radio and television network to be run in competition with the state system.

Finance

(cap. = capital; p.u. = paid up; dep. = deposits; m. = million; res = reserves; brs = branches)

BANKING

Central Bank

Bank of Israel: Bank of Israel Bldg, Kiryat Ben Gurion, POB 780, Jerusalem 91007; tel. 02-552211; telex 26316; fax 02-528805; f. 1954 as the Central Bank of the State of Israel; cap. 60m. new shekels (dep. 21,388m. new shekels (Dec. 1990); Gov. Prof. MICHAEL BRUNO; Senior Exec. Board M. FRAENKEL, A. GOLDSCHMIDT, D. KLEIN, Y. RAHAV; 2 brs.

ISRAEL — Directory

Principal Israeli Banks

American Israel Bank Ltd: 28A Rothschild Blvd, POB 1346, Tel-Aviv 61013; tel. 03-614656; telex 341217; fax 03-263195; f. 1933; subsidiary of Bank Hapoalim BM; total assets 1,172.3m. new shekels, dep. 1,090.2m. new shekels (Dec. 1989); Chair. A. BRENNER; Man. Dir A. SCHER; 19 brs.

Bank Hapoalim BM: 50 Rothschild Blvd, POB 27, Tel-Aviv 65124; tel. 03-5673333; telex 342342; fax 03-622028; f. 1921 as the Workers' Bank, name changed as above 1961; total assets 65,343.7m. new shekels, dep. 47,056m. new shekels (Dec. 1989); Chair. Bd of Man. AMIRAM SIVAN; 344 brs and offices.

Bank Leumi le-Israel BM: 24–32 Yehuda Halevi St, Tel-Aviv 65546; tel. 03-632111; telex 33586; fax 03-664496; f. 1902 as Anglo-Palestine Co; renamed Anglo-Palestine Bank 1930; reincorporated as above 1951; total assets 55,924m. new shekels, dep. 46,882m. new shekels (Dec. 1989); Chair. MOSHE SANBAR; Gen. Man. DAVID FRIEDMAN; 239 brs.

First International Bank of Israel Ltd: Shalom Mayer Tower, 9 Ahad Ha'am St, POB 29036, Tel-Aviv 65251; tel. 03-636111; telex 341252; fax 03-5100316; f. 1972 as a result of a merger between The Foreign Trade Bank Ltd and Export Bank Ltd; total assets 7,414m. new shekels, cap. 525m. new shekels, dep. 5,072m. new shekels (Dec. 1989); Chair. YIGAL ARNON; Gen. Man. SHALOM SINGER; 86 brs.

Industrial Development Bank of Israel Ltd: 2 Dafna St, Tel-Aviv 61334; tel. 03-430611; telex 033646; f. 1957; Chair. A. FRIEDMANN; Man. Dir JOSEPH SARIG.

Israel Ampal Industrial Development Bank Ltd: 111 Arlosoroff St, POB 27, Tel-Aviv 61000; f. 1956; cap. p.u. 9,752m. shekels, dep. 379m. shekels (Dec. 1986); Chair. M. OLENIK; Man. Dirs M. BACHAR, M. ARNON.

Israel Bank of Agriculture Ltd: 83 Hahashmonaim St, POB 2440, Tel-Aviv 61024; tel. (03) 285141; telex 35739; f. 1951; total assets 620.3m. new shekels, cap. p.u. 11m. new shekels, dep. 563.7m. new shekels (Dec. 1986); Chair. GIDON MAKOFF; Gen. Man. ISRAEL RAUCH.

Israel Continental Bank Ltd: 65 Rothschild Blvd, POB 37406, Tel-Aviv 61373; tel. 03-204148; telex 341447; fax 03-200399; f. 1974; capital held jointly by Bank Hapoalim BM (62%) and Bank für Gemeinwirtschaft AG (38%); total assets 533m. new shekels, cap. p.u. 5,613m. new shekels, dep. 450.5m. new shekels (Dec. 1989); Chair. A. SIVAN; CEO Y. YAROM; 3 brs.

Israel Discount Bank Ltd: 27-31 Yehuda Halevi St, Tel-Aviv 65546; tel. 03-637111; telex 33724; fax 03-638027; f. 1935; cap. p.u. 934,146 new shekels, dep. 28,463m. new shekels (June 1990); Chair. JOSEF CIECHANOVER; Man. Dir GIDEON LAHAV; more than 250 brs in Israel and abroad.

Israel General Bank Ltd: 38 Rothschild Blvd, POB 677, Tel-Aviv 61006; tel. 03-5645645; telex 33515; fax 03-5645210; f. 1934 as Palestine Credit Utility Bank Ltd, name changed as above 1964; total assets $330.7m., dep. $301.6m.; Chair. Baron EDMOND DE ROTHSCHILD; Man. Dir ABRAHAM BIGGER; 3 brs.

Leumi Agricultural Development Bank Ltd: 19 Rothschild Blvd, POB 2, Tel-Aviv 65121; tel. 03-5149918; telex 33586; fax 03-659514; f. 1922; subsidiary of Bank Leumi le-Israel BM; cap. and res 77.8m. new shekels (Dec. 1989), debentures and dep. 1,079.5m. new shekels (Dec. 1989); Chair. S. WEINSHAL; Gen. Man. E. HASSON.

Leumi Industrial Development Bank Ltd: 19 Rothschild Blvd, POB 2, Tel-Aviv 65121; tel. 03-5149918; telex 33586; fax 03-659514; f. 1944; subsidiary of Bank Leumi le-Israel BM; cap. and res 18m. new shekels, dep. 1,481.7m. new shekels; Chair. S. WEINSHAL; Gen. Man. E. HASSON.

Maritime Bank of Israel Ltd: 16 Ahad Ha'am St, POB 29373, Tel-Aviv 61293; tel. 03-663111; telex 33507; fax 03-661735; f. 1962; total assets 200.7m. new shekels, dep. 170.9m. new shekels (Dec. 1989); Chair. EITAN RAFF; Man. Dir JOSEPH WEGRZYN.

North American Bank Ltd: 116 Allenby St, POB 30218, Tel-Aviv 61301; f. 1978; Man. Dir. D. ZAFRIR; 4 brs.

Union Bank of Israel Ltd: 6–8 Ahuzat Bayit St, POB 2428, Tel-Aviv 65143; tel. 03-631631; telex 033493; fax 03-631274; f. 1951; subsidiary of Bank Leumi le-Israel BM; total assets 3,347.4m. new shekels, dep. 3,124m. new shekels (Dec. 1989); Chair. D. FRIEDMANN; Gen. Man. and CEO A. HEIFETZ; 25 brs.

United Mizrahi Bank Ltd: 13 Rothschild Blvd, Tel-Aviv 61002; tel. 03-629211; telex 3625; fax 03-614780; f. 1923 as Mizrahi Bank Ltd; 1969 absorbed Hapoel Hamizrahi Bank Ltd and name changed as above; total assets 14,035.3m. new shekels, dep. 12,180.6m. new shekels (Dec. 1989); Chair. CHAIM KUBERSKY; Man. Dir ITZHAK JAEGER; 80 brs.

Mortgage Banks

Israel Development and Mortgage Bank Ltd: 16–18 Simtat Beit Hashoeva, Tel-Aviv 65814; tel. 03-5643111; telex 32368; fax 03-5661104; f. 1959; subsidiary of Israel Discount Bank Ltd; cap. p.u. 1.3m. new shekels, res 65m. new shekels (Dec. 1989); Chair. M. B. GITTER; Jt Gen. Mans M. ELDAR, J. SHEMESH.

Leumi Mortgage Bank Ltd: 31–37 Montefiore St, POB 69, Tel-Aviv 65201; tel. 03-202444; fax 03-202348; f. 1921; subsidiary of Bank Leumi le-Israel BM; total assets 2,484.6m. new shekels, dep. 1,609.3m. new shekels (Dec. 1989); Chair. A. ZELDMAN; Gen. Man. B. AVITAL; 2 brs.

Merav Mortgage and Savings Bank Ltd: 49 Rothschild Blvd, POB 116, Tel-Aviv 61000; f. 1922; subsidiary of First International Bank of Israel Ltd; cap. and res 1,558m. shekels (Dec. 1983); Chair. A. SACHAROV; Man. Dir E. SHANOON.

Mishkan-Hapoalim Mortgage Bank Ltd: 2 Ibn Gvirol St, POB 1610, Tel-Aviv 64077; tel. 03-430111; f. 1950; subsidiary of Bank Hapoalim BM; total assets 4,221.3m. new shekels, dep. 4,133.3m. new shekels (Dec. 1989); Chair. M. OLENIK; Man. Dir A. KROIZER.

Tefahot, Israel Mortgage Bank Ltd: 9 Heleni Hamalka St, POB 93, Jerusalem 91000; tel. 02-219111; fax 02-219344; f. 1945; subsidiary of United Mizrahi Bank Ltd; cap. and res 175m. new shekels, total assets 4,755m. new shekels (Dec. 1989); Chair. H. KUBERSKY; Man. Dir DAVID BLUMBERG; 27 brs.

Foreign Banks

Barclays Discount Bank Ltd: 103 Allenby Rd, POB 1292, Tel-Aviv 61012; tel. 03-643333; telex 33550; f. 1971 by Barclays Bank International Ltd and Israel Discount Bank Ltd to incorporate Israel brs of Barclays; total assets 2,036m. new shekels, dep. 1,837.8m. new shekels (Dec. 1989); Chair. GIDEON LAHAV; Gen. Man. MOSHE NEUDORFER; 70 brs; wholly owned subsidiary: **Mercantile Bank of Israel Ltd,** POB 512, 24 Rothschild Blvd, Tel-Aviv; tel. 03-622541; telex 341344; f. 1924; cap. and res 12.4m. new shekels, dep. 79.3m. new shekels, (Dec. 1989); Chair. and Gen. Man. SHLOMO MAGRISO.

Four branches of the Jordan-based Cairo-Amman Bank were opened in the occupied West Bank, between November 1986 and August 1987 to provide financial services for the Palestinian community. The branches operated in both Jordanian dinars and Israeli shekels and were subject to dual Jordanian and Israeli regulatory authority. The Palestinian uprising in the Occupied Territories and Jordan's severance of legal and administrative links with the West Bank in July 1988 may result in the closure of these branches.

STOCK EXCHANGE

Tel-Aviv Stock Exchange: 54 Ahad Ha'am St, POB 29060, Tel-Aviv 61290; tel. 03-627411; telex 341762; fax 03-662704; f. 1953; Chair. HAIM STOESSEL; Gen. Man. JOSEPH NITZANI.

INSURANCE

The Israel Insurance Association lists 35 companies, a selection of which are listed below; not all companies are members of the association.

Ararat Insurance Co Ltd: Ararat House, 13 Montefiore St, Tel-Aviv 65164; tel. 03-640888; telex 341484; f. 1949; Co-Chair. AHARON DOVRAT, PHILIP ZUCKERMAN; Gen. Man. PINCHAS COHEN.

Aryeh Insurance Co of Israel Ltd: 9 Ahad Ha'am St, Tel-Aviv 65251; tel. 03-652671; telex 342125; fax 03-659337; f. 1948; Chair. AVINOAM M. TOCATLY.

Clal Insurance Co Ltd: 42 Rothschild Blvd, POB 326, Tel-Aviv 61002; tel. 03-627711; telex 341701; fax 03-622666; f. 1962; Man. Dir R. BEN-SHAOUL.

Hassneh Insurance Co of Israel Ltd: 115 Allenby St, POB 805, Tel-Aviv 61007; tel. 03-5649111; telex 341105; f. 1924; Man. Dir M. MICHAEL MILLER.

Israel Phoenix Assurance Co Ltd, The: 30 Levontin St, Tel-Aviv 65116; tel. 03-620111; telex 341199; fax 03-611242; f. 1949; Chair. of Board DAVID J. HACKMEY; Man. Dir JOSEPH D. HACKMEY.

Israel Reinsurance Co Ltd, The: 5 Drujanov St, POB 11589, Tel-Aviv 61114; tel. 03-296141; telex 342677; f. 1951; Chair. N. MISHOR; Man. Dir S. JANNAI.

Maoz Insurance Co Ltd: Tel-Aviv; f. 1945; formerly Binyan Insurance Co Ltd; Chair. B. YEKUTIELI.

Menorah Insurance Co Ltd: Menorah House, 73 Rothschild Blvd, Tel-Aviv 65786; tel. 03-294771; telex 341433; f. 1935; Pres. DAVID HIRSCHFELD.

Migdal Insurance Co Ltd: 26 Sa'adiya Ga'on St, POB 37633, Tel-Aviv 61375; tel. 03-298129; telex 342331; part of Bank Leumi Group; f. 1934; Chair. B. YEKUTIELI; Gen. Mans U. E. LEVY, M. ZANGEN.

Palglass Palestine Plate Glass Insurance Co Ltd: Tel-Aviv 65541; f. 1934; Gen. Man. AKIVA ZALZMAN.

ISRAEL

Sahar Israel Insurance Co Ltd: Sahar House, 23 Ben-Yehuda St, POB 26222, Tel-Aviv 63806; tel. 03-5140311; telex 33759; f. 1949; Chair. Y. HAMBURGER (acting); Gen. Man. M. HARPAZ.

Samson Insurance Co Ltd: Avgad Bldg, 5 Jabotinski Rd, Ramat-Gan 52520, POB 33678, Tel-Aviv; tel. 03-7521616; fax 03-7516644; f. 1933; Chair. E. BEN-AMRAM; Gen. Man. GIORA SAGI.

Sela Insurance Co Ltd: 53 Rothschild Blvd, Tel-Aviv 65124; tel. 03-61028; telex 35744; f. 1938; Man. Dir E. SHANI.

Shiloah Co Ltd: 2 Pinsker St, Tel-Aviv 63322; f. 1933; Gen. Man. Dr S. BAMIRAH; Man. Mme BAMIRAH.

Yardenia Insurance Co Ltd: 22 Maze St, Tel-Aviv 65213; f. 1948; Man. Dir H. LEBANON.

Zion Insurance Co Ltd: 120 Allenby Rd, Tel-Aviv 65128; f. 1935; Chair. A. R. TAIBER.

Trade and Industry

CHAMBERS OF COMMERCE

Federation of Israeli Chambers of Commerce: 84 Hahashmonaim St, POB 501, Tel-Aviv 67011; tel. 03-5612444; telex 33484; fax 03-5612614; co-ordinates the Tel-Aviv, Jerusalem, Haifa and Beersheba Chambers of Commerce; Dir ZVI AMIT.

Jerusalem Chamber of Commerce: POB 2083, 10 Hillel St, Jerusalem 91020; tel. 02-254333; fax 02-254335; f. 1908; c. 300 mems; Pres. JOSEPH PERLMAN; Dir-Gen. SHLOMO NAHMIAS.

Haifa Chamber of Commerce and Industry (Haifa and District): 53 Haatzmaut Rd, POB 33176, Haifa 31331; tel. 04-663471; telex 46653; fax 04-645428; f. 1921; 700 mems; Pres. GAD SASSOWER; Gen. Sec. A. MEHULAL.

Chamber of Commerce, Tel-Aviv-Jaffa: 84 Hahashmonaim St, POB 20027, Tel-Aviv 61200; tel. 03-5612444; telex 33484; fax 03-5612614; f. 1919; 1,800 mems; Pres. DAN GILLERMAN; Man. Dir ZVI AMIT.

Federation of Bi-National Chambers of Commerce with and in Israel: Tel-Aviv; federates: Israel-America Chamber of Commerce and Industry; Israel-British Chamber of Commerce; Australia-Israel Chambers of Commerce; Chamber of Commerce and Industry Israel-Africa; Chamber of Commerce Israel-Belgique-Luxembourg; Canada-Israel Chamber of Commerce and Industry; Israel-Danish Chamber of Commerce; Chambre de Commerce Israel-France; Chamber of Commerce and Industry Israel-Germany; Camera di Commercio Israeli-Italia; Israel-Japan Chamber of Commerce; Israel-Latin America, Spain and Portugal Chamber of Commerce; Netherlands-Israel Chamber of Commerce; Israel-Norway Chamber of Commerce; Handelskammer Israel-Schweiz; Israel-South Africa Chamber of Commerce; Israel-Sweden Chamber of Commerce; also incorporates Bi-National Chamber of Commerce existing in 20 foreign countries with Israel.

Israel-British Chamber of Commerce: POB 16065, Tel-Aviv 61160; tel. 03-259732; telex 342315; fax 03-221783; f. 1951; 440 mems; Chair. BARUCH GROSS; Gen. Sec. FELIX KIPPER.

TRADE AND INDUSTRIAL ORGANIZATIONS

Agricultural Export Co (AGREXCO): Tel-Aviv; state-owned agricultural marketing organization; Dir-Gen. AMOTZ AMIAD.

The Agricultural Union: Tchlenov 20, Tel-Aviv; consists of more than 50 agricultural settlements and is connected with marketing and supplying organizations, and Bahan Ltd, controllers and auditors.

Central Union of Artisans and Small Manufacturers: POB 4041, Tel-Aviv 61040; f. 1907; has a membership of more than 40,000 divided into 70 groups according to trade; the union is led by a 17-man Presidium; Chair. JACOB FRANK; Sec. ITZHAK HASSON; 30 brs.

Citrus Marketing Board: 6 Wissotzky St, POB 21371, Tel-Aviv 61213; tel. 03-430711; telex 341601; fax 03-5468989; f. 1942; the growers' institution for the control of the Israel citrus industry; jointly owned by the Government and the growers. Functions: control of plantations, supervision of picking and packing operations, marketing of the crop overseas and on the home markets; shipping; supply of fertilizers, insecticides, equipment for orchards and packing houses and of packing materials, technical research and extension work; long-term financial assistance to growers; Chair. I. EZRA; Gen. Man. Y. WEINBERG.

Cotton Production and Marketing Board: 10 Carlebach St, POB 20206, Tel-Aviv 67132; tel. 03-5613411; telex 32120; fax 03-5610860.

Export Institute: Tel-Aviv; tel. 03-630830; fax 03-630902; gives advice and financial backing to Israeli exporters; Dir-Gen. DAVID LIVAR.

Farmers' Union of Israel: 8 Kaplan St, POB 209, Tel-Aviv; tel. 03-252227; f. 1913; membership of 7,000 independent farmers, citrus and winegrape growers; Pres. ELIAHU IZAKSON; Dir-Gen. SHLOMO REISMAN.

General Association of Merchants in Israel: 6 Rothschild Blvd, Tel-Aviv; the organization of retail traders; has a membership of 30,000 in 60 brs.

Israel Diamond Exchange Ltd: POB 3222, Ramat-Gan; tel. 03-5760211; fax 03-5750652; f. 1937; production, export, import and finance facilities; estimated exports (1990) US $3,000m.; Pres. MOSHE SCHNITZER.

Israel Export Institute: 29 Rehov Hamered, POB 50084, Tel-Aviv 61500; tel. 03-630830; telex 35613; fax 03-630902; gives advice and financial backing to Israeli exporters; Dir-Gen. YOSSI GINOSSAR.

Israel Fruit Production Board: 119 Rehov Hahashmonaim, Tel-Aviv 61070; tel. 03-5610811; fax 03-5614672; Dir-Gen. EZRA MEIR.

Israel Journalists' Association Ltd: 4 Kaplan St, Tel-Aviv; tel. 03-256141; Sec. YONA SHIMSHI.

Kibbutz Industries Association: 8 Rehov Shaul Hamelech, Tel-Aviv 64733; tel. 03-252171; fax 03-251464; responsible for marketing and export of the goods produced by Israel's 268 kibbutzim (Dec. 1985); Pres. A. EPSTEIN.

Manufacturers' Association of Israel: Industry House, 29 Hamered St, POB 50022, Tel-Aviv 68125; tel. 03-5128800; telex 342651; fax 03-662026; 1,000 mem.-enterprises employing nearly 72% of industrial workers in Israel; Pres. DOV LAUTMAN; Dir-Gen. YORAM BLIZOVSKY.

The Histadrut

Hahistadrut Haklalit shel Haovdim Beeretz Israel (General Federation of Labour in Israel): 93 Arlosoroff St, Tel-Aviv 62098; tel. 03-431111; telex 342488; fax 03-269906; f. 1920; publs *Labour in Israel* (quarterly) in English, French, Spanish and German.

The General Federation of Labour in Israel, usually known as the Histadrut, is the largest voluntary organization in Israel, and the most important economic body in the State. It is open to all workers, including the self-employed, members of co-operatives and of the liberal professions, as well as wives, students and pensioners. Members of two religious labour organizations, Histadrut Hapoel Hamizrahi and Histadrut Poalei Agudat Israel, also belong to the trade union section and welfare service of the Histadrut, which thus extends to c. 85% of all workers. Dues—between 3.6% and 5.2% of wages—cover all its trade union, health insurance and social service activities. The Histadrut engages in four main fields of activity: trade union organization (with some 50 affiliated trade unions and 64 local labour councils operating throughout the country); social services (including a comprehensive health insurance scheme 'Kupat Holim', pension and welfare funds, etc.); educational and cultural activities (vocational schools, workers' colleges, theatre and dance groups, sports clubs, youth movement); and economic development (undertaken by Hevrat Ovdim (Labour Economy), which includes Histadrut-owned industries, agricultural and transport co-operatives, workers' bank, etc.). A women's organization, Na'amat, which also belongs to the Histadrut, operates nursery homes and kindergartens, provides vocational education and promotes legislation for the protection and benefit of working women. The Histadrut publishes its own daily newspaper, *Davar*, in Hebrew. The Histadrut is a member of the ICFTU and its affiliated trade secretariats, APRO, ICA and various international professional organizations.

Secretary-General: ISRAEL KESSAR.

ORGANIZATION

In 1989 the Histadrut had a membership of 1,630,000. In addition some 110,000 young people under 18 years of age belong to the Organization of Working and Student Youth, a direct affiliate of the Histadrut.

All members take part in elections to the Histadrut Convention (Veida), which elects the General Council (Moetsa) and the Executive Committee (Vaad Hapoel). The latter elects the 41-member Executive Bureau (Vaada Merakezet), which is responsible for day-to-day implementation of policy. The Executive Committee also elects the Secretary-General, who acts as its chairman as well as head of the organization as a whole and chairman of the Executive Bureau. Nearly all political parties are represented on the Histadrut Executive Committee.

The Executive Committee has the following departments: Trade Union, Organization and Labour Councils, Education and Culture, Social Security, Industrial Democracy, Students, Youth and Sports, Consumer Protection, Administration, Finance and International.

ISRAEL

TRADE UNION ACTIVITIES

Collective agreements with employers fix wage scales, which are linked with the retail price index; provide for social benefits, including paid sick leave and employers' contributions to sick and pension and provident funds; and regulate dismissals. Dismissal compensation is regulated by law. The Histadrut actively promotes productivity through labour management boards and the National Productivity Institute, and supports incentive pay schemes. There are some 50 trade unions affiliated to the Histadrut.

There are unions for the following groups: clerical workers, building workers, teachers, engineers, agricultural workers, technicians, textile workers, printing workers, diamond workers, metal workers, food and bakery workers, wood workers, government employees, seamen, nurses, civilian employees of the armed forces, actors, musicians and variety artists, social workers, watchmen, cinema technicians, institutional and school staffs, pharmacy employees, medical laboratory workers, X-ray technicians, physiotherapists, social scientists, microbiologists, psychologists, salaried lawyers, pharmacists, physicians, occupational therapists, truck and taxi drivers, hotel and restaurant workers, workers in Histadrut-owned industry, garment, shoe and leather workers, plastic and rubber workers, editors of periodicals, painters and sculptors and industrial workers.

Histadrut Trade Union Department: Dir HAIM HABERFELD.

ECONOMIC ACTIVITIES AND SOCIAL SERVICES

These include Hevrat Haovdim (Economic Sector, literally, 'the Workers' Company', employing 260,000 workers in 1983), Kupat Holim (the Sick Fund, covering almost 77% of Israel's population), seven pension funds, and NA'AMAT (women's organization which runs nursery homes and kindergartens, organizes vocational education and promotes legislation for the protection and benefit of working women).

Other Trade Unions

General Federation of West Bank Trade Unions: Sec.-Gen. SHAHER SAAD.

Histadrut Haovdim Haleumit (National Labour Federation): 23 Sprintzak St, Tel-Aviv 64738; tel. 03-258351; fax 03-261753; f. 1934; 150,000 mems.

Histadrut Hapoel Hamizrahi (National Religious Workers' Party): 166 Even Gavirol St, Tel-Aviv 62023; tel. 03-444151; fax 03-5468942; 125,000 mems in 81 settlements.

Histadrut Poale Agudat Israel (Agudat Israel Workers' Organization): 64 Frishman St, POB 11044, Tel-Aviv; tel. 03-242126; has 33,000 members in 16 settlements and 8 educational insts.

Transport

RAILWAYS

Freight traffic consists mainly of grain, phosphates, potash, containers, oil and building materials. Rail service serves Haifa and Ashdod, ports on the Mediterranean Sea, while a combined railroad service extends to Eilat port on the Red Sea. Passenger services operate between the main towns: Nahariya, Haifa, Tel-Aviv and Jerusalem. In 1988 the National Ports Authority assumed responsibility for the rail system.

Israel State Railways: Central Station, POB 18085, Tel-Aviv 61180; tel. 03-55421515; telex 371946; fax 03-258176; the total length of main line is 528 km and there are 337 km of branch line; gauge 1,435 mm; Gen. Man. ELIAHU BARAK; Deputy Gen. Man. (Admin.) D. GUY; Deputy Gen. Man. (Tech.) LEON HEYMAN.

Underground Railway

Haifa Underground Funicular Railway: 124 Hanassi Ave, Haifa; opened 1959; 2 km in operation; Man. D. SCHARF.

ROADS

In 1988 there were 12,980 km of paved roads, of which 3,995 km were inter-urban, out of which 284 km were motorways with four or more lanes.

Ministry of Housing and Construction: Public Works Dept, 23 Hillel St, Jerusalem.

SHIPPING

In 1988 Israel had a merchant fleet of 81 ships.

Haifa and Ashdod are the main ports in Israel. The former is a natural harbour, enclosed by two main breakwaters and dredged to 45 ft below mean sea-level. In 1965 the deep water port was completed at Ashdod which had a capacity of about 8.6m. tons in 1988.

The port of Eilat is Israel's gate to the Red Sea. It is a natural harbour, operated from a wharf. Another port, to the south of the original one, started operating in 1965. Gaza port fulfils the needs of the Gaza Strip.

The Israel Ports and Railways Authority: Maya Building, 74 Petach Tikva Rd, POB 20121, Tel-Aviv 61201; tel. 03-5121995; fax 03-5697142; f. 1961; to plan, build, develop, administer, maintain and operate the ports. In 1988/89 investment plans amounted to US $68m. for the development budget in Haifa, Ashdod and Eilat ports. Cargo traffic April 1989–March 1990 amounted to 16.2m. tons (oil excluded); Chair. ZVI KEINAN; Dir-Gen. Ing. SHAUL RAZIEL.

ZIM Israel Navigation Co Ltd: 7-9 Pal-Yam Ave, POB 1723, Haifa 31000; tel. 04-652111; telex 46501; f. 1945; runs cargo and container services in the Mediterranean and to N Europe, N and S America, Far East, Africa and Australia; operates about 80 ships (including 30 general cargo ships and one oil tanker) totalling 1.8m. dwt; total dry cargo carried: 8.2m. metric tons in 1988; Chair. ZVI ZUR; Man. Dir MATTY MORGENSTERN.

CIVIL AVIATION

Israel Airports Authority: Ben-Gurion Airport, Tel-Aviv; tel. 03-9712804; Dir-Gen. ZVI GOV-ARI.

El Al Israel Airlines Ltd: POB 41, Ben Gurion Airport, Lod, Tel-Aviv; tel. 03-9716111; telex 381007; fax 03-9721442; f. 1948; the Government is the major stockholder; daily services to most capitals of Europe; over 20 flights weekly to New York; services to the USA, Canada, Egypt, Kenya, South Africa and Turkey; fleet of 5 Boeing 747-200B, 2 Boeing 747-200B Combi, 1 Boeing 747-200F, 1 Boeing 747-100F, 3 Boeing 757-200, 2 Boeing 737-200, 4 Boeing 767-200; Pres. RAFAEL HAR-LEV.

Arkia Israeli Airlines Ltd: Sde-Dov Airport, POB 39301, Tel-Aviv 61392; tel. 03-422777; telex 341749; fax 03-5411390; f. 1980 through merger of Kanaf-Arkia Airlines and Aviation Services; scheduled passenger services linking Tel-Aviv, Jerusalem, Haifa, Eilat, Rosh Pina and Masada; cargo services to European destinations; fleet of 3 Boeing B-707, 2 Boeing B-737, 3 Cessna 337, 4 De Haviland Dash-7, 1 De Haviland Dash-6, 5 Navajo Chieftain, 1 Islander, 1 Aero Commander; Chair. S. ZIV; Pres. ISRAEL BOROVICH.

Tourism

In 1989 a total of 1,424,000 tourists visited Israel.

Ministry of Tourism: 24 King George St, POB 1018, Jerusalem 91000; tel. 02-237311; telex 26115; fax 02-382148; Minister of Tourism GIDEON PATT; Dir-Gen. ABRAHAM ROSENTAL.

Atomic Energy

Israel Atomic Energy Commission: 26 Rehov Hauniversita, Ramat Aviv, POB 7061, Tel-Aviv; tel. 03-422922; telex 33450; fax 02-422974; f. 1952; advises the Government on long term policies and priorities in the advancement of nuclear research and development; supervises the implementation of policies approved by the Government, including the licensing of nuclear power plants and the promotion of technological and industrial applications; represents Israel in its relations with scientific institutions abroad and international organizations engaged in nuclear research and development (Israel is a member of IAEA); Chair. The Prime Minister; Dir-Gen. YONA S. ETTINGER.

The Atomic Energy Commission has two research and development centres: the Nahal Soreq Nuclear Research Centre and the Negev Nuclear Research Centre near Dimona. The main fields of research are: nuclear physics and chemistry, plasma physics, solid state physics and chemistry, optics and electro-optics, reactor physics and engineering, radiation chemistry and biology, metallurgy and materials engineering, nuclear medicine and radio-pharmaceutics, non-destructive testing and environmental studies. Research and development projects and work with industrial applications include studies in isotopes, radiopharmaceuticals, medical and solid state lasers, crystal growth, high-tech. materials (including ceramics, ultra-pure electro-optical materials, infra-red glasses), mineral prospecting and the recovery of uranium from phosphates, use of intense sources of radiation in the medical, chemical and food industries, and the engineering and design of equipment for use in highly corrosive environments. The centres also provide national services: radiation protection, production and distribution of radioactive and stable isotopes, molecule and radio-pharmaceutical labelling, high vacuum engineering, training of personnel, information and documentation, etc.

Nuclear Research Centre-Negev (NRCN): POB 9001, Beersheba; equipped with a natural uranium-fuelled and heavy water-moderated reactor IRR-2 of 25 MW thermal; Dir GIORA AMIR.

Soreq Nuclear Research Centre: Yavne 70600; tel. 08-434211; telex 381455; f. 1954; equipped with a 'swimming pool' type research reactor IRR-1 of 5 MW thermal; Dir Dr U. HALAVEE.

Weizmann Institute of Science: POB 26, Rehovot; tel. 08-483111; telex 381300; fax 08-466966; f. 1949; incorporates the Daniel Sieff Research Institute (f. 1934); includes 21 research units grouped into 5 faculties (Mathematical Sciences, Physics, Chemistry, Biophysics-Biochemistry, Biology), and a department of science teaching within the Feinberg Graduate School; 300 teachers; 651 graduate students; Chair. Bd of Govs MURRAY B. KOFFLER; Pres. Prof. HAIM HARARI; Chair. Scientific Council N. SHARON.

ITALY

Introductory Survey

Location, Climate, Language, Religion, Flag, Capital
The Italian Republic comprises a peninsula, extending from southern Europe into the Mediterranean Sea, and a number of adjacent islands. The two principal islands are Sicily, to the south-west, and Sardinia, to the west. The Alps form a natural boundary to the north, where the bordering countries are France to the north-west, Switzerland and Austria to the north and Yugoslavia to the north-east. The climate is temperate in the north and Mediterranean in the south, with mild winters and long, dry summers. The average temperature in Rome is 7.4°C (45.3°F) in January and 25.7°C (78.3°F) in July. The principal language is Italian. German and Ladin are spoken in the Alto Adige region on the Austrian border, and French in the Valle d'Aosta region (bordering France and Switzerland), while in the Basilicata region of south-eastern Italy there is an Albanian-speaking minority. Catalan is spoken in north-western Sardinia. Almost all of the inhabitants profess Christianity: more than 90% are adherents of the Roman Catholic Church. There is freedom of expression for other Christian denominations and for non-Christian religions. The national flag (proportions 3 by 2) has three equal vertical stripes, of green, white and red. The capital is Rome.

Recent History
The Kingdom of Italy, under the House of Savoy, was proclaimed in 1861 and the country was unified in 1870. Italy subsequently acquired an overseas empire, comprising the African colonies of Eritrea (now part of Ethiopia), Italian Somaliland and Libya. Benito Mussolini, leader of the Fascist Party, became Prime Minister in October 1922 and assumed dictatorial powers in 1925-26. Relations between the Italian state and the Roman Catholic Church, a subject of bitter controversy since Italy's unification, were codified in 1929 by a series of agreements, including the Lateran Treaty, which recognized the sovereignty of the State of the Vatican City (q.v.), a small enclave within the city of Rome, under the jurisdiction of the Pope. Italian forces from Eritrea and Somaliland attacked and occupied neighbouring Ethiopia in 1935-36. Under Mussolini, Italy supported the Fascist forces in the Spanish Civil War of 1936-39, and annexed Albania in April 1939. From June 1940, Italy supported Nazi Germany in the Second World War. Italian forces from Albania attacked Greece in October 1940, but were defeated and forced to withdraw. In 1941 British forces captured Eritrea and Italian Somaliland, and ended Italy's occupation of Ethiopia, and in 1942 British and French forces occupied Libya. As forces from the allied powers invaded Italy, the Fascist regime crumbled. King Victor Emmanuel III dismissed Mussolini, and the Fascist Party was dissolved, in July 1943. With Italy's effective withdrawal from the war, German forces assumed the occupation of Albania. In Italy itself, anti-Fascist partisans joined allied forces in resisting the occupation by the remaining German troops. German forces in Italy surrendered, and Mussolini was killed, in April 1945. Italy's overseas empire was dissolved. In 1950, however, the British military administration of Italian Somaliland ended and the pre-war colony became a UN Trust Territory, with Italy returning as the administering power, until its merger with neighbouring British Somaliland, to form the independent state of Somalia, in 1960.

In May 1946 King Victor Emmanuel abdicated in favour of his son, Umberto II. However, he reigned for only one month. On 10 June, following a referendum, the monarchy was abolished and Italy became a republic. Until 1963 the monopoly of power held by the Partito della Democrazia Cristiana (DC) was unchallenged; industry expanded rapidly in a liberal economic system supported by capital from the USA. By 1963, however, low wage rates and lack of social reforms had increased discontent, and in the elections of that year the Partito Comunista Italiano (PCI), together with other parties of the extreme right and left, made considerable gains at the expense of the DC. The result of these losses was a rapid succession of mainly coalition governments involving the DC and one or more of the other major parties.

Aldo Moro's coalition Government of the DC and the Partito Repubblicano Italiano (PRI), formed in November 1974, resigned in January 1976 after the withdrawal of support by the Partito Socialista Italiano (PSI). Moro formed a minority DC administration in February, but this Government was forced to resign in April. General elections for both Legislative chambers took place in June, at which the PCI won 34.4% of the votes for the Chamber of Deputies. Although the DC still led the poll with 38.7% (the same as in the 1972 election), the PCI increased its strength in the 630-member Chamber from 179 to 228 seats, and continued to press for the 'historic compromise', a plan for a broad-based government with representatives from the DC, PSI and PCI, based on an alliance between Communism and Roman Catholicism. This was rejected by the DC, which insisted on excluding the PCI from power, although the DC could no longer govern against PCI opposition in Parliament. In July a minority DC Government was formed by Giulio Andreotti, a former Prime Minister, with the assurance of the abstention of the PCI deputies, and proceeded to introduce severe austerity measures to cope with the continuing economic crisis. In July 1977 the PCI, after four months of negotiations, was allowed a voice in policy-making but no direct role in the Government. The minority Government was forced to resign in January 1978, owing to pressure from the PCI, which wanted a more active participation in government, but Andreotti formed a new, almost identical administration in March, with PCI support. In May of the same year Aldo Moro, the former Prime Minister, was murdered by the Brigate Rosse (Red Brigades), a terrorist group. In the following month the President, Giovanni Leone, resigned as a result of allegations of corruption. A series of inconclusive ballots finally ended in July, with the inauguration of Alessandro Pertini, a former President of the Chamber of Deputies, as the first Socialist President of the Republic.

The Andreotti administration collapsed in January 1979, when the PCI withdrew from the official parliamentary majority, subsequently renewing its claim to posts in the Council of Ministers. A new coalition Government was formed by Andreotti in March, only to be defeated within 10 days on a vote of confidence. At elections in June the PCI's share of the vote for the Chamber of Deputies declined to 30.4%, and it returned to the role of opposition in the next Parliament.

In August 1979 Francesco Cossiga, a former Minister of the Interior, formed a minority 'Government of truce', composed of the DC, the Partito Liberale Italiano (PLI) and the Partito Socialista Democratico Italiano (PSDI), relying on the abstention of the PSI. In spite of its mandate, the new Government's initiatives were repeatedly thwarted by obstructionism in Parliament. Cossiga's second administration, formed in April 1980, admitted the PSI to the Government, for the first time in six years, in a majority coalition with the DC and the PRI. The deliberate exclusion of the PCI led to an open campaign by its representatives in Parliament to bring down the new coalition. In September the Government was forced out of office in a secret ballot on its economic programme. In October Arnaldo Forlani, the Chairman of the DC, assembled a coalition of members of the DC, PSI, PRI and PSDI. The new administration's integrity was damaged by a series of scandalous allegations, and it was finally forced to resign in May 1981, after it had been made known that more than 1,000 of Italy's foremost establishment figures belonged to a secret masonic lodge named P-2 ('Propaganda Due') which had extensive criminal connections both in Italy and abroad. The lodge was linked with many political and financial scandals and with right-wing terrorism (kown as 'black' terrorism), culminating in the summer of 1982 with the collapse of one of the leading Italian banks, Banco Ambrosiano, and the death of its President, Roberto Calvi. In January 1989 a Milan court ruled that Calvi had been murdered, and in April it was announced that the former head of P-2, Licio Gelli, and 34 other people were to be tried on charges connected with the Banco Ambrosiano bankruptcy.

In June 1981 Senator Giovanni Spadolini, leader of the PRI, formed a majority coalition of members of the PSI, PRI, DC, PSDI and PLI, thus becoming the first non-DC Prime Minister since 1946. This Government fell in August 1982, after the defection of the PSI, but was reconstituted later that month with the same ministers. In November Spadolini resigned, following a dispute between DC and PSI ministers concerning the worsening economic situation. A new Government was formed in December by Amintore Fanfani, a former DC Prime Minister, leading a coalition of the DC, PSI, PSDI and PLI, committed to controlling the economy by increasing taxes and reducing public expenditure. This administration lasted until April 1983, when the PSI withdrew its support and demanded a general election. Parliament was dissolved in May, despite attempts by President Pertini to secure the formation of a new government. At elections in June, the DC, which had rarely won less than 38% of the total vote in any poll since 1946, received only 32.9% of valid votes for the Chamber of Deputies. This loss of support meant that several of the smaller parties increased their shares of the vote. The PSI made a small advance, taking 11.4% of the total vote. This increase, combined with the loss of support for the DC, resulted in the accession of Bettino Craxi, the leader of the PSI, as the first Socialist Prime Minister in the history of the Republic. The new administration, a five-party coalition of the DC, PSI, PRI, PSDI and PLI, took office in August, committed to cutting the budget deficit and to economic reform. Its anti-inflation measures included a Government decree, imposed in February 1984, to reduce automatic index-linked wage increases (the 'scala mobile'). Despite opposition, the decree became law in June.

The repercussions of the P-2 scandals (see above) continued in July 1984, when Pietro Longo, leader of the PSDI in the coalition Government, resigned from his post as Budget Minister, after allegations that he was a member of the P-2 lodge. Craxi continued to consolidate his position by winning votes of confidence in the Senate and the Chamber of Deputies for his programme of economic reforms. In local and regional elections, held in May 1985, the PCI's share of the vote fell sharply, to 30.2%, while support for the DC and PSI increased. The result of a referendum, held in June and sponsored by the Communists, on the Government's decree of the previous year reducing the 'scala mobile', further vindicated the coalition's policies, when 54.3% of votes cast supported the Government.

In July 1985 Francesco Cossiga, President of the Senate and a former DC Prime Minister, succeeded Alessandro Pertini as President of the Republic. The repercussions of the seizure of an Italian cruise ship, the *Achille Lauro*, in the eastern Mediterranean by four Palestinian Arabs, believed to be members of the Palestine Liberation Front, in October, precipitated the collapse of the Government when the PRI withdrew from the coalition, claiming that it had not been fully consulted on policy decisions. A reconciliation was achieved within a few days, and Craxi's resignation as Prime Minister was revoked. In June 1986, however, Craxi resigned, following a vote of 'no confidence' in the Chamber of Deputies, thus bringing to an end Italy's longest administration (1,060 days) since the Second World War. President Cossiga subsequently nominated former Prime Minister Giulio Andreotti, a DC member and hitherto Minister of Foreign Affairs, to form a new government. However, the refusal of the other coalition parties to support Andreotti's nomination led to Craxi's return to power in July, on condition that he transfer the premiership to a DC member in March 1987.

Craxi duly submitted his resignation, and that of his Government, in March 1987. President Cossiga nominated Giulio Andreotti to form a new government. However, the bitter rivalry between the DC and the PSI caused Andreotti to abandon his attempt to form a government, and Nilde Jotti, the PCI President of the Chamber of Deputies, was subsequently selected for the task by President Cossiga. Her failure to reconcile the two parties led President Cossiga to request Bettino Craxi to revive his former coalition Government for a vote of confidence. However, the DC ministers resigned from the Government in protest against PSI proposals to hold referendums on nuclear issues and judicial reforms. Oscar Scalfaro, the DC Minister of the Interior, in turn failed to form a new government, and in April Amintore Fanfani, the DC President of the Senate, was appointed as the head of a 'caretaker' administration, comprising 16 former DC ministers and nine unallied members. Following a vote of 'no confidence' in the Chamber of Deputies, a general election was called for June, when the DC obtained 34.3% of the votes and the PSI obtained 14.3%. The PCI suffered its worst post-war electoral result, obtaining 26.6% of the votes, and thereby losing 21 seats in the Chamber of Deputies. The Green Party obtained 2.5% of the votes and entered the Chamber for the first time, occupying 13 seats. Fanfani resigned in July, when Giovanni Goria, a DC member and the former Minister of the Treasury, became Prime Minister, and reappointed a five-party coalition government. In November Goria resigned, following the withdrawal of the PLI from the coalition, owing to a dispute over economic policy. Although Goria's resignation was rejected by President Cossiga, a series of strikes and other economic problems had seriously weakened the Government by the end of 1987. In February 1988, following difficulties in enacting financial legislation, Goria again announced his resignation, which was rejected by President Cossiga, who requested him to remain as 'caretaker' Prime Minister pending the approval of the 1988 budget and the formation of a new government. Despite the Senate's approval of the budget in the following month, Goria's resignation was precipitated by opposition to the Government's decision to resume construction of the Montalto di Castro nuclear power station (suspended in 1987 because of public concern over environmental risks). Ciriaco De Mita, the Secretary-General of the DC, was requested to form a government. After five weeks of inter-party consultations, the formation of a coalition of the same five parties was agreed upon, and in April De Mita was sworn in at the head of a new administration which included nine newly-appointed ministers and six ministers with changed portfolios. In October 1988 a crisis was narrowly averted when the Government secured a majority of votes in favour of abolishing the secret ballot in Parliament. The reform of parliamentary voting procedures had become a matter of priority for De Mita, who regarded the secret ballot as a source of instability in Italy's political life: henceforth, open voting was to be applied in both chambers of Parliament, except in extraordinary circumstances, such as issues of conscience.

In May 1988 local elections were held throughout the country, in which the DC's share of the votes increased to 36.8% and the PSI's share increased to 18.3%, while the PCI's share decreased to 21.9%, signifying their worst defeat in local polls for 35 years. In the same month the Council of Ministers' decision to give its final approval to a regional autonomy accord for the Alto Adige resulted in a series of bombings, perpetrated by German-speaking extremists in the provincial capital of Bolzano. At provincial elections held in November 1988, the neo-Fascist Movimento Sociale Italiano-Destra Nazionale (MSI-DN) almost doubled its share of the votes, thereby replacing the DC as the largest Italian-language grouping in the region.

In February 1989 the DC elected Arnaldo Forlani to replace De Mita (who became the party's President) as its Secretary-General. In March the PCI offered to form a left-wing alliance with the PSI, but this proposal was rejected by Craxi. In early May an estimated 16m. workers, led by the three major trade unions, participated in a general strike in protest against a proposal to introduce health service charges. A few days later Craxi, his position strengthened by his re-election to the post of Secretary-General of the PSI, severely criticized De Mita. This criticism led to the collapse of the coalition Government and to De Mita's resignation, after 13 months in office. President Cossiga invited the President of the Senate, Giovanni Spadolini, to mediate in the political crisis.

In mid-June 1989 President Cossiga nominated De Mita to form a new government. In early July, however, De Mita announced that he had been unsuccessful, and Cossiga selected Giulio Andreotti to form a government. Andreotti immediately obtained the support of the PSI. The formation of a coalition of the same five parties was agreed in late July, and Andreotti was sworn in as the head of his sixth administration. His success in forming the Government represented a triumph for the conservative elders of the DC over the reformist wing (represented by De Mita). The PSI also secured gains. Gianni De Michelis became the first Socialist Minister of Foreign Affairs for many years, while Craxi's deputy, Claudio Martelli, became the Deputy Prime Minister. In the same month the PCI leader, Achille Occhetto, established a 21-member 'shadow cabinet', based on the British model.

Municipal elections took place in late May 1989, in which the DC's share of the vote increased to 39.6%. The PSI's share increased to 19.1%, thus obtaining for the Socialists a larger proportion of the vote than the PCI for the first time in 40 years. In the elections to the European Parliament in June, the DC received 32.9% of the votes cast, and the PSI increased its share to 14.8%, 3.6% higher than in the 1984 European elections. The PCI received 27.6% of the votes, 5.7% lower than the 1984 result. The repression of the pro-democracy movement in the People's Republic of China by the Communist Government and the crisis of Eastern European communism were considered to be contributory factors in this decline in support.

In August 1989 it was discovered that a US branch (in Atlanta, Georgia) of the Banca Nazionale del Lavoro, Italy's largest state-owned bank, had made unauthorized loan commitments, totalling nearly US $3,000m., to Iraq. It was believed that $1,000m. of the loans had been used for the procurement of military equipment. The Chairman and the Director-General of the bank resigned as a result of the scandal. In January 1990, however, an accord effectively legitimizing the majority of the loans was signed in Geneva, Switzerland.

In February 1990 an internal party dispute prompted De Mita to resign from the presidency of the DC. Supporters of De Mita, who together constituted a left-wing alliance within the DC, also withdrew from party posts, but pledged their continued support for the Andreotti Government. The cohesion of the coalition Government was, none the less, severely undermined in early 1990 by the response of the PRI to an emergency decree, initiated in late 1989 by Claudio Martelli (the Socialist Deputy Prime Minister), that aimed, for the first time, to impose restrictions on immigration levels. Representatives of the PRI claimed that the terms of the decree, which included an 'amnesty' for all clandestine immigrants who were already living in Italy, were inadequate, and tabled numerous amendments in an attempt to delay the successful passage of the legislation. However, the proposals received parliamentary approval in late February 1990.

Local government elections took place in 15 regions, 87 provinces and more than 6,700 communes in May 1991, at which the DC secured 33.6% of the votes cast. However, the PCI, which was, at that time, undergoing a period of radical internal reform (see below), won the support of only 24% of voters (significantly less than in equivalent elections in earlier years). The PSI won 15% of the votes. The most significant electoral gains were enjoyed by the Lega Nord, a grouping of federalist, anti-Mezzogiorno and anti-immigration 'leagues', which denounced what they alleged to be 'Roman colonialism' and the 'southern hegemony' of the central Government. One such league, the Lega Lombarda, won almost 20% of votes in the Lombardy region, while the Lega Nord secured 5.6% of the overall national vote.

In late July 1990 five members of the DC, including the Minister of Defence, Mino Martinazzoli, and the Minister of Education, Sergio Matarella, resigned from the Council of Ministers, in protest against proposals for legislation that would regulate the administration of public and private television networks. New ministers were appointed to the vacant posts, and the new administration was endorsed, in a vote of confidence, by a large parliamentary majority, while the legislation that had provoked the resignations similarly received approval. In October Vincenzo Scotti was appointed Minister of the Interior, following the resignation, for reasons of ill-health, of Antonio Gava (who had recently been the subject of considerable criticism, owing to a resurgence of acts of violence that had allegedly been perpetrated by the Mafia).

In early November 1990 it was made known that the existence of a secret defence organization, code-named 'Operation Gladio', had recently been discovered. The Gladio network had been established in the late 1950s by the US Central Intelligence Agency, in co-operation with NATO, to plan for a counter-rebellion in the event of an invasion by forces of the Warsaw Pact, or of the rise to prominence of a domestic Communist movement. It was subsequently revealed that similar networks had been established in other NATO countries in Europe. Links were alleged between members of Gladio and the right-wing P-2 organization, and it was alleged that the network had been involved in acts of 'black' terrorism in the early 1980s. As doubts were expressed concerning the constitutional legitimacy of the existence of the clandestine organization, the PCI demanded the resignation of President Cossiga, who stated that, as an official at the Ministry of Defence during the late 1960s, he had been involved in the administration of the Gladio network. In late November 1990 it was announced that Gladio had been formally dissolved. However, the repercussions of the incident continued to undermine the integrity of President Cossiga when, in the following month, it was alleged that he had, during the late 1960s, been involved in a conspiracy to tamper with evidence that implicated senior intelligence officers in a plot to thwart the political ambitions of the PCI.

The Central Committee of the PCI had, in November 1989, voted to renounce the party's Communist identity, and to initiate a process by which the PCI would transform itself into a mass social democratic party, which would be eligible to join the Socialist International. A series of party conferences took place during 1990, at which delegates debated proposals for reform. The final congress of the PCI was convened in Rimini in late January and early February 1991: delegates endorsed Occhetto's suggestion that the party rename itself the Partito Democratico della Sinistra (PDS—Democratic Party of the Left) by a large majority. About one-third of the party's membership had previously expressed opposition to the programme of reform; none the less, it was believed that most members would remain loyal to Occhetto, although a small minority were expected to form a new political organization that would embrace orthodox Marxist doctrine. In a ballot to elect a general secretary of the PDS, Occhetto (the sole candidate) failed to secure the votes necessary to ensure his appointment. He was, however, successful in a second ballot. Despite earlier signs that Occhetto's party would seek to co-operate closely with the PSI, the PDS policy of unequivocal opposition to military intervention in response to Iraq's forcible annexation of Kuwait (see below) was expected to delay any *rapprochement* of the two parties.

In the late 1980s the Italian authorities intensified their efforts to combat organized crime. There were mass trials of Mafia suspects in December 1987 and November 1988, resulting in the conviction of a total of 468 defendants. A third mass trial of Mafia suspects culminated in April 1989 with the conviction of 40 defendants. However, 82 defendants were acquitted, including the head of the Sicilian Mafia's governing 'commission', Michele Greco. In June 42 mayors in Calabria, in the south of the country, resigned in protest against the alleged failure of the Government to prevent kidnappings by the Mafia in the region. In the same month the Mafia attempted to assassinate Giovanni Falcone, Italy's most prominent anti-Mafia investigator, indicating a renewed escalation of the conflict between the perpetrators of organized crime and the authorities. In August a Christian Democratic politician, Lodovico Ligato, was murdered by the Calabrian Mafia. Acts of violence by the Mafia escalated during 1990: it was reported that 2,000 people were killed by Mafia organizations in that year. In September the Government announced measures that were intended to strengthen the powers of the police and judiciary in their efforts to combat organized crime.

In October 1989 11 alleged members of the Brigate Rosse were charged in connection with the assassination of Prof. Roberto Ruffilli, a DC senator, in April 1988. Nine of the accused were sentenced to life imprisonment in June 1990. Also in October 1989 253 Brigate Rosse guerrillas, many already imprisoned for other terrorist crimes, were acquitted of armed insurrection, while Enzo Calvitti, allegedly one of the principal members of the Brigate Rosse in the late 1970s and early 1980s, was arrested in Paris. The successful conviction, during 1990, of several members of terrorist organizations, in connection with acts of terrorism that had been committed in earlier decades, was, in part, overshadowed by the release of other convicted terrorists (including alleged perpetrators of the bombing of the railway station in Bologna in 1980, together with members of the group that seized the *Achille Lauro* in 1982).

Italy's foreign policy has traditionally been governed by its firm commitment to Europe, through participation in the EEC, and by its role in NATO. As a consequence of the US air raid on Libya in April 1986, Italian armed forces took control of Lampedusa island, lying south of Sicily (of which region it forms a part) and about 300 km north of Tripoli, following an unsuccessful Libyan attack on the island's US radar facilities. In May eight Libyan diplomats were expelled from Italy in response to Libya's expulsion of 25 Italian diplomats from Tripoli earlier in the month. In March 1987 Gen. Licio Giorgieri, an Italian air force officer in charge of the procurement of air and space weapons, was assassinated by the Brigate Rosse in what was believed to be part of a wider anti-NATO campaign, protesting against European participation in the USA's Strategic Defense Initiative. In September the Italian Government dispatched a task force of eight naval vessels to defend its merchant ships in the Persian Gulf, following allegations of the involvement of an Italian business executive in the supply of arms to Iran. (Italy obtained 45% of its petroleum requirements via the Strait of Hormuz.) In November 1988 it was announced that the task force was to return to Italy. In June, despite strenuous opposition from left-wing parties, the Government agreed to accept the transfer to Italy of 72 American fighter aircraft which, under an agreement between the USA and Spain, were to be withdrawn from their base in Spain by 1991. It was reported in April 1989 that the fighter aircraft were likely to prove superfluous, owing to an agreement by the USSR and the USA to withdraw missiles.

Following Iraq's forcible annexation of Kuwait, in August 1990, the Italian coalition Government demonstrated initial reluctance to contribute to the ensuing deployment of military forces in the region of the Persian (Arabian) Gulf by foreign powers that opposed the Iraqi action. Despite the opposition of the PCI (later the PDS), Italian aircraft and naval vessels were subsequently dispatched to the Gulf region, as part of a co-ordinated military effort by members of the Western European Union (WEU, see p. 212). In mid-January 1991, shortly after the outbreak of hostilities in the Gulf region, the participation of Italian forces in military action was given parliamentary authorization. Later in the same month, however, Vice-Admiral Mario Buracchia, who had hitherto had responsibility for the Italian naval deployment in the Gulf, relinquished his command, following the publication of an interview in which he apparently expressed reservations concerning the policy of military intervention.

Government

Under the 1948 Constitution, legislative power is held by the bicameral Parliament, elected by universal suffrage for five years (subject to dissolution) on the basis of proportional representation. The Senate has 315 elected members (seats allocated on a regional basis) and seven life Senators. The Chamber of Deputies has 630 members. The minimum voting age is 25 years for the Senate and 18 years for the Chamber. The two houses have equal power.

The President of the Republic is a constitutional Head of State elected for seven years by an electoral college comprising both Houses of Parliament and 58 regional representatives. Executive power is exercised by the Council of Ministers. The Head of State appoints the President of the Council (Prime Minister) and, on the latter's recommendation, other Ministers. The Council is responsible to Parliament.

The country is divided into 20 regions, of which five (Sicily, Sardinia, Trentino-Alto Adige, Friuli-Venezia Giulia and Valle d'Aosta) enjoy a special status. There is a large degree of regional autonomy. Each region has a regional council elected every five years by universal suffrage and a Giunta regionale responsible to the regional council. The regional council is a legislative assembly, while the Giunta holds executive power. The regions are subdivided into a total of 95 provinces.

Defence

Italy has been a member of NATO since 1949. In June 1990 it maintained armed forces totalling 389,600 (including 259,000 conscripts): an army of 260,000, a navy of 50,000 and an air force of 79,600. Military service lasts 12 months in all the services. The 1989 state budget allocated 23,996,310m. lire to the Ministry of Defence (5.2% of total expenditure by the central Government).

Economic Affairs

In 1989, according to estimates by the World Bank, Italy's gross national product (GNP), measured at average 1987–89 prices, was US $871,955m., equivalent to $15,150 per head. During 1980–89, it was estimated, GNP increased, in real terms, at an average annual rate of 2.4%, while real GNP per head increased by 2.1% per year over the same period. During 1980–89 the population increased by an annual average of 0.2%. Italy's gross domestic product (GDP) increased, in real terms, by an annual average of 2.2% in 1980–88. The Government forecast real GDP growth of 0.5% in 1990.

Agriculture (including forestry and fishing) contributed 4.1% of GDP in 1989. In 1990 about 8.9% of the employed labour force were engaged in the agricultural sector. The principal crops are sugar beet, grapes, wheat, maize and tomatoes. Italy is a leading producer and exporter of wine. In 1989 agricultural production was less than 0.2% higher than in 1980. Italy's total catch of fish (including crustaceans and molluscs) was 559,249 metric tons in 1988.

Industry (including mining, manufacturing, construction and power) contributed 32.1% of GDP in 1989. Some 32.1% of the employed labour force were engaged in industrial activities in 1990. The State plays a major role in the development of heavy industry. During 1980–87 industrial production increased by an annual average of 1.1%. Industrial output increased by 6% in 1988.

The major product of the mining sector is petroleum, followed by lignite, pyrites, fluorspar and barytes. Italy also has reserves of bauxite, lead and zinc.

Manufacturing contributed 27% of GDP in 1988, according to World Bank estimates. About 22.3% of the employed labour force were engaged in the sector in 1990. The most important branches of manufacturing, measured by gross value of output, are machinery and transport equipment, textiles and clothing, and chemicals.

More than 80% of energy requirements are imported. In 1988 58% of requirements were derived from petroleum; coal-fired electricity generating stations provided 14.6%, natural gas-fired stations provided 12.6%, and nuclear power stations provided 4.6%. In 1989 imports of mineral fuels and lubricants accounted for 11.7% of the value of total imports.

There are more than 1,100 banks in Italy, with over 12,000 branches. In 1988 there was a 29% increase in the net profits of the Italian banking sector, to a record 5,363,000m. lire.

Tourism is an important source of income, and in 1989 55.1m. foreigners visited Italy. Tourist receipts totalled 16,138,880m. lire in 1988. There were 1.7m. hotel beds at December 1989.

In 1989 Italy recorded a visible trade deficit of US $1,990m., and there was a deficit of $6,190m. on the current account of the balance of payments. In 1989 the principal source of imports (21.2%) was the Federal Republic of Germany, which was also the principal market for exports (16.9%). Other major trading partners in that year were France, the USA and the United Kingdom. The principal exports in 1989 were machinery and transport equipment, clothing and footwear, basic manufactures and chemicals. The principal imports were machinery and transport equipment and basic manufactures.

In 1989 Italy recorded a budget deficit of 118,259,037m. lire. The budgetary deficit for 1991 was forecast at approximately 130,000,000m. lire. Italy's total external debt at December 1988 was 1,035,500,000m. lire, equivalent to 96.5% of annual GDP. The annual rate of inflation averaged 11.0% in 1980–88. Consumer prices increased by an average of 5.0% in 1988, and by 6.2% in 1989. As a percentage of the total labour force, unemployment averaged almost 11% in 1990.

Italy is a member of numerous economic organizations of the European Community (see p. 135). The inaugural meeting of the 'Pentagonal Initiative', which envisages political and economic co-operation between Italy, Austria, Czechoslovakia, Hungary and Yugoslavia, took place in Venice in mid-1990.

During the late 1980s, Italy enjoyed sustained economic growth and strong industrial output. However, high levels of government expenditure on social services and industry, which for many years were not equalled by revenue and taxation, have produced a large public-sector deficit. There are also long-term structural problems, principally the underdevelopment of the southern part of the country, a low level of agricultural productivity, and heavy dependence on imported energy supplies. The success of attempts to address such problems has frequently been undermined by the need to ensure cohesion in the country's coalition governments. None the less, Italy is committed to the principle of European economic integration.

Social Welfare

Italy has a comprehensive system of social benefits covering unemployment and disability as well as retirement pensions and family allowances. These benefits are all provided by the social security system (Istituto Nazionale della Previdenza Sociale). There is also an industrial injuries scheme, operated by the Istituto Nazionale per l'Assicurazione contro gli Infortuni sul Lavoro.

A comprehensive national health service, aiming to provide free medical care for all citizens, was introduced in 1980. However, minimum charges are still made for essential medicines, medical examinations and hospital treatment. All workers are eligible for benefits under a unified national medical insurance scheme. In 1986 Italy had 1,752 hospital establishments, with a total of 450,377 beds: equivalent to one for every 79 inhabitants. In 1986 there were 84,339 registered physicians working in Italy. Of total expenditure by the central Government in 1987, 48,410,000m. lire (9.7%) was for health and 175,621,000m. lire (35.1%) for social security and welfare. In 1988 57,218,000m. lire was allocated to health (10.4% of expenditure by the central Government), and 191,883,000m. lire to social security and welfare (34.9%).

Education

Education is free and compulsory between the ages of six and 13 years. The curricula of all Italian schools are standardized by the Ministry of Education. After primary school, for children aged six to 11 years, the pupil enters the lower secondary school (scuola media unificata). An examination at the end of three years leads to a lower secondary school certificate, which gives access to all higher secondary schools. Pupils wishing to enter a classical lycée (liceo classico) must also pass an examination in Latin.

Higher secondary education is provided by classical, artistic and scientific lycées, training schools for elementary teachers and technical and vocational institutes (industrial, commercial, nautical, etc.). After five years at a lycée, the student sits an examination for the higher secondary school certificate (maturità), which allows automatic entry into any university faculty. Special four-year courses are provided at the teachers' training schools and the diploma obtained permits entry to a special university faculty of education, the magistero, and a few other faculties. The technical institutes provide practical courses which prepare students for a specialized university faculty.

In 1988 the total enrolment at primary and secondary schools was equivalent to 82% of the school-age population. Primary enrolment in that year was equivalent to 95% of all children in the relevant age-group, while the comparable ratio for secondary enrolment was 76%. In 1990, according to UNESCO estimates, the average rate of adult illiteracy was 2.9% (males 2.2%; females 3.6%).

University courses last for a minimum of four years. Study allowances are awarded to students according to their means and merit. Expenditure on education by the central Government was 37,053,000m. lire (7.4% of total spending) in 1987. The 1989 state budget allocated 43,158,897m. lire to the Ministry of Education (9.3% of total expenditure by the central Government).

Public Holidays

1991: 1 January (New Year's Day), 6 January (Epiphany), 1 April (Easter Monday), 25 April (Liberation Day), 1 May (Labour Day), 12 May (Festival of the Tricolour), 15 August (Assumption), 1 November (All Saints' Day), 5 November (National Unity Day), 8 December (Immaculate Conception), 25 December (Christmas Day), 26 December (St Stephen).

1992: 1 January (New Year's Day), 6 January (Epiphany), 20 April (Easter Monday), 25 April (Liberation Day), 1 May (Labour Day), 12 May (Festival of the Tricolour), 15 August (Assumption), 1 November (All Saints' Day), 5 November (National Unity Day), 8 December (Immaculate Conception), 25 December (Christmas Day), 26 December (St Stephen).

There are also numerous local public holidays, held on the feast day of the patron saint of each town.

Weights and Measures

The metric system is in force.

Statistical Survey

Source (unless otherwise stated): Istituto Centrale di Statistica, Via Cesare Balbo 16, 00100 Rome; tel. (06) 4673; telex 610338; fax (06) 46733196.

Area and Population

AREA, POPULATION AND DENSITY

Area (sq km)	301,277*
Population (census results)	
24 October 1971	54,136,547
25 October 1981	
Males	27,506,354
Females	29,050,557
Total	56,556,911
Population (official estimates at 31 December)	
1987	57,399,108
1988	57,504,691
1989	57,576,429
Density (per sq km) at 31 December 1989	191.1

* 116,324 sq miles.

REGIONS (31 December 1989)

Region	Area ('000 hectares)	Population	Regional capital	Population of capital
Abruzzi	1,079	1,266,448	L'Aquila	67,348
Basilicata	999	523,175	Potenza	68,046
Calabria	1,508	2,152,539	Catanzaro	103,521
Campania	1,360	5,808,705	Napoli (Naples)	1,204,149
Emilia-Romagna	2,212	3,921,597	Bologna	417,410
Friuli-Venezia Giulia	784	1,202,877	Trieste	233,047
Lazio	1,720	5,170,672	Roma (Rome)	2,803,931
Liguria	542	1,727,212	Genova (Genoa)	706,754
Lombardia (Lombardy)	2,386	8,911,995	Milano (Milan)	1,449,403
Marche	969	1,430,726	Ancona	103,454
Molise	444	335,348	Campobasso	51,206
Piemonte (Piedmont)	2,540	4,357,559	Torino (Turin)	1,002,863
Puglia	1,936	4,069,359	Bari	355,352
Sardegna (Sardinia)	2,409	1,657,562	Cagliari	219,095
Sicilia (Sicily)	2,571	5,172,785	Palermo	731,418
Toscana (Tuscany)	2,299	3,560,582	Firenze (Florence)	413,069
Trentino-Alto Adige	1,362	886,679	Bolzano (Bozen)* / Trento (Trent, Trient)*	100,707 / 101,416
Umbria	846	820,316	Perugia	149,261
Valle d'Aosta	326	115,270	Aosta	36,339
Veneto	1,837	4,385,023	Venezia (Venice)	320,990

* Joint regional capitals.

PRINCIPAL TOWNS (population at 31 December 1989)

Roma (Rome, the capital)	2,803,931	Perugia	149,261
Milano (Milan)	1,449,403	Ferrara	141,404
Napoli (Naples)	1,204,147	Ravenna	136,166
Torino (Turin)	1,002,863	Reggio nell' Emilia	130,825
Palermo	731,418	Rimini	130,638
Genova (Genoa)	706,754	Pescara	128,695
Bologna	417,410	Siracusa (Syracuse)	124,606
Firenze (Florence)	413,069	Monza	123,073
Catania	366,226	Sassari	119,717
Bari	355,352	Bergamo	117,584
Venezia (Venice)	320,990	Terni	110,020
Messina	273,570	Forlí	109,986
Verona	258,476	Vicenza	109,109
Taranto	244,512	Consenza	105,349
Trieste	233,047	La Spezia	104,511
Padova (Padua)	220,358	Piacenza	104,023
Cagliari	219,095	Torre del Greco	103,577
Brescia	196,935	Catanzaro	103,521
Reggio di Calabria	178,620	Ancona	103,454
Modena	176,857	Novara	103,088
Parma	174,341	Pisa	102,150
Livorno (Leghorn)	171,346	Lecce	101,957
Prato	165,888	Latina	101,936
Foggia	159,199	Trento (Trent, Trient)	101,416
Salerno	152,159	Bolzano (Bozen)	100,707

BIRTHS, MARRIAGES AND DEATHS

	Registered live births		Registered marriages		Registered deaths	
	Number	Rate (per 1,000)	Number	Rate (per 1,000)	Number	Rate (per 1,000)
1981	623,103	11.0	316,953	5.6	545,291	9.7
1982	619,097	10.9	312,486	5.5	534,935	9.4
1983	601,928	10.6	303,663	5.3	564,330	9.9
1984	587,871	10.3	300,889	5.3	534,676	9.4
1985	577,345	10.1	298,523	5.2	547,436	9.6
1986	555,445	9.7	297,450	5.2	544,489	9.5
1987	551,539	9.6	305,264	5.3	532,771	9.3
1988	569,698	9.9	318,296	5.5	539,426	9.4
1989*	555,686	9.7	311,613	5.4	525,960	9.5

* Provisional.

Average expectation of life (1983): Males 71.43 years; females 78.14 years.

EMIGRATION

Destination	1985	1986	1987
Belgium	2,402	1,996	1,638
France	4,057	3,808	3,274
Germany, Federal Repub.	21,092	19,793	17,921
Switzerland	17,091	14,021	13,587
United Kingdom	2,350	1,710	1,770
Other European Countries	3,594	3,319	2,393
Argentina	882	852	885
Brazil	545	502	522
Canada	1,818	1,391	1,300
USA	3,541	3,062	2,844
Venezuela	890	723	600
Oceania	1,243	1,053	1,057
Other Countries	7,232	5,632	6,803
Total	66,737	57,862	54,594

ITALY

ECONOMICALLY ACTIVE POPULATION*
(annual averages, '000 persons aged 14 years and over)

	1988	1989	1990
Agriculture, forestry, hunting and fishing	2,052	1,946	1,895
Energy and water	228	224	229
Manufacturing	4,699	4,729	4,757
Construction	1,823	1,800	1,859
Trade, restaurants and hotels	4,500	4,474	4,537
Transport, storage and communications	1,157	1,155	1,146
Financing, insurance, real estate and business services	831	859	895
Community, social and personal services	5,693	5,817	5,986
Total employed	20,983	21,004	21,304
Persons seeking work for the first time	1,398	1,405	1,266
Other unemployed	1,471	1,461	1,356
Total labour force	23,852	23,870	23,925
Males	15,136	15,071	15,053
Females	8,716	8,799	8,872

* Figures exclude permanent members of institutional households (150,000 in 1988; 150,000 in 1989) and persons on compulsory military service (225,000 in 1988; 236,000 in 1989).

Agriculture

PRINCIPAL CROPS ('000 metric tons)

	1987	1988	1989
Wheat	9,359.1	7,945.0	7,412.9
Barley	1,707.9	1,567.0	1,643.8
Oats	360.8	382.7	295.5
Rice (paddy)	1,043.9	1,093.5	1,245.9
Maize	5,761.9	6,319.4	6,359.5
Dry broad beans	159.6	132.5	122.6
Green broad beans	109.2	108.6	94.3
Dry beans	55.4	52.8	41.7
Soybeans (Soya beans)	1,589	1,393	1,623.6
Green beans	256.3	228.5	228.0
Green peas	198.3	179.7	175.3
Potatoes	2,463.9	2,340.9	2,457.5
Onions	477.4	460.9	472.7
Carrots	374.6	299.3	431.0
Turnips	43.3	46.6	42.7
Artichokes	453.2	499.2	453.4
Fennel	350.1	355.5	396.3
Celery	137.1	172.7	147.2
Cabbages	494.4	492.9	457.3
Cauliflowers	422.7	459.5	412.6
Endives, lettuces, radishes	850.8	854.3	666.9
Spinach	101.1	89.7	82.7
Aubergines (Egg-plants)	295.9	222.4	224.3
Tomatoes	4,770.5	4,188.9	5,566.4
Pumpkins	344.4	276.6	280.9
Water melons	714.5	676.4	645.0
Melons	356.3	275.1	289.3
Sugar beet	15,483.3	13,627.6	16,690.7
Tobacco	160.3	138.9	197.3
Grapes	11,497.5	9,545.5	9,449.1
Olives	3,457.4	4,132.0	5,655.7
Oranges	1,342.9	2,109.9	2,066.6
Lemons	591.8	708.4	666.9
Apples	2,234.2	2,331.7	1,924.2
Pears	892.5	986.7	754.2
Peaches	1,513.7	1,055.1	1,166.1
Fresh figs	42.7	44.3	36.8
Dried figs	3.9	5.1	5.2
Almonds (unshelled)	121.8	114.4	95.1

LIVESTOCK ('000 head, year ending September)

	1987	1988	1989
Cattle	8,819	8,794	8,737
Buffaloes	102	104	105*
Sheep	11,451	11,457	11,623
Goats	1,201	1,206	1,214
Pigs	9,278	9,383	9,359
Horses	253	250	250*
Mules	52	50	50*
Asses	91	86	86*

Chickens: (FAO estimates, million, year ending September): 140 in 1987; 132 in 1988; 128 in 1989.

* FAO estimates.

Source: FAO, *Production Yearbook*.

LIVESTOCK PRODUCTS ('000 metric tons)

	1987	1988	1989
Beef and veal	1,175	1,164	1,146
Mutton and lamb	67	69	74
Goats' meat	3.3	3.7	5.0
Pig meat	1,231	1,269	1,295
Horse meat	54	53	54
Poultry meat	1,052	1,076	1,081
Other meat	206	210	214
Edible offals	214	195	138
Lard	213	240	232
Cows' milk	10,899	10,786	10,576
Buffaloes' milk	75	80	98
Sheep's milk	616	611	622
Goats' milk	126	124	125
Butter	84	86	81
Cheese	678	657	702
Hen eggs	607	659	602
Wool: greasy	13.3	13.6	13.8

Forestry

ROUNDWOOD REMOVALS ('000 cubic metres, excl. bark)

	1987	1988	1989
Sawlogs, veneer logs and logs for sleepers	2,599	2,737	2,670
Pulpwood	706	738	865
Other industrial wood	1,159	1,205	1,065
Fuel wood	4,440	4,357	4,041
Total	8,902	9,037	8,641

SAWNWOOD PRODUCTION ('000 cubic metres)

	1986	1987	1988
Coniferous (soft wood)	854	729	900
Broadleaved (hard wood)	1,001	1,098	1,100
Total	1,855	1,827	2,000

Railway sleepers ('000 cubic metres): 64 in 1986; 78 in 1987; 78 in 1988.

Source: FAO, *Yearbook of Forest Products*.

ITALY   Statistical Survey

Fishing

('000 metric tons, live weight)

	1986	1987	1988
Freshwater fishes	9.4	10.7	10.5
Trouts	35.5	39.1	41.2
Flounders, halibuts, soles, etc.	11.7	11.5	11.4
European hake	24.4	26.6	29.5
Surmullets (Red mullets)	10.9	11.0	11.1
Mullets	9.5	10.7	9.0
Jack and horse mackerels	10.8	10.6	9.3
European pilchard (sardine)	52.2	47.5	42.8
European anchovy	32.4	19.7	20.8
Tunas	12.1	9.0	8.7
Swordfish	10.2	11.0	11.6
Other fishes (incl. unspecified)	144.6	129.8	126.8
Total fish	363.5	337.1	332.6
Shrimps, prawns, etc.	14.6	12.1	16.4
Other crustaceans	15.5	15.5	15.4
Mediterranean mussel	78.6	85.4	85.4
Striped venus	26.5	37.3	33.5
Cuttlefishes	15.4	13.7	15.8
Squids	17.3	16.9	16.6
Octopuses	14.3	15.5	16.6
Other molluscs	22.7	27.0	26.9
Total catch	568.2	560.4	559.2
Inland waters	50.6	55.2	58.2
Mediterranean and Black Sea	470.0	446.3	435.7
Atlantic Ocean	47.6	52.9	60.8
Indian Ocean	—	6.0	4.5

Source: FAO, *Yearbook of Fishery Statistics*.

Mining

('000 metric tons)

	1987	1988	1989
Bauxite	15.1	17.9	20.2
Lead concentrates*	21.0	28.4	23.3
Zinc concentrates*	67.8	72.0	81.0
Barytes	82.2	77.3	60.3
Fluorspar	135.6	140.9	118.4
Pyrites	784.9	720.1	835.7
Petroleum	3,904.5	4,839.2	4,568.4
Asphalt and bituminous rock	71.0	56.4	60.1
Lignite	1,641.7	1,600.4	1,485.6

* Figures refer to gross weight of ores and concentrates. The metal content (in '000 metric tons) was: Lead 12.2 in 1987, 13.5 in 1989; Zinc 33.2 in 1987, 39.7 in 1989.

Industry

SELECTED PRODUCTS
('000 metric tons, unless otherwise indicated)

	1987	1988	1989
Wine ('000 hectolitres)	75,820	61,680	n.a.
Pig iron	11,334.9	11,345.6	11,761.3
Steel	22,858.7	23,760.4	25,212.9
Rolled iron	20,846.5	22,275.6	23,443.0
Other iron and steel-finished manufactures	865.0	983.0	1,022.4
Iron alloys and *spiegel-eisen* special pig irons	238.2	243.5	247.1
Fuel oil	21,504.7	21,541.2	21,484.3
Synthetic ammonia	1,745.1	1,747.7	1,160.6
Sulphuric acid at 50° Bé	4,358.7	4,307.7	3,534.4
Synthetic organic dyes	17.5	16.8	18.3
Tanning materials	37.0	34.3	n.a.
Caustic soda	1,216.2	1,189.9	1,178.0

—continued	1987	1988	1989
Rayon and acetate filament yarn	29.5	n.a.	n.a.
Cotton yarn	261.3	258.6	267.1
Natural methane gas (million cu m)	16,217.6	16,510.8	16,765.9
Sewing machines ('000)	327.2	174.7	165.4
Typewriters ('000)	383.4	485.1	326.0
Passenger motor cars ('000)	1,711.8	1,883.5	1,970.7
Lorries (Trucks) ('000)	200.4	230.6	253.9
Hydroelectric power (million kWh)*	42,076	43,017	37,004
Thermoelectric power (million kWh)*	148,820	150,158	162,698

* Net production.

Finance

CURRENCY AND EXCHANGE RATES

Monetary Units
100 centesimi = 1 Italian lira (plural: lire).

Denominations
Coins: 5, 10, 20, 50, 100, 200, 500 and 1,000 lire.
Notes: 1,000, 2,000, 5,000, 10,000, 20,000, 50,000, 100,000 and 500,000 lire.

Sterling and Dollar Equivalents (30 September 1990)
£1 sterling = 2,196.25 lire;
US $1 = 1,172.25 lire;
10,000 lire = £4.553 = $8.531.

Average Exchange Rate (lire per US $)
1987   1,296.1
1988   1,301.6
1989   1,372.1

STATE BUDGET (million lire—1989)

Revenue	
Property and income taxes	163,044,978
Business taxation and duties	81,140,380
Customs and frontier charges	} 30,111,544
Taxes on manufacturing and consumption	
Public lottery and sweepstakes	2,323,093
State monopolies	6,103,399
Other ordinary revenue	62,579,618
Total real revenue	345,303,012
Capital movements	1,086,950
General total	346,389,962

Expenditure	
Ministry of the Treasury	250,842,473
Ministry of Finance	13,259,381
Ministry of Justice	3,836,632
Ministry of Education	43,158,897
Ministry of the Interior	49,949,684
Ministry of Public Works	4,379,083
Ministry of Agriculture and Forests	3,319,224
Ministry of Defence	23,996,310
Ministry of Labour and Social Welfare	31,416,451
Other Ministries	40,490,864
General total	464,648,999

ITALY

Statistical Survey

INTERNATIONAL RESERVES (US $ million at 31 December)*

	1987	1988	1989
Gold†	34,050	28,521	26,496
IMF special drawing rights	948	949	998
Reserve position in IMF	1,447	1,266	1,444
Foreign exchange	27,819	32,500	44,278
Total	64,264	63,236	73,216

* Excluding deposits made with the European Monetary Co-operation Fund.
† Valued at market-related prices.
Source: IMF, *International Financial Statistics*.

MONEY SUPPLY ('000 million lire at 31 December)

	1987	1988	1990
Currency outside banks	52,646	56,980	67,473
Demand deposits at commercial banks	292,894	319,715	353,570

Source: IMF, *International Financial Statistics*.

COST OF LIVING (Consumer Price Index; base: 1980 = 100)

	1987	1988	1989
Food	198.3	206.1	219.1
Fuel and light	205.1	214.3	227.7
Clothing	219.9	232.7	246.9
Rent	312.9	326.4	344.6
All items (incl. others)	211.0	221.7	235.6

Source: ILO, *Year Book of Labour Statistics*.

NATIONAL ACCOUNTS ('000 million lire)

	1987	1988	1989
Gross domestic product at factor cost	909,673	998,676	1,091,990
of which:			
Agriculture, forestry and fisheries	43,599	43,457	46,805
Industry	305,445	337,087	365,925
Other activities	474,732	522,139	573,517
Less imputed bank service charge	40,215	45,757	49,144
Public administration	126,112	141,750	154,887
Net factor income from abroad	−6,722	−7,504	−10,573
Gross national product at factor cost	902,951	991,172	1,081,417
Indirect taxes, *less* subsidies	69,185	84,250	95,998
Gross national product in market prices	972,136	1,075,422	1,177,415
Balance of exports and imports of goods and services	283	5,502	11,593
Available resources	972,419	1,080,924	1,189,008
of which:			
Private consumption expenditure	602,644	662,219	730,124
Government consumption expenditure	166,648	186,944	202,491
Gross fixed capital formation	193,606	216,627	240,241
Increase in stocks	9,521	15,134	16,152

BALANCE OF PAYMENTS (US $ million)

	1987	1988	1989
Merchandise exports f.o.b.	115,866	127,416	140,302
Merchandise imports f.o.b.	−115,939	−128,778	−142,292
Trade balance	−73	−1,362	−1,990
Exports of services	39,596	42,430	48,646
Imports of services	−40,146	−46,049	−55,050
Balance on goods and services	−623	−4,981	−8,394
Private unrequited transfers (net)	1,278	1,445	1,300
Government unrequited transfers (net)	−2,319	−2,654	−3,538
Current balance	−1,663	−6,190	−10,632
Direct capital investment (net)	1,753	1,270	529
Other long-term capital (net)	1,596	6,372	14,767
Short-term capital (net)	6,175	5,960	11,052
Net errors and omissions	−2,459	22	−4,602
Total (net monetary movements)	5,401	7,434	11,115
Valuation changes (net)	3,894	−2,448	1,531
Exceptional financing	34	33	18
Changes in reserves	9,329	5,020	12,664

Source: IMF, *International Financial Statistics*.

External Trade

Note: Data refer to the trade of Italy (excluding the communes of Livigno and Campione) and San Marino, with which Italy maintains a customs union. The figures include trade in second-hand ships, and stores and bunkers for foreign ships and aircraft, but exclude manufactured gas, surplus military equipment, war reparations and repayments and gift parcels by post. Also excluded are imports of military goods and exports of fish landed abroad directly from Italian vessels. Figures include gold ingots for non-monetary uses.

PRINCIPAL COMMODITIES
(distribution by SITC, '000 million lire)

Imports c.i.f.	1987	1988	1989
Food and live animals	19,646.2	21,078.6	23,274.1
Live animals	2,261.7	2,459.9	2,741.8
Bovine cattle	1,643.4	1,766.4	1,980.4
Meat and meat preparations	4,167.4	4,108.5	5,053.3
Fresh, chilled or frozen meat	4,002.2	2,222.0	2,695.3
Meat of bovine cattle	2,307.5	2,114.2	2,556.5
Dairy products and eggs	3,280.4	3,517.8	3,609.3
Cereals and cereal preparations	2,500.5	2,690.0	2,951.7
Maize (unmilled)	412.6	506.0	294.1
Beverages and tobacco	1,688.1	1,892.1	2,172.3
Crude materials (inedible) except fuels	13,063.3	15,894.3	18,378.0
Wood, lumber and cork	2,259.3	2,514.5	2,855.5
Shaped or simply worked wood	1,590.4	1,786.7	2,051.5
Textile fibres and waste	2,537.2	3,576.0	3,956.8
Metalliferous ores and metal scrap	2,079.5	2,727.6	3,806.8
Mineral fuels and lubricants	22,785.8	19,239.2	24,489.3
Petroleum and petroleum products	17,463.8	13,615.6	18,097.4
Crude petroleum	11,483.5	9,171.3	12,013.5
Animal and vegetable oils and fats	1,256.3	1,044.2	1,176.9
Chemicals	17,686.3	20,882.1	23,556.1
Chemical elements and compounds	5,858.9	6,749.3	7,833.7
Organic chemicals	4,710.0	5,597.0	6,526.1
Plastic materials, etc.	4,851.1	1,154.6	1,293.4

ITALY   Statistical Survey

Imports c.i.f.—continued	1987	1988	1989
Basic manufactures	25,093.3	29,699.9	36,100.2
Textile yarn, fabrics, etc.	6,121.9	6,252.3	7,179.8
Iron and steel	5,394.6	6,873.8	9,153.8
Non-ferrous metals	3,609.5	5,139.1	6,500.3
Copper and copper alloys	1,451.2	2,159.6	2,874.7
Machinery and transport equipment	43,938.0	52,122.3	59,947.7
Non-electric machinery } Electrical machinery, apparatus, etc.	27,919.1	33,916.3	37,404.4
Transport equipment	16,018.9	18,206.0	22,543.2
Road motor vehicles and parts	14,075.5	16,279.0	19,716.8
Passenger cars (excl. buses)	9,532.9	10,730.0	13,222.6
Miscellaneous manufactured articles	11,799.2	14,097.1	15,973.5
Scientific instruments, watches, etc.	4,916.3	5,637.2	6,459.6
Other commodities and transactions	5,396.4	4,063.7	4,851.2
Total	162,352.9	180,013.5	209,919.3

Exports f.o.b.	1987	1988	1989
Food and live animals	7,659.9	9,145.2	9,966.7
Fruit and vegetables	4,025.3	3,970.1	4,176.3
Fresh fruit and nuts	1,848.8	1,921.5	1,966.1
Beverages and tobacco	1,686.2	1,857.3	2,169.9
Crude materials (inedible) except fuels	2,345.4	2,806.7	3,074.2
Mineral fuels, lubricants, etc.	3,754.6	2,786.3	3,312.5
Petroleum products	3,513.1	2,578.8	3,083.1
Animal and vegetable oils and fats	464.5	509.4	667.1
Chemicals	11,334.3	13,232.3	14,539.1
Chemical elements and compounds	3,449.7	3,940.0	4,357.5
Plastic materials, etc.	3,659.7	1,755.8	1,935.0
Basic manufactures	33,573.6	37,181.0	43,493.5
Textile yarn, fabrics, etc.	8,945.8	9,681.7	10,925.6
Textile yarn and thread	2,287.9	2,373.5	2,571.3
Woven non-cotton fabrics (excl. narrow or special fabrics)	4,479.3	5,060.7	5,790.3
Non-metallic mineral manufactures	5,549.1	6,531.0	7,486.4
Iron and steel	5,308.4	5,842.2	7,299.1
Machinery and transport equipment	52,380.6	59,598.1	71,165.9
Non-electric machinery } Electrical machinery, apparatus, etc.	39,095.5	44,286.0	52,850.8
Domestic electrical equipment	2,805.8	3,339.8	3,762.6
Transport equipment	13,285.1	15,312.1	18,315.1
Road motor vehicles and parts	11,268.1	12,745.6	15,157.8
Passenger cars (excl. buses)	4,814.4	5,261.0	6,596.8
Miscellaneous manufactured articles	36,508.4	39,228.0	44,551.3
Clothing (excl. footwear)	11,630.1	11,795.4	12,961.2
Clothing not of fur	10,875.0	10,998.4	12,105.1
Footwear	6,825.8	6,915.6	7,751.3
Other commodities and transactions	1,171.5	35.8	108.9
Total	150,879.0	166,380.1	193,049.8

PRINCIPAL TRADING PARTNERS* ('000 million lire)

Imports c.i.f.	1987	1988	1989
Algeria	2,309.4	2,074.1	2,913.9
Argentina	455.5	592.9	611.4
Australia	863.1	1,272.1	1,373.0
Austria	3,732.4	4,311.5	4,847.1
Belgium/Luxembourg	8,037.6	8,800.8	10,391.7
Brazil	1,910.1	2,179.2	2,892.2
Canada	1,077.8	1,263.3	1,573.0
Denmark	1,692.9	1,767.5	1,975.5
Egypt	1,307.7	1,315.8	1,949.3
France	23,764.0	26,721.7	30,843.1
Germany, Federal Republic	34,167.5	39,202.7	44,497.4
Iran	1,365.5	716.3	1,110.1
Iraq	1,583.9	1,300.7	924.9
Japan	3,472.0	4,549.4	4,842.8
Kuwait	1,257.5	608.6	694.0
Libya	3,095.1	3,307.0	4,216.0
Netherlands	9,065.8	10,305.6	11,536.1
Saudi Arabia	1,707.4	1,368.9	1,619.6
South Africa	2,317.8	2,823.8	3,594.8
Spain (excl. Canary Is)	3,625.7	4,347.0	5,076.9
Sweden	2,273.4	2,587.5	3,194.6
Switzerland	7,728.4	8,059.4	9,067.3
USSR	3,689.6	4,087.8	4,941.3
United Kingdom	8,584.1	9,165.4	10,176.0
USA	8,700.7	10,090.6	11,453.8
Yugoslavia	2,366.1	2,922.3	3,497.1
Total (incl. others)	162,352.9	180,013.5	209,919.3

Exports f.o.b.	1987	1988	1989
Algeria	1,007.4	1,035.9	1,617.1
Austria	3,779.4	4,094.6	4,647.6
Belgium/Luxembourg	5,089.7	5,616.7	6,316.0
Canada	1,751.2	1,861.2	2,137.3
Denmark	1,287.7	1,297.5	1,457.2
France	24,629.2	27,598.0	31,439.5
Germany, Federal Republic	27,999.4	30,058.3	32,761.8
Greece	2,201.4	2,686.8	3,530.3
Iran	658.7	484.9	760.8
Japan	2,408.9	3,140.4	4,418.7
Libya	1,456.4	1,637.3	1,580.8
Netherlands	4,663.1	5,124.1	5,981.6
Nigeria	416.4	392.1	353.5
Saudi Arabia	1,898.2	1,873.9	1,880.7
Spain (excl. Canary Is)	5,295.0	6,751.5	9,161.1
Sweden	2,044.3	2,169.3	2,633.2
Switzerland	7,098.5	7,838.3	8,635.5
Turkey	1,364.7	1,194.4	1,391.4
USSR	2,874.7	2,725.7	3,535.3
United Kingdom	11,232.2	13,370.7	15,211.8
USA	14,514.4	14,791.5	16,631.5
Venezuela	619.3	777.1	737.6
Yugoslavia	1,868.8	2,035.3	2,605.5
Total (incl. others)	150,879.0	166,380.1	193,049.8

* Imports by country of production; exports by country of consumption.

Transport

STATE RAILWAYS (traffic)

	1987	1988	1989
Passenger journeys ('000)	394,200	410,000	418,700
Passenger-km (million)	41,395	43,344	44,442
Freight ton-km (million)	18,427	19,566	20,587

ITALY

ROAD TRAFFIC (licensed vehicles at 31 December)

	1986	1987*	1988
Passenger motor cars	23,495,460	24,307,000	25,290,250
Buses and coaches	77,891	82,100	75,820
Goods vehicles	1,887,415	1,906,000	2,058,008
Tractors (non-agricultural)	42,767	572,500	57,064
Trailers and semi-trailers	534,101		613,520
Motorcycles and scooters	2,204,275	6,285,000	2,871,069
Mopeds	3,594,703		3,357,726

* Provisional (Source: IRF, *World Road Statistics*).

SHIPPING
Merchant Fleet ('000 gross registered tons)

	1987	1988	1989
Total	8,024	7,565	7,922

Sea-borne Freight Traffic (international and coastwise)

	1987	1988	1989
Vessels entered ('000 n.r.t.)	332,024	354,390	366,203
Vessels cleared ('000 n.r.t.)	331,931	353,547	365,924
Goods loaded ('000 metric tons)	99,207	104,211	100,071
Goods unloaded ('000 metric tons)	269,225	271,266	277,836

CIVIL AVIATION (traffic on scheduled services)

	1986	1987	1988
Passengers carried ('000)	13,811.1	15,268.1	15,649.2
Passenger-km (million)	16,921.0	18,647.4	19,168.0
Freight ton-km (million)	844.1	911.6	1,029.0

Tourism

	1987	1988	1989
Foreign tourist arrivals*	52,724,941	55,690,434	55,131,098
Amount spent (million lire)	15,782,808	16,138,880	16,442,500

* Including excursionists and cruise passengers. Arrivals at accommodation establishments were 21,349,188 in 1987; 21,851,403 in 1988; 21,607,711 in 1989.

Number of hotel beds: 1,665,319 in 1987; 1,670,451 in 1988; 1,678,910 in 1989.

TOURIST ARRIVALS BY COUNTRY OF ORIGIN
(including excursionists)

	1987	1988	1989
Austria	5,542,812	6,174,611	6,083,370
Belgium	990,069	1,005,567	1,048,930
France	9,042,482	8,975,273	9,390,152
Germany, Federal Republic	9,617,677	10,479,061	10,134,213
Netherlands	1,388,693	1,802,684	1,840,844
Switzerland	10,452,491	11,754,847	10,190,559
United Kingdom	1,999,353	1,819,232	1,906,236
USA	1,482,607	1,351,257	1,356,662
Yugoslavia	4,835,022	5,467,441	5,909,741
Total (incl. others)	52,724,941	55,690,434	55,131,098

Communications Media

	1987	1988	1989
Telephones in use	28,050,000	29,299,000	30,755,940
Radio licences	15,230,000†	14,901,097	15,009,268
Television licences	14,687,000†	14,717,013	14,851,310
Book titles produced*	17,109†	19,620	22,647

* Excluding reprints.
† Source: UNESCO, *Statistical Yearbook*.

Education

(1989/90)

	Schools	Teachers	Students
Pre-primary	28,038	109,565	1,566,364
Primary	25,163	257,961	3,140,113
Secondary:			
Scuola Media	10,021	277,341	2,392,130
Secondaria Superiore	7,879	294,266	2,853,002
of which:			
Technical	2,871	136,702	1,304,899
Vocational	1,723	62,827	539,209
Teacher training	849	21,578	188,994
Art Licei	285	12,855	95,025
Classical, linguistic and scientific Licei	2,151	60,304	724,875
Higher	82	53,760	1,288,881

Directory

The Constitution

The Constitution of the Italian Republic was approved by the Constituent Assembly on 22 December 1947 and came into force on 1 January 1948. The fundamental principles are declared in Articles 1-12, as follows:

Italy is a democratic republic based on the labour of the people.

The Republic recognizes and guarantees as inviolable the rights of its citizens, either as individuals or in a community, and it expects, in return, devotion to duty and the fulfilment of political, economic and social obligations.

All citizens shall enjoy equal status and shall be regarded as equal before the law, without distinction of sex, race, language or religion, and without regard to the political opinions which they may hold or their personal or social standing.

It shall be the function of the Republic to remove the economic and social inequalities which, by restricting the liberty of the individual, impede the full development of the human personality, thereby reducing the effective participation of the citizen in the political, economic and social life of the country.

The Republic recognizes the right of all citizens to work and shall do all in its power to give effect to this right.

The Republic, while remaining one and indivisible, shall recognize and promote local autonomy, fostering the greatest possible decentralization in those services which are administered by the State, and subordinating legislative methods and principles to the exigencies of decentralized and autonomous areas.

The State and the Catholic Church shall be sovereign and independent, each in its own sphere. Their relations shall be governed by the Lateran Pact ('Patti Lateranensi'), and any modification in the pact agreed upon by both parties shall not necessitate any revision of the Constitution.

All religious denominations shall have equal liberty before the law, denominations other than the Catholic having the right to worship according to their beliefs, in so far as they do not conflict with the common law of the country.

The Republic shall do all in its power to promote the development of culture and scientific and technical research. It shall also protect and preserve the countryside and the historical and artistic monuments which are the inheritance of the nation.

The juridical system of the Italian Republic shall be in conformity with the generally recognized practice of international law. The legal rights of foreigners in the country shall be regulated by law in accordance with international practice.

Any citizen of a foreign country who is deprived of democratic liberty such as is guaranteed under the Italian Constitution, has the right of asylum within the territory of the Republic in accordance with the terms of the law, and his extradition for political offences will not be granted.

Italy repudiates war as an instrument of offence against the liberty of other nations and as a means of resolving international disputes. Italy accepts, under parity with other nations, the limitations of sovereignty necessary for the preservation of peace and justice between nations. To that end, it will support and promote international organizations.

The Constitution is further divided into Parts I and II, in which are set forth respectively the rights and responsibilities of the citizen and the administration of the Republic.

PART ONE

Civic Clauses

Section I (Articles 13-28). The liberty of the individual is inviolable and no form of detention, restriction or inspection is permitted unless it be for juridical purposes and in accordance with the provisions of the law. The domicile of a person is likewise inviolable and shall be immune from forced inspection or sequestration, except according to the provisions of the law. Furthermore, all citizens shall be free to move wheresoever they will throughout the country, and may leave it and return to it without let or hinderance. Right of public meeting, if peaceful and without arms, is guaranteed. Secret organizations of a directly or indirectly political or military nature are, however, prohibited.

Freedom in the practice of religious faith is guaranteed.

The Constitution further guarantees complete freedom of thought, speech and writing, and lays down that the Press shall be entirely free from all control or censorship. No person may be deprived of civic or legal rights on political grounds.

The death penalty is not allowed under the Constitution except in case of martial law. The accused shall be considered 'not guilty' until he is otherwise proven. All punishment shall be consistent with humanitarian practice and shall be directed towards the re-education of the criminal.

Ethical and Social Clauses

Section II (Articles 29-34). The Republic regards the family as the fundamental basis of society and considers the parents to be responsible for the maintenance, instruction and education of the children. The Republic shall provide economic assistance for the family, with special regard to large families, and shall make provision for maternity, infancy and youth, subject always to the liberty and freedom of choice of the individuals as envisaged under the law.

Education, the arts and science shall be free, the function of the State being merely to indicate the general lines of instruction. Private entities and individuals shall have the right to conduct educational institutions without assistance from the State, but such non-state institutions must ensure to their pupils liberty and instruction equal to that in the state schools. Institutions of higher culture, universities and academies shall be autonomous within the limitations prescribed by the law.

Education is available to all and is free and obligatory for at least eight years. Higher education for students of proven merit shall be aided by scholarships and other allowances made by the Republic.

Economic Clauses

Section III (Articles 35-47). The Republic shall safeguard the right to work in all its aspects, and shall promote agreement and co-operation with international organizations in matters pertaining to the regulation of labour and the rights of workers. The rights of Italian workers abroad shall be protected.

All workers shall be entitled to remuneration proportionate to the quantity and quality of their work, and in any case shall be ensured of sufficient to provide freedom and a dignified standard of life for themselves and their families.

The maximum working hours shall be fixed by law, and the worker shall be entitled to a weekly day of rest and an annual holiday of nine days with pay.

Women shall have the same rights and, for equal work, the same remuneration as men. Conditions of work shall be regulated by their special family requirements and the needs of mother and child. The work of minors shall be specially protected.

All citizens have the right to sickness, unemployment and disability maintenance.

Liberty to organize in trade unions is guaranteed and any union may register as a legal entity, provided it is organized on a democratic basis. The right to strike is admitted within the limitations of the relevant legislation.

Private enterprise is permitted in so far as it does not run counter to the well-being of society nor constitute a danger to security, freedom and human dignity.

Ownership of private property is permitted and guaranteed within the limitations laid down by the law regarding the acquisition, extent and enjoyment of private property. Inheritance and testamentary bequests shall be regulated by law.

Limitation is placed by law on private ownership of land and on its use, with a view to its best exploitation for the benefit of the community.

The Republic recognizes the value of mutual co-operation and the right of the workers to participate in management.

The Republic shall encourage all forms of saving, by house purchase, by co-operative ownership and by investment in the public utility undertakings of the country.

Political Clauses

Section IV (Articles 48-54). The electorate comprises all citizens, both men and women, who have attained their majority. Voting is free, equal and secret, and its exercise is a civic duty. All citizens have the right to associate freely together in political parties, and may also petition the Chambers to legislate as may be deemed necessary.

All citizens of both sexes may hold public office on equal terms.

Defence of one's country is a sacred duty of the citizen, and military service is obligatory within the limits prescribed by law. Its fulfilment shall in no way prejudice the position of the worker nor hinder the exercise of political rights. The organization of the armed forces shall be imbued with the spirit of democracy.

All citizens must contribute to the public expenditure, in proportion to their capacity.

ITALY

All citizens must be loyal to the Republic and observe the terms of the law and the Constitution.

PART TWO

Sections I, II and III (Articles 55-100). These sections are devoted to a detailed exposition of the Legislature and legislative procedure of the Republic.

Parliament shall comprise two Chambers, namely the Chamber of Deputies (Camera dei Deputati) and the Senate of the Republic (Senato).

The Chamber of Deputies is elected by direct universal suffrage, the number of Deputies being 630. All voters who on the day of the elections are 25 years of age, may be elected Deputies.

Seats are apportioned by dividing the number of inhabitants of the Republic, as shown in the last general census by 630, and allocating the seats proportionally to the population of each constituency.

The Senate of the Republic is elected on regional basis, the number of eligible Senators being 315. No region shall have less than seven Senators. Valle d'Aosta has only one Senator.

Seats are allocated proportionally among the Regions in the same way as the Chamber of Deputies.

The Chamber of Deputies and the Senate of the Republic are elected for five years.

The term of each House cannot be extended except by law and only in the case of war.

Members of Parliament shall receive remuneration fixed by law.

The President of the Republic must be a citizen of at least fifty years of age and in full enjoyment of all civic and political rights. The person shall be elected for a period of seven years (Articles 84-85).

The Government shall consist of the President of the Council and the Ministers who themselves shall form the Council. The President of the Council, or Prime Minister, shall be nominated by the President of the Republic, who shall also appoint the ministers on the recommendation of the Prime Minister (Article 92).

Section IV (Articles 101-113). Sets forth the judicial system and procedure.

Section V (Articles 114-133). Deals with the division of the Republic into regions, provinces and communes, and sets forth the limits and extent of autonomy enjoyed by the regions. Under Article 131 the regions are enumerated as follows:

Piemonte (Piedmont)	Marche
Lombardia (Lombardy)	Lazio
Veneto	Abruzzi
Liguria	Molise
Emilia-Romagna	Campania
Toscana (Tuscany)	Puglia
Umbria	Basilicata
Calabria	Trentino-Alto Adige*
Sicilia (Sicily)*	Friuli-Venezia Giulia*
Sardegna (Sardinia)*	Valle d'Aosta*

*These five regions have a wider form of autonomy based on constitutional legislation specially adapted to their regional characteristics (Article 116). Each region shall be administered by a Regional Council, in which is vested the legislative power and which may make suggestions for legislation to the Chambers, and the Giunta regionale which holds the executive power (Article 121).

The final articles provide for the establishment of the Corte Costituzionale to deal with constitutional questions and any revisions which may be found necessary after the Constitution has come into operation.

The Government

(February 1991)

HEAD OF STATE

President of the Republic: FRANCESCO COSSIGA (took office 3 July 1985).

COUNCIL OF MINISTERS

A coalition of Christian Democrats (DC), Socialists (PSI), Social Democrats (PSDI), Liberals (PLI) and Republicans (PRI).

Prime Minister: GIULIO ANDREOTTI (DC).
Deputy Prime Minister: CLAUDIO MARTELLI (PSI).
Minister of Foreign Affairs: GIANNI DE MICHELIS (PSI).
Minister of the Interior: VINCENZO SCOTTI (DC).
Minister of Justice: Prof. GIULIANO VASSALLI (PSI).
Minister of Finance: RINO FORMICA (PSI).
Minister of the Budget and of Economic Planning: PAOLO CIRINO POMICINO (DC).
Minister of the Treasury: GUIDO CARLI (DC).
Minister of Defence: VIRGINIO ROGNONI (DC).
Minister of Education: GERARDO BIANCO (DC).
Minister of Public Works: GIANNI PRANDINI (DC).
Minister of Transport: CARLO BERNINI (DC).
Minister of Agriculture and Forests: Prof. VITO SACCOMANDI (DC).
Minister of Posts and Telecommunications: Dott. OSCAR MAMMÌ (PRI).
Minister of Industry: Dott. ADOLFO BATTAGLIA (PRI).
Minister of Labour and Social Security: CARLO DONAT-CATTIN (DC).
Minister of State Participation: (vacant).
Minister of Foreign Trade: Dott. RENATO RUGGIERO (PSI).
Minister of Health: FRANCESO DE LORENZO (PLI).
Minister of Tourism and of the Performing Arts: Carlo Tognoli (PSI).
Minister of Culture: FERDINANDO FACCHIANO (PSDI).
Minister of the Merchant Navy: CARLO VIZZINI (PSDI).
Minister of Scientific and Technological Research: Prof. ANTONIO RUBERTI (PSI).
Minister of the Environment: Dott. GIORGIO RUFFOLO (PSI).
Ministers without Portfolio:
  Regional Affairs and Institutional Reforms: Dott. ANTONIO MACCANICO (pro PRI).
  Relations with Parliament: EGIDIO STERPA (PLI).
  Civil Defence: VITO LATTANZIO (DC).
  Public Administration: REMO GASPARI (DC).
  EEC Affairs: PIER LUIGI ROMITA (pro PSI/PSDI).
  Urban Areas: CARMELO CONTE (PSI).
  Social Affairs: ROSA RUSSO JERVOLINO (DC).
  Minister with responsibility for the South (Mezzogiorno): Prof. GIOVANNI MARONGIU (DC).

MINISTRIES

Office of the President: Palazzo del Quirinale, 00187 Rome; tel. (06) 4699; telex 611440.
Office of the Prime Minister: Palazzo Chigi, Piazza Colonna 370, 00100 Rome; tel. (06) 6779; telex 613199.
Ministry of Agriculture and Forests: Via XX Settembre, 00187 Rome; tel. (06) 4665; telex 610148.
Ministry of the Budget and of Economic Planning: Via XX Settembre 97, 00187 Rome; tel. (06) 47611; telex 626432.
Ministry of Culture: Via del Collegio Romano 27, 00186 Rome; tel. (06) 6723; telex 621407.
Ministry of Defence: Palazzo Baracchini, Via XX Settembre, 00187 Rome; tel. (06) 4759841; telex 611438.
Ministry of the Environment: Piazza Venezia 11, 00187 Rome; tel. (06) 6797124.
Ministry of Education: Viale Trastevere 76A, 00153 Rome; tel. (06) 58491; telex 613181.
Ministry of Finance: Viale Europa 242, 00144 Rome; tel. (06) 59971; telex 614460.
Ministry of Foreign Affairs: Piazzale della Farnesina 1, 00194 Rome; tel. (06) 36911; telex 610611.
Ministry of Foreign Trade: Viale America 341, EUR, 00144 Rome; tel. (06) 5993; telex 610083.
Ministry of Health: Viale dell'Industria 20, 00144 Rome; tel. (06) 5994.
Ministry of Industry: Via Vittorio Veneto 33, 00187 Rome; tel. (06) 4705; telex 622550.
Ministry of the Interior: Piazza Viminale, Palazzo Viminale, Via Depretis, 00184 Rome; tel. (06) 46671.
Ministry of Justice: Via Arenula 70, 00186 Rome; tel. (06) 65101; telex 623072.
Ministry of Labour and Social Security: Via Flavia 6, 00187 Rome; tel. (06) 4683; telex 626144.
Ministry of the Merchant Navy: Via dell'Arte 16, EUR, 00144 Rome; tel. (06) 5908.
Ministry of Posts and Telecommunications: Viale America, EUR, 00187 Rome; tel. (06) 54601; telex 616082.

ITALY — Directory

Ministry of Public Works: Piazza Porta Pia 1, 00198 Rome; tel. (06) 84821.

Ministry of Scientific and Technological Research: Lungotevere Thaon di Rebel 76, 00100 Rome; tel. (06) 3969941.

Ministry of State Participation: Via Sallustiana 53, 00187 Rome; tel. (06) 4750420; telex 614229.

Ministry of Tourism and Performing Arts: Via della Ferratella in Laterano 51, 00184 Rome; tel. (06) 77321; telex 616400.

Ministry of Transport: Piazza della Croce Rossa 1, 00161 Rome; tel. (06) 84901; telex 613111.

Ministry of the Treasury: Via XX Settembre 97, 00187 Rome; tel. (06) 47611; telex 623139.

Legislature

PARLAMENTO
(Parliament)

Senato
(Senate)

President: GIOVANNI SPADOLINI (Republican).

General Election, 14–15 June 1987

Parties	Votes	%	Seats
Christian Democrats (DC)	10,870,056	33.6	125
Communists (PCI)*	9,171,180	28.3	100
Socialists (PSI)	3,531,312	10.9	36
Italian Social Movement-National Right (MSI-DN)	2,115,196	6.5	17
PSI/PSDI/PR lists	961,323	3.0	9
Republicans (PRI)	1,247,204	3.9	8
Social Democrats (PSDI)	762,670	2.4	5
Liberals (PLI)	699,980	2.2	3
Radicals (PR)	571,339	1.8	3
Greens	632,856	2.0	1
Proletarian Democracy (DP)	493,290	1.5	1
Others	1,300,111	4.0	7
Total	32,356,517	100.0	315

In addition to the 315 elected members, there are seven life members.

Camera dei Deputati
(Chamber of Deputies)

President: Signora NILDE JOTTI (Communist).

General Election, 14–15 June 1987

Parties	Votes	%	Seats
Christian Democrats (DC)	13,231,960	34.3	234
Communists (PCI)*	10,249,690	26.6	177
Socialists (PSI)	5,501,980	14.3	94
Italian Social Movement-National Right (MSI-DN)	2,282,212	5.9	35
Republicans (PRI)	1,428,358	3.7	21
Social Democrats (PSDI)	1,140,086	3.0	17
Radicals (PR)	987,675	2.6	13
Greens	969,534	2.5	13
Liberals (PLI)	810,961	2.1	11
Proletarian Democracy (DP)	642,021	1.7	8
Others	1,328,577	3.4	7
Total	38,573,054	100.0	630

* Renamed the Democratic Party of the Left in 1991.

Political Organizations

Federazione Nazionale per Le Liste Verdi (Green Party): Rome; tel. (06) 4957383; f. 1987; advocates environmentalist and anti-nuclear policies; branch of the European Green movement.

Movimento Sociale Italiano-Destra Nazionale (MSI-DN) (Italian Social Movement-National Right): Via della Scrofa 19, 00186 Rome; tel. (06) 6543014; f. 1946; neo-Fascist party; Pres. PINO ROMUALDI; Sec.-Gen. PINO RAUTI; 400,000 mems.

Partito Democratico della Sinistra (PDS) (Democratic Party of the Left, formerly Italian Communist Party): Central Office: Via delle Botteghe Oscure 4, 00186 Rome; tel. (06) 6711; f. 1921 as the Partito Comunista Italiano; in early 1991 party delegates met in Rimini, where they voted to change the party's name; advocates a democratic and libertarian society; Gen. Sec. ACHILLE OCCHETTO; approx. 1.4m. mems.

Partito della Democrazia Cristiana (DC) (Christian Democrat Party): Central Office: Piazza Don Luigi Sturzo 15, EUR, 001441 Rome; tel. (06) 59011; f. 1943, the successor to the pre-Fascist Popular Party; while extending its appeal to voters of all classes, the party attempts to maintain a centre position; it is openly and militantly anti-communist; Pres. (vacant); Sec.-Gen. ARNALDO FORLANI; Admin. Sec. SEVERINO CITARISTI.

Partito Liberale Italiano (PLI) (Liberal Party): Via Frattina 89, 00187 Rome; tel. (06) 6796951; f. 1848 by Cavour, its chief aim is the realization of the principle of freedom in all public and private matters; Sec.-Gen. RENATO ALTISSIMO; 153,000 mems.

Partito Radicale (PR) (Radical Party): Via Torre Argentina 18, 00186 Rome; tel. (06) 6547771; telex 610495; campaigns on civil rights issues; Pres MARCO PANNELLA, DOMENICO MODUGNO; Sec.-Gen. SERGIO STANZANI; 5,382 mems.

Partito Repubblicano Italiano (PRI) (Republican Party): Piazza dei Caprettari 70, 00186 Rome; tel. (06) 6544641; f. 1897; followers of the principles of Mazzini (social justice in a modern free society) and modern liberalism; Pres. BRUNO VISENTINI; Political Sec. GIORGIO LA MALFA; 110,000 mems.

Partito Socialista Democratico Italiano (PSDI) (Social Democrat Party): Via Santa Maria in Via 12, 00187 Rome; tel. (06) 67271; f. 1969 after breaking away from the former United Socialist Party, of which it had been part since 1966; composed of former Social Democrats and stands to the right of the PSI; Pres. GIUSEPPE SARAGAT; Sec. ANTONIO CARIGLIA; 200,000 mems.

Partito Socialista Italiano (PSI) (Socialist Party): Via del Corso 476, 00186 Rome; tel. (06) 67781; telex 616300; f. 1892; in 1921 a group broke away to found Italian Communist Party; a further rift in 1947 led to the foundation of the Italian Social Democrat Party; in 1966 merged with the Democratic Socialist Party to form the United Socialist Party, but in 1969 the Democratic Socialists broke away; a centre-left party at the service of the workers and of the civil life of the nation, aiming to create conditions for greater prosperity, freedom and social justice in the country; it adheres to the Socialist International and believes that socialism is inseparable from democracy and individual freedom; Sec.-Gen. BETTINO CRAXI.

Südtiroler Volkspartei (SVP) (South Tyrol People's Party): Brennerstrasse 7A, 39100 Bozen/Bolzano; tel. (0471) 974484; regional party of the German and Ladin-speaking people in the South Tyrol; Pres. SILVIUS MAGNANO; Gen. Sec. HARTMANN GALLMETZER.

There are also numerous small political parties, including the following: Union Valdôtaine (regional party for the French minority in the Valle d'Aosta); Partito Sardo d'Azione (Sardinian autonomy party); Democrazia Proletaria (left-wing); and Lotta Continua (left-wing). In local government elections that took place in May 1990, the Lega Nord, a grouping of federalist, anti-Mezzogiorno and anti-immigration 'leagues', enjoyed considerable successes.

Diplomatic Representation

EMBASSIES IN ITALY

Afghanistan: Via Carlo Fea 1, 00161 Rome; tel. (06) 8322972; Chargé d'affaires a.i.: (vacant).

Albania: Via Asmara 9, 00199 Rome; tel. (06) 8380725; telex 614169; Ambassador: DASHNOR DERVISHI.

Algeria: Via Barnaba Oriani 26, 00197; Rome; tel. (06) 804141; telex 680846; Ambassador: MOURAD BENCHEIKH.

Angola: Via Filippo Bernardini 21, 00165 Rome; tel. (06) 6374325; telex 614505; Ambassador: ARMINDO FERNANDES DO ESPIRITO SANTO VIEIRA.

Argentina: Piazza dell'Esquilino 2, 00185 Rome; tel. (06) 4871422; telex 610386; fax 4819787; Ambassador: CARLOS F. RUCKAUF.

Australia: Via Alessandria 215, 00198 Rome; tel. (06) 832721; telex 610165; fax 83272300; Ambassador: ARCHIBALD DUNCAN CAMPBELL.

Austria: Via G.B. Pergolesi 3, 00198 Rome; tel. (06) 868241; telex 610139; Ambassador: Dr FRIEDRICH FRÖLICHSTHAL.

Bangladesh: Via Antonio Bertoloni 14, 00197 Rome; tel. (06) 878541; telex 614615; Ambassador: WALIUR RAHMAN.

Belgium: Via dei Monti Parioli 49, 00197 Rome; tel. (06) 3609441; telex 610425; Ambassador: MARCEL VAN DE KERKCHOVE.

Bolivia: Via Toscana 30, 00187 Rome; tel. (06) 4817438; telex 620221; fax 4821975; Ambassador: JULIO PANTOJA SALAMANCA.

Brazil: Palazzo Pamphili, Piazza Navona 14, 00186 Rome; tel. (06) 6589341; telex 610099; Ambassador: CARLOS ALBERTO LEITE BARBOSA.

ITALY

Bulgaria: Via Pietro P. Rubens 21, 00197 Rome; tel. (06) 3609640; telex 610234; Ambassador: RAYKO NIKOLOV.

Cameroon: Via di Pieta 82/A, 00186 Rome; tel. (06) 6783546; telex 611558; Ambassador: FÉLIX SABAL LECCO.

Canada: Via G. B. de Rossi 27, 00161 Rome; tel. 8415341; telex 610056; fax 8848752; Ambassador: ALAN W. SULLIVAN.

Chile: Via Nazionale 54, 2nd Floor, 00184 Rome; tel. (06) 4742258; telex 611420; Ambassador: MARIANO FONTECILLA DE SANTIAGO CONCHA.

China, People's Republic: Via Bruxelles 56, 00198 Rome; tel. (06) 8448186; telex 680159; Ambassador: LI BAOCHENG.

Colombia: Via Giuseppe Pisanelli 4, 00197 Rome; tel. (06) 6799586; telex 611266; Ambassador: Dr OSCAR MEJÍA VALLEJO.

Congo: Via Modena 50, 00184 Rome; tel. (06) 4746163; telex 626645; Ambassador: JOSEPH TCHICAYA.

Costa Rica: Piazza della Torretta 26, 00186 Rome; tel. (06) 6871291; telex 623300; Ambassador: OCTAVIO TORREALBA.

Côte d'Ivoire: Via Lazzaro Spallanzani 4-6, 00161 Rome; tel. (06) 868040; telex 610396; Ambassador: SOULEJMANE SAKO.

Cuba: Via Licinia 7, 00153 Rome; tel. (06) 5755984; telex 610677; Ambassador: JAVIER ARDIZONES CEBALLOS.

Cyprus: Via Francesco Denza 15, 00197 Rome; tel. (06) 8870365; telex 621033; fax 8870338; Ambassador: ANDROS NICOLAIDES.

Czechoslovakia: Via Colli della Farnesina 144, 00194 Rome; tel. (06) 3278742; telex 610306; Ambassador: NORBERT ŽÍDEK.

Denmark: Via dei Monti Parioli 50, 00197 Rome; tel. (06) 3600441; telex 624696; fax 3610290; Ambassador: IB RITIO ANDREASEN.

Dominican Republic: Via Domenico Chelini 9, 00197 Rome; tel. (06) 874665; Ambassador: GUIDO EMILIO D'ALESSANDRO TAVAREZ.

Ecuador: Via Guido d'Arezzo 14, 00198 Rome; tel. (06) 851784; telex 613256; Ambassador: ROQUE CAÑADAS PORTILLA.

Egypt: 119 Roma Villa Savoia, Via Salaria 267, 00199 Rome; tel. (06) 856193; telex 610044; Ambassador: YEHIA RIFAAT.

El Salvador: Via Castellini 13, 00197 Rome; tel. (06) 3601853; Ambassador: DAVID TREJO.

Ethiopia: Via Nicolò Tartaglia 11, 00197 Rome; tel. (06) 803057; telex 614414; Ambassador: TESFAYE ABDI.

Finland: Via Lisbona 3, 00198 Rome; tel. (06) 8548329; telex 625600; fax 8540362; Ambassador: OSSI SUNELL.

France: Piazza Farnese 67, 00186 Rome; tel. (06) 6565241; telex 610093; fax 6547859; Ambassador: GILBERT PÉROL.

Gabon: No. 31 Largo A. Vessela, 00199 Rome; tel. (06) 3012449; telex 612264; Ambassador: EDOUARD TEALE.

Germany: Via Po 25C, 00198 Rome; tel. (06) 884741; telex 610179; fax 8441812; Ambassador: Dr FRIEDRICH RUTH.

Ghana: Via Ostriana 4, 00199 Rome; tel. (06) 8391200; telex 610270; Ambassador: GEORGE ODARTEY LAMPTEY.

Greece: Via Mercadente 36, 00198 Rome; tel. (06) 8549630; telex 610416; fax 8415927; Ambassador: KONSTANTINOS GEORGIOU.

Guatemala: Via dei Colli della Farnesina 128, 00194 Rome; tel. (06) 3272632; Ambassador: OSCAR ERNESTO PADILLA VIDAURRE.

Guinea: Via Adelaide Ristori 9/13, 00198 Rome; tel. (06) 878989; telex 611487; Ambassador: ABD AN-NIOUMA SANDOUNO.

Haiti: Via Ruggero Fauro 59, 00197 Rome; tel. (06) 872777; Ambassador: NICHOLAS LEMITHE.

Holy See: Via Po 27-29, 00198 Rome; tel. (06) 8546287; Apostolic Nuncio: Mgr LUIGI POGGI.

Honduras: Via Bafile 5/4, 00195 Rome; tel. (06) 3581453; telex 622014; Ambassador: ARTURO GUILLERMO LÓPEZ LUNA.

Hungary: Via dei Villini 14, 00161 Rome; tel. (06) 860241; Ambassador: GYÖRGY MISUR.

India: Via XX Settembre 5, 00187 Rome; tel. (06) 464642; telex 611274; fax 4819539; Ambassador: KULDIP SAHDEV.

Indonesia: Via Campania 55, 00187 Rome; tel. (06) 4755951; telex 610317; Ambassador: RACHADI ISKANDAR.

Iran: Via della Camilluccia 651, 00135 Rome; tel. (06) 3294294; telex 611337; fax (06) 3273757; Ambassador: HAMID ABUTALEBI.

Iraq: Via della Camilluccia 355, 00135 Rome; tel. (06) 346357; telex 622678; Ambassador: HISHAM FAKHRI NAFEI AT-TABAQCHALI.

Ireland: Largo del Nazareno 3, 00187 Rome; tel. (06) 6782541; telex 626030; Ambassador: CHRISTOPHER P. FOGARTY.

Israel: Via M. Mercati 12, 00197 Rome; tel. (06) 874541; telex 610412; Ambassador: MORDECHAI DRORY.

Japan: Via Quintino Sella 60, 00187 Rome; tel. (06) 4757151; telex 610063; Ambassador: SEIYA NISHIDA.

Jordan: Via Guido d'Arezzo 5, 00198 Rome; tel. (06) 857396; telex 612573; Ambassador: TAREK K. MADI.

Kenya: Via Icilio 14, 00153 Rome; tel. (06) 5781192; telex 626537; Ambassador: Dr DON NANIRA.

Korea, Republic: Via Barnaba Oriani 30, 00197 Rome; tel. (06) 805292; telex 610182; Ambassador: SUK KYU KIM.

Kuwait: Via Archimede 124, 00197 Rome; tel. (06) 874419; telex 620426; Ambassador: AHMAD GHAITH ABDULLAH.

Lebanon: Via Giacomino Carissimi 38, 00198 Rome; tel. (06) 867119; telex 622476; Ambassador: KHALIL MAKKAWI.

Lesotho: Via di Porta Pertusa 4, 00165 Rome; tel. (06) 6378183; telex 610053; Ambassador: GERARD PHIRINYANE KHOJANE.

Liberia: Viale Bruno Buozzi 64, 00197 Rome; tel. (06) 805810; telex 612569; Ambassador: GABRIEL TARR MYERS.

Libya: Via Nomentana 365, 00162 Rome; tel. (06) 830951; telex 611114; Ambassador: ABD UR-RAHMAN M. SHALGAM.

Luxembourg: Via Guerrieri 3, 00153 Rome; tel. (06) 5780456; telex 622532; Ambassador: PAUL MERTZ.

Madagascar: Via Riccardo Zandonai 84A, 00194 Rome; tel. (06) 3277797; telex 622526; fax 3294306; Ambassador: NELSON VICTOR ANDRIAMANOHISOA RANAIVO.

Malaysia: Via Nomentana 297, 00162 Rome; tel. (06) 855764; telex 611035; Ambassador: Datuk ISMAIL BIN BUDIN.

Malta: Lungotevere Marzio 12, 00186 Rome; tel. (06) 6879990; telex 611205; Ambassador: MAURICE ABELA.

Mexico: Via Lazzaro Spallanzani 16, 00161 Rome; tel. (06) 4402757; telex 625279; fax 4403876; Ambassador: FRANCISCO JAVIER ALEJO.

Monaco: Via Bertoloni 36, 00197 Rome: tel. (06) 8083361; fax 877692; Ambassador: RENÉ NOVELLA.

Morocco: Via Lazzaro Spallanzani 8, 00196 Rome; tel. (06) 8448653; telex 620854; Ambassador: M. M. YAHIA BENSLIMANE.

Myanmar: Via Bellini 20, 00198 Rome; tel. (06) 8549374; telex 625103; fax 8413167; Ambassador: U THEIN TOE.

Netherlands: Via Michele Mercati 8, 00197 Rome; tel. (06) 873141; telex 610138; Ambassador: Baron W. VAN PALLANDT.

New Zealand: Via Zara 28, 00198 Rome; tel. (06) 4402928; telex 626615; fax 4402984; Ambassador: PETER ROBERT BENNETT.

Nicaragua: Via Brescia 16, 00198 Rome; tel. (06) 865476; telex 626575; Ambassador: ORESTES PAPI.

Nigeria: Via Orazio 14-18, 00198 Rome; tel. (06) 6531048; telex 610666; Ambassador: JUDITH ATTAH.

Norway: Via delle Terme Deciane 71, 00153 Rome; tel. (06) 5755833; telex 610585; fax 5742115; Ambassador: TORBJØRN CHRISTIANSEN.

Oman: Via Enrico Petrella 4, 00198 Rome; tel. (06) 8848038; telex 612524; Ambassador: MUHAMMAD BIN TAHER AIDEED.

Pakistan: Via della Camilluccia 682, 00135 Rome; tel. (06) 3276775; telex 622083; Ambassador: M. AFZAL QADIR.

Panama: Via del Vignola 39, 00196 Rome; tel. (06) 3619587; telex 622670; Ambassador: NELVA TORRIJOS DE SOLER.

Paraguay: Via Emilio de Cavalieri 12, 00198 Rome; tel. (06) 8448236; Ambassador: ANÍBAL FERNÁNDEZ.

Peru: Via Po 22, 00198 Rome; tel. (06) 8417265; telex 612298; fax 8444496; Ambassador: MANUEL A. ROCA-ZELA.

Philippines: Via San Valentino 12-14, 00197 Rome; tel. (06) 803530; telex 612104; Ambassador: JOSÉ M. ZALDARRIAGA.

Poland: Via Pietro Paolo Rubens 20, 00197 Rome; tel. (06) 3224455; telex 610325; fax 3217895; Ambassador: BOLESŁAW MICHAŁEK.

Portugal: Via Giacinta Pezzana 9, 00197 Rome; tel. (06) 878016; telex 612304; Ambassador: TOMAS ANDRESEN.

Romania: Via Nicolò Tartaglia 36, 00197 Rome; tel. (06) 804567; Ambassador: CONSTANTIN TUDOR.

San Marino: Via Eleonora Duse 35, 00197 Rome; tel. (06) 8084567; fax 870072; Ambassador: Dott. SAVINA ZAFFERANI.

Saudi Arabia: Via G. B. Pergolesi 9, 00198 Rome; tel. (06) 868161; telex 613115; Ambassador: KHALED AN-NASSER AT-TURKI.

Senegal: Via Lisbona 3, 00198 Rome; tel. (06) 859497; telex 612522; Ambassador: HENRI PIERRE ARPHANG SENGHOR.

Somalia: Via dei Villini 9-11, 00161 Rome; tel. (06) 853740; telex 613123; Ambassador: MUHAMMAD MUHAMOUD ABDULLAH.

South Africa: Via Tanaro 14, 00198 Rome; tel. (06) 8443246; telex 621667; Ambassador: DAVID DE V. DU BUISSON.

Spain: Palazzo Borghese, Largo Fontenella Borghese 19, 00186 Rome; tel. (06) 6878172; telex 626126; fax 6872256; Ambassador: EMILIO MENÉNDEZ DEL VALLE.

Sri Lanka: Via Giuseppe Cuboni 618, 00197 Rome; tel. (06) 805362; telex 612602; Ambassador: CHANDRA NAWARATNE DE ZOYSA.

Sudan: Via di Porta Ardeatina 1, 00184 Rome; tel. (06) 7573344; telex 610302; Ambassador: ABD AL-A'AS-SINADA.

Sweden: CP 7201, 00100 Rome; Piazza Rio de Janeiro 3, 00161 Rome; tel. (06) 4402721; telex 610264; Ambassador: SVEN FREDRIK HEDIN.

Switzerland: Via Barnaba Oriani 61; 00197 Rome; tel. (06) 803641; telex 610304; Ambassador: FRANCESCA POMETTA.

Syria: Piazza dell' Ara Coeli, 00186 Rome; tel. (06) 6797791; telex 613083; Ambassador: BURHAN KAIAL.

Tanzania: Via G.B. Vico 9, 00196 Rome; tel. (06) 3610901; telex 612286; fax 3222079; Ambassador: ABBAS KLEIST SYKES.

Thailand: Via Nomentana 132, 00162 Rome; tel. (06) 8320729; telex 616297; Ambassador: NISSAI VEJJAJIVA.

Tunisia: Via Asmara 7, 00199 Rome; tel. (06) 8390748; telex 610190; Ambassador: NOUREDDINE MEJDOUB.

Turkey: Via Palestro 28, 00185 Rome; tel. (06) 4941549; telex 612131; Ambassador: NECDET TEZEL.

USSR: Via Gaeta 5, 00185 Rome; tel. (06) 4743989; telex 611286; Ambassador: ANATOLI L. ADAMISHIN.

United Arab Emirates: Via S. Crescenziano 25, 00199 Rome; tel. (06) 8394839; telex 622671; Chargé d'afffaires a.i.: MUHAMMAD SAID AL-JARRAH.

United Kingdom: Via XX Settembre 80A, 00187 Rome; tel. (06) 4825551; telex 626119; fax 4873324; Ambassador: Sir STEPHEN EGERTON.

USA: Via Vittorio Veneto 119A, 00187 Rome; tel. (06) 4674; telex 622322; Ambassador: PETER F. SECCHIA.

Uruguay: Via Vittorio Veneto 183, 00187 Rome; tel. (06) 492796; telex 611201; Ambassador: MATEO MÁRQUEZ SERÉ.

Venezuela: Viale Bruno Buozzi 109, Apto 6, 00197 Rome; tel. (06) 3221998; telex 610361; fax 6799161; Ambassador: JOSÉ FRANCISCO SUCRE FIGARELLA.

Viet-Nam: Piazza Barberini 12, 00187 Rome; tel. (06) 4754098; telex 610121; Ambassador: HUYNH CONG TAM.

Yemen Arab Republic: Via Verona 3, 00161 Rome; tel. (06) 4270811; telex 621447; Ambassador: AHMAD MUHAMMAD ASH-SHIJNI.

Yugoslavia: Via dei Monti Parioli 20, 00197 Rome; tel. (06) 3600796; telex 616303; Ambassador: ANTE SKATARETIKO.

Zaire: Via Annone 71/79, 00199 Rome; tel. (06) 8393665; telex 611104; Ambassador: KITSHODI NZEKELE.

Zambia: Via Ennio Quirino Visconti 8, 00193 Rome; tel. (06) 3213805; telex 611421; Ambassador: Dr LEONARD S. CHIVUNO.

Judicial System

The Constitutional Court was established in 1956 and is an autonomous constitutional body, standing apart from the judicial system. Its most important function is to pronounce on the constitutionality of legislation both subsequent and prior to the present Constitution of 1948. It also judges accusations brought against the President of the Republic or ministers.

At the base of the system of penal jurisdiction are the Preture (District Courts), where offences carrying a sentence of up to three years' imprisonment are tried. Above the Preture are the Tribunali (Tribunals) and the Corti di Assise presso i Tribunali (Assize Courts attached to the Tribunals), where graver offences are dealt with. From these courts appeal lies to the Corti d'Appello (Courts of Appeal) and the parallel Corti di Assise d'Appello (Assize Courts of Appeal). Final appeal may be made, on juridical grounds only, to the Corte Suprema di Cassazione.

Civil cases may be taken in the first instance to the Giudici Conciliatori (Justices of the Peace), Preture or Tribunali, according to the economic value of the case. Appeal from the Giudici Conciliatori lies to the Preture, from the Preture to the Tribunali, from the Tribunali to the Corti d'Appello, and finally, as in penal justice, to the Corte Suprema di Cassazione on juridical grounds only.

Special divisions for cases concerning labour relations are attached to civil courts. Cases concerned with the public service and its employees are tried by Tribunali Amministrativi Regionali and the Consiglio di Stato. Juvenile courts have criminal and civil jurisdiction.

A new penal code was introduced in late 1989.

Consiglio Superiore della Magistratura (CSM): Piazza dell' Indipendenza 6, 00185 Rome; f. 1958; tel. (06) 497981; supervisory body of judicial system; 33 mems.

President: FRANCESCO COSSIGA.

Vice-President: CESARE MIRABELLI.

CONSTITUTIONAL COURT

Corte Costituzionale: Palazzo della Consulta, Piazza del Quirinale 41, 00187 Rome; tel. (06) 46981; consists of 15 judges, one-third appointed by the President of the Republic, one-third elected by Parliament in joint session, one-third by the ordinary and administrative supreme courts.

President: FRANCESCO SAJA.

Vice-President: GUGLIELMO ROHERSSEN.

ADMINISTRATIVE COURTS

Consiglio di Stato: Palazzo Spada, Piazza Capo di Ferro 13, 00186 Rome; tel. (06) 67771; established in accordance with Article 10 of the Constitution; has both consultative and judicial functions.

President: GIORGIO CRISCO.

Corte dei Conti: Via Baiamonti 25, Rome; tel. (06) 48951, and Via Barberini 38, Rome; functions as the court of public auditors for the state.

President: GIUSEPPE CARBONE.

SUPREME COURT OF APPEAL

Corte Suprema di Cassazione: Palazzo di Giustizia, 00100 Rome; tel. (06) 686001; telex 626069; fax 6874170; supreme court of civil and criminal appeal.

First President: ANTONIO BRANCACCIO.

Vice-President: FERDINANDO ZUCCONI GALLI FONSECA.

Religion

More than 90% of the population of Italy are adherents of the Roman Catholic Church.

Under the terms of the Concordat signed in 1929, Roman Catholicism was recognized as the official religion of Italy. However, a new Concordat was signed in February 1984 between the Prime Minister and Cardinal Agostino Casaroli, the Papal Secretary of State, to replace the earlier agreement. Following approval by both chambers of the Italian Parliament, the new Concordat was formally ratified in June 1985. The Concordat stated that Roman Catholicism would no longer be the state religion, abolished compulsory religious instruction in schools and reduced state financial contributions. The Vatican City's sovereign rights as an independent state, under the terms of the Lateran Treaty of 1929, were not affected.

Several Protestant churches also exist in Italy, with a total membership of about 50,000. There is a small Jewish community, and in 1987 an agreement between the state and Jewish representatives recognized certain rights for the Jewish community, including the right to observe religious festivals on Saturdays by not attending school or work.

CHRISTIANITY

The Roman Catholic Church

For ecclesiastical purposes, Italy comprises the Papal See of Rome, the Patriarchate of Venice, 59 archdioceses (including six directly responsible to the Holy See), 158 dioceses (including seven within the jurisdiction of the Pope, as Archbishop of the Roman Province, and 17 directly responsible to the Holy See), two territorial prelatures (including one directly responsible to the Holy See) and seven territorial abbacies (including four directly responsible to the Holy See). Almost all adherents follow the Latin rite, but there are two dioceses and one abbacy (all directly responsible to the Holy See) for Catholics of the Italo-Albanian (Byzantine) rite.

Bishops' Conference: Conferenza Episcopale Italiana, Circonvallazione Aurelia 50, 00165 Rome; tel. (06) 6237141; f. 1985; Pres. Most Rev. CAMILLO RUINI, Vicar-General of Rome.

Primate of Italy, Archbishop and Metropolitan of the Roman Province and Bishop of Rome: His Holiness Pope JOHN PAUL II.

Patriarch of Venice: HE Cardinal MARCO CÈ.

Archbishops:
Acerenza: Most Rev. MICHELE SCANDIFFIO.
Amalfi-Cava de' Tirreni: Most Rev. FERDINANDO PALATUCCI.
Ancona-Osimo: Most Rev. DIONIGI TETTAMANZI.
Bari-Bitonto: Most Rev. ANDREA MARIANO MAGRASSI.
Benevento: Most Rev. CARLO MINCHIATTI.
Bologna: HE Cardinal GIACOMO BIFFI.
Brindisi-Ostuni: Most Rev. SETTIMIO TODISCO.
Cagliari: Most Rev. OTTORINO PIETRO ALBERTI.
Camerino-San Severino Marche: (vacant).
Campobasso-Boiano: Most Rev. ETTORE DI FILIPPO.
Capua: Most Rev. LUIGI DILIGENZA.
Catania: Most Rev. LUIGI BOMMARITO.
Catanzaro-Squillace: Most Rev. ANTONIO CANTISANI.
Chioti-Vasto: Most Rev. ANTONIO VALENTINI.
Cosenza-Bisignano: Most Rev. DINO TRABALZINI.
Crotone-Santa Severina: Most Rev. GIUSEPPE AGOSTINO.

ITALY

Fermo: Most Rev. CLETO BELLUCCI.
Ferrara-Comacchio: Most Rev. LUIGI MAVERNA.
Florence: HE Cardinal SILVANO PIOVANELLI.
Foggia-Bovino: GIUSEPPE CASALE.
Gaeta: Most Rev. VINCENZO MARIA FARANO.
Genoa: HE Cardinal GIOVANNI CANESTRI.
Gorizia: Most Rev. ANTONIO VITALE BOMMARCO.
Lanciano-Ortona: Most Rev. ENZIO D'ANTONIO.
L'Aquila: Most Rev. MARIO PERESSIN.
Lecce: Most Rev. COSMO FRANCESCO RUPPI.
Lucca: Most Rev. GIULIANO AGRESTI.
Manfredonia-Vieste: Most Rev. VALENTINO VAILATI.
Matera-Irsina: ENNIO APPIGNANESI.
Messina-Lipari-Santa Lucia del Mela: Most Rev. IGNAZIO CANNAVÓ.
Milan: HE Cardinal CARLO MARIA MARTINI.
Modena-Nonantola: Most Rev. SANTO BARTOLOMEO QUADRI.
Monreale: Most Rev. SALVATORE CASSISA.
Naples: HE Cardinal MICHELE GIORDANO.
Oristano: Most Rev. PIER GIULIANO TIDDIA.
Otranto: Most Rev. VINCENZO FRANCO.
Palermo: HE Cardinal SALVATORE PAPPALARDO.
Perugia-Città della Pieve: Most Rev. ENNIO ANTONELLI.
Pescara-Penne: Most Rev. ANTONIO IANNUCCI.
Pisa: Most Rev. ALESSANDRO PLOTTI.
Potenza-Muro Lucano-Marsico Nuovo: Most Rev. GIUSEPPE VAIRO.
Ravenna-Cervia: Most Rev. ERSILIO TONINI.
Reggio Calabria-Bova: Most Rev. AURELIO SORRENTINO.
Rossano-Cariati: Most Rev. SERAFINO SPROVIERI.
Salerno-Campagna-Acerno: Most Rev. GUERINO GRIMALDI.
Sant' Angelo dei Lombardi-Conza-Nusco-Bisaccia: Most Rev. MARIO MILANO.
Siena-Colle di Val d'Elsa-Montalcino: Most Rev. GAETANO BONICELLI.
Sorrento-Castellammare di Stabia: Most Rev. FELICE CECE.
Spoleto-Norcia: ANTONIO AMBROSANIO.
Syracuse: Most Rev. GIUSEPPE COSTANZO.
Taranto: Most Rev. SALVATORE DE GIORGI.
Trani-Barletta-Bisceglie: Most Rev. GIUSEPPE CARATA.
Trento: Most Rev. GIOVANNI MARIA SARTORI.
Turin: Most Rev. GIOVANNI SALDARINI.
Udine: Most Rev. ALFREDO BATTISTI.
Urbino-Urbania-Sant' Angelo in Vado: Most Rev. UGO DONATO BIANCHI.
Vercelli: Most Rev. ALBINO MENSA.

In addition, the Most Rev. FRANCESCO CUCCARESE, the Bishop of Caserta, has been granted the personal title of Archbishop.

Azione Cattolica Italiana (ACI) (Catholic Action): Via della Conciliazione 1, 00193 Rome; tel. (06) 6868751; fax 6542088; most of the nation-wide lay Catholic organizations in Italy are affiliated to Catholic Action, which has a total membership of about one million and is organized in the following divisions: Settore Adulti (Adult Section), Settore Giovani (Youth Section), Azione Cattolica Ragazzi (Children's Catholic Action), Federazione Universitaria Cattolica Italiana—FUCI (University Federation), Movimento Ecclesiale di Impegno Culturale (Ecclesiastical Culture Movement), Movimento di Impegno Educativo (Education Movement), Movimento Lavoratori (Workers' Movement) and Movimento Studenti (Students' Movement). Each division has its own National President. The Presidency-National is the supreme executive body and co-ordinator of the different branches of Catholic Action. Pres. Avv. RAFFAELE CANANZI; Chaplain Mgr SALVATORE DEGIORGI; Sec.-Gen. Dott. MARIA GRAZIA TIBALDI.

Protestant Churches

Federazione delle Chiese Evangeliche in Italio (Federation of the Protestant Churches in Italy): Via Firenze 38, 00184 Rome; tel. (06) 4825120; fax 4828728; the Federation was formed in 1967; total mems more than 50,000; Pres. Pastor GIORGIO BOUCHARD; Sec. Dr RENATO MAIOCCHI; includes the following organizations:

Chiesa Apostolica Italiana

Comunione delle Chiese Cristiane Libere

Comunitá Ecumenica di Ispra-Varese

Chiesa Evangelica Luterana in Italia (Lutheran Church): Via Toscana 7, 00187 Rome; tel. (06) 4817519; Via Palestrina 14, 20124 Milan; Dean HANS GERCH PHILIPPI; 20,100 mems.

Chiesa Evangelica Metodista d'Italia (Evangelical Methodist Church of Italy): Via Firenze 38, 00184 Rome; tel. (06) 4743695; f. 1861; Pres. Pastor CLAUDIO MARTELLI; 4,000 mems.

Tavola Valdese (Waldensian Church): Via Firenze 38, 00184 Rome; tel. (06) 4745537; Moderator Pastor FRANCO GIAMPICCOLI; Sec.-Treas. ROSELLA PANZIRONI; 22,000 mems.

Unione Cristiana Evangelica Battista d'Italia (Italian Baptist Union): Piazza in Lucina 35, 00186 Rome; tel. (06) 6876124; fax 6872261; f. 1873; Pres. Pastor PAOLO SPANU; Admin. Sec. FRANCO CLEMENTE; 5,000 mems.

Associated Organizations

Salvation Army (Esercito della Salvezza): Via dei Marrucini 40, 00185 Rome; tel. (06) 4462614; fax 4456306; Officer Commanding for Italy Lt-Col EMMANUEL MIAGLIA; 17 regional centres.

Seventh-day Adventists: Lungotevere Michelangelo 7, 00192 Rome; tel. (06) 3211207; fax 3210575; represents 89 communities in Italy; Supt PAOLO BENINI; Sec. IGNAZIO BARBUSCIA.

JUDAISM

Union of Italian Jewish Communities: Lungotevere Sanzio 9, 00153 Rome; tel. (06) 5803667; fax 5899569; f. 1930; represents 21 Jewish communities in Italy; Pres. TULLIA ZEVI; Chief Rabbi of Rome Dr ELIO TOAFF.

Rabbinical Council: Chief Rabbi Dott. ELIO R. TOAFF (Via Catalana 1A, Rome), Rabbi Dott. GIUSEPPE LARAS (Via Guastalla 19, Milan), Rabbi Dott. SERGIO SIERRA (Via San Pio V 12, Turin), Rabbi Dott. LUCIANO CARO (Via Mazzini 95, Ferrara), Rabbi Dott. ISIDORO KAHN (Via del Tempioz, Livorno).

BAHÁ'Í FAITH

Assemblea Spirituale Nazionale: Via della Fontanella 4, 00187 Rome; tel. (06) 3225037; fax (06) 3611536; mems resident in 270 localities.

The Press

Relative to the size of Italy's population, the number of daily newspapers is rather small (about 80 titles), most of which appear in the industrial north. The average total daily circulation in 1989 was about 9.8m., while sales totalled about 6.8m. copies per day; sales in the north and centre of the country accounted for 80% of this figure, in the south for 20%. Between 1980 and 1989, sales of daily newspapers increased by approximately 36%.

Rome and Milan are the main press centres. The most important national dailies are *Corriere della Sera* in Milan and Rome and *La Repubblica* in Rome, followed by Turin's *La Stampa*, *Il Giorno* in Milan and *Il Giornale*, which circulates mainly in the north. The other large dailies circulate in and reflect their own region; e.g. *La Nazione* serves Florence and its region, *Il Messaggero* and *Il Tempo* Rome and the centre, *Il Secolo XIX*, based in Genova, extends throughout the Italian riviera, *Il Mattino* serves the Naples region, *La Gazzetta del Mezzogiorno* serves the Bari region and *La Sicilia* and *Giornale di Sicilia* serve Sicily.

For many years the daily press experienced financial difficulties. During the 1980s, however, measures were undertaken to promote improved production methods and higher editorial quality. The dailies have become entirely dependent on financial support from large industrial companies, financial institutions, political parties or other groups with substantial capital. All the political parties represented in Parliament have a daily or weekly paper as party organ. The most important are *L'Unità*, the organ of the Partito Democratico della Sinistra (formerly the Partito Comunista Italiano), the Socialist *Avanti!* and the Christian Democrat *Il Popolo*. In addition, political parties own or have a holding in papers which are not run as party organs. The Christian Democrats, for example, control seven provincial dailies. Catholic organizations have a controlling interest in several papers and *Avvenire* is wholly owned by the Church.

The most important dailies in terms of circulation are: Milan's *Corriere della Sera* (851,000), Turin's *La Stampa* (571,000 with *Stampa Sera*), Rome's *La Repubblica* (about 810,000), *Il Messaggero* (390,000) and *L'Unità* (257,000), Milan's *Il Giorno* (184,000) and *Il Giornale* (247,000), Florence's *La Nazione* (266,000), Bologna's *Il Resto del Carlino* (307,000), and the sports newspapers, Milan's *Gazzetta dello Sport* (830,000) and Rome's *Corriere dello Sport* (622,000). The five dailies accorded most prestige for the standard of their articles and news coverage are *Corriere della Sera*, *Il Giorno*, *Il Giornale*, *La Stampa* and *La Repubblica*. The leading financial paper, Milan's *Il Sole/24 Ore*, has a circulation of 341,000.

In 1988 there were 9,158 periodical titles, with a combined annual circulation of some 2,000m. Many illustrated weekly papers and magazines maintain very high levels of circulation, with *Famiglia Cristiana* enjoying one of the highest figures (1,044,000). Other very popular general-interest weeklies are *Gente* (901,000) and *Oggi* (696,000). Many tend towards sensationalism. Other women's interest and fashion magazines also enjoy wide readership. Among the serious and influential magazines are *Panorama* (504,000), *L'Espresso* (373,000), *Epoca* (192,000), *L'Europeo* (172,000) and the financial *Il Mondo* (83,000).

ITALY

PRINCIPAL DAILIES

Ancona
Corriere Adriatico: Via Berti 20, 60100 Ancona; tel. (071) 42985; f. 1860; Dir Dott. Paolo Biagi; circ. 21,500.

Bari
La Gazzetta del Mezzogiorno: Viale Scipione l'Africano 264, 70124 Bari; tel. (080) 270215; telex 810844; f. 1887; independent; Pres. Stefano Romanazzi; Man. Dir Giuseppe Gorjux; circ. 111,000.

Bergamo
L'Eco di Bergamo: Viale Papa Giovanni XXIII 118, 24100 Bergamo; tel. (035) 212344; f. 1880; Catholic; Dir Gino Carrara; circ 72,500.

Il Giornale di Bergamo-Oggi: Via Paleocapa 18, 24100 Bergamo; tel. (035) 247196; f. 1981; Dir Giulio Scarrone; circ. 10,500.

Bologna
Il Resto del Carlino: Via Enrico Mattei 106, 40138 Bologna; tel. (051) 536111; telex 510037; fax 6570099; f. 1885; independent; Dir Marco Leonelli; circ. 307,000.

Bolzano
Alto Adige: Lungotalvera S. Quirino 26, 39100 Bolzano; tel. (0471) 904111; f. 1945; independent; Dir Ennio Simeone; circ. 56,000.

Dolomiten: Via del Vigneto 7, 39100 Bolzano; tel. (0471) 925111; telex 400161; fax 925440; f. 1926; independent; German language; Editor Dr Josef Rampold; circ. 44,000.

Brescia
Bresciaoggi Nuovo: Via Malla 4, 25126 Brescia; tel. (030) 22941; fax 2294229; f. 1974; Dir Piero Agostini; circ. 16,900.

Il Giornale di Brescia: Via Solferino 22, 25121 Brescia; tel. (030) 29901; telex 303 165; fax 292226; f. 1947; Editor Gian Battista Lanzani; Man. Dir. Francesco Passerini Glazel; circ. 71,000.

Cagliari
L'Unione Sarda: Viale Regina Elena 12, 09100 Cagliari; tel. (070) 6013; f. 1889; independent; Dir Arturo Clavuot; circ. 121,000.

Catania
La Sicilia: Viale Odorico da Pordenone 50, 95126 Catania; tel. (095) 330544; telex 971321; fax 337077; f. 1945; independent; Dir Dott. Mario Cianacio Sanfilippo; circ. 87,000.

Como
La Provincia: Via Anzani 52, 22100 Como; tel. (031) 3121; f. 1892; independent; Dir Sergio Gervasutti; circ. 47,000.

Cremona
La Provincia: Via delle Industrie 2, 26100 Cremona; tel. (0372) 411221; fax (0372) 28487; f. 1946; independent; Pres. Angelo Duchi; Man. Editor Francesco Tartara; circ. 25,000.

Florence
La Nazione: Via Ferdinando Paolieri 2, 50121 Florence; tel. (055) 24851; f. 1859; independent; Dir Roberto Gelmini; circ. 266,000.

Genova
L'Avvisatore Marittimo: Via San Vincenzo 42, 16121 Genova; tel. (010) 562929; telex 283155; fax 566415; f. 1945; shipping and financial; Editor Carlo Bellio; circ. 4,000.

Corriere Mercantile: Via Archimede 169, 16142 Genova; tel. (010) 517851; fax 504148; f. 1824; political and financial; independent; Editor Mimmo Angeli; circ. 32,500.

Il Lavoro: Via Donghi 38, 16132 Genova, tel. (010) 35331; fax 3533263; f. 1903; independent; Publr Selpi SpA; circ. 29,100.

Il Secolo XIX: Via Varese 2, 16122 Genova; tel. (010) 53881; f. 1886; independent; Dir Carlo Rognoni; circ. 204,500.

Lecce
Quotidiano di Lecce/Brindisi/Taranto: Viale degli Studenti (Palazzo Casto), 73100 Lecce; tel. (099) 25855; f. 1978; Man. Editor Vittorio Bruno Stammerra; circ. 23,000.

Livorno
Il Tirreno: Viale Alfieri 9, 57100 Livorno; tel. (0586) 416511; fax 402066; f. 1877; independent; Editor Luigi Bianchi; circ. 137,000.

Mantova
Gazzetta di Mantova: Via Fratelli Bandiera 22, 46100 Mantova; tel. (0376) 303270; f. 1664; independent; Man. Editor Rino Bulbarelli; circ. 41,500.

Messina
Gazzetta del Sud: Via Taormina 15, 98100 Messina; tel. (090) 21801; f. 1952; independent; Dir Nino Calarco; circ. 98,000.

Milan
Avvenire: Via Mauro Macchi 61, 20124 Milan; tel. (02) 67801; telex 3250096; f. 1968; Catholic; Dir Guido Lindrizzi; circ. 130,500.

Corriere della Sera: Via Solferino 28, 20121 Milan; tel. (02) 6353; telex 310031; f. 1876; independent; contains weekly supplement, *Il Sette*; Dir Ugo Stille; circ. 851,000.

La Gazzetta dello Sport: Via Solferino 28, 20121 Milan; tel. (02) 6353; telex 321697; fax (02) 6598936; f. 1896; sport; Dir Candido Cannavò; circ. 830,000.

Il Giornale: Via Gaetano Negri 4, 20123 Milan; tel. (02) 85661; telex 333279; fax 72023859; f. 1973; independent, controlled by staff; Man. Editor Indro Montanelli; circ. 247,000.

Il Giorno: Piazza Cavour 2, 20121 Milan; tel. (02) 77681; telex 330390; Rome office: Largo Goldoni 44; tel. (06) 6780304; f. 1965; owned by ENI, a state-owned energy conglomerate; Editor Francesco Damato; circ. 184,000.

Italia Oggi: Via S. Maria Segreta 7, 20123 Milan; tel. (02) 822791; telex 321191; f. 1986; independent; financial; Editor Antonio Mereu; circ. 69,000.

La Notte: Piazza Cavour 2, 20121 Milan; tel. (02) 77391; f. 1952; evening; independent; Editor Cesare Lanza; circ. 98,000.

Il Sole/24 Ore: Via Paolo Lomazzo 52, 20154 Milan; tel. (02) 31031; telex 331325; f. 1865; financial, political, economic; Dir Gianni Locatelli; circ. 341,000.

Modena
Nuova Gazzetta di Modena: Via del Taglio 22, 41100 Modena; tel. (059) 223707; Dir Antonio Mascolo; circ. 16,000.

Naples
Il Giornale di Napoli: Via Dioclegano 109, 80121 Naples.

Il Mattino: Via Chiatamone 65, 80121 Naples; tel. (081) 7947111; f. 1892, reformed 1950; independent; Dir Pasquale Nonno; circ. 227,000.

Roma: Centro Direz. Isola B/3, 80133 Naples; tel. (081) 7727111; Editor Ottorino Gurgo; circ. 44,029.

Padova
Il Mattino di Padova: Via Pelizzo 15, 35100 Padova; tel. (049) 8292611; f. 1978; Dir Maurizio De Luca; circ. 45,100.

Palermo
Giornale di Sicilia: Via Lincoln 21, 90133 Palermo; tel. (091) 6165355; telex 911088; f. 1860; independent; Dir Antonio Ardizzone; circ. 86,000.

L'Ora: Piazza Napoli 5, 90141 Palermo; tel. (091) 6047111; f. 1900; independent; Dir Tito Cortese; circ. 18,100.

Parma
Gazzetta di Parma: Via Emilio Casa 5, 43100 Parma; tel. (0521) 2159; f. 1735; Pres. Giampaolo Pellegrini; Dir N. H. Baldassarre Molossi; circ. 58,200.

Pavia
La Provincia Pavese: Canton Ticino 16–18, 27100 Pavia; tel. (0382) 472101; f. 1870; independent; Editor Sergio Baraldo; circ. 28,200.

Perugia
Corriere dell' Umbria: Via Pievaiola km 5.8, 06080 Perugia; tel. (075) 788331; fax 74183; f. 1982; independent; Editor Sergio Benincasa; circ. 31,000.

Pescara
Il Centro: Corso Vittorio Emanuele 372, 651000 Pescara; tel. (085) 20521; fax 375205; f, 1986; independent; Editor Andrea Barberi; circ. 31,000.

Piacenza
Libertà: Via Benedettine 68, 29100 Piacenza; tel. (0523) 21718; f. 1883; Dir Ernesto Prati; circ. 40,400.

Reggio Emilia
Gazzetta di Reggio: Via Sessi 1, 42100 Reggio Emilia; tel. (0552) 430745; Dir Umberto Bonafini; circ. 21,000.

Rome
Avanti!: Via Tomacelli 146, 00186 Rome, tel. (06) 686041; fax (06) 6879099; f. 1896; organ of Socialist Party; Dir Roberto Villetti; circ. 60,000.

ITALY

Corriere dello Sport: Piazza Indipendenza 11B, 00185 Rome, tel. (06) 4992; telex 614472; f. 1924; 13 regional editions; Editor Dr Domenico Morale; circ. 622,000.

Il Fiorino: Via Parigi 11, 00185 Rome; tel. (06) 47490; f. 1969; business; Editor Luigi d'Amato; circ. 17,000.

Gazzetta: Via Archimede 57, 00197 Rome; tel. (06) 3602644; fax 3602645; f. 1986; independent; Editor Guiseppe Crescimbeni; circ. 53,000.

Il Giornale d'Italia: Via Parigi 11, 00185 Rome; tel. (06) 47490; Dir Luigi d'Amato; circ. 33,000.

Il Manifesto: Via Tomacelli 146, 00186 Rome; tel. (06) 6790151; telex 626158; f. 1971; splinter communist; Man. Editor Sandro Medici; circ. 82,000.

Il Messaggero: Via del Tritone 152, 00187 Rome; tel. (06) 47201; telex 624644; f. 1878; independent; Editor Mario Pendinelli; circ. 390,000.

Ore 12: Via Alfana 39, 00198 Rome; tel. (06) 3965473; financial; independent; Dir Enzo Caretti; circ. 14,000.

Il Popolo: Corso Rinascimento 113, 00186 Rome; tel. (06) 65151; telex 613276; f. 1944; organ of Christian Democrat Party; Editor Sandro Fontano; circ. 43,800.

Puglia: Via due Macelli 23, 00187 Rome; tel. (06) 6787751; fax 6787755; Dir Mario Gismondi; circ. 7,500.

La Repubblica: Piazza Indipendenza 11b, 00185 Rome; tel. (06) 49821; telex 620660; fax 49822923; f. 1976; left-wing; contains weekly supplements, *Affari e Finanza* and *Venerdi di Repubblica*, on Friday, *Il TrovaRoma* on Thursday and Saturday (in Rome edition only); Editor Eugenio Scalfari; circ. 810,000.

Il Secolo d'Italia: Via della Mercede 33, 00187 Rome; tel. (06) 6840290; fax 6786522; f. 1951; organ of the MSI-DN; Editor Aldo Giorleo; circ. 32,500.

Il Tempo: Piazza Colonna 366, 00187 Rome; tel. (06) 65041; telex 614087; f. 1944; right-wing; Editor Franco Cangini; circ. 158,000.

L'Umanità: Via S. Maria in Via 12, 00187 Rome; tel. (06) 6727230; f. 1948; organ of the Social Democrat Party; Dir Prof. Antonio Casanova; circ. 17,200.

L'Unità: Via dei Taurini 19, 00185 Rome; tel. (06) 404901; telex 613461; f. 1924; newspaper of the Democratic Party of the Left (formerly the Italian Communist Party); Dir Emanuele Macaluso; circ. 257,000 (weekday), 800,000 (Sunday).

La Voce Repubblicana: Piazza dei Capprettari 70, 00186 Rome; tel. (06) 6875297; f. 1921; organ of the Republican Party; circ. 15,400.

Sassari

La Nuova Sardegna: Via Porcellana 9, 07100 Sassari; tel. (079) 22400; f. 1891; independent; Editor Sergio Milani; circ. 101,000.

Taranto

Corriere del Giorno: Piazza Dante 5, Zona 'Bestat', 74100 Taranto; tel. (099) 3203; f. 1947; Editor Riccardo Catacchio; circ. 11,000.

Trento

L'Adige: Via Missioni Africane 17, 38100 Trento; tel. (0461) 985111; f. 1945; Christian Democrat; Editor-in-Chief Paolo Pagliaro; circ. 27,000.

Treviso

La Tribuna de Treviso: Corso del Popolo 42, 31100 Treviso; tel. (0422) 50801; Dir Maurizio De Luca; circ. 27,000.

Trieste

Il Piccolo (Giornale di Trieste): Via Guido Reni 1, 34122 Trieste; tel. (040) 77861; f. 1881; independent; Dir Riccardo Berti; circ. 68,000.

Primorski Dnevnik: Via dei Montecchi 6, 34137 Trieste; tel. (040) 7796600; telex 460894; fax 772418; f. 1945; Slovene; Man. Dir Marko Waltrisch; Editor-in-Chief Dušan Udovič.

Turin

La Stampa and **Stampa Sera:** Via Marenco 32, 10126 Turin; tel. (011) 65681; telex 221121; f. 1868; independent; morning edition, *La Stampa;* evening edition, *Stampa Sera;* circ. 571,000; Dirs Paolo Mieli (morning), Luca Bernardelli (evening).

Tuttosport: Corso Srizzera 185, 10147 Turin; tel. (011) 31081; telex 224230; f. 1945; sport; Dir Piero Dardanello; circ. 195,000.

Udine

Messaggero Veneto: Viale Palmanova 290, 33100 Udine; tel. (0432) 600312; telex 450449; f. 1946; Editor Vittorino Meloni; circ. 67,500.

Varese

La Prealpina: Viale Tamagno 13, 21100 Varese; tel. (0332) 64000; f. 1888; Dir Mino Durand; circ. 34,000.

Venice

Il Gazzettino: Via Torino 110, 30172 Venezia-Mestre; tel. (041) 665111; f. 1887; independent; Dir Giorgio Lago; circ. 180,000.

La Nuova Venezia: Salizzada S. Lio, 5620 Castello, 30122 Venice; tel. (041) 980666; Dir Paolo Ojetti; circ. 23,000.

Verona

L'Arena: Viale del Lavoro 11, 37036 S. Martino Buon Albergo, Verona; tel. (045) 8094000; telex 481815; fax 994527; f. 1866; independent; Dir Giuseppe Brugnoli; circ. 69,000.

Vicenza

Il Giornale di Vicenza: Viale S. Lazzaro 89, 36100 Vicenza; tel. (0444) 564533; f. 1946; Editor Mino Allione; circ. 54,000.

SELECTED PERIODICALS

Fine Arts

Casabella: Via Trentacoste 7, 20134 Milan; tel. (02) 2131851; f. 1928; 11 a year; architecture and interior design; Editor Vittorio Gregotti; circ. 54,000.

Domus: Via A. Grandi 5/7, 20089 Rozzano, Milan; tel. (02) 824721; telex 313589; f. 1928; 11 a year; architecture, interior design and art; Editor Mario Bellini; circ. 60,000.

Flash Art/Heute Kunst: Via Solferino 11, 20121 Milan; tel. (02) 2364133; bi-monthly; Dir Giancarlo Politi.

Il Fotografo: Via Rivoltana 8, 20090 Segrate, Milan; tel. (02) 75421; monthly; photography; Dir Giorgio Coppin.

Graphicus and Graphicus News: Viale Mattioli 39 (Castello del Valentino), 10125 Turin; tel. (011) 6509659; f. 1911; 20 a year; graphic arts; Dir Stefano Ajani; Editor Luciano Lovera; circ. 4,600/5,500.

L'Illustrazione Italiana: Via Gen. Biancardi 1 bis, 21052 Busto Arsizio (VA); f. 1873; quarterly; fine arts.

Interni: Via Trentacoste 7, 20134 Milan; tel. (02) 215631; telex 350523; fax 26410847; monthly; interior decoration and design; Editor Dorothea Balluff; circ. 60,000.

Lotus International: Via Trentacoste 7, 20134 Milan; tel. (02) 21563240; telex 350523; fax (02) 26412586; f. 1960; quarterly; architecture, town-planning; Editor Pierluigi Nicolin.

Rivista Italiana di Musicologia: Leo S. Olschki, Viuzzo del Pozzetto, 50126 Florence; tel. (055) 6530684; fax 6530214; f. 1966; every 6 months; music; Editors A. L. Bellina, A. Collisani, F. della Seta, R. di Benedetto, G. Morelli, A. Pompilio, T. Walker.

Storia dell'Arte: Viale Carso 46, 00195 Rome; tel. (361) 2441; fax 3251055; quarterly; art history; Dir Giulio Carlo Argan.

General, Literary and Political

Archivio Storico Italiano: Leo S. Olschki, Viuzzo del Pozzetto, 50126 Florence; tel. (055) 6530684; fax 6530214; f. 1842; quarterly; history; Editor Arnaldo d'Addario.

Belfagor: POB 66, 50100 Florence; tel. (055) 6530684; fax 6530214; f. 1946; every 2 months; historical and literary criticism; Editor Carlo Ferdinando Russo; circ. 5,000.

La Bibliofilia: Leo S. Olschki, Viuzzo del Pozzetto, 50126 Florence; tel. (055) 6530684; fax 6530214; f. 1899; every 4 months; bibliography; Editor L. Balsamo.

Il Borghese: Viale Regina Margherita 7, 20122 Milan; tel. (02) 592966; f. 1950; weekly; extreme right-wing, political and cultural; Editor Mario Tedeschi.

Civitas: Via Tirso 92, 00198 Rome; tel. (06) 865651; f. 1919; monthly; magazine of political studies; Dir Paolo Emilio Taviani.

Comunità: Milan; tel. (02) 790957; f. 1945; quarterly; culture; Editor Renzo Zorzi; circ. 9,000.

Critica Letteraria: Via Stazio 15, 80123 Napoli; f. 1973; quarterly; literary criticism; Editor P. Giannantonio; circ. 3,000.

Critica Marxista: Via dei Polacchi 41, 00186 Rome; tel. (06) 6789680; f. 1962; 6 a year; Dir Aldo Zanardo.

Critica Sociale: Milan; tel. (02) 806319; f. 1891; monthly; Socialist; Dir Carlo Tognoli; circ. 25,000.

La Discussione: Piazzale Luigi Sturzo 31, 00144 Rome; tel. (06) 5901353; f. 1953; weekly; Christian Democrat; Dir Pierluigi Magnaschi; circ. 50,000.

Epoca: Arnoldo Mondadori Editore SpA, Via Marconi 27, 20090 Segrate, Milan; tel. (02) 7542; telex 310119; f. 1950; illustrated; topical weekly; Dir Carlo Rognoni; circ. 192,000.

ITALY

L'Espresso: Via Po 12, 00198 Rome; tel. (06) 84781; telex 610629; weekly; independent left; political; illustrated; Editor GIOVANNI VALENTINI; circ. 373,900.

L'Europeo: Via Rizzoli, Milan; tel. (02) 2588; f. 1945; weekly; Liberal; political and news; Dir LAMFRANCO VACCARI; circ. 172,000.

Famiglia Cristiana: Via Giotto 36, 20145 Milan; tel. (02) 467071; telex 332232; fax 48008247; f. 1931; weekly; Catholic; illustrated; Dir LEONARDO ZEGA; circ. 1,044,074.

Gazzetta del Lunedì: Via Varese 2, Genova; tel. (010) 517851; f. 1945; weekly; political; Dir MIMMO ANGELI; circ. 150,000.

Gente: Via Vitruvio 43, 20124 Milan; tel. (02) 27751; f. 1957; weekly; illustrated political, cultural and current events; Editor A. TERZI; circ. 901,000.

Giornale della Libreria: Viale Vittorio Veneto 24, 20124 Milan; tel. (02) 6597950; f. 1888; monthly; organ of the Associazione Italiana Editori; bibliographical; Editor SERGIO POLILLO.

Il Giornale del Mezzogiorno: Via Messina 31, 00198 Rome; tel. (06) 8443151; telex 621401; fax 8417595; f. 1946; weekly; politics, economics; Dir VITO BLANCO.

Giorni: Via Zuretti 34, 20125 Milan; tel. (02) 6883151; left-wing weekly; Dir DAVIDE LAJOLO; circ. 180,000.

The International Spectator: Rome; tel. (06) 354456; fax 319806; quarterly; English journal of the Istituto Affari Internazionale; Editor GIANNI BONVICINI.

Lettere Italiane: Leo S. Olschki, POB 66, 50100 Florence; tel. (055) 6530684; fax 6530214; f. 1949; quarterly; literary; Dirs V. BRANCA, CARLO OSSOLA.

Il Mondo: Gruppo Rizzoli, Corso Garibaldi 86, 20121 Milan; tel. (02) 665941; weekly; business and commerce; circ. 83,000.

Mondo Economico: Via P. Lomazzo 47, 20154 Milan; tel. (02) 331211; fax 316905; f. 1948; weekly; economics; business, finance; Editor GIANNI LOCATELLI; circ. 50,000.

Il Mulino: Strada Maggiore 37, 40125 Bologna; tel. (051) 222419; fax 256034; f. 1951; every 2 months; culture and politics; Editor NICOLA MATTEUCCI.

Nuovi Argomenti: Via Sicilia 136, 00187 Rome; tel. (06) 47497376; f. 1953; quarterly; Liberal; Editors FRANCESCA SANVITALE, ENZO SICILIANO.

Oggi: Gruppo Rizzoli, Corso Garibaldi 86, 20121 Milan; tel. (02) 665941; f. 1945; weekly; topical, literary; illustrated; Dir WILLY MOLCO; circ. 696,000.

Panorama: Arnoldo Mondadori Editore SpA, Via Marconi 27, 20090 Segrate, Milan; tel. (02) 7542; f. 1962; weekly; current affairs; Editor ANDREA MONTI; circ. 504,000.

Il Pensiero Politico: Leo S. Olschki, Viuzzo del Pozzetto, 50126 Florence, tel. (055) 6530684; fax 6530214; f. 1968; every 4 months; political and social history; Editor S. MASTELLONE.

Il Ponte: Viale A. Giacomini 8, 50132 Florence; tel. (055) 473964; f. 1945; monthly; politics, art and literature; Publr Vallecchi Editore SpA; Editor MARCELLO ROSSI.

Rinascita: Via dei Taurini 19, 00185 Rome; tel. (06) 4951251; f. 1944; weekly; Communist; Dir GIUSEPPE CHIARANTE; Editor LUCIANO BARCA; circ. 80,000.

Rivista di Storia della Filosofia: Via Albricci 9, 20122 Milan; tel. (02) 8052538; f. 1946; quarterly; philosophy; Publr Franco Angel Editore Srl; Editor Prof. MARIO DAL PRA.

Scuola e Didattica: Via L. Cadorna 11, 25186 Brescia; tel. (030) 29931; telex 300836; 19 a year; education.

Selezione dal Reader's Digest: Via Alserio 10, 20173 Milan; tel. (02) 69871; telex 330378; fax 66800070; monthly; Editor-in-Chief PIETRO MARIANO BENNI.

Storia Illustrata: Via Marconi 27, 20090 Segrate, Milan; tel. (02) 75421; f. 1957; monthly; history; Publr Mondadori Editore; circ. 105,701.

Tempo: Via S. Valeria 5, 20100 Milan; f. 1938; topical illustrated weekly; Dir CARLO GREGORETTI; circ. 230,000.

Visto: Via Rizzoli 4, 20132 Milan; tel. (02) 2588; telex 312119; fax 25843683; f. 1989; illustrated weekly review; Editor-in-Chief MARCELLO MINERBI; circ. 350,000.

Volksbote: Via del Vigneto 7, 39100 Bolzano; tel. (0471) 925111; organ of the Südtiroler Volkspartei; German language.

Religion

Città di Vita: Piazza Santa Croce 16, 50122 Florence; tel. (055) 242783; f. 1946; every 2 months; cultural review of religious research in theology, art and science; Dir P. M. GIUSEPPE ROSITO; circ. 2,000.

La Civiltà Cattolica: Via di Porta Pinciana 1, 00187 Rome; tel. (06) 6798351; f. 1850; fortnightly; Catholic; Editor GIAN PAOLO SALVINI.

Il Fuoco: Via Giacinto Carini 28, 00152 Rome; tel. (06) 5810969; every 2 months; art, literature, science, philosophy, psychology, theology; Dir PASQUALE MAGNI.

Humanitas: Via G. Rosa 71, 25100 Brescia; tel. (030) 46451; f. 1946; every 2 months; religion, philosophy, science, politics, history, sociology, literature, etc.; Dir STEFANO MINELLI.

Protestantesimo: Via Pietro Cossa 42, 00193 Rome; tel. (06) 3204802; fax 3201040; f. 1946; quarterly; theology and current problems, book reviews; Prof. BRUNO CORSANI.

La Rivista del Clero Italiano: Largo Gemelli 1, 20123 Milan; tel. (02) 8856369; telex 321033; f. 1920; monthly; Dir BRUNO MAGGIONI.

Rivista di Storia della Chiesa in Italia: c/o Herder Editrice e Libreria, Piazza Montecitorio 117-120, 00186 Rome; f. 1947; 2 a year.

Rivista di Storia e Letteratura Religiosa: Biblioteca Erik Peterson, Università di Torino, Via S. Ottavio 20, 10124 Turin; tel. (011) 830556; f. 1965; every 4 months; religious history and literature; Dir FRANCO BOLGIANI.

Science and Technology

L'Automobile: Viale Regina Margherita 290, 00198 Rome; tel. (06) 4402061; fax 8840926; f. 1945; monthly; motor mechanics, tourism; Dir CARLO LUNA; circ. 1,500,000.

Fonderia: Via Roncaglia 14, 20146 Milan; tel. (02) 48010095; telex 321655; fax 48010011; f. 1951; every 2 months; foundry techniques; Dir ANTONIO URTI; circ. 3,500.

Gazzetta Medica Italiana-Archivio per le Scienze Mediche: Corso Bramante 83-85, 10126 Turin; tel. (011) 678282; monthly; medical science; Dir ALBERTO OLIARO.

Il Giornale dell' Officina: Via Roncaglia 14, 20146 Milan; tel. (02) 48010095; telex 321655; fax 48010011; f. 1948; monthly; mechanical industry magazine; Dir ANTONIO URTI; circ. 4,500.

L'Italia Agricola: Via Nazionale 89/A, 00184 Rome; tel. (06) 463651; fax 4747206; f. 1864; quarterly; agriculture; Dir BORIS FISCHETTI; circ. 20,000.

Macchine: Via Roncaglia 14, 20146 Milan; tel. (02) 48010095; telex 321655; fax 48010011; f. 1948; monthly; technical review of mechanical engineering industry; Dir ANTONIO URTI; circ. 10,000.

Meccanica: Piazza Leonardo da Vinci 32, 20133 Milan; tel. (02) 23994209; telex 333467; quarterly; Journal of Italian Association of Theoretical and Applied Mechanics; Dir Prof. CARLO CERCIGNANI.

Il Medico d'Italia: Piazza Cola di Rienzo 80A, 00192 Rome; tel. (06) 6874034; fax 6876739; daily; medical science; Editor-in-Chief Dr ANDREA SERTIONTI.

Minerva Medica: Corso Bramante 83-85, 10126 Turin; tel. (011) 678282; monthly; medical science; Dir ALBERTO OLIARO.

Monti e Boschi: Via Emilia Levante 31/2, 40139 Bologna; tel. (051) 492211; telex 510336; f. 1949; 2 a month; ecology and forestry; Pubr Edagricole; Editor UMBERTO BAGNARESI; circ. 15,600.

Motor: Piazza Antonio Mancini 4G, 00196 Rome; tel. (06) 390962; fax 3965431; f. 1942; monthly; motor mechanics; Dir SERGIO FAVIA DEL CORE; circ. 120,000.

Physis: Leo S. Olschki, CP 66, 50100 Florence; Viuzzo del Pozzetto, 50126 Florence; tel. (055) 6530684; fax 6530214; f. 1959; 3 a year; history of science; Editor V. CAPPELLETTI.

La Rivista dei Combustibili: Viale De Gasperi 3, 20097 S. Donato Milanese; tel. (02) 510031; telex 321622; fax 514286; f. 1947; monthly; fuels review; Dir Prof. ALBERTO GIRELLI; circ. 2,000.

Rivista Geografica Italiana: Via Curtatone 1, 50123 Florence; tel. (055) 282150; fax (055) 218993; f. 1894; quarterly geographical review; Editor PIERO INNOCENTI.

Utensil: Via Roncaglia 14, 20146 Milan; tel. (02) 48010095; telex 321655; fax 48010011; f. 1978; 9 a year; technology and marketing in the tool industry; Dir ANTONIO URTI; circ. 12,000.

Women's Publications

Amica: Via Scarsellini 17, 20161 Milan; tel. (02) 6339; telex 310031; f. 1962; weekly; Editor P. PIETRONI; circ. 211,000.

Annabella: Via Civitavecchia 102, Milan; tel. (02) 25843213; telex 312119; f. 1932; weekly; Editor M. VENTURI; circ. 270,000.

Confidenze: Arnoldo Mondadori Editore SpA, Via Marconi 27, 20090 Segrate, Milan; tel. (02) 75421; telex 320457; f. 1946; weekly; Dir ALDO GUSTAVO CIMARELLI; circ. 363,000.

Gioia: Via Vitruvio 43, 20124 Milan; f. 1938; weekly; Editor SILVANA GIACOBINI; circ. 351,000.

Grazia: Arnoldo Mondadori Editore SpA, Via Marconi 27, 20090 Segrate, Milan; f. 1938; weekly; Dir ANDREINA VANNI; circ. 360,000.

Intimità: Via Borgogna 5, 20122 Milan; tel. (02) 701051; weekly; published by Cino del Duca; Dir G. GALLUZZO; circ. 468,000.

ITALY

Mille Idee per la Donna: Rizzoli Editore SpA, Via Angelo Rizzoli 2, 20132 Milan; tel. (02) 2588; monthly; Dir MARA SANTINI; circ. 362,800.

Vogue Italia: Piazza Castello 27, 20121 Milan; tel. (02) 85611; telex 313454; fax 870686; monthly; Editor FRANCA SOZZANI.

Miscellaneous

Annali della Scuola Normale Superiore di Pisa: Scuola Normale Superiore, Pisa; tel. (050) 597111; telex 590548; fax 563513; f. 1873; quarterly; mathematics, philosophy, philology, history, literature; Editor (Mathematics) Prof. EDOARDO VESENTINI; Editor (literature and philosophy) Prof. GIUSEPPE NENCI; circ. 1,300.

Atlante: Via G. Gozzi 1A, 20129 Milan; tel. (02) 700231; telex 333183; fax 70100319; published by Istituto Geografico de Agostini Rizzoli Periodici (Milano); travel, art, geography, ethnology, archaeology; Dir Dott. MASSIMO MORELLO.

Comunità Mediterranea: Lungotevere Flaminio 34, 00196 Rome; quarterly; legal; Editor ENRICO NOUNÈ.

Cooperazione Educativa: La Nuova Italia, Via dei Piceni 16, 00185 Rome; tel. (06) 4940228; f. 1952; monthly; education; Dir GIORGIO TESTA.

Il Maestro: Clivo Monte del Gallo 48, 00165 Rome; f. 1945; fortnightly; Catholic teachers' magazine; Dir MARIANGELA PRIORESCHI; circ. 40,000.

Milano Finanza: Milan; tel. (02) 809161; f. 1986; weekly; financial; Dir PAOLO PANERAI; circ. 90,000.

Quattroruote: Via A. Grandi 5/7, 20089 Rozzano, Milan; telex 316822; fax 26863093; f. 1956; motoring; monthly; Editor RAFFAELE MASTROSTEFANO; circ. 700,000.

Qui Touring: Touring Club Italiano, Corso Italia 10, 20122 Milan; tel. (02) 85261; telex 321160; f. 1971; monthly; travel, art, geography; Editor TCI; circ. 510,000.

Radiocorriere-TV: Via Arsenale 41, 10121 Turin; tel. (011) 5710; weekly; RAI official guide to radio and television programmes; Dir GINO NEBIOLO.

NEWS AGENCIES

Agenzia Giornalistica Italia (AGI): Via Nomentana 92, 00161 Rome; tel. (06) 84361; telex 610512; fax 8416072; owned by ENI, a state-owned energy conglomerate; Editor FRANCO ANGRISANI.

Agenzia Nazionale Stampa Associata (ANSA): Via della Dataria 94, 00187 Rome; tel. (06) 67741; telex 610242; fax 6782408; f. 1945; 20 regional offices in Italy and 90 branches all over the world; service in Italian, Spanish, French, English; Pres. GIOVANNI GIOVANNINI; Man. Dir and Gen. Man. PAOLO DE PALMA; Chief Editor BRUNO CASELLI.

Inter Press Service (IPS): Via Panisperna 207, 00184 Rome; tel. (06) 485692; telex 610574; fax 4817877; f. 1964; Editor-in-Chief GIOVANNI SPINELLI.

Foreign Bureaux

Agencia EFE (Spain): Via dei Canestrari 5, 00186 Rome; tel. (06) 6548802; telex 612323; fax 6874918; Bureau Chief NEMESIO RODRÍGUEZ.

Agence France-Presse (AFP): Piazza Santi-Apostoli 66, 00187 Rome; tel. (06) 6793623; telex 613303; fax 6793588; Bureau Chief YVES GACON.

Associated Press (AP) (USA): Piazza Grazioli 5, 00186 Rome; tel. (06) 6789936; telex 610196; Bureau Chief DENNIS F. REDMONT.

Československá tisková kancelář (ČTK) (Czechoslovakia): Via di Vigna Stelluti 150/13, 00191 Rome; tel. (06) 3270777; telex 43625664.

Deutsche Presse-Agentur (dpa) (Germany): Via della Mercede 55, Int. 15, 00187 Rome; tel. (06) 6789810; telex 610046; Bureau Chief FRANK RAFALSKI.

Kyodo Tsushin (Japan): Rome, tel. (06) 8440709; telex 680840; Bureau Chief KATSUO UEDA.

Magyar Távirati Iroda (MTI) (Hungary): Via Topino 29, 00199 Rome; Correspondent FERENC GARZO.

Reuters (UK): Via della Cordonata 7, 00187 Rome; tel. (06) 6782501; telex 621065; fax 6794248.

Telegrafnoye Agentstvo Sovetskovo Soyuza (TASS) (USSR): Viale dell'Umanesimo 172, 00144 Rome; tel. (06) 5915883; telex 610034; Correspondent NIKOLAJ TETERIN.

United Press International (UPI) (USA): Via della Mercede 55, 00187 Rome; tel. (06) 6795747; telex 624580; fax 6781540; Correspondent CHARLES RIDLEY.

Xinhua (New China) News Agency (People's Republic of China): Via Bruxelles 59, 00198 Rome; tel. (06) 865028; telex 612208; fax 8450575; Bureau Chief HUANG CHANGRUI.

The following are also represented: CNA (Taiwan) and Jiji Tsushin-Sha (Japan).

PRESS ASSOCIATIONS

Associazione della Stampa Estera in Italia: Via della Mercede 55, 00187 Rome; tel. (06) 6786005; foreign correspondents' assen; Pres. DENNIS REDMONT; Sec. SANTIAGO FERNÁNDEZ ARDANAZ.

Federazione Italiana Editori Giornali (FIEG): Via Piemonte 64, 00187 Rome; tel. (06) 461683; telex 625361; fax 4871109; f. 1950; association of newspaper publishers; Pres. GIOVANNI GIOVANNINI; Dir-Gen. SEBASTIANO SORTINO; 276 mems.

Federazione Nazionale della Stampa Italiana: Corso Vittorio Emanuele 349, 00186 Rome; tel. (06) 6547741; fax 6871444; f. 1877; 17 affiliated unions; Pres. GILBERTO EVANGELISTI; Nat. Sec. GIULIANA DEL BUFALO; 16,000 mems.

Unione Stampa Periodica Italiana (USPI): Via Nazionale 163, 00187 Rome; tel. (06) 6783117; fax 6795798; Pres. Avv. VITTORIO CIAMPI; Sec.-Gen. GIAN DOMENICO ZUCCALÀ; 4,500 mems.

Publishers

There are more than 300 major publishing houses and many smaller ones.

Bologna

Edizioni Calderini: Via Emilia Levante 31/2, 40139 Bologna; tel. (051) 492211; telex 510336; fax 490200; f. 1954; art, sport, electronics, mechanics, university and school textbooks, travel guides, nursing, architecture; Man. Dir LUISA PERDISA.

Capitol Dischi CEB: Via Ronchi Vecchia 11, 4006 Iminerbio, Bologna; tel. (051) 660410; telex 511039; f. 1956; children's fiction, textbooks, reference, medicine, art, biography, educational nursing, architecture; Man. Dir LUISA PERDISA.

Capitol Dischi CEB: Via Ronchi Vecchia 11, 4006 Iminerbio, Bologna; tel. (051) 660410; telex 511039; f. 1956; children's fiction, textbooks, reference, medicine, art, biography, educational films and records; Chair. MAURIZIO MALIPIERO; Gen. Man. RAFFAELE MALIPIERO.

Nuova Casa Editrice Licinio Cappelli GEM SrL: Via Farini 14, 40124 Bologna; tel. (051) 239060; fax 239286; f. 1948; medical science, history, politics, literature, textbooks; Chair. and Man. Dir MARIO MUSSO.

Edagricole: Via Emilia Levante 31, 40139 Bologna; tel. (051) 492211; telex 510336; f. 1936; agriculture, veterinary science, gardening, biology, textbooks, directories; Man. Dir SERGIO PERDISA; Editor LUISA MANZONI.

Malipiero Editore SpA: Via Liguria 8–10, CP 788, 40100 Bologna; tel. (051) 792111; telex 510260; fax 792356; f. 1969; albums and books for children and young people, dictionaries, pocket dictionaries, stamp albums, etc.; Chair. GIUSEPPE MALIPIERO; Man. Dir PIERPAOLO MALIPIERO.

Società Editrice Il Mulino: Strada Maggiore 37, 40125 Bologna; tel. (051) 256011; fax (051) 256034; f. 1954; politics, history, philosophy, social sciences, linguistics, literary criticism, law, music, theatre, psychology, economics, journals; Gen. Man. GIOVANNI EVANGELISTI.

Nicola Zanichelli Editore: Via Irnerio 34, 40126 Bologna; tel. (051) 293111; telex 521587; fax 249782; f. 1859; educational, history, literature, philosophy, science, technical books, law, psychology, architecture, reference books, atlases, earth sciences, linguistics, medicine and economics; Chair. and Gen. Man. FEDERICO ENRIQUES; Vice-Chair. and Man. Dir LORENZO ENRIQUES.

Brescia

Editrice La Scuola SpA: Via Cadorna 11, Brescia; tel. (030) 29931; telex 300836; fax 2993299; f. 1904; educational magazines, educational textbooks, audiovisual aids and toys; Chair. Dr Ing. LUCIANO SILVERI; Man. Dir Dr Ing. ADOLFO LOMBARDI.

Busto Arsizio

Bramante Editrice: Via Biancardi 1 bis, 21052 Busto Arsizio; tel. (0331) 620324; fax 322052; f. 1958; art, history, encyclopaedias, natural sciences, interior decoration, arms and armour, music; Chair. Dr GUIDO CERIOTTI.

Florence

Casa Editrice Bonechi: Via dei Cairoli 18B, 50131 Florence; tel. (055) 576841; telex 571323; fax 576844; f. 1973; art, travel, reference; Man. Dir GIAMPAOLO BONECHI; Gen. Man. MARCO BANTI.

Cremonese: Borgo Santa Croce 17, 50122 Florence; tel. (055) 2476371; fax 2476372; f. 1929; history, reference, engineering, science, textbooks, architecture, mathematics, aviation; Chair. ALBERTO STIANTI.

ITALY

Giunti Barbera Editore: Via Vincenzo Gioberti 34, 50121 Florence; tel. (055) 66791; telex 571438; f. 1839; art, psychology, literature, science, law; Dir Dott. SERGIO GIUNTI.

Le Monnier: Via A. Meucci 2, 50015 Grassina, Florence; tel. (055) 6813801; fax 643983; f. 1836; academic and cultural books, textbooks, dictionaries; Man. Dirs Dott. MARCO PAOLETTI, Dott. VANNI PAOLETTI, Dott. ENRICO PAOLETTI.

La Nuova Italia Editrice SpA: Via Ernesto Codignola 1, 50018 Florence; tel. (055) 75901; fax 7590208; f. 1926; biography, psychology, philosophy, philology, education, history, politics, belles-lettres, art, music and science; Man. Dirs FEDERICO CODIGNOLA, MARIO ERMINI, SERGIO PICCIONI.

Casa Editrice Leo S. Olschki: CP 66, 50100 Florence; tel. (055) 6530684; fax 6530214; f. 1886; reference, periodicals, textbooks, humanities; Man. ALESSANDRO OLSCHKI.

Adriano Salani Editore SpA: Via del Giglio 15, 50123 Florence; tel. (055) 263288; fax 263288; f. 1988; art, classics, history, children's books; Editor MARIO SPAGNOL.

Edizioni Remo Sandron: Via L.C. Farini 10, 50121 Florence; tel. (055) 245231; f. 1839; textbooks; Pres. E. MULINACCI.

RCS Sansoni Editore SpA: Via Benedetto Varchi 47, 50132 Florence; tel. (055) 243334; telex 57466; f. 1873; art, archaeology, literature, philology, philosophy, essays, science, social sciences, natural sciences, history, law, teach-yourself books, magazines; Chair. and Man. Dir SANDRO ALFIERI.

Vallecchi Editore SpA: Viale Giovanni Milton 7, 50129 Florence; tel. (055) 473964; telex 573084; fax 499195; f. 1918; art, fiction, classics; Chair. LUIGI VECCHIA.

Genova

Casa Editrice Marietti SpA: Via Palestro 10/8, 16122 Genova; tel. (010) 891254; fax 873749; f. 1820; liturgy, theology, fiction, history, politics, literature, philosophy, psychology, art, children's books; Editor ANTONIO BALLETTO.

Libreria degli Studi (formerly LUPA): Via Balbi 42, Genova; f. 1943; textbooks, fine arts; Dir MARIO BOZZI.

Milan

Adelphi Edizioni SpA: Via S. Giovanni sul Muro 14, 20121 Milan; tel. (02) 72000975; fax 89010337; f. 1962; classics, philosophy, biography, music, art, psychology, religion and fiction; Man. Dirs GIUSEPPE LUCIANO FOÀ, ROBERTO CALASSO.

Editrice Àncora: Via G. B. Niccolini 8, 20154 Milan; tel. (02) 33608941; fax 33608944; f. 1934; religious, educational; Dir SEVERINO MEDICI.

Franco Angeli Srl: Viale Monza 106, CP 17130, 20127, Milan; tel. (02) 2827651; fax 2891515; f. 1956; general; Man. Dir FRANCO ANGELI.

Carisch SpA: Via General Fara 39, 20124 Milan; tel. (02) 66981814; telex 326397; fax 6692682; f. 1884; music and musicology; records; educational musical instruments; Pres. PIETRO MERAVIGLIA MANTEGAZZA.

Gruppo Editoriale Fabbri SpA: Via Mecenate 91, 20138 Milan; tel. (02) 50951; telex 311321; fax 5065361; f. 1947; juveniles, education, textbooks, reference, literature, maps and encyclopaedia series, art books; Chair. GIOVANNI GIOVANNINI; Man. Dir MARIO SPERANZA.

Bompiani: Via Mecenate 91, 20138 Milan; tel. (02) 50951; telex 311321; fax ; f. 1929; modern literature, biographies, theatre, science, art, history, classics, dictionaries, pocket books; Dir MARIO ANDREOSE.

Sonzogno: Via Mecenate 91, 20138 Milan; tel (02) 50951; telex 311321; f. 1861; fiction, non-fiction, illustrated, guides; Dir MARIO ANDREOSE.

Feltrinelli SpA: Via Andegari 6, 20121 Milan; tel. (02) 808346; f. 1954; fiction, juvenile, science, technology, textbooks, poetry, art, music, history, literature, political science, philosophy, reprint editions of periodicals; Chair. INGE FELTRINELLI; Man. Dir GIUSEPPE ANTONINI.

Garzanti Editore: Via Senato 25, 20121 Milan; tel. (02) 77871; telex 325218; fax 76009233; f. 1938; literature, poetry, science, art, history, politics, encyclopaedias, dictionaries, scholastic and children's books; Chair. GUGLIELMO MAGATTI; Man. Dir FRANCO RAMPINI; Gen. Man. FILIPPO TAMBORINI.

Ghisetti e Corvi Editori SpA: Corso Concordia 7, 20129 Milan; tel. (02) 7060232; fax (02) 76009468; f. 1937; educational textbooks.

Casa Editrice Libraria Ulrico Hoepli: Via Hoepli 5, 20121 Milan; tel. (02) 865446; telex 313395; fax 8052886; f. 1870; grammars, art, technical, scientific and school books, encyclopaedias; Chair. ULRICO HOEPLI; Man. Dir GIANNI HOEPLI.

Longanesi e C.: Via T. Salvini 3, 20122 Milan; tel. (02) 700551; telex 353273; fax 781422; f. 1946; religion, music, art, history, philosophy, fiction; Pres. S. PASSIGLI; Man. Dir M. SPAGNOL.

Massimo: Viale Bacchiglione 20/A, 20139 Milan; tel. (02) 55210800; fax 55211315; f. 1955; fiction, biography, history, social science, philosophy, pedagogy, theology, school texts; Chair. CESARE CRESPI.

Arnoldo Mondadori Editore: Via Mondadori 27, 20090 Segrate, Milan; tel. (02) 75421; telex 320457; fax (02) 75422302; f. 1907; literature, fiction, politics, science, music, art, religion, philosophy, children's books, magazines; Man. Dir MARCO POLILLO.

Gruppo Ugo Mursia Editore SpA: Via Tadino 29, 20124, Milan; tel. (02) 29403030; telex 325294; fax (02) 2041557; f. 1922; general fiction and non-fiction, textbooks, reference, art, history, nautical books, philosophy, biography, sports, children's books; Gen. Man. Dott. GIANCARLA MURSIA.

Nuova Accademia Editrice: Via Cavalcabò 9, 20146 Milan; tel. (02) 464884; f. 1946; books on general culture; Pres. LUIGI PINELLI.

Editore dall'Oglio: Via Santa Croce 20/2, 20122 Milan; tel. (02) 58101575; f. 1925; general literature, biography, history, fiction; Gen. Man. BRUNO ROMANO.

Edizioni Paoline: Piazza Soncino 5, 20092 Cinisello Balsamo—Milan; tel. (02) 6600621; telex 325183; fax 6189266; f. 1914; religious; Gen. Man. ANTONIO TARZIA.

Etas Periodici SpA: Via Mecenate 86/7, 20138 Milan; tel. (02) 5075; telex 331342; technical periodicals; Man. Dir Dott. EUGENIO DE ROSA.

Editrice Piccoli Srl: Via Santa Sofia 10, 20122 Milan; tel. (02) 861847; telex 332599; fax 89010743; f. 1944; children's books; Chair. AURELIO PICCO.

Rcs Rizzoli: Via 5 Scarsellini 13/17, 20161 Milan; tel. 2588; fax 6469155; f. 1929; newspapers, magazines and books; Chair. ANTONIO COPPI; Man. Dir GIORGIO FATTORI.

Riccardo Ricciardi Editore SpA: Via Alessandro Manzoni 10, 20121 Milan; tel (02) 875155; f. 1907; classics, philology, history, literature; Gen. Man. Dott. MAURIZIO MATTIOLI.

Ricordi SpA: Via Berchet 2, 20121 Milan; tel. (02) 88811; telex 310177; f. 1808; academic, art, music; Chair. GIANNI BABINI; Man. Dir GUIDO RIGNANO.

Rusconi Libri SpA: Via Livraghi 1B, 20126 Milan; tel. (02) 2574141; telex 312233; fax 2552098; f. 1969; fiction and non-fiction including history, biography, music, philosophy, archaeology, religion and art; Pres. EDILIO RUSCONI; Gen. Man. FERRUCCIO VIVIANI.

Libri Scheiwiller: Via Sacchi 3, 20121 Milan; tel. (02) 865590; fax 72023167; f. 1977; art, literature and archaeology; Chair. GIANCARLO LUNATI; Man. Dir VANNI SCHEIWILLER.

L'Editrice Scientifica: Via Ariberto 20, 20123 Milan; tel. (02) 8390274; f. 1949; university publications in chemistry and medicine; Dirs Dotts. LEONARDA and GUIDO GUADAGNI.

Edizioni Scolastiche Bruno Mondadori: Via Archimede 23, 20129 Milan; tel. (02) 76009881; fax 76014294; f. 1946; textbooks and educational books; Chair. ROBERTA MONDADORI; Man. Dir ROBERTO GULLI; Gen. Man. AGOSTINO CATTANEO.

Selezione dal Reader's Digest SpA: Via Alserio 10, 20173 Milan; tel. (02) 69871; telex 330378; fax 6987401; f. 1948; educational, reference, general interest; Man. Dir EDOARDO LUCHESCHI.

Carlo Signorelli SpA: Via Siusi 7, 20132 Milan; tel. (02) 2896541; fax 2619259; children's and textbooks, dictionaries.

La Sorgente: Via Garofalo 44, 20133 Milan; tel. (02) 230720; fax 2666685; f. 1936; children's books; Man. Dir Dr GIORGIO VIGNATI.

Sugarco Edizioni: Viale Tunisia 41, 20124 Milan; tel. (02) 652192; f. 1957; fiction, biography, history, philosophy, guidebooks; Chair. PAOLO PILLITTERI; Gen. Man. VINCENZO NAGARI.

Casa Editrice Luigi Trevisini: Via Tito Livio 12, Milan; tel. (02) 5450704; f. 1849; school textbooks; Dirs ENRICO TREVISINI, LUIGI TREVISINI.

Il Vaglio Cultura Arte: Via Vitruvio 39, 20124 Milan; tel. (02) 2846903; f. 1985; art and architecture; *Arte Lombarda nuova serie* (quarterly); Man. Prof. MARIA LUISA GATTI PERER.

Vita e Pensiero: Largo A. Gemelli 1, 20123 Milan; tel. (02) 8856335; telex 321033; fax 8856260; f. 1918; publisher to the Catholic University of the Sacred Heart; cultural, scientific, children's books and magazines.

Naples

Casa Editrice Libraria Idelson: Via Alcide De Gasperi 55, 80133 Naples; tel. (081) 5524733; fax 5518295; f. 1908; medicine, psychology, biology; CEO GUIDO GNOCCHI.

Liguori Editore: Via Mezzocannone 19, 80134 Naples; tel. (081) 5527139; f. 1949; linguistics, mathematics, engineering, economics, law, history, philosophy, sociology; Man. Dir Dott. ROLANDO LIGUORI.

Gaetano Macchiaroli Editore: Via Michetti 11, 80127, Naples, tel. (081) 5783129; fax 5780568; archaeology, classical studies, history, philosophy, political science.

Società Editrice Napoletana: Corso Umberto I 34, 80138 Naples; tel. (081) 206602; f. 1973; art, poetry, literature, history; Dir A. DE DOMINICIS.

Novara

Instituto Geografico De Agostini-Novara: Via Giovanni da Verrazano 15, 28100 Novara; tel. (0321) 4241; telex 200290; fax 471286; geography, maps, encyclopaedias, dictionaries, art, literature, textbooks, science; Chair. ADOLFO BOROLI; Man. Dirs MARCO BOROLI, MARCO DRAGO.

Padova

CEDAM—Casa Editrice Dr A. Milani: Via Jappelli 5/6, 35121 Padova; tel. (049) 656677; fax 8752900; f. 1902; law, economics, political and social sciences, engineering, science, medicine, literature, philosophy, textbooks; Dirs ANTONIO MILANI, CARLO PORTA.

Libreria Editrice Gregoriana: Via Roma 82, 35122 Padova; tel. (049) 661033; f. 1922; *Lexicon Totius Latinitatis*, religion, philosophy, psychology, social studies; Dir DON GIANCARLO MINOZZI.

Libreria Editrice Internazionale Zannoni e Figlio: Corso Garibaldi 14, 35122 Padova; tel. (049) 44170; f. 1919; medicine, technical books, scholastic books, miscellaneous; Dir GIULIANA ZANNONI.

Liviana Editrice: Via L. Dottesio 1, 35138 Padova; tel. (049) 8710099; fax 8710261; f. 1948; secondary-school and university textbooks, journals and essays; Pres. LUIGI VECCHIA.

Piccin Nuova Libraria SpA: Via Altinate 107, 35100 Padova; tel. (049) 655566; telex 432074; fax 8750693; f. 1980; scientific textbooks and journals; Man. Dir Dr MASSIMO PICCIN.

Valmartina Editore: Via L. Dottesio 1, 35138 Padova; tel. (049) 8710195; fax 8710261; foreign languages, guide books; Pres. Rag. LUIGI VECCHIA; Gen. Man. Dr GIORGIO RACCIS.

Rome

Armando Armando Editore Srl: Piazza Sidney Sonnino 13, 00153 Rome; tel. (06) 5806420; fax 5818564; philosophy, psychology, social sciences, languages, ecology, education; Man. Dir ENRICO JACOMETTI.

Edizioni Borla Srl: Via delle Fornaci 50, 00165 Rome; tel. (06) 6381618; fax 6376620; f. 1863; religion, philosophy, psychoanalysis, ethnology, literature, novels for teenagers; Man. Dir VINCENZO D'AGOSTINO.

Edizioni d'Arte di Carlo E. Bestetti & C. Sas: Via di San Giacomo 18, 00187 Rome; tel. (06) 6790174; f. 1947; art, architecture, industry; Man. Dir CARLO BESTETTI.

Ausonia: Rome; tel. (06) 595959; f. 1919; textbooks; Pres. E. LUCCHINI; Gen. Man. G. LUCCHINI.

AVE (Anonima Veritas Editrice): Via Aurelia 481, 00165 Rome; tel. (06) 6233041; fax (06) 6620207; f. 1935; theology, sociology, pedagogy, psychology, essays, learned journals, religious textbooks; Man. Dir ANTONIO SANTANGELO.

Vito Bianco Editore: Via Messina 31, 00198 Rome; tel. (06) 8443151; telex 621401; fax 8417595; various, especially marine publications; Chair. Dott. VITO BIANCO.

Bulzoni Editore—Le edizioni universitarie d'Italia: Via dei Liburni 14, 00185 Rome; tel. (06) 4455207; fax 4450355; f. 1969; science, arts, fiction, textbooks; Man. Dir MARIO BULZONI.

E. Calzono: Via del Collegio Romano 9, Rome; f. 1872; art, archaeology, philosophy, science, religion, economics; Dir Dr RICCARDO GAMBERINI MONGENET.

Editrice Ciranna: Via Capograssa 115, 04010 Borgo San Michele-Latina, Rome; tel. (0773) 250746; f. 1940; school textbooks; Man. Dir LIDIA FABIANO.

Armando Curcio Editore SpA: Via Arno 64, 00198 Rome; tel. (06) 84871; telex 614666; f. 1954; encyclopaedias, classics, history, music, science, reference, geography, art, video series; Chair. Dr MARIO SCHIMBERNI; Man. Dir Dr MATILDE BERNABEI.

Editrice Dante Alighieri (Albrighi, Segati & C.): Via Timavo 3, 00195 Rome; tel. (06) 3201656; fax 3614167; f. 1928; school textbooks, science and general culture; Pres. SALVATORE SPINELLI; Man. Dir SILVANO SPINELLI.

Edizioni Europa: Via G.B. Martini 6, 00198 Rome; tel. (06) 8449124; f. 1944; essays, literature, art, history, politics, music, economics; Chair. Prof. PIER FAUSTO PALUMBO.

Hermes Edizioni Srl: Via Flaminia 158, 00196 Rome; tel. (06) 3207656; fax 3614167; f. 1979; alternative medicine, astrology, nature, dietetics; Gen. Man. GIOVANNI CANONICO.

Giuseppe Laterza e Figli SpA: Via Dante 51, 70121 Bari; tel. (080) 5213413; fax 5243461; f. 1885; belles lettres, biography, reference, religion, art, classics, history, economics, philosophy, social science; Man. Dir VITO LATERZA; Editorial Dir ENRICO MISTRETTA.

Le Edizioni del Lavoro: Via Boncompagni 19, 00187 Rome; tel. (06) 4746420; fax 4821976; f. 1982; history, politics, political philosophy, sociology, African literature; Chair. LUIGI COCILOVO; Man. Dir MARIO BERTIN.

Guida Monaci SpA: Via Vitorchiano 107, 00189 Rome; tel. (06) 3288805; telex 623234; fax 3275693; f. 1870; commercial and industrial, financial, administrative and medical directories; publishes *Annuario Generale Italiano*, *Annuario Amministrativo Italiano*, *Chi Sono Nelle Attività Italiane*, *Chi Sono Nelle Attività Amministrative*, *Chi Sono Nelle Attività Sanitarie*, *Annuario Sanitario*, *Il Siglario Italiano*, *Agenda* Ediz. Nazionale e Regionali e Provinciali (yearly); Dir ALBERTO ZAPPONINI.

Fratelli Palombi Srl: Via dei Gracchi 181-185, 00192 Rome; tel. (06) 354960; f. 1914; history, art, etc. of Rome; Man. Dir Dott. MARIO PALOMBI.

Jandi Sapi Editori Srl: Via Crescenzio 62, 00193 Rome; tel. (06) 6545515; f. 1941; industrial and legal publications, art books; Dir Dr CHIARA BASSANINI.

Angelo Signorelli: Via Falconieri 84, 00152 Rome; tel. (06) 5314942; fax 531492; f. 1912; science, general literature, textbooks; Man. Dirs GIORGIO SIGNORELLI, GILBERTA ALPA.

Edizioni Studium: CP 30100, 00100 Rome 47; tel. (06) 6875456; f. 1927; philosophy, literature, sociology, pedagogy, religion, economics, law, science, history, psychology; periodical *Studium*.

Stresa

Libraria Editoriale Sodalitas Sas: Centro Internazionale Studi Rosminiani, Corso Umberto 15, 28049 Stresa; tel. (0323) 31623; f. 1925; philosophy, theology, *Rivista Rosminiana* (quarterly); Dir Prof. PIER PAOLO OTTONELLO.

Trento

G.B. Monauni: Trento; tel. (0461) 21445; f. 1725; art, archaeology, ethnology, folklore, science, history; Man. Dir Dott. G. B. MONAUNI.

Turin

Editrice L'Artist Modern: Via Garibaldi 59, 10121 Turin; tel. (011) 541371; f. 1901; art; Dir. F. NELVA.

Bollati Boringhieri Editore SpA: Corso Vittorio Emanuele II 86, 10121 Turin; tel. (011) 5611951; telex 225444; fax 543024; f. 1957; psychology, social and human sciences, fiction and classical literature; Chair. ROMILDA BOLLATI; Man. Dir GIULIO BOLLATI.

Giulio Einaudi Editore SpA; Via Umberto Biancamano 1, CP 245, 10121 Turin; tel. (011) 533653; telex 220344; f. 1933; fiction, classics, general; Gen. Man. GIULIO EINAUDI.

Giorgio Giappichelli Editore Sas: Via Po 21, 10124 Turin; tel. (011) 8397019; f. 1921; university publications on literature, law, economics, politics and sociology.

Lattes S. e C. Editori: Via Confienza 6, 10121 Turin; f. 1893; tel. (011) 515335; fax 530042; technical, textbooks; Pres. MARIO LATTES.

Levrotto e Bella, Libreria Editrice Universitaria: Corso Vittorio Emanuele II 26, 10123 Turin; tel. (011) 832535; f. 1942; university textbooks; Man. Dir TERENZIO GUALINI.

Loescher: Via Vittorio Amedeo II 18, 10121 Turin; tel. (011) 549333; fax 547614; f. 1867; school textbooks, general literature, academic books; Chair. MAURIZIO PAVIA.

Edizioni Minerva Medica: Corso Bramante 83-85, 10126 Turin; tel. (011) 678282; medical books and journals; Dir PAOLO OLIARO.

Petrini: Corso Trapani 48, 10139 Turin; tel. (011) 3358641; f. 1872; school textbooks; Dir VITTORIO GALLEA.

Rosenberg & Sellier: Via Andrea Doria 14, 10123 Turin; tel. (011) 532150; fax 532188; f. 1979; philology, social sciences, literature, philosophy; Chair. UGO GIANNI ROSENBERG; Man. Dir KATIE ROGGERO.

Società Editrice Internazionale SpA (SEI): Corso Regina Margherita 176, 10152 Turin; tel. (011) 52271; telex 216216; fax 5211320; f. 1908; textbooks, fiction, art, literature, philosophy, children's books, etc.; Man. Dir Dr GIAN NICOLA PIVANO.

Unione Tipografico-Editrice Torinese (UTET): Corso Raffaello 28, 10125 Turin; tel. (011) 65291; telex 225553; fax 6529240; f. 1791; university and specialized editions on history, geography, art, literature, economics, law, sciences, encyclopaedias, dictionaries, etc.; Pres. Dott. GIANNI MERLINI.

Venice

Alfieri Edizioni d'Arte: San Marco 1991, Cannaregio 6099, 30124 Venice; tel. (041) 5223323; f. 1939; modern art, Venetian art, architecture, periodicals; Chair. GIORGIO FANTONI; Gen. Man. MASSIMO VITTA ZELMAN.

Marsilio Editori: S. Croce 518A, Fondamenta S. Chiara, 30135 Venice; tel. (041) 5207188; fax 5238352; f. 1961; literature, arts, fiction, history, music, cinema, philosophy, social sciences; Man.

ITALY

Dirs Dott. EMANUELA BASSETTI, Dott. PAOLO LENARDA, Dott. MARIA CONCETIA FOZZER.

Verona
Bertani Editore Srl: Via Interr. Acqua Morta 31, 37129 Verona; tel. (045) 32686; f. 1973; politics, literature, anthropology, sociology, theatre, cinema, geography, humanities, history of Verona, psychology, cultural journals; Man. Dir MARIO QUARANTA; Editorial Dir GIORGIO BERTANI.

Arnoldo Mondadori Editore: Via Arnoldo Mondadori 15, 37131 Verona; tel. (045) 934602; telex 480071; fax 934566; f. 1946; children's books; Man. Editor MARGHERITA FORESTAN.

Vicenza
Neri Pozza Editore sdf—Folli Pozza: Contrà Oratorio dei Servi 19–21, 36100 Vicenza; tel. (0444) 320787; f. 1946; art, fiction, history, politics; Man. Dir NERI POZZA.

Government Publishing House
Istituto Poligrafico e Zecca dello Stato: Piazza Verdi 10, 00198 Rome; tel. (06) 85081; f. 1928; State publishing house (Italian State Stationery Office); art, literary, scientific, technical books and reproductions; Chair. Dr GIOVANNI RUGGERI; Gen. Dir ALFREDO MAGGI.

PUBLISHERS' ASSOCIATION
Associazione Italiana Editori: Via Delle Erbe 2, 20121 Milan; tel. (02) 8059244; telex 335550; fax 89010863; f. 1869; Via Crescenzio 19, 00193 Rome; tel. (06) 6540298; fax 6872426; Pres. SERGIO POLILLO; Dir PIETRO PIZZONI.

Radio and Television

In 1989 there were 15,009,268 licensed radio receivers and 14,851,310 licensed television receivers.

In April 1975 a law was designed to guarantee the political independence of the RAI and the objectivity of its news coverage. Notably, the new law sought to increase the autonomy of the two existing television channels and to reinforce parliamentary supervision of programme planning. Since the state monopoly on broadcasting was abolished in 1976, approximately 450 local private commercial television stations have been set up all over Italy. Although electronically-transmitted national networks in competition to RAI are technically illegal, seven stations in particular are national networks. In 1989 a Catholic television network was inaugurated. More than one thousand private local radio stations have also begun broadcasting since a court case in 1975 established the right of every citizen to free local information. In 1987 the Italian Constitutional Court granted private radio stations permission to launch commercial international stations.

Radiotelevisione Italiana (RAI-TV): Viale Mazzini 14, 00195 Rome; tel. (06) 3878; telex 61142; fax 3606070; f. 1924; a public share capital company; a permanent parliamentary commission of senators and deputies from all political groups formulates and oversees general guidelines for programmes; the board of directors nominates the President and Vice-President from within its members and appoints the Director-General; Pres. ENRICO MANCA; Vice-Pres. LEO BIRZOLI; Dir-Gen. GIANNI PASQUARELLI.

RADIO
Programmes comprise the National Programme (general), Second Programme (recreational), Third Programme (educational); there are also regional programmes in Italian and in the languages of ethnic minorities. The Foreign and Overseas Service (Radio Roma) broadcasts in 27 languages to Africa, the Americas, Australia, Europe, Japan, the Near East and South Asia.

TELEVISION
There are three RAI television channels, RAI Uno, RAI Due and RAI Tre. There are local programmes in Italian and also in German for the Alto Adige. Seven private stations (Canale 5, Dee Jay TV, Video Music, Euro TV, Italia Uno, Rete A and Rete Quattro) have nationwide networks.

Canale 5: Palazzo dei Cigni, Milano 2, 20090 Segrate, Milan; tel. (02) 21621; telex 316197; f. 1979.

Italia Uno: Via F. Testi 7, 200090 Milan; tel. 6073881.

Rete Quattro: Via Marconi 27, 20090 Segrate, Milan; tel. 216001.

Finance

(cap. = capital; p.u. = paid up; res = reserves; dep. = deposits; m. = million; brs = branches; amounts in lire)

There are more than 1,100 banks in Italy, with a total of over 12,000 branches. Many of them are state controlled, including the majority of the large banks. There are more than 100 private banks, and a large number of co-operative and savings banks (*banche popolari, casse di risparmio, casse rurali*) of widely ranging size and importance. In addition, there are 90 specialized credit institutions which provide medium- and long-term finance, together with other services outside the scope of the banks. In early 1987 reforms giving the Central Bank the right to authorize commercial banks to establish merchant banking subsidiaries were announced.

BANKING
Central Bank
Banca d'Italia: Via Nazionale 91, 00184 Rome; tel. (06) 47921; telex 630045; fax 4747820; f. 1893; cap. 300m., res 3,791,624m. (Dec. 1989); since 1926 the Bank has had the sole right to issue notes in Italy; Gov. Dott. CARLO AZEGLIO CIAMPI; Gen. Man. Dott. LAMBERTO DINI; 98 brs.

Major Commercial Banks
Banca Agricola Mantovana SpA: Corso Vittorio Emanuele 30, 46100 Mantova; tel. (0376) 3311; telex 304265; fax 331261; f. 1871; cap. and res 676,231m., dep. 3,592,529m. (Dec. 1989); Chair. PIERMARIA PACCHIONI; Gen. Man. MARCELLO MELANI; 100 brs.

Banca Agricola Milanese SpA: Via Mazzini 9-11, 20123 Milan; tel. (02) 88091; telex 310608; fax 8693745; f. 1874; cap. 34,500m., res 274,378m., dep. 1,741,385m. (Dec. 1989); Pres. FRANCESCO CESARINI; Gen. Man. GIULIO PALUMBO; 47 brs.

Banca d'America e d'Italia SpA (BAI): Via Borgogna 8, 20122 Milan; tel. (02) 77951; telex 311350; fax 77952439; f. 1917; cap. 46,246m., res 437,342m., dep. 4,401,662m. (Dec. 1989); Chair. EUGENIO CONFALONIERI; Man. Dir GIANEMILIO OSCULATI; 98 brs.

Banca Antoniana: Via 8 Febbraio 5, 35100 Padova; tel. (049) 839111; telex 430252; fax 839658; f. 1893; cap. 6,087m., res 369,851m., dep. 2,709,463m. (Dec. 1989); Pres. Dr DINO MARCHIORELLO; Gen. Man. SILVANO PONTELLO; 54 brs.

Banca Commerciale Italiana SpA—COMIT: Piazza della Scala 6, 20121 Milan; tel. (02) 88501; telex 310080; fax 88503026; f. 1894; cap. 1,050,000m., res 2,487,432m., dep. 434,848,765m. (Dec. 1989); Chair. SERGIO SIGLIENTI; Gen. Mans M. ARCARI, L. FAUSTI; 536 brs, and many overseas brs.

Banca Credito Agrario Bresciano SpA: Via Trieste 8, 25175 Brescia; tel. (030) 22931; telex 301558; fax 2293802; f. 1883; cap. 87,500m., res 213,006m., dep. 5,387,887m. (Dec. 1989); Chair. DOMENICO BIANCHI; Gen. Man. VOLFANGO SOMMAZZI; 81 brs.

Banca del Friuli SpA: Via Vittorio Veneto 20, 33100 Udine; tel. (0432) 4921; telex 450152; fax 482294; f. 1872; cap. 30,000m., res 268,823m., dep. 382,505m. (Dec. 1989); Pres. Dott. PAOLO MALIGNANI; Gen. Man. FLAVIO BOVO; 81 brs.

Banca Nazionale dell'Agricoltura SpA: Via Salaria 231, 00199 Rome; tel. (06) 85881; telex 625330; fax 85883396; f. 1921; cap. 171,000m., res 1,588,067m., dep. 12,330,936m. (Dec. 1989); Chair. Count Dott. GIOVANNI AULETTA ARMENISE; Man. Dirs Dott. ANTONIO CASSELLA, LUCIANO CHRISTOFANI; 238 brs including brs abroad.

Banca Nazionale delle Comunicazioni: Via S. Martino della Battaglia 4, 00185 Rome; tel. (06) 46761; telex 625593; fax 46763555; f. 1927; cap. 10,509m., res 80,644m., dep. 1,966,453m. (Dec. 1989); Pres. Prof. LUIGI CAPPUGI; Gen. Man. Dott. NATALE GILIO; 51 brs.

Banca Nazionale del Lavoro: Via Vittorio Veneto 119, 00187 Rome; tel. (06) 47021; telex 621030; f. 1913; cap. 1,579,295m., res 2,778,965m., dep. 82,373,487m. (1989); Chair. of the Board Prof. GIAMPIERO CANTONI; Mans Dr UMBERTO D'ADDOSIO, Dr PIER DOMENICO GALLO, Prof. PAOLO SAVONA; 449 brs incl. 12 overseas brs.

Banca Popolare Commercio e Industria Srl: Via della Moscova 33, 20121 Milan; tel. (02) 62751; telex 310276; fax 6599072; f. 1888; cap. 13,206m., res 248,089m., dep. 2,444,419m. (Dec. 1989); Chair. ENRICO GIANZINI; Gen. Man. GIUSEPPE VIGORELLI; 30 brs.

Banca Popolare dell' Emilia Srl: Via San Carlo 8/20, 41100 Modena; tel. (059) 202111; telex 511392; fax 220537; f. 1867; cap. 2,532m., res 313,588m., dep. 3,558,175m. (Dec. 1989); Chair. Avv. PIER LUIGI COLIZZI; Gen. Man. Avv. FAUSTO BATTINI; 78 brs.

Banca Popolare di Bergamo Srl: Piazza Vittorio Veneto 8, 24100 Bergamo; tel. (035) 392111; telex 300410; fax 221417; f. 1869; co-operative bank; cap. 28,273m., res 1,425,826m., dep. 8,629,463m. (Dec. 1989); Chair. E. ZANETTI; Gen. Man. GIUSEPPE A. BANFI; 133 brs.

Banca Popolare di Cremona Srl: Via Cesare Battisti 14, 26100 Cremona; tel. (0372) 4041; telex 321099; fax 404362; f. 1865; cap. 7,545m., res 111,775m., dep. 1,854,382m. (Dec. 1989); Pres. Dott. ANGELO DUCHI; Gen. Man. Dott. FRANCO MICHELOTTI; 31 brs.

Banca Popolare di Lecco SpA: Piazza Garibaldi 10, 00059 Lecco; tel. (0341) 480111; telex 380003; fax 480279; f. 1872; cap. 64,444m.,

ITALY
Directory

res 153,142m., dep. 2,134,459m. (Dec. 1989); Pres. Prof. ROBERTO RUOZI; Gen. Man. CESARI CALETTI; 71 brs.

Banca Popolare di Milano Srl: Piazza F. Meda 4, 20121 Milan; tel. (02) 77001; telex 310202; fax 77002993; f. 1865; cap. 72,580m., res 1,097,794m., dep. 11,061,391m. (Dec. 1989); Pres. PIERO SCHLESINGER; Gen. Man. ALDO COVA; 22 brs.

Banca Popolare di Novara Srl: Via Carlo Negroni 12, 28100 Novara; tel. (0321) 4451; telex 200371; fax 29012; f. 1871; co-operative bank; cap. 65,183m., res 1,684,901m., dep. 11,895,405m. (Dec. 1989); Chair. ROBERTO DI TIERI; Man. Dirs PIERO BONGIANINO, CARLO PIANTANIDA; 404 brs and agencies.

Banca Popolare Veneta Srl: Piazza Salvemini 18, 35131 Padova; tel. (049) 8296111; telex 430664; fax 843225; f. 1866; cap. 23,656m., res 359,482m., dep. 2,754,895m. (Dec. 1989); Chair. Dott. GIORGIO DE BENEDETTI; Gen. Man. Dott. ANTONIO CEOLA; 92 brs and agencies.

Banca Popolare di Verona Srl: Piazza Nogara 2, 37121 Verona; tel. (045) 930111; telex 480009; fax 930424; f. 1867; cap. 9,760,996m., res 1,054,209m., dep. 3,901,133m. (Dec. 1989); Pres. Prof. GIORGIO ZANOTTO; Gen. Man. FEDERICO PEPE; 109 brs and agencies.

Banca Provinciale Lombarda SpA: Via Gennaro Sora 4, 24100 Bergamo; tel. (035) 394111; telex 300140; fax 394292; f. 1932; cap. 160,000m., res 166,098m., dep. 4,742,783m. (Dec. 1989); Chair. CARLO GAY; Man. Dir GIUSEPPE MAZZARELLO; 143 brs.

Banca San Paolo-Brescia SpA: POB 346, Corso Martiri della Libertà 13, 25100 Brescia; tel. (030) 29921; telex 300010; fax 2992734; f. 1888; cap. 85,000m., res 184,070m., dep. 3,313,414m. (Dec. 1989); Pres. Dott. Ing. ADOLFO LOMBARDI; Gen. Man. Dott. ALBERTO VALDEMBRI; 85 brs.

Banca Toscana SpA: Via del Corso 6, 50122 Florence; tel. (055) 43911; telex 570507; f. 1904; cap. 276,000m., res 772,287m., dep. 11,297,900m. (Dec. 1989); Pres. GIUSEPPE BARTOLOMEI; Man. Dir. Rag. MARIO VASETTI; 205 brs.

Banca Popolare Vicentina Srl (fmrly Banca Popolare di Vicenza): Via Battaglione Framarin 18, 36100 Vicenza; tel. (0444) 991111; telex 480092; fax 991215; f. 1866; cap. 6,202m., res 282,626m., dep. 1,827,366m. (Dec. 1989); Pres. GIUSEPPE NARDINI; Gen. Man. LUCIANO GENTILINI; 64 brs and agencies.

Banco Ambrosiano Veneto SpA: Piazza Paolo Ferrari 10, 20121 Milan; tel. (02) 85941; telex 321520; fax (02) 807276; f. 1989 by merger of Banca Cattolica del Veneto and Nuovo Banco Ambrosiano; commercial bank; share cap. 606,116m., res 802,151m., total assets 12,316,135m. (Dec. 1989); Chair. Prof. Avv. GIOVANNI BAZOLI; Gen. Man. Dott. CARLO SALVATORI; 336 brs.

Banco Lariano SpA: Piazza Cavour 15, 22100 Como; tel. (031) 3181; telex 311046; fax 451895; f. 1908; cap. 250,000m., res 394,034m., dep. 5,580,654m. (Dec. 1989); Chair. Dr ROBERTO ARDIGO; Gen. Man. Dott. GIORGIO BRAMBILLA; 126 brs.

Banco di Napoli: Via Toledo 177-178, 80132 Naples; tel. (081) 7911111; telex 710227; f. 1539; chartered public institution with no shareholders; cap. 752,425m., res 483,768m., dep. 20,542,160m. (Dec. 1989); Chair. Prof. LUIGI COCCIOLI; Man. Dir Prof. FERDINANDO VENTRIGLIA; 499 brs.

Banco di Roma SpA: Viale U. Tupini 180, 00144 Rome; tel. (06) 54451; telex 616184; fax 54453154; f. 1880; cap. 1,200,000m., res 3,427,649m., dep. 55,085,818m. (Dec. 1989); Chair. ANTONIO ZURZULO; Man. Dirs Dott. GIUSEPPE GRECO, Dott. ANTONIO NOTTOLA, Dott. MARCELLO TACCI; 365 brs including agencies and overseas brs.

Banco San Geminiano e San Prospero SpA: Via Mondatora 14, 41100 Modena; tel. (059) 200111; telex 510603; fax 200571; f. 1897; cap. 32,400m., res 405,187m., dep. 3,961,965m. (Dec. 1989); Chair. VITTORINO CARETTI; Gen. Man. FRANCO FRANCESCHINI; 82 brs.

Banco di Santo Spirito SpA: Largo A. Fochetti 16, 00154 Rome; tel. (06) 51721; telex 623270; fax 51722850; f. 1605; 54.6% owned by Cassa di Risparmio di Roma; cap. 1,229,316m., dep. 21,609,830m. (Dec. 1989); Chair. PELLEGRINO CAPALDO; Man. Dir CESARE GERONZI; 240 brs.

Banco di Sardegna: Viale Umberto 36, 07100 Sassari; tel. (079) 226000; telex 790049; f. 1953; public credit institution; cap. 183,480m., res 487,979m., dep. 6,109,188m. (1989); Pres. and Chair. Prof. LORENZO IDDA; Gen. Man. Dr ANGELO GIAGU DE MARTINI; 90 brs.

Banco di Sicilia: Via Generale Magliocco 1, 90141 Palermo; tel. (091) 274111; telex 910050; f. 1951; public credit institution; cap. 186,222m., res 416,603m., dep. 10,718,986m. (Dec. 1989); Chair. Prof. GIANNINO PARRAVICINI; Gen. Man. Dr OTTAVIO SALAMONE; 351 brs.

Cassa Centrale di Risparmio VE per le Province Siciliane: Via F. Cordova 76, 90143 Palermo; tel. (091) 6291111; telex 910029; fax 6292550; f. 1861; savings bank; cap. and res 330,216m., dep. 7,281,589m. (Dec. 1989); Pres. Dott. GIOVANNI FERRARO; Gen. Man. Dott. FELICE SCORDINO; 238 brs.

Cassa di Risparmio di Firenze: Via Bufalini 4/6, 50122 Florence; tel. (055) 27801; telex 572391; fax 289508; f. 1829; cap. 312,000m., res 12,175m., dep. 6,892,866m. (Dec. 1989); Chair. and Pres. LAPO MAZZEI; Gen. Man. GIOVANNI PAGLIAI; 177 brs.

Cassa di Risparmio di Genova e Imperia: Via Cassa di Risparmio 15, 16123 Genova; tel. (010) 20911; telex 270089; fax 280013; f. 1846; cap. 382,600m., res 54,529m., dep. 5,075,750m. (Dec. 1989); Pres. Avv. GIOVANNI DAGNINO; Gen. Man. Dott. GIOVANNI BERNESCHI; 137 brs.

Cassa di Risparmio di Prato: Via degli Alberti 2, 50047 Prato; tel. (0574) 4921; telex 572382; fax 492507; f. 1830; savings bank; cap. 1,067,030m., res 177,638m., dep. 1,502,928m. (Dec. 1989); Pres. Avv. MAURO GIOVANNELLI; Gen. Man. BRUNO BIANCHI; 23 brs.

Cassa di Risparmio della Provincia di Bolzano—Südtiroler Landessparkasse: Via Cassa di Risparmio 12B, 39100 Bolzano; tel. (0471) 901111; telex 400090; fax 901202; f. 1854; cap. and res 202,175m., dep. 2,277,413m. (Dec. 1987); Pres. Dott. FRANZ SPÖGLER; Gen. Man. Dott. FRANZ OBERMAIR; 52 brs.

Cassa di Risparmio delle Provincie Lombarde (CARIPLO): Via Monte di Pietà 8, 20121 Milan; tel. (02) 88661; telex 313010; fax 88662356; f. 1823; savings bank; res 3,835,429m., dep. 30,859,714m., total assets 70,685m., (Dec. 1988); Chair. ROBERTO MAZZOTTA; Man. Dir SANDRO MOLINARI; 435 brs.

Cassa di Risparmio di Roma: Via del Corso 320, 00186 Rome; tel. (06) 67071; telex 613541; fax 67072464; f. 1836; savings bank; cap. 25,000m., res 928,742m., dep. 11,181,285m. (Dec. 1989); Chair. Prof. PELLEGRINO CAPALDO; Gen. Man. CESARE GERONZI; 183 brs.

Cassa di Risparmio di Torino: Via XX Settembre 31, 10121 Turin; tel. (011) 6921692; telex 212278; fax 638203; f. 1827; savings bank; cap. 700,000m., res 527,558m., dep. 12,504,169m. (Dec. 1989); Chair. Prof. ENRICO FILIPPI; Gen. Man. Dir Dott. GIORGIO GIOVANDO; 225 brs.

Cassa di Risparmio di Venezia: San Marco 4216, 30124 Venice; tel. (041) 5291111; telex 410660; fax 5292459; f. 1822; cap. and res 728,424m., dep. 4,184,607m. (Dec. 1989); Pres. Prof. GIULIANO SEGRE; Gen. Man. Rag. PAOLO BORTOLUZZI; 72 brs.

Cassa di Risparmio di Verona, Vicenza, Belluno e Ancona: Via G. Garibaldi 1, 37121 Verona; tel. (045) 936111; telex 480056; fax 591516; f. 1825; cap. 1,097,336m., res 2,553m., dep. 8,311,270m. (Dec. 1989); Pres. Avv. ALBERTO PAVESI; Gen. Man. Rag. ANTONIO FINOTTI; 183 brs.

Credito Commerciale SpA: Via Armorari 4, 20123 Milan; tel. (02) 88241; telex 321573; fax 780218; f. 1907; subsidiary of Monte dei Paschi de Siena; cap. 100,000m., res 184,165m., dep. 3,262,416m. (Dec. 1989); Pres. ALBERTO QUADRIO CURZIO; Gen. Man. Dott. BENITO BRONZETTI; 87 brs.

Credito Emiliano: Via Emilia S. Pietro 4, 42100 Reggio-Emilia; tel. (0522) 4501; telex 530305; fax 33969; f. 1910; cap. 38,433m., res 202,880m., dep. 1,629,718m. (Dec. 1989); Pres. GIORGIO FERRARI; Gen. Man. FRANCO BIZZOCHI; 53 brs.

Credito Italiano SpA: Piazza Cordusio, 20123 Milan; tel. (02) 88621; telex 310103; f. 1870; cap. 800,000m., res 27,722m., dep. 33,070,664m. (Dec. 1989); Chair. Prof. NATALINO IRTI; Man. Dirs Prof. PIERO BARUCCI, PIER CARLO MARENGO; 535 brs.

Credito Lombardo SpA: Via San Pietro all'Orto 24, 20121 Milan; tel. (02) 77361; telex 334889; fax 7736306; f. 1924; cap. 64,000m., res 153,733m., dep. 1,373,102m. (Dec. 1989); Pres. Dr VIRGILIO DAGNINO; Gen. Man. Rag. ALFREDO NERI; 8 brs.

Credito Romagnolo SpA: POB 775, Via Zamboni 20, 40126 Bologna; tel. (051) 338111; telex 510148; f. 1896; cap. 137,085m., res 865,494m., dep. 6,932,077m. (Dec. 1989); Pres. Prof. FRANCESCO BIGNARDI; Gen. Man. Dott. ROMANO CERONI; 206 brs.

Credito Varesino SpA: Via Vittorio Veneto 2, 21100 Varese; tel. (0332) 829111; telex 326695; fax 829455; f. 1898; cap. 60,000m., res 199,290m., dep. 3,075,615m. (Dec. 1989); Chair. RINALDO OSSOLA; Chief Gen. Man. ANDREA GIBELLINI; 68 brs.

Istituto Bancario Italiano SpA (IBI): Via Manzoni 3, 20121 Milan; tel. (02) 88901; telex 310676; fax 88904520; f. 1918; cap. 200,000m., res 261,515m., dep. 4,727,945m. (Dec. 1989); Chair. MARIO TALAMONA; Gen. Man. Rag. ANTONIO GRU; 74 brs.

Istituto Bancario San Paolo di Torino: Piazza San Carlo 156, 10121 Turin; tel. (011) 5551; telex 212040; fax 513826; Public Law Bank; f. 1563; cap. 2,389,730m., res 1,054,740m., dep. 24,907,919m. (Dec. 1989); Chair. Prof. GIOVANNI ZANDANO; Chief Gen. Man. Prof. ZEFFERINO FRANCO; 435 brs.

Monte dei Paschi di Siena: Piazza Salimbeni 3, 53100 Siena; tel. (0577) 294111; telex 572346; fax 294985; f. 1472; public law credit institution; res 2,566,405m., dep. 24,191,831m. (Dec. 1989); Chair. PIERO BARUCCI; Chief Gen. Man. CARLO ZINI; 531 brs.

FINANCIAL INSTITUTIONS

CENTROBANCA (Banca Centrale di Credito Popolare) SpA: Corso Europa 20, 20122 Milan; tel. (02) 77811; telex 320387; f. 1946; cap. 150,000m., res 537,117m., dep. 8,007,100m. (Dec. 1988); central organization for medium- and long-term operations of Banche Popolari (co-operative banks) throughout Italy; Chair. LINO VENINI; Gen. Man. GIAN GIACOMO FAVERIO; 322 brs.

Consorzio di Credito per le Opere Pubbliche—CREDIOP: Via XX Settembre 30, 00187 Rome; tel. (06) 47711; telex 620317; fax 47715950; f. 1919; cap. and res 2,095,000m.; provides loans to industrial, commercial and service companies, medium- and long-term loans to public authorities and their agencies, and export credits; Pres. and Chair. Ing. PAOLO BARATTA; Gen. Man. Ing. LUIGI MAZZONI.

INTERBANCA (Banca per Finanziamenti a Medio e Lungo Termine SpA): Corso Venezia 56, 20121 Milan; tel. (02) 77311; telex 312649; f. 1961; cap. 88,466m., res 278,826m. (1989); Pres. Dott. ALBERTO RICCARDI; Gen. Man. Dott. EMANUELE DE BERNARDI.

Istituto Mobiliare Italiano (IMI): Viale dell'Arte 25, 00144 Rome; tel. (06) 54501; telex 610256; f. 1931; public-law credit institute; provides medium- and long-term financing to domestic manufacturing and service sector companies, and offers financial services in Europe and the USA; outstanding loans US $29,675m. (March 1990); Pres. Dr LUIGI ARCUTI; Dir-Gen. RAINER MASERA; 10 regional offices in Italy.

Istituto per l'Assistenza allo Sviluppo del Mezzogiorno (IASM) (Institute for assistance in the development of southern Italy): Viale Pilsudski 124, 00197 Rome; tel. (06) 84721; telex 622424; f. 1962; aids investment to promote economic development in the South; Pres. Prof. ANDREA SABA.

Istituto Regionale per il Finanziamento alle Industrie in Sicilia (IRFIS): Via Giovanni Bonanno 47, 90143 Palermo; tel. (091) 300342; telex 910332; fax 6655909; f. 1950; provides credit facilities for business ventures in Sicily, credit for domestic and export trade and for developing tourist facilities; Pres. Dott. ANTONIO MUCCIOLI; Dir-Gen. GIUSEPPE BIONDO.

Istituto per lo Sviluppo Economico dell'Italia Meridionale—ISVEIMER: Via A. De Gasperi 71, 80133 Naples; tel. (081) 7853111; telex 711020; fax 420043; f. 1938; public credit institution granting medium-term loans in mainland southern Italy; cap. and res 457,800m.; Pres. GIUSEPPE DI VAGNO; Dir-Gen. Dott. BENITO PLOTINO; 8 brs.

Mediobanca SpA, Banca di Credito Finanziario: Via Filodrammatici 10, 20121 Milan; tel. (02) 88291; telex 311093; f. 1946; deals in all medium- and long-term credit transactions; accepts medium-term time deposits either direct or through all the branches (approx. 1,100) of Banca Commerciale Italiana, Credito Italiano and Banco di Roma, and their subsidiaries. It grants advances of any type, provided they have a duration of from one to 20 years. It also promotes and manages syndicates to underwrite and/or place bond issues and syndicates to underwrite capital increases; cap. 170,000m. listed on the Italian Stock Exchanges; total res 906,495m. (June 1986); 'privatization' authorized in 1988. Chair. FRANCESCO CINGANO; Gen. Man. VICENZO MARANGHI.

BANKERS' ORGANIZATIONS

Associazione Bancaria Italiana: Piazza del Gesú 49, 00186 Rome; tel. (06) 67671; telex 622107; fax 6767457; Via della Posta 3, 20123 Milan; tel. (02) 806689; telex 324195; fax 878684; f. 1919; Pres. Prof. PIERO BARUCCI; Gen. Man. Dr FELICE GIANANI; membership (1,110 mems) is comprised of the following institutions: public credit institutions; banks of national interest (big commercial banks); private banks and bankers; co-operative banks; saving banks; rural banks; agricultural credit institutions; mortgage banks; industrial credit institutions; leasing and factoring; finance houses.

Associazione fra le Casse di Risparmio Italiane: Viale di Villa Grazioli 23, 00198 Rome; tel. (06) 8841261; telex 622033; fax 8540192; f. 1912; Pres. ROBERTO MAZZOTTA; Gen. Man. Dott. EDOARDO FATTORINI.

Associazione fra gli Istituti Regionale Di Mediocredito: Piazza della Marina 1, 00196 Rome; tel (06) 3225150; telex 620311; fax 3225135; Pres. Prof. ANGELO CALOIA; Gen. Man. Dott. ANTONIO DE VITO.

Associazione fra le Società di Factoring Italiene: Corso Europa 13, 20122 Milan; tel. (02) 7704217; fax 7704205; Pres. Prof. ROBERTO RUOZI; Sec. Gen. Prof. ALESSANDRO CARRETTA.

Associazione Nazionale Aziende Ordinarie di Credito—ASSBANK: Via Domenichino 5, 20149 Milan; tel. (02) 48018137; telex 334355; fax 48010278; Piazza di Spagna 20, 00187 Rome; Pres. Dott. Prof. TANCREDI BIANCHI; Dir-Gen. Dott. GIOVANNI LA SCALA.

Associazione Nazionale fra le Banche Popolari: Via Nazionale 230, 00184 Rome; tel. (06) 464447; Pres. Dott. GIULIANO MONTERASTELLI; Dir-Gen. Dott. GIORGIO CARDUCCI.

Associazione Nazionale fra gli Istituti di Credito Agrario (ANICA): Via A. Bertoloni 3, 00197 Rome; tel. (06) 877506; telex 620311; fax 877506; f. 1946; Pres. Prof. GIUSEPPE GUERRIERI; Sec.-Gen. Dr ERNESTO DE MEDIO.

Associazione Sindacale fra le Aziende del Credito—ASSICREDITO: Via G. Paisiello 5, 00198 Rome; tel. (06) 858041; f. 1947; Via della Posta 7, 20123 Milan; Pres. Dott. CARMELO PETYX; Dir Dott. GIUSEPPE CAPO.

Associazione Italiana delle Società Edenti Digestione Mobiliareed Immobiliare: Via In Lucina 12, 00186 Rome; tel. (06) 6893203; telex 630274; fax 6893262; Pres. Prof. GUSTAVO VISENTINI; Sec. Gen. Prof. GUIDO CAMMARANO.

Associazione Italiana Leasing—ASSILBA: Piazza di Priscilla 4, 00199 Rome; tel. (06) 8390741; telex 626186; fax 2389045; Pres. (vacant); Sec. Gen. Prof. RENATO CLARIZIA.

THE STOCK EXCHANGE

Commissione Nazionale per le Società e la Borsa (CONSOB) (Commission for Companies and the Stock Exchange): Via Isonzo 19, 00198 Rome; tel. (06) 84771; telex 612434; f. 1974 to have regulatory control over companies quoted on stock exchanges, convertible bonds, unlisted securities, insider trading. A law passed in April 1983 extended its powers to all forms of public saving except bank deposits and mutual funds; Chair. Dott. BRUNO PAZZI; Governors ALDO POLINETTI, MARIO BESSONE, VINCENZO MATTURRI. There are 10 stock exchanges, of which the following are the most important:

Genova: Borsa Valori, Via G. Boccardo 1; tel. (010) 2094400; f. 1855; Pres. PAOLO M. PASINI.

Milan: Borsa Valori, Via Camperio 4; tel. (02) 85341; telex 321430; Foreign Relations Dept, tel. (02) 8057674; Pres. ATTILIO VENTURA.

Naples: Borsa Valori, Palazzo Borsa, Piazza Bovio; tel. (081) 269151; Pres. GIORGIO FOCAS.

Rome: Borsa Valori, Via dei Burro 147, 00186; tel. (06) 6792701; f. 1821; Pres. ALBERTO BORTI.

Turin: Borsa Valori, Via San Francesco da Paola 28; tel. (011) 547743; telex 220614; fax 5612193; f. 1850; Pres. Dott. FRANCO CELLINO.

INSURANCE

L'Abeille SpA: Via Leopardi 15, 20123 Milan; tel. (02) 480841; telex 316029; fax 4804331; f. 1956; cap. 8,211m. (July 1986); Chair. Dott. ANTONIO SOZZANI; Man. Dir Dott. PIERRE MERCIER.

Alleanza Assicurazioni SpA: Viale Luigi Sturzo 37, 20154 Milan; tel. (02) 62961; telex 331303; fax 653718; f. 1898; cap. 172,800m. (Sept. 1989); Chair. Dr ALFONSO DESIATA; Vice-Chair. Avv. ENRICO RANDONE; Gen. Mans Dott. VALERIO FLORIO, Dott. DANTE LAMPERTI.

Allianz Pace, Assicurazioni e Riassicurazioni SpA: Piazza Cavour 5, 20121 Milan; tel. (02) 62421; telex 311636; fax 6572684; f. 1919; cap. 15,000m.; Chair. Dott. RAFFAELE DURANTE; Man. Dir CARLO CARLIN.

Assicuratrice Edile SpA: Via A. De Togni 2, 20123 Milan; tel. (02) 88411; telex 334697; fax 8841292; f. 1960; cap. 8,000m. (June 1987); Chair. Dott. GIAN CARLO BORINI; Vice-Pres. Dott. CLAUDIO REICHLIN; Man. Dir Rag. GIAMPIERO SVEVO.

Assicurazioni Generali SpA: Central Head Office: Piazza Duca degli Abruzzi 2, 34132 Trieste; tel. (040) 6711; telex 460190; fax 43863243; Head offices: Piazza San Marco 105, 30124 Venice; Via Tiziano 32, 20145 Milan; f. 1831; cap. 1,166,000m. (June 1990); Chair. and Man. Dir Avv. ENRICO RANDONE; Vice-Chair. ANTOINE BERNHEIM, Dott. FRANCESCO CINGANO, Dott. EUGENIO COPPOLA DI CANZANO, Prince CARLO TORRE e TASSO; Man. Dirs Dott. EUGENIO COPPOLA DI CANZANO, FABIO FEGITZ.

Le Assicurazioni d'Italia (ASSITALIA) SpA: Corso d'Italia 33, 00198 Rome; tel. (06) 84831; telex 611051; f. 1923; cap. 150,000m. (June 1987); Pres. Avv. PIER LUIGI CASSIETTI; Man. Dir Prof. Avv. VINCENZO MUNGARI.

Aurora Assicurazioni SpA: Via R. Montecuccoli 20, 20147 Milan; tel. (02) 41441; telex 312562; fax 48300451; f. 1947; cap. 50,000m. (July 1987); Chair. Avv. EMILIO DUSI; Vice-Chair. Dott. CAMILLO GIUSSANI; Man. Dir AUGUSTO TRAINA.

Ausonia Assicurazioni SpA: Palazzo Ausonia, Milanofiori, 20089 Rozzano, Milan; tel. (02) 824731; telex 321225; fax 8240641; f. 1907; cap. 296,302m. (June 1990); Chair. Dott. GAETANO LAZZATI; Vice-Chair. Dott. FRANCESCO DUSI; Man. Dir DELLA GIULIO GRAZIOLI.

Compagnia Assicuratrice Unipol SpA: Via Stalingrado 45, 40128 Bologna; tel. (051) 507111; telex 510674; fax 375349; f. 1962; cap.

ITALY

96,806m. (June 1990); Chair. Dott. ENEA MAZZOLI; Vice-Chair. and Man. Dir Dott. GIACINTO MILITELLO.

Compagnia Italiana di Assicurazioni—COMITAS SpA: Via Martin Piaggio 13/A, 16122 Genova; tel. (010) 55261; telex 270543; fax 876728; f. 1948; cap. 30,000m. (June 1990); Chair. Dott. GIACOMO MUSSETTI; Vice-Chair. Dott. JODY VENDER; Man. Dir Dott. MANILO VISCONTI.

Compagnia Latina di Assicurazioni SpA: Strada 6, Palazzo A, 20090 Assago, (M1), Milanofiori; tel. (02) 824731; telex 310083; fax 8240644; f. 1958; cap. 58,367m. (January 1990); Chair. Prof. LUIGI SPAVENTA; Vice-Chair Dott. FRANCESCO DOSI; Man. Dir SILLA GIULIO GRAZIOLI.

Compagnia Tirrena: Via Massimi 158, 00136 Rome; tel. (06) 33071; telex 621394; fax 33073382; f. 1945; cap. 175,000m. (Feb. 1990); Chair. and Gen. Man. Dott. GIOVANNI AMABILE.

Compagnie Riunite di Assicurazione (CRA): Via Consolata 3, 10122 Turin; tel. (011) 57741; telex 212597; fax 545281; f. 1935; cap. 40,000m. (June 1987); Chair. Ing. M. LUC BROSSIER; Man. Dir Dott. MARIO PASCUCCI.

L'Edera SpA: Piazzale de Matthaeis 41, 03100 Frosinone; tel. (0775) 872579; telex 626152; fax 873052; f. 1960; cap. 1,000m. (March 1986); Pres. Avv. GIUSEPPE TODINI; Man. Dir Dott. GUISEPPE ZEPPIERI.

FATA (Fondo Assicurativo Tra Agricoltori) SpA: Via Urbana 169/A, 00184 Rome; tel. (06) 47651; telex 620838; fax 4871187; f. 1927; cap. 20,000m. (June 1987); Chair. ARCANGELO LOBIANCO; Man. Dir LUIGI SCOTTI; Gen. Man. FRANCO RIZZI.

LA FENICE RI. SpA—Compagnia di Riassicurazioni: Via Assarotti 5, 16122 Genova; tel. (010) 870293; telex 271297; fax 817955; cap. 50,000m. (May 1988); Chair. Dott. CARLO GALEAZZI; Man. Dir Dott. SERGIO CHIOSTRI; Gen. Man. EDOARDO DANTI.

La Fiduciaria: Via A. Finelli 8, 40126 Bologna; tel. (051) 240901; telex 511491; fax 243030; f. 1970; cap. 8,000m. (June 1990); Chair. JEAN PERROUD; Vice-Chair. PIER UGO ANDREINI; Man. Dir Dott. Ing. SERGIO BEDINI.

Firs Italiana di Assicurazioni SpA: Via Adelmo Niccolai 24, 00155 Rome; tel. (06) 406911; telex 620185; fax 4061459; f. 1965; cap. 36,120m. (1990); Chair. Avv. CARLO BALESTRA; Vice-Chair. Dott. SANDRO CALLONI; Man. Dir GIANCARLO CANEVARI.

La Fondiaria Assicurazioni SpA: Via Lorenzo il Magnifico 1, 50129 Florence; tel. (055) 47941; telex 570430; fax 476026; cap. 104,878m. (1990); Chair. ALFONSO SCARPA; Vice-Chair. Dott CARLO GALEAZZI; Man. Dir Dott. SERGIO CHIOSTRI.

Intercontinentale Assicurazioni SpA: Via di Priscilla 101, 00199 Rome; tel. (06) 83001; telex 611155; fax 8319903; f. 1961; cap. 100,000m. (June 1990); Chair. WALTER GEISER; Man. Dir Dott. ENNIO BAIOCCHI.

Istituto Nazionale delle Assicurazioni (INA): Via Sallustiana 51, 00187 Rome; tel. (06) 47221; telex 610336; fax 47224559; f. 1912; National Insurance Institute; a state institute with an autonomous management; Chair. Avv. LORENZO PALLESI; Gen. Man. Dott. MARIO FORNARI.

Italia Assicurazioni SpA: Via Fieschi 9, 16121 Genova; tel. (010) 53801; telex 270136; fax 592856; f. 1872; cap. 40,000m.; Chair. ALFONSO SCARPA; Vice-Chair. Dott. CARLO GALEAZZI; Man. Dir Dott. CLAUDIO REICHLIN.

ITAS, Istituto Trentino-Alto Adige per Assicurazioni: Via Mantova 67, 38100 Trento; tel. (0461) 982112; telex 400884; fax 980297; f. 1821; cap. 25,000m. (March 1988); Chair. Dott. EDO BENEDETTI; Dir-Gen. Dott. ETTORE LOMBARDO.

Latina Renana Assicurazioni SpA: Via Nazario Sauro 26, 40121 Bologna; tel. (051) 266567; telex 214661; f. 1959; cap. 16,500m. (May 1986); Chair. Prof. Avv. ALBERTO CALTABIANO; Man. Dir SILLA GIULIO GRAZIOLI.

Lavoro e Sicurtà SpA: Piazza Erculea 13–15, 20122 Milan; tel. (02) 85751; telex 320038; fax 72021420; f. 1963; cap. 5,000m. (June 1986); Chair. and Man. Dir ENZO ZENI; Vice-Chair. Dott. GIOVANNI BIANCHI.

Lloyd Adriatico SpA: Largo Ugo Irneri 1, 34123 Trieste; tel. (040) 77811; telex 460350; fax 7781311; f. 1936; cap. 60,000m. (Dec. 1989); Chair. and Man. Dir Dott. ANTONIO SODARO; Vice-Chair. Avv. MARCO GAMBAZZI.

Lloyd Internazionale SpA: Via Massimi 158, 00136 Rome; tel. (06) 33071; telex 621394; f. 1959; cap. 16,000m. (May 1986); Chair. Prof. ROBERTO TANA; Gen. Man. Dott. LUIGI APUZZO.

Lloyd Italico (Divisione dell'Italia Assicurazioni): Via Fieschi 9, 16121 Genova; tel. (010) 53801; telex 270136; fax 592856; f. 1917; cap. 40,000m.; Chair. ALFONSO SCARPA; Man. Dir Dott. CLAUDIO REICHLIN.

MAA Assicurazioni Auto e Rischi Diversi SpA: Via Tonale 26, 20125 Milan; tel. (02) 69791; telex 334397; f. 1952; cap. 30,000m.; Pres. Dott. Ing. ENRICO BONZANO; Vice-Chair. and Man. Dir GIANCARLO GORRINI; Dirs-Gen. Rag. CARLO GIUSSANI, Dott. RAFFAELE PELLINO.

Minerva Assicurazioni SpA: Via Milano 2, 20090 Segrate, Milan; tel. (02) 216081; telex 321284; fax 21608200; f. 1943; cap. 8,000m. (Sept. 1988); Chair. Dott. CHARLES WYNIGER; Man. Dirs Dott. GIUSEPPE PICCIOLA, Dott. GIAN PIERO PORTIGLIA.

La Nationale Assicurazioni SpA: Piazza del Porto di Ripetta 1, 00186 Rome; tel. (06) 67701; telex 611032; fax 6834089; f. 1962; cap. 20,000m. (June 1987); Pres. M. JEAN PERROUD; Vice-Pres. PIER UGO ANDREINI.

Norditalia Assicurazioni SpA: Viale Certosa 222, 20156 Milan; tel. (02) 30761; telex 331345; fax 3086125; f. 1963; cap. 176,800m. (May 1989); Man. Dir Dott. FERDINANDO MENCONI.

La Previdente Assicurazioni SpA: Via Copernico 38, 20125 Milan; tel. (02) 69561; telex 330488; fax 6889995; f. 1917; cap. 25,000m. (June 1988); Chair. Ing. GIUSEPPE GAROFANO; Man. Dir Dott. ROBERTO PONTREMOLI.

RAS-Riunione Adriatica di Sicurtà: Corso Italia 23, 20122 Milan; tel. (02) 88441; telex 320065; and Piazza della Repubblica 1, 34122 Trieste; tel. (040) 7692; telex 460006; f. 1838; cap. 217,000m., res 995,725m. (Dec. 1988); Chair. and Man. Dir Dott. UMBERTO ZANNI.

SAI—Società Assicuratrice Industriale SpA: Corso Galileo Galilei 12, 10126 Turin; tel. (011) 65621; telex 212080; f. 1921; cap. 165,000m. (June 1987); Chair. Dr Ing. SALVATORE LIGRESTI; Man. Dir Dott. GIORGIO BRINATTI.

SAPA (Security and Property Assurance) SpA: Via Riva Villasanta 3, 20145 Milan; tel. (02) 38841; telex 312061; fax 3490492; f. 1965; cap. 21,879m. (June 1990); Chair. WALTER GEISER; Man. Dir ALDO COSMI.

SARA assicurazioni SpA: Via Po 20, 00198 Rome; tel. (06) 84751; telex 614526; fax 8475223; f. 1924; official insurer for Automobile Club d'Italia; cap. 27,000m. (March 1989); Chair. FILIPPO CARPI DE RESMINI; Gen. Man. MARCO ROCCA.

Savoia: Via S. Vigilio 1, 20142 Milan; tel. (02) 84421; telex 311270; fax 8442388; cap. 24,000m. (Sept. 1986); Chair. Avv. GIOVANNI BONELLI; Dir-Gen. Dr GIORGIO OPPEZZI.

Società Cattolica di Assicurazione: Lungadige Cangrande 16, 37126 Verona; tel. (045) 938711; telex 480482; fax 938601; f. 1896; cap. 13,658m. (Dec. 1989); Chair. Ing. GIULIO BISOFFI; Gen. Man. Dott. EZIO PAOLO REGGIA.

Società Italiana di Assicurazioni, SpA (SIDA): Via Massimi 158, 00136 Rome; tel. (06) 33071; telex 621394; f. 1914; cap. 12,000m.; Chair. ALBERTO PUGLIESE; Gen. Man. Dott. GIOVANNI AMABILE.

Società Italiana Assicurazioni e Riassicurazioni (SIAT): Via B. Bosco 15, 16121 Genova; tel. (010) 55461; telex 270307; fax 562638; f. 1967; cap. 13,125m. (March 1989); Chair. Dott. GIORGIO BUDA; Gen. Man. Dott. GIANCARLO CAMERA.

Società Italiana Cauzioni SpA (SIC): Via Crescenzio 12, 00193 Rome; tel. (06) 6896848; telex 611050; fax 6874418; f. 1948; cap. 15,000m. (Nov. 1989); Chair. Avv. Conte CARLO D'AMELIO; Man. Dir GIANLUIGI BOCCIA.

Società Reale Mutua di Assicurazioni: Via Corte d'Appello 11, 10122 Turin; tel. (011) 55961; telex 215105; fax 546580; f. 1828; res 1,555,966m. (1989); Chair. PIER CARLO ROMAGNOLI; Gen. Mans ITI MIHALICH and GIUSEPPE SOLINAS; Dep. Gen. Mans SERGIO CHIABERTO, LUCIANO CORRADI.

Toro Assicurazioni SpA: Via Arcivescovado 16, 10121 Turin; tel. (011) 57331; telex 221567; f. 1833; cap. 110,000m. (April 1986); Chair. Dott. UMBERTO AGNELLI; Man. Dir Rag. FRANCESCO TORRI.

Unione Italiana di Riassicurazione SpA: Via dei Giuochi Istmici 40, 00194 Rome; tel. (06) 323931; telex 610348; fax 3273398; f. 1922; cap. 100,000m. (Nov. 1987); Chair. Dott. MARIO LUZZATTO; Man. Dir ARRIGO BIANCHI DI LAVAGNA.

Unione Subalpina di Assicurazioni SpA: Via Alfieri 22, 10121 Turin; tel. (011) 55121; telex 221201; fax 549756; f. 1928; cap. 9,187.5m. (June 1986); Chair. Avv. VITTORIO BADINI CONFALONIERI; Man. Dir Dott. ROBERTO GAVAZZI.

Unipol: Via Stalingrado 45, Bologna; tel. (051) 507111; telex 510674; Pres. ENEA MAZZOLI.

Universo Assicurazioni SpA: Via del Pilastro 52, 40127 Bologna; tel. (051) 6431111; telex 511170; fax 6431401; f. 1984; cap. 42,500m. (June 1990); Chair. and Man. Dir Rag. SERGIO GETICI; Gen. Man. Dott. GIORGIO DI GIANSANTE.

Veneta Assicurazioni SpA: Via Enrico degli Scrovegni, 35131 Padova; tel. (049) 848111; telex 430482; fax 848230; f. 1961; cap. 38,000m. (June 1990); Chair. Dott. WALTER GEISER; Man. Dir Dott. GASPARE MASARACCHIA.

Vittoria Assicurazioni SpA: Piazza San Babila 3, 20122 Milan; tel. (02) 77901; telex 331030; fax 780329; cap. 12,000m. (June 1988); Chair. Prof. LUIGI GUATRI; Vice-Chair. Dott. CARLOS ACUTIS; Man. Dir Dott. GIUSEPPE DE'CHIARA.

ITALY

INSURANCE ASSOCIATIONS

Associazione Nazionale fra le Imprese Assicuratrici (ANIA): Head Office: Piazza S. Babila 1, 20122 Milan; tel. (02) 77641; telex 333288; fax 780870; Deputation: Via della Frezza 70, 00186 Rome; tel. (06) 3227141; telex 613621; fax 3227135; f. 1944; Chair. Dott. ENRICO TONELLI; 207 mems.

Trade and Industry

CHAMBERS OF COMMERCE

Unione Italiana delle Camere di Commercio, Industria, Artigianato e Agricoltura (Italian Union of Chambers of Commerce, Industry, Crafts and Agriculture): Piazza Sallustio 21, 00187 Rome; tel. (06) 47041; telex 622327; f. 1954 to promote the development of chambers of commerce, industry, trade and agriculture; Pres. PIERO BASSETTI; Sec.-Gen. Dott. GIUSEPPE CERRONI; 765 mems.

EXPORT INSTITUTE

Istituto Nazionale per il Commercio Estero (ICE) (National Institute for Foreign Trade): Via Liszt 21, EUR, 00100 Rome; tel. (06) 59921; telex 610160; fax 5910508; f. 1919; government agency for the promotion of foreign trade; Pres. Dott. MARCELLO INGHILESI; Dir-Gen. Dott. FERRUCCIO SORTI.

EMPLOYERS' ASSOCIATION

Confederazione Generale dell'Industria Italiana—CONFINDUSTRIA (General Confederation of Italian Industry): Viale dell'Astronomia 30, EUR, 00144 Rome; tel. (06) 59031; telex 611393; f. 1919, re-established 1944; mems: 106 territorial asscns and 98 branch asscns, totalling 100,000 firms and 3,000,000 employers; office in Brussels; Pres. Dott. SERGIO PININFARINA; Dir-Gen. Dott. PAOLO ANNIBALDI.

Principal Affiliated Industrial Organizations

Associazione degli Industriali della Birra e del Malto (Brewers): Via Savoia 29, 00198 Rome; tel. (06) 8413409; telex 614486; fax 8417383; Pres. Ing. ALDO BASSETTI; Pres. Del. CESARE MARTIN; Dir Dott. LUCIANO FONTANELLI.

Associazione Industrie Aerospaziali (AIA) (Aerospace Industries): Via Nazionale 200, 00184 Rome; tel. (06) 460247; telex 622250; fax 4827476; f. 1947; Pres. Dr FABRIZIO FORESIO; Gen. Sec. Dott. SERGIO LIBERI.

Associazione Industrie Siderurgiche Italiane—ASSIDER (Iron and Steel Industries): Via XX Settembre 1, 00187 Rome; tel. (06) 463867; f. 1946; Pres. Ing. ADAMO ADAMI; Dir Gen. Dr GIANCARLO LONGHI; 140 mems.

Associazione Italiana degli Industriali dell' Abbigliamento (Clothing Manufacturers): Foro Buonaparte 70, 20121 Milan; tel. (02) 809016; telex 333594; fax 72002178; f. 1945; produces weekly, fortnightly and annual periodicals; Pres. TINO COSMA; Sec.-Gen. Dott. ADRIANO BENVENUTO; 650 mems.

Associazione Italiana Industriali Prodotti Alimentari (AIIPA) (Food Manufacturers): Milan; tel. (02) 708660; telex 330881; Viale Umberto Tupini 103, 00144 Rome; tel. (06) 5924449; f. 1946; Pres. Dott. DEMETRIO CORNO; Dir Dott. GIOVANNI FRANCO CRIPPA; 300 mems.

Associazione Italiana Tecnico Economica del Cemento (AITEC) (Cement): Via di S. Teresa 23, 00198 Rome; tel. (06) 864714; Via Borgonuovo 12, 20121 Milan; tel. (02) 6571861; f. 1959; Pres. Dott. Ing. MARIO FEDERICI; Dir Dott. ANTONIO TRIFOGLI.

Associazione Mineraria Italiana (Mining): Via Cola di Rienzo 297, 00192 Rome; tel. (06) 352261; telex 622264; fax (06) 354543; f. 1144; Pres. VITO GUARRASI; Dir Dott. FRANCESCO SAVERIO GUIDI; 150 mems.

Associazione Nazionale Calzaturifici Italiani (ANCI) (Footwear Manufacturers): Via Dogana 1, 20123 Milan; tel. (02) 809721; telex 320018; fax 72020112; f. 1945; Pres. NATALINO PANCALDI; Dir LEONARDO SOANA.

Associazione Nazionale Costruttori Edili (ANCE) (Builders): Via Guattani 16, 00161 Rome; tel. (06) 84881; telex 623151; fax 8444364; f. 1946; Pres. RICCARDO PISA; Man. Dir CARLO FERRONI; mems: 19,000 firms in 99 provincial and 20 regional asscns.

Associazione Nazionale delle Fonderie—ASSOFOND (Foundries): Via Copernico 54, 20090 Trezzano Sul Naviglio; tel. (0382) 308403; telex 326344; fax (02) 48400967; f. 1948; Pres. Dott. Ing. GIAMPIERO BECCARIA; Dir Dott. GIUSEPPE MAZZONE.

Associazione Nazionale dell'Industria Farmaceutica—FARMINDUSTRIA (Pharmaceutical Industry): Piazza di Pietra 34, 00186 Rome; tel. (06) 650081; telex 614281; fax 6786494; f. 1978; Pres. Dott. CLAUDIO CAVAZZA; Dir Avv. FRANCO ZACCHIA; 265 mem. firms.

Associazione Nazionale fra Industrie Automobilistiche (ANFIA) (Motor Vehicle Industries): Corso Galileo Ferraris 61, 10128 Turin; tel. (011) 57611; telex 221334; fax 545986; f. 1912; Pres. Dott. GREGORIO RAMPA; Dir-Gen. Dott. EMILIO DI CAMILLO; 220 mems.

Associazione Nazionale Industria Meccanica Varia ed Affine (ANIMA) (Engineering and Allied Industries): Piazza Diaz 2, 20123 Milan; tel. (02) 721311; telex 310392; f. 1945; Pres. LUIGI CAZZANIGA; Sec.-Gen. Dott. Ing. ENRICO MALCOVATI; 1,500 mems.

Associazione Nazionale Industrie Elettrotecniche ed Elettroniche (ANIE) (Electrotechnic and Electronic Industries): Via Algardi 2, 20148 Milan; tel. (02) 32641; telex 321616; fax (02) 3264212; Pres. GIO BATTA CLAVARINO; Sec.-Gen. LORENZO TRINGALI-CASANUOVA.

Associazione Nazionale Italiana Industrie Grafiche, Cartotecniche e Trasformatrici (Printing, Paper-Making and Processing Industries): Piazza Conciliazione 1, 20123 Milan; tel. (02) 4981051; telex 331674; fax 4816947; f. 1946; Pres. Dott. PIERFRANCO GIUNCAIOLI; Sec.-Gen. Dott. FELICE SCIOMACHEN; 1,066 mems.

Federazione Italiana delle Industrie delle Acque Minerali, delle Terme e delle Bevande Analcooliche (Mineral Water and Non-Alcoholic Beverage Industries): Via Sicilia 186, 00187 Rome; tel. (06) 4557251; telex 626063; f. 1919; Pres. Dr CARLO VIOLATI; Dir Dr CARMELO CALLIPO.

Federazione Italiana Industriali Produttori Esportatori ed Importatori di Vini, Acquaviti, Liquori, Sciroppi, Aceti ed Affini—FEDERVINI (Producers, Importers and Exporters of Wines, Brandies, Liqueurs, Syrups, Vinegars and Allied Products): Via Mentana 2B, 00185 Rome; tel. (06) 4941488; telex 626436; fax 4941566; f. 1921; Pres. VITTORIO VALLARINO GAUCIA; Dir-Gen. FEDERICO CASTELLUCCI.

Federazione Nazionale dell'Industria Chimica—FEDERCHIMICA (Chemical Industry): Via Accademia 33, 20131 Milan; tel. (02) 63621; telex 332488; fax 6362310; Via Tomacelli 132, 00186 Rome; tel. (06) 6878683; telex 612504; fax 6878337; f. 1945; Pres. GIORGIO PORTA; Dir-Gen. Dott. GUIDO VENTURINI.

Unione Industriali Pastai Italiani—UNIPI (Pasta Manufacturers): Via Po 102, 00198 Rome; tel. (06) 853291; telex 611540; Pres. Ing. GIANFRANCO CARLONE; Dir Dr GIUSEPPE MENCONI.

Unione Nazionale Cantieri e Industrie Nautiche ed Affini (UCINA) (Shipyard and Nautical Industries): Via G. Giardino 4, 20123 Milan; Via Vincenzo Renieri 23, 00143 Rome; tel. (06) 5919744; telex 611585; Pres. GIORGIO ADREANI.

Unione Petrolifera (Petroleum Industries): Viale Civiltà del Lavoro 38, 00144 Rome; tel. (06) 5914841; telex 626568; fax (06) 5919843; f. 1948; Pres. Dott. GIAN MARCO MORATTI; Dir-Gen. Ing. BRUNO DATTILO; 43 mems.

Other Employers' and Industrial Organizations

Associazione Nazionale Comuni Italiani (ANCI): Via dei Prefetti 46, 00186 Rome; tel. (06) 6873501; telex 621313; fax 6873547; Pres. Sen. RICCARDO TRIGLIA; Sec.-Gen. LUCIO D'UBALDO.

Associazione Nazionale fra i Concessionari del Servizio di Riscossione del Tributi (ASCOTRIBUTI) (Services relating to Collection of Payments): Via Parigi 11, 00185 Rome; tel. (06) 485764; telex 628519; fax 463202; Pres. Sen. RICCARDO TRIGLIA; Dir-Gen. Dr GERARDO CHIRO.

Associazione Sindacale Intersind: Via Cristoforo Colombo 98, 00147 Rome; tel. (06) 51751; f. 1960; represents state-controlled firms; Pres. Dr AGOSTINO PACI; Dir-Gen. Dr ETTORE ATTOLINI.

Associazione Sindacale per le Aziende Petrochimiche e Collegate a Partecipazione Statale (State-controlled Petrochemical Companies): Via Due Macelli 66, 00187 Rome; tel. (06) 67341; telex 310246; fax 6734242; f. 1960; draws up labour and union contracts and represents the companies in legal matters; Pres. Avv. GUIDO FANTONI; Vice-Pres. and Dir-Gen. Dott. MODESTINO FUSCO.

Associazione fra le Società Italiane per Azioni—ASSONIME (Limited Companies): Piazza Venezia 11, 00187 Rome; tel. (06) 6784413; telex 613381; fax (06) 6790487; f. 1936; Pres. Dott. GUIDO CARLI; Dir-Gen. ALFONSO DE TOMMASI.

Confederazione Generale della Agricoltura Italiana (General Agricultural): Corso Vittorio Emanuele 101, 00186 Rome; tel. (06) 65121; telex 612533; f. 1945; Pres. STEFANO WALLNER; Dir-Gen. GIUSEPPE PRICOLO; Sec.-Gen. ARCANGELO MAFRICI.

Confederazione Generale Italiana del Commercio e del Turismo—CONFCOMMERCIO (Commerce and Tourism): Piazza G.G. Belli 2, 00153 Rome; tel. (06) 58661; telex 614217; fax 5809425; f. 1946; Pres. Dott. FRANCESCO COLUCCI; Sec.-Gen. Dott. PIETRO ALFONSI; 125 national and 97 territorial asscns affiliated.

Confederazione Italiana della Piccola e Media Industria—CONFAPI (Small and Medium Industry): Via Colonna Antonina 52, 00186 Rome; tel. (06) 6789441; f. 1947; Pres. Dr GIUSEPPE SPINELLA; Sec.-Gen. CARLO BAGNI; 20,000 mems.

ITALY

Confederazione Italiana della Proprietà Edilizia—CONFEDILIZIA (Property and Building): Via Pisanelli 25, 00196 Rome; tel. (06) 3606764; Pres. Dott. Ing. ATTILIO VIZIANO; Man. Dir Dott. Ing. ADRIANO PASTA.

Delegazione Sindacale Industriale Autonoma della Valle d'Aosta (Autonomous Industrial Delegation of the Valle d'Aosta): Via G. Elter 6, 11100 Aosta; Pres. Dr ETTORE FORTUNA; Sec. Dr ROBERTO ANSALDO.

Federazione Associazioni Industriali (Industrial Ascns): Via Petitti 16, 20149 Milan; tel. (02) 324846; telex 331098; fax 33003819; Pres. Ing. PAOLO SORINI; Dir-Gen. Dott. UMBERTO MALTAGLIATI.

Federazione delle Associazioni Italiane Alberghi e Turismo (FAIAT) (Hotels and Tourism): Via Toscana 1, 00187 Rome; tel. (06) 4741151; telex 613116; f. 1950; Pres. GIOVANNI COLOMBO; Gen. Man. ALESSANDRO CIANELLA; 25,000 mems.

Federazione Italiana della Pubblicità (FIP) (Advertisers): Via Maurizio Gonzaga 4, 20123 Milan; tel. (02) 865262; Pres. GIANFRANCO MAI; Sec.-Gen. MARIO CORNELIO.

Federazione Nazionale Imprese Trasporti—FENIT (Transport Undertakings): Via Parigi 11, 00185 Rome; tel. (06) 4741043; f. 1946; Pres. ANGELO MARIA SANZA; Gen. Man. Dr CARLO GIZZI; 234 mems.

Unione Nazionale Aziende Autoproduttrici e Consumatrici di Energia Elettrica—UNAPACE (Concerns producing and consuming their own Electrical Power): Via Paraguay 2, 00198 Rome; tel. (06) 864602; telex 616387; f. 1946; Pres. Dr Ing. LODOVICO PRIORI; Dir Dr Ing. ALDO BUSCAGLIONE.

TRADE UNIONS

There are three main federations of Italian trade unions, CGIL, CISL and UIL, all of which have close ties with political parties. The CGIL is dominated by the Communists, the CISL has links with the Christian Democrats and the UIL is associated with the Socialists. In 1972 all the confederations formally agreed that union leadership and holding party political office were not compatible with independence from party line and a united front between the confederations was seen as crucial to the success of the unions.

National Federations

Confederazione Autonomi Sindacati Artigiani (CASA): V. Flaminio Ponzio 2, 00153 Rome; tel. (06) 5758081; f. 1958; federation of artisans' unions and regional and provincial associations; Pres. GIUSEPPE GUARINO; Sec.-Gen. GIACOMO BASSO.

Confederazione Generale Italiana dell' Artigianato (Artisans): Piazza Venezia 11, 00187 Rome; telex 616261; f. 1945; independent; 157 mem. unions; 600,000 associate enterprises; Pres. MANLIO GERMOZZI.

Confederazione Generale Italiana del Lavoro (CGIL) (General Union of Italian Workers): Corso d'Italia 25, 00198 Rome; tel. (06) 84761; telex 623083; f. 1944; Communist and Socialist; federation of 17 unions; Gen. Sec. BRUNO TRENTIN; 4,556,000 mems.

Confederazione Italiana Dirigenti di Azienda (CIDA): Via Nazionale 75, 00184 Rome; tel. (06) 4818551; federation of six managers' unions; Pres. Dott. FAUSTO D'ELIA; Sec.-Gen. RAFFAELE CIABATTINI.

Confederazione Italiana dei Professionisti e Artisti (CIPA) (Artists and Professional People): Via S. Nicola da Tolentino 21, 00187 Rome; tel. (06) 461849; federation of 19 unions; Pres. Rag. SERGIO SPLENDORI.

Confederazione Italiana dei Sindacati Autonomi Lavoratori (CISAL): Via Cavour 310, 00184 Rome; tel. (06) 6785402; f. 1957; no international affiliations; federation of 67 unions; Gen. Sec. Dr GUSSONI GERMANO; 1,423,000 mems.

Confederazione Italiana dei Sindacati Lavoratori (CISL): Via Po 21, 00198 Rome; tel. (06) 84731; telex 614045; fax 8413782; f. 1950; affiliated to the International Confederation of Free Trade Unions and the European Trade Union Confederation; federation of 17 unions; Sec.-Gen. FRANCO MARINI; 3,080,000 mems.

Confederazione Italiana Sindacati Nazionali dei Lavoratori—CISNAL: Via P. Amedeo 42, 00185 Rome; tel. (06) 4817919; f. 1950; upholds traditions of national syndicalism; federation of 64 unions, 90 provincial unions; Gen. Sec. IVO LAGHI; 1,969,635 mems.

Confederazione Nazionale dell' Artigianato (CNA): Via di S. Prassede 24, 00187 Rome; tel. (06) 4757441; telex 622543; provincial associations; Pres. BRUNO MARIANI; Gen. Sec. Dr MAURO TOGNONI.

Federazione fra le Associazioni e i Sindacati Nazionali dei Quadri Direttivi dell'amministrazione dello Stato—DIRSTAT: Via Ezio 12, 00192 Rome; tel. (06) 3211535; f. 1948; federation of 33 unions and associations of civil service executives and officers; Sec.-Gen. EDUARDO MAZZONE; Treas. Dr V. DONATO.

Unione Italiana del Lavoro (UIL): Via Lucullo 6, 00187 Rome; tel. (06) 49731; telex 622425; fax 4973208; f. 1950; Socialist, Social Democrat and Republican; affiliated to the International Confederation of Free Trade Unions and European Trade Union Confederation; 35 national trade union federations and 95 provincial union councils; Gen. Sec. GIORGIO BENVENUTO; 1,541,404 mems.

Principal Unions
Banking and Insurance

Federazione Autonoma Bancari Italiana (FABI) (Bank Workers): Via Tevere 46, Rome; tel. (06) 8415751; f. 1948; independent; Sec. LUIGI MARMIROLI; 63,000 mems.

Federazione Autonoma Lavoratori Casse di Risparmio Italiane (FALCRI) (Savings Banks Workers): Via Mercato 5, Milan; Via Carducci 4, Rome.

Federazione Italiana Bancari e Assicuratori (FIBA): Via Modena 5, 00184 Rome; tel. (06) 4741245; fax 4746136; affiliated to the CISL; Gen. Sec. SERGIO AMMANNATI; 58,980 mems.

Federazione Italiana Sindacale Lavoratori Assicurazioni Credito (Employees of Credit Institutions): Via Vicenza 5A, 00184 Rome; tel. (06) 4958261; affiliated to the CGIL; Sec. NICOLETTA ROCCHI; 60,000 mems.

Federazione Nazionale Assicuratori—FISAC (Insurance Workers): Via Vincenzo Monti 25, Milan; Via Val d'Ossola 100, Rome; independent; Pres. GIUSEPPE PAGANI; Sec.-Gen. EZIO MARTONE.

Unione Italiana Lavoratori Assicurazioni—UILAS (Assurance Co Workers): Via Piemonte 39/A, Rome; affiliated to the UIL; National Sec. GUGLIELMO BRONZI; 13,000 mems.

Building and Building Materials

Federazione Autonoma Italiana Lavoratori Cemento, Legno, Edilizia ed Affini (FAILCLEA) (Workers in Cement, Wood, Construction and Related Industries): Piazza E. Duse 3, Milan; affiliated to the CISAL; Sec. ENZO BOZZI.

Federazione Lavoratori delle Costruzioni (FLC): includes the following three organizations:

Federazione Italiana Lavoratori delle Costruzioni a Affini (FILCA) (Building Industries' Workers): Via dei Mille 23, Rome; tel. (06) 497801; f. 1955; affiliated to the CISL; Sec.-Gen. CARLO MITRA; 194,493 mems.

Federazione Nazionale Lavoratori Edili Affini e del Legno (FeNEAL) (Builders and Woodworkers): Via dei Mille 23, Rome; affiliated to the UIL and the FLC; Sec.-Gen. GIANCARLO SERAFINI; 135,000 mems.

Federazione Italiana Lavoratori del Legno, Edili ed Affini (FILLEA) (Wood-workers, Construction Workers and Allied Trades): Via dei Mille 23, 00184 Rome; tel. (06) 497801; affiliated to the CGIL; Sec. ANNIO BRESCHI; 434,154 mems.

Chemical, Mining and Allied Industries

Federazione Unitaria Lavoratori Chimici (FULC) (Chemical and Allied Workers): Via Bolzano 16, Rome; affiliated to the CGIL, CISL and UIL; Secs.-Gen. FAUSTO VIGEVANI, DANILO BERETTA, ERNESTO CORNELLI; 450,000 mems.

Unione Italiana Lavoratori Miniere e Cave (Mine Workers): Rome; independent; National Sec. BACCI LUCIANO; 16,000 mems.

Clothing and Textiles

Federazione Italiana Lavoratori Tessili Abbigliamento, Calzaturieri (FILTEA) (Textile and Clothing Workers and Shoe Manufacturers): Via Leopoldo Serra 31, 00153 Rome; tel. (06) 55431; f. 1966; affiliated to the CGIL; Gen. Sec. ALDO AMORETTI; 180,000 mems.

Federazione Italiana dei Lavoratori Tessili e Abbigliamento (FILTA-CISL): Via Goito 39, 00185 Rome; tel. (06) 4270041; fax 492544; affiliated to the CISL; Gen. Sec. AUGUSTA RESTELLI; 125,084 mems.

Engineering and Metallurgy

Confederazione Sindacale Italiana Libere Professioni—CONSILP (Liberal Professions): Via Leopoldo Traversi 40, 00154 Rome; Sec.-Gen. Dott. UBALDO PROCACCINI.

Federazione Architetti—FEDERARCHITETTI (Architects): Piazza Sallustio 24, 00187 Rome; Pres. Dott. Arch. GIANCARLO CAMPIOLI; Sec.-Gen. Dott. Arch. NICOLA D'ERRICO.

Federazione Impiegati Operai Metallurgici (FIOM—CGIL) (Metalworkers): Corso Trieste 36, 00198 Rome; tel. (06) 8471; f. 1902; affiliated to the CGIL; Sec. SERGIO GARAVINI; 450,000 mems.

Federazione Italiana Metalmeccanici (FIM) (Metal Mechanic Workers): Corso Trieste 36, 00198 Rome; tel. (06) 84711; fax (06) 8471305; affiliated to the CISL; Sec. Gen. GIANNI ITALIA; 277,789 mems.

Sindacato Nazionale Ingegneri Liberi Professionisti Italiana (SNILPI) (Liberal Professionals-Engineers): Via Salaria 292, 00199

ITALY

Rome; Pres. Dott. Ing. LUIGI LUCHERINI; Sec.-Gen. Dott. Ing. GIUSEPPE MILONE.

Unione Italiana Lavoratori Metallurgici (UILM) (Metalworkers): Corso Trieste 36, 00198 Rome; tel. (06) 8442757; f. 1950; affiliated to the UIL; Sec. FRANCO LOTITO; 139,000 mems.

Food and Agriculture

Confederazione Generale dell' Agricoltura Italiana—CONFAGRICOLTURA (Farmers): Corso Vittorio Emanuele 101, 00186 Rome; tel. (06) 65121; telex 612533; fax (06) 6548578; Pres. Dr GIUSEPPE GIOIA.

Confederazione Italiana Coltivatori (Farmers): Via Mariano Fortuny 20, 00196 Rome; tel. (06) 3969931; fax 3604761; independent; Pres. GIUSEPPE AVOLIO; Vice-Pres. MASSIMO BELLOTTI.

Confederazione Nazionale Coltivatori Diretti—CONACOLTIVATORI (Small-holders): Via XXIV Maggio 43, 00187 Rome; tel. (06) 46821; telex 6751055; independent; Pres. On. ARCANGELO LOBIANCO; Sec. PIETRO GNISCI.

Federazione Italiana Salariati Braccianti Agricoli e Maestranze Specializzate (FISBA) (Permanent Unskilled and Skilled Agricultural Workers): Via Tevere 20, 00198 Rome; tel. (06) 855455; f. 1950; Sec. CIRINO BRANCATO; 347,265 mems.

Federazione Lavoratori dell' Agroindustria (Workers in the Agricultural Industry): Via Leopoldo Serra 31, 00153 Rome; tel. (06) 5543531; fax (06) 5880585; f. 1988; affiliated to the CGIL; Sec.-Gen. ANGELO LANA; 438,000 mems.

Federazione Nazionale Braccianti, Salariati, Tecnici,—FEDERBRACCIANTI (Agricultural Workers): Rome; tel. (06) 461760; affiliated to the CGIL; Sec. ANDREA GIANFAGNA; 600,000 mems.

Federazione Unitaria Lavoratori Prodotti Industrie Alimentari (Workers in the Manufactured Food Industry): Rome; affiliated to the CISL and the IUF; Sec. Dr E. CREA; 40,000 mems.

Unione Coltivatori Italiana (UCI) (Farmers): Via in Lucina 10, 00186 Rome.

Unione Generale Coltivatori (UGC): Via Tevere 20, 00198 Rome; tel. (06) 8552383; fax 8553891; affiliated to the CISL; Pres. SANTE RICCI; 131,562 mems.

Unione Italiana Lavoratori Industrie Alimentari Saccariferi (UILIAS) (Food Workers): Via del Viminale 43, 00184 Rome; tel. (06) 463486; affiliated to the UIL; Sec. LIVIO CAUDURO.

Unione Italiana Mezzadri e Coltivatori Diretti—UIMEC (Land Workers): Via Salaria 222, 00198 Rome; tel. (06) 8418044; fax 8413968; affiliated to the UIL; Sec. FURIO VENARUCCI; 100,000 mems.

Medical

Federazione Italiana Sindacati Ospedalieri—FISOS (Hospital Workers' Unions): Via Salaria 89, 00198 Rome; tel. (06) 8414815; affiliated to the CISL; Sec. Gen. GIACOMO MUSCOLINO; 150,501 mems.

Sindacato Nazionale Medici (SNM) (Doctors): Rome; affiliated to the CISNAL; Sec. VINCENZO AGAMENNONE.

Papermaking, Printing and Publishing

Federazione Italiana Lavoratori del Libro—FEDERLIBRO: Via Fabio Massimo 57, 00192 Rome; tel. (06) 318202; affiliated to the CISL; Gen. Sec. GIUSEPPE SURRENTI; 35,000 mems.

Federazione Italiana Lavoratori Poligrafici e Cartai (Printing Workers and Papermakers): Via Piemonte 39, 00186 Rome; affiliated to the CGIL; Sec.-Gen. GIORGIO COLZI; 80,000 mems.

Public Services

Federazione Autonoma Italiana Lavoratori Elettrici (FAILE) (Electrical Workers): Via Cavour 310, Rome; affiliated to CISAL; Sec. ANGELO ISERNIA.

Federazione della Funzione Pubblica (FP): Via Rovereto 11, 00198 Rome; tel. (06) 869578; affiliated to the CISL; Sec. Gen. DARIO PAPPUCIA; 244,835 mems.

Federazione Italiana Dipendenti Enti Locali (Local Government Employees): Via XX Settembre 40, Rome; tel. (06) 4759295; f. 1951; affiliated to the CISL; Sec. CRISTOFORO MELINELLI; 150,000 mems.

Federazione Italiana Lavoratori Esattoriali (Tax Collectors): Via A. Poliziano 80, 00184 Rome; tel. (06) 732246; affiliated to the UIL; Sec. LUCIANO PARODI.

Federazione Italiana Lavoratori Statali (State Employees): Via Livenza 7, 00198 Rome; affiliated to the CISL; Gen. Sec. MARZIO BASTIANONI; 60,605 mems.

Federazione Lavoratori Aziende Elettriche Italiane (FLAEI) (Workers in Italian Electrical Undertakings): Via Salaria 83, 00198 Rome; tel. (06) 862352; f. 1948; affiliated to the CISL; Sec. FIORINDO FUMAGALLI; 41,210 mems.

Federazione Nazionale Dipendenti Enti Locali (Employers of Local Authorities): Via Principe Amadeo 42, 00185 Rome; tel. (06) 4750202; affiliated to the CISNAL; Sec. Dott. ARMANDO LA ROCCA.

Federazione Nazionale Dipendenti Enti Pubblici—UILDEP (Public Employees): Via Lucullo 6, Rome; f. 1962; affiliated to the UIL; Gen. Sec. GIAMPIETRO SESTINI; 30,000 mems.

Federazione Nazionale Lavoratori Funzione Pubblica: Via Leopoldo Serra 31, 00153 Rome; tel. (06) 55431; affiliated to the CGIL and Public Services International; Sec.-Gen. ALDO GIUNTI.

Federazione Nazionale Lavoratori Energia (Gas, Water and Electricity): Via Piemonte 32, 00187 Rome; tel. (06) 4746153; affiliated to the CGIL; Sec. ANDREA AMARO; 72,000 mems.

Unione Italiana Lavoratori Pubblico Impiego (UILPI) (Public Office Workers): Via Lucullo 6, 00187 Rome; tel. (06) 49731; fax 4973208; affiliated to the UIL; Sec. GIANCARLO FONTANELLI; 238,000 mems.

Unione Italiana Lavoratori Servizi Pubblici (Public Services Workers): Via Nizza 33, 00198 Rome; tel. (06) 865303; f. 1958; affiliated to the UIL; Sec. GIUSEPPE AUGIERI; 15,500 mems.

Unione Nazionale Dipendenti Enti Locali—UNDEL (Local Authority Employees): Via Po 162, 00198 Rome; tel. (06) 852340; affiliated to the UIL; Gen. Sec. FABRIZIO LUCARINI; 85,000 mems.

Teachers

Federazione Italiana Scuola Università e Ricerca (University Teachers): Via S. Croce in Gerusalemme 107, 00185 Rome; tel. (06) 757941; affiliated to the CISL; Gen. Secs GIORGIO ALESSANDRINI, PIETRO TALAMO; 184,235 mems.

Sindacato Nazionale Autonomo Lavoratori della Scuola (SNALS): Via Leopoldo Serra 5, 00153 Rome; tel. (06) 5898741; f. 1976; grouping of all independent teachers' unions; National Sec. NINO GALLOTTA.

Sindacato Nazionale Scuola Elementare (Elementary School Teachers): Via Santa Croce in Gerusalemme 91, 00185 Rome; tel. (06) 7574856; f. 1944; affiliated to the CISL; Sec.-Gen. LUIGI PICCINATO; 124,000 mems.

Tourism and Entertainments

Federazione Informazione e Spettacolo (FIS) (Actors, Artists and Media Workers): Via Boncompagni 19, 00187 Rome; tel. (06) 4823731; fax 4747263; affiliated to the CISL; Gen. Sec. GIUSEPPE SURRENTI; 43,388 mems.

Federazione Italiana Lavoratori Commercio Albergo Mensa e Servizi—FILCAMS (Hotel and Catering Workers): Rome; tel. (06) 4750300; f. 1960; affiliated to the CGIL; Sec.-Gen. GILBERTO PASCUCCI; 189,000 mems.

Federazione Italiana Lavoratori Informazione Spettacolo (FILIS) (Theatre Workers): Via E. Manfredi 10A, 00197 Rome; tel. (06) 877532; affiliated to the CGIL; Gen. Sec. GUGLIELMO EPIFANI.

Federazione Italiana Personale Aviazione Civile (Aviation Employees): Via Ostiense 224, Rome; affiliated to the CGIL; Sec. PIERRO TORINO.

Federazione Italiana Sindacati Addetti Servizi Commerciali Affini e del Turismo (Commercial and Tourist Unions): Via Livenza 7, 00198 Rome; tel. (06) 8541042; fax 868057; affiliated to the CISL; Sec.-Gen. MARIO CESINO; 99,860 mems.

Unione Italiana Lavoratori Turismo Commercio e Servizi (UIL-TuCS): Via Nizza 59, 00198 Rome; tel. (06) 8844947; f. 1977; affiliated to the UIL; Gen. Sec. RAFFAELE VANNI; 140,000 mems.

Transport and Telecommunications

Federazione Italiana Dipendenti Aziende Telecomunicazioni (FIDAT) (Employees of Telecommunications Undertakings): Via Po 102, 00198 Rome; tel. (06) 855651; affiliated to the CGIL; Sec. GIANFRANCO TESTI; 12,000 mems.

Federazione Italiana Lavoratori Trasporti e Ausiliari del Traffico (FILTAT) (Transport and Associated Workers): Via Nizza 45, Rome; tel. (06) 8448640; affiliated to the CISL; Sec. PIETRO LOMBARDI; 60,000 mems.

Federazione Italiana dei Postelegrafonici (Postal, Telegraph and Telephone Workers): Via Cavour 185, 00187 Rome; tel. (06) 461321; affiliated to the CGIL; Sec. GIUSEPPE MASTRACCHI; 35,000 mems.

Federazione Italiana Trasporti Settore Marittimi (Italian Maritime): Via Boncompagni 19, 00187 Rome; tel. (06) 497881; telex 622005; fax 4750300; affiliated to the International Transport Workers' Federation; Nat. Sec. MARIO GUIDI.

Federazione Nazionale Autoferrotranvieri Internavigatori (FNAI) (Bus, Railway and Tram Workers): Rome; tel. (06) 483783; affiliated to the UIL; Sec. BRUNO MONOSILIO.

Federazione Italiana Sindacati dei Trasporti (FILT): Via G. B. Morgagni 27, 00100 Rome; tel. (06) 89961; affiliated to the CGIL; Sec. LUCIO DE CARLINI.

ITALY — *Directory*

Federazione Italiana Trasporti (FIT): Rome; tel. (06) 866742; affiliated to the CISL; Sec.-Gen. GAETANO ARCONTI; 152,085 mems.

Federazione Nazionale Lavoratori Auto-Ferrotramvieri e Internavigatori—FENLAI: Rome; affiliated to the CISL; Gen. Sec. LAURO MORRA; 28,091 mems.

Federazione Poste e Telecomunicazioni (FPT): Via dell'Esquilino 38, 00185 Rome; tel. (06) 4820264; f. 1981; affiliated to the CISL; Sec.-Gen. ERMINIO CHIOFFI; 133,696 mems.

Federazione dei Sindacati Dipendenti Aziende di Navigazione—FEDERSINDAN: Via Tevere 48, Rome; independent; Sec.-Gen. Dott. GIUSEPPE AURICCHIO.

Sindacato Autonomo Unificato Ferrovieri Italiani (Railway Workers): Via Boncompagni 19, 00187 Rome; tel. (06) 497881; fax (06) 4824300; f. 1950; affiliated to the CISL; National Sec. ANGELO EVANGELISTELLA; 43,000 mems.

Sindacato Italiano Lavoratori Uffici Locali ed Agenzie Postelegrafoniche (Post and Telegraph Workers): Via Esquilino 38, 00185 Rome; affiliated to the CISL; Gen. Sec. GIOVANNI MARIA NIEDDU; 62,268 mems.

UILTRASPORTI: Via Gaeta 15, 00185 Rome; tel. (06) 479911; affiliated to the UIL; Sec. RAFFAELE LIGUORI.

Unione Italiana Lavoratori Trasporti Ausiliari Traffico e Portuali (UILTATEP) (Transport and Associated Workers): Via Palestro 78, 00185 Rome; tel. (06) 4950698; f. 1950; affiliated to the UIL; Sec.-Gen. RAFFAELE LIGOURI; 134,280 mems.

Unione Italiana Marittimi (UIM) (Seamen): Rome; tel. (06) 422800; affiliated to the UIL; National Sec. GIORGIO MARANGONI; 12,500 mems.

Miscellaneous

Federazione Italiana Agenti Rappresentanti Viaggia-tori-Piazzisti 'Fiarvep' (Commercial Travellers and Representatives): Corso Porta Vittoria 43, Milan; affiliated to the CGIL; Sec. LIONELLO GIANNINI.

Federazione Nazionale Pensionati (FNP) (Pensioners): Via Alessandria 26, 00198 Rome; tel. (06) 861218; f. 1952; affiliated to the CISL; Sec. GIANFRANCO CHIAPELLA; 800,000 mems.

Sindacato Nazionale Musicisti (Musicians): Rome; tel. (06) 490467; independent; National Sec. Maestro SALVATORE ALLEGRA.

Sindacato Pensionati Italiani (Pensioners): Via Morgagni 27, 00161 Rome; tel. (06) 869451; fax (06) 8411654; affiliated to the CGIL; Gen. Sec. GIANFRANCO RASTRELLI; 2,350,000 mems.

Co-operative Unions

Confederazione Cooperative Italiane—CONFCOOPERATIVE: Borgo S. Spirito 78, 00193 Rome; tel. (06) 650861; telex 622465; fax 6868595; f. 1945; federation of co-operative unions; Pres. DARIO MENGOZZI; Sec.-Gen. VINCENZO MANNINO.

Associazione Generale delle Cooperative Italiane (AGCI): Viale Somalia 164, 00199 Rome; tel. (06) 8313753; telex 622285; f. 1952; Pres. RENATO ASCARI RACCAGNI; Sec.-Gen. GINO MARINONI.

Federazione Italiana dei Consorzi Agari—FEDERCONCORZI (Landowners' Consortia): Via Curtatone 3, 00185 Rome; tel. (06) 46641; telex 610010; Pres. FERNANDINO TRUZZI; Dir-Gen. LUIGI SCOTTI.

Federazione Nazionale della Cooperazione Agricola (Agricultural Co-operatives): Via Nazionale 69, 00184 Rome; tel. (06) 483824; Pres. CARLO FORCELLA; Dir Dr SANRO ROSSI.

Lega Nazionale delle Cooperative e Mutue (National League of Co-operative and Friendly Societies): Via Guattani 9, 00161 Rome; tel. (06) 844391; telex 611346; 10 affiliated unions; Pres. LANFRANCO TURCI.

STATE HOLDINGS AND NATIONALIZED BODIES

Ente Nazionale Idrocarburi (ENI): Piazzale Enrico Mattei 1, 00144 Rome; tel. (06) 59001; telex 610082; state-owned energy corporation with subsidiaries including AGIP, AGIP Petroli, SNAM and AGIP Carbone operating in the energy sector; Enimont in chemicals; SAMIM in mining and metallurgy; SNAMPROGETTI and SAIPEM in engineering and services; Nuovo Pignone in machines and instruments; SOFID and ENI International Holding SA in the financial sector; Chair. GABRIELE CAGLIARI.

Ente Nazionale per l'Energia Elettrica (ENEL): Via Giovanni Battista Martini 3, 00198 Rome; tel. (06) 85091; telex 610518; fax (06) 85092162; f. 1962 to generate and distribute electrical power throughout various areas of the country and to work in conjunction with the Ministry of Industry and Trade; Chair. FRANCO VIEZZOLI; Gen. Man. Ing. ALBERTO NEGRONI.

Ente Partecipazioni e Finanziamento Industria Manifatturiera (EFIM): Via XXIV Maggio 43/45, 00187 Rome; tel. (06) 47101; telex 621381; f. 1962 as a state law agency, managing three holding companies and more than 100 companies. Its main fields of activity are on-land transports, aeronautics, armaments and defence systems, glass, aluminium and plant engineering; Pres. ROLANDO VALIANI.

Istituto per la Ricostruzione Industriale (IRI): Via Vittorio Veneto 89, 00187 Rome; tel. (06) 47271; f. 1933 as an autonomous agency controlling banking and industrial undertakings, IRI is responsible for many of the companies in which the State participates, including the national airline Alitalia, the road company ANAS, the RAI television service, the SIP telephone network, the three main commercial banks, the iron and steel producer Ilva, the shipping company Italmare and the holding company SPA; Pres. FRANCO NOBILI.

Società Italiana per l'esercizio telefonico SpA (SIP): Via San Dalmazzo 15, 10122 Turin; tel. (011) 5771; telex 610467; cap. 880,000m. (1980); operates, under government licence, the telephone system over the entire country except for intertoll system; 21.7m. telephones (1983).

Transport

Direzione Generale della Motorizzazione Civile e del Trasporti in Concessione: Via dei Monti di Pietralata 137, 00157 Rome; tel. (06) 45181; fax 45182211; controls road transport and traffic, and public transport services (railways operated by private companies, motor-buses, trolley-buses, funicular railways and inland waterways); Dir-Gen. Dott. GIORGIO BERRUTI.

RAILWAYS

The majority of Italian lines are controlled by the State. The first railway line (Naples–Portici) was opened in 1839. The present-day Italian State Railways comprise an amalgamation, begun in 1905 and completed in 1907, of three private companies. In 1988 the total length of the network was 15,983 km, 57% of which is electrified. Apart from the state railway system there are 27 local and municipal railway companies, many of whose lines are narrow gauge. There are metro systems in Rome, Milan and Naples; and a metro system is planned for Turin. A high-speed service with tilting trains is in operation on the following routes: Rome–Milan–Turin, Naples–Rome and Rome–Venice.

Ente Ferrovie dello Stato: Piazza della Croce Rossa 1, 00161 Rome; tel. (06) 84901; telex 622345; fax 8831108; a public enterprise which administers the State Railways, headed by an Administrative Board; Special Commissioner Dott. LORENZO NECCI; Dir-Gen. Dott. BENEDETTO DE CESARIS.

ROADS

In 1986 there were 301,846 km of road in Italy, including 45,779 km of major roads, 108,404 km of secondary roads and 5,997 km of motorway. All the *autostrade* (motorways) are toll roads except for the one between Salerno and Reggio Calabria and motorways in Sicily. By law ANAS is responsible for the planning, construction and management of the motorway network. The 13-km Mount Frejus highway tunnel, linking Italy and France through the Alps, opened in 1980.

Azienda Nazionale Autonoma delle Strade Statali (ANAS) (National Autonomous Road Corporation): Via Monzambano 10, 00185 Rome; tel. (06) 46661; f. 1928, reorganized 1946; responsible for the administration of state roads and their improvement and extension; the president is the Minister of Public Works.

SHIPPING

At 30 June 1989 the Italian merchant fleet (1,571 vessels) had a displacement of 7,602,032 grt.

Genova

Costa Armatori SpA (Linea C): Via Gabriele D'Annunzio 2, 16100 Genova; tel. (010) 54831; telex 270068; passenger and cargo service; Mediterranean–North, Central and South America; Caribbean cruises; Chair. NICOLA COSTA.

Franconia Srl: POB 607, Via XX Settembre 37-11, 16121 Genova; tel. (010) 818851; telex 270017; Chair. FRIGERIO BRUNO; Man. Dir EMANUELE RAVANO.

'Garibaldi' Società Cooperativa di Navigazione Srl: Piazza Dante 8, 16121 Genova; tel. (010) 581635; telex 270548; fax 581637; f. 1918; tanker and cargo services; Pres. GIAN FRANCO VIALE; Man. Dir MARIO DI LELLA.

Industriale Marittima SpA: Via Porta d'Archi 10/21, 16121 Genova; tramp; Man. Dir A. PORTA FIGARI.

'Italia di Navigazione' SpA: Torre WTC, Via de Marini 1, Genova; tel. (010) 24021; telex 270032; fax 2402445; f. 1932; freight services to Mediterranean, North, South and Central America and South

Pacific; Chair. LUCIO DE GIACOMO; Man. Dir ROBERTO COLONNELLO.

Messina, Ignazio and C. SpA: Via G. d'Annunzio 91, 16121 Genova; tel. (010) 53961; tel. 270450; services to Arabian Gulf, Nigeria, North, East and West Africa, Libya and Near East, Red Sea, Malta, Europe; Chair. I. MESSINA; Man. Dirs GINAFRANCO MESSINA, GIORGIO MESSINA, P. MESSINA.

Navigazione Alta Italia, SpA: Via Corsica 19, 16128 Genova; tel. (010) 56331; telex 270181; f. 1906; worldwide dry and bulk cargo; Chair. and Man. Dir SEBASTIANO CAMELI; Gen. Man. ROMANO GUGLIELMINI.

Sidermar di Navigazione SpA: Via XX Settembre 41, Genova; tel. (010) 56341; telex 270412; f. 1956; cargo; Chair. Dott. DARIO DEL BUONO; Man. Dir Dott. CARLO CIONI.

Naples

Garolla Fratelli SpA: Pontile Falvio Giola 45, 80133 Naples; tel. (081) 5534477; telex 710256; Chair. R. GAROLLA; Dirs F. GAROLLA, C. GAROLLA.

Fratelli Grimaldi Armatori: Via M. Campodisola 13, 80133 Naples; tel. (081) 205466; telex 710058; passenger, cargo, containers and tramp to Europe, Middle East, South, Central and North America; Dirs M. GRIMALDI, G. GRIMALDI, A. GRIMALDI, U. GRIMALDI.

Tirrenia di Navigazione SpA: Head Office: Palazzo Sirignano, Rione Sirignano 2, 80121 Naples; tel. (081) 7201111; telex 710028; fax 7201441; Man. Dir FRANCO PECORINI; Dir Gen. GIUSEPPE RAVERA.

Palermo

Sicilia Regionale Marittima SpA—SIREMAR: Via Francesco Crispi 120, 90139 Palermo; tel. (091) 582688; telex 910135; ferry services; Pres. DOMENICO CANGIALOSI; Man. Dir LUIGI FIORENTINO.

Sicula Oceanicas SA—SIOSA: Via Mariano Stabile 179, 90139 Palermo; tel. (091) 217939; telex 910098; f. 1941; cruises, passenger and cargo; Italy to North Europe, South, Central, North America; Dir G. GRIMALDI.

Rome

D'Amico Fratelli, Armatori, SpA: Via Liguria 36, 00187 Rome; tel. (06) 4671; telex 614545; dry cargo, tankers and fruit transport; Dirs GIUSEPPE D'AMICO, VITTORIO D'AMICO.

D'Amico Società di Navigazione SpA: Corso d'Italia 35B, 00198 Rome; tel. (06) 8841061; telex 611118; fax 8553943; f. 1954; liner and tanker trade; Mans ANTONIO D'AMICO, CESARE D'AMICO, PAOLO D'AMICO.

Linee Marittime dell'Adriatico SpA: Via del Nuoto 11, 00194 Rome; tel. (06) 3272312; telex 611034.

Trieste

Fratelli Cosulich, SpA: Piazza S. Antonio 4, 34122 Trieste; tel. (040) 61583; telex 460018; fax 630844; f. 1854; shipowners and shipping agents; cargo to Near East, Red Sea, Far East and South America; brs in Catania, Genoa, Hong Kong, Livorno, Messina, Milan, Naples, Salerno, Savona, Turin, Zürich; Chair. and Man. Dir GEROLIMICH COSULICH.

Lloyd Triestino di Navigazione SpA: Palazzo del Lloyd Triestino, Piazza dell'Unità d'Italia 1, 34121 Trieste; tel. (040) 7785; telex 460321; fax 7785424; f. 1836; cargo services by container, roll on/roll off and conventional vessels to Africa, Australasia and Far East; Pres. Dott. ROBERTO JUCCI; Dir-Gen. Ing. TOMMASO RICCI.

Other Towns

Adriatica di Navigazione SpA: Zattere 1411, CP 705, 30123 Venice; tel. (041) 781611; telex 410045; fax 781894; f. 1937; passenger and freight services from Italy to Eastern Mediterranean, Egypt, Greece, Yugoslavia and Albania; Pres. EMIDIO MASSI; Man. Dir CLAUDIO BONICIOLLI.

Snam SpA: Piazza Vanoni 1, San Donato Milanese, POB 12060, 20097 Milan; tel. (02) 5201; telex 310246; f. 1941; purchase, transport and sale of natural gas, transport of crude oil and petroleum products by means of pipeline and tanker fleet; Pres. Ing. PIO PIGORINI; Vice-Pres. and Man. Dir Ing. LUIGI MEANTI; Man. Dirs Ing. VITTORIO MEAZZINI, Dr ANGELO FERRARI.

SHIPPING ASSOCIATIONS

Associazione Italiana dell' Armamento di Linea—FEDARLINEA: Via Ferdinando di Savoia 8, 00196 Rome; tel. (06) 3603447; f. 1967; Pres. Dr MARIO BONACCHI; Dir Dr GIUSEPPE RAVERA.

Confederazione Italiana Armatori—CONFITARMA: Via dei Sabini 7, 00187 Rome; tel. (06) 6787041; telex 620195; fax 6780473;
f. 1901; Pres. ANTONIO D'AMICO; Dir GIUSEPPE PERASSO; 305 mems.

CIVIL AVIATION

National Airline

Alitalia (Linee Aeree Italiane): Palazzo Alitalia, Piazzale Giulio Pastore 6, 00144 Rome; tel. (06) 54441; telex 626211; fax 5914948; f. 1946; state-owned airline; international services throughout Europe and to Africa, North and South America, the Middle East, the Far East and Australia; Chair. MICHELE PRINCIPE; Dep. Chair. VITTORIO VACCARI; Man. Dir GIOVANNI BISAGNANI; fleet of 14 Airbus A300B4, 11 ATR42, 12 Boeing 747, 1 747F, 43 McDonnell Douglas DC-9-30, 51 MD-80.

Other Airlines

Aero Trasporti Italiani SpA (ATI): Aeroporto Capodichino, 80144 Naples; tel. (081) 7091111; telex 711005; f. 1963; subsidiary of Alitalia; operates scheduled domestic services and services and charter flights to the Middle East, North Africa and Canary Islands and within Europe; Chair. Prof. CARLO BERNINI; Man. Dir Dr MARIO FRANCHI; fleet of 17 DC-9-30, 9 ATR 42, 12 MD-82.

Alisarda SpA: 193 Corso Umberto, 07026 Olbia, Sardinia; tel. (0789) 52600; telex 790043; f. 1963; scheduled services between Olbia and Milan, Rome, Pisa, Bologna, Naples, Genova and Cagliari, other connections from Rome to Catania, Milan Malpensa, Palermo and Venice, seasonal services between Olbia, Turin, Bergamo, Verona, Nice, Paris, Geneva, Zürich, Frankfurt and Munich; Pres. Avv. SERGIO PERALDA; Man. Dir FRANCO TRIVI; Commercial Man. ALFREDO PICCINATO; fleet of 5 MD-82, 6 DC-9-51.

Tourism

A great number of tourists are attracted to Italy by its Alpine and Mediterranean scenery, sunny climate, Roman buildings, medieval and Baroque churches, Renaissance towns and palaces, paintings and sculpture and famous opera houses. Each of the 95 Provinces has a Board of Tourism; there are also about 300 Aziende Autonome di Cura, Soggiorno e Turismo, with information about tourist accommodation and health treatment, and about 2,000 Pro Loco Associations concerned with local amenities. In 1989 55.1m. foreign visitors (including excursionists) arrived in Italy. In that year there were about 1.7m. tourist beds. A plague of algae in the coastal waters of the Adriatic contributed to a significant reduction in the number of tourist arrivals.

Ministero del Turismo e dello Spettacolo: Via della Ferratella in Laterano 51, 00100 Rome; tel. (06) 77321; telex 616400; fax 7732352; the government department for tourism; Dirs-Gen. Dott. STEFANO LUIGI TORDA (Tourism and Sport), Prof. Dott. CARMELO ROCCA (Performing Arts).

Ente Nazionale Italiano per il Turismo (ENIT) (National Tourist Board): Via Marghera 2, 00185 Rome; tel. (06) 49711; telex 680123; fax 4963379; f. 1919; Pres. Dott. MARINO CORONA; Dir-Gen. Dott. MARIO FALCONE.

Atomic Energy

The operation of Italy's two nuclear power stations (with a total generating capacity of 1,130 MW) has been suspended. In accordance with the results of a national referendum, which took place in November 1987, a five-year moratorium was imposed on the construction of nuclear-power installations. Nuclear power provided only 0.1% of total electricity in 1987.

ENEA—Comitato Nazionale per la Ricerca e per lo Sviluppo dell'Energia Nucleare e delle Energie Alternative: Viale Regina Margherita 125, 00198 Rome; tel. (06) 85281; telex 610183; fax 85282591; f. 1960; supervises pure and applied research into nuclear-power plants, provides technical and economic evaluations and supervision of health and environmental protection; promotes energy saving and the use of renewable energy sources; implements advanced technologies in agriculture, controls on nuclear safety; Chair. UMBERTO COLOMBO; Vice-Pres. Prof. LUIGI NOÉ; Dir-Gen. Dr FABIO PISTELLA.

Ente Nazionale per l'Energia Elettrica (ENEL): Via G.B. Martini 3 (Piazza Verdi), 00198 Rome; tel. (06) 85091; state electricity authority; has nuclear power stations in operation in the following areas: Caorso: a 882 MWe plant; Latina: a 160 MWe (MAGNOX) plant; Trino Vercellese: a 270 MWe (PWR) plant; Pres. Dr FRANCO VIEZZOLI; Dir-Gen. Ing. ALBERTO NEGRONI.

JAMAICA

Introductory Survey

Location, Climate, Language, Religion, Flag, Capital

Jamaica is the third largest island in the Caribbean Sea, lying 145 km (90 miles) to the south of Cuba and 160 km (100 miles) to the south-west of Haiti. The climate varies with altitude, being tropical at sea-level and temperate in the mountain areas. The average annual temperature is 27°C (80°F) and mean annual rainfall is 198 cm (78 inches). The official language is English, although a local patois is widely spoken. The majority of the population belong to Christian denominations, the Church of God being the most numerous. The national flag (proportions 2 by 1) consists of a diagonal gold cross on a background of black (left and right) and green (above and below). The capital is Kingston.

Recent History

Jamaica became a British colony in 1655. Slaves, transported from Africa to work on the sugar plantations, formed the basis of the island's economy until the abolition of slavery in 1834. Plans for independence were made in the 1940s. Internal self-government was introduced in 1959, and full independence, within the Commonwealth, was achieved on 6 August 1962. In 1958 Jamaica joined with Trinidad, Barbados, the Leeward Islands and the Windward Islands to form the West Indies Federation. Jamaica seceded in 1961, following a referendum, and the Federation was dissolved.

The two dominant political figures after the Second World War were the late Sir Alexander Bustamante, leader of the Jamaica Labour Party (JLP), who retired as Prime Minister in 1967, and Norman Manley, a former Premier and leader of the People's National Party (PNP), who died in 1969. The JLP won the elections of 1962 and 1967 but, under the premiership of Hugh Shearer, it lost the elections of February 1972 to the PNP, led by Michael Manley, the son of Norman Manley. Michael Manley was an advocate of democratic socialism and his Government put great emphasis on social reform and economic independence.

The early 1970s were marked by escalating street violence and crime, with gang warfare rife in the slum areas of Kingston. Between January and June 1976 162 people were killed, and in June the Government declared a state of public emergency. Despite the unrest, high unemployment and severe economic stagnation, the PNP was returned to power in December 1976 with an increased majority. The state of emergency was lifted in June 1977. By January 1979, however, there was again widespread political unrest, and violent demonstrations signalled growing discontent with the Manley Government.

In February 1980, with a worsening economic crisis, Manley rejected the IMF's stipulation that economic austerity measures (including reductions in government spending) should be undertaken, as a condition of its making further loans to Jamaica. He called a general election to seek support for his economic policies and his decision to end dependence on the IMF. The electoral campaign was one of the most violent in Jamaica's history. In the October election the JLP received about 57% of the total votes and won 51 of the 60 seats in the House of Representatives. Edward Seaga, the leader of the JLP, became Prime Minister; he supported closer political and economic links with the USA and the promotion of free enterprise. Seaga severed diplomatic relations with Cuba in October 1981, and secured valuable US financial support for the economy. Negotiations on IMF assistance were resumed. The PNP dissociated itself from the communist Workers' Party of Jamaica (WPJ) in an attempt to regain the support of more moderate voters. In February 1981 Manley offered to resign as PNP leader, and agreed to continue only upon the expulsion of extreme left-wing members from the party.

In November 1983, before the completion of a new electoral roll, Seaga called an early election, to be held on 15 December. Only four days were allowed for the nomination of candidates. The PNP, unable to present candidates at such short notice, refused to take part and declared the elections void. The JLP, opposed in only six constituencies (by independent candidates), won all 60 seats in the House of Representatives and formed a one-party legislature. Manley announced that the PNP would undertake extraparliamentary opposition to the JLP Government. At the inauguration of the new Parliament in January 1984, he led violent demonstrations by about 7,000 PNP supporters.

Devaluations of the Jamaican dollar, and the withdrawal of food subsidies, provoked demonstrations and sporadic violence in 1984, as the prices of foodstuffs and energy increased by between 50% and 100%. In order to offset the effects of these economic austerity measures, imposed at the instigation of the IMF, the Government extended its programme of food stamps to cover more than one-half of the population. Unemployment, and the consequences of illicit trading in drugs, contributed to a rise in the incidence of crime and violence, especially in Kingston. The Government increased its powers to combat political and violent crime, although the measures were criticized as autocratic by the PNP. The PNP warned of social instability as a result of Seaga's economic policies, and argued for the need to hold fresh elections after the completion of the new electoral roll. In 1985 there were further violent demonstrations in Kingston, after another increase in fuel prices, followed by widespread industrial unrest in the public sector, but Seaga continued to stress the necessity for further austerity. In May 1986, however, Seaga defied recommendations by the IMF and other aid agencies, and introduced an expansionary budget for 1986/87, in an attempt to stimulate economic growth. Large debt arrears to the IMF led to the suspension, in September 1986, of the Fund's loan agreement, but a new stand-by arrangement was agreed in January 1987.

Municipal elections, originally scheduled for June 1984, were held in July 1986, having been postponed three times. The PNP obtained control of 11 of the 13 municipalities in which polling took place, winning 57% of the total votes. During 1987 several members of the JLP left the party, and in July there was a serious outbreak of drug-related violence. In October the Government presented a plan intended to combat crime, which included proposals for the imposition of harsher punishments on persons convicted of drugs-trafficking and the provision of improved equipment for the Jamaica Defence Force.

In September 1988 Jamaica was struck by Hurricane Gilbert, the most damaging storm in the country's recorded history. More than 100,000 homes were destroyed, while the economy, particularly agriculture, was severely disrupted. Seaga's successful efforts to secure international aid won him some initial support, but this soon declined, particularly following controversy over the alleged preferential allocation of relief resources to JLP supporters.

After a brief, and relatively peaceful, campaign, a general election was held on 9 February 1989. The PNP received about 56% of the votes cast and won 45 of the 60 seats in the House of Representatives. Michael Manley, who had developed a more moderate image during his years in opposition, again became Prime Minister.

The PNP Government committed itself to continuing the JLP's economic structural adjustment programme, although this caused some dissatisfaction in the organized labour movement. The Government conceded the necessity for a devaluation of the Jamaican dollar, which was announced in October 1989. Unusually for Jamaican politics, the two main parties achieved a limited consensus on the pursuit of an economic policy of austerity, despite its unpopularity. There was also agreement that further action should be taken against the drug trade, and during 1989 Manley made several appeals for international co-operation. The Government was particularly anxious to prevent the use of Jamaican shipping and aviation for the smuggling of illegal drugs, and demanded further security measures, despite the consequent impediment to normal trade movements.

In January 1990 Manley dismissed the Minister of Industry and Commerce from the Government for failing to adhere to the principle of collective cabinet responsibility (over the rise in food prices). Manley had recently denied rumours that he

JAMAICA

intended to retire from politics, and he continued to do so in 1990, despite being incapacitated by illness between May and September. At local elections, held in March, the PNP was again successful, winning control of 12 of the 13 local councils, and obtaining some 60% of the votes cast. During 1990 there was disagreement within the opposition JLP: five MPs criticized Seaga's style of leadership as being autocratic, and were banned by him from standing as JLP candidates at the next general election. New economic adjustment measures were adopted in January 1990 (including another devaluation of the Jamaican dollar in relation to the US dollar, increases in taxes and in the price of basic foodstuffs and electricity, and restrictions on wage increases), in order to secure another IMF stand-by arrangement, worth US $107m. This agreement was suspended in March because the measures had failed to bring reserves of foreign exchange to the stipulated level, but assistance was resumed in November; nevertheless, in 1990 Jamaica was due to give the IMF and the World Bank US $200m. more in repayments than it received from them. In June a five-year economic development plan was announced (see Economic Affairs), and in November the Cabinet was reorganized, with the aim of increasing economic efficiency: the Deputy Prime Minister, P. J. Patterson, became Minister of Finance (retaining the portfolio of development and planning that he had previously held), while a new ministry of industry, production and commerce was created.

In October 1983 Jamaica contributed troops to the US-led invasion of Grenada and led the Caribbean force which remained, after the removal of the majority of the American forces, to keep the peace and to assist in training the new Grenadian police force.

Prior to his re-election as Prime Minister in February 1989, Michael Manley announced his intention of maintaining good relations with the USA. In May 1990 Manley made an official visit to the USA, requesting assistance for the strengthening of Jamaica's economy and for relieving the country's indebtedness. In July diplomatic relations with Cuba were resumed, and it was also announced in 1990 that the Government intended to strengthen diplomatic relations with Latin American and Asian countries.

Government

The Head of State is the British monarch, who is represented locally by a Governor-General, appointed on the recommendation of the Prime Minister. The Governor-General acts, in almost all matters, on the advice of the Cabinet.

Legislative power is vested in the bicameral Parliament: a Senate, with 21 appointed members, and a House of Representatives, with 60 elected members. Thirteen members of the Senate are appointed by the Governor-General on the advice of the Prime Minister and eight on the advice of the Leader of the Opposition. Members of the House are elected by universal adult suffrage for five years (subject to dissolution). Executive power lies with the Cabinet. The Governor-General appoints the Prime Minister and, on the latter's recommendation, other Ministers. The Cabinet is responsible to Parliament.

Defence

In June 1990 the Jamaica Defence Force consisted of 3,350 men on active service, including an army of 3,000, a coastguard of 200 and an air wing of 150 men. There are reserves of some 870. Defence expenditure in 1987/88 was estimated to be US $25.06m.

Economic Affairs

In 1989, according to estimates by the World Bank, Jamaica's gross national product (GNP), measured at average 1987–89 prices, was US $3,011m., equivalent to $1,260 per head. Between 1980 and 1989 GNP was estimated to have fallen, in real terms, by an average of 0.4% per year, but, over the same period, the population had increased by an annual average of 1.3%. GNP per head, therefore, was estimated to have declined by an average of 1.7% per year. Jamaica's gross domestic product (GDP) increased, in real terms, by an annual average of 0.6% in 1980–88.

Agriculture (including forestry and fishing) contributed 6% of GDP in 1988. In 1989 an estimated 27.4% of the total labour force were employed in the sector. The principal cash crops are sugar cane (sugar accounted for 10.8% of total export earnings in 1988), bananas, citrus fruit, coffee and cocoa. The cultivation of vegetables, fruit and rice is being encouraged, in an attempt to reduce imports and diversify agricultural exports. Goats, cattle and pigs are the principal livestock. During 1980–88 agricultural production increased by an annual average of 0.9%. Production was severely affected by Hurricane Gilbert in 1988.

Industry (including mining, manufacturing, public utilities and construction) contributed 37.4% of GDP in 1986. Average annual growth was recorded at zero in the sector during 1980–88.

Mining and quarrying contributed 6.4% of GDP in 1986 but, with the associated refineries, employed only 0.5% of the labour force in 1987. Mining is the principal productive sector of the economy, and in 1989 bauxite and its derivative, alumina (aluminium oxide), accounted for more than 60% of total export earnings. Bauxite, of which Jamaica is one of the world's leading producers, is the major mineral mined, but there are also reserves of marble, gypsum, silica and clay.

Manufacturing contributed 20.9% of GDP in 1986, and engaged 16.2% of the employed labour force in 1987. Much of the activity in the sector is dependent upon the processing of agricultural products and bauxite. Food, beverages and tobacco together accounted for some 70% of industrial output in 1988, mainly for domestic use. Petroleum-refining is also important. The export of garments, mainly to the USA, became increasingly important during the 1980s, providing 23% of total export earnings in 1989.

Energy is derived principally from imported hydrocarbon fuels (about 20% of total imports in 1989). Most of Jamaica's petroleum requirements are fulfilled by imports from Venezuela and Mexico.

The principal earner of foreign exchange is tourism. Tourist arrivals exceeded 1m. for the first time in 1987 and totalled 1.16m. in 1989. The largest proportion of tourists are from the USA (45% in 1988). Earnings from tourism increased in 1989 to an estimated US $607m., equivalent to some two-thirds of the value of total commodity exports.

In 1988 Jamaica recorded a visible trade deficit of US $551.9m., and a deficit of US $213.6m. on the current account of the balance of payments. In 1988 the principal source of imports (52.0%) and the principal market for exports (45.5%) was the USA. The United Kingdom (15.3% of exports, 5.7% of imports) and Canada (12.5% of exports and 6.8% of imports) were also important trading partners. The principal exports are bauxite and alumina, garments, sugar, rum and bananas. The principal imports in 1987 were machinery, transport equipment and mineral fuels. Between 1987 and 1989 domestic production of hemp (marijuana) and the use of the island as a transit centre for other illegal drugs, from Latin America, were believed to have generated more revenue than the country's legitimate exports.

For the financial year ending 31 March 1990 the Government projected a surplus of J$ 1,392m. in the current budget, but capital expenditure of J$ 3,523m. was planned. In that year the actual budgetary deficit was estimated to be equivalent to 4.4% of Jamaica's GDP. Total external debt in 1988 was US $4,304m., of which $3,554m. was long-term debt. The cost of servicing long-term debt in 1988 was equivalent to 24.8% of the value of exports of goods and services, and in the budget for 1990/91 about 39% of total expenditure was allocated to debt-servicing. The average annual rate of inflation was 18.7% in 1980–88, and stood at 17.2% in 1989. Some 18% of the labour force were unemployed in 1989.

Jamaica is a founding member of CARICOM (see p. 108), of the Inter-American Development bank (see p. 158) and of the International Bauxite Association (which is based in Jamaica—see p. 228).

During the 1980s the development of Jamaica's economy was hampered by a persistent trade deficit, a shortage of foreign exchange, and a high level of external indebtedness. Throughout the decade attempts at economic reform, on which assistance from the IMF was conditional, entailed credit restrictions, devaluations of the currency, and limits on government spending; these measures resulted in economic expansion in the late 1980s, but also caused hardship for the poorer Jamaicans. The hurricane of September 1988 severely affected the economy, but agricultural production and tourism quickly recovered, and growth of 4.6% in GDP (in real terms) was reported for 1989. In June 1990 a five-year development plan was announced, envisaging real annual growth of 3% in GDP, chiefly by encouraging tourism and expanding production of bauxite; the

JAMAICA

plan involved development spending of J $17,000m., of which 42% was to be financed externally. In September the Government announced the deregulation of the foreign exchange market and allowed the currency to 'float' in relation to the US dollar, thus effectively devaluing it for the second time that year; further measures of economic liberalization, including the privatization of some government services and a lessening of restrictions on investment by non-resident Jamaicans, were announced later in the year.

Social Welfare

Social welfare is undertaken by the Government. The Social Development Commission arranges and co-ordinates social welfare in the villages. Contributory national insurance and housing trust schemes are administered by the Government. In 1979 Jamaica had 30 government-controlled hospitals, with a total of 7,648 beds, and there were 759 physicians working in the country. In the 1988/89 budget, projected expenditure on health was J $128.9m., representing about 2% of total expenditure. In 1990 the Inter-American Development Bank approved a credit of US $70.5m. for the rehabilitation of the health service.

Education

Primary education is compulsory in certain districts, and free education is ensured. The education system consists of a primary cycle of six years, followed by two secondary cycles of three and four years respectively. In 1987 about 95% of children between six and 11 years of age were enrolled at primary schools, while 62% of those aged 12 to 18 attended secondary schools. In 1990 an estimated 1.6% of the adult population had received no schooling. Higher education is provided by technical colleges and by the University of the West Indies, which has five faculties situated at its Mona campus in Kingston. Expenditure on education by the central Government in the financial year 1988/89 was estimated to be J $133.6m., some 2% of total expenditure.

Public Holidays

1991: 1 January (New Year's Day), 13 February (Ash Wednesday), 29 March (Good Friday), 1 April (Easter Monday), 23 May (National Labour Day), 5 August (Independence Day), 21 October (National Heroes' Day), 25-26 December (Christmas).

1992: 1 January (New Year's Day), 4 March (Ash Wednesday), 17 April (Good Friday), 20 April (Easter Monday), 25 May (for National Labour Day), 3 August (Independence Day), 19 October (National Heroes' Day), 25-26 December (Christmas).

Weights and Measures

Both the imperial and the metric systems are in use.

Statistical Survey

Sources (unless otherwise stated): Department of Statistics, 9 Swallowfield Rd, Kingston 5, Jamaica; tel. 926-2175; Jamaica Information Service, Jamaica High Commission, 1-2 Prince Consort Rd, London, SW7 2BZ, United Kingdom; tel. (071) 823-9911.

Area and Population

AREA, POPULATION AND DENSITY

Area (sq km)	10,991*
Population (census results)	
7 April 1970	1,848,512
8 June 1982	
Males	1,079,640
Females	1,125,867
Total	2,205,507
Population (official estimates at 31 December)	
1987	2,355,400
1988	2,358,000
1989	2,392,000
Density (per sq km) at 31 December 1989	217.6

* 4,243.6 sq miles.

PARISHES

	Area (sq miles)	Population (31 Dec. 1986)
Kingston	8.406	641,500
St Andrew	186.308	
St Thomas	286.800	85,300
Portland	314.347	77,100
St Mary	235.745	111,600
St Ann	468.213	147,100
Trelawny	337.651	73,200
St James	229.728	149,500
Hanover	173.855	65,200
Westmorland	311.604	126,600
St Elizabeth	468.085	144,400
Manchester	320.482	157,800
Clarendon	461.864	214,400
St Catherine	460.396	353,200
Total	**4,263.484***	**2,346,900**

* Other sources give the total area of the country as 4,243.6 square miles.

Capital: Kingston (population 104,041 at 1982 census).

Other towns (1970 census): Montego Bay (42,800); Spanish Town (41,600).

JAMAICA

Statistical Survey

BIRTHS AND DEATHS*

	Registered live births		Registered deaths	
	Number	Rate (per 1,000)	Number	Rate (per 1,000)
1983	61,436	27.4	12,588	5.6
1984	57,533	25.2	13,405	5.9
1985	56,210	24.3	13,918	6.0
1986	54,067	23.1	13,341	5.7
1987	52,300	22.2	12,400	5.3
1988	53,623	21.9	12,167	5.0
1989	59,104	24.9	14,315	6.0

Registered marriages: 10,536 in 1987; 10,429 in 1988.

* Data are tabulated by year of registration rather than by year of occurrence.

CIVILIAN LABOUR FORCE
(persons aged 14 years and over, at October)

	1985	1986	1987
Agriculture, forestry and fishing	278,900	267,200	269,300
Mining, quarrying and refining	6,000	6,300	5,300
Manufacturing	100,600	115,300	138,200
Construction and installation	34,800	35,400	38,600
Transport, communications and public utilities	34,700	38,300	42,100
Commerce	115,300	125,100	128,100
Public administration	81,100	79,900	72,800
Other services	127,200	150,100	158,600
Activities not adequately defined	2,400	3,000	2,000
Total employed	781,000	820,600	855,000
Unemployed	268,800	234,900	224,200
Total labour force	1,049,800	1,055,500*	1,079,200

* Comprising 566,900 males (491,400 employed, 75,500 unemployed) and 488,600 females (329,200 employed, 159,400 unemployed).

Agriculture

PRINCIPAL CROPS ('000 metric tons)

	1987	1988	1989
Sweet potatoes	24	20	22
Cassava	17	14	10
Yams	176	167	133
Other roots and tubers	36	35	41
Coconuts	192	205	200*
Pumpkins, squash and gourds	27	22	24
Other vegetables and melons	121	92	106
Sugar cane	2,014	2,603	2,548†
Oranges	49	63	60*
Lemons and limes*	24	24	24
Grapefruit and pomelo	31	39	39
Bananas*	180	120	130
Plantains	28	26	26*
Other fruit*	89	95	95
Coffee (green)	2	2	1†
Cocoa beans	3	2	2†
Tobacco (leaves)†	2	2	2

* FAO estimate(s). † Unofficial estimate(s).
Source: FAO, *Production Yearbook*.

LIVESTOCK
(FAO estimates, '000 head, year ending September)

	1987	1988	1989
Horses	4	4	4
Mules	10	10	10
Asses	23	23	23
Cattle	290	290	290
Pigs	246	250	250
Sheep	3	3	3
Goats	440	440	440
Poultry	6,000	6,000	3,000

Source: FAO, *Production Yearbook*.

LIVESTOCK PRODUCTS ('000 metric tons)

	1987	1988	1989*
Beef and veal	14	14	14
Goats' meat*	2	2	2
Pig meat	6	8	6
Poultry meat	38	34	23
Cows' milk*	49	49	49
Hen eggs*	17.6	17.0	12.0

* FAO estimates.
Source: FAO, *Production Yearbook*.

Forestry

ROUNDWOOD REMOVALS ('000 cubic metres, excl. bark)

	1986	1987	1988
Sawlogs, veneer logs and logs for sleepers	96	127	134
Other industrial wood	76	77	73
Fuelwood*	13	13	13
Total	185	217	220

* FAO estimates.
Source: FAO, *Yearbook of Forest Products*.

SAWNWOOD PRODUCTION ('000 cubic metres)

	1986	1987	1988
Total	26	30	44

Source: FAO, *Yearbook of Forest Products*.

Fishing
('000 metric tons, live weight)

	1986	1987	1988*
Total catch	10.8	9.3	10.0

* FAO estimate.
Source: FAO, *Yearbook of Fishery Statistics*.

JAMAICA

Mining

('000 metric tons)

	1985	1986	1987
Bauxite*	6,119.4	5,522.4	7,802.1
Alumina	1,461.7	1,314.8	1,613.0
Gypsum (crude)	176	142	126

1988 ('000 metric tons): Bauxite* 7,410, Alumina 1,580.
1989 ('000 metric tons): Bauxite* 9,400, Alumina 2,400.
1990 ('000 metric tons): Bauxite* 10,920, Alumina (exports) 2,880.

* Dried equivalent of crude ore.

Industry

SELECTED PRODUCTS
('000 metric tons, unless otherwise indicated)

	1985	1986	1987
Margarine and lard	8.9	10.7	10.0
Wheat flour	132	138	137
Sugar	222	203	186
Animal foodstuffs	165	163	221
Rum and gin ('000 hectolitres)	148	n.a.	n.a.
Beer ('000 hectolitres)	568	632	700
Soft drinks ('000 hectolitres)	372	729	677
Cigars (million)	21	19	22
Cigarettes (million)	1,314	1,140*	1,273
Jet fuels	47	40	25
Motor gasoline—Petrol	116	98	70
Kerosene	62	52	35
Distillate fuel oils	176	139	100
Residual fuel oils	484	483	400
Lubricating oils	18	20	15
Rubber tyres ('000)	210	217	265
Quicklime†	86	91	n.a.
Cement	241	247	261
Electric energy (million kWh)	2,286	2,371	2,380

* Estimate.
† Estimates from the US Bureau of Mines.
Source: UN, *Industrial Statistics Yearbook*.

1988 ('000 metric tons): Raw sugar 222; Motor gasoline 75; Kerosene and jet fuels 65; Distillate fuel oils 110; Residual fuel oils 390.
1989 ('000 metric tons): Wheat flour 284; Raw sugar 192 (estimate).

Finance

CURRENCY AND EXCHANGE RATES
Monetary Units
 100 cents = 1 Jamaican dollar (J $).

Denominations
 Coins: 1, 5, 10, 20, 25 and 50 cents.
 Notes: 1, 2, 5, 10, 20, 50 and 100 dollars.

Sterling and US Dollar Equivalents (30 September 1990)
 £1 sterling = J $14.733;
 US $1 = J $7.864;
 J $1,000 = £67.87 = US $127.16.

Average Exchange Rate (J $ per US $)
 1987 5.4867
 1988 5.4886
 1989 5.7446

BUDGET (J $ million, year ending 31 March)

Revenue	1986/87
Recurrent Revenue:	
Customs	231.5
Excise duties	31.0
Income tax	1,514.6
Land and property tax	26.2
Stamp duties	522.8
Motor vehicle licences	62.6
Consumption duty	858.0
Betting and gaming tax	32.8
Retail sales tax	49.4
Other taxes and duties	166.4
Sub-total	**3,495.1**
Non-tax receipts	83.4
Transfer from Capital Development Fund	20.0
Total	**3,598.7**

Expenditure	1986/87
Recurrent Expenditure:	
Interest on public debt	1,078.6
General administration	437.3
Public order and safety	395.2
Agriculture	55.9
Education and social welfare	691.8
Public health	313.6
Trade and industry	26.9
Public utilities and transport	66.0
Housing	58.6
Other	28.2
Sub-total	**3,152.1**
Capital Expenditure:	
General administration	316.5
Agriculture	67.5
Education and social welfare	28.5
Housing	248.4
Health	16.5
Public utilities and transport	64.7
Financing of public enterprises	50.8
Public debt	1,043.7
Sub-total	**1,836.6**
Total	**4,988.7**

1987/88 (J $ million): Revenue 5,400; Current expenditure 4,140; Capital expenditure 1,200.
1988/89 (J $ million): Revenue 6,200; Current expenditure 5,200; Capital expenditure 1,700.
1989/90 (government estimates, J $ million): Revenue 6,920.8; Current expenditure 5,528.8; Capital expenditure 3,522.8.
1990/91 (government estimates, J $ million): Current expenditure 7,049; Capital expenditure 4,068.

CENTRAL BANK RESERVES (US $ million)

	1987	1988	1989
IMF special drawing rights	1.4	—	—
Foreign exchange	172.9	147.2	107.5
Total	**174.3**	**147.2**	**107.5**

Source: IMF, *International Financial Statistics*.

MONEY SUPPLY (J $ million at 31 December)

	1987	1988	1989
Currency outside banks	844	1,288	1,378
Demand deposits at commercial banks	1,407	2,157	1,775
Total money	**2,252**	**3,445**	**3,153**

Source: IMF, *International Financial Statistics*.

JAMAICA

COST OF LIVING (Consumer Price Index; end of December. Base: January 1975 = 100)

	1985	1986	1987*
Food and drink	729.6	818.4	839.9
Fuel and household supplies	863.2	915.0	925.4
Housing	423.1	458.6	476.3
Household furnishings and furniture	761.6	835.8	885.7
Personal clothing and accessories	541.3	639.5	659.2
Personal expenses	728.4	806.4	844.0
Transport	575.4	579.5	578.7
Miscellaneous expenses	523.8	542.8	549.9
All items	**670.7**	**742.5**	**762.9**

* Preliminary.

NATIONAL ACCOUNTS (J $ million at current prices)

Expenditure on the Gross Domestic Product

	1987	1988	1989
Government final consumption expenditure	2,436.0	3,015.6	3,150.0
Private final consumption expenditure	9,801.0	11,767.1	13,467.0
Increase in stocks	160.1	498.6	47.2
Gross fixed capital formation	3,144.7	4,865.3	6,503.0
Total domestic expenditure	**15,541.7**	**20,146.6**	**23,167.2**
Exports of goods and services	8,404.5	8,849.4	10,589.3
Less Imports of goods and services	8,344.0	10,248.0	11,441.7
GDP in purchasers' values	**16,002.1**	**18,748.0**	**22,314.9**
GDP at constant 1985 prices	**12,101.3**	**12,279.5**	**12,839.6**

Source: IMF, *International Financial Statistics*.

Gross Domestic Product by Economic Activity*

	1984	1985	1986
Agriculture, hunting, forestry and fishing	542.4	669.5	818.1
Mining and quarrying	664.2	569.3	901.8
Manufacturing	1,698.5	2,276.1	2,949.0
Electricity, gas and water	287.7	346.4	403.5
Construction	841.5	953.4	1,027.8
Wholesale and retail trade, restaurants and hotels	2,122.9	2,741.8	3,142.3
Transport, storage and communication	693.6	939.3	1,076.0
Finance, insurance, real estate and business services	1,401.8	1,620.2	2,083.1
Producers of government services	1,108.9	1,168.9	1,319.9
Other community, social and personal services	211.8	256.6	290.5
Other producers	70.0	84.5	111.3
Sub-total	**9,643.5**	**11,626.1**	**14,123.2**
Less Imputed bank service charge	320.1	382.5	794.0
GDP in purchasers' values	**9,323.4**	**11,243.6**	**13,329.2**

* Figures are provisional. Revised totals (in J $ million) are: 9,358.4 in 1984; 11,202.6 in 1985; 13,388.5 in 1986.

Source: UN, *National Accounts Statistics*.

BALANCE OF PAYMENTS (US $ million)

	1987	1988	1989
Merchandise exports f.o.b.	708.4	833.5	1,017.0
Merchandise imports f.o.b.	−1,065.1	−1,228.5	−1,568.9
Trade balance	**−356.7**	**−395.0**	**−551.9**
Exports of services	925.0	897.7	1,208.7
Imports of services	−876.0	−931.3	−1,166.7
Balance on goods and services	**−307.7**	**−428.6**	**−509.9**
Private unrequited transfers (net)	117.2	435.6	141.1
Government unrequited transfers (net)	53.5	69.1	155.2
Current balance	**−137.0**	**76.1**	**−213.6**
Direct capital investment (net)	53.4	−12.0	28.1
Other long-term capital (net)	201.9	24.4	211.3
Short-term capital (net)	97.9	84.8	−149.2
Net errors and omissions	82.8	−100.7	34.8
Total (net monetary movements)	**299.0**	**72.6**	**−88.6**
Valuation changes (net)	−86.3	33.4	13.8
Exceptional financing	−134.1	57.0	13.4
Official financing (net)	−3.0	4.8	115.0
Changes in reserves	**75.6**	**167.7**	**53.6**

Source: IMF, *International Financial Statistics*.

External Trade

COMMODITY GROUPS (US $ '000)

Imports	1986	1987
Food and live animals	166,180	181,923
Beverages and tobacco	9,865	12,028
Crude materials (inedible) except fuels	30,150	37,008
Mineral fuels, lubricants, etc.	202,666	219,524
Animal and vegetable oils and fats	10,583	15,475
Chemicals	107,765	119,424
Basic manufactures	168,871	n.a.
Machinery and transport equipment	174,583	245,822
Miscellaneous manufactured articles	87,237	135,527
Other commodities and transactions	18,498	22,223
Total	**976,398**	**1,216,067**

Exports	1986	1987
Food and live animals	122,907	150,596
Beverages and tobacco	29,637	33,855
Crude materials (inedible) except fuels	314,732	333,387
Mineral fuels, lubricants, etc.	18,273	14,111
Animal and vegetable oils and fats	71	303
Chemicals	18,558	20,830
Basic manufactures	8,634	n.a.
Machinery and transport equipment	19,249	11,159
Miscellaneous manufactured articles	65,483	15,038
Other commodities and transactions	32	—
Total	**597,576**	**696,057**

1988 (US $ '000): Total imports 1,427,700; Total exports 823,600.
1989 (US $ '000): Total imports 1,520,000; Total exports 970,400.

JAMAICA

PRINCIPAL TRADING PARTNERS (J $'000)

Imports c.i.f.	1984	1985	1986
Canada	246,344	223,000	282,492
Ecuador	30,131	45,847	148,284
Germany, Federal Republic	73,549	66,321	78,754
Japan	130,276	433,552	196,829
Mexico	49,091	277,044	82,991
Netherlands	42,056	84,793	76,621
Netherlands Dependencies	604,546	507,506	74,367
Trinidad and Tobago	89,852	181,356	103,751
United Kingdom	244,989	326,951	362,584
USA	2,036,052	2,545,619	2,675,854
Total (incl. others)	4,509,548	6,146,681	5,322,277

Exports f.o.b.*	1984	1985	1986
Barbados	38,949	65,665	62,063
Canada	409,085	511,792	500,208
Ghana	—	92,244	36,154
Guyana	12,288	20,978	23,143
Japan	—	46,537	34,632
Netherlands	171	72,480	232,492
Norway	33,036	72,767	92,649
Sweden	101,708	17,720	22,573
Trinidad and Tobago	124,298	85,910	86,755
USSR	145,099	157,082	137,270
United Kingdom	369,089	525,690	609,688
USA	1,375,586	1,022,644	1,052,768
Total (incl. others)	2,675,758	2,958,815	3,089,238

* Excluding re-exports.

Transport

RAILWAYS (traffic)

1988: 1.2m. passenger journeys; 115m. metric ton-km.

ROAD TRAFFIC
(vehicles in use at 31 December 1986)

Passenger cars	42,888
Buses and coaches	
Goods vehicles	26,486
Tractors (non-agricultural)	
Motorcycles and scooters	5,605

SHIPPING

International Sea-borne Freight Traffic
(estimates, '000 metric tons)

	1986	1987	1988
Goods loaded	5,150	5,061	6,549
Goods unloaded	3,946	3,943	4,477

Source: UN, *Monthly Bulletin of Statistics*.

CIVIL AVIATION (traffic on scheduled services)

	1983	1984	1985
Kilometres flown (million)	9.8	10.4	11.9
Passengers carried ('000)	716.0	826.0	888.0
Passenger-km (million)	1,079	1,303	1,482.0
Freight ton-km (million)	16.6	19.6	19.1

Source: UN, *Statistical Yearbook*.

Tourism

	1986	1987	1988
Visitor arrivals	942,100	1,030,413	1,016,605
Stop-overs	663,593	738,827	648,873
Cruise-ship passengers	278,507	291,586	367,732
Hotel rooms	13,371	14,031	n.a.

1989: Total tourist arrivals 1.16m.

Communications Media

(units in use, unless otherwise indicated)

	1985	1986	1987
Radio receivers	900,000*	1,373,577	1,448,122
Television receivers	215,000*	436,000	462,055
Telephones	n.a.	152,295	n.a.
Daily newspapers (number)	2	2	2
Circulation (estimates, '000)	n.a.	n.a.	84
Book production (number of titles)	71†	n.a.	n.a.

* Estimates by UNESCO.
† Including 48 pamphlets (UNESCO figures).

1988: 4 daily newspapers, circulation 155,000 (UNESCO figure).

Education

(1988)

	Institutions	Teachers	Students
Pre-primary	1,673	4,197	136,415
Primary	893	10,251	339,163
Secondary	141*	9,061	241,000
Tertiary	14*	627†	7,420†
University	1	401†	4,634†

* 1984 figures.
† 1986 figures.

Source: mainly UNESCO, *Statistical Yearbook*.

Directory

The Constitution

The Constitution came into force at the independence of Jamaica on 6 August 1962.

HEAD OF STATE

The Head of State is the British monarch, who is locally represented by a Governor-General, appointed on the recommendation of the Jamaican Prime Minister.

THE LEGISLATURE

The Senate or Upper House consists of 21 Senators of whom 13 will be appointed by the Governor-General on the advice of the Prime Minister and eight by the Governor-General on the advice of the Leader of the Opposition. (Legislation enacted in 1984 provided for eight independent Senators to be appointed, after consultations with the Prime Minister, in the eventuality of there being no Leader of the Opposition.)

The House of Representatives consists of 60 elected members called Members of Parliament.

A person is qualified for appointment to the Senate or for election to the House of Representatives if he or she is a citizen of Jamaica or other Commonwealth country, of the age of 21 or more and has been ordinarily resident in Jamaica for the immediately preceding 12 months.

THE PRIVY COUNCIL

The Privy Council consists of six members appointed by the Governor-General after consultation with the Prime Minister, of whom at least two are persons who hold or who have held public office. The functions of the Council are to advise the Governor-General on the exercise of the Royal Prerogative of Mercy and on appeals on disciplinary matters from the three Service Commissions.

THE EXECUTIVE

The Prime Minister is appointed from the House of Representatives by the Governor-General as the person who, in the Governor-General's judgement, is best able to command the support of the majority of the members of that House.

The Leader of the Opposition is appointed by the Governor-General as the member of the House of Representatives who, in the Governor-General's judgement, is best able to command the support of the majority of those members of the House who do not support the Government.

The Cabinet consists of the Prime Minister and not fewer than 11 other Ministers, not more than four of whom may sit in the Senate. The members of the Cabinet are appointed by the Governor-General on the advice of the Prime Minister.

THE JUDICATURE

The Judicature consists of a Supreme Court, a Court of Appeal and minor courts. Judicial matters, notably advice to the Governor-General on appointments, are considered by a Judicial Service Commission, the Chairman of which is the Chief Justice, members being the President of the Court of Appeal, the Chairman of the Public Service Commission and three others.

CITIZENSHIP

All persons born in Jamaica after independence automatically acquire Jamaican citizenship and there is also provision for the acquisition of citizenship by persons born outside Jamaica of Jamaican parents. Persons born in Jamaica (or persons born outside Jamaica of Jamaican parents) before independence who immediately prior to independence were citizens of the United Kingdom and colonies also automatically become citizens of Jamaica.

Appropriate provision is made which permits persons who do not automatically become citizens of Jamaica to be registered as such.

FUNDAMENTAL RIGHTS AND FREEDOMS

The Constitution includes provisions safeguarding the fundamental freedoms of the individual, irrespective of race, place of origin, political opinions, colour, creed or sex, subject only to respect for the rights and freedoms of others and for the public interest. The fundamental freedoms include the rights of life, liberty, security of the person and protection from arbitrary arrest or restriction of movement, the enjoyment of property and the protection of the law, freedom of conscience, of expression and of peaceful assembly and association, and respect for private and family life.

The Government

Head of State: HM Queen ELIZABETH II.
Governor-General: (vacant).

PRIVY COUNCIL OF JAMAICA

Dr VERNON LINDO, EWART FORREST, G. OWEN, W. H. SWABY, Dr DOUGLAS FLETCHER.

THE CABINET
(February 1991)

Prime Minister: MICHAEL MANLEY.
Deputy Prime Minister and Minister of Finance, Development and Planning: PERCIVAL J. PATTERSON.
Attorney-General and Minister of Justice: CARL RATTRAY.
Minister of Foreign Affairs and Foreign Trade: Senator DAVID COORE.
Minister of Agriculture: SEYMOUR MULLINGS.
Minister of National Security: K. D. KNIGHT.
Minister of Industry, Production and Commerce: HUGH SMALL.
Minister of Construction: O. D. RAMTALLIE.
Minister of Education: Senator CARLYLE DUNKLEY.
Minister of Health: EASTON DOUGLAS.
Minister of Labour, Welfare and Sports: PORTIA SIMPSON.
Minister of Local Government: RALPH BROWN.
Minister of Mining and Energy: HORACE CLARKE.
Minister of Public Utilities and Transport: ROBERT PICKERSGILL.
Minister of Tourism: Senator FRANK PRINGLE.
Minister of Youth and Community Development: DOUGLAS MANLEY.
Minister of Information and Culture: Senator Dr PAUL ROBERTSON.
Minister of the Public Service and Leader of the House of Representatives: Dr KENNETH MCNEIL.

MINISTRIES

Office of the Governor-General: King's House, Hope Rd, Kingston 10; tel. 927-6424.

Office of the Prime Minister: 1 Devon Rd, POB 272, Kingston 10; tel. 927-9941; telex 2398; fax 929-0005.

Ministry of Agriculture: Hope Gardens, Kingston 6; tel. 927-1731.

Ministry of Construction: 2 Hagley Park Rd, Kingston 10; tel. 926-1590.

Ministry of Education: 2 National Heroes Circle, Kingston 4; tel. 922-1400.

Ministry of Finance, Development and Planning: 30 National Heroes Circle, Kingston 4; tel. 922-8600; telex 2447.

Ministry of Foreign Affairs and Foreign Trade: 63 Knutsford Blvd, Kingston 5; tel. 926-4220; telex 2114.

Ministry of Health: 10 Caledonia Ave, Kingston 5; tel. 926-9220.

Ministry of Industry, Production and Commerce: 4 Winchester Rd, Kingston 10; tel. 929-1540.

Ministry of Information and Culture: 1 Devon Rd, Kingston 10; tel. 927-9941.

Ministry of Justice: 12 Ocean Blvd, Kingston Mall, Kingston; tel. 922-0080.

Ministry of Labour, Welfare and Sports: 14 National Heroes Circle, POB 10, Kingston 5; tel. 922-8000.

Ministry of Local Government: Ocean Blvd, Kingston; tel. 922-1670.

Ministry of Mining and Energy: 36 Trafalgar Rd, Kingston 10; tel. 926-9170; fax 926-2835.

Ministry of National Security: 12 Ocean Blvd, Kingston Mall, Kingston; tel. 922-0080.

Ministry of the Public Service: Citibank Bldg, 63–67 Knutsford Blvd, Kingston 5; tel. 926-3235.

JAMAICA   Directory

Ministry of Public Utilities and Transport: POB 9000, 2 St Lucia Ave, Kingston 5; tel. 926-8130; fax 929-3375.

Ministry of Tourism: Petrojam Bldg, 36 Trafalgar Rd., Kingston 10; tel. 926-9170.

Ministry of Youth and Community Development: 12 Ocean Blvd, Kingston Mall, POB 503, Kingston; tel. 922-1710.

Legislature

PARLIAMENT

Houses of Parliament: Gordon House, Duke St, Kingston; tel. 922-0200.

Senate

President: HOWARD COOKE.
The Senate has 20 other members.

House of Representatives

Speaker: HEADLEY CUNNINGHAM.

General Election, 9 February 1989

	Votes cast		Seats
	Number	%	
People's National Party (PNP)	463,080	55.8	45
Jamaica Labour Party (JLP)	366,509	44.1	15
Others	623	0.1	—
Total	830,212	100.0	60

Political Organizations

African Comprehensive Party (ACP): Kingston; f. 1988 as political branch of a Rastafarian sect, the Royal Ethiopian Judah Coptic church; opposes IMF and 'capitalist banking system'; advocates legalizing the use of marijuana for religious purposes; Leader ABUNA STEDWICK WHYTE.

Jamaica American Party: Kingston; f. 1986; advocates US statehood for Jamaica; Leader JAMES CHISHOLM.

Jamaica Labour Party (JLP): 20 Belmont Rd, Kingston 5; f. 1943 as political wing of the Bustamante Industrial Trade Union; supports free enterprise in a mixed economy and close co-operation with the USA; Leader EDWARD SEAGA; Chair. BRUCE GOLDING; Gen. Sec. RYAN PERALTO.

People's National Party (PNP): 89 Old Hope Rd, Kingston 5; f. 1938; socialist principles; affiliated with the National Workers' Union; Pres. MICHAEL MANLEY; Chair. P. J. PATTERSON; Gen. Sec. Senator Dr PAUL ROBERTSON.

Workers' Party of Jamaica (WPJ): f. 1978 out of the Workers Liberation League; traditional Marxist-Leninist ideology rejected in 1990; Gen. Sec. Dr TREVOR MUNROE.

Diplomatic Representation

EMBASSIES AND HIGH COMMISSIONS IN JAMAICA

Argentina: 40 Knutsford Blvd, Kingston 5; tel. 926-5588; telex 2107; Ambassador: PAULINO MUSSACCHIO.

Australia: First Life Bldg, 64 Knutsford Blvd, Kingston 5; tel. 926-3550; telex 2355; High Commissioner: MICHAEL LANDALE.

Brazil: First Life Bldg, 64 Knutsford Blvd, Kingston 5; tel. 929-8607; telex 2221; Ambassador: EDMUNDO RADWANSKI.

Canada: Mutual Security Bank Bldg, 30 Knutsford Blvd, POB 1500, Kingston 10; tel. 926-1500; telex 2130; High Commissioner: KATHRYN MCCALLION.

China, People's Republic: 8 Seaview Ave, Kingston 10; tel. 927-0850; telex 2202; Chargé d'affaires: HUANG DONGBI.

Colombia: 53 Knutsford Blvd, Victoria Mutual Bldg, 3 floor, Kingston 5; tel. 929 1702; telex 2200; fax 929-1701, Ambassador: NINON MILLAN.

Costa Rica: 21 John Wesley Ave, Kingston 6; tel. 927-4493; Ambassador: Dr ROGER CHURNSIDE.

Cuba: Kingston; Ambassador: DARÍO DE URRA.

France: 13 Hillcrest Ave, Kingston 6; tel. 927-9811; telex 2367; Ambassador: MICHEL REUILARD.

Germany: 10 Waterloo Rd, Kingston 10; tel. 926-5665; telex 2146; Ambassador: Dr NILS GRUEBER.

India: 4 Retreat Ave, POB 446, Kingston 6; tel. 927-0486; High Commissioner: KHIANGTE C. LALVUNGA.

Israel: Pan Jamaican Bldg, 60 Knutsford Blvd, Kingston 5; tel. 926-8768; telex 2466; Ambassador: URI PROSOR.

Japan: 3rd Floor, 'The Atrium', 32 Trafalgar Rd, Kingston 5; tel. 929-3338; telex 2304; Chargé d'affaires a.i.: NOBORU KAWAGISHI.

Korea, Democratic People's Republic: 18 New Haven Ave, Kingston 6; tel. 927-7087; telex 2491; Ambassador: SHIN MYONG HO.

Korea, Republic: 2nd Floor, Pan Jamaican Bldg, 60 Knutsford Blvd, Kingston 5; tel. 929-3035; Ambassador: KIE YUL MOON.

Mexico: PCJ Bldg, 36 Trafalgar Rd, Kingston 10; tel. 926-4242; telex 2255; Ambassador: GUSTAVO EVARISTO IRUEGAS.

Netherlands: Xerox Bldg, 53 Knutsford Blvd, Kingston 5; tel. 926-1247; telex 2177; Chargé d'affaires a.i.: HANS VAN DEN DOOL.

Nicaragua: Kingston; Ambassador: (vacant).

Nigeria: 5 Waterloo Rd, Kingston 10; tel. 926-6400; telex 2443; High Commissioner: Prof. ADE ADEFUYE.

Panama: 7 Trafalgar Rd, Kingston 5; tel. 927-6970; Ambassador: JACINTA DE BAYARD.

Peru: 2nd Floor, Oxford House, 6 Oxford Rd, Kingston 5; tel. 929-1151; telex 3597; Ambassador: VÍCTOR FERNÁNDEZ-DÁVILA.

Spain: 3rd Floor, Xerox Bldg, 53 Knutsford Blvd, Kingston 5; tel. 929-6710; telex 2364; Ambassador: IGNACIO MASFERRER.

Trinidad and Tobago: 60 Knutsford Blvd, Kingston 5; tel. 926-5730; telex 2387; High Commissioner: KNOWLSON W. GIFT.

USSR: 22 Norbrook Drive, Kingston 8; tel. 924-1048; telex 2216; Ambassador: VLADIMIR ALEKSANDROVICH ROMANCHENKO.

United Kingdom: Trafalgar Rd, POB 575, Kingston 10; tel. 926-9050; telex 2110; fax 929-7869; High Commissioner: DEREK FRANCIS MILTON.

USA: Mutual Life Centre, 2 Oxford Rd, Kingston 5; tel. 929-4850; Ambassador: GLEN HOLDEN.

Venezuela: 5th Floor, Royal Bank Bldg, 30–36 Knutsford Blvd, Kingston 5; tel. 926-5510; telex 2179; Chargé d'affaires: CARLOS GRISANTI.

Judicial System

The Judicial System is based on English common law and practice. Final appeal is to the Judicial Committee of the Privy Council in the United Kingdom.

Justice is administered by the Privy Council, Court of Appeal, Supreme Court (which includes the Revenue Court and the Gun Court), Resident Magistrates' Court (which includes the Traffic Court), two Family Courts and the Courts of Petty Sessions.

Judicial Service Commission: Supreme Court Bldg, POB 491, Kingston; advises the Governor-General on judicial appointments, etc.; chaired by the Chief Justice.

THE SUPREME COURT

Chief Justice: EDWARD ZACCA.
Senior Puisne Judge: C. F. B. ORR.
Master: B. H. B. REID.
Registrars: H. HARRIS, M. K. S. HARRISON (acting).

COURT OF APPEAL

President: I. D. ROWE.
Registrar: A. G. HENDRICKS.

Religion

CHRISTIANITY

There are more than 100 Christian denominations active in Jamaica. According to the 1982 census, the largest religious bodies were the Church of God, Baptists, Anglicans and Seventh-day Adventists. Other denominations include the Methodist and Congregational Churches, the Ethiopian Orthodox Church, the Disciples of Christ, the Moravian Church, the Salvation Army and the Society of Friends (Quakers).

Jamaica Council of Churches: 14 South Ave, POB 30, Kingston 10; tel. 926-0974; f. 1941; 11 member churches and seven agencies; Pres. Rev. OLIVER DALEY; Gen. Sec. CYNTHIA CLAIR.

The Anglican Communion

Anglicans in Jamaica are adherents of the Church in the Province of the West Indies, comprising eight dioceses. The Archbishop of

JAMAICA

the Province is the Bishop of the North East Caribbean and Aruba. The Bishop of Jamaica, whose jurisdiction also includes Grand Cayman (in the Cayman Islands), is assisted by three suffragan Bishops (of Kingston, Mandeville and Montego Bay). The 1982 census recorded 154,548 Anglicans.

Bishop of Jamaica: Rt Rev. NEVILLE WORDSWORTH DESOUZA, Church House, 2 Caledonia Ave, Kingston 5; tel. 926-6609.

The Roman Catholic Church

Jamaica comprises the archdiocese of Kingston in Jamaica (also including the Cayman Islands) and the diocese of Montego Bay. At 31 December 1988 the estimated total of adherents in Jamaica and the Cayman Islands was 86,619, representing about 3.7% of the total population.

Bishops' Conference: Antilles Episcopal Conference, 21 Hopefield Ave, POB 43, Kingston 6; tel. 927-9915; f. 1975; 17 mems from the Caribbean region and Bermuda; Pres. Most Rev. SAMUEL EMMANUEL CARTER, Archbishop of Kingston in Jamaica.

Archbishop of Kingston in Jamaica: Most Rev. SAMUEL EMMANUEL CARTER, Archbishop's Residence, 21 Hopefield Ave, POB 43, Kingston 6; tel. 927-9915.

Other Christian Churches

Assembly of God: Evangel Temple, 3 Friendship Park Rd, Kingston 3; tel. 928-2728; Pastor WILSON.

Baptist Union: 6 Hope Rd, Kingston 10; tel. 926-1395; Pres. Rev. Dr GEORGE V. SIMPSON; Gen. Sec. Rev. CAWLEY BOLT.

Church of God in Jamaica: 35A Hope Rd, Kingston 10; tel. 927-8128; 400,379 adherents (1982 census).

First Church of Christ, Scientist: 17 National Heroes Circle, Kingston.

Methodist Church (Jamaica District): 143 Constant Spring Rd, POB 892, Kingston 8; tel. 925-6768; f. 1789; 18,193 mems; Chair. Rev. C. EVANS BAILEY; Synod Sec. Rev. GILBERT G. BOWEN.

Moravian Church in Jamaica: 3 Hector St, Kingston 5; tel. 928-1861; f. 1754; 25,000 mems; Pres. Rev. ROBERT G. FOSTER.

Seventh-day Adventist Church: 56 James St, Kingston; tel. 922-7440; f. 1901; 150,722 adherents (1982 census); Pastor Rev. E. H. THOMAS.

United Church of Jamaica and Grand Cayman: 12 Carlton Cres, POB 359, Kingston 10; tel. 926-8734; f. 1965 by merger of the Congregational Union of Jamaica (f. 1877) and the Presbyterian Church of Jamaica and Grand Cayman; 13,450 mems; Gen. Sec. Rev. SAM H. SMELLIE.

RASTAFARIANISM

Rastafarianism is an important influence in Jamaican culture. The cult is derived from Christianity and a belief in the divinity of Ras (Prince) Tafari Makonnen (later Emperor Haile Selassie) of Ethiopia. It advocates racial equality and non-violence, but causes controversy by the use of 'ganja' (marijuana) as a sacrament. The 1982 census recorded 14,249 Rastafarians (0.7% of the total population). Although the religion is largely unorganized, there are some denominations.

Royal Ethiopian Judah Coptic Church: Kingston; not officially incorporated, on account of its alleged use of marijuana; Leader ABUNA S. WHYTE.

BAHÁ'Í FAITH

National Spiritual Assembly: 208 Mountain View Ave, Kingston 6; tel. 927-7051; 6,300 mems resident in 320 localities.

ISLAM

At the 1982 census there were 2,238 Muslims.

JUDAISM

The 1982 census recorded 412 Jews.

United Congregation of Israelites: 92 Duke St, Kingston; tel. 922-5931; f. 1655; c. 250 mems; Spiritual Leader and Sec. ERNEST H. DE SOUZA; Pres. LLOYD ALBERGA.

The Press

DAILIES

Daily Gleaner: 7 North St, POB 40, Kingston; tel. 922-3400; telex 2319; fax 922-2058; f. 1834; morning; Independent; Chair. and Man. Dir OLIVER CLARKE; Editor Dr DUDLEY STOKES; circ. 42,100.

Daily Star: 7 North St, POB 40, Kingston; tel. 922-3400; evening; Editor Dr DUDLEY STOKES; circ. 49,500.

The Jamaica Record: 7-11 West St, Kingston; tel. 922-3952; fax 922-1055; f. 1988; Exec. Chair. NEVILL BLYTHE; Editor MILVERTON WALLACE; circ. 30,000.

PERIODICALS

Caribbean Challenge: 55 Church St, POB 186, Kingston; tel. 922-5636; f. 1957; monthly; Editor JOHN KEANE; circ. 24,000.

Caribbean Shipping: Creative Communications Inc, 29 Munroe Rd, POB 105, Kingston 6; tel. 927-4271; fax 927-4996; quarterly.

Catholic Opinion: 11 Duke St, Kingston; monthly; religious.

Children's Own: 7 North St, POB 40, Kingston; weekly; distributed during term time; circ. 99,443.

Government Gazette: POB 487, Kingston; f. 1868; Government Printer EARL BROWN; circ. 4,817.

Inquirer: 7-11 West St, Kingston; tel. 922-3952; weekly; Man. Dir and Exec. Editor MARK RICKETTS; circ. 200,000.

Jamaica Chamber of Commerce Journal: 7-8 East Parade, Kingston; 2 a year; circ. 2,000.

Jamaica Churchman: 2 Caledonia Ave, Kingston 5; quarterly; Editor BARBARA GLOUDON; circ. 6,000.

Jamaican Housewife: Kingston; weekly.

Jamaica Journal: 12-16 East St, Kingston; tel. 922-0620; f. 1967; quarterly; literary, historical and cultural review.

Jamaica Manufacturer: 85A Duke St, Kingston; quarterly; published by The Jamaica Manufacturers' Association Ltd; circ. 3,000.

Jamaica Weekly Gleaner: 7 North St, POB 40, Kingston; tel. 922-3400; weekly; overseas; Chair. and Man. Dir OLIVER CLARKE; circ. 13,599.

The Siren: 1 River Bay Rd, POB 614, Montego Bay; tel. 952-0997; f. 1990; weekly; news review; Man. Editor EVELYN L. ROBINSON; circ. 6,000.

Sunday Gleaner: 7 North St, POB 40, Kingston; tel. 922-3400; weekly; Editor Dr DUDLEY STOKES; circ. 106,900.

Swing: 102 East St, Kingston; f. 1968; monthly; entertainment and culture; Editor ANDELL FORGIE; circ. 12,000.

The Vacationer: POB 614, Montego Bay; tel. 952-0997; f. 1987; weekly; Man. Editor EVELYN L. ROBINSON; circ. 8,000.

Weekend Star: 7 North St, POB 40, Kingston; tel. 922-3400; weekly; Editor LOLITA LONG; circ. 92,000.

The Western Mirror: Westgate Plaza, POB 1258, Montego Bay; tel. 952-5253; f. 1980; 2 a week; Gen. Man. and Editor LLOYD B. SMITH; circ. 12,000.

West Indian Medical Journal: Faculty of Medical Sciences, University of the West Indies, Kingston 7; tel. 927-1214; fax 927-2556; f. 1951; quarterly; Editor Dr VASIL PERSAUD; Asst Editor BRIDGET WILLIAMS; circ. 2,000.

PRESS ASSOCIATION

Press Association of Jamaica (PAJ): 2B Ruthven Rd, Kingston 10; tel. 926-2434; f. 1943; 220 mems; Pres. FRANKLYN MCKNIGHT; Sec. CLAIRE FORRESTER.

NEWS AGENCIES

Jampress Ltd: 3 Chelsea Ave, Kingston 10; tel. 926-3740; telex 3552; fax 929-6727; f. 1984; govt news agency; Editor-in-Chief DESMOND ALLEN.

Foreign Bureaux

Inter Press Service (IPS) (Italy): 21 Central Ave, Kingston 10; tel. 929-2973; fax 929-6889; Third World news agency; Regional Dir BEVERLEY LEWIS.

Associated Press (USA) and CANA (Caribbean News Agency) are also represented in Jamaica.

Publishers

Caribbean Publishing Co Ltd: 18 East Kings House Rd, Kingston 6; tel. 927-0810.

Caribbean Universities Press Jamaica Ltd: POB 83, Kingston 7; tel. 926-2628; academic; Man. Dir VIVALYN LATTY-SCOTT.

Hallmark Publishers Ltd: 10 Hagley Park Plaza, Kingston 10; tel. 929-4823.

Jamaica Publishing House Ltd: 97 Church St, Kingston; tel. 922-1385; f. 1909; wholly-owned subsidiary of Jamaica Teachers' Assen; educational, English language and literature, mathematics, history, geography, social sciences, music; Chair. ELLORINE WALKER; Man. LEO A. OAKLEY.

JAMAICA — Directory

Kingston Publishers Ltd: 1A Norwood Ave, Kingston 5; tel. 926-0091; telex 2293; fax 926-0042; f. 1970; educational textbooks, general, travel, atlases, fiction, non-fiction; Chair. L. MICHAEL HENRY.

Unique Publications Ltd: 18 East Kings House Rd, Kingston 6; tel. 927-0810.

Government Publishing House

Government Printing Office: 77 Duke St, Kingston; tel. 922-5950; law; Government Printer EARL BROWN.

Radio and Television

In 1990 there were an estimated 1,481,000 radio receivers and 484,000 television receivers in use.

Jamaica Broadcasting Corpn (JBC): 5 South Odeon Ave, POB 100, Kingston 10; tel. 926-5620; telex 2218; fax 929-1029; f. 1959; a publicly-owned statutory corporation; semi-commercial radio and television; Chair. IAN RAMSAY; Gen. Man. B. C. (TINO) BAROVIER (acting).

Radio 1 and Radio 2 FM Stereo are both broadcast island-wide for 24 hrs a day.

JBC Television (Programme Dir D. BUCKNER) broadcasts commercially for 54½ hrs a week.

Educational Broadcasting Service: Multi-Media Centre, 37 Arnold Road, Kingston 4; tel. 922-9370; f. 1964; radio broadcasts during school term; Pres. OUIDA HYLTON-TOMLINSON.

Island Broadcasting System: 19 Caledonian Rd, Mandeville; tel. 962-2002; fax 962-2004; commercial; broadcasts 24 hrs a day on FM; Chief Exec. NEVILLE JAMES.

Radio Jamaica Ltd (RJR): Broadcasting House, 32 Lyndhurst Rd, POB 23, Kingston 5; tel. 926-1100; telex 3661; fax 929-7467; f. 1947; commercial, public service; Man. Dir J. A. LESTER SPAULDING.

RJR the Supreme Sound (Programme Dir DONALD TOPPING) broadcasts on AM, island-wide, for 24 hrs a day.

FAME FM (Programme Dir NORMA BROWN BELL) broadcasts on FM, island-wide, for 24 hrs a day.

Finance

(cap. = capital; p.u. = paid up; res = reserves; dep. = deposits; m. = million; amounts in Jamaican dollars; brs = branches)

BANKING

Central Bank

Bank of Jamaica: Nethersole Place, POB 621, Kingston; tel. 922-0750; telex 2165; fax 922-0854; f. 1960; cap. p.u. 4m., res 12m., dep. 13,038m. (Dec. 1989); Gov. G. ARTHUR.

Commercial Banks

Bank of Credit and Commerce International (Overseas) Ltd (Cayman Is): 59 Knutsford Blvd, POB 178, Kingston 5; tel. 929-2890; telex 2363.

Bank of Nova Scotia Jamaica Ltd (Canada): Scotiabank Centre Bldg, Duke and Port Royal Sts, POB 709, Kingston; tel. 922-1000; telex 2297; fax 924-9294; f. 1967; cap. p.u. 81.3m., res. 71.2m., dep. 4,135.1m. (Oct. 1989); Chair. CEDRIC ELMER RITCHIE; Gen. Man. A. B. LINDO; 44 brs.

CIBC Jamaica Ltd (Canada): Victoria Mutual Bldg, 53 Knutsford Blvd, POB 762, Kingston 5; tel. 929-7742; telex 2169; fax 929-7751; subsidiary of Canadian Imperial Bank of Commerce; authorized cap. p.u. 14.5m., res. 59.1m., dep. 719.7m. (Aug. 1989); Man. Dir G. S. NIESEN; 13 brs.

First Jamaica National Bank Ltd: 88 Harbour St, POB 115, Kingston; tel. 922-0110; telex 3515; cap. p.u. 5.0m., res 0.5m., dep. 23.6m. (1988); Man. Dir L. F. REYNOLDS; 1 br.

Jamaica Citizens Bank Ltd: 4 King St, POB 483, Kingston 1; tel. 922-5850; telex 2129; fax 922-7625; f. 1967; cap. p.u. 13.2m., res 13.2m., dep. 676.2m. (Dec. 1989); Chair. R. DANVERS WILLIAMS; Gen. Man. ELON BECKFORD; 8 brs.

Mutual Security Bank: 30–36 Knutsford Blvd, POB 612, Kingston 5; tel. 929-8950; telex 2306; fmrly Royal Bank Jamaica Ltd; cap. p.u. 19.2m., res 13.8m., dep. 750.6m. (1986); Chair. RICHARD ASENHEIM; Man. Dir DOUGLAS FOLKES.

National Commercial Bank Jamaica Ltd: 'The Atrium', 32 Trafalgar Rd, POB 88, Kingston; tel. 929-9089; telex 2139; fax 929-8399; f. 1977; cap. 70m., res. 78.0m., dep. 3,610.9m. (Sept. 1989); Chair. DON A. BANKS; Man. Dir REX JAMES; 44 brs and agencies.

National Export-Import Bank of Jamaica: 48 Duke St, POB 3, Kingston; tel. 922-9690; telex 2165; replaces Jamaica Export Credit Insurance Corpn.

Workers Savings and Loan Bank: 134 Tower St, POB 270, Kingston; tel. 922-8650; telex 2226; f. 1973; cap. p.u. 14.7m., res 4.5m., dep. 413.7m. (1986); Gen. Man. EVERETTE PALMER (acting); 10 brs.

Development Banks

Jamaica Mortgage Bank: 33 Tobago Ave, POB 950, Kingston 5; tel. 929-6350; f. 1971 by the Jamaican Govt and the US Agency for Int. Devt; wholly govt-owned statutory organization since 1973; intended to function primarily as a secondary market facility for home mortgages and to mobilize long-term funds for housing developments in Jamaica; also insures home mortgage loans made by approved financial institutions, thus transferring risk of default on a loan to the govt.

National Development Bank of Jamaica Ltd: 11A–15 Oxford Rd, Kingston 5; tel. 929-6124; telex 2381; fax 929-6996; replaced Jamaica Development Bank, f. 1969; provides funds for medium- and long-term development-orientated projects in the tourism, industrial, agro-industrial and mining sectors through financial intermediaries; Chair. NATAN RICHARDS; Man. Dir Dr NOEL A. LYON.

Agricultural Credit Bank of Jamaica: 11A–15 Oxford Rd, Kingston 5; tel. 929-6124; fax 929-6055.

Banking Association

Bankers' Association of Jamaica: c/o POB 483, Kingston; Pres. ELON BECKFORD.

STOCK EXCHANGE

Jamaica Stock Exchange Ltd: Bank of Jamaica Tower, Nethersole Place, POB 621, Kingston; tel. 922-0806; f. 1968; in 1989 the Governments of Jamaica, Barbados and Trinidad and Tobago agreed to combine their national exchanges into a regional stock exchange, which was expected to begin operations in 1990; Chair. DONALD BANKS; Gen. Man. WAIN ITON.

INSURANCE

Government Supervisory Authority: Office of the Superintendent of Insurance, 51 St Lucia Ave, POB 800, Kingston 5; tel. 926-1790; f. 1972; Superintendent E. W. TAYLOR.

Jamaica Association of General Insurance Companies: 58 Half Way Tree Rd, POB 459, Kingston 10; tel. 92-98404; Man. GLORIA M. GRANT.

Principal Companies

British Caribbean Insurance Co Ltd: 36 Duke St, POB 170, Kingston; tel. 922-1260; fax 922-4475; f. 1962; general insurance; Gen. Man. LESLIE W. CHUNG.

Dyoll Insurance Co Ltd: 40–46 Knutsford Blvd, POB 313, Kingston 5; tel. 926-4711; telex 2208; f. 1965; Pres. PETER J. C. THWAITES; Vice-Pres. PAUL BIGNELL.

Globe Insurance Co of the West Indies Ltd: 60 Knutsford Blvd, POB 401, Kingston 5; tel. 926-3720; telex 2150; fax 929-2727.

Insurance Co of the West Indies Ltd (ICWI): ICWI Building, 2 St Lucia Ave, POB 306, Kingston 5; tel. 926-9182; telex 2246; Chair. and CEO DENNIS LALOR; Gen. Man. JENNIFER COX.

Jamaica General Insurance Co Ltd: 9 Duke St, POB 408, Kingston; tel. 922-6420; fax 922-2073.

Jamaica Mutual Life Assurance Society: 2 Oxford Rd, POB 430, Kingston 5; tel. 926-9024; telex 291-2450; fax 929-7098; f. 1844; Pres. GLORIA D. KNIGHT.

Life of Jamaica Ltd: 17 Dominica Drive, Kingston 5; tel. 929-8920; fax 929-4730; f. 1970; life insurance, pensions; Pres. R. DANNY WILLIAMS; Exec. Vice-Pres. H. A. HALL.

NEM Insurance Co (Jamaica) Ltd: NEM House, 9 King St, Kingston; tel. 922-1460; fax 922-4045; fmrly the National Employers' Mutual General Insurance Asscn.

Trade and Industry

CHAMBERS OF COMMERCE

Associated Chambers of Commerce of Jamaica: 7–8 East Parade, POB 172, Kingston; tel. 922-0150; f. 1974; 12 associated Chambers of Commerce; Pres. WINSTON MEEKS.

Jamaica Chamber of Commerce: 7–8 East Parade, POB 172, Kingston; tel. 922-0150; fax 924-9056; f. 1779; 768 mems; Pres. SAMEER YOUNIS.

ASSOCIATIONS

All-Island Banana Growers' Association Ltd: Banana Industry Bldg, 10 South Ave, Kingston 4; tel. 922-5492; f. 1946; 3,000 mems (1990); Chair. BOBBY POTTINGER; Sec. I. CHANG.

All-Island Jamaica Cane Farmers' Association: 4 North Ave, Kingston 4; tel. 922-3010; fax 922-2077; f. 1941; registered cane farmers; 22,895 mems; Chair. TREVOR G. MIGNOTT; Man. D. D. MCCALLA.

Banana Export Co (BECO): 10 South Ave, Kingston 4; tel. 922-5490; telex 2148; f. 1985 to replace Banana Co of Jamaica; oversees the development of the banana industry; Chair. MARSHALL HALL.

Citrus Growers' Association Ltd: 1A North Ave, Kingston Gdns, POB 159, Kingston; tel. 922-8230; fax 985-2221; f. 1944; 16,000 mems; Chair. IVAN H. TOMLINSON.

Jamaica Banana Producers' Association Ltd: 6A Oxford Rd, POB 237, Kingston 5; tel. 926-3503; telex 2278; fax 929-3636; f. 1927; Chair. C. H. JOHNSTON; Man. Dir MARSHALL HALL.

Jamaica Exporters' Association (JEA): 13 Dominica Drive, POB 9, Kingston 5; tel. 929-1292; telex 2421; fax 929-3831; Pres. KARL JAMES; Exec. Dir MARCIA BENNETT.

Jamaica Livestock Association: Newport East, POB 36, Kingston; f. 1941; tel. 922-7130; telex 2382; fax 923-5046; 7,316 mems; Chair. Brig. DAVID SMITH; Man. Dir and CEO HENRY J. RAINFORD.

Jamaica Manufacturers' Association Ltd: 85A Duke St, Kingston; tel. 922-8880; f. 1947; 640 mems; Pres. ANTHONY ROBINSON.

Jamaican Association of Sugar Technologists: c/o Sugar Industry Research Institute, Mandeville; tel. 962-2241; f. 1936; 265 mems; Pres. C. A. GORDON; Hon. Sec. H. M. THOMPSON.

Private Sector Organization of Jamaica (PSOJ) Ltd: 39 Hope Rd, POB 236, Kingston 10; tel. 927-6238; fax 927-5137; federative body of private business individuals, companies and associations; Pres. DENNIS LALOR; Exec. Dir DELROY F. LINDSAY.

Small Businesses' Association (SBA): 2 Trafalgar Rd, Kingston 10; tel. 927-7071; Pres. ERROL DUNKLEY.

Sugar Manufacturing Corpn of Jamaica Ltd: 5 Trevennion Park Rd, Kingston 5; tel. 926-5930; telex 2113; fax 926-6149; established to represent the sugar manufacturers in Jamaica; deals with all aspects of the sugar industry and its by-products; provides liaison between the Govt, the Sugar Industry Authority and the All-Island Jamaica Cane Farmers' Assen; 9 mems; Chair. CHRISTOPHER BOVELL; Gen. Man. Lt-Col DELROY C. M. ORMSBY.

GOVERNMENT ORGANIZATIONS

Agricultural Development Corpn (ADC): 46 Trinidad Terrace, Kingston; tel. 926-9160; f. 1952; Chair. Dr C. L. BENT; Sec. D. FORRESTER.

Agro 21 Corpn Ltd (ADC Group of Cos): Jamaica Conference Centre, 14–20 Port Royal St, POB 552, GPO Kingston, Kingston; tel. 922-1470; telex 2341; fax 922-2178; f. 1989; monitors activities of state-owned commercial agricultural enterprises, including the production of bananas, orchard crops, livestock development and marketing of local and export agricultural produce; maintains an information centre which provides a wide range of publications on agriculture; Chair. CEZLEY SAMPSON; Man. Dir CLAUDE STEWART.

Cocoa Industry Board: Marcus Garvey Drive, POB 68, Kingston 15; tel. 923-6411; telex 3658; f. 1957; has statutory powers to regulate and develop the industry; owns and operates four central fermentaries; Chair. K. A. HAUGHTON; Man./Sec. V. V. WRIGHT (acting).

Coconut Industry Board: 18 Waterloo Rd, Half Way Tree, Kingston 10; tel. 926-1770; f. 1945; 9 mems; Chair. R. A. JONES; Gen. Man. ROY A. WILLIAMS; Sec. JAMES S. JOYLES.

Coffee Industry Board: Marcus Garvey Drive, POB 508, Kingston 15; tel. 923-7211; fax 923-7587; f. 1950; 9 mems; has wide statutory powers to regulate and develop the industry; Chair. KEBLE MUNN; Man. JOHN PICKERSGILL; Sec. JOYCE CHANG.

Coffee Industry Development Co: Marcus Garvey Drive, Kingston 15; tel. 923-7211; f. 1981; to implement a coffee expansion programme financed by the Commonwealth Development Corporation.

Jamaica Bauxite Institute: Hope Gdns, POB 355, Kingston 6; tel. 927-2073; telex 2309; fax 927-1159; f. 1975; adviser to the Government in the negotiation of agreements, consultancy services to clients in the bauxite/alumina and related industries, laboratory services for mineral and soil-related services, Pilot Plant services for materials and equipment testing, research and development; Exec. Chair. Dr CARLTON DAVIS.

Jamaica Commodity Trading Co Ltd: 8 Ocean Blvd, POB 1021, Kingston; tel. 922-0971; telex 2318; f. 1981 as successor to State Trading Corpn; oversees all importing on behalf of state; Chair. DAVID GAYNAIR; Man. Dir. ANDREE NEMBHARD.

Jamaica Export Trading Co Ltd: 6 Waterloo Rd, POB 645, Kingston 10; tel. 929-4390; telex 2233; f. 1977; export trading in non-traditional products, incl. spices, fresh produce, furniture, garments, processed foods, etc.

Jamaica Information Service (JIS): 58A Halfway Tree Rd, POB 2222, Kingston 10; tel. 926-3740; telex 2393; fax 926-6715; f. 1963; information agency for government policies and programmes, ministries and public sector agencies; Exec. Dir. FRED WILMOT; Dir, Operations KEN WILLIAMS; Dir, Finance and Admin. FESTUS RICHARDS.

Jamaica International Telecommunications Ltd: 15 North St, Kingston; tel. 922-6031; telex 112; fax 921-5329; f. 1971; external telecommunications; Pres. and Chief Exec. TREVOR O. MINOTT.

Jamaica Promotions (JAMPRO) Ltd: 35 Trafalgar Rd, Kingston 10; tel. 929-7190; telex 2222; fax 924-9650; f. 1988 by merger of Jamaica Industrial Development Corpn, Jamaica National Export Corpn and Jamaica National Investment Promotion Ltd; economic development agency; Pres. G. E. TATHAM; Chair. Senator BARCLAY EWART.

National Development Agency Ltd: 12 Ocean Blvd, Kingston; tel. 922-5445; telex 2444.

Petroleum Corpn of Jamaica (PCJ): 36 Trafalgar Rd, POB 597, Kingston 10; tel. 929-5380; telex 2356; fax 929-2409; state oil company; owns and operates petroleum refinery; holds exploration and exploitation rights to local petroleum and gas reserves; Exec. Chair. ELI MATALON.

Planning Institute of Jamaica: 39–41 Barbados Ave, POB 634, Kingston 5; tel. 926-14808; telex 3529; fax 926-4670; f. 1955 as the Central Planning Unit, became Planning Institute of Jamaica in 1984; economic planning; monitoring performance of the economy; publishing of economic surveys; Dir-Gen. Dr. OMAR DAVIES.

Post and Telecommunications Department: Central Sorting Office, South Camp Rd, POB 7000, Kingston; tel. 922-9430; telex 2133; operates Postal Service of Jamaica; exercises regulatory responsibility for telecommunication services in Jamaica; Postmaster-Gen. BERTRAM G. HENRY; Chief Telecommunications Eng. ROY HUMES.

Sugar Industry Authority: 5 Trevennion Park Rd, POB 127, Kingston 5; tel. 926-5930; telex 2113; fax 926-6149; f. 1970; statutory body under portfolio of Ministry of Agriculture; responsible for regulation and control of sugar industry and sugar marketing; conducts research through Sugar Industry Research Institute; Exec. Chair. FRANK G. DOWNIE; Sec. ALVIN A. BURNETT.

Trade Administration Department: The Office Centre, 12 Ocean Blvd, POB 25, Kingston; tel. 922-1840; Admin. TOTLYN GRANT.

Urban Development Corpn: The Office Centre, 8th Floor, 12 Ocean Blvd, Kingston; tel. 922-8310; telex 2281; fax 922-9326; f. 1968; responsibility for urban renewal and development within designated areas; Chair. Dr VINCENT LAWRENCE; Gen. Man. CLINTON WOODSTOCK.

TRADE UNIONS

Bustamante Industrial Trade Union (BITU): 98 Duke St, Kingston; tel. 922-2443; f. 1938; Pres. HUGH SHEARER; Gen. Sec. GEORGE FYFFE; 100,459 mems.

National Workers' Union of Jamaica (NWU): 130–132 East St, Kingston 16; tel. 922-1150; f. 1952; affiliated to ICFTU, ORIT, etc.; Pres. MICHAEL MANLEY; Gen. Sec. LLOYD GOODLEIGH; 102,000 mems.

Trades Union Congress of Jamaica: 25 Sutton St, POB 19, Kingston; tel. 922-5313; affiliated to CCL and ICFTU; Pres. E. SMITH; 20,000 mems.

Principal Independent Unions

Dockers' and Marine Workers' Union: 48 East St, Kingston; tel. 922-6067; Pres. MILTON A. SCOTT.

Industrial Trade Union Action Council: 2 Wildman St, Kingston; Pres. RODERICK FRANCIS.

Jamaica Federation of Musicians' and Artistes' Unions: POB 1125, Montego Bay 1; tel. 952-3238; f. 1958; Pres. HEDLEY H. G. JONES; Sec. CARL AYTON; 2,000 mems.

Jamaica Local Government Officers' Union: c/o Public Service Commission, Knutsford Blvd, Kingston; Pres. E. LLOYD TAYLOR.

Jamaica Teachers' Association: 97 Church St, Kingston; tel. 922-1385; Pres. DOROTHY RAYMOND.

Master Printers' Association of Jamaica: Kingston 11; f. 1943; 11 mems; Pres. HERMON SPOERRI; Sec. RALPH GORDON.

National Union of Democratic Teachers (NUDT): 69 Church St, Kingston; tel. 922-3902; f. 1978; Pres. PAULETTE CHEVANNES; Gen. Sec. JOHN HAUGHTON.

JAMAICA

Union of School and Agricultural Workers (USAW): 2 Wildman St, Kingston; tel. 922-1483; f. 1978; Pres. DUNSTON WHITTINGHAM; Gen. Sec. KEITH COMRIE.

United Portworkers' and Seamen's Union: 20 West St, Kingston.

University and Allied Workers' Union (UAWU): Students' Union, University of West Indies, Mona; affiliated to the WPJ; Gen. Sec. Dr TREVOR MUNROE.

There are also 17 employers' associations registered as trade unions.

CO-OPERATIVES

The Jamaica Social Welfare Commission promotes Co-operative Societies in the following categories: Consumer, Co-operative Farming, Credit, Credit and Marketing, Fishermen's Irrigation, Land Lease, Land Purchase, Marketing, Supplies Co-ops, Thrift, Transport and Tillage.

Transport

RAILWAYS

There are about 339 km (211 miles) of railway, all standard gauge, in Jamaica. Most of the system is operated by the Jamaica Railway Corpn, which is subsidized by the Government. The main lines are from Kingston to Montego Bay and Spanish Town to Ewarton and Port Antonio. There are also four railways for the transport of bauxite.

Jamaica Railway Corporation (JRC): 142 Barry St, POB 489, Kingston; tel. 922-6621; telex 2190; fax 922-7290; f. 1845 as Jamaica Railway Co, the earliest British colonial railway; transferred to JRC in 1960; govt-owned, but autonomous, statutory corpn until 1990, when it was partly leased to Alcan Jamaica Co Ltd, as the first stage of a privatization scheme; 207 km of railway; Gen. Man. OWEN CROOKS.

Alcoa Railroads: Alcoa Minerals of Jamaica Inc, May Pen PO; tel. 986-2561; fax 986-2026; 40 km of standard-gauge railway; transport of bauxite; Superintendents J. SHIM YOU (Railroad Operations), H. O. THOMSEN (Maintenance).

Kaiser Jamaica Bauxite Co Railway: Discovery Bay PO, St Ann; tel. 973-2221; telex 7404; 25 km of standard-gauge railway; transport of bauxite; Gen. Man. R. D. HONIBALL.

ROADS

Jamaica has a good network of tar-surfaced and metalled motoring roads. In 1988 there were 2,944 miles (4,738 km) of main road, 7,264 miles (11,690 km) of parochial and subsidiary roads and 930 miles (1,497 km) of road in the Kingston metropolitan region. In 1990 the Government announced a five-year plan to improve 12,000 miles (19,300 km) of roads, at a cost of US $302m., with assistance from the World Bank and the IDB.

SHIPPING

The principal ports are Kingston and Montego Bay. The port at Kingston has four container berths, and is a major transhipment terminal for the Caribbean area. Jamaica has interests in the multinational shipping line WISCO (West Indies Shipping Corpn—based in Trinidad and Tobago). Services are also provided by most major foreign lines serving the region.

Port Authority of Jamaica: 15–17 Duke St, Kingston; tel. 922-0290; telex 2386; fax 924-9437; f. 1966; Govt's principal maritime agency; responsible for monitoring and regulating the navigation of all vessels berthing at Jamaican ports, for regulating the tariffs on public wharves, and for the development of industrial Free Zones in Jamaica; Chair. NOEL HYLTON; Gen. Man. LUCIEN RATTRAY.

Kingston Free Zone Co Ltd: 27 Shannon Drive, POB 16, Kingston 15; tel. 923-5274; telex 2124; fax 923-6023; f. 1976; subsidiary of Port Authority of Jamaica; management and promotion of an export-orientated industrial free trade zone for companies from various countries; Chair. PETER C. V. KING; Gen. Man. ERROL HEWITT.

Montego Bay Export Free Zone: c/o Port Authority of Jamaica, 15–17 Duke St, Kingston; tel. 922-0290; telex 2386.

Shipping Association of Jamaica: 5–7 King St, POB 40, Kingston 15; tel. 922-8220; telex 2431; fax 922-6221; f. 1939; 40 mems; Pres. LUDLOW A. STEWART; Gen. Man. ALVIN C. HENRY.

Principal Shipping Companies

Jamaica Freight and Shipping Co Ltd (JFS): 80–82 Second St, Port Bustamante, POB 167, Kingston 13; tel. 923-9371; telex 2260; fax 923-4091; cargo services to and from the USA, Caribbean, Central and South America, the United Kingdom, Japan and Canada; Exec. Chair. CHARLES JOHNSTON; Man. Dir GRANTLEY STEPHENSON.

Jamaica Merchant Marine (JMM): 7th floor, Dyoll Bldg, 40–46 Knutsford Blvd, Kingston 5; tel. 922-0290; telex 2483; f. 1975; carries grain from USA and general cargo from the United Kingdom; Chair. NOEL A. HYLTON; Sec. GRANTLEY STEPHENSON.

CIVIL AVIATION

There are two international airports linking Jamaica with North America, Europe, and other Caribbean islands. The Norman Manley International Airport is situated 22.5 km (14 miles) outside Kingston. The Donald Sangster International Airport is 5 km (3 miles) from Montego Bay.

Airports Authority of Jamaica: National Life Bldg, 64 Knutsford Blvd, POB 567, Kingston 5; tel. 926-1622; telex 2441; Chair. GEOFFREY MORRIS; Gen. Man. HOWARD TAYLOR (acting).

Air Jamaica Ltd: 72–76 Harbour St, Kingston; tel. 922-3460; telex 2389; fax 922-0107; f. 1968; fully govt-owned since 1980; services to Canada, the Cayman Islands, Haiti, Puerto Rico, the USA and, in co-operation with British Airways, the United Kingdom; Chair. ANTHONY K. HART; Pres. MIKE FENNEL; fleet of 4 Airbus A300B4, 4 Boeing 727-200.

Civil Aviation Department: 9 Trinidad Terrace, Kingston 5; tel. 926-9115.

Trans-Jamaican Airlines: POB 218, Montego Bay; tel. 952-5401; internal services between Kingston, Montego Bay, Negril, Ocho Rios and Port Antonio; government corporation; Chair. LOTSE HARVEY; Admin. Dir B. G. OSBORNE.

Tourism

Tourists, mainly from the USA, visit Jamaica for its beaches, mountains, historic buildings and cultural heritage. In 1989 there were 1.16m. visitors (of whom about 739,000 were 'stop-over' visitors) and tourist receipts were estimated to be US $593m.

Jamaica Tourist Board (JTB): 21 Dominica Drive, POB 360, Kingston 5; tel. 929-9200; telex 2140; fax 929-9375; f. 1955; a statutory body set up by the govt to develop all aspects of the tourist industry through marketing, promotional and advertising efforts; Chair. O. K. MELHADO; Dir of Tourism ROBERT STEPHENS.

Jamaica Hotel and Tourist Association: 2 Ardenne Rd, Kingston 10; f. 1961; trade association for hoteliers and other companies involved in Jamaican tourism; tel. 926-3635; telex 2426; fax 910-54; Pres. PETER ROUSSEAU; Gen. Man. CAMILLE NEEDHAM.

JAPAN

Introductory Survey

Location, Climate, Language, Religion, Flag, Capital

Japan lies in eastern Asia and comprises a curved chain of more than 3,000 islands. Four large islands, named (from north to south) Hokkaido, Honshu, Shikoku and Kyushu, account for about 98% of the land area. Hokkaido lies just to the south of Sakhalin, a large Soviet island, and about 1,300 km (800 miles) east of the USSR's mainland port of Vladivostok. Southern Japan is about 150 km (93 miles) east of Korea. Although summers are temperate everywhere, the climate in winter varies sharply from cold in the north to mild in the south. Temperatures in Tokyo are generally between −6°C (21°F) and 30°C (86°F). Typhoons and heavy rains are common in summer. The language is Japanese. The major religions are Shintoism and Buddhism, and there is a minority of Christians. The national flag (proportions usually 3 by 2) is white, with a red disc (a sun without rays) in the centre. The capital is Tokyo.

Recent History

Following Japan's defeat in the Second World War, Japanese forces surrendered in August 1945. Japan signed an armistice in September 1945, agreeing to cede control over many of its outer islands, and the country was placed under US military occupation. A new democratic constitution, which took effect from May 1947, renounced war and abandoned the doctrine of the Emperor's divinity. Following the peace treaty of September 1951, Japan regained its sovereignty on 28 April 1952. The Tokara Archipelago and the Amami Islands (parts of the Ryukyu group) were restored to Japanese sovereignty in December 1951 and December 1953 respectively. Rival conservative political groups merged in November 1955 to form the Liberal-Democratic Party (LDP), which has held power ever since. The Bonin Islands and the remainder of the Ryukyu Islands (including Okinawa), administered by the USA from 1945, were returned to Japan in June 1968 and May 1972 respectively.

Nobusuke Kishi became Prime Minister in February 1957 and held office until July 1960, when he was succeeded by Hayato Ikeda. In November 1964 Ikeda resigned, owing to ill health, and was replaced by Eisaku Sato, who was to become the longest-serving Prime Minister in Japanese history. Sato remained in office until July 1972, when he was succeeded by Kakuei Tanaka, hitherto the Minister of International Trade and Industry. Tanaka visited Beijing in September 1972, when he agreed to Japan's recognition of the People's Republic of China and a consequent severance of Japanese diplomatic (though not commercial) relations with Taiwan. After some electoral set-backs, Tanaka resigned as Prime Minister in December 1974. He was succeeded by Takeo Miki, a former Deputy Prime Minister.

During his premiership, Tanaka allegedly accepted bribes, totalling 500m. yen, from the Marubeni Corporation, a representative in Japan of the Lockheed Aircraft Corporation (a leading US aerospace company), in return for using his influence to promote the purchase of Lockheed TriStar airliners by All Nippon Airways, Japan's principal domestic airline. In July 1976 Tanaka was arrested, on charges of accepting bribes, and resigned from the LDP. In December a general election for the House of Representatives (the lower house of the Diet) resulted in a major set-back for the LDP, which lost its overall majority for the first time. Miki resigned as Prime Minister, and was succeeded by Takeo Fukuda, who had resigned in November as Deputy Prime Minister.

The LDP suffered another reversal in July 1977, at elections for one-half of the seats in the House of Councillors (the upper house of the Diet), and in November Fukuda carried out a major reshuffle of the Cabinet, giving ministerial office to some economic experts. In the LDP presidential election of November 1978 Fukuda was unexpectedly defeated by Masayoshi Ohira, the LDP Secretary-General. Ohira became Prime Minister in December, and a new cabinet was formed. Lacking an overall majority in the lower house and facing increasing opposition to proposed tax increases, the Government's legislative programme was seriously hindered.

At elections to the lower house in October 1979 the LDP again failed to win an overall majority, and significant gains were made by the Communists. Ohira survived a challenge to his leadership of the LDP, but in May 1980 the Government was defeated in a motion of 'no confidence', proposed by the Japan Socialist Party (JSP), and Ohira dissolved the lower house. Ohira died before the elections in June, when the LDP won 284 of the 511 seats, although obtaining only a minority of the votes cast. In July Zenko Suzuki, a relatively little-known compromise candidate, was elected President of the LDP and subsequently appointed Prime Minister. He encountered a series of crises during 1981, including a set-back in relations with the USA and criticism from the opposition over Japan's defence policy. In November 1981 Suzuki reorganized the Cabinet, distributing major posts among the five feuding LDP factions. The growing factionalism of the LDP and the worsening economic crisis prompted the resignation of Suzuki as Prime Minister and LDP President in October 1982.

Suzuki's successor was Yasuhiro Nakasone, who was supported by the Suzuki and Tanaka factions of the LDP. In his former post, as Minister of State and Director-General of the Administrative Management Agency, Nakasone had been responsible for implementing the Suzuki Government's expenditure cuts. At elections in June 1983 for one-half of the seats in the upper house, a new electoral system was used. Of the 126 contested seats, 50 were filled on the basis of proportional representation. As a result, two small parties entered the House of Councillors for the first time. Nevertheless, the LDP increased its strength from 134 to 137 members in the 252-seat chamber. This result was seen as an endorsement of Nakasone's policies of increased spending on defence, closer ties with the USA and greater Japanese involvement in international affairs.

In October 1983, after judicial proceedings lasting nearly seven years, a Tokyo court found Kakuei Tanaka, the former Prime Minister, guilty of accepting bribes. In September 1985 he began appeal proceedings against the conviction and the sentence (a heavy fine and four years' imprisonment), and he continued to be an 'independent' member of the Diet. Despite resigning from the LDP, Tanaka remained a major influence on the party, and members of the Tanaka faction held important positions in Nakasone's Cabinet. Tanaka's refusal to resign his legislative seat led to a boycott of the Diet by the opposition, which forced Nakasone to dissolve the House of Representatives in preparation for a premature general election in December 1983. The election campaign was dominated by the issues of political ethics and Nakasone's forthright style of leadership. The LDP suffered the worst defeat in its history, losing 36 seats (and its majority) in the lower house. Nakasone came second (behind Takeo Fukuda) in his district, whereas Tanaka was returned with an overwhelming majority. The Komeito (Clean Government Party), the Democratic Socialist Party (DSP) and the JSP gained seats, while the Communists and the New Liberal Club (NLC) lost influence. The LDP formed a coalition with the NLC (which had split from the LDP over the Tanaka affair in 1976) and several independents, and Nakasone remained as President of the LDP after promising to reduce Tanaka's influence. Six members of Tanaka's faction held posts in Nakasone's new Cabinet, including that of Minister of Finance.

Following the trial of Tanaka, reforms were introduced, whereby cabinet members were required to disclose the extent of their personal assets. Nakasone's domestic policy was based on the 'Three Reforms': administrative reforms, particularly of government-run enterprises such as the railways; fiscal reforms, to enable the Government to balance its budget after many years of persistent deficit; and educational reforms, to liberalize the rigid examination-dominated system. In March 1984 Nakasone introduced Japan's most austere budget since 1955.

In November 1984 Nakasone was re-elected as President of the LDP, guaranteeing him two further years in office as Prime Minister, the first to serve a second term since Eisaku Sato (1964–72). The unexpected late challenge to his leadership by part of the Tanaka faction (headed by Susumu Nikaido, Vice-President of the LDP) was indicative of the widespread disaffection with Nakasone's assertive style of leadership. The continued importance of the Tanaka faction was emphasized when six members were awarded portfolios in the new Cabinet. (However, Tanaka suffered a cerebral haemorrhage in February 1985, and was too ill to contest the general election in July 1986.)

In December 1985 Nakasone reshuffled his Cabinet, preserving a balance among the five major factions. In March 1986 plans to denationalize the Japanese National Railways in 1987 were approved by the Cabinet but strongly opposed by the JSP (the transfer to the private sector was implemented in April 1987). In June 1986 Nakasone secured approval for the dissolution of the Diet in spite of objections from the opposition parties. This enabled the Prime Minister to announce the holding of a premature general election for the House of Representatives (18 months ahead of schedule) to coincide with the triennial election for one-half of the seats in the House of Councillors on 6 July. The Government hoped to benefit from the higher level of participation that was expected to arise from the holding of both polls on the same day. The polling resulted in decisive victories for the LDP. In the election to the House of Representatives, the LDP obtained 49.4% of the votes, its highest level of electoral support since 1963, and won a record 304 of the 512 seats. The increased LDP majority was achieved largely at the expense of the JSP and the DSP. Of the main opposition parties, only the Komeito and the Communists maintained their strength in the House of Representatives. The LDP, therefore, was able to dispense with its coalition partner, the NLC (which disbanded in August and rejoined the LDP). The new Cabinet was composed entirely of LDP members. In September the leaders of the LDP agreed to alter bylaws to allow party presidents one-year extensions beyond the normal limit of two terms of two years each, and then applied this provision to Nakasone. Nakasone could thus retain the posts of President of the LDP and Prime Minister of Japan until 30 October 1987. In December 1986 the tax committee of the LDP issued proposals for a new programme of tax reforms, including the introduction of 5% value-added tax (VAT) and the abolition of tax-free savings schemes. Because of widespread opposition, however, the VAT proposal was withdrawn from the programme before it was approved as legislation by the Diet in September 1987. In 1986 a record trade surplus was registered. In an attempt to correct this imbalance, to reflate the domestic economy and to stabilize the Japanese currency, Nakasone relaxed his policy of domestic fiscal austerity in May 1987.

In July 1987 the Secretary-General of the LDP, Noboru Takeshita, left the Tanaka faction, with 113 other members, and announced the formation of a major new grouping within the ruling party, the Takeshita faction. Susumu Nikaido, a former Vice-President of the LDP and the second most powerful man in the Tanaka faction, retained only about 20 supporters. The remainder of the Tanaka faction comprised a small group of independents who were uncommitted to either side. In the same month, Tanaka's political influence was further weakened when the Tokyo high court upheld the decision, taken in 1983, which found him guilty of accepting bribes.

In October 1987 three senior politicians presented themselves as candidates to succeed Nakasone when he resigned from his post as President of the LDP: Takeshita, the Secretary-General of the LDP; Kiichi Miyazawa, the Minister of Finance; and Shintaro Abe, the Chairman of the Executive Council of the LDP and a former Minister of Foreign Affairs. After negotiations with the three candidates, Nakasone nominated Takeshita as his successor. It was widely believed that Nakasone had chosen this nomination procedure, rather than putting the selection of the new President to the vote of the LDP Diet members, because he feared that the latter procedure might cause further divisions in the ruling party. On 6 November the Diet was convened and Takeshita was formally elected as Prime Minister. In the new Cabinet, Takeshita carefully maintained a balance among the five major factions of the LDP. He retained only two members of Nakasone's previous Cabinet, but appointed four members of the Nakasone faction to senior ministerial posts (including Nakasone's staunch ally, Sosuke Uno, to the post of Minister of Foreign Affairs). At the request of Nakasone, Kiichi Miyazawa was appointed Deputy Prime Minister and Minister of Finance, and Shintaro Abe was assigned the important post of Secretary-General of the LDP. Takeshita claimed that he would work to continue Nakasone's domestic and foreign policies, with particular emphasis on correcting the external trade imbalance and further liberalizing the financial market.

The implementation of a programme of taxation reforms, which Nakasone had failed to achieve, was one of the most important issues confronting Takeshita's Government. In June 1988 the LDP's tax deliberation council proposed the introduction of a new indirect tax (a general consumption tax or a type of VAT), which was to be levied at a rate of 3%. This proposal, however, encountered widespread opposition. In the same month, the Prime Minister and the LDP suffered a serious set-back when several leading figures in the party, including Nakasone, Shintaro Abe, Kiichi Miyazawa and Takeshita himself, were alleged to have been indirectly involved, through secretaries and political aides, in share-trading irregularities with the Recruit Cosmos Company. Despite strenuous denials by these politicians of any knowledge of or involvement in such transactions, the Recruit scandal enabled the opposition parties to postpone consideration by the Diet of the tax reform proposals (which also included the reduction of income taxes). As the situation became increasingly serious, the opposition began to demand the resignation of the alleged participants and a full parliamentary investigation into the alleged share transactions. In November, shortly after the LDP had agreed to establish a 50-member committee to investigate the affair, the House of Representatives approved the tax reform measures (which constituted the most wide-ranging revision of the tax system for 40 years). The legislation was approved by the House of Councillors in December. In the same month Takeshita effected a reorganization of ministerial portfolios, which was widely viewed as an attempt to restore public confidence in the Government; however, three Ministers were forced to resign from their posts in December 1988 and January 1989, owing to their alleged involvement in the Recruit scandal. In February 1989 the Chairman of the DSP, Saburo Tsukamoto, was also obliged to resign, following his implication in the Recruit affair.

Meanwhile, the Showa era came to an end when, after a long illness, Emperor Hirohito, who had reigned since 1926, died in January 1989. He was succeeded by his son, Akihito, and the new era was named Heisei ('achievement of universal peace').

In April 1989, as the allegations of share-trading irregularities among politicians degenerated into a scandal involving charges of bribery and malpractice, Takeshita announced his resignation. Takeshita was himself found to have received political contributions worth more than 150m. yen from the Recruit organization, while there was a growing consensus among LDP officials that Takeshita's continued leadership would adversely affect the party's prospects in elections to the House of Councillors that were scheduled to take place at the end of July. After Masayoshi Ito, the Chairman of the LDP's General Council, refused to accept the post of party leader, Takeshita nominated the Minister of Foreign Affairs, Sosuke Uno. Uno was elected Prime Minister by the Diet on 2 June; a new Cabinet was appointed on the same day. Uno thus became the first Japanese Prime Minister since the foundation of the LDP not to command his own political faction. At the end of May, following an eight-month investigation undertaken by the LDP's special committee, public prosecutors indicted 13 people (eight on charges of offering bribes, and five for allegedly accepting them). Among those indicted were two senior politicians: Takao Fujinami of the LDP and Katsuya Ikeda of the opposition Komeito. At the same time, Nakasone resigned from his faction and from the LDP, assuming complete moral responsibility for the Recruit affair, since it had occurred during his administration. He admitted to having benefited from the sale of Recruit shares; however, he announced that he would continue to undertake his political activities and that he would not resign his seat in the Diet.

Scepticism regarding the new Prime Minister's political independence increased when Uno appointed Ryutaro Hashimoto, one of Takeshita's closest aides, as the new Secretary-General of the LDP. In his first speech on policy, Uno declared that his main priority was to institute political changes aimed at restoring public confidence in the Government. The proposed measures included more effective legislation to monitor and control political funding. A few days later, however, a Japanese magazine published allegations of sexual impropriety involving Uno, which precipitated demands for the Prime Minister's resignation. Further allegations of other extramarital liaisons, in conjunction with serious losses suffered by the LDP in Tokyo's municipal elections in early July 1989, further discredited Uno. The JSP made impressive gains in the Tokyo elections, owing partly to its use of a large number of female candidates in an attempt to capitalize on both male and female voters' growing aversion to corruption in the male-dominated world of politics. This campaign also proved to be highly successful in the elections for one-half of the seats in the upper house, which were held at the end of July. As a result of this considerable increase in support for the JSP, led by Takako Doi (who stressed her opposition to the unpopular consumption tax throughout her election campaign), the LDP lost its majority in the upper house for the first time in its history. The JSP received 35% of the total votes, while the LDP obtained only 27%. Consequently, Uno, who assumed total responsibility for his party's defeat, offered to resign as soon as the LDP had decided on a suitable successor. In early August 1989 the LDP chose the relatively unknown Toshiki Kaifu, a former Minister of Education and a member of the small faction led by Toshio Komoto, to replace Uno as the party's President and as the new Prime Minister. Although the House of Councillors' ballot rejected Kaifu as the new Prime Minister in favour of Takako Doi, the decision of the lower house was adopted (in accordance with stipulations embodied in the Constitution). This was the first time in 41 years that the two houses of the Diet had disagreed over whom should be chosen as Prime Minister. On assuming his new post, Kaifu reiterated his intention to tighten existing controls on fund-raising and to reform the electoral system in order to increase public confidence. He also promised to modify the consumption tax. In recognition of the growing importance of women in Japanese politics, he appointed two women to his Cabinet.

In late August 1989 the LDP suffered another reversal when the Minister of State and Chief Cabinet Secretary, Tojuo Yamashita, was forced to resign from his post, following his admission of sexual misconduct. He was replaced by Mayumi Moriyama, hitherto Minister of State and Director-General of the Environment Agency, who became the first woman to hold such a senior position in the Japanese Government. A few days later, the opposition parties submitted four items of legislation to the House of Councillors, demanding the abolition of the consumption tax. The opposition hoped to achieve the passage of the legislation through the upper house and to force the Government to dissolve the House of Representatives. In early October Kaifu rejected opposition demands for the abolition of the consumption tax, but promised to outline a revised version by the end of November.

The JSP's swift rise was later undermined by disagreements between it and the other opposition parties over defence policies and the opposition's failure to present alternative policies to those of the LDP. In October 1989 both the LDP's and the JSP's standing was affected by allegations that both parties had received funds from pachinko parlours (gaming establishments featuring pin-ball machines) in return for forestalling moves to prevent tax evasion by the industry. Kaifu's popularity increased as a result of a successful visit to North America and Mexico, and his attempts to address the problem of the consumption tax, and in October 1989 he was re-elected as President of the LDP for a further two-year term.

At a general election, held on 18 February 1990, the LDP was returned to power with an unexpectedly large measure of support. The LDP received 46.1% of the votes cast and secured 275 of the 512 seats in the lower house. Despite substantial gains by the JSP (which won 136 seats), the LDP's strength was considered sufficient for it to elect its nominees to preside over all 18 standing committees of the lower house and thus ensure the smooth passage of future legislation. Kaifu interpreted the electoral victory as public endorsement of his performance as Prime Minister, and later received somewhat reserved confirmation of his future in that capacity from the LDP itself. Although all but one of those who had been linked to the Recruit bribery scandal were re-elected to the House of Representatives, Kaifu himself stipulated that politicians tainted by the scandal would not be represented in the new Cabinet, the composition of which was announced at the end of the month.

The three most urgent issues which the new Cabinet had to address were considered to be an early conclusion to negotiations with the USA on structural economic issues (which had been under discussion since September 1989 for the purpose of alleviating bilateral trade friction), the amendment of the consumption tax and political reform.

In May 1990 Prime Minister Kaifu announced his commitment to the implementation of electoral reforms that had been proposed in April by the Election System Council, an advisory body to the Prime Minister. The proposals, for the House of Representatives, included a plan to replace the present multi-seat constituencies with a combination of single seats and proportional representation. Although the proposals were presented as an attempt to counter electoral corruption and to end factionalism within the LDP itself, opposition supporters expressed fears that the changes would invest more power in party committees responsible for nominating candidates and therefore increase the possibility of bribery.

In July 1990 the Government announced a new 10-year plan for industrial and social development, reflecting Japan's expanding international role and focusing on the contribution of the individual and the social implications of Japan's economic pre-eminence. The proposals, which had been prepared by an advisory council to the Ministry of International Trade and Industry, pointed to the importance of increasing public investment, improving the system of distribution of competitively-priced, imported goods, reforming policy regarding land use and catering to consumer needs more effectively.

In October 1990 violent clashes between security forces and some 1,500 rioters in a district of Osaka were prompted by the arrest of a police officer for alleged involvement with several local crime syndicates. Disturbances persisted for five successive nights, resulting in some 200 injuries and more than 50 arrests. Events had been exacerbated by widespread criticism of the public expense, and the alleged unconstitutional nature, of the forthcoming ceremony for the enthronement of Emperor Akihito. Demonstrations (including a series of bomb attacks on Shinto and military targets) continued throughout preparations for the ceremony and during the enthronement itself, which took place, amid stringent security measures, on 12 November 1990.

In December 1990, in a move that was widely interpreted as an attempt to placate disaffected constituent faction leaders and thereby to reinforce his own security, Kaifu announced the reallocation of all but three of the existing government portfolios.

Financial scandals continued to dominate domestic affairs in late 1990. In October Hisashi Shinto, the former chairman of the Nippon Telegraph and Telephone Corporation, became the first person to be convicted in the Recruit scandal trial. Although Shinto's two-year prison sentence was suspended (owing largely to his extreme old age), the ruling that Recruit shares had been intended as bribes was expected seriously to undermine the defence of those still awaiting trial in connection with the affair. In December Toshiyuki Inamura, a long-serving member of the lower house and a former cabinet member (as Director-General of the Environment Agency in the late 1980s), resigned from the LDP after having been charged with large-scale tax evasion and accused of complicity in a new stock-manipulation scandal.

Following a three-day party conference, in January 1991, the Japan Socialist Party leadership announced its intention to alter the English rendering of the party name to the Social Democratic Party of Japan (SDPJ) in accordance with a decision, taken in January 1990, to pursue less interventionist political policies.

In September 1990 Japan announced a US $4,000m. contribution to the international effort to force an unconditional Iraqi withdrawal from Kuwait. A controversial LDP-sponsored Peace Co-operation Bill, which provided for the dispatch to the Persian (Arabian) Gulf area of some 2,000 non-combatant personnel, encountered severe political opposition and provoked widespread discussion on the constitutional legitimacy of the deployment of Japanese personnel (in any capacity) in the context of such a conflict. In November a narrow margin of victory for the LDP candidate in a by-election to the upper house (which had been unofficially designated as a referendum on the Peace Co-operation Bill) convinced the LDP that public support for the bill was not sufficient to counter strong political opposition, and the proposals were withdrawn. In January 1991, in the context of repeated demands by the USA for a greater financial commitment to the Gulf crisis (and a swifter disbursement of monies already pledged), the Kaifu Government announced plans to increase its contribution by US $9,000m. and to provide aircraft for the transportation of refugees in the region. Political opposition to the proposal was again vociferous, particularly in response to the Government's plan to fund the increased contribution by temporarily increasing corporate taxes and duties on petroleum products and cigarettes. By mid-February 1991, however, the Government had secured the support of several centrist parties (including the Komeito), by pledging that any financial aid from Japan would be employed in a 'non-lethal' capacity and by announcing that 43% of the new contribution would be funded by reductions in government expenditure (including a 10% reduction in salary for the Prime Minister and the Cabinet), and it was expected that legislation to approve the new contribution would be successfully adopted by the Diet in late February.

Both Nakasone and Takeshita were committed to raising Japan's international status, and made many successful tours to numerous countries to promote political and social links. However, there is continued concern in the EEC over trade protectionism in Japan, and in the USA over the steadily worsening imbalance of bilateral trade. Partial deregulation of the financial markets has been introduced in an attempt to alleviate the problem, and several measures to stimulate imports were introduced in 1986–90. Relations between Japan and the USA deteriorated in April 1987, when it was discovered that the Toshiba Machine Company had illegally exported sophisticated submarine equipment to the USSR between 1982 and 1984. The USA claimed that these sales had endangered the security of both countries. In February 1989, however, Takeshita was the first foreign leader to hold an official meeting with the new US President, George Bush, following the latter's inauguration in January. In view of the persistent trade imbalance with Japan, the Bush Administration proposed the bilateral Structural Impediments Initiative (SII), which began in September 1989. The US intention was to remove impediments to the penetration of the Japanese market by foreign goods and services. At a two-day meeting of the two countries, convened in January 1991 to review the success of the initiative, the US Assistant Treasury Secretary recognized that trade reforms implemented by the Japanese Government as a result of the SII talks had opened Japanese markets to greater foreign participation; however, he was critical of many Japanese government officials for their failure to acknowledge that corporate groupings (or 'keiretsu') presented a serious obstacle to any further significant penetration of Japanese markets.

Japan continues to receive military support from the USA. Since 1982 Japan has been under continued pressure from the USA to increase its defence spending (which was equivalent to about 0.9% of the country's gross national product in 1983–85) and to assume greater responsibility for security in the Western Pacific area. In 1986 the Japanese Government decided to exceed the self-imposed limit on defence expenditure of 1% of the gross national product (GNP), set in 1976. The Government proposed defence spending equivalent to 1.004% of the forecast GNP in 1987/88, and also announced that it would maintain defence expenditure at around this level until 1991. This increase was welcomed by the USA, but Nakasone stressed that Japan would not become a major military power.

In December 1990, in the context of recent political changes in Eastern Europe and the more conciliatory posture adopted by the USSR in the Pacific region, the Japanese Government announced a new five-year national defence capability development programme (to begin in the fiscal year ending in March 1992). The average annual increase in total military expenditure over the five-year period was expected to be 3%, in comparison with the 5% average annual increase during the previous five-year programme. The new programme, to be implemented at an estimated total cost of US $172,000m., also envisaged that Japan would assume a larger share of the cost of maintaining US troops stationed in Japan, together with an increase in the Japanese contribution to support costs (from about 40% in the late 1980s to some 50% of the total by 1995).

Stability in South-East Asia is a vital consideration in Japanese foreign policy, since Japan depends on Asia for about one-third of its foreign trade, including imports of vital raw materials. In 1978 a treaty of peace and friendship was signed with the People's Republic of China. A meeting between Chinese and Japanese leaders, held in Beijing in June 1986, ended with a pledge by both sides to reduce China's large trade deficit with Japan. This pledge was reiterated when the Japanese Prime Minister visited China in November. In 1987, however, China expressed growing concern about Japan's increased expenditure on defence and its more assertive military stance. In August 1988 Takeshita undertook an official visit to China, which was aimed at further improving relations between the two countries. During the visit, the Japanese Prime Minister announced that Japan would advance 810,000m. yen in loans to China between 1990 and 1995. Following the massacre of pro-democracy demonstrators by Chinese troops in Tian An Men Square, in Beijing, in June 1989, however, Japanese aid to China was suspended indefinitely. In July 1990 Japan announced its intention to resume aid to China, following the Chinese Government's declaration, in January 1990, that a state of martial law no longer existed in that country. In November 1990 Japan duly announced the resumption of a US $6,200m. development loan for China, and in January 1991 Kaifu announced that he was to undertake a visit to China during 1991.

Japan has a long-standing territorial dispute with the People's Republic of China and Taiwan regarding the sovereignty of five uninhabited islands in the East China Sea, 200 km to the north-east of Taiwan, known as the Senkaku Islands in Japan and the Diayoyutai group in China.

In May 1990 Japan's relations with the Republic of Korea were greatly improved following a visit by President Roh Tae-Woo of that country, during which Kaifu offered an unequivocal apology for Japanese colonial aggressions on the Korean Peninsula in the past. In addition, Kaifu promised to improve legislation protecting the basic rights of Koreans and their descendants who were resident in Japan. Attempts to establish full diplomatic relations with the Democratic People's Republic of Korea (DPRK) in early 1991 were hindered by the insistence of the DPRK that Japan should make financial reparations for losses sustained during and following Japan's colonial rule of Korea in 1910–45. Further discussions were scheduled for March 1991.

Japan has demanded from the USSR the return of four small islands (the 'Northern Territories') lying a few kilometres from Hokkaido, which were annexed in 1945 by the USSR. Japan claims sovereignty over the islands under the provisions of an 1855 treaty between Japan and Russia. The Soviet claims are based on possession and on the 1945 Yalta agreement, in which the USA and the United Kingdom agreed that the Kurile Islands would be occupied by the USSR. Japan, supported since the early 1950s by the USA, argues that the islands are not part of the Kuriles. There has been no substantial progress in the matter since 1956, when Japan and the USSR resumed diplomatic relations. Consequently, the two countries have still not signed a peace treaty formally ending the Second World War. In July 1990 Kaifu announced that Japan would not consider extending any form of aid to the USSR as long as the territorial dispute remained unresolved. Hopes of an early settlement, following a visit to Japan by the Soviet Minister of Foreign Affairs, Eduard Shevardnadze, in September, were largely frustrated by the resignation, in December, of Shevardnadze (who had been instrumental in effecting a noticeable improvement in relations between the two countries in the late 1980s) and by Japanese condemnation of Moscow's armed response to political instability in the Baltic region. In late December 1990, however, the Japanese Government confirmed that, in keeping with financial policies adopted by Western Governments, some 14,000m. yen in financial aid had been allocated to the Soviet Union for the fiscal year ending March 1992.

Government

Under the Constitution of 1947, the Emperor is Head of State but has no governing power. Legislative power is vested in the bicameral Diet, consisting of the House of Representatives or lower house (512 seats), whose members are elected for a four-year term, and the House of Councillors or upper house (252 seats), members of which are elected for six years, one-half being elected every three years. At the upper house election of June 1983, an element of proportional representation was introduced, when 50 national seats were determined according to the number of votes for each party. There is universal suffrage for all adults from 20 years of age. Executive power is vested in the Cabinet. The Prime Minister is appointed by the Emperor (on designation by the Diet) and

JAPAN

himself appoints the other Ministers. The Cabinet is responsible to the Diet.

Japan has 47 prefectures, each administered by an elected Governor.

Defence

Although the Constitution renounces war and the use of force, the right of self-defence is not excluded. Japan maintains ground, maritime and air self-defence forces. Military service is voluntary. The USA provides equipment and training staff and also maintains bases. The total strength of the self-defence forces in June 1990 was 249,000, including army 156,200, navy 46,400 and air force 46,400. Proposed expenditure on defence for 1990/91 was 4,159,300m. yen. A five-year defence programme, which was to begin in April 1991, was expected to cost a total of US $172,000m.

Economic Affairs

In 1989, according to estimates by the World Bank, Japan's gross national product (GNP), measured at average 1987–89 prices, was US $2,920,310m., equivalent to US $23,730 per head. During 1980–89, it was estimated, GNP increased, in real terms, at an average annual rate of 4.1%, and GNP per head increased by an annual average of 3.5%. Over the same period, the population increased by an annual average of 0.6%. In 1980–88 Japan's gross domestic product (GDP) increased, in real terms, by an annual average of 3.9%.

In 1988 agriculture (including forestry and fishing) contributed 2.5% of GDP. In that year 7.9% of the employed labour force were engaged in agricultural activities. The principal crops are rice, potatoes, cabbages, sugar beets, and citrus fruits. Japan produces about 71% of its food requirements. Japan is one of the world's leading fishing nations. In 1988 the total catch was 11.9m. metric tons (of which 14.8% were crustaceans and molluscs).

Industry (including mining, manufacturing, construction and power) contributed 39.7% of GDP in 1988. In that year 34.1% of the employed labour force were engaged in the industrial sector. Heavy industries predominate in the manufacturing sector, particularly motor vehicles, steel, machinery, electrical equipment and chemicals. In 1990 Japan was the world's leading manufacturer of passenger cars, trucks and buses, producing a record 13.49m.

Mining and quarrying contributed 0.4% of GDP in 1988. Only 0.1% of the employed labour force were engaged in extractive activities in that year. While the domestic output of limestone and sulphur is sufficient to meet domestic demand, all of Japan's requirements of bauxite, crude petroleum and iron ore, 95% of its requirements of copper ore and 88% of coking coal had to be met by imports in 1987.

In 1988 manufacturing contributed 28.1% of GDP. In that year some 24.2% of the employed labour force were engaged in the sector. The most important sub-sectors, measured by gross value of output, are machinery and transport equipment, which provided 69.4% of total exports in 1988. Electrical machinery is becoming increasingly important, representing just over one-third, by value, of total exports of machinery and transport equipment in 1988.

Japan produced 2,096.9m. cu m of natural gas in 1988, but the country imports most of its energy requirements. Imports of petroleum and petroleum products comprised 13.8% of the value of total imports in 1988. Nuclear energy accounted for 25.5% of electricity output in 1990. The Government has undertaken an ambitious plan to promote and develop nuclear energy, which it is hoped will provide 36% of Japan's electricity requirements by 1995.

In 1989 Japan recorded a visible trade surplus of US $76,850m., and there was a surplus of $56,940m. on the current account of the balance of payments. In 1989 the principal source of imports was the USA (22.9%), which was also the principal market for exports (33.9%). Other major suppliers in that year were the Republic of Korea (6.2%), Australia (5.5%), the People's Republic of China (5.3%), Indonesia (5.2%), the Federal Republic of Germany (4.3%), Taiwan (4.3%) and Canada (4.1%). Other major purchasers of Japanese exports were the Republic of Korea (6.0%), the Federal Republic of Germany (5.8%), Taiwan (5.6%), Hong Kong (4.2%) and the United Kingdom (3.9%). The principal imports in 1988 were mineral fuels and lubricants (20.5% of the value of total imports), crude inedible materials except fuels (14.7%), basic manufactures (14.6%) and food and live animals (14.4%).

The budget for the financial year ending 31 March 1990 was balanced at 60,414,000m. yen. Of the gross long-term capital outflow in 1988, 62% was invested in foreign securities, 23% in foreign direct investment, and 15% in loans. A major part of the investment in foreign securities was in US government bonds, and 46% of the foreign direct investment was effected within the USA. Direct investment abroad in the fiscal year ended March 1990 was estimated at US $67,500m. The annual rate of inflation averaged 1.3% in 1980–88. Consumer prices increased by an average of 0.7% in 1988 and by 2.3% in 1989. An estimated 2.0% of the labour force were unemployed in August 1990.

Japan's main problem is the size of its balance of payments current account surplus, which causes much friction between Japan and its trading partners, and is the subject of discussions with the USA. In December 1989 Japan announced plans, including tax incentives and financial support for Japanese companies that are seen to be raising imports, to reduce the country's massive trade surplus. In 1990 Japan's imbalance of trade with the USA decreased by some 15%, but still accounted for more than 70% of the total surplus. Rising interest rates and fears of higher inflation, together with a temporary increase in international prices for petroleum (following the forcible annexation of Kuwait by Iraq in August 1990), contributed to wide fluctuations in share prices and in the value of the yen throughout 1990.

Social Welfare

Almost all of the population are insured under the various schemes covering health, welfare annuities, unemployment and industrial accidents. Workers normally retire at 55 years of age, with the average pension being about 40% of salary. In 1982 Japan had 9,403 hospital establishments, with a total of 1,401,999 beds (equivalent to one for every 84 inhabitants), and there were 161,260 physicians working in the country. Central government expenditure on social security was expected to increase by 4.8% to 12,180,000m. yen, for the 1991/92 financial year.

Education

A kindergarten system provides education for children aged between three and five years of age, although the majority of kindergartens are privately controlled. At the age of six, children are required to attend elementary schools (shogakko), from which they proceed, after six years, to lower secondary schools (chugakko) for a further three years. Education is compulsory to the age of 15, and there are plans to increase the age limit to 18. In 1988 all children aged six to 11 were enrolled at primary schools, while 95% of those aged 12 to 17 received secondary education. Upper secondary schools provide a three-year course in general topics or a vocational course in subjects such as agriculture, commerce, fine art and technical studies. Higher education is divided into three types of institution. Universities (daigaku) offer a four-year degree course, as well as post-graduate courses. Japan has more than 400 universities, both public and private. Junior colleges (tanki-daigaku) provide less specialized two- to three-year courses. Both universities and junior colleges provide facilities for teacher-training. Technical colleges (tokushu-kyoiku-gakko) offer a five-year specialized training for technicians in many fields of engineering.

Public Holidays

1991: 1 January (New Year's Day), 15 January (Coming of Age Day), 11 February (National Foundation Day), 21 March (Vernal Equinox Day), 29 April (Greenery Day), 3 May (Constitution Day), 5 May (Children's Day), 15 September (Respect for the Aged Day), 23 September (Autumnal Equinox), 10 October (Sports Day), 3 November (Culture Day), 23 November (Labour Thanksgiving Day), 23 December (Emperor's Birthday).

1992: 1 January (New Year's Day), 15 January (Coming of Age Day), 11 February (National Foundation Day), 21 March (Vernal Equinox Day), 29 April (Greenery Day), 3 May (Constitution Day), 5 May (Children's Day), 15 September (Respect for the Aged Day), 23 September (Autumnal Equinox), 10 October (Sports Day), 3 November (Culture Day), 23 November (Labour Thanksgiving Day), 23 December (Emperor's Birthday).

Weights and Measures

The metric system is in force.

Statistical Survey

Source (unless otherwise stated): Japan Center for Economic Research (JCER), 6-1, Nihombashi Kayabacho 2-chome, Chuo-ku, Tokyo 103, tel. (03) 639-2801; fax (03) 639-2839.

Area and Population

AREA, POPULATION AND DENSITY

Area (sq km)	377,815*
Population (census results)†	
1 October 1985	
Males	59,497,316
Females	61,551,607
Total	121,048,923
1 October 1990	123,611,541
Density (per sq km) at 1 October 1990	327.2

* 145,875 sq miles.
† Excluding foreign military and diplomatic personnel and their dependants.

PRINCIPAL CITIES (population at 31 March 1988)*

City	Population	City	Population
Tokyo (capital)†	8,155,781	Oita	392,566
Yokohama	3,121,601	Urawa	391,530
Osaka	2,543,520	Hirakata	385,739
Nagoya	2,099,564	Omiya	383,720
Sapporo	1,582,073	Fukuyama	363,123
Kobe	1,426,838	Asahikawa	362,523
Kyoto	1,419,390	Iwaki	357,056
Fukuoka	1,157,111	Takatsuki	353,940
Kawasaki	1,114,173	Suita	341,590
Hiroshima	1,042,629	Nagano	341,074
Kitakyushu	1,035,053	Nara	338,842
Sendai	865,630	Fujisawa	336,892
Sakai	807,680	Machida	335,347
Chiba	800,620	Takamatsu	327,538
Okayama	575,837	Toyohashi	325,862
Kumamoto	554,904	Toyama	316,061
Kagoshima	527,979	Toyoda	314,996
Hamamatsu	522,299	Kochi	311,710
Funabashi	515,295	Hakodate	311,591
Higashiosaka	502,893	Naha	309,641
Sagamihara	498,995	Koriyama	303,418
Amagasaki	497,212	Akita	294,536
Shizuoka	469,782	Okazaki	292,302
Niigata	469,521	Aomori	292,264
Himeji	450,374	Kawagoe	290,828
Nagasaki	445,814	Kashiwa	290,762
Matsudo	439,106	Tokorozawa	288,747
Matsuyama	433,886	Miyazaki	281,990
Hachioji	432,731	Maebashi	280,639
Yokosuka	430,656	Fukushima	271,226
Kanazawa	422,751	Koshigaya	270,854
Kawaguchi	418,880	Yao	269,439
Kurashiki	415,780	Yokkaichi	267,850
Utsunomiya	415,695	Akashi	261,035
Nishinomiya	412,267	Shimonoseki	260,219
Ichikawa	412,214	Kasugai	259,393
Gifu	407,827	Ichinomiya	258,584
Toyonaka	405,859	Tokushima	257,531
Wakayama	401,194	Neyagawa	256,168

* Except for Tokyo, the data for each city refer to an urban county (*shi*), an administrative division which may include some scattered or rural population as well as an urban centre.
† The figure refers to the 23 wards (*ku*) of Tokyo. The population of Tokyo-to (Tokyo Prefecture) was 11,680,282.

BIRTHS, MARRIAGES AND DEATHS*

	Registered live births		Registered marriages†		Registered deaths	
	Number	Rate (per '000)	Number	Rate (per '000)	Number	Rate (per '000)
1980	1,576,889	13.6	774,702	6.7	722,801	6.2
1981	1,529,455	13.0	776,531	6.6	720,262	6.1
1982	1,515,392	12.8	781,252	6.6	711,883	6.0
1983	1,508,687	12.7	762,552	6.4	740,038	6.2
1984	1,489,780	12.5	739,991	6.2	740,247	6.2
1985	1,431,577	11.9	735,850	6.1	752,283	6.3
1986	1,382,946	11.4	710,962	5.9	750,620	6.2
1987	1,346,658	11.1	696,173	5.7	751,172	6.2

1988 (provisional): Live births 1,314,006 (birth rate 10.7 per 1,000); Deaths 793,045 (death rate 6.5 per 1,000).
1989 (provisional): Live births 1,246,802 (birth rate 10.2 per 1,000).

* Figures relate only to Japanese nationals in Japan.
† Data are tabulated by year of registration rather than by year of occurrence.

Source: Ministry of Health and Welfare.

ECONOMICALLY ACTIVE POPULATION*
(annual averages, '000 persons aged 15 and over)

	1986	1987	1988
Agriculture and forestry	4,500	4,460	4,340
Fishing and aquatic culture	450	430	400
Mining and quarrying	80	80	70
Manufacturing	14,440	14,250	14,540
Electricity, gas and water	320	310	310
Construction	5,340	5,330	5,600
Trade and restaurants	13,390	13,660	13,890
Transport, storage and communications	3,530	3,480	3,530
Financing, insurance, real estate and business services	4,150	4,380	17,140
Community, social and personal services (incl. hotels)	12,120	12,490	
Activities not adequately defined	210	240	
Total employed	58,530	59,110	60,110
Unemployed	1,670	1,730	1,550
Total labour force	60,200	60,840	61,660
Males	36,260	36,550	36,930
Females	23,950	24,290	24,730

* All figures are rounded, so totals may not always be the sum of their component parts.

Source: Management and Co-ordination Agency, *Annual Report on the Labour Force Survey*.

JAPAN

Agriculture

PRINCIPAL CROPS ('000 metric tons)*

	1987	1988	1989
Wheat	864	1,021	985‡
Rice (paddy)	13,284	12,419	12,934‡
Barley	353	399	371‡
Potatoes	3,955	3,763	3,700†
Sweet potatoes	1,423	1,326	1,330†
Yams	166	168†	169†
Taro (Coco yam)	392	397	400†
Dry beans	132	132	135†
Soybeans (Soya beans)	287	277	275†
Groundnuts (in shell)	46	32	30†
Cabbages	3,063	2,874	2,900†
Tomatoes	837	775	780†
Cauliflowers	141	134	135†
Pumpkins, squash and gourds	277	284	285†
Cucumbers and gherkins	1,026	975	980†
Aubergines (Eggplants)	607	563	580†
Chillies and peppers (green)	172	171	169†
Onions (dry)	1,307	1,250	1,274‡
Carrots	669	679	690†
Watermelons	863	790	790†
Melons	411	403	410†
Grapes	308	296	297‡
Sugar cane	2,374	2,297	2,290‡
Sugar beets	3,827	3,849	3,850‡
Apples	998	1,042	1,075†
Pears	477	454	472†
Peaches and nectarines	212	203	205†
Oranges	355	353	297‡
Tangerines, mandarins, clementines and satsumas	2,518	1,998	2,072‡
Other citrus fruit	423	389	405‡
Strawberries	207	219	220†
Tea (green)	96	90	90†
Tobacco (leaves)	104	103‡	90‡

* Data at harvest time.
† FAO estimate.
‡ Unofficial figure.

Source: FAO, *Production Yearbook*.

LIVESTOCK ('000 head, unless otherwise indicated)

	1987	1988	1989
Cattle	4,694	4,667	4,682†
Sheep	27	29	27*
Goats	48	41	40*
Horses	22	22	21*
Pigs	11,354	11,725	11,866†
Chickens (million)	343	334	330*

* FAO estimate.
† Unofficial estimate.

Source: FAO, *Production Yearbook*.

LIVESTOCK PRODUCTS ('000 metric tons)

	1987	1988	1989
Beef and veal	565	569	550‡
Pig meat	1,582	1,578	1,570‡
Poultry meat	1,432	1,471	1,475
Cows' milk	7,335	7,608	7,750‡
Butter*	68.9	68.5	85.0‡
Cheese*	76.6	81.7	83.0†
Hen eggs	2,375.8	2,375.8	2,408.2
Honey	6.0‡	4.9	6.0‡
Raw silk	7.9	6.9	7.0†
Cattle hides (fresh)†	31.1	30.1	29.0

* Industrial production only (i.e. butter and cheese manufactured at milk plants), excluding farm production.
† FAO estimate(s).
‡ Unofficial figure.

Source: FAO, *Production Yearbook*.

Forestry

INDUSTRIAL ROUNDWOOD ('000 cubic metres)

	1985*	1986	1987
Sawn timber	18,814	18,397	18,774
Pulp	1,789	1,856	1,698
Veneer sheets and plywood	433	404	395
Others	11,908	10,863	10,026
Total	32,944	31,520	30,893

* Source: Ministry of Agriculture, Forestry and Fisheries, *Report on Demand and Supply of Lumber*.

Fuel wood ('000 cubic metres): 545 in 1985; 587 in 1986; 581 in 1987; 581 (FAO estimate) in 1988 (Source for 1987–88: FAO, *Yearbook of Forest Products*).

SAWNWOOD PRODUCTION ('000 cubic metres)

	1986	1987	1988*
Coniferous (soft wood)	25,246	26,180	26,164
Broadleaved (hard wood)	3,792	3,932	3,930
Total	29,038	30,112	30,094

* Estimates.

Source: FAO, *Yearbook of Forest Products*.

Fishing

('000 metric tons, live weight)

	1986	1987	1988*
Freshwater fishes	61.3	90.8	57.0
Chum salmon (Keta or Dog salmon)	151.5	144.1	159.3
Flounders, halibuts, soles, etc.	167.1	101.8	88.3
Pacific cod	100.5	111.8	59.1
Alaska pollack	1,421.8	1,312.5	1,259.1
Pacific sandlance	141.3	122.4	82.9
Atka mackerel	89.0	99.4	104.2
Pacific saury (Skipper)	217.2	197.1	291.6
Japanese jack mackerel	114.6	187.0	234.2
Japanese amberjack	145.9	158.9	165.9
Japanese pilchard (sardine)	4,209.5	4,362.0	4,488.4
Japanese anchovy	210.6	140.5	177.5
Skipjack tuna (Oceanic skipjack)	412.1	330.9	434.4
Yellowfin tuna	124.6	121.8	93.8
Bigeye tuna	169.8	160.6	107.8
Other tuna-like fishes	176.0	168.3	145.0
Chub mackerel	944.8	701.4	648.6
Other fishes (incl. unspecified)	1,511.8	1,398.8	1,442.5
Total fish	10,369.6	9,909.9	10,039.6
Marine crabs	94.7	78.1	70.2
Other crustaceans	114.3	131.2	127.5
Pacific cupped oyster	251.6	258.8	270.9
Japanese scallop	249.6	297.8	341.6
Japanese (Manila) clam	120.5	99.5	88.2
Other marine clams	103.4	92.2	115.9
Japanese flying squid	90.4	182.5	156.0
Other squids and cuttlefishes	372.9	572.1	505.3
Other molluscs	86.9	91.1	89.1
Other sea creatures†	122.5	135.3	92.7
Total catch†	11,976.3	11,848.6	11,896.9
Inland waters	198.7	226.0	196.8
Atlantic Ocean‡	273.3	447.0	418.3
Indian Ocean	53.0	44.0	32.3
Pacific Ocean	11,451.3	11,131.6	11,249.6

* Provisional
† Excluding aquatic mammals (including whales, see below).
‡ Including the Mediterranean and Black Sea.

Source: FAO, *Yearbook of Fishery Statistics*.

JAPAN

WHALING*

	1986	1987	1988
Number of whales caught	20,618	23,373	49,822

* Figures include whales caught during the Antarctic summer season beginning in the year prior to the year stated.

Aquatic plants ('000 metric tons): 780.2 in 1986; 664.1 in 1987; 799.9 in 1988.

Source: FAO, *Yearbook of Fishery Statistics*.

Mining

('000 metric tons, unless otherwise indicated)

	1986	1987	1988
Coal	16,012	13,049	11,223
Zinc ore	222	166	147
Iron	291	266	96
Manganese	6	n.a.	n.a.
Silica stone	13,637	14,291	16,198
Limestone	162,358	165,957	182,001
Chromite (metric tons)	10,642	11,815	9,508
Copper ore (metric tons)	34,978	23,817	16,666
Lead (metric tons)	40,327	27,870	26,741
Gold ore (kg)	10,280	8,590	7,310
Crude petroleum (million litres)	736	707	692
Natural gas ('000 cu m)	2,105,385	2,167,746	2,096,855

Source: Ministry of International Trade and Industry.

Industry

SELECTED PRODUCTS

('000 metric tons, unless otherwise indicated)

	1986	1987	1988
Wheat flour[1]	4,524	4,499	n.a.
Refined sugar	2,583	2,596	n.a.
Distilled alcoholic beverages ('000 hectolitres)[1]	8,824	8,725	n.a.
Beer ('000 hectolitres)[1]	50,754	54,927	n.a.
Cigarettes (million)[1]	309,200	309,100*	n.a.
Cotton yarn—pure (metric tons)	399,156	415,500*	n.a.
Cotton yarn—mixed (metric tons)	45,527	46,449	46,386
Woven cotton fabrics—pure and mixed (million sq m)	1,974.2	1,837.0	1,884.8
Flax, ramie and hemp yarn (metric tons)	8,848	10,100*	n.a.
Jute yarn (metric tons)	5,669	4,300*	3,700*
Linen fabrics ('000 sq m)	34,229	36,800*	n.a.
Jute fabrics ('000 sq m)	327	200*	n.a.
Woven silk fabrics—pure and mixed ('000 sq m)	108,221	99,933	103,021
Wool yarn—pure and mixed (metric tons)	112,109	123,254	119,720
Woven woollen fabrics—pure and mixed ('000 sq m)[2]	312,964	331,425	353,119
Rayon continuous filaments (metric tons)	75,787	99,400*	n.a.
Acetate continuous filaments (metric tons)	26,986		n.a.
Rayon discontinuous fibres (metric tons)	217,210	240,216	232,736
Acetate discontinuous fibres (metric tons)[3]	36,972	n.a.	n.a.
Woven rayon fabrics—pure and mixed (million sq m)[2]	638.8	635.5	668.3
Woven acetate fabrics—pure and mixed (million sq m)[2]	61.5		
Non-cellulosic continuous filaments (metric tons)	615,571	619,710	632,575
Non-cellulosic discontinuous fibres (metric tons)	787,240	767,996	770,770
Woven synthetic fabrics (million sq m)[2,4]	2,859.4	2,677.6	2,671.7
Leather footwear ('000 pairs)[5]	51,975	51,984	56,023
Mechanical wood pulp	9,240.0	9,732.7	10,414.9
Chemical wood pulp[6]			
Newsprint	2,640.6	2,668.1	3,066.8
Other printing and writing paper	4,949.5	n.a.	7,598.8
Other paper	4,681.9	2,341.4	3,678.6
Paperboard	8,789.9	9,740.1	10,292.6
Synthetic rubber	1,153.4	1,191.9	1,298.0
Motor vehicle tyres ('000)	147,517	149,212	161,348
Rubber footwear ('000 pairs)	58,064	51,135	49,714
Ethylene—Ethene	4,291.4	4,584.8	n.a.
Propylene—Propene	3,166.9	3,368.3	n.a.
Benzene—Benzol	2,260.9	2,225.5	2,374.1
Toluene—Toluol	830.3	1,005.8	1,018.9
Xylenes—Xylol	1,570.2	1,767.3	1,987.9
Methyl alcohol—Methanol	220.8	181.3	n.a.
Ethyl alcohol—95% (kilolitres)	168,782	n.a.	n.a.
Sulphuric acid—100%	6,562.4	6,541	6,766
Caustic soda—Sodium hydroxide	3,076.4	3,227	3,508
Soda ash—Sodium carbonate	1,020.8	1,098	1,083
Ammonium sulphate	1,783.4	1,083	1,834
Nitrogenous fertilizers (a)[7]	1,054	988	986
Phosphate fertilizers (b)[7]	623	577	531
Liquefied petroleum gas	7,831	8,214	4,100
Naphtha (million litres)	9,672	8,733	8,754
Motor spirit—Gasoline (million litres)[8]	34,332	34,520	35,591
Kerosene (million litres)	24,089	20,054	21,037
Jet fuel (million litres)	4,020	4,038	3,857
Gas oil (million litres)	26,123	25,236	25,554
Heavy fuel oil (million litres)	61,589	60,344	63,746
Lubricating oil (million litres)	2,233	2,284	2,372
Petroleum bitumen—Asphalt	5,587	6,600	n.a.
Coke-oven coke	48,139	n.a.	n.a.
Cement	71,264	71,550	77,556
Pig-iron	74,651	73,418	79,295
Ferro-alloys[9]	1,105	973	1,107
Crude steel	98,275	98,513	105,681
Aluminium—unwrought: primary	104.2	1,032.3	1,305.3
secondary[10]	865.3		
Electrolytic copper	943.0	980.3	955.1
Refined lead—unwrought (metric tons)	283,142	268,500*	n.a.
Electrolytic, distilled and rectified zinc—unwrought (metric tons)	708,032	665,600*	678,200*
Calculating machines ('000)	64,211	53,874	68,119
Radio receivers ('000)	13,911	8,396	8,552
Television receivers ('000)	13,863	14,286	13,388
Merchant vessels launched ('000 g.r.t.)	7,739	4,236	4,554
Passenger motor cars ('000)	7,809.8	7,891.1	8,198.4
Lorries and trucks ('000)	4,407.6	4,347.7	4,488.5
Motorcycles, scooters and mopeds ('000)	3,396.6	2,630.6	2,945.6
Cameras: photographic ('000)	17,383	16,399	15,561
cinematographic ('000)	7.8	n.a.	n.a.
Watches and clocks ('000)	281,703	285,072	352,652
Construction: new dwellings started ('000)[11]	1,536.1	1,838.3	1,836.2
Electric energy (million kWh)[1]	671,770	698,970	753,730*
Town gas (teracalories)	130,673	132,992	n.a.

* Provisional.
[1] Twelve months beginning 1 April of the year stated.
[2] Including finished fabrics.
[3] Including cigarette filtration tow.
[4] Including blankets made of synthetic fibres.   [5] Sales.
[6] Including pulp prepared by semi-chemical processes.
[7] Figures refer to the 12 months ending 30 June of the year stated and are in terms of (a) nitrogen, 100%, and (b) phosphoric acid, 100%.   [8] Including aviation gasoline.
[9] Including silico-chromium.   [10] Including alloys.
[11] Including buildings and dwelling units created by conversion.

Sources: Ministry of Agriculture, Forestry and Fisheries, Ministry of International Trade and Industry, Ministry of Finance and Ministry of Construction.

JAPAN

Finance

CURRENCY AND EXCHANGE RATES

Monetary Units
1,000 rin = 100 sen = 1 yen.

Denominations
Coins: 1, 5, 10, 50 and 100 yen.
Notes: 500, 1,000, 5,000 and 10,000 yen.

Sterling and Dollar Equivalents (30 September 1990)
£1 sterling = 259.00 yen;
US $1 = 138.25 yen;
1,000 yen = £3.861 = $7.233.

Average Exchange Rate (yen per US $)
1987   144.64
1988   128.15
1989   137.96

GENERAL BUDGET ESTIMATES
('000 million yen, year ending 31 March)

Revenue	1987/88	1988/89	1989/90
Taxes and stamps	41,194	45,090	51,010
Public bonds	10,501	8,841	7,111
Others	2,406	2,769	2,293
Total	54,101	56,700	60,414

Expenditure	1987/88	1988/89	1989/90
Social security	10,090	10,385	10,895
Education and science	4,850	4,858	4,937
Government bond servicing	11,334	11,512	11,665
Defence	3,517	3,700	3,920
Public works	6,082	7,382	7,427
Local finance	10,184	10,906	13,369
Pensions	1,896	1,880	1,856
Total (incl. others)	54,101	55,700	60,414

INTERNATIONAL RESERVES (US $ million at 31 December)

	1987	1988	1989
Gold*	1,203	1,141	1,114
IMF special drawing rights	2,463	2,936	2,447
Reserve position in IMF	2,853	3,278	3,518
Foreign exchange	75,657	90,514	77,992
Total	82,176	97,869	85,071

* Valued at 35 SDRs per troy ounce.
Source: IMF, *International Financial Statistics*.

MONEY SUPPLY ('000 million yen at 31 December)

	1987	1988	1989
Currency outside banks	28,583	31,521	36,681
Demand deposits at deposit money banks	74,390	80,323	77,793
Total money	102,973	111,844	114,474

Source: IMF, *International Financial Statistics*.

COST OF LIVING (Consumer Price Index; average of monthly figures. Base: 1985 = 100)

	1986	1987	1988
Food (incl. beverages)	100.2	99.3	100.0
Housing	102.5	105.4	107.6
Rent	102.6	105.8	107.8*
Fuel, light and water charges	95.0	88.0	85.9
Clothing and footwear	102.2	103.3	104.5
Miscellaneous	102.0	103.2	103.6
All items	100.6	100.7	101.4

* Estimate.
Source: Management and Co-ordination Agency, *Annual Report on the Consumer Price Index*.
1989: All items 103.7.

NATIONAL ACCOUNTS ('000 million yen at current prices)

	1986	1987	1988
Government final consumption expenditure	32,424.3	33,015.2	34,283.2
Private final consumption expenditure	191,495.7	199,291.4	209,367.8
Increase in stocks	1,585.7	834.0	1,616.4
Gross fixed capital formation	91,219.9	99,266.9	111,400.9
Total domestic expenditure	316,725.6	332,407.5	356,668.4
Exports of goods and services	38,089.9	36,209.6	37,483.2
Less Imports of goods and services	24,791.1	25,194.9	29,065.1
Gross domestic product (GDP)	330,024.3	343,422.3	365,086.5
Factor income received from abroad	5,337.5	7,607.0	10,123.9
Less Factor income paid abroad	4,108.3	5,553.1	7,821.8
Gross national product (GNP)	331,253.5	345,476.2	367,388.6
Less Consumption of fixed capital	46,073.8	48,738.7	52,100.4
Statistical discrepancy	−1,583.5	−1,305.3	−1,018.7
National income in market prices	283,596.2	295,432.2	314,269.5

Source: Economic Planning Agency, *Annual Report on National Accounts*.

Gross Domestic Product by Economic Activity

	1986	1987	1988
Agriculture, forestry and fishing	9,546.8	9,308.5	9,325.6
Mining and quarrying	1,281.2	1,226.4	1,369.1
Manufacturing	96,380.3	99,593.5	106,593.7
Electricity, gas and water	11,533.8	11,460.8	11,677.1
Construction	24,827.3	27,344.0	30,835.9
Wholesale and retail trade	43,672.5	45,876.7	48,210.5
Transport, storage and communications	20,146.7	20,990.9	21,925.0
Finance and insurance	18,354.4	19,917.1	21,586.5
Real estate	32,895.7	35,557.9	38,086.0
Public administration	15,025.6	15,428.9	14,822.6
Other services	67,772.4	70,046.3	75,049.2
Sub-total	341,436.6	356,751.0	379,481.2
Import duties	942.4	1,043.3	1,146.4
Less Imputed bank service charge	13,938.2	15,677.3	16,559.8
Total	328,440.9	342,116.9	364,067.8
Statistical discrepancy	1,583.5	1,305.3	1,018.7
Gross domestic product	330,024.3	343,422.3	365,086.5

JAPAN

BALANCE OF PAYMENTS (US $ million)*

	1987	1988	1989
Merchandise exports f.o.b.	224,620	259,770	269,590
Merchandise imports f.o.b.	−128,200	−164,770	−192,740
Trade balance	96,420	95,000	76,850
Exports of services	28,850	35,030	39,700
Imports of services	−48,420	−63,530	−75,010
Other income received	50,810	76,750	104,210
Other income paid	−36,960	−59,520	−84,520
Private unrequited transfers (net)	−990	−1,120	−990
Government unrequited transfers (net)	−2,690	−3,000	−3,300
Current balance	87,020	79,610	56,940
Direct capital investment (net)	−18,350	−34,730	−45,220
Portfolio investment (net)	−91,330	−52,750	−32,530
Other capital (net)	64,310	21,260	30,000
Net errors and omissions	−3,710	3,130	−21,950
Overall balance	37,940	16,520	−12,760

* Figures are rounded to the nearest $10 million.
Source: IMF, *International Financial Statistics*.

JAPANESE DEVELOPMENT ASSISTANCE (US $ million)

	1985	1986	1987
Official:			
Bilateral grants:			
Donations	1,185	1,703	2,221
Reparations	636	855	1,154
Technical assistance	549	849	1,067
Direct loans	1,372	2,143	3,027
Total	2,557	3,846	5,248
Capital subscriptions or grants to international agencies	1,240	1,788	2,207
Total	3,797	5,634	7,454
Other Government capital:			
Export credits	−152	−858	−2,047
Direct investment capital	−1	332	287
Loans to international agencies	−148	−198	−47
Total	−302	−724	−1,808
Total official	3,495	4,910	5,646
Private:			
Export credits	−994	273	1,081
Direct investments	1,046	2,902	7,421
Other bilateral security investments	5,138	5,315	4,357
Loans to international agencies	2,832	1,326	1,865
Donations to non-profit organizations	101	82	92
Total private	8,123	9,898	14,816
Grand total	11,618	14,809	20,462

Source: Ministry of International Trade and Industry.

External Trade

PRINCIPAL COMMODITIES (US $ million)

Imports c.i.f.	1986	1987	1988
Food and live animals	18,245.9	20,752.0	26,960.1
Meat and meat preparations	2,586.9	3,338.4	4,313.3
Fresh, chilled or frozen meat	2,477.7	3,197.7	n.a.
Fish and fish preparations*	6,426.4	7,992.2	10,460.7
Crustacea and molluscs (fresh and simply preserved)	3,196.5	3,947.1	n.a.
Cereals and cereal preparations	3,485.2	3,160.4	4,241.0
Wheat and meslin (unmilled)	885.5	784.8	1,033.7
Maize (unmilled) for feeding	1,158.1	1,100.5	1,490.0
Fruit and vegetables	2,363.8	2,832.4	3,705.0
Sugar, sugar preparations and honey	452.8	477.0	654.8
Raw sugar	278.9	289.6	456.3
Coffee, tea, cocoa and spices	1,593.1	1,359.4	1,502.3
Beverages and tobacco	940.5	1,643.2	2,159.5
Crude materials (inedible) except fuels	17,292.0	21,751.1	27,632.9
Oil-seeds, oil nuts and oil kernels	1,567.7	1,616.7	2,152.5
Soya beans (excl. flour)	1,072.4	1,086.5	1,425.6
Wood, lumber and cork	4,044.4	6,245.6	7,140.1
Rough or roughly squared wood	2,922.8	4,347.9	4,545.8
Textile fibres and waste	1,863.3	2,702.0	3,308.8
Cotton	818.4	1,136.7	1,317.7
Raw cotton (excl. linters)	797.1	1,114.4	1,288.4
Metalliferous ores and metal scrap	5,763.4	6,120.1	8,487.6
Iron ore and concentrates	2,759.3	2,618.4	2,832.7
Non-ferrous ores and concentrates	2,080.0	772.9	4,103.8
Copper ores and concentrates (excl. matte)	1,227.5	1,475.7	2,472.2
Mineral fuels, lubricants, etc.	36,903.8	39,136.8	38,356.1
Coal, coke and briquettes	4,943.9	4,669.7	5,421.1
Coal (excl. briquettes)	4,926.5	4,633.5	5,375.3
Petroleum and petroleum products	24,116.6	27,445.3	25,807.0
Crude and partly refined petroleum	19,480.8	20,663.4	18,852.3
Petroleum products	4,635.8	6,781.9	6,954.7
Residual fuel oils	1,093.2	1,476.8	1,164.9
Gas (natural and manufactured)	7,843.3	7,021.8	7,128.0
Animal and vegetable oils and fats	244.7	270.8	406.7
Chemicals	9,733.1	11,844.9	14,829.9
Chemical elements and compounds	4,566.0	5,470.3	6,888.9
Organic chemicals	2,849.0	3,494.0	4,555.0
Inorganic chemicals	766.6	868.6	1,129.5
Medicinal and pharmaceutical products	1,724.4	2,110.0	2,657.7
Basic manufactures	12,389.5	18,055.2	27,339.8
Textile yarn, fabrics, etc.	2,173.9	2,974.9	3,929.1
Non-metallic mineral manufactures	1,927.9	2,847.4	4,149.6
Iron and steel	1,761.8	2,483.8	4,624.7
Non-ferrous metals	3,654.7	5,644.0	9,312.1
Aluminium and aluminium alloys	1,641.0	2,669.4	5,030.1

JAPAN
Statistical Survey

Imports c.i.f.—continued	1986	1987	1988
Machinery and transport equipment	13,283.1	17,263.5	24,727.0
Non-electric machinery	5,317.8	6,745.5	9,321.7
Electrical machinery, apparatus, etc.	4,506.1	5,893.8	9,288.7
Transport equipment	3,459.2	4,624.3	6,116.6
Aircraft and parts†	1,776.8	1,742.0	2,024.1
Miscellaneous manufactured articles	8,633.4	13,396.0	18,702.3
Clothing (excl. footwear)	2,852.7	4,649.4	6,702.0
Other commodities and transactions	8,741.7	5,401.7	6,239.5
Re-imports	1,544.5	1,736.5	1,991.3
Non-monetary gold	6,983.9	3,467.1	4,101.7
Total	126,407.8	149,515.1	187,353.7

* Including crustacea and molluscs.
† Excluding tyres, engines and electrical parts.

Exports f.o.b.	1986	1987	1988
Food and live animals	1,365.9	1,424.2	1,567.5
Beverages and tobacco	110.4	121.3	128.8
Crude materials (inedible) except fuels	1,414.1	1,489.5	1,761.1
Mineral fuels, lubricants, etc.	588.1	782.2	596.1
Animal and vegetable oils and fats	90.5	85.1	157.1
Chemicals	9,483.8	11,662.3	13,964.4
Chemical elements and compounds	3,953.4	4,998.7	6,000.1
Organic chemicals	3,141.3	4,017.3	4,891.7
Plastic materials, etc.	2,842.6	3,405.5	4,002.3
Basic manufactures	29,600.0	30,126.1	35,212.6
Rubber manufactures	2,040.3	2,240.0	3,085.1
Rubber tyres and tubes	1,642.2	1,807.2	2,218.5
Textile yarn, fabrics, etc.	5,444.8	5,544.7	5,472.4
Woven textile fabrics (excl. narrow or special fabrics)	3,706.4	3,741.5	3,598.2
Fabrics of synthetic (excl. regenerated) fibres	2,133.3	2,003.6	1,828.0
Non-metallic mineral manufactures	2,362.3	2,522.5	2,936.1
Iron and steel	12,706.2	12,610.0	15,321.5
Bars, rods, angles, shapes, etc.	1,437.1	1,058.6	2,026.7
Universals, plates and sheets	5,249.9	6,077.7	8,882.9
Thin plates and sheets (uncoated)	2,581.2	3,027.5	3,116.2
Tubes, pipes and fittings	3,398.7	2,567.5	4,189.5
Non-ferrous metals	1,563.7	1,771.9	2,142.0
Other metal manufactures	3,912.8	3,635.7	4,287.3
Machinery and transport equipment	133,325.6	149,562.7	183,764.6
Non-electric machinery	38,380.7	44,754.7	56,047.9
Power generating machinery	4,939.0	5,904.0	6,738.1
Internal combustion engines (non-aircraft)	3,841.8	4,876.0	5,939.3
Office machines	11,305.4	14,391.9	18,405.9
Metalworking machinery	3,636.9	3,475.1	3,927.0
Heating and cooling equipment	1,793.1	2,031.8	2,530.3
Electrical machinery, apparatus, etc.	35,518.5	40,883.1	61,975.4
Electric power machinery	2,453.2	2,724.0	3,405.4
Telecommunications apparatus	13,643.6	15,071.3	6,629.1
Television receivers	1,727.2	1,422.3	1,778.8
Radio receivers	2,755.5	2,463.5	2,211.5
Thermionic valves, tubes, etc.	6,342.4	8,312.3	12,326.9

Exports f.o.b.—continued	1986	1987	1988
Transport equipment	59,426.4	63,925.0	65,741.3
Road motor vehicles and parts*	50,929.4	44,942.2	48,786.9
Passenger cars (excl. buses)	32,945.2	35,693.2	38,671.4
Lorries and trucks (incl. ambulances)	8,021.8	7,324.2	9,627.5
Parts for cars, buses, etc.*	8,253.3	10,713.8	9,130.8
Motor cycles and parts	2,686.3	2,628.3	2,367.8
Motor cycles	2,064.1	1,884.2	1,973.5
Ships and boats	4,878.5	4,359.7	3,946.7
Miscellaneous manufactured articles	31,125.0	31,599.2	24,174.0
Scientific instruments, watches, etc.	12,407.8	13,722.6	13,200.1
Scientific instruments and photographic equipment	8,509.3	9,447.9	10,834.9
Watches, clocks and parts	1,963.4	1,980.8	2,365.1
Musical instruments, sound recorders, etc.	17,559.7	16,828.9	n.a.
Sound recorders, phonographs and parts	11,228.6	10,085.2	n.a.
Sound recorders and phonographs	9,909.6	8,406.0	n.a.
Other commodities and transactions	2,047.8	2,368.6	3,590.5
Re-exports	1,975.0	2,198.9	3,442.5
Total	209,151.2	229,221.2	264,916.8

* Excluding tyres, engines and electrical parts.

PRINCIPAL TRADING PARTNERS* (US $ million)

Imports c.i.f.	1987	1988	1989
Australia	7,869.3	10,284.6	11,604.6
Brazil	2,032.4	2,950.4	2,999.3
Brunei	1,300.5	1,116.9	1,086.4
Canada	6,072.9	8,308.1	8,645.0
China, People's Republic	7,401.4	9,858.8	11,145.8
France	2,871.3	4,315.1	5,545.7
Germany, Federal Republic	6,150.3	8,100.6	8,995.1
Hong Kong	1,560.5	2,108.8	2,218.9
India	1,530.1	1,804.4	1,977.5
Indonesia	8,427.3	9,496.8	11,021.1
Iran	1,555.6	1,164.2	1,792.3
Italy	2,134.8	2,895.0	3,806.1
Korea, Republic	8,075.5	11,810.6	12,994.2
Kuwait	1,795.8	1,590.4	2,338.9
Malaysia	4,771.9	4,710.0	5,106.9
Mexico	1,625.2	1,590.7	1,729.9
Oman	1,555.6	1,689.7	1,530.3
Philippines	1,352.9	2,044.1	2,059.5
Qatar	879.7	1,139.1	1,546.0
Saudi Arabia	7,311.1	6,348.2	7,048.3
Singapore	2,047.6	2,339.2	2,952.2
South Africa	2,259.2	1,933.2	2,034.8
Switzerland	3,101.4	3,565.4	3,863.0
Taiwan	7,128.1	8,743.5	8,979.3
Thailand	1,796.0	2,751.4	3,582.6
USSR	2,351.9	2,765.8	3,004.5
United Arab Emirates	5,926.3	5,323.6	6,051.4
United Kingdom	3,057.0	4,193.0	4,466.0
USA	31,499.5	42,037.3	48,245.8
Total (incl. others)	149,515.1	187,353.7	210,846.6

JAPAN

Exports f.o.b.	1987	1988	1989
Australia	5,146.2	6,680.4	7,805.0
Belgium	2,696.6	3,390.2	3,454.5
Canada	5,610.9	6,424.1	6,807.0
China, People's Republic	8,249.8	9,476.0	8,515.9
France	4,014.4	4,986.7	5,298.4
Germany, Federal Republic	12,832.6	15,792.7	15,920.3
Hong Kong	8,872.0	11,706.3	11,525.6
India	1,957.3	2,081.6	2,018.1
Indonesia	2,990.0	3,053.7	3,301.1
Italy	2,102.7	2,787.4	2,783.4
Korea, Republic	13,229.3	15,441.4	16,561.0
Malaysia	2,167.8	3,060.2	4,124.0
Mexico	1,388.9	1,772.3	1,907.7
Netherlands	4,070.9	5,054.3	5,112.4
New Zealand	1,127.5	1,038.5	1,346.3
Panama	2,416.4	2,652.6	2,512.1
Philippines	1,414.7	1,739.8	2,380.5
Saudi Arabia	3,239.4	3,142.2	2,763.2
Singapore	6,008.1	8,310.8	9,238.9
South Africa	1,863.3	2,046.7	1,717.2
Spain	1,343.3	1,860.3	1,941.5
Sweden	1,931.3	2,319.5	2,174.2
Switzerland	2,266.1	2,775.1	2,664.0
Taiwan	11,346.3	14,354.4	15,421.3
Thailand	2,953.3	5,161.8	6,838.4
USSR	2,563.3	3,129.9	3,081.7
United Arab Emirates	1,117.7	1,286.1	1,296.2
United Kingdom	8,400.3	10,632.2	10,740.9
USA	83,580.0	89,634.1	93,188.5
Total (incl. others)	229,221.2	264,916.8	275,174.6

* Imports by country of production; exports by country of last consignment.

Source: Japan Tariff Association, *The Summary Report on the Trade of Japan*.

Transport

RAILWAYS (traffic, year ending 31 March)

	1984/85	1985/86	1986/87
National railways			
Passengers (million)	6,884	6,941	7,104
Freight ton-km (million)	22,721	21,625	20,146
Private railways			
Passengers (million)	11,869	12,048	12,310
Freight ton-km (million)	513	509	471

Source: Ministry of Transport.

ROAD TRAFFIC ('000 motor vehicles in use at 31 December)

	1987	1988	1989
Cars	29,478	30,776	32,621
Buses and coaches	234	238	242
Goods vehicles	20,194	21,440	22,235
Tractors and trailers	70	75	81
Total	49,976	52,529	55,179

Source: IRF, *World Road Statistics*.

SHIPPING
Merchant Fleet (registered at 1 July)

	1985	1986	1987
Vessels	10,288	15,054	14,884
Displacement ('000 gt)	39,940	33,659	31,223

Source: Ministry of Transport.

International Sea-borne Traffic

	1984	1985	1986
Vessels entered:			
Number	38,980	39,856	40,129
Displacement ('000 net tons)	347,907	352,589	345,284
Goods ('000 metric tons):			
Loaded	94,800	94,307	88,123
Unloaded	603,159	603,684	598,908

Source: Ministry of Finance.

CIVIL AVIATION (domestic and international services)

	1984	1985	1986
Passengers carried ('000)	51,018	50,337	53,640
Passenger/km (million)	64,601	65,529	70,934
Freight ton/km* ('000)	2,699,260	3,089,530	3,589,650

* Including excess baggage.
Original Source: Ministry of Transport.

Tourism

	1986	1987	1988
Foreign visitors	2,061,526	2,154,864	2,355,412
Money received (US $ million)	1,463	2,097	2,893

Communications Media

('000)

	1984	1985	1986
Television subscribers*	31,062	31,509	31,955
Daily newspaper circulation†	48,232	48,232	48,569

* At 31 March. † In October.

In 1988 there were an estimated 72.0m. television receivers and 105.5m. radio receivers in use (Source: UNESCO, *Statistical Yearbook*).

Education

(1988)

	Institutions	Teachers	Students
Primary schools	24,901	449,347	9,872,520
Lower secondary schools	11,266	304,192	5,896,080
High schools	5,512	336,974	5,533,393
Technological colleges	62	6,034	50,934
Junior colleges	571	50,765	450,436
Graduate schools and universities	490	202,439	1,994,616

Directory

The Constitution

The Constitution of Japan was promulgated on 3 November 1946 and came into force on 3 May 1947. The following is a summary of its major provisions:

THE EMPEROR

Articles 1–8. The Emperor derives his position from the will of the people. In the performance of any state act as defined in the Constitution, he must seek the advice and approval of the Cabinet though he may delegate the exercise of his functions, which include: (i) the appointment of the Prime Minister and the Chief Justice of the Supreme Court; (ii) promulgation of laws, cabinet orders, treaties and constitutional amendments; (iii) the convocation of the Diet, dissolution of the House of Representatives and proclamation of elections to the Diet; (iv) the appointment and dismissal of Ministers of State and as well as the granting of amnesties, reprieves and pardons and the ratification of treaties, conventions or protocols; (v) the awarding of honours and performance of ceremonial functions.

RENUNCIATION OF WAR

Article 9. Japan renounces for ever the use of war as a means of settling international disputes.

Articles 10–40 refer to the legal and human rights of individuals guaranteed by the Constitution.

THE DIET

Articles 41–64. The Diet is convened once a year, is the highest organ of state power and has exclusive legislative authority. It comprises the House of Representatives (511 seats) and the House of Councillors (252 seats). The members of the former are elected for four years whilst those of the latter are elected for six years and election for half the members takes place every three years. If the House of Representatives is dissolved, a general election must take place within 40 days and the Diet must be convoked within 30 days of the date of the election. Extraordinary sessions of the Diet may be convened by the Cabinet when one quarter or more of the members of either House request it. Emergency sessions of the House of Councillors may also be held. A quorum of at least one third of the Diet members is needed to carry on Parliamentary business. Any decision arising therefrom must be passed by a majority vote of those present. A bill becomes law having passed both Houses except as provided by the Constitution. If the House of Councillors either vetoes or fails to take action within 60 days upon a bill already passed by the House of Representatives, the bill becomes law when passed a second time by the House of Representatives, by at least a two-thirds majority of those members present.

The Budget must first be submitted to the House of Representatives. If, when it is approved by the House of Representatives, the House of Councillors votes against it or fails to take action on it within 30 days, or failing agreement being reached by a joint committee of both Houses, a decision of the House of Representatives shall be the decision of the Diet. The above procedure also applies in respect of the conclusion of treaties.

THE EXECUTIVE

Articles 65–75. Executive power is vested in the cabinet consisting of a Prime Minister and such other Ministers as may be appointed. The Cabinet is collectively responsible to the Diet. The Prime Minister is designated from among members of the Diet by a resolution thereof.

If the House of Representatives and the House of Councillors disagree on the designation of the Prime Minister, and if no agreement can be reached even through a joint committee of both Houses, provided for by law, or if the House of Councillors fails to make designation within 10 days, exclusive of the period of recess, after the House of Representatives has made designation, the decision of the House of Representatives shall be the decision of the Diet.

The Prime Minister appoints and may remove other Ministers, a majority of whom must be from the Diet. If the House of Representatives passes a no-confidence motion or rejects a confidence motion, the whole Cabinet resigns unless the House of Representatives is dissolved within 10 days. When there is a vacancy in the post of Prime Minister, or upon the first convocation of the Diet after a general election of members of the House of Representatives, the whole Cabinet resigns.

The Prime Minister submits bills, reports on national affairs and foreign relations to the Diet. He exercises control and supervision over various administrative branches of the Government. The Cabinet's primary functions (in addition to administrative ones) are to: (a) administer the law faithfully; (b) conduct State affairs; (c) conclude treaties subject to prior (or subsequent) Diet approval; (d) administer the civil service in accordance with law; (e) prepare and present the budget to the Diet; (f) enact Cabinet orders in order to make effective legal and constitutional provisions; (g) decide on amnesties, reprieves or pardons. All laws and Cabinet orders are signed by the competent Minister of State and countersigned by the Prime Minister. The Ministers of State, during their tenure of office, are not subject to legal action without the consent of the Prime Minister. However, the right to take that action is not impaired.

Articles 76–95. Relate to the Judiciary, Finance and Local Government.

AMENDMENTS

Article 96. Amendments to the Constitution are initiated by the Diet, through a concurring vote of two-thirds or more of all the members of each House and are submitted to the people for ratification, which requires the affirmative vote of a majority of all votes cast at a special referendum or at such election as the Diet may specify.

Amendments when so ratified must immediately be promulgated by the Emperor in the name of the people, as an integral part of the Constitution.

Articles 97–99 outline the Supreme Law, while Articles 100–103 consist of Supplementary Provisions.

The Government

HEAD OF STATE

His Imperial Majesty AKIHITO, Emperor of Japan (succeeded to the throne 7 January 1989).

THE CABINET
(February 1991)

Prime Minister: TOSHIKI KAIFU.
Minister of Finance: RYUTARO HASHIMOTO.
Minister of Justice: MEGUMU SATO.
Minister of Foreign Affairs: TARO NAKAYAMA.
Minister of Education: YUTAKA INOUE.
Minister of Health and Welfare: SHIN'ICHIRO SHIMOJO.
Minister of Agriculture, Forestry and Fisheries: MOTOJI KONDO.
Minister of International Trade and Industry: EIICHI NAKAO.
Minister of Transport: KANEZO MURAOKA.
Minister of Posts and Telecommunications: KATSUTSUGA SEKIYA.
Minister of Labour: SADATOSHI OZATO.
Minister of Construction: YUJI OTSUKA.
Minister of Home Affairs and Chairman of the Public Safety Commission: AKIRA FUKIDA.
Minister of State and Chief Cabinet Secretary: MISOJI SAKAMOTO.
Minister of State and Director-General of the Management and Co-ordination Agency: MAN SASAKI.
Minister of State and Director-General of the Hokkaido Development and Okinawa Development Agencies: YOICHI TANI.
Minister of State and Director-General of the Defence Agency: YUKIHIKO IKEDA.
Minister of State and Director-General of the Economic Planning Agency: MICHIO OCHI.
Minister of State, Director-General of the Science and Technology Agency and Chairman of the Atomic Energy Commission: AKIKO SANTO.
Minister of State and Director-General of the Environment Agency: KAZUO AICHI.
Minister of State and Director-General of the National Land Agency: MAMORU NISHIDA.

MINISTRIES

Imperial Household Agency: 1-1, Chiyoda, Chiyoda-ku, Tokyo 100; tel. (03) 3213-1111.

JAPAN

Prime Minister's Office: 1-6, Nagata-cho, Chiyoda-ku, Tokyo; tel. (03) 3581-2361.

Ministry of Agriculture, Forestry and Fisheries: 1-2, Kasumigaseki, Chiyoda-ku, Tokyo; tel.(03) 3502-8111.

Ministry of Construction: 2-1, Kasumigaseki, Chiyoda-ku, Tokyo; tel. (03) 3580-4311.

Ministry of Education: 3-2, Kasumigaseki, Chiyoda-ku, Tokyo; tel. (03) 3581-4211.

Ministry of Finance: 3-1-1, Kasumigaseki, Chiyoda-ku, Tokyo; tel. (03) 3581-4111; telex 24980.

Ministry of Foreign Affairs: 2-2, Kasumigaseki, Chiyoda-ku, Tokyo; tel. (03) 3580-3311; telex 22350.

Ministry of Health and Welfare: 1-2-2, Kasumigaseki, Chiyoda-ku, Tokyo 100; tel. (03) 3503-1711.

Ministry of Home Affairs: 2-1, Kasumigaseki, Chiyoda-ku, Tokyo; tel. (03) 3581-5311.

Ministry of International Trade and Industry: 1-3, Kasumigaseki, Chiyoda-ku, Tokyo; tel. (03) 3501-1511; telex 22916.

Ministry of Justice: 1-1-1, Kasumigaseki, Chiyoda-ku, Tokyo 100; tel. (03) 3580-4111.

Ministry of Labour: 2-2, Kasumigaseki 1-chome, Chiyoda-ku, Tokyo; tel. (03) 3593-1211.

Ministry of Posts and Telecommunications: 3-2, Kasumigaseki, Chiyoda-ku, Tokyo 100; tel. (03) 3504-4411; telex 32538.

Ministry of Transport: 1-3, 2-chome, Kasumigaseki, Chiyoda-ku, Tokyo; tel. (03) 3580-3111.

Defence Agency: 9-7, Akasaka, Minato-ku, Tokyo; tel. (03) 3408-5211.

Economic Planning Agency: 3-1, Kasumigaseki, Chiyoda-ku, Tokyo; tel. (03) 3581-0261; fax (03) 3581-3907.

Environment Agency: 1-2-2, Kasumigaseki, Chiyoda-ku, Tokyo; tel. (03) 3581-3351; telex 33855; fax (03) 3508-9573.

Hokkaido Development Agency: 3-1-1, Kasumigaseki, Chiyoda-ku, Tokyo 100; tel. (03) 3581-9111.

Management and Co-ordination Agency: 3-1-1, Kasumigaseki, Chiyoda-ku, Tokyo; tel. (03) 3581-6361.

National Land Agency: 1-2-2, Kasumigaseki, Chiyoda-ku, Tokyo 100; tel. (03) 3593-3311.

Okinawa Development Agency: 1-6, Nagata-cho, Chiyoda-ku, Tokyo; tel. (03) 3581-2361.

Science and Technology Agency: 2-2, Kasumigaseki, Chiyoda-ku, Tokyo; tel. (03) 3581-5271.

Legislature

KOKKAI
(Diet)

The Diet consists of two Chambers: the House of Councillors (Upper House) and the House of Representatives (Lower House). The 512 members of the House of Representatives are elected for a period of four years (subject to dissolution). For the House of Councillors, which has 252 members, the term of office is six years, with one-half of the members elected every three years.

House of Councillors
Speaker: YOSHIHIKO TSUCHIYA.

Party	Seats after elections* 6 July 1986	23 July 1989
Liberal-Democratic Party†	142	109
Japan Socialist Party	41	66
Komeito	25	20
Japanese Communist Party	16	14
Democratic Socialist Party	12	8
New Liberal Club†	2	—
Independents	4	13
Second Chamber Club	3	14
Salaried Workers' Party	3	
Tax Party	2	8
Social Democratic Federation	1	
Others	—	
Vacant	1	—
Total	**252**	**252**

* One-half of the 252 seats are renewable every three years. At each election, 50 of the 126 seats were allocated on the basis of proportional representation.

† In August 1986 the New Liberal Club rejoined the Liberal-Democratic Party, from which it had separated in 1976.

House of Representatives
Speaker: KENZABURO HARA.

General Election, 18 February 1990

Party	Votes	% of votes	Seats
Liberal-Democratic Party	30,315,410	46.14	275
Japan Socialist Party	16,025,468	24.39	136
Komeito	5,242,674	7.98	45
Japanese Communist Party	5,226,985	7.96	16
Democratic Socialist Party	3,178,949	4.84	14
Social Democratic Federation	566,957	0.86	4
Progressive Party	281,793	0.43	1
Other parties	58,534	0.09	—
Independents	4,807,520	7.32	21
Total	**65,704,290**	**100.00**	**512**

Political Organizations

The Political Funds Regulation Law provides that any organization which wishes to support a candidate for an elective public office must be registered as a political party. There are over 10,000 registered parties in the country, mostly of local or regional significance. The conservative Liberal-Democratic Party has the support of big business and the rural population and is also by far the richest of the political parties. The proportion of votes for the two socialist parties increased slowly at each election after 1952. The split between the two parties reflects a long-standing division between supporters of a mass popular party (now represented by the DSP) and those seeking a class party on Socialist lines. The Communist Party of Japan split in 1964, the official party being independent and supporting neither the USSR nor the People's Republic of China.

Democratic Socialist Party—DSP (Minshato): 18 Mori Bldg, 2-3-13, Toranomon, Minato-ku, Tokyo 105; tel. (03) 3501-5111; f. 1960 by a right-wing breakaway faction of the Socialist Party of Japan; advocates an independent foreign policy; 72,000 mems (1983); Chair. KEIGO OOUCHI; Sec.-Gen. TAKASHI YONEZAWA.

Japanese Communist Party—JCP: 4-26-7 Sendagaya, Shibuya-ku, Tokyo 151; tel. (03) 3403-6111; telex 34652; fax (03) 3746-0767; f. 1922; 490,000 mems (1988); Chair. Cen. Cttee KENJI MIYAMOTO; Chair. of the Presidium TETSUZO FUWA; Head of Secr. MITSUHIRO KANEKO.

Komeito (Clean Government Party): 17, Minami-Motomachi, Shinjuku-ku, Tokyo 160; tel. (03) 3353-0111; f. 1964; advocates political moderation, humanitarian socialism, and policies respecting 'dignity of human life'; 213,000 mems (1989); Founder DAISAKU IKEDA; Chair. KOSHIRO ISHIDA; Sec.-Gen. YUICHI ICHIKAWA.

Liberal-Democratic Party—LDP (Jiyu-Minshuto): 1-11-23, Nagata-cho, Chiyoda-ku, Tokyo 100; tel. (03) 3581-0111; f. 1955; advocates the establishment of a welfare state, the promotion of industrial development, the improvement of educational and cultural facilities and constitutional reform as needed; follows a foreign policy of alignment with the USA; 2,963,312m. mems (Sept. 1989); Pres. TOSHIKI KAIFU; Sec.-Gen. ICHIRO OZAWA; Chair. of Gen. Council TAKEO NISHIOKA.

Ni-In Club, Kakushin Kyoto (Second Chamber Club): Broadway Corp. 1015, 5-52-15, Nakano, Nakano-ku, Tokyo 164; tel. (03) 3508-8629; successor to the Green Wind Club (Ryukufukai), which originated in the House of Councillors in 1946–47; Sec. YUKIO AOSHIMA.

Progressive Party (Shinpoto): Matsuzaki Bldg, 1-2-2, Atago, Minato-ku, Tokyo 105; tel. (03) 3578-7001; f. 1987 by breakaway group from the New Liberal Club (a breakaway group of the LDP, which rejoined the LDP in Aug. 1986); Leader SEIICHI TAGAWA.

Salaried Workers' New Party (Sarariman Shinto): Hanzomon Co-op. 608, 2-12, Hayabusa-cho, Chiyoda-ku, Tokyo 102; tel. (03) 3234-8669; f. 1983; advocates reform of the tax system; Leader SHIGERU AOKI.

Social Democratic Federation—SDF (Shaminren): c/o House of Representatives, Tokyo; tel. (03) 3405-5644; f. 1977 as the Socialist Citizens' League; Leader SATSUKI EDA.

Social Democratic Party of Japan—SDPJ (Nippon Shakaito): 1-8-1, Nagata-cho, Chiyoda-ku, Tokyo 100; tel. (03) 3580-1171; f. 1945; formerly Japan Socialist Party (JSP); seeks the establishment of collective non-agression and a mutual security system, including Japan, the USA, the USSR and the People's Republic of China; 55,000 mems (1983); Chair. TAKAKO DOI; Sec.-Gen. TSURUO YAMAGUCHI.

Sports Peace Party (Supotsu Heiwato): Inoue Bldg 7F, 6-7-13, Minami Aoyama, Minato-ku, Tokyo 107; tel. (03) 5485-0071; Leader KANJI INOKI.

Taxpayers' Party (Zeikinto): c/o 331 House of Councillors, 1-7-1, Nagata-cho, Chiyoda-ku, Tokyo 100; tel. (03) 3508-8331; Sec. CHIN-PEI NOZUE.

United Social Democratic Party—USDP (Shakai Minshu Rengo): Akasaka Moatside Bldg 502, 1-1-7, Moto-Akasaka, Minato-ku, Tokyo 107; tel. (03) 3405-5644; Pres. SATSUKI EDA; Sec.-Gen. SHOGO ABE.

Several unofficial left-wing (principally Marxist) organizations are also active, including the Revolutionary Marxists (Kakumaruha), the Fourth Internationals (Daiyo Inta) and the Liberation Faction (Kaihoha). The largest of these groups, the Middle Core Faction (Chukakuha), had an estimated membership of 5,000 in early 1991.

Diplomatic Representation

EMBASSIES IN JAPAN

Algeria: 10-67, Mita 2-chome, Meguro-ku, Tokyo 153; tel. (03) 3711-2661; telex 23260; Ambassador: NOURREDINE Y. ZERHOUNI.

Argentina: Chiyoda House, 17-8, Nagata-cho 2-chome, Chiyoda-ku, Tokyo 100; tel. (03) 3592-C321; telex 22489; fax (03) 3506-8469; Ambassador: ERNESTO DE LA GUARDIA.

Australia: 1-12, Shiba Koen 1-chome, Minato-ku, Tokyo 105; tel. (03) 3453-0971; telex 22298; Ambassador: GEOFFREY MILLER.

Austria: 1-20, Moto Azabu 1-chome, Minato-ku, Tokyo 106; tel. (03) 3451-8281; telex 26361; Ambassador: Dr MICHAEL FITZ.

Bangladesh: 7-45, Shirogane 2-chome, Minato-ku, Tokyo 108; tel. (03) 3442-1501; telex 28826; Ambassador: A. K. M. HEDAYETUL.

Belgium: 5, Niban-cho, Chiyoda-ku, Tokyo 102; tel. (03) 3262-0191; telex 24979; fax (03) 3262-0651; Ambassador: Baron PATRICK NOTHOMB.

Bolivia: Kowa Bldg, No. 38, Room 804, 8th Floor, 12-24, Nishi-Azabu 4-chome, Minato-ku, Tokyo 106; tel. (03) 3499-5441; telex 32177; fax (03) 3499-5443; Ambassador: GONZALO MONTENEGRO.

Brazil: 11-12, Kita Aoyama 2-chome, Minato-ku, Tokyo 107; tel. (03) 3404-5211; telex 22590; Ambassador: CARLOS A. B. BUENO.

Brunei: 5-2, Kita Shinagawa 6-chome, Shinagawa-ku, Tokyo 141; tel. (03) 3447-7997; Ambassador: P. D. H. IDRISS.

Bulgaria: 36-3A, Yoyogi 5-chome, Shibuya-ku, Tokyo 151; tel. (03) 3465-1021; Ambassador: PETAR BASHIKAROV.

Burundi: Tokyo; Ambassador: ANTOINE NTAMOBWA.

Cameroon: 9-12, Minami Nanpeidai-cho, Shibuya-ku, Tokyo 150; tel. (03) 3496-1125; telex 28032; Ambassador: ETIENNE NTSAMA.

Canada: 3-38, Akasaka 7-chome, Minato-ku, Tokyo 107; tel. (03) 3408-2101; telex 22218; Ambassador: JAMES H. TAYLOR.

Central African Republic: 32-2, Ohyama-cho, Shibuya-ku, Tokyo 151; tel. (03) 3460-8341; telex 24793; Ambassador: NOEL EREGANI.

Chile: Nihon Seimei Akabanebashi Bldg, 8th Floor, 3-1-14, Shiba, Minato-ku, Tokyo 105; tel. (03) 3452-7561; telex 24585; Ambassador: GUSTAVO PONCE LEROU.

China, People's Republic: 3-4-33, Moto Azabu, Minato-ku, Tokyo 106; tel. (03) 3403-3380; telex 28705; Ambassador: YANG ZHENYA.

Colombia: 10-53, Kami Osaki 3-chome, Shinagawa-ku, Tokyo 141; tel. (03) 3440-6491; Ambassador: FIDEL DUQUE RAMÍREZ.

Costa Rica: Kowa Bldg, No. 38, Room 901, 12-24, Nishi Azabu 4-chome, Minato-ku, Tokyo 106; tel. (03) 3486-1812; Chargé d'affaires (a.i.): ANA LUCÍA NASSAR SOTO.

Côte d'Ivoire: Kowa Bldg, No. 38, Room 701, 12-24, Nishi Azabu 4-chome, Minato-ku, Tokyo 106; tel. (03) 3499-7021; telex 26631; fax (03) 3498-4269; Ambassador: PIERRE NELSON COFFI.

Cuba: 3-16-23, Higashi-Gotanda, Shinagawa-ku, Tokyo 141; tel. (03) 3449-7511; telex 22369; Ambassador: AMADEO BLANCO VALDÉS-FAULY.

Czechoslovakia: 16-14, Hiroo 2-chome, Shibuya-ku, Tokyo 150; tel. (03) 3400-8122; telex 24595; fax (03) 3406-6215; Ambassador: JAN WINKELHÖFER.

Denmark: 29-6, Sarugaku-cho, Shibuya-ku, Tokyo 150; tel.(03) 3496-3001; telex 24417; fax (03) 3496-3440; Ambassador: W. THUNE ANDERSEN.

Dominican Republic: Kowa Bldg, No. 38, Room 904, 12-24, Nishi Azabu 4-chome, Minato-ku, Tokyo 106; tel. (03) 3499-6020; telex 33701; Ambassador: JUAN EMILIO CANÓ DE LA MOTA.

Ecuador: Kowa Bldg, No. 38, Room 806, 12-24, Nishi Azabu 4-chome, Minato-ku, Tokyo 106; tel. (03) 3499-2800; telex 25880; fax (03) 3499-4400; Ambassador: MARCELO AVILA.

Egypt: 5-4, Aobadai 1-chome, Meguro-ku, Tokyo 153; tel. (03) 3770-8021; telex 23240; Ambassador: W. F. ELMENIAWY.

El Salvador: Kowa Bldg, No. 38, 8th Floor, 12-24, Nishi Azabu 4-chome, Minato-ku, Tokyo 106; tel. (03) 3499-4461; telex 25829; Ambassador: Dr ERNESTO ARRIETA PERALTA.

Ethiopia: Roppongi Hilltop House, B-1, 4-25, Roppongi 3-chome, Minato-ku, Tokyo 106; tel. (03) 3585-3151; telex 28402; Ambassador: WORKU MOGES.

Fiji: Noa Bldg, 10th Floor, 3-5, Azabudai 2-chome, Minato-ku, Tokyo 106; tel. (03) 3587-2038; fax (03) 3587-2563; Ambassador: CHARLES WALKER.

Finland: 3-5-39, Minami Azabu, Minato-ku, Tokyo 106; tel. (03) 3442-2231; telex 26277; fax (03) 3442-2175; Ambassador: HEIKKI KALHA.

France: 11-44, Minami Azabu 4-chome, Minato-ku, Tokyo 106; tel. (03) 3473-0171; Ambassador: LOÏC HENNEKINNE.

Gabon: 12-11, Higashi Gotanda 3-chome, Shinagawa-ku, Tokyo 141; tel. (03) 3448-9540; telex 24812; Ambassador: PATRICE MAKIKA.

Germany: 5-10, Minami Azabu 4-chome, Minato-ku, Tokyo 106; tel. (03) 3473-0151; telex 22292; fax (03) 3473-4244; Ambassador: Dr HANS-JOACHIM HALLIER.

Ghana: Mori Bldg, No. 28, 11th Floor, 16-13, Nishi Azabu 4-chome, Minato-ku, Tokyo 106; tel. (03) 3409-3861; telex 22487; Ambassador: JAMES LESLIE MAYNE AMISSAH.

Greece: 16-30, Nishi Azabu 3-chome, Minato-ku, Tokyo 106; tel. (03) 3403-0871; Ambassador: Dr GEORGE LIANIS.

Guatemala: 38 Kowa Bldg, Room 905, 4-12-24, Nishi Azabu, Minato-ku, Tokyo 106; tel. (03) 3400-1830; Ambassador: RODOLFO R. MURALLES.

Guinea: 12-6, Minami Azabu 1-chome, Minato-ku, Tokyo 106; tel. (03) 3769-0451; telex 24165; fax (03) 3769-0453; Ambassador: BOUBACAR BARRY.

Haiti: Kowa Bldg, No. 38, Room 906, 12-24, Nishi Azabu 4-chome, Minato-ku, Tokyo 106; tel. (03) 3486-7070; telex 29601; Chargé d'affaires a.i.: FRITZNEL LAFONTANT.

Holy See: Apostolic Nunciature, 9-2, Sanban-cho, Chiyoda-ku, Tokyo 102; tel. (03) 3263-6851; Apostolic Pro-Nuncio: Archbishop WILLIAM AQUIN CAREW.

Honduras: Kowa Bldg, No. 38, Room 802, 8th Floor, 12-24, Nishi Azabu 4-chome, Minato-ku, Tokyo 106; tel. (03) 3409-1150; telex 28591; Ambassador: ANÍBAL ENRIQUE QUIÑÓNEZ ABARCA.

Hungary: 3-1, Aobadai 2-chome, Meguro-ku, Tokyo 153; tel. (03) 3476-6061; telex 22688; Ambassador: ANDRÁS FORGÁCS.

India: 2-11, Kudan Minami 2-chome, Chiyoda-ku, Tokyo 102; tel. (03) 3262-2391; fax (03) 3234-4866; Ambassador: ARJUN GOBINDRAM ASRANI.

Indonesia: 2-9, Higashi Gotanda 5-chome, Shinagawa-ku, Tokyo 141; tel. (03) 3441-4201; telex 22920; Ambassador: Lt-Gen. (retd) YOGI SUPARDI.

Iran: 10-32, Minami Azabu 3-chome, Minato-ku, Tokyo 106; tel. (03) 3446-8011; telex 22753; Ambassador: SEYED MUHAMMAD HOSSEIN ADELI.

Iraq: 4-7, Akasaka 8-chome, Minato-ku, Tokyo 107; tel. (03) 3423-1727; telex 28825; Ambassador: Dr RASHID M. S. AL-RISAI.

Ireland: Kowa Bldg, No. 25, 8-7, Sanban-cho, Chiyoda-ku, Tokyo 102; tel. (03) 3263-0695; telex 23926; Ambassador: JAMES A. SHARKEY.

Israel: 3, Niban-cho, Chiyoda-ku, Tokyo 102; tel. (03) 3264-0911; telex 22636; Ambassador: NAHUM ESHKOL.

Italy: 5-4, Mita 2-chome, Minato-ku, Tokyo 108; tel. (03) 3453-5291; telex 22433; fax (03) 3456-2319; Ambassador: BARTOLOMEO ATTOLICO.

Jordan: 4A, B, Chiyoda House, 4th Floor, 17-8, Nagata-cho 2-chome, Chiyoda-ku, Tokyo 100; tel. (03) 3580-5856; telex 23708; Ambassador: KHALED MADADHA.

Kenya: 24-3, Yakumo 3-chome, Meguro-ku, Tokyo 152; tel. (03) 3723-4006; telex 22378; Ambassador: STEPHEN K. OLE LEKEN.

Korea, Republic: 2-5, Minami Azabu 1-chome, Minato-ku, Tokyo 106; tel. (03) 3452-7611; telex 22045; Ambassador: LEE WON-KYUNG.

Kuwait: 13-12, Mita 4-chome, Minato-ku, Tokyo 108; tel. (03) 3455-0361; telex 25501; Ambassador: ABDUL-AZIZ ABDULLATIF AL-SHARIKH.

Laos: 3-6-2, Minami-magome, Ota-ku, Tokyo 143; tel. (03) 3778-1660; fax (03) 3778-1661; Ambassador: K. SAYAKONE.

Lebanon: Chiyoda House, 5th Floor, 17-8, Nagata-cho 2-chome, Chiyoda-ku, Tokyo 100; tel. (03) 3580-1227; telex 25356; Ambassador: SAMIR EL-KHOURY.

Liberia: Odakyu Fudosan Minami Aoyama Bldg, 6th Floor, 8-1 Minami Aoyama 7-chome, Minato-ku, Tokyo 107; tel. (03) 3499-2451; Ambassador: STEPHEN J. KOFFA, Sr.

Libya: 10-14, Daikanyama-cho, Shibuya-ku, Tokyo 150; tel. (03) 3477-0701; telex 22181; Secretary of the People's Bureau: Wanis M. Aburwela.

Luxembourg: Niban-cho TS Bldg, 2-1, Niban-cho, Chiyoda-ku, Tokyo 102; tel. (03) 3265-9621; telex 28822; Ambassador: Jean-Louis Wolzfeld.

Madagascar: 3-23, Moto Azabu 2-chome, Minato-ku, Tokyo 106; tel. (03) 3446-7252; telex 25941; Ambassador: Hubert M. Rajaobelina.

Malaysia: 1-11 Minami Azabu 2-chome, Minato-ku, Tokyo 106; tel. (03) 3280-7601; telex 24221; fax (03) 3280-7606; Ambassador: Datuk H. M. Khatib.

Mexico: 15-1, Nagata-cho 2-chome, Chiyoda-ku, Tokyo 100; tel. (03) 3581-1131; telex 26875; Ambassador: Dr Sergio González Gálvez.

Mongolia: Pine Crest Mansion, 21-4, Shoto, Kamiyama-cho, Shibuya-ku, Tokyo 150; tel. (03) 3469-2088; Ambassador: Buyantyn Dashtseren.

Morocco: Silva Kingdom Bldg, 5th and 6th Floors, 16-3, Sendagaya 3-chome, Shibuya-ku, Tokyo 151; tel. (03) 3478-3271; telex 23451; Ambassador: Saad Eddine Taieb.

Myanmar: 8-26, Kita Shinagawa 4-chome, Shinagawa-ku, Tokyo 140; tel. (03) 3441-9291; telex 32289; Ambassador: U Mya Thein.

Nepal: 14-9, Todoroki 7-chome, Setagaya-ku, Tokyo 158; tel. (03) 3705-5558; telex 23936; fax (03) 3705-8264; Ambassador: Narayan Prasad Arjal.

Netherlands: 6-3, Shiba Koen 3-chome, Minato-ku, Tokyo 105; tel. (03) 3431-5126; telex 22855; fax (03) 3432-7560; Ambassador: Herman C. Posthumus Meyjes.

New Zealand: 20-40, Kamiyama-cho, Shibuya-ku, Tokyo 150; tel. (03) 3467-2271; Ambassador: Rodney J. Gates.

Nicaragua: Kowa Bldg, No. 38, Room 903, 9th Floor, 12-24, Nishi Azabu 4-chome, Minato-ku, Tokyo 106; tel. (03) 3499-0400; telex 28119; Ambassador: Jorge Huezo Castrillo.

Nigeria: 2-19-7, Uehara, Shibuya-ku, Tokyo 151; tel. (03) 3468-5531; telex 24397; Ambassador: Mai-Bukar Garba Dogon-Yaro.

Norway: 12-2, Minami Azabu 5-chome, Minato-ku, Tokyo 106; tel. (03) 3440-2611; telex 26440; Ambassador: Terje Johannessen.

Oman: Silva Kingdom Bldg, 3rd Floor, 3-16-3, Sendagaya, Shibuya-ku, Tokyo 151; tel. (03) 3402-0877; Chargé d'affaires a.i.: Mohamed Said Rajad al-Ajeel.

Pakistan: 14-9, Moto Azabu 2-chome, Minato-ku, Tokyo 106; tel. (03) 3454-4861; Ambassador: Mansur Ahmed.

Panama: Kowa Bldg, No. 38, Room 902, 12-24, Nishi Azabu 4-chome, Minato-ku, Tokyo 106; tel. (03) 3499-3741; telex 22157; fax (03) 5485-3548; Ambassador: Alberto A. Boyd Arias.

Papua New Guinea: Mita Kokusai Bldg, Room 313, 3rd Floor, 1-4-28, Mita, Minato-ku, Tokyo 108; tel. (03) 3454-7801; telex 25488; Ambassador: Joseph Kaal Nombri.

Paraguay: Asahi Kami Osaki Bldg, 5th Floor, 5-8, Kami Osaki 3-chome, Shinagawa-ku, Tokyo 141; tel. (03) 3447-7496; telex 27496; Ambassador: Juan Carlos A. Hrase von Bargen.

Peru: 4-27, Higashi 4-chome, Shibuya-ku, Tokyo 150; tel. (03) 3406-4240; telex 26435; Ambassador: Luis Macchiavello Amoros.

Philippines: 11-24, Nampeidai-machi, Shibuya-ku, Tokyo 150; tel. (03) 3496-2731; telex 22694; Ambassador: Ramon V. del Rosario.

Poland: 13-5, Mita 2-chome, Meguro-ku, Tokyo 153; tel. (03) 3711-5224; Ambassador: Ryszard Frackiewicz.

Portugal: Olympia Annex, Apt 304-306, 31-21, Jingumae 6-chome, Shibuya-ku, Tokyo 150; tel. (03) 3400-7907; Ambassador: Dr José Eduardo Mello Gouveia.

Qatar: 16-22, Shirogane 6-chome, Minato-ku, Tokyo 108; tel. (03) 3446-7561; telex 24877; Ambassador: Mohamed Ali al-Ansari.

Romania: 16-19, Nishi Azabu 3-chome, Minato-ku, Tokyo 106; tel. (03) 3479-0311; telex 22664; Ambassador: Prof. Dr Constantin Vlad.

Rwanda: Kowa Bldg, No. 38, Room 702, 12-24, Nishi Azabu 4-chome, Minato-ku, Tokyo 106; tel. (03) 3486-7800; telex 27701; Ambassador: Joseph Nizeyimana.

Saudi Arabia: 1-53, Azabu Nagasaka-cho, Minato-ku, Tokyo 106; tel. (03) 3589-5241; telex 25731; Ambassador: Fawzi bin Abdul Majeed Shobokshi.

Senegal: 3-4, Aobadai 1-chome, Meguro-ku, Tokyo 153; tel. (03) 3464-8451; telex 25493; fax (03) 3464-8452; Ambassador: Kéba Birane Cissé.

Singapore: 12-3, Roppongi 5-chome, Minato-ku, Tokyo 106; tel. (03) 3586-9111; telex 22404; Ambassador: Cheng Tong Fatt.

Somalia: 9-10, Shiroganedai 5-chome, Minato-ku, Tokyo 108; tel. (03) 3442-7138; telex 33160; Ambassador: Hassan Abshir Farah.

Spain: 3-20, Roppongi 1-chome, Minato-ku, Tokyo 106; tel. (03) 3583-8531; telex 22471; fax (03) 3582-8627; Ambassador: Antonio Oyarzábal.

Sri Lanka: 14-1, Akasaka 1-chome, Minato-ku, Tokyo 107; tel. (03) 3585-7431; telex 24524; Ambassador: C. Mahendran.

Sudan: Yada Mansion, 6-20, Minami-Aoyama 6-chome, Minato-ku, Tokyo 107; tel. (03) 3406-0811; telex 23876; fax (03) 3400-1925; Ambassador: Dr Musa Mohammed Omer.

Sweden: 10-3, Roppongi 1-chome, Minato-ku, Tokyo 106; tel. (03) 5562-5350; telex 24586; fax (03) 5562-9095; Ambassador: Ove F. Heyman.

Switzerland: 9-12, Minami Azabu 5-chome, Minato-ku, Tokyo 106; tel. (03) 3473-0121; telex 24282; fax (03) 3473-6090; Ambassador: Dr Roger Bär.

Syria: Hornat Jade 19-45, Akasaka 6-chome, Minato-ku, Tokyo 107; tel. (03) 3586-8977; telex 29405; Ambassador: Dr Amin Esber.

Tanzania: 21-9, Kami Yoga 4-chome, Setagaya-ku, Tokyo 158; tel. (03) 3425-4531; telex 22121; fax (03) 3425-7844; Ambassador: Ali Said Mchumo.

Thailand: 14-6, Kami Osaki 3-chome, Shinagawa-ku, Tokyo 141; tel. (03) 3441-7352; Ambassador: M. L. Birabhongge Kasemsri.

Tunisia: 1-18-8, Wakaba-cho, Shinjuku-ku, Tokyo 160; tel. (03) 3353-4111; telex 27146; Ambassador: Ben Messaouda.

Turkey: 33-6, Jingumae 2-chome, Shibuya-ku, Tokyo 150; tel. (03) 3470-5131; telex 22856; Ambassador: Umut Arik.

USSR: 2-1-1, Azabudai, Minato-ku, Tokyo 106; tel. (03) 3583-4224; Ambassador: Ludvig Chizhov.

United Arab Emirates: Kotsu Anzen Kyoiku Centre Bldg, 7th Floor, 24-20, Nishi Azabu 3-chome, Minato-ku, Tokyo 106; tel. (03) 3478-0650; telex 23552; Ambassador: Hamad Salem al-Makami.

United Kingdom: 1, Ichiban-cho, Chiyoda-ku, Tokyo 102; tel. (03) 3265-5511; telex 22755; fax (03) 3265-5580; Ambassador: Sir John Whitehead.

USA: 10-1, Akasaka 1-chome, Minato-ku, Tokyo 107; tel. (03) 3224-5000; telex 22118; Ambassador: Michael H. Armacost.

Uruguay: Kowa Bldg, No. 38, Room 908, 12-24, Nishi Azabu 4-chome, Minato-ku, Tokyo 106; tel. (03) 3486-1888; telex 22843; fax (03) 3486-9872; Ambassador: Alfredo Giró Pintos.

Venezuela: Kowa Bldg, No. 38, 7th Floor, 12-24, Nishi Azabu 4-chome, Minato-ku, Tokyo 106; tel. (03) 3409-1501; telex 25255; Ambassador: Fernando Báez-Duarte.

Viet-Nam: 50-11, Moto Yoyogi-cho, Shibuya-ku, Tokyo 151; tel. (03) 3466-3311; Ambassador: Vo Van Sung.

Yemen: Kowa Bldg, No. 38, Room 807, 12-24, Nishi Azabu 4-chome, Minato-ku, Tokyo 106; tel. (03) 3499-7151; telex 32431; Ambassador: Muhammad Abdul Koddos Alwazir.

Yugoslavia: 7-24, Kita Shinagawa 4-chome, Shinagawa-ku, Tokyo 140; tel. (03) 3447-3571; telex 22360; Ambassador: Tarik Ajanović.

Zaire: Harajuku Green Heights, Room 701, 53-17, Sendagaya 3-chome, Shibuya-ku, Tokyo 151; tel. (03) 3423-3981; telex 24211; Ambassador: Murairi Mitima Kaneno.

Zambia: 3-9-19, Ebisu, Shibuya-ku, Tokyo 150; tel. (03) 3445-1043; telex 25210; Ambassador: Boniface Salimu Zulu.

Zimbabwe: 5-9-19, Shiroganedai, Minato-ku, Tokyo 108; tel. (03) 3280-0331; telex 32975; fax (03) 3280-0466; Ambassador: Dr T. Mutunhu.

Japan also recognizes the embassy of the Federated States of Micronesia (Ambassador: Masao Nakayama).

Judicial System

The basic principles of the legal system are set forth in the Constitution, which lays down that the whole judicial power is vested in a Supreme Court and in such inferior courts as are established by law, and enunciates the principle that no organ or agency of the Executive shall be given final judicial power. Judges are to be independent in the exercise of their conscience, and may not be removed except by public impeachment, unless judicially declared mentally or physically incompetent to perform official duties. The justices of the Supreme Court are appointed by the Cabinet, the sole exception being the Chief Justice, who is appointed by the Emperor after designation by the Cabinet.

The Court Organization Law, which came into force on 3 May 1947, decreed the constitution of the Supreme Court and the establishment of four types of inferior court—High, District, Family (established 1 January 1949), and Summary Courts. The constitution and functions of the courts are as follows:

THE SUPREME COURT

This court is the highest legal authority in the land, and consists of a Chief Justice and 14 associate justices. It has jurisdiction over

Jokoku (appeals) and Kokoku (complaints), prescribed specially in codes of procedure. It conducts its hearings and renders decisions through a Grand Bench or three Petty Benches. Both are collegiate bodies, the former consisting of all justices of the Court, and the latter of five justices. A Supreme Court Rule prescribes which cases are to be handled by the respective Benches. It is, however, laid down by law that the Petty Bench cannot make decisions as to the constitutionality of a statute, ordinance, regulation, or disposition, or as to cases in which an opinion concerning the interpretation and application of the Constitution or of any laws or ordinances is at variance with a previous decision of the Supreme Court.

Chief Justice: RYOHACHI KUSABA.

INFERIOR COURTS

High Court

A High Court conducts its hearings and renders decisions through a collegiate body, consisting of three judges, though for cases of insurrection the number of judges must be five. The Court has jurisdiction over the following matters:

Koso appeals from judgments in the first instance rendered by District Courts, from judgments rendered by Family Courts, and from judgments concerning criminal cases rendered by Summary Courts.

Kokoku complaints against rulings and orders rendered by District Courts and Family Courts, and against rulings and orders concerning criminal cases rendered by Summary Courts, except those coming within the jurisdiction of the Supreme Court.

Jokoku appeals from judgments in the second instance rendered by District Courts and from judgments rendered by Summary Courts, except those concerning criminal cases.

Actions in the first instance relating to cases of insurrection.

District Court

A District Court conducts hearings and renders decisions through a single judge or, for certain types of cases, through a collegiate body of three judges. It has jurisdiction over the following matters:

Actions in the first instance, except offences relating to insurrection, claims where the subject matter of the action does not exceed 900,000 yen, and offences liable to a fine or lesser penalty.

Koso appeals from judgments rendered by Summary Courts, except those concerning criminal cases.

Kokoku complaints against rulings and orders rendered by Summary Courts, except those coming within the jurisdiction of the Supreme Court and High Courts.

Family Court

A Family Court handles cases through a single judge in case of rendering judgments or decisions. However, in accordance with the provisions of other statutes it conducts its hearings and renders decisions through a collegiate body of three judges. A conciliation is effected through a collegiate body consisting of a judge and two or more members of the conciliation committee selected from among citizens.

It has jurisdiction over the following matters:

Judgment and conciliation with regard to cases relating to family as provided for by the Law for Adjudgment of Domestic Relations.

Judgment with regard to the matters of protection of juveniles as provided for by the Juvenile Law.

Actions in the first instance relating to adult criminal cases of violation of the Labour Standard Law, the Law for Prohibiting Liquors to Minors, or other laws especially enacted for protection of juveniles.

Summary Court

A Summary Court handles cases through a single judge, and has jurisdiction in the first instance over the following matters:

Claims where the value of the subject matter does not exceed 900,000 yen (excluding claims for cancellation or change of administrative dispositions).

Actions which relate to offences liable to fine or lesser penalty, offences liable to a fine as an optional penalty, and certain specified offences such as habitual gambling and larceny.

A Summary Court cannot impose imprisonment or a graver penalty. When it deems proper the imposition of a sentence of imprisonment or a graver penalty, it must transfer such cases to a District Court, but it can impose imprisonment with hard labour not exceeding three years for certain specified offences.

A Procurator's Office, with its complement of procurators, is established for each of these courts. The procurators conduct searches, institute prosecutions and supervise the execution of judgments in criminal cases, and act as representatives of the public interests in civil cases of public concern.

Religion

The traditional religions of Japan are Shintoism and Buddhism. Neither is exclusive, and many Japanese subscribe at least nominally to both. Since 1945 a number of new religions (Shinko Shukyo) have evolved, based on a fusion of Shinto, Buddhist, Daoist, Confucian and Christian beliefs.

SHINTOISM

Shintoism is an indigenous religious system embracing the worship of ancestors and of nature. It is divided into two cults: national Shintoism, which is represented by the shrines; and sectarian Shintoism, which developed during the second half of the 19th century. In 1868 Shinto was designated a national religion, and all Shinto shrines acquired the privileged status of a national institution. Complete freedom of religion was introduced in 1947, and state support of Shinto was banned. There are an estimated 81,000 shrines, 101,000 priests and c. 90m. adherents.

BUDDHISM

World Buddhist Fellowship: Rev. FUJI NAKAYAMA, Hozenji Buddhist Temple, 3-24-2 Akabane-dai, Kita-ku, Tokyo.

CHRISTIANITY

In 1988 the Christian population was estimated at 1,081,387.

National Christian Council in Japan: Japan Christian Centre, 2-3-18-24, Nishi Waseda, Shinjuku-ku, Tokyo 169; tel. (03) 3203-0372; fax (03) 3204-9495; f. 1923; 14 mems (churches and other bodies), 20 assoc. mems; Chair. Rev. KENTARO TAKEUCHI; Gen. Sec. Rev. MUNETOSHI MAEJIMA.

The Anglican Communion

Anglican Church in Japan (Nippon Sei Ko Kai): 4-21, Higashi 1-chome, Shibuya-ku, Tokyo 150; tel. (03) 3400-2314; fax (03) 3400-2895; f. 1887; 11 dioceses; Primate of Japan Most Rev. CHRISTOPHER ICHIRO KIKAWADA, Bishop of Osaka; Gen. Sec. Rev. JINTARO UEDA; 57,538 mems (1989).

The Orthodox Church

Japanese Orthodox Church (Nippon Haristosu Seikyoukai): Holy Resurrection Cathedral (Nicolai-Do), 1-3, 4-chome, Surugadai Kanda, Chiyoda-ku, Tokyo 101; tel. (03) 3291-1885; fax (03) 3291-1886; three dioceses; Archbishop of Tokyo, Primate and Metropolitan of All Japan Most Rev. THEODOSIUS; 24,783 mems.

Protestant Church

United Church of Christ in Japan (Nihon Kirisuto Kyodan): Japan Christian Center, Room 31, 3-18, Nishi Waseda 2-chome, Shinjuku-ku, Tokyo 169; tel. (03) 3202-0541; f. 1941; union of 34 Congregational, Methodist, Presbyterian, Reformed and other Protestant denominations; Moderator Rev. TSUJI NOBUMICHI; Gen. Sec Rev. JOHN M. NAKAJIMA; 201,468 mems (March 1989).

The Roman Catholic Church

Japan comprises three archdioceses and 13 dioceses. There were about 440,000 adherents in 1988.

Catholic Bishops' Conference of Japan (Chuo Kyogikai): 10-1, Rokubancho, Chiyoda-ku, Tokyo 102; tel. (03) 3262-3691; telex 32624; f. 1973; Pres. Most Rev. PETER SEIICHI SHIRAYANAGI, Archbishop of Tokyo; Gen. Sec. Rev. PETER JUNICHI IWAHASHI.

Archbishop of Nagasaki: Cardinal JOSEPH ASAJIRO SATOWAKI, Catholic Center, 10-34 Ueno-machi, Nagasaki-shi 852; tel. (0958) 46-4246.

Archbishop of Osaka: Most Rev. PAUL HISAO YASUDA, Archbishop's House, Koyoen Nishiyama-cho 1-55, Nishinomiya-shi 662, Hyogo-ken; tel. (0798) 73-0921.

Archbishop of Tokyo: Most Rev. PETER SEIICHI SHIRAYANAGI, Archbishop's House, 16-15, Sekiguchi 3-chome, Bunkyo-ku, Tokyo 112; tel. (03) 3943-2301; fax (03) 3944-8511.

Other Christian Churches

Among other denominations active in the country are the Christian Catholic Church, the German Evangelical Church, the Japan Baptist Convention, the Japan Baptist Union, the Japan Evangelical Lutheran Church, the Korean Christian Church in Japan (10,000 mems) and the Tokyo Union Church.

OTHER COMMUNITIES

Bahá'í Faith

The National Spiritual Assembly of the Bahá'ís of Japan: 2-13, 7-chome, Shinjuku Shinjuku-ku, Tokyo 160; tel. (03) 3209-7521.

JAPAN   Directory

Islam

Islam has been active in Japan since the late 19th century. There is a small Japanese and foreign Muslim community, maintaining a mosque at Kobe and an Islamic centre in Tokyo.

Islamic Center, Japan: 1-16-11, Ohara, Setagaya-ku, Tokyo 156; tel. (03) 3460-6169; telex 25329; fax (03) 3460-6105; f. 1965.

The New Religions

Many new cults have emerged in Japan since the end of the Second World War. Collectively these are known as the New Religions (Shinko Shukyo), of which the following are the most important:

Rissho Kosei-kai: 2-11-1, Wada Suginami-ku, Tokyo 166; tel. (03) 3383-1111; telex 22455; fax (03) 3229-1781; f. 1938; Buddhist lay organization based on the teaching of the Lotus Sutra, active interfaith co-operation towards peace; Pres. Rev. Dr NIKKYO NIWANO; 6.2m. mems with 236 brs world-wide (1989).

Soka Gakkai: 32, Shinano-machi, Shinjuku-ku, Tokyo 160; tel. (03) 3353-0616; telex 33145; fax (03) 3353-5431; f. 1930; the lay society of Nichiren Shoshu (Orthodox Nichiren Buddhism); membership of 7.95m. households (1987); Buddhist groups promoting education, international cultural exchange and world peace; Hon. Pres. DAISAKU IKEDA; Pres. EINOSUKE AKIYA.

The Press

The average circulation of Japanese daily newspapers is the highest in the world after the USSR and the USA, and the circulation per head of population is also among the highest, at 566 copies per 1,000 inhabitants in 1986. The large number of weekly news journals is a notable feature of the Japanese press. In 1984 a total of 2,700 magazines were published by 1,200 magazine publishing companies. Technically the Japanese press is highly advanced, and the major newspapers are issued in simultaneous editions in the main centres.

The two newspapers with the largest circulations are the *Asahi Shimbun* and *Yomiuri Shimbun*. Other influential papers include *Mainichi Shimbun*, *Nihon Keizai Shimbun*, *Chunichi Shimbun* and *Sankei Shimbun*.

PRINCIPAL DAILIES

Tokyo

Asahi Evening News: 8-5, Tsukiji 7-chome, Chuo-ku, Tokyo 104; tel. (03) 3546-7111; telex 22306; fax (03) 3543-1660; f. 1954; evening; English; Editor-in-Chief TERUO KUNUGI; circ. 33,000.

Asahi Shimbun: 3-2, Tsukiji 5-chome, Chuo-ku, Tokyo 104-11; tel. (03) 3545-0131; telex 22226; fax (03) 3545-0358; f. 1879; Pres. TOSHITADA NAKAE, Man. Editor MUNEYUKI MATSUSHITA; circ. morning 8.1m., evening 4.8m.

Daily Sports: 1-1-17, Higashi-Shinbashi, Minato-ku, Tokyo 105; tel. (03) 3571-6681; f. 1948; morning; Man. Editor TAKASHI KONDO; circ. 410,000.

The Daily Yomiuri: 7-1, 1-chome, Ohtemachi, Chiyoda-ku, Tokyo 100-55; tel. (03) 3242-1111; f. 1955; morning; English; Editor HIRONOBU ISHIKAWA; circ. 55,000.

Dempa Shimbun: 11-15, Higashi Gotanda 1-chome, Shinagawa-ku, Tokyo 141; tel. (03) 3445-6111; telex 24461; f. 1950; morning; Man. Editor HAJIME NINOMIYA; circ. 285,000.

Fuji: Tokyo; evening.

Gendai: Tokyo; evening.

Hochi Shimbun: 1-1, 2-chome, Hirakawa-cho, Chiyoda-ku, Tokyo 102; tel. (03) 3265-2311; f. 1872; morning; Man. Editor TOKUTEI ENDO; circ. 654,000.

The Japan Times: 5-4, 4-chome, Shibaura, Minato-ku, Tokyo 108; tel. (03) 5453-5312; telex 22319; f. 1897; morning; English; Chair. TOSHIAKI OGASAWARA; Pres. J. SUZUKI; circ. 75,000.

Komei Shimbun: 17, Minami-motomachi, Shinjuku-ku, Tokyo 160; tel. (03) 3353-0111; organ of the Komeito political party; circ. 800,000, Sunday edn 1.4m.

The Mainichi Daily News: 1-1-1, Hitotsubashi, Chiyoda-ku, Tokyo 100; tel. (03) 3212-3266; f. 1922; morning; English; also publ. from Osaka; Pres. NOBORU WATANABE; Man. Editor TAKAHARU YOSHIZAWA; combined circ. 45,000.

Mainichi Shimbun: 1-1, 1-chome, Hitotsubashi, Chiyoda-ku, Tokyo 100-51; tel. (03) 3212-0321; telex 22324; fax (03) 3211-3598; f. 1872; Pres. NOBORYU WATANABE; Gen. Man. and Editor KEN KONDO; circ. morning 4.2m., evening 2.1m.

Naigai Times: 14-14, 7-chome, Ginza, Chuo-ku, Tokyo 104; tel. (03) 3543-1061; f. 1949; evening; Editor-in-Chief KENICHI TOUYA; circ. 296,000.

Nihon Keizai Shimbun: 9-5, 1-chome, Ohtemachi, Chiyoda-ku, Tokyo 100-66; tel. (03) 3270-0251; telex 22308; f. 1876; morning, evening and weekly (English edn: *The Japan Economic Journal*); economic news; Pres. AKIRA ARAI, circ. morning 1.37m., evening 1.36m.

Nihon Kogyo Shimbun: 7-2, 1-chome, Ohtemachi, Chiyoda-ku, Tokyo 100; tel. (03) 3231-7111; f. 1933; morning; business and financial; Pres. TERUMI NAGATA; Man. Editor HIROSHI KONDO; circ. 409,000.

Nihon Nohgyo Shimbun (Agriculture): 2-3, Akihabara, Taito-ku, Tokyo 110; tel. (03) 3257-7140; fax (03) 3253-0980; f. 1928; morning; Pres. SAKON TANOOKA; Man. Editor MASAO OKU; circ. 570,000.

Nikkan Kogyo Shimbun (Industrial Daily News): 8-10, Kudan-kita 1-chome, Chiyoda-ku, Tokyo 100; tel. (03) 3222-7111; telex 29687; fax (03) 3262-6031; f. 1915; morning; Pres. TOSHIO FUJIYOSHI; circ. 546,000.

Nikkan Sports: 5-10, 3-chome, Tsukiji, Chuo-ku, Tokyo 104; tel. (03) 3542-2111; f. 1946; morning; Editor FUMIKI OKAZAKI; circ. 728,000.

Nikkan Suisan Keizai Shimbun (Fisheries): 6-8-19, Roppongi, Minato-ku, Tokyo 106; tel. (03) 3404-6531; fax (03) 3404-0863; f. 1948; morning; Man. Editor KOHSI TORINOUMI; circ. 58,000.

The Red Flag: Tokyo; organ of the Japan Communist Party (JCP); circ. 600,000.

Sankei Shimbun: 7-2, 1-chome, Ohtemachi, Chiyoda-ku, Tokyo 100; tel. (03) 3231-7111; f. 1950; Pres. SHINYA UEDA; Man. Editor Y. HOSOYA; circ. morning 802,000, evening 355,000.

Sankei Sports: 7-2, 1-chome, Ohtemachi, Chiyoda-ku, Tokyo 100; tel. (03) 3231-7111; f. 1963; morning; Man. Editor SHUNICHIRO KONDO; circ. 649,000.

Seikyo Shimbun: 18, Shinano-machi, Shinjuku-ku, Tokyo 160; tel. (03) 3353-6111; telex 33145; f. 1951; organ of Soka Gakkai religious movement; Prin. Officer TORU AOKI; circ. 5.5m.

Shipping and Trade News: Tokyo News Service Ltd, Tsukiji Hamarikyu Bldg, 3-3, Tsukiji 5-chome, Chuo-ku, Tokyo 104; tel. (03) 3542-8521; telex 23285; fax (03) 3542-5086; f. 1949; English; Man. Editor S. YASUDA; Editor T. TAKEDA; circ. 15,000.

Sports Nippon: Palace Side Bldg, 1-1, 1-chome, Hitotsubashi, Chiyoda-ku, Tokyo 100; tel. (03) 3213-3351; f. 1949; morning; Man. Editor JANSUKE EGUMA; circ. 785,000.

Tokyo Lady Kong: Tokyo; evening.

Tokyo Shimbun: 3-13, 2-chome, Konan, Minato-ku, Tokyo 108; tel. (03) 3471-2211; f. 1942; Man. Editor TSUYOSHI SATO; circ. morning 803,181, evening 590,000.

Tokyo Sports: 5-10, 3-chome, Tsukiji, Chuo-ku, Tokyo 104; tel. (03) 3543-6760; f. 1959; evening; Man. Editor MASAAKI WAKITA; circ. 872,000.

Tokyo Times: 2-4-20, Shiohama, Koto-ku, Tokyo 135; tel. (03) 3569-1155; f. 1946; morning; Man. Editor TAKAHARU YOSHIZAWA; circ. 200,000.

Yomiuri Shimbun: 7-1, 1-chome, Ohtemachi, Chiyoda-ku, Tokyo 100-55; tel. (03) 3242-1111; fax (03) 3246-0455; f. 1874; Pres. YOSOJI KOBAYASHI; Man. Editor KENYA MIZUKAMI; circ. morning 5.43m., evening 3.12m.

Yukan Fuji: 7-2, 1-chome, Ohtemachi, Chiyoda-ku, Tokyo 100; tel. (03) 3231-7111; f. 1969; evening; Pres. SHINYA UEDA; Editor T. MAMIZUKA; circ. 1.2m.

Osaka District

Asahi Shimbun: 2-4, 3-chome, Nakano-shima, Kita-ku, Osaka 530; tel. (06) 231-0131; f. 1879; Man. Editor T. SHIBATA; circ. morning 2.18m., evening 1.37m.

Daily Sports: 1-18-11, Edobori, Nishi-ku, Osaka 550; tel. (06) 443-0421; f. 1948; morning; Editor SABURO NAKAZATO; circ. 585,000.

Hochi Shimbun: 2-22-17, Honjo-Nishi, Oyodo-ku, Osaka 531; tel. (06) 374-2311; f. 1964; morning; Man. Editor S. SUZUKI; circ. 336,000.

The Mainichi Daily News: 1-6-20, Dojima, Kita-ku, Osaka 530; tel. (06) 343-1121; fax (06) 348-8829; f. 1922; morning; English; Man. Editor YUTAKA FURUTANI; circ. 50,000.

Mainichi Shimbun: 1-6-20, Dojima, Kita-ku, Osaka 530; tel. (06) 343-1121; f. 1882; Man. Editor FUTOSHI SAKOTA; circ. morning 1.61m., evening 932,000.

Nihon Keizai Shimbun: 1-1, Kyobashi-maeno-cho, Higashi-ku, Osaka 540; tel. (06) 943-7111; f. 1950; Man. Editor KEIJI SAMEJIMA; circ. morning 596,000, evening 387,000.

Nikkan Sports: 92-1, 5-chome, Hattori-kotubuki-cho, Toyonaka City 561; tel. (06) 862-1011; f. 1950; morning; Editor YOUJI KUGAI; circ. 452,000.

Osaka Nichi-nichi Shimbun: 1-5-13, Kitadori, Edobori, Nishi-ku, Osaka 550; tel. (06) 441-5551; f. 1946; evening; Man. Editor Mitsuke Kishimoto; circ. 89,000.

Osaka Shimbun: 2-4-9, Umeda, Kita-ku, Osaka 530; tel. (06) 343-1221; f. 1922; evening; Man. Editor Terukazu Higashiyama; circ. 163,000.

Osaka Sports: 4th Floor, Osaka Ekimae Daiichi Bldg, 1-3-1-400, Umeda, Kita-ku, Osaka 530; tel. (06) 345-7657; f. 1968; evening; Editor Sen Asano; circ. 510,000.

Sankei Shimbun: 2-4-9, Umeda, Kita-ku, Osaka 530; tel. (06) 343-1221; f. 1933; Man. Editor A. Sawa; circ. morning 1.19m., evening 708,000.

Sankei Sports: 2-4-9, Umeda, Kita-ku, Osaka 530; tel. (06) 343-1221; f. 1955; morning; Editor Hiroshi Tanaka; circ. 500,000.

Sports Nippon: 3-2-25, Oyodo-minami, Oyodo-ku, Osaka 531; tel. (06) 458-5981; f. 1949; morning; Man. Editor Jiro Tanaka; circ. 555,000.

Yomiuri Shimbun: 8-10, Nozaki-cho, Kita-ku, Osaka 530; tel. (06) 361-1111; f. 1952; Pres. G. Sakata; Man. Editor Koutaro Furusawa; circ. morning 2.21m., evening 1.4m.

Kanto District

Chiba Nippo (Chiba Daily News): 4-14-10, Chuo, Chiba City 280; tel. (0472) 22-9211; f. 1957; morning; Man. Editor Masaki Ishibashi; circ. 129,000.

Ibaraki: 2-15, Kitami-machi, Mito City 310; tel. (0292) 21-3121; f. 1891; morning; Man. Editor Isamu Murofushi; circ. 122,000.

Jyomo Shimbun: 1-50-21, Furuichi-machi, Maebashi City 371; tel. (0272) 51-4341; f. 1887; morning; Man. Editor Toshio Higuchi; circ. 199,000.

Kanagawa Shimbun: 23, 2-chome, Ohtemachi, Naka-ku, Yokohama City 231; tel. (045) 201-0831; f. 1942; morning; Man. Editor Rikuo Uchiyama; circ. 211,000.

Shimotsuke Shimbun: 1-8-11, Showa, Utsunomiya City 320; tel. (0286) 25-1111; f. 1884; morning; Man. Editor Michiyoshi Yasunaga; circ. 235,000.

Tochigi Shimbun: 45, Shimoto-matsuri 1-chome, Utsunomiya City 320; tel. (0286) 22-5291; f. 1950; morning; Man. Editor Tadashi Toyosaka; circ. 76,000.

Tohoku District
(North-east Honshu)

Akita Sakigake Shimpo: 2-6, 1-chome, Ohtemachi, Akita 010; tel. (0188) 62-1231; f. 1874; Man. Editor Saburo Washio; circ. morning and evening each 231,000.

Daily Tohoku: 1-3-12, Jyoka, Hachinoe 031; tel. (0178) 44-5111; f. 1945; morning; Editor Hiroaki Niiyama; circ. 84,000.

Fukushima Mimpo: 13-17, Ohtemachi, Fukushima City 960; tel. (0245) 31-4111; f. 1892; Man. Editor Shigeo Takahashi; circ. morning 248,000, evening 12,000.

Fukushima Minyu: 9-9, Nakamachi, Fukushima City 960; tel. (0245) 23-1191; f. 1895; Man. Editor Teruo Abe; circ. morning 168,000, evening 9,000.

Iwate Nippo: 3-2, Uchimaru, Morioka City 020; tel. (0196) 53-4111; f. 1938; Man. Editor Gen-ichiro Murata; circ. morning and evening each 210,000.

Kahoku Shimpo: 2-28, 1-chome, Itsutsubashi, Sendai City 980; tel. (0222) 22-6121; f. 1897; Man. Editor T. Suzuki; circ. morning 450,000, evening 175,000.

Too Nippoh: 2-11, 2-chome, Shinmachi, Aomori City 030; tel. (0177) 73-1111; f. 1888; Man. Editor Kouji Yamada; circ. morning 241,000, evening 236,000.

Yamagata Shimbun: 5-12, 2-chome, Hatago-cho, Yamagata City 990; tel. (0236) 22-5271; f. 1876; Man. Editor Kenichi Sohma; circ. morning and evening each 216,000.

Chubu District
(Central Honshu)

Asahi Shimbun: 3-3, 1-chome, Sakae, Naka-ku, Nagoya City 460; tel. (052) 231-8131; telex 22226; f. 1935; Editor Youichi Hosokawa; circ. morning 485,000, evening 247,000.

Chubu Keizai Shimbun: 4-4-12, Meieki, Nakamura-ku, Nagoya City 450; tel. (052) 561-5211; f. 1946; morning; Man. Editor Tadanori Kato; circ. 96,000.

Chukyo Sports: Chukei Bldg, 4-4-12, Meieki, Nakamura-ku, Nagoya City 450; tel. (052) 582-4076; f. 1968; evening; Man. Editor Ryotaro Motoyama; circ. 299,000.

Chunichi Shimbun: 6-1, 1-chome, Sannomaru, Naka-ku, Nagoya City 460; tel. (052) 201-8811; f. 1942; Man. Editor Tadashi Yamaguchi; circ. morning 1.98m., evening 830,000.

Chunichi Sports: 6-1, 1-chome, Sannomaru, Naka-ku, Nagoya City 460; tel. (052) 201-8811; f. 1954; evening: Dir Yasuo Mizutani; circ. 579,000.

Gifu Nichi-nichi Shimbun: 9, Imakomachi, Gifu City 500; tel. (0582) 64-1151; f. 1879; Pres. Mikio Sugiyama; Man. Editor Kiminori Muto; circ. morning 123,000, evening 31,000.

Mainichi Shimbun: 4-7-35, Meieki, Nakamura-ku, Nagoya City 450; tel. (052) 561-2211; f. 1935; Man. Editor Akira Horikoshi; circ. morning 221,000, evening 101,000.

Nagoya Times: 3-10, 1-chome, Marunouchi, Naka-ku, Nagoya City 460; tel. (052) 231-1331; f. 1946; evening; Man. Editor Isao Kimi; circ. 143,000.

Shinano Mainichi Shimbun: 657, Minamiagata-cho, Nagano City 380; tel. (0262) 36-3111; telex 22444; f. 1873; Man. Editor K. Taga; circ. morning 417,000, evening 61,000.

Shizuoka Shimbun: 3-1-1, Toro, Shizuoka City 422; tel. (0542) 82-1111; f. 1941; Man. Editor Kakuji Oishi; circ. morning 621,000, evening 621,000.

Yamanashi Nichi-Nichi Shimbun: 6-10, 2-chome, Kitaguchi, Kofu City 400, tel. (0552) 31-3000; f. 1872; morning; Man. Editor Takehisa Nakagomi; circ. 158,000.

Hokuriku District
(North Coastal Honshu)

Fukui Shimbun: 1-14, 1-chome, Haruyama, Fukui City 910; tel. (0776) 23-5111; f. 1899; morning; Man. Editor Makoto Tsuchida; circ. 150,000.

Hokkoku Shimbun: 5-1, 2-chome, Korinbo, Kanazawa City 920; tel. (0762) 63-2111; f. 1893; Man. Editor S. Arai; circ. morning 244,000, evening 84,000.

Hokuriku Chunichi Shimbun: 7-15, 2-chome, Korinbo, Kanazawa City 920; f. 1960; Editor K. Oyaizu; circ. morning 120,000, evening 20,000.

Kita Nihon Shimbun: 2-14, Yasuzumi-cho, Toyama City 930; tel. (0763) 32-1111; f. 1940; Man. Editor Ruuzo Ueno; circ. morning 197,000, evening 32,000.

Niigata Nippo: 274-1, Niban-cho, Higashinaka-dori, Niigata City 951; tel. (0252) 29-2211; f. 1942; Man. Editor Sachio Igarashi; circ. morning 418,000, evening 98,000.

Yomiuri Shimbun: 4-5, Shimonoseki-machi, Takaoka City 933; tel. (0766) 23-1234; f. 1961; Editor M. Nagahara; circ. morning 146,000, evening 11,000.

Kinki District
(West Central Honshu)

Ise Shimbun: 34-6, Hon-cho, Tsu City 514; tel. (0592) 24-0003; f. 1878; morning; Man. Editor Masao Kobayashi; circ. 97,000.

Kobe Shimbun: 1-1, 7-chome, Kumoidori, Chuo-ku, Kobe City 651; tel. (078) 221-4121; f. 1898; Man. Editor Tadao Tanaka; circ. morning 473,000, evening 277,000.

Kyoto Shimbun: 239, Shoshoi-machi Ebisugawa-kitairu, Karasuma-dori, Nakakyo-ku, Kyoto 604; tel. (075) 222-2111; f. 1879; Man. Editor T. Adachi; circ. morning 467,000, evening 355,000.

Nara Shimbun: 606, Sanjo-machi, Nara City 630; tel. (0742) 26-1331; f. 1946; morning; Man. Editor Yoshikata Hiroshiba; circ. 87,000.

Chugoku District
(Western Honshu)

Chugoku Shimbun: 7-1, Dobashi-cho, Naka-ku, Hiroshima City 730; tel. (082) 236-2111; fax (082) 236-2377; f. 1892; Pres. Akira Yamamoto; Man. Editor Yukio Ogata; circ. morning 680,000, evening 105,000.

Oka-Nichi: 6-30, Hon-cho, Okayama 700; tel. (0862) 31-4211; f. 1946; evening; Man. Editor Keiji Fukuhara; circ. 40,000.

San-In Chuo Shimpo: 383, Tono-machi, Matsue 690; tel. (0852) 21-4491; f. 1882; morning; Man. Editor Tadashi Sugitani; circ. 150,000.

Sanyo Shimbun: 1-23, 2-chome, Yanagi-cho, Okayama 700; tel. (0862) 31-2211; f. 1879; Man. Editor Hitoshi Kawai; circ. morning 396,000, evening 83,000.

Yamaguchi Shimbun: 1-1-7, Higashi-Yamato-cho, Shimonoseki 750; tel. (0832) 66-3211; f. 1946; morning; Pres. Kazuyugi Ogawa; Editor Atsumu Yoshikura; circ. 58,000.

Shikoku Island

Ehime Shimbun: 12-1, 1-chome, Ohtemachi, Matsuyama, 790; tel. (0899) 41-8111; f. 1941; Man. Editor Akira Yamada; circ. morning 213,000, evening 24,000.

Kochi Shimbun: 2-15, 3-chome, Honcho, Kochi City 780; tel. (0888) 25-1111, f. 1904; Man. Editor Shoroku Hashii; circ. morning 212,000, evening 127,000.

Shikoku Shimbun: 15-1, Nakano-machi, Takamatsu 760; tel. (0878) 33-1111; f. 1889; Man. Editor TASUO MURAI; circ. morning 179,000, evening 20,000.

Tokushima Shimbun: 6, 1-chome, Saiwai-cho, Tokushima 770; tel. (0886) 23-2121; f. 1941; Editor-in-Chief YOSHIMI IBATA; circ. morning 212,000, evening 39,000.

Hokkaido Island

Asahi Shimbun: 1-1, 1-chome, Nishi, Kita-Nijo, Chuo-ku, Sapporo 060; tel. (011) 281-2131; f. 1959; Editor A. ISHIZUKA; circ. morning 178,000, evening 117,000.

Hokkai Times: 6, 10-chome, Nishi, Minami-Ichijo, Chuo-ku, Sapporo 060; tel. (011) 231-0131; f. 1946; Man. Editor KIICHI SHIOGUCHI; circ. morning 167,000, evening 40,000.

Hokkaido Shimbun: 6, 3-chome, Odori-Nishi, Chuo-ku, Sapporo 060; tel. (011) 221-2111; f. 1942; Editor K. SAKUTA; circ. morning 1.1m, evening 800,000.

Mainichi Shimbun: 1, Nishi 6, Kita-Yojo, Chuo-ku, Sapporo 060; tel. (011) 221-4141; f. 1959; Rep. ISAO MIYASIMA; circ. morning 101,000, evening 47,000.

Nikkan Sports: Times Bldg, 10-6, Nishi, Minami-Ichijo, Chuo-ku, Sapporo 060; tel. (011) 231-5120; fax (011) 231-5470; f. 1962; morning; Man. Editor AKIRA ABE; circ. 159,000.

Yomiuri Shimbun: 1, 4-chome, Kita-yojo, Chuo-ku, Sapporo 060; tel. (011) 231-7611; f. 1959; Editor A. SHIDARA; circ. morning 260,000, evening 133,000.

Kyushu Island

Asahi Shimbun: 12-1, 1-chome, Sunatsu, Kokura Kita-ku, Kita-Kyushu City 802; tel. (093) 531-1131; f. 1935; Man. Editor TOMONORI MATSUMOTO; circ. morning 824,000, evening 223,000.

Fukunichi: 2-1, 1-chome, Imaizumi, Chuo-ku, Fukuoka 810; tel. (092) 711-2520; f. 1946; morning; Man. Editor TAKAAKI SATANI; circ. 135,000.

Kagoshima Shimpo: 7-28, Jonan-cho, Kagoshima 892; tel. (0992) 26-2100; f. 1959; morning; Man. Editor MOTOYOSH HAGIWARA; circ. 57,000.

Kumamoto Nichi-nichi Shimbun: 2-33, Kamidori-machi, Kumamoto 860; tel. (096) 326-1111; f. 1942; Editor KEISUKE HISANO; circ. morning 332,000, evening 107,000.

Kyushu Sports: Fukuoka Tenjin Centre Bldg, 2-14-8, Tenjin-cho, Chuo-ku, Fukuoka 810; tel. (092) 781-7452; f. 1966; morning; Man. Editor T. OKAMIYA; circ. 262,000.

Mainichi Shimbun: 13-1, Konya-machi, Kokura Kita-ku, Kitakyushu 802; tel. (093) 541-3131; f. 1935; Man. Editor HARUJI SHINOHARA; circ. morning 652,000, evening 166,000.

Minami Nihon Shinbun: 1-2, Yasui-cho, Kagoshima-shi, Kagoshima 892; tel. (0992) 26-4111; f. 1881; Man. Editor JUNICHI SAKOU; circ. morning 362,672, evening 30,050.

Miyazaki Nichi-nichi Shimbun: 1-33, 1-chome, Takachihodori, Miyazaki 880; tel. (0985) 26-9312; f. 1940; Man. Editor MASAKI NAKAMURA; morning; circ. 207,000.

Nagasaki Shimbun: 3-1, Morimachi, Nagasaki 852; tel. (0958) 44-2111; f. 1889; Man. Editor HISASHI IWANAGA; circ. morning 167,000, evening 54,000.

Nihon Keizai Shimbun: 3-1, 2-chome, Sumiyoshi, Hakata-ku, Fukuoka City; tel. (092) 281-4931; f. 1964; Editor TAKESHI INOUE; circ. morning 157,000, evening 62,000.

Nishi Nippon Shimbun: 4-1, 1-chome, Tenjin, Chuo-ku, Fukuoka 810; tel. (092) 711-5555; f. 1877; Man. Editor TSUNEO TAKIGUCHI; circ. morning 771,000, evening 217,000.

Oita Godo Shimbun: 9-15, 3-chome, Fudai-cho, Oita 870; tel. (0975) 36-2121; f. 1886; Man. Editor MOTOO ASAKUNO; circ. morning 202,000, evening 202,000.

Okinawa Times: 2-2-2, Kumoji, Naha City, 900; tel. (0988) 67-3111; f. 1948; Man. Editor TAKAO MIYAGI; circ. morning 245,000, evening 244,000.

Ryukyu Shimpo: 1-10-3, Izumizaki, Naha City, Okinawa 900; tel. (0988) 65-5111; f. 1893; Editor-in-Chief TATSUHIRO HIGA; circ. morning 173,000, evening 173,000.

Saga Shimbun: 3-18, 1-chome, Matsubara, Saga City 840; tel. (0952) 25-4811; fax (0952) 29-5760; f. 1884; morning; Man. Editor HIROFUMI KAWAHARA; circ. 127,000.

Sports Nippon: 4-1, 1-chome, Kiyotaki, Moji-ku, Kita-kyushu 801; tel. (093) 321-4001; f. 1955; morning; Man. Editor T. DOI; circ. 230,000.

Yomiuri Shimbun: 1-11, Meiwa-machi, Kokurakita-ku, Kitakyushu 802; tel. (093) 531-5131; f. 1964; Man. Editor MAKOTO WATARAI; circ. morning 887,000, evening 156,000.

WEEKLIES

An-An: Magazine House, 3-13-10, Ginza, Chuo-ku, Tokyo 104; tel. (03) 3545-7100; telex 22982; fax (03) 3546-0034; f. 1970; fashion; Editor MIYOKO YODOGAWA; circ. 500,000.

Asahi Graphic: Asahi Shimbun Publishing Dept, 5-3-2, Tsukiji, Chuo-ku, Tokyo 104; tel. (03) 3545-0131; telex 22226; f. 1923; pictorial review; Editor ATSUSHI TAKEUCHI; circ. 120,000.

Asahi Journal: Asahi Shimbun Publishing Dept, 5-3-2, Tsukiji, Chuo-ku, Tokyo 104; tel. (03) 3545-0131; telex 22226; f. 1959; review; Editor MITSUKO SHIMOMURA; circ. 83,000.

Economist: Mainichi Newspapers Publishing Dept, 1-1-1, Hitotsubashi, Chiyoda-ku, Tokyo 100-51; tel. (03) 3212-0321; telex 24851; f. 1923; Editorial Chief SABURO ZUSHI; circ. 85,000.

Focus: Shincho-Sha, 71 Yaraicho, Shinjuku-ku, Tokyo; tel. (03) 3266-5211; fax (03) 3266-5235; politics, economics, sport; Editor AKIO GOTO; circ. 850,000.

Friday: Kodan-Sha Ltd, 12-21, Otowa 2-chome, Bunkyo-ku, Tokyo 112-01; tel. (03) 3945-1111; fax (03) 3943-7815; current affairs; circ. 1m.

Hanako: Magazine House, 3-13-10, Ginza, Chuo-ku, Tokyo 104; tel. (03) 3545-7100; telex 22982; fax (03) 3546-0034; f. 1988; consumer guide; Editor YAMATO SHIINE; circ. 300,000.

Shukan Asahi: Asahi Shimbun Publishing Dept, 5-3-2, Tsukiji, Chuo-ku, Tokyo 104; tel. (03) 3545-0131; telex 22226; f. 1922; general interest; Editor J. KAWAMURA; circ. 482,000.

Shukan Bunshun: Bungei-Shunju Ltd., 3-23, Kioicho, Chiyoda-ku, Tokyo 102; tel. (03) 3265-1211; f. 1959; general interest; Editor KAZUYOSHI HANADA; circ. 610,000.

Shukan Daiyamondo: Diamond Inc, 1-4-2, Kasumigaseki, Chiyoda-ku, Tokyo 100; tel. (03) 3504-6519; telex 24461; f. 1913; economics; Editor TEIJI KAJIMA; circ. 81,000.

Shukan Gendai: Kodan-Sha Co Ltd, 2-12-21, Otowa, Bunkyo-ku, Tokyo 112-01; tel. (03) 3945-1111; fax (03) 3943-7815; f. 1959; general; Editor YASUO DOMON; circ. 606,000.

Shukan Josei: Shufu-To-Seikatsu Sha Ltd, 5-7, Kyobashi 3-chome, Chuo-ku, Tokyo 104; tel. (03) 3563-5131; fax (03) 3567-7893; f. 1957; women's interest; circ. 800,000.

Shukan Post: Shogakukan Publishing Co Ltd, 2-3-1, Hitotsubashi, Chiyoda-ku, Tokyo 101; tel. (03) 3230-5217; telex 22192; f. 1969; general; Editor AKIRA YAMAMOTO; circ. 693,000.

Shukan Shincho: Shincho-Sha, 71, Yarai-cho, Shinjuku-ku, Tokyo 162; tel. (03) 3266-5211; fax (03) 3266-5235; f. 1956; general interest; Editor HIKOYA YAMADA; circ. 599,000.

Shukan Spa!: Fuso-Sha Co, 6 Ichigaya-daimachi, Shinjuku-ku, Tokyo 162-80; tel. (03) 3226-8880; f. 1952; general interest; Editor NAOKI WATANABE; circ. 400,000.

Shukan Toyo Keizai: Toyo Keizai Inc., 1-2-1, Hongoku-cho, Nihombashi, Chuo-ku, Tokyo 103; tel. (03) 3246-5492; fax (03) 3270-0159; f. 1895; business and economics; Editor YUTAKA HOSHIKA; circ. 62,000.

Shukan Yomiuri: Yomiuri Shimbun Publication Dept, 1-7-1, Ohtemachi, Chiyoda-ku, Tokyo 100-55; tel. (03) 3242-1111; telex 22228; f. 1938; general interest; Editor TAKAO OHUCHI; circ. 453,000.

Student Times: Japan Times Inc, 4-5-4, Shibaura, Minato-ku, Tokyo 108; tel. (03) 3453-5311; f. 1951; English and Japanese; Editor YUKIO KAKUCHI; circ. 200,000.

Sunday Mainichi: Mainichi Newspapers Publishing Dept, 1-1-1, Hitotsubashi, Chiyoda-ku, Tokyo 100-51; tel. (03) 3212-0321; telex 22324; fax (03) 3211-0895; f. 1922; general interest; Editor TARO MAKI; circ. 258,000.

Tenji Mainichi: Mainichi Newspapers Publishing Dept, 1-6-20, Dōjima, Kita-ku, Osaka; tel. (06) 3348-8826; telex 22324; fax (06) 3348-8966; f. 1922; in Japanese braille; Editor TSUNEYUKI TAKEUCHI; circ. 12,000.

PERIODICALS

All Yomimono: Bungei-Shunju Ltd, 3-23, Kioicho, Chiyoda-ku, Tokyo 102; tel. (03) 3265-1211; f. 1930; monthly; popular fiction; Editor KENICHI FUJINO; circ. 122,000.

Any: S. S. Communications Inc., Cosmo Hirakawacho Bldg, 3-14, Hirakawa cho 1-chome, Chiyoda-ku, Tokyo 102; tel. (03) 3527-62220; fax (03) 3527-62229; f. 1989; every 2 weeks; women's interest; Editor YUKIO MIWA; circ. 380,000.

Asahi Camera: Asahi Shimbun Publishing Dept, 5-3-2, Tsukiji, Chuo-ku, Tokyo 104-11; tel. (03) 3545-0131; telex 22226; f. 1926; monthly; photography; Editor YASUSHI SATO; circ. 80,000.

Balloon: Shufunotomo Co Ltd, 2-9 Kanda Surugadai, Chiyoda-ku, Tokyo; tel. (03) 3294-1137; telex 26925; fax (03) 3291-5093; f. 1986; monthly; expectant mothers; Editor MARIKO HOSODA; circ. 250,000.

JAPAN

Bijutsu Techô: Bijutsu Shuppan-Sha, Inaoka Bldg, 2-36, Kanda, Jinbo-cho, Chiyoda-ku, Tokyo 101; tel. (03) 3234-2155; fax (03) 3234-1365; ; f. 1948; monthly; fine arts; Editor Norio Ohashi; circ. 60,000.

Brutus: Magazine House, 3-13-10, Ginza, Chuo-ku, Tokyo 104; tel. (03) 3545-7100; telex 22982; fax (03) 3546-0034; f. 1980; every 2 weeks; men's interest; Editor Giichiro Hata; circ. 200,000.

Bungei-Shunju: Bungei-Shunju Ltd, 3-23, Kioicho, Chiyoda-ku, Tokyo 102; tel. (03) 3265-1211; fax (03) 3239-5481; f. 1923; monthly; general; Pres. Kengo Tanaka; Editor Masaru Shiraishi; circ. 656,000.

Business JAPAN: Nihon Kogyo Shimbun Co, Sankei Bldg, 1-7-2, Ohtemachi, Chiyoda-ku, Tokyo 100; tel. (03) 3231-7111; f. 1955; monthly; Pres. Y. Hosoya; Editor Shimji Umemura; circ. 63,000.

Business Tokyo: Keizaikai Co Ltd, 2-13-18 Minami Aoyama, Minato-ku, Tokyo 107; tel. (03) 3423-8500; telex 32707; fax (03) 3423-8505; f. 1987; monthly; Chair. Seichu Sato; Editor Anthony Paul; circ. 136,500.

Chuokoron: Chuokoron-Sha Inc, 2-8-7, Kyobashi, Chuo-ku, Tokyo 104; tel. (03) 3563-1866; telex 32505; fax (03) 3561-5920; f. 1887; monthly; general interest; Chief Editor Takashi Hirabayashi; circ. 180,000.

Clique: Magazine House, 3-13-10, Ginza, Chuo-ku, Tokyo 104; tel. (03) 3545-7100; telex 22982; fax (03) 3546-0034; f. 1989; every 2 weeks; women's interest; Editor Hitoshi Akiba; circ. 250,000.

Croissant: Magazine House, 3-13-10, Ginza, Chuo-ku, Tokyo 104; tel. (03) 3545-7100; telex 22982; fax (03) 3546-0034; f. 1977; every 2 weeks; home; Editor Noriko Noshimori; circ. 600,000.

Fujinkoron: Chuokoron-Sha Inc, 2-8-7, Kyobashi, Chuo-ku, Tokyo 104; tel. (03) 3563-1261; f. 1916; women's literary monthly; Editor Kazuo Matsumura; circ. 257,000.

Gakujin (Alpinist): Tokyo Shimbun Publications Dept, 2-3-13, Konan, Minato-ku, Tokyo 108; f. 1947; monthly; Editor Takao Nakazono; circ. 150,000.

Geijutsu Shincho: Shincho-Sha, 71, Yaraicho, Shinjuku-ku, Tokyo 162; tel. (03) 3266-5381; telex 27433; fax (03) 3266-5387; f. 1950; monthly; fine arts, music, architecture, drama and design; Editor-in-Chief Midori Yamakawa; circ. 150,000.

Gendai: Kodan-Sha Co Ltd, 2-12-21, Otowa, Bunkyo-ku, Tokyo 112; tel. (03) 3945-1111; telex 22570; f. 1966; monthly; cultural and political; Editor Yoshisuke Sasaki; circ. 300,000.

Gunzo: Kodan-Sha Co Ltd, 2-12-21, Otowa, Bunkyo-ku, Tokyo 112; tel. (03) 3945-1111; telex 45509; fax (03) 3943-7814; f. 1946; literary monthly; Editor Katsuo Watanabe; circ. 30,000.

Hot-Dog Press: Kodan Sha Ltd, 12-21, Otowa 2-chome, Bunkyo-ku, Tokyo 112-01; tel. (03) 3945-1111; fax (03) 3943-7815; every 2 weeks; men's interest; circ. 650,000.

Ie-no-Hikari (Light of Home): Ie-no-Hikari Asscn, 11, Ichigaya Funagawara-cho, Shinjuku-ku, Tokyo 162; tel. (03) 3266-9000; telex 22367; fax (03) 3266-9048; f. 1925; monthly; rural and general interest; Pres. Shigenori Tokonabe; Editor Toshio Horie; circ. 1.1m.

Iwa-To-Yuki (Rock and Snow): Yama-kei Publrs Co, 1-1-33, Shiba-Daimon, Minato-ku, Tokyo 105; tel. (03) 3436-4026; fax (03) 5472-4430; f. 1958; every 2 months; mountaineering; Editor Tsunemichi Ikeda; circ. 50,000.

Japan Company Handbook: Toyo Keizai Shinpo-Sha, 1-2-1, Nihonbashi Hongoku-cho, Chuo-ku, Tokyo 103; tel. (03) 3246-5621; fax (03) 3241-5543; f. 1974; 2 vols a year; English; Editor Shihiro Nakashima; total circ. 100,000.

Japan Quarterly: Asahi Shimbun Publishing Dept, 5-3-2, Tsukiji, Chuo-ku, Tokyo 104-11; tel. (03) 3545-0131 Ext. 5440; fax (03) 3544-1428; f. 1954; English; political, economic and cultural; Editor Yuji Ohishi; circ. 6,000.

Jitsugyo No Nihon: Jitsugyo No Nihon-Sha Ltd, 1-3-9, Ginza, Chuo-ku, Tokyo 104; tel. (03) 3535-4441; f. 1897; every 2 months; economics and business; Editor Masabumi Noji; circ. 48,000.

Journal of Electronic Engineering: Dempa Publications Inc, 1-11-15, Higashi Gotanda, Shinagawa-ku, Tokyo 141; tel. (03) 3445-6111; telex 24461; f. 1964; monthly; Editor Hideo Hirayama; circ. 51,000.

Journal of the Electronics Industry: Dempa Publications Inc, 1-11-15, Higashi Gotanda, Shinagawa-ku, Tokyo 141; tel. (03) 3445-6111; telex 24461; f. 1953; monthly; Editor Hideo Hirayama; circ. 109,000.

Junon: Shufu-To-Seikatsu Sha Ltd, 5-7, Kyobashi 3-chome, Chuo-ku, Tokyo 104; tel. (03) 3563-5131; fax (03) 3567-7893; f. 1973; monthly; television and entertainment; circ. 480,000.

Kagaku (Science): Iwanami Shoten Publishers, 2-5-5, Hitotsubashi, Chiyoda-ku, Tokyo 101; tel. (03) 3265-4111; telex 29495; f. 1931; Editor Shigeki Kobayashi; circ. 29,000.

Kagaku Asahi: Asahi Shimbun Publishing Dept, 5-3-2, Tsukiji, Chuo-ku, Tokyo 104; tel. (03) 3545-0131; telex 22226; f. 1941; monthly; scientific; Editor Shinkichi Nagatsuka; circ. 95,000.

Kaisha Shikiho: Toyo Keizai Shinpo-Sha, 1-2-1, Nihombashi Hongoku-cho, Chuo-ku, Tokyo 103; tel. (03) 3246-5470; f. 1936; quarterly; corporate data and information; Editor Shihiro Nakashima; circ. 1.3m.

Keizaijin: Kansai Economic Federation, Nakanoshima Center Bldg, 6-2-27, Nakanoshima, Kita-ku, Osaka 530; tel. (06) 441-0105; telex 48208; fax (06) 443-5347; f. 1947; monthly; economics; Editor K. Kojima; circ. 2,600.

Lettuce Club: S.S. Communications Inc, Cosmo Hirakawacho Bldg, 3-14, Hirakawa-cho 1-chome, Chiyoda-ku, Tokyo 102; tel. (03) 3527-62220; fax (03) 3527-62229; f. 1988; every 2 weeks; cookery; Editor Kazuko Sasaki; circ. 800,000.

Liberal Star: 1-11-23, Nagata-cho, Chiyoda-ku, Tokyo 100; tel. (03) 3581-6211; f. 1972; monthly; publ. by the LDP; Editor Koichi Yamaguchi; circ. 500,000.

Mizue: Bijutsu Shuppan-Sha Ltd, Inaoka Bldg, 2-36, Kanda, Jimbo-cho, Chiyoda-ku, Tokyo 101; tel. (03) 3234-2151; fax (03) 3234-9451; f. 1905; quarterly; fine arts; Chief Editor Tatsumi Shinoda; circ. 30,000.

Money Japan: S.S. Communications Inc, Cosmo Hirakawacho Bldg, 3-14, Hirakawa-cho 1-chome, Chiyoda-ku, Tokyo 102; tel. (03) 3527-62220; fax (03) 3527-62229; f. 1985; monthly; finance; Editor Masatoshi Takeuchi; circ. 500,000.

Nikkei Business: Nikkei Business Publications Inc, 3 Mitoshiro-cho, Kanda, Chiyoda-ku, Tokyo 101; tel. (03) 3233-8311; fax (03) 3219-7354; f. 1969; every 2 weeks; Editor Tomio Satoh; circ. 240,168.

Ongaku No Tomo (Friends of Music): Ongaku No Tomo-Sha Corpn, 6-30, Kagurazaka, Shinjuku-ku, Tokyo 162; tel. (03) 3235-2111; telex 23718; fax (03) 3235-2129; f. 1941; monthly; classical music; Editor Hiroshi Asakawa; circ. 120,000.

Popeye: Magazine House, 3-13-10, Ginza, Chuo-ku, Tokyo 104; tel. (03) 3545-7100; telex 22982; fax (03) 3546-0034; f. 1976; every 2 weeks; fashion, teenage interest; Editor Giichiro Hata; circ. 600,000.

President: President Inc, Bridgestone Hirakawacho Bldg, 2-13-12 Hirakawa-cho, Chiyoda-ku, Tokyo 102; tel. (03) 3237-3721; telex 24914; fax (03) 3237-3748; f. 1963; monthly; business; circ. 273,956.

Ray: Shufunotomo Co Ltd, 2-9 Kanda Surugadai, Chiyoda-ku, Tokyo; tel. (03) 3294-1137; telex 26925; fax (03) 3291-5093; f. 1988; monthly; women's interest; Editor Kouichi Murata; circ. 350,000.

Ryoko Yomiuri: Ryoko Yomiuri Publications Inc, 2-2-15, Ginza, Chou-ku, Tokyo; tel. (03) 3561-8956; fax (03) 3561-8950; f. 1965; monthly; travel; Editor Osamu Sakai; circ. 470,000.

Sekai: Iwanami Shoten Publishers, 2-5-5, Hitotsubashi, Tokyo 101; tel. (03) 3265-4111; telex 29495; f. 1946; monthly; review of world and domestic affairs; Editor Akio Yamaguchi; circ. 120,000.

Shinkenchiku: Shinkenchiku Co, 2-31-2, Yushima, Bunkyo-ku, Tokyo 113; tel. (03) 3811-7101; f. 1925; monthly; architecture; Editor Takeshi Ishido; circ. 87,000.

Shiso (Thought): Iwanami Shoten Publishers, 2-5-5, Hitotsubashi, Chiyoda-ku, Tokyo 101-02; tel. (03) 3265-4111; telex 29495; fax (03) 3221-8998; f. 1921; monthly; philosophy, social sciences and humanities; Editor Atsushi Aiba; circ. 25,000.

Shosetsu Shincho: Shincho-Sha, 71, Yarai-cho, Shinjuku-ku, Tokyo 162; tel. (03) 3266-5211; fax (03) 3266-5235; f. 1947; monthly; literature; Chief Editor Masaji Yokoyama; circ. 360,000.

Shufu-To-Seikatsu: Shufu-To-Seikatsu Sha Ltd, 5-7, Kyobashi 3-chome, Chuo-ku, Tokyo 104; tel. (03) 3563-5131; fax (03) 3567-7893; monthly; women's interest; circ. 368,999.

Shufunotomo: Shufunotomo Co Ltd, 2-9 Kanda Surugadai, Chiyoda-ku, Tokyo; tel. (03) 3294-1137; telex 26925; fax (03) 3291-5093; f. 1917; monthly; home and lifestyle; Editor Sachiko Hayashi; circ. 250,000.

Shukan FM: Ongaku No Tomo-Sha Corpn, 6-30, Kagurazaka, Shinjuku-ku, Tokyo 162; tel. (03) 3235-2111; telex 52129; f. 1971; fortnightly; guide to music broadcasts; Editor Nobuyuki Maeyama; circ. 90,000.

So-en: Bunka Publishing Bureau, 3-22-1, Yoyogi, Shibuya-ku, Tokyo 151; tel. (03) 3370-3111; telex 32475; f. 1936; fashion monthly; Editor Tamae Ejima; circ. 230,000.

Statistics Monthly: Toyo Keizai Inc, 1-2-1, Nihonbashi Hongoku-cho, Chuo-ku, Tokyo 103; tel. (03) 3246-5575; fax (03) 3242-4068; f. 1939; monthly; Editor Masaki Hara; circ. 15,000.

Stereo: Ongaku No Tomo-Sha Corpn, 6-30, Kagurazaka, Shinjuku-ku, Tokyo 162; tel. (03) 3235-2111; telex 52129; f. 1963; monthly; records and audio; Editor Seizaburo Mogami; circ. 100,000.

JAPAN
Directory

Tokyo Business Today: Toyo Keizai Inc., 1-2-1, Nihonbashi Hongoku-cho, Chuo-ku, Tokyo 103; tel. (03) 3246-5655; fax (03) 3241-5543; f. 1934; monthly; English; business and finance; Editor YASUO FUJIGANE; circ. 60,000.

The-Yama-To-Keikoku (Mountain and Valley): Yama-Kei Publishers Co, 1-1-33, Shiba-Daimon, Minato-ku, Tokyo 105; tel. (03) 3436-4023; f. 1930; monthly; mountaineering; Editor AKIRA YAMAGUCHI; circ. 230,000.

NEWS AGENCIES

Jiji Tsushin-Sha (Jiji Press): Shisei Kaikan, 1-3, Hibiya Park, Chiyoda-ku, Tokyo 100; tel. (03) 3591-1111; telex 22270; f. 1945; Pres. KAZUO HARANO.

Kyodo Tsushin (Kyodo News Service): 2-2-5, Toranomon, Minato-ku, Tokyo 105; tel. (03) 3584-4111; telex 22207; f. 1945; Pres. SHINJI SAKAI; Man. Dir YASUHIKO INUKAI; Man. Editor ASAHI KAMIYAMA.

Radiopress Inc: R-Bldg Shinjuku, 33-8, Wakamatsu-cho, Shinjuku-ku, Tokyo 162; tel. (03) 5273-2171; fax (03) 5273-2180; f. 1945; provides news from China, the USSR, Democratic People's Repub. of Korea, Viet-Nam and elsewhere to the press and govt offices; Pres. SHOTARO TAKAHASHI.

Sun Telephoto: Palaceside Bldg, 1-1, 1-chome, Hitotsubashi, Chiyoda-ku, Tokyo 100; tel. (03) 3213-6771; f. 1952; Pres. KEN-ICHIRO MATSUOKA; Man. Editor YU YAMAMOTO.

Foreign Bureaux

Agence France-Presse (AFP): Asahi Shimbun Bldg, 11th Floor, 5-3-2, Tsukiji, Chuo-ku, Tokyo 104; tel. (03) 3545-3061; telex 22368; fax (03) 3546-2594; Bureau Chief DIDIER FAUQUEUX.

Agencia EFE (Spain): Kyodo Tsushin Kaikan, 9th Floor, 2-2-5, Toranomon, Minato-ku, Tokyo 105; tel. (03) 3585-8940; telex 34502; Bureau Chief RAMÓN SANTAULARIA.

Agenzia Nazionale Stampa Associata (ANSA) (Italy): Kyodo Tsushin Kaikan, 2-2-5, Toranomon, Minato-ku, Tokyo 105; tel. (03) 3584-6667; telex 28286; fax (03) 3584-5114; Correspondent ROBERTO MAGGI.

Allgemeiner Deutscher Nachrichtendienst (ADN) (Germany): 4-9-3, Jingumae, Shibuya-ku, Tokyo 150; tel. (03) 3478-3842; Correspondent RAINER KÖHLER.

Antara (Indonesia): Kyodo Tsushin Bldg, 9th Floor, 2-2-5, Toranomon, Minato-ku, Tokyo 107; tel. (03) 3584-4234; Correspondent PIDWAN SURYANTHO.

Associated Press (AP) (USA): Asahi Shimbun Bldg, 11th Floor, 5-3-2, Tsukiji, Chuo-ku, Tokyo 104; tel. (03) 3545-5901; telex 22260; Bureau Chief THOMAS J. DYGARD.

Bulgarska Telegrafna Agentsia (BTA): Daiichi Aoyama Mansion, Room 802, 1-10, 5-chome, Minami Aoyama, Minato-ku, Tokyo 107; tel. (03) 3407-6926; Correspondent IVAN A. GAYTANDJIEV.

Central News Agency (Taiwan): Tokyo; tel. (03) 3264-4717; Bureau Chief CHIEM CHAO HUNG.

Deutsche Presse-Agentur (dpa) (Germany): Shisei Kaikan, Room 202, 1-3, Hibiya Koen, Chiyoda-ku, CPOB 1512, Tokyo 100; tel. (03) 3580-6629; telex 22533; Bureau Chief HELMUT RÄTHER.

Informatsionnoye Agentstvo Novosti (IAN) (USSR): 3-9-13, Higashigotanda, Shinagawa-ku, Tokyo 141; tel. (03) 3447-3536; telex 22958; Bureau Chief ALEXEI K. PANTELEYEV.

Inter Press Service (IPS) (Italy): 1-5-9, Yakumo, Meguro-ku, Tokyo; tel. (03) 3211-3161; fax (03) 3211-3168; Correspondent SUVENDRINI KAKUCHI.

Keystone Press Agency (UK): Kaneda Bldg, 3-17-2, Shibuya, Shibuya-ku, Tokyo 150; tel. (03) 3407-0375; Pres. JUNZO SUZUKI.

Magyar Távirati Iroda (MTI) (Hungary): 22-1, Minami-Aoyama 4-chome, Minato-ku, Tokyo 107; tel. (03) 3405-7087; telex 28446; fax (03) 3423-7533; Bureau Chief JÁNOS MARTON.

Prensa Latina (Cuba): Tokyo; tel. (03) 3421-9455; telex 29962; Correspondent JOSÉ AGUILAR.

Reuters (UK): Shuwa Kamiya-cho Bldg, 5th Floor, 4-3-13, Toranomon, Minato-ku, Tokyo 105; tel. (03) 3432-4141; telex 22349; Man. Dir MICHAEL SALAMON.

Telegrafnoye Agentstvo Sovetskovo Soyuza (TASS) (USSR): 5-1, 1-chome, Hon-cho, Shibuya-ku, Tokyo 151; tel. (03) 3377-0380; Correspondent VIKTOR ZATSEPIN.

United Press International (UPI) (USA): Palaceside Bldg, 1-1, Hitusbashi 1-chome, Chiyoda-ku, Tokyo 100; tel. (03) 3212-7911; telex 22364; fax (03) 3213-5053; Bureau Chief STEWART SLAVIN.

Viet-Nam News Agency (VNA): Tokyo; Bureau Chief NGUYEN DAI PHUONG.

Xinhua (New China) News Agency (People's Republic of China): 3-35-23, Ebisu, Shibuya-ku, Tokyo 150; tel. (03) 3441-3766; Correspondent LIU WENYU.

Yonhap (United) News Agency (Republic of Korea): Kyodo Tsushin Bldg, 2-2-5, Toranomon, Minato-ku, Tokyo 105; tel. (03) 3584-4681; f. 1945; Bureau Chief JUNG KIL.

PRESS ASSOCIATIONS

Foreign Press Center: Nippon Press Centre Bldg, 6th Floor, 2-2-1, Uchisaiwai-cho, Chiyoda-ku, Tokyo 100; tel. (03) 3501-3401; fax (03) 3501-3622; f. 1976; est. by Japan Newspaper Publrs' and Editors' Asscn and the Japan Fed. of Economic Orgs; provides services to the foreign press; Pres. TERUJI AKIYAMA; Man. Dir FUMIO KITAMURA.

Foreign Press in Japan: 20F Yuraku-cho Denki Bldg, 1-7-1, Yuraku-cho, Chiyoda-ku, Tokyo 100; tel. (03) 3211-3161; f. 1960; 140 companies; Chair. JAMES COLLIGAN; Man. NOBUYOSHI YAMADA.

Nihon Shinbun Kyokai (Japan Newspaper Publishers' and Editors' Asscn): Nippon Press Center Bldg, 2-1, Uchisaiwai-cho 2-chome, Chiyoda-ku, Tokyo 100; tel. (03) 3591-4401; telex 27504; fax (03) 3591-6149; f. 1946; mems include 170 companies, including 115 daily newspapers, 4 news agencies and 51 radio and TV companies; Pres. YOSOJI KOBAYASHI; Man. Dir TOSHIE YAMADA.

Nihon Zasshi Kyokai (Japan Magazine Publishers Asscn): 1-7, Kanda Surugadai, Chiyoda-ku, Tokyo 101; tel. (03) 3291-0775; fax (03) 3293-6239; f. 1956; 73 mems; Pres. TETSUO OGA; Sec. JUN TANAKA.

Publishers

Akane Shobo Co Ltd: 3-2-1, Nishikanda, Chiyoda-ku, Tokyo; tel. (03) 3263-0641; f. 1949; juvenile; Pres. MASAHARU OKAMOTO.

Akita Publishing Shoten Co Ltd: 2-10-8, Iidabashi, Chiyoda-ku, Tokyo 102; tel. (03) 3264-7011; f. 1948; social sciences, history, juvenile; Chair. SADAO AKITA; Man. Dir SADAMI AKITA.

Asahi Shimbun Publications Dept: 5-3-2, Tsukiji, Chuo-ku, Tokyo; tel. (03) 3545-0131; telex 22226; f. 1879; general; Pres. TOSHITADA NAKAE; Dir of Publications NOBUYUKI KAWAGUCHI.

Baifukan Co Ltd: 3-12, Kudan Minami 4-chome, Chiyoda-ku, Tokyo 102; tel. (03) 3262-5256; f. 1924; engineering, natural and social sciences, psychology; Pres. ITARU YAMAMOTO.

Bijutsu Shuppan-Sha: Inaoka Bldg, 6th Floor, 2-36, Kanda Jimbo-cho, Chiyoda-ku, Tokyo 101; tel. (03) 3234-2151; fax (03) 3234-9451; f. 1905; art and architecture; Pres. ATSUSHI OSHITA.

Chikuma Shobo Publishing Co Ltd: Masudaya Bldg, 6-4, Kuramae 2-chome, Taito-ku, Tokyo 111; tel. (03) 3291-7651; f. 1940; general fiction and non-fiction; Rep. HIDESATO SEKINE.

Chuokoron-Sha Inc: 2-8-7, Kyobashi, Chuo-ku, Tokyo; tel. (03) 3563-1261; telex 32505; f. 1887; philosophy, history, economic, political and natural science, literature, fine arts; Pres. HOJI SHIMANAKA; Man. Dir SHIGERU TAKANASHI.

Froebel-Kan Co Ltd: 3-1, Kanda Ogawa-machi; Chiyoda-ku, Tokyo 101; tel. (03) 3292-7786; telex 24907; fax (03) 3292-7748; f. 1907; juvenile, educational, music; Pres. FUMIO HASE; Dir HARRY IDICHI.

Fukuinkan Shoten: 6-6-3, Honkomagome, Bunkyo-ku, Tokyo 113; tel. (03) 3942-0032; telex 33597; f. 1950; juvenile; Pres. KATSUMI SATO; Man. Dir TADASHI MATSUI.

Gakken Co Ltd: 4-40-5, Kamiikedai, Ohta-ku, Tokyo 145; tel. (03) 3726-8131; telex 27771; f. 1946; fiction, juvenile, educational, art, history, reference, encyclopaedias, dictionaries, languages; Pres. HIROSHI FURUOKA; Chair. HIDETO FURUOKA.

Hakusui-Sha: 3-24, Kanda Ogawa-machi, Chiyoda-ku, Tokyo; tel. (03) 3291-7811; f. 1915; general literature, science and languages; Pres. TAKASHI TAKAHASHI.

Heibonsha Ltd Publishers: 5, Sanban-cho, Chiyoda-ku, Tokyo 102; tel. (03) 3265-0451; fax (03) 3265-0477; f. 1914; encyclopaedias, art, history, geography, Japanese and Chinese literature; Pres. HIROSHI SHIMONAKA.

Hirokawa Publishing Co: 3-27-14, Hongo, Bunkyo-ku, Tokyo; tel. (03) 3815-3651; f. 1926; natural sciences, medicine, textbooks; Pres. SETSUO HIROKAWA.

The Hokuseido Press: 32-4, Honkomagome 3-chome, Bunkyo-ku, Tokyo 113; tel. (03) 3827-0511; fax (03) 3827-0567; f. 1914; regional non-fiction, dictionaries, textbooks; Pres. MASAZO YAMAMOTO.

Ie-No-Hikari Association: 11, Funagawara-cho, Ichigaya, Shinjuku-ku, Tokyo 162; tel. (03) 3266-9000; telex 22367; f. 1925; social science, agriculture; Pres. SHIGENORI TOKONABE; Man. Dir AKIRA SUZUKI.

Iwanami Shoten Publishers: 2-5-5, Hitotsubashi, Chiyoda-ku, Tokyo 101; tel. (03) 3265-4111; telex 29495; f. 1913; natural and social sciences, literature, history, geography; Chair. YUJIRO IWANAMI; Pres. RYOSUKE YASUE.

Jimbun Shoin: Takakura-Nishi-iru, Bukkoji-dori, Shimogyo-ku, Kyoto; tel. (075) 3351-3343; f. 1922; literary, philosophy, history, fine arts; Pres. MUTSUHISA WATANABE.

Kanehara & Co Ltd: 31-14, Yushima 2-chome, Bunkyo-ku, Tokyo; tel. (03) 3811-0285; f. 1875; medical, agricultural, engineering and scientific; Pres. HIDEO KANEHARA.

Kodansha Ltd: 12-21, Otowa 2-chome, Bunkyo-ku, Tokyo 112-01; tel. (03) 3945-1111; telex 34509; fax (03) 3944-9915; f. 1909; art, educational, illustrated children's, fiction, cookery, encyclopaedias, natural science, paperbacks, magazines; Pres. SAWAKO NOMA; Chair. TOSHIYUKI HATTORI.

Kyoritsu Shuppan Co Ltd: 4-6-19, Kobinata 4-chome, Bunkyo-ku, Tokyo 112; tel. (03) 3947-2511; f. 1926; scientific and technical; Pres. MASAO NANJO; Gen. Man. Publishing Division MITSUAKI NANJO.

Maruzen Co Ltd: 3-10, Nihombashi 2-chome, Chuo-ku, Tokyo 103; tel. (03) 3272-7211; telex 26516; fax (03) 3274-3238; f. 1869; general; Pres. KUMAO EBIHARA; Chair. SHINGO IIZUMI.

Minerva Shobo Co Ltd: 1, Tsutsumidani-cho, Hinooka, Yamashina-ku, Kyoto 607; tel. (075) 3581-5191; fax (075) 3581-0589; f. 1948; general non-fiction and reference; Pres. NOBUO SUGITA.

Misuzu Shobo Publishing Co: 3-17-15, Hongo, Bunkyo-ku, Tokyo 113; tel. (03) 3815-9181; fax (03) 3818-8497; f. 1947; general, philosophy, history, literature, science, art; Pres. YUJI OGUMA; Man. Dir KEIJI KATO.

Nanzando Co Ltd: 4-1-11, Yushima, Bunkyo-ku, Tokyo; tel. (03) 3814-3681; medical reference, paperbacks; Man. Dir KIMIO SUZUKI.

Obun-Sha Co Ltd: 55, Yokodera-cho, Shinjuku-ku, Tokyo; tel. (03) 3266-6000; f. 1931; textbooks, reference, general science and fiction, magazines, encyclopaedias, dictionaries; software; audio-visual aids; Pres. FUMIO AKAO; Man. Dir M. ARAI.

Ohm-Sha Ltd: 3-1, Kanda Nishiki-cho, Chiyoda-ku, Tokyo 101; tel. (03) 3233-0641; telex 23125; f. 1914; engineering, technical and scientific; Pres. S. SATO; Dir M. MORI.

Ongaku No Tomo-Sha Corpn (ONT): 6-30, Kagurazaka, Shinjuku-ku, Tokyo 162; tel. (03) 3235-2111; telex 23718; fax (03) 3235-2119; f. 1941; folios, concert hall, music magazines, music textbooks; Pres. SUNAO ASAKA.

Sankei Shimbun Shuppankyoku Co: Tokyo; tel. (03) 3231-7111; f. 1950; history, social sciences, politics, juvenile; Man. Dir SHINYA UEDA.

Sanseido Co Ltd: 2-22-14, Misaki-cho, Chiyoda-ku, Tokyo 101; tel. (03) 3230-9411; f. 1881; dictionaries, educational, languages, social and natural science; Chair. HISANORI UENO; Pres. MASAAKI MORIYA.

Seibundo-Shinko-Sha Publishing Co Ltd: 1-5-5, Kanda Nishiki-cho, Chiyoda-ku, Tokyo; tel. (03) 3292-1211; f. 1912; technical, scientific, general non-fiction; Pres. and Man. Dir SHIGEO OGAWA.

Shinkenchiku-Sha Ltd: 31-2, Yushima 2-chome, Bunkyo-ku, Tokyo; tel. (03) 3811-7101; f. 1925; architecture; Editor SHOZO BABA; Publr YOSHIO YOSHIDA.

Shogakukan Inc.: 2-3-1, Hitotsubashi, Chiyoda-ku, Tokyo 101-01; tel. (03) 3230-5658; telex 22192; fax (03) 3230-5818; f. 1922; juvenile, education, geography, history, encyclopaedias, dictionaries; Pres. TETSUO OHGA.

Shokokusha Publishing Co Ltd: 25, Sakamachi, Shinjuku-ku, Tokyo 160; tel. (03) 3359-3231; f. 1932; architectural, technical and fine arts; Chair. and Pres. TAISHIRO YAMAMOTO.

Shufunotomo Co Ltd: 9, Kanda Surugadai 2-chome, Chiyoda-ku, Tokyo 101; tel. (03) 3294-1118; telex 26925; fax (03) 3293-3926; f. 1916; domestic science, fine arts, gardening, handicraft, cookery and magazines; Pres. HARUHIKO ISHIKAWA.

Shunjusha Co Ltd: 2-18-6, Sotokanda, Chiyoda-ku, Tokyo 101; tel. (03) 3255-9614; fax (03) 3255-5418; f. 1918; philosophy, religion, literary, economics, music; Pres. AKIRA KANDA; Man. YOSHIKAZU SAWAHATA.

Taishukan Shoten: 3-24, Kanda Nishiki-cho, Chiyoda-ku, Tokyo 101; tel. (03) 3294-2221; fax (03) 3295-4108; f. 1918; reference, Japanese and foreign languages, sports, dictionaries, audio-visual aids; Man. Dir SHIGEO SUZUKI.

Tokyo News Service Ltd: Tsukiji Hamarikyu Bldg, 10th Floor, 3-3, Tsukiji 5-chome, Chuo-ku, Tokyo 104; tel. (03) 3542-6511; telex 23285; f. 1947; shipping, trade and shipbuilding, television and video guides; Pres. T. OKUYAMA.

University of Tokyo Press: 7-3-1, Hongo, Bunkyo-ku, Tokyo 113; tel. (03) 3811-0964; fax (03) 3812-6958; f. 1951; natural and social sciences, humanities; Japanese and English; Man. Dir NORIHIRO SAITO.

Tamused Publishing Co Ltd: 1-1-33, Shiba-Daimon, Minato-ku, Tokyo 105; tel. (03) 3436-4021; f. 1930; natural science, geography, mountaineering; Pres. YOSHIMITSU KAWASAKI.

Yuhikaku Publishing Co Ltd: 2-17, Kanda Jimbo-cho, Chiyoda-ku, Tokyo; tel. (03) 3264-1311; f. 1877; social sciences, law, economics; Chair. SHIRO EGUSA; Pres. TADATAKA EGUSA.

Zoshindo Juken Kenkyusha: 2-19-15, Shinmachi, Nishi-ku, Osaka 550; tel. (06) 3532-1581; f. 1890; educational, juvenile; Pres. SHIGETOSHI OKAMOTO.

Government Publishing House

Government Publications' Service Centre: 2-1, 1-chome, Kasumigaseki, Chiyoda-ku, Tokyo 100; tel. (03) 3504-3885.

PUBLISHERS' ASSOCIATIONS

Japan Book Publishers Association: 6, Fukuro-machi, Shinjuku-ku, Tokyo 162; tel. (03) 3268-1301; fax (03) 3268-1196; f. 1957; 465 mems; Pres. TOSHIYUKI HATTORI; Exec. Dir TOSHIKAZU GOMI.

Publishers' Association for Cultural Exchange: 2-1, Sarugaku-cho 1-chome, Chiyoda-ku, Tokyo 101; tel. (03) 3291-5685; fax (03) 3233-3645; f. 1953; 135 mems; Pres. Dr TATSURO MATSUMAE; Dir YASUKO KORENAGA.

Radio and Television

There were an estimated 105.5m. radio receivers and 72.0m. television receivers in use in 1988.

Nippon Hoso Kyokai, NHK (Japan Broadcasting Corporation): Broadcasting Centre, NHK Hoso Centre, 2-2-1, Jinnan, Shibuya-ku, Tokyo 150; tel. (03) 3465-1234; telex 22377; fax (03) 3481-1576; f. 1925; non-commercial public corpn; operates five (two TV and three radio) networks and 2 DBS TV services; TV channels equally divided between general and educational networks; central stations at Tokyo, Osaka, Nagoya, Hiroshima, Kumamoto, Sendai, Sapporo and Matsuyama, and over 6,000 local stations; overseas service in 21 languages; Chair. Board of Govs ICHIRO ISODA; Pres. Y. IKEDA.

National Association of Commercial Broadcasters in Japan (MINPOREN): Floor 5, Bungei Shunju Bldg, 3-23, Kioi-cho, Chiyoda-ku, Tokyo 102; tel. (03) 3265-7481; telex 29889; Pres. SUNAO NAKAGAWA; Sec.-Gen. SEIGO NAGATAKE; asscn of 137 companies (103 TV cos, 34 radio cos). Among the TV cos, 36 operate radio and TV, with 307 radio stations and 6,284 TV stations. These include:

Asahi Hoso—Asahi Broadcasting Corpn: 2-2-48, Oyodo-Minami, Oyodo-ku, Osaka 531; tel. (06) 3458-5321; Chair. TSUNEJIRO HIRAI; Pres. Y. FUKUDA.

Bunka Hoso—Nippon Cultural Broadcasting, Inc: 1-5, Wakaba, Shinjuku-ku, Tokyo 160; tel. (03) 3357-1111; telex 22941; f. 1952; Pres. MASATOSHI IWAMOTO.

Nihon Tanpa Hoso—Nihon Short-Wave Broadcasting Co: 9-15, Akasaka 1-chome, Minato-ku, Tokyo 107; tel. (03) 3583-8151; f. 1954; Pres. KINYA SEKIGUCHI.

Nippon Hoso—Nippon Broadcasting System, Inc: 1-9-3, Yuraku-cho, Chiyoda-ku, Tokyo 100-87; tel. (03) 3287-1111; f. 1954; Pres. S. HIRAYAMA.

Okinawa Televi Hoso—Okinawa Television Broadcasting Co Ltd: 1-2-20, Kumaji, Naha City 900, Okinawa; tel. (0988) 63-2111; fax (0988) 61-0193; f. 1959; Pres. KAZUO KOISO.

Ryukyu Hoso—Ryukyus Broadcasting Co: 2-3-1, Kumoji, Naha 900, Okinawa; tel. (0988) 67-2151; telex 5247; f. 1954; Pres. KUNIO OROKU.

Tokyo Hoso—Tokyo Broadcasting System, Inc: 5-3-6, Akasaka, Minato-ku, Tokyo 107-06; tel. (03) 3584-3111; telex 24883; f. 1951; Pres. IZUMI TANAKA.

There are also 92 commercial television stations operated by Asahi Broadcasting Co, Nippon TV Network Co, Fuji Telecasting Co and others, including:

Fuji Television Network Inc: 3-1 Kawada-cho, Shinjuku-ku, Tokyo 162; tel. (03) 3353-1111; telex 22560; fax (03) 3358-8038; f. 1958; Pres. HISASHI HIEDA.

Televi Asahi—Asahi National Broadcasting Co Ltd: 1-1-1, Roppongi, Minato-ku, Tokyo 106; tel. (03) 405-3211; telex 22520; fax (03) 3505-3539; f. 1959; Chair. YOSHIO AKAO; Pres. KIKUO TASHIRO.

Yomiuri Televi Hoso—Yomiuri Telecasting Corporation: 2-33, Shiromi 2-chome, Chuo-ku, Osaka 540-10; tel. (06) 3947-2298; f. 1958; 20 hrs colour broadcasting daily; Chair. MITSUO MUTAI; Pres. IKUO AOYAMA.

Television News Agencies

Asahi Video Projects Ltd: 6-4-10, Roppongi, Minato-ku, Tokyo; tel. (03) 3405-3003; f. 1958; Pres. K. SAMESHIMA.

Kyodo Television Ltd: 28, Sanban-cho, Chiyoda-ku, Tokyo 102; tel. (03) 3263-4161; telex 22906; f. 1958; Pres. TOSHIKANE BUJO.

Finance

(cap. = capital; p.u. = paid up; res = reserves; dep. = deposits; m. = million; brs = branches; amounts in yen)

BANKING

Japan's central bank and bank of issue is the Bank of Japan. More than half the credit business of the country is handled by 142 private commercial banks, seven trust banks and three long-term credit banks, collectively designated 'All Banks'.

Of the latter category, the most important are the city banks, some of which have a long and distinguished history, originating in the time of the *zaibatsu*, the private entrepreneurial organizations on which Japan's capital wealth was built up before the Second World War. Although the *zaibatsu* were abolished as integral industrial and commercial enterprises during the Allied Occupation, the several businesses and industries which bear the former *zaibatsu* names, such as Mitsubishi, Mitsui and Sumitomo, continue to flourish and to give each other mutual assistance through their respective banks and trust corporations.

Among the commercial banks, the Bank of Tokyo, specializes in foreign exchange business, while the Industrial Bank of Japan provides a large proportion of the finance for capital investment by industry. The Long-Term Credit Bank of Japan and Nippon Credit Bank Ltd also specialize in industrial finance; the work of these three privately-owned banks is supplemented by the government-controlled Japan Development Bank.

The Government has established a number of other specialized organs to supply essential services not performed by the private banks. Thus the Japan Export-Import Bank advances credits for exports of heavy industrial products and imports of raw materials in bulk. A Housing Loan Corporation assists firms building housing for their employees, while the Agriculture, Forestry and Fisheries Finance Corporation provides loans to the named industries for equipment purchases. Similar services are provided for small businesses by the Small Business Finance Corporation.

An important financial role is played by co-operatives and by the many small enterprise institutions. Each prefecture has its own federation of co-operatives, with the Central Co-operative Bank of Agriculture and Forestry as the common central financial institution. This bank also acts as an agent for the government-controlled Agriculture, Forestry and Fisheries Finance Corporation.

There are also two types of private financial institutions for small business. There are 407 Credit Co-operatives and 452 Shinkin Banks (credit associations), which lend only to members. The latter also receive deposits.

The commonest form of savings is through the government-operated Postal Savings System, which collects small savings from the public by means of the post office network. Total deposits stood at 132,926,000m. yen in December 1989. The funds thus made available are used as loan funds by government financial institutions, through the Ministry of Finance's Trust Fund Bureau.

Clearing houses operate in each major city of Japan, and total 182 institutions. The largest are those of Tokyo and Osaka.

Japan's 66 Sogo Banks (mutual loan and savings banks) converted to commercial banks in 1989.

Central Bank

Nippon Ginko (Bank of Japan): 1-1, Hongoku-cho 2-chome, Nihonbashi, Chuo-ku, Tokyo 103; tel. (03) 3279-1111; telex 22763; fax (03) 3245-0358; f. 1882; cap. and res 1,121,300m., dep. 9,555,500m. (March 1990); Gov. M. YASUSHI MIENO; 34 brs.

Principal Commercial Banks

Ashikaga Bank Ltd: 1-25, Sakura 4-chome, Utsonomiya, Tochigi 320; tel. (0286) 22-0111; f. 1895; cap. 24,186m., res 150,488m., dep. 3,807,089m. (March 1987); Chair. YASUO MORI; Pres. HISAO MUKAE; 121 brs.

Bank of Tokyo Ltd: 3-2, Nihonbashi, Hongoku-cho 1-chome, Chuo-ku, Tokyo 103; tel. (03) 3245-1111; telex 22220; fax (03) 3279-3926; f. 1946; specializes in international banking and financial business; cap. p.u. 926,233m., dep. 19,761,286m. (March 1990); Chair. YUSUKE KASHIWAGI; Pres. TASUKU TAKAGAKI; 332 brs.

Bank of Yokohama Ltd: 47, Honcho 5-chome, Naka-ku, Yokohama Kanagawa 231; tel. (045) 201-2211; telex 24945; fax (03) 273-6324; f. 1920; cap. p.u. 133,740m., dep. 9,930,649m. (March 1990); Chair. JIRO YOSHIKUNI; Pres. TAKASHI TANAKA; 201 brs.

Chiba Bank Ltd: 1-2, Chiba-minato, Chiba; tel. (0472) 45-1111; f. 1943; cap. 48,467m., dep. 6,295,499m. (March 1989); Chair. TARO OGATA; Pres. TAKASHI TAMAKI; 170 brs.

Dai-Ichi Kangyo Bank Ltd: 1-5, Uchisaiwai-cho 1-chome, Chiyoda-ku, Tokyo 100; tel. (03) 3596-1111; telex 22315; f. 1971; cap. 457,844m., dep. 50,052,496m. (March 1990); Chair. ICHIRO NAKAMURA; Pres. KUNIJI MIYAZAKI; 380 brs.

Daiwa Bank Ltd: 1-8, Bingo-machi 2-chome, Chuo-ku, Osaka 541; tel. (06) 271-1221; telex 63977; f. 1918; cap. 167,777m., dep. 20,154,948m. (March 1990); Pres. SUMIO ABEKAWA; 250 brs.

Fuji Bank Ltd: 5-5, Ohtemachi 1-chome, Chiyoda-ku, Tokyo 100; tel. (03) 3216-2211; telex 22367; f. 1880; cap. 418,240m., dep. 44,306,334m. (March 1990); Pres. TAIZO HASHIDA; 324 brs.

Hokkaido Takushoku Bank Ltd: 7, Odori-Nishi 3-chome, Chuo-ku, Sapporo 060; tel. (011) 271-2111; telex 32533; f. 1900; cap. 74,679m., dep. 7,995,023m. (Sept. 1989); Chair. SHIGERU SUZUKI; Pres. HIROSHI YAMAUCHI; 214 brs.

Hokuriku Bank Ltd: 2-26, Tsutsumichodori 1-chome, Toyama 930; tel. (0764) 23-7111; f. 1943; cap. 82,295m., dep. 7,298,119m. (March 1990); Chair. SEISUKE MASE; Pres. TERUO KUBOTA; 196 brs.

Joyo Bank Ltd: 5-5, Minamimachi 2-chome, Mito, Ibaraki 310, tel. (0292) 31-2151; f. 1935; cap. 44,605m., dep. 5,832,255m. (March 1989); Chair. MEISHI AOSHIKA; Pres. ITARU ISHIKAWA; 160 brs.

Kyowa Bank Ltd: 1-2, Ohtemachi 1-chome, Chiyoda-ku, Tokyo 100; tel. (03) 3287-2111; telex 24275; f. 1948; to merge with Saitama Bank Ltd in March 1991; cap. 141,172m., dep. 12,473,138m. (March 1990); Chair. TETSUO YAMANAKA; Pres. KOUSUKE YOKOTE; 239 brs.

Mitsubishi Bank Ltd: 7-1, Marunouchi, 2-chome, Chiyoda-ku, Tokyo 100; tel. (03) 3240-1111; telex 22358; fax (03) 3240-3879; f. 1919; cap. 379,866m., dep. 39,534,120m. (Sept. 1989); Pres. TSUNEO WAKAI; 245 brs.

Mitsui Taiyo Kobe Bank Ltd: 3-1, Kudan-Minami 1-chome, Chiyoda-ku, Tokyo 100-91; tel. (03) 3230-3111; telex 22285; f. 1990; Chair. YASUO MATSUSHITA; Pres. KENICHI SUEMATSU; 534 brs.

Saitama Bank Ltd: 4-1, Tokiwa 7-chome, Urawa, Saitama 336; tel. (048) 824-2411; telex 22811; f. 1943; to merge with Kyowa Bank Ltd in March 1991; cap. 97,347m., dep. 10,727,728m. (Sept. 1989); Chair. and Pres. SHIGETAKE IJICHI; 209 brs.

Sanwa Bank Ltd: 10-4, Fushimi-machi, Higashi-ku, Osaka 541; tel. (06) 202-2281; telex 63234; f. 1933; cap. 459,765m., dep. 42,978,366m. (March 1990); Chair. KENJI KAWAKATSU; Pres. HIROSHI WATANABE; 250 brs.

Shizuoka Bank Ltd: 10 Gofukucho 1-chome, Shizuokashi, Shizuoka 420; tel. (0542) 61-3131; telex 28450; f. 1943; cap. 51,090m., dep. 5,344,346m. (March 1989); Pres. JIKICHIRO SAKAI; 193 brs.

Sumitomo Bank Ltd: 22-5, Kitahama, Higashi-ku, Osaka 541; tel. (06) 227-2111; telex 63266; f. 1895; cap. 257,756m., dep. 41,392,280m. (Sept. 1989); Chair. (vacant); Pres. SOTOO TATSUMI; 313 brs.

Tokai Bank Ltd: 21-24, Nishiki 3-chome, Naka-ku, Nagoya 460; tel. (052) 211-1111; telex 59930; fax (052) 211-0931; f. 1941; cap. 309,567m., dep. 28,375,831m. (March 1990); Chair. RYUICHI KATO; Pres. KIICHIRO ITOH; 269 brs.

Principal Trust Banks

Chuo Trust and Banking Co Ltd: 7-1, Kyobashi 1-chome, Chuo-ku, Tokyo 104; tel. (03) 3567-1451; telex 33368; f. 1962; cap. and res 61,215m., dep. 9,907,819m. (Sept. 1989); Chair. TAKESHI SEKIGUCHI; Pres. KEI SAKANOUE; 55 brs.

Mitsubishi Trust and Banking Corporation: 4-5, Marunouchi 1-chome, Chiyoda-ku, Tokyo 100; tel. (03) 3212-1211; telex 24259; f. 1927; cap. 191,638.0m., dep. 13,106,147.5m. (March 1990); Pres. HIROSHI HAYASHI; 59 brs.

Mitsui Trust and Banking Co Ltd: 1-1, Nihonbashi-Muromachi 2-chome, Chuo-ku, Tokyo 103; tel. (03) 270-9511; telex 26397; fax (03) 3245-0459; f. 1924; cap. 168,835m., dep. 22,875,163m. (March 1990); Chair. and Pres. SEIICHI KAWASAKI; 58 brs.

Sumitomo Trust and Banking Co Ltd: Sumitomo Bldg, 5-33, Kitahama 4-chome, Chuo-ku, Osaka 541; tel. (06) 220-2121; telex 63775; f. 1925; cap. 181,137m., dep. 10,653,322m. (March 1990); Chair. OSAMU SAKURAI; Pres. HIROSHI HAYASAKI; 56 brs.

Toyo Trust and Banking Co Ltd: 4-3, Marunouchi 1-chome, Chiyoda-ku, Tokyo 100; tel. (03) 3287-2211; telex 22123; fax (03) 3201-1448; f. 1959; cap. p.u. 113,243m., dep. 4,443,063m. (March 1990); Chair. CHIGAZO MORITA; Pres. MITSUO IMOSE; 58 brs.

Yasuda Trust and Banking Co Ltd: 2-1, Yaesu 1-chome, Chuo-ku, Tokyo 103; tel. (03) 3278-8111; telex 23720; fax (03) 3281-6947; f. 1925; cap. 129,772m., dep. 19,502,123. (Sept. 1989); Chair. YOSHIO YAMAGUCHI; Pres. FUJIO TAKAYAMA; 56 brs.

Long-Term Credit Banks

The Long-Term Credit Bank of Japan Ltd: 2-4, Ohtemachi 1-chome, Chiyoda-ku, Tokyo 100; tel. (03) 3211-5111; telex 24308; f. 1952; cap. 318,528m., dep. and debentures 23,596,495m. (March 1990); Chair. MAMORU SAKAI; Pres. TETSUYA HORIE; 32 brs.

The Nippon Credit Bank Ltd: 13-10, Kudan-kita 1-chome, Chiyoda-ku, Tokyo 102; tel. (03) 3263-1111; telex 26921; f. 1957; cap. 148,377m., dep. and debentures 14,028,138m. (Sept. 1989); Chair. SHIRO EGAWA; Pres. SEISHI MATSUOKA; 25 brs.

JAPAN

Nippon Kogyo Ginko (The Industrial Bank of Japan, Ltd): 3-3, Marunouchi 1-chome, Chiyoda-ku, Tokyo 100; tel. (03) 3214-1111; telex 22325; f. 1902; medium- and long-term financing; cap. p.u. 352,045m., dep. and debentures 32,928,639m., loans and discounts 23,017,483m. (March 1990); Chair. KANEO NAKAMURA; Pres. YO KUROSAWA; 25 brs.

Co-operative Bank

Zenshinren Bank: 8-1, Kyobashi 3-chome, Chuo-ku, Tokyo 104; tel. (03) 3563-4111; telex 24336; f. 1950; cap. 100,000m., dep. 10,354,431m. (March 1989); Chair. ISAMU YAMAGUCHI; 17 brs.

Principal Government Credit Institutions

Agriculture, Forestry and Fisheries Finance Corporation: Koko Bldg, 9-3, Ohtemachi 1-chome, Chiyoda-ku, Tokyo 100; tel. (03) 3270-2261; f. 1953; finances plant and equipment investment; cap. 168,200m. (April 1990); Pres. SAKUE MATSUMOTO; Vice-Pres. YASUTAKA MIYAMOTO; 22 brs.

The Export-Import Bank of Japan: 4-1, Ohtemachi 1-chome, Chiyoda-ku, Tokyo 100; tel. (03) 3287-9108; telex 23728; fax (03) 3287-9540; f. 1950 to supplement and encourage the financing of exports, imports, overseas investment and capital contributions by private financial institutions; cap. p.u. 967,300m. (March 1990); Pres. MITSUHIDE YAMAGUCHI; Dep. Pres. AKIRA AOKI; 2 br.

Government Housing Loan Corporation: 4-10, Koraku 1-chome, Bunkyo-ku, Tokyo 112; tel. (03) 3812-1111; f. 1950 to provide long-term capital for the construction of housing at low interest rates; cap. 97,200m. (March 1990); Pres. SUSUMU TAKAHASHI; Vice-Pres. KAZUMOTO ADACHI; 14 brs.

The Japan Development Bank: 9-1, Ohtemachi 1-chome, Chiyoda-ku, Tokyo 100; tel. (03) 3270-3211; telex 24343; fax (03) 3245-1938; f. 1951; provides long-term loans; subscribes for corporate bonds; guarantees corporate obligations; invests in specific projects; borrows funds from govt and abroad; issues external bonds and notes; cap. 233,900m.; loans outstanding 84,991,000m. (April 1990); Gov. Gen. TAKAHASHI; Dep. Gov. SHIJURO OGATA; 8 brs.

The People's Finance Corporation: Koko Bldg, 9-3, Ohtemachi 1-chome, Chiyoda-ku, Tokyo 100; tel. (03) 3270-1361; f. 1949 to provide business funds, particularly to very small enterprises unable to obtain loans from banks and other private financial institutions; cap. 35,300m. (Feb. 1990); Gov. YOSHIHIKO YOSHINO; Dep. Gov. HIROSHI KUBOTA; 152 brs.

Norinchukin Bank (Central Co-operative Bank for Agriculture, Forestry and Fisheries) 8-3, Ohtemachi 1-chome, Chiyoda-ku, Tokyo 100; tel. (03) 3279-0111; telex 23918; fax (03) 3245-0564; f. 1923; main banker to agricultural, forestry and fisheries co-operatives; receives deposits from individual co-operatives, federations and agricultural enterprises; extends loans to these and to local govt authorities and public corpns; adjusts excess and shortage of funds within co-operative system; issues debentures, invests funds and engages in other regular banking business; cap. 45,000m., dep. and debentures 24,322,800m. (April 1990); Pres. OSAMU MORIMOTO; Dep. Pres. SHINICHI KAMIYAMA; 30 brs.

The Overseas Economic Co-operation Fund: 4-1, Ohtemachi 1-chome, Chiyoda-ku, Tokyo 100; tel. (03) 3215-1311; telex 28790; f. 1961 to provide long-term loans or investments for projects in developing countries; cap. 2,430,544m. (1989); Chair. AKIRA NISHIGAKI; Pres. SHOUICHI TANIMURA.

Shoko Chukin Bank (Central Co-operative Bank for Commerce and Industry): 10-17, Yaesu 2-chome, Chuo-ku, Tokyo 104; tel. (03) 3272-6111; telex 25388; f. 1936 to provide general banking services to facilitate finance for smaller enterprise co-operatives and other organizations formed mainly by small- and medium-sized enterprises; issues debentures; cap. 251,500m., dep. and debentures 11,880,200m. (April 1990); Pres. SHIRO MIYAMOTO; Dep. Pres. KENZO SAKAI; 92 brs.

Small Business Finance Corporation: Koko Bldg, 9-3, Ohtemachi 1-chome, Chiyoda-ku, Tokyo 100; tel. (03) 3270-1261; f. 1953 to lend plant and equipment funds and long-term operating funds to small businesses (capital not more than 100m., or not more than 300 employees) which are not easily secured from other financial institutions; cap. p.u. 68,200m. (March 1990) wholly subscribed by govt; Gov. KIICHI WATANABE; Vice-Gov. MINORU HARADA; 59 brs.

Other government financial institutions include the Hokkaido and Tohoku Development Corps, the Japan Finance Corpn for Municipal Enterprises, the Small Business Credit Insurance Corpn and the Okinawa Development Finance Corpn.

Principal Foreign Banks

In 1989 there were 83 foreign banks operating in Japan.

Algemene Bank Nederland NV (Netherlands): Fuji Bldg, 2-3, Marunouchi 3-chome, Chiyoda-ku, Tokyo 100-91; tel. (03) 3211-1760; fax (03) 3216-5420; Rep. (Japan) P. K. GROSS; brs in Kobe, Osaka, Fukuoka.

American Express Bank Ltd (USA): Toranomon Mitsui Bldg, 8-1, Kasumigaseki 3-chome, Chiyoda-ku, Tokyo 100; tel. (03) 3595-4571; telex 24880; Sr Rep. (Japan) and Sr Vice-Pres. RYUSUKE PAUL FUKUDA.

Amro Bank (Netherlands): South Tower, Yurakucho Denki Bldg, 7-1, Yuraku-cho 1-chome, Chiyoda-ku, Tokyo 100; tel. (03) 3284-0701; telex 25830; fax (03) 3284-0718; Gen. Man. C. J. DE KONING.

Bangkok Bank Ltd (Thailand): Bangkok Bank Bldg, 8-10, Nishi-shinbashi 2-chome, Minato-ku, Tokyo 105; tel. (03) 3503-3333; telex 24373; Sr Vice-Pres. and Gen. Man. SUPONG SOTTHITADA; br. in Osaka.

Bank of America NT & SA: Ark Mori Bldg, 12-32, Akasaka 1-chome, Minato-ku, Tokyo 107; tel. (03) 3587-3111; telex 22272; Vice-Pres. and Area Gen. Man. (East Asia) M. L. GREENBERG; br. in Osaka.

Bank of India: Mitsubishi Denki Bldg, 2-3, Marunouchi 2-chome, Chiyoda-ku, Tokyo 100; tel. (03) 3212-0911; telex 28356; fax (03) 3214-8667; Chief Man. (Japan) N. V. SUBRAMANIAN; br in Osaka.

Bank Indonesia: Hibiya Park Bldg, 8-1, Yuraku-cho 1-chome, Chiyoda-ku, Tokyo 100; tel. (03) 3271-3415; Chief Rep. SUTEDJA TRISNAATMADJA.

Bank Negara Indonesia 1946: Kokusai Bldg, 1-1, Marunouchi 3-chome, Chiyoda-ku, Tokyo 100; tel. (03) 3214-5621; telex 26249; fax (03) 3201-2633; Gen. Man. HERMANSJAH DJAMALUDIN.

Bankers Trust Co (USA): Kishimoto Bldg, 2-1, Marunouchi 2-chome, Chiyoda-ku, Tokyo 100; tel. (03) 3214-7171; Man. Dir and Gen. Man. MASAYUKI YASUOKA.

Banque Indosuez (France): Banque Indosuez Bldg, 1-2, Akasaka 1-chome, Minato-ku, Tokyo 107; tel. (03) 3582-0271; telex 24309; Gen. Man. (Japan) MARC COURET; brs in Osaka and Nagoya.

Banque Nationale de Paris (France): Yusen Bldg, 3-2, Marunouchi 2-chome, Chiyoda-ku, Tokyo 100-91; tel. (03) 3214-2882; telex 24825; Gen. Man. GHILAIN MARTIN DE BEAUCE; br in Osaka.

Banque Paribas (France): Yuraku-cho Denki Bldg, 7-1, Yuraku-cho 1-chome, Chiyoda-ku, Tokyo 100; tel. (03) 3214-5881; Gen. Man. JACQUES TRAUMAN.

Barclays Bank (UK): Mitsubishi Bldg, 5-2, Marunouchi 2-chome, Chiyoda-ku, Tokyo 100; tel. (03) 3214-3611; telex 24968; Dir (Japan) ALAN BROWN.

Bayerische Vereinsbank AG (Federal Republic of Germany): Togin Bldg, 1-4-2, Marunouchi 1-chome, Chiyoda-ku, Tokyo 100; tel. (03) 3284-1341; telex 26351; fax (03) 3284-1370; Gen. Man. Dr PETER BARON.

Chang Hwa Commercial Bank (Taiwan): Tokyo 100.

Chase Manhattan Bank, NA (USA): New Tokyo Kaijo Bldg, 2-1, Marunouchi 1-chome, Chiyoda-ku, Tokyo 100; tel. (03) 3287-4000; telex 22294; Sr Vice-Pres. and Gen. Man. JAYME GARCIA DOS SANTOS; br. in Osaka.

Chemical Bank (USA): Yusen Bldg, 3-2, Marunouchi 2-chome, Chiyoda-ku, Tokyo 100; tel. (03) 3214-1351; Sr Rep. MARC M. MORRISON.

Citibank NA (USA): 2-1, Ohtemachi 2-chome, Chiyoda-ku, Tokyo 100; tel. (03) 3273-6610; Divisional Exec. JAMES J. COLLINS; brs in Kobe, Osaka, Yokohama, Nagoya, Aoyama, Akasaka, Ohtemachi.

Commerzbank AG (Federal Republic of Germany): Nippon Press Center Bldg, 2-1, Uchisaiwai-cho 2-chome, Chiyoda-ku, Tokyo 100; tel. (03) 3502-4371; Gen. Mans FOLKER STREIB, HEINRICH ROEHRS.

Continental Bank, National Association (USA): Mitsui Seimei Bldg, 2-3, Ohtemachi 1-chome, Chiyoda-ku, Tokyo 100; tel. (03) 3216-1661; telex 22265; Man. Dir and Business Man. C. TIMOTHY WOOD.

Deutsche Bank AG (Germany): ARK Mori Bldg, 12-32, Akasaka 1-chome, Minato-ku, Tokyo 107; tel. (03) 3588-1971; telex 24814; Gen. Man. JÜRGEN HINRICH FITSCHEN; br. in Osaka.

Dresdner Bank AG (Federal Republic of Germany): Nihombashi-Muromachi Center Bldg, 2-15, Nihonbashi-Muromachi 3-chome, Chuo-ku, Tokyo 103; tel. (03) 3241-6411; telex 25295; Chief Gen. Man. Dr PETER-JÖRG KLEIN.

First National Bank of Chicago (USA): Hibiya Central Bldg, 2-9, Nishi Shimbashi 1-chome, Minato-ku, Tokyo 105; tel. (03) 3596-8700; telex 24977; fax (03) 3596-8744; Sr Vice-Pres. and Gen. Man. THOMAS H. HODGES.

The Hongkong and Shanghai Banking Corpn (UK): 1-2, Marunouchi 2-chome, Chiyoda-ku, POB 336, Tokyo 100; tel. (03) 3216-0101; telex 22372; CEO C. J. CROOK; brs in Osaka, Nagoya and Fukuoka.

International Commercial Bank of China (Taiwan): Togin Bldg, 4-2, Marunouchi 1-chome, Chiyoda-ku, Tokyo 100; tel. (03) 3211-2501; telex 22917; Sr Vice Pres. and Gen. Man. LARRY Y. CHANG; br. in Osaka.

JAPAN   Directory

Korea Exchange Bank (Republic of Korea): Shin Kokusai Bldg, 4-1, Marunouchi 3-chome, Chiyoda-ku, Tokyo 100; tel. (03) 3216-3561; telex 24243; fax (03) 3214-4491; f. 1967; Regional Sr Vice-Pres. (North East Asia) Chang-Hwa Park; brs in Osaka and Fukuoka.

Lloyds Bank PLC (UK): Ohte Center Bldg, 1-3, Ohtemachi 1-chome, Chiyoda-ku, Tokyo 100; tel. (03) 3214-6771; telex 23521; Chief Man. (Japan) Graham M. Harris.

Manufacturers Hanover Trust Co (USA): Asahi Tokai Bldg, 6-1, Ohtemachi 2-chome, Chiyoda-ku, Tokyo 100; tel. (03) 3242-6511; telex 22687; fax (03) 3270-4340; Vice-Pres. and Gen. Man. Norman J. T. Scott; brs in Osaka.

Midland Bank PLC (UK): AIU Bldg, 1-3, Marunouchi 1-chome, Chiyoda-ku, Tokyo 100; tel. (03) 3284-1861; telex 26137; Gen. Man. Matthew Paine.

Morgan Guaranty Trust Co of New York (USA): Shin Yuraku-cho Bldg, 12-1, Yurakucho 1-chome, Chiyoda-ku, Tokyo 100; tel. (03) 3282-0230; Man. Dir and Gen. Man. James H. Higgins III.

National Bank of Pakistan: 20 Mori Bldg, 7-4, Nishi Shinbashi 2-chome, Minato-ku, Tokyo 105; tel. (30) 3502-0331; f. 1949; Man. Hafiz M. Iqbal.

National Westminster Bank PLC (UK): AIU Bldg, 1-3, Marunouchi 1-chome, Chiyoda-ku, Tokyo 100; tel. (03) 3216-5301; telex 28292; fax (03) 3214-6693; Dir (Japan) J. S. Chester.

Oversea-Chinese Banking Corpn, Ltd (Singapore): Shin Tokyo Bldg, 3-1, Marunouchi 3-chome, Chiyoda-ku, Tokyo 100; tel. (03) 3214-2841; telex 26186; Man. C. S. Chua; br. in Osaka.

Security Pacific National Bank (USA): Ark Mori Bldg, 12-32, Akasaka 1-chome, Minato-ku, Tokyo 107; tel. (03) 3587-4800; telex 24981; Vice-Pres. and Gen. Man. Stephen Campbell.

Société Générale (France): Hibiya Central Bldg, 2-9, Nishi Shinbashi 1-chome, Minato-ku, Tokyo 105; tel. (03) 3503-9781; telex 28611; fax (03) 3595-1880; Gen. Man. for Japan Yannick Chagnon; br. in Osaka.

Standard Chartered Bank (UK): Fuji Bldg, 2-3, Marunouchi 3-chome, Chiyoda-ku, Tokyo 100; tel. (03) 3213-6541; telex 22484; Man. in Japan D. J. Morgan; br. in Osaka.

State Bank of India: South Tower, Yuraku-cho Denki Bldg, 7-1, Yuraku-cho 1-chome, Chiyoda-ku, Tokyo 100; tel. (03) 3284-0085; telex 27377; fax (03) 3201-5750; Chief Man. A. K. Dam; br. in Osaka.

Swiss Bank Corpn: 1-8, Toranomon 4-chome, Minato-ku, Tokyo 105; tel. (03) 5473-5000; telex 24842; fax (03) 5473-5175; First Vice-Pres. and Gen. Man. Hans Pieren.

Union Bank of Switzerland: Yamato Seimei Bldg, 1-7, Uchisaiwai-cho 1-chome, Chiyoda-ku, Tokyo 100; tel. (03) 3595-0121; telex 22730; fax (03) 3595-0117; Exec. Vice-Pres. (Japan) Peter Brutsche.

Union de Banques Arabes et Françaises (UBAF) (France): Fukoku Seimei Bldg, 2-2 Uchisaiwai-cho 2-chome, Chiyoda-ku, POB 5190, Tokyo 100-31; tel. (03) 3595-0801; Gen. Man. in Japan Maxime Roche; br. in Osaka.

Westdeutsche Landesbank Girozentrale (Federal Republic of Germany): Kokusai Bldg, 1-1, Marunouchi 3-chome, Chiyoda-ku, Tokyo 100; tel. (03) 3216-0581; telex 23859; Gen. Mans Klaus R. Pesch, Georg Bissen; br. in Osaka.

Bankers' Associations

Federation of Bankers Associations of Japan: 3-1, Marunouchi 1-chome, Chiyoda-ku, Tokyo 100; tel. (03) 3216-3761; telex 26830; fax (03) 201-5608; f. 1945; 72 mem. asscns; Chair. Taizo Hashida; Man. Dir Koichiro Mizutani.

  Tokyo Bankers' Association Inc: 3-1, Marunouchi 1-chome, Chiyoda-ku, Tokyo 100; tel. (03) 3216-3761; telex 26830; fax (03) 3201-5608; f. 1945; 132 mem. banks; conducts the above Federation's administrative business; Chair. Taizo Hashida; Vice-Chair. Kenichi Suematsu, Tetsuya Horie, Chiaki Kurahara.

Regional Banks Association of Japan: 1-2, Uchikanda 3-chome, Chiyoda-ku, Tokyo 101; tel. (03) 3252-5171; f. 1936; 64 mem. banks; Pres. and Chair. Osamu Hashiguchi.

Second Association of Regional Banks: 5 Sanban-cho, Chiyoda-ku, Tokyo 102; tel. (03) 3262-2181; f. 1989 (fmrly Sogo Banks Asscn); 66 commercial banks and 2 Sogo banks; Chair. Takaya Kousaka.

STOCK EXCHANGES

Fukuoka Stock Exchange: 2-14-12, Tenjin, Chuo-ku, Fukuoka 810.

Hiroshima Stock Exchange: 14-18, Kanayama-cho, Hiroshima 730; f. 1949; 20 mems; Prin. Officer Fubito Shimomura.

Nagoya Stock Exchange: 3-17, Sakae 3-chome, Naka-ku, Nagoya 460; tel. (052) 241-1521; f. 1949; Pres. Junichiro Kumada; Man. Dir Ichiro Kawai.

Osaka Securities Exchange: 8-16, Kitahama 1-chome, Chuo-ku, Osaka 541; tel. (06) 229-8643; telex 22215; fax (06) 231-2639; f. 1949; 99 regular mems, one Nakadachi mem. and nine special mems; Chair. Kazumasa Saito; Pres. Hiroshi Yamanouchi.

Sapporo Stock Exchange: 5-14-1, Nishi, Minami Ichijo, Chuo-ku, Sapporo.

Tokyo Stock Exchange: 2-1, Nihombashi-Kabuto-cho, Chuo-ku, Tokyo 103; tel. (03) 3666-0141; telex 22759; fax (03) 3663-0625; f. 1949; 124 mems (incl. 25 foreign mems); invitations were issued to 10 new members (including 3 foreign brokerages) in March 1990; Pres. Minoru Nagaoka; Sr Man. Dir Mitsuo Sato.

There are also Stock Exchanges at Kyoto and Niigata.

INSURANCE
Principal Life Companies

Asahi Mutual Life Insurance Co: 7-3, Nishishinjuku 1-chome, Shinjuku-ku, Tokyo 163-91; tel. (03) 3342-3111; telex 23229; f. 1888; Pres. Yasuyuki Wakahara.

Chiyoda Mutual Life Insurance Co: 19-18, 2-chome, Kamimeguro Meguro-Ku, Tokyo 153; tel. (03) 5704-5111; telex 67660; f. 1904; Pres. Yasutaro Kanzaki.

Daido Mutual Life Insurance Co: 23-101, 1-chome, Esakacho, Suita-shi, Osaka 564; tel. (06) 3385-1130; telex 33311; f. 1902; Pres. Shiro Kawahara.

Daihyaku Mutual Life Insurance Co: 34-1, Kokuryo-cho 4-chome, Chofu-shi, Tokyo 182; tel. (0424) 85-8111; telex 23063; f. 1914; Chair. Minoru Kawasaki; Pres. Katsuo Fukuchi.

Dai-ichi Mutual Life Insurance Co: 13-1, Yuraku-cho 1-chome, Chiyoda-ku, Tokyo 100; tel. (03) 3216-1211; telex 29848; f. 1902; Chair. Shin-ichi Nishio; Pres. Takahide Sakurai.

Equitable Life Insurance Co Ltd: Togin Kurita Bldg, 3-26 Kanda Nishiki-cho, Chiyoda-ku, Tokyo 101; tel. (03) 3233-3911; f. 1986; Pres. and CEO Donald P. Kanak.

Fukoku Mutual Life Insurance Co: 2-2, Uchisaiwai-cho 2-chome, Chiyoda-ku, Tokyo 100; tel. (03) 3508-1101; f. 1923; Pres. Tetsuo Furuya.

Heiwa Life Insurance Co Ltd: 2-16, Ginza 3-chome, Chuo-ku, Tokyo 104; tel. (03) 3563-8111; f. 1907; Pres. Yutaka Takemoto.

INA Life Insurance Co Ltd: Shinjuku Center Bldg, 48F, 1-25-1, Nishi-Shinjuku, Shinjuku-ku, Tokyo 163; tel. (03) 3348-7011; telex 32471; f. 1981; Pres. Noboru Oka; 7 brs.

Kyoei Life Insurance Co Ltd: 4-4-1, Hongoku-cho, Nihombashi, Chuo-ku, Tokyo 103; tel. (03) 3270-8511; telex 26826; f. 1947; Chair. Masayuki Kitoku; Pres. Yoshio Tayama.

Meiji Mutual Life Insurance Co: 1-1, Marunouchi 2-chome, Chiyoda-ku, Tokyo 100; tel. (03) 3283-8111; telex 27386; f. 1881; Chair. Terumichi Tsuchida; Pres. Kenjiro Hata.

Mitsui Mutual Life Insurance Co: 2-3, Ohtemachi 1-chome, Chiyoda-ku, Tokyo 100; tel. (03) 3211-6111; telex 23261; f. 1927; Chair. Masami Onizawa; Pres. Koshiro Sakata.

Nippon Dantai Life Insurance Co Ltd: 1-2-19, Higashi, Shibuyaku, Tokyo 150; tel. (03) 3407-6211; telex 23342; f. 1934; Chair. Sakae Sawabe; Pres. Hajime Odaka.

Nippon Life Insurance Co (Nissei): 5-12, Imabashi 3-chome, Chuo-ku, Osaka 541-01; tel. (06) 209-4500; telex 28783; f. 1889; Chair. Gentaro Kawase; Pres. Josei Ito.

Nissan Mutual Life Insurance Co: 6-30, Aobadai 3-chome, Meguro-ku, Tokyo 153; tel. (03) 3463-1101; f. 1909; Pres. Ichirozaemon Sakamoto.

Prudential Life Insurance Co Ltd: 1-7, Kojimachi, Chiyoda-ku, Tokyo 102, tel. (03) 3221-0961; f. 1987; Pres. Kiyofumi Sakaguchi.

Seibu Allstate Insurance Co Ltd: Saison Life Insurance Co, Sunshine Sixty Bldg, 38th-39th Floors, 1-1, Higashi Ikebukuro 3-chome, Toshima-ku, Tokyo 170; tel. (03) 3983-6666; f. 1975; Chair. Shigeo Ikuno; Pres. Mikio Matsubara.

Sony Pruco Life Insurance Co Ltd: 1-1, Minami-aoyama 1-chome, Minato-ku, Tokyo 107; tel. (03) 3475-8811; Pres. Kimio Okura.

Sumitomo Life Insurance Co: 2-5, Nakanoshima 2-chome, Kita-ku, Osaka 530; tel. (06) 231-8401; telex 22584; f. 1926; Chair. Kenji Chishiro; Pres. Yasuhiko Ueyama.

Taisho Life Insurance Co Ltd: Taisho Seimei Akasaka Bldg, 17-47 Akasaka 2-chome, Minato-ku, Tokyo 107; tel. (03) 3281-7651; f. 1913; Pres. Toshiyuki Koyama.

Taiyo Mutual Life Insurance Co: 11-2, Nihombashi 2-chome, Chuo-ku, Tokyo 103; tel. (03) 3272-6211; Chair. Magodayu Daibu; Pres. Kyojiro Nishiwaki.

Toho Mutual Life Insurance Co: 15-1, Shibuya 2-chome, Shibuya-ku, Tokyo 150; tel. (03) 3499-1111; telex 28069; f. 1898; Chair. Makoto Yasui; Pres. and CEO Seizo Ota.

JAPAN   *Directory*

Tokyo Mutual Life Insurance Co: 5–2, Uchisaiwai-cho 1-chome, Chiyoda-ku, Tokyo 100; tel. (03) 3504-2211; telex 28517; f. 1895; Pres. MASAKAZU YOGAI.

Yamato Mutual Life Insurance Co: 1-7, Uchisaiwai-cho 1-chome, Chiyoda-ku, Tokyo 100; tel. (03) 3508-3111; f. 1911; Pres. YOSHIO KOHARA.

Yasuda Mutual Life Insurance Co: 9–1, Nishi-shinjuku 1-chome, Shinjuku-ku, Tokyo 160; tel. (03) 3342-7111; telex 22790; f. 1894; Chair. HAJIME YASUDA; Pres. NORIKAZU OKAMOTO.

Principal Non-Life Companies

Allstate Automobile and Fire Insurance Co Ltd: Sunshine Sixty Bldg, 1-1, Higashi Ikebukuro 3-chome, Toshima-ku, Tokyo 170; tel. (03) 3988-2711; telex 22056; fax (03) 3985-8534; Chair. RAYMOND H. KIEFER; Pres. TETSO OTAKI.

Asahi Fire and Marine Insurance Co Ltd: 6–2, Kaji-cho 2-chome, Chiyoda-ku, Tokyo 101; tel. (03) 3254-2211; telex 26974; fax (03) 3254-2211; f. 1951; Pres. KAZUO OCHI.

Chiyoda Fire and Marine Insurance Co Ltd: Kyobashi Chiyoda Bldg, 1-9, Kyobashi 2-chome, Chuo-ku, Tokyo 104; tel. (03) 3281-3311; telex 24975; fax (03) 3272-4987; f. 1897; Chair. TSUTOMU OHSHIMA; Pres. TAKASHI TOYABE.

Daido Fire and Marine Insurance Co Ltd: 2-20, 2-chome, Kume, Naha-shi, Okinawa; tel. (0988) 67-1161; fax (0988) 62-8362; f. 1971; Pres. YUSHO UEZU.

Daiichi Mutual Fire and Marine Insurance Co: 5–1, Niban-cho, Chiyoda-ku, Tokyo; tel. (03) 3239-0011; telex 26554; f. 1949; Chair. SABURO KANEKO; Pres. FUJIO MATSUMURO.

Dai-Tokyo Fire and Marine Insurance Co Ltd: 1-6, Nihonbashi 3-chome, Chuo-ku, Tokyo 103; tel. (03) 3272-8811; telex 26968; fax (03) 3271-4156; f. 1918; Chair. SEI-ICHI SORIMACHI; Pres. ISAO KOSAKA.

Dowa Fire and Marine Insurance Co Ltd: 5-15, Nihonbashi 3-chome, Chuo-ku, Tokyo; tel. (03) 3274-5511; telex 22852; fax (03) 3258-7370; f. 1944; Pres. MASAO OKAZAKI.

Fuji Fire and Marine Insurance Co Ltd: 18-11, Minamisenba 1-chome, Chuo-ku, Osaka; tel. (06) 271-2741; telex 22620; fax (06) 266-7102; f. 1918; Chair. ISAMU WATANABE; Pres. HIROSHI KUZUHARA.

Japan Earthquake Reinsurance Co Ltd: Taishokaijo Bekkan 3–11, Kanda Surugadai, Chiyoda-ku, Tokyo; tel. (03) 3253-4820; fax (03) 3255-0363; f. 1966; Pres. KENJI ATSUMI.

Japan International Accident & Fire Insurance Co Ltd: Shuwa Onarimon Bldg, 1-11, 6-chome, Shimbashi, Minato-ku, Tokyo 106; tel. (03) 3547-6111; fax (03) 3547-6116; f. 1989; Pres. TAKAKI SAKAI.

Koa Fire and Marine Insurance Co Ltd: 7-3, 3-chome, Kasumigaseki, Chiyoda-ku, Tokyo; tel. (03) 3593-3111; telex 23467; f. 1944; Chair. MINORU HOKARI; Pres. TETSUZO SASA.

Kyoei Mutual Fire and Marine Insurance Co: 18-6, 1-chome, Shimbashi, Minato-ku, Tokyo; tel. (03) 3504-0131; telex 22977; fax (03) 3508-7680; f. 1942; Chair. HIDEYUKI TAKAGI; Pres. KATSUMI GYOTOKU.

Mitsui Marine and Fire Insurance Co Ltd: 9, Kanda Surugadai 3-chome, Chiyoda-ku, Tokyo; tel. (03) 3259-3111; telex 24670; fax (03) 3291-5466; f. 1918; Pres. KO MATSUKATA.

Nichido Fire and Marine Insurance Co Ltd: 3-16, 5-chome, Ginza, Chuo-ku, Tokyo; tel. (03) 3571-5141; telex 26920; fax (03) 3574-0646; f. 1914; Chair. YOSHIKAZU SATO; Pres. IKUO EGASHIRA.

Nippon Fire and Marine Insurance Co Ltd: 2-10, Nihombashi 2-chome, Chuo-ku, Tokyo 103; tel. (03) 3272-8111; telex 24214; fax (03) 3281-1788; f. 1892; Chair. MASAJI SHINAGAWA; Pres. YOSHIAKI SANO.

Nissan Fire and Marine Insurance Co Ltd: 9–5, 2-chome, Kita-Aoyama, Minato-ku, Tokyo; tel. (03) 3404-4111; telex 24983; fax (03) 3470-1308; f. 1911; Chair. KEINOSUKE KONDO; Pres. FUMIYA KAWATE.

Nisshin Fire and Marine Insurance Co Ltd: Shiba Tokio Kaijo Bldg, 3–3, Shiba 2-chome, Minato-ku, Tokyo 105; tel. (03) 769-2311; telex 24037; fax (03) 3769-2341; f. 1908; Pres. TOMOICHI NAWAFUNE.

Sumitomo Marine and Fire Insurance Co Ltd: 27-2, Shinkawa 2-chome, Chuo-ku, Tokyo 104; tel. (03) 3297-1111; telex 23051; f. 1944; Pres. TAKASHI ONODA.

Taisei Fire and Marine Insurance Co Ltd: 2-1, 4-chome, Kudan-kita, Chiyoda-ku, Tokyo 102; tel. (03) 3234-3111; telex 28351; fax (03) 3234-4073; f. 1950; Chair. YUTAKA SHIBAIKE; Pres. FUMIO SATO.

Taiyo Fire and Marine Insurance Co Ltd: 18, Kanda Nishiki-cho 3-chome, Chiyoda-ku, Tokyo 101; tel. (03) 3293-6511; telex 25379; fax (03) 3293-6546; f. 1951; Chair. TAMOTSU YOKOTA; Pres. KIYOSHI YANAKI.

Toa Fire and Marine Reinsurance Co Ltd: 11, Kanda Surugadai 3-chome, Chiyoda-ku, Tokyo 101; tel. (03) 3253-3171; telex 24384; fax (03) 3257-1448; f. 1940; Pres. SUMIYOSHI KUSAKABE.

Tokio Marine and Fire Insurance Co Ltd (Tokio Kaijo): 2-1, Marunouchi 1-chome, Chiyoda-ku, Tokyo 100; tel. (03) 3212-6211; telex 24858; f. 1879; Chair. HARUO TAKEDA; Pres. SUNJI KONO.

Toyo Fire and Marine Insurance Co Ltd: 9-15, 1-chome, Nihombashi-Honcho, Chuo-ku, Tokyo 103; tel. (03) 3245-1411; telex 26334; fax (03) 3246-0672; f. 1950; Chair. TSUNEKAZU SAKANO; Pres. EIZO TAKAO.

Yasuda Fire and Marine Insurance Co Ltd: 26–1, Nishi-Shinjuku 1-chome, Shinjuku-ku, Tokyo 160; tel. (03) 3349-3111; telex 22790; fax (03) 3348-3041; f. 1887; Pres. YASUO GOTO.

The Post Office also operates life insurance and annuity plans.

Insurance Associations

Fire and Marine Insurance Rating Association of Japan: Non-Life Insurance Bldg, 9, Kanda Awaji-cho 2-chome, Chiyoda-ku, Tokyo 101; tel. (03) 3255-4991; telex 24829; fax (03) 3255-5376; f. 1948; Chair. IKUO EGASHIRA; Pres. HIROSHI NOMURA.

Life Insurance Association of Japan (Seimei Hoken Kyokai): Shin Kokusai Bldg, 4-1, Marunouchi 3-chome, Chiyoda-ku, Tokyo 100; tel. (03) 3286-2733; f. 1908; 30 mem. cos; Chair. JOSEI ITO; Man. Dir HIROO MASUDA.

Marine and Fire Insurance Association of Japan Inc: Non-Life Insurance Bldg, 9, Kanda Awaji-cho 2-chome, Chiyoda-ku, Tokyo 101; tel. (03) 3255-1211; telex 24829; fax (03) 3255-5376; f. 1917; 24 mems; Pres. SHUNJI KONO; Exec. Dir SHOZO MATSUTA.

Trade and Industry

CHAMBERS OF COMMERCE AND INDUSTRY

The Japan Chamber of Commerce and Industry (Nippon Shoko Kaigi-sho): 2-2, 3-chome, Marunouchi, Chiyoda-ku, Tokyo; tel. (03) 3283-7851; f. 1922; the cen. org. of all chambers of commerce and industry in Japan; mems 489 local chambers of commerce and industry; Chair. ROKURO ISHIKAWA.

Principal chambers include:

Kobe Chamber of Commerce and Industry: 1, Minatojima-nakamachi, 6-Chome, Chuo-ku, Kobe 650; tel. (078) 303-5806; fax (078) 303-2312; f. 1878; 11,543 mems; Chair. SHINICHI ISHINO; Pres. TAKUJI ISHIHARA.

Kyoto Chamber of Commerce and Industry: 240, Shoshoi-cho, Ebisugawa-agaru, Karasumadori, Nakakyo-ku, Kyoto 604; tel. (075) 231-0181; telex 22222; f. 1882; 9,942 mems; Pres. KOICHI TSUKAMOTO; Sr Man. Dir HIROSHI UNO.

Nagoya Chamber of Commerce and Industry: 10–19, Sakae 2-chome, Naka-ku, Nagoya, Aichi 460; tel. (052) 221-7211; telex 24836; f. 1881; 10,235 mems; Pres. KOTARO TAKEDA; Sr Man. Dir YOSHIHISA HARADA.

Naha Chamber of Commerce and Industry: 2-2-4, Kume Naha, Okinawa; tel. 68-3758; f. 1950; 2,856 mems; Pres. KOTARO KOKUBA.

Osaka Chamber of Commerce and Industry: 58–7, Uchi-honmachi Hashizume-cho, Higashi-ku, Osaka; tel. (06) 944-6215; f. 1878; 25,850 mems; Pres. SUSUMU FURUKAWA; Sr Man. Dir HIRONARI MASAGO.

Tokyo Chamber of Commerce and Industry: 2-2, Marunouchi 3-chome, Chiyoda-ku, Tokyo; tel. (03) 3283-7500; telex 24920; f. 1878; 60,000 mems; Pres. ROKURO ISHIKAWA; Man. Dir HIROSHI IKAWA.

Yokohama Chamber of Commerce and Industry: 2, Yamashita-cho, Naka-ku, Yokohama; tel. 671-7400; f. 1880; 13,185 mems; Pres. YUTAKA UYENO; Sr Man. Dir HIROCHIKA KOBAYASHI.

FOREIGN TRADE ORGANIZATIONS

The Association for the Promotion of International Trade, Japan (JAPIT): Nippon Bldg, 5th Floor, 2-6-2, Ohtemachi, Chiyoda-ku, Tokyo; tel. (03) 3245-1561; telex 28471; f. 1954 to promote trade with the People's Repub. of China; Chair. TAKAMARU MORITA; Pres. Y. SAKURAUCHI.

Japan External Trade Organization (JETRO): 2-5, Toranomon 2-chome, Minato-ku, Tokyo 105; tel. (03) 3582-5522; telex 24378; fax (03) 3587-0219; f. 1958; information for foreign firms, investigation of foreign markets, exhbns of Japanese commodities abroad, import promotion, etc.; Chair. MINORU MASUDA; Pres. TERUAKI MIZUNOUE.

Nihon Boeki-Kai (Japan Foreign Trade Council, Inc): 6th Floor, World Trade Center Bldg, 4-1, 2-chome, Hamamatsu-cho, Minato-ku, Tokyo 105; tel. (03) 3435-5952; f. 1947; 307 mems; Pres. YOHEI MIMURA; Exec. Man. Dir MASAO SAITO; Man. Dir TOSHINORI HAYASHI.

TRADE ASSOCIATIONS

Japan Canned Foods Exporters' Association: Fuji Bldg, 6th Floor, 3-3, Yaesu 1-chome, Chuo-ku, Tokyo; tel. (03) 3281-5241; fax (03) 3281-5344.

JAPAN

Japan General Merchandise Exporters' Association: 4-1, Hamamatsu-cho 2-chome, Minato-ku, Tokyo; tel. (03) 3435-3471; f. 1953; 320 mems; Pres. HIROSHI TOYAMA.

Japan Hardwood Exporters' Association: Matsuda Bldg 9-1, 1-chome, Ironai, Otaru, Hokkaido 047; tel. (0134) 23-8411; telex 52701; fax (0134) 22-7150.

Japan Iron and Steel Exporters' Association: 3-2-10, Nihombashi-Kayaba-cho, Chuo-ku, Tokyo; tel. (03) 3669-4811.

Japan Lumber Importers' Association: Yushi Kogyo Bldg, 13-11, Nihombashi 3-chome, Chuo-ku, Tokyo 103; tel. (03) 3271-0926; f. 1950; 118 mems; Pres. S. OTSUBO.

Japan Machinery Exporters' Association: Kikai Shinko Kaikan Bldg, 5-8, Shiba Koen 3-chome, Minato-ku, Tokyo 105; tel. (03) 3431-9507; telex 24744; fax (03) 3436-6455; Pres. TAIICHIRO MATSUO.

Japan Machinery Importers' Association: Koyo Bldg, 8th Floor, 2-11, Toranomon 1-chome, Minato-ku, Tokyo; tel. (03) 3503-9736; f. 1957; 122 mems; Pres. TAIICHIRO MATSUO.

Japan Paper Exporters' Association: Kami Parupu Bldg, 5-6 Nihonbashi Hisamatsu-cho, Chuo-ku, Tokyo 103; tel. (03) 3249-4831; fax (03) 3546-1686; f. 1959; 65 mems; Chair. SHIGERU UCHIMURA.

Japan Paper Importers' Association: Kami Parupu Bldg, 5-6 Nihonbashi Hisamatsu-cho, Chuo-ku, Tokyo 103; tel. (03) 3249-4831; fax (03) 3546-1686; f. 1981; 48 mems; Chair. TAKAHARU MATSUI.

Japan Pearl Exporters' Association: 122 Higashi-machi, Chuo-ku, Kobe; Tokyo branch: 6-15, 3-chome, Kyobashi, Chuo-ku; tel. (03) 3561-7807; f. 1954; Pres. HIRO OTSUKI.

Japan Pharmaceutical, Medical and Dental Supply Exporters' Association: 7-1, Nihombashi-Honcho 4-chome, Chuo-ku, Tokyo 103; tel. (03) 3241-2106; fax (03) 3241-2109; f. 1953; 160 mem. firms; Pres. SHIGEO MORIOKA; Man. Dir KUNIICHIRO OHNO.

Japan Ship Exporters' Association: Senpaku-Shinko Bldg, 1-15-16, Toranomon, Minato-ku, Tokyo 105; tel. (03) 3502-2094; telex 26421; Sr Man. Dir YUICHI WATANABE.

Japan Sugar Import and Export Council: Ginza Gas-Hall, 9-15, 7-chome, Ginza, Chuo-ku, Tokyo; tel. (03) 3571-2362.

Japan Tea Exporters' Association: 81, Kitaban-cho, Shizuoka, Shizuoka Prefecture 420; tel. (0542) 71-3428; telex 20331.

TRADE FAIR

Tokyo International Trade Fair Commission: 7-24, Harumi 4-chome, Chuo-ku, CPOB 1201, Tokyo 104; tel. (03) 3531-3371; telex 23935.

PRINCIPAL INDUSTRIAL ORGANIZATIONS

General

Industry Club of Japan: 4-6, Marunouchi 1-chome, Chiyoda-ku, Tokyo; tel. (03) 3281-1711; f. 1917 to develop closer relations between industrialists at home and abroad and promote expansion of Japanese business activities; c. 1,600 mems; Pres. BUNPEI OTSUKI; Exec. Dir TAKASHI DAI.

Japan Association of Corporate Executives (Keizai Doyukai): Nippon Kogyo Club Bldg, 1-4-6, Marunouchi, Chiyoda-ku, Tokyo 100; tel. (03) 3211-1271; telex 32531; fax (03) 3213-2946; f. 1946; mems: corporate executives concerned with national and international economic and social policies; Chair. TAKASHI ISHIHARA.

Japan Commercial Arbitration Association: Izumi Shiba Koen Bldg, 6-8, Shiba Koen 1-chome, Minato-ku, Tokyo 105; tel. (03) 3435-0710; fax (03) 3435-0702; f. 1950; 1,110 mems; provides facilities for mediation, conciliation and arbitration in international trade disputes; Pres. ROKURO ISHIKAWA.

Japan Federation of Economic Organizations (KEIDANREN) (Keizaidantai Rengo-Kai): 9-4, Ohtemachi 1-chome, Chiyoda-ku, Tokyo, 100; tel. (03) 3279-1411; telex 23188; f. 1946; private non-profit asscn studying domestic and international economic problems; mems 121 industrial orgs, 877 corpns (1986); Chair. GAISHI HIRAIWA; Exec. Vice-Chair. NIHACHIRO HANAMURA.

Japan Federation of Employers' Associations (NIKKEIREN) (Nihon Keieisha Dantai Renmei): 4-6, Marunouchi 1-chome, Chiyoda-ku, Tokyo 100; tel. (03) 3213-4463; telex 23244; f. 1948; 100 mem. asscns; Dir-Gen. YASUICHI OGAWA; Sec.-Gen. HIROSHI KITAMURA.

Japan Federation of Smaller Enterprise Organizations (JFSEO): 2-8-4 Nihombashi, Kayaba-cho, Chuo-ku, Tokyo 103; tel. (03) 3668-2481; f. 1948; 18 mems and c. 1,000 co-operative socs; Pres. MASATAKA TOYODA; Chair. of Int. Affairs SEIICHI ONO.

Japan Productivity Centre (Nihon Seisansei Honbu): 3-1-1 Shibuya, Shibuya-ku, Tokyo 150; tel. (03) 3409-1111; telex 23296; fax (03) 3409-5880; f. 1955; 10,000 mems; concerned with management problems; Chair. TOMITARO HIRATA; Pres. JINNOSUKE MIYAI.

Chemicals

Federation of Pharmaceutical Manufacturers' Associations of Japan: 9, 2-chome, Nihombashi Hon-chu, Chuo-ku, Tokyo; tel. (03) 3270-0581.

Japan Perfumery and Flavouring Association: Nitta Bldg, 2-1, Ginza 8-chome, Chuo-ku, Tokyo 104; tel. (03) 3571-3855; f. 1947; Chair. EIICHI TOGASHI.

Japan Chemical Industry Association: Tokyo Club Bldg, 2-6, 3-chome, Kasumigaseki, Chiyoda-ku, Tokyo 100; tel. (03) 3580-0751; telex 23557; f. 1948; 252 mems; Pres. SEIJI SUZUKI.

Japan Cosmetic Industry Association: Hatsumei Bldg, 9-14, Toranomon 2-chome, Minato-ku, Tokyo 105; tel. (03) 3502-0576; fax (03) 3502-0829; f. 1959; 549 mem. cos; Pres. YOSHIHARU FUKUHARA; Man. Dir KAORU MIYAZAWA.

Japan Gas Association: 15-12, Toranomon 1-chome, Minato-ku, Tokyo 105; tel. (03) 3502-0111; telex 22374; f. 1952; Pres. MASAFUMI OHNISHI; Vice-Pres. YOSHIMITSU SHIBASAKI.

Japan Inorganic Chemical Industry Association: Sanko Bldg, 1-13-1, Ginza Chuo-ku, Tokyo; tel. (03) 3563-1326; f. 1948; Pres. KAN-ICHI TANAHASHI.

Photo-Sensitized Materials Manufacturers' Association: Kyodo Bldg, 2, 2-chome, Kanda Nishiki-cho, Chiyoda-ku, Tokyo 101; tel. (03) 3291-6626; f. 1948; Pres. MINORU OHNISHI.

Fishing and Pearl Cultivation

Japan Fisheries Association (Dai-nippon Suisan Kai): Sankaido Bldg, 9-13, Akasaka 1, Minato-ku, Tokyo; tel. (03) 3585-6683; fax (03) 3582-2337; Pres. YOSHIHIDE UCHIMURA.

Japan Pearl Export and Processing Co-operative Association: 7, 3-chome, Kyobashi, Chuo-ko, Tokyo; f. 1951; 130 mems.

National Federation of Medium Trawlers: Toranomon Chuo Bldg, 1-16, Toranomon 1, Minato-ku, Tokyo; tel. (03) 3508-0361; telex 25404; f. 1948.

Paper and Printing

Japan Federation of Printing Industries: 1-16-8, Shintomi, Chuo-ku, Tokyo 104; tel. (03) 3553-6051; fax (03) 3553-6079; Chair. KAZUO SUZUKI.

Japan Paper Association: Kami-Parupu Kaikan Bldg, Ginza 3-chome, 9-11 Chuo-ku, Tokyo; tel. (03) 3543-2411; telex 22907; f. 1946; 62 mems; Chair. A. SUHARA; Pres. S. HOSHINO.

Japan Paper Products Manufacturers' Association: 2-6, Kotobuki 4-chome, Taito-ku, Tokyo; tel. (03) 3543-2411; f. 1949; Exec. Dir KIYOSHI SATOH.

Mining and Petroleum

Asbestos Cement Products Association: Takahashi Bldg, 10-8, 7-chome, Ginza, Chuo-ku, Tokyo; tel. (03) 3571-1359; f. 1937; Chair. KOSHIRO SHIMIZU.

Cement Association of Japan: Hattori Bldg, 10-3, Kyobashi 1-chome, Chuo-ku, Tokyo 104; tel. (03) 3561-8632; telex 22439; f. 1948; 23 mem. cos; Chair. KAZUSUKE IMAMURA; Exec. Man. Dir M. ONO.

Japan Coal Association: Hibiya Park Bldg, 1-8-1, Yuraku-cho Chiyoda-ku, Tokyo 100; tel. (03) 3214-0581.

Japan Mining Industry Association: Shin-hibiya Bldg, 3-6, Uchisaiwai-cho 1-chome, Chiyoda-ku, Tokyo 100; tel. (03) 3502-7451; f. 1948; 59 mem. cos; Pres. S. NIRATANI; Dir-Gen. T. ISHIKAWA.

Japan Petroleum Development Association: Keidanren Kaikan, 9-4, 1-chome, Ohtemachi, Chiyoda-ku, Tokyo 100; tel. (03) 3279-5841; telex 29400; fax (03) 3279-5844; f. 1961; Chair. TOSHINOBU WADA; Pres. YASUOKI TAKEUCHI.

Metals

Japan Brass Makers' Association: 12-22, 1-chome, Tsukiji, Chuo-ku, Tokyo; f. 1948; 30 mems; Pres. T. SAISHOJI; Man. Dir T. KAWAI.

Japan Iron and Steel Federation: Keidanren Kaikan, 1-9-4, Ohtemachi, Chiyoda-ku, Tokyo; tel. (03) 3279-3611; telex 24210; f. 1948; Chair. H. SAITO.

Japan Light Metal Association: Nihombashi Asahiseimei Bldg, 1-3, Nihonbashi 2-chome, Chuo-ku, Tokyo 103; tel. (03) 3273-3041; fax (03) 3213-2918; f. 1947; 175 mems.

Japan Stainless Steel Association: Tekko Kaikan Bldg, 2-10, Nihombashi Kayaba-cho 3-chome, Chuo-ku, Tokyo 103; tel. (03) 3669-4431; Pres. MITSUNOBU KURITA; Exec. Dir KENICHIRO AOKI.

The Kozai Club: c/o Tekko Kaikan, 3-2-10, Nihombashi Kayaba-cho, Chuo-ku, Tokyo 103; tel. (03) 3669-4811; telex 23607; fax (03) 3667-0245; f. 1947; mems 39 mfrs, 83 dealers; Chair. HIROSHI SAITO.

Steel Castings and Forgings Association of Japan (JSCFA): Tekko Bldg, 8-2, 1-chome, Marunouchi, Chiyoda-ku, Tokyo 100; tel. (03) 3201-0461; f. 1972; mems 59 cos, 67 plants; Exec. Dir SADAO HARA.

Machinery and Precision Equipment

Electronic Industries Association of Japan: Tosho Bldg, 2-2, 3-chome, Marunouchi, Chiyoda-ku, Tokyo; tel. (03) 3211-2765; f. 1948; mems 580 firms; Pres. KATSUSHIGE MITA.

Japan Camera Industry Association: Mori Bldg, No 9, 2-2, Atago 1-chome, Minato-ku, Tokyo 105; tel. (03) 3434-2631; f. 1954; Pres. RYUZABURO KAKU.

Japan Clock and Watch Association: Uchikanda Nishio Bldg., 1-4-15, Uchikanda, Chiyoda-ku, Tokyo 101; tel. (03) 3219-4811.

Japan Electric Association: 1-7-1, Yuraku-cho, Chiyoda-ku, Tokyo 100; tel. (03) 3216-0551; f. 1921; 4,385 mems; Pres. SEIZO YOSHIMURA.

Japan Electric Measuring Instruments Manufacturers' Association: 1-9-10, Toranomon, Minato-ku, Tokyo 105; tel. (03) 3502-0601; fax (03) 3502-0600.

Japan Electrical Manufacturers' Association: 4-15, 2-chome, Nagata-cho, Chiyoda-ku, Tokyo 100; tel. (03) 3581-4844; telex 22619; f. 1948; mems 245 firms; Chair. KATSUSHIGE MITA.

Japan Energy Association: Uchisaiwai Bldg, 1-4-2, Uchisaiwai-cho, Chiyoda-ku, Tokyo 100; tel. (03) 3501-3988; telex 28599; f. 1950; 114 mems; Pres. ICHIRO HORI; Dir FUJIO SAKAGAMI.

Japan Machine Tool Builders' Association: Kikai Shinko Bldg, 3-5-8, Shiba Koen, Minato-ku, Tokyo 105; tel. (03) 3434-3961; telex 22943; f. 1951; 112 mems; Exec. Dir S. ABE.

The Japan Machinery Federation: Kikai Shinko Bldg, 5-8, 3-Chome, Shiba Koen, Minato-ku, Tokyo 105; tel. (03) 3434-5381; fax (03) 3434-6698; f. 1952; Exec. Vice-Pres. SHINICHI NAKANISHI.

Japan Microscope Manufacturers' Association: c/o Olympus Optical Co Ltd, 43-2, Hatagaya 2-chome, Shibuya-ku, Tokyo 151; tel. (03) 3377-2139; fax (03) 3377-2139; f. 1954; 25 mem. firms; Chair. T. SHIMOYAMA.

Japan Motion Picture Equipment Industrial Association: Kikai-Shinko Bldg, 5-8, Shiba Koen 3-chome, Minato-ku, Tokyo 105; tel. (03) 3434-3911; Pres. MASAO SHIKATA; Gen. Sec. TERUHIRO KATO.

Japan Optical Industry Association: Kikai-Shinko Bldg, 3-5-8, Shiba Koen, Minato-ku, Tokyo 105; tel. (03) 3431-7073; f. 1946; 200 mems; Exec. Dir M. SUZUKI.

Japan Society of Industrial Machinery Manufacturers: Kikai Shinko Bldg, 3-5-8, Shiba Koen, Minato-ku, Tokyo 105; tel. (03) 3434-6821; fax (03) 3434-4767; f. 1948; 256 mems; Chair. TSUNESABURO NISHIMURA.

Japan Textile Machinery Association: Kikai Shinko Kaikan, Room 310, 3-5-8, Shiba Koen, Minato-ku, Tokyo 105; tel. (03) 3434-3821; fax (03) 3434-3821; f. 1951; Pres. YOSHITOSHI TOYODA.

Textiles

Central Raw Silk Association of Japan: 7, 1-chome, Yuraku-cho, Chiyoda-ku, Tokyo.

Japan Chemical Fibres Association: 1-20, Nihombashi-Muromachi, 3-chome, Chuo-ku, Tokyo 103; tel. (03) 3241-2311; telex 22304; f. 1948; 55 mems, 17 assoc. mems; Pres. YOSHIKAZU ITO; Dir-Gen. RYOHEI SUZUKI.

Japan Cotton and Staple Fibre Weavers' Association: 8-7, Nishi-Azabu 1-chome, Minato-ku, Tokyo; tel. (03) 3403-9671.

Japan Silk and Rayon Weavers' Association: 15-12, Kudankita 1-chome, Chiyoda-ku, Tokyo; tel. (03) 3262-4101.

Japan Silk Spinners' Association: Mengyo Kaikan Bldg, 8, 3-chome, Bingomachi, Higashi-ku, Osaka; tel. (06) 232-3886; f. 1948; 95 mem. firms; Chair. ICHIJI OHTANI.

Japan Wool Spinners' Association: Sen-i-Kaikan Ueno DK Bldg, 4-15, Ueno 1-chome, Taitoh-ku, Tokyo; tel. (03) 3837-7916; f. 1948; Chair. Y. NISHIMURA.

Japan Worsted and Woollen Weavers' Association: Tokyo; f. 1948; Chair. S. OGAWA; Man. Dir K. OHTANI.

Transport Machinery

Japan Association of Rolling Stock Industries: Daiichi Tekko Bldg, 8-2, Marunouchi 1-chome, Chiyoda-ku, Tokyo; tel. (03) 3201-1911.

Japan Auto Parts Industries Association: 1-16-15, Takanawa, Minato-ku, Tokyo 108; tel. (03) 3445-4211; telex 2829; fax (03) 3447-5372; f. 1948; 390 mem. firms; Chair. K. TODA; Exec. Dir Y. NAKAMURA.

Japan Automobile Manufacturers Association, Inc: Ohtemachi Bldg, 6-1, Ohtemachi 1-chome, Chiyoda-ku, Tokyo 100; tel. (03) 3216-5771; telex 23410; f. 1967; 13 mem. firms; Chair. YUTAKA KUME; Exec. Man. Dir TAKAO TUMINAGA.

Japan Bicycle Manufacturers' Association: 9-3, Akasaka 1-chome, Minato-ku, Tokyo 107; tel. (03) 3583-3123; f. 1955.

Japanese Shipowners' Association: Kaiun Bldg, 6-4, Hirakawa-cho 2-chome, Chiyoda-ku, Tokyo; tel. (03) 3264-7171; telex 22148; fax (03) 3262-4760.

Shipbuilders' Association of Japan: Senpaku Shinko Bldg, 1-15-16, Toranomon, Minato-ku, Tokyo 105; tel. (03) 3502-2010; telex 27056; fax (03) 3502-2816; f. 1947; 40 mems; Chair. KOSAKU INABA; Exec. Man. Dir TAKUJI SHINDO.

Ship-Machinery Manufacturers' Association of Japan: Senpaku-Shinko Bldg, 1-15-16, Toranomon, Minato-ku, Tokyo 105; tel. (03) 3502-2041; fax (03) 3591-2206; f. 1956; 239 mems; Pres. HIDEO WASHIO.

Society of Japanese Aerospace Companies Inc (SJAC): Hibiya Park Bldg, Suite 518, 8-1, Yuraku-cho 1-chome, Chiyoda-ku, Tokyo 100; tel. (03) 3211-5678; fax (03) 3211-5018; f. 1952; reorg. 1974; 148 mems, 39 assoc. mems; Chair. KOSAKU INABA; Exec. Dir EIICHI ONO.

Miscellaneous

Communications Industry Association of Japan (CIA-J): Sankei Bldg Annex, 1-7-2, Ohtemachi, Chiyoda-ku, Tokyo 100; tel. (03) 3231-3156; f. 1948; non-profit org. of telecommunications equipment mfrs; Chair. TADAHIRO SEKIMOTO; Pres. HARUO OZAWA; 240 mems.

Japan Canners' Association: Marunouchi Bldg, 4-1, Marunouchi 2-chome, Chiyoda-ku, Tokyo; tel. (03) 3213-4751.

Japan Fur Association: Ginza-Toshin Bldg, 3-11-15, Ginza, Chuo-ku, Tokyo; tel. (03) 3541-6987; f. 1950; Chair. AKIRA SAITOH; Sec. NORIHIDE SATOH.

Japan Plastics Industry Federation: Tokyo Club Bldg, 2-6, Kasumigaseki 3-chome, Chiyoda-ku, Tokyo; tel. (03) 3580-0771.

Japan Plywood Manufacturers' Association: Meisan Bldg, 18-17, 1-chome, Nishi-Shimbashi, Minato-ku, Tokyo; tel. (03) 3591-9246; fax (03) 3591-9240; f. 1965; 105 mems; Pres. ZENETSU KONNO.

Japan Pottery Manufacturers' Federation: Toto Bldg, 1-28, Toranomon 1-chome, Minato-ku, Tokyo; tel. (03) 3503-6761.

The Japan Rubber Manufacturers Association: Tobu Bldg, 1-5-26, Moto Akasaka, Minato-ku, Tokyo 107; tel. (03) 3408-7101; fax (03) 3408-7106; f. 1950; 160 mems; Pres. HISAAKI SUZUKI.

Japan Spirits and Liquors Makers' Association: Koura Dai-ichi Bldg, 7th Floor, 1-6, Nihombashi-Kayaba-cho 1-chome, Chuo-ku, Tokyo 103; tel. (03) 3668-4621.

Japan Sugar Refiners' Association: 5-7, Sanban-cho, Chiyoda-ku, Tokyo 102; tel. (03) 3262-0176; f. 1949; 18 mems; Sr Man. Dir EIICHI FUJITA.

Motion Picture Producers' Association of Japan: Sankei Bldg, 7-2, 1-chome, Ohtemachi, Chiyoda-ku, Tokyo 100; tel. (03) 3231-6417; fax (03) 3231-6420; Pres. SHIGERU OKADA.

Tokyo Toy Manufacturers' Association: 4-16-3, Higashi-Komagata Sumida-ku, Tokyo 130; tel. (03) 3624-0461.

TRADE UNIONS

A feature of Japan's trade union movement is that the unions are in general based on single enterprises, embracing workers of different occupations in that enterprise. In 1989 union membership stood at 12.2m. workers (25.9% of the total labour force). In November 1989 it was reported that the two largest confederations, SOHYO and RENGO, had merged to form the Japan Trade Union Confederation (Shin-Rengo) with a membership of approximately 9m.

Principal Federations

General Council of Trade Unions of Japan (SOHYO) (Nihon Rodo Kumiai Sohyogikai): Sohyo Kaikan Bldg, 2-11, Kanda Surugadai 3-chome, Chiyoda-ku, Tokyo; tel. (03) 3251-0311; f. 1950; c. 4m. mems; Pres. TAKESHI KUROKAWA; Sec.-Gen. EIKICHI MAGARA.

Major affiliated unions:

All-Japan Express Workers' Union (Zennitsu): Zennitsu Kasumigaseki Bldg, 3-3-3 Kasumigaseki, Chiyoda-ku, Tokyo; tel. (03) 3581-2261; 45,100 mems; Pres. M. OHNISHI.

Federation of Telecommunications Electronic Information and Allied Workers (Dentsuroren): 2-19, Soto Kanda 2-chome, Chiyoda-ku, Tokyo; tel. (03) 3253-3214; 331,897 mems; Pres. AKIRA YAMAGISHI.

General Federation of Private Railway and Bus Workers' Unions (Shitetsusoren): Shitetsu Kaikan Bldg 3-5, Takanawa 4-chome, Minato-ku, Tokyo; tel. (03) 3473-0166; 200,000 mems; Pres. TAKESHI KUROKAWA.

Japan Postal Workers' Union (Zentei): Zentei Kaikan Bldg, 2-7, Koraku 1-chome, Bunkyo-ku, Tokyo; tel. (03) 3812-4261; 186,170 mems; Pres. M. MORIHARA.

Japan Teachers' Union (Nikkyoso): Kyoiku Kaikan Bldg, 6-2, Hitotsubashi 2-chome, Chiyoda-ku, Tokyo; tel. (03) 3265-2171; fax (03) 3230-0172; 677,300 mems; Pres. S. OHBA.

Japanese Federation of Steel Workers' Unions (Tekko Roren): Tokyo; tel. (03) 3555-0401; 211,886 mems; Pres. K. NIINUMA.

National Council of Local and Municipal Government Workers' Unions (Jichiro): Jichiro Kaikan Bldg, 1 Rokuban-cho, Chiyoda-ku, Tokyo; tel. (03) 3263-0261; f. 1951; 1.3m. mems; Pres. Y. MARUYAMA; Gen. Sec. NOBORU CHIBA.

National Federation of Chemical and Synthetic Chemical Industry Workers' Unions (Gokaroren): Senbai Bldg, 26–30, Shiba 5-chome, Minato-ku, Tokyo; tel. (03) 3452-5591; 125,292 mems; Pres. T. MIYAUCHI.

National Metal and Machinery Workers' Union (Kinzoku-Kikai): 6-2, Sakuragaoka, Shibuya-ku, Tokyo 150; tel. (03) 3463-4231; fax (03) 3463-7391; f. 1989; 200,000 mems; Pres. AKIKAZU IKEDA.

National Railway Workers' Union (Kokuro): Kokuro Kaikan Bldg, 11-4, Marunouchi 1-chome, Chiyoda-ku, Tokyo; tel. (03) 3212-0580; 45,000 mems; Pres. T. ROPPONGI.

National Union of General Workers, Sohyo (Zenkoku Ippan): 5-6, Misaki-cho 3-chome, Chiyoda-ku, Tokyo; tel. (03) 3230-4071; 80,125 mems; Pres. I. TOMIOKA.

Japanese Private Sector Trade Union Confederation (RENGO): 1-10-3, Mita, Minato-ku, Tokyo; tel. (03) 3769-6545; telex 25908; f. 1987; 8.2m. mems; 87 unions; affiliated to ICFTU; Pres. TOSHIFUMI TATEYAMA; Gen. Sec. SEIGO YAMADA.

Major affiliated unions:

All-Japan Postal Labour Union (Zenyusei): 20-6, Sandagaya 1-chome, Shibuya-ku, Tokyo 151; tel. (03) 3478-7101; 60,962 mems; Pres. HIDEMASA FUKUI; Gen. Sec. KENJI HACHISU.

All-Japan Seamen's Union (Kaiin Kumiai): 15-26, Roppongi 7-chome, Minato-ku, Tokyo; tel. (03) 3403-6261; telex 25112; fax (03) 3478-0025; 65,000 mems; Pres. S. NAKANISHI.

Federation of All Nissan and General Workers' Unions (Nissan Roren): 4-26, Kaigan 1-chome, Minato-ku, Tokyo 105; tel. (03) 3434-4721; telex 22385; 220,000 mems; Pres. HARUKI SHIMIZU; Gen. Sec. KATSUNARI AKITA.

Federation of Electric Power Workers' Unions of Japan (Denryokuroren): 7-15, Mita 2-chome, Minato-ku, Tokyo 108; tel. (03) 3454-0231; 136,704 mems; Pres. SHIZUKA KATAYAMA; Gen. Sec. YUJI FUKUDA.

Japan Confederation of Shipbuilding and Engineering Workers' Unions (Zosenjukiroren): 2-20-12, Shiba, Minato-ku, Tokyo 105; tel. (03) 3451-6783; fax (03) 3451-6935; 127,560 mems; Pres. SUKESADA ITO; Gen. Sec. MASAYUKI YOSHII.

Japan Federation of Transport Workers' Unions (Kotsuroren): 2-20-12, Shiba, Minato-ku, Tokyo 105; tel. (03) 3451-7243; 101,388 mems; Pres. HIROO MITSUOKA; Gen. Sec. BUNICHI TAMURA.

Japan Railway Workers' Union (Tetsuro): 2-20-12, Shiba, Minato-ku, Tokyo; tel. (03) 3453-9081; 46,247 mems; Pres. SHIGEYUKI TSUJIMOTO; Gen. Sec. YOSHITATSU SHIMA.

Japanese Federation of Chemical and General Trade Unions (Zenkadomei): 2-20-12, Shiba, Minato-ku, Tokyo 105; tel. (03) 3453-3801; fax (03) 3454-2236; f. 1951; 115,000 mems; Pres. HIROICHI HONDA; Gen. Sec. YOSHIKAZU UENO.

Japanese Federation of Electrical Machine Workers' Unions (Denki Roren): Denkiroren Kaikan Bldg, 10-3, 1-chome, Mita, Minato-ku, Tokyo; tel. (03) 3455-6911; f. 1953; 609,197 mems; Chair. and Pres. MITSUHARU WARASHINA.

Japanese Federation of Food and Allied Workers' Unions (Shokuhin Roren): Hiroo Office Bldg, 3-18, Hiroo 1-chome, Shibuya-ku, Tokyo; tel. (03) 3446-2082; f. 1965; 68,979 mems; Pres. KENICHI TAMURA; Gen. Sec. EIJI TAKADA.

Japanese Federation of Textile, Garment, Chemical, Mercantile and Allied Industry Workers' Unions (Zensen): 8-16, Kudan Minami 4-chome, Chiyoda-ku, Tokyo 102; tel. (03) 3265-7521; f. 1946; 1,497 affiliates; 515,029 mems; Pres. USAMI TADANOBU; Gen. Sec. JINNOSUKE ASHIDA.

Japanese Metal Industrial Workers' Union (Zenkin Domei): 2-20-12, Shiba, Minato-ku, Tokyo 105; tel. (03) 3451-2141; f. 1951; 300,000 mems; Pres. TORU EGUCHI; Gen. Sec. AKIRA IMAIZUMI.

Kyoto-Shiga-block Workers' Federation (Keijichiren): Kyoto Rodosha Sogokaikan Bldg, 30-2, Mibusennen-cho, Nakagyo-ku, Kyoto-shi, Tokyo; 10,615 mems; Pres. MEIWA IKEDA.

National Federation of Construction Workers' Unions (Zenkensoren): 7-15, Takadanobaba 2-chome, Shinjuku-ku, Tokyo; tel. (03) 3200-6221; f. 1960; 502,243 mems; Pres. TADAYOSHI KATHO.

National Federation of General Workers' Unions (Ippan Domei): 2-20-12, Shiba, Minato-ku, Tokyo 105; tel. (03) 3453-5869; fax (03) 3769-3738; 113,408 mems; Pres. AKASHI OHKI; Gen. Sec. YOSHIO TSUJIMURA.

National Federation of Life Insurance Workers' Unions (Seiho Roren): Hiroo Office Bldg, 3-18, Hiroo 1-chome, Shibuya-ku, Tokyo; tel. (03) 3446-2031; 359,440 mems; Pres. SHIRO YAMANOBE.

National Organization of All Chemical Workers (Shinkagaku): 9-7, Nishi Shinbashi 3-chome, Minato-ku, Tokyo; tel. (03) 3433-6486; 11,430 mems; Pres. AKIHIRO KAWAI.

Major Non-Affiliated Unions

All-Japan Federation of Transport Workers' Unions (Unyu Roren): 3-3-3, Kasumigaseki, Chiyoda-ku, Tokyo 100; tel. (03) 3503-2171; f. 1968; 124,481 mems; Pres. JIRO TAI.

Confederation of Japan Automobile Workers' Unions (JAW—Jidoshasoren): Kokuryu Shiba Koen Bldg, 6-15, Shiba Koen 2-chome, Minato-ku, Tokyo; tel. (03) 3434-7641; fax (03) 3434-7428; f. 1972; 750,000 mems; Pres. TERUHITO TOKUMOTO.

Federation of City Bank Employees' Unions (Shiginren): Ida Bldg, 3-8, Yaesu 1-chome, Chuo-ku, Tokyo; tel. (03) 3274-5611; 174,135 mems; Pres. Y. OKUMOTO.

Japan Council of Construction Industry Employees' Unions (Nikkenkyo): Dai-7 Daikyo Bldg, 30-8, Sendagaya 1-chome, Shibuya-ku, Tokyo; tel. (03) 3403-7976; f. 1954; 65,479 mems; Pres. MASANORI OKAMURA.

Japan Federation of Commercial Workers' Unions (Shogyororen): 2-23-1, Yoyogi, Shibuya-ku, Tokyo; tel. (03) 3370-4121; telex 29575; 140,000 mems; Pres. MAMORU SHIBATA.

National Federation of Agricultural Mutual Aid Societies Employees' Unions (Zennokyororen): Shinkuku Nokyo Kaikan Bldg, 5-5, Yoyogi 2-chome, Shibuya-ku, Tokyo; tel. (03) 3370-8327; 93,382 mems; Pres. HIDEO GOTO.

National Councils

Co-ordinating bodies for unions whose members are in the same industry or have the same employer.

Council of National Enterprise Workers' Unions (Korokyo): Sohyo Kaikan, 2-11, Kanda Surugadai 3-chome, Chiyoda-ku, Tokyo; tel. (03) 3251-7471; 211,000 mems; Gen. Sec. S. KAWASHUZAKI.

Council of SOHYO-affiliated Federations in the Private Sector (Sohyo Minkan Tansan Kaigi): Sohyo Kaikan, 2-11, Kanda Surugadai 3-chome, Chiyoda-ku, Tokyo; tel. (03) 3251-0311; 1,479,942 mems; Gen. Sec. SIZUO MISHIMA.

FIET Japanese Liaison Council (FIET-JLC): 2-23-1, Yoyogi, Shibuya-ku, Tokyo 151; tel. (03) 3370-4121; telex 29575; f. 1981; 319,000 mems; Gen. Sec. TADASHI MIURA.

Japan Council of Metalworkers' Unions (Zen Nihon Kinzoku Sangyo Rodokumiai Kyogikai): Santoku Yaesu Bldg, 6-21, Yaesu 2-chome, Chuo-ku, Tokyo 104; tel. (03) 3274-2461; telex 22534; fax (03) 3274-2476; f. 1964; 2.41m. mems; Pres. TERUHITO TOKUMOTO; Gen. Sec. SHIRO UMEHARA.

Japan Council of Public Service Workers' Unions (Nihon Komuin Rodo Kumiai Kyoto Kaigi): Sohyo Kaikan, 2-11, Kanda Surugadai 3-chome, Chiyoda-ku, Tokyo; tel. (03) 3251-6263; 2,303,107 mems; Gen. Sec. YASUO MARUYAMA.

Trade Union Council for Policy Promotion (Seisaku Suishin Roso Kaigi): c/o Denryokuroren, 7-15, Mita 2-chome, Minato-ku, Tokyo 108; 5m. mems; Gen. Secs KOICHIRO HASHIMOTO, TOSHIFUMI TATEYAMA.

Trade Union Council for Multinational Companies (Takokuseki-Kigyo Taisaku Rodo Kumiai Kaigi): c/o IMF-JC, Santoku Yaesu Bldg, 6-21, Yaesu 2-chome, Chuo-ku, Tokyo 104; tel. (03) 3274-2288; telex 22534; fax (03) 3274-2476; 3.5m. mems; Standing Reps TERUHITO TOKUMOTO and ICHIRO SETO; Gen. Sec. SEIGO KOJIMA.

CO-OPERATIVE ORGANIZATION

National Federation of Agricultural Co-operative Associations (ZEN-NOH): 8-3, Ohtemachi 1-chome, Chiyoda-ku, Tokyo 100; tel. (03) 3245-0746; telex 23686; fax (03) 3245-7442; purchasers of agricultural materials and marketers of agricultural products.

Transport

RAILWAYS

Japan Railways Group: 6-5, Marunouchi 1-chome, Chiyoda-ku, Tokyo 100; tel. (03) 3215-9649; telex 24873; fmrly the state-controlled Japanese National Railways (JNR); reorg. and transferred to private-sector control in 1987, and divided into six passenger railway cos, one freight railway co, and five other organizations (see list below); very high-speed Tokaido-Sanyo Shinkansen line (1,069 km) links Tokyo with Shin-Yokohama, Nagoya, Kyoto, Shin-Osaka, Okayama, Hiroshima and Hakata. Tohoku Shinkansen (493 km) links Ueno in Tokyo with Omiya, Koriyama, Fukushima, Sendai and Morioka. Joetsu Shinkansen (297 km) links Ueno (Tokyo) with Omiya, Takasaki, Nagaoka and Niigata. A section between Ueno (Tokyo) and Omiya (27 km) was opened in March 1985. The 4-km link between Ueno and Tokyo stations was under construction in the early 1990s. In 1987 the total railway route length was about 20,083 km, of which 10,524 km was electrified. Work began in 1971 on a new 'super express' railway network, linking all the major cities. To be completed by the end of the century, it will total 7,000 km in length.

Central Japan Railway Co: 1-4, Meieki 1-chome, Nakamura-ku, Nagoya 450; tel. (052) 564-2316; fax (052) 564-2331; Chair. SHIGEMITSU MIYAKE; Pres. HIROSHI SUDA.

East Japan Railway Co: 6-5, Marunouchi 1-chome, Chiyoda-ku, Tokyo 100; tel. (03) 3215-9648; telex 24873; fax (03) 3213 5291; f. 1987; Chair. ISAMU YAMASHITA; Pres. SHOJI SUMITA.

Hokkaido Railway Co: Nishi 4-chome, Kita 5-jo, Chuo-ku, Sapporo 060; tel. (011) 222-6123; fax (011) 222-5676; Chair. TAKEI TOJO; Pres. YOSHIHIRO OHMORI.

Japan Freight Railway Co: 6-5, Marunouchi 1-chome, Chiyoda-ku, Tokyo 100; tel. (03) 3285-0071; fax (03) 3216-2089; Chair. SUNAO MACHIDA; Pres. MASASHI HASHIMOTO.

Japan Telecom Co Ltd: 1-7, Kudan-kita 4-chome, Chiyoda-ku, Tokyo 102; tel. (03) 3222-6651; fax (03) 3222-6659; f. 1989; merged with Railway Telecommunications Co Ltd in 1989; Chair. KAZUMASA MAWATARI; Pres. KOICHI SAKATA.

JNR Settlement Corpn: 6-5, Marunouchi 1-chome, Chiyoda-ku, Tokyo 100; tel. (03) 3240-5701; Pres. SHOJI ISHIZUKI.

Kyushu Railway Co: 1-1, Chuogai, Hakataeki, Hakata-ku, Fukuoka 812; tel. (092) 474-2501; fax (092) 473-4805; Chair. MASASUKE NAKAGAWA; Pres. YOSHITAKA ISHII.

Railway Information Systems Co Ltd: 6-5, Marunouchi 1-chome, Chiyoda-ku, Tokyo 100; tel. (03) 3240-9686; f. 1986; Pres. YOSHISUKE MUTO.

Railway Technical Research Institute: 2-8-38, Hikari-cho, Kokubunji, Tokyo 185; tel. (0425) 73-7237; fax (0425) 73-7356; Chair. MASARU IBUKA; Pres. MASANORI OZEKI.

Shikoku Railway Co: 1-10, Hamano-cho, Takamatsu, Kagawa 760; tel. (0878) 51-1880; telex 2266; fax (0878) 51-0497; Pres. HIROATSU ITO.

West Japan Railway Co: 1-1, Ofuka-cho, Kita-ku, Osaka 530; tel. (06) 375-8917; fax (06) 374-6068; f. 1987; Chair. TSUTOMU MURAI; Pres. TATSUO TSUNODA; Vice-Pres. MASATAKA IDE.

Other Principal Private Companies

Hankyu Corporation: 8-8, Kakuda-cho, Kita-ku, Osaka 530; tel. (06) 373-5088; telex 65617; f. 1907; links Osaka, Kyoto, Kobe and Takarazuka; Pres. KOHEI KOBAYASHI.

Hanshin Electric Railway Co Ltd: 3-19, Umeda 2-chome, Kita-ku, Osaka 530; tel. (06) 347-6035; f. 1899; Chair. C. NODA; Pres. T. TANAKA.

Keihan Electric Railway Co Ltd: 7-24, Otemae 1-chome, Chuo-ku, Osaka 540; tel. (06) 944-2521; fax (06) 944-2501; f. 1906; Chair. HIROSHI SUMITA; Pres. MINORU MIYASHITA.

Keihin Electric Express Railway Co Ltd: 20-20, Takanawa 2-chome, Minato-ku, Tokyo 140; tel. (03) 3443-5111; fax (03) 3280-9199; Pres. MORITOSHI SERIZAWA.

Keio Teito Electric Railway Co Ltd: Tokyo; tel. (0423) 37-3200; Pres. KENICHI KUWAYAMA.

Keisei Electric Railway Co Ltd: 10-3, Oshiage 1-chome, Sumida-ku, Tokyo 131; tel. (03) 3621-2231; f. 1909; Pres. M. SATO.

Kinki Nippon Railway Co Ltd: 1-55, Ue-hommachi 6-chome, Tennoji-ku, Osaka 543; tel. (06) 775-3444; fax (06) 775-3468; f. 1910; Chair. YOSHINORI UEYAMA; Pres. SHIGEICHIROU KANAMORI.

Nagoya Railroad Co Ltd: 2-4, 1-chome, Meieki, Nakamura-ku, Nagoya-shi 450; tel. (0571) 2111; Chair. KOTARO TAKEDA; Pres. K. KAJII.

Nankai Electric Railway Co Ltd: 1-60, Nanba 5-chome, Minami-ku, Osaka 542; tel. (06) 631-1151; Pres. SHIGERU YOSHIMURA; Vice-Pres. K. OKAMOTO.

Nishi-Nippon Railroad Co Ltd: 11-17, Tenjin-cho 1-chome, Chuo-ku, Fukuoka 810; tel. (092) 761-6631; serves northern Kyushu; Chair. H. YOSHIMOTO; Pres. G. KIMOTO.

Odakyu Electric Railway Co Ltd: 8-3, Nishi Shinjuku 1-chome, Shinjuku-ku, Tokyo 160; tel. (03) 3349-2301; f. 1948; Pres. TATSUZO TOSHIMITSU.

Seibu Railway Co Ltd: 16-15, Minami-Ikebukuro 1-chome, Toshima-ku, Tokyo 171; tel. (03) 3989-2035; f. 1912; Pres. Y. TSUTSUMI.

Tobu Railway Co Ltd: 1-2, 1-chome, Oshiage, Sumida-ku, Tokyo 131; tel. (03) 0001-5057; Pres. KAICHIRO NEZU.

Tokyu Corporation: 26-20, Sakuragaoka-cho, Shibuya, Tokyo 150; tel. (03) 3477-6075; telex 23395; f. 1922; Pres. JIRO YOKOTA.

Subways, Monorails and Tunnels

Subway service is available in Tokyo, Osaka, Kobe, Nagoya, Sapporo, Yokohama, Kyoto, Sendai and Fukuoka with a combined network of about 500 km. Most new subway lines are directly linked with existing private railway terminals which connect the cities with suburban areas.

Japan started its first monorail system on a commercial scale in 1964 with straddle-type cars between central Tokyo and Tokyo International Airport, a distance of 13 km. In 1988 the total length of monorail was 38.6 km.

In 1985 the 54-km Seikan Tunnel (the world's longest undersea tunnel), linking the islands of Honshu and Hokkaido, was completed at an estimated cost of 690,000m. yen. Electric rail services through the tunnel began operating in March 1988.

Fukuoka City Subway: Fukuoka Municipal Transportation Bureau, 5-31 Daimyo 2-chome, Chuo-ku Fukuoka 810; tel. (092) 714-3211; 2 lines of 14.5 km open; Dir SUKEAKI TATSUICHI.

Kobe Rapid Transit: 5-1, Kanocho 6-chome, Chuo-ku, Kobe 650; tel. (078) 331-8181; 22.6 km open; Dir T. YAMANAKA.

Kyoto Rapid Transit: 48 Bojocho Mibu, Nakakyo-ku, Kyoto 604; tel. (075) 841-9361; 11.4 km open; Dir. NISUHARU NAKABO.

Nagoya Underground Railway: Nagoya Municipal Transportation Bureau, City Hall Annexe, 1-1, Sannomaru 3-chome, Naka-ku, Nagoya 460; tel. (052) 961-1111; 66.5 km open (1989); Gen. Man. KOSUKE TOMATSU.

Osaka Underground Railway: Osaka Municipal Transportation Bureau, 11-53, 1-chome, Kujo Minami, Nishi-ku, Osaka; tel. (06) 582-1101; f. 1933; 99.1 km open in 1989 and the 6.6 km computer-controlled 'New Tram' service began between Suminoekoen and Nakafuto in 1984; a seventh line between Kyobashi and Tsurumi-ryokuchi is to be opened in 1990; Gen. Man. EIICHI SAKAGUCHI.

Sapporo Transportation Bureau: Higashi, 2-4-1 Oyachi, Shiroishi-ku, Sapporo, Hokkaido; tel. (011) 892-1133; 39.7 km metro commenced operations in 1987; line 3 opened in 1988; Dir KOICHI OSABE.

Sendai City Subway: Sendai Municipal Transportation Bureau, 4-15 Kimachidori 1-chome, Aoba-ku, Sendai-shi, Miyagi-ken 980; tel. (022) 224-5111; 14.4 km open; Dir. KOSUKE OGAWA.

Tokyo Underground Railway: Teito Rapid Transit Authority, 19-6, Higashi Ueno 3-chome, Taito-ku, Tokyo 110; tel. (03) 3837-7046; fax (03) 3837-7048; f. 1941; Pres. SHIRO NAKAMURA; 154.6 km open; and Transportation Bureau of Tokyo Metropolitan Govt, 2-10-1, Yuraku-cho, Chiyoda-ku, Tokyo 100; f. 1960; tel. (03) 3216-1411; Dir-Gen. TSUNEHARU OCHI; 64.3 km open; combined length of underground system 218.9 km (1989).

Yokohama Rapid Transit: Municipal Transportation Bureau, 1-1, Minato-cho, Naka-ku, Yokohama 231; 22.1 km open; Dir-Gen. MIKIO KAWAHARA.

ROADS

In April 1989 Japan's road network extended to 1,109,981 km, including 4,407 km of motorways. Plans have been made to cover the country with a trunk automobile highway network with a total length of 7,600 km, of which 4,330 km were expected to be completed by 1989. In mid-1988 work was completed on the world's longest suspension bridge, a 9.4-km multi-section structure spanning the Seto inland sea between Honshu and Shikoku.

There is a national omnibus service, 60 publicly operated services and 298 privately operated services.

SHIPPING

Shipping in Japan is subject to the supervision of the Ministry of Transport. At 30 June 1989 the Japanese merchant fleet (9,830 vessels) had a total displacement of 28,030,425 grt. The main ports are Yokohama, Nagoya and Kobe.

Principal Companies

Daiichi Chuo Kisen Kaisha: Dowa Bldg, 5-15, Nihombashi 3-chome, Chuo-ku, Tokyo 103; tel. (03) 3278-6800; telex 24322; f. 1960; fleet of 14 vessels; liner and tramp services; Chair. K. YAMADA; Pres. K. MORITA.

Iino Kaiun KK: 1-1, 2-chome, Uchisaiwai-cho, Chiyoda-ku, Tokyo 100; tel. (03) 3506-3066; telex 22238; f. 1918; fleet of 10 vessels; cargo and tanker services; Pres. T. CHIBA.

Kansai Kisen KK: Osaka Bldg, 6-32, 3-chome, Nakanoshima, Kita-ku, Osaka 552; tel. (06) 574-9171; telex 37284; f. 1942; fleet of 9 vessels; domestic passenger services; Pres. M. OKI.

Kawasaki Kisen Kaisha Ltd (K Line): 2-9, NishiShinbashi 1-chome, Minato-ku, Tokyo 105; tel. (03) 3595-5000; telex 22361; fax (03) 3595-6111; f. 1919; fleet of 37 vessels; containers, cars, LNG, LPG and oil tankers, bulk ore-carrying, Chair. K. ITOH; Pres. H. MATSUNARI.

JAPAN

Mitsui OSK Lines Ltd: 1-1, Toranomon 2-chome, Minato-ku, Tokyo 105; tel. (03) 3587-7015; telex 22266; f. 1952; 54 vessels; world-wide container, liner, tramp and specialized carrier and tanker services; Chair. KIICHIRO AIURA; Pres. SUSUMU TEMPORIN.

Navix Line Ltd: Palaceside Bldg, 1-1, Hitotsubashi 1-chome, Chiyoda-ku, Tokyo 100; tel. (03) 3282-7500; telex 22345; f. 1989 as a merger between Japan Line Ltd and Yamashita-Shinnihon Steamship Co Ltd (Y. S. Line); fleet of 216 vessels (16m. dwt); tramp, specialized carrier and tanker services; Pres. S. MAGOSHI.

Nippon Yusen Kaisha Line (NYK): CPOB 1250, 3-2, Marunouchi 2-chome, Chiyoda-ku, Tokyo 100; tel. (03) 3284-5151; telex 22236; f. 1885; 115 vessels; world-wide container, cargo, tanker and bulk carrying services; Chair. SUSUMU ONO; Pres. KIMIO MIYAOKA.

Nissho Shipping Co Ltd: 7th Floor, 33 Mori Bldg, 8-21, Toranomon 3-chome, Minato-ku, Tokyo 105; tel. (03) 3438-3511; telex 22573; fax (03) 3438-3566; f. 1943; fleet of 11 vessels; Pres. MINORU IKEDA.

Ryukyu Kaiun KK: POB 98, 1-1, 4-chome, Nishi-honmachi, Naha, Okinawa 900; tel. (0988) 688161; telex 5217; fleet of 6 vessels; cargo and passenger services on domestic routes; Pres. M. AZAMA.

Sankyo Kaiun Kabushiki Kaisha: Miki Bldg, 12-1, 3-chome, Nihombashi, Chuo-ku, Tokyo 103; tel. (03) 3273-1811; telex 22109; f. 1959; fleet of 22 vessels; liner and tramp services; Pres. SADAO KAWAI; Chair. TAIJI HOSOKAWA.

Shinwa Kaiun Kaisha Ltd: Fukoku Seimei Bldg, 2-2, 2-chome, Uchisaiwai-cho, Chiyoda-ku, Tokyo 100; tel. (03) 3597-6076; telex 22348; f. 1950; fleet of 17 vessels; ore carriers, dry cargo and tankers; Pres. MICHIO HAKKAKU.

Showa Line Ltd: Hibiya Kokusai Bldg, 2-3, 2-chome, Uchisaiwai-cho, Chiyoda-ku, Tokyo 100; tel. (03) 3595-2211; telex 22310; f. 1944; fleet of 11 vessels; cargo, tanker, tramping and container services world-wide; Chair. and Pres. DAIJIRO ISHII; Man. Dir AKIRA YAMADA.

Taiheiyo Kaiun KK: Room 316, Marunouchi Bldg, 4-1, 2-chome, Chiyoda-ku, Tokyo 100; tel. (03) 3201-2166; telex 23434; f. 1951; fleet of 20 vessels; cargo and tanker services; Pres. H. CHIBA.

CIVIL AVIATION

There are international airports at Tokyo, Osaka and Narita. In July 1986 construction of the world's first offshore international airport (to be called New Kansai International Airport) began in Osaka Bay. This airport is due to open in March 1994.

Air Nippon: Dai 2, Akiyama Bldg, 3-6-2, Toranomon, Minato-ku, Tokyo 105, tel. (03) 3432-7471; telex 22124; f. 1974; formerly Nihon Kinkyori Airways; domestic services; Pres. KANICHI MARUI; fleet of 1 Boeing 737, 10 YS-11, 2 Twin Otter.

All Nippon Airways—ANA: Kasumigaseki Bldg, 2-5, Kasumigaseki 3-chome, Chiyoda-ku, Tokyo 100; tel. (03) 3592-3035; telex 33670; fax (03) 3592-3239; f. 1952; operates domestic passenger and freight services; scheduled international services to Guam, Beijing, Dalian, Saipan (Northern Mariana Islands), Hong Kong, Los Angeles, Washington DC, Seoul, Sydney, Paris, Brussels ,Vienna, Stockholm, Bangkok, London and Moscow; charter services world-wide; Chair. TOKUJI WAKASA; Pres. AKIO KONDO; fleet of 24 Boeing 747, 11 Lockheed Tristar 1, 34 Boeing 767, 6 Boeing 727, 14 Boeing 737, 17 YS-11A.

Japan Air Lines—JAL (Nihon Koku Kabushiki Kaisha): Tokyo Bldg, 7-3, Marunouchi 2-chome, Chiyoda-ku, Tokyo 100; tel. (03) 3284-2039; telex 24827; fax (03) 3284-3100; f. 1951; fully transferred to private-sector control in 1987; domestic and international services, from Tokyo to Australia, Bahrain, Brazil, Canada, People's Republic of China, Denmark, Egypt, Fiji, France, Federal Republic of Germany, Greece, Hong Kong, India, Indonesia, Italy, the Republic of Korea, Kuwait, Malaysia, Mexico, Netherlands, New Zealand, Pakistan, the Philippines, Saudi Arabia, Singapore, Spain, Switzerland, Thailand, USSR, United Arab Emirates, the UK and the USA; a charter flight subsidiary company is planned for 1991; Chair. FUMIO WATANABE; Pres. MATSUO TOSHIMITSU; fleet of 59 Boeing 747, 13 Boeing 767, 17 DC-10.

Japan Air System: 18 Mori Bldg, 3-13, Toranomon 2-chome, Minato-ku, Tokyo 105; tel. (03) 3507-8030; telex 25182; fax (03) 3592-0115; f. 1971; domestic services and international charter flights; Chair. ISAMU TANAKA; Pres. TAKESHI MASHIMA; fleet of 14 Airbus A-300, 14 DC-9-40, 33 YS-11, 15 MD-81, 1 MD-87.

Japan Asia Airways Co: South Wing, Yuraku-cho Denki Bldg, 7-1, Yuraku-cho 1-chome, Chiyoda-ku, Tokyo 100; tel. (03) 3284-2672; telex 25440; f. 1975; wholly-owned subsidiary of JAL; international services from Tokyo, Osaka and Okinawa to Hong Kong, Guam, Saipan and Taiwan; Chair. TOSHIO ITAKURA; Pres. TAKESHI TSUNOGAE; fleet of 3 Boeing 747, 3 DC-10.

Southwest Air Lines Co Ltd (Nansei Koku KK): 3-1, Yamashita-cho, Naha-shi, Okinawa 900; tel. 572112; telex 795477; f. 1967; subsidiary of JAL; inter-island service in Okinawa; Chair. KAMAKICHI OSHIRO; Pres. MICHIHISA IHARA; fleet of 6 YS-11A, 4 Twin Otter, 7 Boeing 737-200.

Tourism

The ancient capital of Kyoto, pagodas and temples, forests and mountains, traditional festivals and the classical Kabuki theatre are some of the many tourist attractions of Japan. In 1988 there were 2,355,412 foreign visitors to Japan, and receipts from tourism totalled US $2,893m.

Department of Tourism: 2-1-3, Kasumigaseki, Chiyoda-ku, Tokyo 100; f. 1946; a dept of the Ministry of Transport; Dir-Gen. HIROKUNI TSUJI.

Japan National Tourist Organization: Tokyo Kotsu Kaikan Bldg, 2-10-1, Yuraku-cho, Chiyoda-ku, Tokyo; tel. (03) 3216-1901; telex 24132; Pres. SHUNICHI SUMITA.

Japan Travel Bureau Inc: 1-13-1, Nihombashi, Chuo-ku, Tokyo 103; tel. (03) 3276-7811; telex 24418; f. 1912; c. 11,000 mems; Chair. T. NAGASE; Pres. H. ISHIDA.

Atomic Energy

Forty-one nuclear power reactors were in operation by December 1990, with a combined capacity of 30,917 MW. A further 10 reactors, with a combined capacity of 9,012 MW, were under construction. Projected generating capacity: 53,500 MW by 2000. In 1990, 25.5% of Japan's electricity was nuclear-generated. A nuclear power plant in Mihama was temporarily closed in early 1991, following the accidental release of radioactive water into the secondary cooling system.

Atomic Energy Bureau (AEB): Science and Technology Agency, 2-2-1, Kasumigaseki, Chiyoda-ku, Tokyo 100; tel. (03) 3581-5271; f. 1956; administers and controls research and development; Dir KENJIRO OGATA.

Japan Atomic Energy Commission (JAEC): 2-2-1, Kasumigaseki, Chiyoda-ku, Tokyo 100; tel. (03) 3581-5271; f. 1955; policy board for research, development and peaceful uses of atomic energy; Chair. MOICHI MIYAZAKI.

Japan Atomic Energy Research Institute (JAERI): Fuko-kuse-imei Bldg, 2-2-2, Uchisaiwai-cho, Chiyoda-ku, Tokyo 100; tel. (03) 3503-6111; telex 24596; f. 1956; all aspects of nuclear research: water reactor safety, fusion, development of nuclear-powered maritime vessels, HTR and utilization of radiation; Pres. TSUNEO FUJINAMI.

Japan Atomic Industrial Forum Inc (JAIF): Toshin Bldg, 1-13, Shinbashi 1-chome, Minato-ku, Tokyo 105; tel. (03) 3508-2411; telex 26623; f. 1956; non-profit org. representing c. 820 orgs involved in atomic energy development in Japan; also c. 120 overseas mems; aims to promote the peaceful use of atomic energy and the acceptance of nuclear power among the public; carries out related field surveys; Chair. JIRO ENJOJI (acting); Exec. Man. Dir KAZUHISA MORI.

Japan Nuclear Safety Commission (JNSC): 2-2-1, Kasumigaseki, Chiyoda-ku, Tokyo 100; tel. (03) 3581-1880; f. 1978; responsible for all matters relating to safety regulations; Chair. HIDEO UCHIDA.

Nuclear Safety Bureau (NSB): Science and Technology Agency, 2-2-1, Kasumigaseki, Chiyoda-ku, Tokyo 100; tel. (03) 3581-5271; telex 26720; fax (03) 3581-2487; f. 1976; admin. agency for nuclear safety and regulatory matters; Dir KENICHI MURAKAMI.

Power Reactor and Nuclear Fuel Development Corporation (PNC): 1-9-13, Akasaka, Minato-ku, Tokyo; tel. (03) 3586-3311; telex 26462; f. 1967; research and development of FBR, ATR and fuel cycle technologies; Pres. TAKAO ISHIIWATARI.

JORDAN

Introductory Survey

Location, Climate, Language, Religion, Flag, Capital

The Hashemite Kingdom of Jordan is an almost land-locked state in western Asia. It is bordered by Israel to the west, by Syria to the north, by Iraq to the east and by Saudi Arabia to the south. The port of Aqaba, in the far south, gives Jordan a narrow outlet to the Red Sea. The climate is hot and dry. The average annual temperature is about 15°C (60°F) but there are wide diurnal variations. Temperatures in Amman are generally between −1°C (30°F) and 32°C (90°F). More extreme conditions are found in the valley of the River Jordan and on the shores of the Dead Sea (a lake on the Israeli-Jordanian frontier), where the temperature may exceed 50°C (122°F) in summer. The official language is Arabic. More than 90% of the population are Sunni Muslims, while there are small communities of Christians and Shi'i Muslims. The national flag (proportions 2 by 1) has three equal horizontal stripes, of black, white and green, with a red triangle, containing a seven-pointed white star, at the hoist. The capital is Amman.

Recent History

Palestine (including the present-day West Bank of Jordan) and Transjordan (the East Bank) were formerly parts of Turkey's Ottoman Empire. During the First World War (1914–18), when Turkey was allied with Germany, the Arabs under Ottoman rule rebelled. British forces, with Arab support, occupied Palestine and Transjordan in 1917–18, when the Turks withdrew.

British occupation continued after the war, when the Ottoman Empire was dissolved. In 1920 Palestine and Transjordan were formally placed under British administration by a League of Nations mandate. In 1921 Abdullah ibn Hussein, a member of the Hashimi (Hashemite) dynasty of Arabia, was proclaimed Amir (Emir) of Transjordan. In the same year, his brother, Faisal, became King of neighbouring Iraq (also administered by the United Kingdom (UK) under a League of Nations mandate). The two new monarchs were sons of Hussein ibn Ali, the Sharif of Mecca, who had proclaimed himself King of the Hejaz (now part of Saudi Arabia) in 1916. The British decision to nominate Hashemite princes to be rulers of Iraq and Transjordan was a reward for Hussein's co-operation in the wartime campaign against Turkey.

During the period of the British mandate, Transjordan (formally separated from Palestine in 1923) gained increasing autonomy. In 1928 the UK acknowledged the nominal independence of Transjordan, although retaining certain financial and military powers. Amir Abdullah followed a generally pro-British policy and supported the Allied cause in the Second World War (1939–45). The mandate was terminated on 22 March 1946, when Transjordan attained full independence. On 25 May Abdullah was proclaimed King, and a new constitution took effect.

When the British Government terminated its mandate in Palestine in May 1948, Jewish leaders in the area proclaimed the State of Israel, but Palestinian Arabs, supported by the armies of Arab states, opposed Israeli claims and hostilities continued until July. Transjordan's forces occupied about 5,900 sq km of Palestine, including East Jerusalem, and this was confirmed by the armistice with Israel in April 1949. In June 1949 the country was renamed Jordan, and in April 1950, following a referendum, King Abdullah formally annexed the West Bank territory, which contained many Arab refugees from Israeli-held areas.

In July 1951 King Abdullah was assassinated in Jerusalem by a Palestinian Arab belonging to an extremist Islamic organization. The murdered king was succeeded by his eldest son, Talal ibn Abdullah, hitherto Crown Prince. Because of Talal's mental illness, however, a joint session of the National Assembly proclaimed him unfit to reign, and deposed him, in August 1952. The crown passed to his son, Hussein ibn Talal, then 16 years of age. King Hussein formally took power in May 1953.

In March 1956, responding to Arab nationalist sentiment, King Hussein dismissed Lieut-Gen. John Glubb ('Glubb Pasha'), the British army officer who had been Chief of Staff of the Arab Legion (the Jordanian armed forces) since 1939. The Legion, with about 20,000 men, had been created in 1920 by the UK and was financed and equipped by the British Government. However, Jordan's treaty relationship with the UK was ended in March 1957. British troops completed their withdrawal from Jordan in July.

The refugee camps in the West Bank became centres of Palestinian Arab nationalism, with the aim of recovering the homeland from which Arabs had been dispossessed (about 400,000 Arab residents of Palestine evacuated their homes prior to May 1948, when the British mandate ended and Israel was established, and a further 400,000 fled subsequently). In the 1950s there were numerous attacks on Israeli territory by groups of Palestinian *fedayeen* ('martyrs'), which developed into guerrilla movements. The principal Palestinian guerrilla organization was the Palestine National Liberation Movement, known as Al-Fatah ('Conquest'), originally based in the Gaza Strip (then under Egyptian administration). In September 1963 the creation of a unified 'Palestinian entity' was approved by the Council of the League of Arab States (the Arab League, see p. 174), despite opposition from the Jordanian Government, which regarded the proposal as a threat to Jordan's sovereignty over the West Bank. The first congress of Palestinian Arab groups was held in the Jordanian sector of Jerusalem in May–June 1964, when the participants unanimously agreed to form the Palestine Liberation Organization (PLO) as 'the only legitimate spokesman for all matters concerning the Palestinian people'. The PLO was to be financed by the Arab League and was to recruit military units, from among refugees, to constitute a Palestine Liberation Army (PLA). From the outset, King Hussein refused to allow the PLA to train forces in Jordan or the PLO to levy taxes from Palestinian refugees in his country.

Despite political upheavals in Jordan and elsewhere in the Middle East, King Hussein has vigorously maintained his personal rule and has survived attempted assassination and revolt. In April 1965 Hussein nominated his brother, Hassan ibn Talal, to be Crown Prince, so excluding the King's own children from succession to the throne.

Jordan and Israel each have a small strip of coastline on the Gulf of Aqaba, providing access to the Red Sea. In May 1967 the United Arab Republic (Egypt) barred Israeli shipping from entering the Red Sea. In retaliation, Israel launched attacks on its Arab neighbours in June 1967, quickly overcoming opposition and making substantial territorial gains. The Six-Day War, as it is known, left Israel in possession of all Jordanian territory on the West Bank. The Old City of Jerusalem was incorporated into Israel, while the remainder of the conquered area has the status of an Israeli 'administered territory'. Many refugees are still housed in camps on the East Bank. Jordan was formerly a base for several Palestinian Arab guerrilla groups, mainly forces of the PLO, which made armed raids on the administered territories. The strength of these organizations frequently constituted a challenge to the Jordanian Government and, after a civil war lasting from September 1970 to July 1971, King Hussein expelled the guerrilla groups. Since then, Hussein has not allowed guerrilla activity from Jordan, but by 1979 he was again on good terms with the PLO.

In September 1971 King Hussein announced the formation of the Jordanian National Union, to be the country's sole permitted political organization. In March 1972 it was renamed the Arab National Union (ANU), but in April 1974 Hussein dissolved its executive committee. The ANU was abolished in February 1976, and since then Jordan has had no formal political parties.

In October 1973 Egypt and Syria launched simultaneous attacks on Israeli-held territory. Units of the Jordanian army were sent to support the Syrian offensive on the Golan Heights. Aid to Jordan from Kuwait and other wealthy Arab states, which had been suspended following the Jordanian action against Palestinian commandos, was restored after the 1973 war.

During early 1974 King Hussein became increasingly estranged from the governments of other Arab states when it became clear that they considered the PLO, rather than Jordan, to be the legitimate representative of the Palestinian Arabs. At an Arab summit meeting in Rabat, Morocco, in October 1974, King Hussein acknowledged this view, and supported a unanimous resolution which gave the PLO the right to establish an independent national authority on any piece of Palestinian land to be liberated.

The summit meeting at Rabat adopted a resolution which recognized the PLO as 'the sole legitimate representative of the Palestinian people'. In November 1974, as a response to this resolution, both chambers of the Jordanian National Assembly (which had equal representation for the East and West Banks) approved constitutional amendments which empowered the King to dissolve the Assembly and to postpone elections for up to 12 months. The Assembly was dissolved later that month, although it was briefly reconvened in February 1976, when it approved a constitutional amendment which gave the King power to postpone elections indefinitely and to convene the Assembly as required. A royal decree of April 1978 provided for the creation of a National Consultative Council, with 60 members appointed for a two-year term by the King, on the Prime Minister's recommendation, to debate proposed legislation. The Council was dissolved, and the National Assembly reconvened, in January 1984 (see below).

After the Israeli invasion of Lebanon in June 1982, President Ronald Reagan of the USA proposed the creation of an autonomous Palestinian authority on the West Bank, in association with Jordan. However, following talks with Hussein, Yasser Arafat, the Chairman of the PLO, rejected the plan. Jordan subsequently gave diplomatic support to Arafat when a Syrian-backed revolt erupted in May 1983 against his leadership of Al-Fatah, the major guerrilla group within the PLO. During the last three months of the year, Jordanian diplomats in several European countries, and targets in Amman, came under attack from terrorists who were thought to be members of a radical Arab group, based in Syria, which was angered by Jordan's support for Arafat, by its demand for Egypt to be readmitted to the community of Arab states and by the possibility of a revival of the Reagan plan.

King Hussein dissolved the National Consultative Council in January 1984 and recalled the National Assembly for its first session since 1967. He thereby created the kind of Palestinian forum (60% of Jordan's population of 2.4m. are Palestinian and there are 1.3m. Palestinians living in the West Bank) which was called for in the Reagan plan, and effectively infringed the Rabat resolution of 1974, which recognized the PLO as the sole representative of the Palestinian people. Israel allowed the surviving West Bank deputies to attend the Assembly, which approved constitutional amendments enabling elections to be held in the East Bank alone, and West Bank deputies to be chosen by the Assembly itself. Also in January, the Jordanian Council of Ministers resigned, and a new one, containing a higher proportion of Palestinians, took office. King Hussein embarked on a series of talks with Yasser Arafat in January 1984. There was strong opposition to the Reagan plan among Jordanian Palestinians, while Hussein and Arafat stood by the resolution which had been adopted at the Arab summit meeting of 1974, recognizing the PLO as 'the sole legitimate representative of the Palestinian people'.

These developments revealed a split in the Arab world between a moderate body of opinion, formed by Jordan, Egypt and Arafat's wing of the PLO, on one side, and a more radical group, including Syria, Libya and the rebel wing of the PLO, on the other. In February 1984 the Jordanian Embassy in Tripoli, Libya, was burnt down during a demonstration, and Jordan responded by severing diplomatic relations with Libya. Attacks by militant Arab groups on Jordanian diplomats around the world took place throughout 1984 and during 1985.

In 1984 the US Government renewed its efforts to gain Congressional support for an 8,000-strong Jordanian strike force, equipped by the USA, which would respond to requests for military assistance from Arab governments within a 2,400-km (1,500-mile) radius of Jordan. King Hussein tried to distance Jordan from any interest or involvement in the creation of such a force. Then, in March, the planned sale to Jordan of 1,613 Stinger anti-aircraft missiles was cancelled by President Reagan, partly owing to pro-Israeli opposition to the plan in the US Congress, but also owing to King Hussein's recent harsh criticism of US policy in the Middle East. In June the Reagan administration abandoned its plans for a Jordanian strike force. Jordan consequently purchased an air defence system from the USSR in January 1985, having already made an agreement to buy French anti-aircraft missiles in September 1984.

In September 1984 Jordan re-established diplomatic relations with Egypt, which had been broken off after the Egypt-Israel peace treaty of 1979. President Mubarak of Egypt has since given his support to King Hussein's proposals for Middle East peace negotiations. Hussein rejected the Israeli offer of direct negotiations, excluding the PLO, in October, calling instead for a conference of all the concerned parties in the Middle East, including the PLO.

The Palestine National Council (PNC), which finally met in Amman in November 1984, replied non-committally to King Hussein's offer of a joint Jordanian-Palestinian peace initiative, with the UN Security Council's Resolution 242, adopted in November 1967, as the basis for negotiations. Until November 1988 the PLO refused to recognize the resolution because it made mention only of a Palestinian 'refugee problem' and not of the right of Palestinians to self-determination.

In February 1985 King Hussein and Yasser Arafat announced the terms of a joint Jordanian-Palestinian agreement, proposing a confederated state of Jordan and Palestine. Both this agreement and King Hussein's quadripartite plan, announced in May, foundered on Israel's refusal to negotiate with the PLO and Israel's rejection of proposals for an international peace conference. The US Government, meanwhile, refused to meet members of the PLO or its nominees until the PLO recognized Israel's right to exist, renounced terrorism and, in essence, accepted Resolution 242.

In July 1985 Israel independently rejected a list of seven Palestinians, five of whom were members of the PLO or had links with the PNC, whom King Hussein had presented to the USA as candidates for a joint Jordanian-Palestinian delegation to preliminary peace talks.

An extraordinary meeting of the Arab states in August 1985 (which was boycotted by Syria, Libya, Lebanon, the PDRY and Algeria) neither condemned nor endorsed the Hussein/Arafat peace initiative but reaffirmed Arab allegiance to the Fez plan of September 1982.

Further progress was hampered by a series of terrorist incidents in which the PLO was implicated. These incidents gave Israel further cause to reject the PLO as a credible partner in peace negotiations. King Hussein was under increasing pressure to advance the peace process, if necessary without the participation of the PLO. In September President Reagan revived the plan to sell military equipment, valued at $1,900m., to Jordan. The proposal was approved by Congress on the condition that Jordan enter into direct talks with Israel before 1 March 1986. However, a *rapprochement* developed between Jordan and Syria. Among other differences, Jordan supported Iraq in the Iran-Iraq War, while Syria supported Iran. Nevertheless, both countries support a Middle East peace settlement through an international conference, and at talks in Riyadh in October 1985 they rejected 'partial and unilateral' solutions and affirmed their adherence to the Fez plan omitting any mention of the Jordanian-Palestinian initiative. Through a reconciliation with Syria, which is opposed to Yasser Arafat's leadership of the PLO, King Hussein may have hoped to exert pressure on Arafat to take the initiative in the peace process and signal PLO acceptance of Resolution 242.

It was rumoured that King Hussein and the Israeli Prime Minister, Shimon Peres, were meeting in secret, and in October 1985 a document outlining possible peace proposals was unofficially disclosed to the Israeli press. The document suggested the establishment of an interim Israeli-Jordanian condominium in the West Bank, granting a form of Palestinian autonomy, and recorded mutual agreement on the desirability of an international forum for peace talks, with Israel consenting to the participation of the USSR (provided that it re-established diplomatic relations with Israel) and Syria but not of the PLO, on whose involvement King Hussein still insisted.

The Jordanian Prime Minister, Ahmad Ubeidat, resigned in April 1985. A new Cabinet was sworn in under the premiership of Zaid ar-Rifai, who had been Prime Minister from 1973-6.

Frustrated by the lack of co-operation from Yasser Arafat in advancing the aims of the Jordanian-PLO peace initiative,

King Hussein publicly severed political links with the PLO on 19 February 1986. In January, according to King Hussein, the USA had undertaken to invite the PLO to an international peace conference (whereas, before, it had agreed only to consider talks with the PLO) if it would officially acknowledge UN Security Council Resolutions 242 and 338 as the basis for negotiations. Arafat refused to make such a commitment without prior acknowledgement by the USA of the Palestinian right to self-determination.

Following King Hussein's announcement, Arafat was ordered to close his main PLO offices in Jordan by 1 April 1986. The activities of the PLO were henceforth to be restricted to an even greater extent than before, and a number of Fatah officers loyal to Arafat were expelled. King Hussein urged the PLO either to change its policies or its leadership. In July Jordan closed all 25 Fatah offices in Amman, so that only 12 belonging to the PLO remained.

Since the termination of political co-ordination with the PLO, Jordan has continued to reject Israeli requests for direct peace talks which exclude a form of PLO representation. However, Jordan's subsequent efforts to strengthen its influence in the Israeli-occupied territories and to foster a Palestinian constituency there, independent of Arafat's PLO, coincided with Israeli measures to grant a limited autonomy to the Palestinian community in the West Bank (for example, by appointing Arab mayors in four towns in place of Israeli military governors). In March 1986 the Jordanian House of Representatives approved a draft law increasing the number of seats in the House from 60 to 142 (71 seats each for the East and West Banks), thereby providing for greater representation for West Bank Palestinians in the National Assembly. Then, in August, with Israeli support, a five-year development plan for the West Bank and the Gaza Strip, involving projected expenditure of US $1,300m., was announced in Amman. The plan was condemned by Yasser Arafat and West Bank Palestinians as representing a normalization of relations with Israel. There is considerable support for Arafat among Palestinians in the Occupied Territories and in Jordan, and this was consolidated when he re-established himself at the head of a reunified PLO at the 18th session of the Palestine National Council in April 1987 (when the Jordan-PLO accord of 1985 was formally abrogated).

In May 1987, following several secret meetings with King Hussein, Shimon Peres (who was now the Israeli Minister of Foreign Affairs) claimed to have made significant progress on the crucial issue of Palestinian representation at a Middle East peace conference, and to have the consent of Egypt, Jordan and the USA to convene an international conference, including the five permanent members of the UN Security Council and a delegation of Palestinians who 'reject terrorism and violence' and accept Security Council Resolutions 242 and 338 as the basis for negotiations. The Jordanian Prime Minister, Zaid ar-Rifai, confirmed Jordan's willingness to participate in a conference in a joint Jordanian-Palestinian delegation, including the PLO, provided that it complied with the stated conditions. King Hussein appeared to have accepted that a conference would have no power to impose a peace settlement and would be only a preliminary to direct negotiations between the main protagonists. However, Peres failed to secure the support of a majority of the Israeli Cabinet for his proposals. The Israeli Prime Minister, Itzhak Shamir, was opposed in principle to an international peace conference and reiterated his alternative proposal of direct regional talks, excluding the PLO.

During 1987 King Hussein pursued his efforts, begun in 1986, to reconcile Syria and Iraq, with the wider aim of securing Arab unity. He was instrumental in arranging the first full 'summit' meeting of the Arab League for eight years, which took place in Amman in November, principally to discuss the Iran-Iraq War. In September Jordan had restored diplomatic relations with Libya, which had modified its support for Iran in the war and urged a cease-fire. The Arab 'summit' unanimously adopted a resolution of solidarity with Iraq, which condemned Iran for its occupation of Arab territory and for prolonging the war with Iraq. King Hussein's appeal for Egypt to be restored to membership of the League was successfully resisted by Syria and Libya, but nine Arab states re-established diplomatic relations with Egypt soon after the 'summit', and these were followed by Tunisia in January 1988 and by the People's Democratic Republic of Yemen in February. President Saddam Hussain of Iraq and President Assad of Syria held two sessions of talks at the summit, and the resumption of co-operation between Jordan and the PLO was announced.

In December 1987 a violent Palestinian uprising (*intifada*) began in the West Bank and the Gaza Strip, in protest against the continuing Israeli occupation of those territories. Security measures were increased in Jordan to prevent pro-Palestinian demonstrations. In April 1988, however, Black September, a Palestinian terrorist group, claimed responsibility for a series of bomb attacks in Amman.

In February 1988 the intensity of the *intifada*, which Israel was unable to suppress, and world-wide condemnation of Israeli tactics prompted renewed peace initiatives, led by George Shultz, the US Secretary of State. The Shultz Plan envisaged the convening of an international peace conference involving all parties in the Arab–Israeli conflict and the five permanent members of the UN Security Council, with the Palestinians being represented by a joint Jordanian-Palestinian delegation containing no representatives of the PLO. However, the exclusion of the PLO, as well as the plan's failure to consider the Palestinians' right to self-determination and to the establishment of an independent Palestinian state in the West Bank, made it unacceptable to the Arab nations.

In June 1988, at an extraordinary 'summit' meeting of the Arab League, King Hussein gave his unconditional support to the *intifada* and disclaimed any ambition to restore Jordanian rule in the West Bank. He also insisted that the PLO must represent the Palestinians at any future peace conference and repeatedly stressed the PLO's status as 'the sole legitimate representative of the Palestinian people'. The 'summit' rejected the Shultz Plan and gave support to the *intifada* and the Palestinians, insisting on PLO participation in any future peace negotiations.

The *intifada* increased international support for the PLO and Palestinian national rights, as well as heightening Palestinian aspirations to statehood. Jordan could no longer present itself as a viable alternative to the PLO. At the end of July 1988, King Hussein cancelled the West Bank development plan, announced in 1986, and severed Jordan's legal and administrative links with the region, in accordance with the agreements reached at the recent Arab League 'summit' meeting, whereby he was to transfer administrative responsibility for the West Bank to the PLO. However, the abruptness of his actions aroused Palestinian opposition, which King Hussein attempted to suppress, especially by means of press censorship. Jordan's disengagement from the West bank effectively rendered the Shultz Plan redundant.

In August 1988 there was a limited cabinet reshuffle, in which the Ministry of Occupied Territories Affairs was downgraded to the status of an independent department attached to the Ministry of Foreign Affairs, to be known as the Palestinian Affairs Department. King Hussein also dissolved the lower house of the National Assembly, the House of Representatives, where one-half of the seats were held by representatives of the West Bank, and in October postponed legislative elections, pending the revision of electoral laws.

On 15 November 1988 the PLO proclaimed the establishment of an independent state of Palestine and, for the first time, endorsed the UN Security Council's Resolution 242 as a basis for a Middle East peace settlement, thus implicitly recognizing Israel. Jordan and 60 other countries recognized the new state. In December Yasser Arafat addressed a special session of the UN General Assembly in Geneva, where he renounced violence on behalf of the PLO. Subsequently, the USA opened a dialogue with the PLO, and it appeared that Israel would have to negotiate directly with the PLO if it wished to seek a solution to the Palestinian question, and that Jordan's future participation in the peace process was likely to be of less significance.

In December 1988 King Hussein again reshuffled his Cabinet. Marwan al-Qassim became Minister of Foreign Affairs, replacing Taher al-Masri, who had been the principal opponent of King Hussein's decision to withdraw from the West Bank and also of the severe economic measures that the Prime Minister, Zaid ar-Rifai, had introduced.

In April 1989 rioting occurred in several cities in southern Jordan, spreading to areas near the capital, after the Government had imposed price rises of between 15% and 50% on basic goods and services. The gravity of the situation was emphasized by reports that only Bedouin and native Jordanians, from whom the Government traditionally draws most support, participated in the riots, while the Palestinians, who form an estimated 60% of the country's population, were uninvolved; and by the early return to Jordan of King Hussein, who had been making an official visit to the USA, and who had been due, subsequently, to visit Europe. The riots led to the resignation of the Prime Minister and (automatically under Jordanian law) that of his Cabinet. On 24 April Field Marshal Sharif Zaid ibn Shakar, who had been Commander-in-Chief of the Jordanian Armed Forces between 1976 and 1988, was appointed Prime Minister, at the head of a new 24-member Cabinet. While King Hussein refused to make any concessions regarding the price increases which had provoked the disturbances (and which had been implemented in accordance with an agreement with the IMF), he announced, immediately prior to the appointment of the new Prime Minister, that a general election would be held for the first time since 1967.

The election to the 80-seat House of Representatives took place on 8 November 1989 and was contested by 647 candidates, most of whom were independent, as the ban on political parties (in force since 1963) had not been withdrawn. However, it was possible for the Muslim Brotherhood (MB) to present candidates for election, owing to its legal status as a charity rather than a political party. At the election, in which 63% of the total electorate (including, for the first time, women) of 877,475 voted, the MB won 20 seats, while it was estimated that a further 12–14 seats were won by independent Islamic candidates who supported the MB. It was estimated that Palestinian or Arab nationalist candidates won seven seats and that candidates who were supporters of 'leftist' political groupings won four seats. The remaining seats were won by candidates who were broadly considered to be supporters of the Government. The strength of support for the opposition candidates was regarded as surprising, both in Jordan and abroad, especially since a disproportionately large number of seats had been assigned to rural areas from which the Government has traditionally drawn most support.

On 4 December 1989 Mudar Badran was appointed Prime Minister by King Hussein. Badran had served as Prime Minister twice previously, during 1976–79 and 1980–84. Badran's new Cabinet was appointed, and approved by royal decree, on 6 December 1989. The new Government did not include any members of the MB who had been elected to the House of Representatives, the MB having declined participation after its demand for the education portfolio had been rejected. Included in the new Cabinet, however, were three independent Muslim deputies and three 'leftists', all of whom were regarded as members of the opposition. A further four deputies appointed to the Cabinet were described as independent nationalists close to the State, while a further six had held office in the previous Cabinet under Field Marshal Sharif Zaid ibn Shakar.

The new Government received a vote of confidence from the House of Representatives on 1 January 1990. During the debate which preceded the vote, the Prime Minister pledged the abolition of martial law (which had been suspended on 19 December 1989) within four to six months, and to liberalize the judicial system. The Prime Minister affirmed continuing support for prevailing austerity measures, and at the end of January announced the abolition of the 1954 anti-communism law.

In November 1989 King Hussein had announced his intention of appointing a royal commission to draft a national charter which would legalize political parties. In April 1990 the King named the 60-member commission, to convene under the chairmanship of a former Prime Minister, Ahmad Ubeidat. The national charter which the commission drafted was approved by the King in January 1991, but the onset of the Gulf War in mid-January 1991 delayed its ratification by the National Assembly.

In early January 1991 King Hussein reshuffled the Cabinet to include five members of the MB, one of whom received the sensitive portfolio of Minister of Education. The MB had been excluded from the Cabinet formed in December 1989, but pressure for its inclusion in government became so great in the following 12 months that appeals for MB representation could no longer be ignored. The reshuffle also included the appointment of Taher al-Masri as Minister of Foreign Affairs, a post that he had held between 1984 and 1988.

Jordan was deeply affected by Iraq's invasion of Kuwait on 2 August 1990, and the consequent imposition of economic sanctions against Iraq, which UN Security Council Resolution 661 of 6 August demanded. Iraq was Jordan's principal trading partner, and Jordan relied on supplies of Iraqi petroleum. Although King Hussein condemned Iraq's invasion of Kuwait, he was slow to do so, and hoped for an 'Arab solution' to the problem. There was considerable support for Saddam Hussain among the Jordanian population, particularly among the Palestinians. King Hussein was therefore critical of the large deployment of multinational military forces in Saudi Arabia and the Gulf region, which he regarded as US-dominated, and throughout the closing months of 1990 he visited numerous Middle Eastern and other capitals in an attempt to avert a war which could be potentially disastrous for Jordan.

In the early stages of the Gulf crisis Jordan experienced the additional problem of a large-scale influx of Arabs and Asians from Iraq and Kuwait. Many of these evacuees travelled to the desert border between Iraq and Jordan, where they were temporarily accommodated in makeshift transit camps with inadequate shelter and very limited facilities. A large number of these migrants were seeking passage through Jordan in an attempt to return to the Indian sub-continent and South-East Asia. According to Jordanian officials, about 470,000 foreigners fled to Jordan in the five weeks following the Iraqi invasion of Kuwait on 2 August 1990. Many of these, particularly non-Arab Asians, remained stranded in overcrowded camps on the Iraqi-Jordanian border, suffering severe privations (including shortages of food, water and medical supplies), while awaiting repatriation. Conditions improved in early September, as new camps were established and chartered aircraft carried some of the refugees to their countries of origin. However, the exodus of evacuees to the border region continued daily, and in September Jordan issued an urgent appeal for international assistance with the costs of accommodating and repatriating them. By late September the number of refugees remaining had been reduced to 30,000.

In addition to foreign arrivals, Jordan received large numbers of its own nationals fleeing from the Gulf region. By mid-November 1990 about 180,000 of the 450,000 Jordanians previously in Kuwait, many of Palestinian origin, had returned to Jordan. The exiled rulers of Kuwait regarded most of the Jordanian and Palestinian residents of the emirate as collaborators with the Iraqi occuantion forces there.

Meanwhile, Jordan's attitude to the Gulf crisis led to a deterioration in the country's traditionally friendly relations with Egypt and Saudi Arabia, which both contributed forces to the anti-Iraq coalition. It was reported that about 50,000 Egyptian workers were deported from Jordan between June and September 1990. Saudi Arabia halted supplies of petroleum to Jordan, and expelled Jordanian diplomats, in September. However, Jordan re-established diplomatic relations with Iran, severed in 1981, and the Jordanian embassy in Teheran was reopened in February 1991.

When Iraq ignored the UN Security Council's ultimatum to withdraw from Kuwait by 15 January 1991, and the multinational forces launched bombing attacks against Iraq on the following day, King Hussein viewed the situation with alarm and sadness. With the onset of the Gulf War, another exodus of refugees from Iraq and Kuwait into Jordan began. Relief officials in Jordan established camps to accommodate more than 50,000 fugitives from the war zone. There were frequent public demonstrations of support for Iraq and hostility to its opponents. As the bombing of Iraq continued, King Hussein's concern grew deeper, and on 6 February, in a televised address to his compatriots, he sharply criticized the coalition for waging a war which was, he claimed, aimed at Iraq's total destruction, and he urged the two sides to agree to a cease-fire. This apparent shift from a position of neutrality to an openly pro-Iraqi stance provoked a response from the USA, in which the Department of State reported that it was reviewing the level of US military and economic assistance to Jordan ($85.6m. in 1990). A series of air attacks by the anti-Iraq forces on the road between Baghdad and Amman resulted in the destruction of more than 30 Jordanian goods vehicles (mainly tanker-trucks carrying oil), and the deaths of nine civilian lorry-drivers, by mid-February. The UN Secretary-General condemned this bombing as 'inadmissible'.

Iraq's conditional offer to withdraw its forces from Kuwait, announced in mid-February 1991, was welcomed by the Jordanian Government. The plan was unacceptable to the coalition because, as with previous Iraqi proposals, it envisaged linkage with other Middle Eastern issues, including the Palestinian problem. After a subsequent Soviet plan for a settlement, excluding reference to the Palestinian dispute, had been endorsed by Iraq, King Hussein agreed to abandon the linkage, which he had advocated hitherto, between the Gulf crisis and wider Middle Eastern issues. When the anti-Iraq forces launched a ground offensive on 24 February to liberate Kuwait, the Jordanian Government condemned the action and again appealed for a cease-fire. Following the successful onslaught against Iraqi forces in Kuwait and the cessation of hostilities on 28 February, Jordan remained economically crippled and politically ostracized by the main powers among Western and Arab countries. In the immediate post-war period the country's prospects appeared to depend heavily on a resolution of the bitter divisions within the Arab world.

Government

Jordan is a constitutional monarchy. Legislative power is vested in a bicameral National Assembly. The Senate (House of Notables) has 30 members, appointed by the King for eight years (one-half of the members retiring every four years), while the House of Representatives (House of Deputies) has 80 members, elected by universal adult suffrage for four years. Executive power is vested in the King, who governs with the assistance of an appointed Council of Ministers, responsible to the Assembly.

There are eight administrative provinces, of which three have been occupied by Israel since June 1967.

Defence

The total strength of the Jordanian armed forces in June 1990 was 84,250. The army had 74,000 men, the air force 10,000 and the navy (coastguard) 250. Reserves number 35,000 (30,000 in the army). There are paramilitary forces of more than 32,000 men: a Civil Militia of more than 15,000 and a Public Security Force of 17,000. Military service is voluntary. The estimated defence budget in 1990 was JD254.8m.

Economic Affairs

In 1989, according to estimates by the World Bank, the East Bank of Jordan's gross national product (GNP), measured at average 1987–89 prices, was US $5,291m., equivalent to $1,730 per head. During 1980–89, it was estimated, the region's GNP increased, in real terms, at an average annual rate of 0.6%, although GNP per head declined by 3.0%. Over the same period, Jordan's population increased by an annual average of 3.7%. The country's gross domestic product (GDP) increased, in real terms, by an annual average of 4.2% in 1980–88.

Agriculture (including forestry and fishing) contributed 7.7% of the East Bank region's GDP in 1987. An estimated 6.2% of the region's labour force were employed in the sector in 1989. The principal cash crops are vegetables, fruit and nuts, which accounted for about 8% of export earnings in 1987. Wheat production is also important. During 1980–88 agricultural production increased by an annual average of 4.6%, but in 1989 it declined by 13%.

Industry (including mining, manufacturing, construction and power) provided 28.6% of the East Bank's GDP in 1987. During 1980–88 industrial production increased by an annual average of 3.6%.

Mining contributed 4.0% of the East Bank's GDP in 1987, but engaged only 1.5% of the total employed labour force in 1979. Phosphates and potash are the major mineral exports. Together they accounted for 38.5% of total export earnings in 1988 and 35.3% in 1989. Jordan also has reserves of oil-bearing shale, but exploitation of this resource is at present undeveloped.

Manufacturing provided 15.3% of the East Bank's GDP in 1987, and engaged 8% of the total employed labour force in 1979. In 1987 the most important branches of manufacturing in the region, measured by the value of output, were petroleum refineries (accounting for 29.5% of the total), chemical products (13.5%), non-metallic mineral products (11.9%), metals and metal products (10.1%) and food products (9.7%).

Energy is derived principally from imported petroleum, but attempts are being made to develop alternative sources of power, including wind and solar power. Imports of mineral fuels comprised 17% of the total value of imports in 1987.

Services (including wholesale and retail trade, restaurants and hotels, transport, financing and community, social and personal services) accounted for 63.7% of the East Bank's GDP in 1987. In 1979 some 63% of the total employed labour force were engaged in the service sector.

In 1989 Jordan recorded a visible trade deficit of US $773.1m., but there was a surplus of $384.9m. on the current account of the balance of payments, caused by the effect of devaluation of the Jordanian dinar in stimulating exports and restraining imports, and increases in foreign aid and earnings from tourism. In 1989 the principal source of imports was Iraq, which was also the principal market for exports. Other major trading partners were the Federal Republic of Germany, Saudi Arabia, India and the USA. The principal exports in 1987 were chemicals and phosphates, and the principal imports were machinery and transport equipment, basic manufactures, mineral fuels and lubricants and food and live animals.

The budget proposals for 1991 projected a deficit of 351.9m. Jordanian dinars (almost twice that of the 1990 budget), but all financial planning was undermined by the Gulf crisis which began in August 1990 and developed into the Gulf War (see Recent History) in January 1991. The annual rate of inflation averaged 4.1% in 1980–88, but increased to 25.7% in 1989. The rate declined to less than 13% in the year ending September 1990. Jordan's external public debt at the end of 1988 was US $3,955m. The cost of debt-servicing in that year was equivalent to 31.9% of exports of goods and services. An estimated 8% of the labour force were unemployed in 1986. The level of unemployment would have been augmented by Jordanians returning from Kuwait in late 1990 (see below).

Jordan is a member of the Arab League (see p. 174), the Arab Co-operation Council (p. 222), the Arab Monetary Fund (p. 98), the Council of Arab Economic Unity (p. 127) and the Organization of the Islamic Conference (p. 198).

Jordan's economic future is inextricably linked to the eventual outcome of the Gulf War between Iraq and the multi-national fgorces, and also to a general settlement of the Palestinian problem. Even before the crisis caused by Iraq's occupation of Kuwait in August 1990, the Jordanian economy was suffering from a decline in remittances from Jordanians working abroad, and its foreign debt had become unmanageably large. The imposition of sanctions against Iraq, demanded by UN Security Council Resolution 661, had an extremely adverse effect on the Jordanian economy. In mid-1990 Iraq was Jordan's principal trading partner, taking at least 23% of Jordan's exports and supplying more than half of Jordan's petroleum imports (at a price below the free market level), mostly as repayment for a debt. In mid-September Saudi Arabia, dissatisfied with Jordan's stance on the Gulf crisis, refused to continue supplying petroleum to Jordan, although supplies from Iraq, in reduced amounts, continued to arrive, in defiance of the UN sanctions. The outbreak of war in January 1991 interrupted even these supplies, as bombing by the multinational forces disrupted road communications between Iraq and Jordan. At the end of January the Government introduced stringent rationing of fuel, but in mid-February Syria and Yemen agreed to sell crude petroleum and refined products to Jordan, to compensate for the loss of Iraqi supplies. Later in February the UN Children's Fund (UNICEF) issued an appeal for humanitarian aid for Jordan, owing to the damaging effects of the Gulf War. As a 'front line' state in the Gulf crisis, Jordan had received about US $1,000m. in aid from the European Community, Germany and Japan. A UNICEF report estimated that, as a result of the crisis, the unemployment rate in Jordan had risen to 30%, with the influx of returning migrant workers from the Gulf region compounding the loss of local jobs resulting from economic disruption. It has been calculated that the annual cost of the crisis to Jordan, as a result of reductions in earnings from trade and tourism, was about $1,500m. in 1990, expected to rise to $3,600m. in 1991. The consequent increase in poverty and malnutrition seems certain to cause severe hardship in the country.

Social Welfare

There is no comprehensive welfare scheme but the Government administers medical and health services. In 1985 the East Bank region had 44 hospital establishments, with 3,578 beds, and 2,576 physicians. A new Social Security Law, providing security for both employers and employees, was put into effect in 1978 and extended in 1981. Of total expenditure by the central Government in 1987, JD 42.5m. (5.5%) was for health services, and a further JD 66.3m. (8.5%) for social security and welfare. In June 1989 there were 899,811 refugees registered with UNRWA in Jordan and a further 398,391 in the West Bank.

JORDAN

Education

Primary education is free and, where possible, compulsory. It starts at the age of five years and eight months and lasts for six years. A further three-year period, known as the preparatory cycle, is also compulsory. The preparatory cycle is followed by the three-year secondary cycle. UNRWA provides schooling for Palestinian Arab refugees. In 1987 there were 1,387 primary schools, with 19,133 teachers and 570,795 pupils. At the secondary level in 1987, there were 21,729 teachers and 357,475 pupils. In 1988 there were 2,658 teachers and 65,979 pupils engaged in higher education. There are nine universities in Jordan. Expenditure on education by the central Government in 1987 was JD 102.2m. (13.2% of total spending).

Public Holidays

1991: 15 January (Arbor Day), 12 February (Leilat al-Meiraj, ascension of Muhammad), 22 March (Arab League Day), 16 April (Id al-Fitr, end of Ramadan), 25 May (Independence Day), 23 June (Id al-Adha, feast of the Sacrifice), 13 July (Islamic New Year), 11 August (King Hussein's Accession), 21 September (Mouloud, birth of Muhammad), 14 November (King Hussein's Birthday).

1992: 15 January (Arbor Day), 1 February (Leilat al-Meiraj, ascension of Muhammad), 22 March (Arab League Day), 4 April (Id al-Fitr, end of Ramadan), 25 May (Independence Day), 11 June (Id al-Adha, feast of the Sacrifice), 2 July (Islamic New Year), 11 August (King Hussein's Accession), 10 September (Mouloud, birth of Muhammad), 14 November (King Hussein's Birthday).

Weights and Measures

The metric system is in force. In Jordan the dunum is 1,000 sq m (0.247 acre).

Statistical Survey

Source: Department of Statistics, Jabal Amman, 1st Circle, POB 2015, Amman; tel. 24313.

Area and Population

AREA, POPULATION AND DENSITY (East and West Banks)

Area (sq km)	97,740*
Population (UN estimates at mid-year)†	
1987	3,790,000
1988	3,943,000
1989	4,102,000
Density (per sq km) at mid-1989	42.0

* 37,738 sq miles.
† Source: UN, *World Population Prospects: 1988*.

East Bank: Area 89,206 sq km; population 2,100,019 (males 1,086,591; females 1,013,428) at census of 10–11 November 1979; estimated population 2,796,100 at 31 December 1986.

GOVERNORATES
(East Bank only; estimated population at 31 December 1986)

Amman	1,160,000
Irbid	680,200
Zarqa	404,500
Balqa	193,800
Karak	120,100
Mafraq	98,600
Ma'an	97,500
Tafiela	41,400
Total	2,796,100

PRINCIPAL TOWNS (including suburbs)
Population in December 1986: Amman (capital) 972,000; Zarqa 392,220; Irbid 271,000; Salt 134,100.

BIRTHS, MARRIAGES AND DEATHS (East Bank only)*

	Live Births	Marriages	Deaths
1982	97,974	17,488	7,741
1983	98,398	17,055	7,860
1984	102,521	18,189	8,303
1985	102,712	20,152	8,731
1986	112,451	19,397	8,853
1987	107,519	23,208	8,591

* Data are tabulated by year of registration rather than by year of occurrence. Registration of births and marriages is reported to be complete, but death registration is incomplete. Figures exclude foreigners, but include registered Palestinian refugees.

ECONOMICALLY ACTIVE POPULATION (Jordanians only)

	1984	1985	1986
Agriculture	34,850	36,833	37,436
Mining and manufacturing	47,414	49,869	52,706
Electricity and water	4,585	5,195	5,418
Construction	52,733	51,947	54,183
Trade	46,487	47,225	49,258
Transport and communications	41,178	44,391	46,302
Financial and insurance services	14,444	16,104	16,748
Social and administrative services	216,848	220,635	230,525
Total employed	458,539	472,199	492,576
Unemployed	n.a.	n.a.	42,864
Total civilian labour force	n.a.	n.a.	535,440

JORDAN   Statistical Survey

Agriculture

PRINCIPAL CROPS (East Bank only; '000 metric tons)

	1987	1988	1989
Barley	33	45	15
Wheat	80	79	50
Pumpkins, squash and gourds	34	31	30*
Oranges	42†	36†	40*
Tangerines, mandarins, clementines and satsumas	31†	27†	30*
Lemons and limes	38†	33†	35*
Grapefruit and pomelo	7†	6†	6*
Bananas	13	33	15*
Grapes	19	22	22*
Olives	20	71	30*
Tomatoes	237	219	220*
Eggplants (Aubergines)	57	73	65*
Cauliflowers	20	19	20*
Cabbages	14	14	14*
Watermelons	63	67	67*
Melons	29	20	21*
Potatoes	62	48	50*
Green beans	9	14	12*
Cucumbers and gherkins	67	67	68*

* FAO estimates.   † Unofficial figures.
Source: FAO, *Production Yearbook*.

LIVESTOCK
(East Bank only; '000 head, year ending September)

	1987	1988	1989*
Horses	3	4	3
Mules	3	3*	3
Asses	19	19	19
Cattle	29	30	29
Camels	14	18	15
Sheep	1,219	1,279	1,255
Goats	460	510	500
Poultry	59,000	60,000*	60,000

* FAO estimates.
Source: FAO, *Production Yearbook*.

Forestry

ROUNDWOOD REMOVALS (FAO estimates, '000 cubic metres)

	1982	1983	1984
Industrial wood	4	4	4
Fuel wood	3	3	4
Total	7	7	8

1985–88: Annual output as in 1984 (FAO estimates).
Source: FAO, *Yearbook of Forest Products*.

Fishing

(metric tons, live weight)

	1986	1987	1988
Total catch	65	70	70

Source: FAO, *Yearbook of Fishery Statistics*.

Mining and Industry

(East Bank only; '000 metric tons, unless otherwise indicated)

	1985	1986	1987
Phosphates	6,067.1	6,249.2	6,845.4
Potash	908.2	1,102.0	1,203.2
Salt	32.2	33.7	n.a.
Petroleum products	2,423.9	2,257.1	2,404.5
Chemical acids	1,007.6	1,024.8	1,103.2
Fertilizers	510.5	551.1	604.0
Cement	2,022.9	1,794.7	2,371.6
Iron	198.4	209.6	217.0
Alcoholic drinks ('000 litres)	5,547.2	5,457.2	5,320.0
Cigarettes (million)	3,538.1	3,327.7	4,000.4
Electricity (million kWh)	2,154.4	2,646.8	3,123.8

1985: Crude petroleum 1,882 metric tons.

Finance

CURRENCY AND EXCHANGE RATES

Monetary Units
1,000 fils = 1 Jordanian dinar (JD).

Denominations
Coins: 1, 5, 10, 20, 25, 50, 100 and 250 fils.
Notes: 500 fils; 1, 5, 10 and 20 dinars.

Sterling and Dollar Equivalents (30 September 1990)
£1 sterling = JD 1.2328;
US $1 = 658.0 fils;
JD 100 = £81.12 = $151.98.

Average Exchange Rates (US $ per JD)
1987 2.9522
1988 2.6916
1989 1.7532

Note: Since 1975 the value of the Jordanian dinar has been linked to the IMF's special drawing right, with a mid-point exchange rate of JD 1 = SDR 2.579. Since October 1988, however, this link has been only nominal, and the exchange rate has been adjusted in relation to the US dollar.

BUDGET ESTIMATES (East Bank only; JD million)

Revenue	1990	1991
Local revenues (taxes, etc)	746.1	702.5
Grants and loans	162.6	150.0
Unused loans	30.0	50.0
Total	**938.7**	**902.5**

Expenditure	1990	1991
Capital and development expenditure	188.3	230.0
Recurrent expenditure	845.4	889.2
Loan repayments	87.4	135.2
Total	**1,121.1**	**1,254.4**

Source: *Middle East Economic Digest*.

CENTRAL BANK RESERVES (US $ million at 31 December)

	1987	1988	1989
Gold*	200.1	138.3	102.5
IMF special drawing rights	12.1	0.1	11.0
Foreign exchange	412.6	109.5	459.7
Total	**624.8**	**247.9**	**573.2**

* National valuation.
Source: IMF, *International Financial Statistics*.

JORDAN

MONEY SUPPLY (JD million at 31 December)

	1987	1988	1989
Currency outside banks	655.78	811.16	871.13
Demand deposits at commercial banks	322.81	353.71	425.38

Source: IMF, *International Financial Statistics*.

COST OF LIVING (Consumer Price Index; base: 1980 = 100)

	1987	1988	1989
Food	121.0	127.6	154.2
Fuel and light	122.3	122.5	126.0
Clothing	129.9	135.3	222.0
Rent	132.9	133.0	133.8
All items (incl. others)	129.8	138.4	174.0

Source: ILO, *Year Book of Labour Statistics*.

NATIONAL ACCOUNTS
(JD million at current prices)
Expenditure on the Gross Domestic Product

	1987	1988	1989
Government final consumption expenditure	566.3	575.7	549.9
Private final consumption expenditure	1,531.7	1,699.9	2,014.1
Increase in stocks	61.7	415.0	465.0
Gross fixed capital formation	411.8		
Total domestic expenditure	2,571.5	2,690.6	3,029.0
Exports of goods and services	753.5	912.5	1,350.5
Less Imports of goods and services	1,251.8	1,413.6	1,822.9
GDP in purchasers' values	2,073.2	2,189.5	2,556.6
GDP at constant 1985 prices	2,128.7	2,083.0	2,001.2

Source: IMF, *International Financial Statistics*.

Gross Domestic Product by Economic Activity
(East Bank only)

	1985	1986	1987
Agriculture, hunting, forestry and fishing	104.7	104.4	123.2
Mining and quarrying	53.2	55.9	64.4
Manufacturing	224.1	215.6	246.9
Electricity, gas and water	43.7	51.2	48.1
Construction	122.7	125.9	101.3
Trade, restaurants and hotels	285.4	271.1	269.8
Transport, storage and communications	170.0	173.9	188.6
Finance, insurance, real estate and business services	161.1	167.1	173.8
Government services	262.5	294.7	308.8
Other community, social and personal services	46.5	48.4	53.0
Non-profit private services	28.8	30.0	31.0
Sub-total	1,502.6	1,538.2	1,608.9
Import duties	133.5	128.2	117.2
Less Imputed bank service charge	33.7	35.0	39.8
GDP in purchasers' values	1,602.4	1,631.4	1,686.3

Source: UN, *National Accounts Statistics*.

BALANCE OF PAYMENTS (US $ million)

	1987	1988	1989
Merchandise exports f.o.b.	933.1	1,007.4	1,109.4
Merchandise imports	−2,400.1	−2,418.7	−1,882.5
Trade balance	−1,467.0	−1,411.3	−773.1
Exports of services	1,350.0	1,461.3	1,278.2
Imports of services	−1,576.9	−1,695.2	−1,298.9
Balance on goods and services	−1,693.9	−1,645.2	−793.8
Private unrequited transfers (net)	742.9	799.8	565.4
Government unrequited transfers (net)	599.1	551.7	613.2
Current balance	−351.8	−293.7	384.9
Direct capital investment (net)	38.3	23.8	−18.1
Other long-term capital (net)	188.2	13.4	202.6
Short-term capital (net)	238.7	337.0	−105.0
Net errors and omissions	27.9	123.4	0.3
Total (net monetary movements)	141.3	203.9	464.7
Monetization of gold (net)	−12.5	0.2	0.7
Valuation changes (net)	120.1	−165.1	−81.3
Changes in reserves	248.9	39.0	384.1

Source: IMF, *International Financial Statistics*.

External Trade

PRINCIPAL COMMODITIES (JD '000)

Imports	1985	1986	1987
Food and live animals	175,784	165,568	155,719
Beverages and tobacco	4,036	6,672	7,999
Crude materials (inedible) except fuels	33,070	28,646	28,528
Mineral fuels, lubricants, etc.	223,270	116,480	156,138
Crude petroleum	192,640	92,832	118,590
Animal and vegetable oils and fats	10,152	9,417	8,018
Chemicals	67,639	74,865	91,671
Basic manufactures	169,597	140,947	169,391
Machinery and transport equipment	207,385	176,604	186,290
Miscellaneous manufactured articles	105,165	79,863	87,734
Other commodities and transactions	78,347	51,137	24,057
Total	1,074,445	850,199	915,545

Total imports (JD million): 1,020.0 in 1988; 1,214.2 in 1989.

Exports	1985	1986	1987
Phosphates	66,084	64,805	61,002
Potash	30,887	31,396	28,003
Chemicals	50,959	54,455	69,932
Cement	7,132	3,975	10,482
Vegetables, fruit and nuts	24,086	21,852	20,010
Cigarettes	1,716	1,297	3,017
Basic manufactures	32,586	15,647	26,861
Machinery and transport equipment	2,104	1,408	2,464
Miscellaneous manufactured articles	18,513	7,320	9,877
Total (incl. others)	255,346	225,615	248,773

Total exports (JD million): 381.5 (of which phosphates and potash 146.9) in 1988; 637.6 (of which phosphates and potash 224.9) in 1989.

JORDAN

Statistical Survey

PRINCIPAL TRADING PARTNERS (JD '000)

Imports	1985	1986	1987
Belgium	21,621	24,356	22,819
China, People's Republic	13,582	11,243	14,363
France	33,938	33,175	34,222
Germany, Fed. Republic	65,638	65,114	70,504
Italy	73,427	50,220	46,647
Iraq	72,951	80,274	99,401
Japan	67,813	66,642	55,664
Korea Republic	8,170	10,293	13,818
Kuwait	2,892	2,404	16,966
Netherlands	26,006	27,383	27,907
Romania	14,667	14,672	21,191
Saudi Arabia	159,058	49,670	76,761
Spain	15,926	11,692	11,251
Switzerland	58,889	11,173	10,068
Taiwan	20,856	18,040	16,794
Turkey	28,583	27,467	35,021
United Kingdom	63,276	68,786	58,303
USA	128,045	75,529	93,389

Exports	1985	1986	1987
China, People's Republic	2,278	7,570	10,044
Egypt	3,033	3,979	13,448
France	5,252	7,070	5,187
India	45,310	34,126	22,034
Indonesia	9,081	7,606	7,993
Iraq	65,850	42,458	59,865
Italy	3,655	7,099	9,266
Japan	5,815	5,690	7,435
Kuwait	7,738	8,813	8,614
Pakistan	5,941	3,456	10,253
Poland	3,287	3,721	7,068
Romania	10,015	7,524	6,418
Saudi Arabia	39,083	27,817	26,204
Syria	3,901	4,570	7,201
United Arab Emirates	805	845	4,861
Yugoslavia	3,069	7,689	6,923

Transport

RAILWAYS (traffic; East Bank only)

	1984	1985	1986
Passengers carried	30,196	34,247	31,304
Freight carried (tons)	3,152,663	2,582,702	2,789,524

ROAD TRAFFIC (motor vehicles registered, East Bank only)

	1984	1985	1986
Cars (private)	118,497	121,502	126,540
Taxis	12,439	12,699	13,208
Buses	3,346	3,513	3,783
Motorcycles	6,377	6,439	6,503
Others*	70,998	77,301	82,327
Total	211,657	221,454	232,361

* Trucks, vans, tankers, agricultural, construction and government vehicles.

SHIPPING (East Bank only; Aqaba port)

	1986	1987	1989*
Number of vessels calling	2,677	2,555	2,446
Freight loaded ('000 tons)	9,696.5	11,271.6	9,986.0
Freight unloaded ('000 tons)	7,153.2	8,743.8	8,695.0

* 1988 figures are unavailable.

CIVIL AVIATION (traffic; East Bank only)

	1984	1985	1986
Passengers (number)	1,346,800	1,290,300	1,132,000
Freight (tons)	37,879	43,095	43,301

Tourism

ARRIVALS OF VISITORS (East Bank only)

	1984	1985	1986
Arabs	1,254,895	1,549,885	1,622,212
Europeans	102,351	108,443	88,805
Asians	133,467	132,795	112,803
Americans	65,215	54,677	31,139
Others	32,267	44,107	57,079
Total	1,588,195	1,889,907	1,912,038

Communications Media

(East Bank only)

	1984	1985	1986
Telephones in use	113,666	147,873	177,894

Radio receivers (1988): 940,000 in use.
Television receivers (1988): 275,000 in use.

Education

(East Bank, 1988)

	Teachers	Pupils
Pre-primary	1,595	37,910
Primary*	19,133	570,795
Secondary: general*	19,265	323,942
Vocational	2,029	29,235
Universities	1,553	34,994
Other higher	1,105	30,985

* 1987 figures.

Source: UNESCO, *Statistical Yearbook*.

Directory

The Constitution

The revised Constitution was approved by King Talal I on 1 January 1952.

The Hashemite Kingdom of Jordan is an independent, indivisible sovereign state. Its official religion is Islam; its official language Arabic.

RIGHTS OF THE INDIVIDUAL

There is to be no discrimination between Jordanians on account of race, religion or language. Work, education and equal opportunities shall be afforded to all as far as is possible. The freedom of the individual is guaranteed, as are his dwelling and property. No Jordanian shall be exiled. Labour shall be made compulsory only in a national emergency, or as a result of a conviction; conditions, hours worked and allowances are under the protection of the State.

The Press, and all opinions, are free, except under martial law. Societies can be formed, within the law. Schools may be established freely, but they must follow a recognized curriculum and educational policy. Elementary education is free and compulsory. All religions are tolerated. Every Jordanian is eligible for public office, and choices are to be made by merit only. Power belongs to the people.

THE LEGISLATIVE POWER

Legislative power is vested in the National Assembly and the King. The National Assembly consists of two houses: the Senate and the House of Representatives.

THE SENATE

The number of Senators is one-half of the number of members of the House of Representatives. Senators must be unrelated to the King, over 40, and are chosen from present and past Prime Ministers and Ministers, past Ambassadors or Ministers Plenipotentiary, past Presidents of the House of Representatives, past Presidents and members of the Court of Cassation and of the Civil and Shari'a Courts of Appeal, retired officers of the rank of General and above, former members of the House of Representatives who have been elected twice to that House, etc. . . . They may not hold public office. Senators are appointed for four years. They may be reappointed. The President of the Senate is appointed for two years.

THE HOUSE OF REPRESENTATIVES

The members of the House of Representatives are elected by secret ballot in a general direct election and retain their mandate for four years. General elections take place during the four months preceding the end of the term. The President of the House is elected by secret ballot each year by the Representatives. Representatives must be Jordanians of over 30, they must have a clean record, no active business interests, and are debarred from public office. Close relatives of the King are not eligible. If the House of Representatives is dissolved, the new House shall assemble in extraordinary session not more than four months after the date of dissolution. The new House cannot be dissolved for the same reason as the last.

GENERAL PROVISIONS FOR THE NATIONAL ASSEMBLY

The King summons the National Assembly to its ordinary session on 1 November each year. This date can be postponed by the King for two months, or he can dissolve the Assembly before the end of its three months' session. Alternatively, he can extend the session up to a total period of six months. Each session is opened by a speech from the throne.

Decisions in the House of Representatives and the Senate are made by a majority vote. The quorum is two-thirds of the total number of members in each House. When the voting concerns the Constitution, or confidence in the Council of Ministers, 'the votes shall be taken by calling the members by name in a loud voice'. Sessions are public, though secret sessions can be held at the request of the Government or of five members. Complete freedom of speech, within the rules of either House, is allowed.

The Prime Minister places proposals before the House of Representatives; if accepted there, they are referred to the Senate and finally sent to the King for confirmation. If one house rejects a law while the other accepts it, a joint session of the House of Representatives and the Senate is called, and a decision made by a two-thirds majority. If the King withholds his approval from a law, he returns it to the Assembly within six months with the reasons for his dissent; a joint session of the Houses then makes a decision, and if the law is accepted by this decision it is promulgated. The Budget is submitted to the National Assembly one month before the beginning of the financial year.

THE KING

The throne of the Hashemite Kingdom devolves by male descent in the dynasty of King Abdullah Ibn al Hussein. The King attains his majority on his eighteenth lunar year; if the throne is inherited by a minor, the powers of the King are exercised by a Regent or a Council of Regency. If the King, through illness or absence, cannot perform his duties, his powers are given to a Deputy, or to a Council of the Throne. This Deputy, or Council, may be appointed by Iradas (decrees) by the King, or, if he is incapable, by the Council of Ministers.

On his accession, the King takes the oath to respect and observe the provisions of the Constitution and to be loyal to the nation. As head of the State he is immune from all liability or responsibility. He approves laws and promulgates them. He declares war, concludes peace and signs treaties; treaties, however, must be approved by the National Assembly. The King is Commander-in-Chief of the Navy, the Army and the Air Force. He orders the holding of elections; convenes, inaugurates, adjourns and prorogues the House of Representatives. The Prime Minister is appointed by him, as are the President and members of the Senate. Military and civil ranks are also granted, or withdrawn, by the King. No death sentence is carried out until he has confirmed it.

MINISTERS

The Council of Ministers consists of the Prime Minister, President of the Council, and of his Ministers. Ministers are forbidden to become members of any company, to receive a salary from any company, or to participate in any financial act of trade. The Council of Ministers is entrusted with the conduct of all affairs of State, internal and external.

The Council of Ministers is responsible to the House of Representatives for matters of general policy. Ministers may speak in either House, and, if they are members of one House, they may also vote in that House. Votes of confidence in the Council are cast in the House of Representatives, and decided by a two-thirds majority. If a vote of 'no confidence' is returned, the Ministers are bound to resign. Every newly-formed Council of Ministers must present its programme to the House of Representatives and ask for a vote of confidence. The House of Representatives can impeach Ministers, as it impeaches its own members.

AMENDMENTS

Two amendments were passed in November 1974 giving the King the right to dissolve the Senate or to take away membership from any of its members, and to postpone general elections for a period not to exceed a year, if there are circumstances in which the Council of Ministers feels that it is impossible to hold elections. A further amendment in February 1976 enabled the King to postpone elections indefinitely. In January 1984 two amendments were passed, allowing elections 'in any part of the country where it is possible to hold them' (effectively, only the East Bank) and empowering the National Assembly to elect deputies from the Israeli-held West Bank.

The Government

HEAD OF STATE

King HUSSEIN IBN TALAL (proclaimed King on 11 August 1952; crowned on 2 May 1953).

CABINET
(March 1991)

Prime Minister and Minister of Defence: MUDAR BADRAN.

Deputy Prime Minister and Minister of the Interior: SALEM MASADEH.

Minister of Foreign Affairs: TAHER AL-MASRI.

Minister of Finance and Customs: BASIL JARDANEH.

Minister of Culture and Youth: KHALED KARAKI.

Minister of Justice: MAJED KHALEIFAH.

JORDAN — Directory

Minister of Agriculture: MUHAMMAD ALAWNEH.
Minister of Water and Irrigation: SAAD HAYEL AS-SROUR.
Minister of Energy and Mineral Resources: THABET AT-TAHER.
Minister of Awqaf (Religious Endowments) and Islamic Affairs: IBRAHIM ZAID KEILANI.
Minister of Trade and Industry: ZIAD FARIS.
Minister of Supply: IBRAHIM AYYOUB.
Minister of Transport and Communications: JAMAL SARAIREH.
Minister of Information: IBRAHIM IZZIEDDIN.
Minister of Health: ADNAN JALJOULI.
Minister of Social Development: YOUSEF ATHEM.
Minister of Public Works and Housing: ABD AR-RAOUF AR-RAWABDEH.
Minister of Labour: ABDEL-KARIM AL-DUGHMI.
Minister of Education: ABDULLAH AKAILEH.
Minister of Planning: KHALED AMIN ABDULLAH.
Minister of Higher Education: SAAD AT-TAL.
Minister of Tourism and Antiquities: DAOUD KHALAF.
Minister of Municipal, Rural and Environmental Affairs: MUHAMMAD AZ-ZABEN.
Minister of State for Parliamentary Affairs: ABD AL-BAQI GAMMO.
Chief of the Royal Court: Field Marshal Sharif ZAID IBN SHAKAR.

MINISTRIES

Office of the Prime Minister: POB 80, 35216, Amman; tel. 641211; telex 21444.
Ministry of Agriculture: POB 2099, Amman; tel. 639391; telex 24176.
Ministry of Awqaf (Religious Endowments) and Islamic Affairs: POB 659, Amman; tel. 666141; telex 21559.
Ministry of Communications: POB 71, Amman; tel. 624301; telex 21666.
Ministry of Defence: POB 1577, Amman; tel. 644361; telex 21200.
Ministry of Education: POB 1646, Amman; tel. 669181; telex 21396.
Ministry of Finance: POB 85, Amman; tel. 636321; telex 23634; fax 643132.
Ministry of Foreign Affairs: POB 1577, Amman; tel. 644361; telex 21255.
Ministry of Health: POB 86, Amman; tel. 665131; telex 21595.
Ministry of Information: POB 1794, Amman; tel. 661147; telex 21749.
Ministry of the Interior: POB 100, Amman; tel. 663111; telex 23162.
Ministry of Justice: POB 6040, Amman; tel. 663101.
Ministry of Labour: POB 9052, Amman; tel. 630343.
Ministry of Municipal, Rural and Environmental Affairs: POB 1799, Amman; tel. 641393.
Ministry of Public Works and Housing: POB 1220, Amman; tel. 668481; telex 21944.
Ministry of Social Development: POB 6720, Amman; tel. 643838.
Ministry of Supply: POB 830, Amman; tel. 630371; telex 21278.
Ministry of Tourism: POB 224, Amman; tel. 642311; telex 21741.
Ministry of Trade and Industry: POB 2019, Amman; tel. 663191; telex 21163.
Ministry of Transport: POB 1929, 35214 Amman; tel. 641461; telex 21541.

Legislature

MAJLIS AL-UMMA
(National Assembly)

Senate

The Senate (House of Notables) consists of 30 members, appointed by the King. A new Senate was appointed by the King on 12 January 1984.
President: AHMAD AL-LOUZI.

House of Representatives

Elections to the then 60-seat House of Representatives (30 from both the East and West Banks) took place in April 1967. There were no political parties. The House was dissolved by Royal Decree on 23 November 1974, but reconvened briefly on 15 February 1976. Elections were postponed indefinitely.

In April 1978 a National Consultative Council was formed by Royal Decree. It consisted of 60 members appointed by the King, and served terms of two years. The third term began on 20 April 1982. The King, by his constitutional right, dissolved the Council on 7 January 1984 and reconvened the House of Representatives. Eight members from the East Bank had died since the House was last convened and by-elections to fill their seats took place on 12 March 1984. The seven vacant seats of members from the Israeli-occupied West Bank, where elections could not take place, were filled by a vote of the members of the House in accordance with a constitutional amendment unanimously approved on 9 January 1984.

In March 1986 the House of Representatives approved a draft electoral law providing for the number of seats in the House to be increased from 60 to 142 (71 from the East Bank and 71 from the West Bank, including 11 from the refugee camps in the East Bank) at the next election. In October 1987, while opening a new session of the National Assembly, King Hussein announced that elections to the House of Representatives were to be postponed for two years. On 30 July 1988 King Hussein dissolved the House of Representatives, (one-half of whose 60 seats were held by deputies for the West Bank) and on 31 July he severed Jordan's legal and administrative links with the West Bank. (Theoretically, the Senate cannot legislate without the House of Representatives.) Legislative elections were postponed in October 1988, pending a revision of the 1986 electoral laws.

Electoral laws, announced in April 1989, propounded plans for a new, 72-seat House of Representatives. The increase in the number of seats was to take into account expansion in the major population centres of Amman, Zarqa and Irbid. A further eight seats were subsequently allocated to the governorates of Amman, Zarqa and Balqa, bringing the total to 80. A general election to the new House took place in November 1989.
Speaker: ABD AL-LATIF ARABIYAT.

Political Organizations

Political parties were banned before the elections of July 1963. In September 1971 King Hussein announced the formation of a Jordanian National Union. This was the only political organization allowed. Communists, Marxists and 'other advocates of imported ideologies' were ineligible for membership. In March 1972 the organization was renamed the Arab National Union. In April 1974 King Hussein dissolved the executive committee of the Arab National Union, and accepted the resignation of the Secretary-General. In February 1976 the Cabinet approved a law abolishing the Union. Membership was estimated at about 100,000. A royal commission was appointed in April 1990 to draft a National Charter, one feature of which was the legalization of political parties. In January 1991 King Hussein approved the National Charter, but it has yet to be ratified by the National Assembly.

Diplomatic Representation

EMBASSIES IN JORDAN

Algeria: 3rd Circle, Jabal Amman; tel. 641271; Ambassador: ABDERRAHMAN SHRAYYET.
Australia: POB 35201, 4th Circle, Jabal Amman; tel. 678246; telex 21743; fax 673260; Ambassador: G. R. BOWKER.
Austria: POB 815368, Amman; tel. 644635; telex 22484; Ambassador: Dr FRANZ PERNEGGER.
Bahrain: Amman; tel. 664148; Ambassador: IBRAHIM ALI IBRAHIM.
Belgium: Amman; tel. 675683; telex 22340; fax 697487; Ambassador: JOHAN BALLEGEER.
Brazil: POB 5497, Amman; tel. 642183; telex 23827; Ambassador: FÉLIX BAPTISTA DE FARIA.
Bulgaria: POB 950578, Um Uzaina al-Janoubi, Amman; tel. 818151; telex 22247; Ambassador: YANTCHO DEMIREV.
Canada: POB 815403, Pearl of Shmeisani Bldg, Shmeisani, Amman; tel. 666124; telex 23080; fax 689227; Ambassador: MICHAEL D. BELL.
Chile: 73 Suez St, Abdoun, Amman; tel. 814263; telex 21696; Ambassador: NELSON HADAD-HERESIM.
China, People's Republic: Shmeisani, Amman; tel. 666139; telex 21770; Ambassador: ZHANG DELIANG.
Czechoslovakia: POB 2213, Amman; tel. 665105; Ambassador: KAREL FISER.
Egypt: POB 35178, Zahran St, 3rd Circle, Jabal Amman; tel. 641375; Ambassador: IHAB SEID WAHBA.

JORDAN
Directory

France: POB 374, Jabal Amman; tel. 641273; telex 21219; Ambassador: PATRICK LECLERCQ.
Germany: 31 Benghazi St, POB 183, Jabal Amman; tel. 689351; telex 21235; fax 685887; Ambassador: Dr HERWIG BARTELS.
Greece: POB 35069, Jabal Amman; tel. 672331; telex 21566; Ambassador: HANNIBAL VELLIADIS.
Hungary: POB 3441, Amman; tel. 674916; telex 21815; Ambassador: Dr EGYED ANDOR.
India: POB 2168, 1st Circle, Jabal Amman; tel. 637262; telex 21068; fax 659540; Ambassador: K. GAJENDRA SINGH.
Iran: POB 173, Jabal Amman; tel. 641281 telex 21218.
Iraq: POB 2025, 1st Circle, Jabal Amman; tel. 639331; telex 21277; Ambassador: NORI AL-WAYES.
Italy: POB 9800, Jabal Luweibdeh, Amman; tel. 638185; telex 21143; fax 659730; Ambassador: FRANCESCO DE COURTEN.
Japan: POB 2835, Jabal Amman; tel. 672486; telex 21518; Ambassador: AKIRA NAKAYAMA.
Korea, Democratic People's Republic: Amman; tel. 666349; Chargé d'affaires: KIM YONG HO.
Korea, Republic: 3rd Circle, Jabal Amman, Abu Tamman St, POB 3060, Amman; tel. 660745; telex 21457; Ambassador: TAE JIN PARK.
Kuwait: POB 2107, Jabal Amman; tel. 641235; telex 21377; Ambassador: SULEIMAN SALEM AL-FASSAM.
Lebanon: 2nd Circle, Jabal Amman; tel. 641381; Ambassador: PIERRE ZIADÉ.
Morocco: Jabal Amman; tel. 641451; telex 21661; Chargé d'affaires: SALEM FANKHAR ASH-SHANFARI.
Oman: Amman; tel. 661131; telex 21550; Ambassador: KHAMIS BIN HAMAD AL-BATASHI.
Pakistan: Amman; tel. 622787; Ambassador: Prof. EHSAN RASHID.
Philippines: POB 925207, Abbas Aqad St, 2nd Circle, Jabal, Amman; tel. 645161; telex 23321; Ambassador: JUAN V. SAEZ.
Poland: POB 2124, 1st Circle, Jabal Amman; tel. 637153; telex 21119; Ambassador: LUDWIK JANCZYSZYN.
Qatar: Amman; tel. 644331; telex 21248; Ambassador: Sheikh HAMAD BIN MUHAMMAD BIN JABER ATH-THANI.
Romania: Amman; tel. 663161; Ambassador: TEODOR COMAN.
Saudi Arabia: POB 2133, 5th Circle, Jabal Amman; tel. 644154; Ambassador: Sheikh IBRAHIM MUHAMMAD AS-SULTAN.
Spain: Jabal Amman; tel. 622140; telex 21224; Ambassador: RAMÓN ARMENGOD.
Sudan: Jabal Amman; tel. 624145; telex 21778; Ambassador: AHMAD DIAB.
Sweden: 4th Circle, POB 830536, Jabal Amman; tel. 669177; telex 22039; fax 669179; Ambassador: LARS LÖNNBACK.
Switzerland: Jabal Amman; tel. 644416; telex 21237; Ambassador: HARALD BORNER.
Syria: POB 1377, 4th Circle, Jabal Amman; tel. 641935; Chargé d'affaires: MAJID ABOU SALEH.
Tunisia: Jabal Amman; tel. 674307; telex 21849; Ambassador: MONGI LAHBIB.
Turkey: POB 2062, Islamic College St, 2nd Circle, Jabal Amman; tel. 641251; telex 23005; fax 612353; Ambassador: OKTAY AKSOY.
USSR: Amman; tel. 641158; Ambassador: ALEKSANDR IVANOVICH ZINCHUK.
United Arab Emirates: Jabal Amman; tel. 644369; telex 21832; Ambassador: ABDULLAH ALI ASH-SHURAFA.
United Kingdom: POB 87, Abdoun, Amman; tel. 823100; telex 22209; Ambassador: ANTHONY REEVE.
USA: POB 354, Jabal Amman; tel. 644371; telex 21510; Ambassador: ROSCOE S. SUDDARTH.
Yemen: Amman; tel. 642381; telex 23526; Ambassador: ALI ABDULLAH ABU LUHOUM.
Yugoslavia: POB 5227, Amman; tel. 665107; telex 21505; Ambassador: ZORAN S. POPOVIĆ.

Judicial System

With the exception of matters of purely personal nature concerning members of non-Muslim communities, the law of Jordan was based on Islamic Law for both civil and criminal matters. During the days of the Ottoman Empire, certain aspects of Continental law, especially French commercial law and civil and criminal procedure, were introduced. Due to British occupation of Palestine and Transjordan from 1917 to 1948, the Palestine territory has adopted, either by statute or case law, much of the English common law. Since the annexation of the non-occupied part of Palestine and the formation of the Hashemite Kingdom of Jordan, there has been a continuous effort to unify the law.

Court of Cassation. The Court of Cassation consists of seven judges, who sit in full panel for exceptionally important cases. In most appeals, however, only five members sit to hear the case. All cases involving amounts of more than JD100 may be reviewed by this Court, as well as cases involving lesser amounts and cases which cannot be monetarily valued. However, for the latter types of cases, review is available only by leave of the Court of Appeal, or, upon refusal by the Court of Appeal, by leave of the President of the Court of Cassation. In addition to these functions as final and Supreme Court of Appeal, the Court of Cassation also sits as High Court of Justice to hear applications in the nature of habeas corpus, mandamus and certiorari dealing with complaints of a citizen against abuse of governmental authority.

Courts of Appeal. There are two Courts of Appeal, each of which is composed of three judges, whether for hearing of appeals or for dealing with Magistrates Courts' judgments in chambers. Jurisdiction of the two Courts is geographical, with the Court for the Western Region sitting in Jerusalem (which has not sat since June 1967) and the Court for the Eastern Region sitting in Amman. The regions are separated by the River Jordan. Appellate review of the Courts of Appeal extends to judgments rendered in the Courts of First Instance, the Magistrates' Courts, and Religious Courts.

Courts of First Instance. The Courts of First Instance are courts of general jurisdiction in all matters civil and criminal except those specifically allocated to the Magistrates' Courts. Three judges sit in all felony trials, while only two judges sit for misdemeanour and civil cases. Each of the seven Courts of First Instance also exercises appellate jurisdiction in cases involving judgments of less than JD20 and fines of less than JD10, rendered by the Magistrates' Courts.

Magistrates' Courts. There are 14 Magistrates' Courts, which exercise jurisdiction in civil cases involving no more than JD250 and in criminal cases involving maximum fines of JD100 or maximum imprisonment of one year.

Religious Courts. There are two types of religious court: The Shari'a Courts (Muslims): and the Ecclesiastical Courts (Eastern Orthodox, Greek Melkite, Roman Catholic and Protestant). Jurisdiction extends to personal (family) matters, such as marriage, divorce, alimony, inheritance, guardianship, wills, interdiction and, for the Muslim community, the constitution of Waqfs (Religious Endowments). When a dispute involves persons of different religious communities, the Civil Courts have jurisdiction in the matter unless the parties agree to submit to the jurisdiction of one or the other of the Religious Courts involved.

Each Shari'a (Muslim) Court consists of one judge (Qadi), while most of the Ecclesiastical (Christian) Courts are normally composed of three judges, who are usually clerics. Shari'a Courts apply the doctrines of Islamic Law, based on the Koran and the Hadith (Precepts of Muhammad), while the Ecclesiastical Courts base their law on various aspects of Canon Law. In the event of conflict between any two Religious Courts or between a Religious Court and a Civil Court, a Special Tribunal of three judges is appointed by the President of the Court of Cassation, to decide which court shall have jurisdiction. Upon the advice of experts on the law of the various communities, this Special Tribunal decides on the venue for the case at hand.

Religion

Over 80% of the population are Sunni Muslims, and the King can trace unbroken descent from the Prophet Muhammad. There is a Christian minority, living mainly in the towns, and there are smaller numbers of non-Sunni Muslims.

ISLAM

Chief Justice and President of the Supreme Muslim Secular Council: Sheikh MUHAMMAD MHELAN.

Director of Shari'a Courts: Sheikh SUBHI AL-MUWQQAT.

Mufti of the Hashemite Kingdom of Jordan: Sheikh MUHAMMAD ABDO HASHEM.

CHRISTIANITY
The Roman Catholic Church

Latin Rite

Jordan forms part of the Patriarchate of Jerusalem (see chapter on Israel).

Vicar-General for Transjordan: Mgr SELIM SAYEGH (Titular Bishop of Aquae in Proconsulari), Latin Vicariate, POB 1317, Amman.

JORDAN — Directory

Melkite Rite

The Greek-Melkite archdiocese of Petra (Wadi Musa), Philadelphia (Amman) and all Transjordan contained an estimated 20,000 adherents at 31 December 1989.

Archbishop of Petra, Philadelphia and all Transjordan: Most Rev. SABA YOUAKIM, Archevêché Grec-Melkite Catholique, POB 2435, Jabal Amman; tel. 624757.

Syrian Rite

The Syrian Catholic Patriarch of Antioch is resident in Beirut, Lebanon.

Patriarchal Vicariate of Jerusalem: Mont Achrafieh, Rue Barto, POB 10041, Amman; Vicar Patriarchal Mgr PIERRE ABD AL-AHAD.

The Anglican Communion

Within the Episcopal Church in Jerusalem and the Middle East, Jordan forms part of the diocese of Jerusalem. The Presiding Bishop of the Church is the Bishop in Jerusalem (see the chapter on Israel).

Assistant Bishop in Amman: Rt Rev. ELIA KHOURY, POB 598, Amman.

Other Christian Churches

The Coptic Orthodox Church, the Greek Orthodox Church (Patriarchate of Jerusalem) and the Evangelical Lutheran Church in Jordan are also active.

The Press

Jordan Press Association: Amman; Pres. RAKAN AL-MAJALI.

DAILIES

Al-Akhbar (News): POB 62420, Amman; f. 1976; Arabic; publ. by the Arab Press Co; Editor RACAN EL-MAJALI; circ. 15,000.

Ad-Dustour (The Constitution): POB 591, Amman; tel. 664153; telex 21392; f. 1967; Arabic; publ. by the Jordan Press and Publishing Co; owns commercial printing facilities; Chair. KAMEL ASH-SHERIF; Editor-in-Chief and Dir-Gen. MAHMOUD ASH-SHERIF; circ. 90,000.

Ar-Rai (Opinion): POB 6710, Amman; tel. 667171; telex 21497; f. 1971; Arabic; independent; published by Jordan Press Establishment; Chair. Dr KHALIL AL-SALEM; Gen. Dir Dr RADI WAQFI; Editor-in-Chief RAKAN AL-MAJALI; circ. 80,000.

The Jordan Times: POB 6710, Amman; tel. 661242; telex 21497; f. 1975; English; published by Jordan Press Establishment; Responsible Editor RAKAN MAJALI; Editor-in-Chief RAMI G. KHOURI; circ. 15,000.

Sawt ash-Shaab (Voice of the People): Amman; f. 1983; Arabic; circ. 30,000.

PERIODICALS

Akhbar al-Usbou (News of the Week): POB 605, Amman; tel. 677881; telex 21644; fax 677882; f. 1959; weekly; Arabic; economic, social, political; Chief Editor and Publr ABD AL-HAFIZ MUHAMMAD; circ. 100,000.

Al-Aqsa (The Ultimate): POB 1957, Amman; weekly; Arabic; armed forces magazines.

Al-Fajr al-Iqtisadi (Economic Dawn): Amman; f. 1982; weekly; economic; owned by Al-Fajr for Press, Publication and Distribution; Dir-Gen. and Editor-in-Chief YOUSUF ABU-LAIL.

Al-Ghad al-Iqtisadi: Media Services International, POB 9313, Amman; tel. and fax 648298; telex 21392; monthly; Arabic; economic; Chief Editor SAIF ASH-SHARIF.

Huda El-Islam (The Right Way of Islam): POB 659, Amman; tel. 666141; telex 21559; f. 1956; monthly; Arabic; scientific and literary; published by the Ministry of Awqaf and Islamic Affairs; Editor Dr AHMAD MUHAMMAD HULAYYEL.

Jordan: POB 224, Amman; telex 21497; f. 1969; published quarterly by Jordan Information Bureau, Washington; circ. 100,000.

Al-Liwa' (The Standard): Amman; f. 1972; weekly; Arabic; Chief Editor HASSAN ATTEL.

Military Magazine: Army Headquarters, Amman; f. 1955; quarterly; dealing with military and literary subjects; published by Armed Forces.

As-Sabah (The Morning): POB 2396, Amman; weekly; Arabic; circ. 6,000.

Shari'a: POB 585, Amman; f. 1959; fortnightly; Islamic affairs; published by Shari'a College; circ. 5,000.

Shehan: Al-Karak; Editor REYAD AL-HROUB.

The Star: Media Services International, POB 9313 Amman; tel. and fax 648298; telex 21392; f. 1982, formerly The Jerusalem Star; weekly; English; Publr and Editor-in-Chief OSAMA ASH-SHERIF; circ. 10,000.

NEWS AGENCIES

Jordan News Agency (PETRA): POB 6845, Amman; tel. 644455; telex 21220; f. 1965; government-controlled; Dir-Gen. ALI SAFADI.

Foreign News Bureaux

Agence France-Presse (AFP): POB 3340, Amman; tel. 642976; telex 21469; fax 654680; Bureau Man. Mrs RANDA HABIB.

Agenzia Nazionale Stampa Associata (ANSA) (Italy): POB 35111, Amman; tel. 642936; telex 21207; Correspondent JOHN HALABI.

Associated Press (AP) (USA): POB 35111, Amman; tel. 644097; telex 23514; Correspondent JOHN RICE.

Deutsche Presse Agentur (dpa) (Germany): POB 35111, Amman; tel. 623907; telex 21207; Correspondent JOHN HALABI.

Reuters (UK): POB 667, Amman; tel. 623776; telex 21414.

Telegrafnoye Agentstvo Sovetskovo Soyuza (TASS) (USSR): Jabal Amman, Nabich Faris St, Block 111/83 124, Amman; Correspondent NIKOLAI LEBEDINSKY.

Central News Agency (Taiwan), Iraqi News Agency, Middle East News Agency (Egypt), Qatar News Agency, Saudi Press Agency and UPI (USA) also maintain bureaux in Amman.

Publishers

Jordan Press and Publishing Co Ltd: Amman; tel. 664153; telex 21392; f. 1967 by *Al-Manar* and *Falastin* dailies; publishes *Ad-Dustour* (daily), and *The Star* (English weekly); Chair. KAMEL ASH-SHARIF; Dir-Gen and Editor-in-Chief MAHMOUD ASH-SHERIF.

Jordan Press Establishment: POB 6710, Amman; tel. 667171; telex 21497; fax 661242; publishes *Ar-Rai* (daily) and the *Jordan Times* (daily); Chair. MAHMOUD KHAYED; Gen. Dir MOHAMAD AMAD.

Other publishers in Amman include: Dairat al-Ihsaat al-Amman, George N. Kawar, Al-Matbaat al-Hashmiya and The National Press.

Radio and Television

In 1988 there were an estimated 940,000 radio receivers and 275,000 television receivers in use (East Bank only).

Jordan Radio and Television Corporation (JRTV): POB 909, Amman; tel. 773111; telex 23544; f. 1968; government TV station broadcasts for 90 hours weekly in Arabic and English; in colour; advertising accepted; Dir-Gen. RADI ALKHAS; Dir of TV MUHAMMAD AMIN; Dir of Radio I. SHAHZADH.

Finance

(cap. = capital; p.u. = paid up; dep. = deposits; m. = million; res = reserves; brs = branches; JD = Jordanian dinars)

BANKING

Central Bank

Central Bank of Jordan: POB 37, King Hussein St, Amman; tel. 630301; telex 21250; fax 638889; f. 1964; cap. p.u. JD6m., dep. JD577.2m., res JD12m., total assets JD1,625.0m. (Dec. 1989); 2 brs; Gov. MUHAMMAD SAID NABULSI.

National Banks

Arab Bank PLC: POB 950545, Shmeisani, Amman; tel. 660131; telex 23091; fax 606793; f. 1930; cap. p.u. JD22m., dep. JD5,917m., res JD230.5m., total assets JD7,560m. (Dec. 1989); 48 brs in Jordan, 46 brs abroad; Chair. ABD AL-MAJID SHOMAN.

Bank of Jordan Ltd: POB 2140, 3rd Circle, Jabal Amman; tel. 644327; telex 22033; fax 656642; f. 1960; cap. p.u. JD5.25m., dep. JD124m., total assets JD159.6m. (Dec. 1989); 29 brs; Chair. TAWFIK SHAKER FAKHOURI; Gen. Man. FAYEZ ABUL ENEIN.

Cairo Amman Bank: POB 715, Shabsough St, Amman; tel. 639321; telex 21240; fax 639328; f. 1960; cap. p.u. JD5m., dep. JD167.4m., res JD11.8m., total assets JD246.9m. (Dec. 1988); associated with Banque du Caire, Cairo, which has a 12% share in the bank, and succeeded their Amman Branch; remaining 88% is owned by local interests; 19 brs; Chair. and Gen. Man. JAWDAT SHASHA'A.

JORDAN

Jordan-Gulf Bank SA: POB 9989, Shmeisani, al-Burj Area, Amman; tel. 603931; telex 21959; fax 664110; f. 1977; cap. p.u. JD6m., dep. JD126.5m., total assets JD167.6m. (Dec. 1988); 60% Jordanian-owned and 40% by Gulf businessmen; 22 brs; Chair. of Management Cttee WALID ASFOUR.

Jordan Islamic Bank for Finance and Investment: POB 926225, Amman; tel. 677377; telex 21125; fax 666326; f. 1978; dep. JD215.7m., cap. and res JD12.1m., total assets JD253.9m. (Dec. 1989); 18 brs; Chair. Sheikh SALEH A. KAMEL; Gen. Man. MUSA A. SHIHADEH.

Jordan Kuwait Bank: POB 9776, Amman; tel. 68814; telex 21994; fax 687452; f. 1976; cap. p.u. JD5m., dep. JD143m. (Dec. 1989); 15 brs; Chair. Sheikh HAMAD A. AS-SABAH; Deputy Chair. and Gen. Man. SUFIAN IBRAHIM YASSIN SARTAWI.

Jordan National Bank SA: POB 1578, Amman; tel. 642391; telex 21820; fax 628809; f. 1955; cap. p.u. JD9.0m., dep. JD195m., res JD13m., total assets JD248m. (1990); 30 brs in Jordan, 4 brs in Lebanon, 1 br in Cyprus; Chair. ABD AL-KADER TASH; Deputy Chair. YOUSUF I. MOU'ASHER.

Syrian Jordanian Bank: POB 926636, King Hussein St, Amman; tel. 661138; telex 22102; fax 661484; f. 1979; cap. p.u. JD1m., dep. 5.7m., total assets JD9.1m. (1989); 1 br; Chair. Management Cttee MUHAMMAD SALEH AL-HORANI; Gen. Man. HISHAM J. SAFADI.

Foreign Banks

ANZ Grindlays Bank: POB 9997, Shmeisani, Amman; tel. 660301; telex 21980; fax 679115; cap. p.u. JD5m., dep. JD80m. (Dec. 1989); brs in Amman (8 brs), Aqaba, Irbid (2 brs), Zerka, Northern Shouneh and Kerak; Gen. Man. in Jordan ALAN JOHN COOPER.

Arab Banking Corporation (Jordan): POB 926691, Amman; tel. 664183; telex 22258; fax 686291; f. 1990; cap. p.u. JD10m., dep. JD21.8m., total assets JD41.1m. (June 1990); Arab Banking Corpn, Bahrain, holds 60% share; Chair. MUHAMMAD AL-MERAIKHU; Vice-Chair. and Gen. Man. JAWAD HADID.

Arab Land Bank (Egypt): POB 6729, Amir Muhammad St, Amman; tel. 628357; telex 21208; wholly-owned subsidiary of the Central Bank of Egypt; cap. JD5m., dep. JD45.7m., res JD2.4m., total assets JD63.7m. (Dec. 1989); 3 brs in Amman; Chair. ABD AR-RAHMAN AN-NADI; Gen. Man. ALA MUHAMMAD ELOUSSIA.

Bank of Credit and Commerce International SA (Luxembourg): POB 7943, King Hussein St, Amman; tel. 621367; telex 21455; 3 brs; Gen. Man. ABRAR HUSSAIN ZAIDI.

The British Bank of the Middle East (Hong Kong): POB 922376, Amman; tel. 660471; telex 21253; f. 1889; cap. p.u. JD5m., dep. JD69m., total assets JD90m. (Dec. 1988); 5 brs; Chair. W. PURVES; Area Man. D. M. TAIT.

Citibank NA (USA): Jordan Insurance Bldg, 3rd Circle, Jabal Amman; tel. 644065; telex 21314; Gen. Man. GHADA DEBBAS.

Rafidain Bank (Iraq): POB 1194, Amman; tel. 624365; telex 21334; f. 1941; cap. p.u. JD3m., res JD548,263, dep. JD10.2m. (Dec. 1983); 4 brs; Gen. Man. ADNAN AL-AZAWI.

Bank Al-Mashrek (Lebanon) also has a branch in Amman.

Specialized Credit Institutions

Agricultural Credit Corporation: POB 77, Amman; tel. 661105; f. 1959; cap. p.u. JD8.7m., dep. JD182,992, res JD3.5m., total assets JD29.5m. (Dec. 1986); 18 brs; Chair. and Man. Dir Dr SAMI SUNA'A.

The Arab Jordan Investment Bank: POB 8797, Amman; tel. 664126; telex 21719; fax 681482; f. 1978; cap. p.u. JD5m., dep. JD151.6m., res JD6.4m., total assets JD184.6m. (Dec. 1989); 2 brs; Chair. and Gen. Man. ABD AL-KADER AL-QADI.

Cities and Villages Development Bank: POB 1572, Amman; tel. 668151; telex 22476; f. 1979; cap. p.u. JD11.5m., gen. res JD6.6m., total assets JD49.4m. (Dec. 1986); Gen. Man. MUHAMMAD SALEH HOURANI.

Housing Bank: Parliament St, Abdali, POB 7693, Amman; tel. 667126; telex 23460; fax 678121; f. 1973; cap. p.u. JD12m., dep. JD507.9m., total assets JD631.6m. (Dec. 1989); 100 brs; Chair. and Dir-Gen. ZUHAIR KHOURI.

Industrial Development Bank: POB 1982, Jabal Amman, Schools of the Islamic College St, Amman; tel. 642216; telex 21349; fax 647821; f. 1965; cap. p.u. JD6m., total assets JD74.6m. (Dec. 1989); Chair. ROUHI EL-KHATIB; Gen. Man. TAHER KANAAN.

Jordan Co-operative Organization: POB 1343, Amman; tel. 665171; telex 21835; f. 1968; cap. p.u. JD1m., dep. JD9.4m., res JD1,038m. (Aug. 1990); Chair. and Dir-Gen. JAMAL AL-BEDOUR.

Jordan Investment and Finance Bank: POB 950601, Khalil Mardam St., Shmeisani, Amman; tel. 665145; telex 23181; fax 681410; f. 1982 as Jordan Investment and Finance Corpn, name changed 1989; cap. p.u. JD4.5m., res JD6.3m., dep. JD71.3m., total assets JD148.1m. (Dec. 1989); Chair. NIZAR JARDANEH.

Social Security Corporation: POB 926031, Amman; tel. 643000; telex 22287; fax 610014; f. 1978; Dir-Gen. MUHAMMAD AS-SAQQAF.

STOCK EXCHANGE

Amman Financial Market: POB 8802, Amman; tel. 663170; telex 21711; f. 1978; Chair. and Gen. Man. Dr HASHIM SABAGH.

INSURANCE

Jordan Insurance Co Ltd: POB 279, Companies Bldg, 3rd Circle, Jabal Amman, Amman; tel. 634161; telex 21486; fax 637905; f. 1951; cap. p.u. JD5m.; Chair. and Man. Dir JAWDAT SHASHA'A; 8 brs (3 in Saudi Arabia, 3 in the United Arab Emirates, 1 in Kuwait, 1 in Lebanon).

Middle East Insurance Co Ltd: POB 1802, Shmeisani, Yaquob Sarrouf St, Amman; tel. 605144; telex 21420; f. 1963; cap. p.u. JD2m.; Man. Dir SAMI I. GAMMOH.

National Ahlia Insurance Co: POB 6156, Sayed Qutub St, Shmeisani, Amman; tel. 677689; telex 21309; fax 684900; f. 1965; cap. p.u. JD1.25m.; Chair. MUSTAFA ABU GOURA; Gen. Man. GHALEB ABU GOURA.

United Insurance Co Ltd: POB 7521, United Insurance Bldg, King Hussein St, Amman; tel. 625828; telex 23153; fax 629417; f. 1972; merged with Ash-Sharq Insurance (Jordan Agency) and New India Insurance (Jordan Agency) January 1988; all types of insurance; cap. JD1.5m.; Chair. RAOUF SA'AD ABUJABER; Gen. Man. NAZEH K. AZAR.

There are 17 local and 11 foreign insurance companies operating in Jordan. The first reinsurance company in the country was registered on 1 January 1987.

Trade and Industry

CHAMBERS OF COMMERCE AND INDUSTRY

Amman Chamber of Commerce: POB 287, Amman; tel. 666151; telex 21543; f. 1923; Pres. MUHAMMAD ASFOUR; Sec.-Gen. MUHAMMAD AL-MUHTASSEB.

Amman Chamber of Industry: POB 1800, Amman; tel. 643001; telex 22079; fax 647852; f. 1962; 5,000 industrial companies registered (1990); Pres. KHALDOUN ABU HASSAN; Gen. Man. MUHAMMAD S. HALAIQAH.

PUBLIC CORPORATIONS

Jordan Valley Authority: POB 2769, Amman; tel. 642472; telex 21692; projects in Stage I of the Jordan Valley Development Plan were completed in 1979. In 1988 about 26,000 ha was under intensive cultivation. Infrastructure projects also completed include 1,100 km of roads, 2,100 housing units, 100 schools, 15 health centres, 14 administration buildings, 4 marketing centres, 2 community centres, 2 vocational training centres. Electricity is now provided to all the towns and villages in the valley from the national network and domestic water is supplied to them from tube wells. Contributions to the cost of development came through loans from Kuwait Fund, Abu Dhabi Fund, Saudi Fund, Arab Fund, USAID, Fed. Germany, World Bank, EEC, Italy, Netherlands, UK, Japan and OPEC Special Fund. Many of the Stage II irrigation projects are now completed or under implementation. Projects under way include the construction of the Wadi al-Arab dam, the raising of the King Talal dam and the 14.5-km extension of the 98-km East Ghor main canal. Stage II will include the irrigation of 4,700 ha in the southern Ghor. The target for the Plan is to irrigate 43,000 ha of land in the Jordan Valley. Future development in irrigation will include the construction of the Maqarin dam and the Wadi Malaha storage dam; Pres. MUHAMMAD BANI HANI.

Agricultural Marketing and Processing Co of Jordan: POB 7314, Amman; tel. 819161; telex 23796; f. 1984; govt-owned; Chair. SAMI SUNA'A; Gen. Man. AYED WIR.

PHOSPHATES

Jordan Phosphate Mines Co Ltd (JPMC): POB 30, Amman; tel. 660141; telex 21223; f. 1930; engaged in production and export of rock phosphate; Chair. ALI KHRAIS; Dir-Gen. WASEF AZAR; Marketing and Sales Man. MAKRAM ZOREKAT; three mines in operation; production 6.5m. tons (1988); exports 4.9m. tons (1990).

Jordan Fertilizer Industries Co (JFIC): Amman; engaged in production and export of phosphate fertilizer and aluminium fluoride; acquired by JPMC in 1986; cap. 55m.; Man. Dir MAHMOUD MARDI.

TRADE UNIONS

The General Federation of Jordanian Trade Unions: Wadi as-Sir Rd, POB 1065, Amman; f. 1954; 33,000 mems; member of Arab

Trade Unions Confederation; Chair. SAMI HASSAN MANSOUR; Gen. Sec. ABD AR-RAZZAQ HAMAD.

There are also a number of independent unions, including:

Drivers' Union: POB 846, Amman; Sec.-Gen. SAMI HASSAN MANSOUR.

Engineers' Association: Amman; Sec.-Gen. LEITH SHUBELLAT.

Union of Petroleum Workers and Employees: POB 1346, Amman; Sec.-Gen. BRAHIM HADI.

Transport

RAILWAYS

Aqaba Railway Corporation: POB 50, Ma'an; tel. 332234; telex 64003; f. 1975; length of track 292 km (1,050-mm gauge); Dir-Gen. A. I. MAITA.

Formerly a division of the Hedjaz–Jordan Railway (see below), the Aqaba Railway was established as a separate entity in 1979; it retains close links with the Hedjaz but there is no regular through traffic between Aqaba and Amman. It comprises the 169-km line south of Menzil (leased from the Hedjaz–Jordan Railway) and the 115-km extension to Aqaba, opened in October 1975, which serves phosphate mines at el-Hasa and Wadi el-Abyad. A development programme is being implemented to increase the transport capacity of the line to 4m. tons of phosphate per year. Plans for connecting the new phosphate mine at Shidiya to the railway system by 1990/91 are under consideration.

Hedjaz–Jordan Railway (administered by the Ministry of Transport): POB 582, Amman; tel. 689541; telex 21541; f. 1902; length of track 496 km (1,050-mm gauge); Dir-Gen. A. H. AD-DJAZI.

This was formerly a section of the Hedjaz Railway (Damascus to Medina) for Muslim pilgrims to Medina and Mecca. It crosses the Syrian border and enters Jordanian territory south of Dera'a, and runs for approximately 366 km to Naqb Ishtar, passing through Zarka, Amman, Qatrana and Ma'an. Some 844 km of the line, from Ma'an to Medina in Saudi Arabia, were abandoned for over sixty years. Reconstruction of the Medina line, begun in 1965, was scheduled to be completed in 1971 at a cost of £15m., divided equally between Jordan, Saudi Arabia and Syria. However, the reconstruction work was suspended at the request of the Arab States concerned, pending further studies on costs. The line between Ma'an and Saudi Arabia (114 km) is now completed, as well as 15 km in Saudi Arabia as far as Halet Ammar Station. A new 115-km extension to Aqaba (owned by the Aqaba Railway Corporation (see above) was opened in 1975. In 1987 a study conducted by Dorsch Consult (Federal Republic of Germany) into the feasibility of reconstructing the Hedjaz Railway to high international specifications to connect Saudi Arabia, Jordan and Syria, concluded that the reopening of the Hedjaz line would be viable only if it were to be connected with European rail networks.

ROADS

Amman is linked by road with all parts of the kingdom and with neighbouring countries. All cities and most towns are connected by a two-lane paved road system. In addition, several thousand km of tracks make all villages accessible to motor transport. In 1987, the latest inventory showed the East Bank of Jordan to have 2,603 km of main roads, 1,519 km of secondary roads (both types asphalted) and 1,503 km of other roads. Road-building schemes valued at JD108m. were to be carried out in the 1986–90 Five-Year Plan. In November 1985 Jordan, Egypt and Iraq signed an agreement providing for the operation of an overland route between Cairo, Amman and Baghdad. In 1989 the Ministry of Public Works and Housing announced plans to introduce tolls on main roads in order to raise funds for road maintenance.

Joint Land Transport Co: Amman; joint venture of govts of Jordan and Iraq; operates about 750 trucks.

Jordan-Syria Land Transport Co: Amman; f. 1981; transports goods between ports in Jordan and Syria; operates 366 trucks and lorries.

SHIPPING

The port of Aqaba is Jordan's only outlet to the sea and has more than 20 modern and specialized berths, and one container terminal (540 m in length). The port has 299,000 sq m of storage area, and is used for Jordan's international trade and regional transit trade (mainly with Iraq). Transit cargo formed 39% of total cargo traffic in 1989. Total cargo handled in 1989 was 18.7m. metric tons. There is a ferry link between Aqaba and the Egyptian port of Nuweibeh.

Arab Bridge Maritime Navigation Co: Aqaba; f. 1987; joint venture by Egypt, Iraq and Jordan to improve economic co-operation; an extension of the company that established a ferry link between Aqaba and the Egyptian port of Nuweibeh in 1985; cap. US $6m.; Chair. Eng. NABIH AL-ABWA; Dir-Gen SABRY K. ABED.

T. Gargour & Fils: POB 419, Amman; tel. 622307; telex 21213; f. 1928; shipping agents and owners; Chair. JOHN GARGOUR.

Jordan Maritime Navigation Co: Amman; privately owned.

Jordan National Shipping Lines Ltd: POB 5406, Shmeisani, Amman; tel. 666214; telex 21730; POB 657 Aqaba; tel. 315342; telex 62276; owned 75% by the government; service from Antwerp, Zeebrugge, Bremen and Sheerness to Aqaba; daily passenger ferry service from Aqaba to Nuweibeh (Egypt); land transportation to destinations in Iraq and elsewhere in the region; two bulk carriers; Chair. WASIF AZAR; Gen. Man. Y. ET-TAL.

Jordanian Shipping Transport Co: Amman; f. 1984; two cargo vessels.

Kawar, Amin, & Sons Co W.L.L.: POB 222, 24 Abd al-Hamid Sharaf St, Shmeisani, Amman; tel. 603703; telex 21212; fax 672170; chartering and shipping agents; operates three general cargo ships; Chair. TAWFIQ A. KAWAR; Gen. Man. GHASSOUB F. KAWAR; Shipping Man. ABD AL-AZIZ KASAJI.

Petra Navigation and International Trading Co Ltd: POB 8362, White Star Bldg, Amman; tel. 662421; telex 21755; fax 601362; two ro/ro cargo vessels; Gen. Man. AHMAD H. ARMOUSH.

Syrian-Jordanian Shipping Co: rue Port Said, BP 148, Latakia, Syria; tel. 316356; telex 451002; operates two general cargo ships; transported 48,000 metric tons of goods in 1987; Chair. OSMAN LEBBADI.

PIPELINES

Two oil pipelines cross Jordan. The former Iraq Petroleum Company pipeline, carrying petroleum from the oilfields in Iraq to Haifa, has not operated since 1967. The 1,717-km (1,067-mile) pipeline, known as the Trans-Arabian Pipeline (Tapline), carries petroleum from the oilfields of Dhahran in Saudi Arabia to Sidon on the Mediterranean seaboard in Lebanon. Tapline traverses Jordan for a distance of 177 km (110 miles) and has frequently been cut by hostile action. Tapline stopped pumping to Syria and Lebanon at the end of 1983, when it was first due to close. It was later scheduled to close in 1985, but in September 1984 Jordan renewed an agreement to receive Saudi Arabian crude oil through Tapline. The agreement can be cancelled by either party at two years' notice.

CIVIL AVIATION

There are international airports at Amman and Aqaba. The new Queen Alia International Airport at Zizya, 40 km south of Amman, was opened in May 1983.

Civil Aviation Authority: Amman; Dir-Gen. AMIN HUSSEINI.

Royal Jordanian Airline: Head Office: Housing Bank Commercial Centre, Shmeisani, POB 302, Amman; tel. 672872; telex 21501; fax 672527; f. 1963; government-owned; services to Middle East, North Africa, Europe, USA and Far East; fleet of three Boeing 707-320C, three Boeing 727-200A, six Lockheed L-1011-500, six Airbus A310-300; two Airbus A320; Pres. and CEO HUSSAM ABU GHAZALEH.

Arab Wings Co Ltd: POB 341018, Amman; tel. 891994; telex 21608; f. 1975; subsidiary of Royal Jordanian; executive jet charter service, air ambulances, priority cargo; Chair. and Man. Dir HE SHARIF GHAZI RAKAN NASSER.

Tourism

The ancient cities of Jerash and Petra, and Jordan's proximity to biblical sites, have encouraged tourism. In 1988 there were 2,391,167 foreign visitors to Jordan. Earnings from tourism in 1987 were US $600m.

Ministry of Tourism: Tourism Authority, POB 224, Amman; tel. 642311; telex 21741; f. 1952; Minister of Tourism DAOUD KHALAF; Dir-Gen. Jordan Tourism Authority NASRI ATALLAH.

INDEX OF INTERNATIONAL ORGANIZATIONS

(Main reference only)

A

ABEDA, 95
Academy of Arab Music, 174
ACP States (Lomé Convention), 151
Acuerdo de Cartagena, 93
Aerospace Medical Association, 243
AFESD, 97
Africa Reinsurance Corporation—Africa-Re, 92
African Airlines Association, 275
— Anti-Apartheid Committee, 192
— Association for Literacy and Adult Education, 231
— — — Public Administration and Management, 235
— Bureau for Educational Sciences, 192
— Centre for Applied Research and Training in Social Development, 30
— — — Monetary Studies, 230
— — of Meteorological Applications for Development, 30
— Civil Aviation Commission—AFCAC, 192
— Commission on Agricultural Statistics (FAO), 56
— Development Bank—ADB, 91
— — Fund—ADF, 91
— Forestry Commission (FAO), 56
— Groundnut Council, 227
— Industrial Development Fund, 30
— Institute for Higher Technical Training and Research, 31
— Insurance Organization, 230
— Organization of Cartography and Remote Sensing, 267
— Petroleum Producers' Association, 227
— Posts and Telecommunications Union, 248
— Regional Centre for Engineering Design and Manufacturing, 30
— — — — Solar Energy, 30
— — — — Technology, 267
— — Organization for Standardization, 271
— Timber Organization, 219
— Training and Research Centre in Administration for Development—CAFRAD, 222
Afro-Asian Housing Organization, 222
— People's Solidarity Organization, 235
— Rural Reconstruction Organization, 222
Agence de coopération culturelle et technique, 222
Agency for the Prohibition of Nuclear Weapons in Latin America and the Caribbean, 235
AGFUND, 222
Agudath Israel World Organisation, 250
Aid to Displaced Persons and its European Villages, 261
ALADI, 172
ALECSO, 175
All Africa Conference of Churches, 250
Alliance Internationale de Tourisme, 270
— Israélite Universelle, 250
Al-Quds Committee (OIC), 198
Amnesty International, 261
Andean Development Corporation, 93
— Group, 93
— Judicial Tribunal, 93
— Parliament, 93
— Reserve Fund, 93
Anti-Slavery International, 261
ANZUS, 235
Arab Administrative Development Organization, 175
— Air Carriers' Organization, 275
— Authority for Agricultural Investment and Development, 222
— Bank for Economic Development in Africa—BADEA, 95
— Bankers Association, 230
— Bureau for Narcotics, 175
— — — Prevention of Crime, 175
— — of Criminal Police, 175
— Centre for the Study of Arid Zones and Dry Lands, 175
— Civil Aviation Council, 175
— Common Market, 127
— Company for Drug Industries and Medical Appliances, 127
— — — Industrial Investment, 127
— — — Livestock Development, 127
— Co-operation Council, 222
— Co-operative Federation, 127
— Deterrent Force, 174
— Drilling and Workover Company, 197
— Federation for Cement and Building Materials, 127
— — of Chemical Fertilizers Producers, 127
— — — Engineering Industries, 127
— — — Leather Industries, 127
— — — Paper Industries, 127
— — — Petroleum, Mining and Chemicals Workers, 238
— — — Shipping Industries, 127
— — — Textile Industries, 127
— Fund for Economic and Social Development—AFESD, 97
— — — Technical Assistance to African and Arab Countries, 175
— Geophysical Exploration Services Company, 197
— Gulf Programme for the United Nations Development Organizations—AGFUND, 222
— Industrial Development Organization, 175
— Iron and Steel Union, 271
— Labour Organization, 175
— League, 174
— — Educational, Cultural and Scientific Organization—ALECSO, 175
— Maritime Petroleum Transport Company, 197
— — Transport Academy, 175
— Mining Company, 127
— Monetary Fund, 98
— Organization for Agricultural Development, 175
— — — Standardization and Metrology, 175
— Petroleum Investments Corporation—APICORP, 197
— — Services Company, 197
— — Training Institute, 197
— Postal Union, 175
— Satellite Communication Organization, 175
— Seaports Federation, 127
— Shipbuilding and Repair Yard Company, 197
— Sports Confederation, 265
— States Broadcasting Union, 175
— Sugar Federation, 127
— Telecommunications Union, 175
— Tourism Organization, 270
— Towns Organization, 259
— Union of Fish Producers, 127
— — — Food Industries, 127
— — — Land Transport, 127
— — — Pharmaceutical Manufacturers and Medical Appliance Manufacturers, 127
— — — Railways, 275
— Well Logging Company, 197
ASEAN, 103
— Reinsurance Corporation, 105
Asia and Pacific Commission on Agricultural Statistics (FAO), 56
— — — Plant Protection Commission (FAO), 56
— Pacific Academy of Ophthalmology, 243
ASIAFEDOP, 213
Asian and Pacific Centre for Transfer of Technology, 26
— — — Coconut Community, 227
— Clearing Union—ACU, 230
— Confederation of Credit Unions, 230
— Development Bank—ADB, 100
— — Fund—ADF, 101
— Highway Network Project, 26
— Productivity Organization, 271
— Reinsurance Corporation, 230
— Students' Association, 277
— Vegetable Research and Development Center, 219
Asia-Pacific Broadcasting Union, 248
— Economic Co-operation—APEC, 222
— Forestry Commission (FAO), 56
— Telecommunity, 248
Asian-African Legal Consultative Committee, 240
Asian-Pacific Dental Federation, 244
— Postal Union, 248
Asistencia Recíproca Petrolera Estatal Latinoamericana, 229
Asociación de Empresas Estatales de Telecomunicaciones, 94
— del Congreso Panamericano de Ferrocarriles, 277
— Interamericana de Bibliotecarios y Documentalistas Agrícolas, 219
— Latinoamericana de Instituciones Financieros de Desarrollo, 223
— — Integración—ALADI, 172
Associated Country Women of the World, 262

Association des universités partiellement ou entièrement de langue française, 232
— for Childhood Education International, 231
— — Paediatric Education in Europe, 244
— — Systems Management, 238
— — the Advancement of Agricultural Science in Africa, 219
— — — Promotion of the International Circulation of the Press, 248
— — — Study of the World Refugee Problem, 259
— — — Taxonomic Study of the Flora of Tropical Africa, 254
— internationale de la Mutualité, 262
— of African Central Banks, 230
— — Development Finance Institutions, 92
— — Geological Surveys, 254
— — Tax Administrators, 230
— — Trade Promotion Organizations, 271
— — Universities, 231
— — Arab Universities, 231
— — Caribbean Universities and Research Institutes, 232
— — Commonwealth Universities, 117
— — Development Financing Institutions in Asia and the Pacific, 222
— — European Airlines, 275
— — — Atomic Forums—FORATOM, 254
— — — Chambers of Commerce, 271
— — — Institutes of Economic Research, 230
— — — Journalists, 248
— — Geoscientists for International Development, 254
— — Institutes for European Studies, 232
— — International Bond Dealers, 230
— — Iron Ore Exporting Countries, 227
— — National European and Mediterranean Societies of Gastro-enterology, 244
— — Natural Rubber Producing Countries, 227
— — Partially or Wholly French-Language Universities, 232
— — Secretaries General of Parliaments, 235
— — Social Work Education in Africa, 262
— — South Pacific Airlines, 208
— — South-east Asian Institutions of Higher Learning, 232
— — — Nations—ASEAN, 103
— — Tin Producing Countries, 228
Assofoto (CMEA), 126
Atlantic Treaty Association, 235
Autorité du bassin du Niger, 224
Aviation sans frontières, 262

B

BADEA, 95
Bahá'í International Community, 250
Balkan Medical Union, 244
Baltic and International Maritime Council, 275
BAM International, 222
Banco Centroamericano de Integración Económica—BCIE, 111
Bangkok Declaration (ASEAN), 103
Bank for International Settlements—BIS, 106
Banque arabe pour le développement économique en Afrique—BADEA, 95
— centrale des états de l'Afrique de l'ouest—BCEAO, 156
— de développement des états de l'Afrique centrale, 157
— des états de l'Afrique centrale, 157
— ouest-africaine de développement—BOAD, 156
Baptist World Alliance, 250
Benelux Economic Union, 222
Berne Union, 87
Biometric Society, 254
BIS, 106
British Commonwealth Ex-services League, 118
Broadcasting Organizations of Non-aligned Countries, 249
Bureau international de la récupération, 267
Business Co-operation Centre (EEC), 146

C

CAB International (Commonwealth), 115
CABI Bureau of Agricultural Economics, 116
— — — Animal Breeding and Genetics, 116
— — — — Health, 116
— — — Crop Protection, 116
— — — Dairy Science and Technology, 116
— — — Horticulture and Plantation Crops, 116
— — — Nutrition, 116
— — — Pastures and Field Crops, 116
— — — Plant Breeding and Genetics, 116
— — — Soils, 116
— Forestry Bureau, 116

CACM, 110
Cadmium Association, 228
CAFRAD, 222
Cairns Group, 271
Caisse centrale de coopération économique—CCCE (Franc Zone), 157
Caribbean Agricultural Research and Development Institute, 109
— Community and Common Market—CARICOM, 108
— Conference of Churches, 250
— Congress of Labour, 238
— Development Bank, 109
— Examinations Council, 109
— Food and Nutrition Institute, 219
— Free Trade Association, 108
— Meteorological Institute, 109
— Plant Protection Commission (FAO), 57
— Tourism Organization, 270
CARICOM, 108
CARIFTA, 108
Caritas Internationalis, 222
Cartagena Agreement (Andean Group), 93
Catholic International Education Office, 232
— — Federation for Physical and Sports Education, 232
— — Union for Social Service, 262
CEAO, 120
CEEAC, 223
Celtic League, 235
Central American Air Navigation Service Corporation, 111
— — Bank for Economic Integration, 111
— — Common Market—CACM, 110
— — Institute for Business Administration, 111
— — — of Public Administration, 111
— — Maritime Transport Commission, 111
— — Monetary Council, 111
— — — Union, 110
— — Railways Commission, 111
— — Research Institute for Industry, 111
— — University Confederation, 111
— Commission for the Navigation of the Rhine, 275
— Dispatching Organization of the Interconnected Power Systems (CMEA), 126
— Office for International Carriage by Rail, 275
Centre africain de formation et de recherches administratives pour le développement—CAFRAD, 222
— de Recherches alimentaires et nutritionnelles (OCCGE), 247
— — — sur les Méningites et les Schistosomiases (OCCGE), 247
— for Educational Research and Innovation (OECD), 186
— — Latin American Monetary Studies, 230
— — the Development of Industry (Lomé Convention), 151
— Muraz (OCCGE), 247
— Régional de Recherches Entomologiques (OCCGE), 247
Centro de Estudios Monetarios Latinoamericanos, 230
— Interamericano de Investigación y Documentación sobre Formación Profesional, 232
— Internacional de Agricultura Tropical, 220
— Regional de Educación de Adultos y Alfabetización Funcional para América Latina, 234
CERN, 254
Chicago Convention (ICAO), 68
Christian Conference of Asia, 250
— Democrat International, 235
— Medical Commission (WCC), 214
— Peace Conference, 250
CILSS, 224
CIOMS, 242
CLASEP, 213
CLTC, 213
Club of Dakar, 222
— — the Sahel, 222
CMEA, 125
Cocoa Producers' Alliance, 228
COCOM, 271
Codex Alimentarius Commission (FAO/WHO), 57
Collaborative International Pesticides Analytical Council Ltd, 219
Colombo Plan for Co-operative Economic and Social Development in Asia and the Pacific, 112
COMECON, 125
Comisión Centroamericana de Ferrocarriles, 111
— — — Transporte Marítimo, 111
— Técnica de las Telecomunicaciones de Centroamérica—COMTELCA, 111
Comité Européen des Assurances, 230
Commission for Controlling the Desert Locust (FAO), 57
— — Inland Fisheries of Latin America (FAO), 57
— of the Churches in International Affairs (WCC), 214
— — — European Communities, 140

— on African Animal Trypanosomiasis (FAO), 57
— — Fertilizers (FAO), 57
— — Inter-Church Aid, Refugee and World Service (WCC), 214
— — Plant Genetic Resources (FAO), 57
— — the Churches' Participation in Development (WCC), 214
Committee for European Construction Equipment, 271
— of European Foundry Associations, 271
Common Organization for the Control of Desert Locust and Bird Pests, 219
Commonwealth, 113
— Advisory Aeronautical Research Council, 118
— Agricultural Bureaux, 115
— Air Transport Council, 117
— Association of Architects, 118
— — — Science, Technology and Mathematics Educators—CASTME, 117
— Broadcasting Association, 117
— Council for Educational Administration, 117
— Countries League, 118
— Engineers' Council, 118
— Forestry Association, 116
— Foundation, 118
— Fund for Technical Co-operation, 115
— Games Federation, 118
— Geological Surveys Consultative Group, 118
— Institute, London, 117
— — (Scotland), Edinburgh, 117
— Journalists' Association, 117
— Lawyers' Association, 117
— Legal Advisory Service, 117
— — Education Association, 118
— Magistrates' Association, 118
— Medical Association, 117
— Parliamentary Association, 118
— Pharmaceutical Association, 117
— Press Union, 117
— Secretariat, 113
— Society for the Deaf, 117
— Telecommunications Organization, 117
— Trade Union Council, 118
— War Graves Commission, 118
— Youth Exchange Council, 118
Communauté économique de l'Afrique de l'Ouest—CEAO, 120
— — des Etats de l'Afrique Centrale, 223
— — — pays des Grands Lacs, 223
— — du bétail et de la viande du Conseil de l'Entente, 122
Comparative Education Society in Europe, 232
Computers (CMEA), 126
Confederación Interamericana de Educación Católica, 232
— Latinoamericana de Asociaciones Cristianas de Jóvenes, 278
— Universitaria Centroamericana, 111
Confederation of Asia-Pacific Chambers of Commerce and Industry, 271
— — European Soft Drinks Associations, 271
— — International Contractors' Associations, 271
— — the Socialist Parties of the European Community, 235
Conference of European Churches, 250
— — International Catholic Organizations, 251
— — Regions in North-West Europe, 223
— on Security and Co-operation in Europe—CSCE, 235
Conférence permanente des Recteurs, Présidents et Vice-chanceliers des Universités européennes, 234
Conseil de l'Entente, 122
— international des radios-télévisions d'expression française, 249
Consejo de Fundaciones Americanas de Desarrollo, 223
— Interamericano de Música, 225
— Latinoamericano de Iglesias, 251
— Monetario Centroamericano, 111
Consultative Council for Postal Studies (UPU), 83
— — of Jewish Organizations, 251
— Group for International Agricultural Research—CGIAR (IBRD), 63
Convention on International Trade in Endangered Species—CITES, 41
Co-operation Council for the Arab States of the Gulf, 123
Co-ordinating Committee for International Voluntary Service, 262
— — — Multilateral Export Controls—COCOM, 271
— — — the Liberation Movements of Africa (OAU), 191
Corporación Andina de Fomento, 93
— Centroamericana de Servicios de Navegación Aérea, 111
Council for International Organisations of Medical Sciences, 242
— — Mutual Economic Assistance—CMEA (COMECON), 125
— — the Development of Economic and Social Research in Africa, 259
— — — International Congresses of Entomology, 254
— of American Development Foundations, 223
— — Arab Economic Unity, 127
— — Europe, 129
— — European National Youth Committees, 277
— — the Bars and Law Societies of the European Community, 240
— on International Educational Exchange, 277
Court of Auditors of the European Communities, 143
— — Justice of the European Communities, 142
CSCE, 235
Customs and Economic Union of Central Africa, 156
— Co-operation Council, 271

D

Dairy Society International, 219
Danube Commission, 275
Desert Locust Control Organization for Eastern Africa, 219
Duke of Edinburgh's Award Scheme, 118

E

East Asia Travel Association, 270
Eastern and Southern African Management Institute, 31
— — — — Mineral Resources Development Centre, 30
— Caribbean Central Bank, 109
— Regional Organisation for Planning and Housing, 259
— — — — Public Administration, 235
EBRD, 223
ECA, 28
ECE, 24
ECLAC, 27
Eco-Bank Transnational, 134
Econometric Society, 230
Economic and Social Commission for Asia and the Pacific—ESCAP (UN), 25
— — — — Western Asia—ESCWA, 31
— Commission for Africa—ECA (UN), 28
— — — Europe—ECE (UN), 24
— — — Latin America and the Caribbean—ECLAC (UN), 27
— Community of Central African States, 223
— — — the Great Lakes Countries, 223
— — — West African States—ECOWAS, 133
— Co-operation Organization—ECO, 223
— Development Institute (IBRD), 64
ECOSOC, 13, 19
ECOWAS, 133
ECSC, 146
EEC, 135
EFTA, 154
EIB, 143
EIRENE—International Christian Service for Peace, 262
EMS, 148
English-speaking Union of the Commonwealth, 259
Entente Council, 122
Entraide Ouvrière Internationale, 264
ESCAP, 25
ESCAP/WMO Typhoon Committee, 26
ESCWA, 31
Euratom, 146
EUROCONTROL, 275
EUROFEDOP, 213
Eurofinas, 230
Euronet DIANE, 146
Europa Nostra, 225
European Agricultural Guidance and Guarantee Fund, 153
— Air Navigation Planning Group (ICAO), 69
— Aluminium Association, 228
— and Mediterranean Plant Protection Organization, 219
— Alliance of Press Agencies, 249
— Association for Animal Production, 219
— — — Cancer Research, 244
— — — Health Education and Libraries, 244
— — — Personnel Management, 238
— — — Population Studies, 260
— — — Research on Plant Breeding, 219
— — — the Study of Diabetes, 244
— — — Trade in Jute and Related Products, 228
— — of Advertising Agencies, 271
— — — Conservatoires, Music Academies and Music High Schools, 225
— — — Exploration Geophysicists, 254
— — — Internal Medicine, 244
— — — Manufacturers of Radiators, 271
— — — Music Festivals, 226
— — — National Productivity Centres, 271
— — — Radiology, 244

– – – Social Medicine, 244
– Atomic Energy Community—Euratom, 146
– – – Society, 254
– Bank for Reconstruction and Development—EBRD, 223
– Baptist Federation, 251
– Brain and Behaviour Society, 244
– Brewery Convention, 271
– Broadcasting Union, 249
– Builders of Thermal and Electric Locomotives, 267
– Bureau of Adult Education, 232
– Chemical Industry Federation, 271
– Civil Aviation Conference, 275
– – Service Federation, 238
– Coal and Steel Community—ECSC, 146
– Commission for the Control of Foot-and-Mouth Disease (FAO), 57
– – of Human Rights, 129
– – on Agriculture (FAO), 57
– Committee for Standardization, 271
– – – the Protection of the Population against the Hazards of Chronic Toxicity, 244
– – of Associations of Manufacturers of Agricultural Machinery, 272
– – – Sugar Manufacturers, 228
– – – Textile Machinery Manufacturers, 272
– Community, 135
– – Commission, 140
– – Council of Ministers, 141
– – Court of Auditors, 143
– – – Justice, 142
– – Joint Research Centre, 145
– Computer Manufacturers Association, 267
– Confederation of Agriculture, 219
– – – Iron and Steel Industries, 272
– – – Paint, Printing Ink and Artists' Colours Manufacturers' Associations, 272
– – – Woodworking Industries, 272
– Conference of Ministers of Transport, 275
– – – Postal and Telecommunications Administrations, 248
– Convention for Constructional Steelwork, 267
– – – the Protection of Human Rights and Fundamental Freedoms, 129
– Co-ordination Centre for Research and Documentation in Social Sciences, 260
– Council, 141
– Court of Human Rights, 130
– Cultural Centre, 225
– – Foundation, 232
– Currency Unit, 149
– Economic Community—EEC, 135
– Federation for Catholic Adult Education, 232
– – – the Welfare of the Elderly, 262
– – of Associations of Insulation Enterprises, 272
– – – – Particle Board Manufacturers, 272
– – – Chemical Engineering, 267
– – – Conference Towns, 238
– – – Corrosion, 267
– – – Financial Analysts' Societies, 230
– – – Handling Industries, 272
– – – Management Consultants' Associations, 272
– – – National Engineering Associations, 267
– – – Plywood Industry, 272
– – – Productivity Services, 272
– – – Tile and Brick Manufacturers, 272
– Financial Management and Marketing Association, 230
– Forestry Commission (FAO), 57
– Foundation for Management Development, 232
– Free Trade Association—EFTA, 154
– Furniture Manufacturers Federation, 272
– General Galvanizers Association, 272
– Glass Container Manufacturers' Committee, 272
– Grassland Federation, 219
– Healthcare Management Association, 244
– Industrial Research Management Association, 238
– Inland Fisheries Advisory Commission (FAO), 57
– Insurance Committee, 230
– Investment Bank, 143
– League Against Rheumatism, 244
– Livestock and Meat Trading Union, 219
– Molecular Biology Organization, 254
– Monetary Co-operation Fund, 148
– – System, 148
– Motor Hotel Federation, 270
– Movement, 236
– Organisation for the Safety of Air Navigation, 275
– Organization for Caries Research, 244

– – – Civil Aviation Equipment, 267
– – – Nuclear Research, 254
– – – Quality, 272
– Orthodontic Society, 244
– Packaging Federation, 272
– Parliament, 142
– Passenger Train Time-Table Conference, 276
– Patent Office, 272
– Railway Wagon Pool, 276
– Regional Development Fund, 153
– Social Fund, 153
– Society for Opinion and Marketing Research, 272
– – – Rural Sociology, 260
– – of Culture, 225
– Space Agency, 254
– Strategic Research Programme in Information Technology—ESPRIT, 145
– Telecommunications Satellite Organization—EUTELSAT, 248
– Trade Union Confederation, 238
– Travel Commission, 270
– Union of Arabic and Islamic Scholars, 232
– – – Coachbuilders, 272
– – – Medical Specialists, 244
– – – the Natural Gas Industry, 272
– – – Women, 236
– Unit of Account, 149
– University Institute, 147
– Venture Capital Association, 230
– Young Christian Democrats, 236
– Youth Centre, 131
– – Foundation, 131
European-Mediterranean Seismological Centre, 254
Eurospace, 267
Eurotransplant Foundation, 244
EUTELSAT, 248
Evangelical Alliance, 251
Experiment in International Living, 260

F

FAO, 55
Federación de Cámaras de Comercio del Istmo Centroamericano, 111
– – – y Asociaciones Industriales Centroamericanas, 111
– Latinoamericana de Bancos, 231
– – – Trabajadores Campesinos y de la Alimentación, 239
Federation of Arab Scientific Research Councils, 254
– – Asian Scientific Academies and Societies, 255
– – – Women's Associations, 262
– – Central American Chambers of Commerce, 111
– – European Biochemical Societies, 255
– – – Marketing Research Associations, 273
– – French-Language Obstetricians and Gynaecologists, 244
– – Industrial Chambers and Associations in Central America, 111
– – International Civil Servants' Associations, 238
– – Scientific and Technical Organizations of the Socialist Countries, 267
– – the European Dental Industry, 244
– – World Health Foundations, 244
Fédération Aéronautique Internationale, 265
– des gynécologues et obstétriciens de langue française, 244
FEOGA, 153
Fondo Andino de Reservas, 93
– Latinoamericano de Reservas, 93
Fonds d'aide et de coopération (Franc Zone), 157
– d'entraide et de garantie des emprunts (Conseil de l'Entente), 122
– de solidarité et d'intervention pour le développement, (CEAO), 120
Food Aid Committee, 223
– and Agriculture Organization—FAO, 55
Foundation for International Scientific Co-ordination, 255
Franc Zone, 156
Frères des Hommes, 222
Friends (Quakers) World Committee for Consultation, 251
Fund for Co-operation, Compensation and Development (ECOWAS), 133

G

Gambia River Basin Development Organization, 223
General Agreement on Tariffs and Trade—GATT, 58
– Association of International Sports Federations, 265
– Municipal Health and Technical Experts, 244
– Fisheries Council for the Mediterranean—GFCM (FAO), 57

INDEX

— Union of Chambers of Commerce, Industry and Agriculture for Arab Countries, 273
Generalized System of Preferences, 38
Geneva Conventions (Red Cross), 169
Gleneagles Agreement on Sporting Contacts with South Africa, 119
Global Environment Monitoring System (UNEP), 41
Graduate Institute of International Studies, 232
Graphical International Federation, 238
Group of Latin American and Caribbean Sugar Exporting Countries, 228
— — Rio, 236
Grupo Andino, 93
Gulf Co-operation Council, 123
— Investment Corporation, 124
— Organization for Industrial Consulting, 273

H

Habitat, 35
Hague Conference on Private International Law, 240
Hansard Society for Parliamentary Government, 236

I

IAEA, 60
IATA, 276
IBEC, 160
IBRD, 62
ICAO, 68
ICC, 161
ICCROM, 226
ICFTU, 163
ICPHS, 259
ICSU, 252
IDA, 66
IDB, 158
IFAD, 70
IFC, 67
ILO, 72
IMCO, 73
IMF, 74
— Institute, 76
IMO, 73
Inca-Fiej Research Association, 249
Indian Ocean Commission, 223
— — Fishery Commission (FAO), 57
Indo-Pacific Fishery Commission (FAO), 57
INMARSAT, 248
Institut d'émission des départements d'outre-mer (Franc Zone), 157
— — d'outre-mer (Franc Zone), 157
— de formation et de recherche démographiques, 29
— — Recherche sur la Tuberculose et les Infections respiratoires aigües (OCCGE), 247
— d'Ophtalmologie tropicale en Afrique (OCCGE), 247
— Marchoux (OCCGE), 247
— Pierre Richet (OCCGE), 247
— universitaire de hautes études internationales, 232
Institute for International Sociological Research, 260
— — Latin American Integration, 159
— — Standardization (CMEA), 126
— of Air Transport, 276
— — Commonwealth Studies, 116
— — International Business Law and Practice (ICC), 162
— — — Law, 240
— — Nutrition of Central America and Panama, 111
Instituto Andino de Estudios Sociales, 213
— Centroamericano de Administración de Empresas, 111
— — — — Pública, 111
— — — Estudios Sociales, 213
— — — Investigación y Tecnología Industrial, 111
— de Formación del Caribe, 213
— — Nutrición de Centro América y Panamá, 111
— del Cono Sur, 213
— para la Integración de América Latina—INTAL, 159
INTELSAT, 248
Inter-African Bureau for Animal Resources, 193
— — — Soils, 193
— Coffee Organization, 228
— Committee for Hydraulic Studies, 267
— Phytosanitary Commission, 193
— Socialists and Democrats, 236
Inter-American Association of Agricultural Librarians and Documentalists, 219
— — — Sanitary and Environmental Engineering, 244
— Bar Association, 240
— Centre for Research and Documentation on Vocational Training, 232
— Children's Institute, 196
— Commercial Arbitration Commission, 273
— Commission of Women, 196
— — on Human Rights, 194
— Confederation for Catholic Education, 232
— Conference on Social Security, 262
— Council for Education, Science and Culture, 194
— Court of Human Rights, 194
— Defense Board, 196
— Development Bank—IDB, 158
— Economic and Social Council, 194
— Indian Institute, 196
— Institute for Co-operation on Agriculture, 196
— — of Capital Markets, 231
— Investment Corporation, 159
— Juridical Committee, 194
— Music Council, 225
— Nuclear Energy Commission, 196
— Planning Society, 223
— Press Association, 249
— Regional Organization of Workers—ORIT, 163
— Tropical Tuna Commission, 220
Inter-Arab Investment Guarantee Corporation, 175
Interatomenergo (CMEA), 126
Interatominstrument (CMEA), 126
Interchim (CMEA), 126
Interchimvolokno (CMEA), 126
Interelektro (CMEA), 126
Interetalonpribor (CMEA), 126
Interfilm, 225
Intergovernmental Authority on Drought and Development—IGADD, 223
— Committee for Migration, 167
— — — Physical Education and Sport, 81
— Copyright Committee, 240
— Council of Copper Exporting Countries, 228
— Maritime Consultative Organization—IMCO, 73
— Oceanographic Commission, 255
— Programme for the Development of Communication (UNESCO), 81
Interkosmos (CMEA), 126
Intermetall (CMEA), 126
International Abolitionist Federation, 262
— Academic Union, 259
— Academy of Astronautics, 255
— — — Aviation and Space Medicine, 244
— — — Cytology, 245
— — — Legal and Social Medicine, 242
— — — Tourism, 270
— Accounting Standards Committee, 231
— Advertising Association Inc., 273
— Aeronautical Federation, 265
— African Institute, 260
— Agency for Research on Cancer, 85
— — — the Prevention of Blindness, 245
— Air Transport Association, 276
— Alliance of Distribution by Cable, 249
— — — Women, 236
— Amateur Athletic Federation, 265
— — Boxing Association, 265
— — Radio Union, 265
— — Swimming Federation, 265
— — Wrestling Federation, 265
— Anatomical Congress, 245
— Association against Noise, 262
— — for Bridge and Structural Engineering, 267
— — — Cereal Science and Technology, 220
— — — Child and Adolescent Psychiatry and Allied Professions, 245
— — — Cybernetics, 267
— — — Dental Research, 245
— — — Earthquake Engineering, 255
— — — Ecology, 255
— — — Education to a Life without Drugs, 262
— — — Educational and Vocational Guidance, 232
— — — Information, 232
— — — Hydraulic Research, 266
— — — Mass Communication Research, 260
— — — Mathematical Geology, 255
— — — Mathematics and Computers in Simulation, 255
— — — Mutual Benefit Funds, 262
— — — Plant Physiology, 255
— — — Taxonomy, 255

INDEX

– – – Religious Freedom, 251
– – – Research in Income and Wealth, 231
– – – Suicide Prevention, 262
– – – the Development of Documentation, Libraries and Archives in Africa, 232
– – – – Exchange of Students for Technical Experience, 277
– – – – History of Religions, 259
– – – – Physical Sciences of the Ocean, 255
– – – – Protection of Industrial Property, 240
– – – – Rhine Vessels Register, 276
– – – – Study of the Liver, 242
– – – – Vegetation Science, 220
– – of Agricultural Economists, 220
– – – – Information Specialists, 220
– – – – Medicine and Rural Health, 245
– – – Allergology and Clinical Immunology, 242
– – – Applied Linguistics, 260
– – – – Psychology, 245
– – – Art (Painting-Sculpture-Graphic Art), 225
– – – – Critics, 225
– – – Asthmology, 245
– – – Bibliophiles, 225
– – – Biological Standardization, 255
– – – Botanic Gardens, 255
– – – Broadcasting, 249
– – – Buddhist Studies, 251
– – – Buying Groups, 273
– – – Chain Stores, 273
– – – Children's International Summer Villages, 262
– – – Conference Interpreters, 238
– – – – Translators, 239
– – – Congress Centres, 273
– – – Crafts and Small and Medium-Sized Enterprises, 239
– – – Democratic Lawyers, 240
– – – Dental Students, 277
– – – Department Stores, 273
– – – Documentalists and Information Officers, 260
– – – Educators for World Peace, 236
– – – Electrical Contractors, 273
– – – Geodesy, 255
– – – Geomagnetism and Aeronomy, 255
– – – Gerontology, 245
– – – Group Psychotherapy, 245
– – – Horticultural Producers, 220
– – – Hydatid Disease, 245
– – – Hydrological Sciences, 255
– – – Insurance and Reinsurance Intermediaries, 273
– – – Islamic Banks, 231
– – – Juvenile and Family Court Magistrates, 240
– – – Law Libraries, 240
– – – Legal Sciences, 240
– – – Lighthouse Authorities, 266
– – – Literary Critics, 225
– – – Logopedics and Phoniatrics, 245
– – – Medical Laboratory Technologists, 239
– – – Medicine and Biology of the Environment, 243
– – – Meteorology and Atmospheric Physics, 255
– – – Metropolitan City Libraries, 260
– – – Museums of Arms and Military History, 225
– – – Music Libraries, Archives and Documentation Centres, 226
– – – Mutual Insurance Companies, 239
– – – Oral and Maxillofacial Surgeons, 245
– – – Papyrologists, 232
– – – Penal Law, 240
– – – Photobiology, 256
– – – Physical Education in Higher Education, 232
– – – Ports and Harbors, 276
– – – Rolling Stock Builders, 268
– – – Scholarly Publishers, 273
– – – Schools of Social Work, 262
– – – Scientific Experts in Tourism, 270
– – – Sedimentologists, 256
– – – Sound Archives, 249
– – – Students in Economics and Management, 277
– – – Technological University Libraries, 268
– – – Textile Dyers and Printers, 273
– – – Theoretical and Applied Limnology, 256
– – – Universities, 233
– – – University Professors and Lecturers, 233
– – – Volcanology and Chemistry of the Earth's Interior, 256
– – – Wood Anatomists, 256
– – – Workers for Troubled Children and Youth, 262
– – on Water Pollution Research and Control, 256
– Astronautical Federation, 256
– Astronomical Union, 253

– Atomic Energy Agency—IAEA, 60
– Automobile Federation, 276
– Baccalaureate Organization, 233
– Bank for Economic Co-operation—IBEC, 160
– – – Reconstruction and Development—IBRD (World Bank), 62
– Bar Association, 240
– Bauxite Association, 228
– Bee Research Association, 220
– Board on Books for Young People, 226
– Booksellers Federation, 273
– Botanical Congress, 256
– Brain Research Organization, 245
– Bridge, Tunnel and Turnpike Association, 266
– Broncoesophagological Society, 245
– Bureau for Epilepsy, 245
– – – the Standardization of Man-Made Fibres, 273
– – of Chambers of Commerce (ICC), 162
– – – Education—IBE, 81
– – – Fiscal Documentation, 231
– – – Weights and Measures, 256
– Cargo Handling Co-ordination Association, 268
– Cartographic Association, 256
– Catholic Migration Commission, 262
– – Union of the Press, 249
– Cell Research Organization, 245
– Centre for Advanced Technical and Vocational Training (ILO), 73
– – – Genetic Engineering and Biotechnology, 82
– – – Local Credit, 231
– – – Scientific and Technological Information (CMEA), 126
– – – Settlement of Investment Disputes (IBRD), 64
– – – Technical Expertise (ICC), 161
– – – the Study of the Preservation and Restoration of Cultural Property—ICCROM, 226
– – – Theoretical Physics (IAEA), 61
– – – Tropical Agriculture, 220
– – of Films for Children and Young People, 226
– – – Insect Physiology and Ecology, 256
– Chamber of Commerce—ICC, 161
– – – Shipping, 276
– Children's Centre, 262
– Chiropractors' Association, 245
– Christian Federation for the Prevention of Alcoholism and Drug Addiction, 263
– – Service for Peace, 262
– Civil Airports Association, 276
– – Aviation Organization—ICAO, 68
– – Defence Organisation, 263
– Cocoa Organization, 228
– Coffee Organization, 228
– College of Surgeons, 242
– Colour Association, 268
– Commission for Agricultural and Food Industries, 220
– – – Optics, 256
– – – Plant-Bee Relationships, 256
– – – the Conservation of Atlantic Tunas, 220
– – – – History of Representative and Parliamentary Institutions, 236
– – – – Islamic Heritage, 199
– – – – Prevention of Alcoholism and Drug Dependency, 263
– – – – Protection of the Rhine against Pollution, 263
– – – – Scientific Exploration of the Mediterranean Sea, 256
– – – – Southeast Atlantic Fisheries, 220
– – of Agricultural Engineering, 266
– – – Jurists, 240
– – – Sugar Technology, 220
– – on Civil Status, 240
– – – Glass, 266
– – – Illumination, 268
– – – Irrigation and Drainage, 266
– – – Large Dams, 268
– – – Occupational Health, 245
– – – Physics Education, 256
– – – Radiation Units and Measurements, 256
– – – Radiological Protection, 245
– – – Zoological Nomenclature, 256
– Committee for Recording the Productivity of Milk Animals, 220
– – – Social Sciences Information and Documentation, 260
– – – the Diffusion of Arts and Literature through the Cinema, 226
– – – the History of Art, 259
– – of Catholic Nurses, 245
– – – Foundry Technical Associations, 266
– – – Historical Sciences, 259
– – – Military Medicine and Pharmacy, 243

- - - the Red Cross—ICRC, 168
- - on Aeronautical Fatigue, 268
- Comparative Literature Association, 226
- Confederation for Printing and Allied Industries, 273
- - of Art Dealers, 273
- - - Catholic Organizations for Charitable and Social Action, 222
- - - European Sugar Beet Growers, 228
- - - Executive and Professional Staffs, 239
- - - Free Trade Unions—ICFTU, 163
- - - Societies of Authors and Composers, 226
- - - the Butchers' and Delicatessen Trade, 273
- Conference on Assistance to Refugees in Africa, 45
- - - Large High-Voltage Electric Systems, 268
- Congress and Convention Association, 270
- - of African Studies, 259
- - on Tropical Medicine and Malaria, 243
- Container Bureau, 276
- Co-operation for Development and Solidarity, 223
- Co-operative Alliance, 273
- Copyright Society, 240
- Cotton Advisory Committee, 228
- Council for Adult Education, 233
- - - Bird Preservation, 256
- - - Building Research, Studies and Documentation, 268
- - - Distance Education, 233
- - - Film, Television and Audiovisual Communication, 249
- - - Health, Physical Education and Recreation, 265
- - - Laboratory Animal Science, 243
- - - Philosophy and Humanistic Studies—ICPHS, 259
- - - Physical Fitness Research, 245
- - - Scientific and Technical Information, 256
- - - the Exploration of the Sea, 257
- - - Traditional Music, 227
- - of Christians and Jews, 251
- - - Environmental Law, 240
- - - French-speaking Radio and Television Organizations, 249
- - - Graphic Design Associations, 226
- - - Jewish Women, 251
- - - Museums, 226
- - - Nurses, 245
- - - Psychologists, 257
- - - Scientific Unions, 252
- - - Shopping Centres, 273
- - - Societies of Industrial Design, 273
- - - Tanners, 273
- - - the Aeronautical Sciences, 257
- - - Voluntary Agencies, 263
- - - Women, 263
- - on Alcohol and Addictions, 263
- - - Archives, 260
- - - Disability, 263
- - - Jewish Social and Welfare Services, 263
- - - Monuments and Sites, 226
- - - Social Welfare, 263
- Court of Justice, 14, 20
- Cricket Council, 265
- Criminal Police Organization, 240
- Crops Research Institute for the Semi-Arid Tropics, 220
- Customs Tariffs Bureau, 241
- Cycling Union, 265
- Cystic Fibrosis (Mucoviscidosis) Association, 246
- Dachau Committee, 263
- Dairy Federation, 220
- Democrat Union, 236
- Dental Federation, 242
- Development Association—IDA, 66
- - Law Institute, 241
- Diabetes Federation, 242
- Earth Rotation Service, 257
- Economic Association, 231
- Electrotechnical Commission, 268
- Emergency Food Reserve, 51
- Energy Agency (OECD), 188
- Epidemiological Association, 246
- Ergonomics Association, 260
- European Construction Federation, 239
- Exhibitions Bureau, 273
- Falcon Movement, 237
- Federation for Cell Biology, 257
- - - European Law, 241
- - - Household Maintenance Products, 274
- - - Housing and Planning, 260
- - - Hygiene, Preventive Medicine and Social Medicine, 246
- - - Information and Documentation, 268
- - - - Processing, 268
- - - Medical and Biological Engineering, 246
- - - - Psychotherapy, 246
- - - Modern Languages and Literatures, 259
- - - Parent Education, 233
- - - the Theory of Machines and Mechanisms, 266
- - - Theatre Research, 226
- - of Accountants, 231
- - - Actors, 239
- - - Agricultural Producers, 220
- - - Air Line Pilots' Associations, 239
- - - Airworthiness, 268
- - - Association Football, 265
- - - Associations of Specialists in Occupational Safety and Industrial Hygiene, 274
- - - - - Textile Chemists and Colourists, 274
- - - Automatic Control, 266
- - - Automotive Engineering Societies, 268
- - - Beekeepers' Associations, 220
- - - Blue Cross Societies, 263
- - - Building and Woodworkers, 163
- - - Business and Professional Women, 239
- - - Catholic Universities, 233
- - - Chemical, Energy and General Workers' Unions, 163
- - - Clinical Chemistry, 243
- - - - Neurophysiology, 242
- - - Commercial, Clerical, Professional and Technical Employees—FIET, 163
- - - Consulting Engineers, 268
- - - Disabled Workers and Civilian Handicapped, 263
- - - 'Ecole Moderne' Movements, 233
- - - Educative Communities, 263
- - - Fertility Societies, 246
- - - Film Archives, 226
- - - - Producers' Associations, 226
- - - Free Teachers' Unions, 164
- - - Freight Forwarders' Associations, 276
- - - Grocers' Associations, 274
- - - Gynecology and Obstetrics, 246
- - - Hospital Engineering, 268
- - - Human Rights, 263
- - - Industrial Energy Consumers, 266
- - - Institutes for Socio-religious Research, 260
- - - 'Jeunesses Musicales', 227
- - - Journalists, 164
- - - Library Associations and Institutions, 233
- - - Medical Students Associations, 277
- - - Multiple Sclerosis Societies, 246
- - - Musicians, 227
- - - Newspaper Publishers, 249
- - - Operational Research Societies, 257
- - - Ophthalmological Societies, 246
- - - Organisations for School Correspondence and Exchange, 233
- - - Oto-Rhino-Laryngological Societies, 242
- - - Park and Recreation Administration, 265
- - - Pharmaceutical Manufacturers Associations, 274
- - - Philosophical Societies, 259
- - - Physical Education, 233
- - - - Medicine and Rehabilitation, 242
- - - Plantation, Agricultural and Allied Workers, 164
- - - Popular Travel Organizations, 270
- - - Press Cutting Agencies, 249
- - - Resistance Movements, 236
- - - Scientific Editors' Associations, 257
- - - Secondary Teachers, 233
- - - Senior Police Officers, 241
- - - Social Science Organizations, 260
- - - - Workers, 263
- - - - - Electron Microscopy, 257
- - - - of Classical Studies, 259
- - - Stock Exchanges, 231
- - - Surgical Colleges, 242
- - - Teachers' Associations, 233
- - - - of Modern Languages, 233
- - - Textile and Clothing Workers, 213
- - - the Cinematographic Press, 249
- - - - Periodical Press, 249
- - - - Phonographic Industry, 274
- - - - Socialist and Democratic Press, 249
- - - Thermalism and Climatism, 246
- - - Tourist Centres, 270
- - - Trade Unions of Employees in Public Service, 213
- - - - - Transport Workers, 213
- - - University Women, 233
- - - Vexillological Associations, 260
- - - Workers' Educational Associations, 233

INDEX

- Fellowship of Former Scouts and Guides, 263
- — — Reconciliation, 251
- Fertilizer Industry Association, 274
- Finance Corporation—IFC, 67
- Fiscal Association, 231
- Food Information Service, 257
- Foundation of the High-Altitude Research Stations Jungfraujoch and Gornergrat, 257
- Fragrance Association, 274
- Frequency Registration Board (ITU), 79
- Fund for Agricultural Development—IFAD, 70
- Fur Trade Federation, 274
- Gas Union, 266
- Geographical Union, 253
- Glaciological Society, 257
- Graphical Federation, 164
- Group of National Associations of Manufacturers of Agrochemical Products, 274
- — — — Scientific, Technical and Medical Publishers, 257
- Guild of Opticians, 246
- Gymnastic Federation, 265
- Ho-Re-Ca, 270
- Hockey Federation, 265
- Hop Growers' Convention, 220
- Hospital Federation, 246
- Hotel Association, 270
- Humanist and Ethical Union, 251
- Hydrographic Organization, 257
- Industrial Relations Association, 239
- Information Management Congress, 268
- Institute for Adult Literacy Methods, 233
- — — — Children's Literature and Reading Research, 226
- — — — Comparative Music Studies and Documentation, 227
- — — — Conservation of Historic and Artistic Works, 226
- — — — Cotton, 228
- — — — Economic Problems of the Socialist World System, 126
- — — — Educational Planning (UNESCO), 81
- — — — Labour Studies (ILO), 73
- — — — Ligurian Studies, 260
- — — — Peace, 236
- — — — Strategic Studies, 236
- — — — Sugar Beet Research, 220
- — — — the Unification of Private Law, 241
- — — of Administrative Sciences, 260
- — — — Biological Control, 116
- — — — Communications, 249
- — — — Entomology, 116
- — — — Parasitology, 116
- — — — Philosophy, 233
- — — — Public Administration, 233
- — — — — Finance, 231
- — — — Refrigeration, 257
- — — — Seismology and Earthquake Engineering, 268
- — — — Sociology, 260
- — — — Space Law, 241
- — — — Tropical Agriculture, 221
- — — — Welding, 266
- Institution for Production Engineering Research, 269
- Interchurch Film Centre, 225
- Investment Bank, 165
- Iron and Steel Institute, 269
- Islamic Law Commission, 199
- — News Agency, 199
- Jazz Federation, 227
- Judo Federation, 265
- Juridical Institute, 241
- Jute Organization, 228
- Laboratory for Research on Animal Diseases, 221
- — of Marine Radioactivity, 60
- Labour Conference (ILO), 72
- — Office (ILO), 72
- — Organisation—ILO, 72
- Law Association, 241
- — Commission, 18
- Lead and Zinc Study Group, 228
- League against Epilepsy, 246
- — — Rheumatism, 242
- — for Human Rights, 236
- — of Societies for Persons with Mental Handicap, 263
- Leprosy Association, 242
- Liaison Centre for Cinema and Television Schools, 226
- Lifeboat Federation, 263
- Livestock Centre for Africa, 221
- Maize and Wheat Improvement Center, 221
- Maritime Arbitration Organization (ICC), 161
- — — Committee, 241

- — Organization—IMO, 73
- — — Radio Association, 249
- — — Satellite Organization, 248
- — Mathematical Union, 253
- — Measurement Confederation, 266
- — Medical Association for the Study of Living Conditions and Health, 246
- — — Society of Paraplegia, 243
- — Metalworkers' Federation, 164
- — Mineralogical Association, 257
- — Molybdenum Association, 228
- — Monetary Fund—IMF, 74
- — Montessori Association, 234
- — Movement of Catholic Students, 251
- — Music Centre, 227
- — — Council, 226
- — Musicology Society, 259
- — Mycological Institute, 116
- — Narcotics Control Board, 246
- — Natural Rubber Organization, 228
- — North Pacific Fisheries Commission, 221
- — Nuclear Information System—INIS, 61
- — — Law Association, 241
- — — Safety Advisory Group, 60
- — Numismatic Commission, 261
- — Olive Oil Council, 229
- — Olympic Committee, 166
- — Optometric and Optical League, 246
- — Organisation of Employers, 239
- — — — Legal Metrology, 257
- — Organization for Biological Control of Noxious Animals and Plants, 221
- — — — Medical Physics, 246
- — — — Migration, 167
- — — — Motor Trades and Repairs, 274
- — — — Standardization, 269
- — — — the Study of the Old Testament, 251
- — — of Citrus Virologists, 221
- — — — Consumers' Unions, 274
- — — — Experts, 239
- — — — Journalists, 249
- — — — Motor Manufacturers, 274
- — — — the Flavour Industry, 274
- — Palaeontological Association, 257
- — Peace Academy, 261
- — — Bureau, 236
- — — Research Association, 261
- — Peat Society, 257
- — Pediatric Association, 242
- — PEN, 227
- — Penal and Penitentiary Foundation, 241
- — Pepper Community, 229
- — Pharmaceutical Federation, 246
- — — Students' Federation, 277
- — Philatelic Federation, 265
- — Phonetic Association, 257
- — Phycological Society, 257
- — Planned Parenthood Federation, 263
- — Police Association, 249
- — Political Science Association, 236
- — Poplar Commission (FAO), 57
- — Press Institute, 249
- — — Telecommunications Council, 250
- — Primatological Society, 258
- — Prisoners' Aid Association, 264
- — Psycho-Analytical Association, 246
- — Public Relations Association, 239
- — Publishers' Association, 274
- — Radiation Protection Association, 258
- — Radio and Television Organization, 249
- — — Consultative Committee (ITU), 79
- — Rail Transport Committee, 276
- — Railway Congress Association, 276
- — Rayon and Synthetic Fibres Committee, 274
- — Reading Association, 234
- — Recycling Bureau, 267
- — Red Cross and Red Crescent Movement, 168
- — — Locust Control Organization for Central and Southern Africa, 221
- — Regional Organization of Plant Protection and Animal Health, 221
- — Rehabilitation Medicine Association, 242
- — Research Group on Wood Preservation, 269
- — Rhinologic Society, 242
- — Rice Commission (FAO), 57
- — — Research Institute, 221

INDEX — *International Organizations*

— Road Federation, 276
— — Safety, 276
— — Transport Union, 276
— Rowing Federation, 265
— Rubber Research and Development Board, 269
— — Study Group, 229
— Savings Banks Institute, 231
— Schools Association, 234
— Scientific Council for Trypanosomiasis Research and Control, 192
— Sea-Bed Authority, 33
— Secretariat for Arts, Mass Media and Entertainment Trade Unions, 164
— Seed Testing Association, 221
— Sericultural Commission, 221
— Service for National Agricultural Research, 221
— Shipowners' Association (CMEA), 126
— Shipping Federation Ltd, 276
— Shooting Union, 266
— Shopfitting Organisation, 274
— Silk Association, 229
— Skating Union, 266
— Ski Federation, 266
— Social Science Council, 261
— — Security Association, 264
— — Service, 264
— Society and Federation of Cardiology, 242
— — for Business Education, 234
— — — Cardiovascular Surgery, 246
— — — Contemporary Music, 227
— — — Education through Art, 234
— — — General Semantics, 258
— — — Horticultural Science, 221
— — — Human and Animal Mycology, 258
— — — Labour Law and Social Security, 241
— — — Mental Imagery Techniques, 246
— — — Music Education, 234
— — — Photogrammetry and Remote Sensing, 269
— — — Research on Civilization Diseases and Environment, 246
— — — Rock Mechanics, 258
— — — Soil Mechanics and Foundation Engineering, 269
— — — Soilless Culture, 221
— — — Stereology, 258
— — — the Study of Medieval Philosophy, 234
— — — Tropical Ecology, 258
— — of Art and Psychopathology, 246
— — — Audiology, 243
— — — Biometeorology, 258
— — — Blood Transfusion, 243
— — — City and Regional Planners, 239
— — — Criminology, 258
— — — Dermatology, 243
— — — Developmental Biologists, 247
— — — Geographical Pathology, 247
— — — Internal Medicine, 242
— — — Lymphology, 247
— — — Neuropathology, 247
— — — Orthopaedic Surgery and Traumatology, 247
— — — Radiology, 247
— — — Social Defence, 261
— — — Soil Science, 221
— — — Surgery, 247
— Sociological Association, 261
— Solar Energy Society, 269
— Solid Wastes and Public Cleansing Association, 269
— Special Committee on Radio Interference, 268
— Spice Group, 229
— Statistical Institute, 261
— Studies Association, 261
— Sugar Organization, 229
— Table Tennis Federation, 266
— Tea Committee, 229
— — Promotion Organization, 229
— Telecommunication Union—ITU, 78
— Telecommunications Satellite Organization, 248
— Telegraph and Telephone Consultative Committee (ITU), 79
— Tennis Federation, 266
— Textile, Garment and Leather Workers' Federation, 164
— — Manufacturers Federation, 274
— Theatre Institute, 227
— Tin Research Institute, 269
— Trade Centre (GATT/UNCTAD), 58
— Translations Centre, 258
— Transport Workers' Federation, 164
— Tropical Timber Organization, 229
— Tungsten Industry Association, 229
— Typographic Association, 227
— Union against Cancer, 243
— — Tuberculosis and Lung Disease, 247
— — for Conservation of Nature and Natural Resources, 258
— — — Electro-heat, 266
— — — Health Education, 247
— — — Inland Navigation, 276
— — — Oriental and Asian Studies, 259
— — — Pure and Applied Biophysics, 252
— — — Quaternary Research, 258
— — — the Protection of Industrial Property (Paris Convention), 87
— — — — — Literary and Artistic Works (Berne Union), 87
— — — — Scientific Study of Population, 261
— — — Vacuum Science, Technique and Applications, 269
— — of Air Pollution Prevention Associations, 267
— — — Anthropological and Ethnological Sciences, 259
— — — Architects, 239
— — — Biochemistry, 253
— — — Biological Sciences, 253
— — — Crystallography, 253
— — — Family Organisations, 264
— — — Food and Allied Workers' Associations, 164
— — — — Science and Technology, 258
— — — Forestry Research Organizations, 221
— — — Geodesy and Geophysics, 253
— — — Geological Sciences, 253
— — — Heat Distributors, 269
— — — Housing Finance Institutions, 231
— — — Immunological Societies, 253
— — — Latin Notaries, 241
— — — Lawyers, 241
— — — Local Authorities, 236
— — — Marine Insurance, 274
— — — Metal, 269
— — — Microbiological Societies, 253
— — — Nutritional Sciences, 253
— — — Pharmacology, 253
— — — Physiological Sciences, 253
— — — Prehistoric and Protohistoric Sciences, 259
— — — Producers and Distributors of Electrical Energy, 267
— — — Psychological Science, 253
— — — Public Transport, 276
— — — Pure and Applied Biophysics, 253
— — — — — Chemistry, 253
— — — — — Physics, 254
— — — Radio Science, 254
— — — Railways, 277
— — — Socialist Youth, 237
— — — Societies for the Aid of Mental Health, 264
— — — Students, 277
— — — Tenants, 264
— — — Testing and Research Laboratories for Materials and Structures, 267
— — — the History and Philosophy of Science, 254
— — — Theoretical and Applied Mechanics, 254
— — — Therapeutics, 247
— — — Young Christian Democrats, 236
— Universities Bureau, 233
— Veterinary Association for Animal Production, 221
— Vine and Wine Office, 229
— Water Resources Association, 269
— — Supply Association, 269
— Waterfowl and Wetlands Research Bureau, 258
— Weightlifting Federation, 266
— Whaling Commission, 274
— Wheat Council, 229
— Wool Secretariat, 229
— — Study Group, 229
— — Textile Organisation, 274
— Workers' Aid, 264
— Wrought Copper Council, 274
— Yacht Racing Union, 266
— Young Christian Workers, 277
— Youth and Student Movement for the United Nations, 278
— — Hostel Federation, 278
— — Library, 234
Interoceanmetall (CMEA), 126
Inter-Parliamentary Union, 236
INTERPOL, 240
Interport (CMEA), 126
Interrobot (CMEA), 126
Intertextilmash (CMEA), 126
Inter-University European Institute on Social Welfare, 264
Inuit Circumpolar Conference, 237
Islamic Capitals Organization, 199

INDEX

— Centre for Technical and Vocational Training and Research, 199
— — — the Development of Trade, 199
— Chamber of Commerce, Industry and Commodity Exchange, 199
— Commission for Economic, Cultural and Social Affairs (OIC), 198
— — — the International Crescent, 199
— Conference, 198
— Council of Europe, 251
— Court of Justice, 199
— Development Bank, 170
— Educational, Scientific and Cultural Organization, 199
— Foundation for Science, Technology and Development, 199
— Institute of Agriculture, 199
— Jurisprudence Academy, 199
— Research and Training Institute, 171
— Solidarity Fund, 199
— States Broadcasting Organization, 199
ITU, 78

J

Jewish Agency for Israel, 237
Joint Commonwealth Societies' Council, 118
— Conference of African Planners, Statisticians and Demographers (ECA), 29
— European Torus—JET, 146
— Institute for Nuclear Research, 126
Junior Chamber International, 278

K

Kagera River Basin Organization, 224

L

LAFTA, 172
Lagos Plan of Action, 29
LAIA, 172
Lake Chad Basin Commission, 223
Latin American and Caribbean Institute for Economic and Social Planning, 28
— — Association of Development Financing Institutions, 223
— — — — National Academies of Medicine, 243
— — Banking Federation, 231
— — Catholic Press Union, 250
— — Commission for Science and Technology, 224
— — Confederation of Tourist Organizations, 270
— — — — Workers (WCL), 213
— — — — Young Men's Christian Associations, 278
— — Council of Churches, 251
— — Demographic Centre, 28
— — Economic System—SELA, 224
— — Energy Organization—OLADE, 269
— — Episcopal Council, 251
— — Features Agency, 224
— — Federation of Agricultural and Food Industry Workers, 239
— — Fisheries Development Organization, 224
— — Forestry Commission (FAO), 57
— — Free Trade Association—LAFTA, 172
— — Housing and Human Settlements Development Organization, 224
— — Integration Association—ALADI, 172
— — Iron and Steel Institute, 269
— — Multinational Fertilizer Marketing Enterprise, 224
— — Parliament, 237
— — Shipping Organization, 224
— — Tourism Training Institute, 224
Law Association for Asia and the Pacific, 241
— of the Sea Convention, 33
Lead Development Association, 229
League for the Exchange of Commonwealth Teachers, 117
— of Arab States, 174
— — European Research Libraries, 234
— — Red Cross and Red Crescent Societies—LRCS, 169
Liaison Group of the European Mechanical, Electrical, Electronic and Metalworking Industries, 275
Liberal International, 237
Lions Clubs International, 264
Liptako Gourma Integrated Development Authority, 224
Lomé Convention, 151
Lusaka Declaration on Racism, 119
Lutheran World Federation, 251

M

Malacological Union, 258
Mano River Union, 224
Marine Environment Protection Committee (IMO), 73
Maritime Safety Committee (IMO), 73
Médecins sans frontières, 264
Medical Women's International Association, 243
Mensa International, 261
Mercado Común Centroamericano, 110
Middle East Council of Churches, 251
— — Neurosurgical Society, 247
Miners' International Federation, 164
Moral Re-Armament, 251
Multi-fibre Arrangement, 59
Multilateral Investment Guarantee Agency—MIGA, 68
Muslim World League, 251
Mutual Aid and Loan Guarantee Fund (Conseil de l'Entente), 122
— Assistance of the Latin-American Government Oil Companies, 229

N

NATO, 183
Near East Forestry Commission (FAO), 57
— — Regional Commission on Agriculture (FAO), 57
— — — Economic and Social Policy Commission (FAO), 57
New World Information and Communication Order—NWICO, 81
Niger Basin Authority, 224
Nigeria Trust Fund (ADB), 92
Non-aligned Movement, 237
Nordic Council, 179
— — of Ministers, 180
— Cultural Fund, 181
— Economic Research Council, 180
— Federation of Factory Workers' Unions, 239
— Industrial Fund, 180
— Investment Bank, 180
— Project Fund, 180
— Society for Cell Biology, 258
NORDTEST, 180
North American Forestry Commission (FAO), 57
— Atlantic Assembly, 237
— — Council, 183
— — Treaty Organisation—NATO, 183
Northern Shipowners' Defence Club, 277
Northwest Atlantic Fisheries Organization, 221
Nuclear Energy Agency (OECD), 188

O

OAPEC, 197
OAS, 194
OAU, 190
ODECA, 237
OECD, 186
OECS, 109
Office de Recherches sur l'Alimentation et la Nutrition africaine (OCCGE), 247
— of the United Nations Disaster Relief Co-ordinator—UNDRO, 34
OIC, 198
OMVG, 223
OMVS, 224
OPEC, 200
— Fund for International Development, 203
— News Agency, 200
Open Door International, 237
Opus Dei, 251
OPW (CMEA), 126
Organisation de mise en valeur du fleuve Gambie—OMVG, 223
— for Economic Co-operation and Development—OECD, 186
— — the Collaboration of Railways, 277
— of Eastern Caribbean States—OECS, 109
— pour la Mise en Valeur du Fleuve Sénégal—OMVS, 224
— — l'aménagement et le développement du bassin de la rivière Kagera, 224
Organismo Internacional Regional de Sanidad Agropecuaria, 221
— para la Proscripción de las Armas Nucleares en la América Latina, 235
Organización de Estados Centroamericanas—ODECA, 237
— — — Iberoamericanos para la Educación, la Ciencia y la Cultura, 234
— — las Cooperativas de América, 237
— — Solidaridad de los Pueblos de Africa, Asia y América Latina, 237
— — Universidades Católicas de América Latina, 234

— Latinoamericana de Energía—OLADE, 269
— Regional Interamericana de Trabajadores—ORIT, 163
Organization for Co-operation in the Roller-Bearings Industry (CMEA), 126
— — Co-ordination and Co-operation in the Struggle against Endemic Diseases, 247
— — — in the Struggle against Endemic Diseases in Central Africa, 247
— — Museums, Monuments and Sites in Africa, 234
— — the Development of the Senegal River, 224
— — — Management and Development of the Kagera River Basin, 224
— of African Unity—OAU, 190
— — — Trade Union Unity—OATUU, 193
— — American States—OAS, 194
— — Arab Petroleum Exporting Countries—OAPEC, 197
— — Asia-Pacific News Agencies, 250
— — Central American States, 237
— — Ibero-American States for Education, Science and Culture, 234
— — Solidarity of the Peoples of Africa, Asia and Latin America, 237
— — the Catholic Universities of Latin America, 234
— — — Cooperatives of America, 237
— — — Islamic Conference, 198
— — — Petroleum Exporting Countries—OPEC, 200
— — — Trade Unions of West Africa, 134
Orient Airlines Association, 277
ORIT, 163

P

Pacific Asia Travel Association, 270
— Basin Economic Council, 224
— Conference of Churches, 251
— Economic Co-operation Conference, 224
— Forum Line, 208
— Science Association, 258
— Telecommunications Council, 248
Pan-African Documentation and Information Service, 29
— Employers' Federation, 239
— Institute for Development, 224
— News Agency, 193
— Postal Union, 193
— Telecommunications Union, 193
— Youth Movement, 278
Pan American Development Foundation, 224
— — Health Organization, 196
— — Railway Congress Association, 277
Pan-American Association of Ophthalmology, 247
— Institute of Geography and History, 196
Pan-Pacific and South East Asia Women's Association, 264
— Surgical Association, 247
Paris Convention, 87
Parlamento Andino, 93
— Latinoamericano, 237
Parliamentary Association for Euro-Arab Co-operation, 237
Pax Romana International Catholic Movement for Intellectual and Cultural Affairs, 251
Permanent Court of Arbitration, 241
— International Association of Navigation Congresses, 267
— — — — Road Congresses, 267
— — Committee of Linguists, 259
— — Inter-State Committee on Drought Control in the Sahel, 224
Population Council, 224
— Information Network for Africa, 29
Postal, Telegraph and Telephone International, 164
— Union of the Americas and Spain, 248
Preferential Trade Area for Eastern and Southern African States—PTA, 224
Press Foundation of Asia, 250
Public Services International, 164
Pugwash Conferences on Science and World Affairs, 258

R

Rabitat al-Alam al-Islami, 251
Red Cross, 168
Regional Animal Production and Health Commission for Asia, the Far East and the South-West Pacific (FAO), 57
— Centre for Consulting Engineering and Management (ECA), 30
— — — Engineering Design and Manufacturing (ECA), 30
— — — Adult Education and Functional Literacy in Latin America, 234
— — — Services in Surveying, Mapping and Remote Sensing, 269
— — — Training in Aerospace Surveys, 269

— Commission on Farm Management for Asia and the Far East (FAO), 57
— — — Food Security for Asia and the Pacific (FAO), 57
— — — Land and Water Use in the Near East (FAO), 57
— Co-ordination Centre for Research and Development of Coarse Grains, Pulses, Roots and Tuber Crops (ESCAP), 26
— Fisheries Advisory Commission for the Southwest Atlantic (FAO), 57
— Food and Nutrition Commission for Africa (FAO/WHO/OAU), 57
— Institute for Population Studies (ECA), 29
— Network for Agricultural Machinery (ESCAP), 26
Rehabilitation International, 243
Research Centre for Islamic History, Art and Culture, 199
Rotary International, 264
Royal Asiatic Society of Great Britain and Ireland, 227
— Commonwealth Society, 118
— — — for the Blind, 117
— Over-Seas League, 118

S

SAARC, 225
SADCC, 209
Salvation Army, 252
Scientific, Technical and Research Commission (OAU), 193
SELA, 224
Service Civil International, 264
Shelter-Afrique, 92
Ship-chartering Co-ordination Bureau (CMEA), 126
SIFIDA, 92
Sight Savers, 117
Sistema Económica Latinoamericano—SELA, 224
Socialist Educational International, 237
— International, 237
— — Women, 237
Sociedad Interamericana de Planificación, 223
— — — Prensa, 249
Société de neuro-chirurgie de langue française, 247
— internationale financière pour les investissements et le développement en Afrique (ADB), 92
Society for International Development, 225
— of African Culture, 227
— — Comparative Legislation, 241
— — French-Speaking Neuro-Surgeons, 247
— — Saint Vincent de Paul, 264
SOLIDARIOS, 223
Soroptimist International, 252
South Asian Association for Regional Co-operation—SAARC, 225
— Commission, 225
— Pacific Bureau for Economic Cooperation—SPEC, 207
— — Commission, 205
— — Conference, 205
— — Forum, 207
— — — Fisheries Agency, 208
— — Regional Environment Programme, 206
— — Trade Commission, 208
Southeast Asian Ministers of Education Organization, 234
Southern African Centre for Cooperation in Agricultural Research, 210
— — Development Co-ordination Conference—SADCC, 209
— — Transport and Communications Commission (SADCC), 209
SPEC, 207
Special Arab Assistance Fund for Africa (BADEA), 95
— Bureau for Boycotting Israel (Arab League), 175
Standing Committee on Commonwealth Forestry, 116
— Conference of Rectors, Presidents and Vice-Chancellors of the European Universities, 234
Statistical, Economic and Social Research and Training Centre for the Islamic Countries, 199
— Institute for Asia and the Pacific, 26
Stockholm International Peace Research Institute, 237
Sugar Association of the Caribbean, Inc., 229
Supreme Council for Sports in Africa, 193

T

Technical Centre for Agricultural and Rural Co-operation (Lomé Convention), 151
— Commission for Telecommunications in Central America, 111
Theosophical Society, 252
Third World Forum, 261
Tourism Council of the South Pacific, 270
Trade Unions International of Agricultural, Forestry and Plantation Workers, 215

– – – – Chemical, Oil and Allied Workers, 215
– – – – Food, Tobacco, Hotel and Allied Industries Workers, 215
– – – – Metal Workers, 215
– – – – Public and Allied Employees, 215
– – – – Textile, Clothing, Leather and Fur Workers, 215
– – – – Transport Workers, 215
– – – – Workers in Commerce, 215
– – – – – – Energy, 215
– – – – – – of the Building, Wood and Building Materials Industries, 215
Transnational Association of Acupuncture and Taoist Medicine, 247
Transplantation Society, 243
Treaty for the Prohibition of Nuclear Weapons in Latin America (Tlatelolco Treaty), 60
– of Brussels (WEU), 212
– – Lagos (ECOWAS), 133
– – Montevideo (ALADI), 172
– – Rome (EEC), 137
– on the Non-Proliferation of Nuclear Weapons—NPT, 61
Tribunal de Justicia del Acuerdo de Cartagena, 93
Trilateral Commission, 237
Trusteeship Council (United Nations), 14, 18

U

UATI, 266
UDEAC, 156
UMOA, 156
UNCHS, 35
UNCTAD, 37
UNDOF, 46
UNDP, 39
UNDRO, 34
UNEP, 41
UNESCO, 79
UNFICYP, 46
UNFPA, 47
UNHCR, 43
UNICEF, 36
UNIDO, 82
UNIFIL, 46
Union douanière et économique de l'Afrique centrale—UDEAC, 156
– mondiale des professions libérales, 239
– – – voix françaises, 227
– monétaire ouest-africaine—UMOA, 156
– of African Railways, 193
– – Arab Jurists, 241
– – Banana Exporting Countries, 229
– – European Railway Industries, 277
– – – – Road Services, 277
– – Industrial and Employers' Confederations of Europe, 275
– – International Associations, 241
– – – Fairs, 275
– – – Technical Associations, 266
– – Latin American Universities, 234
– – National Radio and Television Organizations of Africa, 250
– – the Arab Maghreb, 225
Unión de Universidades de América Latina, 234
– Internacional del Notariado Latino, 241
– Postal de las Américas y España, 248
UNITAR, 21
Unitas Malacologica, 258
United Bible Societies, 252
– Lodge of Theosophists, 252
– Nations, 3
– – Angola Verification Mission, 47
– – Budget, 7
– – Capital Development Fund, 40
– – Centre against Apartheid, 17
– – – for Human Settlements—UNCHS (Habitat), 35
– – Charter, 9
– – Children's Fund—UNICEF, 36
– – Commission on Human Settlements, 35
– – Conference on the Law of the Sea—UNCLOS, 33
– – – – Trade and Development—UNCTAD, 37
– – Conferences, 17
– – Co-ordinator for Humanitarian and Economic Assistance to Afghanistan, 44
– – Development Fund for Women, 40
– – – Programme—UNDP, 39
– – Disaster Relief Co-ordinator's Office—UNDRO, 34
– – Disengagement Observer Force—UNDOF, 46
– – Economic and Social Commission for Asia and the Pacific—ESCAP, 25
– – – – – – – Western Asia—ESCWA, 31
– – – – – Council—ECOSOC, 13, 19
– – – Commission for Africa—ECA, 28
– – – – – Europe—ECE, 24
– – – – – Latin America and the Caribbean—ECLAC, 27
– – Educational, Scientific and Cultural Organization—UNESCO, 79
– – Environment Programme—UNEP, 41
– – Fund for Population Activities—UNFPA, 47
– – – – Science and Technology for Development—UNFSTD, 40
– – General Assembly, 9, 18
– – Good Offices Mission in Afghanistan and Pakistan—UNGOMAP, 46
– – High Commissioner for Refugees—UNHCR, 43
– – Industrial Development Fund, 82
– – – – Organization—UNIDO, 82
– – Information Centres, 7
– – Institute for Disarmament Research, 21
– – – – Training and Research—UNITAR, 21
– – Interim Force in Lebanon—UNIFIL, 46
– – International Research and Training Institute for the Advancement of Women—INSTRAW, 22
– – Iran-Iraq Military Observer Group—UNIIMOG, 46
– – Military Observer Group in India and Pakistan—UNMOGIP, 47
– – Observer Group in Central America—ONUCA, 47
– – – Missions and Peace-Keeping Forces, 46
– – Observers, 6
– – Peace-Keeping Force in Cyprus—UNFICYP, 46
– – Population Fund—UNFPA, 47
– – Relief and Works Agency for Palestine Refugees in the Near East—UNRWA, 48
– – Research Institute for Social Development—UNRISD, 22
– – Revolving Fund for Natural Resources Exploration, 40
– – Secretariat, 15, 17
– – Security Council, 10, 19
– – Sudano-Sahelian Office, 40
– – Transition Assistance Group—UNTAG, 47
– – Transport and Communications Decade in Africa, 29
– – Truce Supervision Organization—UNTSO, 46
– – Trusteeship Council, 14, 18
– – University, 22
– – Volunteers, 40
– Towns Organization, 227
Universal Alliance of Diamond Workers, 164
– Esperanto Association, 234
– Federation of Travel Agents' Associations, 270
– Postal Union—UPU, 83
Universidad de Trabajadores de América Latina, 213
University for Peace, 23
UNRISD, 22
UNRWA, 48
UNTSO, 46
UPU, 83

V

Victoria League for Commonwealth Friendship, 118
Vienna Institute for Development and Co-operation, 225

W

War Resisters' International, 238
Warsaw Treaty of Friendship, Co-operation and Mutual Assistance—Warsaw Pact, 211
Watch Tower Bible and Tract Society, 252
WCC, 214
WCL, 213
West Africa Rice Development Association, 229
– – Women's Association, 134
– African Clearing House, 231
– – Development Bank, 156
– – Economic Community—CEAO, 120
– – Monetary Union, 156
– – Universities' Association, 134
– – Youth Association, 134
– Indian Sea Island Cotton Association Inc., 229
– Indies Shipping Corporation, 109
Western Central Atlantic Fishery Commission (FAO), 57
– European Union—WEU, 212
WFC, 50
WFP, 51
WFTU, 215
WHO, 84
WIPO, 86

INDEX

WMO, 88
WMO/ESCAP Panel on Tropical Cyclones, 26
Women's International Democratic Federation, 238
World Administrative Radio Conference (ITU), 78
— — Telegraph and Telephone Conference, 78
— Airlines Clubs Association, 277
— Alliance of Reformed Churches (Presbyterian and Congregational), 252
— — — Young Men's Christian Associations, 278
— Assembly of Youth, 278
— Association for Animal Production, 221
— — — Christian Communication, 250
— — — Educational Research, 235
— — — Public Opinion Research, 261
— — — World Federation, 238
— — of Girl Guides and Girl Scouts, 278
— — — Industrial and Technological Research Organizations, 269
— — — Judges, 242
— — — Law Professors, 242
— — — Lawyers, 242
— — — Nuclear Operators, 270
— — — Societies of (Anatomic and Clinical) Pathology, 247
— — — Travel Agencies, 270
— — — Veterinary Food-Hygienists, 222
— — — — Microbiologists, Immunologists and Specialists in Infectious Diseases, 222
— Bank—IBRD, 62
— Blind Union, 264
— Bridge Federation, 266
— Bureau of Metal Statistics, 270
— Chess Federation, 266
— Confederation for Physical Therapy, 248
— — of Labour—WCL, 213
— — — Organizations of the Teaching Profession, 235
— — — Teachers, 213
— Conference on Religion and Peace, 252
— Congress of Authors and Composers, 226
— — — Faiths, 252
— Council of Churches, 214
— — — Credit Unions, 231
— — — Indigenous Peoples, 238
— — — Management, 275
— — — Service Clubs, 278
— Crafts Council, 227
— Disarmament Campaign, 238
— Education Fellowship, 235
— Employment Programme, 72
— Energy Council, 267
— Federation for Medical Education, 243
— — — Mental Health, 248
— — of Advertisers, 275
— — — Agriculture and Food Workers, 213
— — — Associations of Clinical Toxicology Centres and Poison Control Centres, 243
— — — — — Paediatric Surgeons, 243
— — — Building and Woodworkers Unions, 213
— — — Christian Life Communities, 252
— — — Clerical Workers, 213
— — — Democratic Youth, 278
— — — Diamond Bourses, 230
— — — Engineering Organizations, 270
— — — Industry Workers, 213
— — — International Music Competitions, 227
— — — Neurology, 243

— — — Neurosurgical Societies, 248
— — — Occupational Therapists, 248
— — — Public Health Associations, 248
— — — Scientific Workers, 239
— — — Societies of Anaesthesiologists, 248
— — — Teachers' Unions, 215
— — — the Deaf, 264
— — — Trade Unions—WFTU, 215
— — — United Nations Associations, 238
— Fellowship of Buddhists, 252
— Food Council, 50
— — Programme—WFP, 51
— Gold Council, 230
— Health Organization—WHO, 84
— Intellectual Property Organization—WIPO, 86
— Jewish Congress, 252
— Jurist Association, 242
— Medical Association, 243
— Meteorological Organization—WMO, 88
— Methodist Council, 252
— Movement of Christian Workers, 239
— Organisation of Systems and Cybernetics, 258
— Organization of Gastroenterology, 243
— — — the Scout Movement, 278
— ORT Union, 264
— Packaging Organisation, 275
— Peace Council, 238
— Petroleum Congresses, 270
— Ploughing Organization, 222
— Poultry Science Association, 222
— Psychiatric Association, 243
— Sephardi Federation, 252
— Society for Ekistics, 261
— — — the Protection of Animals, 264
— Student Christian Federation, 252
— Tourism Organization, 270
— Trade Centers Association, 275
— — Union Congress, 215
— Underwater Federation, 266
— Union for Progressive Judaism, 252
— — of Catholic Philosophical Societies, 261
— — — Teachers, 235
— — — — Women's Organisations, 252
— — — French Speakers, 227
— — — Jewish Students, 278
— — — Professions, 239
— University Service, 225
— Veterans Federation, 265
— Veterinary Association, 222
— Wide Fund for Nature, 259
— Wildlife Fund, 259
— Young Women's Christian Association, 278

Y

Youth for Development and Co-operation, 278

Z

Zinc Development Association, 230
Zone Franc, 156
Zonta International, 265